2005 Supple

MW01267556

O*NET 7.0 Database Revision and 8.0 proposed updates to Dictionary of Occupational Titles with O*NET™ Definitions
5th Edition

Volumes I-III

Table II

Published and for sale by:
CLAITOR'S PUBLISHING DIVISION
P.O. Box 261333, Baton Rouge, LA 70826-1333
800-274-1403 (In LA 225-344-0476)
Fax: 225-344-0480
Internet address:
e mail: claitors@claitors.com
World Wide Web: http://www.claitors.com

Published and for sale by:
CLAITOR'S PUBLISHING DIVISION
P.O. Box 261333, Baton Rouge, LA 70826-1333
800-274-1403 (In LA 225-344-0476)
Fax: 225-344-0480
Internet address:
e mail: claitors@claitors.com
World Wide Web: http://www.claitors.com

*We acknowlege the input and assistance of the U. S. Department of Labor, since much of the following is extracted from their website at http://online.onetcenter.org.

Introduction

Highlights of the new O*NET 7.0 Database

This second major update from the O*NET Data Collection Program brings the number of comprehensively updated occupations to 280. Highlights of this update include:

- Addition of **Task Statement ratings** (importance, relevance, and frequency) for 100 O*NET-SOC occupations
- Updated **Abilities, Work Activities, Knowledge, Skills, Job Zones**, and **Work Context** data for 100 occupations
- Additional **Work Context** data for 100 occupations
- Addition of **Training and Work Experience** and **Education** data for 100 occupations
- Addition of **Work Styles** data for 100 occupations

Highlights of the new O*NET 6.0 Database

This second major update from the O*NET Data Collection Program brings the number of changes

- Updated Tasks for 69 Occupations
- Updated Job Zones for 54 Occupations

O*NET 5.0 Database Changes

The O*NET 5.0 database represents a major milestone for the O*NET project. The major data collection underway has resulted in a significant update to the database. Highlights include:

- New and revised Task Statements for 455 O*NET-SOC occupations
- Addition of Task Statement ratings (importance and frequency) for 54 O*NET-SOC occupations
- Updated Abilities, Work Activities, Knowledge, Skills, and Work Context data for 54 occupations
- Addition of Training and Work Experience, and Education data for 54 occupations (not reflected in this Supplement as yet)
- Addition of Work Styles data for 54 occupations

- Addition of metadata to the file structure to specify source of data and date of update
- Addition of Emerging Task Statements
- Addition of Detailed Work Activities

All of the above is incorporated in this Revision #3 of O*NET™ Database 7.0 with proposed 8.0 Database to enable the user to be as current as possible. As the O*NET organization continues with Revisions 4, 5, etc., at semi-annual to annual periods over the next contemplated years until Revision is completed, we will keep pace with cumulative Revisions, each replacing the prior Revision, to maintain a current sourcebook for the user. Please register with us if you would like to receive these future Revisions, which will be available at moderate cost depending on size.

How to Use This Revision

1. Research the O*NET-SOC Code Number of your interest in Table II of basic volumes I-III.
2. Then go to the same number in this Revision #3 to see changes, if any. If Code Number is not listed in the proper numbering sequence, this means no changes to same in Revision #3 (changes to follow as future Revisions are released).
3. Check 8.0 Proposed Database Revision at the rear of this Supplement for expected forthcoming changes if these would be of interest.

This material is mostly downloaded from the O*NET website at www.onetcenter.org, and the user is encouraged to go to this site for even further information. We express our appreciation and congratulations to the talented and hardworking O*NET organization for this giant step forward in the vocational field. Many thanks from all of us laboring in this arena for your "sea change" approach and improvements enabling us more capability to better serve the community!

-- Claitor's Publishing Division

Table II

O*NET™—SOC 7.0 Definitions by Code Number

Table II
O*NET – SOC 7.0 Definitions by Code Number

11-1011.00 - Chief Executives

Determine and formulate policies and provide the overall direction of companies or private and public sector organizations within the guidelines set up by a board of directors or similar governing body. Plan, direct, or coordinate operational activities at the highest level of management with the help of subordinate executives and staff managers.

Tasks

11-1011.00 - Chief Executives

Determine and formulate policies and provide the overall direction of companies or private and public sector organizations within the guidelines set up by a board of directors or similar governing body. Plan, direct, or coordinate operational activities at the highest level of management with the help of subordinate executives and staff managers.

Tasks

1) Coordinate the development and implementation of budgetary control systems, record-keeping systems, and other administrative control processes.

2) Direct and coordinate an organization's financial and budget activities in order to fund operations, maximize investments, and increase efficiency.

3) Direct human resources activities, including the approval of human resource plans and activities, the selection of directors and other high-level staff, and establishment and organization of major departments.

4) Direct non-merchandising departments such as advertising, purchasing, credit, and accounting.

5) Appoint department heads or managers, and assign or delegate responsibilities to them.

6) Deliver speeches, write articles, and present information at meetings or conventions in order to promote services, exchange ideas, and accomplish objectives.

7) Attend and participate in meetings of municipal councils and council committees.

8) Preside over or serve on boards of directors, management committees, or other governing boards.

9) Represent organizations and promote their objectives at official functions, or delegate representatives to do so.

10) Serve as liaisons between organizations, shareholders, and outside organizations.

11) Administer programs for selection of sites, construction of buildings, and provision of equipment and supplies.

12) Direct, plan, and implement policies, objectives, and activities of organizations or businesses in order to ensure continuing operations, to maximize returns on investments, and to increase productivity.

13) Conduct or direct investigations or hearings to resolve complaints and violations of laws, or testify at such hearings.

14) Establish departmental responsibilities, and coordinate functions among departments and sites.

15) Direct and conduct studies and research on issues affecting areas of responsibility.

16) Direct and coordinate activities of businesses or departments concerned with production, pricing, sales, and/or distribution of products.

17) Interpret and explain policies, rules, regulations, and laws to organizations, government and corporate officials, and individuals.

18) Make presentations to legislative and other government committees regarding policies, programs, or budgets.

19) Implement corrective action plans to solve organizational or departmental problems.

20) Organize and approve promotional campaigns.

21) Review reports submitted by staff members in order to recommend approval or to suggest changes.

22) Direct and coordinate activities of businesses involved with buying and selling investment products and financial services.

23) Direct and coordinate activities between the United States Government and foreign entities in order to provide information and promote international interests and harmony.

24) Nominate citizens to boards and commissions.

25) Prepare bylaws approved by elected officials, and ensure that bylaws are enforced.

26) Refer major policy matters to elected representatives for final decisions.

27) Review and analyze legislation, laws, and public policy, and recommend changes to promote and support interests of both the general population and special groups.

28) Analyze operations to evaluate performance of a company and its staff in meeting objectives, and to determine areas of potential cost reduction, program improvement, or policy change.

29) Prepare budgets for approval, including those for funding and implementation of programs.

30) Negotiate or approve contracts and agreements with suppliers, distributors, federal and state agencies, and other organizational entities.

11-1021.00 - General and Operations Managers

Plan, direct, or coordinate the operations of companies or public and private sector organizations. Duties and responsibilities include formulating policies, managing daily operations, and planning the use of materials and human resources, but are too diverse and general in nature to be classified in any one functional area of management or administration, such as personnel, purchasing, or administrative services. Includes owners and managers who head small business establishments whose duties are primarily managerial.

Tasks

1) Determine staffing requirements, and interview, hire and train new employees, or oversee those personnel processes.

2) Review financial statements, sales and activity reports, and other performance data to measure productivity and goal achievement and to determine areas needing cost reduction and program improvement.

3) Establish and implement departmental policies, goals, objectives, and procedures, conferring with board members, organization officials, and staff members as necessary.

4) Monitor businesses and agencies to ensure that they efficiently and effectively provide needed services while staying within budgetary limits.

5) Direct and coordinate activities of businesses or departments concerned with the production, pricing, sales, and/or distribution of products.

6) Oversee activities directly related to making products or providing services.

7) Direct and coordinate organization's financial and budget activities to fund operations, maximize investments, and increase efficiency.

8) Perform sales floor work such as greeting and assisting customers, stocking shelves, and taking inventory.

9) Plan and direct activities such as sales promotions, coordinating with other department heads as required.

10) Direct non-merchandising departments of businesses, such as advertising and purchasing.

11) Determine goods and services to be sold, and set prices and credit terms, based on forecasts of customer demand.

12) Locate, select, and procure merchandise for resale, representing management in purchase negotiations.

13) Develop and implement product marketing strategies including advertising campaigns and sales promotions.

14) Manage the movement of goods into and out of production facilities.

15) Recommend locations for new facilities or oversee the remodeling of current facilities.

16) Plan store layouts, and design displays.

Knowledge	Knowledge Definitions
Administration and Management	Knowledge of business and management principles involved in strategic planning, resource allocation, human resources modeling, leadership technique, production methods, and coordination of people and resources.
Customer and Personal Service	Knowledge of principles and processes for providing customer and personal services. This includes customer needs assessment, meeting quality standards for services, and evaluation of customer satisfaction.

English Language	Knowledge of the structure and content of the English language including the meaning and spelling of words, rules of composition, and grammar.
Law and Government	Knowledge of laws, legal codes, court procedures, precedents, government regulations, executive orders, agency rules, and the democratic political process.
Personnel and Human Resources	Knowledge of principles and procedures for personnel recruitment, selection, training, compensation and benefits, labor relations and negotiation, and personnel information systems.
Sales and Marketing	Knowledge of principles and methods for showing, promoting, and selling products or services. This includes marketing strategy and tactics, product demonstration, sales techniques, and sales control systems.
Mathematics	Knowledge of arithmetic, algebra, geometry, calculus, statistics, and their applications.
Public Safety and Security	Knowledge of relevant equipment, policies, procedures, and strategies to promote effective local, state, or national security operations for the protection of people, data, property, and institutions.
Economics and Accounting	Knowledge of economic and accounting principles and practices, the financial markets, banking and the analysis and reporting of financial data.
Production and Processing	Knowledge of raw materials, production processes, quality control, costs, and other techniques for maximizing the effective manufacture and distribution of goods.
Communications and Media	Knowledge of media production, communication, and dissemination techniques and methods. This includes alternative ways to inform and entertain via written, oral, and visual media.
Computers and Electronics	Knowledge of circuit boards, processors, chips, electronic equipment, and computer hardware and software, including applications and programming.
Education and Training	Knowledge of principles and methods for curriculum and training design, teaching and instruction for individuals and groups, and the measurement of training effects.
Transportation	Knowledge of principles and methods for moving people or goods by air, rail, sea, or road, including the relative costs and benefits.
Clerical	Knowledge of administrative and clerical procedures and systems such as word processing, managing files and records, stenography and transcription, designing forms, and other office procedures and terminology.
Psychology	Knowledge of human behavior and performance; individual differences in ability, personality, and interests; learning and motivation; psychological research methods; and the assessment and treatment of behavioral and affective disorders.
Engineering and Technology	Knowledge of the practical application of engineering science and technology. This includes applying principles, techniques, procedures, and equipment to the design and production of various goods and services.
Mechanical	Knowledge of machines and tools, including their designs, uses, repair, and maintenance.
Therapy and Counseling	Knowledge of principles, methods, and procedures for diagnosis, treatment, and rehabilitation of physical and mental dysfunctions, and for career counseling and guidance.
Telecommunications	Knowledge of transmission, broadcasting, switching, control, and operation of telecommunications systems.
Design	Knowledge of design techniques, tools, and principles involved in production of precision technical plans, blueprints, drawings, and models.
Sociology and Anthropology	Knowledge of group behavior and dynamics, societal trends and influences, human migrations, ethnicity, cultures and their history and origins.
Philosophy and Theology	Knowledge of different philosophical systems and religions. This includes their basic principles, values, ethics, ways of thinking, customs, practices, and their impact on human culture.
Geography	Knowledge of principles and methods for describing the features of land, sea, and air masses, including their physical characteristics, locations, interrelationships, and distribution of plant, animal, and human life.
Medicine and Dentistry	Knowledge of the information and techniques needed to diagnose and treat human injuries, diseases, and deformities. This includes symptoms, treatment alternatives, drug properties and interactions, and preventive health-care measures.

Building and Construction	Knowledge of materials, methods, and the tools involved in the construction or repair of houses, buildings, or other structures such as highways and roads.
Food Production	Knowledge of techniques and equipment for planting, growing, and harvesting food products (both plant and animal) for consumption, including storage/handling techniques.
Chemistry	Knowledge of the chemical composition, structure, and properties of substances and of the chemical processes and transformations that they undergo. This includes uses of chemicals and their interactions, danger signs, production techniques, and disposal methods.
Biology	Knowledge of plant and animal organisms, their tissues, cells, functions, interdependencies, and interactions with each other and the environment.
Physics	Knowledge and prediction of physical principles, laws, their interrelationships, and applications to understanding fluid, material, and atmospheric dynamics, and mechanical, electrical, atomic and sub-atomic structures and processes.
Foreign Language	Knowledge of the structure and content of a foreign (non-English) language including the meaning and spelling of words, rules of composition and grammar, and pronunciation.
History and Archeology	Knowledge of historical events and their causes, indicators, and effects on civilizations and cultures.
Fine Arts	Knowledge of the theory and techniques required to compose, produce, and perform works of music, dance, visual arts, drama, and sculpture.

Skills	Skills Definitions
Active Listening	Giving full attention to what other people are saying, taking time to understand the points being made, asking questions as appropriate, and not interrupting at inappropriate times.
Management of Personnel Resources	Motivating, developing, and directing people as they work, identifying the best people for the job.
Time Management	Managing one's own time and the time of others.
Monitoring	Monitoring/Assessing performance of yourself, other individuals, or organizations to make improvements or take corrective action.
Judgment and Decision Making	Considering the relative costs and benefits of potential actions to choose the most appropriate one.
Reading Comprehension	Understanding written sentences and paragraphs in work related documents.
Speaking	Talking to others to convey information effectively.
Management of Financial Resources	Determining how money will be spent to get the work done, and accounting for these expenditures.
Active Learning	Understanding the implications of new information for both current and future problem-solving and decision-making.
Persuasion	Persuading others to change their minds or behavior.
Coordination	Adjusting actions in relation to others' actions.
Negotiation	Bringing others together and trying to reconcile differences.
Critical Thinking	Using logic and reasoning to identify the strengths and weaknesses of alternative solutions, conclusions or approaches to problems.
Writing	Communicating effectively in writing as appropriate for the needs of the audience.
Instructing	Teaching others how to do something.
Management of Material Resources	Obtaining and seeing to the appropriate use of equipment, facilities, and materials needed to do certain work.
Learning Strategies	Selecting and using training/instructional methods and procedures appropriate for the situation when learning or teaching new things.
Service Orientation	Actively looking for ways to help people.
Social Perceptiveness	Being aware of others' reactions and understanding why they react as they do.
Mathematics	Using mathematics to solve problems.
Quality Control Analysis	Conducting tests and inspections of products, services, or processes to evaluate quality or performance.
Complex Problem Solving	Identifying complex problems and reviewing related information to develop and evaluate options and implement solutions.
Troubleshooting	Determining causes of operating errors and deciding what to do about it.
Equipment Selection	Determining the kind of tools and equipment needed to do a job.
Operations Analysis	Analyzing needs and product requirements to create a design.
Systems Analysis	Determining how a system should work and how changes in conditions, operations, and the environment will affect outcomes.

Systems Evaluation	Identifying measures or indicators of system performance and the actions needed to improve or correct performance, relative to the goals of the system.
Science	Using scientific rules and methods to solve problems.
Equipment Maintenance	Performing routine maintenance on equipment and determining when and what kind of maintenance is needed.
Technology Design	Generating or adapting equipment and technology to serve user needs.
Operation and Control	Controlling operations of equipment or systems.
Repairing	Repairing machines or systems using the needed tools.
Operation Monitoring	Watching gauges, dials, or other indicators to make sure a machine is working properly.
Installation	Installing equipment, machines, wiring, or programs to meet specifications.
Programming	Writing computer programs for various purposes.

Ability	Ability Definitions
Oral Expression	The ability to communicate information and ideas in speaking so others will understand.
Oral Comprehension	The ability to listen to and understand information and ideas presented through spoken words and sentences.
Problem Sensitivity	The ability to tell when something is wrong or is likely to go wrong. It does not involve solving the problem, only recognizing there is a problem.
Written Comprehension	The ability to read and understand information and ideas presented in writing.
Speech Clarity	The ability to speak clearly so others can understand you.
Speech Recognition	The ability to identify and understand the speech of another person.
Inductive Reasoning	The ability to combine pieces of information to form general rules or conclusions (includes finding a relationship among seemingly unrelated events).
Deductive Reasoning	The ability to apply general rules to specific problems to produce answers that make sense.
Written Expression	The ability to communicate information and ideas in writing so others will understand.
Near Vision	The ability to see details at close range (within a few feet of the observer).
Originality	The ability to come up with unusual or clever ideas about a given topic or situation, or to develop creative ways to solve a problem.
Fluency of Ideas	The ability to come up with a number of ideas about a topic (the number of ideas is important, not their quality, correctness, or creativity).
Category Flexibility	The ability to generate or use different sets of rules for combining or grouping things in different ways.
Mathematical Reasoning	The ability to choose the right mathematical methods or formulas to solve a problem.
Information Ordering	The ability to arrange things or actions in a certain order or pattern according to a specific rule or set of rules (e.g., patterns of numbers, letters, words, pictures, mathematical operations).
Time Sharing	The ability to shift back and forth between two or more activities or sources of information (such as speech, sounds, touch, or other sources).
Flexibility of Closure	The ability to identify or detect a known pattern (a figure, object, word, or sound) that is hidden in other distracting material.
Selective Attention	The ability to concentrate on a task over a period of time without being distracted.
Visualization	The ability to imagine how something will look after it is moved around or when its parts are moved or rearranged.
Number Facility	The ability to add, subtract, multiply, or divide quickly and correctly.
Perceptual Speed	The ability to quickly and accurately compare similarities and differences among sets of letters, numbers, objects, pictures, or patterns. The things to be compared may be presented at the same time or one after the other. This ability also includes comparing a presented object with a remembered object.
Far Vision	The ability to see details at a distance.
Visual Color Discrimination	The ability to match or detect differences between colors, including shades of color and brightness.
Depth Perception	The ability to judge which of several objects is closer or farther away from you, or to judge the distance between you and an object.
Memorization	The ability to remember information such as words, numbers, pictures, and procedures.

Trunk Strength	The ability to use your abdominal and lower back muscles to support part of the body repeatedly or continuously over time without 'giving out' or fatiguing.
Finger Dexterity	The ability to make precisely coordinated movements of the fingers of one or both hands to grasp, manipulate, or assemble very small objects.
Auditory Attention	The ability to focus on a single source of sound in the presence of other distracting sounds.
Speed of Closure	The ability to quickly make sense of, combine, and organize information into meaningful patterns.
Stamina	The ability to exert yourself physically over long periods of time without getting winded or out of breath.
Hearing Sensitivity	The ability to detect or tell the differences between sounds that vary in pitch and loudness.
Speed of Limb Movement	The ability to quickly move the arms and legs.
Control Precision	The ability to quickly and repeatedly adjust the controls of a machine or a vehicle to exact positions.
Multilimb Coordination	The ability to coordinate two or more limbs (for example, two arms, two legs, or one leg and one arm) while sitting, standing, or lying down. It does not involve performing the activities while the whole body is in motion.
Gross Body Coordination	The ability to coordinate the movement of your arms, legs, and torso together when the whole body is in motion.
Spatial Orientation	The ability to know your location in relation to the environment or to know where other objects are in relation to you.
Response Orientation	The ability to choose quickly between two or more movements in response to two or more different signals (lights, sounds, pictures). It includes the speed with which the correct response is started with the hand, foot, or other body part.
Static Strength	The ability to exert maximum muscle force to lift, push, pull, or carry objects.
Manual Dexterity	The ability to quickly move your hand, your hand together with your arm, or your two hands to grasp, manipulate, or assemble objects.
Extent Flexibility	The ability to bend, stretch, twist, or reach with your body, arms, and/or legs.
Peripheral Vision	The ability to see objects or movement of objects to one's side when the eyes are looking ahead.
Sound Localization	The ability to tell the direction from which a sound originated.
Night Vision	The ability to see under low light conditions.
Wrist-Finger Speed	The ability to make fast, simple, repeated movements of the fingers, hands, and wrists.
Arm-Hand Steadiness	The ability to keep your hand and arm steady while moving your arm or while holding your arm and hand in one position.
Gross Body Equilibrium	The ability to keep or regain your body balance or stay upright when in an unstable position.
Glare Sensitivity	The ability to see objects in the presence of glare or bright lighting.
Dynamic Flexibility	The ability to quickly and repeatedly bend, stretch, twist, or reach out with your body, arms, and/or legs.
Reaction Time	The ability to quickly respond (with the hand, finger, or foot) to a signal (sound, light, picture) when it appears.
Explosive Strength	The ability to use short bursts of muscle force to propel oneself (as in jumping or sprinting), or to throw an object.
Dynamic Strength	The ability to exert muscle force repeatedly or continuously over time. This involves muscular endurance and resistance to muscle fatigue.
Rate Control	The ability to time your movements or the movement of a piece of equipment in anticipation of changes in the speed and/or direction of a moving object or scene.

Work_Activity	Work_Activity Definitions
Getting Information	Observing, receiving, and otherwise obtaining information from all relevant sources.
Communicating with Supervisors, Peers, or Subordin	Providing information to supervisors, co-workers, and subordinates by telephone, in written form, e-mail, or in person.
Establishing and Maintaining Interpersonal Relatio	Developing constructive and cooperative working relationships with others, and maintaining them over time.
Resolving Conflicts and Negotiating with Others	Handling complaints, settling disputes, and resolving grievances and conflicts, or otherwise negotiating with others.
Evaluating Information to Determine Compliance wit	Using relevant information and individual judgment to determine whether events or processes comply with laws, regulations, or standards.
Making Decisions and Solving Problems	Analyzing information and evaluating results to choose the best solution and solve problems.

3

Performing for or Working Directly with the Public	Performing for people or dealing directly with the public. This includes serving customers in restaurants and stores, and receiving clients or guests.
Developing and Building Teams	Encouraging and building mutual trust, respect, and cooperation among team members.
Coaching and Developing Others	Identifying the developmental needs of others and coaching, mentoring, or otherwise helping others to improve their knowledge or skills.
Updating and Using Relevant Knowledge	Keeping up-to-date technically and applying new knowledge to your job.
Scheduling Work and Activities	Scheduling events, programs, and activities, as well as the work of others.
Monitoring and Controlling Resources	Monitoring and controlling resources and overseeing the spending of money.
Guiding, Directing, and Motivating Subordinates	Providing guidance and direction to subordinates, including setting performance standards and monitoring performance.
Training and Teaching Others	Identifying the educational needs of others, developing formal educational or training programs or classes, and teaching or instructing others.
Analyzing Data or Information	Identifying the underlying principles, reasons, or facts of information by breaking down information or data into separate parts.
Processing Information	Compiling, coding, categorizing, calculating, tabulating, auditing, or verifying information or data.
Organizing, Planning, and Prioritizing Work	Developing specific goals and plans to prioritize, organize, and accomplish your work.
Communicating with Persons Outside Organization	Communicating with people outside the organization, representing the organization to customers, the public, government, and other external sources. This information can be exchanged in person, in writing, or by telephone or e-mail.
Documenting/Recording Information	Entering, transcribing, recording, storing, or maintaining information in written or electronic/magnetic form.
Performing Administrative Activities	Performing day-to-day administrative tasks such as maintaining information files and processing paperwork.
Identifying Objects, Actions, and Events'	Identifying information by categorizing, estimating, recognizing differences or similarities, and detecting changes in circumstances or events.
Staffing Organizational Units	Recruiting, interviewing, selecting, hiring, and promoting employees in an organization.
Interacting With Computers	Using computers and computer systems (including hardware and software) to program, write software, set up functions, enter data, or process information.
Monitor Processes, Materials, or Surroundings	Monitoring and reviewing information from materials, events, or the environment, to detect or assess problems.
Judging the Qualities of Things, Services, or Peop	Assessing the value, importance, or quality of things or people.
Provide Consultation and Advice to Others	Providing guidance and expert advice to management or other groups on technical, systems-, or process-related topics.
Coordinating the Work and Activities of Others	Getting members of a group to work together to accomplish tasks.
Developing Objectives and Strategies	Establishing long-range objectives and specifying the strategies and actions to achieve them.
Thinking Creatively	Developing, designing, or creating new applications, ideas, relationships, systems, or products, including artistic contributions.
Interpreting the Meaning of Information for Others	Translating or explaining what information means and how it can be used.
Estimating the Quantifiable Characteristics of Pro	Estimating sizes, distances, and quantities; or determining time, costs, resources, or materials needed to perform a work activity.
Inspecting Equipment, Structures, or Material	Inspecting equipment, structures, or materials to identify the cause of errors or other problems or defects.
Assisting and Caring for Others	Providing personal assistance, medical attention, emotional support, or other personal care to others such as coworkers, customers, or patients.
Selling or Influencing Others	Convincing others to buy merchandise/goods or to otherwise change their minds or actions.
Controlling Machines and Processes	Using either control mechanisms or direct physical activity to operate machines or processes (not including computers or vehicles).
Performing General Physical Activities	Performing physical activities that require considerable use of your arms and legs and moving your whole body, such as climbing, lifting, balancing, walking, stooping, and handling of materials.
Handling and Moving Objects	Using hands and arms in handling, installing, positioning, and moving materials, and manipulating things.
Drafting, Laying Out, and Specifying Technical Dev	Providing documentation, detailed instructions, drawings, or specifications to tell others about how devices, parts, equipment, or structures are to be fabricated, constructed, assembled, modified, maintained, or used.
Operating Vehicles, Mechanized Devices, or Equipme	Running, maneuvering, navigating, or driving vehicles or mechanized equipment, such as forklifts, passenger vehicles, aircraft, or water craft.
Repairing and Maintaining Mechanical Equipment	Servicing, repairing, adjusting, and testing machines, devices, moving parts, and equipment that operate primarily on the basis of mechanical (not electronic) principles.
Repairing and Maintaining Electronic Equipment	Servicing, repairing, calibrating, regulating, fine-tuning, or testing machines, devices, and equipment that operate primarily on the basis of electrical or electronic (not mechanical) principles.

Work_Context	Work_Context Definitions
Telephone	How often do you have telephone conversations in this job?
Work With Work Group or Team	How important is it to work with others in a group or team in this job?
Face-to-Face Discussions	How often do you have to have face-to-face discussions with individuals or teams in this job?
Contact With Others	How much does this job require the worker to be in contact with others (face-to-face, by telephone, or otherwise) in order to perform it?
Frequency of Decision Making	How frequently is the worker required to make decisions that affect other people, the financial resources, and/or the image and reputation of the organization?
Freedom to Make Decisions	How much decision making freedom, without supervision, does the job offer?
Importance of Being Exact or Accurate	How important is being very exact or highly accurate in performing this job?
Indoors, Environmentally Controlled	How often does this job require working indoors in environmentally controlled conditions?
Impact of Decisions on Co-workers or Company Resul	How do the decisions an employee makes impact the results of co-workers, clients or the company?
Responsibility for Outcomes and Results	How responsible is the worker for work outcomes and results of other workers?
Deal With External Customers	How important is it to work with external customers or the public in this job?
Structured versus Unstructured Work	To what extent is this job structured for the worker, rather than allowing the worker to determine tasks, priorities, and goals?
Coordinate or Lead Others	How important is it to coordinate or lead others in accomplishing work activities in this job?
Time Pressure	How often does this job require the worker to meet strict deadlines?
Responsible for Others' Health and Safety	How much responsibility is there for the health and safety of others in this job?
Electronic Mail	How often do you use electronic mail in this job?
Deal With Unpleasant or Angry People	How frequently does the worker have to deal with unpleasant, angry, or discourteous individuals as part of the job requirements?
Letters and Memos	How often does the job require written letters and memos?
Importance of Repeating Same Tasks	How important is repeating the same physical activities (e.g., key entry) or mental activities (e.g., checking entries in a ledger) over and over, without stopping, to performing this job?
Frequency of Conflict Situations	How often are there conflict situations the employee has to face in this job?
Sounds, Noise Levels Are Distracting or Uncomforta	How often does this job require working exposed to sounds and noise levels that are distracting or uncomfortable?
Spend Time Standing	How much does this job require standing?
Consequence of Error	How serious would the result usually be if the worker made a mistake that was not readily correctable?
Physical Proximity	To what extent does this job require the worker to perform job tasks in close physical proximity to other people?
Spend Time Walking and Running	How much does this job require walking and running?
Spend Time Sitting	How much does this job require sitting?
Spend Time Making Repetitive Motions	How much does this job require making repetitive motions?
Level of Competition	To what extent does this job require the worker to compete or to be aware of competitive pressures?
Indoors, Not Environmentally Controlled	How often does this job require working indoors in non-controlled environmental conditions (e.g., warehouse without heat)?
In an Enclosed Vehicle or Equipment	How often does this job require working in a closed vehicle or equipment (e.g., car)?

Outdoors, Exposed to Weather	How often does this job require working outdoors, exposed to all weather conditions?
Public Speaking	How often do you have to perform public speaking in this job?
Degree of Automation	How automated is the job?
Spend Time Using Your Hands to Handle, Control, or	How much does this job require using your hands to handle, control, or feel objects, tools or controls?
Wear Common Protective or Safety Equipment such as	How much does this job require wearing common protective or safety equipment such as safety shoes, glasses, gloves, hard hats or live jackets?
Very Hot or Cold Temperatures	How often does this job require working in very hot (above 90 F degrees) or very cold (below 32 F degrees) temperatures?
Exposed to Contaminants	How often does this job require working exposed to contaminants (such as pollutants, gases, dust or odors)?
In an Open Vehicle or Equipment	How often does this job require working in an open vehicle or equipment (e.g., tractor)?
Spend Time Bending or Twisting the Body	How much does this job require bending or twisting your body?
Pace Determined by Speed of Equipment	How important is it to this job that the pace is determined by the speed of equipment or machinery? (This does not refer to keeping busy at all times on this job.)
Spend Time Kneeling, Crouching, Stooping, or Crawl	How much does this job require kneeling, crouching, stooping or crawling?
Extremely Bright or Inadequate Lighting	How often does this job require working in extremely bright or inadequate lighting conditions?
Exposed to Hazardous Equipment	How often does this job require exposure to hazardous equipment?
Deal With Physically Aggressive People	How frequently does this job require the worker to deal with physical aggression of violent individuals?
Cramped Work Space, Awkward Positions	How often does this job require working in cramped work spaces that requires getting into awkward positions?
Spend Time Climbing Ladders, Scaffolds, or Poles	How much does this job require climbing ladders, scaffolds, or poles?
Exposed to High Places	How often does this job require exposure to high places?
Exposed to Minor Burns, Cuts, Bites, or Stings	How often does this job require exposure to minor burns, cuts, bites, or stings?
Outdoors, Under Cover	How often does this job require working outdoors, under cover (e.g., structure with roof but no walls)?
Exposed to Whole Body Vibration	How often does this job require exposure to whole body vibration (e.g., operate a jackhammer)?
Exposed to Disease or Infections	How often does this job require exposure to disease/infections?
Exposed to Hazardous Conditions	How often does this job require exposure to hazardous conditions?
Exposed to Radiation	How often does this job require exposure to radiation?
Wear Specialized Protective or Safety Equipment su	How much does this job require wearing specialized protective or safety equipment such as breathing apparatus, safety harness, full protection suits, or radiation protection?
Spend Time Keeping or Regaining Balance	How much does this job require keeping or regaining your balance?

Job Zone Component	Job Zone Component Definitions
Title	Job Zone Four: Considerable Preparation Needed
Overall Experience	A minimum of two to four years of work-related skill, knowledge, or experience is needed for these occupations. For example, an accountant must complete four years of college and work for several years in accounting to be considered qualified.
Job Training	Employees in these occupations usually need several years of work-related experience, on-the-job training, and/or vocational training.
Job Zone Examples	Many of these occupations involve coordinating, supervising, managing, or training others. Examples include accountants, chefs and head cooks, computer programmers, historians, pharmacists, and police detectives.
SVP Range	(7.0 to < 8.0)
Education	Most of these occupations require a four - year bachelor's degree, but some do not.

Work_Styles	Work_Styles Definitions
Dependability	Job requires being reliable, responsible, and dependable, and fulfilling obligations.
Leadership	Job requires a willingness to lead, take charge, and offer opinions and direction.
Integrity	Job requires being honest and ethical.
Attention to Detail	Job requires being careful about detail and thorough in completing work tasks.
Initiative	Job requires a willingness to take on responsibilities and challenges.
Self Control	Job requires maintaining composure, keeping emotions in check, controlling anger, and avoiding aggressive behavior, even in very difficult situations.
Cooperation	Job requires being pleasant with others on the job and displaying a good-natured, cooperative attitude.
Concern for Others	Job requires being sensitive to others' needs and feelings and being understanding and helpful on the job.
Analytical Thinking	Job requires analyzing information and using logic to address work-related issues and problems.
Independence	Job requires developing one's own ways of doing things, guiding oneself with little or no supervision, and depending on oneself to get things done.
Stress Tolerance	Job requires accepting criticism and dealing calmly and effectively with high stress situations.
Social Orientation	Job requires preferring to work with others rather than alone, and being personally connected with others on the job.
Innovation	Job requires creativity and alternative thinking to develop new ideas for and answers to work-related problems.
Adaptability/Flexibility	Job requires being open to change (positive or negative) and to considerable variety in the workplace.
Persistence	Job requires persistence in the face of obstacles.
Achievement/Effort	Job requires establishing and maintaining personally challenging achievement goals and exerting effort toward mastering tasks.

11-2011.00 - Advertising and Promotions Managers

Plan and direct advertising policies and programs or produce collateral materials, such as posters, contests, coupons, or give-aways, to create extra interest in the purchase of a product or service for a department, an entire organization, or on an account basis.

Tasks

1) Read trade journals and professional literature to stay informed on trends, innovations, and changes that affect media planning.

2) Gather and organize information to plan advertising campaigns.

3) Plan and prepare advertising and promotional material to increase sales of products or services, working with customers, company officials, sales departments and advertising agencies.

4) Prepare and negotiate advertising and sales contracts.

5) Inspect layouts and advertising copy and edit scripts, audio and video tapes, and other promotional material for adherence to specifications.

6) Identify and develop contacts for promotional campaigns and industry programs that meet identified buyer targets such as dealers, distributors, or consumers.

7) Coordinate activities of departments, such as sales, graphic arts, media, finance, and research.

8) Prepare budgets and submit estimates for program costs as part of campaign plan development.

9) Assist with annual budget development.

10) Monitor and analyze sales promotion results to determine cost effectiveness of promotion campaigns.

11) Confer with clients to provide marketing or technical advice.

12) Represent company at trade association meetings to promote products.

13) Formulate plans to extend business with established accounts and to transact business as agent for advertising accounts.

14) Provide presentation and product demonstration support during the introduction of new products and services to field staff and customers.

15) Plan and execute advertising policies and strategies for organizations.

16) Coordinate with the media to disseminate advertising.

17) Direct, motivate, and monitor the mobilization of a campaign team to advance campaign goals.

18) Track program budgets and expenses and campaign response rates to evaluate each campaign based on program objectives and industry norms.

19) Contact organizations to explain services and facilities offered.

20) Train and direct workers engaged in developing and producing advertisements.

21) Consult publications to learn about conventions and social functions and to organize prospect files for promotional purposes.

22) Direct and coordinate product research and development.

23) Assemble and communicate with a strong, diverse coalition of organizations and/or public figures, securing their cooperation, support and action, to further campaign goals.

Knowledge	Knowledge Definitions
English Language	Knowledge of the structure and content of the English language including the meaning and spelling of words, rules of composition, and grammar.
Sales and Marketing	Knowledge of principles and methods for showing, promoting, and selling products or services. This includes marketing strategy and tactics, product demonstration, sales techniques, and sales control systems.
Communications and Media	Knowledge of media production, communication, and dissemination techniques and methods. This includes alternative ways to inform and entertain via written, oral, and visual media.
Customer and Personal Service	Knowledge of principles and processes for providing customer and personal services. This includes customer needs assessment, meeting quality standards for services, and evaluation of customer satisfaction.
Administration and Management	Knowledge of business and management principles involved in strategic planning, resource allocation, human resources modeling, leadership technique, production methods, and coordination of people and resources.
Design	Knowledge of design techniques, tools, and principles involved in production of precision technical plans, blueprints, drawings, and models.
Computers and Electronics	Knowledge of circuit boards, processors, chips, electronic equipment, and computer hardware and software, including applications and programming.
Production and Processing	Knowledge of raw materials, production processes, quality control, costs, and other techniques for maximizing the effective manufacture and distribution of goods.
Fine Arts	Knowledge of the theory and techniques required to compose, produce, and perform works of music, dance, visual arts, drama, and sculpture.
Clerical	Knowledge of administrative and clerical procedures and systems such as word processing, managing files and records, stenography and transcription, designing forms, and other office procedures and terminology.
Law and Government	Knowledge of laws, legal codes, court procedures, precedents, government regulations, executive orders, agency rules, and the democratic political process.
Mathematics	Knowledge of arithmetic, algebra, geometry, calculus, statistics, and their applications.
Education and Training	Knowledge of principles and methods for curriculum and training design, teaching and instruction for individuals and groups, and the measurement of training effects.
Transportation	Knowledge of principles and methods for moving people or goods by air, rail, sea, or road, including the relative costs and benefits.
Public Safety and Security	Knowledge of relevant equipment, policies, procedures, and strategies to promote effective local, state, or national security operations for the protection of people, data, property, and institutions.
Sociology and Anthropology	Knowledge of group behavior and dynamics, societal trends and influences, human migrations, ethnicity, cultures and their history and origins.
Personnel and Human Resources	Knowledge of principles and procedures for personnel recruitment, selection, training, compensation and benefits, labor relations and negotiation, and personnel information systems.
Economics and Accounting	Knowledge of economic and accounting principles and practices, the financial markets, banking and the analysis and reporting of financial data.
Telecommunications	Knowledge of transmission, broadcasting, switching, control, and operation of telecommunications systems.
Psychology	Knowledge of human behavior and performance; individual differences in ability, personality, and interests; learning and motivation; psychological research methods; and the assessment and treatment of behavioral and affective disorders.
History and Archeology	Knowledge of historical events and their causes, indicators, and effects on civilizations and cultures.
Philosophy and Theology	Knowledge of different philosophical systems and religions. This includes their basic principles, values, ethics, ways of thinking, customs, practices, and their impact on human culture.
Mechanical	Knowledge of machines and tools, including their designs, uses, repair, and maintenance.
Foreign Language	Knowledge of the structure and content of a foreign (non-English) language including the meaning and spelling of words, rules of composition and grammar, and pronunciation.
Engineering and Technology	Knowledge of the practical application of engineering science and technology. This includes applying principles, techniques, procedures, and equipment to the design and production of various goods and services.
Building and Construction	Knowledge of materials, methods, and the tools involved in the construction or repair of houses, buildings, or other structures such as highways and roads.
Geography	Knowledge of principles and methods for describing the features of land, sea, and air masses, including their physical characteristics, locations, interrelationships, and distribution of plant, animal, and human life.
Therapy and Counseling	Knowledge of principles, methods, and procedures for diagnosis, treatment, and rehabilitation of physical and mental dysfunctions, and for career counseling and guidance.
Chemistry	Knowledge of the chemical composition, structure, and properties of substances and of the chemical processes and transformations that they undergo. This includes uses of chemicals and their interactions, danger signs, production techniques, and disposal methods.
Physics	Knowledge and prediction of physical principles, laws, their interrelationships, and applications to understanding fluid, material, and atmospheric dynamics, and mechanical, electrical, atomic and sub- atomic structures and processes.
Medicine and Dentistry	Knowledge of the information and techniques needed to diagnose and treat human injuries, diseases, and deformities. This includes symptoms, treatment alternatives, drug properties and interactions, and preventive health-care measures.
Biology	Knowledge of plant and animal organisms, their tissues, cells, functions, interdependencies, and interactions with each other and the environment.
Food Production	Knowledge of techniques and equipment for planting, growing, and harvesting food products (both plant and animal) for consumption, including storage/handling techniques.

Skills	Skills Definitions
Writing	Communicating effectively in writing as appropriate for the needs of the audience.
Service Orientation	Actively looking for ways to help people.
Active Listening	Giving full attention to what other people are saying, taking time to understand the points being made, asking questions as appropriate, and not interrupting at inappropriate times.
Reading Comprehension	Understanding written sentences and paragraphs in work related documents.
Time Management	Managing one's own time and the time of others.
Speaking	Talking to others to convey information effectively.
Judgment and Decision Making	Considering the relative costs and benefits of potential actions to choose the most appropriate one.
Persuasion	Persuading others to change their minds or behavior.
Critical Thinking	Using logic and reasoning to identify the strengths and weaknesses of alternative solutions, conclusions or approaches to problems.
Management of Financial Resources	Determining how money will be spent to get the work done, and accounting for these expenditures.
Coordination	Adjusting actions in relation to others' actions.
Instructing	Teaching others how to do something.
Active Learning	Understanding the implications of new information for both current and future problem-solving and decision-making.
Mathematics	Using mathematics to solve problems.
Social Perceptiveness	Being aware of others' reactions and understanding why they react as they do.
Negotiation	Bringing others together and trying to reconcile differences.
Monitoring	Monitoring/Assessing performance of yourself, other individuals, or organizations to make improvements or take corrective action.
Management of Personnel Resources	Motivating, developing, and directing people as they work, identifying the best people for the job.

Complex Problem Solving	Identifying complex problems and reviewing related information to develop and evaluate options and implement solutions.
Learning Strategies	Selecting and using training/instructional methods and procedures appropriate for the situation when learning or teaching new things.
Operations Analysis	Analyzing needs and product requirements to create a design.
Equipment Selection	Determining the kind of tools and equipment needed to do a job.
Technology Design	Generating or adapting equipment and technology to serve user needs.
Management of Material Resources	Obtaining and seeing to the appropriate use of equipment, facilities, and materials needed to do certain work.
Quality Control Analysis	Conducting tests and inspections of products, services, or processes to evaluate quality or performance.
Troubleshooting	Determining causes of operating errors and deciding what to do about it.
Systems Evaluation	Identifying measures or indicators of system performance and the actions needed to improve or correct performance, relative to the goals of the system.
Operation and Control	Controlling operations of equipment or systems.
Systems Analysis	Determining how a system should work and how changes in conditions, operations, and the environment will affect outcomes.
Science	Using scientific rules and methods to solve problems.
Operation Monitoring	Watching gauges, dials, or other indicators to make sure a machine is working properly.
Installation	Installing equipment, machines, wiring, or programs to meet specifications.
Repairing	Repairing machines or systems using the needed tools.
Equipment Maintenance	Performing routine maintenance on equipment and determining when and what kind of maintenance is needed.
Programming	Writing computer programs for various purposes.

Ability	Ability Definitions
Oral Comprehension	The ability to listen to and understand information and ideas presented through spoken words and sentences.
Oral Expression	The ability to communicate information and ideas in speaking so others will understand.
Speech Clarity	The ability to speak clearly so others can understand you.
Problem Sensitivity	The ability to tell when something is wrong or is likely to go wrong. It does not involve solving the problem, only recognizing there is a problem.
Written Expression	The ability to communicate information and ideas in writing so others will understand.
Inductive Reasoning	The ability to combine pieces of information to form general rules or conclusions (includes finding a relationship among seemingly unrelated events).
Speech Recognition	The ability to identify and understand the speech of another person.
Written Comprehension	The ability to read and understand information and ideas presented in writing.
Originality	The ability to come up with unusual or clever ideas about a given topic or situation, or to develop creative ways to solve a problem.
Deductive Reasoning	The ability to apply general rules to specific problems to produce answers that make sense.
Fluency of Ideas	The ability to come up with a number of ideas about a topic (the number of ideas is important, not their quality, correctness, or creativity).
Near Vision	The ability to see details at close range (within a few feet of the observer).
Category Flexibility	The ability to generate or use different sets of rules for combining or grouping things in different ways.
Information Ordering	The ability to arrange things or actions in a certain order or pattern according to a specific rule or set of rules (e.g., patterns of numbers, letters, words, pictures, mathematical operations).
Number Facility	The ability to add, subtract, multiply, or divide quickly and correctly.
Selective Attention	The ability to concentrate on a task over a period of time without being distracted.
Mathematical Reasoning	The ability to choose the right mathematical methods or formulas to solve a problem.
Speed of Closure	The ability to quickly make sense of, combine, and organize information into meaningful patterns.
Visual Color Discrimination	The ability to match or detect differences between colors, including shades of color and brightness.

Time Sharing	The ability to shift back and forth between two or more activities or sources of information (such as speech, sounds, touch, or other sources).
Memorization	The ability to remember information such as words, numbers, pictures, and procedures.
Visualization	The ability to imagine how something will look after it is moved around or when its parts are moved or rearranged.
Far Vision	The ability to see details at a distance.
Perceptual Speed	The ability to quickly and accurately compare similarities and differences among sets of letters, numbers, objects, pictures, or patterns. The things to be compared may be presented at the same time or one after the other. This ability also includes comparing a presented object with a remembered object.
Flexibility of Closure	The ability to identify or detect a known pattern (a figure, object, word, or sound) that is hidden in other distracting material.
Hearing Sensitivity	The ability to detect or tell the differences between sounds that vary in pitch and loudness.
Depth Perception	The ability to judge which of several objects is closer or farther away from you, or to judge the distance between you and an object.
Finger Dexterity	The ability to make precisely coordinated movements of the fingers of one or both hands to grasp, manipulate, or assemble very small objects.
Auditory Attention	The ability to focus on a single source of sound in the presence of other distracting sounds.
Multilimb Coordination	The ability to coordinate two or more limbs (for example, two arms, two legs, or one leg and one arm) while sitting, standing, or lying down. It does not involve performing the activities while the whole body is in motion.
Arm-Hand Steadiness	The ability to keep your hand and arm steady while moving your arm or while holding your arm and hand in one position.
Manual Dexterity	The ability to quickly move your hand, your hand together with your arm, or your two hands to grasp, manipulate, or assemble objects.
Control Precision	The ability to quickly and repeatedly adjust the controls of a machine or a vehicle to exact positions.
Trunk Strength	The ability to use your abdominal and lower back muscles to support part of the body repeatedly or continuously over time without 'giving out' or fatiguing.
Spatial Orientation	The ability to know your location in relation to the environment or to know where other objects are in relation to you.
Peripheral Vision	The ability to see objects or movement of objects to one's side when the eyes are looking ahead.
Dynamic Strength	The ability to exert muscle force repeatedly or continuously over time. This involves muscular endurance and resistance to muscle fatigue.
Gross Body Coordination	The ability to coordinate the movement of your arms, legs, and torso together when the whole body is in motion.
Response Orientation	The ability to choose quickly between two or more movements in response to two or more different signals (lights, sounds, pictures). It includes the speed with which the correct response is started with the hand, foot, or other body part.
Rate Control	The ability to time your movements or the movement of a piece of equipment in anticipation of changes in the speed and/or direction of a moving object or scene.
Reaction Time	The ability to quickly respond (with the hand, finger, or foot) to a signal (sound, light, picture) when it appears.
Wrist-Finger Speed	The ability to make fast, simple, repeated movements of the fingers, hands, and wrists.
Speed of Limb Movement	The ability to quickly move the arms and legs.
Glare Sensitivity	The ability to see objects in the presence of glare or bright lighting.
Explosive Strength	The ability to use short bursts of muscle force to propel oneself (as in jumping or sprinting), or to throw an object.
Stamina	The ability to exert yourself physically over long periods of time without getting winded or out of breath.
Dynamic Flexibility	The ability to quickly and repeatedly bend, stretch, twist, or reach out with your body, arms, and/or legs.
Gross Body Equilibrium	The ability to keep or regain your body balance or stay upright when in an unstable position.
Sound Localization	The ability to tell the direction from which a sound originated.
Night Vision	The ability to see under low light conditions.
Extent Flexibility	The ability to bend, stretch, twist, or reach with your body, arms, and/or legs.
Static Strength	The ability to exert maximum muscle force to lift, push, pull, or carry objects.

7

Work_Activity	Work_Activity Definitions
Organizing, Planning, and Prioritizing Work	Developing specific goals and plans to prioritize, organize, and accomplish your work.
Getting Information	Observing, receiving, and otherwise obtaining information from all relevant sources.
Making Decisions and Solving Problems	Analyzing information and evaluating results to choose the best solution and solve problems.
Performing for or Working Directly with the Public	Performing for people or dealing directly with the public. This includes serving customers in restaurants and stores, and receiving clients or guests.
Establishing and Maintaining Interpersonal Relatio	Developing constructive and cooperative working relationships with others, and maintaining them over time.
Interacting With Computers	Using computers and computer systems (including hardware and software) to program, write software, set up functions, enter data, or process information.
Performing Administrative Activities	Performing day-to-day administrative tasks such as maintaining information files and processing paperwork.
Communicating with Persons Outside Organization	Communicating with people outside the organization, representing the organization to customers, the public, government, and other external sources. This information can be exchanged in person, in writing, or by telephone or e-mail.
Thinking Creatively	Developing, designing, or creating new applications, ideas, relationships, systems, or products, including artistic contributions.
Identifying Objects, Actions, and Events	Identifying information by categorizing, estimating, recognizing differences or similarities, and detecting changes in circumstances or events.
Communicating with Supervisors, Peers, or Subordin	Providing information to supervisors, co-workers, and subordinates by telephone, in written form, e-mail, or in person.
Selling or Influencing Others	Convincing others to buy merchandise/goods or to otherwise change their minds or actions.
Scheduling Work and Activities	Scheduling events, programs, and activities, as well as the work of others.
Coordinating the Work and Activities of Others	Getting members of a group to work together to accomplish tasks.
Resolving Conflicts and Negotiating with Others	Handling complaints, settling disputes, and resolving grievances and conflicts, or otherwise negotiating with others.
Developing and Building Teams	Encouraging and building mutual trust, respect, and cooperation among team members.
Developing Objectives and Strategies	Establishing long-range objectives and specifying the strategies and actions to achieve them.
Analyzing Data or Information	Identifying the underlying principles, reasons, or facts of information by breaking down information or data into separate parts.
Guiding, Directing, and Motivating Subordinates	Providing guidance and direction to subordinates, including setting performance standards and monitoring performance.
Judging the Qualities of Things, Services, or Peop	Assessing the value, importance, or quality of things or people.
Updating and Using Relevant Knowledge	Keeping up-to-date technically and applying new knowledge to your job.
Provide Consultation and Advice to Others	Providing guidance and expert advice to management or other groups on technical, systems-, or process-related topics.
Monitoring and Controlling Resources	Monitoring and controlling resources and overseeing the spending of money.
Documenting/Recording Information	Entering, transcribing, recording, storing, or maintaining information in written or electronic/magnetic form.
Training and Teaching Others	Identifying the educational needs of others, developing formal educational or training programs or classes, and teaching or instructing others.
Coaching and Developing Others	Identifying the developmental needs of others and coaching, mentoring, or otherwise helping others to improve their knowledge or skills.
Estimating the Quantifiable Characteristics of Pro	Estimating sizes, distances, and quantities; or determining time, costs, resources, or materials needed to perform a work activity.
Interpreting the Meaning of Information for Others	Translating or explaining what information means and how it can be used.
Staffing Organizational Units	Recruiting, interviewing, selecting, hiring, and promoting employees in an organization.
Inspecting Equipment, Structures, or Material	Inspecting equipment, structures, or materials to identify the cause of errors or other problems or defects.
Monitor Processes, Materials, or Surroundings	Monitoring and reviewing information from materials, events, or the environment, to detect or assess problems.

Processing Information	Compiling, coding, categorizing, calculating, tabulating, auditing, or verifying information or data.
Evaluating Information to Determine Compliance wit	Using relevant information and individual judgment to determine whether events or processes comply with laws, regulations, or standards.
Assisting and Caring for Others	Providing personal assistance, medical attention, emotional support, or other personal care to others such as coworkers, customers, or patients.
Operating Vehicles, Mechanized Devices, or Equipme	Running, maneuvering, navigating, or driving vehicles or mechanized equipment, such as forklifts, passenger vehicles, aircraft, or water craft.
Performing General Physical Activities	Performing physical activities that require considerable use of your arms and legs and moving your whole body, such as climbing, lifting, balancing, walking, stooping, and handling of materials.
Controlling Machines and Processes	Using either control mechanisms or direct physical activity to operate machines or processes (not including computers or vehicles).
Handling and Moving Objects	Using hands and arms in handling, installing, positioning, and moving materials, and manipulating things.
Drafting, Laying Out, and Specifying Technical Dev	Providing documentation, detailed instructions, drawings, or specifications to tell others about how devices, parts, equipment, or structures are to be fabricated, constructed, assembled, modified, maintained, or used.
Repairing and Maintaining Electronic Equipment	Servicing, repairing, calibrating, regulating, fine-tuning, or testing machines, devices, and equipment that operate primarily on the basis of electrical or electronic (not mechanical) principles.
Repairing and Maintaining Mechanical Equipment	Servicing, repairing, adjusting, and testing machines, devices, moving parts, and equipment that operate primarily on the basis of mechanical (not electronic) principles.

Work_Context	Work_Context Definitions
Telephone	How often do you have telephone conversations in this job?
Contact With Others	How much does this job require the worker to be in contact with others (face-to-face, by telephone, or otherwise) in order to perform it?
Work With Work Group or Team	How important is it to work with others in a group or team in this job?
Deal With External Customers	How important is it to work with external customers or the public in this job?
Structured versus Unstructured Work	To what extent is this job structured for the worker, rather than allowing the worker to determine tasks, priorities, and goals?
Face-to-Face Discussions	How often do you have to have face-to-face discussions with individuals or teams in this job?
Freedom to Make Decisions	How much decision making freedom, without supervision, does the job offer?
Impact of Decisions on Co-workers or Company Resul	How do the decisions an employee makes impact the results of co-workers, clients or the company?
Coordinate or Lead Others	How important is it to coordinate or lead others in accomplishing work activities in this job?
Letters and Memos	How often does the job require written letters and memos?
Responsibility for Outcomes and Results	How responsible is the worker for work outcomes and results of other workers?
Level of Competition	To what extent does this job require the worker to compete or to be aware of competitive pressures?
Time Pressure	How often does this job require the worker to meet strict deadlines?
Importance of Being Exact or Accurate	How important is being very exact or highly accurate in performing this job?
Spend Time Sitting	How much does this job require sitting?
Importance of Repeating Same Tasks	How important is repeating the same physical activities (e.g., key entry) or mental activities (e.g., checking entries in a ledger) over and over, without stopping, to performing this job?
Frequency of Conflict Situations	How often are there conflict situations the employee has to face in this job?
Responsible for Others' Health and Safety	How much responsibility is there for the health and safety of others in this job?
Spend Time Making Repetitive Motions	How much does this job require making repetitive motions?
Deal With Unpleasant or Angry People	How frequently does the worker have to deal with unpleasant, angry, or discourteous individuals as part of the job requirements?
Electronic Mail	How often do you use electronic mail in this job?
In an Enclosed Vehicle or Equipment	How often does this job require working in a closed vehicle or equipment (e.g., car)?

Spend Time Using Your Hands to Handle, Control, or	How much does this job require using your hands to handle, control, or feel objects, tools or controls?
Outdoors, Exposed to Weather	How often does this job require working outdoors, exposed to all weather conditions?
Frequency of Decision Making	How frequently is the worker required to make decisions that affect other people, the financial resources, and/or the image and reputation of the organization?
Exposed to Contaminants	How often does this job require working exposed to contaminants (such as pollutants, gases, dust or odors)?
Public Speaking	How often do you have to perform public speaking in this job?
Physical Proximity	To what extent does this job require the worker to perform job tasks in close physical proximity to other people?
Outdoors, Under Cover	How often does this job require working outdoors, under cover (e.g., structure with roof but no walls)?
Spend Time Walking and Running	How much does this job require walking and running?
Spend Time Keeping or Regaining Balance	How much does this job require keeping or regaining your balance?
Spend Time Standing	How much does this job require standing?
Very Hot or Cold Temperatures	How often does this job require working in very hot (above 90 F degrees) or very cold (below 32 F degrees) temperatures?
Degree of Automation	How automated is the job?
Spend Time Bending or Twisting the Body	How much does this job require bending or twisting your body?
Consequence of Error	How serious would the result usually be if the worker made a mistake that was not readily correctable?
Indoors, Environmentally Controlled	How often does this job require working indoors in environmentally controlled conditions?
Spend Time Kneeling, Crouching, Stooping, or Crawl	How much does this job require kneeling, crouching, stooping or crawling?
Sounds, Noise Levels Are Distracting or Uncomforta	How often does this job require working exposed to sounds and noise levels that are distracting or uncomfortable?
Exposed to Minor Burns, Cuts, Bites, or Stings	How often does this job require exposure to minor burns, cuts, bites, or stings?
Deal With Physically Aggressive People	How frequently does this job require the worker to deal with physical aggression of violent individuals?
Spend Time Climbing Ladders, Scaffolds, or Poles	How much does this job require climbing ladders, scaffolds, or poles?
Wear Common Protective or Safety Equipment such as	How much does this job require wearing common protective or safety equipment such as safety shoes, glasses, gloves, hard hats or live jackets?
Cramped Work Space, Awkward Positions	How often does this job require working in cramped work spaces that requires getting into awkward positions?
Indoors, Not Environmentally Controlled	How often does this job require working indoors in non-controlled environmental conditions (e.g., warehouse without heat)?
Exposed to Hazardous Equipment	How often does this job require exposure to hazardous equipment?
Exposed to Radiation	How often does this job require exposure to radiation?
Exposed to Disease or Infections	How often does this job require exposure to disease/infections?
Pace Determined by Speed of Equipment	How important is it to this job that the pace is determined by the speed of equipment or machinery? (This does not refer to keeping busy at all times on this job.)
Extremely Bright or Inadequate Lighting	How often does this job require working in extremely bright or inadequate lighting conditions?
Exposed to High Places	How often does this job require exposure to high places?
In an Open Vehicle or Equipment	How often does this job require working in an open vehicle or equipment (e.g., tractor)?
Wear Specialized Protective or Safety Equipment su	How much does this job require wearing specialized protective or safety equipment such as breathing apparatus, safety harness, full protection suits, or radiation protection?
Exposed to Hazardous Conditions	How often does this job require exposure to hazardous conditions?
Exposed to Whole Body Vibration	How often does this job require exposure to whole body vibration (e.g., operate a jackhammer)?

Job Zone Component	Job Zone Component Definitions
Title	Job Zone Four: Considerable Preparation Needed
	A minimum of two to four years of work-related skill, knowledge, or experience is needed for these occupations. For example, an accountant must complete four years of college
Overall Experience	and work for several years in accounting to be considered qualified.

Job Training	Employees in these occupations usually need several years of work-related experience, on-the-job training, and/or vocational training.
Job Zone Examples	Many of these occupations involve coordinating, supervising, managing, or training others. Examples include accountants, chefs and head cooks, computer programmers, historians, pharmacists, and police detectives.
SVP Range	(7.0 to < 8.0)
Education	Most of these occupations require a four - year bachelor's degree, but some do not.

Work_Styles	Work_Styles Definitions
Attention to Detail	Job requires being careful about detail and thorough in completing work tasks.
Dependability	Job requires being reliable, responsible, and dependable, and fulfilling obligations.
Integrity	Job requires being honest and ethical.
Innovation	Job requires creativity and alternative thinking to develop new ideas for and answers to work-related problems.
Adaptability/Flexibility	Job requires being open to change (positive or negative) and to considerable variety in the workplace.
Initiative	Job requires a willingness to take on responsibilities and challenges.
Self Control	Job requires maintaining composure, keeping emotions in check, controlling anger, and avoiding aggressive behavior, even in very difficult situations.
Cooperation	Job requires being pleasant with others on the job and displaying a good-natured, cooperative attitude.
Stress Tolerance	Job requires accepting criticism and dealing calmly and effectively with high stress situations.
Persistence	Job requires persistence in the face of obstacles.
Achievement/Effort	Job requires establishing and maintaining personally challenging achievement goals and exerting effort toward mastering tasks.
Independence	Job requires developing one's own ways of doing things, guiding oneself with little or no supervision, and depending on oneself to get things done.
Leadership	Job requires a willingness to lead, take charge, and offer opinions and direction.
Concern for Others	Job requires being sensitive to others' needs and feelings and being understanding and helpful on the job.
Analytical Thinking	Job requires analyzing information and using logic to address work-related issues and problems.
Social Orientation	Job requires preferring to work with others rather than alone, and being personally connected with others on the job.

11-2021.00 - Marketing Managers

Determine the demand for products and services offered by a firm and its competitors and identify potential customers. Develop pricing strategies with the goal of maximizing the firm's profits or share of the market while ensuring the firm's customers are satisfied. Oversee product development or monitor trends that indicate the need for new products and services.

Tasks

1) Compile lists describing product or service offerings.

2) Develop pricing strategies, balancing firm objectives and customer satisfaction.

3) Formulate, direct and coordinate marketing activities and policies to promote products and services, working with advertising and promotion managers.

4) Evaluate the financial aspects of product development, such as budgets, expenditures, research and development appropriations, and return-on-investment and profit-loss projections.

5) Use sales forecasting and strategic planning to ensure the sale and profitability of products, lines, or services, analyzing business developments and monitoring market trends.

6) Coordinate and participate in promotional activities and trade shows, working with developers, advertisers, and production managers, to market products and services.

7) Consult with product development personnel on product specifications such as design, color, and packaging.

8) Negotiate contracts with vendors and distributors to manage product distribution, establishing distribution networks and developing distribution strategies.

9) Select products and accessories to be displayed at trade or special production shows.

10) Confer with legal staff to resolve problems, such as copyright infringement and royalty sharing with outside producers and distributors.

11) Direct the hiring, training, and performance evaluations of marketing and sales staff and oversee their daily activities.

12) Initiate market research studies and analyze their findings.

13) Consult with buying personnel to gain advice regarding the types of products or services expected to be in demand.

14) Conduct economic and commercial surveys to identify potential markets for products and services.

15) Advise business and other groups on local, national, and international factors affecting the buying and selling of products and services.

Knowledge	Knowledge Definitions
Sales and Marketing	Knowledge of principles and methods for showing, promoting, and selling products or services. This includes marketing strategy and tactics, product demonstration, sales techniques, and sales control systems.
Customer and Personal Service	Knowledge of principles and processes for providing customer and personal services. This includes customer needs assessment, meeting quality standards for services, and evaluation of customer satisfaction.
English Language	Knowledge of the structure and content of the English language including the meaning and spelling of words, rules of composition, and grammar.
Administration and Management	Knowledge of business and management principles involved in strategic planning, resource allocation, human resources modeling, leadership technique, production methods, and coordination of people and resources.
Communications and Media	Knowledge of media production, communication, and dissemination techniques and methods. This includes alternative ways to inform and entertain via written, oral, and visual media.
Psychology	Knowledge of human behavior and performance; individual differences in ability, personality, and interests; learning and motivation; psychological research methods; and the assessment and treatment of behavioral and affective disorders.
Computers and Electronics	Knowledge of circuit boards, processors, chips, electronic equipment, and computer hardware and software, including applications and programming.
Education and Training	Knowledge of principles and methods for curriculum and training design, teaching and instruction for individuals and groups, and the measurement of training effects.
Clerical	Knowledge of administrative and clerical procedures and systems such as word processing, managing files and records, stenography and transcription, designing forms, and other office procedures and terminology.
Personnel and Human Resources	Knowledge of principles and procedures for personnel recruitment, selection, training, compensation and benefits, labor relations and negotiation, and personnel information systems.
Mathematics	Knowledge of arithmetic, algebra, geometry, calculus, statistics, and their applications.
Economics and Accounting	Knowledge of economic and accounting principles and practices, the financial markets, banking and the analysis and reporting of financial data.
Telecommunications	Knowledge of transmission, broadcasting, switching, control, and operation of telecommunications systems.
Law and Government	Knowledge of laws, legal codes, court procedures, precedents, government regulations, executive orders, agency rules, and the democratic political process.
Sociology and Anthropology	Knowledge of group behavior and dynamics, societal trends and influences, human migrations, ethnicity, cultures and their history and origins.
Transportation	Knowledge of principles and methods for moving people or goods by air, rail, sea, or road, including the relative costs and benefits.
Therapy and Counseling	Knowledge of principles, methods, and procedures for diagnosis, treatment, and rehabilitation of physical and mental dysfunctions, and for career counseling and guidance.
Public Safety and Security	Knowledge of relevant equipment, policies, procedures, and strategies to promote effective local, state, or national security operations for the protection of people, data, property, and institutions.
Production and Processing	Knowledge of raw materials, production processes, quality control, costs, and other techniques for maximizing the effective manufacture and distribution of goods.
Geography	Knowledge of principles and methods for describing the features of land, sea, and air masses, including their physical characteristics, locations, interrelationships, and distribution of plant, animal, and human life.
Foreign Language	Knowledge of the structure and content of a foreign (non-English) language including the meaning and spelling of words, rules of composition and grammar, and pronunciation.
Design	Knowledge of design techniques, tools, and principles involved in production of precision technical plans, blueprints, drawings, and models.
Philosophy and Theology	Knowledge of different philosophical systems and religions. This includes their basic principles, values, ethics, ways of thinking, customs, practices, and their impact on human culture.
Medicine and Dentistry	Knowledge of the information and techniques needed to diagnose and treat human injuries, diseases, and deformities. This includes symptoms, treatment alternatives, drug properties and interactions, and preventive health-care measures.
Fine Arts	Knowledge of the theory and techniques required to compose, produce, and perform works of music, dance, visual arts, drama, and sculpture.
History and Archeology	Knowledge of historical events and their causes, indicators, and effects on civilizations and cultures.
Physics	Knowledge and prediction of physical principles, laws, their interrelationships, and applications to understanding fluid, material, and atmospheric dynamics, and mechanical, electrical, atomic and sub-atomic structures and processes.
Engineering and Technology	Knowledge of the practical application of engineering science and technology. This includes applying principles, techniques, procedures, and equipment to the design and production of various goods and services.
Mechanical	Knowledge of machines and tools, including their designs, uses, repair, and maintenance.
Building and Construction	Knowledge of materials, methods, and the tools involved in the construction or repair of houses, buildings, or other structures such as highways and roads.
Food Production	Knowledge of techniques and equipment for planting, growing, and harvesting food products (both plant and animal) for consumption, including storage/handling techniques.
Biology	Knowledge of plant and animal organisms, their tissues, cells, functions, interdependencies, and interactions with each other and the environment.
Chemistry	Knowledge of the chemical composition, structure, and properties of substances and of the chemical processes and transformations that they undergo. This includes uses of chemicals and their interactions, danger signs, production techniques, and disposal methods.

Skills	Skills Definitions
Critical Thinking	Using logic and reasoning to identify the strengths and weaknesses of alternative solutions, conclusions or approaches to problems.
Coordination	Adjusting actions in relation to others' actions.
Active Learning	Understanding the implications of new information for both current and future problem-solving and decision-making.
Reading Comprehension	Understanding written sentences and paragraphs in work related documents.
Writing	Communicating effectively in writing as appropriate for the needs of the audience.
Speaking	Talking to others to convey information effectively.
Judgment and Decision Making	Considering the relative costs and benefits of potential actions to choose the most appropriate one.
Time Management	Managing one's own time and the time of others.
Negotiation	Bringing others together and trying to reconcile differences.
Persuasion	Persuading others to change their minds or behavior.
Active Listening	Giving full attention to what other people are saying, taking time to understand the points being made, asking questions as appropriate, and not interrupting at inappropriate times.
Learning Strategies	Selecting and using training/instructional methods and procedures appropriate for the situation when learning or teaching new things.
Management of Personnel Resources	Motivating, developing, and directing people as they work, identifying the best people for the job.

Monitoring	Monitoring/Assessing performance of yourself, other individuals, or organizations to make improvements or take corrective action.
Management of Financial Resources	Determining how money will be spent to get the work done, and accounting for these expenditures.
Operations Analysis	Analyzing needs and product requirements to create a design.
Complex Problem Solving	Identifying complex problems and reviewing related information to develop and evaluate options and implement solutions.
Instructing	Teaching others how to do something.
Social Perceptiveness	Being aware of others' reactions and understanding why they react as they do.
Service Orientation	Actively looking for ways to help people.
Mathematics	Using mathematics to solve problems.
Science	Using scientific rules and methods to solve problems.
Quality Control Analysis	Conducting tests and inspections of products, services, or processes to evaluate quality or performance.
Troubleshooting	Determining causes of operating errors and deciding what to do about it.
Equipment Selection	Determining the kind of tools and equipment needed to do a job.
Management of Material Resources	Obtaining and seeing to the appropriate use of equipment, facilities, and materials needed to do certain work.
Systems Evaluation	Identifying measures or indicators of system performance and the actions needed to improve or correct performance, relative to the goals of the system.
Equipment Maintenance	Performing routine maintenance on equipment and determining when and what kind of maintenance is needed.
Programming	Writing computer programs for various purposes.
Systems Analysis	Determining how a system should work and how changes in conditions, operations, and the environment will affect outcomes.
Operation and Control	Controlling operations of equipment or systems.
Technology Design	Generating or adapting equipment and technology to serve user needs.
Operation Monitoring	Watching gauges, dials, or other indicators to make sure a machine is working properly.
Installation	Installing equipment, machines, wiring, or programs to meet specifications.
Repairing	Repairing machines or systems using the needed tools.

Ability	Ability Definitions
Written Comprehension	The ability to read and understand information and ideas presented in writing.
Oral Comprehension	The ability to listen to and understand information and ideas presented through spoken words and sentences.
Oral Expression	The ability to communicate information and ideas in speaking so others will understand.
Speech Clarity	The ability to speak clearly so others can understand you.
Deductive Reasoning	The ability to apply general rules to specific problems to produce answers that make sense.
Fluency of Ideas	The ability to come up with a number of ideas about a topic (the number of ideas is important, not their quality, correctness, or creativity).
Inductive Reasoning	The ability to combine pieces of information to form general rules or conclusions (includes finding a relationship among seemingly unrelated events).
Speech Recognition	The ability to identify and understand the speech of another person.
Problem Sensitivity	The ability to tell when something is wrong or is likely to go wrong. It does not involve solving the problem, only recognizing there is a problem.
Written Expression	The ability to communicate information and ideas in writing so others will understand.
Near Vision	The ability to see details at close range (within a few feet of the observer).
Mathematical Reasoning	The ability to choose the right mathematical methods or formulas to solve a problem.
Originality	The ability to come up with unusual or clever ideas about a given topic or situation, or to develop creative ways to solve a problem.
Information Ordering	The ability to arrange things or actions in a certain order or pattern according to a specific rule or set of rules (e.g., patterns of numbers, letters, words, pictures, mathematical operations).
Category Flexibility	The ability to generate or use different sets of rules for combining or grouping things in different ways.

Selective Attention	The ability to concentrate on a task over a period of time without being distracted.
Memorization	The ability to remember information such as words, numbers, pictures, and procedures.
Visualization	The ability to imagine how something will look after it is moved around or when its parts are moved or rearranged.
Time Sharing	The ability to shift back and forth between two or more activities or sources of information (such as speech, sounds, touch, or other sources).
Number Facility	The ability to add, subtract, multiply, or divide quickly and correctly.
Flexibility of Closure	The ability to identify or detect a known pattern (a figure, object, word, or sound) that is hidden in other distracting material.
Speed of Closure	The ability to quickly make sense of, combine, and organize information into meaningful patterns.
Visual Color Discrimination	The ability to match or detect differences between colors, including shades of color and brightness.
Perceptual Speed	The ability to quickly and accurately compare similarities and differences among sets of letters, numbers, objects, pictures, or patterns. The things to be compared may be presented at the same time or one after the other. This ability also includes comparing a presented object with a remembered object.
Auditory Attention	The ability to focus on a single source of sound in the presence of other distracting sounds.
Depth Perception	The ability to judge which of several objects is closer or farther away from you, or to judge the distance between you and an object.
Far Vision	The ability to see details at a distance.
Wrist-Finger Speed	The ability to make fast, simple, repeated movements of the fingers, hands, and wrists.
Hearing Sensitivity	The ability to detect or tell the differences between sounds that vary in pitch and loudness.
Finger Dexterity	The ability to make precisely coordinated movements of the fingers of one or both hands to grasp, manipulate, or assemble very small objects.
Trunk Strength	The ability to use your abdominal and lower back muscles to support part of the body repeatedly or continuously over time without 'giving out' or fatiguing.
Response Orientation	The ability to choose quickly between two or more movements in response to two or more different signals (lights, sounds, pictures). It includes the speed with which the correct response is started with the hand, foot, or other body part.
Stamina	The ability to exert yourself physically over long periods of time without getting winded or out of breath.
Extent Flexibility	The ability to bend, stretch, twist, or reach with your body, arms, and/or legs.
Dynamic Strength	The ability to exert muscle force repeatedly or continuously over time. This involves muscular endurance and resistance to muscle fatigue.
Sound Localization	The ability to tell the direction from which a sound originated.
Explosive Strength	The ability to use short bursts of muscle force to propel oneself (as in jumping or sprinting), or to throw an object.
Spatial Orientation	The ability to know your location in relation to the environment or to know where other objects are in relation to you.
Static Strength	The ability to exert maximum muscle force to lift, push, pull, or carry objects.
Speed of Limb Movement	The ability to quickly move the arms and legs.
Reaction Time	The ability to quickly respond (with the hand, finger, or foot) to a signal (sound, light, picture) when it appears.
Control Precision	The ability to quickly and repeatedly adjust the controls of a machine or a vehicle to exact positions.
Manual Dexterity	The ability to quickly move your hand, your hand together with your arm, or your two hands to grasp, manipulate, or assemble objects.
Arm-Hand Steadiness	The ability to keep your hand and arm steady while moving your arm or while holding your arm and hand in one position.
Dynamic Flexibility	The ability to quickly and repeatedly bend, stretch, twist, or reach out with your body, arms, and/or legs.
Rate Control	The ability to time your movements or the movement of a piece of equipment in anticipation of changes in the speed and/or direction of a moving object or scene.
Gross Body Equilibrium	The ability to keep or regain your body balance or stay upright when in an unstable position.
Night Vision	The ability to see under low light conditions.
Peripheral Vision	The ability to see objects or movement of objects to one's side when the eyes are looking ahead.

11

Gross Body Coordination	The ability to coordinate the movement of your arms, legs, and torso together when the whole body is in motion.
Multilimb Coordination	The ability to coordinate two or more limbs (for example, two arms, two legs, or one leg and one arm) while sitting, standing, or lying down. It does not involve performing the activities while the whole body is in motion.
Glare Sensitivity	The ability to see objects in the presence of glare or bright lighting.

Work_Activity	Work_Activity Definitions
Communicating with Persons Outside Organization	Communicating with people outside the organization, representing the organization to customers, the public, government, and other external sources. This information can be exchanged in person, in writing, or by telephone or e-mail.
Communicating with Supervisors, Peers, or Subordin	Providing information to supervisors, co-workers, and subordinates by telephone, in written form, e-mail, or in person.
Making Decisions and Solving Problems	Analyzing information and evaluating results to choose the best solution and solve problems.
Establishing and Maintaining Interpersonal Relatio	Developing constructive and cooperative working relationships with others, and maintaining them over time.
Interacting With Computers	Using computers and computer systems (including hardware and software) to program, write software, set up functions, enter data, or process information.
Getting Information	Observing, receiving, and otherwise obtaining information from all relevant sources.
Organizing, Planning, and Prioritizing Work	Developing specific goals and plans to prioritize, organize, and accomplish your work.
Selling or Influencing Others	Convincing others to buy merchandise/goods or to otherwise change their minds or actions.
Judging the Qualities of Things, Services, or Peop	Assessing the value, importance, or quality of things or people.
Processing Information	Compiling, coding, categorizing, calculating, tabulating, auditing, or verifying information or data.
Identifying Objects, Actions, and Events	Identifying information by categorizing, estimating, recognizing differences or similarities, and detecting changes in circumstances or events.
Updating and Using Relevant Knowledge	Keeping up-to-date technically and applying new knowledge to your job.
Documenting/Recording Information	Entering, transcribing, recording, storing, or maintaining information in written or electronic/magnetic form.
Interpreting the Meaning of Information for Others	Translating or explaining what information means and how it can be used.
Resolving Conflicts and Negotiating with Others	Handling complaints, settling disputes, and resolving grievances and conflicts, or otherwise negotiating with others.
Performing for or Working Directly with the Public	Performing for people or dealing directly with the public. This includes serving customers in restaurants and stores, and receiving clients or guests.
Thinking Creatively	Developing, designing, or creating new applications, ideas, relationships, systems, or products, including artistic contributions.
Coordinating the Work and Activities of Others	Getting members of a group to work together to accomplish tasks.
Developing and Building Teams	Encouraging and building mutual trust, respect, and cooperation among team members.
Scheduling Work and Activities	Scheduling events, programs, and activities, as well as the work of others.
Provide Consultation and Advice to Others	Providing guidance and expert advice to management or other groups on technical, systems-, or process-related topics.
Training and Teaching Others	Identifying the educational needs of others, developing formal educational or training programs or classes, and teaching or instructing others.
Developing Objectives and Strategies	Establishing long-range objectives and specifying the strategies and actions to achieve them.
Guiding, Directing, and Motivating Subordinates	Providing guidance and direction to subordinates, including setting performance standards and monitoring performance.
Performing Administrative Activities	Performing day-to-day administrative tasks such as maintaining information files and processing paperwork.
Analyzing Data or Information	Identifying the underlying principles, reasons, or facts of information by breaking down information or data into separate parts.
Monitoring and Controlling Resources	Monitoring and controlling resources and overseeing the spending of money.
Coaching and Developing Others	Identifying the developmental needs of others and coaching, mentoring, or otherwise helping others to improve their knowledge or skills.

Monitor Processes, Materials, or Surroundings	Monitoring and reviewing information from materials, events, or the environment, to detect or assess problems.
Evaluating Information to Determine Compliance wit	Using relevant information and individual judgment to determine whether events or processes comply with laws, regulations, or standards.
Staffing Organizational Units	Recruiting, interviewing, selecting, hiring, and promoting employees in an organization.
Estimating the Quantifiable Characteristics of Pro	Estimating sizes, distances, and quantities; or determining time, costs, resources, or materials needed to perform a work activity.
Assisting and Caring for Others	Providing personal assistance, medical attention, emotional support, or other personal care to others such as coworkers, customers, or patients.
Inspecting Equipment, Structures, or Material	Inspecting equipment, structures, or materials to identify the cause of errors or other problems or defects.
Handling and Moving Objects	Using hands and arms in handling, installing, positioning, and moving materials, and manipulating things.
Performing General Physical Activities	Performing physical activities that require considerable use of your arms and legs and moving your whole body, such as climbing, lifting, balancing, walking, stooping, and handling of materials.
Operating Vehicles, Mechanized Devices, or Equipme	Running, maneuvering, navigating, or driving vehicles or mechanized equipment, such as forklifts, passenger vehicles, aircraft, or water craft.
Repairing and Maintaining Electronic Equipment	Servicing, repairing, calibrating, regulating, fine-tuning, or testing machines, devices, and equipment that operate primarily on the basis of electrical or electronic (not mechanical) principles.
Drafting, Laying Out, and Specifying Technical Dev	Providing documentation, detailed instructions, drawings, or specifications to tell others about how devices, parts, equipment, or structures are to be fabricated, constructed, assembled, modified, maintained, or used.
Controlling Machines and Processes	Using either control mechanisms or direct physical activity to operate machines or processes (not including computers or vehicles).
Repairing and Maintaining Mechanical Equipment	Servicing, repairing, adjusting, and testing machines, devices, moving parts, and equipment that operate primarily on the basis of mechanical (not electronic) principles.

Work_Context	Work_Context Definitions
Electronic Mail	How often do you use electronic mail in this job?
Telephone	How often do you have telephone conversations in this job?
Contact With Others	How much does this job require the worker to be in contact with others (face-to-face, by telephone, or otherwise) in order to perform it?
Deal With External Customers	How important is it to work with external customers or the public in this job?
Structured versus Unstructured Work	To what extent is this job structured for the worker, rather than allowing the worker to determine tasks, priorities, and goals?
Face-to-Face Discussions	How often do you have to have face-to-face discussions with individuals or teams in this job?
Freedom to Make Decisions	How much decision making freedom, without supervision, does the job offer?
Spend Time Sitting	How much does this job require sitting?
Letters and Memos	How often does the job require written letters and memos?
Work With Work Group or Team	How important is it to work with others in a group or team in this job?
Coordinate or Lead Others	How important is it to coordinate or lead others in accomplishing work activities in this job?
Indoors, Environmentally Controlled	How often does this job require working indoors in environmentally controlled conditions?
Impact of Decisions on Co-workers or Company Resul	How do the decisions an employee makes impact the results of co-workers, clients or the company?
Frequency of Decision Making	How frequently is the worker required to make decisions that affect other people, the financial resources, and/or the image and reputation of the organization?
Importance of Being Exact or Accurate	How important is being very exact or highly accurate in performing this job?
Time Pressure	How often does this job require the worker to meet strict deadlines?
Level of Competition	To what extent does this job require the worker to compete or to be aware of competitive pressures?
Responsibility for Outcomes and Results	How responsible is the worker for work outcomes and results of other workers?

Consequence of Error	How serious would the result usually be if the worker made a mistake that was not readily correctable?
Deal With Unpleasant or Angry People	How frequently does the worker have to deal with unpleasant, angry, or discourteous individuals as part of the job requirements?
Spend Time Making Repetitive Motions	How much does this job require making repetitive motions?
Frequency of Conflict Situations	How often are there conflict situations the employee has to face in this job?
Degree of Automation	How automated is the job?
Importance of Repeating Same Tasks	How important is repeating the same physical activities (e.g., key entry) or mental activities (e.g., checking entries in a ledger) over and over, without stopping, to performing this job?
In an Enclosed Vehicle or Equipment	How often does this job require working in a closed vehicle or equipment (e.g., car)?
Public Speaking	How often do you have to perform public speaking in this job?
Responsible for Others' Health and Safety	How much responsibility is there for the health and safety of others in this job?
Physical Proximity	To what extent does this job require the worker to perform job tasks in close physical proximity to other people?
Spend Time Standing	How much does this job require standing?
Indoors, Not Environmentally Controlled	How often does this job require working indoors in non-controlled environmental conditions (e.g., warehouse without heat)?
Spend Time Walking and Running	How much does this job require walking and running?
Outdoors, Exposed to Weather	How often does this job require working outdoors, exposed to all weather conditions?
Sounds, Noise Levels Are Distracting or Uncomforta	How often does this job require working exposed to sounds and noise levels that are distracting or uncomfortable?
Spend Time Using Your Hands to Handle, Control, or	How much does this job require using your hands to handle, control, or feel objects, tools or controls?
Wear Common Protective or Safety Equipment such as	How much does this job require wearing common protective or safety equipment such as safety shoes, glasses, gloves, hard hats or live jackets?
Exposed to Hazardous Conditions	How often does this job require exposure to hazardous conditions?
Very Hot or Cold Temperatures	How often does this job require working in very hot (above 90 F degrees) or very cold (below 32 F degrees) temperatures?
Exposed to Hazardous Equipment	How often does this job require exposure to hazardous equipment?
Extremely Bright or Inadequate Lighting	How often does this job require working in extremely bright or inadequate lighting conditions?
Exposed to Contaminants	How often does this job require working exposed to contaminants (such as pollutants, gases, dust or odors)?
Spend Time Bending or Twisting the Body	How much does this job require bending or twisting your body?
Outdoors, Under Cover	How often does this job require working outdoors, under cover (e.g., structure with roof but no walls)?
Spend Time Kneeling, Crouching, Stooping, or Crawl	How much does this job require kneeling, crouching, stooping or crawling?
Cramped Work Space, Awkward Positions	How often does this job require working in cramped work spaces that requires getting into awkward positions?
Exposed to Minor Burns, Cuts, Bites, or Stings	How often does this job require exposure to minor burns, cuts, bites, or stings?
In an Open Vehicle or Equipment	How often does this job require working in an open vehicle or equipment (e.g., tractor)?
Exposed to High Places	How often does this job require exposure to high places?
Spend Time Climbing Ladders, Scaffolds, or Poles	How much does this job require climbing ladders, scaffolds, or poles?
Pace Determined by Speed of Equipment	How important is it to this job that the pace is determined by the speed of equipment or machinery? (This does not refer to keeping busy at all times on this job.)
Wear Specialized Protective or Safety Equipment su	How much does this job require wearing specialized protective or safety equipment such as breathing apparatus, safety harness, full protection suits, or radiation protection?
Exposed to Radiation	How often does this job require exposure to radiation?
Exposed to Disease or Infections	How often does this job require exposure to disease/infections?
Spend Time Keeping or Regaining Balance	How much does this job require keeping or regaining your balance?
Exposed to Whole Body Vibration	How often does this job require exposure to whole body vibration (e.g., operate a jackhammer)?
Deal With Physically Aggressive People	How frequently does this job require the worker to deal with physical aggression of violent individuals?

Job Zone Component	Job Zone Component Definitions
Title	Job Zone Four: Considerable Preparation Needed
Overall Experience	A minimum of two to four years of work-related skill, knowledge, or experience is needed for these occupations. For example, an accountant must complete four years of college and work for several years in accounting to be considered qualified.
Job Training	Employees in these occupations usually need several years of work-related experience, on-the-job training, and/or vocational training.
Job Zone Examples	Many of these occupations involve coordinating, supervising, managing, or training others. Examples include accountants, chefs and head cooks, computer programmers, historians, pharmacists, and police detectives.
SVP Range	(7.0 to < 8.0)
Education	Most of these occupations require a four - year bachelor's degree, but some do not.

Work_Styles	Work_Styles Definitions
Leadership	Job requires a willingness to lead, take charge, and offer opinions and direction.
Adaptability/Flexibility	Job requires being open to change (positive or negative) and to considerable variety in the workplace.
Initiative	Job requires a willingness to take on responsibilities and challenges.
Persistence	Job requires persistence in the face of obstacles.
Integrity	Job requires being honest and ethical.
Dependability	Job requires being reliable, responsible, and dependable, and fulfilling obligations.
Achievement/Effort	Job requires establishing and maintaining personally challenging achievement goals and exerting effort toward mastering tasks.
Independence	Job requires developing one's own ways of doing things, guiding oneself with little or no supervision, and depending on oneself to get things done.
Cooperation	Job requires being pleasant with others on the job and displaying a good-natured, cooperative attitude.
Social Orientation	Job requires preferring to work with others rather than alone, and being personally connected with others on the job.
Innovation	Job requires creativity and alternative thinking to develop new ideas for and answers to work-related problems.
Stress Tolerance	Job requires accepting criticism and dealing calmly and effectively with high stress situations.
Attention to Detail	Job requires being careful about detail and thorough in completing work tasks.
Self Control	Job requires maintaining composure, keeping emotions in check, controlling anger, and avoiding aggressive behavior, even in very difficult situations.
Concern for Others	Job requires being sensitive to others' needs and feelings and being understanding and helpful on the job.
Analytical Thinking	Job requires analyzing information and using logic to address work-related issues and problems.

11-2022.00 - Sales Managers

Direct the actual distribution or movement of a product or service to the customer. Coordinate sales distribution by establishing sales territories, quotas, and goals and establish training programs for sales representatives. Analyze sales statistics gathered by staff to determine sales potential and inventory requirements and monitor the preferences of customers.

Tasks

1) Determine price schedules and discount rates.

2) Review operational records and reports to project sales and determine profitability.

3) Direct and coordinate activities involving sales of manufactured products, services, commodities, real estate or other subjects of sale.

4) Monitor customer preferences to determine focus of sales efforts.

5) Direct, coordinate, and review activities in sales and service accounting and record keeping, and in receiving and shipping operations.

6) Represent company at trade association meetings to promote products.

7) Advise dealers and distributors on policies and operating procedures to ensure functional effectiveness of business.

8) Confer or consult with department heads to plan advertising services and to secure information on equipment and customer specifications.

9) Prepare budgets and approve budget expenditures.

10) Confer with potential customers regarding equipment needs and advise customers on types of equipment to purchase.

11) Plan and direct staffing, training, and performance evaluations to develop and control sales and service programs.

12) Direct clerical staff to keep records of export correspondence, bid requests, and credit collections, and to maintain current information on tariffs, licenses, and restrictions.

13) Assess marketing potential of new and existing store locations, considering statistics and expenditures.

14) Oversee regional and local sales managers and their staffs.

15) Visit franchised dealers to stimulate interest in establishment or expansion of leasing programs.

16) Direct foreign sales and service outlets of an organization.

Knowledge	Knowledge Definitions
Mathematics	Knowledge of arithmetic, algebra, geometry, calculus, statistics, and their applications.
Sales and Marketing	Knowledge of principles and methods for showing, promoting, and selling products or services. This includes marketing strategy and tactics, product demonstration, sales techniques, and sales control systems.
Computers and Electronics	Knowledge of circuit boards, processors, chips, electronic equipment, and computer hardware and software, including applications and programming.
English Language	Knowledge of the structure and content of the English language including the meaning and spelling of words, rules of composition, and grammar.
Customer and Personal Service	Knowledge of principles and processes for providing customer and personal services. This includes customer needs assessment, meeting quality standards for services, and evaluation of customer satisfaction.
Administration and Management	Knowledge of business and management principles involved in strategic planning, resource allocation, human resources modeling, leadership technique, production methods, and coordination of people and resources.
Transportation	Knowledge of principles and methods for moving people or goods by air, rail, sea, or road, including the relative costs and benefits.
Clerical	Knowledge of administrative and clerical procedures and systems such as word processing, managing files and records, stenography and transcription, designing forms, and other office procedures and terminology.
Law and Government	Knowledge of laws, legal codes, court procedures, precedents, government regulations, executive orders, agency rules, and the democratic political process.
Communications and Media	Knowledge of media production, communication, and dissemination techniques and methods. This includes alternative ways to inform and entertain via written, oral, and visual media.
Personnel and Human Resources	Knowledge of principles and procedures for personnel recruitment, selection, training, compensation and benefits, labor relations and negotiation, and personnel information systems.
Education and Training	Knowledge of principles and methods for curriculum and training design, teaching and instruction for individuals and groups, and the measurement of training effects.
Economics and Accounting	Knowledge of economic and accounting principles and practices, the financial markets, banking and the analysis and reporting of financial data.
Engineering and Technology	Knowledge of the practical application of engineering science and technology. This includes applying principles, techniques, procedures, and equipment to the design and production of various goods and services.
Geography	Knowledge of principles and methods for describing the features of land, sea, and air masses, including their physical characteristics, locations, interrelationships, and distribution of plant, animal, and human life.
Building and Construction	Knowledge of materials, methods, and the tools involved in the construction or repair of houses, buildings, or other structures such as highways and roads.
Production and Processing	Knowledge of raw materials, production processes, quality control, costs, and other techniques for maximizing the effective manufacture and distribution of goods.
Mechanical	Knowledge of machines and tools, including their designs, uses, repair, and maintenance.
Design	Knowledge of design techniques, tools, and principles involved in production of precision technical plans, blueprints, drawings, and models.
Chemistry	Knowledge of the chemical composition, structure, and properties of substances and of the chemical processes and transformations that they undergo. This includes uses of chemicals and their interactions, danger signs, production techniques, and disposal methods.
Psychology	Knowledge of human behavior and performance; individual differences in ability, personality, and interests; learning and motivation; psychological research methods; and the assessment and treatment of behavioral and affective disorders.
Telecommunications	Knowledge of transmission, broadcasting, switching, control, and operation of telecommunications systems.
Physics	Knowledge and prediction of physical principles, laws, their interrelationships, and applications to understanding fluid, material, and atmospheric dynamics, and mechanical, electrical, atomic and sub- atomic structures and processes.
Food Production	Knowledge of techniques and equipment for planting, growing, and harvesting food products (both plant and animal) for consumption, including storage/handling techniques.
Biology	Knowledge of plant and animal organisms, their tissues, cells, functions, interdependencies, and interactions with each other and the environment.
Public Safety and Security	Knowledge of relevant equipment, policies, procedures, and strategies to promote effective local, state, or national security operations for the protection of people, data, property, and institutions.
Sociology and Anthropology	Knowledge of group behavior and dynamics, societal trends and influences, human migrations, ethnicity, cultures and their history and origins.
Foreign Language	Knowledge of the structure and content of a foreign (non-English) language including the meaning and spelling of words, rules of composition and grammar, and pronunciation.
Therapy and Counseling	Knowledge of principles, methods, and procedures for diagnosis, treatment, and rehabilitation of physical and mental dysfunctions, and for career counseling and guidance.
Philosophy and Theology	Knowledge of different philosophical systems and religions. This includes their basic principles, values, ethics, ways of thinking, customs, practices, and their impact on human culture.
Fine Arts	Knowledge of the theory and techniques required to compose, produce, and perform works of music, dance, visual arts, drama, and sculpture.
Medicine and Dentistry	Knowledge of the information and techniques needed to diagnose and treat human injuries, diseases, and deformities. This includes symptoms, treatment alternatives, drug properties and interactions, and preventive health-care measures.
History and Archeology	Knowledge of historical events and their causes, indicators, and effects on civilizations and cultures.

Skills	Skills Definitions
Active Listening	Giving full attention to what other people are saying, taking time to understand the points being made, asking questions as appropriate, and not interrupting at inappropriate times.
Speaking	Talking to others to convey information effectively.
Mathematics	Using mathematics to solve problems.
Time Management	Managing one's own time and the time of others.
Service Orientation	Actively looking for ways to help people.
Persuasion	Persuading others to change their minds or behavior.
Social Perceptiveness	Being aware of others' reactions and understanding why they react as they do.
Monitoring	Monitoring/Assessing performance of yourself, other individuals, or organizations to make improvements or take corrective action.
Reading Comprehension	Understanding written sentences and paragraphs in work related documents.
Negotiation	Bringing others together and trying to reconcile differences.

Active Learning	Understanding the implications of new information for both current and future problem-solving and decision-making.
Judgment and Decision Making	Considering the relative costs and benefits of potential actions to choose the most appropriate one.
Coordination	Adjusting actions in relation to others' actions.
Instructing	Teaching others how to do something.
Critical Thinking	Using logic and reasoning to identify the strengths and weaknesses of alternative solutions, conclusions or approaches to problems.
Management of Personnel Resources	Motivating, developing, and directing people as they work, identifying the best people for the job.
Complex Problem Solving	Identifying complex problems and reviewing related information to develop and evaluate options and implement solutions.
Writing	Communicating effectively in writing as appropriate for the needs of the audience.
Learning Strategies	Selecting and using training/instructional methods and procedures appropriate for the situation when learning or teaching new things.
Operations Analysis	Analyzing needs and product requirements to create a design.
Management of Financial Resources	Determining how money will be spent to get the work done, and accounting for these expenditures.
Troubleshooting	Determining causes of operating errors and deciding what to do about it.
Management of Material Resources	Obtaining and seeing to the appropriate use of equipment, facilities, and materials needed to do certain work.
Systems Evaluation	Identifying measures or indicators of system performance and the actions needed to improve or correct performance, relative to the goals of the system.
Science	Using scientific rules and methods to solve problems.
Systems Analysis	Determining how a system should work and how changes in conditions, operations, and the environment will affect outcomes.
Operation and Control	Controlling operations of equipment or systems.
Quality Control Analysis	Conducting tests and inspections of products, services, or processes to evaluate quality or performance.
Equipment Selection	Determining the kind of tools and equipment needed to do a job.
Equipment Maintenance	Performing routine maintenance on equipment and determining when and what kind of maintenance is needed.
Technology Design	Generating or adapting equipment and technology to serve user needs.
Operation Monitoring	Watching gauges, dials, or other indicators to make sure a machine is working properly.
Repairing	Repairing machines or systems using the needed tools.
Installation	Installing equipment, machines, wiring, or programs to meet specifications.
Programming	Writing computer programs for various purposes.

Ability	Ability Definitions
Oral Expression	The ability to communicate information and ideas in speaking so others will understand.
Oral Comprehension	The ability to listen to and understand information and ideas presented through spoken words and sentences.
Speech Clarity	The ability to speak clearly so others can understand you.
Speech Recognition	The ability to identify and understand the speech of another person.
Problem Sensitivity	The ability to tell when something is wrong or is likely to go wrong. It does not involve solving the problem, only recognizing there is a problem.
Written Comprehension	The ability to read and understand information and ideas presented in writing.
Originality	The ability to come up with unusual or clever ideas about a given topic or situation, or to develop creative ways to solve a problem.
Deductive Reasoning	The ability to apply general rules to specific problems to produce answers that make sense.
Inductive Reasoning	The ability to combine pieces of information to form general rules or conclusions (includes finding a relationship among seemingly unrelated events).
Information Ordering	The ability to arrange things or actions in a certain order or pattern according to a specific rule or set of rules (e.g., patterns of numbers, letters, words, pictures, mathematical operations).
Written Expression	The ability to communicate information and ideas in writing so others will understand.

Fluency of Ideas	The ability to come up with a number of ideas about a topic (the number of ideas is important, not their quality, correctness or creativity).
Near Vision	The ability to see details at close range (within a few feet of the observer).
Category Flexibility	The ability to generate or use different sets of rules for combining or grouping things in different ways.
Mathematical Reasoning	The ability to choose the right mathematical methods or formulas to solve a problem.
Number Facility	The ability to add, subtract, multiply, or divide quickly and correctly.
Speed of Closure	The ability to quickly make sense of, combine, and organize information into meaningful patterns.
Selective Attention	The ability to concentrate on a task over a period of time without being distracted.
Finger Dexterity	The ability to make precisely coordinated movements of the fingers of one or both hands to grasp, manipulate, or assemble very small objects.
Time Sharing	The ability to shift back and forth between two or more activities or sources of information (such as speech, sounds, touch, or other sources).
Perceptual Speed	The ability to quickly and accurately compare similarities and differences among sets of letters, numbers, objects, pictures, or patterns. The things to be compared may be presented at the same time or one after the other. This ability also includes comparing a presented object with a remembered object.
Flexibility of Closure	The ability to identify or detect a known pattern (a figure, object, word, or sound) that is hidden in other distracting material.
Depth Perception	The ability to judge which of several objects is closer or farther away from you, or to judge the distance between you and an object.
Memorization	The ability to remember information such as words, numbers, pictures, and procedures.
Multilimb Coordination	The ability to coordinate two or more limbs (for example, two arms, two legs, or one leg and one arm) while sitting, standing, or lying down. It does not involve performing the activities while the whole body is in motion.
Static Strength	The ability to exert maximum muscle force to lift, push, pull, or carry objects.
Auditory Attention	The ability to focus on a single source of sound in the presence of other distracting sounds.
Control Precision	The ability to quickly and repeatedly adjust the controls of a machine or a vehicle to exact positions.
Stamina	The ability to exert yourself physically over long periods of time without getting winded or out of breath.
Far Vision	The ability to see details at a distance.
Manual Dexterity	The ability to quickly move your hand, your hand together with your arm, or your two hands to grasp, manipulate, or assemble objects.
Trunk Strength	The ability to use your abdominal and lower back muscles to support part of the body repeatedly or continuously over time without 'giving out' or fatiguing.
Gross Body Coordination	The ability to coordinate the movement of your arms, legs, and torso together when the whole body is in motion.
Speed of Limb Movement	The ability to quickly move the arms and legs.
Arm-Hand Steadiness	The ability to keep your hand and arm steady while moving your arm or while holding your arm and hand in one position.
Visualization	The ability to imagine how something will look after it is moved around or when its parts are moved or rearranged.
Extent Flexibility	The ability to bend, stretch, twist, or reach with your body, arms, and/or legs.
Visual Color Discrimination	The ability to match or detect differences between colors, including shades of color and brightness.
Gross Body Equilibrium	The ability to keep or regain your body balance or stay upright when in an unstable position.
Hearing Sensitivity	The ability to detect or tell the differences between sounds that vary in pitch and loudness.
Dynamic Strength	The ability to exert muscle force repeatedly or continuously over time. This involves muscular endurance and resistance to muscle fatigue.
Wrist-Finger Speed	The ability to make fast, simple, repeated movements of the fingers, hands, and wrists.
Spatial Orientation	The ability to know your location in relation to the environment or to know where other objects are in relation to you.
Sound Localization	The ability to tell the direction from which a sound originated.
Night Vision	The ability to see under low light conditions.

Explosive Strength	The ability to use short bursts of muscle force to propel oneself (as in jumping or sprinting), or to throw an object.
Peripheral Vision	The ability to see objects or movement of objects to one's side when the eyes are looking ahead.
Reaction Time	The ability to quickly respond (with the hand, finger, or foot) to a signal (sound, light, picture) when it appears.
Dynamic Flexibility	The ability to quickly and repeatedly bend, stretch, twist, or reach out with your body, arms, and/or legs.
Response Orientation	The ability to choose quickly between two or more movements in response to two or more different signals (lights, sounds, pictures). It includes the speed with which the correct response is started with the hand, foot, or other body part.
Glare Sensitivity	The ability to see objects in the presence of glare or bright lighting.
Rate Control	The ability to time your movements or the movement of a piece of equipment in anticipation of changes in the speed and/or direction of a moving object or scene.

Work_Activity	Work_Activity Definitions
Communicating with Persons Outside Organization	Communicating with people outside the organization, representing the organization to customers, the public, government, and other external sources. This information can be exchanged in person, in writing, or by telephone or e-mail.
Organizing, Planning, and Prioritizing Work	Developing specific goals and plans to prioritize, organize, and accomplish your work.
Interacting With Computers	Using computers and computer systems (including hardware and software) to program, write software, set up functions, enter data, or process information.
Communicating with Supervisors, Peers, or Subordin	Providing information to supervisors, co-workers, and subordinates by telephone, in written form, e-mail, or in person.
Making Decisions and Solving Problems	Analyzing information and evaluating results to choose the best solution and solve problems.
Establishing and Maintaining Interpersonal Relatio	Developing constructive and cooperative working relationships with others, and maintaining them over time.
Updating and Using Relevant Knowledge	Keeping up-to-date technically and applying new knowledge to your job.
Getting Information	Observing, receiving, and otherwise obtaining information from all relevant sources.
Identifying Objects, Actions, and Events	Identifying information by categorizing, estimating, recognizing differences or similarities, and detecting changes in circumstances or events.
Selling or Influencing Others	Convincing others to buy merchandise/goods or to otherwise change their minds or actions.
Developing Objectives and Strategies	Establishing long-range objectives and specifying the strategies and actions to achieve them.
Guiding, Directing, and Motivating Subordinates	Providing guidance and direction to subordinates, including setting performance standards and monitoring performance.
Analyzing Data or Information	Identifying the underlying principles, reasons, or facts of information by breaking down information or data into separate parts.
Performing for or Working Directly with the Public	Performing for people or dealing directly with the public. This includes serving customers in restaurants and stores, and receiving clients or guests.
Processing Information	Compiling, coding, categorizing, calculating, tabulating, auditing, or verifying information or data.
Coordinating the Work and Activities of Others	Getting members of a group to work together to accomplish tasks.
Thinking Creatively	Developing, designing, or creating new applications, ideas, relationships, systems, or products, including artistic contributions.
Scheduling Work and Activities	Scheduling events, programs, and activities, as well as the work of others.
Staffing Organizational Units	Recruiting, interviewing, selecting, hiring, and promoting employees in an organization.
Resolving Conflicts and Negotiating with Others	Handling complaints, settling disputes, and resolving grievances and conflicts, or otherwise negotiating with others.
Monitoring and Controlling Resources	Monitoring and controlling resources and overseeing the spending of money.
Training and Teaching Others	Identifying the educational needs of others, developing formal educational or training programs or classes, and teaching or instructing others.
Developing and Building Teams	Encouraging and building mutual trust, respect, and cooperation among team members.
Estimating the Quantifiable Characteristics of Pro	Estimating sizes, distances, and quantities; or determining time, costs, resources, or materials needed to perform a work activity.
Interpreting the Meaning of Information for Others	Translating or explaining what information means and how it can be used.
Coaching and Developing Others	Identifying the developmental needs of others and coaching, mentoring, or otherwise helping others to improve their knowledge or skills.
Judging the Qualities of Things, Services, or Peop	Assessing the value, importance, or quality of things or people.
Provide Consultation and Advice to Others	Providing guidance and expert advice to management or other groups on technical, systems-, or process-related topics.
Performing Administrative Activities	Performing day-to-day administrative tasks such as maintaining information files and processing paperwork.
Documenting/Recording Information	Entering, transcribing, recording, storing, or maintaining information in written or electronic/magnetic form.
Monitor Processes, Materials, or Surroundings	Monitoring and reviewing information from materials, events, or the environment, to detect or assess problems.
Inspecting Equipment, Structures, or Material	Inspecting equipment, structures, or materials to identify the cause of errors or other problems or defects.
Handling and Moving Objects	Using hands and arms in handling, installing, positioning, and moving materials, and manipulating things.
Evaluating Information to Determine Compliance wit	Using relevant information and individual judgment to determine whether events or processes comply with laws, regulations, or standards.
Assisting and Caring for Others	Providing personal assistance, medical attention, emotional support, or other personal care to others such as coworkers, customers, or patients.
Performing General Physical Activities	Performing physical activities that require considerable use of your arms and legs and moving your whole body, such as climbing, lifting, balancing, walking, stooping, and handling of materials.
Repairing and Maintaining Electronic Equipment	Servicing, repairing, calibrating, regulating, fine-tuning, or testing machines, devices, and equipment that operate primarily on the basis of electrical or electronic (not mechanical) principles.
Operating Vehicles, Mechanized Devices, or Equipme	Running, maneuvering, navigating, or driving vehicles or mechanized equipment, such as forklifts, passenger vehicles, aircraft, or water craft.
Controlling Machines and Processes	Using either control mechanisms or direct physical activity to operate machines or processes (not including computers or vehicles).
Drafting, Laying Out, and Specifying Technical Dev	Providing documentation, detailed instructions, drawings, or specifications to tell others about how devices, parts, equipment, or structures are to be fabricated, constructed, assembled, modified, maintained, or used.
Repairing and Maintaining Mechanical Equipment	Servicing, repairing, adjusting, and testing machines, devices, moving parts, and equipment that operate primarily on the basis of mechanical (not electronic) principles.

Work_Context	Work_Context Definitions
Telephone	How often do you have telephone conversations in this job?
Contact With Others	How much does this job require the worker to be in contact with others (face-to-face, by telephone, or otherwise) in order to perform it?
Electronic Mail	How often do you use electronic mail in this job?
Freedom to Make Decisions	How much decision making freedom, without supervision, does the job offer?
Frequency of Decision Making	How frequently is the worker required to make decisions that affect other people, the financial resources, and/or the image and reputation of the organization?
Structured versus Unstructured Work	To what extent is this job structured for the worker, rather than allowing the worker to determine tasks, priorities, and goals?
Letters and Memos	How often does the job require written letters and memos?
Work With Work Group or Team	How important is it to work with others in a group or team in this job?
Coordinate or Lead Others	How important is it to coordinate or lead others in accomplishing work activities in this job?
Deal With External Customers	How important is it to work with external customers or the public in this job?
Impact of Decisions on Co-workers or Company Resul	How do the decisions an employee makes impact the results of co-workers, clients or the company?
Indoors, Environmentally Controlled	How often does this job require working indoors in environmentally controlled conditions?

Time Pressure	How often does this job require the worker to meet strict deadlines?
Level of Competition	To what extent does this job require the worker to compete or to be aware of competitive pressures?
Importance of Being Exact or Accurate	How important is being very exact or highly accurate in performing this job?
Responsibility for Outcomes and Results	How responsible is the worker for work outcomes and results of other workers?
Face-to-Face Discussions	How often do you have to have face-to-face discussions with individuals or teams in this job?
Frequency of Conflict Situations	How often are there conflict situations the employee has to face in this job?
In an Enclosed Vehicle or Equipment	How often does this job require working in a closed vehicle or equipment (e.g., car)?
Spend Time Sitting	How much does this job require sitting?
Responsible for Others' Health and Safety	How much responsibility is there for the health and safety of others in this job?
Physical Proximity	To what extent does this job require the worker to perform job tasks in close physical proximity to other people?
Importance of Repeating Same Tasks	How important is repeating the same physical activities (e.g., key entry) or mental activities (e.g., checking entries in a ledger) over and over, without stopping, to performing this job?
Deal With Unpleasant or Angry People	How frequently does the worker have to deal with unpleasant, angry, or discourteous individuals as part of the job requirements?
Sounds, Noise Levels Are Distracting or Uncomforta	How often does this job require working exposed to sounds and noise levels that are distracting or uncomfortable?
Public Speaking	How often do you have to perform public speaking in this job?
Degree of Automation	How automated is the job?
Spend Time Walking and Running	How much does this job require walking and running?
Consequence of Error	How serious would the result usually be if the worker made a mistake that was not readily correctable?
Outdoors, Exposed to Weather	How often does this job require working outdoors, exposed to all weather conditions?
Indoors, Not Environmentally Controlled	How often does this job require working indoors in non-controlled environmental conditions (e.g., warehouse without heat)?
Pace Determined by Speed of Equipment	How important is it to this job that the pace is determined by the speed of equipment or machinery? (This does not refer to keeping busy at all times on this job.)
Spend Time Standing	How much does this job require standing?
Outdoors, Under Cover	How often does this job require working outdoors, under cover (e.g., structure with roof but no walls)?
Very Hot or Cold Temperatures	How often does this job require working in very hot (above 90 F degrees) or very cold (below 32 F degrees) temperatures?
Spend Time Using Your Hands to Handle, Control, or	How much does this job require using your hands to handle, control, or feel objects, tools or controls?
Extremely Bright or Inadequate Lighting	How often does this job require working in extremely bright or inadequate lighting conditions?
Exposed to Hazardous Equipment	How often does this job require exposure to hazardous equipment?
Wear Common Protective or Safety Equipment such as	How much does this job require wearing common protective or safety equipment such as safety shoes, glasses, gloves, hard hats or live jackets?
Exposed to Hazardous Conditions	How often does this job require exposure to hazardous conditions?
Exposed to Contaminants	How often does this job require working exposed to contaminants (such as pollutants, gases, dust or odors)?
Cramped Work Space, Awkward Positions	How often does this job require working in cramped work spaces that requires getting into awkward positions?
Spend Time Making Repetitive Motions	How much does this job require making repetitive motions?
Spend Time Bending or Twisting the Body	How much does this job require bending or twisting your body?
Spend Time Kneeling, Crouching, Stooping, or Crawl	How much does this job require kneeling, crouching, stooping, or crawling?
Wear Specialized Protective or Safety Equipment su	How much does this job require wearing specialized protective or safety equipment such as breathing apparatus, safety harness, full protection suits, or radiation protection?
Exposed to High Places	How often does this job require exposure to high places?
Spend Time Keeping or Regaining Balance	How much does this job require keeping or regaining your balance?
Spend Time Climbing Ladders, Scaffolds, or Poles	How much does this job require climbing ladders, scaffolds, or poles?
Exposed to Whole Body Vibration	How often does this job require exposure to whole body vibration (e.g., operate a jackhammer)?
Deal With Physically Aggressive People	How frequently does this job require the worker to deal with physical aggression of violent individuals?
In an Open Vehicle or Equipment	How often does this job require working in an open vehicle or equipment (e.g., tractor)?
Exposed to Minor Burns, Cuts, Bites, or Stings	How often does this job require exposure to minor burns, cuts, bites, or stings?
Exposed to Disease or Infections	How often does this job require exposure to disease/infections?
Exposed to Radiation	How often does this job require exposure to radiation?

Job Zone Component	Job Zone Component Definitions
Title	Job Zone Four: Considerable Preparation Needed
Overall Experience	A minimum of two to four years of work-related skill, knowledge, or experience is needed for these occupations. For example, an accountant must complete four years of college and work for several years in accounting to be considered qualified.
Job Training	Employees in these occupations usually need several years of work-related experience, on-the-job training, and/or vocational training.
Job Zone Examples	Many of these occupations involve coordinating, supervising, managing, or training others. Examples include accountants, chefs and head cooks, computer programmers, historians, pharmacists, and police detectives.
SVP Range	(7.0 to < 8.0)
Education	Most of these occupations require a four - year bachelor's degree, but some do not.

Work_Styles	Work_Styles Definitions
Attention to Detail	Job requires being careful about detail and thorough in completing work tasks.
Integrity	Job requires being honest and ethical.
Self Control	Job requires maintaining composure, keeping emotions in check, controlling anger, and avoiding aggressive behavior, even in very difficult situations.
Analytical Thinking	Job requires analyzing information and using logic to address work-related issues and problems.
Concern for Others	Job requires being sensitive to others' needs and feelings and being understanding and helpful on the job.
Independence	Job requires developing one's own ways of doing things, guiding oneself with little or no supervision, and depending on oneself to get things done.
Cooperation	Job requires being pleasant with others on the job and displaying a good-natured, cooperative attitude.
Innovation	Job requires creativity and alternative thinking to develop new ideas for and answers to work-related problems.
Persistence	Job requires persistence in the face of obstacles.
Adaptability/Flexibility	Job requires being open to change (positive or negative) and to considerable variety in the workplace.
Dependability	Job requires being reliable, responsible, and dependable, and fulfilling obligations.
Initiative	Job requires a willingness to take on responsibilities and challenges.
Leadership	Job requires a willingness to lead, take charge, and offer opinions and direction.
Stress Tolerance	Job requires accepting criticism and dealing calmly and effectively with high stress situations.
Achievement/Effort	Job requires establishing and maintaining personally challenging achievement goals and exerting effort toward mastering tasks.
Social Orientation	Job requires preferring to work with others rather than alone, and being personally connected with others on the job.

11-2031.00 - Public Relations Managers

Plan and direct public relations programs designed to create and maintain a favorable public image for employer or client; or if engaged in fundraising, plan and direct activities to solicit and maintain funds for special projects and nonprofit organizations.

17

Tasks

1) Identify main client groups and audiences and determine the best way to communicate publicity information to them.

2) Evaluate advertising and promotion programs for compatibility with public relations efforts.

3) Develop and maintain the company's corporate image and identity, which includes the use of logos and signage.

4) Write interesting and effective press releases, prepare information for media kits and develop and maintain company internet or intranet web pages.

5) Assign, supervise and review the activities of public relations staff.

6) Direct activities of external agencies, establishments and departments that develop and implement communication strategies and information programs.

7) Formulate policies and procedures related to public information programs, working with public relations executives.

8) Manage communications budgets.

9) Manage special events such as sponsorship of races, parties introducing new products, or other activities the firm supports in order to gain public attention through the media without advertising directly.

10) Observe and report on social, economic and political trends that might affect employers.

11) Respond to requests for information about employers' activities or status.

12) Confer with labor relations managers to develop internal communications that keep employees informed of company activities.

13) Draft speeches for company executives, and arrange interviews and other forms of contact for them.

14) Facilitate consumer relations, or the relationship between parts of the company such as the managers and employees, or different branch offices.

15) Maintain company archives.

16) Produce films and other video products, regulate their distribution, and operate film library.

17) Manage in-house communication courses.

18) Establish goals for soliciting funds, develop policies for collection and safeguarding of contributions, and coordinate disbursement of funds.

Knowledge	Knowledge Definitions
English Language	Knowledge of the structure and content of the English language including the meaning and spelling of words, rules of composition, and grammar.
Law and Government	Knowledge of laws, legal codes, court procedures, precedents, government regulations, executive orders, agency rules, and the democratic political process.
Administration and Management	Knowledge of business and management principles involved in strategic planning, resource allocation, human resources modeling, leadership technique, production methods, and coordination of people and resources.
Customer and Personal Service	Knowledge of principles and processes for providing customer and personal services. This includes customer needs assessment, meeting quality standards for services, and evaluation of customer satisfaction.
Education and Training	Knowledge of principles and methods for curriculum and training design, teaching and instruction for individuals and groups, and the measurement of training effects.
Foreign Language	Knowledge of the structure and content of a foreign (non-English) language including the meaning and spelling of words, rules of composition and grammar, and pronunciation.
Sales and Marketing	Knowledge of principles and methods for showing, promoting, and selling products or services. This includes marketing strategy and tactics, product demonstration, sales techniques, and sales control systems.
Mathematics	Knowledge of arithmetic, algebra, geometry, calculus, statistics, and their applications.
Clerical	Knowledge of administrative and clerical procedures and systems such as word processing, managing files and records, stenography and transcription, designing forms, and other office procedures and terminology.
Economics and Accounting	Knowledge of economic and accounting principles and practices, the financial markets, banking and the analysis and reporting of financial data.
Communications and Media	Knowledge of media production, communication, and dissemination techniques and methods. This includes alternative ways to inform and entertain via written, oral, and visual media.
Computers and Electronics	Knowledge of circuit boards, processors, chips, electronic equipment, and computer hardware and software, including applications and programming.
Production and Processing	Knowledge of raw materials, production processes, quality control, costs, and other techniques for maximizing the effective manufacture and distribution of goods.
Therapy and Counseling	Knowledge of principles, methods, and procedures for diagnosis, treatment, and rehabilitation of physical and mental dysfunctions, and for career counseling and guidance.
Psychology	Knowledge of human behavior and performance; individual differences in ability, personality, and interests; learning and motivation; psychological research methods; and the assessment and treatment of behavioral and affective disorders.
Sociology and Anthropology	Knowledge of group behavior and dynamics, societal trends and influences, human migrations, ethnicity, cultures and their history and origins.
Philosophy and Theology	Knowledge of different philosophical systems and religions. This includes their basic principles, values, ethics, ways of thinking, customs, practices, and their impact on human culture.
Personnel and Human Resources	Knowledge of principles and procedures for personnel recruitment, selection, training, compensation and benefits, labor relations and negotiation, and personnel information systems.
History and Archeology	Knowledge of historical events and their causes, indicators, and effects on civilizations and cultures.
Public Safety and Security	Knowledge of relevant equipment, policies, procedures, and strategies to promote effective local, state, or national security operations for the protection of people, data, property, and institutions.
Telecommunications	Knowledge of transmission, broadcasting, switching, control, and operation of telecommunications systems.
Medicine and Dentistry	Knowledge of the information and techniques needed to diagnose and treat human injuries, diseases, and deformities. This includes symptoms, treatment alternatives, drug properties and interactions, and preventive health-care measures.
Fine Arts	Knowledge of the theory and techniques required to compose, produce, and perform works of music, dance, visual arts, drama, and sculpture.
Engineering and Technology	Knowledge of the practical application of engineering science and technology. This includes applying principles, techniques, procedures, and equipment to the design and production of various goods and services.
Transportation	Knowledge of principles and methods for moving people or goods by air, rail, sea, or road, including the relative costs and benefits.
Geography	Knowledge of principles and methods for describing the features of land, sea, and air masses, including their physical characteristics, locations, interrelationships, and distribution of plant, animal, and human life.
Design	Knowledge of design techniques, tools, and principles involved in production of precision technical plans, blueprints, drawings, and models.
Building and Construction	Knowledge of materials, methods, and the tools involved in the construction or repair of houses, buildings, or other structures such as highways and roads.
Mechanical	Knowledge of machines and tools, including their designs, uses, repair, and maintenance.
Food Production	Knowledge of techniques and equipment for planting, growing, and harvesting food products (both plant and animal) for consumption, including storage/handling techniques.
Biology	Knowledge of plant and animal organisms, their tissues, cells, functions, interdependencies, and interactions with each other and the environment.
Physics	Knowledge and prediction of physical principles, laws, their interrelationships, and applications to understanding fluid, material, and atmospheric dynamics, and mechanical, electrical, atomic and sub-atomic structures and processes.
Chemistry	Knowledge of the chemical composition, structure, and properties of substances and of the chemical processes and transformations that they undergo. This includes uses of chemicals and their interactions, danger signs, production techniques, and disposal methods.

Skills	Skills Definitions
Speaking	Talking to others to convey information effectively.
Time Management	Managing one's own time and the time of others.
Writing	Communicating effectively in writing as appropriate for the needs of the audience.
Reading Comprehension	Understanding written sentences and paragraphs in work related documents.
Active Listening	Giving full attention to what other people are saying, taking time to understand the points being made, asking questions as appropriate, and not interrupting at inappropriate times.
Coordination	Adjusting actions in relation to others' actions.
Service Orientation	Actively looking for ways to help people.
Social Perceptiveness	Being aware of others' reactions and understanding why they react as they do.
Persuasion	Persuading others to change their minds or behavior.
Critical Thinking	Using logic and reasoning to identify the strengths and weaknesses of alternative solutions, conclusions or approaches to problems.
Judgment and Decision Making	Considering the relative costs and benefits of potential actions to choose the most appropriate one.
Active Learning	Understanding the implications of new information for both current and future problem-solving and decision-making.
Monitoring	Monitoring/Assessing performance of yourself, other individuals, or organizations to make improvements or take corrective action.
Negotiation	Bringing others together and trying to reconcile differences.
Complex Problem Solving	Identifying complex problems and reviewing related information to develop and evaluate options and implement solutions.
Management of Personnel Resources	Motivating, developing, and directing people as they work, identifying the best people for the job.
Instructing	Teaching others how to do something.
Management of Financial Resources	Determining how money will be spent to get the work done, and accounting for these expenditures.
Operations Analysis	Analyzing needs and product requirements to create a design.
Learning Strategies	Selecting and using training/instructional methods and procedures appropriate for the situation when learning or teaching new things.
Systems Evaluation	Identifying measures or indicators of system performance and the actions needed to improve or correct performance, relative to the goals of the system.
Mathematics	Using mathematics to solve problems.
Systems Analysis	Determining how a system should work and how changes in conditions, operations, and the environment will affect outcomes.
Equipment Selection	Determining the kind of tools and equipment needed to do a job.
Quality Control Analysis	Conducting tests and inspections of products, services, or processes to evaluate quality or performance.
Science	Using scientific rules and methods to solve problems.
Troubleshooting	Determining causes of operating errors and deciding what to do about it.
Management of Material Resources	Obtaining and seeing to the appropriate use of equipment, facilities, and materials needed to do certain work.
Operation and Control	Controlling operations of equipment or systems.
Technology Design	Generating or adapting equipment and technology to serve user needs.
Installation	Installing equipment, machines, wiring, or programs to meet specifications.
Operation Monitoring	Watching gauges, dials, or other indicators to make sure a machine is working properly.
Equipment Maintenance	Performing routine maintenance on equipment and determining when and what kind of maintenance is needed.
Repairing	Repairing machines or systems using the needed tools.
Programming	Writing computer programs for various purposes.

Ability	Ability Definitions
Oral Comprehension	The ability to listen to and understand information and ideas presented through spoken words and sentences.
Problem Sensitivity	The ability to tell when something is wrong or is likely to go wrong. It does not involve solving the problem, only recognizing there is a problem.
Speech Recognition	The ability to identify and understand the speech of another person.
Speech Clarity	The ability to speak clearly so others can understand you.

Oral Expression	The ability to communicate information and ideas in speaking so others will understand.
Written Comprehension	The ability to read and understand information and ideas presented in writing.
Written Expression	The ability to communicate information and ideas in writing so others will understand.
Deductive Reasoning	The ability to apply general rules to specific problems to produce answers that make sense.
Inductive Reasoning	The ability to combine pieces of information to form general rules or conclusions (includes finding a relationship among seemingly unrelated events).
Originality	The ability to come up with unusual or clever ideas about a given topic or situation, or to develop creative ways to solve a problem.
Fluency of Ideas	The ability to come up with a number of ideas about a topic (the number of ideas is important, not their quality, correctness, or creativity).
Category Flexibility	The ability to generate or use different sets of rules for combining or grouping things in different ways.
Near Vision	The ability to see details at close range (within a few feet of the observer).
Information Ordering	The ability to arrange things or actions in a certain order or pattern according to a specific rule or set of rules (e.g., patterns of numbers, letters, words, pictures, mathematical operations).
Selective Attention	The ability to concentrate on a task over a period of time without being distracted.
Far Vision	The ability to see details at a distance.
Memorization	The ability to remember information such as words, numbers, pictures, and procedures.
Time Sharing	The ability to shift back and forth between two or more activities or sources of information (such as speech, sounds, touch, or other sources).
Number Facility	The ability to add, subtract, multiply, or divide quickly and correctly.
Mathematical Reasoning	The ability to choose the right mathematical methods or formulas to solve a problem.
Flexibility of Closure	The ability to identify or detect a known pattern (a figure, object, word, or sound) that is hidden in other distracting material.
Visual Color Discrimination	The ability to match or detect differences between colors, including shades of color and brightness.
Visualization	The ability to imagine how something will look after it is moved around or when its parts are moved or rearranged.
Perceptual Speed	The ability to quickly and accurately compare similarities and differences among sets of letters, numbers, objects, pictures, or patterns. The things to be compared may be presented at the same time or one after the other. This ability also includes comparing a presented object with a remembered object.
Hearing Sensitivity	The ability to detect or tell the differences between sounds that vary in pitch and loudness.
Speed of Closure	The ability to quickly make sense of, combine, and organize information into meaningful patterns.
Auditory Attention	The ability to focus on a single source of sound in the presence of other distracting sounds.
Depth Perception	The ability to judge which of several objects is closer or farther away from you, or to judge the distance between you and an object.
Finger Dexterity	The ability to make precisely coordinated movements of the fingers of one or both hands to grasp, manipulate, or assemble very small objects.
Control Precision	The ability to quickly and repeatedly adjust the controls of a machine or a vehicle to exact positions.
Multilimb Coordination	The ability to coordinate two or more limbs (for example, two arms, two legs, or one leg and one arm) while sitting, standing, or lying down. It does not involve performing the activities while the whole body is in motion.
Trunk Strength	The ability to use your abdominal and lower back muscles to support part of the body repeatedly or continuously over time without 'giving out' or fatiguing.
Sound Localization	The ability to tell the direction from which a sound originated.
Speed of Limb Movement	The ability to quickly move the arms and legs.
Wrist-Finger Speed	The ability to make fast, simple, repeated movements of the fingers, hands, and wrists.
Reaction Time	The ability to quickly respond (with the hand, finger, or foot) to a signal (sound, light, picture) when it appears.

Response Orientation	The ability to choose quickly between two or more movements in response to two or more different signals (lights, sounds, pictures). It includes the speed with which the correct response is started with the hand, foot, or other body part.
Gross Body Coordination	The ability to coordinate the movement of your arms, legs, and torso together when the whole body is in motion.
Arm-Hand Steadiness	The ability to keep your hand and arm steady while moving your arm or while holding your arm and hand in one position.
Spatial Orientation	The ability to know your location in relation to the environment or to know where other objects are in relation to you.
Rate Control	The ability to time your movements or the movement of a piece of equipment in anticipation of changes in the speed and/or direction of a moving object or scene.
Dynamic Strength	The ability to exert muscle force repeatedly or continuously over time. This involves muscular endurance and resistance to muscle fatigue.
Extent Flexibility	The ability to bend, stretch, twist, or reach with your body, arms, and/or legs.
Gross Body Equilibrium	The ability to keep or regain your body balance or stay upright when in an unstable position.
Night Vision	The ability to see under low light conditions.
Peripheral Vision	The ability to see objects or movement of objects to one's side when the eyes are looking ahead.
Glare Sensitivity	The ability to see objects in the presence of glare or bright lighting.
Dynamic Flexibility	The ability to quickly and repeatedly bend, stretch, twist, or reach out with your body, arms, and/or legs.
Static Strength	The ability to exert maximum muscle force to lift, push, pull, or carry objects.
Stamina	The ability to exert yourself physically over long periods of time without getting winded or out of breath.
Manual Dexterity	The ability to quickly move your hand, your hand together with your arm, or your two hands to grasp, manipulate, or assemble objects.
Explosive Strength	The ability to use short bursts of muscle force to propel oneself (as in jumping or sprinting), or to throw an object.

Work_Activity	Work_Activity Definitions
Getting Information	Observing, receiving, and otherwise obtaining information from all relevant sources.
Establishing and Maintaining Interpersonal Relatio	Developing constructive and cooperative working relationships with others, and maintaining them over time.
Communicating with Persons Outside Organization	Communicating with people outside the organization, representing the organization to customers, the public, government, and other external sources. This information can be exchanged in person, in writing, or by telephone or e-mail.
Thinking Creatively	Developing, designing, or creating new applications, ideas, relationships, systems, or products, including artistic contributions.
Making Decisions and Solving Problems	Analyzing information and evaluating results to choose the best solution and solve problems.
Interacting With Computers	Using computers and computer systems (including hardware and software) to program, write software, set up functions, enter data, or process information.
Performing for or Working Directly with the Public	Performing for people or dealing directly with the public. This includes serving customers in restaurants and stores, and receiving clients or guests.
Identifying Objects, Actions, and Events	Identifying information by categorizing, estimating, recognizing differences or similarities, and detecting changes in circumstances or events.
Judging the Qualities of Things, Services, or Peop	Assessing the value, importance, or quality of things or people.
Communicating with Supervisors, Peers, or Subordin	Providing information to supervisors, co-workers, and subordinates by telephone, in written form, e-mail, or in person.
Guiding, Directing, and Motivating Subordinates	Providing guidance and direction to subordinates, including setting performance standards and monitoring performance.
Organizing, Planning, and Prioritizing Work	Developing specific goals and plans to prioritize, organize, and accomplish your work.
Selling or Influencing Others	Convincing others to buy merchandise/goods or to otherwise change their minds or actions.
Updating and Using Relevant Knowledge	Keeping up-to-date technically and applying new knowledge to your job.
Scheduling Work and Activities	Scheduling events, programs, and activities, as well as the work of others.

Developing and Building Teams	Encouraging and building mutual trust, respect, and cooperation among team members.
Monitor Processes, Materials, or Surroundings	Monitoring and reviewing information from materials, events, or the environment, to detect or assess problems.
Processing Information	Compiling, coding, categorizing, calculating, tabulating, auditing, or verifying information or data.
Developing Objectives and Strategies	Establishing long-range objectives and specifying the strategies and actions to achieve them.
Analyzing Data or Information	Identifying the underlying principles, reasons, or facts of information by breaking down information or data into separate parts.
Interpreting the Meaning of Information for Others	Translating or explaining what information means and how it can be used.
Provide Consultation and Advice to Others	Providing guidance and expert advice to management or other groups on technical, systems-, or process-related topics.
Coaching and Developing Others	Identifying the developmental needs of others and coaching, mentoring, or otherwise helping others to improve their knowledge or skills.
Estimating the Quantifiable Characteristics of Pro	Estimating sizes, distances, and quantities; or determining time, costs, resources, or materials needed to perform a work activity.
Training and Teaching Others	Identifying the educational needs of others, developing formal educational or training programs or classes, and teaching or instructing others.
Documenting/Recording Information	Entering, transcribing, recording, storing, or maintaining information in written or electronic/magnetic form.
Performing Administrative Activities	Performing day-to-day administrative tasks such as maintaining information files and processing paperwork.
Coordinating the Work and Activities of Others	Getting members of a group to work together to accomplish tasks.
Resolving Conflicts and Negotiating with Others	Handling complaints, settling disputes, and resolving grievances and conflicts, or otherwise negotiating with others.
Monitoring and Controlling Resources	Monitoring and controlling resources and overseeing the spending of money.
Assisting and Caring for Others	Providing personal assistance, medical attention, emotional support, or other personal care to others such as coworkers, customers, or patients.
Evaluating Information to Determine Compliance wit	Using relevant information and individual judgment to determine whether events or processes comply with laws, regulations, or standards.
Staffing Organizational Units	Recruiting, interviewing, selecting, hiring, and promoting employees in an organization.
Inspecting Equipment, Structures, or Material	Inspecting equipment, structures, or materials to identify the cause of errors or other problems or defects.
Performing General Physical Activities	Performing physical activities that require considerable use of your arms and legs and moving your whole body, such as climbing, lifting, balancing, walking, stooping, and handling of materials.
Handling and Moving Objects	Using hands and arms in handling, installing, positioning, and moving materials, and manipulating things.
Controlling Machines and Processes	Using either control mechanisms or direct physical activity to operate machines or processes (not including computers or vehicles).
Operating Vehicles, Mechanized Devices, or Equipme	Running, maneuvering, navigating, or driving vehicles or mechanized equipment, such as forklifts, passenger vehicles, aircraft, or water craft.
Repairing and Maintaining Electronic Equipment	Servicing, repairing, calibrating, regulating, fine-tuning, or testing machines, devices, and equipment that operate primarily on the basis of electrical or electronic (not mechanical) principles.
Drafting, Laying Out, and Specifying Technical Dev	Providing documentation, detailed instructions, drawings, or specifications to tell others about how devices, parts, equipment, or structures are to be fabricated, constructed, assembled, modified, maintained, or used.
Repairing and Maintaining Mechanical Equipment	Servicing, repairing, adjusting, and testing machines, devices, moving parts, and equipment that operate primarily on the basis of mechanical (not electronic) principles.

Work_Context	Work_Context Definitions
Telephone	How often do you have telephone conversations in this job?
Structured versus Unstructured Work	To what extent is this job structured for the worker, rather than allowing the worker to determine tasks, priorities, and goals?
Face-to-Face Discussions	How often do you have to have face-to-face discussions with individuals or teams in this job?
Indoors, Environmentally Controlled	How often does this job require working indoors in environmentally controlled conditions?

Electronic Mail	How often do you use electronic mail in this job?
Freedom to Make Decisions	How much decision making freedom, without supervision, does the job offer?
Contact With Others	How much does this job require the worker to be in contact with others (face-to-face, by telephone, or otherwise) in order to perform it?
Letters and Memos	How often does the job require written letters and memos?
Deal With External Customers	How important is it to work with external customers or the public in this job?
Coordinate or Lead Others	How important is it to coordinate or lead others in accomplishing work activities in this job?
Frequency of Decision Making	How frequently is the worker required to make decisions that affect other people, the financial resources, and/or the image and reputation of the organization?
Impact of Decisions on Co-workers or Company Resul	How do the decisions an employee makes impact the results of co-workers, clients or the company?
Work With Work Group or Team	How important is it to work with others in a group or team in this job?
Importance of Being Exact or Accurate	How important is being very exact or highly accurate in performing this job?
Time Pressure	How often does this job require the worker to meet strict deadlines?
Spend Time Sitting	How much does this job require sitting?
Responsibility for Outcomes and Results	How responsible is the worker for work outcomes and results of other workers?
Public Speaking	How often do you have to perform public speaking in this job?
Deal With Unpleasant or Angry People	How frequently does the worker have to deal with unpleasant, angry, or discourteous individuals as part of the job requirements?
Frequency of Conflict Situations	How often are there conflict situations the employee has to face in this job?
Level of Competition	To what extent does this job require the worker to compete or to be aware of competitive pressures?
Physical Proximity	To what extent does this job require the worker to perform job tasks in close physical proximity to other people?
In an Enclosed Vehicle or Equipment	How often does this job require working in a closed vehicle or equipment (e.g., car)?
Degree of Automation	How automated is the job?
Responsible for Others' Health and Safety	How much responsibility is there for the health and safety of others in this job?
Spend Time Standing	How much does this job require standing?
Outdoors, Exposed to Weather	How often does this job require working outdoors, exposed to all weather conditions?
Importance of Repeating Same Tasks	How important is repeating the same physical activities (e.g., key entry) or mental activities (e.g., checking entries in a ledger) over and over, without stopping, to performing this job?
Indoors, Not Environmentally Controlled	How often does this job require working indoors in non-controlled environmental conditions (e.g., warehouse without heat)?
Consequence of Error	How serious would the result usually be if the worker made a mistake that was not readily correctable?
Spend Time Using Your Hands to Handle, Control, or	How much does this job require using your hands to handle, control, or feel objects, tools or controls?
Spend Time Making Repetitive Motions	How much does this job require making repetitive motions?
Sounds, Noise Levels Are Distracting or Uncomforta	How often does this job require working exposed to sounds and noise levels that are distracting or uncomfortable?
Outdoors, Under Cover	How often does this job require working outdoors, under cover (e.g., structure with roof but no walls)?
Extremely Bright or Inadequate Lighting	How often does this job require working in extremely bright or inadequate lighting conditions?
Spend Time Walking and Running	How much does this job require walking and running?
Deal With Physically Aggressive People	How frequently does this job require the worker to deal with physical aggression of violent individuals?
Very Hot or Cold Temperatures	How often does this job require working in very hot (above 90 F degrees) or very cold (below 32 F degrees) temperatures?
Exposed to Contaminants	How often does this job require working exposed to contaminants (such as pollutants, gases, dust or odors)?
Exposed to Disease or Infections	How often does this job require exposure to disease/infections?
Spend Time Bending or Twisting the Body	How much does this job require bending or twisting your body?
Cramped Work Space, Awkward Positions	How often does this job require working in cramped work spaces that requires getting into awkward positions?

In an Open Vehicle or Equipment	How often does this job require working in an open vehicle or equipment (e.g., tractor)?
Exposed to Hazardous Equipment	How often does this job require exposure to hazardous equipment?
Spend Time Kneeling, Crouching, Stooping, or Crawl	How much does this job require kneeling, crouching, stooping or crawling?
Exposed to Minor Burns, Cuts, Bites, or Stings	How often does this job require exposure to minor burns, cuts, bites, or stings?
Exposed to High Places	How often does this job require exposure to high places?
Wear Common Protective or Safety Equipment such as	How much does this job require wearing common protective or safety equipment such as safety shoes, glasses, gloves, hard hats or live jackets?
Spend Time Keeping or Regaining Balance	How much does this job require keeping or regaining your balance?
Pace Determined by Speed of Equipment	How important is it to this job that the pace is determined by the speed of equipment or machinery? (This does not refer to keeping busy at all times on this job.)
Exposed to Radiation	How often does this job require exposure to radiation?
Exposed to Whole Body Vibration	How often does this job require exposure to whole body vibration (e.g., operate a jackhammer)?
Exposed to Hazardous Conditions	How often does this job require exposure to hazardous conditions?
Spend Time Climbing Ladders, Scaffolds, or Poles	How much does this job require climbing ladders, scaffolds, or poles?
Wear Specialized Protective or Safety Equipment su	How much does this job require wearing specialized protective or safety equipment such as breathing apparatus, safety harness, full protection suits, or radiation protection?

Job Zone Component	Job Zone Component Definitions
Title	Job Zone Four: Considerable Preparation Needed
Overall Experience	A minimum of two to four years of work-related skill, knowledge, or experience is needed for these occupations. For example, an accountant must complete four years of college and work for several years in accounting to be considered qualified.
Job Training	Employees in these occupations usually need several years of work-related experience, on-the-job training, and/or vocational training.
Job Zone Examples	Many of these occupations involve coordinating, supervising, managing, or training others. Examples include accountants, chefs and head cooks, computer programmers, historians, pharmacists, and police detectives.
SVP Range	(7.0 to < 8.0)
Education	Most of these occupations require a four - year bachelor's degree, but some do not.

Work_Styles	Work_Styles Definitions
Dependability	Job requires being reliable, responsible, and dependable, and fulfilling obligations.
Attention to Detail	Job requires being careful about detail and thorough in completing work tasks.
Leadership	Job requires a willingness to lead, take charge, and offer opinions and direction.
Cooperation	Job requires being pleasant with others on the job and displaying a good-natured, cooperative attitude.
Concern for Others	Job requires being sensitive to others' needs and feelings and being understanding and helpful on the job.
Initiative	Job requires a willingness to take on responsibilities and challenges.
Integrity	Job requires being honest and ethical.
Analytical Thinking	Job requires analyzing information and using logic to address work-related issues and problems.
Innovation	Job requires creativity and alternative thinking to develop new ideas for and answers to work-related problems.
Independence	Job requires developing one's own ways of doing things, guiding oneself with little or no supervision, and depending on oneself to get things done.
Adaptability/Flexibility	Job requires being open to change (positive or negative) and to considerable variety in the workplace.
Achievement/Effort	Job requires establishing and maintaining personally challenging achievement goals and exerting effort toward mastering tasks.
Stress Tolerance	Job requires accepting criticism and dealing calmly and effectively with high stress situations.

Self Control	Job requires maintaining composure, keeping emotions in check, controlling anger, and avoiding aggressive behavior, even in very difficult situations.
Social Orientation	Job requires preferring to work with others rather than alone, and being personally connected with others on the job.
Persistence	Job requires persistence in the face of obstacles.

11-3011.00 - Administrative Services Managers

Plan, direct, or coordinate supportive services of an organization, such as recordkeeping, mail distribution, telephone operator/receptionist, and other office support services. May oversee facilities planning and maintenance and custodial operations.

Tasks

1) Direct or coordinate the supportive services department of a business, agency, or organization.

2) Analyze internal processes and recommend and implement procedural or policy changes to improve operations, such as supply changes or the disposal of records.

3) Set goals and deadlines for the department.

4) Acquire, distribute and store supplies.

5) Monitor the facility to ensure that it remains safe, secure, and well-maintained.

6) Hire and terminate clerical and administrative personnel.

7) Plan, administer and control budgets for contracts, equipment and supplies.

8) Conduct classes to teach procedures to staff.

9) Oversee the maintenance and repair of machinery, equipment, and electrical and mechanical systems.

10) Oversee construction and renovation projects to improve efficiency and to ensure that facilities meet environmental, health, and security standards, and comply with government regulations.

11) Dispose of, or oversee the disposal of, surplus or unclaimed property.

12) Participate in architectural and engineering planning and design, including space and installation management.

13) Manage leasing of facility space.

Knowledge	Knowledge Definitions
Clerical	Knowledge of administrative and clerical procedures and systems such as word processing, managing files and records, stenography and transcription, designing forms, and other office procedures and terminology.
Administration and Management	Knowledge of business and management principles involved in strategic planning, resource allocation, human resources modeling, leadership technique, production methods, and coordination of people and resources.
Customer and Personal Service	Knowledge of principles and processes for providing customer and personal services. This includes customer needs assessment, meeting quality standards for services, and evaluation of customer satisfaction.
Personnel and Human Resources	Knowledge of principles and procedures for personnel recruitment, selection, training, compensation and benefits, labor relations and negotiation, and personnel information systems.
English Language	Knowledge of the structure and content of the English language including the meaning and spelling of words, rules of composition, and grammar.
Law and Government	Knowledge of laws, legal codes, court procedures, precedents, government regulations, executive orders, agency rules, and the democratic political process.
Mathematics	Knowledge of arithmetic, algebra, geometry, calculus, statistics, and their applications.
Economics and Accounting	Knowledge of economic and accounting principles and practices, the financial markets, banking and the analysis and reporting of financial data.
Public Safety and Security	Knowledge of relevant equipment, policies, procedures, and strategies to promote effective local, state, or national security operations for the protection of people, data, property, and institutions.

Communications and Media	Knowledge of media production, communication, and dissemination techniques and methods. This includes alternative ways to inform and entertain via written, oral, and visual media.
Computers and Electronics	Knowledge of circuit boards, processors, chips, electronic equipment, and computer hardware and software, including applications and programming.
Production and Processing	Knowledge of raw materials, production processes, quality control, costs, and other techniques for maximizing the effective manufacture and distribution of goods.
Education and Training	Knowledge of principles and methods for curriculum and training design, teaching and instruction for individuals and groups, and the measurement of training effects.
Transportation	Knowledge of principles and methods for moving people or goods by air, rail, sea, or road, including the relative costs and benefits.
Psychology	Knowledge of human behavior and performance; individual differences in ability, personality, and interests; learning and motivation; psychological research methods; and the assessment and treatment of behavioral and affective disorders.
Sales and Marketing	Knowledge of principles and methods for showing, promoting, and selling products or services. This includes marketing strategy and tactics, product demonstration, sales techniques, and sales control systems.
Sociology and Anthropology	Knowledge of group behavior and dynamics, societal trends and influences, human migrations, ethnicity, cultures and their history and origins.
Engineering and Technology	Knowledge of the practical application of engineering science and technology. This includes applying principles, techniques, procedures, and equipment to the design and production of various goods and services.
Telecommunications	Knowledge of transmission, broadcasting, switching, control, and operation of telecommunications systems.
Mechanical	Knowledge of machines and tools, including their designs, uses, repair, and maintenance.
Food Production	Knowledge of techniques and equipment for planting, growing, and harvesting food products (both plant and animal) for consumption, including storage/handling techniques.
Chemistry	Knowledge of the chemical composition, structure, and properties of substances and of the chemical processes and transformations that they undergo. This includes uses of chemicals and their interactions, danger signs, production techniques, and disposal methods.
Therapy and Counseling	Knowledge of principles, methods, and procedures for diagnosis, treatment, and rehabilitation of physical and mental dysfunctions, and for career counseling and guidance.
Foreign Language	Knowledge of the structure and content of a foreign (non-English) language including the meaning and spelling of words, rules of composition and grammar, and pronunciation.
Medicine and Dentistry	Knowledge of the information and techniques needed to diagnose and treat human injuries, diseases, and deformities. This includes symptoms, treatment alternatives, drug properties and interactions, and preventive health-care measures.
Physics	Knowledge and prediction of physical principles, laws, their interrelationships, and applications to understanding fluid, material, and atmospheric dynamics, and mechanical, electrical, atomic and sub-atomic structures and processes.
Philosophy and Theology	Knowledge of different philosophical systems and religions. This includes their basic principles, values, ethics, ways of thinking, customs, practices, and their impact on human culture.
Geography	Knowledge of principles and methods for describing the features of land, sea, and air masses, including their physical characteristics, locations, interrelationships, and distribution of plant, animal, and human life.
Design	Knowledge of design techniques, tools, and principles involved in production of precision technical plans, blueprints, drawings, and models.
Building and Construction	Knowledge of materials, methods, and the tools involved in the construction or repair of houses, buildings, or other structures such as highways and roads.
History and Archeology	Knowledge of historical events and their causes, indicators, and effects on civilizations and cultures.
Biology	Knowledge of plant and animal organisms, their tissues, cells, functions, interdependencies, and interactions with each other and the environment.

Fine Arts	Knowledge of the theory and techniques required to compose, produce, and perform works of music, dance, visual arts, drama, and sculpture.

Skills	Skills Definitions
Social Perceptiveness	Being aware of others' reactions and understanding why they react as they do.
Time Management	Managing one's own time and the time of others.
Reading Comprehension	Understanding written sentences and paragraphs in work related documents.
Coordination	Adjusting actions in relation to others' actions.
Service Orientation	Actively looking for ways to help people.
Active Listening	Giving full attention to what other people are saying, taking time to understand the points being made, asking questions as appropriate, and not interrupting at inappropriate times.
Active Learning	Understanding the implications of new information for both current and future problem-solving and decision-making.
Instructing	Teaching others how to do something.
Writing	Communicating effectively in writing as appropriate for the needs of the audience.
Speaking	Talking to others to convey information effectively.
Monitoring	Monitoring/Assessing performance of yourself, other individuals, or organizations to make improvements or take corrective action.
Critical Thinking	Using logic and reasoning to identify the strengths and weaknesses of alternative solutions, conclusions or approaches to problems.
Management of Personnel Resources	Motivating, developing, and directing people as they work, identifying the best people for the job.
Management of Financial Resources	Determining how money will be spent to get the work done, and accounting for these expenditures.
Judgment and Decision Making	Considering the relative costs and benefits of potential actions to choose the most appropriate one.
Mathematics	Using mathematics to solve problems.
Complex Problem Solving	Identifying complex problems and reviewing related information to develop and evaluate options and implement solutions.
Learning Strategies	Selecting and using training/instructional methods and procedures appropriate for the situation when learning or teaching new things.
Operation and Control	Controlling operations of equipment or systems.
Negotiation	Bringing others together and trying to reconcile differences.
Persuasion	Persuading others to change their minds or behavior.
Management of Material Resources	Obtaining and seeing to the appropriate use of equipment, facilities, and materials needed to do certain work.
Systems Evaluation	Identifying measures or indicators of system performance and the actions needed to improve or correct performance, relative to the goals of the system.
Operations Analysis	Analyzing needs and product requirements to create a design.
Systems Analysis	Determining how a system should work and how changes in conditions, operations, and the environment will affect outcomes.
Equipment Selection	Determining the kind of tools and equipment needed to do a job.
Operation Monitoring	Watching gauges, dials, or other indicators to make sure a machine is working properly.
Troubleshooting	Determining causes of operating errors and deciding what to do about it.
Programming	Writing computer programs for various purposes.
Quality Control Analysis	Conducting tests and inspections of products, services, or processes to evaluate quality or performance.
Equipment Maintenance	Performing routine maintenance on equipment and determining when and what kind of maintenance is needed.
Technology Design	Generating or adapting equipment and technology to serve user needs.
Science	Using scientific rules and methods to solve problems.
Repairing	Repairing machines or systems using the needed tools.
Installation	Installing equipment, machines, wiring, or programs to meet specifications.

Ability	Ability Definitions
Oral Expression	The ability to communicate information and ideas in speaking so others will understand.
Oral Comprehension	The ability to listen to and understand information and ideas presented through spoken words and sentences.
Written Comprehension	The ability to read and understand information and ideas presented in writing.
Written Expression	The ability to communicate information and ideas in writing so others will understand.
Speech Clarity	The ability to speak clearly so others can understand you.
Speech Recognition	The ability to identify and understand the speech of another person.
Problem Sensitivity	The ability to tell when something is wrong or is likely to go wrong. It does not involve solving the problem, only recognizing there is a problem.
Information Ordering	The ability to arrange things or actions in a certain order or pattern according to a specific rule or set of rules (e.g., patterns of numbers, letters, words, pictures, mathematical operations).
Inductive Reasoning	The ability to combine pieces of information to form general rules or conclusions (includes finding a relationship among seemingly unrelated events).
Near Vision	The ability to see details at close range (within a few feet of the observer).
Deductive Reasoning	The ability to apply general rules to specific problems to produce answers that make sense.
Selective Attention	The ability to concentrate on a task over a period of time without being distracted.
Category Flexibility	The ability to generate or use different sets of rules for combining or grouping things in different ways.
Originality	The ability to come up with unusual or clever ideas about a given topic or situation, or to develop creative ways to solve a problem.
Far Vision	The ability to see details at a distance.
Finger Dexterity	The ability to make precisely coordinated movements of the fingers of one or both hands to grasp, manipulate, or assemble very small objects.
Trunk Strength	The ability to use your abdominal and lower back muscles to support part of the body repeatedly or continuously over time without 'giving out' or fatiguing.
Number Facility	The ability to add, subtract, multiply, or divide quickly and correctly.
Fluency of Ideas	The ability to come up with a number of ideas about a topic (the number of ideas is important, not their quality, correctness, or creativity).
Time Sharing	The ability to shift back and forth between two or more activities or sources of information (such as speech, sounds, touch, or other sources).
Mathematical Reasoning	The ability to choose the right mathematical methods or formulas to solve a problem.
Memorization	The ability to remember information such as words, numbers, pictures, and procedures.
Flexibility of Closure	The ability to identify or detect a known pattern (a figure, object, word, or sound) that is hidden in other distracting material.
Visualization	The ability to imagine how something will look after it is moved around or when its parts are moved or rearranged.
Auditory Attention	The ability to focus on a single source of sound in the presence of other distracting sounds.
Speed of Closure	The ability to quickly make sense of, combine, and organize information into meaningful patterns.
Perceptual Speed	The ability to quickly and accurately compare similarities and differences among sets of letters, numbers, objects, pictures, or patterns. The things to be compared may be presented at the same time or one after the other. This ability also includes comparing a presented object with a remembered object.
Depth Perception	The ability to judge which of several objects is closer or farther away from you, or to judge the distance between you and an object.
Manual Dexterity	The ability to quickly move your hand, your hand together with your arm, or your two hands to grasp, manipulate, or assemble objects.
Multilimb Coordination	The ability to coordinate two or more limbs (for example, two arms, two legs, or one leg and one arm) while sitting, standing, or lying down. It does not involve performing the activities while the whole body is in motion.
Hearing Sensitivity	The ability to detect or tell the differences between sounds that vary in pitch and loudness.
Control Precision	The ability to quickly and repeatedly adjust the controls of a machine or a vehicle to exact positions.
Arm-Hand Steadiness	The ability to keep your hand and arm steady while moving your arm or while holding your arm and hand in one position.
Visual Color Discrimination	The ability to match or detect differences between colors, including shades of color and brightness.

23

Spatial Orientation	The ability to know your location in relation to the environment or to know where other objects are in relation to you.
Static Strength	The ability to exert maximum muscle force to lift, push, pull, or carry objects.
Extent Flexibility	The ability to bend, stretch, twist, or reach with your body, arms, and/or legs.
Wrist-Finger Speed	The ability to make fast, simple, repeated movements of the fingers, hands, and wrists.
Sound Localization	The ability to tell the direction from which a sound originated.
Rate Control	The ability to time your movements or the movement of a piece of equipment in anticipation of changes in the speed and/or direction of a moving object or scene.
Reaction Time	The ability to quickly respond (with the hand, finger, or foot) to a signal (sound, light, picture) when it appears.
Glare Sensitivity	The ability to see objects in the presence of glare or bright lighting.
Explosive Strength	The ability to use short bursts of muscle force to propel oneself (as in jumping or sprinting), or to throw an object.
Night Vision	The ability to see under low light conditions.
Gross Body Coordination	The ability to coordinate the movement of your arms, legs, and torso together when the whole body is in motion.
Dynamic Flexibility	The ability to quickly and repeatedly bend, stretch, twist, or reach out with your body, arms, and/or legs.
Stamina	The ability to exert yourself physically over long periods of time without getting winded or out of breath.
Response Orientation	The ability to choose quickly between two or more movements in response to two or more different signals (lights, sounds, pictures). It includes the speed with which the correct response is started with the hand, foot, or other body part.
Dynamic Strength	The ability to exert muscle force repeatedly or continuously over time. This involves muscular endurance and resistance to muscle fatigue.
Peripheral Vision	The ability to see objects or movement of objects to one's side when the eyes are looking ahead.
Speed of Limb Movement	The ability to quickly move the arms and legs.
Gross Body Equilibrium	The ability to keep or regain your body balance or stay upright when in an unstable position.

Work_Activity	Work_Activity Definitions
Getting Information	Observing, receiving, and otherwise obtaining information from all relevant sources.
Making Decisions and Solving Problems	Analyzing information and evaluating results to choose the best solution and solve problems.
Communicating with Supervisors, Peers, or Subordin	Providing information to supervisors, co-workers, and subordinates by telephone, in written form, e-mail, or in person.
Communicating with Persons Outside Organization	Communicating with people outside the organization, representing the organization to customers, the public, government, and other external sources. This information can be exchanged in person, in writing, or by telephone or e-mail.
Organizing, Planning, and Prioritizing Work	Developing specific goals and plans to prioritize, organize, and accomplish your work.
Performing for or Working Directly with the Public	Performing for people or dealing directly with the public. This includes serving customers in restaurants and stores, and receiving clients or guests.
Performing Administrative Activities	Performing day-to-day administrative tasks such as maintaining information files and processing paperwork.
Establishing and Maintaining Interpersonal Relatio	Developing constructive and cooperative working relationships with others, and maintaining them over time.
Interacting With Computers	Using computers and computer systems (including hardware and software) to program, write software, set up functions, enter data, or process information.
Documenting/Recording Information	Entering, transcribing, recording, storing, or maintaining information in written or electronic/magnetic form.
Identifying Objects, Actions, and Events	Identifying information by categorizing, estimating, recognizing differences or similarities, and detecting changes in circumstances or events.
Analyzing Data or Information	Identifying the underlying principles, reasons, or facts of information by breaking down information or data into separate parts.
Judging the Qualities of Things, Services, or Peop	Assessing the value, importance, or quality of things or people.
Resolving Conflicts and Negotiating with Others	Handling complaints, settling disputes, and resolving grievances and conflicts, or otherwise negotiating with others.
Monitoring and Controlling Resources	Monitoring and controlling resources and overseeing the spending of money.

Evaluating Information to Determine Compliance wit	Using relevant information and individual judgment to determine whether events or processes comply with laws, regulations, or standards.
Processing Information	Compiling, coding, categorizing, calculating, tabulating, auditing, or verifying information or data.
Thinking Creatively	Developing, designing, or creating new applications, ideas, relationships, systems, or products, including artistic contributions.
Scheduling Work and Activities	Scheduling events, programs, and activities, as well as the work of others.
Coordinating the Work and Activities of Others	Getting members of a group to work together to accomplish tasks.
Updating and Using Relevant Knowledge	Keeping up-to-date technically and applying new knowledge to your job.
Interpreting the Meaning of Information for Others	Translating or explaining what information means and how it can be used.
Provide Consultation and Advice to Others	Providing guidance and expert advice to management or other groups on technical, systems-, or process-related topics.
Monitor Processes, Materials, or Surroundings	Monitoring and reviewing information from materials, events, or the environment, to detect or assess problems.
Coaching and Developing Others	Identifying the developmental needs of others and coaching, mentoring, or otherwise helping others to improve their knowledge or skills.
Assisting and Caring for Others	Providing personal assistance, medical attention, emotional support, or other personal care to others such as coworkers, customers, or patients.
Developing Objectives and Strategies	Establishing long-range objectives and specifying the strategies and actions to achieve them.
Staffing Organizational Units	Recruiting, interviewing, selecting, hiring, and promoting employees in an organization.
Inspecting Equipment, Structures, or Material	Inspecting equipment, structures, or materials to identify the cause of errors or other problems or defects.
Guiding, Directing, and Motivating Subordinates	Providing guidance and direction to subordinates, including setting performance standards and monitoring performance.
Training and Teaching Others	Identifying the educational needs of others, developing formal educational or training programs or classes, and teaching or instructing others.
Developing and Building Teams	Encouraging and building mutual trust, respect, and cooperation among team members.
Selling or Influencing Others	Convincing others to buy merchandise/goods or to otherwise change their minds or actions.
Estimating the Quantifiable Characteristics of Pro	Estimating sizes, distances, and quantities; or determining time, costs, resources, or materials needed to perform a work activity.
Performing General Physical Activities	Performing physical activities that require considerable use of your arms and legs and moving your whole body, such as climbing, lifting, balancing, walking, stooping, and handling of materials.
Handling and Moving Objects	Using hands and arms in handling, installing, positioning, and moving materials, and manipulating things.
Operating Vehicles, Mechanized Devices, or Equipme	Running, maneuvering, navigating, or driving vehicles or mechanized equipment, such as forklifts, passenger vehicles, aircraft, or water craft.
Controlling Machines and Processes	Using either control mechanisms or direct physical activity to operate machines or processes (not including computers or vehicles).
Repairing and Maintaining Mechanical Equipment	Servicing, repairing, adjusting, and testing machines, devices, moving parts, and equipment that operate primarily on the basis of mechanical (not electronic) principles.
Drafting, Laying Out, and Specifying Technical Dev	Providing documentation, detailed instructions, drawings, or specifications to tell others about how devices, parts, equipment, or structures are to be fabricated, constructed, assembled, modified, maintained, or used.
Repairing and Maintaining Electronic Equipment	Servicing, repairing, calibrating, regulating, fine-tuning, or testing machines, devices, and equipment that operate primarily on the basis of electrical or electronic (not mechanical) principles.

Work_Context	Work_Context Definitions
Telephone	How often do you have telephone conversations in this job?
Face-to-Face Discussions	How often do you have to have face-to-face discussions with individuals or teams in this job?
Contact With Others	How much does this job require the worker to be in contact with others (face-to-face, by telephone, or otherwise) in order to perform it?
Letters and Memos	How often does the job require written letters and memos?

Structured versus Unstructured Work	To what extent is this job structured for the worker, rather than allowing the worker to determine tasks, priorities, and goals?
Electronic Mail	How often do you use electronic mail in this job?
Work With Work Group or Team	How important is it to work with others in a group or team in this job?
Freedom to Make Decisions	How much decision making freedom, without supervision, does the job offer?
Coordinate or Lead Others	How important is it to coordinate or lead others in accomplishing work activities in this job?
Frequency of Decision Making	How frequently is the worker required to make decisions that affect other people, the financial resources, and/or the image and reputation of the organization?
Responsibility for Outcomes and Results	How responsible is the worker for work outcomes and results of other workers?
Indoors, Environmentally Controlled	How often does this job require working indoors in environmentally controlled conditions?
Deal With External Customers	How important is it to work with external customers or the public in this job?
Impact of Decisions on Co-workers or Company Resul	How do the decisions an employee makes impact the results of co-workers, clients or the company?
Responsible for Others' Health and Safety	How much responsibility is there for the health and safety of others in this job?
Importance of Being Exact or Accurate	How important is being very exact or highly accurate in performing this job?
Time Pressure	How often does this job require the worker to meet strict deadlines?
Deal With Unpleasant or Angry People	How frequently does the worker have to deal with unpleasant, angry, or discourteous individuals as part of the job requirements?
Importance of Repeating Same Tasks	How important is repeating the same physical activities (e.g., key entry) or mental activities (e.g., checking entries in a ledger) over and over, without stopping, to performing this job?
Frequency of Conflict Situations	How often are there conflict situations the employee has to face in this job?
Spend Time Standing	How much does this job require standing?
Consequence of Error	How serious would the result usually be if the worker made a mistake that was not readily correctable?
Degree of Automation	How automated is the job?
Spend Time Sitting	How much does this job require sitting?
Spend Time Using Your Hands to Handle, Control, or	How much does this job require using your hands to handle, control, or feel objects, tools or controls?
Sounds, Noise Levels Are Distracting or Uncomforta	How often does this job require working exposed to sounds and noise levels that are distracting or uncomfortable?
Spend Time Making Repetitive Motions	How much does this job require making repetitive motions?
Exposed to Contaminants	How often does this job require working exposed to contaminants (such as pollutants, gases, dust or odors)?
In an Enclosed Vehicle or Equipment	How often does this job require working in a closed vehicle or equipment (e.g., car)?
Physical Proximity	To what extent does this job require the worker to perform job tasks in close physical proximity to other people?
Spend Time Walking and Running	How much does this job require walking and running?
Outdoors, Exposed to Weather	How often does this job require working outdoors, exposed to all weather conditions?
Level of Competition	To what extent does this job require the worker to compete or to be aware of competitive pressures?
Public Speaking	How often do you have to perform public speaking in this job?
Spend Time Bending or Twisting the Body	How much does this job require bending or twisting your body?
Wear Common Protective or Safety Equipment such as	How much does this job require wearing common protective or safety equipment such as safety shoes, glasses, gloves, hard hats or live jackets?
Deal With Physically Aggressive People	How frequently does this job require the worker to deal with physical aggression of violent individuals?
Very Hot or Cold Temperatures	How often does this job require working in very hot (above 90 F degrees) or very cold (below 32 F degrees) temperatures?
Exposed to Disease or Infections	How often does this job require exposure to disease/infections?
Cramped Work Space, Awkward Positions	How often does this job require working in cramped work spaces that requires getting into awkward positions?
Spend Time Kneeling, Crouching, Stooping, or Crawl	How much does this job require kneeling, crouching, stooping or crawling?
Exposed to Minor Burns, Cuts, Bites, or Stings	How often does this job require exposure to minor burns, cuts, bites, or stings?

Spend Time Climbing Ladders, Scaffolds, or Poles	How much does this job require climbing ladders, scaffolds, or poles?
Exposed to Hazardous Conditions	How often does this job require exposure to hazardous conditions?
In an Open Vehicle or Equipment	How often does this job require working in an open vehicle or equipment (e.g., tractor)?
Exposed to Hazardous Equipment	How often does this job require exposure to hazardous equipment?
Indoors, Not Environmentally Controlled	How often does this job require working indoors in non-controlled environmental conditions (e.g.: warehouse without heat)?
Extremely Bright or Inadequate Lighting	How often does this job require working in extremely bright or inadequate lighting conditions?
Pace Determined by Speed of Equipment	How important is it to this job that the pace is determined by the speed of equipment or machinery? (This does not refer to keeping busy at all times on this job.)
Exposed to High Places	How often does this job require exposure to high places?
Exposed to Radiation	How often does this job require exposure to radiation?
Outdoors, Under Cover	How often does this job require working outdoors, under cover (e.g., structure with roof but no walls)?
Wear Specialized Protective or Safety Equipment su	How much does this job require wearing specialized protective or safety equipment such as breathing apparatus, safety harness, full protection suits, or radiation protection?
Spend Time Keeping or Regaining Balance	How much does this job require keeping or regaining your balance?
Exposed to Whole Body Vibration	How often does this job require exposure to whole body vibration (e.g., operate a jackhammer)?

Job Zone Component / Job Zone Component Definitions

Job Zone Component	Job Zone Component Definitions
Title	Job Zone Four: Considerable Preparation Needed
Overall Experience	A minimum of two to four years of work-related skill, knowledge, or experience is needed for these occupations. For example, an accountant must complete four years of college and work for several years in accounting to be considered qualified.
Job Training	Employees in these occupations usually need several years of work-related experience, on-the-job training, and/or vocational training.
Job Zone Examples	Many of these occupations involve coordinating, supervising, managing, or training others. Examples include accountants, chefs and head cooks, computer programmers, historians, pharmacists, and police detectives.
SVP Range	(7.0 to < 8.0)
Education	Most of these occupations require a four - year bachelor's degree, but some do not.

Work_Styles / Work_Styles Definitions

Work_Styles	Work_Styles Definitions
Integrity	Job requires being honest and ethical.
Dependability	Job requires being reliable, responsible, and dependable, and fulfilling obligations.
Leadership	Job requires a willingness to lead, take charge, and offer opinions and direction.
Independence	Job requires developing one's own ways of doing things, guiding oneself with little or no supervision, and depending on oneself to get things done.
Attention to Detail	Job requires being careful about detail and thorough in completing work tasks.
Cooperation	Job requires being pleasant with others on the job and displaying a good-natured, cooperative attitude.
Self Control	Job requires maintaining composure, keeping emotions in check, controlling anger, and avoiding aggressive behavior, even in very difficult situations.
Social Orientation	Job requires preferring to work with others rather than alone, and being personally connected with others on the job.
Concern for Others	Job requires being sensitive to others' needs and feelings and being understanding and helpful on the job.
Adaptability/Flexibility	Job requires being open to change (positive or negative) and to considerable variety in the workplace.
Stress Tolerance	Job requires accepting criticism and dealing calmly and effectively with high stress situations.
Analytical Thinking	Job requires analyzing information and using logic to address work-related issues and problems.
Initiative	Job requires a willingness to take on responsibilities and challenges.

Innovation	Job requires creativity and alternative thinking to develop new ideas for and answers to work-related problems.
Persistence	Job requires persistence in the face of obstacles.
Achievement/Effort	Job requires establishing and maintaining personally challenging achievement goals and exerting effort toward mastering tasks.

11-3021.00 - Computer and Information Systems Managers

Plan, direct, or coordinate activities in such fields as electronic data processing, information systems, systems analysis, and computer programming.

Tasks

1) Consult with users, management, vendors, and technicians to assess computing needs and system requirements.

2) Direct daily operations of department, analyzing workflow, establishing priorities, developing standards and setting deadlines.

3) Evaluate the organization's technology use and needs and recommend improvements, such as hardware and software upgrades.

4) Evaluate data processing proposals to assess project feasibility and requirements.

5) Develop computer information resources, providing for data security and control, strategic computing, and disaster recovery.

6) Recruit, hire, train and supervise staff, and/or participate in staffing decisions.

7) Assign and review the work of systems analysts, programmers, and other computer-related workers.

8) Meet with department heads, managers, supervisors, vendors, and others, to solicit cooperation and resolve problems.

9) Prepare and review operational reports or project progress reports.

10) Purchase necessary equipment.

11) Manage backup, security and user help systems.

12) Review project plans in order to plan and coordinate project activity.

13) Develop and interpret organizational goals, policies, and procedures.

14) Review and approve all systems charts and programs prior to their implementation.

15) Control operational budget and expenditures.

Knowledge	Knowledge Definitions
Computers and Electronics	Knowledge of circuit boards, processors, chips, electronic equipment, and computer hardware and software, including applications and programming.
Administration and Management	Knowledge of business and management principles involved in strategic planning, resource allocation, human resources modeling, leadership technique, production methods, and coordination of people and resources.
Mathematics	Knowledge of arithmetic, algebra, geometry, calculus, statistics, and their applications.
English Language	Knowledge of the structure and content of the English language including the meaning and spelling of words, rules of composition, and grammar.
Design	Knowledge of design techniques, tools, and principles involved in production of precision technical plans, blueprints, drawings, and models.
Clerical	Knowledge of administrative and clerical procedures and systems such as word processing, managing files and records, stenography and transcription, designing forms, and other office procedures and terminology.
Engineering and Technology	Knowledge of the practical application of engineering science and technology. This includes applying principles, techniques, procedures, and equipment to the design and production of various goods and services.
Economics and Accounting	Knowledge of economic and accounting principles and practices, the financial markets, banking and the analysis and reporting of financial data.
Education and Training	Knowledge of principles and methods for curriculum and training design, teaching and instruction for individuals and groups, and the measurement of training effects.
Personnel and Human Resources	Knowledge of principles and procedures for personnel recruitment, selection, training, compensation and benefits, labor relations and negotiation, and personnel information systems.
Telecommunications	Knowledge of transmission, broadcasting, switching, control, and operation of telecommunications systems.
Psychology	Knowledge of human behavior and performance; individual differences in ability, personality, and interests; learning and motivation; psychological research methods; and the assessment and treatment of behavioral and affective disorders.
Public Safety and Security	Knowledge of relevant equipment, policies, procedures, and strategies to promote effective local, state, or national security operations for the protection of people, data, property, and institutions.
Customer and Personal Service	Knowledge of principles and processes for providing customer and personal services. This includes customer needs assessment, meeting quality standards for services, and evaluation of customer satisfaction.
Communications and Media	Knowledge of media production, communication, and dissemination techniques and methods. This includes alternative ways to inform and entertain via written, oral, and visual media.
Production and Processing	Knowledge of raw materials, production processes, quality control, costs, and other techniques for maximizing the effective manufacture and distribution of goods.
Law and Government	Knowledge of laws, legal codes, court procedures, precedents, government regulations, executive orders, agency rules, and the democratic political process.
Therapy and Counseling	Knowledge of principles, methods, and procedures for diagnosis, treatment, and rehabilitation of physical and mental dysfunctions, and for career counseling and guidance.
Transportation	Knowledge of principles and methods for moving people or goods by air, rail, sea, or road, including the relative costs and benefits.
Sales and Marketing	Knowledge of principles and methods for showing, promoting, and selling products or services. This includes marketing strategy and tactics, product demonstration, sales techniques, and sales control systems.
Geography	Knowledge of principles and methods for describing the features of land, sea, and air masses, including their physical characteristics, locations, interrelationships, and distribution of plant, animal, and human life.
Mechanical	Knowledge of machines and tools, including their designs, uses, repair, and maintenance.
Sociology and Anthropology	Knowledge of group behavior and dynamics, societal trends and influences, human migrations, ethnicity, cultures and their history and origins.
Fine Arts	Knowledge of the theory and techniques required to compose, produce, and perform works of music, dance, visual arts, drama, and sculpture.
Physics	Knowledge and prediction of physical principles, laws, their interrelationships, and applications to understanding fluid, material, and atmospheric dynamics, and mechanical, electrical, atomic and sub- atomic structures and processes.
Philosophy and Theology	Knowledge of different philosophical systems and religions. This includes their basic principles, values, ethics, ways of thinking, customs, practices, and their impact on human culture.
Chemistry	Knowledge of the chemical composition, structure, and properties of substances and of the chemical processes and transformations that they undergo. This includes uses of chemicals and their interactions, danger signs, production techniques, and disposal methods.
Building and Construction	Knowledge of materials, methods, and the tools involved in the construction or repair of houses, buildings, or other structures such as highways and roads.
Foreign Language	Knowledge of the structure and content of a foreign (non-English) language including the meaning and spelling of words, rules of composition and grammar, and pronunciation.
History and Archeology	Knowledge of historical events and their causes, indicators, and effects on civilizations and cultures.
Medicine and Dentistry	Knowledge of the information and techniques needed to diagnose and treat human injuries, diseases, and deformities. This includes symptoms, treatment alternatives, drug properties and interactions, and preventive health-care measures.
Biology	Knowledge of plant and animal organisms, their tissues, cells, functions, interdependencies, and interactions with each other and the environment.

| Food Production | Knowledge of techniques and equipment for planting. growing. and harvesting food products (both plant and animal) for consumption. including storage/handling techniques. |

Skills	**Skills Definitions**
Reading Comprehension	Understanding written sentences and paragraphs in work related documents.
Critical Thinking	Using logic and reasoning to identify the strengths and weaknesses of alternative solutions, conclusions or approaches to problems.
Active Listening	Giving full attention to what other people are saying, taking time to understand the points being made, asking questions as appropriate, and not interrupting at inappropriate times.
Judgment and Decision Making	Considering the relative costs and benefits of potential actions to choose the most appropriate one.
Active Learning	Understanding the implications of new information for both current and future problem-solving and decision-making.
Negotiation	Bringing others together and trying to reconcile differences.
Management of Financial Resources	Determining how money will be spent to get the work done, and accounting for these expenditures.
Complex Problem Solving	Identifying complex problems and reviewing related information to develop and evaluate options and implement solutions.
Time Management	Managing one's own time and the time of others.
Systems Evaluation	Identifying measures or indicators of system performance and the actions needed to improve or correct performance, relative to the goals of the system.
Coordination	Adjusting actions in relation to others' actions.
Mathematics	Using mathematics to solve problems.
Operations Analysis	Analyzing needs and product requirements to create a design.
Technology Design	Generating or adapting equipment and technology to serve user needs.
Systems Analysis	Determining how a system should work and how changes in conditions, operations, and the environment will affect outcomes.
Quality Control Analysis	Conducting tests and inspections of products, services, or processes to evaluate quality or performance.
Writing	Communicating effectively in writing as appropriate for the needs of the audience.
Speaking	Talking to others to convey information effectively.
Persuasion	Persuading others to change their minds or behavior.
Service Orientation	Actively looking for ways to help people.
Social Perceptiveness	Being aware of others' reactions and understanding why they react as they do.
Troubleshooting	Determining causes of operating errors and deciding what to do about it.
Management of Material Resources	Obtaining and seeing to the appropriate use of equipment, facilities, and materials needed to do certain work.
Learning Strategies	Selecting and using training/instructional methods and procedures appropriate for the situation when learning or teaching new things.
Management of Personnel Resources	Motivating, developing, and directing people as they work, identifying the best people for the job.
Monitoring	Monitoring/Assessing performance of yourself, other individuals, or organizations to make improvements or take corrective action.
Equipment Selection	Determining the kind of tools and equipment needed to do a job.
Instructing	Teaching others how to do something.
Programming	Writing computer programs for various purposes.
Operation and Control	Controlling operations of equipment or systems.
Installation	Installing equipment, machines, wiring, or programs to meet specifications.
Operation Monitoring	Watching gauges, dials, or other indicators to make sure a machine is working properly.
Repairing	Repairing machines or systems using the needed tools.
Equipment Maintenance	Performing routine maintenance on equipment and determining when and what kind of maintenance is needed.
Science	Using scientific rules and methods to solve problems.

Ability	**Ability Definitions**
Oral Expression	The ability to communicate information and ideas in speaking so others will understand.
Problem Sensitivity	The ability to tell when something is wrong or is likely to go wrong. It does not involve solving the problem, only recognizing there is a problem.

Oral Comprehension	The ability to listen to and understand information and ideas presented through spoken words and sentences.
Written Comprehension	The ability to read and understand information and ideas presented in writing.
Near Vision	The ability to see details at close range (within a few feet of the observer).
Deductive Reasoning	The ability to apply general rules to specific problems to produce answers that make sense.
Speech Clarity	The ability to speak clearly so others can understand you.
Inductive Reasoning	The ability to combine pieces of information to form general rules or conclusions (includes finding a relationship among seemingly unrelated events).
Speech Recognition	The ability to identify and understand the speech of another person.
Written Expression	The ability to communicate information and ideas in writing so others will understand.
Information Ordering	The ability to arrange things or actions in a certain order or pattern according to a specific rule or set of rules (e.g., patterns of numbers, letters, words, pictures, mathematical operations).
Category Flexibility	The ability to generate or use different sets of rules for combining or grouping things in different ways.
Originality	The ability to come up with unusual or clever ideas about a given topic or situation, or to develop creative ways to solve a problem.
Fluency of Ideas	The ability to come up with a number of ideas about a topic (the number of ideas is important, not their quality, correctness, or creativity).
Selective Attention	The ability to concentrate on a task over a period of time without being distracted.
Flexibility of Closure	The ability to identify or detect a known pattern (a figure, object, word, or sound) that is hidden in other distracting material.
Memorization	The ability to remember information such as words, numbers, pictures, and procedures.
Visualization	The ability to imagine how something will look after it is moved around or when its parts are moved or rearranged.
Mathematical Reasoning	The ability to choose the right mathematical methods or formulas to solve a problem.
Time Sharing	The ability to shift back and forth between two or more activities or sources of information (such as speech, sounds, touch, or other sources).
Speed of Closure	The ability to quickly make sense of, combine, and organize information into meaningful patterns.
Perceptual Speed	The ability to quickly and accurately compare similarities and differences among sets of letters, numbers, objects, pictures, or patterns. The things to be compared may be presented at the same time or one after the other. This ability also includes comparing a presented object with a remembered object.
Auditory Attention	The ability to focus on a single source of sound in the presence of other distracting sounds.
Number Facility	The ability to add, subtract, multiply, or divide quickly and correctly.
Far Vision	The ability to see details at a distance.
Trunk Strength	The ability to use your abdominal and lower back muscles to support part of the body repeatedly or continuously over time without 'giving out' or fatiguing.
Multilimb Coordination	The ability to coordinate two or more limbs (for example, two arms, two legs, or one leg and one arm) while sitting, standing, or lying down. It does not involve performing the activities while the whole body is in motion.
Extent Flexibility	The ability to bend, stretch, twist, or reach with your body, arms, and/or legs.
Stamina	The ability to exert yourself physically over long periods of time without getting winded or out of breath.
Arm-Hand Steadiness	The ability to keep your hand and arm steady while moving your arm or while holding your arm and hand in one position.
Dynamic Strength	The ability to exert muscle force repeatedly or continuously over time. This involves muscular endurance and resistance to muscle fatigue.
Static Strength	The ability to exert maximum muscle force to lift, push, pull, or carry objects.
Manual Dexterity	The ability to quickly move your hand, your hand together with your arm, or your two hands to grasp, manipulate, or assemble objects.
Gross Body Coordination	The ability to coordinate the movement of your arms, legs, and torso together when the whole body is in motion.

Depth Perception	The ability to judge which of several objects is closer or farther away from you, or to judge the distance between you and an object.
Control Precision	The ability to quickly and repeatedly adjust the controls of a machine or a vehicle to exact positions.
Visual Color Discrimination	The ability to match or detect differences between colors, including shades of color and brightness.
Finger Dexterity	The ability to make precisely coordinated movements of the fingers of one or both hands to grasp, manipulate, or assemble very small objects.
Hearing Sensitivity	The ability to detect or tell the differences between sounds that vary in pitch and loudness.
Gross Body Equilibrium	The ability to keep or regain your body balance or stay upright when in an unstable position.
Glare Sensitivity	The ability to see objects in the presence of glare or bright lighting.
Reaction Time	The ability to quickly respond (with the hand, finger, or foot) to a signal (sound, light, picture) when it appears.
Explosive Strength	The ability to use short bursts of muscle force to propel oneself (as in jumping or sprinting), or to throw an object.
Response Orientation	The ability to choose quickly between two or more movements in response to two or more different signals (lights, sounds, pictures). It includes the speed with which the correct response is started with the hand, foot, or other body part.
Spatial Orientation	The ability to know your location in relation to the environment or to know where other objects are in relation to you.
Wrist-Finger Speed	The ability to make fast, simple, repeated movements of the fingers, hands, and wrists.
Rate Control	The ability to time your movements or the movement of a piece of equipment in anticipation of changes in the speed and/or direction of a moving object or scene.
Peripheral Vision	The ability to see objects or movement of objects to one's side when the eyes are looking ahead.
Sound Localization	The ability to tell the direction from which a sound originated.
Speed of Limb Movement	The ability to quickly move the arms and legs.
Night Vision	The ability to see under low light conditions.
Dynamic Flexibility	The ability to quickly and repeatedly bend, stretch, twist, or reach out with your body, arms, and/or legs.

Work_Activity	Work_Activity Definitions
Getting Information	Observing, receiving, and otherwise obtaining information from all relevant sources.
Interacting With Computers	Using computers and computer systems (including hardware and software) to program, write software, set up functions, enter data, or process information.
Identifying Objects, Actions, and Events	Identifying information by categorizing, estimating, recognizing differences or similarities, and detecting changes in circumstances or events.
Interpreting the Meaning of Information for Others	Translating or explaining what information means and how it can be used.
Scheduling Work and Activities	Scheduling events, programs, and activities, as well as the work of others.
Making Decisions and Solving Problems	Analyzing information and evaluating results to choose the best solution and solve problems.
Establishing and Maintaining Interpersonal Relatio	Developing constructive and cooperative working relationships with others, and maintaining them over time.
Thinking Creatively	Developing, designing, or creating new applications, ideas, relationships, systems, or products, including artistic contributions.
Judging the Qualities of Things, Services, or Peop	Assessing the value, importance, or quality of things or people.
Processing Information	Compiling, coding, categorizing, calculating, tabulating, auditing, or verifying information or data.
Evaluating Information to Determine Compliance wit	Using relevant information and individual judgment to determine whether events or processes comply with laws, regulations, or standards.
Communicating with Supervisors, Peers, or Subordin	Providing information to supervisors, co-workers, and subordinates by telephone, in written form, e-mail, or in person.
Documenting/Recording Information	Entering, transcribing, recording, storing, or maintaining information in written or electronic/magnetic form.
Coordinating the Work and Activities of Others	Getting members of a group to work together to accomplish tasks.
Training and Teaching Others	Identifying the educational needs of others, developing formal educational or training programs or classes, and teaching or instructing others.

Analyzing Data or Information	Identifying the underlying principles, reasons, or facts of information by breaking down information or data into separate parts.
Developing Objectives and Strategies	Establishing long-range objectives and specifying the strategies and actions to achieve them.
Communicating with Persons Outside Organization	Communicating with people outside the organization, representing the organization to customers, the public, government, and other external sources. This information can be exchanged in person, in writing, or by telephone or e-mail.
Coaching and Developing Others	Identifying the developmental needs of others and coaching, mentoring, or otherwise helping others to improve their knowledge or skills.
Updating and Using Relevant Knowledge	Keeping up-to-date technically and applying new knowledge to your job.
Resolving Conflicts and Negotiating with Others	Handling complaints, settling disputes, and resolving grievances and conflicts, or otherwise negotiating with others.
Provide Consultation and Advice to Others	Providing guidance and expert advice to management or other groups on technical, systems-, or process-related topics.
Organizing, Planning, and Prioritizing Work	Developing specific goals and plans to prioritize, organize, and accomplish your work.
Estimating the Quantifiable Characteristics of Pro	Estimating sizes, distances, and quantities; or determining time, costs, resources, or materials needed to perform a work activity.
Guiding, Directing, and Motivating Subordinates	Providing guidance and direction to subordinates, including setting performance standards and monitoring performance.
Monitor Processes, Materials, or Surroundings	Monitoring and reviewing information from materials, events, or the environment, to detect or assess problems.
Staffing Organizational Units	Recruiting, interviewing, selecting, hiring, and promoting employees in an organization.
Selling or Influencing Others	Convincing others to buy merchandise/goods or to otherwise change their minds or actions.
Monitoring and Controlling Resources	Monitoring and controlling resources and overseeing the spending of money.
Developing and Building Teams	Encouraging and building mutual trust, respect, and cooperation among team members.
Assisting and Caring for Others	Providing personal assistance, medical attention, emotional support, or other personal care to others such as coworkers, customers, or patients.
Performing for or Working Directly with the Public	Performing for people or dealing directly with the public. This includes serving customers in restaurants and stores, and receiving clients or guests.
Inspecting Equipment, Structures, or Material	Inspecting equipment, structures, or materials to identify the cause of errors or other problems or defects.
Performing General Physical Activities	Performing physical activities that require considerable use of your arms and legs and moving your whole body, such as climbing, lifting, balancing, walking, stooping, and handling of materials.
Handling and Moving Objects	Using hands and arms in handling, installing, positioning, and moving materials, and manipulating things.
Performing Administrative Activities	Performing day-to-day administrative tasks such as maintaining information files and processing paperwork.
Drafting, Laying Out, and Specifying Technical Dev	Providing documentation, detailed instructions, drawings, or specifications to tell others about how devices, parts, equipment, or structures are to be fabricated, constructed, assembled, modified, maintained, or used.
Repairing and Maintaining Electronic Equipment	Servicing, repairing, calibrating, regulating, fine-tuning, or testing machines, devices, and equipment that operate primarily on the basis of electrical or electronic (not mechanical) principles.
Controlling Machines and Processes	Using either control mechanisms or direct physical activity to operate machines or processes (not including computers or vehicles).
Repairing and Maintaining Mechanical Equipment	Servicing, repairing, adjusting, and testing machines, devices, moving parts, and equipment that operate primarily on the basis of mechanical (not electronic) principles.
Operating Vehicles, Mechanized Devices, or Equipme	Running, maneuvering, navigating, or driving vehicles or mechanized equipment, such as forklifts, passenger vehicles, aircraft, or water craft.

Work_Context	Work_Context Definitions
Telephone	How often do you have telephone conversations in this job?
Electronic Mail	How often do you use electronic mail in this job?
Face-to-Face Discussions	How often do you have to have face-to-face discussions with individuals or teams in this job?
Work With Work Group or Team	How important is it to work with others in a group or team in this job?

Contact With Others	How much does this job require the worker to be in contact with others (face-to-face, by telephone, or otherwise) in order to perform it?
Freedom to Make Decisions	How much decision making freedom, without supervision, does the job offer?
Spend Time Sitting	How much does this job require sitting?
Structured versus Unstructured Work	To what extent is this job structured for the worker, rather than allowing the worker to determine tasks, priorities, and goals?
Indoors, Environmentally Controlled	How often does this job require working indoors in environmentally controlled conditions?
Importance of Being Exact or Accurate	How important is being very exact or highly accurate in performing this job?
Letters and Memos	How often does the job require written letters and memos?
Coordinate or Lead Others	How important is it to coordinate or lead others in accomplishing work activities in this job?
Responsibility for Outcomes and Results	How responsible is the worker for work outcomes and results of other workers?
Impact of Decisions on Co-workers or Company Resul	How do the decisions an employee makes impact the results of co-workers, clients or the company?
Frequency of Decision Making	How frequently is the worker required to make decisions that affect other people, the financial resources, and/or the image and reputation of the organization?
Sounds, Noise Levels Are Distracting or Uncomforta	How often does this job require working exposed to sounds and noise levels that are distracting or uncomfortable?
Level of Competition	To what extent does this job require the worker to compete or to be aware of competitive pressures?
Spend Time Making Repetitive Motions	How much does this job require making repetitive motions?
Time Pressure	How often does this job require the worker to meet strict deadlines?
Spend Time Using Your Hands to Handle, Control, or	How much does this job require using your hands to handle, control, or feel objects, tools or controls?
Importance of Repeating Same Tasks	How important is repeating the same physical activities (e.g., key entry) or mental activities (e.g., checking entries in a ledger) over and over, without stopping, to performing this job?
Responsible for Others' Health and Safety	How much responsibility is there for the health and safety of others in this job?
Deal With External Customers	How important is it to work with external customers or the public in this job?
Frequency of Conflict Situations	How often are there conflict situations the employee has to face in this job?
Physical Proximity	To what extent does this job require the worker to perform job tasks in close physical proximity to other people?
Deal With Unpleasant or Angry People	How frequently does the worker have to deal with unpleasant, angry, or discourteous individuals as part of the job requirements?
Consequence of Error	How serious would the result usually be if the worker made a mistake that was not readily correctable?
Degree of Automation	How automated is the job?
Public Speaking	How often do you have to perform public speaking in this job?
Spend Time Standing	How much does this job require standing?
Cramped Work Space, Awkward Positions	How often does this job require working in cramped work spaces that requires getting into awkward positions?
Wear Common Protective or Safety Equipment such as	How much does this job require wearing common protective or safety equipment such as safety shoes, glasses, gloves, hard hats or life jackets?
Spend Time Walking and Running	How much does this job require walking and running?
Indoors, Not Environmentally Controlled	How often does this job require working indoors in non-controlled environmental conditions (e.g., warehouse without heat)?
Spend Time Bending or Twisting the Body	How much does this job require bending or twisting your body?
In an Enclosed Vehicle or Equipment	How often does this job require working in a closed vehicle or equipment (e.g., car)?
Spend Time Kneeling, Crouching, Stooping, or Crawl	How much does this job require kneeling, crouching, stooping, or crawling?
Extremely Bright or Inadequate Lighting	How often does this job require working in extremely bright or inadequate lighting conditions?
Spend Time Keeping or Regaining Balance	How much does this job require keeping or regaining your balance?
Very Hot or Cold Temperatures	How often does this job require working in very hot (above 90 F degrees) or very cold (below 32 F degrees) temperatures?
Exposed to Contaminants	How often does this job require working exposed to contaminants (such as pollutants, gases, dust or odors)?
Outdoors, Exposed to Weather	How often does this job require working outdoors, exposed to all weather conditions?
Exposed to Hazardous Equipment	How often does this job require exposure to hazardous equipment?
Exposed to High Places	How often does this job require exposure to high places?
Outdoors, Under Cover	How often does this job require working outdoors, under cover (e.g., structure with roof but no walls)?
Spend Time Climbing Ladders, Scaffolds, or Poles	How much does this job require climbing ladders, scaffolds, or poles?
Deal With Physically Aggressive People	How frequently does this job require the worker to deal with physical aggression of violent individuals?
Pace Determined by Speed of Equipment	How important is it to this job that the pace is determined by the speed of equipment or machinery? (This does not refer to keeping busy at all times on this job.)
Exposed to Hazardous Conditions	How often does this job require exposure to hazardous conditions?
Exposed to Minor Burns, Cuts, Bites, or Stings	How often does this job require exposure to minor burns, cuts, bites, or stings?
Exposed to Radiation	How often does this job require exposure to radiation?
Exposed to Disease or Infections	How often does this job require exposure to disease/infections?
Wear Specialized Protective or Safety Equipment su	How much does this job require wearing specialized protective or safety equipment such as breathing apparatus, safety harness, full protection suits, or radiation protection?
Exposed to Whole Body Vibration	How often does this job require exposure to whole body vibration (e.g., operate a jackhammer)?
In an Open Vehicle or Equipment	How often does this job require working in an open vehicle or equipment (e.g., tractor)?

Job Zone Component	Job Zone Component Definitions
Title	Job Zone Five: Extensive Preparation Needed Extensive skill, knowledge, and experience are needed for these occupations. Many require more than five years of experience.
Overall Experience	For example, surgeons must complete four years of college and an additional five to seven years of specialized medical training to be able to do their job.
Job Training	Employees may need some on-the-job training, but most of these occupations assume that the person will already have the required skills, knowledge, work-related experience, and/or training.
Job Zone Examples	These occupations often involve coordinating, training, supervising, or managing the activities of others to accomplish goals. Very advanced communication and organizational skills are required. Examples include athletic trainers, lawyers, managing editors, physicists, social psychologists, and surgeons.
SVP Range	(8.0 and above)
Education	A bachelor's degree is the minimum formal education required for these occupations. However, many also require graduate school. For example, they may require a master's degree, and some require a Ph.D., M.D., or J.D. (law degree).

Work_Styles	Work_Styles Definitions
Dependability	Job requires being reliable, responsible, and dependable, and fulfilling obligations.
Self Control	Job requires maintaining composure, keeping emotions in check, controlling anger, and avoiding aggressive behavior, even in very difficult situations.
Integrity	Job requires being honest and ethical.
Adaptability/Flexibility	Job requires being open to change (positive or negative) and to considerable variety in the workplace.
Persistence	Job requires persistence in the face of obstacles.
Independence	Job requires developing one's own ways of doing things, guiding oneself with little or no supervision, and depending on oneself to get things done.
Analytical Thinking	Job requires analyzing information and using logic to address work-related issues and problems.
Leadership	Job requires a willingness to lead, take charge, and offer opinions and direction.
Cooperation	Job requires being pleasant with others on the job and displaying a good-natured, cooperative attitude.
Initiative	Job requires a willingness to take on responsibilities and challenges.
Attention to Detail	Job requires being careful about detail and thorough in completing work tasks.

Stress Tolerance	Job requires accepting criticism and dealing calmly and effectively with high stress situations.
Achievement/Effort	Job requires establishing and maintaining personally challenging achievement goals and exerting effort toward mastering tasks.
Innovation	Job requires creativity and alternative thinking to develop new ideas for and answers to work-related problems.
Concern for Others	Job requires being sensitive to others' needs and feelings and being understanding and helpful on the job.
Social Orientation	Job requires preferring to work with others rather than alone, and being personally connected with others on the job.

11-3031.01 - Treasurers, Controllers, and Chief Financial Officers

Plan, direct, and coordinate the financial activities of an organization at the highest level of management. Includes financial reserve officers.

Tasks

1) Monitor financial activities and details such as reserve levels to ensure that all legal and regulatory requirements are met.

2) Evaluate needs for procurement of funds and investment of surpluses, and make appropriate recommendations.

3) Lead staff training and development in budgeting and financial management areas.

4) Maintain current knowledge of organizational policies and procedures, federal and state policies and directives, and current accounting standards.

5) Supervise employees performing financial reporting, accounting, billing, collections, payroll, and budgeting duties.

6) Conduct or coordinate audits of company accounts and financial transactions to ensure compliance with state and federal requirements and statutes.

7) Develop and maintain relationships with banking, insurance, and non-organizational accounting personnel in order to facilitate financial activities.

8) Advise management on short-term and long-term financial objectives, policies, and actions.

9) Analyze the financial details of past, present, and expected operations in order to identify development opportunities and areas where improvement is needed.

10) Monitor and evaluate the performance of accounting and other financial staff; recommend and implement personnel actions such as promotions and dismissals.

11) Receive cash and checks, and deposit funds.

12) Prepare or direct preparation of financial statements, business activity reports, financial position forecasts, annual budgets, and/or reports required by regulatory agencies.

13) Develop internal control policies, guidelines, and procedures for activities such as budget administration, cash and credit management, and accounting.

14) Coordinate and direct the financial planning, budgeting, procurement, or investment activities of all or part of an organization.

15) Delegate authority for the receipt, disbursement, banking, protection, and custody of funds, securities, and financial instruments.

16) Perform tax planning work.

17) Receive and record requests for disbursements; authorize disbursements in accordance with policies and procedures.

18) Determine depreciation rates to apply to capitalized items, and advise management on actions regarding the purchase, lease, or disposal of such items.

19) Compute, withhold, and account for all payroll deductions.

20) Prepare and file annual tax returns, or prepare financial information so that outside accountants can complete tax returns.

11-3031.02 - Financial Managers, Branch or Department

Direct and coordinate financial activities of workers in a branch, office, or department of an establishment, such as branch bank, brokerage firm, risk and insurance department, or credit department.

Tasks

1) Examine, evaluate, and process loan applications.

2) Review collection reports to determine the status of collections and the amounts of outstanding balances.

3) Prepare financial and regulatory reports required by laws, regulations, and boards of directors.

4) Oversee the flow of cash and financial instruments.

5) Plan, direct, and coordinate risk and insurance programs of establishments to control risks and losses.

6) Direct insurance negotiations, select insurance brokers and carriers, and place insurance.

7) Communicate with stockholders and other investors to provide information, and to raise capital.

8) Network within communities to find and attract new business.

9) Monitor order flow and transactions that brokerage firm executes on the floor of exchange.

10) Approve or reject, or coordinate the approval and rejection of, lines of credit and commercial, real estate, and personal loans.

11) Establish and maintain relationships with individual and business customers, and provide assistance with problems these customers may encounter.

12) Evaluate financial reporting systems, accounting and collection procedures, and investment activities, and make recommendations for changes to procedures, operating systems, budgets, and other financial control functions.

13) Review reports of securities transactions and price lists in order to analyze market conditions.

14) Analyze and classify risks and investments to determine their potential impacts on companies.

15) Develop and analyze information to assess the current and future financial status of firms.

16) Establish procedures for custody and control of assets, records, loan collateral, and securities, in order to ensure safekeeping.

17) Evaluate data pertaining to costs in order to plan budgets.

18) Recruit staff members, and oversee training programs.

19) Submit delinquent accounts to attorneys or outside agencies for collection.

20) Plan, direct, and coordinate the activities of workers in branches, offices, or departments of such establishments as branch banks, brokerage firms, risk and insurance departments, or credit departments.

21) Prepare operational and risk reports for management analysis.

11-3040.00 - Human Resources Managers

Plan, direct, and coordinate human resource management activities of an organization to maximize the strategic use of human resources and maintain functions such as employee compensation, recruitment, personnel policies, and regulatory compliance.

Tasks

1) Provide current and prospective employees with information about policies, job duties, working conditions, wages, opportunities for promotion and employee benefits.

2) Administer compensation, benefits and performance management systems, and safety and recreation programs.

3) Maintain records and compile statistical reports concerning personnel-related data such as hires, transfers, performance appraisals, and absenteeism rates.

4) Advise managers on organizational policy matters such as equal employment opportunity and sexual harassment, and recommend needed changes.

5) Plan and conduct new employee orientation to foster positive attitude toward organizational objectives.

6) Perform difficult staffing duties, including dealing with understaffing, refereeing disputes, firing employees, and administering disciplinary procedures.

7) Identify staff vacancies and recruit, interview and select applicants.

8) Conduct exit interviews to identify reasons for employee termination.

9) Analyze training needs to design employee development, language training and health and safety programs.

10) Plan, direct, supervise, and coordinate work activities of subordinates and staff relating to employment, compensation, labor relations, and employee relations.

11) Allocate human resources, ensuring appropriate matches between personnel.

12) Analyze statistical data and reports to identify and determine causes of personnel problems and develop recommendations for improvement of organization's personnel policies and practices.

13) Plan, organize, direct, control or coordinate the personnel, training, or labor relations activities of an organization.

14) Analyze and modify compensation and benefits policies to establish competitive programs and ensure compliance with legal requirements.

15) Oversee the evaluation, classification and rating of occupations and job positions.

16) Develop and/or administer special projects in areas such as pay equity, savings bond programs, day-care, and employee awards.

17) Prepare and follow budgets for personnel operations.

18) Investigate and report on industrial accidents for insurance carriers.

19) Represent organization at personnel-related hearings and investigations.

20) Develop, administer and evaluate applicant tests.

21) Prepare personnel forecast to project employment needs.

22) Study legislation, arbitration decisions, and collective bargaining contracts to assess industry trends.

23) Contract with vendors to provide employee services, such as food service, transportation, or relocation service.

24) Provide terminated employees with outplacement or relocation assistance.

25) Negotiate bargaining agreements and help interpret labor contracts.

Knowledge	Knowledge Definitions
Personnel and Human Resources	Knowledge of principles and procedures for personnel recruitment, selection, training, compensation and benefits, labor relations and negotiation, and personnel information systems.
English Language	Knowledge of the structure and content of the English language including the meaning and spelling of words, rules of composition, and grammar.
Customer and Personal Service	Knowledge of principles and processes for providing customer and personal services. This includes customer needs assessment, meeting quality standards for services, and evaluation of customer satisfaction.
Administration and Management	Knowledge of business and management principles involved in strategic planning, resource allocation, human resources modeling, leadership technique, production methods, and coordination of people and resources.
Law and Government	Knowledge of laws, legal codes, court procedures, precedents, government regulations, executive orders, agency rules, and the democratic political process.
Clerical	Knowledge of administrative and clerical procedures and systems such as word processing, managing files and records, stenography and transcription, designing forms, and other office procedures and terminology.
Education and Training	Knowledge of principles and methods for curriculum and training design, teaching and instruction for individuals and groups, and the measurement of training effects.
Economics and Accounting	Knowledge of economic and accounting principles and practices, the financial markets, banking and the analysis and reporting of financial data.
Psychology	Knowledge of human behavior and performance; individual differences in ability, personality, and interests; learning and motivation; psychological research methods; and the assessment and treatment of behavioral and affective disorders.
Mathematics	Knowledge of arithmetic, algebra, geometry, calculus, statistics, and their applications.
Public Safety and Security	Knowledge of relevant equipment, policies, procedures, and strategies to promote effective local, state, or national security operations for the protection of people, data, property, and institutions.
Computers and Electronics	Knowledge of circuit boards, processors, chips, electronic equipment, and computer hardware and software, including applications and programming.
Production and Processing	Knowledge of raw materials, production processes, quality control, costs, and other techniques for maximizing the effective manufacture and distribution of goods.
Communications and Media	Knowledge of media production, communication, and dissemination techniques and methods. This includes alternative ways to inform and entertain via written, oral, and visual media.
Sociology and Anthropology	Knowledge of group behavior and dynamics, societal trends and influences, human migrations, ethnicity, cultures and their history and origins.
Therapy and Counseling	Knowledge of principles, methods, and procedures for diagnosis, treatment, and rehabilitation of physical and mental dysfunctions, and for career counseling and guidance.
Sales and Marketing	Knowledge of principles and methods for showing, promoting, and selling products or services. This includes marketing strategy and tactics, product demonstration, sales techniques, and sales control systems.
Telecommunications	Knowledge of transmission, broadcasting, switching, control, and operation of telecommunications systems.
Design	Knowledge of design techniques, tools, and principles involved in production of precision technical plans, blueprints, drawings, and models.
Transportation	Knowledge of principles and methods for moving people or goods by air, rail, sea, or road, including the relative costs and benefits.
Geography	Knowledge of principles and methods for describing the features of land, sea, and air masses, including their physical characteristics, locations, interrelationships, and distribution of plant, animal, and human life.
Philosophy and Theology	Knowledge of different philosophical systems and religions. This includes their basic principles, values, ethics, ways of thinking, customs, practices, and their impact on human culture.
Medicine and Dentistry	Knowledge of the information and techniques needed to diagnose and treat human injuries, diseases, and deformities. This includes symptoms, treatment alternatives, drug properties and interactions, and preventive health-care measures.
Engineering and Technology	Knowledge of the practical application of engineering science and technology. This includes applying principles, techniques, procedures, and equipment to the design and production of various goods and services.
Foreign Language	Knowledge of the structure and content of a foreign (non-English) language including the meaning and spelling of words, rules of composition and grammar, and pronunciation.
Mechanical	Knowledge of machines and tools, including their designs, uses, repair, and maintenance.
Chemistry	Knowledge of the chemical composition, structure, and properties of substances and of the chemical processes and transformations that they undergo. This includes uses of chemicals and their interactions, danger signs, production techniques, and disposal methods.
History and Archeology	Knowledge of historical events and their causes, indicators, and effects on civilizations and cultures.
Food Production	Knowledge of techniques and equipment for planting, growing, and harvesting food products (both plant and animal) for consumption, including storage/handling techniques.
Fine Arts	Knowledge of the theory and techniques required to compose, produce, and perform works of music, dance, visual arts, drama, and sculpture.
Physics	Knowledge and prediction of physical principles, laws, their interrelationships, and applications to understanding fluid, material, and atmospheric dynamics, and mechanical, electrical, atomic and sub-atomic structures and processes.
Building and Construction	Knowledge of materials, methods, and the tools involved in the construction or repair of houses, buildings, or other structures such as highways and roads.
Biology	Knowledge of plant and animal organisms, their tissues, cells, functions, interdependencies, and interactions with each other and the environment.

Skills	Skills Definitions
Active Listening	Giving full attention to what other people are saying, taking time to understand the points being made, asking questions as appropriate, and not interrupting at inappropriate times.
Management of Personnel Resources	Motivating, developing, and directing people as they work, identifying the best people for the job.
Writing	Communicating effectively in writing as appropriate for the needs of the audience.
Reading Comprehension	Understanding written sentences and paragraphs in work related documents.

Speaking	Talking to others to convey information effectively.
Negotiation	Bringing others together and trying to reconcile differences.
Time Management	Managing one's own time and the time of others.
Social Perceptiveness	Being aware of others' reactions and understanding why they react as they do.
Monitoring	Monitoring/Assessing performance of yourself, other individuals, or organizations to make improvements or take corrective action.
Critical Thinking	Using logic and reasoning to identify the strengths and weaknesses of alternative solutions, conclusions or approaches to problems.
Instructing	Teaching others how to do something.
Persuasion	Persuading others to change their minds or behavior.
Active Learning	Understanding the implications of new information for both current and future problem-solving and decision-making.
Judgment and Decision Making	Considering the relative costs and benefits of potential actions to choose the most appropriate one.
Learning Strategies	Selecting and using training/instructional methods and procedures appropriate for the situation when learning or teaching new things.
Mathematics	Using mathematics to solve problems.
Complex Problem Solving	Identifying complex problems and reviewing related information to develop and evaluate options and implement solutions.
Coordination	Adjusting actions in relation to others' actions.
Service Orientation	Actively looking for ways to help people.
Management of Financial Resources	Determining how money will be spent to get the work done, and accounting for these expenditures.
Quality Control Analysis	Conducting tests and inspections of products, services, or processes to evaluate quality or performance.
Operations Analysis	Analyzing needs and product requirements to create a design.
Management of Material Resources	Obtaining and seeing to the appropriate use of equipment, facilities, and materials needed to do certain work.
Systems Evaluation	Identifying measures or indicators of system performance and the actions needed to improve or correct performance, relative to the goals of the system.
Equipment Selection	Determining the kind of tools and equipment needed to do a job.
Systems Analysis	Determining how a system should work and how changes in conditions, operations, and the environment will affect outcomes.
Troubleshooting	Determining causes of operating errors and deciding what to do about it.
Science	Using scientific rules and methods to solve problems.
Technology Design	Generating or adapting equipment and technology to serve user needs.
Operation and Control	Controlling operations of equipment or systems.
Equipment Maintenance	Performing routine maintenance on equipment and determining when and what kind of maintenance is needed.
Installation	Installing equipment, machines, wiring, or programs to meet specifications.
Operation Monitoring	Watching gauges, dials, or other indicators to make sure a machine is working properly.
Repairing	Repairing machines or systems using the needed tools.
Programming	Writing computer programs for various purposes.

Ability	Ability Definitions
Oral Comprehension	The ability to listen to and understand information and ideas presented through spoken words and sentences.
Oral Expression	The ability to communicate information and ideas in speaking so others will understand.
Speech Clarity	The ability to speak clearly so others can understand you.
Written Expression	The ability to communicate information and ideas in writing so others will understand.
Written Comprehension	The ability to read and understand information and ideas presented in writing.
Speech Recognition	The ability to identify and understand the speech of another person.
Problem Sensitivity	The ability to tell when something is wrong or is likely to go wrong. It does not involve solving the problem, only recognizing there is a problem.
Deductive Reasoning	The ability to apply general rules to specific problems to produce answers that make sense.
Inductive Reasoning	The ability to combine pieces of information to form general rules or conclusions (includes finding a relationship among seemingly unrelated events).

Near Vision	The ability to see details at close range (within a few feet of the observer).
Originality	The ability to come up with unusual or clever ideas about a given topic or situation, or to develop creative ways to solve a problem.
Category Flexibility	The ability to generate or use different sets of rules for combining or grouping things in different ways.
Fluency of Ideas	The ability to come up with a number of ideas about a topic (the number of ideas is important, not their quality, correctness, or creativity).
Information Ordering	The ability to arrange things or actions in a certain order or pattern according to a specific rule or set of rules (e.g., patterns of numbers, letters, words, pictures, mathematical operations).
Mathematical Reasoning	The ability to choose the right mathematical methods or formulas to solve a problem.
Speed of Closure	The ability to quickly make sense of, combine, and organize information into meaningful patterns.
Memorization	The ability to remember information such as words, numbers, pictures, and procedures.
Selective Attention	The ability to concentrate on a task over a period of time without being distracted.
Flexibility of Closure	The ability to identify or detect a known pattern (a figure, object, word, or sound) that is hidden in other distracting material.
Number Facility	The ability to add, subtract, multiply, or divide quickly and correctly.
Visualization	The ability to imagine how something will look after it is moved around or when its parts are moved or rearranged.
Time Sharing	The ability to shift back and forth between two or more activities or sources of information (such as speech, sounds, touch, or other sources).
Far Vision	The ability to see details at a distance.
Finger Dexterity	The ability to make precisely coordinated movements of the fingers of one or both hands to grasp, manipulate, or assemble very small objects.
Auditory Attention	The ability to focus on a single source of sound in the presence of other distracting sounds.
Perceptual Speed	The ability to quickly and accurately compare similarities and differences among sets of letters, numbers, objects, pictures, or patterns. The things to be compared may be presented at the same time or one after the other. This ability also includes comparing a presented object with a remembered object.
Hearing Sensitivity	The ability to detect or tell the differences between sounds that vary in pitch and loudness.
Visual Color Discrimination	The ability to match or detect differences between colors, including shades of color and brightness.
Depth Perception	The ability to judge which of several objects is closer or farther away from you, or to judge the distance between you and an object.
Trunk Strength	The ability to use your abdominal and lower back muscles to support part of the body repeatedly or continuously over time without 'giving out' or fatiguing.
Wrist-Finger Speed	The ability to make fast, simple, repeated movements of the fingers, hands, and wrists.
Control Precision	The ability to quickly and repeatedly adjust the controls of a machine or a vehicle to exact positions.
Extent Flexibility	The ability to bend, stretch, twist, or reach with your body, arms, and/or legs.
Multilimb Coordination	The ability to coordinate two or more limbs (for example, two arms, two legs, or one leg and one arm) while sitting, standing, or lying down. It does not involve performing the activities while the whole body is in motion.
Response Orientation	The ability to choose quickly between two or more movements in response to two or more different signals (lights, sounds, pictures). It includes the speed with which the correct response is started with the hand, foot, or other body part.
Spatial Orientation	The ability to know your location in relation to the environment or to know where other objects are in relation to you.
Static Strength	The ability to exert maximum muscle force to lift, push, pull, or carry objects.
Speed of Limb Movement	The ability to quickly move the arms and legs.
Manual Dexterity	The ability to quickly move your hand, your hand together with your arm, or your two hands to grasp, manipulate, or assemble objects.
Night Vision	The ability to see under low light conditions.
Rate Control	The ability to time your movements or the movement of a piece of equipment in anticipation of changes in the speed and/or direction of a moving object or scene.

Gross Body Equilibrium	The ability to keep or regain your body balance or stay upright when in an unstable position.
Reaction Time	The ability to quickly respond (with the hand, finger, or foot) to a signal (sound, light, picture) when it appears.
Stamina	The ability to exert yourself physically over long periods of time without getting winded or out of breath.
Explosive Strength	The ability to use short bursts of muscle force to propel oneself (as in jumping or sprinting), or to throw an object.
Dynamic Strength	The ability to exert muscle force repeatedly or continuously over time. This involves muscular endurance and resistance to muscle fatigue.
Gross Body Coordination	The ability to coordinate the movement of your arms, legs, and torso together when the whole body is in motion.
Glare Sensitivity	The ability to see objects in the presence of glare or bright lighting.
Peripheral Vision	The ability to see objects or movement of objects to one's side when the eyes are looking ahead.
Sound Localization	The ability to tell the direction from which a sound originated.
Arm-Hand Steadiness	The ability to keep your hand and arm steady while moving your arm or while holding your arm and hand in one position.
Dynamic Flexibility	The ability to quickly and repeatedly bend, stretch, twist, or reach out with your body, arms, and/or legs.

Work_Activity	**Work_Activity Definitions**
Establishing and Maintaining Interpersonal Relatio	Developing constructive and cooperative working relationships with others, and maintaining them over time.
Communicating with Supervisors, Peers, or Subordin	Providing information to supervisors, co-workers, and subordinates by telephone, in written form, e-mail, or in person.
Making Decisions and Solving Problems	Analyzing information and evaluating results to choose the best solution and solve problems.
Staffing Organizational Units	Recruiting, interviewing, selecting, hiring, and promoting employees in an organization.
Getting Information	Observing, receiving, and otherwise obtaining information from all relevant sources.
Judging the Qualities of Things, Services, or Peop	Assessing the value, importance, or quality of things or people.
Resolving Conflicts and Negotiating with Others	Handling complaints, settling disputes, and resolving grievances and conflicts, or otherwise negotiating with others.
Guiding, Directing, and Motivating Subordinates	Providing guidance and direction to subordinates, including setting performance standards and monitoring performance.
Evaluating Information to Determine Compliance wit	Using relevant information and individual judgment to determine whether events or processes comply with laws, regulations, or standards.
Coaching and Developing Others	Identifying the developmental needs of others and coaching, mentoring, or otherwise helping others to improve their knowledge or skills.
Training and Teaching Others	Identifying the educational needs of others, developing formal educational or training programs or classes, and teaching or instructing others.
Provide Consultation and Advice to Others	Providing guidance and expert advice to management or other groups on technical, systems-, or process-related topics.
Organizing, Planning, and Prioritizing Work	Developing specific goals and plans to prioritize, organize, and accomplish your work.
Interacting With Computers	Using computers and computer systems (including hardware and software) to program, write software, set up functions, enter data, or process information.
Documenting/Recording Information	Entering, transcribing, recording, storing, or maintaining information in written or electronic/magnetic form.
Updating and Using Relevant Knowledge	Keeping up-to-date technically and applying new knowledge to your job.
Communicating with Persons Outside Organization	Communicating with people outside the organization, representing the organization to customers, the public, government, and other external sources. This information can be exchanged in person, in writing, or by telephone or e-mail.
Processing Information	Compiling, coding, categorizing, calculating, tabulating, auditing, or verifying information or data.
Scheduling Work and Activities	Scheduling events, programs, and activities, as well as the work of others.
Assisting and Caring for Others	Providing personal assistance, medical attention, emotional support, or other personal care to others such as coworkers, customers, or patients.
Interpreting the Meaning of Information for Others	Translating or explaining what information means and how it can be used.
Developing and Building Teams	Encouraging and building mutual trust, respect, and cooperation among team members.

Thinking Creatively	Developing, designing, or creating new applications, ideas, relationships, systems, or products, including artistic contributions.
Performing Administrative Activities	Performing day-to-day administrative tasks such as maintaining information files and processing paperwork.
Identifying Objects, Actions, and Events	Identifying information by categorizing, estimating, recognizing differences or similarities, and detecting changes in circumstances or events.
Monitoring and Controlling Resources	Monitoring and controlling resources and overseeing the spending of money.
Developing Objectives and Strategies	Establishing long-range objectives and specifying the strategies and actions to achieve them.
Coordinating the Work and Activities of Others	Getting members of a group to work together to accomplish tasks.
Performing for or Working Directly with the Public	Performing for people or dealing directly with the public. This includes serving customers in restaurants and stores, and receiving clients or guests.
Monitor Processes, Materials, or Surroundings	Monitoring and reviewing information from materials, events, or the environment, to detect or assess problems.
Analyzing Data or Information	Identifying the underlying principles, reasons, or facts of information by breaking down information or data into separate parts.
Estimating the Quantifiable Characteristics of Pro	Estimating sizes, distances, and quantities; or determining time, costs, resources, or materials needed to perform a work activity.
Selling or Influencing Others	Convincing others to buy merchandise/goods or to otherwise change their minds or actions.
Performing General Physical Activities	Performing physical activities that require considerable use of your arms and legs and moving your whole body, such as climbing, lifting, balancing, walking, stooping, and handling of materials.
Inspecting Equipment, Structures, or Material	Inspecting equipment, structures, or materials to identify the cause of errors or other problems or defects.
Handling and Moving Objects	Using hands and arms in handling, installing, positioning, and moving materials, and manipulating things.
Repairing and Maintaining Electronic Equipment	Servicing, repairing, calibrating, regulating, fine-tuning, or testing machines, devices, and equipment that operate primarily on the basis of electrical or electronic (not mechanical) principles.
Controlling Machines and Processes	Using either control mechanisms or direct physical activity to operate machines or processes (not including computers or vehicles).
Operating Vehicles, Mechanized Devices, or Equipme	Running, maneuvering, navigating, or driving vehicles or mechanized equipment, such as forklifts, passenger vehicles, aircraft, or water craft.
Drafting, Laying Out, and Specifying Technical Dev	Providing documentation, detailed instructions, drawings, or specifications to tell others about how devices, parts, equipment, or structures are to be fabricated, constructed, assembled, modified, maintained, or used.
Repairing and Maintaining Mechanical Equipment	Servicing, repairing, adjusting, and testing machines, devices, moving parts, and equipment that operate primarily on the basis of mechanical (not electronic) principles.

Work_Context	**Work_Context Definitions**
Telephone	How often do you have telephone conversations in this job?
Indoors, Environmentally Controlled	How often does this job require working indoors in environmentally controlled conditions?
Structured versus Unstructured Work	To what extent is this job structured for the worker, rather than allowing the worker to determine tasks, priorities, and goals?
Contact With Others	How much does this job require the worker to be in contact with others (face-to-face, by telephone, or otherwise) in order to perform it?
Electronic Mail	How often do you use electronic mail in this job?
Spend Time Sitting	How much does this job require sitting?
Freedom to Make Decisions	How much decision making freedom, without supervision, does the job offer?
Importance of Being Exact or Accurate	How important is being very exact or highly accurate in performing this job?
Face-to-Face Discussions	How often do you have to have face-to-face discussions with individuals or teams in this job?
Letters and Memos	How often does the job require written letters and memos?
Work With Work Group or Team	How important is it to work with others in a group or team in this job?
Impact of Decisions on Co-workers or Company Resul	How do the decisions an employee makes impact the results of co-workers, clients or the company?

Frequency of Decision Making	How frequently is the worker required to make decisions that affect other people. the financial resources. and/or the image and reputation of the organization?
Deal With External Customers	How important is it to work with external customers or the public in this job?
Time Pressure	How often does this job require the worker to meet strict deadlines?
Coordinate or Lead Others	How important is it to coordinate or lead others in accomplishing work activities in this job?
Deal With Unpleasant or Angry People	How frequently does the worker have to deal with unpleasant. angry. or discourteous individuals as part of the job requirements?
Responsible for Others' Health and Safety	How much responsibility is there for the health and safety of others in this job?
Degree of Automation	How automated is the job?
Frequency of Conflict Situations	How often are there conflict situations the employee has to face in this job?
Importance of Repeating Same Tasks	How important is repeating the same physical activities (e.g., key entry) or mental activities (e.g.. checking entries in a ledger) over and over, without stopping. to performing this job?
Consequence of Error	How serious would the result usually be if the worker made a mistake that was not readily correctable?
Spend Time Making Repetitive Motions	How much does this job require making repetitive motions?
Responsibility for Outcomes and Results	How responsible is the worker for work outcomes and results of other workers?
Sounds, Noise Levels Are Distracting or Uncomforta	How much does this job require working exposed to sounds and noise levels that are distracting or uncomfortable?
Level of Competition	To what extent does this job require the worker to compete or to be aware of competitive pressures?
Physical Proximity	To what extent does this job require the worker to perform job tasks in close physical proximity to other people?
Spend Time Using Your Hands to Handle, Control, or	How much does this job require using your hands to handle, control, or feel objects, tools or controls?
Public Speaking	How often do you have to perform public speaking in this job?
Deal With Physically Aggressive People	How frequently does this job require the worker to deal with physical aggression of violent individuals?
Spend Time Walking and Running	How much does this job require walking and running?
Spend Time Standing	How much does this job require standing?
Exposed to Contaminants	How often does this job require working exposed to contaminants (such as pollutants, gases, dust or odors)?
Very Hot or Cold Temperatures	How often does this job require working in very hot (above 90 F degrees) or very cold (below 32 F degrees) temperatures?
In an Enclosed Vehicle or Equipment	How often does this job require working in a closed vehicle or equipment (e.g., car)?
Spend Time Bending or Twisting the Body	How much does this job require bending or twisting your body?
Spend Time Keeping or Regaining Balance	How much does this job require keeping or regaining your balance?
Spend Time Kneeling, Crouching, Stooping, or Crawl	How much does this job require kneeling, crouching, stooping or crawling?
Cramped Work Space, Awkward Positions	How often does this job require working in cramped work spaces that requires getting into awkward positions?
Extremely Bright or Inadequate Lighting	How often does this job require working in extremely bright or inadequate lighting conditions?
Exposed to Disease or Infections	How often does this job require exposure to disease/infections?
Exposed to Minor Burns, Cuts, Bites, or Stings	How often does this job require exposure to minor burns, cuts, bites, or stings?
Indoors, Not Environmentally Controlled	How often does this job require working indoors in non-controlled environmental conditions (e.g., warehouse without heat)?
Wear Common Protective or Safety Equipment such as	How much does this job require wearing common protective or safety equipment such as safety shoes, glasses, gloves, hard hats or live jackets?
Pace Determined by Speed of Equipment	How important is it to this job that the pace is determined by the speed of equipment or machinery? (This does not refer to keeping busy at all times on this job.)
Exposed to Hazardous Equipment	How often does this job require exposure to hazardous equipment?
Outdoors, Exposed to Weather	How often does this job require working outdoors, exposed to all weather conditions?
Wear Specialized Protective or Safety Equipment su	How much does this job require wearing specialized protective or safety equipment such as breathing apparatus, safety harness, full protection suits, or radiation protection?

Exposed to Hazardous Conditions	How often does this job require exposure to hazardous conditions?
Exposed to High Places	How often does this job require exposure to high places?
Exposed to Radiation	How often does this job require exposure to radiation?
Exposed to Whole Body Vibration	How often does this job require exposure to whole body vibration (e.g.. operate a jackhammer)?
Outdoors. Under Cover	How often does this job require working outdoors. under cover (e.g.. structure with roof but no walls)?
Spend Time Climbing Ladders. Scaffolds. or Poles	How much does this job require climbing ladders, scaffolds, or poles?
In an Open Vehicle or Equipment	How often does this job require working in an open vehicle or equipment (e.g., tractor)?

Job Zone Component	Job Zone Component Definitions
Title	Job Zone Four: Considerable Preparation Needed
Overall Experience	A minimum of two to four years of work-related skill, knowledge, or experience is needed for these occupations. For example, an accountant must complete four years of college and work for several years in accounting to be considered qualified.
Job Training	Employees in these occupations usually need several years of work-related experience, on-the-job training, and/or vocational training.
Job Zone Examples	Many of these occupations involve coordinating, supervising, managing, or training others. Examples include accountants, chefs and head cooks, computer programmers, historians, pharmacists, and police detectives.
SVP Range	(7.0 to < 8.0)
Education	Most of these occupations require a four - year bachelor's degree, but some do not.

Work_Styles	Work_Styles Definitions
Attention to Detail	Job requires being careful about detail and thorough in completing work tasks.
Concern for Others	Job requires being sensitive to others' needs and feelings and being understanding and helpful on the job.
Integrity	Job requires being honest and ethical.
Independence	Job requires developing one's own ways of doing things, guiding oneself with little or no supervision, and depending on oneself to get things done.
Initiative	Job requires a willingness to take on responsibilities and challenges.
Persistence	Job requires persistence in the face of obstacles.
Dependability	Job requires being reliable, responsible, and dependable, and fulfilling obligations.
Stress Tolerance	Job requires accepting criticism and dealing calmly and effectively with high stress situations.
Leadership	Job requires a willingness to lead, take charge, and offer opinions and direction.
Self Control	Job requires maintaining composure, keeping emotions in check, controlling anger, and avoiding aggressive behavior, even in very difficult situations.
Cooperation	Job requires being pleasant with others on the job and displaying a good-natured, cooperative attitude.
Adaptability/Flexibility	Job requires being open to change (positive or negative) and to considerable variety in the workplace.
Achievement/Effort	Job requires establishing and maintaining personally challenging achievement goals and exerting effort toward mastering tasks.
Innovation	Job requires creativity and alternative thinking to develop new ideas for and answers to work-related problems.
Social Orientation	Job requires preferring to work with others rather than alone, and being personally connected with others on the job.
Analytical Thinking	Job requires analyzing information and using logic to address work-related issues and problems.

11-3041.00 - Compensation and Benefits Managers

Plan, direct, or coordinate compensation and benefits activities and staff of an organization.

Tasks

1) Design, evaluate and modify benefits policies to ensure that programs are current, competitive and in compliance with legal requirements.

2) Mediate between benefits providers and employees, such as by assisting in handling employees' benefits-related questions or taking suggestions.

3) Develop methods to improve employment policies, processes, and practices, and recommend changes to management.

4) Analyze statistical data and reports to identify and determine causes of personnel problems and develop recommendations for improvement of organization's personnel policies and practices.

5) Fulfill all reporting requirements of all relevant government rules and regulations, including the Employee Retirement Income Security Act (ERISA).

6) Analyze compensation policies, government regulations, and prevailing wage rates to develop competitive compensation plan.

7) Formulate policies, procedures and programs for recruitment, testing, placement, classification, orientation, benefits and compensation, and labor and industrial relations.

8) Plan and conduct new employee orientations to foster positive attitude toward organizational objectives.

9) Maintain records and compile statistical reports concerning personnel-related data such as hires, transfers, performance appraisals, and absenteeism rates.

10) Plan, direct, supervise, and coordinate work activities of subordinates and staff relating to employment, compensation, labor relations, and employee relations.

11) Identify and implement benefits to increase the quality of life for employees, by working with brokers and researching benefits issues.

12) Advise management on such matters as equal employment opportunity, sexual harassment and discrimination.

13) Manage the design and development of tools to assist employees in benefits selection, and to guide managers through compensation decisions.

14) Prepare detailed job descriptions and classification systems and define job levels and families, in partnership with other managers.

15) Prepare budgets for personnel operations.

16) Represent organization at personnel-related hearings and investigations.

17) Investigate and report on industrial accidents for insurance carriers.

18) Prepare personnel forecasts to project employment needs.

19) Conduct exit interviews to identify reasons for employee termination.

20) Study legislation, arbitration decisions, and collective bargaining contracts to assess industry trends.

21) Resolve labor disputes and grievances.

22) Contract with vendors to provide employee services, such as food services, transportation, or relocation service.

23) Negotiate bargaining agreements.

24) Direct preparation and distribution of written and verbal information to inform employees of benefits, compensation, and personnel policies.

Knowledge

Knowledge	Knowledge Definitions
Personnel and Human Resources	Knowledge of principles and procedures for personnel recruitment, selection, training, compensation and benefits, labor relations and negotiation, and personnel information systems.
Administration and Management	Knowledge of business and management principles involved in strategic planning, resource allocation, human resources modeling, leadership technique, production methods, and coordination of people and resources.
English Language	Knowledge of the structure and content of the English language including the meaning and spelling of words, rules of composition, and grammar.
Law and Government	Knowledge of laws, legal codes, court procedures, precedents, government regulations, executive orders, agency rules, and the democratic political process.
Clerical	Knowledge of administrative and clerical procedures and systems such as word processing, managing files and records, stenography and transcription, designing forms, and other office procedures and terminology.
Economics and Accounting	Knowledge of economic and accounting principles and practices, the financial markets, banking and the analysis and reporting of financial data.
Customer and Personal Service	Knowledge of principles and processes for providing customer and personal services. This includes customer needs assessment, meeting quality standards for services, and evaluation of customer satisfaction.
Mathematics	Knowledge of arithmetic, algebra, geometry, calculus, statistics, and their applications.
Education and Training	Knowledge of principles and methods for curriculum and training design, teaching and instruction for individuals and groups, and the measurement of training effects.
Psychology	Knowledge of human behavior and performance; individual differences in ability, personality, and interests; learning and motivation; psychological research methods; and the assessment and treatment of behavioral and affective disorders.
Public Safety and Security	Knowledge of relevant equipment, policies, procedures, and strategies to promote effective local, state, or national security operations for the protection of people, data, property, and institutions.
Computers and Electronics	Knowledge of circuit boards, processors, chips, electronic equipment, and computer hardware and software, including applications and programming.
Sociology and Anthropology	Knowledge of group behavior and dynamics, societal trends and influences, human migrations, ethnicity, cultures and their history and origins.
Communications and Media	Knowledge of media production, communication, and dissemination techniques and methods. This includes alternative ways to inform and entertain via written, oral, and visual media.
Therapy and Counseling	Knowledge of principles, methods, and procedures for diagnosis, treatment, and rehabilitation of physical and mental dysfunctions, and for career counseling and guidance.
Telecommunications	Knowledge of transmission, broadcasting, switching, control, and operation of telecommunications systems.
Medicine and Dentistry	Knowledge of the information and techniques needed to diagnose and treat human injuries, diseases, and deformities. This includes symptoms, treatment alternatives, drug properties and interactions, and preventive health-care measures.
Sales and Marketing	Knowledge of principles and methods for showing, promoting, and selling products or services. This includes marketing strategy and tactics, product demonstration, sales techniques, and sales control systems.
Transportation	Knowledge of principles and methods for moving people or goods by air, rail, sea, or road, including the relative costs and benefits.
Philosophy and Theology	Knowledge of different philosophical systems and religions. This includes their basic principles, values, ethics, ways of thinking, customs, practices, and their impact on human culture.
Building and Construction	Knowledge of materials, methods, and the tools involved in the construction or repair of houses, buildings, or other structures such as highways and roads.
History and Archeology	Knowledge of historical events and their causes, indicators, and effects on civilizations and cultures.
Production and Processing	Knowledge of raw materials, production processes, quality control, costs, and other techniques for maximizing the effective manufacture and distribution of goods.
Foreign Language	Knowledge of the structure and content of a foreign (non-English) language including the meaning and spelling of words, rules of composition and grammar, and pronunciation.
Chemistry	Knowledge of the chemical composition, structure, and properties of substances and of the chemical processes and transformations that they undergo. This includes uses of chemicals and their interactions, danger signs, production techniques, and disposal methods.
Mechanical	Knowledge of machines and tools, including their designs, uses, repair, and maintenance.
Design	Knowledge of design techniques, tools, and principles involved in production of precision technical plans, blueprints, drawings, and models.
Geography	Knowledge of principles and methods for describing the features of land, sea, and air masses, including their physical characteristics, locations, interrelationships, and distribution of plant, animal, and human life.
Fine Arts	Knowledge of the theory and techniques required to compose, produce, and perform works of music, dance, visual arts, drama, and sculpture.

Physics	Knowledge and prediction of physical principles, laws, their interrelationships, and applications to understanding fluid, material, and atmospheric dynamics, and mechanical, electrical, atomic and sub- atomic structures and processes.
Biology	Knowledge of plant and animal organisms, their tissues, cells, functions, interdependencies, and interactions with each other and the environment.
Food Production	Knowledge of techniques and equipment for planting, growing, and harvesting food products (both plant and animal) for consumption, including storage/handling techniques.
Engineering and Technology	Knowledge of the practical application of engineering science and technology. This includes applying principles, techniques, procedures, and equipment to the design and production of various goods and services.

Skills	Skills Definitions
Active Listening	Giving full attention to what other people are saying, taking time to understand the points being made, asking questions as appropriate, and not interrupting at inappropriate times.
Critical Thinking	Using logic and reasoning to identify the strengths and weaknesses of alternative solutions, conclusions or approaches to problems.
Time Management	Managing one's own time and the time of others.
Reading Comprehension	Understanding written sentences and paragraphs in work related documents.
Management of Personnel Resources	Motivating, developing, and directing people as they work, identifying the best people for the job.
Writing	Communicating effectively in writing as appropriate for the needs of the audience.
Social Perceptiveness	Being aware of others' reactions and understanding why they react as they do.
Speaking	Talking to others to convey information effectively.
Monitoring	Monitoring/Assessing performance of yourself, other individuals, or organizations to make improvements or take corrective action.
Management of Financial Resources	Determining how money will be spent to get the work done, and accounting for these expenditures.
Learning Strategies	Selecting and using training/instructional methods and procedures appropriate for the situation when learning or teaching new things.
Instructing	Teaching others how to do something.
Judgment and Decision Making	Considering the relative costs and benefits of potential actions to choose the most appropriate one.
Coordination	Adjusting actions in relation to others' actions.
Active Learning	Understanding the implications of new information for both current and future problem-solving and decision-making.
Persuasion	Persuading others to change their minds or behavior.
Mathematics	Using mathematics to solve problems.
Negotiation	Bringing others together and trying to reconcile differences.
Complex Problem Solving	Identifying complex problems and reviewing related information to develop and evaluate options and implement solutions.
Management of Material Resources	Obtaining and seeing to the appropriate use of equipment, facilities, and materials needed to do certain work.
Operations Analysis	Analyzing needs and product requirements to create a design.
Service Orientation	Actively looking for ways to help people.
Quality Control Analysis	Conducting tests and inspections of products, services, or processes to evaluate quality or performance.
Systems Evaluation	Identifying measures or indicators of system performance and the actions needed to improve or correct performance, relative to the goals of the system.
Equipment Selection	Determining the kind of tools and equipment needed to do a job.
Systems Analysis	Determining how a system should work and how changes in conditions, operations, and the environment will affect outcomes.
Troubleshooting	Determining causes of operating errors and deciding what to do about it.
Operation and Control	Controlling operations of equipment or systems.
Technology Design	Generating or adapting equipment and technology to serve user needs.
Programming	Writing computer programs for various purposes.
Operation Monitoring	Watching gauges, dials, or other indicators to make sure a machine is working properly.
Science	Using scientific rules and methods to solve problems.
Installation	Installing equipment, machines, wiring, or programs to meet specifications.

Equipment Maintenance	Performing routine maintenance on equipment and determining when and what kind of maintenance is needed.
Repairing	Repairing machines or systems using the needed tools.

Ability	Ability Definitions
Problem Sensitivity	The ability to tell when something is wrong or is likely to go wrong. It does not involve solving the problem, only recognizing there is a problem.
Written Comprehension	The ability to read and understand information and ideas presented in writing.
Oral Expression	The ability to communicate information and ideas in speaking so others will understand.
Oral Comprehension	The ability to listen to and understand information and ideas presented through spoken words and sentences.
Speech Clarity	The ability to speak clearly so others can understand you.
Deductive Reasoning	The ability to apply general rules to specific problems to produce answers that make sense.
Information Ordering	The ability to arrange things or actions in a certain order or pattern according to a specific rule or set of rules (e.g., patterns of numbers, letters, words, pictures, mathematical operations).
Speech Recognition	The ability to identify and understand the speech of another person.
Written Expression	The ability to communicate information and ideas in writing so others will understand.
Inductive Reasoning	The ability to combine pieces of information to form general rules or conclusions (includes finding a relationship among seemingly unrelated events).
Near Vision	The ability to see details at close range (within a few feet of the observer).
Category Flexibility	The ability to generate or use different sets of rules for combining or grouping things in different ways.
Selective Attention	The ability to concentrate on a task over a period of time without being distracted.
Mathematical Reasoning	The ability to choose the right mathematical methods or formulas to solve a problem.
Originality	The ability to come up with unusual or clever ideas about a given topic or situation, or to develop creative ways to solve a problem.
Number Facility	The ability to add, subtract, multiply, or divide quickly and correctly.
Fluency of Ideas	The ability to come up with a number of ideas about a topic (the number of ideas is important, not their quality, correctness, or creativity).
Perceptual Speed	The ability to quickly and accurately compare similarities and differences among sets of letters, numbers, objects, pictures, or patterns. The things to be compared may be presented at the same time or one after the other. This ability also includes comparing a presented object with a remembered object.
Speed of Closure	The ability to quickly make sense of, combine, and organize information into meaningful patterns.
Flexibility of Closure	The ability to identify or detect a known pattern (a figure, object, word, or sound) that is hidden in other distracting material.
Memorization	The ability to remember information such as words, numbers, pictures, and procedures.
Far Vision	The ability to see details at a distance.
Time Sharing	The ability to shift back and forth between two or more activities or sources of information (such as speech, sounds, touch, or other sources).
Finger Dexterity	The ability to make precisely coordinated movements of the fingers of one or both hands to grasp, manipulate, or assemble very small objects.
Auditory Attention	The ability to focus on a single source of sound in the presence of other distracting sounds.
Visualization	The ability to imagine how something will look after it is moved around or when its parts are moved or rearranged.
Hearing Sensitivity	The ability to detect or tell the differences between sounds that vary in pitch and loudness.
Visual Color Discrimination	The ability to match or detect differences between colors, including shades of color and brightness.
Arm-Hand Steadiness	The ability to keep your hand and arm steady while moving your arm or while holding your arm and hand in one position.
Control Precision	The ability to quickly and repeatedly adjust the controls of a machine or a vehicle to exact positions.
Manual Dexterity	The ability to quickly move your hand, your hand together with your arm, or your two hands to grasp, manipulate, or assemble objects.

Depth Perception	The ability to judge which of several objects is closer or farther away from you, or to judge the distance between you and an object.
Wrist-Finger Speed	The ability to make fast, simple, repeated movements of the fingers, hands, and wrists.
Trunk Strength	The ability to use your abdominal and lower back muscles to support part of the body repeatedly or continuously over time without 'giving out' or fatiguing.
Spatial Orientation	The ability to know your location in relation to the environment or to know where other objects are in relation to you.
Gross Body Equilibrium	The ability to keep or regain your body balance or stay upright when in an unstable position.
Sound Localization	The ability to tell the direction from which a sound originated.
Glare Sensitivity	The ability to see objects in the presence of glare or bright lighting.
Peripheral Vision	The ability to see objects or movement of objects to one's side when the eyes are looking ahead.
Night Vision	The ability to see under low light conditions.
Stamina	The ability to exert yourself physically over long periods of time without getting winded or out of breath.
Dynamic Flexibility	The ability to quickly and repeatedly bend, stretch, twist, or reach out with your body, arms, and/or legs.
Extent Flexibility	The ability to bend, stretch, twist, or reach with your body, arms, and/or legs.
Multilimb Coordination	The ability to coordinate two or more limbs (for example, two arms, two legs, or one leg and one arm) while sitting, standing, or lying down. It does not involve performing the activities while the whole body is in motion.
Response Orientation	The ability to choose quickly between two or more movements in response to two or more different signals (lights, sounds, pictures). It includes the speed with which the correct response is started with the hand, foot, or other body part.
Gross Body Coordination	The ability to coordinate the movement of your arms, legs, and torso together when the whole body is in motion.
Dynamic Strength	The ability to exert muscle force repeatedly or continuously over time. This involves muscular endurance and resistance to muscle fatigue.
Explosive Strength	The ability to use short bursts of muscle force to propel oneself (as in jumping or sprinting), or to throw an object.
Static Strength	The ability to exert maximum muscle force to lift, push, pull, or carry objects.
Rate Control	The ability to time your movements or the movement of a piece of equipment in anticipation of changes in the speed and/or direction of a moving object or scene.
Speed of Limb Movement	The ability to quickly move the arms and legs.
Reaction Time	The ability to quickly respond (with the hand, finger, or foot) to a signal (sound, light, picture) when it appears.

Work_Activity	Work_Activity Definitions
Communicating with Supervisors, Peers, or Subordin	Providing information to supervisors, co-workers, and subordinates by telephone, in written form, e-mail, or in person.
Processing Information	Compiling, coding, categorizing, calculating, tabulating, auditing, or verifying information or data.
Interacting With Computers	Using computers and computer systems (including hardware and software) to program, write software, set up functions, enter data, or process information.
Getting Information	Observing, receiving, and otherwise obtaining information from all relevant sources.
Making Decisions and Solving Problems	Analyzing information and evaluating results to choose the best solution and solve problems.
Evaluating Information to Determine Compliance wit	Using relevant information and individual judgment to determine whether events or processes comply with laws, regulations, or standards.
Communicating with Persons Outside Organization	Communicating with people outside the organization, representing the organization to customers, the public, government, and other external sources. This information can be exchanged in person, in writing, or by telephone or e-mail.
Organizing, Planning, and Prioritizing Work	Developing specific goals and plans to prioritize, organize, and accomplish your work.
Updating and Using Relevant Knowledge	Keeping up-to-date technically and applying new knowledge to your job.
Establishing and Maintaining Interpersonal Relatio	Developing constructive and cooperative working relationships with others, and maintaining them over time.

Identifying Objects, Actions, and Events	Identifying information by categorizing, estimating, recognizing differences or similarities, and detecting changes in circumstances or events.
Interpreting the Meaning of Information for Others	Translating or explaining what information means and how it can be used.
Analyzing Data or Information	Identifying the underlying principles, reasons, or facts of information by breaking down information or data into separate parts.
Thinking Creatively	Developing, designing, or creating new applications, ideas, relationships, systems, or products, including artistic contributions.
Documenting/Recording Information	Entering, transcribing, recording, storing, or maintaining information in written or electronic/magnetic form.
Scheduling Work and Activities	Scheduling events, programs, and activities, as well as the work of others.
Resolving Conflicts and Negotiating with Others	Handling complaints, settling disputes, and resolving grievances and conflicts, or otherwise negotiating with others.
Developing and Building Teams	Encouraging and building mutual trust, respect, and cooperation among team members.
Performing Administrative Activities	Performing day-to-day administrative tasks such as maintaining information files and processing paperwork.
Judging the Qualities of Things, Services, or Peop	Assessing the value, importance, or quality of things or people.
Coordinating the Work and Activities of Others	Getting members of a group to work together to accomplish tasks.
Training and Teaching Others	Identifying the educational needs of others, developing formal educational or training programs or classes, and teaching or instructing others.
Provide Consultation and Advice to Others	Providing guidance and expert advice to management or other groups on technical, systems-, or process-related topics.
Coaching and Developing Others	Identifying the developmental needs of others and coaching, mentoring, or otherwise helping others to improve their knowledge or skills.
Monitor Processes, Materials, or Surroundings	Monitoring and reviewing information from materials, events, or the environment, to detect or assess problems.
Estimating the Quantifiable Characteristics of Pro	Estimating sizes, distances, and quantities; or determining time, costs, resources, or materials needed to perform a work activity.
Assisting and Caring for Others	Providing personal assistance, medical attention, emotional support, or other personal care to others such as coworkers, customers, or patients.
Developing Objectives and Strategies	Establishing long-range objectives and specifying the strategies and actions to achieve them.
Guiding, Directing, and Motivating Subordinates	Providing guidance and direction to subordinates, including setting performance standards and monitoring performance.
Monitoring and Controlling Resources	Monitoring and controlling resources and overseeing the spending of money.
Performing for or Working Directly with the Public	Performing for people or dealing directly with the public. This includes serving customers in restaurants and stores, and receiving clients or guests.
Controlling Machines and Processes	Using either control mechanisms or direct physical activity to operate machines or processes (not including computers or vehicles).
Staffing Organizational Units	Recruiting, interviewing, selecting, hiring, and promoting employees in an organization.
Selling or Influencing Others	Convincing others to buy merchandise/goods or to otherwise change their minds or actions.
Inspecting Equipment, Structures, or Material	Inspecting equipment, structures, or materials to identify the cause of errors or other problems or defects.
Performing General Physical Activities	Performing physical activities that require considerable use of your arms and legs and moving your whole body, such as climbing, lifting, balancing, walking, stooping, and handling of materials.
Handling and Moving Objects	Using hands and arms in handling, installing, positioning, and moving materials, and manipulating things.
Operating Vehicles, Mechanized Devices, or Equipme	Running, maneuvering, navigating, or driving vehicles or mechanized equipment, such as forklifts, passenger vehicles, aircraft, or water craft.
Drafting, Laying Out, and Specifying Technical Dev	Providing documentation, detailed instructions, drawings, or specifications to tell others about how devices, parts, equipment, or structures are to be fabricated, constructed, assembled, modified, maintained, or used.
Repairing and Maintaining Electronic Equipment	Servicing, repairing, calibrating, regulating, fine-tuning, or testing machines, devices, and equipment that operate primarily on the basis of electrical or electronic (not mechanical) principles.

Repairing and Maintaining Mechanical Equipment	Servicing, repairing, adjusting, and testing machines, devices, moving parts, and equipment that operate primarily on the basis of mechanical (not electronic) principles.

Work_Context	Work_Context Definitions
Telephone	How often do you have telephone conversations in this job?
Contact With Others	How much does this job require the worker to be in contact with others (face-to-face, by telephone, or otherwise) in order to perform it?
Indoors, Environmentally Controlled	How often does this job require working indoors in environmentally controlled conditions?
Electronic Mail	How often do you use electronic mail in this job?
Work With Work Group or Team	How important is it to work with others in a group or team in this job?
Face-to-Face Discussions	How often do you have to have face-to-face discussions with individuals or teams in this job?
Importance of Being Exact or Accurate	How important is being very exact or highly accurate in performing this job?
Freedom to Make Decisions	How much decision making freedom, without supervision, does the job offer?
Structured versus Unstructured Work	To what extent is this job structured for the worker, rather than allowing the worker to determine tasks, priorities, and goals?
Spend Time Sitting	How much does this job require sitting?
Letters and Memos	How often does the job require written letters and memos?
Impact of Decisions on Co-workers or Company Resul	How do the decisions an employee makes impact the results of co-workers, clients or the company?
Deal With External Customers	How important is it to work with external customers or the public in this job?
Frequency of Conflict Situations	How often are there conflict situations the employee has to face in this job?
Frequency of Decision Making	How frequently is the worker required to make decisions that affect other people, the financial resources, and/or the image and reputation of the organization?
Responsibility for Outcomes and Results	How responsible is the worker for work outcomes and results of other workers?
Coordinate or Lead Others	How important is it to coordinate or lead others in accomplishing work activities in this job?
Importance of Repeating Same Tasks	How important is repeating the same physical activities (e.g., key entry) or mental activities (e.g., checking entries in a ledger) over and over, without stopping, to performing this job?
Responsible for Others' Health and Safety	How much responsibility is there for the health and safety of others in this job?
Time Pressure	How often does this job require the worker to meet strict deadlines?
Deal With Unpleasant or Angry People	How frequently does the worker have to deal with unpleasant, angry, or discourteous individuals as part of the job requirements?
Physical Proximity	To what extent does this job require the worker to perform job tasks in close physical proximity to other people?
Level of Competition	To what extent does this job require the worker to compete or to be aware of competitive pressures?
Spend Time Making Repetitive Motions	How much does this job require making repetitive motions?
Degree of Automation	How automated is the job?
Spend Time Using Your Hands to Handle, Control, or	How much does this job require using your hands to handle, control, or feel objects, tools or controls?
Consequence of Error	How serious would the result usually be if the worker made a mistake that was not readily correctable?
Public Speaking	How often do you have to perform public speaking in this job?
Spend Time Standing	How much does this job require standing?
Sounds, Noise Levels Are Distracting or Uncomforta	How often does this job require working exposed to sounds and noise levels that are distracting or uncomfortable?
Exposed to Contaminants	How often does this job require working exposed to contaminants (such as pollutants, gases, dust or odors)?
In an Enclosed Vehicle or Equipment	How often does this job require working in a closed vehicle or equipment (e.g., car)?
Spend Time Walking and Running	How much does this job require walking and running?
Outdoors, Exposed to Weather	How often does this job require working outdoors, exposed to all weather conditions?
Indoors, Not Environmentally Controlled	How often does this job require working indoors in non-controlled environmental conditions (e.g., warehouse without heat)?

Wear Common Protective or Safety Equipment such as	How much does this job require wearing common protective or safety equipment such as safety shoes, glasses, gloves, hard hats or life jackets?
Deal With Physically Aggressive People	How frequently does this job require the worker to deal with physical aggression of violent individuals?
Spend Time Bending or Twisting the Body	How much does this job require bending or twisting your body?
Pace Determined by Speed of Equipment	How important is it to this job that the pace is determined by the speed of equipment or machinery? (This does not refer to keeping busy at all times on this job.)
Outdoors, Under Cover	How often does this job require working outdoors, under cover (e.g., structure with roof but no walls)?
Exposed to Disease or Infections	How often does this job require exposure to disease/infections?
Spend Time Kneeling, Crouching, Stooping, or Crawl	How much does this job require kneeling, crouching, stooping or crawling?
Exposed to Minor Burns, Cuts, Bites, or Stings	How often does this job require exposure to minor burns, cuts, bites, or stings?
Very Hot or Cold Temperatures	How often does this job require working in very hot (above 90 F degrees) or very cold (below 32 F degrees) temperatures?
Cramped Work Space, Awkward Positions	How often does this job require working in cramped work spaces that requires getting into awkward positions?
Extremely Bright or Inadequate Lighting	How often does this job require working in extremely bright or inadequate lighting conditions?
Exposed to Hazardous Conditions	How often does this job require exposure to hazardous conditions?
Exposed to Hazardous Equipment	How often does this job require exposure to hazardous equipment?
Wear Specialized Protective or Safety Equipment su	How much does this job require wearing specialized protective or safety equipment such as breathing apparatus, safety harness, full protection suits, or radiation protection?
Spend Time Keeping or Regaining Balance	How much does this job require keeping or regaining your balance?
In an Open Vehicle or Equipment	How often does this job require working in an open vehicle or equipment (e.g., tractor)?
Exposed to Whole Body Vibration	How often does this job require exposure to whole body vibration (e.g., operate a jackhammer)?
Spend Time Climbing Ladders, Scaffolds, or Poles	How much does this job require climbing ladders, scaffolds, or poles?
Exposed to High Places	How often does this job require exposure to high places?
Exposed to Radiation	How often does this job require exposure to radiation?

Job Zone Component	Job Zone Component Definitions
Title	Job Zone Three: Medium Preparation Needed
Overall Experience	Previous work-related skill, knowledge, or experience is required for these occupations. For example, an electrician must have completed three or four years of apprenticeship or several years of vocational training, and often must have passed a licensing exam, in order to perform the job.
Job Training	Employees in these occupations usually need one or two years of training involving both on-the-job experience and informal training with experienced workers.
Job Zone Examples	These occupations usually involve using communication and organizational skills to coordinate, supervise, manage, or train others to accomplish goals. Examples include dental assistants, electricians, fish and game wardens, legal secretaries, personnel recruiters, and recreation workers.
SVP Range	(6.0 to < 7.0)
Education	Most occupations in this zone require training in vocational schools, related on-the-job experience, or an associate's degree. Some may require a bachelor's degree.

Work_Styles	Work_Styles Definitions
Integrity	Job requires being honest and ethical.
Dependability	Job requires being reliable, responsible, and dependable, and fulfilling obligations.
Self Control	Job requires maintaining composure, keeping emotions in check, controlling anger, and avoiding aggressive behavior, even in very difficult situations.
Cooperation	Job requires being pleasant with others on the job and displaying a good-natured, cooperative attitude.
Concern for Others	Job requires being sensitive to others' needs and feelings and being understanding and helpful on the job.

Attention to Detail	Job requires being careful about detail and thorough in completing work tasks.
Adaptability/Flexibility	Job requires being open to change (positive or negative) and to considerable variety in the workplace.
Leadership	Job requires a willingness to lead, take charge, and offer opinions and direction.
Stress Tolerance	Job requires accepting criticism and dealing calmly and effectively with high stress situations.
Initiative	Job requires a willingness to take on responsibilities and challenges.
Persistence	Job requires persistence in the face of obstacles.
Social Orientation	Job requires preferring to work with others rather than alone, and being personally connected with others on the job.
Analytical Thinking	Job requires analyzing information and using logic to address work-related issues and problems.
Achievement/Effort	Job requires establishing and maintaining personally challenging achievement goals and exerting effort toward mastering tasks.
Independence	Job requires developing one's own ways of doing things, guiding oneself with little or no supervision, and depending on oneself to get things done.
Innovation	Job requires creativity and alternative thinking to develop new ideas for and answers to work-related problems.

11-3042.00 - Training and Development Managers

Plan, direct, or coordinate the training and development activities and staff of an organization.

Tasks

1) Conduct orientation sessions and arrange on-the-job training for new hires.

2) Analyze training needs to develop new training programs or modify and improve existing programs.

3) Conduct or arrange for ongoing technical training and personal development classes for staff members.

4) Confer with management and conduct surveys to identify training needs based on projected production processes, changes, and other factors.

5) Develop testing and evaluation procedures.

6) Plan, develop, and provide training and staff development programs, using knowledge of the effectiveness of methods such as classroom training, demonstrations, on-the-job training, meetings, conferences, and workshops.

7) Evaluate instructor performance and the effectiveness of training programs, providing recommendations for improvement.

8) Train instructors and supervisors in techniques and skills for training and dealing with employees.

9) Prepare training budget for department or organization.

10) Review and evaluate training and apprenticeship programs for compliance with government standards.

11) Coordinate established courses with technical and professional courses provided by community schools and designate training procedures.

Knowledge	Knowledge Definitions
Personnel and Human Resources	Knowledge of principles and procedures for personnel recruitment, selection, training, compensation and benefits, labor relations and negotiation, and personnel information systems.
Public Safety and Security	Knowledge of relevant equipment, policies, procedures, and strategies to promote effective local, state, or national security operations for the protection of people, data, property, and institutions.
Administration and Management	Knowledge of business and management principles involved in strategic planning, resource allocation, human resources modeling, leadership technique, production methods, and coordination of people and resources.
Computers and Electronics	Knowledge of circuit boards, processors, chips, electronic equipment, and computer hardware and software, including applications and programming.
Education and Training	Knowledge of principles and methods for curriculum and training design, teaching and instruction for individuals and groups, and the measurement of training effects.
Customer and Personal Service	Knowledge of principles and processes for providing customer and personal services. This includes customer needs assessment, meeting quality standards for services, and evaluation of customer satisfaction.
Law and Government	Knowledge of laws, legal codes, court procedures, precedents, government regulations, executive orders, agency rules, and the democratic political process.
English Language	Knowledge of the structure and content of the English language including the meaning and spelling of words, rules of composition, and grammar.
Clerical	Knowledge of administrative and clerical procedures and systems such as word processing, managing files and records, stenography and transcription, designing forms, and other office procedures and terminology.
Psychology	Knowledge of human behavior and performance; individual differences in ability, personality, and interests; learning and motivation; psychological research methods; and the assessment and treatment of behavioral and affective disorders.
Mathematics	Knowledge of arithmetic, algebra, geometry, calculus, statistics, and their applications.
Economics and Accounting	Knowledge of economic and accounting principles and practices, the financial markets, banking and the analysis and reporting of financial data.
Sales and Marketing	Knowledge of principles and methods for showing, promoting, and selling products or services. This includes marketing strategy and tactics, product demonstration, sales techniques, and sales control systems.
Communications and Media	Knowledge of media production, communication, and dissemination techniques and methods. This includes alternative ways to inform and entertain via written, oral, and visual media.
Production and Processing	Knowledge of raw materials, production processes, quality control, costs, and other techniques for maximizing the effective manufacture and distribution of goods.
Therapy and Counseling	Knowledge of principles, methods, and procedures for diagnosis, treatment, and rehabilitation of physical and mental dysfunctions, and for career counseling and guidance.
Sociology and Anthropology	Knowledge of group behavior and dynamics, societal trends and influences, human migrations, ethnicity, cultures and their history and origins.
Telecommunications	Knowledge of transmission, broadcasting, switching, control, and operation of telecommunications systems.
Foreign Language	Knowledge of the structure and content of a foreign (non-English) language including the meaning and spelling of words, rules of composition and grammar, and pronunciation.
Engineering and Technology	Knowledge of the practical application of engineering science and technology. This includes applying principles, techniques, procedures, and equipment to the design and production of various goods and services.
Philosophy and Theology	Knowledge of different philosophical systems and religions. This includes their basic principles, values, ethics, ways of thinking, customs, practices, and their impact on human culture.
Medicine and Dentistry	Knowledge of the information and techniques needed to diagnose and treat human injuries, diseases, and deformities. This includes symptoms, treatment alternatives, drug properties and interactions, and preventive health-care measures.
Transportation	Knowledge of principles and methods for moving people or goods by air, rail, sea, or road, including the relative costs and benefits.
Geography	Knowledge of principles and methods for describing the features of land, sea, and air masses, including their physical characteristics, locations, interrelationships, and distribution of plant, animal, and human life.
Mechanical	Knowledge of machines and tools, including their designs, uses, repair, and maintenance.
Food Production	Knowledge of techniques and equipment for planting, growing, and harvesting food products (both plant and animal) for consumption, including storage/handling techniques.
History and Archeology	Knowledge of historical events and their causes, indicators, and effects on civilizations and cultures.

Chemistry	Knowledge of the chemical composition, structure, and properties of substances and of the chemical processes and transformations that they undergo. This includes uses of chemicals and their interactions, danger signs, production techniques, and disposal methods.
Biology	Knowledge of plant and animal organisms, their tissues, cells, functions, interdependencies, and interactions with each other and the environment.
Physics	Knowledge and prediction of physical principles, laws, their interrelationships, and applications to understanding fluid, material, and atmospheric dynamics, and mechanical, electrical, atomic and sub- atomic structures and processes.
Building and Construction	Knowledge of materials, methods, and the tools involved in the construction or repair of houses, buildings, or other structures such as highways and roads.
Design	Knowledge of design techniques, tools, and principles involved in production of precision technical plans, blueprints, drawings, and models.
Fine Arts	Knowledge of the theory and techniques required to compose, produce, and perform works of music, dance, visual arts, drama, and sculpture.

Skills	Skills Definitions
Speaking	Talking to others to convey information effectively.
Reading Comprehension	Understanding written sentences and paragraphs in work related documents.
Instructing	Teaching others how to do something.
Management of Personnel Resources	Motivating, developing, and directing people as they work, identifying the best people for the job.
Active Listening	Giving full attention to what other people are saying, taking time to understand the points being made, asking questions as appropriate, and not interrupting at inappropriate times.
Time Management	Managing one's own time and the time of others.
Critical Thinking	Using logic and reasoning to identify the strengths and weaknesses of alternative solutions, conclusions or approaches to problems.
Persuasion	Persuading others to change their minds or behavior.
Judgment and Decision Making	Considering the relative costs and benefits of potential actions to choose the most appropriate one.
Service Orientation	Actively looking for ways to help people.
Learning Strategies	Selecting and using training/instructional methods and procedures appropriate for the situation when learning or teaching new things.
Monitoring	Monitoring/Assessing performance of yourself, other individuals, or organizations to make improvements or take corrective action.
Social Perceptiveness	Being aware of others' reactions and understanding why they react as they do.
Writing	Communicating effectively in writing as appropriate for the needs of the audience.
Active Learning	Understanding the implications of new information for both current and future problem-solving and decision-making.
Coordination	Adjusting actions in relation to others' actions.
Negotiation	Bringing others together and trying to reconcile differences.
Management of Financial Resources	Determining how money will be spent to get the work done, and accounting for these expenditures.
Mathematics	Using mathematics to solve problems.
Complex Problem Solving	Identifying complex problems and reviewing related information to develop and evaluate options and implement solutions.
Equipment Selection	Determining the kind of tools and equipment needed to do a job.
Management of Material Resources	Obtaining and seeing to the appropriate use of equipment, facilities, and materials needed to do certain work.
Operations Analysis	Analyzing needs and product requirements to create a design.
Systems Analysis	Determining how a system should work and how changes in conditions, operations, and the environment will affect outcomes.
Systems Evaluation	Identifying measures or indicators of system performance and the actions needed to improve or correct performance, relative to the goals of the system.
Quality Control Analysis	Conducting tests and inspections of products, services, or processes to evaluate quality or performance.
Science	Using scientific rules and methods to solve problems.
Troubleshooting	Determining causes of operating errors and deciding what to do about it.
Operation and Control	Controlling operations of equipment or systems.

Technology Design	Generating or adapting equipment and technology to serve user needs.
Repairing	Repairing machines or systems using the needed tools.
Equipment Maintenance	Performing routine maintenance on equipment and determining when and what kind of maintenance is needed.
Operation Monitoring	Watching gauges, dials, or other indicators to make sure a machine is working properly.
Installation	Installing equipment, machines, wiring, or programs to meet specifications.
Programming	Writing computer programs for various purposes.

Ability	Ability Definitions
Speech Clarity	The ability to speak clearly so others can understand you.
Oral Expression	The ability to communicate information and ideas in speaking so others will understand.
Oral Comprehension	The ability to listen to and understand information and ideas presented through spoken words and sentences.
Speech Recognition	The ability to identify and understand the speech of another person.
Deductive Reasoning	The ability to apply general rules to specific problems to produce answers that make sense.
Originality	The ability to come up with unusual or clever ideas about a given topic or situation, or to develop creative ways to solve a problem.
Inductive Reasoning	The ability to combine pieces of information to form general rules or conclusions (includes finding a relationship among seemingly unrelated events).
Information Ordering	The ability to arrange things or actions in a certain order or pattern according to a specific rule or set of rules (e.g., patterns of numbers, letters, words, pictures, mathematical operations).
Problem Sensitivity	The ability to tell when something is wrong or is likely to go wrong. It does not involve solving the problem, only recognizing there is a problem.
Fluency of Ideas	The ability to come up with a number of ideas about a topic (the number of ideas is important, not their quality, correctness, or creativity).
Written Comprehension	The ability to read and understand information and ideas presented in writing.
Written Expression	The ability to communicate information and ideas in writing so others will understand.
Near Vision	The ability to see details at close range (within a few feet of the observer).
Category Flexibility	The ability to generate or use different sets of rules for combining or grouping things in different ways.
Selective Attention	The ability to concentrate on a task over a period of time without being distracted.
Memorization	The ability to remember information such as words, numbers, pictures, and procedures.
Far Vision	The ability to see details at a distance.
Time Sharing	The ability to shift back and forth between two or more activities or sources of information (such as speech, sounds, touch, or other sources).
Flexibility of Closure	The ability to identify or detect a known pattern (a figure, object, word, or sound) that is hidden in other distracting material.
Speed of Closure	The ability to quickly make sense of, combine, and organize information into meaningful patterns.
Mathematical Reasoning	The ability to choose the right mathematical methods or formulas to solve a problem.
Visualization	The ability to imagine how something will look after it is moved around or when its parts are moved or rearranged.
Auditory Attention	The ability to focus on a single source of sound in the presence of other distracting sounds.
Finger Dexterity	The ability to make precisely coordinated movements of the fingers of one or both hands to grasp, manipulate, or assemble very small objects.
Perceptual Speed	The ability to quickly and accurately compare similarities and differences among sets of letters, numbers, objects, pictures, or patterns. The things to be compared may be presented at the same time or one after the other. This ability also includes comparing a presented object with a remembered object.
Visual Color Discrimination	The ability to match or detect differences between colors, including shades of color and brightness.
Control Precision	The ability to quickly and repeatedly adjust the controls of a machine or a vehicle to exact positions.
Number Facility	The ability to add, subtract, multiply, or divide quickly and correctly.

Trunk Strength	The ability to use your abdominal and lower back muscles to support part of the body repeatedly or continuously over time without 'giving out' or fatiguing.
Depth Perception	The ability to judge which of several objects is closer or farther away from you, or to judge the distance between you and an object.
Arm-Hand Steadiness	The ability to keep your hand and arm steady while moving your arm or while holding your arm and hand in one position.
Manual Dexterity	The ability to quickly move your hand, your hand together with your arm, or your two hands to grasp, manipulate, or assemble objects.
Hearing Sensitivity	The ability to detect or tell the differences between sounds that vary in pitch and loudness.
Multilimb Coordination	The ability to coordinate two or more limbs (for example, two arms, two legs, or one leg and one arm) while sitting, standing, or lying down. It does not involve performing the activities while the whole body is in motion.
Static Strength	The ability to exert maximum muscle force to lift, push, pull, or carry objects.
Stamina	The ability to exert yourself physically over long periods of time without getting winded or out of breath.
Sound Localization	The ability to tell the direction from which a sound originated.
Extent Flexibility	The ability to bend, stretch, twist, or reach with your body, arms, and/or legs.
Night Vision	The ability to see under low light conditions.
Wrist-Finger Speed	The ability to make fast, simple, repeated movements of the fingers, hands, and wrists.
Response Orientation	The ability to choose quickly between two or more movements in response to two or more different signals (lights, sounds, pictures). It includes the speed with which the correct response is started with the hand, foot, or other body part.
Gross Body Coordination	The ability to coordinate the movement of your arms, legs, and torso together when the whole body is in motion.
Speed of Limb Movement	The ability to quickly move the arms and legs.
Spatial Orientation	The ability to know your location in relation to the environment or to know where other objects are in relation to you.
Reaction Time	The ability to quickly respond (with the hand, finger, or foot) to a signal (sound, light, picture) when it appears.
Glare Sensitivity	The ability to see objects in the presence of glare or bright lighting.
Explosive Strength	The ability to use short bursts of muscle force to propel oneself (as in jumping or sprinting), or to throw an object.
Gross Body Equilibrium	The ability to keep or regain your body balance or stay upright when in an unstable position.
Peripheral Vision	The ability to see objects or movement of objects to one's side when the eyes are looking ahead.
Dynamic Flexibility	The ability to quickly and repeatedly bend, stretch, twist, or reach out with your body, arms, and/or legs.
Dynamic Strength	The ability to exert muscle force repeatedly or continuously over time. This involves muscular endurance and resistance to muscle fatigue.
Rate Control	The ability to time your movements or the movement of a piece of equipment in anticipation of changes in the speed and/or direction of a moving object or scene.

Work_Activity	Work_Activity Definitions
Training and Teaching Others	Identifying the educational needs of others, developing formal educational or training programs or classes, and teaching or instructing others.
Guiding, Directing, and Motivating Subordinates	Providing guidance and direction to subordinates, including setting performance standards and monitoring performance.
Coaching and Developing Others	Identifying the developmental needs of others and coaching, mentoring, or otherwise helping others to improve their knowledge or skills.
Organizing, Planning, and Prioritizing Work	Developing specific goals and plans to prioritize, organize, and accomplish your work.
Communicating with Supervisors, Peers, or Subordin	Providing information to supervisors, co-workers, and subordinates by telephone, in written form, e-mail, or in person.
Establishing and Maintaining Interpersonal Relatio	Developing constructive and cooperative working relationships with others, and maintaining them over time.
Making Decisions and Solving Problems	Analyzing information and evaluating results to choose the best solution and solve problems.
Identifying Objects, Actions, and Events	Identifying information by categorizing, estimating, recognizing differences or similarities, and detecting changes in circumstances or events.

Provide Consultation and Advice to Others	Providing guidance and expert advice to management or other groups on technical, systems-, or process-related topics.
Thinking Creatively	Developing, designing, or creating new applications, ideas, relationships, systems, or products, including artistic contributions.
Getting Information	Observing, receiving, and otherwise obtaining information from all relevant sources.
Updating and Using Relevant Knowledge	Keeping up-to-date technically and applying new knowledge to your job.
Monitor Processes, Materials, or Surroundings	Monitoring and reviewing information from materials, events, or the environment, to detect or assess problems.
Scheduling Work and Activities	Scheduling events, programs, and activities, as well as the work of others.
Interacting With Computers	Using computers and computer systems (including hardware and software) to program, write software, set up functions, enter data, or process information.
Evaluating Information to Determine Compliance wit	Using relevant information and individual judgment to determine whether events or processes comply with laws, regulations, or standards.
Resolving Conflicts and Negotiating with Others	Handling complaints, settling disputes, and resolving grievances and conflicts, or otherwise negotiating with others.
Coordinating the Work and Activities of Others	Getting members of a group to work together to accomplish tasks.
Communicating with Persons Outside Organization	Communicating with people outside the organization, representing the organization to customers, the public, government, and other external sources. This information can be exchanged in person, in writing, or by telephone or e-mail.
Developing and Building Teams	Encouraging and building mutual trust, respect, and cooperation among team members.
Processing Information	Compiling, coding, categorizing, calculating, tabulating, auditing, or verifying information or data.
Interpreting the Meaning of Information for Others	Translating or explaining what information means and how it can be used.
Assisting and Caring for Others	Providing personal assistance, medical attention, emotional support, or other personal care to others such as coworkers, customers, or patients.
Analyzing Data or Information	Identifying the underlying principles, reasons, or facts of information by breaking down information or data into separate parts.
Selling or Influencing Others	Convincing others to buy merchandise/goods or to otherwise change their minds or actions.
Performing for or Working Directly with the Public	Performing for people or dealing directly with the public. This includes serving customers in restaurants and stores, and receiving clients or guests.
Judging the Qualities of Things, Services, or Peop	Assessing the value, importance, or quality of things or people.
Developing Objectives and Strategies	Establishing long-range objectives and specifying the strategies and actions to achieve them.
Documenting/Recording Information	Entering, transcribing, recording, storing, or maintaining information in written or electronic/magnetic form.
Performing Administrative Activities	Performing day-to-day administrative tasks such as maintaining information files and processing paperwork.
Staffing Organizational Units	Recruiting, interviewing, selecting, hiring, and promoting employees in an organization.
Estimating the Quantifiable Characteristics of Pro	Estimating sizes, distances, and quantities; or determining time, costs, resources, or materials needed to perform a work activity.
Monitoring and Controlling Resources	Monitoring and controlling resources and overseeing the spending of money.
Inspecting Equipment, Structures, or Material	Inspecting equipment, structures, or materials to identify the cause of errors or other problems or defects.
Performing General Physical Activities	Performing physical activities that require considerable use of your arms and legs and moving your whole body, such as climbing, lifting, balancing, walking, stooping, and handling of materials.
Handling and Moving Objects	Using hands and arms in handling, installing, positioning, and moving materials, and manipulating things.
Controlling Machines and Processes	Using either control mechanisms or direct physical activity to operate machines or processes (not including computers or vehicles).
Operating Vehicles, Mechanized Devices, or Equipme	Running, maneuvering, navigating, or driving vehicles or mechanized equipment, such as forklifts, passenger vehicles, aircraft, or water craft.
Drafting, Laying Out, and Specifying Technical Dev	Providing documentation, detailed instructions, drawings, or specifications to tell others about how devices, parts, equipment, or structures are to be fabricated, constructed, assembled, modified, maintained, or used.

Repairing and Maintaining Electronic Equipment	Servicing, repairing, calibrating, regulating, fine-tuning, or testing machines, devices, and equipment that operate primarily on the basis of electrical or electronic (not mechanical) principles.
Repairing and Maintaining Mechanical Equipment	Servicing, repairing, adjusting, and testing machines, devices, moving parts, and equipment that operate primarily on the basis of mechanical (not electronic) principles.

Work_Context	**Work_Context Definitions**
Telephone	How often do you have telephone conversations in this job?
Face-to-Face Discussions	How often do you have to have face-to-face discussions with individuals or teams in this job?
Contact With Others	How much does this job require the worker to be in contact with others (face-to-face, by telephone, or otherwise) in order to perform it?
Freedom to Make Decisions	How much decision making freedom, without supervision, does the job offer?
Work With Work Group or Team	How important is it to work with others in a group or team in this job?
Coordinate or Lead Others	How important is it to coordinate or lead others in accomplishing work activities in this job?
Impact of Decisions on Co-workers or Company Resul	How do the decisions an employee makes impact the results of co-workers, clients or the company?
Responsibility for Outcomes and Results	How responsible is the worker for work outcomes and results of other workers?
Structured versus Unstructured Work	To what extent is this job structured for the worker, rather than allowing the worker to determine tasks, priorities, and goals?
Frequency of Decision Making	How frequently is the worker required to make decisions that affect other people, the financial resources, and/or the image and reputation of the organization?
Indoors, Environmentally Controlled	How much does this job require working indoors in environmentally controlled conditions?
Electronic Mail	How often do you use electronic mail in this job?
Time Pressure	How often does this job require the worker to meet strict deadlines?
Deal With External Customers	How important is it to work with external customers or the public in this job?
Consequence of Error	How serious would the result usually be if the worker made a mistake that was not readily correctable?
Frequency of Conflict Situations	How often are there conflict situations the employee has to face in this job?
Letters and Memos	How often does the job require written letters and memos?
Responsible for Others' Health and Safety	How much responsibility is there for the health and safety of others in this job?
Physical Proximity	To what extent does this job require the worker to perform job tasks in close physical proximity to other people?
Importance of Being Exact or Accurate	How important is being very exact or highly accurate in performing this job?
Spend Time Using Your Hands to Handle, Control, or	How much does this job require using your hands to handle, control, or feel objects, tools or controls?
Deal With Unpleasant or Angry People	How frequently does the worker have to deal with unpleasant, angry, or discourteous individuals as part of the job requirements?
Spend Time Sitting	How much does this job require sitting?
Importance of Repeating Same Tasks	How important is repeating the same physical activities (e.g., key entry) or mental activities (e.g., checking entries in a ledger) over and over, without stopping, to performing this job?
Public Speaking	How often do you have to perform public speaking in this job?
Spend Time Making Repetitive Motions	How much does this job require making repetitive motions?
In an Enclosed Vehicle or Equipment	How often does this job require working in a closed vehicle or equipment (e.g., car)?
Spend Time Standing	How much does this job require standing?
Sounds, Noise Levels Are Distracting or Uncomforta	How often does this job require working exposed to sounds and noise levels that are distracting or uncomfortable?
Outdoors, Exposed to Weather	How often does this job require working outdoors, exposed to all weather conditions?
Exposed to Contaminants	How often does this job require working exposed to contaminants (such as pollutants, gases, dust or odors)?
Exposed to Hazardous Equipment	How often does this job require exposure to hazardous equipment?
Exposed to Minor Burns, Cuts, Bites, or Stings	How often does this job require exposure to minor burns, cuts, bites, or stings?

Exposed to Disease or Infections	How often does this job require exposure to disease/infections?
Very Hot or Cold Temperatures	How often does this job require working in very hot (above 90 F degrees) or very cold (below 32 F degrees) temperatures?
Wear Common Protective or Safety Equipment such as	How much does this job require wearing common protective or safety equipment such as safety shoes, glasses, gloves, hard hats or life jackets?
Extremely Bright or Inadequate Lighting	How often does this job require working in extremely bright or inadequate lighting conditions?
Deal With Physically Aggressive People	How frequently does this job require the worker to deal with physical aggression of violent individuals?
Degree of Automation	How automated is the job?
Outdoors, Under Cover	How often does this job require working outdoors, under cover (e.g., structure with roof but no walls)?
Level of Competition	To what extent does this job require the worker to compete or to be aware of competitive pressures?
Spend Time Bending or Twisting the Body	How much does this job require bending or twisting your body?
Exposed to Hazardous Conditions	How often does this job require exposure to hazardous conditions?
Cramped Work Space, Awkward Positions	How often does this job require working in cramped work spaces that requires getting into awkward positions?
Spend Time Walking and Running	How much does this job require walking and running?
In an Open Vehicle or Equipment	How often does this job require working in an open vehicle or equipment (e.g., tractor)?
Pace Determined by Speed of Equipment	How important is it to this job that the pace is determined by the speed of equipment or machinery? (This does not refer to keeping busy at all times on this job?)
Exposed to High Places	How often does this job require exposure to high places?
Exposed to Whole Body Vibration	How often does this job require exposure to whole body vibration (e.g., operate a jackhammer)?
Indoors, Not Environmentally Controlled	How often does this job require working indoors in non-controlled environmental conditions (e.g., warehouse without heat)?
Spend Time Kneeling, Crouching, Stooping, or Crawl	How much does this job require kneeling, crouching, stooping or crawling?
Spend Time Keeping or Regaining Balance	How much does this job require keeping or regaining your balance?
Spend Time Climbing Ladders, Scaffolds, or Poles	How much does this job require climbing ladders, scaffolds, or poles?
Wear Specialized Protective or Safety Equipment su	How much does this job require wearing specialized protective or safety equipment such as breathing apparatus, safety harness, full protection suits, or radiation protection?
Exposed to Radiation	How often does this job require exposure to radiation?

Job Zone Component	**Job Zone Component Definitions**
Title	Job Zone Four: Considerable Preparation Needed
Overall Experience	A minimum of two to four years of work-related skill, knowledge, or experience is needed for these occupations. For example, an accountant must complete four years of college and work for several years in accounting to be considered qualified.
Job Training	Employees in these occupations usually need several years of work-related experience, on-the-job training, and/or vocational training.
Job Zone Examples	Many of these occupations involve coordinating, supervising, managing, or training others. Examples include accountants, chefs and head cooks, computer programmers, historians, pharmacists, and police detectives.
SVP Range	(7.0 to < 8.0)
Education	Most of these occupations require a four-year bachelor's degree, but some do not.

Work_Styles	**Work_Styles Definitions**
Integrity	Job requires being honest and ethical.
Attention to Detail	Job requires being careful about detail and thorough in completing work tasks.
Cooperation	Job requires being pleasant with others on the job and displaying a good-natured, cooperative attitude.
Dependability	Job requires being reliable, responsible, and dependable, and fulfilling obligations.

Self Control	Job requires maintaining composure. keeping emotions in check. controlling anger. and avoiding aggressive behavior. even in very difficult situations.
Initiative	Job requires a willingness to take on responsibilities and challenges.
Concern for Others	Job requires being sensitive to others' needs and feelings and being understanding and helpful on the job.
Social Orientation	Job requires preferring to work with others rather than alone. and being personally connected with others on the job.
Independence	Job requires developing one's own ways of doing things. guiding oneself with little or no supervision. and depending on oneself to get things done.
Analytical Thinking	Job requires analyzing information and using logic to address work-related issues and problems.
Adaptability/Flexibility	Job requires being open to change (positive or negative) and to considerable variety in the workplace.
Leadership	Job requires a willingness to lead. take charge. and offer opinions and direction.
Innovation	Job requires creativity and alternative thinking to develop new ideas for and answers to work-related problems.
Stress Tolerance	Job requires accepting criticism and dealing calmly and effectively with high stress situations.
Achievement/Effort	Job requires establishing and maintaining personally challenging achievement goals and exerting effort toward mastering tasks.
Persistence	Job requires persistence in the face of obstacles.

11-3051.00 - Industrial Production Managers

Plan, direct, or coordinate the work activities and resources necessary for manufacturing products in accordance with cost, quality, and quantity specifications.

Tasks

1) Review processing schedules and production orders to make decisions concerning inventory requirements, staffing requirements, work procedures, and duty assignments, considering budgetary limitations and time constraints.

2) Direct and coordinate production, processing, distribution, and marketing activities of industrial organization.

3) Hire, train, evaluate, and discharge staff, and resolve personnel grievances.

4) Develop and implement production tracking and quality control systems, analyzing production, quality control, maintenance, and other operational reports, to detect production problems.

5) Coordinate and recommend procedures for facility and equipment maintenance or modification, including the replacement of machines.

6) Set and monitor product standards, examining samples of raw products or directing testing during processing, to ensure finished products are of prescribed quality.

7) Develop budgets and approve expenditures for supplies, materials, and human resources, ensuring that materials, labor and equipment are used efficiently to meet production targets.

8) Institute employee suggestion or involvement programs.

9) Prepare and maintain production reports and personnel records.

10) Maintain current knowledge of the quality control field, relying on current literature pertaining to materials use, technological advances, and statistical studies.

11) Initiate and coordinate inventory and cost control programs.

12) Review plans and confer with research and support staff to develop new products and processes.

13) Negotiate materials prices with suppliers.

Knowledge	Knowledge Definitions
Production and Processing	Knowledge of raw materials, production processes, quality control, costs, and other techniques for maximizing the effective manufacture and distribution of goods.
Administration and Management	Knowledge of business and management principles involved in strategic planning, resource allocation, human resources modeling, leadership technique, production methods, and coordination of people and resources.
Mathematics	Knowledge of arithmetic, algebra, geometry, calculus, statistics, and their applications.
Education and Training	Knowledge of principles and methods for curriculum and training design. teaching and instruction for individuals and groups. and the measurement of training effects.
Mechanical	Knowledge of machines and tools. including their designs. uses. repair. and maintenance.
Personnel and Human Resources	Knowledge of principles and procedures for personnel recruitment, selection, training. compensation and benefits, labor relations and negotiation, and personnel information systems.
English Language	Knowledge of the structure and content of the English language including the meaning and spelling of words. rules of composition, and grammar.
Customer and Personal Service	Knowledge of principles and processes for providing customer and personal services. This includes customer needs assessment, meeting quality standards for services, and evaluation of customer satisfaction.
Engineering and Technology	Knowledge of the practical application of engineering science and technology. This includes applying principles, techniques, procedures, and equipment to the design and production of various goods and services.
Design	Knowledge of design techniques. tools. and principles involved in production of precision technical plans. blueprints, drawings, and models.
Psychology	Knowledge of human behavior and performance; individual differences in ability, personality, and interests; learning and motivation; psychological research methods; and the assessment and treatment of behavioral and affective disorders.
Sales and Marketing	Knowledge of principles and methods for showing. promoting, and selling products or services. This includes marketing strategy and tactics, product demonstration, sales techniques, and sales control systems.
Economics and Accounting	Knowledge of economic and accounting principles and practices, the financial markets, banking and the analysis and reporting of financial data.
Clerical	Knowledge of administrative and clerical procedures and systems such as word processing, managing files and records, stenography and transcription, designing forms, and other office procedures and terminology.
Public Safety and Security	Knowledge of relevant equipment, policies, procedures, and strategies to promote effective local, state, or national security operations for the protection of people, data, property, and institutions.
Transportation	Knowledge of principles and methods for moving people or goods by air, rail, sea, or road, including the relative costs and benefits.
Chemistry	Knowledge of the chemical composition, structure, and properties of substances and of the chemical processes and transformations that they undergo. This includes uses of chemicals and their interactions, danger signs, production techniques, and disposal methods.
Law and Government	Knowledge of laws, legal codes, court procedures, precedents, government regulations, executive orders, agency rules, and the democratic political process.
Computers and Electronics	Knowledge of circuit boards, processors, chips, electronic equipment, and computer hardware and software, including applications and programming.
Communications and Media	Knowledge of media production, communication, and dissemination techniques and methods. This includes alternative ways to inform and entertain via written, oral, and visual media.
Physics	Knowledge and prediction of physical principles, laws, their interrelationships, and applications to understanding fluid, material, and atmospheric dynamics, and mechanical, electrical, atomic and sub- atomic structures and processes.
Telecommunications	Knowledge of transmission, broadcasting, switching, control, and operation of telecommunications systems.
Building and Construction	Knowledge of materials, methods, and the tools involved in the construction or repair of houses, buildings, or other structures such as highways and roads.
Food Production	Knowledge of techniques and equipment for planting, growing, and harvesting food products (both plant and animal) for consumption, including storage/handling techniques.
Geography	Knowledge of principles and methods for describing the features of land, sea, and air masses, including their physical characteristics, locations, interrelationships, and distribution of plant, animal, and human life.

Sociology and Anthropology	Knowledge of group behavior and dynamics, societal trends and influences, human migrations, ethnicity, cultures and their history and origins.
Therapy and Counseling	Knowledge of principles, methods, and procedures for diagnosis, treatment, and rehabilitation of physical and mental dysfunctions, and for career counseling and guidance.
Biology	Knowledge of plant and animal organisms, their tissues, cells, functions, interdependencies, and interactions with each other and the environment.
Foreign Language	Knowledge of the structure and content of a foreign (non-English) language including the meaning and spelling of words, rules of composition and grammar, and pronunciation.
Medicine and Dentistry	Knowledge of the information and techniques needed to diagnose and treat human injuries, diseases, and deformities. This includes symptoms, treatment alternatives, drug properties and interactions, and preventive health-care measures.
Philosophy and Theology	Knowledge of different philosophical systems and religions. This includes their basic principles, values, ethics, ways of thinking, customs, practices, and their impact on human culture.
History and Archeology	Knowledge of historical events and their causes, indicators, and effects on civilizations and cultures.
Fine Arts	Knowledge of the theory and techniques required to compose, produce, and perform works of music, dance, visual arts, drama, and sculpture.

Skills	Skills Definitions
Active Listening	Giving full attention to what other people are saying, taking time to understand the points being made, asking questions as appropriate, and not interrupting at inappropriate times.
Judgment and Decision Making	Considering the relative costs and benefits of potential actions to choose the most appropriate one.
Critical Thinking	Using logic and reasoning to identify the strengths and weaknesses of alternative solutions, conclusions or approaches to problems.
Reading Comprehension	Understanding written sentences and paragraphs in work related documents.
Management of Personnel Resources	Motivating, developing, and directing people as they work, identifying the best people for the job.
Coordination	Adjusting actions in relation to others' actions.
Monitoring	Monitoring/Assessing performance of yourself, other individuals, or organizations to make improvements or take corrective action.
Time Management	Managing one's own time and the time of others.
Complex Problem Solving	Identifying complex problems and reviewing related information to develop and evaluate options and implement solutions.
Speaking	Talking to others to convey information effectively.
Instructing	Teaching others how to do something.
Quality Control Analysis	Conducting tests and inspections of products, services, or processes to evaluate quality or performance.
Management of Material Resources	Obtaining and seeing to the appropriate use of equipment, facilities, and materials needed to do certain work.
Equipment Selection	Determining the kind of tools and equipment needed to do a job.
Persuasion	Persuading others to change their minds or behavior.
Operations Analysis	Analyzing needs and product requirements to create a design.
Active Learning	Understanding the implications of new information for both current and future problem-solving and decision-making.
Social Perceptiveness	Being aware of others' reactions and understanding why they react as they do.
Systems Evaluation	Identifying measures or indicators of system performance and the actions needed to improve or correct performance, relative to the goals of the system.
Mathematics	Using mathematics to solve problems.
Writing	Communicating effectively in writing as appropriate for the needs of the audience.
Learning Strategies	Selecting and using training/instructional methods and procedures appropriate for the situation when learning or teaching new things.
Systems Analysis	Determining how a system should work and how changes in conditions, operations, and the environment will affect outcomes.
Service Orientation	Actively looking for ways to help people.
Negotiation	Bringing others together and trying to reconcile differences.
Troubleshooting	Determining causes of operating errors and deciding what to do about it.

Management of Financial Resources	Determining how money will be spent to get the work done, and accounting for these expenditures.
Operation and Control	Controlling operations of equipment or systems.
Operation Monitoring	Watching gauges, dials, or other indicators to make sure a machine is working properly.
Equipment Maintenance	Performing routine maintenance on equipment and determining when and what kind of maintenance is needed.
Technology Design	Generating or adapting equipment and technology to serve user needs.
Science	Using scientific rules and methods to solve problems.
Repairing	Repairing machines or systems using the needed tools.
Installation	Installing equipment, machines, wiring, or programs to meet specifications.
Programming	Writing computer programs for various purposes.

Ability	Ability Definitions
Oral Expression	The ability to communicate information and ideas in speaking so others will understand.
Oral Comprehension	The ability to listen to and understand information and ideas presented through spoken words and sentences.
Problem Sensitivity	The ability to tell when something is wrong or is likely to go wrong. It does not involve solving the problem, only recognizing there is a problem.
Written Comprehension	The ability to read and understand information and ideas presented in writing.
Inductive Reasoning	The ability to combine pieces of information to form general rules or conclusions (includes finding a relationship among seemingly unrelated events).
Deductive Reasoning	The ability to apply general rules to specific problems to produce answers that make sense.
Speech Clarity	The ability to speak clearly so others can understand you.
Near Vision	The ability to see details at close range (within a few feet of the observer).
Information Ordering	The ability to arrange things or actions in a certain order or pattern according to a specific rule or set of rules (e.g., patterns of numbers, letters, words, pictures, mathematical operations).
Speech Recognition	The ability to identify and understand the speech of another person.
Perceptual Speed	The ability to quickly and accurately compare similarities and differences among sets of letters, numbers, objects, pictures, or patterns. The things to be compared may be presented at the same time or one after the other. This ability also includes comparing a presented object with a remembered object.
Category Flexibility	The ability to generate or use different sets of rules for combining or grouping things in different ways.
Written Expression	The ability to communicate information and ideas in writing so others will understand.
Originality	The ability to come up with unusual or clever ideas about a given topic or situation, or to develop creative ways to solve a problem.
Mathematical Reasoning	The ability to choose the right mathematical methods or formulas to solve a problem.
Selective Attention	The ability to concentrate on a task over a period of time without being distracted.
Far Vision	The ability to see details at a distance.
Visualization	The ability to imagine how something will look after it is moved around or when its parts are moved or rearranged.
Number Facility	The ability to add, subtract, multiply, or divide quickly and correctly.
Fluency of Ideas	The ability to come up with a number of ideas about a topic (the number of ideas is important, not their quality, correctness, or creativity).
Speed of Closure	The ability to quickly make sense of, combine, and organize information into meaningful patterns.
Flexibility of Closure	The ability to identify or detect a known pattern (a figure, object, word, or sound) that is hidden in other distracting material.
Memorization	The ability to remember information such as words, numbers, pictures, and procedures.
Time Sharing	The ability to shift back and forth between two or more activities or sources of information (such as speech, sounds, touch, or other sources).
Depth Perception	The ability to judge which of several objects is closer or farther away from you, or to judge the distance between you and an object.

Finger Dexterity	The ability to make precisely coordinated movements of the fingers of one or both hands to grasp, manipulate, or assemble very small objects.
Auditory Attention	The ability to focus on a single source of sound in the presence of other distracting sounds.
Hearing Sensitivity	The ability to detect or tell the differences between sounds that vary in pitch and loudness.
Trunk Strength	The ability to use your abdominal and lower back muscles to support part of the body repeatedly or continuously over time without 'giving out' or fatiguing.
Control Precision	The ability to quickly and repeatedly adjust the controls of a machine or a vehicle to exact positions.
Arm-Hand Steadiness	The ability to keep your hand and arm steady while moving your arm or while holding your arm and hand in one position.
Visual Color Discrimination	The ability to match or detect differences between colors, including shades of color and brightness.
Multilimb Coordination	The ability to coordinate two or more limbs (for example, two arms, two legs, or one leg and one arm) while sitting, standing, or lying down. It does not involve performing the activities while the whole body is in motion.
Manual Dexterity	The ability to quickly move your hand, your hand together with your arm, or your two hands to grasp, manipulate, or assemble objects.
Reaction Time	The ability to quickly respond (with the hand, finger, or foot) to a signal (sound, light, picture) when it appears.
Response Orientation	The ability to choose quickly between two or more movements in response to two or more different signals (lights, sounds, pictures). It includes the speed with which the correct response is started with the hand, foot, or other body part.
Wrist-Finger Speed	The ability to make fast, simple, repeated movements of the fingers, hands, and wrists.
Rate Control	The ability to time your movements or the movement of a piece of equipment in anticipation of changes in the speed and/or direction of a moving object or scene.
Dynamic Strength	The ability to exert muscle force repeatedly or continuously over time. This involves muscular endurance and resistance to muscle fatigue.
Stamina	The ability to exert yourself physically over long periods of time without getting winded or out of breath.
Gross Body Coordination	The ability to coordinate the movement of your arms, legs, and torso together when the whole body is in motion.
Static Strength	The ability to exert maximum muscle force to lift, push, pull, or carry objects.
Gross Body Equilibrium	The ability to keep or regain your body balance or stay upright when in an unstable position.
Extent Flexibility	The ability to bend, stretch, twist, or reach with your body, arms, and/or legs.
Spatial Orientation	The ability to know your location in relation to the environment or to know where other objects are in relation to you.
Speed of Limb Movement	The ability to quickly move the arms and legs.
Sound Localization	The ability to tell the direction from which a sound originated.
Peripheral Vision	The ability to see objects or movement of objects to one's side when the eyes are looking ahead.
Dynamic Flexibility	The ability to quickly and repeatedly bend, stretch, twist, or reach out with your body, arms, and/or legs.
Night Vision	The ability to see under low light conditions.
Explosive Strength	The ability to use short bursts of muscle force to propel oneself (as in jumping or sprinting), or to throw an object.
Glare Sensitivity	The ability to see objects in the presence of glare or bright lighting.

Work_Activity	Work_Activity Definitions
Getting Information	Observing, receiving, and otherwise obtaining information from all relevant sources.
Communicating with Supervisors, Peers, or Subordin	Providing information to supervisors, co-workers, and subordinates by telephone, in written form, e-mail, or in person.
Guiding, Directing, and Motivating Subordinates	Providing guidance and direction to subordinates, including setting performance standards and monitoring performance.
Making Decisions and Solving Problems	Analyzing information and evaluating results to choose the best solution and solve problems.
Coordinating the Work and Activities of Others	Getting members of a group to work together to accomplish tasks.
Organizing, Planning, and Prioritizing Work	Developing specific goals and plans to prioritize, organize, and accomplish your work.
Scheduling Work and Activities	Scheduling events, programs, and activities, as well as the work of others.

Identifying Objects, Actions, and Events	Identifying information by categorizing, estimating, recognizing differences or similarities, and detecting changes in circumstances or events.
Inspecting Equipment, Structures, or Material	Inspecting equipment, structures, or materials to identify the cause of errors or other problems or defects.
Monitor Processes, Materials, or Surroundings	Monitoring and reviewing information from materials, events, or the environment, to detect or assess problems.
Interacting With Computers	Using computers and computer systems (including hardware and software) to program, write software, set up functions, enter data, or process information.
Coaching and Developing Others	Identifying the developmental needs of others and coaching, mentoring, or otherwise helping others to improve their knowledge or skills.
Analyzing Data or Information	Identifying the underlying principles, reasons, or facts of information by breaking down information or data into separate parts.
Monitoring and Controlling Resources	Monitoring and controlling resources and overseeing the spending of money.
Training and Teaching Others	Identifying the educational needs of others, developing formal educational or training programs or classes, and teaching or instructing others.
Establishing and Maintaining Interpersonal Relatio	Developing constructive and cooperative working relationships with others, and maintaining them over time.
Judging the Qualities of Things, Services, or Peop	Assessing the value, importance, or quality of things or people.
Developing and Building Teams	Encouraging and building mutual trust, respect, and cooperation among team members.
Resolving Conflicts and Negotiating with Others	Handling complaints, settling disputes, and resolving grievances and conflicts, or otherwise negotiating with others.
Evaluating Information to Determine Compliance wit	Using relevant information and individual judgment to determine whether events or processes comply with laws, regulations, or standards.
Updating and Using Relevant Knowledge	Keeping up-to-date technically and applying new knowledge to your job.
Controlling Machines and Processes	Using either control mechanisms or direct physical activity to operate machines or processes (not including computers or vehicles).
Thinking Creatively	Developing, designing, or creating new applications, ideas, relationships, systems, or products, including artistic contributions.
Provide Consultation and Advice to Others	Providing guidance and expert advice to management or other groups on technical, systems-, or process-related topics.
Estimating the Quantifiable Characteristics of Pro	Estimating sizes, distances, and quantities; or determining time, costs, resources, or materials needed to perform a work activity.
Documenting/Recording Information	Entering, transcribing, recording, storing, or maintaining information in written or electronic/magnetic form.
Interpreting the Meaning of Information for Others	Translating or explaining what information means and how it can be used.
Processing Information	Compiling, coding, categorizing, calculating, tabulating, auditing, or verifying information or data.
Developing Objectives and Strategies	Establishing long-range objectives and specifying the strategies and actions to achieve them.
Performing Administrative Activities	Performing day-to-day administrative tasks such as maintaining information files and processing paperwork.
Performing General Physical Activities	Performing physical activities that require considerable use of your arms and legs and moving your whole body, such as climbing, lifting, balancing, walking, stooping, and handling of materials.
Staffing Organizational Units	Recruiting, interviewing, selecting, hiring, and promoting employees in an organization.
Selling or Influencing Others	Convincing others to buy merchandise/goods or to otherwise change their minds or actions.
Communicating with Persons Outside Organization	Communicating with people outside the organization, representing the organization to customers, the public, government, and other external sources. This information can be exchanged in person, in writing, or by telephone or e-mail.
Repairing and Maintaining Mechanical Equipment	Servicing, repairing, adjusting, and testing machines, devices, moving parts, and equipment that operate primarily on the basis of mechanical (not electronic) principles.
Assisting and Caring for Others	Providing personal assistance, medical attention, emotional support, or other personal care to others such as coworkers, customers, or patients.

Repairing and Maintaining Electronic Equipment	Servicing, repairing, calibrating, regulating, fine-tuning, or testing machines, devices, and equipment that operate primarily on the basis of electrical or electronic (not mechanical) principles.
Drafting, Laying Out, and Specifying Technical Dev	Providing documentation, detailed instructions, drawings, or specifications to tell others about how devices, parts, equipment, or structures are to be fabricated, constructed, assembled, modified, maintained, or used.
Handling and Moving Objects	Using hands and arms in handling, installing, positioning, and moving materials, and manipulating things.
Performing for or Working Directly with the Public	Performing for people or dealing directly with the public. This includes serving customers in restaurants and stores, and receiving clients or guests.
Operating Vehicles, Mechanized Devices, or Equipme	Running, maneuvering, navigating, or driving vehicles or mechanized equipment, such as forklifts, passenger vehicles, aircraft, or water craft.

Work_Context	**Work_Context Definitions**
Face-to-Face Discussions	How often do you have to have face-to-face discussions with individuals or teams in this job?
Telephone	How often do you have telephone conversations in this job?
Freedom to Make Decisions	How much decision making freedom, without supervision, does the job offer?
Contact With Others	How much does this job require the worker to be in contact with others (face-to-face, by telephone, or otherwise) in order to perform it?
Structured versus Unstructured Work	To what extent is this job structured for the worker, rather than allowing the worker to determine tasks, priorities, and goals?
Responsibility for Outcomes and Results	How responsible is the worker for work outcomes and results of other workers?
Work With Work Group or Team	How important is it to work with others in a group or team in this job?
Electronic Mail	How often do you use electronic mail in this job?
Indoors, Environmentally Controlled	How often does this job require working indoors in environmentally controlled conditions?
Coordinate or Lead Others	How important is it to coordinate or lead others in accomplishing work activities in this job?
Frequency of Decision Making	How frequently is the worker required to make decisions that affect other people, the financial resources, and/or the image and reputation of the organization?
Time Pressure	How often does this job require the worker to meet strict deadlines?
Impact of Decisions on Co-workers or Company Resul	How do the decisions an employee makes impact the results of co-workers, clients or the company?
Importance of Being Exact or Accurate	How important is being very exact or highly accurate in performing this job?
Responsible for Others' Health and Safety	How much responsibility is there for the health and safety of others in this job?
Letters and Memos	How often does the job require written letters and memos?
Wear Common Protective or Safety Equipment such as	How much does this job require wearing common protective or safety equipment such as safety shoes, glasses, gloves, hard hats or live jackets?
Level of Competition	To what extent does this job require the worker to compete or to be aware of competitive pressures?
Spend Time Sitting	How much does this job require sitting?
Deal With External Customers	How important is it to work with external customers or the public in this job?
Frequency of Conflict Situations	How often are there conflict situations the employee has to face in this job?
Deal With Unpleasant or Angry People	How frequently does the worker have to deal with unpleasant, angry, or discourteous individuals as part of the job requirements?
Physical Proximity	To what extent does this job require the worker to perform job tasks in close physical proximity to other people?
Importance of Repeating Same Tasks	How important is repeating the same physical activities (e.g., key entry) or mental activities (e.g., checking entries in a ledger) over and over, without stopping, to performing this job?
Sounds, Noise Levels Are Distracting or Uncomforta	How often does this job require working exposed to sounds and noise levels that are distracting or uncomfortable?
Indoors, Not Environmentally Controlled	How often does this job require working indoors in non-controlled environmental conditions (e.g., warehouse without heat)?
Exposed to Contaminants	How often does this job require working exposed to contaminants (such as pollutants, gases, dust or odors)?
Consequence of Error	How serious would the result usually be if the worker made a mistake that was not readily correctable?

Spend Time Standing	How much does this job require standing?
Exposed to Hazardous Equipment	How often does this job require exposure to hazardous equipment?
In an Enclosed Vehicle or Equipment	How often does this job require working in a closed vehicle or equipment (e.g., car)?
Public Speaking	How often do you have to perform public speaking in this job?
Spend Time Walking and Running	How much does this job require walking and running?
Spend Time Using Your Hands to Handle, Control, or	How much does this job require using your hands to handle, control, or feel objects, tools or controls?
Exposed to Minor Burns, Cuts, Bites, or Stings	How often does this job require exposure to minor burns, cuts, bites, or stings?
Outdoors, Exposed to Weather	How often does this job require working outdoors, exposed to all weather conditions?
Degree of Automation	How automated is the job?
Exposed to Hazardous Conditions	How often does this job require exposure to hazardous conditions?
Outdoors, Under Cover	How often does this job require working outdoors, under cover (e.g., structure with roof but no walls)?
Very Hot or Cold Temperatures	How often does this job require working in very hot (above 90 F degrees) or very cold (below 32 F degrees) temperatures?
Extremely Bright or Inadequate Lighting	How often does this job require working in extremely bright or inadequate lighting conditions?
Pace Determined by Speed of Equipment	How important is it to this job that the pace is determined by the speed of equipment or machinery? (This does not refer to keeping busy at all times on this job.)
Spend Time Making Repetitive Motions	How much does this job require making repetitive motions?
Spend Time Bending or Twisting the Body	How much does this job require bending or twisting your body?
Spend Time Keeping or Regaining Balance	How much does this job require keeping or regaining your balance?
Exposed to High Places	How often does this job require exposure to high places?
In an Open Vehicle or Equipment	How often does this job require working in an open vehicle or equipment (e.g., tractor)?
Exposed to Whole Body Vibration	How often does this job require exposure to whole body vibration (e.g., operate a jackhammer)?
Spend Time Kneeling, Crouching, Stooping, or Crawl	How much does this job require kneeling, crouching, stooping, or crawling?
Deal With Physically Aggressive People	How frequently does this job require the worker to deal with physical aggression of violent individuals?
Spend Time Climbing Ladders, Scaffolds, or Poles	How much does this job require climbing ladders, scaffolds, or poles?
Cramped Work Space, Awkward Positions	How often does this job require working in cramped work spaces that requires getting into awkward positions?
Wear Specialized Protective or Safety Equipment su	How much does this job require wearing specialized protective or safety equipment such as breathing apparatus, safety harness, full protection suits, or radiation protection?
Exposed to Radiation	How often does this job require exposure to radiation?
Exposed to Disease or Infections	How often does this job require exposure to disease/infections?

Job Zone Component	**Job Zone Component Definitions**
Title	Job Zone Four: Considerable Preparation Needed
Overall Experience	A minimum of two to four years of work-related skill, knowledge, or experience is needed for these occupations. For example, an accountant must complete four years of college and work for several years in accounting to be considered qualified.
Job Training	Employees in these occupations usually need several years of work-related experience, on-the-job training, and/or vocational training.
Job Zone Examples	Many of these occupations involve coordinating, supervising, managing, or training others. Examples include accountants, chefs and head cooks, computer programmers, historians, pharmacists, and police detectives.
SVP Range	(7.0 to < 8.0)
Education	Most of these occupations require a four - year bachelor's degree, but some do not.

Work_Styles	**Work_Styles Definitions**
Leadership	Job requires a willingness to lead, take charge, and offer opinions and direction.

Attention to Detail	Job requires being careful about detail and thorough in completing work tasks.
Adaptability/Flexibility	Job requires being open to change (positive or negative) and to considerable variety in the workplace.
Integrity	Job requires being honest and ethical.
Initiative	Job requires a willingness to take on responsibilities and challenges.
Dependability	Job requires being reliable, responsible, and dependable, and fulfilling obligations.
Self Control	Job requires maintaining composure, keeping emotions in check, controlling anger, and avoiding aggressive behavior, even in very difficult situations.
Cooperation	Job requires being pleasant with others on the job and displaying a good-natured, cooperative attitude.
Stress Tolerance	Job requires accepting criticism and dealing calmly and effectively with high stress situations.
Independence	Job requires developing one's own ways of doing things, guiding oneself with little or no supervision, and depending on oneself to get things done.
Achievement/Effort	Job requires establishing and maintaining personally challenging achievement goals and exerting effort toward mastering tasks.
Persistence	Job requires persistence in the face of obstacles.
Analytical Thinking	Job requires analyzing information and using logic to address work-related issues and problems.
Concern for Others	Job requires being sensitive to others' needs and feelings and being understanding and helpful on the job.
Innovation	Job requires creativity and alternative thinking to develop new ideas for and answers to work-related problems.
Social Orientation	Job requires preferring to work with others rather than alone, and being personally connected with others on the job.

11-3061.00 - Purchasing Managers

Plan, direct, or coordinate the activities of buyers, purchasing officers, and related workers involved in purchasing materials, products, and services.

Tasks

1) Maintain records of goods ordered and received.

2) Control purchasing department budgets.

3) Resolve vendor or contractor grievances, and claims against suppliers.

4) Prepare and process requisitions and purchase orders for supplies and equipment.

5) Participate in the development of specifications for equipment, products or substitute materials.

6) Develop and implement purchasing and contract management instructions, policies, and procedures.

7) Arrange for disposal of surplus materials.

8) Analyze market and delivery systems in order to assess present and future material availability.

9) Interview and hire staff, and oversee staff training.

10) Review purchase order claims and contracts for conformance to company policy.

11) Prepare reports regarding market conditions and merchandise costs.

12) Direct and coordinate activities of personnel engaged in buying, selling, and distributing materials, equipment, machinery, and supplies.

13) Review, evaluate, and approve specifications for issuing and awarding bids.

14) Represent companies in negotiating contracts and formulating policies with suppliers.

15) Administer on-line purchasing systems.

16) Prepare bid awards requiring board approval.

Knowledge	Knowledge Definitions
English Language	Knowledge of the structure and content of the English language including the meaning and spelling of words, rules of composition, and grammar.
Administration and Management	Knowledge of business and management principles involved in strategic planning, resource allocation, human resources modeling, leadership technique, production methods, and coordination of people and resources.
Production and Processing	Knowledge of raw materials, production processes, quality control, costs, and other techniques for maximizing the effective manufacture and distribution of goods.
Mathematics	Knowledge of arithmetic, algebra, geometry, calculus, statistics, and their applications.
Personnel and Human Resources	Knowledge of principles and procedures for personnel recruitment, selection, training, compensation and benefits, labor relations and negotiation, and personnel information systems.
Economics and Accounting	Knowledge of economic and accounting principles and practices, the financial markets, banking and the analysis and reporting of financial data.
Computers and Electronics	Knowledge of circuit boards, processors, chips, electronic equipment, and computer hardware and software, including applications and programming.
Customer and Personal Service	Knowledge of principles and processes for providing customer and personal services. This includes customer needs assessment, meeting quality standards for services, and evaluation of customer satisfaction.
Education and Training	Knowledge of principles and methods for curriculum and training design, teaching and instruction for individuals and groups, and the measurement of training effects.
Design	Knowledge of design techniques, tools, and principles involved in production of precision technical plans, blueprints, drawings, and models.
Clerical	Knowledge of administrative and clerical procedures and systems such as word processing, managing files and records, stenography and transcription, designing forms, and other office procedures and terminology.
Transportation	Knowledge of principles and methods for moving people or goods by air, rail, sea, or road, including the relative costs and benefits.
Engineering and Technology	Knowledge of the practical application of engineering science and technology. This includes applying principles, techniques, procedures, and equipment to the design and production of various goods and services.
Communications and Media	Knowledge of media production, communication, and dissemination techniques and methods. This includes alternative ways to inform and entertain via written, oral, and visual media.
Law and Government	Knowledge of laws, legal codes, court procedures, precedents, government regulations, executive orders, agency rules, and the democratic political process.
Psychology	Knowledge of human behavior and performance; individual differences in ability, personality, and interests; learning and motivation; psychological research methods; and the assessment and treatment of behavioral and affective disorders.
Telecommunications	Knowledge of transmission, broadcasting, switching, control, and operation of telecommunications systems.
Mechanical	Knowledge of machines and tools, including their designs, uses, repair, and maintenance.
Sales and Marketing	Knowledge of principles and methods for showing, promoting, and selling products or services. This includes marketing strategy and tactics, product demonstration, sales techniques, and sales control systems.
Public Safety and Security	Knowledge of relevant equipment, policies, procedures, and strategies to promote effective local, state, or national security operations for the protection of people, data, property, and institutions.
Geography	Knowledge of principles and methods for describing the features of land, sea, and air masses, including their physical characteristics, locations, interrelationships, and distribution of plant, animal, and human life.
Chemistry	Knowledge of the chemical composition, structure, and properties of substances and of the chemical processes and transformations that they undergo. This includes uses of chemicals and their interactions, danger signs, production techniques, and disposal methods.
Therapy and Counseling	Knowledge of principles, methods, and procedures for diagnosis, treatment, and rehabilitation of physical and mental dysfunctions, and for career counseling and guidance.

Physics	Knowledge and prediction of physical principles, laws, their interrelationships, and applications to understanding fluid, material, and atmospheric dynamics, and mechanical, electrical, atomic and sub-atomic structures and processes.
Food Production	Knowledge of techniques and equipment for planting, growing, and harvesting food products (both plant and animal) for consumption, including storage/handling techniques.
Sociology and Anthropology	Knowledge of group behavior and dynamics, societal trends and influences, human migrations, ethnicity, cultures and their history and origins.
Foreign Language	Knowledge of the structure and content of a foreign (non-English) language including the meaning and spelling of words, rules of composition and grammar, and pronunciation.
Building and Construction	Knowledge of materials, methods, and the tools involved in the construction or repair of houses, buildings, or other structures such as highways and roads.
Biology	Knowledge of plant and animal organisms, their tissues, cells, functions, interdependencies, and interactions with each other and the environment.
Philosophy and Theology	Knowledge of different philosophical systems and religions. This includes their basic principles, values, ethics, ways of thinking, customs, practices, and their impact on human culture.
Medicine and Dentistry	Knowledge of the information and techniques needed to diagnose and treat human injuries, diseases, and deformities. This includes symptoms, treatment alternatives, drug properties and interactions, and preventive health-care measures.
History and Archeology	Knowledge of historical events and their causes, indicators, and effects on civilizations and cultures.
Fine Arts	Knowledge of the theory and techniques required to compose, produce, and perform works of music, dance, visual arts, drama, and sculpture.

Skills	**Skills Definitions**
Active Listening	Giving full attention to what other people are saying, taking time to understand the points being made, asking questions as appropriate, and not interrupting at inappropriate times.
Critical Thinking	Using logic and reasoning to identify the strengths and weaknesses of alternative solutions, conclusions or approaches to problems.
Judgment and Decision Making	Considering the relative costs and benefits of potential actions to choose the most appropriate one.
Reading Comprehension	Understanding written sentences and paragraphs in work related documents.
Active Learning	Understanding the implications of new information for both current and future problem-solving and decision-making.
Management of Material Resources	Obtaining and seeing to the appropriate use of equipment, facilities, and materials needed to do certain work.
Negotiation	Bringing others together and trying to reconcile differences.
Mathematics	Using mathematics to solve problems.
Time Management	Managing one's own time and the time of others.
Operations Analysis	Analyzing needs and product requirements to create a design.
Learning Strategies	Selecting and using training/instructional methods and procedures appropriate for the situation when learning or teaching new things.
Coordination	Adjusting actions in relation to others' actions.
Management of Financial Resources	Determining how money will be spent to get the work done, and accounting for these expenditures.
Speaking	Talking to others to convey information effectively.
Monitoring	Monitoring/Assessing performance of yourself, other individuals, or organizations to make improvements or take corrective action.
Writing	Communicating effectively in writing as appropriate for the needs of the audience.
Troubleshooting	Determining causes of operating errors and deciding what to do about it.
Service Orientation	Actively looking for ways to help people.
Persuasion	Persuading others to change their minds or behavior.
Operation Monitoring	Watching gauges, dials, or other indicators to make sure a machine is working properly.
Complex Problem Solving	Identifying complex problems and reviewing related information to develop and evaluate options and implement solutions.
Equipment Selection	Determining the kind of tools and equipment needed to do a job.

Systems Evaluation	Identifying measures or indicators of system performance and the actions needed to improve or correct performance, relative to the goals of the system.
Operation and Control	Controlling operations of equipment or systems.
Instructing	Teaching others how to do something.
Social Perceptiveness	Being aware of others' reactions and understanding why they react as they do.
Management of Personnel Resources	Motivating, developing, and directing people as they work, identifying the best people for the job.
Quality Control Analysis	Conducting tests and inspections of products, services, or processes to evaluate quality or performance.
Systems Analysis	Determining how a system should work and how changes in conditions, operations, and the environment will affect outcomes.
Technology Design	Generating or adapting equipment and technology to serve user needs.
Repairing	Repairing machines or systems using the needed tools.
Science	Using scientific rules and methods to solve problems.
Installation	Installing equipment, machines, wiring, or programs to meet specifications.
Programming	Writing computer programs for various purposes.
Equipment Maintenance	Performing routine maintenance on equipment and determining when and what kind of maintenance is needed.

Ability	**Ability Definitions**
Speech Clarity	The ability to speak clearly so others can understand you.
Oral Comprehension	The ability to listen to and understand information and ideas presented through spoken words and sentences.
Speech Recognition	The ability to identify and understand the speech of another person.
Written Comprehension	The ability to read and understand information and ideas presented in writing.
Oral Expression	The ability to communicate information and ideas in speaking so others will understand.
Written Expression	The ability to communicate information and ideas in writing so others will understand.
Problem Sensitivity	The ability to tell when something is wrong or is likely to go wrong. It does not involve solving the problem, only recognizing there is a problem.
Near Vision	The ability to see details at close range (within a few feet of the observer).
Deductive Reasoning	The ability to apply general rules to specific problems to produce answers that make sense.
Inductive Reasoning	The ability to combine pieces of information to form general rules or conclusions (includes finding a relationship among seemingly unrelated events).
Fluency of Ideas	The ability to come up with a number of ideas about a topic (the number of ideas is important, not their quality, correctness, or creativity).
Category Flexibility	The ability to generate or use different sets of rules for combining or grouping things in different ways.
Information Ordering	The ability to arrange things or actions in a certain order or pattern according to a specific rule or set of rules (e.g., patterns of numbers, letters, words, pictures, mathematical operations).
Number Facility	The ability to add, subtract, multiply, or divide quickly and correctly.
Selective Attention	The ability to concentrate on a task over a period of time without being distracted.
Mathematical Reasoning	The ability to choose the right mathematical methods or formulas to solve a problem.
Finger Dexterity	The ability to make precisely coordinated movements of the fingers of one or both hands to grasp, manipulate, or assemble very small objects.
Perceptual Speed	The ability to quickly and accurately compare similarities and differences among sets of letters, numbers, objects, pictures, or patterns. The things to be compared may be presented at the same time or one after the other. This ability also includes comparing a presented object with a remembered object.
Originality	The ability to come up with unusual or clever ideas about a given topic or situation, or to develop creative ways to solve a problem.
Flexibility of Closure	The ability to identify or detect a known pattern (a figure, object, word, or sound) that is hidden in other distracting material.
Memorization	The ability to remember information such as words, numbers, pictures, and procedures.

Visualization	The ability to imagine how something will look after it is moved around or when its parts are moved or rearranged.
Speed of Closure	The ability to quickly make sense of, combine, and organize information into meaningful patterns.
Far Vision	The ability to see details at a distance.
Time Sharing	The ability to shift back and forth between two or more activities or sources of information (such as speech, sounds, touch, or other sources).
Auditory Attention	The ability to focus on a single source of sound in the presence of other distracting sounds.
Arm-Hand Steadiness	The ability to keep your hand and arm steady while moving your arm or while holding your arm and hand in one position.
Trunk Strength	The ability to use your abdominal and lower back muscles to support part of the body repeatedly or continuously over time without 'giving out' or fatiguing.
Depth Perception	The ability to judge which of several objects is closer or farther away from you, or to judge the distance between you and an object.
Visual Color Discrimination	The ability to match or detect differences between colors, including shades of color and brightness.
Hearing Sensitivity	The ability to detect or tell the differences between sounds that vary in pitch and loudness.
Stamina	The ability to exert yourself physically over long periods of time without getting winded or out of breath.
Manual Dexterity	The ability to quickly move your hand, your hand together with your arm, or your two hands to grasp, manipulate, or assemble objects.
Multilimb Coordination	The ability to coordinate two or more limbs (for example, two arms, two legs, or one leg and one arm) while sitting, standing, or lying down. It does not involve performing the activities while the whole body is in motion.
Static Strength	The ability to exert maximum muscle force to lift, push, pull, or carry objects.
Control Precision	The ability to quickly and repeatedly adjust the controls of a machine or a vehicle to exact positions.
Gross Body Coordination	The ability to coordinate the movement of your arms, legs, and torso together when the whole body is in motion.
Speed of Limb Movement	The ability to quickly move the arms and legs.
Reaction Time	The ability to quickly respond (with the hand, finger, or foot) to a signal (sound, light, picture) when it appears.
Response Orientation	The ability to choose quickly between two or more movements in response to two or more different signals (lights, sounds, pictures). It includes the speed with which the correct response is started with the hand, foot, or other body part.
Spatial Orientation	The ability to know your location in relation to the environment or to know where other objects are in relation to you.
Wrist-Finger Speed	The ability to make fast, simple, repeated movements of the fingers, hands, and wrists.
Peripheral Vision	The ability to see objects or movement of objects to one's side when the eyes are looking ahead.
Extent Flexibility	The ability to bend, stretch, twist, or reach with your body, arms, and/or legs.
Rate Control	The ability to time your movements or the movement of a piece of equipment in anticipation of changes in the speed and/or direction of a moving object or scene.
Night Vision	The ability to see under low light conditions.
Glare Sensitivity	The ability to see objects in the presence of glare or bright lighting.
Sound Localization	The ability to tell the direction from which a sound originated.
Gross Body Equilibrium	The ability to keep or regain your body balance or stay upright when in an unstable position.
Dynamic Strength	The ability to exert muscle force repeatedly or continuously over time. This involves muscular endurance and resistance to muscle fatigue.
Dynamic Flexibility	The ability to quickly and repeatedly bend, stretch, twist, or reach out with your body, arms, and/or legs.
Explosive Strength	The ability to use short bursts of muscle force to propel oneself (as in jumping or sprinting), or to throw an object.

Work_Activity	Work_Activity Definitions
Communicating with Supervisors, Peers, or Subordin	Providing information to supervisors, co-workers, and subordinates by telephone, in written form, e-mail, or in person.
Making Decisions and Solving Problems	Analyzing information and evaluating results to choose the best solution and solve problems.
Organizing, Planning, and Prioritizing Work	Developing specific goals and plans to prioritize, organize, and accomplish your work.
Judging the Qualities of Things, Services, or Peop	Assessing the value, importance, or quality of things or people.
Getting Information	Observing, receiving, and otherwise obtaining information from all relevant sources.
Interacting With Computers	Using computers and computer systems (including hardware and software) to program, write software, set up functions, enter data, or process information.
Performing Administrative Activities	Performing day-to-day administrative tasks such as maintaining information files and processing paperwork.
Establishing and Maintaining Interpersonal Relatio	Developing constructive and cooperative working relationships with others, and maintaining them over time.
Developing and Building Teams	Encouraging and building mutual trust, respect, and cooperation among team members.
Documenting/Recording Information	Entering, transcribing, recording, storing, or maintaining information in written or electronic/magnetic form.
Identifying Objects, Actions, and Events	Identifying information by categorizing, estimating, recognizing differences or similarities, and detecting changes in circumstances or events.
Training and Teaching Others	Identifying the educational needs of others, developing formal educational or training programs or classes, and teaching or instructing others.
Provide Consultation and Advice to Others	Providing guidance and expert advice to management or other groups on technical, systems-, or process-related topics.
Scheduling Work and Activities	Scheduling events, programs, and activities, as well as the work of others.
Processing Information	Compiling, coding, categorizing, calculating, tabulating, auditing, or verifying information or data.
Updating and Using Relevant Knowledge	Keeping up-to-date technically and applying new knowledge to your job.
Monitoring and Controlling Resources	Monitoring and controlling resources and overseeing the spending of money.
Performing for or Working Directly with the Public	Performing for people or dealing directly with the public. This includes serving customers in restaurants and stores, and receiving clients or guests.
Resolving Conflicts and Negotiating with Others	Handling complaints, settling disputes, and resolving grievances and conflicts, or otherwise negotiating with others.
Coaching and Developing Others	Identifying the developmental needs of others and coaching, mentoring, or otherwise helping others to improve their knowledge or skills.
Guiding, Directing, and Motivating Subordinates	Providing guidance and direction to subordinates, including setting performance standards and monitoring performance.
Evaluating Information to Determine Compliance wit	Using relevant information and individual judgment to determine whether events or processes comply with laws, regulations, or standards.
Inspecting Equipment, Structures, or Material	Inspecting equipment, structures, or materials to identify the cause of errors or other problems or defects.
Interpreting the Meaning of Information for Others	Translating or explaining what information means and how it can be used.
Analyzing Data or Information	Identifying the underlying principles, reasons, or facts of information by breaking down information or data into separate parts.
Thinking Creatively	Developing, designing, or creating new applications, ideas, relationships, systems, or products, including artistic contributions.
Selling or Influencing Others	Convincing others to buy merchandise/goods or to otherwise change their minds or actions.
Monitor Processes, Materials, or Surroundings	Monitoring and reviewing information from materials, events, or the environment, to detect or assess problems.
Communicating with Persons Outside Organization	Communicating with people outside the organization, representing the organization to customers, the public, government, and other external sources. This information can be exchanged in person, in writing, or by telephone or e-mail.
Developing Objectives and Strategies	Establishing long-range objectives and specifying the strategies and actions to achieve them.
Coordinating the Work and Activities of Others	Getting members of a group to work together to accomplish tasks.
Staffing Organizational Units	Recruiting, interviewing, selecting, hiring, and promoting employees in an organization.
Assisting and Caring for Others	Providing personal assistance, medical attention, emotional support, or other personal care to others such as coworkers, customers, or patients.
Estimating the Quantifiable Characteristics of Pro	Estimating sizes, distances, and quantities; or determining time, costs, resources, or materials needed to perform a work activity.
Handling and Moving Objects	Using hands and arms in handling, installing, positioning, and moving materials, and manipulating things.

Operating Vehicles. Mechanized Devices. or Equipme	Running. maneuvering. navigating. or driving vehicles or mechanized equipment. such as forklifts. passenger vehicles. aircraft. or water craft.
Repairing and Maintaining Mechanical Equipment	Servicing. repairing. adjusting. and testing machines. devices. moving parts. and equipment that operate primarily on the basis of mechanical (not electronic) principles.
Controlling Machines and Processes	Using either control mechanisms or direct physical activity to operate machines or processes (not including computers or vehicles).
Performing General Physical Activities	Performing physical activities that require considerable use of your arms and legs and moving your whole body. such as climbing. lifting. balancing. walking. stooping. and handling of materials.
Repairing and Maintaining Electronic Equipment	Servicing. repairing. calibrating. regulating. fine-tuning. or testing machines. devices. and equipment that operate primarily on the basis of electrical or electronic (not mechanical) principles.
Drafting. Laying Out. and Specifying Technical Dev	Providing documentation. detailed instructions. drawings. or specifications to tell others about how devices. parts. equipment. or structures are to be fabricated. constructed. assembled. modified. maintained. or used.

Work_Context	Work_Context Definitions
Telephone	How often do you have telephone conversations in this job?
Face-to-Face Discussions	How often do you have to have face-to-face discussions with individuals or teams in this job?
Contact With Others	How much does this job require the worker to be in contact with others (face-to-face, by telephone, or otherwise) in order to perform it?
Electronic Mail	How often do you use electronic mail in this job?
Frequency of Decision Making	How frequently is the worker required to make decisions that affect other people, the financial resources, and/or the image and reputation of the organization?
Indoors, Environmentally Controlled	How often does this job require working indoors in environmentally controlled conditions?
Importance of Being Exact or Accurate	How important is being very exact or highly accurate in performing this job?
Time Pressure	How often does this job require the worker to meet strict deadlines?
Freedom to Make Decisions	How much decision making freedom, without supervision, does the job offer?
Work With Work Group or Team	How important is it to work with others in a group or team in this job?
Impact of Decisions on Co-workers or Company Resul	How do the decisions an employee makes impact the results of co-workers, clients or the company?
Structured versus Unstructured Work	To what extent is this job structured for the worker, rather than allowing the worker to determine tasks, priorities, and goals?
Coordinate or Lead Others	How important is it to coordinate or lead others in accomplishing work activities in this job?
Deal With External Customers	How important is it to work with external customers or the public in this job?
Responsibility for Outcomes and Results	How responsible is the worker for work outcomes and results of other workers?
Frequency of Conflict Situations	How often are there conflict situations the employee has to face in this job?
Deal With Unpleasant or Angry People	How frequently does the worker have to deal with unpleasant, angry, or discourteous individuals as part of the job requirements?
Letters and Memos	How often does the job require written letters and memos?
Spend Time Sitting	How much does this job require sitting?
Responsible for Others' Health and Safety	How much responsibility is there for the health and safety of others in this job?
Level of Competition	To what extent does this job require the worker to compete or to be aware of competitive pressures?
Sounds, Noise Levels Are Distracting or Uncomforta	How often does this job require working exposed to sounds and noise levels that are distracting or uncomfortable?
Importance of Repeating Same Tasks	How important is repeating the same physical activities (e.g., key entry) or mental activities (e.g., checking entries in a ledger) over and over, without stopping, to performing this job?
Physical Proximity	To what extent does this job require the worker to perform job tasks in close physical proximity to other people?
Spend Time Making Repetitive Motions	How much does this job require making repetitive motions?
Spend Time Standing	How much does this job require standing?
Degree of Automation	How automated is the job?

Consequence of Error	How serious would the result usually be if the worker made a mistake that was not readily correctable?
Indoors. Not Environmentally Controlled	How often does this job require working indoors in non-controlled environmental conditions (e.g., warehouse without heat)?
Spend Time Walking and Running	How much does this job require walking and running?
Public Speaking	How often do you have to perform public speaking in this job?
Spend Time Using Your Hands to Handle. Control. or	How much does this job require using your hands to handle, control, or feel objects. tools or controls?
Exposed to Contaminants	How often does this job require working exposed to contaminants (such as pollutants, gases, dust or odors)?
Outdoors, Exposed to Weather	How often does this job require working outdoors, exposed to all weather conditions?
Very Hot or Cold Temperatures	How often does this job require working in very hot (above 90 F degrees) or very cold (below 32 F degrees) temperatures?
Wear Common Protective or Safety Equipment such as	How much does this job require wearing common protective or safety equipment such as safety shoes, glasses, gloves, hard hats or life jackets?
Spend Time Bending or Twisting the Body	How much does this job require bending or twisting your body?
Cramped Work Space. Awkward Positions	How often does this job require working in cramped work spaces that requires getting into awkward positions?
In an Enclosed Vehicle or Equipment	How often does this job require working in a closed vehicle or equipment (e.g., car)?
Spend Time Keeping or Regaining Balance	How much does this job require keeping or regaining your balance?
Exposed to Minor Burns. Cuts, Bites, or Stings	How often does this job require exposure to minor burns, cuts, bites, or stings?
Pace Determined by Speed of Equipment	How important is it to this job that the pace is determined by the speed of equipment or machinery? (This does not refer to keeping busy at all times on this job.)
Spend Time Kneeling. Crouching, Stooping. or Crawl	How much does this job require kneeling, crouching, stooping, or crawling?
Extremely Bright or Inadequate Lighting	How often does this job require working in extremely bright or inadequate lighting conditions?
Exposed to Hazardous Equipment	How often does this job require exposure to hazardous equipment?
Deal With Physically Aggressive People	How frequently does this job require the worker to deal with physical aggression of violent individuals?
Exposed to Hazardous Conditions	How often does this job require exposure to hazardous conditions?
Outdoors, Under Cover	How often does this job require working outdoors, under cover (e.g., structure with roof but no walls)?
Exposed to Disease or Infections	How often does this job require exposure to disease/infections?
Exposed to High Places	How often does this job require exposure to high places?
Spend Time Climbing Ladders, Scaffolds, or Poles	How much does this job require climbing ladders, scaffolds, or poles?
In an Open Vehicle or Equipment	How often does this job require working in an open vehicle or equipment (e.g., tractor)?
Exposed to Whole Body Vibration	How often does this job require exposure to whole body vibration (e.g., operate a jackhammer)?
Wear Specialized Protective or Safety Equipment su	How much does this job require wearing specialized protective or safety equipment such as breathing apparatus, safety harness, full protection suits, or radiation protection?
Exposed to Radiation	How often does this job require exposure to radiation?

Job Zone Component	Job Zone Component Definitions
Title	Job Zone Four: Considerable Preparation Needed
Overall Experience	A minimum of two to four years of work-related skill, knowledge, or experience is needed for these occupations. For example, an accountant must complete four years of college and work for several years in accounting to be considered qualified.
Job Training	Employees in these occupations usually need several years of work-related experience, on-the-job training, and/or vocational training.
Job Zone Examples	Many of these occupations involve coordinating, supervising, managing, or training others. Examples include accountants, chefs and head cooks, computer programmers, historians, pharmacists, and police detectives.
SVP Range	(7.0 to < 8.0)

Education	Most of these occupations require a four - year bachelor's degree. but some do not.

Work_Styles	Work_Styles Definitions
Integrity	Job requires being honest and ethical.
Dependability	Job requires being reliable. responsible, and dependable, and fulfilling obligations.
Achievement/Effort	Job requires establishing and maintaining personally challenging achievement goals and exerting effort toward mastering tasks.
Stress Tolerance	Job requires accepting criticism and dealing calmly and effectively with high stress situations.
Attention to Detail	Job requires being careful about detail and thorough in completing work tasks.
Persistence	Job requires persistence in the face of obstacles.
Initiative	Job requires a willingness to take on responsibilities and challenges.
Leadership	Job requires a willingness to lead, take charge, and offer opinions and direction.
Adaptability/Flexibility	Job requires being open to change (positive or negative) and to considerable variety in the workplace.
Cooperation	Job requires being pleasant with others on the job and displaying a good-natured, cooperative attitude.
Self Control	Job requires maintaining composure, keeping emotions in check, controlling anger, and avoiding aggressive behavior, even in very difficult situations.
Independence	Job requires developing one's own ways of doing things, guiding oneself with little or no supervision, and depending on oneself to get things done.
Innovation	Job requires creativity and alternative thinking to develop new ideas for and answers to work-related problems.
Analytical Thinking	Job requires analyzing information and using logic to address work-related issues and problems.
Concern for Others	Job requires being sensitive to others' needs and feelings and being understanding and helpful on the job.
Social Orientation	Job requires preferring to work with others rather than alone, and being personally connected with others on the job.

11-3071.01 - Transportation Managers

Plan, direct, and coordinate the transportation operations within an organization or the activities of organizations that provide transportation services.

Tasks

1) Collaborate with other managers and staff members in order to formulate and implement policies, procedures, goals, and objectives.

2) Serve as contact persons for all workers within assigned territories.

3) Direct activities related to dispatching, routing, and tracking transportation vehicles, such as aircraft and railroad cars.

4) Promote safe work activities by conducting safety audits, attending company safety meetings, and meeting with individual staff members.

5) Monitor operations to ensure that staff members comply with administrative policies and procedures, safety rules, union contracts, and government regulations.

6) Implement schedule and policy changes.

7) Plan, organize and manage the work of subordinate staff to ensure that the work is accomplished in a manner consistent with organizational requirements.

8) Conduct employee training sessions on subjects such as hazardous material handling, employee orientation, quality improvement and computer use.

9) Supervise workers assigning tariff classifications and preparing billing.

10) Direct and coordinate, through subordinates, activities of operations department in order to obtain use of equipment, facilities, and human resources.

11) Monitor spending to ensure that expenses are consistent with approved budgets.

12) Prepare management recommendations, such as proposed fee and tariff increases or schedule changes.

13) Direct procurement processes, including equipment research and testing, vendor contracts, and requisitions approval.

14) Analyze expenditures and other financial information in order to develop plans. policies. and budgets for increasing profits and improving services.

15) Negotiate and authorize contracts with equipment and materials suppliers, and monitor contract fulfillment.

16) Direct activities of staff performing repairs and maintenance to equipment. vehicles, and facilities.

17) Recommend or authorize capital expenditures for acquisition of new equipment or property in order to increase efficiency and services of operations department.

18) Conduct investigations in cooperation with government agencies to determine causes of transportation accidents and to improve safety procedures.

19) Set operations policies and standards, including determination of safety procedures for the handling of dangerous goods.

20) Participate in union contract negotiations and settlements of grievances.

21) Develop criteria, application instructions, procedural manuals, and contracts for federal and state public transportation programs.

22) Provide administrative and technical assistance to those receiving transportation-related grants.

Knowledge	Knowledge Definitions
Transportation	Knowledge of principles and methods for moving people or goods by air, rail, sea, or road. including the relative costs and benefits.
Customer and Personal Service	Knowledge of principles and processes for providing customer and personal services. This includes customer needs assessment, meeting quality standards for services, and evaluation of customer satisfaction.
Administration and Management	Knowledge of business and management principles involved in strategic planning, resource allocation, human resources modeling, leadership technique, production methods, and coordination of people and resources.
Clerical	Knowledge of administrative and clerical procedures and systems such as word processing. managing files and records, stenography and transcription, designing forms, and other office procedures and terminology.
English Language	Knowledge of the structure and content of the English language including the meaning and spelling of words. rules of composition, and grammar.
Mathematics	Knowledge of arithmetic, algebra, geometry. calculus, statistics, and their applications.
Education and Training	Knowledge of principles and methods for curriculum and training design, teaching and instruction for individuals and groups, and the measurement of training effects.
Public Safety and Security	Knowledge of relevant equipment, policies, procedures, and strategies to promote effective local, state, or national security operations for the protection of people, data, property, and institutions.
Psychology	Knowledge of human behavior and performance; individual differences in ability, personality, and interests; learning and motivation; psychological research methods; and the assessment and treatment of behavioral and affective disorders.
Telecommunications	Knowledge of transmission, broadcasting, switching, control, and operation of telecommunications systems.
Sales and Marketing	Knowledge of principles and methods for showing, promoting, and selling products or services. This includes marketing strategy and tactics, product demonstration, sales techniques, and sales control systems.
Computers and Electronics	Knowledge of circuit boards, processors, chips, electronic equipment, and computer hardware and software. including applications and programming.
Production and Processing	Knowledge of raw materials, production processes, quality control, costs, and other techniques for maximizing the effective manufacture and distribution of goods.
Economics and Accounting	Knowledge of economic and accounting principles and practices, the financial markets, banking and the analysis and reporting of financial data.
Personnel and Human Resources	Knowledge of principles and procedures for personnel recruitment, selection, training, compensation and benefits, labor relations and negotiation, and personnel information systems.
Communications and Media	Knowledge of media production, communication, and dissemination techniques and methods. This includes alternative ways to inform and entertain via written, oral, and visual media.

Geography	Knowledge of principles and methods for describing the features of land, sea, and air masses, including their physical characteristics, locations, interrelationships, and distribution of plant, animal, and human life.
Sociology and Anthropology	Knowledge of group behavior and dynamics, societal trends and influences, human migrations, ethnicity, cultures and their history and origins.
Mechanical	Knowledge of machines and tools, including their designs, uses, repair, and maintenance.
Law and Government	Knowledge of laws, legal codes, court procedures, precedents, government regulations, executive orders, agency rules, and the democratic political process.
Design	Knowledge of design techniques, tools, and principles involved in production of precision technical plans, blueprints, drawings, and models.
Engineering and Technology	Knowledge of the practical application of engineering science and technology. This includes applying principles, techniques, procedures, and equipment to the design and production of various goods and services.
Therapy and Counseling	Knowledge of principles, methods, and procedures for diagnosis, treatment, and rehabilitation of physical and mental dysfunctions, and for career counseling and guidance.
Foreign Language	Knowledge of the structure and content of a foreign (non-English) language including the meaning and spelling of words, rules of composition and grammar, and pronunciation.
Chemistry	Knowledge of the chemical composition, structure, and properties of substances and of the chemical processes and transformations that they undergo. This includes uses of chemicals and their interactions, danger signs, production techniques, and disposal methods.
Philosophy and Theology	Knowledge of different philosophical systems and religions. This includes their basic principles, values, ethics, ways of thinking, customs, practices, and their impact on human culture.
Food Production	Knowledge of techniques and equipment for planting, growing, and harvesting food products (both plant and animal) for consumption, including storage/handling techniques.
History and Archeology	Knowledge of historical events and their causes, indicators, and effects on civilizations and cultures.
Building and Construction	Knowledge of materials, methods, and the tools involved in the construction or repair of houses, buildings, or other structures such as highways and roads.
Medicine and Dentistry	Knowledge of the information and techniques needed to diagnose and treat human injuries, diseases, and deformities. This includes symptoms, treatment alternatives, drug properties and interactions, and preventive health-care measures.
Biology	Knowledge of plant and animal organisms, their tissues, cells, functions, interdependencies, and interactions with each other and the environment.
Physics	Knowledge and prediction of physical principles, laws, their interrelationships, and applications to understanding fluid, material, and atmospheric dynamics, and mechanical, electrical, atomic and sub-atomic structures and processes.
Fine Arts	Knowledge of the theory and techniques required to compose, produce, and perform works of music, dance, visual arts, drama, and sculpture.

Skills	Skills Definitions
Reading Comprehension	Understanding written sentences and paragraphs in work related documents.
Time Management	Managing one's own time and the time of others.
Coordination	Adjusting actions in relation to others' actions.
Active Listening	Giving full attention to what other people are saying, taking time to understand the points being made, asking questions as appropriate, and not interrupting at inappropriate times.
Critical Thinking	Using logic and reasoning to identify the strengths and weaknesses of alternative solutions, conclusions or approaches to problems.
Speaking	Talking to others to convey information effectively.
Active Learning	Understanding the implications of new information for both current and future problem-solving and decision-making.
Learning Strategies	Selecting and using training/instructional methods and procedures appropriate for the situation when learning or teaching new things.
Writing	Communicating effectively in writing as appropriate for the needs of the audience.

Judgment and Decision Making	Considering the relative costs and benefits of potential actions to choose the most appropriate one.
Mathematics	Using mathematics to solve problems.
Service Orientation	Actively looking for ways to help people.
Instructing	Teaching others how to do something.
Negotiation	Bringing others together and trying to reconcile differences.
Monitoring	Monitoring/Assessing performance of yourself, other individuals, or organizations to make improvements or take corrective action.
Complex Problem Solving	Identifying complex problems and reviewing related information to develop and evaluate options and implement solutions.
Equipment Selection	Determining the kind of tools and equipment needed to do a job.
Social Perceptiveness	Being aware of others' reactions and understanding why they react as they do.
Troubleshooting	Determining causes of operating errors and deciding what to do about it.
Operation and Control	Controlling operations of equipment or systems.
Management of Personnel Resources	Motivating, developing, and directing people as they work, identifying the best people for the job.
Management of Material Resources	Obtaining and seeing to the appropriate use of equipment, facilities, and materials needed to do certain work.
Technology Design	Generating or adapting equipment and technology to serve user needs.
Operations Analysis	Analyzing needs and product requirements to create a design.
Management of Financial Resources	Determining how money will be spent to get the work done, and accounting for these expenditures.
Quality Control Analysis	Conducting tests and inspections of products, services, or processes to evaluate quality or performance.
Persuasion	Persuading others to change their minds or behavior.
Systems Analysis	Determining how a system should work and how changes in conditions, operations, and the environment will affect outcomes.
Systems Evaluation	Identifying measures or indicators of system performance and the actions needed to improve or correct performance, relative to the goals of the system.
Equipment Maintenance	Performing routine maintenance on equipment and determining when and what kind of maintenance is needed.
Operation Monitoring	Watching gauges, dials, or other indicators to make sure a machine is working properly.
Repairing	Repairing machines or systems using the needed tools.
Programming	Writing computer programs for various purposes.
Installation	Installing equipment, machines, wiring, or programs to meet specifications.
Science	Using scientific rules and methods to solve problems.

Ability	Ability Definitions
Oral Expression	The ability to communicate information and ideas in speaking so others will understand.
Problem Sensitivity	The ability to tell when something is wrong or is likely to go wrong. It does not involve solving the problem, only recognizing there is a problem.
Oral Comprehension	The ability to listen to and understand information and ideas presented through spoken words and sentences.
Speech Clarity	The ability to speak clearly so others can understand you.
Speech Recognition	The ability to identify and understand the speech of another person.
Deductive Reasoning	The ability to apply general rules to specific problems to produce answers that make sense.
Inductive Reasoning	The ability to combine pieces of information to form general rules or conclusions (includes finding a relationship among seemingly unrelated events).
Written Comprehension	The ability to read and understand information and ideas presented in writing.
Written Expression	The ability to communicate information and ideas in writing so others will understand.
Near Vision	The ability to see details at close range (within a few feet of the observer).
Information Ordering	The ability to arrange things or actions in a certain order or pattern according to a specific rule or set of rules (e.g., patterns of numbers, letters, words, pictures, mathematical operations).
Fluency of Ideas	The ability to come up with a number of ideas about a topic (the number of ideas is important, not their quality, correctness, or creativity).
Selective Attention	The ability to concentrate on a task over a period of time without being distracted.

Category Flexibility	The ability to generate or use different sets of rules for combining or grouping things in different ways.
Originality	The ability to come up with unusual or clever ideas about a given topic or situation, or to develop creative ways to solve a problem.
Flexibility of Closure	The ability to identify or detect a known pattern (a figure, object, word, or sound) that is hidden in other distracting material.
Mathematical Reasoning	The ability to choose the right mathematical methods or formulas to solve a problem.
Far Vision	The ability to see details at a distance.
Time Sharing	The ability to shift back and forth between two or more activities or sources of information (such as speech, sounds, touch, or other sources).
Speed of Closure	The ability to quickly make sense of, combine, and organize information into meaningful patterns.
Memorization	The ability to remember information such as words, numbers, pictures, and procedures.
Number Facility	The ability to add, subtract, multiply, or divide quickly and correctly.
Visualization	The ability to imagine how something will look after it is moved around or when its parts are moved or rearranged.
Perceptual Speed	The ability to quickly and accurately compare similarities and differences among sets of letters, numbers, objects, pictures, or patterns. The things to be compared may be presented at the same time or one after the other. This ability also includes comparing a presented object with a remembered object.
Auditory Attention	The ability to focus on a single source of sound in the presence of other distracting sounds.
Finger Dexterity	The ability to make precisely coordinated movements of the fingers of one or both hands to grasp, manipulate, or assemble very small objects.
Hearing Sensitivity	The ability to detect or tell the differences between sounds that vary in pitch and loudness.
Depth Perception	The ability to judge which of several objects is closer or farther away from you, or to judge the distance between you and an object.
Visual Color Discrimination	The ability to match or detect differences between colors, including shades of color and brightness.
Trunk Strength	The ability to use your abdominal and lower back muscles to support part of the body repeatedly or continuously over time without 'giving out' or fatiguing.
Wrist-Finger Speed	The ability to make fast, simple, repeated movements of the fingers, hands, and wrists.
Arm-Hand Steadiness	The ability to keep your hand and arm steady while moving your arm or while holding your arm and hand in one position.
Response Orientation	The ability to choose quickly between two or more movements in response to two or more different signals (lights, sounds, pictures). It includes the speed with which the correct response is started with the hand, foot, or other body part.
Spatial Orientation	The ability to know your location in relation to the environment or to know where other objects are in relation to you.
Stamina	The ability to exert yourself physically over long periods of time without getting winded or out of breath.
Gross Body Coordination	The ability to coordinate the movement of your arms, legs, and torso together when the whole body is in motion.
Speed of Limb Movement	The ability to quickly move the arms and legs.
Manual Dexterity	The ability to quickly move your hand, your hand together with your arm, or your two hands to grasp, manipulate, or assemble objects.
Sound Localization	The ability to tell the direction from which a sound originated.
Static Strength	The ability to exert maximum muscle force to lift, push, pull, or carry objects.
Gross Body Equilibrium	The ability to keep or regain your body balance or stay upright when in an unstable position.
Extent Flexibility	The ability to bend, stretch, twist, or reach with your body, arms, and/or legs.
Glare Sensitivity	The ability to see objects in the presence of glare or bright lighting.
Multilimb Coordination	The ability to coordinate two or more limbs (for example, two arms, two legs, or one leg and one arm) while sitting, standing, or lying down. It does not involve performing the activities while the whole body is in motion.
Night Vision	The ability to see under low light conditions.
Control Precision	The ability to quickly and repeatedly adjust the controls of a machine or a vehicle to exact positions.
Dynamic Flexibility	The ability to quickly and repeatedly bend, stretch, twist, or reach out with your body, arms, and/or legs.

Reaction Time	The ability to quickly respond (with the hand, finger, or foot) to a signal (sound, light, picture) when it appears.
Dynamic Strength	The ability to exert muscle force repeatedly or continuously over time. This involves muscular endurance and resistance to muscle fatigue.
Explosive Strength	The ability to use short bursts of muscle force to propel oneself (as in jumping or sprinting), or to throw an object.
Peripheral Vision	The ability to see objects or movement of objects to one's side when the eyes are looking ahead.
Rate Control	The ability to time your movements or the movement of a piece of equipment in anticipation of changes in the speed and/or direction of a moving object or scene.

Work_Activity	Work_Activity Definitions
Making Decisions and Solving Problems	Analyzing information and evaluating results to choose the best solution and solve problems.
Getting Information	Observing, receiving, and otherwise obtaining information from all relevant sources.
Documenting/Recording Information	Entering, transcribing, recording, storing, or maintaining information in written or electronic/magnetic form.
Updating and Using Relevant Knowledge	Keeping up to-date technically and applying new knowledge to your job.
Communicating with Supervisors, Peers, or Subordin	Providing information to supervisors, co-workers, and subordinates by telephone, in written form, e-mail, or in person.
Communicating with Persons Outside Organization	Communicating with people outside the organization, representing the organization to customers, the public, government, and other external sources. This information can be exchanged in person, in writing, or by telephone or e-mail.
Evaluating Information to Determine Compliance wit	Using relevant information and individual judgment to determine whether events or processes comply with laws, regulations, or standards.
Scheduling Work and Activities	Scheduling events, programs, and activities, as well as the work of others.
Organizing, Planning, and Prioritizing Work	Developing specific goals and plans to prioritize, organize, and accomplish your work.
Judging the Qualities of Things, Services, or Peop	Assessing the value, importance, or quality of things or people.
Guiding, Directing, and Motivating Subordinates	Providing guidance and direction to subordinates, including setting performance standards and monitoring performance.
Coordinating the Work and Activities of Others	Getting members of a group to work together to accomplish tasks.
Resolving Conflicts and Negotiating with Others	Handling complaints, settling disputes, and resolving grievances and conflicts, or otherwise negotiating with others.
Training and Teaching Others	Identifying the educational needs of others, developing formal educational or training programs or classes, and teaching or instructing others.
Monitor Processes, Materials, or Surroundings	Monitoring and reviewing information from materials, events, or the environment, to detect or assess problems.
Performing Administrative Activities	Performing day-to-day administrative tasks such as maintaining information files and processing paperwork.
Inspecting Equipment, Structures, or Material	Inspecting equipment, structures, or materials to identify the cause of errors or other problems or defects.
Establishing and Maintaining Interpersonal Relatio	Developing constructive and cooperative working relationships with others, and maintaining them over time.
Performing for or Working Directly with the Public	Performing for people or dealing directly with the public. This includes serving customers in restaurants and stores, and receiving clients or guests.
Provide Consultation and Advice to Others	Providing guidance and expert advice to management or other groups on technical, systems-, or process-related topics.
Identifying Objects, Actions, and Events	Identifying information by categorizing, estimating, recognizing differences or similarities, and detecting changes in circumstances or events.
Analyzing Data or Information	Identifying the underlying principles, reasons, or facts of information by breaking down information or data into separate parts.
Estimating the Quantifiable Characteristics of Pro	Estimating sizes, distances, and quantities; or determining time, costs, resources, or materials needed to perform a work activity.
Interacting With Computers	Using computers and computer systems (including hardware and software) to program, write software, set up functions, enter data, or process information.
Developing and Building Teams	Encouraging and building mutual trust, respect, and cooperation among team members.

Processing Information	Compiling, coding, categorizing, calculating, tabulating, auditing, or verifying information or data.
Interpreting the Meaning of Information for Others	Translating or explaining what information means and how it can be used.
Thinking Creatively	Developing, designing, or creating new applications, ideas, relationships, systems, or products, including artistic contributions.
Monitoring and Controlling Resources	Monitoring and controlling resources and overseeing the spending of money.
Coaching and Developing Others	Identifying the developmental needs of others and coaching, mentoring, or otherwise helping others to improve their knowledge or skills.
Selling or Influencing Others	Convincing others to buy merchandise/goods or to otherwise change their minds or actions.
Developing Objectives and Strategies	Establishing long-range objectives and specifying the strategies and actions to achieve them.
Staffing Organizational Units	Recruiting, interviewing, selecting, hiring, and promoting employees in an organization.
Operating Vehicles, Mechanized Devices, or Equipme	Running, maneuvering, navigating, or driving vehicles or mechanized equipment, such as forklifts, passenger vehicles, aircraft, or water craft.
Assisting and Caring for Others	Providing personal assistance, medical attention, emotional support, or other personal care to others such as coworkers, customers, or patients.
Performing General Physical Activities	Performing physical activities that require considerable use of your arms and legs and moving your whole body, such as climbing, lifting, balancing, walking, stooping, and handling of materials.
Repairing and Maintaining Mechanical Equipment	Servicing, repairing, adjusting, and testing machines, devices, moving parts, and equipment that operate primarily on the basis of mechanical (not electronic) principles.
Drafting, Laying Out, and Specifying Technical Dev	Providing documentation, detailed instructions, drawings, or specifications to tell others about how devices, parts, equipment, or structures are to be fabricated, constructed, assembled, modified, maintained, or used.
Handling and Moving Objects	Using hands and arms in handling, installing, positioning, and moving materials, and manipulating things.
Controlling Machines and Processes	Using either control mechanisms or direct physical activity to operate machines or processes (not including computers or vehicles).
Repairing and Maintaining Electronic Equipment	Servicing, repairing, calibrating, regulating, fine-tuning, or testing machines, devices, and equipment that operate primarily on the basis of electrical or electronic (not mechanical) principles.

Work_Context	Work_Context Definitions
Telephone	How often do you have telephone conversations in this job?
Indoors, Environmentally Controlled	How often does this job require working indoors in environmentally controlled conditions?
Face-to-Face Discussions	How often do you have to have face-to-face discussions with individuals or teams in this job?
Contact With Others	How much does this job require the worker to be in contact with others (face-to-face, by telephone, or otherwise) in order to perform it?
Structured versus Unstructured Work	To what extent is this job structured for the worker, rather than allowing the worker to determine tasks, priorities, and goals?
Freedom to Make Decisions	How much decision making freedom, without supervision, does the job offer?
Work With Work Group or Team	How important is it to work with others in a group or team in this job?
Frequency of Decision Making	How frequently is the worker required to make decisions that affect other people, the financial resources, and/or the image and reputation of the organization?
Deal With External Customers	How important is it to work with external customers or the public in this job?
Time Pressure	How often does this job require the worker to meet strict deadlines?
Responsibility for Outcomes and Results	How responsible is the worker for work outcomes and results of other workers?
Spend Time Sitting	How much does this job require sitting?
Electronic Mail	How often do you use electronic mail in this job?
Importance of Being Exact or Accurate	How important is being very exact or highly accurate in performing this job?
Impact of Decisions on Co-workers or Company Resul	How do the decisions an employee makes impact the results of co-workers, clients or the company?

Responsible for Others' Health and Safety	How much responsibility is there for the health and safety of others in this job?
Letters and Memos	How often does the job require written letters and memos?
Frequency of Conflict Situations	How often are there conflict situations the employee has to face in this job?
Deal With Unpleasant or Angry People	How frequently does the worker have to deal with unpleasant, angry, or discourteous individuals as part of the job requirements?
Coordinate or Lead Others	How important is it to coordinate or lead others in accomplishing work activities in this job?
Importance of Repeating Same Tasks	How important is repeating the same physical activities (e.g., key entry) or mental activities (e.g., checking entries in a ledger) over and over, without stopping, to performing this job?
Physical Proximity	To what extent does this job require the worker to perform job tasks in close physical proximity to other people?
Sounds, Noise Levels Are Distracting or Uncomforta	How often does this job require working exposed to sounds and noise levels that are distracting or uncomfortable?
Consequence of Error	How serious would the result usually be if the worker made a mistake that was not readily correctable?
Level of Competition	To what extent does this job require the worker to compete or to be aware of competitive pressures?
Very Hot or Cold Temperatures	How often does this job require working in very hot (above 90 F degrees) or very cold (below 32 F degrees) temperatures?
Spend Time Making Repetitive Motions	How much does this job require making repetitive motions?
Exposed to Contaminants	How often does this job require working exposed to contaminants (such as pollutants, gases, dust or odors)?
Exposed to Hazardous Equipment	How often does this job require exposure to hazardous equipment?
In an Enclosed Vehicle or Equipment	How often does this job require working in a closed vehicle or equipment (e.g., car)?
Outdoors, Exposed to Weather	How often does this job require working outdoors, exposed to all weather conditions?
Spend Time Standing	How much does this job require standing?
Wear Common Protective or Safety Equipment such as	How much does this job require wearing common protective or safety equipment such as safety shoes, glasses, gloves, hard hats or live jackets?
Spend Time Using Your Hands to Handle, Control, or	How much does this job require using your hands to handle, control, or feel objects, tools or controls?
Public Speaking	How often do you have to perform public speaking in this job?
Degree of Automation	How automated is the job?
Deal With Physically Aggressive People	How frequently does this job require the worker to deal with physical aggression of violent individuals?
Spend Time Walking and Running	How much does this job require walking and running?
Outdoors, Under Cover	How often does this job require working outdoors, under cover (e.g., structure with roof but no walls)?
Extremely Bright or Inadequate Lighting	How often does this job require working in extremely bright or inadequate lighting conditions?
Pace Determined by Speed of Equipment	How important is it to this job that the pace is determined by the speed of equipment or machinery? (This does not refer to keeping busy at all times on this job.)
Exposed to Minor Burns, Cuts, Bites, or Stings	How often does this job require exposure to minor burns, cuts, bites, or stings?
Indoors, Not Environmentally Controlled	How often does this job require working indoors in non-controlled environmental conditions (e.g., warehouse without heat)?
Spend Time Bending or Twisting the Body	How much does this job require bending or twisting your body?
In an Open Vehicle or Equipment	How often does this job require working in an open vehicle or equipment (e.g., tractor)?
Spend Time Kneeling, Crouching, Stooping, or Crawl	How much does this job require kneeling, crouching, stooping, or crawling?
Exposed to Hazardous Conditions	How often does this job require exposure to hazardous conditions?
Exposed to Disease or Infections	How often does this job require exposure to disease/infections?
Spend Time Climbing Ladders, Scaffolds, or Poles	How much does this job require climbing ladders, scaffolds, or poles?
Exposed to High Places	How often does this job require exposure to high places?
Cramped Work Space, Awkward Positions	How often does this job require working in cramped work spaces that requires getting into awkward positions?
Spend Time Keeping or Regaining Balance	How much does this job require keeping or regaining your balance?

Wear Specialized Protective or Safety Equipment su	How much does this job require wearing specialized protective or safety equipment such as breathing apparatus, safety harness, full protection suits, or radiation protection?
Exposed to Whole Body Vibration	How often does this job require exposure to whole body vibration (e.g., operate a jackhammer)?
Exposed to Radiation	How often does this job require exposure to radiation?

Job Zone Component	Job Zone Component Definitions
Title	Job Zone Three: Medium Preparation Needed
Overall Experience	Previous work-related skill, knowledge, or experience is required for these occupations. For example, an electrician must have completed three or four years of apprenticeship or several years of vocational training, and often must have passed a licensing exam, in order to perform the job.
Job Training	Employees in these occupations usually need one or two years of training involving both on-the-job experience and informal training with experienced workers.
Job Zone Examples	These occupations usually involve using communication and organizational skills to coordinate, supervise, manage, or train others to accomplish goals. Examples include dental assistants, electricians, fish and game wardens, legal secretaries, personnel recruiters, and recreation workers.
SVP Range	(6.0 to < 7.0)
Education	Most occupations in this zone require training in vocational schools, related on-the-job experience, or an associate's degree. Some may require a bachelor's degree.

Work_Styles	Work_Styles Definitions
Dependability	Job requires being reliable, responsible, and dependable, and fulfilling obligations.
Self Control	Job requires maintaining composure, keeping emotions in check, controlling anger, and avoiding aggressive behavior, even in very difficult situations.
Cooperation	Job requires being pleasant with others on the job and displaying a good-natured, cooperative attitude.
Concern for Others	Job requires being sensitive to others' needs and feelings and being understanding and helpful on the job.
Attention to Detail	Job requires being careful about detail and thorough in completing work tasks.
Stress Tolerance	Job requires accepting criticism and dealing calmly and effectively with high stress situations.
Integrity	Job requires being honest and ethical.
Leadership	Job requires a willingness to lead, take charge, and offer opinions and direction.
Social Orientation	Job requires preferring to work with others rather than alone, and being personally connected with others on the job.
Independence	Job requires developing one's own ways of doing things, guiding oneself with little or no supervision, and depending on oneself to get things done.
Adaptability/Flexibility	Job requires being open to change (positive or negative) and to considerable variety in the workplace.
Initiative	Job requires a willingness to take on responsibilities and challenges.
Achievement/Effort	Job requires establishing and maintaining personally challenging achievement goals and exerting effort toward mastering tasks.
Analytical Thinking	Job requires analyzing information and using logic to address work-related issues and problems.
Persistence	Job requires persistence in the face of obstacles.
Innovation	Job requires creativity and alternative thinking to develop new ideas for and answers to work-related problems.

11-3071.02 - Storage and Distribution Managers

Plan, direct, and coordinate the storage and distribution operations within an organization or the activities of organizations that are engaged in storing and distributing materials and products.

Tasks

1) Confer with department heads to coordinate warehouse activities, such as production, sales, records control, and purchasing.

2) Develop and document standard and emergency operating procedures for receiving, handling, storing, shipping, or salvaging products or materials.

3) Review invoices, work orders, consumption reports, and demand forecasts in order to estimate peak delivery periods and to issue work assignments.

4) Inspect physical conditions of warehouses, vehicle fleets and equipment, and order testing, maintenance, repair, or replacement as necessary.

5) Respond to customers' or shippers' questions and complaints regarding storage and distribution services.

6) Plan, develop, and implement warehouse safety and security programs and activities.

7) Interview, select, and train warehouse and supervisory personnel.

8) Examine products or materials in order to estimate quantities or weight and type of container required for storage or transport.

9) Schedule and monitor air or surface pickup, delivery, or distribution of products or materials.

10) Develop and implement plans for facility modification or expansion, such as equipment purchase or changes in space allocation or structural design.

11) Advise sales and billing departments of transportation charges for customers' accounts.

12) Issue shipping instructions and provide routing information to ensure that delivery times and locations are coordinated.

13) Arrange for storage facilities when required.

14) Track and trace goods while they are en route to their destinations, expediting orders when necessary.

15) Arrange for necessary shipping documentation, and contact customs officials in order to effect release of shipments.

16) Prepare and manage departmental budgets.

17) Evaluate freight costs and the inventory costs associated with transit times in order to ensure that costs are appropriate.

18) Prepare or direct preparation of correspondence, reports, and operations, maintenance, and safety manuals.

19) Examine invoices and shipping manifests for conformity to tariff and customs regulations.

20) Evaluate locations for new warehouses and distribution networks in order to determine their potential usefulness.

21) Participate in setting transportation and service rates.

22) Negotiate with carriers, warehouse operators and insurance company representatives for services and preferential rates.

Knowledge	Knowledge Definitions
Customer and Personal Service	Knowledge of principles and processes for providing customer and personal services. This includes customer needs assessment, meeting quality standards for services, and evaluation of customer satisfaction.
English Language	Knowledge of the structure and content of the English language including the meaning and spelling of words, rules of composition, and grammar.
Administration and Management	Knowledge of business and management principles involved in strategic planning, resource allocation, human resources modeling, leadership technique, production methods, and coordination of people and resources.
Mathematics	Knowledge of arithmetic, algebra, geometry, calculus, statistics, and their applications.
Personnel and Human Resources	Knowledge of principles and procedures for personnel recruitment, selection, training, compensation and benefits, labor relations and negotiation, and personnel information systems.
Clerical	Knowledge of administrative and clerical procedures and systems such as word processing, managing files and records, stenography and transcription, designing forms, and other office procedures and terminology.
Computers and Electronics	Knowledge of circuit boards, processors, chips, electronic equipment, and computer hardware and software, including applications and programming.
Production and Processing	Knowledge of raw materials, production processes, quality control, costs, and other techniques for maximizing the effective manufacture and distribution of goods.

Sales and Marketing	Knowledge of principles and methods for showing, promoting, and selling products or services. This includes marketing strategy and tactics, product demonstration, sales techniques, and sales control systems.
Public Safety and Security	Knowledge of relevant equipment, policies, procedures, and strategies to promote effective local, state, or national security operations for the protection of people, data, property, and institutions.
Economics and Accounting	Knowledge of economic and accounting principles and practices, the financial markets, banking and the analysis and reporting of financial data.
Education and Training	Knowledge of principles and methods for curriculum and training design, teaching and instruction for individuals and groups, and the measurement of training effects.
Engineering and Technology	Knowledge of the practical application of engineering science and technology. This includes applying principles, techniques, procedures, and equipment to the design and production of various goods and services.
Psychology	Knowledge of human behavior and performance; individual differences in ability, personality, and interests; learning and motivation; psychological research methods; and the assessment and treatment of behavioral and affective disorders.
Transportation	Knowledge of principles and methods for moving people or goods by air, rail, sea, or road, including the relative costs and benefits.
Mechanical	Knowledge of machines and tools, including their designs, uses, repair, and maintenance.
Law and Government	Knowledge of laws, legal codes, court procedures, precedents, government regulations, executive orders, agency rules, and the democratic political process.
Telecommunications	Knowledge of transmission, broadcasting, switching, control, and operation of telecommunications systems.
Therapy and Counseling	Knowledge of principles, methods, and procedures for diagnosis, treatment, and rehabilitation of physical and mental dysfunctions, and for career counseling and guidance.
Sociology and Anthropology	Knowledge of group behavior and dynamics, societal trends and influences, human migrations, ethnicity, cultures and their history and origins.
Geography	Knowledge of principles and methods for describing the features of land, sea, and air masses, including their physical characteristics, locations, interrelationships, and distribution of plant, animal, and human life.
Foreign Language	Knowledge of the structure and content of a foreign (non-English) language including the meaning and spelling of words, rules of composition and grammar, and pronunciation.
Communications and Media	Knowledge of media production, communication, and dissemination techniques and methods. This includes alternative ways to inform and entertain via written, oral, and visual media.
Food Production	Knowledge of techniques and equipment for planting, growing, and harvesting food products (both plant and animal) for consumption, including storage/handling techniques.
Design	Knowledge of design techniques, tools, and principles involved in production of precision technical plans, blueprints, drawings, and models.
Building and Construction	Knowledge of materials, methods, and the tools involved in the construction or repair of houses, buildings, or other structures such as highways and roads.
Chemistry	Knowledge of the chemical composition, structure, and properties of substances and of the chemical processes and transformations that they undergo. This includes uses of chemicals and their interactions, danger signs, production techniques, and disposal methods.
Physics	Knowledge and prediction of physical principles, laws, their interrelationships, and applications to understanding fluid, material, and atmospheric dynamics, and mechanical, electrical, atomic and sub-atomic structures and processes.
Fine Arts	Knowledge of the theory and techniques required to compose, produce, and perform works of music, dance, visual arts, drama, and sculpture.
Philosophy and Theology	Knowledge of different philosophical systems and religions. This includes their basic principles, values, ethics, ways of thinking, customs, practices, and their impact on human culture.
Medicine and Dentistry	Knowledge of the information and techniques needed to diagnose and treat human injuries, diseases, and deformities. This includes symptoms, treatment alternatives, drug properties and interactions, and preventive health-care measures.
Biology	Knowledge of plant and animal organisms, their tissues, cells, functions, interdependencies, and interactions with each other and the environment.
History and Archeology	Knowledge of historical events and their causes, indicators, and effects on civilizations and cultures.

Skills	Skills Definitions
Management of Personnel Resources	Motivating, developing, and directing people as they work, identifying the best people for the job.
Time Management	Managing one's own time and the time of others.
Reading Comprehension	Understanding written sentences and paragraphs in work related documents.
Speaking	Talking to others to convey information effectively.
Critical Thinking	Using logic and reasoning to identify the strengths and weaknesses of alternative solutions, conclusions or approaches to problems.
Monitoring	Monitoring/Assessing performance of yourself, other individuals, or organizations to make improvements or take corrective action.
Active Listening	Giving full attention to what other people are saying, taking time to understand the points being made, asking questions as appropriate, and not interrupting at inappropriate times.
Instructing	Teaching others how to do something.
Judgment and Decision Making	Considering the relative costs and benefits of potential actions to choose the most appropriate one.
Active Learning	Understanding the implications of new information for both current and future problem-solving and decision-making.
Negotiation	Bringing others together and trying to reconcile differences.
Coordination	Adjusting actions in relation to others' actions.
Learning Strategies	Selecting and using training/instructional methods and procedures appropriate for the situation when learning or teaching new things.
Service Orientation	Actively looking for ways to help people.
Social Perceptiveness	Being aware of others' reactions and understanding why they react as they do.
Complex Problem Solving	Identifying complex problems and reviewing related information to develop and evaluate options and implement solutions.
Operations Analysis	Analyzing needs and product requirements to create a design.
Mathematics	Using mathematics to solve problems.
Quality Control Analysis	Conducting tests and inspections of products, services, or processes to evaluate quality or performance.
Writing	Communicating effectively in writing as appropriate for the needs of the audience.
Management of Material Resources	Obtaining and seeing to the appropriate use of equipment, facilities, and materials needed to do certain work.
Equipment Selection	Determining the kind of tools and equipment needed to do a job.
Systems Analysis	Determining how a system should work and how changes in conditions, operations, and the environment will affect outcomes.
Persuasion	Persuading others to change their minds or behavior.
Systems Evaluation	Identifying measures or indicators of system performance and the actions needed to improve or correct performance, relative to the goals of the system.
Operation and Control	Controlling operations of equipment or systems.
Troubleshooting	Determining causes of operating errors and deciding what to do about it.
Management of Financial Resources	Determining how money will be spent to get the work done, and accounting for these expenditures.
Technology Design	Generating or adapting equipment and technology to serve user needs.
Equipment Maintenance	Performing routine maintenance on equipment and determining when and what kind of maintenance is needed.
Operation Monitoring	Watching gauges, dials, or other indicators to make sure a machine is working properly.
Installation	Installing equipment, machines, wiring, or programs to meet specifications.
Science	Using scientific rules and methods to solve problems.
Programming	Writing computer programs for various purposes.
Repairing	Repairing machines or systems using the needed tools.

Ability	Ability Definitions
Oral Expression	The ability to communicate information and ideas in speaking so others will understand.

Speech Recognition	The ability to identify and understand the speech of another person.
Speech Clarity	The ability to speak clearly so others can understand you.
Oral Comprehension	The ability to listen to and understand information and ideas presented through spoken words and sentences.
Problem Sensitivity	The ability to tell when something is wrong or is likely to go wrong. It does not involve solving the problem, only recognizing there is a problem.
Inductive Reasoning	The ability to combine pieces of information to form general rules or conclusions (includes finding a relationship among seemingly unrelated events).
Deductive Reasoning	The ability to apply general rules to specific problems to produce answers that make sense.
Near Vision	The ability to see details at close range (within a few feet of the observer).
Written Comprehension	The ability to read and understand information and ideas presented in writing.
Information Ordering	The ability to arrange things or actions in a certain order or pattern according to a specific rule or set of rules (e.g., patterns of numbers, letters, words, pictures, mathematical operations).
Category Flexibility	The ability to generate or use different sets of rules for combining or grouping things in different ways.
Written Expression	The ability to communicate information and ideas in writing so others will understand.
Selective Attention	The ability to concentrate on a task over a period of time without being distracted.
Fluency of Ideas	The ability to come up with a number of ideas about a topic (the number of ideas is important, not their quality, correctness, or creativity).
Originality	The ability to come up with unusual or clever ideas about a given topic or situation, or to develop creative ways to solve a problem.
Perceptual Speed	The ability to quickly and accurately compare similarities and differences among sets of letters, numbers, objects, pictures, or patterns. The things to be compared may be presented at the same time or one after the other. This ability also includes comparing a presented object with a remembered object.
Mathematical Reasoning	The ability to choose the right mathematical methods or formulas to solve a problem.
Visualization	The ability to imagine how something will look after it is moved around or when its parts are moved or rearranged.
Far Vision	The ability to see details at a distance.
Number Facility	The ability to add, subtract, multiply, or divide quickly and correctly.
Speed of Closure	The ability to quickly make sense of, combine, and organize information into meaningful patterns.
Flexibility of Closure	The ability to identify or detect a known pattern (a figure, object, word, or sound) that is hidden in other distracting material.
Visual Color Discrimination	The ability to match or detect differences between colors, including shades of color and brightness.
Time Sharing	The ability to shift back and forth between two or more activities or sources of information (such as speech, sounds, touch, or other sources).
Hearing Sensitivity	The ability to detect or tell the differences between sounds that vary in pitch and loudness.
Auditory Attention	The ability to focus on a single source of sound in the presence of other distracting sounds.
Memorization	The ability to remember information such as words, numbers, pictures, and procedures.
Gross Body Equilibrium	The ability to keep or regain your body balance or stay upright when in an unstable position.
Finger Dexterity	The ability to make precisely coordinated movements of the fingers of one or both hands to grasp, manipulate, or assemble very small objects.
Arm-Hand Steadiness	The ability to keep your hand and arm steady while moving your arm or while holding your arm and hand in one position.
Depth Perception	The ability to judge which of several objects is closer or farther away from you, or to judge the distance between you and an object.
Stamina	The ability to exert yourself physically over long periods of time without getting winded or out of breath.
Gross Body Coordination	The ability to coordinate the movement of your arms, legs, and torso together when the whole body is in motion.
Static Strength	The ability to exert maximum muscle force to lift, push, pull, or carry objects.
Reaction Time	The ability to quickly respond (with the hand, finger, or foot) to a signal (sound, light, picture) when it appears.

Rate Control	The ability to time your movements or the movement of a piece of equipment in anticipation of changes in the speed and/or direction of a moving object or scene.
Multilimb Coordination	The ability to coordinate two or more limbs (for example, two arms, two legs, or one leg and one arm) while sitting, standing, or lying down. It does not involve performing the activities while the whole body is in motion.
Trunk Strength	The ability to use your abdominal and lower back muscles to support part of the body repeatedly or continuously over time without 'giving out' or fatiguing.
Manual Dexterity	The ability to quickly move your hand, your hand together with your arm, or your two hands to grasp, manipulate, or assemble objects.
Speed of Limb Movement	The ability to quickly move the arms and legs.
Extent Flexibility	The ability to bend, stretch, twist, or reach with your body, arms, and/or legs.
Dynamic Strength	The ability to exert muscle force repeatedly or continuously over time. This involves muscular endurance and resistance to muscle fatigue.
Spatial Orientation	The ability to know your location in relation to the environment or to know where other objects are in relation to you.
Wrist-Finger Speed	The ability to make fast, simple, repeated movements of the fingers, hands, and wrists.
Glare Sensitivity	The ability to see objects in the presence of glare or bright lighting.
Dynamic Flexibility	The ability to quickly and repeatedly bend, stretch, twist, or reach out with your body, arms, and/or legs.
Response Orientation	The ability to choose quickly between two or more movements in response to two or more different signals (lights, sounds, pictures). It includes the speed with which the correct response is started with the hand, foot, or other body part.
Night Vision	The ability to see under low light conditions.
Peripheral Vision	The ability to see objects or movement of objects to one's side when the eyes are looking ahead.
Control Precision	The ability to quickly and repeatedly adjust the controls of a machine or a vehicle to exact positions.
Sound Localization	The ability to tell the direction from which a sound originated.
Explosive Strength	The ability to use short bursts of muscle force to propel oneself (as in jumping or sprinting), or to throw an object.

Work_Activity	Work_Activity Definitions
Communicating with Supervisors, Peers, or Subordin	Providing information to supervisors, co-workers, and subordinates by telephone, in written form, e-mail, or in person.
Making Decisions and Solving Problems	Analyzing information and evaluating results to choose the best solution and solve problems.
Getting Information	Observing, receiving, and otherwise obtaining information from all relevant sources.
Interacting With Computers	Using computers and computer systems (including hardware and software) to program, write software, set up functions, enter data, or process information.
Organizing, Planning, and Prioritizing Work	Developing specific goals and plans to prioritize, organize, and accomplish your work.
Processing Information	Compiling, coding, categorizing, calculating, tabulating, auditing, or verifying information or data.
Identifying Objects, Actions, and Events	Identifying information by categorizing, estimating, recognizing differences or similarities, and detecting changes in circumstances or events.
Communicating with Persons Outside Organization	Communicating with people outside the organization, representing the organization to customers, the public, government, and other external sources. This information can be exchanged in person, in writing, or by telephone or e-mail.
Coordinating the Work and Activities of Others	Getting members of a group to work together to accomplish tasks.
Guiding, Directing, and Motivating Subordinates	Providing guidance and direction to subordinates, including setting performance standards and monitoring performance.
Judging the Qualities of Things, Services, or Peop	Assessing the value, importance, or quality of things or people.
Establishing and Maintaining Interpersonal Relatio	Developing constructive and cooperative working relationships with others, and maintaining them over time.
Coaching and Developing Others	Identifying the developmental needs of others and coaching, mentoring, or otherwise helping others to improve their knowledge or skills.
Monitor Processes, Materials, or Surroundings	Monitoring and reviewing information from materials, events, or the environment, to detect or assess problems.

Updating and Using Relevant Knowledge	Keeping up-to-date technically and applying new knowledge to your job.
Monitoring and Controlling Resources	Monitoring and controlling resources and overseeing the spending of money.
Developing and Building Teams	Encouraging and building mutual trust, respect, and cooperation among team members.
Resolving Conflicts and Negotiating with Others	Handling complaints, settling disputes, and resolving grievances and conflicts, or otherwise negotiating with others.
Analyzing Data or Information	Identifying the underlying principles, reasons, or facts of information by breaking down information or data into separate parts.
Documenting/Recording Information	Entering, transcribing, recording, storing, or maintaining information in written or electronic/magnetic form.
Performing Administrative Activities	Performing day-to-day administrative tasks such as maintaining information files and processing paperwork.
Training and Teaching Others	Identifying the educational needs of others, developing formal educational or training programs or classes, and teaching or instructing others.
Performing for or Working Directly with the Public	Performing for people or dealing directly with the public. This includes serving customers in restaurants and stores, and receiving clients or guests.
Thinking Creatively	Developing, designing, or creating new applications, ideas, relationships, systems, or products, including artistic contributions.
Developing Objectives and Strategies	Establishing long-range objectives and specifying the strategies and actions to achieve them.
Estimating the Quantifiable Characteristics of Pro	Estimating sizes, distances, and quantities; or determining time, costs, resources, or materials needed to perform a work activity.
Scheduling Work and Activities	Scheduling events, programs, and activities, as well as the work of others.
Inspecting Equipment, Structures, or Material	Inspecting equipment, structures, or materials to identify the cause of errors or other problems or defects.
Evaluating Information to Determine Compliance wit	Using relevant information and individual judgment to determine whether events or processes comply with laws, regulations, or standards.
Handling and Moving Objects	Using hands and arms in handling, installing, positioning, and moving materials, and manipulating things.
Performing General Physical Activities	Performing physical activities that require considerable use of your arms and legs and moving your whole body, such as climbing, lifting, balancing, walking, stooping, and handling of materials.
Interpreting the Meaning of Information for Others	Translating or explaining what information means and how it can be used.
Provide Consultation and Advice to Others	Providing guidance and expert advice to management or other groups on technical, systems-, or process-related topics.
Selling or Influencing Others	Convincing others to buy merchandise/goods or to otherwise change their minds or actions.
Staffing Organizational Units	Recruiting, interviewing, selecting, hiring, and promoting employees in an organization.
Assisting and Caring for Others	Providing personal assistance, medical attention, emotional support, or other personal care to others such as coworkers, customers, or patients.
Operating Vehicles, Mechanized Devices, or Equipme	Running, maneuvering, navigating, or driving vehicles or mechanized equipment, such as forklifts, passenger vehicles, aircraft, or water craft.
Controlling Machines and Processes	Using either control mechanisms or direct physical activity to operate machines or processes (not including computers or vehicles).
Repairing and Maintaining Mechanical Equipment	Servicing, repairing, adjusting, and testing machines, devices, moving parts, and equipment that operate primarily on the basis of mechanical (not electronic) principles.
Drafting, Laying Out, and Specifying Technical Dev	Providing documentation, detailed instructions, drawings, or specifications to tell others about how devices, parts, equipment, or structures are to be fabricated, constructed, assembled, modified, maintained, or used.
Repairing and Maintaining Electronic Equipment	Servicing, repairing, calibrating, regulating, fine-tuning, or testing machines, devices, and equipment that operate primarily on the basis of electrical or electronic (not mechanical) principles.

Work_Context	Work_Context Definitions
Telephone	How often do you have telephone conversations in this job?
Face-to-Face Discussions	How often do you have to have face-to-face discussions with individuals or teams in this job?

Contact With Others	How much does this job require the worker to be in contact with others (face-to-face, by telephone, or otherwise) in order to perform it?
Time Pressure	How often does this job require the worker to meet strict deadlines?
Freedom to Make Decisions	How much decision making freedom, without supervision, does the job offer?
Work With Work Group or Team	How important is it to work with others in a group or team in this job?
Structured versus Unstructured Work	To what extent is this job structured for the worker, rather than allowing the worker to determine tasks, priorities, and goals?
Importance of Being Exact or Accurate	How important is being very exact or highly accurate in performing this job?
Responsibility for Outcomes and Results	How responsible is the worker for work outcomes and results of other workers?
Responsible for Others' Health and Safety	How much responsibility is there for the health and safety of others in this job?
Electronic Mail	How often do you use electronic mail in this job?
Importance of Repeating Same Tasks	How important is repeating the same physical activities (e.g., key entry) or mental activities (e.g., checking entries in a ledger) over and over, without stopping, to performing this job?
Frequency of Decision Making	How frequently is the worker required to make decisions that affect other people, the financial resources, and/or the image and reputation of the organization?
Impact of Decisions on Co-workers or Company Resul	How do the decisions an employee makes impact the results of co-workers, clients or the company?
Level of Competition	To what extent does this job require the worker to compete or to be aware of competitive pressures?
Deal With Unpleasant or Angry People	How frequently does the worker have to deal with unpleasant, angry, or discourteous individuals as part of the job requirements?
Frequency of Conflict Situations	How often are there conflict situations the employee has to face in this job?
Letters and Memos	How often does the job require written letters and memos?
Coordinate or Lead Others	How important is it to coordinate or lead others in accomplishing work activities in this job?
Indoors, Not Environmentally Controlled	How often does this job require working indoors in non-controlled environmental conditions (e.g., warehouse without heat)?
Indoors, Environmentally Controlled	How often does this job require working indoors in environmentally controlled conditions?
Wear Common Protective or Safety Equipment such as	How much does this job require wearing common protective or safety equipment such as safety shoes, glasses, gloves, hard hats or life jackets?
Spend Time Standing	How much does this job require standing?
Physical Proximity	To what extent does this job require the worker to perform job tasks in close physical proximity to other people?
Sounds, Noise Levels Are Distracting or Uncomforta	How often does this job require working exposed to sounds and noise levels that are distracting or uncomfortable?
Spend Time Sitting	How much does this job require sitting?
Exposed to Contaminants	How often does this job require working exposed to contaminants (such as pollutants, gases, dust or odors)?
Deal With External Customers	How important is it to work with external customers or the public in this job?
Very Hot or Cold Temperatures	How often does this job require working in very hot (above 90 F degrees) or very cold (below 32 F degrees) temperatures?
Degree of Automation	How automated is the job?
Exposed to Hazardous Equipment	How often does this job require exposure to hazardous equipment?
Spend Time Walking and Running	How much does this job require walking and running?
Exposed to High Places	How often does this job require exposure to high places?
Consequence of Error	How serious would the result usually be if the worker made a mistake that was not readily correctable?
Public Speaking	How often do you have to perform public speaking in this job?
Pace Determined by Speed of Equipment	How important is it to this job that the pace is determined by the speed of equipment or machinery? (This does not refer to keeping busy at all times on this job.)
Spend Time Using Your Hands to Handle, Control, or	How much does this job require using your hands to handle, control, or feel objects, tools or controls?
Spend Time Making Repetitive Motions	How much does this job require making repetitive motions?
Wear Specialized Protective or Safety Equipment su	How much does this job require wearing specialized protective or safety equipment such as breathing apparatus, safety harness, full protection suits, or radiation protection?

Extremely Bright or Inadequate Lighting	How often does this job require working in extremely bright or inadequate lighting conditions?
Exposed to Minor Burns, Cuts, Bites, or Stings	How often does this job require exposure to minor burns, cuts, bites, or stings?
Spend Time Bending or Twisting the Body	How much does this job require bending or twisting your body?
Deal With Physically Aggressive People	How frequently does this job require the worker to deal with physical aggression of violent individuals?
Cramped Work Space, Awkward Positions	How often does this job require working in cramped work spaces that requires getting into awkward positions?
Exposed to Hazardous Conditions	How often does this job require exposure to hazardous conditions?
In an Enclosed Vehicle or Equipment	How often does this job require working in a closed vehicle or equipment (e.g., car)?
Outdoors, Exposed to Weather	How often does this job require working outdoors, exposed to all weather conditions?
Spend Time Kneeling, Crouching, Stooping, or Crawl	How much does this job require kneeling, crouching, stooping, or crawling?
Exposed to Whole Body Vibration	How often does this job require exposure to whole body vibration (e.g., operate a jackhammer)?
Outdoors, Under Cover	How often does this job require working outdoors, under cover (e.g., structure with roof but no walls)?
In an Open Vehicle or Equipment	How often does this job require working in an open vehicle or equipment (e.g., tractor)?
Spend Time Keeping or Regaining Balance	How much does this job require keeping or regaining your balance?
Spend Time Climbing Ladders, Scaffolds, or Poles	How much does this job require climbing ladders, scaffolds, or poles?
Exposed to Radiation	How often does this job require exposure to radiation?
Exposed to Disease or Infections	How often does this job require exposure to disease/infections?

Job Zone Component	Job Zone Component Definitions
Title	Job Zone Three: Medium Preparation Needed
Overall Experience	Previous work-related skill, knowledge, or experience is required for these occupations. For example, an electrician must have completed three or four years of apprenticeship or several years of vocational training, and often must have passed a licensing exam, in order to perform the job.
Job Training	Employees in these occupations usually need one or two years of training involving both on-the-job experience and informal training with experienced workers.
Job Zone Examples	These occupations usually involve using communication and organizational skills to coordinate, supervise, manage, or train others to accomplish goals. Examples include dental assistants, electricians, fish and game wardens, legal secretaries, personnel recruiters, and recreation workers.
SVP Range	(6.0 to < 7.0)
Education	Most occupations in this zone require training in vocational schools, related on-the-job experience, or an associate's degree. Some may require a bachelor's degree.

Work_Styles	Work_Styles Definitions
Initiative	Job requires a willingness to take on responsibilities and challenges.
Integrity	Job requires being honest and ethical.
Leadership	Job requires a willingness to lead, take charge, and offer opinions and direction.
Dependability	Job requires being reliable, responsible, and dependable, and fulfilling obligations.
Adaptability/Flexibility	Job requires being open to change (positive or negative) and to considerable variety in the workplace.
Cooperation	Job requires being pleasant with others on the job and displaying a good-natured, cooperative attitude.
Attention to Detail	Job requires being careful about detail and thorough in completing work tasks.
Stress Tolerance	Job requires accepting criticism and dealing calmly and effectively with high stress situations.
Self Control	Job requires maintaining composure, keeping emotions in check, controlling anger, and avoiding aggressive behavior, even in very difficult situations.

Achievement/Effort	Job requires establishing and maintaining personally challenging achievement goals and exerting effort toward mastering tasks.
Independence	Job requires developing one's own ways of doing things, guiding oneself with little or no supervision, and depending on oneself to get things done.
Social Orientation	Job requires preferring to work with others rather than alone, and being personally connected with others on the job.
Persistence	Job requires persistence in the face of obstacles.
Concern for Others	Job requires being sensitive to others' needs and feelings and being understanding and helpful on the job.
Analytical Thinking	Job requires analyzing information and using logic to address work-related issues and problems.
Innovation	Job requires creativity and alternative thinking to develop new ideas for and answers to work-related problems.

11-9011.01 - Nursery and Greenhouse Managers

Plan, organize, direct, control, and coordinate activities of workers engaged in propagating, cultivating, and harvesting horticultural specialties, such as trees, shrubs, flowers, mushrooms, and other plants.

Tasks

1) Manage nurseries that grow horticultural plants for sale to trade or retail customers, for display or exhibition, or for research.

2) Inspect facilities and equipment for signs of disrepair, and perform necessary maintenance work.

3) Negotiate contracts such as those for land leases or tree purchases.

4) Position and regulate plant irrigation systems, and program environmental and irrigation control computers.

5) Prepare soil for planting, and plant or transplant seeds, bulbs, and cuttings.

6) Determine plant growing conditions, such as greenhouses, hydroponics, or natural settings, and set planting and care schedules.

7) Determine types and quantities of horticultural plants to be grown, based on budgets, projected sales volumes, and/or executive directives.

8) Cut and prune trees, shrubs, flowers, and plants.

9) Provide information to customers on the care of trees, shrubs, flowers, plants, and lawns.

10) Hire employees, and train them in gardening techniques.

11) Construct structures and accessories such as greenhouses and benches.

12) Explain and enforce safety regulations and policies.

13) Apply pesticides and fertilizers to plants.

14) Tour work areas to observe work being done, to inspect crops, and to evaluate plant and soil conditions.

15) Select and purchase seeds, plant nutrients, disease control chemicals, and garden and lawn care equipment.

16) Identify plants as well as problems such as diseases, weeds, and insect pests.

17) Coordinate clerical, recordkeeping, inventory, requisitioning, and marketing activities.

18) Graft plants.

19) Confer with horticultural personnel in order to plan facility renovations or additions.

11-9021.00 - Construction Managers

Plan, direct, coordinate, or budget, usually through subordinate supervisory personnel, activities concerned with the construction and maintenance of structures, facilities, and systems. Participate in the conceptual development of a construction project and oversee its organization, scheduling, and implementation.

Tasks

1) Confer with supervisory personnel, owners, contractors, and design professionals to discuss and resolve matters such as work procedures, complaints, and construction problems.

2) Take actions to deal with the results of delays, bad weather, or emergencies at construction site.

3) Interpret and explain plans and contract terms to administrative staff, workers, and clients, representing the owner or developer.

4) Study job specifications to determine appropriate construction methods.

5) Plan, organize, and direct activities concerned with the construction and maintenance of structures, facilities, and systems.

6) Prepare contracts and negotiate revisions, changes and additions to contractual agreements with architects, consultants, clients, suppliers and subcontractors.

7) Determine labor requirements and dispatch workers to construction sites.

8) Prepare and submit budget estimates and progress and cost tracking reports.

9) Direct and supervise workers.

10) Investigate damage, accidents, or delays at construction sites, to ensure that proper procedures are being carried out.

11) Inspect and review projects to monitor compliance with building and safety codes, and other regulations.

12) Requisition supplies and materials to complete construction projects.

13) Select, contract, and oversee workers who complete specific pieces of the project, such as painting or plumbing.

14) Obtain all necessary permits and licenses.

15) Develop and implement quality control programs.

16) Evaluate construction methods and determine cost-effectiveness of plans, using computers.

17) Direct acquisition of land for construction projects.

Knowledge	Knowledge Definitions
Building and Construction	Knowledge of materials, methods, and the tools involved in the construction or repair of houses, buildings, or other structures such as highways and roads.
Mathematics	Knowledge of arithmetic, algebra, geometry, calculus, statistics, and their applications.
Design	Knowledge of design techniques, tools, and principles involved in production of precision technical plans, blueprints, drawings, and models.
English Language	Knowledge of the structure and content of the English language including the meaning and spelling of words, rules of composition, and grammar.
Public Safety and Security	Knowledge of relevant equipment, policies, procedures, and strategies to promote effective local, state, or national security operations for the protection of people, data, property, and institutions.
Administration and Management	Knowledge of business and management principles involved in strategic planning, resource allocation, human resources modeling, leadership technique, production methods, and coordination of people and resources.
Customer and Personal Service	Knowledge of principles and processes for providing customer and personal services. This includes customer needs assessment, meeting quality standards for services, and evaluation of customer satisfaction.
Mechanical	Knowledge of machines and tools, including their designs, uses, repair, and maintenance.
Engineering and Technology	Knowledge of the practical application of engineering science and technology. This includes applying principles, techniques, procedures, and equipment to the design and production of various goods and services.
Economics and Accounting	Knowledge of economic and accounting principles and practices, the financial markets, banking and the analysis and reporting of financial data.
Sales and Marketing	Knowledge of principles and methods for showing, promoting, and selling products or services. This includes marketing strategy and tactics, product demonstration, sales techniques, and sales control systems.
Law and Government	Knowledge of laws, legal codes, court procedures, precedents, government regulations, executive orders, agency rules, and the democratic political process.
Clerical	Knowledge of administrative and clerical procedures and systems such as word processing, managing files and records, stenography and transcription, designing forms, and other office procedures and terminology.

Personnel and Human Resources	Knowledge of principles and procedures for personnel recruitment, selection, training, compensation and benefits, labor relations and negotiation, and personnel information systems.
Computers and Electronics	Knowledge of circuit boards, processors, chips, electronic equipment, and computer hardware and software, including applications and programming.
Communications and Media	Knowledge of media production, communication, and dissemination techniques and methods. This includes alternative ways to inform and entertain via written, oral, and visual media.
Education and Training	Knowledge of principles and methods for curriculum and training design, teaching and instruction for individuals and groups, and the measurement of training effects.
Chemistry	Knowledge of the chemical composition, structure, and properties of substances and of the chemical processes and transformations that they undergo. This includes uses of chemicals and their interactions, danger signs, production techniques, and disposal methods.
Physics	Knowledge and prediction of physical principles, laws, their interrelationships, and applications to understanding fluid, material, and atmospheric dynamics, and mechanical, electrical, atomic and sub- atomic structures and processes.
Production and Processing	Knowledge of raw materials, production processes, quality control, costs, and other techniques for maximizing the effective manufacture and distribution of goods.
Telecommunications	Knowledge of transmission, broadcasting, switching, control, and operation of telecommunications systems.
Psychology	Knowledge of human behavior and performance; individual differences in ability, personality, and interests; learning and motivation; psychological research methods; and the assessment and treatment of behavioral and affective disorders.
Geography	Knowledge of principles and methods for describing the features of land, sea, and air masses, including their physical characteristics, locations, interrelationships, and distribution of plant, animal, and human life.
Transportation	Knowledge of principles and methods for moving people or goods by air, rail, sea, or road, including the relative costs and benefits.
Sociology and Anthropology	Knowledge of group behavior and dynamics, societal trends and influences, human migrations, ethnicity, cultures and their history and origins.
Foreign Language	Knowledge of the structure and content of a foreign (non-English) language including the meaning and spelling of words, rules of composition and grammar, and pronunciation.
Philosophy and Theology	Knowledge of different philosophical systems and religions. This includes their basic principles, values, ethics, ways of thinking, customs, practices, and their impact on human culture.
Therapy and Counseling	Knowledge of principles, methods, and procedures for diagnosis, treatment, and rehabilitation of physical and mental dysfunctions, and for career counseling and guidance.
Biology	Knowledge of plant and animal organisms, their tissues, cells, functions, interdependencies, and interactions with each other and the environment.
Medicine and Dentistry	Knowledge of the information and techniques needed to diagnose and treat human injuries, diseases, and deformities. This includes symptoms, treatment alternatives, drug properties and interactions, and preventive health-care measures.
History and Archeology	Knowledge of historical events and their causes, indicators, and effects on civilizations and cultures.
Fine Arts	Knowledge of the theory and techniques required to compose, produce, and perform works of music, dance, visual arts, drama, and sculpture.
Food Production	Knowledge of techniques and equipment for planting, growing, and harvesting food products (both plant and animal) for consumption, including storage/handling techniques.

Skills	Skills Definitions
Reading Comprehension	Understanding written sentences and paragraphs in work related documents.
Critical Thinking	Using logic and reasoning to identify the strengths and weaknesses of alternative solutions, conclusions or approaches to problems.
Coordination	Adjusting actions in relation to others' actions.
Instructing	Teaching others how to do something.
Mathematics	Using mathematics to solve problems.

Active Listening	Giving full attention to what other people are saying, taking time to understand the points being made, asking questions as appropriate, and not interrupting at inappropriate times.
Writing	Communicating effectively in writing as appropriate for the needs of the audience.
Judgment and Decision Making	Considering the relative costs and benefits of potential actions to choose the most appropriate one.
Active Learning	Understanding the implications of new information for both current and future problem-solving and decision-making.
Negotiation	Bringing others together and trying to reconcile differences.
Troubleshooting	Determining causes of operating errors and deciding what to do about it.
Complex Problem Solving	Identifying complex problems and reviewing related information to develop and evaluate options and implement solutions.
Time Management	Managing one's own time and the time of others.
Monitoring	Monitoring/Assessing performance of yourself, other individuals, or organizations to make improvements or take corrective action.
Installation	Installing equipment, machines, wiring, or programs to meet specifications.
Social Perceptiveness	Being aware of others' reactions and understanding why they react as they do.
Service Orientation	Actively looking for ways to help people.
Equipment Selection	Determining the kind of tools and equipment needed to do a job.
Persuasion	Persuading others to change their minds or behavior.
Learning Strategies	Selecting and using training/instructional methods and procedures appropriate for the situation when learning or teaching new things.
Speaking	Talking to others to convey information effectively.
Repairing	Repairing machines or systems using the needed tools.
Management of Material Resources	Obtaining and seeing to the appropriate use of equipment, facilities, and materials needed to do certain work.
Operations Analysis	Analyzing needs and product requirements to create a design.
Management of Financial Resources	Determining how money will be spent to get the work done, and accounting for these expenditures.
Management of Personnel Resources	Motivating, developing, and directing people as they work, identifying the best people for the job.
Operation Monitoring	Watching gauges, dials, or other indicators to make sure a machine is working properly.
Equipment Maintenance	Performing routine maintenance on equipment and determining when and what kind of maintenance is needed.
Quality Control Analysis	Conducting tests and inspections of products, services, or processes to evaluate quality or performance.
Systems Analysis	Determining how a system should work and how changes in conditions, operations, and the environment will affect outcomes.
Operation and Control	Controlling operations of equipment or systems.
Systems Evaluation	Identifying measures or indicators of system performance and the actions needed to improve or correct performance, relative to the goals of the system.
Science	Using scientific rules and methods to solve problems.
Programming	Writing computer programs for various purposes.
Technology Design	Generating or adapting equipment and technology to serve user needs.

Ability	Ability Definitions
Oral Expression	The ability to communicate information and ideas in speaking so others will understand.
Oral Comprehension	The ability to listen to and understand information and ideas presented through spoken words and sentences.
Problem Sensitivity	The ability to tell when something is wrong or is likely to go wrong. It does not involve solving the problem, only recognizing there is a problem.
Inductive Reasoning	The ability to combine pieces of information to form general rules or conclusions (includes finding a relationship among seemingly unrelated events).
Speech Clarity	The ability to speak clearly so others can understand you.
Speech Recognition	The ability to identify and understand the speech of another person.
Information Ordering	The ability to arrange things or actions in a certain order or pattern according to a specific rule or set of rules (e.g., patterns of numbers, letters, words, pictures, mathematical operations).
Deductive Reasoning	The ability to apply general rules to specific problems to produce answers that make sense.

Written Comprehension	The ability to read and understand information and ideas presented in writing.
Near Vision	The ability to see details at close range (within a few feet of the observer).
Written Expression	The ability to communicate information and ideas in writing so others will understand.
Visualization	The ability to imagine how something will look after it is moved around or when its parts are moved or rearranged.
Fluency of Ideas	The ability to come up with a number of ideas about a topic (the number of ideas is important, not their quality, correctness, or creativity).
Originality	The ability to come up with unusual or clever ideas about a given topic or situation, or to develop creative ways to solve a problem.
Category Flexibility	The ability to generate or use different sets of rules for combining or grouping things in different ways.
Mathematical Reasoning	The ability to choose the right mathematical methods or formulas to solve a problem.
Selective Attention	The ability to concentrate on a task over a period of time without being distracted.
Far Vision	The ability to see details at a distance.
Number Facility	The ability to add, subtract, multiply, or divide quickly and correctly.
Time Sharing	The ability to shift back and forth between two or more activities or sources of information (such as speech, sounds, touch, or other sources).
Flexibility of Closure	The ability to identify or detect a known pattern (a figure, object, word, or sound) that is hidden in other distracting material.
Perceptual Speed	The ability to quickly and accurately compare similarities and differences among sets of letters, numbers, objects, pictures, or patterns. The things to be compared may be presented at the same time or one after the other. This ability also includes comparing a presented object with a remembered object.
Memorization	The ability to remember information such as words, numbers, pictures, and procedures.
Depth Perception	The ability to judge which of several objects is closer or farther away from you, or to judge the distance between you and an object.
Auditory Attention	The ability to focus on a single source of sound in the presence of other distracting sounds.
Multilimb Coordination	The ability to coordinate two or more limbs (for example, two arms, two legs, or one leg and one arm) while sitting, standing, or lying down. It does not involve performing the activities while the whole body is in motion.
Control Precision	The ability to quickly and repeatedly adjust the controls of a machine or a vehicle to exact positions.
Reaction Time	The ability to quickly respond (with the hand, finger, or foot) to a signal (sound, light, picture) when it appears.
Trunk Strength	The ability to use your abdominal and lower back muscles to support part of the body repeatedly or continuously over time without 'giving out' or fatiguing.
Static Strength	The ability to exert maximum muscle force to lift, push, pull, or carry objects.
Speed of Closure	The ability to quickly make sense of, combine, and organize information into meaningful patterns.
Manual Dexterity	The ability to quickly move your hand, your hand together with your arm, or your two hands to grasp, manipulate, or assemble objects.
Arm-Hand Steadiness	The ability to keep your hand and arm steady while moving your arm or while holding your arm and hand in one position.
Spatial Orientation	The ability to know your location in relation to the environment or to know where other objects are in relation to you.
Visual Color Discrimination	The ability to match or detect differences between colors, including shades of color and brightness.
Gross Body Coordination	The ability to coordinate the movement of your arms, legs, and torso together when the whole body is in motion.
Finger Dexterity	The ability to make precisely coordinated movements of the fingers of one or both hands to grasp, manipulate, or assemble very small objects.
Hearing Sensitivity	The ability to detect or tell the differences between sounds that vary in pitch and loudness.
Night Vision	The ability to see under low light conditions.
Peripheral Vision	The ability to see objects or movement of objects to one's side when the eyes are looking ahead.
Extent Flexibility	The ability to bend, stretch, twist, or reach with your body, arms, and/or legs.

Stamina	The ability to exert yourself physically over long periods of time without getting winded or out of breath.
Dynamic Strength	The ability to exert muscle force repeatedly or continuously over time. This involves muscular endurance and resistance to muscle fatigue.
Wrist-Finger Speed	The ability to make fast, simple, repeated movements of the fingers, hands, and wrists.
Sound Localization	The ability to tell the direction from which a sound originated.
Gross Body Equilibrium	The ability to keep or regain your body balance or stay upright when in an unstable position.
Rate Control	The ability to time your movements or the movement of a piece of equipment in anticipation of changes in the speed and/or direction of a moving object or scene.
Glare Sensitivity	The ability to see objects in the presence of glare or bright lighting.
Speed of Limb Movement	The ability to quickly move the arms and legs.
Response Orientation	The ability to choose quickly between two or more movements in response to two or more different signals (lights, sounds, pictures). It includes the speed with which the correct response is started with the hand, foot, or other body part.
Explosive Strength	The ability to use short bursts of muscle force to propel oneself (as in jumping or sprinting), or to throw an object.
Dynamic Flexibility	The ability to quickly and repeatedly bend, stretch, twist, or reach out with your body, arms, and/or legs.

Work_Activity	Work_Activity Definitions
Making Decisions and Solving Problems	Analyzing information and evaluating results to choose the best solution and solve problems.
Monitor Processes, Materials, or Surroundings	Monitoring and reviewing information from materials, events, or the environment, to detect or assess problems.
Organizing, Planning, and Prioritizing Work	Developing specific goals and plans to prioritize, organize, and accomplish your work.
Inspecting Equipment, Structures, or Material	Inspecting equipment, structures, or materials to identify the cause of errors or other problems or defects.
Scheduling Work and Activities	Scheduling events, programs, and activities, as well as the work of others.
Getting Information	Observing, receiving, and otherwise obtaining information from all relevant sources.
Communicating with Persons Outside Organization	Communicating with people outside the organization, representing the organization to customers, the public, government, and other external sources. This information can be exchanged in person, in writing, or by telephone or e-mail.
Coordinating the Work and Activities of Others	Getting members of a group to work together to accomplish tasks.
Communicating with Supervisors, Peers, or Subordin	Providing information to supervisors, co-workers, and subordinates by telephone, in written form, e-mail, or in person.
Evaluating Information to Determine Compliance wit	Using relevant information and individual judgment to determine whether events or processes comply with laws, regulations, or standards.
Estimating the Quantifiable Characteristics of Pro	Estimating sizes, distances, and quantities; or determining time, costs, resources, or materials needed to perform a work activity.
Establishing and Maintaining Interpersonal Relatio	Developing constructive and cooperative working relationships with others, and maintaining them over time.
Resolving Conflicts and Negotiating with Others	Handling complaints, settling disputes, and resolving grievances and conflicts, or otherwise negotiating with others.
Updating and Using Relevant Knowledge	Keeping up-to-date technically and applying new knowledge to your job.
Thinking Creatively	Developing, designing, or creating new applications, ideas, relationships, systems, or products, including artistic contributions.
Interpreting the Meaning of Information for Others	Translating or explaining what information means and how it can be used.
Performing Administrative Activities	Performing day-to-day administrative tasks such as maintaining information files and processing paperwork.
Developing Objectives and Strategies	Establishing long-range objectives and specifying the strategies and actions to achieve them.
Documenting/Recording Information	Entering, transcribing, recording, storing, or maintaining information in written or electronic/magnetic form.
Judging the Qualities of Things, Services, or Peop	Assessing the value, importance, or quality of things or people.
Identifying Objects, Actions, and Events	Identifying information by categorizing, estimating, recognizing differences or similarities, and detecting changes in circumstances or events.

Guiding, Directing, and Motivating Subordinates	Providing guidance and direction to subordinates, including setting performance standards and monitoring performance.
Monitoring and Controlling Resources	Monitoring and controlling resources and overseeing the spending of money.
Processing Information	Compiling, coding, categorizing, calculating, tabulating, auditing, or verifying information or data.
Developing and Building Teams	Encouraging and building mutual trust, respect, and cooperation among team members.
Analyzing Data or Information	Identifying the underlying principles, reasons, or facts of information by breaking down information or data into separate parts.
Performing for or Working Directly with the Public	Performing for people or dealing directly with the public. This includes serving customers in restaurants and stores, and receiving clients or guests.
Selling or Influencing Others	Convincing others to buy merchandise/goods or to otherwise change their minds or actions.
Operating Vehicles, Mechanized Devices, or Equipme	Running, maneuvering, navigating, or driving vehicles or mechanized equipment, such as forklifts, passenger vehicles, aircraft, or water craft.
Handling and Moving Objects	Using hands and arms in handling, installing, positioning, and moving materials, and manipulating things.
Provide Consultation and Advice to Others	Providing guidance and expert advice to management or other groups on technical, systems-, or process-related topics.
Coaching and Developing Others	Identifying the developmental needs of others and coaching, mentoring, or otherwise helping others to improve their knowledge or skills.
Interacting With Computers	Using computers and computer systems (including hardware and software) to program, write software, set up functions, enter data, or process information.
Performing General Physical Activities	Performing physical activities that require considerable use of your arms and legs and moving your whole body, such as climbing, lifting, balancing, walking, stooping, and handling of materials.
Controlling Machines and Processes	Using either control mechanisms or direct physical activity to operate machines or processes (not including computers or vehicles).
Training and Teaching Others	Identifying the educational needs of others, developing formal educational or training programs or classes, and teaching or instructing others.
Drafting, Laying Out, and Specifying Technical Dev	Providing documentation, detailed instructions, drawings, or specifications to tell others about how devices, parts, equipment, or structures are to be fabricated, constructed, assembled, modified, maintained, or used.
Repairing and Maintaining Mechanical Equipment	Servicing, repairing, adjusting, and testing machines, devices, moving parts, and equipment that operate primarily on the basis of mechanical (not electronic) principles.
Assisting and Caring for Others	Providing personal assistance, medical attention, emotional support, or other personal care to others such as coworkers, customers, or patients.
Staffing Organizational Units	Recruiting, interviewing, selecting, hiring, and promoting employees in an organization.
Repairing and Maintaining Electronic Equipment	Servicing, repairing, calibrating, regulating, fine-tuning, or testing machines, devices, and equipment that operate primarily on the basis of electrical or electronic (not mechanical) principles.

Job Zone Component	Job Zone Component Definitions
Title	Job Zone Three: Medium Preparation Needed
Overall Experience	Previous work-related skill, knowledge, or experience is required for these occupations. For example, an electrician must have completed three or four years of apprenticeship or several years of vocational training, and often must have passed a licensing exam, in order to perform the job.
Job Training	Employees in these occupations usually need one or two years of training involving both on-the-job experience and informal training with experienced workers.
Job Zone Examples	These occupations usually involve using communication and organizational skills to coordinate, supervise, manage, or train others to accomplish goals. Examples include dental assistants, electricians, fish and game wardens, legal secretaries, personnel recruiters, and recreation workers.
SVP Range	(6.0 to < 7.0)
Education	Most occupations in this zone require training in vocational schools, related on-the-job experience, or an associate's degree. Some may require a bachelor's degree.

Work_Context	Work_Context Definitions
Telephone	How often do you have telephone conversations in this job?
Face-to-Face Discussions	How often do you have to have face-to-face discussions with individuals or teams in this job?
Freedom to Make Decisions	How much decision making freedom, without supervision, does the job offer?
Structured versus Unstructured Work	To what extent is this job structured for the worker, rather than allowing the worker to determine tasks, priorities, and goals?
Work With Work Group or Team	How important is it to work with others in a group or team in this job?
Coordinate or Lead Others	How important is it to coordinate or lead others in accomplishing work activities in this job?
Letters and Memos	How often does the job require written letters and memos?
Impact of Decisions on Co-workers or Company Resul	How do the decisions an employee makes impact the results of co-workers, clients or the company?
Contact With Others	How much does this job require the worker to be in contact with others (face-to-face, by telephone, or otherwise) in order to perform it?
Frequency of Decision Making	How frequently is the worker required to make decisions that affect other people, the financial resources, and/or the image and reputation of the organization?
In an Enclosed Vehicle or Equipment	How often does this job require working in a closed vehicle or equipment (e.g., car)?
Responsibility for Outcomes and Results	How responsible is the worker for work outcomes and results of other workers?
Electronic Mail	How often do you use electronic mail in this job?
Importance of Being Exact or Accurate	How important is being very exact or highly accurate in performing this job?
Time Pressure	How often does this job require the worker to meet strict deadlines?
Frequency of Conflict Situations	How often are there conflict situations the employee has to face in this job?
Responsible for Others' Health and Safety	How much responsibility is there for the health and safety of others in this job?
Deal With External Customers	How important is it to work with external customers or the public in this job?
Indoors, Environmentally Controlled	How often does this job require working indoors in environmentally controlled conditions?
Consequence of Error	How serious would the result usually be if the worker made a mistake that was not readily correctable?
Level of Competition	To what extent does this job require the worker to compete or to be aware of competitive pressures?
Sounds, Noise Levels Are Distracting or Uncomforta	How often does this job require working exposed to sounds and noise levels that are distracting or uncomfortable?
Wear Common Protective or Safety Equipment such as	How much does this job require wearing common protective or safety equipment such as safety shoes, glasses, gloves, hard hats or live jackets?
Spend Time Sitting	How much does this job require sitting?
Importance of Repeating Same Tasks	How important is repeating the same physical activities (e.g., key entry) or mental activities (e.g., checking entries in a ledger) over and over, without stopping, to performing this job?
Physical Proximity	To what extent does this job require the worker to perform job tasks in close physical proximity to other people?
Indoors, Not Environmentally Controlled	How often does this job require working indoors in non-controlled environmental conditions (e.g., warehouse without heat)?
Deal With Unpleasant or Angry People	How frequently does the worker have to deal with unpleasant, angry, or discourteous individuals as part of the job requirements?
Exposed to Contaminants	How often does this job require working exposed to contaminants (such as pollutants, gases, dust or odors)?
Spend Time Standing	How much does this job require standing?
Outdoors, Exposed to Weather	How often does this job require working outdoors, exposed to all weather conditions?
Exposed to Hazardous Equipment	How often does this job require exposure to hazardous equipment?
Public Speaking	How often do you have to perform public speaking in this job?
Spend Time Making Repetitive Motions	How much does this job require making repetitive motions?
Spend Time Using Your Hands to Handle, Control, or	How much does this job require using your hands to handle, control, or feel objects, tools or controls?
Very Hot or Cold Temperatures	How often does this job require working in very hot (above 90 F degrees) or very cold (below 32 F degrees) temperatures?
Degree of Automation	How automated is the job?
Spend Time Walking and Running	How much does this job require walking and running?
Spend Time Bending or Twisting the Body	How much does this job require bending or twisting your body?
Pace Determined by Speed of Equipment	How important is it to this job that the pace is determined by the speed of equipment or machinery? (This does not refer to keeping busy at all times on this job.)
Wear Specialized Protective or Safety Equipment su	How much does this job require wearing specialized protective or safety equipment such as breathing apparatus, safety harness, full protection suits, or radiation protection?
Exposed to Hazardous Conditions	How often does this job require exposure to hazardous conditions?
Extremely Bright or Inadequate Lighting	How often does this job require working in extremely bright or inadequate lighting conditions?
Cramped Work Space, Awkward Positions	How often does this job require working in cramped work spaces that requires getting into awkward positions?
Spend Time Kneeling, Crouching, Stooping, or Crawl	How much does this job require kneeling, crouching, stooping, or crawling?
Exposed to High Places	How often does this job require exposure to high places?
Exposed to Whole Body Vibration	How often does this job require exposure to whole body vibration (e.g., operate a jackhammer)?
Exposed to Minor Burns, Cuts, Bites, or Stings	How often does this job require exposure to minor burns, cuts, bites, or stings?
Outdoors, Under Cover	How often does this job require working outdoors, under cover (e.g., structure with roof but no walls)?
In an Open Vehicle or Equipment	How often does this job require working in an open vehicle or equipment (e.g., tractor)?
Spend Time Keeping or Regaining Balance	How much does this job require keeping or regaining your balance?
Spend Time Climbing Ladders, Scaffolds, or Poles	How much does this job require climbing ladders, scaffolds, or poles?
Deal With Physically Aggressive People	How frequently does this job require the worker to deal with physical aggression of violent individuals?
Exposed to Disease or Infections	How often does this job require exposure to disease/infections?
Exposed to Radiation	How often does this job require exposure to radiation?

Work_Styles	Work_Styles Definitions
Integrity	Job requires being honest and ethical.
Attention to Detail	Job requires being careful about detail and thorough in completing work tasks.
Dependability	Job requires being reliable, responsible, and dependable, and fulfilling obligations.
Leadership	Job requires a willingness to lead, take charge, and offer opinions and direction.
Self Control	Job requires maintaining composure, keeping emotions in check, controlling anger, and avoiding aggressive behavior, even in very difficult situations.
Stress Tolerance	Job requires accepting criticism and dealing calmly and effectively with high stress situations.
Innovation	Job requires creativity and alternative thinking to develop new ideas for and answers to work-related problems.
Cooperation	Job requires being pleasant with others on the job and displaying a good-natured, cooperative attitude.
Adaptability/Flexibility	Job requires being open to change (positive or negative) and to considerable variety in the workplace.
Initiative	Job requires a willingness to take on responsibilities and challenges.
Analytical Thinking	Job requires analyzing information and using logic to address work-related issues and problems.
Persistence	Job requires persistence in the face of obstacles.
Concern for Others	Job requires being sensitive to others' needs and feelings and being understanding and helpful on the job.
Independence	Job requires developing one's own ways of doing things, guiding oneself with little or no supervision, and depending on oneself to get things done.
Social Orientation	Job requires preferring to work with others rather than alone, and being personally connected with others on the job.
Achievement/Effort	Job requires establishing and maintaining personally challenging achievement goals and exerting effort toward mastering tasks.

11-9041.00 - Engineering Managers

Plan, direct, or coordinate activities in such fields as architecture and engineering or research and development in these fields.

Tasks

1) Coordinate and direct projects, making detailed plans to accomplish goals and directing the integration of technical activities.

2) Confer with management, production, and marketing staff to discuss project specifications and procedures.

3) Develop and implement policies, standards and procedures for the engineering and technical work performed in the department, service, laboratory or firm.

4) Set scientific and technical goals within broad outlines provided by top management.

5) Consult or negotiate with clients to prepare project specifications.

6) Direct, review, and approve product design and changes.

7) Analyze technology, resource needs, and market demand, to plan and assess the feasibility of projects.

8) Review and recommend or approve contracts and cost estimates.

9) Plan and direct the installation, testing, operation, maintenance, and repair of facilities and equipment.

10) Prepare budgets, bids, and contracts, and direct the negotiation of research contracts.

11) Recruit employees; assign, direct, and evaluate their work; and oversee the development and maintenance of staff competence.

12) Present and explain proposals, reports, and findings to clients.

13) Confer with and report to officials and the public to provide information and solicit support for projects.

14) Direct the engineering of water control, treatment, and distribution projects.

15) Plan, direct, and coordinate survey work with other staff activities, certifying survey work, and writing land legal descriptions.

16) Administer highway planning, construction, and maintenance.

Knowledge	Knowledge Definitions
Engineering and Technology	Knowledge of the practical application of engineering science and technology. This includes applying principles, techniques, procedures, and equipment to the design and production of various goods and services.
Mathematics	Knowledge of arithmetic, algebra, geometry, calculus, statistics, and their applications.
Design	Knowledge of design techniques, tools, and principles involved in production of precision technical plans, blueprints, drawings, and models.
Computers and Electronics	Knowledge of circuit boards, processors, chips, electronic equipment, and computer hardware and software, including applications and programming.
English Language	Knowledge of the structure and content of the English language including the meaning and spelling of words, rules of composition, and grammar.
Physics	Knowledge and prediction of physical principles, laws, their interrelationships, and applications to understanding fluid, material, and atmospheric dynamics, and mechanical, electrical, atomic and sub-atomic structures and processes.
Administration and Management	Knowledge of business and management principles involved in strategic planning, resource allocation, human resources modeling, leadership technique, production methods, and coordination of people and resources.
Customer and Personal Service	Knowledge of principles and processes for providing customer and personal services. This includes customer needs assessment, meeting quality standards for services, and evaluation of customer satisfaction.
Building and Construction	Knowledge of materials, methods, and the tools involved in the construction or repair of houses, buildings, or other structures such as highways and roads.
Public Safety and Security	Knowledge of relevant equipment, policies, procedures, and strategies to promote effective local, state, or national security operations for the protection of people, data, property, and institutions.
Personnel and Human Resources	Knowledge of principles and procedures for personnel recruitment, selection, training, compensation and benefits, labor relations and negotiation, and personnel information systems.
Education and Training	Knowledge of principles and methods for curriculum and training design, teaching and instruction for individuals and groups, and the measurement of training effects.
Law and Government	Knowledge of laws, legal codes, court procedures, precedents, government regulations, executive orders, agency rules, and the democratic political process.
Economics and Accounting	Knowledge of economic and accounting principles and practices, the financial markets, banking and the analysis and reporting of financial data.
Production and Processing	Knowledge of raw materials, production processes, quality control, costs, and other techniques for maximizing the effective manufacture and distribution of goods.
Mechanical	Knowledge of machines and tools, including their designs, uses, repair, and maintenance.
Communications and Media	Knowledge of media production, communication, and dissemination techniques and methods. This includes alternative ways to inform and entertain via written, oral, and visual media.
Geography	Knowledge of principles and methods for describing the features of land, sea, and air masses, including their physical characteristics, locations, interrelationships, and distribution of plant, animal, and human life.
Psychology	Knowledge of human behavior and performance; individual differences in ability, personality, and interests; learning and motivation; psychological research methods; and the assessment and treatment of behavioral and affective disorders.
Telecommunications	Knowledge of transmission, broadcasting, switching, control, and operation of telecommunications systems.
Clerical	Knowledge of administrative and clerical procedures and systems such as word processing, managing files and records, stenography and transcription, designing forms, and other office procedures and terminology.
Sales and Marketing	Knowledge of principles and methods for showing, promoting, and selling products or services. This includes marketing strategy and tactics, product demonstration, sales techniques, and sales control systems.
Chemistry	Knowledge of the chemical composition, structure, and properties of substances and of the chemical processes and transformations that they undergo. This includes uses of chemicals and their interactions, danger signs, production techniques, and disposal methods.
Transportation	Knowledge of principles and methods for moving people or goods by air, rail, sea, or road, including the relative costs and benefits.
Sociology and Anthropology	Knowledge of group behavior and dynamics, societal trends and influences, human migrations, ethnicity, cultures and their history and origins.
Biology	Knowledge of plant and animal organisms, their tissues, cells, functions, interdependencies, and interactions with each other and the environment.
Therapy and Counseling	Knowledge of principles, methods, and procedures for diagnosis, treatment, and rehabilitation of physical and mental dysfunctions, and for career counseling and guidance.
Philosophy and Theology	Knowledge of different philosophical systems and religions. This includes their basic principles, values, ethics, ways of thinking, customs, practices, and their impact on human culture.
History and Archeology	Knowledge of historical events and their causes, indicators, and effects on civilizations and cultures.
Fine Arts	Knowledge of the theory and techniques required to compose, produce, and perform works of music, dance, visual arts, drama, and sculpture.
Medicine and Dentistry	Knowledge of the information and techniques needed to diagnose and treat human injuries, diseases, and deformities. This includes symptoms, treatment alternatives, drug properties and interactions, and preventive health-care measures.
Foreign Language	Knowledge of the structure and content of a foreign (non-English) language including the meaning and spelling of words, rules of composition and grammar, and pronunciation.
Food Production	Knowledge of techniques and equipment for planting, growing, and harvesting food products (both plant and animal) for consumption, including storage/handling techniques.

Skills	Skills Definitions
Reading Comprehension	Understanding written sentences and paragraphs in work related documents.
Mathematics	Using mathematics to solve problems.
Active Listening	Giving full attention to what other people are saying, taking time to understand the points being made, asking questions as appropriate, and not interrupting at inappropriate times.
Critical Thinking	Using logic and reasoning to identify the strengths and weaknesses of alternative solutions, conclusions or approaches to problems.
Complex Problem Solving	Identifying complex problems and reviewing related information to develop and evaluate options and implement solutions.
Coordination	Adjusting actions in relation to others' actions.
Active Learning	Understanding the implications of new information for both current and future problem-solving and decision-making.
Operations Analysis	Analyzing needs and product requirements to create a design.
Judgment and Decision Making	Considering the relative costs and benefits of potential actions to choose the most appropriate one.
Time Management	Managing one's own time and the time of others.
Technology Design	Generating or adapting equipment and technology to serve user needs.
Writing	Communicating effectively in writing as appropriate for the needs of the audience.
Speaking	Talking to others to convey information effectively.
Science	Using scientific rules and methods to solve problems.
Quality Control Analysis	Conducting tests and inspections of products, services, or processes to evaluate quality or performance.
Negotiation	Bringing others together and trying to reconcile differences.
Monitoring	Monitoring/Assessing performance of yourself, other individuals, or organizations to make improvements or take corrective action.
Learning Strategies	Selecting and using training/instructional methods and procedures appropriate for the situation when learning or teaching new things.
Troubleshooting	Determining causes of operating errors and deciding what to do about it.
Persuasion	Persuading others to change their minds or behavior.
Installation	Installing equipment, machines, wiring, or programs to meet specifications.
Service Orientation	Actively looking for ways to help people.
Instructing	Teaching others how to do something.
Management of Financial Resources	Determining how money will be spent to get the work done, and accounting for these expenditures.
Systems Analysis	Determining how a system should work and how changes in conditions, operations, and the environment will affect outcomes.
Social Perceptiveness	Being aware of others' reactions and understanding why they react as they do.
Equipment Selection	Determining the kind of tools and equipment needed to do a job.
Management of Personnel Resources	Motivating, developing, and directing people as they work, identifying the best people for the job.
Systems Evaluation	Identifying measures or indicators of system performance and the actions needed to improve or correct performance, relative to the goals of the system.
Management of Material Resources	Obtaining and seeing to the appropriate use of equipment, facilities, and materials needed to do certain work.
Operation and Control	Controlling operations of equipment or systems.
Programming	Writing computer programs for various purposes.
Operation Monitoring	Watching gauges, dials, or other indicators to make sure a machine is working properly.
Equipment Maintenance	Performing routine maintenance on equipment and determining when and what kind of maintenance is needed.
Repairing	Repairing machines or systems using the needed tools.

Ability	Ability Definitions
Written Comprehension	The ability to read and understand information and ideas presented in writing.
Oral Comprehension	The ability to listen to and understand information and ideas presented through spoken words and sentences.
Speech Recognition	The ability to identify and understand the speech of another person.
Oral Expression	The ability to communicate information and ideas in speaking so others will understand.

Inductive Reasoning	The ability to combine pieces of information to form general rules or conclusions (includes finding a relationship among seemingly unrelated events).
Information Ordering	The ability to arrange things or actions in a certain order or pattern according to a specific rule or set of rules (e.g., patterns of numbers, letters, words, pictures, mathematical operations).
Deductive Reasoning	The ability to apply general rules to specific problems to produce answers that make sense.
Speech Clarity	The ability to speak clearly so others can understand you.
Problem Sensitivity	The ability to tell when something is wrong or is likely to go wrong. It does not involve solving the problem, only recognizing there is a problem.
Near Vision	The ability to see details at close range (within a few feet of the observer).
Written Expression	The ability to communicate information and ideas in writing so others will understand.
Originality	The ability to come up with unusual or clever ideas about a given topic or situation, or to develop creative ways to solve a problem.
Fluency of Ideas	The ability to come up with a number of ideas about a topic (the number of ideas is important, not their quality, correctness, or creativity).
Category Flexibility	The ability to generate or use different sets of rules for combining or grouping things in different ways.
Far Vision	The ability to see details at a distance.
Visualization	The ability to imagine how something will look after it is moved around or when its parts are moved or rearranged.
Perceptual Speed	The ability to quickly and accurately compare similarities and differences among sets of letters, numbers, objects, pictures, or patterns. The things to be compared may be presented at the same time or one after the other. This ability also includes comparing a presented object with a remembered object.
Flexibility of Closure	The ability to identify or detect a known pattern (a figure, object, word, or sound) that is hidden in other distracting material.
Selective Attention	The ability to concentrate on a task over a period of time without being distracted.
Time Sharing	The ability to shift back and forth between two or more activities or sources of information (such as speech, sounds, touch, or other sources).
Speed of Closure	The ability to quickly make sense of, combine, and organize information into meaningful patterns.
Number Facility	The ability to add, subtract, multiply, or divide quickly and correctly.
Mathematical Reasoning	The ability to choose the right mathematical methods or formulas to solve a problem.
Memorization	The ability to remember information such as words, numbers, pictures, and procedures.
Depth Perception	The ability to judge which of several objects is closer or farther away from you, or to judge the distance between you and an object.
Auditory Attention	The ability to focus on a single source of sound in the presence of other distracting sounds.
Visual Color Discrimination	The ability to match or detect differences between colors, including shades of color and brightness.
Hearing Sensitivity	The ability to detect or tell the differences between sounds that vary in pitch and loudness.
Finger Dexterity	The ability to make precisely coordinated movements of the fingers of one or both hands to grasp, manipulate, or assemble very small objects.
Glare Sensitivity	The ability to see objects in the presence of glare or bright lighting.
Trunk Strength	The ability to use your abdominal and lower back muscles to support part of the body repeatedly or continuously over time without 'giving out' or fatiguing.
Reaction Time	The ability to quickly respond (with the hand, finger, or foot) to a signal (sound, light, picture) when it appears.
Multilimb Coordination	The ability to coordinate two or more limbs (for example, two arms, two legs, or one leg and one arm) while sitting, standing, or lying down. It does not involve performing the activities while the whole body is in motion.
Stamina	The ability to exert yourself physically over long periods of time without getting winded or out of breath.
Control Precision	The ability to quickly and repeatedly adjust the controls of a machine or a vehicle to exact positions.
Gross Body Coordination	The ability to coordinate the movement of your arms, legs, and torso together when the whole body is in motion.
Speed of Limb Movement	The ability to quickly move the arms and legs.

Spatial Orientation	The ability to know your location in relation to the environment or to know where other objects are in relation to you.
Wrist-Finger Speed	The ability to make fast, simple, repeated movements of the fingers, hands, and wrists.
Static Strength	The ability to exert maximum muscle force to lift, push, pull, or carry objects.
Arm-Hand Steadiness	The ability to keep your hand and arm steady while moving your arm or while holding your arm and hand in one position.
Peripheral Vision	The ability to see objects or movement of objects to one's side when the eyes are looking ahead.
Night Vision	The ability to see under low light conditions.
Sound Localization	The ability to tell the direction from which a sound originated.
Gross Body Equilibrium	The ability to keep or regain your body balance or stay upright when in an unstable position.
Manual Dexterity	The ability to quickly move your hand, your hand together with your arm, or your two hands to grasp, manipulate, or assemble objects.
Extent Flexibility	The ability to bend, stretch, twist, or reach with your body, arms, and/or legs.
Dynamic Flexibility	The ability to quickly and repeatedly bend, stretch, twist, or reach out with your body, arms, and/or legs.
Dynamic Strength	The ability to exert muscle force repeatedly or continuously over time. This involves muscular endurance and resistance to muscle fatigue.
Explosive Strength	The ability to use short bursts of muscle force to propel oneself (as in jumping or sprinting), or to throw an object.
Rate Control	The ability to time your movements or the movement of a piece of equipment in anticipation of changes in the speed and/or direction of a moving object or scene.
Response Orientation	The ability to choose quickly between two or more movements in response to two or more different signals (lights, sounds, pictures). It includes the speed with which the correct response is started with the hand, foot, or other body part.

Work_Activity	**Work_Activity Definitions**
Communicating with Supervisors, Peers, or Subordin	Providing information to supervisors, co-workers, and subordinates by telephone, in written form, e-mail, or in person.
Making Decisions and Solving Problems	Analyzing information and evaluating results to choose the best solution and solve problems.
Getting Information	Observing, receiving, and otherwise obtaining information from all relevant sources.
Communicating with Persons Outside Organization	Communicating with people outside the organization, representing the organization to customers, the public, government, and other external sources. This information can be exchanged in person, in writing, or by telephone or e-mail.
Updating and Using Relevant Knowledge	Keeping up-to-date technically and applying new knowledge to your job.
Coordinating the Work and Activities of Others	Getting members of a group to work together to accomplish tasks.
Establishing and Maintaining Interpersonal Relatio	Developing constructive and cooperative working relationships with others, and maintaining them over time.
Identifying Objects, Actions, and Events	Identifying information by categorizing, estimating, recognizing differences or similarities, and detecting changes in circumstances or events.
Monitoring and Controlling Resources	Monitoring and controlling resources and overseeing the spending of money.
Analyzing Data or Information	Identifying the underlying principles, reasons, or facts of information by breaking down information or data into separate parts.
Organizing, Planning, and Prioritizing Work	Developing specific goals and plans to prioritize, organize, and accomplish your work.
Guiding, Directing, and Motivating Subordinates	Providing guidance and direction to subordinates, including setting performance standards and monitoring performance.
Resolving Conflicts and Negotiating with Others	Handling complaints, settling disputes, and resolving grievances and conflicts, or otherwise negotiating with others.
Evaluating Information to Determine Compliance wit	Using relevant information and individual judgment to determine whether events or processes comply with laws, regulations, or standards.
Scheduling Work and Activities	Scheduling events, programs, and activities, as well as the work of others.
Monitor Processes, Materials, or Surroundings	Monitoring and reviewing information from materials, events, or the environment, to detect or assess problems.

Thinking Creatively	Developing, designing, or creating new applications, ideas, relationships, systems, or products, including artistic contributions.
Judging the Qualities of Things, Services, or Peop	Assessing the value, importance, or quality of things or people.
Developing Objectives and Strategies	Establishing long-range objectives and specifying the strategies and actions to achieve them.
Interacting With Computers	Using computers and computer systems (including hardware and software) to program, write software, set up functions, enter data, or process information.
Estimating the Quantifiable Characteristics of Pro	Estimating sizes, distances, and quantities; or determining time, costs, resources, or materials needed to perform a work activity.
Provide Consultation and Advice to Others	Providing guidance and expert advice to management or other groups on technical, systems-, or process-related topics.
Processing Information	Compiling, coding, categorizing, calculating, tabulating, auditing, or verifying information or data.
Interpreting the Meaning of Information for Others	Translating or explaining what information means and how it can be used.
Documenting/Recording Information	Entering, transcribing, recording, storing, or maintaining information in written or electronic/magnetic form.
Developing and Building Teams	Encouraging and building mutual trust, respect, and cooperation among team members.
Coaching and Developing Others	Identifying the developmental needs of others and coaching, mentoring, or otherwise helping others to improve their knowledge or skills.
Inspecting Equipment, Structures, or Material	Inspecting equipment, structures, or materials to identify the cause of errors or other problems or defects.
Training and Teaching Others	Identifying the educational needs of others, developing formal educational or training programs or classes, and teaching or instructing others.
Performing Administrative Activities	Performing day-to-day administrative tasks such as maintaining information files and processing paperwork.
Staffing Organizational Units	Recruiting, interviewing, selecting, hiring, and promoting employees in an organization.
Drafting, Laying Out, and Specifying Technical Dev	Providing documentation, detailed instructions, drawings, or specifications to tell others about how devices, parts, equipment, or structures are to be fabricated, constructed, assembled, modified, maintained, or used.
Performing for or Working Directly with the Public	Performing for people or dealing directly with the public. This includes serving customers in restaurants and stores, and receiving clients or guests.
Selling or Influencing Others	Convincing others to buy merchandise/goods or to otherwise change their minds or actions.
Performing General Physical Activities	Performing physical activities that require considerable use of your arms and legs and moving your whole body, such as climbing, lifting, balancing, walking, stooping, and handling of materials.
Repairing and Maintaining Mechanical Equipment	Servicing, repairing, adjusting, and testing machines, devices, moving parts, and equipment that operate primarily on the basis of mechanical (not electronic) principles.
Repairing and Maintaining Electronic Equipment	Servicing, repairing, calibrating, regulating, fine-tuning, or testing machines, devices, and equipment that operate primarily on the basis of electrical or electronic (not mechanical) principles.
Assisting and Caring for Others	Providing personal assistance, medical attention, emotional support, or other personal care to others such as coworkers, customers, or patients.
Handling and Moving Objects	Using hands and arms in handling, installing, positioning, and moving materials, and manipulating things.
Operating Vehicles, Mechanized Devices, or Equipme	Running, maneuvering, navigating, or driving vehicles or mechanized equipment, such as forklifts, passenger vehicles, aircraft, or water craft.
Controlling Machines and Processes	Using either control mechanisms or direct physical activity to operate machines or processes (not including computers or vehicles).

Work_Context	**Work_Context Definitions**
Telephone	How often do you have telephone conversations in this job?
Face-to-Face Discussions	How often do you have to have face-to-face discussions with individuals or teams in this job?
Electronic Mail	How often do you use electronic mail in this job?
Freedom to Make Decisions	How much decision making freedom, without supervision, does the job offer?
Structured versus Unstructured Work	To what extent is this job structured for the worker, rather than allowing the worker to determine tasks, priorities, and goals?

Frequency of Decision Making	How frequently is the worker required to make decisions that affect other people. the financial resources. and/or the image and reputation of the organization?
Indoors, Environmentally Controlled	How often does this job require working indoors in environmentally controlled conditions?
Contact With Others	How much does this job require the worker to be in contact with others (face-to-face, by telephone, or otherwise) in order to perform it?
Importance of Being Exact or Accurate	How important is being very exact or highly accurate in performing this job?
Impact of Decisions on Co-workers or Company Resul	How do the decisions an employee makes impact the results of co-workers, clients or the company?
Indoors, Not Environmentally Controlled	How often does this job require working indoors in non-controlled environmental conditions (e.g., warehouse without heat)?
Coordinate or Lead Others	How important is it to coordinate or lead others in accomplishing work activities in this job?
Responsibility for Outcomes and Results	How responsible is the worker for work outcomes and results of other workers?
Letters and Memos	How often does the job require written letters and memos?
Time Pressure	How often does this job require the worker to meet strict deadlines?
Responsible for Others' Health and Safety	How much responsibility is there for the health and safety of others in this job?
Work With Work Group or Team	How important is it to work with others in a group or team in this job?
Wear Common Protective or Safety Equipment such as	How much does this job require wearing common protective or safety equipment such as safety shoes. glasses. gloves, hard hats or live jackets?
Sounds, Noise Levels Are Distracting or Uncomforta	How much does this job require working exposed to sounds and noise levels that are distracting or uncomfortable?
Spend Time Sitting	How much does this job require sitting?
Deal With External Customers	How important is it to work with external customers or the public in this job?
Importance of Repeating Same Tasks	How important is repeating the same physical activities (e.g., key entry) or mental activities (e.g., checking entries in a ledger) over and over, without stopping, to performing this job?
Exposed to Hazardous Equipment	How often does this job require exposure to hazardous equipment?
Frequency of Conflict Situations	How often are there conflict situations the employee has to face in this job?
Exposed to Contaminants	How often does this job require working exposed to contaminants (such as pollutants, gases, dust or odors)?
Spend Time Standing	How much does this job require standing?
Degree of Automation	How automated is the job?
Extremely Bright or Inadequate Lighting	How often does this job require working in extremely bright or inadequate lighting conditions?
In an Enclosed Vehicle or Equipment	How often does this job require working in a closed vehicle or equipment (e.g., car)?
Physical Proximity	To what extent does this job require the worker to perform job tasks in close physical proximity to other people?
Very Hot or Cold Temperatures	How often does this job require working in very hot (above 90 F degrees) or very cold (below 32 F degrees) temperatures?
Level of Competition	To what extent does this job require the worker to compete or to be aware of competitive pressures?
Deal With Unpleasant or Angry People	How frequently does the worker have to deal with unpleasant, angry, or discourteous individuals as part of the job requirements?
Pace Determined by Speed of Equipment	How important is it to this job that the pace is determined by the speed of equipment or machinery? (This does not refer to keeping busy at all times on this job.)
Spend Time Making Repetitive Motions	How much does this job require making repetitive motions?
Exposed to Hazardous Conditions	How often does this job require exposure to hazardous conditions?
Spend Time Walking and Running	How much does this job require walking and running?
Public Speaking	How often do you have to perform public speaking in this job?
Outdoors, Exposed to Weather	How often does this job require working outdoors, exposed to all weather conditions?
Consequence of Error	How serious would the result usually be if the worker made a mistake that was not readily correctable?
Exposed to High Places	How often does this job require exposure to high places?
Exposed to Minor Burns, Cuts, Bites, or Stings	How often does this job require exposure to minor burns, cuts, bites, or stings?
Cramped Work Space, Awkward Positions	How often does this job require working in cramped work spaces that requires getting into awkward positions?

Wear Specialized Protective or Safety Equipment su	How much does this job require wearing specialized protective or safety equipment such as breathing apparatus. safety harness. full protection suits, or radiation protection?
Spend Time Using Your Hands to Handle, Control, or	How much does this job require using your hands to handle. control, or feel objects, tools or controls?
Outdoors, Under Cover	How often does this job require working outdoors, under cover (e.g.. structure with roof but no walls)?
In an Open Vehicle or Equipment	How often does this job require working in an open vehicle or equipment (e.g.. tractor)?
Spend Time Climbing Ladders. Scaffolds. or Poles	How much does this job require climbing ladders. scaffolds. or poles?
Spend Time Bending or Twisting the Body	How much does this job require bending or twisting your body?
Spend Time Kneeling. Crouching. Stooping, or Crawl	How much does this job require kneeling, crouching. stooping or crawling?
Spend Time Keeping or Regaining Balance	How much does this job require keeping or regaining your balance?
Deal With Physically Aggressive People	How frequently does this job require the worker to deal with physical aggression of violent individuals?
Exposed to Whole Body Vibration	How often does this job require exposure to whole body vibration (e.g., operate a jackhammer)?
Exposed to Disease or Infections	How often does this job require exposure to disease/infections?
Exposed to Radiation	How often does this job require exposure to radiation?

Job Zone Component	Job Zone Component Definitions
Title	Job Zone Five: Extensive Preparation Needed
Overall Experience	Extensive skill, knowledge, and experience are needed for these occupations. Many require more than five years of experience. For example. surgeons must complete four years of college and an additional five to seven years of specialized medical training to be able to do their job.
Job Training	Employees may need some on-the-job training, but most of these occupations assume that the person will already have the required skills, knowledge, work-related experience. and/or training.
Job Zone Examples	These occupations often involve coordinating, training. supervising, or managing the activities of others to accomplish goals. Very advanced communication and organizational skills are required. Examples include athletic trainers, lawyers, managing editors, phyicists, social psychologists, and surgeons.
SVP Range	(8.0 and above)
Education	A bachelor's degree is the minimum formal education required for these occupations. However, many also require graduate school. For example, they may require a master's degree, and some require a Ph.D., M.D., or J.D. (law degree).

Work_Styles	Work_Styles Definitions
Analytical Thinking	Job requires analyzing information and using logic to address work-related issues and problems.
Dependability	Job requires being reliable, responsible, and dependable, and fulfilling obligations.
Integrity	Job requires being honest and ethical.
Attention to Detail	Job requires being careful about detail and thorough in completing work tasks.
Stress Tolerance	Job requires accepting criticism and dealing calmly and effectively with high stress situations.
Achievement/Effort	Job requires establishing and maintaining personally challenging achievement goals and exerting effort toward mastering tasks.
Self Control	Job requires maintaining composure, keeping emotions in check, controlling anger, and avoiding aggressive behavior. even in very difficult situations.
Persistence	Job requires persistence in the face of obstacles.
Adaptability/Flexibility	Job requires being open to change (positive or negative) and to considerable variety in the workplace.
Cooperation	Job requires being pleasant with others on the job and displaying a good-natured, cooperative attitude.
Leadership	Job requires a willingness to lead, take charge, and offer opinions and direction.
Initiative	Job requires a willingness to take on responsibilities and challenges.

Innovation	Job requires creativity and alternative thinking to develop new ideas for and answers to work-related problems.
Concern for Others	Job requires being sensitive to others' needs and feelings and being understanding and helpful on the job.
Independence	Job requires developing one's own ways of doing things, guiding oneself with little or no supervision, and depending on oneself to get things done.
Social Orientation	Job requires preferring to work with others rather than alone, and being personally connected with others on the job.

11-9051.00 - Food Service Managers

Plan, direct, or coordinate activities of an organization or department that serves food and beverages.

Tasks

1) Investigate and resolve complaints regarding food quality, service, or accommodations.

2) Monitor compliance with health and fire regulations regarding food preparation and serving, and building maintenance in lodging and dining facilities.

3) Test cooked food by tasting and smelling it in order to ensure palatability and flavor conformity.

4) Establish standards for personnel performance and customer service.

5) Schedule and receive food and beverage deliveries, checking delivery contents in order to verify product quality and quantity.

6) Review work procedures and operational problems in order to determine ways to improve service, performance, and/or safety.

7) Perform some food preparation or service tasks such as cooking, clearing tables, and serving food and drinks when necessary.

8) Order and purchase equipment and supplies.

9) Schedule staff hours and assign duties.

10) Organize and direct worker training programs, resolve personnel problems, hire new staff, and evaluate employee performance in dining and lodging facilities.

11) Maintain food and equipment inventories, and keep inventory records.

12) Estimate food, liquor, wine, and other beverage consumption in order to anticipate amounts to be purchased or requisitioned.

13) Keep records required by government agencies regarding sanitation, and food subsidies when appropriate.

14) Arrange for equipment maintenance and repairs, and coordinate a variety of services such as waste removal and pest control.

15) Monitor budgets and payroll records, and review financial transactions in order to ensure that expenditures are authorized and budgeted.

16) Coordinate assignments of cooking personnel in order to ensure economical use of food and timely preparation.

17) Review menus and analyze recipes in order to determine labor and overhead costs, and assign prices to menu items.

18) Record the number, type, and cost of items sold in order to determine which items may be unpopular or less profitable.

19) Assess staffing needs, and recruit staff using methods such as newspaper advertisements or attendance at job fairs.

20) Plan menus and food utilization based on anticipated number of guests, nutritional value, palatability, popularity, and costs.

21) Greet guests, escort them to their seats, and present them with menus and wine lists.

22) Schedule use of facilities or catering services for events such as banquets or receptions, and negotiate details of arrangements with clients.

23) Establish and enforce nutritional standards for dining establishments based on accepted industry standards.

24) Monitor employee and patron activities in order to ensure liquor regulations are obeyed.

25) Take dining reservations.

26) Create specialty dishes and develop recipes to be used in dining facilities.

Knowledge	Knowledge Definitions
Customer and Personal Service	Knowledge of principles and processes for providing customer and personal services. This includes customer needs assessment, meeting quality standards for services, and evaluation of customer satisfaction.
Administration and Management	Knowledge of business and management principles involved in strategic planning, resource allocation, human resources modeling, leadership technique, production methods, and coordination of people and resources.
Production and Processing	Knowledge of raw materials, production processes, quality control, costs, and other techniques for maximizing the effective manufacture and distribution of goods.
Sales and Marketing	Knowledge of principles and methods for showing, promoting, and selling products or services. This includes marketing strategy and tactics, product demonstration, sales techniques, and sales control systems.
Food Production	Knowledge of techniques and equipment for planting, growing, and harvesting food products (both plant and animal) for consumption, including storage/handling techniques.
Mathematics	Knowledge of arithmetic, algebra, geometry, calculus, statistics, and their applications.
Clerical	Knowledge of administrative and clerical procedures and systems such as word processing, managing files and records, stenography and transcription, designing forms, and other office procedures and terminology.
Public Safety and Security	Knowledge of relevant equipment, policies, procedures, and strategies to promote effective local, state, or national security operations for the protection of people, data, property, and institutions.
English Language	Knowledge of the structure and content of the English language including the meaning and spelling of words, rules of composition, and grammar.
Education and Training	Knowledge of principles and methods for curriculum and training design, teaching and instruction for individuals and groups, and the measurement of training effects.
Personnel and Human Resources	Knowledge of principles and procedures for personnel recruitment, selection, training, compensation and benefits, labor relations and negotiation, and personnel information systems.
Economics and Accounting	Knowledge of economic and accounting principles and practices, the financial markets, banking and the analysis and reporting of financial data.
Psychology	Knowledge of human behavior and performance; individual differences in ability, personality, and interests; learning and motivation; psychological research methods; and the assessment and treatment of behavioral and affective disorders.
Law and Government	Knowledge of laws, legal codes, court procedures, precedents, government regulations, executive orders, agency rules, and the democratic political process.
Computers and Electronics	Knowledge of circuit boards, processors, chips, electronic equipment, and computer hardware and software, including applications and programming.
Mechanical	Knowledge of machines and tools, including their designs, uses, repair, and maintenance.
Communications and Media	Knowledge of media production, communication, and dissemination techniques and methods. This includes alternative ways to inform and entertain via written, oral, and visual media.
Chemistry	Knowledge of the chemical composition, structure, and properties of substances and of the chemical processes and transformations that they undergo. This includes uses of chemicals and their interactions, danger signs, production techniques, and disposal methods.
Sociology and Anthropology	Knowledge of group behavior and dynamics, societal trends and influences, human migrations, ethnicity, cultures and their history and origins.
Telecommunications	Knowledge of transmission, broadcasting, switching, control, and operation of telecommunications systems.
Foreign Language	Knowledge of the structure and content of a foreign (non-English) language including the meaning and spelling of words, rules of composition and grammar, and pronunciation.
Transportation	Knowledge of principles and methods for moving people or goods by air, rail, sea, or road, including the relative costs and benefits.

Engineering and Technology	Knowledge of the practical application of engineering science and technology. This includes applying principles, techniques, procedures, and equipment to the design and production of various goods and services.
Philosophy and Theology	Knowledge of different philosophical systems and religions. This includes their basic principles, values, ethics, ways of thinking, customs, practices, and their impact on human culture.
Design	Knowledge of design techniques, tools, and principles involved in production of precision technical plans, blueprints, drawings, and models.
Geography	Knowledge of principles and methods for describing the features of land, sea, and air masses, including their physical characteristics, locations, interrelationships, and distribution of plant, animal, and human life.
Therapy and Counseling	Knowledge of principles, methods, and procedures for diagnosis, treatment, and rehabilitation of physical and mental dysfunctions, and for career counseling and guidance.
Building and Construction	Knowledge of materials, methods, and the tools involved in the construction or repair of houses, buildings, or other structures such as highways and roads.
Physics	Knowledge and prediction of physical principles, laws, their interrelationships, and applications to understanding fluid, material, and atmospheric dynamics, and mechanical, electrical, atomic and sub-atomic structures and processes.
Medicine and Dentistry	Knowledge of the information and techniques needed to diagnose and treat human injuries, diseases, and deformities. This includes symptoms, treatment alternatives, drug properties and interactions, and preventive health-care measures.
Biology	Knowledge of plant and animal organisms, their tissues, cells, functions, interdependencies, and interactions with each other and the environment.
History and Archeology	Knowledge of historical events and their causes, indicators, and effects on civilizations and cultures.
Fine Arts	Knowledge of the theory and techniques required to compose, produce, and perform works of music, dance, visual arts, drama, and sculpture.

Skills	Skills Definitions
Active Listening	Giving full attention to what other people are saying, taking time to understand the points being made, asking questions as appropriate, and not interrupting at inappropriate times.
Instructing	Teaching others how to do something.
Speaking	Talking to others to convey information effectively.
Time Management	Managing one's own time and the time of others.
Monitoring	Monitoring/Assessing performance of yourself, other individuals, or organizations to make improvements or take corrective action.
Learning Strategies	Selecting and using training/instructional methods and procedures appropriate for the situation when learning or teaching new things.
Critical Thinking	Using logic and reasoning to identify the strengths and weaknesses of alternative solutions, conclusions or approaches to problems.
Management of Personnel Resources	Motivating, developing, and directing people as they work, identifying the best people for the job.
Judgment and Decision Making	Considering the relative costs and benefits of potential actions to choose the most appropriate one.
Social Perceptiveness	Being aware of others' reactions and understanding why they react as they do.
Active Learning	Understanding the implications of new information for both current and future problem-solving and decision-making.
Reading Comprehension	Understanding written sentences and paragraphs in work related documents.
Service Orientation	Actively looking for ways to help people.
Coordination	Adjusting actions in relation to others' actions.
Management of Financial Resources	Determining how money will be spent to get the work done, and accounting for these expenditures.
Quality Control Analysis	Conducting tests and inspections of products, services, or processes to evaluate quality or performance.
Mathematics	Using mathematics to solve problems.
Writing	Communicating effectively in writing as appropriate for the needs of the audience.
Troubleshooting	Determining causes of operating errors and deciding what to do about it.
Management of Material Resources	Obtaining and seeing to the appropriate use of equipment, facilities, and materials needed to do certain work.

Negotiation	Bringing others together and trying to reconcile differences.
Complex Problem Solving	Identifying complex problems and reviewing related information to develop and evaluate options and implement solutions.
Equipment Maintenance	Performing routine maintenance on equipment and determining when and what kind of maintenance is needed.
Persuasion	Persuading others to change their minds or behavior.
Operations Analysis	Analyzing needs and product requirements to create a design.
Systems Evaluation	Identifying measures or indicators of system performance and the actions needed to improve or correct performance, relative to the goals of the system.
Equipment Selection	Determining the kind of tools and equipment needed to do a job.
Operation and Control	Controlling operations of equipment or systems.
Operation Monitoring	Watching gauges, dials, or other indicators to make sure a machine is working properly.
Systems Analysis	Determining how a system should work and how changes in conditions, operations, and the environment will affect outcomes.
Repairing	Repairing machines or systems using the needed tools.
Technology Design	Generating or adapting equipment and technology to serve user needs.
Installation	Installing equipment, machines, wiring, or programs to meet specifications.
Science	Using scientific rules and methods to solve problems.
Programming	Writing computer programs for various purposes.

Ability	Ability Definitions
Oral Comprehension	The ability to listen to and understand information and ideas presented through spoken words and sentences.
Oral Expression	The ability to communicate information and ideas in speaking so others will understand.
Problem Sensitivity	The ability to tell when something is wrong or is likely to go wrong. It does not involve solving the problem, only recognizing there is a problem.
Speech Clarity	The ability to speak clearly so others can understand you.
Deductive Reasoning	The ability to apply general rules to specific problems to produce answers that make sense.
Written Comprehension	The ability to read and understand information and ideas presented in writing.
Speech Recognition	The ability to identify and understand the speech of another person.
Inductive Reasoning	The ability to combine pieces of information to form general rules or conclusions (includes finding a relationship among seemingly unrelated events).
Information Ordering	The ability to arrange things or actions in a certain order or pattern according to a specific rule or set of rules (e.g., patterns of numbers, letters, words, pictures, mathematical operations).
Near Vision	The ability to see details at close range (within a few feet of the observer).
Perceptual Speed	The ability to quickly and accurately compare similarities and differences among sets of letters, numbers, objects, pictures, or patterns. The things to be compared may be presented at the same time or one after the other. This ability also includes comparing a presented object with a remembered object.
Category Flexibility	The ability to generate or use different sets of rules for combining or grouping things in different ways.
Selective Attention	The ability to concentrate on a task over a period of time without being distracted.
Time Sharing	The ability to shift back and forth between two or more activities or sources of information (such as speech, sounds, touch, or other sources).
Flexibility of Closure	The ability to identify or detect a known pattern (a figure, object, word, or sound) that is hidden in other distracting material.
Written Expression	The ability to communicate information and ideas in writing so others will understand.
Fluency of Ideas	The ability to come up with a number of ideas about a topic (the number of ideas is important, not their quality, correctness, or creativity).
Number Facility	The ability to add, subtract, multiply, or divide quickly and correctly.
Visualization	The ability to imagine how something will look after it is moved around or when its parts are moved or rearranged.
Far Vision	The ability to see details at a distance.
Mathematical Reasoning	The ability to choose the right mathematical methods or formulas to solve a problem.

Originality	The ability to come up with unusual or clever ideas about a given topic or situation, or to develop creative ways to solve a problem.
Visual Color Discrimination	The ability to match or detect differences between colors, including shades of color and brightness.
Speed of Closure	The ability to quickly make sense of, combine, and organize information into meaningful patterns.
Memorization	The ability to remember information such as words, numbers, pictures, and procedures.
Auditory Attention	The ability to focus on a single source of sound in the presence of other distracting sounds.
Arm-Hand Steadiness	The ability to keep your hand and arm steady while moving your arm or while holding your arm and hand in one position.
Hearing Sensitivity	The ability to detect or tell the differences between sounds that vary in pitch and loudness.
Manual Dexterity	The ability to quickly move your hand, your hand together with your arm, or your two hands to grasp, manipulate, or assemble objects.
Gross Body Coordination	The ability to coordinate the movement of your arms, legs, and torso together when the whole body is in motion.
Trunk Strength	The ability to use your abdominal and lower back muscles to support part of the body repeatedly or continuously over time without 'giving out' or fatiguing.
Extent Flexibility	The ability to bend, stretch, twist, or reach with your body, arms, and/or legs.
Static Strength	The ability to exert maximum muscle force to lift, push, pull, or carry objects.
Finger Dexterity	The ability to make precisely coordinated movements of the fingers of one or both hands to grasp, manipulate, or assemble very small objects.
Stamina	The ability to exert yourself physically over long periods of time without getting winded or out of breath.
Multilimb Coordination	The ability to coordinate two or more limbs (for example, two arms, two legs, or one leg and one arm) while sitting, standing, or lying down. It does not involve performing the activities while the whole body is in motion.
Depth Perception	The ability to judge which of several objects is closer or farther away from you, or to judge the distance between you and an object.
Speed of Limb Movement	The ability to quickly move the arms and legs.
Control Precision	The ability to quickly and repeatedly adjust the controls of a machine or a vehicle to exact positions.
Wrist-Finger Speed	The ability to make fast, simple, repeated movements of the fingers, hands, and wrists.
Dynamic Strength	The ability to exert muscle force repeatedly or continuously over time. This involves muscular endurance and resistance to muscle fatigue.
Reaction Time	The ability to quickly respond (with the hand, finger, or foot) to a signal (sound, light, picture) when it appears.
Response Orientation	The ability to choose quickly between two or more movements in response to two or more different signals (lights, sounds, pictures). It includes the speed with which the correct response is started with the hand, foot, or other body part.
Gross Body Equilibrium	The ability to keep or regain your body balance or stay upright when in an unstable position.
Rate Control	The ability to time your movements or the movement of a piece of equipment in anticipation of changes in the speed and/or direction of a moving object or scene.
Spatial Orientation	The ability to know your location in relation to the environment or to know where other objects are in relation to you.
Peripheral Vision	The ability to see objects or movement of objects to one's side when the eyes are looking ahead.
Dynamic Flexibility	The ability to quickly and repeatedly bend, stretch, twist, or reach out with your body, arms, and/or legs.
Sound Localization	The ability to tell the direction from which a sound originated.
Glare Sensitivity	The ability to see objects in the presence of glare or bright lighting.
Night Vision	The ability to see under low light conditions.
Explosive Strength	The ability to use short bursts of muscle force to propel oneself (as in jumping or sprinting), or to throw an object.

Work_Activity	Work_Activity Definitions
Making Decisions and Solving Problems	Analyzing information and evaluating results to choose the best solution and solve problems.
Resolving Conflicts and Negotiating with Others	Handling complaints, settling disputes, and resolving grievances and conflicts, or otherwise negotiating with others.

Communicating with Supervisors, Peers, or Subordin	Providing information to supervisors, co-workers, and subordinates by telephone, in written form, e-mail, or in person.
Establishing and Maintaining Interpersonal Relatio	Developing constructive and cooperative working relationships with others, and maintaining them over time.
Organizing, Planning, and Prioritizing Work	Developing specific goals and plans to prioritize, organize, and accomplish your work.
Getting Information	Observing, receiving, and otherwise obtaining information from all relevant sources.
Monitoring and Controlling Resources	Monitoring and controlling resources and overseeing the spending of money.
Evaluating Information to Determine Compliance wit	Using relevant information and individual judgment to determine whether events or processes comply with laws, regulations, or standards.
Guiding, Directing, and Motivating Subordinates	Providing guidance and direction to subordinates, including setting performance standards and monitoring performance.
Training and Teaching Others	Identifying the educational needs of others, developing formal educational or training programs or classes, and teaching or instructing others.
Monitor Processes, Materials, or Surroundings	Monitoring and reviewing information from materials, events, or the environment, to detect or assess problems.
Performing for or Working Directly with the Public	Performing for people or dealing directly with the public. This includes serving customers in restaurants and stores, and receiving clients or guests.
Coaching and Developing Others	Identifying the developmental needs of others and coaching, mentoring, or otherwise helping others to improve their knowledge or skills.
Scheduling Work and Activities	Scheduling events, programs, and activities, as well as the work of others.
Developing and Building Teams	Encouraging and building mutual trust, respect, and cooperation among team members.
Coordinating the Work and Activities of Others	Getting members of a group to work together to accomplish tasks.
Inspecting Equipment, Structures, or Material	Inspecting equipment, structures, or materials to identify the cause of errors or other problems or defects.
Identifying Objects, Actions, and Events	Identifying information by categorizing, estimating, recognizing differences or similarities, and detecting changes in circumstances or events.
Performing Administrative Activities	Performing day-to-day administrative tasks such as maintaining information files and processing paperwork.
Judging the Qualities of Things, Services, or Peop	Assessing the value, importance, or quality of things or people.
Assisting and Caring for Others	Providing personal assistance, medical attention, emotional support, or other personal care to others such as coworkers, customers, or patients.
Communicating with Persons Outside Organization	Communicating with people outside the organization, representing the organization to customers, the public, government, and other external sources. This information can be exchanged in person, in writing, or by telephone or e-mail.
Staffing Organizational Units	Recruiting, interviewing, selecting, hiring, and promoting employees in an organization.
Updating and Using Relevant Knowledge	Keeping up-to-date technically and applying new knowledge to your job.
Thinking Creatively	Developing, designing, or creating new applications, ideas, relationships, systems, or products, including artistic contributions.
Estimating the Quantifiable Characteristics of Pro	Estimating sizes, distances, and quantities; or determining time, costs, resources, or materials needed to perform a work activity.
Performing General Physical Activities	Performing physical activities that require considerable use of your arms and legs and moving your whole body, such as climbing, lifting, balancing, walking, stooping, and handling of materials.
Selling or Influencing Others	Convincing others to buy merchandise/goods or to otherwise change their minds or actions.
Processing Information	Compiling, coding, categorizing, calculating, tabulating, auditing, or verifying information or data.
Interacting With Computers	Using computers and computer systems (including hardware and software) to program, write software, set up functions, enter data, or process information.
Documenting/Recording Information	Entering, transcribing, recording, storing, or maintaining information in written or electronic/magnetic form.
Controlling Machines and Processes	Using either control mechanisms or direct physical activity to operate machines or processes (not including computers or vehicles).

Analyzing Data or Information	Identifying the underlying principles, reasons, or facts of information by breaking down information or data into separate parts.
Handling and Moving Objects	Using hands and arms in handling, installing, positioning, and moving materials, and manipulating things.
Developing Objectives and Strategies	Establishing long-range objectives and specifying the strategies and actions to achieve them.
Interpreting the Meaning of Information for Others	Translating or explaining what information means and how it can be used.
Provide Consultation and Advice to Others	Providing guidance and expert advice to management or other groups on technical, systems-, or process-related topics.
Repairing and Maintaining Mechanical Equipment	Servicing, repairing, adjusting, and testing machines, devices, moving parts, and equipment that operate primarily on the basis of mechanical (not electronic) principles.
Repairing and Maintaining Electronic Equipment	Servicing, repairing, calibrating, regulating, fine-tuning, or testing machines, devices, and equipment that operate primarily on the basis of electrical or electronic (not mechanical) principles.
Operating Vehicles, Mechanized Devices, or Equipme	Running, maneuvering, navigating, or driving vehicles or mechanized equipment, such as forklifts, passenger vehicles, aircraft, or water craft.
Drafting, Laying Out, and Specifying Technical Dev	Providing documentation, detailed instructions, drawings, or specifications to tell others about how devices, parts, equipment, or structures are to be fabricated, constructed, assembled, modified, maintained, or used.

Work_Context	Work_Context Definitions
Work With Work Group or Team	How important is it to work with others in a group or team in this job?
Responsibility for Outcomes and Results	How responsible is the worker for work outcomes and results of other workers?
Contact With Others	How much does this job require the worker to be in contact with others (face-to-face, by telephone, or otherwise) in order to perform it?
Deal With External Customers	How important is it to work with external customers or the public in this job?
Responsible for Others' Health and Safety	How much responsibility is there for the health and safety of others in this job?
Telephone	How often do you have telephone conversations in this job?
Face-to-Face Discussions	How often do you have to have face-to-face discussions with individuals or teams in this job?
Freedom to Make Decisions	How much decision making freedom, without supervision, does the job offer?
Structured versus Unstructured Work	To what extent is this job structured for the worker, rather than allowing the worker to determine tasks, priorities, and goals?
Frequency of Decision Making	How frequently is the worker required to make decisions that affect other people, the financial resources, and/or the image and reputation of the organization?
Spend Time Standing	How much does this job require standing?
Importance of Being Exact or Accurate	How important is being very exact or highly accurate in performing this job?
Physical Proximity	To what extent does this job require the worker to perform job tasks in close physical proximity to other people?
Coordinate or Lead Others	How important is it to coordinate or lead others in accomplishing work activities in this job?
Indoors, Environmentally Controlled	How often does this job require working indoors in environmentally controlled conditions?
Impact of Decisions on Co-workers or Company Resul	How do the decisions an employee makes impact the results of co-workers, clients or the company?
Spend Time Using Your Hands to Handle, Control, or	How much does this job require using your hands to handle, control, or feel objects, tools or controls?
Spend Time Walking and Running	How much does this job require walking and running?
Time Pressure	How often does this job require the worker to meet strict deadlines?
Deal With Unpleasant or Angry People	How frequently does the worker have to deal with unpleasant, angry, or discourteous individuals as part of the job requirements?
Very Hot or Cold Temperatures	How often does this job require working in very hot (above 90 F degrees) or very cold (below 32 F degrees) temperatures?
Wear Common Protective or Safety Equipment such as	How much does this job require wearing common protective or safety equipment such as safety shoes, glasses, gloves, hard hats or live jackets?
Spend Time Making Repetitive Motions	How much does this job require making repetitive motions?

Frequency of Conflict Situations	How often are there conflict situations the employee has to face in this job?
Exposed to Minor Burns, Cuts, Bites, or Stings	How often does this job require exposure to minor burns, cuts, bites, or stings?
Letters and Memos	How often does the job require written letters and memos?
Importance of Repeating Same Tasks	How important is repeating the same physical activities (e.g., key entry) or mental activities (e.g., checking entries in a ledger) over and over, without stopping, to performing this job?
Level of Competition	To what extent does this job require the worker to compete or to be aware of competitive pressures?
Sounds, Noise Levels Are Distracting or Uncomforta	How often does this job require working exposed to sounds and noise levels that are distracting or uncomfortable?
Spend Time Bending or Twisting the Body	How much does this job require bending or twisting your body?
Electronic Mail	How often do you use electronic mail in this job?
Degree of Automation	How automated is the job?
Consequence of Error	How serious would the result usually be if the worker made a mistake that was not readily correctable?
Exposed to Contaminants	How often does this job require working exposed to contaminants (such as pollutants, gases, dust or odors)?
Public Speaking	How often do you have to perform public speaking in this job?
Spend Time Kneeling, Crouching, Stooping, or Crawl	How much does this job require kneeling, crouching, stooping or crawling?
Outdoors, Exposed to Weather	How often does this job require working outdoors, exposed to all weather conditions?
Pace Determined by Speed of Equipment	How important is it to this job that the pace is determined by the speed of equipment or machinery? (This does not refer to keeping busy at all times on this job.)
Deal With Physically Aggressive People	How frequently does this job require the worker to deal with physical aggression of violent individuals?
Spend Time Sitting	How much does this job require sitting?
Cramped Work Space, Awkward Positions	How often does this job require working in cramped work spaces that requires getting into awkward positions?
Spend Time Keeping or Regaining Balance	How much does this job require keeping or regaining your balance?
Indoors, Not Environmentally Controlled	How often does this job require working indoors in non-controlled environmental conditions (e.g., warehouse without heat)?
In an Enclosed Vehicle or Equipment	How often does this job require working in a closed vehicle or equipment (e.g., car)?
Exposed to Hazardous Conditions	How often does this job require exposure to hazardous conditions?
Extremely Bright or Inadequate Lighting	How often does this job require working in extremely bright or inadequate lighting conditions?
Exposed to Hazardous Equipment	How often does this job require exposure to hazardous equipment?
Exposed to Radiation	How often does this job require exposure to radiation?
Exposed to High Places	How often does this job require exposure to high places?
Outdoors, Under Cover	How often does this job require working outdoors, under cover (e.g., structure with roof but no walls)?
Spend Time Climbing Ladders, Scaffolds, or Poles	How much does this job require climbing ladders, scaffolds, or poles?
Exposed to Disease or Infections	How often does this job require exposure to disease/infections?
Exposed to Whole Body Vibration	How often does this job require exposure to whole body vibration (e.g., operate a jackhammer)?
Wear Specialized Protective or Safety Equipment su	How much does this job require wearing specialized protective or safety equipment such as breathing apparatus, safety harness, full protection suits, or radiation protection?
In an Open Vehicle or Equipment	How often does this job require working in an open vehicle or equipment (e.g., tractor)?

Job Zone Component	Job Zone Component Definitions
Title	Job Zone Three: Medium Preparation Needed
Overall Experience	Previous work-related skill, knowledge, or experience is required for these occupations. For example, an electrician must have completed three or four years of apprenticeship or several years of vocational training, and often must have passed a licensing exam, in order to perform the job.
Job Training	Employees in these occupations usually need one or two years of training involving both on-the-job experience and informal training with experienced workers.

Job Zone Examples	These occupations usually involve using communication and organizational skills to coordinate, supervise, manage, or train others to accomplish goals. Examples include dental assistants, electricians, fish and game wardens, legal secretaries, personnel recruiters, and recreation workers.
SVP Range	(6.0 to < 7.0)
Education	Most occupations in this zone require training in vocational schools, related on-the-job experience, or an associate's degree. Some may require a bachelor's degree.

Work_Styles	Work_Styles Definitions
Dependability	Job requires being reliable, responsible, and dependable, and fulfilling obligations.
Leadership	Job requires a willingness to lead, take charge, and offer opinions and direction.
Attention to Detail	Job requires being careful about detail and thorough in completing work tasks.
Self Control	Job requires maintaining composure, keeping emotions in check, controlling anger, and avoiding aggressive behavior, even in very difficult situations.
Adaptability/Flexibility	Job requires being open to change (positive or negative) and to considerable variety in the workplace.
Stress Tolerance	Job requires accepting criticism and dealing calmly and effectively with high stress situations.
Initiative	Job requires a willingness to take on responsibilities and challenges.
Cooperation	Job requires being pleasant with others on the job and displaying a good-natured, cooperative attitude.
Concern for Others	Job requires being sensitive to others' needs and feelings and being understanding and helpful on the job.
Independence	Job requires developing one's own ways of doing things, guiding oneself with little or no supervision, and depending on oneself to get things done.
Integrity	Job requires being honest and ethical.
Analytical Thinking	Job requires analyzing information and using logic to address work-related issues and problems.
Social Orientation	Job requires preferring to work with others rather than alone, and being personally connected with others on the job.
Persistence	Job requires persistence in the face of obstacles.
Achievement/Effort	Job requires establishing and maintaining personally challenging achievement goals and exerting effort toward mastering tasks.
Innovation	Job requires creativity and alternative thinking to develop new ideas for and answers to work-related problems.

11-9061.00 - Funeral Directors

Perform various tasks to arrange and direct funeral services, such as coordinating transportation of body to mortuary for embalming, interviewing family or other authorized person to arrange details, selecting pallbearers, procuring official for religious rites, and providing transportation for mourners.

Tasks

1) Close caskets and lead funeral corteges to churches or burial sites.

2) Arrange for clergy members to perform needed services.

3) Provide or arrange transportation between sites for the remains, mourners, pallbearers, clergy, and flowers.

4) Contact cemeteries to schedule the opening and closing of graves.

5) Consult with families and/or friends of the deceased to arrange funeral details such as obituary notice wording, casket selection, and plans for services.

6) Obtain information needed to complete legal documents such as death certificates and burial permits.

7) Provide information on funeral service options, products, and merchandise, and maintain a casket display area.

8) Arrange for pallbearers, and inform pallbearers and honorary groups of their duties.

9) Receive and usher people to their seats for services.

10) Plan placement of caskets at funeral sites, and place and adjust lights, fixtures, and floral displays.

11) Direct preparations and shipment of bodies for out-of-state burial.

12) Offer counsel and comfort to bereaved families and friends.

13) Inform survivors of benefits for which they may be eligible.

14) Maintain financial records, order merchandise, and prepare accounts.

15) Discuss and negotiate pre-arranged funerals with clients.

16) Oversee the preparation and care of the remains of people who have died.

17) Perform embalming duties as necessary.

18) Manage funeral home operations, including hiring and supervising embalmers, funeral attendants, and other staff.

Knowledge	Knowledge Definitions
Customer and Personal Service	Knowledge of principles and processes for providing customer and personal services. This includes customer needs assessment, meeting quality standards for services, and evaluation of customer satisfaction.
Administration and Management	Knowledge of business and management principles involved in strategic planning, resource allocation, human resources modeling, leadership technique, production methods, and coordination of people and resources.
English Language	Knowledge of the structure and content of the English language including the meaning and spelling of words, rules of composition, and grammar.
Clerical	Knowledge of administrative and clerical procedures and systems such as word processing, managing files and records, stenography and transcription, designing forms, and other office procedures and terminology.
Psychology	Knowledge of human behavior and performance; individual differences in ability, personality, and interests; learning and motivation; psychological research methods; and the assessment and treatment of behavioral and affective disorders.
Sales and Marketing	Knowledge of principles and methods for showing, promoting, and selling products or services. This includes marketing strategy and tactics, product demonstration, sales techniques, and sales control systems.
Law and Government	Knowledge of laws, legal codes, court procedures, precedents, government regulations, executive orders, agency rules, and the democratic political process.
Personnel and Human Resources	Knowledge of principles and procedures for personnel recruitment, selection, training, compensation and benefits, labor relations and negotiation, and personnel information systems.
Economics and Accounting	Knowledge of economic and accounting principles and practices, the financial markets, banking and the analysis and reporting of financial data.
Therapy and Counseling	Knowledge of principles, methods, and procedures for diagnosis, treatment, and rehabilitation of physical and mental dysfunctions, and for career counseling and guidance.
Philosophy and Theology	Knowledge of different philosophical systems and religions. This includes their basic principles, values, ethics, ways of thinking, customs, practices, and their impact on human culture.
Education and Training	Knowledge of principles and methods for curriculum and training design, teaching and instruction for individuals and groups, and the measurement of training effects.
Mathematics	Knowledge of arithmetic, algebra, geometry, calculus, statistics, and their applications.
Transportation	Knowledge of principles and methods for moving people or goods by air, rail, sea, or road, including the relative costs and benefits.
Chemistry	Knowledge of the chemical composition, structure, and properties of substances and of the chemical processes and transformations that they undergo. This includes uses of chemicals and their interactions, danger signs, production techniques, and disposal methods.
Computers and Electronics	Knowledge of circuit boards, processors, chips, electronic equipment, and computer hardware and software, including applications and programming.
Sociology and Anthropology	Knowledge of group behavior and dynamics, societal trends and influences, human migrations, ethnicity, cultures and their history and origins.
Biology	Knowledge of plant and animal organisms, their tissues, cells, functions, interdependencies, and interactions with each other and the environment.

Public Safety and Security	Knowledge of relevant equipment, policies, procedures, and strategies to promote effective local, state, or national security operations for the protection of people, data, property, and institutions.
Communications and Media	Knowledge of media production, communication, and dissemination techniques and methods. This includes alternative ways to inform and entertain via written, oral, and visual media.
Production and Processing	Knowledge of raw materials, production processes, quality control, costs, and other techniques for maximizing the effective manufacture and distribution of goods.
Telecommunications	Knowledge of transmission, broadcasting, switching, control, and operation of telecommunications systems.
Medicine and Dentistry	Knowledge of the information and techniques needed to diagnose and treat human injuries, diseases, and deformities. This includes symptoms, treatment alternatives, drug properties and interactions, and preventive health-care measures.
Mechanical	Knowledge of machines and tools, including their designs, uses, repair, and maintenance.
Geography	Knowledge of principles and methods for describing the features of land, sea, and air masses, including their physical characteristics, locations, interrelationships, and distribution of plant, animal, and human life.
Foreign Language	Knowledge of the structure and content of a foreign (non-English) language including the meaning and spelling of words, rules of composition and grammar, and pronunciation.
History and Archeology	Knowledge of historical events and their causes, indicators, and effects on civilizations and cultures.
Design	Knowledge of design techniques, tools, and principles involved in production of precision technical plans, blueprints, drawings, and models.
Engineering and Technology	Knowledge of the practical application of engineering science and technology. This includes applying principles, techniques, procedures, and equipment to the design and production of various goods and services.
Physics	Knowledge and prediction of physical principles, laws, their interrelationships, and applications to understanding fluid, material, and atmospheric dynamics, and mechanical, electrical, atomic and sub- atomic structures and processes.
Building and Construction	Knowledge of materials, methods, and the tools involved in the construction or repair of houses, buildings, or other structures such as highways and roads.
Fine Arts	Knowledge of the theory and techniques required to compose, produce, and perform works of music, dance, visual arts, drama, and sculpture.
Food Production	Knowledge of techniques and equipment for planting, growing, and harvesting food products (both plant and animal) for consumption, including storage/handling techniques.

Skills	Skills Definitions
Active Listening	Giving full attention to what other people are saying, taking time to understand the points being made, asking questions as appropriate, and not interrupting at inappropriate times.
Service Orientation	Actively looking for ways to help people.
Coordination	Adjusting actions in relation to others' actions.
Social Perceptiveness	Being aware of others' reactions and understanding why they react as they do.
Speaking	Talking to others to convey information effectively.
Time Management	Managing one's own time and the time of others.
Reading Comprehension	Understanding written sentences and paragraphs in work related documents.
Writing	Communicating effectively in writing as appropriate for the needs of the audience.
Judgment and Decision Making	Considering the relative costs and benefits of potential actions to choose the most appropriate one.
Critical Thinking	Using logic and reasoning to identify the strengths and weaknesses of alternative solutions, conclusions or approaches to problems.
Management of Financial Resources	Determining how money will be spent to get the work done, and accounting for these expenditures.
Active Learning	Understanding the implications of new information for both current and future problem-solving and decision-making.
Management of Personnel Resources	Motivating, developing, and directing people as they work, identifying the best people for the job.
Monitoring	Monitoring/Assessing performance of yourself, other individuals, or organizations to make improvements or take corrective action.

Instructing	Teaching others how to do something.
Negotiation	Bringing others together and trying to reconcile differences.
Mathematics	Using mathematics to solve problems.
Learning Strategies	Selecting and using training/instructional methods and procedures appropriate for the situation when learning or teaching new things.
Equipment Selection	Determining the kind of tools and equipment needed to do a job.
Science	Using scientific rules and methods to solve problems.
Management of Material Resources	Obtaining and seeing to the appropriate use of equipment, facilities, and materials needed to do certain work.
Complex Problem Solving	Identifying complex problems and reviewing related information to develop and evaluate options and implement solutions.
Quality Control Analysis	Conducting tests and inspections of products, services, or processes to evaluate quality or performance.
Operations Analysis	Analyzing needs and product requirements to create a design.
Troubleshooting	Determining causes of operating errors and deciding what to do about it.
Equipment Maintenance	Performing routine maintenance on equipment and determining when and what kind of maintenance is needed.
Persuasion	Persuading others to change their minds or behavior.
Operation and Control	Controlling operations of equipment or systems.
Operation Monitoring	Watching gauges, dials, or other indicators to make sure a machine is working properly.
Repairing	Repairing machines or systems using the needed tools.
Systems Evaluation	Identifying measures or indicators of system performance and the actions needed to improve or correct performance, relative to the goals of the system.
Systems Analysis	Determining how a system should work and how changes in conditions, operations, and the environment will affect outcomes.
Technology Design	Generating or adapting equipment and technology to serve user needs.
Installation	Installing equipment, machines, wiring, or programs to meet specifications.
Programming	Writing computer programs for various purposes.

Ability	Ability Definitions
Oral Expression	The ability to communicate information and ideas in speaking so others will understand.
Problem Sensitivity	The ability to tell when something is wrong or is likely to go wrong. It does not involve solving the problem, only recognizing there is a problem.
Oral Comprehension	The ability to listen to and understand information and ideas presented through spoken words and sentences.
Speech Clarity	The ability to speak clearly so others can understand you.
Speech Recognition	The ability to identify and understand the speech of another person.
Deductive Reasoning	The ability to apply general rules to specific problems to produce answers that make sense.
Information Ordering	The ability to arrange things or actions in a certain order or pattern according to a specific rule or set of rules (e.g., patterns of numbers, letters, words, pictures, mathematical operations).
Written Comprehension	The ability to read and understand information and ideas presented in writing.
Near Vision	The ability to see details at close range (within a few feet of the observer).
Inductive Reasoning	The ability to combine pieces of information to form general rules or conclusions (includes finding a relationship among seemingly unrelated events).
Category Flexibility	The ability to generate or use different sets of rules for combining or grouping things in different ways.
Written Expression	The ability to communicate information and ideas in writing so others will understand.
Number Facility	The ability to add, subtract, multiply, or divide quickly and correctly.
Selective Attention	The ability to concentrate on a task over a period of time without being distracted.
Time Sharing	The ability to shift back and forth between two or more activities or sources of information (such as speech, sounds, touch, or other sources).
Fluency of Ideas	The ability to come up with a number of ideas about a topic (the number of ideas is important, not their quality, correctness, or creativity).

Depth Perception	The ability to judge which of several objects is closer or farther away from you, or to judge the distance between you and an object.
Far Vision	The ability to see details at a distance.
Visualization	The ability to imagine how something will look after it is moved around or when its parts are moved or rearranged.
Memorization	The ability to remember information such as words, numbers, pictures, and procedures.
Flexibility of Closure	The ability to identify or detect a known pattern (a figure, object, word, or sound) that is hidden in other distracting material.
Speed of Closure	The ability to quickly make sense of, combine, and organize information into meaningful patterns.
Mathematical Reasoning	The ability to choose the right mathematical methods or formulas to solve a problem.
Visual Color Discrimination	The ability to match or detect differences between colors, including shades of color and brightness.
Originality	The ability to come up with unusual or clever ideas about a given topic or situation, or to develop creative ways to solve a problem.
Multilimb Coordination	The ability to coordinate two or more limbs (for example, two arms, two legs, or one leg and one arm) while sitting, standing, or lying down. It does not involve performing the activities while the whole body is in motion.
Hearing Sensitivity	The ability to detect or tell the differences between sounds that vary in pitch and loudness.
Manual Dexterity	The ability to quickly move your hand, your hand together with your arm, or your two hands to grasp, manipulate, or assemble objects.
Auditory Attention	The ability to focus on a single source of sound in the presence of other distracting sounds.
Perceptual Speed	The ability to quickly and accurately compare similarities and differences among sets of letters, numbers, objects, pictures, or patterns. The things to be compared may be presented at the same time or one after the other. This ability also includes comparing a presented object with a remembered object.
Arm-Hand Steadiness	The ability to keep your hand and arm steady while moving your arm or while holding your arm and hand in one position.
Control Precision	The ability to quickly and repeatedly adjust the controls of a machine or a vehicle to exact positions.
Trunk Strength	The ability to use your abdominal and lower back muscles to support part of the body repeatedly or continuously over time without 'giving out' or fatiguing.
Finger Dexterity	The ability to make precisely coordinated movements of the fingers of one or both hands to grasp, manipulate, or assemble very small objects.
Static Strength	The ability to exert maximum muscle force to lift, push, pull, or carry objects.
Glare Sensitivity	The ability to see objects in the presence of glare or bright lighting.
Peripheral Vision	The ability to see objects or movement of objects to one's side when the eyes are looking ahead.
Response Orientation	The ability to choose quickly between two or more movements in response to two or more different signals (lights, sounds, pictures). It includes the speed with which the correct response is started with the hand, foot, or other body part.
Rate Control	The ability to time your movements or the movement of a piece of equipment in anticipation of changes in the speed and/or direction of a moving object or scene.
Sound Localization	The ability to tell the direction from which a sound originated.
Reaction Time	The ability to quickly respond (with the hand, finger, or foot) to a signal (sound, light, picture) when it appears.
Speed of Limb Movement	The ability to quickly move the arms and legs.
Spatial Orientation	The ability to know your location in relation to the environment or to know where other objects are in relation to you.
Gross Body Coordination	The ability to coordinate the movement of your arms, legs, and torso together when the whole body is in motion.
Extent Flexibility	The ability to bend, stretch, twist, or reach with your body, arms, and/or legs.
Stamina	The ability to exert yourself physically over long periods of time without getting winded or out of breath.
Dynamic Strength	The ability to exert muscle force repeatedly or continuously over time. This involves muscular endurance and resistance to muscle fatigue.
Gross Body Equilibrium	The ability to keep or regain your body balance or stay upright when in an unstable position.
Night Vision	The ability to see under low light conditions.

Explosive Strength	The ability to use short bursts of muscle force to propel oneself (as in jumping or sprinting), or to throw an object.
Wrist-Finger Speed	The ability to make fast, simple, repeated movements of the fingers, hands, and wrists.
Dynamic Flexibility	The ability to quickly and repeatedly bend, stretch, twist, or reach out with your body, arms, and/or legs.

Work_Activity	Work_Activity Definitions
Performing for or Working Directly with the Public	Performing for people or dealing directly with the public. This includes serving customers in restaurants and stores, and receiving clients or guests.
Getting Information	Observing, receiving, and otherwise obtaining information from all relevant sources.
Assisting and Caring for Others	Providing personal assistance, medical attention, emotional support, or other personal care to others such as coworkers, customers, or patients.
Establishing and Maintaining Interpersonal Relatio	Developing constructive and cooperative working relationships with others, and maintaining them over time.
Making Decisions and Solving Problems	Analyzing information and evaluating results to choose the best solution and solve problems.
Communicating with Supervisors, Peers, or Subordin	Providing information to supervisors, co-workers, and subordinates by telephone, in written form, e-mail, or in person.
Evaluating Information to Determine Compliance wit	Using relevant information and individual judgment to determine whether events or processes comply with laws, regulations, or standards.
Communicating with Persons Outside Organization	Communicating with people outside the organization, representing the organization to customers, the public, government, and other external sources. This information can be exchanged in person, in writing, or by telephone or e-mail.
Documenting/Recording Information	Entering, transcribing, recording, storing, or maintaining information in written or electronic/magnetic form.
Updating and Using Relevant Knowledge	Keeping up-to-date technically and applying new knowledge to your job.
Identifying Objects, Actions, and Events	Identifying information by categorizing, estimating, recognizing differences or similarities, and detecting changes in circumstances or events.
Coordinating the Work and Activities of Others	Getting members of a group to work together to accomplish tasks.
Judging the Qualities of Things, Services, or Peop	Assessing the value, importance, or quality of things or people.
Processing Information	Compiling, coding, categorizing, calculating, tabulating, auditing, or verifying information or data.
Organizing, Planning, and Prioritizing Work	Developing specific goals and plans to prioritize, organize, and accomplish your work.
Resolving Conflicts and Negotiating with Others	Handling complaints, settling disputes, and resolving grievances and conflicts, or otherwise negotiating with others.
Performing Administrative Activities	Performing day-to-day administrative tasks such as maintaining information files and processing paperwork.
Scheduling Work and Activities	Scheduling events, programs, and activities, as well as the work of others.
Monitor Processes, Materials, or Surroundings	Monitoring and reviewing information from materials, events, or the environment, to detect or assess problems.
Monitoring and Controlling Resources	Monitoring and controlling resources and overseeing the spending of money.
Interacting With Computers	Using computers and computer systems (including hardware and software) to program, write software, set up functions, enter data, or process information.
Operating Vehicles, Mechanized Devices, or Equipme	Running, maneuvering, navigating, or driving vehicles or mechanized equipment, such as forklifts, passenger vehicles, aircraft, or water craft.
Thinking Creatively	Developing, designing, or creating new applications, ideas, relationships, systems, or products, including artistic contributions.
Guiding, Directing, and Motivating Subordinates	Providing guidance and direction to subordinates, including setting performance standards and monitoring performance.
Developing and Building Teams	Encouraging and building mutual trust, respect, and cooperation among team members.
Developing Objectives and Strategies	Establishing long-range objectives and specifying the strategies and actions to achieve them.
Handling and Moving Objects	Using hands and arms in handling, installing, positioning, and moving materials, and manipulating things.
Coaching and Developing Others	Identifying the developmental needs of others and coaching, mentoring, or otherwise helping others to improve their knowledge or skills.

Estimating the Quantifiable Characteristics of Pro	Estimating sizes, distances, and quantities; or determining time, costs, resources, or materials needed to perform a work activity.
Selling or Influencing Others	Convincing others to buy merchandise/goods or to otherwise change their minds or actions.
Training and Teaching Others	Identifying the educational needs of others, developing formal educational or training programs or classes, and teaching or instructing others.
Analyzing Data or Information	Identifying the underlying principles, reasons, or facts of information by breaking down information or data into separate parts.
Provide Consultation and Advice to Others	Providing guidance and expert advice to management or other groups on technical, systems-, or process-related topics.
Performing General Physical Activities	Performing physical activities that require considerable use of your arms and legs and moving your whole body, such as climbing, lifting, balancing, walking, stooping, and handling of materials.
Interpreting the Meaning of Information for Others	Translating or explaining what information means and how it can be used.
Inspecting Equipment, Structures, or Material	Inspecting equipment, structures, or materials to identify the cause of errors or other problems or defects.
Staffing Organizational Units	Recruiting, interviewing, selecting, hiring, and promoting employees in an organization.
Controlling Machines and Processes	Using either control mechanisms or direct physical activity to operate machines or processes (not including computers or vehicles).
Repairing and Maintaining Mechanical Equipment	Servicing, repairing, adjusting, and testing machines, devices, moving parts, and equipment that operate primarily on the basis of mechanical (not electronic) principles.
Repairing and Maintaining Electronic Equipment	Servicing, repairing, calibrating, regulating, fine-tuning, or testing machines, devices, and equipment that operate primarily on the basis of electrical or electronic (not mechanical) principles.
Drafting, Laying Out, and Specifying Technical Dev	Providing documentation, detailed instructions, drawings, or specifications to tell others about how devices, parts, equipment, or structures are to be fabricated, constructed, assembled, modified, maintained, or used.

Work_Context	Work_Context Definitions
Telephone	How often do you have telephone conversations in this job?
Face-to-Face Discussions	How often do you have to have face-to-face discussions with individuals or teams in this job?
Contact With Others	How much does this job require the worker to be in contact with others (face-to-face, by telephone, or otherwise) in order to perform it?
Deal With External Customers	How important is it to work with external customers or the public in this job?
Freedom to Make Decisions	How much decision making freedom, without supervision, does the job offer?
Work With Work Group or Team	How important is it to work with others in a group or team in this job?
Importance of Being Exact or Accurate	How important is being very exact or highly accurate in performing this job?
In an Enclosed Vehicle or Equipment	How often does this job require working in a closed vehicle or equipment (e.g., car)?
Impact of Decisions on Co-workers or Company Resul	How do the decisions an employee makes impact the results of co-workers, clients or the company?
Indoors, Environmentally Controlled	How often does this job require working indoors in environmentally controlled conditions?
Structured versus Unstructured Work	To what extent is this job structured for the worker, rather than allowing the worker to determine tasks, priorities, and goals?
Frequency of Decision Making	How frequently is the worker required to make decisions that affect other people, the financial resources, and/or the image and reputation of the organization?
Responsibility for Outcomes and Results	How responsible is the worker for work outcomes and results of other workers?
Coordinate or Lead Others	How important is it to coordinate or lead others in accomplishing work activities in this job?
Time Pressure	How often does this job require the worker to meet strict deadlines?
Letters and Memos	How often does the job require written letters and memos?
Physical Proximity	To what extent does this job require the worker to perform job tasks in close physical proximity to other people?
Outdoors, Exposed to Weather	How often does this job require working outdoors, exposed to all weather conditions?

Responsible for Others' Health and Safety	How much responsibility is there for the health and safety of others in this job?
Exposed to Disease or Infections	How often does this job require exposure to disease/infections?
Exposed to Contaminants	How often does this job require working exposed to contaminants (such as pollutants, gases, dust or odors)?
Level of Competition	To what extent does this job require the worker to compete or to be aware of competitive pressures?
Importance of Repeating Same Tasks	How important is repeating the same physical activities (e.g., key entry) or mental activities (e.g., checking entries in a ledger) over and over, without stopping, to performing this job?
Wear Common Protective or Safety Equipment such as	How much does this job require wearing common protective or safety equipment such as safety shoes, glasses, gloves, hard hats or life jackets?
Spend Time Standing	How much does this job require standing?
Exposed to Hazardous Conditions	How often does this job require exposure to hazardous conditions?
Consequence of Error	How serious would the result usually be if the worker made a mistake that was not readily correctable?
Public Speaking	How often do you have to perform public speaking in this job?
Electronic Mail	How often do you use electronic mail in this job?
Frequency of Conflict Situations	How often are there conflict situations the employee has to face in this job?
Very Hot or Cold Temperatures	How often does this job require working in very hot (above 90 F degrees) or very cold (below 32 F degrees) temperatures?
Spend Time Sitting	How much does this job require sitting?
Deal With Unpleasant or Angry People	How frequently does the worker have to deal with unpleasant, angry, or discourteous individuals as part of the job requirements?
Indoors, Not Environmentally Controlled	How often does this job require working indoors in non-controlled environmental conditions (e.g., warehouse without heat)?
Outdoors, Under Cover	How often does this job require working outdoors, under cover (e.g., structure with roof but no walls)?
Spend Time Using Your Hands to Handle, Control, or	How much does this job require using your hands to handle, control, or feel objects, tools or controls?
Spend Time Walking and Running	How much does this job require walking and running?
Wear Specialized Protective or Safety Equipment su	How much does this job require wearing specialized protective or safety equipment such as breathing apparatus, safety harness, full protection suits, or radiation protection?
Spend Time Making Repetitive Motions	How much does this job require making repetitive motions?
Exposed to Minor Burns, Cuts, Bites, or Stings	How often does this job require exposure to minor burns, cuts, bites, or stings?
Spend Time Bending or Twisting the Body	How much does this job require bending or twisting your body?
Sounds, Noise Levels Are Distracting or Uncomforta	How often does this job require working exposed to sounds and noise levels that are distracting or uncomfortable?
Degree of Automation	How automated is the job?
Extremely Bright or Inadequate Lighting	How often does this job require working in extremely bright or inadequate lighting conditions?
Exposed to Hazardous Equipment	How often does this job require exposure to hazardous equipment?
Cramped Work Space, Awkward Positions	How often does this job require working in cramped work spaces that requires getting into awkward positions?
Deal With Physically Aggressive People	How frequently does this job require the worker to deal with physical aggression of violent individuals?
Spend Time Kneeling, Crouching, Stooping, or Crawl	How much does this job require kneeling, crouching, stooping, or crawling?
Pace Determined by Speed of Equipment	How important is it to this job that the pace is determined by the speed of equipment or machinery? (This does not refer to keeping busy at all times on this job.)
Spend Time Keeping or Regaining Balance	How much does this job require keeping or regaining your balance?
Exposed to High Places	How often does this job require exposure to high places?
In an Open Vehicle or Equipment	How often does this job require working in an open vehicle or equipment (e.g., tractor)?
Exposed to Radiation	How often does this job require exposure to radiation?
Spend Time Climbing Ladders, Scaffolds, or Poles	How much does this job require climbing ladders, scaffolds, or poles?
Exposed to Whole Body Vibration	How often does this job require exposure to whole body vibration (e.g., operate a jackhammer)?

Job Zone Component	Job Zone Component Definitions
Title	Job Zone Three: Medium Preparation Needed
Overall Experience	Previous work-related skill, knowledge, or experience is required for these occupations. For example, an electrician must have completed three or four years of apprenticeship or several years of vocational training, and often must have passed a licensing exam, in order to perform the job.
Job Training	Employees in these occupations usually need one or two years of training involving both on-the-job experience and informal training with experienced workers.
Job Zone Examples	These occupations usually involve using communication and organizational skills to coordinate, supervise, manage, or train others to accomplish goals. Examples include dental assistants, electricians, fish and game wardens, legal secretaries, personnel recruiters, and recreation workers.
SVP Range	(6.0 to < 7.0)
Education	Most occupations in this zone require training in vocational schools, related on-the-job experience, or an associate's degree. Some may require a bachelor's degree.

Work_Styles	Work_Styles Definitions
Attention to Detail	Job requires being careful about detail and thorough in completing work tasks.
Integrity	Job requires being honest and ethical.
Concern for Others	Job requires being sensitive to others' needs and feelings and being understanding and helpful on the job.
Dependability	Job requires being reliable, responsible, and dependable, and fulfilling obligations.
Self Control	Job requires maintaining composure, keeping emotions in check, controlling anger, and avoiding aggressive behavior, even in very difficult situations.
Cooperation	Job requires being pleasant with others on the job and displaying a good-natured, cooperative attitude.
Stress Tolerance	Job requires accepting criticism and dealing calmly and effectively with high stress situations.
Social Orientation	Job requires preferring to work with others rather than alone, and being personally connected with others on the job.
Adaptability/Flexibility	Job requires being open to change (positive or negative) and to considerable variety in the workplace.
Initiative	Job requires a willingness to take on responsibilities and challenges.
Leadership	Job requires a willingness to lead, take charge, and offer opinions and direction.
Achievement/Effort	Job requires establishing and maintaining personally challenging achievement goals and exerting effort toward mastering tasks.
Independence	Job requires developing one's own ways of doing things, guiding oneself with little or no supervision, and depending on oneself to get things done.
Persistence	Job requires persistence in the face of obstacles.
Innovation	Job requires creativity and alternative thinking to develop new ideas for and answers to work-related problems.
Analytical Thinking	Job requires analyzing information and using logic to address work-related issues and problems.

11-9071.00 - Gaming Managers

Plan, organize, direct, control, or coordinate gaming operations in a casino. Formulate gaming policies for their area of responsibility.

Tasks

1) Establish policies on issues such as the type of gambling offered and the odds, the extension of credit, and the serving of food and beverages.

2) Direct the distribution of complimentary hotel rooms, meals, and other discounts or free items given to players based on their length of play and betting totals.

3) Maintain familiarity with all games used at a facility, as well as strategies and tricks employed in those games.

4) Circulate among gaming tables to ensure that operations are conducted properly, that dealers follow house rules, and that players are not cheating

5) Interview and hire workers.

6) Prepare work schedules and station assignments, and keep attendance records.

7) Resolve customer complaints regarding problems such as payout errors.

8) Direct workers compiling summary sheets that show wager amounts and payoffs for races and events.

9) Set and maintain a bank and table limit for each game.

10) Record, collect, and pay off bets, issuing receipts as necessary.

11) Monitor credit extended to players.

12) Remove suspected cheaters, such as card counters and other players who may have systems that shift the odds of winning to their favor.

13) Notify board attendants of table vacancies so that waiting patrons can play.

14) Explain and interpret house rules, such as game rules and betting limits.

15) Train new workers and evaluate their performance.

16) Track supplies of money to tables, and perform any required paperwork.

17) Review operational expenses, budget estimates, betting accounts, and collection reports for accuracy.

11-9081.00 - Lodging Managers

Plan, direct, or coordinate activities of an organization or department that provides lodging and other accommodations.

Tasks

1) Inspect guest rooms, public areas, and grounds for cleanliness and appearance.

2) Train staff members in their duties.

3) Prepare required paperwork pertaining to departmental functions.

4) Develop and implement policies and procedures for the operation of a department or establishment.

5) Participate in financial activities such as the setting of room rates, the establishment of budgets, and the allocation of funds to departments.

6) Observe and monitor staff performance in order to ensure efficient operations and adherence to facility's policies and procedures.

7) Show, rent, or assign accommodations.

8) Purchase supplies, and arrange for outside services, such as deliveries, laundry, maintenance and repair, and trash collection.

9) Manage and maintain temporary or permanent lodging facilities.

10) Confer and cooperate with other managers in order to ensure coordination of hotel activities.

11) Coordinate front-office activities of hotels or motels, and resolve problems.

12) Arrange telephone answering services, deliver mail and packages, and answer questions regarding locations for eating and entertainment.

13) Interview and hire applicants.

14) Collect payments, and record data pertaining to funds and expenditures.

15) Assign duties to workers, and schedule shifts.

16) Greet and register guests.

17) Perform marketing and public relations activities.

18) Meet with clients in order to schedule and plan details of conventions, banquets, receptions and other functions.

19) Receive and process advance registration payments, send out letters of confirmation, and return checks when registrations cannot be accepted.

20) Provide assistance to staff members by performing activities such as inspecting rooms, setting tables and doing laundry.

21) Book tickets for guests for local tours and attractions.

22) Organize and coordinate the work of staff and convention personnel for meetings to be held at a particular facility.

Knowledge	Knowledge Definitions
Customer and Personal Service	Knowledge of principles and processes for providing customer and personal services. This includes customer needs assessment, meeting quality standards for services, and evaluation of customer satisfaction.
Administration and Management	Knowledge of business and management principles involved in strategic planning, resource allocation, human resources modeling, leadership technique, production methods, and coordination of people and resources.
English Language	Knowledge of the structure and content of the English language including the meaning and spelling of words, rules of composition, and grammar.
Sales and Marketing	Knowledge of principles and methods for showing, promoting, and selling products or services. This includes marketing strategy and tactics, product demonstration, sales techniques, and sales control systems.
Personnel and Human Resources	Knowledge of principles and procedures for personnel recruitment, selection, training, compensation and benefits, labor relations and negotiation, and personnel information systems.
Clerical	Knowledge of administrative and clerical procedures and systems such as word processing, managing files and records, stenography and transcription, designing forms, and other office procedures and terminology.
Economics and Accounting	Knowledge of economic and accounting principles and practices, the financial markets, banking and the analysis and reporting of financial data.
Psychology	Knowledge of human behavior and performance; individual differences in ability, personality, and interests; learning and motivation; psychological research methods; and the assessment and treatment of behavioral and affective disorders.
Mathematics	Knowledge of arithmetic, algebra, geometry, calculus, statistics, and their applications.
Education and Training	Knowledge of principles and methods for curriculum and training design, teaching and instruction for individuals and groups, and the measurement of training effects.
Computers and Electronics	Knowledge of circuit boards, processors, chips, electronic equipment, and computer hardware and software, including applications and programming.
Public Safety and Security	Knowledge of relevant equipment, policies, procedures, and strategies to promote effective local, state, or national security operations for the protection of people, data, property, and institutions.
Law and Government	Knowledge of laws, legal codes, court procedures, precedents, government regulations, executive orders, agency rules, and the democratic political process.
Geography	Knowledge of principles and methods for describing the features of land, sea, and air masses, including their physical characteristics, locations, interrelationships, and distribution of plant, animal, and human life.
Communications and Media	Knowledge of media production, communication, and dissemination techniques and methods. This includes alternative ways to inform and entertain via written, oral, and visual media.
Production and Processing	Knowledge of raw materials, production processes, quality control, costs, and other techniques for maximizing the effective manufacture and distribution of goods.
Sociology and Anthropology	Knowledge of group behavior and dynamics, societal trends and influences, human migrations, ethnicity, cultures and their history and origins.
Telecommunications	Knowledge of transmission, broadcasting, switching, control, and operation of telecommunications systems.
Transportation	Knowledge of principles and methods for moving people or goods by air, rail, sea, or road, including the relative costs and benefits.
Foreign Language	Knowledge of the structure and content of a foreign (non-English) language including the meaning and spelling of words, rules of composition and grammar, and pronunciation.
Food Production	Knowledge of techniques and equipment for planting, growing, and harvesting food products (both plant and animal) for consumption, including storage/handling techniques.
Philosophy and Theology	Knowledge of different philosophical systems and religions. This includes their basic principles, values, ethics, ways of thinking, customs, practices, and their impact on human culture.

Medicine and Dentistry	Knowledge of the information and techniques needed to diagnose and treat human injuries, diseases, and deformities. This includes symptoms, treatment alternatives, drug properties and interactions, and preventive health-care measures.
Therapy and Counseling	Knowledge of principles, methods, and procedures for diagnosis, treatment, and rehabilitation of physical and mental dysfunctions, and for career counseling and guidance.
Fine Arts	Knowledge of the theory and techniques required to compose, produce, and perform works of music, dance, visual arts, drama, and sculpture.
Mechanical	Knowledge of machines and tools, including their designs, uses, repair, and maintenance.
Chemistry	Knowledge of the chemical composition, structure, and properties of substances and of the chemical processes and transformations that they undergo. This includes uses of chemicals and their interactions, danger signs, production techniques, and disposal methods.
Building and Construction	Knowledge of materials, methods, and the tools involved in the construction or repair of houses, buildings, or other structures such as highways and roads.
Biology	Knowledge of plant and animal organisms, their tissues, cells, functions, interdependencies, and interactions with each other and the environment.
History and Archeology	Knowledge of historical events and their causes, indicators, and effects on civilizations and cultures.
Engineering and Technology	Knowledge of the practical application of engineering science and technology. This includes applying principles, techniques, procedures, and equipment to the design and production of various goods and services.
Design	Knowledge of design techniques, tools, and principles involved in production of precision technical plans, blueprints, drawings, and models.
Physics	Knowledge and prediction of physical principles, laws, their interrelationships, and applications to understanding fluid, material, and atmospheric dynamics, and mechanical, electrical, atomic and sub-atomic structures and processes.

Skills	Skills Definitions
Active Listening	Giving full attention to what other people are saying, taking time to understand the points being made, asking questions as appropriate, and not interrupting at inappropriate times.
Speaking	Talking to others to convey information effectively.
Social Perceptiveness	Being aware of others' reactions and understanding why they react as they do.
Critical Thinking	Using logic and reasoning to identify the strengths and weaknesses of alternative solutions, conclusions or approaches to problems.
Reading Comprehension	Understanding written sentences and paragraphs in work related documents.
Monitoring	Monitoring/Assessing performance of yourself, other individuals, or organizations to make improvements or take corrective action.
Active Learning	Understanding the implications of new information for both current and future problem-solving and decision-making.
Service Orientation	Actively looking for ways to help people.
Time Management	Managing one's own time and the time of others.
Instructing	Teaching others how to do something.
Management of Financial Resources	Determining how money will be spent to get the work done, and accounting for these expenditures.
Management of Personnel Resources	Motivating, developing, and directing people as they work, identifying the best people for the job.
Judgment and Decision Making	Considering the relative costs and benefits of potential actions to choose the most appropriate one.
Learning Strategies	Selecting and using training/instructional methods and procedures appropriate for the situation when learning or teaching new things.
Coordination	Adjusting actions in relation to others' actions.
Writing	Communicating effectively in writing as appropriate for the needs of the audience.
Management of Material Resources	Obtaining and seeing to the appropriate use of equipment, facilities, and materials needed to do certain work.
Equipment Selection	Determining the kind of tools and equipment needed to do a job.
Negotiation	Bringing others together and trying to reconcile differences.
Complex Problem Solving	Identifying complex problems and reviewing related information to develop and evaluate options and implement solutions.

Mathematics	Using mathematics to solve problems.
Persuasion	Persuading others to change their minds or behavior.
Operations Analysis	Analyzing needs and product requirements to create a design.
Quality Control Analysis	Conducting tests and inspections of products, services, or processes to evaluate quality or performance.
Technology Design	Generating or adapting equipment and technology to serve user needs.
Troubleshooting	Determining causes of operating errors and deciding what to do about it.
Equipment Maintenance	Performing routine maintenance on equipment and determining when and what kind of maintenance is needed.
Systems Evaluation	Identifying measures or indicators of system performance and the actions needed to improve or correct performance, relative to the goals of the system.
Systems Analysis	Determining how a system should work and how changes in conditions, operations, and the environment will affect outcomes.
Operation and Control	Controlling operations of equipment or systems.
Installation	Installing equipment, machines, wiring, or programs to meet specifications.
Operation Monitoring	Watching gauges, dials, or other indicators to make sure a machine is working properly.
Science	Using scientific rules and methods to solve problems.
Repairing	Repairing machines or systems using the needed tools.
Programming	Writing computer programs for various purposes.

Ability	Ability Definitions
Oral Expression	The ability to communicate information and ideas in speaking so others will understand.
Oral Comprehension	The ability to listen to and understand information and ideas presented through spoken words and sentences.
Speech Clarity	The ability to speak clearly so others can understand you.
Speech Recognition	The ability to identify and understand the speech of another person.
Problem Sensitivity	The ability to tell when something is wrong or is likely to go wrong. It does not involve solving the problem, only recognizing there is a problem.
Deductive Reasoning	The ability to apply general rules to specific problems to produce answers that make sense.
Written Comprehension	The ability to read and understand information and ideas presented in writing.
Inductive Reasoning	The ability to combine pieces of information to form general rules or conclusions (includes finding a relationship among seemingly unrelated events).
Information Ordering	The ability to arrange things or actions in a certain order or pattern according to a specific rule or set of rules (e.g., patterns of numbers, letters, words, pictures, mathematical operations).
Written Expression	The ability to communicate information and ideas in writing so others will understand.
Near Vision	The ability to see details at close range (within a few feet of the observer).
Category Flexibility	The ability to generate or use different sets of rules for combining or grouping things in different ways.
Fluency of Ideas	The ability to come up with a number of ideas about a topic (the number of ideas is important, not their quality, correctness, or creativity).
Time Sharing	The ability to shift back and forth between two or more activities or sources of information (such as speech, sounds, touch, or other sources).
Mathematical Reasoning	The ability to choose the right mathematical methods or formulas to solve a problem.
Originality	The ability to come up with unusual or clever ideas about a given topic or situation, or to develop creative ways to solve a problem.
Selective Attention	The ability to concentrate on a task over a period of time without being distracted.
Memorization	The ability to remember information such as words, numbers, pictures, and procedures.
Far Vision	The ability to see details at a distance.
Trunk Strength	The ability to use your abdominal and lower back muscles to support part of the body repeatedly or continuously over time without 'giving out' or fatiguing.
Visualization	The ability to imagine how something will look after it is moved around or when its parts are moved or rearranged.

Multilimb Coordination	The ability to coordinate two or more limbs (for example, two arms, two legs, or one leg and one arm) while sitting, standing, or lying down. It does not involve performing the activities while the whole body is in motion.
Speed of Closure	The ability to quickly make sense of, combine, and organize information into meaningful patterns.
Flexibility of Closure	The ability to identify or detect a known pattern (a figure, object, word, or sound) that is hidden in other distracting material.
Number Facility	The ability to add, subtract, multiply, or divide quickly and correctly.
Control Precision	The ability to quickly and repeatedly adjust the controls of a machine or a vehicle to exact positions.
Visual Color Discrimination	The ability to match or detect differences between colors, including shades of color and brightness.
Depth Perception	The ability to judge which of several objects is closer or farther away from you, or to judge the distance between you and an object.
Perceptual Speed	The ability to quickly and accurately compare similarities and differences among sets of letters, numbers, objects, pictures, or patterns. The things to be compared may be presented at the same time or one after the other. This ability also includes comparing a presented object with a remembered object.
Finger Dexterity	The ability to make precisely coordinated movements of the fingers of one or both hands to grasp, manipulate, or assemble very small objects.
Manual Dexterity	The ability to quickly move your hand, your hand together with your arm, or your two hands to grasp, manipulate, or assemble objects.
Spatial Orientation	The ability to know your location in relation to the environment or to know where other objects are in relation to you.
Response Orientation	The ability to choose quickly between two or more movements in response to two or more different signals (lights, sounds, pictures). It includes the speed with which the correct response is started with the hand, foot, or other body part.
Auditory Attention	The ability to focus on a single source of sound in the presence of other distracting sounds.
Hearing Sensitivity	The ability to detect or tell the differences between sounds that vary in pitch and loudness.
Wrist-Finger Speed	The ability to make fast, simple, repeated movements of the fingers, hands, and wrists.
Static Strength	The ability to exert maximum muscle force to lift, push, pull, or carry objects.
Gross Body Equilibrium	The ability to keep or regain your body balance or stay upright when in an unstable position.
Speed of Limb Movement	The ability to quickly move the arms and legs.
Gross Body Coordination	The ability to coordinate the movement of your arms, legs, and torso together when the whole body is in motion.
Dynamic Flexibility	The ability to quickly and repeatedly bend, stretch, twist, or reach out with your body, arms, and/or legs.
Stamina	The ability to exert yourself physically over long periods of time without getting winded or out of breath.
Peripheral Vision	The ability to see objects or movement of objects to one's side when the eyes are looking ahead.
Glare Sensitivity	The ability to see objects in the presence of glare or bright lighting.
Rate Control	The ability to time your movements or the movement of a piece of equipment in anticipation of changes in the speed and/or direction of a moving object or scene.
Dynamic Strength	The ability to exert muscle force repeatedly or continuously over time. This involves muscular endurance and resistance to muscle fatigue.
Arm-Hand Steadiness	The ability to keep your hand and arm steady while moving your arm or while holding your arm and hand in one position.
Sound Localization	The ability to tell the direction from which a sound originated.
Reaction Time	The ability to quickly respond (with the hand, finger, or foot) to a signal (sound, light, picture) when it appears.
Explosive Strength	The ability to use short bursts of muscle force to propel oneself (as in jumping or sprinting), or to throw an object.
Extent Flexibility	The ability to bend, stretch, twist, or reach with your body, arms, and/or legs.
Night Vision	The ability to see under low light conditions.

Work_Activity	Work_Activity Definitions
Getting Information	Observing, receiving, and otherwise obtaining information from all relevant sources.

Performing for or Working Directly with the Public	Performing for people or dealing directly with the public. This includes serving customers in restaurants and stores, and receiving clients or guests.
Establishing and Maintaining Interpersonal Relatio	Developing constructive and cooperative working relationships with others, and maintaining them over time.
Making Decisions and Solving Problems	Analyzing information and evaluating results to choose the best solution and solve problems.
Documenting/Recording Information	Entering, transcribing, recording, storing, or maintaining information in written or electronic/magnetic form.
Interacting With Computers	Using computers and computer systems (including hardware and software) to program, write software, set up functions, enter data, or process information.
Communicating with Supervisors, Peers, or Subordin	Providing information to supervisors, co-workers, and subordinates by telephone, in written form, e-mail, or in person.
Resolving Conflicts and Negotiating with Others	Handling complaints, settling disputes, and resolving grievances and conflicts, or otherwise negotiating with others.
Selling or Influencing Others	Convincing others to buy merchandise/goods or to otherwise change their minds or actions.
Organizing, Planning, and Prioritizing Work	Developing specific goals and plans to prioritize, organize, and accomplish your work.
Processing Information	Compiling, coding, categorizing, calculating, tabulating, auditing, or verifying information or data.
Performing Administrative Activities	Performing day-to-day administrative tasks such as maintaining information files and processing paperwork.
Communicating with Persons Outside Organization	Communicating with people outside the organization, representing the organization to customers, the public, government, and other external sources. This information can be exchanged in person, in writing, or by telephone or e-mail.
Coordinating the Work and Activities of Others	Getting members of a group to work together to accomplish tasks.
Monitoring and Controlling Resources	Monitoring and controlling resources and overseeing the spending of money.
Judging the Qualities of Things, Services, or Peop	Assessing the value, importance, or quality of things or people.
Updating and Using Relevant Knowledge	Keeping up-to-date technically and applying new knowledge to your job.
Developing Objectives and Strategies	Establishing long-range objectives and specifying the strategies and actions to achieve them.
Scheduling Work and Activities	Scheduling events, programs, and activities, as well as the work of others.
Identifying Objects, Actions, and Events	Identifying information by categorizing, estimating, recognizing differences or similarities, and detecting changes in circumstances or events.
Evaluating Information to Determine Compliance wit	Using relevant information and individual judgment to determine whether events or processes comply with laws, regulations, or standards.
Monitor Processes, Materials, or Surroundings	Monitoring and reviewing information from materials, events, or the environment, to detect or assess problems.
Guiding, Directing, and Motivating Subordinates	Providing guidance and direction to subordinates, including setting performance standards and monitoring performance.
Analyzing Data or Information	Identifying the underlying principles, reasons, or facts of information by breaking down information or data into separate parts.
Thinking Creatively	Developing, designing, or creating new applications, ideas, relationships, systems, or products, including artistic contributions.
Developing and Building Teams	Encouraging and building mutual trust, respect, and cooperation among team members.
Interpreting the Meaning of Information for Others	Translating or explaining what information means and how it can be used.
Inspecting Equipment, Structures, or Material	Inspecting equipment, structures, or materials to identify the cause of errors or other problems or defects.
Training and Teaching Others	Identifying the educational needs of others, developing formal educational or training programs or classes, and teaching or instructing others.
Estimating the Quantifiable Characteristics of Pro	Estimating sizes, distances, and quantities; or determining time, costs, resources, or materials needed to perform a work activity.
Staffing Organizational Units	Recruiting, interviewing, selecting, hiring, and promoting employees in an organization.
Assisting and Caring for Others	Providing personal assistance, medical attention, emotional support, or other personal care to others such as coworkers, customers, or patients.
Provide Consultation and Advice to Others	Providing guidance and expert advice to management or other groups on technical, systems-, or process-related topics.
Coaching and Developing Others	Identifying the developmental needs of others and coaching, mentoring, or otherwise helping others to improve their knowledge or skills.
Performing General Physical Activities	Performing physical activities that require considerable use of your arms and legs and moving your whole body, such as climbing, lifting, balancing, walking, stooping, and handling of materials.
Controlling Machines and Processes	Using either control mechanisms or direct physical activity to operate machines or processes (not including computers or vehicles).
Handling and Moving Objects	Using hands and arms in handling, installing, positioning, and moving materials, and manipulating things.
Operating Vehicles, Mechanized Devices, or Equipme	Running, maneuvering, navigating, or driving vehicles or mechanized equipment, such as forklifts, passenger vehicles, aircraft, or water craft.
Repairing and Maintaining Electronic Equipment	Servicing, repairing, calibrating, regulating, fine-tuning, or testing machines, devices, and equipment that operate primarily on the basis of electrical or electronic (not mechanical) principles.
Drafting, Laying Out, and Specifying Technical Dev	Providing documentation, detailed instructions, drawings, or specifications to tell others about how devices, parts, equipment, or structures are to be fabricated, constructed, assembled, modified, maintained, or used.
Repairing and Maintaining Mechanical Equipment	Servicing, repairing, adjusting, and testing machines, devices, moving parts, and equipment that operate primarily on the basis of mechanical (not electronic) principles.

Work_Context	Work_Context Definitions
Telephone	How often do you have telephone conversations in this job?
Face-to-Face Discussions	How often do you have to have face-to-face discussions with individuals or teams in this job?
Indoors, Environmentally Controlled	How often does this job require working indoors in environmentally controlled conditions?
Frequency of Decision Making	How frequently is the worker required to make decisions that affect other people, the financial resources, and/or the image and reputation of the organization?
Contact With Others	How much does this job require the worker to be in contact with others (face-to-face, by telephone, or otherwise) in order to perform it?
Freedom to Make Decisions	How much decision making freedom, without supervision, does the job offer?
Impact of Decisions on Co-workers or Company Resul	How do the decisions an employee makes impact the results of co-workers, clients or the company?
Deal With External Customers	How important is it to work with external customers or the public in this job?
Structured versus Unstructured Work	To what extent is this job structured for the worker, rather than allowing the worker to determine tasks, priorities, and goals?
Responsibility for Outcomes and Results	How responsible is the worker for work outcomes and results of other workers?
Letters and Memos	How often does the job require written letters and memos?
Importance of Repeating Same Tasks	How important is repeating the same physical activities (e.g., key entry) or mental activities (e.g., checking entries in a ledger) over and over, without stopping, to performing this job?
Work With Work Group or Team	How important is it to work with others in a group or team in this job?
Coordinate or Lead Others	How important is it to coordinate or lead others in accomplishing work activities in this job?
Time Pressure	How often does this job require the worker to meet strict deadlines?
Importance of Being Exact or Accurate	How important is being very exact or highly accurate in performing this job?
Responsible for Others' Health and Safety	How much responsibility is there for the health and safety of others in this job?
Level of Competition	To what extent does this job require the worker to compete or to be aware of competitive pressures?
Deal With Unpleasant or Angry People	How frequently does the worker have to deal with unpleasant, angry, or discourteous individuals as part of the job requirements?
Physical Proximity	To what extent does this job require the worker to perform job tasks in close physical proximity to other people?
Electronic Mail	How often do you use electronic mail in this job?
Spend Time Sitting	How much does this job require sitting?
Spend Time Standing	How much does this job require standing?
Frequency of Conflict Situations	How often are there conflict situations the employee has to face in this job?

In an Enclosed Vehicle or Equipment	How often does this job require working in a closed vehicle or equipment (e.g., car)?
Degree of Automation	How automated is the job?
Outdoors, Exposed to Weather	How often does this job require working outdoors, exposed to all weather conditions?
Sounds, Noise Levels Are Distracting or Uncomforta	How often does this job require working exposed to sounds and noise levels that are distracting or uncomfortable?
Spend Time Making Repetitive Motions	How much does this job require making repetitive motions?
Spend Time Walking and Running	How much does this job require walking and running?
Public Speaking	How often do you have to perform public speaking in this job?
Spend Time Using Your Hands to Handle, Control, or	How much does this job require using your hands to handle, control, or feel objects, tools or controls?
Exposed to Minor Burns, Cuts, Bites, or Stings	How often does this job require exposure to minor burns, cuts, bites, or stings?
Spend Time Bending or Twisting the Body	How much does this job require bending or twisting your body?
Very Hot or Cold Temperatures	How often does this job require working in very hot (above 90 F degrees) or very cold (below 32 F degrees) temperatures?
Consequence of Error	How serious would the result usually be if the worker made a mistake that was not readily correctable?
Outdoors, Under Cover	How often does this job require working outdoors, under cover (e.g., structure with roof but no walls)?
Exposed to Contaminants	How often does this job require working exposed to contaminants (such as pollutants, gases, dust or odors)?
Indoors, Not Environmentally Controlled	How often does this job require working indoors in non-controlled environmental conditions (e.g., warehouse without heat)?
Deal With Physically Aggressive People	How frequently does this job require the worker to deal with physical aggression of violent individuals?
Extremely Bright or Inadequate Lighting	How often does this job require working in extremely bright or inadequate lighting conditions?
Cramped Work Space, Awkward Positions	How often does this job require working in cramped work spaces that requires getting into awkward positions?
Wear Common Protective or Safety Equipment such as	How much does this job require wearing common protective or safety equipment such as safety shoes, glasses, gloves, hard hats or life jackets?
Exposed to Hazardous Conditions	How often does this job require exposure to hazardous conditions?
Spend Time Keeping or Regaining Balance	How much does this job require keeping or regaining your balance?
Spend Time Kneeling, Crouching, Stooping, or Crawl	How much does this job require kneeling, crouching, stooping or crawling?
Exposed to High Places	How often does this job require exposure to high places?
Exposed to Disease or Infections	How often does this job require exposure to disease/infections?
Exposed to Hazardous Equipment	How often does this job require exposure to hazardous equipment?
Spend Time Climbing Ladders, Scaffolds, or Poles	How much does this job require climbing ladders, scaffolds, or poles?
Pace Determined by Speed of Equipment	How important is it to this job that the pace is determined by the speed of equipment or machinery? (This does not refer to keeping busy at all times on this job.)
Exposed to Whole Body Vibration	How often does this job require exposure to whole body vibration (e.g., operate a jackhammer)?
Wear Specialized Protective or Safety Equipment su	How much does this job require wearing specialized protective or safety equipment such as breathing apparatus, safety harness, full protection suits, or radiation protection?
Exposed to Radiation	How often does this job require exposure to radiation?
In an Open Vehicle or Equipment	How often does this job require working in an open vehicle or equipment (e.g., tractor)?

Job Zone Component	Job Zone Component Definitions
Title	Job Zone Three: Medium Preparation Needed
Overall Experience	Previous work-related skill, knowledge, or experience is required for these occupations. For example, an electrician must have completed three or four years of apprenticeship or several years of vocational training, and often must have passed a licensing exam, in order to perform the job.
Job Training	Employees in these occupations usually need one or two years of training involving both on-the-job experience and informal training with experienced workers.

	These occupations usually involve using communication and organizational skills to coordinate, supervise, manage, or train others to accomplish goals.
Job Zone Examples	Examples include dental assistants, electricians, fish and game wardens, legal secretaries, personnel recruiters, and recreation workers.
SVP Range	(6.0 to < 7.0)
Education	Most occupations in this zone require training in vocational schools, related on-the-job experience, or an associate's degree. Some may require a bachelor's degree.

Work_Styles	Work_Styles Definitions
Cooperation	Job requires being pleasant with others on the job and displaying a good-natured, cooperative attitude.
Self Control	Job requires maintaining composure, keeping emotions in check, controlling anger, and avoiding aggressive behavior, even in very difficult situations.
Social Orientation	Job requires preferring to work with others rather than alone, and being personally connected with others on the job.
Concern for Others	Job requires being sensitive to others' needs and feelings and being understanding and helpful on the job.
Attention to Detail	Job requires being careful about detail and thorough in completing work tasks.
Independence	Job requires developing one's own ways of doing things, guiding oneself with little or no supervision, and depending on oneself to get things done.
Stress Tolerance	Job requires accepting criticism and dealing calmly and effectively with high stress situations.
Dependability	Job requires being reliable, responsible, and dependable, and fulfilling obligations.
Integrity	Job requires being honest and ethical.
Adaptability/Flexibility	Job requires being open to change (positive or negative) and to considerable variety in the workplace.
Leadership	Job requires a willingness to lead, take charge, and offer opinions and direction.
Analytical Thinking	Job requires analyzing information and using logic to address work-related issues and problems.
Initiative	Job requires a willingness to take on responsibilities and challenges.
Achievement/Effort	Job requires establishing and maintaining personally challenging achievement goals and exerting effort toward mastering tasks.
Innovation	Job requires creativity and alternative thinking to develop new ideas for and answers to work-related problems.
Persistence	Job requires persistence in the face of obstacles.

11-9111.00 - Medical and Health Services Managers

Plan, direct, or coordinate medicine and health services in hospitals, clinics, managed care organizations, public health agencies, or similar organizations.

Tasks

1) Establish work schedules and assignments for staff, according to workload, space and equipment availability.

2) Direct or conduct recruitment, hiring and training of personnel.

3) Develop and implement organizational policies and procedures for the facility or medical unit.

4) Prepare activity reports to inform management of the status and implementation plans of programs, services, and quality initiatives.

5) Establish objectives and evaluative or operational criteria for units they manage.

6) Conduct and administer fiscal operations, including accounting, planning budgets, authorizing expenditures, establishing rates for services, and coordinating financial reporting.

7) Maintain awareness of advances in medicine, computerized diagnostic and treatment equipment, data processing technology, government regulations, health insurance changes, and financing options.

8) Manage change in integrated health care delivery systems, such as work restructuring, technological innovations, and shifts in the focus of care.

9) Maintain communication between governing boards, medical staff, and department heads by attending board meetings and coordinating interdepartmental functioning.

10) Monitor the use of diagnostic services, inpatient beds, facilities, and staff to ensure effective use of resources and assess the need for additional staff, equipment, and services.

11) Review and analyze facility activities and data to aid planning and cash and risk management and to improve service utilization.

12) Consult with medical, business, and community groups to discuss service problems, respond to community needs, enhance public relations, coordinate activities and plans, and promote health programs.

13) Plan, implement and administer programs and services in a health care or medical facility, including personnel administration, training, and coordination of medical, nursing and physical plant staff.

14) Develop and maintain computerized record management systems to store and process data, such as personnel activities and information, and to produce reports.

15) Develop instructional materials and conduct in-service and community-based educational programs.

16) Inspect facilities and recommend building or equipment modifications to ensure emergency readiness and compliance to access, safety, and sanitation regulations.

17) Develop or expand and implement medical programs or health services that promote research, rehabilitation, and community health.

Knowledge	Knowledge Definitions
Customer and Personal Service	Knowledge of principles and processes for providing customer and personal services. This includes customer needs assessment, meeting quality standards for services, and evaluation of customer satisfaction.
Administration and Management	Knowledge of business and management principles involved in strategic planning, resource allocation, human resources modeling, leadership technique, production methods, and coordination of people and resources.
Personnel and Human Resources	Knowledge of principles and procedures for personnel recruitment, selection, training, compensation and benefits, labor relations and negotiation, and personnel information systems.
English Language	Knowledge of the structure and content of the English language including the meaning and spelling of words, rules of composition, and grammar.
Public Safety and Security	Knowledge of relevant equipment, policies, procedures, and strategies to promote effective local, state, or national security operations for the protection of people, data, property, and institutions.
Medicine and Dentistry	Knowledge of the information and techniques needed to diagnose and treat human injuries, diseases, and deformities. This includes symptoms, treatment alternatives, drug properties and interactions, and preventive health-care measures.
Education and Training	Knowledge of principles and methods for curriculum and training design, teaching and instruction for individuals and groups, and the measurement of training effects.
Computers and Electronics	Knowledge of circuit boards, processors, chips, electronic equipment, and computer hardware and software, including applications and programming.
Law and Government	Knowledge of laws, legal codes, court procedures, precedents, government regulations, executive orders, agency rules, and the democratic political process.
Therapy and Counseling	Knowledge of principles, methods, and procedures for diagnosis, treatment, and rehabilitation of physical and mental dysfunctions, and for career counseling and guidance.
Psychology	Knowledge of human behavior and performance; individual differences in ability, personality, and interests; learning and motivation; psychological research methods; and the assessment and treatment of behavioral and affective disorders.
Mathematics	Knowledge of arithmetic, algebra, geometry, calculus, statistics, and their applications.
Communications and Media	Knowledge of media production, communication, and dissemination techniques and methods. This includes alternative ways to inform and entertain via written, oral, and visual media.
Production and Processing	Knowledge of raw materials, production processes, quality control, costs, and other techniques for maximizing the effective manufacture and distribution of goods.
Economics and Accounting	Knowledge of economic and accounting principles and practices, the financial markets, banking and the analysis and reporting of financial data.
Sociology and Anthropology	Knowledge of group behavior and dynamics, societal trends and influences, human migrations, ethnicity, cultures and their history and origins.
Philosophy and Theology	Knowledge of different philosophical systems and religions. This includes their basic principles, values, ethics, ways of thinking, customs, practices, and their impact on human culture.
Sales and Marketing	Knowledge of principles and methods for showing, promoting, and selling products or services. This includes marketing strategy and tactics, product demonstration, sales techniques, and sales control systems.
Telecommunications	Knowledge of transmission, broadcasting, switching, control, and operation of telecommunications systems.
Chemistry	Knowledge of the chemical composition, structure, and properties of substances and of the chemical processes and transformations that they undergo. This includes uses of chemicals and their interactions, danger signs, production techniques, and disposal methods.
Clerical	Knowledge of administrative and clerical procedures and systems such as word processing, managing files and records, stenography and transcription, designing forms, and other office procedures and terminology.
Biology	Knowledge of plant and animal organisms, their tissues, cells, functions, interdependencies, and interactions with each other and the environment.
Physics	Knowledge and prediction of physical principles, laws, their interrelationships, and applications to understanding fluid, material, and atmospheric dynamics, and mechanical, electrical, atomic and sub-atomic structures and processes.
Building and Construction	Knowledge of materials, methods, and the tools involved in the construction or repair of houses, buildings, or other structures such as highways and roads.
Engineering and Technology	Knowledge of the practical application of engineering science and technology. This includes applying principles, techniques, procedures, and equipment to the design and production of various goods and services.
Design	Knowledge of design techniques, tools, and principles involved in production of precision technical plans, blueprints, drawings, and models.
Food Production	Knowledge of techniques and equipment for planting, growing, and harvesting food products (both plant and animal) for consumption, including storage/handling techniques.
Foreign Language	Knowledge of the structure and content of a foreign (non-English) language including the meaning and spelling of words, rules of composition and grammar, and pronunciation.
Transportation	Knowledge of principles and methods for moving people or goods by air, rail, sea, or road, including the relative costs and benefits.
History and Archeology	Knowledge of historical events and their causes, indicators, and effects on civilizations and cultures.
Mechanical	Knowledge of machines and tools, including their designs, uses, repair, and maintenance.
Fine Arts	Knowledge of the theory and techniques required to compose, produce, and perform works of music, dance, visual arts, drama, and sculpture.
Geography	Knowledge of principles and methods for describing the features of land, sea, and air masses, including their physical characteristics, locations, interrelationships, and distribution of plant, animal, and human life.

Skills	Skills Definitions
Active Listening	Giving full attention to what other people are saying, taking time to understand the points being made, asking questions as appropriate, and not interrupting at inappropriate times.
Reading Comprehension	Understanding written sentences and paragraphs in work related documents.
Critical Thinking	Using logic and reasoning to identify the strengths and weaknesses of alternative solutions, conclusions or approaches to problems.
Speaking	Talking to others to convey information effectively.
Monitoring	Monitoring/Assessing performance of yourself, other individuals, or organizations to make improvements or take corrective action.
Time Management	Managing one's own time and the time of others.
Judgment and Decision Making	Considering the relative costs and benefits of potential actions to choose the most appropriate one.
Service Orientation	Actively looking for ways to help people.
Writing	Communicating effectively in writing as appropriate for the needs of the audience.

Active Learning	Understanding the implications of new information for both current and future problem-solving and decision-making.
Management of Personnel Resources	Motivating, developing, and directing people as they work, identifying the best people for the job.
Coordination	Adjusting actions in relation to others' actions.
Social Perceptiveness	Being aware of others' reactions and understanding why they react as they do.
Learning Strategies	Selecting and using training/instructional methods and procedures appropriate for the situation when learning or teaching new things.
Persuasion	Persuading others to change their minds or behavior.
Instructing	Teaching others how to do something.
Complex Problem Solving	Identifying complex problems and reviewing related information to develop and evaluate options and implement solutions.
Management of Financial Resources	Determining how money will be spent to get the work done, and accounting for these expenditures.
Operations Analysis	Analyzing needs and product requirements to create a design.
Systems Evaluation	Identifying measures or indicators of system performance and the actions needed to improve or correct performance, relative to the goals of the system.
Quality Control Analysis	Conducting tests and inspections of products, services, or processes to evaluate quality or performance.
Management of Material Resources	Obtaining and seeing to the appropriate use of equipment, facilities, and materials needed to do certain work.
Equipment Selection	Determining the kind of tools and equipment needed to do a job.
Negotiation	Bringing others together and trying to reconcile differences.
Mathematics	Using mathematics to solve problems.
Troubleshooting	Determining causes of operating errors and deciding what to do about it.
Systems Analysis	Determining how a system should work and how changes in conditions, operations, and the environment will affect outcomes.
Science	Using scientific rules and methods to solve problems.
Operation Monitoring	Watching gauges, dials, or other indicators to make sure a machine is working properly.
Technology Design	Generating or adapting equipment and technology to serve user needs.
Operation and Control	Controlling operations of equipment or systems.
Equipment Maintenance	Performing routine maintenance on equipment and determining when and what kind of maintenance is needed.
Programming	Writing computer programs for various purposes.
Installation	Installing equipment, machines, wiring, or programs to meet specifications.
Repairing	Repairing machines or systems using the needed tools.

Ability	**Ability Definitions**
Oral Comprehension	The ability to listen to and understand information and ideas presented through spoken words and sentences.
Deductive Reasoning	The ability to apply general rules to specific problems to produce answers that make sense.
Written Comprehension	The ability to read and understand information and ideas presented in writing.
Problem Sensitivity	The ability to tell when something is wrong or is likely to go wrong. It does not involve solving the problem, only recognizing there is a problem.
Oral Expression	The ability to communicate information and ideas in speaking so others will understand.
Inductive Reasoning	The ability to combine pieces of information to form general rules or conclusions (includes finding a relationship among seemingly unrelated events).
Written Expression	The ability to communicate information and ideas in writing so others will understand.
Information Ordering	The ability to arrange things or actions in a certain order or pattern according to a specific rule or set of rules (e.g., patterns of numbers, letters, words, pictures, mathematical operations).
Speech Recognition	The ability to identify and understand the speech of another person.
Speech Clarity	The ability to speak clearly so others can understand you.
Category Flexibility	The ability to generate or use different sets of rules for combining or grouping things in different ways.
Near Vision	The ability to see details at close range (within a few feet of the observer).
Mathematical Reasoning	The ability to choose the right mathematical methods or formulas to solve a problem.

Time Sharing	The ability to shift back and forth between two or more activities or sources of information (such as speech, sounds, touch, or other sources).
Selective Attention	The ability to concentrate on a task over a period of time without being distracted.
Originality	The ability to come up with unusual or clever ideas about a given topic or situation, or to develop creative ways to solve a problem.
Fluency of Ideas	The ability to come up with a number of ideas about a topic (the number of ideas is important, not their quality, correctness, or creativity).
Perceptual Speed	The ability to quickly and accurately compare similarities and differences among sets of letters, numbers, objects, pictures, or patterns. The things to be compared may be presented at the same time or one after the other. This ability also includes comparing a presented object with a remembered object.
Flexibility of Closure	The ability to identify or detect a known pattern (a figure, object, word, or sound) that is hidden in other distracting material.
Far Vision	The ability to see details at a distance.
Number Facility	The ability to add, subtract, multiply, or divide quickly and correctly.
Speed of Closure	The ability to quickly make sense of, combine, and organize information into meaningful patterns.
Visualization	The ability to imagine how something will look after it is moved around or when its parts are moved or rearranged.
Trunk Strength	The ability to use your abdominal and lower back muscles to support part of the body repeatedly or continuously over time without 'giving out' or fatiguing.
Memorization	The ability to remember information such as words, numbers, pictures, and procedures.
Auditory Attention	The ability to focus on a single source of sound in the presence of other distracting sounds.
Depth Perception	The ability to judge which of several objects is closer or farther away from you, or to judge the distance between you and an object.
Finger Dexterity	The ability to make precisely coordinated movements of the fingers of one or both hands to grasp, manipulate, or assemble very small objects.
Manual Dexterity	The ability to quickly move your hand, your hand together with your arm, or your two hands to grasp, manipulate, or assemble objects.
Hearing Sensitivity	The ability to detect or tell the differences between sounds that vary in pitch and loudness.
Gross Body Coordination	The ability to coordinate the movement of your arms, legs, and torso together when the whole body is in motion.
Visual Color Discrimination	The ability to match or detect differences between colors, including shades of color and brightness.
Control Precision	The ability to quickly and repeatedly adjust the controls of a machine or a vehicle to exact positions.
Stamina	The ability to exert yourself physically over long periods of time without getting winded or out of breath.
Speed of Limb Movement	The ability to quickly move the arms and legs.
Arm-Hand Steadiness	The ability to keep your hand and arm steady while moving your arm or while holding your arm and hand in one position.
Wrist-Finger Speed	The ability to make fast, simple, repeated movements of the fingers, hands, and wrists.
Spatial Orientation	The ability to know your location in relation to the environment or to know where other objects are in relation to you.
Extent Flexibility	The ability to bend, stretch, twist, or reach with your body, arms, and/or legs.
Gross Body Equilibrium	The ability to keep or regain your body balance or stay upright when in an unstable position.
Rate Control	The ability to time your movements or the movement of a piece of equipment in anticipation of changes in the speed and/or direction of a moving object or scene.
Explosive Strength	The ability to use short bursts of muscle force to propel oneself (as in jumping or sprinting), or to throw an object.
Sound Localization	The ability to tell the direction from which a sound originated.
Night Vision	The ability to see under low light conditions.
Reaction Time	The ability to quickly respond (with the hand, finger, or foot) to a signal (sound, light, picture) when it appears.
Multilimb Coordination	The ability to coordinate two or more limbs (for example, two arms, two legs, or one leg and one arm) while sitting, standing, or lying down. It does not involve performing the activities while the whole body is in motion.
Peripheral Vision	The ability to see objects or movement of objects to one's side when the eyes are looking ahead.

Dynamic Flexibility	The ability to quickly and repeatedly bend. stretch. twist. or reach out with your body, arms. and/or legs.
Response Orientation	The ability to choose quickly between two or more movements in response to two or more different signals (lights. sounds. pictures). It includes the speed with which the correct response is started with the hand, foot, or other body part.
Dynamic Strength	The ability to exert muscle force repeatedly or continuously over time. This involves muscular endurance and resistance to muscle fatigue.
Static Strength	The ability to exert maximum muscle force to lift, push, pull. or carry objects.
Glare Sensitivity	The ability to see objects in the presence of glare or bright lighting.

Work_Activity	Work_Activity Definitions
Establishing and Maintaining Interpersonal Relatio	Developing constructive and cooperative working relationships with others, and maintaining them over time.
Making Decisions and Solving Problems	Analyzing information and evaluating results to choose the best solution and solve problems.
Monitor Processes. Materials. or Surroundings	Monitoring and reviewing information from materials. events. or the environment. to detect or assess problems.
Coordinating the Work and Activities of Others	Getting members of a group to work together to accomplish tasks.
Communicating with Supervisors, Peers. or Subordin	Providing information to supervisors, co-workers, and subordinates by telephone. in written form, e-mail, or in person.
Evaluating Information to Determine Compliance wit	Using relevant information and individual judgment to determine whether events or processes comply with laws. regulations, or standards.
Analyzing Data or Information	Identifying the underlying principles, reasons, or facts of information by breaking down information or data into separate parts.
Monitoring and Controlling Resources	Monitoring and controlling resources and overseeing the spending of money.
Updating and Using Relevant Knowledge	Keeping up-to-date technically and applying new knowledge to your job.
Resolving Conflicts and Negotiating with Others	Handling complaints, settling disputes, and resolving grievances and conflicts, or otherwise negotiating with others.
Staffing Organizational Units	Recruiting, interviewing, selecting, hiring, and promoting employees in an organization.
Getting Information	Observing, receiving, and otherwise obtaining information from all relevant sources.
Guiding, Directing, and Motivating Subordinates	Providing guidance and direction to subordinates, including setting performance standards and monitoring performance.
Organizing, Planning, and Prioritizing Work	Developing specific goals and plans to prioritize, organize, and accomplish your work.
Developing and Building Teams	Encouraging and building mutual trust, respect, and cooperation among team members.
Documenting/Recording Information	Entering, transcribing, recording, storing, or maintaining information in written or electronic/magnetic form.
Interacting With Computers	Using computers and computer systems (including hardware and software) to program, write software, set up functions, enter data, or process information.
Processing Information	Compiling, coding, categorizing, calculating, tabulating. auditing, or verifying information or data.
Developing Objectives and Strategies	Establishing long-range objectives and specifying the strategies and actions to achieve them.
Performing Administrative Activities	Performing day-to-day administrative tasks such as maintaining information files and processing paperwork.
Identifying Objects, Actions, and Events	Identifying information by categorizing, estimating. recognizing differences or similarities, and detecting changes in circumstances or events.
Communicating with Persons Outside Organization	Communicating with people outside the organization, representing the organization to customers, the public, government, and other external sources. This information can be exchanged in person, in writing, or by telephone or e-mail.
Thinking Creatively	Developing, designing, or creating new applications, ideas. relationships, systems, or products, including artistic contributions.
Scheduling Work and Activities	Scheduling events, programs, and activities, as well as the work of others.
Judging the Qualities of Things. Services, or Peop	Assessing the value, importance, or quality of things or people.
Provide Consultation and Advice to Others	Providing guidance and expert advice to management or other groups on technical, systems-, or process-related topics.

Selling or Influencing Others	Convincing others to buy merchandise/goods or to otherwise change their minds or actions.
Estimating the Quantifiable Characteristics of Pro	Estimating sizes, distances, and quantities; or determining time. costs, resources. or materials needed to perform a work activity.
Coaching and Developing Others	Identifying the developmental needs of others and coaching, mentoring, or otherwise helping others to improve their knowledge or skills.
Inspecting Equipment, Structures, or Material	Inspecting equipment, structures, or materials to identify the cause of errors or other problems or defects.
Training and Teaching Others	Identifying the educational needs of others, developing formal educational or training programs or classes, and teaching or instructing others.
Assisting and Caring for Others	Providing personal assistance. medical attention, emotional support, or other personal care to others such as coworkers, customers, or patients.
Interpreting the Meaning of Information for Others	Translating or explaining what information means and how it can be used.
Performing General Physical Activities	Performing physical activities that require considerable use of your arms and legs and moving your whole body, such as climbing, lifting, balancing, walking, stooping, and handling of materials.
Performing for or Working Directly with the Public	Performing for people or dealing directly with the public. This includes serving customers in restaurants and stores, and receiving clients or guests.
Handling and Moving Objects	Using hands and arms in handling, installing, positioning, and moving materials, and manipulating things.
Controlling Machines and Processes	Using either control mechanisms or direct physical activity to operate machines or processes (not including computers or vehicles).
Repairing and Maintaining Electronic Equipment	Servicing, repairing, calibrating. regulating, fine-tuning, or testing machines, devices. and equipment that operate primarily on the basis of electrical or electronic (not mechanical) principles.
Operating Vehicles, Mechanized Devices, or Equipme	Running, maneuvering, navigating. or driving vehicles or mechanized equipment, such as forklifts, passenger vehicles, aircraft, or water craft.
Repairing and Maintaining Mechanical Equipment	Servicing, repairing, adjusting, and testing machines, devices, moving parts, and equipment that operate primarily on the basis of mechanical (not electronic) principles.
Drafting, Laying Out, and Specifying Technical Dev	Providing documentation, detailed instructions, drawings, or specifications to tell others about how devices, parts, equipment, or structures are to be fabricated, constructed, assembled, modified, maintained, or used.

Work_Context	Work_Context Definitions
Telephone	How often do you have telephone conversations in this job?
Face-to-Face Discussions	How often do you have to have face-to-face discussions with individuals or teams in this job?
Structured versus Unstructured Work	To what extent is this job structured for the worker, rather than allowing the worker to determine tasks, priorities, and goals?
Contact With Others	How much does this job require the worker to be in contact with others (face-to-face, by telephone, or otherwise) in order to perform it?
Indoors, Environmentally Controlled	How often does this job require working indoors in environmentally controlled conditions?
Frequency of Decision Making	How frequently is the worker required to make decisions that affect other people, the financial resources, and/or the image and reputation of the organization?
Coordinate or Lead Others	How important is it to coordinate or lead others in accomplishing work activities in this job?
Freedom to Make Decisions	How much decision making freedom, without supervision, does the job offer?
Work With Work Group or Team	How important is it to work with others in a group or team in this job?
Impact of Decisions on Co-workers or Company Resul	How do the decisions an employee makes impact the results of co-workers, clients or the company?
Importance of Being Exact or Accurate	How important is being very exact or highly accurate in performing this job?
Time Pressure	How often does this job require the worker to meet strict deadlines?
Frequency of Conflict Situations	How often are there conflict situations the employee has to face in this job?
Responsibility for Outcomes and Results	How responsible is the worker for work outcomes and results of other workers?
Letters and Memos	How often does the job require written letters and memos?

Deal With External Customers	How important is it to work with external customers or the public in this job?
Deal With Unpleasant or Angry People	How frequently does the worker have to deal with unpleasant, angry, or discourteous individuals as part of the job requirements?
Exposed to Disease or Infections	How often does this job require exposure to disease/infections?
Responsible for Others' Health and Safety	How much responsibility is there for the health and safety of others in this job?
Physical Proximity	To what extent does this job require the worker to perform job tasks in close physical proximity to other people?
Electronic Mail	How often do you use electronic mail in this job?
Level of Competition	To what extent does this job require the worker to compete or to be aware of competitive pressures?
Spend Time Sitting	How much does this job require sitting?
Sounds, Noise Levels Are Distracting or Uncomforta	How often does this job require working exposed to sounds and noise levels that are distracting or uncomfortable?
Wear Common Protective or Safety Equipment such as	How much does this job require wearing common protective or safety equipment such as safety shoes, glasses, gloves, hard hats or life jackets?
Spend Time Walking and Running	How much does this job require walking and running?
Exposed to Radiation	How often does this job require exposure to radiation?
Spend Time Using Your Hands to Handle, Control, or	How much does this job require using your hands to handle, control, or feel objects, tools or controls?
Spend Time Standing	How much does this job require standing?
Importance of Repeating Same Tasks	How important is repeating the same physical activities (e.g., key entry) or mental activities (e.g., checking entries in a ledger) over and over, without stopping, to performing this job?
Consequence of Error	How serious would the result usually be if the worker made a mistake that was not readily correctable?
Degree of Automation	How automated is the job?
Exposed to Contaminants	How often does this job require working exposed to contaminants (such as pollutants, gases, dust or odors)?
Wear Specialized Protective or Safety Equipment su	How much does this job require wearing specialized protective or safety equipment such as breathing apparatus, safety harness, full protection suits, or radiation protection?
Deal With Physically Aggressive People	How frequently does this job require the worker to deal with physical aggression of violent individuals?
Spend Time Bending or Twisting the Body	How much does this job require bending or twisting your body?
Spend Time Making Repetitive Motions	How much does this job require making repetitive motions?
Public Speaking	How often do you have to perform public speaking in this job?
Spend Time Kneeling, Crouching, Stooping, or Crawl	How much does this job require kneeling, crouching, stooping, or crawling?
Extremely Bright or Inadequate Lighting	How often does this job require working in extremely bright or inadequate lighting conditions?
Indoors, Not Environmentally Controlled	How often does this job require working indoors in non-controlled environmental conditions (e.g., warehouse without heat)?
Exposed to Minor Burns, Cuts, Bites, or Stings	How often does this job require exposure to minor burns, cuts, bites, or stings?
In an Enclosed Vehicle or Equipment	How often does this job require working in a closed vehicle or equipment (e.g., car)?
Outdoors, Exposed to Weather	How often does this job require working outdoors, exposed to all weather conditions?
Very Hot or Cold Temperatures	How often does this job require working in very hot (above 90 F degrees) or very cold (below 32 F degrees) temperatures?
Pace Determined by Speed of Equipment	How important is it to this job that the pace is determined by the speed of equipment or machinery? (This does not refer to keeping busy at all times on this job.)
Exposed to Hazardous Conditions	How often does this job require exposure to hazardous conditions?
Spend Time Keeping or Regaining Balance	How much does this job require keeping or regaining your balance?
Cramped Work Space, Awkward Positions	How often does this job require working in cramped work spaces that requires getting into awkward positions?
Exposed to Hazardous Equipment	How often does this job require exposure to hazardous equipment?
Outdoors, Under Cover	How often does this job require working outdoors, under cover (e.g., structure with roof but no walls)?
Spend Time Climbing Ladders, Scaffolds, or Poles	How much does this job require climbing ladders, scaffolds, or poles?

Exposed to Whole Body Vibration	How often does this job require exposure to whole body vibration (e.g., operate a jackhammer)?
In an Open Vehicle or Equipment	How often does this job require working in an open vehicle or equipment (e.g., tractor)?
Exposed to High Places	How often does this job require exposure to high places?

Job Zone Component	Job Zone Component Definitions
Title	Job Zone Five: Extensive Preparation Needed
Overall Experience	Extensive skill, knowledge, and experience are needed for these occupations. Many require more than five years of experience. For example, surgeons must complete four years of college and an additional five to seven years of specialized medical training to be able to do their job.
Job Training	Employees may need some on-the-job training, but most of these occupations assume that the person will already have the required skills, knowledge, work-related experience, and/or training.
Job Zone Examples	These occupations often involve coordinating, training, supervising, or managing the activities of others to accomplish goals. Very advanced communication and organizational skills are required. Examples include athletic trainers, lawyers, managing editors, physicists, social psychologists, and surgeons.
SVP Range	(8.0 and above)
Education	A bachelor's degree is the minimum formal education required for these occupations. However, many also require graduate school. For example, they may require a master's degree, and some require a Ph.D., M.D., or J.D. (law degree).

Work_Styles	Work_Styles Definitions
Attention to Detail	Job requires being careful about detail and thorough in completing work tasks.
Leadership	Job requires a willingness to lead, take charge, and offer opinions and direction.
Dependability	Job requires being reliable, responsible, and dependable, and fulfilling obligations.
Integrity	Job requires being honest and ethical.
Adaptability/Flexibility	Job requires being open to change (positive or negative) and to considerable variety in the workplace.
Cooperation	Job requires being pleasant with others on the job and displaying a good-natured, cooperative attitude.
Concern for Others	Job requires being sensitive to others' needs and feelings and being understanding and helpful on the job.
Self Control	Job requires maintaining composure, keeping emotions in check, controlling anger, and avoiding aggressive behavior, even in very difficult situations.
Independence	Job requires developing one's own ways of doing things, guiding oneself with little or no supervision, and depending on oneself to get things done.
Social Orientation	Job requires preferring to work with others rather than alone, and being personally connected with others on the job.
Initiative	Job requires a willingness to take on responsibilities and challenges.
Stress Tolerance	Job requires accepting criticism and dealing calmly and effectively with high stress situations.
Persistence	Job requires persistence in the face of obstacles.
Achievement/Effort	Job requires establishing and maintaining personally challenging achievement goals and exerting effort toward mastering tasks.
Innovation	Job requires creativity and alternative thinking to develop new ideas for and answers to work-related problems.
Analytical Thinking	Job requires analyzing information and using logic to address work-related issues and problems.

11-9121.00 - Natural Sciences Managers

Plan, direct, or coordinate activities in such fields as life sciences, physical sciences, mathematics, statistics, and research and development in these fields.

Tasks

1) Hire, supervise and evaluate engineers, technicians, researchers and other staff.

2) Recruit personnel and oversee the development and maintenance of staff competence.

3) Determine scientific and technical goals within broad outlines provided by top management and make detailed plans to accomplish these goals.

4) Develop and implement policies, standards and procedures for the architectural, scientific and technical work performed, to ensure regulatory compliance and operations enhancement.

5) Plan and direct research, development, and production activities.

6) Prepare project proposals.

7) Advise and assist in obtaining patents or meeting other legal requirements.

8) Develop innovative technology and train staff for its implementation.

9) Confer with scientists, engineers, regulators, and others, to plan and review projects, and to provide technical assistance.

10) Prepare and administer budget, approve and review expenditures, and prepare financial reports.

11) Review project activities, and prepare and review research, testing, and operational reports.

12) Make presentations at professional meetings to further knowledge in the field.

13) Provide for stewardship of plant and animal resources and habitats, studying land use, monitoring animal populations and/or providing shelter, resources, and medical treatment for animals.

14) Design and coordinate successive phases of problem analysis, solution proposals, and testing.

15) Develop client relationships and communicate with clients to explain proposals, present research findings, establish specifications or discuss project status.

11-9141.00 - Property, Real Estate, and Community Association Managers

Plan, direct, or coordinate selling, buying, leasing, or governance activities of commercial, industrial, or residential real estate properties.

Tasks

1) Clean common areas, change light bulbs, and make minor property repairs.

2) Direct and coordinate the activities of staff and contract personnel, and evaluate their performance.

3) Purchase building and maintenance supplies, equipment, or furniture.

4) Prepare detailed budgets and financial reports for properties.

5) Prepare and administer contracts for provision of property services such as cleaning, maintenance, and security services.

6) Plan, schedule, and coordinate general maintenance, major repairs, and remodeling or construction projects for commercial or residential properties.

7) Negotiate the sale, lease, or development of property, and complete or review appropriate documents and forms.

8) Meet with prospective tenants to show properties, explain terms of occupancy, and provide information about local areas.

9) Investigate complaints, disturbances and violations, and resolve problems, following management rules and regulations.

10) Manage and oversee operations, maintenance, administration, and improvement of commercial, industrial, or residential properties.

11) Confer with legal authorities to ensure that renting and advertising practices are not discriminatory and that properties comply with state and federal regulations.

12) Market vacant space to prospective tenants through leasing agents, advertising, or other methods.

13) Confer regularly with community association members to ensure their needs are being met.

14) Maintain contact with insurance carriers, fire and police departments, and other agencies to ensure protection and compliance with codes and regulations.

15) Maintain records of sales, rental or usage activity, special permits issued, maintenance and operating costs, or property availability.

16) Determine and certify the eligibility of prospective tenants, following government regulations.

17) Direct collection of monthly assessments, rental fees, and deposits and payment of insurance premiums, mortgage, taxes, and incurred operating expenses.

18) Analyze information on property values, taxes, zoning, population growth, and traffic volume and patterns in order to determine if properties should be acquired.

19) Negotiate with government leaders, businesses, special interest representatives, and utility companies to gain support for new projects and to eliminate potential obstacles.

20) Contract with architectural firms to draw up detailed plans for new structures.

21) Solicit and analyze bids from contractors for repairs, renovations, and maintenance.

22) Review rents to ensure that they are in line with rental markets.

23) Act as liaisons between on-site managers or tenants and owners.

24) Meet with clients to negotiate management and service contracts, determine priorities, and discuss the financial and operational status of properties.

25) Meet with boards of directors and committees to discuss and resolve legal and environmental issues or disputes between neighbors.

26) Negotiate short- and long-term loans to finance construction and ownership of structures.

11-9151.00 - Social and Community Service Managers

Plan, organize, or coordinate the activities of a social service program or community outreach organization. Oversee the program or organization's budget and policies regarding participant involvement, program requirements, and benefits. Work may involve directing social workers, counselors, or probation officers.

Tasks

1) Research and analyze member or community needs in order to determine program directions and goals.

2) Prepare and maintain records and reports, such as budgets, personnel records, or training manuals.

3) Recruit, interview, and hire or sign up volunteers and staff.

4) Speak to community groups to explain and interpret agency purposes, programs, and policies.

5) Direct activities of professional and technical staff members and volunteers.

6) Evaluate the work of staff and volunteers in order to ensure that programs are of appropriate quality and that resources are used effectively.

7) Participate in the determination of organizational policies regarding such issues as participant eligibility, program requirements, and program benefits.

8) Establish and oversee administrative procedures to meet objectives set by boards of directors or senior management.

9) Represent organizations in relations with governmental and media institutions.

10) Act as consultants to agency staff and other community programs regarding the interpretation of program-related federal, state, and county regulations and policies.

11) Implement and evaluate staff training programs.

12) Analyze proposed legislation, regulations, or rule changes in order to determine how agency services could be impacted.

13) Plan and administer budgets for programs, equipment and support services.

14) Direct fund-raising activities and the preparation of public relations materials.

Knowledge	Knowledge Definitions
English Language	Knowledge of the structure and content of the English language including the meaning and spelling of words, rules of composition, and grammar.
Education and Training	Knowledge of principles and methods for curriculum and training design, teaching and instruction for individuals and groups, and the measurement of training effects.
Psychology	Knowledge of human behavior and performance; individual differences in ability, personality, and interests; learning and motivation; psychological research methods; and the assessment and treatment of behavioral and affective disorders.
Customer and Personal Service	Knowledge of principles and processes for providing customer and personal services. This includes customer needs assessment, meeting quality standards for services, and evaluation of customer satisfaction.

Sociology and Anthropology	Knowledge of group behavior and dynamics, societal trends and influences, human migrations, ethnicity, cultures and their history and origins.
Clerical	Knowledge of administrative and clerical procedures and systems such as word processing, managing files and records, stenography and transcription, designing forms, and other office procedures and terminology.
Administration and Management	Knowledge of business and management principles involved in strategic planning, resource allocation, human resources modeling, leadership technique, production methods, and coordination of people and resources.
Therapy and Counseling	Knowledge of principles, methods, and procedures for diagnosis, treatment, and rehabilitation of physical and mental dysfunctions, and for career counseling and guidance.
Personnel and Human Resources	Knowledge of principles and procedures for personnel recruitment, selection, training, compensation and benefits, labor relations and negotiation, and personnel information systems.
Communications and Media	Knowledge of media production, communication, and dissemination techniques and methods. This includes alternative ways to inform and entertain via written, oral, and visual media.
Computers and Electronics	Knowledge of circuit boards, processors, chips, electronic equipment, and computer hardware and software, including applications and programming.
Mathematics	Knowledge of arithmetic, algebra, geometry, calculus, statistics, and their applications.
Law and Government	Knowledge of laws, legal codes, court procedures, precedents, government regulations, executive orders, agency rules, and the democratic political process.
Philosophy and Theology	Knowledge of different philosophical systems and religions. This includes their basic principles, values, ethics, ways of thinking, customs, practices, and their impact on human culture.
Public Safety and Security	Knowledge of relevant equipment, policies, procedures, and strategies to promote effective local, state, or national security operations for the protection of people, data, property, and institutions.
Economics and Accounting	Knowledge of economic and accounting principles and practices, the financial markets, banking and the analysis and reporting of financial data.
Foreign Language	Knowledge of the structure and content of a foreign (non-English) language including the meaning and spelling of words, rules of composition and grammar, and pronunciation.
Medicine and Dentistry	Knowledge of the information and techniques needed to diagnose and treat human injuries, diseases, and deformities. This includes symptoms, treatment alternatives, drug properties and interactions, and preventive health-care measures.
Telecommunications	Knowledge of transmission, broadcasting, switching, control, and operation of telecommunications systems.
Transportation	Knowledge of principles and methods for moving people or goods by air, rail, sea, or road, including the relative costs and benefits.
Sales and Marketing	Knowledge of principles and methods for showing, promoting, and selling products or services. This includes marketing strategy and tactics, product demonstration, sales techniques, and sales control systems.
Geography	Knowledge of principles and methods for describing the features of land, sea, and air masses, including their physical characteristics, locations, interrelationships, and distribution of plant, animal, and human life.
Biology	Knowledge of plant and animal organisms, their tissues, cells, functions, interdependencies, and interactions with each other and the environment.
Fine Arts	Knowledge of the theory and techniques required to compose, produce, and perform works of music, dance, visual arts, drama, and sculpture.
History and Archeology	Knowledge of historical events and their causes, indicators, and effects on civilizations and cultures.
Design	Knowledge of design techniques, tools, and principles involved in production of precision technical plans, blueprints, drawings, and models.
Engineering and Technology	Knowledge of the practical application of engineering science and technology. This includes applying principles, techniques, procedures, and equipment to the design and production of various goods and services.

Chemistry	Knowledge of the chemical composition, structure, and properties of substances and of the chemical processes and transformations that they undergo. This includes uses of chemicals and their interactions, danger signs, production techniques, and disposal methods.
Mechanical	Knowledge of machines and tools, including their designs, uses, repair, and maintenance.
Production and Processing	Knowledge of raw materials, production processes, quality control, costs, and other techniques for maximizing the effective manufacture and distribution of goods.
Building and Construction	Knowledge of materials, methods, and the tools involved in the construction or repair of houses, buildings, or other structures such as highways and roads.
Physics	Knowledge and prediction of physical principles, laws, their interrelationships, and applications to understanding fluid, material, and atmospheric dynamics, and mechanical, electrical, atomic and sub-atomic structures and processes.
Food Production	Knowledge of techniques and equipment for planting, growing, and harvesting food products (both plant and animal) for consumption, including storage/handling techniques.

Skills	Skills Definitions
Active Listening	Giving full attention to what other people are saying, taking time to understand the points being made, asking questions as appropriate, and not interrupting at inappropriate times.
Speaking	Talking to others to convey information effectively.
Social Perceptiveness	Being aware of others' reactions and understanding why they react as they do.
Time Management	Managing one's own time and the time of others.
Instructing	Teaching others how to do something.
Monitoring	Monitoring/Assessing performance of yourself, other individuals, or organizations to make improvements or take corrective action.
Reading Comprehension	Understanding written sentences and paragraphs in work related documents.
Service Orientation	Actively looking for ways to help people.
Active Learning	Understanding the implications of new information for both current and future problem-solving and decision-making.
Negotiation	Bringing others together and trying to reconcile differences.
Learning Strategies	Selecting and using training/instructional methods and procedures appropriate for the situation when learning or teaching new things.
Critical Thinking	Using logic and reasoning to identify the strengths and weaknesses of alternative solutions, conclusions or approaches to problems.
Writing	Communicating effectively in writing as appropriate for the needs of the audience.
Management of Personnel Resources	Motivating, developing, and directing people as they work, identifying the best people for the job.
Coordination	Adjusting actions in relation to others' actions.
Persuasion	Persuading others to change their minds or behavior.
Complex Problem Solving	Identifying complex problems and reviewing related information to develop and evaluate options and implement solutions.
Judgment and Decision Making	Considering the relative costs and benefits of potential actions to choose the most appropriate one.
Systems Evaluation	Identifying measures or indicators of system performance and the actions needed to improve or correct performance, relative to the goals of the system.
Management of Financial Resources	Determining how money will be spent to get the work done, and accounting for these expenditures.
Mathematics	Using mathematics to solve problems.
Operations Analysis	Analyzing needs and product requirements to create a design.
Quality Control Analysis	Conducting tests and inspections of products, services, or processes to evaluate quality or performance.
Systems Analysis	Determining how a system should work and how changes in conditions, operations, and the environment will affect outcomes.
Management of Material Resources	Obtaining and seeing to the appropriate use of equipment, facilities, and materials needed to do certain work.
Science	Using scientific rules and methods to solve problems.
Equipment Maintenance	Performing routine maintenance on equipment and determining when and what kind of maintenance is needed.
Equipment Selection	Determining the kind of tools and equipment needed to do a job.
Troubleshooting	Determining causes of operating errors and deciding what to do about it.

Technology Design	Generating or adapting equipment and technology to serve user needs.
Operation and Control	Controlling operations of equipment or systems.
Programming	Writing computer programs for various purposes.
Installation	Installing equipment, machines, wiring, or programs to meet specifications.
Repairing	Repairing machines or systems using the needed tools.
Operation Monitoring	Watching gauges, dials, or other indicators to make sure a machine is working properly.

Ability	Ability Definitions
Oral Comprehension	The ability to listen to and understand information and ideas presented through spoken words and sentences.
Speech Clarity	The ability to speak clearly so others can understand you.
Written Comprehension	The ability to read and understand information and ideas presented in writing.
Oral Expression	The ability to communicate information and ideas in speaking so others will understand.
Problem Sensitivity	The ability to tell when something is wrong or is likely to go wrong. It does not involve solving the problem, only recognizing there is a problem.
Written Expression	The ability to communicate information and ideas in writing so others will understand.
Speech Recognition	The ability to identify and understand the speech of another person.
Deductive Reasoning	The ability to apply general rules to specific problems to produce answers that make sense.
Inductive Reasoning	The ability to combine pieces of information to form general rules or conclusions (includes finding a relationship among seemingly unrelated events).
Originality	The ability to come up with unusual or clever ideas about a given topic or situation, or to develop creative ways to solve a problem.
Near Vision	The ability to see details at close range (within a few feet of the observer).
Fluency of Ideas	The ability to come up with a number of ideas about a topic (the number of ideas is important, not their quality, correctness, or creativity).
Information Ordering	The ability to arrange things or actions in a certain order or pattern according to a specific rule or set of rules (e.g., patterns of numbers, letters, words, pictures, mathematical operations).
Category Flexibility	The ability to generate or use different sets of rules for combining or grouping things in different ways.
Mathematical Reasoning	The ability to choose the right mathematical methods or formulas to solve a problem.
Selective Attention	The ability to concentrate on a task over a period of time without being distracted.
Time Sharing	The ability to shift back and forth between two or more activities or sources of information (such as speech, sounds, touch, or other sources).
Finger Dexterity	The ability to make precisely coordinated movements of the fingers of one or both hands to grasp, manipulate, or assemble very small objects.
Memorization	The ability to remember information such as words, numbers, pictures, and procedures.
Visualization	The ability to imagine how something will look after it is moved around or when its parts are moved or rearranged.
Flexibility of Closure	The ability to identify or detect a known pattern (a figure, object, word, or sound) that is hidden in other distracting material.
Far Vision	The ability to see details at a distance.
Perceptual Speed	The ability to quickly and accurately compare similarities and differences among sets of letters, numbers, objects, pictures, or patterns. The things to be compared may be presented at the same time or one after the other. This ability also includes comparing a presented object with a remembered object.
Number Facility	The ability to add, subtract, multiply, or divide quickly and correctly.
Speed of Closure	The ability to quickly make sense of, combine, and organize information into meaningful patterns.
Auditory Attention	The ability to focus on a single source of sound in the presence of other distracting sounds.
Hearing Sensitivity	The ability to detect or tell the differences between sounds that vary in pitch and loudness.
Visual Color Discrimination	The ability to match or detect differences between colors, including shades of color and brightness.

Depth Perception	The ability to judge which of several objects is closer or farther away from you, or to judge the distance between you and an object.
Trunk Strength	The ability to use your abdominal and lower back muscles to support part of the body repeatedly or continuously over time without 'giving out' or fatiguing.
Stamina	The ability to exert yourself physically over long periods of time without getting winded or out of breath.
Static Strength	The ability to exert maximum muscle force to lift, push, pull, or carry objects.
Extent Flexibility	The ability to bend, stretch, twist, or reach with your body, arms, and/or legs.
Night Vision	The ability to see under low light conditions.
Spatial Orientation	The ability to know your location in relation to the environment or to know where other objects are in relation to you.
Wrist-Finger Speed	The ability to make fast, simple, repeated movements of the fingers, hands, and wrists.
Response Orientation	The ability to choose quickly between two or more movements in response to two or more different signals (lights, sounds, pictures). It includes the speed with which the correct response is started with the hand, foot, or other body part.
Sound Localization	The ability to tell the direction from which a sound originated.
Gross Body Coordination	The ability to coordinate the movement of your arms, legs, and torso together when the whole body is in motion.
Arm-Hand Steadiness	The ability to keep your hand and arm steady while moving your arm or while holding your arm and hand in one position.
Gross Body Equilibrium	The ability to keep or regain your body balance or stay upright when in an unstable position.
Explosive Strength	The ability to use short bursts of muscle force to propel oneself (as in jumping or sprinting), or to throw an object.
Dynamic Flexibility	The ability to quickly and repeatedly bend, stretch, twist, or reach out with your body, arms, and/or legs.
Dynamic Strength	The ability to exert muscle force repeatedly or continuously over time. This involves muscular endurance and resistance to muscle fatigue.
Speed of Limb Movement	The ability to quickly move the arms and legs.
Reaction Time	The ability to quickly respond (with the hand, finger, or foot) to a signal (sound, light, picture) when it appears.
Manual Dexterity	The ability to quickly move your hand, your hand together with your arm, or your two hands to grasp, manipulate, or assemble objects.
Rate Control	The ability to time your movements or the movement of a piece of equipment in anticipation of changes in the speed and/or direction of a moving object or scene.
Control Precision	The ability to quickly and repeatedly adjust the controls of a machine or a vehicle to exact positions.
Peripheral Vision	The ability to see objects or movement of objects to one's side when the eyes are looking ahead.
Glare Sensitivity	The ability to see objects in the presence of glare or bright lighting.
Multilimb Coordination	The ability to coordinate two or more limbs (for example, two arms, two legs, or one leg and one arm) while sitting, standing, or lying down. It does not involve performing the activities while the whole body is in motion.

Work_Activity	Work_Activity Definitions
Establishing and Maintaining Interpersonal Relatio	Developing constructive and cooperative working relationships with others, and maintaining them over time.
Making Decisions and Solving Problems	Analyzing information and evaluating results to choose the best solution and solve problems.
Communicating with Supervisors, Peers, or Subordin	Providing information to supervisors, co-workers, and subordinates by telephone, in written form, e-mail, or in person.
Performing for or Working Directly with the Public	Performing for people or dealing directly with the public. This includes serving customers in restaurants and stores, and receiving clients or guests.
Getting Information	Observing, receiving, and otherwise obtaining information from all relevant sources.
Communicating with Persons Outside Organization	Communicating with people outside the organization, representing the organization to customers, the public, government, and other external sources. This information can be exchanged in person, in writing, or by telephone or e-mail.
Organizing, Planning, and Prioritizing Work	Developing specific goals and plans to prioritize, organize, and accomplish your work.

Thinking Creatively	Developing, designing, or creating new applications, ideas, relationships, systems, or products, including artistic contributions.
Resolving Conflicts and Negotiating with Others	Handling complaints, settling disputes, and resolving grievances and conflicts, or otherwise negotiating with others.
Developing and Building Teams	Encouraging and building mutual trust, respect, and cooperation among team members.
Judging the Qualities of Things, Services, or Peop	Assessing the value, importance, or quality of things or people.
Interacting With Computers	Using computers and computer systems (including hardware and software) to program, write software, set up functions, enter data, or process information.
Coordinating the Work and Activities of Others	Getting members of a group to work together to accomplish tasks.
Assisting and Caring for Others	Providing personal assistance, medical attention, emotional support, or other personal care to others such as coworkers, customers, or patients.
Updating and Using Relevant Knowledge	Keeping up-to-date technically and applying new knowledge to your job.
Developing Objectives and Strategies	Establishing long-range objectives and specifying the strategies and actions to achieve them.
Documenting/Recording Information	Entering, transcribing, recording, storing, or maintaining information in written or electronic/magnetic form.
Interpreting the Meaning of Information for Others	Translating or explaining what information means and how it can be used.
Processing Information	Compiling, coding, categorizing, calculating, tabulating, auditing, or verifying information or data.
Provide Consultation and Advice to Others	Providing guidance and expert advice to management or other groups on technical, systems-, or process-related topics.
Scheduling Work and Activities	Scheduling events, programs, and activities, as well as the work of others.
Performing Administrative Activities	Performing day-to-day administrative tasks such as maintaining information files and processing paperwork.
Selling or Influencing Others	Convincing others to buy merchandise/goods or to otherwise change their minds or actions.
Analyzing Data or Information	Identifying the underlying principles, reasons, or facts of information by breaking down information or data into separate parts.
Evaluating Information to Determine Compliance wit	Using relevant information and individual judgment to determine whether events or processes comply with laws, regulations, or standards.
Training and Teaching Others	Identifying the educational needs of others, developing formal educational or training programs or classes, and teaching or instructing others.
Identifying Objects, Actions, and Events	Identifying information by categorizing, estimating, recognizing differences or similarities, and detecting changes in circumstances or events.
Guiding, Directing, and Motivating Subordinates	Providing guidance and direction to subordinates, including setting performance standards and monitoring performance.
Coaching and Developing Others	Identifying the developmental needs of others and coaching, mentoring, or otherwise helping others to improve their knowledge or skills.
Monitor Processes, Materials, or Surroundings	Monitoring and reviewing information from materials, events, or the environment, to detect or assess problems.
Estimating the Quantifiable Characteristics of Pro	Estimating sizes, distances, and quantities; or determining time, costs, resources, or materials needed to perform a work activity.
Staffing Organizational Units	Recruiting, interviewing, selecting, hiring, and promoting employees in an organization.
Monitoring and Controlling Resources	Monitoring and controlling resources and overseeing the spending of money.
Operating Vehicles, Mechanized Devices, or Equipme	Running, maneuvering, navigating, or driving vehicles or mechanized equipment, such as forklifts, passenger vehicles, aircraft, or water craft.
Inspecting Equipment, Structures, or Material	Inspecting equipment, structures, or materials to identify the cause of errors or other problems or defects.
Handling and Moving Objects	Using hands and arms in handling, installing, positioning, and moving materials, and manipulating things.
Performing General Physical Activities	Performing physical activities that require considerable use of your arms and legs and moving your whole body, such as climbing, lifting, balancing, walking, stooping, and handling of materials.
Controlling Machines and Processes	Using either control mechanisms or direct physical activity to operate machines or processes (not including computers or vehicles).

Drafting, Laying Out, and Specifying Technical Dev	Providing documentation, detailed instructions, drawings, or specifications to tell others about how devices, parts, equipment, or structures are to be fabricated, constructed, assembled, modified, or used.
Repairing and Maintaining Electronic Equipment	Servicing, repairing, calibrating, regulating, fine-tuning, or testing machines, devices, and equipment that operate primarily on the basis of electrical or electronic (not mechanical) principles.
Repairing and Maintaining Mechanical Equipment	Servicing, repairing, adjusting, and testing machines, devices, moving parts, and equipment that operate primarily on the basis of mechanical (not electronic) principles.

Work_Context	Work_Context Definitions
Face-to-Face Discussions	How often do you have to have face-to-face discussions with individuals or teams in this job?
Telephone	How often do you have telephone conversations in this job?
Contact With Others	How much does this job require the worker to be in contact with others (face-to-face, by telephone, or otherwise) in order to perform it?
Work With Work Group or Team	How important is it to work with others in a group or team in this job?
Electronic Mail	How often do you use electronic mail in this job?
Structured versus Unstructured Work	To what extent is this job structured for the worker, rather than allowing the worker to determine tasks, priorities, and goals?
Freedom to Make Decisions	How much decision making freedom, without supervision, does the job offer?
Coordinate or Lead Others	How important is it to coordinate or lead others in accomplishing work activities in this job?
Deal With External Customers	How important is it to work with external customers or the public in this job?
Frequency of Decision Making	How frequently is the worker required to make decisions that affect other people, the financial resources, and/or the image and reputation of the organization?
Indoors, Environmentally Controlled	How often does this job require working indoors in environmentally controlled conditions?
Impact of Decisions on Co-workers or Company Resul	How do the decisions an employee makes impact the results of co-workers, clients or the company?
Time Pressure	How often does this job require the worker to meet strict deadlines?
Letters and Memos	How often does the job require written letters and memos?
Spend Time Sitting	How much does this job require sitting?
Responsibility for Outcomes and Results	How responsible is the worker for work outcomes and results of other workers?
Importance of Being Exact or Accurate	How important is being very exact or highly accurate in performing this job?
Sounds, Noise Levels Are Distracting or Uncomforta	How often does this job require working exposed to sounds and noise levels that are distracting or uncomfortable?
Responsible for Others' Health and Safety	How much responsibility is there for the health and safety of others in this job?
Deal With Unpleasant or Angry People	How frequently does the worker have to deal with unpleasant, angry, or discourteous individuals as part of the job requirements?
In an Enclosed Vehicle or Equipment	How often does this job require working in a closed vehicle or equipment (e.g., car)?
Frequency of Conflict Situations	How often are there conflict situations the employee has to face in this job?
Public Speaking	How often do you have to perform public speaking in this job?
Physical Proximity	To what extent does this job require the worker to perform job tasks in close physical proximity to other people?
Level of Competition	To what extent does this job require the worker to compete or to be aware of competitive pressures?
Importance of Repeating Same Tasks	How important is repeating the same physical activities (e.g., key entry) or mental activities (e.g., checking entries in a ledger) over and over, without stopping, to performing this job?
Consequence of Error	How serious would the result usually be if the worker made a mistake that was not readily correctable?
Degree of Automation	How automated is the job?
Spend Time Making Repetitive Motions	How much does this job require making repetitive motions?
Indoors, Not Environmentally Controlled	How often does this job require working indoors in non-controlled environmental conditions (e.g., warehouse without heat)?
Spend Time Standing	How much does this job require standing?
Outdoors, Exposed to Weather	How often does this job require working outdoors, exposed to all weather conditions?

Exposed to Disease or Infections	How often does this job require exposure to disease/infections?
Deal With Physically Aggressive People	How frequently does this job require the worker to deal with physical aggression of violent individuals?
Spend Time Walking and Running	How much does this job require walking and running?
Spend Time Bending or Twisting the Body	How much does this job require bending or twisting your body?
Spend Time Using Your Hands to Handle, Control, or	How much does this job require using your hands to handle, control, or feel objects, tools or controls?
Outdoors, Under Cover	How often does this job require working outdoors, under cover (e.g., structure with roof but no walls)?
Extremely Bright or Inadequate Lighting	How often does this job require working in extremely bright or inadequate lighting conditions?
Wear Common Protective or Safety Equipment such as	How much does this job require wearing common protective or safety equipment such as safety shoes, glasses, gloves, hard hats or live jackets?
Exposed to Contaminants	How often does this job require working exposed to contaminants (such as pollutants, gases, dust or odors)?
Pace Determined by Speed of Equipment	How important is it to this job that the pace is determined by the speed of equipment or machinery? (This does not refer to keeping busy at all times on this job.)
Spend Time Kneeling, Crouching, Stooping, or Crawl	How much does this job require kneeling, crouching, stooping or crawling?
Cramped Work Space, Awkward Positions	How often does this job require working in cramped work spaces that requires getting into awkward positions?
Very Hot or Cold Temperatures	How often does this job require working in very hot (above 90 F degrees) or very cold (below 32 F degrees) temperatures?
Exposed to Minor Burns, Cuts, Bites, or Stings	How often does this job require exposure to minor burns, cuts, bites, or stings?
Spend Time Climbing Ladders, Scaffolds, or Poles	How much does this job require climbing ladders, scaffolds, or poles?
Exposed to Hazardous Equipment	How often does this job require exposure to hazardous equipment?
Spend Time Keeping or Regaining Balance	How much does this job require keeping or regaining your balance?
Exposed to High Places	How often does this job require exposure to high places?
Exposed to Hazardous Conditions	How often does this job require exposure to hazardous conditions?
Exposed to Whole Body Vibration	How often does this job require exposure to whole body vibration (e.g., operate a jackhammer)?
In an Open Vehicle or Equipment	How often does this job require working in an open vehicle or equipment (e.g., tractor)?
Wear Specialized Protective or Safety Equipment su	How much does this job require wearing specialized protective or safety equipment such as breathing apparatus, safety harness, full protection suits, or radiation protection?
Exposed to Radiation	How often does this job require exposure to radiation?

Job Zone Component	Job Zone Component Definitions
Title	Job Zone Four: Considerable Preparation Needed
Overall Experience	A minimum of two to four years of work-related skill, knowledge, or experience is needed for these occupations. For example, an accountant must complete four years of college and work for several years in accounting to be considered qualified.
Job Training	Employees in these occupations usually need several years of work-related experience, on-the-job training, and/or vocational training.
Job Zone Examples	Many of these occupations involve coordinating, supervising, managing, or training others. Examples include accountants, chefs and head cooks, computer programmers, historians, pharmacists, and police detectives.
SVP Range	(7.0 to < 8.0)
Education	Most of these occupations require a four - year bachelor's degree, but some do not.

Work_Styles	Work_Styles Definitions
Dependability	Job requires being reliable, responsible, and dependable, and fulfilling obligations.
Integrity	Job requires being honest and ethical.
Adaptability/Flexibility	Job requires being open to change (positive or negative) and to considerable variety in the workplace.
Concern for Others	Job requires being sensitive to others' needs and feelings and being understanding and helpful on the job.
Cooperation	Job requires being pleasant with others on the job and displaying a good-natured, cooperative attitude.
Initiative	Job requires a willingness to take on responsibilities and challenges.
Self Control	Job requires maintaining composure, keeping emotions in check, controlling anger, and avoiding aggressive behavior, even in very difficult situations.
Stress Tolerance	Job requires accepting criticism and dealing calmly and effectively with high stress situations.
Persistence	Job requires persistence in the face of obstacles.
Attention to Detail	Job requires being careful about detail and thorough in completing work tasks.
Leadership	Job requires a willingness to lead, take charge, and offer opinions and direction.
Independence	Job requires developing one's own ways of doing things, guiding oneself with little or no supervision, and depending on oneself to get things done.
Achievement/Effort	Job requires establishing and maintaining personally challenging achievement goals and exerting effort toward mastering tasks.
Innovation	Job requires creativity and alternative thinking to develop new ideas for and answers to work-related problems.
Social Orientation	Job requires preferring to work with others rather than alone, and being personally connected with others on the job.
Analytical Thinking	Job requires analyzing information and using logic to address work-related issues and problems.

13-1011.00 - Agents and Business Managers of Artists, Performers, and Athletes

Represent and promote artists, performers, and athletes to prospective employers. May handle contract negotiation and other business matters for clients.

Tasks

1) Arrange meetings concerning issues involving their clients.

2) Keep informed of industry trends and deals.

3) Prepare periodic accounting statements for clients.

4) Hire trainers or coaches to advise clients on performance matters such as training techniques or performance presentations.

5) Schedule promotional or performance engagements for clients.

6) Negotiate with managers, promoters, union officials, and other persons regarding clients' contractual rights and obligations.

7) Manage business and financial affairs for clients, such as arranging travel and lodging, selling tickets, and directing marketing and advertising activities.

8) Confer with clients to develop strategies for their careers, and to explain actions taken on their behalf.

9) Conduct auditions or interviews in order to evaluate potential clients.

10) Collect fees, commissions, or other payments, according to contract terms.

11) Develop contacts with individuals and organizations, and apply effective strategies and techniques to ensure their clients' success.

12) Advise clients on financial and legal matters such as investments and taxes.

13-1021.00 - Purchasing Agents and Buyers, Farm Products

Purchase farm products either for further processing or resale.

Tasks

1) Purchase for further processing or for resale farm products such as milk, grains, and Christmas trees.

2) Coordinate and direct activities of workers engaged in cutting, transporting, storing, or milling products and in maintaining records.

3) Arrange for processing and/or resale of purchased products.

4) Arrange for transportation and/or storage of purchased products.

5) Examine and test crops and products to estimate their value, determine their grade, and locate any evidence of disease or insect damage.

6) Advise farm groups and growers on land preparation and livestock care techniques that will maximize the quantity and quality of production.

7) Estimate land production possibilities, surveying property and studying factors such as crop rotation history, soil fertility, and irrigation facilities.

8) Sell supplies such as seed, feed, fertilizers, and insecticides, arranging for loans or financing as necessary.

9) Calculate applicable government grain quotas.

10) Maintain records of business transactions and product inventories, reporting data to companies or government agencies as necessary.

11) Review orders to determine product types and quantities required to meet demand.

13-1022.00 - Wholesale and Retail Buyers, Except Farm Products

Buy merchandise or commodities, other than farm products, for resale to consumers at the wholesale or retail level, including both durable and nondurable goods. Analyze past buying trends, sales records, price, and quality of merchandise to determine value and yield. Select, order, and authorize payment for merchandise according to contractual agreements. May conduct meetings with sales personnel and introduce new products.

Tasks

1) Negotiate prices, discount terms and transportation arrangements for merchandise.

2) Interview and work closely with vendors to obtain and develop desired products.

3) Authorize payment of invoices or return of merchandise.

4) Analyze and monitor sales records, trends and economic conditions to anticipate consumer buying patterns and determine what the company will sell and how much inventory is needed.

5) Confer with sales and purchasing personnel to obtain information about customer needs and preferences.

6) Conduct staff meetings with sales personnel to introduce new merchandise.

7) Set or recommend mark-up rates, mark-down rates, and selling prices for merchandise.

8) Inspect merchandise or products to determine value or yield.

9) Consult with store or merchandise managers about budget and goods to be purchased.

10) Use computers to organize and locate inventory, and operate spreadsheet and word processing software.

11) Monitor competitors' sales activities by following their advertisements in newspapers and other media.

12) Determine which products should be featured in advertising, the advertising medium to be used, and when the ads should be run.

13) Train and supervise sales and clerical staff.

14) Provide clerks with information to print on price tags, such as price, mark-ups or mark-downs, manufacturer number, season code, and style number.

15) Manage the department for which they buy.

Knowledge	Knowledge Definitions
Sales and Marketing	Knowledge of principles and methods for showing, promoting, and selling products or services. This includes marketing strategy and tactics, product demonstration, sales techniques, and sales control systems.
Customer and Personal Service	Knowledge of principles and processes for providing customer and personal services. This includes customer needs assessment, meeting quality standards for services, and evaluation of customer satisfaction.
Economics and Accounting	Knowledge of economic and accounting principles and practices, the financial markets, banking and the analysis and reporting of financial data.
English Language	Knowledge of the structure and content of the English language including the meaning and spelling of words, rules of composition, and grammar.
Clerical	Knowledge of administrative and clerical procedures and systems such as word processing, managing files and records, stenography and transcription, designing forms, and other office procedures and terminology.
Administration and Management	Knowledge of business and management principles involved in strategic planning, resource allocation, human resources modeling, leadership technique, production methods, and coordination of people and resources.
Mathematics	Knowledge of arithmetic, algebra, geometry, calculus, statistics, and their applications.
Transportation	Knowledge of principles and methods for moving people or goods by air, rail, sea, or road, including the relative costs and benefits.
Computers and Electronics	Knowledge of circuit boards, processors, chips, electronic equipment, and computer hardware and software, including applications and programming.
Communications and Media	Knowledge of media production, communication, and dissemination techniques and methods. This includes alternative ways to inform and entertain via written, oral, and visual media.
Telecommunications	Knowledge of transmission, broadcasting, switching, control, and operation of telecommunications systems.
Education and Training	Knowledge of principles and methods for curriculum and training design, teaching and instruction for individuals and groups, and the measurement of training effects.
Production and Processing	Knowledge of raw materials, production processes, quality control, costs, and other techniques for maximizing the effective manufacture and distribution of goods.
Building and Construction	Knowledge of materials, methods, and the tools involved in the construction or repair of houses, buildings, or other structures such as highways and roads.
Personnel and Human Resources	Knowledge of principles and procedures for personnel recruitment, selection, training, compensation and benefits, labor relations and negotiation, and personnel information systems.
Psychology	Knowledge of human behavior and performance; individual differences in ability, personality, and interests; learning and motivation; psychological research methods; and the assessment and treatment of behavioral and affective disorders.
Law and Government	Knowledge of laws, legal codes, court procedures, precedents, government regulations, executive orders, agency rules, and the democratic political process.
Public Safety and Security	Knowledge of relevant equipment, policies, procedures, and strategies to promote effective local, state, or national security operations for the protection of people, data, property, and institutions.
Mechanical	Knowledge of machines and tools, including their designs, uses, repair, and maintenance.
Design	Knowledge of design techniques, tools, and principles involved in production of precision technical plans, blueprints, drawings, and models.
Geography	Knowledge of principles and methods for describing the features of land, sea, and air masses, including their physical characteristics, locations, interrelationships, and distribution of plant, animal, and human life.
Chemistry	Knowledge of the chemical composition, structure, and properties of substances and of the chemical processes and transformations that they undergo. This includes uses of chemicals and their interactions, danger signs, production techniques, and disposal methods.
Sociology and Anthropology	Knowledge of group behavior and dynamics, societal trends and influences, human migrations, ethnicity, cultures and their history and origins.
Engineering and Technology	Knowledge of the practical application of engineering science and technology. This includes applying principles, techniques, procedures, and equipment to the design and production of various goods and services.
Physics	Knowledge and prediction of physical principles, laws, their interrelationships, and applications to understanding fluid, material, and atmospheric dynamics, and mechanical, electrical, atomic and sub-atomic structures and processes.
Foreign Language	Knowledge of the structure and content of a foreign (non-English) language including the meaning and spelling of words, rules of composition and grammar, and pronunciation.
Fine Arts	Knowledge of the theory and techniques required to compose, produce, and perform works of music, dance, visual arts, drama, and sculpture.

Biology	Knowledge of plant and animal organisms, their tissues, cells, functions, interdependencies, and interactions with each other and the environment.
Therapy and Counseling	Knowledge of principles, methods, and procedures for diagnosis, treatment, and rehabilitation of physical and mental dysfunctions, and for career counseling and guidance.
Philosophy and Theology	Knowledge of different philosophical systems and religions. This includes their basic principles, values, ethics, ways of thinking, customs, practices, and their impact on human culture.
Medicine and Dentistry	Knowledge of the information and techniques needed to diagnose and treat human injuries, diseases, and deformities. This includes symptoms, treatment alternatives, drug properties and interactions, and preventive health-care measures.
History and Archeology	Knowledge of historical events and their causes, indicators, and effects on civilizations and cultures.
Food Production	Knowledge of techniques and equipment for planting, growing, and harvesting food products (both plant and animal) for consumption, including storage/handling techniques.

Skills — Skills Definitions

Active Listening	Giving full attention to what other people are saying, taking time to understand the points being made, asking questions as appropriate, and not interrupting at inappropriate times.
Speaking	Talking to others to convey information effectively.
Reading Comprehension	Understanding written sentences and paragraphs in work related documents.
Critical Thinking	Using logic and reasoning to identify the strengths and weaknesses of alternative solutions, conclusions or approaches to problems.
Time Management	Managing one's own time and the time of others.
Service Orientation	Actively looking for ways to help people.
Judgment and Decision Making	Considering the relative costs and benefits of potential actions to choose the most appropriate one.
Mathematics	Using mathematics to solve problems.
Instructing	Teaching others how to do something.
Management of Material Resources	Obtaining and seeing to the appropriate use of equipment, facilities, and materials needed to do certain work.
Management of Financial Resources	Determining how money will be spent to get the work done, and accounting for these expenditures.
Coordination	Adjusting actions in relation to others' actions.
Writing	Communicating effectively in writing as appropriate for the needs of the audience.
Monitoring	Monitoring/Assessing performance of yourself, other individuals, or organizations to make improvements or take corrective action.
Quality Control Analysis	Conducting tests and inspections of products, services, or processes to evaluate quality or performance.
Social Perceptiveness	Being aware of others' reactions and understanding why they react as they do.
Operations Analysis	Analyzing needs and product requirements to create a design.
Active Learning	Understanding the implications of new information for both current and future problem-solving and decision-making.
Negotiation	Bringing others together and trying to reconcile differences.
Learning Strategies	Selecting and using training/instructional methods and procedures appropriate for the situation when learning or teaching new things.
Management of Personnel Resources	Motivating, developing, and directing people as they work, identifying the best people for the job.
Equipment Selection	Determining the kind of tools and equipment needed to do a job.
Persuasion	Persuading others to change their minds or behavior.
Complex Problem Solving	Identifying complex problems and reviewing related information to develop and evaluate options and implement solutions.
Troubleshooting	Determining causes of operating errors and deciding what to do about it.
Operation and Control	Controlling operations of equipment or systems.
Systems Evaluation	Identifying measures or indicators of system performance and the actions needed to improve or correct performance, relative to the goals of the system.
Installation	Installing equipment, machines, wiring, or programs to meet specifications.
Technology Design	Generating or adapting equipment and technology to serve user needs.

Systems Analysis	Determining how a system should work and how changes in conditions, operations, and the environment will affect outcomes.
Operation Monitoring	Watching gauges, dials, or other indicators to make sure a machine is working properly.
Equipment Maintenance	Performing routine maintenance on equipment and determining when and what kind of maintenance is needed.
Repairing	Repairing machines or systems using the needed tools.
Science	Using scientific rules and methods to solve problems.
Programming	Writing computer programs for various purposes.

Ability — Ability Definitions

Oral Expression	The ability to communicate information and ideas in speaking so others will understand.
Oral Comprehension	The ability to listen to and understand information and ideas presented through spoken words and sentences.
Speech Clarity	The ability to speak clearly so others can understand you.
Written Comprehension	The ability to read and understand information and ideas presented in writing.
Inductive Reasoning	The ability to combine pieces of information to form general rules or conclusions (includes finding a relationship among seemingly unrelated events).
Speech Recognition	The ability to identify and understand the speech of another person.
Mathematical Reasoning	The ability to choose the right mathematical methods or formulas to solve a problem.
Deductive Reasoning	The ability to apply general rules to specific problems to produce answers that make sense.
Problem Sensitivity	The ability to tell when something is wrong or is likely to go wrong. It does not involve solving the problem, only recognizing there is a problem.
Near Vision	The ability to see details at close range (within a few feet of the observer).
Information Ordering	The ability to arrange things or actions in a certain order or pattern according to a specific rule or set of rules (e.g., patterns of numbers, letters, words, pictures, mathematical operations).
Category Flexibility	The ability to generate or use different sets of rules for combining or grouping things in different ways.
Fluency of Ideas	The ability to come up with a number of ideas about a topic (the number of ideas is important, not their quality, correctness, or creativity).
Written Expression	The ability to communicate information and ideas in writing so others will understand.
Flexibility of Closure	The ability to identify or detect a known pattern (a figure, object, word, or sound) that is hidden in other distracting material.
Number Facility	The ability to add, subtract, multiply, or divide quickly and correctly.
Originality	The ability to come up with unusual or clever ideas about a given topic or situation, or to develop creative ways to solve a problem.
Selective Attention	The ability to concentrate on a task over a period of time without being distracted.
Speed of Closure	The ability to quickly make sense of, combine, and organize information into meaningful patterns.
Time Sharing	The ability to shift back and forth between two or more activities or sources of information (such as speech, sounds, touch, or other sources).
Memorization	The ability to remember information such as words, numbers, pictures, and procedures.
Far Vision	The ability to see details at a distance.
Perceptual Speed	The ability to quickly and accurately compare similarities and differences among sets of letters, numbers, objects, pictures, or patterns. The things to be compared may be presented at the same time or one after the other. This ability also includes comparing a presented object with a remembered object.
Arm-Hand Steadiness	The ability to keep your hand and arm steady while moving your arm or while holding your arm and hand in one position.
Auditory Attention	The ability to focus on a single source of sound in the presence of other distracting sounds.
Visual Color Discrimination	The ability to match or detect differences between colors, including shades of color and brightness.
Finger Dexterity	The ability to make precisely coordinated movements of the fingers of one or both hands to grasp, manipulate, or assemble very small objects.
Visualization	The ability to imagine how something will look after it is moved around or when its parts are moved or rearranged.

Manual Dexterity	The ability to quickly move your hand, your hand together with your arm, or your two hands to grasp, manipulate, or assemble objects.
Control Precision	The ability to quickly and repeatedly adjust the controls of a machine or a vehicle to exact positions.
Static Strength	The ability to exert maximum muscle force to lift, push, pull, or carry objects.
Trunk Strength	The ability to use your abdominal and lower back muscles to support part of the body repeatedly or continuously over time without 'giving out' or fatiguing.
Extent Flexibility	The ability to bend, stretch, twist, or reach with your body, arms, and/or legs.
Depth Perception	The ability to judge which of several objects is closer or farther away from you, or to judge the distance between you and an object.
Hearing Sensitivity	The ability to detect or tell the differences between sounds that vary in pitch and loudness.
Dynamic Strength	The ability to exert muscle force repeatedly or continuously over time. This involves muscular endurance and resistance to muscle fatigue.
Multilimb Coordination	The ability to coordinate two or more limbs (for example, two arms, two legs, or one leg and one arm) while sitting, standing, or lying down. It does not involve performing the activities while the whole body is in motion.
Stamina	The ability to exert yourself physically over long periods of time without getting winded or out of breath.
Gross Body Equilibrium	The ability to keep or regain your body balance or stay upright when in an unstable position.
Gross Body Coordination	The ability to coordinate the movement of your arms, legs, and torso together when the whole body is in motion.
Wrist-Finger Speed	The ability to make fast, simple, repeated movements of the fingers, hands, and wrists.
Night Vision	The ability to see under low light conditions.
Spatial Orientation	The ability to know your location in relation to the environment or to know where other objects are in relation to you.
Dynamic Flexibility	The ability to quickly and repeatedly bend, stretch, twist, or reach out with your body, arms, and/or legs.
Speed of Limb Movement	The ability to quickly move the arms and legs.
Explosive Strength	The ability to use short bursts of muscle force to propel oneself (as in jumping or sprinting), or to throw an object.
Peripheral Vision	The ability to see objects or movement of objects to one's side when the eyes are looking ahead.
Glare Sensitivity	The ability to see objects in the presence of glare or bright lighting.
Rate Control	The ability to time your movements or the movement of a piece of equipment in anticipation of changes in the speed and/or direction of a moving object or scene.
Reaction Time	The ability to quickly respond (with the hand, finger, or foot) to a signal (sound, light, picture) when it appears.
Response Orientation	The ability to choose quickly between two or more movements in response to two or more different signals (lights, sounds, pictures). It includes the speed with which the correct response is started with the hand, foot, or other body part.
Sound Localization	The ability to tell the direction from which a sound originated.

Work_Activity	**Work_Activity Definitions**
Selling or Influencing Others	Convincing others to buy merchandise/goods or to otherwise change their minds or actions.
Establishing and Maintaining Interpersonal Relatio	Developing constructive and cooperative working relationships with others, and maintaining them over time.
Updating and Using Relevant Knowledge	Keeping up-to-date technically and applying new knowledge to your job.
Organizing, Planning, and Prioritizing Work	Developing specific goals and plans to prioritize, organize, and accomplish your work.
Resolving Conflicts and Negotiating with Others	Handling complaints, settling disputes, and resolving grievances and conflicts, or otherwise negotiating with others.
Thinking Creatively	Developing, designing, or creating new applications, ideas, relationships, systems, or products, including artistic contributions.
Judging the Qualities of Things, Services, or Peop	Assessing the value, importance, or quality of things or people.
Estimating the Quantifiable Characteristics of Pro	Estimating sizes, distances, and quantities; or determining time, costs, resources, or materials needed to perform a work activity
Making Decisions and Solving Problems	Analyzing information and evaluating results to choose the best solution and solve problems.
Performing for or Working Directly with the Public	Performing for people or dealing directly with the public. This includes serving customers in restaurants and stores, and receiving clients or guests.
Communicating with Supervisors, Peers, or Subordin	Providing information to supervisors, co-workers, and subordinates by telephone, in written form, e-mail, or in person.
Communicating with Persons Outside Organization	Communicating with people outside the organization, representing the organization to customers, the public, government, and other external sources. This information can be exchanged in person, in writing, or by telephone or e-mail.
Performing Administrative Activities	Performing day-to-day administrative tasks such as maintaining information files and processing paperwork.
Scheduling Work and Activities	Scheduling events, programs, and activities, as well as the work of others.
Interacting With Computers	Using computers and computer systems (including hardware and software) to program, write software, set up functions, enter data, or process information.
Getting Information	Observing, receiving, and otherwise obtaining information from all relevant sources.
Processing Information	Compiling, coding, categorizing, calculating, tabulating, auditing, or verifying information or data.
Developing Objectives and Strategies	Establishing long-range objectives and specifying the strategies and actions to achieve them.
Training and Teaching Others	Identifying the educational needs of others, developing formal educational or training programs or classes, and teaching or instructing others.
Guiding, Directing, and Motivating Subordinates	Providing guidance and direction to subordinates, including setting performance standards and monitoring performance.
Developing and Building Teams	Encouraging and building mutual trust, respect, and cooperation among team members.
Interpreting the Meaning of Information for Others	Translating or explaining what information means and how it can be used.
Monitor Processes, Materials, or Surroundings	Monitoring and reviewing information from materials, events, or the environment, to detect or assess problems.
Coordinating the Work and Activities of Others	Getting members of a group to work together to accomplish tasks.
Coaching and Developing Others	Identifying the developmental needs of others and coaching, mentoring, or otherwise helping others to improve their knowledge or skills.
Performing General Physical Activities	Performing physical activities that require considerable use of your arms and legs and moving your whole body, such as climbing, lifting, balancing, walking, stooping, and handling of materials.
Inspecting Equipment, Structures, or Material	Inspecting equipment, structures, or materials to identify the cause of errors or other problems or defects.
Handling and Moving Objects	Using hands and arms in handling, installing, positioning, and moving materials, and manipulating things.
Monitoring and Controlling Resources	Monitoring and controlling resources and overseeing the spending of money.
Identifying Objects, Actions, and Events	Identifying information by categorizing, estimating, recognizing differences or similarities, and detecting changes in circumstances or events.
Assisting and Caring for Others	Providing personal assistance, medical attention, emotional support, or other personal care to others such as coworkers, customers, or patients.
Analyzing Data or Information	Identifying the underlying principles, reasons, or facts of information by breaking down information or data into separate parts.
Provide Consultation and Advice to Others	Providing guidance and expert advice to management or other groups on technical, systems-, or process-related topics.
Evaluating Information to Determine Compliance wit	Using relevant information and individual judgment to determine whether events or processes comply with laws, regulations, or standards.
Staffing Organizational Units	Recruiting, interviewing, selecting, hiring, and promoting employees in an organization.
Controlling Machines and Processes	Using either control mechanisms or direct physical activity to operate machines or processes (not including computers or vehicles).
Repairing and Maintaining Mechanical Equipment	Servicing, repairing, adjusting, and testing machines, devices, moving parts, and equipment that operate primarily on the basis of mechanical (not electronic) principles.
Documenting/Recording Information	Entering, transcribing, recording, storing, or maintaining information in written or electronic/magnetic form.
Repairing and Maintaining Electronic Equipment	Servicing, repairing, calibrating, regulating, fine-tuning, or testing machines, devices, and equipment that operate primarily on the basis of electrical or electronic (not mechanical) principles.

Drafting. Laying Out. and Specifying Technical Dev	Providing documentation. detailed instructions. drawings. or specifications to tell others about how devices, parts. equipment. or structures are to be fabricated, constructed. assembled, modified, maintained, or used.
Operating Vehicles. Mechanized Devices. or Equipme	Running, maneuvering, navigating, or driving vehicles or mechanized equipment, such as forklifts, passenger vehicles. aircraft, or water craft.

Work_Context	Work_Context Definitions
Telephone	How often do you have telephone conversations in this job?
Contact With Others	How much does this job require the worker to be in contact with others (face-to-face, by telephone, or otherwise) in order to perform it?
Importance of Being Exact or Accurate	How important is being very exact or highly accurate in performing this job?
Freedom to Make Decisions	How much decision making freedom, without supervision. does the job offer?
Indoors, Environmentally Controlled	How often does this job require working indoors in environmentally controlled conditions?
Importance of Repeating Same Tasks	How important is repeating the same physical activities (e.g.. key entry) or mental activities (e.g., checking entries in a ledger) over and over, without stopping, to performing this job?
Spend Time Sitting	How much does this job require sitting?
Face-to-Face Discussions	How often do you have to have face-to-face discussions with individuals or teams in this job?
Time Pressure	How often does this job require the worker to meet strict deadlines?
Electronic Mail	How often do you use electronic mail in this job?
Spend Time Making Repetitive Motions	How much does this job require making repetitive motions?
Deal With Unpleasant or Angry People	How frequently does the worker have to deal with unpleasant. angry, or discourteous individuals as part of the job requirements?
Frequency of Decision Making	How frequently is the worker required to make decisions that affect other people, the financial resources, and/or the image and reputation of the organization?
Letters and Memos	How often does the job require written letters and memos?
Deal With External Customers	How important is it to work with external customers or the public in this job?
Work With Work Group or Team	How important is it to work with others in a group or team in this job?
Physical Proximity	To what extent does this job require the worker to perform job tasks in close physical proximity to other people?
Frequency of Conflict Situations	How often are there conflict situations the employee has to face in this job?
Structured versus Unstructured Work	To what extent is this job structured for the worker, rather than allowing the worker to determine tasks, priorities, and goals?
Impact of Decisions on Co-workers or Company Resul	How do the decisions an employee makes impact the results of co-workers, clients or the company?
Level of Competition	To what extent does this job require the worker to compete or to be aware of competitive pressures?
Coordinate or Lead Others	How important is it to coordinate or lead others in accomplishing work activities in this job?
Degree of Automation	How automated is the job?
Spend Time Using Your Hands to Handle, Control, or	How much does this job require using your hands to handle, control, or feel objects, tools or controls?
Sounds, Noise Levels Are Distracting or Uncomforta	How often does this job require working exposed to sounds and noise levels that are distracting or uncomfortable?
Consequence of Error	How serious would the result usually be if the worker made a mistake that was not readily correctable?
Spend Time Standing	How much does this job require standing?
Responsibility for Outcomes and Results	How responsible is the worker for work outcomes and results of other workers?
Pace Determined by Speed of Equipment	How important is it to this job that the pace is determined by the speed of equipment or machinery? (This does not refer to keeping busy at all times on this job.)
Responsible for Others' Health and Safety	How much responsibility is there for the health and safety of others in this job?
Exposed to Contaminants	How often does this job require working exposed to contaminants (such as pollutants, gases, dust or odors)?
Spend Time Walking and Running	How much does this job require walking and running?
Spend Time Kneeling, Crouching, Stooping, or Crawl	How much does this job require kneeling, crouching, stooping, or crawling?

Spend Time Climbing Ladders. Scaffolds. or Poles	How much does this job require climbing ladders. scaffolds. or poles?
Outdoors. Under Cover	How often does this job require working outdoors. under cover (e.g.. structure with roof but no walls)?
Exposed to High Places	How often does this job require exposure to high places?
Public Speaking	How often do you have to perform public speaking in this job?
Indoors. Not Environmentally Controlled	How often does this job require working indoors in non-controlled environmental conditions (e.g.. warehouse without heat)?
Exposed to Hazardous Equipment	How often does this job require exposure to hazardous equipment?
Outdoors. Exposed to Weather	How often does this job require working outdoors, exposed to all weather conditions?
Spend Time Bending or Twisting the Body	How much does this job require bending or twisting your body?
In an Enclosed Vehicle or Equipment	How often does this job require working in a closed vehicle or equipment (e.g., car)?
Deal With Physically Aggressive People	How frequently does this job require the worker to deal with physical aggression of violent individuals?
Very Hot or Cold Temperatures	How often does this job require working in very hot (above 90 F degrees) or very cold (below 32 F degrees) temperatures?
Wear Common Protective or Safety Equipment such as	How much does this job require wearing common protective or safety equipment such as safety shoes, glasses, gloves, hard hats or live jackets?
Exposed to Minor Burns. Cuts, Bites. or Stings	How often does this job require exposure to minor burns, cuts, bites, or stings?
In an Open Vehicle or Equipment	How often does this job require working in an open vehicle or equipment (e.g., tractor)?
Cramped Work Space. Awkward Positions	How often does this job require working in cramped work spaces that requires getting into awkward positions?
Exposed to Disease or Infections	How often does this job require exposure to disease/infections?
Extremely Bright or Inadequate Lighting	How often does this job require working in extremely bright or inadequate lighting conditions?
Spend Time Keeping or Regaining Balance	How much does this job require keeping or regaining your balance?
Exposed to Hazardous Conditions	How often does this job require exposure to hazardous conditions?
Wear Specialized Protective or Safety Equipment su	How much does this job require wearing specialized protective or safety equipment such as breathing apparatus, safety harness, full protection suits, or radiation protection?
Exposed to Radiation	How often does this job require exposure to radiation?
Exposed to Whole Body Vibration	How often does this job require exposure to whole body vibration (e.g., operate a jackhammer)?

Job Zone Component	Job Zone Component Definitions
Title	Job Zone Three: Medium Preparation Needed
Overall Experience	Previous work-related skill, knowledge, or experience is required for these occupations. For example, an electrician must have completed three or four years of apprenticeship or several years of vocational training, and often must have passed a licensing exam, in order to perform the job.
Job Training	Employees in these occupations usually need one or two years of training involving both on-the-job experience and informal training with experienced workers.
Job Zone Examples	These occupations usually involve using communication and organizational skills to coordinate, supervise, manage, or train others to accomplish goals. Examples include dental assistants, electricians, fish and game wardens, legal secretaries, personnel recruiters, and recreation workers.
SVP Range	(6.0 to < 7.0)
Education	Most occupations in this zone require training in vocational schools, related on-the-job experience, or an associate's degree. Some may require a bachelor's degree.

Work_Styles	Work_Styles Definitions
Dependability	Job requires being reliable, responsible, and dependable, and fulfilling obligations.
Integrity	Job requires being honest and ethical.
Cooperation	Job requires being pleasant with others on the job and displaying a good-natured, cooperative attitude.
Attention to Detail	Job requires being careful about detail and thorough in completing work tasks.
Persistence	Job requires persistence in the face of obstacles.

Stress Tolerance	Job requires accepting criticism and dealing calmly and effectively with high stress situations.
Initiative	Job requires a willingness to take on responsibilities and challenges.
Achievement/Effort	Job requires establishing and maintaining personally challenging achievement goals and exerting effort toward mastering tasks.
Self Control	Job requires maintaining composure, keeping emotions in check, controlling anger, and avoiding aggressive behavior, even in very difficult situations.
Adaptability/Flexibility	Job requires being open to change (positive or negative) and to considerable variety in the workplace.
Concern for Others	Job requires being sensitive to others' needs and feelings and being understanding and helpful on the job.
Leadership	Job requires a willingness to lead, take charge, and offer opinions and direction.
Independence	Job requires developing one's own ways of doing things, guiding oneself with little or no supervision, and depending on oneself to get things done.
Innovation	Job requires creativity and alternative thinking to develop new ideas for and answers to work-related problems.
Analytical Thinking	Job requires analyzing information and using logic to address work-related issues and problems.
Social Orientation	Job requires preferring to work with others rather than alone, and being personally connected with others on the job.

13-1023.00 - Purchasing Agents, Except Wholesale, Retail, and Farm Products

Purchase machinery, equipment, tools, parts, supplies, or services necessary for the operation of an establishment. Purchase raw or semi-finished materials for manufacturing.

Tasks

1) Review catalogs, industry periodicals, directories, trade journals, and Internet sites, and consult with other department personnel to locate necessary goods and services.

2) Purchase the highest quality merchandise at the lowest possible price and in correct amounts.

3) Monitor shipments to ensure that goods come in on time, and in the event of problems trace shipments and follow up undelivered goods.

4) Prepare purchase orders, solicit bid proposals and review requisitions for goods and services.

5) Confer with staff, users, and vendors to discuss defective or unacceptable goods or services and determine corrective action.

6) Negotiate, or renegotiate, and administer contracts with suppliers, vendors, and other representatives.

7) Research and evaluate suppliers based on price, quality, selection, service, support, availability, reliability, production and distribution capabilities, and the supplier's reputation and history.

8) Study sales records and inventory levels of current stock to develop strategic purchasing programs that facilitate employee access to supplies.

9) Interview vendors and visit suppliers' plants and distribution centers to examine and learn about products, services and prices.

10) Analyze price proposals, financial reports, and other data and information to determine reasonable prices.

11) Evaluate and monitor contract performance to ensure compliance with contractual obligations and to determine need for changes.

12) Monitor and follow applicable laws and regulations.

13) Attend meetings, trade shows, conferences, conventions and seminars to network with people in other purchasing departments.

14) Write and review product specifications, maintaining a working technical knowledge of the goods or services to be purchased.

15) Formulate policies and procedures for bid proposals and procurement of goods and services.

16) Arrange the payment of duty and freight charges.

17) Monitor changes affecting supply and demand, tracking market conditions, price trends, or futures markets.

18) Hire, train and/or supervise purchasing clerks, buyers, and expediters.

Knowledge	Knowledge Definitions
Mathematics	Knowledge of arithmetic, algebra, geometry, calculus, statistics, and their applications.
Clerical	Knowledge of administrative and clerical procedures and systems such as word processing, managing files and records, stenography and transcription, designing forms, and other office procedures and terminology.
Administration and Management	Knowledge of business and management principles involved in strategic planning, resource allocation, human resources modeling, leadership technique, production methods, and coordination of people and resources.
Economics and Accounting	Knowledge of economic and accounting principles and practices, the financial markets, banking and the analysis and reporting of financial data.
Production and Processing	Knowledge of raw materials, production processes, quality control, costs, and other techniques for maximizing the effective manufacture and distribution of goods.
English Language	Knowledge of the structure and content of the English language including the meaning and spelling of words, rules of composition, and grammar.
Computers and Electronics	Knowledge of circuit boards, processors, chips, electronic equipment, and computer hardware and software, including applications and programming.
Customer and Personal Service	Knowledge of principles and processes for providing customer and personal services. This includes customer needs assessment, meeting quality standards for services, and evaluation of customer satisfaction.
Transportation	Knowledge of principles and methods for moving people or goods by air, rail, sea, or road, including the relative costs and benefits.
Communications and Media	Knowledge of media production, communication, and dissemination techniques and methods. This includes alternative ways to inform and entertain via written, oral, and visual media.
Personnel and Human Resources	Knowledge of principles and procedures for personnel recruitment, selection, training, compensation and benefits, labor relations and negotiation, and personnel information systems.
Telecommunications	Knowledge of transmission, broadcasting, switching, control, and operation of telecommunications systems.
Sales and Marketing	Knowledge of principles and methods for showing, promoting, and selling products or services. This includes marketing strategy and tactics, product demonstration, sales techniques, and sales control systems.
Public Safety and Security	Knowledge of relevant equipment, policies, procedures, and strategies to promote effective local, state, or national security operations for the protection of people, data, property, and institutions.
Education and Training	Knowledge of principles and methods for curriculum and training design, teaching and instruction for individuals and groups, and the measurement of training effects.
Psychology	Knowledge of human behavior and performance; individual differences in ability, personality, and interests; learning and motivation; psychological research methods; and the assessment and treatment of behavioral and affective disorders.
Law and Government	Knowledge of laws, legal codes, court procedures, precedents, government regulations, executive orders, agency rules, and the democratic political process.
Engineering and Technology	Knowledge of the practical application of engineering science and technology. This includes applying principles, techniques, procedures, and equipment to the design and production of various goods and services.
Mechanical	Knowledge of machines and tools, including their designs, uses, repair, and maintenance.
Geography	Knowledge of principles and methods for describing the features of land, sea, and air masses, including their physical characteristics, locations, interrelationships, and distribution of plant, animal, and human life.
Physics	Knowledge and prediction of physical principles, laws, their interrelationships, and applications to understanding fluid, material, and atmospheric dynamics, and mechanical, electrical, atomic and sub-atomic structures and processes.

Building and Construction	Knowledge of materials, methods, and the tools involved in the construction or repair of houses, buildings, or other structures such as highways and roads.
Philosophy and Theology	Knowledge of different philosophical systems and religions. This includes their basic principles, values, ethics, ways of thinking, customs, practices, and their impact on human culture.
Chemistry	Knowledge of the chemical composition, structure, and properties of substances and of the chemical processes and transformations that they undergo. This includes uses of chemicals and their interactions, danger signs, production techniques, and disposal methods.
Sociology and Anthropology	Knowledge of group behavior and dynamics, societal trends and influences, human migrations, ethnicity, cultures and their history and origins.
Design	Knowledge of design techniques, tools, and principles involved in production of precision technical plans, blueprints, drawings, and models.
Foreign Language	Knowledge of the structure and content of a foreign (non-English) language including the meaning and spelling of words, rules of composition and grammar, and pronunciation.
Therapy and Counseling	Knowledge of principles, methods, and procedures for diagnosis, treatment, and rehabilitation of physical and mental dysfunctions, and for career counseling and guidance.
Medicine and Dentistry	Knowledge of the information and techniques needed to diagnose and treat human injuries, diseases, and deformities. This includes symptoms, treatment alternatives, drug properties and interactions, and preventive health-care measures.
History and Archeology	Knowledge of historical events and their causes, indicators, and effects on civilizations and cultures.
Food Production	Knowledge of techniques and equipment for planting, growing, and harvesting food products (both plant and animal) for consumption, including storage/handling techniques.
Fine Arts	Knowledge of the theory and techniques required to compose, produce, and perform works of music, dance, visual arts, drama, and sculpture.
Biology	Knowledge of plant and animal organisms, their tissues, cells, functions, interdependencies, and interactions with each other and the environment.

Skills	Skills Definitions
Speaking	Talking to others to convey information effectively.
Active Listening	Giving full attention to what other people are saying, taking time to understand the points being made, asking questions as appropriate, and not interrupting at inappropriate times.
Judgment and Decision Making	Considering the relative costs and benefits of potential actions to choose the most appropriate one.
Critical Thinking	Using logic and reasoning to identify the strengths and weaknesses of alternative solutions, conclusions or approaches to problems.
Reading Comprehension	Understanding written sentences and paragraphs in work related documents.
Writing	Communicating effectively in writing as appropriate for the needs of the audience.
Time Management	Managing one's own time and the time of others.
Mathematics	Using mathematics to solve problems.
Active Learning	Understanding the implications of new information for both current and future problem-solving and decision-making.
Negotiation	Bringing others together and trying to reconcile differences.
Coordination	Adjusting actions in relation to others' actions.
Monitoring	Monitoring/Assessing performance of yourself, other individuals, or organizations to make improvements or take corrective action.
Persuasion	Persuading others to change their minds or behavior.
Equipment Selection	Determining the kind of tools and equipment needed to do a job.
Learning Strategies	Selecting and using training/instructional methods and procedures appropriate for the situation when learning or teaching new things.
Management of Financial Resources	Determining how money will be spent to get the work done, and accounting for these expenditures.
Operations Analysis	Analyzing needs and product requirements to create a design.
Complex Problem Solving	Identifying complex problems and reviewing related information to develop and evaluate options and implement solutions.
Instructing	Teaching others how to do something.

Management of Personnel Resources	Motivating, developing, and directing people as they work, identifying the best people for the job.
Social Perceptiveness	Being aware of others' reactions and understanding why they react as they do.
Management of Material Resources	Obtaining and seeing to the appropriate use of equipment, facilities, and materials needed to do certain work.
Troubleshooting	Determining causes of operating errors and deciding what to do about it.
Service Orientation	Actively looking for ways to help people.
Quality Control Analysis	Conducting tests and inspections of products, services, or processes to evaluate quality or performance.
Operation Monitoring	Watching gauges, dials, or other indicators to make sure a machine is working properly.
Systems Evaluation	Identifying measures or indicators of system performance and the actions needed to improve or correct performance, relative to the goals of the system.
Installation	Installing equipment, machines, wiring, or programs to meet specifications.
Technology Design	Generating or adapting equipment and technology to serve user needs.
Operation and Control	Controlling operations of equipment or systems.
Systems Analysis	Determining how a system should work and how changes in conditions, operations, and the environment will affect outcomes.
Science	Using scientific rules and methods to solve problems.
Equipment Maintenance	Performing routine maintenance on equipment and determining when and what kind of maintenance is needed.
Repairing	Repairing machines or systems using the needed tools.
Programming	Writing computer programs for various purposes.

Ability	Ability Definitions
Oral Expression	The ability to communicate information and ideas in speaking so others will understand.
Oral Comprehension	The ability to listen to and understand information and ideas presented through spoken words and sentences.
Inductive Reasoning	The ability to combine pieces of information to form general rules or conclusions (includes finding a relationship among seemingly unrelated events).
Deductive Reasoning	The ability to apply general rules to specific problems to produce answers that make sense.
Written Comprehension	The ability to read and understand information and ideas presented in writing.
Problem Sensitivity	The ability to tell when something is wrong or is likely to go wrong. It does not involve solving the problem, only recognizing there is a problem.
Speech Clarity	The ability to speak clearly so others can understand you.
Speech Recognition	The ability to identify and understand the speech of another person.
Written Expression	The ability to communicate information and ideas in writing so others will understand.
Near Vision	The ability to see details at close range (within a few feet of the observer).
Information Ordering	The ability to arrange things or actions in a certain order or pattern according to a specific rule or set of rules (e.g., patterns of numbers, letters, words, pictures, mathematical operations).
Mathematical Reasoning	The ability to choose the right mathematical methods or formulas to solve a problem.
Category Flexibility	The ability to generate or use different sets of rules for combining or grouping things in different ways.
Originality	The ability to come up with unusual or clever ideas about a given topic or situation, or to develop creative ways to solve a problem.
Selective Attention	The ability to concentrate on a task over a period of time without being distracted.
Perceptual Speed	The ability to quickly and accurately compare similarities and differences among sets of letters, numbers, objects, pictures, or patterns. The things to be compared may be presented at the same time or one after the other. This ability also includes comparing a presented object with a remembered object.
Fluency of Ideas	The ability to come up with a number of ideas about a topic (the number of ideas is important, not their quality, correctness, or creativity).
Speed of Closure	The ability to quickly make sense of, combine, and organize information into meaningful patterns.
Time Sharing	The ability to shift back and forth between two or more activities or sources of information (such as speech, sounds, touch, or other sources).

Flexibility of Closure	The ability to identify or detect a known pattern (a figure, object, word, or sound) that is hidden in other distracting material.
Memorization	The ability to remember information such as words, numbers, pictures, and procedures.
Number Facility	The ability to add, subtract, multiply, or divide quickly and correctly.
Visualization	The ability to imagine how something will look after it is moved around or when its parts are moved or rearranged.
Manual Dexterity	The ability to quickly move your hand, your hand together with your arm, or your two hands to grasp, manipulate, or assemble objects.
Auditory Attention	The ability to focus on a single source of sound in the presence of other distracting sounds.
Far Vision	The ability to see details at a distance.
Control Precision	The ability to quickly and repeatedly adjust the controls of a machine or a vehicle to exact positions.
Arm-Hand Steadiness	The ability to keep your hand and arm steady while moving your arm or while holding your arm and hand in one position.
Finger Dexterity	The ability to make precisely coordinated movements of the fingers of one or both hands to grasp, manipulate, or assemble very small objects.
Spatial Orientation	The ability to know your location in relation to the environment or to know where other objects are in relation to you.
Depth Perception	The ability to judge which of several objects is closer or farther away from you, or to judge the distance between you and an object.
Visual Color Discrimination	The ability to match or detect differences between colors, including shades of color and brightness.
Hearing Sensitivity	The ability to detect or tell the differences between sounds that vary in pitch and loudness.
Wrist-Finger Speed	The ability to make fast, simple, repeated movements of the fingers, hands, and wrists.
Multilimb Coordination	The ability to coordinate two or more limbs (for example, two arms, two legs, or one leg and one arm) while sitting, standing, or lying down. It does not involve performing the activities while the whole body is in motion.
Explosive Strength	The ability to use short bursts of muscle force to propel oneself (as in jumping or sprinting), or to throw an object.
Gross Body Coordination	The ability to coordinate the movement of your arms, legs, and torso together when the whole body is in motion.
Response Orientation	The ability to choose quickly between two or more movements in response to two or more different signals (lights, sounds, pictures). It includes the speed with which the correct response is started with the hand, foot, or other body part.
Rate Control	The ability to time your movements or the movement of a piece of equipment in anticipation of changes in the speed and/or direction of a moving object or scene.
Reaction Time	The ability to quickly respond (with the hand, finger, or foot) to a signal (sound, light, picture) when it appears.
Static Strength	The ability to exert maximum muscle force to lift, push, pull, or carry objects.
Dynamic Strength	The ability to exert muscle force repeatedly or continuously over time. This involves muscular endurance and resistance to muscle fatigue.
Trunk Strength	The ability to use your abdominal and lower back muscles to support part of the body repeatedly or continuously over time without 'giving out' or fatiguing.
Sound Localization	The ability to tell the direction from which a sound originated.
Speed of Limb Movement	The ability to quickly move the arms and legs.
Stamina	The ability to exert yourself physically over long periods of time without getting winded or out of breath.
Glare Sensitivity	The ability to see objects in the presence of glare or bright lighting.
Peripheral Vision	The ability to see objects or movement of objects to one's side when the eyes are looking ahead.
Night Vision	The ability to see under low light conditions.
Gross Body Equilibrium	The ability to keep or regain your body balance or stay upright when in an unstable position.
Dynamic Flexibility	The ability to quickly and repeatedly bend, stretch, twist, or reach out with your body, arms, and/or legs.
Extent Flexibility	The ability to bend, stretch, twist, or reach with your body, arms, and/or legs.

Work_Activity	**Work_Activity Definitions**
Interacting With Computers	Using computers and computer systems (including hardware and software) to program, write software, set up functions, enter data, or process information.
Communicating with Supervisors, Peers, or Subordin	Providing information to supervisors, co-workers, and subordinates by telephone, in written form, e-mail, or in person.
Getting Information	Observing, receiving, and otherwise obtaining information from all relevant sources.
Communicating with Persons Outside Organization	Communicating with people outside the organization, representing the organization to customers, the public, government, and other external sources. This information can be exchanged in person, in writing, or by telephone or e-mail.
Organizing, Planning, and Prioritizing Work	Developing specific goals and plans to prioritize, organize, and accomplish your work.
Making Decisions and Solving Problems	Analyzing information and evaluating results to choose the best solution and solve problems.
Establishing and Maintaining Interpersonal Relatio	Developing constructive and cooperative working relationships with others, and maintaining them over time.
Processing Information	Compiling, coding, categorizing, calculating, tabulating, auditing, or verifying information or data.
Performing Administrative Activities	Performing day-to-day administrative tasks such as maintaining information files and processing paperwork.
Monitor Processes, Materials, or Surroundings	Monitoring and reviewing information from materials, events, or the environment, to detect or assess problems.
Resolving Conflicts and Negotiating with Others	Handling complaints, settling disputes, and resolving grievances and conflicts, or otherwise negotiating with others.
Updating and Using Relevant Knowledge	Keeping up-to-date technically and applying new knowledge to your job.
Identifying Objects, Actions, and Events	Identifying information by categorizing, estimating, recognizing differences or similarities, and detecting changes in circumstances or events.
Analyzing Data or Information	Identifying the underlying principles, reasons, or facts of information by breaking down information or data into separate parts.
Scheduling Work and Activities	Scheduling events, programs, and activities, as well as the work of others.
Developing and Building Teams	Encouraging and building mutual trust, respect, and cooperation among team members.
Evaluating Information to Determine Compliance wit	Using relevant information and individual judgment to determine whether events or processes comply with laws, regulations, or standards.
Documenting/Recording Information	Entering, transcribing, recording, storing, or maintaining information in written or electronic/magnetic form.
Interpreting the Meaning of Information for Others	Translating or explaining what information means and how it can be used.
Judging the Qualities of Things, Services, or Peop	Assessing the value, importance, or quality of things or people.
Monitoring and Controlling Resources	Monitoring and controlling resources and overseeing the spending of money.
Estimating the Quantifiable Characteristics of Pro	Estimating sizes, distances, and quantities; or determining time, costs, resources, or materials needed to perform a work activity.
Thinking Creatively	Developing, designing, or creating new applications, ideas, relationships, systems, or products, including artistic contributions.
Training and Teaching Others	Identifying the educational needs of others, developing formal educational or training programs or classes, and teaching or instructing others.
Provide Consultation and Advice to Others	Providing guidance and expert advice to management or other groups on technical, systems-, or process-related topics.
Coordinating the Work and Activities of Others	Getting members of a group to work together to accomplish tasks.
Selling or Influencing Others	Convincing others to buy merchandise/goods or to otherwise change their minds or actions.
Coaching and Developing Others	Identifying the developmental needs of others and coaching, mentoring, or otherwise helping others to improve their knowledge or skills.
Developing Objectives and Strategies	Establishing long-range objectives and specifying the strategies and actions to achieve them.
Performing for or Working Directly with the Public	Performing for people or dealing directly with the public. This includes serving customers in restaurants and stores, and receiving clients or guests.
Guiding, Directing, and Motivating Subordinates	Providing guidance and direction to subordinates, including setting performance standards and monitoring performance.
Inspecting Equipment, Structures, or Material	Inspecting equipment, structures, or materials to identify the cause of errors or other problems or defects.

Drafting. Laying Out, and Specifying Technical Dev	Providing documentation, detailed instructions, drawings, or specifications to tell others about how devices, parts, equipment, or structures are to be fabricated, constructed, assembled, modified, maintained, or used.
Assisting and Caring for Others	Providing personal assistance, medical attention, emotional support, or other personal care to others such as coworkers, customers, or patients.
Staffing Organizational Units	Recruiting, interviewing, selecting, hiring, and promoting employees in an organization.
Performing General Physical Activities	Performing physical activities that require considerable use of your arms and legs and moving your whole body, such as climbing, lifting, balancing, walking, stooping, and handling of materials.
Handling and Moving Objects	Using hands and arms in handling, installing, positioning, and moving materials, and manipulating things.
Controlling Machines and Processes	Using either control mechanisms or direct physical activity to operate machines or processes (not including computers or vehicles).
Repairing and Maintaining Electronic Equipment	Servicing, repairing, calibrating, regulating, fine-tuning, or testing machines, devices, and equipment that operate primarily on the basis of electrical or electronic (not mechanical) principles.
Operating Vehicles, Mechanized Devices, or Equipme	Running, maneuvering, navigating, or driving vehicles or mechanized equipment, such as forklifts, passenger vehicles, aircraft, or water craft.
Repairing and Maintaining Mechanical Equipment	Servicing, repairing, adjusting, and testing machines, devices, moving parts, and equipment that operate primarily on the basis of mechanical (not electronic) principles.

Work_Context **Work_Context Definitions**

Telephone	How often do you have telephone conversations in this job?
Importance of Being Exact or Accurate	How important is being very exact or highly accurate in performing this job?
Structured versus Unstructured Work	To what extent is this job structured for the worker, rather than allowing the worker to determine tasks, priorities, and goals?
Contact With Others	How much does this job require the worker to be in contact with others (face-to-face, by telephone, or otherwise) in order to perform it?
Electronic Mail	How often do you use electronic mail in this job?
Time Pressure	How often does this job require the worker to meet strict deadlines?
Indoors, Environmentally Controlled	How often does this job require working indoors in environmentally controlled conditions?
Freedom to Make Decisions	How much decision making freedom, without supervision, does the job offer?
Work With Work Group or Team	How important is it to work with others in a group or team in this job?
Spend Time Sitting	How much does this job require sitting?
Face-to-Face Discussions	How often do you have to have face-to-face discussions with individuals or teams in this job?
Frequency of Decision Making	How frequently is the worker required to make decisions that affect other people, the financial resources, and/or the image and reputation of the organization?
Impact of Decisions on Co-workers or Company Resul	How do the decisions an employee makes impact the results of co-workers, clients or the company?
Importance of Repeating Same Tasks	How important is repeating the same physical activities (e.g., key entry) or mental activities (e.g., checking entries in a ledger) over and over, without stopping, to performing this job?
Deal With External Customers	How important is it to work with external customers or the public in this job?
Letters and Memos	How often does the job require written letters and memos?
Degree of Automation	How automated is the job?
Spend Time Using Your Hands to Handle, Control, or	How much does this job require using your hands to handle, control, or feel objects, tools or controls?
Spend Time Making Repetitive Motions	How much does this job require making repetitive motions?
Coordinate or Lead Others	How important is it to coordinate or lead others in accomplishing work activities in this job?
Physical Proximity	To what extent does this job require the worker to perform job tasks in close physical proximity to other people?
Level of Competition	To what extent does this job require the worker to compete or to be aware of competitive pressures?
Responsibility for Outcomes and Results	How responsible is the worker for work outcomes and results of other workers?

Frequency of Conflict Situations	How often are there conflict situations the employee has to face in this job?
Spend Time Standing	How much does this job require standing?
Indoors, Not Environmentally Controlled	How often does this job require working indoors in non-controlled environmental conditions (e.g., warehouse without heat)?
Sounds, Noise Levels Are Distracting or Uncomforta	How often does this job require working exposed to sounds and noise levels that are distracting or uncomfortable?
Responsible for Others' Health and Safety	How much responsibility is there for the health and safety of others in this job?
Deal With Unpleasant or Angry People	How frequently does the worker have to deal with unpleasant, angry, or discourteous individuals as part of the job requirements?
Pace Determined by Speed of Equipment	How important is it to this job that the pace is determined by the speed of equipment or machinery? (This does not refer to keeping busy at all times on this job.)
Cramped Work Space, Awkward Positions	How often does this job require working in cramped work spaces that requires getting into awkward positions?
In an Enclosed Vehicle or Equipment	How often does this job require working in a closed vehicle or equipment (e.g., car)?
Spend Time Walking and Running	How much does this job require walking and running?
Very Hot or Cold Temperatures	How often does this job require working in very hot (above 90 F degrees) or very cold (below 32 F degrees) temperatures?
Exposed to Contaminants	How often does this job require working exposed to contaminants (such as pollutants, gases, dust or odors)?
Consequence of Error	How serious would the result usually be if the worker made a mistake that was not readily correctable?
Wear Common Protective or Safety Equipment such as	How much does this job require wearing common protective or safety equipment such as safety shoes, glasses, gloves, hard hats or life jackets?
Outdoors, Exposed to Weather	How often does this job require working outdoors, exposed to all weather conditions?
Public Speaking	How often do you have to perform public speaking in this job?
Extremely Bright or Inadequate Lighting	How often does this job require working in extremely bright or inadequate lighting conditions?
Spend Time Bending or Twisting the Body	How much does this job require bending or twisting your body?
Exposed to Minor Burns, Cuts, Bites, or Stings	How often does this job require exposure to minor burns, cuts, bites, or stings?
In an Open Vehicle or Equipment	How often does this job require working in an open vehicle or equipment (e.g., tractor)?
Spend Time Kneeling, Crouching, Stooping, or Crawl	How much does this job require kneeling, crouching, stooping or crawling?
Outdoors, Under Cover	How often does this job require working outdoors, under cover (e.g., structure with roof but no walls)?
Exposed to Hazardous Equipment	How often does this job require exposure to hazardous equipment?
Exposed to Hazardous Conditions	How often does this job require exposure to hazardous conditions?
Spend Time Climbing Ladders, Scaffolds, or Poles	How much does this job require climbing ladders, scaffolds, or poles?
Exposed to Whole Body Vibration	How often does this job require exposure to whole body vibration (e.g., operate a jackhammer)?
Exposed to High Places	How often does this job require exposure to high places?
Exposed to Disease or Infections	How often does this job require exposure to disease/infections?
Deal With Physically Aggressive People	How frequently does this job require the worker to deal with physical aggression of violent individuals?
Wear Specialized Protective or Safety Equipment su	How much does this job require wearing specialized protective or safety equipment such as breathing apparatus, safety harness, full protection suits, or radiation protection?
Spend Time Keeping or Regaining Balance	How much does this job require keeping or regaining your balance?
Exposed to Radiation	How often does this job require exposure to radiation?

Job Zone Component **Job Zone Component Definitions**

Title	Job Zone Three: Medium Preparation Needed
	Previous work-related skill, knowledge, or experience is required for these occupations. For example, an electrician must
Overall Experience	have completed three or four years of apprenticeship or several years of vocational training, and often must have passed a licensing exam, in order to perform the job.

Job Training	Employees in these occupations usually need one or two years of training involving both on-the-job experience and informal training with experienced workers.
Job Zone Examples	These occupations usually involve using communication and organizational skills to coordinate, supervise, manage, or train others to accomplish goals. Examples include dental assistants, electricians, fish and game wardens, legal secretaries, personnel recruiters, and recreation workers.
SVP Range	(6.0 to < 7.0)
Education	Most occupations in this zone require training in vocational schools, related on-the-job experience, or an associate's degree. Some may require a bachelor's degree.

Work_Styles	Work_Styles Definitions
Integrity	Job requires being honest and ethical.
Attention to Detail	Job requires being careful about detail and thorough in completing work tasks.
Dependability	Job requires being reliable, responsible, and dependable, and fulfilling obligations.
Cooperation	Job requires being pleasant with others on the job and displaying a good-natured, cooperative attitude.
Self Control	Job requires maintaining composure, keeping emotions in check, controlling anger, and avoiding aggressive behavior, even in very difficult situations.
Adaptability/Flexibility	Job requires being open to change (positive or negative) and to considerable variety in the workplace.
Initiative	Job requires a willingness to take on responsibilities and challenges.
Analytical Thinking	Job requires analyzing information and using logic to address work-related issues and problems.
Concern for Others	Job requires being sensitive to others' needs and feelings and being understanding and helpful on the job.
Stress Tolerance	Job requires accepting criticism and dealing calmly and effectively with high stress situations.
Independence	Job requires developing one's own ways of doing things, guiding oneself with little or no supervision, and depending on oneself to get things done.
Achievement/Effort	Job requires establishing and maintaining personally challenging achievement goals and exerting effort toward mastering tasks.
Persistence	Job requires persistence in the face of obstacles.
Social Orientation	Job requires preferring to work with others rather than alone, and being personally connected with others on the job.
Leadership	Job requires a willingness to lead, take charge, and offer opinions and direction.
Innovation	Job requires creativity and alternative thinking to develop new ideas for and answers to work-related problems.

13-1031.02 - Insurance Adjusters, Examiners, and Investigators

Investigate, analyze, and determine the extent of insurance company's liability concerning personal, casualty, or property loss or damages, and attempt to effect settlement with claimants. Correspond with or interview medical specialists, agents, witnesses, or claimants to compile information. Calculate benefit payments and approve payment of claims within a certain monetary limit.

Tasks

1) Negotiate claim settlements and recommend litigation when settlement cannot be negotiated.

2) Examine claims form and other records to determine insurance coverage.

3) Interview or correspond with claimant and witnesses, consult police and hospital records, and inspect property damage to determine extent of liability.

4) Interview or correspond with agents and claimants to correct errors or omissions and to investigate questionable claims.

5) Refer questionable claims to investigator or claims adjuster for investigation or settlement.

6) Collect evidence to support contested claims in court.

7) Prepare report of findings of investigation.

8) Investigate and assess damage to property.

9) Examine titles to property to determine validity and act as company agent in transactions with property owners.

10) Obtain credit information from banks and other credit services.

11) Communicate with former associates to verify employment record and to obtain background information regarding persons or businesses applying for credit.

Knowledge	Knowledge Definitions
Customer and Personal Service	Knowledge of principles and processes for providing customer and personal services. This includes customer needs assessment, meeting quality standards for services, and evaluation of customer satisfaction.
English Language	Knowledge of the structure and content of the English language including the meaning and spelling of words, rules of composition, and grammar.
Mathematics	Knowledge of arithmetic, algebra, geometry, calculus, statistics, and their applications.
Computers and Electronics	Knowledge of circuit boards, processors, chips, electronic equipment, and computer hardware and software, including applications and programming.
Law and Government	Knowledge of laws, legal codes, court procedures, precedents, government regulations, executive orders, agency rules, and the democratic political process.
Clerical	Knowledge of administrative and clerical procedures and systems such as word processing, managing files and records, stenography and transcription, designing forms, and other office procedures and terminology.
Administration and Management	Knowledge of business and management principles involved in strategic planning, resource allocation, human resources modeling, leadership technique, production methods, and coordination of people and resources.
Personnel and Human Resources	Knowledge of principles and procedures for personnel recruitment, selection, training, compensation and benefits, labor relations and negotiation, and personnel information systems.
Medicine and Dentistry	Knowledge of the information and techniques needed to diagnose and treat human injuries, diseases, and deformities. This includes symptoms, treatment alternatives, drug properties and interactions, and preventive health-care measures.
Education and Training	Knowledge of principles and methods for curriculum and training design, teaching and instruction for individuals and groups, and the measurement of training effects.
Psychology	Knowledge of human behavior and performance; individual differences in ability, personality, and interests; learning and motivation; psychological research methods; and the assessment and treatment of behavioral and affective disorders.
Therapy and Counseling	Knowledge of principles, methods, and procedures for diagnosis, treatment, and rehabilitation of physical and mental dysfunctions, and for career counseling and guidance.
Building and Construction	Knowledge of materials, methods, and the tools involved in the construction or repair of houses, buildings, or other structures such as highways and roads.
Communications and Media	Knowledge of media production, communication, and dissemination techniques and methods. This includes alternative ways to inform and entertain via written, oral, and visual media.
Sales and Marketing	Knowledge of principles and methods for showing, promoting, and selling products or services. This includes marketing strategy and tactics, product demonstration, sales techniques, and sales control systems.
Economics and Accounting	Knowledge of economic and accounting principles and practices, the financial markets, banking and the analysis and reporting of financial data.
Production and Processing	Knowledge of raw materials, production processes, quality control, costs, and other techniques for maximizing the effective manufacture and distribution of goods.
Telecommunications	Knowledge of transmission, broadcasting, switching, control, and operation of telecommunications systems.
Transportation	Knowledge of principles and methods for moving people or goods by air, rail, sea, or road, including the relative costs and benefits.
Biology	Knowledge of plant and animal organisms, their tissues, cells, functions, interdependencies, and interactions with each other and the environment.
Public Safety and Security	Knowledge of relevant equipment, policies, procedures, and strategies to promote effective local, state, or national security operations for the protection of people, data, property, and institutions.

Sociology and Anthropology	Knowledge of group behavior and dynamics, societal trends and influences, human migrations, ethnicity, cultures and their history and origins.
Mechanical	Knowledge of machines and tools, including their designs, uses, repair, and maintenance.
Foreign Language	Knowledge of the structure and content of a foreign (non-English) language including the meaning and spelling of words, rules of composition and grammar, and pronunciation.
Fine Arts	Knowledge of the theory and techniques required to compose, produce, and perform works of music, dance, visual arts, drama, and sculpture.
Geography	Knowledge of principles and methods for describing the features of land, sea, and air masses, including their physical characteristics, locations, interrelationships, and distribution of plant, animal, and human life.
Chemistry	Knowledge of the chemical composition, structure, and properties of substances and of the chemical processes and transformations that they undergo. This includes uses of chemicals and their interactions, danger signs, production techniques, and disposal methods.
Engineering and Technology	Knowledge of the practical application of engineering science and technology. This includes applying principles, techniques, procedures, and equipment to the design and production of various goods and services.
Philosophy and Theology	Knowledge of different philosophical systems and religions. This includes their basic principles, values, ethics, ways of thinking, customs, practices, and their impact on human culture.
Physics	Knowledge and prediction of physical principles, laws, their interrelationships, and applications to understanding fluid, material, and atmospheric dynamics, and mechanical, electrical, atomic and sub-atomic structures and processes.
History and Archeology	Knowledge of historical events and their causes, indicators, and effects on civilizations and cultures.
Design	Knowledge of design techniques, tools, and principles involved in production of precision technical plans, blueprints, drawings, and models.
Food Production	Knowledge of techniques and equipment for planting, growing, and harvesting food products (both plant and animal) for consumption, including storage/handling techniques.

Skills	**Skills Definitions**
Reading Comprehension	Understanding written sentences and paragraphs in work related documents.
Active Listening	Giving full attention to what other people are saying, taking time to understand the points being made, asking questions as appropriate, and not interrupting at inappropriate times.
Time Management	Managing one's own time and the time of others.
Critical Thinking	Using logic and reasoning to identify the strengths and weaknesses of alternative solutions, conclusions or approaches to problems.
Judgment and Decision Making	Considering the relative costs and benefits of potential actions to choose the most appropriate one.
Writing	Communicating effectively in writing as appropriate for the needs of the audience.
Negotiation	Bringing others together and trying to reconcile differences.
Persuasion	Persuading others to change their minds or behavior.
Speaking	Talking to others to convey information effectively.
Social Perceptiveness	Being aware of others' reactions and understanding why they react as they do.
Active Learning	Understanding the implications of new information for both current and future problem-solving and decision-making.
Complex Problem Solving	Identifying complex problems and reviewing related information to develop and evaluate options and implement solutions.
Coordination	Adjusting actions in relation to others' actions.
Service Orientation	Actively looking for ways to help people.
Mathematics	Using mathematics to solve problems.
Monitoring	Monitoring/Assessing performance of yourself, other individuals, or organizations to make improvements or take corrective action.
Learning Strategies	Selecting and using training/instructional methods and procedures appropriate for the situation when learning or teaching new things.
Management of Financial Resources	Determining how money will be spent to get the work done, and accounting for these expenditures.
Instructing	Teaching others how to do something

Management of Personnel Resources	Motivating, developing, and directing people as they work, identifying the best people for the job.
Operations Analysis	Analyzing needs and product requirements to create a design.
Quality Control Analysis	Conducting tests and inspections of products, services, or processes to evaluate quality or performance.
Troubleshooting	Determining causes of operating errors and deciding what to do about it.
Science	Using scientific rules and methods to solve problems.
Equipment Selection	Determining the kind of tools and equipment needed to do a job.
Management of Material Resources	Obtaining and seeing to the appropriate use of equipment, facilities, and materials needed to do certain work.
Technology Design	Generating or adapting equipment and technology to serve user needs.
Operation Monitoring	Watching gauges, dials, or other indicators to make sure a machine is working properly.
Systems Evaluation	Identifying measures or indicators of system performance and the actions needed to improve or correct performance, relative to the goals of the system.
Systems Analysis	Determining how a system should work and how changes in conditions, operations, and the environment will affect outcomes.
Installation	Installing equipment, machines, wiring, or programs to meet specifications.
Operation and Control	Controlling operations of equipment or systems.
Programming	Writing computer programs for various purposes.
Equipment Maintenance	Performing routine maintenance on equipment and determining when and what kind of maintenance is needed.
Repairing	Repairing machines or systems using the needed tools.

Ability	**Ability Definitions**
Oral Comprehension	The ability to listen to and understand information and ideas presented through spoken words and sentences.
Written Comprehension	The ability to read and understand information and ideas presented in writing.
Oral Expression	The ability to communicate information and ideas in speaking so others will understand.
Speech Clarity	The ability to speak clearly so others can understand you.
Inductive Reasoning	The ability to combine pieces of information to form general rules or conclusions (includes finding a relationship among seemingly unrelated events).
Near Vision	The ability to see details at close range (within a few feet of the observer).
Deductive Reasoning	The ability to apply general rules to specific problems to produce answers that make sense.
Speech Recognition	The ability to identify and understand the speech of another person.
Written Expression	The ability to communicate information and ideas in writing so others will understand.
Problem Sensitivity	The ability to tell when something is wrong or is likely to go wrong. It does not involve solving the problem, only recognizing there is a problem.
Information Ordering	The ability to arrange things or actions in a certain order or pattern according to a specific rule or set of rules (e.g., patterns of numbers, letters, words, pictures, mathematical operations).
Selective Attention	The ability to concentrate on a task over a period of time without being distracted.
Flexibility of Closure	The ability to identify or detect a known pattern (a figure, object, word, or sound) that is hidden in other distracting material.
Far Vision	The ability to see details at a distance.
Category Flexibility	The ability to generate or use different sets of rules for combining or grouping things in different ways.
Originality	The ability to come up with unusual or clever ideas about a given topic or situation, or to develop creative ways to solve a problem.
Mathematical Reasoning	The ability to choose the right mathematical methods or formulas to solve a problem.
Time Sharing	The ability to shift back and forth between two or more activities or sources of information (such as speech, sounds, touch, or other sources).
Speed of Closure	The ability to quickly make sense of, combine, and organize information into meaningful patterns.
Memorization	The ability to remember information such as words, numbers, pictures, and procedures.

Ability	Definition
Fluency of Ideas	The ability to come up with a number of ideas about a topic (the number of ideas is important, not their quality, correctness, or creativity).
Auditory Attention	The ability to focus on a single source of sound in the presence of other distracting sounds.
Depth Perception	The ability to judge which of several objects is closer or farther away from you, or to judge the distance between you and an object.
Number Facility	The ability to add, subtract, multiply, or divide quickly and correctly.
Visualization	The ability to imagine how something will look after it is moved around or when its parts are moved or rearranged.
Visual Color Discrimination	The ability to match or detect differences between colors, including shades of color and brightness.
Multilimb Coordination	The ability to coordinate two or more limbs (for example, two arms, two legs, or one leg and one arm) while sitting, standing, or lying down. It does not involve performing the activities while the whole body is in motion.
Control Precision	The ability to quickly and repeatedly adjust the controls of a machine or a vehicle to exact positions.
Perceptual Speed	The ability to quickly and accurately compare similarities and differences among sets of letters, numbers, objects, pictures, or patterns. The things to be compared may be presented at the same time or one after the other. This ability also includes comparing a presented object with a remembered object.
Spatial Orientation	The ability to know your location in relation to the environment or to know where other objects are in relation to you.
Finger Dexterity	The ability to make precisely coordinated movements of the fingers of one or both hands to grasp, manipulate, or assemble very small objects.
Manual Dexterity	The ability to quickly move your hand, your hand together with your arm, or your two hands to grasp, manipulate, or assemble objects.
Arm-Hand Steadiness	The ability to keep your hand and arm steady while moving your arm or while holding your arm and hand in one position.
Peripheral Vision	The ability to see objects or movement of objects to one's side when the eyes are looking ahead.
Hearing Sensitivity	The ability to detect or tell the differences between sounds that vary in pitch and loudness.
Glare Sensitivity	The ability to see objects in the presence of glare or bright lighting.
Rate Control	The ability to time your movements or the movement of a piece of equipment in anticipation of changes in the speed and/or direction of a moving object or scene.
Reaction Time	The ability to quickly respond (with the hand, finger, or foot) to a signal (sound, light, picture) when it appears.
Sound Localization	The ability to tell the direction from which a sound originated.
Response Orientation	The ability to choose quickly between two or more movements in response to two or more different signals (lights, sounds, pictures). It includes the speed with which the correct response is started with the hand, foot, or other body part.
Speed of Limb Movement	The ability to quickly move the arms and legs.
Night Vision	The ability to see under low light conditions.
Extent Flexibility	The ability to bend, stretch, twist, or reach with your body, arms, and/or legs.
Dynamic Flexibility	The ability to quickly and repeatedly bend, stretch, twist, or reach out with your body, arms, and/or legs.
Stamina	The ability to exert yourself physically over long periods of time without getting winded or out of breath.
Wrist-Finger Speed	The ability to make fast, simple, repeated movements of the fingers, hands, and wrists.
Static Strength	The ability to exert maximum muscle force to lift, push, pull, or carry objects.
Explosive Strength	The ability to use short bursts of muscle force to propel oneself (as in jumping or sprinting), or to throw an object.
Trunk Strength	The ability to use your abdominal and lower back muscles to support part of the body repeatedly or continuously over time without 'giving out' or fatiguing.
Gross Body Coordination	The ability to coordinate the movement of your arms, legs, and torso together when the whole body is in motion.
Gross Body Equilibrium	The ability to keep or regain your body balance or stay upright when in an unstable position.
Dynamic Strength	The ability to exert muscle force repeatedly or continuously over time. This involves muscular endurance and resistance to muscle fatigue.

Work_Activity	Work_Activity Definitions
Getting Information	Observing, receiving, and otherwise obtaining information from all relevant sources.
Communicating with Persons Outside Organization	Communicating with people outside the organization, representing the organization to customers, the public, government, and other external sources. This information can be exchanged in person, in writing, or by telephone or e-mail.
Communicating with Supervisors, Peers, or Subordin	Providing information to supervisors, co-workers, and subordinates by telephone, in written form, e-mail, or in person.
Establishing and Maintaining Interpersonal Relatio	Developing constructive and cooperative working relationships with others, and maintaining them over time.
Interacting With Computers	Using computers and computer systems (including hardware and software) to program, write software, set up functions, enter data, or process information.
Organizing, Planning, and Prioritizing Work	Developing specific goals and plans to prioritize, organize, and accomplish your work.
Making Decisions and Solving Problems	Analyzing information and evaluating results to choose the best solution and solve problems.
Documenting/Recording Information	Entering, transcribing, recording, storing, or maintaining information in written or electronic/magnetic form.
Performing Administrative Activities	Performing day-to-day administrative tasks such as maintaining information files and processing paperwork.
Judging the Qualities of Things, Services, or Peop	Assessing the value, importance, or quality of things or people.
Identifying Objects, Actions, and Events	Identifying information by categorizing, estimating, recognizing differences or similarities, and detecting changes in circumstances or events.
Evaluating Information to Determine Compliance wit	Using relevant information and individual judgment to determine whether events or processes comply with laws, regulations, or standards.
Updating and Using Relevant Knowledge	Keeping up-to-date technically and applying new knowledge to your job.
Performing for or Working Directly with the Public	Performing for people or dealing directly with the public. This includes serving customers in restaurants and stores, and receiving clients or guests.
Processing Information	Compiling, coding, categorizing, calculating, tabulating, auditing, or verifying information or data.
Resolving Conflicts and Negotiating with Others	Handling complaints, settling disputes, and resolving grievances and conflicts, or otherwise negotiating with others.
Interpreting the Meaning of Information for Others	Translating or explaining what information means and how it can be used.
Analyzing Data or Information	Identifying the underlying principles, reasons, or facts of information by breaking down information or data into separate parts.
Estimating the Quantifiable Characteristics of Pro	Estimating sizes, distances, and quantities; or determining time, costs, resources, or materials needed to perform a work activity.
Monitor Processes, Materials, or Surroundings	Monitoring and reviewing information from materials, events, or the environment, to detect or assess problems.
Scheduling Work and Activities	Scheduling events, programs, and activities, as well as the work of others.
Thinking Creatively	Developing, designing, or creating new applications, ideas, relationships, systems, or products, including artistic contributions.
Developing Objectives and Strategies	Establishing long-range objectives and specifying the strategies and actions to achieve them.
Operating Vehicles, Mechanized Devices, or Equipme	Running, maneuvering, navigating, or driving vehicles or mechanized equipment, such as forklifts, passenger vehicles, aircraft, or water craft.
Developing and Building Teams	Encouraging and building mutual trust, respect, and cooperation among team members.
Assisting and Caring for Others	Providing personal assistance, medical attention, emotional support, or other personal care to others such as coworkers, customers, or patients.
Monitoring and Controlling Resources	Monitoring and controlling resources and overseeing the spending of money.
Selling or Influencing Others	Convincing others to buy merchandise/goods or to otherwise change their minds or actions.
Coordinating the Work and Activities of Others	Getting members of a group to work together to accomplish tasks.
Inspecting Equipment, Structures, or Material	Inspecting equipment, structures, or materials to identify the cause of errors or other problems or defects.
Provide Consultation and Advice to Others	Providing guidance and expert advice to management or other groups on technical, systems-, or process-related topics.

Performing General Physical Activities	Performing physical activities that require considerable use of your arms and legs and moving your whole body, such as climbing, lifting, balancing, walking, stooping, and handling of materials.
Coaching and Developing Others	Identifying the developmental needs of others and coaching, mentoring, or otherwise helping others to improve their knowledge or skills.
Handling and Moving Objects	Using hands and arms in handling, installing, positioning, and moving materials, and manipulating things.
Guiding, Directing, and Motivating Subordinates	Providing guidance and direction to subordinates, including setting performance standards and monitoring performance.
Training and Teaching Others	Identifying the educational needs of others, developing formal educational or training programs or classes, and teaching or instructing others.
Drafting, Laying Out, and Specifying Technical Dev	Providing documentation, detailed instructions, drawings, or specifications to tell others about how devices, parts, equipment, or structures are to be fabricated, constructed, assembled, modified, maintained, or used.
Controlling Machines and Processes	Using either control mechanisms or direct physical activity to operate machines or processes (not including computers or vehicles).
Staffing Organizational Units	Recruiting, interviewing, selecting, hiring, and promoting employees in an organization.
Repairing and Maintaining Mechanical Equipment	Servicing, repairing, adjusting, and testing machines, devices, moving parts, and equipment that operate primarily on the basis of mechanical (not electronic) principles.
Repairing and Maintaining Electronic Equipment	Servicing, repairing, calibrating, regulating, fine-tuning, or testing machines, devices, and equipment that operate primarily on the basis of electrical or electronic (not mechanical) principles.

Work_Context	Work_Context Definitions
Contact With Others	How much does this job require the worker to be in contact with others (face-to-face, by telephone, or otherwise) in order to perform it?
Letters and Memos	How often does the job require written letters and memos?
Electronic Mail	How often do you use electronic mail in this job?
Telephone	How often do you have telephone conversations in this job?
Frequency of Decision Making	How frequently is the worker required to make decisions that affect other people, the financial resources, and/or the image and reputation of the organization?
Deal With External Customers	How important is it to work with external customers or the public in this job?
Impact of Decisions on Co-workers or Company Resul	How do the decisions an employee makes impact the results of co-workers, clients or the company?
Spend Time Sitting	How much does this job require sitting?
Face-to-Face Discussions	How often do you have to have face-to-face discussions with individuals or teams in this job?
Indoors, Environmentally Controlled	How often does this job require working indoors in environmentally controlled conditions?
Deal With Unpleasant or Angry People	How frequently does the worker have to deal with unpleasant, angry, or discourteous individuals as part of the job requirements?
Frequency of Conflict Situations	How often are there conflict situations the employee has to face in this job?
Importance of Being Exact or Accurate	How important is being very exact or highly accurate in performing this job?
Work With Work Group or Team	How important is it to work with others in a group or team in this job?
Time Pressure	How often does this job require the worker to meet strict deadlines?
Freedom to Make Decisions	How much decision making freedom, without supervision, does the job offer?
Structured versus Unstructured Work	To what extent is this job structured for the worker, rather than allowing the worker to determine tasks, priorities, and goals?
Importance of Repeating Same Tasks	How important is repeating the same physical activities (e.g., key entry) or mental activities (e.g., checking entries in a ledger) over and over, without stopping, to performing this job?
Spend Time Making Repetitive Motions	How much does this job require making repetitive motions?
Sounds, Noise Levels Are Distracting or Uncomforta	How often does this job require working exposed to sounds and noise levels that are distracting or uncomfortable?
Physical Proximity	To what extent does this job require the worker to perform job tasks in close physical proximity to other people?
Coordinate or Lead Others	How important is it to coordinate or lead others in accomplishing work activities in this job?

Level of Competition	To what extent does this job require the worker to compete or to be aware of competitive pressures?
Consequence of Error	How serious would the result usually be if the worker made a mistake that was not readily correctable?
Degree of Automation	How automated is the job?
Spend Time Using Your Hands to Handle, Control, or	How much does this job require using your hands to handle, control, or feel objects, tools or controls?
Responsibility for Outcomes and Results	How responsible is the worker for work outcomes and results of other workers?
Extremely Bright or Inadequate Lighting	How often does this job require working in extremely bright or inadequate lighting conditions?
In an Enclosed Vehicle or Equipment	How often does this job require working in a closed vehicle or equipment (e.g., car)?
Public Speaking	How often do you have to perform public speaking in this job?
Spend Time Bending or Twisting the Body	How much does this job require bending or twisting your body?
Exposed to Contaminants	How often does this job require working exposed to contaminants (such as pollutants, gases, dust or odors)?
Spend Time Standing	How much does this job require standing?
Spend Time Walking and Running	How much does this job require walking and running?
Outdoors, Exposed to Weather	How often does this job require working outdoors, exposed to all weather conditions?
Responsible for Others' Health and Safety	How much responsibility is there for the health and safety of others in this job?
Indoors, Not Environmentally Controlled	How often does this job require working indoors in non-controlled environmental conditions (e.g., warehouse without heat)?
Outdoors, Under Cover	How often does this job require working outdoors, under cover (e.g., structure with roof but no walls)?
Spend Time Kneeling, Crouching, Stooping, or Crawl	How much does this job require kneeling, crouching, stooping or crawling?
Very Hot or Cold Temperatures	How often does this job require working in very hot (above 90 F degrees) or very cold (below 32 F degrees) temperatures?
Deal With Physically Aggressive People	How frequently does this job require the worker to deal with physical aggression of violent individuals?
Exposed to High Places	How often does this job require exposure to high places?
Exposed to Hazardous Equipment	How often does this job require exposure to hazardous equipment?
Cramped Work Space, Awkward Positions	How often does this job require working in cramped work spaces that requires getting into awkward positions?
Exposed to Minor Burns, Cuts, Bites, or Stings	How often does this job require exposure to minor burns, cuts, bites, or stings?
Spend Time Keeping or Regaining Balance	How much does this job require keeping or regaining your balance?
Pace Determined by Speed of Equipment	How important is it to this job that the pace is determined by the speed of equipment or machinery? (This does not refer to keeping busy at all times on this job.)
Wear Common Protective or Safety Equipment such as	How much does this job require wearing common protective or safety equipment such as safety shoes, glasses, gloves, hard hats or live jackets?
Spend Time Climbing Ladders, Scaffolds, or Poles	How much does this job require climbing ladders, scaffolds, or poles?
Exposed to Hazardous Conditions	How often does this job require exposure to hazardous conditions?
Exposed to Radiation	How often does this job require exposure to radiation?
Wear Specialized Protective or Safety Equipment su	How much does this job require wearing specialized protective or safety equipment such as breathing apparatus, safety harness, full protection suits, or radiation protection?
In an Open Vehicle or Equipment	How often does this job require working in an open vehicle or equipment (e.g., tractor)?
Exposed to Disease or Infections	How often does this job require exposure to disease/infections?
Exposed to Whole Body Vibration	How often does this job require exposure to whole body vibration (e.g., operate a jackhammer)?

Job Zone Component	Job Zone Component Definitions
Title	Job Zone Three: Medium Preparation Needed
Overall Experience	Previous work-related skill, knowledge, or experience is required for these occupations. For example, an electrician must have completed three or four years of apprenticeship or several years of vocational training, and often must have passed a licensing exam, in order to perform the job.

Job Training	Employees in these occupations usually need one or two years of training involving both on-the-job experience and informal training with experienced workers.
Job Zone Examples	These occupations usually involve using communication and organizational skills to coordinate, supervise, manage, or train others to accomplish goals. Examples include dental assistants, electricians, fish and game wardens, legal secretaries, personnel recruiters, and recreation workers.
SVP Range	(6.0 to < 7.0)
Education	Most occupations in this zone require training in vocational schools, related on-the-job experience, or an associate's degree. Some may require a bachelor's degree.

Work_Styles	Work_Styles Definitions
Integrity	Job requires being honest and ethical.
Attention to Detail	Job requires being careful about detail and thorough in completing work tasks.
Self Control	Job requires maintaining composure, keeping emotions in check, controlling anger, and avoiding aggressive behavior, even in very difficult situations.
Dependability	Job requires being reliable, responsible, and dependable, and fulfilling obligations.
Stress Tolerance	Job requires accepting criticism and dealing calmly and effectively with high stress situations.
Achievement/Effort	Job requires establishing and maintaining personally challenging achievement goals and exerting effort toward mastering tasks.
Cooperation	Job requires being pleasant with others on the job and displaying a good-natured, cooperative attitude.
Initiative	Job requires a willingness to take on responsibilities and challenges.
Analytical Thinking	Job requires analyzing information and using logic to address work-related issues and problems.
Leadership	Job requires a willingness to lead, take charge, and offer opinions and direction.
Persistence	Job requires persistence in the face of obstacles.
Independence	Job requires developing one's own ways of doing things, guiding oneself with little or no supervision, and depending on oneself to get things done.
Concern for Others	Job requires being sensitive to others' needs and feelings and being understanding and helpful on the job.
Adaptability/Flexibility	Job requires being open to change (positive or negative) and to considerable variety in the workplace.
Innovation	Job requires creativity and alternative thinking to develop new ideas for and answers to work-related problems.
Social Orientation	Job requires preferring to work with others rather than alone, and being personally connected with others on the job.

13-1032.00 - Insurance Appraisers, Auto Damage

Appraise automobile or other vehicle damage to determine cost of repair for insurance claim settlement and seek agreement with automotive repair shop on cost of repair. Prepare insurance forms to indicate repair cost or cost estimates and recommendations.

Tasks

1) Arrange to have damage appraised by another appraiser to resolve disagreement with shop on repair cost.

2) Examine damaged vehicle to determine extent of structural, body, mechanical, electrical, or interior damage.

3) Estimate parts and labor to repair damage, using standard automotive labor and parts-cost manuals and knowledge of automotive repair.

4) Determine salvage value on total-loss vehicle.

5) Review repair-cost estimates with automobile-repair shop to secure agreement on cost of repairs.

6) Evaluate practicality of repair as opposed to payment of market value of vehicle before accident.

13-1041.02 - Licensing Examiners and Inspectors

Examine, evaluate, and investigate eligibility for, conformity with, or liability under licenses or permits.

Tasks

1) Prepare correspondence to inform concerned parties of licensing decisions and of appeals processes.

2) Visit establishments to verify that valid licenses and permits are displayed, and that licensing standards are being upheld.

3) Advise licensees and other individuals or groups concerning licensing, permit, or passport regulations.

4) Issue licenses to individuals meeting standards.

5) Warn violators of infractions or penalties.

6) Report law or regulation violations to appropriate boards and agencies.

7) Confer with and interview officials, technical or professional specialists, and applicants, in order to obtain information or to clarify facts relevant to licensing decisions.

8) Prepare reports of activities, evaluations, recommendations, and decisions.

9) Score tests and observe equipment operation and control in order to rate ability of applicants.

10) Administer oral, written, road, or flight tests to license applicants.

13-1041.03 - Equal Opportunity Representatives and Officers

Monitor and evaluate compliance with equal opportunity laws, guidelines, and policies to ensure that employment practices and contracting arrangements give equal opportunity without regard to race, religion, color, national origin, sex, age, or disability.

Tasks

1) Provide information, technical assistance, and training to supervisors, managers, and employees on topics such as employee supervision, hiring, grievance procedures, and staff development.

2) Verify that all job descriptions are submitted for review and approval, and that descriptions meet regulatory standards.

3) Conduct surveys and evaluate findings in order to determine if systematic discrimination exists.

4) Investigate employment practices and alleged violations of laws, in order to document and correct discriminatory factors.

5) Meet with persons involved in equal opportunity complaints in order to verify case information, and to arbitrate and settle disputes.

6) Prepare reports of selection, survey, and other statistics, and recommendations for corrective action.

7) Consult with community representatives to develop technical assistance agreements in accordance with governmental regulations.

8) Counsel newly hired members of minority and disadvantaged groups, informing them about details of civil rights laws.

9) Act as liaisons between minority placement agencies and employers, or between job search committees and other equal opportunity administrators.

10) Study equal opportunity complaints in order to clarify issues.

11) Meet with job search committees or coordinators to explain the role of the equal opportunity coordinator, to provide resources for advertising, and to explain expectations for future contacts.

12) Review company contracts to determine actions required to meet governmental equal opportunity provisions.

13) Participate in the recruitment of employees through job fairs, career days, and advertising plans.

14) Develop guidelines for non-discriminatory employment practices, and monitor their implementation and impact.

15) Coordinate, monitor, and revise complaint procedures to ensure timely processing and review of complaints.

13-1051.00 - Cost Estimators

Prepare cost estimates for product manufacturing, construction projects, or services to aid management in bidding on or determining price of product or service. May specialize according to particular service performed or type of product manufactured.

Tasks

1) Consult with clients, vendors, personnel in other departments or construction foremen to discuss and formulate estimates and resolve issues.

2) Confer with engineers, architects, owners, contractors and subcontractors on changes and adjustments to cost estimates.

3) Prepare and maintain a directory of suppliers, contractors and subcontractors.

4) Prepare estimates for use in selecting vendors or subcontractors.

5) Prepare estimates used by management for purposes such as planning, organizing, and scheduling work.

6) Analyze blueprints and other documentation to prepare time, cost, materials, and labor estimates.

7) Review material and labor requirements, to decide whether it is more cost-effective to produce or purchase components.

8) Prepare cost and expenditure statements and other necessary documentation at regular intervals for the duration of the project.

9) Conduct special studies to develop and establish standard hour and related cost data or to effect cost reduction.

10) Set up cost monitoring and reporting systems and procedures.

11) Establish and maintain tendering process, and conduct negotiations.

12) Visit site and record information about access, drainage and topography, and availability of services such as water and electricity.

Knowledge	Knowledge Definitions
Mathematics	Knowledge of arithmetic, algebra, geometry, calculus, statistics, and their applications.
Administration and Management	Knowledge of business and management principles involved in strategic planning, resource allocation, human resources modeling, leadership technique, production methods, and coordination of people and resources.
English Language	Knowledge of the structure and content of the English language including the meaning and spelling of words, rules of composition, and grammar.
Customer and Personal Service	Knowledge of principles and processes for providing customer and personal services. This includes customer needs assessment, meeting quality standards for services, and evaluation of customer satisfaction.
Production and Processing	Knowledge of raw materials, production processes, quality control, costs, and other techniques for maximizing the effective manufacture and distribution of goods.
Clerical	Knowledge of administrative and clerical procedures and systems such as word processing, managing files and records, stenography and transcription, designing forms, and other office procedures and terminology.
Economics and Accounting	Knowledge of economic and accounting principles and practices, the financial markets, banking and the analysis and reporting of financial data.
Sales and Marketing	Knowledge of principles and methods for showing, promoting, and selling products or services. This includes marketing strategy and tactics, product demonstration, sales techniques, and sales control systems.
Personnel and Human Resources	Knowledge of principles and procedures for personnel recruitment, selection, training, compensation and benefits, labor relations and negotiation, and personnel information systems.
Education and Training	Knowledge of principles and methods for curriculum and training design, teaching and instruction for individuals and groups, and the measurement of training effects.
Communications and Media	Knowledge of media production, communication, and dissemination techniques and methods. This includes alternative ways to inform and entertain via written, oral, and visual media.
Building and Construction	Knowledge of materials, methods, and the tools involved in the construction or repair of houses, buildings, or other structures such as highways and roads.
Computers and Electronics	Knowledge of circuit boards, processors, chips, electronic equipment, and computer hardware and software, including applications and programming.
Law and Government	Knowledge of laws, legal codes, court procedures, precedents, government regulations, executive orders, agency rules, and the democratic political process.
Design	Knowledge of design techniques, tools, and principles involved in production of precision technical plans, blueprints, drawings, and models.
Public Safety and Security	Knowledge of relevant equipment, policies, procedures, and strategies to promote effective local, state, or national security operations for the protection of people, data, property, and institutions.
Engineering and Technology	Knowledge of the practical application of engineering science and technology. This includes applying principles, techniques, procedures, and equipment to the design and production of various goods and services.
Transportation	Knowledge of principles and methods for moving people or goods by air, rail, sea, or road, including the relative costs and benefits.
Mechanical	Knowledge of machines and tools, including their designs, uses, repair, and maintenance.
Chemistry	Knowledge of the chemical composition, structure, and properties of substances and of the chemical processes and transformations that they undergo. This includes uses of chemicals and their interactions, danger signs, production techniques, and disposal methods.
Physics	Knowledge and prediction of physical principles, laws, their interrelationships, and applications to understanding fluid, material, and atmospheric dynamics, and mechanical, electrical, atomic and sub-atomic structures and processes.
Telecommunications	Knowledge of transmission, broadcasting, switching, control, and operation of telecommunications systems.
Psychology	Knowledge of human behavior and performance; individual differences in ability, personality, and interests; learning and motivation; psychological research methods; and the assessment and treatment of behavioral and affective disorders.
Geography	Knowledge of principles and methods for describing the features of land, sea, and air masses, including their physical characteristics, locations, interrelationships, and distribution of plant, animal, and human life.
History and Archeology	Knowledge of historical events and their causes, indicators, and effects on civilizations and cultures.
Foreign Language	Knowledge of the structure and content of a foreign (non-English) language including the meaning and spelling of words, rules of composition and grammar, and pronunciation.
Medicine and Dentistry	Knowledge of the information and techniques needed to diagnose and treat human injuries, diseases, and deformities. This includes symptoms, treatment alternatives, drug properties and interactions, and preventive health-care measures.
Therapy and Counseling	Knowledge of principles, methods, and procedures for diagnosis, treatment, and rehabilitation of physical and mental dysfunctions, and for career counseling and guidance.
Philosophy and Theology	Knowledge of different philosophical systems and religions. This includes their basic principles, values, ethics, ways of thinking, customs, practices, and their impact on human culture.
Biology	Knowledge of plant and animal organisms, their tissues, cells, functions, interdependencies, and interactions with each other and the environment.
Sociology and Anthropology	Knowledge of group behavior and dynamics, societal trends and influences, human migrations, ethnicity, cultures and their history and origins.
Fine Arts	Knowledge of the theory and techniques required to compose, produce, and perform works of music, dance, visual arts, drama, and sculpture.
Food Production	Knowledge of techniques and equipment for planting, growing, and harvesting food products (both plant and animal) for consumption, including storage/handling techniques.

Skills	Skills Definitions
Active Listening	Giving full attention to what other people are saying, taking time to understand the points being made, asking questions as appropriate, and not interrupting at inappropriate times.
Reading Comprehension	Understanding written sentences and paragraphs in work related documents.
Mathematics	Using mathematics to solve problems.
Time Management	Managing one's own time and the time of others.
Writing	Communicating effectively in writing as appropriate for the needs of the audience.

Management of Personnel Resources	Motivating, developing, and directing people as they work, identifying the best people for the job.
Critical Thinking	Using logic and reasoning to identify the strengths and weaknesses of alternative solutions, conclusions or approaches to problems.
Active Learning	Understanding the implications of new information for both current and future problem-solving and decision-making.
Speaking	Talking to others to convey information effectively.
Equipment Selection	Determining the kind of tools and equipment needed to do a job.
Complex Problem Solving	Identifying complex problems and reviewing related information to develop and evaluate options and implement solutions.
Coordination	Adjusting actions in relation to others' actions.
Social Perceptiveness	Being aware of others' reactions and understanding why they react as they do.
Judgment and Decision Making	Considering the relative costs and benefits of potential actions to choose the most appropriate one.
Monitoring	Monitoring/Assessing performance of yourself, other individuals, or organizations to make improvements or take corrective action.
Negotiation	Bringing others together and trying to reconcile differences.
Instructing	Teaching others how to do something.
Management of Financial Resources	Determining how money will be spent to get the work done, and accounting for these expenditures.
Learning Strategies	Selecting and using training/instructional methods and procedures appropriate for the situation when learning or teaching new things.
Quality Control Analysis	Conducting tests and inspections of products, services, or processes to evaluate quality or performance.
Service Orientation	Actively looking for ways to help people.
Persuasion	Persuading others to change their minds or behavior.
Technology Design	Generating or adapting equipment and technology to serve user needs.
Operations Analysis	Analyzing needs and product requirements to create a design.
Management of Material Resources	Obtaining and seeing to the appropriate use of equipment, facilities, and materials needed to do certain work.
Troubleshooting	Determining causes of operating errors and deciding what to do about it.
Installation	Installing equipment, machines, wiring, or programs to meet specifications.
Science	Using scientific rules and methods to solve problems.
Operation Monitoring	Watching gauges, dials, or other indicators to make sure a machine is working properly.
Equipment Maintenance	Performing routine maintenance on equipment and determining when and what kind of maintenance is needed.
Systems Evaluation	Identifying measures or indicators of system performance and the actions needed to improve or correct performance, relative to the goals of the system.
Operation and Control	Controlling operations of equipment or systems.
Systems Analysis	Determining how a system should work and how changes in conditions, operations, and the environment will affect outcomes.
Repairing	Repairing machines or systems using the needed tools.
Programming	Writing computer programs for various purposes.

Ability	Ability Definitions
Oral Comprehension	The ability to listen to and understand information and ideas presented through spoken words and sentences.
Oral Expression	The ability to communicate information and ideas in speaking so others will understand.
Information Ordering	The ability to arrange things or actions in a certain order or pattern according to a specific rule or set of rules (e.g., patterns of numbers, letters, words, pictures, mathematical operations).
Written Comprehension	The ability to read and understand information and ideas presented in writing.
Near Vision	The ability to see details at close range (within a few feet of the observer).
Speech Clarity	The ability to speak clearly so others can understand you.
Speech Recognition	The ability to identify and understand the speech of another person.
Mathematical Reasoning	The ability to choose the right mathematical methods or formulas to solve a problem.
Inductive Reasoning	The ability to combine pieces of information to form general rules or conclusions (includes finding a relationship among seemingly unrelated events).

Deductive Reasoning	The ability to apply general rules to specific problems to produce answers that make sense.
Problem Sensitivity	The ability to tell when something is wrong or is likely to go wrong. It does not involve solving the problem, only recognizing there is a problem.
Written Expression	The ability to communicate information and ideas in writing so others will understand.
Category Flexibility	The ability to generate or use different sets of rules for combining or grouping things in different ways.
Number Facility	The ability to add, subtract, multiply, or divide quickly and correctly.
Selective Attention	The ability to concentrate on a task over a period of time without being distracted.
Originality	The ability to come up with unusual or clever ideas about a given topic or situation, or to develop creative ways to solve a problem.
Fluency of Ideas	The ability to come up with a number of ideas about a topic (the number of ideas is important, not their quality, correctness, or creativity).
Visualization	The ability to imagine how something will look after it is moved around or when its parts are moved or rearranged.
Far Vision	The ability to see details at a distance.
Memorization	The ability to remember information such as words, numbers, pictures, and procedures.
Flexibility of Closure	The ability to identify or detect a known pattern (a figure, object, word, or sound) that is hidden in other distracting material.
Speed of Closure	The ability to quickly make sense of, combine, and organize information into meaningful patterns.
Perceptual Speed	The ability to quickly and accurately compare similarities and differences among sets of letters, numbers, objects, pictures, or patterns. The things to be compared may be presented at the same time or one after the other. This ability also includes comparing a presented object with a remembered object.
Time Sharing	The ability to shift back and forth between two or more activities or sources of information (such as speech, sounds, touch, or other sources).
Depth Perception	The ability to judge which of several objects is closer or farther away from you, or to judge the distance between you and an object.
Finger Dexterity	The ability to make precisely coordinated movements of the fingers of one or both hands to grasp, manipulate, or assemble very small objects.
Trunk Strength	The ability to use your abdominal and lower back muscles to support part of the body repeatedly or continuously over time without 'giving out' or fatiguing.
Auditory Attention	The ability to focus on a single source of sound in the presence of other distracting sounds.
Reaction Time	The ability to quickly respond (with the hand, finger, or foot) to a signal (sound, light, picture) when it appears.
Control Precision	The ability to quickly and repeatedly adjust the controls of a machine or a vehicle to exact positions.
Multilimb Coordination	The ability to coordinate two or more limbs (for example, two arms, two legs, or one leg and one arm) while sitting, standing, or lying down. It does not involve performing the activities while the whole body is in motion.
Visual Color Discrimination	The ability to match or detect differences between colors, including shades of color and brightness.
Hearing Sensitivity	The ability to detect or tell the differences between sounds that vary in pitch and loudness.
Wrist-Finger Speed	The ability to make fast, simple, repeated movements of the fingers, hands, and wrists.
Spatial Orientation	The ability to know your location in relation to the environment or to know where other objects are in relation to you.
Manual Dexterity	The ability to quickly move your hand, your hand together with your arm, or your two hands to grasp, manipulate, or assemble objects.
Sound Localization	The ability to tell the direction from which a sound originated.
Gross Body Coordination	The ability to coordinate the movement of your arms, legs, and torso together when the whole body is in motion.
Response Orientation	The ability to choose quickly between two or more movements in response to two or more different signals (lights, sounds, pictures). It includes the speed with which the correct response is started with the hand, foot, or other body part.
Arm-Hand Steadiness	The ability to keep your hand and arm steady while moving your arm or while holding your arm and hand in one position.
Static Strength	The ability to exert maximum muscle force to lift, push, pull, or carry objects.

Stamina	The ability to exert yourself physically over long periods of time without getting winded or out of breath.
Speed of Limb Movement	The ability to quickly move the arms and legs.
Explosive Strength	The ability to use short bursts of muscle force to propel oneself (as in jumping or sprinting), or to throw an object.
Dynamic Strength	The ability to exert muscle force repeatedly or continuously over time. This involves muscular endurance and resistance to muscle fatigue.
Rate Control	The ability to time your movements or the movement of a piece of equipment in anticipation of changes in the speed and/or direction of a moving object or scene.
Dynamic Flexibility	The ability to quickly and repeatedly bend, stretch, twist, or reach out with your body, arms, and/or legs.
Gross Body Equilibrium	The ability to keep or regain your body balance or stay upright when in an unstable position.
Night Vision	The ability to see under low light conditions.
Peripheral Vision	The ability to see objects or movement of objects to one's side when the eyes are looking ahead.
Glare Sensitivity	The ability to see objects in the presence of glare or bright lighting.
Extent Flexibility	The ability to bend, stretch, twist, or reach with your body, arms, and/or legs.

Work_Activity	Work_Activity Definitions
Communicating with Persons Outside Organization	Communicating with people outside the organization, representing the organization to customers, the public, government, and other external sources. This information can be exchanged in person, in writing, or by telephone or e-mail.
Scheduling Work and Activities	Scheduling events, programs, and activities, as well as the work of others.
Communicating with Supervisors, Peers, or Subordin	Providing information to supervisors, co-workers, and subordinates by telephone, in written form, e-mail, or in person.
Getting Information	Observing, receiving, and otherwise obtaining information from all relevant sources.
Establishing and Maintaining Interpersonal Relatio	Developing constructive and cooperative working relationships with others, and maintaining them over time.
Performing for or Working Directly with the Public	Performing for people or dealing directly with the public. This includes serving customers in restaurants and stores, and receiving clients or guests.
Estimating the Quantifiable Characteristics of Pro	Estimating sizes, distances, and quantities; or determining time, costs, resources, or materials needed to perform a work activity.
Coordinating the Work and Activities of Others	Getting members of a group to work together to accomplish tasks.
Making Decisions and Solving Problems	Analyzing information and evaluating results to choose the best solution and solve problems.
Resolving Conflicts and Negotiating with Others	Handling complaints, settling disputes, and resolving grievances and conflicts, or otherwise negotiating with others.
Organizing, Planning, and Prioritizing Work	Developing specific goals and plans to prioritize, organize, and accomplish your work.
Selling or Influencing Others	Convincing others to buy merchandise/goods or to otherwise change their minds or actions.
Thinking Creatively	Developing, designing, or creating new applications, ideas, relationships, systems, or products, including artistic contributions.
Developing and Building Teams	Encouraging and building mutual trust, respect, and cooperation among team members.
Identifying Objects, Actions, and Events	Identifying information by categorizing, estimating, recognizing differences or similarities, and detecting changes in circumstances or events.
Evaluating Information to Determine Compliance wit	Using relevant information and individual judgment to determine whether events or processes comply with laws, regulations, or standards.
Interacting With Computers	Using computers and computer systems (including hardware and software) to program, write software, set up functions, enter data, or process information.
Updating and Using Relevant Knowledge	Keeping up-to-date technically and applying new knowledge to your job.
Performing Administrative Activities	Performing day-to-day administrative tasks such as maintaining information files and processing paperwork.
Monitor Processes, Materials, or Surroundings	Monitoring and reviewing information from materials, events, or the environment, to detect or assess problems.
Inspecting Equipment, Structures, or Material	Inspecting equipment, structures, or materials to identify the cause of errors or other problems or defects.

Judging the Qualities of Things, Services, or Peop	Assessing the value, importance, or quality of things or people.
Drafting, Laying Out, and Specifying Technical Dev	Providing documentation, detailed instructions, drawings, or specifications to tell others about how devices, parts, equipment, or structures are to be fabricated, constructed, assembled, modified, maintained, or used.
Processing Information	Compiling, coding, categorizing, calculating, tabulating, auditing, or verifying information or data.
Developing Objectives and Strategies	Establishing long-range objectives and specifying the strategies and actions to achieve them.
Guiding, Directing, and Motivating Subordinates	Providing guidance and direction to subordinates, including setting performance standards and monitoring performance.
Interpreting the Meaning of Information for Others	Translating or explaining what information means and how it can be used.
Coaching and Developing Others	Identifying the developmental needs of others and coaching, mentoring, or otherwise helping others to improve their knowledge or skills.
Documenting/Recording Information	Entering, transcribing, recording, storing, or maintaining information in written or electronic/magnetic form.
Monitoring and Controlling Resources	Monitoring and controlling resources and overseeing the spending of money.
Provide Consultation and Advice to Others	Providing guidance and expert advice to management or other groups on technical, systems-, or process-related topics.
Analyzing Data or Information	Identifying the underlying principles, reasons, or facts of information by breaking down information or data into separate parts.
Staffing Organizational Units	Recruiting, interviewing, selecting, hiring, and promoting employees in an organization.
Training and Teaching Others	Identifying the educational needs of others, developing formal educational or training programs or classes, and teaching or instructing others.
Operating Vehicles, Mechanized Devices, or Equipme	Running, maneuvering, navigating, or driving vehicles or mechanized equipment, such as forklifts, passenger vehicles, aircraft, or water craft.
Assisting and Caring for Others	Providing personal assistance, medical attention, emotional support, or other personal care to others such as coworkers, customers, or patients.
Performing General Physical Activities	Performing physical activities that require considerable use of your arms and legs and moving your whole body, such as climbing, lifting, balancing, walking, stooping, and handling of materials.
Handling and Moving Objects	Using hands and arms in handling, installing, positioning, and moving materials, and manipulating things.
Repairing and Maintaining Mechanical Equipment	Servicing, repairing, adjusting, and testing machines, devices, moving parts, and equipment that operate primarily on the basis of mechanical (not electronic) principles.
Controlling Machines and Processes	Using either control mechanisms or direct physical activity to operate machines or processes (not including computers or vehicles).
Repairing and Maintaining Electronic Equipment	Servicing, repairing, calibrating, regulating, fine-tuning, or testing machines, devices, and equipment that operate primarily on the basis of electrical or electronic (not mechanical) principles.

Work_Context	Work_Context Definitions
Telephone	How often do you have telephone conversations in this job?
Face-to-Face Discussions	How often do you have to have face-to-face discussions with individuals or teams in this job?
Freedom to Make Decisions	How much decision making freedom, without supervision, does the job offer?
Structured versus Unstructured Work	To what extent is this job structured for the worker, rather than allowing the worker to determine tasks, priorities, and goals?
Impact of Decisions on Co-workers or Company Resul	How do the decisions an employee makes impact the results of co-workers, clients or the company?
Contact With Others	How much does this job require the worker to be in contact with others (face-to-face, by telephone, or otherwise) in order to perform it?
Work With Work Group or Team	How important is it to work with others in a group or team in this job?
Importance of Being Exact or Accurate	How important is being very exact or highly accurate in performing this job?
Frequency of Decision Making	How frequently is the worker required to make decisions that affect other people, the financial resources, and/or the image and reputation of the organization?
Time Pressure	How often does this job require the worker to meet strict deadlines?

Coordinate or Lead Others	How important is it to coordinate or lead others in accomplishing work activities in this job?
Deal With External Customers	How important is it to work with external customers or the public in this job?
Responsibility for Outcomes and Results	How responsible is the worker for work outcomes and results of other workers?
Indoors, Environmentally Controlled	How often does this job require working indoors in environmentally controlled conditions?
Electronic Mail	How often do you use electronic mail in this job?
Frequency of Conflict Situations	How often are there conflict situations the employee has to face in this job?
Letters and Memos	How often does the job require written letters and memos?
Responsible for Others' Health and Safety	How much responsibility is there for the health and safety of others in this job?
Consequence of Error	How serious would the result usually be if the worker made a mistake that was not readily correctable?
Level of Competition	To what extent does this job require the worker to compete or to be aware of competitive pressures?
In an Enclosed Vehicle or Equipment	How often does this job require working in a closed vehicle or equipment (e.g., car)?
Physical Proximity	To what extent does this job require the worker to perform job tasks in close physical proximity to other people?
Spend Time Sitting	How much does this job require sitting?
Importance of Repeating Same Tasks	How important is repeating the same physical activities (e.g., key entry) or mental activities (e.g., checking entries in a ledger) over and over, without stopping, to performing this job?
Exposed to Contaminants	How often does this job require working exposed to contaminants (such as pollutants, gases, dust or odors)?
Deal With Unpleasant or Angry People	How frequently does the worker have to deal with unpleasant, angry, or discourteous individuals as part of the job requirements?
Indoors, Not Environmentally Controlled	How often does this job require working indoors in non-controlled environmental conditions (e.g., warehouse without heat)?
Outdoors, Exposed to Weather	How often does this job require working outdoors, exposed to all weather conditions?
Exposed to Hazardous Equipment	How often does this job require exposure to hazardous equipment?
Spend Time Standing	How much does this job require standing?
Sounds, Noise Levels Are Distracting or Uncomforta	How often does this job require working exposed to sounds and noise levels that are distracting or uncomfortable?
Very Hot or Cold Temperatures	How often does this job require working in very hot (above 90 F degrees) or very cold (below 32 F degrees) temperatures?
Wear Common Protective or Safety Equipment such as	How much does this job require wearing common protective or safety equipment such as safety shoes, glasses, gloves, hard hats or live jackets?
Spend Time Using Your Hands to Handle, Control, or	How much does this job require using your hands to handle, control, or feel objects, tools or controls?
Outdoors, Under Cover	How often does this job require working outdoors, under cover (e.g., structure with roof but no walls)?
Degree of Automation	How automated is the job?
Spend Time Making Repetitive Motions	How much does this job require making repetitive motions?
Exposed to Minor Burns, Cuts, Bites, or Stings	How often does this job require exposure to minor burns, cuts, bites, or stings?
Spend Time Walking and Running	How much does this job require walking and running?
Public Speaking	How often do you have to perform public speaking in this job?
Exposed to High Places	How often does this job require exposure to high places?
Spend Time Kneeling, Crouching, Stooping, or Crawl	How much does this job require kneeling, crouching, stooping or crawling?
Extremely Bright or Inadequate Lighting	How often does this job require working in extremely bright or inadequate lighting conditions?
Pace Determined by Speed of Equipment	How important is it to this job that the pace is determined by the speed of equipment or machinery? (This does not refer to keeping busy at all times on this job.)
Exposed to Hazardous Conditions	How often does this job require exposure to hazardous conditions?
Spend Time Bending or Twisting the Body	How much does this job require bending or twisting your body?
Spend Time Climbing Ladders, Scaffolds, or Poles	How much does this job require climbing ladders, scaffolds, or poles?
Cramped Work Space, Awkward Positions	How often does this job require working in cramped work spaces that requires getting into awkward positions?
Deal With Physically Aggressive People	How frequently does this job require the worker to deal with physical aggression of violent individuals?
Spend Time Keeping or Regaining Balance	How much does this job require keeping or regaining your balance?
Exposed to Whole Body Vibration	How often does this job require exposure to whole body vibration (e.g., operate a jackhammer)?
In an Open Vehicle or Equipment	How often does this job require working in an open vehicle or equipment (e.g., tractor)?
Wear Specialized Protective or Safety Equipment su	How much does this job require wearing specialized protective or safety equipment such as breathing apparatus, safety harness, full protection suits, or radiation protection?
Exposed to Disease or Infections	How often does this job require exposure to disease/infections?
Exposed to Radiation	How often does this job require exposure to radiation?

Job Zone Component	Job Zone Component Definitions
Title	Job Zone Four: Considerable Preparation Needed
Overall Experience	A minimum of two to four years of work-related skill, knowledge, or experience is needed for these occupations. For example, an accountant must complete four years of college and work for several years in accounting to be considered qualified.
Job Training	Employees in these occupations usually need several years of work-related experience, on-the-job training, and/or vocational training.
Job Zone Examples	Many of these occupations involve coordinating, supervising, managing, or training others. Examples include accountants, chefs and head cooks, computer programmers, historians, pharmacists, and police detectives.
SVP Range	(7.0 to < 8.0)
Education	Most of these occupations require a four - year bachelor's degree, but some do not.

Work_Styles	Work_Styles Definitions
Attention to Detail	Job requires being careful about detail and thorough in completing work tasks.
Dependability	Job requires being reliable, responsible, and dependable, and fulfilling obligations.
Integrity	Job requires being honest and ethical.
Cooperation	Job requires being pleasant with others on the job and displaying a good-natured, cooperative attitude.
Concern for Others	Job requires being sensitive to others' needs and feelings and being understanding and helpful on the job.
Independence	Job requires developing one's own ways of doing things, guiding oneself with little or no supervision, and depending on oneself to get things done.
Self Control	Job requires maintaining composure, keeping emotions in check, controlling anger, and avoiding aggressive behavior, even in very difficult situations.
Analytical Thinking	Job requires analyzing information and using logic to address work-related issues and problems.
Stress Tolerance	Job requires accepting criticism and dealing calmly and effectively with high stress situations.
Adaptability/Flexibility	Job requires being open to change (positive or negative) and to considerable variety in the workplace.
Leadership	Job requires a willingness to lead, take charge, and offer opinions and direction.
Innovation	Job requires creativity and alternative thinking to develop new ideas for and answers to work-related problems.
Initiative	Job requires a willingness to take on responsibilities and challenges.
Persistence	Job requires persistence in the face of obstacles.
Achievement/Effort	Job requires establishing and maintaining personally challenging achievement goals and exerting effort toward mastering tasks.
Social Orientation	Job requires preferring to work with others rather than alone, and being personally connected with others on the job.

13-1061.00 - Emergency Management Specialists

Coordinate disaster response or crisis management activities, provide disaster preparedness training, and prepare emergency plans and procedures for natural (e.g., hurricanes, floods, earthquakes), wartime, or technological (e.g., nuclear power plant emergencies, hazardous materials spills) disasters or hostage situations.

Tasks

1) Train local groups in the preparation of long-term plans that are compatible with federal and state plans.

2) Inventory and distribute nuclear, biological, and chemical detection and contamination equipment, providing instruction in its maintenance and use.

3) Propose alteration of emergency response procedures based on regulatory changes, technological changes, or knowledge gained from outcomes of previous emergency situations.

4) Prepare plans that outline operating procedures to be used in response to disasters/emergencies such as hurricanes, nuclear accidents, and terrorist attacks, and in recovery from these events.

5) Develop and maintain liaisons with municipalities, county departments, and similar entities in order to facilitate plan development, response effort coordination, and exchanges of personnel and equipment.

6) Develop instructional materials for the public, and make presentations to citizens' groups in order to provide information on emergency plans and their implementation process.

7) Maintain and update all resource materials associated with emergency preparedness plans.

8) Provide communities with assistance in applying for federal funding for emergency management facilities, radiological instrumentation, and other related items.

9) Develop and implement training procedures and strategies for radiological protection, detection, and decontamination.

10) Keep informed of activities or changes that could affect the likelihood of an emergency, as well as those that could affect response efforts and details of plan implementation.

11) Attend meetings, conferences, and workshops related to emergency management in order to learn new information and to develop working relationships with other emergency management specialists.

12) Prepare emergency situation status reports that describe response and recovery efforts, needs, and preliminary damage assessments.

13) Inspect facilities and equipment such as emergency management centers and communications equipment in order to determine their operational and functional capabilities in emergency situations.

14) Develop and perform tests and evaluations of emergency management plans in accordance with state and federal regulations.

15) Study emergency plans used elsewhere in order to gather information for plan development.

16) Review emergency plans of individual organizations such as medical facilities in order to ensure their adequacy.

17) Collaborate with other officials in order to prepare and analyze damage assessments following disasters or emergencies.

18) Conduct surveys to determine the types of emergency-related needs that will need to be addressed in disaster planning, or provide technical support to others conducting such surveys.

19) Consult with officials of local and area governments, schools, hospitals, and other institutions in order to determine their needs and capabilities in the event of a natural disaster or other emergency.

20) Coordinate disaster response or crisis management activities such as ordering evacuations, opening public shelters, and implementing special needs plans and programs

21) Design and administer emergency/disaster preparedness training courses that teach people how to effectively respond to major emergencies and disasters.

22) Apply for federal funding for emergency management related needs; administer such grants and report on their progress.

13-1071.01 - Employment Interviewers, Private or Public Employment Service

Interview job applicants in employment office and refer them to prospective employers for consideration. Search application files, notify selected applicants of job openings, and refer qualified applicants to prospective employers. Contact employers to verify referral results. Record and evaluate various pertinent data.

Tasks

1) Inform applicants of job openings and details such as duties and responsibilities, compensation, benefits, schedules, working conditions, and promotion opportunities.

2) Maintain records of applicants not selected for employment.

3) Perform reference and background checks on applicants.

4) Select qualified applicants or refer them to employers, according to organization policy.

5) Review employment applications and job orders to match applicants with job requirements, using manual or computerized file searches.

6) Conduct or arrange for skill, intelligence, or psychological testing of applicants and current employees.

7) Search for and recruit applicants for open positions through campus job fairs and advertisements.

8) Instruct job applicants in presenting a positive image by providing help with resume writing, personal appearance, and interview techniques.

9) Provide background information on organizations with which interviews are scheduled.

10) Refer applicants to services such as vocational counseling, literacy or language instruction, transportation assistance, vocational training and child care.

11) Contact employers to solicit orders for job vacancies, determining their requirements and recording relevant data such as job descriptions.

12) Administer assessment tests to identify skill building needs.

13) Conduct workshops and demonstrate the use of job listings to assist applicants with skill building.

14) Hire workers and place them with employers needing temporary help.

15) Evaluate selection and testing techniques by conducting research or follow-up activities and conferring with management and supervisory personnel.

Knowledge	Knowledge Definitions
English Language	Knowledge of the structure and content of the English language including the meaning and spelling of words, rules of composition, and grammar.
Customer and Personal Service	Knowledge of principles and processes for providing customer and personal services. This includes customer needs assessment, meeting quality standards for services, and evaluation of customer satisfaction.
Clerical	Knowledge of administrative and clerical procedures and systems such as word processing, managing files and records, stenography and transcription, designing forms, and other office procedures and terminology.
Administration and Management	Knowledge of business and management principles involved in strategic planning, resource allocation, human resources modeling, leadership technique, production methods, and coordination of people and resources.
Foreign Language	Knowledge of the structure and content of a foreign (non-English) language including the meaning and spelling of words, rules of composition and grammar, and pronunciation.
Personnel and Human Resources	Knowledge of principles and procedures for personnel recruitment, selection, training, compensation and benefits, labor relations and negotiation, and personnel information systems.
Mathematics	Knowledge of arithmetic, algebra, geometry, calculus, statistics, and their applications.
Sales and Marketing	Knowledge of principles and methods for showing, promoting, and selling products or services. This includes marketing strategy and tactics, product demonstration, sales techniques, and sales control systems.
Education and Training	Knowledge of principles and methods for curriculum and training design, teaching and instruction for individuals and groups, and the measurement of training effects.
Telecommunications	Knowledge of transmission, broadcasting, switching, control, and operation of telecommunications systems.
Computers and Electronics	Knowledge of circuit boards, processors, chips, electronic equipment, and computer hardware and software, including applications and programming.
Sociology and Anthropology	Knowledge of group behavior and dynamics, societal trends and influences, human migrations, ethnicity, cultures and their history and origins.
Psychology	Knowledge of human behavior and performance; individual differences in ability, personality, and interests; learning and motivation; psychological research methods; and the assessment and treatment of behavioral and affective disorders.

Economics and Accounting	Knowledge of economic and accounting principles and practices, the financial markets, banking and the analysis and reporting of financial data.
Production and Processing	Knowledge of raw materials, production processes, quality control, costs, and other techniques for maximizing the effective manufacture and distribution of goods.
Communications and Media	Knowledge of media production, communication, and dissemination techniques and methods. This includes alternative ways to inform and entertain via written, oral, and visual media.
Law and Government	Knowledge of laws, legal codes, court procedures, precedents, government regulations, executive orders, agency rules, and the democratic political process.
Public Safety and Security	Knowledge of relevant equipment, policies, procedures, and strategies to promote effective local, state, or national security operations for the protection of people, data, property, and institutions.
Biology	Knowledge of plant and animal organisms, their tissues, cells, functions, interdependencies, and interactions with each other and the environment.
Therapy and Counseling	Knowledge of principles, methods, and procedures for diagnosis, treatment, and rehabilitation of physical and mental dysfunctions, and for career counseling and guidance.
Transportation	Knowledge of principles and methods for moving people or goods by air, rail, sea, or road, including the relative costs and benefits.
Engineering and Technology	Knowledge of the practical application of engineering science and technology. This includes applying principles, techniques, procedures, and equipment to the design and production of various goods and services.
Medicine and Dentistry	Knowledge of the information and techniques needed to diagnose and treat human injuries, diseases, and deformities. This includes symptoms, treatment alternatives, drug properties and interactions, and preventive health-care measures.
Design	Knowledge of design techniques, tools, and principles involved in production of precision technical plans, blueprints, drawings, and models.
Food Production	Knowledge of techniques and equipment for planting, growing, and harvesting food products (both plant and animal) for consumption, including storage/handling techniques.
Philosophy and Theology	Knowledge of different philosophical systems and religions. This includes their basic principles, values, ethics, ways of thinking, customs, practices, and their impact on human culture.
Geography	Knowledge of principles and methods for describing the features of land, sea, and air masses, including their physical characteristics, locations, interrelationships, and distribution of plant, animal, and human life.
Chemistry	Knowledge of the chemical composition, structure, and properties of substances and of the chemical processes and transformations that they undergo. This includes uses of chemicals and their interactions, danger signs, production techniques, and disposal methods.
Fine Arts	Knowledge of the theory and techniques required to compose, produce, and perform works of music, dance, visual arts, drama, and sculpture.
Mechanical	Knowledge of machines and tools, including their designs, uses, repair, and maintenance.
Physics	Knowledge and prediction of physical principles, laws, their interrelationships, and applications to understanding fluid, material, and atmospheric dynamics, and mechanical, electrical, atomic and sub-atomic structures and processes.
History and Archeology	Knowledge of historical events and their causes, indicators, and effects on civilizations and cultures.
Building and Construction	Knowledge of materials, methods, and the tools involved in construction or repair of houses, buildings, or other structures such as highways and roads.

Skills	Skills Definitions
Reading Comprehension	Understanding written sentences and paragraphs in work related documents.
Service Orientation	Actively looking for ways to help people.
Speaking	Talking to others to convey information effectively.
Active Listening	Giving full attention to what other people are saying, taking time to understand the points being made, asking questions as appropriate, and not interrupting at inappropriate times.
Persuasion	Persuading others to change their minds or behavior.

Writing	Communicating effectively in writing as appropriate for the needs of the audience.
Critical Thinking	Using logic and reasoning to identify the strengths and weaknesses of alternative solutions, conclusions or approaches to problems.
Management of Personnel Resources	Motivating, developing, and directing people as they work, identifying the best people for the job.
Social Perceptiveness	Being aware of others' reactions and understanding why they react as they do.
Active Learning	Understanding the implications of new information for both current and future problem-solving and decision-making.
Instructing	Teaching others how to do something.
Time Management	Managing one's own time and the time of others.
Monitoring	Monitoring/Assessing performance of yourself, other individuals, or organizations to make improvements or take corrective action.
Learning Strategies	Selecting and using training/instructional methods and procedures appropriate for the situation when learning or teaching new things.
Coordination	Adjusting actions in relation to others' actions.
Negotiation	Bringing others together and trying to reconcile differences.
Judgment and Decision Making	Considering the relative costs and benefits of potential actions to choose the most appropriate one.
Complex Problem Solving	Identifying complex problems and reviewing related information to develop and evaluate options and implement solutions.
Operations Analysis	Analyzing needs and product requirements to create a design.
Equipment Selection	Determining the kind of tools and equipment needed to do a job.
Mathematics	Using mathematics to solve problems.
Management of Financial Resources	Determining how money will be spent to get the work done, and accounting for these expenditures.
Technology Design	Generating or adapting equipment and technology to serve user needs.
Troubleshooting	Determining causes of operating errors and deciding what to do about it.
Management of Material Resources	Obtaining and seeing to the appropriate use of equipment, facilities, and materials needed to do certain work.
Systems Evaluation	Identifying measures or indicators of system performance and the actions needed to improve or correct performance, relative to the goals of the system.
Operation and Control	Controlling operations of equipment or systems.
Installation	Installing equipment, machines, wiring, or programs to meet specifications.
Quality Control Analysis	Conducting tests and inspections of products, services, or processes to evaluate quality or performance.
Equipment Maintenance	Performing routine maintenance on equipment and determining when and what kind of maintenance is needed.
Systems Analysis	Determining how a system should work and how changes in conditions, operations, and the environment will affect outcomes.
Repairing	Repairing machines or systems using the needed tools.
Operation Monitoring	Watching gauges, dials, or other indicators to make sure a machine is working properly.
Science	Using scientific rules and methods to solve problems.
Programming	Writing computer programs for various purposes.

Ability	Ability Definitions
Oral Comprehension	The ability to listen to and understand information and ideas presented through spoken words and sentences.
Oral Expression	The ability to communicate information and ideas in speaking so others will understand.
Speech Clarity	The ability to speak clearly so others can understand you.
Written Comprehension	The ability to read and understand information and ideas presented in writing.
Speech Recognition	The ability to identify and understand the speech of another person.
Inductive Reasoning	The ability to combine pieces of information to form general rules or conclusions (includes finding a relationship among seemingly unrelated events).
Problem Sensitivity	The ability to tell when something is wrong or is likely to go wrong. It does not involve solving the problem, only recognizing there is a problem.
Near Vision	The ability to see details at close range (within a few feet of the observer).
Deductive Reasoning	The ability to apply general rules to specific problems to produce answers that make sense.

Written Expression	The ability to communicate information and ideas in writing so others will understand.
Information Ordering	The ability to arrange things or actions in a certain order or pattern according to a specific rule or set of rules (e.g., patterns of numbers, letters, words, pictures, mathematical operations).
Category Flexibility	The ability to generate or use different sets of rules for combining or grouping things in different ways.
Selective Attention	The ability to concentrate on a task over a period of time without being distracted.
Time Sharing	The ability to shift back and forth between two or more activities or sources of information (such as speech, sounds, touch, or other sources).
Originality	The ability to come up with unusual or clever ideas about a given topic or situation, or to develop creative ways to solve a problem.
Memorization	The ability to remember information such as words, numbers, pictures, and procedures.
Fluency of Ideas	The ability to come up with a number of ideas about a topic (the number of ideas is important, not their quality, correctness, or creativity).
Flexibility of Closure	The ability to identify or detect a known pattern (a figure, object, word, or sound) that is hidden in other distracting material.
Speed of Closure	The ability to quickly make sense of, combine, and organize information into meaningful patterns.
Auditory Attention	The ability to focus on a single source of sound in the presence of other distracting sounds.
Depth Perception	The ability to judge which of several objects is closer or farther away from you, or to judge the distance between you and an object.
Multilimb Coordination	The ability to coordinate two or more limbs (for example, two arms, two legs, or one leg and one arm) while sitting, standing, or lying down. It does not involve performing the activities while the whole body is in motion.
Mathematical Reasoning	The ability to choose the right mathematical methods or formulas to solve a problem.
Control Precision	The ability to quickly and repeatedly adjust the controls of a machine or a vehicle to exact positions.
Manual Dexterity	The ability to quickly move your hand, your hand together with your arm, or your two hands to grasp, manipulate, or assemble objects.
Perceptual Speed	The ability to quickly and accurately compare similarities and differences among sets of letters, numbers, objects, pictures, or patterns. The things to be compared may be presented at the same time or one after the other. This ability also includes comparing a presented object with a remembered object.
Visualization	The ability to imagine how something will look after it is moved around or when its parts are moved or rearranged.
Far Vision	The ability to see details at a distance.
Finger Dexterity	The ability to make precisely coordinated movements of the fingers of one or both hands to grasp, manipulate, or assemble very small objects.
Static Strength	The ability to exert maximum muscle force to lift, push, pull, or carry objects.
Number Facility	The ability to add, subtract, multiply, or divide quickly and correctly.
Trunk Strength	The ability to use your abdominal and lower back muscles to support part of the body repeatedly or continuously over time without 'giving out' or fatiguing.
Visual Color Discrimination	The ability to match or detect differences between colors, including shades of color and brightness.
Arm-Hand Steadiness	The ability to keep your hand and arm steady while moving your arm or while holding your arm and hand in one position.
Hearing Sensitivity	The ability to detect or tell the differences between sounds that vary in pitch and loudness.
Wrist-Finger Speed	The ability to make fast, simple, repeated movements of the fingers, hands, and wrists.
Response Orientation	The ability to choose quickly between two or more movements in response to two or more different signals (lights, sounds, pictures). It includes the speed with which the correct response is started with the hand, foot, or other body part.
Rate Control	The ability to time your movements or the movement of a piece of equipment in anticipation of changes in the speed and/or direction of a moving object or scene.
Reaction Time	The ability to quickly respond (with the hand, finger, or foot) to a signal (sound, light, picture) when it appears.

Dynamic Strength	The ability to exert muscle force repeatedly or continuously over time. This involves muscular endurance and resistance to muscle fatigue.
Glare Sensitivity	The ability to see objects in the presence of glare or bright lighting.
Extent Flexibility	The ability to bend, stretch, twist, or reach with your body, arms, and/or legs.
Dynamic Flexibility	The ability to quickly and repeatedly bend, stretch, twist, or reach out with your body, arms, and/or legs.
Gross Body Equilibrium	The ability to keep or regain your body balance or stay upright when in an unstable position.
Explosive Strength	The ability to use short bursts of muscle force to propel oneself (as in jumping or sprinting), or to throw an object.
Night Vision	The ability to see under low light conditions.
Gross Body Coordination	The ability to coordinate the movement of your arms, legs, and torso together when the whole body is in motion.
Peripheral Vision	The ability to see objects or movement of objects to one's side when the eyes are looking ahead.
Stamina	The ability to exert yourself physically over long periods of time without getting winded or out of breath.
Spatial Orientation	The ability to know your location in relation to the environment or to know where other objects are in relation to you.
Sound Localization	The ability to tell the direction from which a sound originated.
Speed of Limb Movement	The ability to quickly move the arms and legs.

Work_Activity	Work_Activity Definitions
Interacting With Computers	Using computers and computer systems (including hardware and software) to program, write software, set up functions, enter data, or process information.
Performing for or Working Directly with the Public	Performing for people or dealing directly with the public. This includes serving customers in restaurants and stores, and receiving clients or guests.
Getting Information	Observing, receiving, and otherwise obtaining information from all relevant sources.
Establishing and Maintaining Interpersonal Relatio	Developing constructive and cooperative working relationships with others, and maintaining them over time.
Judging the Qualities of Things, Services, or Peop	Assessing the value, importance, or quality of things or people.
Organizing, Planning, and Prioritizing Work	Developing specific goals and plans to prioritize, organize, and accomplish your work.
Performing Administrative Activities	Performing day-to-day administrative tasks such as maintaining information files and processing paperwork.
Communicating with Persons Outside Organization	Communicating with people outside the organization, representing the organization to customers, the public, government, and other external sources. This information can be exchanged in person, in writing, or by telephone or e-mail.
Resolving Conflicts and Negotiating with Others	Handling complaints, settling disputes, and resolving grievances and conflicts, or otherwise negotiating with others.
Making Decisions and Solving Problems	Analyzing information and evaluating results to choose the best solution and solve problems.
Coaching and Developing Others	Identifying the developmental needs of others and coaching, mentoring, or otherwise helping others to improve their knowledge or skills.
Developing and Building Teams	Encouraging and building mutual trust, respect, and cooperation among team members.
Communicating with Supervisors, Peers, or Subordin	Providing information to supervisors, co-workers, and subordinates by telephone, in written form, e-mail, or in person.
Guiding, Directing, and Motivating Subordinates	Providing guidance and direction to subordinates, including setting performance standards and monitoring performance.
Processing Information	Compiling, coding, categorizing, calculating, tabulating, auditing, or verifying information or data.
Analyzing Data or Information	Identifying the underlying principles, reasons, or facts of information by breaking down information or data into separate parts.
Assisting and Caring for Others	Providing personal assistance, medical attention, emotional support, or other personal care to others such as coworkers, customers, or patients.
Identifying Objects, Actions, and Events	Identifying information by categorizing, estimating, recognizing differences or similarities, and detecting changes in circumstances or events.
Scheduling Work and Activities	Scheduling events, programs, and activities, as well as the work of others.
Coordinating the Work and Activities of Others	Getting members of a group to work together to accomplish tasks.

Training and Teaching Others	Identifying the educational needs of others, developing formal educational or training programs or classes, and teaching or instructing others.
Monitor Processes, Materials, or Surroundings	Monitoring and reviewing information from materials, events, or the environment, to detect or assess problems.
Evaluating Information to Determine Compliance wit	Using relevant information and individual judgment to determine whether events or processes comply with laws, regulations, or standards.
Provide Consultation and Advice to Others	Providing guidance and expert advice to management or other groups on technical, systems-, or process-related topics.
Updating and Using Relevant Knowledge	Keeping up-to-date technically and applying new knowledge to your job.
Selling or Influencing Others	Convincing others to buy merchandise/goods or to otherwise change their minds or actions.
Developing Objectives and Strategies	Establishing long-range objectives and specifying the strategies and actions to achieve them.
Interpreting the Meaning of Information for Others	Translating or explaining what information means and how it can be used.
Estimating the Quantifiable Characteristics of Pro	Estimating sizes, distances, and quantities; or determining time, costs, resources, or materials needed to perform a work activity.
Thinking Creatively	Developing, designing, or creating new applications, ideas, relationships, systems, or products, including artistic contributions.
Controlling Machines and Processes	Using either control mechanisms or direct physical activity to operate machines or processes (not including computers or vehicles).
Documenting/Recording Information	Entering, transcribing, recording, storing, or maintaining information in written or electronic/magnetic form.
Staffing Organizational Units	Recruiting, interviewing, selecting, hiring, and promoting employees in an organization.
Handling and Moving Objects	Using hands and arms in handling, installing, positioning, and moving materials, and manipulating things.
Performing General Physical Activities	Performing physical activities that require considerable use of your arms and legs and moving your whole body, such as climbing, lifting, balancing, walking, stooping, and handling of materials.
Monitoring and Controlling Resources	Monitoring and controlling resources and overseeing the spending of money.
Drafting, Laying Out, and Specifying Technical Dev	Providing documentation, detailed instructions, drawings, or specifications to tell others about how devices, parts, equipment, or structures are to be fabricated, constructed, assembled, modified, maintained, or used.
Inspecting Equipment, Structures, or Material	Inspecting equipment, structures, or materials to identify the cause of errors or other problems or defects.
Operating Vehicles, Mechanized Devices, or Equipme	Running, maneuvering, navigating, or driving vehicles or mechanized equipment, such as forklifts, passenger vehicles, aircraft, or water craft.
Repairing and Maintaining Electronic Equipment	Servicing, repairing, calibrating, regulating, fine-tuning, or testing machines, devices, and equipment that operate primarily on the basis of electrical or electronic (not mechanical) principles.
Repairing and Maintaining Mechanical Equipment	Servicing, repairing, adjusting, and testing machines, devices, moving parts, and equipment that operate primarily on the basis of mechanical (not electronic) principles.

Work_Context	Work_Context Definitions
Contact With Others	How much does this job require the worker to be in contact with others (face-to-face, by telephone, or otherwise) in order to perform it?
Telephone	How often do you have telephone conversations in this job?
Face-to-Face Discussions	How often do you have to have face-to-face discussions with individuals or teams in this job?
Deal With External Customers	How important is it to work with external customers or the public in this job?
Spend Time Sitting	How much does this job require sitting?
Work With Work Group or Team	How important is it to work with others in a group or team in this job?
Frequency of Decision Making	How frequently is the worker required to make decisions that affect other people, the financial resources, and/or the image and reputation of the organization?
Letters and Memos	How often does the job require written letters and memos?
Coordinate or Lead Others	How important is it to coordinate or lead others in accomplishing work activities in this job?
Indoors, Environmentally Controlled	How often does this job require working indoors in environmentally controlled conditions?

Importance of Being Exact or Accurate	How important is being very exact or highly accurate in performing this job?
Electronic Mail	How often do you use electronic mail in this job?
Time Pressure	How often does this job require the worker to meet strict deadlines?
Impact of Decisions on Co-workers or Company Resul	How do the decisions an employee makes impact the results of co-workers, clients or the company?
Freedom to Make Decisions	How much decision making freedom, without supervision, does the job offer?
Structured versus Unstructured Work	To what extent is this job structured for the worker, rather than allowing the worker to determine tasks, priorities, and goals?
Responsibility for Outcomes and Results	How responsible is the worker for work outcomes and results of other workers?
Frequency of Conflict Situations	How often are there conflict situations the employee has to face in this job?
Importance of Repeating Same Tasks	How important is repeating the same physical activities (e.g., key entry) or mental activities (e.g., checking entries in a ledger) over and over, without stopping, to performing this job?
Deal With Unpleasant or Angry People	How frequently does the worker have to deal with unpleasant, angry, or discourteous individuals as part of the job requirements?
Responsible for Others' Health and Safety	How much responsibility is there for the health and safety of others in this job?
Physical Proximity	To what extent does this job require the worker to perform job tasks in close physical proximity to other people?
Spend Time Making Repetitive Motions	How much does this job require making repetitive motions?
Level of Competition	To what extent does this job require the worker to compete or to be aware of competitive pressures?
Public Speaking	How often do you have to perform public speaking in this job?
Spend Time Using Your Hands to Handle, Control, or	How much does this job require using your hands to handle, control, or feel objects, tools or controls?
Degree of Automation	How automated is the job?
Sounds, Noise Levels Are Distracting or Uncomforta	How often does this job require working exposed to sounds and noise levels that are distracting or uncomfortable?
In an Enclosed Vehicle or Equipment	How often does this job require working in a closed vehicle or equipment (e.g., car)?
Consequence of Error	How serious would the result usually be if the worker made a mistake that was not readily correctable?
Extremely Bright or Inadequate Lighting	How often does this job require working in extremely bright or inadequate lighting conditions?
Exposed to Contaminants	How often does this job require working exposed to contaminants (such as pollutants, gases, dust or odors)?
Exposed to Disease or Infections	How often does this job require exposure to disease/infections?
Deal With Physically Aggressive People	How frequently does this job require the worker to deal with physical aggression of violent individuals?
Spend Time Standing	How much does this job require standing?
Indoors, Not Environmentally Controlled	How often does this job require working indoors in non-controlled environmental conditions (e.g., warehouse without heat)?
Spend Time Walking and Running	How much does this job require walking and running?
Outdoors, Exposed to Weather	How often does this job require working outdoors, exposed to all weather conditions?
Spend Time Bending or Twisting the Body	How much does this job require bending or twisting your body?
Pace Determined by Speed of Equipment	How important is it to this job that the pace is determined by the speed of equipment or machinery? (This does not refer to keeping busy at all times on this job.)
Exposed to Minor Burns, Cuts, Bites, or Stings	How often does this job require exposure to minor burns, cuts, bites, or stings?
Wear Common Protective or Safety Equipment such as	How much does this job require wearing common protective or safety equipment such as safety shoes, glasses, gloves, hard hats or live jackets?
Exposed to Hazardous Conditions	How often does this job require exposure to hazardous conditions?
Exposed to Hazardous Equipment	How often does this job require exposure to hazardous equipment?
Spend Time Kneeling, Crouching, Stooping, or Crawl	How much does this job require kneeling, crouching, stooping, or crawling?
Very Hot or Cold Temperatures	How often does this job require working in very hot (above 90 F degrees) or very cold (below 32 F degrees) temperatures?
Cramped Work Space, Awkward Positions	How often does this job require working in cramped work spaces that requires getting into awkward positions?

Outdoors, Under Cover	How often does this job require working outdoors, under cover (e.g., structure with roof but no walls)?
In an Open Vehicle or Equipment	How often does this job require working in an open vehicle or equipment (e.g., tractor)?
Wear Specialized Protective or Safety Equipment su	How much does this job require wearing specialized protective or safety equipment such as breathing apparatus, safety harness, full protection suits, or radiation protection?
Spend Time Keeping or Regaining Balance	How much does this job require keeping or regaining your balance?
Exposed to High Places	How often does this job require exposure to high places?
Exposed to Whole Body Vibration	How often does this job require exposure to whole body vibration (e.g., operate a jackhammer)?
Exposed to Radiation	How often does this job require exposure to radiation?
Spend Time Climbing Ladders, Scaffolds, or Poles	How much does this job require climbing ladders, scaffolds, or poles?

Job Zone Component	Job Zone Component Definitions
Title	Job Zone Three: Medium Preparation Needed
Overall Experience	Previous work-related skill, knowledge, or experience is required for these occupations. For example, an electrician must have completed three or four years of apprenticeship or several years of vocational training, and often must have passed a licensing exam, in order to perform the job.
Job Training	Employees in these occupations usually need one or two years of training involving both on-the-job experience and informal training with experienced workers.
Job Zone Examples	These occupations usually involve using communication and organizational skills to coordinate, supervise, manage, or train others to accomplish goals. Examples include dental assistants, electricians, fish and game wardens, legal secretaries, personnel recruiters, and recreation workers.
SVP Range	(6.0 to < 7.0)
Education	Most occupations in this zone require training in vocational schools, related on-the-job experience, or an associate's degree. Some may require a bachelor's degree.

Work_Styles	Work_Styles Definitions
Attention to Detail	Job requires being careful about detail and thorough in completing work tasks.
Dependability	Job requires being reliable, responsible, and dependable, and fulfilling obligations.
Stress Tolerance	Job requires accepting criticism and dealing calmly and effectively with high stress situations.
Self Control	Job requires maintaining composure, keeping emotions in check, controlling anger, and avoiding aggressive behavior, even in very difficult situations.
Integrity	Job requires being honest and ethical.
Initiative	Job requires a willingness to take on responsibilities and challenges.
Concern for Others	Job requires being sensitive to others' needs and feelings and being understanding and helpful on the job.
Cooperation	Job requires being pleasant with others on the job and displaying a good-natured, cooperative attitude.
Achievement/Effort	Job requires establishing and maintaining personally challenging achievement goals and exerting effort toward mastering tasks.
Persistence	Job requires persistence in the face of obstacles.
Social Orientation	Job requires preferring to work with others rather than alone, and being personally connected with others on the job.
Leadership	Job requires a willingness to lead, take charge, and offer opinions and direction.
Adaptability/Flexibility	Job requires being open to change (positive or negative) and to considerable variety in the workplace.
Independence	Job requires developing one's own ways of doing things, guiding oneself with little or no supervision, and depending on oneself to get things done.
Innovation	Job requires creativity and alternative thinking to develop new ideas for and answers to work-related problems.
Analytical Thinking	Job requires analyzing information and using logic to address work-related issues and problems.

13-1071.02 - Personnel Recruiters

Seek out, interview, and screen applicants to fill existing and future job openings and promote career opportunities within an organization.

Tasks

1) Inform potential applicants about facilities, operations, benefits, and job or career opportunities in organizations.

2) Advise managers and employees on staffing policies and procedures.

3) Maintain current knowledge of Equal Employment Opportunity (EEO) and affirmative action guidelines and laws, such as the Americans with Disabilities Act.

4) Interview applicants to obtain information on work history, training, education, and job skills.

5) Conduct reference and background checks on applicants.

6) Advise management on organizing, preparing, and implementing recruiting and retention programs.

7) Evaluate recruitment and selection criteria to ensure conformance to professional, statistical, and testing standards, recommending revision as needed.

8) Establish and maintain relationships with hiring managers to stay abreast of current and future hiring and business needs.

9) Screen and refer applicants to hiring personnel in the organization, making hiring recommendations when appropriate.

10) Arrange for interviews and provide travel arrangements as necessary.

11) Perform searches for qualified candidates according to relevant job criteria, using computer databases, networking, Internet recruiting resources, cold calls, media, recruiting firms, and employee referrals.

12) Recruit applicants for open positions, arranging job fairs with college campus representatives.

13) Hire applicants and authorize paperwork assigning them to positions.

14) Prepare and maintain employment records.

15) Review and evaluate applicant qualifications or eligibility for specified licensing, according to established guidelines and designated licensing codes.

16) Address civic and social groups and attend conferences to disseminate information concerning possible job openings and career opportunities.

17) Supervise personnel clerks performing filing, typing and record-keeping duties.

18) Project yearly recruitment expenditures for budgetary consideration and control.

19) Serve on selection and examination boards to evaluate applicants according to test scores, contacting promising candidates for interviews.

Knowledge	Knowledge Definitions
Administration and Management	Knowledge of business and management principles involved in strategic planning, resource allocation, human resources modeling, leadership technique, production methods, and coordination of people and resources.
Personnel and Human Resources	Knowledge of principles and procedures for personnel recruitment, selection, training, compensation and benefits, labor relations and negotiation, and personnel information systems.
English Language	Knowledge of the structure and content of the English language including the meaning and spelling of words, rules of composition, and grammar.
Education and Training	Knowledge of principles and methods for curriculum and training design, teaching and instruction for individuals and groups, and the measurement of training effects.
Clerical	Knowledge of administrative and clerical procedures and systems such as word processing, managing files and records, stenography and transcription, designing forms, and other office procedures and terminology.
Communications and Media	Knowledge of media production, communication, and dissemination techniques and methods. This includes alternative ways to inform and entertain via written, oral, and visual media.
Computers and Electronics	Knowledge of circuit boards, processors, chips, electronic equipment, and computer hardware and software, including applications and programming.
Customer and Personal Service	Knowledge of principles and processes for providing customer and personal services. This includes customer needs assessment, meeting quality standards for services, and evaluation of customer satisfaction.

Sales and Marketing	Knowledge of principles and methods for showing, promoting, and selling products or services. This includes marketing strategy and tactics, product demonstration, sales techniques, and sales control systems.
Mathematics	Knowledge of arithmetic, algebra, geometry, calculus, statistics, and their applications.
Telecommunications	Knowledge of transmission, broadcasting, switching, control, and operation of telecommunications systems.
Law and Government	Knowledge of laws, legal codes, court procedures, precedents, government regulations, executive orders, agency rules, and the democratic political process.
Therapy and Counseling	Knowledge of principles, methods, and procedures for diagnosis, treatment, and rehabilitation of physical and mental dysfunctions, and for career counseling and guidance.
Psychology	Knowledge of human behavior and performance; individual differences in ability, personality, and interests; learning and motivation; psychological research methods; and the assessment and treatment of behavioral and affective disorders.
Economics and Accounting	Knowledge of economic and accounting principles and practices, the financial markets, banking and the analysis and reporting of financial data.
Sociology and Anthropology	Knowledge of group behavior and dynamics, societal trends and influences, human migrations, ethnicity, cultures and their history and origins.
Geography	Knowledge of principles and methods for describing the features of land, sea, and air masses, including their physical characteristics, locations, interrelationships, and distribution of plant, animal, and human life.
Public Safety and Security	Knowledge of relevant equipment, policies, procedures, and strategies to promote effective local, state, or national security operations for the protection of people, data, property, and institutions.
Foreign Language	Knowledge of the structure and content of a foreign (non-English) language including the meaning and spelling of words, rules of composition and grammar, and pronunciation.
Transportation	Knowledge of principles and methods for moving people or goods by air, rail, sea, or road, including the relative costs and benefits.
Production and Processing	Knowledge of raw materials, production processes, quality control, costs, and other techniques for maximizing the effective manufacture and distribution of goods.
Philosophy and Theology	Knowledge of different philosophical systems and religions. This includes their basic principles, values, ethics, ways of thinking, customs, practices, and their impact on human culture.
Engineering and Technology	Knowledge of the practical application of engineering science and technology. This includes applying principles, techniques, procedures, and equipment to the design and production of various goods and services.
Mechanical	Knowledge of machines and tools, including their designs, uses, repair, and maintenance.
Medicine and Dentistry	Knowledge of the information and techniques needed to diagnose and treat human injuries, diseases, and deformities. This includes symptoms, treatment alternatives, drug properties and interactions, and preventive health-care measures.
History and Archeology	Knowledge of historical events and their causes, indicators, and effects on civilizations and cultures.
Chemistry	Knowledge of the chemical composition, structure, and properties of substances and of the chemical processes and transformations that they undergo. This includes uses of chemicals and their interactions, danger signs, production techniques, and disposal methods.
Physics	Knowledge and prediction of physical principles, laws, their interrelationships, and applications to understanding fluid, material, and atmospheric dynamics, and mechanical, electrical, atomic and sub-atomic structures and processes.
Building and Construction	Knowledge of materials, methods, and the tools involved in the construction or repair of houses, buildings, or other structures such as highways and roads.
Design	Knowledge of design techniques, tools, and principles involved in production of precision technical plans, blueprints, drawings, and models.
Biology	Knowledge of plant and animal organisms, their tissues, cells, functions, interdependencies, and interactions with each other and the environment.
Fine Arts	Knowledge of the theory and techniques required to compose, produce, and perform works of music, dance, visual arts, drama, and sculpture.

Food Production	Knowledge of techniques and equipment for planting, growing, and harvesting food products (both plant and animal) for consumption, including storage/handling techniques.

Skills	Skills Definitions
Active Listening	Giving full attention to what other people are saying, taking time to understand the points being made, asking questions as appropriate, and not interrupting at inappropriate times.
Reading Comprehension	Understanding written sentences and paragraphs in work related documents.
Speaking	Talking to others to convey information effectively.
Service Orientation	Actively looking for ways to help people.
Negotiation	Bringing others together and trying to reconcile differences.
Time Management	Managing one's own time and the time of others.
Writing	Communicating effectively in writing as appropriate for the needs of the audience.
Judgment and Decision Making	Considering the relative costs and benefits of potential actions to choose the most appropriate one.
Critical Thinking	Using logic and reasoning to identify the strengths and weaknesses of alternative solutions, conclusions or approaches to problems.
Management of Personnel Resources	Motivating, developing, and directing people as they work, identifying the best people for the job.
Persuasion	Persuading others to change their minds or behavior.
Active Learning	Understanding the implications of new information for both current and future problem-solving and decision-making.
Social Perceptiveness	Being aware of others' reactions and understanding why they react as they do.
Instructing	Teaching others how to do something.
Monitoring	Monitoring/Assessing performance of yourself, other individuals, or organizations to make improvements or take corrective action.
Learning Strategies	Selecting and using training/instructional methods and procedures appropriate for the situation when learning or teaching new things.
Complex Problem Solving	Identifying complex problems and reviewing related information to develop and evaluate options and implement solutions.
Coordination	Adjusting actions in relation to others' actions.
Management of Financial Resources	Determining how money will be spent to get the work done, and accounting for these expenditures.
Equipment Selection	Determining the kind of tools and equipment needed to do a job.
Operations Analysis	Analyzing needs and product requirements to create a design.
Management of Material Resources	Obtaining and seeing to the appropriate use of equipment, facilities, and materials needed to do certain work.
Troubleshooting	Determining causes of operating errors and deciding what to do about it.
Systems Evaluation	Identifying measures or indicators of system performance and the actions needed to improve or correct performance, relative to the goals of the system.
Mathematics	Using mathematics to solve problems.
Technology Design	Generating or adapting equipment and technology to serve user needs.
Quality Control Analysis	Conducting tests and inspections of products, services, or processes to evaluate quality or performance.
Systems Analysis	Determining how a system should work and how changes in conditions, operations, and the environment will affect outcomes.
Operation Monitoring	Watching gauges, dials, or other indicators to make sure a machine is working properly.
Operation and Control	Controlling operations of equipment or systems.
Programming	Writing computer programs for various purposes.
Equipment Maintenance	Performing routine maintenance on equipment and determining when and what kind of maintenance is needed.
Repairing	Repairing machines or systems using the needed tools.
Science	Using scientific rules and methods to solve problems.
Installation	Installing equipment, machines, wiring, or programs to meet specifications.

Ability	Ability Definitions
Oral Comprehension	The ability to listen to and understand information and ideas presented through spoken words and sentences.
Speech Clarity	The ability to speak clearly so others can understand you.
Oral Expression	The ability to communicate information and ideas in speaking so others will understand.

Speech Recognition	The ability to identify and understand the speech of another person.
Written Comprehension	The ability to read and understand information and ideas presented in writing.
Inductive Reasoning	The ability to combine pieces of information to form general rules or conclusions (includes finding a relationship among seemingly unrelated events).
Problem Sensitivity	The ability to tell when something is wrong or is likely to go wrong. It does not involve solving the problem, only recognizing there is a problem.
Written Expression	The ability to communicate information and ideas in writing so others will understand.
Deductive Reasoning	The ability to apply general rules to specific problems to produce answers that make sense.
Near Vision	The ability to see details at close range (within a few feet of the observer).
Flexibility of Closure	The ability to identify or detect a known pattern (a figure, object, word, or sound) that is hidden in other distracting material.
Category Flexibility	The ability to generate or use different sets of rules for combining or grouping things in different ways.
Information Ordering	The ability to arrange things or actions in a certain order or pattern according to a specific rule or set of rules (e.g., patterns of numbers, letters, words, pictures, mathematical operations).
Speed of Closure	The ability to quickly make sense of, combine, and organize information into meaningful patterns.
Selective Attention	The ability to concentrate on a task over a period of time without being distracted.
Memorization	The ability to remember information such as words, numbers, pictures, and procedures.
Fluency of Ideas	The ability to come up with a number of ideas about a topic (the number of ideas is important, not their quality, correctness, or creativity).
Originality	The ability to come up with unusual or clever ideas about a given topic or situation, or to develop creative ways to solve a problem.
Mathematical Reasoning	The ability to choose the right mathematical methods or formulas to solve a problem.
Finger Dexterity	The ability to make precisely coordinated movements of the fingers of one or both hands to grasp, manipulate, or assemble very small objects.
Time Sharing	The ability to shift back and forth between two or more activities or sources of information (such as speech, sounds, touch, or other sources).
Number Facility	The ability to add, subtract, multiply, or divide quickly and correctly.
Far Vision	The ability to see details at a distance.
Perceptual Speed	The ability to quickly and accurately compare similarities and differences among sets of letters, numbers, objects, pictures, or patterns. The things to be compared may be presented at the same time or one after the other. This ability also includes comparing a presented object with a remembered object.
Auditory Attention	The ability to focus on a single source of sound in the presence of other distracting sounds.
Visualization	The ability to imagine how something will look after it is moved around or when its parts are moved or rearranged.
Visual Color Discrimination	The ability to match or detect differences between colors, including shades of color and brightness.
Hearing Sensitivity	The ability to detect or tell the differences between sounds that vary in pitch and loudness.
Trunk Strength	The ability to use your abdominal and lower back muscles to support part of the body repeatedly or continuously over time without 'giving out' or fatiguing.
Wrist-Finger Speed	The ability to make fast, simple, repeated movements of the fingers, hands, and wrists.
Extent Flexibility	The ability to bend, stretch, twist, or reach with your body, arms, and/or legs.
Depth Perception	The ability to judge which of several objects is closer or farther away from you, or to judge the distance between you and an object.
Control Precision	The ability to quickly and repeatedly adjust the controls of a machine or a vehicle to exact positions.
Static Strength	The ability to exert maximum muscle force to lift, push, pull, or carry objects.
Arm-Hand Steadiness	The ability to keep your hand and arm steady while moving your arm or while holding your arm and hand in one position.
Multilimb Coordination	The ability to coordinate two or more limbs (for example, two arms, two legs, or one leg and one arm) while sitting, standing, or lying down. It does not involve performing the activities while the whole body is in motion.
Sound Localization	The ability to tell the direction from which a sound originated.
Response Orientation	The ability to choose quickly between two or more movements in response to two or more different signals (lights, sounds, pictures). It includes the speed with which the correct response is started with the hand, foot, or other body part.
Gross Body Coordination	The ability to coordinate the movement of your arms, legs, and torso together when the whole body is in motion.
Rate Control	The ability to time your movements or the movement of a piece of equipment in anticipation of changes in the speed and/or direction of a moving object or scene.
Gross Body Equilibrium	The ability to keep or regain your body balance or stay upright when in an unstable position.
Speed of Limb Movement	The ability to quickly move the arms and legs.
Explosive Strength	The ability to use short bursts of muscle force to propel oneself (as in jumping or sprinting), or to throw an object.
Dynamic Strength	The ability to exert muscle force repeatedly or continuously over time. This involves muscular endurance and resistance to muscle fatigue.
Stamina	The ability to exert yourself physically over long periods of time without getting winded or out of breath.
Night Vision	The ability to see under low light conditions.
Glare Sensitivity	The ability to see objects in the presence of glare or bright lighting.
Reaction Time	The ability to quickly respond (with the hand, finger, or foot) to a signal (sound, light, picture) when it appears.
Spatial Orientation	The ability to know your location in relation to the environment or to know where other objects are in relation to you.
Peripheral Vision	The ability to see objects or movement of objects to one's side when the eyes are looking ahead.
Manual Dexterity	The ability to quickly move your hand, your hand together with your arm, or your two hands to grasp, manipulate, or assemble objects.
Dynamic Flexibility	The ability to quickly and repeatedly bend, stretch, twist, or reach out with your body, arms, and/or legs.

Work_Activity	Work_Activity Definitions
Communicating with Supervisors, Peers, or Subordin	Providing information to supervisors, co-workers, and subordinates by telephone, in written form, e-mail, or in person.
Establishing and Maintaining Interpersonal Relatio	Developing constructive and cooperative working relationships with others, and maintaining them over time.
Getting Information	Observing, receiving, and otherwise obtaining information from all relevant sources.
Communicating with Persons Outside Organization	Communicating with people outside the organization, representing the organization to customers, the public, government, and other external sources. This information can be exchanged in person, in writing, or by telephone or e-mail.
Organizing, Planning, and Prioritizing Work	Developing specific goals and plans to prioritize, organize, and accomplish your work.
Making Decisions and Solving Problems	Analyzing information and evaluating results to choose the best solution and solve problems.
Staffing Organizational Units	Recruiting, interviewing, selecting, hiring, and promoting employees in an organization.
Documenting/Recording Information	Entering, transcribing, recording, storing, or maintaining information in written or electronic/magnetic form.
Interacting With Computers	Using computers and computer systems (including hardware and software) to program, write software, set up functions, enter data, or process information.
Evaluating Information to Determine Compliance wit	Using relevant information and individual judgment to determine whether events or processes comply with laws, regulations, or standards.
Resolving Conflicts and Negotiating with Others	Handling complaints, settling disputes, and resolving grievances and conflicts, or otherwise negotiating with others.
Judging the Qualities of Things, Services, or Peop	Assessing the value, importance, or quality of things or people.
Processing Information	Compiling, coding, categorizing, calculating, tabulating, auditing, or verifying information or data.
Updating and Using Relevant Knowledge	Keeping up-to-date technically and applying new knowledge to your job.
Thinking Creatively	Developing, designing, or creating new applications, ideas, relationships, systems, or products, including artistic contributions.

113

Scheduling Work and Activities	Scheduling events, programs, and activities, as well as the work of others.
Developing and Building Teams	Encouraging and building mutual trust, respect, and cooperation among team members.
Performing for or Working Directly with the Public	Performing for people or dealing directly with the public. This includes serving customers in restaurants and stores, and receiving clients or guests.
Performing Administrative Activities	Performing day-to-day administrative tasks such as maintaining information files and processing paperwork.
Coaching and Developing Others	Identifying the developmental needs of others and coaching, mentoring, or otherwise helping others to improve their knowledge or skills.
Coordinating the Work and Activities of Others	Getting members of a group to work together to accomplish tasks.
Identifying Objects, Actions, and Events	Identifying information by categorizing, estimating, recognizing differences or similarities, and detecting changes in circumstances or events.
Developing Objectives and Strategies	Establishing long-range objectives and specifying the strategies and actions to achieve them.
Provide Consultation and Advice to Others	Providing guidance and expert advice to management or other groups on technical, systems-, or process-related topics.
Monitor Processes, Materials, or Surroundings	Monitoring and reviewing information from materials, events, or the environment, to detect or assess problems.
Selling or Influencing Others	Convincing others to buy merchandise/goods or to otherwise change their minds or actions.
Guiding, Directing, and Motivating Subordinates	Providing guidance and direction to subordinates, including setting performance standards and monitoring performance.
Interpreting the Meaning of Information for Others	Translating or explaining what information means and how it can be used.
Assisting and Caring for Others	Providing personal assistance, medical attention, emotional support, or other personal care to others such as coworkers, customers, or patients.
Analyzing Data or Information	Identifying the underlying principles, reasons, or facts of information by breaking down information or data into separate parts.
Training and Teaching Others	Identifying the educational needs of others, developing formal educational or training programs or classes, and teaching or instructing others.
Monitoring and Controlling Resources	Monitoring and controlling resources and overseeing the spending of money.
Estimating the Quantifiable Characteristics of Pro	Estimating sizes, distances, and quantities; or determining time, costs, resources, or materials needed to perform a work activity.
Inspecting Equipment, Structures, or Material	Inspecting equipment, structures, or materials to identify the cause of errors or other problems or defects.
Handling and Moving Objects	Using hands and arms in handling, installing, positioning, and moving materials, and manipulating things.
Performing General Physical Activities	Performing physical activities that require considerable use of your arms and legs and moving your whole body, such as climbing, lifting, balancing, walking, stooping, and handling of materials.
Controlling Machines and Processes	Using either control mechanisms or direct physical activity to operate machines or processes (not including computers or vehicles).
Repairing and Maintaining Electronic Equipment	Servicing, repairing, calibrating, regulating, fine-tuning, or testing machines, devices, and equipment that operate primarily on the basis of electrical or electronic (not mechanical) principles.
Operating Vehicles, Mechanized Devices, or Equipme	Running, maneuvering, navigating, or driving vehicles or mechanized equipment, such as forklifts, passenger vehicles, aircraft, or water craft.
Drafting, Laying Out, and Specifying Technical Dev	Providing documentation, detailed instructions, drawings, or specifications to tell others about how devices, parts, equipment, or structures are to be fabricated, constructed, assembled, modified, maintained, or used.
Repairing and Maintaining Mechanical Equipment	Servicing, repairing, adjusting, and testing machines, devices, moving parts, and equipment that operate primarily on the basis of mechanical (not electronic) principles.

Work_Context	**Work_Context Definitions**
Telephone	How often do you have telephone conversations in this job?
Electronic Mail	How much does this job require you use electronic mail in this job?
Contact With Others	How much does this job require the worker to be in contact with others (face-to-face, by telephone, or otherwise) in order to perform it?

Structured versus Unstructured Work	To what extent is this job structured for the worker, rather than allowing the worker to determine tasks, priorities, and goals?
Spend Time Sitting	How much does this job require sitting?
Indoors, Environmentally Controlled	How often does this job require working indoors in environmentally controlled conditions?
Frequency of Decision Making	How frequently is the worker required to make decisions that affect other people, the financial resources, and/or the image and reputation of the organization?
Face-to-Face Discussions	How often do you have to have face-to-face discussions with individuals or teams in this job?
Freedom to Make Decisions	How much decision making freedom, without supervision, does the job offer?
Work With Work Group or Team	How important is it to work with others in a group or team in this job?
Importance of Being Exact or Accurate	How important is being very exact or highly accurate in performing this job?
Letters and Memos	How often does the job require written letters and memos?
Deal With External Customers	How important is it to work with external customers or the public in this job?
Impact of Decisions on Co-workers or Company Resul	How do the decisions an employee makes impact the results of co-workers, clients or the company?
Time Pressure	How often does this job require the worker to meet strict deadlines?
Deal With Unpleasant or Angry People	How frequently does the worker have to deal with unpleasant, angry, or discourteous individuals as part of the job requirements?
Importance of Repeating Same Tasks	How important is repeating the same physical activities (e.g., key entry) or mental activities (e.g., checking entries in a ledger) over and over, without stopping, to performing this job?
Frequency of Conflict Situations	How often are there conflict situations the employee has to face in this job?
Level of Competition	To what extent does this job require the worker to compete or to be aware of competitive pressures?
Coordinate or Lead Others	How important is it to coordinate or lead others in accomplishing work activities in this job?
Sounds, Noise Levels Are Distracting or Uncomforta	How often does this job require working exposed to sounds and noise levels that are distracting or uncomfortable?
Degree of Automation	How automated is the job?
Spend Time Making Repetitive Motions	How much does this job require making repetitive motions?
Physical Proximity	To what extent does this job require the worker to perform job tasks in close physical proximity to other people?
Responsibility for Outcomes and Results	How responsible is the worker for work outcomes and results of other workers?
Exposed to Contaminants	How often does this job require working exposed to contaminants (such as pollutants, gases, dust or odors)?
Spend Time Using Your Hands to Handle, Control, or	How much does this job require using your hands to handle, control, or feel objects, tools or controls?
Spend Time Standing	How much does this job require standing?
Public Speaking	How often do you have to perform public speaking in this job?
Responsible for Others' Health and Safety	How much responsibility is there for the health and safety of others in this job?
Consequence of Error	How serious would the result usually be if the worker made a mistake that was not readily correctable?
Cramped Work Space, Awkward Positions	How often does this job require working in cramped work spaces that requires getting into awkward positions?
In an Enclosed Vehicle or Equipment	How often does this job require working in a closed vehicle or equipment (e.g., car)?
Spend Time Walking and Running	How much does this job require walking and running?
Spend Time Kneeling, Crouching, Stooping, or Crawl	How much does this job require kneeling, crouching, stooping or crawling?
Deal With Physically Aggressive People	How frequently does this job require the worker to deal with physical aggression of violent individuals?
Wear Common Protective or Safety Equipment such as	How much does this job require wearing common protective or safety equipment such as safety shoes, glasses, gloves, hard hats or live jackets?
Spend Time Bending or Twisting the Body	How much does this job require bending or twisting your body?
Outdoors, Exposed to Weather	How often does this job require working outdoors, exposed to all weather conditions?
Exposed to Disease or Infections	How often does this job require exposure to disease/infections?
Spend Time Keeping or Regaining Balance	How much does this job require keeping or regaining your balance?

Extremely Bright or Inadequate Lighting	How often does this job require working in extremely bright or inadequate lighting conditions?
Indoors, Not Environmentally Controlled	How often does this job require working indoors in non-controlled environmental conditions (e.g., warehouse without heat)?
Exposed to Hazardous Conditions	How often does this job require exposure to hazardous conditions?
Wear Specialized Protective or Safety Equipment su	How much does this job require wearing specialized protective or safety equipment such as breathing apparatus, safety harness, full protection suits, or radiation protection?
Pace Determined by Speed of Equipment	How important is it to this job that the pace is determined by the speed of equipment or machinery? (This does not refer to keeping busy at all times on this job.)
Very Hot or Cold Temperatures	How often does this job require working in very hot (above 90 F degrees) or very cold (below 32 F degrees) temperatures?
Exposed to High Places	How often does this job require exposure to high places?
Exposed to Radiation	How often does this job require exposure to radiation?
Exposed to Minor Burns, Cuts, Bites, or Stings	How often does this job require exposure to minor burns, cuts, bites, or stings?
Exposed to Hazardous Equipment	How often does this job require exposure to hazardous equipment?
In an Open Vehicle or Equipment	How often does this job require working in an open vehicle or equipment (e.g., tractor)?
Spend Time Climbing Ladders, Scaffolds, or Poles	How much does this job require climbing ladders, scaffolds, or poles?
Exposed to Whole Body Vibration	How often does this job require exposure to whole body vibration (e.g., operate a jackhammer)?
Outdoors, Under Cover	How often does this job require working outdoors, under cover (e.g., structure with roof but no walls)?

Job Zone Component	Job Zone Component Definitions
Title	Job Zone Four: Considerable Preparation Needed
Overall Experience	A minimum of two to four years of work-related skill, knowledge, or experience is needed for these occupations. For example, an accountant must complete four years of college and work for several years in accounting to be considered qualified.
Job Training	Employees in these occupations usually need several years of work-related experience, on-the-job training, and/or vocational training.
Job Zone Examples	Many of these occupations involve coordinating, supervising, managing, or training others. Examples include accountants, chefs and head cooks, computer programmers, historians, pharmacists, and police detectives.
SVP Range	(7.0 to < 8.0)
Education	Most of these occupations require a four - year bachelor's degree, but some do not.

Work_Styles	Work_Styles Definitions
Integrity	Job requires being honest and ethical.
Attention to Detail	Job requires being careful about detail and thorough in completing work tasks.
Cooperation	Job requires being pleasant with others on the job and displaying a good-natured, cooperative attitude.
Dependability	Job requires being reliable, responsible, and dependable, and fulfilling obligations.
Adaptability/Flexibility	Job requires being open to change (positive or negative) and to considerable variety in the workplace.
Concern for Others	Job requires being sensitive to others' needs and feelings and being understanding and helpful on the job.
Independence	Job requires developing one's own ways of doing things, guiding oneself with little or no supervision, and depending on oneself to get things done.
Self Control	Job requires maintaining composure, keeping emotions in check, controlling anger, and avoiding aggressive behavior, even in very difficult situations.
Stress Tolerance	Job requires accepting criticism and dealing calmly and effectively with high stress situations.
Initiative	Job requires a willingness to take on responsibilities and challenges.
Leadership	Job requires a willingness to lead, take charge, and offer opinions and direction.
Social Orientation	Job requires preferring to work with others rather than alone, and being personally connected with others on the job.

Persistence	Job requires persistence in the face of obstacles.
Achievement/Effort	Job requires establishing and maintaining personally challenging achievement goals and exerting effort toward mastering tasks.
Analytical Thinking	Job requires analyzing information and using logic to address work-related issues and problems.
Innovation	Job requires creativity and alternative thinking to develop new ideas for and answers to work-related problems.

13-1072.00 - Compensation, Benefits, and Job Analysis Specialists

Conduct programs of compensation and benefits and job analysis for employer. May specialize in specific areas, such as position classification and pension programs.

Tasks

1) Ensure company compliance with federal and state laws, including reporting requirements.

2) Assist in preparing and maintaining personnel records and handbooks.

3) Plan, develop, evaluate, improve, and communicate methods and techniques for selecting, promoting, compensating, evaluating, and training workers.

4) Evaluate job positions, determining classification, exempt or non-exempt status, and salary.

5) Provide advice on the resolution of classification and salary complaints.

6) Prepare reports, such as organization and flow charts, and career path reports, to summarize job analysis and evaluation and compensation analysis information.

7) Prepare occupational classifications, job descriptions and salary scales.

8) Consult with or serve as a technical liaison between business, industry, government, and union officials.

9) Research employee benefit and health and safety practices and recommend changes or modifications to existing policies.

10) Develop, implement, administer and evaluate personnel and labor relations programs, including performance appraisal, affirmative action and employment equity programs.

11) Advise staff of individuals' qualifications.

12) Plan and develop curricula and materials for training programs and conduct training.

13) Assess need for and develop job analysis instruments and materials.

14) Administer employee insurance, pension and savings plans, working with insurance brokers and plan carriers.

15) Analyze organizational, occupational, and industrial data to facilitate organizational functions and provide technical information to business, industry, and government.

16) Observe, interview, and survey employees and conduct focus group meetings to collect job, organizational, and occupational information.

17) Perform multifactor data and cost analyses that may be used in areas such as support of collective bargaining agreements.

18) Research job and worker requirements, structural and functional relationships among jobs and occupations, and occupational trends.

19) Work with the Department of Labor and promote its use with employers.

20) Prepare research results for publication in form of journals, books, manuals, and film.

21) Negotiate collective agreements on behalf of employers or workers, and mediate labor disputes and grievances.

22) Speak at conferences and events to promote apprenticeships and related training programs.

23) Review occupational data on Alien Employment Certification Applications to determine the appropriate occupational title and code, and provide local offices with information about immigration and occupations.

Knowledge	Knowledge Definitions
Personnel and Human Resources	Knowledge of principles and procedures for personnel recruitment, selection, training, compensation and benefits, labor relations and negotiation, and personnel information systems.

English Language	Knowledge of the structure and content of the English language including the meaning and spelling of words, rules of composition, and grammar.
Customer and Personal Service	Knowledge of principles and processes for providing customer and personal services. This includes customer needs assessment, meeting quality standards for services, and evaluation of customer satisfaction.
Clerical	Knowledge of administrative and clerical procedures and systems such as word processing, managing files and records, stenography and transcription, designing forms, and other office procedures and terminology.
Administration and Management	Knowledge of business and management principles involved in strategic planning, resource allocation, human resources modeling, leadership technique, production methods, and coordination of people and resources.
Mathematics	Knowledge of arithmetic, algebra, geometry, calculus, statistics, and their applications.
Law and Government	Knowledge of laws, legal codes, court procedures, precedents, government regulations, executive orders, agency rules, and the democratic political process.
Computers and Electronics	Knowledge of circuit boards, processors, chips, electronic equipment, and computer hardware and software, including applications and programming.
Education and Training	Knowledge of principles and methods for curriculum and training design, teaching and instruction for individuals and groups, and the measurement of training effects.
Psychology	Knowledge of human behavior and performance; individual differences in ability, personality, and interests; learning and motivation; psychological research methods; and the assessment and treatment of behavioral and affective disorders.
Communications and Media	Knowledge of media production, communication, and dissemination techniques and methods. This includes alternative ways to inform and entertain via written, oral, and visual media.
Economics and Accounting	Knowledge of economic and accounting principles and practices, the financial markets, banking and the analysis and reporting of financial data.
Public Safety and Security	Knowledge of relevant equipment, policies, procedures, and strategies to promote effective local, state, or national security operations for the protection of people, data, property, and institutions.
Sociology and Anthropology	Knowledge of group behavior and dynamics, societal trends and influences, human migrations, ethnicity, cultures and their history and origins.
Therapy and Counseling	Knowledge of principles, methods, and procedures for diagnosis, treatment, and rehabilitation of physical and mental dysfunctions, and for career counseling and guidance.
Sales and Marketing	Knowledge of principles and methods for showing, promoting, and selling products or services. This includes marketing strategy and tactics, product demonstration, sales techniques, and sales control systems.
History and Archeology	Knowledge of historical events and their causes, indicators, and effects on civilizations and cultures.
Foreign Language	Knowledge of the structure and content of a foreign (non-English) language including the meaning and spelling of words, rules of composition and grammar, and pronunciation.
Philosophy and Theology	Knowledge of different philosophical systems and religions. This includes their basic principles, values, ethics, ways of thinking, customs, practices, and their impact on human culture.
Telecommunications	Knowledge of transmission, broadcasting, switching, control, and operation of telecommunications systems.
Transportation	Knowledge of principles and methods for moving people or goods by air, rail, sea, or road, including the relative costs and benefits.
Medicine and Dentistry	Knowledge of the information and techniques needed to diagnose and treat human injuries, diseases, and deformities. This includes symptoms, treatment alternatives, drug properties and interactions, and preventive health-care measures.
Geography	Knowledge of principles and methods for describing the features of land, sea, and air masses, including their physical characteristics, locations, interrelationships, and distribution of plant, animal, and human life.
Fine Arts	Knowledge of the theory and techniques required to compose, produce, and perform works of music, dance, visual arts, drama, and sculpture.

Chemistry	Knowledge of the chemical composition, structure, and properties of substances and of the chemical processes and transformations that they undergo. This includes uses of chemicals and their interactions, danger signs, production techniques, and disposal methods.
Mechanical	Knowledge of machines and tools, including their designs, uses, repair, and maintenance.
Biology	Knowledge of plant and animal organisms, their tissues, cells, functions, interdependencies, and interactions with each other and the environment.
Production and Processing	Knowledge of raw materials, production processes, quality control, costs, and other techniques for maximizing the effective manufacture and distribution of goods.
Engineering and Technology	Knowledge of the practical application of engineering science and technology. This includes applying principles, techniques, procedures, and equipment to the design and production of various goods and services.
Design	Knowledge of design techniques, tools, and principles involved in production of precision technical plans, blueprints, drawings, and models.
Physics	Knowledge and prediction of physical principles, laws, their interrelationships, and applications to understanding fluid, material, and atmospheric dynamics, and mechanical, electrical, atomic and sub- atomic structures and processes.
Food Production	Knowledge of techniques and equipment for planting, growing, and harvesting food products (both plant and animal) for consumption, including storage/handling techniques.
Building and Construction	Knowledge of materials, methods, and the tools involved in the construction or repair of houses, buildings, or other structures such as highways and roads.

Skills	Skills Definitions
Reading Comprehension	Understanding written sentences and paragraphs in work related documents.
Active Listening	Giving full attention to what other people are saying, taking time to understand the points being made, asking questions as appropriate, and not interrupting at inappropriate times.
Critical Thinking	Using logic and reasoning to identify the strengths and weaknesses of alternative solutions, conclusions or approaches to problems.
Writing	Communicating effectively in writing as appropriate for the needs of the audience.
Judgment and Decision Making	Considering the relative costs and benefits of potential actions to choose the most appropriate one.
Speaking	Talking to others to convey information effectively.
Service Orientation	Actively looking for ways to help people.
Time Management	Managing one's own time and the time of others.
Active Learning	Understanding the implications of new information for both current and future problem-solving and decision-making.
Coordination	Adjusting actions in relation to others' actions.
Monitoring	Monitoring/Assessing performance of yourself, other individuals, or organizations to make improvements or take corrective action.
Mathematics	...ng mathematics to solve problems.
Complex Problem Solving	...fying complex problems and reviewing related information to develop and evaluate options and implement solutions.
Social Perceptiveness	Being aware of others' reactions and understanding why they react as they do.
Learning Strategies	Selecting and using training/instructional methods and procedures appropriate for the situation when learning or teaching new things.
Persuasion	Persuading others to change their minds or behavior.
Negotiation	Bringing others together and trying to reconcile differences.
Instructing	Teaching others how to do something.
Operations Analysis	Analyzing needs and product requirements to create a design.
Management of Financial Resources	Determining how money will be spent to get the work done, and accounting for these expenditures.
Management of Personnel Resources	Motivating, developing, and directing people as they work, identifying the best people for the job.
Equipment Selection	Determining the kind of tools and equipment needed to do a job.
Quality Control Analysis	Conducting tests and inspections of products, services, or processes to evaluate quality or performance.
Systems Evaluation	Identifying measures or indicators of system performance and the actions needed to improve or correct performance, relative to the goals of the system.

Management of Material Resources	Obtaining and seeing to the appropriate use of equipment, facilities, and materials needed to do certain work.
Troubleshooting	Determining causes of operating errors and deciding what to do about it.
Systems Analysis	Determining how a system should work and how changes in conditions, operations, and the environment will affect outcomes.
Operation and Control	Controlling operations of equipment or systems.
Technology Design	Generating or adapting equipment and technology to serve user needs.
Science	Using scientific rules and methods to solve problems.
Installation	Installing equipment, machines, wiring, or programs to meet specifications.
Operation Monitoring	Watching gauges, dials, or other indicators to make sure a machine is working properly.
Equipment Maintenance	Performing routine maintenance on equipment and determining when and what kind of maintenance is needed.
Programming	Writing computer programs for various purposes.
Repairing	Repairing machines or systems using the needed tools.

Ability	Ability Definitions
Oral Expression	The ability to communicate information and ideas in speaking so others will understand.
Oral Comprehension	The ability to listen to and understand information and ideas presented through spoken words and sentences.
Speech Clarity	The ability to speak clearly so others can understand you.
Written Comprehension	The ability to read and understand information and ideas presented in writing.
Problem Sensitivity	The ability to tell when something is wrong or is likely to go wrong. It does not involve solving the problem, only recognizing there is a problem.
Speech Recognition	The ability to identify and understand the speech of another person.
Deductive Reasoning	The ability to apply general rules to specific problems to produce answers that make sense.
Inductive Reasoning	The ability to combine pieces of information to form general rules or conclusions (includes finding a relationship among seemingly unrelated events).
Written Expression	The ability to communicate information and ideas in writing so others will understand.
Information Ordering	The ability to arrange things or actions in a certain order or pattern according to a specific rule or set of rules (e.g., patterns of numbers, letters, words, pictures, mathematical operations).
Near Vision	The ability to see details at close range (within a few feet of the observer).
Category Flexibility	The ability to generate or use different sets of rules for combining or grouping things in different ways.
Selective Attention	The ability to concentrate on a task over a period of time without being distracted.
Originality	The ability to come up with unusual or clever ideas about a given topic or situation, or to develop creative ways to solve a problem.
Mathematical Reasoning	The ability to choose the right mathematical methods or formulas to solve a problem.
Number Facility	The ability to add, subtract, multiply, or divide quickly and correctly.
Fluency of Ideas	The ability to come up with a number of ideas about a topic (the number of ideas is important, not their quality, correctness, or creativity).
Speed of Closure	The ability to quickly make sense of, combine, and organize information into meaningful patterns.
Flexibility of Closure	The ability to identify or detect a known pattern (a figure, object, word, or sound) that is hidden in other distracting material.
Memorization	The ability to remember information such as words, numbers, pictures, and procedures.
Far Vision	The ability to see details at a distance.
Perceptual Speed	The ability to quickly and accurately compare similarities and differences among sets of letters, numbers, objects, pictures, or patterns. The things to be compared may be presented at the same time or one after the other. This ability also includes comparing a presented object with a remembered object.
Time Sharing	The ability to shift back and forth between two or more activities or sources of information (such as speech, sounds, touch, or other sources).

Finger Dexterity	The ability to make precisely coordinated movements of the fingers of one or both hands to grasp, manipulate, or assemble very small objects.
Visualization	The ability to imagine how something will look after it is moved around or when its parts are moved or rearranged.
Auditory Attention	The ability to focus on a single source of sound in the presence of other distracting sounds.
Hearing Sensitivity	The ability to detect or tell the differences between sounds that vary in pitch and loudness.
Visual Color Discrimination	The ability to match or detect differences between colors, including shades of color and brightness.
Manual Dexterity	The ability to quickly move your hand, your hand together with your arm, or your two hands to grasp, manipulate, or assemble objects.
Arm-Hand Steadiness	The ability to keep your hand and arm steady while moving your arm or while holding your arm and hand in one position.
Control Precision	The ability to quickly and repeatedly adjust the controls of a machine or a vehicle to exact positions.
Depth Perception	The ability to judge which of several objects is closer or farther away from you, or to judge the distance between you and an object.
Trunk Strength	The ability to use your abdominal and lower back muscles to support part of the body repeatedly or continuously over time without 'giving out' or fatiguing.
Wrist-Finger Speed	The ability to make fast, simple, repeated movements of the fingers, hands, and wrists.
Speed of Limb Movement	The ability to quickly move the arms and legs.
Reaction Time	The ability to quickly respond (with the hand, finger, or foot) to a signal (sound, light, picture) when it appears.
Explosive Strength	The ability to use short bursts of muscle force to propel oneself (as in jumping or sprinting), or to throw an object.
Dynamic Strength	The ability to exert muscle force repeatedly or continuously over time. This involves muscular endurance and resistance to muscle fatigue.
Stamina	The ability to exert yourself physically over long periods of time without getting winded or out of breath.
Extent Flexibility	The ability to bend, stretch, twist, or reach with your body, arms, and/or legs.
Gross Body Coordination	The ability to coordinate the movement of your arms, legs, and torso together when the whole body is in motion.
Rate Control	The ability to time your movements or the movement of a piece of equipment in anticipation of changes in the speed and/or direction of a moving object or scene.
Gross Body Equilibrium	The ability to keep or regain your body balance or stay upright when in an unstable position.
Dynamic Flexibility	The ability to quickly and repeatedly bend, stretch, twist, or reach out with your body, arms, and/or legs.
Static Strength	The ability to exert maximum muscle force to lift, push, pull, or carry objects.
Spatial Orientation	The ability to know your location in relation to the environment or to know where other objects are in relation to you.
Night Vision	The ability to see under low light conditions.
Glare Sensitivity	The ability to see objects in the presence of glare or bright lighting.
Response Orientation	The ability to choose quickly between two or more movements in response to two or more different signals (lights, sounds, pictures). It includes the speed with which the correct response is started with the hand, foot, or other body part.
Multilimb Coordination	The ability to coordinate two or more limbs (for example, two arms, two legs, or one leg and one arm) while sitting, standing, or lying down. It does not involve performing the activities while the whole body is in motion.
Sound Localization	The ability to tell the direction from which a sound originated.
Peripheral Vision	The ability to see objects or movement of objects to one's side when the eyes are looking ahead.

Work_Activity	Work_Activity Definitions
Getting Information	Observing, receiving, and otherwise obtaining information from all relevant sources.
Communicating with Supervisors, Peers, or Subordin	Providing information to supervisors, co-workers, and subordinates by telephone, in written form, e-mail, or in person.
Interacting With Computers	Using computers and computer systems (including hardware and software) to program, write software, set up functions, enter data, or process information.

117

Establishing and Maintaining Interpersonal Relatio	Developing constructive and cooperative working relationships with others, and maintaining them over time.
Processing Information	Compiling, coding, categorizing, calculating, tabulating, auditing, or verifying information or data.
Evaluating Information to Determine Compliance wit	Using relevant information and individual judgment to determine whether events or processes comply with laws, regulations, or standards.
Identifying Objects, Actions, and Events	Identifying information by categorizing, estimating, recognizing differences or similarities, and detecting changes in circumstances or events.
Updating and Using Relevant Knowledge	Keeping up-to-date technically and applying new knowledge to your job.
Performing Administrative Activities	Performing day-to-day administrative tasks such as maintaining information files and processing paperwork.
Organizing, Planning, and Prioritizing Work	Developing specific goals and plans to prioritize, organize, and accomplish your work.
Documenting/Recording Information	Entering, transcribing, recording, storing, or maintaining information in written or electronic/magnetic form.
Making Decisions and Solving Problems	Analyzing information and evaluating results to choose the best solution and solve problems.
Interpreting the Meaning of Information for Others	Translating or explaining what information means and how it can be used.
Analyzing Data or Information	Identifying the underlying principles, reasons, or facts of information by breaking down information or data into separate parts.
Communicating with Persons Outside Organization	Communicating with people outside the organization, representing the organization to customers, the public, government, and other external sources. This information can be exchanged in person, in writing, or by telephone or e-mail.
Monitor Processes, Materials, or Surroundings	Monitoring and reviewing information from materials, events, or the environment, to detect or assess problems.
Resolving Conflicts and Negotiating with Others	Handling complaints, settling disputes, and resolving grievances and conflicts, or otherwise negotiating with others.
Provide Consultation and Advice to Others	Providing guidance and expert advice to management or other groups on technical, systems-, or process-related topics.
Scheduling Work and Activities	Scheduling events, programs, and activities, as well as the work of others.
Training and Teaching Others	Identifying the educational needs of others, developing formal educational or training programs or classes, and teaching or instructing others.
Assisting and Caring for Others	Providing personal assistance, medical attention, emotional support, or other personal care to others such as coworkers, customers, or patients.
Thinking Creatively	Developing, designing, or creating new applications, ideas, relationships, systems, or products, including artistic contributions.
Developing Objectives and Strategies	Establishing long-range objectives and specifying the strategies and actions to achieve them.
Judging the Qualities of Things, Services, or Peop	Assessing the value, importance, or quality of things or people.
Developing and Building Teams	Encouraging and building mutual trust, respect, and cooperation among team members.
Coordinating the Work and Activities of Others	Getting members of a group to work together to accomplish tasks.
Coaching and Developing Others	Identifying the developmental needs of others and coaching, mentoring, or otherwise helping others to improve their knowledge or skills.
Estimating the Quantifiable Characteristics of Pro	Estimating sizes, distances, and quantities; or determining time, costs, resources, or materials needed to perform a work activity.
Selling or Influencing Others	Convincing others to buy merchandise/goods or to otherwise change their minds or actions.
Guiding, Directing, and Motivating Subordinates	Providing guidance and direction to subordinates, including setting performance standards and monitoring performance.
Monitoring and Controlling Resources	Monitoring and controlling resources and overseeing the spending of money.
Staffing Organizational Units	Recruiting, interviewing, selecting, hiring, and promoting employees in an organization.
Performing for or Working Directly with the Public	Performing for people or dealing directly with the public. This includes serving customers in restaurants and stores, and receiving clients or guests.
Inspecting Equipment, Structures, or Material	Inspecting equipment, structures, or materials to identify the cause of errors or other problems or defects.
Performing General Physical Activities	Performing physical activities that require considerable use of your arms and legs and moving your whole body, such as climbing, lifting, balancing, walking, stooping, and handling of materials.
Handling and Moving Objects	Using hands and arms in handling, installing, positioning, and moving materials, and manipulating things.
Controlling Machines and Processes	Using either control mechanisms or direct physical activity to operate machines or processes (not including computers or vehicles).
Repairing and Maintaining Electronic Equipment	Servicing, repairing, calibrating, regulating, fine-tuning, or testing machines, devices, and equipment that operate primarily on the basis of electrical or electronic (not mechanical) principles.
Drafting, Laying Out, and Specifying Technical Dev	Providing documentation, detailed instructions, drawings, or specifications to tell others about how devices, parts, equipment, or structures are to be fabricated, constructed, assembled, modified, maintained, or used.
Repairing and Maintaining Mechanical Equipment	Servicing, repairing, adjusting, and testing machines, devices, moving parts, and equipment that operate primarily on the basis of mechanical (not electronic) principles.
Operating Vehicles, Mechanized Devices, or Equipme	Running, maneuvering, navigating, or driving vehicles or mechanized equipment, such as forklifts, passenger vehicles, aircraft, or water craft.

Work_Context	Work_Context Definitions
Electronic Mail	How often do you use electronic mail in this job?
Telephone	How often do you have telephone conversations in this job?
Indoors, Environmentally Controlled	How often does this job require working indoors in environmentally controlled conditions?
Importance of Being Exact or Accurate	How important is being very exact or highly accurate in performing this job?
Structured versus Unstructured Work	To what extent is this job structured for the worker, rather than allowing the worker to determine tasks, priorities, and goals?
Letters and Memos	How often does the job require written letters and memos?
Contact With Others	How much does this job require the worker to be in contact with others (face-to-face, by telephone, or otherwise) in order to perform it?
Spend Time Sitting	How much does this job require sitting?
Time Pressure	How often does this job require the worker to meet strict deadlines?
Frequency of Decision Making	How frequently is the worker required to make decisions that affect other people, the financial resources, and/or the image and reputation of the organization?
Face-to-Face Discussions	How often do you have to have face-to-face discussions with individuals or teams in this job?
Freedom to Make Decisions	How much decision making freedom, without supervision, does the job offer?
Impact of Decisions on Co-workers or Company Resul	How do the decisions an employee makes impact the results of co-workers, clients or the company?
Work With Work Group or Team	How important is it to work with others in a group or team in this job?
Importance of Repeating Same Tasks	How important is repeating the same physical activities (e.g., key entry) or mental activities (e.g., checking entries in a ledger) over and over, without stopping, to performing this job?
Frequency of Conflict Situations	How often are there conflict situations the employee has to face in this job?
Spend Time Making Repetitive Motions	How much does this job require making repetitive motions?
Coordinate or Lead Others	How important is it to coordinate or lead others in accomplishing work activities in this job?
Deal With Unpleasant or Angry People	How frequently does the worker have to deal with unpleasant, angry, or discourteous individuals as part of the job requirements?
Sounds, Noise Levels Are Distracting or Uncomforta	How often does this job require working exposed to sounds and noise levels that are distracting or uncomfortable?
Spend Time Using Your Hands to Handle, Control, or	How much does this job require using your hands to handle, control, or feel objects, tools or controls?
Deal With External Customers	How important is it to work with external customers or the public in this job?
Degree of Automation	How automated is the job?
Consequence of Error	How serious would the result usually be if the worker made a mistake that was not readily correctable?
Responsibility for Outcomes and Results	How responsible is the worker for work outcomes and results of other workers?

Physical Proximity	To what extent does this job require the worker to perform job tasks in close physical proximity to other people?
Level of Competition	To what extent does this job require the worker to compete or to be aware of competitive pressures?
Exposed to Contaminants	How often does this job require working exposed to contaminants (such as pollutants, gases, dust or odors)?
Responsible for Others' Health and Safety	How much responsibility is there for the health and safety of others in this job?
Public Speaking	How often do you have to perform public speaking in this job?
Spend Time Standing	How much does this job require standing?
Spend Time Bending or Twisting the Body	How much does this job require bending or twisting your body?
Spend Time Walking and Running	How much does this job require walking and running?
In an Enclosed Vehicle or Equipment	How often does this job require working in a closed vehicle or equipment (e.g., car)?
Deal With Physically Aggressive People	How frequently does this job require the worker to deal with physical aggression of violent individuals?
Wear Common Protective or Safety Equipment such as	How much does this job require wearing common protective or safety equipment such as safety shoes, glasses, gloves, hard hats or life jackets?
Spend Time Kneeling, Crouching, Stooping, or Crawl	How much does this job require kneeling, crouching, stooping or crawling?
Cramped Work Space, Awkward Positions	How much does this job require working in cramped work spaces that requires getting into awkward positions?
Pace Determined by Speed of Equipment	How important is it to this job that the pace is determined by the speed of equipment or machinery? (This does not refer to keeping busy at all times on this job.)
Exposed to Minor Burns, Cuts, Bites, or Stings	How often does this job require exposure to minor burns, cuts, bites, or stings?
Very Hot or Cold Temperatures	How often does this job require working in very hot (above 90 F degrees) or very cold (below 32 F degrees) temperatures?
Extremely Bright or Inadequate Lighting	How often does this job require working in extremely bright or inadequate lighting conditions?
Indoors, Not Environmentally Controlled	How often does this job require working indoors in non-controlled environmental conditions (e.g., warehouse without heat)?
Outdoors, Under Cover	How often does this job require working outdoors, under cover (e.g., structure with roof but no walls)?
Spend Time Keeping or Regaining Balance	How much does this job require keeping or regaining your balance?
Exposed to Hazardous Equipment	How often does this job require exposure to hazardous equipment?
Spend Time Climbing Ladders, Scaffolds, or Poles	How much does this job require climbing ladders, scaffolds, or poles?
Exposed to Hazardous Conditions	How often does this job require exposure to hazardous conditions?
Outdoors, Exposed to Weather	How often does this job require working outdoors, exposed to all weather conditions?
Exposed to Disease or Infections	How often does this job require exposure to disease/infections?
Wear Specialized Protective or Safety Equipment su	How much does this job require wearing specialized protective or safety equipment such as breathing apparatus, safety harness, full protection suits, or radiation protection?
Exposed to High Places	How often does this job require exposure to high places?
Exposed to Radiation	How often does this job require exposure to radiation?
Exposed to Whole Body Vibration	How often does this job require exposure to whole body vibration (e.g., operate a jackhammer)?
In an Open Vehicle or Equipment	How often does this job require working in an open vehicle or equipment (e.g., tractor)?

Job Zone Component	Job Zone Component Definitions
Title	Job Zone Four: Considerable Preparation Needed
Overall Experience	A minimum of two to four years of work-related skill, knowledge, or experience is needed for these occupations. For example, an accountant must complete four years of college and work for several years in accounting to be considered qualified.
Job Training	Employees in these occupations usually need several years of work-related experience, on-the-job training, and/or vocational training.

Job Zone Examples	Many of these occupations involve coordinating, supervising, managing, or training others. Examples include accountants, chefs and head cooks, computer programmers, historians, pharmacists, and police detectives.
SVP Range	(7.0 to 8.0)
Education	Most of these occupations require a four-year bachelor's degree, but some do not.

Work_Styles	Work_Styles Definitions
Integrity	Job requires being honest and ethical.
Cooperation	Job requires being pleasant with others on the job and displaying a good-natured, cooperative attitude.
Dependability	Job requires being reliable, responsible, and dependable, and fulfilling obligations.
Attention to Detail	Job requires being careful about detail and thorough in completing work tasks.
Initiative	Job requires a willingness to take on responsibilities and challenges.
Adaptability/Flexibility	Job requires being open to change (positive or negative) and to considerable variety in the workplace.
Concern for Others	Job requires being sensitive to others' needs and feelings and being understanding and helpful on the job.
Stress Tolerance	Job requires accepting criticism and dealing calmly and effectively with high stress situations.
Achievement/Effort	Job requires establishing and maintaining personally challenging achievement goals and exerting effort toward mastering tasks.
Analytical Thinking	Job requires analyzing information and using logic to address work-related issues and problems.
Self Control	Job requires maintaining composure, keeping emotions in check, controlling anger, and avoiding aggressive behavior, even in very difficult situations.
Leadership	Job requires a willingness to lead, take charge, and offer opinions and direction.
Independence	Job requires developing one's own ways of doing things, guiding oneself with little or no supervision, and depending on oneself to get things done.
Persistence	Job requires persistence in the face of obstacles.
Innovation	Job requires creativity and alternative thinking to develop new ideas for and answers to work-related problems.
Social Orientation	Job requires preferring to work with others rather than alone, and being personally connected with others on the job.

13-1073.00 - Training and Development Specialists

Conduct training and development programs for employees.

Tasks

1) Keep up with developments in area of expertise by reading current journals, books and magazine articles.

2) Assess training needs through surveys, interviews with employees, focus groups, and/or consultation with managers, instructors or customer representatives.

3) Present information, using a variety of instructional techniques and formats such as role playing, simulations, team exercises, group discussions, videos and lectures.

4) Organize and develop, or obtain, training procedure manuals and guides and course materials such as handouts and visual materials.

5) Monitor, evaluate and record training activities and program effectiveness.

6) Develop alternative training methods if expected improvements are not seen.

7) Evaluate training materials prepared by instructors, such as outlines, text, and handouts.

8) Offer specific training programs to help workers maintain or improve job skills.

9) Coordinate recruitment and placement of training program participants.

10) Schedule classes based on availability of classrooms, equipment, and instructors.

11) Design, plan, organize and direct orientation and training for employees or customers of industrial or commercial establishment.

12) Select and assign instructors to conduct training.

13) Monitor training costs to ensure budget is not exceeded, and prepare budget reports to

justify expenditures.

14) Screen, hire, and assign workers to positions based on qualifications.

15) Supervise instructors, evaluate instructor performance, and refer instructors to classes for skill development.

16) Devise programs to develop executive potential among employees in lower-level positions.

17) Negotiate contracts with clients, including desired training outcomes, fees and expenses.

18) Refer trainees to employer relations representatives, to locations offering job placement assistance, or to appropriate social services agencies if warranted.

Knowledge	Knowledge Definitions
Customer and Personal Service	Knowledge of principles and processes for providing customer and personal services. This includes customer needs assessment, meeting quality standards for services, and evaluation of customer satisfaction.
Personnel and Human Resources	Knowledge of principles and procedures for personnel recruitment, selection, training, compensation and benefits, labor relations and negotiation, and personnel information systems.
Education and Training	Knowledge of principles and methods for curriculum and training design, teaching and instruction for individuals and groups, and the measurement of training effects.
Clerical	Knowledge of administrative and clerical procedures and systems such as word processing, managing files and records, stenography and transcription, designing forms, and other office procedures and terminology.
English Language	Knowledge of the structure and content of the English language including the meaning and spelling of words, rules of composition, and grammar.
Psychology	Knowledge of human behavior and performance; individual differences in ability, personality, and interests; learning and motivation; psychological research methods; and the assessment and treatment of behavioral and affective disorders.
Administration and Management	Knowledge of business and management principles involved in strategic planning, resource allocation, human resources modeling, leadership technique, production methods, and coordination of people and resources.
Computers and Electronics	Knowledge of circuit boards, processors, chips, electronic equipment, and computer hardware and software, including applications and programming.
Public Safety and Security	Knowledge of relevant equipment, policies, procedures, and strategies to promote effective local, state, or national security operations for the protection of people, data, property, and institutions.
Communications and Media	Knowledge of media production, communication, and dissemination techniques and methods. This includes alternative ways to inform and entertain via written, oral, and visual media.
Sociology and Anthropology	Knowledge of group behavior and dynamics, societal trends and influences, human migrations, ethnicity, cultures and their history and origins.
Law and Government	Knowledge of laws, legal codes, court procedures, precedents, government regulations, executive orders, agency rules, and the democratic political process.
Therapy and Counseling	Knowledge of principles, methods, and procedures for diagnosis, treatment, and rehabilitation of physical and mental dysfunctions, and for career counseling and guidance.
Mathematics	Knowledge of arithmetic, algebra, geometry, calculus, statistics, and their applications.
Medicine and Dentistry	Knowledge of the information and techniques needed to diagnose and treat human injuries, diseases, and deformities. This includes symptoms, treatment alternatives, drug properties and interactions, and preventive health-care measures.
Sales and Marketing	Knowledge of principles and methods for showing, promoting, and selling products or services. This includes marketing strategy and tactics, product demonstration, sales techniques, and sales control systems.
Economics and Accounting	Knowledge of economic and accounting principles and practices, the financial markets, banking and the analysis and reporting of financial data.
Telecommunications	Knowledge of transmission, broadcasting, switching, control, and operation of telecommunications systems.
Philosophy and Theology	Knowledge of different philosophical systems and religions. This includes their basic principles, values, ethics, ways of thinking, customs, practices, and their impact on human culture.
Foreign Language	Knowledge of the structure and content of a foreign (non-English) language including the meaning and spelling of words, rules of composition and grammar, and pronunciation.
Mechanical	Knowledge of machines and tools, including their designs, uses, repair, and maintenance.
Transportation	Knowledge of principles and methods for moving people or goods by air, rail, sea, or road, including the relative costs and benefits.
Engineering and Technology	Knowledge of the practical application of engineering science and technology. This includes applying principles, techniques, procedures, and equipment to the design and production of various goods and services.
Design	Knowledge of design techniques, tools, and principles involved in production of precision technical plans, blueprints, drawings, and models.
Biology	Knowledge of plant and animal organisms, their tissues, cells, functions, interdependencies, and interactions with each other and the environment.
Physics	Knowledge and prediction of physical principles, laws, their interrelationships, and applications to understanding fluid, material, and atmospheric dynamics, and mechanical, electrical, atomic and sub-atomic structures and processes.
History and Archeology	Knowledge of historical events and their causes, indicators, and effects on civilizations and cultures.
Chemistry	Knowledge of the chemical composition, structure, and properties of substances and of the chemical processes and transformations that they undergo. This includes uses of chemicals and their interactions, danger signs, production techniques, and disposal methods.
Production and Processing	Knowledge of raw materials, production processes, quality control, costs, and other techniques for maximizing the effective manufacture and distribution of goods.
Fine Arts	Knowledge of the theory and techniques required to compose, produce, and perform works of music, dance, visual arts, drama, and sculpture.
Geography	Knowledge of principles and methods for describing the features of land, sea, and air masses, including their physical characteristics, locations, interrelationships, and distribution of plant, animal, and human life.
Food Production	Knowledge of techniques and equipment for planting, growing, and harvesting food products (both plant and animal) for consumption, including storage/handling techniques.
Building and Construction	Knowledge of materials, methods, and the tools involved in the construction or repair of houses, buildings, or other structures such as highways and roads.

Skills	Skills Definitions
Active Listening	Giving full attention to what other people are saying, taking time to understand the points being made, asking questions as appropriate, and not interrupting at inappropriate times.
Speaking	Talking to others to convey information effectively.
Time Management	Managing one's own time and the time of others.
Writing	Communicating effectively in writing as appropriate for the needs of the audience.
Reading Comprehension	Understanding written sentences and paragraphs in work related documents.
Critical Thinking	Using logic and reasoning to identify the strengths and weaknesses of alternative solutions, conclusions or approaches to problems.
Instructing	Teaching others how to do something.
Learning Strategies	Selecting and using training/instructional methods and procedures appropriate for the situation when learning or teaching new things.
Service Orientation	Actively looking for ways to help people.
Active Learning	Understanding the implications of new information for both current and future problem-solving and decision-making.
Monitoring	Monitoring/Assessing performance of yourself, other individuals, or organizations to make improvements or take corrective action.
Coordination	Adjusting actions in relation to others' actions.
Social Perceptiveness	Being aware of others' reactions and understanding why they react as they do.
Persuasion	Persuading others to change their minds or behavior.

Mathematics	Using mathematics to solve problems.
Judgment and Decision Making	Considering the relative costs and benefits of potential actions to choose the most appropriate one.
Management of Personnel Resources	Motivating, developing, and directing people as they work, identifying the best people for the job.
Complex Problem Solving	Identifying complex problems and reviewing related information to develop and evaluate options and implement solutions.
Negotiation	Bringing others together and trying to reconcile differences.
Quality Control Analysis	Conducting tests and inspections of products, services, or processes to evaluate quality or performance.
Equipment Maintenance	Performing routine maintenance on equipment and determining when and what kind of maintenance is needed.
Operations Analysis	Analyzing needs and product requirements to create a design.
Management of Material Resources	Obtaining and seeing to the appropriate use of equipment, facilities, and materials needed to do certain work.
Equipment Selection	Determining the kind of tools and equipment needed to do a job.
Systems Evaluation	Identifying measures or indicators of system performance and the actions needed to improve or correct performance, relative to the goals of the system.
Science	Using scientific rules and methods to solve problems.
Troubleshooting	Determining causes of operating errors and deciding what to do about it.
Installation	Installing equipment, machines, wiring, or programs to meet specifications.
Technology Design	Generating or adapting equipment and technology to serve user needs.
Management of Financial Resources	Determining how money will be spent to get the work done, and accounting for these expenditures.
Repairing	Repairing machines or systems using the needed tools.
Systems Analysis	Determining how a system should work and how changes in conditions, operations, and the environment will affect outcomes.
Operation and Control	Controlling operations of equipment or systems.
Operation Monitoring	Watching gauges, dials, or other indicators to make sure a machine is working properly.
Programming	Writing computer programs for various purposes.

Ability	**Ability Definitions**
Oral Expression	The ability to communicate information and ideas in speaking so others will understand.
Speech Clarity	The ability to speak clearly so others can understand you.
Oral Comprehension	The ability to listen to and understand information and ideas presented through spoken words and sentences.
Written Comprehension	The ability to read and understand information and ideas presented in writing.
Deductive Reasoning	The ability to apply general rules to specific problems to produce answers that make sense.
Originality	The ability to come up with unusual or clever ideas about a given topic or situation, or to develop creative ways to solve a problem.
Speech Recognition	The ability to identify and understand the speech of another person.
Written Expression	The ability to communicate information and ideas in writing so others will understand.
Information Ordering	The ability to arrange things or actions in a certain order or pattern according to a specific rule or set of rules (e.g., patterns of numbers, letters, words, pictures, mathematical operations).
Problem Sensitivity	The ability to tell when something is wrong or is likely to go wrong. It does not involve solving the problem, only recognizing there is a problem.
Near Vision	The ability to see details at close range (within a few feet of the observer).
Fluency of Ideas	The ability to come up with a number of ideas about a topic (the number of ideas is important, not their quality, correctness, or creativity).
Inductive Reasoning	The ability to combine pieces of information to form general rules or conclusions (includes finding a relationship among seemingly unrelated events).
Category Flexibility	The ability to generate or use different sets of rules for combining or grouping things in different ways.
Selective Attention	The ability to concentrate on a task over a period of time without being distracted.
Time Sharing	The ability to shift back and forth between two or more activities or sources of information (such as speech, sounds, touch, or other sources).

Memorization	The ability to remember information such as words, numbers, pictures, and procedures.
Far Vision	The ability to see details at a distance.
Flexibility of Closure	The ability to identify or detect a known pattern (a figure, object, word, or sound) that is hidden in other distracting material.
Finger Dexterity	The ability to make precisely coordinated movements of the fingers of one or both hands to grasp, manipulate, or assemble very small objects.
Auditory Attention	The ability to focus on a single source of sound in the presence of other distracting sounds.
Speed of Closure	The ability to quickly make sense of, combine, and organize information into meaningful patterns.
Perceptual Speed	The ability to quickly and accurately compare similarities and differences among sets of letters, numbers, objects, pictures, or patterns. The things to be compared may be presented at the same time or one after the other. This ability also includes comparing a presented object with a remembered object.
Mathematical Reasoning	The ability to choose the right mathematical methods or formulas to solve a problem.
Depth Perception	The ability to judge which of several objects is closer or farther away from you, or to judge the distance between you and an object.
Trunk Strength	The ability to use your abdominal and lower back muscles to support part of the body repeatedly or continuously over time without 'giving out' or fatiguing.
Visualization	The ability to imagine how something will look after it is moved around or when its parts are moved or rearranged.
Control Precision	The ability to quickly and repeatedly adjust the controls of a machine or a vehicle to exact positions.
Extent Flexibility	The ability to bend, stretch, twist, or reach with your body, arms, and/or legs.
Number Facility	The ability to add, subtract, multiply, or divide quickly and correctly.
Gross Body Coordination	The ability to coordinate the movement of your arms, legs, and torso together when the whole body is in motion.
Stamina	The ability to exert yourself physically over long periods of time without getting winded or out of breath.
Multilimb Coordination	The ability to coordinate two or more limbs (for example, two arms, two legs, or one leg and one arm) while sitting, standing, or lying down. It does not involve performing the activities while the whole body is in motion.
Arm-Hand Steadiness	The ability to keep your hand and arm steady while moving your arm or while holding your arm and hand in one position.
Manual Dexterity	The ability to quickly move your hand, your hand together with your arm, or your two hands to grasp, manipulate, or assemble objects.
Visual Color Discrimination	The ability to match or detect differences between colors, including shades of color and brightness.
Speed of Limb Movement	The ability to quickly move the arms and legs.
Hearing Sensitivity	The ability to detect or tell the differences between sounds that vary in pitch and loudness.
Night Vision	The ability to see under low light conditions.
Wrist-Finger Speed	The ability to make fast, simple, repeated movements of the fingers, hands, and wrists.
Sound Localization	The ability to tell the direction from which a sound originated.
Glare Sensitivity	The ability to see objects in the presence of glare or bright lighting.
Static Strength	The ability to exert maximum muscle force to lift, push, pull, or carry objects.
Response Orientation	The ability to choose quickly between two or more movements in response to two or more different signals (lights, sounds, pictures). It includes the speed with which the correct response is started with the hand, foot, or other body part.
Reaction Time	The ability to quickly respond (with the hand, finger, or foot) to a signal (sound, light, picture) when it appears.
Gross Body Equilibrium	The ability to keep or regain your body balance or stay upright when in an unstable position.
Explosive Strength	The ability to use short bursts of muscle force to propel oneself (as in jumping or sprinting), or to throw an object.
Dynamic Strength	The ability to exert muscle force repeatedly or continuously over time. This involves muscular endurance and resistance to muscle fatigue.
Rate Control	The ability to time your movements or the movement of a piece of equipment in anticipation of changes in the speed and/or direction of a moving object or scene.
Peripheral Vision	The ability to see objects or movement of objects to one's side when the eyes are looking ahead.

Spatial Orientation	The ability to know your location in relation to the environment or to know where other objects are in relation to you.
Dynamic Flexibility	The ability to quickly and repeatedly bend, stretch, twist, or reach out with your body, arms, and/or legs.

Work_Activity	**Work_Activity Definitions**
Communicating with Supervisors, Peers, or Subordin	Providing information to supervisors, co-workers, and subordinates by telephone, in written form, e-mail, or in person.
Getting Information	Observing, receiving, and otherwise obtaining information from all relevant sources.
Training and Teaching Others	Identifying the educational needs of others, developing formal educational or training programs or classes, and teaching or instructing others.
Organizing, Planning, and Prioritizing Work	Developing specific goals and plans to prioritize, organize, and accomplish your work.
Developing Objectives and Strategies	Establishing long-range objectives and specifying the strategies and actions to achieve them.
Interacting With Computers	Using computers and computer systems (including hardware and software) to program, write software, set up functions, enter data, or process information.
Making Decisions and Solving Problems	Analyzing information and evaluating results to choose the best solution and solve problems.
Updating and Using Relevant Knowledge	Keeping up-to-date technically and applying new knowledge to your job.
Establishing and Maintaining Interpersonal Relatio	Developing constructive and cooperative working relationships with others, and maintaining them over time.
Performing for or Working Directly with the Public	Performing for people or dealing directly with the public. This includes serving customers in restaurants and stores, and receiving clients or guests.
Developing and Building Teams	Encouraging and building mutual trust, respect, and cooperation among team members.
Evaluating Information to Determine Compliance wit	Using relevant information and individual judgment to determine whether events or processes comply with laws, regulations, or standards.
Coaching and Developing Others	Identifying the developmental needs of others and coaching, mentoring, or otherwise helping others to improve their knowledge or skills.
Processing Information	Compiling, coding, categorizing, calculating, tabulating, auditing, or verifying information or data.
Judging the Qualities of Things, Services, or Peop	Assessing the value, importance, or quality of things or people.
Scheduling Work and Activities	Scheduling events, programs, and activities, as well as the work of others.
Coordinating the Work and Activities of Others	Getting members of a group to work together to accomplish tasks.
Thinking Creatively	Developing, designing, or creating new applications, ideas, relationships, systems, or products, including artistic contributions.
Analyzing Data or Information	Identifying the underlying principles, reasons, or facts of information by breaking down information or data into separate parts.
Identifying Objects, Actions, and Events	Identifying information by categorizing, estimating, recognizing differences or similarities, and detecting changes in circumstances or events.
Communicating with Persons Outside Organization	Communicating with people outside the organization, representing the organization to customers, the public, government, and other external sources. This information can be exchanged in person, in writing, or by telephone or e-mail.
Provide Consultation and Advice to Others	Providing guidance and expert advice to management or other groups on technical, systems-, or process-related topics.
Interpreting the Meaning of Information for Others	Translating or explaining what information means and how it can be used.
Guiding, Directing, and Motivating Subordinates	Providing guidance and direction to subordinates, including setting performance standards and monitoring performance.
Documenting/Recording Information	Entering, transcribing, recording, storing, or maintaining information in written or electronic/magnetic form.
Monitor Processes, Materials, or Surroundings	Monitoring and reviewing information from materials, events, or the environment, to detect or assess problems.
Estimating the Quantifiable Characteristics of Pro	Estimating sizes, distances, and quantities; or determining time, costs, resources, or materials needed to perform a work activity.
Performing Administrative Activities	Performing day-to-day administrative tasks such as maintaining information files and processing paperwork.

Assisting and Caring for Others	Providing personal assistance, medical attention, emotional support, or other personal care to others such as co-workers, customers, or patients.
Selling or Influencing Others	Convincing others to buy merchandise/goods or to otherwise change their minds or actions.
Inspecting Equipment, Structures, or Material	Inspecting equipment, structures, or materials to identify the cause of errors or other problems or defects.
Resolving Conflicts and Negotiating with Others	Handling complaints, settling disputes, and resolving grievances and conflicts, or otherwise negotiating with others.
Monitoring and Controlling Resources	Monitoring and controlling resources and overseeing the spending of money.
Staffing Organizational Units	Recruiting, interviewing, selecting, hiring, and promoting employees in an organization.
Handling and Moving Objects	Using hands and arms in handling, installing, positioning, and moving materials, and manipulating things.
Controlling Machines and Processes	Using either control mechanisms or direct physical activity to operate machines or processes (not including computers or vehicles).
Performing General Physical Activities	Performing physical activities that require considerable use of your arms and legs and moving your whole body, such as climbing, lifting, balancing, walking, stooping, and handling of materials.
Operating Vehicles, Mechanized Devices, or Equipme	Running, maneuvering, navigating, or driving vehicles or mechanized equipment, such as forklifts, passenger vehicles, aircraft, or water craft.
Repairing and Maintaining Electronic Equipment	Servicing, repairing, calibrating, regulating, fine-tuning, or testing machines, devices, and equipment that operate primarily on the basis of electrical or electronic (not mechanical) principles.
Repairing and Maintaining Mechanical Equipment	Servicing, repairing, adjusting, and testing machines, devices, moving parts, and equipment that operate primarily on the basis of mechanical (not electronic) principles.
Drafting, Laying Out, and Specifying Technical Dev	Providing documentation, detailed instructions, drawings, or specifications to tell others about how devices, parts, equipment, or structures are to be fabricated, constructed, assembled, modified, maintained, or used.

Work_Context	**Work_Context Definitions**
Telephone	How often do you have telephone conversations in this job?
Electronic Mail	How often do you use electronic mail in this job?
Freedom to Make Decisions	How much decision making freedom, without supervision, does the job offer?
Face-to-Face Discussions	How often do you have to have face-to-face discussions with individuals or teams in this job?
Indoors, Environmentally Controlled	How often does this job require working indoors in environmentally controlled conditions?
Coordinate or Lead Others	How important is it to coordinate or lead others in accomplishing work activities in this job?
Deal With External Customers	How important is it to work with external customers or the public in this job?
Letters and Memos	How often does the job require written letters and memos?
Importance of Being Exact or Accurate	How important is being very exact or highly accurate in performing this job?
Contact With Others	How much does this job require the worker to be in contact with others (face-to-face, by telephone, or otherwise) in order to perform it?
Impact of Decisions on Co-workers or Company Resul	How do the decisions an employee makes impact the results of co-workers, clients or the company?
Public Speaking	How often do you have to perform public speaking in this job?
Structured versus Unstructured Work	To what extent is this job structured for the worker, rather than allowing the worker to determine tasks, priorities, and goals?
Work With Work Group or Team	How important is it to work with others in a group or team in this job?
Physical Proximity	To what extent does this job require the worker to perform job tasks in close physical proximity to other people?
Frequency of Decision Making	How frequently is the worker required to make decisions that affect other people, the financial resources, and/or the image and reputation of the organization?
Time Pressure	How often does this job require the worker to meet strict deadlines?
In an Enclosed Vehicle or Equipment	How often does this job require working in a closed vehicle or equipment (e.g., car)?
Spend Time Standing	How much does this job require standing?
Deal With Unpleasant or Angry People	How frequently does the worker have to deal with unpleasant, angry, or discourteous individuals as part of the job requirements?

Sounds, Noise Levels Are Distracting or Uncomforta	How often does this job require working exposed to sounds and noise levels that are distracting or uncomfortable?
Spend Time Making Repetitive Motions	How much does this job require making repetitive motions?
Degree of Automation	How automated is the job?
Spend Time Sitting	How much does this job require sitting?
Importance of Repeating Same Tasks	How important is repeating the same physical activities (e.g., key entry) or mental activities (e.g., checking entries in a ledger) over and over, without stopping, to performing this job?
Consequence of Error	How serious would the result usually be if the worker made a mistake that was not readily correctable?
Spend Time Using Your Hands to Handle, Control, or	How much does this job require using your hands to handle, control, or feel objects, tools or controls?
Frequency of Conflict Situations	How often are there conflict situations the employee has to face in this job?
Responsibility for Outcomes and Results	How responsible is the worker for work outcomes and results of other workers?
Cramped Work Space, Awkward Positions	How often does this job require working in cramped work spaces that requires getting into awkward positions?
Spend Time Walking and Running	How much does this job require walking and running?
Responsible for Others' Health and Safety	How much responsibility is there for the health and safety of others in this job?
Level of Competition	To what extent does this job require the worker to compete or to be aware of competitive pressures?
Exposed to Contaminants	How often does this job require working exposed to contaminants (such as pollutants, gases, dust or odors)?
Exposed to Disease or Infections	How often does this job require exposure to disease/infections?
Wear Common Protective or Safety Equipment such as	How much does this job require wearing common protective or safety equipment such as safety shoes, glasses, gloves, hard hats or life jackets?
Wear Specialized Protective or Safety Equipment su	How much does this job require wearing specialized protective or safety equipment such as breathing apparatus, safety harness, full protection suits, or radiation protection?
Exposed to Radiation	How often does this job require exposure to radiation?
Deal With Physically Aggressive People	How frequently does this job require the worker to deal with physical aggression of violent individuals?
Spend Time Bending or Twisting the Body	How much does this job require bending or twisting your body?
Very Hot or Cold Temperatures	How often does this job require working in very hot (above 90 F degrees) or very cold (below 32 F degrees) temperatures?
Outdoors, Exposed to Weather	How often does this job require working outdoors, exposed to all weather conditions?
Pace Determined by Speed of Equipment	How important is it to this job that the pace is determined by the speed of equipment or machinery? (This does not refer to keeping busy at all times on this job.)
Outdoors, Under Cover	How often does this job require working outdoors, under cover (e.g., structure with roof but no walls)?
Spend Time Kneeling, Crouching, Stooping, or Crawl	How much does this job require kneeling, crouching, stooping or crawling?
Extremely Bright or Inadequate Lighting	How often does this job require working in extremely bright or inadequate lighting conditions?
Exposed to Minor Burns, Cuts, Bites, or Stings	How often does this job require exposure to minor burns, cuts, bites, or stings?
Exposed to Hazardous Conditions	How often does this job require exposure to hazardous conditions?
Indoors, Not Environmentally Controlled	How often does this job require working indoors in non-controlled environmental conditions (e.g., warehouse without heat)?
Spend Time Climbing Ladders, Scaffolds, or Poles	How much does this job require climbing ladders, scaffolds, or poles?
Exposed to High Places	How often does this job require exposure to high places?
Exposed to Hazardous Equipment	How often does this job require exposure to hazardous equipment?
Spend Time Keeping or Regaining Balance	How much does this job require keeping or regaining your balance?
In an Open Vehicle or Equipment	How often does this job require working in an open vehicle or equipment (e.g., tractor)?
Exposed to Whole Body Vibration	How often does this job require exposure to whole body vibration (e.g., operate a jackhammer)?

Job Zone Component	Job Zone Component Definitions
Title	Job Zone Four: Considerable Preparation Needed A minimum of two to four years of work-related skill, knowledge, or experience is needed for these occupations. For
Overall Experience	example, an accountant must complete four years of college and work for several years in accounting to be considered qualified.
Job Training	Employees in these occupations usually need several years of work-related experience, on-the-job training, and/or vocational training.
Job Zone Examples	Many of these occupations involve coordinating, supervising, managing, or training others. Examples include accountants, chefs and head cooks, computer programmers, historians, pharmacists, and police detectives.
SVP Range	(7.0 to < 8.0)
Education	Most of these occupations require a four - year bachelor's degree, but some do not.

Work_Styles	Work_Styles Definitions
Integrity	Job requires being honest and ethical.
Dependability	Job requires being reliable, responsible, and dependable, and fulfilling obligations.
Cooperation	Job requires being pleasant with others on the job and displaying a good-natured, cooperative attitude.
Concern for Others	Job requires being sensitive to others' needs and feelings and being understanding and helpful on the job.
Stress Tolerance	Job requires accepting criticism and dealing calmly and effectively with high stress situations.
Social Orientation	Job requires preferring to work with others rather than alone, and being personally connected with others on the job.
Self Control	Job requires maintaining composure, keeping emotions in check, controlling anger, and avoiding aggressive behavior, even in very difficult situations.
Adaptability/Flexibility	Job requires being open to change (positive or negative) and to considerable variety in the workplace.
Attention to Detail	Job requires being careful about detail and thorough in completing work tasks.
Leadership	Job requires a willingness to lead, take charge, and offer opinions and direction.
Initiative	Job requires a willingness to take on responsibilities and challenges.
Independence	Job requires developing one's own ways of doing things, guiding oneself with little or no supervision, and depending on oneself to get things done.
Analytical Thinking	Job requires analyzing information and using logic to address work-related issues and problems.
Persistence	Job requires persistence in the face of obstacles.
Achievement/Effort	Job requires establishing and maintaining personally challenging achievement goals and exerting effort toward mastering tasks.
Innovation	Job requires creativity and alternative thinking to develop new ideas for and answers to work-related problems.

13-1081.00 - Logisticians

Analyze and coordinate the logistical functions of a firm or organization. Responsible for the entire life cycle of a product, including acquisition, distribution, internal allocation, delivery, and final disposal of resources.

Tasks

1) Perform system life-cycle cost analysis, and develop component studies.

2) Plan, organize, and execute logistics support activities such as maintenance planning, repair analysis, and test equipment recommendations.

3) Provide project management services, including the provision and analysis of technical data.

4) Protect and control proprietary materials.

5) Redesign the movement of goods in order to maximize value and minimize costs.

6) Report project plans, progress, and results.

7) Develop an understanding of customers' needs, and take actions to ensure that such needs

are met.

8) Direct availability and allocation of materials, supplies, and finished products.

9) Participate in the assessment and review of design alternatives and design change proposal impacts.

10) Stay informed of logistics technology advances, and apply appropriate technology in order to improve logistics processes.

11) Maintain and develop positive business relationships with a customer's key personnel involved in or directly relevant to a logistics activity.

12) Support the development of training materials and technical manuals.

13) Direct team activities, establishing task priorities, scheduling and tracking work assignments, providing guidance, and ensuring the availability of resources.

14) Explain proposed solutions to customers, management, or other interested parties through written proposals and oral presentations.

15) Manage subcontractor activities, reviewing proposals, developing performance specifications, and serving as liaisons between subcontractors and organizations.

16) Review logistics performance with customers against targets, benchmarks and service agreements.

17) Develop proposals that include documentation for estimates.

18) Direct and support the compilation and analysis of technical source data necessary for product development.

19) Develop and implement technical project management tools such as plans, schedules, and responsibility and compliance matrices.

20) Manage the logistical aspects of product life cycles, including coordination or provisioning of samples, and the minimization of obsolescence.

13-1111.00 - Management Analysts

Conduct organizational studies and evaluations, design systems and procedures, conduct work simplifications and measurement studies, and prepare operations and procedures manuals to assist management in operating more efficiently and effectively. Includes program analysts and management consultants.

Tasks

1) Review forms and reports, and confer with management and users about format, distribution, and purpose, and to identify problems and improvements.

2) Analyze data gathered and develop solutions or alternative methods of proceeding.

3) Plan study of work problems and procedures, such as organizational change, communications, information flow, integrated production methods, inventory control, or cost analysis.

4) Gather and organize information on problems or procedures.

5) Design, evaluate, recommend, and approve changes of forms and reports.

6) Document findings of study and prepare recommendations for implementation of new systems, procedures, or organizational changes.

7) Prepare manuals and train workers in use of new forms, reports, procedures or equipment, according to organizational policy.

8) Develop and implement records management program for filing, protection, and retrieval of records, and assure compliance with program.

9) Confer with personnel concerned to ensure successful functioning of newly implemented systems or procedures.

10) Interview personnel and conduct on-site observation to ascertain unit functions, work performed, and methods, equipment, and personnel used.

13-1121.00 - Meeting and Convention Planners

Coordinate activities of staff and convention personnel to make arrangements for group meetings and conventions.

Tasks

1) Arrange the availability of audio-visual equipment, transportation, displays, and other

event needs.

2) Consult with customers in order to determine objectives and requirements for events such as meetings, conferences, and conventions.

3) Coordinate services for events, such as accommodation and transportation for participants, facilities, catering, signage, displays, special needs requirements, printing and event security.

4) Monitor event activities in order to ensure compliance with applicable regulations and laws, satisfaction of participants, and resolution of any problems that arise.

5) Conduct post-event evaluations in order to determine how future events could be improved.

6) Confer with staff at a chosen event site in order to coordinate details.

7) Evaluate and select providers of services according to customer requirements.

8) Plan and develop programs, agendas, budgets, and services according to customer requirements.

9) Read trade publications, attend seminars, and consult with other meeting professionals in order to keep abreast of meeting management standards and trends.

10) Review event bills for accuracy, and approve payment.

11) Inspect event facilities in order to ensure that they conform to customer requirements.

12) Negotiate contracts with such service providers and suppliers as hotels, convention centers, and speakers.

13) Direct administrative details such as financial operations, dissemination of promotional materials, and responses to inquiries.

14) Meet with sponsors and organizing committees in order to plan scope and format of events, to establish and monitor budgets, and to review administrative procedures and event progress.

15) Organize registration of event participants.

16) Design and implement efforts to publicize events and promote sponsorships.

17) Promote conference, convention and trades show services by performing tasks such as meeting with professional and trade associations, and producing brochures and other publications.

18) Hire, train, and supervise volunteers and support staff required for events.

19) Obtain permits from fire and health departments to erect displays and exhibits and serve food at events.

20) Develop event topics and choose featured speakers.

Knowledge	Knowledge Definitions
Customer and Personal Service	Knowledge of principles and processes for providing customer and personal services. This includes customer needs assessment, meeting quality standards for services, and evaluation of customer satisfaction.
Administration and Management	Knowledge of business and management principles involved in strategic planning, resource allocation, human resources modeling, leadership technique, production methods, and coordination of people and resources.
English Language	Knowledge of the structure and content of the English language including the meaning and spelling of words, rules of composition, and grammar.
Sales and Marketing	Knowledge of principles and methods for showing, promoting, and selling products or services. This includes marketing strategy and tactics, product demonstration, sales techniques, and sales control systems.
Clerical	Knowledge of administrative and clerical procedures and systems such as word processing, managing files and records, stenography and transcription, designing forms, and other office procedures and terminology.
Communications and Media	Knowledge of media production, communication, and dissemination techniques and methods. This includes alternative ways to inform and entertain via written, oral, and visual media.
Computers and Electronics	Knowledge of circuit boards, processors, chips, electronic equipment, and computer hardware and software, including applications and programming.
Education and Training	Knowledge of principles and methods for curriculum and training design, teaching and instruction for individuals and groups, and the measurement of training effects.
Mathematics	Knowledge of arithmetic, algebra, geometry, calculus, statistics, and their applications.

Economics and Accounting	Knowledge of economic and accounting principles and practices, the financial markets, banking and the analysis and reporting of financial data.
Psychology	Knowledge of human behavior and performance; individual differences in ability, personality, and interests; learning and motivation; psychological research methods; and the assessment and treatment of behavioral and affective disorders.
Personnel and Human Resources	Knowledge of principles and procedures for personnel recruitment, selection, training, compensation and benefits, labor relations and negotiation, and personnel information systems.
Public Safety and Security	Knowledge of relevant equipment, policies, procedures, and strategies to promote effective local, state, or national security operations for the protection of people, data, property, and institutions.
Law and Government	Knowledge of laws, legal codes, court procedures, precedents, government regulations, executive orders, agency rules, and the democratic political process.
Telecommunications	Knowledge of transmission, broadcasting, switching, control, and operation of telecommunications systems.
Production and Processing	Knowledge of raw materials, production processes, quality control, costs, and other techniques for maximizing the effective manufacture and distribution of goods.
Transportation	Knowledge of principles and methods for moving people or goods by air, rail, sea, or road, including the relative costs and benefits.
Geography	Knowledge of principles and methods for describing the features of land, sea, and air masses, including their physical characteristics, locations, interrelationships, and distribution of plant, animal, and human life.
Sociology and Anthropology	Knowledge of group behavior and dynamics, societal trends and influences, human migrations, ethnicity, cultures and their history and origins.
Foreign Language	Knowledge of the structure and content of a foreign (non-English) language including the meaning and spelling of words, rules of composition and grammar, and pronunciation.
Design	Knowledge of design techniques, tools, and principles involved in production of precision technical plans, blueprints, drawings, and models.
Food Production	Knowledge of techniques and equipment for planting, growing, and harvesting food products (both plant and animal) for consumption, including storage/handling techniques.
Fine Arts	Knowledge of the theory and techniques required to compose, produce, and perform works of music, dance, visual arts, drama, and sculpture.
History and Archeology	Knowledge of historical events and their causes, indicators, and effects on civilizations and cultures.
Therapy and Counseling	Knowledge of principles, methods, and procedures for diagnosis, treatment, and rehabilitation of physical and mental dysfunctions, and for career counseling and guidance.
Mechanical	Knowledge of machines and tools, including their designs, uses, repair, and maintenance.
Engineering and Technology	Knowledge of the practical application of engineering science and technology. This includes applying principles, techniques, procedures, and equipment to the design and production of various goods and services.
Philosophy and Theology	Knowledge of different philosophical systems and religions. This includes their basic principles, values, ethics, ways of thinking, customs, practices, and their impact on human culture.
Medicine and Dentistry	Knowledge of the information and techniques needed to diagnose and treat human injuries, diseases, and deformities. This includes symptoms, treatment alternatives, drug properties and interactions, and preventive health-care measures.
Building and Construction	Knowledge of materials, methods, and the tools involved in the construction or repair of houses, buildings, or other structures such as highways and roads.
Physics	Knowledge and prediction of physical principles, laws, their interrelationships, and applications to understanding fluid, material, and atmospheric dynamics, and mechanical, electrical, atomic and sub-atomic structures and processes.
Biology	Knowledge of plant and animal organisms, their tissues, cells, functions, interdependencies, and interactions with each other and the environment.

Chemistry	Knowledge of the chemical composition, structure, and properties of substances and of the chemical processes and transformations that they undergo. This includes uses of chemicals and their interactions, danger signs, production techniques, and disposal methods.

Skills	Skills Definitions
Active Listening	Giving full attention to what other people are saying, taking time to understand the points being made, asking questions as appropriate, and not interrupting at inappropriate times.
Reading Comprehension	Understanding written sentences and paragraphs in work related documents.
Social Perceptiveness	Being aware of others' reactions and understanding why they react as they do.
Service Orientation	Actively looking for ways to help people.
Time Management	Managing one's own time and the time of others.
Speaking	Talking to others to convey information effectively.
Critical Thinking	Using logic and reasoning to identify the strengths and weaknesses of alternative solutions, conclusions or approaches to problems.
Coordination	Adjusting actions in relation to others' actions.
Writing	Communicating effectively in writing as appropriate for the needs of the audience.
Active Learning	Understanding the implications of new information for both current and future problem-solving and decision-making.
Complex Problem Solving	Identifying complex problems and reviewing related information to develop and evaluate options and implement solutions.
Judgment and Decision Making	Considering the relative costs and benefits of potential actions to choose the most appropriate one.
Negotiation	Bringing others together and trying to reconcile differences.
Instructing	Teaching others how to do something.
Persuasion	Persuading others to change their minds or behavior.
Learning Strategies	Selecting and using training/instructional methods and procedures appropriate for the situation when learning or teaching new things.
Monitoring	Monitoring/Assessing performance of yourself, other individuals, or organizations to make improvements or take corrective action.
Operations Analysis	Analyzing needs and product requirements to create a design.
Management of Personnel Resources	Motivating, developing, and directing people as they work, identifying the best people for the job.
Management of Financial Resources	Determining how money will be spent to get the work done, and accounting for these expenditures.
Troubleshooting	Determining causes of operating errors and deciding what to do about it.
Management of Material Resources	Obtaining and seeing to the appropriate use of equipment, facilities, and materials needed to do certain work.
Mathematics	Using mathematics to solve problems.
Equipment Selection	Determining the kind of tools and equipment needed to do a job.
Quality Control Analysis	Conducting tests and inspections of products, services, or processes to evaluate quality or performance.
Technology Design	Generating or adapting equipment and technology to serve user needs.
Operation and Control	Controlling operations of equipment or systems.
Systems Analysis	Determining how a system should work and how changes in conditions, operations, and the environment will affect outcomes.
Installation	Installing equipment, machines, wiring, or programs to meet specifications.
Systems Evaluation	Identifying measures or indicators of system performance and the actions needed to improve or correct performance, relative to the goals of the system.
Programming	Writing computer programs for various purposes.
Equipment Maintenance	Performing routine maintenance on equipment and determining when and what kind of maintenance is needed.
Operation Monitoring	Watching gauges, dials, or other indicators to make sure a machine is working properly.
Science	Using scientific rules and methods to solve problems.
Repairing	Repairing machines or systems using the needed tools.

Ability	Ability Definitions
Oral Comprehension	The ability to listen to and understand information and ideas presented through spoken words and sentences.

Oral Expression	The ability to communicate information and ideas in speaking so others will understand.
Speech Clarity	The ability to speak clearly so others can understand you.
Problem Sensitivity	The ability to tell when something is wrong or is likely to go wrong. It does not involve solving the problem, only recognizing there is a problem.
Speech Recognition	The ability to identify and understand the speech of another person.
Written Comprehension	The ability to read and understand information and ideas presented in writing.
Inductive Reasoning	The ability to combine pieces of information to form general rules or conclusions (includes finding a relationship among seemingly unrelated events).
Originality	The ability to come up with unusual or clever ideas about a given topic or situation, or to develop creative ways to solve a problem.
Near Vision	The ability to see details at close range (within a few feet of the observer).
Written Expression	The ability to communicate information and ideas in writing so others will understand.
Visualization	The ability to imagine how something will look after it is moved around or when its parts are moved or rearranged.
Information Ordering	The ability to arrange things or actions in a certain order or pattern according to a specific rule or set of rules (e.g., patterns of numbers, letters, words, pictures, mathematical operations).
Deductive Reasoning	The ability to apply general rules to specific problems to produce answers that make sense.
Fluency of Ideas	The ability to come up with a number of ideas about a topic (the number of ideas is important, not their quality, correctness, or creativity).
Category Flexibility	The ability to generate or use different sets of rules for combining or grouping things in different ways.
Flexibility of Closure	The ability to identify or detect a known pattern (a figure, object, word, or sound) that is hidden in other distracting material.
Far Vision	The ability to see details at a distance.
Selective Attention	The ability to concentrate on a task over a period of time without being distracted.
Mathematical Reasoning	The ability to choose the right mathematical methods or formulas to solve a problem.
Time Sharing	The ability to shift back and forth between two or more activities or sources of information (such as speech, sounds, touch, or other sources).
Perceptual Speed	The ability to quickly and accurately compare similarities and differences among sets of letters, numbers, objects, pictures, or patterns. The things to be compared may be presented at the same time or one after the other. This ability also includes comparing a presented object with a remembered object.
Number Facility	The ability to add, subtract, multiply, or divide quickly and correctly.
Memorization	The ability to remember information such as words, numbers, pictures, and procedures.
Finger Dexterity	The ability to make precisely coordinated movements of the fingers of one or both hands to grasp, manipulate, or assemble very small objects.
Speed of Closure	The ability to quickly make sense of, combine, and organize information into meaningful patterns.
Visual Color Discrimination	The ability to match or detect differences between colors, including shades of color and brightness.
Auditory Attention	The ability to focus on a single source of sound in the presence of other distracting sounds.
Hearing Sensitivity	The ability to detect or tell the differences between sounds that vary in pitch and loudness.
Depth Perception	The ability to judge which of several objects is closer or farther away from you, or to judge the distance between you and an object.
Spatial Orientation	The ability to know your location in relation to the environment or to know where other objects are in relation to you.
Static Strength	The ability to exert maximum muscle force to lift, push, pull, or carry objects.
Trunk Strength	The ability to use your abdominal and lower back muscles to support part of the body repeatedly or continuously over time without 'giving out' or fatiguing.
Stamina	The ability to exert yourself physically over long periods of time without getting winded or out of breath.
Arm-Hand Steadiness	The ability to keep your hand and arm steady while moving your arm or while holding your arm and hand in one position.
Sound Localization	The ability to tell the direction from which a sound originated.

Extent Flexibility	The ability to bend, stretch, twist, or reach with your body, arms, and/or legs.
Wrist-Finger Speed	The ability to make fast, simple, repeated movements of the fingers, hands, and wrists.
Gross Body Coordination	The ability to coordinate the movement of your arms, legs, and torso together when the whole body is in motion.
Multilimb Coordination	The ability to coordinate two or more limbs (for example, two arms, two legs, or one leg and one arm) while sitting, standing, or lying down. It does not involve performing the activities while the whole body is in motion.
Night Vision	The ability to see under low light conditions.
Response Orientation	The ability to choose quickly between two or more movements in response to two or more different signals (lights, sounds, pictures). It includes the speed with which the correct response is started with the hand, foot, or other body part.
Reaction Time	The ability to quickly respond (with the hand, finger, or foot) to a signal (sound, light, picture) when it appears.
Glare Sensitivity	The ability to see objects in the presence of glare or bright lighting.
Speed of Limb Movement	The ability to quickly move the arms and legs.
Manual Dexterity	The ability to quickly move your hand, your hand together with your arm, or your two hands to grasp, manipulate, or assemble objects.
Explosive Strength	The ability to use short bursts of muscle force to propel oneself (as in jumping or sprinting), or to throw an object.
Control Precision	The ability to quickly and repeatedly adjust the controls of a machine or a vehicle to exact positions.
Gross Body Equilibrium	The ability to keep or regain your body balance or stay upright when in an unstable position.
Rate Control	The ability to time your movements or the movement of a piece of equipment in anticipation of changes in the speed and/or direction of a moving object or scene.
Dynamic Strength	The ability to exert muscle force repeatedly or continuously over time. This involves muscular endurance and resistance to muscle fatigue.
Peripheral Vision	The ability to see objects or movement of objects to one's side when the eyes are looking ahead.
Dynamic Flexibility	The ability to quickly and repeatedly bend, stretch, twist, or reach out with your body, arms, and/or legs.

Work_Activity	Work_Activity Definitions
Establishing and Maintaining Interpersonal Relatio	Developing constructive and cooperative working relationships with others, and maintaining them over time.
Communicating with Supervisors, Peers, or Subordin	Providing information to supervisors, co-workers, and subordinates by telephone, in written form, e-mail, or in person.
Getting Information	Observing, receiving, and otherwise obtaining information from all relevant sources.
Interacting With Computers	Using computers and computer systems (including hardware and software) to program, write software, set up functions, enter data, or process information.
Organizing, Planning, and Prioritizing Work	Developing specific goals and plans to prioritize, organize, and accomplish your work.
Communicating with Persons Outside Organization	Communicating with people outside the organization, representing the organization to customers, the public, government, and other external sources. This information can be exchanged in person, in writing, or by telephone or e-mail.
Performing for or Working Directly with the Public	Performing for people or dealing directly with the public. This includes serving customers in restaurants and stores, and receiving clients or guests.
Making Decisions and Solving Problems	Analyzing information and evaluating results to choose the best solution and solve problems.
Performing Administrative Activities	Performing day-to-day administrative tasks such as maintaining information files and processing paperwork.
Scheduling Work and Activities	Scheduling events, programs, and activities, as well as the work of others.
Processing Information	Compiling, coding, categorizing, calculating, tabulating, auditing, or verifying information or data.
Judging the Qualities of Things, Services, or Peop	Assessing the value, importance, or quality of things or people.
Identifying Objects, Actions, and Events	Identifying information by categorizing, estimating, recognizing differences or similarities, and detecting changes in circumstances or events.
Coordinating the Work and Activities of Others	Getting members of a group to work together to accomplish tasks.

Thinking Creatively	Developing, designing, or creating new applications, ideas, relationships, systems, or products, including artistic contributions.
Estimating the Quantifiable Characteristics of Pro	Estimating sizes, distances, and quantities; or determining time, costs, resources, or materials needed to perform a work activity.
Selling or Influencing Others	Convincing others to buy merchandise/goods or to otherwise change their minds or actions.
Resolving Conflicts and Negotiating with Others	Handling complaints, settling disputes, and resolving grievances and conflicts, or otherwise negotiating with others.
Guiding, Directing, and Motivating Subordinates	Providing guidance and direction to subordinates, including setting performance standards and monitoring performance.
Assisting and Caring for Others	Providing personal assistance, medical attention, emotional support, or other personal care to others such as coworkers, customers, or patients.
Documenting/Recording Information	Entering, transcribing, recording, storing, or maintaining information in written or electronic/magnetic form.
Updating and Using Relevant Knowledge	Keeping up-to-date technically and applying new knowledge to your job.
Developing Objectives and Strategies	Establishing long-range objectives and specifying the strategies and actions to achieve them.
Coaching and Developing Others	Identifying the developmental needs of others and coaching, mentoring, or otherwise helping others to improve their knowledge or skills.
Monitoring and Controlling Resources	Monitoring and controlling resources and overseeing the spending of money.
Monitor Processes, Materials, or Surroundings	Monitoring and reviewing information from materials, events, or the environment, to detect or assess problems.
Interpreting the Meaning of Information for Others	Translating or explaining what information means and how it can be used.
Developing and Building Teams	Encouraging and building mutual trust, respect, and cooperation among team members.
Provide Consultation and Advice to Others	Providing guidance and expert advice to management or other groups on technical, systems-, or process-related topics.
Evaluating Information to Determine Compliance wit	Using relevant information and individual judgment to determine whether events or processes comply with laws, regulations, or standards.
Analyzing Data or Information	Identifying the underlying principles, reasons, or facts of information by breaking down information or data into separate parts.
Training and Teaching Others	Identifying the educational needs of others, developing formal educational or training programs or classes, and teaching or instructing others.
Performing General Physical Activities	Performing physical activities that require considerable use of your arms and legs and moving your whole body, such as climbing, lifting, balancing, walking, stooping, and handling of materials.
Inspecting Equipment, Structures, or Material	Inspecting equipment, structures, or materials to identify the cause of errors or other problems or defects.
Staffing Organizational Units	Recruiting, interviewing, selecting, hiring, and promoting employees in an organization.
Handling and Moving Objects	Using hands and arms in handling, installing, positioning, and moving materials, and manipulating things.
Drafting, Laying Out, and Specifying Technical Dev	Providing documentation, detailed instructions, drawings, or specifications to tell others about how devices, parts, equipment, or structures are to be fabricated, constructed, assembled, modified, maintained, or used.
Repairing and Maintaining Electronic Equipment	Servicing, repairing, calibrating, regulating, fine-tuning, or testing machines, devices, and equipment that operate primarily on the basis of electrical or electronic (not mechanical) principles.
Controlling Machines and Processes	Using either control mechanisms or direct physical activity to operate machines or processes (not including computers or vehicles).
Repairing and Maintaining Mechanical Equipment	Servicing, repairing, adjusting, and testing machines, devices, moving parts, and equipment that operate primarily on the basis of mechanical (not electronic) principles.
Operating Vehicles, Mechanized Devices, or Equipme	Running, maneuvering, navigating, or driving vehicles or mechanized equipment, such as forklifts, passenger vehicles, aircraft, or water craft.

Work_Context	Work_Context Definitions
Telephone	How often do you have telephone conversations in this job?
Contact With Others	How much does this job require the worker to be in contact with others (face-to-face, by telephone, or otherwise) in order to perform it?

Electronic Mail	How often do you use electronic mail in this job?
Structured versus Unstructured Work	To what extent is this job structured for the worker, rather than allowing the worker to determine tasks, priorities, and goals?
Work With Work Group or Team	How important is it to work with others in a group or team in this job?
Face-to-Face Discussions	How often do you have to have face-to-face discussions with individuals or teams in this job?
Deal With External Customers	How important is it to work with external customers or the public in this job?
Impact of Decisions on Co-workers or Company Resul	How do the decisions an employee makes impact the results of co-workers, clients or the company?
Coordinate or Lead Others	How important is it to coordinate or lead others in accomplishing work activities in this job?
Freedom to Make Decisions	How much decision making freedom, without supervision, does the job offer?
Frequency of Decision Making	How frequently is the worker required to make decisions that affect other people, the financial resources, and/or the image and reputation of the organization?
Letters and Memos	How often does the job require written letters and memos?
Time Pressure	How often does this job require the worker to meet strict deadlines?
Importance of Being Exact or Accurate	How important is being very exact or highly accurate in performing this job?
Responsibility for Outcomes and Results	How responsible is the worker for work outcomes and results of other workers?
Indoors, Environmentally Controlled	How often does this job require working indoors in environmentally controlled conditions?
Spend Time Sitting	How much does this job require sitting?
Frequency of Conflict Situations	How often are there conflict situations the employee has to face in this job?
Importance of Repeating Same Tasks	How important is repeating the same physical activities (e.g., key entry) or mental activities (e.g., checking entries in a ledger) over and over, without stopping, to performing this job?
Deal With Unpleasant or Angry People	How frequently does the worker have to deal with unpleasant, angry, or discourteous individuals as part of the job requirements?
Level of Competition	To what extent does this job require the worker to compete or to be aware of competitive pressures?
Responsible for Others' Health and Safety	How much responsibility is there for the health and safety of others in this job?
Spend Time Making Repetitive Motions	How much does this job require making repetitive motions?
Consequence of Error	How serious would the result usually be if the worker made a mistake that was not readily correctable?
Degree of Automation	How automated is the job?
Sounds, Noise Levels Are Distracting or Uncomforta	How often does this job require working exposed to sounds and noise levels that are distracting or uncomfortable?
Public Speaking	How often do you have to perform public speaking in this job?
Spend Time Using Your Hands to Handle, Control, or	How much does this job require using your hands to handle, control, or feel objects, tools or controls?
Spend Time Standing	How much does this job require standing?
Spend Time Walking and Running	How much does this job require walking and running?
Physical Proximity	To what extent does this job require the worker to perform job tasks in close physical proximity to other people?
In an Enclosed Vehicle or Equipment	How often does this job require working in a closed vehicle or equipment (e.g., car)?
Extremely Bright or Inadequate Lighting	How often does this job require working in extremely bright or inadequate lighting conditions?
Exposed to Contaminants	How often does this job require working exposed to contaminants (such as pollutants, gases, dust or odors)?
Indoors, Not Environmentally Controlled	How often does this job require working indoors in non-controlled environmental conditions (e.g., warehouse without heat)?
Outdoors, Exposed to Weather	How often does this job require working outdoors, exposed to all weather conditions?
Spend Time Bending or Twisting the Body	How much does this job require bending or twisting your body?
Spend Time Kneeling, Crouching, Stooping, or Crawl	How much does this job require kneeling, crouching, stooping or crawling?
Deal With Physically Aggressive People	How frequently does this job require the worker to deal with physical aggression of violent individuals?
Cramped Work Space, Awkward Positions	How often does this job require working in cramped work spaces that requires getting into awkward positions?

Very Hot or Cold Temperatures	How often does this job require working in very hot (above 90 F degrees) or very cold (below 32 F degrees) temperatures?
Exposed to High Places	How often does this job require exposure to high places?
Pace Determined by Speed of Equipment	How important is it to this job that the pace is determined by the speed of equipment or machinery? (This does not refer to keeping busy at all times on this job.)
Outdoors, Under Cover	How often does this job require working outdoors, under cover (e.g., structure with roof but no walls)?
Exposed to Minor Burns, Cuts, Bites, or Stings	How often does this job require exposure to minor burns, cuts, bites, or stings?
Spend Time Keeping or Regaining Balance	How much does this job require keeping or regaining your balance?
Exposed to Hazardous Conditions	How often does this job require exposure to hazardous conditions?
Wear Common Protective or Safety Equipment such as	How much does this job require wearing common protective or safety equipment such as safety shoes, glasses, gloves, hard hats or life jackets?
In an Open Vehicle or Equipment	How often does this job require working in an open vehicle or equipment (e.g., tractor)?
Exposed to Whole Body Vibration	How often does this job require exposure to whole body vibration (e.g., operate a jackhammer)?
Exposed to Disease or Infections	How often does this job require exposure to disease/infections?
Exposed to Hazardous Equipment	How often does this job require exposure to hazardous equipment?
Spend Time Climbing Ladders, Scaffolds, or Poles	How much does this job require climbing ladders, scaffolds, or poles?
Wear Specialized Protective or Safety Equipment su	How much does this job require wearing specialized protective or safety equipment such as breathing apparatus, safety harness, full protection suits, or radiation protection?
Exposed to Radiation	How often does this job require exposure to radiation?

Job Zone Component	Job Zone Component Definitions
Title	Job Zone Four: Considerable Preparation Needed
Overall Experience	A minimum of two to four years of work-related skill, knowledge, or experience is needed for these occupations. For example, an accountant must complete four years of college and work for several years in accounting to be considered qualified.
Job Training	Employees in these occupations usually need several years of work-related experience, on-the-job training, and/or vocational training.
Job Zone Examples	Many of these occupations involve coordinating, supervising, managing, or training others. Examples include accountants, chefs and head cooks, computer programmers, historians, pharmacists, and police detectives.
SVP Range	(7.0 to < 8.0)
Education	Most of these occupations require a four - year bachelor's degree, but some do not.

Work_Styles	Work_Styles Definitions
Cooperation	Job requires being pleasant with others on the job and displaying a good-natured, cooperative attitude.
Attention to Detail	Job requires being careful about detail and thorough in completing work tasks.
Dependability	Job requires being reliable, responsible, and dependable, and fulfilling obligations.
Self Control	Job requires maintaining composure, keeping emotions in check, controlling anger, and avoiding aggressive behavior, even in very difficult situations.
Adaptability/Flexibility	Job requires being open to change (positive or negative) and to considerable variety in the workplace.
Integrity	Job requires being honest and ethical.
Initiative	Job requires a willingness to take on responsibilities and challenges.
Stress Tolerance	Job requires accepting criticism and dealing calmly and effectively with high stress situations.
Concern for Others	Job requires being sensitive to others' needs and feelings and being understanding and helpful on the job.
Leadership	Job requires a willingness to lead, take charge, and offer opinions and direction.
Social Orientation	Job requires preferring to work with others rather than alone, and being personally connected with others on the job.

Innovation	Job requires creativity and alternative thinking to develop new ideas for and answers to work-related problems.
Independence	Job requires developing one's own ways of doing things, guiding oneself with little or no supervision, and depending on oneself to get things done.
Achievement/Effort	Job requires establishing and maintaining personally challenging achievement goals and exerting effort toward mastering tasks.
Persistence	Job requires persistence in the face of obstacles.
Analytical Thinking	Job requires analyzing information and using logic to address work-related issues and problems.

13-2011.01 - Accountants

Analyze financial information and prepare financial reports to determine or maintain record of assets, liabilities, profit and loss, tax liability, or other financial activities within an organization.

Tasks

1) Establish tables of accounts, and assign entries to proper accounts.

2) Develop, implement, modify, and document record keeping and accounting systems, making use of current computer technology.

3) Survey operations to ascertain accounting needs and to recommend, develop, and maintain solutions to business and financial problems.

4) Report to management regarding the finances of establishment.

5) Compute taxes owed and prepare tax returns, ensuring compliance with payment, reporting and other tax requirements.

6) Analyze business operations, trends, costs, revenues, financial commitments, and obligations, to project future revenues and expenses or to provide advice.

7) Develop, maintain, and analyze budgets, preparing periodic reports that compare budgeted costs to actual costs.

8) Prepare forms and manuals for accounting and bookkeeping personnel, and direct their work activities.

9) Appraise, evaluate, and inventory real property and equipment, recording information such as the property's description, value, and location.

10) Advise management about issues such as resource utilization, tax strategies, and the assumptions underlying budget forecasts.

11) Advise clients in areas such as compensation, employee health care benefits, the design of accounting and data processing systems, and long-range tax and estate plans.

12) Provide internal and external auditing services for businesses and individuals.

13) Investigate bankruptcies and other complex financial transactions and prepare reports summarizing the findings.

14) Represent clients before taxing authorities and provide support during litigation involving financial issues.

15) Maintain and examine the records of government agencies.

16) Serve as bankruptcy trustees and business valuators.

17) Work as Internal Revenue Service agents.

Knowledge	Knowledge Definitions
Mathematics	Knowledge of arithmetic, algebra, geometry, calculus, statistics, and their applications.
Economics and Accounting	Knowledge of economic and accounting principles and practices, the financial markets, banking and the analysis and reporting of financial data.
English Language	Knowledge of the structure and content of the English language including the meaning and spelling of words, rules of composition, and grammar.
Customer and Personal Service	Knowledge of principles and processes for providing customer and personal services. This includes customer needs assessment, meeting quality standards for services, and evaluation of customer satisfaction.
Computers and Electronics	Knowledge of circuit boards, processors, chips, electronic equipment, and computer hardware and software, including applications and programming.

Law and Government	Knowledge of laws. legal codes. court procedures. precedents. government regulations. executive orders. agency rules. and the democratic political process.
Clerical	Knowledge of administrative and clerical procedures and systems such as word processing. managing files and records. stenography and transcription. designing forms. and other office procedures and terminology.
Personnel and Human Resources	Knowledge of principles and procedures for personnel recruitment, selection. training. compensation and benefits. labor relations and negotiation, and personnel information systems.
Administration and Management	Knowledge of business and management principles involved in strategic planning. resource allocation, human resources modeling. leadership technique. production methods. and coordination of people and resources.
Production and Processing	Knowledge of raw materials, production processes, quality control, costs, and other techniques for maximizing the effective manufacture and distribution of goods.
Education and Training	Knowledge of principles and methods for curriculum and training design, teaching and instruction for individuals and groups, and the measurement of training effects.
Public Safety and Security	Knowledge of relevant equipment, policies, procedures, and strategies to promote effective local, state, or national security operations for the protection of people, data, property, and institutions.
Telecommunications	Knowledge of transmission, broadcasting, switching, control, and operation of telecommunications systems.
Communications and Media	Knowledge of media production, communication, and dissemination techniques and methods. This includes alternative ways to inform and entertain via written, oral, and visual media.
Engineering and Technology	Knowledge of the practical application of engineering science and technology. This includes applying principles, techniques, procedures, and equipment to the design and production of various goods and services.
Sales and Marketing	Knowledge of principles and methods for showing, promoting, and selling products or services. This includes marketing strategy and tactics, product demonstration, sales techniques, and sales control systems.
Psychology	Knowledge of human behavior and performance; individual differences in ability, personality, and interests; learning and motivation; psychological research methods; and the assessment and treatment of behavioral and affective disorders.
Foreign Language	Knowledge of the structure and content of a foreign (non-English) language including the meaning and spelling of words, rules of composition and grammar, and pronunciation.
Transportation	Knowledge of principles and methods for moving people or goods by air, rail, sea, or road, including the relative costs and benefits.
Sociology and Anthropology	Knowledge of group behavior and dynamics, societal trends and influences, human migrations, ethnicity, cultures and their history and origins.
Building and Construction	Knowledge of materials, methods, and the tools involved in the construction or repair of houses, buildings, or other structures such as highways and roads.
Philosophy and Theology	Knowledge of different philosophical systems and religions. This includes their basic principles, values, ethics, ways of thinking, customs, practices, and their impact on human culture.
Design	Knowledge of design techniques, tools, and principles involved in production of precision technical plans, blueprints, drawings, and models.
Therapy and Counseling	Knowledge of principles, methods, and procedures for diagnosis, treatment, and rehabilitation of physical and mental dysfunctions, and for career counseling and guidance.
Geography	Knowledge of principles and methods for describing the features of land, sea, and air masses, including their physical characteristics, locations, interrelationships, and distribution of plant, animal, and human life.
Medicine and Dentistry	Knowledge of the information and techniques needed to diagnose and treat human injuries, diseases, and deformities. This includes symptoms, treatment alternatives, drug properties and interactions, and preventive health-care measures.
Food Production	Knowledge of techniques and equipment for planting, growing, and harvesting food products (both plant and animal) for consumption, including storage/handling techniques.
Mechanical	Knowledge of machines and tools, including their designs, uses, repair, and maintenance.

History and Archeology	Knowledge of historical events and their causes. indicators. and effects on civilizations and cultures.
Chemistry	Knowledge of the chemical composition. structure. and properties of substances and of the chemical processes and transformations that they undergo. This includes uses of chemicals and their interactions. danger signs. production techniques. and disposal methods.
Physics	Knowledge and prediction of physical principles, laws, their interrelationships, and applications to understanding fluid, material. and atmospheric dynamics. and mechanical, electrical. atomic and sub-atomic structures and processes.
Biology	Knowledge of plant and animal organisms. their tissues, cells, functions, interdependencies, and interactions with each other and the environment.
Fine Arts	Knowledge of the theory and techniques required to compose, produce, and perform works of music, dance, visual arts, drama, and sculpture.

Skills	Skills Definitions
Mathematics	Using mathematics to solve problems.
Active Listening	Giving full attention to what other people are saying, taking time to understand the points being made, asking questions as appropriate, and not interrupting at inappropriate times.
Critical Thinking	Using logic and reasoning to identify the strengths and weaknesses of alternative solutions, conclusions or approaches to problems.
Monitoring	Monitoring/Assessing performance of yourself, other individuals, or organizations to make improvements or take corrective action.
Judgment and Decision Making	Considering the relative costs and benefits of potential actions to choose the most appropriate one.
Active Learning	Understanding the implications of new information for both current and future problem-solving and decision-making.
Reading Comprehension	Understanding written sentences and paragraphs in work related documents.
Systems Analysis	Determining how a system should work and how changes in conditions, operations, and the environment will affect outcomes.
Systems Evaluation	Identifying measures or indicators of system performance and the actions needed to improve or correct performance, relative to the goals of the system.
Coordination	Adjusting actions in relation to others' actions.
Management of Financial Resources	Determining how money will be spent to get the work done, and accounting for these expenditures.
Time Management	Managing one's own time and the time of others.
Social Perceptiveness	Being aware of others' reactions and understanding why they react as they do.
Operations Analysis	Analyzing needs and product requirements to create a design.
Speaking	Talking to others to convey information effectively.
Complex Problem Solving	Identifying complex problems and reviewing related information to develop and evaluate options and implement solutions.
Learning Strategies	Selecting and using training/instructional methods and procedures appropriate for the situation when learning or teaching new things.
Writing	Communicating effectively in writing as appropriate for the needs of the audience.
Troubleshooting	Determining causes of operating errors and deciding what to do about it.
Service Orientation	Actively looking for ways to help people.
Instructing	Teaching others how to do something.
Negotiation	Bringing others together and trying to reconcile differences.
Persuasion	Persuading others to change their minds or behavior.
Quality Control Analysis	Conducting tests and inspections of products, services, or processes to evaluate quality or performance.
Equipment Selection	Determining the kind of tools and equipment needed to do a job.
Operation Monitoring	Watching gauges, dials, or other indicators to make sure a machine is working properly.
Programming	Writing computer programs for various purposes.
Management of Material Resources	Obtaining and seeing to the appropriate use of equipment, facilities, and materials needed to do certain work.
Management of Personnel Resources	Motivating, developing, and directing people as they work, identifying the best people for the job.
Operation and Control	Controlling operations of equipment or systems.
Equipment Maintenance	Performing routine maintenance on equipment and determining when and what kind of maintenance is needed.

Technology Design	Generating or adapting equipment and technology to serve user needs.
Installation	Installing equipment, machines, wiring, or programs to meet specifications.
Science	Using scientific rules and methods to solve problems.
Repairing	Repairing machines or systems using the needed tools.

Ability	Ability Definitions
Problem Sensitivity	The ability to tell when something is wrong or is likely to go wrong. It does not involve solving the problem, only recognizing there is a problem.
Deductive Reasoning	The ability to apply general rules to specific problems to produce answers that make sense.
Oral Expression	The ability to communicate information and ideas in speaking so others will understand.
Information Ordering	The ability to arrange things or actions in a certain order or pattern according to a specific rule or set of rules (e.g., patterns of numbers, letters, words, pictures, mathematical operations).
Written Expression	The ability to communicate information and ideas in writing so others will understand.
Mathematical Reasoning	The ability to choose the right mathematical methods or formulas to solve a problem.
Written Comprehension	The ability to read and understand information and ideas presented in writing.
Near Vision	The ability to see details at close range (within a few feet of the observer).
Inductive Reasoning	The ability to combine pieces of information to form general rules or conclusions (includes finding a relationship among seemingly unrelated events).
Speech Clarity	The ability to speak clearly so others can understand you.
Speech Recognition	The ability to identify and understand the speech of another person.
Oral Comprehension	The ability to listen to and understand information and ideas presented through spoken words and sentences.
Number Facility	The ability to add, subtract, multiply, or divide quickly and correctly.
Flexibility of Closure	The ability to identify or detect a known pattern (a figure, object, word, or sound) that is hidden in other distracting material.
Perceptual Speed	The ability to quickly and accurately compare similarities and differences among sets of letters, numbers, objects, pictures, or patterns. The things to be compared may be presented at the same time or one after the other. This ability also includes comparing a presented object with a remembered object.
Selective Attention	The ability to concentrate on a task over a period of time without being distracted.
Category Flexibility	The ability to generate or use different sets of rules for combining or grouping things in different ways.
Finger Dexterity	The ability to make precisely coordinated movements of the fingers of one or both hands to grasp, manipulate, or assemble very small objects.
Speed of Closure	The ability to quickly make sense of, combine, and organize information into meaningful patterns.
Originality	The ability to come up with unusual or clever ideas about a given topic or situation, or to develop creative ways to solve a problem.
Memorization	The ability to remember information such as words, numbers, pictures, and procedures.
Fluency of Ideas	The ability to come up with a number of ideas about a topic (the number of ideas is important, not their quality, correctness, or creativity).
Far Vision	The ability to see details at a distance.
Visualization	The ability to imagine how something will look after it is moved around or when its parts are moved or rearranged.
Time Sharing	The ability to shift back and forth between two or more activities or sources of information (such as speech, sounds, touch, or other sources).
Trunk Strength	The ability to use your abdominal and lower back muscles to support part of the body repeatedly or continuously over time without 'giving out' or fatiguing.
Hearing Sensitivity	The ability to detect or tell the differences between sounds that vary in pitch and loudness.
Visual Color Discrimination	The ability to match or detect differences between colors, including shades of color and brightness.
Depth Perception	The ability to judge which of several objects is closer or farther away from you, or to judge the distance between you and an object.

Auditory Attention	The ability to focus on a single source of sound in the presence of other distracting sounds.
Wrist-Finger Speed	The ability to make fast, simple, repeated movements of the fingers, hands, and wrists.
Manual Dexterity	The ability to quickly move your hand, your hand together with your arm, or your two hands to grasp, manipulate, or assemble objects.
Arm-Hand Steadiness	The ability to keep your hand and arm steady while moving your arm or while holding your arm and hand in one position.
Speed of Limb Movement	The ability to quickly move the arms and legs.
Sound Localization	The ability to tell the direction from which a sound originated.
Static Strength	The ability to exert maximum muscle force to lift, push, pull, or carry objects.
Stamina	The ability to exert yourself physically over long periods of time without getting winded or out of breath.
Extent Flexibility	The ability to bend, stretch, twist, or reach with your body, arms, and/or legs.
Dynamic Flexibility	The ability to quickly and repeatedly bend, stretch, twist, or reach out with your body, arms, and/or legs.
Gross Body Coordination	The ability to coordinate the movement of your arms, legs, and torso together when the whole body is in motion.
Gross Body Equilibrium	The ability to keep or regain your body balance or stay upright when in an unstable position.
Dynamic Strength	The ability to exert muscle force repeatedly or continuously over time. This involves muscular endurance and resistance to muscle fatigue.
Night Vision	The ability to see under low light conditions.
Spatial Orientation	The ability to know your location in relation to the environment or to know where other objects are in relation to you.
Rate Control	The ability to time your movements or the movement of a piece of equipment in anticipation of changes in the speed and/or direction of a moving object or scene.
Multilimb Coordination	The ability to coordinate two or more limbs (for example, two arms, two legs, or one leg and one arm) while sitting, standing, or lying down. It does not involve performing the activities while the whole body is in motion.
Peripheral Vision	The ability to see objects or movement of objects to one's side when the eyes are looking ahead.
Glare Sensitivity	The ability to see objects in the presence of glare or bright lighting.
Control Precision	The ability to quickly and repeatedly adjust the controls of a machine or a vehicle to exact positions.
Explosive Strength	The ability to use short bursts of muscle force to propel oneself (as in jumping or sprinting), or to throw an object.
Response Orientation	The ability to choose quickly between two or more movements in response to two or more different signals (lights, sounds, pictures). It includes the speed with which the correct response is started with the hand, foot, or other body part.
Reaction Time	The ability to quickly respond (with the hand, finger, or foot) to a signal (sound, light, picture) when it appears.

Work_Activity	Work_Activity Definitions
Interacting With Computers	Using computers and computer systems (including hardware and software) to program, write software, set up functions, enter data, or process information.
Analyzing Data or Information	Identifying the underlying principles, reasons, or facts of information by breaking down information or data into separate parts.
Processing Information	Compiling, coding, categorizing, calculating, tabulating, auditing, or verifying information or data.
Getting Information	Observing, receiving, and otherwise obtaining information from all relevant sources.
Documenting/Recording Information	Entering, transcribing, recording, storing, or maintaining information in written or electronic/magnetic form.
Establishing and Maintaining Interpersonal Relatio	Developing constructive and cooperative working relationships with others, and maintaining them over time.
Organizing, Planning, and Prioritizing Work	Developing specific goals and plans to prioritize, organize, and accomplish your work.
Communicating with Supervisors, Peers, or Subordin	Providing information to supervisors, co-workers, and subordinates by telephone, in written form, e-mail, or in person.
Making Decisions and Solving Problems	Analyzing information and evaluating results to choose the best solution and solve problems.
Interpreting the Meaning of Information for Others	Translating or explaining what information means and how it can be used.

Evaluating Information to Determine Compliance wit	Using relevant information and individual judgment to determine whether events or processes comply with laws, regulations, or standards.
Updating and Using Relevant Knowledge	Keeping up-to-date technically and applying new knowledge to your job.
Communicating with Persons Outside Organization	Communicating with people outside the organization, representing the organization to customers, the public, government, and other external sources. This information can be exchanged in person, in writing, or by telephone or e-mail.
Identifying Objects, Actions, and Events	Identifying information by categorizing, estimating, recognizing differences or similarities, and detecting changes in circumstances or events.
Developing Objectives and Strategies	Establishing long-range objectives and specifying the strategies and actions to achieve them.
Thinking Creatively	Developing, designing, or creating new applications, ideas, relationships, systems, or products, including artistic contributions.
Developing and Building Teams	Encouraging and building mutual trust, respect, and cooperation among team members.
Coordinating the Work and Activities of Others	Getting members of a group to work together to accomplish tasks.
Performing Administrative Activities	Performing day-to-day administrative tasks such as maintaining information files and processing paperwork.
Monitoring and Controlling Resources	Monitoring and controlling resources and overseeing the spending of money.
Guiding, Directing, and Motivating Subordinates	Providing guidance and direction to subordinates, including setting performance standards and monitoring performance.
Scheduling Work and Activities	Scheduling events, programs, and activities, as well as the work of others.
Estimating the Quantifiable Characteristics of Pro	Estimating sizes, distances, and quantities; or determining time, costs, resources, or materials needed to perform a work activity.
Resolving Conflicts and Negotiating with Others	Handling complaints, settling disputes, and resolving grievances and conflicts, or otherwise negotiating with others.
Training and Teaching Others	Identifying the educational needs of others, developing formal educational or training programs or classes, and teaching or instructing others.
Coaching and Developing Others	Identifying the developmental needs of others and coaching, mentoring, or otherwise helping others to improve their knowledge or skills.
Provide Consultation and Advice to Others	Providing guidance and expert advice to management or other groups on technical, systems-, or process-related topics.
Staffing Organizational Units	Recruiting, interviewing, selecting, hiring, and promoting employees in an organization.
Judging the Qualities of Things, Services, or Peop	Assessing the value, importance, or quality of things or people.
Assisting and Caring for Others	Providing personal assistance, medical attention, emotional support, or other personal care to others such as coworkers, customers, or patients.
Selling or Influencing Others	Convincing others to buy merchandise/goods or to otherwise change their minds or actions.
Controlling Machines and Processes	Using either control mechanisms or direct physical activity to operate machines or processes (not including computers or vehicles).
Monitor Processes, Materials, or Surroundings	Monitoring and reviewing information from materials, events, or the environment, to detect or assess problems.
Handling and Moving Objects	Using hands and arms in handling, installing, positioning, and moving materials, and manipulating things.
Performing General Physical Activities	Performing physical activities that require considerable use of your arms and legs and moving your whole body, such as climbing, lifting, balancing, walking, stooping, and handling of materials.
Performing for or Working Directly with the Public	Performing for people or dealing directly with the public. This includes serving customers in restaurants and stores, and receiving clients or guests.
Operating Vehicles, Mechanized Devices, or Equipme	Running, maneuvering, navigating, or driving vehicles or mechanized equipment, such as forklifts, passenger vehicles, aircraft, or water craft.
Inspecting Equipment, Structures, or Material	Inspecting equipment, structures, or materials to identify the cause of errors or other problems or defects.
Repairing and Maintaining Electronic Equipment	Servicing, repairing, calibrating, regulating, fine-tuning, or testing machines, devices, and equipment that operate primarily on the basis of electrical or electronic (not mechanical) principles.
Drafting, Laying Out, and Specifying Technical Dev	Providing documentation, detailed instructions, drawings, or specifications to tell others about how devices, parts, equipment, or structures are to be fabricated, constructed, assembled, modified, maintained, or used.
Repairing and Maintaining Mechanical Equipment	Servicing, repairing, adjusting, and testing machines, devices, moving parts, and equipment that operate primarily on the basis of mechanical (not electronic) principles.

Work_Context	Work_Context Definitions
Telephone	How often do you have telephone conversations in this job?
Electronic Mail	How often do you use electronic mail in this job?
Indoors, Environmentally Controlled	How often does this job require working indoors in environmentally controlled conditions?
Face-to-Face Discussions	How often do you have to have face-to-face discussions with individuals or teams in this job?
Structured versus Unstructured Work	To what extent is this job structured for the worker, rather than allowing the worker to determine tasks, priorities, and goals?
Spend Time Sitting	How much does this job require sitting?
Freedom to Make Decisions	How much decision making freedom, without supervision, does the job offer?
Importance of Being Exact or Accurate	How important is being very exact or highly accurate in performing this job?
Work With Work Group or Team	How important is it to work with others in a group or team in this job?
Letters and Memos	How often does the job require written letters and memos?
Contact With Others	How much does this job require the worker to be in contact with others (face-to-face, by telephone, or otherwise) in order to perform it?
Degree of Automation	How automated is the job?
Importance of Repeating Same Tasks	How important is repeating the same physical activities (e.g., key entry) or mental activities (e.g., checking entries in a ledger) over and over, without stopping, to performing this job?
Impact of Decisions on Co-workers or Company Resul	How do the decisions an employee makes impact the results of co-workers, clients or the company?
Time Pressure	How often does this job require the worker to meet strict deadlines?
Frequency of Decision Making	How frequently is the worker required to make decisions that affect other people, the financial resources, and/or the image and reputation of the organization?
Physical Proximity	To what extent does this job require the worker to perform job tasks in close physical proximity to other people?
Spend Time Making Repetitive Motions	How much does this job require making repetitive motions?
Responsibility for Outcomes and Results	How responsible is the worker for work outcomes and results of other workers?
Deal With Unpleasant or Angry People	How frequently does the worker have to deal with unpleasant, angry, or discourteous individuals as part of the job requirements?
Level of Competition	To what extent does this job require the worker to compete or to be aware of competitive pressures?
Deal With External Customers	How important is it to work with external customers or the public in this job?
Coordinate or Lead Others	How important is it to coordinate or lead others in accomplishing work activities in this job?
Spend Time Using Your Hands to Handle, Control, or	How much does this job require using your hands to handle, control, or feel objects, tools or controls?
Spend Time Standing	How much does this job require standing?
Frequency of Conflict Situations	How often are there conflict situations the employee has to face in this job?
Responsible for Others' Health and Safety	How much responsibility is there for the health and safety of others in this job?
Consequence of Error	How serious would the result usually be if the worker made a mistake that was not readily correctable?
Spend Time Walking and Running	How much does this job require walking and running?
Sounds, Noise Levels Are Distracting or Uncomforta	How often does this job require working exposed to sounds and noise levels that are distracting or uncomfortable?
Very Hot or Cold Temperatures	How often does this job require working in very hot (above 90 F degrees) or very cold (below 32 F degrees) temperatures?
In an Enclosed Vehicle or Equipment	How often does this job require working in a closed vehicle or equipment (e.g., car)?
Public Speaking	How often do you have to perform public speaking in this job?
Exposed to Minor Burns, Cuts, Bites, or Stings	How often does this job require exposure to minor burns, cuts, bites, or stings?

Spend Time Kneeling. Crouching. Stooping. or Crawl	How much does this job require kneeling. crouching. stooping or crawling?
Extremely Bright or Inadequate Lighting	How often does this job require working in extremely bright or inadequate lighting conditions?
Spend Time Bending or Twisting the Body	How much does this job require bending or twisting your body?
Exposed to Contaminants	How often does this job require working exposed to contaminants (such as pollutants. gases. dust or odors)?
Deal With Physically Aggressive People	How frequently does this job require the worker to deal with physical aggression of violent individuals?
Indoors. Not Environmentally Controlled	How often does this job require working indoors in non-controlled environmental conditions (e.g.. warehouse without heat)?
Exposed to High Places	How often does this job require exposure to high places?
Outdoors. Exposed to Weather	How often does this job require working outdoors. exposed to all weather conditions?
Spend Time Climbing Ladders. Scaffolds. or Poles	How much does this job require climbing ladders. scaffolds. or poles?
Outdoors. Under Cover	How often does this job require working outdoors. under cover (e.g., structure with roof but no walls)?
Wear Common Protective or Safety Equipment such as	How much does this job require wearing common protective or safety equipment such as safety shoes. glasses. gloves. hard hats or live jackets?
Spend Time Keeping or Regaining Balance	How much does this job require keeping or regaining your balance?
Cramped Work Space. Awkward Positions	How often does this job require working in cramped work spaces that requires getting into awkward positions?
Wear Specialized Protective or Safety Equipment su	How much does this job require wearing specialized protective or safety equipment such as breathing apparatus, safety harness, full protection suits, or radiation protection?
In an Open Vehicle or Equipment	How often does this job require working in an open vehicle or equipment (e.g., tractor)?
Exposed to Whole Body Vibration	How often does this job require exposure to whole body vibration (e.g., operate a jackhammer)?
Exposed to Radiation	How often does this job require exposure to radiation?
Exposed to Disease or Infections	How often does this job require exposure to disease/infections?
Exposed to Hazardous Conditions	How often does this job require exposure to hazardous conditions?
Pace Determined by Speed of Equipment	How important is it to this job that the pace is determined by the speed of equipment or machinery? (This does not refer to keeping busy at all times on this job.)
Exposed to Hazardous Equipment	How often does this job require exposure to hazardous equipment?

Job Zone Component	Job Zone Component Definitions
Title	Job Zone Four: Considerable Preparation Needed
Overall Experience	A minimum of two to four years of work-related skill, knowledge, or experience is needed for these occupations. For example, an accountant must complete four years of college and work for several years in accounting to be considered qualified.
Job Training	Employees in these occupations usually need several years of work-related experience. on-the-job training. and/or vocational training.
Job Zone Examples	Many of these occupations involve coordinating, supervising, managing, or training others. Examples include accountants. chefs and head cooks, computer programmers. historians, pharmacists, and police detectives.
SVP Range	(7.0 to < 8.0)
Education	Most of these occupations require a four - year bachelor's degree, but some do not.

Work_Styles	Work_Styles Definitions
Attention to Detail	Job requires being careful about detail and thorough in completing work tasks.
Dependability	Job requires being reliable. responsible, and dependable, and fulfilling obligations.
Integrity	Job requires being honest and ethical.
Analytical Thinking	Job requires analyzing information and using logic to address work-related issues and problems
Stress Tolerance	Job requires accepting criticism and dealing calmly and effectively with high stress situations.

Cooperation	Job requires being pleasant with others on the job and displaying a good-natured. cooperative attitude.
Achievement/Effort	Job requires establishing and maintaining personally challenging achievement goals and exerting effort toward mastering tasks.
Adaptability/Flexibility	Job requires being open to change (positive or negative) and to considerable variety in the workplace.
Independence	Job requires developing one's own ways of doing things. guiding oneself with little or no supervision, and depending on oneself to get things done.
Self Control	Job requires maintaining composure, keeping emotions in check. controlling anger. and avoiding aggressive behavior. even in very difficult situations.
Persistence	Job requires persistence in the face of obstacles.
Concern for Others	Job requires being sensitive to others' needs and feelings and being understanding and helpful on the job.
Initiative	Job requires a willingness to take on responsibilities and challenges.
Leadership	Job requires a willingness to lead, take charge, and offer opinions and direction.
Innovation	Job requires creativity and alternative thinking to develop new ideas for and answers to work-related problems.
Social Orientation	Job requires preferring to work with others rather than alone. and being personally connected with others on the job.

13-2011.02 - Auditors

Examine and analyze accounting records to determine financial status of establishment and prepare financial reports concerning operating procedures.

Tasks

1) Inspect account books and accounting systems for efficiency, effectiveness, and use of accepted accounting procedures to record transactions.

2) Examine records and interview workers to ensure recording of transactions and compliance with laws and regulations.

3) Collect and analyze data to detect deficient controls, duplicated effort, extravagance, fraud, or non-compliance with laws, regulations, and management policies.

4) Prepare, analyze, and verify annual reports, financial statements, and other records, using accepted accounting and statistical procedures to assess financial condition and facilitate financial planning.

5) Prepare detailed reports on audit findings.

6) Report to management about asset utilization and audit results, and recommend changes in operations and financial activities.

7) Inspect cash on hand, notes receivable and payable, negotiable securities, and canceled checks to confirm records are accurate.

8) Review data about material assets, net worth, liabilities, capital stock, surplus, income, and expenditures.

9) Confer with company officials about financial and regulatory matters.

10) Examine inventory to verify journal and ledger entries.

11) Supervise auditing of establishments, and determine scope of investigation required.

12) Audit payroll and personnel records to determine unemployment insurance premiums, workers' compensation coverage, liabilities, and compliance with tax laws.

13) Examine whether the organization's objectives are reflected in its management activities. and whether employees understand the objectives.

14) Direct activities of personnel engaged in filing, recording, compiling and transmitting financial records.

15) Conduct pre-implementation audits to determine if systems and programs under development will work as planned.

16) Produce up-to-the-minute information, using internal computer systems, to allow management to base decisions on actual, not historical, data.

17) Evaluate taxpayer finances to determine tax liability, using knowledge of interest and discount rates, annuities, valuation of stocks and bonds, and amortization valuation of depletable assets.

18) Examine records, tax returns, and related documents pertaining to settlement of decedent's estate.

19) Review taxpayer accounts, and conduct audits on-site, by correspondence, or by summoning taxpayer to office.

Knowledge	Knowledge Definitions
Economics and Accounting	Knowledge of economic and accounting principles and practices, the financial markets, banking and the analysis and reporting of financial data.
English Language	Knowledge of the structure and content of the English language including the meaning and spelling of words, rules of composition, and grammar.
Customer and Personal Service	Knowledge of principles and processes for providing customer and personal services. This includes customer needs assessment, meeting quality standards for services, and evaluation of customer satisfaction.
Mathematics	Knowledge of arithmetic, algebra, geometry, calculus, statistics, and their applications.
Computers and Electronics	Knowledge of circuit boards, processors, chips, electronic equipment, and computer hardware and software, including applications and programming.
Administration and Management	Knowledge of business and management principles involved in strategic planning, resource allocation, human resources modeling, leadership technique, production methods, and coordination of people and resources.
Law and Government	Knowledge of laws, legal codes, court procedures, precedents, government regulations, executive orders, agency rules, and the democratic political process.
Education and Training	Knowledge of principles and methods for curriculum and training design, teaching and instruction for individuals and groups, and the measurement of training effects.
Sales and Marketing	Knowledge of principles and methods for showing, promoting, and selling products or services. This includes marketing strategy and tactics, product demonstration, sales techniques, and sales control systems.
Clerical	Knowledge of administrative and clerical procedures and systems such as word processing, managing files and records, stenography and transcription, designing forms, and other office procedures and terminology.
Personnel and Human Resources	Knowledge of principles and procedures for personnel recruitment, selection, training, compensation and benefits, labor relations and negotiation, and personnel information systems.
Communications and Media	Knowledge of media production, communication, and dissemination techniques and methods. This includes alternative ways to inform and entertain via written, oral, and visual media.
Production and Processing	Knowledge of raw materials, production processes, quality control, costs, and other techniques for maximizing the effective manufacture and distribution of goods.
Telecommunications	Knowledge of transmission, broadcasting, switching, control, and operation of telecommunications systems.
Psychology	Knowledge of human behavior and performance; individual differences in ability, personality, and interests; learning and motivation; psychological research methods; and the assessment and treatment of behavioral and affective disorders.
Transportation	Knowledge of principles and methods for moving people or goods by air, rail, sea, or road, including the relative costs and benefits.
Philosophy and Theology	Knowledge of different philosophical systems and religions. This includes their basic principles, values, ethics, ways of thinking, customs, practices, and their impact on human culture.
Therapy and Counseling	Knowledge of principles, methods, and procedures for diagnosis, treatment, and rehabilitation of physical and mental dysfunctions, and for career counseling and guidance.
Sociology and Anthropology	Knowledge of group behavior and dynamics, societal trends and influences, human migrations, ethnicity, cultures and their history and origins.
Foreign Language	Knowledge of the structure and content of a foreign (non-English) language including the meaning and spelling of words, rules of composition and grammar, and pronunciation.
Public Safety and Security	Knowledge of relevant equipment, policies, procedures, and strategies to promote effective local, state, or national security operations for the protection of people, data, property, and institutions.
Food Production	Knowledge of techniques and equipment for planting, growing, and harvesting food products (both plant and animal) for consumption, including storage/handling techniques.
Geography	Knowledge of principles and methods for describing the features of land, sea, and air masses, including their physical characteristics, locations, interrelationships, and distribution of plant, animal, and human life.
Engineering and Technology	Knowledge of the practical application of engineering science and technology. This includes applying principles, techniques, procedures, and equipment to the design and production of various goods and services.
Building and Construction	Knowledge of materials, methods, and the tools involved in the construction or repair of houses, buildings, or other structures such as highways and roads.
Mechanical	Knowledge of machines and tools, including their designs, uses, repair, and maintenance.
History and Archeology	Knowledge of historical events and their causes, indicators, and effects on civilizations and cultures.
Design	Knowledge of design techniques, tools, and principles involved in production of precision technical plans, blueprints, drawings, and models.
Fine Arts	Knowledge of the theory and techniques required to compose, produce, and perform works of music, dance, visual arts, drama, and sculpture.
Medicine and Dentistry	Knowledge of the information and techniques needed to diagnose and treat human injuries, diseases, and deformities. This includes symptoms, treatment alternatives, drug properties and interactions, and preventive health-care measures.
Chemistry	Knowledge of the chemical composition, structure, and properties of substances and of the chemical processes and transformations that they undergo. This includes uses of chemicals and their interactions, danger signs, production techniques, and disposal methods.
Physics	Knowledge and prediction of physical principles, laws, their interrelationships, and applications to understanding fluid, material, and atmospheric dynamics, and mechanical, electrical, atomic and sub-atomic structures and processes.
Biology	Knowledge of plant and animal organisms, their tissues, cells, functions, interdependencies, and interactions with each other and the environment.

Skills	Skills Definitions
Time Management	Managing one's own time and the time of others.
Mathematics	Using mathematics to solve problems.
Active Learning	Understanding the implications of new information for both current and future problem-solving and decision-making.
Critical Thinking	Using logic and reasoning to identify the strengths and weaknesses of alternative solutions, conclusions or approaches to problems.
Reading Comprehension	Understanding written sentences and paragraphs in work related documents.
Active Listening	Giving full attention to what other people are saying, taking time to understand the points being made, asking questions as appropriate, and not interrupting at inappropriate times.
Writing	Communicating effectively in writing as appropriate for the needs of the audience.
Speaking	Talking to others to convey information effectively.
Coordination	Adjusting actions in relation to others' actions.
Judgment and Decision Making	Considering the relative costs and benefits of potential actions to choose the most appropriate one.
Monitoring	Monitoring/Assessing performance of yourself, other individuals, or organizations to make improvements or take corrective action.
Instructing	Teaching others how to do something.
Social Perceptiveness	Being aware of others' reactions and understanding why they react as they do.
Complex Problem Solving	Identifying complex problems and reviewing related information to develop and evaluate options and implement solutions.
Management of Personnel Resources	Motivating, developing, and directing people as they work, identifying the best people for the job.
Service Orientation	Actively looking for ways to help people.
Learning Strategies	Selecting and using training/instructional methods and procedures appropriate for the situation when learning or teaching new things.
Negotiation	Bringing others together and trying to reconcile differences.
Management of Financial Resources	Determining how money will be spent to get the work done, and accounting for these expenditures.
Persuasion	Persuading others to change their minds or behavior.
Operations Analysis	Analyzing needs and product requirements to create a design.

Quality Control Analysis	Conducting tests and inspections of products, services, or processes to evaluate quality or performance.
Management of Material Resources	Obtaining and seeing to the appropriate use of equipment, facilities, and materials needed to do certain work.
Systems Evaluation	Identifying measures or indicators of system performance and the actions needed to improve or correct performance, relative to the goals of the system.
Troubleshooting	Determining causes of operating errors and deciding what to do about it.
Technology Design	Generating or adapting equipment and technology to serve user needs.
Systems Analysis	Determining how a system should work and how changes in conditions, operations, and the environment will affect outcomes.
Equipment Selection	Determining the kind of tools and equipment needed to do a job.
Operation Monitoring	Watching gauges, dials, or other indicators to make sure a machine is working properly.
Operation and Control	Controlling operations of equipment or systems.
Installation	Installing equipment, machines, wiring, or programs to meet specifications.
Programming	Writing computer programs for various purposes.
Equipment Maintenance	Performing routine maintenance on equipment and determining when and what kind of maintenance is needed.
Repairing	Repairing machines or systems using the needed tools.
Science	Using scientific rules and methods to solve problems.

Ability	**Ability Definitions**
Written Comprehension	The ability to read and understand information and ideas presented in writing.
Near Vision	The ability to see details at close range (within a few feet of the observer).
Oral Comprehension	The ability to listen to and understand information and ideas presented through spoken words and sentences.
Inductive Reasoning	The ability to combine pieces of information to form general rules or conclusions (includes finding a relationship among seemingly unrelated events).
Problem Sensitivity	The ability to tell when something is wrong or is likely to go wrong. It does not involve solving the problem, only recognizing there is a problem.
Oral Expression	The ability to communicate information and ideas in speaking so others will understand.
Speech Clarity	The ability to speak clearly so others can understand you.
Speech Recognition	The ability to identify and understand the speech of another person.
Mathematical Reasoning	The ability to choose the right mathematical methods or formulas to solve a problem.
Number Facility	The ability to add, subtract, multiply, or divide quickly and correctly.
Written Expression	The ability to communicate information and ideas in writing so others will understand.
Deductive Reasoning	The ability to apply general rules to specific problems to produce answers that make sense.
Information Ordering	The ability to arrange things or actions in a certain order or pattern according to a specific rule or set of rules (e.g., patterns of numbers, letters, words, pictures, mathematical operations).
Flexibility of Closure	The ability to identify or detect a known pattern (a figure, object, word, or sound) that is hidden in other distracting material.
Selective Attention	The ability to concentrate on a task over a period of time without being distracted.
Category Flexibility	The ability to generate or use different sets of rules for combining or grouping things in different ways.
Perceptual Speed	The ability to quickly and accurately compare similarities and differences among sets of letters, numbers, objects, pictures, or patterns. The things to be compared may be presented at the same time or one after the other. This ability also includes comparing a presented object with a remembered object.
Finger Dexterity	The ability to make precisely coordinated movements of the fingers of one or both hands to grasp, manipulate, or assemble very small objects
Time Sharing	The ability to shift back and forth between two or more activities or sources of information (such as speech, sounds, touch, or other sources).
Speed of Closure	The ability to quickly make sense of, combine, and organize information into meaningful patterns.

Memorization	The ability to remember information such as words, numbers, pictures, and procedures.
Fluency of Ideas	The ability to come up with a number of ideas about a topic (the number of ideas is important, not their quality, correctness, or creativity).
Far Vision	The ability to see details at a distance.
Originality	The ability to come up with unusual or clever ideas about a given topic or situation, or to develop creative ways to solve a problem.
Auditory Attention	The ability to focus on a single source of sound in the presence of other distracting sounds.
Arm-Hand Steadiness	The ability to keep your hand and arm steady while moving your arm or while holding your arm and hand in one position.
Visual Color Discrimination	The ability to match or detect differences between colors, including shades of color and brightness.
Visualization	The ability to imagine how something will look after it is moved around or when its parts are moved or rearranged.
Manual Dexterity	The ability to quickly move your hand, your hand together with your arm, or your two hands to grasp, manipulate, or assemble objects.
Control Precision	The ability to quickly and repeatedly adjust the controls of a machine or a vehicle to exact positions.
Hearing Sensitivity	The ability to detect or tell the differences between sounds that vary in pitch and loudness.
Depth Perception	The ability to judge which of several objects is closer or farther away from you, or to judge the distance between you and an object.
Multilimb Coordination	The ability to coordinate two or more limbs (for example, two arms, two legs, or one leg and one arm) while sitting, standing, or lying down. It does not involve performing the activities while the whole body is in motion.
Trunk Strength	The ability to use your abdominal and lower back muscles to support part of the body repeatedly or continuously over time without 'giving out' or fatiguing.
Wrist-Finger Speed	The ability to make fast, simple, repeated movements of the fingers, hands, and wrists.
Static Strength	The ability to exert maximum muscle force to lift, push, pull, or carry objects.
Extent Flexibility	The ability to bend, stretch, twist, or reach with your body, arms, and/or legs.
Glare Sensitivity	The ability to see objects in the presence of glare or bright lighting.
Gross Body Coordination	The ability to coordinate the movement of your arms, legs, and torso together when the whole body is in motion.
Speed of Limb Movement	The ability to quickly move the arms and legs.
Night Vision	The ability to see under low light conditions.
Peripheral Vision	The ability to see objects or movement of objects to one's side when the eyes are looking ahead.
Rate Control	The ability to time your movements or the movement of a piece of equipment in anticipation of changes in the speed and/or direction of a moving object or scene.
Dynamic Flexibility	The ability to quickly and repeatedly bend, stretch, twist, or reach out with your body, arms, and/or legs.
Stamina	The ability to exert yourself physically over long periods of time without getting winded or out of breath.
Dynamic Strength	The ability to exert muscle force repeatedly or continuously over time. This involves muscular endurance and resistance to muscle fatigue.
Response Orientation	The ability to choose quickly between two or more movements in response to two or more different signals (lights, sounds, pictures). It includes the speed with which the correct response is started with the hand, foot, or other body part.
Sound Localization	The ability to tell the direction from which a sound originated.
Spatial Orientation	The ability to know your location in relation to the environment or to know where other objects are in relation to you.
Gross Body Equilibrium	The ability to keep or regain your body balance or stay upright when in an unstable position.
Reaction Time	The ability to quickly respond (with the hand, finger, or foot) to a signal (sound, light, picture) when it appears.
Explosive Strength	The ability to use short bursts of muscle force to propel oneself (as in jumping or sprinting), or to throw an object.

Work_Activity	**Work_Activity Definitions**
Getting Information	Observing, receiving, and otherwise obtaining information from all relevant sources.

Evaluating Information to Determine Compliance wit	Using relevant information and individual judgment to determine whether events or processes comply with laws, regulations, or standards.
Analyzing Data or Information	Identifying the underlying principles, reasons, or facts of information by breaking down information or data into separate parts.
Interacting With Computers	Using computers and computer systems (including hardware and software) to program, write software, set up functions, enter data, or process information.
Establishing and Maintaining Interpersonal Relatio	Developing constructive and cooperative working relationships with others, and maintaining them over time.
Communicating with Supervisors, Peers, or Subordin	Providing information to supervisors, co-workers, and subordinates by telephone, in written form, e-mail, or in person.
Processing Information	Compiling, coding, categorizing, calculating, tabulating, auditing, or verifying information or data.
Identifying Objects, Actions, and Events	Identifying information by categorizing, estimating, recognizing differences or similarities, and detecting changes in circumstances or events.
Organizing, Planning, and Prioritizing Work	Developing specific goals and plans to prioritize, organize, and accomplish your work.
Monitor Processes, Materials, or Surroundings	Monitoring and reviewing information from materials, events, or the environment, to detect or assess problems.
Judging the Qualities of Things, Services, or Peop	Assessing the value, importance, or quality of things or people.
Making Decisions and Solving Problems	Analyzing information and evaluating results to choose the best solution and solve problems.
Updating and Using Relevant Knowledge	Keeping up-to-date technically and applying new knowledge to your job.
Documenting/Recording Information	Entering, transcribing, recording, storing, or maintaining information in written or electronic/magnetic form.
Communicating with Persons Outside Organization	Communicating with people outside the organization, representing the organization to customers, the public, government, and other external sources. This information can be exchanged in person, in writing, or by telephone or e-mail.
Interpreting the Meaning of Information for Others	Translating or explaining what information means and how it can be used.
Resolving Conflicts and Negotiating with Others	Handling complaints, settling disputes, and resolving grievances and conflicts, or otherwise negotiating with others.
Provide Consultation and Advice to Others	Providing guidance and expert advice to management or other groups on technical, systems-, or process-related topics.
Estimating the Quantifiable Characteristics of Pro	Estimating sizes, distances, and quantities; or determining time, costs, resources, or materials needed to perform a work activity.
Thinking Creatively	Developing, designing, or creating new applications, ideas, relationships, systems, or products, including artistic contributions.
Developing Objectives and Strategies	Establishing long-range objectives and specifying the strategies and actions to achieve them.
Scheduling Work and Activities	Scheduling events, programs, and activities, as well as the work of others.
Monitoring and Controlling Resources	Monitoring and controlling resources and overseeing the spending of money.
Guiding, Directing, and Motivating Subordinates	Providing guidance and direction to subordinates, including setting performance standards and monitoring performance.
Performing Administrative Activities	Performing day-to-day administrative tasks such as maintaining information files and processing paperwork.
Coordinating the Work and Activities of Others	Getting members of a group to work together to accomplish tasks.
Developing and Building Teams	Encouraging and building mutual trust, respect, and cooperation among team members.
Training and Teaching Others	Identifying the educational needs of others, developing formal educational or training programs or classes, and teaching or instructing others.
Coaching and Developing Others	Identifying the developmental needs of others and coaching, mentoring, or otherwise helping others to improve their knowledge or skills.
Selling or Influencing Others	Convincing others to buy merchandise/goods or to otherwise change their minds or actions.
Assisting and Caring for Others	Providing personal assistance, medical attention, emotional support, or other personal care to others such as coworkers, customers, or patients.
Performing for or Working Directly with the Public	Performing for people or dealing directly with the public. This includes serving customers in restaurants and stores, and receiving clients or guests.

Inspecting Equipment, Structures, or Material	Inspecting equipment, structures, or materials to identify the cause of errors or other problems or defects.
Controlling Machines and Processes	Using either control mechanisms or direct physical activity to operate machines or processes (not including computers or vehicles).
Performing General Physical Activities	Performing physical activities that require considerable use of your arms and legs and moving your whole body, such as climbing, lifting, balancing, walking, stooping, and handling of materials.
Staffing Organizational Units	Recruiting, interviewing, selecting, hiring, and promoting employees in an organization.
Handling and Moving Objects	Using hands and arms in handling, installing, positioning, and moving materials, and manipulating things.
Operating Vehicles, Mechanized Devices, or Equipme	Running, maneuvering, navigating, or driving vehicles or mechanized equipment, such as forklifts, passenger vehicles, aircraft, or water craft.
Drafting, Laying Out, and Specifying Technical Dev	Providing documentation, detailed instructions, drawings, or specifications to tell others about how devices, parts, equipment, or structures are to be fabricated, constructed, assembled, modified, maintained, or used.
Repairing and Maintaining Electronic Equipment	Servicing, repairing, calibrating, regulating, fine-tuning, or testing machines, devices, and equipment that operate primarily on the basis of electrical or electronic (not mechanical) principles.
Repairing and Maintaining Mechanical Equipment	Servicing, repairing, adjusting, and testing machines, devices, moving parts, and equipment that operate primarily on the basis of mechanical (not electronic) principles.

Work_Context	Work_Context Definitions
Telephone	How often do you have telephone conversations in this job?
Face-to-Face Discussions	How often do you have to have face-to-face discussions with individuals or teams in this job?
Electronic Mail	How often do you use electronic mail in this job?
Importance of Being Exact or Accurate	How important is being very exact or highly accurate in performing this job?
Contact With Others	How much does this job require the worker to be in contact with others (face-to-face, by telephone, or otherwise) in order to perform it?
Work With Work Group or Team	How important is it to work with others in a group or team in this job?
Spend Time Sitting	How much does this job require sitting?
Indoors, Environmentally Controlled	How often does this job require working indoors in environmentally controlled conditions?
Structured versus Unstructured Work	To what extent is this job structured for the worker, rather than allowing the worker to determine tasks, priorities, and goals?
Frequency of Decision Making	How frequently is the worker required to make decisions that affect other people, the financial resources, and/or the image and reputation of the organization?
Letters and Memos	How often does the job require written letters and memos?
Time Pressure	How often does the job require the worker to meet strict deadlines?
Impact of Decisions on Co-workers or Company Resul	How do the decisions an employee makes impact the results of co-workers, clients or the company?
Freedom to Make Decisions	How much decision making freedom, without supervision, does the job offer?
Importance of Repeating Same Tasks	How important is repeating the same physical activities (e.g., key entry) or mental activities (e.g., checking entries in a ledger) over and over, without stopping, to performing this job?
Consequence of Error	How serious would the result usually be if the worker made a mistake that was not readily correctable?
Coordinate or Lead Others	How important is it to coordinate or lead others in accomplishing work activities in this job?
Spend Time Making Repetitive Motions	How much does this job require making repetitive motions?
Level of Competition	To what extent does this job require the worker to compete or to be aware of competitive pressures?
Degree of Automation	How automated is the job?
Spend Time Using Your Hands to Handle, Control, or	How much does this job require using your hands to handle, control, or feel objects, tools or controls?
In an Enclosed Vehicle or Equipment	How often does this job require working in a closed vehicle or equipment (e.g., car)?
Frequency of Conflict Situations	How often are there conflict situations the employee has to face in this job?
Responsibility for Outcomes and Results	How responsible is the worker for work outcomes and results of other workers?

135

Sounds, Noise Levels Are Distracting or Uncomforta	How often does this job require working exposed to sounds and noise levels that are distracting or uncomfortable?
Deal With External Customers	How important is it to work with external customers or the public in this job?
Deal With Unpleasant or Angry People	How frequently does the worker have to deal with unpleasant, angry, or discourteous individuals as part of the job requirements?
Responsible for Others' Health and Safety	How much responsibility is there for the health and safety of others in this job?
Physical Proximity	To what extent does this job require the worker to perform job tasks in close physical proximity to other people?
Public Speaking	How often do you have to perform public speaking in this job?
Spend Time Standing	How much does this job require standing?
Exposed to Hazardous Equipment	How often does this job require exposure to hazardous equipment?
Spend Time Walking and Running	How much does this job require walking and running?
Wear Common Protective or Safety Equipment such as	How much does this job require wearing common protective or safety equipment such as safety shoes, glasses, gloves, hard hats or life jackets?
Pace Determined by Speed of Equipment	How important is it to this job that the pace is determined by the speed of equipment or machinery? (This does not refer to keeping busy at all times on this job.)
Spend Time Bending or Twisting the Body	How much does this job require bending or twisting your body?
Indoors, Not Environmentally Controlled	How often does this job require working indoors in non-controlled environmental conditions (e.g., warehouse without heat)?
Cramped Work Space, Awkward Positions	How often does this job require working in cramped work spaces that requires getting into awkward positions?
Extremely Bright or Inadequate Lighting	How often does this job require working in extremely bright or inadequate lighting conditions?
Deal With Physically Aggressive People	How frequently does this job require the worker to deal with physical aggression of violent individuals?
Very Hot or Cold Temperatures	How often does this job require working in very hot (above 90 F degrees) or very cold (below 32 F degrees) temperatures?
In an Open Vehicle or Equipment	How often does this job require working in an open vehicle or equipment (e.g., tractor)?
Exposed to Contaminants	How often does this job require working exposed to contaminants (such as pollutants, gases, dust or odors)?
Outdoors, Exposed to Weather	How often does this job require working outdoors, exposed to all weather conditions?
Outdoors, Under Cover	How often does this job require working outdoors, under cover (e.g., structure with roof but no walls)?
Spend Time Kneeling, Crouching, Stooping, or Crawl	How much does this job require kneeling, crouching, stooping, or crawling?
Exposed to Minor Burns, Cuts, Bites, or Stings	How often does this job require exposure to minor burns, cuts, bites, or stings?
Exposed to Disease or Infections	How often does this job require exposure to disease/infections?
Spend Time Keeping or Regaining Balance	How much does this job require keeping or regaining your balance?
Spend Time Climbing Ladders, Scaffolds, or Poles	How much does this job require climbing ladders, scaffolds, or poles?
Exposed to Whole Body Vibration	How often does this job require exposure to whole body vibration (e.g., operate a jackhammer)?
Exposed to Hazardous Conditions	How often does this job require exposure to hazardous conditions?
Exposed to High Places	How often does this job require exposure to high places?
Exposed to Radiation	How often does this job require exposure to radiation?
Wear Specialized Protective or Safety Equipment su	How much does this job require wearing specialized protective or safety equipment such as breathing apparatus, safety harness, full protection suits, or radiation protection?

Job Zone Component	Job Zone Component Definitions
Title	Job Zone Four: Considerable Preparation Needed
Overall Experience	A minimum of two to four years of work-related skill, knowledge, or experience is needed for these occupations. For example, an accountant must complete four years of college and work for several years in accounting to be considered qualified.
Job Training	Employees in these occupations usually need several years of work-related experience, on-the-job training, and/or vocational training.

Job Zone Examples	Many of these occupations involve coordinating, supervising, managing, or training others. Examples include accountants, chefs and head cooks, computer programmers, historians, pharmacists, and police detectives.
SVP Range	(7.0 to < 8.0)
Education	Most of these occupations require a four - year bachelor's degree, but some do not.

Work_Styles	Work_Styles Definitions
Analytical Thinking	Job requires analyzing information and using logic to address work-related issues and problems.
Integrity	Job requires being honest and ethical.
Attention to Detail	Job requires being careful about detail and thorough in completing work tasks.
Initiative	Job requires a willingness to take on responsibilities and challenges.
Achievement/Effort	Job requires establishing and maintaining personally challenging achievement goals and exerting effort toward mastering tasks.
Dependability	Job requires being reliable, responsible, and dependable, and fulfilling obligations.
Leadership	Job requires a willingness to lead, take charge, and offer opinions and direction.
Independence	Job requires developing one's own ways of doing things, guiding oneself with little or no supervision, and depending on oneself to get things done.
Stress Tolerance	Job requires accepting criticism and dealing calmly and effectively with high stress situations.
Cooperation	Job requires being pleasant with others on the job and displaying a good-natured, cooperative attitude.
Adaptability/Flexibility	Job requires being open to change (positive or negative) and to considerable variety in the workplace.
Self Control	Job requires maintaining composure, keeping emotions in check, controlling anger, and avoiding aggressive behavior, even in very difficult situations.
Persistence	Job requires persistence in the face of obstacles.
Innovation	Job requires creativity and alternative thinking to develop new ideas for and answers to work-related problems.
Social Orientation	Job requires preferring to work with others rather than alone, and being personally connected with others on the job.
Concern for Others	Job requires being sensitive to others' needs and feelings and being understanding and helpful on the job.

13-2021.01 - Assessors

Appraise real and personal property to determine its fair value. May assess taxes in accordance with prescribed schedules.

Tasks

1) Inspect properties, considering factors such as market value, location, and building or replacement costs to determine appraisal value.

2) Explain assessed values to property owners and defend appealed assessments at public hearings.

3) Inspect new construction and major improvements to existing structures in order to determine values.

4) Analyze trends in sales prices, construction costs, and rents, in order to assess property values and/or determine the accuracy of assessments.

5) Prepare and maintain current data on each parcel assessed, including maps of boundaries, inventories of land and structures, property characteristics, and any applicable exemptions.

6) Review information about transfers of property to ensure its accuracy, checking basic information on buyers, sellers, and sales prices and making corrections as necessary.

7) Maintain familiarity with aspects of local real estate markets.

8) Conduct regular reviews of property within jurisdictions in order to determine changes in property due to construction or demolition.

9) Complete and maintain assessment rolls that show the assessed values and status of all property in a municipality.

10) Identify the ownership of each piece of taxable property.

11) Approve applications for property tax exemptions or deductions.

12) Issue notices of assessments and taxes.

13) Calculate tax bills for properties by multiplying assessed values by jurisdiction tax rates.

14) Establish uniform and equitable systems for assessing all classes and kinds of property.

15) Write and submit appraisal and tax reports for public record.

16) Provide sales analyses to be used for equalization of school aid.

17) Hire staff members.

18) Serve on assessment review boards.

Knowledge	Knowledge Definitions
Customer and Personal Service	Knowledge of principles and processes for providing customer and personal services. This includes customer needs assessment, meeting quality standards for services, and evaluation of customer satisfaction.
Mathematics	Knowledge of arithmetic, algebra, geometry, calculus, statistics, and their applications.
Building and Construction	Knowledge of materials, methods, and the tools involved in the construction or repair of houses, buildings, or other structures such as highways and roads.
Law and Government	Knowledge of laws, legal codes, court procedures, precedents, government regulations, executive orders, agency rules, and the democratic political process.
Computers and Electronics	Knowledge of circuit boards, processors, chips, electronic equipment, and computer hardware and software, including applications and programming.
English Language	Knowledge of the structure and content of the English language including the meaning and spelling of words, rules of composition, and grammar.
Clerical	Knowledge of administrative and clerical procedures and systems such as word processing, managing files and records, stenography and transcription, designing forms, and other office procedures and terminology.
Geography	Knowledge of principles and methods for describing the features of land, sea, and air masses, including their physical characteristics, locations, interrelationships, and distribution of plant, animal, and human life.
Economics and Accounting	Knowledge of economic and accounting principles and practices, the financial markets, banking and the analysis and reporting of financial data.
Administration and Management	Knowledge of business and management principles involved in strategic planning, resource allocation, human resources modeling, leadership technique, production methods, and coordination of people and resources.
Communications and Media	Knowledge of media production, communication, and dissemination techniques and methods. This includes alternative ways to inform and entertain via written, oral, and visual media.
Public Safety and Security	Knowledge of relevant equipment, policies, procedures, and strategies to promote effective local, state, or national security operations for the protection of people, data, property, and institutions.
Education and Training	Knowledge of principles and methods for curriculum and training design, teaching and instruction for individuals and groups, and the measurement of training effects.
Design	Knowledge of design techniques, tools, and principles involved in production of precision technical plans, blueprints, drawings, and models.
Transportation	Knowledge of principles and methods for moving people or goods by air, rail, sea, or road, including the relative costs and benefits.
Personnel and Human Resources	Knowledge of principles and procedures for personnel recruitment, selection, training, compensation and benefits, labor relations and negotiation, and personnel information systems.
Psychology	Knowledge of human behavior and performance; individual differences in ability, personality, and interests; learning and motivation; psychological research methods; and the assessment and treatment of behavioral and affective disorders.
Production and Processing	Knowledge of raw materials, production processes, quality control, costs, and other techniques for maximizing the effective manufacture and distribution of goods.
Sales and Marketing	Knowledge of principles and methods for showing, promoting, and selling products or services. This includes marketing strategy and tactics, product demonstration, sales techniques, and sales control systems.
Telecommunications	Knowledge of transmission, broadcasting, switching, control, and operation of telecommunications systems.
History and Archeology	Knowledge of historical events and their causes, indicators, and effects on civilizations and cultures.
Sociology and Anthropology	Knowledge of group behavior and dynamics, societal trends and influences, human migrations, ethnicity, cultures and their history and origins.
Engineering and Technology	Knowledge of the practical application of engineering science and technology. This includes applying principles, techniques, procedures, and equipment to the design and production of various goods and services.
Physics	Knowledge and prediction of physical principles, laws, their interrelationships, and applications to understanding fluid, material, and atmospheric dynamics, and mechanical, electrical, atomic and sub-atomic structures and processes.
Mechanical	Knowledge of machines and tools, including their designs, uses, repair, and maintenance.
Therapy and Counseling	Knowledge of principles, methods, and procedures for diagnosis, treatment, and rehabilitation of physical and mental dysfunctions, and for career counseling and guidance.
Foreign Language	Knowledge of the structure and content of a foreign (non-English) language including the meaning and spelling of words, rules of composition and grammar, and pronunciation.
Philosophy and Theology	Knowledge of different philosophical systems and religions. This includes their basic principles, values, ethics, ways of thinking, customs, practices, and their impact on human culture.
Food Production	Knowledge of techniques and equipment for planting, growing, and harvesting food products (both plant and animal) for consumption, including storage/handling techniques.
Medicine and Dentistry	Knowledge of the information and techniques needed to diagnose and treat human injuries, diseases, and deformities. This includes symptoms, treatment alternatives, drug properties and interactions, and preventive health-care measures.
Chemistry	Knowledge of the chemical composition, structure, and properties of substances and of the chemical processes and transformations that they undergo. This includes uses of chemicals and their interactions, danger signs, production techniques, and disposal methods.
Fine Arts	Knowledge of the theory and techniques required to compose, produce, and perform works of music, dance, visual arts, drama, and sculpture.
Biology	Knowledge of plant and animal organisms, their tissues, cells, functions, interdependencies, and interactions with each other and the environment.

Skills	Skills Definitions
Active Listening	Giving full attention to what other people are saying, taking time to understand the points being made, asking questions as appropriate, and not interrupting at inappropriate times.
Reading Comprehension	Understanding written sentences and paragraphs in work related documents.
Speaking	Talking to others to convey information effectively.
Mathematics	Using mathematics to solve problems.
Time Management	Managing one's own time and the time of others.
Active Learning	Understanding the implications of new information for both current and future problem-solving and decision-making.
Social Perceptiveness	Being aware of others' reactions and understanding why they react as they do.
Critical Thinking	Using logic and reasoning to identify the strengths and weaknesses of alternative solutions, conclusions or approaches to problems.
Writing	Communicating effectively in writing as appropriate for the needs of the audience.
Coordination	Adjusting actions in relation to others' actions.
Service Orientation	Actively looking for ways to help people.
Persuasion	Persuading others to change their minds or behavior.
Complex Problem Solving	Identifying complex problems and reviewing related information to develop and evaluate options and implement solutions.
Judgment and Decision Making	Considering the relative costs and benefits of potential actions to choose the most appropriate one.
Negotiation	Bringing others together and trying to reconcile differences.

Learning Strategies	Selecting and using training/instructional methods and procedures appropriate for the situation when learning or teaching new things.
Instructing	Teaching others how to do something.
Monitoring	Monitoring/Assessing performance of yourself, other individuals, or organizations to make improvements or take corrective action.
Systems Analysis	Determining how a system should work and how changes in conditions, operations, and the environment will affect outcomes.
Equipment Selection	Determining the kind of tools and equipment needed to do a job.
Management of Personnel Resources	Motivating, developing, and directing people as they work, identifying the best people for the job.
Operations Analysis	Analyzing needs and product requirements to create a design.
Systems Evaluation	Identifying measures or indicators of system performance and the actions needed to improve or correct performance, relative to the goals of the system.
Management of Financial Resources	Determining how money will be spent to get the work done, and accounting for these expenditures.
Quality Control Analysis	Conducting tests and inspections of products, services, or processes to evaluate quality or performance.
Technology Design	Generating or adapting equipment and technology to serve user needs.
Operation Monitoring	Watching gauges, dials, or other indicators to make sure a machine is working properly.
Management of Material Resources	Obtaining and seeing to the appropriate use of equipment, facilities, and materials needed to do certain work.
Troubleshooting	Determining causes of operating errors and deciding what to do about it.
Operation and Control	Controlling operations of equipment or systems.
Science	Using scientific rules and methods to solve problems.
Programming	Writing computer programs for various purposes.
Equipment Maintenance	Performing routine maintenance on equipment and determining when and what kind of maintenance is needed.
Installation	Installing equipment, machines, wiring, or programs to meet specifications.
Repairing	Repairing machines or systems using the needed tools.

Ability — Ability Definitions

Ability	Ability Definitions
Inductive Reasoning	The ability to combine pieces of information to form general rules or conclusions (includes finding a relationship among seemingly unrelated events).
Oral Comprehension	The ability to listen to and understand information and ideas presented through spoken words and sentences.
Deductive Reasoning	The ability to apply general rules to specific problems to produce answers that make sense.
Written Comprehension	The ability to read and understand information and ideas presented in writing.
Oral Expression	The ability to communicate information and ideas in speaking so others will understand.
Near Vision	The ability to see details at close range (within a few feet of the observer).
Speech Clarity	The ability to speak clearly so others can understand you.
Problem Sensitivity	The ability to tell when something is wrong or is likely to go wrong. It does not involve solving the problem, only recognizing there is a problem.
Speech Recognition	The ability to identify and understand the speech of another person.
Information Ordering	The ability to arrange things or actions in a certain order or pattern according to a specific rule or set of rules (e.g., patterns of numbers, letters, words, pictures, mathematical operations).
Category Flexibility	The ability to generate or use different sets of rules for combining or grouping things in different ways.
Selective Attention	The ability to concentrate on a task over a period of time without being distracted.
Written Expression	The ability to communicate information and ideas in writing so others will understand.
Perceptual Speed	The ability to quickly and accurately compare similarities and differences among sets of letters, numbers, objects, pictures, or patterns. The things to be compared may be presented at the same time or one after the other. This ability also includes comparing a presented object with a remembered object.
Mathematical Reasoning	The ability to choose the right mathematical methods or formulas to solve a problem.
Number Facility	The ability to add, subtract, multiply, or divide quickly and correctly.

Far Vision	The ability to see details at a distance.
Fluency of Ideas	The ability to come up with a number of ideas about a topic (the number of ideas is important, not their quality, correctness, or creativity).
Originality	The ability to come up with unusual or clever ideas about a given topic or situation, or to develop creative ways to solve a problem.
Speed of Closure	The ability to quickly make sense of, combine, and organize information into meaningful patterns.
Time Sharing	The ability to shift back and forth between two or more activities or sources of information (such as speech, sounds, touch, or other sources).
Flexibility of Closure	The ability to identify or detect a known pattern (a figure, object, word, or sound) that is hidden in other distracting material.
Depth Perception	The ability to judge which of several objects is closer or farther away from you, or to judge the distance between you and an object.
Visualization	The ability to imagine how something will look after it is moved around or when its parts are moved or rearranged.
Finger Dexterity	The ability to make precisely coordinated movements of the fingers of one or both hands to grasp, manipulate, or assemble very small objects.
Visual Color Discrimination	The ability to match or detect differences between colors, including shades of color and brightness.
Trunk Strength	The ability to use your abdominal and lower back muscles to support part of the body repeatedly or continuously over time without 'giving out' or fatiguing.
Control Precision	The ability to quickly and repeatedly adjust the controls of a machine or a vehicle to exact positions.
Memorization	The ability to remember information such as words, numbers, pictures, and procedures.
Arm-Hand Steadiness	The ability to keep your hand and arm steady while moving your arm or while holding your arm and hand in one position.
Stamina	The ability to exert yourself physically over long periods of time without getting winded or out of breath.
Hearing Sensitivity	The ability to detect or tell the differences between sounds that vary in pitch and loudness.
Gross Body Coordination	The ability to coordinate the movement of your arms, legs, and torso together when the whole body is in motion.
Auditory Attention	The ability to focus on a single source of sound in the presence of other distracting sounds.
Multilimb Coordination	The ability to coordinate two or more limbs (for example, two arms, two legs, or one leg and one arm) while sitting, standing, or lying down. It does not involve performing the activities while the whole body is in motion.
Extent Flexibility	The ability to bend, stretch, twist, or reach with your body, arms, and/or legs.
Gross Body Equilibrium	The ability to keep or regain your body balance or stay upright when in an unstable position.
Manual Dexterity	The ability to quickly move your hand, your hand together with your arm, or your two hands to grasp, manipulate, or assemble objects.
Dynamic Strength	The ability to exert muscle force repeatedly or continuously over time. This involves muscular endurance and resistance to muscle fatigue.
Static Strength	The ability to exert maximum muscle force to lift, push, pull, or carry objects.
Speed of Limb Movement	The ability to quickly move the arms and legs.
Spatial Orientation	The ability to know your location in relation to the environment or to know where other objects are in relation to you.
Night Vision	The ability to see under low light conditions.
Wrist-Finger Speed	The ability to make fast, simple, repeated movements of the fingers, hands, and wrists.
Peripheral Vision	The ability to see objects or movement of objects to one's side when the eyes are looking ahead.
Reaction Time	The ability to quickly respond (with the hand, finger, or foot) to a signal (sound, light, picture) when it appears.
Response Orientation	The ability to choose quickly between two or more movements in response to two or more different signals (lights, sounds, pictures). It includes the speed with which the correct response is started with the hand, foot, or other body part.
Glare Sensitivity	The ability to see objects in the presence of glare or bright lighting.
Sound Localization	The ability to tell the direction from which a sound originated.
Dynamic Flexibility	The ability to quickly and repeatedly bend, stretch, twist, or reach out with your body, arms, and/or legs.

Explosive Strength	The ability to use short bursts of muscle force to propel oneself (as in jumping or sprinting), or to throw an object.
Rate Control	The ability to time your movements or the movement of a piece of equipment in anticipation of changes in the speed and/or direction of a moving object or scene.

Work_Activity	Work_Activity Definitions
Getting Information	Observing, receiving, and otherwise obtaining information from all relevant sources.
Documenting/Recording Information	Entering, transcribing, recording, storing, or maintaining information in written or electronic/magnetic form.
Interacting With Computers	Using computers and computer systems (including hardware and software) to program, write software, set up functions, enter data, or process information.
Performing for or Working Directly with the Public	Performing for people or dealing directly with the public. This includes serving customers in restaurants and stores, and receiving clients or guests.
Judging the Qualities of Things, Services, or Peop	Assessing the value, importance, or quality of things or people.
Processing Information	Compiling, coding, categorizing, calculating, tabulating, auditing, or verifying information or data.
Updating and Using Relevant Knowledge	Keeping up-to-date technically and applying new knowledge to your job.
Communicating with Supervisors, Peers, or Subordin	Providing information to supervisors, co-workers, and subordinates by telephone, in written form, e-mail, or in person.
Communicating with Persons Outside Organization	Communicating with people outside the organization, representing the organization to customers, the public, government, and other external sources. This information can be exchanged in person, in writing, or by telephone or e-mail.
Analyzing Data or Information	Identifying the underlying principles, reasons, or facts of information by breaking down information or data into separate parts.
Identifying Objects, Actions, and Events	Identifying information by categorizing, estimating, recognizing differences or similarities, and detecting changes in circumstances or events.
Evaluating Information to Determine Compliance wit	Using relevant information and individual judgment to determine whether events or processes comply with laws, regulations, or standards.
Resolving Conflicts and Negotiating with Others	Handling complaints, settling disputes, and resolving grievances and conflicts, or otherwise negotiating with others.
Making Decisions and Solving Problems	Analyzing information and evaluating results to choose the best solution and solve problems.
Organizing, Planning, and Prioritizing Work	Developing specific goals and plans to prioritize, organize, and accomplish your work.
Estimating the Quantifiable Characteristics of Pro	Estimating sizes, distances, and quantities; or determining time, costs, resources, or materials needed to perform a work activity.
Performing Administrative Activities	Performing day-to-day administrative tasks such as maintaining information files and processing paperwork.
Establishing and Maintaining Interpersonal Relatio	Developing constructive and cooperative working relationships with others, and maintaining them over time.
Interpreting the Meaning of Information for Others	Translating or explaining what information means and how it can be used.
Monitor Processes, Materials, or Surroundings	Monitoring and reviewing information from materials, events, or the environment, to detect or assess problems.
Performing General Physical Activities	Performing physical activities that require considerable use of your arms and legs and moving your whole body, such as climbing, lifting, balancing, walking, stooping, and handling of materials.
Inspecting Equipment, Structures, or Material	Inspecting equipment, structures, or materials to identify the cause of errors or other problems or defects.
Scheduling Work and Activities	Scheduling events, programs, and activities, as well as the work of others.
Thinking Creatively	Developing, designing, or creating new applications, ideas, relationships, systems, or products, including artistic contributions.
Developing and Building Teams	Encouraging and building mutual trust, respect, and cooperation among team members.
Guiding, Directing, and Motivating Subordinates	Providing guidance and direction to subordinates, including setting performance standards and monitoring performance.
Developing Objectives and Strategies	Establishing long-range objectives and specifying the strategies and actions to achieve them.
Provide Consultation and Advice to Others	Providing guidance and expert advice to management or other groups on technical, systems-, or process-related topics.

Operating Vehicles, Mechanized Devices, or Equipme	Running, maneuvering, navigating, or driving vehicles or mechanized equipment, such as forklifts, passenger vehicles, aircraft, or water craft.
Training and Teaching Others	Identifying the educational needs of others, developing formal educational or training programs or classes, and teaching or instructing others.
Coordinating the Work and Activities of Others	Getting members of a group to work together to accomplish tasks.
Monitoring and Controlling Resources	Monitoring and controlling resources and overseeing the spending of money.
Coaching and Developing Others	Identifying the developmental needs of others and coaching, mentoring, or otherwise helping others to improve their knowledge or skills.
Handling and Moving Objects	Using hands and arms in handling, installing, positioning, and moving materials, and manipulating things.
Drafting, Laying Out, and Specifying Technical Dev	Providing documentation, detailed instructions, drawings, or specifications to tell others about how devices, parts, equipment, or structures are to be fabricated, constructed, assembled, modified, maintained, or used.
Staffing Organizational Units	Recruiting, interviewing, selecting, hiring, and promoting employees in an organization.
Selling or Influencing Others	Convincing others to buy merchandise/goods or to otherwise change their minds or actions.
Assisting and Caring for Others	Providing personal assistance, medical attention, emotional support, or other personal care to others such as coworkers, customers, or patients.
Controlling Machines and Processes	Using either control mechanisms or direct physical activity to operate machines or processes (not including computers or vehicles).
Repairing and Maintaining Electronic Equipment	Servicing, repairing, calibrating, regulating, fine-tuning, or testing machines, devices, and equipment that operate primarily on the basis of electrical or electronic (not mechanical) principles.
Repairing and Maintaining Mechanical Equipment	Servicing, repairing, adjusting, and testing machines, devices, moving parts, and equipment that operate primarily on the basis of mechanical (not electronic) principles.

Work_Context	Work_Context Definitions
Telephone	How often do you have telephone conversations in this job?
Contact With Others	How much does this job require the worker to be in contact with others (face-to-face, by telephone, or otherwise) in order to perform it?
Face-to-Face Discussions	How often do you have to have face-to-face discussions with individuals or teams in this job?
Indoors, Environmentally Controlled	How often does this job require working indoors in environmentally controlled conditions?
Deal With External Customers	How important is it to work with external customers or the public in this job?
Frequency of Decision Making	How frequently is the worker required to make decisions that affect other people, the financial resources, and/or the image and reputation of the organization?
Importance of Being Exact or Accurate	How important is being very exact or highly accurate in performing this job?
Work With Work Group or Team	How important is it to work with others in a group or team in this job?
Freedom to Make Decisions	How much decision making freedom, without supervision, does the job offer?
Impact of Decisions on Co-workers or Company Resul	How do the decisions an employee makes impact the results of co-workers, clients or the company?
Structured versus Unstructured Work	To what extent is this job structured for the worker, rather than allowing the worker to determine tasks, priorities, and goals?
In an Enclosed Vehicle or Equipment	How often does this job require working in a closed vehicle or equipment (e.g., car)?
Coordinate or Lead Others	How important is it to coordinate or lead others in accomplishing work activities in this job?
Letters and Memos	How often does the job require written letters and memos?
Deal With Unpleasant or Angry People	How frequently does the worker have to deal with unpleasant, angry, or discourteous individuals as part of the job requirements?
Importance of Repeating Same Tasks	How important is repeating the same physical activities (e.g., key entry) or mental activities (e.g., checking entries in a ledger) over and over, without stopping, to performing this job?
Electronic Mail	How often do you use electronic mail in this job?
Physical Proximity	To what extent does this job require the worker to perform job tasks in close physical proximity to other people?

Time Pressure	How often does this job require the worker to meet strict deadlines?
Outdoors, Exposed to Weather	How often does this job require working outdoors, exposed to all weather conditions?
Frequency of Conflict Situations	How often are there conflict situations the employee has to face in this job?
Spend Time Sitting	How much does this job require sitting?
Responsibility for Outcomes and Results	How responsible is the worker for work outcomes and results of other workers?
Spend Time Making Repetitive Motions	How much does this job require making repetitive motions?
Degree of Automation	How automated is the job?
Spend Time Using Your Hands to Handle, Control, or	How much does this job require using your hands to handle, control, or feel objects, tools or controls?
Consequence of Error	How serious would the result usually be if the worker made a mistake that was not readily correctable?
Exposed to Contaminants	How often does this job require working exposed to contaminants (such as pollutants, gases, dust or odors)?
Very Hot or Cold Temperatures	How often does this job require working in very hot (above 90 F degrees) or very cold (below 32 F degrees) temperatures?
Spend Time Standing	How much does this job require standing?
Spend Time Walking and Running	How much does this job require walking and running?
Level of Competition	To what extent does this job require the worker to compete or to be aware of competitive pressures?
Sounds, Noise Levels Are Distracting or Uncomfortable	How often does this job require working exposed to sounds and noise levels that are distracting or uncomfortable?
Responsible for Others' Health and Safety	How much responsibility is there for the health and safety of others in this job?
Exposed to Minor Burns, Cuts, Bites, or Stings	How often does this job require exposure to minor burns, cuts, bites, or stings?
Public Speaking	How often do you have to perform public speaking in this job?
Indoors, Not Environmentally Controlled	How often does this job require working indoors in non-controlled environmental conditions (e.g., warehouse without heat)?
Extremely Bright or Inadequate Lighting	How often does this job require working in extremely bright or inadequate lighting conditions?
Spend Time Bending or Twisting the Body	How much does this job require bending or twisting your body?
Deal With Physically Aggressive People	How frequently does this job require the worker to deal with physical aggression of violent individuals?
Cramped Work Space, Awkward Positions	How often does this job require working in cramped work spaces that requires getting into awkward positions?
Spend Time Kneeling, Crouching, Stooping, or Crawl	How much does this job require kneeling, crouching, stooping, or crawling?
Spend Time Keeping or Regaining Balance	How much does this job require keeping or regaining your balance?
Pace Determined by Speed of Equipment	How important is it to this job that the pace is determined by the speed of equipment or machinery? (This does not refer to keeping busy at all times on this job.)
Outdoors, Under Cover	How often does this job require working outdoors, under cover (e.g., structure with roof but no walls)?
Exposed to High Places	How often does this job require exposure to high places?
Wear Common Protective or Safety Equipment such as	How much does this job require wearing common protective or safety equipment such as safety shoes, glasses, gloves, hard hats or live jackets?
Exposed to Hazardous Equipment	How often does this job require exposure to hazardous equipment?
Exposed to Hazardous Conditions	How often does this job require exposure to hazardous conditions?
Exposed to Disease or Infections	How often does this job require exposure to disease/infections?
Spend Time Climbing Ladders, Scaffolds, or Poles	How much does this job require climbing ladders, scaffolds, or poles?
In an Open Vehicle or Equipment	How often does this job require working in an open vehicle or equipment (e.g., tractor)?
Exposed to Whole Body Vibration	How often does this job require exposure to whole body vibration (e.g., operate a jackhammer)?
Wear Specialized Protective or Safety Equipment su	How much does this job require wearing specialized protective or safety equipment such as breathing apparatus, safety harness, full protection suits, or radiation protection?
Exposed to Radiation	How often does this job require exposure to radiation?

Job Zone Component	Job Zone Component Definitions
Title	Job Zone Three: Medium Preparation Needed
Overall Experience	Previous work-related skill, knowledge, or experience is required for these occupations. For example, an electrician must have completed three or four years of apprenticeship or several years of vocational training, and often must have passed a licensing exam, in order to perform the job.
Job Training	Employees in these occupations usually need one or two years of training involving both on-the-job experience and informal training with experienced workers.
Job Zone Examples	These occupations usually involve using communication and organizational skills to coordinate, supervise, manage, or train others to accomplish goals. Examples include dental assistants, electricians, fish and game wardens, legal secretaries, personnel recruiters, and recreation workers.
SVP Range	(6.0 to < 7.0)
Education	Most occupations in this zone require training in vocational schools, related on-the-job experience, or an associate's degree. Some may require a bachelor's degree.

Work_Styles	Work_Styles Definitions
Integrity	Job requires being honest and ethical.
Attention to Detail	Job requires being careful about detail and thorough in completing work tasks.
Dependability	Job requires being reliable, responsible, and dependable, and fulfilling obligations.
Self Control	Job requires maintaining composure, keeping emotions in check, controlling anger, and avoiding aggressive behavior, even in very difficult situations.
Stress Tolerance	Job requires accepting criticism and dealing calmly and effectively with high stress situations.
Independence	Job requires developing one's own ways of doing things, guiding oneself with little or no supervision, and depending on oneself to get things done.
Cooperation	Job requires being pleasant with others on the job and displaying a good-natured, cooperative attitude.
Analytical Thinking	Job requires analyzing information and using logic to address work-related issues and problems.
Adaptability/Flexibility	Job requires being open to change (positive or negative) and to considerable variety in the workplace.
Initiative	Job requires a willingness to take on responsibilities and challenges.
Concern for Others	Job requires being sensitive to others' needs and feelings and being understanding and helpful on the job.
Achievement/Effort	Job requires establishing and maintaining personally challenging achievement goals and exerting effort toward mastering tasks.
Persistence	Job requires persistence in the face of obstacles.
Innovation	Job requires creativity and alternative thinking to develop new ideas for and answers to work-related problems.
Leadership	Job requires a willingness to lead, take charge, and offer opinions and direction.
Social Orientation	Job requires preferring to work with others rather than alone, and being personally connected with others on the job.

13-2021.02 - Appraisers, Real Estate

Appraise real property to determine its value for purchase, sales, investment, mortgage, or loan purposes.

Tasks

1) Interview persons familiar with properties and immediate surroundings, such as contractors, home owners, and realtors, in order to obtain pertinent information.

2) Testify in court as to the value of a piece of real estate property.

3) Verify legal descriptions of properties by comparing them to county records.

4) Compute final estimation of property values, taking into account such factors as depreciation, replacement costs, value comparisons of similar properties, and income potential.

5) Check building codes and zoning bylaws in order to determine any effects on the properties being appraised.

6) Search public records for transactions such as sales, leases, and assessments.

7) Prepare written reports that estimate property values, outline methods by which the estimations were made, and meet appraisal standards.

8) Obtain county land values and sales information about nearby properties in order to aid in establishment of property values.

9) Inspect properties to evaluate construction, condition, special features, and functional design, and to take property measurements.

10) Examine the type and location of nearby services such as shopping centers, schools, parks, and other neighborhood features in order to evaluate their impact on property values.

11) Evaluate land and neighborhoods where properties are situated, considering locations and trends or impending changes that could influence future values.

12) Draw land diagrams that will be used in appraisal reports to support findings.

13) Examine income records and operating costs of income properties.

14) Estimate building replacement costs using building valuation manuals and professional cost estimators.

13-2031.00 - Budget Analysts

Examine budget estimates for completeness, accuracy, and conformance with procedures and regulations. Analyze budgeting and accounting reports for the purpose of maintaining expenditure controls.

Tasks

1) Review operating budgets to analyze trends affecting budget needs.

2) Provide advice and technical assistance with cost analysis, fiscal allocation, and budget preparation.

3) Analyze monthly department budgeting and accounting reports to maintain expenditure controls.

4) Consult with managers to ensure that budget adjustments are made in accordance with program changes.

5) Compile and analyze accounting records and other data to determine the financial resources required to implement a program.

6) Direct the preparation of regular and special budget reports.

7) Summarize budgets and submit recommendations for the approval or disapproval of funds requests.

8) Interpret budget directives and establish policies for carrying out directives.

9) Perform cost-benefits analyses to compare operating programs, review financial requests, and explore alternative financing methods.

10) Seek new ways to improve efficiency and increase profits.

11) Match appropriations for specific programs with appropriations for broader programs, including items for emergency funds.

12) Testify before examining and fund-granting authorities, clarifying and promoting the proposed budgets.

Knowledge	Knowledge Definitions
English Language	Knowledge of the structure and content of the English language including the meaning and spelling of words, rules of composition, and grammar.
Computers and Electronics	Knowledge of circuit boards, processors, chips, electronic equipment, and computer hardware and software, including applications and programming.
Economics and Accounting	Knowledge of economic and accounting principles and practices, the financial markets, banking and the analysis and reporting of financial data.
Mathematics	Knowledge of arithmetic, algebra, geometry, calculus, statistics, and their applications.
Administration and Management	Knowledge of business and management principles involved in strategic planning, resource allocation, human resources modeling, leadership technique, production methods, and coordination of people and resources.
Clerical	Knowledge of administrative and clerical procedures and systems such as word processing, managing files and records, stenography and transcription, designing forms, and other office procedures and terminology.
Personnel and Human Resources	Knowledge of principles and procedures for personnel recruitment, selection, training, compensation and benefits, labor relations and negotiation, and personnel information systems.
Law and Government	Knowledge of laws, legal codes, court procedures, precedents, government regulations, executive orders, agency rules, and the democratic political process.
Production and Processing	Knowledge of raw materials, production processes, quality control, costs, and other techniques for maximizing the effective manufacture and distribution of goods.
Education and Training	Knowledge of principles and methods for curriculum and training design, teaching and instruction for individuals and groups, and the measurement of training effects.
Telecommunications	Knowledge of transmission, broadcasting, switching, control, and operation of telecommunications systems.
Engineering and Technology	Knowledge of the practical application of engineering science and technology. This includes applying principles, techniques, procedures, and equipment to the design and production of various goods and services.
Public Safety and Security	Knowledge of relevant equipment, policies, procedures, and strategies to promote effective local, state, or national security operations for the protection of people, data, property, and institutions.
Transportation	Knowledge of principles and methods for moving people or goods by air, rail, sea, or road, including the relative costs and benefits.
Communications and Media	Knowledge of media production, communication, and dissemination techniques and methods. This includes alternative ways to inform and entertain via written, oral, and visual media.
Geography	Knowledge of principles and methods for describing the features of land, sea, and air masses, including their physical characteristics, locations, interrelationships, and distribution of plant, animal, and human life.
Design	Knowledge of design techniques, tools, and principles involved in production of precision technical plans, blueprints, drawings, and models.
Therapy and Counseling	Knowledge of principles, methods, and procedures for diagnosis, treatment, and rehabilitation of physical and mental dysfunctions, and for career counseling and guidance.
Customer and Personal Service	Knowledge of principles and processes for providing customer and personal services. This includes customer needs assessment, meeting quality standards for services, and evaluation of customer satisfaction.
Medicine and Dentistry	Knowledge of the information and techniques needed to diagnose and treat human injuries, diseases, and deformities. This includes symptoms, treatment alternatives, drug properties and interactions, and preventive health-care measures.
Mechanical	Knowledge of machines and tools, including their designs, uses, repair, and maintenance.
Sociology and Anthropology	Knowledge of group behavior and dynamics, societal trends and influences, human migrations, ethnicity, cultures and their history and origins.
Psychology	Knowledge of human behavior and performance; individual differences in ability, personality, and interests; learning and motivation; psychological research methods; and the assessment and treatment of behavioral and affective disorders.
History and Archeology	Knowledge of historical events and their causes, indicators, and effects on civilizations and cultures.
Building and Construction	Knowledge of materials, methods, and the tools involved in the construction or repair of houses, buildings, or other structures such as highways and roads.
Sales and Marketing	Knowledge of principles and methods for showing, promoting, and selling products or services. This includes marketing strategy and tactics, product demonstration, sales techniques, and sales control systems.
Food Production	Knowledge of techniques and equipment for planting, growing, and harvesting food products (both plant and animal) for consumption, including storage/handling techniques.
Foreign Language	Knowledge of the structure and content of a foreign (non-English) language including the meaning and spelling of words, rules of composition and grammar, and pronunciation.
Chemistry	Knowledge of the chemical composition, structure, and properties of substances and of the chemical processes and transformations that they undergo. This includes uses of chemicals and their interactions, danger signs, production techniques, and disposal methods.

Philosophy and Theology	Knowledge of different philosophical systems and religions. This includes their basic principles, values, ethics, ways of thinking, customs, practices, and their impact on human culture.
Biology	Knowledge of plant and animal organisms, their tissues, cells, functions, interdependencies, and interactions with each other and the environment.
Fine Arts	Knowledge of the theory and techniques required to compose, produce, and perform works of music, dance, visual arts, drama, and sculpture.
Physics	Knowledge and prediction of physical principles, laws, their interrelationships, and applications to understanding fluid, material, and atmospheric dynamics, and mechanical, electrical, atomic and sub-atomic structures and processes.

Skills	Skills Definitions
Management of Financial Resources	Determining how money will be spent to get the work done, and accounting for these expenditures.
Critical Thinking	Using logic and reasoning to identify the strengths and weaknesses of alternative solutions, conclusions or approaches to problems.
Speaking	Talking to others to convey information effectively.
Complex Problem Solving	Identifying complex problems and reviewing related information to develop and evaluate options and implement solutions.
Writing	Communicating effectively in writing as appropriate for the needs of the audience.
Mathematics	Using mathematics to solve problems.
Coordination	Adjusting actions in relation to others' actions.
Judgment and Decision Making	Considering the relative costs and benefits of potential actions to choose the most appropriate one.
Time Management	Managing one's own time and the time of others.
Active Learning	Understanding the implications of new information for both current and future problem-solving and decision-making.
Active Listening	Giving full attention to what other people are saying, taking time to understand the points being made, asking questions as appropriate, and not interrupting at inappropriate times.
Social Perceptiveness	Being aware of others' reactions and understanding why they react as they do.
Reading Comprehension	Understanding written sentences and paragraphs in work related documents.
Learning Strategies	Selecting and using training/instructional methods and procedures appropriate for the situation when learning or teaching new things.
Instructing	Teaching others how to do something.
Operations Analysis	Analyzing needs and product requirements to create a design.
Monitoring	Monitoring/Assessing performance of yourself, other individuals, or organizations to make improvements or take corrective action.
Service Orientation	Actively looking for ways to help people.
Quality Control Analysis	Conducting tests and inspections of products, services, or processes to evaluate quality or performance.
Negotiation	Bringing others together and trying to reconcile differences.
Technology Design	Generating or adapting equipment and technology to serve user needs.
Persuasion	Persuading others to change their minds or behavior.
Management of Personnel Resources	Motivating, developing, and directing people as they work, identifying the best people for the job.
Systems Analysis	Determining how a system should work and how changes in conditions, operations, and the environment will affect outcomes.
Equipment Selection	Determining the kind of tools and equipment needed to do a job.
Systems Evaluation	Identifying measures or indicators of system performance and the actions needed to improve or correct performance, relative to the goals of the system.
Science	Using scientific rules and methods to solve problems.
Management of Material Resources	Obtaining and seeing to the appropriate use of equipment, facilities, and materials needed to do certain work.
Troubleshooting	Determining causes of operating errors and deciding what to do about it.
Operation and Control	Controlling operations of equipment or systems.
Programming	Writing computer programs for various purposes.
Installation	Installing equipment, machines, wiring, or programs to meet specifications.
Operation Monitoring	Watching gauges, dials, or other indicators to make sure a machine is working properly.

Equipment Maintenance	Performing routine maintenance on equipment and determining when and what kind of maintenance is needed.
Repairing	Repairing machines or systems using the needed tools.

Ability	Ability Definitions
Problem Sensitivity	The ability to tell when something is wrong or is likely to go wrong. It does not involve solving the problem, only recognizing there is a problem.
Written Comprehension	The ability to read and understand information and ideas presented in writing.
Oral Comprehension	The ability to listen to and understand information and ideas presented through spoken words and sentences.
Information Ordering	The ability to arrange things or actions in a certain order or pattern according to a specific rule or set of rules (e.g., patterns of numbers, letters, words, pictures, mathematical operations).
Inductive Reasoning	The ability to combine pieces of information to form general rules or conclusions (includes finding a relationship among seemingly unrelated events).
Deductive Reasoning	The ability to apply general rules to specific problems to produce answers that make sense.
Oral Expression	The ability to communicate information and ideas in speaking so others will understand.
Mathematical Reasoning	The ability to choose the right mathematical methods or formulas to solve a problem.
Speech Recognition	The ability to identify and understand the speech of another person.
Speech Clarity	The ability to speak clearly so others can understand you.
Near Vision	The ability to see details at close range (within a few feet of the observer).
Category Flexibility	The ability to generate or use different sets of rules for combining or grouping things in different ways.
Number Facility	The ability to add, subtract, multiply, or divide quickly and correctly.
Written Expression	The ability to communicate information and ideas in writing so others will understand.
Selective Attention	The ability to concentrate on a task over a period of time without being distracted.
Fluency of Ideas	The ability to come up with a number of ideas about a topic (the number of ideas is important, not their quality, correctness, or creativity).
Perceptual Speed	The ability to quickly and accurately compare similarities and differences among sets of letters, numbers, objects, pictures, or patterns. The things to be compared may be presented at the same time or one after the other. This ability also includes comparing a presented object with a remembered object.
Originality	The ability to come up with unusual or clever ideas about a given topic or situation, or to develop creative ways to solve a problem.
Speed of Closure	The ability to quickly make sense of, combine, and organize information into meaningful patterns.
Flexibility of Closure	The ability to identify or detect a known pattern (a figure, object, word, or sound) that is hidden in other distracting material.
Memorization	The ability to remember information such as words, numbers, pictures, and procedures.
Finger Dexterity	The ability to make precisely coordinated movements of the fingers of one or both hands to grasp, manipulate, or assemble very small objects.
Time Sharing	The ability to shift back and forth between two or more activities or sources of information (such as speech, sounds, touch, or other sources).
Far Vision	The ability to see details at a distance.
Visualization	The ability to imagine how something will look after it is moved around or when its parts are moved or rearranged.
Auditory Attention	The ability to focus on a single source of sound in the presence of other distracting sounds.
Visual Color Discrimination	The ability to match or detect differences between colors, including shades of color and brightness.
Hearing Sensitivity	The ability to detect or tell the differences between sounds that vary in pitch and loudness.
Trunk Strength	The ability to use your abdominal and lower back muscles to support part of the body repeatedly or continuously over time without 'giving out' or fatiguing.
Arm-Hand Steadiness	The ability to keep your hand and arm steady while moving your arm or while holding your arm and hand in one position.

Response Orientation	The ability to choose quickly between two or more movements in response to two or more different signals (lights, sounds, pictures). It includes the speed with which the correct response is started with the hand, foot, or other body part.
Sound Localization	The ability to tell the direction from which a sound originated.
Wrist-Finger Speed	The ability to make fast, simple, repeated movements of the fingers, hands, and wrists.
Manual Dexterity	The ability to quickly move your hand, your hand together with your arm, or your two hands to grasp, manipulate, or assemble objects.
Speed of Limb Movement	The ability to quickly move the arms and legs.
Reaction Time	The ability to quickly respond (with the hand, finger, or foot) to a signal (sound, light, picture) when it appears.
Spatial Orientation	The ability to know your location in relation to the environment or to know where other objects are in relation to you.
Dynamic Flexibility	The ability to quickly and repeatedly bend, stretch, twist, or reach out with your body, arms, and/or legs.
Gross Body Coordination	The ability to coordinate the movement of your arms, legs, and torso together when the whole body is in motion.
Stamina	The ability to exert yourself physically over long periods of time without getting winded or out of breath.
Dynamic Strength	The ability to exert muscle force repeatedly or continuously over time. This involves muscular endurance and resistance to muscle fatigue.
Explosive Strength	The ability to use short bursts of muscle force to propel oneself (as in jumping or sprinting), or to throw an object.
Static Strength	The ability to exert maximum muscle force to lift, push, pull, or carry objects.
Rate Control	The ability to time your movements or the movement of a piece of equipment in anticipation of changes in the speed and/or direction of a moving object or scene.
Glare Sensitivity	The ability to see objects in the presence of glare or bright lighting.
Gross Body Equilibrium	The ability to keep or regain your body balance or stay upright when in an unstable position.
Control Precision	The ability to quickly and repeatedly adjust the controls of a machine or a vehicle to exact positions.
Extent Flexibility	The ability to bend, stretch, twist, or reach with your body, arms, and/or legs.
Night Vision	The ability to see under low light conditions.
Peripheral Vision	The ability to see objects or movement of objects to one's side when the eyes are looking ahead.
Depth Perception	The ability to judge which of several objects is closer or farther away from you, or to judge the distance between you and an object.
Multilimb Coordination	The ability to coordinate two or more limbs (for example, two arms, two legs, or one leg and one arm) while sitting, standing, or lying down. It does not involve performing the activities while the whole body is in motion.

Work_Activity	Work_Activity Definitions
Analyzing Data or Information	Identifying the underlying principles, reasons, or facts of information by breaking down information or data into separate parts.
Interacting With Computers	Using computers and computer systems (including hardware and software) to program, write software, set up functions, enter data, or process information.
Monitoring and Controlling Resources	Monitoring and controlling resources and overseeing the spending of money.
Getting Information	Observing, receiving, and otherwise obtaining information from all relevant sources.
Communicating with Supervisors, Peers, or Subordin	Providing information to supervisors, co-workers, and subordinates by telephone, in written form, e-mail, or in person.
Processing Information	Compiling, coding, categorizing, calculating, tabulating, auditing, or verifying information or data.
Organizing, Planning, and Prioritizing Work	Developing specific goals and plans to prioritize, organize, and accomplish your work.
Interpreting the Meaning of Information for Others	Translating or explaining what information means and how it can be used.
Making Decisions and Solving Problems	Analyzing information and evaluating results to choose the best solution and solve problems.
Updating and Using Relevant Knowledge	Keeping up-to-date technically and applying new knowledge to your job.
Establishing and Maintaining Interpersonal Relatio	Developing constructive and cooperative working relationships with others, and maintaining them over time.

Coordinating the Work and Activities of Others	Getting members of a group to work together to accomplish tasks.
Provide Consultation and Advice to Others	Providing guidance and expert advice to management or other groups on technical, systems-, or process-related topics.
Evaluating Information to Determine Compliance wit	Using relevant information and individual judgment to determine whether events or processes comply with laws, regulations, or standards.
Identifying Objects, Actions, and Events	Identifying information by categorizing, estimating, recognizing differences or similarities, and detecting changes in circumstances or events.
Performing Administrative Activities	Performing day-to-day administrative tasks such as maintaining information files and processing paperwork.
Monitor Processes, Materials, or Surroundings	Monitoring and reviewing information from materials, events, or the environment, to detect or assess problems.
Coaching and Developing Others	Identifying the developmental needs of others and coaching, mentoring, or otherwise helping others to improve their knowledge or skills.
Documenting/Recording Information	Entering, transcribing, recording, storing, or maintaining information in written or electronic/magnetic form.
Resolving Conflicts and Negotiating with Others	Handling complaints, settling disputes, and resolving grievances and conflicts, or otherwise negotiating with others.
Scheduling Work and Activities	Scheduling events, programs, and activities, as well as the work of others.
Developing Objectives and Strategies	Establishing long-range objectives and specifying the strategies and actions to achieve them.
Communicating with Persons Outside Organization	Communicating with people outside the organization, representing the organization to customers, the public, government, and other external sources. This information can be exchanged in person, in writing, or by telephone or e-mail.
Guiding, Directing, and Motivating Subordinates	Providing guidance and direction to subordinates, including setting performance standards and monitoring performance.
Assisting and Caring for Others	Providing personal assistance, medical attention, emotional support, or other personal care to others such as coworkers, customers, or patients.
Thinking Creatively	Developing, designing, or creating new applications, ideas, relationships, systems, or products, including artistic contributions.
Training and Teaching Others	Identifying the educational needs of others, developing formal educational or training programs or classes, and teaching or instructing others.
Staffing Organizational Units	Recruiting, interviewing, selecting, hiring, and promoting employees in an organization.
Developing and Building Teams	Encouraging and building mutual trust, respect, and cooperation among team members.
Selling or Influencing Others	Convincing others to buy merchandise/goods or to otherwise change their minds or actions.
Judging the Qualities of Things, Services, or Peop	Assessing the value, importance, or quality of things or people.
Controlling Machines and Processes	Using either control mechanisms or direct physical activity to operate machines or processes (not including computers or vehicles).
Performing for or Working Directly with the Public	Performing for people or dealing directly with the public. This includes serving customers in restaurants and stores, and receiving clients or guests.
Estimating the Quantifiable Characteristics of Pro	Estimating sizes, distances, and quantities; or determining time, costs, resources, or materials needed to perform a work activity.
Handling and Moving Objects	Using hands and arms in handling, installing, positioning, and moving materials, and manipulating things.
Repairing and Maintaining Mechanical Equipment	Servicing, repairing, adjusting, and testing machines, devices, moving parts, and equipment that operate primarily on the basis of mechanical (not electronic) principles.
Inspecting Equipment, Structures, or Material	Inspecting equipment, structures, or materials to identify the cause of errors or other problems or defects.
Performing General Physical Activities	Performing physical activities that require considerable use of your arms and legs and moving your whole body, such as climbing, lifting, balancing, walking, stooping, and handling of materials.
Operating Vehicles, Mechanized Devices, or Equipme	Running, maneuvering, navigating, or driving vehicles or mechanized equipment, such as forklifts, passenger vehicles, aircraft, or water craft.
Drafting, Laying Out, and Specifying Technical Dev	Providing documentation, detailed instructions, drawings, or specifications to tell others about how devices, parts, equipment, or structures are to be fabricated, constructed, assembled, modified, maintained, or used.

Repairing and Maintaining Electronic Equipment	Servicing, repairing, calibrating, regulating, fine-tuning, or testing machines, devices, and equipment that operate primarily on the basis of electrical or electronic (not mechanical) principles.

Work_Context	**Work_Context Definitions**
Face-to-Face Discussions	How often do you have to have face-to-face discussions with individuals or teams in this job?
Telephone	How often do you have telephone conversations in this job?
Electronic Mail	How often do you use electronic mail in this job?
Indoors, Environmentally Controlled	How often does this job require working indoors in environmentally controlled conditions?
Structured versus Unstructured Work	To what extent is this job structured for the worker, rather than allowing the worker to determine tasks, priorities, and goals?
Spend Time Sitting	How much does this job require sitting?
Freedom to Make Decisions	How much decision making freedom, without supervision, does the job offer?
Importance of Being Exact or Accurate	How important is being very exact or highly accurate in performing this job?
Letters and Memos	How often does the job require written letters and memos?
Contact With Others	How much does this job require the worker to be in contact with others (face-to-face, by telephone, or otherwise) in order to perform it?
Work With Work Group or Team	How important is it to work with others in a group or team in this job?
Time Pressure	How often does this job require the worker to meet strict deadlines?
Importance of Repeating Same Tasks	How important is repeating the same physical activities (e.g., key entry) or mental activities (e.g., checking entries in a ledger) over and over, without stopping, to performing this job?
Impact of Decisions on Co-workers or Company Resul	How do the decisions an employee makes impact the results of co-workers, clients or the company?
Frequency of Decision Making	How frequently is the worker required to make decisions that affect other people, the financial resources, and/or the image and reputation of the organization?
Coordinate or Lead Others	How important is it to coordinate or lead others in accomplishing work activities in this job?
Level of Competition	To what extent does this job require the worker to compete or to be aware of competitive pressures?
Degree of Automation	How automated is the job?
Deal With External Customers	How important is it to work with external customers or the public in this job?
Physical Proximity	To what extent does this job require the worker to perform job tasks in close physical proximity to other people?
Responsibility for Outcomes and Results	How responsible is the worker for work outcomes and results of other workers?
Spend Time Making Repetitive Motions	How much does this job require making repetitive motions?
Frequency of Conflict Situations	How often are there conflict situations the employee has to face in this job?
Consequence of Error	How serious would the result usually be if the worker made a mistake that was not readily correctable?
Deal With Unpleasant or Angry People	How frequently does the worker have to deal with unpleasant, angry, or discourteous individuals as part of the job requirements?
Spend Time Using Your Hands to Handle, Control, or	How much does this job require using your hands to handle, control, or feel objects, tools or controls?
Responsible for Others' Health and Safety	How much responsibility is there for the health and safety of others in this job?
Sounds, Noise Levels Are Distracting or Uncomforta	How often does this job require working exposed to sounds and noise levels that are distracting or uncomfortable?
Spend Time Standing	How much does this job require standing?
Public Speaking	How often do you have to perform public speaking in this job?
Spend Time Walking and Running	How much does this job require walking and running?
Exposed to Contaminants	How often does this job require working exposed to contaminants (such as pollutants, gases, dust or odors)?
Exposed to Hazardous Equipment	How often does this job require exposure to hazardous equipment?
In an Enclosed Vehicle or Equipment	How often does this job require working in a closed vehicle or equipment (e.g., car)?
Spend Time Bending or Twisting the Body	How much does this job require bending or twisting your body?

Wear Common Protective or Safety Equipment such as	How much does this job require wearing common protective or safety equipment such as safety shoes, glasses, gloves, hard hats or life jackets?
Pace Determined by Speed of Equipment	How important is it to this job that the pace is determined by the speed of equipment or machinery? (This does not refer to keeping busy at all times on this job.)
Cramped Work Space, Awkward Positions	How often does this job require working in cramped work spaces that requires getting into awkward positions?
Spend Time Kneeling, Crouching, Stooping, or Crawl	How much does this job require kneeling, crouching, stooping, or crawling?
Exposed to High Places	How often does this job require exposure to high places?
Exposed to Disease or Infections	How often does this job require exposure to disease/infections?
Exposed to Whole Body Vibration	How often does this job require exposure to whole body vibration (e.g., operate a jackhammer)?
Indoors, Not Environmentally Controlled	How often does this job require working indoors in non-controlled environmental conditions (e.g., warehouse without heat)?
Deal With Physically Aggressive People	How frequently does this job require the worker to deal with physical aggression of violent individuals?
Exposed to Minor Burns, Cuts, Bites, or Stings	How often does this job require exposure to minor burns, cuts, bites, or stings?
Very Hot or Cold Temperatures	How often does this job require working in very hot (above 90 F degrees) or very cold (below 32 F degrees) temperatures?
Extremely Bright or Inadequate Lighting	How often does this job require working in extremely bright or inadequate lighting conditions?
Outdoors, Under Cover	How often does this job require working outdoors, under cover (e.g., structure with roof but no walls)?
Outdoors, Exposed to Weather	How often does this job require working outdoors, exposed to all weather conditions?
Exposed to Radiation	How often does this job require exposure to radiation?
Wear Specialized Protective or Safety Equipment su	How much does this job require wearing specialized protective or safety equipment such as breathing apparatus, safety harness, full protection suits, or radiation protection?
Spend Time Keeping or Regaining Balance	How much does this job require keeping or regaining your balance?
In an Open Vehicle or Equipment	How often does this job require working in an open vehicle or equipment (e.g., tractor)?
Spend Time Climbing Ladders, Scaffolds, or Poles	How much does this job require climbing ladders, scaffolds, or poles?
Exposed to Hazardous Conditions	How often does this job require exposure to hazardous conditions?

Job Zone Component	**Job Zone Component Definitions**
Title	Job Zone Four: Considerable Preparation Needed
Overall Experience	A minimum of two to four years of work-related skill, knowledge, or experience is needed for these occupations. For example, an accountant must complete four years of college and work for several years in accounting to be considered qualified.
Job Training	Employees in these occupations usually need several years of work-related experience, on-the-job training, and/or vocational training.
Job Zone Examples	Many of these occupations involve coordinating, supervising, managing, or training others. Examples include accountants, chefs and head cooks, computer programmers, historians, pharmacists, and police detectives.
SVP Range	(7.0 to < 8.0)
Education	Most of these occupations require a four - year bachelor's degree, but some do not.

Work_Styles	**Work_Styles Definitions**
Attention to Detail	Job requires being careful about detail and thorough in completing work tasks.
Analytical Thinking	Job requires analyzing information and using logic to address work-related issues and problems.
Adaptability/Flexibility	Job requires being open to change (positive or negative) and to considerable variety in the workplace.
Cooperation	Job requires being pleasant with others on the job and displaying a good-natured, cooperative attitude.
Dependability	Job requires being reliable, responsible, and dependable, and fulfilling obligations.

Achievement/Effort	Job requires establishing and maintaining personally challenging achievement goals and exerting effort toward mastering tasks.
Integrity	Job requires being honest and ethical.
Persistence	Job requires persistence in the face of obstacles.
Independence	Job requires developing one's own ways of doing things, guiding oneself with little or no supervision, and depending on oneself to get things done.
Stress Tolerance	Job requires accepting criticism and dealing calmly and effectively with high stress situations.
Self Control	Job requires maintaining composure, keeping emotions in check, controlling anger, and avoiding aggressive behavior, even in very difficult situations.
Leadership	Job requires a willingness to lead, take charge, and offer opinions and direction.
Initiative	Job requires a willingness to take on responsibilities and challenges.
Concern for Others	Job requires being sensitive to others' needs and feelings and being understanding and helpful on the job.
Innovation	Job requires creativity and alternative thinking to develop new ideas for and answers to work-related problems.
Social Orientation	Job requires preferring to work with others rather than alone, and being personally connected with others on the job.

13-2041.00 - Credit Analysts

Analyze current credit data and financial statements of individuals or firms to determine the degree of risk involved in extending credit or lending money. Prepare reports with this credit information for use in decision-making.

Tasks

1) Confer with credit association and other business representatives to exchange credit information.

2) Evaluate customer records and recommend payment plans based on earnings, savings data, payment history, and purchase activity.

3) Prepare reports that include the degree of risk involved in extending credit or lending money.

4) Generate financial ratios, using computer programs, to evaluate customers' financial status.

5) Consult with customers to resolve complaints and verify financial and credit transactions.

6) Compare liquidity, profitability, and credit histories of establishments being evaluated with those of similar establishments in the same industries and geographic locations.

7) Review individual or commercial customer files to identify and select delinquent accounts for collection.

8) Complete loan applications, including credit analyses and summaries of loan requests, and submit to loan committees for approval.

9) Analyze financial data such as income growth, quality of management, and market share to determine expected profitability of loans.

Knowledge	Knowledge Definitions
Economics and Accounting	Knowledge of economic and accounting principles and practices, the financial markets, banking and the analysis and reporting of financial data.
English Language	Knowledge of the structure and content of the English language including the meaning and spelling of words, rules of composition, and grammar.
Clerical	Knowledge of administrative and clerical procedures and systems such as word processing, managing files and records, stenography and transcription, designing forms, and other office procedures and terminology.
Mathematics	Knowledge of arithmetic, algebra, geometry, calculus, statistics, and their applications.
Customer and Personal Service	Knowledge of principles and processes for providing customer and personal services. This includes customer needs assessment, meeting quality standards for services, and evaluation of customer satisfaction.
Administration and Management	Knowledge of business and management principles involved in strategic planning, resource allocation, human resources modeling, leadership technique, production methods, and coordination of people and resources.

Education and Training	Knowledge of principles and methods for curriculum and training design, teaching and instruction for individuals and groups, and the measurement of training effects.
Computers and Electronics	Knowledge of circuit boards, processors, chips, electronic equipment, and computer hardware and software, including applications and programming.
Law and Government	Knowledge of laws, legal codes, court procedures, precedents, government regulations, executive orders, agency rules, and the democratic political process.
Sales and Marketing	Knowledge of principles and methods for showing, promoting, and selling products or services. This includes marketing strategy and tactics, product demonstration, sales techniques, and sales control systems.
Production and Processing	Knowledge of raw materials, production processes, quality control, costs, and other techniques for maximizing the effective manufacture and distribution of goods.
Personnel and Human Resources	Knowledge of principles and procedures for personnel recruitment, selection, training, compensation and benefits, labor relations and negotiation, and personnel information systems.
Communications and Media	Knowledge of media production, communication, and dissemination techniques and methods. This includes alternative ways to inform and entertain via written, oral, and visual media.
Psychology	Knowledge of human behavior and performance; individual differences in ability, personality, and interests; learning and motivation; psychological research methods; and the assessment and treatment of behavioral and affective disorders.
Foreign Language	Knowledge of the structure and content of a foreign (non-English) language including the meaning and spelling of words, rules of composition and grammar, and pronunciation.
Sociology and Anthropology	Knowledge of group behavior and dynamics, societal trends and influences, human migrations, ethnicity, cultures and their history and origins.
Geography	Knowledge of principles and methods for describing the features of land, sea, and air masses, including their physical characteristics, locations, interrelationships, and distribution of plant, animal, and human life.
Telecommunications	Knowledge of transmission, broadcasting, switching, control, and operation of telecommunications systems.
Public Safety and Security	Knowledge of relevant equipment, policies, procedures, and strategies to promote effective local, state, or national security operations for the protection of people, data, property, and institutions.
Design	Knowledge of design techniques, tools, and principles involved in production of precision technical plans, blueprints, drawings, and models.
Transportation	Knowledge of principles and methods for moving people or goods by air, rail, sea, or road, including the relative costs and benefits.
Philosophy and Theology	Knowledge of different philosophical systems and religions. This includes their basic principles, values, ethics, ways of thinking, customs, practices, and their impact on human culture.
Engineering and Technology	Knowledge of the practical application of engineering science and technology. This includes applying principles, techniques, procedures, and equipment to the design and production of various goods and services.
History and Archeology	Knowledge of historical events and their causes, indicators, and effects on civilizations and cultures.
Chemistry	Knowledge of the chemical composition, structure, and properties of substances and of the chemical processes and transformations that they undergo. This includes uses of chemicals and their interactions, danger signs, production techniques, and disposal methods.
Physics	Knowledge and prediction of physical principles, laws, their interrelationships, and applications to understanding fluid, material, and atmospheric dynamics, and mechanical, electrical, atomic and sub-atomic structures and processes.
Building and Construction	Knowledge of materials, methods, and the tools involved in the construction or repair of houses, buildings, or other structures such as highways and roads.
Food Production	Knowledge of techniques and equipment for planting, growing, and harvesting food products (both plant and animal) for consumption, including storage/handling techniques.
Therapy and Counseling	Knowledge of principles, methods, and procedures for diagnosis, treatment, and rehabilitation of physical and mental dysfunctions, and for career counseling and guidance.

Fine Arts	Knowledge of the theory and techniques required to compose, produce, and perform works of music, dance, visual arts, drama, and sculpture.	Operation Monitoring	Watching gauges, dials, or other indicators to make sure a machine is working properly.
Mechanical	Knowledge of machines and tools, including their designs, uses, repair, and maintenance.	**Ability**	**Ability Definitions**
Biology	Knowledge of plant and animal organisms, their tissues, cells, functions, interdependencies, and interactions with each other and the environment.	Written Comprehension	The ability to read and understand information and ideas presented in writing.
Medicine and Dentistry	Knowledge of the information and techniques needed to diagnose and treat human injuries, diseases, and deformities. This includes symptoms, treatment alternatives, drug properties and interactions, and preventive health-care measures.	Problem Sensitivity	The ability to tell when something is wrong or is likely to go wrong. It does not involve solving the problem, only recognizing there is a problem.
		Oral Comprehension	The ability to listen to and understand information and ideas presented through spoken words and sentences.
Skills	**Skills Definitions**	Oral Expression	The ability to communicate information and ideas in speaking so others will understand.
Active Listening	Giving full attention to what other people are saying, taking time to understand the points being made, asking questions as appropriate, and not interrupting at inappropriate times.	Deductive Reasoning	The ability to apply general rules to specific problems to produce answers that make sense.
Speaking	Talking to others to convey information effectively.	Near Vision	The ability to see details at close range (within a few feet of the observer).
Reading Comprehension	Understanding written sentences and paragraphs in work related documents.	Mathematical Reasoning	The ability to choose the right mathematical methods or formulas to solve a problem.
Critical Thinking	Using logic and reasoning to identify the strengths and weaknesses of alternative solutions, conclusions or approaches to problems.	Speech Recognition	The ability to identify and understand the speech of another person.
Social Perceptiveness	Being aware of others' reactions and understanding why they react as they do.	Written Expression	The ability to communicate information and ideas in writing so others will understand.
Instructing	Teaching others how to do something.	Inductive Reasoning	The ability to combine pieces of information to form general rules or conclusions (includes finding a relationship among seemingly unrelated events).
Writing	Communicating effectively in writing as appropriate for the needs of the audience.	Selective Attention	The ability to concentrate on a task over a period of time without being distracted.
Learning Strategies	Selecting and using training/instructional methods and procedures appropriate for the situation when learning or teaching new things.	Speech Clarity	The ability to speak clearly so others can understand you.
Judgment and Decision Making	Considering the relative costs and benefits of potential actions to choose the most appropriate one.	Flexibility of Closure	The ability to identify or detect a known pattern (a figure, object, word, or sound) that is hidden in other distracting material.
Active Learning	Understanding the implications of new information for both current and future problem-solving and decision-making.	Information Ordering	The ability to arrange things or actions in a certain order or pattern according to a specific rule or set of rules (e.g., patterns of numbers, letters, words, pictures, mathematical operations).
Monitoring	Monitoring/Assessing performance of yourself, other individuals, or organizations to make improvements or take corrective action.	Category Flexibility	The ability to generate or use different sets of rules for combining or grouping things in different ways.
Mathematics	Using mathematics to solve problems.	Number Facility	The ability to add, subtract, multiply, or divide quickly and correctly.
Complex Problem Solving	Identifying complex problems and reviewing related information to develop and evaluate options and implement solutions.	Fluency of Ideas	The ability to come up with a number of ideas about a topic (the number of ideas is important, not their quality, correctness, or creativity).
Negotiation	Bringing others together and trying to reconcile differences.	Perceptual Speed	The ability to quickly and accurately compare similarities and differences among sets of letters, numbers, objects, pictures, or patterns. The things to be compared may be presented at the same time or one after the other. This ability also includes comparing a presented object with a remembered object.
Time Management	Managing one's own time and the time of others.		
Systems Evaluation	Identifying measures or indicators of system performance and the actions needed to improve or correct performance, relative to the goals of the system.	Memorization	The ability to remember information such as words, numbers, pictures, and procedures.
Coordination	Adjusting actions in relation to others' actions.	Finger Dexterity	The ability to make precisely coordinated movements of the fingers of one or both hands to grasp, manipulate, or assemble very small objects.
Service Orientation	Actively looking for ways to help people.		
Persuasion	Persuading others to change their minds or behavior.	Originality	The ability to come up with unusual or clever ideas about a given topic or situation, or to develop creative ways to solve a problem.
Equipment Selection	Determining the kind of tools and equipment needed to do a job.		
Operations Analysis	Analyzing needs and product requirements to create a design.	Speed of Closure	The ability to quickly make sense of, combine, and organize information into meaningful patterns.
Troubleshooting	Determining causes of operating errors and deciding what to do about it.	Time Sharing	The ability to shift back and forth between two or more activities or sources of information (such as speech, sounds, touch, or other sources).
Systems Analysis	Determining how a system should work and how changes in conditions, operations, and the environment will affect outcomes.		
Repairing	Repairing machines or systems using the needed tools.	Visualization	The ability to imagine how something will look after it is moved around or when its parts are moved or rearranged.
Quality Control Analysis	Conducting tests and inspections of products, services, or processes to evaluate quality or performance.	Far Vision	The ability to see details at a distance.
Installation	Installing equipment, machines, wiring, or programs to meet specifications.	Manual Dexterity	The ability to quickly move your hand, your hand together with your arm, or your two hands to grasp, manipulate, or assemble objects.
Equipment Maintenance	Performing routine maintenance on equipment and determining when and what kind of maintenance is needed.	Arm-Hand Steadiness	The ability to keep your hand and arm steady while moving your arm or while holding your arm and hand in one position.
Management of Personnel Resources	Motivating, developing, and directing people as they work, identifying the best people for the job.	Trunk Strength	The ability to use your abdominal and lower back muscles to support part of the body repeatedly or continuously over time without 'giving out' or fatiguing.
Technology Design	Generating or adapting equipment and technology to serve user needs.		
Operation and Control	Controlling operations of equipment or systems.	Control Precision	The ability to quickly and repeatedly adjust the controls of a machine or a vehicle to exact positions.
Programming	Writing computer programs for various purposes.		
Science	Using scientific rules and methods to solve problems.	Visual Color Discrimination	The ability to match or detect differences between colors, including shades of color and brightness.
Management of Material Resources	Obtaining and seeing to the appropriate use of equipment, facilities, and materials needed to do certain work.		
Management of Financial Resources	Determining how money will be spent to get the work done, and accounting for these expenditures.	Auditory Attention	The ability to focus on a single source of sound in the presence of other distracting sounds.

Wrist-Finger Speed	The ability to make fast, simple, repeated movements of the fingers, hands, and wrists.
Extent Flexibility	The ability to bend, stretch, twist, or reach with your body, arms, and/or legs.
Hearing Sensitivity	The ability to detect or tell the differences between sounds that vary in pitch and loudness.
Stamina	The ability to exert yourself physically over long periods of time without getting winded or out of breath.
Speed of Limb Movement	The ability to quickly move the arms and legs.
Glare Sensitivity	The ability to see objects in the presence of glare or bright lighting.
Multilimb Coordination	The ability to coordinate two or more limbs (for example, two arms, two legs, or one leg and one arm) while sitting, standing, or lying down. It does not involve performing the activities while the whole body is in motion.
Gross Body Coordination	The ability to coordinate the movement of your arms, legs, and torso together when the whole body is in motion.
Static Strength	The ability to exert maximum muscle force to lift, push, pull, or carry objects.
Spatial Orientation	The ability to know your location in relation to the environment or to know where other objects are in relation to you.
Gross Body Equilibrium	The ability to keep or regain your body balance or stay upright when in an unstable position.
Reaction Time	The ability to quickly respond (with the hand, finger, or foot) to a signal (sound, light, picture) when it appears.
Depth Perception	The ability to judge which of several objects is closer or farther away from you, or to judge the distance between you and an object.
Explosive Strength	The ability to use short bursts of muscle force to propel oneself (as in jumping or sprinting), or to throw an object.
Dynamic Strength	The ability to exert muscle force repeatedly or continuously over time. This involves muscular endurance and resistance to muscle fatigue.
Dynamic Flexibility	The ability to quickly and repeatedly bend, stretch, twist, or reach out with your body, arms, and/or legs.
Peripheral Vision	The ability to see objects or movement of objects to one's side when the eyes are looking ahead.
Response Orientation	The ability to choose quickly between two or more movements in response to two or more different signals (lights, sounds, pictures). It includes the speed with which the correct response is started with the hand, foot, or other body part.
Sound Localization	The ability to tell the direction from which a sound originated.
Night Vision	The ability to see under low light conditions.
Rate Control	The ability to time your movements or the movement of a piece of equipment in anticipation of changes in the speed and/or direction of a moving object or scene.

Work_Activity	Work_Activity Definitions
Interacting With Computers	Using computers and computer systems (including hardware and software) to program, write software, set up functions, enter data, or process information.
Getting Information	Observing, receiving, and otherwise obtaining information from all relevant sources.
Making Decisions and Solving Problems	Analyzing information and evaluating results to choose the best solution and solve problems.
Evaluating Information to Determine Compliance wit	Using relevant information and individual judgment to determine whether events or processes comply with laws, regulations, or standards.
Communicating with Supervisors, Peers, or Subordin	Providing information to supervisors, co-workers, and subordinates by telephone, in written form, e-mail, or in person.
Documenting/Recording Information	Entering, transcribing, recording, storing, or maintaining information in written or electronic/magnetic form.
Processing Information	Compiling, coding, categorizing, calculating, tabulating, auditing, or verifying information or data.
Establishing and Maintaining Interpersonal Relatio	Developing constructive and cooperative working relationships with others, and maintaining them over time.
Analyzing Data or Information	Identifying the underlying principles, reasons, or facts of information by breaking down information or data into separate parts.
Updating and Using Relevant Knowledge	Keeping up-to-date technically and applying new knowledge to your job.
Organizing, Planning, and Prioritizing Work	Developing specific goals and plans to prioritize, organize, and accomplish your work.

Identifying Objects, Actions, and Events	Identifying information by categorizing, estimating, recognizing differences or similarities, and detecting changes in circumstances or events.
Communicating with Persons Outside Organization	Communicating with people outside the organization, representing the organization to customers, the public, government, and other external sources. This information can be exchanged in person, in writing, or by telephone or e-mail.
Thinking Creatively	Developing, designing, or creating new applications, ideas, relationships, systems, or products, including artistic contributions.
Judging the Qualities of Things, Services, or Peop	Assessing the value, importance, or quality of things or people.
Interpreting the Meaning of Information for Others	Translating or explaining what information means and how it can be used.
Performing Administrative Activities	Performing day-to-day administrative tasks such as maintaining information files and processing paperwork.
Training and Teaching Others	Identifying the educational needs of others, developing formal educational or training programs or classes, and teaching or instructing others.
Scheduling Work and Activities	Scheduling events, programs, and activities, as well as the work of others.
Developing and Building Teams	Encouraging and building mutual trust, respect, and cooperation among team members.
Assisting and Caring for Others	Providing personal assistance, medical attention, emotional support, or other personal care to others such as coworkers, customers, or patients.
Monitor Processes, Materials, or Surroundings	Monitoring and reviewing information from materials, events, or the environment, to detect or assess problems.
Resolving Conflicts and Negotiating with Others	Handling complaints, settling disputes, and resolving grievances and conflicts, or otherwise negotiating with others.
Developing Objectives and Strategies	Establishing long-range objectives and specifying the strategies and actions to achieve them.
Selling or Influencing Others	Convincing others to buy merchandise/goods or to otherwise change their minds or actions.
Provide Consultation and Advice to Others	Providing guidance and expert advice to management or other groups on technical, systems-, or process-related topics.
Coordinating the Work and Activities of Others	Getting members of a group to work together to accomplish tasks.
Coaching and Developing Others	Identifying the developmental needs of others and coaching, mentoring, or otherwise helping others to improve their knowledge or skills.
Guiding, Directing, and Motivating Subordinates	Providing guidance and direction to subordinates, including setting performance standards and monitoring performance.
Estimating the Quantifiable Characteristics of Pro	Estimating sizes, distances, and quantities; or determining time, costs, resources, or materials needed to perform a work activity.
Staffing Organizational Units	Recruiting, interviewing, selecting, hiring, and promoting employees in an organization.
Monitoring and Controlling Resources	Monitoring and controlling resources and overseeing the spending of money.
Performing for or Working Directly with the Public	Performing for people or dealing directly with the public. This includes serving customers in restaurants and stores, and receiving clients or guests.
Handling and Moving Objects	Using hands and arms in handling, installing, positioning, and moving materials, and manipulating things.
Inspecting Equipment, Structures, or Material	Inspecting equipment, structures, or materials to identify the cause of errors or other problems or defects.
Operating Vehicles, Mechanized Devices, or Equipme	Running, maneuvering, navigating, or driving vehicles or mechanized equipment, such as forklifts, passenger vehicles, aircraft, or water craft.
Controlling Machines and Processes	Using either control mechanisms or direct physical activity to operate machines or processes (not including computers or vehicles).
Performing General Physical Activities	Performing physical activities that require considerable use of your arms and legs and moving your whole body, such as climbing, lifting, balancing, walking, stooping, and handling of materials.
Repairing and Maintaining Mechanical Equipment	Servicing, repairing, adjusting, and testing machines, devices, moving parts, and equipment that operate primarily on the basis of mechanical (not electronic) principles.
Drafting, Laying Out, and Specifying Technical Dev	Providing documentation, detailed instructions, drawings, or specifications to tell others about how devices, parts, equipment, or structures are to be fabricated, constructed, assembled, modified, maintained, or used.

Repairing and Maintaining Electronic Equipment	Servicing, repairing, calibrating, regulating, fine-tuning, or testing machines, devices, and equipment that operate primarily on the basis of electrical or electronic (not mechanical) principles.

Work_Context	Work_Context Definitions
Indoors, Environmentally Controlled	How often does this job require working indoors in environmentally controlled conditions?
Telephone	How often do you have telephone conversations in this job?
Spend Time Sitting	How much does this job require sitting?
Face-to-Face Discussions	How often do you have to have face-to-face discussions with individuals or teams in this job?
Importance of Being Exact or Accurate	How important is being very exact or highly accurate in performing this job?
Spend Time Making Repetitive Motions	How much does this job require making repetitive motions?
Work With Work Group or Team	How important is it to work with others in a group or team in this job?
Freedom to Make Decisions	How much decision making freedom, without supervision, does the job offer?
Letters and Memos	How often does the job require written letters and memos?
Electronic Mail	How often do you use electronic mail in this job?
Importance of Repeating Same Tasks	How important is repeating the same physical activities (e.g., key entry) or mental activities (e.g., checking entries in a ledger) over and over, without stopping, to performing this job?
Structured versus Unstructured Work	To what extent is this job structured for the worker, rather than allowing the worker to determine tasks, priorities, and goals?
Time Pressure	How often does this job require the worker to meet strict deadlines?
Contact With Others	How much does this job require the worker to be in contact with others (face-to-face, by telephone, or otherwise) in order to perform it?
Frequency of Decision Making	How frequently is the worker required to make decisions that affect other people, the financial resources, and/or the image and reputation of the organization?
Impact of Decisions on Co-workers or Company Result	How do the decisions an employee makes impact the results of co-workers, clients or the company?
Deal With External Customers	How important is it to work with external customers or the public in this job?
Physical Proximity	To what extent does this job require the worker to perform job tasks in close physical proximity to other people?
Coordinate or Lead Others	How important is it to coordinate or lead others in accomplishing work activities in this job?
Level of Competition	To what extent does this job require the worker to compete or to be aware of competitive pressures?
Deal With Unpleasant or Angry People	How frequently does the worker have to deal with unpleasant, angry, or discourteous individuals as part of the job requirements?
Spend Time Using Your Hands to Handle, Control, or	How much does this job require using your hands to handle, control, or feel objects, tools or controls?
Sounds, Noise Levels Are Distracting or Uncomforta	How often does this job require working exposed to sounds and noise levels that are distracting or uncomfortable?
Responsibility for Outcomes and Results	How responsible is the worker for work outcomes and results of other workers?
Degree of Automation	How automated is the job?
Consequence of Error	How serious would the result usually be if the worker made a mistake that was not readily correctable?
Frequency of Conflict Situations	How often are there conflict situations the employee has to face in this job?
Responsible for Others' Health and Safety	How much responsibility is there for the health and safety of others in this job?
Spend Time Standing	How much does this job require standing?
Extremely Bright or Inadequate Lighting	How often does this job require working in extremely bright or inadequate lighting conditions?
In an Enclosed Vehicle or Equipment	How often does this job require working in a closed vehicle or equipment (e.g., car)?
Cramped Work Space, Awkward Positions	How often does this job require working in cramped work spaces that requires getting into awkward positions?
Exposed to Contaminants	How often does this job require working exposed to contaminants (such as pollutants, gases, dust or odors)?
Very Hot or Cold Temperatures	How often does this job require working in very hot (above 90 F degrees) or very cold (below 32 F degrees) temperatures?
Spend Time Walking and Running	How much does this job require walking and running?
Public Speaking	How often do you have to perform public speaking in this job?
Spend Time Bending or Twisting the Body	How much does this job require bending or twisting your body?
Outdoors, Exposed to Weather	How often does this job require working outdoors, exposed to all weather conditions?
Spend Time Kneeling, Crouching, Stooping, or Crawl	How much does this job require kneeling, crouching, stooping, or crawling?
Pace Determined by Speed of Equipment	How important is it to this job that the pace is determined by the speed of equipment or machinery? (This does not refer to keeping busy at all times on this job.)
Exposed to Disease or Infections	How often does this job require exposure to disease/infections?
Exposed to Radiation	How often does this job require exposure to radiation?
Indoors, Not Environmentally Controlled	How often does this job require working indoors in non-controlled environmental conditions (e.g., warehouse without heat)?
Outdoors, Under Cover	How often does this job require working outdoors, under cover (e.g., structure with roof but no walls)?
Wear Specialized Protective or Safety Equipment su	How much does this job require wearing specialized protective or safety equipment such as breathing apparatus, safety harness, full protection suits, or radiation protection?
Exposed to Hazardous Equipment	How often does this job require exposure to hazardous equipment?
In an Open Vehicle or Equipment	How often does this job require working in an open vehicle or equipment (e.g., tractor)?
Exposed to Whole Body Vibration	How often does this job require exposure to whole body vibration (e.g., operate a jackhammer)?
Exposed to High Places	How often does this job require exposure to high places?
Exposed to Hazardous Conditions	How often does this job require exposure to hazardous conditions?
Exposed to Minor Burns, Cuts, Bites, or Stings	How often does this job require exposure to minor burns, cuts, bites, or stings?
Spend Time Keeping or Regaining Balance	How much does this job require keeping or regaining your balance?
Deal With Physically Aggressive People	How frequently does this job require the worker to deal with physical aggression of violent individuals?
Wear Common Protective or Safety Equipment such as	How much does this job require wearing common protective or safety equipment such as safety shoes, glasses, gloves, hard hats or live jackets?
Spend Time Climbing Ladders, Scaffolds, or Poles	How much does this job require climbing ladders, scaffolds, or poles?

Job Zone Component	Job Zone Component Definitions
Title	Job Zone Four: Considerable Preparation Needed
Overall Experience	A minimum of two to four years of work-related skill, knowledge, or experience is needed for these occupations. For example, an accountant must complete four years of college and work for several years in accounting to be considered qualified.
Job Training	Employees in these occupations usually need several years of work-related experience, on-the-job training, and/or vocational training.
Job Zone Examples	Many of these occupations involve coordinating, supervising, managing, or training others. Examples include accountants, chefs and head cooks, computer programmers, historians, pharmacists, and police detectives.
SVP Range	(7.0 to < 8.0)
Education	Most of these occupations require a four - year bachelor's degree, but some do not.

Work_Styles	Work_Styles Definitions
Attention to Detail	Job requires being careful about detail and thorough in completing work tasks.
Integrity	Job requires being honest and ethical.
Analytical Thinking	Job requires analyzing information and using logic to address work-related issues and problems.
Dependability	Job requires being reliable, responsible, and dependable, and fulfilling obligations.
Independence	Job requires developing one's own ways of doing things, guiding oneself with little or no supervision, and depending on oneself to get things done.
Cooperation	Job requires being pleasant with others on the job and displaying a good-natured, cooperative attitude.

Achievement/Effort	Job requires establishing and maintaining personally challenging achievement goals and exerting effort toward mastering tasks.
Self Control	Job requires maintaining composure, keeping emotions in check, controlling anger, and avoiding aggressive behavior, even in very difficult situations.
Concern for Others	Job requires being sensitive to others' needs and feelings and being understanding and helpful on the job.
Persistence	Job requires persistence in the face of obstacles.
Stress Tolerance	Job requires accepting criticism and dealing calmly and effectively with high stress situations.
Initiative	Job requires a willingness to take on responsibilities and challenges.
Adaptability/Flexibility	Job requires being open to change (positive or negative) and to considerable variety in the workplace.
Innovation	Job requires creativity and alternative thinking to develop new ideas for and answers to work-related problems.
Leadership	Job requires a willingness to lead, take charge, and offer opinions and direction.
Social Orientation	Job requires preferring to work with others rather than alone, and being personally connected with others on the job.

13-2051.00 - Financial Analysts

Conduct quantitative analyses of information affecting investment programs of public or private institutions.

Tasks

1) Evaluate and compare the relative quality of various securities in a given industry.

2) Contact brokers and purchase investments for companies, according to company policy.

3) Recommend investments and investment timing to companies, investment firm staff, or the investing public.

4) Prepare plans of action for investment based on financial analyses.

5) Monitor fundamental economic, industrial, and corporate developments through the analysis of information obtained from financial publications and services, investment banking firms, government agencies, trade publications, company sources, and personal interviews.

6) Collaborate with investment bankers to attract new corporate clients to securities firms.

7) Assemble spreadsheets and draw charts and graphs used to illustrate technical reports, using computer.

8) Analyze financial information to produce forecasts of business, industry, and economic conditions for use in making investment decisions.

9) Maintain knowledge and stay abreast of developments in the fields of industrial technology, business, finance, and economic theory.

10) Present oral and written reports on general economic trends, individual corporations, and entire industries.

11) Interpret data affecting investment programs, such as price, yield, stability, future trends in investment risks, and economic influences.

13-2052.00 - Personal Financial Advisors

Advise clients on financial plans utilizing knowledge of tax and investment strategies, securities, insurance, pension plans, and real estate. Duties include assessing clients' assets, liabilities, cash flow, insurance coverage, tax status, and financial objectives to establish investment strategies.

Tasks

1) Implement financial planning recommendations, or refer clients to someone who can assist them with plan implementation.

2) Conduct seminars and workshops on financial planning topics such as retirement planning, estate planning, and the evaluation of severance packages.

3) Monitor financial market trends to ensure that plans are effective, and to identify any necessary updates.

4) Prepare and interpret for clients information such as investment performance reports,

financial document summaries, and income projections.

5) Recommend strategies clients can use to achieve their financial goals and objectives, including specific recommendations in such areas as cash management, insurance coverage, and investment planning.

6) Research and investigate available investment opportunities to determine whether they fit into financial plans.

7) Sell financial products such as stocks, bonds, mutual funds, and insurance if licensed to do so.

8) Build and maintain client bases, keeping current client plans up-to-date and recruiting new clients on an ongoing basis.

9) Guide clients in the gathering of information such as bank account records, income tax returns, life and disability insurance records, pension plan information, and wills.

10) Authorize release of financial aid funds to students.

11) Review clients' accounts and plans regularly to determine whether life changes, economic changes, or financial performance indicate a need for plan reassessment.

12) Explain to individuals and groups the details of financial assistance available to college and university students, such as loans, grants, and scholarships.

13) Contact clients periodically to determine if there have been changes in their financial status.

14) Answer clients' questions about the purposes and details of financial plans and strategies.

15) Analyze financial information obtained from clients to determine strategies for meeting clients' financial objectives.

16) Meet with clients' other advisors, including attorneys, accountants, trust officers, and investment bankers, to fully understand clients' financial goals and circumstances.

17) Interview clients to determine their current income, expenses, insurance coverage, tax status, financial objectives, risk tolerance, and other information needed to develop a financial plan.

18) Determine amounts of aid to be granted to students, considering such factors as funds available, extent of demand, and financial needs.

19) Open accounts for clients, and disburse funds from account to creditors as agents for clients.

20) Participate in the selection of candidates for specific financial aid awards.

21) Contact clients' creditors to arrange for payment adjustments so that payments are feasible for clients and agreeable to creditors.

22) Devise debt liquidation plans that include payoff priorities and timelines.

23) Explain and document for clients the types of services that are to be provided, and the responsibilities to be taken by the personal financial advisor.

13-2053.00 - Insurance Underwriters

Review individual applications for insurance to evaluate degree of risk involved and determine acceptance of applications.

Tasks

1) Decline excessive risks.

2) Evaluate possibility of losses due to catastrophe or excessive insurance.

3) Write to field representatives, medical personnel, and others to obtain further information, quote rates, or explain company underwriting policies.

4) Decrease value of policy when risk is substandard and specify applicable endorsements or apply rating to ensure safe profitable distribution of risks, using reference materials.

5) Review company records to determine amount of insurance in force on single risk or group of closely related risks.

6) Authorize reinsurance of policy when risk is high.

Knowledge	Knowledge Definitions
Customer and Personal Service	Knowledge of principles and processes for providing customer and personal services. This includes customer needs assessment, meeting quality standards for services, and evaluation of customer satisfaction.
English Language	Knowledge of the structure and content of the English language including the meaning and spelling of words, rules of composition, and grammar.

Clerical	Knowledge of administrative and clerical procedures and systems such as word processing, managing files and records, stenography and transcription, designing forms, and other office procedures and terminology.
Mathematics	Knowledge of arithmetic, algebra, geometry, calculus, statistics, and their applications.
Sales and Marketing	Knowledge of principles and methods for showing, promoting, and selling products or services. This includes marketing strategy and tactics, product demonstration, sales techniques, and sales control systems.
Economics and Accounting	Knowledge of economic and accounting principles and practices, the financial markets, banking and the analysis and reporting of financial data.
Computers and Electronics	Knowledge of circuit boards, processors, chips, electronic equipment, and computer hardware and software, including applications and programming.
Law and Government	Knowledge of laws, legal codes, court procedures, precedents, government regulations, executive orders, agency rules, and the democratic political process.
Administration and Management	Knowledge of business and management principles involved in strategic planning, resource allocation, human resources modeling, leadership technique, production methods, and coordination of people and resources.
Education and Training	Knowledge of principles and methods for curriculum and training design, teaching and instruction for individuals and groups, and the measurement of training effects.
Communications and Media	Knowledge of media production, communication, and dissemination techniques and methods. This includes alternative ways to inform and entertain via written, oral, and visual media.
Personnel and Human Resources	Knowledge of principles and procedures for personnel recruitment, selection, training, compensation and benefits, labor relations and negotiation, and personnel information systems.
Public Safety and Security	Knowledge of relevant equipment, policies, procedures, and strategies to promote effective local, state, or national security operations for the protection of people, data, property, and institutions.
Telecommunications	Knowledge of transmission, broadcasting, switching, control, and operation of telecommunications systems.
Psychology	Knowledge of human behavior and performance; individual differences in ability, personality, and interests; learning and motivation; psychological research methods; and the assessment and treatment of behavioral and affective disorders.
Building and Construction	Knowledge of materials, methods, and the tools involved in the construction or repair of houses, buildings, or other structures such as highways and roads.
Production and Processing	Knowledge of raw materials, production processes, quality control, costs, and other techniques for maximizing the effective manufacture and distribution of goods.
Philosophy and Theology	Knowledge of different philosophical systems and religions. This includes their basic principles, values, ethics, ways of thinking, customs, practices, and their impact on human culture.
Geography	Knowledge of principles and methods for describing the features of land, sea, and air masses, including their physical characteristics, locations, interrelationships, and distribution of plant, animal, and human life.
Medicine and Dentistry	Knowledge of the information and techniques needed to diagnose and treat human injuries, diseases, and deformities. This includes symptoms, treatment alternatives, drug properties and interactions, and preventive health-care measures.
Sociology and Anthropology	Knowledge of group behavior and dynamics, societal trends and influences, human migrations, ethnicity, cultures and their history and origins.
Mechanical	Knowledge of machines and tools, including their designs, uses, repair, and maintenance.
Engineering and Technology	Knowledge of the practical application of engineering science and technology. This includes applying principles, techniques, procedures, and equipment to the design and production of various goods and services.
Transportation	Knowledge of principles and methods for moving people or goods by air, rail, sea, or road, including the relative costs and benefits.
Design	Knowledge of design techniques, tools, and principles involved in production of precision technical plans, blueprints, drawings, and models.

Food Production	Knowledge of techniques and equipment for planting, growing, and harvesting food products (both plant and animal) for consumption, including storage/handling techniques.
Therapy and Counseling	Knowledge of principles, methods, and procedures for diagnosis, treatment, and rehabilitation of physical and mental dysfunctions, and for career counseling and guidance.
Chemistry	Knowledge of the chemical composition, structure, and properties of substances and of the chemical processes and transformations that they undergo. This includes uses of chemicals and their interactions, danger signs, production techniques, and disposal methods.
Physics	Knowledge and prediction of physical principles, laws, their interrelationships, and applications to understanding fluid, material, and atmospheric dynamics, and mechanical, electrical, atomic and sub-atomic structures and processes.
Biology	Knowledge of plant and animal organisms, their tissues, cells, functions, interdependencies, and interactions with each other and the environment.
Foreign Language	Knowledge of the structure and content of a foreign (non-English) language including the meaning and spelling of words, rules of composition and grammar, and pronunciation.
Fine Arts	Knowledge of the theory and techniques required to compose, produce, and perform works of music, dance, visual arts, drama, and sculpture.
History and Archeology	Knowledge of historical events and their causes, indicators, and effects on civilizations and cultures.

Skills	Skills Definitions
Active Listening	Giving full attention to what other people are saying, taking time to understand the points being made, asking questions as appropriate, and not interrupting at inappropriate times.
Critical Thinking	Using logic and reasoning to identify the strengths and weaknesses of alternative solutions, conclusions or approaches to problems.
Reading Comprehension	Understanding written sentences and paragraphs in work related documents.
Writing	Communicating effectively in writing as appropriate for the needs of the audience.
Speaking	Talking to others to convey information effectively.
Active Learning	Understanding the implications of new information for both current and future problem-solving and decision-making.
Judgment and Decision Making	Considering the relative costs and benefits of potential actions to choose the most appropriate one.
Time Management	Managing one's own time and the time of others.
Complex Problem Solving	Identifying complex problems and reviewing related information to develop and evaluate options and implement solutions.
Service Orientation	Actively looking for ways to help people.
Monitoring	Monitoring/Assessing performance of yourself, other individuals, or organizations to make improvements or take corrective action.
Learning Strategies	Selecting and using training/instructional methods and procedures appropriate for the situation when learning or teaching new things.
Social Perceptiveness	Being aware of others' reactions and understanding why they react as they do.
Coordination	Adjusting actions in relation to others' actions.
Negotiation	Bringing others together and trying to reconcile differences.
Instructing	Teaching others how to do something.
Mathematics	Using mathematics to solve problems.
Persuasion	Persuading others to change their minds or behavior.
Management of Personnel Resources	Motivating, developing, and directing people as they work, identifying the best people for the job.
Quality Control Analysis	Conducting tests and inspections of products, services, or processes to evaluate quality or performance.
Operations Analysis	Analyzing needs and product requirements to create a design.
Management of Financial Resources	Determining how money will be spent to get the work done, and accounting for these expenditures.
Systems Evaluation	Identifying measures or indicators of system performance and the actions needed to improve or correct performance, relative to the goals of the system.
Systems Analysis	Determining how a system should work and how changes in conditions, operations, and the environment will affect outcomes.
Troubleshooting	Determining causes of operating errors and deciding what to do about it.

Management of Material Resources	Obtaining and seeing to the appropriate use of equipment, facilities, and materials needed to do certain work.
Programming	Writing computer programs for various purposes.
Science	Using scientific rules and methods to solve problems.
Equipment Selection	Determining the kind of tools and equipment needed to do a job.
Operation Monitoring	Watching gauges, dials, or other indicators to make sure a machine is working properly.
Technology Design	Generating or adapting equipment and technology to serve user needs.
Installation	Installing equipment, machines, wiring, or programs to meet specifications.
Operation and Control	Controlling operations of equipment or systems.
Equipment Maintenance	Performing routine maintenance on equipment and determining when and what kind of maintenance is needed.
Repairing	Repairing machines or systems using the needed tools.

Ability	Ability Definitions
Written Comprehension	The ability to read and understand information and ideas presented in writing.
Inductive Reasoning	The ability to combine pieces of information to form general rules or conclusions (includes finding a relationship among seemingly unrelated events).
Deductive Reasoning	The ability to apply general rules to specific problems to produce answers that make sense.
Near Vision	The ability to see details at close range (within a few feet of the observer).
Problem Sensitivity	The ability to tell when something is wrong or is likely to go wrong. It does not involve solving the problem, only recognizing there is a problem.
Speech Recognition	The ability to identify and understand the speech of another person.
Oral Comprehension	The ability to listen to and understand information and ideas presented through spoken words and sentences.
Oral Expression	The ability to communicate information and ideas in speaking so others will understand.
Flexibility of Closure	The ability to identify or detect a known pattern (a figure, object, word, or sound) that is hidden in other distracting material.
Information Ordering	The ability to arrange things or actions in a certain order or pattern according to a specific rule or set of rules (e.g., patterns of numbers, letters, words, pictures, mathematical operations).
Speech Clarity	The ability to speak clearly so others can understand you.
Written Expression	The ability to communicate information and ideas in writing so others will understand.
Category Flexibility	The ability to generate or use different sets of rules for combining or grouping things in different ways.
Number Facility	The ability to add, subtract, multiply, or divide quickly and correctly.
Mathematical Reasoning	The ability to choose the right mathematical methods or formulas to solve a problem.
Selective Attention	The ability to concentrate on a task over a period of time without being distracted.
Speed of Closure	The ability to quickly make sense of, combine, and organize information into meaningful patterns.
Perceptual Speed	The ability to quickly and accurately compare similarities and differences among sets of letters, numbers, objects, pictures, or patterns. The things to be compared may be presented at the same time or one after the other. This ability also includes comparing a presented object with a remembered object.
Originality	The ability to come up with unusual or clever ideas about a given topic or situation, or to develop creative ways to solve a problem.
Fluency of Ideas	The ability to come up with a number of ideas about a topic (the number of ideas is important, not their quality, correctness, or creativity).
Memorization	The ability to remember information such as words, numbers, pictures, and procedures.
Finger Dexterity	The ability to make precisely coordinated movements of the fingers of one or both hands to grasp, manipulate, or assemble very small objects.
Far Vision	The ability to see details at a distance.
Visualization	The ability to imagine how something will look after it is moved around or when its parts are moved or rearranged.
Time Sharing	The ability to shift back and forth between two or more activities or sources of information (such as speech, sounds, touch, or other sources).

Auditory Attention	The ability to focus on a single source of sound in the presence of other distracting sounds.
Visual Color Discrimination	The ability to match or detect differences between colors, including shades of color and brightness.
Manual Dexterity	The ability to quickly move your hand, your hand together with your arm, or your two hands to grasp, manipulate, or assemble objects.
Arm-Hand Steadiness	The ability to keep your hand and arm steady while moving your arm or while holding your arm and hand in one position.
Hearing Sensitivity	The ability to detect or tell the differences between sounds that vary in pitch and loudness.
Trunk Strength	The ability to use your abdominal and lower back muscles to support part of the body repeatedly or continuously over time without 'giving out' or fatiguing.
Control Precision	The ability to quickly and repeatedly adjust the controls of a machine or a vehicle to exact positions.
Depth Perception	The ability to judge which of several objects is closer or farther away from you, or to judge the distance between you and an object.
Wrist-Finger Speed	The ability to make fast, simple, repeated movements of the fingers, hands, and wrists.
Speed of Limb Movement	The ability to quickly move the arms and legs.
Multilimb Coordination	The ability to coordinate two or more limbs (for example, two arms, two legs, or one leg and one arm) while sitting, standing, or lying down. It does not involve performing the activities while the whole body is in motion.
Static Strength	The ability to exert maximum muscle force to lift, push, pull, or carry objects.
Explosive Strength	The ability to use short bursts of muscle force to propel oneself (as in jumping or sprinting), or to throw an object.
Rate Control	The ability to time your movements or the movement of a piece of equipment in anticipation of changes in the speed and/or direction of a moving object or scene.
Gross Body Equilibrium	The ability to keep or regain your body balance or stay upright when in an unstable position.
Gross Body Coordination	The ability to coordinate the movement of your arms, legs, and torso together when the whole body is in motion.
Dynamic Flexibility	The ability to quickly and repeatedly bend, stretch, twist, or reach out with your body, arms, and/or legs.
Extent Flexibility	The ability to bend, stretch, twist, or reach with your body, arms, and/or legs.
Stamina	The ability to exert yourself physically over long periods of time without getting winded or out of breath.
Dynamic Strength	The ability to exert muscle force repeatedly or continuously over time. This involves muscular endurance and resistance to muscle fatigue.
Response Orientation	The ability to choose quickly between two or more movements in response to two or more different signals (lights, sounds, pictures). It includes the speed with which the correct response is started with the hand, foot, or other body part.
Sound Localization	The ability to tell the direction from which a sound originated.
Night Vision	The ability to see under low light conditions.
Peripheral Vision	The ability to see objects or movement of objects to one's side when the eyes are looking ahead.
Glare Sensitivity	The ability to see objects in the presence of glare or bright lighting.
Spatial Orientation	The ability to know your location in relation to the environment or to know where other objects are in relation to you.
Reaction Time	The ability to quickly respond (with the hand, finger, or foot) to a signal (sound, light, picture) when it appears.

Work_Activity	Work_Activity Definitions
Getting Information	Observing, receiving, and otherwise obtaining information from all relevant sources.
Interacting With Computers	Using computers and computer systems (including hardware and software) to program, write software, set up functions, enter data, or process information.
Making Decisions and Solving Problems	Analyzing information and evaluating results to choose the best solution and solve problems.
Communicating with Persons Outside Organization	Communicating with people outside the organization, representing the organization to customers, the public, government, and other external sources. This information can be exchanged in person, in writing, or by telephone or e-mail.
Establishing and Maintaining Interpersonal Relatio	Developing constructive and cooperative working relationships with others, and maintaining them over time.

Communicating with Supervisors, Peers, or Subordin	Providing information to supervisors, co-workers, and subordinates by telephone, in written form, e-mail, or in person.
Analyzing Data or Information	Identifying the underlying principles, reasons, or facts of information by breaking down information or data into separate parts.
Processing Information	Compiling, coding, categorizing, calculating, tabulating, auditing, or verifying information or data.
Evaluating Information to Determine Compliance wit	Using relevant information and individual judgment to determine whether events or processes comply with laws, regulations, or standards.
Updating and Using Relevant Knowledge	Keeping up-to-date technically and applying new knowledge to your job.
Organizing, Planning, and Prioritizing Work	Developing specific goals and plans to prioritize, organize, and accomplish your work.
Resolving Conflicts and Negotiating with Others	Handling complaints, settling disputes, and resolving grievances and conflicts, or otherwise negotiating with others.
Identifying Objects, Actions, and Events	Identifying information by categorizing, estimating, recognizing differences or similarities, and detecting changes in circumstances or events.
Developing and Building Teams	Encouraging and building mutual trust, respect, and cooperation among team members.
Interpreting the Meaning of Information for Others	Translating or explaining what information means and how it can be used.
Coaching and Developing Others	Identifying the developmental needs of others and coaching, mentoring, or otherwise helping others to improve their knowledge or skills.
Monitor Processes, Materials, or Surroundings	Monitoring and reviewing information from materials, events, or the environment, to detect or assess problems.
Performing Administrative Activities	Performing day-to-day administrative tasks such as maintaining information files and processing paperwork.
Documenting/Recording Information	Entering, transcribing, recording, storing, or maintaining information in written or electronic/magnetic form.
Selling or Influencing Others	Convincing others to buy merchandise/goods or to otherwise change their minds or actions.
Developing Objectives and Strategies	Establishing long-range objectives and specifying the strategies and actions to achieve them.
Training and Teaching Others	Identifying the educational needs of others, developing formal educational or training programs or classes, and teaching or instructing others.
Judging the Qualities of Things, Services, or Peop	Assessing the value, importance, or quality of things or people.
Scheduling Work and Activities	Scheduling events, programs, and activities, as well as the work of others.
Thinking Creatively	Developing, designing, or creating new applications, ideas, relationships, systems, or products, including artistic contributions.
Provide Consultation and Advice to Others	Providing guidance and expert advice to management or other groups on technical, systems-, or process-related topics.
Estimating the Quantifiable Characteristics of Pro	Estimating sizes, distances, and quantities; or determining time, costs, resources, or materials needed to perform a work activity.
Coordinating the Work and Activities of Others	Getting members of a group to work together to accomplish tasks.
Guiding, Directing, and Motivating Subordinates	Providing guidance and direction to subordinates, including setting performance standards and monitoring performance.
Performing for or Working Directly with the Public	Performing for people or dealing directly with the public. This includes serving customers in restaurants and stores, and receiving clients or guests.
Inspecting Equipment, Structures, or Material	Inspecting equipment, structures, or materials to identify the cause of errors or other problems or defects.
Assisting and Caring for Others	Providing personal assistance, medical attention, emotional support, or other personal care to others such as coworkers, customers, or patients.
Monitoring and Controlling Resources	Monitoring and controlling resources and overseeing the spending of money.
Performing General Physical Activities	Performing physical activities that require considerable use of your arms and legs and moving your whole body, such as climbing, lifting, balancing, walking, stooping, and handling of materials.
Handling and Moving Objects	Using hands and arms in handling, installing, positioning, and moving materials, and manipulating things.
Controlling Machines and Processes	Using either control mechanisms or direct physical activity to operate machines or processes (not including computers or vehicles).

Drafting, Laying Out, and Specifying Technical Dev	Providing documentation, detailed instructions, drawings, or specifications to tell others about how devices, parts, equipment, or structures are to be fabricated, constructed, assembled, modified, maintained, or used.
Staffing Organizational Units	Recruiting, interviewing, selecting, hiring, and promoting employees in an organization.
Repairing and Maintaining Electronic Equipment	Servicing, repairing, calibrating, regulating, fine-tuning, or testing machines, devices, and equipment that operate primarily on the basis of electrical or electronic (not mechanical) principles.
Operating Vehicles, Mechanized Devices, or Equipme	Running, maneuvering, navigating, or driving vehicles or mechanized equipment, such as forklifts, passenger vehicles, aircraft, or water craft.
Repairing and Maintaining Mechanical Equipment	Servicing, repairing, adjusting, and testing machines, devices, moving parts, and equipment that operate primarily on the basis of mechanical (not electronic) principles.

Work_Context	Work_Context Definitions
Telephone	How often do you have telephone conversations in this job?
Contact With Others	How much does this job require the worker to be in contact with others (face-to-face, by telephone, or otherwise) in order to perform it?
Spend Time Sitting	How much does this job require sitting?
Freedom to Make Decisions	How much decision making freedom, without supervision, does the job offer?
Structured versus Unstructured Work	To what extent is this job structured for the worker, rather than allowing the worker to determine tasks, priorities, and goals?
Face-to-Face Discussions	How often do you have to have face-to-face discussions with individuals or teams in this job?
Time Pressure	How often does this job require the worker to meet strict deadlines?
Importance of Being Exact or Accurate	How important is being very exact or highly accurate in performing this job?
Letters and Memos	How often does the job require written letters and memos?
Indoors, Environmentally Controlled	How often does this job require working indoors in environmentally controlled conditions?
Electronic Mail	How often do you use electronic mail in this job?
Work With Work Group or Team	How important is it to work with others in a group or team in this job?
Impact of Decisions on Co-workers or Company Resul	How do the decisions an employee makes impact the results of co-workers, clients or the company?
Spend Time Making Repetitive Motions	How much does this job require making repetitive motions?
Frequency of Decision Making	How frequently is the worker required to make decisions that affect other people, the financial resources, and/or the image and reputation of the organization?
Importance of Repeating Same Tasks	How important is repeating the same physical activities (e.g., key entry) or mental activities (e.g., checking entries in a ledger) over and over, without stopping, to performing this job?
Coordinate or Lead Others	How important is it to coordinate or lead others in accomplishing work activities in this job?
Physical Proximity	To what extent does this job require the worker to perform job tasks in close physical proximity to other people?
Spend Time Using Your Hands to Handle, Control, or	How much does this job require using your hands to handle, control, or feel objects, tools or controls?
Level of Competition	To what extent does this job require the worker to compete or to be aware of competitive pressures?
Deal With External Customers	How important is it to work with external customers or the public in this job?
Deal With Unpleasant or Angry People	How frequently does the worker have to deal with unpleasant, angry, or discourteous individuals as part of the job requirements?
Frequency of Conflict Situations	How often are there conflict situations the employee has to face in this job?
Consequence of Error	How serious would the result usually be if the worker made a mistake that was not readily correctable?
Degree of Automation	How automated is the job?
Responsibility for Outcomes and Results	How responsible is the worker for work outcomes and results of other workers?
Sounds, Noise Levels Are Distracting or Uncomforta	How often does this job require working exposed to sounds and noise levels that are distracting or uncomfortable?
In an Enclosed Vehicle or Equipment	How often does this job require working in a closed vehicle or equipment (e.g., car)?
Spend Time Standing	How much does this job require standing?

Deal With Physically Aggressive People	How frequently does this job require the worker to deal with physical aggression of violent individuals?
Cramped Work Space, Awkward Positions	How often does this job require working in cramped work spaces that requires getting into awkward positions?
Spend Time Walking and Running	How much does this job require walking and running?
Public Speaking	How often do you have to perform public speaking in this job?
Responsible for Others' Health and Safety	How much responsibility is there for the health and safety of others in this job?
Spend Time Bending or Twisting the Body	How much does this job require bending or twisting your body?
Very Hot or Cold Temperatures	How often does this job require working in very hot (above 90 F degrees) or very cold (below 32 F degrees) temperatures?
Pace Determined by Speed of Equipment	How important is it to this job that the pace is determined by the speed of equipment or machinery? (This does not refer to keeping busy at all times on this job.)
Exposed to Contaminants	How often does this job require working exposed to contaminants (such as pollutants, gases, dust or odors)?
Exposed to Disease or Infections	How often does this job require exposure to disease/infections?
Outdoors, Exposed to Weather	How often does this job require working outdoors, exposed to all weather conditions?
Extremely Bright or Inadequate Lighting	How often does this job require working in extremely bright or inadequate lighting conditions?
Wear Common Protective or Safety Equipment such as	How much does this job require wearing common protective or safety equipment such as safety shoes, glasses, gloves, hard hats or live jackets?
Spend Time Kneeling, Crouching, Stooping, or Crawl	How much does this job require kneeling, crouching, stooping or crawling?
Indoors, Not Environmentally Controlled	How often does this job require working indoors in non-controlled environmental conditions (e.g., warehouse without heat)?
Wear Specialized Protective or Safety Equipment su	How much does this job require wearing specialized protective or safety equipment such as breathing apparatus, safety harness, full protection suits, or radiation protection?
Exposed to Radiation	How often does this job require exposure to radiation?
Exposed to Hazardous Equipment	How often does this job require exposure to hazardous equipment?
Exposed to Whole Body Vibration	How often does this job require exposure to whole body vibration (e.g., operate a jackhammer)?
Spend Time Keeping or Regaining Balance	How much does this job require keeping or regaining your balance?
Outdoors, Under Cover	How often does this job require working outdoors, under cover (e.g., structure with roof but no walls)?
In an Open Vehicle or Equipment	How often does this job require working in an open vehicle or equipment (e.g., tractor)?
Spend Time Climbing Ladders, Scaffolds, or Poles	How much does this job require climbing ladders, scaffolds, or poles?
Exposed to Minor Burns, Cuts, Bites, or Stings	How often does this job require exposure to minor burns, cuts, bites, or stings?
Exposed to Hazardous Conditions	How often does this job require exposure to hazardous conditions?
Exposed to High Places	How often does this job require exposure to high places?

Job Zone Component	Job Zone Component Definitions
Title	Job Zone Three: Medium Preparation Needed
Overall Experience	Previous work-related skill, knowledge, or experience is required for these occupations. For example, an electrician must have completed three or four years of apprenticeship or several years of vocational training, and often must have passed a licensing exam, in order to perform the job.
Job Training	Employees in these occupations usually need one or two years of training involving both on-the-job experience and informal training with experienced workers.
Job Zone Examples	These occupations usually involve using communication and organizational skills to coordinate, supervise, manage, or train others to accomplish goals. Examples include dental assistants, electricians, fish and game wardens, legal secretaries, personnel recruiters, and recreation workers.
SVP Range	(6.0 to < 7.0)
Education	Most occupations in this zone require training in vocational schools, related on-the-job experience, or an associate's degree. Some may require a bachelor's degree.

Work_Styles	Work_Styles Definitions
Integrity	Job requires being honest and ethical.
Cooperation	Job requires being pleasant with others on the job and displaying a good-natured, cooperative attitude.
Attention to Detail	Job requires being careful about detail and thorough in completing work tasks.
Dependability	Job requires being reliable, responsible, and dependable, and fulfilling obligations.
Independence	Job requires developing one's own ways of doing things, guiding oneself with little or no supervision, and depending on oneself to get things done.
Analytical Thinking	Job requires analyzing information and using logic to address work-related issues and problems.
Self Control	Job requires maintaining composure, keeping emotions in check, controlling anger, and avoiding aggressive behavior, even in very difficult situations.
Adaptability/Flexibility	Job requires being open to change (positive or negative) and to considerable variety in the workplace.
Initiative	Job requires a willingness to take on responsibilities and challenges.
Concern for Others	Job requires being sensitive to others' needs and feelings and being understanding and helpful on the job.
Achievement/Effort	Job requires establishing and maintaining personally challenging achievement goals and exerting effort toward mastering tasks.
Persistence	Job requires persistence in the face of obstacles.
Stress Tolerance	Job requires accepting criticism and dealing calmly and effectively with high stress situations.
Innovation	Job requires creativity and alternative thinking to develop new ideas for and answers to work-related problems.
Social Orientation	Job requires preferring to work with others rather than alone, and being personally connected with others on the job.
Leadership	Job requires a willingness to lead, take charge, and offer opinions and direction.

13-2061.00 - Financial Examiners

Enforce or ensure compliance with laws and regulations governing financial and securities institutions and financial and real estate transactions. May examine, verify correctness of, or establish authenticity of records.

Tasks

1) Direct and participate in formal and informal meetings with bank directors, trustees, senior management, counsels, outside accountants and consultants in order to gather information and discuss findings.

2) Verify and inspect cash reserves, assigned collateral, and bank-owned securities in order to check internal control procedures.

3) Prepare reports, exhibits and other supporting schedules that detail an institution's safety and soundness, compliance with laws and regulations, and recommended solutions to questionable financial conditions.

4) Recommend actions to ensure compliance with laws and regulations, or to protect solvency of institutions.

5) Resolve problems concerning the overall financial integrity of banking institutions including loan investment portfolios, capital, earnings, and specific or large troubled accounts.

6) Review audit reports of internal and external auditors in order to monitor adequacy of scope of reports or to discover specific weaknesses in internal routines.

7) Establish guidelines for procedures and policies that comply with new and revised regulations, and direct their implementation.

8) Confer with officials of real estate, securities, or financial institution industries in order to exchange views and discuss issues or pending cases.

9) Evaluate data processing applications for institutions under examination in order to develop recommendations for coordinating existing systems with examination procedures.

10) Plan, supervise, and review work of assigned subordinates.

11) Review and analyze new, proposed, or revised laws, regulations, policies, and procedures in order to interpret their meaning and determine their impact.

12) Review applications for mergers, acquisitions, establishment of new institutions.

acceptance in Federal Reserve System, or registration of securities sales in order to determine their public interest value and conformance to regulations, and recommend acceptance or rejection.

13) Train other examiners in the financial examination process.

14) Examine the minutes of meetings of directors, stockholders and committees in order to investigate the specific authority extended at various levels of management.

15) Review balance sheets, operating income and expense accounts, and loan documentation in order to confirm institution assets and liabilities.

13-2071.00 - Loan Counselors

Provide guidance to prospective loan applicants who have problems qualifying for traditional loans. Guidance may include determining the best type of loan and explaining loan requirements or restrictions.

Tasks

1) Submit applications to credit analysts for verification and recommendation.

2) Contact borrowers with delinquent accounts to obtain payment in full or to negotiate repayment plans.

3) Refer loans to loan committees for approval.

4) Interview applicants and request specified information for loan applications.

5) Assist in selection of financial award candidates, using electronic databases to certify loan eligibility.

6) Arrange for maintenance and liquidation of delinquent properties.

7) Maintain and review account records, updating and recategorizing them according to status changes.

8) Contact applicants or creditors to resolve questions about applications or to assist with completion of paperwork.

9) Check loan agreements to ensure that they are complete and accurate, according to policies.

10) Confer with underwriters to resolve mortgage application problems.

11) Analyze applicants' financial status, credit, and property evaluations to determine feasibility of granting loans.

12) Authorize and sign mail collection letters.

13) Compare data on student aid applications with eligibility requirements of assistance programs.

14) Establish payment priorities according to credit terms and interest rates in order to reduce clients' overall costs.

15) Review billing for accuracy.

16) Counsel clients on personal and family financial problems, such as excessive spending and borrowing of funds.

17) Inform individuals and groups about the financial assistance available to college or university students.

18) Locate debtors using post office directories, utility services account listings, and mailing lists.

19) Match students' needs and eligibility with available financial aid programs in order to provide informed recommendations.

20) Open accounts for clients and disburse funds from clients' accounts to creditors.

21) Approve loans within specified limits.

22) Contact creditors to explain clients' financial situations and to arrange for payment adjustments so that payments are feasible for clients and agreeable to creditors.

23) Maintain current knowledge of credit regulations.

24) Calculate amount of debt and funds available in order to plan methods of payoff and to estimate time for debt liquidation.

25) Analyze potential loan markets to find opportunities to promote loans and financial services.

26) Supervise loan personnel.

27) Petition courts to transfer titles and deeds of collateral to banks.

13-2072.00 - Loan Officers

Evaluate, authorize, or recommend approval of commercial, real estate, or credit loans. Advise borrowers on financial status and methods of payments. Includes mortgage loan officers and agents, collection analysts, loan servicing officers, and loan underwriters.

Tasks

1) Analyze applicants' financial status, credit, and property evaluations to determine feasibility of granting loans.

2) Obtain and compile copies of loan applicants' credit histories, corporate financial statements, and other financial information.

3) Stay abreast of new types of loans and other financial services and products in order to better meet customers' needs.

4) Explain to customers the different types of loans and credit options that are available, as well as the terms of those services.

5) Compute payment schedules.

6) Review and update credit and loan files.

7) Submit applications to credit analysts for verification and recommendation.

8) Handle customer complaints and take appropriate action to resolve them.

9) Work with clients to identify their financial goals and to find ways of reaching those goals.

10) Approve loans within specified limits, and refer loan applications outside those limits to management for approval.

11) Review loan agreements to ensure that they are complete and accurate according to policy.

12) Confer with underwriters to aid in resolving mortgage application problems.

13) Negotiate payment arrangements with customers who have delinquent loans.

14) Analyze potential loan markets and develop referral networks in order to locate prospects for loans.

15) Interview, hire, and train new employees.

16) Arrange for maintenance and liquidation of delinquent properties.

17) Market bank products to individuals and firms, promoting bank services that may meet customers' needs.

18) Supervise loan personnel.

19) Prepare reports to send to customers whose accounts are delinquent, and forward irreconcilable accounts for collector action.

20) Set credit policies, credit lines, procedures and standards in conjunction with senior managers.

21) Petition courts to transfer titles and deeds of collateral to banks.

22) Provide special services such as investment banking for clients with more specialized needs.

Knowledge	Knowledge Definitions
Sales and Marketing	Knowledge of principles and methods for showing, promoting, and selling products or services. This includes marketing strategy and tactics, product demonstration, sales techniques, and sales control systems.
Customer and Personal Service	Knowledge of principles and processes for providing customer and personal services. This includes customer needs assessment, meeting quality standards for services, and evaluation of customer satisfaction.
Economics and Accounting	Knowledge of economic and accounting principles and practices, the financial markets, banking and the analysis and reporting of financial data.
English Language	Knowledge of the structure and content of the English language including the meaning and spelling of words, rules of composition, and grammar.
Mathematics	Knowledge of arithmetic, algebra, geometry, calculus, statistics, and their applications.
Clerical	Knowledge of administrative and clerical procedures and systems such as word processing, managing files and records, stenography and transcription, designing forms, and other office procedures and terminology.

Law and Government	Knowledge of laws, legal codes. court procedures. precedents. government regulations, executive orders. agency rules. and the democratic political process.
Personnel and Human Resources	Knowledge of principles and procedures for personnel recruitment, selection, training, compensation and benefits. labor relations and negotiation, and personnel information systems.
Administration and Management	Knowledge of business and management principles involved in strategic planning, resource allocation, human resources modeling, leadership technique, production methods, and coordination of people and resources.
Computers and Electronics	Knowledge of circuit boards, processors. chips. electronic equipment, and computer hardware and software, including applications and programming.
Psychology	Knowledge of human behavior and performance; individual differences in ability, personality, and interests; learning and motivation; psychological research methods; and the assessment and treatment of behavioral and affective disorders.
Education and Training	Knowledge of principles and methods for curriculum and training design, teaching and instruction for individuals and groups, and the measurement of training effects.
Public Safety and Security	Knowledge of relevant equipment. policies, procedures. and strategies to promote effective local, state, or national security operations for the protection of people. data, property, and institutions.
Communications and Media	Knowledge of media production, communication, and dissemination techniques and methods. This includes alternative ways to inform and entertain via written, oral, and visual media.
Telecommunications	Knowledge of transmission, broadcasting, switching, control, and operation of telecommunications systems.
Transportation	Knowledge of principles and methods for moving people or goods by air, rail, sea, or road, including the relative costs and benefits.
Production and Processing	Knowledge of raw materials, production processes, quality control, costs, and other techniques for maximizing the effective manufacture and distribution of goods.
Geography	Knowledge of principles and methods for describing the features of land, sea, and air masses, including their physical characteristics, locations, interrelationships, and distribution of plant, animal, and human life.
Sociology and Anthropology	Knowledge of group behavior and dynamics, societal trends and influences, human migrations, ethnicity, cultures and their history and origins.
Building and Construction	Knowledge of materials, methods, and the tools involved in the construction or repair of houses, buildings, or other structures such as highways and roads.
Philosophy and Theology	Knowledge of different philosophical systems and religions. This includes their basic principles, values, ethics, ways of thinking, customs, practices, and their impact on human culture.
Therapy and Counseling	Knowledge of principles, methods, and procedures for diagnosis, treatment, and rehabilitation of physical and mental dysfunctions, and for career counseling and guidance.
Food Production	Knowledge of techniques and equipment for planting, growing, and harvesting food products (both plant and animal) for consumption, including storage/handling techniques.
History and Archeology	Knowledge of historical events and their causes, indicators, and effects on civilizations and cultures.
Mechanical	Knowledge of machines and tools, including their designs, uses, repair, and maintenance.
Foreign Language	Knowledge of the structure and content of a foreign (non-English) language including the meaning and spelling of words, rules of composition and grammar, and pronunciation.
Biology	Knowledge of plant and animal organisms, their tissues, cells, functions, interdependencies, and interactions with each other and the environment.
Fine Arts	Knowledge of the theory and techniques required to compose, produce, and perform works of music, dance, visual arts, drama, and sculpture.
Physics	Knowledge and prediction of physical principles, laws, their interrelationships, and applications to understanding fluid, material, and atmospheric dynamics, and mechanical, electrical, atomic and sub-atomic structures and processes.
Engineering and Technology	Knowledge of the practical application of engineering science and technology. This includes applying principles, techniques, procedures, and equipment to the design and production of various goods and services.
Medicine and Dentistry	Knowledge of the information and techniques needed to diagnose and treat human injuries. diseases. and deformities. This includes symptoms. treatment alternatives. drug properties and interactions, and preventive health-care measures.
Design	Knowledge of design techniques. tools. and principles involved in production of precision technical plans. blueprints. drawings, and models.
Chemistry	Knowledge of the chemical composition, structure, and properties of substances and of the chemical processes and transformations that they undergo. This includes uses of chemicals and their interactions. danger signs, production techniques. and disposal methods.

Skills	Skills Definitions
Active Listening	Giving full attention to what other people are saying, taking time to understand the points being made. asking questions as appropriate, and not interrupting at inappropriate times.
Time Management	Managing one's own time and the time of others.
Reading Comprehension	Understanding written sentences and paragraphs in work related documents.
Persuasion	Persuading others to change their minds or behavior.
Speaking	Talking to others to convey information effectively.
Social Perceptiveness	Being aware of others' reactions and understanding why they react as they do.
Coordination	Adjusting actions in relation to others' actions.
Service Orientation	Actively looking for ways to help people.
Complex Problem Solving	Identifying complex problems and reviewing related information to develop and evaluate options and implement solutions.
Active Learning	Understanding the implications of new information for both current and future problem-solving and decision-making.
Judgment and Decision Making	Considering the relative costs and benefits of potential actions to choose the most appropriate one.
Monitoring	Monitoring/Assessing performance of yourself, other individuals, or organizations to make improvements or take corrective action.
Learning Strategies	Selecting and using training/instructional methods and procedures appropriate for the situation when learning or teaching new things.
Critical Thinking	Using logic and reasoning to identify the strengths and weaknesses of alternative solutions, conclusions or approaches to problems.
Negotiation	Bringing others together and trying to reconcile differences.
Instructing	Teaching others how to do something.
Writing	Communicating effectively in writing as appropriate for the needs of the audience.
Mathematics	Using mathematics to solve problems.
Management of Personnel Resources	Motivating, developing, and directing people as they work, identifying the best people for the job.
Quality Control Analysis	Conducting tests and inspections of products, services, or processes to evaluate quality or performance.
Operations Analysis	Analyzing needs and product requirements to create a design.
Management of Financial Resources	Determining how money will be spent to get the work done, and accounting for these expenditures.
Systems Evaluation	Identifying measures or indicators of system performance and the actions needed to improve or correct performance, relative to the goals of the system.
Management of Material Resources	Obtaining and seeing to the appropriate use of equipment, facilities, and materials needed to do certain work.
Troubleshooting	Determining causes of operating errors and deciding what to do about it.
Operation Monitoring	Watching gauges, dials, or other indicators to make sure a machine is working properly.
Technology Design	Generating or adapting equipment and technology to serve user needs.
Operation and Control	Controlling operations of equipment or systems.
Systems Analysis	Determining how a system should work and how changes in conditions, operations, and the environment will affect outcomes.
Equipment Selection	Determining the kind of tools and equipment needed to do a job.
Equipment Maintenance	Performing routine maintenance on equipment and determining when and what kind of maintenance is needed.
Installation	Installing equipment, machines, wiring, or programs to meet specifications.
Programming	Writing computer programs for various purposes.
Science	Using scientific rules and methods to solve problems.

Ability	Ability Definitions
Repairing	Repairing machines or systems using the needed tools.
Oral Comprehension	The ability to listen to and understand information and ideas presented through spoken words and sentences.
Oral Expression	The ability to communicate information and ideas in speaking so others will understand.
Speech Clarity	The ability to speak clearly so others can understand you.
Written Comprehension	The ability to read and understand information and ideas presented in writing.
Inductive Reasoning	The ability to combine pieces of information to form general rules or conclusions (includes finding a relationship among seemingly unrelated events).
Speech Recognition	The ability to identify and understand the speech of another person.
Problem Sensitivity	The ability to tell when something is wrong or is likely to go wrong. It does not involve solving the problem, only recognizing there is a problem.
Near Vision	The ability to see details at close range (within a few feet of the observer).
Deductive Reasoning	The ability to apply general rules to specific problems to produce answers that make sense.
Written Expression	The ability to communicate information and ideas in writing so others will understand.
Information Ordering	The ability to arrange things or actions in a certain order or pattern according to a specific rule or set of rules (e.g., patterns of numbers, letters, words, pictures, mathematical operations).
Mathematical Reasoning	The ability to choose the right mathematical methods or formulas to solve a problem.
Number Facility	The ability to add, subtract, multiply, or divide quickly and correctly.
Selective Attention	The ability to concentrate on a task over a period of time without being distracted.
Category Flexibility	The ability to generate or use different sets of rules for combining or grouping things in different ways.
Fluency of Ideas	The ability to come up with a number of ideas about a topic (the number of ideas is important, not their quality, correctness, or creativity).
Flexibility of Closure	The ability to identify or detect a known pattern (a figure, object, word, or sound) that is hidden in other distracting material.
Time Sharing	The ability to shift back and forth between two or more activities or sources of information (such as speech, sounds, touch, or other sources).
Originality	The ability to come up with unusual or clever ideas about a given topic or situation, or to develop creative ways to solve a problem.
Perceptual Speed	The ability to quickly and accurately compare similarities and differences among sets of letters, numbers, objects, pictures, or patterns. The things to be compared may be presented at the same time or one after the other. This ability also includes comparing a presented object with a remembered object.
Speed of Closure	The ability to quickly make sense of, combine, and organize information into meaningful patterns.
Memorization	The ability to remember information such as words, numbers, pictures, and procedures.
Auditory Attention	The ability to focus on a single source of sound in the presence of other distracting sounds.
Finger Dexterity	The ability to make precisely coordinated movements of the fingers of one or both hands to grasp, manipulate, or assemble very small objects.
Manual Dexterity	The ability to quickly move your hand, your hand together with your arm, or your two hands to grasp, manipulate, or assemble objects.
Trunk Strength	The ability to use your abdominal and lower back muscles to support part of the body repeatedly or continuously over time without 'giving out' or fatiguing.
Far Vision	The ability to see details at a distance.
Arm-Hand Steadiness	The ability to keep your hand and arm steady while moving your arm or while holding your arm and hand in one position.
Control Precision	The ability to quickly and repeatedly adjust the controls of a machine or a vehicle to exact positions.
Wrist-Finger Speed	The ability to make fast, simple, repeated movements of the fingers, hands, and wrists.
Visualization	The ability to imagine how something will look after it is moved around or when its parts are moved or rearranged.
Hearing Sensitivity	The ability to detect or tell the differences between sounds that vary in pitch and loudness.
Visual Color Discrimination	The ability to match or detect differences between colors, including shades of color and brightness.
Reaction Time	The ability to quickly respond (with the hand, finger, or foot) to a signal (sound, light, picture) when it appears.
Response Orientation	The ability to choose quickly between two or more movements in response to two or more different signals (lights, sounds, pictures). It includes the speed with which the correct response is started with the hand, foot, or other body part.
Static Strength	The ability to exert maximum muscle force to lift, push, pull, or carry objects.
Rate Control	The ability to time your movements or the movement of a piece of equipment in anticipation of changes in the speed and/or direction of a moving object or scene.
Dynamic Strength	The ability to exert muscle force repeatedly or continuously over time. This involves muscular endurance and resistance to muscle fatigue.
Stamina	The ability to exert yourself physically over long periods of time without getting winded or out of breath.
Speed of Limb Movement	The ability to quickly move the arms and legs.
Dynamic Flexibility	The ability to quickly and repeatedly bend, stretch, twist, or reach out with your body, arms, and/or legs.
Gross Body Coordination	The ability to coordinate the movement of your arms, legs, and torso together when the whole body is in motion.
Extent Flexibility	The ability to bend, stretch, twist, or reach with your body, arms, and/or legs.
Night Vision	The ability to see under low light conditions.
Multilimb Coordination	The ability to coordinate two or more limbs (for example, two arms, two legs, or one leg and one arm) while sitting, standing, or lying down. It does not involve performing the activities while the whole body is in motion.
Spatial Orientation	The ability to know your location in relation to the environment or to know where other objects are in relation to you.
Sound Localization	The ability to tell the direction from which a sound originated.
Glare Sensitivity	The ability to see objects in the presence of glare or bright lighting.
Peripheral Vision	The ability to see objects or movement of objects to one's side when the eyes are looking ahead.
Gross Body Equilibrium	The ability to keep or regain your body balance or stay upright when in an unstable position.
Explosive Strength	The ability to use short bursts of muscle force to propel oneself (as in jumping or sprinting), or to throw an object.
Depth Perception	The ability to judge which of several objects is closer or farther away from you, or to judge the distance between you and an object.

Work_Activity	Work_Activity Definitions
Making Decisions and Solving Problems	Analyzing information and evaluating results to choose the best solution and solve problems.
Processing Information	Compiling, coding, categorizing, calculating, tabulating, auditing, or verifying information or data.
Analyzing Data or Information	Identifying the underlying principles, reasons, or facts of information by breaking down information or data into separate parts.
Performing for or Working Directly with the Public	Performing for people or dealing directly with the public. This includes serving customers in restaurants and stores, and receiving clients or guests.
Getting Information	Observing, receiving, and otherwise obtaining information from all relevant sources.
Establishing and Maintaining Interpersonal Relatio	Developing constructive and cooperative working relationships with others, and maintaining them over time.
Communicating with Persons Outside Organization	Communicating with people outside the organization, representing the organization to customers, the public, government, and other external sources. This information can be exchanged in person, in writing, or by telephone or e-mail.
Judging the Qualities of Things, Services, or Peop	Assessing the value, importance, or quality of things or people.
Communicating with Supervisors, Peers, or Subordin	Providing information to supervisors, co-workers, and subordinates by telephone, in written form, e-mail, or in person.
Documenting/Recording Information	Entering, transcribing, recording, storing, or maintaining information in written or electronic/magnetic form.
Interacting With Computers	Using computers and computer systems (including hardware and software) to program, write software, set up functions, enter data, or process information.

Evaluating Information to Determine Compliance wit	Using relevant information and individual judgment to determine whether events or processes comply with laws, regulations, or standards.
Organizing, Planning, and Prioritizing Work	Developing specific goals and plans to prioritize, organize, and accomplish your work.
Selling or Influencing Others	Convincing others to buy merchandise/goods or to otherwise change their minds or actions.
Performing Administrative Activities	Performing day-to-day administrative tasks such as maintaining information files and processing paperwork.
Interpreting the Meaning of Information for Others	Translating or explaining what information means and how it can be used.
Updating and Using Relevant Knowledge	Keeping up-to-date technically and applying new knowledge to your job.
Monitor Processes, Materials, or Surroundings	Monitoring and reviewing information from materials, events, or the environment, to detect or assess problems.
Identifying Objects, Actions, and Events	Identifying information by categorizing, estimating, recognizing differences or similarities, and detecting changes in circumstances or events.
Resolving Conflicts and Negotiating with Others	Handling complaints, settling disputes, and resolving grievances and conflicts, or otherwise negotiating with others.
Coaching and Developing Others	Identifying the developmental needs of others and coaching, mentoring, or otherwise helping others to improve their knowledge or skills.
Developing and Building Teams	Encouraging and building mutual trust, respect, and cooperation among team members.
Scheduling Work and Activities	Scheduling events, programs, and activities, as well as the work of others.
Assisting and Caring for Others	Providing personal assistance, medical attention, emotional support, or other personal care to others such as coworkers, customers, or patients.
Thinking Creatively	Developing, designing, or creating new applications, ideas, relationships, systems, or products, including artistic contributions.
Coordinating the Work and Activities of Others	Getting members of a group to work together to accomplish tasks.
Provide Consultation and Advice to Others	Providing guidance and expert advice to management or other groups on technical, systems-, or process-related topics.
Guiding, Directing, and Motivating Subordinates	Providing guidance and direction to subordinates, including setting performance standards and monitoring performance.
Training and Teaching Others	Identifying the educational needs of others, developing formal educational or training programs or classes, and teaching or instructing others.
Developing Objectives and Strategies	Establishing long-range objectives and specifying the strategies and actions to achieve them.
Monitoring and Controlling Resources	Monitoring and controlling resources and overseeing the spending of money.
Estimating the Quantifiable Characteristics of Pro	Estimating sizes, distances, and quantities; or determining time, costs, resources, or materials needed to perform a work activity.
Controlling Machines and Processes	Using either control mechanisms or direct physical activity to operate machines or processes (not including computers or vehicles).
Inspecting Equipment, Structures, or Material	Inspecting equipment, structures, or materials to identify the cause of errors or other problems or defects.
Performing General Physical Activities	Performing physical activities that require considerable use of your arms and legs and moving your whole body, such as climbing, lifting, balancing, walking, stooping, and handling of materials.
Handling and Moving Objects	Using hands and arms in handling, installing, positioning, and moving materials, and manipulating things.
Staffing Organizational Units	Recruiting, interviewing, selecting, hiring, and promoting employees in an organization.
Repairing and Maintaining Electronic Equipment	Servicing, repairing, calibrating, regulating, fine-tuning, or testing machines, devices, and equipment that operate primarily on the basis of electrical or electronic (not mechanical) principles.
Operating Vehicles, Mechanized Devices, or Equipme	Running, maneuvering, navigating, or driving vehicles or mechanized equipment, such as forklifts, passenger vehicles, aircraft, or water craft.
Repairing and Maintaining Mechanical Equipment	Servicing, repairing, adjusting, and testing machines, devices, moving parts, and equipment that operate primarily on the basis of mechanical (not electronic) principles.
Drafting, Laying Out, and Specifying Technical Dev	Providing documentation, detailed instructions, drawings, or specifications to tell others about how devices, parts, equipment, or structures are to be fabricated, constructed, assembled, modified, maintained, or used.

Work_Context	Work_Context Definitions
Face-to-Face Discussions	How often do you have to have face-to-face discussions with individuals or teams in this job?
Telephone	How often do you have telephone conversations in this job?
Contact With Others	How much does this job require the worker to be in contact with others (face-to-face, by telephone, or otherwise) in order to perform it?
Work With Work Group or Team	How important is it to work with others in a group or team in this job?
Frequency of Decision Making	How frequently is the worker required to make decisions that affect other people, the financial resources, and/or the image and reputation of the organization?
Impact of Decisions on Co-workers or Company Resul	How do the decisions an employee makes impact the results of co-workers, clients or the company?
Freedom to Make Decisions	How much decision making freedom, without supervision, does the job offer?
Spend Time Sitting	How much does this job require sitting?
Structured versus Unstructured Work	To what extent is this job structured for the worker, rather than allowing the worker to determine tasks, priorities, and goals?
Importance of Being Exact or Accurate	How important is being very exact or highly accurate in performing this job?
Electronic Mail	How often do you use electronic mail in this job?
Importance of Repeating Same Tasks	How important is repeating the same physical activities (e.g., key entry) or mental activities (e.g., checking entries in a ledger) over and over, without stopping, to performing this job?
Responsibility for Outcomes and Results	How responsible is the worker for work outcomes and results of other workers?
Deal With External Customers	How important is it to work with external customers or the public in this job?
Indoors, Environmentally Controlled	How often does this job require working indoors in environmentally controlled conditions?
Letters and Memos	How often does the job require written letters and memos?
Time Pressure	How often does this job require the worker to meet strict deadlines?
Deal With Unpleasant or Angry People	How frequently does the worker have to deal with unpleasant, angry, or discourteous individuals as part of the job requirements?
Coordinate or Lead Others	How important is it to coordinate or lead others in accomplishing work activities in this job?
Spend Time Making Repetitive Motions	How much does this job require making repetitive motions?
Level of Competition	To what extent does this job require the worker to compete or to be aware of competitive pressures?
Degree of Automation	How automated is the job?
Frequency of Conflict Situations	How often are there conflict situations the employee has to face in this job?
Physical Proximity	To what extent does this job require the worker to perform job tasks in close physical proximity to other people?
Spend Time Using Your Hands to Handle, Control, or	How much does this job require using your hands to handle, control, or feel objects, tools or controls?
Sounds, Noise Levels Are Distracting or Uncomforta	How often does this job require working exposed to sounds and noise levels that are distracting or uncomfortable?
Consequence of Error	How serious would the result usually be if the worker made a mistake that was not readily correctable?
Responsibility for Others' Health and Safety	How much responsibility is there for the health and safety of others in this job?
In an Enclosed Vehicle or Equipment	How often does this job require working in a closed vehicle or equipment (e.g., car)?
Spend Time Standing	How much does this job require standing?
Public Speaking	How often do you have to perform public speaking in this job?
Outdoors, Exposed to Weather	How often does this job require working outdoors, exposed to all weather conditions?
Very Hot or Cold Temperatures	How often does this job require working in very hot (above 90 F degrees) or very cold (below 32 F degrees) temperatures?
Deal With Physically Aggressive People	How frequently does this job require the worker to deal with physical aggression of violent individuals?
Spend Time Walking and Running	How much does this job require walking and running?
Spend Time Bending or Twisting the Body	How much does this job require bending or twisting your body?
Spend Time Kneeling, Crouching, Stooping, or Crawl	How much does this job require kneeling, crouching, stooping or crawling?
Exposed to Contaminants	How often does this job require working exposed to contaminants (such as pollutants, gases, dust or odors)?

Exposed to Minor Burns, Cuts, Bites, or Stings	How often does this job require exposure to minor burns, cuts, bites, or stings?
Outdoors, Under Cover	How often does this job require working outdoors, under cover (e.g., structure with roof but no walls)?
Extremely Bright or Inadequate Lighting	How often does this job require working in extremely bright or inadequate lighting conditions?
Indoors, Not Environmentally Controlled	How often does this job require working indoors in non-controlled environmental conditions (e.g., warehouse without heat)?
Cramped Work Space, Awkward Positions	How often does this job require working in cramped work spaces that requires getting into awkward positions?
Exposed to Radiation	How often does this job require exposure to radiation?
Spend Time Climbing Ladders, Scaffolds, or Poles	How much does this job require climbing ladders, scaffolds, or poles?
Exposed to High Places	How often does this job require exposure to high places?
Exposed to Disease or Infections	How often does this job require exposure to disease/infections?
Wear Specialized Protective or Safety Equipment su	How much does this job require wearing specialized protective or safety equipment such as breathing apparatus, safety harness, full protection suits, or radiation protection?
Spend Time Keeping or Regaining Balance	How much does this job require keeping or regaining your balance?
Exposed to Hazardous Equipment	How often does this job require exposure to hazardous equipment?
Exposed to Hazardous Conditions	How often does this job require exposure to hazardous conditions?
In an Open Vehicle or Equipment	How often does this job require working in an open vehicle or equipment (e.g., tractor)?
Wear Common Protective or Safety Equipment such as	How much does this job require wearing common protective or safety equipment such as safety shoes, glasses, gloves, hard hats or life jackets?
Pace Determined by Speed of Equipment	How important is it to this job that the pace is determined by the speed of equipment or machinery? (This does not refer to keeping busy at all times on this job.)
Exposed to Whole Body Vibration	How often does this job require exposure to whole body vibration (e.g., operate a jackhammer)?

13-2072.00

Job Zone Component	Job Zone Component Definitions
Title	Job Zone Three: Medium Preparation Needed
Overall Experience	Previous work-related skill, knowledge, or experience is required for these occupations. For example, an electrician must have completed three or four years of apprenticeship or several years of vocational training, and often must have passed a licensing exam, in order to perform the job.
Job Training	Employees in these occupations usually need one or two years of training involving both on-the-job experience and informal training with experienced workers.
Job Zone Examples	These occupations usually involve using communication and organizational skills to coordinate, supervise, manage, or train others to accomplish goals. Examples include dental assistants, electricians, fish and game wardens, legal secretaries, personnel recruiters, and recreation workers.
SVP Range	(6.0 to < 7.0)
Education	Most occupations in this zone require training in vocational schools, related on-the-job experience, or an associate's degree. Some may require a bachelor's degree.

Work_Styles	Work_Styles Definitions
Integrity	Job requires being honest and ethical.
Social Orientation	Job requires preferring to work with others rather than alone, and being personally connected with others on the job.
Dependability	Job requires being reliable, responsible, and dependable, and fulfilling obligations.
Analytical Thinking	Job requires analyzing information and using logic to address work-related issues and problems.
Attention to Detail	Job requires being careful about detail and thorough in completing work tasks.
Independence	Job requires developing one's own ways of doing things, guiding oneself with little or no supervision, and depending on oneself to get things done.
Initiative	Job requires a willingness to take on responsibilities and challenges.
Cooperation	Job requires being pleasant with others on the job and displaying a good-natured, cooperative attitude.

Adaptability/Flexibility	Job requires being open to change (positive or negative) and to considerable variety in the workplace.
Leadership	Job requires a willingness to lead, take charge, and offer opinions and direction.
Innovation	Job requires creativity and alternative thinking to develop new ideas for and answers to work-related problems.
Self Control	Job requires maintaining composure, keeping emotions in check, controlling anger, and avoiding aggressive behavior, even in very difficult situations.
Persistence	Job requires persistence in the face of obstacles.
Concern for Others	Job requires being sensitive to others' needs and feelings and being understanding and helpful on the job.
Achievement/Effort	Job requires establishing and maintaining personally challenging achievement goals and exerting effort toward mastering tasks.
Stress Tolerance	Job requires accepting criticism and dealing calmly and effectively with high stress situations.

13-2082.00 - Tax Preparers

Prepare tax returns for individuals or small businesses but do not have the background or responsibilities of an accredited or certified public accountant.

Tasks

1) Check data input or verify totals on forms prepared by others to detect errors in arithmetic, data entry, or procedures.

2) Compute taxes owed or overpaid, using adding machines or personal computers, and complete entries on forms, following tax form instructions and tax tables.

3) Interview clients to obtain additional information on taxable income and deductible expenses and allowances.

4) Use all appropriate adjustments, deductions, and credits to keep clients' taxes to a minimum.

5) Review financial records such as income statements and documentation of expenditures in order to determine forms needed to prepare tax returns.

6) Consult tax law handbooks or bulletins in order to determine procedures for preparation of atypical returns.

7) Furnish taxpayers with sufficient information and advice in order to ensure correct tax form completion.

8) Calculate form preparation fees according to return complexity and processing time required.

15-1021.00 - Computer Programmers

Convert project specifications and statements of problems and procedures to detailed logical flow charts for coding into computer language. Develop and write computer programs to store, locate, and retrieve specific documents, data, and information. May program web sites.

Tasks

1) Compile and write documentation of program development and subsequent revisions, inserting comments in the coded instructions so others can understand the program.

2) Perform or direct revision, repair, or expansion of existing programs to increase operating efficiency or adapt to new requirements.

3) Consult with and assist computer operators or system analysts to define and resolve problems in running computer programs.

4) Write, update, and maintain computer programs or software packages to handle specific jobs, such as tracking inventory, storing or retrieving data, or controlling other equipment.

5) Write, analyze, review, and rewrite programs, using workflow chart and diagram, and applying knowledge of computer capabilities, subject matter, and symbolic logic.

6) Prepare detailed workflow charts and diagrams that describe input, output, and logical operation, and convert them into a series of instructions coded in a computer language.

7) Investigate whether networks, workstations, the central processing unit of the system, and/or peripheral equipment are responding to a program's instructions.

8) Write or contribute to instructions or manuals to guide end users.

9) Perform systems analysis and programming tasks to maintain and control the use of computer systems software as a systems programmer.

10) Assign, coordinate, and review work and activities of programming personnel.

11) Train subordinates in programming and program coding.

12) Collaborate with computer manufacturers and other users to develop new programming methods.

13) Correct errors by making appropriate changes and then rechecking the program to ensure that the desired results are produced.

14) Conduct trial runs of programs and software applications to be sure they will produce the desired information and that the instructions are correct.

Knowledge	Knowledge Definitions
Computers and Electronics	Knowledge of circuit boards, processors, chips, electronic equipment, and computer hardware and software, including applications and programming.
English Language	Knowledge of the structure and content of the English language including the meaning and spelling of words, rules of composition, and grammar.
Mathematics	Knowledge of arithmetic, algebra, geometry, calculus, statistics, and their applications.
Design	Knowledge of design techniques, tools, and principles involved in production of precision technical plans, blueprints, drawings, and models.
Engineering and Technology	Knowledge of the practical application of engineering science and technology. This includes applying principles, techniques, procedures, and equipment to the design and production of various goods and services.
Telecommunications	Knowledge of transmission, broadcasting, switching, control, and operation of telecommunications systems.
Clerical	Knowledge of administrative and clerical procedures and systems such as word processing, managing files and records, stenography and transcription, designing forms, and other office procedures and terminology.
Customer and Personal Service	Knowledge of principles and processes for providing customer and personal services. This includes customer needs assessment, meeting quality standards for services, and evaluation of customer satisfaction.
Economics and Accounting	Knowledge of economic and accounting principles and practices, the financial markets, banking and the analysis and reporting of financial data.
Communications and Media	Knowledge of media production, communication, and dissemination techniques and methods. This includes alternative ways to inform and entertain via written, oral, and visual media.
Administration and Management	Knowledge of business and management principles involved in strategic planning, resource allocation, human resources modeling, leadership technique, production methods, and coordination of people and resources.
Education and Training	Knowledge of principles and methods for curriculum and training design, teaching and instruction for individuals and groups, and the measurement of training effects.
Public Safety and Security	Knowledge of relevant equipment, policies, procedures, and strategies to promote effective local, state, or national security operations for the protection of people, data, property, and institutions.
Law and Government	Knowledge of laws, legal codes, court procedures, precedents, government regulations, executive orders, agency rules, and the democratic political process.
Physics	Knowledge and prediction of physical principles, laws, their interrelationships, and applications to understanding fluid, material, and atmospheric dynamics, and mechanical, electrical, atomic and sub-atomic structures and processes.
Mechanical	Knowledge of machines and tools, including their designs, uses, repair, and maintenance.
Psychology	Knowledge of human behavior and performance; individual differences in ability, personality, and interests; learning and motivation; psychological research methods; and the assessment and treatment of behavioral and affective disorders.
Sales and Marketing	Knowledge of principles and methods for showing, promoting, and selling products or services. This includes marketing strategy and tactics, product demonstration, sales techniques, and sales control systems.
Production and Processing	Knowledge of raw materials, production processes, quality control, costs, and other techniques for maximizing the effective manufacture and distribution of goods.
Personnel and Human Resources	Knowledge of principles and procedures for personnel recruitment, selection, training, compensation and benefits, labor relations and negotiation, and personnel information systems.
Sociology and Anthropology	Knowledge of group behavior and dynamics, societal trends and influences, human migrations, ethnicity, cultures and their history and origins.
Transportation	Knowledge of principles and methods for moving people or goods by air, rail, sea, or road, including the relative costs and benefits.
Foreign Language	Knowledge of the structure and content of a foreign (non-English) language including the meaning and spelling of words, rules of composition and grammar, and pronunciation.
Geography	Knowledge of principles and methods for describing the features of land, sea, and air masses, including their physical characteristics, locations, interrelationships, and distribution of plant, animal, and human life.
Philosophy and Theology	Knowledge of different philosophical systems and religions. This includes their basic principles, values, ethics, ways of thinking, customs, practices, and their impact on human culture.
Building and Construction	Knowledge of materials, methods, and the tools involved in the construction or repair of houses, buildings, or other structures such as highways and roads.
History and Archeology	Knowledge of historical events and their causes, indicators, and effects on civilizations and cultures.
Medicine and Dentistry	Knowledge of the information and techniques needed to diagnose and treat human injuries, diseases, and deformities. This includes symptoms, treatment alternatives, drug properties and interactions, and preventive health-care measures.
Therapy and Counseling	Knowledge of principles, methods, and procedures for diagnosis, treatment, and rehabilitation of physical and mental dysfunctions, and for career counseling and guidance.
Biology	Knowledge of plant and animal organisms, their tissues, cells, functions, interdependencies, and interactions with each other and the environment.
Chemistry	Knowledge of the chemical composition, structure, and properties of substances and of the chemical processes and transformations that they undergo. This includes uses of chemicals and their interactions, danger signs, production techniques, and disposal methods.
Fine Arts	Knowledge of the theory and techniques required to compose, produce, and perform works of music, dance, visual arts, drama, and sculpture.
Food Production	Knowledge of techniques and equipment for planting, growing, and harvesting food products (both plant and animal) for consumption, including storage/handling techniques.

Skills	Skills Definitions
Programming	Writing computer programs for various purposes.
Critical Thinking	Using logic and reasoning to identify the strengths and weaknesses of alternative solutions, conclusions or approaches to problems.
Complex Problem Solving	Identifying complex problems and reviewing related information to develop and evaluate options and implement solutions.
Active Learning	Understanding the implications of new information for both current and future problem-solving and decision-making.
Reading Comprehension	Understanding written sentences and paragraphs in work related documents.
Learning Strategies	Selecting and using training/instructional methods and procedures appropriate for the situation when learning or teaching new things.
Operations Analysis	Analyzing needs and product requirements to create a design.
Active Listening	Giving full attention to what other people are saying, taking time to understand the points being made, asking questions as appropriate, and not interrupting at inappropriate times.
Technology Design	Generating or adapting equipment and technology to serve user needs.
Troubleshooting	Determining causes of operating errors and deciding what to do about it.
Coordination	Adjusting actions in relation to others' actions.
Time Management	Managing one's own time and the time of others.
Systems Analysis	Determining how a system should work and how changes in conditions, operations, and the environment will affect outcomes.
Speaking	Talking to others to convey information effectively.

Equipment Selection	Determining the kind of tools and equipment needed to do a job.
Quality Control Analysis	Conducting tests and inspections of products, services, or processes to evaluate quality or performance.
Installation	Installing equipment, machines, wiring, or programs to meet specifications.
Mathematics	Using mathematics to solve problems.
Judgment and Decision Making	Considering the relative costs and benefits of potential actions to choose the most appropriate one.
Instructing	Teaching others how to do something.
Monitoring	Monitoring/Assessing performance of yourself, other individuals, or organizations to make improvements or take corrective action.
Repairing	Repairing machines or systems using the needed tools.
Social Perceptiveness	Being aware of others' reactions and understanding why they react as they do.
Writing	Communicating effectively in writing as appropriate for the needs of the audience.
Persuasion	Persuading others to change their minds or behavior.
Systems Evaluation	Identifying measures or indicators of system performance and the actions needed to improve or correct performance, relative to the goals of the system.
Equipment Maintenance	Performing routine maintenance on equipment and determining when and what kind of maintenance is needed.
Operation and Control	Controlling operations of equipment or systems.
Service Orientation	Actively looking for ways to help people.
Operation Monitoring	Watching gauges, dials, or other indicators to make sure a machine is working properly.
Negotiation	Bringing others together and trying to reconcile differences.
Science	Using scientific rules and methods to solve problems.
Management of Personnel Resources	Motivating, developing, and directing people as they work, identifying the best people for the job.
Management of Material Resources	Obtaining and seeing to the appropriate use of equipment, facilities, and materials needed to do certain work.
Management of Financial Resources	Determining how money will be spent to get the work done, and accounting for these expenditures.

Ability	Ability Definitions
Information Ordering	The ability to arrange things or actions in a certain order or pattern according to a specific rule or set of rules (e.g., patterns of numbers, letters, words, pictures, mathematical operations).
Deductive Reasoning	The ability to apply general rules to specific problems to produce answers that make sense.
Near Vision	The ability to see details at close range (within a few feet of the observer).
Written Expression	The ability to communicate information and ideas in writing so others will understand.
Written Comprehension	The ability to read and understand information and ideas presented in writing.
Oral Comprehension	The ability to listen to and understand information and ideas presented through spoken words and sentences.
Oral Expression	The ability to communicate information and ideas in speaking so others will understand.
Inductive Reasoning	The ability to combine pieces of information to form general rules or conclusions (includes finding a relationship among seemingly unrelated events).
Problem Sensitivity	The ability to tell when something is wrong or is likely to go wrong. It does not involve solving the problem, only recognizing there is a problem.
Speech Clarity	The ability to speak clearly so others can understand you.
Speech Recognition	The ability to identify and understand the speech of another person.
Flexibility of Closure	The ability to identify or detect a known pattern (a figure, object, word, or sound) that is hidden in other distracting material.
Category Flexibility	The ability to generate or use different sets of rules for combining or grouping things in different ways.
Fluency of Ideas	The ability to come up with a number of ideas about a topic (the number of ideas is important, not their quality, correctness, or creativity).
Selective Attention	The ability to concentrate on a task over a period of time without being distracted.
Originality	The ability to come up with unusual or clever ideas about a given topic or situation, or to develop creative ways to solve a problem.

Perceptual Speed	The ability to quickly and accurately compare similarities and differences among sets of letters, numbers, objects, pictures, or patterns. The things to be compared may be presented at the same time or one after the other. This ability also includes comparing a presented object with a remembered object.
Memorization	The ability to remember information such as words, numbers, pictures, and procedures.
Speed of Closure	The ability to quickly make sense of, combine, and organize information into meaningful patterns.
Visualization	The ability to imagine how something will look after it is moved around or when its parts are moved or rearranged.
Mathematical Reasoning	The ability to choose the right mathematical methods or formulas to solve a problem.
Arm-Hand Steadiness	The ability to keep your hand and arm steady while moving your arm or while holding your arm and hand in one position.
Finger Dexterity	The ability to make precisely coordinated movements of the fingers of one or both hands to grasp, manipulate, or assemble very small objects.
Manual Dexterity	The ability to quickly move your hand, your hand together with your arm, or your two hands to grasp, manipulate, or assemble objects.
Wrist-Finger Speed	The ability to make fast, simple, repeated movements of the fingers, hands, and wrists.
Time Sharing	The ability to shift back and forth between two or more activities or sources of information (such as speech, sounds, touch, or other sources).
Auditory Attention	The ability to focus on a single source of sound in the presence of other distracting sounds.
Far Vision	The ability to see details at a distance.
Visual Color Discrimination	The ability to match or detect differences between colors, including shades of color and brightness.
Number Facility	The ability to add, subtract, multiply, or divide quickly and correctly.
Control Precision	The ability to quickly and repeatedly adjust the controls of a machine or a vehicle to exact positions.
Hearing Sensitivity	The ability to detect or tell the differences between sounds that vary in pitch and loudness.
Depth Perception	The ability to judge which of several objects is closer or farther away from you, or to judge the distance between you and an object.
Trunk Strength	The ability to use your abdominal and lower back muscles to support part of the body repeatedly or continuously over time without 'giving out' or fatiguing.
Stamina	The ability to exert yourself physically over long periods of time without getting winded or out of breath.
Gross Body Coordination	The ability to coordinate the movement of your arms, legs, and torso together when the whole body is in motion.
Explosive Strength	The ability to use short bursts of muscle force to propel oneself (as in jumping or sprinting), or to throw an object.
Extent Flexibility	The ability to bend, stretch, twist, or reach with your body, arms, and/or legs.
Dynamic Strength	The ability to exert muscle force repeatedly or continuously over time. This involves muscular endurance and resistance to muscle fatigue.
Static Strength	The ability to exert maximum muscle force to lift, push, pull, or carry objects.
Speed of Limb Movement	The ability to quickly move the arms and legs.
Reaction Time	The ability to quickly respond (with the hand, finger, or foot) to a signal (sound, light, picture) when it appears.
Response Orientation	The ability to choose quickly between two or more movements in response to two or more different signals (lights, sounds, pictures). It includes the speed with which the correct response is started with the hand, foot, or other body part.
Gross Body Equilibrium	The ability to keep or regain your body balance or stay upright when in an unstable position.
Spatial Orientation	The ability to know your location in relation to the environment or to know where other objects are in relation to you.
Sound Localization	The ability to tell the direction from which a sound originated.
Multilimb Coordination	The ability to coordinate two or more limbs (for example, two arms, two legs, or one leg and one arm) while sitting, standing, or lying down. It does not involve performing the activities while the whole body is in motion.
Dynamic Flexibility	The ability to quickly and repeatedly bend, stretch, twist, or reach out with your body, arms, and/or legs.
Night Vision	The ability to see under low light conditions.
Peripheral Vision	The ability to see objects or movement of objects to one's side when the eyes are looking ahead.

Glare Sensitivity	The ability to see objects in the presence of glare or bright lighting.
Rate Control	The ability to time your movements or the movement of a piece of equipment in anticipation of changes in the speed and/or direction of a moving object or scene.

Work_Activity	Work_Activity Definitions
Interacting With Computers	Using computers and computer systems (including hardware and software) to program, write software, set up functions, enter data, or process information.
Organizing, Planning, and Prioritizing Work	Developing specific goals and plans to prioritize, organize, and accomplish your work.
Making Decisions and Solving Problems	Analyzing information and evaluating results to choose the best solution and solve problems.
Getting Information	Observing, receiving, and otherwise obtaining information from all relevant sources.
Updating and Using Relevant Knowledge	Keeping up-to-date technically and applying new knowledge to your job.
Communicating with Supervisors, Peers, or Subordin	Providing information to supervisors, co-workers, and subordinates by telephone, in written form, e-mail, or in person.
Analyzing Data or Information	Identifying the underlying principles, reasons, or facts of information by breaking down information or data into separate parts.
Establishing and Maintaining Interpersonal Relatio	Developing constructive and cooperative working relationships with others, and maintaining them over time.
Processing Information	Compiling, coding, categorizing, calculating, tabulating, auditing, or verifying information or data.
Documenting/Recording Information	Entering, transcribing, recording, storing, or maintaining information in written or electronic/magnetic form.
Identifying Objects, Actions, and Events	Identifying information by categorizing, estimating, recognizing differences or similarities, and detecting changes in circumstances or events.
Interpreting the Meaning of Information for Others	Translating or explaining what information means and how it can be used.
Monitor Processes, Materials, or Surroundings	Monitoring and reviewing information from materials, events, or the environment, to detect or assess problems.
Thinking Creatively	Developing, designing, or creating new applications, ideas, relationships, systems, or products, including artistic contributions.
Provide Consultation and Advice to Others	Providing guidance and expert advice to management or other groups on technical, systems-, or process-related topics.
Resolving Conflicts and Negotiating with Others	Handling complaints, settling disputes, and resolving grievances and conflicts, or otherwise negotiating with others.
Estimating the Quantifiable Characteristics of Pro	Estimating sizes, distances, and quantities; or determining time, costs, resources, or materials needed to perform a work activity.
Developing Objectives and Strategies	Establishing long-range objectives and specifying the strategies and actions to achieve them.
Communicating with Persons Outside Organization	Communicating with people outside the organization, representing the organization to customers, the public, government, and other external sources. This information can be exchanged in person, in writing, or by telephone or e-mail.
Coordinating the Work and Activities of Others	Getting members of a group to work together to accomplish tasks.
Assisting and Caring for Others	Providing personal assistance, medical attention, emotional support, or other personal care to others such as coworkers, customers, or patients.
Evaluating Information to Determine Compliance wit	Using relevant information and individual judgment to determine whether events or processes comply with laws, regulations, or standards.
Developing and Building Teams	Encouraging and building mutual trust, respect, and cooperation among team members.
Inspecting Equipment, Structures, or Material	Inspecting equipment, structures, or materials to identify the cause of errors or other problems or defects.
Training and Teaching Others	Identifying the educational needs of others, developing formal educational or training programs or classes, and teaching or instructing others.
Judging the Qualities of Things, Services, or Peop	Assessing the value, importance, or quality of things or people.
Coaching and Developing Others	Identifying the developmental needs of others and coaching, mentoring, or otherwise helping others to improve their knowledge or skills.
Selling or Influencing Others	Convincing others to buy merchandise/goods or to otherwise change their minds or actions.

Guiding, Directing, and Motivating Subordinates	Providing guidance and direction to subordinates, including setting performance standards and monitoring performance.
Performing Administrative Activities	Performing day-to-day administrative tasks such as maintaining information files and processing paperwork.
Scheduling Work and Activities	Scheduling events, programs, and activities, as well as the work of others.
Repairing and Maintaining Electronic Equipment	Servicing, repairing, calibrating, regulating, fine-tuning, or testing machines, devices, and equipment that operate primarily on the basis of electrical or electronic (not mechanical) principles.
Staffing Organizational Units	Recruiting, interviewing, selecting, hiring, and promoting employees in an organization.
Controlling Machines and Processes	Using either control mechanisms or direct physical activity to operate machines or processes (not including computers or vehicles).
Monitoring and Controlling Resources	Monitoring and controlling resources and overseeing the spending of money.
Repairing and Maintaining Mechanical Equipment	Servicing, repairing, adjusting, and testing machines, devices, moving parts, and equipment that operate primarily on the basis of mechanical (not electronic) principles.
Performing General Physical Activities	Performing physical activities that require considerable use of your arms and legs and moving your whole body, such as climbing, lifting, balancing, walking, stooping, and handling of materials.
Handling and Moving Objects	Using hands and arms in handling, installing, positioning, and moving materials, and manipulating things.
Drafting, Laying Out, and Specifying Technical Dev	Providing documentation, detailed instructions, drawings, or specifications to tell others about how devices, parts, equipment, or structures are to be fabricated, constructed, assembled, modified, maintained, or used.
Operating Vehicles, Mechanized Devices, or Equipme	Running, maneuvering, navigating, or driving vehicles or mechanized equipment, such as forklifts, passenger vehicles, aircraft, or water craft.
Performing for or Working Directly with the Public	Performing for people or dealing directly with the public. This includes serving customers in restaurants and stores, and receiving clients or guests.

Work_Context	Work_Context Definitions
Electronic Mail	How often do you use electronic mail in this job?
Face-to-Face Discussions	How often do you have to have face-to-face discussions with individuals or teams in this job?
Telephone	How often do you have telephone conversations in this job?
Importance of Being Exact or Accurate	How important is being very exact or highly accurate in performing this job?
Work With Work Group or Team	How important is it to work with others in a group or team in this job?
Spend Time Sitting	How much does this job require sitting?
Indoors, Environmentally Controlled	How often does this job require working indoors in environmentally controlled conditions?
Freedom to Make Decisions	How much decision making freedom, without supervision, does the job offer?
Contact With Others	How much does this job require the worker to be in contact with others (face-to-face, by telephone, or otherwise) in order to perform it?
Structured versus Unstructured Work	To what extent is this job structured for the worker, rather than allowing the worker to determine tasks, priorities, and goals?
Time Pressure	How often does this job require the worker to meet strict deadlines?
Spend Time Using Your Hands to Handle, Control, or	How much does this job require using your hands to handle, control, or feel objects, tools or controls?
Letters and Memos	How often does the job require written letters and memos?
Spend Time Making Repetitive Motions	How much does this job require making repetitive motions?
Coordinate or Lead Others	How important is it to coordinate or lead others in accomplishing work activities in this job?
Impact of Decisions on Co-workers or Company Resul	How do the decisions an employee makes impact the results of co-workers, clients or the company?
Physical Proximity	To what extent does this job require the worker to perform job tasks in close physical proximity to other people?
Responsibility for Outcomes and Results	How responsible is the worker for work outcomes and results of other workers?
Consequence of Error	How serious would the result usually be if the worker made a mistake that was not readily correctable?
Frequency of Conflict Situations	How often are there conflict situations the employee has to face in this job?

Frequency of Decision Making	How frequently is the worker required to make decisions that affect other people, the financial resources, and/or the image and reputation of the organization?
Degree of Automation	How automated is the job?
Level of Competition	To what extent does this job require the worker to compete or to be aware of competitive pressures?
Deal With External Customers	How important is it to work with external customers or the public in this job?
Sounds, Noise Levels Are Distracting or Uncomforta	How often does this job require working exposed to sounds and noise levels that are distracting or uncomfortable?
Importance of Repeating Same Tasks	How important is repeating the same physical activities (e.g., key entry) or mental activities (e.g., checking entries in a ledger) over and over, without stopping, to performing this job?
In an Enclosed Vehicle or Equipment	How often does this job require working in a closed vehicle or equipment (e.g., car)?
Deal With Unpleasant or Angry People	How frequently does the worker have to deal with unpleasant, angry, or discourteous individuals as part of the job requirements?
Public Speaking	How often do you have to perform public speaking in this job?
Responsible for Others' Health and Safety	How much responsibility is there for the health and safety of others in this job?
Spend Time Standing	How much does this job require standing?
Spend Time Bending or Twisting the Body	How much does this job require bending or twisting your body?
Wear Common Protective or Safety Equipment such as	How much does this job require wearing common protective or safety equipment such as safety shoes, glasses, gloves, hard hats or live jackets?
Spend Time Walking and Running	How much does this job require walking and running?
Deal With Physically Aggressive People	How frequently does this job require the worker to deal with physical aggression of violent individuals?
Pace Determined by Speed of Equipment	How important is it to this job that the pace is determined by the speed of equipment or machinery? (This does not refer to keeping busy at all times on this job.)
Very Hot or Cold Temperatures	How often does this job require working in very hot (above 90 F degrees) or very cold (below 32 F degrees) temperatures?
Exposed to Contaminants	How often does this job require working exposed to contaminants (such as pollutants, gases, dust or odors)?
Spend Time Kneeling, Crouching, Stooping, or Crawl	How much does this job require kneeling, crouching, stooping or crawling?
Exposed to Hazardous Equipment	How often does this job require exposure to hazardous equipment?
Extremely Bright or Inadequate Lighting	How often does this job require working in extremely bright or inadequate lighting conditions?
Cramped Work Space, Awkward Positions	How often does this job require working in cramped work spaces that requires getting into awkward positions?
Indoors, Not Environmentally Controlled	How often does this job require working indoors in non-controlled environmental conditions (e.g., warehouse without heat)?
Outdoors, Under Cover	How often does this job require working outdoors, under cover (e.g., structure with roof but no walls)?
Spend Time Keeping or Regaining Balance	How much does this job require keeping or regaining your balance?
Outdoors, Exposed to Weather	How often does this job require working outdoors, exposed to all weather conditions?
Exposed to Hazardous Conditions	How often does this job require exposure to hazardous conditions?
Exposed to Disease or Infections	How often does this job require exposure to disease/infections?
Exposed to Radiation	How often does this job require exposure to radiation?
Spend Time Climbing Ladders, Scaffolds, or Poles	How much does this job require climbing ladders, scaffolds, or poles?
Exposed to High Places	How often does this job require exposure to high places?
Exposed to Whole Body Vibration	How often does this job require exposure to whole body vibration (e.g., operate a jackhammer)?
In an Open Vehicle or Equipment	How often does this job require working in an open vehicle or equipment (e.g., tractor)?
Exposed to Minor Burns, Cuts, Bites, or Stings	How often does this job require exposure to minor burns, cuts, bites, or stings?
Wear Specialized Protective or Safety Equipment su	How much does this job require wearing specialized protective or safety equipment such as breathing apparatus, safety harness, full protection suits, or radiation protection?

Job Zone Component	Job Zone Component Definitions
Title	Job Zone Four: Considerable Preparation Needed A minimum of two to four years of work-related skill, knowledge, or experience is needed for these occupations. For example, an accountant must complete four years of college and work for several years in accounting to be considered qualified.
Overall Experience	
Job Training	Employees in these occupations usually need several years of work-related experience, on-the-job training, and/or vocational training.
Job Zone Examples	Many of these occupations involve coordinating, supervising, managing, or training others. Examples include accountants, chefs and head cooks, computer programmers, historians, pharmacists, and police detectives.
SVP Range	(7.0 to < 8.0)
Education	Most of these occupations require a four - year bachelor's degree, but some do not.

Work_Styles	Work_Styles Definitions
Attention to Detail	Job requires being careful about detail and thorough in completing work tasks.
Analytical Thinking	Job requires analyzing information and using logic to address work-related issues and problems.
Dependability	Job requires being reliable, responsible, and dependable, and fulfilling obligations.
Initiative	Job requires a willingness to take on responsibilities and challenges.
Independence	Job requires developing one's own ways of doing things, guiding oneself with little or no supervision, and depending on oneself to get things done.
Integrity	Job requires being honest and ethical.
Achievement/Effort	Job requires establishing and maintaining personally challenging achievement goals and exerting effort toward mastering tasks.
Adaptability/Flexibility	Job requires being open to change (positive or negative) and to considerable variety in the workplace.
Persistence	Job requires persistence in the face of obstacles.
Cooperation	Job requires being pleasant with others on the job and displaying a good-natured, cooperative attitude.
Stress Tolerance	Job requires accepting criticism and dealing calmly and effectively with high stress situations.
Innovation	Job requires creativity and alternative thinking to develop new ideas for and answers to work-related problems.
Concern for Others	Job requires being sensitive to others' needs and feelings and being understanding and helpful on the job.
Leadership	Job requires a willingness to lead, take charge, and offer opinions and direction.
Self Control	Job requires maintaining composure, keeping emotions in check, controlling anger, and avoiding aggressive behavior, even in very difficult situations.
Social Orientation	Job requires preferring to work with others rather than alone, and being personally connected with others on the job.

15-1031.00 - Computer Software Engineers, Applications

Develop, create, and modify general computer applications software or specialized utility programs. Analyze user needs and develop software solutions. Design software or customize software for client use with the aim of optimizing operational efficiency. May analyze and design databases within an application area, working individually or coordinating database development as part of a team.

Tasks

1) Modify existing software to correct errors, allow it to adapt to new hardware, or to improve its performance.

2) Develop and direct software system testing and validation procedures, programming, and documentation.

.3) Analyze user needs and software requirements to determine feasibility of design within time and cost constraints.

4) Store, retrieve, and manipulate data for analysis of system capabilities and requirements.

5) Design, develop and modify software systems, using scientific analysis and mathematical

models to predict and measure outcome and consequences of design.

6) Analyze information to determine, recommend, and plan computer specifications and layouts, and peripheral equipment modifications.

7) Determine system performance standards.

8) Coordinate software system installation and monitor equipment functioning to ensure specifications are met.

9) Consult with customers about software system design and maintenance.

10) Obtain and evaluate information on factors such as reporting formats required, costs, and security needs to determine hardware configuration.

11) Train users to use new or modified equipment.

12) Supervise the work of programmers, technologists and technicians and other engineering and scientific personnel.

13) Specify power supply requirements and configuration.

14) Recommend purchase of equipment to control dust, temperature, and humidity in area of system installation.

Knowledge	Knowledge Definitions
Computers and Electronics	Knowledge of circuit boards, processors, chips, electronic equipment, and computer hardware and software, including applications and programming.
Engineering and Technology	Knowledge of the practical application of engineering science and technology. This includes applying principles, techniques, procedures, and equipment to the design and production of various goods and services.
Telecommunications	Knowledge of transmission, broadcasting, switching, control, and operation of telecommunications systems.
Mathematics	Knowledge of arithmetic, algebra, geometry, calculus, statistics, and their applications.
English Language	Knowledge of the structure and content of the English language including the meaning and spelling of words, rules of composition, and grammar.
Design	Knowledge of design techniques, tools, and principles involved in production of precision technical plans, blueprints, drawings, and models.
Education and Training	Knowledge of principles and methods for curriculum and training design, teaching and instruction for individuals and groups, and the measurement of training effects.
Physics	Knowledge and prediction of physical principles, laws, their interrelationships, and applications to understanding fluid, material, and atmospheric dynamics, and mechanical, electrical, atomic and sub-atomic structures and processes.
Customer and Personal Service	Knowledge of principles and processes for providing customer and personal services. This includes customer needs assessment, meeting quality standards for services, and evaluation of customer satisfaction.
Public Safety and Security	Knowledge of relevant equipment, policies, procedures, and strategies to promote effective local, state, or national security operations for the protection of people, data, property, and institutions.
Production and Processing	Knowledge of raw materials, production processes, quality control, costs, and other techniques for maximizing the effective manufacture and distribution of goods.
Communications and Media	Knowledge of media production, communication, and dissemination techniques and methods. This includes alternative ways to inform and entertain via written, oral, and visual media.
Clerical	Knowledge of administrative and clerical procedures and systems such as word processing, managing files and records, stenography and transcription, designing forms, and other office procedures and terminology.
Mechanical	Knowledge of machines and tools, including their designs, uses, repair, and maintenance.
Sociology and Anthropology	Knowledge of group behavior and dynamics, societal trends and influences, human migrations, ethnicity, cultures and their history and origins.
Chemistry	Knowledge of the chemical composition, structure, and properties of substances and of the chemical processes and transformations that they undergo. This includes uses of chemicals and their interactions, danger signs, production techniques, and disposal methods.
Law and Government	Knowledge of laws, legal codes, court procedures, precedents, government regulations, executive orders, agency rules, and the democratic political process.

Psychology	Knowledge of human behavior and performance; individual differences in ability, personality, and interests; learning and motivation; psychological research methods; and the assessment and treatment of behavioral and affective disorders.
Sales and Marketing	Knowledge of principles and methods for showing, promoting, and selling products or services. This includes marketing strategy and tactics, product demonstration, sales techniques, and sales control systems.
Building and Construction	Knowledge of materials, methods, and the tools involved in the construction or repair of houses, buildings, or other structures such as highways and roads.
Administration and Management	Knowledge of business and management principles involved in strategic planning, resource allocation, human resources modeling, leadership technique, production methods, and coordination of people and resources.
Foreign Language	Knowledge of the structure and content of a foreign (non-English) language including the meaning and spelling of words, rules of composition and grammar, and pronunciation.
History and Archeology	Knowledge of historical events and their causes, indicators, and effects on civilizations and cultures.
Economics and Accounting	Knowledge of economic and accounting principles and practices, the financial markets, banking and the analysis and reporting of financial data.
Geography	Knowledge of principles and methods for describing the features of land, sea, and air masses, including their physical characteristics, locations, interrelationships, and distribution of plant, animal, and human life.
Fine Arts	Knowledge of the theory and techniques required to compose, produce, and perform works of music, dance, visual arts, drama, and sculpture.
Personnel and Human Resources	Knowledge of principles and procedures for personnel recruitment, selection, training, compensation and benefits, labor relations and negotiation, and personnel information systems.
Philosophy and Theology	Knowledge of different philosophical systems and religions. This includes their basic principles, values, ethics, ways of thinking, customs, practices, and their impact on human culture.
Therapy and Counseling	Knowledge of principles, methods, and procedures for diagnosis, treatment, and rehabilitation of physical and mental dysfunctions, and for career counseling and guidance.
Biology	Knowledge of plant and animal organisms, their tissues, cells, functions, interdependencies, and interactions with each other and the environment.
Transportation	Knowledge of principles and methods for moving people or goods by air, rail, sea, or road, including the relative costs and benefits.
Food Production	Knowledge of techniques and equipment for planting, growing, and harvesting food products (both plant and animal) for consumption, including storage/handling techniques.
Medicine and Dentistry	Knowledge of the information and techniques needed to diagnose and treat human injuries, diseases, and deformities. This includes symptoms, treatment alternatives, drug properties and interactions, and preventive health-care measures.

Skills	Skills Definitions
Programming	Writing computer programs for various purposes.
Critical Thinking	Using logic and reasoning to identify the strengths and weaknesses of alternative solutions, conclusions or approaches to problems.
Complex Problem Solving	Identifying complex problems and reviewing related information to develop and evaluate options and implement solutions.
Troubleshooting	Determining causes of operating errors and deciding what to do about it.
Active Learning	Understanding the implications of new information for both current and future problem-solving and decision-making.
Judgment and Decision Making	Considering the relative costs and benefits of potential actions to choose the most appropriate one.
Technology Design	Generating or adapting equipment and technology to serve user needs.
Reading Comprehension	Understanding written sentences and paragraphs in work related documents.
Operations Analysis	Analyzing needs and product requirements to create a design.
Systems Analysis	Determining how a system should work and how changes in conditions, operations, and the environment will affect outcomes.

Quality Control Analysis	Conducting tests and inspections of products, services, or processes to evaluate quality or performance.
Active Listening	Giving full attention to what other people are saying, taking time to understand the points being made, asking questions as appropriate, and not interrupting at inappropriate times.
Speaking	Talking to others to convey information effectively.
Time Management	Managing one's own time and the time of others.
Coordination	Adjusting actions in relation to others' actions.
Learning Strategies	Selecting and using training/instructional methods and procedures appropriate for the situation when learning or teaching new things.
Instructing	Teaching others how to do something.
Writing	Communicating effectively in writing as appropriate for the needs of the audience.
Systems Evaluation	Identifying measures or indicators of system performance and the actions needed to improve or correct performance, relative to the goals of the system.
Equipment Selection	Determining the kind of tools and equipment needed to do a job.
Installation	Installing equipment, machines, wiring, or programs to meet specifications.
Persuasion	Persuading others to change their minds or behavior.
Monitoring	Monitoring/Assessing performance of yourself, other individuals, or organizations to make improvements or take corrective action.
Mathematics	Using mathematics to solve problems.
Science	Using scientific rules and methods to solve problems.
Service Orientation	Actively looking for ways to help people.
Negotiation	Bringing others together and trying to reconcile differences.
Management of Personnel Resources	Motivating, developing, and directing people as they work, identifying the best people for the job.
Social Perceptiveness	Being aware of others' reactions and understanding why they react as they do.
Operation Monitoring	Watching gauges, dials, or other indicators to make sure a machine is working properly.
Management of Financial Resources	Determining how money will be spent to get the work done, and accounting for these expenditures.
Operation and Control	Controlling operations of equipment or systems.
Equipment Maintenance	Performing routine maintenance on equipment and determining when and what kind of maintenance is needed.
Repairing	Repairing machines or systems using the needed tools.
Management of Material Resources	Obtaining and seeing to the appropriate use of equipment, facilities, and materials needed to do certain work.

Ability	Ability Definitions
Deductive Reasoning	The ability to apply general rules to specific problems to produce answers that make sense.
Oral Comprehension	The ability to listen to and understand information and ideas presented through spoken words and sentences.
Near Vision	The ability to see details at close range (within a few feet of the observer).
Problem Sensitivity	The ability to tell when something is wrong or is likely to go wrong. It does not involve solving the problem, only recognizing there is a problem.
Inductive Reasoning	The ability to combine pieces of information to form general rules or conclusions (includes finding a relationship among seemingly unrelated events).
Speech Clarity	The ability to speak clearly so others can understand you.
Written Comprehension	The ability to read and understand information and ideas presented in writing.
Information Ordering	The ability to arrange things or actions in a certain order or pattern according to a specific rule or set of rules (e.g., patterns of numbers, letters, words, pictures, mathematical operations).
Oral Expression	The ability to communicate information and ideas in speaking so others will understand.
Speech Recognition	The ability to identify and understand the speech of another person.
Mathematical Reasoning	The ability to choose the right mathematical methods or formulas to solve a problem.
Category Flexibility	The ability to generate or use different sets of rules for combining or grouping things in different ways.
Originality	The ability to come up with unusual or clever ideas about a given topic or situation, or to develop creative ways to solve a problem.
Selective Attention	The ability to concentrate on a task over a period of time without being distracted.

Written Expression	The ability to communicate information and ideas in writing so others will understand.
Number Facility	The ability to add, subtract, multiply, or divide quickly and correctly.
Fluency of Ideas	The ability to come up with a number of ideas about a topic (the number of ideas is important, not their quality, correctness, or creativity).
Perceptual Speed	The ability to quickly and accurately compare similarities and differences among sets of letters, numbers, objects, pictures, or patterns. The things to be compared may be presented at the same time or one after the other. This ability also includes comparing a presented object with a remembered object.
Flexibility of Closure	The ability to identify or detect a known pattern (a figure, object, word, or sound) that is hidden in other distracting material.
Finger Dexterity	The ability to make precisely coordinated movements of the fingers of one or both hands to grasp, manipulate, or assemble very small objects.
Visualization	The ability to imagine how something will look after it is moved around or when its parts are moved or rearranged.
Memorization	The ability to remember information such as words, numbers, pictures, and procedures.
Speed of Closure	The ability to quickly make sense of, combine, and organize information into meaningful patterns.
Time Sharing	The ability to shift back and forth between two or more activities or sources of information (such as speech, sounds, touch, or other sources).
Far Vision	The ability to see details at a distance.
Hearing Sensitivity	The ability to detect or tell the differences between sounds that vary in pitch and loudness.
Auditory Attention	The ability to focus on a single source of sound in the presence of other distracting sounds.
Visual Color Discrimination	The ability to match or detect differences between colors, including shades of color and brightness.
Arm-Hand Steadiness	The ability to keep your hand and arm steady while moving your arm or while holding your arm and hand in one position.
Response Orientation	The ability to choose quickly between two or more movements in response to two or more different signals (lights, sounds, pictures). It includes the speed with which the correct response is started with the hand, foot, or other body part.
Wrist-Finger Speed	The ability to make fast, simple, repeated movements of the fingers, hands, and wrists.
Manual Dexterity	The ability to quickly move your hand, your hand together with your arm, or your two hands to grasp, manipulate, or assemble objects.
Rate Control	The ability to time your movements or the movement of a piece of equipment in anticipation of changes in the speed and/or direction of a moving object or scene.
Reaction Time	The ability to quickly respond (with the hand, finger, or foot) to a signal (sound, light, picture) when it appears.
Control Precision	The ability to quickly and repeatedly adjust the controls of a machine or a vehicle to exact positions.
Depth Perception	The ability to judge which of several objects is closer or farther away from you, or to judge the distance between you and an object.
Multilimb Coordination	The ability to coordinate two or more limbs (for example, two arms, two legs, or one leg and one arm) while sitting, standing, or lying down. It does not involve performing the activities while the whole body is in motion.
Trunk Strength	The ability to use your abdominal and lower back muscles to support part of the body repeatedly or continuously over time without 'giving out' or fatiguing.
Night Vision	The ability to see under low light conditions.
Gross Body Equilibrium	The ability to keep or regain your body balance or stay upright when in an unstable position.
Speed of Limb Movement	The ability to quickly move the arms and legs.
Static Strength	The ability to exert maximum muscle force to lift, push, pull, or carry objects.
Explosive Strength	The ability to use short bursts of muscle force to propel oneself (as in jumping or sprinting), or to throw an object.
Dynamic Strength	The ability to exert muscle force repeatedly or continuously over time. This involves muscular endurance and resistance to muscle fatigue.
Stamina	The ability to exert yourself physically over long periods of time without getting winded or out of breath.
Gross Body Coordination	The ability to coordinate the movement of your arms, legs, and torso together when the whole body is in motion.
Sound Localization	The ability to tell the direction from which a sound originated.

Spatial Orientation	The ability to know your location in relation to the environment or to know where other objects are in relation to you.
Peripheral Vision	The ability to see objects or movement of objects to one's side when the eyes are looking ahead.
Dynamic Flexibility	The ability to quickly and repeatedly bend. stretch. twist. or reach out with your body. arms. and/or legs.
Glare Sensitivity	The ability to see objects in the presence of glare or bright lighting.
Extent Flexibility	The ability to bend. stretch. twist. or reach with your body. arms. and/or legs.

Work_Activity	Work_Activity Definitions
Interacting With Computers	Using computers and computer systems (including hardware and software) to program. write software. set up functions. enter data. or process information.
Updating and Using Relevant Knowledge	Keeping up-to-date technically and applying new knowledge to your job.
Getting Information	Observing. receiving. and otherwise obtaining information from all relevant sources.
Making Decisions and Solving Problems	Analyzing information and evaluating results to choose the best solution and solve problems.
Communicating with Supervisors, Peers, or Subordin	Providing information to supervisors. co-workers. and subordinates by telephone. in written form. e-mail. or in person.
Thinking Creatively	Developing. designing. or creating new applications. ideas. relationships. systems. or products. including artistic contributions.
Identifying Objects, Actions, and Events	Identifying information by categorizing. estimating. recognizing differences or similarities. and detecting changes in circumstances or events.
Analyzing Data or Information	Identifying the underlying principles, reasons, or facts of information by breaking down information or data into separate parts.
Processing Information	Compiling, coding, categorizing, calculating, tabulating, auditing, or verifying information or data.
Interpreting the Meaning of Information for Others	Translating or explaining what information means and how it can be used.
Organizing, Planning, and Prioritizing Work	Developing specific goals and plans to prioritize, organize, and accomplish your work.
Evaluating Information to Determine Compliance wit	Using relevant information and individual judgment to determine whether events or processes comply with laws, regulations, or standards.
Documenting/Recording Information	Entering, transcribing, recording, storing, or maintaining information in written or electronic/magnetic form.
Developing Objectives and Strategies	Establishing long-range objectives and specifying the strategies and actions to achieve them.
Performing Administrative Activities	Performing day-to-day administrative tasks such as maintaining information files and processing paperwork.
Communicating with Persons Outside Organization	Communicating with people outside the organization, representing the organization to customers, the public, government, and other external sources. This information can be exchanged in person, in writing, or by telephone or e-mail.
Establishing and Maintaining Interpersonal Relatio	Developing constructive and cooperative working relationships with others, and maintaining them over time.
Scheduling Work and Activities	Scheduling events, programs, and activities, as well as the work of others.
Resolving Conflicts and Negotiating with Others	Handling complaints, settling disputes, and resolving grievances and conflicts, or otherwise negotiating with others.
Monitor Processes, Materials, or Surroundings	Monitoring and reviewing information from materials, events, or the environment, to detect or assess problems.
Judging the Qualities of Things, Services, or Peop	Assessing the value, importance, or quality of things or people.
Provide Consultation and Advice to Others	Providing guidance and expert advice to management or other groups on technical, systems-, or process-related topics.
Controlling Machines and Processes	Using either control mechanisms or direct physical activity to operate machines or processes (not including computers or vehicles).
Estimating the Quantifiable Characteristics of Pro	Estimating sizes, distances, and quantities; or determining time. costs. resources. or materials needed to perform a work activity.
Coordinating the Work and Activities of Others	Getting members of a group to work together to accomplish tasks.
Training and Teaching Others	Identifying the educational needs of others. developing formal educational programs or classes. and teaching or instructing others.

Inspecting Equipment. Structures. or Material	Inspecting equipment. structures. or materials to identify the cause of errors or other problems or defects.
Guiding. Directing. and Motivating Subordinates	Providing guidance and direction to subordinates. including setting performance standards and monitoring performance.
Repairing and Maintaining Electronic Equipment	Servicing. repairing. calibrating. regulating. fine-tuning. or testing machines. devices. and equipment that operate primarily on the basis of electrical or electronic (not mechanical) principles.
Selling or Influencing Others	Convincing others to buy merchandise/goods or to otherwise change their minds or actions.
Developing and Building Teams	Encouraging and building mutual trust, respect, and cooperation among team members.
Assisting and Caring for Others	Providing personal assistance, medical attention, emotional support, or other personal care to others such as coworkers. customers. or patients.
Drafting. Laying Out. and Specifying Technical Dev	Providing documentation, detailed instructions, drawings, or specifications to tell others about how devices, parts, equipment, or structures are to be fabricated, constructed, assembled, modified, maintained, or used.
Performing for or Working Directly with the Public	Performing for people or dealing directly with the public. This includes serving customers in restaurants and stores, and receiving clients or guests.
Handling and Moving Objects	Using hands and arms in handling, installing, positioning, and moving materials, and manipulating things.
Coaching and Developing Others	Identifying the developmental needs of others and coaching, mentoring, or otherwise helping others to improve their knowledge or skills.
Repairing and Maintaining Mechanical Equipment	Servicing, repairing, adjusting, and testing machines, devices, moving parts, and equipment that operate primarily on the basis of mechanical (not electronic) principles.
Performing General Physical Activities	Performing physical activities that require considerable use of your arms and legs and moving your whole body, such as climbing, lifting, balancing, walking, stooping, and handling of materials.
Monitoring and Controlling Resources	Monitoring and controlling resources and overseeing the spending of money.
Staffing Organizational Units	Recruiting, interviewing, selecting, hiring, and promoting employees in an organization.
Operating Vehicles. Mechanized Devices, or Equipme	Running, maneuvering, navigating, or driving vehicles or mechanized equipment, such as forklifts, passenger vehicles. aircraft. or water craft.

Work_Context	Work_Context Definitions
Face-to-Face Discussions	How often do you have to have face-to-face discussions with individuals or teams in this job?
Electronic Mail	How often do you use electronic mail in this job?
Spend Time Sitting	How much does this job require sitting?
Work With Work Group or Team	How important is it to work with others in a group or team in this job?
Freedom to Make Decisions	How much decision making freedom, without supervision, does the job offer?
Indoors, Environmentally Controlled	How often does this job require working indoors in environmentally controlled conditions?
Importance of Being Exact or Accurate	How important is being very exact or highly accurate in performing this job?
Coordinate or Lead Others	How important is it to coordinate or lead others in accomplishing work activities in this job?
Structured versus Unstructured Work	To what extent is this job structured for the worker, rather than allowing the worker to determine tasks, priorities, and goals?
Contact With Others	How much does this job require the worker to be in contact with others (face-to-face, by telephone, or otherwise) in order to perform it?
Impact of Decisions on Co-workers or Company Resul	How do the decisions an employee makes impact the results of co-workers, clients or the company?
Telephone	How often do you have telephone conversations in this job?
Level of Competition	To what extent does this job require the worker to compete or to be aware of competitive pressures?
Spend Time Making Repetitive Motions	How much does this job require making repetitive motions?
Spend Time Using Your Hands to Handle, Control, or	How much does this job require using your hands to handle. control. or feel objects, tools or controls?
Frequency of Decision Making	How frequently is the worker required to make decisions that affect other people, the financial resources, and/or the image and reputation of the organization?

Consequence of Error	How serious would the result usually be if the worker made a mistake that was not readily correctable?
Importance of Repeating Same Tasks	How important is repeating the same physical activities (e.g., key entry) or mental activities (e.g., checking entries in a ledger) over and over, without stopping, to performing this job?
Frequency of Conflict Situations	How often are there conflict situations the employee has to face in this job?
Time Pressure	How often does this job require the worker to meet strict deadlines?
Physical Proximity	To what extent does this job require the worker to perform job tasks in close physical proximity to other people?
Sounds, Noise Levels Are Distracting or Uncomforta	How often does this job require working exposed to sounds and noise levels that are distracting or uncomfortable?
Responsibility for Outcomes and Results	How responsible is the worker for work outcomes and results of other workers?
Letters and Memos	How often does the job require written letters and memos?
Degree of Automation	How automated is the job?
Deal With Unpleasant or Angry People	How frequently does the worker have to deal with unpleasant, angry, or discourteous individuals as part of the job requirements?
Deal With External Customers	How important is it to work with external customers or the public in this job?
Spend Time Standing	How much does this job require standing?
Responsible for Others' Health and Safety	How much responsibility is there for the health and safety of others in this job?
Public Speaking	How often do you have to perform public speaking in this job?
Spend Time Walking and Running	How much does this job require walking and running?
Spend Time Kneeling, Crouching, Stooping, or Crawl	How much does this job require kneeling, crouching, stooping, or crawling?
Exposed to Contaminants	How often does this job require working exposed to contaminants (such as pollutants, gases, dust or odors)?
Pace Determined by Speed of Equipment	How important is it to this job that the pace is determined by the speed of equipment or machinery? (This does not refer to keeping busy at all times on this job.)
Exposed to Radiation	How often does this job require exposure to radiation?
Extremely Bright or Inadequate Lighting	How often does this job require working in extremely bright or inadequate lighting conditions?
Spend Time Bending or Twisting the Body	How much does this job require bending or twisting your body?
Deal With Physically Aggressive People	How frequently does this job require the worker to deal with physical aggression of violent individuals?
Very Hot or Cold Temperatures	How often does this job require working in very hot (above 90 F degrees) or very cold (below 32 F degrees) temperatures?
Exposed to Hazardous Conditions	How often does this job require exposure to hazardous conditions?
In an Enclosed Vehicle or Equipment	How often does this job require working in a closed vehicle or equipment (e.g., car)?
Cramped Work Space, Awkward Positions	How often does this job require working in cramped work spaces that requires getting into awkward positions?
Outdoors, Exposed to Weather	How often does this job require working outdoors, exposed to all weather conditions?
In an Open Vehicle or Equipment	How often does this job require working in an open vehicle or equipment (e.g., tractor)?
Spend Time Climbing Ladders, Scaffolds, or Poles	How much does this job require climbing ladders, scaffolds, or poles?
Exposed to Minor Burns, Cuts, Bites, or Stings	How often does this job require exposure to minor burns, cuts, bites, or stings?
Outdoors, Under Cover	How often does this job require working outdoors, under cover (e.g., structure with roof but no walls)?
Exposed to Disease or Infections	How often does this job require exposure to disease/infections?
Spend Time Keeping or Regaining Balance	How much does this job require keeping or regaining your balance?
Exposed to High Places	How often does this job require exposure to high places?
Indoors, Not Environmentally Controlled	How often does this job require working indoors in non-controlled environmental conditions (e.g., warehouse without heat)?
Wear Common Protective or Safety Equipment such as	How much does this job require wearing common protective or safety equipment such as safety shoes, glasses, gloves, hard hats or life jackets?
Exposed to Whole Body Vibration	How often does this job require exposure to whole body vibration (e.g., operate a jackhammer)?
Exposed to Hazardous Equipment	How often does this job require exposure to hazardous equipment?

Wear Specialized Protective or Safety Equipment su	How much does this job require wearing specialized protective or safety equipment such as breathing apparatus, safety harness, full protection suits, or radiation protection?

Job Zone Component	Job Zone Component Definitions
Title	Job Zone Four: Considerable Preparation Needed
Overall Experience	A minimum of two to four years of work-related skill, knowledge, or experience is needed for these occupations. For example, an accountant must complete four years of college and work for several years in accounting to be considered qualified.
Job Training	Employees in these occupations usually need several years of work-related experience, on-the-job training, and/or vocational training.
Job Zone Examples	Many of these occupations involve coordinating, supervising, managing, or training others. Examples include accountants, chefs and head cooks, computer programmers, historians, pharmacists, and police detectives.
SVP Range	(7.0 to < 8.0)
Education	Most of these occupations require a four-year bachelor's degree, but some do not.

Work_Styles	Work_Styles Definitions
Analytical Thinking	Job requires analyzing information and using logic to address work-related issues and problems.
Attention to Detail	Job requires being careful about detail and thorough in completing work tasks.
Dependability	Job requires being reliable, responsible, and dependable, and fulfilling obligations.
Cooperation	Job requires being pleasant with others on the job and displaying a good-natured, cooperative attitude.
Achievement/Effort	Job requires establishing and maintaining personally challenging achievement goals and exerting effort toward mastering tasks.
Innovation	Job requires creativity and alternative thinking to develop new ideas for and answers to work-related problems.
Adaptability/Flexibility	Job requires being open to change (positive or negative) and to considerable variety in the workplace.
Persistence	Job requires persistence in the face of obstacles.
Initiative	Job requires a willingness to take on responsibilities and challenges.
Stress Tolerance	Job requires accepting criticism and dealing calmly and effectively with high stress situations.
Integrity	Job requires being honest and ethical.
Independence	Job requires developing one's own ways of doing things, guiding oneself with little or no supervision, and depending on oneself to get things done.
Self Control	Job requires maintaining composure, keeping emotions in check, controlling anger, and avoiding aggressive behavior, even in very difficult situations.
Concern for Others	Job requires being sensitive to others' needs and feelings and being understanding and helpful on the job.
Leadership	Job requires a willingness to lead, take charge, and offer opinions and direction.
Social Orientation	Job requires preferring to work with others rather than alone, and being personally connected with others on the job.

15-1032.00 - Computer Software Engineers, Systems Software

Research, design, develop, and test operating systems-level software, compilers, and network distribution software for medical, industrial, military, communications, aerospace, business, scientific, and general computing applications. Set operational specifications and formulate and analyze software requirements. Apply principles and techniques of computer science, engineering, and mathematical analysis.

Tasks

1) Prepare reports and correspondence concerning project specifications, activities and status.

2) Consult with engineering staff to evaluate interface between hardware and software, develop specifications and performance requirements and resolve customer problems.

3) Coordinate installation of software system.

4) Modify existing software to correct errors, to adapt it to new hardware or to upgrade interfaces and improve performance.

5) Consult with customers and/or other departments on project status, proposals and technical issues such as software system design and maintenance.

6) Develop and direct software system testing and validation procedures.

7) Advise customer about, or perform, maintenance of software system.

8) Store, retrieve, and manipulate data for analysis of system capabilities and requirements.

9) Direct software programming and development of documentation.

10) Monitor functioning of equipment to ensure system operates in conformance with specifications.

11) Confer with data processing and project managers to obtain information on limitations and capabilities for data processing projects.

12) Design and develop software systems, using scientific analysis and mathematical models to predict and measure outcome and consequences of design.

13) Evaluate factors such as reporting formats required, cost constraints, and need for security restrictions to determine hardware configuration.

14) Train users to use new or modified equipment.

15) Supervise and assign work to programmers, designers, technologists and technicians and other engineering and scientific personnel.

16) Specify power supply requirements and configuration.

17) Recommend purchase of equipment to control dust, temperature, and humidity in area of system installation.

18) Utilize microcontrollers to develop control signals, implement control algorithms and measure process variables such as temperatures, pressures and positions.

Knowledge	Knowledge Definitions
Computers and Electronics	Knowledge of circuit boards, processors, chips, electronic equipment, and computer hardware and software, including applications and programming.
Mathematics	Knowledge of arithmetic, algebra, geometry, calculus, statistics, and their applications.
English Language	Knowledge of the structure and content of the English language including the meaning and spelling of words, rules of composition, and grammar.
Engineering and Technology	Knowledge of the practical application of engineering science and technology. This includes applying principles, techniques, procedures, and equipment to the design and production of various goods and services.
Design	Knowledge of design techniques, tools, and principles involved in production of precision technical plans, blueprints, drawings, and models.
Customer and Personal Service	Knowledge of principles and processes for providing customer and personal services. This includes customer needs assessment, meeting quality standards for services, and evaluation of customer satisfaction.
Education and Training	Knowledge of principles and methods for curriculum and training design, teaching and instruction for individuals and groups, and the measurement of training effects.
Communications and Media	Knowledge of media production, communication, and dissemination techniques and methods. This includes alternative ways to inform and entertain via written, oral, and visual media.
Clerical	Knowledge of administrative and clerical procedures and systems such as word processing, managing files and records, stenography and transcription, designing forms, and other office procedures and terminology.
Telecommunications	Knowledge of transmission, broadcasting, switching, control, and operation of telecommunications systems.
Administration and Management	Knowledge of business and management principles involved in strategic planning, resource allocation, human resources modeling, leadership technique, production methods, and coordination of people and resources.
Public Safety and Security	Knowledge of relevant equipment, policies, procedures, and strategies to promote effective local, state, or national security operations for the protection of people, data, property, and institutions.

Physics	Knowledge and prediction of physical principles, laws, their interrelationships, and applications to understanding fluid, material, and atmospheric dynamics, and mechanical, electrical, atomic and sub-atomic structures and processes.
Psychology	Knowledge of human behavior and performance: individual differences in ability, personality, and interests; learning and motivation; psychological research methods; and the assessment and treatment of behavioral and affective disorders.
Production and Processing	Knowledge of raw materials, production processes, quality control, costs, and other techniques for maximizing the effective manufacture and distribution of goods.
Economics and Accounting	Knowledge of economic and accounting principles and practices, the financial markets, banking and the analysis and reporting of financial data.
Law and Government	Knowledge of laws, legal codes, court procedures, precedents, government regulations, executive orders, agency rules, and the democratic political process.
Sales and Marketing	Knowledge of principles and methods for showing, promoting, and selling products or services. This includes marketing strategy and tactics, product demonstration, sales techniques, and sales control systems.
Fine Arts	Knowledge of the theory and techniques required to compose, produce, and perform works of music, dance, visual arts, drama, and sculpture.
Mechanical	Knowledge of machines and tools, including their designs, uses, repair, and maintenance.
Foreign Language	Knowledge of the structure and content of a foreign (non-English) language including the meaning and spelling of words, rules of composition and grammar, and pronunciation.
Personnel and Human Resources	Knowledge of principles and procedures for personnel recruitment, selection, training, compensation and benefits, labor relations and negotiation, and personnel information systems.
Sociology and Anthropology	Knowledge of group behavior and dynamics, societal trends and influences, human migrations, ethnicity, cultures and their history and origins.
Therapy and Counseling	Knowledge of principles, methods, and procedures for diagnosis, treatment, and rehabilitation of physical and mental dysfunctions, and for career counseling and guidance.
Transportation	Knowledge of principles and methods for moving people or goods by air, rail, sea, or road, including the relative costs and benefits.
Philosophy and Theology	Knowledge of different philosophical systems and religions. This includes their basic principles, values, ethics, ways of thinking, customs, practices, and their impact on human culture.
History and Archeology	Knowledge of historical events and their causes, indicators, and effects on civilizations and cultures.
Chemistry	Knowledge of the chemical composition, structure, and properties of substances and of the chemical processes and transformations that they undergo. This includes uses of chemicals and their interactions, danger signs, production techniques, and disposal methods.
Geography	Knowledge of principles and methods for describing the features of land, sea, and air masses, including their physical characteristics, locations, interrelationships, and distribution of plant, animal, and human life.
Biology	Knowledge of plant and animal organisms, their tissues, cells, functions, interdependencies, and interactions with each other and the environment.
Building and Construction	Knowledge of materials, methods, and the tools involved in the construction or repair of houses, buildings, or other structures such as highways and roads.
Medicine and Dentistry	Knowledge of the information and techniques needed to diagnose and treat human injuries, diseases, and deformities. This includes symptoms, treatment alternatives, drug properties and interactions, and preventive health-care measures.
Food Production	Knowledge of techniques and equipment for planting, growing, and harvesting food products (both plant and animal) for consumption, including storage/handling techniques.

Skills	Skills Definitions
Complex Problem Solving	Identifying complex problems and reviewing related information to develop and evaluate options and implement solutions.
Technology Design	Generating or adapting equipment and technology to serve user needs.

Troubleshooting	Determining causes of operating errors and deciding what to do about it.
Critical Thinking	Using logic and reasoning to identify the strengths and weaknesses of alternative solutions, conclusions or approaches to problems.
Active Learning	Understanding the implications of new information for both current and future problem-solving and decision-making.
Programming	Writing computer programs for various purposes.
Reading Comprehension	Understanding written sentences and paragraphs in work related documents.
Systems Analysis	Determining how a system should work and how changes in conditions, operations, and the environment will affect outcomes.
Mathematics	Using mathematics to solve problems.
Operations Analysis	Analyzing needs and product requirements to create a design.
Active Listening	Giving full attention to what other people are saying, taking time to understand the points being made, asking questions as appropriate, and not interrupting at inappropriate times.
Time Management	Managing one's own time and the time of others.
Coordination	Adjusting actions in relation to others' actions.
Learning Strategies	Selecting and using training/instructional methods and procedures appropriate for the situation when learning or teaching new things.
Judgment and Decision Making	Considering the relative costs and benefits of potential actions to choose the most appropriate one.
Quality Control Analysis	Conducting tests and inspections of products, services, or processes to evaluate quality or performance.
Installation	Installing equipment, machines, wiring, or programs to meet specifications.
Speaking	Talking to others to convey information effectively.
Equipment Selection	Determining the kind of tools and equipment needed to do a job.
Instructing	Teaching others how to do something.
Operation and Control	Controlling operations of equipment or systems.
Systems Evaluation	Identifying measures or indicators of system performance and the actions needed to improve or correct performance, relative to the goals of the system.
Science	Using scientific rules and methods to solve problems.
Writing	Communicating effectively in writing as appropriate for the needs of the audience.
Social Perceptiveness	Being aware of others' reactions and understanding why they react as they do.
Monitoring	Monitoring/Assessing performance of yourself, other individuals, or organizations to make improvements or take corrective action.
Service Orientation	Actively looking for ways to help people.
Persuasion	Persuading others to change their minds or behavior.
Operation Monitoring	Watching gauges, dials, or other indicators to make sure a machine is working properly.
Repairing	Repairing machines or systems using the needed tools.
Management of Material Resources	Obtaining and seeing to the appropriate use of equipment, facilities, and materials needed to do certain work.
Negotiation	Bringing others together and trying to reconcile differences.
Management of Financial Resources	Determining how money will be spent to get the work done, and accounting for these expenditures.
Management of Personnel Resources	Motivating, developing, and directing people as they work, identifying the best people for the job.
Equipment Maintenance	Performing routine maintenance on equipment and determining when and what kind of maintenance is needed.

Ability	Ability Definitions
Deductive Reasoning	The ability to apply general rules to specific problems to produce answers that make sense.
Inductive Reasoning	The ability to combine pieces of information to form general rules or conclusions (includes finding a relationship among seemingly unrelated events).
Information Ordering	The ability to arrange things or actions in a certain order or pattern according to a specific rule or set of rules (e.g., patterns of numbers, letters, words, pictures, mathematical operations).
Oral Expression	The ability to communicate information and ideas in speaking so others will understand.
Oral Comprehension	The ability to listen to and understand information and ideas presented through spoken words and sentences.
Problem Sensitivity	The ability to tell when something is wrong or is likely to go wrong. It does not involve solving the problem, only recognizing there is a problem.

Mathematical Reasoning	The ability to choose the right mathematical methods or formulas to solve a problem.
Near Vision	The ability to see details at close range (within a few feet of the observer).
Originality	The ability to come up with unusual or clever ideas about a given topic or situation, or to develop creative ways to solve a problem.
Written Comprehension	The ability to read and understand information and ideas presented in writing.
Speech Recognition	The ability to identify and understand the speech of another person.
Speech Clarity	The ability to speak clearly so others can understand you.
Written Expression	The ability to communicate information and ideas in writing so others will understand.
Selective Attention	The ability to concentrate on a task over a period of time without being distracted.
Number Facility	The ability to add, subtract, multiply, or divide quickly and correctly.
Category Flexibility	The ability to generate or use different sets of rules for combining or grouping things in different ways.
Fluency of Ideas	The ability to come up with a number of ideas about a topic (the number of ideas is important, not their quality, correctness, or creativity).
Perceptual Speed	The ability to quickly and accurately compare similarities and differences among sets of letters, numbers, objects, pictures, or patterns. The things to be compared may be presented at the same time or one after the other. This ability also includes comparing a presented object with a remembered object.
Memorization	The ability to remember information such as words, numbers, pictures, and procedures.
Flexibility of Closure	The ability to identify or detect a known pattern (a figure, object, word, or sound) that is hidden in other distracting material.
Finger Dexterity	The ability to make precisely coordinated movements of the fingers of one or both hands to grasp, manipulate, or assemble very small objects.
Visualization	The ability to imagine how something will look after it is moved around or when its parts are moved or rearranged.
Hearing Sensitivity	The ability to detect or tell the differences between sounds that vary in pitch and loudness.
Far Vision	The ability to see details at a distance.
Speed of Closure	The ability to quickly make sense of, combine, and organize information into meaningful patterns.
Visual Color Discrimination	The ability to match or detect differences between colors, including shades of color and brightness.
Time Sharing	The ability to shift back and forth between two or more activities or sources of information (such as speech, sounds, touch, or other sources).
Auditory Attention	The ability to focus on a single source of sound in the presence of other distracting sounds.
Manual Dexterity	The ability to quickly move your hand, your hand together with your arm, or your two hands to grasp, manipulate, or assemble objects.
Arm-Hand Steadiness	The ability to keep your hand and arm steady while moving your arm or while holding your arm and hand in one position.
Depth Perception	The ability to judge which of several objects is closer or farther away from you, or to judge the distance between you and an object.
Control Precision	The ability to quickly and repeatedly adjust the controls of a machine or a vehicle to exact positions.
Wrist-Finger Speed	The ability to make fast, simple, repeated movements of the fingers, hands, and wrists.
Trunk Strength	The ability to use your abdominal and lower back muscles to support part of the body repeatedly or continuously over time without 'giving out' or fatiguing.
Reaction Time	The ability to quickly respond (with the hand, finger, or foot) to a signal (sound, light, picture) when it appears.
Speed of Limb Movement	The ability to quickly move the arms and legs.
Explosive Strength	The ability to use short bursts of muscle force to propel oneself (as in jumping or sprinting), or to throw an object.
Peripheral Vision	The ability to see objects or movement of objects to one's side when the eyes are looking ahead.
Dynamic Strength	The ability to exert muscle force repeatedly or continuously over time. This involves muscular endurance and resistance to muscle fatigue.
Stamina	The ability to exert yourself physically over long periods of time without getting winded or out of breath.

Extent Flexibility	The ability to bend, stretch, twist, or reach with your body, arms, and/or legs.
Dynamic Flexibility	The ability to quickly and repeatedly bend, stretch, twist, or reach out with your body, arms, and/or legs.
Gross Body Coordination	The ability to coordinate the movement of your arms, legs, and torso together when the whole body is in motion.
Static Strength	The ability to exert maximum muscle force to lift, push, pull, or carry objects.
Response Orientation	The ability to choose quickly between two or more movements in response to two or more different signals (lights, sounds, pictures). It includes the speed with which the correct response is started with the hand, foot, or other body part.
Night Vision	The ability to see under low light conditions.
Multilimb Coordination	The ability to coordinate two or more limbs (for example, two arms, two legs, or one leg and one arm) while sitting, standing, or lying down. It does not involve performing the activities while the whole body is in motion.
Sound Localization	The ability to tell the direction from which a sound originated.
Rate Control	The ability to time your movements or the movement of a piece of equipment in anticipation of changes in the speed and/or direction of a moving object or scene.
Spatial Orientation	The ability to know your location in relation to the environment or to know where other objects are in relation to you.
Glare Sensitivity	The ability to see objects in the presence of glare or bright lighting.
Gross Body Equilibrium	The ability to keep or regain your body balance or stay upright when in an unstable position.

Work_Activity	**Work_Activity Definitions**
Interacting With Computers	Using computers and computer systems (including hardware and software) to program, write software, set up functions, enter data, or process information.
Making Decisions and Solving Problems	Analyzing information and evaluating results to choose the best solution and solve problems.
Analyzing Data or Information	Identifying the underlying principles, reasons, or facts of information by breaking down information or data into separate parts.
Updating and Using Relevant Knowledge	Keeping up-to-date technically and applying new knowledge to your job.
Organizing, Planning, and Prioritizing Work	Developing specific goals and plans to prioritize, organize, and accomplish your work.
Getting Information	Observing, receiving, and otherwise obtaining information from all relevant sources.
Communicating with Supervisors, Peers, or Subordin	Providing information to supervisors, co-workers, and subordinates by telephone, in written form, e-mail, or in person.
Evaluating Information to Determine Compliance wit	Using relevant information and individual judgment to determine whether events or processes comply with laws, regulations, or standards.
Documenting/Recording Information	Entering, transcribing, recording, storing, or maintaining information in written or electronic/magnetic form.
Identifying Objects, Actions, and Events	Identifying information by categorizing, estimating, recognizing differences or similarities, and detecting changes in circumstances or events.
Interpreting the Meaning of Information for Others	Translating or explaining what information means and how it can be used.
Processing Information	Compiling, coding, categorizing, calculating, tabulating, auditing, or verifying information or data
Thinking Creatively	Developing, designing, or creating new applications, ideas, relationships, systems, or products, including artistic contributions.
Scheduling Work and Activities	Scheduling events, programs, and activities, as well as the work of others.
Developing Objectives and Strategies	Establishing long-range objectives and specifying the strategies and actions to achieve them.
Establishing and Maintaining Interpersonal Relatio	Developing constructive and cooperative working relationships with others, and maintaining them over time.
Provide Consultation and Advice to Others	Providing guidance and expert advice to management or other groups on technical, systems-, or process-related topics.
Monitor Processes, Materials, or Surroundings	Monitoring and reviewing information from materials, events, or the environment, to detect or assess problems.
Estimating the Quantifiable Characteristics of Pro	Estimating sizes, distances, and quantities; or determining time, costs, resources, or materials needed to perform a work activity.

Judging the Qualities of Things, Services, or Peop	Assessing the value, importance, or quality of things or people.
Communicating with Persons Outside Organization	Communicating with people outside the organization, representing the organization to customers, the public, government, and other external sources. This information can be exchanged in person, in writing, or by telephone or e-mail.
Coordinating the Work and Activities of Others	Getting members of a group to work together to accomplish tasks.
Developing and Building Teams	Encouraging and building mutual trust, respect, and cooperation among team members.
Inspecting Equipment, Structures, or Material	Inspecting equipment, structures, or materials to identify the cause of errors or other problems or defects.
Resolving Conflicts and Negotiating with Others	Handling complaints, settling disputes, and resolving grievances and conflicts, or otherwise negotiating with others.
Drafting, Laying Out, and Specifying Technical Dev	Providing documentation, detailed instructions, drawings, or specifications to tell others about how devices, parts, equipment, or structures are to be fabricated, constructed, assembled, modified, maintained, or used.
Training and Teaching Others	Identifying the educational needs of others, developing formal educational or training programs or classes, and teaching or instructing others.
Repairing and Maintaining Electronic Equipment	Servicing, repairing, calibrating, regulating, fine-tuning, or testing machines, devices, and equipment that operate primarily on the basis of electrical or electronic (not mechanical) principles.
Guiding, Directing, and Motivating Subordinates	Providing guidance and direction to subordinates, including setting performance standards and monitoring performance.
Coaching and Developing Others	Identifying the developmental needs of others and coaching, mentoring, or otherwise helping others to improve their knowledge or skills.
Performing Administrative Activities	Performing day-to-day administrative tasks such as maintaining information files and processing paperwork.
Monitoring and Controlling Resources	Monitoring and controlling resources and overseeing the spending of money.
Assisting and Caring for Others	Providing personal assistance, medical attention, emotional support, or other personal care to others such as coworkers, customers, or patients.
Selling or Influencing Others	Convincing others to buy merchandise/goods or to otherwise change their minds or actions.
Staffing Organizational Units	Recruiting, interviewing, selecting, hiring, and promoting employees in an organization.
Controlling Machines and Processes	Using either control mechanisms or direct physical activity to operate machines or processes (not including computers or vehicles).
Performing General Physical Activities	Performing physical activities that require considerable use of your arms and legs and moving your whole body, such as climbing, lifting, balancing, walking, stooping, and handling of materials.
Performing for or Working Directly with the Public	Performing for people or dealing directly with the public. This includes serving customers in restaurants and stores, and receiving clients or guests.
Handling and Moving Objects	Using hands and arms in handling, installing, positioning, and moving materials, and manipulating things.
Repairing and Maintaining Mechanical Equipment	Servicing, repairing, adjusting, and testing machines, devices, moving parts, and equipment that operate primarily on the basis of mechanical (not electronic) principles.
Operating Vehicles, Mechanized Devices, or Equipme	Running, maneuvering, navigating, or driving vehicles or mechanized equipment, such as forklifts, passenger vehicles, aircraft, or water craft.

Work_Context	**Work_Context Definitions**
Face-to-Face Discussions	How often do you have to have face-to-face discussions with individuals or teams in this job?
Electronic Mail	How often do you use electronic mail in this job?
Work With Work Group or Team	How important is it to work with others in a group or team in this job?
Importance of Being Exact or Accurate	How important is being very exact or highly accurate in performing this job?
Structured versus Unstructured Work	To what extent is this job structured for the worker, rather than allowing the worker to determine tasks, priorities, and goals?
Spend Time Sitting	How much does this job require sitting?
Indoors, Environmentally Controlled	How often does this job require working indoors in environmentally controlled conditions?
Telephone	How often do you have telephone conversations in this job?
Freedom to Make Decisions	How much decision making freedom, without supervision, does the job offer?

Contact With Others	How much does this job require the worker to be in contact with others (face-to-face, by telephone, or otherwise) in order to perform it?
Importance of Repeating Same Tasks	How important is repeating the same physical activities (e.g., key entry) or mental activities (e.g., checking entries in a ledger) over and over, without stopping, to performing this job?
Time Pressure	How often does this job require the worker to meet strict deadlines?
Spend Time Making Repetitive Motions	How much does this job require making repetitive motions?
Frequency of Decision Making	How frequently is the worker required to make decisions that affect other people, the financial resources, and/or the image and reputation of the organization?
Spend Time Using Your Hands to Handle, Control, or	How much does this job require using your hands to handle, control, or feel objects, tools or controls?
Coordinate or Lead Others	How important is it to coordinate or lead others in accomplishing work activities in this job?
Consequence of Error	How serious would the result usually be if the worker made a mistake that was not readily correctable?
Impact of Decisions on Co-workers or Company Resul	How do the decisions an employee makes impact the results of co-workers, clients or the company?
Level of Competition	To what extent does this job require the worker to compete or to be aware of competitive pressures?
Letters and Memos	How often does the job require written letters and memos?
Physical Proximity	To what extent does this job require the worker to perform job tasks in close physical proximity to other people?
Public Speaking	How often do you have to perform public speaking in this job?
Deal With External Customers	How important is it to work with external customers or the public in this job?
Responsibility for Outcomes and Results	How responsible is the worker for work outcomes and results of other workers?
Degree of Automation	How automated is the job?
Sounds, Noise Levels Are Distracting or Uncomforta	How often does this job require working exposed to sounds and noise levels that are distracting or uncomfortable?
Extremely Bright or Inadequate Lighting	How often does this job require working in extremely bright or inadequate lighting conditions?
Deal With Unpleasant or Angry People	How frequently does the worker have to deal with unpleasant, angry, or discourteous individuals as part of the job requirements?
Spend Time Standing	How much does this job require standing?
Responsible for Others' Health and Safety	How much responsibility is there for the health and safety of others in this job?
Frequency of Conflict Situations	How often are there conflict situations the employee has to face in this job?
In an Enclosed Vehicle or Equipment	How often does this job require working in a closed vehicle or equipment (e.g., car)?
Spend Time Kneeling, Crouching, Stooping, or Crawl	How much does this job require kneeling, crouching, stooping or crawling?
Spend Time Walking and Running	How much does this job require walking and running?
Pace Determined by Speed of Equipment	How important is it to this job that the pace is determined by the speed of equipment or machinery? (This does not refer to keeping busy at all times on this job.)
Exposed to Contaminants	How often does this job require working exposed to contaminants (such as pollutants, gases, dust or odors)?
Cramped Work Space, Awkward Positions	How often does this job require working in cramped work spaces that requires getting into awkward positions?
Spend Time Bending or Twisting the Body	How much does this job require bending or twisting your body?
Outdoors, Under Cover	How often does this job require working outdoors, under cover (e.g., structure with roof but no walls)?
Exposed to High Places	How often does this job require exposure to high places?
Spend Time Climbing Ladders, Scaffolds, or Poles	How much does this job require climbing ladders, scaffolds, or poles?
Indoors, Not Environmentally Controlled	How often does this job require working indoors in non-controlled environmental conditions (e.g., warehouse without heat)?
Deal With Physically Aggressive People	How frequently does this job require the worker to deal with physical aggression of violent individuals?
Very Hot or Cold Temperatures	How often does this job require working in very hot (above 90 F degrees) or very cold (below 32 F degrees) temperatures?
Exposed to Radiation	How often does this job require exposure to radiation?
Spend Time Keeping or Regaining Balance	How much does this job require keeping or regaining your balance?

Outdoors, Exposed to Weather	How often does this job require working outdoors, exposed to all weather conditions?
Exposed to Hazardous Conditions	How often does this job require exposure to hazardous conditions?
Exposed to Hazardous Equipment	How often does this job require exposure to hazardous equipment?
Exposed to Disease or Infections	How often does this job require exposure to disease/infections?
Exposed to Whole Body Vibration	How often does this job require exposure to whole body vibration (e.g., operate a jackhammer)?
Wear Specialized Protective or Safety Equipment su	How much does this job require wearing specialized protective or safety equipment such as breathing apparatus, safety harness, full protection suits, or radiation protection?
Exposed to Minor Burns, Cuts, Bites, or Stings	How often does this job require exposure to minor burns, cuts, bites, or stings?
Wear Common Protective or Safety Equipment such as	How much does this job require wearing common protective or safety equipment such as safety shoes, glasses, gloves, hard hats or live jackets?
In an Open Vehicle or Equipment	How often does this job require working in an open vehicle or equipment (e.g., tractor)?

Job Zone Component	Job Zone Component Definitions
Title	Job Zone Four: Considerable Preparation Needed
Overall Experience	A minimum of two to four years of work-related skill, knowledge, or experience is needed for these occupations. For example, an accountant must complete four years of college and work for several years in accounting to be considered qualified.
Job Training	Employees in these occupations usually need several years of work-related experience, on-the-job training, and/or vocational training.
Job Zone Examples	Many of these occupations involve coordinating, supervising, managing, or training others. Examples include accountants, chefs and head cooks, computer programmers, historians, pharmacists, and police detectives.
SVP Range	(7.0 to < 8.0)
Education	Most of these occupations require a four - year bachelor's degree, but some do not.

Work_Styles	Work_Styles Definitions
Analytical Thinking	Job requires analyzing information and using logic to address work-related issues and problems.
Attention to Detail	Job requires being careful about detail and thorough in completing work tasks.
Cooperation	Job requires being pleasant with others on the job and displaying a good-natured, cooperative attitude.
Initiative	Job requires a willingness to take on responsibilities and challenges.
Achievement/Effort	Job requires establishing and maintaining personally challenging achievement goals and exerting effort toward mastering tasks.
Innovation	Job requires creativity and alternative thinking to develop new ideas for and answers to work-related problems.
Integrity	Job requires being honest and ethical.
Adaptability/Flexibility	Job requires being open to change (positive or negative) and to considerable variety in the workplace.
Dependability	Job requires being reliable, responsible, and dependable, and fulfilling obligations.
Persistence	Job requires persistence in the face of obstacles.
Stress Tolerance	Job requires accepting criticism and dealing calmly and effectively with high stress situations.
Leadership	Job requires a willingness to lead, take charge, and offer opinions and direction.
Independence	Job requires developing one's own ways of doing things, guiding oneself with little or no supervision, and depending on oneself to get things done.
Self Control	Job requires maintaining composure, keeping emotions in check, controlling anger, and avoiding aggressive behavior, even in very difficult situations.
Social Orientation	Job requires preferring to work with others rather than alone, and being personally connected with others on the job.
Concern for Others	Job requires being sensitive to others' needs and feelings and being understanding and helpful on the job.

15-1041.00 - Computer Support Specialists

Provide technical assistance to computer system users. Answer questions or resolve computer problems for clients in person, via telephone or from remote location. May provide assistance concerning the use of computer hardware and software, including printing, installation, word processing, electronic mail, and operating systems.

Tasks

1) Read technical manuals, confer with users, and conduct computer diagnostics to investigate and resolve problems and to provide technical assistance and support.

2) Enter commands and observe system functioning to verify correct operations and detect errors.

3) Develop training materials and procedures, and/or train users in the proper use of hardware and software.

4) Install and perform minor repairs to hardware, software, and peripheral equipment, following design or installation specifications.

5) Refer major hardware or software problems or defective products to vendors or technicians for service.

6) Read trade magazines and technical manuals, and attend conferences and seminars to maintain knowledge of hardware and software.

7) Set up equipment for employee use, performing or ensuring proper installation of cable, operating systems, and appropriate software.

8) Maintain record of daily data communication transactions, problems and remedial action taken, and installation activities.

9) Oversee the daily performance of computer systems.

10) Prepare evaluations of software or hardware, and recommend improvements or upgrades.

11) Confer with staff, users, and management to establish requirements for new systems or modifications.

12) Inspect equipment and read order sheets to prepare for delivery to users.

13) Supervise and coordinate workers engaged in problem-solving, monitoring, and installing data communication equipment and software.

14) Modify and customize commercial programs for internal needs.

15) Conduct office automation feasibility studies, including workflow analysis, space design, and cost comparison analysis.

Knowledge	Knowledge Definitions
Computers and Electronics	Knowledge of circuit boards, processors, chips, electronic equipment, and computer hardware and software, including applications and programming.
Customer and Personal Service	Knowledge of principles and processes for providing customer and personal services. This includes customer needs assessment, meeting quality standards for services, and evaluation of customer satisfaction.
Engineering and Technology	Knowledge of the practical application of engineering science and technology. This includes applying principles, techniques, procedures, and equipment to the design and production of various goods and services.
English Language	Knowledge of the structure and content of the English language including the meaning and spelling of words, rules of composition, and grammar.
Telecommunications	Knowledge of transmission, broadcasting, switching, control, and operation of telecommunications systems.
Mathematics	Knowledge of arithmetic, algebra, geometry, calculus, statistics, and their applications.
Administration and Management	Knowledge of business and management principles involved in strategic planning, resource allocation, human resources modeling, leadership technique, production methods, and coordination of people and resources.
Production and Processing	Knowledge of raw materials, production processes, quality control, costs, and other techniques for maximizing the effective manufacture and distribution of goods.
Design	Knowledge of design techniques, tools, and principles involved in production of precision technical plans, blueprints, drawings, and models.
Psychology	Knowledge of human behavior and performance; individual differences in ability, personality, and interests; learning and motivation; psychological research methods; and the assessment and treatment of behavioral and affective disorders.
Education and Training	Knowledge of principles and methods for curriculum and training design, teaching and instruction for individuals and groups, and the measurement of training effects.
Mechanical	Knowledge of machines and tools, including their designs, uses, repair, and maintenance.
Clerical	Knowledge of administrative and clerical procedures and systems such as word processing, managing files and records, stenography and transcription, designing forms, and other office procedures and terminology.
Communications and Media	Knowledge of media production, communication, and dissemination techniques and methods. This includes alternative ways to inform and entertain via written, oral, and visual media.
Transportation	Knowledge of principles and methods for moving people or goods by air, rail, sea, or road, including the relative costs and benefits.
Physics	Knowledge and prediction of physical principles, laws, their interrelationships, and applications to understanding fluid, material, and atmospheric dynamics, and mechanical, electrical, atomic and sub-atomic structures and processes.
Public Safety and Security	Knowledge of relevant equipment, policies, procedures, and strategies to promote effective local, state, or national security operations for the protection of people, data, property, and institutions.
Law and Government	Knowledge of laws, legal codes, court procedures, precedents, government regulations, executive orders, agency rules, and the democratic political process.
Foreign Language	Knowledge of the structure and content of a foreign (non-English) language including the meaning and spelling of words, rules of composition and grammar, and pronunciation.
Personnel and Human Resources	Knowledge of principles and procedures for personnel recruitment, selection, training, compensation and benefits, labor relations and negotiation, and personnel information systems.
Sociology and Anthropology	Knowledge of group behavior and dynamics, societal trends and influences, human migrations, ethnicity, cultures and their history and origins.
History and Archeology	Knowledge of historical events and their causes, indicators, and effects on civilizations and cultures.
Sales and Marketing	Knowledge of principles and methods for showing, promoting, and selling products or services. This includes marketing strategy and tactics, product demonstration, sales techniques, and sales control systems.
Economics and Accounting	Knowledge of economic and accounting principles and practices, the financial markets, banking and the analysis and reporting of financial data.
Geography	Knowledge of principles and methods for describing the features of land, sea, and air masses, including their physical characteristics, locations, interrelationships, and distribution of plant, animal, and human life.
Chemistry	Knowledge of the chemical composition, structure, and properties of substances and of the chemical processes and transformations that they undergo. This includes uses of chemicals and their interactions, danger signs, production techniques, and disposal methods.
Medicine and Dentistry	Knowledge of the information and techniques needed to diagnose and treat human injuries, diseases, and deformities. This includes symptoms, treatment alternatives, drug properties and interactions, and preventive health-care measures.
Food Production	Knowledge of techniques and equipment for planting, growing, and harvesting food products (both plant and animal) for consumption, including storage/handling techniques.
Building and Construction	Knowledge of materials, methods, and the tools involved in the construction or repair of houses, buildings, or other structures such as highways and roads.
Therapy and Counseling	Knowledge of principles, methods, and procedures for diagnosis, treatment, and rehabilitation of physical and mental dysfunctions, and for career counseling and guidance.
Philosophy and Theology	Knowledge of different philosophical systems and religions. This includes their basic principles, values, ethics, ways of thinking, customs, practices, and their impact on human culture.
Biology	Knowledge of plant and animal organisms, their tissues, cells, functions, interdependencies, and interactions with each other and the environment.
Fine Arts	Knowledge of the theory and techniques required to compose, produce, and perform works of music, dance, visual arts, drama, and sculpture.

Skills	Skills Definitions
Troubleshooting	Determining causes of operating errors and deciding what to do about it.
Reading Comprehension	Understanding written sentences and paragraphs in work related documents.
Critical Thinking	Using logic and reasoning to identify the strengths and weaknesses of alternative solutions, conclusions or approaches to problems.
Active Listening	Giving full attention to what other people are saying, taking time to understand the points being made, asking questions as appropriate, and not interrupting at inappropriate times.
Writing	Communicating effectively in writing as appropriate for the needs of the audience.
Speaking	Talking to others to convey information effectively.
Learning Strategies	Selecting and using training/instructional methods and procedures appropriate for the situation when learning or teaching new things.
Active Learning	Understanding the implications of new information for both current and future problem-solving and decision-making.
Instructing	Teaching others how to do something.
Complex Problem Solving	Identifying complex problems and reviewing related information to develop and evaluate options and implement solutions.
Social Perceptiveness	Being aware of others' reactions and understanding why they react as they do.
Repairing	Repairing machines or systems using the needed tools.
Equipment Maintenance	Performing routine maintenance on equipment and determining when and what kind of maintenance is needed.
Time Management	Managing one's own time and the time of others.
Coordination	Adjusting actions in relation to others' actions.
Equipment Selection	Determining the kind of tools and equipment needed to do a job.
Persuasion	Persuading others to change their minds or behavior.
Judgment and Decision Making	Considering the relative costs and benefits of potential actions to choose the most appropriate one.
Service Orientation	Actively looking for ways to help people.
Installation	Installing equipment, machines, wiring, or programs to meet specifications.
Monitoring	Monitoring/Assessing performance of yourself, other individuals, or organizations to make improvements or take corrective action.
Mathematics	Using mathematics to solve problems.
Systems Evaluation	Identifying measures or indicators of system performance and the actions needed to improve or correct performance, relative to the goals of the system.
Operations Analysis	Analyzing needs and product requirements to create a design.
Technology Design	Generating or adapting equipment and technology to serve user needs.
Systems Analysis	Determining how a system should work and how changes in conditions, operations, and the environment will affect outcomes.
Negotiation	Bringing others together and trying to reconcile differences.
Management of Personnel Resources	Motivating, developing, and directing people as they work, identifying the best people for the job.
Operation and Control	Controlling operations of equipment or systems.
Quality Control Analysis	Conducting tests and inspections of products, services, or processes to evaluate quality or performance.
Management of Material Resources	Obtaining and seeing to the appropriate use of equipment, facilities, and materials needed to do certain work.
Operation Monitoring	Watching gauges, dials, or other indicators to make sure a machine is working properly.
Science	Using scientific rules and methods to solve problems.
Management of Financial Resources	Determining how money will be spent to get the work done, and accounting for these expenditures.
Programming	Writing computer programs for various purposes.

Ability	Ability Definitions
Oral Expression	The ability to communicate information and ideas in speaking so others will understand.
Inductive Reasoning	The ability to combine pieces of information to form general rules or conclusions (includes finding a relationship among seemingly unrelated events).
Deductive Reasoning	The ability to apply general rules to specific problems to produce answers that make sense.
Oral Comprehension	The ability to listen to and understand information and ideas presented through spoken words and sentences.
Written Comprehension	The ability to read and understand information and ideas presented in writing.
Problem Sensitivity	The ability to tell when something is wrong or is likely to go wrong. It does not involve solving the problem, only recognizing there is a problem.
Speech Clarity	The ability to speak clearly so others can understand you.
Information Ordering	The ability to arrange things or actions in a certain order or pattern according to a specific rule or set of rules (e.g., patterns of numbers, letters, words, pictures, mathematical operations).
Speech Recognition	The ability to identify and understand the speech of another person.
Near Vision	The ability to see details at close range (within a few feet of the observer).
Written Expression	The ability to communicate information and ideas in writing so others will understand.
Fluency of Ideas	The ability to come up with a number of ideas about a topic (the number of ideas is important, not their quality, correctness, or creativity).
Visualization	The ability to imagine how something will look after it is moved around or when its parts are moved or rearranged.
Selective Attention	The ability to concentrate on a task over a period of time without being distracted.
Category Flexibility	The ability to generate or use different sets of rules for combining or grouping things in different ways.
Flexibility of Closure	The ability to identify or detect a known pattern (a figure, object, word, or sound) that is hidden in other distracting material.
Originality	The ability to come up with unusual or clever ideas about a given topic or situation, or to develop creative ways to solve a problem.
Finger Dexterity	The ability to make precisely coordinated movements of the fingers of one or both hands to grasp, manipulate, or assemble very small objects.
Time Sharing	The ability to shift back and forth between two or more activities or sources of information (such as speech, sounds, touch, or other sources).
Manual Dexterity	The ability to quickly move your hand, your hand together with your arm, or your two hands to grasp, manipulate, or assemble objects.
Arm-Hand Steadiness	The ability to keep your hand and arm steady while moving your arm or while holding your arm and hand in one position.
Perceptual Speed	The ability to quickly and accurately compare similarities and differences among sets of letters, numbers, objects, pictures, or patterns. The things to be compared may be presented at the same time or one after the other. This ability also includes comparing a presented object with a remembered object.
Memorization	The ability to remember information such as words, numbers, pictures, and procedures.
Visual Color Discrimination	The ability to match or detect differences between colors, including shades of color and brightness.
Speed of Closure	The ability to quickly make sense of, combine, and organize information into meaningful patterns.
Auditory Attention	The ability to focus on a single source of sound in the presence of other distracting sounds.
Control Precision	The ability to quickly and repeatedly adjust the controls of a machine or a vehicle to exact positions.
Far Vision	The ability to see details at a distance.
Wrist-Finger Speed	The ability to make fast, simple, repeated movements of the fingers, hands, and wrists.
Mathematical Reasoning	The ability to choose the right mathematical methods or formulas to solve a problem.
Multilimb Coordination	The ability to coordinate two or more limbs (for example, two arms, two legs, or one leg and one arm) while sitting, standing, or lying down. It does not involve performing the activities while the whole body is in motion.
Depth Perception	The ability to judge which of several objects is closer or farther away from you, or to judge the distance between you and an object.
Trunk Strength	The ability to use your abdominal and lower back muscles to support part of the body repeatedly or continuously over time without 'giving out' or fatiguing.
Static Strength	The ability to exert maximum muscle force to lift, push, pull, or carry objects.
Hearing Sensitivity	The ability to detect or tell the differences between sounds that vary in pitch and loudness.

Number Facility	The ability to add, subtract, multiply, or divide quickly and correctly.
Extent Flexibility	The ability to bend, stretch, twist, or reach with your body, arms, and/or legs.
Peripheral Vision	The ability to see objects or movement of objects to one's side when the eyes are looking ahead.
Night Vision	The ability to see under low light conditions.
Speed of Limb Movement	The ability to quickly move the arms and legs.
Explosive Strength	The ability to use short bursts of muscle force to propel oneself (as in jumping or sprinting), or to throw an object.
Dynamic Strength	The ability to exert muscle force repeatedly or continuously over time. This involves muscular endurance and resistance to muscle fatigue.
Stamina	The ability to exert yourself physically over long periods of time without getting winded or out of breath.
Dynamic Flexibility	The ability to quickly and repeatedly bend, stretch, twist, or reach out with your body, arms, and/or legs.
Gross Body Coordination	The ability to coordinate the movement of your arms, legs, and torso together when the whole body is in motion.
Response Orientation	The ability to choose quickly between two or more movements in response to two or more different signals (lights, sounds, pictures). It includes the speed with which the correct response is started with the hand, foot, or other body part.
Rate Control	The ability to time your movements or the movement of a piece of equipment in anticipation of changes in the speed and/or direction of a moving object or scene.
Glare Sensitivity	The ability to see objects in the presence of glare or bright lighting.
Spatial Orientation	The ability to know your location in relation to the environment or to know where other objects are in relation to you.
Sound Localization	The ability to tell the direction from which a sound originated.
Reaction Time	The ability to quickly respond (with the hand, finger, or foot) to a signal (sound, light, picture) when it appears.
Gross Body Equilibrium	The ability to keep or regain your body balance or stay upright when in an unstable position.

Work_Activity	Work_Activity Definitions
Interacting With Computers	Using computers and computer systems (including hardware and software) to program, write software, set up functions, enter data, or process information.
Getting Information	Observing, receiving, and otherwise obtaining information from all relevant sources.
Updating and Using Relevant Knowledge	Keeping up-to-date technically and applying new knowledge to your job.
Making Decisions and Solving Problems	Analyzing information and evaluating results to choose the best solution and solve problems.
Communicating with Persons Outside Organization	Communicating with people outside the organization, representing the organization to customers, the public, government, and other external sources. This information can be exchanged in person, in writing, or by telephone or e-mail.
Communicating with Supervisors, Peers, or Subordin	Providing information to supervisors, co-workers, and subordinates by telephone, in written form, e-mail, or in person.
Establishing and Maintaining Interpersonal Relatio	Developing constructive and cooperative working relationships with others, and maintaining them over time.
Identifying Objects, Actions, and Events	Identifying information by categorizing, estimating, recognizing differences or similarities, and detecting changes in circumstances or events.
Interpreting the Meaning of Information for Others	Translating or explaining what information means and how it can be used.
Documenting/Recording Information	Entering, transcribing, recording, storing, or maintaining information in written or electronic/magnetic form.
Developing and Building Teams	Encouraging and building mutual trust, respect, and cooperation among team members.
Inspecting Equipment, Structures, or Material	Inspecting equipment, structures, or materials to identify the cause of errors or other problems or defects.
Resolving Conflicts and Negotiating with Others	Handling complaints, settling disputes, and resolving grievances and conflicts, or otherwise negotiating with others.
Monitor Processes, Materials, or Surroundings	Monitoring and reviewing information from materials, events, or the environment, to detect or assess problems.
Repairing and Maintaining Electronic Equipment	Servicing, repairing, calibrating, regulating, fine-tuning, or testing machines, devices, and equipment that operate primarily on the basis of electrical or electronic (not mechanical) principles.

Organizing, Planning, and Prioritizing Work	Developing specific goals and plans to prioritize, organize, and accomplish your work.
Performing General Physical Activities	Performing physical activities that require considerable use of your arms and legs and moving your whole body, such as climbing, lifting, balancing, walking, stooping, and handling of materials.
Analyzing Data or Information	Identifying the underlying principles, reasons, or facts of information by breaking down information or data into separate parts.
Coordinating the Work and Activities of Others	Getting members of a group to work together to accomplish tasks.
Evaluating Information to Determine Compliance wit	Using relevant information and individual judgment to determine whether events or processes comply with laws, regulations, or standards.
Scheduling Work and Activities	Scheduling events, programs, and activities, as well as the work of others.
Handling and Moving Objects	Using hands and arms in handling, installing, positioning, and moving materials, and manipulating things.
Processing Information	Compiling, coding, categorizing, calculating, tabulating, auditing, or verifying information or data.
Selling or Influencing Others	Convincing others to buy merchandise/goods or to otherwise change their minds or actions.
Provide Consultation and Advice to Others	Providing guidance and expert advice to management or other groups on technical, systems-, or process-related topics.
Repairing and Maintaining Mechanical Equipment	Servicing, repairing, adjusting, and testing machines, devices, moving parts, and equipment that operate primarily on the basis of mechanical (not electronic) principles.
Drafting, Laying Out, and Specifying Technical Dev	Providing documentation, detailed instructions, drawings, or specifications to tell others about how devices, parts, equipment, or structures are to be fabricated, constructed, assembled, modified, maintained, or used.
Performing Administrative Activities	Performing day-to-day administrative tasks such as maintaining information files and processing paperwork.
Assisting and Caring for Others	Providing personal assistance, medical attention, emotional support, or other personal care to others such as coworkers, customers, or patients.
Estimating the Quantifiable Characteristics of Pro	Estimating sizes, distances, and quantities; or determining time, costs, resources, or materials needed to perform a work activity.
Developing Objectives and Strategies	Establishing long-range objectives and specifying the strategies and actions to achieve them.
Operating Vehicles, Mechanized Devices, or Equipme	Running, maneuvering, navigating, or driving vehicles or mechanized equipment, such as forklifts, passenger vehicles, aircraft, or water craft.
Thinking Creatively	Developing, designing, or creating new applications, ideas, relationships, systems, or products, including artistic contributions.
Judging the Qualities of Things, Services, or Peop	Assessing the value, importance, or quality of things or people.
Training and Teaching Others	Identifying the educational needs of others, developing formal educational or training programs or classes, and teaching or instructing others.
Performing for or Working Directly with the Public	Performing for people or dealing directly with the public. This includes serving customers in restaurants and stores, and receiving clients or guests.
Controlling Machines and Processes	Using either control mechanisms or direct physical activity to operate machines or processes (not including computers or vehicles).
Monitoring and Controlling Resources	Monitoring and controlling resources and overseeing the spending of money.
Guiding, Directing, and Motivating Subordinates	Providing guidance and direction to subordinates, including setting performance standards and monitoring performance.
Coaching and Developing Others	Identifying the developmental needs of others and coaching, mentoring, or otherwise helping others to improve their knowledge or skills.
Staffing Organizational Units	Recruiting, interviewing, selecting, hiring, and promoting employees in an organization.

Work_Context	Work_Context Definitions
Face-to-Face Discussions	How often do you have to have face-to-face discussions with individuals or teams in this job?
Indoors, Environmentally Controlled	How often does this job require working indoors in environmentally controlled conditions?
Telephone	How often do you have telephone conversations in this job?
Contact With Others	How much does this job require the worker to be in contact with others (face-to-face, by telephone, or otherwise) in order to perform it?

Electronic Mail	How often do you use electronic mail in this job?
Structured versus Unstructured Work	To what extent is this job structured for the worker, rather than allowing the worker to determine tasks, priorities, and goals?
Physical Proximity	To what extent does this job require the worker to perform job tasks in close physical proximity to other people?
Deal With Unpleasant or Angry People	How frequently does the worker have to deal with unpleasant, angry, or discourteous individuals as part of the job requirements?
Work With Work Group or Team	How important is it to work with others in a group or team in this job?
Importance of Repeating Same Tasks	How important is repeating the same physical activities (e.g., key entry) or mental activities (e.g., checking entries in a ledger) over and over, without stopping, to performing this job?
Frequency of Conflict Situations	How often are there conflict situations the employee has to face in this job?
Freedom to Make Decisions	How much decision making freedom, without supervision, does the job offer?
Spend Time Sitting	How much does this job require sitting?
Importance of Being Exact or Accurate	How important is being very exact or highly accurate in performing this job?
Sounds, Noise Levels Are Distracting or Uncomforta	How often does this job require working exposed to sounds and noise levels that are distracting or uncomfortable?
Frequency of Decision Making	How frequently is the worker required to make decisions that affect other people, the financial resources, and/or the image and reputation of the organization?
Deal With External Customers	How important is it to work with external customers or the public in this job?
Spend Time Making Repetitive Motions	How much does this job require making repetitive motions?
Impact of Decisions on Co-workers or Company Resul	How do the decisions an employee makes impact the results of co-workers, clients or the company?
Coordinate or Lead Others	How important is it to coordinate or lead others in accomplishing work activities in this job?
Letters and Memos	How often does the job require written letters and memos?
Time Pressure	How often does this job require the worker to meet strict deadlines?
Spend Time Using Your Hands to Handle, Control, or	How much does this job require using your hands to handle, control, or feel objects, tools or controls?
Consequence of Error	How serious would the result usually be if the worker made a mistake that was not readily correctable?
Responsibility for Outcomes and Results	How responsible is the worker for work outcomes and results of other workers?
Level of Competition	To what extent does this job require the worker to compete or to be aware of competitive pressures?
Spend Time Standing	How much does this job require standing?
Degree of Automation	How automated is the job?
Spend Time Kneeling, Crouching, Stooping, or Crawl	How much does this job require kneeling, crouching, stooping, or crawling?
Spend Time Walking and Running	How much does this job require walking and running?
Public Speaking	How often do you have to perform public speaking in this job?
Spend Time Bending or Twisting the Body	How much does this job require bending or twisting your body?
Exposed to Contaminants	How often does this job require working exposed to contaminants (such as pollutants, gases, dust or odors)?
In an Enclosed Vehicle or Equipment	How often does this job require working in a closed vehicle or equipment (e.g., car)?
Cramped Work Space, Awkward Positions	How often does this job require working in cramped work spaces that requires getting into awkward positions?
Spend Time Keeping or Regaining Balance	How much does this job require keeping or regaining your balance?
Deal With Physically Aggressive People	How frequently does this job require the worker to deal with physical aggression of violent individuals?
Indoors, Not Environmentally Controlled	How often does this job require working indoors in non-controlled environmental conditions (e.g., warehouse without heat)?
Exposed to Minor Burns, Cuts, Bites, or Stings	How often does this job require exposure to minor burns, cuts, bites, or stings?
Extremely Bright or Inadequate Lighting	How often does this job require working in extremely bright or inadequate lighting conditions?
Responsible for Others' Health and Safety	How much responsibility is there for the health and safety of others in this job?
Very Hot or Cold Temperatures	How often does this job require working in very hot (above 90 F degrees) or very cold (below 32 F degrees) temperatures?
Pace Determined by	How important is it to this job that the pace is determined by

Exposed to Hazardous Equipment	How often does this job require exposure to hazardous equipment?
Exposed to Hazardous Conditions	How often does this job require exposure to hazardous conditions?
Wear Common Protective or Safety Equipment such as	How much does this job require wearing common protective or safety equipment such as safety shoes, glasses, gloves, hard hats or live jackets?
Exposed to Disease or Infections	How often does this job require exposure to disease/infections?
Wear Specialized Protective or Safety Equipment su	How much does this job require wearing specialized protective or safety equipment such as breathing apparatus, safety harness, full protection suits, or radiation protection?
Spend Time Climbing Ladders, Scaffolds, or Poles	How much does this job require climbing ladders, scaffolds, or poles?
Exposed to Radiation	How often does this job require exposure to radiation?
Exposed to High Places	How often does this job require exposure to high places?
Outdoors, Exposed to Weather	How often does this job require working outdoors, exposed to all weather conditions?
In an Open Vehicle or Equipment	How often does this job require working in an open vehicle or equipment (e.g., tractor)?
Outdoors, Under Cover	How often does this job require working outdoors, under cover (e.g., structure with roof but no walls)?
Exposed to Whole Body Vibration	How often does this job require exposure to whole body vibration (e.g., operate a jackhammer)?

Job Zone Component	Job Zone Component Definitions
Title	Job Zone Three: Medium Preparation Needed
Overall Experience	Previous work-related skill, knowledge, or experience is required for these occupations. For example, an electrician must have completed three or four years of apprenticeship or several years of vocational training, and often must have passed a licensing exam, in order to perform the job.
Job Training	Employees in these occupations usually need one or two years of training involving both on-the-job experience and informal training with experienced workers.
Job Zone Examples	These occupations usually involve using communication and organizational skills to coordinate, supervise, manage, or train others to accomplish goals. Examples include dental assistants, electricians, fish and game wardens, legal secretaries, personnel recruiters, and recreation workers.
SVP Range	(6.0 to < 7.0)
Education	Most occupations in this zone require training in vocational schools, related on-the-job experience, or an associate's degree. Some may require a bachelor's degree.

Work_Styles	Work_Styles Definitions
Attention to Detail	Job requires being careful about detail and thorough in completing work tasks.
Analytical Thinking	Job requires analyzing information and using logic to address work-related issues and problems.
Adaptability/Flexibility	Job requires being open to change (positive or negative) and to considerable variety in the workplace.
Dependability	Job requires being reliable, responsible, and dependable, and fulfilling obligations.
Cooperation	Job requires being pleasant with others on the job and displaying a good-natured, cooperative attitude.
Independence	Job requires developing one's own ways of doing things, guiding oneself with little or no supervision, and depending on oneself to get things done.
Integrity	Job requires being honest and ethical.
Persistence	Job requires persistence in the face of obstacles.
Initiative	Job requires a willingness to take on responsibilities and challenges.
Concern for Others	Job requires being sensitive to others' needs and feelings and being understanding and helpful on the job.
Innovation	Job requires creativity and alternative thinking to develop new ideas for and answers to work-related problems.
Stress Tolerance	Job requires accepting criticism and dealing calmly and effectively with high stress situations.
Self Control	Job requires maintaining composure, keeping emotions in check, controlling anger, and avoiding aggressive behavior, even in very difficult situations.
Leadership	Job requires a willingness to lead, take charge, and offer opinions and direction.

Achievement/Effort	Job requires establishing and maintaining personally challenging achievement goals and exerting effort toward mastering tasks.
Social Orientation	Job requires preferring to work with others rather than alone, and being personally connected with others on the job.

15-1051.00 - Computer Systems Analysts

Analyze science, engineering, business, and all other data processing problems for application to electronic data processing systems. Analyze user requirements, procedures, and problems to automate or improve existing systems and review computer system capabilities, workflow, and scheduling limitations. May analyze or recommend commercially available software. May supervise computer programmers.

Tasks

1) Test, maintain, and monitor computer programs and systems, including coordinating the installation of computer programs and systems.

2) Expand or modify system to serve new purposes or improve work flow.

3) Confer with clients regarding the nature of the information processing or computation needs a computer program is to address.

4) Train staff and users to work with computer systems and programs.

5) Determine computer software or hardware needed to set up or alter system.

6) Develop, document and revise system design procedures, test procedures, and quality standards.

7) Read manuals, periodicals, and technical reports to learn how to develop programs that meet staff and user requirements.

8) Analyze information processing or computation needs and plan and design computer systems, using techniques such as structured analysis, data modeling and information engineering.

9) Use object-oriented programming languages, as well as client/server applications development processes and multimedia and Internet technology.

10) Assess the usefulness of pre-developed application packages and adapt them to a user environment.

11) Interview or survey workers, observe job performance and/or perform the job in order to determine what information is processed and how it is processed.

12) Consult with management to ensure agreement on system principles.

13) Recommend new equipment or software packages.

14) Review and analyze computer printouts and performance indicators to locate code problems, and correct errors by correcting codes.

15) Define the goals of the system and devise flow charts and diagrams describing logical operational steps of programs.

16) Specify inputs accessed by the system and plan the distribution and use of the results.

17) Coordinate and link the computer systems within an organization to increase compatibility and so information can be shared.

18) Utilize the computer in the analysis and solution of business problems such as development of integrated production and inventory control and cost analysis systems.

19) Supervise computer programmers or other systems analysts or serve as project leaders for particular systems projects.

20) Prepare cost-benefit and return-on-investment analyses to aid in decisions on system implementation.

Knowledge	Knowledge Definitions
Computers and Electronics	Knowledge of circuit boards, processors, chips, electronic equipment, and computer hardware and software, including applications and programming.
English Language	Knowledge of the structure and content of the English language including the meaning and spelling of words, rules of composition, and grammar.
Customer and Personal Service	Knowledge of principles and processes for providing customer and personal services. This includes customer needs assessment, meeting quality standards for services, and evaluation of customer satisfaction.
Design	Knowledge of design techniques, tools, and principles involved in production of precision technical plans, blueprints, drawings, and models.
Telecommunications	Knowledge of transmission, broadcasting, switching, control, and operation of telecommunications systems.
Mathematics	Knowledge of arithmetic, algebra, geometry, calculus, statistics, and their applications.
Education and Training	Knowledge of principles and methods for curriculum and training design, teaching and instruction for individuals and groups, and the measurement of training effects.
Engineering and Technology	Knowledge of the practical application of engineering science and technology. This includes applying principles, techniques, procedures, and equipment to the design and production of various goods and services.
Communications and Media	Knowledge of media production, communication, and dissemination techniques and methods. This includes alternative ways to inform and entertain via written, oral, and visual media.
Administration and Management	Knowledge of business and management principles involved in strategic planning, resource allocation, human resources modeling, leadership technique, production methods, and coordination of people and resources.
Clerical	Knowledge of administrative and clerical procedures and systems such as word processing, managing files and records, stenography and transcription, designing forms, and other office procedures and terminology.
Law and Government	Knowledge of laws, legal codes, court procedures, precedents, government regulations, executive orders, agency rules, and the democratic political process.
Public Safety and Security	Knowledge of relevant equipment, policies, procedures, and strategies to promote effective local, state, or national security operations for the protection of people, data, property, and institutions.
Personnel and Human Resources	Knowledge of principles and procedures for personnel recruitment, selection, training, compensation and benefits, labor relations and negotiation, and personnel information systems.
Economics and Accounting	Knowledge of economic and accounting principles and practices, the financial markets, banking and the analysis and reporting of financial data.
Psychology	Knowledge of human behavior and performance; individual differences in ability, personality, and interests; learning and motivation; psychological research methods; and the assessment and treatment of behavioral and affective disorders.
Production and Processing	Knowledge of raw materials, production processes, quality control, costs, and other techniques for maximizing the effective manufacture and distribution of goods.
Sociology and Anthropology	Knowledge of group behavior and dynamics, societal trends and influences, human migrations, ethnicity, cultures and their history and origins.
Transportation	Knowledge of principles and methods for moving people or goods by air, rail, sea, or road, including the relative costs and benefits.
Sales and Marketing	Knowledge of principles and methods for showing, promoting, and selling products or services. This includes marketing strategy and tactics, product demonstration, sales techniques, and sales control systems.
Physics	Knowledge and prediction of physical principles, laws, their interrelationships, and applications to understanding fluid, material, and atmospheric dynamics, and mechanical, electrical, atomic and sub-atomic structures and processes.
Geography	Knowledge of principles and methods for describing the features of land, sea, and air masses, including their physical characteristics, locations, interrelationships, and distribution of plant, animal, and human life.
Mechanical	Knowledge of machines and tools, including their designs, uses, repair, and maintenance.
Therapy and Counseling	Knowledge of principles, methods, and procedures for diagnosis, treatment, and rehabilitation of physical and mental dysfunctions, and for career counseling and guidance.
Philosophy and Theology	Knowledge of different philosophical systems and religions. This includes their basic principles, values, ethics, ways of thinking, customs, practices, and their impact on human culture.
Foreign Language	Knowledge of the structure and content of a foreign (non-English) language including the meaning and spelling of words, rules of composition and grammar, and pronunciation.

Medicine and Dentistry	Knowledge of the information and techniques needed to diagnose and treat human injuries, diseases, and deformities. This includes symptoms, treatment alternatives, drug properties and interactions, and preventive health-care measures.
Biology	Knowledge of plant and animal organisms, their tissues, cells, functions, interdependencies, and interactions with each other and the environment.
History and Archeology	Knowledge of historical events and their causes, indicators, and effects on civilizations and cultures.
Building and Construction	Knowledge of materials, methods, and the tools involved in the construction or repair of houses, buildings, or other structures such as highways and roads.
Chemistry	Knowledge of the chemical composition, structure, and properties of substances and of the chemical processes and transformations that they undergo. This includes uses of chemicals and their interactions, danger signs, production techniques, and disposal methods.
Fine Arts	Knowledge of the theory and techniques required to compose, produce, and perform works of music, dance, visual arts, drama, and sculpture.
Food Production	Knowledge of techniques and equipment for planting, growing, and harvesting food products (both plant and animal) for consumption, including storage/handling techniques.

Skills	**Skills Definitions**
Active Learning	Understanding the implications of new information for both current and future problem-solving and decision-making.
Reading Comprehension	Understanding written sentences and paragraphs in work related documents.
Complex Problem Solving	Identifying complex problems and reviewing related information to develop and evaluate options and implement solutions.
Critical Thinking	Using logic and reasoning to identify the strengths and weaknesses of alternative solutions, conclusions or approaches to problems.
Active Listening	Giving full attention to what other people are saying, taking time to understand the points being made, asking questions as appropriate, and not interrupting at inappropriate times.
Troubleshooting	Determining causes of operating errors and deciding what to do about it.
Time Management	Managing one's own time and the time of others.
Service Orientation	Actively looking for ways to help people.
Monitoring	Monitoring/Assessing performance of yourself, other individuals, or organizations to make improvements or take corrective action.
Quality Control Analysis	Conducting tests and inspections of products, services, or processes to evaluate quality or performance.
Coordination	Adjusting actions in relation to others' actions.
Systems Analysis	Determining how a system should work and how changes in conditions, operations, and the environment will affect outcomes.
Technology Design	Generating or adapting equipment and technology to serve user needs.
Judgment and Decision Making	Considering the relative costs and benefits of potential actions to choose the most appropriate one.
Equipment Selection	Determining the kind of tools and equipment needed to do a job.
Learning Strategies	Selecting and using training/instructional methods and procedures appropriate for the situation when learning or teaching new things.
Installation	Installing equipment, machines, wiring, or programs to meet specifications.
Operations Analysis	Analyzing needs and product requirements to create a design.
Writing	Communicating effectively in writing as appropriate for the needs of the audience.
Instructing	Teaching others how to do something.
Speaking	Talking to others to convey information effectively.
Systems Evaluation	Identifying measures or indicators of system performance and the actions needed to improve or correct performance, relative to the goals of the system.
Repairing	Repairing machines or systems using the needed tools.
Operation Monitoring	Watching gauges, dials, or other indicators to make sure a machine is working properly.
Persuasion	Persuading others to change their minds or behavior.
Operation and Control	Controlling operations of equipment or systems.
Programming	Writing computer programs for various purposes.
Mathematics	Using mathematics to solve problems.

Social Perceptiveness	Being aware of others' reactions and understanding why they react as they do.
Equipment Maintenance	Performing routine maintenance on equipment and determining when and what kind of maintenance is needed.
Negotiation	Bringing others together and trying to reconcile differences.
Management of Personnel Resources	Motivating, developing, and directing people as they work, identifying the best people for the job.
Management of Material Resources	Obtaining and seeing to the appropriate use of equipment, facilities, and materials needed to do certain work.
Science	Using scientific rules and methods to solve problems.
Management of Financial Resources	Determining how money will be spent to get the work done, and accounting for these expenditures.

Ability	**Ability Definitions**
Problem Sensitivity	The ability to tell when something is wrong or is likely to go wrong. It does not involve solving the problem, only recognizing there is a problem.
Oral Comprehension	The ability to listen to and understand information and ideas presented through spoken words and sentences.
Deductive Reasoning	The ability to apply general rules to specific problems to produce answers that make sense.
Inductive Reasoning	The ability to combine pieces of information to form general rules or conclusions (includes finding a relationship among seemingly unrelated events).
Written Comprehension	The ability to read and understand information and ideas presented in writing.
Near Vision	The ability to see details at close range (within a few feet of the observer).
Speech Recognition	The ability to identify and understand the speech of another person.
Oral Expression	The ability to communicate information and ideas in speaking so others will understand.
Speech Clarity	The ability to speak clearly so others can understand you.
Information Ordering	The ability to arrange things or actions in a certain order or pattern according to a specific rule or set of rules (e.g., patterns of numbers, letters, words, pictures, mathematical operations).
Selective Attention	The ability to concentrate on a task over a period of time without being distracted.
Originality	The ability to come up with unusual or clever ideas about a given topic or situation, or to develop creative ways to solve a problem.
Category Flexibility	The ability to generate or use different sets of rules for combining or grouping things in different ways.
Memorization	The ability to remember information such as words, numbers, pictures, and procedures.
Perceptual Speed	The ability to quickly and accurately compare similarities and differences among sets of letters, numbers, objects, pictures, or patterns. The things to be compared may be presented at the same time or one after the other. This ability also includes comparing a presented object with a remembered object.
Mathematical Reasoning	The ability to choose the right mathematical methods or formulas to solve a problem.
Flexibility of Closure	The ability to identify or detect a known pattern (a figure, object, word, or sound) that is hidden in other distracting material.
Fluency of Ideas	The ability to come up with a number of ideas about a topic (the number of ideas is important, not their quality, correctness, or creativity).
Written Expression	The ability to communicate information and ideas in writing so others will understand.
Time Sharing	The ability to shift back and forth between two or more activities or sources of information (such as speech, sounds, touch, or other sources).
Number Facility	The ability to add, subtract, multiply, or divide quickly and correctly.
Finger Dexterity	The ability to make precisely coordinated movements of the fingers of one or both hands to grasp, manipulate, or assemble very small objects.
Far Vision	The ability to see details at a distance.
Speed of Closure	The ability to quickly make sense of, combine, and organize information into meaningful patterns.
Visualization	The ability to imagine how something will look after it is moved around or when its parts are moved or rearranged.
Visual Color Discrimination	The ability to match or detect differences between colors, including shades of color and brightness.
Auditory Attention	The ability to focus on a single source of sound in the presence of other distracting sounds.

Hearing Sensitivity	The ability to detect or tell the differences between sounds that vary in pitch and loudness.
Depth Perception	The ability to judge which of several objects is closer or farther away from you, or to judge the distance between you and an object.
Control Precision	The ability to quickly and repeatedly adjust the controls of a machine or a vehicle to exact positions.
Arm-Hand Steadiness	The ability to keep your hand and arm steady while moving your arm or while holding your arm and hand in one position.
Manual Dexterity	The ability to quickly move your hand, your hand together with your arm, or your two hands to grasp, manipulate, or assemble objects.
Wrist-Finger Speed	The ability to make fast, simple, repeated movements of the fingers, hands, and wrists.
Trunk Strength	The ability to use your abdominal and lower back muscles to support part of the body repeatedly or continuously over time without 'giving out' or fatiguing.
Spatial Orientation	The ability to know your location in relation to the environment or to know where other objects are in relation to you.
Multilimb Coordination	The ability to coordinate two or more limbs (for example, two arms, two legs, or one leg and one arm) while sitting, standing, or lying down. It does not involve performing the activities while the whole body is in motion.
Dynamic Flexibility	The ability to quickly and repeatedly bend, stretch, twist, or reach out with your body, arms, and/or legs.
Extent Flexibility	The ability to bend, stretch, twist, or reach with your body, arms, and/or legs.
Stamina	The ability to exert yourself physically over long periods of time without getting winded or out of breath.
Explosive Strength	The ability to use short bursts of muscle force to propel oneself (as in jumping or sprinting), or to throw an object.
Speed of Limb Movement	The ability to quickly move the arms and legs.
Response Orientation	The ability to choose quickly between two or more movements in response to two or more different signals (lights, sounds, pictures). It includes the speed with which the correct response is started with the hand, foot, or other body part.
Gross Body Coordination	The ability to coordinate the movement of your arms, legs, and torso together when the whole body is in motion.
Sound Localization	The ability to tell the direction from which a sound originated.
Glare Sensitivity	The ability to see objects in the presence of glare or bright lighting.
Peripheral Vision	The ability to see objects or movement of objects to one's side when the eyes are looking ahead.
Night Vision	The ability to see under low light conditions.
Static Strength	The ability to exert maximum muscle force to lift, push, pull, or carry objects.
Reaction Time	The ability to quickly respond (with the hand, finger, or foot) to a signal (sound, light, picture) when it appears.
Gross Body Equilibrium	The ability to keep or regain your body balance or stay upright when in an unstable position.
Dynamic Strength	The ability to exert muscle force repeatedly or continuously over time. This involves muscular endurance and resistance to muscle fatigue.
Rate Control	The ability to time your movements or the movement of a piece of equipment in anticipation of changes in the speed and/or direction of a moving object or scene.

Work_Activity	Work_Activity Definitions
Interacting With Computers	Using computers and computer systems (including hardware and software) to program, write software, set up functions, enter data, or process information.
Processing Information	Compiling, coding, categorizing, calculating, tabulating, auditing, or verifying information or data.
Making Decisions and Solving Problems	Analyzing information and evaluating results to choose the best solution and solve problems.
Getting Information	Observing, receiving, and otherwise obtaining information from all relevant sources.
Updating and Using Relevant Knowledge	Keeping up-to-date technically and applying new knowledge to your job.
Identifying Objects, Actions, and Events	Identifying information by categorizing, estimating, recognizing differences or similarities, and detecting changes in circumstances or events.
Analyzing Data or Information	Identifying the underlying principles, reasons, or facts of information by breaking down information or data into separate parts.

Communicating with Supervisors, Peers, or Subordin	Providing information to supervisors, co-workers, and subordinates by telephone, in written form, e-mail, or in person.
Thinking Creatively	Developing, designing, or creating new applications, ideas, relationships, systems, or products, including artistic contributions.
Interpreting the Meaning of Information for Others	Translating or explaining what information means and how it can be used.
Establishing and Maintaining Interpersonal Relatio	Developing constructive and cooperative working relationships with others, and maintaining them over time.
Monitor Processes, Materials, or Surroundings	Monitoring and reviewing information from materials, events, or the environment, to detect or assess problems.
Communicating with Persons Outside Organization	Communicating with people outside the organization, representing the organization to customers, the public, government, and other external sources. This information can be exchanged in person, in writing, or by telephone or e-mail
Documenting/Recording Information	Entering, transcribing, recording, storing, or maintaining information in written or electronic/magnetic form.
Organizing, Planning, and Prioritizing Work	Developing specific goals and plans to prioritize, organize, and accomplish your work.
Provide Consultation and Advice to Others	Providing guidance and expert advice to management or other groups on technical, systems-, or process-related topics.
Developing Objectives and Strategies	Establishing long-range objectives and specifying the strategies and actions to achieve them.
Training and Teaching Others	Identifying the educational needs of others, developing formal educational or training programs or classes, and teaching or instructing others.
Estimating the Quantifiable Characteristics of Pro	Estimating sizes, distances, and quantities; or determining time, costs, resources, or materials needed to perform a work activity
Scheduling Work and Activities	Scheduling events, programs, and activities, as well as the work of others.
Developing and Building Teams	Encouraging and building mutual trust, respect, and cooperation among team members.
Evaluating Information to Determine Compliance wit	Using relevant information and individual judgment to determine whether events or processes comply with laws, regulations, or standards.
Coordinating the Work and Activities of Others	Getting members of a group to work together to accomplish tasks.
Performing Administrative Activities	Performing day-to-day administrative tasks such as maintaining information files and processing paperwork.
Judging the Qualities of Things, Services, or Peop	Assessing the value, importance, or quality of things or people.
Guiding, Directing, and Motivating Subordinates	Providing guidance and direction to subordinates, including setting performance standards and monitoring performance.
Resolving Conflicts and Negotiating with Others	Handling complaints, settling disputes, and resolving grievances and conflicts, or otherwise negotiating with others.
Inspecting Equipment, Structures, or Material	Inspecting equipment, structures, or materials to identify the cause of errors or other problems or defects.
Controlling Machines and Processes	Using either control mechanisms or direct physical activity to operate machines or processes (not including computers or vehicles).
Coaching and Developing Others	Identifying the developmental needs of others and coaching, mentoring, or otherwise helping others to improve their knowledge or skills.
Monitoring and Controlling Resources	Monitoring and controlling resources and overseeing the spending of money.
Assisting and Caring for Others	Providing personal assistance, medical attention, emotional support, or other personal care to others such as coworkers, customers, or patients.
Selling or Influencing Others	Convincing others to buy merchandise/goods or to otherwise change their minds or actions.
Drafting, Laying Out, and Specifying Technical Dev	Providing documentation, detailed instructions, drawings, or specifications to tell others about how devices, parts, equipment, or structures are to be fabricated, constructed, assembled, modified, maintained, or used.
Repairing and Maintaining Electronic Equipment	Servicing, repairing, calibrating, regulating, fine-tuning, or testing machines, devices, and equipment that operate primarily on the basis of electrical or electronic (not mechanical) principles.
Handling and Moving Objects	Using hands and arms in handling, installing, positioning, and moving materials, and manipulating things.
Performing General Physical Activities	Performing physical activities that require considerable use of your arms and legs and moving your whole body, such as climbing, lifting, balancing, walking, stooping, and handling of materials.

Performing for or Working Directly with the Public | Performing for people or dealing directly with the public. This includes serving customers in restaurants and stores. and receiving clients or guests.

Staffing Organizational Units | Recruiting. interviewing. selecting. hiring. and promoting employees in an organization.

Repairing and Maintaining Mechanical Equipment | Servicing. repairing. adjusting. and testing machines. devices. moving parts. and equipment that operate primarily on the basis of mechanical (not electronic) principles.

Operating Vehicles, Mechanized Devices, or Equipme | Running. maneuvering. navigating. or driving vehicles or mechanized equipment. such as forklifts. passenger vehicles. aircraft. or water craft.

Work_Context — Work_Context Definitions

Electronic Mail | How often do you use electronic mail in this job?

Freedom to Make Decisions | How much decision making freedom. without supervision. does the job offer?

Structured versus Unstructured Work | To what extent is this job structured for the worker. rather than allowing the worker to determine tasks. priorities. and goals?

Telephone | How often do you have telephone conversations in this job?

Spend Time Sitting | How much does this job require sitting?

Face-to-Face Discussions | How often do you have to have face-to-face discussions with individuals or teams in this job?

Importance of Being Exact or Accurate | How important is being very exact or highly accurate in performing this job?

Work With Work Group or Team | How important is it to work with others in a group or team in this job?

Indoors. Environmentally Controlled | How often does this job require working indoors in environmentally controlled conditions?

Impact of Decisions on Co-workers or Company Resul | How do the decisions an employee makes impact the results of co-workers, clients or the company?

Contact With Others | How much does this job require the worker to be in contact with others (face-to-face, by telephone, or otherwise) in order to perform it?

Coordinate or Lead Others | How important is it to coordinate or lead others in accomplishing work activities in this job?

Time Pressure | How often does this job require the worker to meet strict deadlines?

Responsibility for Outcomes and Results | How responsible is the worker for work outcomes and results of other workers?

Importance of Repeating Same Tasks | How important is repeating the same physical activities (e.g., key entry) or mental activities (e.g., checking entries in a ledger) over and over, without stopping, to performing this job?

Consequence of Error | How serious would the result usually be if the worker made a mistake that was not readily correctable?

Frequency of Decision Making | How frequently is the worker required to make decisions that affect other people, the financial resources, and/or the image and reputation of the organization?

Deal With External Customers | How important is it to work with external customers or the public in this job?

Spend Time Using Your Hands to Handle, Control, or | How much does this job require using your hands to handle, control, or feel objects, tools or controls?

Level of Competition | To what extent does this job require the worker to compete or to be aware of competitive pressures?

Physical Proximity | To what extent does this job require the worker to perform job tasks in close physical proximity to other people?

Letters and Memos | How often does the job require written letters and memos?

Deal With Unpleasant or Angry People | How frequently does the worker have to deal with unpleasant, angry, or discourteous individuals as part of the job requirements?

Degree of Automation | How automated is the job?

Spend Time Making Repetitive Motions | How much does this job require making repetitive motions?

Frequency of Conflict Situations | How often are there conflict situations the employee has to face in this job?

Responsible for Others' Health and Safety | How much responsibility is there for the health and safety of others in this job?

Sounds, Noise Levels Are Distracting or Uncomforta | How often does this job require working exposed to sounds and noise levels that are distracting or uncomfortable?

Spend Time Standing | How much does this job require standing?

Public Speaking | How often do you have to perform public speaking in this job?

Cramped Work Space, Awkward Positions | How often does this job require working in cramped work spaces that requires getting into awkward positions?

Very Hot or Cold Temperatures | How often does this job require working in very hot (above 90 F degrees) or very cold (below 32 F degrees) temperatures?

Extremely Bright or Inadequate Lighting | How often does this job require working in extremely bright or inadequate lighting conditions?

In an Enclosed Vehicle or Equipment | How often does this job require working in a closed vehicle or equipment (e.g., car)?

Spend Time Walking and Running | How much does this job require walking and running?

Spend Time Bending or Twisting the Body | How much does this job require bending or twisting your body?

Indoors, Not Environmentally Controlled | How often does this job require working indoors in non-controlled environmental conditions (e.g., warehouse without heat)?

Exposed to Contaminants | How often does this job require working exposed to contaminants (such as pollutants. gases. dust or odors)?

Spend Time Kneeling. Crouching, Stooping, or Crawl | How much does this job require kneeling, crouching, stooping or crawling?

Exposed to Hazardous Conditions | How often does this job require exposure to hazardous conditions?

Exposed to Hazardous Equipment | How often does this job require exposure to hazardous equipment?

Wear Common Protective or Safety Equipment such as | How much does this job require wearing common protective or safety equipment such as safety shoes, glasses, gloves, hard hats or life jackets?

Exposed to High Places | How often does this job require exposure to high places?

Outdoors, Exposed to Weather | How often does this job require working outdoors, exposed to all weather conditions?

Outdoors, Under Cover | How often does this job require working outdoors, under cover (e.g., structure with roof but no walls)?

Spend Time Climbing Ladders, Scaffolds, or Poles | How much does this job require climbing ladders, scaffolds, or poles?

Exposed to Minor Burns. Cuts, Bites, or Stings | How often does this job require exposure to minor burns, cuts, bites. or stings?

Exposed to Radiation | How often does this job require exposure to radiation?

Exposed to Whole Body Vibration | How often does this job require exposure to whole body vibration (e.g., operate a jackhammer)?

Pace Determined by Speed of Equipment | How important is it to this job that the pace is determined by the speed of equipment or machinery? (This does not refer to keeping busy at all times on this job.)

Spend Time Keeping or Regaining Balance | How much does this job require keeping or regaining your balance?

Wear Specialized Protective or Safety Equipment su | How much does this job require wearing specialized protective or safety equipment such as breathing apparatus, safety harness, full protection suits, or radiation protection?

In an Open Vehicle or Equipment | How often does this job require working in an open vehicle or equipment (e.g., tractor)?

Deal With Physically Aggressive People | How frequently does this job require the worker to deal with physical aggression of violent individuals?

Exposed to Disease or Infections | How often does this job require exposure to disease/infections?

Job Zone Component — Job Zone Component Definitions

Title | Job Zone Four: Considerable Preparation Needed

Overall Experience | A minimum of two to four years of work-related skill, knowledge, or experience is needed for these occupations. For example, an accountant must complete four years of college and work for several years in accounting to be considered qualified.

Job Training | Employees in these occupations usually need several years of work-related experience, on-the-job training, and/or vocational training.

Job Zone Examples | Many of these occupations involve coordinating, supervising, managing, or training others. Examples include accountants, chefs and head cooks, computer programmers, historians, pharmacists, and police detectives.

SVP Range | (7.0 to < 8.0)

Education | Most of these occupations require a four - year bachelor's degree, but some do not.

Work_Styles — Work_Styles Definitions

Adaptability/Flexibility | Job requires being open to change (positive or negative) and to considerable variety in the workplace.

Attention to Detail | Job requires being careful about detail and thorough in completing work tasks.

Analytical Thinking	Job requires analyzing information and using logic to address work-related issues and problems.
Persistence	Job requires persistence in the face of obstacles.
Dependability	Job requires being reliable, responsible, and dependable, and fulfilling obligations.
Initiative	Job requires a willingness to take on responsibilities and challenges.
Integrity	Job requires being honest and ethical.
Cooperation	Job requires being pleasant with others on the job and displaying a good-natured, cooperative attitude.
Stress Tolerance	Job requires accepting criticism and dealing calmly and effectively with high stress situations.
Achievement/Effort	Job requires establishing and maintaining personally challenging achievement goals and exerting effort toward mastering tasks.
Independence	Job requires developing one's own ways of doing things, guiding oneself with little or no supervision, and depending on oneself to get things done.
Self Control	Job requires maintaining composure, keeping emotions in check, controlling anger, and avoiding aggressive behavior, even in very difficult situations.
Leadership	Job requires a willingness to lead, take charge, and offer opinions and direction.
Concern for Others	Job requires being sensitive to others' needs and feelings and being understanding and helpful on the job.
Innovation	Job requires creativity and alternative thinking to develop new ideas for and answers to work-related problems.
Social Orientation	Job requires preferring to work with others rather than alone, and being personally connected with others on the job.

15-1061.00 - Database Administrators

Coordinate changes to computer databases, test and implement the database applying knowledge of database management systems. May plan, coordinate, and implement security measures to safeguard computer databases.

Tasks

1) Modify existing databases and database management systems or direct programmers and analysts to make changes.

2) Test programs or databases, correct errors and make necessary modifications.

3) Plan, coordinate and implement security measures to safeguard information in computer files against accidental or unauthorized damage, modification or disclosure.

4) Develop data model describing data elements and how they are used, following procedures and using pen, template or computer software.

5) Review procedures in database management system manuals for making changes to database.

6) Develop standards and guidelines to guide the use and acquisition of software and to protect vulnerable information.

7) Review project requests describing database user needs to estimate time and cost required to accomplish project.

8) Specify users and user access levels for each segment of database.

9) Work as part of a project team to coordinate database development and determine project scope and limitations.

10) Develop methods for integrating different products so they work properly together, such as customizing commercial databases to fit specific needs.

11) Approve, schedule, plan, and supervise the installation and testing of new products and improvements to computer systems, such as the installation of new databases.

12) Establish and calculate optimum values for database parameters, using manuals and calculator.

13) Select and enter codes to monitor database performance and to create production database.

14) Write and code logical and physical database descriptions and specify identifiers of database to management system or direct others in coding descriptions.

15) Revise company definition of data as defined in data dictionary.

16) Review workflow charts developed by programmer analyst to understand tasks computer will perform, such as updating records.

17) Identify and evaluate industry trends in database systems to serve as a source of information and advice for upper management.

Knowledge	Knowledge Definitions
Computers and Electronics	Knowledge of circuit boards, processors, chips, electronic equipment, and computer hardware and software, including applications and programming.
Mathematics	Knowledge of arithmetic, algebra, geometry, calculus, statistics, and their applications.
Administration and Management	Knowledge of business and management principles involved in strategic planning, resource allocation, human resources modeling, leadership technique, production methods, and coordination of people and resources.
Customer and Personal Service	Knowledge of principles and processes for providing customer and personal services. This includes customer needs assessment, meeting quality standards for services, and evaluation of customer satisfaction.
Education and Training	Knowledge of principles and methods for curriculum and training design, teaching and instruction for individuals and groups, and the measurement of training effects.
English Language	Knowledge of the structure and content of the English language including the meaning and spelling of words, rules of composition, and grammar.
Economics and Accounting	Knowledge of economic and accounting principles and practices, the financial markets, banking and the analysis and reporting of financial data.
Clerical	Knowledge of administrative and clerical procedures and systems such as word processing, managing files and records, stenography and transcription, designing forms, and other office procedures and terminology.
Telecommunications	Knowledge of transmission, broadcasting, switching, control, and operation of telecommunications systems.
Engineering and Technology	Knowledge of the practical application of engineering science and technology. This includes applying principles, techniques, procedures, and equipment to the design and production of various goods and services.
Design	Knowledge of design techniques, tools, and principles involved in production of precision technical plans, blueprints, drawings, and models.
Personnel and Human Resources	Knowledge of principles and procedures for personnel recruitment, selection, training, compensation and benefits, labor relations and negotiation, and personnel information systems.
Communications and Media	Knowledge of media production, communication, and dissemination techniques and methods. This includes alternative ways to inform and entertain via written, oral, and visual media.
Production and Processing	Knowledge of raw materials, production processes, quality control, costs, and other techniques for maximizing the effective manufacture and distribution of goods.
Law and Government	Knowledge of laws, legal codes, court procedures, precedents, government regulations, executive orders, agency rules, and the democratic political process.
Public Safety and Security	Knowledge of relevant equipment, policies, procedures, and strategies to promote effective local, state, or national security operations for the protection of people, data, property, and institutions.
Psychology	Knowledge of human behavior and performance; individual differences in ability, personality, and interests; learning and motivation; psychological research methods; and the assessment and treatment of behavioral and affective disorders.
Foreign Language	Knowledge of the structure and content of a foreign (non-English) language including the meaning and spelling of words, rules of composition and grammar, and pronunciation.
Sales and Marketing	Knowledge of principles and methods for showing, promoting, and selling products or services. This includes marketing strategy and tactics, product demonstration, sales techniques, and sales control systems.
Mechanical	Knowledge of machines and tools, including their designs, uses, repair, and maintenance.
Transportation	Knowledge of principles and methods for moving people or goods by air, rail, sea, or road, including the relative costs and benefits.
Physics	Knowledge and prediction of physical principles, laws, their interrelationships, and applications to understanding fluid, material, and atmospheric dynamics, and mechanical, electrical, atomic and sub-atomic structures and processes.

Geography	Knowledge of principles and methods for describing the features of land, sea, and air masses, including their physical characteristics, locations, interrelationships, and distribution of plant, animal, and human life.
Biology	Knowledge of plant and animal organisms, their tissues, cells, functions, interdependencies, and interactions with each other and the environment.
Chemistry	Knowledge of the chemical composition, structure, and properties of substances and of the chemical processes and transformations that they undergo. This includes uses of chemicals and their interactions, danger signs, production techniques, and disposal methods.
Sociology and Anthropology	Knowledge of group behavior and dynamics, societal trends and influences, human migrations, ethnicity, cultures and their history and origins.
History and Archeology	Knowledge of historical events and their causes, indicators, and effects on civilizations and cultures.
Building and Construction	Knowledge of materials, methods, and the tools involved in the construction or repair of houses, buildings, or other structures such as highways and roads.
Medicine and Dentistry	Knowledge of the information and techniques needed to diagnose and treat human injuries, diseases, and deformities. This includes symptoms, treatment alternatives, drug properties and interactions, and preventive health-care measures.
Philosophy and Theology	Knowledge of different philosophical systems and religions. This includes their basic principles, values, ethics, ways of thinking, customs, practices, and their impact on human culture.
Food Production	Knowledge of techniques and equipment for planting, growing, and harvesting food products (both plant and animal) for consumption, including storage/handling techniques.
Therapy and Counseling	Knowledge of principles, methods, and procedures for diagnosis, treatment, and rehabilitation of physical and mental dysfunctions, and for career counseling and guidance.
Fine Arts	Knowledge of the theory and techniques required to compose, produce, and perform works of music, dance, visual arts, drama, and sculpture.

Skills	Skills Definitions
Active Learning	Understanding the implications of new information for both current and future problem-solving and decision-making.
Troubleshooting	Determining causes of operating errors and deciding what to do about it.
Critical Thinking	Using logic and reasoning to identify the strengths and weaknesses of alternative solutions, conclusions or approaches to problems.
Coordination	Adjusting actions in relation to others' actions.
Active Listening	Giving full attention to what other people are saying, taking time to understand the points being made, asking questions as appropriate, and not interrupting at inappropriate times.
Reading Comprehension	Understanding written sentences and paragraphs in work related documents.
Complex Problem Solving	Identifying complex problems and reviewing related information to develop and evaluate options and implement solutions.
Time Management	Managing one's own time and the time of others.
Operations Analysis	Analyzing needs and product requirements to create a design.
Instructing	Teaching others how to do something.
Persuasion	Persuading others to change their minds or behavior.
Systems Analysis	Determining how a system should work and how changes in conditions, operations, and the environment will affect outcomes.
Negotiation	Bringing others together and trying to reconcile differences.
Monitoring	Monitoring/Assessing performance of yourself, other individuals, or organizations to make improvements or take corrective action.
Social Perceptiveness	Being aware of others' reactions and understanding why they react as they do.
Writing	Communicating effectively in writing as appropriate for the needs of the audience.
Quality Control Analysis	Conducting tests and inspections of products, services, or processes to evaluate quality or performance.
Systems Evaluation	Identifying measures or indicators of system performance and the actions needed to improve or correct performance, relative to the goals of the system.
Judgment and Decision Making	Considering the relative costs and benefits of potential actions to choose the most appropriate one.

Technology Design	Generating or adapting equipment and technology to serve user needs.
Management of Personnel Resources	Motivating, developing, and directing people as they work, identifying the best people for the job.
Speaking	Talking to others to convey information effectively.
Learning Strategies	Selecting and using training/instructional methods and procedures appropriate for the situation when learning or teaching new things.
Service Orientation	Actively looking for ways to help people.
Programming	Writing computer programs for various purposes.
Operation and Control	Controlling operations of equipment or systems.
Management of Financial Resources	Determining how money will be spent to get the work done, and accounting for these expenditures.
Installation	Installing equipment, machines, wiring, or programs to meet specifications.
Mathematics	Using mathematics to solve problems.
Equipment Selection	Determining the kind of tools and equipment needed to do a job.
Equipment Maintenance	Performing routine maintenance on equipment and determining when and what kind of maintenance is needed.
Management of Material Resources	Obtaining and seeing to the appropriate use of equipment, facilities, and materials needed to do certain work.
Operation Monitoring	Watching gauges, dials, or other indicators to make sure a machine is working properly.
Repairing	Repairing machines or systems using the needed tools.
Science	Using scientific rules and methods to solve problems.

Ability	Ability Definitions
Problem Sensitivity	The ability to tell when something is wrong or is likely to go wrong. It does not involve solving the problem, only recognizing there is a problem.
Deductive Reasoning	The ability to apply general rules to specific problems to produce answers that make sense.
Information Ordering	The ability to arrange things or actions in a certain order or pattern according to a specific rule or set of rules (e.g., patterns of numbers, letters, words, pictures, mathematical operations).
Inductive Reasoning	The ability to combine pieces of information to form general rules or conclusions (includes finding a relationship among seemingly unrelated events).
Written Comprehension	The ability to read and understand information and ideas presented in writing.
Near Vision	The ability to see details at close range (within a few feet of the observer).
Oral Expression	The ability to communicate information and ideas in speaking so others will understand.
Oral Comprehension	The ability to listen to and understand information and ideas presented through spoken words and sentences.
Originality	The ability to come up with unusual or clever ideas about a given topic or situation, or to develop creative ways to solve a problem.
Flexibility of Closure	The ability to identify or detect a known pattern (a figure, object, word, or sound) that is hidden in other distracting material.
Category Flexibility	The ability to generate or use different sets of rules for combining or grouping things in different ways.
Fluency of Ideas	The ability to come up with a number of ideas about a topic (the number of ideas is important, not their quality, correctness, or creativity).
Written Expression	The ability to communicate information and ideas in writing so others will understand.
Speech Clarity	The ability to speak clearly so others can understand you.
Speech Recognition	The ability to identify and understand the speech of another person.
Selective Attention	The ability to concentrate on a task over a period of time without being distracted.
Mathematical Reasoning	The ability to choose the right mathematical methods or formulas to solve a problem.
Visualization	The ability to imagine how something will look after it is moved around or when its parts are moved or rearranged.
Perceptual Speed	The ability to quickly and accurately compare similarities and differences among sets of letters, numbers, objects, pictures, or patterns. The things to be compared may be presented at the same time or one after the other. This ability also includes comparing a presented object with a remembered object.
Finger Dexterity	The ability to make precisely coordinated movements of the fingers of one or both hands to grasp, manipulate, or assemble very small objects.

Far Vision	The ability to see details at a distance.
Memorization	The ability to remember information such as words, numbers, pictures, and procedures.
Visual Color Discrimination	The ability to match or detect differences between colors, including shades of color and brightness.
Number Facility	The ability to add, subtract, multiply, or divide quickly and correctly.
Speed of Closure	The ability to quickly make sense of, combine, and organize information into meaningful patterns.
Time Sharing	The ability to shift back and forth between two or more activities or sources of information (such as speech, sounds, touch, or other sources).
Arm-Hand Steadiness	The ability to keep your hand and arm steady while moving your arm or while holding your arm and hand in one position.
Manual Dexterity	The ability to quickly move your hand, your hand together with your arm, or your two hands to grasp, manipulate, or assemble objects.
Auditory Attention	The ability to focus on a single source of sound in the presence of other distracting sounds.
Hearing Sensitivity	The ability to detect or tell the differences between sounds that vary in pitch and loudness.
Wrist-Finger Speed	The ability to make fast, simple, repeated movements of the fingers, hands, and wrists.
Control Precision	The ability to quickly and repeatedly adjust the controls of a machine or a vehicle to exact positions.
Multilimb Coordination	The ability to coordinate two or more limbs (for example, two arms, two legs, or one leg and one arm) while sitting, standing, or lying down. It does not involve performing the activities while the whole body is in motion.
Static Strength	The ability to exert maximum muscle force to lift, push, pull, or carry objects.
Depth Perception	The ability to judge which of several objects is closer or farther away from you, or to judge the distance between you and an object.
Trunk Strength	The ability to use your abdominal and lower back muscles to support part of the body repeatedly or continuously over time without 'giving out' or fatiguing.
Speed of Limb Movement	The ability to quickly move the arms and legs.
Gross Body Coordination	The ability to coordinate the movement of your arms, legs, and torso together when the whole body is in motion.
Extent Flexibility	The ability to bend, stretch, twist, or reach with your body, arms, and/or legs.
Glare Sensitivity	The ability to see objects in the presence of glare or bright lighting.
Night Vision	The ability to see under low light conditions.
Sound Localization	The ability to tell the direction from which a sound originated.
Explosive Strength	The ability to use short bursts of muscle force to propel oneself (as in jumping or sprinting), or to throw an object.
Dynamic Strength	The ability to exert muscle force repeatedly or continuously over time. This involves muscular endurance and resistance to muscle fatigue.
Spatial Orientation	The ability to know your location in relation to the environment or to know where other objects are in relation to you.
Stamina	The ability to exert yourself physically over long periods of time without getting winded or out of breath.
Response Orientation	The ability to choose quickly between two or more movements in response to two or more different signals (lights, sounds, pictures). It includes the speed with which the correct response is started with the hand, foot, or other body part.
Dynamic Flexibility	The ability to quickly and repeatedly bend, stretch, twist, or reach out with your body, arms, and/or legs.
Rate Control	The ability to time your movements or the movement of a piece of equipment in anticipation of changes in the speed and/or direction of a moving object or scene.
Reaction Time	The ability to quickly respond (with the hand, finger, or foot) to a signal (sound, light, picture) when it appears.
Gross Body Equilibrium	The ability to keep or regain your body balance or stay upright when in an unstable position.
Peripheral Vision	The ability to see objects or movement of objects to one's side when the eyes are looking ahead.

Work_Activity	Work_Activity Definitions
Interacting With Computers	Using computers and computer systems (including hardware and software) to program, write software, set up functions, enter data, or process information.
Processing Information	Compiling, coding, categorizing, calculating, tabulating, auditing, or verifying information or data.
Analyzing Data or Information	Identifying the underlying principles, reasons, or facts of information by breaking down information or data into separate parts.
Communicating with Supervisors, Peers, or Subordin	Providing information to supervisors, co-workers, and subordinates by telephone, in written form, e-mail, or in person.
Identifying Objects, Actions, and Events	Identifying information by categorizing, estimating, recognizing differences or similarities, and detecting changes in circumstances or events.
Making Decisions and Solving Problems	Analyzing information and evaluating results to choose the best solution and solve problems.
Thinking Creatively	Developing, designing, or creating new applications, ideas, relationships, systems, or products, including artistic contributions.
Getting Information	Observing, receiving, and otherwise obtaining information from all relevant sources.
Interpreting the Meaning of Information for Others	Translating or explaining what information means and how it can be used.
Documenting/Recording Information	Entering, transcribing, recording, storing, or maintaining information in written or electronic/magnetic form.
Updating and Using Relevant Knowledge	Keeping up-to-date technically and applying new knowledge to your job.
Performing Administrative Activities	Performing day-to-day administrative tasks such as maintaining information files and processing paperwork.
Organizing, Planning, and Prioritizing Work	Developing specific goals and plans to prioritize, organize, and accomplish your work.
Monitor Processes, Materials, or Surroundings	Monitoring and reviewing information from materials, events, or the environment, to detect or assess problems.
Establishing and Maintaining Interpersonal Relatio	Developing constructive and cooperative working relationships with others, and maintaining them over time.
Estimating the Quantifiable Characteristics of Pro	Estimating sizes, distances, and quantities; or determining time, costs, resources, or materials needed to perform a work activity.
Training and Teaching Others	Identifying the educational needs of others, developing formal educational or training programs or classes, and teaching or instructing others.
Evaluating Information to Determine Compliance wit	Using relevant information and individual judgment to determine whether events or processes comply with laws, regulations, or standards.
Judging the Qualities of Things, Services, or Peop	Assessing the value, importance, or quality of things or people.
Communicating with Persons Outside Organization	Communicating with people outside the organization, representing the organization to customers, the public, government, and other external sources. This information can be exchanged in person, in writing, or by telephone or e-mail.
Provide Consultation and Advice to Others	Providing guidance and expert advice to management or other groups on technical, systems-, or process-related topics.
Developing Objectives and Strategies	Establishing long-range objectives and specifying the strategies and actions to achieve them.
Coordinating the Work and Activities of Others	Getting members of a group to work together to accomplish tasks.
Coaching and Developing Others	Identifying the developmental needs of others and coaching, mentoring, or otherwise helping others to improve their knowledge or skills.
Monitoring and Controlling Resources	Monitoring and controlling resources and overseeing the spending of money.
Handling and Moving Objects	Using hands and arms in handling, installing, positioning, and moving materials, and manipulating things.
Scheduling Work and Activities	Scheduling events, programs, and activities, as well as the work of others.
Drafting, Laying Out, and Specifying Technical Dev	Providing documentation, detailed instructions, drawings, or specifications to tell others about how devices, parts, equipment, or structures are to be fabricated, constructed, assembled, modified, maintained, or used.
Resolving Conflicts and Negotiating with Others	Handling complaints, settling disputes, and resolving grievances and conflicts, or otherwise negotiating with others.
Developing and Building Teams	Encouraging and building mutual trust, respect, and cooperation among team members.
Controlling Machines and Processes	Using either control mechanisms or direct physical activity to operate machines or processes (not including computers or vehicles).
Staffing Organizational Units	Recruiting, interviewing, selecting, hiring, and promoting employees in an organization.
Assisting and Caring for Others	Providing personal assistance, medical attention, emotional support, or other personal care to others such as coworkers, customers, or patients.

Selling or Influencing Others	Convincing others to buy merchandise/goods or to otherwise change their minds or actions.
Inspecting Equipment, Structures, or Material	Inspecting equipment, structures, or materials to identify the cause of errors or other problems or defects.
Guiding, Directing, and Motivating Subordinates	Providing guidance and direction to subordinates, including setting performance standards and monitoring performance.
Performing for or Working Directly with the Public	Performing for people or dealing directly with the public. This includes serving customers in restaurants and stores, and receiving clients or guests.
Repairing and Maintaining Electronic Equipment	Servicing, repairing, calibrating, regulating, fine-tuning, or testing machines, devices, and equipment that operate primarily on the basis of electrical or electronic (not mechanical) principles.
Repairing and Maintaining Mechanical Equipment	Servicing, repairing, adjusting, and testing machines, devices, moving parts, and equipment that operate primarily on the basis of mechanical (not electronic) principles.
Operating Vehicles, Mechanized Devices, or Equipme	Running, maneuvering, navigating, or driving vehicles or mechanized equipment, such as forklifts, passenger vehicles, aircraft, or water craft.
Performing General Physical Activities	Performing physical activities that require considerable use of your arms and legs and moving your whole body, such as climbing, lifting, balancing, walking, stooping, and handling of materials.

Work_Context	Work_Context Definitions
Electronic Mail	How often do you use electronic mail in this job?
Spend Time Sitting	How much does this job require sitting?
Importance of Being Exact or Accurate	How important is being very exact or highly accurate in performing this job?
Letters and Memos	How often does the job require written letters and memos?
Telephone	How often do you have telephone conversations in this job?
Time Pressure	How often does this job require the worker to meet strict deadlines?
Face-to-Face Discussions	How often do you have to have face-to-face discussions with individuals or teams in this job?
Freedom to Make Decisions	How much decision making freedom, without supervision, does the job offer?
Importance of Repeating Same Tasks	How important is repeating the same physical activities (e.g., key entry) or mental activities (e.g., checking entries in a ledger) over and over, without stopping, to performing this job?
Contact With Others	How much does this job require the worker to be in contact with others (face-to-face, by telephone, or otherwise) in order to perform it?
Indoors, Environmentally Controlled	How often does this job require working indoors in environmentally controlled conditions?
Structured versus Unstructured Work	To what extent is this job structured for the worker, rather than allowing the worker to determine tasks, priorities, and goals?
Spend Time Making Repetitive Motions	How much does this job require making repetitive motions?
Impact of Decisions on Co-workers or Company Resul	How do the decisions an employee makes impact the results of co-workers, clients or the company?
Physical Proximity	To what extent does this job require the worker to perform job tasks in close physical proximity to other people?
Consequence of Error	How serious would the result usually be if the worker made a mistake that was not readily correctable?
Sounds, Noise Levels Are Distracting or Uncomforta	How often does this job require working exposed to sounds and noise levels that are distracting or uncomfortable?
Level of Competition	To what extent does this job require the worker to compete or to be aware of competitive pressures?
Frequency of Decision Making	How frequently is the worker required to make decisions that affect other people, the financial resources, and/or the image and reputation of the organization?
Work With Work Group or Team	How important is it to work with others in a group or team in this job?
Spend Time Using Your Hands to Handle, Control, or	How much does this job require using your hands to handle, control, or feel objects, tools or controls?
Frequency of Conflict Situations	How often are there conflict situations the employee has to face in this job?
Coordinate or Lead Others	How important is it to coordinate or lead others in accomplishing work activities in this job?
Responsibility for Outcomes and Results	How responsible is the worker for work outcomes and results of other workers?
Degree of Automation	How automated is the job?

Deal With Unpleasant or Angry People	How frequently does the worker have to deal with unpleasant, angry, or discourteous individuals as part of the job requirements?
Spend Time Standing	How much does this job require standing?
Cramped Work Space, Awkward Positions	How often does this job require working in cramped work spaces that requires getting into awkward positions?
Deal With External Customers	How important is it to work with external customers or the public in this job?
Responsible for Others' Health and Safety	How much responsibility is there for the health and safety of others in this job?
Spend Time Walking and Running	How much does this job require walking and running?
Public Speaking	How often do you have to perform public speaking in this job?
Exposed to Contaminants	How often does this job require working exposed to contaminants (such as pollutants, gases, dust or odors)?
Spend Time Bending or Twisting the Body	How much does this job require bending or twisting your body?
Spend Time Kneeling, Crouching, Stooping, or Crawl	How much does this job require kneeling, crouching, stooping or crawling?
In an Enclosed Vehicle or Equipment	How often does this job require working in a closed vehicle or equipment (e.g., car)?
Indoors, Not Environmentally Controlled	How often does this job require working indoors in non-controlled environmental conditions (e.g., warehouse without heat)?
Extremely Bright or Inadequate Lighting	How often does this job require working in extremely bright or inadequate lighting conditions?
Exposed to Minor Burns, Cuts, Bites, or Stings	How often does this job require exposure to minor burns, cuts, bites, or stings?
Pace Determined by Speed of Equipment	How important is it to this job that the pace is determined by the speed of equipment or machinery? (This does not refer to keeping busy at all times on this job.)
Very Hot or Cold Temperatures	How often does this job require working in very hot (above 90 F degrees) or very cold (below 32 F degrees) temperatures?
Exposed to Radiation	How often does this job require exposure to radiation?
Outdoors, Under Cover	How often does this job require working outdoors, under cover (e.g., structure with roof but no walls)?
Outdoors, Exposed to Weather	How often does this job require working outdoors, exposed to all weather conditions?
In an Open Vehicle or Equipment	How often does this job require working in an open vehicle or equipment (e.g., tractor)?
Deal With Physically Aggressive People	How frequently does this job require the worker to deal with physical aggression of violent individuals?
Wear Common Protective or Safety Equipment such as	How much does this job require wearing common protective or safety equipment such as safety shoes, glasses, gloves, hard hats or live jackets?
Exposed to Whole Body Vibration	How often does this job require exposure to whole body vibration (e.g., operate a jackhammer)?
Exposed to Hazardous Equipment	How often does this job require exposure to hazardous equipment?
Spend Time Climbing Ladders, Scaffolds, or Poles	How much does this job require climbing ladders, scaffolds, or poles?
Spend Time Keeping or Regaining Balance	How much does this job require keeping or regaining your balance?
Exposed to Disease or Infections	How often does this job require exposure to disease/infections?
Wear Specialized Protective or Safety Equipment su	How much does this job require wearing specialized protective or safety equipment such as breathing apparatus, safety harness, full protection suits, or radiation protection?
Exposed to Hazardous Conditions	How often does this job require exposure to hazardous conditions?
Exposed to High Places	How often does this job require exposure to high places?

Job Zone Component	Job Zone Component Definitions
Title	Job Zone Four: Considerable Preparation Needed
Overall Experience	A minimum of two to four years of work-related skill, knowledge, or experience is needed for these occupations. For example, an accountant must complete four years of college and work for several years in accounting to be considered qualified.
Job Training	Employees in these occupations usually need several years of work-related experience, on-the-job training, and/or vocational training.

Job Zone Examples	Many of these occupations involve coordinating. supervising. managing. or training others. Examples include accountants. chefs and head cooks. computer programmers, historians. pharmacists. and police detectives.
SVP Range	(7.0 to < 8.0)
Education	Most of these occupations require a four - year bachelor's degree, but some do not.

Work_Styles	Work_Styles Definitions
Attention to Detail	Job requires being careful about detail and thorough in completing work tasks.
Analytical Thinking	Job requires analyzing information and using logic to address work-related issues and problems.
Dependability	Job requires being reliable, responsible, and dependable, and fulfilling obligations.
Cooperation	Job requires being pleasant with others on the job and displaying a good-natured, cooperative attitude.
Integrity	Job requires being honest and ethical.
Initiative	Job requires a willingness to take on responsibilities and challenges.
Adaptability/Flexibility	Job requires being open to change (positive or negative) and to considerable variety in the workplace.
Independence	Job requires developing one's own ways of doing things. guiding oneself with little or no supervision, and depending on oneself to get things done.
Innovation	Job requires creativity and alternative thinking to develop new ideas for and answers to work-related problems.
Self Control	Job requires maintaining composure, keeping emotions in check, controlling anger, and avoiding aggressive behavior. even in very difficult situations.
Stress Tolerance	Job requires accepting criticism and dealing calmly and effectively with high stress situations.
Persistence	Job requires persistence in the face of obstacles.
Achievement/Effort	Job requires establishing and maintaining personally challenging achievement goals and exerting effort toward mastering tasks.
Concern for Others	Job requires being sensitive to others' needs and feelings and being understanding and helpful on the job.
Leadership	Job requires a willingness to lead, take charge, and offer opinions and direction.
Social Orientation	Job requires preferring to work with others rather than alone, and being personally connected with others on the job.

15-1071.00 - Network and Computer Systems Administrators

Install, configure, and support an organization's local area network (LAN), wide area network (WAN), and Internet system or a segment of a network system. Maintain network hardware and software. Monitor network to ensure network availability to all system users and perform necessary maintenance to support network availability. May supervise other network support and client server specialists and plan, coordinate, and implement network security measures.

Tasks

1) Recommend changes to improve systems and network configurations, and determine hardware or software requirements related to such changes.

2) Research new technology, and implement it or recommend its implementation.

3) Maintain and administer computer networks and related computing environments, including computer hardware, systems software, applications software, and all configurations.

4) Train people in computer system use.

5) Confer with network users about how to solve existing system problems.

6) Gather data pertaining to customer needs, and use the information to identify, predict, interpret, and evaluate system and network requirements.

7) Design, configure, and test computer hardware, networking software and operating system software.

8) Perform data backups and disaster recovery operations.

9) Perform routine network startup and shutdown procedures, and maintain control records.

10) Load computer tapes and disks, and install software and printer paper or forms.

11) Plan, coordinate, and implement network security measures in order to protect data, software. and hardware.

12) Coordinate with vendors and with company personnel in order to facilitate purchases.

13) Monitor network performance in order to determine whether adjustments need to be made, and to determine where changes will need to be made in the future.

14) Maintain logs related to network functions. as well as maintenance and repair records.

15) Analyze equipment performance records in order to determine the need for repair or replacement.

16) Operate master consoles in order to monitor the performance of computer systems and networks. and to coordinate computer network access and use.

17) Maintain an inventory of parts for emergency repairs.

Knowledge	Knowledge Definitions
Computers and Electronics	Knowledge of circuit boards, processors, chips, electronic equipment, and computer hardware and software, including applications and programming.
Customer and Personal Service	Knowledge of principles and processes for providing customer and personal services. This includes customer needs assessment, meeting quality standards for services, and evaluation of customer satisfaction.
Telecommunications	Knowledge of transmission, broadcasting, switching, control, and operation of telecommunications systems.
English Language	Knowledge of the structure and content of the English language including the meaning and spelling of words, rules of composition, and grammar.
Education and Training	Knowledge of principles and methods for curriculum and training design, teaching and instruction for individuals and groups, and the measurement of training effects.
Engineering and Technology	Knowledge of the practical application of engineering science and technology. This includes applying principles, techniques. procedures, and equipment to the design and production of various goods and services.
Administration and Management	Knowledge of business and management principles involved in strategic planning, resource allocation, human resources modeling, leadership technique, production methods, and coordination of people and resources.
Mathematics	Knowledge of arithmetic, algebra, geometry, calculus, statistics, and their applications.
Public Safety and Security	Knowledge of relevant equipment, policies, procedures, and strategies to promote effective local, state, or national security operations for the protection of people, data, property, and institutions.
Communications and Media	Knowledge of media production, communication, and dissemination techniques and methods. This includes alternative ways to inform and entertain via written, oral, and visual media.
Clerical	Knowledge of administrative and clerical procedures and systems such as word processing, managing files and records, stenography and transcription, designing forms, and other office procedures and terminology.
Design	Knowledge of design techniques, tools, and principles involved in production of precision technical plans, blueprints, drawings, and models.
Production and Processing	Knowledge of raw materials, production processes, quality control, costs, and other techniques for maximizing the effective manufacture and distribution of goods.
Law and Government	Knowledge of laws, legal codes, court procedures, precedents, government regulations, executive orders, agency rules, and the democratic political process.
Mechanical	Knowledge of machines and tools, including their designs, uses, repair, and maintenance.
Personnel and Human Resources	Knowledge of principles and procedures for personnel recruitment, selection, training, compensation and benefits, labor relations and negotiation, and personnel information systems.
Psychology	Knowledge of human behavior and performance; individual differences in ability, personality, and interests; learning and motivation; psychological research methods; and the assessment and treatment of behavioral and affective disorders.
Economics and Accounting	Knowledge of economic and accounting principles and practices, the financial markets, banking and the analysis and reporting of financial data.
Physics	Knowledge and prediction of physical principles, laws, their interrelationships, and applications to understanding fluid, material, and atmospheric dynamics, and mechanical, electrical, atomic and sub-atomic structures and processes.

Sales and Marketing	Knowledge of principles and methods for showing, promoting, and selling products or services. This includes marketing strategy and tactics, product demonstration, sales techniques, and sales control systems.
Building and Construction	Knowledge of materials, methods, and the tools involved in the construction or repair of houses, buildings, or other structures such as highways and roads.
Transportation	Knowledge of principles and methods for moving people or goods by air, rail, sea, or road, including the relative costs and benefits.
Geography	Knowledge of principles and methods for describing the features of land, sea, and air masses, including their physical characteristics, locations, interrelationships, and distribution of plant, animal, and human life.
Therapy and Counseling	Knowledge of principles, methods, and procedures for diagnosis, treatment, and rehabilitation of physical and mental dysfunctions, and for career counseling and guidance.
Sociology and Anthropology	Knowledge of group behavior and dynamics, societal trends and influences, human migrations, ethnicity, cultures and their history and origins.
History and Archeology	Knowledge of historical events and their causes, indicators, and effects on civilizations and cultures.
Philosophy and Theology	Knowledge of different philosophical systems and religions. This includes their basic principles, values, ethics, ways of thinking, customs, practices, and their impact on human culture.
Chemistry	Knowledge of the chemical composition, structure, and properties of substances and of the chemical processes and transformations that they undergo. This includes uses of chemicals and their interactions, danger signs, production techniques, and disposal methods.
Medicine and Dentistry	Knowledge of the information and techniques needed to diagnose and treat human injuries, diseases, and deformities. This includes symptoms, treatment alternatives, drug properties and interactions, and preventive health-care measures.
Fine Arts	Knowledge of the theory and techniques required to compose, produce, and perform works of music, dance, visual arts, drama, and sculpture.
Foreign Language	Knowledge of the structure and content of a foreign (non-English) language including the meaning and spelling of words, rules of composition and grammar, and pronunciation.
Biology	Knowledge of plant and animal organisms, their tissues, cells, functions, interdependencies, and interactions with each other and the environment.
Food Production	Knowledge of techniques and equipment for planting, growing, and harvesting food products (both plant and animal) for consumption, including storage/handling techniques.

Skills	Skills Definitions
Troubleshooting	Determining causes of operating errors and deciding what to do about it.
Reading Comprehension	Understanding written sentences and paragraphs in work related documents.
Active Listening	Giving full attention to what other people are saying, taking time to understand the points being made, asking questions as appropriate, and not interrupting at inappropriate times.
Active Learning	Understanding the implications of new information for both current and future problem-solving and decision-making.
Critical Thinking	Using logic and reasoning to identify the strengths and weaknesses of alternative solutions, conclusions or approaches to problems.
Complex Problem Solving	Identifying complex problems and reviewing related information to develop and evaluate options and implement solutions.
Service Orientation	Actively looking for ways to help people.
Equipment Selection	Determining the kind of tools and equipment needed to do a job.
Coordination	Adjusting actions in relation to others' actions.
Installation	Installing equipment, machines, wiring, or programs to meet specifications.
Time Management	Managing one's own time and the time of others.
Repairing	Repairing machines or systems using the needed tools.
Technology Design	Generating or adapting equipment and technology to serve user needs.
Systems Analysis	Determining how a system should work and how changes in conditions, operations, and the environment will affect outcomes.

Systems Evaluation	Identifying measures or indicators of system performance and the actions needed to improve or correct performance, relative to the goals of the system.
Instructing	Teaching others how to do something.
Learning Strategies	Selecting and using training/instructional methods and procedures appropriate for the situation when learning or teaching new things.
Speaking	Talking to others to convey information effectively.
Judgment and Decision Making	Considering the relative costs and benefits of potential actions to choose the most appropriate one.
Operations Analysis	Analyzing needs and product requirements to create a design.
Monitoring	Monitoring/Assessing performance of yourself, other individuals, or organizations to make improvements or take corrective action.
Writing	Communicating effectively in writing as appropriate for the needs of the audience.
Equipment Maintenance	Performing routine maintenance on equipment and determining when and what kind of maintenance is needed.
Operation and Control	Controlling operations of equipment or systems.
Mathematics	Using mathematics to solve problems.
Negotiation	Bringing others together and trying to reconcile differences.
Persuasion	Persuading others to change their minds or behavior.
Social Perceptiveness	Being aware of others' reactions and understanding why they react as they do.
Quality Control Analysis	Conducting tests and inspections of products, services, or processes to evaluate quality or performance.
Operation Monitoring	Watching gauges, dials, or other indicators to make sure a machine is working properly.
Programming	Writing computer programs for various purposes.
Management of Material Resources	Obtaining and seeing to the appropriate use of equipment, facilities, and materials needed to do certain work.
Management of Personnel Resources	Motivating, developing, and directing people as they work, identifying the best people for the job.
Science	Using scientific rules and methods to solve problems.
Management of Financial Resources	Determining how money will be spent to get the work done, and accounting for these expenditures.

Ability	Ability Definitions
Near Vision	The ability to see details at close range (within a few feet of the observer).
Problem Sensitivity	The ability to tell when something is wrong or is likely to go wrong. It does not involve solving the problem, only recognizing there is a problem.
Inductive Reasoning	The ability to combine pieces of information to form general rules or conclusions (includes finding a relationship among seemingly unrelated events).
Oral Comprehension	The ability to listen to and understand information and ideas presented through spoken words and sentences.
Information Ordering	The ability to arrange things or actions in a certain order or pattern according to a specific rule or set of rules (e.g., patterns of numbers, letters, words, pictures, mathematical operations).
Written Comprehension	The ability to read and understand information and ideas presented in writing.
Oral Expression	The ability to communicate information and ideas in speaking so others will understand.
Deductive Reasoning	The ability to apply general rules to specific problems to produce answers that make sense.
Finger Dexterity	The ability to make precisely coordinated movements of the fingers of one or both hands to grasp, manipulate, or assemble very small objects.
Selective Attention	The ability to concentrate on a task over a period of time without being distracted.
Flexibility of Closure	The ability to identify or detect a known pattern (a figure, object, word, or sound) that is hidden in other distracting material.
Originality	The ability to come up with unusual or clever ideas about a given topic or situation, or to develop creative ways to solve a problem.
Visualization	The ability to imagine how something will look after it is moved around or when its parts are moved or rearranged.
Written Expression	The ability to communicate information and ideas in writing so others will understand.
Category Flexibility	The ability to generate or use different sets of rules for combining or grouping things in different ways.
Memorization	The ability to remember information such as words, numbers, pictures, and procedures.

Fluency of Ideas	The ability to come up with a number of ideas about a topic (the number of ideas is important, not their quality, correctness, or creativity).
Speech Clarity	The ability to speak clearly so others can understand you.
Speech Recognition	The ability to identify and understand the speech of another person.
Perceptual Speed	The ability to quickly and accurately compare similarities and differences among sets of letters, numbers, objects, pictures, or patterns. The things to be compared may be presented at the same time or one after the other. This ability also includes comparing a presented object with a remembered object.
Visual Color Discrimination	The ability to match or detect differences between colors, including shades of color and brightness.
Time Sharing	The ability to shift back and forth between two or more activities or sources of information (such as speech, sounds, touch, or other sources).
Arm-Hand Steadiness	The ability to keep your hand and arm steady while moving your arm or while holding your arm and hand in one position.
Mathematical Reasoning	The ability to choose the right mathematical methods or formulas to solve a problem.
Manual Dexterity	The ability to quickly move your hand, your hand together with your arm, or your two hands to grasp, manipulate, or assemble objects.
Speed of Closure	The ability to quickly make sense of, combine, and organize information into meaningful patterns.
Far Vision	The ability to see details at a distance.
Static Strength	The ability to exert maximum muscle force to lift, push, pull, or carry objects.
Auditory Attention	The ability to focus on a single source of sound in the presence of other distracting sounds.
Number Facility	The ability to add, subtract, multiply, or divide quickly and correctly.
Control Precision	The ability to quickly and repeatedly adjust the controls of a machine or a vehicle to exact positions.
Depth Perception	The ability to judge which of several objects is closer or farther away from you, or to judge the distance between you and an object.
Trunk Strength	The ability to use your abdominal and lower back muscles to support part of the body repeatedly or continuously over time without 'giving out' or fatiguing.
Hearing Sensitivity	The ability to detect or tell the differences between sounds that vary in pitch and loudness.
Multilimb Coordination	The ability to coordinate two or more limbs (for example, two arms, two legs, or one leg and one arm) while sitting, standing, or lying down. It does not involve performing the activities while the whole body is in motion.
Extent Flexibility	The ability to bend, stretch, twist, or reach with your body, arms, and/or legs.
Gross Body Coordination	The ability to coordinate the movement of your arms, legs, and torso together when the whole body is in motion.
Dynamic Strength	The ability to exert muscle force repeatedly or continuously over time. This involves muscular endurance and resistance to muscle fatigue.
Stamina	The ability to exert yourself physically over long periods of time without getting winded or out of breath.
Wrist-Finger Speed	The ability to make fast, simple, repeated movements of the fingers, hands, and wrists.
Gross Body Equilibrium	The ability to keep or regain your body balance or stay upright when in an unstable position.
Night Vision	The ability to see under low light conditions.
Reaction Time	The ability to quickly respond (with the hand, finger, or foot) to a signal (sound, light, picture) when it appears.
Sound Localization	The ability to tell the direction from which a sound originated.
Speed of Limb Movement	The ability to quickly move the arms and legs.
Response Orientation	The ability to choose quickly between two or more movements in response to two or more different signals (lights, sounds, pictures). It includes the speed with which the correct response is started with the hand, foot, or other body part.
Dynamic Flexibility	The ability to quickly and repeatedly bend, stretch, twist, or reach out with your body, arms, and/or legs.
Glare Sensitivity	The ability to see objects in the presence of glare or bright lighting.
Rate Control	The ability to time your movements or the movement of a piece of equipment in anticipation of changes in the speed and/or direction of a moving object or scene.
Peripheral Vision	The ability to see objects or movement of objects to one's side when the eyes are looking ahead.

Explosive Strength	The ability to use short bursts of muscle force to propel oneself (as in jumping or sprinting), or to throw an object.
Spatial Orientation	The ability to know your location in relation to the environment or to know where other objects are in relation to you.

Work_Activity	Work_Activity Definitions
Interacting With Computers	Using computers and computer systems (including hardware and software) to program, write software, set up functions, enter data, or process information.
Updating and Using Relevant Knowledge	Keeping up-to-date technically and applying new knowledge to your job.
Making Decisions and Solving Problems	Analyzing information and evaluating results to choose the best solution and solve problems.
Getting Information	Observing, receiving, and otherwise obtaining information from all relevant sources.
Communicating with Supervisors, Peers, or Subordin	Providing information to supervisors, co-workers, and subordinates by telephone, in written form, e-mail, or in person.
Processing Information	Compiling, coding, categorizing, calculating, tabulating, auditing, or verifying information or data.
Identifying Objects, Actions, and Events	Identifying information by categorizing, estimating, recognizing differences or similarities, and detecting changes in circumstances or events.
Analyzing Data or Information	Identifying the underlying principles, reasons, or facts of information by breaking down information or data into separate parts.
Thinking Creatively	Developing, designing, or creating new applications, ideas, relationships, systems, or products, including artistic contributions.
Repairing and Maintaining Electronic Equipment	Servicing, repairing, calibrating, regulating, fine-tuning, or testing machines, devices, and equipment that operate primarily on the basis of electrical or electronic (not mechanical) principles.
Organizing, Planning, and Prioritizing Work	Developing specific goals and plans to prioritize, organize, and accomplish your work.
Monitor Processes, Materials, or Surroundings	Monitoring and reviewing information from materials, events, or the environment, to detect or assess problems.
Documenting/Recording Information	Entering, transcribing, recording, storing, or maintaining information in written or electronic/magnetic form.
Establishing and Maintaining Interpersonal Relatio	Developing constructive and cooperative working relationships with others, and maintaining them over time.
Training and Teaching Others	Identifying the educational needs of others, developing formal educational or training programs or classes, and teaching or instructing others.
Inspecting Equipment, Structures, or Material	Inspecting equipment, structures, or materials to identify the cause of errors or other problems or defects.
Evaluating Information to Determine Compliance wit	Using relevant information and individual judgment to determine whether events or processes comply with laws, regulations, or standards.
Interpreting the Meaning of Information for Others	Translating or explaining what information means and how it can be used.
Provide Consultation and Advice to Others	Providing guidance and expert advice to management or other groups on technical, systems-, or process-related topics.
Scheduling Work and Activities	Scheduling events, programs, and activities, as well as the work of others.
Developing Objectives and Strategies	Establishing long-range objectives and specifying the strategies and actions to achieve them.
Judging the Qualities of Things, Services, or Peop	Assessing the value, importance, or quality of things or people.
Resolving Conflicts and Negotiating with Others	Handling complaints, settling disputes, and resolving grievances and conflicts, or otherwise negotiating with others.
Coordinating the Work and Activities of Others	Getting members of a group to work together to accomplish tasks.
Communicating with Persons Outside Organization	Communicating with people outside the organization, representing the organization to customers, the public, government, and other external sources. This information can be exchanged in person, in writing, or by telephone or e-mail.
Developing and Building Teams	Encouraging and building mutual trust, respect, and cooperation among team members.
Coaching and Developing Others	Identifying the developmental needs of others and coaching, mentoring, or otherwise helping others to improve their knowledge or skills.
Handling and Moving Objects	Using hands and arms in handling, installing, positioning, and moving materials, and manipulating things.

Estimating the Quantifiable Characteristics of Pro	Estimating sizes, distances, and quantities; or determining time, costs, resources, or materials needed to perform a work activity.
Drafting, Laying Out, and Specifying Technical Dev	Providing documentation, detailed instructions, drawings, or specifications to tell others about how devices, parts, equipment, or structures are to be fabricated, constructed, assembled, modified, maintained, or used.
Performing Administrative Activities	Performing day-to-day administrative tasks such as maintaining information files and processing paperwork.
Assisting and Caring for Others	Providing personal assistance, medical attention, emotional support, or other personal care to others such as coworkers, customers, or patients.
Guiding, Directing, and Motivating Subordinates	Providing guidance and direction to subordinates, including setting performance standards and monitoring performance.
Performing General Physical Activities	Performing physical activities that require considerable use of your arms and legs and moving your whole body, such as climbing, lifting, balancing, walking, stooping, and handling of materials.
Monitoring and Controlling Resources	Monitoring and controlling resources and overseeing the spending of money.
Controlling Machines and Processes	Using either control mechanisms or direct physical activity to operate machines or processes (not including computers or vehicles).
Repairing and Maintaining Mechanical Equipment	Servicing, repairing, adjusting, and testing machines, devices, moving parts, and equipment that operate primarily on the basis of mechanical (not electronic) principles.
Selling or Influencing Others	Convincing others to buy merchandise/goods or to otherwise change their minds or actions.
Performing for or Working Directly with the Public	Performing for people or dealing directly with the public. This includes serving customers in restaurants and stores, and receiving clients or guests.
Operating Vehicles, Mechanized Devices, or Equipme	Running, maneuvering, navigating, or driving vehicles or mechanized equipment, such as forklifts, passenger vehicles, aircraft, or water craft.
Staffing Organizational Units	Recruiting, interviewing, selecting, hiring, and promoting employees in an organization.

Work_Context	Work_Context Definitions
Electronic Mail	How often do you use electronic mail in this job?
Telephone	How often do you have telephone conversations in this job?
Face-to-Face Discussions	How often do you have to have face-to-face discussions with individuals or teams in this job?
Indoors, Environmentally Controlled	How often does this job require working indoors in environmentally controlled conditions?
Contact With Others	How much does this job require the worker to be in contact with others (face-to-face, by telephone, or otherwise) in order to perform it?
Structured versus Unstructured Work	To what extent is this job structured for the worker, rather than allowing the worker to determine tasks, priorities, and goals?
Importance of Being Exact or Accurate	How important is being very exact or highly accurate in performing this job?
Freedom to Make Decisions	How much decision making freedom, without supervision, does the job offer?
Work With Work Group or Team	How important is it to work with others in a group or team in this job?
Spend Time Sitting	How much does this job require sitting?
Time Pressure	How often does this job require the worker to meet strict deadlines?
Impact of Decisions on Co-workers or Company Resul	How do the decisions an employee makes impact the results of co-workers, clients or the company?
Coordinate or Lead Others	How important is it to coordinate or lead others in accomplishing work activities in this job?
Frequency of Decision Making	How frequently is the worker required to make decisions that affect other people, the financial resources, and/or the image and reputation of the organization?
Physical Proximity	To what extent does this job require the worker to perform job tasks in close physical proximity to other people?
Consequence of Error	How serious would the result usually be if the worker made a mistake that was not readily correctable?
Spend Time Using Your Hands to Handle, Control, or	How much does this job require using your hands to handle, control, or feel objects, tools or controls?
Importance of Repeating Same Tasks	How important is repeating the same physical activities (e.g., key entry) or mental activities (e.g., checking entries in a ledger) over and over, without stopping, to performing this job?

Deal With Unpleasant or Angry People	How frequently does the worker have to deal with unpleasant, angry, or discourteous individuals as part of the job requirements?
Frequency of Conflict Situations	How often are there conflict situations the employee has to face in this job?
Letters and Memos	How often does the job require written letters and memos?
Responsibility for Outcomes and Results	How responsible is the worker for work outcomes and results of other workers?
Level of Competition	To what extent does this job require the worker to compete or to be aware of competitive pressures?
Spend Time Making Repetitive Motions	How much does this job require making repetitive motions?
Deal With External Customers	How important is it to work with external customers or the public in this job?
Sounds, Noise Levels Are Distracting or Uncomforta	How often does this job require working exposed to sounds and noise levels that are distracting or uncomfortable?
Spend Time Standing	How much does this job require standing?
Cramped Work Space, Awkward Positions	How often does this job require working in cramped work spaces that requires getting into awkward positions?
Degree of Automation	How automated is the job?
Exposed to Contaminants	How often does this job require working exposed to contaminants (such as pollutants, gases, dust or odors)?
Public Speaking	How often do you have to perform public speaking in this job?
Responsible for Others' Health and Safety	How much responsibility is there for the health and safety of others in this job?
Spend Time Walking and Running	How much does this job require walking and running?
Pace Determined by Speed of Equipment	How important is it to this job that the pace is determined by the speed of equipment or machinery? (This does not refer to keeping busy at all times on this job.)
Spend Time Bending or Twisting the Body	How much does this job require bending or twisting your body?
Spend Time Kneeling, Crouching, Stooping, or Crawl	How much does this job require kneeling, crouching, stooping or crawling?
Indoors, Not Environmentally Controlled	How often does this job require working indoors in non-controlled environmental conditions (e.g., warehouse without heat)?
Exposed to Minor Burns, Cuts, Bites, or Stings	How often does this job require exposure to minor burns, cuts, bites, or stings?
In an Enclosed Vehicle or Equipment	How often does this job require working in a closed vehicle or equipment (e.g., car)?
Extremely Bright or Inadequate Lighting	How often does this job require working in extremely bright or inadequate lighting conditions?
Exposed to Hazardous Equipment	How often does this job require exposure to hazardous equipment?
Exposed to Hazardous Conditions	How often does this job require exposure to hazardous conditions?
Very Hot or Cold Temperatures	How often does this job require working in very hot (above 90 F degrees) or very cold (below 32 F degrees) temperatures?
Exposed to Radiation	How often does this job require exposure to radiation?
Spend Time Climbing Ladders, Scaffolds, or Poles	How much does this job require climbing ladders, scaffolds, or poles?
Outdoors, Exposed to Weather	How often does this job require working outdoors, exposed to all weather conditions?
Wear Common Protective or Safety Equipment such as	How much does this job require wearing common protective or safety equipment such as safety shoes, glasses, gloves, hard hats or live jackets?
Spend Time Keeping or Regaining Balance	How much does this job require keeping or regaining your balance?
Exposed to High Places	How often does this job require exposure to high places?
Outdoors, Under Cover	How often does this job require working outdoors, under cover (e.g., structure with roof but no walls)?
Deal With Physically Aggressive People	How frequently does this job require the worker to deal with physical aggression of violent individuals?
Exposed to Disease or Infections	How often does this job require exposure to disease/infections?
Wear Specialized Protective or Safety Equipment su	How much does this job require wearing specialized protective or safety equipment such as breathing apparatus, safety harness, full protection suits, or radiation protection?
In an Open Vehicle or Equipment	How often does this job require working in an open vehicle or equipment (e.g., tractor)?
Exposed to Whole Body Vibration	How often does this job require exposure to whole body vibration (e.g., operate a jackhammer)?

Job Zone Component	Job Zone Component Definitions
Title	Job Zone Four: Considerable Preparation Needed
Overall Experience	A minimum of two to four years of work-related skill, knowledge, or experience is needed for these occupations. For example, an accountant must complete four years of college and work for several years in accounting to be considered qualified.
Job Training	Employees in these occupations usually need several years of work-related experience, on-the-job training, and/or vocational training.
Job Zone Examples	Many of these occupations involve coordinating, supervising, managing, or training others. Examples include accountants, chefs and head cooks, computer programmers, historians, pharmacists, and police detectives.
SVP Range	(7.0 to < 8.0)
Education	Most of these occupations require a four - year bachelor's degree, but some do not.

Work_Styles	Work_Styles Definitions
Dependability	Job requires being reliable, responsible, and dependable, and fulfilling obligations.
Attention to Detail	Job requires being careful about detail and thorough in completing work tasks.
Analytical Thinking	Job requires analyzing information and using logic to address work-related issues and problems.
Cooperation	Job requires being pleasant with others on the job and displaying a good-natured, cooperative attitude.
Initiative	Job requires a willingness to take on responsibilities and challenges.
Stress Tolerance	Job requires accepting criticism and dealing calmly and effectively with high stress situations.
Adaptability/Flexibility	Job requires being open to change (positive or negative) and to considerable variety in the workplace.
Integrity	Job requires being honest and ethical.
Independence	Job requires developing one's own ways of doing things, guiding oneself with little or no supervision, and depending on oneself to get things done.
Achievement/Effort	Job requires establishing and maintaining personally challenging achievement goals and exerting effort toward mastering tasks.
Persistence	Job requires persistence in the face of obstacles.
Innovation	Job requires creativity and alternative thinking to develop new ideas for and answers to work-related problems.
Self Control	Job requires maintaining composure, keeping emotions in check, controlling anger, and avoiding aggressive behavior, even in very difficult situations.
Leadership	Job requires a willingness to lead, take charge, and offer opinions and direction.
Concern for Others	Job requires being sensitive to others' needs and feelings and being understanding and helpful on the job.
Social Orientation	Job requires preferring to work with others rather than alone, and being personally connected with others on the job.

15-1081.00 - Network Systems and Data Communications Analysts

Analyze, design, test, and evaluate network systems, such as local area networks (LAN), wide area networks (WAN), Internet, intranet, and other data communications systems. Perform network modeling, analysis, and planning. Research and recommend network and data communications hardware and software. Includes telecommunications specialists who deal with the interfacing of computer and communications equipment. May supervise computer programmers.

Tasks

1) Monitor system performance and provide security measures, troubleshooting and maintenance as needed.

2) Design and implement network configurations, network architecture (including hardware and software technology, site locations, and integration of technologies), and systems.

3) Identify areas of operation that need upgraded equipment such as modems, fiber optic cables, and telephone wires.

4) Test and evaluate hardware and software to determine efficiency, reliability, and compatibility with existing system, and make purchase recommendations.

5) Maintain needed files by adding and deleting files on the network server and backing up files to guarantee their safety in the event of problems with the network.

6) Train users in use of equipment.

7) Visit vendors, attend conferences or training and study technical journals to keep up with changes in technology.

8) Consult customers, visit workplaces or conduct surveys to determine present and future user needs.

9) Read technical manuals and brochures to determine which equipment meets establishment requirements.

10) Work with other engineers, systems analysts, programmers, technicians, scientists and top-level managers in the design, testing and evaluation of systems.

11) Set up user accounts, regulating and monitoring file access to ensure confidentiality and proper use.

12) Develop and write procedures for installation, use, and troubleshooting of communications hardware and software.

13) Maintain the peripherals, such as printers, that are connected to the network.

14) Adapt and modify existing software to meet specific needs.

Knowledge	Knowledge Definitions
Computers and Electronics	Knowledge of circuit boards, processors, chips, electronic equipment, and computer hardware and software, including applications and programming.
Customer and Personal Service	Knowledge of principles and processes for providing customer and personal services. This includes customer needs assessment, meeting quality standards for services, and evaluation of customer satisfaction.
Telecommunications	Knowledge of transmission, broadcasting, switching, control, and operation of telecommunications systems.
Education and Training	Knowledge of principles and methods for curriculum and training design, teaching and instruction for individuals and groups, and the measurement of training effects.
Administration and Management	Knowledge of business and management principles involved in strategic planning, resource allocation, human resources modeling, leadership technique, production methods, and coordination of people and resources.
English Language	Knowledge of the structure and content of the English language including the meaning and spelling of words, rules of composition, and grammar.
Engineering and Technology	Knowledge of the practical application of engineering science and technology. This includes applying principles, techniques, procedures, and equipment to the design and production of various goods and services.
Mathematics	Knowledge of arithmetic, algebra, geometry, calculus, statistics, and their applications.
Public Safety and Security	Knowledge of relevant equipment, policies, procedures, and strategies to promote effective local, state, or national security operations for the protection of people, data, property, and institutions.
Sales and Marketing	Knowledge of principles and methods for showing, promoting, and selling products or services. This includes marketing strategy and tactics, product demonstration, sales techniques, and sales control systems.
Clerical	Knowledge of administrative and clerical procedures and systems such as word processing, managing files and records, stenography and transcription, designing forms, and other office procedures and terminology.
Design	Knowledge of design techniques, tools, and principles involved in production of precision technical plans, blueprints, drawings, and models.
Communications and Media	Knowledge of media production, communication, and dissemination techniques and methods. This includes alternative ways to inform and entertain via written, oral, and visual media.
Mechanical	Knowledge of machines and tools, including their designs, uses, repair, and maintenance.
Economics and Accounting	Knowledge of economic and accounting principles and practices, the financial markets, banking and the analysis and reporting of financial data.

Personnel and Human Resources	Knowledge of principles and procedures for personnel recruitment, selection, training, compensation and benefits, labor relations and negotiation, and personnel information systems.
Production and Processing	Knowledge of raw materials, production processes, quality control, costs, and other techniques for maximizing the effective manufacture and distribution of goods.
Law and Government	Knowledge of laws, legal codes, court procedures, precedents, government regulations, executive orders, agency rules, and the democratic political process.
Psychology	Knowledge of human behavior and performance; individual differences in ability, personality, and interests; learning and motivation; psychological research methods; and the assessment and treatment of behavioral and affective disorders.
Transportation	Knowledge of principles and methods for moving people or goods by air, rail, sea, or road, including the relative costs and benefits.
Geography	Knowledge of principles and methods for describing the features of land, sea, and air masses, including their physical characteristics, locations, interrelationships, and distribution of plant, animal, and human life.
Foreign Language	Knowledge of the structure and content of a foreign (non-English) language including the meaning and spelling of words, rules of composition and grammar, and pronunciation.
Sociology and Anthropology	Knowledge of group behavior and dynamics, societal trends and influences, human migrations, ethnicity, cultures and their history and origins.
Building and Construction	Knowledge of materials, methods, and the tools involved in the construction or repair of houses, buildings, or other structures such as highways and roads.
Physics	Knowledge and prediction of physical principles, laws, their interrelationships, and applications to understanding fluid, material, and atmospheric dynamics, and mechanical, electrical, atomic and sub-atomic structures and processes.
Therapy and Counseling	Knowledge of principles, methods, and procedures for diagnosis, treatment, and rehabilitation of physical and mental dysfunctions, and for career counseling and guidance.
Philosophy and Theology	Knowledge of different philosophical systems and religions. This includes their basic principles, values, ethics, ways of thinking, customs, practices, and their impact on human culture.
Medicine and Dentistry	Knowledge of the information and techniques needed to diagnose and treat human injuries, diseases, and deformities. This includes symptoms, treatment alternatives, drug properties and interactions, and preventive health-care measures.
Chemistry	Knowledge of the chemical composition, structure, and properties of substances and of the chemical processes and transformations that they undergo. This includes uses of chemicals and their interactions, danger signs, production techniques, and disposal methods.
Fine Arts	Knowledge of the theory and techniques required to compose, produce, and perform works of music, dance, visual arts, drama, and sculpture.
Food Production	Knowledge of techniques and equipment for planting, growing, and harvesting food products (both plant and animal) for consumption, including storage/handling techniques.
Biology	Knowledge of plant and animal organisms, their tissues, cells, functions, interdependencies, and interactions with each other and the environment.
History and Archeology	Knowledge of historical events and their causes, indicators, and effects on civilizations and cultures.

Skills	Skills Definitions
Equipment Selection	Determining the kind of tools and equipment needed to do a job.
Troubleshooting	Determining causes of operating errors and deciding what to do about it.
Complex Problem Solving	Identifying complex problems and reviewing related information to develop and evaluate options and implement solutions.
Active Listening	Giving full attention to what other people are saying, taking time to understand the points being made, asking questions as appropriate, and not interrupting at inappropriate times.
Active Learning	Understanding the implications of new information for both current and future problem-solving and decision-making.

Critical Thinking	Using logic and reasoning to identify the strengths and weaknesses of alternative solutions, conclusions or approaches to problems.
Installation	Installing equipment, machines, wiring, or programs to meet specifications.
Reading Comprehension	Understanding written sentences and paragraphs in work related documents.
Technology Design	Generating or adapting equipment and technology to serve user needs.
Judgment and Decision Making	Considering the relative costs and benefits of potential actions to choose the most appropriate one.
Systems Analysis	Determining how a system should work and how changes in conditions, operations, and the environment will affect outcomes.
Coordination	Adjusting actions in relation to others' actions.
Operations Analysis	Analyzing needs and product requirements to create a design.
Systems Evaluation	Identifying measures or indicators of system performance and the actions needed to improve or correct performance, relative to the goals of the system.
Equipment Maintenance	Performing routine maintenance on equipment and determining when and what kind of maintenance is needed.
Instructing	Teaching others how to do something.
Persuasion	Persuading others to change their minds or behavior.
Learning Strategies	Selecting and using training/instructional methods and procedures appropriate for the situation when learning or teaching new things.
Speaking	Talking to others to convey information effectively.
Operation and Control	Controlling operations of equipment or systems.
Operation Monitoring	Watching gauges, dials, or other indicators to make sure a machine is working properly.
Quality Control Analysis	Conducting tests and inspections of products, services, or processes to evaluate quality or performance.
Time Management	Managing one's own time and the time of others.
Management of Material Resources	Obtaining and seeing to the appropriate use of equipment, facilities, and materials needed to do certain work.
Management of Financial Resources	Determining how money will be spent to get the work done, and accounting for these expenditures.
Writing	Communicating effectively in writing as appropriate for the needs of the audience.
Monitoring	Monitoring/Assessing performance of yourself, other individuals, or organizations to make improvements or take corrective action.
Repairing	Repairing machines or systems using the needed tools.
Service Orientation	Actively looking for ways to help people.
Social Perceptiveness	Being aware of others' reactions and understanding why they react as they do.
Programming	Writing computer programs for various purposes.
Mathematics	Using mathematics to solve problems.
Negotiation	Bringing others together and trying to reconcile differences.
Management of Personnel Resources	Motivating, developing, and directing people as they work, identifying the best people for the job.
Science	Using scientific rules and methods to solve problems.

Ability	Ability Definitions
Near Vision	The ability to see details at close range (within a few feet of the observer).
Written Comprehension	The ability to read and understand information and ideas presented in writing.
Deductive Reasoning	The ability to apply general rules to specific problems to produce answers that make sense.
Problem Sensitivity	The ability to tell when something is wrong or is likely to go wrong. It does not involve solving the problem, only recognizing there is a problem.
Oral Comprehension	The ability to listen to and understand information and ideas presented through spoken words and sentences.
Inductive Reasoning	The ability to combine pieces of information to form general rules or conclusions (includes finding a relationship among seemingly unrelated events).
Information Ordering	The ability to arrange things or actions in a certain order or pattern according to a specific rule or set of rules (e.g., patterns of numbers, letters, words, pictures, mathematical operations).
Category Flexibility	The ability to generate or use different sets of rules for combining or grouping things in different ways.
Oral Expression	The ability to communicate information and ideas in speaking so others will understand.

Originality	The ability to come up with unusual or clever ideas about a given topic or situation, or to develop creative ways to solve a problem.
Selective Attention	The ability to concentrate on a task over a period of time without being distracted.
Finger Dexterity	The ability to make precisely coordinated movements of the fingers of one or both hands to grasp, manipulate, or assemble very small objects.
Speech Recognition	The ability to identify and understand the speech of another person.
Written Expression	The ability to communicate information and ideas in writing so others will understand.
Number Facility	The ability to add, subtract, multiply, or divide quickly and correctly.
Flexibility of Closure	The ability to identify or detect a known pattern (a figure, object, word, or sound) that is hidden in other distracting material.
Speech Clarity	The ability to speak clearly so others can understand you.
Mathematical Reasoning	The ability to choose the right mathematical methods or formulas to solve a problem.
Fluency of Ideas	The ability to come up with a number of ideas about a topic (the number of ideas is important, not their quality, correctness, or creativity).
Perceptual Speed	The ability to quickly and accurately compare similarities and differences among sets of letters, numbers, objects, pictures, or patterns. The things to be compared may be presented at the same time or one after the other. This ability also includes comparing a presented object with a remembered object.
Visualization	The ability to imagine how something will look after it is moved around or when its parts are moved or rearranged.
Far Vision	The ability to see details at a distance.
Speed of Closure	The ability to quickly make sense of, combine, and organize information into meaningful patterns.
Memorization	The ability to remember information such as words, numbers, pictures, and procedures.
Visual Color Discrimination	The ability to match or detect differences between colors, including shades of color and brightness.
Arm-Hand Steadiness	The ability to keep your hand and arm steady while moving your arm or while holding your arm and hand in one position.
Time Sharing	The ability to shift back and forth between two or more activities or sources of information (such as speech, sounds, touch, or other sources).
Hearing Sensitivity	The ability to detect or tell the differences between sounds that vary in pitch and loudness.
Auditory Attention	The ability to focus on a single source of sound in the presence of other distracting sounds.
Manual Dexterity	The ability to quickly move your hand, your hand together with your arm, or your two hands to grasp, manipulate, or assemble objects.
Depth Perception	The ability to judge which of several objects is closer or farther away from you, or to judge the distance between you and an object.
Control Precision	The ability to quickly and repeatedly adjust the controls of a machine or a vehicle to exact positions.
Trunk Strength	The ability to use your abdominal and lower back muscles to support part of the body repeatedly or continuously over time without 'giving out' or fatiguing.
Wrist-Finger Speed	The ability to make fast, simple, repeated movements of the fingers, hands, and wrists.
Response Orientation	The ability to choose quickly between two or more movements in response to two or more different signals (lights, sounds, pictures). It includes the speed with which the correct response is started with the hand, foot, or other body part.
Extent Flexibility	The ability to bend, stretch, twist, or reach with your body, arms, and/or legs.
Reaction Time	The ability to quickly respond (with the hand, finger, or foot) to a signal (sound, light, picture) when it appears.
Multilimb Coordination	The ability to coordinate two or more limbs (for example, two arms, two legs, or one leg and one arm) while sitting, standing, or lying down. It does not involve performing the activities while the whole body is in motion.
Rate Control	The ability to time your movements or the movement of a piece of equipment in anticipation of changes in the speed and/or direction of a moving object or scene.
Sound Localization	The ability to tell the direction from which a sound originated.
Dynamic Strength	The ability to exert muscle force repeatedly or continuously over time. This involves muscular endurance and resistance to muscle fatigue.

Explosive Strength	The ability to use short bursts of muscle force to propel oneself (as in jumping or sprinting), or to throw an object.
Static Strength	The ability to exert maximum muscle force to lift, push, pull, or carry objects.
Peripheral Vision	The ability to see objects or movement of objects to one's side when the eyes are looking ahead.
Speed of Limb Movement	The ability to quickly move the arms and legs.
Glare Sensitivity	The ability to see objects in the presence of glare or bright lighting.
Spatial Orientation	The ability to know your location in relation to the environment or to know where other objects are in relation to you.
Night Vision	The ability to see under low light conditions.
Stamina	The ability to exert yourself physically over long periods of time without getting winded or out of breath.
Dynamic Flexibility	The ability to quickly and repeatedly bend, stretch, twist, or reach out with your body, arms, and/or legs.
Gross Body Equilibrium	The ability to keep or regain your body balance or stay upright when in an unstable position.
Gross Body Coordination	The ability to coordinate the movement of your arms, legs, and torso together when the whole body is in motion.

Work_Activity	Work_Activity Definitions
Interacting With Computers	Using computers and computer systems (including hardware and software) to program, write software, set up functions, enter data, or process information.
Communicating with Supervisors, Peers, or Subordin	Providing information to supervisors, co-workers, and subordinates by telephone, in written form, e-mail, or in person.
Getting Information	Observing, receiving, and otherwise obtaining information from all relevant sources.
Thinking Creatively	Developing, designing, or creating new applications, ideas, relationships, systems, or products, including artistic contributions.
Communicating with Persons Outside Organization	Communicating with people outside the organization, representing the organization to customers, the public, government, and other external sources. This information can be exchanged in person, in writing, or by telephone or e-mail.
Establishing and Maintaining Interpersonal Relatio	Developing constructive and cooperative working relationships with others, and maintaining them over time.
Organizing, Planning, and Prioritizing Work	Developing specific goals and plans to prioritize, organize, and accomplish your work.
Identifying Objects, Actions, and Events	Identifying information by categorizing, estimating, recognizing differences or similarities, and detecting changes in circumstances or events.
Making Decisions and Solving Problems	Analyzing information and evaluating results to choose the best solution and solve problems.
Monitor Processes, Materials, or Surroundings	Monitoring and reviewing information from materials, events, or the environment, to detect or assess problems.
Updating and Using Relevant Knowledge	Keeping up-to-date technically and applying new knowledge to your job.
Judging the Qualities of Things, Services, or Peop	Assessing the value, importance, or quality of things or people.
Evaluating Information to Determine Compliance wit	Using relevant information and individual judgment to determine whether events or processes comply with laws, regulations, or standards.
Analyzing Data or Information	Identifying the underlying principles, reasons, or facts of information by breaking down information or data into separate parts.
Processing Information	Compiling, coding, categorizing, calculating, tabulating, auditing, or verifying information or data.
Interpreting the Meaning of Information for Others	Translating or explaining what information means and how it can be used.
Documenting/Recording Information	Entering, transcribing, recording, storing, or maintaining information in written or electronic/magnetic form.
Estimating the Quantifiable Characteristics of Pro	Estimating sizes, distances, and quantities; or determining time, costs, resources, or materials needed to perform a work activity.
Developing Objectives and Strategies	Establishing long-range objectives and specifying the strategies and actions to achieve them.
Performing Administrative Activities	Performing day-to-day administrative tasks such as maintaining information files and processing paperwork.
Repairing and Maintaining Electronic Equipment	Servicing, repairing, calibrating, regulating, fine-tuning, or testing machines, devices, and equipment that operate primarily on the basis of electrical or electronic (not mechanical) principles.

Training and Teaching Others	Identifying the educational needs of others, developing formal educational or training programs or classes, and teaching or instructing others.
Inspecting Equipment, Structures, or Material	Inspecting equipment, structures, or materials to identify the cause of errors or other problems or defects.
Developing and Building Teams	Encouraging and building mutual trust, respect, and cooperation among team members.
Scheduling Work and Activities	Scheduling events, programs, and activities, as well as the work of others.
Coordinating the Work and Activities of Others	Getting members of a group to work together to accomplish tasks.
Monitoring and Controlling Resources	Monitoring and controlling resources and overseeing the spending of money.
Controlling Machines and Processes	Using either control mechanisms or direct physical activity to operate machines or processes (not including computers or vehicles).
Resolving Conflicts and Negotiating with Others	Handling complaints, settling disputes, and resolving grievances and conflicts, or otherwise negotiating with others.
Provide Consultation and Advice to Others	Providing guidance and expert advice to management or other groups on technical, systems-, or process-related topics.
Drafting, Laying Out, and Specifying Technical Dev	Providing documentation, detailed instructions, drawings, or specifications to tell others about how devices, parts, equipment, or structures are to be fabricated, constructed, assembled, modified, maintained, or used.
Selling or Influencing Others	Convincing others to buy merchandise/goods or to otherwise change their minds or actions.
Guiding, Directing, and Motivating Subordinates	Providing guidance and direction to subordinates, including setting performance standards and monitoring performance.
Staffing Organizational Units	Recruiting, interviewing, selecting, hiring, and promoting employees in an organization.
Assisting and Caring for Others	Providing personal assistance, medical attention, emotional support, or other personal care to others such as coworkers, customers, or patients.
Coaching and Developing Others	Identifying the developmental needs of others and coaching, mentoring, or otherwise helping others to improve their knowledge or skills.
Performing for or Working Directly with the Public	Performing for people or dealing directly with the public. This includes serving customers in restaurants and stores, and receiving clients or guests.
Repairing and Maintaining Mechanical Equipment	Servicing, repairing, adjusting, and testing machines, devices, moving parts, and equipment that operate primarily on the basis of mechanical (not electronic) principles.
Handling and Moving Objects	Using hands and arms in handling, installing, positioning, and moving materials, and manipulating things.
Performing General Physical Activities	Performing physical activities that require considerable use of your arms and legs and moving your whole body, such as climbing, lifting, balancing, walking, stooping, and handling of materials.
Operating Vehicles, Mechanized Devices, or Equipme	Running, maneuvering, navigating, or driving vehicles or mechanized equipment, such as forklifts, passenger vehicles, aircraft, or water craft.

Work_Context

Work_Context Definitions

Telephone	How often do you have telephone conversations in this job?
Electronic Mail	How often do you use electronic mail in this job?
Indoors, Environmentally Controlled	How often does this job require working indoors in environmentally controlled conditions?
Face-to-Face Discussions	How often do you have to have face-to-face discussions with individuals or teams in this job?
Importance of Being Exact or Accurate	How important is being very exact or highly accurate in performing this job?
Structured versus Unstructured Work	To what extent is this job structured for the worker, rather than allowing the worker to determine tasks, priorities, and goals?
Freedom to Make Decisions	How much decision making freedom, without supervision, does the job offer?
Work With Work Group or Team	How important is it to work with others in a group or team in this job?
Contact With Others	How much does this job require the worker to be in contact with others (face-to-face, by telephone, or otherwise) in order to perform it?
Spend Time Sitting	How much does this job require sitting?
Time Pressure	How often does this job require the worker to meet strict deadlines?
Physical Proximity	To what extent does this job require the worker to perform job tasks in close physical proximity to other people?

Importance of Repeating Same Task's	How important is repeating the same physical activities (e.g., key entry) or mental activities (e.g., checking entries in a ledger) over and over, without stopping, to performing this job?
Impact of Decisions on Co-workers or Company Resul	How do the decisions an employee makes impact the results of co-workers, clients or the company?
Consequence of Error	How serious would the result usually be if the worker made a mistake that was not readily correctable?
Coordinate or Lead Others	How important is it to coordinate or lead others in accomplishing work activities in this job?
Frequency of Decision Making	How frequently is the worker required to make decisions that affect other people, the financial resources, and/or the image and reputation of the organization?
Cramped Work Space, Awkward Positions	How often does this job require working in cramped work spaces that requires getting into awkward positions?
Letters and Memos	How often does the job require written letters and memos?
Spend Time Using Your Hands to Handle, Control, or	How much does this job require using your hands to handle, control, or feel objects, tools or controls?
Level of Competition	To what extent does this job require the worker to compete or to be aware of competitive pressures?
Spend Time Standing	How much does this job require standing?
Responsibility for Outcomes and Results	How responsible is the worker for work outcomes and results of other workers?
Deal With External Customers	How important is it to work with external customers or the public in this job?
Spend Time Making Repetitive Motions	How much does this job require making repetitive motions?
Frequency of Conflict Situations	How often are there conflict situations the employee has to face in this job?
Sounds, Noise Levels Are Distracting or Uncomforta	How often does this job require working exposed to sounds and noise levels that are distracting or uncomfortable?
Deal With Unpleasant or Angry People	How frequently does the worker have to deal with unpleasant, angry, or discourteous individuals as part of the job requirements?
In an Enclosed Vehicle or Equipment	How often does this job require working in a closed vehicle or equipment (e.g., car)?
Public Speaking	How often do you have to perform public speaking in this job?
Spend Time Walking and Running	How much does this job require walking and running?
Degree of Automation	How automated is the job?
Spend Time Kneeling, Crouching, Stooping, or Crawl	How much does this job require kneeling, crouching, stooping or crawling?
Spend Time Bending or Twisting the Body	How much does this job require bending or twisting your body?
Responsible for Others' Health and Safety	How much responsibility is there for the health and safety of others in this job?
Exposed to Contaminants	How often does this job require working exposed to contaminants (such as pollutants, gases, dust or odors)?
Exposed to Minor Burns, Cuts, Bites, or Stings	How often does this job require exposure to minor burns, cuts, bites, or stings?
Extremely Bright or Inadequate Lighting	How often does this job require working in extremely bright or inadequate lighting conditions?
Indoors, Not Environmentally Controlled	How often does this job require working indoors in non-controlled environmental conditions (e.g., warehouse without heat)?
Exposed to High Places	How often does this job require exposure to high places?
Pace Determined by Speed of Equipment	How important is it to this job that the pace is determined by the speed of equipment or machinery? (This does not refer to keeping busy at all times on this job.)
Deal With Physically Aggressive People	How frequently does this job require the worker to deal with physical aggression of violent individuals?
Spend Time Keeping or Regaining Balance	How much does this job require keeping or regaining your balance?
Very Hot or Cold Temperatures	How often does this job require working in very hot (above 90 F degrees) or very cold (below 32 F degrees) temperatures?
Outdoors, Exposed to Weather	How often does this job require working outdoors, exposed to all weather conditions?
Outdoors, Under Cover	How often does this job require working outdoors, under cover (e.g., structure with roof but no walls)?
Exposed to Hazardous Equipment	How often does this job require exposure to hazardous equipment?
Wear Common Protective or Safety Equipment such as	How much does this job require wearing common protective or safety equipment such as safety shoes, glasses, gloves, hard hats or live jackets?

Spend Time Climbing Ladders. Scaffolds. or Poles	How much does this job require climbing ladders. scaffolds. or poles?
Exposed to Hazardous Conditions	How often does this job require exposure to hazardous conditions?
Exposed to Radiation	How often does this job require exposure to radiation?
Exposed to Disease or Infections	How often does this job require exposure to disease/infections?
In an Open Vehicle or Equipment	How often does this job require working in an open vehicle or equipment (e.g.. tractor)?
Exposed to Whole Body Vibration	How often does this job require exposure to whole body vibration (e.g.. operate a jackhammer)?
Wear Specialized Protective or Safety Equipment su	How much does this job require wearing specialized protective or safety equipment such as breathing apparatus. safety harness. full protection suits, or radiation protection?

15-2011.00 - Actuaries

Analyze statistical data. such as mortality. accident. sickness. disability. and retirement rates and construct probability tables to forecast risk and liability for payment of future benefits. May ascertain premium rates required and cash reserves necessary to ensure payment of future benefits.

Tasks

1) Ascertain premium rates required and cash reserves and liabilities necessary to ensure payment of future benefits.

2) Collaborate with programmers, underwriters, accounts. claims experts. and senior management to help companies develop plans for new lines of business or improving existing business.

3) Design, review and help administer insurance. annuity and pension plans, determining financial soundness and calculating premiums.

4) Determine or help determine company policy, and explain complex technical matters to company executives. government officials, shareholders, policyholders, and/or the public.

5) Determine policy contract provisions for each type of insurance.

6) Construct probability tables for events such as fires, natural disasters, and unemployment. based on analysis of statistical data and other pertinent information.

7) Provide advice to clients on a contract basis, working as a consultant.

8) Explain changes in contract provisions to customers.

9) Testify in court as expert witness or to provide legal evidence on matters such as the value of potential lifetime earnings of a person who is disabled or killed in an accident.

10) Manage credit and help price corporate security offerings.

11) Testify before public agencies on proposed legislation affecting businesses.

12) Provide expertise to help financial institutions manage risks and maximize returns associated with investment products or credit offerings.

13) Determine equitable basis for distributing surplus earnings under participating insurance and annuity contracts in mutual companies.

Job Zone Component / Job Zone Component Definitions

Job Zone Component	Job Zone Component Definitions
Title	Job Zone Three: Medium Preparation Needed
Overall Experience	Previous work-related skill, knowledge, or experience is required for these occupations. For example. an electrician must have completed three or four years of apprenticeship or several years of vocational training, and often must have passed a licensing exam. in order to perform the job.
Job Training	Employees in these occupations usually need one or two years of training involving both on-the-job experience and informal training with experienced workers.
Job Zone Examples	These occupations usually involve using communication and organizational skills to coordinate, supervise, manage, or train others to accomplish goals. Examples include dental assistants. electricians,fish and game wardens, legal secretaries. personnel recruiters, and recreation workers.
SVP Range	(6.0 to < 7.0)
Education	Most occupations in this zone require training in vocational schools, related on-the-job experience, or an associate's degree. Some may require a bachelor's degree.

Work_Styles / Work_Styles Definitions

Work_Styles	Work_Styles Definitions
Attention to Detail	Job requires being careful about detail and thorough in completing work tasks.
Dependability	Job requires being reliable, responsible, and dependable, and fulfilling obligations.
Stress Tolerance	Job requires accepting criticism and dealing calmly and effectively with high stress situations.
Analytical Thinking	Job requires analyzing information and using logic to address work-related issues and problems.
Initiative	Job requires a willingness to take on responsibilities and challenges.
Adaptability/Flexibility	Job requires being open to change (positive or negative) and to considerable variety in the workplace.
Persistence	Job requires persistence in the face of obstacles.
Achievement/Effort	Job requires establishing and maintaining personally challenging achievement goals and exerting effort toward mastering tasks.
Self Control	Job requires maintaining composure, keeping emotions in check, controlling anger, and avoiding aggressive behavior, even in very difficult situations.
Cooperation	Job requires being pleasant with others on the job and displaying a good-natured, cooperative attitude.
Independence	Job requires developing one's own ways of doing things, guiding oneself with little or no supervision, and depending on oneself to get things done.
Integrity	Job requires being honest and ethical.
Leadership	Job requires a willingness to lead, take charge, and offer opinions and direction.
Innovation	Job requires creativity and alternative thinking to develop new ideas for and answers to work-related problems.
Concern for Others	Job requires being sensitive to others' needs and feelings and being understanding and helpful on the job.
Social Orientation	Job requires preferring to work with others rather than alone. and being personally connected with others on the job.

Knowledge / Knowledge Definitions

Knowledge	Knowledge Definitions
Mathematics	Knowledge of arithmetic, algebra, geometry, calculus, statistics, and their applications.
English Language	Knowledge of the structure and content of the English language including the meaning and spelling of words, rules of composition, and grammar.
Economics and Accounting	Knowledge of economic and accounting principles and practices, the financial markets, banking and the analysis and reporting of financial data.
Computers and Electronics	Knowledge of circuit boards, processors, chips, electronic equipment, and computer hardware and software, including applications and programming.
Administration and Management	Knowledge of business and management principles involved in strategic planning, resource allocation, human resources modeling, leadership technique, production methods, and coordination of people and resources.
Law and Government	Knowledge of laws, legal codes, court procedures, precedents, government regulations, executive orders, agency rules, and the democratic political process.
Sales and Marketing	Knowledge of principles and methods for showing, promoting. and selling products or services. This includes marketing strategy and tactics, product demonstration, sales techniques, and sales control systems.
Clerical	Knowledge of administrative and clerical procedures and systems such as word processing. managing files and records, stenography and transcription, designing forms, and other office procedures and terminology.
Customer and Personal Service	Knowledge of principles and processes for providing customer and personal services. This includes customer needs assessment, meeting quality standards for services, and evaluation of customer satisfaction.
Personnel and Human Resources	Knowledge of principles and procedures for personnel recruitment, selection, training, compensation and benefits, labor relations and negotiation, and personnel information systems.
Education and Training	Knowledge of principles and methods for curriculum and training design, teaching and instruction for individuals and groups, and the measurement of training effects.

Communications and Media	Knowledge of media production, communication, and dissemination techniques and methods. This includes alternative ways to inform and entertain via written, oral, and visual media.
Medicine and Dentistry	Knowledge of the information and techniques needed to diagnose and treat human injuries, diseases, and deformities. This includes symptoms, treatment alternatives, drug properties and interactions, and preventive health-care measures.
Production and Processing	Knowledge of raw materials, production processes, quality control, costs, and other techniques for maximizing the effective manufacture and distribution of goods.
Engineering and Technology	Knowledge of the practical application of engineering science and technology. This includes applying principles, techniques, procedures, and equipment to the design and production of various goods and services.
Telecommunications	Knowledge of transmission, broadcasting, switching, control, and operation of telecommunications systems.
Psychology	Knowledge of human behavior and performance; individual differences in ability, personality, and interests; learning and motivation; psychological research methods; and the assessment and treatment of behavioral and affective disorders.
Geography	Knowledge of principles and methods for describing the features of land, sea, and air masses, including their physical characteristics, locations, interrelationships, and distribution of plant, animal, and human life.
Design	Knowledge of design techniques, tools, and principles involved in production of precision technical plans, blueprints, drawings, and models.
Therapy and Counseling	Knowledge of principles, methods, and procedures for diagnosis, treatment, and rehabilitation of physical and mental dysfunctions, and for career counseling and guidance.
Sociology and Anthropology	Knowledge of group behavior and dynamics, societal trends and influences, human migrations, ethnicity, cultures and their history and origins.
Public Safety and Security	Knowledge of relevant equipment, policies, procedures, and strategies to promote effective local, state, or national security operations for the protection of people, data, property, and institutions.
History and Archeology	Knowledge of historical events and their causes, indicators, and effects on civilizations and cultures.
Foreign Language	Knowledge of the structure and content of a foreign (non-English) language including the meaning and spelling of words, rules of composition and grammar, and pronunciation.
Transportation	Knowledge of principles and methods for moving people or goods by air, rail, sea, or road, including the relative costs and benefits.
Physics	Knowledge and prediction of physical principles, laws, their interrelationships, and applications to understanding fluid, material, and atmospheric dynamics, and mechanical, electrical, atomic and sub-atomic structures and processes.
Biology	Knowledge of plant and animal organisms, their tissues, cells, functions, interdependencies, and interactions with each other and the environment.
Philosophy and Theology	Knowledge of different philosophical systems and religions. This includes their basic principles, values, ethics, ways of thinking, customs, practices, and their impact on human culture.
Mechanical	Knowledge of machines and tools, including their designs, uses, repair, and maintenance.
Fine Arts	Knowledge of the theory and techniques required to compose, produce, and perform works of music, dance, visual arts, drama, and sculpture.
Building and Construction	Knowledge of materials, methods, and the tools involved in the construction or repair of houses, buildings, or other structures such as highways and roads.
Food Production	Knowledge of techniques and equipment for planting, growing, and harvesting food products (both plant and animal) for consumption, including storage/handling techniques.
Chemistry	Knowledge of the chemical composition, structure, and properties of substances and of the chemical processes and transformations that they undergo. This includes uses of chemicals and their interactions, danger signs, production techniques, and disposal methods.

Skills	Skills Definitions
Mathematics	Using mathematics to solve problems.

Active Learning	Understanding the implications of new information for both current and future problem-solving and decision-making.
Complex Problem Solving	Identifying complex problems and reviewing related information to develop and evaluate options and implement solutions.
Critical Thinking	Using logic and reasoning to identify the strengths and weaknesses of alternative solutions, conclusions or approaches to problems.
Active Listening	Giving full attention to what other people are saying, taking time to understand the points being made, asking questions as appropriate, and not interrupting at inappropriate times.
Time Management	Managing one's own time and the time of others.
Reading Comprehension	Understanding written sentences and paragraphs in work related documents.
Judgment and Decision Making	Considering the relative costs and benefits of potential actions to choose the most appropriate one.
Coordination	Adjusting actions in relation to others' actions.
Speaking	Talking to others to convey information effectively.
Writing	Communicating effectively in writing as appropriate for the needs of the audience.
Learning Strategies	Selecting and using training/instructional methods and procedures appropriate for the situation when learning or teaching new things.
Instructing	Teaching others how to do something.
Operations Analysis	Analyzing needs and product requirements to create a design.
Monitoring	Monitoring/Assessing performance of yourself, other individuals, or organizations to make improvements or take corrective action.
Troubleshooting	Determining causes of operating errors and deciding what to do about it.
Quality Control Analysis	Conducting tests and inspections of products, services, or processes to evaluate quality or performance.
Programming	Writing computer programs for various purposes.
Persuasion	Persuading others to change their minds or behavior.
Management of Personnel Resources	Motivating, developing, and directing people as they work, identifying the best people for the job.
Management of Financial Resources	Determining how money will be spent to get the work done, and accounting for these expenditures.
Systems Analysis	Determining how a system should work and how changes in conditions, operations, and the environment will affect outcomes.
Negotiation	Bringing others together and trying to reconcile differences.
Equipment Selection	Determining the kind of tools and equipment needed to do a job.
Social Perceptiveness	Being aware of others' reactions and understanding why they react as they do.
Service Orientation	Actively looking for ways to help people.
Systems Evaluation	Identifying measures or indicators of system performance and the actions needed to improve or correct performance, relative to the goals of the system.
Technology Design	Generating or adapting equipment and technology to serve user needs.
Science	Using scientific rules and methods to solve problems.
Operation Monitoring	Watching gauges, dials, or other indicators to make sure a machine is working properly.
Operation and Control	Controlling operations of equipment or systems.
Management of Material Resources	Obtaining and seeing to the appropriate use of equipment, facilities, and materials needed to do certain work.
Installation	Installing equipment, machines, wiring, or programs to meet specifications.
Equipment Maintenance	Performing routine maintenance on equipment and determining when and what kind of maintenance is needed.
Repairing	Repairing machines or systems using the needed tools.

Ability	Ability Definitions
Mathematical Reasoning	The ability to choose the right mathematical methods or formulas to solve a problem.
Inductive Reasoning	The ability to combine pieces of information to form general rules or conclusions (includes finding a relationship among seemingly unrelated events).
Deductive Reasoning	The ability to apply general rules to specific problems to produce answers that make sense.
Information Ordering	The ability to arrange things or actions in a certain order or pattern according to a specific rule or set of rules (e.g., patterns of numbers, letters, words, pictures, mathematical operations).
Oral Expression	The ability to communicate information and ideas in speaking so others will understand.

Written Expression	The ability to communicate information and ideas in writing so others will understand.
Written Comprehension	The ability to read and understand information and ideas presented in writing.
Oral Comprehension	The ability to listen to and understand information and ideas presented through spoken words and sentences.
Problem Sensitivity	The ability to tell when something is wrong or is likely to go wrong. It does not involve solving the problem, only recognizing there is a problem.
Category Flexibility	The ability to generate or use different sets of rules for combining or grouping things in different ways.
Near Vision	The ability to see details at close range (within a few feet of the observer).
Speech Clarity	The ability to speak clearly so others can understand you.
Number Facility	The ability to add, subtract, multiply, or divide quickly and correctly.
Originality	The ability to come up with unusual or clever ideas about a given topic or situation, or to develop creative ways to solve a problem.
Speech Recognition	The ability to identify and understand the speech of another person.
Fluency of Ideas	The ability to come up with a number of ideas about a topic (the number of ideas is important, not their quality, correctness, or creativity).
Flexibility of Closure	The ability to identify or detect a known pattern (a figure, object, word, or sound) that is hidden in other distracting material.
Selective Attention	The ability to concentrate on a task over a period of time without being distracted.
Perceptual Speed	The ability to quickly and accurately compare similarities and differences among sets of letters, numbers, objects, pictures, or patterns. The things to be compared may be presented at the same time or one after the other. This ability also includes comparing a presented object with a remembered object.
Visualization	The ability to imagine how something will look after it is moved around or when its parts are moved or rearranged.
Memorization	The ability to remember information such as words, numbers, pictures, and procedures.
Far Vision	The ability to see details at a distance.
Finger Dexterity	The ability to make precisely coordinated movements of the fingers of one or both hands to grasp, manipulate, or assemble very small objects.
Speed of Closure	The ability to quickly make sense of, combine, and organize information into meaningful patterns.
Auditory Attention	The ability to focus on a single source of sound in the presence of other distracting sounds.
Time Sharing	The ability to shift back and forth between two or more activities or sources of information (such as speech, sounds, touch, or other sources).
Manual Dexterity	The ability to quickly move your hand, your hand together with your arm, or your two hands to grasp, manipulate, or assemble objects.
Arm-Hand Steadiness	The ability to keep your hand and arm steady while moving your arm or while holding your arm and hand in one position.
Trunk Strength	The ability to use your abdominal and lower back muscles to support part of the body repeatedly or continuously over time without 'giving out' or fatiguing.
Visual Color Discrimination	The ability to match or detect differences between colors, including shades of color and brightness.
Control Precision	The ability to quickly and repeatedly adjust the controls of a machine or a vehicle to exact positions.
Hearing Sensitivity	The ability to detect or tell the differences between sounds that vary in pitch and loudness.
Depth Perception	The ability to judge which of several objects is closer or farther away from you, or to judge the distance between you and an object.
Response Orientation	The ability to choose quickly between two or more movements in response to two or more different signals (lights, sounds, pictures). It includes the speed with which the correct response is started with the hand, foot, or other body part.
Static Strength	The ability to exert maximum muscle force to lift, push, pull, or carry objects.
Explosive Strength	The ability to use short bursts of muscle force to propel oneself (as in jumping or sprinting), or to throw an object.
Dynamic Strength	The ability to exert muscle force repeatedly or continuously over time. This involves muscular endurance and resistance to muscle fatigue.

Stamina	The ability to exert yourself physically over long periods of time without getting winded or out of breath.
Dynamic Flexibility	The ability to quickly and repeatedly bend, stretch, twist, or reach out with your body, arms, and/or legs.
Sound Localization	The ability to tell the direction from which a sound originated.
Reaction Time	The ability to quickly respond (with the hand, finger, or foot) to a signal (sound, light, picture) when it appears.
Extent Flexibility	The ability to bend, stretch, twist, or reach with your body, arms, and/or legs.
Glare Sensitivity	The ability to see objects in the presence of glare or bright lighting.
Rate Control	The ability to time your movements or the movement of a piece of equipment in anticipation of changes in the speed and/or direction of a moving object or scene.
Spatial Orientation	The ability to know your location in relation to the environment or to know where other objects are in relation to you.
Peripheral Vision	The ability to see objects or movement of objects to one's side when the eyes are looking ahead.
Night Vision	The ability to see under low light conditions.
Gross Body Equilibrium	The ability to keep or regain your body balance or stay upright when in an unstable position.
Wrist-Finger Speed	The ability to make fast, simple, repeated movements of the fingers, hands, and wrists.
Speed of Limb Movement	The ability to quickly move the arms and legs.
Gross Body Coordination	The ability to coordinate the movement of your arms, legs, and torso together when the whole body is in motion.
Multilimb Coordination	The ability to coordinate two or more limbs (for example, two arms, two legs, or one leg and one arm) while sitting, standing, or lying down. It does not involve performing the activities while the whole body is in motion.

Work_Activity	Work_Activity Definitions
Getting Information	Observing, receiving, and otherwise obtaining information from all relevant sources.
Processing Information	Compiling, coding, categorizing, calculating, tabulating, auditing, or verifying information or data.
Analyzing Data or Information	Identifying the underlying principles, reasons, or facts of information by breaking down information or data into separate parts.
Interacting With Computers	Using computers and computer systems (including hardware and software) to program, write software, set up functions, enter data, or process information.
Identifying Objects, Actions, and Events	Identifying information by categorizing, estimating, recognizing differences or similarities, and detecting changes in circumstances or events.
Making Decisions and Solving Problems	Analyzing information and evaluating results to choose the best solution and solve problems.
Updating and Using Relevant Knowledge	Keeping up-to-date technically and applying new knowledge to your job.
Organizing, Planning, and Prioritizing Work	Developing specific goals and plans to prioritize, organize, and accomplish your work.
Documenting/Recording Information	Entering, transcribing, recording, storing, or maintaining information in written or electronic/magnetic form.
Evaluating Information to Determine Compliance wit	Using relevant information and individual judgment to determine whether events or processes comply with laws, regulations, or standards.
Estimating the Quantifiable Characteristics of Pro	Estimating sizes, distances, and quantities; or determining time, costs, resources, or materials needed to perform a work activity.
Interpreting the Meaning of Information for Others	Translating or explaining what information means and how it can be used.
Thinking Creatively	Developing, designing, or creating new applications, ideas, relationships, systems, or products, including artistic contributions.
Communicating with Supervisors, Peers, or Subordin	Providing information to supervisors, co-workers, and subordinates by telephone, in written form, e-mail, or in person.
Developing Objectives and Strategies	Establishing long-range objectives and specifying the strategies and actions to achieve them.
Coordinating the Work and Activities of Others	Getting members of a group to work together to accomplish tasks.
Guiding, Directing, and Motivating Subordinates	Providing guidance and direction to subordinates, including setting performance standards and monitoring performance.
Establishing and Maintaining Interpersonal Relatio	Developing constructive and cooperative working relationships with others, and maintaining them over time.

Coaching and Developing Others	Identifying the developmental needs of others and coaching, mentoring, or otherwise helping others to improve their knowledge or skills.
Provide Consultation and Advice to Others	Providing guidance and expert advice to management or other groups on technical, systems-, or process-related topics.
Training and Teaching Others	Identifying the educational needs of others, developing formal educational or training programs or classes, and teaching or instructing others.
Judging the Qualities of Things, Services, or Peop	Assessing the value, importance, or quality of things or people.
Communicating with Persons Outside Organization	Communicating with people outside the organization, representing the organization to customers, the public, government, and other external sources. This information can be exchanged in person, in writing, or by telephone or e-mail.
Selling or Influencing Others	Convincing others to buy merchandise/goods or to otherwise change their minds or actions.
Monitor Processes, Materials, or Surroundings	Monitoring and reviewing information from materials, events, or the environment, to detect or assess problems.
Performing Administrative Activities	Performing day-to-day administrative tasks such as maintaining information files and processing paperwork.
Developing and Building Teams	Encouraging and building mutual trust, respect, and cooperation among team members.
Scheduling Work and Activities	Scheduling events, programs, and activities, as well as the work of others.
Monitoring and Controlling Resources	Monitoring and controlling resources and overseeing the spending of money.
Resolving Conflicts and Negotiating with Others	Handling complaints, settling disputes, and resolving grievances and conflicts, or otherwise negotiating with others.
Staffing Organizational Units	Recruiting, interviewing, selecting, hiring, and promoting employees in an organization.
Assisting and Caring for Others	Providing personal assistance, medical attention, emotional support, or other personal care to others such as coworkers, customers, or patients.
Controlling Machines and Processes	Using either control mechanisms or direct physical activity to operate machines or processes (not including computers or vehicles).
Inspecting Equipment, Structures, or Material	Inspecting equipment, structures, or materials to identify the cause of errors or other problems or defects.
Repairing and Maintaining Electronic Equipment	Servicing, repairing, calibrating, regulating, fine-tuning, or testing machines, devices, and equipment that operate primarily on the basis of electrical or electronic (not mechanical) principles.
Performing for or Working Directly with the Public	Performing for people or dealing directly with the public. This includes serving customers in restaurants and stores, and receiving clients or guests.
Repairing and Maintaining Mechanical Equipment	Servicing, repairing, adjusting, and testing machines, devices, moving parts, and equipment that operate primarily on the basis of mechanical (not electronic) principles.
Performing General Physical Activities	Performing physical activities that require considerable use of your arms and legs and moving your whole body, such as climbing, lifting, balancing, walking, stooping, and handling of materials.
Drafting, Laying Out, and Specifying Technical Dev	Providing documentation, detailed instructions, drawings, or specifications to tell others about how devices, parts, equipment, or structures are to be fabricated, constructed, assembled, modified, maintained, or used.
Handling and Moving Objects	Using hands and arms in handling, installing, positioning, and moving materials, and manipulating things.
Operating Vehicles, Mechanized Devices, or Equipme	Running, maneuvering, navigating, or driving vehicles or mechanized equipment, such as forklifts, passenger vehicles, aircraft, or water craft.

Work_Context | Work_Context Definitions

Electronic Mail	How often do you use electronic mail in this job?
Indoors, Environmentally Controlled	How often does this job require working indoors in environmentally controlled conditions?
Spend Time Sitting	How much does this job require sitting?
Importance of Being Exact or Accurate	How important is being very exact or highly accurate in performing this job?
Face-to-Face Discussions	How often do you have to have face-to-face discussions with individuals or teams in this job?
Telephone	How often do you have telephone conversations in this job?
Structured versus Unstructured Work	To what extent is this job structured for the worker, rather than allowing the worker to determine tasks, priorities, and goals?
Freedom to Make Decisions	How much decision making freedom, without supervision, does the job offer?

Work With Work Group or Team	How important is it to work with others in a group or team in this job?
Impact of Decisions on Co-workers or Company Resul	How do the decisions an employee makes impact the results of co-workers, clients or the company?
Importance of Repeating Same Tasks	How important is repeating the same physical activities (e.g., key entry) or mental activities (e.g., checking entries in a ledger) over and over, without stopping, to performing this job?
Contact With Others	How much does this job require the worker to be in contact with others (face-to-face, by telephone, or otherwise) in order to perform it?
Frequency of Decision Making	How frequently is the worker required to make decisions that affect other people, the financial resources, and/or the image and reputation of the organization?
Letters and Memos	How often does the job require written letters and memos?
Spend Time Using Your Hands to Handle, Control, or	How much does this job require using your hands to handle, control, or feel objects, tools or controls?
Coordinate or Lead Others	How important is it to coordinate or lead others in accomplishing work activities in this job?
Spend Time Making Repetitive Motions	How much does this job require making repetitive motions?
Time Pressure	How often does this job require the worker to meet strict deadlines?
Responsibility for Outcomes and Results	How responsible is the worker for work outcomes and results of other workers?
Consequence of Error	How serious would the result usually be if the worker made a mistake that was not readily correctable?
Physical Proximity	To what extent does this job require the worker to perform job tasks in close physical proximity to other people?
Degree of Automation	How automated is the job?
Sounds, Noise Levels Are Distracting or Uncomforta	How often does this job require working exposed to sounds and noise levels that are distracting or uncomfortable?
Level of Competition	To what extent does this job require the worker to compete or to be aware of competitive pressures?
Frequency of Conflict Situations	How often are there conflict situations the employee has to face in this job?
Deal With External Customers	How important is it to work with external customers or the public in this job?
Deal With Unpleasant or Angry People	How frequently does the worker have to deal with unpleasant, angry, or discourteous individuals as part of the job requirements?
Spend Time Standing	How much does this job require standing?
Public Speaking	How often do you have to perform public speaking in this job?
Spend Time Walking and Running	How much does this job require walking and running?
Responsible for Others' Health and Safety	How much responsibility is there for the health and safety of others in this job?
Extremely Bright or Inadequate Lighting	How often does this job require working in extremely bright or inadequate lighting conditions?
Pace Determined by Speed of Equipment	How important is it to this job that the pace is determined by the speed of equipment or machinery? (This does not refer to keeping busy at all times on this job.)
Deal With Physically Aggressive People	How frequently does this job require the worker to deal with physical aggression of violent individuals?
Cramped Work Space, Awkward Positions	How often does this job require working in cramped work spaces that requires getting into awkward positions?
In an Enclosed Vehicle or Equipment	How often does this job require working in a closed vehicle or equipment (e.g., car)?
Exposed to Disease or Infections	How often does this job require exposure to disease/infections?
Exposed to Contaminants	How often does this job require working exposed to contaminants (such as pollutants, gases, dust or odors)?
Spend Time Kneeling, Crouching, Stooping, or Crawl	How much does this job require kneeling, crouching, stooping, or crawling?
Spend Time Keeping or Regaining Balance	How much does this job require keeping or regaining your balance?
Very Hot or Cold Temperatures	How often does this job require working in very hot (above 90 F degrees) or very cold (below 32 F degrees) temperatures?
In an Open Vehicle or Equipment	How often does this job require working in an open vehicle or equipment (e.g., tractor)?
Spend Time Climbing Ladders, Scaffolds, or Poles	How much does this job require climbing ladders, scaffolds, or poles?
Exposed to Hazardous Equipment	How often does this job require exposure to hazardous equipment?

Exposed to Hazardous Conditions	How often does this job require exposure to hazardous conditions?
Exposed to High Places	How often does this job require exposure to high places?
Exposed to Radiation	How often does this job require exposure to radiation?
Wear Specialized Protective or Safety Equipment su	How much does this job require wearing specialized protective or safety equipment such as breathing apparatus, safety harness, full protection suits, or radiation protection?
Outdoors, Under Cover	How often does this job require working outdoors, under cover (e.g., structure with roof but no walls)?
Outdoors, Exposed to Weather	How often does this job require working outdoors, exposed to all weather conditions?
Indoors, Not Environmentally Controlled	How often does this job require working indoors in non-controlled environmental conditions (e.g., warehouse without heat)?
Exposed to Minor Burns, Cuts, Bites, or Stings	How often does this job require exposure to minor burns, cuts, bites, or stings?
Exposed to Whole Body Vibration	How often does this job require exposure to whole body vibration (e.g., operate a jackhammer)?
Wear Common Protective or Safety Equipment such as	How much does this job require wearing common protective or safety equipment such as safety shoes, glasses, gloves, hard hats or live jackets?
Spend Time Bending or Twisting the Body	How much does this job require bending or twisting your body?

Job Zone Component	Job Zone Component Definitions
Title	Job Zone Five: Extensive Preparation Needed
	Extensive skill, knowledge, and experience are needed for these occupations. Many require more than five years of experience.
Overall Experience	For example, surgeons must complete four years of college and an additional five to seven years of specialized medical training to be able to do their job.
Job Training	Employees may need some on-the-job training, but most of these occupations assume that the person will already have the required skills, knowledge, work-related experience, and/or training.
Job Zone Examples	These occupations often involve coordinating, training, supervising, or managing the activities of others to accomplish goals. Very advanced communication and organizational skills are required. Examples include athletic trainers, lawyers, managing editors, phyicists, social psychologists, and surgeons.
SVP Range	(8.0 and above)
Education	A bachelor's degree is the minimum formal education required for these occupations. However, many also require graduate school. For example, they may require a master's degree, and some require a Ph.D., M.D., or J.D. (law degree).

Work_Styles	Work_Styles Definitions
Attention to Detail	Job requires being careful about detail and thorough in completing work tasks.
Analytical Thinking	Job requires analyzing information and using logic to address work-related issues and problems.
Integrity	Job requires being honest and ethical.
Dependability	Job requires being reliable, responsible, and dependable, and fulfilling obligations.
Initiative	Job requires a willingness to take on responsibilities and challenges.
Cooperation	Job requires being pleasant with others on the job and displaying a good-natured, cooperative attitude.
Achievement/Effort	Job requires establishing and maintaining personally challenging achievement goals and exerting effort toward mastering tasks.
Leadership	Job requires a willingness to lead, take charge, and offer opinions and direction.
Innovation	Job requires creativity and alternative thinking to develop new ideas for and answers to work-related problems.
Independence	Job requires developing one's own ways of doing things, guiding oneself with little or no supervision, and depending on oneself to get things done.
Persistence	Job requires persistence in the face of obstacles.
Adaptability/Flexibility	Job requires being open to change (positive or negative) and to considerable variety in the workplace.
Concern for Others	Job requires being sensitive to others' needs and feelings and being understanding and helpful on the job.
Stress Tolerance	Job requires accepting criticism and dealing calmly and effectively with high stress situations.

Self Control	Job requires maintaining composure, keeping emotions in check, controlling anger, and avoiding aggressive behavior, even in very difficult situations.
Social Orientation	Job requires preferring to work with others rather than alone, and being personally connected with others on the job.

15-2021.00 - Mathematicians

Conduct research in fundamental mathematics or in application of mathematical techniques to science, management, and other fields. Solve or direct solutions to problems in various fields by mathematical methods.

Tasks

1) Conduct research to extend mathematical knowledge in traditional areas, such as algebra, geometry, probability, and logic.

2) Maintain knowledge in the field by reading professional journals, talking with other mathematicians, and attending professional conferences.

3) Design, analyze, and decipher encryption systems designed to transmit military, political, financial, or law-enforcement-related information in code.

4) Develop new principles, and new relationships between existing mathematical principles, to advance mathematical science.

5) Address the relationships of quantities, magnitudes, and forms through the use of numbers and symbols.

6) Assemble sets of assumptions and explore the consequences of each set.

7) Apply mathematical theories and techniques to the solution of practical problems in business, engineering, or the sciences.

15-2041.00 - Statisticians

Engage in the development of mathematical theory or apply statistical theory and methods to collect, organize, interpret, and summarize numerical data to provide usable information. May specialize in fields, such as bio-statistics, agricultural statistics, business statistics, economic statistics, or other fields.

Tasks

1) Evaluate the statistical methods and procedures used to obtain data in order to ensure validity, applicability, efficiency, and accuracy.

2) Evaluate sources of information in order to determine any limitations in terms of reliability or usability.

3) Adapt statistical methods in order to solve specific problems in many fields, such as economics, biology and engineering.

4) Analyze and interpret statistical data in order to identify significant differences in relationships among sources of information.

5) Apply sampling techniques or utilize complete enumeration bases in order to determine and define groups to be surveyed.

6) Develop and test experimental designs, sampling techniques, and analytical methods.

7) Plan data collection methods for specific projects, and determine the types and sizes of sample groups to be used.

8) Process large amounts of data for statistical modeling and graphic analysis, using computers.

9) Report results of statistical analyses, including information in the form of graphs, charts, and tables.

10) Develop an understanding of fields to which statistical methods are to be applied in order to determine whether methods and results are appropriate.

11) Design research projects that apply valid scientific techniques and utilize information obtained from baselines or historical data in order to structure uncompromised and efficient analyses.

12) Supervise and provide instructions for workers collecting and tabulating data.

13) Identify relationships and trends in data, as well as any factors that could affect the results of research.

14) Examine theories, such as those of probability and inference in order to discover mathematical bases for new or improved methods of obtaining and evaluating numerical data.

15-2091.00 - Mathematical Technicians

Apply standardized mathematical formulas, principles, and methodology to technological problems in engineering and physical sciences in relation to specific industrial and research objectives, processes, equipment, and products.

Tasks

1) Reduce raw data to meaningful terms, using the most practical and accurate combination and sequence of computational methods.

2) Process data for analysis, using computers.

3) Apply standardized mathematical formulas, principles, and methodology to the solution of technological problems involving engineering or physical science.

4) Translate data into numbers, equations, flow charts, graphs, or other forms.

5) Confer with scientific or engineering personnel to plan projects.

17-1011.00 - Architects, Except Landscape and Naval

Plan and design structures, such as private residences, office buildings, theaters, factories, and other structural property.

Tasks

1) Plan layout of project.

2) Conduct periodic on-site observation of work during construction to monitor compliance with plans.

3) Consult with client to determine functional and spatial requirements of structure.

4) Direct activities of workers engaged in preparing drawings and specification documents.

5) Prepare scale drawings.

6) Integrate engineering element into unified design.

7) Prepare contract documents for building contractors.

8) Represent client in obtaining bids and awarding construction contracts.

9) Administer construction contracts.

10) Prepare operating and maintenance manuals, studies, and reports.

Knowledge	Knowledge Definitions
Building and Construction	Knowledge of materials, methods, and the tools involved in the construction or repair of houses, buildings, or other structures such as highways and roads.
Design	Knowledge of design techniques, tools, and principles involved in production of precision technical plans, blueprints, drawings, and models.
Engineering and Technology	Knowledge of the practical application of engineering science and technology. This includes applying principles, techniques, procedures, and equipment to the design and production of various goods and services.
English Language	Knowledge of the structure and content of the English language including the meaning and spelling of words, rules of composition, and grammar.
Mathematics	Knowledge of arithmetic, algebra, geometry, calculus, statistics, and their applications.
Administration and Management	Knowledge of business and management principles involved in strategic planning, resource allocation, human resources modeling, leadership technique, production methods, and coordination of people and resources.
Computers and Electronics	Knowledge of circuit boards, processors, chips, electronic equipment, and computer hardware and software, including applications and programming.
Customer and Personal Service	Knowledge of principles and processes for providing customer and personal services. This includes customer needs assessment, meeting quality standards for services, and evaluation of customer satisfaction.
Public Safety and Security	Knowledge of relevant equipment, policies, procedures, and strategies to promote effective local, state, or national security operations for the protection of people, data, property, and institutions.
Law and Government	Knowledge of laws, legal codes, court procedures, precedents, government regulations, executive orders, agency rules, and the democratic political process.
Clerical	Knowledge of administrative and clerical procedures and systems such as word processing, managing files and records, stenography and transcription, designing forms, and other office procedures and terminology.
Sales and Marketing	Knowledge of principles and methods for showing, promoting, and selling products or services. This includes marketing strategy and tactics, product demonstration, sales techniques, and sales control systems.
Mechanical	Knowledge of machines and tools, including their designs, uses, repair, and maintenance.
Communications and Media	Knowledge of media production, communication, and dissemination techniques and methods. This includes alternative ways to inform and entertain via written, oral, and visual media.
Economics and Accounting	Knowledge of economic and accounting principles and practices, the financial markets, banking and the analysis and reporting of financial data.
Education and Training	Knowledge of principles and methods for curriculum and training design, teaching and instruction for individuals and groups, and the measurement of training effects.
Physics	Knowledge and prediction of physical principles, laws, their interrelationships, and applications to understanding fluid, material, and atmospheric dynamics, and mechanical, electrical, atomic and sub- atomic structures and processes.
Fine Arts	Knowledge of the theory and techniques required to compose, produce, and perform works of music, dance, visual arts, drama, and sculpture.
Production and Processing	Knowledge of raw materials, production processes, quality control, costs, and other techniques for maximizing the effective manufacture and distribution of goods.
Telecommunications	Knowledge of transmission, broadcasting, switching, control, and operation of telecommunications systems.
Personnel and Human Resources	Knowledge of principles and procedures for personnel recruitment, selection, training, compensation and benefits, labor relations and negotiation, and personnel information systems.
Geography	Knowledge of principles and methods for describing the features of land, sea, and air masses, including their physical characteristics, locations, interrelationships, and distribution of plant, animal, and human life.
History and Archeology	Knowledge of historical events and their causes, indicators, and effects on civilizations and cultures.
Psychology	Knowledge of human behavior and performance; individual differences in ability, personality, and interests; learning and motivation; psychological research methods; and the assessment and treatment of behavioral and affective disorders.
Chemistry	Knowledge of the chemical composition, structure, and properties of substances and of the chemical processes and transformations that they undergo. This includes uses of chemicals and their interactions, danger signs, production techniques, and disposal methods.
Sociology and Anthropology	Knowledge of group behavior and dynamics, societal trends and influences, human migrations, ethnicity, cultures and their history and origins.
Transportation	Knowledge of principles and methods for moving people or goods by air, rail, sea, or road, including the relative costs and benefits.
Biology	Knowledge of plant and animal organisms, their tissues, cells, functions, interdependencies, and interactions with each other and the environment.
Philosophy and Theology	Knowledge of different philosophical systems and religions. This includes their basic principles, values, ethics, ways of thinking, customs, practices, and their impact on human culture.
Foreign Language	Knowledge of the structure and content of a foreign (non-English) language including the meaning and spelling of words, rules of composition and grammar, and pronunciation.
Medicine and Dentistry	Knowledge of the information and techniques needed to diagnose and treat human injuries, diseases, and deformities. This includes symptoms, treatment alternatives, drug properties and interactions, and preventive health-care measures.

Therapy and Counseling	Knowledge of principles, methods, and procedures for diagnosis, treatment, and rehabilitation of physical and mental dysfunctions, and for career counseling and guidance.
Food Production	Knowledge of techniques and equipment for planting, growing, and harvesting food products (both plant and animal) for consumption, including storage/handling techniques.

Skills	Skills Definitions
Active Listening	Giving full attention to what other people are saying, taking time to understand the points being made, asking questions as appropriate, and not interrupting at inappropriate times.
Critical Thinking	Using logic and reasoning to identify the strengths and weaknesses of alternative solutions, conclusions or approaches to problems.
Complex Problem Solving	Identifying complex problems and reviewing related information to develop and evaluate options and implement solutions.
Time Management	Managing one's own time and the time of others.
Reading Comprehension	Understanding written sentences and paragraphs in work related documents.
Management of Personnel Resources	Motivating, developing, and directing people as they work, identifying the best people for the job.
Coordination	Adjusting actions in relation to others' actions.
Writing	Communicating effectively in writing as appropriate for the needs of the audience.
Speaking	Talking to others to convey information effectively.
Operations Analysis	Analyzing needs and product requirements to create a design.
Active Learning	Understanding the implications of new information for both current and future problem-solving and decision-making.
Judgment and Decision Making	Considering the relative costs and benefits of potential actions to choose the most appropriate one.
Mathematics	Using mathematics to solve problems.
Monitoring	Monitoring/Assessing performance of yourself, other individuals, or organizations to make improvements or take corrective action.
Persuasion	Persuading others to change their minds or behavior.
Management of Financial Resources	Determining how money will be spent to get the work done, and accounting for these expenditures.
Negotiation	Bringing others together and trying to reconcile differences.
Quality Control Analysis	Conducting tests and inspections of products, services, or processes to evaluate quality or performance.
Instructing	Teaching others how to do something.
Social Perceptiveness	Being aware of others' reactions and understanding why they react as they do.
Learning Strategies	Selecting and using training/instructional methods and procedures appropriate for the situation when learning or teaching new things.
Troubleshooting	Determining causes of operating errors and deciding what to do about it.
Service Orientation	Actively looking for ways to help people.
Science	Using scientific rules and methods to solve problems.
Technology Design	Generating or adapting equipment and technology to serve user needs.
Systems Evaluation	Identifying measures or indicators of system performance and the actions needed to improve or correct performance, relative to the goals of the system.
Management of Material Resources	Obtaining and seeing to the appropriate use of equipment, facilities, and materials needed to do certain work.
Equipment Selection	Determining the kind of tools and equipment needed to do a job.
Systems Analysis	Determining how a system should work and how changes in conditions, operations, and the environment will affect outcomes.
Repairing	Repairing machines or systems using the needed tools.
Operation and Control	Controlling operations of equipment or systems.
Installation	Installing equipment, machines, wiring, or programs to meet specifications.
Equipment Maintenance	Performing routine maintenance on equipment and determining when and what kind of maintenance is needed.
Operation Monitoring	Watching gauges, dials, or other indicators to make sure a machine is working properly.
Programming	Writing computer programs for various purposes.

Ability	Ability Definitions
Oral Expression	The ability to communicate information and ideas in speaking so others will understand.

Oral Comprehension	The ability to listen to and understand information and ideas presented through spoken words and sentences.
Problem Sensitivity	The ability to tell when something is wrong or is likely to go wrong. It does not involve solving the problem, only recognizing there is a problem.
Near Vision	The ability to see details at close range (within a few feet of the observer).
Information Ordering	The ability to arrange things or actions in a certain order or pattern according to a specific rule or set of rules (e.g., patterns of numbers, letters, words, pictures, mathematical operations).
Written Expression	The ability to communicate information and ideas in writing so others will understand.
Speech Clarity	The ability to speak clearly so others can understand you.
Speech Recognition	The ability to identify and understand the speech of another person.
Deductive Reasoning	The ability to apply general rules to specific problems to produce answers that make sense.
Visualization	The ability to imagine how something will look after it is moved around or when its parts are moved or rearranged.
Originality	The ability to come up with unusual or clever ideas about a given topic or situation, or to develop creative ways to solve a problem.
Written Comprehension	The ability to read and understand information and ideas presented in writing.
Category Flexibility	The ability to generate or use different sets of rules for combining or grouping things in different ways.
Inductive Reasoning	The ability to combine pieces of information to form general rules or conclusions (includes finding a relationship among seemingly unrelated events).
Fluency of Ideas	The ability to come up with a number of ideas about a topic (the number of ideas is important, not their quality, correctness, or creativity).
Selective Attention	The ability to concentrate on a task over a period of time without being distracted.
Finger Dexterity	The ability to make precisely coordinated movements of the fingers of one or both hands to grasp, manipulate, or assemble very small objects.
Arm-Hand Steadiness	The ability to keep your hand and arm steady while moving your arm or while holding your arm and hand in one position.
Visual Color Discrimination	The ability to match or detect differences between colors, including shades of color and brightness.
Far Vision	The ability to see details at a distance.
Mathematical Reasoning	The ability to choose the right mathematical methods or formulas to solve a problem.
Flexibility of Closure	The ability to identify or detect a known pattern (a figure, object, word, or sound) that is hidden in other distracting material.
Depth Perception	The ability to judge which of several objects is closer or farther away from you, or to judge the distance between you and an object.
Memorization	The ability to remember information such as words, numbers, pictures, and procedures.
Manual Dexterity	The ability to quickly move your hand, your hand together with your arm, or your two hands to grasp, manipulate, or assemble objects.
Control Precision	The ability to quickly and repeatedly adjust the controls of a machine or a vehicle to exact positions.
Number Facility	The ability to add, subtract, multiply, or divide quickly and correctly.
Time Sharing	The ability to shift back and forth between two or more activities or sources of information (such as speech, sounds, touch, or other sources).
Auditory Attention	The ability to focus on a single source of sound in the presence of other distracting sounds.
Speed of Closure	The ability to quickly make sense of, combine, and organize information into meaningful patterns.
Perceptual Speed	The ability to quickly and accurately compare similarities and differences among sets of letters, numbers, objects, pictures, or patterns. The things to be compared may be presented at the same time or one after the other. This ability also includes comparing a presented object with a remembered object.
Multilimb Coordination	The ability to coordinate two or more limbs (for example, two arms, two legs, or one leg and one arm) while sitting, standing, or lying down. It does not involve performing the activities while the whole body is in motion.
Trunk Strength	The ability to use your abdominal and lower back muscles to support part of the body repeatedly or continuously over time without 'giving out' or fatiguing.

Spatial Orientation	The ability to know your location in relation to the environment or to know where other objects are in relation to you.
Hearing Sensitivity	The ability to detect or tell the differences between sounds that vary in pitch and loudness.
Wrist-Finger Speed	The ability to make fast, simple, repeated movements of the fingers, hands, and wrists.
Static Strength	The ability to exert maximum muscle force to lift, push, pull, or carry objects.
Explosive Strength	The ability to use short bursts of muscle force to propel oneself (as in jumping or sprinting), or to throw an object.
Stamina	The ability to exert yourself physically over long periods of time without getting winded or out of breath.
Extent Flexibility	The ability to bend, stretch, twist, or reach with your body, arms, and/or legs.
Dynamic Flexibility	The ability to quickly and repeatedly bend, stretch, twist, or reach out with your body, arms, and/or legs.
Gross Body Coordination	The ability to coordinate the movement of your arms, legs, and torso together when the whole body is in motion.
Gross Body Equilibrium	The ability to keep or regain your body balance or stay upright when in an unstable position.
Speed of Limb Movement	The ability to quickly move the arms and legs.
Night Vision	The ability to see under low light conditions.
Peripheral Vision	The ability to see objects or movement of objects to one's side when the eyes are looking ahead.
Response Orientation	The ability to choose quickly between two or more movements in response to two or more different signals (lights, sounds, pictures). It includes the speed with which the correct response is started with the hand, foot, or other body part.
Rate Control	The ability to time your movements or the movement of a piece of equipment in anticipation of changes in the speed and/or direction of a moving object or scene.
Sound Localization	The ability to tell the direction from which a sound originated.
Reaction Time	The ability to quickly respond (with the hand, finger, or foot) to a signal (sound, light, picture) when it appears.
Glare Sensitivity	The ability to see objects in the presence of glare or bright lighting.
Dynamic Strength	The ability to exert muscle force repeatedly or continuously over time. This involves muscular endurance and resistance to muscle fatigue.

Work_Activity	**Work_Activity Definitions**
Interacting With Computers	Using computers and computer systems (including hardware and software) to program, write software, set up functions, enter data, or process information.
Thinking Creatively	Developing, designing, or creating new applications, ideas, relationships, systems, or products, including artistic contributions.
Making Decisions and Solving Problems	Analyzing information and evaluating results to choose the best solution and solve problems.
Drafting, Laying Out, and Specifying Technical Dev	Providing documentation, detailed instructions, drawings, or specifications to tell others about how devices, parts, equipment, or structures are to be fabricated, constructed, assembled, modified, maintained, or used.
Organizing, Planning, and Prioritizing Work	Developing specific goals and plans to prioritize, organize, and accomplish your work.
Communicating with Supervisors, Peers, or Subordin	Providing information to supervisors, co-workers, and subordinates by telephone, in written form, e-mail, or in person.
Updating and Using Relevant Knowledge	Keeping up-to-date technically and applying new knowledge to your job.
Communicating with Persons Outside Organization	Communicating with people outside the organization, representing the organization to customers, the public, government, and other external sources. This information can be exchanged in person, in writing, or by telephone or e-mail.
Getting Information	Observing, receiving, and otherwise obtaining information from all relevant sources.
Evaluating Information to Determine Compliance wit	Using relevant information and individual judgment to determine whether events or processes comply with laws, regulations, or standards.
Coordinating the Work and Activities of Others	Getting members of a group to work together to accomplish tasks.
Identifying Objects, Actions, and Events	Identifying information by categorizing, estimating, recognizing differences or similarities, and detecting changes in circumstances or events.
Establishing and Maintaining Interpersonal Relatio	Developing constructive and cooperative working relationships with others, and maintaining them over time.

Developing and Building Teams	Encouraging and building mutual trust, respect, and cooperation among team members.
Scheduling Work and Activities	Scheduling events, programs, and activities, as well as the work of others.
Analyzing Data or Information	Identifying the underlying principles, reasons, or facts of information by breaking down information or data into separate parts.
Monitor Processes, Materials, or Surroundings	Monitoring and reviewing information from materials, events, or the environment, to detect or assess problems.
Judging the Qualities of Things, Services, or Peop	Assessing the value, importance, or quality of things or people.
Documenting/Recording Information	Entering, transcribing, recording, storing, or maintaining information in written or electronic/magnetic form.
Performing Administrative Activities	Performing day-to-day administrative tasks such as maintaining information files and processing paperwork.
Interpreting the Meaning of Information for Others	Translating or explaining what information means and how it can be used.
Inspecting Equipment, Structures, or Material	Inspecting equipment, structures, or materials to identify the cause of errors or other problems or defects.
Processing Information	Compiling, coding, categorizing, calculating, tabulating, auditing, or verifying information or data.
Monitoring and Controlling Resources	Monitoring and controlling resources and overseeing the spending of money.
Resolving Conflicts and Negotiating with Others	Handling complaints, settling disputes, and resolving grievances and conflicts, or otherwise negotiating with others.
Developing Objectives and Strategies	Establishing long-range objectives and specifying the strategies and actions to achieve them.
Provide Consultation and Advice to Others	Providing guidance and expert advice to management or other groups on technical, systems-, or process-related topics.
Coaching and Developing Others	Identifying the developmental needs of others and coaching, mentoring, or otherwise helping others to improve their knowledge or skills.
Guiding, Directing, and Motivating Subordinates	Providing guidance and direction to subordinates, including setting performance standards and monitoring performance.
Performing for or Working Directly with the Public	Performing for people or dealing directly with the public. This includes serving customers in restaurants and stores, and receiving clients or guests.
Training and Teaching Others	Identifying the educational needs of others, developing formal educational or training programs or classes, and teaching or instructing others.
Estimating the Quantifiable Characteristics of Pro	Estimating sizes, distances, and quantities; or determining time, costs, resources, or materials needed to perform a work activity.
Selling or Influencing Others	Convincing others to buy merchandise/goods or to otherwise change their minds or actions.
Controlling Machines and Processes	Using either control mechanisms or direct physical activity to operate machines or processes (not including computers or vehicles).
Staffing Organizational Units	Recruiting, interviewing, selecting, hiring, and promoting employees in an organization.
Repairing and Maintaining Electronic Equipment	Servicing, repairing, calibrating, regulating, fine-tuning, or testing machines, devices, and equipment that operate primarily on the basis of electrical or electronic (not mechanical) principles.
Assisting and Caring for Others	Providing personal assistance, medical attention, emotional support, or other personal care to others such as coworkers, customers, or patients.
Performing General Physical Activities	Performing physical activities that require considerable use of your arms and legs and moving your whole body, such as climbing, lifting, balancing, walking, stooping, and handling of materials.
Handling and Moving Objects	Using hands and arms in handling, installing, positioning, and moving materials, and manipulating things.
Operating Vehicles, Mechanized Devices, or Equipme	Running, maneuvering, navigating, or driving vehicles or mechanized equipment, such as forklifts, passenger vehicles, aircraft, or water craft.
Repairing and Maintaining Mechanical Equipment	Servicing, repairing, adjusting, and testing machines, devices, moving parts, and equipment that operate primarily on the basis of mechanical (not electronic) principles.

Work_Context	**Work_Context Definitions**
Telephone	How often do you have telephone conversations in this job?
Face-to-Face Discussions	How often do you have to have face-to-face discussions with individuals or teams in this job?
Freedom to Make Decisions	How much decision making freedom, without supervision, does the job offer?

Letters and Memos	How often does the job require written letters and memos?
Work With Work Group or Team	How important is it to work with others in a group or team in this job?
Structured versus Unstructured Work	To what extent is this job structured for the worker, rather than allowing the worker to determine tasks, priorities, and goals?
Importance of Being Exact or Accurate	How important is being very exact or highly accurate in performing this job?
Contact With Others	How much does this job require the worker to be in contact with others (face-to-face, by telephone, or otherwise) in order to perform it?
Indoors, Environmentally Controlled	How often does this job require working indoors in environmentally controlled conditions?
Electronic Mail	How often do you use electronic mail in this job?
Frequency of Decision Making	How frequently is the worker required to make decisions that affect other people, the financial resources, and/or the image and reputation of the organization?
Coordinate or Lead Others	How important is it to coordinate or lead others in accomplishing work activities in this job?
Impact of Decisions on Co-workers or Company Resul	How do the decisions an employee makes impact the results of co-workers, clients or the company?
Spend Time Sitting	How much does this job require sitting?
Level of Competition	To what extent does this job require the worker to compete or to be aware of competitive pressures?
Responsibility for Outcomes and Results	How responsible is the worker for work outcomes and results of other workers?
Time Pressure	How often does this job require the worker to meet strict deadlines?
Importance of Repeating Same Tasks	How important is repeating the same physical activities (e.g., key entry) or mental activities (e.g., checking entries in a ledger) over and over, without stopping, to performing this job?
Physical Proximity	To what extent does this job require the worker to perform job tasks in close physical proximity to other people?
Deal With External Customers	How important is it to work with external customers or the public in this job?
Consequence of Error	How serious would the result usually be if the worker made a mistake that was not readily correctable?
In an Enclosed Vehicle or Equipment	How often does this job require working in a closed vehicle or equipment (e.g., car)?
Spend Time Using Your Hands to Handle, Control, or	How much does this job require using your hands to handle, control, or feel objects, tools or controls?
Frequency of Conflict Situations	How often are there conflict situations the employee has to face in this job?
Spend Time Making Repetitive Motions	How much does this job require making repetitive motions?
Outdoors, Exposed to Weather	How often does this job require working outdoors, exposed to all weather conditions?
Sounds, Noise Levels Are Distracting or Uncomforta	How often does this job require working exposed to sounds and noise levels that are distracting or uncomfortable?
Indoors, Not Environmentally Controlled	How often does this job require working indoors in non-controlled environmental conditions (e.g., warehouse without heat)?
Responsible for Others' Health and Safety	How much responsibility is there for the health and safety of others in this job?
Degree of Automation	How automated is the job?
Deal With Unpleasant or Angry People	How frequently does the worker have to deal with unpleasant, angry, or discourteous individuals as part of the job requirements?
Extremely Bright or Inadequate Lighting	How often does this job require working in extremely bright or inadequate lighting conditions?
Wear Common Protective or Safety Equipment such as	How much does this job require wearing common protective or safety equipment such as safety shoes, glasses, gloves, hard hats or life jackets?
Public Speaking	How often do you have to perform public speaking in this job?
Spend Time Standing	How much does this job require standing?
Very Hot or Cold Temperatures	How often does this job require working in very hot (above 90 F degrees) or very cold (below 32 F degrees) temperatures?
Outdoors, Under Cover	How often does this job require working outdoors, under cover (e.g., structure with roof but no walls)?
Exposed to Contaminants	How often does this job require working exposed to contaminants (such as pollutants, gases, dust or odors)?
Spend Time Walking and Running	How much does this job require walking and running?
Exposed to High Places	How often does this job require exposure to high places?
Spend Time Bending or Twisting the Body	How often does this job require bending or twisting your body?
Cramped Work Space.	How often does this job require working in cramped work

Spend Time Kneeling, Crouching, Stooping, or Crawl	How much does this job require kneeling, crouching, stooping, or crawling?
Exposed to Hazardous Equipment	How often does this job require exposure to hazardous equipment?
Spend Time Climbing Ladders, Scaffolds, or Poles	How much does this job require climbing ladders, scaffolds, or poles?
Exposed to Hazardous Conditions	How often does this job require exposure to hazardous conditions?
Pace Determined by Speed of Equipment	How important is it to this job that the pace is determined by the speed of equipment or machinery? (This does not refer to keeping busy at all times on this job.)
Deal With Physically Aggressive People	How frequently does this job require the worker to deal with physical aggression of violent individuals?
Exposed to Disease or Infections	How often does this job require exposure to disease/infections?
Exposed to Minor Burns, Cuts, Bites, or Stings	How often does this job require exposure to minor burns, cuts, bites, or stings?
Spend Time Keeping or Regaining Balance	How much does this job require keeping or regaining your balance?
Wear Specialized Protective or Safety Equipment su	How much does this job require wearing specialized protective or safety equipment such as breathing apparatus, safety harness, full protection suits, or radiation protection?
Exposed to Whole Body Vibration	How often does this job require exposure to whole body vibration (e.g., operate a jackhammer)?
Exposed to Radiation	How often does this job require exposure to radiation?
In an Open Vehicle or Equipment	How often does this job require working in an open vehicle or equipment (e.g., tractor)?

Job Zone Component	Job Zone Component Definitions
Title	Job Zone Five: Extensive Preparation Needed
	Extensive skill, knowledge, and experience are needed for these occupations. Many require more than five years of experience.
Overall Experience	For example, surgeons must complete four years of college and an additional five to seven years of specialized medical training to be able to do their job.
Job Training	Employees may need some on-the-job training, but most of these occupations assume that the person will already have the required skills, knowledge, work-related experience, and/or training.
Job Zone Examples	These occupations often involve coordinating, training, supervising, or managing the activities of others to accomplish goals. Very advanced communication and organizational skills are required. Examples include athletic trainers, lawyers, managing editors, physicists, social psychologists, and surgeons.
SVP Range	(8.0 and above)
Education	A bachelor's degree is the minimum formal education required for these occupations. However, many also require graduate school. For example, they may require a master's degree, and some require a Ph.D., M.D., or J.D. (law degree).

Work_Styles	Work_Styles Definitions
Attention to Detail	Job requires being careful about detail and thorough in completing work tasks.
Dependability	Job requires being reliable, responsible, and dependable, and fulfilling obligations.
Analytical Thinking	Job requires analyzing information and using logic to address work-related issues and problems.
Innovation	Job requires creativity and alternative thinking to develop new ideas for and answers to work-related problems.
Initiative	Job requires a willingness to take on responsibilities and challenges.
Stress Tolerance	Job requires accepting criticism and dealing calmly and effectively with high stress situations.
Integrity	Job requires being honest and ethical.
Cooperation	Job requires being pleasant with others on the job and displaying a good-natured, cooperative attitude.
Leadership	Job requires a willingness to lead, take charge, and offer opinions and direction.
Adaptability/Flexibility	Job requires being open to change (positive or negative) and to considerable variety in the workplace.
Achievement/Effort	Job requires establishing and maintaining personally challenging achievement goals and exerting effort toward mastering tasks.

Persistence	Job requires persistence in the face of obstacles.
Self Control	Job requires maintaining composure, keeping emotions in check, controlling anger, and avoiding aggressive behavior, even in very difficult situations.
Independence	Job requires developing one's own ways of doing things, guiding oneself with little or no supervision, and depending on oneself to get things done.
Concern for Others	Job requires being sensitive to others' needs and feelings and being understanding and helpful on the job.
Social Orientation	Job requires preferring to work with others rather than alone, and being personally connected with others on the job.

17-1012.00 - Landscape Architects

Plan and design land areas for such projects as parks and other recreational facilities, airports, highways, hospitals, schools, land subdivisions, and commercial, industrial, and residential sites.

Tasks

1) Compile and analyze data on conditions, such as location, drainage, and location of structures for environmental reports and landscaping plans.

2) Prepare site plans, specifications, and cost estimates for land development, coordinating arrangement of existing and proposed land features and structures.

3) Confer with clients, engineering personnel, and architects on overall program.

Knowledge	Knowledge Definitions
Design	Knowledge of design techniques, tools, and principles involved in production of precision technical plans, blueprints, drawings, and models.
Building and Construction	Knowledge of materials, methods, and the tools involved in the construction or repair of houses, buildings, or other structures such as highways and roads.
Administration and Management	Knowledge of business and management principles involved in strategic planning, resource allocation, human resources modeling, leadership technique, production methods, and coordination of people and resources.
Engineering and Technology	Knowledge of the practical application of engineering science and technology. This includes applying principles, techniques, procedures, and equipment to the design and production of various goods and services.
Computers and Electronics	Knowledge of circuit boards, processors, chips, electronic equipment, and computer hardware and software, including applications and programming.
Mathematics	Knowledge of arithmetic, algebra, geometry, calculus, statistics, and their applications.
Geography	Knowledge of principles and methods for describing the features of land, sea, and air masses, including their physical characteristics, locations, interrelationships, and distribution of plant, animal, and human life.
English Language	Knowledge of the structure and content of the English language including the meaning and spelling of words, rules of composition, and grammar.
Sales and Marketing	Knowledge of principles and methods for showing, promoting, and selling products or services. This includes marketing strategy and tactics, product demonstration, sales techniques, and sales control systems.
Public Safety and Security	Knowledge of relevant equipment, policies, procedures, and strategies to promote effective local, state, or national security operations for the protection of people, data, property, and institutions.
Law and Government	Knowledge of laws, legal codes, court procedures, precedents, government regulations, executive orders, agency rules, and the democratic political process.
Biology	Knowledge of plant and animal organisms, their tissues, cells, functions, interdependencies, and interactions with each other and the environment.
Fine Arts	Knowledge of the theory and techniques required to compose, produce, and perform works of music, dance, visual arts, drama, and sculpture.
Customer and Personal Service	Knowledge of principles and processes for providing customer and personal services. This includes customer needs assessment, meeting quality standards for services, and evaluation of customer satisfaction.
Clerical	Knowledge of administrative and clerical procedures and systems such as word processing, managing files and records, stenography and transcription, designing forms, and other office procedures and terminology.
Communications and Media	Knowledge of media production, communication, and dissemination techniques and methods. This includes alternative ways to inform and entertain via written, oral, and visual media.
Transportation	Knowledge of principles and methods for moving people or goods by air, rail, sea, or road, including the relative costs and benefits.
Education and Training	Knowledge of principles and methods for curriculum and training design, teaching and instruction for individuals and groups, and the measurement of training effects.
Personnel and Human Resources	Knowledge of principles and procedures for personnel recruitment, selection, training, compensation and benefits, labor relations and negotiation, and personnel information systems.
Physics	Knowledge and prediction of physical principles, laws, their interrelationships, and applications to understanding fluid, material, and atmospheric dynamics, and mechanical, electrical, atomic and sub-atomic structures and processes.
Psychology	Knowledge of human behavior and performance; individual differences in ability, personality, and interests; learning and motivation; psychological research methods; and the assessment and treatment of behavioral and affective disorders.
History and Archeology	Knowledge of historical events and their causes, indicators, and effects on civilizations and cultures.
Production and Processing	Knowledge of raw materials, production processes, quality control, costs, and other techniques for maximizing the effective manufacture and distribution of goods.
Economics and Accounting	Knowledge of economic and accounting principles and practices, the financial markets, banking and the analysis and reporting of financial data.
Telecommunications	Knowledge of transmission, broadcasting, switching, control, and operation of telecommunications systems.
Chemistry	Knowledge of the chemical composition, structure, and properties of substances and of the chemical processes and transformations that they undergo. This includes uses of chemicals and their interactions, danger signs, production techniques, and disposal methods.
Sociology and Anthropology	Knowledge of group behavior and dynamics, societal trends and influences, human migrations, ethnicity, cultures and their history and origins.
Mechanical	Knowledge of machines and tools, including their designs, uses, repair, and maintenance.
Philosophy and Theology	Knowledge of different philosophical systems and religions. This includes their basic principles, values, ethics, ways of thinking, customs, practices, and their impact on human culture.
Therapy and Counseling	Knowledge of principles, methods, and procedures for diagnosis, treatment, and rehabilitation of physical and mental dysfunctions, and for career counseling and guidance.
Foreign Language	Knowledge of the structure and content of a foreign (non-English) language including the meaning and spelling of words, rules of composition and grammar, and pronunciation.
Food Production	Knowledge of techniques and equipment for planting, growing, and harvesting food products (both plant and animal) for consumption, including storage/handling techniques.
Medicine and Dentistry	Knowledge of the information and techniques needed to diagnose and treat human injuries, diseases, and deformities. This includes symptoms, treatment alternatives, drug properties and interactions, and preventive health-care measures.

Skills	Skills Definitions
Time Management	Managing one's own time and the time of others.
Coordination	Adjusting actions in relation to others' actions.
Active Listening	Giving full attention to what other people are saying, taking time to understand the points being made, asking questions as appropriate, and not interrupting at inappropriate times.
Reading Comprehension	Understanding written sentences and paragraphs in work related documents.

Judgment and Decision Making	Considering the relative costs and benefits of potential actions to choose the most appropriate one.
Critical Thinking	Using logic and reasoning to identify the strengths and weaknesses of alternative solutions, conclusions or approaches to problems.
Active Learning	Understanding the implications of new information for both current and future problem-solving and decision-making.
Writing	Communicating effectively in writing as appropriate for the needs of the audience.
Complex Problem Solving	Identifying complex problems and reviewing related information to develop and evaluate options and implement solutions.
Mathematics	Using mathematics to solve problems.
Speaking	Talking to others to convey information effectively.
Operations Analysis	Analyzing needs and product requirements to create a design.
Monitoring	Monitoring/Assessing performance of yourself, other individuals, or organizations to make improvements or take corrective action.
Social Perceptiveness	Being aware of others' reactions and understanding why they react as they do.
Management of Financial Resources	Determining how money will be spent to get the work done, and accounting for these expenditures.
Management of Personnel Resources	Motivating, developing, and directing people as they work, identifying the best people for the job.
Negotiation	Bringing others together and trying to reconcile differences.
Instructing	Teaching others how to do something.
Persuasion	Persuading others to change their minds or behavior.
Service Orientation	Actively looking for ways to help people.
Learning Strategies	Selecting and using training/instructional methods and procedures appropriate for the situation when learning or teaching new things.
Technology Design	Generating or adapting equipment and technology to serve user needs.
Science	Using scientific rules and methods to solve problems.
Equipment Selection	Determining the kind of tools and equipment needed to do a job.
Systems Evaluation	Identifying measures or indicators of system performance and the actions needed to improve or correct performance, relative to the goals of the system.
Troubleshooting	Determining causes of operating errors and deciding what to do about it.
Quality Control Analysis	Conducting tests and inspections of products, services, or processes to evaluate quality or performance.
Management of Material Resources	Obtaining and seeing to the appropriate use of equipment, facilities, and materials needed to do certain work.
Systems Analysis	Determining how a system should work and how changes in conditions, operations, and the environment will affect outcomes.
Equipment Maintenance	Performing routine maintenance on equipment and determining when and what kind of maintenance is needed.
Operation and Control	Controlling operations of equipment or systems.
Repairing	Repairing machines or systems using the needed tools.
Installation	Installing equipment, machines, wiring, or programs to meet specifications.
Programming	Writing computer programs for various purposes.
Operation Monitoring	Watching gauges, dials, or other indicators to make sure a machine is working properly.

Ability	Ability Definitions
Written Expression	The ability to communicate information and ideas in writing so others will understand.
Oral Comprehension	The ability to listen to and understand information and ideas presented through spoken words and sentences.
Oral Expression	The ability to communicate information and ideas in speaking so others will understand.
Originality	The ability to come up with unusual or clever ideas about a given topic or situation, or to develop creative ways to solve a problem.
Fluency of Ideas	The ability to come up with a number of ideas about a topic (the number of ideas is important, not their quality, correctness, or creativity).
Information Ordering	The ability to arrange things or actions in a certain order or pattern according to a specific rule or set of rules (e.g., patterns of numbers, letters, words, pictures, mathematical operations).
Visualization	The ability to imagine how something will look after it is moved around or when its parts are moved or rearranged.

Written Comprehension	The ability to read and understand information and ideas presented in writing.
Problem Sensitivity	The ability to tell when something is wrong or is likely to go wrong. It does not involve solving the problem, only recognizing there is a problem.
Deductive Reasoning	The ability to apply general rules to specific problems to produce answers that make sense.
Speech Clarity	The ability to speak clearly so others can understand you.
Inductive Reasoning	The ability to combine pieces of information to form general rules or conclusions (includes finding a relationship among seemingly unrelated events).
Near Vision	The ability to see details at close range (within a few feet of the observer).
Speech Recognition	The ability to identify and understand the speech of another person.
Category Flexibility	The ability to generate or use different sets of rules for combining or grouping things in different ways.
Far Vision	The ability to see details at a distance.
Mathematical Reasoning	The ability to choose the right mathematical methods or formulas to solve a problem.
Perceptual Speed	The ability to quickly and accurately compare similarities and differences among sets of letters, numbers, objects, pictures, or patterns. The things to be compared may be presented at the same time or one after the other. This ability also includes comparing a presented object with a remembered object.
Selective Attention	The ability to concentrate on a task over a period of time without being distracted.
Flexibility of Closure	The ability to identify or detect a known pattern (a figure, object, word, or sound) that is hidden in other distracting material.
Time Sharing	The ability to shift back and forth between two or more activities or sources of information (such as speech, sounds, touch, or other sources).
Depth Perception	The ability to judge which of several objects is closer or farther away from you, or to judge the distance between you and an object.
Visual Color Discrimination	The ability to match or detect differences between colors, including shades of color and brightness.
Number Facility	The ability to add, subtract, multiply, or divide quickly and correctly.
Speed of Closure	The ability to quickly make sense of, combine, and organize information into meaningful patterns.
Finger Dexterity	The ability to make precisely coordinated movements of the fingers of one or both hands to grasp, manipulate, or assemble very small objects.
Memorization	The ability to remember information such as words, numbers, pictures, and procedures.
Auditory Attention	The ability to focus on a single source of sound in the presence of other distracting sounds.
Multilimb Coordination	The ability to coordinate two or more limbs (for example, two arms, two legs, or one leg and one arm) while sitting, standing, or lying down. It does not involve performing the activities while the whole body is in motion.
Control Precision	The ability to quickly and repeatedly adjust the controls of a machine or a vehicle to exact positions.
Arm-Hand Steadiness	The ability to keep your hand and arm steady while moving your arm or while holding your arm and hand in one position.
Manual Dexterity	The ability to quickly move your hand, your hand together with your arm, or your two hands to grasp, manipulate, or assemble objects.
Hearing Sensitivity	The ability to detect or tell the differences between sounds that vary in pitch and loudness.
Glare Sensitivity	The ability to see objects in the presence of glare or bright lighting.
Reaction Time	The ability to quickly respond (with the hand, finger, or foot) to a signal (sound, light, picture) when it appears.
Gross Body Equilibrium	The ability to keep or regain your body balance or stay upright when in an unstable position.
Spatial Orientation	The ability to know your location in relation to the environment or to know where other objects are in relation to you.
Extent Flexibility	The ability to bend, stretch, twist, or reach with your body, arms, and/or legs.
Gross Body Coordination	The ability to coordinate the movement of your arms, legs, and torso together when the whole body is in motion.
Trunk Strength	The ability to use your abdominal and lower back muscles to support part of the body repeatedly or continuously over time without 'giving out' or fatiguing.

Wrist-Finger Speed	The ability to make fast, simple, repeated movements of the fingers, hands, and wrists.
Dynamic Flexibility	The ability to quickly and repeatedly bend, stretch, twist, or reach out with your body, arms, and/or legs.
Peripheral Vision	The ability to see objects or movement of objects to one's side when the eyes are looking ahead.
Stamina	The ability to exert yourself physically over long periods of time without getting winded or out of breath.
Static Strength	The ability to exert maximum muscle force to lift, push, pull, or carry objects.
Speed of Limb Movement	The ability to quickly move the arms and legs.
Night Vision	The ability to see under low light conditions.
Rate Control	The ability to time your movements or the movement of a piece of equipment in anticipation of changes in the speed and/or direction of a moving object or scene.
Dynamic Strength	The ability to exert muscle force repeatedly or continuously over time. This involves muscular endurance and resistance to muscle fatigue.
Sound Localization	The ability to tell the direction from which a sound originated.
Explosive Strength	The ability to use short bursts of muscle force to propel oneself (as in jumping or sprinting), or to throw an object.
Response Orientation	The ability to choose quickly between two or more movements in response to two or more different signals (lights, sounds, pictures). It includes the speed with which the correct response is started with the hand, foot, or other body part.

Work_Activity	**Work_Activity Definitions**
Thinking Creatively	Developing, designing, or creating new applications, ideas, relationships, systems, or products, including artistic contributions.
Making Decisions and Solving Problems	Analyzing information and evaluating results to choose the best solution and solve problems.
Drafting, Laying Out, and Specifying Technical Dev	Providing documentation, detailed instructions, drawings, or specifications to tell others about how devices, parts, equipment, or structures are to be fabricated, constructed, assembled, modified, maintained, or used.
Getting Information	Observing, receiving, and otherwise obtaining information from all relevant sources.
Communicating with Persons Outside Organization	Communicating with people outside the organization, representing the organization to customers, the public, government, and other external sources. This information can be exchanged in person, in writing, or by telephone or e-mail.
Communicating with Supervisors, Peers, or Subordin	Providing information to supervisors, co-workers, and subordinates by telephone, in written form, e-mail, or in person.
Identifying Objects, Actions, and Events	Identifying information by categorizing, estimating, recognizing differences or similarities, and detecting changes in circumstances or events.
Organizing, Planning, and Prioritizing Work	Developing specific goals and plans to prioritize, organize, and accomplish your work.
Establishing and Maintaining Interpersonal Relatio	Developing constructive and cooperative working relationships with others, and maintaining them over time.
Performing for or Working Directly with the Public	Performing for people or dealing directly with the public. This includes serving customers in restaurants and stores, and receiving clients or guests.
Evaluating Information to Determine Compliance wit	Using relevant information and individual judgment to determine whether events or processes comply with laws, regulations, or standards.
Updating and Using Relevant Knowledge	Keeping up-to-date technically and applying new knowledge to your job.
Scheduling Work and Activities	Scheduling events, programs, and activities, as well as the work of others.
Coordinating the Work and Activities of Others	Getting members of a group to work together to accomplish tasks.
Interacting With Computers	Using computers and computer systems (including hardware and software) to program, write software, set up functions, enter data, or process information.
Provide Consultation and Advice to Others	Providing guidance and expert advice to management or other groups on technical, systems-, or process-related topics.
Inspecting Equipment, Structures, or Material	Inspecting equipment, structures, or materials to identify the cause of errors or other problems or defects.
Developing and Building Teams	Encouraging and building mutual trust, respect, and cooperation among team members.
Monitor Processes, Materials, or Surroundings	Monitoring and reviewing information from materials, events, or the environment, to detect or assess problems.

Analyzing Data or Information	Identifying the underlying principles, reasons, or facts of information by breaking down information or data into separate parts.
Judging the Qualities of Things, Services, or Peop	Assessing the value, importance, or quality of things or people.
Resolving Conflicts and Negotiating with Others	Handling complaints, settling disputes, and resolving grievances and conflicts, or otherwise negotiating with others.
Developing Objectives and Strategies	Establishing long-range objectives and specifying the strategies and actions to achieve them.
Processing Information	Compiling, coding, categorizing, calculating, tabulating, auditing, or verifying information or data.
Training and Teaching Others	Identifying the educational needs of others, developing formal educational or training programs or classes, and teaching or instructing others.
Guiding, Directing, and Motivating Subordinates	Providing guidance and direction to subordinates, including setting performance standards and monitoring performance.
Estimating the Quantifiable Characteristics of Pro	Estimating sizes, distances, and quantities; or determining time, costs, resources, or materials needed to perform a work activity.
Performing Administrative Activities	Performing day-to-day administrative tasks such as maintaining information files and processing paperwork.
Interpreting the Meaning of Information for Others	Translating or explaining what information means and how it can be used.
Selling or Influencing Others	Convincing others to buy merchandise/goods or to otherwise change their minds or actions.
Documenting/Recording Information	Entering, transcribing, recording, storing, or maintaining information in written or electronic/magnetic form.
Monitoring and Controlling Resources	Monitoring and controlling resources and overseeing the spending of money.
Coaching and Developing Others	Identifying the developmental needs of others and coaching, mentoring, or otherwise helping others to improve their knowledge or skills.
Staffing Organizational Units	Recruiting, interviewing, selecting, hiring, and promoting employees in an organization.
Handling and Moving Objects	Using hands and arms in handling, installing, positioning, and moving materials, and manipulating things.
Operating Vehicles, Mechanized Devices, or Equipme	Running, maneuvering, navigating, or driving vehicles or mechanized equipment, such as forklifts, passenger vehicles, aircraft, or water craft.
Assisting and Caring for Others	Providing personal assistance, medical attention, emotional support, or other personal care to others such as coworkers, customers, or patients.
Repairing and Maintaining Mechanical Equipment	Servicing, repairing, adjusting, and testing machines, devices, moving parts, and equipment that operate primarily on the basis of mechanical (not electronic) principles.
Repairing and Maintaining Electronic Equipment	Servicing, repairing, calibrating, regulating, fine-tuning, or testing machines, devices, and equipment that operate primarily on the basis of electrical or electronic (not mechanical) principles.
Performing General Physical Activities	Performing physical activities that require considerable use of your arms and legs and moving your whole body, such as climbing, lifting, balancing, walking, stooping, and handling of materials.
Controlling Machines and Processes	Using either control mechanisms or direct physical activity to operate machines or processes (not including computers or vehicles).

Work_Context	**Work_Context Definitions**
Telephone	How often do you have telephone conversations in this job?
Face-to-Face Discussions	How often do you have to have face-to-face discussions with individuals or teams in this job?
Contact With Others	How much does this job require the worker to be in contact with others (face-to-face, by telephone, or otherwise) in order to perform it?
Importance of Being Exact or Accurate	How important is being very exact or highly accurate in performing this job?
Indoors, Environmentally Controlled	How often does this job require working indoors in environmentally controlled conditions?
Letters and Memos	How often does the job require written letters and memos?
Coordinate or Lead Others	How important is it to coordinate or lead others in accomplishing work activities in this job?
Structured versus Unstructured Work	To what extent is this job structured for the worker, rather than allowing the worker to determine tasks, priorities, and goals?
Freedom to Make Decisions	How much decision making freedom, without supervision, does the job offer?
Time Pressure	How often does this job require the worker to meet strict deadlines?

Frequency of Decision Making	How frequently is the worker required to make decisions that affect other people. the financial resources. and/or the image and reputation of the organization?	Spend Time Keeping or Regaining Balance	How much does this job require keeping or regaining your balance?
Responsibility for Outcomes and Results	How responsible is the worker for work outcomes and results of other workers?	Spend Time Climbing Ladders. Scaffolds. or Poles	How much does this job require climbing ladders. scaffolds. or poles?
Deal With External Customers	How important is it to work with external customers or the public in this job?	In an Open Vehicle or Equipment	How often does this job require working in an open vehicle or equipment (e.g.. tractor)?
Electronic Mail	How often do you use electronic mail in this job?	Deal With Physically Aggressive People	How frequently does this job require the worker to deal with physical aggression of violent individuals?
Impact of Decisions on Co-workers or Company Resul	How do the decisions an employee makes impact the results of co-workers. clients or the company?	Pace Determined by Speed of Equipment	How important is it to this job that the pace is determined by the speed of equipment or machinery? (This does not refer to keeping busy at all times on this job.)
Level of Competition	To what extent does this job require the worker to compete or to be aware of competitive pressures?	Exposed to Whole Body Vibration	How often does this job require exposure to whole body vibration (e.g.. operate a jackhammer)?
Work With Work Group or Team	How important is it to work with others in a group or team in this job?	Exposed to Disease or Infections	How often does this job require exposure to disease/infections?
In an Enclosed Vehicle or Equipment	How often does this job require working in a closed vehicle or equipment (e.g.. car)?	Exposed to Radiation	How often does this job require exposure to radiation?
Consequence of Error	How serious would the result usually be if the worker made a mistake that was not readily correctable?		
Outdoors, Exposed to Weather	How often does this job require working outdoors. exposed to all weather conditions?		

Responsible for Others' Health and Safety	How much responsibility is there for the health and safety of others in this job?	**Job Zone Component**	**Job Zone Component Definitions**
Spend Time Sitting	How much does this job require sitting?	Title	Job Zone Four: Considerable Preparation Needed
Frequency of Conflict Situations	How often are there conflict situations the employee has to face in this job?		A minimum of two to four years of work-related skill, knowledge. or experience is needed for these occupations. For example. an accountant must complete four years of college
Physical Proximity	To what extent does this job require the worker to perform job tasks in close physical proximity to other people?	Overall Experience	and work for several years in accounting to be considered qualified.
Indoors, Not Environmentally Controlled	How often does this job require working indoors in non-controlled environmental conditions (e.g.. warehouse without heat)?	Job Training	Employees in these occupations usually need several years of work-related experience. on-the-job training. and/or vocational training.
Very Hot or Cold Temperatures	How often does this job require working in very hot (above 90 F degrees) or very cold (below 32 F degrees) temperatures?	Job Zone Examples	Many of these occupations involve coordinating, supervising, managing, or training others. Examples include accountants, chefs and head cooks. computer programmers, historians, pharmacists, and police detectives.
Deal With Unpleasant or Angry People	How frequently does the worker have to deal with unpleasant, angry. or discourteous individuals as part of the job requirements?	SVP Range	(7.0 to < 8.0)
Exposed to Hazardous Equipment	How often does this job require exposure to hazardous equipment?	Education	Most of these occupations require a four - year bachelor's degree, but some do not.
Exposed to Minor Burns, Cuts, Bites, or Stings	How often does this job require exposure to minor burns, cuts, bites, or stings?		
Sounds, Noise Levels Are Distracting or Uncomforta	How often does this job require working exposed to sounds and noise levels that are distracting or uncomfortable?	**Work_Styles**	**Work_Styles Definitions**
Importance of Repeating Same Tasks	How important is repeating the same physical activities (e.g., key entry) or mental activities (e.g., checking entries in a ledger) over and over, without stopping, to performing this job?	Attention to Detail	Job requires being careful about detail and thorough in completing work tasks.
Exposed to Hazardous Conditions	How often does this job require exposure to hazardous conditions?	Dependability	Job requires being reliable, responsible, and dependable, and fulfilling obligations.
Outdoors, Under Cover	How often does this job require working outdoors, under cover (e.g., structure with roof but no walls)?	Stress Tolerance	Job requires accepting criticism and dealing calmly and effectively with high stress situations.
Extremely Bright or Inadequate Lighting	How often does this job require working in extremely bright or inadequate lighting conditions?	Innovation	Job requires creativity and alternative thinking to develop new ideas for and answers to work-related problems.
Exposed to High Places	How often does this job require exposure to high places?	Independence	Job requires developing one's own ways of doing things, guiding oneself with little or no supervision, and depending on oneself to get things done.
Spend Time Using Your Hands to Handle, Control, or	How much does this job require using your hands to handle, control, or feel objects, tools or controls?	Leadership	Job requires a willingness to lead, take charge, and offer opinions and direction.
Spend Time Standing	How much does this job require standing?	Persistence	Job requires persistence in the face of obstacles.
Public Speaking	How often do you have to perform public speaking in this job?	Analytical Thinking	Job requires analyzing information and using logic to address work-related issues and problems.
Spend Time Making Repetitive Motions	How much does this job require making repetitive motions?	Integrity	Job requires being honest and ethical.
Cramped Work Space, Awkward Positions	How often does this job require working in cramped work spaces that requires getting into awkward positions?	Cooperation	Job requires being pleasant with others on the job and displaying a good-natured, cooperative attitude.
Wear Common Protective or Safety Equipment such as	How much does this job require wearing common protective or safety equipment such as safety shoes, glasses, gloves, hard hats or live jackets?	Adaptability/Flexibility	Job requires being open to change (positive or negative) and to considerable variety in the workplace.
Spend Time Walking and Running	How much does this job require walking and running?	Initiative	Job requires a willingness to take on responsibilities and challenges.
Exposed to Contaminants	How often does this job require working exposed to contaminants (such as pollutants, gases, dust or odors)?	Achievement/Effort	Job requires establishing and maintaining personally challenging achievement goals and exerting effort toward mastering tasks.
Degree of Automation	How automated is the job?	Self Control	Job requires maintaining composure, keeping emotions in check, controlling anger, and avoiding aggressive behavior. even in very difficult situations.
Wear Specialized Protective or Safety Equipment su	How much does this job require wearing specialized protective or safety equipment such as breathing apparatus, safety harness, full protection suits, or radiation protection?	Social Orientation	Job requires preferring to work with others rather than alone, and being personally connected with others on the job.
Spend Time Bending or Twisting the Body	How much does this job require bending or twisting your body?	Concern for Others	Job requires being sensitive to others' needs and feelings and being understanding and helpful on the job.
Spend Time Kneeling, Crouching, Stooping, or Crawl	How much does this job require kneeling, crouching, stooping or crawling?		

17-1021.00 - Cartographers and Photogrammetrists

Collect, analyze, and interpret geographic information provided by geodetic surveys, aerial photographs, and satellite data. Research, study, and prepare maps and other spatial data in digital or graphic form for legal, social, political, educational, and design purposes. May work with Geographic Information Systems (GIS). May design and evaluate algorithms, data structures, and user interfaces for GIS and mapping systems.

Tasks

1) Compile data required for map preparation, including aerial photographs, survey notes, records, reports, and original maps.

2) Inspect final compositions in order to ensure completeness and accuracy.

3) Examine and analyze data from ground surveys, reports, aerial photographs, and satellite images in order to prepare topographic maps, aerial-photograph mosaics, and related charts.

4) Determine map content and layout, as well as production specifications such as scale, size, projection, and colors, and direct production in order to ensure that specifications are followed.

5) Identify, scale, and orient geodetic points, elevations, and other planimetric or topographic features, applying standard mathematical formulas.

6) Collect information about specific features of the Earth, using aerial photography and other digital remote sensing techniques.

7) Select aerial photographic and remote sensing techniques and plotting equipment needed to meet required standards of accuracy.

8) Delineate aerial photographic detail, such as control points, hydrography, topography, and cultural features, using precision stereoplotting apparatus or drafting instruments.

9) Build and update digital databases.

10) Prepare and alter trace maps, charts, tables, detailed drawings, and three-dimensional optical models of terrain, using stereoscopic plotting and computer graphics equipment.

11) Determine guidelines that specify which source material is acceptable for use.

12) Study legal records in order to establish boundaries of local, national, and international properties.

13) Travel over photographed areas in order to observe, identify, record, and verify all relevant features.

Knowledge	Knowledge Definitions
Geography	Knowledge of principles and methods for describing the features of land, sea, and air masses, including their physical characteristics, locations, interrelationships, and distribution of plant, animal, and human life.
Computers and Electronics	Knowledge of circuit boards, processors, chips, electronic equipment, and computer hardware and software, including applications and programming.
Engineering and Technology	Knowledge of the practical application of engineering science and technology. This includes applying principles, techniques, procedures, and equipment to the design and production of various goods and services.
Mathematics	Knowledge of arithmetic, algebra, geometry, calculus, statistics, and their applications.
Design	Knowledge of design techniques, tools, and principles involved in production of precision technical plans, blueprints, drawings, and models.
Production and Processing	Knowledge of raw materials, production processes, quality control, costs, and other techniques for maximizing the effective manufacture and distribution of goods.
Customer and Personal Service	Knowledge of principles and processes for providing customer and personal services. This includes customer needs assessment, meeting quality standards for services, and evaluation of customer satisfaction.
Administration and Management	Knowledge of business and management principles involved in strategic planning, resource allocation, human resources modeling, leadership technique, production methods, and coordination of people and resources.
English Language	Knowledge of the structure and content of the English language including the meaning and spelling of words, rules of composition, and grammar.
Clerical	Knowledge of administrative and clerical procedures and systems such as word processing, managing files and records, stenography and transcription, designing forms, and other office procedures and terminology.
Education and Training	Knowledge of principles and methods for curriculum and training design, teaching and instruction for individuals and groups, and the measurement of training effects.
Personnel and Human Resources	Knowledge of principles and procedures for personnel recruitment, selection, training, compensation and benefits, labor relations and negotiation, and personnel information systems.
Sales and Marketing	Knowledge of principles and methods for showing, promoting, and selling products or services. This includes marketing strategy and tactics, product demonstration, sales techniques, and sales control systems.
Mechanical	Knowledge of machines and tools, including their designs, uses, repair, and maintenance.
Communications and Media	Knowledge of media production, communication, and dissemination techniques and methods. This includes alternative ways to inform and entertain via written, oral, and visual media.
Law and Government	Knowledge of laws, legal codes, court procedures, precedents, government regulations, executive orders, agency rules, and the democratic political process.
Transportation	Knowledge of principles and methods for moving people or goods by air, rail, sea, or road, including the relative costs and benefits.
Physics	Knowledge and prediction of physical principles, laws, their interrelationships, and applications to understanding fluid, material, and atmospheric dynamics, and mechanical, electrical, atomic and sub- atomic structures and processes.
Public Safety and Security	Knowledge of relevant equipment, policies, procedures, and strategies to promote effective local, state, or national security operations for the protection of people, data, property, and institutions.
History and Archeology	Knowledge of historical events and their causes, indicators, and effects on civilizations and cultures.
Telecommunications	Knowledge of transmission, broadcasting, switching, control, and operation of telecommunications systems.
Economics and Accounting	Knowledge of economic and accounting principles and practices, the financial markets, banking and the analysis and reporting of financial data.
Building and Construction	Knowledge of materials, methods, and the tools involved in the construction or repair of houses, buildings, or other structures such as highways and roads.
Chemistry	Knowledge of the chemical composition, structure, and properties of substances and of the chemical processes and transformations that they undergo. This includes uses of chemicals and their interactions, danger signs, production techniques, and disposal methods.
Psychology	Knowledge of human behavior and performance; individual differences in ability, personality, and interests; learning and motivation; psychological research methods; and the assessment and treatment of behavioral and affective disorders.
Biology	Knowledge of plant and animal organisms, their tissues, cells, functions, interdependencies, and interactions with each other and the environment.
Sociology and Anthropology	Knowledge of group behavior and dynamics, societal trends and influences, human migrations, ethnicity, cultures and their history and origins.
Fine Arts	Knowledge of the theory and techniques required to compose, produce, and perform works of music, dance, visual arts, drama, and sculpture.
Foreign Language	Knowledge of the structure and content of a foreign (non-English) language including the meaning and spelling of words, rules of composition and grammar, and pronunciation.
Philosophy and Theology	Knowledge of different philosophical systems and religions. This includes their basic principles, values, ethics, ways of thinking, customs, practices, and their impact on human culture.
Therapy and Counseling	Knowledge of principles, methods, and procedures for diagnosis, treatment, and rehabilitation of physical and mental dysfunctions, and for career counseling and guidance.
Medicine and Dentistry	Knowledge of the information and techniques needed to diagnose and treat human injuries, diseases, and deformities. This includes symptoms, treatment alternatives, drug properties and interactions, and preventive health-care measures.
Food Production	Knowledge of techniques and equipment for planting, growing, and harvesting food products (both plant and animal) for consumption, including storage/handling techniques.

Skills	Skills Definitions
Active Learning	Understanding the implications of new information for both current and future problem-solving and decision-making.
Reading Comprehension	Understanding written sentences and paragraphs in work related documents.
Writing	Communicating effectively in writing as appropriate for the needs of the audience.
Critical Thinking	Using logic and reasoning to identify the strengths and weaknesses of alternative solutions, conclusions or approaches to problems.
Mathematics	Using mathematics to solve problems.
Troubleshooting	Determining causes of operating errors and deciding what to do about it.
Technology Design	Generating or adapting equipment and technology to serve user needs.
Active Listening	Giving full attention to what other people are saying, taking time to understand the points being made, asking questions as appropriate, and not interrupting at inappropriate times.
Complex Problem Solving	Identifying complex problems and reviewing related information to develop and evaluate options and implement solutions.
Learning Strategies	Selecting and using training/instructional methods and procedures appropriate for the situation when learning or teaching new things.
Science	Using scientific rules and methods to solve problems.
Speaking	Talking to others to convey information effectively.
Quality Control Analysis	Conducting tests and inspections of products, services, or processes to evaluate quality or performance.
Service Orientation	Actively looking for ways to help people.
Time Management	Managing one's own time and the time of others.
Negotiation	Bringing others together and trying to reconcile differences.
Monitoring	Monitoring/Assessing performance of yourself, other individuals, or organizations to make improvements or take corrective action.
Equipment Selection	Determining the kind of tools and equipment needed to do a job.
Operation and Control	Controlling operations of equipment or systems.
Coordination	Adjusting actions in relation to others' actions.
Social Perceptiveness	Being aware of others' reactions and understanding why they react as they do.
Equipment Maintenance	Performing routine maintenance on equipment and determining when and what kind of maintenance is needed.
Instructing	Teaching others how to do something.
Persuasion	Persuading others to change their minds or behavior.
Judgment and Decision Making	Considering the relative costs and benefits of potential actions to choose the most appropriate one.
Repairing	Repairing machines or systems using the needed tools.
Operations Analysis	Analyzing needs and product requirements to create a design.
Operation Monitoring	Watching gauges, dials, or other indicators to make sure a machine is working properly.
Systems Evaluation	Identifying measures or indicators of system performance and the actions needed to improve or correct performance, relative to the goals of the system.
Systems Analysis	Determining how a system should work and how changes in conditions, operations, and the environment will affect outcomes.
Management of Personnel Resources	Motivating, developing, and directing people as they work, identifying the best people for the job.
Installation	Installing equipment, machines, wiring, or programs to meet specifications.
Management of Material Resources	Obtaining and seeing to the appropriate use of equipment, facilities, and materials needed to do certain work.
Programming	Writing computer programs for various purposes.
Management of Financial Resources	Determining how money will be spent to get the work done, and accounting for these expenditures.

Ability	Ability Definitions
Near Vision	The ability to see details at close range (within a few feet of the observer).
Problem Sensitivity	The ability to tell when something is wrong or is likely to go wrong. It does not involve solving the problem, only recognizing there is a problem.
Information Ordering	The ability to arrange things or actions in a certain order or pattern according to a specific rule or set of rules (e.g., patterns of numbers, letters, words, pictures, mathematical operations).

Inductive Reasoning	The ability to combine pieces of information to form general rules or conclusions (includes finding a relationship among seemingly unrelated events).
Written Comprehension	The ability to read and understand information and ideas presented in writing.
Mathematical Reasoning	The ability to choose the right mathematical methods or formulas to solve a problem.
Deductive Reasoning	The ability to apply general rules to specific problems to produce answers that make sense.
Category Flexibility	The ability to generate or use different sets of rules for combining or grouping things in different ways.
Flexibility of Closure	The ability to identify or detect a known pattern (a figure, object, word, or sound) that is hidden in other distracting material.
Selective Attention	The ability to concentrate on a task over a period of time without being distracted.
Oral Comprehension	The ability to listen to and understand information and ideas presented through spoken words and sentences.
Number Facility	The ability to add, subtract, multiply, or divide quickly and correctly.
Visual Color Discrimination	The ability to match or detect differences between colors, including shades of color and brightness.
Perceptual Speed	The ability to quickly and accurately compare similarities and differences among sets of letters, numbers, objects, pictures, or patterns. The things to be compared may be presented at the same time or one after the other. This ability also includes comparing a presented object with a remembered object.
Speech Recognition	The ability to identify and understand the speech of another person.
Oral Expression	The ability to communicate information and ideas in speaking so others will understand.
Written Expression	The ability to communicate information and ideas in writing so others will understand.
Speech Clarity	The ability to speak clearly so others can understand you.
Visualization	The ability to imagine how something will look after it is moved around or when its parts are moved or rearranged.
Speed of Closure	The ability to quickly make sense of, combine, and organize information into meaningful patterns.
Far Vision	The ability to see details at a distance.
Finger Dexterity	The ability to make precisely coordinated movements of the fingers of one or both hands to grasp, manipulate, or assemble very small objects.
Originality	The ability to come up with unusual or clever ideas about a given topic or situation, or to develop creative ways to solve a problem.
Arm-Hand Steadiness	The ability to keep your hand and arm steady while moving your arm or while holding your arm and hand in one position.
Fluency of Ideas	The ability to come up with a number of ideas about a topic (the number of ideas is important, not their quality, correctness, or creativity).
Memorization	The ability to remember information such as words, numbers, pictures, and procedures.
Manual Dexterity	The ability to quickly move your hand, your hand together with your arm, or your two hands to grasp, manipulate, or assemble objects.
Depth Perception	The ability to judge which of several objects is closer or farther away from you, or to judge the distance between you and an object.
Control Precision	The ability to quickly and repeatedly adjust the controls of a machine or a vehicle to exact positions.
Time Sharing	The ability to shift back and forth between two or more activities or sources of information (such as speech, sounds, touch, or other sources).
Hearing Sensitivity	The ability to detect or tell the differences between sounds that vary in pitch and loudness.
Spatial Orientation	The ability to know your location in relation to the environment or to know where other objects are in relation to you.
Auditory Attention	The ability to focus on a single source of sound in the presence of other distracting sounds.
Glare Sensitivity	The ability to see objects in the presence of glare or bright lighting.
Trunk Strength	The ability to use your abdominal and lower back muscles to support part of the body repeatedly or continuously over time without 'giving out' or fatiguing.
Wrist-Finger Speed	The ability to make fast, simple, repeated movements of the fingers, hands, and wrists.
Explosive Strength	The ability to use short bursts of muscle force to propel oneself (as in jumping or sprinting), or to throw an object.

Speed of Limb Movement	The ability to quickly move the arms and legs.
Stamina	The ability to exert yourself physically over long periods of time without getting winded or out of breath.
Extent Flexibility	The ability to bend, stretch, twist, or reach with your body, arms, and/or legs.
Gross Body Coordination	The ability to coordinate the movement of your arms, legs, and torso together when the whole body is in motion.
Static Strength	The ability to exert maximum muscle force to lift, push, pull, or carry objects.
Night Vision	The ability to see under low light conditions.
Peripheral Vision	The ability to see objects or movement of objects to one's side when the eyes are looking ahead.
Gross Body Equilibrium	The ability to keep or regain your body balance or stay upright when in an unstable position.
Rate Control	The ability to time your movements or the movement of a piece of equipment in anticipation of changes in the speed and/or direction of a moving object or scene.
Dynamic Flexibility	The ability to quickly and repeatedly bend, stretch, twist, or reach out with your body, arms, and/or legs.
Response Orientation	The ability to choose quickly between two or more movements in response to two or more different signals (lights, sounds, pictures). It includes the speed with which the correct response is started with the hand, foot, or other body part.
Dynamic Strength	The ability to exert muscle force repeatedly or continuously over time. This involves muscular endurance and resistance to muscle fatigue.
Sound Localization	The ability to tell the direction from which a sound originated.
Multilimb Coordination	The ability to coordinate two or more limbs (for example, two arms, two legs, or one leg and one arm) while sitting, standing, or lying down. It does not involve performing the activities while the whole body is in motion.
Reaction Time	The ability to quickly respond (with the hand, finger, or foot) to a signal (sound, light, picture) when it appears.

Work_Activity	**Work_Activity Definitions**
Interacting With Computers	Using computers and computer systems (including hardware and software) to program, write software, set up functions, enter data, or process information.
Processing Information	Compiling, coding, categorizing, calculating, tabulating, auditing, or verifying information or data.
Getting Information	Observing, receiving, and otherwise obtaining information from all relevant sources.
Documenting/Recording Information	Entering, transcribing, recording, storing, or maintaining information in written or electronic/magnetic form.
Updating and Using Relevant Knowledge	Keeping up-to-date technically and applying new knowledge to your job.
Communicating with Supervisors, Peers, or Subordin	Providing information to supervisors, co-workers, and subordinates by telephone, in written form, e-mail, or in person.
Evaluating Information to Determine Compliance wit	Using relevant information and individual judgment to determine whether events or processes comply with laws, regulations, or standards.
Analyzing Data or Information	Identifying the underlying principles, reasons, or facts of information by breaking down information or data into separate parts.
Making Decisions and Solving Problems	Analyzing information and evaluating results to choose the best solution and solve problems.
Identifying Objects, Actions, and Events	Identifying information by categorizing, estimating, recognizing differences or similarities, and detecting changes in circumstances or events.
Organizing, Planning, and Prioritizing Work	Developing specific goals and plans to prioritize, organize, and accomplish your work.
Estimating the Quantifiable Characteristics of Pro	Estimating sizes, distances, and quantities; or determining time, costs, resources, or materials needed to perform a work activity.
Establishing and Maintaining Interpersonal Relatio	Developing constructive and cooperative working relationships with others, and maintaining them over time.
Interpreting the Meaning of Information for Others	Translating or explaining what information means and how it can be used.
Thinking Creatively	Developing, designing, or creating new applications, ideas, relationships, systems, or products, including artistic contributions.
Monitor Processes, Materials, or Surroundings	Monitoring and reviewing information from materials, events, or the environment, to detect or assess problems.

Scheduling Work and Activities	Scheduling events, programs, and activities, as well as the work of others.
Communicating with Persons Outside Organization	Communicating with people outside the organization, representing the organization to customers, the public, government, and other external sources. This information can be exchanged in person, in writing, or by telephone or e-mail.
Training and Teaching Others	Identifying the educational needs of others, developing formal educational or training programs or classes, and teaching or instructing others.
Drafting, Laying Out, and Specifying Technical Dev	Providing documentation, detailed instructions, drawings, or specifications to tell others about how devices, parts, equipment, or structures are to be fabricated, constructed, assembled, modified, maintained, or used.
Coordinating the Work and Activities of Others	Getting members of a group to work together to accomplish tasks.
Judging the Qualities of Things, Services, or Peop	Assessing the value, importance, or quality of things or people.
Developing and Building Teams	Encouraging and building mutual trust, respect, and cooperation among team members.
Developing Objectives and Strategies	Establishing long-range objectives and specifying the strategies and actions to achieve them.
Performing Administrative Activities	Performing day-to-day administrative tasks such as maintaining information files and processing paperwork.
Coaching and Developing Others	Identifying the developmental needs of others and coaching, mentoring, or otherwise helping others to improve their knowledge or skills.
Repairing and Maintaining Electronic Equipment	Servicing, repairing, calibrating, regulating, fine-tuning, or testing machines, devices, and equipment that operate primarily on the basis of electrical or electronic (not mechanical) principles.
Provide Consultation and Advice to Others	Providing guidance and expert advice to management or other groups on technical, systems-, or process-related topics.
Inspecting Equipment, Structures, or Material	Inspecting equipment, structures, or materials to identify the cause of errors or other problems or defects.
Guiding, Directing, and Motivating Subordinates	Providing guidance and direction to subordinates, including setting performance standards and monitoring performance.
Resolving Conflicts and Negotiating with Others	Handling complaints, settling disputes, and resolving grievances and conflicts, or otherwise negotiating with others.
Monitoring and Controlling Resources	Monitoring and controlling resources and overseeing the spending of money.
Controlling Machines and Processes	Using either control mechanisms or direct physical activity to operate machines or processes (not including computers or vehicles).
Handling and Moving Objects	Using hands and arms in handling, installing, positioning, and moving materials, and manipulating things.
Selling or Influencing Others	Convincing others to buy merchandise/goods or to otherwise change their minds or actions.
Assisting and Caring for Others	Providing personal assistance, medical attention, emotional support, or other personal care to others such as coworkers, customers, or patients.
Operating Vehicles, Mechanized Devices, or Equipme	Running, maneuvering, navigating, or driving vehicles or mechanized equipment, such as forklifts, passenger vehicles, aircraft, or water craft.
Performing General Physical Activities	Performing physical activities that require considerable use of your arms and legs and moving your whole body, such as climbing, lifting, balancing, walking, stooping, and handling of materials.
Staffing Organizational Units	Recruiting, interviewing, selecting, hiring, and promoting employees in an organization.
Performing for or Working Directly with the Public	Performing for people or dealing directly with the public. This includes serving customers in restaurants and stores, and receiving clients or guests.
Repairing and Maintaining Mechanical Equipment	Servicing, repairing, adjusting, and testing machines, devices, moving parts, and equipment that operate primarily on the basis of mechanical (not electronic) principles.

Work_Context	**Work_Context Definitions**
Importance of Being Exact or Accurate	How important is being very exact or highly accurate in performing this job?
Indoors, Environmentally Controlled	How often does this job require working indoors in environmentally controlled conditions?
Freedom to Make Decisions	How much decision making freedom, without supervision, does the job offer?
Spend Time Sitting	How much does this job require sitting?
Importance of Repeating Same Tasks	How important is repeating the same physical activities (e.g., key entry) or mental activities (e.g., checking entries in a ledger) over and over, without stopping, to performing this job?

Electronic Mail	How often do you use electronic mail in this job?
Spend Time Using Your Hands to Handle, Control, or	How much does this job require using your hands to handle, control, or feel objects, tools or controls?
Face-to-Face Discussions	How often do you have to have face-to-face discussions with individuals or teams in this job?
Structured versus Unstructured Work	To what extent is this job structured for the worker, rather than allowing the worker to determine tasks, priorities, and goals?
Telephone	How often do you have telephone conversations in this job?
Work With Work Group or Team	How important is it to work with others in a group or team in this job?
Spend Time Making Repetitive Motions	How much does this job require making repetitive motions?
Impact of Decisions on Co-workers or Company Resul	How do the decisions an employee makes impact the results of co-workers, clients or the company?
Time Pressure	How often does this job require the worker to meet strict deadlines?
Frequency of Decision Making	How frequently is the worker required to make decisions that affect other people, the financial resources, and/or the image and reputation of the organization?
Contact With Others	How much does this job require the worker to be in contact with others (face-to-face, by telephone, or otherwise) in order to perform it?
Coordinate or Lead Others	How important is it to coordinate or lead others in accomplishing work activities in this job?
Responsibility for Outcomes and Results	How responsible is the worker for work outcomes and results of other workers?
Level of Competition	To what extent does this job require the worker to compete or to be aware of competitive pressures?
Degree of Automation	How automated is the job?
Letters and Memos	How often does the job require written letters and memos?
Deal With External Customers	How important is it to work with external customers or the public in this job?
Frequency of Conflict Situations	How often are there conflict situations the employee has to face in this job?
Physical Proximity	To what extent does this job require the worker to perform job tasks in close physical proximity to other people?
Consequence of Error	How serious would the result usually be if the worker made a mistake that was not readily correctable?
Sounds, Noise Levels Are Distracting or Uncomforta	How often does this job require working exposed to sounds and noise levels that are distracting or uncomfortable?
Deal With Unpleasant or Angry People	How frequently does the worker have to deal with unpleasant, angry, or discourteous individuals as part of the job requirements?
Public Speaking	How often do you have to perform public speaking in this job?
Pace Determined by Speed of Equipment	How important is it to this job that the pace is determined by the speed of equipment or machinery? (This does not refer to keeping busy at all times on this job.)
In an Enclosed Vehicle or Equipment	How often does this job require working in a closed vehicle or equipment (e.g., car)?
Responsible for Others' Health and Safety	How much responsibility is there for the health and safety of others in this job?
Spend Time Standing	How much does this job require standing?
Indoors, Not Environmentally Controlled	How often does this job require working indoors in non-controlled environmental conditions (e.g., warehouse without heat)?
Spend Time Walking and Running	How much does this job require walking and running?
Outdoors, Exposed to Weather	How often does this job require working outdoors, exposed to all weather conditions?
Extremely Bright or Inadequate Lighting	How often does this job require working in extremely bright or inadequate lighting conditions?
Exposed to Contaminants	How often does this job require working exposed to contaminants (such as pollutants, gases, dust or odors)?
Spend Time Bending or Twisting the Body	How much does this job require bending or twisting your body?
Very Hot or Cold Temperatures	How often does this job require working in very hot (above 90 F degrees) or very cold (below 32 F degrees) temperatures?
Exposed to Hazardous Equipment	How often does this job require exposure to hazardous equipment?
Cramped Work Space, Awkward Positions	How often does this job require working in cramped work spaces that requires getting into awkward positions?
Exposed to Minor Burns, Cuts, Bites, or Stings	How often does this job require exposure to minor burns, cuts, bites, or stings?
Wear Common Protective or Safety Equipment such as	How much does this job require wearing common protective or safety equipment such as safety shoes, glasses, gloves, hard hats or life jackets?

Outdoors, Under Cover	How often does this job require working outdoors, under cover (e.g., structure with roof but no walls)?
Exposed to Hazardous Conditions	How often does this job require exposure to hazardous conditions?
Spend Time Kneeling, Crouching, Stooping, or Crawl	How much does this job require kneeling, crouching, stooping or crawling?
Exposed to Whole Body Vibration	How often does this job require exposure to whole body vibration (e.g., operate a jackhammer)?
Exposed to Radiation	How often does this job require exposure to radiation?
Exposed to High Places	How often does this job require exposure to high places?
Spend Time Keeping or Regaining Balance	How much does this job require keeping or regaining your balance?
In an Open Vehicle or Equipment	How often does this job require working in an open vehicle or equipment (e.g., tractor)?
Deal With Physically Aggressive People	How frequently does this job require the worker to deal with physical aggression of violent individuals?
Spend Time Climbing Ladders, Scaffolds, or Poles	How much does this job require climbing ladders, scaffolds, or poles?
Exposed to Disease or Infections	How often does this job require exposure to disease/infections?
Wear Specialized Protective or Safety Equipment su	How much does this job require wearing specialized protective or safety equipment such as breathing apparatus, safety harness, full protection suits, or radiation protection?

Job Zone Component	Job Zone Component Definitions
Title	Job Zone Three: Medium Preparation Needed
Overall Experience	Previous work-related skill, knowledge, or experience is required for these occupations. For example, an electrician must have completed three or four years of apprenticeship or several years of vocational training, and often must have passed a licensing exam, in order to perform the job.
Job Training	Employees in these occupations usually need one or two years of training involving both on-the-job experience and informal training with experienced workers.
Job Zone Examples	These occupations usually involve using communication and organizational skills to coordinate, supervise, manage, or train others to accomplish goals. Examples include dental assistants, electricians, fish and game wardens, legal secretaries, personnel recruiters, and recreation workers.
SVP Range	(6.0 to < 7.0)
Education	Most occupations in this zone require training in vocational schools, related on-the-job experience, or an associate's degree. Some may require a bachelor's degree.

Work_Styles	Work_Styles Definitions
Attention to Detail	Job requires being careful about detail and thorough in completing work tasks.
Dependability	Job requires being reliable, responsible, and dependable, and fulfilling obligations.
Integrity	Job requires being honest and ethical.
Persistence	Job requires persistence in the face of obstacles.
Achievement/Effort	Job requires establishing and maintaining personally challenging achievement goals and exerting effort toward mastering tasks.
Analytical Thinking	Job requires analyzing information and using logic to address work-related issues and problems.
Initiative	Job requires a willingness to take on responsibilities and challenges.
Adaptability/Flexibility	Job requires being open to change (positive or negative) and to considerable variety in the workplace.
Cooperation	Job requires being pleasant with others on the job and displaying a good-natured, cooperative attitude.
Independence	Job requires developing one's own ways of doing things, guiding oneself with little or no supervision, and depending on oneself to get things done.
Stress Tolerance	Job requires accepting criticism and dealing calmly and effectively with high stress situations.
Innovation	Job requires creativity and alternative thinking to develop new ideas for and answers to work-related problems.
Self Control	Job requires maintaining composure, keeping emotions in check, controlling anger, and avoiding aggressive behavior, even in very difficult situations.

Leadership	Job requires a willingness to lead, take charge, and offer opinions and direction.
Concern for Others	Job requires being sensitive to others' needs and feelings and being understanding and helpful on the job.
Social Orientation	Job requires preferring to work with others rather than alone, and being personally connected with others on the job.

17-1022.00 - Surveyors

Make exact measurements and determine property boundaries. Provide data relevant to the shape, contour, gravitation, location, elevation, or dimension of land or land features on or near the earth's surface for engineering, mapmaking, mining, land evaluation, construction, and other purposes.

Tasks

1) Train assistants and helpers, and direct their work in such activities as performing surveys or drafting maps.

2) Calculate heights, depths, relative positions, property lines, and other characteristics of terrain.

3) Plan and conduct ground surveys designed to establish baselines, elevations, and other geodetic measurements.

4) Direct or conduct surveys in order to establish legal boundaries for properties, based on legal deeds and titles.

5) Search legal records, survey records, and land titles in order to obtain information about property boundaries in areas to be surveyed.

6) Record the results of surveys, including the shape, contour, location, elevation, and dimensions of land or land features.

7) Analyze survey objectives and specifications in order to prepare survey proposals or to direct others in survey proposal preparation.

8) Coordinate findings with the work of engineering and architectural personnel, clients, and others concerned with projects.

9) Establish fixed points for use in making maps, using geodetic and engineering instruments.

10) Prepare and maintain sketches, maps, reports, and legal descriptions of surveys in order to describe, certify, and assume liability for work performed.

11) Prepare or supervise preparation of all data, charts, plots, maps, records, and documents related to surveys.

12) Write descriptions of property boundary surveys for use in deeds, leases, or other legal documents.

13) Adjust surveying instruments in order to maintain their accuracy.

14) Develop criteria for survey methods and procedures.

15) Compute geodetic measurements and interpret survey data in order to determine positions, shapes, and elevations of geomorphic and topographic features.

16) Determine longitudes and latitudes of important features and boundaries in survey areas, using theodolites, transits, levels, and satellite-based global positioning systems (GPS).

17) Direct aerial surveys of specified geographical areas.

18) Conduct research in surveying and mapping methods, using knowledge of techniques of photogrammetric map compilation and electronic data processing.

19) Survey bodies of water in order to determine navigable channels and to secure data for construction of breakwaters, piers, and other marine structures.

20) Develop criteria for the design and modification of survey instruments.

21) Locate and mark sites selected for geophysical prospecting activities, such as efforts to locate petroleum or other mineral products.

22) Determine specifications for photographic equipment to be used for aerial photography, as well as altitudes from which to photograph terrain.

Knowledge	Knowledge Definitions
Mathematics	Knowledge of arithmetic, algebra, geometry, calculus, statistics, and their applications.
Engineering and Technology	Knowledge of the practical application of engineering science and technology. This includes applying principles, techniques, procedures, and equipment to the design and production of various goods and services.
Building and Construction	Knowledge of materials, methods, and the tools involved in the construction or repair of houses, buildings, or other structures such as highways and roads.
Design	Knowledge of design techniques, tools, and principles involved in production of precision technical plans, blueprints, drawings, and models.
Geography	Knowledge of principles and methods for describing the features of land, sea, and air masses, including their physical characteristics, locations, interrelationships, and distribution of plant, animal, and human life.
Computers and Electronics	Knowledge of circuit boards, processors, chips, electronic equipment, and computer hardware and software, including applications and programming.
Law and Government	Knowledge of laws, legal codes, court procedures, precedents, government regulations, executive orders, agency rules, and the democratic political process.
English Language	Knowledge of the structure and content of the English language including the meaning and spelling of words, rules of composition, and grammar.
Administration and Management	Knowledge of business and management principles involved in strategic planning, resource allocation, human resources modeling, leadership technique, production methods, and coordination of people and resources.
Customer and Personal Service	Knowledge of principles and processes for providing customer and personal services. This includes customer needs assessment, meeting quality standards for services, and evaluation of customer satisfaction.
Personnel and Human Resources	Knowledge of principles and procedures for personnel recruitment, selection, training, compensation and benefits, labor relations and negotiation, and personnel information systems.
Education and Training	Knowledge of principles and methods for curriculum and training design, teaching and instruction for individuals and groups, and the measurement of training effects.
Clerical	Knowledge of administrative and clerical procedures and systems such as word processing, managing files and records, stenography and transcription, designing forms, and other office procedures and terminology.
Economics and Accounting	Knowledge of economic and accounting principles and practices, the financial markets, banking and the analysis and reporting of financial data.
Sales and Marketing	Knowledge of principles and methods for showing, promoting, and selling products or services. This includes marketing strategy and tactics, product demonstration, sales techniques, and sales control systems.
Mechanical	Knowledge of machines and tools, including their designs, uses, repair, and maintenance.
Transportation	Knowledge of principles and methods for moving people or goods by air, rail, sea, or road, including the relative costs and benefits.
Physics	Knowledge and prediction of physical principles, laws, their interrelationships, and applications to understanding fluid, material, and atmospheric dynamics, and mechanical, electrical, atomic and sub-atomic structures and processes.
Biology	Knowledge of plant and animal organisms, their tissues, cells, functions, interdependencies, and interactions with each other and the environment.
Public Safety and Security	Knowledge of relevant equipment, policies, procedures, and strategies to promote effective local, state, or national security operations for the protection of people, data, property, and institutions.
Telecommunications	Knowledge of transmission, broadcasting, switching, control, and operation of telecommunications systems.
Production and Processing	Knowledge of raw materials, production processes, quality control, costs, and other techniques for maximizing the effective manufacture and distribution of goods.
Psychology	Knowledge of human behavior and performance; individual differences in ability, personality, and interests; learning and motivation; psychological research methods; and the assessment and treatment of behavioral and affective disorders.
Communications and Media	Knowledge of media production, communication, and dissemination techniques and methods. This includes alternative ways to inform and entertain via written, oral, and visual media.
History and Archeology	Knowledge of historical events and their causes, indicators, and effects on civilizations and cultures.

Chemistry	Knowledge of the chemical composition, structure, and properties of substances and of the chemical processes and transformations that they undergo. This includes uses of chemicals and their interactions, danger signs, production techniques, and disposal methods.
Sociology and Anthropology	Knowledge of group behavior and dynamics, societal trends and influences, human migrations, ethnicity, cultures and their history and origins.
Therapy and Counseling	Knowledge of principles, methods, and procedures for diagnosis, treatment, and rehabilitation of physical and mental dysfunctions, and for career counseling and guidance.
Philosophy and Theology	Knowledge of different philosophical systems and religions. This includes their basic principles, values, ethics, ways of thinking, customs, practices, and their impact on human culture.
Medicine and Dentistry	Knowledge of the information and techniques needed to diagnose and treat human injuries, diseases, and deformities. This includes symptoms, treatment alternatives, drug properties and interactions, and preventive health-care measures.
Foreign Language	Knowledge of the structure and content of a foreign (non-English) language including the meaning and spelling of words, rules of composition and grammar, and pronunciation.
Fine Arts	Knowledge of the theory and techniques required to compose, produce, and perform works of music, dance, visual arts, drama, and sculpture.
Food Production	Knowledge of techniques and equipment for planting, growing, and harvesting food products (both plant and animal) for consumption, including storage/handling techniques.

Skills	Skills Definitions
Mathematics	Using mathematics to solve problems.
Active Listening	Giving full attention to what other people are saying, taking time to understand the points being made, asking questions as appropriate, and not interrupting at inappropriate times.
Critical Thinking	Using logic and reasoning to identify the strengths and weaknesses of alternative solutions, conclusions or approaches to problems.
Writing	Communicating effectively in writing as appropriate for the needs of the audience.
Reading Comprehension	Understanding written sentences and paragraphs in work related documents.
Coordination	Adjusting actions in relation to others' actions.
Time Management	Managing one's own time and the time of others.
Speaking	Talking to others to convey information effectively.
Judgment and Decision Making	Considering the relative costs and benefits of potential actions to choose the most appropriate one.
Active Learning	Understanding the implications of new information for both current and future problem-solving and decision-making.
Complex Problem Solving	Identifying complex problems and reviewing related information to develop and evaluate options and implement solutions.
Equipment Selection	Determining the kind of tools and equipment needed to do a job.
Monitoring	Monitoring/Assessing performance of yourself, other individuals, or organizations to make improvements or take corrective action.
Instructing	Teaching others how to do something.
Learning Strategies	Selecting and using training/instructional methods and procedures appropriate for the situation when learning or teaching new things.
Equipment Maintenance	Performing routine maintenance on equipment and determining when and what kind of maintenance is needed.
Troubleshooting	Determining causes of operating errors and deciding what to do about it.
Quality Control Analysis	Conducting tests and inspections of products, services, or processes to evaluate quality or performance.
Operation and Control	Controlling operations of equipment or systems.
Social Perceptiveness	Being aware of others' reactions and understanding why they react as they do.
Negotiation	Bringing others together and trying to reconcile differences.
Management of Personnel Resources	Motivating, developing, and directing people as they work, identifying the best people for the job.
Science	Using scientific rules and methods to solve problems.
Service Orientation	Actively looking for ways to help people.
Technology Design	Generating or adapting equipment and technology to serve user needs.

Management of Material Resources	Obtaining and seeing to the appropriate use of equipment, facilities, and materials needed to do certain work.
Management of Financial Resources	Determining how money will be spent to get the work done, and accounting for these expenditures.
Persuasion	Persuading others to change their minds or behavior.
Operations Analysis	Analyzing needs and product requirements to create a design.
Operation Monitoring	Watching gauges, dials, or other indicators to make sure a machine is working properly.
Systems Evaluation	Identifying measures or indicators of system performance and the actions needed to improve or correct performance, relative to the goals of the system.
Installation	Installing equipment, machines, wiring, or programs to meet specifications.
Systems Analysis	Determining how a system should work and how changes in conditions, operations, and the environment will affect outcomes.
Repairing	Repairing machines or systems using the needed tools.
Programming	Writing computer programs for various purposes.

Ability	Ability Definitions
Problem Sensitivity	The ability to tell when something is wrong or is likely to go wrong. It does not involve solving the problem, only recognizing there is a problem.
Written Comprehension	The ability to read and understand information and ideas presented in writing.
Information Ordering	The ability to arrange things or actions in a certain order or pattern according to a specific rule or set of rules (e.g., patterns of numbers, letters, words, pictures, mathematical operations).
Oral Comprehension	The ability to listen to and understand information and ideas presented through spoken words and sentences.
Near Vision	The ability to see details at close range (within a few feet of the observer).
Deductive Reasoning	The ability to apply general rules to specific problems to produce answers that make sense.
Oral Expression	The ability to communicate information and ideas in speaking so others will understand.
Speech Clarity	The ability to speak clearly so others can understand you.
Far Vision	The ability to see details at a distance.
Written Expression	The ability to communicate information and ideas in writing so others will understand.
Number Facility	The ability to add, subtract, multiply, or divide quickly and correctly.
Inductive Reasoning	The ability to combine pieces of information to form general rules or conclusions (includes finding a relationship among seemingly unrelated events).
Speech Recognition	The ability to identify and understand the speech of another person.
Mathematical Reasoning	The ability to choose the right mathematical methods or formulas to solve a problem.
Category Flexibility	The ability to generate or use different sets of rules for combining or grouping things in different ways.
Finger Dexterity	The ability to make precisely coordinated movements of the fingers of one or both hands to grasp, manipulate, or assemble very small objects.
Perceptual Speed	The ability to quickly and accurately compare similarities and differences among sets of letters, numbers, objects, pictures, or patterns. The things to be compared may be presented at the same time or one after the other. This ability also includes comparing a presented object with a remembered object.
Visualization	The ability to imagine how something will look after it is moved around or when its parts are moved or rearranged.
Selective Attention	The ability to concentrate on a task over a period of time without being distracted.
Flexibility of Closure	The ability to identify or detect a known pattern (a figure, object, word, or sound) that is hidden in other distracting material.
Originality	The ability to come up with unusual or clever ideas about a given topic or situation, or to develop creative ways to solve a problem.
Visual Color Discrimination	The ability to match or detect differences between colors, including shades of color and brightness.
Depth Perception	The ability to judge which of several objects is closer or farther away from you, or to judge the distance between you and an object.
Control Precision	The ability to quickly and repeatedly adjust the controls of a machine or a vehicle to exact positions.

Spatial Orientation	The ability to know your location in relation to the environment or to know where other objects are in relation to you.
Speed of Closure	The ability to quickly make sense of, combine, and organize information into meaningful patterns.
Fluency of Ideas	The ability to come up with a number of ideas about a topic (the number of ideas is important, not their quality, correctness, or creativity).
Time Sharing	The ability to shift back and forth between two or more activities or sources of information (such as speech, sounds, touch, or other sources).
Arm-Hand Steadiness	The ability to keep your hand and arm steady while moving your arm or while holding your arm and hand in one position.
Auditory Attention	The ability to focus on a single source of sound in the presence of other distracting sounds.
Hearing Sensitivity	The ability to detect or tell the differences between sounds that vary in pitch and loudness.
Manual Dexterity	The ability to quickly move your hand, your hand together with your arm, or your two hands to grasp, manipulate, or assemble objects.
Multilimb Coordination	The ability to coordinate two or more limbs (for example, two arms, two legs, or one leg and one arm) while sitting, standing, or lying down. It does not involve performing the activities while the whole body is in motion.
Memorization	The ability to remember information such as words, numbers, pictures, and procedures.
Gross Body Coordination	The ability to coordinate the movement of your arms, legs, and torso together when the whole body is in motion.
Extent Flexibility	The ability to bend, stretch, twist, or reach with your body, arms, and/or legs.
Trunk Strength	The ability to use your abdominal and lower back muscles to support part of the body repeatedly or continuously over time without 'giving out' or fatiguing.
Peripheral Vision	The ability to see objects or movement of objects to one's side when the eyes are looking ahead.
Glare Sensitivity	The ability to see objects in the presence of glare or bright lighting.
Stamina	The ability to exert yourself physically over long periods of time without getting winded or out of breath.
Static Strength	The ability to exert maximum muscle force to lift, push, pull, or carry objects.
Response Orientation	The ability to choose quickly between two or more movements in response to two or more different signals (lights, sounds, pictures). It includes the speed with which the correct response is started with the hand, foot, or other body part.
Reaction Time	The ability to quickly respond (with the hand, finger, or foot) to a signal (sound, light, picture) when it appears.
Dynamic Strength	The ability to exert muscle force repeatedly or continuously over time. This involves muscular endurance and resistance to muscle fatigue.
Speed of Limb Movement	The ability to quickly move the arms and legs.
Sound Localization	The ability to tell the direction from which a sound originated.
Rate Control	The ability to time your movements or the movement of a piece of equipment in anticipation of changes in the speed and/or direction of a moving object or scene.
Night Vision	The ability to see under low light conditions.
Gross Body Equilibrium	The ability to keep or regain your body balance or stay upright when in an unstable position.
Wrist-Finger Speed	The ability to make fast, simple, repeated movements of the fingers, hands, and wrists.
Explosive Strength	The ability to use short bursts of muscle force to propel oneself (as in jumping or sprinting), or to throw an object.
Dynamic Flexibility	The ability to quickly and repeatedly bend, stretch, twist, or reach out with your body, arms, and/or legs.

Work_Activity	Work_Activity Definitions
Getting Information	Observing, receiving, and otherwise obtaining information from all relevant sources.
Processing Information	Compiling, coding, categorizing, calculating, tabulating, auditing, or verifying information or data.
Making Decisions and Solving Problems	Analyzing information and evaluating results to choose the best solution and solve problems.
Analyzing Data or Information	Identifying the underlying principles, reasons, or facts of information by breaking down information or data into separate parts.
Interacting With Computers	Using computers and computer systems (including hardware and software) to program, write software, set up functions, enter data, or process information.
Documenting/Recording Information	Entering, transcribing, recording, storing, or maintaining information in written or electronic/magnetic form.
Performing for or Working Directly with the Public	Performing for people or dealing directly with the public. This includes serving customers in restaurants and stores, and receiving clients or guests.
Evaluating Information to Determine Compliance wit	Using relevant information and individual judgment to determine whether events or processes comply with laws, regulations, or standards.
Identifying Objects, Actions, and Events	Identifying information by categorizing, estimating, recognizing differences or similarities, and detecting changes in circumstances or events.
Communicating with Supervisors, Peers, or Subordin	Providing information to supervisors, co-workers, and subordinates by telephone, in written form, e-mail, or in person.
Communicating with Persons Outside Organization	Communicating with people outside the organization, representing the organization to customers, the public, government, and other external sources. This information can be exchanged in person, in writing, or by telephone or e-mail.
Scheduling Work and Activities	Scheduling events, programs, and activities, as well as the work of others.
Organizing, Planning, and Prioritizing Work	Developing specific goals and plans to prioritize, organize, and accomplish your work.
Inspecting Equipment, Structures, or Material	Inspecting equipment, structures, or materials to identify the cause of errors or other problems or defects.
Coordinating the Work and Activities of Others	Getting members of a group to work together to accomplish tasks.
Drafting, Laying Out, and Specifying Technical Dev	Providing documentation, detailed instructions, drawings, or specifications to tell others about how devices, parts, equipment, or structures are to be fabricated, constructed, assembled, modified, maintained, or used.
Monitoring and Controlling Resources	Monitoring and controlling resources and overseeing the spending of money.
Monitor Processes, Materials, or Surroundings	Monitoring and reviewing information from materials, events, or the environment, to detect or assess problems.
Resolving Conflicts and Negotiating with Others	Handling complaints, settling disputes, and resolving grievances and conflicts, or otherwise negotiating with others.
Updating and Using Relevant Knowledge	Keeping up-to-date technically and applying new knowledge to your job.
Guiding, Directing, and Motivating Subordinates	Providing guidance and direction to subordinates, including setting performance standards and monitoring performance.
Training and Teaching Others	Identifying the educational needs of others, developing formal educational or training programs or classes, and teaching or instructing others.
Operating Vehicles, Mechanized Devices, or Equipme	Running, maneuvering, navigating, or driving vehicles or mechanized equipment, such as forklifts, passenger vehicles, aircraft, or water craft.
Performing General Physical Activities	Performing physical activities that require considerable use of your arms and legs and moving your whole body, such as climbing, lifting, balancing, walking, stooping, and handling of materials.
Establishing and Maintaining Interpersonal Relatio	Developing constructive and cooperative working relationships with others, and maintaining them over time.
Estimating the Quantifiable Characteristics of Pro	Estimating sizes, distances, and quantities; or determining time, costs, resources, or materials needed to perform a work activity.
Performing Administrative Activities	Performing day-to-day administrative tasks such as maintaining information files and processing paperwork.
Coaching and Developing Others	Identifying the developmental needs of others and coaching, mentoring, or otherwise helping others to improve their knowledge or skills.
Developing Objectives and Strategies	Establishing long-range objectives and specifying the strategies and actions to achieve them.
Developing and Building Teams	Encouraging and building mutual trust, respect, and cooperation among team members.
Staffing Organizational Units	Recruiting, interviewing, selecting, hiring, and promoting employees in an organization.
Judging the Qualities of Things, Services, or Peop	Assessing the value, importance, or quality of things or people.
Controlling Machines and Processes	Using either control mechanisms or direct physical activity to operate machines or processes (not including computers or vehicles).
Interpreting the Meaning of Information for Others	Translating or explaining what information means and how it can be used.
Thinking Creatively	Developing, designing, or creating new applications, ideas, relationships, systems, or products, including artistic contributions.

Provide Consultation and Advice to Others	Providing guidance and expert advice to management or other groups on technical, systems-, or process-related topics.
Repairing and Maintaining Electronic Equipment	Servicing, repairing, calibrating, regulating, fine-tuning, or testing machines, devices, and equipment that operate primarily on the basis of electrical or electronic (not mechanical) principles.
Handling and Moving Objects	Using hands and arms in handling, installing, positioning, and moving materials, and manipulating things.
Assisting and Caring for Others	Providing personal assistance, medical attention, emotional support, or other personal care to others such as coworkers, customers, or patients.
Repairing and Maintaining Mechanical Equipment	Servicing, repairing, adjusting, and testing machines, devices, moving parts, and equipment that operate primarily on the basis of mechanical (not electronic) principles.
Selling or Influencing Others	Convincing others to buy merchandise/goods or to otherwise change their minds or actions.

Work_Context	Work_Context Definitions
Telephone	How often do you have telephone conversations in this job?
Face-to-Face Discussions	How often do you have to have face-to-face discussions with individuals or teams in this job?
Structured versus Unstructured Work	To what extent is this job structured for the worker, rather than allowing the worker to determine tasks, priorities, and goals?
Importance of Being Exact or Accurate	How important is being very exact or highly accurate in performing this job?
Outdoors, Exposed to Weather	How often does this job require working outdoors, exposed to all weather conditions?
Freedom to Make Decisions	How much decision making freedom, without supervision, does the job offer?
Importance of Repeating Same Tasks	How important is repeating the same physical activities (e.g., key entry) or mental activities (e.g., checking entries in a ledger) over and over, without stopping, to performing this job?
Frequency of Decision Making	How frequently is the worker required to make decisions that affect other people, the financial resources, and/or the image and reputation of the organization?
Contact With Others	How much does this job require the worker to be in contact with others (face-to-face, by telephone, or otherwise) in order to perform it?
Time Pressure	How often does this job require the worker to meet strict deadlines?
Work With Work Group or Team	How important is it to work with others in a group or team in this job?
Exposed to Minor Burns, Cuts, Bites, or Stings	How often does this job require exposure to minor burns, cuts, bites, or stings?
Very Hot or Cold Temperatures	How often does this job require working in very hot (above 90 F degrees) or very cold (below 32 F degrees) temperatures?
In an Enclosed Vehicle or Equipment	How often does this job require working in a closed vehicle or equipment (e.g., car)?
Indoors, Environmentally Controlled	How often does this job require working indoors in environmentally controlled conditions?
Coordinate or Lead Others	How important is it to coordinate or lead others in accomplishing work activities in this job?
Impact of Decisions on Co-workers or Company Resul	How do the decisions an employee makes impact the results of co-workers, clients or the company?
Electronic Mail	How often do you use electronic mail in this job?
Responsibility for Outcomes and Results	How responsible is the worker for work outcomes and results of other workers?
Wear Common Protective or Safety Equipment such as	How much does this job require wearing common protective or safety equipment such as safety shoes, glasses, gloves, hard hats or live jackets?
Responsible for Others' Health and Safety	How much responsibility is there for the health and safety of others in this job?
Spend Time Standing	How much does this job require standing?
Letters and Memos	How often does the job require written letters and memos?
Exposed to Hazardous Equipment	How often does this job require exposure to hazardous equipment?
Sounds, Noise Levels Are Distracting or Uncomforta	How often does this job require working exposed to sounds and noise levels that are distracting or uncomfortable?
Deal With External Customers	How important is it to work with external customers or the public in this job?
Spend Time Using Your Hands to Handle, Control, or	How much does this job require using your hands to handle, control, or feel objects, tools or controls?
Frequency of Conflict Situations	How often are there conflict situations the employee has to face in this job?
Level of Competition	To what extent does this job require the worker to compete or to be aware of competitive pressures?
Spend Time Bending or Twisting the Body	How much does this job require bending or twisting your body?
Physical Proximity	To what extent does this job require the worker to perform job tasks in close physical proximity to other people?
Exposed to Contaminants	How often does this job require working exposed to contaminants (such as pollutants, gases, dust or odors)?
Extremely Bright or Inadequate Lighting	How often does this job require working in extremely bright or inadequate lighting conditions?
Spend Time Making Repetitive Motions	How much does this job require making repetitive motions?
Consequence of Error	How serious would the result usually be if the worker made a mistake that was not readily correctable?
Degree of Automation	How automated is the job?
Indoors, Not Environmentally Controlled	How often does this job require working indoors in non-controlled environmental conditions (e.g., warehouse without heat)?
Spend Time Sitting	How much does this job require sitting?
Spend Time Walking and Running	How much does this job require walking and running?
Deal With Unpleasant or Angry People	How frequently does the worker have to deal with unpleasant, angry, or discourteous individuals as part of the job requirements?
Spend Time Kneeling, Crouching, Stooping, or Crawl	How much does this job require kneeling, crouching, stooping or crawling?
Cramped Work Space, Awkward Positions	How often does this job require working in cramped work spaces that requires getting into awkward positions?
Outdoors, Under Cover	How often does this job require working outdoors, under cover (e.g., structure with roof but no walls)?
Exposed to High Places	How often does this job require exposure to high places?
Exposed to Hazardous Conditions	How often does this job require exposure to hazardous conditions?
Public Speaking	How often do you have to perform public speaking in this job?
Spend Time Keeping or Regaining Balance	How much does this job require keeping or regaining your balance?
Pace Determined by Speed of Equipment	How important is it to this job that the pace is determined by the speed of equipment or machinery? (This does not refer to keeping busy at all times on this job.)
Spend Time Climbing Ladders, Scaffolds, or Poles	How much does this job require climbing ladders, scaffolds, or poles?
Deal With Physically Aggressive People	How frequently does this job require the worker to deal with physical aggression of violent individuals?
Exposed to Whole Body Vibration	How often does this job require exposure to whole body vibration (e.g., operate a jackhammer)?
In an Open Vehicle or Equipment	How often does this job require working in an open vehicle or equipment (e.g., tractor)?
Wear Specialized Protective or Safety Equipment su	How much does this job require wearing specialized protective or safety equipment such as breathing apparatus, safety harness, full protection suits, or radiation protection?
Exposed to Disease or Infections	How often does this job require exposure to disease/infections?
Exposed to Radiation	How often does this job require exposure to radiation?

Job Zone Component	Job Zone Component Definitions
Title	Job Zone Three: Medium Preparation Needed
Overall Experience	Previous work-related skill, knowledge, or experience is required for these occupations. For example, an electrician must have completed three or four years of apprenticeship or several years of vocational training, and often must have passed a licensing exam, in order to perform the job.
Job Training	Employees in these occupations usually need one or two years of training involving both on-the-job experience and informal training with experienced workers.
Job Zone Examples	These occupations usually involve using communication and organizational skills to coordinate, supervise, manage, or train others to accomplish goals. Examples include dental assistants, electricians, fish and game wardens, legal secretaries, personnel recruiters, and recreation workers.
SVP Range	(6.0 to < 7.0)
Education	Most occupations in this zone require training in vocational schools, related on-the-job experience, or an associate's degree. Some may require a bachelor's degree.

Work_Styles	Work_Styles Definitions
Attention to Detail	Job requires being careful about detail and thorough in completing work tasks.
Integrity	Job requires being honest and ethical.
Cooperation	Job requires being pleasant with others on the job and displaying a good-natured, cooperative attitude.
Analytical Thinking	Job requires analyzing information and using logic to address work-related issues and problems.
Independence	Job requires developing one's own ways of doing things, guiding oneself with little or no supervision, and depending on oneself to get things done.
Adaptability/Flexibility	Job requires being open to change (positive or negative) and to considerable variety in the workplace.
Dependability	Job requires being reliable, responsible, and dependable, and fulfilling obligations.
Stress Tolerance	Job requires accepting criticism and dealing calmly and effectively with high stress situations.
Persistence	Job requires persistence in the face of obstacles.
Initiative	Job requires a willingness to take on responsibilities and challenges.
Concern for Others	Job requires being sensitive to others' needs and feelings and being understanding and helpful on the job.
Leadership	Job requires a willingness to lead, take charge, and offer opinions and direction.
Innovation	Job requires creativity and alternative thinking to develop new ideas for and answers to work-related problems.
Achievement/Effort	Job requires establishing and maintaining personally challenging achievement goals and exerting effort toward mastering tasks.
Self Control	Job requires maintaining composure, keeping emotions in check, controlling anger, and avoiding aggressive behavior, even in very difficult situations.
Social Orientation	Job requires preferring to work with others rather than alone, and being personally connected with others on the job.

17-2011.00 - Aerospace Engineers

Perform a variety of engineering work in designing, constructing, and testing aircraft, missiles, and spacecraft. May conduct basic and applied research to evaluate adaptability of materials and equipment to aircraft design and manufacture. May recommend improvements in testing equipment and techniques.

Tasks

1) Formulate conceptual design of aeronautical or aerospace products or systems to meet customer requirements.

2) Direct and coordinate activities of engineering or technical personnel designing, fabricating, modifying, or testing of aircraft or aerospace products.

3) Analyze project requests and proposals and engineering data to determine feasibility, productibility, cost, and production time of aerospace or aeronautical product.

4) Evaluate product data and design from inspections and reports for conformance to engineering principles, customer requirements, and quality standards.

5) Evaluate and approve selection of vendors by study of past performance and new advertisements.

6) Formulate mathematical models or other methods of computer analysis to develop, evaluate, or modify design according to customer engineering requirements.

7) Direct research and development programs.

8) Write technical reports and other documentation, such as handbooks and bulletins, for use by engineering staff, management, and customers.

9) Review performance reports and documentation from customers and field engineers, and inspect malfunctioning or damaged products to determine problem.

10) Plan and conduct experimental, environmental, operational and stress tests on models and prototypes of aircraft and aerospace systems and equipment.

11) Maintain records of performance reports for future reference.

12) Plan and coordinate activities concerned with investigating and resolving customers' reports of technical problems with aircraft or aerospace vehicles.

Knowledge	Knowledge Definitions
Engineering and Technology	Knowledge of the practical application of engineering science and technology. This includes applying principles, techniques, procedures, and equipment to the design and production of various goods and services.
Design	Knowledge of design techniques, tools, and principles involved in production of precision technical plans, blueprints, drawings, and models.
Computers and Electronics	Knowledge of circuit boards, processors, chips, electronic equipment, and computer hardware and software, including applications and programming.
Physics	Knowledge and prediction of physical principles, laws, their interrelationships, and applications to understanding fluid, material, and atmospheric dynamics, and mechanical, electrical, atomic and sub-atomic structures and processes.
Production and Processing	Knowledge of raw materials, production processes, quality control, costs, and other techniques for maximizing the effective manufacture and distribution of goods.
Mechanical	Knowledge of machines and tools, including their designs, uses, repair, and maintenance.
English Language	Knowledge of the structure and content of the English language including the meaning and spelling of words, rules of composition, and grammar.
Mathematics	Knowledge of arithmetic, algebra, geometry, calculus, statistics, and their applications.
Customer and Personal Service	Knowledge of principles and processes for providing customer and personal services. This includes customer needs assessment, meeting quality standards for services, and evaluation of customer satisfaction.
Education and Training	Knowledge of principles and methods for curriculum and training design, teaching and instruction for individuals and groups, and the measurement of training effects.
Administration and Management	Knowledge of business and management principles involved in strategic planning, resource allocation, human resources modeling, leadership technique, production methods, and coordination of people and resources.
Law and Government	Knowledge of laws, legal codes, court procedures, precedents, government regulations, executive orders, agency rules, and the democratic political process.
Transportation	Knowledge of principles and methods for moving people or goods by air, rail, sea, or road, including the relative costs and benefits.
Telecommunications	Knowledge of transmission, broadcasting, switching, control, and operation of telecommunications systems.
Sales and Marketing	Knowledge of principles and methods for showing, promoting, and selling products or services. This includes marketing strategy and tactics, product demonstration, sales techniques, and sales control systems.
Communications and Media	Knowledge of media production, communication, and dissemination techniques and methods. This includes alternative ways to inform and entertain via written, oral, and visual media.
Public Safety and Security	Knowledge of relevant equipment, policies, procedures, and strategies to promote effective local, state, or national security operations for the protection of people, data, property, and institutions.
Chemistry	Knowledge of the chemical composition, structure, and properties of substances and of the chemical processes and transformations that they undergo. This includes uses of chemicals and their interactions, danger signs, production techniques, and disposal methods.
Personnel and Human Resources	Knowledge of principles and procedures for personnel recruitment, selection, training, compensation and benefits, labor relations and negotiation, and personnel information systems.
Clerical	Knowledge of administrative and clerical procedures and systems such as word processing, managing files and records, stenography and transcription, designing forms, and other office procedures and terminology.
Geography	Knowledge of principles and methods for describing the features of land, sea, and air masses, including their physical characteristics, locations, interrelationships, and distribution of plant, animal, and human life.
Economics and Accounting	Knowledge of economic and accounting principles and practices, the financial markets, banking and the analysis and reporting of financial data.

Building and Construction	Knowledge of materials, methods, and the tools involved in the construction or repair of houses, buildings, or other structures such as highways and roads.
Psychology	Knowledge of human behavior and performance; individual differences in ability, personality, and interests; learning and motivation; psychological research methods; and the assessment and treatment of behavioral and affective disorders.
Foreign Language	Knowledge of the structure and content of a foreign (non-English) language including the meaning and spelling of words, rules of composition and grammar, and pronunciation.
Sociology and Anthropology	Knowledge of group behavior and dynamics, societal trends and influences, human migrations, ethnicity, cultures and their history and origins.
History and Archeology	Knowledge of historical events and their causes, indicators, and effects on civilizations and cultures.
Philosophy and Theology	Knowledge of different philosophical systems and religions. This includes their basic principles, values, ethics, ways of thinking, customs, practices, and their impact on human culture.
Biology	Knowledge of plant and animal organisms, their tissues, cells, functions, interdependencies, and interactions with each other and the environment.
Medicine and Dentistry	Knowledge of the information and techniques needed to diagnose and treat human injuries, diseases, and deformities. This includes symptoms, treatment alternatives, drug properties and interactions, and preventive health-care measures.
Fine Arts	Knowledge of the theory and techniques required to compose, produce, and perform works of music, dance, visual arts, drama, and sculpture.
Therapy and Counseling	Knowledge of principles, methods, and procedures for diagnosis, treatment, and rehabilitation of physical and mental dysfunctions, and for career counseling and guidance.
Food Production	Knowledge of techniques and equipment for planting, growing, and harvesting food products (both plant and animal) for consumption, including storage/handling techniques.

Skills | Skills Definitions

Critical Thinking	Using logic and reasoning to identify the strengths and weaknesses of alternative solutions, conclusions or approaches to problems.
Judgment and Decision Making	Considering the relative costs and benefits of potential actions to choose the most appropriate one.
Time Management	Managing one's own time and the time of others.
Active Learning	Understanding the implications of new information for both current and future problem-solving and decision-making.
Writing	Communicating effectively in writing as appropriate for the needs of the audience.
Reading Comprehension	Understanding written sentences and paragraphs in work related documents.
Monitoring	Monitoring/Assessing performance of yourself, other individuals, or organizations to make improvements or take corrective action.
Speaking	Talking to others to convey information effectively.
Systems Evaluation	Identifying measures or indicators of system performance and the actions needed to improve or correct performance, relative to the goals of the system.
Management of Personnel Resources	Motivating, developing, and directing people as they work, identifying the best people for the job.
Active Listening	Giving full attention to what other people are saying, taking time to understand the points being made, asking questions as appropriate, and not interrupting at inappropriate times.
Persuasion	Persuading others to change their minds or behavior.
Coordination	Adjusting actions in relation to others' actions.
Science	Using scientific rules and methods to solve problems.
Systems Analysis	Determining how a system should work and how changes in conditions, operations, and the environment will affect outcomes.
Negotiation	Bringing others together and trying to reconcile differences.
Technology Design	Generating or adapting equipment and technology to serve user needs.
Social Perceptiveness	Being aware of others' reactions and understanding why they react as they do.
Instructing	Teaching others how to do something.
Complex Problem Solving	Identifying complex problems and reviewing related information to develop and evaluate options and implement solutions.

Equipment Selection	Determining the kind of tools and equipment needed to do a job.
Mathematics	Using mathematics to solve problems.
Management of Financial Resources	Determining how money will be spent to get the work done, and accounting for these expenditures.
Operations Analysis	Analyzing needs and product requirements to create a design.
Learning Strategies	Selecting and using training/instructional methods and procedures appropriate for the situation when learning or teaching new things.
Quality Control Analysis	Conducting tests and inspections of products, services, or processes to evaluate quality or performance.
Troubleshooting	Determining causes of operating errors and deciding what to do about it.
Service Orientation	Actively looking for ways to help people.
Management of Material Resources	Obtaining and seeing to the appropriate use of equipment, facilities, and materials needed to do certain work.
Operation Monitoring	Watching gauges, dials, or other indicators to make sure a machine is working properly.
Operation and Control	Controlling operations of equipment or systems.
Programming	Writing computer programs for various purposes.
Installation	Installing equipment, machines, wiring, or programs to meet specifications.
Equipment Maintenance	Performing routine maintenance on equipment and determining when and what kind of maintenance is needed.
Repairing	Repairing machines or systems using the needed tools.

Ability | Ability Definitions

Problem Sensitivity	The ability to tell when something is wrong or is likely to go wrong. It does not involve solving the problem, only recognizing there is a problem.
Deductive Reasoning	The ability to apply general rules to specific problems to produce answers that make sense.
Mathematical Reasoning	The ability to choose the right mathematical methods or formulas to solve a problem.
Written Comprehension	The ability to read and understand information and ideas presented in writing.
Written Expression	The ability to communicate information and ideas in writing so others will understand.
Inductive Reasoning	The ability to combine pieces of information to form general rules or conclusions (includes finding a relationship among seemingly unrelated events).
Near Vision	The ability to see details at close range (within a few feet of the observer).
Visualization	The ability to imagine how something will look after it is moved around or when its parts are moved or rearranged.
Information Ordering	The ability to arrange things or actions in a certain order or pattern according to a specific rule or set of rules (e.g., patterns of numbers, letters, words, pictures, mathematical operations).
Oral Comprehension	The ability to listen to and understand information and ideas presented through spoken words and sentences.
Oral Expression	The ability to communicate information and ideas in speaking so others will understand.
Speech Clarity	The ability to speak clearly so others can understand you.
Originality	The ability to come up with unusual or clever ideas about a given topic or situation, or to develop creative ways to solve a problem.
Fluency of Ideas	The ability to come up with a number of ideas about a topic (the number of ideas is important, not their quality, correctness, or creativity).
Speech Recognition	The ability to identify and understand the speech of another person.
Flexibility of Closure	The ability to identify or detect a known pattern (a figure, object, word, or sound) that is hidden in other distracting material.
Category Flexibility	The ability to generate or use different sets of rules for combining or grouping things in different ways.
Selective Attention	The ability to concentrate on a task over a period of time without being distracted.
Memorization	The ability to remember information such as words, numbers, pictures, and procedures.
Time Sharing	The ability to shift back and forth between two or more activities or sources of information (such as speech, sounds, touch, or other sources).
Speed of Closure	The ability to quickly make sense of, combine, and organize information into meaningful patterns.

Perceptual Speed	The ability to quickly and accurately compare similarities and differences among sets of letters, numbers, objects, pictures, or patterns. The things to be compared may be presented at the same time or one after the other. This ability also includes comparing a presented object with a remembered object.
Number Facility	The ability to add, subtract, multiply, or divide quickly and correctly.
Far Vision	The ability to see details at a distance.
Auditory Attention	The ability to focus on a single source of sound in the presence of other distracting sounds.
Visual Color Discrimination	The ability to match or detect differences between colors, including shades of color and brightness.
Hearing Sensitivity	The ability to detect or tell the differences between sounds that vary in pitch and loudness.
Spatial Orientation	The ability to know your location in relation to the environment or to know where other objects are in relation to you.
Reaction Time	The ability to quickly respond (with the hand, finger, or foot) to a signal (sound, light, picture) when it appears.
Depth Perception	The ability to judge which of several objects is closer or farther away from you, or to judge the distance between you and an object.
Control Precision	The ability to quickly and repeatedly adjust the controls of a machine or a vehicle to exact positions.
Multilimb Coordination	The ability to coordinate two or more limbs (for example, two arms, two legs, or one leg and one arm) while sitting, standing, or lying down. It does not involve performing the activities while the whole body is in motion.
Wrist-Finger Speed	The ability to make fast, simple, repeated movements of the fingers, hands, and wrists.
Sound Localization	The ability to tell the direction from which a sound originated.
Finger Dexterity	The ability to make precisely coordinated movements of the fingers of one or both hands to grasp, manipulate, or assemble very small objects.
Extent Flexibility	The ability to bend, stretch, twist, or reach with your body, arms, and/or legs.
Manual Dexterity	The ability to quickly move your hand, your hand together with your arm, or your two hands to grasp, manipulate, or assemble objects.
Speed of Limb Movement	The ability to quickly move the arms and legs.
Arm-Hand Steadiness	The ability to keep your hand and arm steady while moving your arm or while holding your arm and hand in one position.
Dynamic Flexibility	The ability to quickly and repeatedly bend, stretch, twist, or reach out with your body, arms, and/or legs.
Gross Body Equilibrium	The ability to keep or regain your body balance or stay upright when in an unstable position.
Response Orientation	The ability to choose quickly between two or more movements in response to two or more different signals (lights, sounds, pictures). It includes the speed with which the correct response is started with the hand, foot, or other body part.
Rate Control	The ability to time your movements or the movement of a piece of equipment in anticipation of changes in the speed and/or direction of a moving object or scene.
Static Strength	The ability to exert maximum muscle force to lift, push, pull, or carry objects.
Explosive Strength	The ability to use short bursts of muscle force to propel oneself (as in jumping or sprinting), or to throw an object.
Dynamic Strength	The ability to exert muscle force repeatedly or continuously over time. This involves muscular endurance and resistance to muscle fatigue.
Stamina	The ability to exert yourself physically over long periods of time without getting winded or out of breath.
Gross Body Coordination	The ability to coordinate the movement of your arms, legs, and torso together when the whole body is in motion.
Night Vision	The ability to see under low light conditions.
Glare Sensitivity	The ability to see objects in the presence of glare or bright lighting.
Peripheral Vision	The ability to see objects or movement of objects to one's side when the eyes are looking ahead.
Trunk Strength	The ability to use your abdominal and lower back muscles to support part of the body repeatedly or continuously over time without 'giving out' or fatiguing.

Work_Activity	Work_Activity Definitions
Making Decisions and Solving Problems	Analyzing information and evaluating results to choose the best solution and solve problems.
Analyzing Data or Information	Identifying the underlying principles, reasons, or facts of information by breaking down information or data into separate parts.
Interacting With Computers	Using computers and computer systems (including hardware and software) to program, write software, set up functions, enter data, or process information.
Evaluating Information to Determine Compliance wit	Using relevant information and individual judgment to determine whether events or processes comply with laws, regulations, or standards.
Updating and Using Relevant Knowledge	Keeping up-to-date technically and applying new knowledge to your job.
Getting Information	Observing, receiving, and otherwise obtaining information from all relevant sources.
Communicating with Supervisors, Peers, or Subordin	Providing information to supervisors, co-workers, and subordinates by telephone, in written form, e-mail, or in person.
Organizing, Planning, and Prioritizing Work	Developing specific goals and plans to prioritize, organize, and accomplish your work.
Thinking Creatively	Developing, designing, or creating new applications, ideas, relationships, systems, or products, including artistic contributions.
Drafting, Laying Out, and Specifying Technical Dev	Providing documentation, detailed instructions, drawings, or specifications to tell others about how devices, parts, equipment, or structures are to be fabricated, constructed, assembled, modified, maintained, or used.
Coordinating the Work and Activities of Others	Getting members of a group to work together to accomplish tasks.
Establishing and Maintaining Interpersonal Relatio	Developing constructive and cooperative working relationships with others, and maintaining them over time.
Monitor Processes, Materials, or Surroundings	Monitoring and reviewing information from materials, events, or the environment, to detect or assess problems.
Processing Information	Compiling, coding, categorizing, calculating, tabulating, auditing, or verifying information or data.
Estimating the Quantifiable Characteristics of Pro	Estimating sizes, distances, and quantities; or determining time, costs, resources, or materials needed to perform a work activity.
Interpreting the Meaning of Information for Others	Translating or explaining what information means and how it can be used.
Identifying Objects, Actions, and Events	Identifying information by categorizing, estimating, recognizing differences or similarities, and detecting changes in circumstances or events.
Communicating with Persons Outside Organization	Communicating with people outside the organization, representing the organization to customers, the public, government, and other external sources. This information can be exchanged in person, in writing, or by telephone or e-mail.
Developing Objectives and Strategies	Establishing long-range objectives and specifying the strategies and actions to achieve them.
Scheduling Work and Activities	Scheduling events, programs, and activities, as well as the work of others.
Developing and Building Teams	Encouraging and building mutual trust, respect, and cooperation among team members.
Provide Consultation and Advice to Others	Providing guidance and expert advice to management or other groups on technical, systems-, or process-related topics.
Documenting/Recording Information	Entering, transcribing, recording, storing, or maintaining information in written or electronic/magnetic form.
Judging the Qualities of Things, Services, or Peop	Assessing the value, importance, or quality of things or people.
Guiding, Directing, and Motivating Subordinates	Providing guidance and direction to subordinates, including setting performance standards and monitoring performance.
Selling or Influencing Others	Convincing others to buy merchandise/goods or to otherwise change their minds or actions.
Training and Teaching Others	Identifying the educational needs of others, developing formal educational or training programs or classes, and teaching or instructing others.
Resolving Conflicts and Negotiating with Others	Handling complaints, settling disputes, and resolving grievances and conflicts, or otherwise negotiating with others.
Monitoring and Controlling Resources	Monitoring and controlling resources and overseeing the spending of money.
Inspecting Equipment, Structures, or Material	Inspecting equipment, structures, or materials to identify the cause of errors or other problems or defects.
Performing Administrative Activities	Performing day-to-day administrative tasks such as maintaining information files and processing paperwork.
Coaching and Developing Others	Identifying the developmental needs of others and coaching, mentoring, or otherwise helping others to improve their knowledge or skills.

Staffing Organizational Units	Recruiting, interviewing, selecting, hiring, and promoting employees in an organization.
Controlling Machines and Processes	Using either control mechanisms or direct physical activity to operate machines or processes (not including computers or vehicles).
Performing for or Working Directly with the Public	Performing for people or dealing directly with the public. This includes serving customers in restaurants and stores, and receiving clients or guests.
Performing General Physical Activities	Performing physical activities that require considerable use of your arms and legs and moving your whole body, such as climbing, lifting, balancing, walking, stooping, and handling of materials.
Assisting and Caring for Others	Providing personal assistance, medical attention, emotional support, or other personal care to others such as coworkers, customers, or patients.
Handling and Moving Objects	Using hands and arms in handling, installing, positioning, and moving materials, and manipulating things.
Repairing and Maintaining Mechanical Equipment	Servicing, repairing, adjusting, and testing machines, devices, moving parts, and equipment that operate primarily on the basis of mechanical (not electronic) principles.
Operating Vehicles, Mechanized Devices, or Equipme	Running, maneuvering, navigating, or driving vehicles or mechanized equipment, such as forklifts, passenger vehicles, aircraft, or water craft.
Repairing and Maintaining Electronic Equipment	Servicing, repairing, calibrating, regulating, fine-tuning, or testing machines, devices, and equipment that operate primarily on the basis of electrical or electronic (not mechanical) principles.

Work_Context	Work_Context Definitions
Indoors, Environmentally Controlled	How often does this job require working indoors in environmentally controlled conditions?
Importance of Being Exact or Accurate	How important is being very exact or highly accurate in performing this job?
Electronic Mail	How often do you use electronic mail in this job?
Freedom to Make Decisions	How much decision making freedom, without supervision, does the job offer?
Telephone	How often do you have telephone conversations in this job?
Spend Time Sitting	How much does this job require sitting?
Face-to-Face Discussions	How often do you have to have face-to-face discussions with individuals or teams in this job?
Impact of Decisions on Co-workers or Company Resul	How do the decisions an employee makes impact the results of co-workers, clients or the company?
Structured versus Unstructured Work	To what extent is this job structured for the worker, rather than allowing the worker to determine tasks, priorities, and goals?
Work With Work Group or Team	How important is it to work with others in a group or team in this job?
Consequence of Error	How serious would the result usually be if the worker made a mistake that was not readily correctable?
Frequency of Decision Making	How frequently is the worker required to make decisions that affect other people, the financial resources, and/or the image and reputation of the organization?
Contact With Others	How much does this job require the worker to be in contact with others (face-to-face, by telephone, or otherwise) in order to perform it?
Responsibility for Outcomes and Results	How responsible is the worker for work outcomes and results of other workers?
Spend Time Making Repetitive Motions	How much does this job require making repetitive motions?
Time Pressure	How often does this job require the worker to meet strict deadlines?
Importance of Repeating Same Tasks	How important is repeating the same physical activities (e.g., key entry) or mental activities (e.g., checking entries in a ledger) over and over, without stopping, to performing this job?
Coordinate or Lead Others	How important is it to coordinate or lead others in accomplishing work activities in this job?
Level of Competition	To what extent does this job require the worker to compete or to be aware of competitive pressures?
Physical Proximity	To what extent does this job require the worker to perform job tasks in close physical proximity to other people?
Sounds, Noise Levels Are Distracting or Uncomforta	How often does this job require working exposed to sounds and noise levels that are distracting or uncomfortable?
Deal With External Customers	How important is it to work with external customers or the public in this job?
Letters and Memos	How often does the job require written letters and memos?
Responsible for Others' Health and Safety	How much responsibility is there for the health and safety of others in this job?

Frequency of Conflict Situations	How often are there conflict situations the employee has to face in this job?
Spend Time Using Your Hands to Handle, Control, or	How much does this job require using your hands to handle, control, or feel objects, tools or controls?
Wear Common Protective or Safety Equipment such as	How much does this job require wearing common protective or safety equipment such as safety shoes, glasses, gloves, hard hats or life jackets?
Degree of Automation	How automated is the job?
Deal With Unpleasant or Angry People	How frequently does the worker have to deal with unpleasant, angry, or discourteous individuals as part of the job requirements?
Spend Time Standing	How much does this job require standing?
Indoors, Not Environmentally Controlled	How often does this job require working indoors in non-controlled environmental conditions (e.g., warehouse without heat)?
Very Hot or Cold Temperatures	How often does this job require working in very hot (above 90 F degrees) or very cold (below 32 F degrees) temperatures?
Exposed to Contaminants	How often does this job require working exposed to contaminants (such as pollutants, gases, dust or odors)?
Public Speaking	How often do you have to perform public speaking in this job?
Exposed to Radiation	How often does this job require exposure to radiation?
Exposed to Hazardous Conditions	How often does this job require exposure to hazardous conditions?
Outdoors, Under Cover	How often does this job require working outdoors, under cover (e.g., structure with roof but no walls)?
Spend Time Walking and Running	How much does this job require walking and running?
In an Enclosed Vehicle or Equipment	How often does this job require working in a closed vehicle or equipment (e.g., car)?
Exposed to Hazardous Equipment	How often does this job require exposure to hazardous equipment?
Exposed to High Places	How often does this job require exposure to high places?
Outdoors, Exposed to Weather	How often does this job require working outdoors, exposed to all weather conditions?
Extremely Bright or Inadequate Lighting	How often does this job require working in extremely bright or inadequate lighting conditions?
In an Open Vehicle or Equipment	How often does this job require working in an open vehicle or equipment (e.g., tractor)?
Pace Determined by Speed of Equipment	How important is it to this job that the pace is determined by the speed of equipment or machinery? (This does not refer to keeping busy at all times on this job.)
Wear Specialized Protective or Safety Equipment su	How much does this job require wearing specialized protective or safety equipment such as breathing apparatus, safety harness, full protection suits, or radiation protection?
Spend Time Bending or Twisting the Body	How often does this job require bending or twisting your body?
Cramped Work Space, Awkward Positions	How often does this job require working in cramped work spaces that requires getting into awkward positions?
Spend Time Climbing Ladders, Scaffolds, or Poles	How much does this job require climbing ladders, scaffolds, or poles?
Spend Time Kneeling, Crouching, Stooping, or Crawl	How much does this job require kneeling, crouching, stooping or crawling?
Exposed to Minor Burns, Cuts, Bites, or Stings	How often does this job require exposure to minor burns, cuts, bites, or stings?
Spend Time Keeping or Regaining Balance	How much does this job require keeping or regaining your balance?
Exposed to Whole Body Vibration	How often does this job require exposure to whole body vibration (e.g., operate a jackhammer)?
Exposed to Disease or Infections	How often does this job require exposure to disease/infections?
Deal With Physically Aggressive People	How frequently does this job require the worker to deal with physical aggression of violent individuals?

Job Zone Component	Job Zone Component Definitions
Title	Job Zone Five: Extensive Preparation Needed
	Extensive skill, knowledge, and experience are needed for these occupations. Many require more than five years of experience.
Overall Experience	For example, surgeons must complete four years of college and an additional five to seven years of specialized medical training to be able to do their job.

Job Training	Employees may need some on-the-job training, but most of these occupations assume that the person will already have the required skills, knowledge, work-related experience, and/or training.
Job Zone Examples	These occupations often involve coordinating, training, supervising, or managing the activities of others to accomplish goals. Very advanced communication and organizational skills are required. Examples include athletic trainers, lawyers, managing editors, physicists, social psychologists, and surgeons.
SVP Range	(8.0 and above)
Education	A bachelor's degree is the minimum formal education required for these occupations. However, many also require graduate school. For example, they may require a master's degree, and some require a Ph.D., M.D., or J.D. (law degree).

Work_Styles	Work_Styles Definitions
Attention to Detail	Job requires being careful about detail and thorough in completing work tasks.
Analytical Thinking	Job requires analyzing information and using logic to address work-related issues and problems.
Dependability	Job requires being reliable, responsible, and dependable, and fulfilling obligations.
Cooperation	Job requires being pleasant with others on the job and displaying a good-natured, cooperative attitude.
Innovation	Job requires creativity and alternative thinking to develop new ideas for and answers to work-related problems.
Integrity	Job requires being honest and ethical.
Adaptability/Flexibility	Job requires being open to change (positive or negative) and to considerable variety in the workplace.
Self Control	Job requires maintaining composure, keeping emotions in check, controlling anger, and avoiding aggressive behavior, even in very difficult situations.
Initiative	Job requires a willingness to take on responsibilities and challenges.
Persistence	Job requires persistence in the face of obstacles.
Independence	Job requires developing one's own ways of doing things, guiding oneself with little or no supervision, and depending on oneself to get things done.
Concern for Others	Job requires being sensitive to others' needs and feelings and being understanding and helpful on the job.
Stress Tolerance	Job requires accepting criticism and dealing calmly and effectively with high stress situations.
Social Orientation	Job requires preferring to work with others rather than alone, and being personally connected with others on the job.
Leadership	Job requires a willingness to lead, take charge, and offer opinions and direction.
Achievement/Effort	Job requires establishing and maintaining personally challenging achievement goals and exerting effort toward mastering tasks.

17-2031.00 - Biomedical Engineers

Apply knowledge of engineering, biology, and biomechanical principles to the design, development, and evaluation of biological and health systems and products, such as artificial organs, prostheses, instrumentation, medical information systems, and health management and care delivery systems.

Tasks

1) Advise hospital administrators on the planning, acquisition, and use of medical equipment.

2) Conduct research, along with life scientists, chemists, and medical scientists, on the engineering aspects of the biological systems of humans and animals.

3) Evaluate the safety, efficiency, and effectiveness of biomedical equipment.

4) Research new materials to be used for products such as implanted artificial organs.

5) Analyze new medical procedures in order to forecast likely outcomes.

6) Adapt or design computer hardware or software for medical science uses.

7) Design and deliver technology to assist people with disabilities.

8) Design and develop medical diagnostic and clinical instrumentation, equipment, and procedures, utilizing the principles of engineering and bio-behavioral sciences.

9) Diagnose and interpret bioelectric data, using signal processing techniques.

10) Install, adjust, maintain, and/or repair biomedical equipment.

11) Teach biomedical engineering, or disseminate knowledge about field through writing or consulting.

12) Develop models or computer simulations of human bio-behavioral systems in order to obtain data for measuring or controlling life processes.

13) Advise and assist in the application of instrumentation in clinical environments.

17-2041.00 - Chemical Engineers

Design chemical plant equipment and devise processes for manufacturing chemicals and products, such as gasoline, synthetic rubber, plastics, detergents, cement, paper, and pulp, by applying principles and technology of chemistry, physics, and engineering.

Tasks

1) Determine most effective arrangement of operations, such as mixing, crushing, heat transfer, distillation, and drying.

2) Develop safety procedures to be employed by workers operating equipment or working in close proximity to on-going chemical reactions.

3) Design and plan layout of equipment.

4) Prepare estimate of production costs and production progress reports for management.

5) Perform laboratory studies of steps in manufacture of new product and test proposed process in small scale operation (pilot plant).

6) Conduct research to develop new and improved chemical manufacturing processes.

7) Develop processes to separate components of liquids or gases or generate electrical currents, using controlled chemical processes.

8) Design measurement and control systems for chemical plants based on data collected in laboratory experiments and in pilot plant operations.

9) Direct activities of workers who operate or who are engaged in constructing and improving absorption, evaporation, or electromagnetic equipment.

Knowledge	Knowledge Definitions
Engineering and Technology	Knowledge of the practical application of engineering science and technology. This includes applying principles, techniques, procedures, and equipment to the design and production of various goods and services.
Chemistry	Knowledge of the chemical composition, structure, and properties of substances and of the chemical processes and transformations that they undergo. This includes uses of chemicals and their interactions, danger signs, production techniques, and disposal methods.
Mathematics	Knowledge of arithmetic, algebra, geometry, calculus, statistics, and their applications.
Physics	Knowledge and prediction of physical principles, laws, their interrelationships, and applications to understanding fluid, material, and atmospheric dynamics, and mechanical, electrical, atomic and sub-atomic structures and processes.
Production and Processing	Knowledge of raw materials, production processes, quality control, costs, and other techniques for maximizing the effective manufacture and distribution of goods.
English Language	Knowledge of the structure and content of the English language including the meaning and spelling of words, rules of composition, and grammar.
Design	Knowledge of design techniques, tools, and principles involved in production of precision technical plans, blueprints, drawings, and models.
Computers and Electronics	Knowledge of circuit boards, processors, chips, electronic equipment, and computer hardware and software, including applications and programming.
Administration and Management	Knowledge of business and management principles involved in strategic planning, resource allocation, human resources modeling, leadership technique, production methods, and coordination of people and resources.
Mechanical	Knowledge of machines and tools, including their designs, uses, repair, and maintenance.

Customer and Personal Service	Knowledge of principles and processes for providing customer and personal services. This includes customer needs assessment, meeting quality standards for services, and evaluation of customer satisfaction.
Law and Government	Knowledge of laws, legal codes, court procedures, precedents, government regulations, executive orders, agency rules, and the democratic political process.
Education and Training	Knowledge of principles and methods for curriculum and training design, teaching and instruction for individuals and groups, and the measurement of training effects.
Economics and Accounting	Knowledge of economic and accounting principles and practices, the financial markets, banking and the analysis and reporting of financial data.
Communications and Media	Knowledge of media production, communication, and dissemination techniques and methods. This includes alternative ways to inform and entertain via written, oral, and visual media.
Public Safety and Security	Knowledge of relevant equipment, policies, procedures, and strategies to promote effective local, state, or national security operations for the protection of people, data, property, and institutions.
Clerical	Knowledge of administrative and clerical procedures and systems such as word processing, managing files and records, stenography and transcription, designing forms, and other office procedures and terminology.
Personnel and Human Resources	Knowledge of principles and procedures for personnel recruitment, selection, training, compensation and benefits, labor relations and negotiation, and personnel information systems.
Transportation	Knowledge of principles and methods for moving people or goods by air, rail, sea, or road, including the relative costs and benefits.
Biology	Knowledge of plant and animal organisms, their tissues, cells, functions, interdependencies, and interactions with each other and the environment.
Sales and Marketing	Knowledge of principles and methods for showing, promoting, and selling products or services. This includes marketing strategy and tactics, product demonstration, sales techniques, and sales control systems.
Building and Construction	Knowledge of materials, methods, and the tools involved in the construction or repair of houses, buildings, or other structures such as highways and roads.
Psychology	Knowledge of human behavior and performance; individual differences in ability, personality, and interests; learning and motivation; psychological research methods; and the assessment and treatment of behavioral and affective disorders.
Telecommunications	Knowledge of transmission, broadcasting, switching, control, and operation of telecommunications systems.
Philosophy and Theology	Knowledge of different philosophical systems and religions. This includes their basic principles, values, ethics, ways of thinking, customs, practices, and their impact on human culture.
Sociology and Anthropology	Knowledge of group behavior and dynamics, societal trends and influences, human migrations, ethnicity, cultures and their history and origins.
Therapy and Counseling	Knowledge of principles, methods, and procedures for diagnosis, treatment, and rehabilitation of physical and mental dysfunctions, and for career counseling and guidance.
Foreign Language	Knowledge of the structure and content of a foreign (non-English) language including the meaning and spelling of words, rules of composition and grammar, and pronunciation.
Geography	Knowledge of principles and methods for describing the features of land, sea, and air masses, including their physical characteristics, locations, interrelationships, and distribution of plant, animal, and human life.
Medicine and Dentistry	Knowledge of the information and techniques needed to diagnose and treat human injuries, diseases, and deformities. This includes symptoms, treatment alternatives, drug properties and interactions, and preventive health-care measures.
History and Archeology	Knowledge of historical events and their causes, indicators, and effects on civilizations and cultures.
Food Production	Knowledge of techniques and equipment for planting, growing, and harvesting food products (both plant and animal) for consumption, including storage/handling techniques.
Fine Arts	Knowledge of the theory and techniques required to compose, produce, and perform works of music, dance, visual arts, drama, and sculpture.

Skills	Skills Definitions
Science	Using scientific rules and methods to solve problems.
Critical Thinking	Using logic and reasoning to identify the strengths and weaknesses of alternative solutions, conclusions or approaches to problems.
Active Listening	Giving full attention to what other people are saying, taking time to understand the points being made, asking questions as appropriate, and not interrupting at inappropriate times.
Complex Problem Solving	Identifying complex problems and reviewing related information to develop and evaluate options and implement solutions.
Reading Comprehension	Understanding written sentences and paragraphs in work related documents.
Troubleshooting	Determining causes of operating errors and deciding what to do about it.
Technology Design	Generating or adapting equipment and technology to serve user needs.
Active Learning	Understanding the implications of new information for both current and future problem-solving and decision-making.
Mathematics	Using mathematics to solve problems.
Writing	Communicating effectively in writing as appropriate for the needs of the audience.
Speaking	Talking to others to convey information effectively.
Equipment Selection	Determining the kind of tools and equipment needed to do a job.
Judgment and Decision Making	Considering the relative costs and benefits of potential actions to choose the most appropriate one.
Operations Analysis	Analyzing needs and product requirements to create a design.
Monitoring	Monitoring/Assessing performance of yourself, other individuals, or organizations to make improvements or take corrective action.
Systems Analysis	Determining how a system should work and how changes in conditions, operations, and the environment will affect outcomes.
Time Management	Managing one's own time and the time of others.
Persuasion	Persuading others to change their minds or behavior.
Coordination	Adjusting actions in relation to others' actions.
Quality Control Analysis	Conducting tests and inspections of products, services, or processes to evaluate quality or performance.
Systems Evaluation	Identifying measures or indicators of system performance and the actions needed to improve or correct performance, relative to the goals of the system.
Operation and Control	Controlling operations of equipment or systems.
Learning Strategies	Selecting and using training/instructional methods and procedures appropriate for the situation when learning or teaching new things.
Operation Monitoring	Watching gauges, dials, or other indicators to make sure a machine is working properly.
Instructing	Teaching others how to do something.
Installation	Installing equipment, machines, wiring, or programs to meet specifications.
Social Perceptiveness	Being aware of others' reactions and understanding why they react as they do.
Management of Material Resources	Obtaining and seeing to the appropriate use of equipment, facilities, and materials needed to do certain work.
Negotiation	Bringing others together and trying to reconcile differences.
Management of Personnel Resources	Motivating, developing, and directing people as they work, identifying the best people for the job.
Programming	Writing computer programs for various purposes.
Management of Financial Resources	Determining how money will be spent to get the work done, and accounting for these expenditures.
Service Orientation	Actively looking for ways to help people.
Equipment Maintenance	Performing routine maintenance on equipment and determining when and what kind of maintenance is needed.
Repairing	Repairing machines or systems using the needed tools.

Ability	Ability Definitions
Problem Sensitivity	The ability to tell when something is wrong or is likely to go wrong. It does not involve solving the problem, only recognizing there is a problem.
Deductive Reasoning	The ability to apply general rules to specific problems to produce answers that make sense.
Information Ordering	The ability to arrange things or actions in a certain order or pattern according to a specific rule or set of rules (e.g., patterns of numbers, letters, words, pictures, mathematical operations).

Inductive Reasoning	The ability to combine pieces of information to form general rules or conclusions (includes finding a relationship among seemingly unrelated events).
Category Flexibility	The ability to generate or use different sets of rules for combining or grouping things in different ways.
Speech Clarity	The ability to speak clearly so others can understand you.
Near Vision	The ability to see details at close range (within a few feet of the observer).
Oral Comprehension	The ability to listen to and understand information and ideas presented through spoken words and sentences.
Written Comprehension	The ability to read and understand information and ideas presented in writing.
Oral Expression	The ability to communicate information and ideas in speaking so others will understand.
Speech Recognition	The ability to identify and understand the speech of another person.
Selective Attention	The ability to concentrate on a task over a period of time without being distracted.
Originality	The ability to come up with unusual or clever ideas about a given topic or situation, or to develop creative ways to solve a problem.
Perceptual Speed	The ability to quickly and accurately compare similarities and differences among sets of letters, numbers, objects, pictures, or patterns. The things to be compared may be presented at the same time or one after the other. This ability also includes comparing a presented object with a remembered object.
Number Facility	The ability to add, subtract, multiply, or divide quickly and correctly.
Written Expression	The ability to communicate information and ideas in writing so others will understand.
Mathematical Reasoning	The ability to choose the right mathematical methods or formulas to solve a problem.
Fluency of Ideas	The ability to come up with a number of ideas about a topic (the number of ideas is important, not their quality, correctness, or creativity).
Visualization	The ability to imagine how something will look after it is moved around or when its parts are moved or rearranged.
Flexibility of Closure	The ability to identify or detect a known pattern (a figure, object, word, or sound) that is hidden in other distracting material.
Finger Dexterity	The ability to make precisely coordinated movements of the fingers of one or both hands to grasp, manipulate, or assemble very small objects.
Time Sharing	The ability to shift back and forth between two or more activities or sources of information (such as speech, sounds, touch, or other sources).
Far Vision	The ability to see details at a distance.
Arm-Hand Steadiness	The ability to keep your hand and arm steady while moving your arm or while holding your arm and hand in one position.
Visual Color Discrimination	The ability to match or detect differences between colors, including shades of color and brightness.
Auditory Attention	The ability to focus on a single source of sound in the presence of other distracting sounds.
Hearing Sensitivity	The ability to detect or tell the differences between sounds that vary in pitch and loudness.
Speed of Closure	The ability to quickly make sense of, combine, and organize information into meaningful patterns.
Control Precision	The ability to quickly and repeatedly adjust the controls of a machine or a vehicle to exact positions.
Memorization	The ability to remember information such as words, numbers, pictures, and procedures.
Depth Perception	The ability to judge which of several objects is closer or farther away from you, or to judge the distance between you and an object.
Multilimb Coordination	The ability to coordinate two or more limbs (for example, two arms, two legs, or one leg and one arm) while sitting, standing, or lying down. It does not involve performing the activities while the whole body is in motion.
Manual Dexterity	The ability to quickly move your hand, your hand together with your arm, or your two hands to grasp, manipulate, or assemble objects.
Reaction Time	The ability to quickly respond (with the hand, finger, or foot) to a signal (sound, light, picture) when it appears.
Response Orientation	The ability to choose quickly between two or more movements in response to two or more different signals (lights, sounds, pictures). It includes the speed with which the correct response is started with the hand, foot, or other body part.

Wrist-Finger Speed	The ability to make fast, simple, repeated movements of the fingers, hands, and wrists.
Rate Control	The ability to time your movements or the movement of a piece of equipment in anticipation of changes in the speed and/or direction of a moving object or scene.
Static Strength	The ability to exert maximum muscle force to lift, push, pull, or carry objects.
Sound Localization	The ability to tell the direction from which a sound originated.
Trunk Strength	The ability to use your abdominal and lower back muscles to support part of the body repeatedly or continuously over time without 'giving out' or fatiguing.
Peripheral Vision	The ability to see objects or movement of objects to one's side when the eyes are looking ahead.
Extent Flexibility	The ability to bend, stretch, twist, or reach with your body, arms, and/or legs.
Explosive Strength	The ability to use short bursts of muscle force to propel oneself (as in jumping or sprinting), or to throw an object.
Spatial Orientation	The ability to know your location in relation to the environment or to know where other objects are in relation to you.
Night Vision	The ability to see under low light conditions.
Dynamic Flexibility	The ability to quickly and repeatedly bend, stretch, twist, or reach out with your body, arms, and/or legs.
Gross Body Coordination	The ability to coordinate the movement of your arms, legs, and torso together when the whole body is in motion.
Gross Body Equilibrium	The ability to keep or regain your body balance or stay upright when in an unstable position.
Glare Sensitivity	The ability to see objects in the presence of glare or bright lighting.
Dynamic Strength	The ability to exert muscle force repeatedly or continuously over time. This involves muscular endurance and resistance to muscle fatigue.
Stamina	The ability to exert yourself physically over long periods of time without getting winded or out of breath.
Speed of Limb Movement	The ability to quickly move the arms and legs.

Work_Activity	**Work_Activity Definitions**
Interacting With Computers	Using computers and computer systems (including hardware and software) to program, write software, set up functions, enter data, or process information.
Analyzing Data or Information	Identifying the underlying principles, reasons, or facts of information by breaking down information or data into separate parts.
Processing Information	Compiling, coding, categorizing, calculating, tabulating, auditing, or verifying information or data.
Monitor Processes, Materials, or Surroundings	Monitoring and reviewing information from materials, events, or the environment, to detect or assess problems.
Making Decisions and Solving Problems	Analyzing information and evaluating results to choose the best solution and solve problems.
Getting Information	Observing, receiving, and otherwise obtaining information from all relevant sources.
Identifying Objects, Actions, and Events	Identifying information by categorizing, estimating, recognizing differences or similarities, and detecting changes in circumstances or events.
Communicating with Supervisors, Peers, or Subordin	Providing information to supervisors, co-workers, and subordinates by telephone, in written form, e-mail, or in person.
Updating and Using Relevant Knowledge	Keeping up-to-date technically and applying new knowledge to your job.
Organizing, Planning, and Prioritizing Work	Developing specific goals and plans to prioritize, organize, and accomplish your work.
Documenting/Recording Information	Entering, transcribing, recording, storing, or maintaining information in written or electronic/magnetic form.
Evaluating Information to Determine Compliance wit	Using relevant information and individual judgment to determine whether events or processes comply with laws, regulations, or standards.
Thinking Creatively	Developing, designing, or creating new applications, ideas, relationships, systems, or products, including artistic contributions.
Establishing and Maintaining Interpersonal Relatio	Developing constructive and cooperative working relationships with others, and maintaining them over time.
Communicating with Persons Outside Organization	Communicating with people outside the organization, representing the organization to customers, the public, government, and other external sources. This information can be exchanged in person, in writing, or by telephone or e-mail.

Provide Consultation and Advice to Others	Providing guidance and expert advice to management or other groups on technical, systems-, or process-related topics.
Interpreting the Meaning of Information for Others	Translating or explaining what information means and how it can be used.
Estimating the Quantifiable Characteristics of Pro	Estimating sizes, distances, and quantities; or determining time, costs, resources, or materials needed to perform a work activity.
Judging the Qualities of Things, Services, or Peop	Assessing the value, importance, or quality of things or people.
Developing Objectives and Strategies	Establishing long-range objectives and specifying the strategies and actions to achieve them.
Inspecting Equipment, Structures, or Material	Inspecting equipment, structures, or materials to identify the cause of errors or other problems or defects.
Developing and Building Teams	Encouraging and building mutual trust, respect, and cooperation among team members.
Training and Teaching Others	Identifying the educational needs of others, developing formal educational or training programs or classes, and teaching or instructing others.
Performing Administrative Activities	Performing day-to-day administrative tasks such as maintaining information files and processing paperwork.
Controlling Machines and Processes	Using either control mechanisms or direct physical activity to operate machines or processes (not including computers or vehicles).
Resolving Conflicts and Negotiating with Others	Handling complaints, settling disputes, and resolving grievances and conflicts, or otherwise negotiating with others.
Scheduling Work and Activities	Scheduling events, programs, and activities, as well as the work of others.
Monitoring and Controlling Resources	Monitoring and controlling resources and overseeing the spending of money.
Coaching and Developing Others	Identifying the developmental needs of others and coaching, mentoring, or otherwise helping others to improve their knowledge or skills.
Coordinating the Work and Activities of Others	Getting members of a group to work together to accomplish tasks.
Selling or Influencing Others	Convincing others to buy merchandise/goods or to otherwise change their minds or actions.
Handling and Moving Objects	Using hands and arms in handling, installing, positioning, and moving materials, and manipulating things.
Drafting, Laying Out, and Specifying Technical Dev	Providing documentation, detailed instructions, drawings, or specifications to tell others about how devices, parts, equipment, or structures are to be fabricated, constructed, assembled, modified, maintained, or used.
Assisting and Caring for Others	Providing personal assistance, medical attention, emotional support, or other personal care to others such as coworkers, customers, or patients.
Guiding, Directing, and Motivating Subordinates	Providing guidance and direction to subordinates, including setting performance standards and monitoring performance.
Performing General Physical Activities	Performing physical activities that require considerable use of your arms and legs and moving your whole body, such as climbing, lifting, balancing, walking, stooping, and handling of materials.
Repairing and Maintaining Electronic Equipment	Servicing, repairing, calibrating, regulating, fine-tuning, or testing machines, devices, and equipment that operate primarily on the basis of electrical or electronic (not mechanical) principles.
Repairing and Maintaining Mechanical Equipment	Servicing, repairing, adjusting, and testing machines, devices, moving parts, and equipment that operate primarily on the basis of mechanical (not electronic) principles.
Operating Vehicles, Mechanized Devices, or Equipme	Running, maneuvering, navigating, or driving vehicles or mechanized equipment, such as forklifts, passenger vehicles, aircraft, or water craft.
Performing for or Working Directly with the Public	Performing for people or dealing directly with the public. This includes serving customers in restaurants and stores, and receiving clients or guests.
Staffing Organizational Units	Recruiting, interviewing, selecting, hiring, and promoting employees in an organization.

Work_Context

	Work_Context Definitions
Telephone	How often do you have telephone conversations in this job?
Electronic Mail	How often do you use electronic mail in this job?
Face-to-Face Discussions	How often do you have to have face-to-face discussions with individuals or teams in this job?
Work With Work Group or Team	How important is it to work with others in a group or team in this job?
Structured versus Unstructured Work	To what extent is this job structured for the worker, rather than allowing the worker to determine tasks, priorities, and goals?

Freedom to Make Decisions	How much decision making freedom, without supervision, does the job offer?
Wear Common Protective or Safety Equipment such as	How much does this job require wearing common protective or safety equipment such as safety shoes, glasses, gloves, hard hats or life jackets?
Contact With Others	How much does this job require the worker to be in contact with others (face-to-face, by telephone, or otherwise) in order to perform it?
Importance of Being Exact or Accurate	How important is being very exact or highly accurate in performing this job?
Coordinate or Lead Others	How important is it to coordinate or lead others in accomplishing work activities in this job?
Indoors, Environmentally Controlled	How often does this job require working indoors in environmentally controlled conditions?
Letters and Memos	How often does the job require written letters and memos?
Spend Time Sitting	How much does this job require sitting?
Frequency of Decision Making	How frequently is the worker required to make decisions that affect other people, the financial resources, and/or the image and reputation of the organization?
Sounds, Noise Levels Are Distracting or Uncomforta	How often does this job require working exposed to sounds and noise levels that are distracting or uncomfortable?
Responsibility for Outcomes and Results	How responsible is the worker for work outcomes and results of other workers?
Impact of Decisions on Co-workers or Company Resul	How do the decisions an employee makes impact the results of co-workers, clients or the company?
Time Pressure	How often does this job require the worker to meet strict deadlines?
Consequence of Error	How serious would the result usually be if the worker made a mistake that was not readily correctable?
Exposed to Hazardous Conditions	How often does this job require exposure to hazardous conditions?
Importance of Repeating Same Tasks	How important is repeating the same physical activities (e.g., key entry) or mental activities (e.g., checking entries in a ledger) over and over, without stopping, to performing this job?
Level of Competition	To what extent does this job require the worker to compete or to be aware of competitive pressures?
Responsible for Others' Health and Safety	How much responsibility is there for the health and safety of others in this job?
Deal With External Customers	How important is it to work with external customers or the public in this job?
Frequency of Conflict Situations	How often are there conflict situations the employee has to face in this job?
Public Speaking	How often do you have to perform public speaking in this job?
Indoors, Not Environmentally Controlled	How often does this job require working indoors in non-controlled environmental conditions (e.g., warehouse without heat)?
In an Enclosed Vehicle or Equipment	How often does this job require working in a closed vehicle or equipment (e.g., car)?
Physical Proximity	To what extent does this job require the worker to perform job tasks in close physical proximity to other people?
Spend Time Standing	How much does this job require standing?
Exposed to Contaminants	How often does this job require working exposed to contaminants (such as pollutants, gases, dust or odors)?
Deal With Unpleasant or Angry People	How frequently does the worker have to deal with unpleasant, angry, or discourteous individuals as part of the job requirements?
Degree of Automation	How automated is the job?
Spend Time Walking and Running	How much does this job require walking and running?
Exposed to Hazardous Equipment	How often does this job require exposure to hazardous equipment?
Very Hot or Cold Temperatures	How often does this job require working in very hot (above 90 F degrees) or very cold (below 32 F degrees) temperatures?
Wear Specialized Protective or Safety Equipment su	How much does this job require wearing specialized protective or safety equipment such as breathing apparatus, safety harness, full protection suits, or radiation protection?
Spend Time Making Repetitive Motions	How much does this job require making repetitive motions?
Cramped Work Space, Awkward Positions	How often does this job require working in cramped work spaces that requires getting into awkward positions?
Outdoors, Exposed to Weather	How often does this job require working outdoors, exposed to all weather conditions?
Spend Time Using Your Hands to Handle, Control, or	How much does this job require using your hands to handle, control, or feel objects, tools or controls?
Extremely Bright or Inadequate Lighting	How often does this job require working in extremely bright or inadequate lighting conditions?

219

Outdoors, Under Cover	How often does this job require working outdoors, under cover (e.g., structure with roof but no walls)?
Exposed to High Places	How often does this job require exposure to high places?
Exposed to Radiation	How often does this job require exposure to radiation?
Pace Determined by Speed of Equipment	How important is it to this job that the pace is determined by the speed of equipment or machinery? (This does not refer to keeping busy at all times on this job.)
Exposed to Minor Burns, Cuts, Bites, or Stings	How often does this job require exposure to minor burns, cuts, bites, or stings?
Spend Time Climbing Ladders, Scaffolds, or Poles	How much does this job require climbing ladders, scaffolds, or poles?
Exposed to Whole Body Vibration	How often does this job require exposure to whole body vibration (e.g., operate a jackhammer)?
Deal With Physically Aggressive People	How frequently does this job require the worker to deal with physical aggression of violent individuals?
Spend Time Bending or Twisting the Body	How much does this job require bending or twisting your body?
Spend Time Kneeling, Crouching, Stooping, or Crawl	How much does this job require kneeling, crouching, stooping or crawling?
Spend Time Keeping or Regaining Balance	How much does this job require keeping or regaining your balance?
In an Open Vehicle or Equipment	How often does this job require working in an open vehicle or equipment (e.g., tractor)?
Exposed to Disease or Infections	How often does this job require exposure to disease/infections?

Job Zone Component	Job Zone Component Definitions
Title	Job Zone Four: Considerable Preparation Needed
Overall Experience	A minimum of two to four years of work-related skill, knowledge, or experience is needed for these occupations. For example, an accountant must complete four years of college and work for several years in accounting to be considered qualified.
Job Training	Employees in these occupations usually need several years of work-related experience, on-the-job training, and/or vocational training.
Job Zone Examples	Many of these occupations involve coordinating, supervising, managing, or training others. Examples include accountants, chefs and head cooks, computer programmers, historians, pharmacists, and police detectives.
SVP Range	(7.0 to < 8.0)
Education	Most of these occupations require a four - year bachelor's degree, but some do not.

Work_Styles	Work_Styles Definitions
Analytical Thinking	Job requires analyzing information and using logic to address work-related issues and problems.
Innovation	Job requires creativity and alternative thinking to develop new ideas for and answers to work-related problems.
Integrity	Job requires being honest and ethical.
Persistence	Job requires persistence in the face of obstacles.
Dependability	Job requires being reliable, responsible, and dependable, and fulfilling obligations.
Leadership	Job requires a willingness to lead, take charge, and offer opinions and direction.
Initiative	Job requires a willingness to take on responsibilities and challenges.
Independence	Job requires developing one's own ways of doing things, guiding oneself with little or no supervision, and depending on oneself to get things done.
Achievement/Effort	Job requires establishing and maintaining personally challenging achievement goals and exerting effort toward mastering tasks.
Adaptability/Flexibility	Job requires being open to change (positive or negative) and to considerable variety in the workplace.
Cooperation	Job requires being pleasant with others on the job and displaying a good-natured, cooperative attitude.
Attention to Detail	Job requires being careful about detail and thorough in completing work tasks.
Social Orientation	Job requires preferring to work with others rather than alone, and being personally connected with others on the job.

Self Control	Job requires maintaining composure, keeping emotions in check, controlling anger, and avoiding aggressive behavior, even in very difficult situations.
Stress Tolerance	Job requires accepting criticism and dealing calmly and effectively with high stress situations.
Concern for Others	Job requires being sensitive to others' needs and feelings and being understanding and helpful on the job.

17-2051.00 - Civil Engineers

Perform engineering duties in planning, designing, and overseeing construction and maintenance of building structures, and facilities, such as roads, railroads, airports, bridges, harbors, channels, dams, irrigation projects, pipelines, power plants, water and sewage systems, and waste disposal units. Includes architectural, structural, traffic, ocean, and geo-technical engineers.

Tasks

1) Plan and design transportation or hydraulic systems and structures, following construction and government standards, using design software and drawing tools.

2) Compute load and grade requirements, water flow rates, and material stress factors to determine design specifications.

3) Inspect project sites to monitor progress and ensure conformance to design specifications and safety or sanitation standards.

4) Provide technical advice regarding design, construction, or program modifications and structural repairs to industrial and managerial personnel.

5) Test soils and materials to determine the adequacy and strength of foundations, concrete, asphalt, or steel.

6) Direct or participate in surveying to lay out installations and establish reference points, grades, and elevations to guide construction.

7) Direct construction, operations, and maintenance activities at project site.

8) Prepare or present public reports, such as bid proposals, deeds, environmental impact statements, and property and right-of-way descriptions.

9) Conduct studies of traffic patterns or environmental conditions to identify engineering problems and assess the potential impact of projects.

10) Analyze survey reports, maps, drawings, blueprints, aerial photography, and other topographical or geologic data to plan projects.

Knowledge	Knowledge Definitions
Engineering and Technology	Knowledge of the practical application of engineering science and technology. This includes applying principles, techniques, procedures, and equipment to the design and production of various goods and services.
Design	Knowledge of design techniques, tools, and principles involved in production of precision technical plans, blueprints, drawings, and models.
Mathematics	Knowledge of arithmetic, algebra, geometry, calculus, statistics, and their applications.
Building and Construction	Knowledge of materials, methods, and the tools involved in the construction or repair of houses, buildings, or other structures such as highways and roads.
English Language	Knowledge of the structure and content of the English language including the meaning and spelling of words, rules of composition, and grammar.
Customer and Personal Service	Knowledge of principles and processes for providing customer and personal services. This includes customer needs assessment, meeting quality standards for services, and evaluation of customer satisfaction.
Administration and Management	Knowledge of business and management principles involved in strategic planning, resource allocation, human resources modeling, leadership technique, production methods, and coordination of people and resources.
Transportation	Knowledge of principles and methods for moving people or goods by air, rail, sea, or road, including the relative costs and benefits.
Public Safety and Security	Knowledge of relevant equipment, policies, procedures, and strategies to promote effective local, state, or national security operations for the protection of people, data, property, and institutions.

Computers and Electronics	Knowledge of circuit boards. processors. chips. electronic equipment. and computer hardware and software. including applications and programming.
Personnel and Human Resources	Knowledge of principles and procedures for personnel recruitment. selection, training, compensation and benefits. labor relations and negotiation, and personnel information systems.
Law and Government	Knowledge of laws, legal codes, court procedures, precedents, government regulations, executive orders, agency rules. and the democratic political process.
Economics and Accounting	Knowledge of economic and accounting principles and practices. the financial markets, banking and the analysis and reporting of financial data.
Clerical	Knowledge of administrative and clerical procedures and systems such as word processing, managing files and records, stenography and transcription, designing forms, and other office procedures and terminology.
Physics	Knowledge and prediction of physical principles, laws, their interrelationships, and applications to understanding fluid. material. and atmospheric dynamics, and mechanical. electrical. atomic and sub- atomic structures and processes.
Education and Training	Knowledge of principles and methods for curriculum and training design, teaching and instruction for individuals and groups. and the measurement of training effects.
Sales and Marketing	Knowledge of principles and methods for showing, promoting. and selling products or services. This includes marketing strategy and tactics, product demonstration, sales techniques, and sales control systems.
Geography	Knowledge of principles and methods for describing the features of land, sea, and air masses, including their physical characteristics, locations, interrelationships, and distribution of plant, animal, and human life.
Psychology	Knowledge of human behavior and performance; individual differences in ability, personality, and interests; learning and motivation; psychological research methods; and the assessment and treatment of behavioral and affective disorders.
Mechanical	Knowledge of machines and tools, including their designs, uses, repair, and maintenance.
Communications and Media	Knowledge of media production, communication, and dissemination techniques and methods. This includes alternative ways to inform and entertain via written, oral, and visual media.
Production and Processing	Knowledge of raw materials, production processes, quality control, costs, and other techniques for maximizing the effective manufacture and distribution of goods.
Biology	Knowledge of plant and animal organisms, their tissues, cells, functions, interdependencies, and interactions with each other and the environment.
Chemistry	Knowledge of the chemical composition, structure, and properties of substances and of the chemical processes and transformations that they undergo. This includes uses of chemicals and their interactions, danger signs, production techniques, and disposal methods.
Telecommunications	Knowledge of transmission, broadcasting, switching, control, and operation of telecommunications systems.
Sociology and Anthropology	Knowledge of group behavior and dynamics, societal trends and influences, human migrations, ethnicity, cultures and their history and origins.
History and Archeology	Knowledge of historical events and their causes, indicators, and effects on civilizations and cultures.
Therapy and Counseling	Knowledge of principles, methods, and procedures for diagnosis, treatment, and rehabilitation of physical and mental dysfunctions, and for career counseling and guidance.
Philosophy and Theology	Knowledge of different philosophical systems and religions. This includes their basic principles, values, ethics, ways of thinking, customs, practices, and their impact on human culture.
Foreign Language	Knowledge of the structure and content of a foreign (non-English) language including the meaning and spelling of words, rules of composition and grammar, and pronunciation.
Medicine and Dentistry	Knowledge of the information and techniques needed to diagnose and treat human injuries, diseases, and deformities. This includes symptoms, treatment alternatives, drug properties and interactions, and preventive health-care measures.
Food Production	Knowledge of techniques and equipment for planting, growing. and harvesting food products (both plant and animal) for consumption, including storage/handling techniques.

Fine Arts	Knowledge of the theory and techniques required to compose. produce, and perform works of music. dance. visual arts. drama, and sculpture.

Skills	**Skills Definitions**
Mathematics	Using mathematics to solve problems.
Critical Thinking	Using logic and reasoning to identify the strengths and weaknesses of alternative solutions. conclusions or approaches to problems.
Science	Using scientific rules and methods to solve problems.
Active Listening	Giving full attention to what other people are saying, taking time to understand the points being made. asking questions as appropriate, and not interrupting at inappropriate times.
Reading Comprehension	Understanding written sentences and paragraphs in work related documents.
Active Learning	Understanding the implications of new information for both current and future problem-solving and decision-making.
Complex Problem Solving	Identifying complex problems and reviewing related information to develop and evaluate options and implement solutions.
Monitoring	Monitoring/Assessing performance of yourself, other individuals, or organizations to make improvements or take corrective action.
Negotiation	Bringing others together and trying to reconcile differences.
Judgment and Decision Making	Considering the relative costs and benefits of potential actions to choose the most appropriate one.
Writing	Communicating effectively in writing as appropriate for the needs of the audience.
Coordination	Adjusting actions in relation to others' actions.
Time Management	Managing one's own time and the time of others.
Operations Analysis	Analyzing needs and product requirements to create a design.
Social Perceptiveness	Being aware of others' reactions and understanding why they react as they do.
Service Orientation	Actively looking for ways to help people.
Speaking	Talking to others to convey information effectively.
Persuasion	Persuading others to change their minds or behavior.
Instructing	Teaching others how to do something.
Technology Design	Generating or adapting equipment and technology to serve user needs.
Learning Strategies	Selecting and using training/instructional methods and procedures appropriate for the situation when learning or teaching new things.
Equipment Selection	Determining the kind of tools and equipment needed to do a job.
Quality Control Analysis	Conducting tests and inspections of products, services, or processes to evaluate quality or performance.
Troubleshooting	Determining causes of operating errors and deciding what to do about it.
Management of Personnel Resources	Motivating, developing, and directing people as they work, identifying the best people for the job.
Systems Evaluation	Identifying measures or indicators of system performance and the actions needed to improve or correct performance, relative to the goals of the system.
Systems Analysis	Determining how a system should work and how changes in conditions, operations, and the environment will affect outcomes.
Operation and Control	Controlling operations of equipment or systems.
Management of Financial Resources	Determining how money will be spent to get the work done, and accounting for these expenditures.
Installation	Installing equipment, machines, wiring, or programs to meet specifications.
Operation Monitoring	Watching gauges, dials, or other indicators to make sure a machine is working properly.
Programming	Writing computer programs for various purposes.
Management of Material Resources	Obtaining and seeing to the appropriate use of equipment, facilities, and materials needed to do certain work.
Equipment Maintenance	Performing routine maintenance on equipment and determining when and what kind of maintenance is needed.
Repairing	Repairing machines or systems using the needed tools.

Ability	**Ability Definitions**
Problem Sensitivity	The ability to tell when something is wrong or is likely to go wrong. It does not involve solving the problem, only recognizing there is a problem.
Oral Expression	The ability to communicate information and ideas in speaking so others will understand.

Deductive Reasoning	The ability to apply general rules to specific problems to produce answers that make sense.
Written Comprehension	The ability to read and understand information and ideas presented in writing.
Near Vision	The ability to see details at close range (within a few feet of the observer).
Oral Comprehension	The ability to listen to and understand information and ideas presented through spoken words and sentences.
Speech Clarity	The ability to speak clearly so others can understand you.
Visualization	The ability to imagine how something will look after it is moved around or when its parts are moved or rearranged.
Information Ordering	The ability to arrange things or actions in a certain order or pattern according to a specific rule or set of rules (e.g., patterns of numbers, letters, words, pictures, mathematical operations).
Originality	The ability to come up with unusual or clever ideas about a given topic or situation, or to develop creative ways to solve a problem.
Inductive Reasoning	The ability to combine pieces of information to form general rules or conclusions (includes finding a relationship among seemingly unrelated events).
Speech Recognition	The ability to identify and understand the speech of another person.
Written Expression	The ability to communicate information and ideas in writing so others will understand.
Fluency of Ideas	The ability to come up with a number of ideas about a topic (the number of ideas is important, not their quality, correctness, or creativity).
Selective Attention	The ability to concentrate on a task over a period of time without being distracted.
Mathematical Reasoning	The ability to choose the right mathematical methods or formulas to solve a problem.
Category Flexibility	The ability to generate or use different sets of rules for combining or grouping things in different ways.
Far Vision	The ability to see details at a distance.
Flexibility of Closure	The ability to identify or detect a known pattern (a figure, object, word, or sound) that is hidden in other distracting material.
Depth Perception	The ability to judge which of several objects is closer or farther away from you, or to judge the distance between you and an object.
Finger Dexterity	The ability to make precisely coordinated movements of the fingers of one or both hands to grasp, manipulate, or assemble very small objects.
Visual Color Discrimination	The ability to match or detect differences between colors, including shades of color and brightness.
Speed of Closure	The ability to quickly make sense of, combine, and organize information into meaningful patterns.
Time Sharing	The ability to shift back and forth between two or more activities or sources of information (such as speech, sounds, touch, or other sources).
Control Precision	The ability to quickly and repeatedly adjust the controls of a machine or a vehicle to exact positions.
Multilimb Coordination	The ability to coordinate two or more limbs (for example, two arms, two legs, or one leg and one arm) while sitting, standing, or lying down. It does not involve performing the activities while the whole body is in motion.
Number Facility	The ability to add, subtract, multiply, or divide quickly and correctly.
Memorization	The ability to remember information such as words, numbers, pictures, and procedures.
Perceptual Speed	The ability to quickly and accurately compare similarities and differences among sets of letters, numbers, objects, pictures, or patterns. The things to be compared may be presented at the same time or one after the other. This ability also includes comparing a presented object with a remembered object.
Arm-Hand Steadiness	The ability to keep your hand and arm steady while moving your arm or while holding your arm and hand in one position.
Auditory Attention	The ability to focus on a single source of sound in the presence of other distracting sounds.
Manual Dexterity	The ability to quickly move your hand, your hand together with your arm, or your two hands to grasp, manipulate, or assemble objects.
Hearing Sensitivity	The ability to detect or tell the differences between sounds that vary in pitch and loudness.
Spatial Orientation	The ability to know your location in relation to the environment or to know where other objects are in relation to you.
Reaction Time	The ability to quickly respond (with the hand, finger, or foot) to a signal (sound, light, picture) when it appears.

Trunk Strength	The ability to use your abdominal and lower back muscles to support part of the body repeatedly or continuously over time without 'giving out' or fatiguing.
Extent Flexibility	The ability to bend, stretch, twist, or reach with your body, arms, and/or legs.
Peripheral Vision	The ability to see objects or movement of objects to one's side when the eyes are looking ahead.
Static Strength	The ability to exert maximum muscle force to lift, push, pull, or carry objects.
Response Orientation	The ability to choose quickly between two or more movements in response to two or more different signals (lights, sounds, pictures). It includes the speed with which the correct response is started with the hand, foot, or other body part.
Dynamic Strength	The ability to exert muscle force repeatedly or continuously over time. This involves muscular endurance and resistance to muscle fatigue.
Wrist-Finger Speed	The ability to make fast, simple, repeated movements of the fingers, hands, and wrists.
Gross Body Coordination	The ability to coordinate the movement of your arms, legs, and torso together when the whole body is in motion.
Stamina	The ability to exert yourself physically over long periods of time without getting winded or out of breath.
Gross Body Equilibrium	The ability to keep or regain your body balance or stay upright when in an unstable position.
Sound Localization	The ability to tell the direction from which a sound originated.
Speed of Limb Movement	The ability to quickly move the arms and legs.
Rate Control	The ability to time your movements or the movement of a piece of equipment in anticipation of changes in the speed and/or direction of a moving object or scene.
Dynamic Flexibility	The ability to quickly and repeatedly bend, stretch, twist, or reach out with your body, arms, and/or legs.
Explosive Strength	The ability to use short bursts of muscle force to propel oneself (as in jumping or sprinting), or to throw an object.
Night Vision	The ability to see under low light conditions.
Glare Sensitivity	The ability to see objects in the presence of glare or bright lighting.

Work_Activity	Work_Activity Definitions
Drafting, Laying Out, and Specifying Technical Dev	Providing documentation, detailed instructions, drawings, or specifications to tell others about how devices, parts, equipment, or structures are to be fabricated, constructed, assembled, modified, maintained, or used.
Making Decisions and Solving Problems	Analyzing information and evaluating results to choose the best solution and solve problems.
Interacting With Computers	Using computers and computer systems (including hardware and software) to program, write software, set up functions, enter data, or process information.
Communicating with Supervisors, Peers, or Subordin	Providing information to supervisors, co-workers, and subordinates by telephone, in written form, e-mail, or in person
Documenting/Recording Information	Entering, transcribing, recording, storing, or maintaining information in written or electronic/magnetic form.
Thinking Creatively	Developing, designing, or creating new applications, ideas, relationships, systems, or products, including artistic contributions.
Organizing, Planning, and Prioritizing Work	Developing specific goals and plans to prioritize, organize, and accomplish your work.
Getting Information	Observing, receiving, and otherwise obtaining information from all relevant sources.
Estimating the Quantifiable Characteristics of Pro	Estimating sizes, distances, and quantities; or determining time, costs, resources, or materials needed to perform a work activity.
Interpreting the Meaning of Information for Others	Translating or explaining what information means and how it can be used.
Analyzing Data or Information	Identifying the underlying principles, reasons, or facts of information by breaking down information or data into separate parts.
Scheduling Work and Activities	Scheduling events, programs, and activities, as well as the work of others.
Evaluating Information to Determine Compliance wit	Using relevant information and individual judgment to determine whether events or processes comply with laws, regulations, or standards.
Updating and Using Relevant Knowledge	Keeping up-to-date technically and applying new knowledge to your job.

Communicating with Persons Outside Organization	Communicating with people outside the organization. representing the organization to customers. the public. government. and other external sources. This information can be exchanged in person. in writing. or by telephone or e-mail.
Judging the Qualities of Things. Services. or Peop	Assessing the value, importance, or quality of things or people.
Developing and Building Teams	Encouraging and building mutual trust, respect, and cooperation among team members.
Resolving Conflicts and Negotiating with Others	Handling complaints, settling disputes, and resolving grievances and conflicts, or otherwise negotiating with others.
Establishing and Maintaining Interpersonal Relatio	Developing constructive and cooperative working relationships with others, and maintaining them over time.
Processing Information	Compiling, coding, categorizing, calculating. tabulating. auditing, or verifying information or data.
Monitor Processes, Materials, or Surroundings	Monitoring and reviewing information from materials, events, or the environment, to detect or assess problems.
Performing for or Working Directly with the Public	Performing for people or dealing directly with the public. This includes serving customers in restaurants and stores, and receiving clients or guests.
Inspecting Equipment, Structures, or Material	Inspecting equipment, structures, or materials to identify the cause of errors or other problems or defects.
Identifying Objects, Actions, and Events	Identifying information by categorizing. estimating. recognizing differences or similarities. and detecting changes in circumstances or events.
Coordinating the Work and Activities of Others	Getting members of a group to work together to accomplish tasks.
Coaching and Developing Others	Identifying the developmental needs of others and coaching, mentoring, or otherwise helping others to improve their knowledge or skills.
Selling or Influencing Others	Convincing others to buy merchandise/goods or to otherwise change their minds or actions.
Training and Teaching Others	Identifying the educational needs of others, developing formal educational or training programs or classes, and teaching or instructing others.
Monitoring and Controlling Resources	Monitoring and controlling resources and overseeing the spending of money.
Developing Objectives and Strategies	Establishing long-range objectives and specifying the strategies and actions to achieve them.
Provide Consultation and Advice to Others	Providing guidance and expert advice to management or other groups on technical, systems-, or process-related topics.
Guiding, Directing, and Motivating Subordinates	Providing guidance and direction to subordinates, including setting performance standards and monitoring performance.
Performing Administrative Activities	Performing day-to-day administrative tasks such as maintaining information files and processing paperwork.
Staffing Organizational Units	Recruiting, interviewing, selecting, hiring, and promoting employees in an organization.
Assisting and Caring for Others	Providing personal assistance, medical attention, emotional support, or other personal care to others such as coworkers, customers, or patients.
Repairing and Maintaining Electronic Equipment	Servicing, repairing, calibrating, regulating, fine-tuning, or testing machines, devices, and equipment that operate primarily on the basis of electrical or electronic (not mechanical) principles.
Operating Vehicles, Mechanized Devices, or Equipme	Running, maneuvering, navigating, or driving vehicles or mechanized equipment, such as forklifts, passenger vehicles, aircraft, or water craft.
Repairing and Maintaining Mechanical Equipment	Servicing, repairing, adjusting, and testing machines, devices, moving parts, and equipment that operate primarily on the basis of mechanical (not electronic) principles.
Performing General Physical Activities	Performing physical activities that require considerable use of your arms and legs and moving your whole body, such as climbing, lifting, balancing, walking, stooping, and handling of materials.
Controlling Machines and Processes	Using either control mechanisms or direct physical activity to operate machines or processes (not including computers or vehicles).
Handling and Moving Objects	Using hands and arms in handling. installing. positioning, and moving materials, and manipulating things.

Work_Context	**Work_Context Definitions**
Telephone	How often do you have telephone conversations in this job?
Freedom to Make Decisions	How much decision making freedom. without supervision, does the job offer?
Face-to-Face Discussions	How often do you have to have face-to-face discussions with individuals or teams in this job?

Importance of Being Exact or Accurate	How important is being very exact or highly accurate in performing this job?
Letters and Memos	How often does the job require written letters and memos?
In an Enclosed Vehicle or Equipment	How often does this job require working in a closed vehicle or equipment (e.g.. car)?
Responsibility for Outcomes and Results	How responsible is the worker for work outcomes and results of other workers?
Structured versus Unstructured Work	To what extent is this job structured for the worker, rather than allowing the worker to determine tasks, priorities, and goals?
Impact of Decisions on Co-workers or Company Resul	How do the decisions an employee makes impact the results of co-workers. clients or the company?
Spend Time Sitting	How much does this job require sitting?
Outdoors. Exposed to Weather	How often does this job require working outdoors, exposed to all weather conditions?
Frequency of Conflict Situations	How often are there conflict situations the employee has to face in this job?
Indoors, Environmentally Controlled	How often does this job require working indoors in environmentally controlled conditions?
Coordinate or Lead Others	How important is it to coordinate or lead others in accomplishing work activities in this job?
Frequency of Decision Making	How frequently is the worker required to make decisions that affect other people, the financial resources, and/or the image and reputation of the organization?
Work With Work Group or Team	How important is it to work with others in a group or team in this job?
Deal With External Customers	How important is it to work with external customers or the public in this job?
Exposed to Contaminants	How often does this job require working exposed to contaminants (such as pollutants, gases, dust or odors)?
Very Hot or Cold Temperatures	How often does this job require working in very hot (above 90 F degrees) or very cold (below 32 F degrees) temperatures?
Indoors, Not Environmentally Controlled	How often does this job require working indoors in non-controlled environmental conditions (e.g., warehouse without heat)?
Contact With Others	How much does this job require the worker to be in contact with others (face-to-face, by telephone, or otherwise) in order to perform it?
Time Pressure	How often does this job require the worker to meet strict deadlines?
Exposed to Hazardous Equipment	How often does this job require exposure to hazardous equipment?
Consequence of Error	How serious would the result usually be if the worker made a mistake that was not readily correctable?
Level of Competition	To what extent does this job require the worker to compete or to be aware of competitive pressures?
Deal With Unpleasant or Angry People	How frequently does the worker have to deal with unpleasant, angry, or discourteous individuals as part of the job requirements?
Sounds, Noise Levels Are Distracting or Uncomforta	How often does this job require working exposed to sounds and noise levels that are distracting or uncomfortable?
Electronic Mail	How often do you use electronic mail in this job?
Wear Common Protective or Safety Equipment such as	How much does this job require wearing common protective or safety equipment such as safety shoes, glasses, gloves, hard hats or live jackets?
Physical Proximity	To what extent does this job require the worker to perform job tasks in close physical proximity to other people?
Spend Time Standing	How much does this job require standing?
Importance of Repeating Same Tasks	How important is repeating the same physical activities (e.g., key entry) or mental activities (e.g., checking entries in a ledger) over and over, without stopping, to performing this job?
Public Speaking	How often do you have to perform public speaking in this job?
Responsible for Others' Health and Safety	How much responsibility is there for the health and safety of others in this job?
Spend Time Using Your Hands to Handle, Control, or	How much does this job require using your hands to handle, control, or feel objects, tools or controls?
Spend Time Walking and Running	How much does this job require walking and running?
Outdoors, Under Cover	How often does this job require working outdoors, under cover (e.g., structure with roof but no walls)?
Exposed to Hazardous Conditions	How often does this job require exposure to hazardous conditions?
Cramped Work Space, Awkward Positions	How often does this job require working in cramped work spaces that requires getting into awkward positions?
Spend Time Making Repetitive Motions	How much does this job require making repetitive motions?
Exposed to Radiation	How often does this job require exposure to radiation?

Exposed to Minor Burns, Cuts, Bites, or Stings	How often does this job require exposure to minor burns, cuts, bites, or stings?
Degree of Automation	How automated is the job?
Exposed to Disease or Infections	How often does this job require exposure to disease/infections?
Spend Time Bending or Twisting the Body	How much does this job require bending or twisting your body?
Extremely Bright or Inadequate Lighting	How often does this job require working in extremely bright or inadequate lighting conditions?
Pace Determined by Speed of Equipment	How important is it to this job that the pace is determined by the speed of equipment or machinery? (This does not refer to keeping busy at all times on this job.)
Deal With Physically Aggressive People	How frequently does this job require the worker to deal with physical aggression of violent individuals?
Exposed to High Places	How often does this job require exposure to high places?
Spend Time Kneeling, Crouching, Stooping, or Crawl	How much does this job require kneeling, crouching, stooping or crawling?
Wear Specialized Protective or Safety Equipment su	How much does this job require wearing specialized protective or safety equipment such as breathing apparatus, safety harness, full protection suits, or radiation protection?
Spend Time Climbing Ladders, Scaffolds, or Poles	How much does this job require climbing ladders, scaffolds, or poles?
Spend Time Keeping or Regaining Balance	How much does this job require keeping or regaining your balance?
Exposed to Whole Body Vibration	How often does this job require exposure to whole body vibration (e.g., operate a jackhammer)?
In an Open Vehicle or Equipment	How often does this job require working in an open vehicle or equipment (e.g., tractor)?

Job Zone Component	Job Zone Component Definitions
Title	Job Zone Four: Considerable Preparation Needed
Overall Experience	A minimum of two to four years of work-related skill, knowledge, or experience is needed for these occupations. For example, an accountant must complete four years of college and work for several years in accounting to be considered qualified.
Job Training	Employees in these occupations usually need several years of work-related experience, on-the-job training, and/or vocational training.
Job Zone Examples	Many of these occupations involve coordinating, supervising, managing, or training others. Examples include accountants, chefs and head cooks, computer programmers, historians, pharmacists, and police detectives.
SVP Range	(7.0 to < 8.0)
Education	Most of these occupations require a four-year bachelor's degree, but some do not.

Work_Styles	Work_Styles Definitions
Dependability	Job requires being reliable, responsible, and dependable, and fulfilling obligations.
Integrity	Job requires being honest and ethical.
Attention to Detail	Job requires being careful about detail and thorough in completing work tasks.
Initiative	Job requires a willingness to take on responsibilities and challenges.
Analytical Thinking	Job requires analyzing information and using logic to address work-related issues and problems.
Leadership	Job requires a willingness to lead, take charge, and offer opinions and direction.
Self Control	Job requires maintaining composure, keeping emotions in check, controlling anger, and avoiding aggressive behavior, even in very difficult situations.
Persistence	Job requires persistence in the face of obstacles.
Achievement/Effort	Job requires establishing and maintaining personally challenging achievement goals and exerting effort toward mastering tasks.
Stress Tolerance	Job requires accepting criticism and dealing calmly and effectively with high stress situations.
Cooperation	Job requires being pleasant with others on the job and displaying a good-natured, cooperative attitude.
Independence	Job requires developing one's own ways of doing things, guiding oneself with little or no supervision, and depending on oneself to get things done.

Adaptability/Flexibility	Job requires being open to change (positive or negative) and to considerable variety in the workplace.
Social Orientation	Job requires preferring to work with others rather than alone, and being personally connected with others on the job.
Innovation	Job requires creativity and alternative thinking to develop new ideas for and answers to work-related problems.
Concern for Others	Job requires being sensitive to others' needs and feelings and being understanding and helpful on the job.

17-2061.00 - Computer Hardware Engineers

Research, design, develop, and test computer or computer-related equipment for commercial, industrial, military, or scientific use. May supervise the manufacturing and installation of computer or computer-related equipment and components.

Tasks

1) Provide technical support to designers, marketing and sales departments, suppliers, engineers and other team members throughout the product development and implementation process.

2) Evaluate factors such as reporting formats required, cost constraints, and need for security restrictions to determine hardware configuration.

3) Test and verify hardware and support peripherals to ensure that they meet specifications and requirements, analyzing and recording test data.

4) Analyze information to determine, recommend, and plan layout, including type of computers and peripheral equipment modifications.

5) Analyze user needs and recommend appropriate hardware.

6) Build, test and modify product prototypes, using working models or theoretical models constructed using computer simulation.

7) Specify power supply requirements and configuration, drawing on system performance expectations and design specifications.

8) Monitor functioning of equipment and make necessary modifications to ensure system operates in conformance with specifications.

9) Store, retrieve, and manipulate data for analysis of system capabilities and requirements.

10) Write detailed functional specifications that document the hardware development process and support hardware introduction.

11) Assemble and modify existing pieces of equipment to meet special needs.

12) Direct technicians, engineering designers or other technical support personnel as needed.

13) Provide training and support to system designers and users.

14) Recommend purchase of equipment to control dust, temperature, and humidity in area of system installation.

15) Select hardware and material, assuring compliance with specifications and product requirements.

16) Update knowledge and skills to keep up with rapid advancements in computer technology.

17) Design and develop computer hardware and support peripherals, including central processing units (CPUs), support logic, microprocessors, custom integrated circuits, and printers and disk drives.

17-2071.00 - Electrical Engineers

Design, develop, test, or supervise the manufacturing and installation of electrical equipment, components, or systems for commercial, industrial, military, or scientific use.

Tasks

1) Direct and coordinate manufacturing, construction, installation, maintenance, support, documentation, and testing activities to ensure compliance with specifications, codes, and customer requirements.

2) Design, implement, maintain, and improve electrical instruments, equipment, facilities, components, products, and systems for commercial, industrial, and domestic purposes.

3) Prepare specifications for purchase of materials and equipment.

224

4) Operate computer-assisted engineering and design software and equipment to perform engineering tasks.

5) Inspect completed installations and observe operations, to ensure conformance to design and equipment specifications and compliance with operational and safety standards.

6) Compile data and write reports regarding existing and potential engineering studies and projects.

7) Plan and implement research methodology and procedures to apply principles of electrical theory to engineering projects.

8) Investigate and test vendors' and competitors' products.

9) Supervise and train project team members as necessary.

10) Perform detailed calculations to compute and establish manufacturing, construction, and installation standards and specifications.

11) Investigate customer or public complaints, determine nature and extent of problem, and recommend remedial measures.

12) Prepare and study technical drawings, specifications of electrical systems, and topographical maps to ensure that installation and operations conform to standards and customer requirements.

13) Oversee project production efforts to assure projects are completed satisfactorily, on time and within budget.

14) Develop budgets, estimating labor, material, and construction costs.

15) Assist in developing capital project programs for new equipment and major repairs.

16) Conduct field surveys and study maps, graphs, diagrams, and other data to identify and correct power system problems.

17) Plan layout of electric power generating plants and distribution lines and stations.

18) Collect data relating to commercial and residential development, population, and power system interconnection to determine operating efficiency of electrical systems.

Knowledge	Knowledge Definitions
Engineering and Technology	Knowledge of the practical application of engineering science and technology. This includes applying principles, techniques, procedures, and equipment to the design and production of various goods and services.
Computers and Electronics	Knowledge of circuit boards, processors, chips, electronic equipment, and computer hardware and software, including applications and programming.
Mathematics	Knowledge of arithmetic, algebra, geometry, calculus, statistics, and their applications.
English Language	Knowledge of the structure and content of the English language including the meaning and spelling of words, rules of composition, and grammar.
Design	Knowledge of design techniques, tools, and principles involved in production of precision technical plans, blueprints, drawings, and models.
Physics	Knowledge and prediction of physical principles, laws, their interrelationships, and applications to understanding fluid, material, and atmospheric dynamics, and mechanical, electrical, atomic and sub- atomic structures and processes.
Telecommunications	Knowledge of transmission, broadcasting, switching, control, and operation of telecommunications systems.
Production and Processing	Knowledge of raw materials, production processes, quality control, costs, and other techniques for maximizing the effective manufacture and distribution of goods.
Customer and Personal Service	Knowledge of principles and processes for providing customer and personal services. This includes customer needs assessment, meeting quality standards for services, and evaluation of customer satisfaction.
Chemistry	Knowledge of the chemical composition, structure, and properties of substances and of the chemical processes and transformations that they undergo. This includes uses of chemicals and their interactions, danger signs, production techniques, and disposal methods.
Administration and Management	Knowledge of business and management principles involved in strategic planning, resource allocation, human resources modeling, leadership technique, production methods, and coordination of people and resources.
Mechanical	Knowledge of machines and tools, including their designs, uses, repair, and maintenance.
Psychology	Knowledge of human behavior and performance; individual differences in ability, personality, and interests; learning and motivation; psychological research methods; and the assessment and treatment of behavioral and affective disorders.
Education and Training	Knowledge of principles and methods for curriculum and training design, teaching and instruction for individuals and groups, and the measurement of training effects.
Clerical	Knowledge of administrative and clerical procedures and systems such as word processing, managing files and records, stenography and transcription, designing forms, and other office procedures and terminology.
Public Safety and Security	Knowledge of relevant equipment, policies, procedures, and strategies to promote effective local, state, or national security operations for the protection of people, data, property, and institutions.
Sales and Marketing	Knowledge of principles and methods for showing, promoting, and selling products or services. This includes marketing strategy and tactics, product demonstration, sales techniques, and sales control systems.
Communications and Media	Knowledge of media production, communication, and dissemination techniques and methods. This includes alternative ways to inform and entertain via written, oral, and visual media.
Transportation	Knowledge of principles and methods for moving people or goods by air, rail, sea, or road, including the relative costs and benefits.
Building and Construction	Knowledge of materials, methods, and the tools involved in the construction or repair of houses, buildings, or other structures such as highways and roads.
Economics and Accounting	Knowledge of economic and accounting principles and practices, the financial markets, banking and the analysis and reporting of financial data.
Personnel and Human Resources	Knowledge of principles and procedures for personnel recruitment, selection, training, compensation and benefits, labor relations and negotiation, and personnel information systems.
Sociology and Anthropology	Knowledge of group behavior and dynamics, societal trends and influences, human migrations, ethnicity, cultures and their history and origins.
Geography	Knowledge of principles and methods for describing the features of land, sea, and air masses, including their physical characteristics, locations, interrelationships, and distribution of plant, animal, and human life.
Law and Government	Knowledge of laws, legal codes, court procedures, precedents, government regulations, executive orders, agency rules, and the democratic political process.
Biology	Knowledge of plant and animal organisms, their tissues, cells, functions, interdependencies, and interactions with each other and the environment.
Therapy and Counseling	Knowledge of principles, methods, and procedures for diagnosis, treatment, and rehabilitation of physical and mental dysfunctions, and for career counseling and guidance.
Foreign Language	Knowledge of the structure and content of a foreign (non-English) language including the meaning and spelling of words, rules of composition and grammar, and pronunciation.
Philosophy and Theology	Knowledge of different philosophical systems and religions. This includes their basic principles, values, ethics, ways of thinking, customs, practices, and their impact on human culture.
Medicine and Dentistry	Knowledge of the information and techniques needed to diagnose and treat human injuries, diseases, and deformities. This includes symptoms, treatment alternatives, drug properties and interactions, and preventive health-care measures.
History and Archeology	Knowledge of historical events and their causes, indicators, and effects on civilizations and cultures.
Fine Arts	Knowledge of the theory and techniques required to compose, produce, and perform works of music, dance, visual arts, drama, and sculpture.
Food Production	Knowledge of techniques and equipment for planting, growing, and harvesting food products (both plant and animal) for consumption, including storage/handling techniques.

Skills	Skills Definitions
Active Listening	Giving full attention to what other people are saying, taking time to understand the points being made, asking questions as appropriate, and not interrupting at inappropriate times.
Troubleshooting	Determining causes of operating errors and deciding what to do about it.
Critical Thinking	Using logic and reasoning to identify the strengths and weaknesses of alternative solutions, conclusions or approaches to problems.

Reading Comprehension	Understanding written sentences and paragraphs in work related documents.
Technology Design	Generating or adapting equipment and technology to serve user needs.
Complex Problem Solving	Identifying complex problems and reviewing related information to develop and evaluate options and implement solutions.
Active Learning	Understanding the implications of new information for both current and future problem-solving and decision-making.
Systems Analysis	Determining how a system should work and how changes in conditions, operations, and the environment will affect outcomes.
Judgment and Decision Making	Considering the relative costs and benefits of potential actions to choose the most appropriate one.
Time Management	Managing one's own time and the time of others.
Coordination	Adjusting actions in relation to others' actions.
Equipment Selection	Determining the kind of tools and equipment needed to do a job.
Learning Strategies	Selecting and using training/instructional methods and procedures appropriate for the situation when learning or teaching new things.
Speaking	Talking to others to convey information effectively.
Systems Evaluation	Identifying measures or indicators of system performance and the actions needed to improve or correct performance, relative to the goals of the system.
Mathematics	Using mathematics to solve problems.
Monitoring	Monitoring/Assessing performance of yourself, other individuals, or organizations to make improvements or take corrective action.
Writing	Communicating effectively in writing as appropriate for the needs of the audience.
Science	Using scientific rules and methods to solve problems.
Service Orientation	Actively looking for ways to help people.
Operation and Control	Controlling operations of equipment or systems.
Management of Personnel Resources	Motivating, developing, and directing people as they work, identifying the best people for the job.
Operations Analysis	Analyzing needs and product requirements to create a design.
Management of Financial Resources	Determining how money will be spent to get the work done, and accounting for these expenditures.
Quality Control Analysis	Conducting tests and inspections of products, services, or processes to evaluate quality or performance.
Management of Material Resources	Obtaining and seeing to the appropriate use of equipment, facilities, and materials needed to do certain work.
Installation	Installing equipment, machines, wiring, or programs to meet specifications.
Social Perceptiveness	Being aware of others' reactions and understanding why they react as they do.
Negotiation	Bringing others together and trying to reconcile differences.
Operation Monitoring	Watching gauges, dials, or other indicators to make sure a machine is working properly.
Instructing	Teaching others how to do something.
Equipment Maintenance	Performing routine maintenance on equipment and determining when and what kind of maintenance is needed.
Persuasion	Persuading others to change their minds or behavior.
Programming	Writing computer programs for various purposes.
Repairing	Repairing machines or systems using the needed tools.

Ability	Ability Definitions
Deductive Reasoning	The ability to apply general rules to specific problems to produce answers that make sense.
Near Vision	The ability to see details at close range (within a few feet of the observer).
Problem Sensitivity	The ability to tell when something is wrong or is likely to go wrong. It does not involve solving the problem, only recognizing there is a problem.
Visualization	The ability to imagine how something will look after it is moved around or when its parts are moved or rearranged.
Mathematical Reasoning	The ability to choose the right mathematical methods or formulas to solve a problem.
Information Ordering	The ability to arrange things or actions in a certain order or pattern according to a specific rule or set of rules (e.g., patterns of numbers, letters, words, pictures, mathematical operations).
Oral Expression	The ability to communicate information and ideas in speaking so others will understand.
Speech Clarity	The ability to speak clearly so others can understand you.
Written Expression	The ability to communicate information and ideas in writing so others will understand.

Oral Comprehension	The ability to listen to and understand information and ideas presented through spoken words and sentences.
Written Comprehension	The ability to read and understand information and ideas presented in writing.
Inductive Reasoning	The ability to combine pieces of information to form general rules or conclusions (includes finding a relationship among seemingly unrelated events).
Speech Recognition	The ability to identify and understand the speech of another person.
Originality	The ability to come up with unusual or clever ideas about a given topic or situation, or to develop creative ways to solve a problem.
Fluency of Ideas	The ability to come up with a number of ideas about a topic (the number of ideas is important, not their quality, correctness, or creativity).
Flexibility of Closure	The ability to identify or detect a known pattern (a figure, object, word, or sound) that is hidden in other distracting material.
Selective Attention	The ability to concentrate on a task over a period of time without being distracted.
Category Flexibility	The ability to generate or use different sets of rules for combining or grouping things in different ways.
Speed of Closure	The ability to quickly make sense of, combine, and organize information into meaningful patterns.
Memorization	The ability to remember information such as words, numbers, pictures, and procedures.
Far Vision	The ability to see details at a distance.
Time Sharing	The ability to shift back and forth between two or more activities or sources of information (such as speech, sounds, touch, or other sources).
Perceptual Speed	The ability to quickly and accurately compare similarities and differences among sets of letters, numbers, objects, pictures, or patterns. The things to be compared may be presented at the same time or one after the other. This ability also includes comparing a presented object with a remembered object.
Number Facility	The ability to add, subtract, multiply, or divide quickly and correctly.
Visual Color Discrimination	The ability to match or detect differences between colors, including shades of color and brightness.
Depth Perception	The ability to judge which of several objects is closer or farther away from you, or to judge the distance between you and an object.
Spatial Orientation	The ability to know your location in relation to the environment or to know where other objects are in relation to you.
Finger Dexterity	The ability to make precisely coordinated movements of the fingers of one or both hands to grasp, manipulate, or assemble very small objects.
Hearing Sensitivity	The ability to detect or tell the differences between sounds that vary in pitch and loudness.
Auditory Attention	The ability to focus on a single source of sound in the presence of other distracting sounds.
Control Precision	The ability to quickly and repeatedly adjust the controls of a machine or a vehicle to exact positions.
Extent Flexibility	The ability to bend, stretch, twist, or reach with your body, arms, and/or legs.
Arm-Hand Steadiness	The ability to keep your hand and arm steady while moving your arm or while holding your arm and hand in one position.
Manual Dexterity	The ability to quickly move your hand, your hand together with your arm, or your two hands to grasp, manipulate, or assemble objects.
Reaction Time	The ability to quickly respond (with the hand, finger, or foot) to a signal (sound, light, picture) when it appears.
Night Vision	The ability to see under low light conditions.
Glare Sensitivity	The ability to see objects in the presence of glare or bright lighting.
Trunk Strength	The ability to use your abdominal and lower back muscles to support part of the body repeatedly or continuously over time without 'giving out' or fatiguing.
Stamina	The ability to exert yourself physically over long periods of time without getting winded or out of breath.
Explosive Strength	The ability to use short bursts of muscle force to propel oneself (as in jumping or sprinting), or to throw an object.
Dynamic Flexibility	The ability to quickly and repeatedly bend, stretch, twist, or reach out with your body, arms, and/or legs.
Gross Body Coordination	The ability to coordinate the movement of your arms, legs, and torso together when the whole body is in motion.
Gross Body Equilibrium	The ability to keep or regain your body balance or stay upright when in an unstable position.

Static Strength	The ability to exert maximum muscle force to lift, push, pull, or carry objects.
Sound Localization	The ability to tell the direction from which a sound originated.
Speed of Limb Movement	The ability to quickly move the arms and legs.
Peripheral Vision	The ability to see objects or movement of objects to one's side when the eyes are looking ahead.
Dynamic Strength	The ability to exert muscle force repeatedly or continuously over time. This involves muscular endurance and resistance to muscle fatigue.
Multilimb Coordination	The ability to coordinate two or more limbs (for example, two arms, two legs, or one leg and one arm) while sitting, standing, or lying down. It does not involve performing the activities while the whole body is in motion.
Response Orientation	The ability to choose quickly between two or more movements in response to two or more different signals (lights, sounds, pictures). It includes the speed with which the correct response is started with the hand, foot, or other body part.
Rate Control	The ability to time your movements or the movement of a piece of equipment in anticipation of changes in the speed and/or direction of a moving object or scene.
Wrist-Finger Speed	The ability to make fast, simple, repeated movements of the fingers, hands, and wrists.

Work_Activity	Work_Activity Definitions
Interacting With Computers	Using computers and computer systems (including hardware and software) to program, write software, set up functions, enter data, or process information.
Organizing, Planning, and Prioritizing Work	Developing specific goals and plans to prioritize, organize, and accomplish your work.
Getting Information	Observing, receiving, and otherwise obtaining information from all relevant sources.
Making Decisions and Solving Problems	Analyzing information and evaluating results to choose the best solution and solve problems.
Analyzing Data or Information	Identifying the underlying principles, reasons, or facts of information by breaking down information or data into separate parts.
Updating and Using Relevant Knowledge	Keeping up-to-date technically and applying new knowledge to your job.
Thinking Creatively	Developing, designing, or creating new applications, ideas, relationships, systems, or products, including artistic contributions.
Documenting/Recording Information	Entering, transcribing, recording, storing, or maintaining information in written or electronic/magnetic form.
Communicating with Supervisors, Peers, or Subordin	Providing information to supervisors, co-workers, and subordinates by telephone, in written form, e-mail, or in person.
Evaluating Information to Determine Compliance wit	Using relevant information and individual judgment to determine whether events or processes comply with laws, regulations, or standards.
Identifying Objects, Actions, and Events	Identifying information by categorizing, estimating, recognizing differences or similarities, and detecting changes in circumstances or events.
Estimating the Quantifiable Characteristics of Pro	Estimating sizes, distances, and quantities; or determining time, costs, resources, or materials needed to perform a work activity.
Judging the Qualities of Things, Services, or Peop	Assessing the value, importance, or quality of things or people.
Scheduling Work and Activities	Scheduling events, programs, and activities, as well as the work of others.
Communicating with Persons Outside Organization	Communicating with people outside the organization, representing the organization to customers, the public, government, and other external sources. This information can be exchanged in person, in writing, or by telephone or e-mail.
Interpreting the Meaning of Information for Others	Translating or explaining what information means and how it can be used.
Establishing and Maintaining Interpersonal Relatio	Developing constructive and cooperative working relationships with others, and maintaining them over time.
Processing Information	Compiling, coding, categorizing, calculating, tabulating, auditing, or verifying information or data.
Developing Objectives and Strategies	Establishing long-range objectives and specifying the strategies and actions to achieve them.
Drafting, Laying Out, and Specifying Technical Dev	Providing documentation, detailed instructions, drawings, or specifications to tell others about how devices, parts, equipment, or structures are to be fabricated, constructed, assembled, modified, maintained, or used.

Provide Consultation and Advice to Others	Providing guidance and expert advice to management or other groups on technical, systems-, or process-related topics.
Monitor Processes, Materials, or Surroundings	Monitoring and reviewing information from materials, events, or the environment, to detect or assess problems.
Developing and Building Teams	Encouraging and building mutual trust, respect, and cooperation among team members.
Coordinating the Work and Activities of Others	Getting members of a group to work together to accomplish tasks.
Inspecting Equipment, Structures, or Material	Inspecting equipment, structures, or materials to identify the cause of errors or other problems or defects.
Training and Teaching Others	Identifying the educational needs of others, developing formal educational or training programs or classes, and teaching or instructing others.
Assisting and Caring for Others	Providing personal assistance, medical attention, emotional support, or other personal care to others such as coworkers, customers, or patients.
Guiding, Directing, and Motivating Subordinates	Providing guidance and direction to subordinates, including setting performance standards and monitoring performance.
Coaching and Developing Others	Identifying the developmental needs of others and coaching, mentoring, or otherwise helping others to improve their knowledge or skills.
Resolving Conflicts and Negotiating with Others	Handling complaints, settling disputes, and resolving grievances and conflicts, or otherwise negotiating with others.
Repairing and Maintaining Electronic Equipment	Servicing, repairing, calibrating, regulating, fine-tuning, or testing machines, devices, and equipment that operate primarily on the basis of electrical or electronic (not mechanical) principles.
Operating Vehicles, Mechanized Devices, or Equipme	Running, maneuvering, navigating, or driving vehicles or mechanized equipment, such as forklifts, passenger vehicles, aircraft, or water craft.
Performing General Physical Activities	Performing physical activities that require considerable use of your arms and legs and moving your whole body, such as climbing, lifting, balancing, walking, stooping, and handling of materials.
Monitoring and Controlling Resources	Monitoring and controlling resources and overseeing the spending of money.
Controlling Machines and Processes	Using either control mechanisms or direct physical activity to operate machines or processes (not including computers or vehicles).
Handling and Moving Objects	Using hands and arms in handling, installing, positioning, and moving materials, and manipulating things.
Selling or Influencing Others	Convincing others to buy merchandise/goods or to otherwise change their minds or actions.
Repairing and Maintaining Mechanical Equipment	Servicing, repairing, adjusting, and testing machines, devices, moving parts, and equipment that operate primarily on the basis of mechanical (not electronic) principles.
Performing Administrative Activities	Performing day-to-day administrative tasks such as maintaining information files and processing paperwork.
Staffing Organizational Units	Recruiting, interviewing, selecting, hiring, and promoting employees in an organization.
Performing for or Working Directly with the Public	Performing for people or dealing directly with the public. This includes serving customers in restaurants and stores, and receiving clients or guests.

Work_Context	Work_Context Definitions
Indoors, Environmentally Controlled	How often does this job require working indoors in environmentally controlled conditions?
Electronic Mail	How often do you use electronic mail in this job?
Freedom to Make Decisions	How much decision making freedom, without supervision, does the job offer?
Structured versus Unstructured Work	To what extent is this job structured for the worker, rather than allowing the worker to determine tasks, priorities, and goals?
Face-to-Face Discussions	How often do you have to have face-to-face discussions with individuals or teams in this job?
Importance of Being Exact or Accurate	How important is being very exact or highly accurate in performing this job?
Telephone	How often do you have telephone conversations in this job?
Spend Time Sitting	How much does this job require sitting?
Work With Work Group or Team	How important is it to work with others in a group or team in this job?
Responsibility for Outcomes and Results	How responsible is the worker for work outcomes and results of other workers?
Level of Competition	To what extent does this job require the worker to compete or to be aware of competitive pressures?

227

Impact of Decisions on Co-workers or Company Resul	How do the decisions an employee makes impact the results of co-workers, clients or the company?
Contact With Others	How much does this job require the worker to be in contact with others (face-to-face, by telephone, or otherwise) in order to perform it?
Letters and Memos	How often does the job require written letters and memos?
Time Pressure	How often does this job require the worker to meet strict deadlines?
Coordinate or Lead Others	How important is it to coordinate or lead others in accomplishing work activities in this job?
Frequency of Decision Making	How frequently is the worker required to make decisions that affect other people, the financial resources, and/or the image and reputation of the organization?
Physical Proximity	To what extent does this job require the worker to perform job tasks in close physical proximity to other people?
Responsible for Others' Health and Safety	How much responsibility is there for the health and safety of others in this job?
Importance of Repeating Same Tasks	How important is repeating the same physical activities (e.g., key entry) or mental activities (e.g., checking entries in a ledger) over and over, without stopping, to performing this job?
Consequence of Error	How serious would the result usually be if the worker made a mistake that was not readily correctable?
Sounds, Noise Levels Are Distracting or Uncomforta	How often does this job require working exposed to sounds and noise levels that are distracting or uncomfortable?
Deal With External Customers	How important is it to work with external customers or the public in this job?
Spend Time Using Your Hands to Handle, Control, or	How much does this job require using your hands to handle, control, or feel objects, tools or controls?
Deal With Unpleasant or Angry People	How frequently does the worker have to deal with unpleasant, angry, or discourteous individuals as part of the job requirements?
Wear Common Protective or Safety Equipment such as	How much does this job require wearing common protective or safety equipment such as safety shoes, glasses, gloves, hard hats or live jackets?
Frequency of Conflict Situations	How often are there conflict situations the employee has to face in this job?
Spend Time Standing	How much does this job require standing?
Degree of Automation	How automated is the job?
Exposed to Contaminants	How often does this job require working exposed to contaminants (such as pollutants, gases, dust or odors)?
Public Speaking	How often do you have to perform public speaking in this job?
Exposed to Hazardous Conditions	How often does this job require exposure to hazardous conditions?
Spend Time Making Repetitive Motions	How much does this job require making repetitive motions?
Spend Time Walking and Running	How much does this job require walking and running?
Exposed to Hazardous Equipment	How often does this job require exposure to hazardous equipment?
Indoors, Not Environmentally Controlled	How often does this job require working indoors in non-controlled environmental conditions (e.g., warehouse without heat)?
Very Hot or Cold Temperatures	How often does this job require working in very hot (above 90 F degrees) or very cold (below 32 F degrees) temperatures?
In an Enclosed Vehicle or Equipment	How often does this job require working in a closed vehicle or equipment (e.g., car)?
Spend Time Bending or Twisting the Body	How much does this job require bending or twisting your body?
Cramped Work Space, Awkward Positions	How often does this job require working in cramped work spaces that requires getting into awkward positions?
Spend Time Kneeling, Crouching, Stooping, or Crawl	How much does this job require kneeling, crouching, stooping, or crawling?
Exposed to Minor Burns, Cuts, Bites, or Stings	How often does this job require exposure to minor burns, cuts, bites, or stings?
Extremely Bright or Inadequate Lighting	How often does this job require working in extremely bright or inadequate lighting conditions?
Exposed to High Places	How often does this job require exposure to high places?
Outdoors, Exposed to Weather	How often does this job require working outdoors, exposed to all weather conditions?
Pace Determined by Speed of Equipment	How important is it to this job that the pace is determined by the speed of equipment or machinery? (This does not refer to keeping busy at all times on this job.)
Outdoors, Under Cover	How often does this job require working outdoors, under cover (e.g., structure with roof but no walls)?

Spend Time Keeping or Regaining Balance	How much does this job require keeping or regaining your balance?
Spend Time Climbing Ladders, Scaffolds, or Poles	How much does this job require climbing ladders, scaffolds, or poles?
Exposed to Disease or Infections	How often does this job require exposure to disease/infections?
In an Open Vehicle or Equipment	How often does this job require working in an open vehicle or equipment (e.g., tractor)?
Exposed to Radiation	How often does this job require exposure to radiation?
Deal With Physically Aggressive People	How frequently does this job require the worker to deal with physical aggression of violent individuals?
Wear Specialized Protective or Safety Equipment su	How much does this job require wearing specialized protective or safety equipment such as breathing apparatus, safety harness, full protection suits, or radiation protection?
Exposed to Whole Body Vibration	How often does this job require exposure to whole body vibration (e.g., operate a jackhammer)?

Job Zone Component	Job Zone Component Definitions
Title	Job Zone Four: Considerable Preparation Needed
Overall Experience	A minimum of two to four years of work-related skill, knowledge, or experience is needed for these occupations. For example, an accountant must complete four years of college and work for several years in accounting to be considered qualified.
Job Training	Employees in these occupations usually need several years of work-related experience, on-the-job training, and/or vocational training.
Job Zone Examples	Many of these occupations involve coordinating, supervising, managing, or training others. Examples include accountants, chefs and head cooks, computer programmers, historians, pharmacists, and police detectives.
SVP Range	(7.0 to < 8.0)
Education	Most of these occupations require a four - year bachelor's degree, but some do not.

Work_Styles	Work_Styles Definitions
Attention to Detail	Job requires being careful about detail and thorough in completing work tasks.
Analytical Thinking	Job requires analyzing information and using logic to address work-related issues and problems.
Integrity	Job requires being honest and ethical.
Dependability	Job requires being reliable, responsible, and dependable, and fulfilling obligations.
Self Control	Job requires maintaining composure, keeping emotions in check, controlling anger, and avoiding aggressive behavior, even in very difficult situations.
Initiative	Job requires a willingness to take on responsibilities and challenges.
Stress Tolerance	Job requires accepting criticism and dealing calmly and effectively with high stress situations.
Cooperation	Job requires being pleasant with others on the job and displaying a good-natured, cooperative attitude.
Achievement/Effort	Job requires establishing and maintaining personally challenging achievement goals and exerting effort toward mastering tasks.
Adaptability/Flexibility	Job requires being open to change (positive or negative) and to considerable variety in the workplace.
Persistence	Job requires persistence in the face of obstacles.
Innovation	Job requires creativity and alternative thinking to develop new ideas for and answers to work-related problems.
Leadership	Job requires a willingness to lead, take charge, and offer opinions and direction.
Independence	Job requires developing one's own ways of doing things, guiding oneself with little or no supervision, and depending on oneself to get things done.
Social Orientation	Job requires preferring to work with others rather than alone, and being personally connected with others on the job.
Concern for Others	Job requires being sensitive to others' needs and feelings and being understanding and helpful on the job.

17-2081.00 - Environmental Engineers

Design, plan, or perform engineering duties in the prevention, control, and remediation of environmental health hazards utilizing various engineering disciplines. Work may include waste treatment, site remediation, or pollution control technology.

Tasks

1) Provide administrative support for projects by collecting data, providing project documentation, training staff, and performing other general administrative duties.

2) Develop proposed project objectives and targets, and report to management on progress in attaining them.

3) Prepare, review, and update environmental investigation and recommendation reports.

4) Request bids from suppliers or consultants.

5) Assist in budget implementation, forecasts, and administration.

6) Monitor progress of environmental improvement programs.

7) Advise industries and government agencies about environmental policies and standards.

8) Provide technical-level support for environmental remediation and litigation projects, including remediation system design and determination of regulatory applicability.

9) Assess the existing or potential environmental impact of land use projects on air, water, and land.

10) Inspect industrial and municipal facilities and programs in order to evaluate operational effectiveness and ensure compliance with environmental regulations.

11) Obtain, update, and maintain plans, permits, and standard operating procedures.

12) Provide environmental engineering assistance in network analysis, regulatory analysis, and planning or reviewing database development.

13) Inform company employees and other interested parties of environmental issues.

14) Advise corporations and government agencies of procedures to follow in cleaning up contaminated sites in order to protect people and the environment.

15) Maintain, write, and revise quality-assurance documentation and procedures.

16) Serve on teams conducting multimedia inspections at complex facilities, providing assistance with planning, quality assurance, safety inspection protocols, and sampling.

17) Develop, implement, and manage plans and programs related to conservation and management of natural resources.

18) Coordinate and manage environmental protection programs and projects, assigning and evaluating work.

19) Develop site-specific health and safety protocols, such as spill contingency plans and methods for loading and transporting waste.

20) Serve as liaison with federal, state, and local agencies and officials on issues pertaining to solid and hazardous waste program requirements.

21) Develop and present environmental compliance training or orientation sessions.

22) Design systems, processes, and equipment for control, management, and remediation of water, air, and soil quality.

23) Assess, sort, characterize, and pack known and unknown materials.

24) Prepare hazardous waste manifests and land disposal restriction notifications.

Knowledge	Knowledge Definitions
Public Safety and Security	Knowledge of relevant equipment, policies, procedures, and strategies to promote effective local, state, or national security operations for the protection of people, data, property, and institutions.
Mathematics	Knowledge of arithmetic, algebra, geometry, calculus, statistics, and their applications.
Law and Government	Knowledge of laws, legal codes, court procedures, precedents, government regulations, executive orders, agency rules, and the democratic political process.
Engineering and Technology	Knowledge of the practical application of engineering science and technology. This includes applying principles, techniques, procedures, and equipment to the design and production of various goods and services.
English Language	Knowledge of the structure and content of the English language including the meaning and spelling of words, rules of composition, and grammar.
Administration and Management	Knowledge of business and management principles involved in strategic planning, resource allocation, human resources modeling, leadership technique, production methods, and coordination of people and resources.
Education and Training	Knowledge of principles and methods for curriculum and training design, teaching and instruction for individuals and groups, and the measurement of training effects.
Chemistry	Knowledge of the chemical composition, structure, and properties of substances and of the chemical processes and transformations that they undergo. This includes uses of chemicals and their interactions, danger signs, production techniques, and disposal methods.
Computers and Electronics	Knowledge of circuit boards, processors, chips, electronic equipment, and computer hardware and software, including applications and programming.
Design	Knowledge of design techniques, tools, and principles involved in production of precision technical plans, blueprints, drawings, and models.
Customer and Personal Service	Knowledge of principles and processes for providing customer and personal services. This includes customer needs assessment, meeting quality standards for services, and evaluation of customer satisfaction.
Clerical	Knowledge of administrative and clerical procedures and systems such as word processing, managing files and records, stenography and transcription, designing forms, and other office procedures and terminology.
Biology	Knowledge of plant and animal organisms, their tissues, cells, functions, interdependencies, and interactions with each other and the environment.
Physics	Knowledge and prediction of physical principles, laws, their interrelationships, and applications to understanding fluid, material, and atmospheric dynamics, and mechanical, electrical, atomic and sub-atomic structures and processes.
Building and Construction	Knowledge of materials, methods, and the tools involved in the construction or repair of houses, buildings, or other structures such as highways and roads.
Communications and Media	Knowledge of media production, communication, and dissemination techniques and methods. This includes alternative ways to inform and entertain via written, oral, and visual media.
Sales and Marketing	Knowledge of principles and methods for showing, promoting, and selling products or services. This includes marketing strategy and tactics, product demonstration, sales techniques, and sales control systems.
Mechanical	Knowledge of machines and tools, including their designs, uses, repair, and maintenance.
Telecommunications	Knowledge of transmission, broadcasting, switching, control, and operation of telecommunications systems.
Production and Processing	Knowledge of raw materials, production processes, quality control, costs, and other techniques for maximizing the effective manufacture and distribution of goods.
Personnel and Human Resources	Knowledge of principles and procedures for personnel recruitment, selection, training, compensation and benefits, labor relations and negotiation, and personnel information systems.
Transportation	Knowledge of principles and methods for moving people or goods by air, rail, sea, or road, including the relative costs and benefits.
Geography	Knowledge of principles and methods for describing the features of land, sea, and air masses, including their physical characteristics, locations, interrelationships, and distribution of plant, animal, and human life.
Psychology	Knowledge of human behavior and performance; individual differences in ability, personality, and interests; learning and motivation; psychological research methods; and the assessment and treatment of behavioral and affective disorders.
Medicine and Dentistry	Knowledge of the information and techniques needed to diagnose and treat human injuries, diseases, and deformities. This includes symptoms, treatment alternatives, drug properties and interactions, and preventive health-care measures.
Economics and Accounting	Knowledge of economic and accounting principles and practices, the financial markets, banking and the analysis and reporting of financial data.
History and Archeology	Knowledge of historical events and their causes, indicators, and effects on civilizations and cultures.
Sociology and Anthropology	Knowledge of group behavior and dynamics, societal trends and influences, human migrations, ethnicity, cultures and their history and origins.

Therapy and Counseling	Knowledge of principles, methods, and procedures for diagnosis, treatment, and rehabilitation of physical and mental dysfunctions, and for career counseling and guidance.
Philosophy and Theology	Knowledge of different philosophical systems and religions. This includes their basic principles, values, ethics, ways of thinking, customs, practices, and their impact on human culture.
Food Production	Knowledge of techniques and equipment for planting, growing, and harvesting food products (both plant and animal) for consumption, including storage/handling techniques.
Foreign Language	Knowledge of the structure and content of a foreign (non-English) language including the meaning and spelling of words, rules of composition and grammar, and pronunciation.
Fine Arts	Knowledge of the theory and techniques required to compose, produce, and perform works of music, dance, visual arts, drama, and sculpture.

Skills	Skills Definitions
Reading Comprehension	Understanding written sentences and paragraphs in work related documents.
Active Listening	Giving full attention to what other people are saying, taking time to understand the points being made, asking questions as appropriate, and not interrupting at inappropriate times.
Science	Using scientific rules and methods to solve problems.
Writing	Communicating effectively in writing as appropriate for the needs of the audience.
Critical Thinking	Using logic and reasoning to identify the strengths and weaknesses of alternative solutions, conclusions or approaches to problems.
Speaking	Talking to others to convey information effectively.
Time Management	Managing one's own time and the time of others.
Active Learning	Understanding the implications of new information for both current and future problem-solving and decision-making.
Complex Problem Solving	Identifying complex problems and reviewing related information to develop and evaluate options and implement solutions.
Coordination	Adjusting actions in relation to others' actions.
Judgment and Decision Making	Considering the relative costs and benefits of potential actions to choose the most appropriate one.
Mathematics	Using mathematics to solve problems.
Negotiation	Bringing others together and trying to reconcile differences.
Learning Strategies	Selecting and using training/instructional methods and procedures appropriate for the situation when learning or teaching new things.
Management of Financial Resources	Determining how money will be spent to get the work done, and accounting for these expenditures.
Technology Design	Generating or adapting equipment and technology to serve user needs.
Persuasion	Persuading others to change their minds or behavior.
Monitoring	Monitoring/Assessing performance of yourself, other individuals, or organizations to make improvements or take corrective action.
Social Perceptiveness	Being aware of others' reactions and understanding why they react as they do.
Systems Evaluation	Identifying measures or indicators of system performance and the actions needed to improve or correct performance, relative to the goals of the system.
Systems Analysis	Determining how a system should work and how changes in conditions, operations, and the environment will affect outcomes.
Operations Analysis	Analyzing needs and product requirements to create a design.
Service Orientation	Actively looking for ways to help people.
Instructing	Teaching others how to do something.
Quality Control Analysis	Conducting tests and inspections of products, services, or processes to evaluate quality or performance.
Equipment Selection	Determining the kind of tools and equipment needed to do a job.
Management of Personnel Resources	Motivating, developing, and directing people as they work, identifying the best people for the job.
Management of Material Resources	Obtaining and seeing to the appropriate use of equipment, facilities, and materials needed to do certain work.
Programming	Writing computer programs for various purposes.
Troubleshooting	Determining causes of operating errors and deciding what to do about it.
Operation and Control	Controlling operations of equipment or systems.
Operation Monitoring	Watching gauges, dials, or other indicators to make sure a machine is working properly.

Equipment Maintenance	Performing routine maintenance on equipment and determining when and what kind of maintenance is needed.
Repairing	Repairing machines or systems using the needed tools.
Installation	Installing equipment, machines, wiring, or programs to meet specifications.

Ability	Ability Definitions
Oral Expression	The ability to communicate information and ideas in speaking so others will understand.
Problem Sensitivity	The ability to tell when something is wrong or is likely to go wrong. It does not involve solving the problem, only recognizing there is a problem.
Oral Comprehension	The ability to listen to and understand information and ideas presented through spoken words and sentences.
Inductive Reasoning	The ability to combine pieces of information to form general rules or conclusions (includes finding a relationship among seemingly unrelated events).
Deductive Reasoning	The ability to apply general rules to specific problems to produce answers that make sense.
Written Comprehension	The ability to read and understand information and ideas presented in writing.
Speech Clarity	The ability to speak clearly so others can understand you.
Speech Recognition	The ability to identify and understand the speech of another person.
Written Expression	The ability to communicate information and ideas in writing so others will understand.
Near Vision	The ability to see details at close range (within a few feet of the observer).
Information Ordering	The ability to arrange things or actions in a certain order or pattern according to a specific rule or set of rules (e.g., patterns of numbers, letters, words, pictures, mathematical operations).
Selective Attention	The ability to concentrate on a task over a period of time without being distracted.
Category Flexibility	The ability to generate or use different sets of rules for combining or grouping things in different ways.
Time Sharing	The ability to shift back and forth between two or more activities or sources of information (such as speech, sounds, touch, or other sources).
Flexibility of Closure	The ability to identify or detect a known pattern (a figure, object, word, or sound) that is hidden in other distracting material.
Originality	The ability to come up with unusual or clever ideas about a given topic or situation, or to develop creative ways to solve a problem.
Mathematical Reasoning	The ability to choose the right mathematical methods or formulas to solve a problem.
Fluency of Ideas	The ability to come up with a number of ideas about a topic (the number of ideas is important, not their quality, correctness, or creativity).
Far Vision	The ability to see details at a distance.
Perceptual Speed	The ability to quickly and accurately compare similarities and differences among sets of letters, numbers, objects, pictures, or patterns. The things to be compared may be presented at the same time or one after the other. This ability also includes comparing a presented object with a remembered object.
Visualization	The ability to imagine how something will look after it is moved around or when its parts are moved or rearranged.
Auditory Attention	The ability to focus on a single source of sound in the presence of other distracting sounds.
Memorization	The ability to remember information such as words, numbers, pictures, and procedures.
Speed of Closure	The ability to quickly make sense of, combine, and organize information into meaningful patterns.
Depth Perception	The ability to judge which of several objects is closer or farther away from you, or to judge the distance between you and an object.
Arm-Hand Steadiness	The ability to keep your hand and arm steady while moving your arm or while holding your arm and hand in one position.
Manual Dexterity	The ability to quickly move your hand, your hand together with your arm, or your two hands to grasp, manipulate, or assemble objects.
Visual Color Discrimination	The ability to match or detect differences between colors, including shades of color and brightness.
Trunk Strength	The ability to use your abdominal and lower back muscles to support part of the body repeatedly or continuously over time without 'giving out' or fatiguing.

Number Facility	The ability to add, subtract, multiply, or divide quickly and correctly.	Analyzing Data or Information	Identifying the underlying principles, reasons, or facts of information by breaking down information or data into separate parts.
Hearing Sensitivity	The ability to detect or tell the differences between sounds that vary in pitch and loudness.	Updating and Using Relevant Knowledge	Keeping up-to-date technically and applying new knowledge to your job.
Stamina	The ability to exert yourself physically over long periods of time without getting winded or out of breath.	Establishing and Maintaining Interpersonal Relatio	Developing constructive and cooperative working relationships with others, and maintaining them over time.
Finger Dexterity	The ability to make precisely coordinated movements of the fingers of one or both hands to grasp, manipulate, or assemble very small objects.	Documenting/Recording Information	Entering, transcribing, recording, storing, or maintaining information in written or electronic/magnetic form.
Control Precision	The ability to quickly and repeatedly adjust the controls of a machine or a vehicle to exact positions.	Organizing, Planning, and Prioritizing Work	Developing specific goals and plans to prioritize, organize, and accomplish your work.
Multilimb Coordination	The ability to coordinate two or more limbs (for example, two arms, two legs, or one leg and one arm) while sitting, standing, or lying down. It does not involve performing the activities while the whole body is in motion.	Estimating the Quantifiable Characteristics of Pro	Estimating sizes, distances, and quantities; or determining time, costs, resources, or materials needed to perform a work activity.
Spatial Orientation	The ability to know your location in relation to the environment or to know where other objects are in relation to you.	Interpreting the Meaning of Information for Others	Translating or explaining what information means and how it can be used.
Gross Body Coordination	The ability to coordinate the movement of your arms, legs, and torso together when the whole body is in motion.	Inspecting Equipment, Structures, or Material	Inspecting equipment, structures, or materials to identify the cause of errors or other problems or defects.
Static Strength	The ability to exert maximum muscle force to lift, push, pull, or carry objects.	Provide Consultation and Advice to Others	Providing guidance and expert advice to management or other groups on technical, systems-, or process-related topics.
Reaction Time	The ability to quickly respond (with the hand, finger, or foot) to a signal (sound, light, picture) when it appears.	Thinking Creatively	Developing, designing, or creating new applications, ideas, relationships, systems, or products, including artistic contributions.
Sound Localization	The ability to tell the direction from which a sound originated.		
Glare Sensitivity	The ability to see objects in the presence of glare or bright lighting.	Developing Objectives and Strategies	Establishing long-range objectives and specifying the strategies and actions to achieve them.
Night Vision	The ability to see under low light conditions.	Scheduling Work and Activities	Scheduling events, programs, and activities, as well as the work of others.
Dynamic Flexibility	The ability to quickly and repeatedly bend, stretch, twist, or reach out with your body, arms, and/or legs.	Performing Administrative Activities	Performing day-to-day administrative tasks such as maintaining information files and processing paperwork.
Gross Body Equilibrium	The ability to keep or regain your body balance or stay upright when in an unstable position.	Judging the Qualities of Things, Services, or Peop	Assessing the value, importance, or quality of things or people.
Speed of Limb Movement	The ability to quickly move the arms and legs.	Coordinating the Work and Activities of Others	Getting members of a group to work together to accomplish tasks.
Wrist-Finger Speed	The ability to make fast, simple, repeated movements of the fingers, hands, and wrists.	Performing for or Working Directly with the Public	Performing for people or dealing directly with the public. This includes serving customers in restaurants and stores, and receiving clients or guests.
Extent Flexibility	The ability to bend, stretch, twist, or reach with your body, arms, and/or legs.	Resolving Conflicts and Negotiating with Others	Handling complaints, settling disputes, and resolving grievances and conflicts, or otherwise negotiating with others.
Response Orientation	The ability to choose quickly between two or more movements in response to two or more different signals (lights, sounds, pictures). It includes the speed with which the correct response is started with the hand, foot, or other body part.	Performing General Physical Activities	Performing physical activities that require considerable use of your arms and legs and moving your whole body, such as climbing, lifting, balancing, walking, stooping, and handling of materials.
Peripheral Vision	The ability to see objects or movement of objects to one's side when the eyes are looking ahead.	Training and Teaching Others	Identifying the educational needs of others, developing formal educational or training programs or classes, and teaching or instructing others.
Dynamic Strength	The ability to exert muscle force repeatedly or continuously over time. This involves muscular endurance and resistance to muscle fatigue.	Controlling Machines and Processes	Using either control mechanisms or direct physical activity to operate machines or processes (not including computers or vehicles).
Explosive Strength	The ability to use short bursts of muscle force to propel oneself (as in jumping or sprinting), or to throw an object.	Operating Vehicles, Mechanized Devices, or Equipme	Running, maneuvering, navigating, or driving vehicles or mechanized equipment, such as forklifts, passenger vehicles, aircraft, or water craft.
Rate Control	The ability to time your movements or the movement of a piece of equipment in anticipation of changes in the speed and/or direction of a moving object or scene.	Selling or Influencing Others	Convincing others to buy merchandise/goods or to otherwise change their minds or actions.

Work_Activity	**Work_Activity Definitions**	Monitoring and Controlling Resources	Monitoring and controlling resources and overseeing the spending of money.
Evaluating Information to Determine Compliance wit	Using relevant information and individual judgment to determine whether events or processes comply with laws, regulations, or standards.	Handling and Moving Objects	Using hands and arms in handling, installing, positioning, and moving materials, and manipulating things.
Getting Information	Observing, receiving, and otherwise obtaining information from all relevant sources.	Assisting and Caring for Others	Providing personal assistance, medical attention, emotional support, or other personal care to others such as coworkers, customers, or patients.
Monitor Processes, Materials, or Surroundings	Monitoring and reviewing information from materials, events, or the environment, to detect or assess problems.	Drafting, Laying Out, and Specifying Technical Dev	Providing documentation, detailed instructions, drawings, or specifications to tell others about how devices, parts, equipment, or structures are to be fabricated, constructed, assembled, modified, maintained, or used.
Making Decisions and Solving Problems	Analyzing information and evaluating results to choose the best solution and solve problems.	Guiding, Directing, and Motivating Subordinates	Providing guidance and direction to subordinates, including setting performance standards and monitoring performance.
Communicating with Supervisors, Peers, or Subordin	Providing information to supervisors, co-workers, and subordinates by telephone, in written form, e-mail, or in person.	Coaching and Developing Others	Identifying the developmental needs of others and coaching, mentoring, or otherwise helping others to improve their knowledge or skills.
Interacting With Computers	Using computers and computer systems (including hardware and software) to program, write software, set up functions, enter data, or process information.	Developing and Building Teams	Encouraging and building mutual trust, respect, and cooperation among team members.
Communicating with Persons Outside Organization	Communicating with people outside the organization, representing the organization to customers, the public, government, and other external sources. This information can be exchanged in person, in writing, or by telephone or e-mail.	Repairing and Maintaining Electronic Equipment	Servicing, repairing, calibrating, regulating, fine-tuning, or testing machines, devices, and equipment that operate primarily on the basis of electrical or electronic (not mechanical) principles.
Identifying Objects, Actions, and Events	Identifying information by categorizing, estimating, recognizing differences or similarities, and detecting changes in circumstances or events.		
Processing Information	Compiling, coding, categorizing, calculating, tabulating, auditing, or verifying information or data.		

231

| Repairing and Maintaining Mechanical Equipment | Servicing, repairing, adjusting, and testing machines, devices, moving parts, and equipment that operate primarily on the basis of mechanical (not electronic) principles. |
| Staffing Organizational Units | Recruiting, interviewing, selecting, hiring, and promoting employees in an organization. |

Work_Context	Work_Context Definitions
Telephone	How often do you have telephone conversations in this job?
Electronic Mail	How often do you use electronic mail in this job?
Face-to-Face Discussions	How often do you have to have face-to-face discussions with individuals or teams in this job?
Contact With Others	How much does this job require the worker to be in contact with others (face-to-face, by telephone, or otherwise) in order to perform it?
Letters and Memos	How often does the job require written letters and memos?
Structured versus Unstructured Work	To what extent is this job structured for the worker, rather than allowing the worker to determine tasks, priorities, and goals?
Indoors, Environmentally Controlled	How often does this job require working indoors in environmentally controlled conditions?
Importance of Being Exact or Accurate	How important is being very exact or highly accurate in performing this job?
Spend Time Sitting	How much does this job require sitting?
Freedom to Make Decisions	How much decision making freedom, without supervision, does the job offer?
Work With Work Group or Team	How important is it to work with others in a group or team in this job?
Coordinate or Lead Others	How important is it to coordinate or lead others in accomplishing work activities in this job?
Impact of Decisions on Co-workers or Company Resul	How do the decisions an employee makes impact the results of co-workers, clients or the company?
Frequency of Decision Making	How frequently is the worker required to make decisions that affect other people, the financial resources, and/or the image and reputation of the organization?
Responsible for Others' Health and Safety	How much responsibility is there for the health and safety of others in this job?
Time Pressure	How often does this job require the worker to meet strict deadlines?
Responsibility for Outcomes and Results	How responsible is the worker for work outcomes and results of other workers?
Deal With External Customers	How important is it to work with external customers or the public in this job?
Importance of Repeating Same Tasks	How important is repeating the same physical activities (e.g., key entry) or mental activities (e.g., checking entries in a ledger) over and over, without stopping, to performing this job?
Wear Common Protective or Safety Equipment such as	How much does this job require wearing common protective or safety equipment such as safety shoes, glasses, gloves, hard hats or life jackets?
Physical Proximity	To what extent does this job require the worker to perform job tasks in close physical proximity to other people?
Frequency of Conflict Situations	How often are there conflict situations the employee has to face in this job?
Indoors, Not Environmentally Controlled	How often does this job require working indoors in non-controlled environmental conditions (e.g., warehouse without heat)?
Sounds, Noise Levels Are Distracting or Uncomforta	How often does this job require working exposed to sounds and noise levels that are distracting or uncomfortable?
Very Hot or Cold Temperatures	How often does this job require working in very hot (above 90 F degrees) or very cold (below 32 F degrees) temperatures?
Level of Competition	To what extent does this job require the worker to compete or to be aware of competitive pressures?
Outdoors, Exposed to Weather	How often does this job require working outdoors, exposed to all weather conditions?
Deal With Unpleasant or Angry People	How frequently does the worker have to deal with unpleasant, angry, or discourteous individuals as part of the job requirements?
Spend Time Using Your Hands to Handle, Control, or	How much does this job require using your hands to handle, control, or feel objects, tools or controls?
Public Speaking	How often do you have to perform public speaking in this job?
Exposed to Hazardous Conditions	How often does this job require exposure to hazardous conditions?
Consequence of Error	How serious would the result usually be if the worker made a mistake that was not readily correctable?
In an Enclosed Vehicle or Equipment	How often does this job require working in a closed vehicle or equipment (e.g., car)?

Exposed to Contaminants	How often does this job require working exposed to contaminants (such as pollutants, gases, dust or odors)?
Spend Time Making Repetitive Motions	How much does this job require making repetitive motions?
Outdoors, Under Cover	How often does this job require working outdoors, under cover (e.g., structure with roof but no walls)?
Exposed to Hazardous Equipment	How often does this job require exposure to hazardous equipment?
Spend Time Standing	How much does this job require standing?
Spend Time Walking and Running	How much does this job require walking and running?
Degree of Automation	How automated is the job?
Spend Time Bending or Twisting the Body	How much does this job require bending or twisting your body?
Exposed to High Places	How often does this job require exposure to high places?
Extremely Bright or Inadequate Lighting	How often does this job require working in extremely bright or inadequate lighting conditions?
Spend Time Keeping or Regaining Balance	How much does this job require keeping or regaining your balance?
Wear Specialized Protective or Safety Equipment su	How much does this job require wearing specialized protective or safety equipment such as breathing apparatus, safety harness, full protection suits, or radiation protection?
Exposed to Minor Burns, Cuts, Bites, or Stings	How often does this job require exposure to minor burns, cuts, bites, or stings?
Cramped Work Space, Awkward Positions	How often does this job require working in cramped work spaces that requires getting into awkward positions?
Spend Time Kneeling, Crouching, Stooping, or Crawl	How much does this job require kneeling, crouching, stooping, or crawling?
Spend Time Climbing Ladders, Scaffolds, or Poles	How much does this job require climbing ladders, scaffolds, or poles?
In an Open Vehicle or Equipment	How often does this job require working in an open vehicle or equipment (e.g., tractor)?
Exposed to Whole Body Vibration	How often does this job require exposure to whole body vibration (e.g., operate a jackhammer)?
Exposed to Disease or Infections	How often does this job require exposure to disease/infections?
Deal With Physically Aggressive People	How frequently does this job require the worker to deal with physical aggression of violent individuals?
Exposed to Radiation	How often does this job require exposure to radiation?
Pace Determined by Speed of Equipment	How important is it to this job that the pace is determined by the speed of equipment or machinery? (This does not refer to keeping busy at all times on this job.)

Job Zone Component	Job Zone Component Definitions
Title	Job Zone Five: Extensive Preparation Needed
Overall Experience	Extensive skill, knowledge, and experience are needed for these occupations. Many require more than five years of experience. For example, surgeons must complete four years of college and an additional five to seven years of specialized medical training to be able to do their job.
Job Training	Employees may need some on-the-job training, but most of these occupations assume that the person will already have the required skills, knowledge, work-related experience, and/or training.
Job Zone Examples	These occupations often involve coordinating, training, supervising, or managing the activities of others to accomplish goals. Very advanced communication and organizational skills are required. Examples include athletic trainers, lawyers, managing editors, physicists, social psychologists, and surgeons.
SVP Range	(8.0 and above)
Education	A bachelor's degree is the minimum formal education required for these occupations. However, many also require graduate school. For example, they may require a master's degree, and some require a Ph.D., M.D., or J.D. (law degree).

Work_Styles	Work_Styles Definitions
Integrity	Job requires being honest and ethical.
Initiative	Job requires a willingness to take on responsibilities and challenges.
Attention to Detail	Job requires being careful about detail and thorough in completing work tasks.
Persistence	Job requires persistence in the face of obstacles.

Achievement/Effort	Job requires establishing and maintaining personally challenging achievement goals and exerting effort toward mastering tasks.
Cooperation	Job requires being pleasant with others on the job and displaying a good-natured, cooperative attitude.
Independence	Job requires developing one's own ways of doing things, guiding oneself with little or no supervision, and depending on oneself to get things done.
Dependability	Job requires being reliable, responsible, and dependable, and fulfilling obligations.
Analytical Thinking	Job requires analyzing information and using logic to address work-related issues and problems.
Self Control	Job requires maintaining composure, keeping emotions in check, controlling anger, and avoiding aggressive behavior, even in very difficult situations.
Leadership	Job requires a willingness to lead, take charge, and offer opinions and direction.
Stress Tolerance	Job requires accepting criticism and dealing calmly and effectively with high stress situations.
Adaptability/Flexibility	Job requires being open to change (positive or negative) and to considerable variety in the workplace.
Innovation	Job requires creativity and alternative thinking to develop new ideas for and answers to work-related problems.
Concern for Others	Job requires being sensitive to others' needs and feelings and being understanding and helpful on the job.
Social Orientation	Job requires preferring to work with others rather than alone, and being personally connected with others on the job.

17-2112.00 - Industrial Engineers

Design, develop, test, and evaluate integrated systems for managing industrial production processes including human work factors, quality control, inventory control, logistics and material flow, cost analysis, and production coordination.

Tasks

1) Confer with vendors, staff, and management personnel regarding purchases, procedures, product specifications, manufacturing capabilities, and project status.

2) Develop manufacturing methods, labor utilization standards, and cost analysis systems to promote efficient staff and facility utilization.

3) Estimate production cost and effect of product design changes for management review, action, and control.

4) Communicate with management and user personnel to develop production and design standards.

5) Review production schedules, engineering specifications, orders, and related information to obtain knowledge of manufacturing methods, procedures, and activities.

6) Plan and establish sequence of operations to fabricate and assemble parts or products and to promote efficient utilization.

7) Draft and design layout of equipment, materials, and workspace to illustrate maximum efficiency, using drafting tools and computer.

8) Study operations sequence, material flow, functional statements, organization charts, and project information to determine worker functions and responsibilities.

9) Coordinate quality control objectives and activities to resolve production problems, maximize product reliability, and minimize cost.

10) Apply statistical methods and perform mathematical calculations to determine manufacturing processes, staff requirements, and production standards.

11) Analyze statistical data and product specifications to determine standards and establish quality and reliability objectives of finished product.

12) Complete production reports, purchase orders, and material, tool, and equipment lists.

13) Record or oversee recording of information to ensure currency of engineering drawings and documentation of production problems.

14) Formulate sampling procedures and designs and develop forms and instructions for recording, evaluating, and reporting quality and reliability data.

15) Direct workers engaged in product measurement, inspection, and testing activities to ensure quality control and reliability.

16) Evaluate precision and accuracy of production and testing equipment and engineering drawings to formulate corrective action plan.

17) Regulate and alter workflow schedules according to established manufacturing sequences and lead times to expedite production operations.

18) Schedule deliveries based on production forecasts, material substitutions, storage and handling facilities, and maintenance requirements.

19) Implement methods and procedures for disposition of discrepant material and defective or damaged parts, and assess cost and responsibility.

Knowledge	Knowledge Definitions
Engineering and Technology	Knowledge of the practical application of engineering science and technology. This includes applying principles, techniques, procedures, and equipment to the design and production of various goods and services.
Production and Processing	Knowledge of raw materials, production processes, quality control, costs, and other techniques for maximizing the effective manufacture and distribution of goods.
Mathematics	Knowledge of arithmetic, algebra, geometry, calculus, statistics, and their applications.
Administration and Management	Knowledge of business and management principles involved in strategic planning, resource allocation, human resources modeling, leadership technique, production methods, and coordination of people and resources.
Mechanical	Knowledge of machines and tools, including their designs, uses, repair, and maintenance.
Computers and Electronics	Knowledge of circuit boards, processors, chips, electronic equipment, and computer hardware and software, including applications and programming.
Design	Knowledge of design techniques, tools, and principles involved in production of precision technical plans, blueprints, drawings, and models.
English Language	Knowledge of the structure and content of the English language including the meaning and spelling of words, rules of composition, and grammar.
Education and Training	Knowledge of principles and methods for curriculum and training design, teaching and instruction for individuals and groups, and the measurement of training effects.
Clerical	Knowledge of administrative and clerical procedures and systems such as word processing, managing files and records, stenography and transcription, designing forms, and other office procedures and terminology.
Customer and Personal Service	Knowledge of principles and processes for providing customer and personal services. This includes customer needs assessment, meeting quality standards for services, and evaluation of customer satisfaction.
Economics and Accounting	Knowledge of economic and accounting principles and practices, the financial markets, banking and the analysis and reporting of financial data.
Physics	Knowledge and prediction of physical principles, laws, their interrelationships, and applications to understanding fluid, material, and atmospheric dynamics, and mechanical, electrical, atomic and sub- atomic structures and processes.
Personnel and Human Resources	Knowledge of principles and procedures for personnel recruitment, selection, training, compensation and benefits, labor relations and negotiation, and personnel information systems.
Public Safety and Security	Knowledge of relevant equipment, policies, procedures, and strategies to promote effective local, state, or national security operations for the protection of people, data, property, and institutions.
Transportation	Knowledge of principles and methods for moving people or goods by air, rail, sea, or road, including the relative costs and benefits.
Psychology	Knowledge of human behavior and performance; individual differences in ability, personality, and interests; learning and motivation; psychological research methods; and the assessment and treatment of behavioral and affective disorders.
Law and Government	Knowledge of laws, legal codes, court procedures, precedents, government regulations, executive orders, agency rules, and the democratic political process.
Building and Construction	Knowledge of materials, methods, and the tools involved in the construction or repair of houses, buildings, or other structures such as highways and roads.
Chemistry	Knowledge of the chemical composition, structure, and properties of substances and of the chemical processes and transformations that they undergo. This includes uses of chemicals and their interactions, danger signs, production techniques, and disposal methods.

Sociology and Anthropology	Knowledge of group behavior and dynamics, societal trends and influences, human migrations, ethnicity, cultures and their history and origins.
Telecommunications	Knowledge of transmission, broadcasting, switching, control, and operation of telecommunications systems.
Communications and Media	Knowledge of media production, communication, and dissemination techniques and methods. This includes alternative ways to inform and entertain via written, oral, and visual media.
Sales and Marketing	Knowledge of principles and methods for showing, promoting, and selling products or services. This includes marketing strategy and tactics, product demonstration, sales techniques, and sales control systems.
Biology	Knowledge of plant and animal organisms, their tissues, cells, functions, interdependencies, and interactions with each other and the environment.
Therapy and Counseling	Knowledge of principles, methods, and procedures for diagnosis, treatment, and rehabilitation of physical and mental dysfunctions, and for career counseling and guidance.
Geography	Knowledge of principles and methods for describing the features of land, sea, and air masses, including their physical characteristics, locations, interrelationships, and distribution of plant, animal, and human life.
Foreign Language	Knowledge of the structure and content of a foreign (non-English) language including the meaning and spelling of words, rules of composition and grammar, and pronunciation.
History and Archeology	Knowledge of historical events and their causes, indicators, and effects on civilizations and cultures.
Fine Arts	Knowledge of the theory and techniques required to compose, produce, and perform works of music, dance, visual arts, drama, and sculpture.
Food Production	Knowledge of techniques and equipment for planting, growing, and harvesting food products (both plant and animal) for consumption, including storage/handling techniques.
Medicine and Dentistry	Knowledge of the information and techniques needed to diagnose and treat human injuries, diseases, and deformities. This includes symptoms, treatment alternatives, drug properties and interactions, and preventive health-care measures.
Philosophy and Theology	Knowledge of different philosophical systems and religions. This includes their basic principles, values, ethics, ways of thinking, customs, practices, and their impact on human culture.

Skills	Skills Definitions
Critical Thinking	Using logic and reasoning to identify the strengths and weaknesses of alternative solutions, conclusions or approaches to problems.
Time Management	Managing one's own time and the time of others.
Active Listening	Giving full attention to what other people are saying, taking time to understand the points being made, asking questions as appropriate, and not interrupting at inappropriate times.
Reading Comprehension	Understanding written sentences and paragraphs in work related documents.
Complex Problem Solving	Identifying complex problems and reviewing related information to develop and evaluate options and implement solutions.
Mathematics	Using mathematics to solve problems.
Writing	Communicating effectively in writing as appropriate for the needs of the audience.
Judgment and Decision Making	Considering the relative costs and benefits of potential actions to choose the most appropriate one.
Speaking	Talking to others to convey information effectively.
Equipment Selection	Determining the kind of tools and equipment needed to do a job.
Active Learning	Understanding the implications of new information for both current and future problem-solving and decision-making.
Coordination	Adjusting actions in relation to others' actions.
Learning Strategies	Selecting and using training/instructional methods and procedures appropriate for the situation when learning or teaching new things.
Instructing	Teaching others how to do something.
Troubleshooting	Determining causes of operating errors and deciding what to do about it.
Negotiation	Bringing others together and trying to reconcile differences.
Persuasion	Persuading others to change their minds or behavior.

Systems Analysis	Determining how a system should work and how changes in conditions, operations, and the environment will affect outcomes.
Quality Control Analysis	Conducting tests and inspections of products, services, or processes to evaluate quality or performance.
Monitoring	Monitoring/Assessing performance of yourself, other individuals, or organizations to make improvements or take corrective action.
Technology Design	Generating or adapting equipment and technology to serve user needs.
Service Orientation	Actively looking for ways to help people.
Systems Evaluation	Identifying measures or indicators of system performance and the actions needed to improve or correct performance, relative to the goals of the system.
Social Perceptiveness	Being aware of others' reactions and understanding why they react as they do.
Management of Financial Resources	Determining how money will be spent to get the work done, and accounting for these expenditures.
Installation	Installing equipment, machines, wiring, or programs to meet specifications.
Operations Analysis	Analyzing needs and product requirements to create a design.
Science	Using scientific rules and methods to solve problems.
Management of Personnel Resources	Motivating, developing, and directing people as they work, identifying the best people for the job.
Management of Material Resources	Obtaining and seeing to the appropriate use of equipment, facilities, and materials needed to do certain work.
Programming	Writing computer programs for various purposes.
Operation and Control	Controlling operations of equipment or systems.
Operation Monitoring	Watching gauges, dials, or other indicators to make sure a machine is working properly.
Repairing	Repairing machines or systems using the needed tools.
Equipment Maintenance	Performing routine maintenance on equipment and determining when and what kind of maintenance is needed.

Ability	Ability Definitions
Oral Expression	The ability to communicate information and ideas in speaking so others will understand.
Deductive Reasoning	The ability to apply general rules to specific problems to produce answers that make sense.
Oral Comprehension	The ability to listen to and understand information and ideas presented through spoken words and sentences.
Problem Sensitivity	The ability to tell when something is wrong or is likely to go wrong. It does not involve solving the problem, only recognizing there is a problem.
Mathematical Reasoning	The ability to choose the right mathematical methods or formulas to solve a problem.
Speech Clarity	The ability to speak clearly so others can understand you.
Information Ordering	The ability to arrange things or actions in a certain order or pattern according to a specific rule or set of rules (e.g., patterns of numbers, letters, words, pictures, mathematical operations).
Inductive Reasoning	The ability to combine pieces of information to form general rules or conclusions (includes finding a relationship among seemingly unrelated events).
Visualization	The ability to imagine how something will look after it is moved around or when its parts are moved or rearranged.
Written Comprehension	The ability to read and understand information and ideas presented in writing.
Near Vision	The ability to see details at close range (within a few feet of the observer).
Written Expression	The ability to communicate information and ideas in writing so others will understand.
Originality	The ability to come up with unusual or clever ideas about a given topic or situation, or to develop creative ways to solve a problem.
Fluency of Ideas	The ability to come up with a number of ideas about a topic (the number of ideas is important, not their quality, correctness, or creativity).
Speech Recognition	The ability to identify and understand the speech of another person.
Category Flexibility	The ability to generate or use different sets of rules for combining or grouping things in different ways.
Selective Attention	The ability to concentrate on a task over a period of time without being distracted.
Auditory Attention	The ability to focus on a single source of sound in the presence of other distracting sounds.

Time Sharing	The ability to shift back and forth between two or more activities or sources of information (such as speech, sounds, touch, or other sources).
Memorization	The ability to remember information such as words, numbers, pictures, and procedures.
Flexibility of Closure	The ability to identify or detect a known pattern (a figure, object, word, or sound) that is hidden in other distracting material.
Number Facility	The ability to add, subtract, multiply, or divide quickly and correctly.
Trunk Strength	The ability to use your abdominal and lower back muscles to support part of the body repeatedly or continuously over time without 'giving out' or fatiguing.
Stamina	The ability to exert yourself physically over long periods of time without getting winded or out of breath.
Perceptual Speed	The ability to quickly and accurately compare similarities and differences among sets of letters, numbers, objects, pictures, or patterns. The things to be compared may be presented at the same time or one after the other. This ability also includes comparing a presented object with a remembered object.
Control Precision	The ability to quickly and repeatedly adjust the controls of a machine or a vehicle to exact positions.
Speed of Closure	The ability to quickly make sense of, combine, and organize information into meaningful patterns.
Far Vision	The ability to see details at a distance.
Arm-Hand Steadiness	The ability to keep your hand and arm steady while moving your arm or while holding your arm and hand in one position.
Depth Perception	The ability to judge which of several objects is closer or farther away from you, or to judge the distance between you and an object.
Finger Dexterity	The ability to make precisely coordinated movements of the fingers of one or both hands to grasp, manipulate, or assemble very small objects.
Manual Dexterity	The ability to quickly move your hand, your hand together with your arm, or your two hands to grasp, manipulate, or assemble objects.
Gross Body Coordination	The ability to coordinate the movement of your arms, legs, and torso together when the whole body is in motion.
Spatial Orientation	The ability to know your location in relation to the environment or to know where other objects are in relation to you.
Multilimb Coordination	The ability to coordinate two or more limbs (for example, two arms, two legs, or one leg and one arm) while sitting, standing, or lying down. It does not involve performing the activities while the whole body is in motion.
Visual Color Discrimination	The ability to match or detect differences between colors, including shades of color and brightness.
Reaction Time	The ability to quickly respond (with the hand, finger, or foot) to a signal (sound, light, picture) when it appears.
Hearing Sensitivity	The ability to detect or tell the differences between sounds that vary in pitch and loudness.
Speed of Limb Movement	The ability to quickly move the arms and legs.
Response Orientation	The ability to choose quickly between two or more movements in response to two or more different signals (lights, sounds, pictures). It includes the speed with which the correct response is started with the hand, foot, or other body part.
Wrist-Finger Speed	The ability to make fast, simple, repeated movements of the fingers, hands, and wrists.
Extent Flexibility	The ability to bend, stretch, twist, or reach with your body, arms, and/or legs.
Rate Control	The ability to time your movements or the movement of a piece of equipment in anticipation of changes in the speed and/or direction of a moving object or scene.
Dynamic Flexibility	The ability to quickly and repeatedly bend, stretch, twist, or reach out with your body, arms, and/or legs.
Static Strength	The ability to exert maximum muscle force to lift, push, pull, or carry objects.
Explosive Strength	The ability to use short bursts of muscle force to propel oneself (as in jumping or sprinting), or to throw an object.
Gross Body Equilibrium	The ability to keep or regain your body balance or stay upright when in an unstable position.
Dynamic Strength	The ability to exert muscle force repeatedly or continuously over time. This involves muscular endurance and resistance to muscle fatigue.
Night Vision	The ability to see under low light conditions.
Peripheral Vision	The ability to see objects or movement of objects to one's side when the eyes are looking ahead.
Sound Localization	The ability to tell the direction from which a sound originated.

Glare Sensitivity	The ability to see objects in the presence of glare or bright lighting.

Work_Activity	Work_Activity Definitions
Communicating with Supervisors, Peers, or Subordin	Providing information to supervisors, co-workers, and subordinates by telephone, in written form, e-mail, or in person.
Making Decisions and Solving Problems	Analyzing information and evaluating results to choose the best solution and solve problems.
Interacting With Computers	Using computers and computer systems (including hardware and software) to program, write software, set up functions, enter data, or process information.
Getting Information	Observing, receiving, and otherwise obtaining information from all relevant sources.
Analyzing Data or Information	Identifying the underlying principles, reasons, or facts of information by breaking down information or data into separate parts.
Establishing and Maintaining Interpersonal Relatio	Developing constructive and cooperative working relationships with others, and maintaining them over time.
Documenting/Recording Information	Entering, transcribing, recording, storing, or maintaining information in written or electronic/magnetic form.
Processing Information	Compiling, coding, categorizing, calculating, tabulating, auditing, or verifying information or data.
Monitor Processes, Materials, or Surroundings	Monitoring and reviewing information from materials, events, or the environment, to detect or assess problems.
Evaluating Information to Determine Compliance wit	Using relevant information and individual judgment to determine whether events or processes comply with laws, regulations, or standards.
Organizing, Planning, and Prioritizing Work	Developing specific goals and plans to prioritize, organize, and accomplish your work.
Identifying Objects, Actions, and Events	Identifying information by categorizing, estimating, recognizing differences or similarities, and detecting changes in circumstances or events.
Drafting, Laying Out, and Specifying Technical Dev	Providing documentation, detailed instructions, drawings, or specifications to tell others about how devices, parts, equipment, or structures are to be fabricated, constructed, assembled, modified, maintained, or used.
Updating and Using Relevant Knowledge	Keeping up-to-date technically and applying new knowledge to your job.
Thinking Creatively	Developing, designing, or creating new applications, ideas, relationships, systems, or products, including artistic contributions.
Estimating the Quantifiable Characteristics of Pro	Estimating sizes, distances, and quantities; or determining time, costs, resources, or materials needed to perform a work activity.
Judging the Qualities of Things, Services, or Peop	Assessing the value, importance, or quality of things or people.
Interpreting the Meaning of Information for Others	Translating or explaining what information means and how it can be used.
Training and Teaching Others	Identifying the educational needs of others, developing formal educational or training programs or classes, and teaching or instructing others.
Developing and Building Teams	Encouraging and building mutual trust, respect, and cooperation among team members.
Coordinating the Work and Activities of Others	Getting members of a group to work together to accomplish tasks.
Developing Objectives and Strategies	Establishing long-range objectives and specifying the strategies and actions to achieve them.
Inspecting Equipment, Structures, or Material	Inspecting equipment, structures, or materials to identify the cause of errors or other problems or defects.
Monitoring and Controlling Resources	Monitoring and controlling resources and overseeing the spending of money.
Provide Consultation and Advice to Others	Providing guidance and expert advice to management or other groups on technical, systems-, or process-related topics.
Resolving Conflicts and Negotiating with Others	Handling complaints, settling disputes, and resolving grievances and conflicts, or otherwise negotiating with others.
Guiding, Directing, and Motivating Subordinates	Providing guidance and direction to subordinates, including setting performance standards and monitoring performance.
Scheduling Work and Activities	Scheduling events, programs, and activities, as well as the work of others.
Coaching and Developing Others	Identifying the developmental needs of others and coaching, mentoring, or otherwise helping others to improve their knowledge or skills.

Communicating with Persons Outside Organization	Communicating with people outside the organization, representing the organization to customers, the public, government, and other external sources. This information can be exchanged in person, in writing, or by telephone or e-mail.
Controlling Machines and Processes	Using either control mechanisms or direct physical activity to operate machines or processes (not including computers or vehicles).
Performing Administrative Activities	Performing day-to-day administrative tasks such as maintaining information files and processing paperwork.
Selling or Influencing Others	Convincing others to buy merchandise/goods or to otherwise change their minds or actions.
Assisting and Caring for Others	Providing personal assistance, medical attention, emotional support, or other personal care to others such as coworkers, customers, or patients.
Staffing Organizational Units	Recruiting, interviewing, selecting, hiring, and promoting employees in an organization.
Performing General Physical Activities	Performing physical activities that require considerable use of your arms and legs and moving your whole body, such as climbing, lifting, balancing, walking, stooping, and handling of materials.
Repairing and Maintaining Electronic Equipment	Servicing, repairing, calibrating, regulating, fine-tuning, or testing machines, devices, and equipment that operate primarily on the basis of electrical or electronic (not mechanical) principles.
Repairing and Maintaining Mechanical Equipment	Servicing, repairing, adjusting, and testing machines, devices, moving parts, and equipment that operate primarily on the basis of mechanical (not electronic) principles.
Operating Vehicles, Mechanized Devices, or Equipme	Running, maneuvering, navigating, or driving vehicles or mechanized equipment, such as forklifts, passenger vehicles, aircraft, or water craft.
Handling and Moving Objects	Using hands and arms in handling, installing, positioning, and moving materials, and manipulating things.
Performing for or Working Directly with the Public	Performing for people or dealing directly with the public. This includes serving customers in restaurants and stores, and receiving clients or guests.

Work_Context	Work_Context Definitions
Face-to-Face Discussions	How often do you have to have face-to-face discussions with individuals or teams in this job?
Telephone	How often do you have telephone conversations in this job?
Importance of Being Exact or Accurate	How important is being very exact or highly accurate in performing this job?
Electronic Mail	How often do you use electronic mail in this job?
Wear Common Protective or Safety Equipment such as	How much does this job require wearing common protective or safety equipment such as safety shoes, glasses, gloves, hard hats or live jackets?
Indoors, Environmentally Controlled	How often does this job require working indoors in environmentally controlled conditions?
Work With Work Group or Team	How important is it to work with others in a group or team in this job?
Contact With Others	How much does this job require the worker to be in contact with others (face-to-face, by telephone, or otherwise) in order to perform it?
Impact of Decisions on Co-workers or Company Resul	How do the decisions an employee makes impact the results of co-workers, clients or the company?
Sounds, Noise Levels Are Distracting or Uncomforta	How often does this job require working exposed to sounds and noise levels that are distracting or uncomfortable?
Structured versus Unstructured Work	To what extent is this job structured for the worker, rather than allowing the worker to determine tasks, priorities, and goals?
Freedom to Make Decisions	How much decision making freedom, without supervision, does the job offer?
Letters and Memos	How often does the job require written letters and memos?
Frequency of Decision Making	How frequently is the worker required to make decisions that affect other people, the financial resources, and/or the image and reputation of the organization?
Time Pressure	How often does this job require the worker to meet strict deadlines?
Responsibility for Outcomes and Results	How responsible is the worker for work outcomes and results of other workers?
Exposed to Contaminants	How often does this job require working exposed to contaminants (such as pollutants, gases, dust or odors)?
Importance of Repeating Same Tasks	How important is repeating the same physical activities (e.g., key entry) or mental activities (e.g., checking entries in a ledger) over and over, without stopping, to performing this job?
Spend Time Sitting	How much does this job require sitting?

Coordinate or Lead Others	How important is it to coordinate or lead others in accomplishing work activities in this job?
Spend Time Standing	How much does this job require standing?
Frequency of Conflict Situations	How often are there conflict situations the employee has to face in this job?
Physical Proximity	To what extent does this job require the worker to perform job tasks in close physical proximity to other people?
Exposed to Hazardous Equipment	How often does this job require exposure to hazardous equipment?
Indoors, Not Environmentally Controlled	How often does this job require working indoors in non-controlled environmental conditions (e.g., warehouse without heat)?
Consequence of Error	How serious would the result usually be if the worker made a mistake that was not readily correctable?
Level of Competition	To what extent does this job require the worker to compete or to be aware of competitive pressures?
Spend Time Walking and Running	How much does this job require walking and running?
Deal With Unpleasant or Angry People	How frequently does the worker have to deal with unpleasant, angry, or discourteous individuals as part of the job requirements?
Public Speaking	How often do you have to perform public speaking in this job?
Spend Time Using Your Hands to Handle, Control, or	How much does this job require using your hands to handle, control, or feel objects, tools or controls?
Responsible for Others' Health and Safety	How much responsibility is there for the health and safety of others in this job?
Deal With External Customers	How important is it to work with external customers or the public in this job?
Extremely Bright or Inadequate Lighting	How often does this job require working in extremely bright or inadequate lighting conditions?
In an Enclosed Vehicle or Equipment	How often does this job require working in a closed vehicle or equipment (e.g., car)?
Cramped Work Space, Awkward Positions	How often does this job require working in cramped work spaces that requires getting into awkward positions?
Exposed to Minor Burns, Cuts, Bites, or Stings	How often does this job require exposure to minor burns, cuts, bites, or stings?
Very Hot or Cold Temperatures	How often does this job require working in very hot (above 90 F degrees) or very cold (below 32 F degrees) temperatures?
Pace Determined by Speed of Equipment	How important is it to this job that the pace is determined by the speed of equipment or machinery? (This does not refer to keeping busy at all times on this job.)
Degree of Automation	How automated is the job?
Spend Time Making Repetitive Motions	How much does this job require making repetitive motions?
Exposed to Hazardous Conditions	How often does this job require exposure to hazardous conditions?
Spend Time Kneeling, Crouching, Stooping, or Crawl	How much does this job require kneeling, crouching, stooping or crawling?
Spend Time Bending or Twisting the Body	How much does this job require bending or twisting your body?
Deal With Physically Aggressive People	How frequently does this job require the worker to deal with physical aggression of violent individuals?
Outdoors, Exposed to Weather	How often does this job require working outdoors, exposed to all weather conditions?
Exposed to High Places	How often does this job require exposure to high places?
Spend Time Climbing Ladders, Scaffolds, or Poles	How much does this job require climbing ladders, scaffolds, or poles?
Exposed to Radiation	How often does this job require exposure to radiation?
In an Open Vehicle or Equipment	How often does this job require working in an open vehicle or equipment (e.g., tractor)?
Outdoors, Under Cover	How often does this job require working outdoors, under cover (e.g., structure with roof but no walls)?
Spend Time Keeping or Regaining Balance	How much does this job require keeping or regaining your balance?
Exposed to Whole Body Vibration	How often does this job require exposure to whole body vibration (e.g., operate a jackhammer)?
Exposed to Disease or Infections	How often does this job require exposure to disease/infections?
Wear Specialized Protective or Safety Equipment su	How much does this job require wearing specialized protective or safety equipment such as breathing apparatus, safety harness, full protection suits, or radiation protection?

Job Zone Component	Job Zone Component Definitions
Title	Job Zone Four: Considerable Preparation Needed
Overall Experience	A minimum of two to four years of work-related skill, knowledge, or experience is needed for these occupations. For example, an accountant must complete four years of college and work for several years in accounting to be considered qualified.
Job Training	Employees in these occupations usually need several years of work-related experience, on-the-job training, and/or vocational training.
Job Zone Examples	Many of these occupations involve coordinating, supervising, managing, or training others. Examples include accountants, chefs and head cooks, computer programmers, historians, pharmacists, and police detectives.
SVP Range	(7.0 to < 8.0)
Education	Most of these occupations require a four-year bachelor's degree, but some do not.

Work_Styles	Work_Styles Definitions
Attention to Detail	Job requires being careful about detail and thorough in completing work tasks.
Analytical Thinking	Job requires analyzing information and using logic to address work-related issues and problems.
Dependability	Job requires being reliable, responsible, and dependable, and fulfilling obligations.
Initiative	Job requires a willingness to take on responsibilities and challenges.
Adaptability/Flexibility	Job requires being open to change (positive or negative) and to considerable variety in the workplace.
Integrity	Job requires being honest and ethical.
Persistence	Job requires persistence in the face of obstacles.
Innovation	Job requires creativity and alternative thinking to develop new ideas for and answers to work-related problems.
Cooperation	Job requires being pleasant with others on the job and displaying a good-natured, cooperative attitude.
Leadership	Job requires a willingness to lead, take charge, and offer opinions and direction.
Achievement/Effort	Job requires establishing and maintaining personally challenging achievement goals and exerting effort toward mastering tasks.
Independence	Job requires developing one's own ways of doing things, guiding oneself with little or no supervision, and depending on oneself to get things done.
Stress Tolerance	Job requires accepting criticism and dealing calmly and effectively with high stress situations.
Self Control	Job requires maintaining composure, keeping emotions in check, controlling anger, and avoiding aggressive behavior, even in very difficult situations.
Concern for Others	Job requires being sensitive to others' needs and feelings and being understanding and helpful on the job.
Social Orientation	Job requires preferring to work with others rather than alone, and being personally connected with others on the job.

17-2121.01 - Marine Engineers

Design, develop, and take responsibility for the installation of ship machinery and related equipment including propulsion machines and power supply systems.

Tasks

1) Maintain contact with, and formulate reports for, contractors and clients in order to ensure completion of work at minimum cost.

2) Design and oversee testing, installation, and repair of marine apparatus and equipment.

3) Evaluate operation of marine equipment during acceptance testing and shakedown cruises.

4) Schedule machine overhauls and the servicing of electrical, heating, ventilation, refrigeration, water, and sewage systems.

5) Confer with research personnel in order to clarify or resolve problems, and to develop or modify designs.

6) Procure materials needed to repair marine equipment and machinery.

7) Investigate and observe tests on machinery and equipment for compliance with standards.

8) Prepare plans, estimates, design and construction schedules, and contract specifications, including any special provisions.

9) Prepare technical reports for use by engineering, management, or sales personnel.

10) Supervise other engineers and crewmembers, and train them for routine and emergency duties.

11) Maintain records of engineering department activities, including expense records and details of equipment maintenance and repairs.

12) Conduct environmental, operational, or performance tests on marine machinery and equipment.

13) Inspect marine equipment and machinery in order to draw up work requests and job specifications.

14) Maintain and coordinate repair of marine machinery and equipment for installation on vessels.

15) Analyze data in order to determine feasibility of product proposals.

16) Determine conditions under which tests are to be conducted, as well as sequences and phases of test operations.

17) Review work requests, and compare them with previous work completed on ships in order to ensure that costs are economically sound.

18) Prepare, or direct the preparation of, product or system layouts and detailed drawings and schematics.

19) Coordinate activities with regulatory bodies in order to ensure repairs and alterations are at minimum cost, consistent with safety.

20) Act as liaisons between ships' captains and shore personnel in order to ensure that schedules and budgets are maintained, and that ships are operated safely and efficiently.

21) Conduct analytical, environmental, operational, or performance studies in order to develop designs for products, such as marine engines, equipment, and structures.

22) Perform monitoring activities in order to ensure that ships comply with international regulations and standards for life saving equipment and pollution preventatives.

17-2121.02 - Marine Architects

Design and oversee construction and repair of marine craft and floating structures such as ships, barges, tugs, dredges, submarines, torpedoes, floats, and buoys. May confer with marine engineers.

Tasks

1) Evaluate performance of craft during dock and sea trials to determine design changes and conformance with national and international standards.

2) Design layout of craft interior, including cargo space, passenger compartments, ladder wells, and elevators.

3) Study design proposals and specifications to establish basic characteristics of craft, such as size, weight, speed, propulsion, displacement, and draft.

4) Confer with marine engineering personnel to establish arrangement of boiler room equipment and propulsion machinery, heating and ventilating systems, refrigeration equipment, piping, and other functional equipment.

5) Design complete hull and superstructure according to specifications and test data, in conformity with standards of safety, efficiency, and economy.

17-2131.00 - Materials Engineers

Evaluate materials and develop machinery and processes to manufacture materials for use in products that must meet specialized design and performance specifications. Develop new uses for known materials. Includes those working with composite materials or specializing in one type of material, such as graphite, metal and metal alloys, ceramics and glass, plastics and polymers, and naturally occurring materials.

Tasks

1) Determine appropriate methods for fabricating and joining materials.

2) Design and direct the testing and/or control of processing procedures.

3) Plan and evaluate new projects, consulting with other engineers and corporate executives

as necessary.

4) Teach in colleges and universities.

5) Supervise the work of technologists, technicians and other engineers and scientists.

6) Replicate the characteristics of materials and their components with computers.

7) Remove metals from ores, and refine and alloy them to obtain useful metal.

8) Conduct or supervise tests on raw materials or finished products in order to ensure their quality.

9) Perform managerial functions such as preparing proposals and budgets, analyzing labor costs, and writing reports.

10) Analyze product failure data and laboratory test results in order to determine causes of problems and develop solutions.

11) Design processing plants and equipment.

12) Conduct training sessions on new material products, applications, or manufacturing methods for customers and their employees.

13) Supervise production and testing processes in industrial settings such as metal refining facilities, smelting or foundry operations, or non-metallic materials production operations.

14) Solve problems in a number of engineering fields, such as mechanical, chemical, electrical, civil, nuclear and aerospace.

15) Review new product plans and make recommendations for material selection based on design objectives, such as strength, weight, heat resistance, electrical conductivity, and cost.

16) Write for technical magazines, journals, and trade association publications.

17) Plan and implement laboratory operations for the purpose of developing material and fabrication procedures that meet cost, product specification, and performance standards.

18) Monitor material performance and evaluate material deterioration.

19) Evaluate technical specifications and economic factors relating to process or product design objectives.

20) Modify properties of metal alloys, using thermal and mechanical treatments.

21) Guide technical staff engaged in developing materials for specific uses in projected products or devices.

17-2141.00 - Mechanical Engineers

Perform engineering duties in planning and designing tools, engines, machines, and other mechanically functioning equipment. Oversee installation, operation, maintenance, and repair of such equipment as centralized heat, gas, water, and steam systems.

Tasks

1) Confer with engineers and other personnel to implement operating procedures, resolve system malfunctions, and provide technical information.

2) Recommend design modifications to eliminate machine or system malfunctions.

3) Specify system components or direct modification of products to ensure conformance with engineering design and performance specifications.

4) Conduct research that tests and analyzes the feasibility, design, operation and performance of equipment, components and systems.

5) Research, design, evaluate, install, operate, and maintain mechanical products, equipment, systems and processes to meet requirements, applying knowledge of engineering principles.

6) Provide feedback to design engineers on customer problems and needs.

7) Research and analyze customer design proposals, specifications, manuals, and other data to evaluate the feasibility, cost, and maintenance requirements of designs or applications.

8) Investigate equipment failures and difficulties to diagnose faulty operation, and to make recommendations to maintenance crew.

9) Assist drafters in developing the structural design of products, using drafting tools or computer-assisted design/drafting equipment and software.

10) Oversee installation, operation, maintenance, and repair to ensure that machines and equipment are installed and functioning according to specifications.

11) Develop and test models of alternate designs and processing methods to assess feasibility, operating condition effects, possible new applications and necessity of modification.

12) Design test control apparatus and equipment and develop procedures for testing products.

13) Establish and coordinate the maintenance and safety procedures, service schedule, and

supply of materials required to maintain machines and equipment in the prescribed condition.

14) Write performance requirements for product development or engineering projects.

15) Perform personnel functions, such as supervision of production workers, technicians, technologists and other engineers, and design of evaluation programs.

16) Estimate costs and submit bids for engineering, construction, or extraction projects, and prepare contract documents.

17) Study industrial processes to determine where and how application of equipment can be made.

18) Solicit new business and provide technical customer service.

19) Develop, coordinate, and monitor all aspects of production, including selection of manufacturing methods, fabrication, and operation of product designs.

20) Apply engineering principles and practices to emerging fields, such as robotics, waste management, and biomedical engineering.

Knowledge	Knowledge Definitions
Engineering and Technology	Knowledge of the practical application of engineering science and technology. This includes applying principles, techniques, procedures, and equipment to the design and production of various goods and services.
Mechanical	Knowledge of machines and tools, including their designs, uses, repair, and maintenance.
Design	Knowledge of design techniques, tools, and principles involved in production of precision technical plans, blueprints, drawings, and models.
Production and Processing	Knowledge of raw materials, production processes, quality control, costs, and other techniques for maximizing the effective manufacture and distribution of goods.
Mathematics	Knowledge of arithmetic, algebra, geometry, calculus, statistics, and their applications.
Administration and Management	Knowledge of business and management principles involved in strategic planning, resource allocation, human resources modeling, leadership technique, production methods, and coordination of people and resources.
English Language	Knowledge of the structure and content of the English language including the meaning and spelling of words, rules of composition, and grammar.
Computers and Electronics	Knowledge of circuit boards, processors, chips, electronic equipment, and computer hardware and software, including applications and programming.
Physics	Knowledge and prediction of physical principles, laws, their interrelationships, and applications to understanding fluid, material, and atmospheric dynamics, and mechanical, electrical, atomic and sub- atomic structures and processes.
Customer and Personal Service	Knowledge of principles and processes for providing customer and personal services. This includes customer needs assessment, meeting quality standards for services, and evaluation of customer satisfaction.
Chemistry	Knowledge of the chemical composition, structure, and properties of substances and of the chemical processes and transformations that they undergo. This includes uses of chemicals and their interactions, danger signs, production techniques, and disposal methods.
Public Safety and Security	Knowledge of relevant equipment, policies, procedures, and strategies to promote effective local, state, or national security operations for the protection of people, data, property, and institutions.
Sales and Marketing	Knowledge of principles and methods for showing, promoting, and selling products or services. This includes marketing strategy and tactics, product demonstration, sales techniques, and sales control systems.
Education and Training	Knowledge of principles and methods for curriculum and training design, teaching and instruction for individuals and groups, and the measurement of training effects.
Communications and Media	Knowledge of media production, communication, and dissemination techniques and methods. This includes alternative ways to inform and entertain via written, oral, and visual media.
Building and Construction	Knowledge of materials, methods, and the tools involved in the construction or repair of houses, buildings, or other structures such as highways and roads.
Clerical	Knowledge of administrative and clerical procedures and systems such as word processing, managing files and records, stenography and transcription, designing forms, and other office procedures and terminology.

Law and Government	Knowledge of laws, legal codes, court procedures, precedents, government regulations, executive orders, agency rules, and the democratic political process.
Transportation	Knowledge of principles and methods for moving people or goods by air, rail, sea, or road, including the relative costs and benefits.
Economics and Accounting	Knowledge of economic and accounting principles and practices, the financial markets, banking and the analysis and reporting of financial data.
Personnel and Human Resources	Knowledge of principles and procedures for personnel recruitment, selection, training, compensation and benefits, labor relations and negotiation, and personnel information systems.
Psychology	Knowledge of human behavior and performance; individual differences in ability, personality, and interests; learning and motivation; psychological research methods; and the assessment and treatment of behavioral and affective disorders.
Telecommunications	Knowledge of transmission, broadcasting, switching, control, and operation of telecommunications systems.
Geography	Knowledge of principles and methods for describing the features of land, sea, and air masses, including their physical characteristics, locations, interrelationships, and distribution of plant, animal, and human life.
Food Production	Knowledge of techniques and equipment for planting, growing, and harvesting food products (both plant and animal) for consumption, including storage/handling techniques.
Sociology and Anthropology	Knowledge of group behavior and dynamics, societal trends and influences, human migrations, ethnicity, cultures and their history and origins.
Philosophy and Theology	Knowledge of different philosophical systems and religions. This includes their basic principles, values, ethics, ways of thinking, customs, practices, and their impact on human culture.
Biology	Knowledge of plant and animal organisms, their tissues, cells, functions, interdependencies, and interactions with each other and the environment.
Medicine and Dentistry	Knowledge of the information and techniques needed to diagnose and treat human injuries, diseases, and deformities. This includes symptoms, treatment alternatives, drug properties and interactions, and preventive health-care measures.
Therapy and Counseling	Knowledge of principles, methods, and procedures for diagnosis, treatment, and rehabilitation of physical and mental dysfunctions, and for career counseling and guidance.
Foreign Language	Knowledge of the structure and content of a foreign (non-English) language including the meaning and spelling of words, rules of composition and grammar, and pronunciation.
Fine Arts	Knowledge of the theory and techniques required to compose, produce, and perform works of music, dance, visual arts, drama, and sculpture.
History and Archeology	Knowledge of historical events and their causes, indicators, and effects on civilizations and cultures.

Skills	**Skills Definitions**
Mathematics	Using mathematics to solve problems.
Complex Problem Solving	Identifying complex problems and reviewing related information to develop and evaluate options and implement solutions.
Critical Thinking	Using logic and reasoning to identify the strengths and weaknesses of alternative solutions, conclusions or approaches to problems.
Science	Using scientific rules and methods to solve problems.
Reading Comprehension	Understanding written sentences and paragraphs in work related documents.
Active Listening	Giving full attention to what other people are saying, taking time to understand the points being made, asking questions as appropriate, and not interrupting at inappropriate times.
Judgment and Decision Making	Considering the relative costs and benefits of potential actions to choose the most appropriate one.
Time Management	Managing one's own time and the time of others.
Writing	Communicating effectively in writing as appropriate for the needs of the audience.
Speaking	Talking to others to convey information effectively.
Operations Analysis	Analyzing needs and product requirements to create a design.
Coordination	Adjusting actions in relation to others' actions.
Active Learning	Understanding the implications of new information for both current and future problem-solving and decision-making.

Monitoring	Monitoring/Assessing performance of yourself, other individuals, or organizations to make improvements or take corrective action.
Systems Analysis	Determining how a system should work and how changes in conditions, operations, and the environment will affect outcomes.
Negotiation	Bringing others together and trying to reconcile differences.
Installation	Installing equipment, machines, wiring, or programs to meet specifications.
Equipment Selection	Determining the kind of tools and equipment needed to do a job.
Social Perceptiveness	Being aware of others' reactions and understanding why they react as they do.
Learning Strategies	Selecting and using training/instructional methods and procedures appropriate for the situation when learning or teaching new things.
Technology Design	Generating or adapting equipment and technology to serve user needs.
Troubleshooting	Determining causes of operating errors and deciding what to do about it.
Management of Financial Resources	Determining how money will be spent to get the work done, and accounting for these expenditures.
Quality Control Analysis	Conducting tests and inspections of products, services, or processes to evaluate quality or performance.
Management of Personnel Resources	Motivating, developing, and directing people as they work, identifying the best people for the job.
Persuasion	Persuading others to change their minds or behavior.
Service Orientation	Actively looking for ways to help people.
Systems Evaluation	Identifying measures or indicators of system performance and the actions needed to improve or correct performance, relative to the goals of the system.
Management of Material Resources	Obtaining and seeing to the appropriate use of equipment, facilities, and materials needed to do certain work.
Instructing	Teaching others how to do something.
Operation Monitoring	Watching gauges, dials, or other indicators to make sure a machine is working properly.
Equipment Maintenance	Performing routine maintenance on equipment and determining when and what kind of maintenance is needed.
Repairing	Repairing machines or systems using the needed tools.
Operation and Control	Controlling operations of equipment or systems.
Programming	Writing computer programs for various purposes.

Ability	**Ability Definitions**
Oral Comprehension	The ability to listen to and understand information and ideas presented through spoken words and sentences.
Written Comprehension	The ability to read and understand information and ideas presented in writing.
Problem Sensitivity	The ability to tell when something is wrong or is likely to go wrong. It does not involve solving the problem, only recognizing there is a problem.
Inductive Reasoning	The ability to combine pieces of information to form general rules or conclusions (includes finding a relationship among seemingly unrelated events).
Near Vision	The ability to see details at close range (within a few feet of the observer).
Information Ordering	The ability to arrange things or actions in a certain order or pattern according to a specific rule or set of rules (e.g., patterns of numbers, letters, words, pictures, mathematical operations).
Deductive Reasoning	The ability to apply general rules to specific problems to produce answers that make sense.
Oral Expression	The ability to communicate information and ideas in speaking so others will understand.
Visualization	The ability to imagine how something will look after it is moved around or when its parts are moved or rearranged.
Speech Clarity	The ability to speak clearly so others can understand you.
Flexibility of Closure	The ability to identify or detect a known pattern (a figure, object, word, or sound) that is hidden in other distracting material.
Speech Recognition	The ability to identify and understand the speech of another person.
Mathematical Reasoning	The ability to choose the right mathematical methods or formulas to solve a problem.
Written Expression	The ability to communicate information and ideas in writing so others will understand.
Selective Attention	The ability to concentrate on a task over a period of time without being distracted.

Fluency of Ideas	The ability to come up with a number of ideas about a topic (the number of ideas is important, not their quality, correctness, or creativity).
Number Facility	The ability to add, subtract, multiply, or divide quickly and correctly.
Category Flexibility	The ability to generate or use different sets of rules for combining or grouping things in different ways.
Perceptual Speed	The ability to quickly and accurately compare similarities and differences among sets of letters, numbers, objects, pictures, or patterns. The things to be compared may be presented at the same time or one after the other. This ability also includes comparing a presented object with a remembered object.
Originality	The ability to come up with unusual or clever ideas about a given topic or situation, or to develop creative ways to solve a problem.
Memorization	The ability to remember information such as words, numbers, pictures, and procedures.
Speed of Closure	The ability to quickly make sense of, combine, and organize information into meaningful patterns.
Finger Dexterity	The ability to make precisely coordinated movements of the fingers of one or both hands to grasp, manipulate, or assemble very small objects.
Far Vision	The ability to see details at a distance.
Time Sharing	The ability to shift back and forth between two or more activities or sources of information (such as speech, sounds, touch, or other sources).
Auditory Attention	The ability to focus on a single source of sound in the presence of other distracting sounds.
Visual Color Discrimination	The ability to match or detect differences between colors, including shades of color and brightness.
Depth Perception	The ability to judge which of several objects is closer or farther away from you, or to judge the distance between you and an object.
Hearing Sensitivity	The ability to detect or tell the differences between sounds that vary in pitch and loudness.
Trunk Strength	The ability to use your abdominal and lower back muscles to support part of the body repeatedly or continuously over time without 'giving out' or fatiguing.
Reaction Time	The ability to quickly respond (with the hand, finger, or foot) to a signal (sound, light, picture) when it appears.
Arm-Hand Steadiness	The ability to keep your hand and arm steady while moving your arm or while holding your arm and hand in one position.
Manual Dexterity	The ability to quickly move your hand, your hand together with your arm, or your two hands to grasp, manipulate, or assemble objects.
Static Strength	The ability to exert maximum muscle force to lift, push, pull, or carry objects.
Control Precision	The ability to quickly and repeatedly adjust the controls of a machine or a vehicle to exact positions.
Multilimb Coordination	The ability to coordinate two or more limbs (for example, two arms, two legs, or one leg and one arm) while sitting, standing, or lying down. It does not involve performing the activities while the whole body is in motion.
Extent Flexibility	The ability to bend, stretch, twist, or reach with your body, arms, and/or legs.
Spatial Orientation	The ability to know your location in relation to the environment or to know where other objects are in relation to you.
Wrist-Finger Speed	The ability to make fast, simple, repeated movements of the fingers, hands, and wrists.
Gross Body Equilibrium	The ability to keep or regain your body balance or stay upright when in an unstable position.
Response Orientation	The ability to choose quickly between two or more movements in response to two or more different signals (lights, sounds, pictures). It includes the speed with which the correct response is started with the hand, foot, or other body part.
Gross Body Coordination	The ability to coordinate the movement of your arms, legs, and torso together when the whole body is in motion.
Rate Control	The ability to time your movements or the movement of a piece of equipment in anticipation of changes in the speed and/or direction of a moving object or scene.
Explosive Strength	The ability to use short bursts of muscle force to propel oneself (as in jumping or sprinting), or to throw an object.
Speed of Limb Movement	The ability to quickly move the arms and legs.
Sound Localization	The ability to tell the direction from which a sound originated.
Peripheral Vision	The ability to see objects or movement of objects to one's side when the eyes are looking ahead.
Stamina	The ability to exert yourself physically over long periods of time without getting winded or out of breath.

Dynamic Flexibility	The ability to quickly and repeatedly bend, stretch, twist, or reach out with your body, arms, and/or legs.
Night Vision	The ability to see under low light conditions.
Dynamic Strength	The ability to exert muscle force repeatedly or continuously over time. This involves muscular endurance and resistance to muscle fatigue.
Glare Sensitivity	The ability to see objects in the presence of glare or bright lighting.

Work_Activity	**Work_Activity Definitions**
Making Decisions and Solving Problems	Analyzing information and evaluating results to choose the best solution and solve problems.
Interacting With Computers	Using computers and computer systems (including hardware and software) to program, write software, set up functions, enter data, or process information.
Getting Information	Observing, receiving, and otherwise obtaining information from all relevant sources.
Communicating with Supervisors, Peers, or Subordin	Providing information to supervisors, co-workers, and subordinates by telephone, in written form, e-mail, or in person.
Evaluating Information to Determine Compliance wit	Using relevant information and individual judgment to determine whether events or processes comply with laws, regulations, or standards.
Organizing, Planning, and Prioritizing Work	Developing specific goals and plans to prioritize, organize, and accomplish your work.
Processing Information	Compiling, coding, categorizing, calculating, tabulating, auditing, or verifying information or data.
Identifying Objects, Actions, and Events	Identifying information by categorizing, estimating, recognizing differences or similarities, and detecting changes in circumstances or events.
Communicating with Persons Outside Organization	Communicating with people outside the organization, representing the organization to customers, the public, government, and other external sources. This information can be exchanged in person, in writing, or by telephone or e-mail.
Analyzing Data or Information	Identifying the underlying principles, reasons, or facts of information by breaking down information or data into separate parts.
Updating and Using Relevant Knowledge	Keeping up-to-date technically and applying new knowledge to your job.
Interpreting the Meaning of Information for Others	Translating or explaining what information means and how it can be used.
Establishing and Maintaining Interpersonal Relatio	Developing constructive and cooperative working relationships with others, and maintaining them over time.
Documenting/Recording Information	Entering, transcribing, recording, storing, or maintaining information in written or electronic/magnetic form.
Monitor Processes, Materials, or Surroundings	Monitoring and reviewing information from materials, events, or the environment, to detect or assess problems.
Drafting, Laying Out, and Specifying Technical Dev	Providing documentation, detailed instructions, drawings, or specifications to tell others about how devices, parts, equipment, or structures are to be fabricated, constructed, assembled, modified, maintained, or used.
Judging the Qualities of Things, Services, or Peop	Assessing the value, importance, or quality of things or people.
Thinking Creatively	Developing, designing, or creating new applications, ideas, relationships, systems, or products, including artistic contributions.
Resolving Conflicts and Negotiating with Others	Handling complaints, settling disputes, and resolving grievances and conflicts, or otherwise negotiating with others.
Performing Administrative Activities	Performing day-to-day administrative tasks such as maintaining information files and processing paperwork.
Scheduling Work and Activities	Scheduling events, programs, and activities, as well as the work of others.
Estimating the Quantifiable Characteristics of Pro	Estimating sizes, distances, and quantities; or determining time, costs, resources, or materials needed to perform a work activity.
Training and Teaching Others	Identifying the educational needs of others, developing formal educational or training programs or classes, and teaching or instructing others.
Inspecting Equipment, Structures, or Material	Inspecting equipment, structures, or materials to identify the cause of errors or other problems or defects.
Coordinating the Work and Activities of Others	Getting members of a group to work together to accomplish tasks.
Provide Consultation and Advice to Others	Providing guidance and expert advice to management or other groups on technical, systems-, or process-related topics.

Assisting and Caring for Others	Providing personal assistance, medical attention, emotional support, or other personal care to others such as coworkers, customers, or patients.
Developing and Building Teams	Encouraging and building mutual trust, respect, and cooperation among team members.
Performing General Physical Activities	Performing physical activities that require considerable use of your arms and legs and moving your whole body, such as climbing, lifting, balancing, walking, stooping, and handling of materials.
Developing Objectives and Strategies	Establishing long-range objectives and specifying the strategies and actions to achieve them.
Handling and Moving Objects	Using hands and arms in handling, installing, positioning, and moving materials, and manipulating things.
Selling or Influencing Others	Convincing others to buy merchandise/goods or to otherwise change their minds or actions.
Guiding, Directing, and Motivating Subordinates	Providing guidance and direction to subordinates, including setting performance standards and monitoring performance.
Coaching and Developing Others	Identifying the developmental needs of others and coaching, mentoring, or otherwise helping others to improve their knowledge or skills.
Controlling Machines and Processes	Using either control mechanisms or direct physical activity to operate machines or processes (not including computers or vehicles).
Monitoring and Controlling Resources	Monitoring and controlling resources and overseeing the spending of money.
Operating Vehicles, Mechanized Devices, or Equipme	Running, maneuvering, navigating, or driving vehicles or mechanized equipment, such as forklifts, passenger vehicles, aircraft, or water craft.
Performing for or Working Directly with the Public	Performing for people or dealing directly with the public. This includes serving customers in restaurants and stores, and receiving clients or guests.
Repairing and Maintaining Electronic Equipment	Servicing, repairing, calibrating, regulating, fine-tuning, or testing machines, devices, and equipment that operate primarily on the basis of electrical or electronic (not mechanical) principles.
Repairing and Maintaining Mechanical Equipment	Servicing, repairing, adjusting, and testing machines, devices, moving parts, and equipment that operate primarily on the basis of mechanical (not electronic) principles.
Staffing Organizational Units	Recruiting, interviewing, selecting, hiring, and promoting employees in an organization.

Work_Context	Work_Context Definitions
Indoors, Environmentally Controlled	How often does this job require working indoors in environmentally controlled conditions?
Face-to-Face Discussions	How often do you have to have face-to-face discussions with individuals or teams in this job?
Electronic Mail	How often do you use electronic mail in this job?
Freedom to Make Decisions	How much decision making freedom, without supervision, does the job offer?
Work With Work Group or Team	How important is it to work with others in a group or team in this job?
Telephone	How often do you have telephone conversations in this job?
Importance of Being Exact or Accurate	How important is being very exact or highly accurate in performing this job?
Contact With Others	How much does this job require the worker to be in contact with others (face-to-face, by telephone, or otherwise) in order to perform it?
Letters and Memos	How often does the job require written letters and memos?
Structured versus Unstructured Work	To what extent is this job structured for the worker, rather than allowing the worker to determine tasks, priorities, and goals?
Impact of Decisions on Co-workers or Company Resul	How do the decisions an employee makes impact the results of co-workers, clients or the company?
Frequency of Decision Making	How frequently is the worker required to make decisions that affect other people, the financial resources, and/or the image and reputation of the organization?
Time Pressure	How often does this job require the worker to meet strict deadlines?
Coordinate or Lead Others	How important is it to coordinate or lead others in accomplishing work activities in this job?
Spend Time Sitting	How much does this job require sitting?
Responsibility for Outcomes and Results	How responsible is the worker for work outcomes and results of other workers?
Level of Competition	To what extent does this job require the worker to compete or to be aware of competitive pressures?
Deal With External Customers	How important is it to work with external customers or the public in this job?

Consequence of Error	How serious would the result usually be if the worker made a mistake that was not readily correctable?
Wear Common Protective or Safety Equipment such as	How much does this job require wearing common protective or safety equipment such as safety shoes, glasses, gloves, hard hats or life jackets?
Sounds, Noise Levels Are Distracting or Uncomforta	How often does this job require working exposed to sounds and noise levels that are distracting or uncomfortable?
Deal With Unpleasant or Angry People	How frequently does the worker have to deal with unpleasant, angry, or discourteous individuals as part of the job requirements?
Physical Proximity	To what extent does this job require the worker to perform job tasks in close physical proximity to other people?
Exposed to Hazardous Equipment	How often does this job require exposure to hazardous equipment?
Responsible for Others' Health and Safety	How much responsibility is there for the health and safety of others in this job?
Frequency of Conflict Situations	How often are there conflict situations the employee has to face in this job?
Importance of Repeating Same Tasks	How important is repeating the same physical activities (e.g., key entry) or mental activities (e.g., checking entries in a ledger) over and over, without stopping, to performing this job?
Spend Time Standing	How much does this job require standing?
Degree of Automation	How automated is the job?
Public Speaking	How often do you have to perform public speaking in this job?
Exposed to Contaminants	How often does this job require working exposed to contaminants (such as pollutants, gases, dust or odors)?
Indoors, Not Environmentally Controlled	How often does this job require working indoors in non-controlled environmental conditions (e.g., warehouse without heat)?
In an Enclosed Vehicle or Equipment	How often does this job require working in a closed vehicle or equipment (e.g., car)?
Spend Time Walking and Running	How much does this job require walking and running?
Spend Time Making Repetitive Motions	How much does this job require making repetitive motions?
Exposed to Minor Burns, Cuts, Bites, or Stings	How often does this job require exposure to minor burns, cuts, bites, or stings?
Spend Time Using Your Hands to Handle, Control, or	How much does this job require using your hands to handle, control, or feel objects, tools or controls?
Exposed to Hazardous Conditions	How often does this job require exposure to hazardous conditions?
Cramped Work Space, Awkward Positions	How often does this job require working in cramped work spaces that requires getting into awkward positions?
Pace Determined by Speed of Equipment	How important is it to this job that the pace is determined by the speed of equipment or machinery? (This does not refer to keeping busy at all times on this job.)
Spend Time Bending or Twisting the Body	How much does this job require bending or twisting your body?
Very Hot or Cold Temperatures	How often does this job require working in very hot (above 90 F degrees) or very cold (below 32 F degrees) temperatures?
Extremely Bright or Inadequate Lighting	How often does this job require working in extremely bright or inadequate lighting conditions?
Outdoors, Exposed to Weather	How often does this job require working outdoors, exposed to all weather conditions?
Outdoors, Under Cover	How often does this job require working outdoors, under cover (e.g., structure with roof but no walls)?
Exposed to High Places	How often does this job require exposure to high places?
Spend Time Climbing Ladders, Scaffolds, or Poles	How much does this job require climbing ladders, scaffolds, or poles?
Spend Time Kneeling, Crouching, Stooping, or Crawl	How much does this job require kneeling, crouching, stooping or crawling?
Wear Specialized Protective or Safety Equipment su	How much does this job require wearing specialized protective or safety equipment such as breathing apparatus, safety harness, full protection suits, or radiation protection?
Deal With Physically Aggressive People	How frequently does this job require the worker to deal with physical aggression of violent individuals?
Exposed to Whole Body Vibration	How often does this job require exposure to whole body vibration (e.g., operate a jackhammer)?
Spend Time Keeping or Regaining Balance	How much does this job require keeping or regaining your balance?
In an Open Vehicle or Equipment	How often does this job require working in an open vehicle or equipment (e.g., tractor)?
Exposed to Radiation	How often does this job require exposure to radiation?
Exposed to Disease or Infections	How often does this job require exposure to disease/infections?

3) Examine maps. deposits. drilling locations. and/or mines in order to determine the location. size. accessibility. contents. value. and potential profitability of mineral. oil. and gas deposits.

4) Monitor mine production rates in order to assess operational effectiveness.

5) Prepare schedules. reports. and estimates of the costs involved in developing and operating mines.

6) Select or develop mineral location, extraction, and production methods. based on factors such as safety, cost, and deposit characteristics.

7) Supervise and coordinate the work of technicians, technologists, survey personnel, engineers. scientists and other mine personnel.

8) Design, implement, and monitor the development of mines. facilities, systems, and equipment.

9) Design, develop, and implement computer applications for use in mining operations such as mine design, modeling, or mapping; or for monitoring mine conditions.

10) Lay out, direct, and supervise mine construction operations, such as the construction of shafts and tunnels.

11) Select or devise materials-handling methods and equipment to transport ore, waste materials, and mineral products efficiently and economically.

12) Devise solutions to problems of land reclamation and water and air pollution, such as methods of storing excavated soil and returning exhausted mine sites to natural states.

13) Conduct or direct mining experiments in order to test or prove research findings.

14) Evaluate data in order to develop new mining products, equipment, or processes.

15) Implement and coordinate mine safety programs, including the design and maintenance of protective and rescue equipment and safety devices.

16) Test air to detect toxic gases and recommend measures to remove them, such as installation of ventilation shafts.

17) Design mining and mineral treatment equipment and machinery in collaboration with other engineering specialists.

Knowledge	Knowledge Definitions
Engineering and Technology	Knowledge of the practical application of engineering science and technology. This includes applying principles, techniques, procedures, and equipment to the design and production of various goods and services.
Production and Processing	Knowledge of raw materials, production processes, quality control, costs, and other techniques for maximizing the effective manufacture and distribution of goods.
Mathematics	Knowledge of arithmetic, algebra, geometry, calculus, statistics, and their applications.
Computers and Electronics	Knowledge of circuit boards, processors, chips, electronic equipment, and computer hardware and software, including applications and programming.
Administration and Management	Knowledge of business and management principles involved in strategic planning, resource allocation, human resources modeling, leadership technique, production methods, and coordination of people and resources.
English Language	Knowledge of the structure and content of the English language including the meaning and spelling of words, rules of composition, and grammar.
Design	Knowledge of design techniques, tools, and principles involved in production of precision technical plans, blueprints, drawings, and models.
Public Safety and Security	Knowledge of relevant equipment, policies, procedures, and strategies to promote effective local, state, or national security operations for the protection of people, data, property, and institutions.
Physics	Knowledge and prediction of physical principles, laws, their interrelationships, and applications to understanding fluid, material, and atmospheric dynamics, and mechanical, electrical, atomic and sub-atomic structures and processes.
Chemistry	Knowledge of the chemical composition, structure, and properties of substances and of the chemical processes and transformations that they undergo. This includes uses of chemicals and their interactions, danger signs, production techniques, and disposal methods.
Law and Government	Knowledge of laws, legal codes, court procedures, precedents, government regulations, executive orders, agency rules, and the democratic political process.
Education and Training	Knowledge of principles and methods for curriculum and training design, teaching and instruction for individuals and groups, and the measurement of training effects.

Job Zone Component	Job Zone Component Definitions
Title	Job Zone Four: Considerable Preparation Needed
Overall Experience	A minimum of two to four years of work-related skill, knowledge, or experience is needed for these occupations. For example, an accountant must complete four years of college and work for several years in accounting to be considered qualified.
Job Training	Employees in these occupations usually need several years of work-related experience, on-the-job training, and/or vocational training.
Job Zone Examples	Many of these occupations involve coordinating, supervising, managing, or training others. Examples include accountants, chefs and head cooks, computer programmers, historians, pharmacists, and police detectives.
SVP Range	(7.0 to < 8.0)
Education	Most of these occupations require a four-year bachelor's degree, but some do not.

Work_Styles	Work_Styles Definitions
Attention to Detail	Job requires being careful about detail and thorough in completing work tasks.
Cooperation	Job requires being pleasant with others on the job and displaying a good-natured, cooperative attitude.
Dependability	Job requires being reliable, responsible, and dependable, and fulfilling obligations.
Leadership	Job requires a willingness to lead, take charge, and offer opinions and direction.
Achievement/Effort	Job requires establishing and maintaining personally challenging achievement goals and exerting effort toward mastering tasks.
Adaptability/Flexibility	Job requires being open to change (positive or negative) and to considerable variety in the workplace.
Analytical Thinking	Job requires analyzing information and using logic to address work-related issues and problems.
Initiative	Job requires a willingness to take on responsibilities and challenges.
Integrity	Job requires being honest and ethical.
Persistence	Job requires persistence in the face of obstacles.
Innovation	Job requires creativity and alternative thinking to develop new ideas for and answers to work-related problems.
Independence	Job requires developing one's own ways of doing things, guiding oneself with little or no supervision, and depending on oneself to get things done.
Self Control	Job requires maintaining composure, keeping emotions in check, controlling anger, and avoiding aggressive behavior, even in very difficult situations.
Stress Tolerance	Job requires accepting criticism and dealing calmly and effectively with high stress situations.
Concern for Others	Job requires being sensitive to others' needs and feelings and being understanding and helpful on the job.
Social Orientation	Job requires preferring to work with others rather than alone, and being personally connected with others on the job.

17-2151.00 - Mining and Geological Engineers, Including Mining Safety Engineers

Determine the location and plan the extraction of coal, metallic ores, nonmetallic minerals, and building materials, such as stone and gravel. Work involves conducting preliminary surveys of deposits or undeveloped mines and planning their development; examining deposits or mines to determine whether they can be worked at a profit; making geological and topographical surveys; evolving methods of mining best suited to character, type, and size of deposits; and supervising mining operations.

Tasks

1) Inspect mining areas for unsafe structures, equipment, and working conditions.

2) Select locations and plan underground or surface mining operations, specifying processes, labor usage, and equipment that will result in safe, economical, and environmentally sound extraction of minerals and ores.

Economics and Accounting	Knowledge of economic and accounting principles and practices, the financial markets, banking and the analysis and reporting of financial data.
Building and Construction	Knowledge of materials, methods, and the tools involved in the construction or repair of houses, buildings, or other structures such as highways and roads.
Clerical	Knowledge of administrative and clerical procedures and systems such as word processing, managing files and records, stenography and transcription, designing forms, and other office procedures and terminology.
Communications and Media	Knowledge of media production, communication, and dissemination techniques and methods. This includes alternative ways to inform and entertain via written, oral, and visual media.
Mechanical	Knowledge of machines and tools, including their designs, uses, repair, and maintenance.
Geography	Knowledge of principles and methods for describing the features of land, sea, and air masses, including their physical characteristics, locations, interrelationships, and distribution of plant, animal, and human life.
Customer and Personal Service	Knowledge of principles and processes for providing customer and personal services. This includes customer needs assessment, meeting quality standards for services, and evaluation of customer satisfaction.
Transportation	Knowledge of principles and methods for moving people or goods by air, rail, sea, or road, including the relative costs and benefits.
Personnel and Human Resources	Knowledge of principles and procedures for personnel recruitment, selection, training, compensation and benefits, labor relations and negotiation, and personnel information systems.
Psychology	Knowledge of human behavior and performance; individual differences in ability, personality, and interests; learning and motivation; psychological research methods; and the assessment and treatment of behavioral and affective disorders.
Biology	Knowledge of plant and animal organisms, their tissues, cells, functions, interdependencies, and interactions with each other and the environment.
Telecommunications	Knowledge of transmission, broadcasting, switching, control, and operation of telecommunications systems.
Sales and Marketing	Knowledge of principles and methods for showing, promoting, and selling products or services. This includes marketing strategy and tactics, product demonstration, sales techniques, and sales control systems.
Therapy and Counseling	Knowledge of principles, methods, and procedures for diagnosis, treatment, and rehabilitation of physical and mental dysfunctions, and for career counseling and guidance.
Medicine and Dentistry	Knowledge of the information and techniques needed to diagnose and treat human injuries, diseases, and deformities. This includes symptoms, treatment alternatives, drug properties and interactions, and preventive health-care measures.
History and Archeology	Knowledge of historical events and their causes, indicators, and effects on civilizations and cultures.
Philosophy and Theology	Knowledge of different philosophical systems and religions. This includes their basic principles, values, ethics, ways of thinking, customs, practices, and their impact on human culture.
Sociology and Anthropology	Knowledge of group behavior and dynamics, societal trends and influences, human migrations, ethnicity, cultures and their history and origins.
Foreign Language	Knowledge of the structure and content of a foreign (non-English) language including the meaning and spelling of words, rules of composition and grammar, and pronunciation.
Food Production	Knowledge of techniques and equipment for planting, growing, and harvesting food products (both plant and animal) for consumption, including storage/handling techniques.
Fine Arts	Knowledge of the theory and techniques required to compose, produce, and perform works of music, dance, visual arts, drama, and sculpture.

Skills	Skills Definitions
Active Listening	Giving full attention to what other people are saying, taking time to understand the points being made, asking questions as appropriate, and not interrupting at inappropriate times.
Time Management	Managing one's own time and the time of others.
Reading Comprehension	Understanding written sentences and paragraphs in work related documents.

Judgment and Decision Making	Considering the relative costs and benefits of potential actions to choose the most appropriate one.
Mathematics	Using mathematics to solve problems.
Critical Thinking	Using logic and reasoning to identify the strengths and weaknesses of alternative solutions, conclusions or approaches to problems.
Speaking	Talking to others to convey information effectively.
Writing	Communicating effectively in writing as appropriate for the needs of the audience.
Active Learning	Understanding the implications of new information for both current and future problem-solving and decision-making.
Monitoring	Monitoring/Assessing performance of yourself, other individuals, or organizations to make improvements or take corrective action.
Complex Problem Solving	Identifying complex problems and reviewing related information to develop and evaluate options and implement solutions.
Science	Using scientific rules and methods to solve problems.
Operations Analysis	Analyzing needs and product requirements to create a design.
Learning Strategies	Selecting and using training/instructional methods and procedures appropriate for the situation when learning or teaching new things.
Persuasion	Persuading others to change their minds or behavior.
Management of Financial Resources	Determining how money will be spent to get the work done, and accounting for these expenditures.
Equipment Selection	Determining the kind of tools and equipment needed to do a job.
Coordination	Adjusting actions in relation to others' actions.
Technology Design	Generating or adapting equipment and technology to serve user needs.
Management of Material Resources	Obtaining and seeing to the appropriate use of equipment, facilities, and materials needed to do certain work.
Negotiation	Bringing others together and trying to reconcile differences.
Systems Analysis	Determining how a system should work and how changes in conditions, operations, and the environment will affect outcomes.
Social Perceptiveness	Being aware of others' reactions and understanding why they react as they do.
Instructing	Teaching others how to do something.
Quality Control Analysis	Conducting tests and inspections of products, services, or processes to evaluate quality or performance.
Management of Personnel Resources	Motivating, developing, and directing people as they work, identifying the best people for the job.
Systems Evaluation	Identifying measures or indicators of system performance and the actions needed to improve or correct performance, relative to the goals of the system.
Troubleshooting	Determining causes of operating errors and deciding what to do about it.
Programming	Writing computer programs for various purposes.
Operation and Control	Controlling operations of equipment or systems.
Service Orientation	Actively looking for ways to help people.
Operation Monitoring	Watching gauges, dials, or other indicators to make sure a machine is working properly.
Installation	Installing equipment, machines, wiring, or programs to meet specifications.
Equipment Maintenance	Performing routine maintenance on equipment and determining when and what kind of maintenance is needed.
Repairing	Repairing machines or systems using the needed tools.

Ability	Ability Definitions
Inductive Reasoning	The ability to combine pieces of information to form general rules or conclusions (includes finding a relationship among seemingly unrelated events).
Problem Sensitivity	The ability to tell when something is wrong or is likely to go wrong. It does not involve solving the problem, only recognizing there is a problem.
Deductive Reasoning	The ability to apply general rules to specific problems to produce answers that make sense.
Oral Comprehension	The ability to listen to and understand information and ideas presented through spoken words and sentences.
Written Comprehension	The ability to read and understand information and ideas presented in writing.
Written Expression	The ability to communicate information and ideas in writing so others will understand.
Near Vision	The ability to see details at close range (within a few feet of the observer).
Speech Clarity	The ability to speak clearly so others can understand you.

Oral Expression	The ability to communicate information and ideas in speaking so others will understand.
Information Ordering	The ability to arrange things or actions in a certain order or pattern according to a specific rule or set of rules (e.g., patterns of numbers, letters, words, pictures, mathematical operations).
Speech Recognition	The ability to identify and understand the speech of another person.
Category Flexibility	The ability to generate or use different sets of rules for combining or grouping things in different ways.
Originality	The ability to come up with unusual or clever ideas about a given topic or situation, or to develop creative ways to solve a problem.
Far Vision	The ability to see details at a distance.
Selective Attention	The ability to concentrate on a task over a period of time without being distracted.
Mathematical Reasoning	The ability to choose the right mathematical methods or formulas to solve a problem.
Number Facility	The ability to add, subtract, multiply, or divide quickly and correctly.
Perceptual Speed	The ability to quickly and accurately compare similarities and differences among sets of letters, numbers, objects, pictures, or patterns. The things to be compared may be presented at the same time or one after the other. This ability also includes comparing a presented object with a remembered object.
Flexibility of Closure	The ability to identify or detect a known pattern (a figure, object, word, or sound) that is hidden in other distracting material.
Fluency of Ideas	The ability to come up with a number of ideas about a topic (the number of ideas is important, not their quality, correctness, or creativity).
Visualization	The ability to imagine how something will look after it is moved around or when its parts are moved or rearranged.
Time Sharing	The ability to shift back and forth between two or more activities or sources of information (such as speech, sounds, touch, or other sources).
Speed of Closure	The ability to quickly make sense of, combine, and organize information into meaningful patterns.
Depth Perception	The ability to judge which of several objects is closer or farther away from you, or to judge the distance between you and an object.
Visual Color Discrimination	The ability to match or detect differences between colors, including shades of color and brightness.
Memorization	The ability to remember information such as words, numbers, pictures, and procedures.
Finger Dexterity	The ability to make precisely coordinated movements of the fingers of one or both hands to grasp, manipulate, or assemble very small objects.
Auditory Attention	The ability to focus on a single source of sound in the presence of other distracting sounds.
Multilimb Coordination	The ability to coordinate two or more limbs (for example, two arms, two legs, or one leg and one arm) while sitting, standing, or lying down. It does not involve performing the activities while the whole body is in motion.
Control Precision	The ability to quickly and repeatedly adjust the controls of a machine or a vehicle to exact positions.
Reaction Time	The ability to quickly respond (with the hand, finger, or foot) to a signal (sound, light, picture) when it appears.
Hearing Sensitivity	The ability to detect or tell the differences between sounds that vary in pitch and loudness.
Static Strength	The ability to exert maximum muscle force to lift, push, pull, or carry objects.
Trunk Strength	The ability to use your abdominal and lower back muscles to support part of the body repeatedly or continuously over time without 'giving out' or fatiguing.
Glare Sensitivity	The ability to see objects in the presence of glare or bright lighting.
Gross Body Coordination	The ability to coordinate the movement of your arms, legs, and torso together when the whole body is in motion.
Arm-Hand Steadiness	The ability to keep your hand and arm steady while moving your arm or while holding your arm and hand in one position.
Stamina	The ability to exert yourself physically over long periods of time without getting winded or out of breath.
Gross Body Equilibrium	The ability to keep or regain your body balance or stay upright when in an unstable position.
Extent Flexibility	The ability to bend, stretch, twist, or reach with your body, arms, and/or legs.

Dynamic Strength	The ability to exert muscle force repeatedly or continuously over time. This involves muscular endurance and resistance to muscle fatigue.
Spatial Orientation	The ability to know your location in relation to the environment or to know where other objects are in relation to you.
Night Vision	The ability to see under low light conditions.
Sound Localization	The ability to tell the direction from which a sound originated.
Peripheral Vision	The ability to see objects or movement of objects to one's side when the eyes are looking ahead.
Manual Dexterity	The ability to quickly move your hand, your hand together with your arm, or your two hands to grasp, manipulate, or assemble objects.
Response Orientation	The ability to choose quickly between two or more movements in response to two or more different signals (lights, sounds, pictures). It includes the speed with which the correct response is started with the hand, foot, or other body part.
Wrist-Finger Speed	The ability to make fast, simple, repeated movements of the fingers, hands, and wrists.
Speed of Limb Movement	The ability to quickly move the arms and legs.
Explosive Strength	The ability to use short bursts of muscle force to propel oneself (as in jumping or sprinting), or to throw an object.
Dynamic Flexibility	The ability to quickly and repeatedly bend, stretch, twist, or reach out with your body, arms, and/or legs.
Rate Control	The ability to time your movements or the movement of a piece of equipment in anticipation of changes in the speed and/or direction of a moving object or scene.

Work_Activity	Work_Activity Definitions
Getting Information	Observing, receiving, and otherwise obtaining information from all relevant sources.
Communicating with Supervisors, Peers, or Subordin	Providing information to supervisors, co-workers, and subordinates by telephone, in written form, e-mail, or in person.
Making Decisions and Solving Problems	Analyzing information and evaluating results to choose the best solution and solve problems.
Interacting With Computers	Using computers and computer systems (including hardware and software) to program, write software, set up functions, enter data, or process information.
Analyzing Data or Information	Identifying the underlying principles, reasons, or facts of information by breaking down information or data into separate parts.
Estimating the Quantifiable Characteristics of Pro	Estimating sizes, distances, and quantities; or determining time, costs, resources, or materials needed to perform a work activity.
Evaluating Information to Determine Compliance wit	Using relevant information and individual judgment to determine whether events or processes comply with laws, regulations, or standards.
Processing Information	Compiling, coding, categorizing, calculating, tabulating, auditing, or verifying information or data.
Organizing, Planning, and Prioritizing Work	Developing specific goals and plans to prioritize, organize, and accomplish your work.
Monitor Processes, Materials, or Surroundings	Monitoring and reviewing information from materials, events, or the environment, to detect or assess problems.
Updating and Using Relevant Knowledge	Keeping up-to-date technically and applying new knowledge to your job.
Establishing and Maintaining Interpersonal Relatio	Developing constructive and cooperative working relationships with others, and maintaining them over time.
Identifying Objects, Actions, and Events	Identifying information by categorizing, estimating, recognizing differences or similarities, and detecting changes in circumstances or events.
Documenting/Recording Information	Entering, transcribing, recording, storing, or maintaining information in written or electronic/magnetic form.
Thinking Creatively	Developing, designing, or creating new applications, ideas, relationships, systems, or products, including artistic contributions.
Developing Objectives and Strategies	Establishing long-range objectives and specifying the strategies and actions to achieve them.
Developing and Building Teams	Encouraging and building mutual trust, respect, and cooperation among team members.
Coordinating the Work and Activities of Others	Getting members of a group to work together to accomplish tasks.
Scheduling Work and Activities	Scheduling events, programs, and activities, as well as the work of others.
Judging the Qualities of Things, Services, or Peop	Assessing the value, importance, or quality of things or people.

Interpreting the Meaning of Information for Others	Translating or explaining what information means and how it can be used.
Communicating with Persons Outside Organization	Communicating with people outside the organization, representing the organization to customers, the public, government, and other external sources. This information can be exchanged in person, in writing, or by telephone or e-mail.
Performing Administrative Activities	Performing day-to-day administrative tasks such as maintaining information files and processing paperwork.
Resolving Conflicts and Negotiating with Others	Handling complaints, settling disputes, and resolving grievances and conflicts, or otherwise negotiating with others.
Drafting, Laying Out, and Specifying Technical Dev	Providing documentation, detailed instructions, drawings, or specifications to tell others about how devices, parts, equipment, or structures are to be fabricated, constructed, assembled, modified, maintained, or used.
Guiding, Directing, and Motivating Subordinates	Providing guidance and direction to subordinates, including setting performance standards and monitoring performance.
Inspecting Equipment, Structures, or Material	Inspecting equipment, structures, or materials to identify the cause of errors or other problems or defects.
Training and Teaching Others	Identifying the educational needs of others, developing formal educational or training programs or classes, and teaching or instructing others.
Provide Consultation and Advice to Others	Providing guidance and expert advice to management or other groups on technical, systems-, or process-related topics.
Monitoring and Controlling Resources	Monitoring and controlling resources and overseeing the spending of money.
Coaching and Developing Others	Identifying the developmental needs of others and coaching, mentoring, or otherwise helping others to improve their knowledge or skills.
Selling or Influencing Others	Convincing others to buy merchandise/goods or to otherwise change their minds or actions.
Performing General Physical Activities	Performing physical activities that require considerable use of your arms and legs and moving your whole body, such as climbing, lifting, balancing, walking, stooping, and handling of materials.
Staffing Organizational Units	Recruiting, interviewing, selecting, hiring, and promoting employees in an organization.
Assisting and Caring for Others	Providing personal assistance, medical attention, emotional support, or other personal care to others such as coworkers, customers, or patients.
Operating Vehicles, Mechanized Devices, or Equipme	Running, maneuvering, navigating, or driving vehicles or mechanized equipment, such as forklifts, passenger vehicles, aircraft, or water craft.
Handling and Moving Objects	Using hands and arms in handling, installing, positioning, and moving materials, and manipulating things.
Performing for or Working Directly with the Public	Performing for people or dealing directly with the public. This includes serving customers in restaurants and stores, and receiving clients or guests.
Controlling Machines and Processes	Using either control mechanisms or direct physical activity to operate machines or processes (not including computers or vehicles).
Repairing and Maintaining Electronic Equipment	Servicing, repairing, calibrating, regulating, fine-tuning, or testing machines, devices, and equipment that operate primarily on the basis of electrical or electronic (not mechanical) principles.
Repairing and Maintaining Mechanical Equipment	Servicing, repairing, adjusting, and testing machines, devices, moving parts, and equipment that operate primarily on the basis of mechanical (not electronic) principles.

Work_Context	**Work_Context Definitions**
Telephone	How often do you have telephone conversations in this job?
Electronic Mail	How often do you use electronic mail in this job?
Face-to-Face Discussions	How often do you have to have face-to-face discussions with individuals or teams in this job?
Structured versus Unstructured Work	To what extent is this job structured for the worker, rather than allowing the worker to determine tasks, priorities, and goals?
Indoors, Environmentally Controlled	How often does this job require working indoors in environmentally controlled conditions?
Work With Work Group or Team	How important is it to work with others in a group or team in this job?
Contact With Others	How much does this job require the worker to be in contact with others (face-to-face, by telephone, or otherwise) in order to perform it?
Importance of Being Exact or Accurate	How important is being very exact or highly accurate in performing this job?
Freedom to Make Decisions	How much decision making freedom, without supervision, does the job offer?

Time Pressure	How often does this job require the worker to meet strict deadlines?
Impact of Decisions on Co-workers or Company Resul	How do the decisions an employee makes impact the results of co-workers, clients or the company?
Wear Common Protective or Safety Equipment such as	How much does this job require wearing common protective or safety equipment such as safety shoes, glasses, gloves, hard hats or live jackets?
Letters and Memos	How often does the job require written letters and memos?
Coordinate or Lead Others	How important is it to coordinate or lead others in accomplishing work activities in this job?
Frequency of Decision Making	How frequently is the worker required to make decisions that affect other people, the financial resources, and/or the image and reputation of the organization?
Responsible for Others' Health and Safety	How much responsibility is there for the health and safety of others in this job?
In an Enclosed Vehicle or Equipment	How often does this job require working in a closed vehicle or equipment (e.g., car)?
Responsibility for Outcomes and Results	How responsible is the worker for work outcomes and results of other workers?
Spend Time Sitting	How much does this job require sitting?
Exposed to Hazardous Equipment	How often does this job require exposure to hazardous equipment?
Exposed to Contaminants	How often does this job require working exposed to contaminants (such as pollutants, gases, dust or odors)?
Outdoors, Exposed to Weather	How often does this job require working outdoors, exposed to all weather conditions?
Consequence of Error	How serious would the result usually be if the worker made a mistake that was not readily correctable?
Indoors, Not Environmentally Controlled	How often does this job require working indoors in non-controlled environmental conditions (e.g., warehouse without heat)?
Deal With External Customers	How important is it to work with external customers or the public in this job?
Importance of Repeating Same Tasks	How important is repeating the same physical activities (e.g., key entry) or mental activities (e.g., checking entries in a ledger) over and over, without stopping, to performing this job?
Physical Proximity	To what extent does this job require the worker to perform job tasks in close physical proximity to other people?
Very Hot or Cold Temperatures	How often does this job require working in very hot (above 90 F degrees) or very cold (below 32 F degrees) temperatures?
Frequency of Conflict Situations	How often are there conflict situations the employee has to face in this job?
Sounds, Noise Levels Are Distracting or Uncomforta	How often does this job require working exposed to sounds and noise levels that are distracting or uncomfortable?
Level of Competition	To what extent does this job require the worker to compete or to be aware of competitive pressures?
Public Speaking	How often do you have to perform public speaking in this job?
Deal With Unpleasant or Angry People	How frequently does the worker have to deal with unpleasant, angry, or discourteous individuals as part of the job requirements?
Degree of Automation	How automated is the job?
Exposed to Hazardous Conditions	How often does this job require exposure to hazardous conditions?
Spend Time Making Repetitive Motions	How much does this job require making repetitive motions?
Extremely Bright or Inadequate Lighting	How often does this job require working in extremely bright or inadequate lighting conditions?
Spend Time Using Your Hands to Handle, Control, or	How much does this job require using your hands to handle, control, or feel objects, tools or controls?
Exposed to High Places	How often does this job require exposure to high places?
Spend Time Standing	How much does this job require standing?
Outdoors, Under Cover	How often does this job require working outdoors, under cover (e.g., structure with roof but no walls)?
In an Open Vehicle or Equipment	How often does this job require working in an open vehicle or equipment (e.g., tractor)?
Spend Time Walking and Running	How much does this job require walking and running?
Cramped Work Space, Awkward Positions	How often does this job require working in cramped work spaces that requires getting into awkward positions?
Spend Time Bending or Twisting the Body	How much does this job require bending or twisting your body?
Exposed to Minor Burns, Cuts, Bites, or Stings	How often does this job require exposure to minor burns, cuts, bites, or stings?
Wear Specialized Protective or Safety Equipment su	How much does this job require wearing specialized protective or safety equipment such as breathing apparatus, safety harness, full protection suits, or radiation protection?

Pace Determined by Speed of Equipment	How important is it to this job that the pace is determined by the speed of equipment or machinery? (This does not refer to keeping busy at all times on this job.)
Exposed to Whole Body Vibration	How often does this job require exposure to whole body vibration (e.g., operate a jackhammer)?
Spend Time Kneeling. Crouching. Stooping. or Crawl	How much does this job require kneeling, crouching, stooping or crawling?
Spend Time Keeping or Regaining Balance	How much does this job require keeping or regaining your balance?
Spend Time Climbing Ladders, Scaffolds. or Poles	How much does this job require climbing ladders, scaffolds, or poles?
Deal With Physically Aggressive People	How frequently does this job require the worker to deal with physical aggression of violent individuals?
Exposed to Disease or Infections	How often does this job require exposure to disease/infections?
Exposed to Radiation	How often does this job require exposure to radiation?

Job Zone Component	Job Zone Component Definitions
Title	Job Zone Four: Considerable Preparation Needed
Overall Experience	A minimum of two to four years of work-related skill, knowledge, or experience is needed for these occupations. For example, an accountant must complete four years of college and work for several years in accounting to be considered qualified.
Job Training	Employees in these occupations usually need several years of work-related experience, on-the-job training, and/or vocational training.
Job Zone Examples	Many of these occupations involve coordinating, supervising, managing, or training others. Examples include accountants, chefs and head cooks, computer programmers, historians, pharmacists, and police detectives.
SVP Range	(7.0 to < 8.0)
Education	Most of these occupations require a four - year bachelor's degree, but some do not.

Work_Styles	Work_Styles Definitions
Dependability	Job requires being reliable, responsible, and dependable, and fulfilling obligations.
Integrity	Job requires being honest and ethical.
Initiative	Job requires a willingness to take on responsibilities and challenges.
Adaptability/Flexibility	Job requires being open to change (positive or negative) and to considerable variety in the workplace.
Analytical Thinking	Job requires analyzing information and using logic to address work-related issues and problems.
Attention to Detail	Job requires being careful about detail and thorough in completing work tasks.
Cooperation	Job requires being pleasant with others on the job and displaying a good-natured, cooperative attitude.
Persistence	Job requires persistence in the face of obstacles.
Independence	Job requires developing one's own ways of doing things, guiding oneself with little or no supervision, and depending on oneself to get things done.
Stress Tolerance	Job requires accepting criticism and dealing calmly and effectively with high stress situations.
Achievement/Effort	Job requires establishing and maintaining personally challenging achievement goals and exerting effort toward mastering tasks.
Self Control	Job requires maintaining composure, keeping emotions in check, controlling anger, and avoiding aggressive behavior, even in very difficult situations.
Leadership	Job requires a willingness to lead, take charge, and offer opinions and direction.
Innovation	Job requires creativity and alternative thinking to develop new ideas for and answers to work-related problems.
Concern for Others	Job requires being sensitive to others' needs and feelings and being understanding and helpful on the job.
Social Orientation	Job requires preferring to work with others rather than alone, and being personally connected with others on the job.

17-2171.00 - Petroleum Engineers

Devise methods to improve oil and gas well production and determine the need for new or modified tool designs. Oversee drilling and offer technical advice to achieve economical and satisfactory progress.

Tasks

1) Monitor production rates, and plan rework processes in order to improve production.

2) Write technical reports for engineering and management personnel.

3) Evaluate findings in order to develop. design. or test equipment or processes.

4) Analyze data in order to recommend placement of wells and supplementary processes to enhance production.

5) Assist engineering and other personnel to solve operating problems.

6) Develop plans for oil and gas field drilling. and for product recovery and treatment.

7) Assign work to staff in order to obtain maximum utilization of personnel.

8) Assess costs and estimate the production capabilities and economic value of oil and gas wells, in order to evaluate the economic viability of potential drilling sites.

9) Direct and monitor the completion and evaluation of wells, well testing, and well surveys.

10) Maintain records of drilling and production operations.

11) Specify and supervise well modification and stimulation programs, in order to maximize oil and gas recovery.

12) Interpret drilling and testing information for personnel.

13) Coordinate activities of workers engaged in research, planning, and development.

14) Design and implement environmental controls on oil and gas operations.

15) Conduct engineering research experiments in order to improve or modify mining and oil machinery and operations.

16) Take samples in order to assess the amount and quality of oil, the depth at which resources lie, and the equipment needed to properly extract them.

17) Simulate reservoir performance for different recovery techniques, using computer models.

18) Inspect oil and gas wells in order to determine that installations are completed.

19) Coordinate the installation, maintenance, and operation of mining and oil field equipment.

20) Test machinery and equipment in order to ensure that it is safe and conforms to performance specifications.

21) Design or modify mining and oil field machinery and tools, applying engineering principles.

22) Supervise the removal of drilling equipment, the removal of any waste, and the safe return of land to structural stability when wells or pockets are exhausted.

Knowledge	Knowledge Definitions
Engineering and Technology	Knowledge of the practical application of engineering science and technology. This includes applying principles, techniques, procedures, and equipment to the design and production of various goods and services.
Mathematics	Knowledge of arithmetic, algebra, geometry, calculus, statistics, and their applications.
English Language	Knowledge of the structure and content of the English language including the meaning and spelling of words, rules of composition, and grammar.
Physics	Knowledge and prediction of physical principles, laws, their interrelationships, and applications to understanding fluid, material, and atmospheric dynamics, and mechanical, electrical, atomic and sub- atomic structures and processes.
Computers and Electronics	Knowledge of circuit boards, processors, chips, electronic equipment, and computer hardware and software, including applications and programming.
Administration and Management	Knowledge of business and management principles involved in strategic planning, resource allocation, human resources modeling, leadership technique, production methods, and coordination of people and resources.
Production and Processing	Knowledge of raw materials, production processes, quality control, costs, and other techniques for maximizing the effective manufacture and distribution of goods.

Chemistry	Knowledge of the chemical composition, structure, and properties of substances and of the chemical processes and transformations that they undergo. This includes uses of chemicals and their interactions, danger signs, production techniques, and disposal methods.
Economics and Accounting	Knowledge of economic and accounting principles and practices, the financial markets, banking and the analysis and reporting of financial data.
Design	Knowledge of design techniques, tools, and principles involved in production of precision technical plans, blueprints, drawings, and models.
Clerical	Knowledge of administrative and clerical procedures and systems such as word processing, managing files and records, stenography and transcription, designing forms, and other office procedures and terminology.
Mechanical	Knowledge of machines and tools, including their designs, uses, repair, and maintenance.
Law and Government	Knowledge of laws, legal codes, court procedures, precedents, government regulations, executive orders, agency rules, and the democratic political process.
Public Safety and Security	Knowledge of relevant equipment, policies, procedures, and strategies to promote effective local, state, or national security operations for the protection of people, data, property, and institutions.
Geography	Knowledge of principles and methods for describing the features of land, sea, and air masses, including their physical characteristics, locations, interrelationships, and distribution of plant, animal, and human life.
Personnel and Human Resources	Knowledge of principles and procedures for personnel recruitment, selection, training, compensation and benefits, labor relations and negotiation, and personnel information systems.
Psychology	Knowledge of human behavior and performance; individual differences in ability, personality, and interests; learning and motivation; psychological research methods; and the assessment and treatment of behavioral and affective disorders.
Building and Construction	Knowledge of materials, methods, and the tools involved in the construction or repair of houses, buildings, or other structures such as highways and roads.
Education and Training	Knowledge of principles and methods for curriculum and training design, teaching and instruction for individuals and groups, and the measurement of training effects.
Sales and Marketing	Knowledge of principles and methods for showing, promoting, and selling products or services. This includes marketing strategy and tactics, product demonstration, sales techniques, and sales control systems.
Telecommunications	Knowledge of transmission, broadcasting, switching, control, and operation of telecommunications systems.
Customer and Personal Service	Knowledge of principles and processes for providing customer and personal services. This includes customer needs assessment, meeting quality standards for services, and evaluation of customer satisfaction.
Transportation	Knowledge of principles and methods for moving people or goods by air, rail, sea, or road, including the relative costs and benefits.
Communications and Media	Knowledge of media production, communication, and dissemination techniques and methods. This includes alternative ways to inform and entertain via written, oral, and visual media.
Foreign Language	Knowledge of the structure and content of a foreign (non-English) language including the meaning and spelling of words, rules of composition and grammar, and pronunciation.
Biology	Knowledge of plant and animal organisms, their tissues, cells, functions, interdependencies, and interactions with each other and the environment.
Philosophy and Theology	Knowledge of different philosophical systems and religions. This includes their basic principles, values, ethics, ways of thinking, customs, practices, and their impact on human culture.
Medicine and Dentistry	Knowledge of the information and techniques needed to diagnose and treat human injuries, diseases, and deformities. This includes symptoms, treatment alternatives, drug properties and interactions, and preventive health-care measures.
Sociology and Anthropology	Knowledge of group behavior and dynamics, societal trends and influences, human migrations, ethnicity, cultures and their history and origins.
History and Archeology	Knowledge of historical events and their causes, indicators, and effects on civilizations and cultures.
Therapy and Counseling	Knowledge of principles, methods, and procedures for diagnosis, treatment, and rehabilitation of physical and mental dysfunctions, and for career counseling and guidance.
Fine Arts	Knowledge of the theory and techniques required to compose, produce, and perform works of music, dance, visual arts, drama, and sculpture.
Food Production	Knowledge of techniques and equipment for planting, growing, and harvesting food products (both plant and animal) for consumption, including storage/handling techniques.

Skills	Skills Definitions
Judgment and Decision Making	Considering the relative costs and benefits of potential actions to choose the most appropriate one.
Critical Thinking	Using logic and reasoning to identify the strengths and weaknesses of alternative solutions, conclusions or approaches to problems.
Active Listening	Giving full attention to what other people are saying, taking time to understand the points being made, asking questions as appropriate, and not interrupting at inappropriate times.
Complex Problem Solving	Identifying complex problems and reviewing related information to develop and evaluate options and implement solutions.
Reading Comprehension	Understanding written sentences and paragraphs in work related documents.
Mathematics	Using mathematics to solve problems.
Coordination	Adjusting actions in relation to others' actions.
Troubleshooting	Determining causes of operating errors and deciding what to do about it.
Science	Using scientific rules and methods to solve problems.
Active Learning	Understanding the implications of new information for both current and future problem-solving and decision-making.
Management of Financial Resources	Determining how money will be spent to get the work done, and accounting for these expenditures.
Writing	Communicating effectively in writing as appropriate for the needs of the audience.
Speaking	Talking to others to convey information effectively.
Operations Analysis	Analyzing needs and product requirements to create a design.
Time Management	Managing one's own time and the time of others.
Persuasion	Persuading others to change their minds or behavior.
Equipment Selection	Determining the kind of tools and equipment needed to do a job.
Negotiation	Bringing others together and trying to reconcile differences.
Monitoring	Monitoring/Assessing performance of yourself, other individuals, or organizations to make improvements or take corrective action.
Operation Monitoring	Watching gauges, dials, or other indicators to make sure a machine is working properly.
Technology Design	Generating or adapting equipment and technology to serve user needs.
Management of Material Resources	Obtaining and seeing to the appropriate use of equipment, facilities, and materials needed to do certain work.
Learning Strategies	Selecting and using training/instructional methods and procedures appropriate for the situation when learning or teaching new things.
Systems Analysis	Determining how a system should work and how changes in conditions, operations, and the environment will affect outcomes.
Systems Evaluation	Identifying measures or indicators of system performance and the actions needed to improve or correct performance, relative to the goals of the system.
Management of Personnel Resources	Motivating, developing, and directing people as they work, identifying the best people for the job.
Social Perceptiveness	Being aware of others' reactions and understanding why they react as they do.
Instructing	Teaching others how to do something.
Quality Control Analysis	Conducting tests and inspections of products, services, or processes to evaluate quality or performance.
Equipment Maintenance	Performing routine maintenance on equipment and determining when and what kind of maintenance is needed.
Programming	Writing computer programs for various purposes.
Operation and Control	Controlling operations of equipment or systems.
Service Orientation	Actively looking for ways to help people.
Repairing	Repairing machines or systems using the needed tools.
Installation	Installing equipment, machines, wiring, or programs to meet specifications.

Ability	Ability Definitions
Problem Sensitivity	The ability to tell when something is wrong or is likely to go wrong. It does not involve solving the problem, only recognizing there is a problem.
Oral Comprehension	The ability to listen to and understand information and ideas presented through spoken words and sentences.
Written Comprehension	The ability to read and understand information and ideas presented in writing.
Deductive Reasoning	The ability to apply general rules to specific problems to produce answers that make sense.
Inductive Reasoning	The ability to combine pieces of information to form general rules or conclusions (includes finding a relationship among seemingly unrelated events).
Oral Expression	The ability to communicate information and ideas in speaking so others will understand.
Information Ordering	The ability to arrange things or actions in a certain order or pattern according to a specific rule or set of rules (e.g., patterns of numbers, letters, words, pictures, mathematical operations).
Speech Clarity	The ability to speak clearly so others can understand you.
Flexibility of Closure	The ability to identify or detect a known pattern (a figure, object, word, or sound) that is hidden in other distracting material.
Near Vision	The ability to see details at close range (within a few feet of the observer).
Mathematical Reasoning	The ability to choose the right mathematical methods or formulas to solve a problem.
Category Flexibility	The ability to generate or use different sets of rules for combining or grouping things in different ways.
Number Facility	The ability to add, subtract, multiply, or divide quickly and correctly.
Speech Recognition	The ability to identify and understand the speech of another person.
Selective Attention	The ability to concentrate on a task over a period of time without being distracted.
Written Expression	The ability to communicate information and ideas in writing so others will understand.
Originality	The ability to come up with unusual or clever ideas about a given topic or situation, or to develop creative ways to solve a problem.
Far Vision	The ability to see details at a distance.
Fluency of Ideas	The ability to come up with a number of ideas about a topic (the number of ideas is important, not their quality, correctness, or creativity).
Visualization	The ability to imagine how something will look after it is moved around or when its parts are moved or rearranged.
Speed of Closure	The ability to quickly make sense of, combine, and organize information into meaningful patterns.
Perceptual Speed	The ability to quickly and accurately compare similarities and differences among sets of letters, numbers, objects, pictures, or patterns. The things to be compared may be presented at the same time or one after the other. This ability also includes comparing a presented object with a remembered object.
Finger Dexterity	The ability to make precisely coordinated movements of the fingers of one or both hands to grasp, manipulate, or assemble very small objects.
Time Sharing	The ability to shift back and forth between two or more activities or sources of information (such as speech, sounds, touch, or other sources).
Hearing Sensitivity	The ability to detect or tell the differences between sounds that vary in pitch and loudness.
Depth Perception	The ability to judge which of several objects is closer or farther away from you, or to judge the distance between you and an object.
Visual Color Discrimination	The ability to match or detect differences between colors, including shades of color and brightness.
Auditory Attention	The ability to focus on a single source of sound in the presence of other distracting sounds.
Memorization	The ability to remember information such as words, numbers, pictures, and procedures.
Control Precision	The ability to quickly and repeatedly adjust the controls of a machine or a vehicle to exact positions.
Multilimb Coordination	The ability to coordinate two or more limbs (for example, two arms, two legs, or one leg and one arm) while sitting, standing, or lying down. It does not involve performing the activities while the whole body is in motion.
Spatial Orientation	The ability to know your location in relation to the environment or to know where other objects are in relation to you.

Manual Dexterity	The ability to quickly move your hand, your hand together with your arm, or your two hands to grasp, manipulate, or assemble objects.
Response Orientation	The ability to choose quickly between two or more movements in response to two or more different signals (lights, sounds, pictures). It includes the speed with which the correct response is started with the hand, foot, or other body part.
Sound Localization	The ability to tell the direction from which a sound originated.
Dynamic Strength	The ability to exert muscle force repeatedly or continuously over time. This involves muscular endurance and resistance to muscle fatigue.
Explosive Strength	The ability to use short bursts of muscle force to propel oneself (as in jumping or sprinting), or to throw an object.
Static Strength	The ability to exert maximum muscle force to lift, push, pull, or carry objects.
Reaction Time	The ability to quickly respond (with the hand, finger, or foot) to a signal (sound, light, picture) when it appears.
Wrist-Finger Speed	The ability to make fast, simple, repeated movements of the fingers, hands, and wrists.
Extent Flexibility	The ability to bend, stretch, twist, or reach with your body, arms, and/or legs.
Arm-Hand Steadiness	The ability to keep your hand and arm steady while moving your arm or while holding your arm and hand in one position.
Rate Control	The ability to time your movements or the movement of a piece of equipment in anticipation of changes in the speed and/or direction of a moving object or scene.
Gross Body Coordination	The ability to coordinate the movement of your arms, legs, and torso together when the whole body is in motion.
Glare Sensitivity	The ability to see objects in the presence of glare or bright lighting.
Speed of Limb Movement	The ability to quickly move the arms and legs.
Dynamic Flexibility	The ability to quickly and repeatedly bend, stretch, twist, or reach out with your body, arms, and/or legs.
Gross Body Equilibrium	The ability to keep or regain your body balance or stay upright when in an unstable position.
Stamina	The ability to exert yourself physically over long periods of time without getting winded or out of breath.
Peripheral Vision	The ability to see objects or movement of objects to one's side when the eyes are looking ahead.
Night Vision	The ability to see under low light conditions.
Trunk Strength	The ability to use your abdominal and lower back muscles to support part of the body repeatedly or continuously over time without 'giving out' or fatiguing.

Work_Activity	Work_Activity Definitions
Making Decisions and Solving Problems	Analyzing information and evaluating results to choose the best solution and solve problems.
Analyzing Data or Information	Identifying the underlying principles, reasons, or facts of information by breaking down information or data into separate parts.
Getting Information	Observing, receiving, and otherwise obtaining information from all relevant sources.
Processing Information	Compiling, coding, categorizing, calculating, tabulating, auditing, or verifying information or data.
Communicating with Supervisors, Peers, or Subordin	Providing information to supervisors, co-workers, and subordinates by telephone, in written form, e-mail, or in person.
Estimating the Quantifiable Characteristics of Pro	Estimating sizes, distances, and quantities; or determining time, costs, resources, or materials needed to perform a work activity.
Identifying Objects, Actions, and Events	Identifying information by categorizing, estimating, recognizing differences or similarities, and detecting changes in circumstances or events.
Monitor Processes, Materials, or Surroundings	Monitoring and reviewing information from materials, events, or the environment, to detect or assess problems.
Organizing, Planning, and Prioritizing Work	Developing specific goals and plans to prioritize, organize, and accomplish your work.
Evaluating Information to Determine Compliance wit	Using relevant information and individual judgment to determine whether events or processes comply with laws, regulations, or standards.
Updating and Using Relevant Knowledge	Keeping up-to-date technically and applying new knowledge to your job.
Interacting With Computers	Using computers and computer systems (including hardware and software) to program, write software, set up functions, enter data, or process information.

Monitoring and Controlling Resources	Monitoring and controlling resources and overseeing the spending of money.
Documenting/Recording Information	Entering, transcribing, recording, storing, or maintaining information in written or electronic/magnetic form.
Interpreting the Meaning of Information for Others	Translating or explaining what information means and how it can be used.
Communicating with Persons Outside Organization	Communicating with people outside the organization, representing the organization to customers, the public, government, and other external sources. This information can be exchanged in person, in writing, or by telephone or e-mail.
Developing Objectives and Strategies	Establishing long-range objectives and specifying the strategies and actions to achieve them.
Scheduling Work and Activities	Scheduling events, programs, and activities, as well as the work of others.
Judging the Qualities of Things, Services, or Peop	Assessing the value, importance, or quality of things or people.
Coordinating the Work and Activities of Others	Getting members of a group to work together to accomplish tasks.
Thinking Creatively	Developing, designing, or creating new applications, ideas, relationships, systems, or products, including artistic contributions.
Provide Consultation and Advice to Others	Providing guidance and expert advice to management or other groups on technical, systems-, or process-related topics.
Establishing and Maintaining Interpersonal Relatio	Developing constructive and cooperative working relationships with others, and maintaining them over time.
Performing Administrative Activities	Performing day-to-day administrative tasks such as maintaining information files and processing paperwork.
Inspecting Equipment, Structures, or Material	Inspecting equipment, structures, or materials to identify the cause of errors or other problems or defects.
Developing and Building Teams	Encouraging and building mutual trust, respect, and cooperation among team members.
Drafting, Laying Out, and Specifying Technical Dev	Providing documentation, detailed instructions, drawings, or specifications to tell others about how devices, parts, equipment, or structures are to be fabricated, constructed, assembled, modified, maintained, or used.
Selling or Influencing Others	Convincing others to buy merchandise/goods or to otherwise change their minds or actions.
Resolving Conflicts and Negotiating with Others	Handling complaints, settling disputes, and resolving grievances and conflicts, or otherwise negotiating with others.
Guiding, Directing, and Motivating Subordinates	Providing guidance and direction to subordinates, including setting performance standards and monitoring performance.
Training and Teaching Others	Identifying the educational needs of others, developing formal educational or training programs or classes, and teaching or instructing others.
Coaching and Developing Others	Identifying the developmental needs of others and coaching, mentoring, or otherwise helping others to improve their knowledge or skills.
Operating Vehicles, Mechanized Devices, or Equipme	Running, maneuvering, navigating, or driving vehicles or mechanized equipment, such as forklifts, passenger vehicles, aircraft, or water craft.
Controlling Machines and Processes	Using either control mechanisms or direct physical activity to operate machines or processes (not including computers or vehicles).
Handling and Moving Objects	Using hands and arms in handling, installing, positioning, and moving materials, and manipulating things.
Staffing Organizational Units	Recruiting, interviewing, selecting, hiring, and promoting employees in an organization.
Performing for or Working Directly with the Public	Performing for people or dealing directly with the public. This includes serving customers in restaurants and stores, and receiving clients or guests.
Performing General Physical Activities	Performing physical activities that require considerable use of your arms and legs and moving your whole body, such as climbing, lifting, balancing, walking, stooping, and handling of materials.
Repairing and Maintaining Electronic Equipment	Servicing, repairing, calibrating, regulating, fine-tuning, or testing machines, devices, and equipment that operate primarily on the basis of electrical or electronic (not mechanical) principles.
Repairing and Maintaining Mechanical Equipment	Servicing, repairing, adjusting, and testing machines, devices, moving parts, and equipment that operate primarily on the basis of mechanical (not electronic) principles.
Assisting and Caring for Others	Providing personal assistance, medical attention, emotional support, or other personal care to others such as coworkers, customers, or patients.

Work_Context	Work_Context Definitions
Telephone	How often do you have telephone conversations in this job?
Face-to-Face Discussions	How often do you have to have face-to-face discussions with individuals or teams in this job?
Indoors, Environmentally Controlled	How often does this job require working indoors in environmentally controlled conditions?
Work With Work Group or Team	How important is it to work with others in a group or team in this job?
Structured versus Unstructured Work	To what extent is this job structured for the worker, rather than allowing the worker to determine tasks, priorities, and goals?
Electronic Mail	How often do you use electronic mail in this job?
Contact With Others	How much does this job require the worker to be in contact with others (face-to-face, by telephone, or otherwise) in order to perform it?
Spend Time Sitting	How much does this job require sitting?
Impact of Decisions on Co-workers or Company Resul	How do the decisions an employee makes impact the results of co-workers, clients or the company?
Coordinate or Lead Others	How important is it to coordinate or lead others in accomplishing work activities in this job?
Importance of Being Exact or Accurate	How important is being very exact or highly accurate in performing this job?
Freedom to Make Decisions	How much decision making freedom, without supervision, does the job offer?
Responsibility for Outcomes and Results	How responsible is the worker for work outcomes and results of other workers?
Time Pressure	How often does this job require the worker to meet strict deadlines?
Frequency of Decision Making	How frequently is the worker required to make decisions that affect other people, the financial resources, and/or the image and reputation of the organization?
Letters and Memos	How often does the job require written letters and memos?
Level of Competition	To what extent does this job require the worker to compete or to be aware of competitive pressures?
Public Speaking	How often do you have to perform public speaking in this job?
Frequency of Conflict Situations	How often are there conflict situations the employee has to face in this job?
Deal With External Customers	How important is it to work with external customers or the public in this job?
In an Enclosed Vehicle or Equipment	How often does this job require working in a closed vehicle or equipment (e.g., car)?
Importance of Repeating Same Tasks	How important is repeating the same physical activities (e.g., key entry) or mental activities (e.g., checking entries in a ledger) over and over, without stopping, to performing this job?
Responsible for Others' Health and Safety	How much responsibility is there for the health and safety of others in this job?
Consequence of Error	How serious would the result usually be if the worker made a mistake that was not readily correctable?
Physical Proximity	To what extent does this job require the worker to perform job tasks in close physical proximity to other people?
Spend Time Making Repetitive Motions	How much does this job require making repetitive motions?
Exposed to Contaminants	How often does this job require working exposed to contaminants (such as pollutants, gases, dust or odors)?
Deal With Unpleasant or Angry People	How frequently does the worker have to deal with unpleasant, angry, or discourteous individuals as part of the job requirements?
Sounds, Noise Levels Are Distracting or Uncomforta	How often does this job require working exposed to sounds and noise levels that are distracting or uncomfortable?
Spend Time Using Your Hands to Handle, Control, or	How much does this job require using your hands to handle, control, or feel objects, tools or controls?
Indoors, Not Environmentally Controlled	How often does this job require working indoors in non-controlled environmental conditions (e.g., warehouse without heat)?
Outdoors, Exposed to Weather	How often does this job require working outdoors, exposed to all weather conditions?
Degree of Automation	How automated is the job?
Spend Time Standing	How much does this job require standing?
Wear Common Protective or Safety Equipment such as	How much does this job require wearing common protective or safety equipment such as safety shoes, glasses, gloves, hard hats or live jackets?
Spend Time Walking and Running	How much does this job require walking and running?
Exposed to Hazardous Conditions	How often does this job require exposure to hazardous conditions?

Very Hot or Cold Temperatures	How often does this job require working in very hot (above 90 F degrees) or very cold (below 32 F degrees) temperatures?
Pace Determined by Speed of Equipment	How important is it to this job that the pace is determined by the speed of equipment or machinery? (This does not refer to keeping busy at all times on this job.)
Extremely Bright or Inadequate Lighting	How often does this job require working in extremely bright or inadequate lighting conditions?
Exposed to Hazardous Equipment	How often does this job require exposure to hazardous equipment?
Cramped Work Space, Awkward Positions	How often does this job require working in cramped work spaces that requires getting into awkward positions?
Spend Time Bending or Twisting the Body	How much does this job require bending or twisting your body?
Exposed to Minor Burns, Cuts, Bites, or Stings	How often does this job require exposure to minor burns, cuts, bites, or stings?
Exposed to Radiation	How often does this job require exposure to radiation?
Outdoors, Under Cover	How often does this job require working outdoors, under cover (e.g., structure with roof but no walls)?
Spend Time Climbing Ladders, Scaffolds, or Poles	How much does this job require climbing ladders, scaffolds, or poles?
Exposed to High Places	How often does this job require exposure to high places?
Deal With Physically Aggressive People	How frequently does this job require the worker to deal with physical aggression of violent individuals?
Spend Time Keeping or Regaining Balance	How much does this job require keeping or regaining your balance?
Wear Specialized Protective or Safety Equipment su	How much does this job require wearing specialized protective or safety equipment such as breathing apparatus, safety harness, full protection suits, or radiation protection?
In an Open Vehicle or Equipment	How often does this job require working in an open vehicle or equipment (e.g., tractor)?
Spend Time Kneeling, Crouching, Stooping, or Crawl	How much does this job require kneeling, crouching, stooping, or crawling?
Exposed to Whole Body Vibration	How often does this job require exposure to whole body vibration (e.g., operate a jackhammer)?
Exposed to Disease or Infections	How often does this job require exposure to disease/infections?

Independence	Job requires developing one's own ways of doing things, guiding oneself with little or no supervision, and depending on oneself to get things done.
Persistence	Job requires persistence in the face of obstacles.
Cooperation	Job requires being pleasant with others on the job and displaying a good-natured, cooperative attitude.
Self Control	Job requires maintaining composure, keeping emotions in check, controlling anger, and avoiding aggressive behavior, even in very difficult situations.
Leadership	Job requires a willingness to lead, take charge, and offer opinions and direction.
Innovation	Job requires creativity and alternative thinking to develop new ideas for and answers to work-related problems.
Social Orientation	Job requires preferring to work with others rather than alone, and being personally connected with others on the job.
Concern for Others	Job requires being sensitive to others' needs and feelings and being understanding and helpful on the job.

17-3011.01 - Architectural Drafters

Prepare detailed drawings of architectural designs and plans for buildings and structures according to specifications provided by architect.

Tasks

1) Obtain and assemble data to complete architectural designs, visiting job sites to compile measurements as necessary.

2) Analyze building codes, by-laws, space and site requirements, and other technical documents and reports to determine their effect on architectural designs.

3) Coordinate structural, electrical and mechanical designs and determine a method of presentation in order to graphically represent building plans.

4) Draw rough and detailed scale plans for foundations, buildings and structures, based on preliminary concepts, sketches, engineering calculations, specification sheets and other data.

5) Lay out and plan interior room arrangements for commercial buildings, using computer-assisted drafting (CAD) equipment and software.

6) Create freehand drawings and lettering to accompany drawings.

7) Check dimensions of materials to be used and assign numbers to lists of materials.

8) Prepare colored drawings of landscape and interior designs for presentation to client.

9) Determine procedures and instructions to be followed, according to design specifications and quantity of required materials.

10) Represent architect on construction site, ensuring builder compliance with design specifications and advising on design corrections, under architect's supervision.

11) Supervise, coordinate, and inspect the work of draftspersons, technicians, and technologists on construction projects.

12) Reproduce drawings on copy machines or trace copies of plans and drawings, using transparent paper or cloth, ink, pencil, and standard drafting instruments.

13) Analyze technical implications of architect's design concept, calculating weights, volumes, and stress factors.

14) Prepare cost estimates, contracts, bidding documents and technical reports for specific projects under an architect's supervision.

15) Build landscape, architectural and display models.

16) Calculate heat loss and gain of buildings and structures to determine required equipment specifications, following standard procedures.

Job Zone Component	Job Zone Component Definitions
Title	Job Zone Four: Considerable Preparation Needed
Overall Experience	A minimum of two to four years of work-related skill, knowledge, or experience is needed for these occupations. For example, an accountant must complete four years of college and work for several years in accounting to be considered qualified.
Job Training	Employees in these occupations usually need several years of work-related experience, on-the-job training, and/or vocational training.
Job Zone Examples	Many of these occupations involve coordinating, supervising, managing, or training others. Examples include accountants, chefs and head cooks, computer programmers, historians, pharmacists, and police detectives.
SVP Range	(7.0 to < 8.0)
Education	Most of these occupations require a four - year bachelor's degree, but some do not.

Work_Styles	Work_Styles Definitions
Analytical Thinking	Job requires analyzing information and using logic to address work-related issues and problems.
Initiative	Job requires a willingness to take on responsibilities and challenges.
Dependability	Job requires being reliable, responsible, and dependable, and fulfilling obligations.
Adaptability/Flexibility	Job requires being open to change (positive or negative) and to considerable variety in the workplace.
Integrity	Job requires being honest and ethical.
Achievement/Effort	Job requires establishing and maintaining personally challenging achievement goals and exerting effort toward mastering tasks.
Attention to Detail	Job requires being careful about detail and thorough in completing work tasks.
Stress Tolerance	Job requires accepting criticism and dealing calmly and effectively with high stress situations.

Knowledge	Knowledge Definitions
Design	Knowledge of design techniques, tools, and principles involved in production of precision technical plans, blueprints, drawings, and models.
Building and Construction	Knowledge of materials, methods, and the tools involved in the construction or repair of houses, buildings, or other structures such as highways and roads.
Mathematics	Knowledge of arithmetic, algebra, geometry, calculus, statistics, and their applications.
Computers and Electronics	Knowledge of circuit boards, processors, chips, electronic equipment, and computer hardware and software, including applications and programming.

English Language	Knowledge of the structure and content of the English language including the meaning and spelling of words, rules of composition, and grammar.
Engineering and Technology	Knowledge of the practical application of engineering science and technology. This includes applying principles, techniques, procedures, and equipment to the design and production of various goods and services.
Customer and Personal Service	Knowledge of principles and processes for providing customer and personal services. This includes customer needs assessment, meeting quality standards for services, and evaluation of customer satisfaction.
Public Safety and Security	Knowledge of relevant equipment, policies, procedures, and strategies to promote effective local, state, or national security operations for the protection of people, data, property, and institutions.
Administration and Management	Knowledge of business and management principles involved in strategic planning, resource allocation, human resources modeling, leadership technique, production methods, and coordination of people and resources.
Law and Government	Knowledge of laws, legal codes, court procedures, precedents, government regulations, executive orders, agency rules, and the democratic political process.
Physics	Knowledge and prediction of physical principles, laws, their interrelationships, and applications to understanding fluid, material, and atmospheric dynamics, and mechanical, electrical, atomic and sub- atomic structures and processes.
Production and Processing	Knowledge of raw materials, production processes, quality control, costs, and other techniques for maximizing the effective manufacture and distribution of goods.
Clerical	Knowledge of administrative and clerical procedures and systems such as word processing, managing files and records, stenography and transcription, designing forms, and other office procedures and terminology.
Mechanical	Knowledge of machines and tools, including their designs, uses, repair, and maintenance.
Psychology	Knowledge of human behavior and performance; individual differences in ability, personality, and interests; learning and motivation; psychological research methods; and the assessment and treatment of behavioral and affective disorders.
Geography	Knowledge of principles and methods for describing the features of land, sea, and air masses, including their physical characteristics, locations, interrelationships, and distribution of plant, animal, and human life.
Education and Training	Knowledge of principles and methods for curriculum and training design, teaching and instruction for individuals and groups, and the measurement of training effects.
Sales and Marketing	Knowledge of principles and methods for showing, promoting, and selling products or services. This includes marketing strategy and tactics, product demonstration, sales techniques, and sales control systems.
Fine Arts	Knowledge of the theory and techniques required to compose, produce, and perform works of music, dance, visual arts, drama, and sculpture.
Telecommunications	Knowledge of transmission, broadcasting, switching, control, and operation of telecommunications systems.
History and Archeology	Knowledge of historical events and their causes, indicators, and effects on civilizations and cultures.
Communications and Media	Knowledge of media production, communication, and dissemination techniques and methods. This includes alternative ways to inform and entertain via written, oral, and visual media.
Personnel and Human Resources	Knowledge of principles and procedures for personnel recruitment, selection, training, compensation and benefits, labor relations and negotiation, and personnel information systems.
Economics and Accounting	Knowledge of economic and accounting principles and practices, the financial markets, banking and the analysis and reporting of financial data.
Sociology and Anthropology	Knowledge of group behavior and dynamics, societal trends and influences, human migrations, ethnicity, cultures and their history and origins.
Transportation	Knowledge of principles and methods for moving people or goods by air, rail, sea, or road, including the relative costs and benefits.
Philosophy and Theology	Knowledge of different philosophical systems and religions. This includes their basic principles, values, ethics, ways of thinking, customs, practices, and their impact on human culture.

Foreign Language	Knowledge of the structure and content of a foreign (non-English) language including the meaning and spelling of words, rules of composition and grammar, and pronunciation.
Chemistry	Knowledge of the chemical composition, structure, and properties of substances and of the chemical processes and transformations that they undergo. This includes uses of chemicals and their interactions, danger signs, production techniques, and disposal methods.
Therapy and Counseling	Knowledge of principles, methods, and procedures for diagnosis, treatment, and rehabilitation of physical and mental dysfunctions, and for career counseling and guidance.
Medicine and Dentistry	Knowledge of the information and techniques needed to diagnose and treat human injuries, diseases, and deformities. This includes symptoms, treatment alternatives, drug properties and interactions, and preventive health-care measures.
Food Production	Knowledge of techniques and equipment for planting, growing, and harvesting food products (both plant and animal) for consumption, including storage/handling techniques.
Biology	Knowledge of plant and animal organisms, their tissues, cells, functions, interdependencies, and interactions with each other and the environment.

Skills	Skills Definitions
Active Listening	Giving full attention to what other people are saying, taking time to understand the points being made, asking questions as appropriate, and not interrupting at inappropriate times.
Coordination	Adjusting actions in relation to others' actions.
Active Learning	Understanding the implications of new information for both current and future problem-solving and decision-making.
Complex Problem Solving	Identifying complex problems and reviewing related information to develop and evaluate options and implement solutions.
Mathematics	Using mathematics to solve problems.
Reading Comprehension	Understanding written sentences and paragraphs in work related documents.
Critical Thinking	Using logic and reasoning to identify the strengths and weaknesses of alternative solutions, conclusions or approaches to problems.
Operations Analysis	Analyzing needs and product requirements to create a design.
Instructing	Teaching others how to do something.
Speaking	Talking to others to convey information effectively.
Time Management	Managing one's own time and the time of others.
Monitoring	Monitoring/Assessing performance of yourself, other individuals, or organizations to make improvements or take corrective action.
Learning Strategies	Selecting and using training/instructional methods and procedures appropriate for the situation when learning or teaching new things.
Technology Design	Generating or adapting equipment and technology to serve user needs.
Writing	Communicating effectively in writing as appropriate for the needs of the audience.
Social Perceptiveness	Being aware of others' reactions and understanding why they react as they do.
Service Orientation	Actively looking for ways to help people.
Persuasion	Persuading others to change their minds or behavior.
Quality Control Analysis	Conducting tests and inspections of products, services, or processes to evaluate quality or performance.
Science	Using scientific rules and methods to solve problems.
Judgment and Decision Making	Considering the relative costs and benefits of potential actions to choose the most appropriate one.
Equipment Selection	Determining the kind of tools and equipment needed to do a job.
Negotiation	Bringing others together and trying to reconcile differences.
Systems Evaluation	Identifying measures or indicators of system performance and the actions needed to improve or correct performance, relative to the goals of the system.
Systems Analysis	Determining how a system should work and how changes in conditions, operations, and the environment will affect outcomes.
Management of Personnel Resources	Motivating, developing, and directing people as they work, identifying the best people for the job.
Troubleshooting	Determining causes of operating errors and deciding what to do about it.
Management of Financial Resources	Determining how money will be spent to get the work done, and accounting for these expenditures.

Installation	Installing equipment. machines. wiring, or programs to meet specifications.
Programming	Writing computer programs for various purposes.
Management of Material Resources	Obtaining and seeing to the appropriate use of equipment, facilities, and materials needed to do certain work.
Operation and Control	Controlling operations of equipment or systems.
Operation Monitoring	Watching gauges. dials. or other indicators to make sure a machine is working properly.
Equipment Maintenance	Performing routine maintenance on equipment and determining when and what kind of maintenance is needed.
Repairing	Repairing machines or systems using the needed tools.

Ability	**Ability Definitions**
Visualization	The ability to imagine how something will look after it is moved around or when its parts are moved or rearranged.
Deductive Reasoning	The ability to apply general rules to specific problems to produce answers that make sense.
Near Vision	The ability to see details at close range (within a few feet of the observer).
Information Ordering	The ability to arrange things or actions in a certain order or pattern according to a specific rule or set of rules (e.g., patterns of numbers, letters, words, pictures, mathematical operations).
Inductive Reasoning	The ability to combine pieces of information to form general rules or conclusions (includes finding a relationship among seemingly unrelated events).
Finger Dexterity	The ability to make precisely coordinated movements of the fingers of one or both hands to grasp, manipulate, or assemble very small objects.
Oral Comprehension	The ability to listen to and understand information and ideas presented through spoken words and sentences.
Written Comprehension	The ability to read and understand information and ideas presented in writing.
Oral Expression	The ability to communicate information and ideas in speaking so others will understand.
Originality	The ability to come up with unusual or clever ideas about a given topic or situation, or to develop creative ways to solve a problem.
Arm-Hand Steadiness	The ability to keep your hand and arm steady while moving your arm or while holding your arm and hand in one position.
Problem Sensitivity	The ability to tell when something is wrong or is likely to go wrong. It does not involve solving the problem, only recognizing there is a problem.
Written Expression	The ability to communicate information and ideas in writing so others will understand.
Selective Attention	The ability to concentrate on a task over a period of time without being distracted.
Speech Clarity	The ability to speak clearly so others can understand you.
Fluency of Ideas	The ability to come up with a number of ideas about a topic (the number of ideas is important, not their quality, correctness, or creativity).
Mathematical Reasoning	The ability to choose the right mathematical methods or formulas to solve a problem.
Visual Color Discrimination	The ability to match or detect differences between colors, including shades of color and brightness.
Category Flexibility	The ability to generate or use different sets of rules for combining or grouping things in different ways.
Speech Recognition	The ability to identify and understand the speech of another person.
Far Vision	The ability to see details at a distance.
Manual Dexterity	The ability to quickly move your hand, your hand together with your arm, or your two hands to grasp, manipulate, or assemble objects.
Flexibility of Closure	The ability to identify or detect a known pattern (a figure, object, word, or sound) that is hidden in other distracting material.
Depth Perception	The ability to judge which of several objects is closer or farther away from you, or to judge the distance between you and an object.
Memorization	The ability to remember information such as words, numbers, pictures, and procedures.
Speed of Closure	The ability to quickly make sense of, combine, and organize information into meaningful patterns.
Control Precision	The ability to quickly and repeatedly adjust the controls of a machine or a vehicle to exact positions.
Number Facility	The ability to add, subtract, multiply, or divide quickly and correctly.

Time Sharing	The ability to shift back and forth between two or more activities or sources of information (such as speech, sounds, touch, or other sources).
Perceptual Speed	The ability to quickly and accurately compare similarities and differences among sets of letters, numbers, objects, pictures, or patterns. The things to be compared may be presented at the same time or one after the other. This ability also includes comparing a presented object with a remembered object.
Auditory Attention	The ability to focus on a single source of sound in the presence of other distracting sounds.
Multilimb Coordination	The ability to coordinate two or more limbs (for example, two arms, two legs, or one leg and one arm) while sitting, standing, or lying down. It does not involve performing the activities while the whole body is in motion.
Trunk Strength	The ability to use your abdominal and lower back muscles to support part of the body repeatedly or continuously over time without 'giving out' or fatiguing.
Wrist-Finger Speed	The ability to make fast, simple, repeated movements of the fingers, hands, and wrists.
Spatial Orientation	The ability to know your location in relation to the environment or to know where other objects are in relation to you.
Hearing Sensitivity	The ability to detect or tell the differences between sounds that vary in pitch and loudness.
Reaction Time	The ability to quickly respond (with the hand, finger, or foot) to a signal (sound, light, picture) when it appears.
Response Orientation	The ability to choose quickly between two or more movements in response to two or more different signals (lights, sounds, pictures). It includes the speed with which the correct response is started with the hand, foot, or other body part.
Rate Control	The ability to time your movements or the movement of a piece of equipment in anticipation of changes in the speed and/or direction of a moving object or scene.
Extent Flexibility	The ability to bend, stretch, twist, or reach with your body, arms, and/or legs.
Dynamic Flexibility	The ability to quickly and repeatedly bend, stretch, twist, or reach out with your body, arms, and/or legs.
Speed of Limb Movement	The ability to quickly move the arms and legs.
Stamina	The ability to exert yourself physically over long periods of time without getting winded or out of breath.
Static Strength	The ability to exert maximum muscle force to lift, push, pull, or carry objects.
Explosive Strength	The ability to use short bursts of muscle force to propel oneself (as in jumping or sprinting), or to throw an object.
Dynamic Strength	The ability to exert muscle force repeatedly or continuously over time. This involves muscular endurance and resistance to muscle fatigue.
Gross Body Equilibrium	The ability to keep or regain your body balance or stay upright when in an unstable position.
Night Vision	The ability to see under low light conditions.
Peripheral Vision	The ability to see objects or movement of objects to one's side when the eyes are looking ahead.
Sound Localization	The ability to tell the direction from which a sound originated.
Glare Sensitivity	The ability to see objects in the presence of glare or bright lighting.
Gross Body Coordination	The ability to coordinate the movement of your arms, legs, and torso together when the whole body is in motion.

Work_Activity	**Work_Activity Definitions**
Interacting With Computers	Using computers and computer systems (including hardware and software) to program, write software, set up functions, enter data, or process information.
Drafting, Laying Out, and Specifying Technical Dev	Providing documentation, detailed instructions, drawings, or specifications to tell others about how devices, parts, equipment, or structures are to be fabricated, constructed, assembled, modified, maintained, or used.
Getting Information	Observing, receiving, and otherwise obtaining information from all relevant sources.
Thinking Creatively	Developing, designing, or creating new applications, ideas, relationships, systems, or products, including artistic contributions.
Estimating the Quantifiable Characteristics of Pro	Estimating sizes, distances, and quantities; or determining time, costs, resources, or materials needed to perform a work activity.
Evaluating Information to Determine Compliance wit	Using relevant information and individual judgment to determine whether events or processes comply with laws, regulations, or standards.

Identifying Objects, Actions, and Events	Identifying information by categorizing, estimating, recognizing differences or similarities, and detecting changes in circumstances or events.
Making Decisions and Solving Problems	Analyzing information and evaluating results to choose the best solution and solve problems.
Organizing, Planning, and Prioritizing Work	Developing specific goals and plans to prioritize, organize, and accomplish your work.
Establishing and Maintaining Interpersonal Relatio	Developing constructive and cooperative working relationships with others, and maintaining them over time.
Communicating with Persons Outside Organization	Communicating with people outside the organization, representing the organization to customers, the public, government, and other external sources. This information can be exchanged in person, in writing, or by telephone or e-mail.
Updating and Using Relevant Knowledge	Keeping up-to-date technically and applying new knowledge to your job.
Communicating with Supervisors, Peers, or Subordin	Providing information to supervisors, co-workers, and subordinates by telephone, in written form, e-mail, or in person.
Analyzing Data or Information	Identifying the underlying principles, reasons, or facts of information by breaking down information or data into separate parts.
Processing Information	Compiling, coding, categorizing, calculating, tabulating, auditing, or verifying information or data.
Interpreting the Meaning of Information for Others	Translating or explaining what information means and how it can be used.
Monitor Processes, Materials, or Surroundings	Monitoring and reviewing information from materials, events, or the environment, to detect or assess problems.
Coordinating the Work and Activities of Others	Getting members of a group to work together to accomplish tasks.
Documenting/Recording Information	Entering, transcribing, recording, storing, or maintaining information in written or electronic/magnetic form.
Inspecting Equipment, Structures, or Material	Inspecting equipment, structures, or materials to identify the cause of errors or other problems or defects.
Scheduling Work and Activities	Scheduling events, programs, and activities, as well as the work of others.
Judging the Qualities of Things, Services, or Peop	Assessing the value, importance, or quality of things or people.
Controlling Machines and Processes	Using either control mechanisms or direct physical activity to operate machines or processes (not including computers or vehicles).
Performing Administrative Activities	Performing day-to-day administrative tasks such as maintaining information files and processing paperwork.
Resolving Conflicts and Negotiating with Others	Handling complaints, settling disputes, and resolving grievances and conflicts, or otherwise negotiating with others.
Provide Consultation and Advice to Others	Providing guidance and expert advice to management or other groups on technical, systems-, or process-related topics.
Developing and Building Teams	Encouraging and building mutual trust, respect, and cooperation among team members.
Developing Objectives and Strategies	Establishing long-range objectives and specifying the strategies and actions to achieve them.
Selling or Influencing Others	Convincing others to buy merchandise/goods or to otherwise change their minds or actions.
Training and Teaching Others	Identifying the educational needs of others, developing formal educational or training programs or classes, and teaching or instructing others.
Guiding, Directing, and Motivating Subordinates	Providing guidance and direction to subordinates, including setting performance standards and monitoring performance.
Monitoring and Controlling Resources	Monitoring and controlling resources and overseeing the spending of money.
Assisting and Caring for Others	Providing personal assistance, medical attention, emotional support, or other personal care to others such as coworkers, customers, or patients.
Performing for or Working Directly with the Public	Performing for people or dealing directly with the public. This includes serving customers in restaurants and stores, and receiving clients or guests.
Repairing and Maintaining Electronic Equipment	Servicing, repairing, calibrating, regulating, fine-tuning, or testing machines, devices, and equipment that operate primarily on the basis of electrical or electronic (not mechanical) principles.
Performing General Physical Activities	Performing physical activities that require considerable use of your arms and legs and moving your whole body, such as climbing, lifting, balancing, walking, stooping, and handling of materials.
Handling and Moving Objects	Using hands and arms in handling, installing, positioning, and moving materials, and manipulating things.
Coaching and Developing Others	Identifying the developmental needs of others and coaching, mentoring, or otherwise helping others to improve their knowledge or skills.
Staffing Organizational Units	Recruiting, interviewing, selecting, hiring, and promoting employees in an organization.
Repairing and Maintaining Mechanical Equipment	Servicing, repairing, adjusting, and testing machines, devices, moving parts, and equipment that operate primarily on the basis of mechanical (not electronic) principles.
Operating Vehicles, Mechanized Devices, or Equipme	Running, maneuvering, navigating, or driving vehicles or mechanized equipment, such as forklifts, passenger vehicles, aircraft, or water craft.

Work_Context	Work_Context Definitions
Indoors, Environmentally Controlled	How often does this job require working indoors in environmentally controlled conditions?
Importance of Being Exact or Accurate	How important is being very exact or highly accurate in performing this job?
Face-to-Face Discussions	How often do you have to have face-to-face discussions with individuals or teams in this job?
Work With Work Group or Team	How important is it to work with others in a group or team in this job?
Letters and Memos	How often does the job require written letters and memos?
Spend Time Sitting	How much does this job require sitting?
Electronic Mail	How often do you use electronic mail in this job?
Telephone	How often do you have telephone conversations in this job?
Contact With Others	How much does this job require the worker to be in contact with others (face-to-face, by telephone, or otherwise) in order to perform it?
Importance of Repeating Same Tasks	How important is repeating the same physical activities (e.g., key entry) or mental activities (e.g., checking entries in a ledger) over and over, without stopping, to performing this job?
Spend Time Using Your Hands to Handle, Control, or	How much does this job require using your hands to handle, control, or feel objects, tools or controls?
Structured versus Unstructured Work	To what extent is this job structured for the worker, rather than allowing the worker to determine tasks, priorities, and goals?
Freedom to Make Decisions	How much decision making freedom, without supervision, does the job offer?
Time Pressure	How often does this job require the worker to meet strict deadlines?
Sounds, Noise Levels Are Distracting or Uncomforta	How often does this job require working exposed to sounds and noise levels that are distracting or uncomfortable?
Spend Time Making Repetitive Motions	How much does this job require making repetitive motions?
Physical Proximity	To what extent does this job require the worker to perform job tasks in close physical proximity to other people?
Coordinate or Lead Others	How important is it to coordinate or lead others in accomplishing work activities in this job?
Deal With External Customers	How important is it to work with external customers or the public in this job?
Frequency of Conflict Situations	How often are there conflict situations the employee has to face in this job?
Level of Competition	To what extent does this job require the worker to compete or to be aware of competitive pressures?
Frequency of Decision Making	How frequently is the worker required to make decisions that affect other people, the financial resources, and/or the image and reputation of the organization?
Consequence of Error	How serious would the result usually be if the worker made a mistake that was not readily correctable?
Impact of Decisions on Co-workers or Company Resul	How do the decisions an employee makes impact the results of co-workers, clients or the company?
Deal With Unpleasant or Angry People	How frequently does the worker have to deal with unpleasant, angry, or discourteous individuals as part of the job requirements?
Responsibility for Outcomes and Results	How responsible is the worker for work outcomes and results of other workers?
Degree of Automation	How automated is the job?
Outdoors, Exposed to Weather	How often does this job require working outdoors, exposed to all weather conditions?
Public Speaking	How often do you have to perform public speaking in this job?
Spend Time Standing	How much does this job require standing?
Indoors, Not Environmentally Controlled	How often does this job require working indoors in non-controlled environmental conditions (e.g., warehouse without heat)?
Exposed to Hazardous Equipment	How often does this job require exposure to hazardous equipment?

Spend Time Walking and Running	How much does this job require walking and running?
Pace Determined by Speed of Equipment	How important is it to this job that the pace is determined by the speed of equipment or machinery? (This does not refer to keeping busy at all times on this job.)
Exposed to Contaminants	How often does this job require working exposed to contaminants (such as pollutants, gases, dust or odors)?
Exposed to High Places	How often does this job require exposure to high places?
Outdoors, Under Cover	How often does this job require working outdoors, under cover (e.g., structure with roof but no walls)?
Very Hot or Cold Temperatures	How often does this job require working in very hot (above 90 F degrees) or very cold (below 32 F degrees) temperatures?
In an Enclosed Vehicle or Equipment	How often does this job require working in a closed vehicle or equipment (e.g., car)?
Exposed to Hazardous Conditions	How often does this job require exposure to hazardous conditions?
Responsible for Others' Health and Safety	How much responsibility is there for the health and safety of others in this job?
Wear Common Protective or Safety Equipment such as	How much does this job require wearing common protective or safety equipment such as safety shoes, glasses, gloves, hard hats or live jackets?
Extremely Bright or Inadequate Lighting	How often does this job require working in extremely bright or inadequate lighting conditions?
Spend Time Bending or Twisting the Body	How much does this job require bending or twisting your body?
Spend Time Kneeling, Crouching, Stooping, or Crawl	How much does this job require kneeling, crouching, stooping, or crawling?
Exposed to Minor Burns, Cuts, Bites, or Stings	How often does this job require exposure to minor burns, cuts, bites, or stings?
Spend Time Climbing Ladders, Scaffolds, or Poles	How much does this job require climbing ladders, scaffolds, or poles?
Cramped Work Space, Awkward Positions	How often does this job require working in cramped work spaces that requires getting into awkward positions?
Deal With Physically Aggressive People	How frequently does this job require the worker to deal with physical aggression of violent individuals?
Spend Time Keeping or Regaining Balance	How much does this job require keeping or regaining your balance?
Wear Specialized Protective or Safety Equipment su	How much does this job require wearing specialized protective or safety equipment such as breathing apparatus, safety harness, full protection suits, or radiation protection?
Exposed to Disease or Infections	How often does this job require exposure to disease/infections?
Exposed to Whole Body Vibration	How often does this job require exposure to whole body vibration (e.g., operate a jackhammer)?
In an Open Vehicle or Equipment	How often does this job require working in an open vehicle or equipment (e.g., tractor)?
Exposed to Radiation	How often does this job require exposure to radiation?

Job Zone Component	Job Zone Component Definitions
Title	Job Zone Three: Medium Preparation Needed
Overall Experience	Previous work-related skill, knowledge, or experience is required for these occupations. For example, an electrician must have completed three or four years of apprenticeship or several years of vocational training, and often must have passed a licensing exam, in order to perform the job.
Job Training	Employees in these occupations usually need one or two years of training involving both on-the-job experience and informal training with experienced workers.
Job Zone Examples	These occupations usually involve using communication and organizational skills to coordinate, supervise, manage, or train others to accomplish goals. Examples include dental assistants, electricians, fish and game wardens, legal secretaries, personnel recruiters, and recreation workers.
SVP Range	(6.0 to < 7.0)
Education	Most occupations in this zone require training in vocational schools, related on-the-job experience, or an associate's degree. Some may require a bachelor's degree.

Work_Styles	Work_Styles Definitions
Attention to Detail	Job requires being careful about detail and thorough in completing work tasks.
Dependability	Job requires being reliable, responsible, and dependable, and fulfilling obligations.

Stress Tolerance	Job requires accepting criticism and dealing calmly and effectively with high stress situations.
Cooperation	Job requires being pleasant with others on the job and displaying a good-natured, cooperative attitude.
Adaptability/Flexibility	Job requires being open to change (positive or negative) and to considerable variety in the workplace.
Analytical Thinking	Job requires analyzing information and using logic to address work-related issues and problems.
Integrity	Job requires being honest and ethical.
Concern for Others	Job requires being sensitive to others' needs and feelings and being understanding and helpful on the job.
Initiative	Job requires a willingness to take on responsibilities and challenges.
Self Control	Job requires maintaining composure, keeping emotions in check, controlling anger, and avoiding aggressive behavior, even in very difficult situations.
Achievement/Effort	Job requires establishing and maintaining personally challenging achievement goals and exerting effort toward mastering tasks.
Independence	Job requires developing one's own ways of doing things, guiding oneself with little or no supervision, and depending on oneself to get things done.
Innovation	Job requires creativity and alternative thinking to develop new ideas for and answers to work-related problems.
Persistence	Job requires persistence in the face of obstacles.
Leadership	Job requires a willingness to lead, take charge, and offer opinions and direction.
Social Orientation	Job requires preferring to work with others rather than alone, and being personally connected with others on the job.

17-3011.02 - Civil Drafters

Prepare drawings and topographical and relief maps used in civil engineering projects, such as highways, bridges, pipelines, flood control projects, and water and sewerage control systems.

Tasks

1) Draft plans and detailed drawings for structures, installations, and construction projects such as highways, sewage disposal systems, and dikes, working from sketches or notes.

2) Finish and duplicate drawings and documentation packages, according to required mediums and specifications for reproduction, using blueprinting, photography, or other duplicating methods.

3) Review rough sketches, drawings, specifications, and other engineering data received from civil engineers to ensure that they conform to design concepts.

4) Correlate, interpret, and modify data obtained from topographical surveys, well logs, and geophysical prospecting reports.

5) Supervise and train other technologists, technicians and drafters.

6) Supervise or conduct field surveys, inspections or technical investigations to obtain data required to revise construction drawings.

7) Calculate excavation tonnage and prepare graphs and fill-hauling diagrams for use in earth-moving operations.

8) Explain drawings to production or construction teams and provide adjustments as necessary.

9) Locate and identify symbols located on topographical surveys to denote geological and geophysical formations or oil field installations.

10) Determine the order of work and method of presentation, such as orthographic or isometric drawing.

11) Determine quality, cost, strength and quantity of required materials, and enter figures on materials lists.

12) Calculate weights, volumes, and stress factors and their implications for technical aspects of designs.

13) Plot characteristics of boreholes for oil and gas wells from photographic subsurface survey recordings and other data, representing depth, degree and direction of inclination.

14) Produce drawings using computer assisted drafting systems (CAD) or drafting machines or by hand using compasses, dividers, protractors, triangles and other drafting devices.

Knowledge	Knowledge Definitions
Computers and Electronics	Knowledge of circuit boards, processors, chips, electronic equipment, and computer hardware and software, including applications and programming.
Mathematics	Knowledge of arithmetic, algebra, geometry, calculus, statistics, and their applications.
Design	Knowledge of design techniques, tools, and principles involved in production of precision technical plans, blueprints, drawings, and models.
Engineering and Technology	Knowledge of the practical application of engineering science and technology. This includes applying principles, techniques, procedures, and equipment to the design and production of various goods and services.
English Language	Knowledge of the structure and content of the English language including the meaning and spelling of words, rules of composition, and grammar.
Geography	Knowledge of principles and methods for describing the features of land, sea, and air masses, including their physical characteristics, locations, interrelationships, and distribution of plant, animal, and human life.
Public Safety and Security	Knowledge of relevant equipment, policies, procedures, and strategies to promote effective local, state, or national security operations for the protection of people, data, property, and institutions.
Law and Government	Knowledge of laws, legal codes, court procedures, precedents, government regulations, executive orders, agency rules, and the democratic political process.
Building and Construction	Knowledge of materials, methods, and the tools involved in the construction or repair of houses, buildings, or other structures such as highways and roads.
Transportation	Knowledge of principles and methods for moving people or goods by air, rail, sea, or road, including the relative costs and benefits.
Education and Training	Knowledge of principles and methods for curriculum and training design, teaching and instruction for individuals and groups, and the measurement of training effects.
Physics	Knowledge and prediction of physical principles, laws, their interrelationships, and applications to understanding fluid, material, and atmospheric dynamics, and mechanical, electrical, atomic and sub- atomic structures and processes.
Communications and Media	Knowledge of media production, communication, and dissemination techniques and methods. This includes alternative ways to inform and entertain via written, oral, and visual media.
Mechanical	Knowledge of machines and tools, including their designs, uses, repair, and maintenance.
Clerical	Knowledge of administrative and clerical procedures and systems such as word processing, managing files and records, stenography and transcription, designing forms, and other office procedures and terminology.
Customer and Personal Service	Knowledge of principles and processes for providing customer and personal services. This includes customer needs assessment, meeting quality standards for services, and evaluation of customer satisfaction.
Administration and Management	Knowledge of business and management principles involved in strategic planning, resource allocation, human resources modeling, leadership technique, production methods, and coordination of people and resources.
Production and Processing	Knowledge of raw materials, production processes, quality control, costs, and other techniques for maximizing the effective manufacture and distribution of goods.
Chemistry	Knowledge of the chemical composition, structure, and properties of substances and of the chemical processes and transformations that they undergo. This includes uses of chemicals and their interactions, danger signs, production techniques, and disposal methods.
Personnel and Human Resources	Knowledge of principles and procedures for personnel recruitment, selection, training, compensation and benefits, labor relations and negotiation, and personnel information systems.
Telecommunications	Knowledge of transmission, broadcasting, switching, control, and operation of telecommunications systems.
Psychology	Knowledge of human behavior and performance; individual differences in ability, personality, and interests; learning and motivation; psychological research methods; and the assessment and treatment of behavioral and affective disorders.
Biology	Knowledge of plant and animal organisms, their tissues, cells, functions, interdependencies, and interactions with each other and the environment.
Sales and Marketing	Knowledge of principles and methods for showing, promoting, and selling products or services. This includes marketing strategy and tactics, product demonstration, sales techniques, and sales control systems.
Economics and Accounting	Knowledge of economic and accounting principles and practices, the financial markets, banking and the analysis and reporting of financial data.
Sociology and Anthropology	Knowledge of group behavior and dynamics, societal trends and influences, human migrations, ethnicity, cultures and their history and origins.
Fine Arts	Knowledge of the theory and techniques required to compose, produce, and perform works of music, dance, visual arts, drama, and sculpture.
Philosophy and Theology	Knowledge of different philosophical systems and religions. This includes their basic principles, values, ethics, ways of thinking, customs, practices, and their impact on human culture.
History and Archeology	Knowledge of historical events and their causes, indicators, and effects on civilizations and cultures.
Foreign Language	Knowledge of the structure and content of a foreign (non-English) language including the meaning and spelling of words, rules of composition and grammar, and pronunciation.
Therapy and Counseling	Knowledge of principles, methods, and procedures for diagnosis, treatment, and rehabilitation of physical and mental dysfunctions, and for career counseling and guidance.
Medicine and Dentistry	Knowledge of the information and techniques needed to diagnose and treat human injuries, diseases, and deformities. This includes symptoms, treatment alternatives, drug properties and interactions, and preventive health-care measures.
Food Production	Knowledge of techniques and equipment for planting, growing, and harvesting food products (both plant and animal) for consumption, including storage/handling techniques.

Skills	Skills Definitions
Mathematics	Using mathematics to solve problems.
Active Listening	Giving full attention to what other people are saying, taking time to understand the points being made, asking questions as appropriate, and not interrupting at inappropriate times.
Active Learning	Understanding the implications of new information for both current and future problem-solving and decision-making.
Time Management	Managing one's own time and the time of others.
Reading Comprehension	Understanding written sentences and paragraphs in work related documents.
Critical Thinking	Using logic and reasoning to identify the strengths and weaknesses of alternative solutions, conclusions or approaches to problems.
Coordination	Adjusting actions in relation to others' actions.
Speaking	Talking to others to convey information effectively.
Instructing	Teaching others how to do something.
Learning Strategies	Selecting and using training/instructional methods and procedures appropriate for the situation when learning or teaching new things.
Judgment and Decision Making	Considering the relative costs and benefits of potential actions to choose the most appropriate one.
Complex Problem Solving	Identifying complex problems and reviewing related information to develop and evaluate options and implement solutions.
Operations Analysis	Analyzing needs and product requirements to create a design.
Equipment Selection	Determining the kind of tools and equipment needed to do a job.
Writing	Communicating effectively in writing as appropriate for the needs of the audience.
Troubleshooting	Determining causes of operating errors and deciding what to do about it.
Service Orientation	Actively looking for ways to help people.
Monitoring	Monitoring/Assessing performance of yourself, other individuals, or organizations to make improvements or take corrective action.
Technology Design	Generating or adapting equipment and technology to serve user needs.
Social Perceptiveness	Being aware of others' reactions and understanding why they react as they do.
Operation and Control	Controlling operations of equipment or systems.

Quality Control Analysis	Conducting tests and inspections of products, services, or processes to evaluate quality or performance.
Persuasion	Persuading others to change their minds or behavior.
Installation	Installing equipment, machines, wiring, or programs to meet specifications.
Equipment Maintenance	Performing routine maintenance on equipment and determining when and what kind of maintenance is needed.
Science	Using scientific rules and methods to solve problems.
Negotiation	Bringing others together and trying to reconcile differences.
Management of Material Resources	Obtaining and seeing to the appropriate use of equipment, facilities, and materials needed to do certain work.
Management of Personnel Resources	Motivating, developing, and directing people as they work, identifying the best people for the job.
Programming	Writing computer programs for various purposes.
Repairing	Repairing machines or systems using the needed tools.
Operation Monitoring	Watching gauges, dials, or other indicators to make sure a machine is working properly.
Systems Analysis	Determining how a system should work and how changes in conditions, operations, and the environment will affect outcomes.
Management of Financial Resources	Determining how money will be spent to get the work done, and accounting for these expenditures.
Systems Evaluation	Identifying measures or indicators of system performance and the actions needed to improve or correct performance, relative to the goals of the system.

Ability	Ability Definitions
Near Vision	The ability to see details at close range (within a few feet of the observer).
Inductive Reasoning	The ability to combine pieces of information to form general rules or conclusions (includes finding a relationship among seemingly unrelated events).
Visualization	The ability to imagine how something will look after it is moved around or when its parts are moved or rearranged.
Written Comprehension	The ability to read and understand information and ideas presented in writing.
Flexibility of Closure	The ability to identify or detect a known pattern (a figure, object, word, or sound) that is hidden in other distracting material.
Problem Sensitivity	The ability to tell when something is wrong or is likely to go wrong. It does not involve solving the problem, only recognizing there is a problem.
Oral Comprehension	The ability to listen to and understand information and ideas presented through spoken words and sentences.
Deductive Reasoning	The ability to apply general rules to specific problems to produce answers that make sense.
Perceptual Speed	The ability to quickly and accurately compare similarities and differences among sets of letters, numbers, objects, pictures, or patterns. The things to be compared may be presented at the same time or one after the other. This ability also includes comparing a presented object with a remembered object.
Oral Expression	The ability to communicate information and ideas in speaking so others will understand.
Mathematical Reasoning	The ability to choose the right mathematical methods or formulas to solve a problem.
Information Ordering	The ability to arrange things or actions in a certain order or pattern according to a specific rule or set of rules (e.g., patterns of numbers, letters, words, pictures, mathematical operations).
Originality	The ability to come up with unusual or clever ideas about a given topic or situation, or to develop creative ways to solve a problem.
Speech Recognition	The ability to identify and understand the speech of another person.
Far Vision	The ability to see details at a distance.
Speech Clarity	The ability to speak clearly so others can understand you.
Selective Attention	The ability to concentrate on a task over a period of time without being distracted.
Category Flexibility	The ability to generate or use different sets of rules for combining or grouping things in different ways.
Fluency of Ideas	The ability to come up with a number of ideas about a topic (the number of ideas is important, not their quality, correctness, or creativity).
Written Expression	The ability to communicate information and ideas in writing so others will understand.
Number Facility	The ability to add, subtract, multiply, or divide quickly and correctly.

Finger Dexterity	The ability to make precisely coordinated movements of the fingers of one or both hands to grasp, manipulate, or assemble very small objects.
Visual Color Discrimination	The ability to match or detect differences between colors, including shades of color and brightness.
Arm-Hand Steadiness	The ability to keep your hand and arm steady while moving your arm or while holding your arm and hand in one position.
Memorization	The ability to remember information such as words, numbers, pictures, and procedures.
Speed of Closure	The ability to quickly make sense of, combine, and organize information into meaningful patterns.
Depth Perception	The ability to judge which of several objects is closer or farther away from you, or to judge the distance between you and an object.
Time Sharing	The ability to shift back and forth between two or more activities or sources of information (such as speech, sounds, touch, or other sources).
Auditory Attention	The ability to focus on a single source of sound in the presence of other distracting sounds.
Control Precision	The ability to quickly and repeatedly adjust the controls of a machine or a vehicle to exact positions.
Manual Dexterity	The ability to quickly move your hand, your hand together with your arm, or your two hands to grasp, manipulate, or assemble objects.
Hearing Sensitivity	The ability to detect or tell the differences between sounds that vary in pitch and loudness.
Spatial Orientation	The ability to know your location in relation to the environment or to know where other objects are in relation to you.
Trunk Strength	The ability to use your abdominal and lower back muscles to support part of the body repeatedly or continuously over time without 'giving out' or fatiguing.
Wrist-Finger Speed	The ability to make fast, simple, repeated movements of the fingers, hands, and wrists.
Speed of Limb Movement	The ability to quickly move the arms and legs.
Static Strength	The ability to exert maximum muscle force to lift, push, pull, or carry objects.
Gross Body Coordination	The ability to coordinate the movement of your arms, legs, and torso together when the whole body is in motion.
Glare Sensitivity	The ability to see objects in the presence of glare or bright lighting.
Stamina	The ability to exert yourself physically over long periods of time without getting winded or out of breath.
Extent Flexibility	The ability to bend, stretch, twist, or reach with your body, arms, and/or legs.
Reaction Time	The ability to quickly respond (with the hand, finger, or foot) to a signal (sound, light, picture) when it appears.
Gross Body Equilibrium	The ability to keep or regain your body balance or stay upright when in an unstable position.
Multilimb Coordination	The ability to coordinate two or more limbs (for example, two arms, two legs, or one leg and one arm) while sitting, standing, or lying down. It does not involve performing the activities while the whole body is in motion.
Rate Control	The ability to time your movements or the movement of a piece of equipment in anticipation of changes in the speed and/or direction of a moving object or scene.
Explosive Strength	The ability to use short bursts of muscle force to propel oneself (as in jumping or sprinting), or to throw an object.
Peripheral Vision	The ability to see objects or movement of objects to one's side when the eyes are looking ahead.
Night Vision	The ability to see under low light conditions.
Response Orientation	The ability to choose quickly between two or more movements in response to two or more different signals (lights, sounds, pictures). It includes the speed with which the correct response is started with the hand, foot, or other body part.
Sound Localization	The ability to tell the direction from which a sound originated.
Dynamic Strength	The ability to exert muscle force repeatedly or continuously over time. This involves muscular endurance and resistance to muscle fatigue.
Dynamic Flexibility	The ability to quickly and repeatedly bend, stretch, twist, or reach out with your body, arms, and/or legs.

Work_Activity	Work_Activity Definitions
Getting Information	Observing, receiving, and otherwise obtaining information from all relevant sources.

Drafting, Laying Out, and Specifying Technical Dev	Providing documentation, detailed instructions, drawings, or specifications to tell others about how devices, parts, equipment, or structures are to be fabricated, constructed, assembled, modified, maintained, or used.
Interacting With Computers	Using computers and computer systems (including hardware and software) to program, write software, set up functions, enter data, or process information.
Making Decisions and Solving Problems	Analyzing information and evaluating results to choose the best solution and solve problems.
Evaluating Information to Determine Compliance wit	Using relevant information and individual judgment to determine whether events or processes comply with laws, regulations, or standards.
Updating and Using Relevant Knowledge	Keeping up-to-date technically and applying new knowledge to your job.
Communicating with Supervisors, Peers, or Subordin	Providing information to supervisors, co-workers, and subordinates by telephone, in written form, e-mail, or in person.
Organizing, Planning, and Prioritizing Work	Developing specific goals and plans to prioritize, organize, and accomplish your work.
Identifying Objects, Actions, and Events	Identifying information by categorizing, estimating, recognizing differences or similarities, and detecting changes in circumstances or events.
Estimating the Quantifiable Characteristics of Pro	Estimating sizes, distances, and quantities; or determining time, costs, resources, or materials needed to perform a work activity.
Processing Information	Compiling, coding, categorizing, calculating, tabulating, auditing, or verifying information or data.
Thinking Creatively	Developing, designing, or creating new applications, ideas, relationships, systems, or products, including artistic contributions.
Establishing and Maintaining Interpersonal Relatio	Developing constructive and cooperative working relationships with others, and maintaining them over time.
Communicating with Persons Outside Organization	Communicating with people outside the organization, representing the organization to customers, the public, government, and other external sources. This information can be exchanged in person, in writing, or by telephone or e-mail.
Documenting/Recording Information	Entering, transcribing, recording, storing, or maintaining information in written or electronic/magnetic form.
Judging the Qualities of Things, Services, or Peop	Assessing the value, importance, or quality of things or people.
Interpreting the Meaning of Information for Others	Translating or explaining what information means and how it can be used.
Analyzing Data or Information	Identifying the underlying principles, reasons, or facts of information by breaking down information or data into separate parts.
Scheduling Work and Activities	Scheduling events, programs, and activities, as well as the work of others.
Inspecting Equipment, Structures, or Material	Inspecting equipment, structures, or materials to identify the cause of errors or other problems or defects.
Monitor Processes, Materials, or Surroundings	Monitoring and reviewing information from materials, events, or the environment, to detect or assess problems.
Developing Objectives and Strategies	Establishing long-range objectives and specifying the strategies and actions to achieve them.
Resolving Conflicts and Negotiating with Others	Handling complaints, settling disputes, and resolving grievances and conflicts, or otherwise negotiating with others.
Coordinating the Work and Activities of Others	Getting members of a group to work together to accomplish tasks.
Training and Teaching Others	Identifying the educational needs of others, developing formal educational or training programs or classes, and teaching or instructing others.
Developing and Building Teams	Encouraging and building mutual trust, respect, and cooperation among team members.
Coaching and Developing Others	Identifying the developmental needs of others and coaching, mentoring, or otherwise helping others to improve their knowledge or skills.
Performing for or Working Directly with the Public	Performing for people or dealing directly with the public. This includes serving customers in restaurants and stores, and receiving clients or guests.
Performing Administrative Activities	Performing day-to-day administrative tasks such as maintaining information files and processing paperwork.
Guiding, Directing, and Motivating Subordinates	Providing guidance and direction to subordinates, including setting performance standards and monitoring performance.
Provide Consultation and Advice to Others	Providing guidance and expert advice to management or other groups on technical, systems-, or process-related topics.

Assisting and Caring for Others	Providing personal assistance, medical attention, emotional support, or other personal care to others such as coworkers, customers, or patients.
Controlling Machines and Processes	Using either control mechanisms or direct physical activity to operate machines or processes (not including computers or vehicles).
Monitoring and Controlling Resources	Monitoring and controlling resources and overseeing the spending of money.
Performing General Physical Activities	Performing physical activities that require considerable use of your arms and legs and moving your whole body, such as climbing, lifting, balancing, walking, stooping, and handling of materials.
Selling or Influencing Others	Convincing others to buy merchandise/goods or to otherwise change their minds or actions.
Handling and Moving Objects	Using hands and arms in handling, installing, positioning, and moving materials, and manipulating things.
Operating Vehicles, Mechanized Devices, or Equipme	Running, maneuvering, navigating, or driving vehicles or mechanized equipment, such as forklifts, passenger vehicles, aircraft, or water craft.
Repairing and Maintaining Electronic Equipment	Servicing, repairing, calibrating, regulating, fine-tuning, or testing machines, devices, and equipment that operate primarily on the basis of electrical or electronic (not mechanical) principles.
Staffing Organizational Units	Recruiting, interviewing, selecting, hiring, and promoting employees in an organization.
Repairing and Maintaining Mechanical Equipment	Servicing, repairing, adjusting, and testing machines, devices, moving parts, and equipment that operate primarily on the basis of mechanical (not electronic) principles.

Work_Context	Work_Context Definitions
Spend Time Sitting	How much does this job require sitting?
Indoors, Environmentally Controlled	How often does this job require working indoors in environmentally controlled conditions?
Importance of Being Exact or Accurate	How important is being very exact or highly accurate in performing this job?
Electronic Mail	How often do you use electronic mail in this job?
Telephone	How often do you have telephone conversations in this job?
Face-to-Face Discussions	How often do you have to have face-to-face discussions with individuals or teams in this job?
Work With Work Group or Team	How important is it to work with others in a group or team in this job?
Time Pressure	How often does this job require the worker to meet strict deadlines?
Freedom to Make Decisions	How much decision making freedom, without supervision, does the job offer?
Contact With Others	How much does this job require the worker to be in contact with others (face-to-face, by telephone, or otherwise) in order to perform it?
Importance of Repeating Same Tasks	How important is repeating the same physical activities (e.g., key entry) or mental activities (e.g., checking entries in a ledger) over and over, without stopping, to performing this job?
Structured versus Unstructured Work	To what extent is this job structured for the worker, rather than allowing the worker to determine tasks, priorities, and goals?
Letters and Memos	How often does the job require written letters and memos?
Spend Time Making Repetitive Motions	How much does this job require making repetitive motions?
Physical Proximity	To what extent does this job require the worker to perform job tasks in close physical proximity to other people?
Degree of Automation	How automated is the job?
Level of Competition	To what extent does this job require the worker to compete or to be aware of competitive pressures?
Impact of Decisions on Co-workers or Company Resul	How do the decisions an employee makes impact the results of co-workers, clients or the company?
Frequency of Decision Making	How frequently is the worker required to make decisions that affect other people, the financial resources, and/or the image and reputation of the organization?
Coordinate or Lead Others	How important is it to coordinate or lead others in accomplishing work activities in this job?
Deal With External Customers	How important is it to work with external customers or the public in this job?
Spend Time Using Your Hands to Handle, Control, or	How much does this job require using your hands to handle, control, or feel objects, tools or controls?
Frequency of Conflict Situations	How often are there conflict situations the employee has to face in this job?

Outdoors, Exposed to Weather	How often does this job require working outdoors, exposed to all weather conditions?
In an Enclosed Vehicle or Equipment	How often does this job require working in a closed vehicle or equipment (e.g., car)?
Responsibility for Outcomes and Results	How responsible is the worker for work outcomes and results of other workers?
Consequence of Error	How serious would the result usually be if the worker made a mistake that was not readily correctable?
Sounds, Noise Levels Are Distracting or Uncomforta	How often does this job require working exposed to sounds and noise levels that are distracting or uncomfortable?
Deal With Unpleasant or Angry People	How frequently does the worker have to deal with unpleasant, angry, or discourteous individuals as part of the job requirements?
Responsible for Others' Health and Safety	How much responsibility is there for the health and safety of others in this job?
Spend Time Standing	How much does this job require standing?
Exposed to Contaminants	How often does this job require working exposed to contaminants (such as pollutants, gases, dust or odors)?
Indoors, Not Environmentally Controlled	How often does this job require working indoors in non-controlled environmental conditions (e.g., warehouse without heat)?
Exposed to Minor Burns, Cuts, Bites, or Stings	How often does this job require exposure to minor burns, cuts, bites, or stings?
Extremely Bright or Inadequate Lighting	How often does this job require working in extremely bright or inadequate lighting conditions?
Wear Common Protective or Safety Equipment such as	How much does this job require wearing common protective or safety equipment such as safety shoes, glasses, gloves, hard hats or live jackets?
Very Hot or Cold Temperatures	How often does this job require working in very hot (above 90 F degrees) or very cold (below 32 F degrees) temperatures?
Spend Time Walking and Running	How much does this job require walking and running?
Spend Time Bending or Twisting the Body	How much does this job require bending or twisting your body?
Cramped Work Space, Awkward Positions	How often does this job require working in cramped work spaces that requires getting into awkward positions?
Public Speaking	How often do you have to perform public speaking in this job?
Exposed to Hazardous Equipment	How often does this job require exposure to hazardous equipment?
Spend Time Kneeling, Crouching, Stooping, or Crawl	How much does this job require kneeling, crouching, stooping or crawling?
Spend Time Keeping or Regaining Balance	How much does this job require keeping or regaining your balance?
Exposed to High Places	How often does this job require exposure to high places?
Outdoors, Under Cover	How often does this job require working outdoors, under cover (e.g., structure with roof but no walls)?
In an Open Vehicle or Equipment	How often does this job require working in an open vehicle or equipment (e.g., tractor)?
Exposed to Hazardous Conditions	How often does this job require exposure to hazardous conditions?
Deal With Physically Aggressive People	How frequently does this job require the worker to deal with physical aggression of violent individuals?
Wear Specialized Protective or Safety Equipment su	How much does this job require wearing specialized protective or safety equipment such as breathing apparatus, safety harness, full protection suits, or radiation protection?
Pace Determined by Speed of Equipment	How important is it to this job that the pace is determined by the speed of equipment or machinery? (This does not refer to keeping busy at all times on this job.)
Exposed to Disease or Infections	How often does this job require exposure to disease/infections?
Exposed to Whole Body Vibration	How often does this job require exposure to whole body vibration (e.g., operate a jackhammer)?
Spend Time Climbing Ladders, Scaffolds, or Poles	How much does this job require climbing ladders, scaffolds, or poles?
Exposed to Radiation	How often does this job require exposure to radiation?

17-3011.02

Job Zone Component	Job Zone Component Definitions
Title	Job Zone Three: Medium Preparation Needed
Overall Experience	Previous work-related skill, knowledge, or experience is required for these occupations. For example, an electrician must have completed three or four years of apprenticeship or several years of vocational training, and often must have passed a licensing exam, in order to perform the job.

Job Training	Employees in these occupations usually need one or two years of training involving both on-the-job experience and informal training with experienced workers.
Job Zone Examples	These occupations usually involve using communication and organizational skills to coordinate, supervise, manage, or train others to accomplish goals. Examples include dental assistants, electricians, fish and game wardens, legal secretaries, personnel recruiters, and recreation workers.
SVP Range	(6.0 to < 7.0)
Education	Most occupations in this zone require training in vocational schools, related on-the-job experience, or an associate's degree. Some may require a bachelor's degree.

Work_Styles	Work_Styles Definitions
Attention to Detail	Job requires being careful about detail and thorough in completing work tasks.
Dependability	Job requires being reliable, responsible, and dependable, and fulfilling obligations.
Analytical Thinking	Job requires analyzing information and using logic to address work-related issues and problems.
Cooperation	Job requires being pleasant with others on the job and displaying a good-natured, cooperative attitude.
Initiative	Job requires a willingness to take on responsibilities and challenges.
Adaptability/Flexibility	Job requires being open to change (positive or negative) and to considerable variety in the workplace.
Persistence	Job requires persistence in the face of obstacles.
Integrity	Job requires being honest and ethical.
Achievement/Effort	Job requires establishing and maintaining personally challenging achievement goals and exerting effort toward mastering tasks.
Stress Tolerance	Job requires accepting criticism and dealing calmly and effectively with high stress situations.
Independence	Job requires developing one's own ways of doing things, guiding oneself with little or no supervision, and depending on oneself to get things done.
Self Control	Job requires maintaining composure, keeping emotions in check, controlling anger, and avoiding aggressive behavior, even in very difficult situations.
Innovation	Job requires creativity and alternative thinking to develop new ideas for and answers to work-related problems.
Social Orientation	Job requires preferring to work with others rather than alone, and being personally connected with others on the job.
Leadership	Job requires a willingness to lead, take charge, and offer opinions and direction.
Concern for Others	Job requires being sensitive to others' needs and feelings and being understanding and helpful on the job.

17-3012.01 - Electronic Drafters

Draw wiring diagrams, circuit board assembly diagrams, schematics, and layout drawings used for manufacture, installation, and repair of electronic equipment.

Tasks

1) Draft detail and assembly drawings of design components, circuitry and printed circuit boards, using computer-assisted equipment or standard drafting techniques and devices.

2) Compare logic element configuration on display screen with engineering schematics and calculate figures to convert, redesign, and modify element.

3) Plot electrical test points on layout sheets, and draw schematics for wiring test fixture heads to frames.

4) Locate files relating to specified design project in database library, load program into computer, and record completed job data.

5) Examine electronic schematics and supporting documents to develop, compute, and verify specifications for drafting data, such as configuration of parts, dimensions, and tolerances.

6) Copy drawings of printed circuit board fabrication, using print machine or blueprinting procedure.

7) Select drill size to drill test head, according to test design and specifications, and submit guide layout to designated department.

8) Supervise and coordinate work activities of workers engaged in drafting, designing

layouts, assembling, and testing printed circuit boards.

9) Key and program specified commands and engineering specifications into computer system to change functions and test final layout.

10) Train students to use drafting machines and to prepare schematic diagrams, block diagrams, control drawings, logic diagrams, integrated circuit drawings, and interconnection diagrams.

11) Review blueprints to determine customer requirements and consult with assembler regarding schematics, wiring procedures, and conductor paths.

12) Review work orders and procedural manuals and confer with vendors and design staff to resolve problems and modify design.

13) Generate computer tapes of final layout design to produce layered photo masks and photo plotting design onto film.

17-3012.02 - Electrical Drafters

Develop specifications and instructions for installation of voltage transformers, overhead or underground cables, and related electrical equipment used to conduct electrical energy from transmission lines or high-voltage distribution lines to consumers.

Tasks

1) Visit proposed installation sites and draw rough sketches of location.

2) Use computer-aided drafting equipment and/or conventional drafting stations, technical handbooks, tables, calculators, and traditional drafting tools such as boards, pencils, protractors, and T-squares.

3) Assemble documentation packages and produce drawing sets which are then checked by an engineer or an architect.

4) Confer with engineering staff and other personnel to resolve problems.

5) Draft working drawings, wiring diagrams, wiring connection specifications or cross-sections of underground cables, as required for instructions to installation crew.

6) Draw master sketches to scale showing relation of proposed installations to existing facilities and exact specifications and dimensions.

7) Measure factors that affect installation and arrangement of equipment, such as distances to be spanned by wire and cable.

8) Study work order requests to determine type of service, such as lighting or power, demanded by installation.

9) Explain drawings to production or construction teams and provide adjustments as necessary.

10) Reproduce working drawings on copy machines or trace drawings in ink.

11) Review completed construction drawings and cost estimates for accuracy and conformity to standards and regulations.

12) Write technical reports and draw charts that display statistics and data.

13) Supervise and train other technologists, technicians and drafters.

14) Determine the order of work and the method of presentation, such as orthographic or isometric drawing.

17-3013.00 - Mechanical Drafters

Prepare detailed working diagrams of machinery and mechanical devices, including dimensions, fastening methods, and other engineering information.

Tasks

1) Coordinate with and consult other workers to design, lay out, or detail components and systems and to resolve design or other problems.

2) Lay out and draw schematic, orthographic, or angle views to depict functional relationships of components, assemblies, systems, and machines.

3) Review and analyze specifications, sketches, drawings, ideas, and related data to assess factors affecting component designs and the procedures and instructions to be followed.

4) Develop detailed design drawings and specifications for mechanical equipment, dies/tools, and controls, using computer-assisted drafting (CAD) equipment.

5) Modify and revise designs to correct operating deficiencies or to reduce production problems.

6) Check dimensions of materials to be used and assign numbers to the materials.

7) Confer with customer representatives to review schematics and answer questions pertaining to installation of systems.

8) Compute mathematical formulas to develop and design detailed specifications for components or machinery, using computer-assisted equipment.

9) Draw freehand sketches of designs, trace finished drawings onto designated paper for the reproduction of blueprints, and reproduce working drawings on copy machines.

10) Design scale or full-size blueprints of specialty items, such as furniture and automobile body or chassis components.

11) Lay out, draw, and reproduce illustrations for reference manuals and technical publications to describe operation and maintenance of mechanical systems.

12) Supervise and train other drafters, technologists, and technicians.

13) Shade or color drawings to clarify and emphasize details and dimensions and eliminate background, using ink, crayon, airbrush, and overlays.

Knowledge	Knowledge Definitions
Design	Knowledge of design techniques, tools, and principles involved in production of precision technical plans, blueprints, drawings, and models.
Engineering and Technology	Knowledge of the practical application of engineering science and technology. This includes applying principles, techniques, procedures, and equipment to the design and production of various goods and services.
Mathematics	Knowledge of arithmetic, algebra, geometry, calculus, statistics, and their applications.
English Language	Knowledge of the structure and content of the English language including the meaning and spelling of words, rules of composition, and grammar.
Building and Construction	Knowledge of materials, methods, and the tools involved in the construction or repair of houses, buildings, or other structures such as highways and roads.
Physics	Knowledge and prediction of physical principles, laws, their interrelationships, and applications to understanding fluid, material, and atmospheric dynamics, and mechanical, electrical, atomic and sub-atomic structures and processes.
Customer and Personal Service	Knowledge of principles and processes for providing customer and personal services. This includes customer needs assessment, meeting quality standards for services, and evaluation of customer satisfaction.
Mechanical	Knowledge of machines and tools, including their designs, uses, repair, and maintenance.
Public Safety and Security	Knowledge of relevant equipment, policies, procedures, and strategies to promote effective local, state, or national security operations for the protection of people, data, property, and institutions.
Computers and Electronics	Knowledge of circuit boards, processors, chips, electronic equipment, and computer hardware and software, including applications and programming.
Administration and Management	Knowledge of business and management principles involved in strategic planning, resource allocation, human resources modeling, leadership technique, production methods, and coordination of people and resources.
Law and Government	Knowledge of laws, legal codes, court procedures, precedents, government regulations, executive orders, agency rules, and the democratic political process.
Clerical	Knowledge of administrative and clerical procedures and systems such as word processing, managing files and records, stenography and transcription, designing forms, and other office procedures and terminology.
Chemistry	Knowledge of the chemical composition, structure, and properties of substances and of the chemical processes and transformations that they undergo. This includes uses of chemicals and their interactions, danger signs, production techniques, and disposal methods.
Production and Processing	Knowledge of raw materials, production processes, quality control, costs, and other techniques for maximizing the effective manufacture and distribution of goods.
Education and Training	Knowledge of principles and methods for curriculum and training design, teaching and instruction for individuals and groups, and the measurement of training effects.

Communications and Media	Knowledge of media production, communication, and dissemination techniques and methods. This includes alternative ways to inform and entertain via written, oral, and visual media.
Telecommunications	Knowledge of transmission, broadcasting, switching, control, and operation of telecommunications systems.
Biology	Knowledge of plant and animal organisms, their tissues, cells, functions, interdependencies, and interactions with each other and the environment.
Sales and Marketing	Knowledge of principles and methods for showing, promoting, and selling products or services. This includes marketing strategy and tactics, product demonstration, sales techniques, and sales control systems.
Economics and Accounting	Knowledge of economic and accounting principles and practices, the financial markets, banking and the analysis and reporting of financial data.
Transportation	Knowledge of principles and methods for moving people or goods by air, rail, sea, or road, including the relative costs and benefits.
Geography	Knowledge of principles and methods for describing the features of land, sea, and air masses, including their physical characteristics, locations, interrelationships, and distribution of plant, animal, and human life.
Personnel and Human Resources	Knowledge of principles and procedures for personnel recruitment, selection, training, compensation and benefits, labor relations and negotiation, and personnel information systems.
Psychology	Knowledge of human behavior and performance; individual differences in ability, personality, and interests; learning and motivation; psychological research methods; and the assessment and treatment of behavioral and affective disorders.
Food Production	Knowledge of techniques and equipment for planting, growing, and harvesting food products (both plant and animal) for consumption, including storage/handling techniques.
Foreign Language	Knowledge of the structure and content of a foreign (non-English) language including the meaning and spelling of words, rules of composition and grammar, and pronunciation.
Medicine and Dentistry	Knowledge of the information and techniques needed to diagnose and treat human injuries, diseases, and deformities. This includes symptoms, treatment alternatives, drug properties and interactions, and preventive health-care measures.
Sociology and Anthropology	Knowledge of group behavior and dynamics, societal trends and influences, human migrations, ethnicity, cultures and their history and origins.
Therapy and Counseling	Knowledge of principles, methods, and procedures for diagnosis, treatment, and rehabilitation of physical and mental dysfunctions, and for career counseling and guidance.
Philosophy and Theology	Knowledge of different philosophical systems and religions. This includes their basic principles, values, ethics, ways of thinking, customs, practices, and their impact on human culture.
History and Archeology	Knowledge of historical events and their causes, indicators, and effects on civilizations and cultures.
Fine Arts	Knowledge of the theory and techniques required to compose, produce, and perform works of music, dance, visual arts, drama, and sculpture.

Skills	Skills Definitions
Reading Comprehension	Understanding written sentences and paragraphs in work related documents.
Mathematics	Using mathematics to solve problems.
Active Listening	Giving full attention to what other people are saying, taking time to understand the points being made, asking questions as appropriate, and not interrupting at inappropriate times.
Instructing	Teaching others how to do something.
Technology Design	Generating or adapting equipment and technology to serve user needs.
Critical Thinking	Using logic and reasoning to identify the strengths and weaknesses of alternative solutions, conclusions or approaches to problems.
Equipment Selection	Determining the kind of tools and equipment needed to do a job.
Complex Problem Solving	Identifying complex problems and reviewing related information to develop and evaluate options and implement solutions.
Speaking	Talking to others to convey information effectively.

Judgment and Decision Making	Considering the relative costs and benefits of potential actions to choose the most appropriate one.
Troubleshooting	Determining causes of operating errors and deciding what to do about it.
Writing	Communicating effectively in writing as appropriate for the needs of the audience.
Operations Analysis	Analyzing needs and product requirements to create a design.
Quality Control Analysis	Conducting tests and inspections of products, services, or processes to evaluate quality or performance.
Active Learning	Understanding the implications of new information for both current and future problem-solving and decision-making.
Installation	Installing equipment, machines, wiring, or programs to meet specifications.
Coordination	Adjusting actions in relation to others' actions.
Learning Strategies	Selecting and using training/instructional methods and procedures appropriate for the situation when learning or teaching new things.
Time Management	Managing one's own time and the time of others.
Systems Evaluation	Identifying measures or indicators of system performance and the actions needed to improve or correct performance, relative to the goals of the system.
Monitoring	Monitoring/Assessing performance of yourself, other individuals, or organizations to make improvements or take corrective action.
Repairing	Repairing machines or systems using the needed tools.
Persuasion	Persuading others to change their minds or behavior.
Social Perceptiveness	Being aware of others' reactions and understanding why they react as they do.
Operation Monitoring	Watching gauges, dials, or other indicators to make sure a machine is working properly.
Negotiation	Bringing others together and trying to reconcile differences.
Science	Using scientific rules and methods to solve problems.
Service Orientation	Actively looking for ways to help people.
Operation and Control	Controlling operations of equipment or systems.
Systems Analysis	Determining how a system should work and how changes in conditions, operations, and the environment will affect outcomes.
Equipment Maintenance	Performing routine maintenance on equipment and determining when and what kind of maintenance is needed.
Management of Personnel Resources	Motivating, developing, and directing people as they work, identifying the best people for the job.
Programming	Writing computer programs for various purposes.
Management of Material Resources	Obtaining and seeing to the appropriate use of equipment, facilities, and materials needed to do certain work.
Management of Financial Resources	Determining how money will be spent to get the work done, and accounting for these expenditures.

Ability	Ability Definitions
Visualization	The ability to imagine how something will look after it is moved around or when its parts are moved or rearranged.
Near Vision	The ability to see details at close range (within a few feet of the observer).
Oral Expression	The ability to communicate information and ideas in speaking so others will understand.
Oral Comprehension	The ability to listen to and understand information and ideas presented through spoken words and sentences.
Written Expression	The ability to communicate information and ideas in writing so others will understand.
Problem Sensitivity	The ability to tell when something is wrong or is likely to go wrong. It does not involve solving the problem, only recognizing there is a problem.
Deductive Reasoning	The ability to apply general rules to specific problems to produce answers that make sense.
Inductive Reasoning	The ability to combine pieces of information to form general rules or conclusions (includes finding a relationship among seemingly unrelated events).
Information Ordering	The ability to arrange things or actions in a certain order or pattern according to a specific rule or set of rules (e.g., patterns of numbers, letters, words, pictures, mathematical operations).
Mathematical Reasoning	The ability to choose the right mathematical methods or formulas to solve a problem.
Written Comprehension	The ability to read and understand information and ideas presented in writing.
Speech Clarity	The ability to speak clearly so others can understand you.
Speech Recognition	The ability to identify and understand the speech of another person.

Fluency of Ideas	The ability to come up with a number of ideas about a topic (the number of ideas is important, not their quality, correctness, or creativity).	Night Vision	The ability to see under low light conditions.
Originality	The ability to come up with unusual or clever ideas about a given topic or situation, or to develop creative ways to solve a problem.	Explosive Strength	The ability to use short bursts of muscle force to propel oneself (as in jumping or sprinting), or to throw an object.
Selective Attention	The ability to concentrate on a task over a period of time without being distracted.	Peripheral Vision	The ability to see objects or movement of objects to one's side when the eyes are looking ahead.
Number Facility	The ability to add, subtract, multiply, or divide quickly and correctly.	Gross Body Equilibrium	The ability to keep or regain your body balance or stay upright when in an unstable position.
Flexibility of Closure	The ability to identify or detect a known pattern (a figure, object, word, or sound) that is hidden in other distracting material.	Glare Sensitivity	The ability to see objects in the presence of glare or bright lighting.
Category Flexibility	The ability to generate or use different sets of rules for combining or grouping things in different ways.	Sound Localization	The ability to tell the direction from which a sound originated.
Finger Dexterity	The ability to make precisely coordinated movements of the fingers of one or both hands to grasp, manipulate, or assemble very small objects.	Rate Control	The ability to time your movements or the movement of a piece of equipment in anticipation of changes in the speed and/or direction of a moving object or scene.

Arm-Hand Steadiness	The ability to keep your hand and arm steady while moving your arm or while holding your arm and hand in one position.	**Work_Activity**	**Work_Activity Definitions**
Speed of Closure	The ability to quickly make sense of, combine, and organize information into meaningful patterns.	Drafting, Laying Out, and Specifying Technical Dev	Providing documentation, detailed instructions, drawings, or specifications to tell others about how devices, parts, equipment, or structures are to be fabricated, constructed, assembled, modified, maintained, or used.
Far Vision	The ability to see details at a distance.	Interacting With Computers	Using computers and computer systems (including hardware and software) to program, write software, set up functions, enter data, or process information.
Perceptual Speed	The ability to quickly and accurately compare similarities and differences among sets of letters, numbers, objects, pictures, or patterns. The things to be compared may be presented at the same time or one after the other. This ability also includes comparing a presented object with a remembered object.	Getting Information	Observing, receiving, and otherwise obtaining information from all relevant sources.
Visual Color Discrimination	The ability to match or detect differences between colors, including shades of color and brightness.	Making Decisions and Solving Problems	Analyzing information and evaluating results to choose the best solution and solve problems.
Time Sharing	The ability to shift back and forth between two or more activities or sources of information (such as speech, sounds, touch, or other sources).	Processing Information	Compiling, coding, categorizing, calculating, tabulating, auditing, or verifying information or data.
		Documenting/Recording Information	Entering, transcribing, recording, storing, or maintaining information in written or electronic/magnetic form.
Manual Dexterity	The ability to quickly move your hand, your hand together with your arm, or your two hands to grasp, manipulate, or assemble objects.	Communicating with Supervisors, Peers, or Subordin	Providing information to supervisors, co-workers, and subordinates by telephone, in written form, e-mail, or in person.
Memorization	The ability to remember information such as words, numbers, pictures, and procedures.	Evaluating Information to Determine Compliance wit	Using relevant information and individual judgment to determine whether events or processes comply with laws, regulations, or standards.
Auditory Attention	The ability to focus on a single source of sound in the presence of other distracting sounds.	Analyzing Data or Information	Identifying the underlying principles, reasons, or facts of information by breaking down information or data into separate parts.
Hearing Sensitivity	The ability to detect or tell the differences between sounds that vary in pitch and loudness.	Establishing and Maintaining Interpersonal Relatio	Developing constructive and cooperative working relationships with others, and maintaining them over time.
Multilimb Coordination	The ability to coordinate two or more limbs (for example, two arms, two legs, or one leg and one arm) while sitting, standing, or lying down. It does not involve performing the activities while the whole body is in motion.	Thinking Creatively	Developing, designing, or creating new applications, ideas, relationships, systems, or products, including artistic contributions.
Control Precision	The ability to quickly and repeatedly adjust the controls of a machine or a vehicle to exact positions.	Updating and Using Relevant Knowledge	Keeping up-to-date technically and applying new knowledge to your job.
Static Strength	The ability to exert maximum muscle force to lift, push, pull, or carry objects.	Identifying Objects, Actions, and Events	Identifying information by categorizing, estimating, recognizing differences or similarities, and detecting changes in circumstances or events.
Wrist-Finger Speed	The ability to make fast, simple, repeated movements of the fingers, hands, and wrists.	Handling and Moving Objects	Using hands and arms in handling, installing, positioning, and moving materials, and manipulating things.
Depth Perception	The ability to judge which of several objects is closer or farther away from you, or to judge the distance between you and an object.	Organizing, Planning, and Prioritizing Work	Developing specific goals and plans to prioritize, organize, and accomplish your work.
Trunk Strength	The ability to use your abdominal and lower back muscles to support part of the body repeatedly or continuously over time without 'giving out' or fatiguing.	Interpreting the Meaning of Information for Others	Translating or explaining what information means and how it can be used.
Spatial Orientation	The ability to know your location in relation to the environment or to know where other objects are in relation to you.	Monitor Processes, Materials, or Surroundings	Monitoring and reviewing information from materials, events, or the environment, to detect or assess problems.
Speed of Limb Movement	The ability to quickly move the arms and legs.	Performing Administrative Activities	Performing day-to-day administrative tasks such as maintaining information files and processing paperwork.
Extent Flexibility	The ability to bend, stretch, twist, or reach with your body, arms, and/or legs.	Communicating with Persons Outside Organization	Communicating with people outside the organization, representing the organization to customers, the public, government, and other external sources. This information can be exchanged in person, in writing, or by telephone or e-mail.
Stamina	The ability to exert yourself physically over long periods of time without getting winded or out of breath.		
Response Orientation	The ability to choose quickly between two or more movements in response to two or more different signals (lights, sounds, pictures). It includes the speed with which the correct response is started with the hand, foot, or other body part.	Training and Teaching Others	Identifying the educational needs of others, developing formal educational or training programs or classes, and teaching or instructing others.
Gross Body Coordination	The ability to coordinate the movement of your arms, legs, and torso together when the whole body is in motion.	Scheduling Work and Activities	Scheduling events, programs, and activities, as well as the work of others.
Reaction Time	The ability to quickly respond (with the hand, finger, or foot) to a signal (sound, light, picture) when it appears.	Judging the Qualities of Things, Services, or Peop	Assessing the value, importance, or quality of things or people.
Dynamic Flexibility	The ability to quickly and repeatedly bend, stretch, twist, or reach out with your body, arms, and/or legs.	Provide Consultation and Advice to Others	Providing guidance and expert advice to management or other groups on technical, systems-, or process-related topics.
Dynamic Strength	The ability to exert muscle force repeatedly or continuously over time. This involves muscular endurance and resistance to muscle fatigue.	Estimating the Quantifiable Characteristics of Pro	Estimating sizes, distances, and quantities; or determining time, costs, resources, or materials needed to perform a work activity.

Inspecting Equipment, Structures, or Material	Inspecting equipment, structures, or materials to identify the cause of errors or other problems or defects.
Monitoring and Controlling Resources	Monitoring and controlling resources and overseeing the spending of money.
Controlling Machines and Processes	Using either control mechanisms or direct physical activity to operate machines or processes (not including computers or vehicles).
Coaching and Developing Others	Identifying the developmental needs of others and coaching, mentoring, or otherwise helping others to improve their knowledge or skills.
Resolving Conflicts and Negotiating with Others	Handling complaints, settling disputes, and resolving grievances and conflicts, or otherwise negotiating with others.
Coordinating the Work and Activities of Others	Getting members of a group to work together to accomplish tasks.
Developing and Building Teams	Encouraging and building mutual trust, respect, and cooperation among team members.
Repairing and Maintaining Mechanical Equipment	Servicing, repairing, adjusting, and testing machines, devices, moving parts, and equipment that operate primarily on the basis of mechanical (not electronic) principles.
Selling or Influencing Others	Convincing others to buy merchandise/goods or to otherwise change their minds or actions.
Developing Objectives and Strategies	Establishing long-range objectives and specifying the strategies and actions to achieve them.
Assisting and Caring for Others	Providing personal assistance, medical attention, emotional support, or other personal care to others such as coworkers, customers, or patients.
Guiding, Directing, and Motivating Subordinates	Providing guidance and direction to subordinates, including setting performance standards and monitoring performance.
Performing General Physical Activities	Performing physical activities that require considerable use of your arms and legs and moving your whole body, such as climbing, lifting, balancing, walking, stooping, and handling of materials.
Repairing and Maintaining Electronic Equipment	Servicing, repairing, calibrating, regulating, fine-tuning, or testing machines, devices, and equipment that operate primarily on the basis of electrical or electronic (not mechanical) principles.
Staffing Organizational Units	Recruiting, interviewing, selecting, hiring, and promoting employees in an organization.
Operating Vehicles, Mechanized Devices, or Equipme	Running, maneuvering, navigating, or driving vehicles or mechanized equipment, such as forklifts, passenger vehicles, aircraft, or water craft.
Performing for or Working Directly with the Public	Performing for people or dealing directly with the public. This includes serving customers in restaurants and stores, and receiving clients or guests.

Work_Context	Work_Context Definitions
Face-to-Face Discussions	How often do you have to have face-to-face discussions with individuals or teams in this job?
Electronic Mail	How often do you use electronic mail in this job?
Indoors, Environmentally Controlled	How often does this job require working indoors in environmentally controlled conditions?
Importance of Being Exact or Accurate	How important is being very exact or highly accurate in performing this job?
Telephone	How often do you have telephone conversations in this job?
Spend Time Sitting	How much does this job require sitting?
Contact With Others	How much does this job require the worker to be in contact with others (face-to-face, by telephone, or otherwise) in order to perform it?
Importance of Repeating Same Tasks	How important is repeating the same physical activities (e.g., key entry) or mental activities (e.g., checking entries in a ledger) over and over, without stopping, to performing this job?
Time Pressure	How often does this job require the worker to meet strict deadlines?
Work With Work Group or Team	How important is it to work with others in a group or team in this job?
Spend Time Making Repetitive Motions	How much does this job require making repetitive motions?
Letters and Memos	How often does the job require written letters and memos?
Consequence of Error	How serious would the result usually be if the worker made a mistake that was not readily correctable?
Freedom to Make Decisions	How much decision making freedom, without supervision, does the job offer?
Deal With External Customers	How important is it to work with external customers or the public in this job?
Coordinate or Lead Others	How important is it to coordinate or lead others in accomplishing work activities in this job?

Impact of Decisions on Co-workers or Company Resul	How do the decisions an employee makes impact the results of co-workers, clients or the company?
Structured versus Unstructured Work	To what extent is this job structured for the worker, rather than allowing the worker to determine tasks, priorities, and goals?
Sounds, Noise Levels Are Distracting or Uncomforta	How often does this job require working exposed to sounds and noise levels that are distracting or uncomfortable?
Frequency of Decision Making	How frequently is the worker required to make decisions that affect other people, the financial resources, and/or the image and reputation of the organization?
Deal With Unpleasant or Angry People	How frequently does the worker have to deal with unpleasant, angry, or discourteous individuals as part of the job requirements?
Wear Common Protective or Safety Equipment such as	How much does this job require wearing common protective or safety equipment such as safety shoes, glasses, gloves, hard hats or live jackets?
Spend Time Using Your Hands to Handle, Control, or	How much does this job require using your hands to handle, control, or feel objects, tools or controls?
Physical Proximity	To what extent does this job require the worker to perform job tasks in close physical proximity to other people?
Indoors, Not Environmentally Controlled	How often does this job require working indoors in non-controlled environmental conditions (e.g., warehouse without heat)?
Frequency of Conflict Situations	How often are there conflict situations the employee has to face in this job?
Degree of Automation	How automated is the job?
Level of Competition	To what extent does this job require the worker to compete or to be aware of competitive pressures?
Public Speaking	How often do you have to perform public speaking in this job?
Exposed to Contaminants	How often does this job require working exposed to contaminants (such as pollutants, gases, dust or odors)?
Responsibility for Outcomes and Results	How responsible is the worker for work outcomes and results of other workers?
Exposed to Hazardous Equipment	How often does this job require exposure to hazardous equipment?
Spend Time Standing	How much does this job require standing?
Responsible for Others' Health and Safety	How much responsibility is there for the health and safety of others in this job?
Exposed to Minor Burns, Cuts, Bites, or Stings	How often does this job require exposure to minor burns, cuts, bites, or stings?
Very Hot or Cold Temperatures	How often does this job require working in very hot (above 90 F degrees) or very cold (below 32 F degrees) temperatures?
In an Enclosed Vehicle or Equipment	How often does this job require working in a closed vehicle or equipment (e.g., car)?
Pace Determined by Speed of Equipment	How important is it to this job that the pace is determined by the speed of equipment or machinery? (This does not refer to keeping busy at all times on this job.)
Spend Time Walking and Running	How much does this job require walking and running?
Cramped Work Space, Awkward Positions	How often does this job require working in cramped work spaces that requires getting into awkward positions?
Extremely Bright or Inadequate Lighting	How often does this job require working in extremely bright or inadequate lighting conditions?
Spend Time Bending or Twisting the Body	How much does this job require bending or twisting your body?
Exposed to High Places	How often does this job require exposure to high places?
Outdoors, Exposed to Weather	How often does this job require working outdoors, exposed to all weather conditions?
Exposed to Hazardous Conditions	How often does this job require exposure to hazardous conditions?
Outdoors, Under Cover	How often does this job require working outdoors, under cover (e.g., structure with roof but no walls)?
Spend Time Kneeling, Crouching, Stooping, or Crawl	How much does this job require kneeling, crouching, stooping, or crawling?
Wear Specialized Protective or Safety Equipment su	How much does this job require wearing specialized protective or safety equipment such as breathing apparatus, safety harness, full protection suits, or radiation protection?
Deal With Physically Aggressive People	How frequently does this job require the worker to deal with physical aggression of violent individuals?
Spend Time Keeping or Regaining Balance	How much does this job require keeping or regaining your balance?
Spend Time Climbing Ladders, Scaffolds, or Poles	How much does this job require climbing ladders, scaffolds, or poles?
Exposed to Radiation	How often does this job require exposure to radiation?

In an Open Vehicle or Equipment	How often does this job require working in an open vehicle or equipment (e.g., tractor)?
Exposed to Whole Body Vibration	How often does this job require exposure to whole body vibration (e.g., operate a jackhammer)?
Exposed to Disease or Infections	How often does this job require exposure to disease/infections?

Job Zone Component	Job Zone Component Definitions
Title	Job Zone Three: Medium Preparation Needed
Overall Experience	Previous work-related skill, knowledge, or experience is required for these occupations. For example, an electrician must have completed three or four years of apprenticeship or several years of vocational training, and often must have passed a licensing exam, in order to perform the job.
Job Training	Employees in these occupations usually need one or two years of training involving both on-the-job experience and informal training with experienced workers.
Job Zone Examples	These occupations usually involve using communication and organizational skills to coordinate, supervise, manage, or train others to accomplish goals. Examples include dental assistants, electricians, fish and game wardens, legal secretaries, personnel recruiters, and recreation workers.
SVP Range	(6.0 to < 7.0)
Education	Most occupations in this zone require training in vocational schools, related on-the-job experience, or an associate's degree. Some may require a bachelor's degree.

Work_Styles	Work_Styles Definitions
Attention to Detail	Job requires being careful about detail and thorough in completing work tasks.
Cooperation	Job requires being pleasant with others on the job and displaying a good-natured, cooperative attitude.
Adaptability/Flexibility	Job requires being open to change (positive or negative) and to considerable variety in the workplace.
Analytical Thinking	Job requires analyzing information and using logic to address work-related issues and problems.
Innovation	Job requires creativity and alternative thinking to develop new ideas for and answers to work-related problems.
Dependability	Job requires being reliable, responsible, and dependable, and fulfilling obligations.
Initiative	Job requires a willingness to take on responsibilities and challenges.
Achievement/Effort	Job requires establishing and maintaining personally challenging achievement goals and exerting effort toward mastering tasks.
Independence	Job requires developing one's own ways of doing things, guiding oneself with little or no supervision, and depending on oneself to get things done.
Stress Tolerance	Job requires accepting criticism and dealing calmly and effectively with high stress situations.
Integrity	Job requires being honest and ethical.
Persistence	Job requires persistence in the face of obstacles.
Leadership	Job requires a willingness to lead, take charge, and offer opinions and direction.
Self Control	Job requires maintaining composure, keeping emotions in check, controlling anger, and avoiding aggressive behavior, even in very difficult situations.
Social Orientation	Job requires preferring to work with others rather than alone, and being personally connected with others on the job.
Concern for Others	Job requires being sensitive to others' needs and feelings and being understanding and helpful on the job.

17-3021.00 - Aerospace Engineering and Operations Technicians

Operate, install, calibrate, and maintain integrated computer/communications systems consoles, simulators, and other data acquisition, test, and measurement instruments and equipment to launch, track, position, and evaluate air and space vehicles. May record and interpret test data.

17-3021.00 - Aerospace Engineering and Operations Technicians

Tasks

1) Record and interpret test data on parts, assemblies, and mechanisms.

2) Identify required data, data acquisition plans and test parameters, setting up equipment to conform to these specifications.

3) Adjust, repair or replace faulty components of test setups and equipment.

4) Construct and maintain test facilities for aircraft parts and systems, according to specifications.

5) Fabricate and install parts and systems to be tested in test equipment, using hand tools, power tools, and test instruments.

6) Confer with engineering personnel regarding details and implications of test procedures and results.

7) Inspect, diagnose, maintain, and operate test setups and equipment to detect malfunctions.

8) Exchange cooling system components in various vehicles.

9) Test aircraft systems under simulated operational conditions, performing systems readiness tests and pre- and post-operational checkouts, to establish design or fabrication parameters.

10) Operate and calibrate computer systems and devices to comply with test requirements and to perform data acquisition and analysis.

17-3022.00 - Civil Engineering Technicians

Apply theory and principles of civil engineering in planning, designing, and overseeing construction and maintenance of structures and facilities under the direction of engineering staff or physical scientists.

Tasks

1) Calculate dimensions, square footage, profile and component specifications, and material quantities, using calculator or computer.

2) Prepare reports and document project activities and data.

3) Analyze proposed site factors and design maps, graphs, tracings, and diagrams to illustrate findings.

4) Draft detailed dimensional drawings and design layouts for projects and to ensure conformance to specifications.

5) Inspect project site and evaluate contractor work to detect design malfunctions and ensure conformance to design specifications and applicable codes.

6) Plan and conduct field surveys to locate new sites and analyze details of project sites.

7) Read and review project blueprints and structural specifications to determine dimensions of structure or system and material requirements.

8) Respond to public suggestions and complaints.

9) Report maintenance problems occurring at project site to supervisor and negotiate changes to resolve system conflicts.

10) Develop plans and estimate costs for installation of systems, utilization of facilities, or construction of structures.

11) Conduct materials test and analysis, using tools and equipment, and applying engineering knowledge.

12) Evaluate facility to determine suitability for occupancy and square footage availability.

Knowledge	Knowledge Definitions
Mathematics	Knowledge of arithmetic, algebra, geometry, calculus, statistics, and their applications.
Engineering and Technology	Knowledge of the practical application of engineering science and technology. This includes applying principles, techniques, procedures, and equipment to the design and production of various goods and services.
Design	Knowledge of design techniques, tools, and principles involved in production of precision technical plans, blueprints, drawings, and models.
Computers and Electronics	Knowledge of circuit boards, processors, chips, electronic equipment, and computer hardware and software, including applications and programming.
English Language	Knowledge of the structure and content of the English language including the meaning and spelling of words, rules of composition, and grammar.

Building and Construction	Knowledge of materials, methods, and the tools involved in the construction or repair of houses, buildings, or other structures such as highways and roads.
Transportation	Knowledge of principles and methods for moving people or goods by air, rail, sea, or road, including the relative costs and benefits.
Customer and Personal Service	Knowledge of principles and processes for providing customer and personal services. This includes customer needs assessment, meeting quality standards for services, and evaluation of customer satisfaction.
Administration and Management	Knowledge of business and management principles involved in strategic planning, resource allocation, human resources modeling, leadership technique, production methods, and coordination of people and resources.
Public Safety and Security	Knowledge of relevant equipment, policies, procedures, and strategies to promote effective local, state, or national security operations for the protection of people, data, property, and institutions.
Education and Training	Knowledge of principles and methods for curriculum and training design, teaching and instruction for individuals and groups, and the measurement of training effects.
Clerical	Knowledge of administrative and clerical procedures and systems such as word processing, managing files and records, stenography and transcription, designing forms, and other office procedures and terminology.
Production and Processing	Knowledge of raw materials, production processes, quality control, costs, and other techniques for maximizing the effective manufacture and distribution of goods.
Law and Government	Knowledge of laws, legal codes, court procedures, precedents, government regulations, executive orders, agency rules, and the democratic political process.
Geography	Knowledge of principles and methods for describing the features of land, sea, and air masses, including their physical characteristics, locations, interrelationships, and distribution of plant, animal, and human life.
Mechanical	Knowledge of machines and tools, including their designs, uses, repair, and maintenance.
Physics	Knowledge and prediction of physical principles, laws, their interrelationships, and applications to understanding fluid, material, and atmospheric dynamics, and mechanical, electrical, atomic and sub-atomic structures and processes.
Telecommunications	Knowledge of transmission, broadcasting, switching, control, and operation of telecommunications systems.
Personnel and Human Resources	Knowledge of principles and procedures for personnel recruitment, selection, training, compensation and benefits, labor relations and negotiation, and personnel information systems.
Communications and Media	Knowledge of media production, communication, and dissemination techniques and methods. This includes alternative ways to inform and entertain via written, oral, and visual media.
History and Archeology	Knowledge of historical events and their causes, indicators, and effects on civilizations and cultures.
Economics and Accounting	Knowledge of economic and accounting principles and practices, the financial markets, banking and the analysis and reporting of financial data.
Psychology	Knowledge of human behavior and performance; individual differences in ability, personality, and interests; learning and motivation; psychological research methods; and the assessment and treatment of behavioral and affective disorders.
Chemistry	Knowledge of the chemical composition, structure, and properties of substances and of the chemical processes and transformations that they undergo. This includes uses of chemicals and their interactions, danger signs, production techniques, and disposal methods.
Biology	Knowledge of plant and animal organisms, their tissues, cells, functions, interdependencies, and interactions with each other and the environment.
Philosophy and Theology	Knowledge of different philosophical systems and religions. This includes their basic principles, values, ethics, ways of thinking, customs, practices, and their impact on human culture.
Medicine and Dentistry	Knowledge of the information and techniques needed to diagnose and treat human injuries, diseases, and deformities. This includes symptoms, treatment alternatives, drug properties and interactions, and preventive health-care measures.

Sociology and Anthropology	Knowledge of group behavior and dynamics, societal trends and influences, human migrations, ethnicity, cultures and their history and origins.
Therapy and Counseling	Knowledge of principles, methods, and procedures for diagnosis, treatment, and rehabilitation of physical and mental dysfunctions, and for career counseling and guidance.
Foreign Language	Knowledge of the structure and content of a foreign (non-English) language including the meaning and spelling of words, rules of composition and grammar, and pronunciation.
Fine Arts	Knowledge of the theory and techniques required to compose, produce, and perform works of music, dance, visual arts, drama, and sculpture.
Sales and Marketing	Knowledge of principles and methods for showing, promoting, and selling products or services. This includes marketing strategy and tactics, product demonstration, sales techniques, and sales control systems.
Food Production	Knowledge of techniques and equipment for planting, growing, and harvesting food products (both plant and animal) for consumption, including storage/handling techniques.

Skills	Skills Definitions
Mathematics	Using mathematics to solve problems.
Active Learning	Understanding the implications of new information for both current and future problem-solving and decision-making.
Reading Comprehension	Understanding written sentences and paragraphs in work related documents.
Critical Thinking	Using logic and reasoning to identify the strengths and weaknesses of alternative solutions, conclusions or approaches to problems.
Time Management	Managing one's own time and the time of others.
Speaking	Talking to others to convey information effectively.
Active Listening	Giving full attention to what other people are saying, taking time to understand the points being made, asking questions as appropriate, and not interrupting at inappropriate times.
Complex Problem Solving	Identifying complex problems and reviewing related information to develop and evaluate options and implement solutions.
Coordination	Adjusting actions in relation to others' actions.
Judgment and Decision Making	Considering the relative costs and benefits of potential actions to choose the most appropriate one.
Instructing	Teaching others how to do something.
Writing	Communicating effectively in writing as appropriate for the needs of the audience.
Learning Strategies	Selecting and using training/instructional methods and procedures appropriate for the situation when learning or teaching new things.
Operations Analysis	Analyzing needs and product requirements to create a design.
Monitoring	Monitoring/Assessing performance of yourself, other individuals, or organizations to make improvements or take corrective action.
Equipment Selection	Determining the kind of tools and equipment needed to do a job.
Science	Using scientific rules and methods to solve problems.
Social Perceptiveness	Being aware of others' reactions and understanding why they react as they do.
Persuasion	Persuading others to change their minds or behavior.
Troubleshooting	Determining causes of operating errors and deciding what to do about it.
Service Orientation	Actively looking for ways to help people.
Negotiation	Bringing others together and trying to reconcile differences.
Management of Material Resources	Obtaining and seeing to the appropriate use of equipment, facilities, and materials needed to do certain work.
Management of Personnel Resources	Motivating, developing, and directing people as they work, identifying the best people for the job.
Technology Design	Generating or adapting equipment and technology to serve user needs.
Quality Control Analysis	Conducting tests and inspections of products, services, or processes to evaluate quality or performance.
Systems Analysis	Determining how a system should work and how changes in conditions, operations, and the environment will affect outcomes.
Programming	Writing computer programs for various purposes.
Systems Evaluation	Identifying measures or indicators of system performance and the actions needed to improve or correct performance, relative to the goals of the system.
Management of Financial Resources	Determining how money will be spent to get the work done, and accounting for these expenditures.

Operation Monitoring	Watching gauges, dials, or other indicators to make sure a machine is working properly.
Equipment Maintenance	Performing routine maintenance on equipment and determining when and what kind of maintenance is needed.
Repairing	Repairing machines or systems using the needed tools.
Operation and Control	Controlling operations of equipment or systems.
Installation	Installing equipment, machines, wiring, or programs to meet specifications.

Ability | Ability Definitions

Written Comprehension	The ability to read and understand information and ideas presented in writing.
Deductive Reasoning	The ability to apply general rules to specific problems to produce answers that make sense.
Oral Comprehension	The ability to listen to and understand information and ideas presented through spoken words and sentences.
Inductive Reasoning	The ability to combine pieces of information to form general rules or conclusions (includes finding a relationship among seemingly unrelated events).
Near Vision	The ability to see details at close range (within a few feet of the observer).
Problem Sensitivity	The ability to tell when something is wrong or is likely to go wrong. It does not involve solving the problem, only recognizing there is a problem.
Information Ordering	The ability to arrange things or actions in a certain order or pattern according to a specific rule or set of rules (e.g., patterns of numbers, letters, words, pictures, mathematical operations).
Mathematical Reasoning	The ability to choose the right mathematical methods or formulas to solve a problem.
Visualization	The ability to imagine how something will look after it is moved around or when its parts are moved or rearranged.
Oral Expression	The ability to communicate information and ideas in speaking so others will understand.
Written Expression	The ability to communicate information and ideas in writing so others will understand.
Originality	The ability to come up with unusual or clever ideas about a given topic or situation, or to develop creative ways to solve a problem.
Number Facility	The ability to add, subtract, multiply, or divide quickly and correctly.
Far Vision	The ability to see details at a distance.
Category Flexibility	The ability to generate or use different sets of rules for combining or grouping things in different ways.
Fluency of Ideas	The ability to come up with a number of ideas about a topic (the number of ideas is important, not their quality, correctness, or creativity).
Speech Clarity	The ability to speak clearly so others can understand you.
Speech Recognition	The ability to identify and understand the speech of another person.
Flexibility of Closure	The ability to identify or detect a known pattern (a figure, object, word, or sound) that is hidden in other distracting material.
Selective Attention	The ability to concentrate on a task over a period of time without being distracted.
Perceptual Speed	The ability to quickly and accurately compare similarities and differences among sets of letters, numbers, objects, pictures, or patterns. The things to be compared may be presented at the same time or one after the other. This ability also includes comparing a presented object with a remembered object.
Finger Dexterity	The ability to make precisely coordinated movements of the fingers of one or both hands to grasp, manipulate, or assemble very small objects.
Time Sharing	The ability to shift back and forth between two or more activities or sources of information (such as speech, sounds, touch, or other sources).
Speed of Closure	The ability to quickly make sense of, combine, and organize information into meaningful patterns.
Visual Color Discrimination	The ability to match or detect differences between colors, including shades of color and brightness.
Memorization	The ability to remember information such as words, numbers, pictures, and procedures.
Arm-Hand Steadiness	The ability to keep your hand and arm steady while moving your arm or while holding your arm and hand in one position.
Auditory Attention	The ability to focus on a single source of sound in the presence of other distracting sounds.

Depth Perception	The ability to judge which of several objects is closer or farther away from you, or to judge the distance between you and an object.
Trunk Strength	The ability to use your abdominal and lower back muscles to support part of the body repeatedly or continuously over time without 'giving out' or fatiguing.
Hearing Sensitivity	The ability to detect or tell the differences between sounds that vary in pitch and loudness.
Control Precision	The ability to quickly and repeatedly adjust the controls of a machine or a vehicle to exact positions.
Manual Dexterity	The ability to quickly move your hand, your hand together with your arm, or your two hands to grasp, manipulate, or assemble objects.
Multilimb Coordination	The ability to coordinate two or more limbs (for example, two arms, two legs, or one leg and one arm) while sitting, standing, or lying down. It does not involve performing the activities while the whole body is in motion.
Spatial Orientation	The ability to know your location in relation to the environment or to know where other objects are in relation to you.
Reaction Time	The ability to quickly respond (with the hand, finger, or foot) to a signal (sound, light, picture) when it appears.
Wrist-Finger Speed	The ability to make fast, simple, repeated movements of the fingers, hands, and wrists.
Speed of Limb Movement	The ability to quickly move the arms and legs.
Peripheral Vision	The ability to see objects or movement of objects to one's side when the eyes are looking ahead.
Glare Sensitivity	The ability to see objects in the presence of glare or bright lighting.
Response Orientation	The ability to choose quickly between two or more movements in response to two or more different signals (lights, sounds, pictures). It includes the speed with which the correct response is started with the hand, foot, or other body part.
Gross Body Coordination	The ability to coordinate the movement of your arms, legs, and torso together when the whole body is in motion.
Gross Body Equilibrium	The ability to keep or regain your body balance or stay upright when in an unstable position.
Stamina	The ability to exert yourself physically over long periods of time without getting winded or out of breath.
Static Strength	The ability to exert maximum muscle force to lift, push, pull, or carry objects.
Night Vision	The ability to see under low light conditions.
Extent Flexibility	The ability to bend, stretch, twist, or reach with your body, arms, and/or legs.
Explosive Strength	The ability to use short bursts of muscle force to propel oneself (as in jumping or sprinting), or to throw an object.
Rate Control	The ability to time your movements or the movement of a piece of equipment in anticipation of changes in the speed and/or direction of a moving object or scene.
Sound Localization	The ability to tell the direction from which a sound originated.
Dynamic Strength	The ability to exert muscle force repeatedly or continuously over time. This involves muscular endurance and resistance to muscle fatigue.
Dynamic Flexibility	The ability to quickly and repeatedly bend, stretch, twist, or reach out with your body, arms, and/or legs.

Work_Activity | Work_Activity Definitions

Getting Information	Observing, receiving, and otherwise obtaining information from all relevant sources.
Interacting With Computers	Using computers and computer systems (including hardware and software) to program, write software, set up functions, enter data, or process information.
Processing Information	Compiling, coding, categorizing, calculating, tabulating, auditing, or verifying information or data.
Analyzing Data or Information	Identifying the underlying principles, reasons, or facts of information by breaking down information or data into separate parts.
Updating and Using Relevant Knowledge	Keeping up-to-date technically and applying new knowledge to your job.
Documenting/Recording Information	Entering, transcribing, recording, storing, or maintaining information in written or electronic/magnetic form.
Communicating with Supervisors, Peers, or Subordin	Providing information to supervisors, co-workers, and subordinates by telephone, in written form, e-mail, or in person.
Evaluating Information to Determine Compliance wit	Using relevant information and individual judgment to determine whether events or processes comply with laws, regulations, or standards.

Thinking Creatively	Developing, designing, or creating new applications, ideas, relationships, systems, or products, including artistic contributions.
Identifying Objects, Actions, and Events	Identifying information by categorizing, estimating, recognizing differences or similarities, and detecting changes in circumstances or events.
Interpreting the Meaning of Information for Others	Translating or explaining what information means and how it can be used.
Making Decisions and Solving Problems	Analyzing information and evaluating results to choose the best solution and solve problems.
Organizing, Planning, and Prioritizing Work	Developing specific goals and plans to prioritize, organize, and accomplish your work.
Communicating with Persons Outside Organization	Communicating with people outside the organization, representing the organization to customers, the public, government, and other external sources. This information can be exchanged in person, in writing, or by telephone or e-mail.
Establishing and Maintaining Interpersonal Relatio	Developing constructive and cooperative working relationships with others, and maintaining them over time.
Estimating the Quantifiable Characteristics of Pro	Estimating sizes, distances, and quantities; or determining time, costs, resources, or materials needed to perform a work activity.
Drafting, Laying Out, and Specifying Technical Dev	Providing documentation, detailed instructions, drawings, or specifications to tell others about how devices, parts, equipment, or structures are to be fabricated, constructed, assembled, modified, maintained, or used.
Judging the Qualities of Things, Services, or Peop	Assessing the value, importance, or quality of things or people.
Performing for or Working Directly with the Public	Performing for people or dealing directly with the public. This includes serving customers in restaurants and stores, and receiving clients or guests.
Monitor Processes, Materials, or Surroundings	Monitoring and reviewing information from materials, events, or the environment, to detect or assess problems.
Training and Teaching Others	Identifying the educational needs of others, developing formal educational or training programs or classes, and teaching or instructing others.
Scheduling Work and Activities	Scheduling events, programs, and activities, as well as the work of others.
Coordinating the Work and Activities of Others	Getting members of a group to work together to accomplish tasks.
Developing Objectives and Strategies	Establishing long-range objectives and specifying the strategies and actions to achieve them.
Developing and Building Teams	Encouraging and building mutual trust, respect, and cooperation among team members.
Provide Consultation and Advice to Others	Providing guidance and expert advice to management or other groups on technical, systems-, or process-related topics.
Resolving Conflicts and Negotiating with Others	Handling complaints, settling disputes, and resolving grievances and conflicts, or otherwise negotiating with others.
Inspecting Equipment, Structures, or Material	Inspecting equipment, structures, or materials to identify the cause of errors or other problems or defects.
Assisting and Caring for Others	Providing personal assistance, medical attention, emotional support, or other personal care to others such as coworkers, customers, or patients.
Guiding, Directing, and Motivating Subordinates	Providing guidance and direction to subordinates, including setting performance standards and monitoring performance.
Monitoring and Controlling Resources	Monitoring and controlling resources and overseeing the spending of money.
Controlling Machines and Processes	Using either control mechanisms or direct physical activity to operate machines or processes (not including computers or vehicles).
Performing Administrative Activities	Performing day-to-day administrative tasks such as maintaining information files and processing paperwork.
Operating Vehicles, Mechanized Devices, or Equipme	Running, maneuvering, navigating, or driving vehicles or mechanized equipment, such as forklifts, passenger vehicles, aircraft, or water craft.
Coaching and Developing Others	Identifying the developmental needs of others and coaching, mentoring, or otherwise helping others to improve their knowledge or skills.
Selling or Influencing Others	Convincing others to buy merchandise/goods or to otherwise change their minds or actions.
Performing General Physical Activities	Performing physical activities that require considerable use of your arms and legs and moving your whole body, such as climbing, lifting, balancing, walking, stooping, and handling of materials.
Handling and Moving Objects	Using hands and arms in handling, installing, positioning, and moving materials, and manipulating things.

Repairing and Maintaining Electronic Equipment	Servicing, repairing, calibrating, regulating, fine-tuning, or testing machines, devices, and equipment that operate primarily on the basis of electrical or electronic (not mechanical) principles.
Staffing Organizational Units	Recruiting, interviewing, selecting, hiring, and promoting employees in an organization.
Repairing and Maintaining Mechanical Equipment	Servicing, repairing, adjusting, and testing machines, devices, moving parts, and equipment that operate primarily on the basis of mechanical (not electronic) principles.

Work_Context	Work_Context Definitions
Face-to-Face Discussions	How often do you have to have face-to-face discussions with individuals or teams in this job?
Telephone	How often do you have telephone conversations in this job?
Contact With Others	How much does this job require the worker to be in contact with others (face-to-face, by telephone, or otherwise) in order to perform it?
Freedom to Make Decisions	How much decision making freedom, without supervision, does the job offer?
Importance of Being Exact or Accurate	How important is being very exact or highly accurate in performing this job?
Impact of Decisions on Co-workers or Company Resul	How do the decisions an employee makes impact the results of co-workers, clients or the company?
Work With Work Group or Team	How important is it to work with others in a group or team in this job?
Indoors, Environmentally Controlled	How often does this job require working indoors in environmentally controlled conditions?
Structured versus Unstructured Work	To what extent is this job structured for the worker, rather than allowing the worker to determine tasks, priorities, and goals?
Letters and Memos	How often does the job require written letters and memos?
Time Pressure	How often does this job require the worker to meet strict deadlines?
Electronic Mail	How often do you use electronic mail in this job?
Spend Time Sitting	How much does this job require sitting?
Physical Proximity	To what extent does this job require the worker to perform job tasks in close physical proximity to other people?
Frequency of Decision Making	How frequently is the worker required to make decisions that affect other people, the financial resources, and/or the image and reputation of the organization?
Consequence of Error	How serious would the result usually be if the worker made a mistake that was not readily correctable?
Outdoors, Exposed to Weather	How often does this job require working outdoors, exposed to all weather conditions?
Coordinate or Lead Others	How important is it to coordinate or lead others in accomplishing work activities in this job?
In an Enclosed Vehicle or Equipment	How often does this job require working in a closed vehicle or equipment (e.g., car)?
Importance of Repeating Same Tasks	How important is repeating the same physical activities (e.g., key entry) or mental activities (e.g., checking entries in a ledger) over and over, without stopping, to performing this job?
Responsibility for Outcomes and Results	How responsible is the worker for work outcomes and results of other workers?
Wear Common Protective or Safety Equipment such as	How much does this job require wearing common protective or safety equipment such as safety shoes, glasses, gloves, hard hats or life jackets?
Sounds, Noise Levels Are Distracting or Uncomforta	How often does this job require working exposed to sounds and noise levels that are distracting or uncomfortable?
Exposed to Hazardous Equipment	How often does this job require exposure to hazardous equipment?
Deal With External Customers	How important is it to work with external customers or the public in this job?
Spend Time Standing	How much does this job require standing?
Responsible for Others' Health and Safety	How much responsibility is there for the health and safety of others in this job?
Frequency of Conflict Situations	How often are there conflict situations the employee has to face in this job?
Deal With Unpleasant or Angry People	How frequently does the worker have to deal with unpleasant, angry, or discourteous individuals as part of the job requirements?
Degree of Automation	How automated is the job?
Spend Time Using Your Hands to Handle, Control, or	How much does this job require using your hands to handle, control, or feel objects, tools or controls?
Spend Time Making Repetitive Motions	How much does this job require making repetitive motions?

Level of Competition	To what extent does this job require the worker to compete or to be aware of competitive pressures?
Very Hot or Cold Temperatures	How often does this job require working in very hot (above 90 F degrees) or very cold (below 32 F degrees) temperatures?
Exposed to Contaminants	How often does this job require working exposed to contaminants (such as pollutants, gases, dust or odors)?
Extremely Bright or Inadequate Lighting	How often does this job require working in extremely bright or inadequate lighting conditions?
Spend Time Walking and Running	How much does this job require walking and running?
Indoors, Not Environmentally Controlled	How often does this job require working indoors in non-controlled environmental conditions (e.g., warehouse without heat)?
Public Speaking	How often do you have to perform public speaking in this job?
Spend Time Bending or Twisting the Body	How much does this job require bending or twisting your body?
Exposed to High Places	How often does this job require exposure to high places?
Outdoors, Under Cover	How often does this job require working outdoors, under cover (e.g., structure with roof but no walls)?
Pace Determined by Speed of Equipment	How important is it to this job that the pace is determined by the speed of equipment or machinery? (This does not refer to keeping busy at all times on this job.)
Exposed to Minor Burns, Cuts, Bites, or Stings	How often does this job require exposure to minor burns, cuts, bites, or stings?
Cramped Work Space, Awkward Positions	How often does this job require working in cramped work spaces that requires getting into awkward positions?
Exposed to Hazardous Conditions	How often does this job require exposure to hazardous conditions?
Spend Time Kneeling, Crouching, Stooping, or Crawl	How much does this job require kneeling, crouching, stooping, or crawling?
Wear Specialized Protective or Safety Equipment su	How much does this job require wearing specialized protective or safety equipment such as breathing apparatus, safety harness, full protection suits, or radiation protection?
Exposed to Whole Body Vibration	How often does this job require exposure to whole body vibration (e.g., operate a jackhammer)?
In an Open Vehicle or Equipment	How often does this job require working in an open vehicle or equipment (e.g., tractor)?
Spend Time Climbing Ladders, Scaffolds, or Poles	How much does this job require climbing ladders, scaffolds, or poles?
Exposed to Radiation	How often does this job require exposure to radiation?
Spend Time Keeping or Regaining Balance	How much does this job require keeping or regaining your balance?
Exposed to Disease or Infections	How often does this job require exposure to disease/infections?
Deal With Physically Aggressive People	How frequently does this job require the worker to deal with physical aggression of violent individuals?

Job Zone Component	Job Zone Component Definitions
Title	Job Zone Three: Medium Preparation Needed
Overall Experience	Previous work-related skill, knowledge, or experience is required for these occupations. For example, an electrician must have completed three or four years of apprenticeship or several years of vocational training, and often must have passed a licensing exam, in order to perform the job.
Job Training	Employees in these occupations usually need one or two years of training involving both on-the-job experience and informal training with experienced workers.
Job Zone Examples	These occupations usually involve using communication and organizational skills to coordinate, supervise, manage, or train others to accomplish goals. Examples include dental assistants, electricians, fish and game wardens, legal secretaries, personnel recruiters, and recreation workers.
SVP Range	(6.0 to < 7.0)
Education	Most occupations in this zone require training in vocational schools, related on-the-job experience, or an associate's degree. Some may require a bachelor's degree.

Work_Styles	Work_Styles Definitions
Attention to Detail	Job requires being careful about detail and thorough in completing work tasks.
Independence	Job requires developing one's own ways of doing things, guiding oneself with little or no supervision, and depending on oneself to get things done.

Integrity	Job requires being honest and ethical.
Adaptability/Flexibility	Job requires being open to change (positive or negative) and to considerable variety in the workplace.
Dependability	Job requires being reliable, responsible, and dependable, and fulfilling obligations.
Cooperation	Job requires being pleasant with others on the job and displaying a good-natured, cooperative attitude.
Analytical Thinking	Job requires analyzing information and using logic to address work-related issues and problems.
Initiative	Job requires a willingness to take on responsibilities and challenges.
Innovation	Job requires creativity and alternative thinking to develop new ideas for and answers to work-related problems.
Stress Tolerance	Job requires accepting criticism and dealing calmly and effectively with high stress situations.
Self Control	Job requires maintaining composure, keeping emotions in check, controlling anger, and avoiding aggressive behavior, even in very difficult situations.
Concern for Others	Job requires being sensitive to others' needs and feelings and being understanding and helpful on the job.
Leadership	Job requires a willingness to lead, take charge, and offer opinions and direction.
Persistence	Job requires persistence in the face of obstacles.
Social Orientation	Job requires preferring to work with others rather than alone, and being personally connected with others on the job.
Achievement/Effort	Job requires establishing and maintaining personally challenging achievement goals and exerting effort toward mastering tasks.

17-3023.01 - Electronics Engineering Technicians

Lay out, build, test, troubleshoot, repair, and modify developmental and production electronic components, parts, equipment, and systems, such as computer equipment, missile control instrumentation, electron tubes, test equipment, and machine tool numerical controls, applying principles and theories of electronics, electrical circuitry, engineering mathematics, electronic and electrical testing, and physics. Usually work under direction of engineering staff.

Tasks

1) Assemble, test, and maintain circuitry or electronic components according to engineering instructions, technical manuals, and knowledge of electronics, using hand and power tools.

2) Adjust and replace defective or improperly functioning circuitry and electronics components, using hand tools and soldering iron.

3) Read blueprints, wiring diagrams, schematic drawings, and engineering instructions for assembling electronics units, applying knowledge of electronic theory and components.

4) Identify and resolve equipment malfunctions, working with manufacturers and field representatives as necessary to procure replacement parts.

5) Maintain system logs and manuals to document testing and operation of equipment.

6) Perform preventative maintenance and calibration of equipment and systems.

7) Maintain working knowledge of state-of-the-art tools, software, etc., through reading and/or attending conferences, workshops or other training.

8) Procure parts and maintain inventory and related documentation.

9) Develop and upgrade preventative maintenance procedures for components, equipment, parts and systems.

10) Provide user applications and engineering support and recommendations for new and existing equipment with regard to installation, upgrades and enhancement.

11) Build prototypes from rough sketches or plans.

12) Write reports and record data on testing techniques, laboratory equipment, and specifications to assist engineers.

13) Research equipment and component needs, sources, competitive prices, delivery times and ongoing operational costs.

14) Provide customer support and education, working with users to identify needs, determine sources of problems and to provide information on product use.

15) Fabricate parts, such as coils, terminal boards, and chassis, using bench lathes, drills, or other machine tools.

16) Design basic circuitry and draft sketches for clarification of details and design

documentation under engineers' direction, using drafting instruments and computer aided design equipment.

17) Write computer or microprocessor software programs.

18) Survey satellite receival sites for proper signal level and provide technical assistance in dish location and installation, transporting dishes as necessary.

Knowledge	Knowledge Definitions
Computers and Electronics	Knowledge of circuit boards, processors, chips, electronic equipment, and computer hardware and software, including applications and programming.
English Language	Knowledge of the structure and content of the English language including the meaning and spelling of words, rules of composition, and grammar.
Engineering and Technology	Knowledge of the practical application of engineering science and technology. This includes applying principles, techniques, procedures, and equipment to the design and production of various goods and services.
Mechanical	Knowledge of machines and tools, including their designs, uses, repair, and maintenance.
Mathematics	Knowledge of arithmetic, algebra, geometry, calculus, statistics, and their applications.
Production and Processing	Knowledge of raw materials, production processes, quality control, costs, and other techniques for maximizing the effective manufacture and distribution of goods.
Design	Knowledge of design techniques, tools, and principles involved in production of precision technical plans, blueprints, drawings, and models.
Education and Training	Knowledge of principles and methods for curriculum and training design, teaching and instruction for individuals and groups, and the measurement of training effects.
Public Safety and Security	Knowledge of relevant equipment, policies, procedures, and strategies to promote effective local, state, or national security operations for the protection of people, data, property, and institutions.
Customer and Personal Service	Knowledge of principles and processes for providing customer and personal services. This includes customer needs assessment, meeting quality standards for services, and evaluation of customer satisfaction.
Clerical	Knowledge of administrative and clerical procedures and systems such as word processing, managing files and records, stenography and transcription, designing forms, and other office procedures and terminology.
Telecommunications	Knowledge of transmission, broadcasting, switching, control, and operation of telecommunications systems.
Physics	Knowledge and prediction of physical principles, laws, their interrelationships, and applications to understanding fluid, material, and atmospheric dynamics, and mechanical, electrical, atomic and sub- atomic structures and processes.
Administration and Management	Knowledge of business and management principles involved in strategic planning, resource allocation, human resources modeling, leadership technique, production methods, and coordination of people and resources.
Chemistry	Knowledge of the chemical composition, structure, and properties of substances and of the chemical processes and transformations that they undergo. This includes uses of chemicals and their interactions, danger signs, production techniques, and disposal methods.
Personnel and Human Resources	Knowledge of principles and procedures for personnel recruitment, selection, training, compensation and benefits, labor relations and negotiation, and personnel information systems.
Psychology	Knowledge of human behavior and performance; individual differences in ability, personality, and interests; learning and motivation; psychological research methods; and the assessment and treatment of behavioral and affective disorders.
Communications and Media	Knowledge of media production, communication, and dissemination techniques and methods. This includes alternative ways to inform and entertain via written, oral, and visual media.
Building and Construction	Knowledge of materials, methods, and the tools involved in the construction or repair of houses, buildings, or other structures such as highways and roads.
Transportation	Knowledge of principles and methods for moving people or goods by air, rail, sea, or road, including the relative costs and benefits.
Law and Government	Knowledge of laws, legal codes, court procedures, precedents, government regulations, executive orders, agency rules, and the democratic political process.
Sales and Marketing	Knowledge of principles and methods for showing, promoting, and selling products or services. This includes marketing strategy and tactics, product demonstration, sales techniques, and sales control systems.
Economics and Accounting	Knowledge of economic and accounting principles and practices, the financial markets, banking and the analysis and reporting of financial data.
Medicine and Dentistry	Knowledge of the information and techniques needed to diagnose and treat human injuries, diseases, and deformities. This includes symptoms, treatment alternatives, drug properties and interactions, and preventive health-care measures.
Therapy and Counseling	Knowledge of principles, methods, and procedures for diagnosis, treatment, and rehabilitation of physical and mental dysfunctions, and for career counseling and guidance.
Sociology and Anthropology	Knowledge of group behavior and dynamics, societal trends and influences, human migrations, ethnicity, cultures and their history and origins.
Geography	Knowledge of principles and methods for describing the features of land, sea, and air masses, including their physical characteristics, locations, interrelationships, and distribution of plant, animal, and human life.
Biology	Knowledge of plant and animal organisms, their tissues, cells, functions, interdependencies, and interactions with each other and the environment.
Foreign Language	Knowledge of the structure and content of a foreign (non-English) language including the meaning and spelling of words, rules of composition and grammar, and pronunciation.
Philosophy and Theology	Knowledge of different philosophical systems and religions. This includes their basic principles, values, ethics, ways of thinking, customs, practices, and their impact on human culture.
History and Archeology	Knowledge of historical events and their causes, indicators, and effects on civilizations and cultures.
Fine Arts	Knowledge of the theory and techniques required to compose, produce, and perform works of music, dance, visual arts, drama, and sculpture.
Food Production	Knowledge of techniques and equipment for planting, growing, and harvesting food products (both plant and animal) for consumption, including storage/handling techniques.

Skills	Skills Definitions
Troubleshooting	Determining causes of operating errors and deciding what to do about it.
Repairing	Repairing machines or systems using the needed tools.
Equipment Maintenance	Performing routine maintenance on equipment and determining when and what kind of maintenance is needed.
Equipment Selection	Determining the kind of tools and equipment needed to do a job.
Time Management	Managing one's own time and the time of others.
Reading Comprehension	Understanding written sentences and paragraphs in work related documents.
Judgment and Decision Making	Considering the relative costs and benefits of potential actions to choose the most appropriate one.
Operation Monitoring	Watching gauges, dials, or other indicators to make sure a machine is working properly.
Complex Problem Solving	Identifying complex problems and reviewing related information to develop and evaluate options and implement solutions.
Installation	Installing equipment, machines, wiring, or programs to meet specifications.
Active Learning	Understanding the implications of new information for both current and future problem-solving and decision-making.
Service Orientation	Actively looking for ways to help people.
Instructing	Teaching others how to do something.
Active Listening	Giving full attention to what other people are saying, taking time to understand the points being made, asking questions as appropriate, and not interrupting at inappropriate times.
Speaking	Talking to others to convey information effectively.
Critical Thinking	Using logic and reasoning to identify the strengths and weaknesses of alternative solutions, conclusions or approaches to problems.
Quality Control Analysis	Conducting tests and inspections of products, services, or processes to evaluate quality or performance.
Mathematics	Using mathematics to solve problems.

Coordination	Adjusting actions in relation to others' actions.
Operation and Control	Controlling operations of equipment or systems.
Systems Analysis	Determining how a system should work and how changes in conditions, operations, and the environment will affect outcomes.
Learning Strategies	Selecting and using training/instructional methods and procedures appropriate for the situation when learning or teaching new things.
Systems Evaluation	Identifying measures or indicators of system performance and the actions needed to improve or correct performance, relative to the goals of the system.
Science	Using scientific rules and methods to solve problems.
Technology Design	Generating or adapting equipment and technology to serve user needs.
Writing	Communicating effectively in writing as appropriate for the needs of the audience.
Management of Personnel Resources	Motivating, developing, and directing people as they work, identifying the best people for the job.
Operations Analysis	Analyzing needs and product requirements to create a design.
Management of Material Resources	Obtaining and seeing to the appropriate use of equipment, facilities, and materials needed to do certain work.
Monitoring	Monitoring/Assessing performance of yourself, other individuals, or organizations to make improvements or take corrective action.
Social Perceptiveness	Being aware of others' reactions and understanding why they react as they do.
Management of Financial Resources	Determining how money will be spent to get the work done, and accounting for these expenditures.
Persuasion	Persuading others to change their minds or behavior.
Programming	Writing computer programs for various purposes.
Negotiation	Bringing others together and trying to reconcile differences.

Ability	Ability Definitions
Deductive Reasoning	The ability to apply general rules to specific problems to produce answers that make sense.
Near Vision	The ability to see details at close range (within a few feet of the observer).
Written Comprehension	The ability to read and understand information and ideas presented in writing.
Problem Sensitivity	The ability to tell when something is wrong or is likely to go wrong. It does not involve solving the problem, only recognizing there is a problem.
Information Ordering	The ability to arrange things or actions in a certain order or pattern according to a specific rule or set of rules (e.g., patterns of numbers, letters, words, pictures, mathematical operations).
Oral Comprehension	The ability to listen to and understand information and ideas presented through spoken words and sentences.
Oral Expression	The ability to communicate information and ideas in speaking so others will understand.
Speech Clarity	The ability to speak clearly so others can understand you.
Inductive Reasoning	The ability to combine pieces of information to form general rules or conclusions (includes finding a relationship among seemingly unrelated events).
Visualization	The ability to imagine how something will look after it is moved around or when its parts are moved or rearranged.
Arm-Hand Steadiness	The ability to keep your hand and arm steady while moving your arm or while holding your arm and hand in one position.
Finger Dexterity	The ability to make precisely coordinated movements of the fingers of one or both hands to grasp, manipulate, or assemble very small objects.
Manual Dexterity	The ability to quickly move your hand, your hand together with your arm, or your two hands to grasp, manipulate, or assemble objects.
Speech Recognition	The ability to identify and understand the speech of another person.
Written Expression	The ability to communicate information and ideas in writing so others will understand.
Flexibility of Closure	The ability to identify or detect a known pattern (a figure, object, word, or sound) that is hidden in other distracting material.
Category Flexibility	The ability to generate or use different sets of rules for combining or grouping things in different ways.
Fluency of Ideas	The ability to come up with a number of ideas about a topic (the number of ideas is important, not their quality, correctness, or creativity).
Visual Color Discrimination	The ability to match or detect differences between colors, including shades of color and brightness.

Control Precision	The ability to quickly and repeatedly adjust the controls of a machine or a vehicle to exact positions.
Selective Attention	The ability to concentrate on a task over a period of time without being distracted.
Mathematical Reasoning	The ability to choose the right mathematical methods or formulas to solve a problem.
Reaction Time	The ability to quickly respond (with the hand, finger, or foot) to a signal (sound, light, picture) when it appears.
Perceptual Speed	The ability to quickly and accurately compare similarities and differences among sets of letters, numbers, objects, pictures, or patterns. The things to be compared may be presented at the same time or one after the other. This ability also includes comparing a presented object with a remembered object.
Originality	The ability to come up with unusual or clever ideas about a given topic or situation, or to develop creative ways to solve a problem.
Multilimb Coordination	The ability to coordinate two or more limbs (for example, two arms, two legs, or one leg and one arm) while sitting, standing, or lying down. It does not involve performing the activities while the whole body is in motion.
Memorization	The ability to remember information such as words, numbers, pictures, and procedures.
Depth Perception	The ability to judge which of several objects is closer or farther away from you, or to judge the distance between you and an object.
Far Vision	The ability to see details at a distance.
Trunk Strength	The ability to use your abdominal and lower back muscles to support part of the body repeatedly or continuously over time without 'giving out' or fatiguing.
Extent Flexibility	The ability to bend, stretch, twist, or reach with your body, arms, and/or legs.
Time Sharing	The ability to shift back and forth between two or more activities or sources of information (such as speech, sounds, touch, or other sources).
Number Facility	The ability to add, subtract, multiply, or divide quickly and correctly.
Speed of Closure	The ability to quickly make sense of, combine, and organize information into meaningful patterns.
Wrist-Finger Speed	The ability to make fast, simple, repeated movements of the fingers, hands, and wrists.
Static Strength	The ability to exert maximum muscle force to lift, push, pull, or carry objects.
Response Orientation	The ability to choose quickly between two or more movements in response to two or more different signals (lights, sounds, pictures). It includes the speed with which the correct response is started with the hand, foot, or other body part.
Auditory Attention	The ability to focus on a single source of sound in the presence of other distracting sounds.
Hearing Sensitivity	The ability to detect or tell the differences between sounds that vary in pitch and loudness.
Spatial Orientation	The ability to know your location in relation to the environment or to know where other objects are in relation to you.
Speed of Limb Movement	The ability to quickly move the arms and legs.
Rate Control	The ability to time your movements or the movement of a piece of equipment in anticipation of changes in the speed and/or direction of a moving object or scene.
Stamina	The ability to exert yourself physically over long periods of time without getting winded or out of breath.
Explosive Strength	The ability to use short bursts of muscle force to propel oneself (as in jumping or sprinting), or to throw an object.
Dynamic Flexibility	The ability to quickly and repeatedly bend, stretch, twist, or reach out with your body, arms, and/or legs.
Night Vision	The ability to see under low light conditions.
Dynamic Strength	The ability to exert muscle force repeatedly or continuously over time. This involves muscular endurance and resistance to muscle fatigue.
Glare Sensitivity	The ability to see objects in the presence of glare or bright lighting.
Sound Localization	The ability to tell the direction from which a sound originated.
Gross Body Equilibrium	The ability to keep or regain your body balance or stay upright when in an unstable position.
Gross Body Coordination	The ability to coordinate the movement of your arms, legs, and torso together when the whole body is in motion.
Peripheral Vision	The ability to see objects or movement of objects to one's side when the eyes are looking ahead.

Work_Activity	Work_Activity Definitions
Interacting With Computers	Using computers and computer systems (including hardware and software) to program, write software, set up functions, enter data, or process information.
Repairing and Maintaining Electronic Equipment	Servicing, repairing, calibrating, regulating, fine-tuning, or testing machines, devices, and equipment that operate primarily on the basis of electrical or electronic (not mechanical) principles.
Analyzing Data or Information	Identifying the underlying principles, reasons, or facts of information by breaking down information or data into separate parts.
Getting Information	Observing, receiving, and otherwise obtaining information from all relevant sources.
Making Decisions and Solving Problems	Analyzing information and evaluating results to choose the best solution and solve problems.
Identifying Objects, Actions, and Events	Identifying information by categorizing, estimating, recognizing differences or similarities, and detecting changes in circumstances or events.
Documenting/Recording Information	Entering, transcribing, recording, storing, or maintaining information in written or electronic/magnetic form.
Inspecting Equipment, Structures, or Material	Inspecting equipment, structures, or materials to identify the cause of errors or other problems or defects.
Communicating with Supervisors, Peers, or Subordin	Providing information to supervisors, co-workers, and subordinates by telephone, in written form, e-mail, or in person.
Organizing, Planning, and Prioritizing Work	Developing specific goals and plans to prioritize, organize, and accomplish your work.
Repairing and Maintaining Mechanical Equipment	Servicing, repairing, adjusting, and testing machines, devices, moving parts, and equipment that operate primarily on the basis of mechanical (not electronic) principles.
Updating and Using Relevant Knowledge	Keeping up-to-date technically and applying new knowledge to your job.
Monitor Processes, Materials, or Surroundings	Monitoring and reviewing information from materials, events, or the environment, to detect or assess problems.
Processing Information	Compiling, coding, categorizing, calculating, tabulating, auditing, or verifying information or data.
Evaluating Information to Determine Compliance wit	Using relevant information and individual judgment to determine whether events or processes comply with laws, regulations, or standards.
Controlling Machines and Processes	Using either control mechanisms or direct physical activity to operate machines or processes (not including computers or vehicles).
Interpreting the Meaning of Information for Others	Translating or explaining what information means and how it can be used.
Judging the Qualities of Things, Services, or Peop	Assessing the value, importance, or quality of things or people.
Thinking Creatively	Developing, designing, or creating new applications, ideas, relationships, systems, or products, including artistic contributions.
Establishing and Maintaining Interpersonal Relatio	Developing constructive and cooperative working relationships with others, and maintaining them over time.
Communicating with Persons Outside Organization	Communicating with people outside the organization, representing the organization to customers, the public, government, and other external sources. This information can be exchanged in person, in writing, or by telephone or e-mail.
Scheduling Work and Activities	Scheduling events, programs, and activities, as well as the work of others.
Handling and Moving Objects	Using hands and arms in handling, installing, positioning, and moving materials, and manipulating things.
Training and Teaching Others	Identifying the educational needs of others, developing formal educational or training programs or classes, and teaching or instructing others.
Provide Consultation and Advice to Others	Providing guidance and expert advice to management or other groups on technical, systems-, or process-related topics.
Estimating the Quantifiable Characteristics of Pro	Estimating sizes, distances, and quantities; or determining time, costs, resources, or materials needed to perform a work activity.
Developing Objectives and Strategies	Establishing long-range objectives and specifying the strategies and actions to achieve them.
Performing General Physical Activities	Performing physical activities that require considerable use of your arms and legs and moving your whole body, such as climbing, lifting, balancing, walking, stooping, and handling of materials.
Drafting, Laying Out, and Specifying Technical Dev	Providing documentation, detailed instructions, drawings, or specifications to tell others about how devices, parts, equipment, or structures are to be fabricated, constructed, assembled, modified, maintained, or used.
Performing Administrative Activities	Performing day-to-day administrative tasks such as maintaining information files and processing paperwork.
Selling or Influencing Others	Convincing others to buy merchandise/goods or to otherwise change their minds or actions.
Coaching and Developing Others	Identifying the developmental needs of others and coaching, mentoring, or otherwise helping others to improve their knowledge or skills.
Coordinating the Work and Activities of Others	Getting members of a group to work together to accomplish tasks.
Operating Vehicles, Mechanized Devices, or Equipme	Running, maneuvering, navigating, or driving vehicles or mechanized equipment, such as forklifts, passenger vehicles, aircraft, or water craft.
Developing and Building Teams	Encouraging and building mutual trust, respect, and cooperation among team members.
Resolving Conflicts and Negotiating with Others	Handling complaints, settling disputes, and resolving grievances and conflicts, or otherwise negotiating with others.
Guiding, Directing, and Motivating Subordinates	Providing guidance and direction to subordinates, including setting performance standards and monitoring performance.
Assisting and Caring for Others	Providing personal assistance, medical attention, emotional support, or other personal care to others such as coworkers, customers, or patients.
Monitoring and Controlling Resources	Monitoring and controlling resources and overseeing the spending of money.
Staffing Organizational Units	Recruiting, interviewing, selecting, hiring, and promoting employees in an organization.
Performing for or Working Directly with the Public	Performing for people or dealing directly with the public. This includes serving customers in restaurants and stores, and receiving clients or guests.

Work_Context	Work_Context Definitions
Face-to-Face Discussions	How often do you have to have face-to-face discussions with individuals or teams in this job?
Indoors, Environmentally Controlled	How often does this job require working indoors in environmentally controlled conditions?
Spend Time Using Your Hands to Handle, Control, or	How much does this job require using your hands to handle, control, or feel objects, tools or controls?
Freedom to Make Decisions	How much decision making freedom, without supervision, does the job offer?
Importance of Being Exact or Accurate	How important is being very exact or highly accurate in performing this job?
Time Pressure	How often does this job require the worker to meet strict deadlines?
Structured versus Unstructured Work	To what extent is this job structured for the worker, rather than allowing the worker to determine tasks, priorities, and goals?
Contact With Others	How much does this job require the worker to be in contact with others (face-to-face, by telephone, or otherwise) in order to perform it?
Exposed to Hazardous Equipment	How often does this job require exposure to hazardous equipment?
Wear Common Protective or Safety Equipment such as	How much does this job require wearing common protective or safety equipment such as safety shoes, glasses, gloves, hard hats or live jackets?
Work With Work Group or Team	How important is it to work with others in a group or team in this job?
Exposed to Contaminants	How often does this job require working exposed to contaminants (such as pollutants, gases, dust or odors)?
Frequency of Decision Making	How frequently is the worker required to make decisions that affect other people, the financial resources, and/or the image and reputation of the organization?
Telephone	How often do you have telephone conversations in this job?
Importance of Repeating Same Tasks	How important is repeating the same physical activities (e.g., key entry) or mental activities (e.g., checking entries in a ledger) over and over, without stopping, to performing this job?
Physical Proximity	To what extent does this job require the worker to perform job tasks in close physical proximity to other people?
Indoors, Not Environmentally Controlled	How often does this job require working indoors in non-controlled environmental conditions (e.g., warehouse without heat)?
Exposed to Hazardous Conditions	How often does this job require exposure to hazardous conditions?
Spend Time Sitting	How much does this job require sitting?

Impact of Decisions on Co-workers or Company Resul	How do the decisions an employee makes impact the results of co-workers, clients or the company?
Electronic Mail	How often do you use electronic mail in this job?
Frequency of Conflict Situations	How often are there conflict situations the employee has to face in this job?
Exposed to Minor Burns, Cuts, Bites, or Stings	How often does this job require exposure to minor burns, cuts, bites, or stings?
Cramped Work Space, Awkward Positions	How often does this job require working in cramped work spaces that requires getting into awkward positions?
Spend Time Standing	How much does this job require standing?
Coordinate or Lead Others	How important is it to coordinate or lead others in accomplishing work activities in this job?
Consequence of Error	How serious would the result usually be if the worker made a mistake that was not readily correctable?
Level of Competition	To what extent does this job require the worker to compete or to be aware of competitive pressures?
Wear Specialized Protective or Safety Equipment su	How much does this job require wearing specialized protective or safety equipment such as breathing apparatus, safety harness, full protection suits, or radiation protection?
Spend Time Making Repetitive Motions	How much does this job require making repetitive motions?
In an Open Vehicle or Equipment	How often does this job require working in an open vehicle or equipment (e.g., tractor)?
Responsible for Others' Health and Safety	How much responsibility is there for the health and safety of others in this job?
Sounds, Noise Levels Are Distracting or Uncomforta	How often does this job require working exposed to sounds and noise levels that are distracting or uncomfortable?
Letters and Memos	How often does the job require written letters and memos?
Spend Time Kneeling, Crouching, Stooping, or Crawl	How much does this job require kneeling, crouching, stooping or crawling?
Spend Time Bending or Twisting the Body	How much does this job require bending or twisting your body?
Deal With External Customers	How important is it to work with external customers or the public in this job?
Spend Time Walking and Running	How much does this job require walking and running?
Very Hot or Cold Temperatures	How often does this job require working in very hot (above 90 F degrees) or very cold (below 32 F degrees) temperatures?
Deal With Unpleasant or Angry People	How frequently does the worker have to deal with unpleasant, angry, or discourteous individuals as part of the job requirements?
Responsibility for Outcomes and Results	How responsible is the worker for work outcomes and results of other workers?
Degree of Automation	How automated is the job?
Pace Determined by Speed of Equipment	How important is it to this job that the pace is determined by the speed of equipment or machinery? (This does not refer to keeping busy at all times on this job.)
Outdoors, Exposed to Weather	How often does this job require working outdoors, exposed to all weather conditions?
In an Enclosed Vehicle or Equipment	How often does this job require working in a closed vehicle or equipment (e.g., car)?
Extremely Bright or Inadequate Lighting	How often does this job require working in extremely bright or inadequate lighting conditions?
Exposed to High Places	How often does this job require exposure to high places?
Exposed to Radiation	How often does this job require exposure to radiation?
Public Speaking	How often do you have to perform public speaking in this job?
Exposed to Disease or Infections	How often does this job require exposure to disease/infections?
Outdoors, Under Cover	How often does this job require working outdoors, under cover (e.g., structure with roof but no walls)?
Spend Time Keeping or Regaining Balance	How much does this job require keeping or regaining your balance?
Deal With Physically Aggressive People	How frequently does this job require the worker to deal with physical aggression of violent individuals?
Spend Time Climbing Ladders, Scaffolds, or Poles	How much does this job require climbing ladders, scaffolds, or poles?
Exposed to Whole Body Vibration	How often does this job require exposure to whole body vibration (e.g., operate a jackhammer)?

Job Zone Component	Job Zone Component Definitions
Title	Job Zone Three: Medium Preparation Needed

Overall Experience	Previous work-related skill, knowledge, or experience is required for these occupations. For example, an electrician must have completed three or four years of apprenticeship or several years of vocational training, and often must have passed a licensing exam, in order to perform the job.
Job Training	Employees in these occupations usually need one or two years of training involving both on-the-job experience and informal training with experienced workers.
Job Zone Examples	These occupations usually involve using communication and organizational skills to coordinate, supervise, manage, or train others to accomplish goals. Examples include dental assistants, electricians, fish and game wardens, legal secretaries, personnel recruiters, and recreation workers.
SVP Range	(6.0 to < 7.0)
Education	Most occupations in this zone require training in vocational schools, related on-the-job experience, or an associate's degree. Some may require a bachelor's degree.

Work_Styles	Work_Styles Definitions
Attention to Detail	Job requires being careful about detail and thorough in completing work tasks.
Integrity	Job requires being honest and ethical.
Dependability	Job requires being reliable, responsible, and dependable, and fulfilling obligations.
Cooperation	Job requires being pleasant with others on the job and displaying a good-natured, cooperative attitude.
Concern for Others	Job requires being sensitive to others' needs and feelings and being understanding and helpful on the job.
Independence	Job requires developing one's own ways of doing things, guiding oneself with little or no supervision, and depending on oneself to get things done.
Self Control	Job requires maintaining composure, keeping emotions in check, controlling anger, and avoiding aggressive behavior, even in very difficult situations.
Initiative	Job requires a willingness to take on responsibilities and challenges.
Analytical Thinking	Job requires analyzing information and using logic to address work-related issues and problems.
Adaptability/Flexibility	Job requires being open to change (positive or negative) and to considerable variety in the workplace.
Stress Tolerance	Job requires accepting criticism and dealing calmly and effectively with high stress situations.
Persistence	Job requires persistence in the face of obstacles.
Achievement/Effort	Job requires establishing and maintaining personally challenging achievement goals and exerting effort toward mastering tasks.
Innovation	Job requires creativity and alternative thinking to develop new ideas for and answers to work-related problems.
Leadership	Job requires a willingness to lead, take charge, and offer opinions and direction.
Social Orientation	Job requires preferring to work with others rather than alone, and being personally connected with others on the job.

17-3023.03 - Electrical Engineering Technicians

Apply electrical theory and related knowledge to test and modify developmental or operational electrical machinery and electrical control equipment and circuitry in industrial or commercial plants and laboratories. Usually work under direction of engineering staff.

Tasks

1) Provide technical assistance and resolution when electrical or engineering problems are encountered before, during, and after construction.

2) Set up and operate test equipment to evaluate performance of developmental parts, assemblies, or systems under simulated operating conditions, and record results.

3) Assemble electrical and electronic systems and prototypes according to engineering data and knowledge of electrical principles, using hand tools and measuring instruments.

4) Analyze and interpret test information to resolve design-related problems.

5) Install and maintain electrical control systems and solid state equipment.

6) Build, calibrate, maintain, troubleshoot and repair electrical instruments or testing equipment.

7) Modify electrical prototypes, parts, assemblies, and systems to correct functional deviations.

8) Plan, schedule and monitor work of support personnel to assist supervisor.

9) Plan method and sequence of operations for developing and testing experimental electronic and electrical equipment.

10) Review existing electrical engineering criteria to identify necessary revisions, deletions or amendments to outdated material.

11) Perform supervisory duties such as recommending work assignments, approving leaves and completing performance evaluations.

12) Draw or modify diagrams and write engineering specifications to clarify design details and functional criteria of experimental electronics units.

13) Evaluate engineering proposals, shop drawings and design comments for sound electrical engineering practice and conformance with established safety and design criteria, and recommend approval or disapproval.

14) Prepare project cost and work-time estimates.

15) Conduct inspections for quality control and assurance programs, reporting findings and recommendations.

16) Visit construction sites to observe conditions impacting design and to identify solutions to technical design problems involving electrical systems equipment that arise during construction.

17) Prepare contracts and initiate, review and coordinate modifications to contract specifications and plans throughout the construction process.

18) Write commissioning procedures for electrical installations.

Knowledge	Knowledge Definitions
Computers and Electronics	Knowledge of circuit boards, processors, chips, electronic equipment, and computer hardware and software, including applications and programming.
Engineering and Technology	Knowledge of the practical application of engineering science and technology. This includes applying principles, techniques, procedures, and equipment to the design and production of various goods and services.
English Language	Knowledge of the structure and content of the English language including the meaning and spelling of words, rules of composition, and grammar.
Mechanical	Knowledge of machines and tools, including their designs, uses, repair, and maintenance.
Design	Knowledge of design techniques, tools, and principles involved in production of precision technical plans, blueprints, drawings, and models.
Mathematics	Knowledge of arithmetic, algebra, geometry, calculus, statistics, and their applications.
Production and Processing	Knowledge of raw materials, production processes, quality control, costs, and other techniques for maximizing the effective manufacture and distribution of goods.
Public Safety and Security	Knowledge of relevant equipment, policies, procedures, and strategies to promote effective local, state, or national security operations for the protection of people, data, property, and institutions.
Customer and Personal Service	Knowledge of principles and processes for providing customer and personal services. This includes customer needs assessment, meeting quality standards for services, and evaluation of customer satisfaction.
Telecommunications	Knowledge of transmission, broadcasting, switching, control, and operation of telecommunications systems.
Physics	Knowledge and prediction of physical principles, laws, their interrelationships, and applications to understanding fluid, material, and atmospheric dynamics, and mechanical, electrical, atomic and sub-atomic structures and processes.
Education and Training	Knowledge of principles and methods for curriculum and training design, teaching and instruction for individuals and groups, and the measurement of training effects.
Clerical	Knowledge of administrative and clerical procedures and systems such as word processing, managing files and records, stenography and transcription, designing forms, and other office procedures and terminology.
Administration and Management	Knowledge of business and management principles involved in strategic planning, resource allocation, human resources modeling, leadership technique, production methods, and coordination of people and resources.

Communications and Media	Knowledge of media production, communication, and dissemination techniques and methods. This includes alternative ways to inform and entertain via written, oral, and visual media.
Building and Construction	Knowledge of materials, methods, and the tools involved in the construction or repair of houses, buildings, or other structures such as highways and roads.
Law and Government	Knowledge of laws, legal codes, court procedures, precedents, government regulations, executive orders, agency rules, and the democratic political process.
Chemistry	Knowledge of the chemical composition, structure, and properties of substances and of the chemical processes and transformations that they undergo. This includes uses of chemicals and their interactions, danger signs, production techniques, and disposal methods.
Personnel and Human Resources	Knowledge of principles and procedures for personnel recruitment, selection, training, compensation and benefits, labor relations and negotiation, and personnel information systems.
Transportation	Knowledge of principles and methods for moving people or goods by air, rail, sea, or road, including the relative costs and benefits.
Psychology	Knowledge of human behavior and performance; individual differences in ability, personality, and interests; learning and motivation; psychological research methods; and the assessment and treatment of behavioral and affective disorders.
Economics and Accounting	Knowledge of economic and accounting principles and practices, the financial markets, banking and the analysis and reporting of financial data.
Sales and Marketing	Knowledge of principles and methods for showing, promoting, and selling products or services. This includes marketing strategy and tactics, product demonstration, sales techniques, and sales control systems.
Geography	Knowledge of principles and methods for describing the features of land, sea, and air masses, including their physical characteristics, locations, interrelationships, and distribution of plant, animal, and human life.
Philosophy and Theology	Knowledge of different philosophical systems and religions. This includes their basic principles, values, ethics, ways of thinking, customs, practices, and their impact on human culture.
Medicine and Dentistry	Knowledge of the information and techniques needed to diagnose and treat human injuries, diseases, and deformities. This includes symptoms, treatment alternatives, drug properties and interactions, and preventive health-care measures.
Sociology and Anthropology	Knowledge of group behavior and dynamics, societal trends and influences, human migrations, ethnicity, cultures and their history and origins.
History and Archeology	Knowledge of historical events and their causes, indicators, and effects on civilizations and cultures.
Foreign Language	Knowledge of the structure and content of a foreign (non-English) language including the meaning and spelling of words, rules of composition and grammar, and pronunciation.
Biology	Knowledge of plant and animal organisms, their tissues, cells, functions, interdependencies, and interactions with each other and the environment.
Fine Arts	Knowledge of the theory and techniques required to compose, produce, and perform works of music, dance, visual arts, drama, and sculpture.
Therapy and Counseling	Knowledge of principles, methods, and procedures for diagnosis, treatment, and rehabilitation of physical and mental dysfunctions, and for career counseling and guidance.
Food Production	Knowledge of techniques and equipment for planting, growing, and harvesting food products (both plant and animal) for consumption, including storage/handling techniques.

Skills	Skills Definitions
Troubleshooting	Determining causes of operating errors and deciding what to do about it.
Mathematics	Using mathematics to solve problems.
Critical Thinking	Using logic and reasoning to identify the strengths and weaknesses of alternative solutions, conclusions or approaches to problems.
Reading Comprehension	Understanding written sentences and paragraphs in work related documents.

Active Listening	Giving full attention to what other people are saying, taking time to understand the points being made, asking questions as appropriate, and not interrupting at inappropriate times.
Active Learning	Understanding the implications of new information for both current and future problem-solving and decision-making.
Repairing	Repairing machines or systems using the needed tools.
Learning Strategies	Selecting and using training/instructional methods and procedures appropriate for the situation when learning or teaching new things.
Equipment Selection	Determining the kind of tools and equipment needed to do a job.
Monitoring	Monitoring/Assessing performance of yourself, other individuals, or organizations to make improvements or take corrective action.
Speaking	Talking to others to convey information effectively.
Installation	Installing equipment, machines, wiring, or programs to meet specifications.
Time Management	Managing one's own time and the time of others.
Operation and Control	Controlling operations of equipment or systems.
Complex Problem Solving	Identifying complex problems and reviewing related information to develop and evaluate options and implement solutions.
Coordination	Adjusting actions in relation to others' actions.
Judgment and Decision Making	Considering the relative costs and benefits of potential actions to choose the most appropriate one.
Service Orientation	Actively looking for ways to help people.
Instructing	Teaching others how to do something.
Operations Analysis	Analyzing needs and product requirements to create a design.
Technology Design	Generating or adapting equipment and technology to serve user needs.
Systems Analysis	Determining how a system should work and how changes in conditions, operations, and the environment will affect outcomes.
Equipment Maintenance	Performing routine maintenance on equipment and determining when and what kind of maintenance is needed.
Writing	Communicating effectively in writing as appropriate for the needs of the audience.
Social Perceptiveness	Being aware of others' reactions and understanding why they react as they do.
Quality Control Analysis	Conducting tests and inspections of products, services, or processes to evaluate quality or performance.
Operation Monitoring	Watching gauges, dials, or other indicators to make sure a machine is working properly.
Systems Evaluation	Identifying measures or indicators of system performance and the actions needed to improve or correct performance, relative to the goals of the system.
Science	Using scientific rules and methods to solve problems.
Management of Material Resources	Obtaining and seeing to the appropriate use of equipment, facilities, and materials needed to do certain work.
Management of Personnel Resources	Motivating, developing, and directing people as they work, identifying the best people for the job.
Programming	Writing computer programs for various purposes.
Persuasion	Persuading others to change their minds or behavior.
Negotiation	Bringing others together and trying to reconcile differences.
Management of Financial Resources	Determining how money will be spent to get the work done, and accounting for these expenditures.

Ability	Ability Definitions
Near Vision	The ability to see details at close range (within a few feet of the observer).
Problem Sensitivity	The ability to tell when something is wrong or is likely to go wrong. It does not involve solving the problem, only recognizing there is a problem.
Deductive Reasoning	The ability to apply general rules to specific problems to produce answers that make sense.
Oral Comprehension	The ability to listen to and understand information and ideas presented through spoken words and sentences.
Written Comprehension	The ability to read and understand information and ideas presented in writing.
Oral Expression	The ability to communicate information and ideas in speaking so others will understand.
Inductive Reasoning	The ability to combine pieces of information to form general rules or conclusions (includes finding a relationship among seemingly unrelated events).
Written Expression	The ability to communicate information and ideas in writing so others will understand.

Finger Dexterity	The ability to make precisely coordinated movements of the fingers of one or both hands to grasp, manipulate, or assemble very small objects.
Information Ordering	The ability to arrange things or actions in a certain order or pattern according to a specific rule or set of rules (e.g., patterns of numbers, letters, words, pictures, mathematical operations).
Visualization	The ability to imagine how something will look after it is moved around or when its parts are moved or rearranged.
Arm-Hand Steadiness	The ability to keep your hand and arm steady while moving your arm or while holding your arm and hand in one position.
Manual Dexterity	The ability to quickly move your hand, your hand together with your arm, or your two hands to grasp, manipulate, or assemble objects.
Speech Clarity	The ability to speak clearly so others can understand you.
Speech Recognition	The ability to identify and understand the speech of another person.
Category Flexibility	The ability to generate or use different sets of rules for combining or grouping things in different ways.
Visual Color Discrimination	The ability to match or detect differences between colors, including shades of color and brightness.
Mathematical Reasoning	The ability to choose the right mathematical methods or formulas to solve a problem.
Selective Attention	The ability to concentrate on a task over a period of time without being distracted.
Flexibility of Closure	The ability to identify or detect a known pattern (a figure, object, word, or sound) that is hidden in other distracting material.
Originality	The ability to come up with unusual or clever ideas about a given topic or situation, or to develop creative ways to solve a problem.
Perceptual Speed	The ability to quickly and accurately compare similarities and differences among sets of letters, numbers, objects, pictures, or patterns. The things to be compared may be presented at the same time or one after the other. This ability also includes comparing a presented object with a remembered object.
Fluency of Ideas	The ability to come up with a number of ideas about a topic (the number of ideas is important, not their quality, correctness, or creativity).
Control Precision	The ability to quickly and repeatedly adjust the controls of a machine or a vehicle to exact positions.
Multilimb Coordination	The ability to coordinate two or more limbs (for example, two arms, two legs, or one leg and one arm) while sitting, standing, or lying down. It does not involve performing the activities while the whole body is in motion.
Depth Perception	The ability to judge which of several objects is closer or farther away from you, or to judge the distance between you and an object.
Memorization	The ability to remember information such as words, numbers, pictures, and procedures.
Static Strength	The ability to exert maximum muscle force to lift, push, pull, or carry objects.
Speed of Closure	The ability to quickly make sense of, combine, and organize information into meaningful patterns.
Time Sharing	The ability to shift back and forth between two or more activities or sources of information (such as speech, sounds, touch, or other sources).
Number Facility	The ability to add, subtract, multiply, or divide quickly and correctly.
Trunk Strength	The ability to use your abdominal and lower back muscles to support part of the body repeatedly or continuously over time without 'giving out' or fatiguing.
Auditory Attention	The ability to focus on a single source of sound in the presence of other distracting sounds.
Far Vision	The ability to see details at a distance.
Wrist-Finger Speed	The ability to make fast, simple, repeated movements of the fingers, hands, and wrists.
Extent Flexibility	The ability to bend, stretch, twist, or reach with your body, arms, and/or legs.
Dynamic Strength	The ability to exert muscle force repeatedly or continuously over time. This involves muscular endurance and resistance to muscle fatigue.
Gross Body Coordination	The ability to coordinate the movement of your arms, legs, and torso together when the whole body is in motion.
Stamina	The ability to exert yourself physically over long periods of time without getting winded or out of breath.

Response Orientation	The ability to choose quickly between two or more movements in response to two or more different signals (lights, sounds, pictures). It includes the speed with which the correct response is started with the hand, foot, or other body part.
Hearing Sensitivity	The ability to detect or tell the differences between sounds that vary in pitch and loudness.
Reaction Time	The ability to quickly respond (with the hand, finger, or foot) to a signal (sound, light, picture) when it appears.
Gross Body Equilibrium	The ability to keep or regain your body balance or stay upright when in an unstable position.
Rate Control	The ability to time your movements or the movement of a piece of equipment in anticipation of changes in the speed and/or direction of a moving object or scene.
Sound Localization	The ability to tell the direction from which a sound originated.
Glare Sensitivity	The ability to see objects in the presence of glare or bright lighting.
Spatial Orientation	The ability to know your location in relation to the environment or to know where other objects are in relation to you.
Dynamic Flexibility	The ability to quickly and repeatedly bend, stretch, twist, or reach out with your body, arms, and/or legs.
Explosive Strength	The ability to use short bursts of muscle force to propel oneself (as in jumping or sprinting), or to throw an object.
Speed of Limb Movement	The ability to quickly move the arms and legs.
Night Vision	The ability to see under low light conditions.
Peripheral Vision	The ability to see objects or movement of objects to one's side when the eyes are looking ahead.

Work_Activity	Work_Activity Definitions
Inspecting Equipment, Structures, or Material	Inspecting equipment, structures, or materials to identify the cause of errors or other problems or defects.
Identifying Objects, Actions, and Events	Identifying information by categorizing, estimating, recognizing differences or similarities, and detecting changes in circumstances or events.
Communicating with Supervisors, Peers, or Subordin	Providing information to supervisors, co-workers, and subordinates by telephone, in written form, e-mail, or in person.
Updating and Using Relevant Knowledge	Keeping up-to-date technically and applying new knowledge to your job.
Processing Information	Compiling, coding, categorizing, calculating, tabulating, auditing, or verifying information or data.
Getting Information	Observing, receiving, and otherwise obtaining information from all relevant sources.
Judging the Qualities of Things, Services, or Peop	Assessing the value, importance, or quality of things or people.
Documenting/Recording Information	Entering, transcribing, recording, storing, or maintaining information in written or electronic/magnetic form.
Evaluating Information to Determine Compliance wit	Using relevant information and individual judgment to determine whether events or processes comply with laws, regulations, or standards.
Handling and Moving Objects	Using hands and arms in handling, installing, positioning, and moving materials, and manipulating things.
Making Decisions and Solving Problems	Analyzing information and evaluating results to choose the best solution and solve problems.
Monitor Processes, Materials, or Surroundings	Monitoring and reviewing information from materials, events, or the environment, to detect or assess problems.
Repairing and Maintaining Electronic Equipment	Servicing, repairing, calibrating, regulating, fine-tuning, or testing machines, devices, and equipment that operate primarily on the basis of electrical or electronic (not mechanical) principles.
Interacting With Computers	Using computers and computer systems (including hardware and software) to program, write software, set up functions, enter data, or process information.
Establishing and Maintaining Interpersonal Relatio	Developing constructive and cooperative working relationships with others, and maintaining them over time.
Thinking Creatively	Developing, designing, or creating new applications, ideas, relationships, systems, or products, including artistic contributions.
Analyzing Data or Information	Identifying the underlying principles, reasons, or facts of information by breaking down information or data into separate parts.
Drafting, Laying Out, and Specifying Technical Dev	Providing documentation, detailed instructions, drawings, or specifications to tell others about how devices, parts, equipment, or structures are to be fabricated, constructed, assembled, modified, maintained, or used.

Organizing, Planning, and Prioritizing Work	Developing specific goals and plans to prioritize, organize, and accomplish your work.
Interpreting the Meaning of Information for Others	Translating or explaining what information means and how it can be used.
Performing General Physical Activities	Performing physical activities that require considerable use of your arms and legs and moving your whole body, such as climbing, lifting, balancing, walking, stooping, and handling of materials.
Developing Objectives and Strategies	Establishing long-range objectives and specifying the strategies and actions to achieve them.
Provide Consultation and Advice to Others	Providing guidance and expert advice to management or other groups on technical, systems-, or process-related topics.
Estimating the Quantifiable Characteristics of Pro	Estimating sizes, distances, and quantities; or determining time, costs, resources, or materials needed to perform a work activity.
Scheduling Work and Activities	Scheduling events, programs, and activities, as well as the work of others.
Controlling Machines and Processes	Using either control mechanisms or direct physical activity to operate machines or processes (not including computers or vehicles).
Training and Teaching Others	Identifying the educational needs of others, developing formal educational or training programs or classes, and teaching or instructing others.
Communicating with Persons Outside Organization	Communicating with people outside the organization, representing the organization to customers, the public, government, and other external sources. This information can be exchanged in person, in writing, or by telephone or e-mail.
Guiding, Directing, and Motivating Subordinates	Providing guidance and direction to subordinates, including setting performance standards and monitoring performance.
Developing and Building Teams	Encouraging and building mutual trust, respect, and cooperation among team members.
Coaching and Developing Others	Identifying the developmental needs of others and coaching, mentoring, or otherwise helping others to improve their knowledge or skills.
Repairing and Maintaining Mechanical Equipment	Servicing, repairing, adjusting, and testing machines, devices, moving parts, and equipment that operate primarily on the basis of mechanical (not electronic) principles.
Assisting and Caring for Others	Providing personal assistance, medical attention, emotional support, or other personal care to others such as coworkers, customers, or patients.
Resolving Conflicts and Negotiating with Others	Handling complaints, settling disputes, and resolving grievances and conflicts, or otherwise negotiating with others.
Coordinating the Work and Activities of Others	Getting members of a group to work together to accomplish tasks.
Selling or Influencing Others	Convincing others to buy merchandise/goods or to otherwise change their minds or actions.
Operating Vehicles, Mechanized Devices, or Equipme	Running, maneuvering, navigating, or driving vehicles or mechanized equipment, such as forklifts, passenger vehicles, aircraft, or water craft.
Performing Administrative Activities	Performing day-to-day administrative tasks such as maintaining information files and processing paperwork.
Monitoring and Controlling Resources	Monitoring and controlling resources and overseeing the spending of money.
Performing for or Working Directly with the Public	Performing for people or dealing directly with the public. This includes serving customers in restaurants and stores, and receiving clients or guests.
Staffing Organizational Units	Recruiting, interviewing, selecting, hiring, and promoting employees in an organization.

Work_Context	Work_Context Definitions
Indoors, Environmentally Controlled	How often does this job require working indoors in environmentally controlled conditions?
Face-to-Face Discussions	How often do you have to have face-to-face discussions with individuals or teams in this job?
Electronic Mail	How often do you use electronic mail in this job?
Importance of Being Exact or Accurate	How important is being very exact or highly accurate in performing this job?
Telephone	How often do you have telephone conversations in this job?
Impact of Decisions on Co-workers or Company Resul	How do the decisions an employee makes impact the results of co-workers, clients or the company?
Freedom to Make Decisions	How much decision making freedom, without supervision, does the job offer?
Contact With Others	How much does this job require the worker to be in contact with others (face-to-face, by telephone, or otherwise) in order to perform it?

Structured versus Unstructured Work	To what extent is this job structured for the worker, rather than allowing the worker to determine tasks, priorities, and goals?
Work With Work Group or Team	How important is it to work with others in a group or team in this job?
Spend Time Using Your Hands to Handle, Control, or	How much does this job require using your hands to handle, control, or feel objects, tools or controls?
Coordinate or Lead Others	How important is it to coordinate or lead others in accomplishing work activities in this job?
Spend Time Sitting	How much does this job require sitting?
Responsibility for Outcomes and Results	How responsible is the worker for work outcomes and results of other workers?
Importance of Repeating Same Tasks	How important is repeating the same physical activities (e.g., key entry) or mental activities (e.g., checking entries in a ledger) over and over, without stopping, to performing this job?
Frequency of Decision Making	How frequently is the worker required to make decisions that affect other people, the financial resources, and/or the image and reputation of the organization?
Time Pressure	How often does this job require the worker to meet strict deadlines?
Consequence of Error	How serious would the result usually be if the worker made a mistake that was not readily correctable?
Letters and Memos	How often does the job require written letters and memos?
Sounds, Noise Levels Are Distracting or Uncomforta	How often does this job require working exposed to sounds and noise levels that are distracting or uncomfortable?
Spend Time Making Repetitive Motions	How much does this job require making repetitive motions?
Physical Proximity	To what extent does this job require the worker to perform job tasks in close physical proximity to other people?
Level of Competition	To what extent does this job require the worker to compete or to be aware of competitive pressures?
Responsible for Others' Health and Safety	How much responsibility is there for the health and safety of others in this job?
Frequency of Conflict Situations	How often are there conflict situations the employee has to face in this job?
Degree of Automation	How automated is the job?
Deal With External Customers	How important is it to work with external customers or the public in this job?
Deal With Unpleasant or Angry People	How frequently does the worker have to deal with unpleasant, angry, or discourteous individuals as part of the job requirements?
Wear Common Protective or Safety Equipment such as	How much does this job require wearing common protective or safety equipment such as safety shoes, glasses, gloves, hard hats or live jackets?
Spend Time Standing	How much does this job require standing?
Exposed to Hazardous Conditions	How often does this job require exposure to hazardous conditions?
Exposed to Contaminants	How often does this job require working exposed to contaminants (such as pollutants, gases, dust or odors)?
Cramped Work Space, Awkward Positions	How often does this job require working in cramped work spaces that requires getting into awkward positions?
Spend Time Kneeling, Crouching, Stooping, or Crawl	How much does this job require kneeling, crouching, stooping or crawling?
Spend Time Walking and Running	How much does this job require walking and running?
In an Enclosed Vehicle or Equipment	How often does this job require working in a closed vehicle or equipment (e.g., car)?
Indoors, Not Environmentally Controlled	How often does this job require working indoors in non-controlled environmental conditions (e.g., warehouse without heat)?
Spend Time Bending or Twisting the Body	How much does this job require bending or twisting your body?
Exposed to Minor Burns, Cuts, Bites, or Stings	How often does this job require exposure to minor burns, cuts, bites, or stings?
Public Speaking	How often do you have to perform public speaking in this job?
Pace Determined by Speed of Equipment	How important is it to this job that the pace is determined by the speed of equipment or machinery? (This does not refer to keeping busy at all times on this job.)
Exposed to Hazardous Equipment	How often does this job require exposure to hazardous equipment?
Extremely Bright or Inadequate Lighting	How often does this job require working in extremely bright or inadequate lighting conditions?
Wear Specialized Protective or Safety Equipment su	How much does this job require wearing specialized protective or safety equipment such as breathing apparatus, safety harness, full protection suits, or radiation protection?
Very Hot or Cold Temperatures	How often does this job require working in very hot (above 90 F degrees) or very cold (below 32 F degrees) temperatures?

Exposed to Radiation	How often does this job require exposure to radiation?
Spend Time Keeping or Regaining Balance	How much does this job require keeping or regaining your balance?
Outdoors, Exposed to Weather	How often does this job require working outdoors, exposed to all weather conditions?
Exposed to High Places	How often does this job require exposure to high places?
Outdoors, Under Cover	How often does this job require working outdoors, under cover (e.g., structure with roof but no walls)?
Spend Time Climbing Ladders, Scaffolds, or Poles	How much does this job require climbing ladders, scaffolds, or poles?
Deal With Physically Aggressive People	How frequently does this job require the worker to deal with physical aggression of violent individuals?
In an Open Vehicle or Equipment	How often does this job require working in an open vehicle or equipment (e.g., tractor)?
Exposed to Whole Body Vibration	How often does this job require exposure to whole body vibration (e.g., operate a jackhammer)?
Exposed to Disease or Infections	How often does this job require exposure to disease/infections?

Job Zone Component	Job Zone Component Definitions
Title	Job Zone Three: Medium Preparation Needed
Overall Experience	Previous work-related skill, knowledge, or experience is required for these occupations. For example, an electrician must have completed three or four years of apprenticeship or several years of vocational training, and often must have passed a licensing exam, in order to perform the job.
Job Training	Employees in these occupations usually need one or two years of training involving both on-the-job experience and informal training with experienced workers.
Job Zone Examples	These occupations usually involve using communication and organizational skills to coordinate, supervise, manage, or train others to accomplish goals. Examples include dental assistants, electricians, fish and game wardens, legal secretaries, personnel recruiters, and recreation workers.
SVP Range	(6.0 to < 7.0)
Education	Most occupations in this zone require training in vocational schools, related on-the-job experience, or an associate's degree. Some may require a bachelor's degree.

Work_Styles	Work_Styles Definitions
Attention to Detail	Job requires being careful about detail and thorough in completing work tasks.
Dependability	Job requires being reliable, responsible, and dependable, and fulfilling obligations.
Cooperation	Job requires being pleasant with others on the job and displaying a good-natured, cooperative attitude.
Initiative	Job requires a willingness to take on responsibilities and challenges.
Integrity	Job requires being honest and ethical.
Analytical Thinking	Job requires analyzing information and using logic to address work-related issues and problems.
Innovation	Job requires creativity and alternative thinking to develop new ideas for and answers to work-related problems.
Persistence	Job requires persistence in the face of obstacles.
Leadership	Job requires a willingness to lead, take charge, and offer opinions and direction.
Achievement/Effort	Job requires establishing and maintaining personally challenging achievement goals and exerting effort toward mastering tasks.
Adaptability/Flexibility	Job requires being open to change (positive or negative) and to considerable variety in the workplace.
Self Control	Job requires maintaining composure, keeping emotions in check, controlling anger, and avoiding aggressive behavior, even in very difficult situations.
Independence	Job requires developing one's own ways of doing things, guiding oneself with little or no supervision, and depending on oneself to get things done.
Social Orientation	Job requires preferring to work with others rather than alone, and being personally connected with others on the job.
Concern for Others	Job requires being sensitive to others' needs and feelings and being understanding and helpful on the job.
Stress Tolerance	Job requires accepting criticism and dealing calmly and effectively with high stress situations.

17-3025.00 - Environmental Engineering Technicians

Apply theory and principles of environmental engineering to modify, test, and operate equipment and devices used in the prevention, control, and remediation of environmental pollution, including waste treatment and site remediation. May assist in the development of environmental pollution remediation devices under direction of engineer.

Tasks

1) Maintain project logbook records and computer program files.

2) Receive, set up, test, and decontaminate equipment.

3) Review technical documents to ensure completeness and conformance to requirements.

4) Conduct pollution surveys, collecting and analyzing samples such as air and ground water.

5) Obtain product information, identify vendors and suppliers, and order materials and equipment to maintain inventory.

6) Review work plans to schedule activities.

7) Perform laboratory work such as logging numerical and visual observations, preparing and packaging samples, recording test results, and performing photo documentation.

8) Maintain process parameters and evaluate process anomalies.

9) Produce environmental assessment reports, tabulating data and preparing charts, graphs and sketches.

10) Develop work plans, including writing specifications and establishing material, manpower and facilities needs.

11) Provide technical engineering support in the planning of projects, such as wastewater treatment plants, to ensure compliance with environmental regulations and policies.

12) Inspect facilities to monitor compliance with regulations governing substances such as asbestos, lead, and wastewater.

13) Oversee support staff.

14) Perform statistical analysis and correction of air and/or water pollution data submitted by industry and other agencies.

15) Assist in the cleanup of hazardous material spills.

16) Arrange for the disposal of lead, asbestos and other hazardous materials.

17) Work with customers to assess the environmental impact of proposed construction and to develop pollution prevention programs.

18) Improve chemical processes to reduce toxic emissions.

Knowledge	Knowledge Definitions
Engineering and Technology	Knowledge of the practical application of engineering science and technology. This includes applying principles, techniques, procedures, and equipment to the design and production of various goods and services.
Customer and Personal Service	Knowledge of principles and processes for providing customer and personal services. This includes customer needs assessment, meeting quality standards for services, and evaluation of customer satisfaction.
Mathematics	Knowledge of arithmetic, algebra, geometry, calculus, statistics, and their applications.
English Language	Knowledge of the structure and content of the English language including the meaning and spelling of words, rules of composition, and grammar.
Mechanical	Knowledge of machines and tools, including their designs, uses, repair, and maintenance.
Building and Construction	Knowledge of materials, methods, and the tools involved in the construction or repair of houses, buildings, or other structures such as highways and roads.
Design	Knowledge of design techniques, tools, and principles involved in production of precision technical plans, blueprints, drawings, and models.
Law and Government	Knowledge of laws, legal codes, court procedures, precedents, government regulations, executive orders, agency rules, and the democratic political process.
Administration and Management	Knowledge of business and management principles involved in strategic planning, resource allocation, human resources modeling, leadership technique, production methods, and coordination of people and resources.

Physics	Knowledge and prediction of physical principles, laws, their interrelationships, and applications to understanding fluid, material, and atmospheric dynamics, and mechanical, electrical, atomic and sub- atomic structures and processes.
Clerical	Knowledge of administrative and clerical procedures and systems such as word processing, managing files and records, stenography and transcription, designing forms, and other office procedures and terminology.
Public Safety and Security	Knowledge of relevant equipment, policies, procedures, and strategies to promote effective local, state, or national security operations for the protection of people, data, property, and institutions.
Biology	Knowledge of plant and animal organisms, their tissues, cells, functions, interdependencies, and interactions with each other and the environment.
Computers and Electronics	Knowledge of circuit boards, processors, chips, electronic equipment, and computer hardware and software, including applications and programming.
Chemistry	Knowledge of the chemical composition, structure, and properties of substances and of the chemical processes and transformations that they undergo. This includes uses of chemicals and their interactions, danger signs, production techniques, and disposal methods.
Geography	Knowledge of principles and methods for describing the features of land, sea, and air masses, including their physical characteristics, locations, interrelationships, and distribution of plant, animal, and human life.
Communications and Media	Knowledge of media production, communication, and dissemination techniques and methods. This includes alternative ways to inform and entertain via written, oral, and visual media.
Education and Training	Knowledge of principles and methods for curriculum and training design, teaching and instruction for individuals and groups, and the measurement of training effects.
Personnel and Human Resources	Knowledge of principles and procedures for personnel recruitment, selection, training, compensation and benefits, labor relations and negotiation, and personnel information systems.
Production and Processing	Knowledge of raw materials, production processes, quality control, costs, and other techniques for maximizing the effective manufacture and distribution of goods.
Telecommunications	Knowledge of transmission, broadcasting, switching, control, and operation of telecommunications systems.
Sales and Marketing	Knowledge of principles and methods for showing, promoting, and selling products or services. This includes marketing strategy and tactics, product demonstration, sales techniques, and sales control systems.
Psychology	Knowledge of human behavior and performance; individual differences in ability, personality, and interests; learning and motivation; psychological research methods; and the assessment and treatment of behavioral and affective disorders.
Transportation	Knowledge of principles and methods for moving people or goods by air, rail, sea, or road, including the relative costs and benefits.
Economics and Accounting	Knowledge of economic and accounting principles and practices, the financial markets, banking and the analysis and reporting of financial data.
History and Archeology	Knowledge of historical events and their causes, indicators, and effects on civilizations and cultures.
Medicine and Dentistry	Knowledge of the information and techniques needed to diagnose and treat human injuries, diseases, and deformities. This includes symptoms, treatment alternatives, drug properties and interactions, and preventive health-care measures.
Food Production	Knowledge of techniques and equipment for planting, growing, and harvesting food products (both plant and animal) for consumption, including storage/handling techniques.
Foreign Language	Knowledge of the structure and content of a foreign (non-English) language including the meaning and spelling of words, rules of composition and grammar, and pronunciation.
Sociology and Anthropology	Knowledge of group behavior and dynamics, societal trends and influences, human migrations, ethnicity, cultures and their history and origins.
Therapy and Counseling	Knowledge of principles, methods, and procedures for diagnosis, treatment, and rehabilitation of physical and mental dysfunctions, and for career counseling and guidance.

Philosophy and Theology	Knowledge of different philosophical systems and religions. This includes their basic principles, values, ethics, ways of thinking, customs, practices, and their impact on human culture.
Fine Arts	Knowledge of the theory and techniques required to compose, produce, and perform works of music, dance, visual arts, drama, and sculpture.

Skills	Skills Definitions
Active Listening	Giving full attention to what other people are saying, taking time to understand the points being made, asking questions as appropriate, and not interrupting at inappropriate times.
Reading Comprehension	Understanding written sentences and paragraphs in work related documents.
Time Management	Managing one's own time and the time of others.
Coordination	Adjusting actions in relation to others' actions.
Writing	Communicating effectively in writing as appropriate for the needs of the audience.
Science	Using scientific rules and methods to solve problems.
Active Learning	Understanding the implications of new information for both current and future problem-solving and decision-making.
Mathematics	Using mathematics to solve problems.
Troubleshooting	Determining causes of operating errors and deciding what to do about it.
Critical Thinking	Using logic and reasoning to identify the strengths and weaknesses of alternative solutions, conclusions or approaches to problems.
Judgment and Decision Making	Considering the relative costs and benefits of potential actions to choose the most appropriate one.
Speaking	Talking to others to convey information effectively.
Quality Control Analysis	Conducting tests and inspections of products, services, or processes to evaluate quality or performance.
Service Orientation	Actively looking for ways to help people.
Monitoring	Monitoring/Assessing performance of yourself, other individuals, or organizations to make improvements or take corrective action.
Complex Problem Solving	Identifying complex problems and reviewing related information to develop and evaluate options and implement solutions.
Equipment Maintenance	Performing routine maintenance on equipment and determining when and what kind of maintenance is needed.
Equipment Selection	Determining the kind of tools and equipment needed to do a job.
Operation Monitoring	Watching gauges, dials, or other indicators to make sure a machine is working properly.
Instructing	Teaching others how to do something.
Learning Strategies	Selecting and using training/instructional methods and procedures appropriate for the situation when learning or teaching new things.
Operation and Control	Controlling operations of equipment or systems.
Repairing	Repairing machines or systems using the needed tools.
Installation	Installing equipment, machines, wiring, or programs to meet specifications.
Management of Material Resources	Obtaining and seeing to the appropriate use of equipment, facilities, and materials needed to do certain work.
Operations Analysis	Analyzing needs and product requirements to create a design.
Negotiation	Bringing others together and trying to reconcile differences.
Management of Personnel Resources	Motivating, developing, and directing people as they work, identifying the best people for the job.
Social Perceptiveness	Being aware of others' reactions and understanding why they react as they do.
Persuasion	Persuading others to change their minds or behavior.
Management of Financial Resources	Determining how money will be spent to get the work done, and accounting for these expenditures.
Technology Design	Generating or adapting equipment and technology to serve user needs.
Systems Analysis	Determining how a system should work and how changes in conditions, operations, and the environment will affect outcomes.
Systems Evaluation	Identifying measures or indicators of system performance and the actions needed to improve or correct performance, relative to the goals of the system.
Programming	Writing computer programs for various purposes.

Ability	Ability Definitions
Near Vision	The ability to see details at close range (within a few feet of the observer).
Problem Sensitivity	The ability to tell when something is wrong or is likely to go wrong. It does not involve solving the problem, only recognizing there is a problem.
Deductive Reasoning	The ability to apply general rules to specific problems to produce answers that make sense.
Written Comprehension	The ability to read and understand information and ideas presented in writing.
Information Ordering	The ability to arrange things or actions in a certain order or pattern according to a specific rule or set of rules (e.g., patterns of numbers, letters, words, pictures, mathematical operations).
Oral Comprehension	The ability to listen to and understand information and ideas presented through spoken words and sentences.
Inductive Reasoning	The ability to combine pieces of information to form general rules or conclusions (includes finding a relationship among seemingly unrelated events).
Speech Clarity	The ability to speak clearly so others can understand you.
Oral Expression	The ability to communicate information and ideas in speaking so others will understand.
Written Expression	The ability to communicate information and ideas in writing so others will understand.
Speech Recognition	The ability to identify and understand the speech of another person.
Far Vision	The ability to see details at a distance.
Category Flexibility	The ability to generate or use different sets of rules for combining or grouping things in different ways.
Selective Attention	The ability to concentrate on a task over a period of time without being distracted.
Number Facility	The ability to add, subtract, multiply, or divide quickly and correctly.
Perceptual Speed	The ability to quickly and accurately compare similarities and differences among sets of letters, numbers, objects, pictures, or patterns. The things to be compared may be presented at the same time or one after the other. This ability also includes comparing a presented object with a remembered object.
Visual Color Discrimination	The ability to match or detect differences between colors, including shades of color and brightness.
Mathematical Reasoning	The ability to choose the right mathematical methods or formulas to solve a problem.
Visualization	The ability to imagine how something will look after it is moved around or when its parts are moved or rearranged.
Arm-Hand Steadiness	The ability to keep your hand and arm steady while moving your arm or while holding your arm and hand in one position.
Manual Dexterity	The ability to quickly move your hand, your hand together with your arm, or your two hands to grasp, manipulate, or assemble objects.
Fluency of Ideas	The ability to come up with a number of ideas about a topic (the number of ideas is important, not their quality, correctness, or creativity).
Time Sharing	The ability to shift back and forth between two or more activities or sources of information (such as speech, sounds, touch, or other sources).
Flexibility of Closure	The ability to identify or detect a known pattern (a figure, object, word, or sound) that is hidden in other distracting material.
Trunk Strength	The ability to use your abdominal and lower back muscles to support part of the body repeatedly or continuously over time without 'giving out' or fatiguing.
Control Precision	The ability to quickly and repeatedly adjust the controls of a machine or a vehicle to exact positions.
Originality	The ability to come up with unusual or clever ideas about a given topic or situation, or to develop creative ways to solve a problem.
Memorization	The ability to remember information such as words, numbers, pictures, and procedures.
Reaction Time	The ability to quickly respond (with the hand, finger, or foot) to a signal (sound, light, picture) when it appears.
Finger Dexterity	The ability to make precisely coordinated movements of the fingers of one or both hands to grasp, manipulate, or assemble very small objects.
Multilimb Coordination	The ability to coordinate two or more limbs (for example, two arms, two legs, or one leg and one arm) while sitting, standing, or lying down. It does not involve performing the activities while the whole body is in motion.

Static Strength	The ability to exert maximum muscle force to lift, push, pull, or carry objects.
Depth Perception	The ability to judge which of several objects is closer or farther away from you, or to judge the distance between you and an object.
Gross Body Coordination	The ability to coordinate the movement of your arms, legs, and torso together when the whole body is in motion.
Auditory Attention	The ability to focus on a single source of sound in the presence of other distracting sounds.
Dynamic Strength	The ability to exert muscle force repeatedly or continuously over time. This involves muscular endurance and resistance to muscle fatigue.
Speed of Closure	The ability to quickly make sense of, combine, and organize information into meaningful patterns.
Extent Flexibility	The ability to bend, stretch, twist, or reach with your body, arms, and/or legs.
Hearing Sensitivity	The ability to detect or tell the differences between sounds that vary in pitch and loudness.
Stamina	The ability to exert yourself physically over long periods of time without getting winded or out of breath.
Gross Body Equilibrium	The ability to keep or regain your body balance or stay upright when in an unstable position.
Glare Sensitivity	The ability to see objects in the presence of glare or bright lighting.
Response Orientation	The ability to choose quickly between two or more movements in response to two or more different signals (lights, sounds, pictures). It includes the speed with which the correct response is started with the hand, foot, or other body part.
Spatial Orientation	The ability to know your location in relation to the environment or to know where other objects are in relation to you.
Wrist-Finger Speed	The ability to make fast, simple, repeated movements of the fingers, hands, and wrists.
Sound Localization	The ability to tell the direction from which a sound originated.
Rate Control	The ability to time your movements or the movement of a piece of equipment in anticipation of changes in the speed and/or direction of a moving object or scene.
Night Vision	The ability to see under low light conditions.
Peripheral Vision	The ability to see objects or movement of objects to one's side when the eyes are looking ahead.
Speed of Limb Movement	The ability to quickly move the arms and legs.
Dynamic Flexibility	The ability to quickly and repeatedly bend, stretch, twist, or reach out with your body, arms, and/or legs.
Explosive Strength	The ability to use short bursts of muscle force to propel oneself (as in jumping or sprinting), or to throw an object.

Work_Activity	**Work_Activity Definitions**
Interacting With Computers	Using computers and computer systems (including hardware and software) to program, write software, set up functions, enter data, or process information.
Documenting/Recording Information	Entering, transcribing, recording, storing, or maintaining information in written or electronic/magnetic form.
Identifying Objects, Actions, and Events	Identifying information by categorizing, estimating, recognizing differences or similarities, and detecting changes in circumstances or events.
Getting Information	Observing, receiving, and otherwise obtaining information from all relevant sources.
Evaluating Information to Determine Compliance wit	Using relevant information and individual judgment to determine whether events or processes comply with laws, regulations, or standards.
Updating and Using Relevant Knowledge	Keeping up-to-date technically and applying new knowledge to your job.
Processing Information	Compiling, coding, categorizing, calculating, tabulating, auditing, or verifying information or data.
Analyzing Data or Information	Identifying the underlying principles, reasons, or facts of information by breaking down information or data into separate parts.
Making Decisions and Solving Problems	Analyzing information and evaluating results to choose the best solution and solve problems.
Communicating with Supervisors, Peers, or Subordin	Providing information to supervisors, co-workers, and subordinates by telephone, in written form, e-mail, or in person.
Communicating with Persons Outside Organization	Communicating with people outside the organization, representing the organization to customers, the public, government, and other external sources. This information can be exchanged in person, in writing, or by telephone or e-mail.

Monitor Processes, Materials, or Surroundings	Monitoring and reviewing information from materials, events, or the environment, to detect or assess problems.
Performing General Physical Activities	Performing physical activities that require considerable use of your arms and legs and moving your whole body, such as climbing, lifting, balancing, walking, stooping, and handling of materials.
Establishing and Maintaining Interpersonal Relatio	Developing constructive and cooperative working relationships with others, and maintaining them over time.
Inspecting Equipment, Structures, or Material	Inspecting equipment, structures, or materials to identify the cause of errors or other problems or defects.
Scheduling Work and Activities	Scheduling events, programs, and activities, as well as the work of others.
Handling and Moving Objects	Using hands and arms in handling, installing, positioning, and moving materials, and manipulating things.
Organizing, Planning, and Prioritizing Work	Developing specific goals and plans to prioritize, organize, and accomplish your work.
Interpreting the Meaning of Information for Others	Translating or explaining what information means and how it can be used.
Thinking Creatively	Developing, designing, or creating new applications, ideas, relationships, systems, or products, including artistic contributions.
Performing Administrative Activities	Performing day-to-day administrative tasks such as maintaining information files and processing paperwork.
Operating Vehicles, Mechanized Devices, or Equipme	Running, maneuvering, navigating, or driving vehicles or mechanized equipment, such as forklifts, passenger vehicles, aircraft, or water craft.
Estimating the Quantifiable Characteristics of Pro	Estimating sizes, distances, and quantities; or determining time, costs, resources, or materials needed to perform a work activity.
Performing for or Working Directly with the Public	Performing for people or dealing directly with the public. This includes serving customers in restaurants and stores, and receiving clients or guests.
Judging the Qualities of Things, Services, or Peop	Assessing the value, importance, or quality of things or people.
Provide Consultation and Advice to Others	Providing guidance and expert advice to management or other groups on technical, systems-, or process-related topics.
Controlling Machines and Processes	Using either control mechanisms or direct physical activity to operate machines or processes (not including computers or vehicles).
Drafting, Laying Out, and Specifying Technical Dev	Providing documentation, detailed instructions, drawings, or specifications to tell others about how devices, parts, equipment, or structures are to be fabricated, constructed, assembled, modified, maintained, or used.
Developing and Building Teams	Encouraging and building mutual trust, respect, and cooperation among team members.
Training and Teaching Others	Identifying the educational needs of others, developing formal educational or training programs or classes, and teaching or instructing others.
Developing Objectives and Strategies	Establishing long-range objectives and specifying the strategies and actions to achieve them.
Monitoring and Controlling Resources	Monitoring and controlling resources and overseeing the spending of money.
Repairing and Maintaining Electronic Equipment	Servicing, repairing, calibrating, regulating, fine-tuning, or testing machines, devices, and equipment that operate primarily on the basis of electrical or electronic (not mechanical) principles.
Coordinating the Work and Activities of Others	Getting members of a group to work together to accomplish tasks.
Resolving Conflicts and Negotiating with Others	Handling complaints, settling disputes, and resolving grievances and conflicts, or otherwise negotiating with others.
Repairing and Maintaining Mechanical Equipment	Servicing, repairing, adjusting, and testing machines, devices, moving parts, and equipment that operate primarily on the basis of mechanical (not electronic) principles.
Selling or Influencing Others	Convincing others to buy merchandise/goods or to otherwise change their minds or actions.
Assisting and Caring for Others	Providing personal assistance, medical attention, emotional support, or other personal care to others such as coworkers, customers, or patients.
Guiding, Directing, and Motivating Subordinates	Providing guidance and direction to subordinates, including setting performance standards and monitoring performance.
Coaching and Developing Others	Identifying the developmental needs of others and coaching, mentoring, or otherwise helping others to improve their knowledge or skills.
Staffing Organizational Units	Recruiting, interviewing, selecting, hiring, and promoting employees in an organization.

Work_Context	Work_Context Definitions
Face-to-Face Discussions	How often do you have to have face-to-face discussions with individuals or teams in this job?
Telephone	How often do you have telephone conversations in this job?
Indoors. Environmentally Controlled	How often does this job require working indoors in environmentally controlled conditions?
Wear Common Protective or Safety Equipment such as	How much does this job require wearing common protective or safety equipment such as safety shoes. glasses, gloves, hard hats or live jackets)?
Indoors, Not Environmentally Controlled	How often does this job require working indoors in non-controlled environmental conditions (e.g., warehouse without heat)?
Structured versus Unstructured Work	To what extent is this job structured for the worker, rather than allowing the worker to determine tasks, priorities, and goals?
Freedom to Make Decisions	How much decision making freedom, without supervision, does the job offer?
Responsible for Others' Health and Safety	How much responsibility is there for the health and safety of others in this job?
Frequency of Decision Making	How frequently is the worker required to make decisions that affect other people, the financial resources, and/or the image and reputation of the organization?
Work With Work Group or Team	How important is it to work with others in a group or team in this job?
Letters and Memos	How often does the job require written letters and memos?
Impact of Decisions on Co-workers or Company Resul	How do the decisions an employee makes impact the results of co-workers, clients or the company?
Importance of Being Exact or Accurate	How important is being very exact or highly accurate in performing this job?
Electronic Mail	How often do you use electronic mail in this job?
Contact With Others	How much does this job require the worker to be in contact with others (face-to-face, by telephone, or otherwise) in order to perform it?
Outdoors, Exposed to Weather	How often does this job require working outdoors, exposed to all weather conditions?
Exposed to Hazardous Equipment	How often does this job require exposure to hazardous equipment?
Exposed to Hazardous Conditions	How often does this job require exposure to hazardous conditions?
Outdoors, Under Cover	How often does this job require working outdoors, under cover (e.g., structure with roof but no walls)?
Time Pressure	How often does this job require the worker to meet strict deadlines?
Consequence of Error	How serious would the result usually be if the worker made a mistake that was not readily correctable?
Coordinate or Lead Others	How important is it to coordinate or lead others in accomplishing work activities in this job?
Exposed to Contaminants	How often does this job require working exposed to contaminants (such as pollutants, gases, dust or odors)?
Spend Time Standing	How much does this job require standing?
Deal With External Customers	How important is it to work with external customers or the public in this job?
Sounds, Noise Levels Are Distracting or Uncomforta	How often does this job require working exposed to sounds and noise levels that are distracting or uncomfortable?
Physical Proximity	To what extent does this job require the worker to perform job tasks in close physical proximity to other people?
In an Enclosed Vehicle or Equipment	How often does this job require working in a closed vehicle or equipment (e.g., car)?
Importance of Repeating Same Tasks	How important is repeating the same physical activities (e.g., key entry) or mental activities (e.g., checking entries in a ledger) over and over, without stopping, to performing this job?
Spend Time Using Your Hands to Handle, Control, or	How much does this job require using your hands to handle, control, or feel objects, tools or controls?
Spend Time Sitting	How much does this job require sitting?
Deal With Unpleasant or Angry People	How frequently does the worker have to deal with unpleasant, angry, or discourteous individuals as part of the job requirements?
Very Hot or Cold Temperatures	How often does this job require working in very hot (above 90 F degrees) or very cold (below 32 F degrees) temperatures?
In an Open Vehicle or Equipment	How often does this job require working in an open vehicle or equipment (e.g., tractor)?
Spend Time Walking and Running	How much does this job require walking and running?
Extremely Bright or Inadequate Lighting	How often does this job require working in extremely bright or inadequate lighting conditions?

Frequency of Conflict Situations	How often are there conflict situations the employee has to face in this job?
Responsibility for Outcomes and Results	How responsible is the worker for work outcomes and results of other workers?
Spend Time Making Repetitive Motions	How much does this job require making repetitive motions?
Spend Time Bending or Twisting the Body	How much does this job require bending or twisting your body?
Cramped Work Space, Awkward Positions	How often does this job require working in cramped work spaces that requires getting into awkward positions?
Degree of Automation	How automated is the job?
Wear Specialized Protective or Safety Equipment su	How much does this job require wearing specialized protective or safety equipment such as breathing apparatus, safety harness, full protection suits, or radiation protection?
Exposed to Minor Burns, Cuts, Bites, or Stings	How often does this job require exposure to minor burns, cuts, bites, or stings?
Spend Time Kneeling, Crouching. Stooping, or Crawl	How much does this job require kneeling, crouching. stooping or crawling?
Exposed to High Places	How often does this job require exposure to high places?
Level of Competition	To what extent does this job require the worker to compete or to be aware of competitive pressures?
Spend Time Climbing Ladders, Scaffolds, or Poles	How much does this job require climbing ladders. scaffolds, or poles?
Public Speaking	How often do you have to perform public speaking in this job?
Spend Time Keeping or Regaining Balance	How much does this job require keeping or regaining your balance?
Exposed to Disease or Infections	How often does this job require exposure to disease/infections?
Pace Determined by Speed of Equipment	How important is it to this job that the pace is determined by the speed of equipment or machinery? (This does not refer to keeping busy at all times on this job.)
Deal With Physically Aggressive People	How frequently does this job require the worker to deal with physical aggression of violent individuals?
Exposed to Radiation	How often does this job require exposure to radiation?
Exposed to Whole Body Vibration	How often does this job require exposure to whole body vibration (e.g., operate a jackhammer)?

Job Zone Component	Job Zone Component Definitions
Title	Job Zone Three: Medium Preparation Needed
Overall Experience	Previous work-related skill, knowledge, or experience is required for these occupations. For example, an electrician must have completed three or four years of apprenticeship or several years of vocational training, and often must have passed a licensing exam, in order to perform the job.
Job Training	Employees in these occupations usually need one or two years of training involving both on-the-job experience and informal training with experienced workers.
Job Zone Examples	These occupations usually involve using communication and organizational skills to coordinate, supervise, manage, or train others to accomplish goals. Examples include dental assistants, electricians, fish and game wardens, legal secretaries, personnel recruiters, and recreation workers.
SVP Range	(6.0 to < 7.0)
Education	Most occupations in this zone require training in vocational schools, related on-the-job experience, or an associate's degree. Some may require a bachelor's degree.

Work_Styles	Work_Styles Definitions
Attention to Detail	Job requires being careful about detail and thorough in completing work tasks.
Dependability	Job requires being reliable, responsible, and dependable, and fulfilling obligations.
Integrity	Job requires being honest and ethical.
Stress Tolerance	Job requires accepting criticism and dealing calmly and effectively with high stress situations.
Self Control	Job requires maintaining composure, keeping emotions in check, controlling anger, and avoiding aggressive behavior, even in very difficult situations.
Independence	Job requires developing one's own ways of doing things, guiding oneself with little or no supervision, and depending on oneself to get things done.
Analytical Thinking	Job requires analyzing information and using logic to address work-related issues and problems.

Adaptability/Flexibility	Job requires being open to change (positive or negative) and to considerable variety in the workplace.
Initiative	Job requires a willingness to take on responsibilities and challenges.
Cooperation	Job requires being pleasant with others on the job and displaying a good-natured, cooperative attitude.
Persistence	Job requires persistence in the face of obstacles.
Achievement/Effort	Job requires establishing and maintaining personally challenging achievement goals and exerting effort toward mastering tasks.
Leadership	Job requires a willingness to lead, take charge, and offer opinions and direction.
Concern for Others	Job requires being sensitive to others' needs and feelings and being understanding and helpful on the job.
Innovation	Job requires creativity and alternative thinking to develop new ideas for and answers to work-related problems.
Social Orientation	Job requires preferring to work with others rather than alone, and being personally connected with others on the job.

17-3026.00 - Industrial Engineering Technicians

Apply engineering theory and principles to problems of industrial layout or manufacturing production, usually under the direction of engineering staff. May study and record time, motion, method, and speed involved in performance of production, maintenance, clerical, and other worker operations for such purposes as establishing standard production rates or improving efficiency.

Tasks

1) Recommend modifications to existing quality or production standards to achieve optimum quality within limits of equipment capability.

2) Observe worker using equipment to verify that equipment is being operated and maintained according to quality assurance standards.

3) Study time, motion, methods, and speed involved in maintenance, production, and other operations to establish standard production rate and improve efficiency.

4) Interpret engineering drawings, schematic diagrams, or formulas and confers with management or engineering staff to determine quality and reliability standards.

5) Prepare graphs or charts of data or enter data into computer for analysis.

6) Prepare charts, graphs, and diagrams to illustrate workflow, routing, floor layouts, material handling, and machine utilization.

7) Observe workers operating equipment or performing tasks to determine time involved and fatigue rate, using timing devices.

8) Aid in planning work assignments in accordance with worker performance, machine capacity, production schedules, and anticipated delays.

9) Evaluate data and write reports to validate or indicate deviations from existing standards.

10) Record test data, applying statistical quality control procedures.

11) Read worker logs, product processing sheets, and specification sheets, to verify that records adhere to quality assurance specifications.

12) Select products for tests at specified stages in production process, and test products for performance characteristics and adherence to specifications.

13) Compile and evaluate statistical data to determine and maintain quality and reliability of products.

Knowledge	Knowledge Definitions
Production and Processing	Knowledge of raw materials, production processes, quality control, costs, and other techniques for maximizing the effective manufacture and distribution of goods.
Engineering and Technology	Knowledge of the practical application of engineering science and technology. This includes applying principles, techniques, procedures, and equipment to the design and production of various goods and services.
Mathematics	Knowledge of arithmetic, algebra, geometry, calculus, statistics, and their applications.
English Language	Knowledge of the structure and content of the English language including the meaning and spelling of words, rules of composition, and grammar.
Clerical	Knowledge of administrative and clerical procedures and systems such as word processing, managing files and records, stenography and transcription, designing forms, and other office procedures and terminology.
Design	Knowledge of design techniques, tools, and principles involved in production of precision technical plans, blueprints, drawings, and models.
Computers and Electronics	Knowledge of circuit boards, processors, chips, electronic equipment, and computer hardware and software, including applications and programming.
Mechanical	Knowledge of machines and tools, including their designs, uses, repair, and maintenance.
Education and Training	Knowledge of principles and methods for curriculum and training design, teaching and instruction for individuals and groups, and the measurement of training effects.
Customer and Personal Service	Knowledge of principles and processes for providing customer and personal services. This includes customer needs assessment, meeting quality standards for services, and evaluation of customer satisfaction.
Administration and Management	Knowledge of business and management principles involved in strategic planning, resource allocation, human resources modeling, leadership technique, production methods, and coordination of people and resources.
Physics	Knowledge and prediction of physical principles, laws, their interrelationships, and applications to understanding fluid, material, and atmospheric dynamics, and mechanical, electrical, atomic and sub- atomic structures and processes.
Personnel and Human Resources	Knowledge of principles and procedures for personnel recruitment, selection, training, compensation and benefits, labor relations and negotiation, and personnel information systems.
Economics and Accounting	Knowledge of economic and accounting principles and practices, the financial markets, banking and the analysis and reporting of financial data.
Psychology	Knowledge of human behavior and performance; individual differences in ability, personality, and interests; learning and motivation; psychological research methods; and the assessment and treatment of behavioral and affective disorders.
Public Safety and Security	Knowledge of relevant equipment, policies, procedures, and strategies to promote effective local, state, or national security operations for the protection of people, data, property, and institutions.
Chemistry	Knowledge of the chemical composition, structure, and properties of substances and of the chemical processes and transformations that they undergo. This includes uses of chemicals and their interactions, danger signs, production techniques, and disposal methods.
Law and Government	Knowledge of laws, legal codes, court procedures, precedents, government regulations, executive orders, agency rules, and the democratic political process.
Transportation	Knowledge of principles and methods for moving people or goods by air, rail, sea, or road, including the relative costs and benefits.
Communications and Media	Knowledge of media production, communication, and dissemination techniques and methods. This includes alternative ways to inform and entertain via written, oral, and visual media.
Sales and Marketing	Knowledge of principles and methods for showing, promoting, and selling products or services. This includes marketing strategy and tactics, product demonstration, sales techniques, and sales control systems.
Building and Construction	Knowledge of materials, methods, and the tools involved in the construction or repair of houses, buildings, or other structures such as highways and roads.
Telecommunications	Knowledge of transmission, broadcasting, switching, control, and operation of telecommunications systems.
Sociology and Anthropology	Knowledge of group behavior and dynamics, societal trends and influences, human migrations, ethnicity, cultures and their history and origins.
Foreign Language	Knowledge of the structure and content of a foreign (non-English) language including the meaning and spelling of words, rules of composition and grammar, and pronunciation.
Therapy and Counseling	Knowledge of principles, methods, and procedures for diagnosis, treatment, and rehabilitation of physical and mental dysfunctions, and for career counseling and guidance.

Geography	Knowledge of principles and methods for describing the features of land, sea, and air masses, including their physical characteristics, locations, interrelationships, and distribution of plant, animal, and human life.
Medicine and Dentistry	Knowledge of the information and techniques needed to diagnose and treat human injuries, diseases, and deformities. This includes symptoms, treatment alternatives, drug properties and interactions, and preventive health-care measures.
History and Archeology	Knowledge of historical events and their causes, indicators, and effects on civilizations and cultures.
Biology	Knowledge of plant and animal organisms, their tissues, cells, functions, interdependencies, and interactions with each other and the environment.
Philosophy and Theology	Knowledge of different philosophical systems and religions. This includes their basic principles, values, ethics, ways of thinking, customs, practices, and their impact on human culture.
Fine Arts	Knowledge of the theory and techniques required to compose, produce, and perform works of music, dance, visual arts, drama, and sculpture.
Food Production	Knowledge of techniques and equipment for planting, growing, and harvesting food products (both plant and animal) for consumption, including storage/handling techniques.

Skills	Skills Definitions
Active Listening	Giving full attention to what other people are saying, taking time to understand the points being made, asking questions as appropriate, and not interrupting at inappropriate times.
Complex Problem Solving	Identifying complex problems and reviewing related information to develop and evaluate options and implement solutions.
Critical Thinking	Using logic and reasoning to identify the strengths and weaknesses of alternative solutions, conclusions or approaches to problems.
Judgment and Decision Making	Considering the relative costs and benefits of potential actions to choose the most appropriate one.
Coordination	Adjusting actions in relation to others' actions.
Active Learning	Understanding the implications of new information for both current and future problem-solving and decision-making.
Reading Comprehension	Understanding written sentences and paragraphs in work related documents.
Instructing	Teaching others how to do something.
Speaking	Talking to others to convey information effectively.
Monitoring	Monitoring/Assessing performance of yourself, other individuals, or organizations to make improvements or take corrective action.
Troubleshooting	Determining causes of operating errors and deciding what to do about it.
Time Management	Managing one's own time and the time of others.
Mathematics	Using mathematics to solve problems.
Learning Strategies	Selecting and using training/instructional methods and procedures appropriate for the situation when learning or teaching new things.
Service Orientation	Actively looking for ways to help people.
Quality Control Analysis	Conducting tests and inspections of products, services, or processes to evaluate quality or performance.
Writing	Communicating effectively in writing as appropriate for the needs of the audience.
Equipment Selection	Determining the kind of tools and equipment needed to do a job.
Operations Analysis	Analyzing needs and product requirements to create a design.
Social Perceptiveness	Being aware of others' reactions and understanding why they react as they do.
Systems Analysis	Determining how a system should work and how changes in conditions, operations, and the environment will affect outcomes.
Systems Evaluation	Identifying measures or indicators of system performance and the actions needed to improve or correct performance, relative to the goals of the system.
Persuasion	Persuading others to change their minds or behavior.
Management of Personnel Resources	Motivating, developing, and directing people as they work, identifying the best people for the job.
Repairing	Repairing machines or systems using the needed tools.
Negotiation	Bringing others together and trying to reconcile differences.
Operation Monitoring	Watching gauges, dials, or other indicators to make sure a machine is working properly.

Technology Design	Generating or adapting equipment and technology to serve user needs.
Operation and Control	Controlling operations of equipment or systems.
Science	Using scientific rules and methods to solve problems.
Equipment Maintenance	Performing routine maintenance on equipment and determining when and what kind of maintenance is needed.
Management of Material Resources	Obtaining and seeing to the appropriate use of equipment, facilities, and materials needed to do certain work.
Installation	Installing equipment, machines, wiring, or programs to meet specifications.
Management of Financial Resources	Determining how money will be spent to get the work done, and accounting for these expenditures.
Programming	Writing computer programs for various purposes.

Ability	Ability Definitions
Deductive Reasoning	The ability to apply general rules to specific problems to produce answers that make sense.
Inductive Reasoning	The ability to combine pieces of information to form general rules or conclusions (includes finding a relationship among seemingly unrelated events).
Near Vision	The ability to see details at close range (within a few feet of the observer).
Oral Comprehension	The ability to listen to and understand information and ideas presented through spoken words and sentences.
Problem Sensitivity	The ability to tell when something is wrong or is likely to go wrong. It does not involve solving the problem, only recognizing there is a problem.
Oral Expression	The ability to communicate information and ideas in speaking so others will understand.
Selective Attention	The ability to concentrate on a task over a period of time without being distracted.
Speech Clarity	The ability to speak clearly so others can understand you.
Speech Recognition	The ability to identify and understand the speech of another person.
Category Flexibility	The ability to generate or use different sets of rules for combining or grouping things in different ways.
Written Expression	The ability to communicate information and ideas in writing so others will understand.
Written Comprehension	The ability to read and understand information and ideas presented in writing.
Information Ordering	The ability to arrange things or actions in a certain order or pattern according to a specific rule or set of rules (e.g., patterns of numbers, letters, words, pictures, mathematical operations).
Originality	The ability to come up with unusual or clever ideas about a given topic or situation, or to develop creative ways to solve a problem.
Visualization	The ability to imagine how something will look after it is moved around or when its parts are moved or rearranged.
Mathematical Reasoning	The ability to choose the right mathematical methods or formulas to solve a problem.
Fluency of Ideas	The ability to come up with a number of ideas about a topic (the number of ideas is important, not their quality, correctness, or creativity).
Far Vision	The ability to see details at a distance.
Number Facility	The ability to add, subtract, multiply, or divide quickly and correctly.
Perceptual Speed	The ability to quickly and accurately compare similarities and differences among sets of letters, numbers, objects, pictures, or patterns. The things to be compared may be presented at the same time or one after the other. This ability also includes comparing a presented object with a remembered object.
Flexibility of Closure	The ability to identify or detect a known pattern (a figure, object, word, or sound) that is hidden in other distracting material.
Speed of Closure	The ability to quickly make sense of, combine, and organize information into meaningful patterns.
Auditory Attention	The ability to focus on a single source of sound in the presence of other distracting sounds.
Time Sharing	The ability to shift back and forth between two or more activities or sources of information (such as speech, sounds, touch, or other sources).
Hearing Sensitivity	The ability to detect or tell the differences between sounds that vary in pitch and loudness.
Visual Color Discrimination	The ability to match or detect differences between colors, including shades of color and brightness.

Finger Dexterity	The ability to make precisely coordinated movements of the fingers of one or both hands to grasp, manipulate, or assemble very small objects.
Depth Perception	The ability to judge which of several objects is closer or farther away from you, or to judge the distance between you and an object.
Memorization	The ability to remember information such as words, numbers, pictures, and procedures.
Reaction Time	The ability to quickly respond (with the hand, finger, or foot) to a signal (sound, light, picture) when it appears.
Arm-Hand Steadiness	The ability to keep your hand and arm steady while moving your arm or while holding your arm and hand in one position.
Trunk Strength	The ability to use your abdominal and lower back muscles to support part of the body repeatedly or continuously over time without 'giving out' or fatiguing.
Control Precision	The ability to quickly and repeatedly adjust the controls of a machine or a vehicle to exact positions.
Response Orientation	The ability to choose quickly between two or more movements in response to two or more different signals (lights, sounds, pictures). It includes the speed with which the correct response is started with the hand, foot, or other body part.
Wrist-Finger Speed	The ability to make fast, simple, repeated movements of the fingers, hands, and wrists.
Multilimb Coordination	The ability to coordinate two or more limbs (for example, two arms, two legs, or one leg and one arm) while sitting, standing, or lying down. It does not involve performing the activities while the whole body is in motion.
Manual Dexterity	The ability to quickly move your hand, your hand together with your arm, or your two hands to grasp, manipulate, or assemble objects.
Rate Control	The ability to time your movements or the movement of a piece of equipment in anticipation of changes in the speed and/or direction of a moving object or scene.
Speed of Limb Movement	The ability to quickly move the arms and legs.
Stamina	The ability to exert yourself physically over long periods of time without getting winded or out of breath.
Gross Body Coordination	The ability to coordinate the movement of your arms, legs, and torso together when the whole body is in motion.
Sound Localization	The ability to tell the direction from which a sound originated.
Peripheral Vision	The ability to see objects or movement of objects to one's side when the eyes are looking ahead.
Spatial Orientation	The ability to know your location in relation to the environment or to know where other objects are in relation to you.
Glare Sensitivity	The ability to see objects in the presence of glare or bright lighting.
Night Vision	The ability to see under low light conditions.
Dynamic Flexibility	The ability to quickly and repeatedly bend, stretch, twist, or reach out with your body, arms, and/or legs.
Static Strength	The ability to exert maximum muscle force to lift, push, pull, or carry objects.
Explosive Strength	The ability to use short bursts of muscle force to propel oneself (as in jumping or sprinting), or to throw an object.
Dynamic Strength	The ability to exert muscle force repeatedly or continuously over time. This involves muscular endurance and resistance to muscle fatigue.
Gross Body Equilibrium	The ability to keep or regain your body balance or stay upright when in an unstable position.
Extent Flexibility	The ability to bend, stretch, twist, or reach with your body, arms, and/or legs.

Work_Activity	Work_Activity Definitions
Communicating with Supervisors, Peers, or Subordin	Providing information to supervisors, co-workers, and subordinates by telephone, in written form, e-mail, or in person.
Identifying Objects, Actions, and Events	Identifying information by categorizing, estimating, recognizing differences or similarities, and detecting changes in circumstances or events.
Establishing and Maintaining Interpersonal Relatio	Developing constructive and cooperative working relationships with others, and maintaining them over time.
Documenting/Recording Information	Entering, transcribing, recording, storing, or maintaining information in written or electronic/magnetic form.
Interacting With Computers	Using computers and computer systems (including hardware and software) to program, write software, set up functions, enter data, or process information.
Getting Information	Observing, receiving, and otherwise obtaining information from all relevant sources.

Monitor Processes, Materials, or Surroundings	Monitoring and reviewing information from materials, events, or the environment, to detect or assess problems.
Analyzing Data or Information	Identifying the underlying principles, reasons, or facts of information by breaking down information or data into separate parts.
Processing Information	Compiling, coding, categorizing, calculating, tabulating, auditing, or verifying information or data.
Thinking Creatively	Developing, designing, or creating new applications, ideas, relationships, systems, or products, including artistic contributions.
Making Decisions and Solving Problems	Analyzing information and evaluating results to choose the best solution and solve problems.
Organizing, Planning, and Prioritizing Work	Developing specific goals and plans to prioritize, organize, and accomplish your work.
Drafting, Laying Out, and Specifying Technical Dev	Providing documentation, detailed instructions, drawings, or specifications to tell others about how devices, parts, equipment, or structures are to be fabricated, constructed, assembled, modified, maintained, or used.
Estimating the Quantifiable Characteristics of Pro	Estimating sizes, distances, and quantities; or determining time, costs, resources, or materials needed to perform a work activity.
Interpreting the Meaning of Information for Others	Translating or explaining what information means and how it can be used.
Scheduling Work and Activities	Scheduling events, programs, and activities, as well as the work of others.
Updating and Using Relevant Knowledge	Keeping up-to-date technically and applying new knowledge to your job.
Coordinating the Work and Activities of Others	Getting members of a group to work together to accomplish tasks.
Judging the Qualities of Things, Services, or Peop	Assessing the value, importance, or quality of things or people.
Inspecting Equipment, Structures, or Material	Inspecting equipment, structures, or materials to identify the cause of errors or other problems or defects.
Evaluating Information to Determine Compliance wit	Using relevant information and individual judgment to determine whether events or processes comply with laws, regulations, or standards.
Performing Administrative Activities	Performing day-to-day administrative tasks such as maintaining information files and processing paperwork.
Developing and Building Teams	Encouraging and building mutual trust, respect, and cooperation among team members.
Monitoring and Controlling Resources	Monitoring and controlling resources and overseeing the spending of money.
Training and Teaching Others	Identifying the educational needs of others, developing formal educational or training programs or classes, and teaching or instructing others.
Communicating with Persons Outside Organization	Communicating with people outside the organization, representing the organization to customers, the public, government, and other external sources. This information can be exchanged in person, in writing, or by telephone or e-mail.
Developing Objectives and Strategies	Establishing long-range objectives and specifying the strategies and actions to achieve them.
Selling or Influencing Others	Convincing others to buy merchandise/goods or to otherwise change their minds or actions.
Controlling Machines and Processes	Using either control mechanisms or direct physical activity to operate machines or processes (not including computers or vehicles).
Guiding, Directing, and Motivating Subordinates	Providing guidance and direction to subordinates, including setting performance standards and monitoring performance.
Resolving Conflicts and Negotiating with Others	Handling complaints, settling disputes, and resolving grievances and conflicts, or otherwise negotiating with others.
Provide Consultation and Advice to Others	Providing guidance and expert advice to management or other groups on technical, systems-, or process-related topics.
Coaching and Developing Others	Identifying the developmental needs of others and coaching, mentoring, or otherwise helping others to improve their knowledge or skills.
Staffing Organizational Units	Recruiting, interviewing, selecting, hiring, and promoting employees in an organization.
Handling and Moving Objects	Using hands and arms in handling, installing, positioning, and moving materials, and manipulating things.
Repairing and Maintaining Mechanical Equipment	Servicing, repairing, adjusting, and testing machines, devices, moving parts, and equipment that operate primarily on the basis of mechanical (not electronic) principles.
Repairing and Maintaining Electronic Equipment	Servicing, repairing, calibrating, regulating, fine-tuning, or testing machines, devices, and equipment that operate primarily on the basis of electrical or electronic (not mechanical) principles.

Performing General Physical Activities	Performing physical activities that require considerable use of your arms and legs and moving your whole body, such as climbing, lifting, balancing, walking, stooping, and handling of materials.
Assisting and Caring for Others	Providing personal assistance, medical attention, emotional support, or other personal care to others such as coworkers, customers, or patients.
Operating Vehicles, Mechanized Devices, or Equipme	Running, maneuvering, navigating, or driving vehicles or mechanized equipment, such as forklifts, passenger vehicles, aircraft, or water craft.
Performing for or Working Directly with the Public	Performing for people or dealing directly with the public. This includes serving customers in restaurants and stores, and receiving clients or guests.

Work_Context	Work_Context Definitions
Face-to-Face Discussions	How often do you have to have face-to-face discussions with individuals or teams in this job?
Contact With Others	How much does this job require the worker to be in contact with others (face-to-face, by telephone, or otherwise) in order to perform it?
Work With Work Group or Team	How important is it to work with others in a group or team in this job?
Telephone	How often do you have telephone conversations in this job?
Wear Common Protective or Safety Equipment such as	How much does this job require wearing common protective or safety equipment such as safety shoes, glasses, gloves, hard hats or live jackets?
Letters and Memos	How often does the job require written letters and memos?
Freedom to Make Decisions	How much decision making freedom, without supervision, does the job offer?
Frequency of Decision Making	How frequently is the worker required to make decisions that affect other people, the financial resources, and/or the image and reputation of the organization?
Indoors, Environmentally Controlled	How often does this job require working indoors in environmentally controlled conditions?
Time Pressure	How often does this job require the worker to meet strict deadlines?
Structured versus Unstructured Work	To what extent is this job structured for the worker, rather than allowing the worker to determine tasks, priorities, and goals?
Importance of Being Exact or Accurate	How important is being very exact or highly accurate in performing this job?
Electronic Mail	How often do you use electronic mail in this job?
Impact of Decisions on Co-workers or Company Resul	How do the decisions an employee makes impact the results of co-workers, clients or the company?
Coordinate or Lead Others	How important is it to coordinate or lead others in accomplishing work activities in this job?
Physical Proximity	To what extent does this job require the worker to perform job tasks in close physical proximity to other people?
Responsibility for Outcomes and Results	How responsible is the worker for work outcomes and results of other workers?
Exposed to Contaminants	How often does this job require working exposed to contaminants (such as pollutants, gases, dust or odors)?
Level of Competition	To what extent does this job require the worker to compete or to be aware of competitive pressures?
Sounds, Noise Levels Are Distracting or Uncomforta	How often does this job require working exposed to sounds and noise levels that are distracting or uncomfortable?
Frequency of Conflict Situations	How often are there conflict situations the employee has to face in this job?
Spend Time Standing	How much does this job require standing?
Deal With Unpleasant or Angry People	How frequently does the worker have to deal with unpleasant, angry, or discourteous individuals as part of the job requirements?
Exposed to Hazardous Equipment	How often does this job require exposure to hazardous equipment?
Responsible for Others' Health and Safety	How much responsibility is there for the health and safety of others in this job?
Spend Time Walking and Running	How much does this job require walking and running?
Indoors, Not Environmentally Controlled	How often does this job require working indoors in non-controlled environmental conditions (e.g., warehouse without heat)?
Importance of Repeating Same Tasks	How important is repeating the same physical activities (e.g., key entry) or mental activities (e.g., checking entries in a ledger) over and over, without stopping, to performing this job?
Deal With External Customers	How important is it to work with external customers or the public in this job?

Consequence of Error	How serious would the result usually be if the worker made a mistake that was not readily correctable?
Degree of Automation	How automated is the job?
Spend Time Sitting	How much does this job require sitting?
Spend Time Using Your Hands to Handle, Control, or	How much does this job require using your hands to handle, control, or feel objects, tools or controls?
Exposed to Minor Burns, Cuts, Bites, or Stings	How often does this job require exposure to minor burns, cuts, bites, or stings?
Public Speaking	How often do you have to perform public speaking in this job?
Pace Determined by Speed of Equipment	How important is it to this job that the pace is determined by the speed of equipment or machinery? (This does not refer to keeping busy at all times on this job.)
Spend Time Making Repetitive Motions	How much does this job require making repetitive motions?
Extremely Bright or Inadequate Lighting	How often does this job require working in extremely bright or inadequate lighting conditions?
Very Hot or Cold Temperatures	How often does this job require working in very hot (above 90 F degrees) or very cold (below 32 F degrees) temperatures?
Spend Time Bending or Twisting the Body	How much does this job require bending or twisting your body?
Exposed to Hazardous Conditions	How often does this job require exposure to hazardous conditions?
Spend Time Kneeling, Crouching, Stooping, or Crawl	How much does this job require kneeling, crouching, stooping or crawling?
In an Enclosed Vehicle or Equipment	How often does this job require working in a closed vehicle or equipment (e.g., car)?
Deal With Physically Aggressive People	How frequently does this job require the worker to deal with physical aggression of violent individuals?
In an Open Vehicle or Equipment	How often does this job require working in an open vehicle or equipment (e.g., tractor)?
Outdoors, Exposed to Weather	How often does this job require working outdoors, exposed to all weather conditions?
Cramped Work Space, Awkward Positions	How often does this job require working in cramped work spaces that requires getting into awkward positions?
Spend Time Keeping or Regaining Balance	How much does this job require keeping or regaining your balance?
Exposed to Disease or Infections	How often does this job require exposure to disease/infections?
Outdoors, Under Cover	How often does this job require working outdoors, under cover (e.g., structure with roof but no walls)?
Wear Specialized Protective or Safety Equipment su	How much does this job require wearing specialized protective or safety equipment such as breathing apparatus, safety harness, full protection suits, or radiation protection?
Spend Time Climbing Ladders, Scaffolds, or Poles	How much does this job require climbing ladders, scaffolds, or poles?
Exposed to High Places	How often does this job require exposure to high places?
Exposed to Whole Body Vibration	How often does this job require exposure to whole body vibration (e.g., operate a jackhammer)?
Exposed to Radiation	How often does this job require exposure to radiation?

Job Zone Component	Job Zone Component Definitions
Title	Job Zone Three: Medium Preparation Needed
Overall Experience	Previous work-related skill, knowledge, or experience is required for these occupations. For example, an electrician must have completed three or four years of apprenticeship or several years of vocational training, and often must have passed a licensing exam, in order to perform the job.
Job Training	Employees in these occupations usually need one or two years of training involving both on-the-job experience and informal training with experienced workers.
Job Zone Examples	These occupations usually involve using communication and organizational skills to coordinate, supervise, manage, or train others to accomplish goals. Examples include dental assistants, electricians, fish and game wardens, legal secretaries, personnel recruiters, and recreation workers.
SVP Range	(6.0 to < 7.0)
Education	Most occupations in this zone require training in vocational schools, related on-the-job experience, or an associate's degree. Some may require a bachelor's degree.

Work_Styles	Work_Styles Definitions
Analytical Thinking	Job requires analyzing information and using logic to address work-related issues and problems.
Dependability	Job requires being reliable, responsible, and dependable, and fulfilling obligations.
Attention to Detail	Job requires being careful about detail and thorough in completing work tasks.
Integrity	Job requires being honest and ethical.
Achievement/Effort	Job requires establishing and maintaining personally challenging achievement goals and exerting effort toward mastering tasks.
Initiative	Job requires a willingness to take on responsibilities and challenges.
Persistence	Job requires persistence in the face of obstacles.
Innovation	Job requires creativity and alternative thinking to develop new ideas for and answers to work-related problems.
Stress Tolerance	Job requires accepting criticism and dealing calmly and effectively with high stress situations.
Adaptability/Flexibility	Job requires being open to change (positive or negative) and to considerable variety in the workplace.
Cooperation	Job requires being pleasant with others on the job and displaying a good-natured, cooperative attitude.
Self Control	Job requires maintaining composure, keeping emotions in check, controlling anger, and avoiding aggressive behavior, even in very difficult situations.
Leadership	Job requires a willingness to lead, take charge, and offer opinions and direction.
Independence	Job requires developing one's own ways of doing things, guiding oneself with little or no supervision, and depending on oneself to get things done.
Concern for Others	Job requires being sensitive to others' needs and feelings and being understanding and helpful on the job.
Social Orientation	Job requires preferring to work with others rather than alone, and being personally connected with others on the job.

17-3027.00 - Mechanical Engineering Technicians

Apply theory and principles of mechanical engineering to modify, develop, and test machinery and equipment under direction of engineering staff or physical scientists.

Tasks

1) Set up and conduct tests of complete units and components under operational conditions to investigate proposals for improving equipment performance.

2) Discuss changes in design, method of manufacture and assembly, and drafting techniques and procedures with staff and coordinate corrections.

3) Review project instructions and specifications to identify, modify and plan requirements fabrication, assembly and testing.

4) Devise, fabricate, and assemble new or modified mechanical components for products, such as industrial machinery or equipment, and measuring instruments.

5) Prepare parts sketches and write work orders and purchase requests to be furnished by outside contractors.

6) Draft detail drawing or sketch for drafting room completion or to request parts fabrication by machine, sheet or wood shops.

7) Analyze test results in relation to design or rated specifications and test objectives, and modify or adjust equipment to meet specifications.

8) Estimate cost factors, including labor and material for purchased and fabricated parts and costs for assembly, testing, and installing.

9) Read dials and meters to determine amperage, voltage, electrical output and input at specific operating temperature to analyze parts performance.

10) Set up prototype and test apparatus and operate test controlling equipment to observe and record prototype test results.

11) Operate drill press, grinders, engine lathe, or other machines to modify parts tested or to fabricate experimental parts for testing.

12) Evaluate tool drawing designs by measuring drawing dimensions and comparing with original specifications for form and function, using engineering skills.

13) Record test procedures and results, numerical and graphical data, and recommendations for changes in product or test methods.

14) Confer with technicians and submit reports of test results to engineering department and recommend design or material changes.

15) Calculate required capacities for equipment of proposed system to obtain specified performance and submit data to engineering personnel for approval.

16) Test equipment, using test devices attached to generator, voltage regulator, or other electrical parts, such as generators or spark plugs.

17) Inspect lines and figures for clarity and return erroneous drawings to designer for correction.

Knowledge	Knowledge Definitions
Engineering and Technology	Knowledge of the practical application of engineering science and technology. This includes applying principles, techniques, procedures, and equipment to the design and production of various goods and services.
Mechanical	Knowledge of machines and tools, including their designs, uses, repair, and maintenance.
Design	Knowledge of design techniques, tools, and principles involved in production of precision technical plans, blueprints, drawings, and models.
Production and Processing	Knowledge of raw materials, production processes, quality control, costs, and other techniques for maximizing the effective manufacture and distribution of goods.
English Language	Knowledge of the structure and content of the English language including the meaning and spelling of words, rules of composition, and grammar.
Computers and Electronics	Knowledge of circuit boards, processors, chips, electronic equipment, and computer hardware and software, including applications and programming.
Mathematics	Knowledge of arithmetic, algebra, geometry, calculus, statistics, and their applications.
Administration and Management	Knowledge of business and management principles involved in strategic planning, resource allocation, human resources modeling, leadership technique, production methods, and coordination of people and resources.
Customer and Personal Service	Knowledge of principles and processes for providing customer and personal services. This includes customer needs assessment, meeting quality standards for services, and evaluation of customer satisfaction.
Physics	Knowledge and prediction of physical principles, laws, their interrelationships, and applications to understanding fluid, material, and atmospheric dynamics, and mechanical, electrical, atomic and sub-atomic structures and processes.
Public Safety and Security	Knowledge of relevant equipment, policies, procedures, and strategies to promote effective local, state, or national security operations for the protection of people, data, property, and institutions.
Clerical	Knowledge of administrative and clerical procedures and systems such as word processing, managing files and records, stenography and transcription, designing forms, and other office procedures and terminology.
Chemistry	Knowledge of the chemical composition, structure, and properties of substances and of the chemical processes and transformations that they undergo. This includes uses of chemicals and their interactions, danger signs, production techniques, and disposal methods.
Building and Construction	Knowledge of materials, methods, and the tools involved in the construction or repair of houses, buildings, or other structures such as highways and roads.
Education and Training	Knowledge of principles and methods for curriculum and training design, teaching and instruction for individuals and groups, and the measurement of training effects.
Communications and Media	Knowledge of media production, communication, and dissemination techniques and methods. This includes alternative ways to inform and entertain via written, oral, and visual media.
Sales and Marketing	Knowledge of principles and methods for showing, promoting, and selling products or services. This includes marketing strategy and tactics, product demonstration, sales techniques, and sales control systems.
Law and Government	Knowledge of laws, legal codes, court procedures, precedents, government regulations, executive orders, agency rules, and the democratic political process.
Personnel and Human Resources	Knowledge of principles and procedures for personnel recruitment, selection, training, compensation and benefits, labor relations and negotiation, and personnel information systems.

Psychology	Knowledge of human behavior and performance; individual differences in ability, personality, and interests; learning and motivation; psychological research methods; and the assessment and treatment of behavioral and affective disorders.
Transportation	Knowledge of principles and methods for moving people or goods by air, rail, sea, or road, including the relative costs and benefits.
Telecommunications	Knowledge of transmission, broadcasting, switching, control, and operation of telecommunications systems.
Economics and Accounting	Knowledge of economic and accounting principles and practices, the financial markets, banking and the analysis and reporting of financial data.
Geography	Knowledge of principles and methods for describing the features of land, sea, and air masses, including their physical characteristics, locations, interrelationships, and distribution of plant, animal, and human life.
Food Production	Knowledge of techniques and equipment for planting, growing, and harvesting food products (both plant and animal) for consumption, including storage/handling techniques.
Fine Arts	Knowledge of the theory and techniques required to compose, produce, and perform works of music, dance, visual arts, drama, and sculpture.
Biology	Knowledge of plant and animal organisms, their tissues, cells, functions, interdependencies, and interactions with each other and the environment.
Medicine and Dentistry	Knowledge of the information and techniques needed to diagnose and treat human injuries, diseases, and deformities. This includes symptoms, treatment alternatives, drug properties and interactions, and preventive health-care measures.
Therapy and Counseling	Knowledge of principles, methods, and procedures for diagnosis, treatment, and rehabilitation of physical and mental dysfunctions, and for career counseling and guidance.
Philosophy and Theology	Knowledge of different philosophical systems and religions. This includes their basic principles, values, ethics, ways of thinking, customs, practices, and their impact on human culture.
Foreign Language	Knowledge of the structure and content of a foreign (non-English) language including the meaning and spelling of words, rules of composition and grammar, and pronunciation.
Sociology and Anthropology	Knowledge of group behavior and dynamics, societal trends and influences, human migrations, ethnicity, cultures and their history and origins.
History and Archeology	Knowledge of historical events and their causes, indicators, and effects on civilizations and cultures.

Skills	Skills Definitions
Reading Comprehension	Understanding written sentences and paragraphs in work related documents.
Active Listening	Giving full attention to what other people are saying, taking time to understand the points being made, asking questions as appropriate, and not interrupting at inappropriate times.
Coordination	Adjusting actions in relation to others' actions.
Judgment and Decision Making	Considering the relative costs and benefits of potential actions to choose the most appropriate one.
Mathematics	Using mathematics to solve problems.
Complex Problem Solving	Identifying complex problems and reviewing related information to develop and evaluate options and implement solutions.
Time Management	Managing one's own time and the time of others.
Troubleshooting	Determining causes of operating errors and deciding what to do about it.
Active Learning	Understanding the implications of new information for both current and future problem-solving and decision-making.
Equipment Selection	Determining the kind of tools and equipment needed to do a job.
Writing	Communicating effectively in writing as appropriate for the needs of the audience.
Critical Thinking	Using logic and reasoning to identify the strengths and weaknesses of alternative solutions, conclusions or approaches to problems.
Speaking	Talking to others to convey information effectively.
Instructing	Teaching others how to do something.
Learning Strategies	Selecting and using training/instructional methods and procedures appropriate for the situation when learning or teaching new things.
Service Orientation	Actively looking for ways to help people.
Operations Analysis	Analyzing needs and product requirements to create a design.

Technology Design	Generating or adapting equipment and technology to serve user needs.
Science	Using scientific rules and methods to solve problems.
Monitoring	Monitoring/Assessing performance of yourself, other individuals, or organizations to make improvements or take corrective action.
Installation	Installing equipment, machines, wiring, or programs to meet specifications.
Systems Evaluation	Identifying measures or indicators of system performance and the actions needed to improve or correct performance, relative to the goals of the system.
Quality Control Analysis	Conducting tests and inspections of products, services, or processes to evaluate quality or performance.
Operation and Control	Controlling operations of equipment or systems.
Operation Monitoring	Watching gauges, dials, or other indicators to make sure a machine is working properly.
Management of Personnel Resources	Motivating, developing, and directing people as they work, identifying the best people for the job.
Repairing	Repairing machines or systems using the needed tools.
Management of Material Resources	Obtaining and seeing to the appropriate use of equipment, facilities, and materials needed to do certain work.
Negotiation	Bringing others together and trying to reconcile differences.
Systems Analysis	Determining how a system should work and how changes in conditions, operations, and the environment will affect outcomes.
Equipment Maintenance	Performing routine maintenance on equipment and determining when and what kind of maintenance is needed.
Persuasion	Persuading others to change their minds or behavior.
Social Perceptiveness	Being aware of others' reactions and understanding why they react as they do.
Management of Financial Resources	Determining how money will be spent to get the work done, and accounting for these expenditures.
Programming	Writing computer programs for various purposes.

Ability	Ability Definitions
Deductive Reasoning	The ability to apply general rules to specific problems to produce answers that make sense.
Written Comprehension	The ability to read and understand information and ideas presented in writing.
Near Vision	The ability to see details at close range (within a few feet of the observer).
Oral Comprehension	The ability to listen to and understand information and ideas presented through spoken words and sentences.
Problem Sensitivity	The ability to tell when something is wrong or is likely to go wrong. It does not involve solving the problem, only recognizing there is a problem.
Information Ordering	The ability to arrange things or actions in a certain order or pattern according to a specific rule or set of rules (e.g., patterns of numbers, letters, words, pictures, mathematical operations).
Inductive Reasoning	The ability to combine pieces of information to form general rules or conclusions (includes finding a relationship among seemingly unrelated events).
Oral Expression	The ability to communicate information and ideas in speaking so others will understand.
Visualization	The ability to imagine how something will look after it is moved around or when its parts are moved or rearranged.
Speech Clarity	The ability to speak clearly so others can understand you.
Finger Dexterity	The ability to make precisely coordinated movements of the fingers of one or both hands to grasp, manipulate, or assemble very small objects.
Flexibility of Closure	The ability to identify or detect a known pattern (a figure, object, word, or sound) that is hidden in other distracting material.
Written Expression	The ability to communicate information and ideas in writing so others will understand.
Mathematical Reasoning	The ability to choose the right mathematical methods or formulas to solve a problem.
Selective Attention	The ability to concentrate on a task over a period of time without being distracted.
Speech Recognition	The ability to identify and understand the speech of another person.
Depth Perception	The ability to judge which of several objects is closer or farther away from you, or to judge the distance between you and an object.
Visual Color Discrimination	The ability to match or detect differences between colors, including shades of color and brightness.

Ability	Definition
Perceptual Speed	The ability to quickly and accurately compare similarities and differences among sets of letters, numbers, objects, pictures, or patterns. The things to be compared may be presented at the same time or one after the other. This ability also includes comparing a presented object with a remembered object.
Category Flexibility	The ability to generate or use different sets of rules for combining or grouping things in different ways.
Far Vision	The ability to see details at a distance.
Originality	The ability to come up with unusual or clever ideas about a given topic or situation, or to develop creative ways to solve a problem.
Fluency of Ideas	The ability to come up with a number of ideas about a topic (the number of ideas is important, not their quality, correctness, or creativity).
Memorization	The ability to remember information such as words, numbers, pictures, and procedures.
Hearing Sensitivity	The ability to detect or tell the differences between sounds that vary in pitch and loudness.
Arm-Hand Steadiness	The ability to keep your hand and arm steady while moving your arm or while holding your arm and hand in one position.
Control Precision	The ability to quickly and repeatedly adjust the controls of a machine or a vehicle to exact positions.
Auditory Attention	The ability to focus on a single source of sound in the presence of other distracting sounds.
Number Facility	The ability to add, subtract, multiply, or divide quickly and correctly.
Reaction Time	The ability to quickly respond (with the hand, finger, or foot) to a signal (sound, light, picture) when it appears.
Time Sharing	The ability to shift back and forth between two or more activities or sources of information (such as speech, sounds, touch, or other sources).
Manual Dexterity	The ability to quickly move your hand, your hand together with your arm, or your two hands to grasp, manipulate, or assemble objects.
Multilimb Coordination	The ability to coordinate two or more limbs (for example, two arms, two legs, or one leg and one arm) while sitting, standing, or lying down. It does not involve performing the activities while the whole body is in motion.
Trunk Strength	The ability to use your abdominal and lower back muscles to support part of the body repeatedly or continuously over time without 'giving out' or fatiguing.
Speed of Closure	The ability to quickly make sense of, combine, and organize information into meaningful patterns.
Static Strength	The ability to exert maximum muscle force to lift, push, pull, or carry objects.
Response Orientation	The ability to choose quickly between two or more movements in response to two or more different signals (lights, sounds, pictures). It includes the speed with which the correct response is started with the hand, foot, or other body part.
Dynamic Strength	The ability to exert muscle force repeatedly or continuously over time. This involves muscular endurance and resistance to muscle fatigue.
Rate Control	The ability to time your movements or the movement of a piece of equipment in anticipation of changes in the speed and/or direction of a moving object or scene.
Stamina	The ability to exert yourself physically over long periods of time without getting winded or out of breath.
Spatial Orientation	The ability to know your location in relation to the environment or to know where other objects are in relation to you.
Peripheral Vision	The ability to see objects or movement of objects to one's side when the eyes are looking ahead.
Gross Body Coordination	The ability to coordinate the movement of your arms, legs, and torso together when the whole body is in motion.
Wrist-Finger Speed	The ability to make fast, simple, repeated movements of the fingers, hands, and wrists.
Extent Flexibility	The ability to bend, stretch, twist, or reach with your body, arms, and/or legs.
Sound Localization	The ability to tell the direction from which a sound originated.
Gross Body Equilibrium	The ability to keep or regain your body balance or stay upright when in an unstable position.
Speed of Limb Movement	The ability to quickly move the arms and legs.
Night Vision	The ability to see under low light conditions.
Glare Sensitivity	The ability to see objects in the presence of glare or bright lighting.
Explosive Strength	The ability to use short bursts of muscle force to propel oneself (as in jumping or sprinting), or to throw an object.
Dynamic Flexibility	The ability to quickly and repeatedly bend, stretch, twist, or reach out with your body, arms, and/or legs.

Work_Activity	Work_Activity Definitions
Getting Information	Observing, receiving, and otherwise obtaining information from all relevant sources.
Interacting With Computers	Using computers and computer systems (including hardware and software) to program, write software, set up functions, enter data, or process information.
Communicating with Supervisors, Peers, or Subordin	Providing information to supervisors, co-workers, and subordinates by telephone, in written form, e-mail, or in person.
Identifying Objects, Actions, and Events	Identifying information by categorizing, estimating, recognizing differences or similarities, and detecting changes in circumstances or events.
Evaluating Information to Determine Compliance wit	Using relevant information and individual judgment to determine whether events or processes comply with laws, regulations, or standards.
Establishing and Maintaining Interpersonal Relatio	Developing constructive and cooperative working relationships with others, and maintaining them over time.
Making Decisions and Solving Problems	Analyzing information and evaluating results to choose the best solution and solve problems.
Drafting, Laying Out, and Specifying Technical Dev	Providing documentation, detailed instructions, drawings, or specifications to tell others about how devices, parts, equipment, or structures are to be fabricated, constructed, assembled, modified, maintained, or used.
Documenting/Recording Information	Entering, transcribing, recording, storing, or maintaining information in written or electronic/magnetic form.
Estimating the Quantifiable Characteristics of Pro	Estimating sizes, distances, and quantities; or determining time, costs, resources, or materials needed to perform a work activity.
Controlling Machines and Processes	Using either control mechanisms or direct physical activity to operate machines or processes (not including computers or vehicles).
Monitor Processes, Materials, or Surroundings	Monitoring and reviewing information from materials, events, or the environment, to detect or assess problems.
Updating and Using Relevant Knowledge	Keeping up-to-date technically and applying new knowledge to your job.
Communicating with Persons Outside Organization	Communicating with people outside the organization, representing the organization to customers, the public, government, and other external sources. This information can be exchanged in person, in writing, or by telephone or e-mail.
Thinking Creatively	Developing, designing, or creating new applications, ideas, relationships, systems, or products, including artistic contributions.
Inspecting Equipment, Structures, or Material	Inspecting equipment, structures, or materials to identify the cause of errors or other problems or defects.
Processing Information	Compiling, coding, categorizing, calculating, tabulating, auditing, or verifying information or data.
Scheduling Work and Activities	Scheduling events, programs, and activities, as well as the work of others.
Repairing and Maintaining Mechanical Equipment	Servicing, repairing, adjusting, and testing machines, devices, moving parts, and equipment that operate primarily on the basis of mechanical (not electronic) principles.
Training and Teaching Others	Identifying the educational needs of others, developing formal educational or training programs or classes, and teaching or instructing others.
Performing General Physical Activities	Performing physical activities that require considerable use of your arms and legs and moving your whole body, such as climbing, lifting, balancing, walking, stooping, and handling of materials.
Interpreting the Meaning of Information for Others	Translating or explaining what information means and how it can be used.
Judging the Qualities of Things, Services, or Peop	Assessing the value, importance, or quality of things or people.
Handling and Moving Objects	Using hands and arms in handling, installing, positioning, and moving materials, and manipulating things.
Coaching and Developing Others	Identifying the developmental needs of others and coaching, mentoring, or otherwise helping others to improve their knowledge or skills.
Guiding, Directing, and Motivating Subordinates	Providing guidance and direction to subordinates, including setting performance standards and monitoring performance.
Operating Vehicles, Mechanized Devices, or Equipme	Running, maneuvering, navigating, or driving vehicles or mechanized equipment, such as forklifts, passenger vehicles, aircraft, or water craft.
Organizing, Planning, and Prioritizing Work	Developing specific goals and plans to prioritize, organize, and accomplish your work.

Repairing and Maintaining Electronic Equipment	Servicing, repairing, calibrating, regulating, fine-tuning, or testing machines, devices, and equipment that operate primarily on the basis of electrical or electronic (not mechanical) principles.
Coordinating the Work and Activities of Others	Getting members of a group to work together to accomplish tasks.
Analyzing Data or Information	Identifying the underlying principles, reasons, or facts of information by breaking down information or data into separate parts.
Performing Administrative Activities	Performing day-to-day administrative tasks such as maintaining information files and processing paperwork.
Developing and Building Teams	Encouraging and building mutual trust, respect, and cooperation among team members.
Provide Consultation and Advice to Others	Providing guidance and expert advice to management or other groups on technical, systems-, or process-related topics.
Resolving Conflicts and Negotiating with Others	Handling complaints, settling disputes, and resolving grievances and conflicts, or otherwise negotiating with others.
Monitoring and Controlling Resources	Monitoring and controlling resources and overseeing the spending of money.
Assisting and Caring for Others	Providing personal assistance, medical attention, emotional support, or other personal care to others such as coworkers, customers, or patients.
Developing Objectives and Strategies	Establishing long-range objectives and specifying the strategies and actions to achieve them.
Selling or Influencing Others	Convincing others to buy merchandise/goods or to otherwise change their minds or actions.
Staffing Organizational Units	Recruiting, interviewing, selecting, hiring, and promoting employees in an organization.
Performing for or Working Directly with the Public	Performing for people or dealing directly with the public. This includes serving customers in restaurants and stores, and receiving clients or guests.

Work_Context   Work_Context Definitions

Face-to-Face Discussions	How often do you have to have face-to-face discussions with individuals or teams in this job?
Telephone	How often do you have telephone conversations in this job?
Wear Common Protective or Safety Equipment such as	How much does this job require wearing common protective or safety equipment such as safety shoes, glasses, gloves, hard hats or life jackets?
Structured versus Unstructured Work	To what extent is this job structured for the worker, rather than allowing the worker to determine tasks, priorities, and goals?
Electronic Mail	How often do you use electronic mail in this job?
Freedom to Make Decisions	How much decision making freedom, without supervision, does the job offer?
Impact of Decisions on Co-workers or Company Resul	How do the decisions an employee makes impact the results of co-workers, clients or the company?
Contact With Others	How much does this job require the worker to be in contact with others (face-to-face, by telephone, or otherwise) in order to perform it?
Responsible for Others' Health and Safety	How much responsibility is there for the health and safety of others in this job?
Consequence of Error	How serious would the result usually be if the worker made a mistake that was not readily correctable?
Coordinate or Lead Others	How important is it to coordinate or lead others in accomplishing work activities in this job?
Work With Work Group or Team	How important is it to work with others in a group or team in this job?
Responsibility for Outcomes and Results	How responsible is the worker for work outcomes and results of other workers?
Letters and Memos	How often does the job require written letters and memos?
Indoors, Environmentally Controlled	How often does this job require working indoors in environmentally controlled conditions?
Importance of Being Exact or Accurate	How important is being very exact or highly accurate in performing this job?
Exposed to Contaminants	How often does this job require working exposed to contaminants (such as pollutants, gases, dust or odors)?
Exposed to Hazardous Equipment	How often does this job require exposure to hazardous equipment?
Sounds, Noise Levels Are Distracting or Uncomforta	How often does this job require working exposed to sounds and noise levels that are distracting or uncomfortable?
Frequency of Decision Making	How frequently is the worker required to make decisions that affect other people, the financial resources, and/or the image and reputation of the organization?
Indoors, Not Environmentally Controlled	How often does this job require working indoors in non-controlled environmental conditions (e.g., warehouse without heat)?

Spend Time Sitting	How much does this job require sitting?
Time Pressure	How often does this job require the worker to meet strict deadlines?
Physical Proximity	To what extent does this job require the worker to perform job tasks in close physical proximity to other people?
Deal With External Customers	How important is it to work with external customers or the public in this job?
Spend Time Standing	How much does this job require standing?
Very Hot or Cold Temperatures	How often does this job require working in very hot (above 90 F degrees) or very cold (below 32 F degrees) temperatures?
Frequency of Conflict Situations	How often are there conflict situations the employee has to face in this job?
Spend Time Using Your Hands to Handle, Control, or	How much does this job require using your hands to handle, control, or feel objects, tools or controls?
Level of Competition	To what extent does this job require the worker to compete or to be aware of competitive pressures?
Extremely Bright or Inadequate Lighting	How often does this job require working in extremely bright or inadequate lighting conditions?
Exposed to High Places	How often does this job require exposure to high places?
Outdoors, Exposed to Weather	How often does this job require working outdoors, exposed to all weather conditions?
Exposed to Hazardous Conditions	How often does this job require exposure to hazardous conditions?
Outdoors, Under Cover	How often does this job require working outdoors, under cover (e.g., structure with roof but no walls)?
Deal With Unpleasant or Angry People	How frequently does the worker have to deal with unpleasant, angry, or discourteous individuals as part of the job requirements?
Spend Time Walking and Running	How much does this job require walking and running?
Cramped Work Space, Awkward Positions	How often does this job require working in cramped work spaces that requires getting into awkward positions?
Exposed to Minor Burns, Cuts, Bites, or Stings	How often does this job require exposure to minor burns, cuts, bites, or stings?
In an Enclosed Vehicle or Equipment	How often does this job require working in a closed vehicle or equipment (e.g., car)?
Spend Time Bending or Twisting the Body	How much does this job require bending or twisting your body?
Spend Time Climbing Ladders, Scaffolds, or Poles	How much does this job require climbing ladders, scaffolds, or poles?
Spend Time Making Repetitive Motions	How much does this job require making repetitive motions?
Degree of Automation	How automated is the job?
Wear Specialized Protective or Safety Equipment su	How much does this job require wearing specialized protective or safety equipment such as breathing apparatus, safety harness, full protection suits, or radiation protection?
Spend Time Kneeling, Crouching, Stooping, or Crawl	How much does this job require kneeling, crouching, stooping, or crawling?
Spend Time Keeping or Regaining Balance	How much does this job require keeping or regaining your balance?
Importance of Repeating Same Tasks	How important is repeating the same physical activities (e.g., key entry) or mental activities (e.g., checking entries in a ledger) over and over, without stopping, or performing this job?
Public Speaking	How often do you have to perform public speaking in this job?
Pace Determined by Speed of Equipment	How important is it to this job that the pace is determined by the speed of equipment or machinery? (This does not refer to keeping busy at all times on this job.)
Exposed to Radiation	How often does this job require exposure to radiation?
Exposed to Whole Body Vibration	How often does this job require exposure to whole body vibration (e.g., operate a jackhammer)?
Deal With Physically Aggressive People	How frequently does this job require the worker to deal with physical aggression of violent individuals?
In an Open Vehicle or Equipment	How often does this job require working in an open vehicle or equipment (e.g., tractor)?
Exposed to Disease or Infections	How often does this job require exposure to disease/infections?

Job Zone Component   Job Zone Component Definitions

Title	Job Zone Three: Medium Preparation Needed

Overall Experience	Previous work-related skill, knowledge, or experience is required for these occupations. For example, an electrician must have completed three or four years of apprenticeship or several years of vocational training, and often must have passed a licensing exam, in order to perform the job.
Job Training	Employees in these occupations usually need one or two years of training involving both on-the-job experience and informal training with experienced workers.
Job Zone Examples	These occupations usually involve using communication and organizational skills to coordinate, supervise, manage, or train others to accomplish goals. Examples include dental assistants, electricians,fish and game wardens, legal secretaries, personnel recruiters, and recreation workers.
SVP Range	(6.0 to < 7.0)
Education	Most occupations in this zone require training in vocational schools, related on-the-job experience, or an associate's degree. Some may require a bachelor's degree.

Work_Styles	Work_Styles Definitions
Attention to Detail	Job requires being careful about detail and thorough in completing work tasks.
Analytical Thinking	Job requires analyzing information and using logic to address work-related issues and problems.
Dependability	Job requires being reliable, responsible, and dependable, and fulfilling obligations.
Cooperation	Job requires being pleasant with others on the job and displaying a good-natured, cooperative attitude.
Innovation	Job requires creativity and alternative thinking to develop new ideas for and answers to work-related problems.
Initiative	Job requires a willingness to take on responsibilities and challenges.
Achievement/Effort	Job requires establishing and maintaining personally challenging achievement goals and exerting effort toward mastering tasks.
Persistence	Job requires persistence in the face of obstacles.
Self Control	Job requires maintaining composure, keeping emotions in check, controlling anger, and avoiding aggressive behavior, even in very difficult situations.
Integrity	Job requires being honest and ethical.
Independence	Job requires developing one's own ways of doing things, guiding oneself with little or no supervision, and depending on oneself to get things done.
Leadership	Job requires a willingness to lead, take charge, and offer opinions and direction.
Stress Tolerance	Job requires accepting criticism and dealing calmly and effectively with high stress situations.
Adaptability/Flexibility	Job requires being open to change (positive or negative) and to considerable variety in the workplace.
Social Orientation	Job requires preferring to work with others rather than alone, and being personally connected with others on the job.
Concern for Others	Job requires being sensitive to others' needs and feelings and being understanding and helpful on the job.

17-3031.02 - Mapping Technicians

Calculate mapmaking information from field notes, and draw and verify accuracy of topographical maps.

Tasks

1) Trim, align, and join prints in order to form photographic mosaics, maintaining scaled distances between reference points.

2) Trace contours and topographic details in order to generate maps that denote specific land and property locations and geographic attributes.

3) Redraw and correct maps, such as revising parcel maps to reflect tax code area changes, using information from official records and surveys.

4) Produce representations of surface and mineral ownership layers, by interpreting legal survey plans.

5) Complete detailed source and method notes detailing the location of routine and complex land parcels.

6) Produce and update overlay maps in order to show information boundaries, water

locations, and topographic features on various base maps and at different scales.

7) Identify, research, and resolve anomalies in legal land descriptions, referring issues to title and survey experts as appropriate.

8) Monitor mapping work and the updating of maps in order to ensure accuracy, the inclusion of new and/or changed information, and compliance with rules and regulations.

9) Lay out and match aerial photographs in sequences in which they were taken, and identify any areas missing from photographs.

10) Check all layers of maps in order to ensure accuracy, identifying and marking errors and making corrections.

11) Create survey description pages and historical records related to the mapping activities and specifications of section plats.

12) Identify and compile database information in order to create maps in response to requests.

13) Research resources such as survey maps and legal descriptions in order to verify property lines and to obtain information needed for mapping.

14) Supervise and coordinate activities of workers engaged in plotting data and drafting maps; or in producing blueprints, photostats, and photographs.

15) Form three-dimensional images of aerial photographs taken from different locations, using mathematical techniques and plotting instruments.

16) Answer questions and provide information to the public and to staff members regarding assessment maps, surveys, boundaries, easements, property ownership, roads, zoning, and similar matters.

17) Enter GPS data, legal deeds, field notes, and land survey reports into GIS workstations so that information can be transformed into graphic land descriptions, such as maps and drawings.

18) Calculate latitudes, longitudes, angles, areas, and other information for mapmaking, using survey field notes and reference tables.

19) Compare topographical features and contour lines with images from aerial photographs, old maps, and other reference materials in order to verify the accuracy of their identification.

20) Compute and measure scaled distances between reference points in order to establish relative positions of adjoining prints and enable the creation of photographic mosaics.

21) Train staff members in duties such as tax mapping, the use of computerized mapping equipment, and the interpretation of source documents.

22) Determine scales, line sizes, and colors to be used for hard copies of computerized maps, using plotters.

23) Analyze aerial photographs in order to detect and interpret significant military, industrial, resource, or topographical data.

19-1012.00 - Food Scientists and Technologists

Use chemistry, microbiology, engineering, and other sciences to study the principles underlying the processing and deterioration of foods; analyze food content to determine levels of vitamins, fat, sugar, and protein; discover new food sources; research ways to make processed foods safe, palatable, and healthful; and apply food science knowledge to determine best ways to process, package, preserve, store, and distribute food.

Tasks

1) Evaluate food processing and storage operations, and assist in the development of quality assurance programs for such operations.

2) Test new products for flavor, texture, color, nutritional content, and adherence to government and industry standards.

3) Inspect food processing areas in order to ensure compliance with government regulations and standards for sanitation, safety, quality, and waste management standards.

4) Confer with process engineers, plant operators, flavor experts, and packaging and marketing specialists in order to resolve problems in product development.

5) Check raw ingredients for maturity or stability for processing, and finished products for safety, quality and nutritional value.

6) Search for substitutes for harmful or undesirable additives, such as nitrites.

7) Develop food standards and production specifications, safety and sanitary regulations, and waste management and water supply specifications.

8) Demonstrate products to clients.

9) Study the structure and composition of food, or the changes foods undergo in storage and processing.

10) Study methods to improve aspects of foods such as chemical composition, flavor, color, texture, nutritional value, and convenience.

19-1020.01 - Biologists

Research or study basic principles of plant and animal life, such as origin, relationship, development, anatomy, and functions.

Tasks

1) Communicate test results to state and federal representatives and general public.

2) Program and use computers to store, process and analyze data.

3) Collect and analyze biological data about relationships among and between organisms and their environment.

4) Develop and maintain liaisons and effective working relations with groups and individuals, agencies, and the public to encourage cooperative management strategies or to develop information and interpret findings.

5) Study aquatic plants and animals and environmental conditions affecting them, such as radioactivity or pollution.

6) Identify, classify, and study structure, behavior, ecology, physiology, nutrition, culture, and distribution of plant and animal species.

7) Prepare environmental impact reports for industry, government, or publication.

8) Measure salinity, acidity, light, oxygen content, and other physical conditions of water to determine their relationship to aquatic life.

9) Study basic principles of plant and animal life, such as origin, relationship, development, anatomy, and functions.

10) Study and manage wild animal populations.

11) Supervise biological technicians and technologists and other scientists.

12) Prepare requests for proposals or statements of work.

13) Develop methods and apparatus for securing representative plant, animal, aquatic, or soil samples.

14) Study reactions of plants, animals, and marine species to parasites.

15) Plan and administer biological research programs for government, research firms, medical industries, or manufacturing firms.

16) Review reports such as those relating to land use classifications and recreational development for accuracy and adequacy.

17) Prepare plans for management of renewable resources.

18) Research environmental effects of present and potential uses of land and water areas, determining methods of improving environmental conditions or such outputs as crop yields.

19) Cultivate, breed, and grow aquatic life, such as lobsters, clams, or fish.

20) Develop pest management and control measures, and conduct risk assessments related to pest exclusion, using scientific methods.

21) Teach, supervise students and perform research at universities and colleges.

Knowledge	Knowledge Definitions
Biology	Knowledge of plant and animal organisms, their tissues, cells, functions, interdependencies, and interactions with each other and the environment.
Law and Government	Knowledge of laws, legal codes, court procedures, precedents, government regulations, executive orders, agency rules, and the democratic political process.
Chemistry	Knowledge of the chemical composition, structure, and properties of substances and of the chemical processes and transformations that they undergo. This includes uses of chemicals and their interactions, danger signs, production techniques, and disposal methods.
English Language	Knowledge of the structure and content of the English language including the meaning and spelling of words, rules of composition, and grammar.
Computers and Electronics	Knowledge of circuit boards, processors, chips, electronic equipment, and computer hardware and software, including applications and programming.
Customer and Personal Service	Knowledge of principles and processes for providing customer and personal services. This includes customer needs assessment, meeting quality standards for services, and evaluation of customer satisfaction.
Public Safety and Security	Knowledge of relevant equipment, policies, procedures, and strategies to promote effective local, state, or national security operations for the protection of people, data, property, and institutions.
Mathematics	Knowledge of arithmetic, algebra, geometry, calculus, statistics, and their applications.
Geography	Knowledge of principles and methods for describing the features of land, sea, and air masses, including their physical characteristics, locations, interrelationships, and distribution of plant, animal, and human life.
Engineering and Technology	Knowledge of the practical application of engineering science and technology. This includes applying principles, techniques, procedures, and equipment to the design and production of various goods and services.
Clerical	Knowledge of administrative and clerical procedures and systems such as word processing, managing files and records, stenography and transcription, designing forms, and other office procedures and terminology.
Administration and Management	Knowledge of business and management principles involved in strategic planning, resource allocation, human resources modeling, leadership technique, production methods, and coordination of people and resources.
Education and Training	Knowledge of principles and methods for curriculum and training design, teaching and instruction for individuals and groups, and the measurement of training effects.
Communications and Media	Knowledge of media production, communication, and dissemination techniques and methods. This includes alternative ways to inform and entertain via written, oral, and visual media.
Physics	Knowledge and prediction of physical principles, laws, their interrelationships, and applications to understanding fluid, material, and atmospheric dynamics, and mechanical, electrical, atomic and sub-atomic structures and processes.
Mechanical	Knowledge of machines and tools, including their designs, uses, repair, and maintenance.
Design	Knowledge of design techniques, tools, and principles involved in production of precision technical plans, blueprints, drawings, and models.
Transportation	Knowledge of principles and methods for moving people or goods by air, rail, sea, or road, including the relative costs and benefits.
Building and Construction	Knowledge of materials, methods, and the tools involved in the construction or repair of houses, buildings, or other structures such as highways and roads.
Medicine and Dentistry	Knowledge of the information and techniques needed to diagnose and treat human injuries, diseases, and deformities. This includes symptoms, treatment alternatives, drug properties and interactions, and preventive health-care measures.
Psychology	Knowledge of human behavior and performance; individual differences in ability, personality, and interests; learning and motivation; psychological research methods; and the assessment and treatment of behavioral and affective disorders.
History and Archeology	Knowledge of historical events and their causes, indicators, and effects on civilizations and cultures.
Personnel and Human Resources	Knowledge of principles and procedures for personnel recruitment, selection, training, compensation and benefits, labor relations and negotiation, and personnel information systems.
Telecommunications	Knowledge of transmission, broadcasting, switching, control, and operation of telecommunications systems.
Economics and Accounting	Knowledge of economic and accounting principles and practices, the financial markets, banking and the analysis and reporting of financial data.
Production and Processing	Knowledge of raw materials, production processes, quality control, costs, and other techniques for maximizing the effective manufacture and distribution of goods.
Sales and Marketing	Knowledge of principles and methods for showing, promoting, and selling products or services. This includes marketing strategy and tactics, product demonstration, sales techniques, and sales control systems.
Foreign Language	Knowledge of the structure and content of a foreign (non-English) language including the meaning and spelling of words, rules of composition and grammar, and pronunciation.

Therapy and Counseling	Knowledge of principles, methods, and procedures for diagnosis, treatment, and rehabilitation of physical and mental dysfunctions, and for career counseling and guidance.
Philosophy and Theology	Knowledge of different philosophical systems and religions. This includes their basic principles, values, ethics, ways of thinking, customs, practices, and their impact on human culture.
Sociology and Anthropology	Knowledge of group behavior and dynamics, societal trends and influences, human migrations, ethnicity, cultures and their history and origins.
Food Production	Knowledge of techniques and equipment for planting, growing, and harvesting food products (both plant and animal) for consumption, including storage/handling techniques.
Fine Arts	Knowledge of the theory and techniques required to compose, produce, and perform works of music, dance, visual arts, drama, and sculpture.

Skills	Skills Definitions
Science	Using scientific rules and methods to solve problems.
Reading Comprehension	Understanding written sentences and paragraphs in work related documents.
Time Management	Managing one's own time and the time of others.
Judgment and Decision Making	Considering the relative costs and benefits of potential actions to choose the most appropriate one.
Critical Thinking	Using logic and reasoning to identify the strengths and weaknesses of alternative solutions, conclusions or approaches to problems.
Active Listening	Giving full attention to what other people are saying, taking time to understand the points being made, asking questions as appropriate, and not interrupting at inappropriate times.
Writing	Communicating effectively in writing as appropriate for the needs of the audience.
Active Learning	Understanding the implications of new information for both current and future problem-solving and decision-making.
Complex Problem Solving	Identifying complex problems and reviewing related information to develop and evaluate options and implement solutions.
Equipment Selection	Determining the kind of tools and equipment needed to do a job.
Persuasion	Persuading others to change their minds or behavior.
Management of Material Resources	Obtaining and seeing to the appropriate use of equipment, facilities, and materials needed to do certain work.
Negotiation	Bringing others together and trying to reconcile differences.
Management of Financial Resources	Determining how money will be spent to get the work done, and accounting for these expenditures.
Coordination	Adjusting actions in relation to others' actions.
Monitoring	Monitoring/Assessing performance of yourself, other individuals, or organizations to make improvements or take corrective action.
Mathematics	Using mathematics to solve problems.
Management of Personnel Resources	Motivating, developing, and directing people as they work, identifying the best people for the job.
Speaking	Talking to others to convey information effectively.
Learning Strategies	Selecting and using training/instructional methods and procedures appropriate for the situation when learning or teaching new things.
Social Perceptiveness	Being aware of others' reactions and understanding why they react as they do.
Instructing	Teaching others how to do something.
Service Orientation	Actively looking for ways to help people.
Troubleshooting	Determining causes of operating errors and deciding what to do about it.
Quality Control Analysis	Conducting tests and inspections of products, services, or processes to evaluate quality or performance.
Operations Analysis	Analyzing needs and product requirements to create a design.
Systems Evaluation	Identifying measures or indicators of system performance and the actions needed to improve or correct performance, relative to the goals of the system.
Systems Analysis	Determining how a system should work and how changes in conditions, operations, and the environment will affect outcomes.
Equipment Maintenance	Performing routine maintenance on equipment and determining when and what kind of maintenance is needed.
Technology Design	Generating or adapting equipment and technology to serve user needs.
Operation Monitoring	Watching gauges, dials, or other indicators to make sure a machine is working properly.

Operation and Control	Controlling operations of equipment or systems.
Repairing	Repairing machines or systems using the needed tools.
Installation	Installing equipment, machines, wiring, or programs to meet specifications.
Programming	Writing computer programs for various purposes.

Ability	Ability Definitions
Oral Expression	The ability to communicate information and ideas in speaking so others will understand.
Inductive Reasoning	The ability to combine pieces of information to form general rules or conclusions (includes finding a relationship among seemingly unrelated events).
Written Expression	The ability to communicate information and ideas in writing so others will understand.
Near Vision	The ability to see details at close range (within a few feet of the observer).
Written Comprehension	The ability to read and understand information and ideas presented in writing.
Category Flexibility	The ability to generate or use different sets of rules for combining or grouping things in different ways.
Speech Clarity	The ability to speak clearly so others can understand you.
Information Ordering	The ability to arrange things or actions in a certain order or pattern according to a specific rule or set of rules (e.g., patterns of numbers, letters, words, pictures, mathematical operations).
Speech Recognition	The ability to identify and understand the speech of another person.
Oral Comprehension	The ability to listen to and understand information and ideas presented through spoken words and sentences.
Problem Sensitivity	The ability to tell when something is wrong or is likely to go wrong. It does not involve solving the problem, only recognizing there is a problem.
Deductive Reasoning	The ability to apply general rules to specific problems to produce answers that make sense.
Flexibility of Closure	The ability to identify or detect a known pattern (a figure, object, word, or sound) that is hidden in other distracting material.
Mathematical Reasoning	The ability to choose the right mathematical methods or formulas to solve a problem.
Finger Dexterity	The ability to make precisely coordinated movements of the fingers of one or both hands to grasp, manipulate, or assemble very small objects.
Selective Attention	The ability to concentrate on a task over a period of time without being distracted.
Auditory Attention	The ability to focus on a single source of sound in the presence of other distracting sounds.
Originality	The ability to come up with unusual or clever ideas about a given topic or situation, or to develop creative ways to solve a problem.
Visual Color Discrimination	The ability to match or detect differences between colors, including shades of color and brightness.
Perceptual Speed	The ability to quickly and accurately compare similarities and differences among sets of letters, numbers, objects, pictures, or patterns. The things to be compared may be presented at the same time or one after the other. This ability also includes comparing a presented object with a remembered object.
Fluency of Ideas	The ability to come up with a number of ideas about a topic (the number of ideas is important, not their quality, correctness, or creativity).
Memorization	The ability to remember information such as words, numbers, pictures, and procedures.
Speed of Closure	The ability to quickly make sense of, combine, and organize information into meaningful patterns.
Far Vision	The ability to see details at a distance.
Number Facility	The ability to add, subtract, multiply, or divide quickly and correctly.
Time Sharing	The ability to shift back and forth between two or more activities or sources of information (such as speech, sounds, touch, or other sources).
Multilimb Coordination	The ability to coordinate two or more limbs (for example, two arms, two legs, or one leg and one arm) while sitting, standing, or lying down. It does not involve performing the activities while the whole body is in motion.
Visualization	The ability to imagine how something will look after it is moved around or when its parts are moved or rearranged.
Control Precision	The ability to quickly and repeatedly adjust the controls of a machine or a vehicle to exact positions.

Arm-Hand Steadiness	The ability to keep your hand and arm steady while moving your arm or while holding your arm and hand in one position.
Depth Perception	The ability to judge which of several objects is closer or farther away from you, or to judge the distance between you and an object.
Hearing Sensitivity	The ability to detect or tell the differences between sounds that vary in pitch and loudness.
Trunk Strength	The ability to use your abdominal and lower back muscles to support part of the body repeatedly or continuously over time without 'giving out' or fatiguing.
Spatial Orientation	The ability to know your location in relation to the environment or to know where other objects are in relation to you.
Manual Dexterity	The ability to quickly move your hand, your hand together with your arm, or your two hands to grasp, manipulate, or assemble objects.
Static Strength	The ability to exert maximum muscle force to lift, push, pull, or carry objects.
Night Vision	The ability to see under low light conditions.
Wrist-Finger Speed	The ability to make fast, simple, repeated movements of the fingers, hands, and wrists.
Peripheral Vision	The ability to see objects or movement of objects to one's side when the eyes are looking ahead.
Response Orientation	The ability to choose quickly between two or more movements in response to two or more different signals (lights, sounds, pictures). It includes the speed with which the correct response is started with the hand, foot, or other body part.
Reaction Time	The ability to quickly respond (with the hand, finger, or foot) to a signal (sound, light, picture) when it appears.
Speed of Limb Movement	The ability to quickly move the arms and legs.
Glare Sensitivity	The ability to see objects in the presence of glare or bright lighting.
Dynamic Strength	The ability to exert muscle force repeatedly or continuously over time. This involves muscular endurance and resistance to muscle fatigue.
Stamina	The ability to exert yourself physically over long periods of time without getting winded or out of breath.
Extent Flexibility	The ability to bend, stretch, twist, or reach with your body, arms, and/or legs.
Dynamic Flexibility	The ability to quickly and repeatedly bend, stretch, twist, or reach out with your body, arms, and/or legs.
Gross Body Equilibrium	The ability to keep or regain your body balance or stay upright when in an unstable position.
Rate Control	The ability to time your movements or the movement of a piece of equipment in anticipation of changes in the speed and/or direction of a moving object or scene.
Explosive Strength	The ability to use short bursts of muscle force to propel oneself (as in jumping or sprinting), or to throw an object.
Sound Localization	The ability to tell the direction from which a sound originated.
Gross Body Coordination	The ability to coordinate the movement of your arms, legs, and torso together when the whole body is in motion.

Work_Activity	**Work_Activity Definitions**
Getting Information	Observing, receiving, and otherwise obtaining information from all relevant sources.
Interacting With Computers	Using computers and computer systems (including hardware and software) to program, write software, set up functions, enter data, or process information.
Documenting/Recording Information	Entering, transcribing, recording, storing, or maintaining information in written or electronic/magnetic form.
Identifying Objects, Actions, and Events	Identifying information by categorizing, estimating, recognizing differences or similarities, and detecting changes in circumstances or events.
Processing Information	Compiling, coding, categorizing, calculating, tabulating, auditing, or verifying information or data.
Monitor Processes, Materials, or Surroundings	Monitoring and reviewing information from materials, events, or the environment, to detect or assess problems.
Updating and Using Relevant Knowledge	Keeping up-to-date technically and applying new knowledge to your job.
Evaluating Information to Determine Compliance wit	Using relevant information and individual judgment to determine whether events or processes comply with laws, regulations, or standards.
Interpreting the Meaning of Information for Others	Translating or explaining what information means and how it can be used.
Organizing, Planning, and Prioritizing Work	Developing specific goals and plans to prioritize, organize, and accomplish your work.

Communicating with Supervisors, Peers, or Subordin	Providing information to supervisors, co-workers, and subordinates by telephone, in written form, e-mail, or in person.
Establishing and Maintaining Interpersonal Relatio	Developing constructive and cooperative working relationships with others, and maintaining them over time.
Analyzing Data or Information	Identifying the underlying principles, reasons, or facts of information by breaking down information or data into separate parts.
Making Decisions and Solving Problems	Analyzing information and evaluating results to choose the best solution and solve problems.
Communicating with Persons Outside Organization	Communicating with people outside the organization, representing the organization to customers, the public, government, and other external sources. This information can be exchanged in person, in writing, or by telephone or e-mail.
Thinking Creatively	Developing, designing, or creating new applications, ideas, relationships, systems, or products, including artistic contributions.
Performing for or Working Directly with the Public	Performing for people or dealing directly with the public. This includes serving customers in restaurants and stores, and receiving clients or guests.
Judging the Qualities of Things, Services, or Peop	Assessing the value, importance, or quality of things or people.
Provide Consultation and Advice to Others	Providing guidance and expert advice to management or other groups on technical, systems-, or process-related topics.
Resolving Conflicts and Negotiating with Others	Handling complaints, settling disputes, and resolving grievances and conflicts, or otherwise negotiating with others.
Scheduling Work and Activities	Scheduling events, programs, and activities, as well as the work of others.
Controlling Machines and Processes	Using either control mechanisms or direct physical activity to operate machines or processes (not including computers or vehicles).
Repairing and Maintaining Electronic Equipment	Servicing, repairing, calibrating, regulating, fine-tuning, or testing machines, devices, and equipment that operate primarily on the basis of electrical or electronic (not mechanical) principles.
Inspecting Equipment, Structures, or Material	Inspecting equipment, structures, or materials to identify the cause of errors or other problems or defects.
Operating Vehicles, Mechanized Devices, or Equipme	Running, maneuvering, navigating, or driving vehicles or mechanized equipment, such as forklifts, passenger vehicles, aircraft, or water craft.
Performing General Physical Activities	Performing physical activities that require considerable use of your arms and legs and moving your whole body, such as climbing, lifting, balancing, walking, stooping, and handling of materials.
Handling and Moving Objects	Using hands and arms in handling, installing, positioning, and moving materials, and manipulating things.
Developing Objectives and Strategies	Establishing long-range objectives and specifying the strategies and actions to achieve them.
Selling or Influencing Others	Convincing others to buy merchandise/goods or to otherwise change their minds or actions.
Coaching and Developing Others	Identifying the developmental needs of others and coaching, mentoring, or otherwise helping others to improve their knowledge or skills.
Performing Administrative Activities	Performing day-to-day administrative tasks such as maintaining information files and processing paperwork.
Estimating the Quantifiable Characteristics of Pro	Estimating sizes, distances, and quantities; or determining time, costs, resources, or materials needed to perform a work activity.
Training and Teaching Others	Identifying the educational needs of others, developing formal educational or training programs or classes, and teaching or instructing others.
Repairing and Maintaining Mechanical Equipment	Servicing, repairing, adjusting, and testing machines, devices, moving parts, and equipment that operate primarily on the basis of mechanical (not electronic) principles.
Coordinating the Work and Activities of Others	Getting members of a group to work together to accomplish tasks.
Assisting and Caring for Others	Providing personal assistance, medical attention, emotional support, or other personal care to others such as coworkers, customers, or patients.
Developing and Building Teams	Encouraging and building mutual trust, respect, and cooperation among team members.
Guiding, Directing, and Motivating Subordinates	Providing guidance and direction to subordinates, including setting performance standards and monitoring performance.
Monitoring and Controlling Resources	Monitoring and controlling resources and overseeing the spending of money.

Drafting, Laying Out, and Specifying Technical Dev	Providing documentation, detailed instructions, drawings, or specifications to tell others about how devices, parts, equipment, or structures are to be fabricated, constructed, assembled, modified, maintained, or used.
Staffing Organizational Units	Recruiting, interviewing, selecting, hiring, and promoting employees in an organization.

Work_Context	Work_Context Definitions
Face-to-Face Discussions	How often do you have to have face-to-face discussions with individuals or teams in this job?
Telephone	How often do you have telephone conversations in this job?
Electronic Mail	How often do you use electronic mail in this job?
Indoors, Environmentally Controlled	How often does this job require working indoors in environmentally controlled conditions?
Spend Time Sitting	How much does this job require sitting?
Sounds, Noise Levels Are Distracting or Uncomforta	How often does this job require working exposed to sounds and noise levels that are distracting or uncomfortable?
Importance of Being Exact or Accurate	How important is being very exact or highly accurate in performing this job?
Work With Work Group or Team	How important is it to work with others in a group or team in this job?
Letters and Memos	How often does the job require written letters and memos?
Structured versus Unstructured Work	To what extent is this job structured for the worker, rather than allowing the worker to determine tasks, priorities, and goals?
Contact With Others	How much does this job require the worker to be in contact with others (face-to-face, by telephone, or otherwise) in order to perform it?
In an Enclosed Vehicle or Equipment	How often does this job require working in a closed vehicle or equipment (e.g., car)?
Outdoors, Exposed to Weather	How often does this job require working outdoors, exposed to all weather conditions?
Physical Proximity	To what extent does this job require the worker to perform job tasks in close physical proximity to other people?
Freedom to Make Decisions	How much decision making freedom, without supervision, does the job offer?
Impact of Decisions on Co-workers or Company Resul	How do the decisions an employee makes impact the results of co-workers, clients or the company?
Deal With External Customers	How important is it to work with external customers or the public in this job?
Responsibility for Outcomes and Results	How responsible is the worker for work outcomes and results of other workers?
Time Pressure	How often does this job require the worker to meet strict deadlines?
Frequency of Decision Making	How frequently is the worker required to make decisions that affect other people, the financial resources, and/or the image and reputation of the organization?
Consequence of Error	How serious would the result usually be if the worker made a mistake that was not readily correctable?
Coordinate or Lead Others	How important is it to coordinate or lead others in accomplishing work activities in this job?
Wear Common Protective or Safety Equipment such as	How much does this job require wearing common protective or safety equipment such as safety shoes, glasses, gloves, hard hats or life jackets?
Exposed to Hazardous Conditions	How often does this job require exposure to hazardous conditions?
Level of Competition	To what extent does this job require the worker to compete or to be aware of competitive pressures?
Deal With Unpleasant or Angry People	How frequently does the worker have to deal with unpleasant, angry, or discourteous individuals as part of the job requirements?
Exposed to Contaminants	How often does this job require working exposed to contaminants (such as pollutants, gases, dust or odors)?
Public Speaking	How often do you have to perform public speaking in this job?
Responsible for Others' Health and Safety	How much responsibility is there for the health and safety of others in this job?
Very Hot or Cold Temperatures	How often does this job require working in very hot (above 90 F degrees) or very cold (below 32 F degrees) temperatures?
Extremely Bright or Inadequate Lighting	How often does this job require working in extremely bright or inadequate lighting conditions?
Spend Time Walking and Running	How much does this job require walking and running?
Exposed to Minor Burns, Cuts, Bites, or Stings	How often does this job require exposure to minor burns, cuts, bites, or stings?
In an Open Vehicle or Equipment	How often does this job require working in an open vehicle or equipment (e.g., tractor)?

Exposed to Hazardous Equipment	How often does this job require exposure to hazardous equipment?
Exposed to Whole Body Vibration	How often does this job require exposure to whole body vibration (e.g., operate a jackhammer)?
Importance of Repeating Same Tasks	How important is repeating the same physical activities (e.g., key entry) or mental activities (e.g., checking entries in a ledger) over and over, without stopping, to performing this job?
Frequency of Conflict Situations	How often are there conflict situations the employee has to face in this job?
Indoors, Not Environmentally Controlled	How often does this job require working indoors in non-controlled environmental conditions (e.g., warehouse without heat)?
Spend Time Making Repetitive Motions	How much does this job require making repetitive motions?
Spend Time Standing	How much does this job require standing?
Spend Time Using Your Hands to Handle, Control, or	How much does this job require using your hands to handle, control, or feel objects, tools or controls?
Exposed to Disease or Infections	How often does this job require exposure to disease/infections?
Spend Time Kneeling, Crouching, Stooping, or Crawl	How much does this job require kneeling, crouching, stooping or crawling?
Cramped Work Space, Awkward Positions	How often does this job require working in cramped work spaces that requires getting into awkward positions?
Spend Time Bending or Twisting the Body	How much does this job require bending or twisting your body?
Outdoors, Under Cover	How often does this job require working outdoors, under cover (e.g., structure with roof but no walls)?
Spend Time Keeping or Regaining Balance	How much does this job require keeping or regaining your balance?
Degree of Automation	How automated is the job?
Exposed to High Places	How often does this job require exposure to high places?
Deal With Physically Aggressive People	How frequently does this job require the worker to deal with physical aggression of violent individuals?
Wear Specialized Protective or Safety Equipment su	How much does this job require wearing specialized protective or safety equipment such as breathing apparatus, safety harness, full protection suits, or radiation protection?
Spend Time Climbing Ladders, Scaffolds, or Poles	How much does this job require climbing ladders, scaffolds, or poles?
Pace Determined by Speed of Equipment	How important is it to this job that the pace is determined by the speed of equipment or machinery? (This does not refer to keeping busy at all times on this job.)
Exposed to Radiation	How often does this job require exposure to radiation?

Job Zone Component	Job Zone Component Definitions
Title	Job Zone Five: Extensive Preparation Needed
Overall Experience	Extensive skill, knowledge, and experience are needed for these occupations. Many require more than five years of experience. For example, surgeons must complete four years of college and an additional five to seven years of specialized medical training to be able to do their job.
Job Training	Employees may need some on-the-job training, but most of these occupations assume that the person will already have the required skills, knowledge, work-related experience, and/or training.
Job Zone Examples	These occupations often involve coordinating, training, supervising, or managing the activities of others to accomplish goals. Very advanced communication and organizational skills are required. Examples include athletic trainers, lawyers, managing editors, phyicists, social psychologists, and surgeons.
SVP Range	(8.0 and above)
Education	A bachelor's degree is the minimum formal education required for these occupations. However, many also require graduate school. For example, they may require a master's degree, and some require a Ph.D., M.D., or J.D. (law degree).

Work_Styles	Work_Styles Definitions
Attention to Detail	Job requires being careful about detail and thorough in completing work tasks.
Analytical Thinking	Job requires analyzing information and using logic to address work-related issues and problems.
Integrity	Job requires being honest and ethical.

Cooperation	Job requires being pleasant with others on the job and displaying a good-natured, cooperative attitude.
Dependability	Job requires being reliable, responsible, and dependable, and fulfilling obligations.
Initiative	Job requires a willingness to take on responsibilities and challenges.
Persistence	Job requires persistence in the face of obstacles.
Stress Tolerance	Job requires accepting criticism and dealing calmly and effectively with high stress situations.
Independence	Job requires developing one's own ways of doing things, guiding oneself with little or no supervision, and depending on oneself to get things done.
Achievement/Effort	Job requires establishing and maintaining personally challenging achievement goals and exerting effort toward mastering tasks.
Leadership	Job requires a willingness to lead, take charge, and offer opinions and direction.
Self Control	Job requires maintaining composure, keeping emotions in check, controlling anger, and avoiding aggressive behavior, even in very difficult situations.
Adaptability/Flexibility	Job requires being open to change (positive or negative) and to considerable variety in the workplace.
Concern for Others	Job requires being sensitive to others' needs and feelings and being understanding and helpful on the job.
Innovation	Job requires creativity and alternative thinking to develop new ideas for and answers to work-related problems.
Social Orientation	Job requires preferring to work with others rather than alone, and being personally connected with others on the job.

19-1021.00 - Biochemists and Biophysicists

Study the chemical composition and physical principles of living cells and organisms, their electrical and mechanical energy, and related phenomena. May conduct research to further understanding of the complex chemical combinations and reactions involved in metabolism, reproduction, growth, and heredity. May determine the effects of foods, drugs, serums, hormones, and other substances on tissues and vital processes of living organisms.

Tasks

1) Analyze brain functions such as learning, thinking, and memory, and the dynamics of seeing and hearing.

2) Design and perform experiments with equipment such as lasers, accelerators, and mass spectrometers.

3) Develop and test new drugs and medications intended for commercial distribution.

4) Isolate, analyze, and synthesize vitamins, hormones, allergens, minerals, and enzymes, and determine their effects on body functions.

5) Determine the three-dimensional structure of biological macromolecules.

6) Develop and execute tests to detect diseases, genetic disorders, or other abnormalities.

7) Investigate damage to cells and tissues caused by x-rays and nuclear particles.

8) Investigate the transmission of electrical impulses along nerves and muscles.

9) Manage laboratory teams, and monitor the quality of a team's work.

10) Research cancer treatment, using radiation and nuclear particles.

11) Prepare reports and recommendations based upon research outcomes.

12) Study how light is absorbed in processes such as photosynthesis or vision.

13) Study spatial configurations of submicroscopic molecules such as proteins, using x-rays and electron microscopes.

14) Analyze foods to determine their nutritional values and the effects of cooking, canning, and processing on these values.

15) Prepare pharmaceutical compounds for commercial distribution.

16) Investigate the nature, composition, and expression of genes, and research how genetic engineering can impact these processes.

17) Teach and advise undergraduate and graduate students, and supervise their research.

18) Research how characteristics of plants and animals are carried through successive generations.

19) Research transformations of substances in cells, using atomic isotopes.

20) Study the mutations in organisms that lead to cancer and other diseases.

21) Study the chemistry of living processes, such as cell development, breathing and digestion, and living energy changes such as growth, aging, and death.

22) Study physical principles of living cells and organisms and their electrical and mechanical energy, applying methods and knowledge of mathematics, physics, chemistry, and biology.

23) Develop new methods to study the mechanisms of biological processes.

24) Develop methods to process, store, and use foods, drugs, and chemical compounds.

25) Share research findings by writing scientific articles and by making presentations at scientific conferences.

26) Research the chemical effects of substances such as drugs, serums, hormones, and food on tissues and vital processes.

27) Design and build laboratory equipment needed for special research projects.

28) Produce pharmaceutically and industrially useful proteins, using recombinant DNA technology.

19-1022.00 - Microbiologists

Investigate the growth, structure, development, and other characteristics of microscopic organisms, such as bacteria, algae, or fungi. Includes medical microbiologists who study the relationship between organisms and disease or the effects of antibiotics on microorganisms.

Tasks

1) Isolate and make cultures of bacteria or other microorganisms in prescribed media, controlling moisture, aeration, temperature, and nutrition.

2) Perform tests on water, food and the environment to detect harmful microorganisms and to obtain information about sources of pollution and contamination.

3) Supervise biological technologists and technicians and other scientists.

4) Prepare technical reports and recommendations based upon research outcomes.

5) Provide laboratory services for health departments, for community environmental health programs and for physicians needing information for diagnosis and treatment.

6) Investigate the relationship between organisms and disease, including the control of epidemics and the effects of antibiotics on microorganisms.

7) Use a variety of specialized equipment such as electron microscopes, gas chromatographs and high pressure liquid chromatographs, electrophoresis units, thermocyclers, fluorescence activated cell sorters and phosphoimagers.

8) Study growth, structure, development, and general characteristics of bacteria and other microorganisms to understand their relationship to human, plant, and animal health.

9) Conduct chemical analyses of substances, such as acids, alcohols, and enzymes.

10) Observe action of microorganisms upon living tissues of plants, higher animals, and other microorganisms, and on dead organic matter.

11) Study the structure and function of human, animal and plant tissues, cells, pathogens and toxins.

12) Research use of bacteria and microorganisms to develop vitamins, antibiotics, amino acids, grain alcohol, sugars, and polymers.

Knowledge	Knowledge Definitions
Biology	Knowledge of plant and animal organisms, their tissues, cells, functions, interdependencies, and interactions with each other and the environment.
English Language	Knowledge of the structure and content of the English language including the meaning and spelling of words, rules of composition, and grammar.
Customer and Personal Service	Knowledge of principles and processes for providing customer and personal services. This includes customer needs assessment, meeting quality standards for services, and evaluation of customer satisfaction.
Mathematics	Knowledge of arithmetic, algebra, geometry, calculus, statistics, and their applications.
Education and Training	Knowledge of principles and methods for curriculum and training design, teaching and instruction for individuals and groups, and the measurement of training effects.

Clerical	Knowledge of administrative and clerical procedures and systems such as word processing, managing files and records, stenography and transcription, designing forms, and other office procedures and terminology.
Production and Processing	Knowledge of raw materials, production processes, quality control, costs, and other techniques for maximizing the effective manufacture and distribution of goods.
Administration and Management	Knowledge of business and management principles involved in strategic planning, resource allocation, human resources modeling, leadership technique, production methods, and coordination of people and resources.
Chemistry	Knowledge of the chemical composition, structure, and properties of substances and of the chemical processes and transformations that they undergo. This includes uses of chemicals and their interactions, danger signs, production techniques, and disposal methods.
Computers and Electronics	Knowledge of circuit boards, processors, chips, electronic equipment, and computer hardware and software, including applications and programming.
Psychology	Knowledge of human behavior and performance; individual differences in ability, personality, and interests; learning and motivation; psychological research methods; and the assessment and treatment of behavioral and affective disorders.
Food Production	Knowledge of techniques and equipment for planting, growing, and harvesting food products (both plant and animal) for consumption, including storage/handling techniques.
Public Safety and Security	Knowledge of relevant equipment, policies, procedures, and strategies to promote effective local, state, or national security operations for the protection of people, data, property, and institutions.
Physics	Knowledge and prediction of physical principles, laws, their interrelationships, and applications to understanding fluid, material, and atmospheric dynamics, and mechanical, electrical, atomic and sub- atomic structures and processes.
Mechanical	Knowledge of machines and tools, including their designs, uses, repair, and maintenance.
Communications and Media	Knowledge of media production, communication, and dissemination techniques and methods. This includes alternative ways to inform and entertain via written, oral, and visual media.
Personnel and Human Resources	Knowledge of principles and procedures for personnel recruitment, selection, training, compensation and benefits, labor relations and negotiation, and personnel information systems.
Medicine and Dentistry	Knowledge of the information and techniques needed to diagnose and treat human injuries, diseases, and deformities. This includes symptoms, treatment alternatives, drug properties and interactions, and preventive health-care measures.
Engineering and Technology	Knowledge of the practical application of engineering science and technology. This includes applying principles, techniques, procedures, and equipment to the design and production of various goods and services.
Telecommunications	Knowledge of transmission, broadcasting, switching, control, and operation of telecommunications systems.
Economics and Accounting	Knowledge of economic and accounting principles and practices, the financial markets, banking and the analysis and reporting of financial data.
Geography	Knowledge of principles and methods for describing the features of land, sea, and air masses, including their physical characteristics, locations, interrelationships, and distribution of plant, animal, and human life.
Foreign Language	Knowledge of the structure and content of a foreign (non-English) language including the meaning and spelling of words, rules of composition and grammar, and pronunciation.
Law and Government	Knowledge of laws, legal codes, court procedures, precedents, government regulations, executive orders, agency rules, and the democratic political process.
Sales and Marketing	Knowledge of principles and methods for showing, promoting, and selling products or services. This includes marketing strategy and tactics, product demonstration, sales techniques, and sales control systems.
Therapy and Counseling	Knowledge of principles, methods, and procedures for diagnosis, treatment, and rehabilitation of physical and mental dysfunctions, and for career counseling and guidance.
History and Archeology	Knowledge of historical events and their causes, indicators, and effects on civilizations and cultures.
Transportation	Knowledge of principles and methods for moving people or goods by air, rail, sea, or road, including the relative costs and benefits.
Design	Knowledge of design techniques, tools, and principles involved in production of precision technical plans, blueprints, drawings, and models.
Philosophy and Theology	Knowledge of different philosophical systems and religions. This includes their basic principles, values, ethics, ways of thinking, customs, practices, and their impact on human culture.
Sociology and Anthropology	Knowledge of group behavior and dynamics, societal trends and influences, human migrations, ethnicity, cultures and their history and origins.
Building and Construction	Knowledge of materials, methods, and the tools involved in the construction or repair of houses, buildings, or other structures such as highways and roads.
Fine Arts	Knowledge of the theory and techniques required to compose, produce, and perform works of music, dance, visual arts, drama, and sculpture.

Skills	Skills Definitions
Science	Using scientific rules and methods to solve problems.
Reading Comprehension	Understanding written sentences and paragraphs in work related documents.
Instructing	Teaching others how to do something.
Active Listening	Giving full attention to what other people are saying, taking time to understand the points being made, asking questions as appropriate, and not interrupting at inappropriate times.
Critical Thinking	Using logic and reasoning to identify the strengths and weaknesses of alternative solutions, conclusions or approaches to problems.
Active Learning	Understanding the implications of new information for both current and future problem-solving and decision-making.
Writing	Communicating effectively in writing as appropriate for the needs of the audience.
Time Management	Managing one's own time and the time of others.
Troubleshooting	Determining causes of operating errors and deciding what to do about it.
Complex Problem Solving	Identifying complex problems and reviewing related information to develop and evaluate options and implement solutions.
Equipment Maintenance	Performing routine maintenance on equipment and determining when and what kind of maintenance is needed.
Mathematics	Using mathematics to solve problems.
Monitoring	Monitoring/Assessing performance of yourself, other individuals, or organizations to make improvements or take corrective action.
Judgment and Decision Making	Considering the relative costs and benefits of potential actions to choose the most appropriate one.
Coordination	Adjusting actions in relation to others' actions.
Equipment Selection	Determining the kind of tools and equipment needed to do a job.
Operation Monitoring	Watching gauges, dials, or other indicators to make sure a machine is working properly.
Operations Analysis	Analyzing needs and product requirements to create a design.
Speaking	Talking to others to convey information effectively.
Quality Control Analysis	Conducting tests and inspections of products, services, or processes to evaluate quality or performance.
Learning Strategies	Selecting and using training/instructional methods and procedures appropriate for the situation when learning or teaching new things.
Operation and Control	Controlling operations of equipment or systems.
Technology Design	Generating or adapting equipment and technology to serve user needs.
Service Orientation	Actively looking for ways to help people.
Social Perceptiveness	Being aware of others' reactions and understanding why they react as they do.
Installation	Installing equipment, machines, wiring, or programs to meet specifications.
Negotiation	Bringing others together and trying to reconcile differences.
Repairing	Repairing machines or systems using the needed tools.
Management of Personnel Resources	Motivating, developing, and directing people as they work, identifying the best people for the job.
Persuasion	Persuading others to change their minds or behavior.
Management of Material Resources	Obtaining and seeing to the appropriate use of equipment, facilities, and materials needed to do certain work.

Management of Financial Resources	Determining how money will be spent to get the work done, and accounting for these expenditures.
Systems Evaluation	Identifying measures or indicators of system performance and the actions needed to improve or correct performance, relative to the goals of the system.
Systems Analysis	Determining how a system should work and how changes in conditions, operations, and the environment will affect outcomes.
Programming	Writing computer programs for various purposes.

Ability	Ability Definitions
Near Vision	The ability to see details at close range (within a few feet of the observer).
Inductive Reasoning	The ability to combine pieces of information to form general rules or conclusions (includes finding a relationship among seemingly unrelated events).
Problem Sensitivity	The ability to tell when something is wrong or is likely to go wrong. It does not involve solving the problem, only recognizing there is a problem.
Information Ordering	The ability to arrange things or actions in a certain order or pattern according to a specific rule or set of rules (e.g., patterns of numbers, letters, words, pictures, mathematical operations).
Written Comprehension	The ability to read and understand information and ideas presented in writing.
Category Flexibility	The ability to generate or use different sets of rules for combining or grouping things in different ways.
Deductive Reasoning	The ability to apply general rules to specific problems to produce answers that make sense.
Written Expression	The ability to communicate information and ideas in writing so others will understand.
Oral Comprehension	The ability to listen to and understand information and ideas presented through spoken words and sentences.
Flexibility of Closure	The ability to identify or detect a known pattern (a figure, object, word, or sound) that is hidden in other distracting material.
Speech Recognition	The ability to identify and understand the speech of another person.
Visual Color Discrimination	The ability to match or detect differences between colors, including shades of color and brightness.
Mathematical Reasoning	The ability to choose the right mathematical methods or formulas to solve a problem.
Arm-Hand Steadiness	The ability to keep your hand and arm steady while moving your arm or while holding your arm and hand in one position.
Selective Attention	The ability to concentrate on a task over a period of time without being distracted.
Oral Expression	The ability to communicate information and ideas in speaking so others will understand.
Speech Clarity	The ability to speak clearly so others can understand you.
Finger Dexterity	The ability to make precisely coordinated movements of the fingers of one or both hands to grasp, manipulate, or assemble very small objects.
Speed of Closure	The ability to quickly make sense of, combine, and organize information into meaningful patterns.
Perceptual Speed	The ability to quickly and accurately compare similarities and differences among sets of letters, numbers, objects, pictures, or patterns. The things to be compared may be presented at the same time or one after the other. This ability also includes comparing a presented object with a remembered object.
Number Facility	The ability to add, subtract, multiply, or divide quickly and correctly.
Originality	The ability to come up with unusual or clever ideas about a given topic or situation, or to develop creative ways to solve a problem.
Fluency of Ideas	The ability to come up with a number of ideas about a topic (the number of ideas is important, not their quality, correctness, or creativity).
Depth Perception	The ability to judge which of several objects is closer or farther away from you, or to judge the distance between you and an object.
Memorization	The ability to remember information such as words, numbers, pictures, and procedures.
Visualization	The ability to imagine how something will look after it is moved around or when its parts are moved or rearranged.
Far Vision	The ability to see details at a distance.
Control Precision	The ability to quickly and repeatedly adjust the controls of a machine or a vehicle to exact positions.
Manual Dexterity	The ability to quickly move your hand, your hand together with your arm, or your two hands to grasp, manipulate, or assemble objects.
Multilimb Coordination	The ability to coordinate two or more limbs (for example, two arms, two legs, or one leg and one arm) while sitting, standing, or lying down. It does not involve performing the activities while the whole body is in motion.
Hearing Sensitivity	The ability to detect or tell the differences between sounds that vary in pitch and loudness.
Time Sharing	The ability to shift back and forth between two or more activities or sources of information (such as speech, sounds, touch, or other sources).
Reaction Time	The ability to quickly respond (with the hand, finger, or foot) to a signal (sound, light, picture) when it appears.
Response Orientation	The ability to choose quickly between two or more movements in response to two or more different signals (lights, sounds, pictures). It includes the speed with which the correct response is started with the hand, foot, or other body part.
Wrist-Finger Speed	The ability to make fast, simple, repeated movements of the fingers, hands, and wrists.
Auditory Attention	The ability to focus on a single source of sound in the presence of other distracting sounds.
Rate Control	The ability to time your movements or the movement of a piece of equipment in anticipation of changes in the speed and/or direction of a moving object or scene.
Trunk Strength	The ability to use your abdominal and lower back muscles to support part of the body repeatedly or continuously over time without 'giving out' or fatiguing.
Static Strength	The ability to exert maximum muscle force to lift, push, pull, or carry objects.
Glare Sensitivity	The ability to see objects in the presence of glare or bright lighting.
Night Vision	The ability to see under low light conditions.
Extent Flexibility	The ability to bend, stretch, twist, or reach with your body, arms, and/or legs.
Explosive Strength	The ability to use short bursts of muscle force to propel oneself (as in jumping or sprinting), or to throw an object.
Dynamic Strength	The ability to exert muscle force repeatedly or continuously over time. This involves muscular endurance and resistance to muscle fatigue.
Spatial Orientation	The ability to know your location in relation to the environment or to know where other objects are in relation to you.
Stamina	The ability to exert yourself physically over long periods of time without getting winded or out of breath.
Speed of Limb Movement	The ability to quickly move the arms and legs.
Dynamic Flexibility	The ability to quickly and repeatedly bend, stretch, twist, or reach out with your body, arms, and/or legs.
Gross Body Coordination	The ability to coordinate the movement of your arms, legs, and torso together when the whole body is in motion.
Gross Body Equilibrium	The ability to keep or regain your body balance or stay upright when in an unstable position.
Sound Localization	The ability to tell the direction from which a sound originated.
Peripheral Vision	The ability to see objects or movement of objects to one's side when the eyes are looking ahead.

Work_Activity	Work_Activity Definitions
Getting Information	Observing, receiving, and otherwise obtaining information from all relevant sources.
Documenting/Recording Information	Entering, transcribing, recording, storing, or maintaining information in written or electronic/magnetic form.
Identifying Objects, Actions, and Events	Identifying information by categorizing, estimating, recognizing differences or similarities, and detecting changes in circumstances or events.
Monitor Processes, Materials, or Surroundings	Monitoring and reviewing information from materials, events, or the environment, to detect or assess problems.
Updating and Using Relevant Knowledge	Keeping up-to-date technically and applying new knowledge to your job.
Communicating with Supervisors, Peers, or Subordin	Providing information to supervisors, co-workers, and subordinates by telephone, in written form, e-mail, or in person.
Evaluating Information to Determine Compliance wit	Using relevant information and individual judgment to determine whether events or processes comply with laws, regulations, or standards.
Making Decisions and Solving Problems	Analyzing information and evaluating results to choose the best solution and solve problems.

Analyzing Data or Information	Identifying the underlying principles, reasons, or facts of information by breaking down information or data into separate parts.
Interacting With Computers	Using computers and computer systems (including hardware and software) to program, write software, set up functions, enter data, or process information.
Processing Information	Compiling, coding, categorizing, calculating, tabulating, auditing, or verifying information or data.
Training and Teaching Others	Identifying the educational needs of others, developing formal educational or training programs or classes, and teaching or instructing others.
Estimating the Quantifiable Characteristics of Pro	Estimating sizes, distances, and quantities; or determining time, costs, resources, or materials needed to perform a work activity.
Interpreting the Meaning of Information for Others	Translating or explaining what information means and how it can be used.
Judging the Qualities of Things, Services, or Peop	Assessing the value, importance, or quality of things or people.
Organizing, Planning, and Prioritizing Work	Developing specific goals and plans to prioritize, organize, and accomplish your work.
Establishing and Maintaining Interpersonal Relatio	Developing constructive and cooperative working relationships with others, and maintaining them over time.
Controlling Machines and Processes	Using either control mechanisms or direct physical activity to operate machines or processes (not including computers or vehicles).
Scheduling Work and Activities	Scheduling events, programs, and activities, as well as the work of others.
Communicating with Persons Outside Organization	Communicating with people outside the organization, representing the organization to customers, the public, government, and other external sources. This information can be exchanged in person, in writing, or by telephone or e-mail.
Inspecting Equipment, Structures, or Material	Inspecting equipment, structures, or materials to identify the cause of errors or other problems or defects.
Thinking Creatively	Developing, designing, or creating new applications, ideas, relationships, systems, or products, including artistic contributions.
Coaching and Developing Others	Identifying the developmental needs of others and coaching, mentoring, or otherwise helping others to improve their knowledge or skills.
Developing Objectives and Strategies	Establishing long-range objectives and specifying the strategies and actions to achieve them.
Provide Consultation and Advice to Others	Providing guidance and expert advice to management or other groups on technical, systems-, or process-related topics.
Coordinating the Work and Activities of Others	Getting members of a group to work together to accomplish tasks.
Performing Administrative Activities	Performing day-to-day administrative tasks such as maintaining information files and processing paperwork.
Handling and Moving Objects	Using hands and arms in handling, installing, positioning, and moving materials, and manipulating things.
Guiding, Directing, and Motivating Subordinates	Providing guidance and direction to subordinates, including setting performance standards and monitoring performance.
Monitoring and Controlling Resources	Monitoring and controlling resources and overseeing the spending of money.
Resolving Conflicts and Negotiating with Others	Handling complaints, settling disputes, and resolving grievances and conflicts, or otherwise negotiating with others.
Assisting and Caring for Others	Providing personal assistance, medical attention, emotional support, or other personal care to others such as coworkers, customers, or patients.
Developing and Building Teams	Encouraging and building mutual trust, respect, and cooperation among team members.
Performing for or Working Directly with the Public	Performing for people or dealing directly with the public. This includes serving customers in restaurants and stores, and receiving clients or guests.
Performing General Physical Activities	Performing physical activities that require considerable use of your arms and legs and moving your whole body, such as climbing, lifting, balancing, walking, stooping, and handling of materials.
Repairing and Maintaining Electronic Equipment	Servicing, repairing, calibrating, regulating, fine-tuning, or testing machines, devices, and equipment that operate primarily on the basis of electrical or electronic (not mechanical) principles.
Repairing and Maintaining Mechanical Equipment	Servicing, repairing, adjusting, and testing machines, devices, moving parts, and equipment that operate primarily on the basis of mechanical (not electronic) principles.
Drafting, Laying Out, and Specifying Technical Dev	Providing documentation, detailed instructions, drawings, or specifications to tell others about how devices, parts, equipment, or structures are to be fabricated, constructed, assembled, modified, maintained, or used.
Selling or Influencing Others	Convincing others to buy merchandise/goods or to otherwise change their minds or actions.
Operating Vehicles, Mechanized Devices, or Equipme	Running, maneuvering, navigating, or driving vehicles or mechanized equipment, such as forklifts, passenger vehicles, aircraft, or water craft.
Staffing Organizational Units	Recruiting, interviewing, selecting, hiring, and promoting employees in an organization.

Work_Context	Work_Context Definitions
Indoors, Environmentally Controlled	How often does this job require working indoors in environmentally controlled conditions?
Importance of Being Exact or Accurate	How important is being very exact or highly accurate in performing this job?
Wear Common Protective or Safety Equipment such as	How much does this job require wearing common protective or safety equipment such as safety shoes, glasses, gloves, hard hats or live jackets?
Electronic Mail	How often do you use electronic mail in this job?
Impact of Decisions on Co-workers or Company Resul	How do the decisions an employee makes impact the results of co-workers, clients or the company?
Structured versus Unstructured Work	To what extent is this job structured for the worker, rather than allowing the worker to determine tasks, priorities, and goals?
Face-to-Face Discussions	How often do you have to have face-to-face discussions with individuals or teams in this job?
Telephone	How often do you have telephone conversations in this job?
Freedom to Make Decisions	How much decision making freedom, without supervision, does the job offer?
Exposed to Disease or Infections	How often does this job require exposure to disease/infections?
Responsible for Others' Health and Safety	How much responsibility is there for the health and safety of others in this job?
Contact With Others	How much does this job require the worker to be in contact with others (face-to-face, by telephone, or otherwise) in order to perform it?
Work With Work Group or Team	How important is it to work with others in a group or team in this job?
Exposed to Contaminants	How often does this job require working exposed to contaminants (such as pollutants, gases, dust or odors)?
Time Pressure	How often does this job require the worker to meet strict deadlines?
Spend Time Using Your Hands to Handle, Control, or	How much does this job require using your hands to handle, control, or feel objects, tools or controls?
Exposed to Hazardous Conditions	How often does this job require exposure to hazardous conditions?
Frequency of Decision Making	How frequently is the worker required to make decisions that affect other people, the financial resources, and/or the image and reputation of the organization?
Consequence of Error	How serious would the result usually be if the worker made a mistake that was not readily correctable?
Responsibility for Outcomes and Results	How responsible is the worker for work outcomes and results of other workers?
Importance of Repeating Same Tasks	How important is repeating the same physical activities (e.g., key entry) or mental activities (e.g., checking entries in a ledger) over and over, without stopping, to performing this job?
Physical Proximity	To what extent does this job require the worker to perform job tasks in close physical proximity to other people?
Spend Time Making Repetitive Motions	How much does this job require making repetitive motions?
Spend Time Sitting	How much does this job require sitting?
Spend Time Standing	How much does this job require standing?
Level of Competition	To what extent does this job require the worker to compete or to be aware of competitive pressures?
Letters and Memos	How often does the job require written letters and memos?
Coordinate or Lead Others	How important is it to coordinate or lead others in accomplishing work activities in this job?
Sounds, Noise Levels Are Distracting or Uncomforta	How often does this job require working exposed to sounds and noise levels that are distracting or uncomfortable?
Deal With External Customers	How important is it to work with external customers or the public in this job?
Spend Time Walking and Running	How much does this job require walking and running?
Degree of Automation	How automated is the job?

Frequency of Conflict Situations	How often are there conflict situations the employee has to face in this job?
Deal With Unpleasant or Angry People	How frequently does the worker have to deal with unpleasant, angry, or discourteous individuals as part of the job requirements?
Wear Specialized Protective or Safety Equipment su	How much does this job require wearing specialized protective or safety equipment such as breathing apparatus, safety harness, full protection suits, or radiation protection?
Public Speaking	How often do you have to perform public speaking in this job?
Very Hot or Cold Temperatures	How often does this job require working in very hot (above 90 F degrees) or very cold (below 32 F degrees) temperatures?
Exposed to Hazardous Equipment	How often does this job require exposure to hazardous equipment?
In an Enclosed Vehicle or Equipment	How often does this job require working in a closed vehicle or equipment (e.g., car)?
Exposed to Minor Burns, Cuts, Bites, or Stings	How often does this job require exposure to minor burns, cuts, bites, or stings?
Exposed to Radiation	How often does this job require exposure to radiation?
Spend Time Bending or Twisting the Body	How much does this job require bending or twisting your body?
Indoors, Not Environmentally Controlled	How often does this job require working indoors in non-controlled environmental conditions (e.g., warehouse without heat)?
Extremely Bright or Inadequate Lighting	How often does this job require working in extremely bright or inadequate lighting conditions?
Spend Time Kneeling, Crouching, Stooping, or Crawl	How much does this job require kneeling, crouching, stooping, or crawling?
Cramped Work Space, Awkward Positions	How often does this job require working in cramped work spaces that requires getting into awkward positions?
Outdoors, Exposed to Weather	How often does this job require working outdoors, exposed to all weather conditions?
Deal With Physically Aggressive People	How frequently does this job require the worker to deal with physical aggression of violent individuals?
Outdoors, Under Cover	How often does this job require working outdoors, under cover (e.g., structure with roof but no walls)?
Spend Time Climbing Ladders, Scaffolds, or Poles	How much does this job require climbing ladders, scaffolds, or poles?
Spend Time Keeping or Regaining Balance	How much does this job require keeping or regaining your balance?
In an Open Vehicle or Equipment	How often does this job require working in an open vehicle or equipment (e.g., tractor)?
Pace Determined by Speed of Equipment	How important is it to this job that the pace is determined by the speed of equipment or machinery? (This does not refer to keeping busy at all times on this job.)
Exposed to Whole Body Vibration	How often does this job require exposure to whole body vibration (e.g., operate a jackhammer)?
Exposed to High Places	How often does this job require exposure to high places?

Job Zone Component	Job Zone Component Definitions
Title	Job Zone Four: Considerable Preparation Needed
Overall Experience	A minimum of two to four years of work-related skill, knowledge, or experience is needed for these occupations. For example, an accountant must complete four years of college and work for several years in accounting to be considered qualified.
Job Training	Employees in these occupations usually need several years of work-related experience, on-the-job training, and/or vocational training.
Job Zone Examples	Many of these occupations involve coordinating, supervising, managing, or training others. Examples include accountants, chefs and head cooks, computer programmers, historians, pharmacists, and police detectives.
SVP Range	(7.0 to < 8.0)
Education	Most of these occupations require a four - year bachelor's degree, but some do not.

Work_Styles	Work_Styles Definitions
Attention to Detail	Job requires being careful about detail and thorough in completing work tasks.
Initiative	Job requires a willingness to take on responsibilities and challenges.
Dependability	Job requires being reliable, responsible, and dependable, and fulfilling obligations.

Persistence	Job requires persistence in the face of obstacles.
Integrity	Job requires being honest and ethical.
Achievement/Effort	Job requires establishing and maintaining personally challenging achievement goals and exerting effort toward mastering tasks.
Analytical Thinking	Job requires analyzing information and using logic to address work-related issues and problems.
Cooperation	Job requires being pleasant with others on the job and displaying a good natured, cooperative attitude.
Leadership	Job requires a willingness to lead, take charge, and offer opinions and direction.
Stress Tolerance	Job requires accepting criticism and dealing calmly and effectively with high stress situations.
Adaptability/Flexibility	Job requires being open to change (positive or negative) and to considerable variety in the workplace.
Self Control	Job requires maintaining composure, keeping emotions in check, controlling anger, and avoiding aggressive behavior, even in very difficult situations.
Concern for Others	Job requires being sensitive to others' needs and feelings and being understanding and helpful on the job.
Innovation	Job requires creativity and alternative thinking to develop new ideas for and answers to work-related problems.
Social Orientation	Job requires preferring to work with others rather than alone, and being personally connected with others on the job.
Independence	Job requires developing one's own ways of doing things, guiding oneself with little or no supervision, and depending on oneself to get things done.

19-1023.00 - Zoologists and Wildlife Biologists

Study the origins, behavior, diseases, genetics, and life processes of animals and wildlife. May specialize in wildlife research and management, including the collection and analysis of biological data to determine the environmental effects of present and potential use of land and water areas.

Tasks

1) Inventory or estimate plant and wildlife populations.

2) Make recommendations on management systems and planning for wildlife populations and habitat, consulting with stakeholders and the public at large to explore options.

3) Study characteristics of animals such as origin, interrelationships, classification, life histories and diseases, development, genetics, and distribution.

4) Analyze characteristics of animals to identify and classify them.

5) Study animals in their natural habitats, assessing effects of environment and industry on animals, interpreting findings and recommending alternative operating conditions for industry.

6) Collect and dissect animal specimens and examine specimens under microscope.

7) Organize and conduct experimental studies with live animals in controlled or natural surroundings.

8) Prepare collections of preserved specimens or microscopic slides for species identification and study of development or disease.

9) Coordinate preventive programs to control the outbreak of wildlife diseases.

10) Perform administrative duties such as fundraising, public relations, budgeting, and supervision of zoo staff.

11) Raise specimens for study and observation or for use in experiments.

12) Oversee the care and distribution of zoo animals, working with curators and zoo directors to determine the best way to contain animals, maintain their habitats and manage facilities.

Knowledge	Knowledge Definitions
Biology	Knowledge of plant and animal organisms, their tissues, cells, functions, interdependencies, and interactions with each other and the environment.
English Language	Knowledge of the structure and content of the English language including the meaning and spelling of words, rules of composition, and grammar.
Computers and Electronics	Knowledge of circuit boards, processors, chips, electronic equipment, and computer hardware and software, including applications and programming.

Mathematics	Knowledge of arithmetic, algebra, geometry, calculus, statistics, and their applications.
Administration and Management	Knowledge of business and management principles involved in strategic planning, resource allocation, human resources modeling, leadership technique, production methods, and coordination of people and resources.
Law and Government	Knowledge of laws, legal codes, court procedures, precedents, government regulations, executive orders, agency rules, and the democratic political process.
Geography	Knowledge of principles and methods for describing the features of land, sea, and air masses, including their physical characteristics, locations, interrelationships, and distribution of plant, animal, and human life.
Customer and Personal Service	Knowledge of principles and processes for providing customer and personal services. This includes customer needs assessment, meeting quality standards for services, and evaluation of customer satisfaction.
Clerical	Knowledge of administrative and clerical procedures and systems such as word processing, managing files and records, stenography and transcription, designing forms, and other office procedures and terminology.
Communications and Media	Knowledge of media production, communication, and dissemination techniques and methods. This includes alternative ways to inform and entertain via written, oral, and visual media.
Personnel and Human Resources	Knowledge of principles and procedures for personnel recruitment, selection, training, compensation and benefits, labor relations and negotiation, and personnel information systems.
Public Safety and Security	Knowledge of relevant equipment, policies, procedures, and strategies to promote effective local, state, or national security operations for the protection of people, data, property, and institutions.
Education and Training	Knowledge of principles and methods for curriculum and training design, teaching and instruction for individuals and groups, and the measurement of training effects.
Mechanical	Knowledge of machines and tools, including their designs, uses, repair, and maintenance.
Engineering and Technology	Knowledge of the practical application of engineering science and technology. This includes applying principles, techniques, procedures, and equipment to the design and production of various goods and services.
Physics	Knowledge and prediction of physical principles, laws, their interrelationships, and applications to understanding fluid, material, and atmospheric dynamics, and mechanical, electrical, atomic and sub-atomic structures and processes.
Psychology	Knowledge of human behavior and performance; individual differences in ability, personality, and interests; learning and motivation; psychological research methods; and the assessment and treatment of behavioral and affective disorders.
Chemistry	Knowledge of the chemical composition, structure, and properties of substances and of the chemical processes and transformations that they undergo. This includes uses of chemicals and their interactions, danger signs, production techniques, and disposal methods.
Transportation	Knowledge of principles and methods for moving people or goods by air, rail, sea, or road, including the relative costs and benefits.
History and Archeology	Knowledge of historical events and their causes, indicators, and effects on civilizations and cultures.
Sociology and Anthropology	Knowledge of group behavior and dynamics, societal trends and influences, human migrations, ethnicity, cultures and their history and origins.
Telecommunications	Knowledge of transmission, broadcasting, switching, control, and operation of telecommunications systems.
Production and Processing	Knowledge of raw materials, production processes, quality control, costs, and other techniques for maximizing the effective manufacture and distribution of goods.
Food Production	Knowledge of techniques and equipment for planting, growing, and harvesting food products (both plant and animal) for consumption, including storage/handling techniques.
Sales and Marketing	Knowledge of principles and methods for showing, promoting, and selling products or services. This includes marketing strategy and tactics, product demonstration, sales techniques, and sales control systems.
Building and Construction	Knowledge of materials, methods, and the tools involved in the construction or repair of houses, buildings, or other structures such as highways and roads.

Design	Knowledge of design techniques, tools, and principles involved in production of precision technical plans, blueprints, drawings, and models.
Economics and Accounting	Knowledge of economic and accounting principles and practices, the financial markets, banking and the analysis and reporting of financial data.
Medicine and Dentistry	Knowledge of the information and techniques needed to diagnose and treat human injuries, diseases, and deformities. This includes symptoms, treatment alternatives, drug properties and interactions, and preventive health-care measures.
Philosophy and Theology	Knowledge of different philosophical systems and religions. This includes their basic principles, values, ethics, ways of thinking, customs, practices, and their impact on human culture.
Therapy and Counseling	Knowledge of principles, methods, and procedures for diagnosis, treatment, and rehabilitation of physical and mental dysfunctions, and for career counseling and guidance.
Foreign Language	Knowledge of the structure and content of a foreign (non-English) language including the meaning and spelling of words, rules of composition and grammar, and pronunciation.
Fine Arts	Knowledge of the theory and techniques required to compose, produce, and perform works of music, dance, visual arts, drama, and sculpture.

Skills	Skills Definitions
Science	Using scientific rules and methods to solve problems.
Writing	Communicating effectively in writing as appropriate for the needs of the audience.
Reading Comprehension	Understanding written sentences and paragraphs in work related documents.
Active Listening	Giving full attention to what other people are saying, taking time to understand the points being made, asking questions as appropriate, and not interrupting at inappropriate times.
Active Learning	Understanding the implications of new information for both current and future problem-solving and decision-making.
Coordination	Adjusting actions in relation to others' actions.
Judgment and Decision Making	Considering the relative costs and benefits of potential actions to choose the most appropriate one.
Complex Problem Solving	Identifying complex problems and reviewing related information to develop and evaluate options and implement solutions.
Critical Thinking	Using logic and reasoning to identify the strengths and weaknesses of alternative solutions, conclusions or approaches to problems.
Time Management	Managing one's own time and the time of others.
Monitoring	Monitoring/Assessing performance of yourself, other individuals, or organizations to make improvements or take corrective action.
Instructing	Teaching others how to do something.
Learning Strategies	Selecting and using training/instructional methods and procedures appropriate for the situation when learning or teaching new things.
Speaking	Talking to others to convey information effectively.
Mathematics	Using mathematics to solve problems.
Management of Financial Resources	Determining how money will be spent to get the work done, and accounting for these expenditures.
Negotiation	Bringing others together and trying to reconcile differences.
Persuasion	Persuading others to change their minds or behavior.
Social Perceptiveness	Being aware of others' reactions and understanding why they react as they do.
Service Orientation	Actively looking for ways to help people.
Management of Personnel Resources	Motivating, developing, and directing people as they work, identifying the best people for the job.
Quality Control Analysis	Conducting tests and inspections of products, services, or processes to evaluate quality or performance.
Equipment Selection	Determining the kind of tools and equipment needed to do a job.
Operations Analysis	Analyzing needs and product requirements to create a design.
Systems Analysis	Determining how a system should work and how changes in conditions, operations, and the environment will affect outcomes.
Management of Material Resources	Obtaining and seeing to the appropriate use of equipment, facilities, and materials needed to do certain work.
Systems Evaluation	Identifying measures or indicators of system performance and the actions needed to improve or correct performance, relative to the goals of the system.

Troubleshooting	Determining causes of operating errors and deciding what to do about it.
Equipment Maintenance	Performing routine maintenance on equipment and determining when and what kind of maintenance is needed.
Technology Design	Generating or adapting equipment and technology to serve user needs.
Operation and Control	Controlling operations of equipment or systems.
Repairing	Repairing machines or systems using the needed tools.
Installation	Installing equipment, machines, wiring, or programs to meet specifications.
Programming	Writing computer programs for various purposes.
Operation Monitoring	Watching gauges, dials, or other indicators to make sure a machine is working properly.

Ability	Ability Definitions
Oral Expression	The ability to communicate information and ideas in speaking so others will understand.
Inductive Reasoning	The ability to combine pieces of information to form general rules or conclusions (includes finding a relationship among seemingly unrelated events).
Deductive Reasoning	The ability to apply general rules to specific problems to produce answers that make sense.
Written Expression	The ability to communicate information and ideas in writing so others will understand.
Oral Comprehension	The ability to listen to and understand information and ideas presented through spoken words and sentences.
Information Ordering	The ability to arrange things or actions in a certain order or pattern according to a specific rule or set of rules (e.g., patterns of numbers, letters, words, pictures, mathematical operations).
Written Comprehension	The ability to read and understand information and ideas presented in writing.
Speech Clarity	The ability to speak clearly so others can understand you.
Problem Sensitivity	The ability to tell when something is wrong or is likely to go wrong. It does not involve solving the problem, only recognizing there is a problem.
Near Vision	The ability to see details at close range (within a few feet of the observer).
Category Flexibility	The ability to generate or use different sets of rules for combining or grouping things in different ways.
Speech Recognition	The ability to identify and understand the speech of another person.
Far Vision	The ability to see details at a distance.
Selective Attention	The ability to concentrate on a task over a period of time without being distracted.
Originality	The ability to come up with unusual or clever ideas about a given topic or situation, or to develop creative ways to solve a problem.
Flexibility of Closure	The ability to identify or detect a known pattern (a figure, object, word, or sound) that is hidden in other distracting material.
Fluency of Ideas	The ability to come up with a number of ideas about a topic (the number of ideas is important, not their quality, correctness, or creativity).
Arm-Hand Steadiness	The ability to keep your hand and arm steady while moving your arm or while holding your arm and hand in one position.
Time Sharing	The ability to shift back and forth between two or more activities or sources of information (such as speech, sounds, touch, or other sources).
Visual Color Discrimination	The ability to match or detect differences between colors, including shades of color and brightness.
Memorization	The ability to remember information such as words, numbers, pictures, and procedures.
Manual Dexterity	The ability to quickly move your hand, your hand together with your arm, or your two hands to grasp, manipulate, or assemble objects.
Speed of Closure	The ability to quickly make sense of, combine, and organize information into meaningful patterns.
Visualization	The ability to imagine how something will look after it is moved around or when its parts are moved or rearranged.
Mathematical Reasoning	The ability to choose the right mathematical methods or formulas to solve a problem.
Multilimb Coordination	The ability to coordinate two or more limbs (for example, two arms, two legs, or one leg and one arm) while sitting, standing, or lying down. It does not involve performing the activities while the whole body is in motion.

Depth Perception	The ability to judge which of several objects is closer or farther away from you, or to judge the distance between you and an object.
Trunk Strength	The ability to use your abdominal and lower back muscles to support part of the body repeatedly or continuously over time without 'giving out' or fatiguing.
Finger Dexterity	The ability to make precisely coordinated movements of the fingers of one or both hands to grasp, manipulate, or assemble very small objects.
Spatial Orientation	The ability to know your location in relation to the environment or to know where other objects are in relation to you.
Perceptual Speed	The ability to quickly and accurately compare similarities and differences among sets of letters, numbers, objects, pictures, or patterns. The things to be compared may be presented at the same time or one after the other. This ability also includes comparing a presented object with a remembered object.
Control Precision	The ability to quickly and repeatedly adjust the controls of a machine or a vehicle to exact positions.
Auditory Attention	The ability to focus on a single source of sound in the presence of other distracting sounds.
Hearing Sensitivity	The ability to detect or tell the differences between sounds that vary in pitch and loudness.
Static Strength	The ability to exert maximum muscle force to lift, push, pull, or carry objects.
Stamina	The ability to exert yourself physically over long periods of time without getting winded or out of breath.
Gross Body Coordination	The ability to coordinate the movement of your arms, legs, and torso together when the whole body is in motion.
Number Facility	The ability to add, subtract, multiply, or divide quickly and correctly.
Wrist-Finger Speed	The ability to make fast, simple, repeated movements of the fingers, hands, and wrists.
Extent Flexibility	The ability to bend, stretch, twist, or reach with your body, arms, and/or legs.
Dynamic Strength	The ability to exert muscle force repeatedly or continuously over time. This involves muscular endurance and resistance to muscle fatigue.
Reaction Time	The ability to quickly respond (with the hand, finger, or foot) to a signal (sound, light, picture) when it appears.
Peripheral Vision	The ability to see objects or movement of objects to one's side when the eyes are looking ahead.
Speed of Limb Movement	The ability to quickly move the arms and legs.
Glare Sensitivity	The ability to see objects in the presence of glare or bright lighting.
Night Vision	The ability to see under low light conditions.
Response Orientation	The ability to choose quickly between two or more movements in response to two or more different signals (lights, sounds, pictures). It includes the speed with which the correct response is started with the hand, foot, or other body part.
Rate Control	The ability to time your movements or the movement of a piece of equipment in anticipation of changes in the speed and/or direction of a moving object or scene.
Sound Localization	The ability to tell the direction from which a sound originated.
Gross Body Equilibrium	The ability to keep or regain your body balance or stay upright when in an unstable position.
Dynamic Flexibility	The ability to quickly and repeatedly bend, stretch, twist, or reach out with your body, arms, and/or legs.
Explosive Strength	The ability to use short bursts of muscle force to propel oneself (as in jumping or sprinting), or to throw an object.

Work_Activity	Work_Activity Definitions
Communicating with Supervisors, Peers, or Subordin	Providing information to supervisors, co-workers, and subordinates by telephone, in written form, e-mail, or in person.
Organizing, Planning, and Prioritizing Work	Developing specific goals and plans to prioritize, organize, and accomplish your work.
Interacting With Computers	Using computers and computer systems (including hardware and software) to program, write software, set up functions, enter data, or process information.
Getting Information	Observing, receiving, and otherwise obtaining information from all relevant sources.
Documenting/Recording Information	Entering, transcribing, recording, storing, or maintaining information in written or electronic/magnetic form.
Processing Information	Compiling, coding, categorizing, calculating, tabulating, auditing, or verifying information or data.
Updating and Using Relevant Knowledge	Keeping up-to-date technically and applying new knowledge to your job.

Analyzing Data or Information — Identifying the underlying principles, reasons, or facts of information by breaking down information or data into separate parts.

Operating Vehicles, Mechanized Devices, or Equipme — Running, maneuvering, navigating, or driving vehicles or mechanized equipment, such as forklifts, passenger vehicles, aircraft, or water craft.

Monitor Processes, Materials, or Surroundings — Monitoring and reviewing information from materials, events, or the environment, to detect or assess problems.

Communicating with Persons Outside Organization — Communicating with people outside the organization, representing the organization to customers, the public, government, and other external sources. This information can be exchanged in person, in writing, or by telephone or e-mail.

Performing for or Working Directly with the Public — Performing for people or dealing directly with the public. This includes serving customers in restaurants and stores, and receiving clients or guests.

Establishing and Maintaining Interpersonal Relatio — Developing constructive and cooperative working relationships with others, and maintaining them over time.

Making Decisions and Solving Problems — Analyzing information and evaluating results to choose the best solution and solve problems.

Scheduling Work and Activities — Scheduling events, programs, and activities, as well as the work of others.

Thinking Creatively — Developing, designing, or creating new applications, ideas, relationships, systems, or products, including artistic contributions.

Identifying Objects, Actions, and Events — Identifying information by categorizing, estimating, recognizing differences or similarities, and detecting changes in circumstances or events.

Developing Objectives and Strategies — Establishing long-range objectives and specifying the strategies and actions to achieve them.

Provide Consultation and Advice to Others — Providing guidance and expert advice to management or other groups on technical, systems-, or process-related topics.

Performing General Physical Activities — Performing physical activities that require considerable use of your arms and legs and moving your whole body, such as climbing, lifting, balancing, walking, stooping, and handling of materials.

Interpreting the Meaning of Information for Others — Translating or explaining what information means and how it can be used.

Coordinating the Work and Activities of Others — Getting members of a group to work together to accomplish tasks.

Estimating the Quantifiable Characteristics of Pro — Estimating sizes, distances, and quantities; or determining time, costs, resources, or materials needed to perform a work activity.

Evaluating Information to Determine Compliance wit — Using relevant information and individual judgment to determine whether events or processes comply with laws, regulations, or standards.

Monitoring and Controlling Resources — Monitoring and controlling resources and overseeing the spending of money.

Performing Administrative Activities — Performing day-to-day administrative tasks such as maintaining information files and processing paperwork.

Resolving Conflicts and Negotiating with Others — Handling complaints, settling disputes, and resolving grievances and conflicts, or otherwise negotiating with others.

Judging the Qualities of Things, Services, or Peop — Assessing the value, importance, or quality of things or people.

Handling and Moving Objects — Using hands and arms in handling, installing, positioning, and moving materials, and manipulating things.

Developing and Building Teams — Encouraging and building mutual trust, respect, and cooperation among team members.

Controlling Machines and Processes — Using either control mechanisms or direct physical activity to operate machines or processes (not including computers or vehicles).

Training and Teaching Others — Identifying the educational needs of others, developing formal educational or training programs or classes, and teaching or instructing others.

Inspecting Equipment, Structures, or Material — Inspecting equipment, structures, or materials to identify the cause of errors or other problems or defects.

Selling or Influencing Others — Convincing others to buy merchandise/goods or to otherwise change their minds or actions.

Guiding, Directing, and Motivating Subordinates — Providing guidance and direction to subordinates, including setting performance standards and monitoring performance.

Coaching and Developing Others — Identifying the developmental needs of others and coaching, mentoring, or otherwise helping others to improve their knowledge or skills.

Repairing and Maintaining Mechanical Equipment — Servicing, repairing, adjusting, and testing machines, devices, moving parts, and equipment that operate primarily on the basis of mechanical (not electronic) principles.

Assisting and Caring for Others — Providing personal assistance, medical attention, emotional support, or other personal care to others such as coworkers, customers, or patients.

Staffing Organizational Units — Recruiting, interviewing, selecting, hiring, and promoting employees in an organization.

Repairing and Maintaining Electronic Equipment — Servicing, repairing, calibrating, regulating, fine-tuning, or testing machines, devices, and equipment that operate primarily on the basis of electrical or electronic (not mechanical) principles.

Drafting, Laying Out, and Specifying Technical Dev — Providing documentation, detailed instructions, drawings, or specifications to tell others about how devices, parts, equipment, or structures are to be fabricated, constructed, assembled, modified, maintained, or used.

Work_Context / Work_Context Definitions

Electronic Mail — How often do you use electronic mail in this job?

Face-to-Face Discussions — How often do you have to have face-to-face discussions with individuals or teams in this job?

Telephone — How often do you have telephone conversations in this job?

Freedom to Make Decisions — How much decision making freedom, without supervision, does the job offer?

Structured versus Unstructured Work — To what extent is this job structured for the worker, rather than allowing the worker to determine tasks, priorities, and goals?

Letters and Memos — How often does the job require written letters and memos?

Contact With Others — How much does this job require the worker to be in contact with others (face-to-face, by telephone, or otherwise) in order to perform it?

Work With Work Group or Team — How important is it to work with others in a group or team in this job?

Indoors, Environmentally Controlled — How often does this job require working indoors in environmentally controlled conditions?

In an Enclosed Vehicle or Equipment — How often does this job require working in a closed vehicle or equipment (e.g., car)?

Impact of Decisions on Co-workers or Company Resul — How do the decisions an employee makes impact the results of co-workers, clients or the company?

Time Pressure — How often does this job require the worker to meet strict deadlines?

Outdoors, Exposed to Weather — How often does this job require working outdoors, exposed to all weather conditions?

Responsibility for Outcomes and Results — How responsible is the worker for work outcomes and results of other workers?

Coordinate or Lead Others — How important is it to coordinate or lead others in accomplishing work activities in this job?

Deal With External Customers — How important is it to work with external customers or the public in this job?

Importance of Being Exact or Accurate — How important is being very exact or highly accurate in performing this job?

Frequency of Decision Making — How frequently is the worker required to make decisions that affect other people, the financial resources, and/or the image and reputation of the organization?

Frequency of Conflict Situations — How often are there conflict situations the employee has to face in this job?

Spend Time Sitting — How much does this job require sitting?

Level of Competition — To what extent does this job require the worker to compete or to be aware of competitive pressures?

Wear Common Protective or Safety Equipment such as — How much does this job require wearing common protective or safety equipment such as safety shoes, glasses, gloves, hard hats or live jackets?

Importance of Repeating Same Tasks — How important is repeating the same physical activities (e.g., key entry) or mental activities (e.g., checking entries in a ledger) over and over, without stopping, to performing this job?

Sounds, Noise Levels Are Distracting or Uncomforta — How often does this job require working exposed to sounds and noise levels that are distracting or uncomfortable?

Deal With Unpleasant or Angry People — How frequently does the worker have to deal with unpleasant, angry, or discourteous individuals as part of the job requirements?

Responsible for Others' Health and Safety — How much responsibility is there for the health and safety of others in this job?

Very Hot or Cold Temperatures — How often does this job require working in very hot (above 90 F degrees) or very cold (below 32 F degrees) temperatures?

Physical Proximity — To what extent does this job require the worker to perform job tasks in close physical proximity to other people?

Indoors, Not Environmentally Controlled — How often does this job require working indoors in non-controlled environmental conditions (e.g., warehouse without heat)?

Exposed to Minor Burns, Cuts, Bites, or Stings	How often does this job require exposure to minor burns, cuts, bites, or stings?
Spend Time Using Your Hands to Handle, Control, or	How much does this job require using your hands to handle, control, or feel objects, tools or controls?
Spend Time Standing	How much does this job require standing?
Consequence of Error	How serious would the result usually be if the worker made a mistake that was not readily correctable?
Spend Time Making Repetitive Motions	How much does this job require making repetitive motions?
Spend Time Walking and Running	How much does this job require walking and running?
Extremely Bright or Inadequate Lighting	How often does this job require working in extremely bright or inadequate lighting conditions?
Spend Time Bending or Twisting the Body	How much does this job require bending or twisting your body?
Exposed to Contaminants	How often does this job require working exposed to contaminants (such as pollutants, gases, dust or odors)?
Outdoors, Under Cover	How often does this job require working outdoors, under cover (e.g., structure with roof but no walls)?
Public Speaking	How often do you have to perform public speaking in this job?
Degree of Automation	How automated is the job?
Exposed to Hazardous Conditions	How often does this job require exposure to hazardous conditions?
Cramped Work Space, Awkward Positions	How often does this job require working in cramped work spaces that requires getting into awkward positions?
Exposed to Hazardous Equipment	How often does this job require exposure to hazardous equipment?
Exposed to High Places	How often does this job require exposure to high places?
In an Open Vehicle or Equipment	How often does this job require working in an open vehicle or equipment (e.g., tractor)?
Spend Time Kneeling, Crouching, Stooping, or Crawl	How much does this job require kneeling, crouching, stooping, or crawling?
Spend Time Keeping or Regaining Balance	How much does this job require keeping or regaining your balance?
Exposed to Disease or Infections	How often does this job require exposure to disease/infections?
Wear Specialized Protective or Safety Equipment su	How much does this job require wearing specialized protective or safety equipment such as breathing apparatus, safety harness, full protection suits, or radiation protection?
Exposed to Whole Body Vibration	How often does this job require exposure to whole body vibration (e.g., operate a jackhammer)?
Spend Time Climbing Ladders, Scaffolds, or Poles	How much does this job require climbing ladders, scaffolds, or poles?
Deal With Physically Aggressive People	How frequently does this job require the worker to deal with physical aggression of violent individuals?
Pace Determined by Speed of Equipment	How important is it to this job that the pace is determined by the speed of equipment or machinery? (This does not refer to keeping busy at all times on this job.)
Exposed to Radiation	How often does this job require exposure to radiation?

Job Zone Component	Job Zone Component Definitions
Title	Job Zone Five: Extensive Preparation Needed
Overall Experience	Extensive skill, knowledge, and experience are needed for these occupations. Many require more than five years of experience. For example, surgeons must complete four years of college and an additional five to seven years of specialized medical training to be able to do their job.
Job Training	Employees may need some on-the-job training, but most of these occupations assume that the person will already have the required skills, knowledge, work-related experience, and/or training.
Job Zone Examples	These occupations often involve coordinating, training, supervising, or managing the activities of others to accomplish goals. Very advanced communication and organizational skills are required. Examples include athletic trainers, lawyers, managing editors, phyicists, social psychologists, and surgeons.
SVP Range	(8.0 and above)
Education	A bachelor's degree is the minimum formal education required for these occupations. However, many also require graduate school. For example, they may require a master's degree, and some require a Ph.D., M.D., or J.D. (law degree).

Work_Styles	Work_Styles Definitions
Integrity	Job requires being honest and ethical.
Dependability	Job requires being reliable, responsible, and dependable, and fulfilling obligations.
Attention to Detail	Job requires being careful about detail and thorough in completing work tasks.
Independence	Job requires developing one's own ways of doing things, guiding oneself with little or no supervision, and depending on oneself to get things done.
Initiative	Job requires a willingness to take on responsibilities and challenges.
Cooperation	Job requires being pleasant with others on the job and displaying a good-natured, cooperative attitude.
Self Control	Job requires maintaining composure, keeping emotions in check, controlling anger, and avoiding aggressive behavior, even in very difficult situations.
Analytical Thinking	Job requires analyzing information and using logic to address work-related issues and problems.
Stress Tolerance	Job requires accepting criticism and dealing calmly and effectively with high stress situations.
Achievement/Effort	Job requires establishing and maintaining personally challenging achievement goals and exerting effort toward mastering tasks.
Persistence	Job requires persistence in the face of obstacles.
Innovation	Job requires creativity and alternative thinking to develop new ideas for and answers to work-related problems.
Leadership	Job requires a willingness to lead, take charge, and offer opinions and direction.
Adaptability/Flexibility	Job requires being open to change (positive or negative) and to considerable variety in the workplace.
Concern for Others	Job requires being sensitive to others' needs and feelings and being understanding and helpful on the job.
Social Orientation	Job requires preferring to work with others rather than alone, and being personally connected with others on the job.

19-1031.01 - Soil Conservationists

Plan and develop coordinated practices for soil erosion control, soil and water conservation, and sound land use.

Tasks

1) Coordinate and implement technical, financial, and administrative assistance programs for local government units to ensure efficient program implementation and timely responses to requests for assistance.

2) Participate on work teams to plan, develop, and implement water and land management programs and policies.

3) Analyze results of investigations to determine measures needed to maintain or restore proper soil management.

4) Compute design specifications for implementation of conservation practices, using survey and field information technical guides, engineering manuals, and calculator.

5) Initiate, schedule and conduct annual audits and compliance checks of program implementation by local government.

6) Compile and interpret wetland biodata to determine extent and type of wetland and to aid in program formulation.

7) Provide access to programs and training to assist in completion of government groundwater protection plans.

8) Manage field offices and involve staff in cooperative ventures.

9) Conduct fact-finding and mediation sessions among government units, landowners, and other agencies in order to resolve disputes.

10) Compute cost estimates of different conservation practices based on needs of land users, maintenance requirements and life expectancy of practices.

11) Develop, conduct and/or participate in surveys, studies and investigations of various land uses, gathering information for use in developing corrective action plans.

12) Survey property to mark locations and measurements, using surveying instruments.

13) Review grant applications and make funding recommendations.

14) Respond to complaints and questions on wetland jurisdiction, providing information and

clarification.

15) Monitor projects during and after construction to ensure projects conform to design specifications.

16) Advise land users such as farmers and ranchers on conservation plans, problems and alternative solutions, and provide technical and planning assistance.

17) Develop and maintain working relationships with local government staff and board members.

18) Visit areas affected by erosion problems to seek sources and solutions.

19) Review proposed wetland restoration easements and provide technical recommendations.

20) Review annual reports of counties, conservation districts, and watershed management organizations, certifying compliance with mandated reporting requirements.

21) Review and approve amendments to comprehensive local water plans and conservation district plans.

22) Plan soil management and conservation practices, such as crop rotation, reforestation, permanent vegetation, contour plowing, or terracing, to maintain soil and conserve water.

23) Revisit land users to view implemented land use practices and plans.

24) Apply principles of specialized fields of science, such as agronomy, soil science, forestry, or agriculture, to achieve conservation objectives.

19-1031.02 - Range Managers

Research or study range land management practices to provide sustained production of forage, livestock, and wildlife.

Tasks

1) Offer advice to rangeland users on water management, forage production methods, and control of brush.

2) Plan and implement revegetation of disturbed sites.

3) Tailor conservation plans to landowners' goals, such as livestock support, wildlife, or recreation.

4) Develop new and improved instruments and techniques for activities such as range reseeding.

5) Study forage plants and their growth requirements to determine varieties best suited to particular range.

6) Manage private livestock operations.

7) Regulate grazing, and help ranchers plan and organize grazing systems in order to manage, improve and protect rangelands and maximize their use.

8) Maintain soil stability and vegetation for non-grazing uses, such as wildlife habitats and outdoor recreation.

9) Study grazing patterns to determine number and kind of livestock that can be most profitably grazed and to determine the best grazing seasons.

10) Measure and assess vegetation resources for biological assessment companies, environmental impact statements, and rangeland monitoring programs.

11) Plan and direct construction and maintenance of range improvements such as fencing, corrals, stock-watering reservoirs and soil-erosion control structures.

12) Mediate agreements among rangeland users and preservationists as to appropriate land use and management.

13) Develop technical standards and specifications used to manage, protect and improve the natural resources of range lands and related grazing lands.

14) Study rangeland management practices and research range problems to provide sustained production of forage, livestock, and wildlife.

15) Manage forage resources through fire, herbicide use, or revegetation to maintain a sustainable yield from the land.

19-1031.03 - Park Naturalists

Plan, develop, and conduct programs to inform public of historical, natural, and scientific features of national, state, or local park.

Tasks

1) Prepare and present illustrated lectures and interpretive talks about park features.

2) Provide visitor services by explaining regulations; answering visitor requests, needs and complaints; and providing information about the park and surrounding areas.

3) Assist with operations of general facilities, such as visitor centers.

4) Compile and maintain official park photographic and information files.

5) Construct historical, scientific, and nature visitor-center displays.

6) Prepare brochures and write newspaper articles.

7) Confer with park staff to determine subjects and schedules for park programs.

8) Research stories regarding the area's natural history or environment.

9) Interview specialists in desired fields to obtain and develop data for park information programs.

10) Perform routine maintenance on park structures.

11) Perform emergency duties to protect human life, government property, and natural features of park.

12) Plan and develop audiovisual devices for public programs.

13) Take photographs and motion pictures for use in lectures and publications and to develop displays.

14) Plan, organize and direct activities of seasonal staff members.

15) Survey park to determine forest conditions and distribution and abundance of fauna and flora.

Knowledge	Knowledge Definitions
Customer and Personal Service	Knowledge of principles and processes for providing customer and personal services. This includes customer needs assessment, meeting quality standards for services, and evaluation of customer satisfaction.
English Language	Knowledge of the structure and content of the English language including the meaning and spelling of words, rules of composition, and grammar.
Biology	Knowledge of plant and animal organisms, their tissues, cells, functions, interdependencies, and interactions with each other and the environment.
Communications and Media	Knowledge of media production, communication, and dissemination techniques and methods. This includes alternative ways to inform and entertain via written, oral, and visual media.
Education and Training	Knowledge of principles and methods for curriculum and training design, teaching and instruction for individuals and groups, and the measurement of training effects.
Public Safety and Security	Knowledge of relevant equipment, policies, procedures, and strategies to promote effective local, state, or national security operations for the protection of people, data, property, and institutions.
Clerical	Knowledge of administrative and clerical procedures and systems such as word processing, managing files and records, stenography and transcription, designing forms, and other office procedures and terminology.
Geography	Knowledge of principles and methods for describing the features of land, sea, and air masses, including their physical characteristics, locations, interrelationships, and distribution of plant, animal, and human life.
Law and Government	Knowledge of laws, legal codes, court procedures, precedents, government regulations, executive orders, agency rules, and the democratic political process.
History and Archeology	Knowledge of historical events and their causes, indicators, and effects on civilizations and cultures.
Psychology	Knowledge of human behavior and performance; individual differences in ability, personality, and interests; learning and motivation; psychological research methods; and the assessment and treatment of behavioral and affective disorders.
Sales and Marketing	Knowledge of principles and methods for showing, promoting, and selling products or services. This includes marketing strategy and tactics, product demonstration, sales techniques, and sales control systems.
Computers and Electronics	Knowledge of circuit boards, processors, chips, electronic equipment, and computer hardware and software, including applications and programming.

Sociology and Anthropology	Knowledge of group behavior and dynamics, societal trends and influences, human migrations, ethnicity, cultures and their history and origins.
Administration and Management	Knowledge of business and management principles involved in strategic planning, resource allocation, human resources modeling, leadership technique, production methods, and coordination of people and resources.
Mathematics	Knowledge of arithmetic, algebra, geometry, calculus, statistics, and their applications.
Personnel and Human Resources	Knowledge of principles and procedures for personnel recruitment, selection, training, compensation and benefits, labor relations and negotiation, and personnel information systems.
Chemistry	Knowledge of the chemical composition, structure, and properties of substances and of the chemical processes and transformations that they undergo. This includes uses of chemicals and their interactions, danger signs, production techniques, and disposal methods.
Physics	Knowledge and prediction of physical principles, laws, their interrelationships, and applications to understanding fluid, material, and atmospheric dynamics, and mechanical, electrical, atomic and sub- atomic structures and processes.
Telecommunications	Knowledge of transmission, broadcasting, switching, control, and operation of telecommunications systems.
Fine Arts	Knowledge of the theory and techniques required to compose, produce, and perform works of music, dance, visual arts, drama, and sculpture.
Mechanical	Knowledge of machines and tools, including their designs, uses, repair, and maintenance.
Design	Knowledge of design techniques, tools, and principles involved in production of precision technical plans, blueprints, drawings, and models.
Engineering and Technology	Knowledge of the practical application of engineering science and technology. This includes applying principles, techniques, procedures, and equipment to the design and production of various goods and services.
Medicine and Dentistry	Knowledge of the information and techniques needed to diagnose and treat human injuries, diseases, and deformities. This includes symptoms, treatment alternatives, drug properties and interactions, and preventive health-care measures.
Building and Construction	Knowledge of materials, methods, and the tools involved in the construction or repair of houses, buildings, or other structures such as highways and roads.
Economics and Accounting	Knowledge of economic and accounting principles and practices, the financial markets, banking and the analysis and reporting of financial data.
Philosophy and Theology	Knowledge of different philosophical systems and religions. This includes their basic principles, values, ethics, ways of thinking, customs, practices, and their impact on human culture.
Transportation	Knowledge of principles and methods for moving people or goods by air, rail, sea, or road, including the relative costs and benefits.
Therapy and Counseling	Knowledge of principles, methods, and procedures for diagnosis, treatment, and rehabilitation of physical and mental dysfunctions, and for career counseling and guidance.
Foreign Language	Knowledge of the structure and content of a foreign (non-English) language including the meaning and spelling of words, rules of composition and grammar, and pronunciation.
Production and Processing	Knowledge of raw materials, production processes, quality control, costs, and other techniques for maximizing the effective manufacture and distribution of goods.
Food Production	Knowledge of techniques and equipment for planting, growing, and harvesting food products (both plant and animal) for consumption, including storage/handling techniques.

Skills	Skills Definitions
Speaking	Talking to others to convey information effectively.
Reading Comprehension	Understanding written sentences and paragraphs in work related documents.
Time Management	Managing one's own time and the time of others.
Instructing	Teaching others how to do something.
Learning Strategies	Selecting and using training/instructional methods and procedures appropriate for the situation when learning or teaching new things.
Social Perceptiveness	Being aware of others' reactions and understanding why they react as they do.

Service Orientation	Actively looking for ways to help people.
Management of Personnel Resources	Motivating, developing, and directing people as they work, identifying the best people for the job.
Coordination	Adjusting actions in relation to others' actions.
Writing	Communicating effectively in writing as appropriate for the needs of the audience.
Active Learning	Understanding the implications of new information for both current and future problem-solving and decision-making.
Active Listening	Giving full attention to what other people are saying, taking time to understand the points being made, asking questions as appropriate, and not interrupting at inappropriate times.
Management of Material Resources	Obtaining and seeing to the appropriate use of equipment, facilities, and materials needed to do certain work.
Critical Thinking	Using logic and reasoning to identify the strengths and weaknesses of alternative solutions, conclusions or approaches to problems.
Monitoring	Monitoring/Assessing performance of yourself, other individuals, or organizations to make improvements or take corrective action.
Science	Using scientific rules and methods to solve problems.
Equipment Maintenance	Performing routine maintenance on equipment and determining when and what kind of maintenance is needed.
Persuasion	Persuading others to change their minds or behavior.
Management of Financial Resources	Determining how money will be spent to get the work done, and accounting for these expenditures.
Judgment and Decision Making	Considering the relative costs and benefits of potential actions to choose the most appropriate one.
Operations Analysis	Analyzing needs and product requirements to create a design.
Complex Problem Solving	Identifying complex problems and reviewing related information to develop and evaluate options and implement solutions.
Troubleshooting	Determining causes of operating errors and deciding what to do about it.
Equipment Selection	Determining the kind of tools and equipment needed to do a job.
Negotiation	Bringing others together and trying to reconcile differences.
Technology Design	Generating or adapting equipment and technology to serve user needs.
Mathematics	Using mathematics to solve problems.
Quality Control Analysis	Conducting tests and inspections of products, services, or processes to evaluate quality or performance.
Installation	Installing equipment, machines, wiring, or programs to meet specifications.
Repairing	Repairing machines or systems using the needed tools.
Operation and Control	Controlling operations of equipment or systems.
Systems Analysis	Determining how a system should work and how changes in conditions, operations, and the environment will affect outcomes.
Operation Monitoring	Watching gauges, dials, or other indicators to make sure a machine is working properly.
Systems Evaluation	Identifying measures or indicators of system performance and the actions needed to improve or correct performance, relative to the goals of the system.
Programming	Writing computer programs for various purposes.

Ability	Ability Definitions
Oral Expression	The ability to communicate information and ideas in speaking so others will understand.
Speech Clarity	The ability to speak clearly so others can understand you.
Speech Recognition	The ability to identify and understand the speech of another person.
Oral Comprehension	The ability to listen to and understand information and ideas presented through spoken words and sentences.
Problem Sensitivity	The ability to tell when something is wrong or is likely to go wrong. It does not involve solving the problem, only recognizing there is a problem.
Written Comprehension	The ability to read and understand information and ideas presented in writing.
Information Ordering	The ability to arrange things or actions in a certain order or pattern according to a specific rule or set of rules (e.g., patterns of numbers, letters, words, pictures, mathematical operations).
Inductive Reasoning	The ability to combine pieces of information to form general rules or conclusions (includes finding a relationship among seemingly unrelated events).
Near Vision	The ability to see details at close range (within a few feet of the observer).

Deductive Reasoning	The ability to apply general rules to specific problems to produce answers that make sense.
Written Expression	The ability to communicate information and ideas in writing so others will understand.
Far Vision	The ability to see details at a distance.
Originality	The ability to come up with unusual or clever ideas about a given topic or situation, or to develop creative ways to solve a problem.
Flexibility of Closure	The ability to identify or detect a known pattern (a figure, object, word, or sound) that is hidden in other distracting material.
Selective Attention	The ability to concentrate on a task over a period of time without being distracted.
Category Flexibility	The ability to generate or use different sets of rules for combining or grouping things in different ways.
Fluency of Ideas	The ability to come up with a number of ideas about a topic (the number of ideas is important, not their quality, correctness, or creativity).
Perceptual Speed	The ability to quickly and accurately compare similarities and differences among sets of letters, numbers, objects, pictures, or patterns. The things to be compared may be presented at the same time or one after the other. This ability also includes comparing a presented object with a remembered object.
Visual Color Discrimination	The ability to match or detect differences between colors, including shades of color and brightness.
Control Precision	The ability to quickly and repeatedly adjust the controls of a machine or a vehicle to exact positions.
Multilimb Coordination	The ability to coordinate two or more limbs (for example, two arms, two legs, or one leg and one arm) while sitting, standing, or lying down. It does not involve performing the activities while the whole body is in motion.
Static Strength	The ability to exert maximum muscle force to lift, push, pull, or carry objects.
Arm-Hand Steadiness	The ability to keep your hand and arm steady while moving your arm or while holding your arm and hand in one position.
Depth Perception	The ability to judge which of several objects is closer or farther away from you, or to judge the distance between you and an object.
Manual Dexterity	The ability to quickly move your hand, your hand together with your arm, or your two hands to grasp, manipulate, or assemble objects.
Finger Dexterity	The ability to make precisely coordinated movements of the fingers of one or both hands to grasp, manipulate, or assemble very small objects.
Hearing Sensitivity	The ability to detect or tell the differences between sounds that vary in pitch and loudness.
Visualization	The ability to imagine how something will look after it is moved around or when its parts are moved or rearranged.
Auditory Attention	The ability to focus on a single source of sound in the presence of other distracting sounds.
Speed of Closure	The ability to quickly make sense of, combine, and organize information into meaningful patterns.
Memorization	The ability to remember information such as words, numbers, pictures, and procedures.
Time Sharing	The ability to shift back and forth between two or more activities or sources of information (such as speech, sounds, touch, or other sources).
Trunk Strength	The ability to use your abdominal and lower back muscles to support part of the body repeatedly or continuously over time without 'giving out' or fatiguing.
Number Facility	The ability to add, subtract, multiply, or divide quickly and correctly.
Mathematical Reasoning	The ability to choose the right mathematical methods or formulas to solve a problem.
Response Orientation	The ability to choose quickly between two or more movements in response to two or more different signals (lights, sounds, pictures). It includes the speed with which the correct response is started with the hand, foot, or other body part.
Spatial Orientation	The ability to know your location in relation to the environment or to know where other objects are in relation to you.
Reaction Time	The ability to quickly respond (with the hand, finger, or foot) to a signal (sound, light, picture) when it appears.
Rate Control	The ability to time your movements or the movement of a piece of equipment in anticipation of changes in the speed and/or direction of a moving object or scene.
Gross Body Coordination	The ability to coordinate the movement of your arms, legs, and torso together when the whole body is in motion.

Extent Flexibility	The ability to bend, stretch, twist, or reach with your body, arms, and/or legs.
Dynamic Strength	The ability to exert muscle force repeatedly or continuously over time. This involves muscular endurance and resistance to muscle fatigue.
Gross Body Equilibrium	The ability to keep or regain your body balance or stay upright when in an unstable position.
Night Vision	The ability to see under low light conditions.
Peripheral Vision	The ability to see objects or movement of objects to one's side when the eyes are looking ahead.
Stamina	The ability to exert yourself physically over long periods of time without getting winded or out of breath.
Glare Sensitivity	The ability to see objects in the presence of glare or bright lighting.
Sound Localization	The ability to tell the direction from which a sound originated.
Wrist-Finger Speed	The ability to make fast, simple, repeated movements of the fingers, hands, and wrists.
Speed of Limb Movement	The ability to quickly move the arms and legs.
Explosive Strength	The ability to use short bursts of muscle force to propel oneself (as in jumping or sprinting), or to throw an object.
Dynamic Flexibility	The ability to quickly and repeatedly bend, stretch, twist, or reach out with your body, arms, and/or legs.

Work_Activity	Work_Activity Definitions
Performing for or Working Directly with the Public	Performing for people or dealing directly with the public. This includes serving customers in restaurants and stores, and receiving clients or guests.
Interpreting the Meaning of Information for Others	Translating or explaining what information means and how it can be used.
Getting Information	Observing, receiving, and otherwise obtaining information from all relevant sources.
Communicating with Supervisors, Peers, or Subordin	Providing information to supervisors, co-workers, and subordinates by telephone, in written form, e-mail, or in person.
Communicating with Persons Outside Organization	Communicating with people outside the organization, representing the organization to customers, the public, government, and other external sources. This information can be exchanged in person, in writing, or by telephone or e-mail.
Identifying Objects, Actions, and Events	Identifying information by categorizing, estimating, recognizing differences or similarities, and detecting changes in circumstances or events.
Thinking Creatively	Developing, designing, or creating new applications, ideas, relationships, systems, or products, including artistic contributions.
Monitor Processes, Materials, or Surroundings	Monitoring and reviewing information from materials, events, or the environment, to detect or assess problems.
Performing General Physical Activities	Performing physical activities that require considerable use of your arms and legs and moving your whole body, such as climbing, lifting, balancing, walking, stooping, and handling of materials.
Establishing and Maintaining Interpersonal Relatio	Developing constructive and cooperative working relationships with others, and maintaining them over time.
Scheduling Work and Activities	Scheduling events, programs, and activities, as well as the work of others.
Documenting/Recording Information	Entering, transcribing, recording, storing, or maintaining information in written or electronic/magnetic form.
Organizing, Planning, and Prioritizing Work	Developing specific goals and plans to prioritize, organize, and accomplish your work.
Updating and Using Relevant Knowledge	Keeping up-to-date technically and applying new knowledge to your job.
Handling and Moving Objects	Using hands and arms in handling, installing, positioning, and moving materials, and manipulating things.
Making Decisions and Solving Problems	Analyzing information and evaluating results to choose the best solution and solve problems.
Training and Teaching Others	Identifying the educational needs of others, developing formal educational or training programs or classes, and teaching or instructing others.
Processing Information	Compiling, coding, categorizing, calculating, tabulating, auditing, or verifying information or data.
Developing Objectives and Strategies	Establishing long-range objectives and specifying the strategies and actions to achieve them.
Analyzing Data or Information	Identifying the underlying principles, reasons, or facts of information by breaking down information or data into separate parts.

Evaluating Information to Determine Compliance wit	Using relevant information and individual judgment to determine whether events or processes comply with laws, regulations, or standards.
Coordinating the Work and Activities of Others	Getting members of a group to work together to accomplish tasks.
Interacting With Computers	Using computers and computer systems (including hardware and software) to program, write software, set up functions, enter data, or process information.
Operating Vehicles, Mechanized Devices, or Equipme	Running, maneuvering, navigating, or driving vehicles or mechanized equipment, such as forklifts, passenger vehicles, aircraft, or water craft.
Judging the Qualities of Things, Services, or Peop	Assessing the value, importance, or quality of things or people.
Guiding, Directing, and Motivating Subordinates	Providing guidance and direction to subordinates, including setting performance standards and monitoring performance.
Inspecting Equipment, Structures, or Material	Inspecting equipment, structures, or materials to identify the cause of errors or other problems or defects.
Resolving Conflicts and Negotiating with Others	Handling complaints, settling disputes, and resolving grievances and conflicts, or otherwise negotiating with others.
Controlling Machines and Processes	Using either control mechanisms or direct physical activity to operate machines or processes (not including computers or vehicles).
Assisting and Caring for Others	Providing personal assistance, medical attention, emotional support, or other personal care to others such as coworkers, customers, or patients.
Monitoring and Controlling Resources	Monitoring and controlling resources and overseeing the spending of money.
Coaching and Developing Others	Identifying the developmental needs of others and coaching, mentoring, or otherwise helping others to improve their knowledge or skills.
Performing Administrative Activities	Performing day-to-day administrative tasks such as maintaining information files and processing paperwork.
Repairing and Maintaining Mechanical Equipment	Servicing, repairing, adjusting, and testing machines, devices, moving parts, and equipment that operate primarily on the basis of mechanical (not electronic) principles.
Selling or Influencing Others	Convincing others to buy merchandise/goods or to otherwise change their minds or actions.
Provide Consultation and Advice to Others	Providing guidance and expert advice to management or other groups on technical, systems-, or process-related topics.
Developing and Building Teams	Encouraging and building mutual trust, respect, and cooperation among team members.
Estimating the Quantifiable Characteristics of Pro	Estimating sizes, distances, and quantities; or determining time, costs, resources, or materials needed to perform a work activity.
Staffing Organizational Units	Recruiting, interviewing, selecting, hiring, and promoting employees in an organization.
Repairing and Maintaining Electronic Equipment	Servicing, repairing, calibrating, regulating, fine-tuning, or testing machines, devices, and equipment that operate primarily on the basis of electrical or electronic (not mechanical) principles.
Drafting, Laying Out, and Specifying Technical Dev	Providing documentation, detailed instructions, drawings, or specifications to tell others about how devices, parts, equipment, or structures are to be fabricated, constructed, assembled, modified, maintained, or used.

Work_Context

Work_Context	Work_Context Definitions
Face-to-Face Discussions	How often do you have to have face-to-face discussions with individuals or teams in this job?
Telephone	How often do you have telephone conversations in this job?
Indoors, Environmentally Controlled	How often does this job require working indoors in environmentally controlled conditions?
Freedom to Make Decisions	How much decision making freedom, without supervision, does the job offer?
Electronic Mail	How often do you use electronic mail in this job?
Work With Work Group or Team	How important is it to work with others in a group or team in this job?
Indoors, Not Environmentally Controlled	How often does this job require working indoors in non-controlled environmental conditions (e.g., warehouse without heat)?
Outdoors, Exposed to Weather	How often does this job require working outdoors, exposed to all weather conditions?
In an Enclosed Vehicle or Equipment	How often does this job require working in a closed vehicle or equipment (e.g., car)?
Contact With Others	How much does this job require the worker to be in contact with others (face-to-face, by telephone, or otherwise) in order to perform it?
Structured versus Unstructured Work	To what extent is this job structured for the worker, rather than allowing the worker to determine tasks, priorities, and goals?
Time Pressure	How often does this job require the worker to meet strict deadlines?
Impact of Decisions on Co-workers or Company Resul	How do the decisions an employee makes impact the results of co-workers, clients or the company?
Deal With External Customers	How important is it to work with external customers or the public in this job?
Frequency of Decision Making	How frequently is the worker required to make decisions that affect other people, the financial resources, and/or the image and reputation of the organization?
Public Speaking	How often do you have to perform public speaking in this job?
Letters and Memos	How often does the job require written letters and memos?
Physical Proximity	To what extent does this job require the worker to perform job tasks in close physical proximity to other people?
Importance of Being Exact or Accurate	How important is being very exact or highly accurate in performing this job?
Importance of Repeating Same Tasks	How important is repeating the same physical activities (e.g., key entry) or mental activities (e.g., checking entries in a ledger) over and over, without stopping, to performing this job?
Deal With Unpleasant or Angry People	How frequently does the worker have to deal with unpleasant, angry, or discourteous individuals as part of the job requirements?
Level of Competition	To what extent does this job require the worker to compete or to be aware of competitive pressures?
Very Hot or Cold Temperatures	How often does this job require working in very hot (above 90 F degrees) or very cold (below 32 F degrees) temperatures?
Coordinate or Lead Others	How important is it to coordinate or lead others in accomplishing work activities in this job?
Exposed to Minor Burns, Cuts, Bites, or Stings	How often does this job require exposure to minor burns, cuts, bites, or stings?
Spend Time Using Your Hands to Handle, Control, or	How much does this job require using your hands to handle, control, or feel objects, tools or controls?
Spend Time Sitting	How much does this job require sitting?
Responsible for Others' Health and Safety	How much responsibility is there for the health and safety of others in this job?
Frequency of Conflict Situations	How often are there conflict situations the employee has to face in this job?
Outdoors, Under Cover	How often does this job require working outdoors, under cover (e.g., structure with roof but no walls)?
Spend Time Standing	How much does this job require standing?
Spend Time Making Repetitive Motions	How much does this job require making repetitive motions?
Consequence of Error	How serious would the result usually be if the worker made a mistake that was not readily correctable?
Responsibility for Outcomes and Results	How responsible is the worker for work outcomes and results of other workers?
Wear Common Protective or Safety Equipment such as	How much does this job require wearing common protective or safety equipment such as safety shoes, glasses, gloves, hard hats or life jackets?
Sounds, Noise Levels Are Distracting or Uncomforta	How often does this job require working exposed to sounds and noise levels that are distracting or uncomfortable?
Exposed to Contaminants	How often does this job require working exposed to contaminants (such as pollutants, gases, dust or odors)?
Spend Time Walking and Running	How much does this job require walking and running?
Exposed to Hazardous Equipment	How often does this job require exposure to hazardous equipment?
Spend Time Bending or Twisting the Body	How much does this job require bending or twisting your body?
Degree of Automation	How automated is the job?
Exposed to Disease or Infections	How often does this job require exposure to disease/infections?
Wear Specialized Protective or Safety Equipment su	How much does this job require wearing specialized protective or safety equipment such as breathing apparatus, safety harness, full protection suits, or radiation protection?
Extremely Bright or Inadequate Lighting	How often does this job require working in extremely bright or inadequate lighting conditions?
Spend Time Kneeling, Crouching, Stooping, or Crawl	How much does this job require kneeling, crouching, stooping or crawling?
Exposed to High Places	How often does this job require exposure to high places?
Deal With Physically Aggressive People	How frequently does this job require the worker to deal with physical aggression of violent individuals?
Cramped Work Space, Awkward Positions	How often does this job require working in cramped work spaces that requires getting into awkward positions?

In an Open Vehicle or Equipment	How often does this job require working in an open vehicle or equipment (e.g., tractor)?
Exposed to Hazardous Conditions	How often does this job require exposure to hazardous conditions?
Spend Time Keeping or Regaining Balance	How much does this job require keeping or regaining your balance?
Spend Time Climbing Ladders, Scaffolds, or Poles	How much does this job require climbing ladders, scaffolds, or poles?
Exposed to Whole Body Vibration	How often does this job require exposure to whole body vibration (e.g., operate a jackhammer)?
Pace Determined by Speed of Equipment	How important is it to this job that the pace is determined by the speed of equipment or machinery? (This does not refer to keeping busy at all times on this job.)
Exposed to Radiation	How often does this job require exposure to radiation?

Job Zone Component	Job Zone Component Definitions
Title	Job Zone Four: Considerable Preparation Needed
Overall Experience	A minimum of two to four years of work-related skill, knowledge, or experience is needed for these occupations. For example, an accountant must complete four years of college and work for several years in accounting to be considered qualified.
Job Training	Employees in these occupations usually need several years of work-related experience, on-the-job training, and/or vocational training.
Job Zone Examples	Many of these occupations involve coordinating, supervising, managing, or training others. Examples include accountants, chefs and head cooks, computer programmers, historians, pharmacists, and police detectives.
SVP Range	(7.0 to < 8.0)
Education	Most of these occupations require a four - year bachelor's degree, but some do not.

Work_Styles	Work_Styles Definitions
Adaptability/Flexibility	Job requires being open to change (positive or negative) and to considerable variety in the workplace.
Cooperation	Job requires being pleasant with others on the job and displaying a good-natured, cooperative attitude.
Dependability	Job requires being reliable, responsible, and dependable, and fulfilling obligations.
Self Control	Job requires maintaining composure, keeping emotions in check, controlling anger, and avoiding aggressive behavior, even in very difficult situations.
Social Orientation	Job requires preferring to work with others rather than alone, and being personally connected with others on the job.
Innovation	Job requires creativity and alternative thinking to develop new ideas for and answers to work-related problems.
Integrity	Job requires being honest and ethical.
Initiative	Job requires a willingness to take on responsibilities and challenges.
Stress Tolerance	Job requires accepting criticism and dealing calmly and effectively with high stress situations.
Attention to Detail	Job requires being careful about detail and thorough in completing work tasks.
Independence	Job requires developing one's own ways of doing things, guiding oneself with little or no supervision, and depending on oneself to get things done.
Achievement/Effort	Job requires establishing and maintaining personally challenging achievement goals and exerting effort toward mastering tasks.
Concern for Others	Job requires being sensitive to others' needs and feelings and being understanding and helpful on the job.
Persistence	Job requires persistence in the face of obstacles.
Leadership	Job requires a willingness to lead, take charge, and offer opinions and direction.
Analytical Thinking	Job requires analyzing information and using logic to address work-related issues and problems.

19-1032.00 - Foresters

Manage forested lands for economic, recreational, and conservation purposes. May inventory the type, amount, and location of standing timber, appraise the timber's worth, negotiate the purchase, and draw up contracts for procurement. May determine how to conserve wildlife habitats, creek beds, water quality, and soil stability, and how best to comply with environmental regulations. May devise plans for planting and growing new trees, monitor trees for healthy growth, and determine the best time for harvesting. Develop forest management plans for public and privately-owned forested lands.

Tasks

1) Direct, and participate in, forest-fire suppression.

2) Establish short- and long-term plans for management of forest lands and forest resources.

3) Supervise activities of other forestry workers.

4) Plan and implement projects for conservation of wildlife habitats and soil and water quality.

5) Plan and direct forest surveys and related studies and prepare reports and recommendations.

6) Choose and prepare sites for new trees, using controlled burning, bulldozers, or herbicides to clear weeds, brush, and logging debris.

7) Plan and supervise forestry projects, such as determining the type, number and placement of trees to be planted, managing tree nurseries, thinning forest and monitoring growth of new seedlings.

8) Analyze effect of forest conditions on tree growth rates and tree species prevalence and the yield, duration, seed production, growth viability, and germination of different species.

9) Perform inspections of forests or forest nurseries.

10) Monitor forest-cleared lands to ensure that they are reclaimed to their most suitable end use.

11) Conduct public educational programs on forest care and conservation.

12) Map forest area soils and vegetation to estimate the amount of standing timber and future value and growth.

13) Negotiate terms and conditions of agreements and contracts for forest harvesting, forest management and leasing of forest lands.

14) Determine methods of cutting and removing timber with minimum waste and environmental damage.

15) Study different tree species' classification, life history, light and soil requirements, adaptation to new environmental conditions and resistance to disease and insects.

16) Monitor wildlife populations and assess the impacts of forest operations on population and habitats.

17) Plan cutting programs and manage timber sales from harvested areas, assisting companies to achieve production goals.

18) Plan and direct construction and maintenance of recreation facilities, fire towers, trails, roads and bridges, ensuring that they comply with guidelines and regulations set for forested public lands.

19) Develop techniques for measuring and identifying trees.

20) Provide advice and recommendations, as a consultant on forestry issues, to private woodlot owners, firefighters, government agencies or to companies.

21) Subcontract with loggers or pulpwood cutters for tree removal and to aid in road layout.

22) Develop new techniques for wood or residue use.

23) Procure timber from private landowners.

24) Contact local forest owners and gain permission to take inventory of the type, amount, and location of all standing timber on the property.

Knowledge	Knowledge Definitions
Biology	Knowledge of plant and animal organisms, their tissues, cells, functions, interdependencies, and interactions with each other and the environment.
English Language	Knowledge of the structure and content of the English language including the meaning and spelling of words, rules of composition, and grammar.
Mathematics	Knowledge of arithmetic, algebra, geometry, calculus, statistics, and their applications.
Administration and Management	Knowledge of business and management principles involved in strategic planning, resource allocation, human resources modeling, leadership technique, production methods, and coordination of people and resources.

Computers and Electronics	Knowledge of circuit boards, processors, chips, electronic equipment, and computer hardware and software, including applications and programming.
Geography	Knowledge of principles and methods for describing the features of land, sea, and air masses, including their physical characteristics, locations, interrelationships, and distribution of plant, animal, and human life.
Customer and Personal Service	Knowledge of principles and processes for providing customer and personal services. This includes customer needs assessment, meeting quality standards for services, and evaluation of customer satisfaction.
Law and Government	Knowledge of laws, legal codes, court procedures, precedents, government regulations, executive orders, agency rules, and the democratic political process.
Education and Training	Knowledge of principles and methods for curriculum and training design, teaching and instruction for individuals and groups, and the measurement of training effects.
Communications and Media	Knowledge of media production, communication, and dissemination techniques and methods. This includes alternative ways to inform and entertain via written, oral, and visual media.
Mechanical	Knowledge of machines and tools, including their designs, uses, repair, and maintenance.
Psychology	Knowledge of human behavior and performance; individual differences in ability, personality, and interests; learning and motivation; psychological research methods; and the assessment and treatment of behavioral and affective disorders.
Clerical	Knowledge of administrative and clerical procedures and systems such as word processing, managing files and records, stenography and transcription, designing forms, and other office procedures and terminology.
Public Safety and Security	Knowledge of relevant equipment, policies, procedures, and strategies to promote effective local, state, or national security operations for the protection of people, data, property, and institutions.
Chemistry	Knowledge of the chemical composition, structure, and properties of substances and of the chemical processes and transformations that they undergo. This includes uses of chemicals and their interactions, danger signs, production techniques, and disposal methods.
Building and Construction	Knowledge of materials, methods, and the tools involved in the construction or repair of houses, buildings, or other structures such as highways and roads.
Transportation	Knowledge of principles and methods for moving people or goods by air, rail, sea, or road, including the relative costs and benefits.
Personnel and Human Resources	Knowledge of principles and procedures for personnel recruitment, selection, training, compensation and benefits, labor relations and negotiation, and personnel information systems.
Telecommunications	Knowledge of transmission, broadcasting, switching, control, and operation of telecommunications systems.
Physics	Knowledge and prediction of physical principles, laws, their interrelationships, and applications to understanding fluid, material, and atmospheric dynamics, and mechanical, electrical, atomic and sub- atomic structures and processes.
Engineering and Technology	Knowledge of the practical application of engineering science and technology. This includes applying principles, techniques, procedures, and equipment to the design and production of various goods and services.
Design	Knowledge of design techniques, tools, and principles involved in production of precision technical plans, blueprints, drawings, and models.
Production and Processing	Knowledge of raw materials, production processes, quality control, costs, and other techniques for maximizing the effective manufacture and distribution of goods.
Economics and Accounting	Knowledge of economic and accounting principles and practices, the financial markets, banking and the analysis and reporting of financial data.
Sales and Marketing	Knowledge of principles and methods for showing, promoting, and selling products or services. This includes marketing strategy and tactics, product demonstration, sales techniques, and sales control systems.
Sociology and Anthropology	Knowledge of group behavior and dynamics, societal trends and influences, human migrations, ethnicity, cultures and their history and origins.
History and Archeology	Knowledge of historical events and their causes, indicators, and effects on civilizations and cultures.

Philosophy and Theology	Knowledge of different philosophical systems and religions. This includes their basic principles, values, ethics, ways of thinking, customs, practices, and their impact on human culture.
Therapy and Counseling	Knowledge of principles, methods, and procedures for diagnosis, treatment, and rehabilitation of physical and mental dysfunctions, and for career counseling and guidance.
Foreign Language	Knowledge of the structure and content of a foreign (non-English) language including the meaning and spelling of words, rules of composition and grammar, and pronunciation.
Food Production	Knowledge of techniques and equipment for planting, growing, and harvesting food products (both plant and animal) for consumption, including storage/handling techniques.
Medicine and Dentistry	Knowledge of the information and techniques needed to diagnose and treat human injuries, diseases, and deformities. This includes symptoms, treatment alternatives, drug properties and interactions, and preventive health-care measures.
Fine Arts	Knowledge of the theory and techniques required to compose, produce, and perform works of music, dance, visual arts, drama, and sculpture.

Skills	Skills Definitions
Time Management	Managing one's own time and the time of others.
Coordination	Adjusting actions in relation to others' actions.
Science	Using scientific rules and methods to solve problems.
Critical Thinking	Using logic and reasoning to identify the strengths and weaknesses of alternative solutions, conclusions or approaches to problems.
Reading Comprehension	Understanding written sentences and paragraphs in work related documents.
Active Listening	Giving full attention to what other people are saying, taking time to understand the points being made, asking questions as appropriate, and not interrupting at inappropriate times.
Active Learning	Understanding the implications of new information for both current and future problem-solving and decision-making.
Mathematics	Using mathematics to solve problems.
Speaking	Talking to others to convey information effectively.
Management of Financial Resources	Determining how money will be spent to get the work done, and accounting for these expenditures.
Writing	Communicating effectively in writing as appropriate for the needs of the audience.
Operations Analysis	Analyzing needs and product requirements to create a design.
Judgment and Decision Making	Considering the relative costs and benefits of potential actions to choose the most appropriate one.
Complex Problem Solving	Identifying complex problems and reviewing related information to develop and evaluate options and implement solutions.
Quality Control Analysis	Conducting tests and inspections of products, services, or processes to evaluate quality or performance.
Equipment Selection	Determining the kind of tools and equipment needed to do a job.
Monitoring	Monitoring/Assessing performance of yourself, other individuals, or organizations to make improvements or take corrective action.
Instructing	Teaching others how to do something.
Social Perceptiveness	Being aware of others' reactions and understanding why they react as they do.
Management of Personnel Resources	Motivating, developing, and directing people as they work, identifying the best people for the job.
Service Orientation	Actively looking for ways to help people.
Persuasion	Persuading others to change their minds or behavior.
Learning Strategies	Selecting and using training/instructional methods and procedures appropriate for the situation when learning or teaching new things.
Troubleshooting	Determining causes of operating errors and deciding what to do about it.
Systems Analysis	Determining how a system should work and how changes in conditions, operations, and the environment will affect outcomes.
Negotiation	Bringing others together and trying to reconcile differences.
Operation Monitoring	Watching gauges, dials, or other indicators to make sure a machine is working properly.
Management of Material Resources	Obtaining and seeing to the appropriate use of equipment, facilities, and materials needed to do certain work.
Programming	Writing computer programs for various purposes.

Systems Evaluation	Identifying measures or indicators of system performance and the actions needed to improve or correct performance, relative to the goals of the system.
Operation and Control	Controlling operations of equipment or systems.
Equipment Maintenance	Performing routine maintenance on equipment and determining when and what kind of maintenance is needed.
Technology Design	Generating or adapting equipment and technology to serve user needs.
Repairing	Repairing machines or systems using the needed tools.
Installation	Installing equipment, machines, wiring, or programs to meet specifications.

Ability	Ability Definitions
Oral Expression	The ability to communicate information and ideas in speaking so others will understand.
Deductive Reasoning	The ability to apply general rules to specific problems to produce answers that make sense.
Problem Sensitivity	The ability to tell when something is wrong or is likely to go wrong. It does not involve solving the problem, only recognizing there is a problem.
Oral Comprehension	The ability to listen to and understand information and ideas presented through spoken words and sentences.
Written Comprehension	The ability to read and understand information and ideas presented in writing.
Speech Clarity	The ability to speak clearly so others can understand you.
Inductive Reasoning	The ability to combine pieces of information to form general rules or conclusions (includes finding a relationship among seemingly unrelated events).
Category Flexibility	The ability to generate or use different sets of rules for combining or grouping things in different ways.
Near Vision	The ability to see details at close range (within a few feet of the observer).
Speech Recognition	The ability to identify and understand the speech of another person.
Originality	The ability to come up with unusual or clever ideas about a given topic or situation, or to develop creative ways to solve a problem.
Information Ordering	The ability to arrange things or actions in a certain order or pattern according to a specific rule or set of rules (e.g., patterns of numbers, letters, words, pictures, mathematical operations).
Written Expression	The ability to communicate information and ideas in writing so others will understand.
Far Vision	The ability to see details at a distance.
Fluency of Ideas	The ability to come up with a number of ideas about a topic (the number of ideas is important, not their quality, correctness, or creativity).
Spatial Orientation	The ability to know your location in relation to the environment or to know where other objects are in relation to you.
Flexibility of Closure	The ability to identify or detect a known pattern (a figure, object, word, or sound) that is hidden in other distracting material.
Selective Attention	The ability to concentrate on a task over a period of time without being distracted.
Time Sharing	The ability to shift back and forth between two or more activities or sources of information (such as speech, sounds, touch, or other sources).
Static Strength	The ability to exert maximum muscle force to lift, push, pull, or carry objects.
Speed of Closure	The ability to quickly make sense of, combine, and organize information into meaningful patterns.
Visualization	The ability to imagine how something will look after it is moved around or when its parts are moved or rearranged.
Depth Perception	The ability to judge which of several objects is closer or farther away from you, or to judge the distance between you and an object.
Multilimb Coordination	The ability to coordinate two or more limbs (for example, two arms, two legs, or one leg and one arm) while sitting, standing, or lying down. It does not involve performing the activities while the whole body is in motion.
Mathematical Reasoning	The ability to choose the right mathematical methods or formulas to solve a problem.
Dynamic Strength	The ability to exert muscle force repeatedly or continuously over time. This involves muscular endurance and resistance to muscle fatigue.
Control Precision	The ability to quickly and repeatedly adjust the controls of a machine or a vehicle to exact positions.

Finger Dexterity	The ability to make precisely coordinated movements of the fingers of one or both hands to grasp, manipulate, or assemble very small objects.
Trunk Strength	The ability to use your abdominal and lower back muscles to support part of the body repeatedly or continuously over time without 'giving out' or fatiguing.
Reaction Time	The ability to quickly respond (with the hand, finger, or foot) to a signal (sound, light, picture) when it appears.
Visual Color Discrimination	The ability to match or detect differences between colors, including shades of color and brightness.
Arm-Hand Steadiness	The ability to keep your hand and arm steady while moving your arm or while holding your arm and hand in one position.
Auditory Attention	The ability to focus on a single source of sound in the presence of other distracting sounds.
Stamina	The ability to exert yourself physically over long periods of time without getting winded or out of breath.
Number Facility	The ability to add, subtract, multiply, or divide quickly and correctly.
Memorization	The ability to remember information such as words, numbers, pictures, and procedures.
Perceptual Speed	The ability to quickly and accurately compare similarities and differences among sets of letters, numbers, objects, pictures, or patterns. The things to be compared may be presented at the same time or one after the other. This ability also includes comparing a presented object with a remembered object.
Manual Dexterity	The ability to quickly move your hand, your hand together with your arm, or your two hands to grasp, manipulate, or assemble objects.
Gross Body Coordination	The ability to coordinate the movement of your arms, legs, and torso together when the whole body is in motion.
Peripheral Vision	The ability to see objects or movement of objects to one's side when the eyes are looking ahead.
Glare Sensitivity	The ability to see objects in the presence of glare or bright lighting.
Extent Flexibility	The ability to bend, stretch, twist, or reach with your body, arms, and/or legs.
Speed of Limb Movement	The ability to quickly move the arms and legs.
Night Vision	The ability to see under low light conditions.
Response Orientation	The ability to choose quickly between two or more movements in response to two or more different signals (lights, sounds, pictures). It includes the speed with which the correct response is started with the hand, foot, or other body part.
Rate Control	The ability to time your movements or the movement of a piece of equipment in anticipation of changes in the speed and/or direction of a moving object or scene.
Wrist-Finger Speed	The ability to make fast, simple, repeated movements of the fingers, hands, and wrists.
Gross Body Equilibrium	The ability to keep or regain your body balance or stay upright when in an unstable position.
Hearing Sensitivity	The ability to detect or tell the differences between sounds that vary in pitch and loudness.
Sound Localization	The ability to tell the direction from which a sound originated.
Dynamic Flexibility	The ability to quickly and repeatedly bend, stretch, twist, or reach out with your body, arms, and/or legs.
Explosive Strength	The ability to use short bursts of muscle force to propel oneself (as in jumping or sprinting), or to throw an object.

Work_Activity	Work_Activity Definitions
Documenting/Recording Information	Entering, transcribing, recording, storing, or maintaining information in written or electronic/magnetic form.
Making Decisions and Solving Problems	Analyzing information and evaluating results to choose the best solution and solve problems.
Organizing, Planning, and Prioritizing Work	Developing specific goals and plans to prioritize, organize, and accomplish your work.
Monitor Processes, Materials, or Surroundings	Monitoring and reviewing information from materials, events, or the environment, to detect or assess problems.
Communicating with Supervisors, Peers, or Subordin	Providing information to supervisors, co-workers, and subordinates by telephone, in written form, e-mail, or in person.
Communicating with Persons Outside Organization	Communicating with people outside the organization, representing the organization to customers, the public, government, and other external sources. This information can be exchanged in person, in writing, or by telephone or e-mail.
Performing for or Working Directly with the Public	Performing for people or dealing directly with the public. This includes serving customers in restaurants and stores, and receiving clients or guests.

Processing Information	Compiling, coding, categorizing, calculating, tabulating, auditing, or verifying information or data.
Getting Information	Observing, receiving, and otherwise obtaining information from all relevant sources.
Evaluating Information to Determine Compliance wit	Using relevant information and individual judgment to determine whether events or processes comply with laws, regulations, or standards.
Performing General Physical Activities	Performing physical activities that require considerable use of your arms and legs and moving your whole body, such as climbing, lifting, balancing, walking, stooping, and handling of materials.
Scheduling Work and Activities	Scheduling events, programs, and activities, as well as the work of others.
Analyzing Data or Information	Identifying the underlying principles, reasons, or facts of information by breaking down information or data into separate parts.
Resolving Conflicts and Negotiating with Others	Handling complaints, settling disputes, and resolving grievances and conflicts, or otherwise negotiating with others.
Interacting With Computers	Using computers and computer systems (including hardware and software) to program, write software, set up functions, enter data, or process information.
Identifying Objects, Actions, and Events	Identifying information by categorizing, estimating, recognizing differences or similarities, and detecting changes in circumstances or events.
Thinking Creatively	Developing, designing, or creating new applications, ideas, relationships, systems, or products, including artistic contributions.
Coordinating the Work and Activities of Others	Getting members of a group to work together to accomplish tasks.
Developing Objectives and Strategies	Establishing long-range objectives and specifying the strategies and actions to achieve them.
Establishing and Maintaining Interpersonal Relatio	Developing constructive and cooperative working relationships with others, and maintaining them over time.
Operating Vehicles, Mechanized Devices, or Equipme	Running, maneuvering, navigating, or driving vehicles or mechanized equipment, such as forklifts, passenger vehicles, aircraft, or water craft.
Estimating the Quantifiable Characteristics of Pro	Estimating sizes, distances, and quantities; or determining time, costs, resources, or materials needed to perform a work activity.
Updating and Using Relevant Knowledge	Keeping up-to-date technically and applying new knowledge to your job.
Judging the Qualities of Things, Services, or Peop	Assessing the value, importance, or quality of things or people.
Developing and Building Teams	Encouraging and building mutual trust, respect, and cooperation among team members.
Selling or Influencing Others	Convincing others to buy merchandise/goods or to otherwise change their minds or actions.
Controlling Machines and Processes	Using either control mechanisms or direct physical activity to operate machines or processes (not including computers or vehicles).
Provide Consultation and Advice to Others	Providing guidance and expert advice to management or other groups on technical, systems-, or process-related topics.
Interpreting the Meaning of Information for Others	Translating or explaining what information means and how it can be used.
Guiding, Directing, and Motivating Subordinates	Providing guidance and direction to subordinates, including setting performance standards and monitoring performance.
Training and Teaching Others	Identifying the educational needs of others, developing formal educational or training programs or classes, and teaching or instructing others.
Handling and Moving Objects	Using hands and arms in handling, installing, positioning, and moving materials, and manipulating things.
Monitoring and Controlling Resources	Monitoring and controlling resources and overseeing the spending of money.
Drafting, Laying Out, and Specifying Technical Dev	Providing documentation, detailed instructions, drawings, or specifications to tell others about how devices, parts, equipment, or structures are to be fabricated, constructed, assembled, modified, maintained, or used.
Assisting and Caring for Others	Providing personal assistance, medical attention, emotional support, or other personal care to others such as coworkers, customers, or patients.
Performing Administrative Activities	Performing day-to-day administrative tasks such as maintaining information files and processing paperwork.
Inspecting Equipment, Structures, or Material	Inspecting equipment, structures, or materials to identify the cause of errors or other problems or defects.
Coaching and Developing Others	Identifying the developmental needs of others and coaching, mentoring, or otherwise helping others to improve their knowledge or skills.

Repairing and Maintaining Mechanical Equipment	Servicing, repairing, adjusting, and testing machines, devices, moving parts, and equipment that operate primarily on the basis of mechanical (not electronic) principles.
Repairing and Maintaining Electronic Equipment	Servicing, repairing, calibrating, regulating, fine-tuning, or testing machines, devices, and equipment that operate primarily on the basis of electrical or electronic (not mechanical) principles.
Staffing Organizational Units	Recruiting, interviewing, selecting, hiring, and promoting employees in an organization.

Work_Context	Work_Context Definitions
Freedom to Make Decisions	How much decision making freedom, without supervision, does the job offer?
Electronic Mail	How often do you use electronic mail in this job?
Telephone	How often do you have telephone conversations in this job?
Structured versus Unstructured Work	To what extent is this job structured for the worker, rather than allowing the worker to determine tasks, priorities, and goals?
Face-to-Face Discussions	How often do you have to have face-to-face discussions with individuals or teams in this job?
Frequency of Decision Making	How frequently is the worker required to make decisions that affect other people, the financial resources, and/or the image and reputation of the organization?
Responsibility for Outcomes and Results	How responsible is the worker for work outcomes and results of other workers?
Work With Work Group or Team	How important is it to work with others in a group or team in this job?
Coordinate or Lead Others	How important is it to coordinate or lead others in accomplishing work activities in this job?
Impact of Decisions on Co-workers or Company Resul	How do the decisions an employee makes impact the results of co-workers, clients or the company?
Responsible for Others' Health and Safety	How much responsibility is there for the health and safety of others in this job?
Indoors, Environmentally Controlled	How often does this job require working indoors in environmentally controlled conditions?
In an Enclosed Vehicle or Equipment	How often does this job require working in a closed vehicle or equipment (e.g., car)?
Consequence of Error	How serious would the result usually be if the worker made a mistake that was not readily correctable?
Contact With Others	How much does this job require the worker to be in contact with others (face-to-face, by telephone, or otherwise) in order to perform it?
Letters and Memos	How often does the job require written letters and memos?
Level of Competition	To what extent does this job require the worker to compete or to be aware of competitive pressures?
Importance of Being Exact or Accurate	How important is being very exact or highly accurate in performing this job?
Deal With External Customers	How important is it to work with external customers or the public in this job?
Spend Time Sitting	How much does this job require sitting?
Outdoors, Exposed to Weather	How often does this job require working outdoors, exposed to all weather conditions?
Indoors, Not Environmentally Controlled	How often does this job require working indoors in non-controlled environmental conditions (e.g., warehouse without heat)?
Sounds, Noise Levels Are Distracting or Uncomforta	How often does this job require working exposed to sounds and noise levels that are distracting or uncomfortable?
Time Pressure	How often does this job require the worker to meet strict deadlines?
Wear Common Protective or Safety Equipment such as	How much does this job require wearing common protective or safety equipment such as safety shoes, glasses, gloves, hard hats or live jackets?
Importance of Repeating Same Tasks	How important is repeating the same physical activities (e.g., key entry) or mental activities (e.g., checking entries in a ledger) over and over, without stopping, to performing this job?
Exposed to Hazardous Equipment	How often does this job require exposure to hazardous equipment?
Exposed to Contaminants	How often does this job require working exposed to contaminants (such as pollutants, gases, dust or odors)?
Frequency of Conflict Situations	How often are there conflict situations the employee has to face in this job?
Very Hot or Cold Temperatures	How often does this job require working in very hot (above 90 F degrees) or very cold (below 32 F degrees) temperatures?
Deal With Unpleasant or Angry People	How frequently does the worker have to deal with unpleasant, angry, or discourteous individuals as part of the job requirements?

Exposed to Minor Burns, Cuts, Bites, or Stings	How often does this job require exposure to minor burns, cuts, bites, or stings?
Spend Time Making Repetitive Motions	How much does this job require making repetitive motions?
Spend Time Standing	How much does this job require standing?
Spend Time Walking and Running	How much does this job require walking and running?
Physical Proximity	To what extent does this job require the worker to perform job tasks in close physical proximity to other people?
Public Speaking	How often do you have to perform public speaking in this job?
Degree of Automation	How automated is the job?
Extremely Bright or Inadequate Lighting	How often does this job require working in extremely bright or inadequate lighting conditions?
Exposed to Hazardous Conditions	How often does this job require exposure to hazardous conditions?
Spend Time Using Your Hands to Handle, Control, or	How much does this job require using your hands to handle, control, or feel objects, tools or controls?
Spend Time Bending or Twisting the Body	How much does this job require bending or twisting your body?
Exposed to High Places	How often does this job require exposure to high places?
Spend Time Keeping or Regaining Balance	How much does this job require keeping or regaining your balance?
Spend Time Kneeling, Crouching, Stooping, or Crawl	How much does this job require kneeling, crouching, stooping or crawling?
Deal With Physically Aggressive People	How frequently does this job require the worker to deal with physical aggression of violent individuals?
Outdoors, Under Cover	How often does this job require working outdoors, under cover (e.g., structure with roof but no walls)?
Wear Specialized Protective or Safety Equipment su	How much does this job require wearing specialized protective or safety equipment such as breathing apparatus, safety harness, full protection suits, or radiation protection?
Cramped Work Space, Awkward Positions	How often does this job require working in cramped work spaces that requires getting into awkward positions?
In an Open Vehicle or Equipment	How often does this job require working in an open vehicle or equipment (e.g., tractor)?
Exposed to Whole Body Vibration	How often does this job require exposure to whole body vibration (e.g., operate a jackhammer)?
Spend Time Climbing Ladders, Scaffolds, or Poles	How much does this job require climbing ladders, scaffolds, or poles?
Exposed to Radiation	How often does this job require exposure to radiation?
Exposed to Disease or Infections	How often does this job require exposure to disease/infections?
Pace Determined by Speed of Equipment	How important is it to this job that the pace is determined by the speed of equipment or machinery? (This does not refer to keeping busy at all times on this job.)

Job Zone Component	Job Zone Component Definitions
Title	Job Zone Four: Considerable Preparation Needed
Overall Experience	A minimum of two to four years of work-related skill, knowledge, or experience is needed for these occupations. For example, an accountant must complete four years of college and work for several years in accounting to be considered qualified.
Job Training	Employees in these occupations usually need several years of work-related experience, on-the-job training, and/or vocational training.
Job Zone Examples	Many of these occupations involve coordinating, supervising, managing, or training others. Examples include accountants, chefs and head cooks, computer programmers, historians, pharmacists, and police detectives.
SVP Range	(7.0 to < 8.0)
Education	Most of these occupations require a four - year bachelor's degree, but some do not.

Work_Styles	Work_Styles Definitions
Cooperation	Job requires being pleasant with others on the job and displaying a good-natured, cooperative attitude.
Independence	Job requires developing one's own ways of doing things, guiding oneself with little or no supervision, and depending on oneself to get things done.
Dependability	Job requires being reliable, responsible, and dependable, and fulfilling obligations.

Integrity	Job requires being honest and ethical.
Initiative	Job requires a willingness to take on responsibilities and challenges.
Attention to Detail	Job requires being careful about detail and thorough in completing work tasks.
Persistence	Job requires persistence in the face of obstacles.
Self Control	Job requires maintaining composure, keeping emotions in check, controlling anger, and avoiding aggressive behavior, even in very difficult situations.
Adaptability/Flexibility	Job requires being open to change (positive or negative) and to considerable variety in the workplace.
Concern for Others	Job requires being sensitive to others' needs and feelings and being understanding and helpful on the job.
Analytical Thinking	Job requires analyzing information and using logic to address work-related issues and problems.
Achievement/Effort	Job requires establishing and maintaining personally challenging achievement goals and exerting effort toward mastering tasks.
Innovation	Job requires creativity and alternative thinking to develop new ideas for and answers to work-related problems.
Leadership	Job requires a willingness to lead, take charge, and offer opinions and direction.
Social Orientation	Job requires preferring to work with others rather than alone, and being personally connected with others on the job.
Stress Tolerance	Job requires accepting criticism and dealing calmly and effectively with high stress situations.

19-1042.00 - Medical Scientists, Except Epidemiologists

Conduct research dealing with the understanding of human diseases and the improvement of human health. Engage in clinical investigation or other research, production, technical writing, or related activities.

Tasks

1) Follow strict safety procedures when handling toxic materials to avoid contamination.

2) Investigate cause, progress, life cycle, or mode of transmission of diseases or parasites.

3) Standardize drug dosages, methods of immunization, and procedures for manufacture of drugs and medicinal compounds.

4) Prepare and analyze organ, tissue and cell samples to identify toxicity, bacteria, or microorganisms, or to study cell structure.

5) Confer with health department, industry personnel, physicians, and others to develop health safety standards and public health improvement programs.

6) Study animal and human health and physiological processes.

7) Consult with and advise physicians, educators, researchers, and others regarding medical applications of physics, biology, and chemistry.

8) Teach principles of medicine and medical and laboratory procedures to physicians, residents, students, and technicians.

9) Plan and direct studies to investigate human or animal disease, preventive methods, and treatments for disease.

10) Use equipment such as atomic absorption spectrometers, electron microscopes, flow cytometers and chromatography systems.

11) Conduct research to develop methodologies, instrumentation and procedures for medical application, analyzing data and presenting findings.

19-2012.00 - Physicists

Conduct research into the phases of physical phenomena, develop theories and laws on the basis of observation and experiments, and devise methods to apply laws and theories to industry and other fields.

Tasks

1) Describe and express observations and conclusions in mathematical terms.

2) Design computer simulations to model physical data so that it can be better understood.

3) Observe the structure and properties of matter, and the transformation and propagation of

energy, using equipment such as masers, lasers, and telescopes, in order to explore and identify the basic principles governing these phenomena.

4) Report experimental results by writing papers for scientific journals or by presenting information at scientific conferences.

5) Collaborate with other scientists in the design, development, and testing of experimental, industrial, or medical equipment, instrumentation, and procedures.

6) Analyze data from research conducted to detect and measure physical phenomena.

7) Develop manufacturing, assembly, and fabrication processes of lasers, masers, infrared, and other light-emitting and light-sensitive devices.

8) Perform complex calculations as part of the analysis and evaluation of data, using computers.

9) Teach physics to students.

10) Conduct research pertaining to potential environmental impacts of atomic energy-related industrial development in order to determine licensing qualifications.

11) Develop standards of permissible concentrations of radioisotopes in liquids and gases.

12) Direct testing and monitoring of contamination of radioactive equipment, and recording of personnel and plant area radiation exposure data.

13) Advise authorities of procedures to be followed in radiation incidents or hazards, and assist in civil defense planning.

14) Develop theories and laws on the basis of observation and experiments, and apply these theories and laws to problems in areas such as nuclear energy, optics, and aerospace technology.

15) Conduct application evaluations and analyze results in order to determine commercial, industrial, scientific, medical, military, or other uses for electro-optical devices.

19-2021.00 - Atmospheric and Space Scientists

Investigate atmospheric phenomena and interpret meteorological data gathered by surface and air stations, satellites, and radar to prepare reports and forecasts for public and other uses.

Tasks

1) Study and interpret data, reports, maps, photographs, and charts to predict long- and short-range weather conditions, using computer models and knowledge of climate theory, physics, and mathematics.

2) Broadcast weather conditions, forecasts, and severe weather warnings to the public via television, radio, and the Internet, and/or provide this information to the news media.

3) Direct forecasting services at weather stations, or at radio or television broadcasting facilities.

4) Teach at colleges or universities.

5) Make scientific presentations, and publish reports, articles, or texts.

6) Measure wind, temperature, and humidity in the upper atmosphere, using weather balloons.

7) Design and develop new equipment and methods for meteorological data collection, remote sensing, or related applications.

8) Consult with agencies, professionals, or researchers regarding the use and interpretation of climatological information.

9) Prepare forecasts and briefings to meet the needs of industry, business, government, and other groups.

10) Operate computer graphic equipment to produce weather reports and maps for analysis, distribution, or use in weather broadcasts.

11) Gather data from sources such as surface and upper air stations, satellites, weather bureaus, and radar for use in meteorological reports and forecasts.

12) Apply meteorological knowledge to problems in areas including agriculture, pollution control, and water management, and to issues such as global warming or ozone depletion.

13) Conduct numerical simulations of climate conditions in order to understand and predict global and regional weather patterns.

14) Collect and analyze historical climate information such as precipitation and temperature records in order to help predict future weather and climate trends.

15) Develop and use weather forecasting tools such as mathematical and computer models.

16) Research and analyze the impact of industrial projects and pollution on climate, air quality, and weather phenomena.

17) Conduct basic or applied meteorological research into the processes and determinants of atmospheric phenomena, weather, and climate.

19-2031.00 - Chemists

Conduct qualitative and quantitative chemical analyses or chemical experiments in laboratories for quality or process control or to develop new products or knowledge.

Tasks

1) Confer with scientists and engineers to conduct analyses of research projects, interpret test results, or develop nonstandard tests.

2) Write technical papers and reports; and prepare standards and specifications for processes, facilities, products, and tests.

3) Compile and analyze test information to determine process or equipment operating efficiency and to diagnose malfunctions.

4) Direct, coordinate, and advise personnel in test procedures for analyzing components and physical properties of materials.

5) Induce changes in composition of substances by introducing heat, light, energy, and chemical catalysts for quantitative and qualitative analysis.

6) Analyze organic and inorganic compounds to determine chemical and physical properties, composition, structure, relationships, and reactions, utilizing chromatography, spectroscopy, and spectrophotometry techniques.

7) Prepare test solutions, compounds, and reagents for laboratory personnel to conduct test.

8) Study effects of various methods of processing, preserving, and packaging on composition and properties of foods.

Knowledge	Knowledge Definitions
Chemistry	Knowledge of the chemical composition, structure, and properties of substances and of the chemical processes and transformations that they undergo. This includes uses of chemicals and their interactions, danger signs, production techniques, and disposal methods.
Mathematics	Knowledge of arithmetic, algebra, geometry, calculus, statistics, and their applications.
English Language	Knowledge of the structure and content of the English language including the meaning and spelling of words, rules of composition, and grammar.
Computers and Electronics	Knowledge of circuit boards, processors, chips, electronic equipment, and computer hardware and software, including applications and programming.
Production and Processing	Knowledge of raw materials, production processes, quality control, costs, and other techniques for maximizing the effective manufacture and distribution of goods.
Engineering and Technology	Knowledge of the practical application of engineering science and technology. This includes applying principles, techniques, procedures, and equipment to the design and production of various goods and services.
Education and Training	Knowledge of principles and methods for curriculum and training design, teaching and instruction for individuals and groups, and the measurement of training effects.
Public Safety and Security	Knowledge of relevant equipment, policies, procedures, and strategies to promote effective local, state, or national security operations for the protection of people, data, property, and institutions.
Law and Government	Knowledge of laws, legal codes, court procedures, precedents, government regulations, executive orders, agency rules, and the democratic political process.
Customer and Personal Service	Knowledge of principles and processes for providing customer and personal services. This includes customer needs assessment, meeting quality standards for services, and evaluation of customer satisfaction.
Communications and Media	Knowledge of media production, communication, and dissemination techniques and methods. This includes alternative ways to inform and entertain via written, oral, and visual media.
Administration and Management	Knowledge of business and management principles involved in strategic planning, resource allocation, human resources modeling, leadership technique, production methods, and coordination of people and resources.

Mechanical	Knowledge of machines and tools, including their designs, uses, repair, and maintenance.
Physics	Knowledge and prediction of physical principles, laws, their interrelationships, and applications to understanding fluid, material, and atmospheric dynamics, and mechanical, electrical, atomic and sub-atomic structures and processes.
Clerical	Knowledge of administrative and clerical procedures and systems such as word processing, managing files and records, stenography and transcription, designing forms, and other office procedures and terminology.
Biology	Knowledge of plant and animal organisms, their tissues, cells, functions, interdependencies, and interactions with each other and the environment.
Telecommunications	Knowledge of transmission, broadcasting, switching, control, and operation of telecommunications systems.
Geography	Knowledge of principles and methods for describing the features of land, sea, and air masses, including their physical characteristics, locations, interrelationships, and distribution of plant, animal, and human life.
Design	Knowledge of design techniques, tools, and principles involved in production of precision technical plans, blueprints, drawings, and models.
Economics and Accounting	Knowledge of economic and accounting principles and practices, the financial markets, banking and the analysis and reporting of financial data.
Personnel and Human Resources	Knowledge of principles and procedures for personnel recruitment, selection, training, compensation and benefits, labor relations and negotiation, and personnel information systems.
Sales and Marketing	Knowledge of principles and methods for showing, promoting, and selling products or services. This includes marketing strategy and tactics, product demonstration, sales techniques, and sales control systems.
Transportation	Knowledge of principles and methods for moving people or goods by air, rail, sea, or road, including the relative costs and benefits.
Medicine and Dentistry	Knowledge of the information and techniques needed to diagnose and treat human injuries, diseases, and deformities. This includes symptoms, treatment alternatives, drug properties and interactions, and preventive health-care measures.
Psychology	Knowledge of human behavior and performance; individual differences in ability, personality, and interests; learning and motivation; psychological research methods; and the assessment and treatment of behavioral and affective disorders.
Building and Construction	Knowledge of materials, methods, and the tools involved in construction or repair of houses, buildings, or other structures such as highways and roads.
History and Archeology	Knowledge of historical events and their causes, indicators, and effects on civilizations and cultures.
Philosophy and Theology	Knowledge of different philosophical systems and religions. This includes their basic principles, values, ethics, ways of thinking, customs, practices, and their impact on human culture.
Therapy and Counseling	Knowledge of principles, methods, and procedures for diagnosis, treatment, and rehabilitation of physical and mental dysfunctions, and for career counseling and guidance.
Sociology and Anthropology	Knowledge of group behavior and dynamics, societal trends and influences, human migrations, ethnicity, cultures and their history and origins.
Foreign Language	Knowledge of the structure and content of a foreign (non-English) language including the meaning and spelling of words, rules of composition and grammar, and pronunciation.
Food Production	Knowledge of techniques and equipment for planting, growing, and harvesting food products (both plant and animal) for consumption, including storage/handling techniques.
Fine Arts	Knowledge of the theory and techniques required to compose, produce, and perform works of music, dance, visual arts, drama, and sculpture.

Skills	Skills Definitions
Science	Using scientific rules and methods to solve problems.
Complex Problem Solving	Identifying complex problems and reviewing related information to develop and evaluate options and implement solutions.
Reading Comprehension	Understanding written sentences and paragraphs in work related documents.

Quality Control Analysis	Conducting tests and inspections of products, services, or processes to evaluate quality or performance.
Writing	Communicating effectively in writing as appropriate for the needs of the audience.
Time Management	Managing one's own time and the time of others.
Active Listening	Giving full attention to what other people are saying, taking time to understand the points being made, asking questions as appropriate, and not interrupting at inappropriate times.
Critical Thinking	Using logic and reasoning to identify the strengths and weaknesses of alternative solutions, conclusions or approaches to problems.
Active Learning	Understanding the implications of new information for both current and future problem-solving and decision-making.
Speaking	Talking to others to convey information effectively.
Equipment Selection	Determining the kind of tools and equipment needed to do a job.
Troubleshooting	Determining causes of operating errors and deciding what to do about it.
Mathematics	Using mathematics to solve problems.
Judgment and Decision Making	Considering the relative costs and benefits of potential actions to choose the most appropriate one.
Coordination	Adjusting actions in relation to others' actions.
Monitoring	Monitoring/Assessing performance of yourself, other individuals, or organizations to make improvements or take corrective action.
Instructing	Teaching others how to do something.
Operation Monitoring	Watching gauges, dials, or other indicators to make sure a machine is working properly.
Management of Material Resources	Obtaining and seeing to the appropriate use of equipment, facilities, and materials needed to do certain work.
Persuasion	Persuading others to change their minds or behavior.
Technology Design	Generating or adapting equipment and technology to serve user needs.
Learning Strategies	Selecting and using training/instructional methods and procedures appropriate for the situation when learning or teaching new things.
Social Perceptiveness	Being aware of others' reactions and understanding why they react as they do.
Systems Analysis	Determining how a system should work and how changes in conditions, operations, and the environment will affect outcomes.
Operations Analysis	Analyzing needs and product requirements to create a design.
Systems Evaluation	Identifying measures or indicators of system performance and the actions needed to improve or correct performance, relative to the goals of the system.
Operation and Control	Controlling operations of equipment or systems.
Negotiation	Bringing others together and trying to reconcile differences.
Equipment Maintenance	Performing routine maintenance on equipment and determining when and what kind of maintenance is needed.
Management of Financial Resources	Determining how money will be spent to get the work done, and accounting for these expenditures.
Service Orientation	Actively looking for ways to help people.
Management of Personnel Resources	Motivating, developing, and directing people as they work, identifying the best people for the job.
Installation	Installing equipment, machines, wiring, or programs to meet specifications.
Repairing	Repairing machines or systems using the needed tools.
Programming	Writing computer programs for various purposes.

Ability	Ability Definitions
Deductive Reasoning	The ability to apply general rules to specific problems to produce answers that make sense.
Inductive Reasoning	The ability to combine pieces of information to form general rules or conclusions (includes finding a relationship among seemingly unrelated events).
Oral Comprehension	The ability to listen to and understand information and ideas presented through spoken words and sentences.
Oral Expression	The ability to communicate information and ideas in speaking so others will understand.
Information Ordering	The ability to arrange things or actions in a certain order or pattern according to a specific rule or set of rules (e.g., patterns of numbers, letters, words, pictures, mathematical operations).
Problem Sensitivity	The ability to tell when something is wrong or is likely to go wrong. It does not involve solving the problem, only recognizing there is a problem.
Speech Clarity	The ability to speak clearly so others can understand you.

Written Comprehension	The ability to read and understand information and ideas presented in writing.
Near Vision	The ability to see details at close range (within a few feet of the observer).
Category Flexibility	The ability to generate or use different sets of rules for combining or grouping things in different ways.
Written Expression	The ability to communicate information and ideas in writing so others will understand.
Speech Recognition	The ability to identify and understand the speech of another person.
Mathematical Reasoning	The ability to choose the right mathematical methods or formulas to solve a problem.
Flexibility of Closure	The ability to identify or detect a known pattern (a figure, object, word, or sound) that is hidden in other distracting material.
Selective Attention	The ability to concentrate on a task over a period of time without being distracted.
Fluency of Ideas	The ability to come up with a number of ideas about a topic (the number of ideas is important, not their quality, correctness, or creativity).
Perceptual Speed	The ability to quickly and accurately compare similarities and differences among sets of letters, numbers, objects, pictures, or patterns. The things to be compared may be presented at the same time or one after the other. This ability also includes comparing a presented object with a remembered object.
Visualization	The ability to imagine how something will look after it is moved around or when its parts are moved or rearranged.
Arm-Hand Steadiness	The ability to keep your hand and arm steady while moving your arm or while holding your arm and hand in one position.
Originality	The ability to come up with unusual or clever ideas about a given topic or situation, or to develop creative ways to solve a problem.
Control Precision	The ability to quickly and repeatedly adjust the controls of a machine or a vehicle to exact positions.
Time Sharing	The ability to shift back and forth between two or more activities or sources of information (such as speech, sounds, touch, or other sources).
Visual Color Discrimination	The ability to match or detect differences between colors, including shades of color and brightness.
Memorization	The ability to remember information such as words, numbers, pictures, and procedures.
Trunk Strength	The ability to use your abdominal and lower back muscles to support part of the body repeatedly or continuously over time without 'giving out' or fatiguing.
Manual Dexterity	The ability to quickly move your hand, your hand together with your arm, or your two hands to grasp, manipulate, or assemble objects.
Speed of Closure	The ability to quickly make sense of, combine, and organize information into meaningful patterns.
Finger Dexterity	The ability to make precisely coordinated movements of the fingers of one or both hands to grasp, manipulate, or assemble very small objects.
Multilimb Coordination	The ability to coordinate two or more limbs (for example, two arms, two legs, or one leg and one arm) while sitting, standing, or lying down. It does not involve performing the activities while the whole body is in motion.
Depth Perception	The ability to judge which of several objects is closer or farther away from you, or to judge the distance between you and an object.
Auditory Attention	The ability to focus on a single source of sound in the presence of other distracting sounds.
Far Vision	The ability to see details at a distance.
Hearing Sensitivity	The ability to detect or tell the differences between sounds that vary in pitch and loudness.
Static Strength	The ability to exert maximum muscle force to lift, push, pull, or carry objects.
Reaction Time	The ability to quickly respond (with the hand, finger, or foot) to a signal (sound, light, picture) when it appears.
Number Facility	The ability to add, subtract, multiply, or divide quickly and correctly.
Spatial Orientation	The ability to know your location in relation to the environment or to know where other objects are in relation to you.
Stamina	The ability to exert yourself physically over long periods of time without getting winded or out of breath.
Extent Flexibility	The ability to bend, stretch, twist, or reach with your body, arms, and/or legs.
Gross Body Coordination	The ability to coordinate the movement of your arms, legs, and torso together when the whole body is in motion.

Dynamic Strength	The ability to exert muscle force repeatedly or continuously over time. This involves muscular endurance and resistance to muscle fatigue.
Gross Body Equilibrium	The ability to keep or regain your body balance or stay upright when in an unstable position.
Rate Control	The ability to time your movements or the movement of a piece of equipment in anticipation of changes in the speed and/or direction of a moving object or scene.
Response Orientation	The ability to choose quickly between two or more movements in response to two or more different signals (lights, sounds, pictures). It includes the speed with which the correct response is started with the hand, foot, or other body part.
Wrist-Finger Speed	The ability to make fast, simple, repeated movements of the fingers, hands, and wrists.
Night Vision	The ability to see under low light conditions.
Peripheral Vision	The ability to see objects or movement of objects to one's side when the eyes are looking ahead.
Explosive Strength	The ability to use short bursts of muscle force to propel oneself (as in jumping or sprinting), or to throw an object.
Glare Sensitivity	The ability to see objects in the presence of glare or bright lighting.
Speed of Limb Movement	The ability to quickly move the arms and legs.
Sound Localization	The ability to tell the direction from which a sound originated.
Dynamic Flexibility	The ability to quickly and repeatedly bend, stretch, twist, or reach out with your body, arms, and/or legs.

Work_Activity	Work_Activity Definitions
Interacting With Computers	Using computers and computer systems (including hardware and software) to program, write software, set up functions, enter data, or process information.
Getting Information	Observing, receiving, and otherwise obtaining information from all relevant sources.
Processing Information	Compiling, coding, categorizing, calculating, tabulating, auditing, or verifying information or data.
Analyzing Data or Information	Identifying the underlying principles, reasons, or facts of information by breaking down information or data into separate parts.
Evaluating Information to Determine Compliance wit	Using relevant information and individual judgment to determine whether events or processes comply with laws, regulations, or standards.
Documenting/Recording Information	Entering, transcribing, recording, storing, or maintaining information in written or electronic/magnetic form.
Organizing, Planning, and Prioritizing Work	Developing specific goals and plans to prioritize, organize, and accomplish your work.
Updating and Using Relevant Knowledge	Keeping up-to-date technically and applying new knowledge to your job.
Monitor Processes, Materials, or Surroundings	Monitoring and reviewing information from materials, events, or the environment, to detect or assess problems.
Making Decisions and Solving Problems	Analyzing information and evaluating results to choose the best solution and solve problems.
Identifying Objects, Actions, and Events	Identifying information by categorizing, estimating, recognizing differences or similarities, and detecting changes in circumstances or events.
Inspecting Equipment, Structures, or Material	Inspecting equipment, structures, or materials to identify the cause of errors or other problems or defects.
Communicating with Supervisors, Peers, or Subordin	Providing information to supervisors, co-workers, and subordinates by telephone, in written form, e-mail, or in person.
Repairing and Maintaining Electronic Equipment	Servicing, repairing, calibrating, regulating, fine-tuning, or testing machines, devices, and equipment that operate primarily on the basis of electrical or electronic (not mechanical) principles.
Handling and Moving Objects	Using hands and arms in handling, installing, positioning, and moving materials, and manipulating things.
Estimating the Quantifiable Characteristics of Pro	Estimating sizes, distances, and quantities; or determining time, costs, resources, or materials needed to perform a work activity.
Establishing and Maintaining Interpersonal Relatio	Developing constructive and cooperative working relationships with others, and maintaining them over time.
Thinking Creatively	Developing, designing, or creating new applications, ideas, relationships, systems, or products, including artistic contributions.
Controlling Machines and Processes	Using either control mechanisms or direct physical activity to operate machines or processes (not including computers or vehicles).

Interpreting the Meaning of Information for Others	Translating or explaining what information means and how it can be used.
Repairing and Maintaining Mechanical Equipment	Servicing, repairing, adjusting, and testing machines, devices, moving parts, and equipment that operate primarily on the basis of mechanical (not electronic) principles.
Scheduling Work and Activities	Scheduling events, programs, and activities, as well as the work of others.
Performing General Physical Activities	Performing physical activities that require considerable use of your arms and legs and moving your whole body, such as climbing, lifting, balancing, walking, stooping, and handling of materials.
Performing Administrative Activities	Performing day-to-day administrative tasks such as maintaining information files and processing paperwork.
Training and Teaching Others	Identifying the educational needs of others, developing formal educational or training programs or classes, and teaching or instructing others.
Provide Consultation and Advice to Others	Providing guidance and expert advice to management or other groups on technical, systems-, or process-related topics.
Judging the Qualities of Things, Services, or Peop	Assessing the value, importance, or quality of things or people.
Coordinating the Work and Activities of Others	Getting members of a group to work together to accomplish tasks.
Monitoring and Controlling Resources	Monitoring and controlling resources and overseeing the spending of money.
Developing Objectives and Strategies	Establishing long-range objectives and specifying the strategies and actions to achieve them.
Coaching and Developing Others	Identifying the developmental needs of others and coaching, mentoring, or otherwise helping others to improve their knowledge or skills.
Communicating with Persons Outside Organization	Communicating with people outside the organization, representing the organization to customers, the public, government, and other external sources. This information can be exchanged in person, in writing, or by telephone or e-mail.
Drafting, Laying Out, and Specifying Technical Dev	Providing documentation, detailed instructions, drawings, or specifications to tell others about how devices, parts, equipment, or structures are to be fabricated, constructed, assembled, modified, maintained, or used.
Performing for or Working Directly with the Public	Performing for people or dealing directly with the public. This includes serving customers in restaurants and stores, and receiving clients or guests.
Developing and Building Teams	Encouraging and building mutual trust, respect, and cooperation among team members.
Resolving Conflicts and Negotiating with Others	Handling complaints, settling disputes, and resolving grievances and conflicts, or otherwise negotiating with others.
Guiding, Directing, and Motivating Subordinates	Providing guidance and direction to subordinates, including setting performance standards and monitoring performance.
Assisting and Caring for Others	Providing personal assistance, medical attention, emotional support, or other personal care to others such as coworkers, customers, or patients.
Staffing Organizational Units	Recruiting, interviewing, selecting, hiring, and promoting employees in an organization.
Selling or Influencing Others	Convincing others to buy merchandise/goods or to otherwise change their minds or actions.
Operating Vehicles, Mechanized Devices, or Equipme	Running, maneuvering, navigating, or driving vehicles or mechanized equipment, such as forklifts, passenger vehicles, aircraft, or water craft.

Work_Context	Work_Context Definitions
Wear Common Protective or Safety Equipment such as	How much does this job require wearing common protective or safety equipment such as safety shoes, glasses, gloves, hard hats or live jackets?
Face-to-Face Discussions	How often do you have to have face-to-face discussions with individuals or teams in this job?
Freedom to Make Decisions	How much decision making freedom, without supervision, does the job offer?
Structured versus Unstructured Work	To what extent is this job structured for the worker, rather than allowing the worker to determine tasks, priorities, and goals?
Indoors, Environmentally Controlled	How often does this job require working indoors in environmentally controlled conditions?
Telephone	How often do you have telephone conversations in this job?
Exposed to Hazardous Conditions	How often does this job require exposure to hazardous conditions?
Importance of Being Exact or Accurate	How important is being very exact or highly accurate in performing this job?
Coordinate or Lead Others	How important is it to coordinate or lead others in accomplishing work activities in this job?

Impact of Decisions on Co-workers or Company Resul	How do the decisions an employee makes impact the results of co-workers, clients or the company?
Responsibility for Outcomes and Results	How responsible is the worker for work outcomes and results of other workers?
Electronic Mail	How often do you use electronic mail in this job?
Work With Work Group or Team	How important is it to work with others in a group or team in this job?
Contact With Others	How much does this job require the worker to be in contact with others (face-to-face, by telephone, or otherwise) in order to perform it?
Level of Competition	To what extent does this job require the worker to compete or to be aware of competitive pressures?
Exposed to Contaminants	How often does this job require working exposed to contaminants (such as pollutants, gases, dust or odors)?
Frequency of Decision Making	How frequently is the worker required to make decisions that affect other people, the financial resources, and/or the image and reputation of the organization?
Responsible for Others' Health and Safety	How much responsibility is there for the health and safety of others in this job?
Time Pressure	How often does this job require the worker to meet strict deadlines?
Physical Proximity	To what extent does this job require the worker to perform job tasks in close physical proximity to other people?
Deal With External Customers	How important is it to work with external customers or the public in this job?
Letters and Memos	How often does the job require written letters and memos?
Consequence of Error	How serious would the result usually be if the worker made a mistake that was not readily correctable?
Spend Time Standing	How much does this job require standing?
Spend Time Sitting	How much does this job require sitting?
Sounds, Noise Levels Are Distracting or Uncomforta	How often does this job require working exposed to sounds and noise levels that are distracting or uncomfortable?
Spend Time Using Your Hands to Handle, Control, or	How much does this job require using your hands to handle, control, or feel objects, tools or controls?
Importance of Repeating Same Tasks	How important is repeating the same physical activities (e.g., key entry) or mental activities (e.g., checking entries in a ledger) over and over, without stopping, to performing this job?
Frequency of Conflict Situations	How often are there conflict situations the employee has to face in this job?
Indoors, Not Environmentally Controlled	How often does this job require working indoors in non-controlled environmental conditions (e.g., warehouse without heat)?
Spend Time Walking and Running	How much does this job require walking and running?
Degree of Automation	How automated is the job?
Wear Specialized Protective or Safety Equipment su	How much does this job require wearing specialized protective or safety equipment such as breathing apparatus, safety harness, full protection suits, or radiation protection?
Exposed to Hazardous Equipment	How often does this job require exposure to hazardous equipment?
Spend Time Making Repetitive Motions	How much does this job require making repetitive motions?
Deal With Unpleasant or Angry People	How frequently does the worker have to deal with unpleasant, angry, or discourteous individuals as part of the job requirements?
Exposed to Minor Burns, Cuts, Bites, or Stings	How often does this job require exposure to minor burns, cuts, bites, or stings?
Pace Determined by Speed of Equipment	How important is it to this job that the pace is determined by the speed of equipment or machinery? (This does not refer to keeping busy at all times on this job.)
Public Speaking	How often do you have to perform public speaking in this job?
In an Enclosed Vehicle or Equipment	How often does this job require working in a closed vehicle or equipment (e.g., car)?
Spend Time Bending or Twisting the Body	How much does this job require bending or twisting your body?
Exposed to Disease or Infections	How often does this job require exposure to disease/infections?
Outdoors, Exposed to Weather	How often does this job require working outdoors, exposed to all weather conditions?
Very Hot or Cold Temperatures	How often does this job require working in very hot (above 90 F degrees) or very cold (below 32 F degrees) temperatures?
Exposed to Radiation	How often does this job require exposure to radiation?
Spend Time Kneeling, Crouching, Stooping, or Crawl	How much does this job require kneeling, crouching, stooping or crawling?

314

Cramped Work Space, Awkward Positions	How often does this job require working in cramped work spaces that requires getting into awkward positions?
Extremely Bright or Inadequate Lighting	How often does this job require working in extremely bright or inadequate lighting conditions?
Spend Time Keeping or Regaining Balance	How much does this job require keeping or regaining your balance?
Spend Time Climbing Ladders, Scaffolds, or Poles	How much does this job require climbing ladders, scaffolds, or poles?
Outdoors, Under Cover	How often does this job require working outdoors, under cover (e.g., structure with roof but no walls)?
Exposed to High Places	How often does this job require exposure to high places?
Deal With Physically Aggressive People	How frequently does this job require the worker to deal with physical aggression of violent individuals?
In an Open Vehicle or Equipment	How often does this job require working in an open vehicle or equipment (e.g., tractor)?
Exposed to Whole Body Vibration	How often does this job require exposure to whole body vibration (e.g., operate a jackhammer)?

Job Zone Component	Job Zone Component Definitions
Title	Job Zone Four: Considerable Preparation Needed
Overall Experience	A minimum of two to four years of work-related skill, knowledge, or experience is needed for these occupations. For example, an accountant must complete four years of college and work for several years in accounting to be considered qualified.
Job Training	Employees in these occupations usually need several years of work-related experience, on-the-job training, and/or vocational training.
Job Zone Examples	Many of these occupations involve coordinating, supervising, managing, or training others. Examples include accountants, chefs and head cooks, computer programmers, historians, pharmacists, and police detectives.
SVP Range	(7.0 to < 8.0)
Education	Most of these occupations require a four - year bachelor's degree, but some do not.

Work_Styles	Work_Styles Definitions
Integrity	Job requires being honest and ethical.
Dependability	Job requires being reliable, responsible, and dependable, and fulfilling obligations.
Attention to Detail	Job requires being careful about detail and thorough in completing work tasks.
Analytical Thinking	Job requires analyzing information and using logic to address work-related issues and problems.
Achievement/Effort	Job requires establishing and maintaining personally challenging achievement goals and exerting effort toward mastering tasks.
Initiative	Job requires a willingness to take on responsibilities and challenges.
Independence	Job requires developing one's own ways of doing things, guiding oneself with little or no supervision, and depending on oneself to get things done.
Cooperation	Job requires being pleasant with others on the job and displaying a good-natured, cooperative attitude.
Persistence	Job requires persistence in the face of obstacles.
Innovation	Job requires creativity and alternative thinking to develop new ideas for and answers to work-related problems.
Adaptability/Flexibility	Job requires being open to change (positive or negative) and to considerable variety in the workplace.
Stress Tolerance	Job requires accepting criticism and dealing calmly and effectively with high stress situations.
Leadership	Job requires a willingness to lead, take charge, and offer opinions and direction.
Self Control	Job requires maintaining composure, keeping emotions in check, controlling anger, and avoiding aggressive behavior, even in very difficult situations.
Concern for Others	Job requires being sensitive to others' needs and feelings and being understanding and helpful on the job.
Social Orientation	Job requires preferring to work with others rather than alone, and being personally connected with others on the job.

19-2032.00 - Materials Scientists

Research and study the structures and chemical properties of various natural and manmade materials, including metals, alloys, rubber, ceramics, semiconductors, polymers, and glass. Determine ways to strengthen or combine materials or develop new materials with new or specific properties for use in a variety of products and applications.

Tasks

1) Conduct research into the structures and properties of materials, such as metals, alloys, polymers, and ceramics in order to obtain information that could be used to develop new products or enhance existing ones.

2) Determine ways to strengthen or combine materials, or develop new materials with new or specific properties for use in a variety of products and applications.

3) Devise testing methods to evaluate the effects of various conditions on particular materials.

4) Plan laboratory experiments to confirm feasibility of processes and techniques used in the production of materials having special characteristics.

5) Prepare reports of materials study findings for the use of other scientists and requestors.

6) Recommend materials for reliable performance in various environments.

7) Research methods of processing, forming, and firing materials in order to develop such products as ceramic fillings for teeth, unbreakable dinner plates, and telescope lenses.

8) Test material samples for tolerance under tension, compression and shear, to determine the cause of metal failures.

9) Monitor production processes in order to ensure that equipment is used efficiently and that projects are completed within appropriate time frames and budgets.

10) Test metals in order to determine whether they meet specifications of mechanical strength, strength-weight ratio, ductility, magnetic and electrical properties, and resistance to abrasion, corrosion, heat and cold.

11) Study the nature, structure and physical properties of metals and their alloys, and their responses to applied forces.

12) Test individual parts and products in order to ensure that manufacturer and governmental quality and safety standards are met.

13) Visit suppliers of materials or users of products in order to gather specific information.

14) Confer with customers in order to determine how materials can be tailored to suit their needs.

15) Teach in colleges and universities.

19-2041.00 - Environmental Scientists and Specialists, Including Health

Conduct research or perform investigation for the purpose of identifying, abating, or eliminating sources of pollutants or hazards that affect either the environment or the health of the population. Utilizing knowledge of various scientific disciplines may collect, synthesize, study, report, and take action based on data derived from measurements or observations of air, food, soil, water, and other sources.

Tasks

1) Communicate scientific and technical information through oral briefings, written documents, workshops, conferences, and public hearings.

2) Provide advice on proper standards and regulations and the development of policies, strategies, and codes of practice for environmental management.

3) Conduct environmental audits and inspections, and investigations of violations.

4) Determine data collection methods to be employed in research projects and surveys.

5) Review and implement environmental technical standards, guidelines, policies, and formal regulations that meet all appropriate requirements.

6) Analyze data to determine validity, quality, and scientific significance, and to interpret correlations between human activities and environmental effects.

7) Prepare charts or graphs from data samples, and provide summary information on the environmental relevance of the data.

8) Evaluate violations or problems discovered during inspections in order to determine appropriate regulatory actions or to provide advice on the development and prosecution of regulatory cases.

315

9) Collect, synthesize, and analyze data derived from pollution emission measurements, atmospheric monitoring, meteorological and mineralogical information, and soil or water samples.

10) Design and direct studies to obtain technical environmental information about planned projects.

11) Monitor effects of pollution and land degradation, and recommend means of prevention or control.

12) Investigate and report on accidents affecting the environment.

13) Monitor environmental impacts of development activities.

14) Develop the technical portions of legal documents, administrative orders, or consent decrees.

15) Develop methods to minimize the impact of production processes on the environment, based on the study and assessment of industrial production, environmental legislation, and physical, biological, and social environments.

16) Conduct applied research on topics such as waste control and treatment and pollution control methods.

17) Supervise environmental technologists and technicians.

18) Research sources of pollution to determine their effects on the environment and to develop theories or methods of pollution abatement or control.

19) Plan and develop research models using knowledge of mathematical and statistical concepts.

20) Develop programs designed to obtain the most productive, non-damaging use of land.

Knowledge	Knowledge Definitions
Law and Government	Knowledge of laws, legal codes, court procedures, precedents, government regulations, executive orders, agency rules, and the democratic political process.
Biology	Knowledge of plant and animal organisms, their tissues, cells, functions, interdependencies, and interactions with each other and the environment.
English Language	Knowledge of the structure and content of the English language including the meaning and spelling of words, rules of composition, and grammar.
Public Safety and Security	Knowledge of relevant equipment, policies, procedures, and strategies to promote effective local, state, or national security operations for the protection of people, data, property, and institutions.
Customer and Personal Service	Knowledge of principles and processes for providing customer and personal services. This includes customer needs assessment, meeting quality standards for services, and evaluation of customer satisfaction.
Chemistry	Knowledge of the chemical composition, structure, and properties of substances and of the chemical processes and transformations that they undergo. This includes uses of chemicals and their interactions, danger signs, production techniques, and disposal methods.
Administration and Management	Knowledge of business and management principles involved in strategic planning, resource allocation, human resources modeling, leadership technique, production methods, and coordination of people and resources.
Geography	Knowledge of principles and methods for describing the features of land, sea, and air masses, including their physical characteristics, locations, interrelationships, and distribution of plant, animal, and human life.
Engineering and Technology	Knowledge of the practical application of engineering science and technology. This includes applying principles, techniques, procedures, and equipment to the design and production of various goods and services.
Mathematics	Knowledge of arithmetic, algebra, geometry, calculus, statistics, and their applications.
Computers and Electronics	Knowledge of circuit boards, processors, chips, electronic equipment, and computer hardware and software, including applications and programming.
Communications and Media	Knowledge of media production, communication, and dissemination techniques and methods. This includes alternative ways to inform and entertain via written, oral, and visual media.
Education and Training	Knowledge of principles and methods for curriculum and training design, teaching and instruction for individuals and groups, and the measurement of training effects.
Clerical	Knowledge of administrative and clerical procedures and systems such as word processing, managing files and records, stenography and transcription, designing forms, and other office procedures and terminology.
Psychology	Knowledge of human behavior and performance; individual differences in ability, personality, and interests; learning and motivation; psychological research methods; and the assessment and treatment of behavioral and affective disorders.
Physics	Knowledge and prediction of physical principles, laws, their interrelationships, and applications to understanding fluid, material, and atmospheric dynamics, and mechanical, electrical, atomic and sub-atomic structures and processes.
Design	Knowledge of design techniques, tools, and principles involved in production of precision technical plans, blueprints, drawings, and models.
Personnel and Human Resources	Knowledge of principles and procedures for personnel recruitment, selection, training, compensation and benefits, labor relations and negotiation, and personnel information systems.
Building and Construction	Knowledge of materials, methods, and the tools involved in the construction or repair of houses, buildings, or other structures such as highways and roads.
Transportation	Knowledge of principles and methods for moving people or goods by air, rail, sea, or road, including the relative costs and benefits.
Mechanical	Knowledge of machines and tools, including their designs, uses, repair, and maintenance.
Sociology and Anthropology	Knowledge of group behavior and dynamics, societal trends and influences, human migrations, ethnicity, cultures and their history and origins.
Telecommunications	Knowledge of transmission, broadcasting, switching, control, and operation of telecommunications systems.
Production and Processing	Knowledge of raw materials, production processes, quality control, costs, and other techniques for maximizing the effective manufacture and distribution of goods.
Economics and Accounting	Knowledge of economic and accounting principles and practices, the financial markets, banking and the analysis and reporting of financial data.
Sales and Marketing	Knowledge of principles and methods for showing, promoting, and selling products or services. This includes marketing strategy and tactics, product demonstration, sales techniques, and sales control systems.
Food Production	Knowledge of techniques and equipment for planting, growing, and harvesting food products (both plant and animal) for consumption, including storage/handling techniques.
Medicine and Dentistry	Knowledge of the information and techniques needed to diagnose and treat human injuries, diseases, and deformities. This includes symptoms, treatment alternatives, drug properties and interactions, and preventive health-care measures.
History and Archeology	Knowledge of historical events and their causes, indicators, and effects on civilizations and cultures.
Foreign Language	Knowledge of the structure and content of a foreign (non-English) language including the meaning and spelling of words, rules of composition and grammar, and pronunciation.
Philosophy and Theology	Knowledge of different philosophical systems and religions. This includes their basic principles, values, ethics, ways of thinking, customs, practices, and their impact on human culture.
Therapy and Counseling	Knowledge of principles, methods, and procedures for diagnosis, treatment, and rehabilitation of physical and mental dysfunctions, and for career counseling and guidance.
Fine Arts	Knowledge of the theory and techniques required to compose, produce, and perform works of music, dance, visual arts, drama, and sculpture.

Skills	Skills Definitions
Reading Comprehension	Understanding written sentences and paragraphs in work related documents.
Active Listening	Giving full attention to what other people are saying, taking time to understand the points being made, asking questions as appropriate, and not interrupting at inappropriate times.
Science	Using scientific rules and methods to solve problems.
Coordination	Adjusting actions in relation to others' actions.
Active Learning	Understanding the implications of new information for both current and future problem-solving and decision-making.
Time Management	Managing one's own time and the time of others.

Critical Thinking	Using logic and reasoning to identify the strengths and weaknesses of alternative solutions, conclusions or approaches to problems.
Writing	Communicating effectively in writing as appropriate for the needs of the audience.
Speaking	Talking to others to convey information effectively.
Service Orientation	Actively looking for ways to help people.
Social Perceptiveness	Being aware of others' reactions and understanding why they react as they do.
Complex Problem Solving	Identifying complex problems and reviewing related information to develop and evaluate options and implement solutions.
Learning Strategies	Selecting and using training/instructional methods and procedures appropriate for the situation when learning or teaching new things.
Monitoring	Monitoring/Assessing performance of yourself, other individuals, or organizations to make improvements or take corrective action.
Negotiation	Bringing others together and trying to reconcile differences.
Judgment and Decision Making	Considering the relative costs and benefits of potential actions to choose the most appropriate one.
Persuasion	Persuading others to change their minds or behavior.
Mathematics	Using mathematics to solve problems.
Instructing	Teaching others how to do something.
Quality Control Analysis	Conducting tests and inspections of products, services, or processes to evaluate quality or performance.
Operations Analysis	Analyzing needs and product requirements to create a design.
Management of Financial Resources	Determining how money will be spent to get the work done, and accounting for these expenditures.
Equipment Selection	Determining the kind of tools and equipment needed to do a job.
Systems Evaluation	Identifying measures or indicators of system performance and the actions needed to improve or correct performance, relative to the goals of the system.
Management of Personnel Resources	Motivating, developing, and directing people as they work, identifying the best people for the job.
Troubleshooting	Determining causes of operating errors and deciding what to do about it.
Systems Analysis	Determining how a system should work and how changes in conditions, operations, and the environment will affect outcomes.
Technology Design	Generating or adapting equipment and technology to serve user needs.
Management of Material Resources	Obtaining and seeing to the appropriate use of equipment, facilities, and materials needed to do certain work.
Operation Monitoring	Watching gauges, dials, or other indicators to make sure a machine is working properly.
Operation and Control	Controlling operations of equipment or systems.
Equipment Maintenance	Performing routine maintenance on equipment and determining when and what kind of maintenance is needed.
Installation	Installing equipment, machines, wiring, or programs to meet specifications.
Programming	Writing computer programs for various purposes.
Repairing	Repairing machines or systems using the needed tools.

Ability	Ability Definitions
Speech Clarity	The ability to speak clearly so others can understand you.
Inductive Reasoning	The ability to combine pieces of information to form general rules or conclusions (includes finding a relationship among seemingly unrelated events).
Deductive Reasoning	The ability to apply general rules to specific problems to produce answers that make sense.
Written Comprehension	The ability to read and understand information and ideas presented in writing.
Oral Expression	The ability to communicate information and ideas in speaking so others will understand.
Written Expression	The ability to communicate information and ideas in writing so others will understand.
Oral Comprehension	The ability to listen to and understand information and ideas presented through spoken words and sentences.
Near Vision	The ability to see details at close range (within a few feet of the observer).
Problem Sensitivity	The ability to tell when something is wrong or is likely to go wrong. It does not involve solving the problem, only recognizing there is a problem.

Information Ordering	The ability to arrange things or actions in a certain order or pattern according to a specific rule or set of rules (e.g., patterns of numbers, letters, words, pictures, mathematical operations).
Mathematical Reasoning	The ability to choose the right mathematical methods or formulas to solve a problem.
Far Vision	The ability to see details at a distance.
Category Flexibility	The ability to generate or use different sets of rules for combining or grouping things in different ways.
Selective Attention	The ability to concentrate on a task over a period of time without being distracted.
Speech Recognition	The ability to identify and understand the speech of another person.
Flexibility of Closure	The ability to identify or detect a known pattern (a figure, object, word, or sound) that is hidden in other distracting material.
Originality	The ability to come up with unusual or clever ideas about a given topic or situation, or to develop creative ways to solve a problem.
Fluency of Ideas	The ability to come up with a number of ideas about a topic (the number of ideas is important, not their quality, correctness, or creativity).
Visual Color Discrimination	The ability to match or detect differences between colors, including shades of color and brightness.
Speed of Closure	The ability to quickly make sense of, combine, and organize information into meaningful patterns.
Perceptual Speed	The ability to quickly and accurately compare similarities and differences among sets of letters, numbers, objects, pictures, or patterns. The things to be compared may be presented at the same time or one after the other. This ability also includes comparing a presented object with a remembered object.
Number Facility	The ability to add, subtract, multiply, or divide quickly and correctly.
Memorization	The ability to remember information such as words, numbers, pictures, and procedures.
Visualization	The ability to imagine how something will look after it is moved around or when its parts are moved or rearranged.
Auditory Attention	The ability to focus on a single source of sound in the presence of other distracting sounds.
Time Sharing	The ability to shift back and forth between two or more activities or sources of information (such as speech, sounds, touch, or other sources).
Hearing Sensitivity	The ability to detect or tell the differences between sounds that vary in pitch and loudness.
Depth Perception	The ability to judge which of several objects is closer or farther away from you, or to judge the distance between you and an object.
Finger Dexterity	The ability to make precisely coordinated movements of the fingers of one or both hands to grasp, manipulate, or assemble very small objects.
Trunk Strength	The ability to use your abdominal and lower back muscles to support part of the body repeatedly or continuously over time without 'giving out' or fatiguing.
Arm-Hand Steadiness	The ability to keep your hand and arm steady while moving your arm or while holding your arm and hand in one position.
Multilimb Coordination	The ability to coordinate two or more limbs (for example, two arms, two legs, or one leg and one arm) while sitting, standing, or lying down. It does not involve performing the activities while the whole body is in motion.
Extent Flexibility	The ability to bend, stretch, twist, or reach with your body, arms, and/or legs.
Stamina	The ability to exert yourself physically over long periods of time without getting winded or out of breath.
Gross Body Coordination	The ability to coordinate the movement of your arms, legs, and torso together when the whole body is in motion.
Static Strength	The ability to exert maximum muscle force to lift, push, pull, or carry objects.
Dynamic Strength	The ability to exert muscle force repeatedly or continuously over time. This involves muscular endurance and resistance to muscle fatigue.
Gross Body Equilibrium	The ability to keep or regain your body balance or stay upright when in an unstable position.
Spatial Orientation	The ability to know your location in relation to the environment or to know where other objects are in relation to you.
Glare Sensitivity	The ability to see objects in the presence of glare or bright lighting.
Night Vision	The ability to see under low light conditions.

Manual Dexterity	The ability to quickly move your hand, your hand together with your arm, or your two hands to grasp, manipulate, or assemble objects.
Peripheral Vision	The ability to see objects or movement of objects to one's side when the eyes are looking ahead.
Wrist-Finger Speed	The ability to make fast, simple, repeated movements of the fingers, hands, and wrists.
Control Precision	The ability to quickly and repeatedly adjust the controls of a machine or a vehicle to exact positions.
Speed of Limb Movement	The ability to quickly move the arms and legs.
Response Orientation	The ability to choose quickly between two or more movements in response to two or more different signals (lights, sounds, pictures). It includes the speed with which the correct response is started with the hand, foot, or other body part.
Reaction Time	The ability to quickly respond (with the hand, finger, or foot) to a signal (sound, light, picture) when it appears.
Rate Control	The ability to time your movements or the movement of a piece of equipment in anticipation of changes in the speed and/or direction of a moving object or scene.
Explosive Strength	The ability to use short bursts of muscle force to propel oneself (as in jumping or sprinting), or to throw an object.
Sound Localization	The ability to tell the direction from which a sound originated.
Dynamic Flexibility	The ability to quickly and repeatedly bend, stretch, twist, or reach out with your body, arms, and/or legs.

Work_Activity	Work_Activity Definitions
Interacting With Computers	Using computers and computer systems (including hardware and software) to program, write software, set up functions, enter data, or process information.
Getting Information	Observing, receiving, and otherwise obtaining information from all relevant sources.
Monitor Processes, Materials, or Surroundings	Monitoring and reviewing information from materials, events, or the environment, to detect or assess problems.
Communicating with Supervisors, Peers, or Subordin	Providing information to supervisors, co-workers, and subordinates by telephone, in written form, e-mail, or in person.
Evaluating Information to Determine Compliance wit	Using relevant information and individual judgment to determine whether events or processes comply with laws, regulations, or standards.
Making Decisions and Solving Problems	Analyzing information and evaluating results to choose the best solution and solve problems.
Analyzing Data or Information	Identifying the underlying principles, reasons, or facts of information by breaking down information or data into separate parts.
Identifying Objects, Actions, and Events	Identifying information by categorizing, estimating, recognizing differences or similarities, and detecting changes in circumstances or events.
Updating and Using Relevant Knowledge	Keeping up-to-date technically and applying new knowledge to your job.
Documenting/Recording Information	Entering, transcribing, recording, storing, or maintaining information in written or electronic/magnetic form.
Establishing and Maintaining Interpersonal Relatio	Developing constructive and cooperative working relationships with others, and maintaining them over time.
Communicating with Persons Outside Organization	Communicating with people outside the organization, representing the organization to customers, the public, government, and other external sources. This information can be exchanged in person, in writing, or by telephone or e-mail.
Processing Information	Compiling, coding, categorizing, calculating, tabulating, auditing, or verifying information or data.
Interpreting the Meaning of Information for Others	Translating or explaining what information means and how it can be used.
Organizing, Planning, and Prioritizing Work	Developing specific goals and plans to prioritize, organize, and accomplish your work.
Estimating the Quantifiable Characteristics of Pro	Estimating sizes, distances, and quantities; or determining time, costs, resources, or materials needed to perform a work activity.
Developing and Building Teams	Encouraging and building mutual trust, respect, and cooperation among team members.
Developing Objectives and Strategies	Establishing long-range objectives and specifying the strategies and actions to achieve them.
Coordinating the Work and Activities of Others	Getting members of a group to work together to accomplish tasks.
Thinking Creatively	Developing, designing, or creating new applications, ideas, relationships, systems, or products, including artistic contributions.

Scheduling Work and Activities	Scheduling events, programs, and activities, as well as the work of others.
Resolving Conflicts and Negotiating with Others	Handling complaints, settling disputes, and resolving grievances and conflicts, or otherwise negotiating with others.
Judging the Qualities of Things, Services, or Peop	Assessing the value, importance, or quality of things or people.
Performing for or Working Directly with the Public	Performing for people or dealing directly with the public. This includes serving customers in restaurants and stores, and receiving clients or guests.
Performing Administrative Activities	Performing day-to-day administrative tasks such as maintaining information files and processing paperwork.
Provide Consultation and Advice to Others	Providing guidance and expert advice to management or other groups on technical, systems-, or process-related topics.
Monitoring and Controlling Resources	Monitoring and controlling resources and overseeing the spending of money.
Training and Teaching Others	Identifying the educational needs of others, developing formal educational or training programs or classes, and teaching or instructing others.
Inspecting Equipment, Structures, or Material	Inspecting equipment, structures, or materials to identify the cause of errors or other problems or defects.
Guiding, Directing, and Motivating Subordinates	Providing guidance and direction to subordinates, including setting performance standards and monitoring performance.
Performing General Physical Activities	Performing physical activities that require considerable use of your arms and legs and moving your whole body, such as climbing, lifting, balancing, walking, stooping, and handling of materials.
Coaching and Developing Others	Identifying the developmental needs of others and coaching, mentoring, or otherwise helping others to improve their knowledge or skills.
Assisting and Caring for Others	Providing personal assistance, medical attention, emotional support, or other personal care to others such as coworkers, customers, or patients.
Operating Vehicles, Mechanized Devices, or Equipme	Running, maneuvering, navigating, or driving vehicles or mechanized equipment, such as forklifts, passenger vehicles, aircraft, or water craft.
Handling and Moving Objects	Using hands and arms in handling, installing, positioning, and moving materials, and manipulating things.
Staffing Organizational Units	Recruiting, interviewing, selecting, hiring, and promoting employees in an organization.
Selling or Influencing Others	Convincing others to buy merchandise/goods or to otherwise change their minds or actions.
Repairing and Maintaining Mechanical Equipment	Servicing, repairing, adjusting, and testing machines, devices, moving parts, and equipment that operate primarily on the basis of mechanical (not electronic) principles.
Drafting, Laying Out, and Specifying Technical Dev	Providing documentation, detailed instructions, drawings, or specifications to tell others about how devices, parts, equipment, or structures are to be fabricated, constructed, assembled, modified, maintained, or used.
Controlling Machines and Processes	Using either control mechanisms or direct physical activity to operate machines or processes (not including computers or vehicles).
Repairing and Maintaining Electronic Equipment	Servicing, repairing, calibrating, regulating, fine-tuning, or testing machines, devices, and equipment that operate primarily on the basis of electrical or electronic (not mechanical) principles.

Work_Context	Work_Context Definitions
Telephone	How often do you have telephone conversations in this job?
Face-to-Face Discussions	How often do you have to have face-to-face discussions with individuals or teams in this job?
Contact With Others	How much does this job require the worker to be in contact with others (face-to-face, by telephone, or otherwise) in order to perform it?
Electronic Mail	How often do you use electronic mail in this job?
Deal With External Customers	How important is it to work with external customers or the public in this job?
Structured versus Unstructured Work	To what extent is this job structured for the worker, rather than allowing the worker to determine tasks, priorities, and goals?
Freedom to Make Decisions	How much decision making freedom, without supervision, does the job offer?
Indoors, Environmentally Controlled	How often does this job require working indoors in environmentally controlled conditions?
Importance of Being Exact or Accurate	How important is being very exact or highly accurate in performing this job?
Work With Work Group or Team	How important is it to work with others in a group or team in this job?
Letters and Memos	How often does the job require written letters and memos?

In an Enclosed Vehicle or Equipment	How often does this job require working in a closed vehicle or equipment (e.g., car)?
Impact of Decisions on Co-workers or Company Resul	How do the decisions an employee makes impact the results of co-workers, clients or the company?
Spend Time Sitting	How much does this job require sitting?
Time Pressure	How often does this job require the worker to meet strict deadlines?
Coordinate or Lead Others	How important is it to coordinate or lead others in accomplishing work activities in this job?
Frequency of Decision Making	How frequently is the worker required to make decisions that affect other people, the financial resources, and/or the image and reputation of the organization?
Importance of Repeating Same Tasks	How important is repeating the same physical activities (e.g., key entry) or mental activities (e.g., checking entries in a ledger) over and over, without stopping, to performing this job?
Outdoors, Exposed to Weather	How often does this job require working outdoors, exposed to all weather conditions?
Sounds, Noise Levels Are Distracting or Uncomforta	How often does this job require working exposed to sounds and noise levels that are distracting or uncomfortable?
Frequency of Conflict Situations	How often are there conflict situations the employee has to face in this job?
Exposed to Contaminants	How often does this job require working exposed to contaminants (such as pollutants, gases, dust or odors)?
Very Hot or Cold Temperatures	How often does this job require working in very hot (above 90 F degrees) or very cold (below 32 F degrees) temperatures?
Exposed to Minor Burns, Cuts, Bites, or Stings	How often does this job require exposure to minor burns, cuts, bites, or stings?
Consequence of Error	How serious would the result usually be if the worker made a mistake that was not readily correctable?
Deal With Unpleasant or Angry People	How frequently does the worker have to deal with unpleasant, angry, or discourteous individuals as part of the job requirements?
Physical Proximity	To what extent does this job require the worker to perform job tasks in close physical proximity to other people?
Wear Common Protective or Safety Equipment such as	How much does this job require wearing common protective or safety equipment such as safety shoes, glasses, gloves, hard hats or live jackets?
Responsible for Others' Health and Safety	How much responsibility is there for the health and safety of others in this job?
Extremely Bright or Inadequate Lighting	How often does this job require working in extremely bright or inadequate lighting conditions?
Responsibility for Outcomes and Results	How responsible is the worker for work outcomes and results of other workers?
Indoors, Not Environmentally Controlled	How often does this job require working indoors in non-controlled environmental conditions (e.g., warehouse without heat)?
Spend Time Walking and Running	How much does this job require walking and running?
Spend Time Making Repetitive Motions	How much does this job require making repetitive motions?
Public Speaking	How often do you have to perform public speaking in this job?
Level of Competition	To what extent does this job require the worker to compete or to be aware of competitive pressures?
Spend Time Standing	How much does this job require standing?
Degree of Automation	How automated is the job?
Exposed to Disease or Infections	How often does this job require exposure to disease/infections?
Outdoors, Under Cover	How often does this job require working outdoors, under cover (e.g., structure with roof but no walls)?
Spend Time Using Your Hands to Handle, Control, or	How much does this job require using your hands to handle, control, or feel objects, tools or controls?
Spend Time Bending or Twisting the Body	How much does this job require bending or twisting your body?
Exposed to Hazardous Equipment	How often does this job require exposure to hazardous equipment?
Exposed to Hazardous Conditions	How often does this job require exposure to hazardous conditions?
Spend Time Kneeling, Crouching, Stooping, or Crawl	How much does this job require kneeling, crouching, stooping or crawling?
Spend Time Keeping or Regaining Balance	How much does this job require keeping or regaining your balance?
Cramped Work Space, Awkward Positions	How often does this job require working in cramped work spaces that requires getting into awkward positions?

Wear Specialized Protective or Safety Equipment su	How much does this job require wearing specialized protective or safety equipment such as breathing apparatus, safety harness, full protection suits, or radiation protection?
Exposed to High Places	How often does this job require exposure to high places?
Exposed to Whole Body Vibration	How often does this job require exposure to whole body vibration (e.g., operate a jackhammer)?
In an Open Vehicle or Equipment	How often does this job require working in an open vehicle or equipment (e.g., tractor)?
Deal With Physically Aggressive People	How frequently does this job require the worker to deal with physical aggression of violent individuals?
Spend Time Climbing Ladders, Scaffolds, or Poles	How much does this job require climbing ladders, scaffolds, or poles?
Exposed to Radiation	How often does this job require exposure to radiation?
Pace Determined by Speed of Equipment	How important is it to this job that the pace is determined by the speed of equipment or machinery? (This does not refer to keeping busy at all times on this job.)

Job Zone Component	Job Zone Component Definitions
Title	Job Zone Five: Extensive Preparation Needed
Overall Experience	Extensive skill, knowledge, and experience are needed for these occupations. Many require more than five years of experience. For example, surgeons must complete four years of college and an additional five to seven years of specialized medical training to be able to do their job.
Job Training	Employees may need some on-the-job training, but most of these occupations assume that the person will already have the required skills, knowledge, work-related experience, and/or training.
Job Zone Examples	These occupations often involve coordinating, training, supervising, or managing the activities of others to accomplish goals. Very advanced communication and organizational skills are required. Examples include athletic trainers, lawyers, managing editors, phyicists, social psychologists, and surgeons.
SVP Range	(8.0 and above)
Education	A bachelor's degree is the minimum formal education required for these occupations. However, many also require graduate school. For example, they may require a master's degree, and some require a Ph.D., M.D., or J.D. (law degree).

Work_Styles	Work_Styles Definitions
Analytical Thinking	Job requires analyzing information and using logic to address work-related issues and problems.
Cooperation	Job requires being pleasant with others on the job and displaying a good-natured, cooperative attitude.
Persistence	Job requires persistence in the face of obstacles.
Attention to Detail	Job requires being careful about detail and thorough in completing work tasks.
Adaptability/Flexibility	Job requires being open to change (positive or negative) and to considerable variety in the workplace.
Initiative	Job requires a willingness to take on responsibilities and challenges.
Integrity	Job requires being honest and ethical.
Stress Tolerance	Job requires accepting criticism and dealing calmly and effectively with high stress situations.
Dependability	Job requires being reliable, responsible, and dependable, and fulfilling obligations.
Self Control	Job requires maintaining composure, keeping emotions in check, controlling anger, and avoiding aggressive behavior, even in very difficult situations.
Achievement/Effort	Job requires establishing and maintaining personally challenging achievement goals and exerting effort toward mastering tasks.
Leadership	Job requires a willingness to lead, take charge, and offer opinions and direction.
Concern for Others	Job requires being sensitive to others' needs and feelings and being understanding and helpful on the job.
Social Orientation	Job requires preferring to work with others rather than alone, and being personally connected with others on the job.
Independence	Job requires developing one's own ways of doing things, guiding oneself with little or no supervision, and depending on oneself to get things done.
Innovation	Job requires creativity and alternative thinking to develop new ideas for and answers to work-related problems.

19-2042.01 - Geologists

Study composition, structure, and history of the earth's crust; examine rocks, minerals, and fossil remains to identify and determine the sequence of processes affecting the development of the earth; apply knowledge of chemistry, physics, biology, and mathematics to explain these phenomena and to help locate mineral and petroleum deposits and underground water resources; prepare geologic reports and maps; and interpret research data to recommend further action for study.

Tasks

1) Plan and conduct geological, geochemical, and geophysical field studies and surveys; sample collection; and drilling and testing programs used to collect data for research and/or application.

2) Prepare geological maps, cross-sectional diagrams, charts, and reports concerning mineral extraction, land use, and resource management, using results of field work and laboratory research.

3) Communicate geological findings by writing research papers, participating in conferences, and/or teaching geological science at universities.

4) Locate and estimate probable natural gas, oil, and mineral ore deposits and underground water resources, using aerial photographs, charts, and research and survey results.

5) Investigate the composition, structure, and history of the Earth's crust through the collection, examination, measurement, and classification of soils, minerals, rocks, and fossil remains.

6) Assess ground and surface water movement in order to provide advice regarding issues such as waste management, route and site selection, and the restoration of contaminated sites.

7) Conduct geological and geophysical studies to provide information for use in regional development, site selection, and the development of public works projects.

8) Advise construction firms and government agencies on dam and road construction, foundation design, and land use and resource management.

9) Inspect construction projects in order to analyze engineering problems, applying geological knowledge and using test equipment and drilling machinery.

10) Measure characteristics of the Earth, such as gravity and magnetic fields, using equipment such as seismographs, gravimeters, torsion balances, and magnetometers.

11) Identify deposits of construction materials, and assess the materials' characteristics and suitability for use as concrete aggregates, road fill, or in other applications.

12) Identify risks for natural disasters such as mud slides, earthquakes, and volcanic eruptions, and provide advice on ways in which potential damage can be mitigated.

13) Develop applied software for the analysis and interpretation of geological data.

14) Test industrial diamonds and abrasives, soil, or rocks in order to determine their geological characteristics, using optical, x-ray, heat, acid, and precision instruments.

Knowledge	Knowledge Definitions
English Language	Knowledge of the structure and content of the English language including the meaning and spelling of words, rules of composition, and grammar.
Geography	Knowledge of principles and methods for describing the features of land, sea, and air masses, including their physical characteristics, locations, interrelationships, and distribution of plant, animal, and human life.
Mathematics	Knowledge of arithmetic, algebra, geometry, calculus, statistics, and their applications.
Engineering and Technology	Knowledge of the practical application of engineering science and technology. This includes applying principles, techniques, procedures, and equipment to the design and production of various goods and services.
Law and Government	Knowledge of laws, legal codes, court procedures, precedents, government regulations, executive orders, agency rules, and the democratic political process.
Chemistry	Knowledge of the chemical composition, structure, and properties of substances and of the chemical processes and transformations that they undergo. This includes uses of chemicals and their interactions, danger signs, production techniques, and disposal methods.
Physics	Knowledge and prediction of physical principles, laws, their interrelationships, and applications to understanding fluid, material, and atmospheric dynamics, and mechanical, electrical, atomic and sub-atomic structures and processes.
Computers and Electronics	Knowledge of circuit boards, processors, chips, electronic equipment, and computer hardware and software, including applications and programming.
Public Safety and Security	Knowledge of relevant equipment, policies, procedures, and strategies to promote effective local, state, or national security operations for the protection of people, data, property, and institutions.
Administration and Management	Knowledge of business and management principles involved in strategic planning, resource allocation, human resources modeling, leadership technique, production methods, and coordination of people and resources.
Customer and Personal Service	Knowledge of principles and processes for providing customer and personal services. This includes customer needs assessment, meeting quality standards for services, and evaluation of customer satisfaction.
Clerical	Knowledge of administrative and clerical procedures and systems such as word processing, managing files and records, stenography and transcription, designing forms, and other office procedures and terminology.
Biology	Knowledge of plant and animal organisms, their tissues, cells, functions, interdependencies, and interactions with each other and the environment.
Design	Knowledge of design techniques, tools, and principles involved in production of precision technical plans, blueprints, drawings, and models.
Communications and Media	Knowledge of media production, communication, and dissemination techniques and methods. This includes alternative ways to inform and entertain via written, oral, and visual media.
Mechanical	Knowledge of machines and tools, including their designs, uses, repair, and maintenance.
Education and Training	Knowledge of principles and methods for curriculum and training design, teaching and instruction for individuals and groups, and the measurement of training effects.
History and Archeology	Knowledge of historical events and their causes, indicators, and effects on civilizations and cultures.
Sales and Marketing	Knowledge of principles and methods for showing, promoting, and selling products or services. This includes marketing strategy and tactics, product demonstration, sales techniques, and sales control systems.
Economics and Accounting	Knowledge of economic and accounting principles and practices, the financial markets, banking and the analysis and reporting of financial data.
Building and Construction	Knowledge of materials, methods, and the tools involved in the construction or repair of houses, buildings, or other structures such as highways and roads.
Psychology	Knowledge of human behavior and performance; individual differences in ability, personality, and interests; learning and motivation; psychological research methods; and the assessment and treatment of behavioral and affective disorders.
Sociology and Anthropology	Knowledge of group behavior and dynamics, societal trends and influences, human migrations, ethnicity, cultures and their history and origins.
Personnel and Human Resources	Knowledge of principles and procedures for personnel recruitment, selection, training, compensation and benefits, labor relations and negotiation, and personnel information systems.
Transportation	Knowledge of principles and methods for moving people or goods by air, rail, sea, or road, including the relative costs and benefits.
Foreign Language	Knowledge of the structure and content of a foreign (non-English) language including the meaning and spelling of words, rules of composition and grammar, and pronunciation.
Telecommunications	Knowledge of transmission, broadcasting, switching, control, and operation of telecommunications systems.
Production and Processing	Knowledge of raw materials, production processes, quality control, costs, and other techniques for maximizing the effective manufacture and distribution of goods.
Therapy and Counseling	Knowledge of principles, methods, and procedures for diagnosis, treatment, and rehabilitation of physical and mental dysfunctions, and for career counseling and guidance.
Medicine and Dentistry	Knowledge of the information and techniques needed to diagnose and treat human injuries, diseases, and deformities. This includes symptoms, treatment alternatives, drug properties and interactions, and preventive health-care measures.
Fine Arts	Knowledge of the theory and techniques required to compose, produce, and perform works of music, dance, visual arts, drama, and sculpture.

Philosophy and Theology	Knowledge of different philosophical systems and religions. This includes their basic principles, values, ethics, ways of thinking, customs, practices, and their impact on human culture.
Food Production	Knowledge of techniques and equipment for planting, growing, and harvesting food products (both plant and animal) for consumption, including storage/handling techniques.

Skills	Skills Definitions
Science	Using scientific rules and methods to solve problems.
Writing	Communicating effectively in writing as appropriate for the needs of the audience.
Reading Comprehension	Understanding written sentences and paragraphs in work related documents.
Critical Thinking	Using logic and reasoning to identify the strengths and weaknesses of alternative solutions, conclusions or approaches to problems.
Judgment and Decision Making	Considering the relative costs and benefits of potential actions to choose the most appropriate one.
Coordination	Adjusting actions in relation to others' actions.
Time Management	Managing one's own time and the time of others.
Active Listening	Giving full attention to what other people are saying, taking time to understand the points being made, asking questions as appropriate, and not interrupting at inappropriate times.
Active Learning	Understanding the implications of new information for both current and future problem-solving and decision-making.
Complex Problem Solving	Identifying complex problems and reviewing related information to develop and evaluate options and implement solutions.
Speaking	Talking to others to convey information effectively.
Management of Financial Resources	Determining how money will be spent to get the work done, and accounting for these expenditures.
Monitoring	Monitoring/Assessing performance of yourself, other individuals, or organizations to make improvements or take corrective action.
Learning Strategies	Selecting and using training/instructional methods and procedures appropriate for the situation when learning or teaching new things.
Equipment Selection	Determining the kind of tools and equipment needed to do a job.
Service Orientation	Actively looking for ways to help people.
Management of Personnel Resources	Motivating, developing, and directing people as they work, identifying the best people for the job.
Persuasion	Persuading others to change their minds or behavior.
Negotiation	Bringing others together and trying to reconcile differences.
Quality Control Analysis	Conducting tests and inspections of products, services, or processes to evaluate quality or performance.
Operations Analysis	Analyzing needs and product requirements to create a design.
Mathematics	Using mathematics to solve problems.
Social Perceptiveness	Being aware of others' reactions and understanding why they react as they do.
Instructing	Teaching others how to do something.
Management of Material Resources	Obtaining and seeing to the appropriate use of equipment, facilities, and materials needed to do certain work.
Systems Evaluation	Identifying measures or indicators of system performance and the actions needed to improve or correct performance, relative to the goals of the system.
Troubleshooting	Determining causes of operating errors and deciding what to do about it.
Systems Analysis	Determining how a system should work and how changes in conditions, operations, and the environment will affect outcomes.
Operation Monitoring	Watching gauges, dials, or other indicators to make sure a machine is working properly.
Installation	Installing equipment, machines, wiring, or programs to meet specifications.
Technology Design	Generating or adapting equipment and technology to serve user needs.
Operation and Control	Controlling operations of equipment or systems.
Repairing	Repairing machines or systems using the needed tools.
Equipment Maintenance	Performing routine maintenance on equipment and determining when and what kind of maintenance is needed.
Programming	Writing computer programs for various purposes.

Ability	Ability Definitions
Written Comprehension	The ability to read and understand information and ideas presented in writing.
Inductive Reasoning	The ability to combine pieces of information to form general rules or conclusions (includes finding a relationship among seemingly unrelated events).
Deductive Reasoning	The ability to apply general rules to specific problems to produce answers that make sense.
Near Vision	The ability to see details at close range (within a few feet of the observer).
Problem Sensitivity	The ability to tell when something is wrong or is likely to go wrong. It does not involve solving the problem, only recognizing there is a problem.
Written Expression	The ability to communicate information and ideas in writing so others will understand.
Oral Comprehension	The ability to listen to and understand information and ideas presented through spoken words and sentences.
Category Flexibility	The ability to generate or use different sets of rules for combining or grouping things in different ways.
Oral Expression	The ability to communicate information and ideas in speaking so others will understand.
Flexibility of Closure	The ability to identify or detect a known pattern (a figure, object, word, or sound) that is hidden in other distracting material.
Information Ordering	The ability to arrange things or actions in a certain order or pattern according to a specific rule or set of rules (e.g., patterns of numbers, letters, words, pictures, mathematical operations).
Speech Clarity	The ability to speak clearly so others can understand you.
Speech Recognition	The ability to identify and understand the speech of another person.
Fluency of Ideas	The ability to come up with a number of ideas about a topic (the number of ideas is important, not their quality, correctness, or creativity).
Mathematical Reasoning	The ability to choose the right mathematical methods or formulas to solve a problem.
Originality	The ability to come up with unusual or clever ideas about a given topic or situation, or to develop creative ways to solve a problem.
Visualization	The ability to imagine how something will look after it is moved around or when its parts are moved or rearranged.
Selective Attention	The ability to concentrate on a task over a period of time without being distracted.
Speed of Closure	The ability to quickly make sense of, combine, and organize information into meaningful patterns.
Far Vision	The ability to see details at a distance.
Memorization	The ability to remember information such as words, numbers, pictures, and procedures.
Visual Color Discrimination	The ability to match or detect differences between colors, including shades of color and brightness.
Perceptual Speed	The ability to quickly and accurately compare similarities and differences among sets of letters, numbers, objects, pictures, or patterns. The things to be compared may be presented at the same time or one after the other. This ability also includes comparing a presented object with a remembered object.
Finger Dexterity	The ability to make precisely coordinated movements of the fingers of one or both hands to grasp, manipulate, or assemble very small objects.
Control Precision	The ability to quickly and repeatedly adjust the controls of a machine or a vehicle to exact positions.
Arm-Hand Steadiness	The ability to keep your hand and arm steady while moving your arm or while holding your arm and hand in one position.
Number Facility	The ability to add, subtract, multiply, or divide quickly and correctly.
Trunk Strength	The ability to use your abdominal and lower back muscles to support part of the body repeatedly or continuously over time without 'giving out' or fatiguing.
Manual Dexterity	The ability to quickly move your hand, your hand together with your arm, or your two hands to grasp, manipulate, or assemble objects.
Depth Perception	The ability to judge which of several objects is closer or farther away from you, or to judge the distance between you and an object.
Auditory Attention	The ability to focus on a single source of sound in the presence of other distracting sounds.
Time Sharing	The ability to shift back and forth between two or more activities or sources of information (such as speech, sounds, touch, or other sources).

Multilimb Coordination	The ability to coordinate two or more limbs (for example, two arms, two legs, or one leg and one arm) while sitting, standing, or lying down. It does not involve performing the activities while the whole body is in motion.
Reaction Time	The ability to quickly respond (with the hand, finger, or foot) to a signal (sound, light, picture) when it appears.
Glare Sensitivity	The ability to see objects in the presence of glare or bright lighting.
Gross Body Coordination	The ability to coordinate the movement of your arms, legs, and torso together when the whole body is in motion.
Static Strength	The ability to exert maximum muscle force to lift, push, pull, or carry objects.
Stamina	The ability to exert yourself physically over long periods of time without getting winded or out of breath.
Extent Flexibility	The ability to bend, stretch, twist, or reach with your body, arms, and/or legs.
Hearing Sensitivity	The ability to detect or tell the differences between sounds that vary in pitch and loudness.
Dynamic Strength	The ability to exert muscle force repeatedly or continuously over time. This involves muscular endurance and resistance to muscle fatigue.
Spatial Orientation	The ability to know your location in relation to the environment or to know where other objects are in relation to you.
Gross Body Equilibrium	The ability to keep or regain your body balance or stay upright when in an unstable position.
Night Vision	The ability to see under low light conditions.
Speed of Limb Movement	The ability to quickly move the arms and legs.
Dynamic Flexibility	The ability to quickly and repeatedly bend, stretch, twist, or reach out with your body, arms, and/or legs.
Explosive Strength	The ability to use short bursts of muscle force to propel oneself (as in jumping or sprinting), or to throw an object.
Response Orientation	The ability to choose quickly between two or more movements in response to two or more different signals (lights, sounds, pictures). It includes the speed with which the correct response is started with the hand, foot, or other body part.
Peripheral Vision	The ability to see objects or movement of objects to one's side when the eyes are looking ahead.
Rate Control	The ability to time your movements or the movement of a piece of equipment in anticipation of changes in the speed and/or direction of a moving object or scene.
Wrist-Finger Speed	The ability to make fast, simple, repeated movements of the fingers, hands, and wrists.
Sound Localization	The ability to tell the direction from which a sound originated.

Work_Activity	Work_Activity Definitions
Getting Information	Observing, receiving, and otherwise obtaining information from all relevant sources.
Interacting With Computers	Using computers and computer systems (including hardware and software) to program, write software, set up functions, enter data, or process information.
Identifying Objects, Actions, and Events	Identifying information by categorizing, estimating, recognizing differences or similarities, and detecting changes in circumstances or events.
Processing Information	Compiling, coding, categorizing, calculating, tabulating, auditing, or verifying information or data.
Analyzing Data or Information	Identifying the underlying principles, reasons, or facts of information by breaking down information or data into separate parts.
Making Decisions and Solving Problems	Analyzing information and evaluating results to choose the best solution and solve problems.
Thinking Creatively	Developing, designing, or creating new applications, ideas, relationships, systems, or products, including artistic contributions.
Interpreting the Meaning of Information for Others	Translating or explaining what information means and how it can be used.
Updating and Using Relevant Knowledge	Keeping up-to-date technically and applying new knowledge to your job.
Monitor Processes, Materials, or Surroundings	Monitoring and reviewing information from materials, events, or the environment, to detect or assess problems.
Documenting/Recording Information	Entering, transcribing, recording, storing, or maintaining information in written or electronic/magnetic form.
Communicating with Supervisors, Peers, or Subordin	Providing information to supervisors, co-workers, and subordinates by telephone, in written form, e-mail, or in person.

Estimating the Quantifiable Characteristics of Pro	Estimating sizes, distances, and quantities; or determining time, costs, resources, or materials needed to perform a work activity.
Establishing and Maintaining Interpersonal Relatio	Developing constructive and cooperative working relationships with others, and maintaining them over time.
Evaluating Information to Determine Compliance wit	Using relevant information and individual judgment to determine whether events or processes comply with laws, regulations, or standards.
Communicating with Persons Outside Organization	Communicating with people outside the organization, representing the organization to customers, the public, government, and other external sources. This information can be exchanged in person, in writing, or by telephone or e-mail.
Organizing, Planning, and Prioritizing Work	Developing specific goals and plans to prioritize, organize, and accomplish your work.
Judging the Qualities of Things, Services, or Peop	Assessing the value, importance, or quality of things or people.
Inspecting Equipment, Structures, or Material	Inspecting equipment, structures, or materials to identify the cause of errors or other problems or defects.
Developing Objectives and Strategies	Establishing long-range objectives and specifying the strategies and actions to achieve them.
Provide Consultation and Advice to Others	Providing guidance and expert advice to management or other groups on technical, systems-, or process-related topics.
Scheduling Work and Activities	Scheduling events, programs, and activities, as well as the work of others.
Monitoring and Controlling Resources	Monitoring and controlling resources and overseeing the spending of money.
Selling or Influencing Others	Convincing others to buy merchandise/goods or to otherwise change their minds or actions.
Resolving Conflicts and Negotiating with Others	Handling complaints, settling disputes, and resolving grievances and conflicts, or otherwise negotiating with others.
Performing General Physical Activities	Performing physical activities that require considerable use of your arms and legs and moving your whole body, such as climbing, lifting, balancing, walking, stooping, and handling of materials.
Coordinating the Work and Activities of Others	Getting members of a group to work together to accomplish tasks.
Performing Administrative Activities	Performing day-to-day administrative tasks such as maintaining information files and processing paperwork.
Training and Teaching Others	Identifying the educational needs of others, developing formal educational or training programs or classes, and teaching or instructing others.
Drafting, Laying Out, and Specifying Technical Dev	Providing documentation, detailed instructions, drawings, or specifications to tell others about how devices, parts, equipment, or structures are to be fabricated, constructed, assembled, modified, maintained, or used.
Developing and Building Teams	Encouraging and building mutual trust, respect, and cooperation among team members.
Operating Vehicles, Mechanized Devices, or Equipme	Running, maneuvering, navigating, or driving vehicles or mechanized equipment, such as forklifts, passenger vehicles, aircraft, or water craft.
Controlling Machines and Processes	Using either control mechanisms or direct physical activity to operate machines or processes (not including computers or vehicles).
Coaching and Developing Others	Identifying the developmental needs of others and coaching, mentoring, or otherwise helping others to improve their knowledge or skills.
Handling and Moving Objects	Using hands and arms in handling, installing, positioning, and moving materials, and manipulating things.
Performing for or Working Directly with the Public	Performing for people or dealing directly with the public. This includes serving customers in restaurants and stores, and receiving clients or guests.
Guiding, Directing, and Motivating Subordinates	Providing guidance and direction to subordinates, including setting performance standards and monitoring performance.
Assisting and Caring for Others	Providing personal assistance, medical attention, emotional support, or other personal care to others such as coworkers, customers, or patients.
Repairing and Maintaining Electronic Equipment	Servicing, repairing, calibrating, regulating, fine-tuning, or testing machines, devices, and equipment that operate primarily on the basis of electrical or electronic (not mechanical) principles.
Repairing and Maintaining Mechanical Equipment	Servicing, repairing, adjusting, and testing machines, devices, moving parts, and equipment that operate primarily on the basis of mechanical (not electronic) principles.
Staffing Organizational Units	Recruiting, interviewing, selecting, hiring, and promoting employees in an organization.

Work_Context	Work_Context Definitions
Telephone	How often do you have telephone conversations in this job?
Electronic Mail	How often do you use electronic mail in this job?
Impact of Decisions on Co-workers or Company Resul	How do the decisions an employee makes impact the results of co-workers, clients or the company?
Indoors, Environmentally Controlled	How often does this job require working indoors in environmentally controlled conditions?
Face-to-Face Discussions	How often do you have to have face-to-face discussions with individuals or teams in this job?
Importance of Being Exact or Accurate	How important is being very exact or highly accurate in performing this job?
Contact With Others	How much does this job require the worker to be in contact with others (face-to-face, by telephone, or otherwise) in order to perform it?
Freedom to Make Decisions	How much decision making freedom, without supervision, does the job offer?
Structured versus Unstructured Work	To what extent is this job structured for the worker, rather than allowing the worker to determine tasks, priorities, and goals?
Letters and Memos	How often does the job require written letters and memos?
Work With Work Group or Team	How important is it to work with others in a group or team in this job?
Frequency of Decision Making	How frequently is the worker required to make decisions that affect other people, the financial resources, and/or the image and reputation of the organization?
Spend Time Sitting	How much does this job require sitting?
Consequence of Error	How serious would the result usually be if the worker made a mistake that was not readily correctable?
Time Pressure	How often does this job require the worker to meet strict deadlines?
Coordinate or Lead Others	How important is it to coordinate or lead others in accomplishing work activities in this job?
Importance of Repeating Same Tasks	How important is repeating the same physical activities (e.g., key entry) or mental activities (e.g., checking entries in a ledger) over and over, without stopping, to performing this job?
Level of Competition	To what extent does this job require the worker to compete or to be aware of competitive pressures?
Responsible for Others' Health and Safety	How much responsibility is there for the health and safety of others in this job?
Deal With External Customers	How important is it to work with external customers or the public in this job?
Responsibility for Outcomes and Results	How responsible is the worker for work outcomes and results of other workers?
In an Enclosed Vehicle or Equipment	How often does this job require working in a closed vehicle or equipment (e.g., car)?
Outdoors, Exposed to Weather	How often does this job require working outdoors, exposed to all weather conditions?
Frequency of Conflict Situations	How often are there conflict situations the employee has to face in this job?
Sounds, Noise Levels Are Distracting or Uncomforta	How often does this job require working exposed to sounds and noise levels that are distracting or uncomfortable?
Spend Time Making Repetitive Motions	How much does this job require making repetitive motions?
Exposed to Contaminants	How often does this job require working exposed to contaminants (such as pollutants, gases, dust or odors)?
Spend Time Standing	How much does this job require standing?
Very Hot or Cold Temperatures	How often does this job require working in very hot (above 90 F degrees) or very cold (below 32 F degrees) temperatures?
Physical Proximity	To what extent does this job require the worker to perform job tasks in close physical proximity to other people?
Indoors, Not Environmentally Controlled	How often does this job require working indoors in non-controlled environmental conditions (e.g., warehouse without heat)?
Exposed to Hazardous Equipment	How often does this job require exposure to hazardous equipment?
Extremely Bright or Inadequate Lighting	How often does this job require working in extremely bright or inadequate lighting conditions?
Exposed to Hazardous Conditions	How often does this job require exposure to hazardous conditions?
Spend Time Using Your Hands to Handle, Control, or	How much does this job require using your hands to handle, control, or feel objects, tools or controls?
Wear Common Protective or Safety Equipment such as	How much does this job require wearing common protective or safety equipment such as safety shoes, glasses, gloves, hard hats or life jackets?

Deal With Unpleasant or Angry People	How frequently does the worker have to deal with unpleasant, angry, or discourteous individuals as part of the job requirements?
Exposed to Minor Burns, Cuts, Bites, or Stings	How often does this job require exposure to minor burns, cuts, bites, or stings?
Public Speaking	How often do you have to perform public speaking in this job?
Cramped Work Space, Awkward Positions	How often does this job require working in cramped work spaces that requires getting into awkward positions?
Spend Time Walking and Running	How much does this job require walking and running?
Spend Time Kneeling, Crouching, Stooping, or Crawl	How much does this job require kneeling, crouching, stooping, or crawling?
Degree of Automation	How automated is the job?
Spend Time Bending or Twisting the Body	How much does this job require bending or twisting your body?
Pace Determined by Speed of Equipment	How important is it to this job that the pace is determined by the speed of equipment or machinery? (This does not refer to keeping busy at all times on this job.)
Deal With Physically Aggressive People	How frequently does this job require the worker to deal with physical aggression of violent individuals?
Spend Time Keeping or Regaining Balance	How much does this job require keeping or regaining your balance?
Exposed to High Places	How often does this job require exposure to high places?
Exposed to Radiation	How often does this job require exposure to radiation?
Exposed to Whole Body Vibration	How often does this job require exposure to whole body vibration (e.g., operate a jackhammer)?
Wear Specialized Protective or Safety Equipment su	How much does this job require wearing specialized protective or safety equipment such as breathing apparatus, safety harness, full protection suits, or radiation protection?
Outdoors, Under Cover	How often does this job require working outdoors, under cover (e.g., structure with roof but no walls)?
Exposed to Disease or Infections	How often does this job require exposure to disease/infections?
In an Open Vehicle or Equipment	How often does this job require working in an open vehicle or equipment (e.g., tractor)?
Spend Time Climbing Ladders, Scaffolds, or Poles	How much does this job require climbing ladders, scaffolds, or poles?

Job Zone Component	Job Zone Component Definitions
Title	Job Zone Five: Extensive Preparation Needed
Overall Experience	Extensive skill, knowledge, and experience are needed for these occupations. Many require more than five years of experience. For example, surgeons must complete four years of college and an additional five to seven years of specialized medical training to be able to do their job.
Job Training	Employees may need some on-the-job training, but most of these occupations assume that the person will already have the required skills, knowledge, work-related experience, and/or training.
Job Zone Examples	These occupations often involve coordinating, training, supervising, or managing the activities of others to accomplish goals. Very advanced communication and organizational skills are required. Examples include athletic trainers, lawyers, managing editors, phyicists, social psychologists, and surgeons.
SVP Range	(8.0 and above)
Education	A bachelor's degree is the minimum formal education required for these occupations. However, many also require graduate school. For example, they may require a master's degree, and some require a Ph.D., M.D., or J.D. (law degree).

Work_Styles	Work_Styles Definitions
Attention to Detail	Job requires being careful about detail and thorough in completing work tasks.
Dependability	Job requires being reliable, responsible, and dependable, and fulfilling obligations.
Integrity	Job requires being honest and ethical.
Analytical Thinking	Job requires analyzing information and using logic to address work-related issues and problems.
Achievement/Effort	Job requires establishing and maintaining personally challenging achievement goals and exerting effort toward mastering tasks.
Cooperation	Job requires being pleasant with others on the job and displaying a good-natured, cooperative attitude.

Adaptability/Flexibility	Job requires being open to change (positive or negative) and to considerable variety in the workplace.
Initiative	Job requires a willingness to take on responsibilities and challenges.
Leadership	Job requires a willingness to lead, take charge, and offer opinions and direction.
Independence	Job requires developing one's own ways of doing things, guiding oneself with little or no supervision, and depending on oneself to get things done.
Stress Tolerance	Job requires accepting criticism and dealing calmly and effectively with high stress situations.
Persistence	Job requires persistence in the face of obstacles.
Innovation	Job requires creativity and alternative thinking to develop new ideas for and answers to work-related problems.
Concern for Others	Job requires being sensitive to others' needs and feelings and being understanding and helpful on the job.
Self Control	Job requires maintaining composure, keeping emotions in check, controlling anger, and avoiding aggressive behavior, even in very difficult situations.
Social Orientation	Job requires preferring to work with others rather than alone, and being personally connected with others on the job.

19-3011.00 - Economists

Conduct research, prepare reports, or formulate plans to aid in solution of economic problems arising from production and distribution of goods and services. May collect and process economic and statistical data using econometric and sampling techniques.

Tasks

1) Supervise research projects and students' study projects.

2) Provide advice and consultation on economic relationships to businesses, public and private agencies, and other employers.

3) Formulate recommendations, policies, or plans to solve economic problems or to interpret markets.

4) Study economic and statistical data in area of specialization, such as finance, labor, or agriculture.

5) Compile, analyze, and report data to explain economic phenomena and forecast market trends, applying mathematical models and statistical techniques.

6) Develop economic guidelines and standards and prepare points of view used in forecasting trends and formulating economic policy.

7) Teach theories, principles, and methods of economics.

8) Forecast production and consumption of renewable resources and supply, consumption and depletion of non-renewable resources.

19-3022.00 - Survey Researchers

Design or conduct surveys. May supervise interviewers who conduct the survey in person or over the telephone. May present survey results to client.

Tasks

1) Determine and specify details of survey projects, including sources of information, procedures to be used, and the design of survey instruments and materials.

2) Conduct surveys and collect data, using methods such as interviews, questionnaires, focus groups, market analysis surveys, public opinion polls, literature reviews, and file reviews.

3) Conduct research in order to gather information about survey topics.

4) Direct and review the work of staff members, including survey support staff and interviewers who gather survey data.

5) Collaborate with other researchers in the planning, implementation, and evaluation of surveys.

6) Analyze data from surveys, old records, and/or case studies, using statistical software programs.

7) Review, classify, and record survey data in preparation for computer analysis.

8) Hire and train recruiters and data collectors.

9) Prepare and present summaries and analyses of survey data, including tables, graphs, and fact sheets that describe survey techniques and results.

10) Support, plan, and coordinate operations for single or multiple surveys.

11) Monitor and evaluate survey progress and performance, using sample disposition reports and response rate calculations.

12) Write training manuals to be used by survey interviewers.

13) Direct updates and changes in survey implementation and methods.

14) Produce documentation of the questionnaire development process, data collection methods, sampling designs, and decisions related to sample statistical weighting.

19-3031.02 - Clinical Psychologists

Diagnose or evaluate mental and emotional disorders of individuals through observation, interview, and psychological tests, and formulate and administer programs of treatment.

Tasks

1) Observe individuals at play, in group interactions, or in other contexts to detect indications of mental deficiency, abnormal behavior, or maladjustment.

2) Interact with clients to assist them in gaining insight, defining goals, and planning action to achieve effective personal, social, educational, and vocational development and adjustment.

3) Identify psychological, emotional, or behavioral issues, and diagnose disorders, using information obtained from interviews, tests, records, and reference materials.

4) Evaluate the effectiveness of counseling or treatments, and the accuracy and completeness of diagnoses, then modify plans and diagnoses as necessary.

5) Discuss the treatment of problems with clients.

6) Consult reference material such as textbooks, manuals, and journals in order to identify symptoms, to make diagnoses, and to develop approaches to treatment.

7) Obtain and study medical, psychological, social, and family histories, by interviewing individuals, couples, or families, and by reviewing records.

8) Refer clients to other specialists, institutions, or support services as necessary.

9) Plan, supervise, and conduct psychological research, and write papers describing research results.

10) Develop and implement individual treatment plans, specifying type, frequency, intensity, and duration of therapy.

11) Provide psychological and/or administrative services and advice to private firms and community agencies regarding mental health programs or individual cases.

12) Utilize a variety of treatment methods such as psychotherapy, hypnosis, behavior modification, stress reduction therapy, psychodrama, and play therapy.

13) Maintain current knowledge of relevant research.

14) Write reports on clients, and maintain required paperwork.

15) Develop, direct, and participate in training programs for staff and students.

16) Plan and develop accredited psychological service programs in psychiatric centers or hospitals, in collaboration with psychiatrists and other professional staff.

17) Direct, coordinate, and evaluate activities of staff and interns engaged in patient assessment and treatment.

18) Select, administer, score, and interpret psychological tests in order to obtain information on individuals' intelligence, achievements, interests, and personalities.

19) Provide occupational, educational, and other information to individuals so that they can make educational and vocational plans.

19-3031.03 - Counseling Psychologists

Assess and evaluate individuals' problems through the use of case history, interview, and observation and provide individual or group counseling services to assist individuals in achieving more effective personal, social, educational, and vocational development and adjustment.

Tasks

1) Collect information about individuals or clients, using interviews, case histories, observational techniques, and other assessment methods.

2) Counsel individuals, groups, or families to help them understand problems, define goals, and develop realistic action plans.

3) Select, administer, and interpret psychological tests to assess intelligence, aptitudes, abilities, or interests.

4) Advise clients on how they could be helped by counseling.

5) Consult with other professionals to discuss therapies, treatments, counseling resources, or techniques, and to share occupational information.

6) Provide consulting services to schools, social service agencies, and businesses.

7) Conduct research to develop or improve diagnostic or therapeutic counseling techniques.

8) Develop therapeutic and treatment plans based on clients' interests, abilities, and needs.

9) Evaluate the results of counseling methods to determine the reliability and validity of treatments.

10) Analyze data such as interview notes, test results, and reference manuals in order to identify symptoms, and to diagnose the nature of clients' problems.

19-3032.00 - Industrial-Organizational Psychologists

Apply principles of psychology to personnel, administration, management, sales, and marketing problems. Activities may include policy planning; employee screening, training and development; and organizational development and analysis. May work with management to reorganize the work setting to improve worker productivity.

Tasks

1) Facilitate organizational development and change.

2) Advise management concerning personnel, managerial, and marketing policies and practices and their potential effects on organizational effectiveness and efficiency.

3) Assess employee performance.

4) Counsel workers about job and career-related issues.

5) Participate in mediation and dispute resolution.

6) Study consumers' reactions to new products and package designs, and to advertising efforts, using surveys and tests.

7) Identify training and development needs.

8) Formulate and implement training programs, applying principles of learning and individual differences.

9) Develop and implement employee selection and placement programs.

10) Observe and interview workers in order to obtain information about the physical, mental, and educational requirements of jobs as well as information about aspects such as job satisfaction.

11) Write reports on research findings and implications in order to contribute to general knowledge and to suggest potential changes in organizational functioning.

12) Analyze data, using statistical methods and applications, in order to evaluate the outcomes and effectiveness of workplace programs.

13) Analyze job requirements and content in order to establish criteria for classification, selection, training, and other related personnel functions.

14) Develop interview techniques, rating scales, and psychological tests used to assess skills, abilities, and interests for the purpose of employee selection, placement, and promotion.

15) Conduct research studies of physical work environments, organizational structures, communication systems, group interactions, morale, and motivation in order to assess organizational functioning.

19-3051.00 - Urban and Regional Planners

Develop comprehensive plans and programs for use of land and physical facilities of local jurisdictions, such as towns, cities, counties, and metropolitan areas.

Tasks

1) Discuss with planning officials the purpose of land use projects such as transportation, conservation, residential, commercial, industrial, and community use.

2) Conduct field investigations, surveys, impact studies or other research in order to compile and analyze data on economic, social, regulatory and physical factors affecting land use.

3) Keep informed about economic and legal issues involved in zoning codes, building codes, and environmental regulations.

4) Assess the feasibility of proposals and identify necessary changes.

5) Determine the effects of regulatory limitations on projects.

6) Create, prepare, or requisition graphic and narrative reports on land use data, including land area maps overlaid with geographic variables such as population density.

7) Hold public meetings and confer with government, social scientists, lawyers, developers, the public, and special interest groups to formulate and develop land use or community plans.

8) Coordinate work with economic consultants and architects during the formulation of plans and the design of large pieces of infrastructure.

9) Design, promote and administer government plans and policies affecting land use, zoning, public utilities, community facilities, housing, and transportation.

10) Recommend approval, denial or conditional approval of proposals.

11) Mediate community disputes and assist in developing alternative plans and recommendations for programs or projects.

12) Review and evaluate environmental impact reports pertaining to private and public planning projects and programs.

13) Investigate property availability.

14) Supervise and coordinate the work of urban planning technicians and technologists.

Knowledge	Knowledge Definitions
Design	Knowledge of design techniques, tools, and principles involved in production of precision technical plans, blueprints, drawings, and models.
Customer and Personal Service	Knowledge of principles and processes for providing customer and personal services. This includes customer needs assessment, meeting quality standards for services, and evaluation of customer satisfaction.
English Language	Knowledge of the structure and content of the English language including the meaning and spelling of words, rules of composition, and grammar.
Law and Government	Knowledge of laws, legal codes, court procedures, precedents, government regulations, executive orders, agency rules, and the democratic political process.
Building and Construction	Knowledge of materials, methods, and the tools involved in the construction or repair of houses, buildings, or other structures such as highways and roads.
Administration and Management	Knowledge of business and management principles involved in strategic planning, resource allocation, human resources modeling, leadership technique, production methods, and coordination of people and resources.
Geography	Knowledge of principles and methods for describing the features of land, sea, and air masses, including their physical characteristics, locations, interrelationships, and distribution of plant, animal, and human life.
Computers and Electronics	Knowledge of circuit boards, processors, chips, electronic equipment, and computer hardware and software, including applications and programming.
Mathematics	Knowledge of arithmetic, algebra, geometry, calculus, statistics, and their applications.
Clerical	Knowledge of administrative and clerical procedures and systems such as word processing, managing files and records, stenography and transcription, designing forms, and other office procedures and terminology.
Engineering and Technology	Knowledge of the practical application of engineering science and technology. This includes applying principles, techniques, procedures, and equipment to the design and production of various goods and services.
Personnel and Human Resources	Knowledge of principles and procedures for personnel recruitment, selection, training, compensation and benefits, labor relations and negotiation, and personnel information systems.
Economics and Accounting	Knowledge of economic and accounting principles and practices, the financial markets, banking and the analysis and reporting of financial data.

Clerical	Knowledge of administrative and clerical procedures and systems such as word processing. managing files and records. stenography and transcription. designing forms, and other office procedures and terminology.
Engineering and Technology	Knowledge of the practical application of engineering science and technology. This includes applying principles. techniques, procedures, and equipment to the design and production of various goods and services.
Personnel and Human Resources	Knowledge of principles and procedures for personnel recruitment, selection, training. compensation and benefits, labor relations and negotiation, and personnel information systems.
Economics and Accounting	Knowledge of economic and accounting principles and practices, the financial markets. banking and the analysis and reporting of financial data.
Transportation	Knowledge of principles and methods for moving people or goods by air, rail, sea, or road, including the relative costs and benefits.
Communications and Media	Knowledge of media production, communication, and dissemination techniques and methods. This includes alternative ways to inform and entertain via written, oral, and visual media.
History and Archeology	Knowledge of historical events and their causes, indicators, and effects on civilizations and cultures.
Sales and Marketing	Knowledge of principles and methods for showing, promoting, and selling products or services. This includes marketing strategy and tactics, product demonstration, sales techniques, and sales control systems.
Education and Training	Knowledge of principles and methods for curriculum and training design, teaching and instruction for individuals and groups, and the measurement of training effects.
Public Safety and Security	Knowledge of relevant equipment, policies, procedures, and strategies to promote effective local, state. or national security operations for the protection of people, data, property, and institutions.
Psychology	Knowledge of human behavior and performance; individual differences in ability, personality, and interests; learning and motivation; psychological research methods; and the assessment and treatment of behavioral and affective disorders.
Sociology and Anthropology	Knowledge of group behavior and dynamics, societal trends and influences, human migrations, ethnicity, cultures and their history and origins.
Telecommunications	Knowledge of transmission, broadcasting, switching, control, and operation of telecommunications systems.
Mechanical	Knowledge of machines and tools, including their designs, uses, repair, and maintenance.
Production and Processing	Knowledge of raw materials, production processes, quality control, costs, and other techniques for maximizing the effective manufacture and distribution of goods.
Biology	Knowledge of plant and animal organisms, their tissues, cells, functions, interdependencies, and interactions with each other and the environment.
Therapy and Counseling	Knowledge of principles, methods, and procedures for diagnosis, treatment, and rehabilitation of physical and mental dysfunctions, and for career counseling and guidance.
Philosophy and Theology	Knowledge of different philosophical systems and religions. This includes their basic principles, values, ethics, ways of thinking, customs, practices, and their impact on human culture.
Chemistry	Knowledge of the chemical composition, structure, and properties of substances and of the chemical processes and transformations that they undergo. This includes uses of chemicals and their interactions, danger signs, production techniques, and disposal methods.
Foreign Language	Knowledge of the structure and content of a foreign (non-English) language including the meaning and spelling of words, rules of composition and grammar, and pronunciation.
Medicine and Dentistry	Knowledge of the information and techniques needed to diagnose and treat human injuries, diseases, and deformities. This includes symptoms, treatment alternatives, drug properties and interactions, and preventive health-care measures.
Fine Arts	Knowledge of the theory and techniques required to compose, produce, and perform works of music, dance, visual arts, drama, and sculpture.
Physics	Knowledge of physical principles, laws, their interrelationships, and applications to understanding fluid, material, and atmospheric dynamics, and mechanical, electrical, atomic and sub- atomic structures and processes.

Food Production	Knowledge of techniques and equipment for planting. growing. and harvesting food products (both plant and animal) for consumption, including storage/handling techniques.

Skills	**Skills Definitions**
Writing	Communicating effectively in writing as appropriate for the needs of the audience.
Active Listening	Giving full attention to what other people are saying, taking time to understand the points being made, asking questions as appropriate, and not interrupting at inappropriate times.
Reading Comprehension	Understanding written sentences and paragraphs in work related documents.
Critical Thinking	Using logic and reasoning to identify the strengths and weaknesses of alternative solutions, conclusions or approaches to problems.
Time Management	Managing one's own time and the time of others.
Speaking	Talking to others to convey information effectively.
Judgment and Decision Making	Considering the relative costs and benefits of potential actions to choose the most appropriate one.
Complex Problem Solving	Identifying complex problems and reviewing related information to develop and evaluate options and implement solutions.
Service Orientation	Actively looking for ways to help people.
Coordination	Adjusting actions in relation to others' actions.
Social Perceptiveness	Being aware of others' reactions and understanding why they react as they do.
Active Learning	Understanding the implications of new information for both current and future problem-solving and decision-making.
Monitoring	Monitoring/Assessing performance of yourself, other individuals, or organizations to make improvements or take corrective action.
Persuasion	Persuading others to change their minds or behavior.
Learning Strategies	Selecting and using training/instructional methods and procedures appropriate for the situation when learning or teaching new things.
Mathematics	Using mathematics to solve problems.
Negotiation	Bringing others together and trying to reconcile differences.
Instructing	Teaching others how to do something.
Management of Personnel Resources	Motivating, developing, and directing people as they work, identifying the best people for the job.
Operations Analysis	Analyzing needs and product requirements to create a design.
Management of Financial Resources	Determining how money will be spent to get the work done, and accounting for these expenditures.
Science	Using scientific rules and methods to solve problems.
Systems Evaluation	Identifying measures or indicators of system performance and the actions needed to improve or correct performance, relative to the goals of the system.
Equipment Selection	Determining the kind of tools and equipment needed to do a job.
Quality Control Analysis	Conducting tests and inspections of products, services, or processes to evaluate quality or performance.
Management of Material Resources	Obtaining and seeing to the appropriate use of equipment, facilities, and materials needed to do certain work.
Systems Analysis	Determining how a system should work and how changes in conditions, operations, and the environment will affect outcomes.
Operation and Control	Controlling operations of equipment or systems.
Technology Design	Generating or adapting equipment and technology to serve user needs.
Troubleshooting	Determining causes of operating errors and deciding what to do about it.
Programming	Writing computer programs for various purposes.
Equipment Maintenance	Performing routine maintenance on equipment and determining when and what kind of maintenance is needed.
Installation	Installing equipment, machines, wiring, or programs to meet specifications.
Operation Monitoring	Watching gauges, dials, or other indicators to make sure a machine is working properly.
Repairing	Repairing machines or systems using the needed tools.

Ability	**Ability Definitions**
Written Comprehension	The ability to read and understand information and ideas presented in writing.
Deductive Reasoning	The ability to apply general rules to specific problems to produce answers that make sense.

Oral Comprehension	The ability to listen to and understand information and ideas presented through spoken words and sentences.	Glare Sensitivity	The ability to see objects in the presence of glare or bright lighting.
Inductive Reasoning	The ability to combine pieces of information to form general rules or conclusions (includes finding a relationship among seemingly unrelated events).	Speed of Limb Movement	The ability to quickly move the arms and legs.
		Hearing Sensitivity	The ability to detect or tell the differences between sounds that vary in pitch and loudness.
Oral Expression	The ability to communicate information and ideas in speaking so others will understand.	Trunk Strength	The ability to use your abdominal and lower back muscles to support part of the body repeatedly or continuously over time without 'giving out' or fatiguing.
Written Expression	The ability to communicate information and ideas in writing so others will understand.	Extent Flexibility	The ability to bend, stretch, twist, or reach with your body, arms, and legs.
Speech Clarity	The ability to speak clearly so others can understand you.		
Problem Sensitivity	The ability to tell when something is wrong or is likely to go wrong. It does not involve solving the problem, only recognizing there is a problem.	Wrist-Finger Speed	The ability to make fast, simple, repeated movements of the fingers, hands, and wrists.
Information Ordering	The ability to arrange things or actions in a certain order or pattern according to a specific rule or set of rules (e.g., patterns of numbers, letters, words, pictures, mathematical operations).	Spatial Orientation	The ability to know your location in relation to the environment or to know where other objects are in relation to you.
		Dynamic Flexibility	The ability to quickly and repeatedly bend, stretch, twist, or reach out with your body, arms, and/or legs.
Near Vision	The ability to see details at close range (within a few feet of the observer).	Gross Body Equilibrium	The ability to keep or regain your body balance or stay upright when in an unstable position.
Category Flexibility	The ability to generate or use different sets of rules for combining or grouping things in different ways.	Dynamic Strength	The ability to exert muscle force repeatedly or continuously over time. This involves muscular endurance and resistance to muscle fatigue.
Speech Recognition	The ability to identify and understand the speech of another person.	Explosive Strength	The ability to use short bursts of muscle force to propel oneself (as in jumping or sprinting), or to throw an object.
Originality	The ability to come up with unusual or clever ideas about a given topic or situation, or to develop creative ways to solve a problem.	Night Vision	The ability to see under low light conditions.
		Peripheral Vision	The ability to see objects or movement of objects to one's side when the eyes are looking ahead.
Fluency of Ideas	The ability to come up with a number of ideas about a topic (the number of ideas is important, not their quality, correctness, or creativity).	Static Strength	The ability to exert maximum muscle force to lift, push, pull, or carry objects.
Selective Attention	The ability to concentrate on a task over a period of time without being distracted.	Reaction Time	The ability to quickly respond (with the hand, finger, or foot) to a signal (sound, light, picture) when it appears.
Visualization	The ability to imagine how something will look after it is moved around or when its parts are moved or rearranged.	Rate Control	The ability to time your movements or the movement of a piece of equipment in anticipation of changes in the speed and/or direction of a moving object or scene.
Flexibility of Closure	The ability to identify or detect a known pattern (a figure, object, word, or sound) that is hidden in other distracting material.	Sound Localization	The ability to tell the direction from which a sound originated.
Far Vision	The ability to see details at a distance.	Response Orientation	The ability to choose quickly between two or more movements in response to two or more different signals (lights, sounds, pictures). It includes the speed with which the correct response is started with the hand, foot, or other body part.
Time Sharing	The ability to shift back and forth between two or more activities or sources of information (such as speech, sounds, touch, or other sources).		
Speed of Closure	The ability to quickly make sense of, combine, and organize information into meaningful patterns.		

Work_Activity	Work_Activity Definitions
Communicating with Persons Outside Organization	Communicating with people outside the organization, representing the organization to customers, the public, government, and other external sources. This information can be exchanged in person, in writing, or by telephone or e-mail.
Getting Information	Observing, receiving, and otherwise obtaining information from all relevant sources.
Evaluating Information to Determine Compliance wit	Using relevant information and individual judgment to determine whether events or processes comply with laws, regulations, or standards.
Performing for or Working Directly with the Public	Performing for people or dealing directly with the public. This includes serving customers in restaurants and stores, and receiving clients or guests.
Making Decisions and Solving Problems	Analyzing information and evaluating results to choose the best solution and solve problems.
Communicating with Supervisors, Peers, or Subordin	Providing information to supervisors, co-workers, and subordinates by telephone, in written form, e-mail, or in person.
Establishing and Maintaining Interpersonal Relatio	Developing constructive and cooperative working relationships with others, and maintaining them over time.
Analyzing Data or Information	Identifying the underlying principles, reasons, or facts of information by breaking down information or data into separate parts.
Processing Information	Compiling, coding, categorizing, calculating, tabulating, auditing, or verifying information or data.
Organizing, Planning, and Prioritizing Work	Developing specific goals and plans to prioritize, organize, and accomplish your work.
Developing Objectives and Strategies	Establishing long-range objectives and specifying the strategies and actions to achieve them.
Interacting With Computers	Using computers and computer systems (including hardware and software) to program, write software, set up functions, enter data, or process information.
Updating and Using Relevant Knowledge	Keeping up-to-date technically and applying new knowledge to your job.
Interpreting the Meaning of Information for Others	Translating or explaining what information means and how it can be used.

The remaining left-column definitions:

Mathematical Reasoning	The ability to choose the right mathematical methods or formulas to solve a problem.
Finger Dexterity	The ability to make precisely coordinated movements of the fingers of one or both hands to grasp, manipulate, or assemble very small objects.
Depth Perception	The ability to judge which of several objects is closer or farther away from you, or to judge the distance between you and an object.
Perceptual Speed	The ability to quickly and accurately compare similarities and differences among sets of letters, numbers, objects, pictures, or patterns. The things to be compared may be presented at the same time or one after the other. This ability also includes comparing a presented object with a remembered object.
Number Facility	The ability to add, subtract, multiply, or divide quickly and correctly.
Memorization	The ability to remember information such as words, numbers, pictures, and procedures.
Visual Color Discrimination	The ability to match or detect differences between colors, including shades of color and brightness.
Control Precision	The ability to quickly and repeatedly adjust the controls of a machine or a vehicle to exact positions.
Multilimb Coordination	The ability to coordinate two or more limbs (for example, two arms, two legs, or one leg and one arm) while sitting, standing, or lying down. It does not involve performing the activities while the whole body is in motion.
Arm-Hand Steadiness	The ability to keep your hand and arm steady while moving your arm or while holding your arm and hand in one position.
Gross Body Coordination	The ability to coordinate the movement of your arms, legs, and torso together when the whole body is in motion.
Auditory Attention	The ability to focus on a single source of sound in the presence of other distracting sounds.
Stamina	The ability to exert yourself physically over long periods of time without getting winded or out of breath.
Manual Dexterity	The ability to quickly move your hand, your hand together with your arm, or your two hands to grasp, manipulate, or assemble objects.

Identifying Objects, Actions, and Events	Identifying information by categorizing, estimating, recognizing differences or similarities, and detecting changes in circumstances or events.
Thinking Creatively	Developing, designing, or creating new applications, ideas, relationships, systems, or products, including artistic contributions.
Resolving Conflicts and Negotiating with Others	Handling complaints, settling disputes, and resolving grievances and conflicts, or otherwise negotiating with others.
Provide Consultation and Advice to Others	Providing guidance and expert advice to management or other groups on technical, systems-, or process-related topics.
Scheduling Work and Activities	Scheduling events, programs, and activities, as well as the work of others.
Performing Administrative Activities	Performing day-to-day administrative tasks such as maintaining information files and processing paperwork.
Documenting/Recording Information	Entering, transcribing, recording, storing, or maintaining information in written or electronic/magnetic form.
Coordinating the Work and Activities of Others	Getting members of a group to work together to accomplish tasks.
Monitor Processes, Materials, or Surroundings	Monitoring and reviewing information from materials, events, or the environment, to detect or assess problems.
Estimating the Quantifiable Characteristics of Pro	Estimating sizes, distances, and quantities; or determining time, costs, resources, or materials needed to perform a work activity.
Developing and Building Teams	Encouraging and building mutual trust, respect, and cooperation among team members.
Judging the Qualities of Things, Services, or Peop	Assessing the value, importance, or quality of things or people.
Training and Teaching Others	Identifying the educational needs of others, developing formal educational or training programs or classes, and teaching or instructing others.
Assisting and Caring for Others	Providing personal assistance, medical attention, emotional support, or other personal care to others such as coworkers, customers, or patients.
Coaching and Developing Others	Identifying the developmental needs of others and coaching, mentoring, or otherwise helping others to improve their knowledge or skills.
Guiding, Directing, and Motivating Subordinates	Providing guidance and direction to subordinates, including setting performance standards and monitoring performance.
Monitoring and Controlling Resources	Monitoring and controlling resources and overseeing the spending of money.
Selling or Influencing Others	Convincing others to buy merchandise/goods or to otherwise change their minds or actions.
Staffing Organizational Units	Recruiting, interviewing, selecting, hiring, and promoting employees in an organization.
Operating Vehicles, Mechanized Devices, or Equipme	Running, maneuvering, navigating, or driving vehicles or mechanized equipment, such as forklifts, passenger vehicles, aircraft, or water craft.
Performing General Physical Activities	Performing physical activities that require considerable use of your arms and legs and moving your whole body, such as climbing, lifting, balancing, walking, stooping, and handling of materials.
Inspecting Equipment, Structures, or Material	Inspecting equipment, structures, or materials to identify the cause of errors or other problems or defects.
Drafting, Laying Out, and Specifying Technical Dev	Providing documentation, detailed instructions, drawings, or specifications to tell others about how devices, parts, equipment, or structures are to be fabricated, constructed, assembled, modified, maintained, or used.
Handling and Moving Objects	Using hands and arms in handling, installing, positioning, and moving materials, and manipulating things.
Controlling Machines and Processes	Using either control mechanisms or direct physical activity to operate machines or processes (not including computers or vehicles).
Repairing and Maintaining Electronic Equipment	Servicing, repairing, calibrating, regulating, fine-tuning, or testing machines, devices, and equipment that operate primarily on the basis of electrical or electronic (not mechanical) principles.
Repairing and Maintaining Mechanical Equipment	Servicing, repairing, adjusting, and testing machines, devices, moving parts, and equipment that operate primarily on the basis of mechanical (not electronic) principles.

Work_Context	Work_Context Definitions
Telephone	How often do you have telephone conversations in this job?
Electronic Mail	How often do you use electronic mail in this job?
Face-to-Face Discussions	How often do you have to have face-to-face discussions with individuals or teams in this job?

Contact With Others	How much does this job require the worker to be in contact with others (face-to-face, by telephone, or otherwise) in order to perform it?
Letters and Memos	How often does the job require written letters and memos?
Indoors, Environmentally Controlled	How often does this job require working indoors in environmentally controlled conditions?
Deal With External Customers	How important is it to work with external customers or the public in this job?
Frequency of Decision Making	How frequently is the worker required to make decisions that affect other people, the financial resources, and/or the image and reputation of the organization?
Spend Time Sitting	How much does this job require sitting?
Coordinate or Lead Others	How important is it to coordinate or lead others in accomplishing work activities in this job?
Structured versus Unstructured Work	To what extent is this job structured for the worker, rather than allowing the worker to determine tasks, priorities, and goals?
Impact of Decisions on Co-workers or Company Resul	How do the decisions an employee makes impact the results of co-workers, clients or the company?
Deal With Unpleasant or Angry People	How frequently does the worker have to deal with unpleasant, angry, or discourteous individuals as part of the job requirements?
Work With Work Group or Team	How important is it to work with others in a group or team in this job?
Freedom to Make Decisions	How much decision making freedom, without supervision, does the job offer?
Time Pressure	How often does this job require the worker to meet strict deadlines?
Frequency of Conflict Situations	How often are there conflict situations the employee has to face in this job?
Responsibility for Outcomes and Results	How responsible is the worker for work outcomes and results of other workers?
Importance of Being Exact or Accurate	How important is being very exact or highly accurate in performing this job?
Spend Time Using Your Hands to Handle, Control, or	How much does this job require using your hands to handle, control, or feel objects, tools or controls?
Public Speaking	How often do you have to perform public speaking in this job?
Spend Time Making Repetitive Motions	How much does this job require making repetitive motions?
Sounds, Noise Levels Are Distracting or Uncomforta	How often does this job require working exposed to sounds and noise levels that are distracting or uncomfortable?
In an Enclosed Vehicle or Equipment	How often does this job require working in a closed vehicle or equipment (e.g., car)?
Extremely Bright or Inadequate Lighting	How often does this job require working in extremely bright or inadequate lighting conditions?
Spend Time Bending or Twisting the Body	How much does this job require bending or twisting your body?
Importance of Repeating Same Tasks	How important is repeating the same physical activities (e.g., key entry) or mental activities (e.g., checking entries in a ledger) over and over, without stopping, to performing this job?
Spend Time Walking and Running	How much does this job require walking and running?
Level of Competition	To what extent does this job require the worker to compete or to be aware of competitive pressures?
Exposed to Contaminants	How often does this job require working exposed to contaminants (such as pollutants, gases, dust or odors)?
Outdoors, Exposed to Weather	How often does this job require working outdoors, exposed to all weather conditions?
Responsible for Others' Health and Safety	How much responsibility is there for the health and safety of others in this job?
Consequence of Error	How serious would the result usually be if the worker made a mistake that was not readily correctable?
Degree of Automation	How automated is the job?
Physical Proximity	To what extent does this job require the worker to perform job tasks in close physical proximity to other people?
Spend Time Standing	How much does this job require standing?
Indoors, Not Environmentally Controlled	How often does this job require working indoors in non-controlled environmental conditions (e.g., warehouse without heat)?
Cramped Work Space, Awkward Positions	How often does this job require working in cramped work spaces that requires getting into awkward positions?
Spend Time Kneeling, Crouching, Stooping, or Crawl	How much does this job require kneeling, crouching, stooping, or crawling?
Deal With Physically Aggressive People	How frequently does this job require the worker to deal with physical aggression of violent individuals?

Very Hot or Cold Temperatures	How often does this job require working in very hot (above 90 F degrees) or very cold (below 32 F degrees) temperatures?
Wear Common Protective or Safety Equipment such as	How much does this job require wearing common protective or safety equipment such as safety shoes, glasses, gloves, hard hats or live jackets?
Outdoors, Under Cover	How often does this job require working outdoors, under cover (e.g., structure with roof but no walls)?
Exposed to Hazardous Conditions	How often does this job require exposure to hazardous conditions?
Spend Time Climbing Ladders, Scaffolds, or Poles	How much does this job require climbing ladders, scaffolds, or poles?
Exposed to Minor Burns, Cuts, Bites, or Stings	How often does this job require exposure to minor burns, cuts, bites, or stings?
Pace Determined by Speed of Equipment	How important is it to this job that the pace is determined by the speed of equipment or machinery? (This does not refer to keeping busy at all times on this job.)
Spend Time Keeping or Regaining Balance	How much does this job require keeping or regaining your balance?
Exposed to Hazardous Equipment	How often does this job require exposure to hazardous equipment?
Exposed to High Places	How often does this job require exposure to high places?
Exposed to Whole Body Vibration	How often does this job require exposure to whole body vibration (e.g., operate a jackhammer)?
Exposed to Disease or Infections	How often does this job require exposure to disease/infections?
Wear Specialized Protective or Safety Equipment su	How much does this job require wearing specialized protective or safety equipment such as breathing apparatus, safety harness, full protection suits, or radiation protection?
Exposed to Radiation	How often does this job require exposure to radiation?
In an Open Vehicle or Equipment	How often does this job require working in an open vehicle or equipment (e.g., tractor)?

Job Zone Component	Job Zone Component Definitions
Title	Job Zone Four: Considerable Preparation Needed
Overall Experience	A minimum of two to four years of work-related skill, knowledge, or experience is needed for these occupations. For example, an accountant must complete four years of college and work for several years in accounting to be considered qualified.
Job Training	Employees in these occupations usually need several years of work-related experience, on-the-job training, and/or vocational training.
Job Zone Examples	Many of these occupations involve coordinating, supervising, managing, or training others. Examples include accountants, chefs and head cooks, computer programmers, historians, pharmacists, and police detectives.
SVP Range	(7.0 to < 8.0)
Education	Most of these occupations require a four - year bachelor's degree, but some do not.

Work_Styles	Work_Styles Definitions
Integrity	Job requires being honest and ethical.
Attention to Detail	Job requires being careful about detail and thorough in completing work tasks.
Initiative	Job requires a willingness to take on responsibilities and challenges.
Self Control	Job requires maintaining composure, keeping emotions in check, controlling anger, and avoiding aggressive behavior, even in very difficult situations.
Dependability	Job requires being reliable, responsible, and dependable, and fulfilling obligations.
Cooperation	Job requires being pleasant with others on the job and displaying a good-natured, cooperative attitude.
Analytical Thinking	Job requires analyzing information and using logic to address work-related issues and problems.
Stress Tolerance	Job requires accepting criticism and dealing calmly and effectively with high stress situations.
Concern for Others	Job requires being sensitive to others' needs and feelings and being understanding and helpful on the job.
Persistence	Job requires persistence in the face of obstacles.
Adaptability/Flexibility	Job requires being open to change (positive or negative) and to considerable variety in the workplace.
Leadership	Job requires a willingness to lead, take charge, and offer opinions and direction.

Innovation	Job requires creativity and alternative thinking to develop new ideas for and answers to work-related problems.
Social Orientation	Job requires preferring to work with others rather than alone, and being personally connected with others on the job.
Independence	Job requires developing one's own ways of doing things, guiding oneself with little or no supervision, and depending on oneself to get things done.
Achievement/Effort	Job requires establishing and maintaining personally challenging achievement goals and exerting effort toward mastering tasks.

19-3091.02 - Archeologists

Conduct research to reconstruct record of past human life and culture from human remains, artifacts, architectural features, and structures recovered through excavation, underwater recovery, or other means of discovery.

Tasks

1) Lead field training sites and train field staff, students, and volunteers in excavation methods.

2) Teach archaeology at colleges and universities.

3) Assess archaeological sites for resource management, development, or conservation purposes, and recommend methods for site protection.

4) Create artifact typologies to organize and make sense of past material cultures.

5) Study objects and structures recovered by excavation to identify, date, and/or authenticate them, and to interpret their significance.

6) Collect artifacts made of stone, bone, metal, and other materials, placing them in bags and marking them to show where they were found.

7) Clean, restore, and preserve artifacts.

8) Create a grid of each site, and draw and update maps of unit profiles, stratum surfaces, features, and findings.

9) Write, present, and publish reports that record site history, methodology and artifact analysis results, along with recommendations for conserving and interpreting findings.

10) Compare findings from one site with archeological data from other sites to find similarities or differences.

11) Research, survey, and assess sites of past societies and cultures in search of answers to specific research questions.

12) Record the exact locations and conditions of artifacts uncovered in diggings or surveys, using drawings and photographs as necessary.

13) Develop and test theories concerning the origin and development of past cultures.

14) Describe artifacts' physical properties or attributes, such as the materials from which artifacts are made, and their size, shape, function, and decoration.

19-3093.00 - Historians

Research, analyze, record, and interpret the past as recorded in sources, such as government and institutional records, newspapers and other periodicals, photographs, interviews, films, and unpublished manuscripts, such as personal diaries and letters.

Tasks

1) Gather historical data from sources such as archives, court records, diaries, news files, and photographs, as well as collect data sources such as books, pamphlets, and periodicals.

2) Conduct historical research, and publish or present findings and theories.

3) Organize data, and analyze and interpret its authenticity and relative significance.

4) Organize information for publication and for other means of dissemination, such as use in CD-ROMs or Internet sites.

5) Research the history of a particular country or region, or of a specific time period.

6) Determine which topics to research, or pursue research topics specified by clients or employers.

7) Prepare publications and exhibits, or review those prepared by others in order to ensure

their historical accuracy.

8) Collect detailed information on individuals for use in biographies.

9) Teach and conduct research in colleges, universities, museums, and other research agencies and schools.

10) Speak to various groups, organizations, and clubs in order to promote the aims and activities of historical societies.

11) Present historical accounts in terms of individuals or social, ethnic, political, economic, or geographic groupings.

12) Advise or consult with individuals and institutions regarding issues such as the historical authenticity of materials or the customs of a specific historical period.

13) Interview people in order to gather information about historical events, and to record oral histories.

14) Translate or request translation of reference materials.

15) Research and prepare manuscripts in support of public programming and the development of exhibits at historic sites, museums, libraries, and archives.

16) Recommend actions related to historical art, such as which items to add to a collection or which items to display in an exhibit.

17) Conduct historical research as a basis for the identification, conservation, and reconstruction of historic places and materials.

18) Coordinate activities of workers engaged in cataloging and filing materials.

19) Edit historical society publications.

Knowledge	Knowledge Definitions
English Language	Knowledge of the structure and content of the English language including the meaning and spelling of words, rules of composition, and grammar.
Computers and Electronics	Knowledge of circuit boards, processors, chips, electronic equipment, and computer hardware and software, including applications and programming.
History and Archeology	Knowledge of historical events and their causes, indicators, and effects on civilizations and cultures.
Administration and Management	Knowledge of business and management principles involved in strategic planning, resource allocation, human resources modeling, leadership technique, production methods, and coordination of people and resources.
Clerical	Knowledge of administrative and clerical procedures and systems such as word processing, managing files and records, stenography and transcription, designing forms, and other office procedures and terminology.
Customer and Personal Service	Knowledge of principles and processes for providing customer and personal services. This includes customer needs assessment, meeting quality standards for services, and evaluation of customer satisfaction.
Engineering and Technology	Knowledge of the practical application of engineering science and technology. This includes applying principles, techniques, procedures, and equipment to the design and production of various goods and services.
Mathematics	Knowledge of arithmetic, algebra, geometry, calculus, statistics, and their applications.
Communications and Media	Knowledge of media production, communication, and dissemination techniques and methods. This includes alternative ways to inform and entertain via written, oral, and visual media.
Design	Knowledge of design techniques, tools, and principles involved in production of precision technical plans, blueprints, drawings, and models.
Geography	Knowledge of principles and methods for describing the features of land, sea, and air masses, including their physical characteristics, locations, interrelationships, and distribution of plant, animal, and human life.
Philosophy and Theology	Knowledge of different philosophical systems and religions. This includes their basic principles, values, ethics, ways of thinking, customs, practices, and their impact on human culture.
Education and Training	Knowledge of principles and methods for curriculum and training design, teaching and instruction for individuals and groups, and the measurement of training effects.
Personnel and Human Resources	Knowledge of principles and procedures for personnel recruitment, selection, training, compensation and benefits, labor relations and negotiation, and personnel information systems.
Mechanical	Knowledge of machines and tools, including their designs, uses, repair, and maintenance.
Public Safety and Security	Knowledge of relevant equipment, policies, procedures, and strategies to promote effective local, state, or national security operations for the protection of people, data, property, and institutions.
Sociology and Anthropology	Knowledge of group behavior and dynamics, societal trends and influences, human migrations, ethnicity, cultures and their history and origins.
Sales and Marketing	Knowledge of principles and methods for showing, promoting, and selling products or services. This includes marketing strategy and tactics, product demonstration, sales techniques, and sales control systems.
Physics	Knowledge and prediction of physical principles, laws, their interrelationships, and applications to understanding fluid, material, and atmospheric dynamics, and mechanical, electrical, atomic and sub-atomic structures and processes.
Law and Government	Knowledge of laws, legal codes, court procedures, precedents, government regulations, executive orders, agency rules, and the democratic political process.
Chemistry	Knowledge of the chemical composition, structure, and properties of substances and of the chemical processes and transformations that they undergo. This includes uses of chemicals and their interactions, danger signs, production techniques, and disposal methods.
Production and Processing	Knowledge of raw materials, production processes, quality control, costs, and other techniques for maximizing the effective manufacture and distribution of goods.
Economics and Accounting	Knowledge of economic and accounting principles and practices, the financial markets, banking and the analysis and reporting of financial data.
Foreign Language	Knowledge of the structure and content of a foreign (non-English) language including the meaning and spelling of words, rules of composition and grammar, and pronunciation.
Telecommunications	Knowledge of transmission, broadcasting, switching, control, and operation of telecommunications systems.
Psychology	Knowledge of human behavior and performance; individual differences in ability, personality, and interests; learning and motivation; psychological research methods; and the assessment and treatment of behavioral and affective disorders.
Biology	Knowledge of plant and animal organisms, their tissues, cells, functions, interdependencies, and interactions with each other and the environment.
Medicine and Dentistry	Knowledge of the information and techniques needed to diagnose and treat human injuries, diseases, and deformities. This includes symptoms, treatment alternatives, drug properties and interactions, and preventive health-care measures.
Building and Construction	Knowledge of materials, methods, and the tools involved in the construction or repair of houses, buildings, or other structures such as highways and roads.
Transportation	Knowledge of principles and methods for moving people or goods by air, rail, sea, or road, including the relative costs and benefits.
Fine Arts	Knowledge of the theory and techniques required to compose, produce, and perform works of music, dance, visual arts, drama, and sculpture.
Therapy and Counseling	Knowledge of principles, methods, and procedures for diagnosis, treatment, and rehabilitation of physical and mental dysfunctions, and for career counseling and guidance.
Food Production	Knowledge of techniques and equipment for planting, growing, and harvesting food products (both plant and animal) for consumption, including storage/handling techniques.

Skills	Skills Definitions
Reading Comprehension	Understanding written sentences and paragraphs in work related documents.
Active Listening	Giving full attention to what other people are saying, taking time to understand the points being made, asking questions as appropriate, and not interrupting at inappropriate times.
Writing	Communicating effectively in writing as appropriate for the needs of the audience.
Speaking	Talking to others to convey information effectively.
Critical Thinking	Using logic and reasoning to identify the strengths and weaknesses of alternative solutions, conclusions or approaches to problems.
Active Learning	Understanding the implications of new information for both current and future problem-solving and decision-making.

Instructing	Teaching others how to do something.
Social Perceptiveness	Being aware of others' reactions and understanding why they react as they do.
Complex Problem Solving	Identifying complex problems and reviewing related information to develop and evaluate options and implement solutions.
Monitoring	Monitoring/Assessing performance of yourself, other individuals, or organizations to make improvements or take corrective action.
Time Management	Managing one's own time and the time of others.
Judgment and Decision Making	Considering the relative costs and benefits of potential actions to choose the most appropriate one.
Management of Personnel Resources	Motivating, developing, and directing people as they work, identifying the best people for the job.
Learning Strategies	Selecting and using training/instructional methods and procedures appropriate for the situation when learning or teaching new things.
Service Orientation	Actively looking for ways to help people.
Coordination	Adjusting actions in relation to others' actions.
Persuasion	Persuading others to change their minds or behavior.
Management of Financial Resources	Determining how money will be spent to get the work done, and accounting for these expenditures.
Equipment Selection	Determining the kind of tools and equipment needed to do a job.
Operations Analysis	Analyzing needs and product requirements to create a design.
Negotiation	Bringing others together and trying to reconcile differences.
Science	Using scientific rules and methods to solve problems.
Systems Analysis	Determining how a system should work and how changes in conditions, operations, and the environment will affect outcomes.
Technology Design	Generating or adapting equipment and technology to serve user needs.
Management of Material Resources	Obtaining and seeing to the appropriate use of equipment, facilities, and materials needed to do certain work.
Troubleshooting	Determining causes of operating errors and deciding what to do about it.
Systems Evaluation	Identifying measures or indicators of system performance and the actions needed to improve or correct performance, relative to the goals of the system.
Quality Control Analysis	Conducting tests and inspections of products, services, or processes to evaluate quality or performance.
Mathematics	Using mathematics to solve problems.
Operation and Control	Controlling operations of equipment or systems.
Equipment Maintenance	Performing routine maintenance on equipment and determining when and what kind of maintenance is needed.
Operation Monitoring	Watching gauges, dials, or other indicators to make sure a machine is working properly.
Programming	Writing computer programs for various purposes.
Installation	Installing equipment, machines, wiring, or programs to meet specifications.
Repairing	Repairing machines or systems using the needed tools.

Ability	Ability Definitions
Written Comprehension	The ability to read and understand information and ideas presented in writing.
Written Expression	The ability to communicate information and ideas in writing so others will understand.
Oral Expression	The ability to communicate information and ideas in speaking so others will understand.
Inductive Reasoning	The ability to combine pieces of information to form general rules or conclusions (includes finding a relationship among seemingly unrelated events).
Oral Comprehension	The ability to listen to and understand information and ideas presented through spoken words and sentences.
Near Vision	The ability to see details at close range (within a few feet of the observer).
Speech Clarity	The ability to speak clearly so others can understand you.
Speech Recognition	The ability to identify and understand the speech of another person.
Deductive Reasoning	The ability to apply general rules to specific problems to produce answers that make sense.
Problem Sensitivity	The ability to tell when something is wrong or is likely to go wrong. It does not involve solving the problem, only recognizing there is a problem.
Category Flexibility	The ability to generate or use different sets of rules for combining or grouping things in different ways.

Selective Attention	The ability to concentrate on a task over a period of time without being distracted.
Information Ordering	The ability to arrange things or actions in a certain order or pattern according to a specific rule or set of rules (e.g., patterns of numbers, letters, words, pictures, mathematical operations).
Originality	The ability to come up with unusual or clever ideas about a given topic or situation, or to develop creative ways to solve a problem.
Fluency of Ideas	The ability to come up with a number of ideas about a topic (the number of ideas is important, not their quality, correctness, or creativity).
Auditory Attention	The ability to focus on a single source of sound in the presence of other distracting sounds.
Flexibility of Closure	The ability to identify or detect a known pattern (a figure, object, word, or sound) that is hidden in other distracting material.
Memorization	The ability to remember information such as words, numbers, pictures, and procedures.
Perceptual Speed	The ability to quickly and accurately compare similarities and differences among sets of letters, numbers, objects, pictures, or patterns. The things to be compared may be presented at the same time or one after the other. This ability also includes comparing a presented object with a remembered object.
Visualization	The ability to imagine how something will look after it is moved around or when its parts are moved or rearranged.
Time Sharing	The ability to shift back and forth between two or more activities or sources of information (such as speech, sounds, touch, or other sources).
Far Vision	The ability to see details at a distance.
Trunk Strength	The ability to use your abdominal and lower back muscles to support part of the body repeatedly or continuously over time without 'giving out' or fatiguing.
Speed of Closure	The ability to quickly make sense of, combine, and organize information into meaningful patterns.
Manual Dexterity	The ability to quickly move your hand, your hand together with your arm, or your two hands to grasp, manipulate, or assemble objects.
Gross Body Coordination	The ability to coordinate the movement of your arms, legs, and torso together when the whole body is in motion.
Stamina	The ability to exert yourself physically over long periods of time without getting winded or out of breath.
Extent Flexibility	The ability to bend, stretch, twist, or reach with your body, arms, and/or legs.
Control Precision	The ability to quickly and repeatedly adjust the controls of a machine or a vehicle to exact positions.
Multilimb Coordination	The ability to coordinate two or more limbs (for example, two arms, two legs, or one leg and one arm) while sitting, standing, or lying down. It does not involve performing the activities while the whole body is in motion.
Glare Sensitivity	The ability to see objects in the presence of glare or bright lighting.
Visual Color Discrimination	The ability to match or detect differences between colors, including shades of color and brightness.
Depth Perception	The ability to judge which of several objects is closer or farther away from you, or to judge the distance between you and an object.
Arm-Hand Steadiness	The ability to keep your hand and arm steady while moving your arm or while holding your arm and hand in one position.
Mathematical Reasoning	The ability to choose the right mathematical methods or formulas to solve a problem.
Speed of Limb Movement	The ability to quickly move the arms and legs.
Reaction Time	The ability to quickly respond (with the hand, finger, or foot) to a signal (sound, light, picture) when it appears.
Number Facility	The ability to add, subtract, multiply, or divide quickly and correctly.
Finger Dexterity	The ability to make precisely coordinated movements of the fingers of one or both hands to grasp, manipulate, or assemble very small objects.
Night Vision	The ability to see under low light conditions.
Wrist-Finger Speed	The ability to make fast, simple, repeated movements of the fingers, hands, and wrists.
Hearing Sensitivity	The ability to detect or tell the differences between sounds that vary in pitch and loudness.
Static Strength	The ability to exert maximum muscle force to lift, push, pull, or carry objects.
Rate Control	The ability to time your movements or the movement of a piece of equipment in anticipation of changes in the speed and/or direction of a moving object or scene.

Explosive Strength	The ability to use short bursts of muscle force to propel oneself (as in jumping or sprinting), or to throw an object.
Spatial Orientation	The ability to know your location in relation to the environment or to know where other objects are in relation to you.
Dynamic Strength	The ability to exert muscle force repeatedly or continuously over time. This involves muscular endurance and resistance to muscle fatigue.
Response Orientation	The ability to choose quickly between two or more movements in response to two or more different signals (lights, sounds, pictures). It includes the speed with which the correct response is started with the hand, foot, or other body part.
Gross Body Equilibrium	The ability to keep or regain your body balance or stay upright when in an unstable position.
Sound Localization	The ability to tell the direction from which a sound originated.
Dynamic Flexibility	The ability to quickly and repeatedly bend, stretch, twist, or reach out with your body, arms, and/or legs.
Peripheral Vision	The ability to see objects or movement of objects to one's side when the eyes are looking ahead.

Work_Activity	Work_Activity Definitions
Processing Information	Compiling, coding, categorizing, calculating, tabulating, auditing, or verifying information or data.
Documenting/Recording Information	Entering, transcribing, recording, storing, or maintaining information in written or electronic/magnetic form.
Getting Information	Observing, receiving, and otherwise obtaining information from all relevant sources.
Communicating with Persons Outside Organization	Communicating with people outside the organization, representing the organization to customers, the public, government, and other external sources. This information can be exchanged in person, in writing, or by telephone or e-mail.
Interpreting the Meaning of Information for Others	Translating or explaining what information means and how it can be used.
Training and Teaching Others	Identifying the educational needs of others, developing formal educational or training programs or classes, and teaching or instructing others.
Establishing and Maintaining Interpersonal Relatio	Developing constructive and cooperative working relationships with others, and maintaining them over time.
Analyzing Data or Information	Identifying the underlying principles, reasons, or facts of information by breaking down information or data into separate parts.
Updating and Using Relevant Knowledge	Keeping up-to-date technically and applying new knowledge to your job.
Performing for or Working Directly with the Public	Performing for people or dealing directly with the public. This includes serving customers in restaurants and stores, and receiving clients or guests.
Identifying Objects, Actions, and Events	Identifying information by categorizing, estimating, recognizing differences or similarities, and detecting changes in circumstances or events.
Thinking Creatively	Developing, designing, or creating new applications, ideas, relationships, systems, or products, including artistic contributions.
Interacting With Computers	Using computers and computer systems (including hardware and software) to program, write software, set up functions, enter data, or process information.
Coaching and Developing Others	Identifying the developmental needs of others and coaching, mentoring, or otherwise helping others to improve their knowledge or skills.
Provide Consultation and Advice to Others	Providing guidance and expert advice to management or other groups on technical, systems-, or process-related topics.
Inspecting Equipment, Structures, or Material	Inspecting equipment, structures, or materials to identify the cause of errors or other problems or defects.
Communicating with Supervisors, Peers, or Subordin	Providing information to supervisors, co-workers, and subordinates by telephone, in written form, e-mail, or in person.
Organizing, Planning, and Prioritizing Work	Developing specific goals and plans to prioritize, organize, and accomplish your work.
Developing Objectives and Strategies	Establishing long-range objectives and specifying the strategies and actions to achieve them.
Scheduling Work and Activities	Scheduling events, programs, and activities, as well as the work of others.
Coordinating the Work and Activities of Others	Getting members of a group to work together to accomplish tasks.
Monitor Processes, Materials, or Surroundings	Monitoring and reviewing information from materials, events, or the environment, to detect or assess problems.

Estimating the Quantifiable Characteristics of Pro	Estimating sizes, distances, and quantities; or determining time, costs, resources, or materials needed to perform a work activity.
Performing Administrative Activities	Performing day-to-day administrative tasks such as maintaining information files and processing paperwork.
Developing and Building Teams	Encouraging and building mutual trust, respect, and cooperation among team members.
Judging the Qualities of Things, Services, or Peop	Assessing the value, importance, or quality of things or people.
Making Decisions and Solving Problems	Analyzing information and evaluating results to choose the best solution and solve problems.
Guiding, Directing, and Motivating Subordinates	Providing guidance and direction to subordinates, including setting performance standards and monitoring performance.
Resolving Conflicts and Negotiating with Others	Handling complaints, settling disputes, and resolving grievances and conflicts, or otherwise negotiating with others.
Evaluating Information to Determine Compliance wit	Using relevant information and individual judgment to determine whether events or processes comply with laws, regulations, or standards.
Performing General Physical Activities	Performing physical activities that require considerable use of your arms and legs and moving your whole body, such as climbing, lifting, balancing, walking, stooping, and handling of materials.
Drafting, Laying Out, and Specifying Technical Dev	Providing documentation, detailed instructions, drawings, or specifications to tell others about how devices, parts, equipment, or structures are to be fabricated, constructed, assembled, modified, maintained, or used.
Selling or Influencing Others	Convincing others to buy merchandise/goods or to otherwise change their minds or actions.
Assisting and Caring for Others	Providing personal assistance, medical attention, emotional support, or other personal care to others such as coworkers, customers, or patients.
Monitoring and Controlling Resources	Monitoring and controlling resources and overseeing the spending of money.
Staffing Organizational Units	Recruiting, interviewing, selecting, hiring, and promoting employees in an organization.
Repairing and Maintaining Mechanical Equipment	Servicing, repairing, adjusting, and testing machines, devices, moving parts, and equipment that operate primarily on the basis of mechanical (not electronic) principles.
Handling and Moving Objects	Using hands and arms in handling, installing, positioning, and moving materials, and manipulating things.
Controlling Machines and Processes	Using either control mechanisms or direct physical activity to operate machines or processes (not including computers or vehicles).
Operating Vehicles, Mechanized Devices, or Equipme	Running, maneuvering, navigating, or driving vehicles or mechanized equipment, such as forklifts, passenger vehicles, aircraft, or water craft.
Repairing and Maintaining Electronic Equipment	Servicing, repairing, calibrating, regulating, fine-tuning, or testing machines, devices, and equipment that operate primarily on the basis of electrical or electronic (not mechanical) principles.

Work_Context	Work_Context Definitions
Electronic Mail	How often do you use electronic mail in this job?
Importance of Being Exact or Accurate	How important is being very exact or highly accurate in performing this job?
Face-to-Face Discussions	How often do you have to have face-to-face discussions with individuals or teams in this job?
Indoors, Environmentally Controlled	How often does this job require working indoors in environmentally controlled conditions?
Telephone	How often do you have telephone conversations in this job?
Structured versus Unstructured Work	To what extent is this job structured for the worker, rather than allowing the worker to determine tasks, priorities, and goals?
Work With Work Group or Team	How important is it to work with others in a group or team in this job?
Contact With Others	How much does this job require the worker to be in contact with others (face-to-face, by telephone, or otherwise) in order to perform it?
Coordinate or Lead Others	How important is it to coordinate or lead others in accomplishing work activities in this job?
Deal With External Customers	How important is it to work with external customers or the public in this job?
Impact of Decisions on Co-workers or Company Resul	How do the decisions an employee makes impact the results of co-workers, clients or the company?
Responsibility for Outcomes and Results	How responsible is the worker for work outcomes and results of other workers?

Frequency of Decision Making	How frequently is the worker required to make decisions that affect other people, the financial resources, and/or the image and reputation of the organization?
Importance of Repeating Same Tasks	How important is repeating the same physical activities (e.g., key entry) or mental activities (e.g., checking entries in a ledger) over and over, without stopping, to performing this job?
Freedom to Make Decisions	How much decision making freedom, without supervision, does the job offer?
Physical Proximity	To what extent does this job require the worker to perform job tasks in close physical proximity to other people?
Letters and Memos	How often does the job require written letters and memos?
Frequency of Conflict Situations	How often are there conflict situations the employee has to face in this job?
Consequence of Error	How serious would the result usually be if the worker made a mistake that was not readily correctable?
Sounds, Noise Levels Are Distracting or Uncomforta	How often does this job require working exposed to sounds and noise levels that are distracting or uncomfortable?
Exposed to Contaminants	How often does this job require working exposed to contaminants (such as pollutants, gases, dust or odors)?
Spend Time Using Your Hands to Handle, Control, or	How much does this job require using your hands to handle, control, or feel objects, tools or controls?
Time Pressure	How often does this job require the worker to meet strict deadlines?
Cramped Work Space, Awkward Positions	How often does this job require working in cramped work spaces that requires getting into awkward positions?
Extremely Bright or Inadequate Lighting	How often does this job require working in extremely bright or inadequate lighting conditions?
Deal With Unpleasant or Angry People	How frequently does the worker have to deal with unpleasant, angry, or discourteous individuals as part of the job requirements?
Exposed to Minor Burns, Cuts, Bites, or Stings	How often does this job require exposure to minor burns, cuts, bites, or stings?
Spend Time Standing	How much does this job require standing?
In an Enclosed Vehicle or Equipment	How often does this job require working in a closed vehicle or equipment (e.g., car)?
Spend Time Walking and Running	How much does this job require walking and running?
Public Speaking	How often do you have to perform public speaking in this job?
Indoors, Not Environmentally Controlled	How often does this job require working indoors in non-controlled environmental conditions (e.g., warehouse without heat)?
Spend Time Sitting	How much does this job require sitting?
Responsible for Others' Health and Safety	How much responsibility is there for the health and safety of others in this job?
Exposed to Hazardous Conditions	How often does this job require exposure to hazardous conditions?
Exposed to Hazardous Equipment	How often does this job require exposure to hazardous equipment?
Very Hot or Cold Temperatures	How often does this job require working in very hot (above 90 F degrees) or very cold (below 32 F degrees) temperatures?
Spend Time Making Repetitive Motions	How much does this job require making repetitive motions?
Level of Competition	To what extent does this job require the worker to compete or to be aware of competitive pressures?
Pace Determined by Speed of Equipment	How important is it to this job that the pace is determined by the speed of equipment or machinery? (This does not refer to keeping busy at all times on this job.)
Degree of Automation	How automated is the job?
Spend Time Bending or Twisting the Body	How much does this job require bending or twisting your body?
Deal With Physically Aggressive People	How frequently does this job require the worker to deal with physical aggression of violent individuals?
Spend Time Kneeling, Crouching, Stooping, or Crawl	How much does this job require kneeling, crouching, stooping or crawling?
Outdoors, Exposed to Weather	How often does this job require working outdoors, exposed to all weather conditions?
Outdoors, Under Cover	How often does this job require working outdoors, under cover (e.g., structure with roof but no walls)?
Wear Common Protective or Safety Equipment such as	How much does this job require wearing common protective or safety equipment such as safety shoes, glasses, gloves, hard hats or live jackets?
Spend Time Climbing Ladders, Scaffolds, or Poles	How much does this job require climbing ladders, scaffolds, or poles?
Spend Time Keeping or Regaining Balance	How much does this job require keeping or regaining your balance?

Wear Specialized Protective or Safety Equipment su	How much does this job require wearing specialized protective or safety equipment such as breathing apparatus, safety harness, full protection suits, or radiation protection?
Exposed to Disease or Infections	How often does this job require exposure to disease/infections?
Exposed to High Places	How often does this job require exposure to high places?
In an Open Vehicle or Equipment	How often does this job require working in an open vehicle or equipment (e.g., tractor)?
Exposed to Radiation	How often does this job require exposure to radiation?
Exposed to Whole Body Vibration	How often does this job require exposure to whole body vibration (e.g., operate a jackhammer)?

Job Zone Component	Job Zone Component Definitions
Title	Job Zone Five: Extensive Preparation Needed
	Extensive skill, knowledge, and experience are needed for these occupations. Many require more than five years of experience.
Overall Experience	For example, surgeons must complete four years of college and an additional five to seven years of specialized medical training to be able to do their job.
Job Training	Employees may need some on-the-job training, but most of these occupations assume that the person will already have the required skills, knowledge, work-related experience, and/or training.
Job Zone Examples	These occupations often involve coordinating, training, supervising, or managing the activities of others to accomplish goals. Very advanced communication and organizational skills are required. Examples include athletic trainers, lawyers, managing editors, phyicists, social psychologists, and surgeons.
SVP Range	(8.0 and above)
Education	A bachelor's degree is the minimum formal education required for these occupations. However, many also require graduate school. For example, they may require a master's degree, and some require a Ph.D., M.D., or J.D. (law degree).

Work_Styles	Work_Styles Definitions
Integrity	Job requires being honest and ethical.
Dependability	Job requires being reliable, responsible, and dependable, and fulfilling obligations.
Persistence	Job requires persistence in the face of obstacles.
Attention to Detail	Job requires being careful about detail and thorough in completing work tasks.
Cooperation	Job requires being pleasant with others on the job and displaying a good-natured, cooperative attitude.
Self Control	Job requires maintaining composure, keeping emotions in check, controlling anger, and avoiding aggressive behavior, even in very difficult situations.
Achievement/Effort	Job requires establishing and maintaining personally challenging achievement goals and exerting effort toward mastering tasks.
Initiative	Job requires a willingness to take on responsibilities and challenges.
Concern for Others	Job requires being sensitive to others' needs and feelings and being understanding and helpful on the job.
Independence	Job requires developing one's own ways of doing things, guiding oneself with little or no supervision, and depending on oneself to get things done.
Adaptability/Flexibility	Job requires being open to change (positive or negative) and to considerable variety in the workplace.
Innovation	Job requires creativity and alternative thinking to develop new ideas for and answers to work-related problems.
Leadership	Job requires a willingness to lead, take charge, and offer opinions and direction.
Stress Tolerance	Job requires accepting criticism and dealing calmly and effectively with high stress situations.
Analytical Thinking	Job requires analyzing information and using logic to address work-related issues and problems.
Social Orientation	Job requires preferring to work with others rather than alone, and being personally connected with others on the job.

19-4011.02 - Food Science Technicians

Perform standardized qualitative and quantitative tests to determine physical or chemical properties of food or beverage products.

Tasks

1) Mix, blend, or cultivate ingredients in order to make reagents or to manufacture food or beverage products.

2) Record and compile test results, and prepare graphs, charts, and reports.

3) Provide assistance to food scientists and technologists in research and development, production technology, and quality control.

4) Prepare slides and incubate slides with cell cultures.

5) Examine chemical and biological samples in order to identify cell structures, and to locate bacteria, or extraneous material, using microscope.

6) Conduct standardized tests on food, beverages, additives, and preservatives in order to ensure compliance with standards and regulations regarding factors such as color, texture, and nutrients.

7) Analyze test results to classify products, or compare results with standard tables.

8) Order supplies needed to maintain inventories in laboratories or in storage facilities of food or beverage processing plants.

9) Compute moisture or salt content, percentages of ingredients, formulas, or other product factors, using mathematical and chemical procedures.

10) Measure, test, and weigh bottles, cans, and other containers in order to ensure hardness, strength, and dimensions that meet specifications.

11) Taste or smell foods or beverages in order to ensure that flavors meet specifications, or to select samples with specific characteristics.

19-4021.00 - Biological Technicians

Assist biological and medical scientists in laboratories. Set up, operate, and maintain laboratory instruments and equipment, monitor experiments, make observations, and calculate and record results. May analyze organic substances, such as blood, food, and drugs.

Tasks

1) Use computers, computer-interfaced equipment, robotics and high-technology industrial applications to perform work duties.

2) Set up, adjust, calibrate, clean, maintain, and troubleshoot laboratory and field equipment.

3) Monitor laboratory work to ensure compliance with set standards.

4) Provide technical support and services for scientists and engineers working in fields such as agriculture, environmental science, resource management, biology, and health sciences.

5) Isolate, identify and prepare specimens for examination.

6) Keep detailed logs of all work-related activities.

7) Conduct, or assist in conducting, research, including the collection of information and samples, such as blood, water, soil, plants and animals.

8) Analyze experimental data and interpret results to write reports and summaries of findings.

9) Monitor and observe experiments, recording production and test data for evaluation by research personnel.

10) Conduct standardized biological, microbiological and biochemical tests and laboratory analyses to evaluate the quantity or quality of physical or chemical substances in food and other products.

11) Measure or weigh compounds and solutions for use in testing or animal feed.

12) Examine animals and specimens to detect the presence of disease or other problems.

13) Participate in the research, development, and manufacturing of medicinal and pharmaceutical preparations.

14) Feed livestock and laboratory animals.

15) Conduct or supervise operational programs such as fish hatcheries, greenhouses and livestock production programs.

Knowledge	Knowledge Definitions
Chemistry	Knowledge of the chemical composition, structure, and properties of substances and of the chemical processes and transformations that they undergo. This includes uses of chemicals and their interactions, danger signs, production techniques, and disposal methods.
Mathematics	Knowledge of arithmetic, algebra, geometry, calculus, statistics, and their applications.
Biology	Knowledge of plant and animal organisms, their tissues, cells, functions, interdependencies, and interactions with each other and the environment.
English Language	Knowledge of the structure and content of the English language including the meaning and spelling of words, rules of composition, and grammar.
Production and Processing	Knowledge of raw materials, production processes, quality control, costs, and other techniques for maximizing the effective manufacture and distribution of goods.
Public Safety and Security	Knowledge of relevant equipment, policies, procedures, and strategies to promote effective local, state, or national security operations for the protection of people, data, property, and institutions.
Computers and Electronics	Knowledge of circuit boards, processors, chips, electronic equipment, and computer hardware and software, including applications and programming.
Education and Training	Knowledge of principles and methods for curriculum and training design, teaching and instruction for individuals and groups, and the measurement of training effects.
Mechanical	Knowledge of machines and tools, including their designs, uses, repair, and maintenance.
Clerical	Knowledge of administrative and clerical procedures and systems such as word processing, managing files and records, stenography and transcription, designing forms, and other office procedures and terminology.
Customer and Personal Service	Knowledge of principles and processes for providing customer and personal services. This includes customer needs assessment, meeting quality standards for services, and evaluation of customer satisfaction.
Administration and Management	Knowledge of business and management principles involved in strategic planning, resource allocation, human resources modeling, leadership technique, production methods, and coordination of people and resources.
Physics	Knowledge and prediction of physical principles, laws, their interrelationships, and applications to understanding fluid, material, and atmospheric dynamics, and mechanical, electrical, atomic and sub-atomic structures and processes.
Geography	Knowledge of principles and methods for describing the features of land, sea, and air masses, including their physical characteristics, locations, interrelationships, and distribution of plant, animal, and human life.
Medicine and Dentistry	Knowledge of the information and techniques needed to diagnose and treat human injuries, diseases, and deformities. This includes symptoms, treatment alternatives, drug properties and interactions, and preventive health-care measures.
Engineering and Technology	Knowledge of the practical application of engineering science and technology. This includes applying principles, techniques, procedures, and equipment to the design and production of various goods and services.
Communications and Media	Knowledge of media production, communication, and dissemination techniques and methods. This includes alternative ways to inform and entertain via written, oral, and visual media.
Law and Government	Knowledge of laws, legal codes, court procedures, precedents, government regulations, executive orders, agency rules, and the democratic political process.
Telecommunications	Knowledge of transmission, broadcasting, switching, control, and operation of telecommunications systems.
Design	Knowledge of design techniques, tools, and principles involved in production of precision technical plans, blueprints, drawings, and models.
Sociology and Anthropology	Knowledge of group behavior and dynamics, societal trends and influences, human migrations, ethnicity, cultures and their history and origins.
Psychology	Knowledge of human behavior and performance; individual differences in ability, personality, and interests; learning and motivation; psychological research methods; and the assessment and treatment of behavioral and affective disorders.

Personnel and Human Resources	Knowledge of principles and procedures for personnel recruitment, selection, training, compensation and benefits, labor relations and negotiation, and personnel information systems.
Building and Construction	Knowledge of materials, methods, and the tools involved in the construction or repair of houses, buildings, or other structures such as highways and roads.
Transportation	Knowledge of principles and methods for moving people or goods by air, rail, sea, or road, including the relative costs and benefits.
History and Archeology	Knowledge of historical events and their causes, indicators, and effects on civilizations and cultures.
Sales and Marketing	Knowledge of principles and methods for showing, promoting, and selling products or services. This includes marketing strategy and tactics, product demonstration, sales techniques, and sales control systems.
Therapy and Counseling	Knowledge of principles, methods, and procedures for diagnosis, treatment, and rehabilitation of physical and mental dysfunctions, and for career counseling and guidance.
Food Production	Knowledge of techniques and equipment for planting, growing, and harvesting food products (both plant and animal) for consumption, including storage/handling techniques.
Economics and Accounting	Knowledge of economic and accounting principles and practices, the financial markets, banking and the analysis and reporting of financial data.
Philosophy and Theology	Knowledge of different philosophical systems and religions. This includes their basic principles, values, ethics, ways of thinking, customs, practices, and their impact on human culture.
Foreign Language	Knowledge of the structure and content of a foreign (non-English) language including the meaning and spelling of words, rules of composition and grammar, and pronunciation.
Fine Arts	Knowledge of the theory and techniques required to compose, produce, and perform works of music, dance, visual arts, drama, and sculpture.

Skills	Skills Definitions
Science	Using scientific rules and methods to solve problems.
Reading Comprehension	Understanding written sentences and paragraphs in work related documents.
Instructing	Teaching others how to do something.
Active Learning	Understanding the implications of new information for both current and future problem-solving and decision-making.
Learning Strategies	Selecting and using training/instructional methods and procedures appropriate for the situation when learning or teaching new things.
Time Management	Managing one's own time and the time of others.
Active Listening	Giving full attention to what other people are saying, taking time to understand the points being made, asking questions as appropriate, and not interrupting at inappropriate times.
Mathematics	Using mathematics to solve problems.
Speaking	Talking to others to convey information effectively.
Quality Control Analysis	Conducting tests and inspections of products, services, or processes to evaluate quality or performance.
Troubleshooting	Determining causes of operating errors and deciding what to do about it.
Critical Thinking	Using logic and reasoning to identify the strengths and weaknesses of alternative solutions, conclusions or approaches to problems.
Judgment and Decision Making	Considering the relative costs and benefits of potential actions to choose the most appropriate one.
Writing	Communicating effectively in writing as appropriate for the needs of the audience.
Complex Problem Solving	Identifying complex problems and reviewing related information to develop and evaluate options and implement solutions.
Coordination	Adjusting actions in relation to others' actions.
Equipment Selection	Determining the kind of tools and equipment needed to do a job.
Service Orientation	Actively looking for ways to help people.
Monitoring	Monitoring/Assessing performance of yourself, other individuals, or organizations to make improvements or take corrective action.
Equipment Maintenance	Performing routine maintenance on equipment and determining when and what kind of maintenance is needed.
Operation Monitoring	Watching gauges, dials, or other indicators to make sure a machine is working properly.

Technology Design	Generating or adapting equipment and technology to serve user needs.
Management of Material Resources	Obtaining and seeing to the appropriate use of equipment, facilities, and materials needed to do certain work.
Management of Personnel Resources	Motivating, developing, and directing people as they work, identifying the best people for the job.
Operation and Control	Controlling operations of equipment or systems.
Social Perceptiveness	Being aware of others' reactions and understanding why they react as they do.
Management of Financial Resources	Determining how money will be spent to get the work done, and accounting for these expenditures.
Systems Analysis	Determining how a system should work and how changes in conditions, operations, and the environment will affect outcomes.
Persuasion	Persuading others to change their minds or behavior.
Repairing	Repairing machines or systems using the needed tools.
Systems Evaluation	Identifying measures or indicators of system performance and the actions needed to improve or correct performance, relative to the goals of the system.
Negotiation	Bringing others together and trying to reconcile differences.
Operations Analysis	Analyzing needs and product requirements to create a design.
Installation	Installing equipment, machines, wiring, or programs to meet specifications.
Programming	Writing computer programs for various purposes.

Ability	Ability Definitions
Information Ordering	The ability to arrange things or actions in a certain order or pattern according to a specific rule or set of rules (e.g., patterns of numbers, letters, words, pictures, mathematical operations).
Problem Sensitivity	The ability to tell when something is wrong or is likely to go wrong. It does not involve solving the problem, only recognizing there is a problem.
Near Vision	The ability to see details at close range (within a few feet of the observer).
Deductive Reasoning	The ability to apply general rules to specific problems to produce answers that make sense.
Oral Expression	The ability to communicate information and ideas in speaking so others will understand.
Selective Attention	The ability to concentrate on a task over a period of time without being distracted.
Speech Recognition	The ability to identify and understand the speech of another person.
Written Comprehension	The ability to read and understand information and ideas presented in writing.
Oral Comprehension	The ability to listen to and understand information and ideas presented through spoken words and sentences.
Category Flexibility	The ability to generate or use different sets of rules for combining or grouping things in different ways.
Written Expression	The ability to communicate information and ideas in writing so others will understand.
Inductive Reasoning	The ability to combine pieces of information to form general rules or conclusions (includes finding a relationship among seemingly unrelated events).
Number Facility	The ability to add, subtract, multiply, or divide quickly and correctly.
Speech Clarity	The ability to speak clearly so others can understand you.
Mathematical Reasoning	The ability to choose the right mathematical methods or formulas to solve a problem.
Arm-Hand Steadiness	The ability to keep your hand and arm steady while moving your arm or while holding your arm and hand in one position.
Perceptual Speed	The ability to quickly and accurately compare similarities and differences among sets of letters, numbers, objects, pictures, or patterns. The things to be compared may be presented at the same time or one after the other. This ability also includes comparing a presented object with a remembered object.
Far Vision	The ability to see details at a distance.
Visual Color Discrimination	The ability to match or detect differences between colors, including shades of color and brightness.
Flexibility of Closure	The ability to identify or detect a known pattern (a figure, object, word, or sound) that is hidden in other distracting material.
Finger Dexterity	The ability to make precisely coordinated movements of the fingers of one or both hands to grasp, manipulate, or assemble very small objects.
Manual Dexterity	The ability to quickly move your hand, your hand together with your arm, or your two hands to grasp, manipulate, or assemble objects.

Visualization	The ability to imagine how something will look after it is moved around or when its parts are moved or rearranged.
Time Sharing	The ability to shift back and forth between two or more activities or sources of information (such as speech, sounds, touch, or other sources).
Originality	The ability to come up with unusual or clever ideas about a given topic or situation, or to develop creative ways to solve a problem.
Control Precision	The ability to quickly and repeatedly adjust the controls of a machine or a vehicle to exact positions.
Fluency of Ideas	The ability to come up with a number of ideas about a topic (the number of ideas is important, not their quality, correctness, or creativity).
Depth Perception	The ability to judge which of several objects is closer or farther away from you, or to judge the distance between you and an object.
Speed of Closure	The ability to quickly make sense of, combine, and organize information into meaningful patterns.
Memorization	The ability to remember information such as words, numbers, pictures, and procedures.
Multilimb Coordination	The ability to coordinate two or more limbs (for example, two arms, two legs, or one leg and one arm) while sitting, standing, or lying down. It does not involve performing the activities while the whole body is in motion.
Auditory Attention	The ability to focus on a single source of sound in the presence of other distracting sounds.
Hearing Sensitivity	The ability to detect or tell the differences between sounds that vary in pitch and loudness.
Static Strength	The ability to exert maximum muscle force to lift, push, pull, or carry objects.
Trunk Strength	The ability to use your abdominal and lower back muscles to support part of the body repeatedly or continuously over time without 'giving out' or fatiguing.
Reaction Time	The ability to quickly respond (with the hand, finger, or foot) to a signal (sound, light, picture) when it appears.
Rate Control	The ability to time your movements or the movement of a piece of equipment in anticipation of changes in the speed and/or direction of a moving object or scene.
Response Orientation	The ability to choose quickly between two or more movements in response to two or more different signals (lights, sounds, pictures). It includes the speed with which the correct response is started with the hand, foot, or other body part.
Dynamic Strength	The ability to exert muscle force repeatedly or continuously over time. This involves muscular endurance and resistance to muscle fatigue.
Peripheral Vision	The ability to see objects or movement of objects to one's side when the eyes are looking ahead.
Spatial Orientation	The ability to know your location in relation to the environment or to know where other objects are in relation to you.
Speed of Limb Movement	The ability to quickly move the arms and legs.
Stamina	The ability to exert yourself physically over long periods of time without getting winded or out of breath.
Gross Body Coordination	The ability to coordinate the movement of your arms, legs, and torso together when the whole body is in motion.
Gross Body Equilibrium	The ability to keep or regain your body balance or stay upright when in an unstable position.
Night Vision	The ability to see under low light conditions.
Glare Sensitivity	The ability to see objects in the presence of glare or bright lighting.
Sound Localization	The ability to tell the direction from which a sound originated.
Wrist-Finger Speed	The ability to make fast, simple, repeated movements of the fingers, hands, and wrists.
Extent Flexibility	The ability to bend, stretch, twist, or reach with your body, arms, and/or legs.
Explosive Strength	The ability to use short bursts of muscle force to propel oneself (as in jumping or sprinting), or to throw an object.
Dynamic Flexibility	The ability to quickly and repeatedly bend, stretch, twist, or reach out with your body, arms, and/or legs.

Work_Activity	Work_Activity Definitions
Interacting With Computers	Using computers and computer systems (including hardware and software) to program, write software, set up functions, enter data, or process information.
Documenting/Recording Information	Entering, transcribing, recording, storing, or maintaining information in written or electronic/magnetic form.
Updating and Using Relevant Knowledge	Keeping up-to-date technically and applying new knowledge to your job.

Processing Information	Compiling, coding, categorizing, calculating, tabulating, auditing, or verifying information or data.
Identifying Objects, Actions, and Events	Identifying information by categorizing, estimating, recognizing differences or similarities, and detecting changes in circumstances or events.
Getting Information	Observing, receiving, and otherwise obtaining information from all relevant sources.
Communicating with Supervisors, Peers, or Subordin	Providing information to supervisors, co-workers, and subordinates by telephone, in written form, e-mail, or in person.
Evaluating Information to Determine Compliance wit	Using relevant information and individual judgment to determine whether events or processes comply with laws, regulations, or standards.
Making Decisions and Solving Problems	Analyzing information and evaluating results to choose the best solution and solve problems.
Analyzing Data or Information	Identifying the underlying principles, reasons, or facts of information by breaking down information or data into separate parts.
Monitor Processes, Materials, or Surroundings	Monitoring and reviewing information from materials, events, or the environment, to detect or assess problems.
Organizing, Planning, and Prioritizing Work	Developing specific goals and plans to prioritize, organize, and accomplish your work.
Estimating the Quantifiable Characteristics of Pro	Estimating sizes, distances, and quantities; or determining time, costs, resources, or materials needed to perform a work activity.
Inspecting Equipment, Structures, or Material	Inspecting equipment, structures, or materials to identify the cause of errors or other problems or defects.
Judging the Qualities of Things, Services, or Peop	Assessing the value, importance, or quality of things or people.
Performing General Physical Activities	Performing physical activities that require considerable use of your arms and legs and moving your whole body, such as climbing, lifting, balancing, walking, stooping, and handling of materials.
Thinking Creatively	Developing, designing, or creating new applications, ideas, relationships, systems, or products, including artistic contributions.
Repairing and Maintaining Electronic Equipment	Servicing, repairing, calibrating, regulating, fine-tuning, or testing machines, devices, and equipment that operate primarily on the basis of electrical or electronic (not mechanical) principles.
Establishing and Maintaining Interpersonal Relatio	Developing constructive and cooperative working relationships with others, and maintaining them over time.
Handling and Moving Objects	Using hands and arms in handling, installing, positioning, and moving materials, and manipulating things.
Developing Objectives and Strategies	Establishing long-range objectives and specifying the strategies and actions to achieve them.
Training and Teaching Others	Identifying the educational needs of others, developing formal educational or training programs or classes, and teaching or instructing others.
Scheduling Work and Activities	Scheduling events, programs, and activities, as well as the work of others.
Controlling Machines and Processes	Using either control mechanisms or direct physical activity to operate machines or processes (not including computers or vehicles).
Assisting and Caring for Others	Providing personal assistance, medical attention, emotional support, or other personal care to others such as coworkers, customers, or patients.
Coaching and Developing Others	Identifying the developmental needs of others and coaching, mentoring, or otherwise helping others to improve their knowledge or skills.
Repairing and Maintaining Mechanical Equipment	Servicing, repairing, adjusting, and testing machines, devices, moving parts, and equipment that operate primarily on the basis of mechanical (not electronic) principles.
Communicating with Persons Outside Organization	Communicating with people outside the organization, representing the organization to customers, the public, government, and other external sources. This information can be exchanged in person, in writing, or by telephone or e-mail.
Operating Vehicles, Mechanized Devices, or Equipme	Running, maneuvering, navigating, or driving vehicles or mechanized equipment, such as forklifts, passenger vehicles, aircraft, or water craft.
Guiding, Directing, and Motivating Subordinates	Providing guidance and direction to subordinates, including setting performance standards and monitoring performance.
Developing and Building Teams	Encouraging and building mutual trust, respect, and cooperation among team members.
Interpreting the Meaning of Information for Others	Translating or explaining what information means and how it can be used.

Coordinating the Work and Activities of Others	Getting members of a group to work together to accomplish tasks.
Performing Administrative Activities	Performing day-to-day administrative tasks such as maintaining information files and processing paperwork.
Staffing Organizational Units	Recruiting, interviewing, selecting, hiring, and promoting employees in an organization.
Provide Consultation and Advice to Others	Providing guidance and expert advice to management or other groups on technical, systems-, or process-related topics.
Drafting, Laying Out, and Specifying Technical Dev	Providing documentation, detailed instructions, drawings, or specifications to tell others about how devices, parts, equipment, or structures are to be fabricated, constructed, assembled, modified, maintained, or used.
Monitoring and Controlling Resources	Monitoring and controlling resources and overseeing the spending of money.
Performing for or Working Directly with the Public	Performing for people or dealing directly with the public. This includes serving customers in restaurants and stores, and receiving clients or guests.
Resolving Conflicts and Negotiating with Others	Handling complaints, settling disputes, and resolving grievances and conflicts, or otherwise negotiating with others.
Selling or Influencing Others	Convincing others to buy merchandise/goods or to otherwise change their minds or actions.

Work_Context	Work_Context Definitions
Electronic Mail	How often do you use electronic mail in this job?
Indoors, Environmentally Controlled	How often does this job require working indoors in environmentally controlled conditions?
Face-to-Face Discussions	How often do you have to have face-to-face discussions with individuals or teams in this job?
Importance of Being Exact or Accurate	How important is being very exact or highly accurate in performing this job?
Work With Work Group or Team	How important is it to work with others in a group or team in this job?
Wear Common Protective or Safety Equipment such as	How much does this job require wearing common protective or safety equipment such as safety shoes, glasses, gloves, hard hats or live jackets?
Telephone	How often do you have telephone conversations in this job?
Contact With Others	How much does this job require the worker to be in contact with others (face-to-face, by telephone, or otherwise) in order to perform it?
Time Pressure	How often does this job require the worker to meet strict deadlines?
Importance of Repeating Same Tasks	How important is repeating the same physical activities (e.g., key entry) or mental activities (e.g., checking entries in a ledger) over and over, without stopping, to performing this job?
Coordinate or Lead Others	How important is it to coordinate or lead others in accomplishing work activities in this job?
Spend Time Using Your Hands to Handle, Control, or	How much does this job require using your hands to handle, control, or feel objects, tools or controls?
Responsibility for Outcomes and Results	How responsible is the worker for work outcomes and results of other workers?
Spend Time Making Repetitive Motions	How much does this job require making repetitive motions?
Responsible for Others' Health and Safety	How much responsibility is there for the health and safety of others in this job?
Frequency of Decision Making	How frequently is the worker required to make decisions that affect other people, the financial resources, and/or the image and reputation of the organization?
Freedom to Make Decisions	How much decision making freedom, without supervision, does the job offer?
Impact of Decisions on Co-workers or Company Resul	How do the decisions an employee makes impact the results of co-workers, clients or the company?
Consequence of Error	How serious would the result usually be if the worker made a mistake that was not readily correctable?
Deal With Unpleasant or Angry People	How frequently does the worker have to deal with unpleasant, angry, or discourteous individuals as part of the job requirements?
Deal With External Customers	How important is it to work with external customers or the public in this job?
Spend Time Standing	How much does this job require standing?
Structured versus Unstructured Work	To what extent is this job structured for the worker, rather than allowing the worker to determine tasks, priorities, and goals?
Physical Proximity	To what extent does this job require the worker to perform job tasks in close physical proximity to other people?
Exposed to Disease or Infections	How often does this job require exposure to disease/infections?

Spend Time Sitting	How much does this job require sitting?
Exposed to Contaminants	How often does this job require working exposed to contaminants (such as pollutants, gases, dust or odors)?
Frequency of Conflict Situations	How often are there conflict situations the employee has to face in this job?
Exposed to Hazardous Conditions	How often does this job require exposure to hazardous conditions?
Letters and Memos	How often does the job require written letters and memos?
Sounds, Noise Levels Are Distracting or Uncomforta	How often does this job require working exposed to sounds and noise levels that are distracting or uncomfortable?
Exposed to Minor Burns, Cuts, Bites, or Stings	How often does this job require exposure to minor burns, cuts, bites, or stings?
Spend Time Walking and Running	How much does this job require walking and running?
Degree of Automation	How automated is the job?
Level of Competition	To what extent does this job require the worker to compete or to be aware of competitive pressures?
Pace Determined by Speed of Equipment	How important is it to this job that the pace is determined by the speed of equipment or machinery? (This does not refer to keeping busy at all times on this job.)
Wear Specialized Protective or Safety Equipment su	How much does this job require wearing specialized protective or safety equipment such as breathing apparatus, safety harness, full protection suits, or radiation protection?
Spend Time Bending or Twisting the Body	How much does this job require bending or twisting your body?
Exposed to Hazardous Equipment	How often does this job require exposure to hazardous equipment?
Public Speaking	How often do you have to perform public speaking in this job?
Spend Time Kneeling, Crouching, Stooping, or Crawl	How much does this job require kneeling, crouching, stooping or crawling?
Very Hot or Cold Temperatures	How often does this job require working in very hot (above 90 F degrees) or very cold (below 32 F degrees) temperatures?
Outdoors, Exposed to Weather	How often does this job require working outdoors, exposed to all weather conditions?
Indoors, Not Environmentally Controlled	How often does this job require working indoors in non-controlled environmental conditions (e.g., warehouse without heat)?
In an Enclosed Vehicle or Equipment	How often does this job require working in a closed vehicle or equipment (e.g., car)?
Exposed to Radiation	How often does this job require exposure to radiation?
Cramped Work Space, Awkward Positions	How often does this job require working in cramped work spaces that requires getting into awkward positions?
Extremely Bright or Inadequate Lighting	How often does this job require working in extremely bright or inadequate lighting conditions?
Outdoors, Under Cover	How often does this job require working outdoors, under cover (e.g., structure with roof but no walls)?
Deal With Physically Aggressive People	How frequently does this job require the worker to deal with physical aggression of violent individuals?
Spend Time Climbing Ladders, Scaffolds, or Poles	How much does this job require climbing ladders, scaffolds, or poles?
Spend Time Keeping or Regaining Balance	How much does this job require keeping or regaining your balance?
Exposed to High Places	How often does this job require exposure to high places?
In an Open Vehicle or Equipment	How often does this job require working in an open vehicle or equipment (e.g., tractor)?
Exposed to Whole Body Vibration	How often does this job require exposure to whole body vibration (e.g., operate a jackhammer)?

Job Zone Component	Job Zone Component Definitions
Title	Job Zone Four: Considerable Preparation Needed
Overall Experience	A minimum of two to four years of work-related skill, knowledge, or experience is needed for these occupations. For example, an accountant must complete four years of college and work for several years in accounting to be considered qualified.
Job Training	Employees in these occupations usually need several years of work-related experience, on-the-job training, and/or vocational training.
Job Zone Examples	Many of these occupations involve coordinating, supervising, managing, or training others. Examples include accountants, chefs and head cooks, computer programmers, historians, pharmacists, and police detectives.
SVP Range	(7.0 to < 8.0)

Education	Most of these occupations require a four - year bachelor's degree, but some do not.

Work_Styles	Work_Styles Definitions
Attention to Detail	Job requires being careful about detail and thorough in completing work tasks.
Dependability	Job requires being reliable, responsible, and dependable, and fulfilling obligations.
Integrity	Job requires being honest and ethical.
Cooperation	Job requires being pleasant with others on the job and displaying a good-natured, cooperative attitude.
Adaptability/Flexibility	Job requires being open to change (positive or negative) and to considerable variety in the workplace.
Independence	Job requires developing one's own ways of doing things, guiding oneself with little or no supervision, and depending on oneself to get things done.
Initiative	Job requires a willingness to take on responsibilities and challenges.
Persistence	Job requires persistence in the face of obstacles.
Analytical Thinking	Job requires analyzing information and using logic to address work-related issues and problems.
Self Control	Job requires maintaining composure, keeping emotions in check, controlling anger, and avoiding aggressive behavior, even in very difficult situations.
Concern for Others	Job requires being sensitive to others' needs and feelings and being understanding and helpful on the job.
Achievement/Effort	Job requires establishing and maintaining personally challenging achievement goals and exerting effort toward mastering tasks.
Stress Tolerance	Job requires accepting criticism and dealing calmly and effectively with high stress situations.
Social Orientation	Job requires preferring to work with others rather than alone, and being personally connected with others on the job.
Leadership	Job requires a willingness to lead, take charge, and offer opinions and direction.
Innovation	Job requires creativity and alternative thinking to develop new ideas for and answers to work-related problems.

19-4031.00 - Chemical Technicians

Conduct chemical and physical laboratory tests to assist scientists in making qualitative and quantitative analyses of solids, liquids, and gaseous materials for purposes, such as research and development of new products or processes, quality control, maintenance of environmental standards, and other work involving experimental, theoretical, or practical application of chemistry and related sciences.

Tasks

1) Monitor product quality to ensure compliance to standards and specifications.

2) Order and inventory materials in order to maintain supplies.

3) Maintain, clean, and sterilize laboratory instruments and equipment.

4) Conduct chemical and physical laboratory tests to assist scientists in making qualitative and quantitative analyses of solids, liquids, and gaseous materials.

5) Write technical reports or prepare graphs and charts to document experimental results.

6) Provide technical support and assistance to chemists and engineers.

7) Prepare chemical solutions for products and processes following standardized formulas, or create experimental formulas.

8) Set up and conduct chemical experiments, tests, and analyses using techniques such as chromatography, spectroscopy, physical and chemical separation techniques, and microscopy.

9) Design and fabricate experimental apparatus to develop new products and processes.

10) Develop and conduct programs of sampling and analysis to maintain quality standards of raw materials, chemical intermediates, and products.

11) Direct or monitor other workers producing chemical products.

12) Develop new chemical engineering processes or production techniques.

13) Operate experimental pilot plants, assisting with experimental design.

Knowledge	Knowledge Definitions
Chemistry	Knowledge of the chemical composition, structure, and properties of substances and of the chemical processes and transformations that they undergo. This includes uses of chemicals and their interactions, danger signs, production techniques, and disposal methods.
English Language	Knowledge of the structure and content of the English language including the meaning and spelling of words, rules of composition, and grammar.
Mathematics	Knowledge of arithmetic, algebra, geometry, calculus, statistics, and their applications.
Mechanical	Knowledge of machines and tools, including their designs, uses, repair, and maintenance.
Computers and Electronics	Knowledge of circuit boards, processors, chips, electronic equipment, and computer hardware and software, including applications and programming.
Customer and Personal Service	Knowledge of principles and processes for providing customer and personal services. This includes customer needs assessment, meeting quality standards for services, and evaluation of customer satisfaction.
Production and Processing	Knowledge of raw materials, production processes, quality control, costs, and other techniques for maximizing the effective manufacture and distribution of goods.
Clerical	Knowledge of administrative and clerical procedures and systems such as word processing, managing files and records, stenography and transcription, designing forms, and other office procedures and terminology.
Administration and Management	Knowledge of business and management principles involved in strategic planning, resource allocation, human resources modeling, leadership technique, production methods, and coordination of people and resources.
Engineering and Technology	Knowledge of the practical application of engineering science and technology. This includes applying principles, techniques, procedures, and equipment to the design and production of various goods and services.
Public Safety and Security	Knowledge of relevant equipment, policies, procedures, and strategies to promote effective local, state, or national security operations for the protection of people, data, property, and institutions.
Physics	Knowledge and prediction of physical principles, laws, their interrelationships, and applications to understanding fluid, material, and atmospheric dynamics, and mechanical, electrical, atomic and sub- atomic structures and processes.
Education and Training	Knowledge of principles and methods for curriculum and training design, teaching and instruction for individuals and groups, and the measurement of training effects.
Communications and Media	Knowledge of media production, communication, and dissemination techniques and methods. This includes alternative ways to inform and entertain via written, oral, and visual media.
Law and Government	Knowledge of laws, legal codes, court procedures, precedents, government regulations, executive orders, agency rules, and the democratic political process.
Transportation	Knowledge of principles and methods for moving people or goods by air, rail, sea, or road, including the relative costs and benefits.
Biology	Knowledge of plant and animal organisms, their tissues, cells, functions, interdependencies, and interactions with each other and the environment.
Personnel and Human Resources	Knowledge of principles and procedures for personnel recruitment, selection, training, compensation and benefits, labor relations and negotiation, and personnel information systems.
Telecommunications	Knowledge of transmission, broadcasting, switching, control, and operation of telecommunications systems.
Design	Knowledge of design techniques, tools, and principles involved in production of precision technical plans, blueprints, drawings, and models.
Economics and Accounting	Knowledge of economic and accounting principles and practices, the financial markets, banking and the analysis and reporting of financial data.
Medicine and Dentistry	Knowledge of the information and techniques needed to diagnose and treat human injuries, diseases, and deformities. This includes symptoms, treatment alternatives, drug properties and interactions, and preventive health-care measures.

Psychology	Knowledge of human behavior and performance; individual differences in ability, personality, and interests; learning and motivation; psychological research methods; and the assessment and treatment of behavioral and affective disorders.
Building and Construction	Knowledge of materials, methods, and the tools involved in the construction or repair of houses, buildings, or other structures such as highways and roads.
Therapy and Counseling	Knowledge of principles, methods, and procedures for diagnosis, treatment, and rehabilitation of physical and mental dysfunctions, and for career counseling and guidance.
Sales and Marketing	Knowledge of principles and methods for showing, promoting, and selling products or services. This includes marketing strategy and tactics, product demonstration, sales techniques, and sales control systems.
Sociology and Anthropology	Knowledge of group behavior and dynamics, societal trends and influences, human migrations, ethnicity, cultures and their history and origins.
Geography	Knowledge of principles and methods for describing the features of land, sea, and air masses, including their physical characteristics, locations, interrelationships, and distribution of plant, animal, and human life.
Foreign Language	Knowledge of the structure and content of a foreign (non-English) language including the meaning and spelling of words, rules of composition and grammar, and pronunciation.
Philosophy and Theology	Knowledge of different philosophical systems and religions. This includes their basic principles, values, ethics, ways of thinking, customs, practices, and their impact on human culture.
Food Production	Knowledge of techniques and equipment for planting, growing, and harvesting food products (both plant and animal) for consumption, including storage/handling techniques.
History and Archeology	Knowledge of historical events and their causes, indicators, and effects on civilizations and cultures.
Fine Arts	Knowledge of the theory and techniques required to compose, produce, and perform works of music, dance, visual arts, drama, and sculpture.

Skills	Skills Definitions
Science	Using scientific rules and methods to solve problems.
Reading Comprehension	Understanding written sentences and paragraphs in work related documents.
Quality Control Analysis	Conducting tests and inspections of products, services, or processes to evaluate quality or performance.
Mathematics	Using mathematics to solve problems.
Operation Monitoring	Watching gauges, dials, or other indicators to make sure a machine is working properly.
Active Listening	Giving full attention to what other people are saying, taking time to understand the points being made, asking questions as appropriate, and not interrupting at inappropriate times.
Critical Thinking	Using logic and reasoning to identify the strengths and weaknesses of alternative solutions, conclusions or approaches to problems.
Writing	Communicating effectively in writing as appropriate for the needs of the audience.
Time Management	Managing one's own time and the time of others.
Operation and Control	Controlling operations of equipment or systems.
Active Learning	Understanding the implications of new information for both current and future problem-solving and decision-making.
Equipment Maintenance	Performing routine maintenance on equipment and determining when and what kind of maintenance is needed.
Troubleshooting	Determining causes of operating errors and deciding what to do about it.
Complex Problem Solving	Identifying complex problems and reviewing related information to develop and evaluate options and implement solutions.
Learning Strategies	Selecting and using training/instructional methods and procedures appropriate for the situation when learning or teaching new things.
Equipment Selection	Determining the kind of tools and equipment needed to do a job.
Instructing	Teaching others how to do something.
Speaking	Talking to others to convey information effectively.
Monitoring	Monitoring/Assessing performance of yourself, other individuals, or organizations to make improvements or take corrective action.
Coordination	Adjusting actions in relation to others' actions.

Systems Evaluation	Identifying measures or indicators of system performance and the actions needed to improve or correct performance, relative to the goals of the system.
Judgment and Decision Making	Considering the relative costs and benefits of potential actions to choose the most appropriate one.
Operations Analysis	Analyzing needs and product requirements to create a design.
Systems Analysis	Determining how a system should work and how changes in conditions, operations, and the environment will affect outcomes.
Repairing	Repairing machines or systems using the needed tools.
Technology Design	Generating or adapting equipment and technology to serve user needs.
Social Perceptiveness	Being aware of others' reactions and understanding why they react as they do.
Persuasion	Persuading others to change their minds or behavior.
Installation	Installing equipment, machines, wiring, or programs to meet specifications.
Service Orientation	Actively looking for ways to help people.
Management of Material Resources	Obtaining and seeing to the appropriate use of equipment, facilities, and materials needed to do certain work.
Negotiation	Bringing others together and trying to reconcile differences.
Management of Personnel Resources	Motivating, developing, and directing people as they work, identifying the best people for the job.
Management of Financial Resources	Determining how money will be spent to get the work done, and accounting for these expenditures.
Programming	Writing computer programs for various purposes.

Ability	Ability Definitions
Deductive Reasoning	The ability to apply general rules to specific problems to produce answers that make sense.
Near Vision	The ability to see details at close range (within a few feet of the observer).
Information Ordering	The ability to arrange things or actions in a certain order or pattern according to a specific rule or set of rules (e.g., patterns of numbers, letters, words, pictures, mathematical operations).
Problem Sensitivity	The ability to tell when something is wrong or is likely to go wrong. It does not involve solving the problem, only recognizing there is a problem.
Written Comprehension	The ability to read and understand information and ideas presented in writing.
Inductive Reasoning	The ability to combine pieces of information to form general rules or conclusions (includes finding a relationship among seemingly unrelated events).
Oral Expression	The ability to communicate information and ideas in speaking so others will understand.
Written Expression	The ability to communicate information and ideas in writing so others will understand.
Oral Comprehension	The ability to listen to and understand information and ideas presented through spoken words and sentences.
Speech Clarity	The ability to speak clearly so others can understand you.
Speech Recognition	The ability to identify and understand the speech of another person.
Mathematical Reasoning	The ability to choose the right mathematical methods or formulas to solve a problem.
Category Flexibility	The ability to generate or use different sets of rules for combining or grouping things in different ways.
Selective Attention	The ability to concentrate on a task over a period of time without being distracted.
Flexibility of Closure	The ability to identify or detect a known pattern (a figure, object, word, or sound) that is hidden in other distracting material.
Arm-Hand Steadiness	The ability to keep your hand and arm steady while moving your arm or while holding your arm and hand in one position.
Control Precision	The ability to quickly and repeatedly adjust the controls of a machine or a vehicle to exact positions.
Memorization	The ability to remember information such as words, numbers, pictures, and procedures.
Perceptual Speed	The ability to quickly and accurately compare similarities and differences among sets of letters, numbers, objects, pictures, or patterns. The things to be compared may be presented at the same time or one after the other. This ability also includes comparing a presented object with a remembered object.
Time Sharing	The ability to shift back and forth between two or more activities or sources of information (such as speech, sounds, touch, or other sources).

Originality	The ability to come up with unusual or clever ideas about a given topic or situation, or to develop creative ways to solve a problem.
Auditory Attention	The ability to focus on a single source of sound in the presence of other distracting sounds.
Trunk Strength	The ability to use your abdominal and lower back muscles to support part of the body repeatedly or continuously over time without 'giving out' or fatiguing.
Visual Color Discrimination	The ability to match or detect differences between colors, including shades of color and brightness.
Finger Dexterity	The ability to make precisely coordinated movements of the fingers of one or both hands to grasp, manipulate, or assemble very small objects.
Multilimb Coordination	The ability to coordinate two or more limbs (for example, two arms, two legs, or one leg and one arm) while sitting, standing, or lying down. It does not involve performing the activities while the whole body is in motion.
Visualization	The ability to imagine how something will look after it is moved around or when its parts are moved or rearranged.
Manual Dexterity	The ability to quickly move your hand, your hand together with your arm, or your two hands to grasp, manipulate, or assemble objects.
Fluency of Ideas	The ability to come up with a number of ideas about a topic (the number of ideas is important, not their quality, correctness, or creativity).
Speed of Closure	The ability to quickly make sense of, combine, and organize information into meaningful patterns.
Depth Perception	The ability to judge which of several objects is closer or farther away from you, or to judge the distance between you and an object.
Wrist-Finger Speed	The ability to make fast, simple, repeated movements of the fingers, hands, and wrists.
Stamina	The ability to exert yourself physically over long periods of time without getting winded or out of breath.
Number Facility	The ability to add, subtract, multiply, or divide quickly and correctly.
Reaction Time	The ability to quickly respond (with the hand, finger, or foot) to a signal (sound, light, picture) when it appears.
Gross Body Coordination	The ability to coordinate the movement of your arms, legs, and torso together when the whole body is in motion.
Spatial Orientation	The ability to know your location in relation to the environment or to know where other objects are in relation to you.
Static Strength	The ability to exert maximum muscle force to lift, push, pull, or carry objects.
Response Orientation	The ability to choose quickly between two or more movements in response to two or more different signals (lights, sounds, pictures). It includes the speed with which the correct response is started with the hand, foot, or other body part.
Hearing Sensitivity	The ability to detect or tell the differences between sounds that vary in pitch and loudness.
Speed of Limb Movement	The ability to quickly move the arms and legs.
Extent Flexibility	The ability to bend, stretch, twist, or reach with your body, arms, and/or legs.
Far Vision	The ability to see details at a distance.
Sound Localization	The ability to tell the direction from which a sound originated.
Gross Body Equilibrium	The ability to keep or regain your body balance or stay upright when in an unstable position.
Dynamic Flexibility	The ability to quickly and repeatedly bend, stretch, twist, or reach out with your body, arms, and/or legs.
Rate Control	The ability to time your movements or the movement of a piece of equipment in anticipation of changes in the speed and/or direction of a moving object or scene.
Dynamic Strength	The ability to exert muscle force repeatedly or continuously over time. This involves muscular endurance and resistance to muscle fatigue.
Peripheral Vision	The ability to see objects or movement of objects to one's side when the eyes are looking ahead.
Glare Sensitivity	The ability to see objects in the presence of glare or bright lighting.
Night Vision	The ability to see under low light conditions.
Explosive Strength	The ability to use short bursts of muscle force to propel oneself (as in jumping or sprinting), or to throw an object.

Work_Activity	Work_Activity Definitions
Documenting/Recording Information	Entering, transcribing, recording, storing, or maintaining information in written or electronic/magnetic form.

Processing Information	Compiling, coding, categorizing, calculating, tabulating, auditing, or verifying information or data.
Getting Information	Observing, receiving, and otherwise obtaining information from all relevant sources.
Identifying Objects, Actions, and Events	Identifying information by categorizing, estimating, recognizing differences or similarities, and detecting changes in circumstances or events.
Monitor Processes, Materials, or Surroundings	Monitoring and reviewing information from materials, events, or the environment, to detect or assess problems.
Analyzing Data or Information	Identifying the underlying principles, reasons, or facts of information by breaking down information or data into separate parts.
Communicating with Supervisors, Peers, or Subordin	Providing information to supervisors, co-workers, and subordinates by telephone, in written form, e-mail, or in person.
Making Decisions and Solving Problems	Analyzing information and evaluating results to choose the best solution and solve problems.
Interacting With Computers	Using computers and computer systems (including hardware and software) to program, write software, set up functions, enter data, or process information.
Inspecting Equipment, Structures, or Material	Inspecting equipment, structures, or materials to identify the cause of errors or other problems or defects.
Organizing, Planning, and Prioritizing Work	Developing specific goals and plans to prioritize, organize, and accomplish your work.
Evaluating Information to Determine Compliance wit	Using relevant information and individual judgment to determine whether events or processes comply with laws, regulations, or standards.
Controlling Machines and Processes	Using either control mechanisms or direct physical activity to operate machines or processes (not including computers or vehicles).
Updating and Using Relevant Knowledge	Keeping up-to-date technically and applying new knowledge to your job.
Establishing and Maintaining Interpersonal Relatio	Developing constructive and cooperative working relationships with others, and maintaining them over time.
Thinking Creatively	Developing, designing, or creating new applications, ideas, relationships, systems, or products, including artistic contributions.
Judging the Qualities of Things, Services, or Peop	Assessing the value, importance, or quality of things or people.
Estimating the Quantifiable Characteristics of Pro	Estimating sizes, distances, and quantities; or determining time, costs, resources, or materials needed to perform a work activity.
Interpreting the Meaning of Information for Others	Translating or explaining what information means and how it can be used.
Scheduling Work and Activities	Scheduling events, programs, and activities, as well as the work of others.
Training and Teaching Others	Identifying the educational needs of others, developing formal educational or training programs or classes, and teaching or instructing others.
Handling and Moving Objects	Using hands and arms in handling, installing, positioning, and moving materials, and manipulating things.
Developing Objectives and Strategies	Establishing long-range objectives and specifying the strategies and actions to achieve them.
Performing Administrative Activities	Performing day-to-day administrative tasks such as maintaining information files and processing paperwork.
Performing General Physical Activities	Performing physical activities that require considerable use of your arms and legs and moving your whole body, such as climbing, lifting, balancing, walking, stooping, and handling of materials.
Communicating with Persons Outside Organization	Communicating with people outside the organization, representing the organization to customers, the public, government, and other external sources. This information can be exchanged in person, in writing, or by telephone or e-mail.
Repairing and Maintaining Mechanical Equipment	Servicing, repairing, adjusting, and testing machines, devices, moving parts, and equipment that operate primarily on the basis of mechanical (not electronic) principles.
Repairing and Maintaining Electronic Equipment	Servicing, repairing, calibrating, regulating, fine-tuning, or testing machines, devices, and equipment that operate primarily on the basis of electrical or electronic (not mechanical) principles.
Resolving Conflicts and Negotiating with Others	Handling complaints, settling disputes, and resolving grievances and conflicts, or otherwise negotiating with others.
Coordinating the Work and Activities of Others	Getting members of a group to work together to accomplish tasks.
Developing and Building Teams	Encouraging and building mutual trust, respect, and cooperation among team members.

Monitoring and Controlling Resources	Monitoring and controlling resources and overseeing the spending of money.
Coaching and Developing Others	Identifying the developmental needs of others and coaching, mentoring, or otherwise helping others to improve their knowledge or skills.
Provide Consultation and Advice to Others	Providing guidance and expert advice to management or other groups on technical, systems-, or process-related topics.
Assisting and Caring for Others	Providing personal assistance, medical attention, emotional support, or other personal care to others such as coworkers, customers, or patients.
Operating Vehicles, Mechanized Devices, or Equipme	Running, maneuvering, navigating, or driving vehicles or mechanized equipment, such as forklifts, passenger vehicles, aircraft, or water craft.
Drafting, Laying Out, and Specifying Technical Dev	Providing documentation, detailed instructions, drawings, or specifications to tell others about how devices, parts, equipment, or structures are to be fabricated, constructed, assembled, modified, maintained, or used.
Guiding, Directing, and Motivating Subordinates	Providing guidance and direction to subordinates, including setting performance standards and monitoring performance.
Selling or Influencing Others	Convincing others to buy merchandise/goods or to otherwise change their minds or actions.
Performing for or Working Directly with the Public	Performing for people or dealing directly with the public. This includes serving customers in restaurants and stores, and receiving clients or guests.
Staffing Organizational Units	Recruiting, interviewing, selecting, hiring, and promoting employees in an organization.

Work_Context	Work_Context Definitions
Wear Common Protective or Safety Equipment such as	How much does this job require wearing common protective or safety equipment such as safety shoes, glasses, gloves, hard hats or live jackets?
Indoors, Environmentally Controlled	How often does this job require working indoors in environmentally controlled conditions?
Importance of Being Exact or Accurate	How important is being very exact or highly accurate in performing this job?
Electronic Mail	How often do you use electronic mail in this job?
Telephone	How often do you have telephone conversations in this job?
Face-to-Face Discussions	How often do you have to have face-to-face discussions with individuals or teams in this job?
Time Pressure	How often does this job require the worker to meet strict deadlines?
Exposed to Hazardous Conditions	How often does this job require exposure to hazardous conditions?
Freedom to Make Decisions	How much decision making freedom, without supervision, does the job offer?
Importance of Repeating Same Tasks	How important is repeating the same physical activities (e.g., key entry) or mental activities (e.g., checking entries in a ledger) over and over, without stopping, to performing this job?
Structured versus Unstructured Work	To what extent is this job structured for the worker, rather than allowing the worker to determine tasks, priorities, and goals?
Exposed to Contaminants	How often does this job require working exposed to contaminants (such as pollutants, gases, dust or odors)?
Sounds, Noise Levels Are Distracting or Uncomforta	How often does this job require working exposed to sounds and noise levels that are distracting or uncomfortable?
Contact With Others	How much does this job require the worker to be in contact with others (face-to-face, by telephone, or otherwise) in order to perform it?
Letters and Memos	How often does the job require written letters and memos?
Spend Time Standing	How much does this job require standing?
Impact of Decisions on Co-workers or Company Resul	How do the decisions an employee makes impact the results of co-workers, clients or the company?
Frequency of Decision Making	How frequently is the worker required to make decisions that affect other people, the financial resources, and/or the image and reputation of the organization?
Work With Work Group or Team	How important is it to work with others in a group or team in this job?
Responsible for Others' Health and Safety	How much responsibility is there for the health and safety of others in this job?
Spend Time Using Your Hands to Handle, Control, or	How much does this job require using your hands to handle, control, or feel objects, tools or controls?
Responsibility for Outcomes and Results	How responsible is the worker for work outcomes and results of other workers?
Spend Time Making Repetitive Motions	How much does this job require making repetitive motions?

Spend Time Walking and Running	How much does this job require walking and running?
Coordinate or Lead Others	How important is it to coordinate or lead others in accomplishing work activities in this job?
Consequence of Error	How serious would the result usually be if the worker made a mistake that was not readily correctable?
Physical Proximity	To what extent does this job require the worker to perform job tasks in close physical proximity to other people?
Spend Time Sitting	How much does this job require sitting?
Exposed to Hazardous Equipment	How often does this job require exposure to hazardous equipment?
Degree of Automation	How automated is the job?
Exposed to Minor Burns, Cuts, Bites, or Stings	How often does this job require exposure to minor burns, cuts, bites, or stings?
Very Hot or Cold Temperatures	How often does this job require working in very hot (above 90 F degrees) or very cold (below 32 F degrees) temperatures?
Frequency of Conflict Situations	How often are there conflict situations the employee has to face in this job?
Deal With External Customers	How important is it to work with external customers or the public in this job?
Level of Competition	To what extent does this job require the worker to compete or to be aware of competitive pressures?
Deal With Unpleasant or Angry People	How frequently does the worker have to deal with unpleasant, angry, or discourteous individuals as part of the job requirements?
Indoors, Not Environmentally Controlled	How often does this job require working indoors in non-controlled environmental conditions (e.g., warehouse without heat)?
Spend Time Bending or Twisting the Body	How much does this job require bending or twisting your body?
In an Enclosed Vehicle or Equipment	How often does this job require working in a closed vehicle or equipment (e.g., car)?
Cramped Work Space, Awkward Positions	How often does this job require working in cramped work spaces that requires getting into awkward positions?
Public Speaking	How often do you have to perform public speaking in this job?
Pace Determined by Speed of Equipment	How important is it to this job that the pace is determined by the speed of equipment or machinery? (This does not refer to keeping busy at all times on this job.)
Wear Specialized Protective or Safety Equipment su	How much does this job require wearing specialized protective or safety equipment such as breathing apparatus, safety harness, full protection suits, or radiation protection?
Exposed to Radiation	How often does this job require exposure to radiation?
Outdoors, Exposed to Weather	How often does this job require working outdoors, exposed to all weather conditions?
Spend Time Kneeling, Crouching, Stooping, or Crawl	How much does this job require kneeling, crouching, stooping or crawling?
Extremely Bright or Inadequate Lighting	How often does this job require working in extremely bright or inadequate lighting conditions?
Spend Time Climbing Ladders, Scaffolds, or Poles	How much does this job require climbing ladders, scaffolds, or poles?
Spend Time Keeping or Regaining Balance	How much does this job require keeping or regaining your balance?
Outdoors, Under Cover	How often does this job require working outdoors, under cover (e.g., structure with roof but no walls)?
Exposed to High Places	How often does this job require exposure to high places?
In an Open Vehicle or Equipment	How often does this job require working in an open vehicle or equipment (e.g., tractor)?
Deal With Physically Aggressive People	How frequently does this job require the worker to deal with physical aggression of violent individuals?
Exposed to Disease or Infections	How often does this job require exposure to disease/infections?
Exposed to Whole Body Vibration	How often does this job require exposure to whole body vibration (e.g., operate a jackhammer)?

Job Zone Component	Job Zone Component Definitions
Title	Job Zone Three: Medium Preparation Needed
Overall Experience	Previous work-related skill, knowledge, or experience is required for these occupations. For example, an electrician must have completed three or four years of apprenticeship or several years of vocational training, and often must have passed a licensing exam, in order to perform the job.
Job Training	Employees in these occupations usually need one or two years of training involving both on-the-job experience and informal training with experienced workers.

341

Job Zone Examples	These occupations usually involve using communication and organizational skills to coordinate, supervise, manage, or train others to accomplish goals. Examples include dental assistants, electricians, fish and game wardens, legal secretaries, personnel recruiters, and recreation workers.
SVP Range	(6.0 to < 7.0)
Education	Most occupations in this zone require training in vocational schools, related on-the-job experience, or an associate's degree. Some may require a bachelor's degree.

Work_Styles	Work_Styles Definitions
Integrity	Job requires being honest and ethical.
Dependability	Job requires being reliable, responsible, and dependable, and fulfilling obligations.
Attention to Detail	Job requires being careful about detail and thorough in completing work tasks.
Cooperation	Job requires being pleasant with others on the job and displaying a good-natured, cooperative attitude.
Independence	Job requires developing one's own ways of doing things, guiding oneself with little or no supervision, and depending on oneself to get things done.
Adaptability/Flexibility	Job requires being open to change (positive or negative) and to considerable variety in the workplace.
Analytical Thinking	Job requires analyzing information and using logic to address work-related issues and problems.
Initiative	Job requires a willingness to take on responsibilities and challenges.
Stress Tolerance	Job requires accepting criticism and dealing calmly and effectively with high stress situations.
Concern for Others	Job requires being sensitive to others' needs and feelings and being understanding and helpful on the job.
Persistence	Job requires persistence in the face of obstacles.
Self Control	Job requires maintaining composure, keeping emotions in check, controlling anger, and avoiding aggressive behavior, even in very difficult situations.
Innovation	Job requires creativity and alternative thinking to develop new ideas for and answers to work-related problems.
Achievement/Effort	Job requires establishing and maintaining personally challenging achievement goals and exerting effort toward mastering tasks.
Leadership	Job requires a willingness to lead, take charge, and offer opinions and direction.
Social Orientation	Job requires preferring to work with others rather than alone, and being personally connected with others on the job.

19-4041.01 - Geological Data Technicians

Measure, record, and evaluate geological data, using sonic, electronic, electrical, seismic, or gravity-measuring instruments to prospect for oil or gas. May collect and evaluate core samples and cuttings.

Tasks

1) Prepare notes, sketches, geological maps and cross-sections.

2) Measure geological characteristics used in prospecting for oil or gas, using measuring instruments.

3) Develop and print photographic recordings of information, using equipment.

4) Plan and direct activities of workers who operate equipment to collect data.

5) Set up, or direct set-up of instruments used to collect geological data.

6) Collect samples and cuttings, using equipment and hand tools.

7) Read and study reports in order to compile information and data for geological and geophysical prospecting.

8) Assemble, maintain, and distribute information for library or record systems.

9) Interview individuals, and research public databases in order to obtain information.

10) Operate and adjust equipment and apparatus used to obtain geological data.

11) Evaluate and interpret core samples and cuttings, and other geological data used in prospecting for oil or gas.

12) Develop and design packing materials and handling procedures for shipping of objects.

13) Supervise oil, water, and gas well drilling activities.

14) Prepare and attach packing instructions to shipping containers.

15) Record readings in order to compile data used in prospecting for oil or gas.

19-4041.02 - Geological Sample Test Technicians

Test and analyze geological samples, crude oil, or petroleum products to detect presence of petroleum, gas, or mineral deposits indicating potential for exploration and production, or to determine physical and chemical properties to ensure that products meet quality standards.

Tasks

1) Collect and prepare solid and fluid samples for analysis.

2) Supervise well exploration and drilling activities, and well completions.

3) Inspect engines for wear and defective parts, using equipment and measuring devices.

4) Test and analyze samples in order to determine their content and characteristics, using laboratory apparatus and testing equipment.

5) Prepare, transcribe, and/or analyze seismic, gravimetric, well log or other geophysical and survey data.

6) Prepare notes, sketches, geological maps, and cross sections.

7) Compile and record testing and operational data for review and further analysis.

8) Participate in geological, geophysical, geochemical, hydrographic or oceanographic surveys, prospecting field trips, exploratory drilling, well logging or underground mine survey programs.

9) Assess the environmental impacts of development projects on subsurface materials.

10) Adjust and repair testing, electrical, and mechanical equipment and devices.

11) Plot information from aerial photographs, well logs, section descriptions, and other databases.

12) Collaborate with hydro-geologists in order to evaluate groundwater and well circulation.

13) Participate in the evaluation of possible mining locations.

19-4051.01 - Nuclear Equipment Operation Technicians

Operate equipment used for the release, control, and utilization of nuclear energy to assist scientists in laboratory and production activities.

Tasks

1) Monitor instruments, gauges, and recording devices in control rooms during operation of equipment, under direction of nuclear experimenters.

2) Modify, devise, and maintain equipment used in operations.

3) Position fuel elements in geometric configurations around tubes in reactors or gamma facilities, according to radiation intensity specifications, using slave manipulators or extension tools.

4) Review experiment schedules in order to determine specifications, such as subatomic particle energy, intensity, and repetition rate parameters.

5) Set control panel switches, according to standard procedures, in order to route electric power from sources and direct particle beams through injector units.

6) Transfer capsules of experimental materials to and from tubes, chambers, or tunnels leading to reactor cores, using slave manipulators or extension tools.

7) Calculate equipment operating factors, such as radiation times, dosages, temperatures, gamma intensities, and pressures, using standard formulas and conversion tables.

8) Collaborate with accelerator and beamline physicists in order to make experimental measurements.

9) Communicate with accelerator maintenance personnel in order to ensure readiness of support systems, such as vacuum, water cooling, and radiofrequency power sources.

10) Diagnose routine problems affecting accelerator performance.

11) Write summaries of activities and record experimental data, such as accelerator performance, systems status, particle beam specification and beam conditions obtained.

12) Disassemble, clean, and decontaminate hot cells and reactor parts during maintenance

shutdowns, using slave manipulators, cranes, and hand tools.

13) Install instrumentation leads in reactor cores in order to measure operating temperatures and pressures, according to mockups, blueprints, and diagrams.

14) Perform testing, maintenance, repair, and upgrading of accelerator systems.

15) Set up and operate machines to cut fuel elements to size to fit into shielding boxes or to polish test pieces, following blueprints and other specifications and using extension tools.

16) Submit computations to supervisors for review.

17) Warn maintenance workers of radiation hazards, and direct workers to vacate hazardous areas.

18) Adjust controls of equipment in order to control particle beam movement, pulse rates, energy and intensity, or radiation, according to specifications.

19) Clear personnel from particle beam areas before operations begin.

20) Control laboratory compounding equipment enclosed in protective hot cells in order to prepare radioisotopes and other radioactive materials.

21) Follow policies and procedures for radiation workers in order to ensure personnel safety.

22) Direct the work of accelerator support service personnel.

23) Notify experimenters in target control rooms when particle beam parameters meet specifications.

19-4051.02 - Nuclear Monitoring Technicians

Collect and test samples to monitor results of nuclear experiments and contamination of humans, facilities, and environment.

Tasks

1) Operate manipulators from outside cells to move specimens into and out of shielded containers, to remove specimens from cells, or to place specimens on benches or equipment work stations.

2) Enter data into computers in order to record characteristics of nuclear events and locating coordinates of particles.

3) Decontaminate objects by cleaning with soap or solvents or by abrading with wire brushes, buffing wheels, or sandblasting machines.

4) Calculate safe radiation exposure times for personnel, using plant contamination readings and prescribed safe levels of radiation.

5) Test materials' physical, chemical, or metallurgical properties, using equipment such as tensile testers, hardness testers, metallographic units, micrometers, and gauges.

6) Set up equipment that automatically detects area radiation deviations, and test detection equipment in order to ensure its accuracy.

7) Determine intensities and types of radiation in work areas, equipment, and materials, using radiation detectors and other instruments.

8) Collect samples of air, water, gases, and solids in order to determine radioactivity levels of contamination.

9) Calibrate and maintain chemical instrumentation sensing elements and sampling system equipment, using calibration instruments and hand tools.

10) Weigh and mix decontamination chemical solutions in tanks, and immerse objects in solutions for specified times, using hoists.

11) Place irradiated nuclear fuel materials in environmental chambers for testing, and observe reactions through cell windows.

12) Instruct personnel in radiation safety procedures, and demonstrate use of protective clothing and equipment.

13) Monitor personnel in order to determine the amounts and intensities of radiation exposure.

14) Inform supervisors when individual exposures or area radiation levels approach maximum permissible limits.

15) Immerse samples in chemical compounds in order to prepare them for testing.

16) Scan photographic emulsions exposed to direct radiation in order to compute track properties from standard formulas, using microscopes with scales and protractors.

17) Confer with scientists directing projects in order to determine significant events to monitor during tests.

18) Set up and operate machines that cut, lap, and polish test pieces, following blueprints,

x-ray negatives, and sketches.

19) Prepare reports describing contamination tests, material and equipment decontaminated, and methods used in decontamination processes.

20) Place radioactive waste, such as sweepings and broken sample bottles, into containers for disposal.

21) Observe projected photographs to locate particle tracks and events, and compile lists of events from particle detectors.

22) Provide initial response to abnormal events and to alarms from radiation monitoring equipment.

19-4061.00 - Social Science Research Assistants

Assist social scientists in laboratory, survey, and other social research. May perform publication activities, laboratory analysis, quality control, or data management. Normally these individuals work under the direct supervision of a social scientist and assist in those activities which are more routine.

Tasks

1) Track research participants, and perform any necessary followup tasks.

2) Administer standardized tests to research subjects, and/or interview them in order to collect research data.

3) Present research findings to groups of people.

4) Develop and implement research quality control procedures.

5) Supervise the work of survey interviewers.

6) Track laboratory supplies, and expenses such as participant reimbursement.

7) Recruit and schedule research participants.

8) Conduct internet-based and library research.

9) Code data in preparation for computer entry.

10) Perform descriptive and multivariate statistical analyses of data, using computer software.

11) Allocate and manage laboratory space and resources.

12) Perform needs assessments and/or consult with clients in order to determine the types of research and information that are required.

13) Design and create special programs for tasks such as statistical analysis and data entry and cleaning.

14) Screen potential subjects in order to determine their suitability as study participants.

15) Verify the accuracy and validity of data entered in databases; correct any errors.

16) Provide assistance with the preparation of project-related reports, manuscripts, and presentations.

17) Provide assistance in the design of survey instruments such as questionnaires.

18) Prepare tables, graphs, fact sheets, and written reports summarizing research results.

19) Obtain informed consent of research subjects and/or their guardians.

20) Perform data entry and other clerical work as required for project completion.

21) Edit and submit protocols and other required research documentation.

22) Collect specimens such as blood samples, as required by research projects.

19-4091.00 - Environmental Science and Protection Technicians, Including Health

Performs laboratory and field tests to monitor the environment and investigate sources of pollution, including those that affect health. Under direction of an environmental scientist or specialist, may collect samples of gases, soil, water, and other materials for testing and take corrective actions as assigned.

Tasks

1) Record test data and prepare reports, summaries, and charts that interpret test results.

2) Provide information and technical and program assistance to government representatives, employers and the general public on the issues of public health, environmental protection or

workplace safety.

3) Respond to and investigate hazardous conditions or spills, or outbreaks of disease or food poisoning, collecting samples for analysis.

4) Calibrate microscopes and test instruments.

5) Make recommendations to control or eliminate unsafe conditions at workplaces or public facilities.

6) Discuss test results and analyses with customers.

7) Perform statistical analysis of environmental data.

8) Calculate amount of pollutant in samples or compute air pollution or gas flow in industrial processes, using chemical and mathematical formulas.

9) Set up equipment or stations to monitor and collect pollutants from sites, such as smoke stacks, manufacturing plants, or mechanical equipment.

10) Prepare samples or photomicrographs for testing and analysis.

11) Develop and implement programs for monitoring of environmental pollution and radiation.

12) Maintain files such as hazardous waste databases, chemical usage data, personnel exposure information and diagrams showing equipment locations.

13) Distribute permits, closure plans and cleanup plans.

14) Weigh, analyze, and measure collected sample particles, such as lead, coal dust, or rock, to determine concentration of pollutants.

15) Initiate procedures to close down or fine establishments violating environmental and/or health regulations.

16) Inspect workplaces to ensure the absence of health and safety hazards such as high noise levels, radiation or potential lighting hazards.

17) Inspect sanitary conditions at public facilities.

18) Determine amounts and kinds of chemicals to use in destroying harmful organisms and removing impurities from purification systems.

19) Examine and analyze material for presence and concentration of contaminants such as asbestos, using variety of microscopes.

20) Develop testing procedures, and direct activities of workers in laboratory.

21) Conduct standardized tests to ensure materials and supplies used throughout power supply systems meet processing and safety specifications.

Knowledge	Knowledge Definitions
Law and Government	Knowledge of laws, legal codes, court procedures, precedents, government regulations, executive orders, agency rules, and the democratic political process.
Public Safety and Security	Knowledge of relevant equipment, policies, procedures, and strategies to promote effective local, state, or national security operations for the protection of people, data, property, and institutions.
Chemistry	Knowledge of the chemical composition, structure, and properties of substances and of the chemical processes and transformations that they undergo. This includes uses of chemicals and their interactions, danger signs, production techniques, and disposal methods.
Customer and Personal Service	Knowledge of principles and processes for providing customer and personal services. This includes customer needs assessment, meeting quality standards for services, and evaluation of customer satisfaction.
Mathematics	Knowledge of arithmetic, algebra, geometry, calculus, statistics, and their applications.
Education and Training	Knowledge of principles and methods for curriculum and training design, teaching and instruction for individuals and groups, and the measurement of training effects.
Biology	Knowledge of plant and animal organisms, their tissues, cells, functions, interdependencies, and interactions with each other and the environment.
Engineering and Technology	Knowledge of the practical application of engineering science and technology. This includes applying principles, techniques, procedures, and equipment to the design and production of various goods and services.
English Language	Knowledge of the structure and content of the English language including the meaning and spelling of words, rules of composition, and grammar.
Computers and Electronics	Knowledge of circuit boards, processors, chips, electronic equipment, and computer hardware and software, including applications and programming.
Clerical	Knowledge of administrative and clerical procedures and systems such as word processing, managing files and records, stenography and transcription, designing forms, and other office procedures and terminology.
Design	Knowledge of design techniques, tools, and principles involved in production of precision technical plans, blueprints, drawings, and models.
Mechanical	Knowledge of machines and tools, including their designs, uses, repair, and maintenance.
Building and Construction	Knowledge of materials, methods, and the tools involved in the construction or repair of houses, buildings, or other structures such as highways and roads.
Economics and Accounting	Knowledge of economic and accounting principles and practices, the financial markets, banking and the analysis and reporting of financial data.
Physics	Knowledge and prediction of physical principles, laws, their interrelationships, and applications to understanding fluid, material, and atmospheric dynamics, and mechanical, electrical, atomic and sub-atomic structures and processes.
Administration and Management	Knowledge of business and management principles involved in strategic planning, resource allocation, human resources modeling, leadership technique, production methods, and coordination of people and resources.
Geography	Knowledge of principles and methods for describing the features of land, sea, and air masses, including their physical characteristics, locations, interrelationships, and distribution of plant, animal, and human life.
Personnel and Human Resources	Knowledge of principles and procedures for personnel recruitment, selection, training, compensation and benefits, labor relations and negotiation, and personnel information systems.
Medicine and Dentistry	Knowledge of the information and techniques needed to diagnose and treat human injuries, diseases, and deformities. This includes symptoms, treatment alternatives, drug properties and interactions, and preventive health-care measures.
Production and Processing	Knowledge of raw materials, production processes, quality control, costs, and other techniques for maximizing the effective manufacture and distribution of goods.
Communications and Media	Knowledge of media production, communication, and dissemination techniques and methods. This includes alternative ways to inform and entertain via written, oral, and visual media.
Telecommunications	Knowledge of transmission, broadcasting, switching, control, and operation of telecommunications systems.
Psychology	Knowledge of human behavior and performance; individual differences in ability, personality, and interests; learning and motivation; psychological research methods; and the assessment and treatment of behavioral and affective disorders.
Sociology and Anthropology	Knowledge of group behavior and dynamics, societal trends and influences, human migrations, ethnicity, cultures and their history and origins.
Transportation	Knowledge of principles and methods for moving people or goods by air, rail, sea, or road, including the relative costs and benefits.
Sales and Marketing	Knowledge of principles and methods for showing, promoting, and selling products or services. This includes marketing strategy and tactics, product demonstration, sales techniques, and sales control systems.
Food Production	Knowledge of techniques and equipment for planting, growing, and harvesting food products (both plant and animal) for consumption, including storage/handling techniques.
Therapy and Counseling	Knowledge of principles, methods, and procedures for diagnosis, treatment, and rehabilitation of physical and mental dysfunctions, and for career counseling and guidance.
Foreign Language	Knowledge of the structure and content of a foreign (non-English) language including the meaning and spelling of words, rules of composition and grammar, and pronunciation.
Philosophy and Theology	Knowledge of different philosophical systems and religions. This includes their basic principles, values, ethics, ways of thinking, customs, practices, and their impact on human culture.
History and Archeology	Knowledge of historical events and their causes, indicators, and effects on civilizations and cultures.
Fine Arts	Knowledge of the theory and techniques required to compose, produce, and perform works of music, dance, visual arts, drama, and sculpture.

Skills	Skills Definitions
Reading Comprehension	Understanding written sentences and paragraphs in work related documents.
Science	Using scientific rules and methods to solve problems.
Critical Thinking	Using logic and reasoning to identify the strengths and weaknesses of alternative solutions, conclusions or approaches to problems.
Active Listening	Giving full attention to what other people are saying, taking time to understand the points being made, asking questions as appropriate, and not interrupting at inappropriate times.
Active Learning	Understanding the implications of new information for both current and future problem-solving and decision-making.
Writing	Communicating effectively in writing as appropriate for the needs of the audience.
Monitoring	Monitoring/Assessing performance of yourself, other individuals, or organizations to make improvements or take corrective action.
Mathematics	Using mathematics to solve problems.
Judgment and Decision Making	Considering the relative costs and benefits of potential actions to choose the most appropriate one.
Social Perceptiveness	Being aware of others' reactions and understanding why they react as they do.
Speaking	Talking to others to convey information effectively.
Persuasion	Persuading others to change their minds or behavior.
Learning Strategies	Selecting and using training/instructional methods and procedures appropriate for the situation when learning or teaching new things.
Instructing	Teaching others how to do something.
Complex Problem Solving	Identifying complex problems and reviewing related information to develop and evaluate options and implement solutions.
Equipment Selection	Determining the kind of tools and equipment needed to do a job.
Quality Control Analysis	Conducting tests and inspections of products, services, or processes to evaluate quality or performance.
Coordination	Adjusting actions in relation to others' actions.
Troubleshooting	Determining causes of operating errors and deciding what to do about it.
Time Management	Managing one's own time and the time of others.
Negotiation	Bringing others together and trying to reconcile differences.
Operation Monitoring	Watching gauges, dials, or other indicators to make sure a machine is working properly.
Operation and Control	Controlling operations of equipment or systems.
Installation	Installing equipment, machines, wiring, or programs to meet specifications.
Systems Analysis	Determining how a system should work and how changes in conditions, operations, and the environment will affect outcomes.
Equipment Maintenance	Performing routine maintenance on equipment and determining when and what kind of maintenance is needed.
Service Orientation	Actively looking for ways to help people.
Operations Analysis	Analyzing needs and product requirements to create a design.
Management of Financial Resources	Determining how money will be spent to get the work done, and accounting for these expenditures.
Systems Evaluation	Identifying measures or indicators of system performance and the actions needed to improve or correct performance, relative to the goals of the system.
Management of Personnel Resources	Motivating, developing, and directing people as they work, identifying the best people for the job.
Technology Design	Generating or adapting equipment and technology to serve user needs.
Repairing	Repairing machines or systems using the needed tools.
Management of Material Resources	Obtaining and seeing to the appropriate use of equipment, facilities, and materials needed to do certain work.
Programming	Writing computer programs for various purposes.

Ability	Ability Definitions
Oral Expression	The ability to communicate information and ideas in speaking so others will understand.
Inductive Reasoning	The ability to combine pieces of information to form general rules or conclusions (includes finding a relationship among seemingly unrelated events).
Problem Sensitivity	The ability to tell when something is wrong or is likely to go wrong. It does not involve solving the problem, only recognizing there is a problem.

Speech Recognition	The ability to identify and understand the speech of another person.
Near Vision	The ability to see details at close range (within a few feet of the observer).
Oral Comprehension	The ability to listen to and understand information and ideas presented through spoken words and sentences.
Speech Clarity	The ability to speak clearly so others can understand you.
Deductive Reasoning	The ability to apply general rules to specific problems to produce answers that make sense.
Information Ordering	The ability to arrange things or actions in a certain order or pattern according to a specific rule or set of rules (e.g., patterns of numbers, letters, words, pictures, mathematical operations).
Mathematical Reasoning	The ability to choose the right mathematical methods or formulas to solve a problem.
Written Expression	The ability to communicate information and ideas in writing so others will understand.
Written Comprehension	The ability to read and understand information and ideas presented in writing.
Flexibility of Closure	The ability to identify or detect a known pattern (a figure, object, word, or sound) that is hidden in other distracting material.
Category Flexibility	The ability to generate or use different sets of rules for combining or grouping things in different ways.
Arm-Hand Steadiness	The ability to keep your hand and arm steady while moving your arm or while holding your arm and hand in one position.
Far Vision	The ability to see details at a distance.
Selective Attention	The ability to concentrate on a task over a period of time without being distracted.
Fluency of Ideas	The ability to come up with a number of ideas about a topic (the number of ideas is important, not their quality, correctness, or creativity).
Control Precision	The ability to quickly and repeatedly adjust the controls of a machine or a vehicle to exact positions.
Originality	The ability to come up with unusual or clever ideas about a given topic or situation, or to develop creative ways to solve a problem.
Speed of Closure	The ability to quickly make sense of, combine, and organize information into meaningful patterns.
Multilimb Coordination	The ability to coordinate two or more limbs (for example, two arms, two legs, or one leg and one arm) while sitting, standing, or lying down. It does not involve performing the activities while the whole body is in motion.
Finger Dexterity	The ability to make precisely coordinated movements of the fingers of one or both hands to grasp, manipulate, or assemble very small objects.
Time Sharing	The ability to shift back and forth between two or more activities or sources of information (such as speech, sounds, touch, or other sources).
Perceptual Speed	The ability to quickly and accurately compare similarities and differences among sets of letters, numbers, objects, pictures, or patterns. The things to be compared may be presented at the same time or one after the other. This ability also includes comparing a presented object with a remembered object.
Memorization	The ability to remember information such as words, numbers, pictures, and procedures.
Depth Perception	The ability to judge which of several objects is closer or farther away from you, or to judge the distance between you and an object.
Manual Dexterity	The ability to quickly move your hand, your hand together with your arm, or your two hands to grasp, manipulate, or assemble objects.
Spatial Orientation	The ability to know your location in relation to the environment or to know where other objects are in relation to you.
Visual Color Discrimination	The ability to match or detect differences between colors, including shades of color and brightness.
Number Facility	The ability to add, subtract, multiply, or divide quickly and correctly.
Trunk Strength	The ability to use your abdominal and lower back muscles to support part of the body repeatedly or continuously over time without 'giving out' or fatiguing.
Visualization	The ability to imagine how something will look after it is moved around or when its parts are moved or rearranged.
Gross Body Coordination	The ability to coordinate the movement of your arms, legs, and torso together when the whole body is in motion.
Glare Sensitivity	The ability to see objects in the presence of glare or bright lighting.
Extent Flexibility	The ability to bend, stretch, twist, or reach with your body, arms, and/or legs.

Peripheral Vision	The ability to see objects or movement of objects to one's side when the eyes are looking ahead.
Static Strength	The ability to exert maximum muscle force to lift, push, pull, or carry objects.
Stamina	The ability to exert yourself physically over long periods of time without getting winded or out of breath.
Auditory Attention	The ability to focus on a single source of sound in the presence of other distracting sounds.
Gross Body Equilibrium	The ability to keep or regain your body balance or stay upright when in an unstable position.
Reaction Time	The ability to quickly respond (with the hand, finger, or foot) to a signal (sound, light, picture) when it appears.
Hearing Sensitivity	The ability to detect or tell the differences between sounds that vary in pitch and loudness.
Speed of Limb Movement	The ability to quickly move the arms and legs.
Rate Control	The ability to time your movements or the movement of a piece of equipment in anticipation of changes in the speed and/or direction of a moving object or scene.
Response Orientation	The ability to choose quickly between two or more movements in response to two or more different signals (lights, sounds, pictures). It includes the speed with which the correct response is started with the hand, foot, or other body part.
Dynamic Strength	The ability to exert muscle force repeatedly or continuously over time. This involves muscular endurance and resistance to muscle fatigue.
Wrist-Finger Speed	The ability to make fast, simple, repeated movements of the fingers, hands, and wrists.
Night Vision	The ability to see under low light conditions.
Dynamic Flexibility	The ability to quickly and repeatedly bend, stretch, twist, or reach out with your body, arms, and/or legs.
Sound Localization	The ability to tell the direction from which a sound originated.
Explosive Strength	The ability to use short bursts of muscle force to propel oneself (as in jumping or sprinting), or to throw an object.

Work_Activity	Work_Activity Definitions
Documenting/Recording Information	Entering, transcribing, recording, storing, or maintaining information in written or electronic/magnetic form.
Getting Information	Observing, receiving, and otherwise obtaining information from all relevant sources.
Identifying Objects, Actions, and Events	Identifying information by categorizing, estimating, recognizing differences or similarities, and detecting changes in circumstances or events.
Communicating with Supervisors, Peers, or Subordin	Providing information to supervisors, co-workers, and subordinates by telephone, in written form, e-mail, or in person.
Establishing and Maintaining Interpersonal Relatio	Developing constructive and cooperative working relationships with others, and maintaining them over time.
Interacting With Computers	Using computers and computer systems (including hardware and software) to program, write software, set up functions, enter data, or process information.
Making Decisions and Solving Problems	Analyzing information and evaluating results to choose the best solution and solve problems.
Processing Information	Compiling, coding, categorizing, calculating, tabulating, auditing, or verifying information or data.
Operating Vehicles, Mechanized Devices, or Equipme	Running, maneuvering, navigating, or driving vehicles or mechanized equipment, such as forklifts, passenger vehicles, aircraft, or water craft.
Evaluating Information to Determine Compliance wit	Using relevant information and individual judgment to determine whether events or processes comply with laws, regulations, or standards.
Communicating with Persons Outside Organization	Communicating with people outside the organization, representing the organization to customers, the public, government, and other external sources. This information can be exchanged in person, in writing, or by telephone or e-mail.
Analyzing Data or Information	Identifying the underlying principles, reasons, or facts of information by breaking down information or data into separate parts.
Organizing, Planning, and Prioritizing Work	Developing specific goals and plans to prioritize, organize, and accomplish your work.
Estimating the Quantifiable Characteristics of Pro	Estimating sizes, distances, and quantities; or determining time, costs, resources, or materials needed to perform a work activity.
Scheduling Work and Activities	Scheduling events, programs, and activities, as well as the work of others.

Monitor Processes, Materials, or Surroundings	Monitoring and reviewing information from materials, events, or the environment, to detect or assess problems.
Updating and Using Relevant Knowledge	Keeping up-to-date technically and applying new knowledge to your job.
Inspecting Equipment, Structures, or Material	Inspecting equipment, structures, or materials to identify the cause of errors or other problems or defects.
Performing General Physical Activities	Performing physical activities that require considerable use of your arms and legs and moving your whole body, such as climbing, lifting, balancing, walking, stooping, and handling of materials.
Thinking Creatively	Developing, designing, or creating new applications, ideas, relationships, systems, or products, including artistic contributions.
Developing Objectives and Strategies	Establishing long-range objectives and specifying the strategies and actions to achieve them.
Controlling Machines and Processes	Using either control mechanisms or direct physical activity to operate machines or processes (not including computers or vehicles).
Provide Consultation and Advice to Others	Providing guidance and expert advice to management or other groups on technical, systems-, or process-related topics.
Developing and Building Teams	Encouraging and building mutual trust, respect, and cooperation among team members.
Interpreting the Meaning of Information for Others	Translating or explaining what information means and how it can be used.
Resolving Conflicts and Negotiating with Others	Handling complaints, settling disputes, and resolving grievances and conflicts, or otherwise negotiating with others.
Coordinating the Work and Activities of Others	Getting members of a group to work together to accomplish tasks.
Handling and Moving Objects	Using hands and arms in handling, installing, positioning, and moving materials, and manipulating things.
Training and Teaching Others	Identifying the educational needs of others, developing formal educational or training programs or classes, and teaching or instructing others.
Judging the Qualities of Things, Services, or Peop	Assessing the value, importance, or quality of things or people.
Repairing and Maintaining Mechanical Equipment	Servicing, repairing, adjusting, and testing machines, devices, moving parts, and equipment that operate primarily on the basis of mechanical (not electronic) principles.
Performing for or Working Directly with the Public	Performing for people or dealing directly with the public. This includes serving customers in restaurants and stores, and receiving clients or guests.
Monitoring and Controlling Resources	Monitoring and controlling resources and overseeing the spending of money.
Drafting, Laying Out, and Specifying Technical Dev	Providing documentation, detailed instructions, drawings, or specifications to tell others about how devices, parts, equipment, or structures are to be fabricated, constructed, assembled, modified, maintained, or used.
Coaching and Developing Others	Identifying the developmental needs of others and coaching, mentoring, or otherwise helping others to improve their knowledge or skills.
Performing Administrative Activities	Performing day-to-day administrative tasks such as maintaining information files and processing paperwork.
Repairing and Maintaining Electronic Equipment	Servicing, repairing, calibrating, regulating, fine-tuning, or testing machines, devices, and equipment that operate primarily on the basis of electrical or electronic (not mechanical) principles.
Guiding, Directing, and Motivating Subordinates	Providing guidance and direction to subordinates, including setting performance standards and monitoring performance.
Assisting and Caring for Others	Providing personal assistance, medical attention, emotional support, or other personal care to others such as coworkers, customers, or patients.
Selling or Influencing Others	Convincing others to buy merchandise/goods or to otherwise change their minds or actions.
Staffing Organizational Units	Recruiting, interviewing, selecting, hiring, and promoting employees in an organization.

Work_Context	Work_Context Definitions
Telephone	How often do you have telephone conversations in this job?
Face-to-Face Discussions	How often do you have to have face-to-face discussions with individuals or teams in this job?
Work With Work Group or Team	How important is it to work with others in a group or team in this job?
Importance of Being Exact or Accurate	How important is being very exact or highly accurate in performing this job?
Structured versus Unstructured Work	To what extent is this job structured for the worker, rather than allowing the worker to determine tasks, priorities, and goals?

Contact With Others	How much does this job require the worker to be in contact with others (face-to-face, by telephone, or otherwise) in order to perform it?
In an Enclosed Vehicle or Equipment	How often does this job require working in a closed vehicle or equipment (e.g., car)?
Freedom to Make Decisions	How much decision making freedom, without supervision, does the job offer?
Indoors, Environmentally Controlled	How often does this job require working indoors in environmentally controlled conditions?
Impact of Decisions on Co-workers or Company Resul	How do the decisions an employee makes impact the results of co-workers, clients or the company?
Letters and Memos	How often does the job require written letters and memos?
Deal With External Customers	How important is it to work with external customers or the public in this job?
Electronic Mail	How often do you use electronic mail in this job?
Time Pressure	How often does this job require the worker to meet strict deadlines?
Outdoors, Exposed to Weather	How often does this job require working outdoors, exposed to all weather conditions?
Frequency of Decision Making	How frequently is the worker required to make decisions that affect other people, the financial resources, and/or the image and reputation of the organization?
Coordinate or Lead Others	How important is it to coordinate or lead others in accomplishing work activities in this job?
Responsible for Others' Health and Safety	How much responsibility is there for the health and safety of others in this job?
Exposed to Contaminants	How often does this job require working exposed to contaminants (such as pollutants, gases, dust or odors)?
Physical Proximity	To what extent does this job require the worker to perform job tasks in close physical proximity to other people?
Very Hot or Cold Temperatures	How often does this job require working in very hot (above 90 F degrees) or very cold (below 32 F degrees) temperatures?
Sounds, Noise Levels Are Distracting or Uncomforta	How often does this job require working exposed to sounds and noise levels that are distracting or uncomfortable?
Wear Common Protective or Safety Equipment such as	How much does this job require wearing common protective or safety equipment such as safety shoes, glasses, gloves, hard hats or live jackets?
Spend Time Sitting	How much does this job require sitting?
Consequence of Error	How serious would the result usually be if the worker made a mistake that was not readily correctable?
Responsibility for Outcomes and Results	How responsible is the worker for work outcomes and results of other workers?
Level of Competition	To what extent does this job require the worker to compete or to be aware of competitive pressures?
Frequency of Conflict Situations	How often are there conflict situations the employee has to face in this job?
Spend Time Using Your Hands to Handle, Control, or	How much does this job require using your hands to handle, control, or feel objects, tools or controls?
Indoors, Not Environmentally Controlled	How often does this job require working indoors in non controlled environmental conditions (e.g., warehouse without heat)?
Deal With Unpleasant or Angry People	How frequently does the worker have to deal with unpleasant, angry, or discourteous individuals as part of the job requirements?
Importance of Repeating Same Tasks	How important is repeating the same physical activities (e.g., key entry) or mental activities (e.g., checking entries in a ledger) over and over, without stopping, to performing this job?
Extremely Bright or Inadequate Lighting	How often does this job require working in extremely bright or inadequate lighting conditions?
Spend Time Standing	How much does this job require standing?
Outdoors, Under Cover	How often does this job require working outdoors, under cover (e.g., structure with roof but no walls)?
Exposed to Hazardous Conditions	How often does this job require exposure to hazardous conditions?
Exposed to Minor Burns, Cuts, Bites, or Stings	How often does this job require exposure to minor burns, cuts, bites, or stings?
Public Speaking	How often do you have to perform public speaking in this job?
Spend Time Walking and Running	How much does this job require walking and running?
Cramped Work Space, Awkward Positions	How often does this job require working in cramped work spaces that requires getting into awkward positions?
Spend Time Bending or Twisting the Body	How much does this job require bending or twisting your body?
Exposed to Hazardous Equipment	How often does this job require exposure to hazardous equipment?
Degree of Automation	How automated is the job?
Spend Time Making Repetitive Motions	How much does this job require making repetitive motions?
Spend Time Kneeling, Crouching, Stooping, or Crawl	How much does this job require kneeling, crouching, stooping or crawling?
Wear Specialized Protective or Safety Equipment su	How much does this job require wearing specialized protective or safety equipment such as breathing apparatus, safety harness, full protection suits, or radiation protection?
Pace Determined by Speed of Equipment	How important is it to this job that the pace is determined by the speed of equipment or machinery? (This does not refer to keeping busy at all times on this job.)
Exposed to Disease or Infections	How often does this job require exposure to disease/infections?
Spend Time Keeping or Regaining Balance	How much does this job require keeping or regaining your balance?
In an Open Vehicle or Equipment	How often does this job require working in an open vehicle or equipment (e.g., tractor)?
Exposed to High Places	How often does this job require exposure to high places?
Exposed to Whole Body Vibration	How often does this job require exposure to whole body vibration (e.g., operate a jackhammer)?
Deal With Physically Aggressive People	How frequently does this job require the worker to deal with physical aggression of violent individuals?
Spend Time Climbing Ladders, Scaffolds, or Poles	How much does this job require climbing ladders, scaffolds, or poles?
Exposed to Radiation	How often does this job require exposure to radiation?

Job Zone Component	Job Zone Component Definitions
Title	Job Zone Four: Considerable Preparation Needed
Overall Experience	A minimum of two to four years of work-related skill, knowledge, or experience is needed for these occupations. For example, an accountant must complete four years of college and work for several years in accounting to be considered qualified.
Job Training	Employees in these occupations usually need several years of work-related experience, on-the-job training, and/or vocational training.
Job Zone Examples	Many of these occupations involve coordinating, supervising, managing, or training others. Examples include accountants, chefs and head cooks, computer programmers, historians, pharmacists, and police detectives.
SVP Range	(7.0 to < 8.0)
Education	Most of these occupations require a four - year bachelor's degree, but some do not.

Work_Styles	Work_Styles Definitions
Analytical Thinking	Job requires analyzing information and using logic to address work-related issues and problems.
Dependability	Job requires being reliable, responsible, and dependable, and fulfilling obligations.
Adaptability/Flexibility	Job requires being open to change (positive or negative) and to considerable variety in the workplace.
Cooperation	Job requires being pleasant with others on the job and displaying a good-natured, cooperative attitude.
Achievement/Effort	Job requires establishing and maintaining personally challenging achievement goals and exerting effort toward mastering tasks.
Attention to Detail	Job requires being careful about detail and thorough in completing work tasks.
Independence	Job requires developing one's own ways of doing things, guiding oneself with little or no supervision, and depending on oneself to get things done.
Initiative	Job requires a willingness to take on responsibilities and challenges.
Persistence	Job requires persistence in the face of obstacles.
Stress Tolerance	Job requires accepting criticism and dealing calmly and effectively with high stress situations.
Self Control	Job requires maintaining composure, keeping emotions in check, controlling anger, and avoiding aggressive behavior, even in very difficult situations.
Concern for Others	Job requires being sensitive to others' needs and feelings and being understanding and helpful on the job.
Innovation	Job requires creativity and alternative thinking to develop new ideas for and answers to work-related problems.
Integrity	Job requires being honest and ethical.

Leadership	Job requires a willingness to lead, take charge, and offer opinions and direction.
Social Orientation	Job requires preferring to work with others rather than alone, and being personally connected with others on the job.

19-4092.00 - Forensic Science Technicians

Collect, identify, classify, and analyze physical evidence related to criminal investigations. Perform tests on weapons or substances, such as fiber, hair, and tissue to determine significance to investigation. May testify as expert witnesses on evidence or crime laboratory techniques. May serve as specialists in area of expertise, such as ballistics, fingerprinting, handwriting, or biochemistry.

Tasks

1) Keep records and prepare reports detailing findings, investigative methods, and laboratory techniques.

2) Operate and maintain laboratory equipment and apparatus.

3) Prepare solutions, reagents, and sample formulations needed for laboratory work.

4) Interpret laboratory findings and test results in order to identify and classify substances, materials, and other evidence collected at crime scenes.

5) Visit morgues, examine scenes of crimes, or contact other sources in order to obtain evidence or information to be used in investigations.

6) Reconstruct crime scenes in order to determine relationships among pieces of evidence.

7) Confer with ballistics, fingerprinting, handwriting, documents, electronics, medical, chemical, or metallurgical experts concerning evidence and its interpretation.

8) Collect evidence from crime scenes, storing it in conditions that preserve its integrity.

9) Collect impressions of dust from surfaces in order to obtain and identify fingerprints.

10) Compare objects such as tools with impression marks in order to determine whether a specific object is responsible for a specific mark.

11) Analyze gunshot residue and bullet paths in order to determine how shootings occurred.

12) Determine types of bullets used in shooting and if fired from a specific weapon.

13) Identify and quantify drugs and poisons found in biological fluids and tissues, in foods, and at crime scenes.

14) Examine physical evidence such as hair, fiber, wood or soil residues in order to obtain information about its source and composition.

15) Interpret the pharmacological effects of a drug or a combination of drugs on an individual.

16) Examine DNA samples to determine if they match other samples.

17) Analyze and classify biological fluids using DNA typing or serological techniques.

18) Examine firearms in order to determine mechanical condition and legal status, performing restoration work on damaged firearms in order to obtain information such as serial numbers.

19) Analyze handwritten and machine-produced textual evidence to decipher altered or obliterated text or to determine authorship, age, and/or source.

Knowledge	Knowledge Definitions
Chemistry	Knowledge of the chemical composition, structure, and properties of substances and of the chemical processes and transformations that they undergo. This includes uses of chemicals and their interactions, danger signs, production techniques, and disposal methods.
Law and Government	Knowledge of laws, legal codes, court procedures, precedents, government regulations, executive orders, agency rules, and the democratic political process.
English Language	Knowledge of the structure and content of the English language including the meaning and spelling of words, rules of composition, and grammar.
Customer and Personal Service	Knowledge of principles and processes for providing customer and personal services. This includes customer needs assessment, meeting quality standards for services, and evaluation of customer satisfaction.
Public Safety and Security	Knowledge of relevant equipment, policies, procedures, and strategies to promote effective local, state, or national security operations for the protection of people, data, property, and institutions.

Mathematics	Knowledge of arithmetic, algebra, geometry, calculus, statistics, and their applications.
Computers and Electronics	Knowledge of circuit boards, processors, chips, electronic equipment, and computer hardware and software, including applications and programming.
Clerical	Knowledge of administrative and clerical procedures and systems such as word processing, managing files and records, stenography and transcription, designing forms, and other office procedures and terminology.
Biology	Knowledge of plant and animal organisms, their tissues, cells, functions, interdependencies, and interactions with each other and the environment.
Psychology	Knowledge of human behavior and performance; individual differences in ability, personality, and interests; learning and motivation; psychological research methods; and the assessment and treatment of behavioral and affective disorders.
Administration and Management	Knowledge of business and management principles involved in strategic planning, resource allocation, human resources modeling, leadership technique, production methods, and coordination of people and resources.
Education and Training	Knowledge of principles and methods for curriculum and training design, teaching and instruction for individuals and groups, and the measurement of training effects.
Engineering and Technology	Knowledge of the practical application of engineering science and technology. This includes applying principles, techniques, procedures, and equipment to the design and production of various goods and services.
Communications and Media	Knowledge of media production, communication, and dissemination techniques and methods. This includes alternative ways to inform and entertain via written, oral, and visual media.
Telecommunications	Knowledge of transmission, broadcasting, switching, control, and operation of telecommunications systems.
Mechanical	Knowledge of machines and tools, including their designs, uses, repair, and maintenance.
Medicine and Dentistry	Knowledge of the information and techniques needed to diagnose and treat human injuries, diseases, and deformities. This includes symptoms, treatment alternatives, drug properties and interactions, and preventive health-care measures.
Physics	Knowledge and prediction of physical principles, laws, their interrelationships, and applications to understanding fluid, material, and atmospheric dynamics, and mechanical, electrical, atomic and sub-atomic structures and processes.
Transportation	Knowledge of principles and methods for moving people or goods by air, rail, sea, or road, including the relative costs and benefits.
Sociology and Anthropology	Knowledge of group behavior and dynamics, societal trends and influences, human migrations, ethnicity, cultures and their history and origins.
Geography	Knowledge of principles and methods for describing the features of land, sea, and air masses, including their physical characteristics, locations, interrelationships, and distribution of plant, animal, and human life.
Personnel and Human Resources	Knowledge of principles and procedures for personnel recruitment, selection, training, compensation and benefits, labor relations and negotiation, and personnel information systems.
Philosophy and Theology	Knowledge of different philosophical systems and religions. This includes their basic principles, values, ethics, ways of thinking, customs, practices, and their impact on human culture.
Foreign Language	Knowledge of the structure and content of a foreign (non-English) language including the meaning and spelling of words, rules of composition and grammar, and pronunciation.
Design	Knowledge of design techniques, tools, and principles involved in production of precision technical plans, blueprints, drawings, and models.
Therapy and Counseling	Knowledge of principles, methods, and procedures for diagnosis, treatment, and rehabilitation of physical and mental dysfunctions, and for career counseling and guidance.
History and Archeology	Knowledge of historical events and their causes, indicators, and effects on civilizations and cultures.
Economics and Accounting	Knowledge of economic and accounting principles and practices, the financial markets, banking and the analysis and reporting of financial data.
Production and Processing	Knowledge of raw materials, production processes, quality control, costs, and other techniques for maximizing the effective manufacture and distribution of goods.

Sales and Marketing	Knowledge of principles and methods for showing, promoting, and selling products or services. This includes marketing strategy and tactics, product demonstration, sales techniques, and sales control systems.
Fine Arts	Knowledge of the theory and techniques required to compose, produce, and perform works of music, dance, visual arts, drama, and sculpture.
Building and Construction	Knowledge of materials, methods, and the tools involved in the construction or repair of houses, buildings, or other structures such as highways and roads.
Food Production	Knowledge of techniques and equipment for planting, growing, and harvesting food products (both plant and animal) for consumption, including storage/handling techniques.

Skills	Skills Definitions
Science	Using scientific rules and methods to solve problems.
Speaking	Talking to others to convey information effectively.
Quality Control Analysis	Conducting tests and inspections of products, services, or processes to evaluate quality or performance.
Reading Comprehension	Understanding written sentences and paragraphs in work related documents.
Critical Thinking	Using logic and reasoning to identify the strengths and weaknesses of alternative solutions, conclusions or approaches to problems.
Active Listening	Giving full attention to what other people are saying, taking time to understand the points being made, asking questions as appropriate, and not interrupting at inappropriate times.
Writing	Communicating effectively in writing as appropriate for the needs of the audience.
Active Learning	Understanding the implications of new information for both current and future problem-solving and decision-making.
Equipment Selection	Determining the kind of tools and equipment needed to do a job.
Coordination	Adjusting actions in relation to others' actions.
Monitoring	Monitoring/Assessing performance of yourself, other individuals, or organizations to make improvements or take corrective action.
Troubleshooting	Determining causes of operating errors and deciding what to do about it.
Learning Strategies	Selecting and using training/instructional methods and procedures appropriate for the situation when learning or teaching new things.
Time Management	Managing one's own time and the time of others.
Equipment Maintenance	Performing routine maintenance on equipment and determining when and what kind of maintenance is needed.
Mathematics	Using mathematics to solve problems.
Instructing	Teaching others how to do something.
Judgment and Decision Making	Considering the relative costs and benefits of potential actions to choose the most appropriate one.
Complex Problem Solving	Identifying complex problems and reviewing related information to develop and evaluate options and implement solutions.
Persuasion	Persuading others to change their minds or behavior.
Operation and Control	Controlling operations of equipment or systems.
Operation Monitoring	Watching gauges, dials, or other indicators to make sure a machine is working properly.
Systems Analysis	Determining how a system should work and how changes in conditions, operations, and the environment will affect outcomes.
Social Perceptiveness	Being aware of others' reactions and understanding why they react as they do.
Management of Financial Resources	Determining how money will be spent to get the work done, and accounting for these expenditures.
Service Orientation	Actively looking for ways to help people.
Operations Analysis	Analyzing needs and product requirements to create a design.
Negotiation	Bringing others together and trying to reconcile differences.
Repairing	Repairing machines or systems using the needed tools.
Management of Material Resources	Obtaining and seeing to the appropriate use of equipment, facilities, and materials needed to do certain work.
Systems Evaluation	Identifying measures or indicators of system performance and the actions needed to improve or correct performance, relative to the goals of the system.
Management of Personnel Resources	Motivating, developing, and directing people as they work, identifying the best people for the job.
Technology Design	Generating or adapting equipment and technology to serve user needs.

| Installation | Installing equipment, machines, wiring, or programs to meet specifications. |
| Programming | Writing computer programs for various purposes. |

Ability	Ability Definitions
Inductive Reasoning	The ability to combine pieces of information to form general rules or conclusions (includes finding a relationship among seemingly unrelated events).
Oral Expression	The ability to communicate information and ideas in speaking so others will understand.
Near Vision	The ability to see details at close range (within a few feet of the observer).
Speech Clarity	The ability to speak clearly so others can understand you.
Oral Comprehension	The ability to listen to and understand information and ideas presented through spoken words and sentences.
Deductive Reasoning	The ability to apply general rules to specific problems to produce answers that make sense.
Information Ordering	The ability to arrange things or actions in a certain order or pattern according to a specific rule or set of rules (e.g., patterns of numbers, letters, words, pictures, mathematical operations).
Written Expression	The ability to communicate information and ideas in writing so others will understand.
Problem Sensitivity	The ability to tell when something is wrong or is likely to go wrong. It does not involve solving the problem, only recognizing there is a problem.
Category Flexibility	The ability to generate or use different sets of rules for combining or grouping things in different ways.
Speech Recognition	The ability to identify and understand the speech of another person.
Flexibility of Closure	The ability to identify or detect a known pattern (a figure, object, word, or sound) that is hidden in other distracting material.
Visualization	The ability to imagine how something will look after it is moved around or when its parts are moved or rearranged.
Written Comprehension	The ability to read and understand information and ideas presented in writing.
Fluency of Ideas	The ability to come up with a number of ideas about a topic (the number of ideas is important, not their quality, correctness, or creativity).
Mathematical Reasoning	The ability to choose the right mathematical methods or formulas to solve a problem.
Finger Dexterity	The ability to make precisely coordinated movements of the fingers of one or both hands to grasp, manipulate, or assemble very small objects.
Arm-Hand Steadiness	The ability to keep your hand and arm steady while moving your arm or while holding your arm and hand in one position.
Depth Perception	The ability to judge which of several objects is closer or farther away from you, or to judge the distance between you and an object.
Selective Attention	The ability to concentrate on a task over a period of time without being distracted.
Time Sharing	The ability to shift back and forth between two or more activities or sources of information (such as speech, sounds, touch, or other sources).
Originality	The ability to come up with unusual or clever ideas about a given topic or situation, or to develop creative ways to solve a problem.
Visual Color Discrimination	The ability to match or detect differences between colors, including shades of color and brightness.
Control Precision	The ability to quickly and repeatedly adjust the controls of a machine or a vehicle to exact positions.
Perceptual Speed	The ability to quickly and accurately compare similarities and differences among sets of letters, numbers, objects, pictures, or patterns. The things to be compared may be presented at the same time or one after the other. This ability also includes comparing a presented object with a remembered object.
Multilimb Coordination	The ability to coordinate two or more limbs (for example, two arms, two legs, or one leg and one arm) while sitting, standing, or lying down. It does not involve performing the activities while the whole body is in motion.
Memorization	The ability to remember information such as words, numbers, pictures, and procedures.
Spatial Orientation	The ability to know your location in relation to the environment or to know where other objects are in relation to you.
Speed of Closure	The ability to quickly make sense of, combine, and organize information into meaningful patterns.
Far Vision	The ability to see details at a distance.

Manual Dexterity	The ability to quickly move your hand, your hand together with your arm, or your two hands to grasp, manipulate, or assemble objects.
Extent Flexibility	The ability to bend, stretch, twist, or reach with your body, arms, and/or legs.
Trunk Strength	The ability to use your abdominal and lower back muscles to support part of the body repeatedly or continuously over time without 'giving out' or fatiguing.
Hearing Sensitivity	The ability to detect or tell the differences between sounds that vary in pitch and loudness.
Reaction Time	The ability to quickly respond (with the hand, finger, or foot) to a signal (sound, light, picture) when it appears.
Auditory Attention	The ability to focus on a single source of sound in the presence of other distracting sounds.
Peripheral Vision	The ability to see objects or movement of objects to one's side when the eyes are looking ahead.
Number Facility	The ability to add, subtract, multiply, or divide quickly and correctly.
Glare Sensitivity	The ability to see objects in the presence of glare or bright lighting.
Static Strength	The ability to exert maximum muscle force to lift, push, pull, or carry objects.
Response Orientation	The ability to choose quickly between two or more movements in response to two or more different signals (lights, sounds, pictures). It includes the speed with which the correct response is started with the hand, foot, or other body part.
Speed of Limb Movement	The ability to quickly move the arms and legs.
Night Vision	The ability to see under low light conditions.
Gross Body Coordination	The ability to coordinate the movement of your arms, legs, and torso together when the whole body is in motion.
Sound Localization	The ability to tell the direction from which a sound originated.
Wrist-Finger Speed	The ability to make fast, simple, repeated movements of the fingers, hands, and wrists.
Rate Control	The ability to time your movements or the movement of a piece of equipment in anticipation of changes in the speed and/or direction of a moving object or scene.
Dynamic Flexibility	The ability to quickly and repeatedly bend, stretch, twist, or reach out with your body, arms, and/or legs.
Stamina	The ability to exert yourself physically over long periods of time without getting winded or out of breath.
Dynamic Strength	The ability to exert muscle force repeatedly or continuously over time. This involves muscular endurance and resistance to muscle fatigue.
Explosive Strength	The ability to use short bursts of muscle force to propel oneself (as in jumping or sprinting), or to throw an object.
Gross Body Equilibrium	The ability to keep or regain your body balance or stay upright when in an unstable position.

Work_Activity	Work_Activity Definitions
Identifying Objects, Actions, and Events	Identifying information by categorizing, estimating, recognizing differences or similarities, and detecting changes in circumstances or events.
Documenting/Recording Information	Entering, transcribing, recording, storing, or maintaining information in written or electronic/magnetic form.
Updating and Using Relevant Knowledge	Keeping up-to-date technically and applying new knowledge to your job.
Getting Information	Observing, receiving, and otherwise obtaining information from all relevant sources.
Interacting With Computers	Using computers and computer systems (including hardware and software) to program, write software, set up functions, enter data, or process information.
Making Decisions and Solving Problems	Analyzing information and evaluating results to choose the best solution and solve problems.
Communicating with Persons Outside Organization	Communicating with people outside the organization, representing the organization to customers, the public, government, and other external sources. This information can be exchanged in person, in writing, or by telephone or e-mail.
Interpreting the Meaning of Information for Others	Translating or explaining what information means and how it can be used.
Scheduling Work and Activities	Scheduling events, programs, and activities, as well as the work of others.
Evaluating Information to Determine Compliance wit	Using relevant information and individual judgment to determine whether events or processes comply with laws, regulations, or standards.
Organizing, Planning, and Prioritizing Work	Developing specific goals and plans to prioritize, organize, and accomplish your work.

Estimating the Quantifiable Characteristics of Pro	Estimating sizes, distances, and quantities; or determining time, costs, resources, or materials needed to perform a work activity.
Processing Information	Compiling, coding, categorizing, calculating, tabulating, auditing, or verifying information or data.
Monitor Processes, Materials, or Surroundings	Monitoring and reviewing information from materials, events, or the environment, to detect or assess problems.
Analyzing Data or Information	Identifying the underlying principles, reasons, or facts of information by breaking down information or data into separate parts.
Communicating with Supervisors, Peers, or Subordin	Providing information to supervisors, co-workers, and subordinates by telephone, in written form, e-mail, or in person.
Establishing and Maintaining Interpersonal Relatio	Developing constructive and cooperative working relationships with others, and maintaining them over time.
Performing Administrative Activities	Performing day-to-day administrative tasks such as maintaining information files and processing paperwork.
Judging the Qualities of Things, Services, or Peop	Assessing the value, importance, or quality of things or people.
Controlling Machines and Processes	Using either control mechanisms or direct physical activity to operate machines or processes (not including computers or vehicles).
Thinking Creatively	Developing, designing, or creating new applications, ideas, relationships, systems, or products, including artistic contributions.
Inspecting Equipment, Structures, or Material	Inspecting equipment, structures, or materials to identify the cause of errors or other problems or defects.
Coordinating the Work and Activities of Others	Getting members of a group to work together to accomplish tasks.
Performing for or Working Directly with the Public	Performing for people or dealing directly with the public. This includes serving customers in restaurants and stores, and receiving clients or guests.
Operating Vehicles, Mechanized Devices, or Equipme	Running, maneuvering, navigating, or driving vehicles or mechanized equipment, such as forklifts, passenger vehicles, aircraft, or water craft.
Developing Objectives and Strategies	Establishing long-range objectives and specifying the strategies and actions to achieve them.
Repairing and Maintaining Mechanical Equipment	Servicing, repairing, adjusting, and testing machines, devices, moving parts, and equipment that operate primarily on the basis of mechanical (not electronic) principles.
Repairing and Maintaining Electronic Equipment	Servicing, repairing, calibrating, regulating, fine-tuning, or testing machines, devices, and equipment that operate primarily on the basis of electrical or electronic (not mechanical) principles.
Performing General Physical Activities	Performing physical activities that require considerable use of your arms and legs and moving your whole body, such as climbing, lifting, balancing, walking, stooping, and handling of materials.
Handling and Moving Objects	Using hands and arms in handling, installing, positioning, and moving materials, and manipulating things.
Provide Consultation and Advice to Others	Providing guidance and expert advice to management or other groups on technical, systems-, or process-related topics.
Drafting, Laying Out, and Specifying Technical Dev	Providing documentation, detailed instructions, drawings, or specifications to tell others about how devices, parts, equipment, or structures are to be fabricated, constructed, assembled, modified, maintained, or used.
Monitoring and Controlling Resources	Monitoring and controlling resources and overseeing the spending of money.
Guiding, Directing, and Motivating Subordinates	Providing guidance and direction to subordinates, including setting performance standards and monitoring performance.
Assisting and Caring for Others	Providing personal assistance, medical attention, emotional support, or other personal care to others such as coworkers, customers, or patients.
Resolving Conflicts and Negotiating with Others	Handling complaints, settling disputes, and resolving grievances and conflicts, or otherwise negotiating with others.
Training and Teaching Others	Identifying the educational needs of others, developing formal educational or training programs or classes, and teaching or instructing others.
Developing and Building Teams	Encouraging and building mutual trust, respect, and cooperation among team members.
Coaching and Developing Others	Identifying the developmental needs of others and coaching, mentoring, or otherwise helping others to improve their knowledge or skills.
Selling or Influencing Others	Convincing others to buy merchandise/goods or to otherwise change their minds or actions.

| Staffing Organizational Units | Recruiting, interviewing, selecting, hiring, and promoting employees in an organization. |

Work_Context	**Work_Context Definitions**
Importance of Being Exact or Accurate	How important is being very exact or highly accurate in performing this job?
Indoors, Environmentally Controlled	How often does this job require working indoors in environmentally controlled conditions?
Face-to-Face Discussions	How often do you have to have face-to-face discussions with individuals or teams in this job?
Telephone	How often do you have telephone conversations in this job?
Contact With Others	How much does this job require the worker to be in contact with others (face-to-face, by telephone, or otherwise) in order to perform it?
Frequency of Decision Making	How frequently is the worker required to make decisions that affect other people, the financial resources, and/or the image and reputation of the organization?
Freedom to Make Decisions	How much decision making freedom, without supervision, does the job offer?
Electronic Mail	How often do you use electronic mail in this job?
Work With Work Group or Team	How important is it to work with others in a group or team in this job?
Deal With External Customers	How important is it to work with external customers or the public in this job?
Impact of Decisions on Co-workers or Company Resul	How do the decisions an employee makes impact the results of co-workers, clients or the company?
Wear Common Protective or Safety Equipment such as	How much does this job require wearing common protective or safety equipment such as safety shoes, glasses, gloves, hard hats or live jackets?
Exposed to Contaminants	How often does this job require working exposed to contaminants (such as pollutants, gases, dust or odors)?
Structured versus Unstructured Work	To what extent is this job structured for the worker, rather than allowing the worker to determine tasks, priorities, and goals?
In an Enclosed Vehicle or Equipment	How often does this job require working in a closed vehicle or equipment (e.g., car)?
Letters and Memos	How often does the job require written letters and memos?
Spend Time Sitting	How much does this job require sitting?
Exposed to Hazardous Conditions	How often does this job require exposure to hazardous conditions?
Time Pressure	How often does this job require the worker to meet strict deadlines?
Coordinate or Lead Others	How important is it to coordinate or lead others in accomplishing work activities in this job?
Physical Proximity	To what extent does this job require the worker to perform job tasks in close physical proximity to other people?
Exposed to Disease or Infections	How often does this job require exposure to disease/infections?
Consequence of Error	How serious would the result usually be if the worker made a mistake that was not readily correctable?
Level of Competition	To what extent does this job require the worker to compete or to be aware of competitive pressures?
Cramped Work Space, Awkward Positions	How often does this job require working in cramped work spaces that requires getting into awkward positions?
Outdoors, Exposed to Weather	How often does this job require working outdoors, exposed to all weather conditions?
Indoors, Not Environmentally Controlled	How often does this job require working indoors in non-controlled environmental conditions (e.g., warehouse without heat)?
Spend Time Using Your Hands to Handle, Control, or	How much does this job require using your hands to handle, control, or feel objects, tools or controls?
Frequency of Conflict Situations	How often are there conflict situations the employee has to face in this job?
Importance of Repeating Same Tasks	How important is repeating the same physical activities (e.g., key entry) or mental activities (e.g., checking entries in a ledger) over and over, without stopping, to performing this job?
Deal With Unpleasant or Angry People	How frequently does the worker have to deal with unpleasant, angry, or discourteous individuals as part of the job requirements?
Responsible for Others' Health and Safety	How much responsibility is there for the health and safety of others in this job?
Public Speaking	How often do you have to perform public speaking in this job?
Responsibility for Outcomes and Results	How responsible is the worker for work outcomes and results of other workers?
Spend Time Standing	How much does this job require standing?

Spend Time Making Repetitive Motions	How much does this job require making repetitive motions?
Sounds, Noise Levels Are Distracting or Uncomforta	How often does this job require working exposed to sounds and noise levels that are distracting or uncomfortable?
Exposed to Minor Burns, Cuts, Bites, or Stings	How often does this job require exposure to minor burns, cuts, bites, or stings?
Very Hot or Cold Temperatures	How often does this job require working in very hot (above 90 F degrees) or very cold (below 32 F degrees) temperatures?
Degree of Automation	How automated is the job?
Extremely Bright or Inadequate Lighting	How often does this job require working in extremely bright or inadequate lighting conditions?
Spend Time Kneeling, Crouching, Stooping, or Crawl	How much does this job require kneeling, crouching, stooping or crawling?
Exposed to Hazardous Equipment	How often does this job require exposure to hazardous equipment?
Outdoors, Under Cover	How often does this job require working outdoors, under cover (e.g., structure with roof but no walls)?
Spend Time Bending or Twisting the Body	How much does this job require bending or twisting your body?
Spend Time Walking and Running	How much does this job require walking and running?
Wear Specialized Protective or Safety Equipment su	How much does this job require wearing specialized protective or safety equipment such as breathing apparatus, safety harness, full protection suits, or radiation protection?
Exposed to High Places	How often does this job require exposure to high places?
Pace Determined by Speed of Equipment	How important is it to this job that the pace is determined by the speed of equipment or machinery? (This does not refer to keeping busy at all times on this job.)
Spend Time Climbing Ladders, Scaffolds, or Poles	How much does this job require climbing ladders, scaffolds, or poles?
Spend Time Keeping or Regaining Balance	How much does this job require keeping or regaining your balance?
Deal With Physically Aggressive People	How frequently does this job require the worker to deal with physical aggression of violent individuals?
In an Open Vehicle or Equipment	How often does this job require working in an open vehicle or equipment (e.g., tractor)?
Exposed to Radiation	How often does this job require exposure to radiation?
Exposed to Whole Body Vibration	How often does this job require exposure to whole body vibration (e.g., operate a jackhammer)?

Job Zone Component	**Job Zone Component Definitions**
Title	Job Zone Four: Considerable Preparation Needed
Overall Experience	A minimum of two to four years of work-related skill, knowledge, or experience is needed for these occupations. For example, an accountant must complete four years of college and work for several years in accounting to be considered qualified.
Job Training	Employees in these occupations usually need several years of work-related experience, on-the-job training, and/or vocational training.
Job Zone Examples	Many of these occupations involve coordinating, supervising, managing, or training others. Examples include accountants, chefs and head cooks, computer programmers, historians, pharmacists, and police detectives.
SVP Range	(7.0 to < 8.0)
Education	Most of these occupations require a four - year bachelor's degree, but some do not.

Work_Styles	**Work_Styles Definitions**
Integrity	Job requires being honest and ethical.
Attention to Detail	Job requires being careful about detail and thorough in completing work tasks.
Stress Tolerance	Job requires accepting criticism and dealing calmly and effectively with high stress situations.
Dependability	Job requires being reliable, responsible, and dependable, and fulfilling obligations.
Cooperation	Job requires being pleasant with others on the job and displaying a good-natured, cooperative attitude.
Self Control	Job requires maintaining composure, keeping emotions in check, controlling anger, and avoiding aggressive behavior, even in very difficult situations.
Adaptability/Flexibility	Job requires being open to change (positive or negative) and to considerable variety in the workplace.

Initiative	Job requires a willingness to take on responsibilities and challenges.
Analytical Thinking	Job requires analyzing information and using logic to address work-related issues and problems.
Persistence	Job requires persistence in the face of obstacles.
Achievement/Effort	Job requires establishing and maintaining personally challenging achievement goals and exerting effort toward mastering tasks.
Leadership	Job requires a willingness to lead, take charge, and offer opinions and direction.
Independence	Job requires developing one's own ways of doing things, guiding oneself with little or no supervision, and depending on oneself to get things done.
Concern for Others	Job requires being sensitive to others' needs and feelings and being understanding and helpful on the job.
Innovation	Job requires creativity and alternative thinking to develop new ideas for and answers to work-related problems.
Social Orientation	Job requires preferring to work with others rather than alone, and being personally connected with others on the job.

21-1013.00 - Marriage and Family Therapists

Diagnose and treat mental and emotional disorders, whether cognitive, affective, or behavioral, within the context of marriage and family systems. Apply psychotherapeutic and family systems theories and techniques in the delivery of professional services to individuals, couples, and families for the purpose of treating such diagnosed nervous and mental disorders.

Tasks

1) Confer with other counselors in order to analyze individual cases and to coordinate counseling services.

2) Follow up on results of counseling programs and clients' adjustments in order to determine effectiveness of programs.

3) Determine whether clients should be counseled or referred to other specialists in such fields as medicine, psychiatry and legal aid.

4) Supervise other counselors, social service staff and assistants.

5) Provide instructions to clients on how to obtain help with legal, financial, and other personal issues.

6) Ask questions that will help clients identify their feelings and behaviors.

7) Confer with clients in order to develop plans for post-treatment activities.

8) Contact doctors, schools, social workers, juvenile counselors, law enforcement personnel and others to gather information in order to make recommendations to courts for the resolution of child custody or visitation disputes.

9) Maintain case files that include activities, progress notes, evaluations, and recommendations.

10) Encourage individuals and family members to develop and use skills and strategies for confronting their problems in a constructive manner.

11) Provide family counseling and treatment services to inmates participating in substance abuse programs.

12) Counsel clients on concerns such as unsatisfactory relationships, divorce and separation, child rearing, home management, and financial difficulties.

13) Provide public education and consultation to other professionals or groups regarding counseling services, issues and methods.

14) Write evaluations of parents and children for use by courts deciding divorce and custody cases, testifying in court if necessary.

15) Develop and implement individualized treatment plans addressing family relationship problems.

21-1014.00 - Mental Health Counselors

Counsel with emphasis on prevention. Work with individuals and groups to promote optimum mental health. May help individuals deal with addictions and substance abuse; family, parenting, and marital problems; suicide; stress management; problems with self-esteem; and issues associated with aging and mental and emotional health.

Tasks

1) Act as client advocates in order to coordinate required services or to resolve emergency problems in crisis situations.

2) Learn about new developments in their field by reading professional literature, attending courses and seminars, and establishing and maintaining contact with other social service agencies.

3) Maintain confidentiality of records relating to clients' treatment.

4) Encourage clients to express their feelings and discuss what is happening in their lives, and help them to develop insight into themselves and their relationships.

5) Counsel family members to assist them in understanding, dealing with, and supporting clients or patients.

6) Prepare and maintain all required treatment records and reports.

7) Collect information about clients through interviews, observation, and tests.

8) Refer patients, clients, or family members to community resources or to specialists as necessary.

9) Discuss with individual patients their plans for life after leaving therapy.

10) Modify treatment activities and approaches as needed in order to comply with changes in clients' status.

11) Evaluate clients' physical or mental condition based on review of client information.

12) Develop and implement treatment plans based on clinical experience and knowledge.

13) Collaborate with other staff members to perform clinical assessments and develop treatment plans.

14) Meet with families, probation officers, police, and other interested parties in order to exchange necessary information during the treatment process.

15) Gather information about community mental health needs and resources that could be used in conjunction with therapy.

16) Plan, organize and lead structured programs of counseling, work, study, recreation and social activities for clients.

17) Evaluate the effectiveness of counseling programs and clients' progress in resolving identified problems and moving towards defined objectives.

18) Counsel clients and patients, individually and in group sessions, to assist in overcoming dependencies, adjusting to life, and making changes.

19) Monitor clients' use of medications.

20) Supervise other counselors, social service staff, and assistants.

21) Plan and conduct programs to prevent substance abuse or improve community health and counseling services.

22) Run workshops and courses about mental health issues.

Knowledge	Knowledge Definitions
Psychology	Knowledge of human behavior and performance; individual differences in ability, personality, and interests; learning and motivation; psychological research methods; and the assessment and treatment of behavioral and affective disorders.
Therapy and Counseling	Knowledge of principles, methods, and procedures for diagnosis, treatment, and rehabilitation of physical and mental dysfunctions, and for career counseling and guidance.
English Language	Knowledge of the structure and content of the English language including the meaning and spelling of words, rules of composition, and grammar.
Education and Training	Knowledge of principles and methods for curriculum and training design, teaching and instruction for individuals and groups, and the measurement of training effects.
Sociology and Anthropology	Knowledge of group behavior and dynamics, societal trends and influences, human migrations, ethnicity, cultures and their history and origins.
Customer and Personal Service	Knowledge of principles and processes for providing customer and personal services. This includes customer needs assessment, meeting quality standards for services, and evaluation of customer satisfaction.
Administration and Management	Knowledge of business and management principles involved in strategic planning, resource allocation, human resources modeling, leadership technique, production methods, and coordination of people and resources.
Clerical	Knowledge of administrative and clerical procedures and systems such as word processing, managing files and records, stenography and transcription, designing forms, and other office procedures and terminology.

Law and Government	Knowledge of laws, legal codes, court procedures, precedents, government regulations, executive orders, agency rules, and the democratic political process.
Public Safety and Security	Knowledge of relevant equipment, policies, procedures, and strategies to promote effective local, state, or national security operations for the protection of people, data, property, and institutions.
Medicine and Dentistry	Knowledge of the information and techniques needed to diagnose and treat human injuries, diseases, and deformities. This includes symptoms, treatment alternatives, drug properties and interactions, and preventive health-care measures.
Philosophy and Theology	Knowledge of different philosophical systems and religions. This includes their basic principles, values, ethics, ways of thinking, customs, practices, and their impact on human culture.
Computers and Electronics	Knowledge of circuit boards, processors, chips, electronic equipment, and computer hardware and software, including applications and programming.
Mathematics	Knowledge of arithmetic, algebra, geometry, calculus, statistics, and their applications.
Personnel and Human Resources	Knowledge of principles and procedures for personnel recruitment, selection, training, compensation and benefits, labor relations and negotiation, and personnel information systems.
Communications and Media	Knowledge of media production, communication, and dissemination techniques and methods. This includes alternative ways to inform and entertain via written, oral, and visual media.
Transportation	Knowledge of principles and methods for moving people or goods by air, rail, sea, or road, including the relative costs and benefits.
Telecommunications	Knowledge of transmission, broadcasting, switching, control, and operation of telecommunications systems.
Geography	Knowledge of principles and methods for describing the features of land, sea, and air masses, including their physical characteristics, locations, interrelationships, and distribution of plant, animal, and human life.
Biology	Knowledge of plant and animal organisms, their tissues, cells, functions, interdependencies, and interactions with each other and the environment.
Economics and Accounting	Knowledge of economic and accounting principles and practices, the financial markets, banking and the analysis and reporting of financial data.
History and Archeology	Knowledge of historical events and their causes, indicators, and effects on civilizations and cultures.
Production and Processing	Knowledge of raw materials, production processes, quality control, costs, and other techniques for maximizing the effective manufacture and distribution of goods.
Foreign Language	Knowledge of the structure and content of a foreign (non-English) language including the meaning and spelling of words, rules of composition and grammar, and pronunciation.
Chemistry	Knowledge of the chemical composition, structure, and properties of substances and of the chemical processes and transformations that they undergo. This includes uses of chemicals and their interactions, danger signs, production techniques, and disposal methods.
Sales and Marketing	Knowledge of principles and methods for showing, promoting, and selling products or services. This includes marketing strategy and tactics, product demonstration, sales techniques, and sales control systems.
Fine Arts	Knowledge of the theory and techniques required to compose, produce, and perform works of music, dance, visual arts, drama, and sculpture.
Design	Knowledge of design techniques, tools, and principles involved in production of precision technical plans, blueprints, drawings, and models.
Mechanical	Knowledge of machines and tools, including their designs, uses, repair, and maintenance.
Food Production	Knowledge of techniques and equipment for planting, growing, and harvesting food products (both plant and animal) for consumption, including storage/handling techniques.
Engineering and Technology	Knowledge of the practical application of engineering science and technology. This includes applying principles, techniques, procedures, and equipment to the design and production of various goods and services.
Physics	Knowledge and prediction of physical principles, laws, their interrelationships, and applications to understanding fluid, material, and atmospheric dynamics, and mechanical, electrical, atomic and sub- atomic structures and processes.
Building and Construction	Knowledge of materials, methods, and the tools involved in the construction or repair of houses, buildings, or other structures such as highways and roads.

Skills	Skills Definitions
Active Listening	Giving full attention to what other people are saying, taking time to understand the points being made, asking questions as appropriate, and not interrupting at inappropriate times.
Social Perceptiveness	Being aware of others' reactions and understanding why they react as they do.
Critical Thinking	Using logic and reasoning to identify the strengths and weaknesses of alternative solutions, conclusions or approaches to problems.
Service Orientation	Actively looking for ways to help people.
Active Learning	Understanding the implications of new information for both current and future problem-solving and decision-making.
Learning Strategies	Selecting and using training/instructional methods and procedures appropriate for the situation when learning or teaching new things.
Speaking	Talking to others to convey information effectively.
Time Management	Managing one's own time and the time of others.
Reading Comprehension	Understanding written sentences and paragraphs in work related documents.
Monitoring	Monitoring/Assessing performance of yourself, other individuals, or organizations to make improvements or take corrective action.
Negotiation	Bringing others together and trying to reconcile differences.
Writing	Communicating effectively in writing as appropriate for the needs of the audience.
Coordination	Adjusting actions in relation to others' actions.
Complex Problem Solving	Identifying complex problems and reviewing related information to develop and evaluate options and implement solutions.
Instructing	Teaching others how to do something.
Judgment and Decision Making	Considering the relative costs and benefits of potential actions to choose the most appropriate one.
Persuasion	Persuading others to change their minds or behavior.
Systems Analysis	Determining how a system should work and how changes in conditions, operations, and the environment will affect outcomes.
Systems Evaluation	Identifying measures or indicators of system performance and the actions needed to improve or correct performance, relative to the goals of the system.
Management of Personnel Resources	Motivating, developing, and directing people as they work, identifying the best people for the job.
Mathematics	Using mathematics to solve problems.
Operations Analysis	Analyzing needs and product requirements to create a design.
Management of Financial Resources	Determining how money will be spent to get the work done, and accounting for these expenditures.
Equipment Selection	Determining the kind of tools and equipment needed to do a job.
Science	Using scientific rules and methods to solve problems.
Troubleshooting	Determining causes of operating errors and deciding what to do about it.
Technology Design	Generating or adapting equipment and technology to serve user needs.
Management of Material Resources	Obtaining and seeing to the appropriate use of equipment, facilities, and materials needed to do certain work.
Quality Control Analysis	Conducting tests and inspections of products, services, or processes to evaluate quality or performance.
Installation	Installing equipment, machines, wiring, or programs to meet specifications.
Operation and Control	Controlling operations of equipment or systems.
Equipment Maintenance	Performing routine maintenance on equipment and determining when and what kind of maintenance is needed.
Repairing	Repairing machines or systems using the needed tools.
Operation Monitoring	Watching gauges, dials, or other indicators to make sure a machine is working properly.
Programming	Writing computer programs for various purposes.

Ability	Ability Definitions

Oral Expression	The ability to communicate information and ideas in speaking so others will understand.
Oral Comprehension	The ability to listen to and understand information and ideas presented through spoken words and sentences.
Problem Sensitivity	The ability to tell when something is wrong or is likely to go wrong. It does not involve solving the problem, only recognizing there is a problem.
Speech Clarity	The ability to speak clearly so others can understand you.
Inductive Reasoning	The ability to combine pieces of information to form general rules or conclusions (includes finding a relationship among seemingly unrelated events).
Written Comprehension	The ability to read and understand information and ideas presented in writing.
Deductive Reasoning	The ability to apply general rules to specific problems to produce answers that make sense.
Written Expression	The ability to communicate information and ideas in writing so others will understand.
Speech Recognition	The ability to identify and understand the speech of another person.
Near Vision	The ability to see details at close range (within a few feet of the observer).
Selective Attention	The ability to concentrate on a task over a period of time without being distracted.
Information Ordering	The ability to arrange things or actions in a certain order or pattern according to a specific rule or set of rules (e.g., patterns of numbers, letters, words, pictures, mathematical operations).
Originality	The ability to come up with unusual or clever ideas about a given topic or situation, or to develop creative ways to solve a problem.
Category Flexibility	The ability to generate or use different sets of rules for combining or grouping things in different ways.
Fluency of Ideas	The ability to come up with a number of ideas about a topic (the number of ideas is important, not their quality, correctness, or creativity).
Time Sharing	The ability to shift back and forth between two or more activities or sources of information (such as speech, sounds, touch, or other sources).
Memorization	The ability to remember information such as words, numbers, pictures, and procedures.
Speed of Closure	The ability to quickly make sense of, combine, and organize information into meaningful patterns.
Flexibility of Closure	The ability to identify or detect a known pattern (a figure, object, word, or sound) that is hidden in other distracting material.
Visualization	The ability to imagine how something will look after it is moved around or when its parts are moved or rearranged.
Perceptual Speed	The ability to quickly and accurately compare similarities and differences among sets of letters, numbers, objects, pictures, or patterns. The things to be compared may be presented at the same time or one after the other. This ability also includes comparing a presented object with a remembered object.
Auditory Attention	The ability to focus on a single source of sound in the presence of other distracting sounds.
Far Vision	The ability to see details at a distance.
Static Strength	The ability to exert maximum muscle force to lift, push, pull, or carry objects.
Reaction Time	The ability to quickly respond (with the hand, finger, or foot) to a signal (sound, light, picture) when it appears.
Mathematical Reasoning	The ability to choose the right mathematical methods or formulas to solve a problem.
Number Facility	The ability to add, subtract, multiply, or divide quickly and correctly.
Finger Dexterity	The ability to make precisely coordinated movements of the fingers of one or both hands to grasp, manipulate, or assemble very small objects.
Stamina	The ability to exert yourself physically over long periods of time without getting winded or out of breath.
Gross Body Equilibrium	The ability to keep or regain your body balance or stay upright when in an unstable position.
Gross Body Coordination	The ability to coordinate the movement of your arms, legs, and torso together when the whole body is in motion.
Hearing Sensitivity	The ability to detect or tell the differences between sounds that vary in pitch and loudness.
Response Orientation	The ability to choose quickly between two or more movements in response to two or more different signals (lights, sounds, pictures). It includes the speed with which the correct response is started with the hand, foot, or other body part.

Explosive Strength	The ability to use short bursts of muscle force to propel oneself (as in jumping or sprinting), or to throw an object.
Visual Color Discrimination	The ability to match or detect differences between colors, including shades of color and brightness.
Trunk Strength	The ability to use your abdominal and lower back muscles to support part of the body repeatedly or continuously over time without 'giving out' or fatiguing.
Spatial Orientation	The ability to know your location in relation to the environment or to know where other objects are in relation to you.
Dynamic Flexibility	The ability to quickly and repeatedly bend, stretch, twist, or reach out with your body, arms, and/or legs.
Dynamic Strength	The ability to exert muscle force repeatedly or continuously over time. This involves muscular endurance and resistance to muscle fatigue.
Speed of Limb Movement	The ability to quickly move the arms and legs.
Multilimb Coordination	The ability to coordinate two or more limbs (for example, two arms, two legs, or one leg and one arm) while sitting, standing, or lying down. It does not involve performing the activities while the whole body is in motion.
Rate Control	The ability to time your movements or the movement of a piece of equipment in anticipation of changes in the speed and/or direction of a moving object or scene.
Control Precision	The ability to quickly and repeatedly adjust the controls of a machine or a vehicle to exact positions.
Extent Flexibility	The ability to bend, stretch, twist, or reach with your body, arms, and/or legs.
Glare Sensitivity	The ability to see objects in the presence of glare or bright lighting.
Arm-Hand Steadiness	The ability to keep your hand and arm steady while moving your arm or while holding your arm and hand in one position.
Wrist-Finger Speed	The ability to make fast, simple, repeated movements of the fingers, hands, and wrists.
Night Vision	The ability to see under low light conditions.
Peripheral Vision	The ability to see objects or movement of objects to one's side when the eyes are looking ahead.
Sound Localization	The ability to tell the direction from which a sound originated.
Depth Perception	The ability to judge which of several objects is closer or farther away from you, or to judge the distance between you and an object.
Manual Dexterity	The ability to quickly move your hand, your hand together with your arm, or your two hands to grasp, manipulate, or assemble objects.

Work_Activity	Work_Activity Definitions
Communicating with Supervisors, Peers, or Subordin	Providing information to supervisors, co-workers, and subordinates by telephone, in written form, e-mail, or in person.
Assisting and Caring for Others	Providing personal assistance, medical attention, emotional support, or other personal care to others such as coworkers, customers, or patients.
Resolving Conflicts and Negotiating with Others	Handling complaints, settling disputes, and resolving grievances and conflicts, or otherwise negotiating with others.
Establishing and Maintaining Interpersonal Relatio	Developing constructive and cooperative working relationships with others, and maintaining them over time.
Documenting/Recording Information	Entering, transcribing, recording, storing, or maintaining information in written or electronic/magnetic form.
Identifying Objects, Actions, and Events	Identifying information by categorizing, estimating, recognizing differences or similarities, and detecting changes in circumstances or events.
Getting Information	Observing, receiving, and otherwise obtaining information from all relevant sources.
Interpreting the Meaning of Information for Others	Translating or explaining what information means and how it can be used.
Making Decisions and Solving Problems	Analyzing information and evaluating results to choose the best solution and solve problems.
Organizing, Planning, and Prioritizing Work	Developing specific goals and plans to prioritize, organize, and accomplish your work.
Monitor Processes, Materials, or Surroundings	Monitoring and reviewing information from materials, events, or the environment, to detect or assess problems.
Communicating with Persons Outside Organization	Communicating with people outside the organization, representing the organization to customers, the public, government, and other external sources. This information can be exchanged in person, in writing, or by telephone or e-mail.
Provide Consultation and Advice to Others	Providing guidance and expert advice to management or other groups on technical, systems-, or process-related topics.

Thinking Creatively	Developing, designing, or creating new applications, ideas, relationships, systems, or products, including artistic contributions.
Coaching and Developing Others	Identifying the developmental needs of others and coaching, mentoring, or otherwise helping others to improve their knowledge or skills.
Developing Objectives and Strategies	Establishing long-range objectives and specifying the strategies and actions to achieve them.
Judging the Qualities of Things, Services, or Peop	Assessing the value, importance, or quality of things or people.
Interacting With Computers	Using computers and computer systems (including hardware and software) to program, write software, set up functions, enter data, or process information.
Updating and Using Relevant Knowledge	Keeping up-to-date technically and applying new knowledge to your job.
Developing and Building Teams	Encouraging and building mutual trust, respect, and cooperation among team members.
Performing for or Working Directly with the Public	Performing for people or dealing directly with the public. This includes serving customers in restaurants and stores, and receiving clients or guests.
Training and Teaching Others	Identifying the educational needs of others, developing formal educational or training programs or classes, and teaching or instructing others.
Evaluating Information to Determine Compliance wit	Using relevant information and individual judgment to determine whether events or processes comply with laws, regulations, or standards.
Performing Administrative Activities	Performing day-to-day administrative tasks such as maintaining information files and processing paperwork.
Guiding, Directing, and Motivating Subordinates	Providing guidance and direction to subordinates, including setting performance standards and monitoring performance.
Processing Information	Compiling, coding, categorizing, calculating, tabulating, auditing, or verifying information or data.
Analyzing Data or Information	Identifying the underlying principles, reasons, or facts of information by breaking down information or data into separate parts.
Scheduling Work and Activities	Scheduling events, programs, and activities, as well as the work of others.
Coordinating the Work and Activities of Others	Getting members of a group to work together to accomplish tasks.
Selling or Influencing Others	Convincing others to buy merchandise/goods or to otherwise change their minds or actions.
Estimating the Quantifiable Characteristics of Pro	Estimating sizes, distances, and quantities; or determining time, costs, resources, or materials needed to perform a work activity.
Staffing Organizational Units	Recruiting, interviewing, selecting, hiring, and promoting employees in an organization.
Monitoring and Controlling Resources	Monitoring and controlling resources and overseeing the spending of money.
Performing General Physical Activities	Performing physical activities that require considerable use of your arms and legs and moving your whole body, such as climbing, lifting, balancing, walking, stooping, and handling of materials.
Operating Vehicles, Mechanized Devices, or Equipme	Running, maneuvering, navigating, or driving vehicles or mechanized equipment, such as forklifts, passenger vehicles, aircraft, or water craft.
Inspecting Equipment, Structures, or Material	Inspecting equipment, structures, or materials to identify the cause of errors or other problems or defects.
Handling and Moving Objects	Using hands and arms in handling, installing, positioning, and moving materials, and manipulating things.
Controlling Machines and Processes	Using either control mechanisms or direct physical activity to operate machines or processes (not including computers or vehicles).
Repairing and Maintaining Electronic Equipment	Servicing, repairing, calibrating, regulating, fine-tuning, or testing machines, devices, and equipment that operate primarily on the basis of electrical or electronic (not mechanical) principles.
Drafting, Laying Out, and Specifying Technical Dev	Providing documentation, detailed instructions, drawings, or specifications to tell others about how devices, parts, equipment, or structures are to be fabricated, constructed, assembled, modified, maintained, or used.
Repairing and Maintaining Mechanical Equipment	Servicing, repairing, adjusting, and testing machines, devices, moving parts, and equipment that operate primarily on the basis of mechanical (not electronic) principles.

Work_Context	**Work_Context Definitions**
Telephone	How often do you have telephone conversations in this job?

Face-to-Face Discussions	How often do you have to have face-to-face discussions with individuals or teams in this job?
Contact With Others	How much does this job require the worker to be in contact with others (face-to-face, by telephone, or otherwise) in order to perform it?
Frequency of Decision Making	How frequently is the worker required to make decisions that affect other people, the financial resources, and/or the image and reputation of the organization?
Work With Work Group or Team	How important is it to work with others in a group or team in this job?
Deal With External Customers	How important is it to work with external customers or the public in this job?
Electronic Mail	How often do you use electronic mail in this job?
Frequency of Conflict Situations	How often are there conflict situations the employee has to face in this job?
Letters and Memos	How often does the job require written letters and memos?
Impact of Decisions on Co-workers or Company Resul	How do the decisions an employee makes impact the results of co-workers, clients or the company?
Coordinate or Lead Others	How important is it to coordinate or lead others in accomplishing work activities in this job?
Freedom to Make Decisions	How much decision making freedom, without supervision, does the job offer?
Structured versus Unstructured Work	To what extent is this job structured for the worker, rather than allowing the worker to determine tasks, priorities, and goals?
Deal With Unpleasant or Angry People	How frequently does the worker have to deal with unpleasant, angry, or discourteous individuals as part of the job requirements?
Physical Proximity	To what extent does this job require the worker to perform job tasks in close physical proximity to other people?
Spend Time Sitting	How much does this job require sitting?
Indoors, Environmentally Controlled	How often does this job require working indoors in environmentally controlled conditions?
Deal With Physically Aggressive People	How frequently does this job require the worker to deal with physical aggression of violent individuals?
Sounds, Noise Levels Are Distracting or Uncomforta	How often does this job require working exposed to sounds and noise levels that are distracting or uncomfortable?
Time Pressure	How often does this job require the worker to meet strict deadlines?
Exposed to Disease or Infections	How often does this job require exposure to disease/infections?
Importance of Being Exact or Accurate	How important is being very exact or highly accurate in performing this job?
Consequence of Error	How serious would the result usually be if the worker made a mistake that was not readily correctable?
Responsible for Others' Health and Safety	How much responsibility is there for the health and safety of others in this job?
Public Speaking	How often do you have to perform public speaking in this job?
Indoors, Not Environmentally Controlled	How often does this job require working indoors in non-controlled environmental conditions (e.g., warehouse without heat)?
Responsibility for Outcomes and Results	How responsible is the worker for work outcomes and results of other workers?
Spend Time Standing	How much does this job require standing?
Spend Time Walking and Running	How much does this job require walking and running?
Spend Time Using Your Hands to Handle, Control, or	How much does this job require using your hands to handle, control, or feel objects, tools or controls?
Exposed to Contaminants	How often does this job require working exposed to contaminants (such as pollutants, gases, dust or odors)?
Importance of Repeating Same Tasks	How important is repeating the same physical activities (e.g., key entry) or mental activities (e.g., checking entries in a ledger) over and over, without stopping, to performing this job?
Level of Competition	To what extent does this job require the worker to compete or to be aware of competitive pressures?
In an Enclosed Vehicle or Equipment	How often does this job require working in a closed vehicle or equipment (e.g., car)?
Spend Time Making Repetitive Motions	How much does this job require making repetitive motions?
Very Hot or Cold Temperatures	How often does this job require working in very hot (above 90 F degrees) or very cold (below 32 F degrees) temperatures?
Extremely Bright or Inadequate Lighting	How often does this job require working in extremely bright or inadequate lighting conditions?
Degree of Automation	How automated is the job?
Outdoors, Exposed to Weather	How often does this job require working outdoors, exposed to all weather conditions?

Spend Time Bending or Twisting the Body	How much does this job require bending or twisting your body?
Wear Common Protective or Safety Equipment such as	How much does this job require wearing common protective or safety equipment such as safety shoes, glasses, gloves, hard hats or live jackets?
Spend Time Kneeling, Crouching, Stooping, or Crawl	How much does this job require kneeling, crouching, stooping or crawling?
Outdoors, Under Cover	How often does this job require working outdoors, under cover (e.g., structure with roof but no walls)?
Spend Time Keeping or Regaining Balance	How much does this job require keeping or regaining your balance?
Cramped Work Space, Awkward Positions	How often does this job require working in cramped work spaces that requires getting into awkward positions?
Exposed to Minor Burns, Cuts, Bites, or Stings	How often does this job require exposure to minor burns, cuts, bites, or stings?
In an Open Vehicle or Equipment	How often does this job require working in an open vehicle or equipment (e.g., tractor)?
Exposed to Hazardous Equipment	How often does this job require exposure to hazardous equipment?
Exposed to Whole Body Vibration	How often does this job require exposure to whole body vibration (e.g., operate a jackhammer)?
Exposed to Radiation	How often does this job require exposure to radiation?
Exposed to Hazardous Conditions	How often does this job require exposure to hazardous conditions?
Spend Time Climbing Ladders, Scaffolds, or Poles	How much does this job require climbing ladders, scaffolds, or poles?
Pace Determined by Speed of Equipment	How important is it to this job that the pace is determined by the speed of equipment or machinery? (This does not refer to keeping busy at all times on this job.)
Wear Specialized Protective or Safety Equipment su	How much does this job require wearing specialized protective or safety equipment such as breathing apparatus, safety harness, full protection suits, or radiation protection?
Exposed to High Places	How often does this job require exposure to high places?

Job Zone Component	Job Zone Component Definitions
Title	Job Zone Five: Extensive Preparation Needed
Overall Experience	Extensive skill, knowledge, and experience are needed for these occupations. Many require more than five years of experience. For example, surgeons must complete four years of college and an additional five to seven years of specialized medical training to be able to do their job.
Job Training	Employees may need some on-the-job training, but most of these occupations assume that the person will already have the required skills, knowledge, work-related experience, and/or training.
Job Zone Examples	These occupations often involve coordinating, training, supervising, or managing the activities of others to accomplish goals. Very advanced communication and organizational skills are required. Examples include athletic trainers, lawyers, managing editors, physicists, social psychologists, and surgeons.
SVP Range	(8.0 and above)
Education	A bachelor's degree is the minimum formal education required for these occupations. However, many also require graduate school. For example, they may require a master's degree, and some require a Ph.D., M.D., or J.D. (law degree).

Work_Styles	Work_Styles Definitions
Integrity	Job requires being honest and ethical.
Concern for Others	Job requires being sensitive to others' needs and feelings and being understanding and helpful on the job.
Stress Tolerance	Job requires accepting criticism and dealing calmly and effectively with high stress situations.
Dependability	Job requires being reliable, responsible, and dependable, and fulfilling obligations.
Self Control	Job requires maintaining composure, keeping emotions in check, controlling anger, and avoiding aggressive behavior, even in very difficult situations.
Cooperation	Job requires being pleasant with others on the job and displaying a good-natured, cooperative attitude.
Persistence	Job requires persistence in the face of obstacles.
Initiative	Job requires a willingness to take on responsibilities and challenges.

Attention to Detail	Job requires being careful about detail and thorough in completing work tasks.
Analytical Thinking	Job requires analyzing information and using logic to address work-related issues and problems.
Independence	Job requires developing one's own ways of doing things, guiding oneself with little or no supervision, and depending on oneself to get things done.
Adaptability/Flexibility	Job requires being open to change (positive or negative) and to considerable variety in the workplace.
Social Orientation	Job requires preferring to work with others rather than alone, and being personally connected with others on the job.
Leadership	Job requires a willingness to lead, take charge, and offer opinions and direction.
Achievement/Effort	Job requires establishing and maintaining personally challenging achievement goals and exerting effort toward mastering tasks.
Innovation	Job requires creativity and alternative thinking to develop new ideas for and answers to work-related problems.

21-1015.00 - Rehabilitation Counselors

Counsel individuals to maximize the independence and employability of persons coping with personal, social, and vocational difficulties that result from birth defects, illness, disease, accidents, or the stress of daily life. Coordinate activities for residents of care and treatment facilities. Assess client needs and design and implement rehabilitation programs that may include personal and vocational counseling, training, and job placement.

Tasks

1) Develop rehabilitation plans that fit clients' aptitudes, education levels, physical abilities, and career goals.

2) Maintain close contact with clients during job training and placements, in order to resolve problems and evaluate placement adequacy.

3) Confer with clients to discuss their options and goals so that rehabilitation programs and plans for accessing needed services can be developed.

4) Arrange for on-site job coaching or assistive devices such as specially equipped wheelchairs in order to help clients adapt to work or school environments.

5) Collaborate with community agencies to establish facilities and programs to assist persons with disabilities.

6) Develop diagnostic procedures for determining clients' needs.

7) Participate in job development and placement programs, contacting prospective employers, placing clients in jobs, and evaluating the success of placements.

8) Analyze information from interviews, educational and medical records, consultation with other professionals, and diagnostic evaluations, in order to assess clients' abilities, needs, and eligibility for services.

9) Collaborate with clients' families to implement rehabilitation plans that include behavioral, residential, social, and/or employment goals.

10) Prepare and maintain records and case files, including documentation such as clients' personal and eligibility information, services provided, narratives of client contacts, and relevant correspondence.

11) Develop and maintain relationships with community referral sources such as schools and community groups.

12) Monitor and record clients' progress in order to ensure that goals and objectives are met.

13) Locate barriers to client employment, such as inaccessible work sites, inflexible schedules, and transportation problems, and work with clients to develop strategies for overcoming these barriers.

14) Confer with physicians, psychologists, occupational therapists, and other professionals, in order to develop and implement client rehabilitation programs.

15) Direct case service allocations, authorizing expenditures and payments.

21-1021.00 - Child, Family, and School Social Workers

Provide social services and assistance to improve the social and psychological functioning of children and their families and to maximize the family well-being and the academic functioning of children. May assist single parents, arrange adoptions, and find foster homes for abandoned or abused children. In schools, they address such problems as teenage pregnancy, misbehavior, and truancy. May also advise teachers on how to deal with problem children.

Tasks

1) Develop and review service plans in consultation with clients, and perform follow-ups assessing the quantity and quality of services provided.

2) Refer clients to community resources for services such as job placement, debt counseling, legal aid, housing, medical treatment, or financial assistance, and provide concrete information, such as where to go and how to apply.

3) Counsel individuals, groups, families, or communities regarding issues including mental health, poverty, unemployment, substance abuse, physical abuse, rehabilitation, social adjustment, child care, and/or medical care.

4) Arrange for medical, psychiatric, and other tests that may disclose causes of difficulties and indicate remedial measures.

5) Collect supplementary information needed to assist client, such as employment records, medical records, or school reports.

6) Maintain case history records and prepare reports.

7) Provide, find, or arrange for support services, such as child care, homemaker service, prenatal care, substance abuse treatment, job training, counseling, or parenting classes, to prevent more serious problems from developing.

8) Consult with parents, teachers, and other school personnel to determine causes of problems such as truancy and misbehavior, and to implement solutions.

9) Counsel parents with child rearing problems, interviewing the child and family to determine whether further action is required.

10) Address legal issues, such as child abuse and discipline, assisting with hearings and providing testimony to inform custody arrangements.

11) Counsel students whose behavior, school progress, or mental or physical impairment indicate a need for assistance, diagnosing students' problems and arranging for needed services.

12) Serve as liaisons between students, homes, schools, family services, child guidance clinics, courts, protective services, doctors, and other contacts, to help children who face problems such as disabilities, abuse, or poverty.

13) Serve on policymaking committees, assist in community development, and assist client groups by lobbying for solutions to problems.

14) Lead group counseling sessions that provide support in such areas as grief, stress, or chemical dependency.

15) Place children in foster or adoptive homes, institutions, or medical treatment centers.

16) Determine clients' eligibility for financial assistance.

17) Recommend temporary foster care and advise foster or adoptive parents.

18) Evaluate personal characteristics and home conditions of foster home or adoption applicants.

19) Supervise other social workers.

20) Conduct social research.

21) Work in child and adolescent residential institutions.

22) Administer welfare programs.

Knowledge	Knowledge Definitions
Psychology	Knowledge of human behavior and performance; individual differences in ability, personality, and interests; learning and motivation; psychological research methods; and the assessment and treatment of behavioral and affective disorders.
Therapy and Counseling	Knowledge of principles, methods, and procedures for diagnosis, treatment, and rehabilitation of physical and mental dysfunctions, and for career counseling and guidance.
Customer and Personal Service	Knowledge of principles and processes for providing customer and personal services. This includes customer needs assessment, meeting quality standards for services, and evaluation of customer satisfaction.
Sociology and Anthropology	Knowledge of group behavior and dynamics, societal trends and influences, human migrations, ethnicity, cultures and their history and origins.
English Language	Knowledge of the structure and content of the English language including the meaning and spelling of words, rules of composition, and grammar.
Law and Government	Knowledge of laws, legal codes, court procedures, precedents, government regulations, executive orders, agency rules, and the democratic political process.
Computers and Electronics	Knowledge of circuit boards, processors, chips, electronic equipment, and computer hardware and software, including applications and programming.
Education and Training	Knowledge of principles and methods for curriculum and training design, teaching and instruction for individuals and groups, and the measurement of training effects.
Clerical	Knowledge of administrative and clerical procedures and systems such as word processing, managing files and records, stenography and transcription, designing forms, and other office procedures and terminology.
Public Safety and Security	Knowledge of relevant equipment, policies, procedures, and strategies to promote effective local, state, or national security operations for the protection of people, data, property, and institutions.
Philosophy and Theology	Knowledge of different philosophical systems and religions. This includes their basic principles, values, ethics, ways of thinking, customs, practices, and their impact on human culture.
Communications and Media	Knowledge of media production, communication, and dissemination techniques and methods. This includes alternative ways to inform and entertain via written, oral, and visual media.
Administration and Management	Knowledge of business and management principles involved in strategic planning, resource allocation, human resources modeling, leadership technique, production methods, and coordination of people and resources.
Transportation	Knowledge of principles and methods for moving people or goods by air, rail, sea, or road, including the relative costs and benefits.
Telecommunications	Knowledge of transmission, broadcasting, switching, control, and operation of telecommunications systems.
Personnel and Human Resources	Knowledge of principles and procedures for personnel recruitment, selection, training, compensation and benefits, labor relations and negotiation, and personnel information systems.
Mathematics	Knowledge of arithmetic, algebra, geometry, calculus, statistics, and their applications.
Medicine and Dentistry	Knowledge of the information and techniques needed to diagnose and treat human injuries, diseases, and deformities. This includes symptoms, treatment alternatives, drug properties and interactions, and preventive health-care measures.
Geography	Knowledge of principles and methods for describing the features of land, sea, and air masses, including their physical characteristics, locations, interrelationships, and distribution of plant, animal, and human life.
Foreign Language	Knowledge of the structure and content of a foreign (non-English) language including the meaning and spelling of words, rules of composition and grammar, and pronunciation.
Biology	Knowledge of plant and animal organisms, their tissues, cells, functions, interdependencies, and interactions with each other and the environment.
Economics and Accounting	Knowledge of economic and accounting principles and practices, the financial markets, banking and the analysis and reporting of financial data.
History and Archeology	Knowledge of historical events and their causes, indicators, and effects on civilizations and cultures.
Sales and Marketing	Knowledge of principles and methods for showing, promoting, and selling products or services. This includes marketing strategy and tactics, product demonstration, sales techniques, and sales control systems.
Chemistry	Knowledge of the chemical composition, structure, and properties of substances and of the chemical processes and transformations that they undergo. This includes uses of chemicals and their interactions, danger signs, production techniques, and disposal methods.
Production and Processing	Knowledge of raw materials, production processes, quality control, costs, and other techniques for maximizing the effective manufacture and distribution of goods.
Mechanical	Knowledge of machines and tools, including their designs, uses, repair, and maintenance.
Fine Arts	Knowledge of the theory and techniques required to compose, produce, and perform works of music, dance, visual arts, drama, and sculpture.

Design	Knowledge of design techniques, tools, and principles involved in production of precision technical plans, blueprints, drawings, and models.
Physics	Knowledge and prediction of physical principles, laws, their interrelationships, and applications to understanding fluid, material, and atmospheric dynamics, and mechanical, electrical, atomic and sub- atomic structures and processes.
Building and Construction	Knowledge of materials, methods, and the tools involved in the construction or repair of houses, buildings, or other structures such as highways and roads.
Engineering and Technology	Knowledge of the practical application of engineering science and technology. This includes applying principles, techniques, procedures, and equipment to the design and production of various goods and services.
Food Production	Knowledge of techniques and equipment for planting, growing, and harvesting food products (both plant and animal) for consumption, including storage/handling techniques.

Skills	Skills Definitions
Speaking	Talking to others to convey information effectively.
Active Listening	Giving full attention to what other people are saying, taking time to understand the points being made, asking questions as appropriate, and not interrupting at inappropriate times.
Monitoring	Monitoring/Assessing performance of yourself, other individuals, or organizations to make improvements or take corrective action.
Social Perceptiveness	Being aware of others' reactions and understanding why they react as they do.
Service Orientation	Actively looking for ways to help people.
Reading Comprehension	Understanding written sentences and paragraphs in work related documents.
Active Learning	Understanding the implications of new information for both current and future problem-solving and decision-making.
Writing	Communicating effectively in writing as appropriate for the needs of the audience.
Critical Thinking	Using logic and reasoning to identify the strengths and weaknesses of alternative solutions, conclusions or approaches to problems.
Judgment and Decision Making	Considering the relative costs and benefits of potential actions to choose the most appropriate one.
Coordination	Adjusting actions in relation to others' actions.
Time Management	Managing one's own time and the time of others.
Negotiation	Bringing others together and trying to reconcile differences.
Persuasion	Persuading others to change their minds or behavior.
Learning Strategies	Selecting and using training/instructional methods and procedures appropriate for the situation when learning or teaching new things.
Complex Problem Solving	Identifying complex problems and reviewing related information to develop and evaluate options and implement solutions.
Instructing	Teaching others how to do something.
Management of Personnel Resources	Motivating, developing, and directing people as they work, identifying the best people for the job.
Mathematics	Using mathematics to solve problems.
Systems Evaluation	Identifying measures or indicators of system performance and the actions needed to improve or correct performance, relative to the goals of the system.
Science	Using scientific rules and methods to solve problems.
Operations Analysis	Analyzing needs and product requirements to create a design.
Management of Financial Resources	Determining how money will be spent to get the work done, and accounting for these expenditures.
Systems Analysis	Determining how a system should work and how changes in conditions, operations, and the environment will affect outcomes.
Quality Control Analysis	Conducting tests and inspections of products, services, or processes to evaluate quality or performance.
Troubleshooting	Determining causes of operating errors and deciding what to do about it.
Equipment Selection	Determining the kind of tools and equipment needed to do a job.
Management of Material Resources	Obtaining and seeing to the appropriate use of equipment, facilities, and materials needed to do certain work.
Technology Design	Generating or adapting equipment and technology to serve user needs.
Operation and Control	Controlling operations of equipment or systems.
Repairing	Repairing machines or systems using the needed tools.

Operation Monitoring	Watching gauges, dials, or other indicators to make sure a machine is working properly.
Programming	Writing computer programs for various purposes.
Installation	Installing equipment, machines, wiring, or programs to meet specifications.
Equipment Maintenance	Performing routine maintenance on equipment and determining when and what kind of maintenance is needed.

Ability	Ability Definitions
Oral Comprehension	The ability to listen to and understand information and ideas presented through spoken words and sentences.
Oral Expression	The ability to communicate information and ideas in speaking so others will understand.
Problem Sensitivity	The ability to tell when something is wrong or is likely to go wrong. It does not involve solving the problem, only recognizing there is a problem.
Speech Clarity	The ability to speak clearly so others can understand you.
Speech Recognition	The ability to identify and understand the speech of another person.
Inductive Reasoning	The ability to combine pieces of information to form general rules or conclusions (includes finding a relationship among seemingly unrelated events).
Written Expression	The ability to communicate information and ideas in writing so others will understand.
Written Comprehension	The ability to read and understand information and ideas presented in writing.
Near Vision	The ability to see details at close range (within a few feet of the observer).
Deductive Reasoning	The ability to apply general rules to specific problems to produce answers that make sense.
Selective Attention	The ability to concentrate on a task over a period of time without being distracted.
Originality	The ability to come up with unusual or clever ideas about a given topic or situation, or to develop creative ways to solve a problem.
Information Ordering	The ability to arrange things or actions in a certain order or pattern according to a specific rule or set of rules (e.g., patterns of numbers, letters, words, pictures, mathematical operations).
Fluency of Ideas	The ability to come up with a number of ideas about a topic (the number of ideas is important, not their quality, correctness, or creativity).
Category Flexibility	The ability to generate or use different sets of rules for combining or grouping things in different ways.
Speed of Closure	The ability to quickly make sense of, combine, and organize information into meaningful patterns.
Time Sharing	The ability to shift back and forth between two or more activities or sources of information (such as speech, sounds, touch, or other sources).
Flexibility of Closure	The ability to identify or detect a known pattern (a figure, object, word, or sound) that is hidden in other distracting material.
Finger Dexterity	The ability to make precisely coordinated movements of the fingers of one or both hands to grasp, manipulate, or assemble very small objects.
Trunk Strength	The ability to use your abdominal and lower back muscles to support part of the body repeatedly or continuously over time without 'giving out' or fatiguing.
Auditory Attention	The ability to focus on a single source of sound in the presence of other distracting sounds.
Memorization	The ability to remember information such as words, numbers, pictures, and procedures.
Depth Perception	The ability to judge which of several objects is closer or farther away from you, or to judge the distance between you and an object.
Far Vision	The ability to see details at a distance.
Multilimb Coordination	The ability to coordinate two or more limbs (for example, two arms, two legs, or one leg and one arm) while sitting, standing, or lying down. It does not involve performing the activities while the whole body is in motion.
Control Precision	The ability to quickly and repeatedly adjust the controls of a machine or a vehicle to exact positions.
Perceptual Speed	The ability to quickly and accurately compare similarities and differences among sets of letters, numbers, objects, pictures, or patterns. The things to be compared may be presented at the same time or one after the other. This ability also includes comparing a presented object with a remembered object.

Mathematical Reasoning	The ability to choose the right mathematical methods or formulas to solve a problem.
Visualization	The ability to imagine how something will look after it is moved around or when its parts are moved or rearranged.
Number Facility	The ability to add, subtract, multiply, or divide quickly and correctly.
Hearing Sensitivity	The ability to detect or tell the differences between sounds that vary in pitch and loudness.
Visual Color Discrimination	The ability to match or detect differences between colors, including shades of color and brightness.
Night Vision	The ability to see under low light conditions.
Wrist-Finger Speed	The ability to make fast, simple, repeated movements of the fingers, hands, and wrists.
Static Strength	The ability to exert maximum muscle force to lift, push, pull, or carry objects.
Arm-Hand Steadiness	The ability to keep your hand and arm steady while moving your arm or while holding your arm and hand in one position.
Manual Dexterity	The ability to quickly move your hand, your hand together with your arm, or your two hands to grasp, manipulate, or assemble objects.
Response Orientation	The ability to choose quickly between two or more movements in response to two or more different signals (lights, sounds, pictures). It includes the speed with which the correct response is started with the hand, foot, or other body part.
Rate Control	The ability to time your movements or the movement of a piece of equipment in anticipation of changes in the speed and/or direction of a moving object or scene.
Glare Sensitivity	The ability to see objects in the presence of glare or bright lighting.
Reaction Time	The ability to quickly respond (with the hand, finger, or foot) to a signal (sound, light, picture) when it appears.
Speed of Limb Movement	The ability to quickly move the arms and legs.
Gross Body Coordination	The ability to coordinate the movement of your arms, legs, and torso together when the whole body is in motion.
Explosive Strength	The ability to use short bursts of muscle force to propel oneself (as in jumping or sprinting), or to throw an object.
Dynamic Strength	The ability to exert muscle force repeatedly or continuously over time. This involves muscular endurance and resistance to muscle fatigue.
Stamina	The ability to exert yourself physically over long periods of time without getting winded or out of breath.
Spatial Orientation	The ability to know your location in relation to the environment or to know where other objects are in relation to you.
Extent Flexibility	The ability to bend, stretch, twist, or reach with your body, arms, and/or legs.
Sound Localization	The ability to tell the direction from which a sound originated.
Gross Body Equilibrium	The ability to keep or regain your body balance or stay upright when in an unstable position.
Peripheral Vision	The ability to see objects or movement of objects to one's side when the eyes are looking ahead.
Dynamic Flexibility	The ability to quickly and repeatedly bend, stretch, twist, or reach out with your body, arms, and/or legs.

Work_Activity	Work_Activity Definitions
Communicating with Supervisors, Peers, or Subordin	Providing information to supervisors, co-workers, and subordinates by telephone, in written form, e-mail, or in person.
Making Decisions and Solving Problems	Analyzing information and evaluating results to choose the best solution and solve problems.
Getting Information	Observing, receiving, and otherwise obtaining information from all relevant sources.
Communicating with Persons Outside Organization	Communicating with people outside the organization, representing the organization to customers, the public, government, and other external sources. This information can be exchanged in person, in writing, or by telephone or e-mail.
Establishing and Maintaining Interpersonal Relatio	Developing constructive and cooperative working relationships with others, and maintaining them over time.
Evaluating Information to Determine Compliance wit	Using relevant information and individual judgment to determine whether events or processes comply with laws, regulations, or standards.
Organizing, Planning, and Prioritizing Work	Developing specific goals and plans to prioritize, organize, and accomplish your work.
Assisting and Caring for Others	Providing personal assistance, medical attention, emotional support, or other personal care to others such as coworkers, customers, or patients.

Documenting/Recording Information	Entering, transcribing, recording, storing, or maintaining information in written or electronic/magnetic form.
Resolving Conflicts and Negotiating with Others	Handling complaints, settling disputes, and resolving grievances and conflicts, or otherwise negotiating with others.
Coordinating the Work and Activities of Others	Getting members of a group to work together to accomplish tasks.
Developing and Building Teams	Encouraging and building mutual trust, respect, and cooperation among team members.
Training and Teaching Others	Identifying the educational needs of others, developing formal educational or training programs or classes, and teaching or instructing others.
Developing Objectives and Strategies	Establishing long-range objectives and specifying the strategies and actions to achieve them.
Scheduling Work and Activities	Scheduling events, programs, and activities, as well as the work of others.
Performing Administrative Activities	Performing day-to-day administrative tasks such as maintaining information files and processing paperwork.
Interacting With Computers	Using computers and computer systems (including hardware and software) to program, write software, set up functions, enter data, or process information.
Coaching and Developing Others	Identifying the developmental needs of others and coaching, mentoring, or otherwise helping others to improve their knowledge or skills.
Judging the Qualities of Things, Services, or Peop	Assessing the value, importance, or quality of things or people.
Thinking Creatively	Developing, designing, or creating new applications, ideas, relationships, systems, or products, including artistic contributions.
Updating and Using Relevant Knowledge	Keeping up-to-date technically and applying new knowledge to your job.
Identifying Objects, Actions, and Events	Identifying information by categorizing, estimating, recognizing differences or similarities, and detecting changes in circumstances or events.
Guiding, Directing, and Motivating Subordinates	Providing guidance and direction to subordinates, including setting performance standards and monitoring performance.
Performing for or Working Directly with the Public	Performing for people or dealing directly with the public. This includes serving customers in restaurants and stores, and receiving clients or guests.
Processing Information	Compiling, coding, categorizing, calculating, tabulating, auditing, or verifying information or data.
Monitor Processes, Materials, or Surroundings	Monitoring and reviewing information from materials, events, or the environment, to detect or assess problems.
Interpreting the Meaning of Information for Others	Translating or explaining what information means and how it can be used.
Staffing Organizational Units	Recruiting, interviewing, selecting, hiring, and promoting employees in an organization.
Provide Consultation and Advice to Others	Providing guidance and expert advice to management or other groups on technical, systems-, or process-related topics.
Monitoring and Controlling Resources	Monitoring and controlling resources and overseeing the spending of money.
Analyzing Data or Information	Identifying the underlying principles, reasons, or facts of information by breaking down information or data into separate parts.
Selling or Influencing Others	Convincing others to buy merchandise/goods or to otherwise change their minds or actions.
Operating Vehicles, Mechanized Devices, or Equipme	Running, maneuvering, navigating, or driving vehicles or mechanized equipment, such as forklifts, passenger vehicles, aircraft, or water craft.
Performing General Physical Activities	Performing physical activities that require considerable use of your arms and legs and moving your whole body, such as climbing, lifting, balancing, walking, stooping, and handling of materials.
Estimating the Quantifiable Characteristics of Pro	Estimating sizes, distances, and quantities; or determining time, costs, resources, or materials needed to perform a work activity.
Inspecting Equipment, Structures, or Material	Inspecting equipment, structures, or materials to identify the cause of errors or other problems or defects.
Controlling Machines and Processes	Using either control mechanisms or direct physical activity to operate machines or processes (not including computers or vehicles).
Handling and Moving Objects	Using hands and arms in handling, installing, positioning, and moving materials, and manipulating things.
Drafting, Laying Out, and Specifying Technical Dev	Providing documentation, detailed instructions, drawings, or specifications to tell others about how devices, parts, equipment, or structures are to be fabricated, constructed, assembled, modified, maintained, or used.

| Repairing and Maintaining Electronic Equipment | Servicing, repairing, calibrating, regulating, fine-tuning, or testing machines. devices, and equipment that operate primarily on the basis of electrical or electronic (not mechanical) principles. |
| Repairing and Maintaining Mechanical Equipment | Servicing, repairing, adjusting, and testing machines, devices, moving parts, and equipment that operate primarily on the basis of mechanical (not electronic) principles. |

Work_Context	**Work_Context Definitions**
Telephone	How often do you have telephone conversations in this job?
Face-to-Face Discussions	How often do you have to have face-to-face discussions with individuals or teams in this job?
Contact With Others	How much does this job require the worker to be in contact with others (face-to-face, by telephone, or otherwise) in order to perform it?
Freedom to Make Decisions	How much decision making freedom, without supervision, does the job offer?
Structured versus Unstructured Work	To what extent is this job structured for the worker, rather than allowing the worker to determine tasks, priorities, and goals?
Deal With External Customers	How important is it to work with external customers or the public in this job?
Work With Work Group or Team	How important is it to work with others in a group or team in this job?
Letters and Memos	How often does the job require written letters and memos?
Impact of Decisions on Co-workers or Company Resul	How do the decisions an employee makes impact the results of co-workers, clients or the company?
Importance of Being Exact or Accurate	How important is being very exact or highly accurate in performing this job?
Frequency of Decision Making	How frequently is the worker required to make decisions that affect other people, the financial resources, and/or the image and reputation of the organization?
Indoors, Environmentally Controlled	How often does this job require working indoors in environmentally controlled conditions?
Time Pressure	How often does this job require the worker to meet strict deadlines?
Spend Time Sitting	How much does this job require sitting?
Electronic Mail	How often do you use electronic mail in this job?
Coordinate or Lead Others	How important is it to coordinate or lead others in accomplishing work activities in this job?
In an Enclosed Vehicle or Equipment	How often does this job require working in a closed vehicle or equipment (e.g., car)?
Physical Proximity	To what extent does this job require the worker to perform job tasks in close physical proximity to other people?
Deal With Unpleasant or Angry People	How frequently does the worker have to deal with unpleasant, angry, or discourteous individuals as part of the job requirements?
Frequency of Conflict Situations	How often are there conflict situations the employee has to face in this job?
Consequence of Error	How serious would the result usually be if the worker made a mistake that was not readily correctable?
Sounds, Noise Levels Are Distracting or Uncomforta	How often does this job require working exposed to sounds and noise levels that are distracting or uncomfortable?
Responsibility for Outcomes and Results	How responsible is the worker for work outcomes and results of other workers?
Outdoors, Exposed to Weather	How often does this job require working outdoors, exposed to all weather conditions?
Spend Time Standing	How much does this job require standing?
Degree of Automation	How automated is the job?
Responsible for Others' Health and Safety	How much responsibility is there for the health and safety of others in this job?
Exposed to Disease or Infections	How often does this job require exposure to disease/infections?
Level of Competition	To what extent does this job require the worker to compete or to be aware of competitive pressures?
Public Speaking	How often do you have to perform public speaking in this job?
Spend Time Walking and Running	How much does this job require walking and running?
Deal With Physically Aggressive People	How frequently does this job require the worker to deal with physical aggression of violent individuals?
Exposed to Contaminants	How often does this job require working exposed to contaminants (such as pollutants, gases, dust or odors)?
Spend Time Using Your Hands to Handle, Control, or	How much does this job require using your hands to handle, control, or feel objects, tools or controls?

Importance of Repeating Same Tasks	How important is repeating the same physical activities (e.g., key entry) or mental activities (e.g., checking entries in a ledger) over and over, without stopping, to performing this job?
Indoors, Not Environmentally Controlled	How often does this job require working indoors in non-controlled environmental conditions (e.g., warehouse without heat)?
Spend Time Making Repetitive Motions	How much does this job require making repetitive motions?
Wear Common Protective or Safety Equipment such as	How much does this job require wearing common protective or safety equipment such as safety shoes, glasses, gloves, hard hats or live jackets?
Very Hot or Cold Temperatures	How often does this job require working in very hot (above 90 F degrees) or very cold (below 32 F degrees) temperatures?
Pace Determined by Speed of Equipment	How important is it to this job that the pace is determined by the speed of equipment or machinery? (This does not refer to keeping busy at all times on this job.)
Exposed to Minor Burns, Cuts, Bites, or Stings	How often does this job require exposure to minor burns, cuts, bites, or stings?
Spend Time Bending or Twisting the Body	How much does this job require bending or twisting your body?
Outdoors, Under Cover	How often does this job require working outdoors, under cover (e.g., structure with roof but no walls)?
Extremely Bright or Inadequate Lighting	How often does this job require working in extremely bright or inadequate lighting conditions?
Spend Time Kneeling, Crouching, Stooping, or Crawl	How much does this job require kneeling, crouching, stooping, or crawling?
Cramped Work Space, Awkward Positions	How often does this job require working in cramped work spaces that requires getting into awkward positions?
Spend Time Climbing Ladders, Scaffolds, or Poles	How much does this job require climbing ladders, scaffolds, or poles?
Exposed to Hazardous Equipment	How often does this job require exposure to hazardous equipment?
In an Open Vehicle or Equipment	How often does this job require working in an open vehicle or equipment (e.g., tractor)?
Exposed to Hazardous Conditions	How often does this job require exposure to hazardous conditions?
Exposed to Radiation	How often does this job require exposure to radiation?
Exposed to High Places	How often does this job require exposure to high places?
Spend Time Keeping or Regaining Balance	How much does this job require keeping or regaining your balance?
Wear Specialized Protective or Safety Equipment su	How much does this job require wearing specialized protective or safety equipment such as breathing apparatus, safety harness, full protection suits, or radiation protection?
Exposed to Whole Body Vibration	How often does this job require exposure to whole body vibration (e.g., operate a jackhammer)?

Job Zone Component	**Job Zone Component Definitions**
Title	Job Zone Five: Extensive Preparation Needed
Overall Experience	Extensive skill, knowledge, and experience are needed for these occupations. Many require more than five years of experience. For example, surgeons must complete four years of college and an additional five to seven years of specialized medical training to be able to do their job.
Job Training	Employees may need some on-the-job training, but most of these occupations assume that the person will already have the required skills, knowledge, work-related experience, and/or training.
Job Zone Examples	These occupations often involve coordinating, training, supervising, or managing the activities of others to accomplish goals. Very advanced communication and organizational skills are required. Examples include athletic trainers, lawyers, managing editors, phyicists, social psychologists, and surgeons.
SVP Range	(8.0 and above)
Education	A bachelor's degree is the minimum formal education required for these occupations. However, many also require graduate school. For example, they may require a master's degree, and some require a Ph.D., M.D., or J.D. (law degree).

Work_Styles	**Work_Styles Definitions**
Integrity	Job requires being honest and ethical.
Concern for Others	Job requires being sensitive to others' needs and feelings and being understanding and helpful on the job.

Stress Tolerance	Job requires accepting criticism and dealing calmly and effectively with high stress situations.
Cooperation	Job requires being pleasant with others on the job and displaying a good-natured, cooperative attitude.
Self Control	Job requires maintaining composure, keeping emotions in check, controlling anger, and avoiding aggressive behavior, even in very difficult situations.
Initiative	Job requires a willingness to take on responsibilities and challenges.
Dependability	Job requires being reliable, responsible, and dependable, and fulfilling obligations.
Adaptability/Flexibility	Job requires being open to change (positive or negative) and to considerable variety in the workplace.
Social Orientation	Job requires preferring to work with others rather than alone, and being personally connected with others on the job.
Persistence	Job requires persistence in the face of obstacles.
Attention to Detail	Job requires being careful about detail and thorough in completing work tasks.
Achievement/Effort	Job requires establishing and maintaining personally challenging achievement goals and exerting effort toward mastering tasks.
Independence	Job requires developing one's own ways of doing things, guiding oneself with little or no supervision, and depending on oneself to get things done.
Leadership	Job requires a willingness to lead, take charge, and offer opinions and direction.
Analytical Thinking	Job requires analyzing information and using logic to address work-related issues and problems.
Innovation	Job requires creativity and alternative thinking to develop new ideas for and answers to work-related problems.

21-1022.00 - Medical and Public Health Social Workers

Provide persons, families, or vulnerable populations with the psychosocial support needed to cope with chronic, acute, or terminal illnesses, such as Alzheimer's, cancer, or AIDS. Services include advising family care givers, providing patient education and counseling, and making necessary referrals for other social services.

Tasks

1) Advocate for clients or patients to resolve crises.

2) Identify environmental impediments to client or patient progress through interviews and review of patient records.

3) Modify treatment plans to comply with changes in clients' status.

4) Refer patient, client, or family to community resources to assist in recovery from mental or physical illness and to provide access to services such as financial assistance, legal aid, housing, job placement or education.

5) Utilize consultation data and social work experience to plan and coordinate client or patient care and rehabilitation, following through to ensure service efficacy.

6) Counsel clients and patients in individual and group sessions to help them overcome dependencies, recover from illness, and adjust to life.

7) Monitor, evaluate, and record client progress according to measurable goals described in treatment and care plan.

8) Organize support groups or counsel family members to assist them in understanding, dealing with, and supporting the client or patient.

9) Investigate child abuse or neglect cases and take authorized protective action when necessary.

10) Plan and conduct programs to combat social problems, prevent substance abuse, or improve community health and counseling services.

11) Develop or advise on social policy and assist in community development.

12) Supervise and direct other workers providing services to clients or patients.

13) Oversee Medicaid- and Medicare-related paperwork and record-keeping in hospitals.

14) Conduct social research to advance knowledge in the social work field.

Knowledge	Knowledge Definitions
Psychology	Knowledge of human behavior and performance; individual differences in ability, personality, and interests; learning and motivation; psychological research methods; and the assessment and treatment of behavioral and affective disorders.
Customer and Personal Service	Knowledge of principles and processes for providing customer and personal services. This includes customer needs assessment, meeting quality standards for services, and evaluation of customer satisfaction.
Therapy and Counseling	Knowledge of principles, methods, and procedures for diagnosis, treatment, and rehabilitation of physical and mental dysfunctions, and for career counseling and guidance.
English Language	Knowledge of the structure and content of the English language including the meaning and spelling of words, rules of composition, and grammar.
Sociology and Anthropology	Knowledge of group behavior and dynamics, societal trends and influences, human migrations, ethnicity, cultures and their history and origins.
Education and Training	Knowledge of principles and methods for curriculum and training design, teaching and instruction for individuals and groups, and the measurement of training effects.
Philosophy and Theology	Knowledge of different philosophical systems and religions. This includes their basic principles, values, ethics, ways of thinking, customs, practices, and their impact on human culture.
Medicine and Dentistry	Knowledge of the information and techniques needed to diagnose and treat human injuries, diseases, and deformities. This includes symptoms, treatment alternatives, drug properties and interactions, and preventive health-care measures.
Law and Government	Knowledge of laws, legal codes, court procedures, precedents, government regulations, executive orders, agency rules, and the democratic political process.
Personnel and Human Resources	Knowledge of principles and procedures for personnel recruitment, selection, training, compensation and benefits, labor relations and negotiation, and personnel information systems.
Clerical	Knowledge of administrative and clerical procedures and systems such as word processing, managing files and records, stenography and transcription, designing forms, and other office procedures and terminology.
Administration and Management	Knowledge of business and management principles involved in strategic planning, resource allocation, human resources modeling, leadership technique, production methods, and coordination of people and resources.
Mathematics	Knowledge of arithmetic, algebra, geometry, calculus, statistics, and their applications.
Computers and Electronics	Knowledge of circuit boards, processors, chips, electronic equipment, and computer hardware and software, including applications and programming.
Transportation	Knowledge of principles and methods for moving people or goods by air, rail, sea, or road, including the relative costs and benefits.
Public Safety and Security	Knowledge of relevant equipment, policies, procedures, and strategies to promote effective local, state, or national security operations for the protection of people, data, property, and institutions.
Biology	Knowledge of plant and animal organisms, their tissues, cells, functions, interdependencies, and interactions with each other and the environment.
Communications and Media	Knowledge of media production, communication, and dissemination techniques and methods. This includes alternative ways to inform and entertain via written, oral, and visual media.
Chemistry	Knowledge of the chemical composition, structure, and properties of substances and of the chemical processes and transformations that they undergo. This includes uses of chemicals and their interactions, danger signs, production techniques, and disposal methods.
Physics	Knowledge and prediction of physical principles, laws, their interrelationships, and applications to understanding fluid, material, and atmospheric dynamics, and mechanical, electrical, atomic and sub- atomic structures and processes.
Sales and Marketing	Knowledge of principles and methods for showing, promoting, and selling products or services. This includes marketing strategy and tactics, product demonstration, sales techniques, and sales control systems.
History and Archeology	Knowledge of historical events and their causes, indicators, and effects on civilizations and cultures.

Production and Processing	Knowledge of raw materials, production processes, quality control, costs, and other techniques for maximizing the effective manufacture and distribution of goods.
Telecommunications	Knowledge of transmission, broadcasting, switching, control, and operation of telecommunications systems.
Geography	Knowledge of principles and methods for describing the features of land, sea, and air masses, including their physical characteristics, locations, interrelationships, and distribution of plant, animal, and human life.
Mechanical	Knowledge of machines and tools, including their designs, uses, repair, and maintenance.
Foreign Language	Knowledge of the structure and content of a foreign (non-English) language including the meaning and spelling of words, rules of composition and grammar, and pronunciation.
Engineering and Technology	Knowledge of the practical application of engineering science and technology. This includes applying principles, techniques, procedures, and equipment to the design and production of various goods and services.
Economics and Accounting	Knowledge of economic and accounting principles and practices, the financial markets, banking and the analysis and reporting of financial data.
Fine Arts	Knowledge of the theory and techniques required to compose, produce, and perform works of music, dance, visual arts, drama, and sculpture.
Building and Construction	Knowledge of materials, methods, and the tools involved in the construction or repair of houses, buildings, or other structures such as highways and roads.
Design	Knowledge of design techniques, tools, and principles involved in production of precision technical plans, blueprints, drawings, and models.
Food Production	Knowledge of techniques and equipment for planting, growing, and harvesting food products (both plant and animal) for consumption, including storage/handling techniques.

Skills	Skills Definitions
Active Listening	Giving full attention to what other people are saying, taking time to understand the points being made, asking questions as appropriate, and not interrupting at inappropriate times.
Writing	Communicating effectively in writing as appropriate for the needs of the audience.
Reading Comprehension	Understanding written sentences and paragraphs in work related documents.
Social Perceptiveness	Being aware of others' reactions and understanding why they react as they do.
Speaking	Talking to others to convey information effectively.
Critical Thinking	Using logic and reasoning to identify the strengths and weaknesses of alternative solutions, conclusions or approaches to problems.
Coordination	Adjusting actions in relation to others' actions.
Time Management	Managing one's own time and the time of others.
Service Orientation	Actively looking for ways to help people.
Active Learning	Understanding the implications of new information for both current and future problem-solving and decision-making.
Judgment and Decision Making	Considering the relative costs and benefits of potential actions to choose the most appropriate one.
Complex Problem Solving	Identifying complex problems and reviewing related information to develop and evaluate options and implement solutions.
Negotiation	Bringing others together and trying to reconcile differences.
Monitoring	Monitoring/Assessing performance of yourself, other individuals, or organizations to make improvements or take corrective action.
Learning Strategies	Selecting and using training/instructional methods and procedures appropriate for the situation when learning or teaching new things.
Instructing	Teaching others how to do something.
Persuasion	Persuading others to change their minds or behavior.
Systems Analysis	Determining how a system should work and how changes in conditions, operations, and the environment will affect outcomes.
Management of Personnel Resources	Motivating, developing, and directing people as they work, identifying the best people for the job.
Systems Evaluation	Identifying measures or indicators of system performance and the actions needed to improve or correct performance, relative to the goals of the system.
Quality Control Analysis	Conducting tests and inspections of products, services, or processes to evaluate quality or performance.

Troubleshooting	Determining causes of operating errors and deciding what to do about it.
Science	Using scientific rules and methods to solve problems.
Operations Analysis	Analyzing needs and product requirements to create a design.
Management of Financial Resources	Determining how money will be spent to get the work done, and accounting for these expenditures.
Mathematics	Using mathematics to solve problems.
Equipment Selection	Determining the kind of tools and equipment needed to do a job.
Technology Design	Generating or adapting equipment and technology to serve user needs.
Operation Monitoring	Watching gauges, dials, or other indicators to make sure a machine is working properly.
Management of Material Resources	Obtaining and seeing to the appropriate use of equipment, facilities, and materials needed to do certain work.
Operation and Control	Controlling operations of equipment or systems.
Installation	Installing equipment, machines, wiring, or programs to meet specifications.
Programming	Writing computer programs for various purposes.
Repairing	Repairing machines or systems using the needed tools.
Equipment Maintenance	Performing routine maintenance on equipment and determining when and what kind of maintenance is needed.

Ability	Ability Definitions
Oral Comprehension	The ability to listen to and understand information and ideas presented through spoken words and sentences.
Problem Sensitivity	The ability to tell when something is wrong or is likely to go wrong. It does not involve solving the problem, only recognizing there is a problem.
Oral Expression	The ability to communicate information and ideas in speaking so others will understand.
Inductive Reasoning	The ability to combine pieces of information to form general rules or conclusions (includes finding a relationship among seemingly unrelated events).
Deductive Reasoning	The ability to apply general rules to specific problems to produce answers that make sense.
Speech Clarity	The ability to speak clearly so others can understand you.
Speech Recognition	The ability to identify and understand the speech of another person.
Written Comprehension	The ability to read and understand information and ideas presented in writing.
Written Expression	The ability to communicate information and ideas in writing so others will understand.
Near Vision	The ability to see details at close range (within a few feet of the observer).
Speed of Closure	The ability to quickly make sense of, combine, and organize information into meaningful patterns.
Category Flexibility	The ability to generate or use different sets of rules for combining or grouping things in different ways.
Information Ordering	The ability to arrange things or actions in a certain order or pattern according to a specific rule or set of rules (e.g., patterns of numbers, letters, words, pictures, mathematical operations).
Flexibility of Closure	The ability to identify or detect a known pattern (a figure, object, word, or sound) that is hidden in other distracting material.
Originality	The ability to come up with unusual or clever ideas about a given topic or situation, or to develop creative ways to solve a problem.
Time Sharing	The ability to shift back and forth between two or more activities or sources of information (such as speech, sounds, touch, or other sources).
Fluency of Ideas	The ability to come up with a number of ideas about a topic (the number of ideas is important, not their quality, correctness, or creativity).
Selective Attention	The ability to concentrate on a task over a period of time without being distracted.
Far Vision	The ability to see details at a distance.
Memorization	The ability to remember information such as words, numbers, pictures, and procedures.
Finger Dexterity	The ability to make precisely coordinated movements of the fingers of one or both hands to grasp, manipulate, or assemble very small objects.
Auditory Attention	The ability to focus on a single source of sound in the presence of other distracting sounds.

Perceptual Speed	The ability to quickly and accurately compare similarities and differences among sets of letters. numbers, objects, pictures, or patterns. The things to be compared may be presented at the same time or one after the other. This ability also includes comparing a presented object with a remembered object.
Visual Color Discrimination	The ability to match or detect differences between colors, including shades of color and brightness.
Hearing Sensitivity	The ability to detect or tell the differences between sounds that vary in pitch and loudness.
Response Orientation	The ability to choose quickly between two or more movements in response to two or more different signals (lights, sounds, pictures). It includes the speed with which the correct response is started with the hand, foot, or other body part.
Number Facility	The ability to add, subtract, multiply, or divide quickly and correctly.
Mathematical Reasoning	The ability to choose the right mathematical methods or formulas to solve a problem.
Stamina	The ability to exert yourself physically over long periods of time without getting winded or out of breath.
Reaction Time	The ability to quickly respond (with the hand, finger, or foot) to a signal (sound, light, picture) when it appears.
Visualization	The ability to imagine how something will look after it is moved around or when its parts are moved or rearranged.
Static Strength	The ability to exert maximum muscle force to lift, push, pull, or carry objects.
Explosive Strength	The ability to use short bursts of muscle force to propel oneself (as in jumping or sprinting), or to throw an object.
Gross Body Coordination	The ability to coordinate the movement of your arms, legs, and torso together when the whole body is in motion.
Gross Body Equilibrium	The ability to keep or regain your body balance or stay upright when in an unstable position.
Trunk Strength	The ability to use your abdominal and lower back muscles to support part of the body repeatedly or continuously over time without 'giving out' or fatiguing.
Extent Flexibility	The ability to bend, stretch, twist, or reach with your body, arms, and/or legs.
Wrist-Finger Speed	The ability to make fast, simple, repeated movements of the fingers, hands, and wrists.
Dynamic Flexibility	The ability to quickly and repeatedly bend, stretch, twist, or reach out with your body, arms, and/or legs.
Arm-Hand Steadiness	The ability to keep your hand and arm steady while moving your arm or while holding your arm and hand in one position.
Manual Dexterity	The ability to quickly move your hand, your hand together with your arm, or your two hands to grasp, manipulate, or assemble objects.
Multilimb Coordination	The ability to coordinate two or more limbs (for example, two arms, two legs, or one leg and one arm) while sitting, standing, or lying down. It does not involve performing the activities while the whole body is in motion.
Night Vision	The ability to see under low light conditions.
Rate Control	The ability to time your movements or the movement of a piece of equipment in anticipation of changes in the speed and/or direction of a moving object or scene.
Control Precision	The ability to quickly and repeatedly adjust the controls of a machine or a vehicle to exact positions.
Speed of Limb Movement	The ability to quickly move the arms and legs.
Dynamic Strength	The ability to exert muscle force repeatedly or continuously over time. This involves muscular endurance and resistance to muscle fatigue.
Glare Sensitivity	The ability to see objects in the presence of glare or bright lighting.
Peripheral Vision	The ability to see objects or movement of objects to one's side when the eyes are looking ahead.
Depth Perception	The ability to judge which of several objects is closer or farther away from you, or to judge the distance between you and an object.
Sound Localization	The ability to tell the direction from which a sound originated.
Spatial Orientation	The ability to know your location in relation to the environment or to know where other objects are in relation to you.

Work_Activity	**Work_Activity Definitions**
Getting Information	Observing, receiving, and otherwise obtaining information from all relevant sources.
Making Decisions and Solving Problems	Analyzing information and evaluating results to choose the best solution and solve problems.

Establishing and Maintaining Interpersonal Relatio	Developing constructive and cooperative working relationships with others. and maintaining them over time.
Identifying Objects. Actions. and Events	Identifying information by categorizing, estimating, recognizing differences or similarities, and detecting changes in circumstances or events.
Assisting and Caring for Others	Providing personal assistance, medical attention, emotional support, or other personal care to others such as coworkers, customers, or patients.
Documenting/Recording Information	Entering. transcribing, recording, storing, or maintaining information in written or electronic/magnetic form.
Communicating with Supervisors, Peers. or Subordin	Providing information to supervisors, co-workers, and subordinates by telephone, in written form, e-mail, or in person.
Updating and Using Relevant Knowledge	Keeping up-to-date technically and applying new knowledge to your job.
Performing for or Working Directly with the Public	Performing for people or dealing directly with the public. This includes serving customers in restaurants and stores, and receiving clients or guests.
Organizing, Planning, and Prioritizing Work	Developing specific goals and plans to prioritize, organize, and accomplish your work.
Judging the Qualities of Things, Services, or Peop	Assessing the value, importance, or quality of things or people.
Communicating with Persons Outside Organization	Communicating with people outside the organization, representing the organization to customers, the public, government, and other external sources. This information can be exchanged in person, in writing, or by telephone or e-mail.
Interacting With Computers	Using computers and computer systems (including hardware and software) to program, write software, set up functions, enter data, or process information.
Resolving Conflicts and Negotiating with Others	Handling complaints, settling disputes, and resolving grievances and conflicts, or otherwise negotiating with others.
Interpreting the Meaning of Information for Others	Translating or explaining what information means and how it can be used.
Developing and Building Teams	Encouraging and building mutual trust, respect, and cooperation among team members.
Thinking Creatively	Developing, designing, or creating new applications, ideas, relationships, systems, or products, including artistic contributions.
Developing Objectives and Strategies	Establishing long-range objectives and specifying the strategies and actions to achieve them.
Processing Information	Compiling, coding, categorizing, calculating, tabulating, auditing, or verifying information or data.
Analyzing Data or Information	Identifying the underlying principles, reasons, or facts of information by breaking down information or data into separate parts.
Training and Teaching Others	Identifying the educational needs of others, developing formal educational or training programs or classes, and teaching or instructing others.
Provide Consultation and Advice to Others	Providing guidance and expert advice to management or other groups on technical, systems-, or process-related topics.
Evaluating Information to Determine Compliance wit	Using relevant information and individual judgment to determine whether events or processes comply with laws, regulations, or standards.
Monitor Processes, Materials, or Surroundings	Monitoring and reviewing information from materials, events, or the environment, to detect or assess problems.
Coaching and Developing Others	Identifying the developmental needs of others and coaching, mentoring, or otherwise helping others to improve their knowledge or skills.
Performing Administrative Activities	Performing day-to-day administrative tasks such as maintaining information files and processing paperwork.
Scheduling Work and Activities	Scheduling events, programs, and activities, as well as the work of others.
Coordinating the Work and Activities of Others	Getting members of a group to work together to accomplish tasks.
Selling or Influencing Others	Convincing others to buy merchandise/goods or to otherwise change their minds or actions.
Guiding, Directing, and Motivating Subordinates	Providing guidance and direction to subordinates, including setting performance standards and monitoring performance.
Performing General Physical Activities	Performing physical activities that require considerable use of your arms and legs and moving your whole body, such as climbing, lifting, balancing, walking, stooping, and handling of materials.
Monitoring and Controlling Resources	Monitoring and controlling resources and overseeing the spending of money.
Staffing Organizational Units	Recruiting, interviewing, selecting, hiring, and promoting employees in an organization.

363

Estimating the Quantifiable Characteristics of Pro	Estimating sizes, distances, and quantities; or determining time, costs, resources, or materials needed to perform a work activity.
Operating Vehicles, Mechanized Devices, or Equipme	Running, maneuvering, navigating, or driving vehicles or mechanized equipment, such as forklifts, passenger vehicles, aircraft, or water craft.
Handling and Moving Objects	Using hands and arms in handling, installing, positioning, and moving materials, and manipulating things.
Controlling Machines and Processes	Using either control mechanisms or direct physical activity to operate machines or processes (not including computers or vehicles).
Inspecting Equipment, Structures, or Material	Inspecting equipment, structures, or materials to identify the cause of errors or other problems or defects.
Repairing and Maintaining Electronic Equipment	Servicing, repairing, calibrating, regulating, fine-tuning, or testing machines, devices, and equipment that operate primarily on the basis of electrical or electronic (not mechanical) principles.
Repairing and Maintaining Mechanical Equipment	Servicing, repairing, adjusting, and testing machines, devices, moving parts, and equipment that operate primarily on the basis of mechanical (not electronic) principles.
Drafting, Laying Out, and Specifying Technical Dev	Providing documentation, detailed instructions, drawings, or specifications to tell others about how devices, parts, equipment, or structures are to be fabricated, constructed, assembled, modified, maintained, or used.

Work_Context	**Work_Context Definitions**
Telephone	How often do you have telephone conversations in this job?
Face-to-Face Discussions	How often do you have to have face-to-face discussions with individuals or teams in this job?
Contact With Others	How much does this job require the worker to be in contact with others (face-to-face, by telephone, or otherwise) in order to perform it?
Work With Work Group or Team	How important is it to work with others in a group or team in this job?
Indoors, Environmentally Controlled	How often does this job require working indoors in environmentally controlled conditions?
Frequency of Decision Making	How frequently is the worker required to make decisions that affect other people, the financial resources, and/or the image and reputation of the organization?
Physical Proximity	To what extent does this job require the worker to perform job tasks in close physical proximity to other people?
Freedom to Make Decisions	How much decision making freedom, without supervision, does the job offer?
Structured versus Unstructured Work	To what extent is this job structured for the worker, rather than allowing the worker to determine tasks, priorities, and goals?
Exposed to Disease or Infections	How often does this job require exposure to disease/infections?
Impact of Decisions on Co-workers or Company Resul	How do the decisions an employee makes impact the results of co-workers, clients or the company?
Letters and Memos	How often does the job require written letters and memos?
Frequency of Conflict Situations	How often are there conflict situations the employee has to face in this job?
Deal With Unpleasant or Angry People	How frequently does the worker have to deal with unpleasant, angry, or discourteous individuals as part of the job requirements?
Electronic Mail	How often do you use electronic mail in this job?
Time Pressure	How often does this job require the worker to meet strict deadlines?
Deal With External Customers	How important is it to work with external customers or the public in this job?
Coordinate or Lead Others	How important is it to coordinate or lead others in accomplishing work activities in this job?
Spend Time Sitting	How much does this job require sitting?
Sounds, Noise Levels Are Distracting or Uncomforta	How often does this job require working exposed to sounds and noise levels that are distracting or uncomfortable?
Importance of Being Exact or Accurate	How important is being very exact or highly accurate in performing this job?
Deal With Physically Aggressive People	How frequently does this job require the worker to deal with physical aggression of violent individuals?
Consequence of Error	How serious would the result usually be if the worker made a mistake that was not readily correctable?
Level of Competition	To what extent does this job require the worker to compete or to be aware of competitive pressures?
Exposed to Contaminants	How often does this job require working exposed to contaminants (such as pollutants, gases, dust or odors)?

Responsible for Others' Health and Safety	How much responsibility is there for the health and safety of others in this job?
Spend Time Standing	How much does this job require standing?
Extremely Bright or Inadequate Lighting	How often does this job require working in extremely bright or inadequate lighting conditions?
Responsibility for Outcomes and Results	How responsible is the worker for work outcomes and results of other workers?
Spend Time Walking and Running	How much does this job require walking and running?
Importance of Repeating Same Tasks	How important is repeating the same physical activities (e.g., key entry) or mental activities (e.g., checking entries in a ledger) over and over, without stopping, to performing this job?
Spend Time Making Repetitive Motions	How much does this job require making repetitive motions?
Wear Common Protective or Safety Equipment such as	How much does this job require wearing common protective or safety equipment such as safety shoes, glasses, gloves, hard hats or live jackets?
Public Speaking	How often do you have to perform public speaking in this job?
Cramped Work Space, Awkward Positions	How often does this job require working in cramped work spaces that requires getting into awkward positions?
Spend Time Bending or Twisting the Body	How much does this job require bending or twisting your body?
Spend Time Kneeling, Crouching, Stooping, or Crawl	How much does this job require kneeling, crouching, stooping, or crawling?
Spend Time Using Your Hands to Handle, Control, or	How much does this job require using your hands to handle, control, or feel objects, tools or controls?
Exposed to Minor Burns, Cuts, Bites, or Stings	How much does this job require exposure to minor burns, cuts, bites, or stings?
Degree of Automation	How automated is the job?
Wear Specialized Protective or Safety Equipment su	How much does this job require wearing specialized protective or safety equipment such as breathing apparatus, safety harness, full protection suits, or radiation protection?
In an Enclosed Vehicle or Equipment	How often does this job require working in a closed vehicle or equipment (e.g., car)?
Exposed to Radiation	How often does this job require exposure to radiation?
Very Hot or Cold Temperatures	How often does this job require working in very hot (above 90 F degrees) or very cold (below 32 F degrees) temperatures?
Indoors, Not Environmentally Controlled	How often does this job require working indoors in non-controlled environmental conditions (e.g., warehouse without heat)?
Outdoors, Exposed to Weather	How often does this job require working outdoors, exposed to all weather conditions?
Exposed to Hazardous Conditions	How often does this job require exposure to hazardous conditions?
Spend Time Keeping or Regaining Balance	How much does this job require keeping or regaining your balance?
Outdoors, Under Cover	How often does this job require working outdoors, under cover (e.g., structure with roof but no walls)?
Pace Determined by Speed of Equipment	How important is it to this job that the pace is determined by the speed of equipment or machinery? (This does not refer to keeping busy at all times on this job.)
Exposed to Whole Body Vibration	How often does this job require exposure to whole body vibration (e.g., operate a jackhammer)?
Exposed to Hazardous Equipment	How often does this job require exposure to hazardous equipment?
Exposed to High Places	How often does this job require exposure to high places?
Spend Time Climbing Ladders, Scaffolds, or Poles	How much does this job require climbing ladders, scaffolds, or poles?
In an Open Vehicle or Equipment	How often does this job require working in an open vehicle or equipment (e.g., tractor)?

Job Zone Component	**Job Zone Component Definitions**
Title	Job Zone Five: Extensive Preparation Needed
	Extensive skill, knowledge, and experience are needed for these occupations. Many require more than five years of experience.
Overall Experience	For example, surgeons must complete four years of college and an additional five to seven years of specialized medical training to be able to do their job.
Job Training	Employees may need some on-the-job training, but most of these occupations assume that the person will already have the required skills, knowledge, work-related experience, and/or training.

Job Zone Examples	These occupations often involve coordinating, training, supervising, or managing the activities of others to accomplish goals. Very advanced communication and organizational skills are required. Examples include athletic trainers, lawyers, managing editors, phyicists, social psychologists, and surgeons. (8.0 and above)
SVP Range	
Education	A bachelor's degree is the minimum formal education required for these occupations. However, many also require graduate school. For example, they may require a master's degree, and some require a Ph.D., M.D., or J.D. (law degree).

Work_Styles	Work_Styles Definitions
Dependability	Job requires being reliable, responsible, and dependable, and fulfilling obligations.
Integrity	Job requires being honest and ethical.
Concern for Others	Job requires being sensitive to others' needs and feelings and being understanding and helpful on the job.
Persistence	Job requires persistence in the face of obstacles.
Self Control	Job requires maintaining composure, keeping emotions in check, controlling anger, and avoiding aggressive behavior, even in very difficult situations.
Attention to Detail	Job requires being careful about detail and thorough in completing work tasks.
Cooperation	Job requires being pleasant with others on the job and displaying a good-natured, cooperative attitude.
Initiative	Job requires a willingness to take on responsibilities and challenges.
Adaptability/Flexibility	Job requires being open to change (positive or negative) and to considerable variety in the workplace.
Stress Tolerance	Job requires accepting criticism and dealing calmly and effectively with high stress situations.
Independence	Job requires developing one's own ways of doing things, guiding oneself with little or no supervision, and depending on oneself to get things done.
Achievement/Effort	Job requires establishing and maintaining personally challenging achievement goals and exerting effort toward mastering tasks.
Innovation	Job requires creativity and alternative thinking to develop new ideas for and answers to work-related problems.
Social Orientation	Job requires preferring to work with others rather than alone, and being personally connected with others on the job.
Analytical Thinking	Job requires analyzing information and using logic to address work-related issues and problems.
Leadership	Job requires a willingness to lead, take charge, and offer opinions and direction.

21-1023.00 - Mental Health and Substance Abuse Social Workers

Assess and treat individuals with mental, emotional, or substance abuse problems, including abuse of alcohol, tobacco, and/or other drugs. Activities may include individual and group therapy, crisis intervention, case management, client advocacy, prevention, and education.

Tasks

1) Interview clients, review records, and confer with other professionals to evaluate mental or physical condition of client or patient.

2) Monitor, evaluate, and record client progress with respect to treatment goals.

3) Modify treatment plans according to changes in client status.

4) Counsel clients in individual and group sessions to assist them in dealing with substance abuse, mental and physical illness, poverty, unemployment, or physical abuse.

5) Collaborate with counselors, physicians, and nurses to plan and coordinate treatment, drawing on social work experience and patient needs.

6) Refer patient, client, or family to community resources for housing or treatment to assist in recovery from mental or physical illness, following through to ensure service efficacy.

7) Plan and conduct programs to prevent substance abuse, to combat social problems, or to improve health and counseling services in community.

8) Supervise and direct other workers who provide services to clients or patients.

9) Develop or advise on social policy and assist in community development.

10) Conduct social research to advance knowledge in the social work field.

Knowledge	Knowledge Definitions
Psychology	Knowledge of human behavior and performance; individual differences in ability, personality, and interests; learning and motivation; psychological research methods; and the assessment and treatment of behavioral and affective disorders.
Therapy and Counseling	Knowledge of principles, methods, and procedures for diagnosis, treatment, and rehabilitation of physical and mental dysfunctions, and for career counseling and guidance.
Customer and Personal Service	Knowledge of principles and processes for providing customer and personal services. This includes customer needs assessment, meeting quality standards for services, and evaluation of customer satisfaction.
Sociology and Anthropology	Knowledge of group behavior and dynamics, societal trends and influences, human migrations, ethnicity, cultures and their history and origins.
English Language	Knowledge of the structure and content of the English language including the meaning and spelling of words, rules of composition, and grammar.
Administration and Management	Knowledge of business and management principles involved in strategic planning, resource allocation, human resources modeling, leadership technique, production methods, and coordination of people and resources.
Personnel and Human Resources	Knowledge of principles and procedures for personnel recruitment, selection, training, compensation and benefits, labor relations and negotiation, and personnel information systems.
Education and Training	Knowledge of principles and methods for curriculum and training design, teaching and instruction for individuals and groups, and the measurement of training effects.
Medicine and Dentistry	Knowledge of the information and techniques needed to diagnose and treat human injuries, diseases, and deformities. This includes symptoms, treatment alternatives, drug properties and interactions, and preventive health-care measures.
Communications and Media	Knowledge of media production, communication, and dissemination techniques and methods. This includes alternative ways to inform and entertain via written, oral, and visual media.
Telecommunications	Knowledge of transmission, broadcasting, switching, control, and operation of telecommunications systems.
Clerical	Knowledge of administrative and clerical procedures and systems such as word processing, managing files and records, stenography and transcription, designing forms, and other office procedures and terminology.
Philosophy and Theology	Knowledge of different philosophical systems and religions. This includes their basic principles, values, ethics, ways of thinking, customs, practices, and their impact on human culture.
Law and Government	Knowledge of laws, legal codes, court procedures, precedents, government regulations, executive orders, agency rules, and the democratic political process.
Public Safety and Security	Knowledge of relevant equipment, policies, procedures, and strategies to promote effective local, state, or national security operations for the protection of people, data, property, and institutions.
Transportation	Knowledge of principles and methods for moving people or goods by air, rail, sea, or road, including the relative costs and benefits.
Mathematics	Knowledge of arithmetic, algebra, geometry, calculus, statistics, and their applications.
Computers and Electronics	Knowledge of circuit boards, processors, chips, electronic equipment, and computer hardware and software, including applications and programming.
Sales and Marketing	Knowledge of principles and methods for showing, promoting, and selling products or services. This includes marketing strategy and tactics, product demonstration, sales techniques, and sales control systems.
Biology	Knowledge of plant and animal organisms, their tissues, cells, functions, interdependencies, and interactions with each other and the environment.
Economics and Accounting	Knowledge of economic and accounting principles and practices, the financial markets, banking and the analysis and reporting of financial data.

Chemistry	Knowledge of the chemical composition, structure, and properties of substances and of the chemical processes and transformations that they undergo. This includes uses of chemicals and their interactions, danger signs, production techniques, and disposal methods.
History and Archeology	Knowledge of historical events and their causes, indicators, and effects on civilizations and cultures.
Foreign Language	Knowledge of the structure and content of a foreign (non-English) language including the meaning and spelling of words, rules of composition and grammar, and pronunciation.
Fine Arts	Knowledge of the theory and techniques required to compose, produce, and perform works of music, dance, visual arts, drama, and sculpture.
Geography	Knowledge of principles and methods for describing the features of land, sea, and air masses, including their physical characteristics, locations, interrelationships, and distribution of plant, animal, and human life.
Mechanical	Knowledge of machines and tools, including their designs, uses, repair, and maintenance.
Food Production	Knowledge of techniques and equipment for planting, growing, and harvesting food products (both plant and animal) for consumption, including storage/handling techniques.
Engineering and Technology	Knowledge of the practical application of engineering science and technology. This includes applying principles, techniques, procedures, and equipment to the design and production of various goods and services.
Design	Knowledge of design techniques, tools, and principles involved in production of precision technical plans, blueprints, drawings, and models.
Production and Processing	Knowledge of raw materials, production processes, quality control, costs, and other techniques for maximizing the effective manufacture and distribution of goods.
Physics	Knowledge and prediction of physical principles, laws, their interrelationships, and applications to understanding fluid, material, and atmospheric dynamics, and mechanical, electrical, atomic and sub- atomic structures and processes.
Building and Construction	Knowledge of materials, methods, and the tools involved in the construction or repair of houses, buildings, or other structures such as highways and roads.

Skills	Skills Definitions
Active Listening	Giving full attention to what other people are saying, taking time to understand the points being made, asking questions as appropriate, and not interrupting at inappropriate times.
Social Perceptiveness	Being aware of others' reactions and understanding why they react as they do.
Critical Thinking	Using logic and reasoning to identify the strengths and weaknesses of alternative solutions, conclusions or approaches to problems.
Speaking	Talking to others to convey information effectively.
Writing	Communicating effectively in writing as appropriate for the needs of the audience.
Reading Comprehension	Understanding written sentences and paragraphs in work related documents.
Active Learning	Understanding the implications of new information for both current and future problem-solving and decision-making.
Coordination	Adjusting actions in relation to others' actions.
Service Orientation	Actively looking for ways to help people.
Judgment and Decision Making	Considering the relative costs and benefits of potential actions to choose the most appropriate one.
Time Management	Managing one's own time and the time of others.
Monitoring	Monitoring/Assessing performance of yourself, other individuals, or organizations to make improvements or take corrective action.
Complex Problem Solving	Identifying complex problems and reviewing related information to develop and evaluate options and implement solutions.
Negotiation	Bringing others together and trying to reconcile differences.
Instructing	Teaching others how to do something.
Learning Strategies	Selecting and using training/instructional methods and procedures appropriate for the situation when learning or teaching new things.
Persuasion	Persuading others to change their minds or behavior.
Systems Evaluation	Identifying measures or indicators of system performance and the actions needed to improve or correct performance, relative to the goals of the system.

Systems Analysis	Determining how a system should work and how changes in conditions, operations, and the environment will affect outcomes.
Quality Control Analysis	Conducting tests and inspections of products, services, or processes to evaluate quality or performance.
Management of Financial Resources	Determining how money will be spent to get the work done, and accounting for these expenditures.
Management of Personnel Resources	Motivating, developing, and directing people as they work, identifying the best people for the job.
Troubleshooting	Determining causes of operating errors and deciding what to do about it.
Science	Using scientific rules and methods to solve problems.
Operations Analysis	Analyzing needs and product requirements to create a design.
Management of Material Resources	Obtaining and seeing to the appropriate use of equipment, facilities, and materials needed to do certain work.
Operation and Control	Controlling operations of equipment or systems.
Equipment Selection	Determining the kind of tools and equipment needed to do a job.
Mathematics	Using mathematics to solve problems.
Operation Monitoring	Watching gauges, dials, or other indicators to make sure a machine is working properly.
Technology Design	Generating or adapting equipment and technology to serve user needs.
Installation	Installing equipment, machines, wiring, or programs to meet specifications.
Repairing	Repairing machines or systems using the needed tools.
Programming	Writing computer programs for various purposes.
Equipment Maintenance	Performing routine maintenance on equipment and determining when and what kind of maintenance is needed.

Ability	Ability Definitions
Oral Expression	The ability to communicate information and ideas in speaking so others will understand.
Oral Comprehension	The ability to listen to and understand information and ideas presented through spoken words and sentences.
Speech Clarity	The ability to speak clearly so others can understand you.
Inductive Reasoning	The ability to combine pieces of information to form general rules or conclusions (includes finding a relationship among seemingly unrelated events).
Problem Sensitivity	The ability to tell when something is wrong or is likely to go wrong. It does not involve solving the problem, only recognizing there is a problem.
Written Comprehension	The ability to read and understand information and ideas presented in writing.
Speech Recognition	The ability to identify and understand the speech of another person.
Written Expression	The ability to communicate information and ideas in writing so others will understand.
Deductive Reasoning	The ability to apply general rules to specific problems to produce answers that make sense.
Selective Attention	The ability to concentrate on a task over a period of time without being distracted.
Near Vision	The ability to see details at close range (within a few feet of the observer).
Originality	The ability to come up with unusual or clever ideas about a given topic or situation, or to develop creative ways to solve a problem.
Information Ordering	The ability to arrange things or actions in a certain order or pattern according to a specific rule or set of rules (e.g., patterns of numbers, letters, words, pictures, mathematical operations).
Flexibility of Closure	The ability to identify or detect a known pattern (a figure, object, word, or sound) that is hidden in other distracting material.
Category Flexibility	The ability to generate or use different sets of rules for combining or grouping things in different ways.
Fluency of Ideas	The ability to come up with a number of ideas about a topic (the number of ideas is important, not their quality, correctness, or creativity).
Auditory Attention	The ability to focus on a single source of sound in the presence of other distracting sounds.
Finger Dexterity	The ability to make precisely coordinated movements of the fingers of one or both hands to grasp, manipulate, or assemble very small objects.
Time Sharing	The ability to shift back and forth between two or more activities or sources of information (such as speech, sounds, touch, or other sources).

			Work_Activity	Work_Activity Definitions

Speed of Closure — The ability to quickly make sense of, combine, and organize information into meaningful patterns.

Establishing and Maintaining Interpersonal Relatio — Developing constructive and cooperative working relationships with others, and maintaining them over time.

Memorization — The ability to remember information such as words, numbers, pictures, and procedures.

Getting Information — Observing, receiving, and otherwise obtaining information from all relevant sources.

Response Orientation — The ability to choose quickly between two or more movements in response to two or more different signals (lights, sounds, pictures). It includes the speed with which the correct response is started with the hand, foot, or other body part.

Assisting and Caring for Others — Providing personal assistance, medical attention, emotional support, or other personal care to others such as coworkers, customers, or patients.

Static Strength — The ability to exert maximum muscle force to lift, push, pull, or carry objects.

Performing for or Working Directly with the Public — Performing for people or dealing directly with the public. This includes serving customers in restaurants and stores, and receiving clients or guests.

Far Vision — The ability to see details at a distance.

Communicating with Supervisors, Peers, or Subordin — Providing information to supervisors, co-workers, and subordinates by telephone, in written form, e-mail, or in person.

Perceptual Speed — The ability to quickly and accurately compare similarities and differences among sets of letters, numbers, objects, pictures, or patterns. The things to be compared may be presented at the same time or one after the other. This ability also includes comparing a presented object with a remembered object.

Documenting/Recording Information — Entering, transcribing, recording, storing, or maintaining information in written or electronic/magnetic form.

Judging the Qualities of Things, Services, or Peop — Assessing the value, importance, or quality of things or people.

Reaction Time — The ability to quickly respond (with the hand, finger, or foot) to a signal (sound, light, picture) when it appears.

Making Decisions and Solving Problems — Analyzing information and evaluating results to choose the best solution and solve problems.

Gross Body Coordination — The ability to coordinate the movement of your arms, legs, and torso together when the whole body is in motion.

Explosive Strength — The ability to use short bursts of muscle force to propel oneself (as in jumping or sprinting), or to throw an object.

Communicating with Persons Outside Organization — Communicating with people outside the organization, representing the organization to customers, the public, government, and other external sources. This information can be exchanged in person, in writing, or by telephone or e-mail.

Mathematical Reasoning — The ability to choose the right mathematical methods or formulas to solve a problem.

Visualization — The ability to imagine how something will look after it is moved around or when its parts are moved or rearranged.

Identifying Objects, Actions, and Events — Identifying information by categorizing, estimating, recognizing differences or similarities, and detecting changes in circumstances or events.

Stamina — The ability to exert yourself physically over long periods of time without getting winded or out of breath.

Resolving Conflicts and Negotiating with Others — Handling complaints, settling disputes, and resolving grievances and conflicts, or otherwise negotiating with others.

Gross Body Equilibrium — The ability to keep or regain your body balance or stay upright when in an unstable position.

Updating and Using Relevant Knowledge — Keeping up-to-date technically and applying new knowledge to your job.

Trunk Strength — The ability to use your abdominal and lower back muscles to support part of the body repeatedly or continuously over time without 'giving out' or fatiguing.

Training and Teaching Others — Identifying the educational needs of others, developing formal educational or training programs or classes, and teaching or instructing others.

Number Facility — The ability to add, subtract, multiply, or divide quickly and correctly.

Organizing, Planning, and Prioritizing Work — Developing specific goals and plans to prioritize, organize, and accomplish your work.

Hearing Sensitivity — The ability to detect or tell the differences between sounds that vary in pitch and loudness.

Interpreting the Meaning of Information for Others — Translating or explaining what information means and how it can be used.

Visual Color Discrimination — The ability to match or detect differences between colors, including shades of color and brightness.

Provide Consultation and Advice to Others — Providing guidance and expert advice to management or other groups on technical, systems-, or process-related topics.

Wrist-Finger Speed — The ability to make fast, simple, repeated movements of the fingers, hands, and wrists.

Thinking Creatively — Developing, designing, or creating new applications, ideas, relationships, systems, or products, including artistic contributions.

Rate Control — The ability to time your movements or the movement of a piece of equipment in anticipation of changes in the speed and/or direction of a moving object or scene.

Selling or Influencing Others — Convincing others to buy merchandise/goods or to otherwise change their minds or actions.

Control Precision — The ability to quickly and repeatedly adjust the controls of a machine or a vehicle to exact positions.

Evaluating Information to Determine Compliance wit — Using relevant information and individual judgment to determine whether events or processes comply with laws, regulations, or standards.

Arm-Hand Steadiness — The ability to keep your hand and arm steady while moving your arm or while holding your arm and hand in one position.

Developing and Building Teams — Encouraging and building mutual trust, respect, and cooperation among team members.

Dynamic Flexibility — The ability to quickly and repeatedly bend, stretch, twist, or reach out with your body, arms, and/or legs

Coaching and Developing Others — Identifying the developmental needs of others and coaching, mentoring, or otherwise helping others to improve their knowledge or skills.

Extent Flexibility — The ability to bend, stretch, twist, or reach with your body, arms, and/or legs.

Developing Objectives and Strategies — Establishing long-range objectives and specifying the strategies and actions to achieve them.

Dynamic Strength — The ability to exert muscle force repeatedly or continuously over time. This involves muscular endurance and resistance to muscle fatigue.

Scheduling Work and Activities — Scheduling events, programs, and activities, as well as the work of others.

Speed of Limb Movement — The ability to quickly move the arms and legs.

Monitor Processes, Materials, or Surroundings — Monitoring and reviewing information from materials, events, or the environment, to detect or assess problems.

Multilimb Coordination — The ability to coordinate two or more limbs (for example, two arms, two legs, or one leg and one arm) while sitting, standing, or lying down. It does not involve performing the activities while the whole body is in motion.

Processing Information — Compiling, coding, categorizing, calculating, tabulating, auditing, or verifying information or data.

Performing Administrative Activities — Performing day-to-day administrative tasks such as maintaining information files and processing paperwork.

Manual Dexterity — The ability to quickly move your hand, your hand together with your arm, or your two hands to grasp, manipulate, or assemble objects.

Analyzing Data or Information — Identifying the underlying principles, reasons, or facts of information by breaking down information or data into separate parts.

Peripheral Vision — The ability to see objects or movement of objects to one's side when the eyes are looking ahead.

Coordinating the Work and Activities of Others — Getting members of a group to work together to accomplish tasks.

Glare Sensitivity — The ability to see objects in the presence of glare or bright lighting.

Night Vision — The ability to see under low light conditions.

Interacting With Computers — Using computers and computer systems (including hardware and software) to program, write software, set up functions, enter data, or process information.

Depth Perception — The ability to judge which of several objects is closer or farther away from you, or to judge the distance between you and an object.

Guiding, Directing, and Motivating Subordinates — Providing guidance and direction to subordinates, including setting performance standards and monitoring performance.

Sound Localization — The ability to tell the direction from which a sound originated.

Spatial Orientation — The ability to know your location in relation to the environment or to know where other objects are in relation to you.

Estimating the Quantifiable Characteristics of Pro	Estimating sizes, distances, and quantities; or determining time, costs, resources, or materials needed to perform a work activity.
Monitoring and Controlling Resources	Monitoring and controlling resources and overseeing the spending of money.
Staffing Organizational Units	Recruiting, interviewing, selecting, hiring, and promoting employees in an organization.
Operating Vehicles, Mechanized Devices, or Equipme	Running, maneuvering, navigating, or driving vehicles or mechanized equipment, such as forklifts, passenger vehicles, aircraft, or water craft.
Inspecting Equipment, Structures, or Material	Inspecting equipment, structures, or materials to identify the cause of errors or other problems or defects.
Performing General Physical Activities	Performing physical activities that require considerable use of your arms and legs and moving your whole body, such as climbing, lifting, balancing, walking, stooping, and handling of materials.
Handling and Moving Objects	Using hands and arms in handling, installing, positioning, and moving materials, and manipulating things.
Controlling Machines and Processes	Using either control mechanisms or direct physical activity to operate machines or processes (not including computers or vehicles).
Repairing and Maintaining Electronic Equipment	Servicing, repairing, calibrating, regulating, fine-tuning, or testing machines, devices, and equipment that operate primarily on the basis of electrical or electronic (not mechanical) principles.
Drafting, Laying Out, and Specifying Technical Dev	Providing documentation, detailed instructions, drawings, or specifications to tell others about how devices, parts, equipment, or structures are to be fabricated, constructed, assembled, modified, maintained, or used.
Repairing and Maintaining Mechanical Equipment	Servicing, repairing, adjusting, and testing machines, devices, moving parts, and equipment that operate primarily on the basis of mechanical (not electronic) principles.

Work_Context	Work_Context Definitions
Face-to-Face Discussions	How often do you have to have face-to-face discussions with individuals or teams in this job?
Telephone	How often do you have telephone conversations in this job?
Contact With Others	How much does this job require the worker to be in contact with others (face-to-face, by telephone, or otherwise) in order to perform it?
Letters and Memos	How often does the job require written letters and memos?
Frequency of Conflict Situations	How often are there conflict situations the employee has to face in this job?
Freedom to Make Decisions	How much decision making freedom, without supervision, does the job offer?
Frequency of Decision Making	How frequently is the worker required to make decisions that affect other people, the financial resources, and/or the image and reputation of the organization?
Deal With Unpleasant or Angry People	How frequently does the worker have to deal with unpleasant, angry, or discourteous individuals as part of the job requirements?
Work With Work Group or Team	How important is it to work with others in a group or team in this job?
Time Pressure	How often does this job require the worker to meet strict deadlines?
Deal With External Customers	How important is it to work with external customers or the public in this job?
Coordinate or Lead Others	How important is it to coordinate or lead others in accomplishing work activities in this job?
Importance of Being Exact or Accurate	How important is being very exact or highly accurate in performing this job?
Spend Time Sitting	How much does this job require sitting?
Structured versus Unstructured Work	To what extent is this job structured for the worker, rather than allowing the worker to determine tasks, priorities, and goals?
Indoors, Environmentally Controlled	How often does this job require working indoors in environmentally controlled conditions?
Sounds, Noise Levels Are Distracting or Uncomforta	How often does this job require working exposed to sounds and noise levels that are distracting or uncomfortable?
Physical Proximity	To what extent does this job require the worker to perform job tasks in close physical proximity to other people?
Deal With Physically Aggressive People	How frequently does this job require the worker to deal with physical aggression of violent individuals?
Impact of Decisions on Co-workers or Company Resul	How do the decisions an employee makes impact the results of co-workers, clients or the company?
Electronic Mail	How often do you use electronic mail in this job?

Responsible for Others' Health and Safety	How much responsibility is there for the health and safety of others in this job?
Responsibility for Outcomes and Results	How responsible is the worker for work outcomes and results of other workers?
Exposed to Disease or Infections	How often does this job require exposure to disease/infections?
Level of Competition	To what extent does this job require the worker to compete or to be aware of competitive pressures?
Importance of Repeating Same Tasks	How important is repeating the same physical activities (e.g., key entry) or mental activities (e.g., checking entries in a ledger) over and over, without stopping, to performing this job?
Consequence of Error	How serious would the result usually be if the worker made a mistake that was not readily correctable?
In an Enclosed Vehicle or Equipment	How often does this job require working in a closed vehicle or equipment (e.g., car)?
Spend Time Standing	How much does this job require standing?
Spend Time Walking and Running	How much does this job require walking and running?
Public Speaking	How often do you have to perform public speaking in this job?
Degree of Automation	How automated is the job?
Exposed to Minor Burns, Cuts, Bites, or Stings	How often does this job require exposure to minor burns, cuts, bites, or stings?
Exposed to Contaminants	How often does this job require working exposed to contaminants (such as pollutants, gases, dust or odors)?
Outdoors, Exposed to Weather	How often does this job require working outdoors, exposed to all weather conditions?
Spend Time Making Repetitive Motions	How much does this job require making repetitive motions?
Indoors, Not Environmentally Controlled	How often does this job require working indoors in non-controlled environmental conditions (e.g., warehouse without heat)?
Extremely Bright or Inadequate Lighting	How often does this job require working in extremely bright or inadequate lighting conditions?
Spend Time Using Your Hands to Handle, Control, or	How much does this job require using your hands to handle, control, or feel objects, tools or controls?
Spend Time Kneeling, Crouching, Stooping, or Crawl	How much does this job require kneeling, crouching, stooping or crawling?
Spend Time Bending or Twisting the Body	How much does this job require bending or twisting your body?
Very Hot or Cold Temperatures	How often does this job require working in very hot (above 90 F degrees) or very cold (below 32 F degrees) temperatures?
Wear Common Protective or Safety Equipment such as	How much does this job require wearing common protective or safety equipment such as safety shoes, glasses, gloves, hard hats or live jackets?
Outdoors, Under Cover	How often does this job require working outdoors, under cover (e.g., structure with roof but no walls)?
Cramped Work Space, Awkward Positions	How often does this job require working in cramped work spaces that requires getting into awkward positions?
Pace Determined by Speed of Equipment	How important is it to this job that the pace is determined by the speed of equipment or machinery? (This does not refer to keeping busy at all times on this job.)
Exposed to Hazardous Conditions	How often does this job require exposure to hazardous conditions?
Spend Time Climbing Ladders, Scaffolds, or Poles	How much does this job require climbing ladders, scaffolds, or poles?
In an Open Vehicle or Equipment	How often does this job require working in an open vehicle or equipment (e.g., tractor)?
Spend Time Keeping or Regaining Balance	How much does this job require keeping or regaining your balance?
Exposed to Hazardous Equipment	How often does this job require exposure to hazardous equipment?
Exposed to Radiation	How often does this job require exposure to radiation?
Wear Specialized Protective or Safety Equipment su	How much does this job require wearing specialized protective or safety equipment such as breathing apparatus, safety harness, full protection suits, or radiation protection?
Exposed to Whole Body Vibration	How often does this job require exposure to whole body vibration (e.g., operate a jackhammer)?
Exposed to High Places	How often does this job require exposure to high places?

Job Zone Component	Job Zone Component Definitions
Title	Job Zone Five: Extensive Preparation Needed

Overall Experience	Extensive skill, knowledge, and experience are needed for these occupations. Many require more than five years of experience. For example, surgeons must complete four years of college and an additional five to seven years of specialized medical training to be able to do their job.
Job Training	Employees may need some on-the-job training, but most of these occupations assume that the person will already have the required skills, knowledge, work-related experience, and/or training.
Job Zone Examples	These occupations often involve coordinating, training, supervising, or managing the activities of others to accomplish goals. Very advanced communication and organizational skills are required. Examples include athletic trainers, lawyers, managing editors, phyicists, social psychologists, and surgeons. (8.0 and above)
SVP Range	
Education	A bachelor's degree is the minimum formal education required for these occupations. However, many also require graduate school. For example, they may require a master's degree, and some require a Ph.D., M.D., or J.D. (law degree).

Work_Styles	Work_Styles Definitions
Concern for Others	Job requires being sensitive to others' needs and feelings and being understanding and helpful on the job.
Integrity	Job requires being honest and ethical.
Self Control	Job requires maintaining composure, keeping emotions in check, controlling anger, and avoiding aggressive behavior, even in very difficult situations.
Dependability	Job requires being reliable, responsible, and dependable, and fulfilling obligations.
Cooperation	Job requires being pleasant with others on the job and displaying a good-natured, cooperative attitude.
Adaptability/Flexibility	Job requires being open to change (positive or negative) and to considerable variety in the workplace.
Stress Tolerance	Job requires accepting criticism and dealing calmly and effectively with high stress situations.
Attention to Detail	Job requires being careful about detail and thorough in completing work tasks.
Independence	Job requires developing one's own ways of doing things, guiding oneself with little or no supervision, and depending on oneself to get things done.
Social Orientation	Job requires preferring to work with others rather than alone, and being personally connected with others on the job.
Initiative	Job requires a willingness to take on responsibilities and challenges.
Analytical Thinking	Job requires analyzing information and using logic to address work-related issues and problems.
Leadership	Job requires a willingness to lead, take charge, and offer opinions and direction.
Persistence	Job requires persistence in the face of obstacles.
Innovation	Job requires creativity and alternative thinking to develop new ideas for and answers to work-related problems.
Achievement/Effort	Job requires establishing and maintaining personally challenging achievement goals and exerting effort toward mastering tasks.

21-1091.00 - Health Educators

Promote, maintain, and improve individual and community health by assisting individuals and communities to adopt healthy behaviors. Collect and analyze data to identify community needs prior to planning, implementing, monitoring, and evaluating programs designed to encourage healthy lifestyles, policies and environments. May also serve as a resource to assist individuals, other professionals, or the community, and may administer fiscal resources for health education programs.

Tasks

1) Develop and maintain health education libraries to provide resources for staff and community agencies.

2) Maintain databases, mailing lists, telephone networks, and other information to facilitate the functioning of health education programs.

3) Collaborate with health specialists and civic groups to determine community health needs and the availability of services, and to develop goals for meeting needs.

4) Provide program information to the public by preparing and presenting press releases, conducting media campaigns, and/or maintaining program-related web sites.

5) Document activities, recording information such as the numbers of applications completed, presentations conducted, and persons assisted.

6) Design and conduct evaluations and diagnostic studies to assess the quality and performance of health education programs.

7) Develop and maintain cooperative working relationships with agencies and organizations interested in public health care.

8) Provide guidance to agencies and organizations in the assessment of health education needs, and in the development and delivery of health education programs.

9) Prepare and distribute health education materials, including reports, bulletins, and visual aids such as films, videotapes, photographs, and posters.

10) Develop, conduct, or coordinate health needs assessments and other public health surveys.

11) Develop operational plans and policies necessary to achieve health education objectives and services.

12) Develop and present health education and promotion programs such as training workshops, conferences, and school or community presentations.

13) Supervise professional and technical staff in implementing health programs, objectives, and goals.

21-1092.00 - Probation Officers and Correctional Treatment Specialists

Provide social services to assist in rehabilitation of law offenders in custody or on probation or parole. Make recommendations for actions involving formulation of rehabilitation plan and treatment of offender, including conditional release and education and employment stipulations.

Tasks

1) Write reports describing offenders' progress.

2) Arrange for medical, mental health, or substance abuse treatment services according to individual needs and/or court orders.

3) Prepare and maintain case folder for each assigned inmate or offender.

4) Develop rehabilitation programs for assigned offenders or inmates, establishing rules of conduct, goals, and objectives.

5) Inform offenders or inmates of requirements of conditional release, such as office visits, restitution payments, or educational and employment stipulations.

6) Gather information about offenders' backgrounds by talking to offenders, their families and friends, and other people who have relevant information.

7) Develop liaisons and networks with other parole officers, community agencies, staff in correctional institutions, psychiatric facilities and after-care agencies in order to make plans for helping offenders with life adjustments.

8) Provide offenders or inmates with assistance in matters concerning detainers, sentences in other jurisdictions, writs, and applications for social assistance.

9) Arrange for post-release services such as employment, housing, counseling, education, and social activities.

10) Develop and prepare packets containing information about social service agencies and assistance organizations and programs that might be useful for inmates or offenders.

11) Recommend remedial action or initiate court action when terms of probation or parole are not complied with.

12) Assess the suitability of penitentiary inmates for release under parole and statutory release programs, and submit recommendations to parole boards.

13) Interview probationers and parolees regularly to evaluate their progress in accomplishing goals and maintaining the terms specified in their probation contracts and rehabilitation plans.

14) Conduct prehearing and presentencing investigations, and testify in court regarding offenders' backgrounds and recommended sentences and sentencing conditions.

15) Supervise people on community-based sentences, including people on electronically monitored home detention.

16) Investigate alleged parole violations, using interviews, surveillance, and search and seizure.

17) Participate in decisions about whether cases should go before courts and which court should hear them.

18) Identify and approve work placements for offenders with community service sentences.

19) Recommend appropriate penitentiary for initial placement of an offender.

Knowledge	Knowledge Definitions
Psychology	Knowledge of human behavior and performance; individual differences in ability, personality, and interests; learning and motivation; psychological research methods; and the assessment and treatment of behavioral and affective disorders.
Public Safety and Security	Knowledge of relevant equipment, policies, procedures, and strategies to promote effective local, state, or national security operations for the protection of people, data, property, and institutions.
Law and Government	Knowledge of laws, legal codes, court procedures, precedents, government regulations, executive orders, agency rules, and the democratic political process.
Therapy and Counseling	Knowledge of principles, methods, and procedures for diagnosis, treatment, and rehabilitation of physical and mental dysfunctions, and for career counseling and guidance.
Sociology and Anthropology	Knowledge of group behavior and dynamics, societal trends and influences, human migrations, ethnicity, cultures and their history and origins.
English Language	Knowledge of the structure and content of the English language including the meaning and spelling of words, rules of composition, and grammar.
Customer and Personal Service	Knowledge of principles and processes for providing customer and personal services. This includes customer needs assessment, meeting quality standards for services, and evaluation of customer satisfaction.
Education and Training	Knowledge of principles and methods for curriculum and training design, teaching and instruction for individuals and groups, and the measurement of training effects.
Administration and Management	Knowledge of business and management principles involved in strategic planning, resource allocation, human resources modeling, leadership technique, production methods, and coordination of people and resources.
Clerical	Knowledge of administrative and clerical procedures and systems such as word processing, managing files and records, stenography and transcription, designing forms, and other office procedures and terminology.
Communications and Media	Knowledge of media production, communication, and dissemination techniques and methods. This includes alternative ways to inform and entertain via written, oral, and visual media.
Philosophy and Theology	Knowledge of different philosophical systems and religions. This includes their basic principles, values, ethics, ways of thinking, customs, practices, and their impact on human culture.
Personnel and Human Resources	Knowledge of principles and procedures for personnel recruitment, selection, training, compensation and benefits, labor relations and negotiation, and personnel information systems.
Computers and Electronics	Knowledge of circuit boards, processors, chips, electronic equipment, and computer hardware and software, including applications and programming.
Telecommunications	Knowledge of transmission, broadcasting, switching, control, and operation of telecommunications systems.
Transportation	Knowledge of principles and methods for moving people or goods by air, rail, sea, or road, including the relative costs and benefits.
Mathematics	Knowledge of arithmetic, algebra, geometry, calculus, statistics, and their applications.
Foreign Language	Knowledge of the structure and content of a foreign (non-English) language including the meaning and spelling of words, rules of composition and grammar, and pronunciation.
Geography	Knowledge of principles and methods for describing the features of land, sea, and air masses, including their physical characteristics, locations, interrelationships, and distribution of plant, animal, and human life.
Medicine and Dentistry	Knowledge of the information and techniques needed to diagnose and treat human injuries, diseases, and deformities. This includes symptoms, treatment alternatives, drug properties and interactions, and preventive health-care measures.
Chemistry	Knowledge of the chemical composition, structure, and properties of substances and of the chemical processes and transformations that they undergo. This includes uses of chemicals and their interactions, danger signs, production techniques, and disposal methods.
Economics and Accounting	Knowledge of economic and accounting principles and practices, the financial markets, banking and the analysis and reporting of financial data.
History and Archeology	Knowledge of historical events and their causes, indicators, and effects on civilizations and cultures.
Mechanical	Knowledge of machines and tools, including their designs, uses, repair, and maintenance.
Production and Processing	Knowledge of raw materials, production processes, quality control, costs, and other techniques for maximizing the effective manufacture and distribution of goods.
Sales and Marketing	Knowledge of principles and methods for showing, promoting, and selling products or services. This includes marketing strategy and tactics, product demonstration, sales techniques, and sales control systems.
Physics	Knowledge and prediction of physical principles, laws, their interrelationships, and applications to understanding fluid, material, and atmospheric dynamics, and mechanical, electrical, atomic and sub-atomic structures and processes.
Design	Knowledge of design techniques, tools, and principles involved in production of precision technical plans, blueprints, drawings, and models.
Engineering and Technology	Knowledge of the practical application of engineering science and technology. This includes applying principles, techniques, procedures, and equipment to the design and production of various goods and services.
Biology	Knowledge of plant and animal organisms, their tissues, cells, functions, interdependencies, and interactions with each other and the environment.
Fine Arts	Knowledge of the theory and techniques required to compose, produce, and perform works of music, dance, visual arts, drama, and sculpture.
Food Production	Knowledge of techniques and equipment for planting, growing, and harvesting food products (both plant and animal) for consumption, including storage/handling techniques.
Building and Construction	Knowledge of materials, methods, and the tools involved in the construction or repair of houses, buildings, or other structures such as highways and roads.

Skills	Skills Definitions
Active Listening	Giving full attention to what other people are saying, taking time to understand the points being made, asking questions as appropriate, and not interrupting at inappropriate times.
Social Perceptiveness	Being aware of others' reactions and understanding why they react as they do.
Writing	Communicating effectively in writing as appropriate for the needs of the audience.
Monitoring	Monitoring/Assessing performance of yourself, other individuals, or organizations to make improvements or take corrective action.
Judgment and Decision Making	Considering the relative costs and benefits of potential actions to choose the most appropriate one.
Critical Thinking	Using logic and reasoning to identify the strengths and weaknesses of alternative solutions, conclusions or approaches to problems.
Time Management	Managing one's own time and the time of others.
Speaking	Talking to others to convey information effectively.
Active Learning	Understanding the implications of new information for both current and future problem-solving and decision-making.
Instructing	Teaching others how to do something.
Negotiation	Bringing others together and trying to reconcile differences.
Reading Comprehension	Understanding written sentences and paragraphs in work related documents.
Learning Strategies	Selecting and using training/instructional methods and procedures appropriate for the situation when learning or teaching new things.
Coordination	Adjusting actions in relation to others' actions.
Persuasion	Persuading others to change their minds or behavior.
Service Orientation	Actively looking for ways to help people.
Management of Personnel Resources	Motivating, developing, and directing people as they work, identifying the best people for the job.

Complex Problem Solving	Identifying complex problems and reviewing related information to develop and evaluate options and implement solutions.
Equipment Selection	Determining the kind of tools and equipment needed to do a job.
Mathematics	Using mathematics to solve problems.
Quality Control Analysis	Conducting tests and inspections of products, services, or processes to evaluate quality or performance.
Troubleshooting	Determining causes of operating errors and deciding what to do about it.
Equipment Maintenance	Performing routine maintenance on equipment and determining when and what kind of maintenance is needed.
Systems Evaluation	Identifying measures or indicators of system performance and the actions needed to improve or correct performance, relative to the goals of the system.
Repairing	Repairing machines or systems using the needed tools.
Operations Analysis	Analyzing needs and product requirements to create a design.
Systems Analysis	Determining how a system should work and how changes in conditions, operations, and the environment will affect outcomes.
Management of Material Resources	Obtaining and seeing to the appropriate use of equipment, facilities, and materials needed to do certain work.
Operation and Control	Controlling operations of equipment or systems.
Science	Using scientific rules and methods to solve problems.
Operation Monitoring	Watching gauges, dials, or other indicators to make sure a machine is working properly.
Installation	Installing equipment, machines, wiring, or programs to meet specifications.
Management of Financial Resources	Determining how money will be spent to get the work done, and accounting for these expenditures.
Technology Design	Generating or adapting equipment and technology to serve user needs.
Programming	Writing computer programs for various purposes.

Ability	**Ability Definitions**
Problem Sensitivity	The ability to tell when something is wrong or is likely to go wrong. It does not involve solving the problem, only recognizing there is a problem.
Oral Expression	The ability to communicate information and ideas in speaking so others will understand.
Oral Comprehension	The ability to listen to and understand information and ideas presented through spoken words and sentences.
Speech Clarity	The ability to speak clearly so others can understand you.
Deductive Reasoning	The ability to apply general rules to specific problems to produce answers that make sense.
Inductive Reasoning	The ability to combine pieces of information to form general rules or conclusions (includes finding a relationship among seemingly unrelated events).
Written Expression	The ability to communicate information and ideas in writing so others will understand.
Speech Recognition	The ability to identify and understand the speech of another person.
Near Vision	The ability to see details at close range (within a few feet of the observer).
Written Comprehension	The ability to read and understand information and ideas presented in writing.
Information Ordering	The ability to arrange things or actions in a certain order or pattern according to a specific rule or set of rules (e.g., patterns of numbers, letters, words, pictures, mathematical operations).
Selective Attention	The ability to concentrate on a task over a period of time without being distracted.
Time Sharing	The ability to shift back and forth between two or more activities or sources of information (such as speech, sounds, touch, or other sources).
Fluency of Ideas	The ability to come up with a number of ideas about a topic (the number of ideas is important, not their quality, correctness, or creativity).
Category Flexibility	The ability to generate or use different sets of rules for combining or grouping things in different ways.
Originality	The ability to come up with unusual or clever ideas about a given topic or situation, or to develop creative ways to solve a problem.
Trunk Strength	The ability to use your abdominal and lower back muscles to support part of the body repeatedly or continuously over time without 'giving out' or fatiguing.
Memorization	The ability to remember information such as words, numbers, pictures, and procedures.

Flexibility of Closure	The ability to identify or detect a known pattern (a figure, object, word, or sound) that is hidden in other distracting material.
Stamina	The ability to exert yourself physically over long periods of time without getting winded or out of breath.
Gross Body Coordination	The ability to coordinate the movement of your arms, legs, and torso together when the whole body is in motion.
Far Vision	The ability to see details at a distance.
Multilimb Coordination	The ability to coordinate two or more limbs (for example, two arms, two legs, or one leg and one arm) while sitting, standing, or lying down. It does not involve performing the activities while the whole body is in motion.
Depth Perception	The ability to judge which of several objects is closer or farther away from you, or to judge the distance between you and an object.
Extent Flexibility	The ability to bend, stretch, twist, or reach with your body, arms, and/or legs.
Reaction Time	The ability to quickly respond (with the hand, finger, or foot) to a signal (sound, light, picture) when it appears.
Static Strength	The ability to exert maximum muscle force to lift, push, pull, or carry objects.
Arm-Hand Steadiness	The ability to keep your hand and arm steady while moving your arm or while holding your arm and hand in one position.
Manual Dexterity	The ability to quickly move your hand, your hand together with your arm, or your two hands to grasp, manipulate, or assemble objects.
Control Precision	The ability to quickly and repeatedly adjust the controls of a machine or a vehicle to exact positions.
Visualization	The ability to imagine how something will look after it is moved around or when its parts are moved or rearranged.
Auditory Attention	The ability to focus on a single source of sound in the presence of other distracting sounds.
Finger Dexterity	The ability to make precisely coordinated movements of the fingers of one or both hands to grasp, manipulate, or assemble very small objects.
Speed of Limb Movement	The ability to quickly move the arms and legs.
Glare Sensitivity	The ability to see objects in the presence of glare or bright lighting.
Gross Body Equilibrium	The ability to keep or regain your body balance or stay upright when in an unstable position.
Response Orientation	The ability to choose quickly between two or more movements in response to two or more different signals (lights, sounds, pictures). It includes the speed with which the correct response is started with the hand, foot, or other body part.
Peripheral Vision	The ability to see objects or movement of objects to one's side when the eyes are looking ahead.
Spatial Orientation	The ability to know your location in relation to the environment or to know where other objects are in relation to you.
Speed of Closure	The ability to quickly make sense of, combine, and organize information into meaningful patterns.
Explosive Strength	The ability to use short bursts of muscle force to propel oneself (as in jumping or sprinting), or to throw an object.
Mathematical Reasoning	The ability to choose the right mathematical methods or formulas to solve a problem.
Night Vision	The ability to see under low light conditions.
Dynamic Strength	The ability to exert muscle force repeatedly or continuously over time. This involves muscular endurance and resistance to muscle fatigue.
Sound Localization	The ability to tell the direction from which a sound originated.
Hearing Sensitivity	The ability to detect or tell the differences between sounds that vary in pitch and loudness.
Perceptual Speed	The ability to quickly and accurately compare similarities and differences among sets of letters, numbers, objects, pictures, or patterns. The things to be compared may be presented at the same time or one after the other. This ability also includes comparing a presented object with a remembered object.
Number Facility	The ability to add, subtract, multiply, or divide quickly and correctly.
Rate Control	The ability to time your movements or the movement of a piece of equipment in anticipation of changes in the speed and/or direction of a moving object or scene.
Visual Color Discrimination	The ability to match or detect differences between colors, including shades of color and brightness.
Dynamic Flexibility	The ability to quickly and repeatedly bend, stretch, twist, or reach out with your body, arms, and/or legs.
Wrist-Finger Speed	The ability to make fast, simple, repeated movements of the fingers, hands, and wrists.

Work_Activity	Work_Activity Definitions
Getting Information	Observing, receiving, and otherwise obtaining information from all relevant sources.
Resolving Conflicts and Negotiating with Others	Handling complaints, settling disputes, and resolving grievances and conflicts, or otherwise negotiating with others.
Communicating with Supervisors, Peers, or Subordin	Providing information to supervisors, co-workers, and subordinates by telephone, in written form, e-mail, or in person.
Organizing, Planning, and Prioritizing Work	Developing specific goals and plans to prioritize, organize, and accomplish your work.
Making Decisions and Solving Problems	Analyzing information and evaluating results to choose the best solution and solve problems.
Establishing and Maintaining Interpersonal Relatio	Developing constructive and cooperative working relationships with others, and maintaining them over time.
Documenting/Recording Information	Entering, transcribing, recording, storing, or maintaining information in written or electronic/magnetic form.
Communicating with Persons Outside Organization	Communicating with people outside the organization, representing the organization to customers, the public, government, and other external sources. This information can be exchanged in person, in writing, or by telephone or e-mail.
Evaluating Information to Determine Compliance wit	Using relevant information and individual judgment to determine whether events or processes comply with laws, regulations, or standards.
Performing Administrative Activities	Performing day-to-day administrative tasks such as maintaining information files and processing paperwork.
Identifying Objects, Actions, and Events	Identifying information by categorizing, estimating, recognizing differences or similarities, and detecting changes in circumstances or events.
Interacting With Computers	Using computers and computer systems (including hardware and software) to program, write software, set up functions, enter data, or process information.
Updating and Using Relevant Knowledge	Keeping up-to-date technically and applying new knowledge to your job.
Performing for or Working Directly with the Public	Performing for people or dealing directly with the public. This includes serving customers in restaurants and stores, and receiving clients or guests.
Judging the Qualities of Things, Services, or Peop	Assessing the value, importance, or quality of things or people.
Scheduling Work and Activities	Scheduling events, programs, and activities, as well as the work of others.
Monitor Processes, Materials, or Surroundings	Monitoring and reviewing information from materials, events, or the environment, to detect or assess problems.
Assisting and Caring for Others	Providing personal assistance, medical attention, emotional support, or other personal care to others such as coworkers, customers, or patients.
Developing Objectives and Strategies	Establishing long-range objectives and specifying the strategies and actions to achieve them.
Interpreting the Meaning of Information for Others	Translating or explaining what information means and how it can be used.
Processing Information	Compiling, coding, categorizing, calculating, tabulating, auditing, or verifying information or data.
Coaching and Developing Others	Identifying the developmental needs of others and coaching, mentoring, or otherwise helping others to improve their knowledge or skills.
Training and Teaching Others	Identifying the educational needs of others, developing formal educational or training programs or classes, and teaching or instructing others.
Thinking Creatively	Developing, designing, or creating new applications, ideas, relationships, systems, or products, including artistic contributions.
Developing and Building Teams	Encouraging and building mutual trust, respect, and cooperation among team members.
Guiding, Directing, and Motivating Subordinates	Providing guidance and direction to subordinates, including setting performance standards and monitoring performance.
Analyzing Data or Information	Identifying the underlying principles, reasons, or facts of information by breaking down information or data into separate parts.
Coordinating the Work and Activities of Others	Getting members of a group to work together to accomplish tasks.
Provide Consultation and Advice to Others	Providing guidance and expert advice to management or other groups on technical, systems-, or process-related topics.
Inspecting Equipment, Structures, or Material	Inspecting equipment, structures, or materials to identify the cause of errors or other problems or defects.
Performing General Physical Activities	Performing physical activities that require considerable use of your arms and legs and moving your whole body, such as climbing, lifting, balancing, walking, stooping, and handling of materials.
Estimating the Quantifiable Characteristics of Pro	Estimating sizes, distances, and quantities; or determining time, costs, resources, or materials needed to perform a work activity.
Operating Vehicles, Mechanized Devices, or Equipme	Running, maneuvering, navigating, or driving vehicles or mechanized equipment, such as forklifts, passenger vehicles, aircraft, or water craft.
Selling or Influencing Others	Convincing others to buy merchandise/goods or to otherwise change their minds or actions.
Monitoring and Controlling Resources	Monitoring and controlling resources and overseeing the spending of money.
Handling and Moving Objects	Using hands and arms in handling, installing, positioning, and moving materials, and manipulating things.
Staffing Organizational Units	Recruiting, interviewing, selecting, hiring, and promoting employees in an organization.
Controlling Machines and Processes	Using either control mechanisms or direct physical activity to operate machines or processes (not including computers or vehicles).
Drafting, Laying Out, and Specifying Technical Dev	Providing documentation, detailed instructions, drawings, or specifications to tell others about how devices, parts, equipment, or structures are to be fabricated, constructed, assembled, modified, maintained, or used.
Repairing and Maintaining Electronic Equipment	Servicing, repairing, calibrating, regulating, fine-tuning, or testing machines, devices, and equipment that operate primarily on the basis of electrical or electronic (not mechanical) principles.
Repairing and Maintaining Mechanical Equipment	Servicing, repairing, adjusting, and testing machines, devices, moving parts, and equipment that operate primarily on the basis of mechanical (not electronic) principles.

Work_Context	Work_Context Definitions
Face-to-Face Discussions	How often do you have to have face-to-face discussions with individuals or teams in this job?
Deal With Unpleasant or Angry People	How frequently does the worker have to deal with unpleasant, angry, or discourteous individuals as part of the job requirements?
Exposed to Disease or Infections	How often does this job require exposure to disease/infections?
Frequency of Conflict Situations	How often are there conflict situations the employee has to face in this job?
Telephone	How often do you have telephone conversations in this job?
Contact With Others	How much does this job require the worker to be in contact with others (face-to-face, by telephone, or otherwise) in order to perform it?
Work With Work Group or Team	How important is it to work with others in a group or team in this job?
Deal With External Customers	How important is it to work with external customers or the public in this job?
Indoors, Environmentally Controlled	How often does this job require working indoors in environmentally controlled conditions?
Impact of Decisions on Co-workers or Company Resul	How do the decisions an employee makes impact the results of co-workers, clients or the company?
Time Pressure	How often does this job require the worker to meet strict deadlines?
Frequency of Decision Making	How frequently is the worker required to make decisions that affect other people, the financial resources, and/or the image and reputation of the organization?
Deal With Physically Aggressive People	How frequently does this job require the worker to deal with physical aggression of violent individuals?
Letters and Memos	How often does the job require written letters and memos?
Importance of Being Exact or Accurate	How important is being very exact or highly accurate in performing this job?
Structured versus Unstructured Work	To what extent is this job structured for the worker, rather than allowing the worker to determine tasks, priorities, and goals?
Coordinate or Lead Others	How important is it to coordinate or lead others in accomplishing work activities in this job?
Consequence of Error	How serious would the result usually be if the worker made a mistake that was not readily correctable?
Electronic Mail	How often do you use electronic mail in this job?
Physical Proximity	To what extent does this job require the worker to perform job tasks in close physical proximity to other people?
Freedom to Make Decisions	How much decision making freedom, without supervision, does the job offer?

Responsible for Others' Health and Safety	How much responsibility is there for the health and safety of others in this job?
Importance of Repeating Same Tasks	How important is repeating the same physical activities (e.g., key entry) or mental activities (e.g., checking entries in a ledger) over and over, without stopping, to performing this job?
In an Enclosed Vehicle or Equipment	How often does this job require working in a closed vehicle or equipment (e.g., car)?
Outdoors, Exposed to Weather	How often does this job require working outdoors, exposed to all weather conditions?
Indoors, Not Environmentally Controlled	How often does this job require working indoors in non-controlled environmental conditions (e.g., warehouse without heat)?
Responsibility for Outcomes and Results	How responsible is the worker for work outcomes and results of other workers?
Very Hot or Cold Temperatures	How often does this job require working in very hot (above 90 F degrees) or very cold (below 32 F degrees) temperatures?
Spend Time Sitting	How much does this job require sitting?
Level of Competition	To what extent does this job require the worker to compete or to be aware of competitive pressures?
Exposed to Contaminants	How often does this job require working exposed to contaminants (such as pollutants, gases, dust or odors)?
Spend Time Using Your Hands to Handle, Control, or	How much does this job require using your hands to handle, control, or feel objects, tools or controls?
Public Speaking	How often do you have to perform public speaking in this job?
Spend Time Walking and Running	How much does this job require walking and running?
Spend Time Standing	How much does this job require standing?
Sounds, Noise Levels Are Distracting or Uncomforta	How often does this job require working exposed to sounds and noise levels that are distracting or uncomfortable?
Degree of Automation	How automated is the job?
Exposed to Minor Burns, Cuts, Bites, or Stings	How often does this job require exposure to minor burns, cuts, bites, or stings?
Wear Common Protective or Safety Equipment such as	How much does this job require wearing common protective or safety equipment such as safety shoes, glasses, gloves, hard hats or life jackets?
Spend Time Making Repetitive Motions	How much does this job require making repetitive motions?
Spend Time Bending or Twisting the Body	How much does this job require bending or twisting your body?
Outdoors, Under Cover	How often does this job require working outdoors, under cover (e.g., structure with roof but no walls)?
Extremely Bright or Inadequate Lighting	How often does this job require working in extremely bright or inadequate lighting conditions?
Spend Time Keeping or Regaining Balance	How much does this job require keeping or regaining your balance?
Spend Time Kneeling, Crouching, Stooping, or Crawl	How much does this job require kneeling, crouching, stooping or crawling?
Exposed to Hazardous Equipment	How often does this job require exposure to hazardous equipment?
Cramped Work Space, Awkward Positions	How often does this job require working in cramped work spaces that requires getting into awkward positions?
In an Open Vehicle or Equipment	How often does this job require working in an open vehicle or equipment (e.g., tractor)?
Exposed to Hazardous Conditions	How often does this job require exposure to hazardous conditions?
Wear Specialized Protective or Safety Equipment su	How much does this job require wearing specialized protective or safety equipment such as breathing apparatus, safety harness, full protection suits, or radiation protection?
Exposed to Radiation	How often does this job require exposure to radiation?
Pace Determined by Speed of Equipment	How important is it to this job that the pace is determined by the speed of equipment or machinery? (This does not refer to keeping busy at all times on this job.)
Spend Time Climbing Ladders, Scaffolds, or Poles	How much does this job require climbing ladders, scaffolds, or poles?
Exposed to High Places	How often does this job require exposure to high places?
Exposed to Whole Body Vibration	How often does this job require exposure to whole body vibration (e.g., operate a jackhammer)?

Job Zone Component	Job Zone Component Definitions
Title	Job Zone Four: Considerable Preparation Needed

Overall Experience	A minimum of two to four years of work-related skill, knowledge, or experience is needed for these occupations. For example, an accountant must complete four years of college and work for several years in accounting to be considered qualified.
Job Training	Employees in these occupations usually need several years of work-related experience, on-the-job training, and/or vocational training.
Job Zone Examples	Many of these occupations involve coordinating, supervising, managing, or training others. Examples include accountants, chefs and head cooks, computer programmers; historians, pharmacists, and police detectives.
SVP Range	(7.0 to < 8.0)
Education	Most of these occupations require a four - year bachelor's degree, but some do not.

Work_Styles	Work_Styles Definitions
Self Control	Job requires maintaining composure, keeping emotions in check, controlling anger, and avoiding aggressive behavior, even in very difficult situations.
Stress Tolerance	Job requires accepting criticism and dealing calmly and effectively with high stress situations.
Integrity	Job requires being honest and ethical.
Dependability	Job requires being reliable, responsible, and dependable, and fulfilling obligations.
Adaptability/Flexibility	Job requires being open to change (positive or negative) and to considerable variety in the workplace.
Cooperation	Job requires being pleasant with others on the job and displaying a good-natured, cooperative attitude.
Attention to Detail	Job requires being careful about detail and thorough in completing work tasks.
Initiative	Job requires a willingness to take on responsibilities and challenges.
Concern for Others	Job requires being sensitive to others' needs and feelings and being understanding and helpful on the job.
Independence	Job requires developing one's own ways of doing things, guiding oneself with little or no supervision, and depending on oneself to get things done.
Leadership	Job requires a willingness to lead, take charge, and offer opinions and direction.
Achievement/Effort	Job requires establishing and maintaining personally challenging achievement goals and exerting effort toward mastering tasks.
Analytical Thinking	Job requires analyzing information and using logic to address work-related issues and problems.
Social Orientation	Job requires preferring to work with others rather than alone, and being personally connected with others on the job.
Persistence	Job requires persistence in the face of obstacles.
Innovation	Job requires creativity and alternative thinking to develop new ideas for and answers to work-related problems.

21-1093.00 - Social and Human Service Assistants

Assist professionals from a wide variety of fields, such as psychology, rehabilitation, or social work, to provide client services, as well as support for families. May assist clients in identifying available benefits and social and community services and help clients obtain them. May assist social workers with developing, organizing, and conducting programs to prevent and resolve problems relevant to substance abuse, human relationships, rehabilitation, or adult daycare.

Tasks

1) Provide information on and refer individuals to public or private agencies and community services for assistance.

2) Visit individuals in homes or attend group meetings to provide information on agency services, requirements and procedures.

3) Advise clients regarding food stamps, child care, food, money management, sanitation, and housekeeping.

4) Keep records and prepare reports for owner or management concerning visits with clients.

5) Interview individuals and family members to compile information on social, educational, criminal, institutional, or drug history.

6) Assist clients with preparation of forms, such as tax or rent forms.

7) Assist in locating housing for displaced individuals.

8) Consult with supervisor concerning programs for individual families.

9) Assist in planning of food budget, utilizing charts and sample budgets.

10) Transport and accompany clients to shopping area and to appointments, using automobile.

11) Explain rules established by owner or management, such as sanitation and maintenance requirements, and parking regulations.

12) Observe and discuss meal preparation and suggest alternate methods of food preparation.

13) Meet with youth groups to acquaint them with consequences of delinquent acts.

14) Observe clients' food selections and recommend alternate economical and nutritional food choices.

15) Oversee day-to-day group activities of residents in institution.

16) Monitor free, supplementary meal program to ensure cleanliness of facility and that eligibility guidelines are met for persons receiving meals.

17) Inform tenants of facilities, such as laundries and playgrounds.

18) Demonstrate use and care of equipment for tenant use.

19) Care for children in client's home during client's appointments.

Knowledge	Knowledge Definitions
Customer and Personal Service	Knowledge of principles and processes for providing customer and personal services. This includes customer needs assessment, meeting quality standards for services, and evaluation of customer satisfaction.
English Language	Knowledge of the structure and content of the English language including the meaning and spelling of words, rules of composition, and grammar.
Psychology	Knowledge of human behavior and performance; individual differences in ability, personality, and interests; learning and motivation; psychological research methods; and the assessment and treatment of behavioral and affective disorders.
Therapy and Counseling	Knowledge of principles, methods, and procedures for diagnosis, treatment, and rehabilitation of physical and mental dysfunctions, and for career counseling and guidance.
Education and Training	Knowledge of principles and methods for curriculum and training design, teaching and instruction for individuals and groups, and the measurement of training effects.
Clerical	Knowledge of administrative and clerical procedures and systems such as word processing, managing files and records, stenography and transcription, designing forms, and other office procedures and terminology.
Sociology and Anthropology	Knowledge of group behavior and dynamics, societal trends and influences, human migrations, ethnicity, cultures and their history and origins.
Public Safety and Security	Knowledge of relevant equipment, policies, procedures, and strategies to promote effective local, state, or national security operations for the protection of people, data, property, and institutions.
Law and Government	Knowledge of laws, legal codes, court procedures, precedents, government regulations, executive orders, agency rules, and the democratic political process.
Personnel and Human Resources	Knowledge of principles and procedures for personnel recruitment, selection, training, compensation and benefits, labor relations and negotiation, and personnel information systems.
Computers and Electronics	Knowledge of circuit boards, processors, chips, electronic equipment, and computer hardware and software, including applications and programming.
Administration and Management	Knowledge of business and management principles involved in strategic planning, resource allocation, human resources modeling, leadership technique, production methods, and coordination of people and resources.
Transportation	Knowledge of principles and methods for moving people or goods by air, rail, sea, or road, including the relative costs and benefits.
Communications and Media	Knowledge of media production, communication, and dissemination techniques and methods. This includes alternative ways to inform and entertain via written, oral, and visual media.
Mathematics	Knowledge of arithmetic, algebra, geometry, calculus, statistics, and their applications.
Philosophy and Theology	Knowledge of different philosophical systems and religions. This includes their basic principles, values, ethics, ways of thinking, customs, practices, and their impact on human culture.
Telecommunications	Knowledge of transmission, broadcasting, switching, control, and operation of telecommunications systems.
Medicine and Dentistry	Knowledge of the information and techniques needed to diagnose and treat human injuries, diseases, and deformities. This includes symptoms, treatment alternatives, drug properties and interactions, and preventive health-care measures.
Sales and Marketing	Knowledge of principles and methods for showing, promoting, and selling products or services. This includes marketing strategy and tactics, product demonstration, sales techniques, and sales control systems.
Economics and Accounting	Knowledge of economic and accounting principles and practices, the financial markets, banking and the analysis and reporting of financial data.
Food Production	Knowledge of techniques and equipment for planting, growing, and harvesting food products (both plant and animal) for consumption, including storage/handling techniques.
Mechanical	Knowledge of machines and tools, including their designs, uses, repair, and maintenance.
Building and Construction	Knowledge of materials, methods, and the tools involved in the construction or repair of houses, buildings, or other structures such as highways and roads.
Geography	Knowledge of principles and methods for describing the features of land, sea, and air masses, including their physical characteristics, locations, interrelationships, and distribution of plant, animal, and human life.
Biology	Knowledge of plant and animal organisms, their tissues, cells, functions, interdependencies, and interactions with each other and the environment.
Engineering and Technology	Knowledge of the practical application of engineering science and technology. This includes applying principles, techniques, procedures, and equipment to the design and production of various goods and services.
Production and Processing	Knowledge of raw materials, production processes, quality control, costs, and other techniques for maximizing the effective manufacture and distribution of goods.
Design	Knowledge of design techniques, tools, and principles involved in production of precision technical plans, blueprints, drawings, and models.
Foreign Language	Knowledge of the structure and content of a foreign (non-English) language including the meaning and spelling of words, rules of composition and grammar, and pronunciation.
Chemistry	Knowledge of the chemical composition, structure, and properties of substances and of the chemical processes and transformations that they undergo. This includes uses of chemicals and their interactions, danger signs, production techniques, and disposal methods.
History and Archeology	Knowledge of historical events and their causes, indicators, and effects on civilizations and cultures.
Physics	Knowledge and prediction of physical principles, laws, their interrelationships, and applications to understanding fluid, material, and atmospheric dynamics, and mechanical, electrical, atomic and sub- atomic structures and processes.
Fine Arts	Knowledge of the theory and techniques required to compose, produce, and perform works of music, dance, visual arts, drama, and sculpture.

Skills	Skills Definitions
Active Listening	Giving full attention to what other people are saying, taking time to understand the points being made, asking questions as appropriate, and not interrupting at inappropriate times.
Speaking	Talking to others to convey information effectively.
Writing	Communicating effectively in writing as appropriate for the needs of the audience.
Reading Comprehension	Understanding written sentences and paragraphs in work related documents.
Social Perceptiveness	Being aware of others' reactions and understanding why they react as they do.
Time Management	Managing one's own time and the time of others.
Critical Thinking	Using logic and reasoning to identify the strengths and weaknesses of alternative solutions, conclusions or approaches to problems.
Service Orientation	Actively looking for ways to help people.

Judgment and Decision Making	Considering the relative costs and benefits of potential actions to choose the most appropriate one.
Monitoring	Monitoring/Assessing performance of yourself, other individuals, or organizations to make improvements or take corrective action.
Management of Financial Resources	Determining how money will be spent to get the work done, and accounting for these expenditures.
Learning Strategies	Selecting and using training/instructional methods and procedures appropriate for the situation when learning or teaching new things.
Coordination	Adjusting actions in relation to others' actions.
Instructing	Teaching others how to do something.
Persuasion	Persuading others to change their minds or behavior.
Active Learning	Understanding the implications of new information for both current and future problem-solving and decision-making.
Mathematics	Using mathematics to solve problems.
Complex Problem Solving	Identifying complex problems and reviewing related information to develop and evaluate options and implement solutions.
Negotiation	Bringing others together and trying to reconcile differences.
Quality Control Analysis	Conducting tests and inspections of products, services, or processes to evaluate quality or performance.
Management of Personnel Resources	Motivating, developing, and directing people as they work, identifying the best people for the job.
Equipment Selection	Determining the kind of tools and equipment needed to do a job.
Systems Evaluation	Identifying measures or indicators of system performance and the actions needed to improve or correct performance, relative to the goals of the system.
Technology Design	Generating or adapting equipment and technology to serve user needs.
Operations Analysis	Analyzing needs and product requirements to create a design.
Systems Analysis	Determining how a system should work and how changes in conditions, operations, and the environment will affect outcomes.
Management of Material Resources	Obtaining and seeing to the appropriate use of equipment, facilities, and materials needed to do certain work.
Troubleshooting	Determining causes of operating errors and deciding what to do about it.
Operation and Control	Controlling operations of equipment or systems.
Installation	Installing equipment, machines, wiring, or programs to meet specifications.
Repairing	Repairing machines or systems using the needed tools.
Equipment Maintenance	Performing routine maintenance on equipment and determining when and what kind of maintenance is needed.
Science	Using scientific rules and methods to solve problems.
Programming	Writing computer programs for various purposes.
Operation Monitoring	Watching gauges, dials, or other indicators to make sure a machine is working properly.

Ability	Ability Definitions
Speech Clarity	The ability to speak clearly so others can understand you.
Speech Recognition	The ability to identify and understand the speech of another person.
Oral Comprehension	The ability to listen to and understand information and ideas presented through spoken words and sentences.
Oral Expression	The ability to communicate information and ideas in speaking so others will understand.
Problem Sensitivity	The ability to tell when something is wrong or is likely to go wrong. It does not involve solving the problem, only recognizing there is a problem.
Written Expression	The ability to communicate information and ideas in writing so others will understand.
Information Ordering	The ability to arrange things or actions in a certain order or pattern according to a specific rule or set of rules (e.g., patterns of numbers, letters, words, pictures, mathematical operations).
Deductive Reasoning	The ability to apply general rules to specific problems to produce answers that make sense.
Written Comprehension	The ability to read and understand information and ideas presented in writing.
Inductive Reasoning	The ability to combine pieces of information to form general rules or conclusions (includes finding a relationship among seemingly unrelated events).
Selective Attention	The ability to concentrate on a task over a period of time without being distracted.
Category Flexibility	The ability to generate or use different sets of rules for combining or grouping things in different ways.

Near Vision	The ability to see details at close range (within a few feet of the observer).
Time Sharing	The ability to shift back and forth between two or more activities or sources of information (such as speech, sounds, touch, or other sources).
Fluency of Ideas	The ability to come up with a number of ideas about a topic (the number of ideas is important, not their quality, correctness, or creativity).
Originality	The ability to come up with unusual or clever ideas about a given topic or situation, or to develop creative ways to solve a problem.
Far Vision	The ability to see details at a distance.
Speed of Closure	The ability to quickly make sense of, combine, and organize information into meaningful patterns.
Flexibility of Closure	The ability to identify or detect a known pattern (a figure, object, word, or sound) that is hidden in other distracting material.
Perceptual Speed	The ability to quickly and accurately compare similarities and differences among sets of letters, numbers, objects, pictures, or patterns. The things to be compared may be presented at the same time or one after the other. This ability also includes comparing a presented object with a remembered object.
Memorization	The ability to remember information such as words, numbers, pictures, and procedures.
Auditory Attention	The ability to focus on a single source of sound in the presence of other distracting sounds.
Hearing Sensitivity	The ability to detect or tell the differences between sounds that vary in pitch and loudness.
Number Facility	The ability to add, subtract, multiply, or divide quickly and correctly.
Mathematical Reasoning	The ability to choose the right mathematical methods or formulas to solve a problem.
Depth Perception	The ability to judge which of several objects is closer or farther away from you, or to judge the distance between you and an object.
Finger Dexterity	The ability to make precisely coordinated movements of the fingers of one or both hands to grasp, manipulate, or assemble very small objects.
Trunk Strength	The ability to use your abdominal and lower back muscles to support part of the body repeatedly or continuously over time without 'giving out' or fatiguing.
Visual Color Discrimination	The ability to match or detect differences between colors, including shades of color and brightness.
Multilimb Coordination	The ability to coordinate two or more limbs (for example, two arms, two legs, or one leg and one arm) while sitting, standing, or lying down. It does not involve performing the activities while the whole body is in motion.
Visualization	The ability to imagine how something will look after it is moved around or when its parts are moved or rearranged.
Static Strength	The ability to exert maximum muscle force to lift, push, pull, or carry objects.
Manual Dexterity	The ability to quickly move your hand, your hand together with your arm, or your two hands to grasp, manipulate, or assemble objects.
Extent Flexibility	The ability to bend, stretch, twist, or reach with your body, arms, and/or legs.
Control Precision	The ability to quickly and repeatedly adjust the controls of a machine or a vehicle to exact positions.
Arm-Hand Steadiness	The ability to keep your hand and arm steady while moving your arm or while holding your arm and hand in one position.
Stamina	The ability to exert yourself physically over long periods of time without getting winded or out of breath.
Gross Body Coordination	The ability to coordinate the movement of your arms, legs, and torso together when the whole body is in motion.
Dynamic Strength	The ability to exert muscle force repeatedly or continuously over time. This involves muscular endurance and resistance to muscle fatigue.
Gross Body Equilibrium	The ability to keep or regain your body balance or stay upright when in an unstable position.
Response Orientation	The ability to choose quickly between two or more movements in response to two or more different signals (lights, sounds, pictures). It includes the speed with which the correct response is started with the hand, foot, or other body part.
Spatial Orientation	The ability to know your location in relation to the environment or to know where other objects are in relation to you.
Sound Localization	The ability to tell the direction from which a sound originated.
Glare Sensitivity	The ability to see objects in the presence of glare or bright lighting.

Reaction Time	The ability to quickly respond (with the hand, finger, or foot) to a signal (sound, light, picture) when it appears.
Peripheral Vision	The ability to see objects or movement of objects to one's side when the eyes are looking ahead.
Night Vision	The ability to see under low light conditions.
Wrist-Finger Speed	The ability to make fast, simple, repeated movements of the fingers, hands, and wrists.
Explosive Strength	The ability to use short bursts of muscle force to propel oneself (as in jumping or sprinting), or to throw an object.
Dynamic Flexibility	The ability to quickly and repeatedly bend, stretch, twist, or reach out with your body, arms, and/or legs.
Speed of Limb Movement	The ability to quickly move the arms and legs.
Rate Control	The ability to time your movements or the movement of a piece of equipment in anticipation of changes in the speed and/or direction of a moving object or scene.

Work_Activity	Work_Activity Definitions
Establishing and Maintaining Interpersonal Relatio	Developing constructive and cooperative working relationships with others, and maintaining them over time.
Assisting and Caring for Others	Providing personal assistance, medical attention, emotional support, or other personal care to others such as coworkers, customers, or patients.
Resolving Conflicts and Negotiating with Others	Handling complaints, settling disputes, and resolving grievances and conflicts, or otherwise negotiating with others.
Getting Information	Observing, receiving, and otherwise obtaining information from all relevant sources.
Making Decisions and Solving Problems	Analyzing information and evaluating results to choose the best solution and solve problems.
Developing and Building Teams	Encouraging and building mutual trust, respect, and cooperation among team members.
Communicating with Supervisors, Peers, or Subordin	Providing information to supervisors, co-workers, and subordinates by telephone, in written form, e-mail, or in person.
Evaluating Information to Determine Compliance wit	Using relevant information and individual judgment to determine whether events or processes comply with laws, regulations, or standards.
Performing for or Working Directly with the Public	Performing for people or dealing directly with the public. This includes serving customers in restaurants and stores, and receiving clients or guests.
Coordinating the Work and Activities of Others	Getting members of a group to work together to accomplish tasks.
Communicating with Persons Outside Organization	Communicating with people outside the organization, representing the organization to customers, the public, government, and other external sources. This information can be exchanged in person, in writing, or by telephone or e-mail.
Identifying Objects, Actions, and Events	Identifying information by categorizing, estimating, recognizing differences or similarities, and detecting changes in circumstances or events.
Monitor Processes, Materials, or Surroundings	Monitoring and reviewing information from materials, events, or the environment, to detect or assess problems.
Interpreting the Meaning of Information for Others	Translating or explaining what information means and how it can be used.
Training and Teaching Others	Identifying the educational needs of others, developing formal educational or training programs or classes, and teaching or instructing others.
Judging the Qualities of Things, Services, or Peop	Assessing the value, importance, or quality of things or people.
Updating and Using Relevant Knowledge	Keeping up-to-date technically and applying new knowledge to your job.
Analyzing Data or Information	Identifying the underlying principles, reasons, or facts of information by breaking down information or data into separate parts.
Provide Consultation and Advice to Others	Providing guidance and expert advice to management or other groups on technical, systems-, or process-related topics.
Documenting/Recording Information	Entering, transcribing, recording, storing, or maintaining information in written or electronic/magnetic form.
Organizing, Planning, and Prioritizing Work	Developing specific goals and plans to prioritize, organize, and accomplish your work.
Inspecting Equipment, Structures, or Material	Inspecting equipment, structures, or materials to identify the cause of errors or other problems or defects.
Performing General Physical Activities	Performing physical activities that require considerable use of your arms and legs and moving your whole body, such as climbing, lifting, balancing, walking, stooping, and handling of materials.

Processing Information	Compiling, coding, categorizing, calculating, tabulating, auditing, or verifying information or data.
Thinking Creatively	Developing, designing, or creating new applications, ideas, relationships, systems, or products, including artistic contributions.
Guiding, Directing, and Motivating Subordinates	Providing guidance and direction to subordinates, including setting performance standards and monitoring performance.
Coaching and Developing Others	Identifying the developmental needs of others and coaching, mentoring, or otherwise helping others to improve their knowledge or skills.
Performing Administrative Activities	Performing day-to-day administrative tasks such as maintaining information files and processing paperwork.
Interacting With Computers	Using computers and computer systems (including hardware and software) to program, write software, set up functions, enter data, or process information.
Scheduling Work and Activities	Scheduling events, programs, and activities, as well as the work of others.
Handling and Moving Objects	Using hands and arms in handling, installing, positioning, and moving materials, and manipulating things.
Monitoring and Controlling Resources	Monitoring and controlling resources and overseeing the spending of money.
Developing Objectives and Strategies	Establishing long-range objectives and specifying the strategies and actions to achieve them.
Estimating the Quantifiable Characteristics of Pro	Estimating sizes, distances, and quantities; or determining time, costs, resources, or materials needed to perform a work activity.
Selling or Influencing Others	Convincing others to buy merchandise/goods or to otherwise change their minds or actions.
Operating Vehicles, Mechanized Devices, or Equipme	Running, maneuvering, navigating, or driving vehicles or mechanized equipment, such as forklifts, passenger vehicles, aircraft, or water craft.
Staffing Organizational Units	Recruiting, interviewing, selecting, hiring, and promoting employees in an organization.
Drafting, Laying Out, and Specifying Technical Dev	Providing documentation, detailed instructions, drawings, or specifications to tell others about how devices, parts, equipment, or structures are to be fabricated, constructed, assembled, modified, maintained, or used.
Controlling Machines and Processes	Using either control mechanisms or direct physical activity to operate machines or processes (not including computers or vehicles).
Repairing and Maintaining Electronic Equipment	Servicing, repairing, calibrating, regulating, fine-tuning, or testing machines, devices, and equipment that operate primarily on the basis of electrical or electronic (not mechanical) principles.
Repairing and Maintaining Mechanical Equipment	Servicing, repairing, adjusting, and testing machines, devices, moving parts, and equipment that operate primarily on the basis of mechanical (not electronic) principles.

Work_Context	Work_Context Definitions
Telephone	How often do you have telephone conversations in this job?
Face-to-Face Discussions	How often do you have to have face-to-face discussions with individuals or teams in this job?
Contact With Others	How much does this job require the worker to be in contact with others (face-to-face, by telephone, or otherwise) in order to perform it?
Freedom to Make Decisions	How much decision making freedom, without supervision, does the job offer?
Work With Work Group or Team	How important is it to work with others in a group or team in this job?
Structured versus Unstructured Work	To what extent is this job structured for the worker, rather than allowing the worker to determine tasks, priorities, and goals?
Impact of Decisions on Co-workers or Company Resul	How do the decisions an employee makes impact the results of co-workers, clients or the company?
Letters and Memos	How often does the job require written letters and memos?
Deal With External Customers	How important is it to work with external customers or the public in this job?
Importance of Being Exact or Accurate	How important is being very exact or highly accurate in performing this job?
Indoors, Environmentally Controlled	How often does this job require working indoors in environmentally controlled conditions?
Frequency of Decision Making	How frequently is the worker required to make decisions that affect other people, the financial resources, and/or the image and reputation of the organization?
Coordinate or Lead Others	How important is it to coordinate or lead others in accomplishing work activities in this job?

Responsibility for Outcomes and Results	How responsible is the worker for work outcomes and results of other workers?
Spend Time Sitting	How much does this job require sitting?
Frequency of Conflict Situations	How often are there conflict situations the employee has to face in this job?
In an Enclosed Vehicle or Equipment	How often does this job require working in a closed vehicle or equipment (e.g., car)?
Time Pressure	How often does this job require the worker to meet strict deadlines?
Deal With Unpleasant or Angry People	How frequently does the worker have to deal with unpleasant, angry, or discourteous individuals as part of the job requirements?
Physical Proximity	To what extent does this job require the worker to perform job tasks in close physical proximity to other people?
Responsible for Others' Health and Safety	How much responsibility is there for the health and safety of others in this job?
Importance of Repeating Same Tasks	How important is repeating the same physical activities (e.g., key entry) or mental activities (e.g., checking entries in a ledger) over and over, without stopping, to performing this job?
Sounds, Noise Levels Are Distracting or Uncomforta	How often does this job require working exposed to sounds and noise levels that are distracting or uncomfortable?
Electronic Mail	How often do you use electronic mail in this job?
Consequence of Error	How serious would the result usually be if the worker made a mistake that was not readily correctable?
Level of Competition	To what extent does this job require the worker to compete or to be aware of competitive pressures?
Exposed to Disease or Infections	How often does this job require exposure to disease/infections?
Degree of Automation	How automated is the job?
Spend Time Making Repetitive Motions	How much does this job require making repetitive motions?
Public Speaking	How often do you have to perform public speaking in this job?
Spend Time Standing	How much does this job require standing?
Extremely Bright or Inadequate Lighting	How often does this job require working in extremely bright or inadequate lighting conditions?
Spend Time Walking and Running	How much does this job require walking and running?
Outdoors, Exposed to Weather	How often does this job require working outdoors, exposed to all weather conditions?
Exposed to Minor Burns, Cuts, Bites, or Stings	How often does this job require exposure to minor burns, cuts, bites, or stings?
Exposed to Contaminants	How often does this job require working exposed to contaminants (such as pollutants, gases, dust or odors)?
Deal With Physically Aggressive People	How frequently does this job require the worker to deal with physical aggression of violent individuals?
Outdoors, Under Cover	How often does this job require working outdoors, under cover (e.g., structure with roof but no walls)?
Spend Time Using Your Hands to Handle, Control, or	How much does this job require using your hands to handle, control, or feel objects, tools or controls?
Spend Time Bending or Twisting the Body	How much does this job require bending or twisting your body?
Indoors, Not Environmentally Controlled	How often does this job require working indoors in non-controlled environmental conditions (e.g., warehouse without heat)?
Very Hot or Cold Temperatures	How often does this job require working in very hot (above 90 F degrees) or very cold (below 32 F degrees) temperatures?
Spend Time Keeping or Regaining Balance	How much does this job require keeping or regaining your balance?
Cramped Work Space, Awkward Positions	How often does this job require working in cramped work spaces that requires getting into awkward positions?
Pace Determined by Speed of Equipment	How important is it to this job that the pace is determined by the speed of equipment or machinery? (This does not refer to keeping busy at all times on this job.)
Wear Common Protective or Safety Equipment such as	How often does this job require wearing common protective or safety equipment such as safety shoes, glasses, gloves, hard hats or life jackets?
Spend Time Kneeling, Crouching, Stooping, or Crawl	How much does this job require kneeling, crouching, stooping or crawling?
Exposed to Hazardous Conditions	How often does this job require exposure to hazardous conditions?
Spend Time Climbing Ladders, Scaffolds, or Poles	How much does this job require climbing ladders, scaffolds, or poles?
Exposed to High Places	How often does this job require exposure to high places?

Wear Specialized Protective or Safety Equipment su	How much does this job require wearing specialized protective or safety equipment such as breathing apparatus, safety harness, full protection suits, or radiation protection?
Exposed to Hazardous Equipment	How often does this job require exposure to hazardous equipment?
In an Open Vehicle or Equipment	How often does this job require working in an open vehicle or equipment (e.g., tractor)?
Exposed to Radiation	How often does this job require exposure to radiation?
Exposed to Whole Body Vibration	How often does this job require exposure to whole body vibration (e.g., operate a jackhammer)?

Job Zone Component	Job Zone Component Definitions
Title	Job Zone Three: Medium Preparation Needed
Overall Experience	Previous work-related skill, knowledge, or experience is required for these occupations. For example, an electrician must have completed three or four years of apprenticeship or several years of vocational training, and often must have passed a licensing exam, in order to perform the job.
Job Training	Employees in these occupations usually need one or two years of training involving both on-the-job experience and informal training with experienced workers.
Job Zone Examples	These occupations usually involve using communication and organizational skills to coordinate, supervise, manage, or train others to accomplish goals. Examples include dental assistants, electricians, fish and game wardens, legal secretaries, personnel recruiters, and recreation workers.
SVP Range	(6.0 to < 7.0)
Education	Most occupations in this zone require training in vocational schools, related on-the-job experience, or an associate's degree. Some may require a bachelor's degree.

Work_Styles	Work_Styles Definitions
Concern for Others	Job requires being sensitive to others' needs and feelings and being understanding and helpful on the job.
Integrity	Job requires being honest and ethical.
Dependability	Job requires being reliable, responsible, and dependable, and fulfilling obligations.
Adaptability/Flexibility	Job requires being open to change (positive or negative) and to considerable variety in the workplace.
Stress Tolerance	Job requires accepting criticism and dealing calmly and effectively with high stress situations.
Cooperation	Job requires being pleasant with others on the job and displaying a good-natured, cooperative attitude.
Self Control	Job requires maintaining composure, keeping emotions in check, controlling anger, and avoiding aggressive behavior, even in very difficult situations.
Initiative	Job requires a willingness to take on responsibilities and challenges.
Attention to Detail	Job requires being careful about detail and thorough in completing work tasks.
Social Orientation	Job requires preferring to work with others rather than alone, and being personally connected with others on the job.
Leadership	Job requires a willingness to lead, take charge, and offer opinions and direction.
Analytical Thinking	Job requires analyzing information and using logic to address work-related issues and problems.
Independence	Job requires developing one's own ways of doing things, guiding oneself with little or no supervision, and depending on oneself to get things done.
Innovation	Job requires creativity and alternative thinking to develop new ideas for and answers to work-related problems.
Persistence	Job requires persistence in the face of obstacles.
Achievement/Effort	Job requires establishing and maintaining personally challenging achievement goals and exerting effort toward mastering tasks.

21-2011.00 - Clergy

Conduct religious worship and perform other spiritual functions associated with beliefs and practices of religious faith or denomination. Provide spiritual and moral guidance and assistance to members.

21-2021.00 - Directors, Religious Activities and Education

Tasks

1) Refer people to community support services, psychologists, and/or doctors as necessary.

2) Visit people in homes, hospitals, and prisons to provide them with comfort and support.

3) Train leaders of church, community, and youth groups.

4) Share information about religious issues by writing articles, giving speeches, or teaching.

5) Respond to requests for assistance during emergencies or crises.

6) Organize and lead regular religious services.

7) Counsel individuals and groups concerning their spiritual, emotional, and personal needs.

8) Administer religious rites or ordinances.

9) Conduct special ceremonies such as weddings, funerals, and confirmations.

10) Participate in fundraising activities to support congregation activities and facilities.

11) Study and interpret religious laws, doctrines, and/or traditions.

12) Plan and lead religious education programs for their congregations.

13) Perform administrative duties such as overseeing building management, ordering supplies, contracting for services and repairs, and supervising the work of staff members and volunteers.

14) Organize and engage in interfaith, community, civic, educational, and recreational activities sponsored by or related to their religion.

15) Devise ways in which congregation membership can be expanded.

16) Collaborate with committees and individuals to address financial and administrative issues pertaining to congregations.

17) Read from sacred texts such as the Bible, Torah, or Koran.

18) Prepare and deliver sermons and other talks.

19) Pray and promote spirituality.

20) Prepare people for participation in religious ceremonies.

21-2021.00 - Directors, Religious Activities and Education

Direct and coordinate activities of a denominational group to meet religious needs of students. Plan, direct, or coordinate church school programs designed to promote religious education among church membership. May provide counseling and guidance relative to marital, health, financial, and religious problems.

Tasks

1) Select appropriate curricula and class structures for educational programs.

2) Locate and distribute resources such as periodicals and curricula in order to enhance the effectiveness of educational programs.

3) Collaborate with other ministry members to establish goals and objectives for religious education programs, and to develop ways to encourage program participation.

4) Interpret religious education activities to the public through speaking, leading discussions, and writing articles for local and national publications.

5) Analyze revenue and program cost data to determine budget priorities.

6) Counsel individuals regarding interpersonal, health, financial, and religious problems.

7) Publicize programs through sources such as newsletters, bulletins, and mailings.

8) Visit congregation members' homes, or arrange for pastoral visits, in order to provide information and resources regarding religious education programs.

9) Implement program plans by ordering needed materials, scheduling speakers, reserving space, and handling other administrative details.

10) Identify and recruit potential volunteer workers.

11) Develop and direct study courses and religious education programs within congregations.

12) Confer with clergy members, congregation officials, and congregation organizations to encourage support of and participation in religious education activities.

13) Schedule special events such as camps, conferences, meetings, seminars, and retreats.

14) Analyze member participation and changes in congregation emphasis to determine needs for religious education.

15) Participate in denominational activities aimed at goals such as promoting interfaith understanding or providing aid to new or small congregations.

16) Attend workshops, seminars, and conferences to obtain program ideas, information, and resources.

17) Train and supervise religious education instructional staff.

23-1011.00 - Lawyers

Represent clients in criminal and civil litigation and other legal proceedings, draw up legal documents, and manage or advise clients on legal transactions. May specialize in a single area or may practice broadly in many areas of law.

Tasks

1) Interpret laws, rulings and regulations for individuals and businesses.

2) Analyze the probable outcomes of cases, using knowledge of legal precedents.

3) Prepare and draft legal documents, such as wills, deeds, patent applications, mortgages, leases, and contracts.

4) Confer with colleagues with specialties in appropriate areas of legal issue to establish and verify bases for legal proceedings.

5) Study Constitution, statutes, decisions, regulations, and ordinances of quasi-judicial bodies to determine ramifications for cases.

6) Negotiate settlements of civil disputes.

7) Examine legal data to determine advisability of defending or prosecuting lawsuit.

8) Perform administrative and management functions related to the practice of law.

9) Evaluate findings and develop strategies and arguments in preparation for presentation of cases.

10) Represent clients in court or before government agencies.

11) Supervise legal assistants.

12) Gather evidence to formulate defense or to initiate legal actions, by such means as interviewing clients and witnesses to ascertain the facts of a case.

13) Present and summarize cases to judges and juries.

14) Prepare legal briefs and opinions, and file appeals in state and federal courts of appeal.

15) Present evidence to defend clients or prosecute defendants in criminal or civil litigation.

16) Search for and examine public and other legal records to write opinions or establish ownership.

17) Select jurors, argue motions, meet with judges and question witnesses during the course of a trial.

18) Act as agent, trustee, guardian, or executor for businesses or individuals.

19) Probate wills and represent and advise executors and administrators of estates.

20) Help develop federal and state programs, draft and interpret laws and legislation, and establish enforcement procedures.

21) Work in environmental law, representing public interest groups, waste disposal companies, or construction firms in their dealings with state and federal agencies.

Knowledge	Knowledge Definitions
Law and Government	Knowledge of laws, legal codes, court procedures, precedents, government regulations, executive orders, agency rules, and the democratic political process.
English Language	Knowledge of the structure and content of the English language including the meaning and spelling of words, rules of composition, and grammar.
Customer and Personal Service	Knowledge of principles and processes for providing customer and personal services. This includes customer needs assessment, meeting quality standards for services, and evaluation of customer satisfaction.
Administration and Management	Knowledge of business and management principles involved in strategic planning, resource allocation, human resources modeling, leadership technique, production methods, and coordination of people and resources.
Computers and Electronics	Knowledge of circuit boards, processors, chips, electronic equipment, and computer hardware and software, including applications and programming.

Personnel and Human Resources	Knowledge of principles and procedures for personnel recruitment, selection, training. compensation and benefits. labor relations and negotiation, and personnel information systems.	Chemistry	Knowledge of the chemical composition, structure, and properties of substances and of the chemical processes and transformations that they undergo. This includes uses of chemicals and their interactions, danger signs, production techniques. and disposal methods.
Clerical	Knowledge of administrative and clerical procedures and systems such as word processing, managing files and records. stenography and transcription, designing forms, and other office procedures and terminology.	Mechanical	Knowledge of machines and tools, including their designs, uses, repair, and maintenance.
Psychology	Knowledge of human behavior and performance; individual differences in ability, personality, and interests; learning and motivation; psychological research methods; and the assessment and treatment of behavioral and affective disorders.	Fine Arts	Knowledge of the theory and techniques required to compose, produce, and perform works of music, dance, visual arts, drama, and sculpture.
Economics and Accounting	Knowledge of economic and accounting principles and practices, the financial markets, banking and the analysis and reporting of financial data.	Physics	Knowledge and prediction of physical principles, laws, their interrelationships, and applications to understanding fluid, material, and atmospheric dynamics, and mechanical, electrical, atomic and sub- atomic structures and processes.
Mathematics	Knowledge of arithmetic, algebra, geometry, calculus, statistics, and their applications.	Food Production	Knowledge of techniques and equipment for planting, growing, and harvesting food products (both plant and animal) for consumption, including storage/handling techniques.
Communications and Media	Knowledge of media production, communication, and dissemination techniques and methods. This includes alternative ways to inform and entertain via written, oral, and visual media.		

Skills	**Skills Definitions**
Reading Comprehension	Understanding written sentences and paragraphs in work related documents.

Public Safety and Security	Knowledge of relevant equipment, policies, procedures, and strategies to promote effective local, state, or national security operations for the protection of people, data, property, and institutions.

Judgment and Decision Making	Considering the relative costs and benefits of potential actions to choose the most appropriate one.
Writing	Communicating effectively in writing as appropriate for the needs of the audience.

Education and Training	Knowledge of principles and methods for curriculum and training design, teaching and instruction for individuals and groups, and the measurement of training effects.

Critical Thinking	Using logic and reasoning to identify the strengths and weaknesses of alternative solutions, conclusions or approaches to problems.

Sales and Marketing	Knowledge of principles and methods for showing, promoting, and selling products or services. This includes marketing strategy and tactics, product demonstration, sales techniques, and sales control systems.

Active Listening	Giving full attention to what other people are saying, taking time to understand the points being made, asking questions as appropriate, and not interrupting at inappropriate times.
Persuasion	Persuading others to change their minds or behavior.
Time Management	Managing one's own time and the time of others.
Negotiation	Bringing others together and trying to reconcile differences.

Transportation	Knowledge of principles and methods for moving people or goods by air, rail, sea, or road, including the relative costs and benefits.
Sociology and Anthropology	Knowledge of group behavior and dynamics, societal trends and influences, human migrations, ethnicity, cultures and their history and origins.
Philosophy and Theology	Knowledge of different philosophical systems and religions. This includes their basic principles, values, ethics, ways of thinking, customs, practices, and their impact on human culture.

Speaking	Talking to others to convey information effectively.
Active Learning	Understanding the implications of new information for both current and future problem-solving and decision-making.
Complex Problem Solving	Identifying complex problems and reviewing related information to develop and evaluate options and implement solutions.
Social Perceptiveness	Being aware of others' reactions and understanding why they react as they do.

Telecommunications	Knowledge of transmission, broadcasting, switching, control, and operation of telecommunications systems.
Therapy and Counseling	Knowledge of principles, methods, and procedures for diagnosis, treatment, and rehabilitation of physical and mental dysfunctions, and for career counseling and guidance.

Learning Strategies	Selecting and using training/instructional methods and procedures appropriate for the situation when learning or teaching new things.
Service Orientation	Actively looking for ways to help people.
Coordination	Adjusting actions in relation to others' actions.
Management of Personnel Resources	Motivating, developing, and directing people as they work, identifying the best people for the job.

History and Archeology	Knowledge of historical events and their causes, indicators, and effects on civilizations and cultures.
Geography	Knowledge of principles and methods for describing the features of land, sea, and air masses, including their physical characteristics, locations, interrelationships, and distribution of plant, animal, and human life.

Monitoring	Monitoring/Assessing performance of yourself, other individuals, or organizations to make improvements or take corrective action.
Instructing	Teaching others how to do something.
Management of Financial Resources	Determining how money will be spent to get the work done, and accounting for these expenditures.
Mathematics	Using mathematics to solve problems.

Medicine and Dentistry	Knowledge of the information and techniques needed to diagnose and treat human injuries, diseases, and deformities. This includes symptoms, treatment alternatives, drug properties and interactions, and preventive health-care measures.
Building and Construction	Knowledge of materials, methods, and the tools involved in the construction or repair of houses, buildings, or other structures such as highways and roads.
Production and Processing	Knowledge of raw materials, production processes, quality control, costs, and other techniques for maximizing the effective manufacture and distribution of goods.

Management of Material Resources	Obtaining and seeing to the appropriate use of equipment, facilities, and materials needed to do certain work.
Operations Analysis	Analyzing needs and product requirements to create a design.
Science	Using scientific rules and methods to solve problems.
Equipment Selection	Determining the kind of tools and equipment needed to do a job.
Systems Analysis	Determining how a system should work and how changes in conditions, operations, and the environment will affect outcomes.

Engineering and Technology	Knowledge of the practical application of engineering science and technology. This includes applying principles, techniques, procedures, and equipment to the design and production of various goods and services.
Design	Knowledge of design techniques, tools, and principles involved in production of precision technical plans, blueprints, drawings, and models.
Foreign Language	Knowledge of the structure and content of a foreign (non-English) language including the meaning and spelling of words, rules of composition and grammar, and pronunciation.
Biology	Knowledge of plant and animal organisms, their tissues, cells, functions, interdependencies, and interactions with each other and the environment.

Quality Control Analysis	Conducting tests and inspections of products, services, or processes to evaluate quality or performance.
Systems Evaluation	Identifying measures or indicators of system performance and the actions needed to improve or correct performance, relative to the goals of the system.
Operation and Control	Controlling operations of equipment or systems.
Troubleshooting	Determining causes of operating errors and deciding what to do about it.
Installation	Installing equipment, machines, wiring, or programs to meet specifications.
Technology Design	Generating or adapting equipment and technology to serve user needs.

Operation Monitoring	Watching gauges, dials, or other indicators to make sure a machine is working properly.
Equipment Maintenance	Performing routine maintenance on equipment and determining when and what kind of maintenance is needed.
Repairing	Repairing machines or systems using the needed tools.
Programming	Writing computer programs for various purposes.

Ability	Ability Definitions
Oral Expression	The ability to communicate information and ideas in speaking so others will understand.
Speech Clarity	The ability to speak clearly so others can understand you.
Problem Sensitivity	The ability to tell when something is wrong or is likely to go wrong. It does not involve solving the problem, only recognizing there is a problem.
Oral Comprehension	The ability to listen to and understand information and ideas presented through spoken words and sentences.
Written Comprehension	The ability to read and understand information and ideas presented in writing.
Inductive Reasoning	The ability to combine pieces of information to form general rules or conclusions (includes finding a relationship among seemingly unrelated events).
Speech Recognition	The ability to identify and understand the speech of another person.
Written Expression	The ability to communicate information and ideas in writing so others will understand.
Deductive Reasoning	The ability to apply general rules to specific problems to produce answers that make sense.
Information Ordering	The ability to arrange things or actions in a certain order or pattern according to a specific rule or set of rules (e.g., patterns of numbers, letters, words, pictures, mathematical operations).
Fluency of Ideas	The ability to come up with a number of ideas about a topic (the number of ideas is important, not their quality, correctness, or creativity).
Near Vision	The ability to see details at close range (within a few feet of the observer).
Originality	The ability to come up with unusual or clever ideas about a given topic or situation, or to develop creative ways to solve a problem.
Flexibility of Closure	The ability to identify or detect a known pattern (a figure, object, word, or sound) that is hidden in other distracting material.
Category Flexibility	The ability to generate or use different sets of rules for combining or grouping things in different ways.
Selective Attention	The ability to concentrate on a task over a period of time without being distracted.
Speed of Closure	The ability to quickly make sense of, combine, and organize information into meaningful patterns.
Far Vision	The ability to see details at a distance.
Memorization	The ability to remember information such as words, numbers, pictures, and procedures.
Time Sharing	The ability to shift back and forth between two or more activities or sources of information (such as speech, sounds, touch, or other sources).
Number Facility	The ability to add, subtract, multiply, or divide quickly and correctly.
Perceptual Speed	The ability to quickly and accurately compare similarities and differences among sets of letters, numbers, objects, pictures, or patterns. The things to be compared may be presented at the same time or one after the other. This ability also includes comparing a presented object with a remembered object.
Mathematical Reasoning	The ability to choose the right mathematical methods or formulas to solve a problem.
Auditory Attention	The ability to focus on a single source of sound in the presence of other distracting sounds.
Visualization	The ability to imagine how something will look after it is moved around or when its parts are moved or rearranged.
Hearing Sensitivity	The ability to detect or tell the differences between sounds that vary in pitch and loudness.
Finger Dexterity	The ability to make precisely coordinated movements of the fingers of one or both hands to grasp, manipulate, or assemble very small objects.
Visual Color Discrimination	The ability to match or detect differences between colors, including shades of color and brightness.
Depth Perception	The ability to judge which of several objects is closer or farther away from you, or to judge the distance between you and an object.

Stamina	The ability to exert yourself physically over long periods of time without getting winded or out of breath.
Trunk Strength	The ability to use your abdominal and lower back muscles to support part of the body repeatedly or continuously over time without 'giving out' or fatiguing.
Arm-Hand Steadiness	The ability to keep your hand and arm steady while moving your arm or while holding your arm and hand in one position.
Dynamic Strength	The ability to exert muscle force repeatedly or continuously over time. This involves muscular endurance and resistance to muscle fatigue.
Explosive Strength	The ability to use short bursts of muscle force to propel oneself (as in jumping or sprinting), or to throw an object.
Static Strength	The ability to exert maximum muscle force to lift, push, pull, or carry objects.
Speed of Limb Movement	The ability to quickly move the arms and legs.
Wrist-Finger Speed	The ability to make fast, simple, repeated movements of the fingers, hands, and wrists.
Rate Control	The ability to time your movements or the movement of a piece of equipment in anticipation of changes in the speed and/or direction of a moving object or scene.
Response Orientation	The ability to choose quickly between two or more movements in response to two or more different signals (lights, sounds, pictures). It includes the speed with which the correct response is started with the hand, foot, or other body part.
Multilimb Coordination	The ability to coordinate two or more limbs (for example, two arms, two legs, or one leg and one arm) while sitting, standing, or lying down. It does not involve performing the activities while the whole body is in motion.
Reaction Time	The ability to quickly respond (with the hand, finger, or foot) to a signal (sound, light, picture) when it appears.
Spatial Orientation	The ability to know your location in relation to the environment or to know where other objects are in relation to you.
Control Precision	The ability to quickly and repeatedly adjust the controls of a machine or a vehicle to exact positions.
Dynamic Flexibility	The ability to quickly and repeatedly bend, stretch, twist, or reach out with your body, arms, and/or legs.
Sound Localization	The ability to tell the direction from which a sound originated.
Gross Body Coordination	The ability to coordinate the movement of your arms, legs, and torso together when the whole body is in motion.
Gross Body Equilibrium	The ability to keep or regain your body balance or stay upright when in an unstable position.
Night Vision	The ability to see under low light conditions.
Peripheral Vision	The ability to see objects or movement of objects to one's side when the eyes are looking ahead.
Glare Sensitivity	The ability to see objects in the presence of glare or bright lighting.
Extent Flexibility	The ability to bend, stretch, twist, or reach with your body, arms, and/or legs.
Manual Dexterity	The ability to quickly move your hand, your hand together with your arm, or your two hands to grasp, manipulate, or assemble objects.

Work_Activity	Work_Activity Definitions
Getting Information	Observing, receiving, and otherwise obtaining information from all relevant sources.
Updating and Using Relevant Knowledge	Keeping up-to-date technically and applying new knowledge to your job.
Resolving Conflicts and Negotiating with Others	Handling complaints, settling disputes, and resolving grievances and conflicts, or otherwise negotiating with others.
Making Decisions and Solving Problems	Analyzing information and evaluating results to choose the best solution and solve problems.
Provide Consultation and Advice to Others	Providing guidance and expert advice to management or other groups on technical, systems-, or process-related topics.
Communicating with Persons Outside Organization	Communicating with people outside the organization, representing the organization to customers, the public, government, and other external sources. This information can be exchanged in person, in writing, or by telephone or e-mail.
Thinking Creatively	Developing, designing, or creating new applications, ideas, relationships, systems, or products, including artistic contributions.
Identifying Objects, Actions, and Events	Identifying information by categorizing, estimating, recognizing differences or similarities, and detecting changes in circumstances or events.
Evaluating Information to Determine Compliance wit	Using relevant information and individual judgment to determine whether events or processes comply with laws, regulations, or standards.

Analyzing Data or Information	Identifying the underlying principles, reasons, or facts of information by breaking down information or data into separate parts.
Interpreting the Meaning of Information for Others	Translating or explaining what information means and how it can be used.
Establishing and Maintaining Interpersonal Relatio	Developing constructive and cooperative working relationships with others, and maintaining them over time.
Organizing, Planning, and Prioritizing Work	Developing specific goals and plans to prioritize, organize, and accomplish your work.
Communicating with Supervisors, Peers, or Subordin	Providing information to supervisors, co-workers, and subordinates by telephone, in written form, e-mail, or in person.
Processing Information	Compiling, coding, categorizing, calculating, tabulating, auditing, or verifying information or data.
Developing Objectives and Strategies	Establishing long-range objectives and specifying the strategies and actions to achieve them.
Performing for or Working Directly with the Public	Performing for people or dealing directly with the public. This includes serving customers in restaurants and stores, and receiving clients or guests.
Scheduling Work and Activities	Scheduling events, programs, and activities, as well as the work of others.
Judging the Qualities of Things, Services, or Peop	Assessing the value, importance, or quality of things or people.
Monitor Processes, Materials, or Surroundings	Monitoring and reviewing information from materials, events, or the environment, to detect or assess problems.
Selling or Influencing Others	Convincing others to buy merchandise/goods or to otherwise change their minds or actions.
Interacting With Computers	Using computers and computer systems (including hardware and software) to program, write software, set up functions, enter data, or process information.
Coordinating the Work and Activities of Others	Getting members of a group to work together to accomplish tasks.
Documenting/Recording Information	Entering, transcribing, recording, storing, or maintaining information in written or electronic/magnetic form.
Performing Administrative Activities	Performing day-to-day administrative tasks such as maintaining information files and processing paperwork.
Guiding, Directing, and Motivating Subordinates	Providing guidance and direction to subordinates, including setting performance standards and monitoring performance.
Estimating the Quantifiable Characteristics of Pro	Estimating sizes, distances, and quantities; or determining time, costs, resources, or materials needed to perform a work activity.
Training and Teaching Others	Identifying the educational needs of others, developing formal educational or training programs or classes, and teaching or instructing others.
Developing and Building Teams	Encouraging and building mutual trust, respect, and cooperation among team members.
Assisting and Caring for Others	Providing personal assistance, medical attention, emotional support, or other personal care to others such as coworkers, customers, or patients.
Monitoring and Controlling Resources	Monitoring and controlling resources and overseeing the spending of money.
Coaching and Developing Others	Identifying the developmental needs of others and coaching, mentoring, or otherwise helping others to improve their knowledge or skills.
Inspecting Equipment, Structures, or Material	Inspecting equipment, structures, or materials to identify the cause of errors or other problems or defects.
Staffing Organizational Units	Recruiting, interviewing, selecting, hiring, and promoting employees in an organization.
Operating Vehicles, Mechanized Devices, or Equipme	Running, maneuvering, navigating, or driving vehicles or mechanized equipment, such as forklifts, passenger vehicles, aircraft, or water craft.
Performing General Physical Activities	Performing physical activities that require considerable use of your arms and legs and moving your whole body, such as climbing, lifting, balancing, walking, stooping, and handling of materials.
Handling and Moving Objects	Using hands and arms in handling, installing, positioning, and moving materials, and manipulating things.
Controlling Machines and Processes	Using either control mechanisms or direct physical activity to operate machines or processes (not including computers or vehicles).
Repairing and Maintaining Electronic Equipment	Servicing, repairing, calibrating, regulating, fine-tuning, or testing machines, devices, and equipment that operate primarily on the basis of electrical or electronic (not mechanical) principles.
Drafting, Laying Out, and Specifying Technical Dev	Providing documentation, detailed instructions, drawings, or specifications to tell others about how devices, parts, equipment, or structures are to be fabricated, constructed, assembled, modified, maintained, or used.
Repairing and Maintaining Mechanical Equipment	Servicing, repairing, adjusting, and testing machines, devices, moving parts, and equipment that operate primarily on the basis of mechanical (not electronic) principles.

Work_Context	Work_Context Definitions
Telephone	How often do you have telephone conversations in this job?
Indoors, Environmentally Controlled	How often does this job require working indoors in environmentally controlled conditions?
Letters and Memos	How often does the job require written letters and memos?
Face-to-Face Discussions	How often do you have to have face-to-face discussions with individuals or teams in this job?
Freedom to Make Decisions	How much decision making freedom, without supervision, does the job offer?
Frequency of Decision Making	How frequently is the worker required to make decisions that affect other people, the financial resources, and/or the image and reputation of the organization?
Importance of Being Exact or Accurate	How important is being very exact or highly accurate in performing this job?
Structured versus Unstructured Work	To what extent is this job structured for the worker, rather than allowing the worker to determine tasks, priorities, and goals?
Impact of Decisions on Co-workers or Company Resul	How do the decisions an employee makes impact the results of co-workers, clients or the company?
Contact With Others	How much does this job require the worker to be in contact with others (face-to-face, by telephone, or otherwise) in order to perform it?
Electronic Mail	How often do you use electronic mail in this job?
Time Pressure	How often does this job require the worker to meet strict deadlines?
Spend Time Sitting	How much does this job require sitting?
Deal With External Customers	How important is it to work with external customers or the public in this job?
Frequency of Conflict Situations	How often are there conflict situations the employee has to face in this job?
Consequence of Error	How serious would the result usually be if the worker made a mistake that was not readily correctable?
Work With Work Group or Team	How important is it to work with others in a group or team in this job?
Coordinate or Lead Others	How important is it to coordinate or lead others in accomplishing work activities in this job?
Level of Competition	To what extent does this job require the worker to compete or to be aware of competitive pressures?
Responsibility for Outcomes and Results	How responsible is the worker for work outcomes and results of other workers?
Deal With Unpleasant or Angry People	How frequently does the worker have to deal with unpleasant, angry, or discourteous individuals as part of the job requirements?
Public Speaking	How often do you have to perform public speaking in this job?
In an Enclosed Vehicle or Equipment	How often does this job require working in a closed vehicle or equipment (e.g., car)?
Physical Proximity	To what extent does this job require the worker to perform job tasks in close physical proximity to other people?
Importance of Repeating Same Tasks	How important is repeating the same physical activities (e.g., key entry) or mental activities (e.g., checking entries in a ledger) over and over, without stopping, to performing this job?
Responsible for Others' Health and Safety	How much responsibility is there for the health and safety of others in this job?
Degree of Automation	How automated is the job?
Spend Time Using Your Hands to Handle, Control, or	How much does this job require using your hands to handle, control, or feel objects, tools or controls?
Spend Time Standing	How much does this job require standing?
Spend Time Making Repetitive Motions	How much does this job require making repetitive motions?
Sounds, Noise Levels Are Distracting or Uncomforta	How often does this job require working exposed to sounds and noise levels that are distracting or uncomfortable?
Spend Time Walking and Running	How much does this job require walking and running?
Indoors, Not Environmentally Controlled	How often does this job require working indoors in non-controlled environmental conditions (e.g., warehouse without heat)?
Exposed to Contaminants	How often does this job require working exposed to contaminants (such as pollutants, gases, dust or odors)?

Deal With Physically Aggressive People	How frequently does this job require the worker to deal with physical aggression of violent individuals?
Exposed to Disease or Infections	How often does this job require exposure to disease/infections?
Extremely Bright or Inadequate Lighting	How often does this job require working in extremely bright or inadequate lighting conditions?
Outdoors, Exposed to Weather	How often does this job require working outdoors, exposed to all weather conditions?
Very Hot or Cold Temperatures	How often does this job require working in very hot (above 90 F degrees) or very cold (below 32 F degrees) temperatures?
Spend Time Bending or Twisting the Body	How much does this job require bending or twisting your body?
Outdoors, Under Cover	How often does this job require working outdoors, under cover (e.g., structure with roof but no walls)?
Spend Time Kneeling, Crouching, Stooping, or Crawl	How much does this job require kneeling, crouching, stooping, or crawling?
Exposed to Minor Burns, Cuts, Bites, or Stings	How often does this job require exposure to minor burns, cuts, bites, or stings?
Cramped Work Space, Awkward Positions	How often does this job require working in cramped work spaces that requires getting into awkward positions?
Pace Determined by Speed of Equipment	How important is it to this job that the pace is determined by the speed of equipment or machinery? (This does not refer to keeping busy at all times on this job.)
Spend Time Keeping or Regaining Balance	How much does this job require keeping or regaining your balance?
Exposed to Hazardous Equipment	How often does this job require exposure to hazardous equipment?
Wear Common Protective or Safety Equipment such as	How much does this job require wearing common protective or safety equipment such as safety shoes, glasses, gloves, hard hats or life jackets?
Exposed to High Places	How often does this job require exposure to high places?
In an Open Vehicle or Equipment	How often does this job require working in an open vehicle or equipment (e.g., tractor)?
Spend Time Climbing Ladders, Scaffolds, or Poles	How much does this job require climbing ladders, scaffolds, or poles?
Exposed to Radiation	How often does this job require exposure to radiation?
Wear Specialized Protective or Safety Equipment su	How much does this job require wearing specialized protective or safety equipment such as breathing apparatus, safety harness, full protection suits, or radiation protection?
Exposed to Whole Body Vibration	How often does this job require exposure to whole body vibration (e.g., operate a jackhammer)?
Exposed to Hazardous Conditions	How often does this job require exposure to hazardous conditions?

Job Zone Component	Job Zone Component Definitions
Title	Job Zone Five: Extensive Preparation Needed
Overall Experience	Extensive skill, knowledge, and experience are needed for these occupations. Many require more than five years of experience. For example, surgeons must complete four years of college and an additional five to seven years of specialized medical training to be able to do their job.
Job Training	Employees may need some on-the-job training, but most of these occupations assume that the person will already have the required skills, knowledge, work-related experience, and/or training.
Job Zone Examples	These occupations often involve coordinating, training, supervising, or managing the activities of others to accomplish goals. Very advanced communication and organizational skills are required. Examples include athletic trainers, lawyers, managing editors, phyicists, social psychologists, and surgeons.
SVP Range	(8.0 and above)
Education	A bachelor's degree is the minimum formal education required for these occupations. However, many also require graduate school. For example, they may require a master's degree, and some require a Ph.D., M.D., or J.D. (law degree).

Work_Styles	Work_Styles Definitions
Integrity	Job requires being honest and ethical.
Attention to Detail	Job requires being careful about detail and thorough in completing work tasks.
Dependability	Job requires being reliable, responsible, and dependable, and fulfilling obligations.

Stress Tolerance	Job requires accepting criticism and dealing calmly and effectively with high stress situations.
Persistence	Job requires persistence in the face of obstacles.
Initiative	Job requires a willingness to take on responsibilities and challenges.
Achievement/Effort	Job requires establishing and maintaining personally challenging achievement goals and exerting effort toward mastering tasks.
Analytical Thinking	Job requires analyzing information and using logic to address work-related issues and problems.
Independence	Job requires developing one's own ways of doing things, guiding oneself with little or no supervision, and depending on oneself to get things done.
Leadership	Job requires a willingness to lead, take charge, and offer opinions and direction.
Self Control	Job requires maintaining composure, keeping emotions in check, controlling anger, and avoiding aggressive behavior, even in very difficult situations.
Cooperation	Job requires being pleasant with others on the job and displaying a good-natured, cooperative attitude.
Adaptability/Flexibility	Job requires being open to change (positive or negative) and to considerable variety in the workplace.
Concern for Others	Job requires being sensitive to others' needs and feelings and being understanding and helpful on the job.
Innovation	Job requires creativity and alternative thinking to develop new ideas for and answers to work-related problems.
Social Orientation	Job requires preferring to work with others rather than alone, and being personally connected with others on the job.

23-1021.00 - Administrative Law Judges, Adjudicators, and Hearing Officers

Conduct hearings to decide or recommend decisions on claims concerning government programs or other government-related matters and prepare decisions. Determine penalties or the existence and the amount of liability, or recommend the acceptance or rejection of claims, or compromise settlements.

Tasks

1) Rule on exceptions, motions, and admissibility of evidence.

2) Explain to claimants how they can appeal rulings that go against them.

3) Conduct hearings to review and decide claims regarding issues such as social program eligibility, environmental protection, and enforcement of health and safety regulations.

4) Research and analyze laws, regulations, policies, and precedent decisions to prepare for hearings and to determine conclusions.

5) Recommend the acceptance or rejection of claims or compromise settlements according to laws, regulations, policies, and precedent decisions.

6) Prepare written opinions and decisions.

7) Authorize payment of valid claims and determine method of payment.

8) Confer with individuals or organizations involved in cases in order to obtain relevant information.

9) Monitor and direct the activities of trials and hearings to ensure that they are conducted fairly and that courts administer justice while safeguarding the legal rights of all involved parties.

10) Issue subpoenas and administer oaths in preparation for formal hearings.

11) Conduct studies of appeals procedures in field agencies to ensure adherence to legal requirements and to facilitate determination of cases.

12) Review and evaluate data on documents such as claim applications, birth or death certificates, and physician or employer records.

23-1022.00 - Arbitrators, Mediators, and Conciliators

Facilitate negotiation and conflict resolution through dialogue. Resolve conflicts outside of the court system by mutual consent of parties involved.

Tasks

1) Authorize payment of valid claims.

2) Interview claimants, agents, or witnesses to obtain information about disputed issues.

3) Analyze evidence and apply relevant laws, regulations, policies, and precedents in order to reach conclusions.

4) Participate in court proceedings.

5) Prepare settlement agreements for disputants to sign.

6) Recommend acceptance or rejection of compromise settlement offers.

7) Research laws, regulations, policies, and precedent decisions to prepare for hearings.

8) Review and evaluate information from documents such as claim applications, birth or death certificates, and physician or employer records.

9) Use mediation techniques to facilitate communication between disputants, to further parties' understanding of different perspectives, and to guide parties toward mutual agreement.

10) Confer with disputants to clarify issues, identify underlying concerns, and develop an understanding of their respective needs and interests.

11) Determine existence and amount of liability, according to evidence, laws, and administrative and judicial precedents.

12) Issue subpoenas and administer oaths to prepare for formal hearings.

13) Conduct initial meetings with disputants to outline the arbitration process, settle procedural matters such as fees, and determine details such as witness numbers and time requirements.

14) Conduct studies of appeals procedures in order to ensure adherence to legal requirements and to facilitate disposition of cases.

15) Notify claimants of denied claims and appeal rights.

16) Organize and deliver public presentations about mediation to organizations such as community agencies and schools.

17) Set up appointments for parties to meet for mediation.

18) Prepare written opinions and decisions regarding cases.

19) Rule on exceptions, motions, and admissibility of evidence.

23-2011.00 - Paralegals and Legal Assistants

Assist lawyers by researching legal precedent, investigating facts, or preparing legal documents. Conduct research to support a legal proceeding, to formulate a defense, or to initiate legal action.

Tasks

1) Prepare affidavits or other documents, maintain document file, and file pleadings with court clerk.

2) Gather and analyze research data, such as statutes, decisions, and legal articles, codes, and documents.

3) Direct and coordinate law office activity, including delivery of subpoenas.

4) Investigate facts and law of cases to determine causes of action and to prepare cases.

5) Call upon witnesses to testify at hearing.

6) Keep and monitor legal volumes to ensure that law library is up-to-date.

7) Arbitrate disputes between parties and assist in real estate closing process.

8) Appraise and inventory real and personal property for estate planning.

Knowledge	Knowledge Definitions
English Language	Knowledge of the structure and content of the English language including the meaning and spelling of words, rules of composition, and grammar.
Law and Government	Knowledge of laws, legal codes, court procedures, precedents, government regulations, executive orders, agency rules, and the democratic political process.
Clerical	Knowledge of administrative and clerical procedures and systems such as word processing, managing files and records, stenography and transcription, designing forms, and other office procedures and terminology.
Computers and Electronics	Knowledge of circuit boards, processors, chips, electronic equipment, and computer hardware and software, including applications and programming.
Customer and Personal Service	Knowledge of principles and processes for providing customer and personal services. This includes customer needs assessment, meeting quality standards for services, and evaluation of customer satisfaction.
Administration and Management	Knowledge of business and management principles involved in strategic planning, resource allocation, human resources modeling, leadership technique, production methods, and coordination of people and resources.
Personnel and Human Resources	Knowledge of principles and procedures for personnel recruitment, selection, training, compensation and benefits, labor relations and negotiation, and personnel information systems.
Mathematics	Knowledge of arithmetic, algebra, geometry, calculus, statistics, and their applications.
Communications and Media	Knowledge of media production, communication, and dissemination techniques and methods. This includes alternative ways to inform and entertain via written, oral, and visual media.
Economics and Accounting	Knowledge of economic and accounting principles and practices, the financial markets, banking and the analysis and reporting of financial data.
Education and Training	Knowledge of principles and methods for curriculum and training design, teaching and instruction for individuals and groups, and the measurement of training effects.
Telecommunications	Knowledge of transmission, broadcasting, switching, control, and operation of telecommunications systems.
Psychology	Knowledge of human behavior and performance; individual differences in ability, personality, and interests; learning and motivation; psychological research methods; and the assessment and treatment of behavioral and affective disorders.
Medicine and Dentistry	Knowledge of the information and techniques needed to diagnose and treat human injuries, diseases, and deformities. This includes symptoms, treatment alternatives, drug properties and interactions, and preventive health-care measures.
Public Safety and Security	Knowledge of relevant equipment, policies, procedures, and strategies to promote effective local, state, or national security operations for the protection of people, data, property, and institutions.
Sociology and Anthropology	Knowledge of group behavior and dynamics, societal trends and influences, human migrations, ethnicity, cultures and their history and origins.
Therapy and Counseling	Knowledge of principles, methods, and procedures for diagnosis, treatment, and rehabilitation of physical and mental dysfunctions, and for career counseling and guidance.
Production and Processing	Knowledge of raw materials, production processes, quality control, costs, and other techniques for maximizing the effective manufacture and distribution of goods.
Design	Knowledge of design techniques, tools, and principles involved in production of precision technical plans, blueprints, drawings, and models.
Foreign Language	Knowledge of the structure and content of a foreign (non-English) language including the meaning and spelling of words, rules of composition and grammar, and pronunciation.
Sales and Marketing	Knowledge of principles and methods for showing, promoting, and selling products or services. This includes marketing strategy and tactics, product demonstration, sales techniques, and sales control systems.
Geography	Knowledge of principles and methods for describing the features of land, sea, and air masses, including their physical characteristics, locations, interrelationships, and distribution of plant, animal, and human life.
Engineering and Technology	Knowledge of the practical application of engineering science and technology. This includes applying principles, techniques, procedures, and equipment to the design and production of various goods and services.
Philosophy and Theology	Knowledge of different philosophical systems and religions. This includes their basic principles, values, ethics, ways of thinking, customs, practices, and their impact on human culture.
Transportation	Knowledge of principles and methods for moving people or goods by air, rail, sea, or road, including the relative costs and benefits.
Building and Construction	Knowledge of materials, methods, and the tools involved in the construction or repair of houses, buildings, or other structures such as highways and roads.

Physics	Knowledge and prediction of physical principles, laws, their interrelationships, and applications to understanding fluid, material, and atmospheric dynamics, and mechanical, electrical, atomic and sub- atomic structures and processes.
Mechanical	Knowledge of machines and tools, including their designs, uses, repair, and maintenance.
Biology	Knowledge of plant and animal organisms, their tissues, cells, functions, interdependencies, and interactions with each other and the environment.
Chemistry	Knowledge of the chemical composition, structure, and properties of substances and of the chemical processes and transformations that they undergo. This includes uses of chemicals and their interactions, danger signs, production techniques, and disposal methods.
Food Production	Knowledge of techniques and equipment for planting, growing, and harvesting food products (both plant and animal) for consumption, including storage/handling techniques.
History and Archeology	Knowledge of historical events and their causes, indicators, and effects on civilizations and cultures.
Fine Arts	Knowledge of the theory and techniques required to compose, produce, and perform works of music, dance, visual arts, drama, and sculpture.

Skills	Skills Definitions
Reading Comprehension	Understanding written sentences and paragraphs in work related documents.
Time Management	Managing one's own time and the time of others.
Active Listening	Giving full attention to what other people are saying, taking time to understand the points being made, asking questions as appropriate, and not interrupting at inappropriate times.
Writing	Communicating effectively in writing as appropriate for the needs of the audience.
Speaking	Talking to others to convey information effectively.
Active Learning	Understanding the implications of new information for both current and future problem-solving and decision-making.
Coordination	Adjusting actions in relation to others' actions.
Critical Thinking	Using logic and reasoning to identify the strengths and weaknesses of alternative solutions, conclusions or approaches to problems.
Monitoring	Monitoring/Assessing performance of yourself, other individuals, or organizations to make improvements or take corrective action.
Judgment and Decision Making	Considering the relative costs and benefits of potential actions to choose the most appropriate one.
Service Orientation	Actively looking for ways to help people.
Social Perceptiveness	Being aware of others' reactions and understanding why they react as they do.
Learning Strategies	Selecting and using training/instructional methods and procedures appropriate for the situation when learning or teaching new things.
Instructing	Teaching others how to do something.
Mathematics	Using mathematics to solve problems.
Complex Problem Solving	Identifying complex problems and reviewing related information to develop and evaluate options and implement solutions.
Equipment Selection	Determining the kind of tools and equipment needed to do a job.
Management of Personnel Resources	Motivating, developing, and directing people as they work, identifying the best people for the job.
Quality Control Analysis	Conducting tests and inspections of products, services, or processes to evaluate quality or performance.
Troubleshooting	Determining causes of operating errors and deciding what to do about it.
Persuasion	Persuading others to change their minds or behavior.
Management of Material Resources	Obtaining and seeing to the appropriate use of equipment, facilities, and materials needed to do certain work.
Management of Financial Resources	Determining how money will be spent to get the work done, and accounting for these expenditures.
Operations Analysis	Analyzing needs and product requirements to create a design.
Technology Design	Generating or adapting equipment and technology to serve user needs.
Operation and Control	Controlling operations of equipment or systems.
Negotiation	Bringing others together and trying to reconcile differences.
Equipment Maintenance	Performing routine maintenance on equipment and determining when and what kind of maintenance is needed.

Systems Analysis	Determining how a system should work and how changes in conditions, operations, and the environment will affect outcomes.
Programming	Writing computer programs for various purposes.
Systems Evaluation	Identifying measures or indicators of system performance and the actions needed to improve or correct performance, relative to the goals of the system.
Installation	Installing equipment, machines, wiring, or programs to meet specifications.
Repairing	Repairing machines or systems using the needed tools.
Science	Using scientific rules and methods to solve problems.
Operation Monitoring	Watching gauges, dials, or other indicators to make sure a machine is working properly.

Ability	Ability Definitions
Written Comprehension	The ability to read and understand information and ideas presented in writing.
Oral Expression	The ability to communicate information and ideas in speaking so others will understand.
Oral Comprehension	The ability to listen to and understand information and ideas presented through spoken words and sentences.
Inductive Reasoning	The ability to combine pieces of information to form general rules or conclusions (includes finding a relationship among seemingly unrelated events).
Written Expression	The ability to communicate information and ideas in writing so others will understand.
Near Vision	The ability to see details at close range (within a few feet of the observer).
Speech Clarity	The ability to speak clearly so others can understand you.
Speech Recognition	The ability to identify and understand the speech of another person.
Deductive Reasoning	The ability to apply general rules to specific problems to produce answers that make sense.
Information Ordering	The ability to arrange things or actions in a certain order or pattern according to a specific rule or set of rules (e.g., patterns of numbers, letters, words, pictures, mathematical operations).
Problem Sensitivity	The ability to tell when something is wrong or is likely to go wrong. It does not involve solving the problem, only recognizing there is a problem.
Category Flexibility	The ability to generate or use different sets of rules for combining or grouping things in different ways.
Flexibility of Closure	The ability to identify or detect a known pattern (a figure, object, word, or sound) that is hidden in other distracting material.
Finger Dexterity	The ability to make precisely coordinated movements of the fingers of one or both hands to grasp, manipulate, or assemble very small objects.
Originality	The ability to come up with unusual or clever ideas about a given topic or situation, or to develop creative ways to solve a problem.
Fluency of Ideas	The ability to come up with a number of ideas about a topic (the number of ideas is important, not their quality, correctness, or creativity).
Selective Attention	The ability to concentrate on a task over a period of time without being distracted.
Speed of Closure	The ability to quickly make sense of, combine, and organize information into meaningful patterns.
Memorization	The ability to remember information such as words, numbers, pictures, and procedures.
Perceptual Speed	The ability to quickly and accurately compare similarities and differences among sets of letters, numbers, objects, pictures, or patterns. The things to be compared may be presented at the same time or one after the other. This ability also includes comparing a presented object with a remembered object.
Auditory Attention	The ability to focus on a single source of sound in the presence of other distracting sounds.
Far Vision	The ability to see details at a distance.
Time Sharing	The ability to shift back and forth between two or more activities or sources of information (such as speech, sounds, touch, or other sources).
Number Facility	The ability to add, subtract, multiply, or divide quickly and correctly.
Mathematical Reasoning	The ability to choose the right mathematical methods or formulas to solve a problem.
Visualization	The ability to imagine how something will look after it is moved around or when its parts are moved or rearranged.

Manual Dexterity	The ability to quickly move your hand, your hand together with your arm, or your two hands to grasp, manipulate, or assemble objects.
Visual Color Discrimination	The ability to match or detect differences between colors, including shades of color and brightness.
Hearing Sensitivity	The ability to detect or tell the differences between sounds that vary in pitch and loudness.
Arm-Hand Steadiness	The ability to keep your hand and arm steady while moving your arm or while holding your arm and hand in one position.
Control Precision	The ability to quickly and repeatedly adjust the controls of a machine or a vehicle to exact positions.
Wrist-Finger Speed	The ability to make fast, simple, repeated movements of the fingers, hands, and wrists.
Trunk Strength	The ability to use your abdominal and lower back muscles to support part of the body repeatedly or continuously over time without 'giving out' or fatiguing.
Speed of Limb Movement	The ability to quickly move the arms and legs.
Extent Flexibility	The ability to bend, stretch, twist, or reach with your body, arms, and/or legs.
Static Strength	The ability to exert maximum muscle force to lift, push, pull, or carry objects.
Spatial Orientation	The ability to know your location in relation to the environment or to know where other objects are in relation to you.
Dynamic Flexibility	The ability to quickly and repeatedly bend, stretch, twist, or reach out with your body, arms, and/or legs.
Depth Perception	The ability to judge which of several objects is closer or farther away from you, or to judge the distance between you and an object.
Stamina	The ability to exert yourself physically over long periods of time without getting winded or out of breath.
Multilimb Coordination	The ability to coordinate two or more limbs (for example, two arms, two legs, or one leg and one arm) while sitting, standing, or lying down. It does not involve performing the activities while the whole body is in motion.
Gross Body Coordination	The ability to coordinate the movement of your arms, legs, and torso together when the whole body is in motion.
Gross Body Equilibrium	The ability to keep or regain your body balance or stay upright when in an unstable position.
Glare Sensitivity	The ability to see objects in the presence of glare or bright lighting.
Dynamic Strength	The ability to exert muscle force repeatedly or continuously over time. This involves muscular endurance and resistance to muscle fatigue.
Response Orientation	The ability to choose quickly between two or more movements in response to two or more different signals (lights, sounds, pictures). It includes the speed with which the correct response is started with the hand, foot, or other body part.
Sound Localization	The ability to tell the direction from which a sound originated.
Rate Control	The ability to time your movements or the movement of a piece of equipment in anticipation of changes in the speed and/or direction of a moving object or scene.
Peripheral Vision	The ability to see objects or movement of objects to one's side when the eyes are looking ahead.
Explosive Strength	The ability to use short bursts of muscle force to propel oneself (as in jumping or sprinting), or to throw an object.
Night Vision	The ability to see under low light conditions.
Reaction Time	The ability to quickly respond (with the hand, finger, or foot) to a signal (sound, light, picture) when it appears.

Work_Activity	Work_Activity Definitions
Getting Information	Observing, receiving, and otherwise obtaining information from all relevant sources.
Organizing, Planning, and Prioritizing Work	Developing specific goals and plans to prioritize, organize, and accomplish your work.
Interacting With Computers	Using computers and computer systems (including hardware and software) to program, write software, set up functions, enter data, or process information.
Communicating with Supervisors, Peers, or Subordin	Providing information to supervisors, co-workers, and subordinates by telephone, in written form, e-mail, or in person.
Processing Information	Compiling, coding, categorizing, calculating, tabulating, auditing, or verifying information or data.
Establishing and Maintaining Interpersonal Relatio	Developing constructive and cooperative working relationships with others, and maintaining them over time.
Documenting/Recording Information	Entering, transcribing, recording, storing, or maintaining information in written or electronic/magnetic form.

Communicating with Persons Outside Organization	Communicating with people outside the organization, representing the organization to customers, the public, government, and other external sources. This information can be exchanged in person, in writing, or by telephone or e-mail.
Updating and Using Relevant Knowledge	Keeping up-to-date technically and applying new knowledge to your job.
Making Decisions and Solving Problems	Analyzing information and evaluating results to choose the best solution and solve problems.
Performing Administrative Activities	Performing day-to-day administrative tasks such as maintaining information files and processing paperwork.
Identifying Objects, Actions, and Events	Identifying information by categorizing, estimating, recognizing differences or similarities, and detecting changes in circumstances or events.
Interpreting the Meaning of Information for Others	Translating or explaining what information means and how it can be used.
Evaluating Information to Determine Compliance wit	Using relevant information and individual judgment to determine whether events or processes comply with laws, regulations, or standards.
Analyzing Data or Information	Identifying the underlying principles, reasons, or facts of information by breaking down information or data into separate parts.
Scheduling Work and Activities	Scheduling events, programs, and activities, as well as the work of others.
Thinking Creatively	Developing, designing, or creating new applications, ideas, relationships, systems, or products, including artistic contributions.
Judging the Qualities of Things, Services, or Peop	Assessing the value, importance, or quality of things or people.
Provide Consultation and Advice to Others	Providing guidance and expert advice to management or other groups on technical, systems-, or process-related topics.
Resolving Conflicts and Negotiating with Others	Handling complaints, settling disputes, and resolving grievances and conflicts, or otherwise negotiating with others.
Monitor Processes, Materials, or Surroundings	Monitoring and reviewing information from materials, events, or the environment, to detect or assess problems.
Performing for or Working Directly with the Public	Performing for people or dealing directly with the public. This includes serving customers in restaurants and stores, and receiving clients or guests.
Guiding, Directing, and Motivating Subordinates	Providing guidance and direction to subordinates, including setting performance standards and monitoring performance.
Developing Objectives and Strategies	Establishing long-range objectives and specifying the strategies and actions to achieve them.
Coordinating the Work and Activities of Others	Getting members of a group to work together to accomplish tasks.
Training and Teaching Others	Identifying the educational needs of others, developing formal educational or training programs or classes, and teaching or instructing others.
Developing and Building Teams	Encouraging and building mutual trust, respect, and cooperation among team members.
Selling or Influencing Others	Convincing others to buy merchandise/goods or to otherwise change their minds or actions.
Coaching and Developing Others	Identifying the developmental needs of others and coaching, mentoring, or otherwise helping others to improve their knowledge or skills.
Estimating the Quantifiable Characteristics of Pro	Estimating sizes, distances, and quantities; or determining time, costs, resources, or materials needed to perform a work activity.
Assisting and Caring for Others	Providing personal assistance, medical attention, emotional support, or other personal care to others such as coworkers, customers, or patients.
Handling and Moving Objects	Using hands and arms in handling, installing, positioning, and moving materials, and manipulating things.
Monitoring and Controlling Resources	Monitoring and controlling resources and overseeing the spending of money.
Performing General Physical Activities	Performing physical activities that require considerable use of your arms and legs and moving your whole body, such as climbing, lifting, balancing, walking, stooping, and handling of materials.
Inspecting Equipment, Structures, or Material	Inspecting equipment, structures, or materials to identify the cause of errors or other problems or defects.
Staffing Organizational Units	Recruiting, interviewing, selecting, hiring, and promoting employees in an organization.
Operating Vehicles, Mechanized Devices, or Equipme	Running, maneuvering, navigating, or driving vehicles or mechanized equipment, such as forklifts, passenger vehicles, aircraft, or water craft.
Controlling Machines and Processes	Using either control mechanisms or direct physical activity to operate machines or processes (not including computers or vehicles).

Repairing and Maintaining Electronic Equipment	Servicing, repairing, calibrating, regulating, fine-tuning, or testing machines, devices, and equipment that operate primarily on the basis of electrical or electronic (not mechanical) principles.
Drafting, Laying Out, and Specifying Technical Dev	Providing documentation, detailed instructions, drawings, or specifications to tell others about how devices, parts, equipment, or structures are to be fabricated, constructed, assembled, modified, maintained, or used.
Repairing and Maintaining Mechanical Equipment	Servicing, repairing, adjusting, and testing machines, devices, moving parts, and equipment that operate primarily on the basis of mechanical (not electronic) principles.

Work_Context	Work_Context Definitions
Telephone	How often do you have telephone conversations in this job?
Face-to-Face Discussions	How often do you have to have face-to-face discussions with individuals or teams in this job?
Electronic Mail	How often do you use electronic mail in this job?
Spend Time Sitting	How much does this job require sitting?
Work With Work Group or Team	How important is it to work with others in a group or team in this job?
Contact With Others	How much does this job require the worker to be in contact with others (face-to-face, by telephone, or otherwise) in order to perform it?
Letters and Memos	How often does the job require written letters and memos?
Importance of Being Exact or Accurate	How important is being very exact or highly accurate in performing this job?
Indoors, Environmentally Controlled	How often does this job require working indoors in environmentally controlled conditions?
Time Pressure	How often does this job require the worker to meet strict deadlines?
Structured versus Unstructured Work	To what extent is this job structured for the worker, rather than allowing the worker to determine tasks, priorities, and goals?
Freedom to Make Decisions	How much decision making freedom, without supervision, does the job offer?
Impact of Decisions on Co-workers or Company Resul	How do the decisions an employee makes impact the results of co-workers, clients or the company?
Spend Time Making Repetitive Motions	How much does this job require making repetitive motions?
Coordinate or Lead Others	How important is it to coordinate or lead others in accomplishing work activities in this job?
Importance of Repeating Same Tasks	How important is repeating the same physical activities (e.g., key entry) or mental activities (e.g., checking entries in a ledger) over and over, without stopping, to performing this job?
Frequency of Decision Making	How frequently is the worker required to make decisions that affect other people, the financial resources, and/or the image and reputation of the organization?
Spend Time Using Your Hands to Handle, Control, or	How much does this job require using your hands to handle, control, or feel objects, tools or controls?
Responsibility for Outcomes and Results	How responsible is the worker for work outcomes and results of other workers?
Deal With External Customers	How important is it to work with external customers or the public in this job?
Deal With Unpleasant or Angry People	How frequently does the worker have to deal with unpleasant, angry, or discourteous individuals as part of the job requirements?
Degree of Automation	How automated is the job?
Consequence of Error	How serious would the result usually be if the worker made a mistake that was not readily correctable?
Level of Competition	To what extent does this job require the worker to compete or to be aware of competitive pressures?
Sounds, Noise Levels Are Distracting or Uncomforta	How often does this job require working exposed to sounds and noise levels that are distracting or uncomfortable?
Frequency of Conflict Situations	How often are there conflict situations the employee has to face in this job?
Physical Proximity	To what extent does this job require the worker to perform job tasks in close physical proximity to other people?
Spend Time Standing	How much does this job require standing?
Spend Time Walking and Running	How much does this job require walking and running?
In an Enclosed Vehicle or Equipment	How often does this job require working in a closed vehicle or equipment (e.g., car)?
Cramped Work Space, Awkward Positions	How often does this job require working in cramped work spaces that requires getting into awkward positions?
Exposed to Contaminants	How often does this job require working exposed to contaminants (such as pollutants, gases, dust or odors)?

Public Speaking	How often do you have to perform public speaking in this job?
Spend Time Kneeling, Crouching, Stooping, or Crawl	How much does this job require kneeling, crouching, stooping or crawling?
Exposed to Minor Burns, Cuts, Bites, or Stings	How often does this job require exposure to minor burns, cuts, bites, or stings?
Indoors, Not Environmentally Controlled	How often does this job require working indoors in non-controlled environmental conditions (e.g., warehouse without heat)?
Spend Time Bending or Twisting the Body	How much does this job require bending or twisting your body?
Very Hot or Cold Temperatures	How often does this job require working in very hot (above 90 F degrees) or very cold (below 32 F degrees) temperatures?
Responsible for Others' Health and Safety	How much responsibility is there for the health and safety of others in this job?
Deal With Physically Aggressive People	How frequently does this job require the worker to deal with physical aggression of violent individuals?
Outdoors, Exposed to Weather	How often does this job require working outdoors, exposed to all weather conditions?
Pace Determined by Speed of Equipment	How important is it to this job that the pace is determined by the speed of equipment or machinery? (This does not refer to keeping busy at all times on this job.)
Spend Time Keeping or Regaining Balance	How much does this job require keeping or regaining your balance?
Outdoors, Under Cover	How often does this job require working outdoors, under cover (e.g., structure with roof but no walls)?
Extremely Bright or Inadequate Lighting	How often does this job require working in extremely bright or inadequate lighting conditions?
Exposed to High Places	How often does this job require exposure to high places?
Spend Time Climbing Ladders, Scaffolds, or Poles	How much does this job require climbing ladders, scaffolds, or poles?
Exposed to Hazardous Equipment	How often does this job require exposure to hazardous equipment?
In an Open Vehicle or Equipment	How often does this job require working in an open vehicle or equipment (e.g., tractor)?
Exposed to Hazardous Conditions	How often does this job require exposure to hazardous conditions?
Exposed to Whole Body Vibration	How often does this job require exposure to whole body vibration (e.g., operate a jackhammer)?
Exposed to Disease or Infections	How often does this job require exposure to disease/infections?
Exposed to Radiation	How often does this job require exposure to radiation?
Wear Common Protective or Safety Equipment such as	How much does this job require wearing common protective or safety equipment such as safety shoes, glasses, gloves, hard hats or live jackets?
Wear Specialized Protective or Safety Equipment su	How much does this job require wearing specialized protective or safety equipment such as breathing apparatus, safety harness, full protection suits, or radiation protection?

Job Zone Component	Job Zone Component Definitions
Title	Job Zone Three: Medium Preparation Needed
Overall Experience	Previous work-related skill, knowledge, or experience is required for these occupations. For example, an electrician must have completed three or four years of apprenticeship or several years of vocational training, and often must have passed a licensing exam, in order to perform the job.
Job Training	Employees in these occupations usually need one or two years of training involving both on-the-job experience and informal training with experienced workers.
Job Zone Examples	These occupations usually involve using communication and organizational skills to coordinate, supervise, manage, or train others to accomplish goals. Examples include dental assistants, electricians, fish and game wardens, legal secretaries, personnel recruiters, and recreation workers.
SVP Range	(6.0 to < 7.0)
Education	Most occupations in this zone require training in vocational schools, related on-the-job experience, or an associate's degree. Some may require a bachelor's degree.

Work_Styles	Work_Styles Definitions
Attention to Detail	Job requires being careful about detail and thorough in completing work tasks.
Dependability	Job requires being reliable, responsible, and dependable, and fulfilling obligations.

Cooperation	Job requires being pleasant with others on the job and displaying a good-natured, cooperative attitude.
Initiative	Job requires a willingness to take on responsibilities and challenges.
Stress Tolerance	Job requires accepting criticism and dealing calmly and effectively with high stress situations.
Persistence	Job requires persistence in the face of obstacles.
Self Control	Job requires maintaining composure, keeping emotions in check, controlling anger, and avoiding aggressive behavior, even in very difficult situations.
Integrity	Job requires being honest and ethical.
Achievement/Effort	Job requires establishing and maintaining personally challenging achievement goals and exerting effort toward mastering tasks.
Adaptability/Flexibility	Job requires being open to change (positive or negative) and to considerable variety in the workplace.
Independence	Job requires developing one's own ways of doing things, guiding oneself with little or no supervision, and depending on oneself to get things done.
Concern for Others	Job requires being sensitive to others' needs and feelings and being understanding and helpful on the job.
Social Orientation	Job requires preferring to work with others rather than alone, and being personally connected with others on the job.
Analytical Thinking	Job requires analyzing information and using logic to address work-related issues and problems.
Leadership	Job requires a willingness to lead, take charge, and offer opinions and direction.
Innovation	Job requires creativity and alternative thinking to develop new ideas for and answers to work-related problems.

23-2091.00 - Court Reporters

Use verbatim methods and equipment to capture, store, retrieve, and transcribe pretrial and trial proceedings or other information. Includes stenocaptioners who operate computerized stenographic captioning equipment to provide captions of live or prerecorded broadcasts for hearing-impaired viewers.

Tasks

1) Ask speakers to clarify inaudible statements.

2) Record symbols on computer disks or CD-ROM, then translate and display them as text in computer-aided transcription process.

3) Caption news, emergency broadcasts, sporting events, and other programming for television networks or cable stations.

4) File a legible transcript of records of a court case with the court clerk's office

5) Provide transcripts of proceedings upon request of judges, lawyers, or the public.

6) Take notes in shorthand or use a stenotype or shorthand machine that prints letters on a paper tape.

7) Record verbatim proceedings of courts, legislative assemblies, committee meetings, and other proceedings, using computerized recording equipment, electronic stenograph machines, or stenomasks.

8) Respond to requests during court sessions to read portions of the proceedings already recorded.

9) Transcribe recorded proceedings in accordance with established formats.

10) Verify accuracy of transcripts by checking copies against original records of proceedings and accuracy of rulings by checking with judges.

11) Record depositions and other proceedings for attorneys.

23-2092.00 - Law Clerks

Assist lawyers or judges by researching or preparing legal documents. May meet with clients or assist lawyers and judges in court.

Tasks

1) Review and file pleadings, petitions and other documents relevant to court actions.

2) Prepare affidavits of documents and maintain document files and case correspondence.

3) Research and analyze law sources to prepare drafts of briefs or arguments for review, approval, and use by attorney.

4) Store, catalog, and maintain currency of legal volumes.

5) Communicate and arbitrate disputes between parties.

6) Prepare real estate closing statements and assist in closing process.

7) Serve copies of pleas to opposing counsel.

8) Deliver or direct delivery of subpoenas to witnesses and parties to action.

9) Arrange transportation and accommodation for witnesses and jurors, if required.

10) Appraise and inventory real and personal property for estate planning.

Knowledge	Knowledge Definitions
Law and Government	Knowledge of laws, legal codes, court procedures, precedents, government regulations, executive orders, agency rules, and the democratic political process.
English Language	Knowledge of the structure and content of the English language including the meaning and spelling of words, rules of composition, and grammar.
Clerical	Knowledge of administrative and clerical procedures and systems such as word processing, managing files and records, stenography and transcription, designing forms, and other office procedures and terminology.
Customer and Personal Service	Knowledge of principles and processes for providing customer and personal services. This includes customer needs assessment, meeting quality standards for services, and evaluation of customer satisfaction.
Computers and Electronics	Knowledge of circuit boards, processors, chips, electronic equipment, and computer hardware and software, including applications and programming.
Public Safety and Security	Knowledge of relevant equipment, policies, procedures, and strategies to promote effective local, state, or national security operations for the protection of people, data, property, and institutions.
Administration and Management	Knowledge of business and management principles involved in strategic planning, resource allocation, human resources modeling, leadership technique, production methods, and coordination of people and resources.
Psychology	Knowledge of human behavior and performance; individual differences in ability, personality, and interests; learning and motivation; psychological research methods; and the assessment and treatment of behavioral and affective disorders.
Economics and Accounting	Knowledge of economic and accounting principles and practices, the financial markets, banking and the analysis and reporting of financial data.
Mathematics	Knowledge of arithmetic, algebra, geometry, calculus, statistics, and their applications.
Sales and Marketing	Knowledge of principles and methods for showing, promoting, and selling products or services. This includes marketing strategy and tactics, product demonstration, sales techniques, and sales control systems.
Personnel and Human Resources	Knowledge of principles and procedures for personnel recruitment, selection, training, compensation and benefits, labor relations and negotiation, and personnel information systems.
Communications and Media	Knowledge of media production, communication, and dissemination techniques and methods. This includes alternative ways to inform and entertain via written, oral, and visual media.
Education and Training	Knowledge of principles and methods for curriculum and training design, teaching and instruction for individuals and groups, and the measurement of training effects.
Sociology and Anthropology	Knowledge of group behavior and dynamics, societal trends and influences, human migrations, ethnicity, cultures and their history and origins.
Design	Knowledge of design techniques, tools, and principles involved in production of precision technical plans, blueprints, drawings, and models.
Telecommunications	Knowledge of transmission, broadcasting, switching, control, and operation of telecommunications systems.
Building and Construction	Knowledge of materials, methods, and the tools involved in the construction or repair of houses, buildings, or other structures such as highways and roads.

Philosophy and Theology	Knowledge of different philosophical systems and religions. This includes their basic principles, values, ethics, ways of thinking, customs, practices, and their impact on human culture.
History and Archeology	Knowledge of historical events and their causes, indicators, and effects on civilizations and cultures.
Therapy and Counseling	Knowledge of principles, methods, and procedures for diagnosis, treatment, and rehabilitation of physical and mental dysfunctions, and for career counseling and guidance.
Mechanical	Knowledge of machines and tools, including their designs, uses, repair, and maintenance.
Geography	Knowledge of principles and methods for describing the features of land, sea, and air masses, including their physical characteristics, locations, interrelationships, and distribution of plant, animal, and human life.
Medicine and Dentistry	Knowledge of the information and techniques needed to diagnose and treat human injuries, diseases, and deformities. This includes symptoms, treatment alternatives, drug properties and interactions, and preventive health-care measures.
Foreign Language	Knowledge of the structure and content of a foreign (non-English) language including the meaning and spelling of words, rules of composition and grammar, and pronunciation.
Transportation	Knowledge of principles and methods for moving people or goods by air, rail, sea, or road, including the relative costs and benefits.
Production and Processing	Knowledge of raw materials, production processes, quality control, costs, and other techniques for maximizing the effective manufacture and distribution of goods.
Engineering and Technology	Knowledge of the practical application of engineering science and technology. This includes applying principles, techniques, procedures, and equipment to the design and production of various goods and services.
Biology	Knowledge of plant and animal organisms, their tissues, cells, functions, interdependencies, and interactions with each other and the environment.
Chemistry	Knowledge of the chemical composition, structure, and properties of substances and of the chemical processes and transformations that they undergo. This includes uses of chemicals and their interactions, danger signs, production techniques, and disposal methods.
Physics	Knowledge and prediction of physical principles, laws, their interrelationships, and applications to understanding fluid, material, and atmospheric dynamics, and mechanical, electrical, atomic and sub-atomic structures and processes.
Fine Arts	Knowledge of the theory and techniques required to compose, produce, and perform works of music, dance, visual arts, drama, and sculpture.
Food Production	Knowledge of techniques and equipment for planting, growing, and harvesting food products (both plant and animal) for consumption, including storage/handling techniques.

Skills	Skills Definitions
Reading Comprehension	Understanding written sentences and paragraphs in work related documents.
Critical Thinking	Using logic and reasoning to identify the strengths and weaknesses of alternative solutions, conclusions or approaches to problems.
Writing	Communicating effectively in writing as appropriate for the needs of the audience.
Active Learning	Understanding the implications of new information for both current and future problem-solving and decision-making.
Active Listening	Giving full attention to what other people are saying, taking time to understand the points being made, asking questions as appropriate, and not interrupting at inappropriate times.
Time Management	Managing one's own time and the time of others.
Judgment and Decision Making	Considering the relative costs and benefits of potential actions to choose the most appropriate one.
Complex Problem Solving	Identifying complex problems and reviewing related information to develop and evaluate options and implement solutions.
Social Perceptiveness	Being aware of others' reactions and understanding why they react as they do.
Persuasion	Persuading others to change their minds or behavior.
Speaking	Talking to others to convey information effectively.
Coordination	Adjusting actions in relation to others' actions.
Negotiation	Bringing others together and trying to reconcile differences.

Monitoring	Monitoring/Assessing performance of yourself, other individuals, or organizations to make improvements or take corrective action.
Learning Strategies	Selecting and using training/instructional methods and procedures appropriate for the situation when learning or teaching new things.
Instructing	Teaching others how to do something.
Service Orientation	Actively looking for ways to help people.
Quality Control Analysis	Conducting tests and inspections of products, services, or processes to evaluate quality or performance.
Mathematics	Using mathematics to solve problems.
Equipment Selection	Determining the kind of tools and equipment needed to do a job.
Troubleshooting	Determining causes of operating errors and deciding what to do about it.
Management of Personnel Resources	Motivating, developing, and directing people as they work, identifying the best people for the job.
Management of Material Resources	Obtaining and seeing to the appropriate use of equipment, facilities, and materials needed to do certain work.
Systems Analysis	Determining how a system should work and how changes in conditions, operations, and the environment will affect outcomes.
Science	Using scientific rules and methods to solve problems.
Operations Analysis	Analyzing needs and product requirements to create a design.
Management of Financial Resources	Determining how money will be spent to get the work done, and accounting for these expenditures.
Operation and Control	Controlling operations of equipment or systems.
Systems Evaluation	Identifying measures or indicators of system performance and the actions needed to improve or correct performance, relative to the goals of the system.
Programming	Writing computer programs for various purposes.
Technology Design	Generating or adapting equipment and technology to serve user needs.
Installation	Installing equipment, machines, wiring, or programs to meet specifications.
Equipment Maintenance	Performing routine maintenance on equipment and determining when and what kind of maintenance is needed.
Repairing	Repairing machines or systems using the needed tools.
Operation Monitoring	Watching gauges, dials, or other indicators to make sure a machine is working properly.

Ability	Ability Definitions
Oral Comprehension	The ability to listen to and understand information and ideas presented through spoken words and sentences.
Problem Sensitivity	The ability to tell when something is wrong or is likely to go wrong. It does not involve solving the problem, only recognizing there is a problem.
Oral Expression	The ability to communicate information and ideas in speaking so others will understand.
Written Comprehension	The ability to read and understand information and ideas presented in writing.
Speech Recognition	The ability to identify and understand the speech of another person.
Speech Clarity	The ability to speak clearly so others can understand you.
Near Vision	The ability to see details at close range (within a few feet of the observer).
Deductive Reasoning	The ability to apply general rules to specific problems to produce answers that make sense.
Inductive Reasoning	The ability to combine pieces of information to form general rules or conclusions (includes finding a relationship among seemingly unrelated events).
Information Ordering	The ability to arrange things or actions in a certain order or pattern according to a specific rule or set of rules (e.g., patterns of numbers, letters, words, pictures, mathematical operations).
Written Expression	The ability to communicate information and ideas in writing so others will understand.
Category Flexibility	The ability to generate or use different sets of rules for combining or grouping things in different ways.
Selective Attention	The ability to concentrate on a task over a period of time without being distracted.
Speed of Closure	The ability to quickly make sense of, combine, and organize information into meaningful patterns.
Flexibility of Closure	The ability to identify or detect a known pattern (a figure, object, word, or sound) that is hidden in other distracting material.

Originality	The ability to come up with unusual or clever ideas about a given topic or situation, or to develop creative ways to solve a problem.
Fluency of Ideas	The ability to come up with a number of ideas about a topic (the number of ideas is important, not their quality, correctness, or creativity).
Perceptual Speed	The ability to quickly and accurately compare similarities and differences among sets of letters, numbers, objects, pictures, or patterns. The things to be compared may be presented at the same time or one after the other. This ability also includes comparing a presented object with a remembered object.
Number Facility	The ability to add, subtract, multiply, or divide quickly and correctly.
Finger Dexterity	The ability to make precisely coordinated movements of the fingers of one or both hands to grasp, manipulate, or assemble very small objects.
Far Vision	The ability to see details at a distance.
Memorization	The ability to remember information such as words, numbers, pictures, and procedures.
Mathematical Reasoning	The ability to choose the right mathematical methods or formulas to solve a problem.
Visualization	The ability to imagine how something will look after it is moved around or when its parts are moved or rearranged.
Hearing Sensitivity	The ability to detect or tell the differences between sounds that vary in pitch and loudness.
Visual Color Discrimination	The ability to match or detect differences between colors, including shades of color and brightness.
Time Sharing	The ability to shift back and forth between two or more activities or sources of information (such as speech, sounds, touch, or other sources).
Wrist-Finger Speed	The ability to make fast, simple, repeated movements of the fingers, hands, and wrists.
Manual Dexterity	The ability to quickly move your hand, your hand together with your arm, or your two hands to grasp, manipulate, or assemble objects.
Auditory Attention	The ability to focus on a single source of sound in the presence of other distracting sounds.
Control Precision	The ability to quickly and repeatedly adjust the controls of a machine or a vehicle to exact positions.
Reaction Time	The ability to quickly respond (with the hand, finger, or foot) to a signal (sound, light, picture) when it appears.
Response Orientation	The ability to choose quickly between two or more movements in response to two or more different signals (lights, sounds, pictures). It includes the speed with which the correct response is started with the hand, foot, or other body part.
Spatial Orientation	The ability to know your location in relation to the environment or to know where other objects are in relation to you.
Glare Sensitivity	The ability to see objects in the presence of glare or bright lighting.
Speed of Limb Movement	The ability to quickly move the arms and legs.
Static Strength	The ability to exert maximum muscle force to lift, push, pull, or carry objects.
Rate Control	The ability to time your movements or the movement of a piece of equipment in anticipation of changes in the speed and/or direction of a moving object or scene.
Arm-Hand Steadiness	The ability to keep your hand and arm steady while moving your arm or while holding your arm and hand in one position.
Gross Body Equilibrium	The ability to keep or regain your body balance or stay upright when in an unstable position.
Multilimb Coordination	The ability to coordinate two or more limbs (for example, two arms, two legs, or one leg and one arm) while sitting, standing, or lying down. It does not involve performing the activities while the whole body is in motion.
Sound Localization	The ability to tell the direction from which a sound originated.
Dynamic Flexibility	The ability to quickly and repeatedly bend, stretch, twist, or reach out with your body, arms, or legs.
Night Vision	The ability to see under low light conditions.
Depth Perception	The ability to judge which of several objects is closer or farther away from you, or to judge the distance between you and an object.
Stamina	The ability to exert yourself physically over long periods of time without getting winded or out of breath.
Peripheral Vision	The ability to see objects or movement of objects to one's side when the eyes are looking ahead.
Dynamic Strength	The ability to exert muscle force repeatedly or continuously over time. This involves muscular endurance and resistance to muscle fatigue.
Extent Flexibility	The ability to bend, stretch, twist, or reach with your body, arms, and/or legs.
Explosive Strength	The ability to use short bursts of muscle force to propel oneself (as in jumping or sprinting), or to throw an object.
Gross Body Coordination	The ability to coordinate the movement of your arms, legs, and torso together when the whole body is in motion.
Trunk Strength	The ability to use your abdominal and lower back muscles to support part of the body repeatedly or continuously over time without 'giving out' or fatiguing.

Work_Activity	Work_Activity Definitions
Getting Information	Observing, receiving, and otherwise obtaining information from all relevant sources.
Establishing and Maintaining Interpersonal Relatio	Developing constructive and cooperative working relationships with others, and maintaining them over time.
Evaluating Information to Determine Compliance wit	Using relevant information and individual judgment to determine whether events or processes comply with laws, regulations, or standards.
Updating and Using Relevant Knowledge	Keeping up-to-date technically and applying new knowledge to your job.
Organizing, Planning, and Prioritizing Work	Developing specific goals and plans to prioritize, organize, and accomplish your work.
Interacting With Computers	Using computers and computer systems (including hardware and software) to program, write software, set up functions, enter data, or process information.
Communicating with Supervisors, Peers, or Subordin	Providing information to supervisors, co-workers, and subordinates by telephone, in written form, e-mail, or in person.
Interpreting the Meaning of Information for Others	Translating or explaining what information means and how it can be used.
Analyzing Data or Information	Identifying the underlying principles, reasons, or facts of information by breaking down information or data into separate parts.
Making Decisions and Solving Problems	Analyzing information and evaluating results to choose the best solution and solve problems.
Resolving Conflicts and Negotiating with Others	Handling complaints, settling disputes, and resolving grievances and conflicts, or otherwise negotiating with others.
Communicating with Persons Outside Organization	Communicating with people outside the organization, representing the organization to customers, the public, government, and other external sources. This information can be exchanged in person, in writing, or by telephone or e-mail.
Documenting/Recording Information	Entering, transcribing, recording, storing, or maintaining information in written or electronic/magnetic form.
Processing Information	Compiling, coding, categorizing, calculating, tabulating, auditing, or verifying information or data.
Developing Objectives and Strategies	Establishing long-range objectives and specifying the strategies and actions to achieve them.
Identifying Objects, Actions, and Events	Identifying information by categorizing, estimating, recognizing differences or similarities, and detecting changes in circumstances or events.
Assisting and Caring for Others	Providing personal assistance, medical attention, emotional support, or other personal care to others such as coworkers, customers, or patients.
Thinking Creatively	Developing, designing, or creating new applications, ideas, relationships, systems, or products, including artistic contributions.
Judging the Qualities of Things, Services, or Peop	Assessing the value, importance, or quality of things or people.
Provide Consultation and Advice to Others	Providing guidance and expert advice to management or other groups on technical, systems-, or process-related topics.
Performing Administrative Activities	Performing day-to-day administrative tasks such as maintaining information files and processing paperwork.
Scheduling Work and Activities	Scheduling events, programs, and activities, as well as the work of others.
Developing and Building Teams	Encouraging and building mutual trust, respect, and cooperation among team members.
Coordinating the Work and Activities of Others	Getting members of a group to work together to accomplish tasks.
Monitor Processes, Materials, or Surroundings	Monitoring and reviewing information from materials, events, or the environment, to detect or assess problems.
Coaching and Developing Others	Identifying the developmental needs of others and coaching, mentoring, or otherwise helping others to improve their knowledge or skills.
Inspecting Equipment, Structures, or Material	Inspecting equipment, structures, or materials to identify the cause of errors or other problems or defects.

Training and Teaching Others	Identifying the educational needs of others, developing formal educational or training programs or classes, and teaching or instructing others.
Estimating the Quantifiable Characteristics of Pro	Estimating sizes, distances, and quantities; or determining time, costs, resources, or materials needed to perform a work activity.
Guiding, Directing, and Motivating Subordinates	Providing guidance and direction to subordinates, including setting performance standards and monitoring performance.
Performing for or Working Directly with the Public	Performing for people or dealing directly with the public. This includes serving customers in restaurants and stores, and receiving clients or guests.
Selling or Influencing Others	Convincing others to buy merchandise/goods or to otherwise change their minds or actions.
Monitoring and Controlling Resources	Monitoring and controlling resources and overseeing the spending of money.
Handling and Moving Objects	Using hands and arms in handling, installing, positioning, and moving materials, and manipulating things.
Controlling Machines and Processes	Using either control mechanisms or direct physical activity to operate machines or processes (not including computers or vehicles).
Drafting, Laying Out, and Specifying Technical Dev	Providing documentation, detailed instructions, drawings, or specifications to tell others about how devices, parts, equipment, or structures are to be fabricated, constructed, assembled, modified, maintained, or used.
Performing General Physical Activities	Performing physical activities that require considerable use of your arms and legs and moving your whole body, such as climbing, lifting, balancing, walking, stooping, and handling of materials.
Staffing Organizational Units	Recruiting, interviewing, selecting, hiring, and promoting employees in an organization.
Operating Vehicles, Mechanized Devices, or Equipme	Running, maneuvering, navigating, or driving vehicles or mechanized equipment, such as forklifts, passenger vehicles, aircraft, or water craft.
Repairing and Maintaining Electronic Equipment	Servicing, repairing, calibrating, regulating, fine-tuning, or testing machines, devices, and equipment that operate primarily on the basis of electrical or electronic (not mechanical) principles.
Repairing and Maintaining Mechanical Equipment	Servicing, repairing, adjusting, and testing machines, devices, moving parts, and equipment that operate primarily on the basis of mechanical (not electronic) principles.

Work_Context	Work_Context Definitions
Indoors, Environmentally Controlled	How often does this job require working indoors in environmentally controlled conditions?
Telephone	How often do you have telephone conversations in this job?
Face-to-Face Discussions	How often do you have to have face-to-face discussions with individuals or teams in this job?
Contact With Others	How much does this job require the worker to be in contact with others (face-to-face, by telephone, or otherwise) in order to perform it?
Importance of Being Exact or Accurate	How important is being very exact or highly accurate in performing this job?
Spend Time Sitting	How much does this job require sitting?
Letters and Memos	How often does the job require written letters and memos?
Structured versus Unstructured Work	To what extent is this job structured for the worker, rather than allowing the worker to determine tasks, priorities, and goals?
Electronic Mail	How often do you use electronic mail in this job?
Freedom to Make Decisions	How much decision making freedom, without supervision, does the job offer?
Time Pressure	How often does this job require the worker to meet strict deadlines?
Deal With Unpleasant or Angry People	How frequently does the worker have to deal with unpleasant, angry, or discourteous individuals as part of the job requirements?
Importance of Repeating Same Tasks	How important is repeating the same physical activities (e.g., key entry) or mental activities (e.g., checking entries in a ledger) over and over, without stopping, to performing this job?
Frequency of Conflict Situations	How often are there conflict situations the employee has to face in this job?
Impact of Decisions on Co-workers or Company Resul	How do the decisions an employee makes impact the results of co-workers, clients or the company?
Work With Work Group or Team	How important is it to work with others in a group or team in this job?
Deal With External Customers	How important is it to work with external customers or the public in this job?

Frequency of Decision Making	How frequently is the worker required to make decisions that affect other people, the financial resources, and/or the image and reputation of the organization?
Physical Proximity	To what extent does this job require the worker to perform job tasks in close physical proximity to other people?
Spend Time Making Repetitive Motions	How much does this job require making repetitive motions?
Degree of Automation	How automated is the job?
Level of Competition	To what extent does this job require the worker to compete or to be aware of competitive pressures?
Consequence of Error	How serious would the result usually be if the worker made a mistake that was not readily correctable?
Coordinate or Lead Others	How important is it to coordinate or lead others in accomplishing work activities in this job?
Spend Time Standing	How much does this job require standing?
Spend Time Using Your Hands to Handle, Control, or	How much does this job require using your hands to handle, control, or feel objects, tools or controls?
Sounds, Noise Levels Are Distracting or Uncomforta	How often does this job require working exposed to sounds and noise levels that are distracting or uncomfortable?
Spend Time Walking and Running	How much does this job require walking and running?
Responsibility for Outcomes and Results	How responsible is the worker for work outcomes and results of other workers?
Deal With Physically Aggressive People	How frequently does this job require the worker to deal with physical aggression of violent individuals?
Responsible for Others' Health and Safety	How much responsibility is there for the health and safety of others in this job?
Public Speaking	How often do you have to perform public speaking in this job?
Spend Time Bending or Twisting the Body	How much does this job require bending or twisting your body?
Cramped Work Space, Awkward Positions	How often does this job require working in cramped work spaces that requires getting into awkward positions?
In an Enclosed Vehicle or Equipment	How often does this job require working in a closed vehicle or equipment (e.g., car)?
Spend Time Kneeling, Crouching, Stooping, or Crawl	How much does this job require kneeling, crouching, stooping, or crawling?
Very Hot or Cold Temperatures	How often does this job require working in very hot (above 90 F degrees) or very cold (below 32 F degrees) temperatures?
Exposed to Contaminants	How often does this job require working exposed to contaminants (such as pollutants, gases, dust or odors)?
Extremely Bright or Inadequate Lighting	How often does this job require working in extremely bright or inadequate lighting conditions?
Exposed to Minor Burns, Cuts, Bites, or Stings	How often does this job require exposure to minor burns, cuts, bites, or stings?
Indoors, Not Environmentally Controlled	How often does this job require working indoors in non-controlled environmental conditions (e.g., warehouse without heat)?
Exposed to Disease or Infections	How often does this job require exposure to disease/infections?
Outdoors, Under Cover	How often does this job require working outdoors, under cover (e.g., structure with roof but no walls)?
Outdoors, Exposed to Weather	How often does this job require working outdoors, exposed to all weather conditions?
Pace Determined by Speed of Equipment	How important is it to this job that the pace is determined by the speed of equipment or machinery? (This does not refer to keeping busy at all times on this job.)
Spend Time Keeping or Regaining Balance	How much does this job require keeping or regaining your balance?
Exposed to Hazardous Equipment	How often does this job require exposure to hazardous equipment?
Spend Time Climbing Ladders, Scaffolds, or Poles	How much does this job require climbing ladders, scaffolds, or poles?
In an Open Vehicle or Equipment	How often does this job require working in an open vehicle or equipment (e.g., tractor)?
Wear Specialized Protective or Safety Equipment su	How much does this job require wearing specialized protective or safety equipment such as breathing apparatus, safety harness, full protection suits, or radiation protection?
Exposed to High Places	How often does this job require exposure to high places?
Exposed to Radiation	How often does this job require exposure to radiation?
Exposed to Whole Body Vibration	How often does this job require exposure to whole body vibration (e.g., operate a jackhammer)?
Wear Common Protective or Safety Equipment such as	How much does this job require wearing common protective or safety equipment such as safety shoes, glasses, gloves, hard hats or live jackets?

Exposed to Hazardous Conditions	How often does this job require exposure to hazardous conditions?

Job Zone Component	Job Zone Component Definitions
Title	Job Zone Four: Considerable Preparation Needed
Overall Experience	A minimum of two to four years of work-related skill, knowledge, or experience is needed for these occupations. For example, an accountant must complete four years of college and work for several years in accounting to be considered qualified.
Job Training	Employees in these occupations usually need several years of work-related experience, on-the-job training, and/or vocational training.
Job Zone Examples	Many of these occupations involve coordinating, supervising, managing, or training others. Examples include accountants, chefs and head cooks, computer programmers, historians, pharmacists, and police detectives.
SVP Range	(7.0 to < 8.0)
Education	Most of these occupations require a four - year bachelor's degree, but some do not.

Work_Styles	Work_Styles Definitions
Analytical Thinking	Job requires analyzing information and using logic to address work-related issues and problems.
Attention to Detail	Job requires being careful about detail and thorough in completing work tasks.
Integrity	Job requires being honest and ethical.
Dependability	Job requires being reliable, responsible, and dependable, and fulfilling obligations.
Independence	Job requires developing one's own ways of doing things, guiding oneself with little or no supervision, and depending on oneself to get things done.
Initiative	Job requires a willingness to take on responsibilities and challenges.
Stress Tolerance	Job requires accepting criticism and dealing calmly and effectively with high stress situations.
Self Control	Job requires maintaining composure, keeping emotions in check, controlling anger, and avoiding aggressive behavior, even in very difficult situations.
Cooperation	Job requires being pleasant with others on the job and displaying a good-natured, cooperative attitude.
Persistence	Job requires persistence in the face of obstacles.
Adaptability/Flexibility	Job requires being open to change (positive or negative) and to considerable variety in the workplace.
Achievement/Effort	Job requires establishing and maintaining personally challenging achievement goals and exerting effort toward mastering tasks.
Concern for Others	Job requires being sensitive to others' needs and feelings and being understanding and helpful on the job.
Innovation	Job requires creativity and alternative thinking to develop new ideas for and answers to work-related problems.
Social Orientation	Job requires preferring to work with others rather than alone, and being personally connected with others on the job.
Leadership	Job requires a willingness to lead, take charge, and offer opinions and direction.

23-2093.00 - Title Examiners, Abstractors, and Searchers

Search real estate records, examine titles, or summarize pertinent legal or insurance details for a variety of purposes. May compile lists of mortgages, contracts, and other instruments pertaining to titles by searching public and private records for law firms, real estate agencies, or title insurance companies.

Tasks

1) Summarize pertinent legal or insurance details, or sections of statutes or case law from reference books so that they can be used in examinations, or as proofs or ready reference.

2) Copy or summarize recorded documents, such as mortgages, trust deeds, and contracts, that affect property titles.

3) Examine individual titles in order to determine if restrictions, such as delinquent taxes, will affect titles and limit property use.

4) Read search requests in order to ascertain types of title evidence required and to obtain descriptions of properties and names of involved parties.

5) Determine whether land-related documents can be registered under the relevant legislation such as the Land Titles Act.

6) Prepare lists of all legal instruments applying to a specific piece of land and the buildings on it.

7) Prepare reports describing any title encumbrances encountered during searching activities, and outlining actions needed to clear titles.

8) Assess fees related to registration of property-related documents.

9) Prepare and issue title commitments and title insurance policies based on information compiled from title searches.

10) Prepare real estate closing statements, utilizing knowledge and expertise in real estate procedures.

11) Examine documentation such as mortgages, liens, judgments, easements, plat books, maps, contracts, and agreements in order to verify factors such as properties' legal descriptions, ownership, or restrictions.

12) Verify accuracy and completeness of land-related documents accepted for registration; prepare rejection notices when documents are not acceptable.

13) Direct activities of workers who search records and examine titles, assigning, scheduling, and evaluating work, and providing technical guidance as necessary.

14) Enter into record-keeping systems appropriate data needed to create new title records or update existing ones.

15) Retrieve and examine real estate closing files for accuracy and to ensure that information included is recorded and executed according to regulations.

16) Obtain maps or drawings delineating properties from company title plants, county surveyors, and/or assessors' offices.

25-1191.00 - Graduate Teaching Assistants

Assist department chairperson, faculty members, or other professional staff members in college or university by performing teaching or teaching-related duties, such as teaching lower level courses, developing teaching materials, preparing and giving examinations, and grading examinations or papers. Graduate assistants must be enrolled in a graduate school program. Graduate assistants who primarily perform non-teaching duties, such as laboratory research, should be reported in the occupational category related to the work performed.

Tasks

1) Provide assistance to faculty members or staff with laboratory or field research.

2) Provide assistance to library staff in maintaining library collections.

3) Assist faculty members or staff with student conferences.

4) Evaluate and grade examinations, assignments, and papers, and record grades.

5) Demonstrate use of laboratory equipment, and enforce laboratory rules.

6) Return assignments to students in accordance with established deadlines.

7) Provide instructors with assistance in the use of audiovisual equipment.

8) Prepare and proctor examinations.

9) Order or obtain materials needed for classes.

10) Meet with supervisors to discuss students' grades, and to complete required grade-related paperwork.

11) Inform students of the procedures for completing and submitting class work such as lab reports.

12) Copy and distribute classroom materials.

13) Lead discussion sections, tutorials, and laboratory sections.

14) Teach undergraduate level courses.

15) Develop teaching materials such as syllabi, visual aids, answer keys, supplementary notes, and course websites.

16) Notify instructors of errors or problems with assignments.

17) Attend lectures given by the instructor whom they are assisting.

18) Schedule and maintain regular office hours to meet with students.

19) Complete laboratory projects prior to assigning them to students so that any needed modifications can be made.

25-3021.00 - Self-Enrichment Education Teachers

Teach or instruct courses other than those that normally lead to an occupational objective or degree. Courses may include self-improvement, nonvocational, and nonacademic subjects. Teaching may or may not take place in a traditional educational institution.

Tasks

1) Select, order, and issue books, materials, and supplies for courses or projects.

2) Participate in publicity planning and student recruitment.

3) Organize and supervise games and other recreational activities to promote physical, mental, and social development.

4) Use computers, audiovisual aids, and other equipment and materials to supplement presentations.

5) Write instructional articles on designated subjects.

6) Establish clear objectives for all lessons, units, and projects, and communicate those objectives to students.

7) Instruct students individually and in groups, using various teaching methods such as lectures, discussions, and demonstrations.

8) Instruct and monitor students in use and care of equipment and materials, in order to prevent injury and damage.

9) Observe and evaluate the performance of other instructors.

10) Enforce policies and rules governing students.

11) Attend professional meetings, conferences, and workshops in order to maintain and improve professional competence.

12) Plan and conduct activities for a balanced program of instruction, demonstration, and work time that provides students with opportunities to observe, question, and investigate.

13) Assign and grade class work and homework.

14) Observe students to determine qualifications, limitations, abilities, interests, and other individual characteristics.

15) Meet with parents and guardians to discuss their children's progress, and to determine their priorities for their children.

16) Confer with other teachers and professionals to plan and schedule lessons promoting learning and development.

17) Prepare instructional program objectives, outlines, and lesson plans.

18) Prepare and implement remedial programs for students requiring extra help.

19) Prepare and administer written, oral, and performance tests, and issue grades in accordance with performance.

20) Monitor students' performance in order to make suggestions for improvement, and to ensure that they satisfy course standards, training requirements, and objectives.

21) Plan and supervise class projects, field trips, visits by guest speakers, contests, or other experiential activities, and guide students in learning from those activities.

22) Conduct classes, workshops, and demonstrations, and provide individual instruction to teach topics and skills such as cooking, dancing, writing, physical fitness, photography, personal finance, and flying.

23) Meet with other instructors to discuss individual students and their progress.

24) Adapt teaching methods and instructional materials to meet students' varying needs and interests.

25) Prepare students for further development by encouraging them to explore learning opportunities and to persevere with challenging tasks.

26) Review instructional content, methods, and student evaluations in order to assess strengths and weaknesses, and to develop recommendations for course revision, development, or elimination.

27) Maintain accurate and complete student records as required by administrative policy.

28) Prepare materials and classrooms for class activities.

29) Attend staff meetings, and serve on committees as required.

25-4011.00 - Archivists

Appraise, edit, and direct safekeeping of permanent records and historically valuable documents. Participate in research activities based on archival materials.

Tasks

1) Authenticate and appraise historical documents and archival materials.

2) Direct activities of workers who assist in arranging, cataloguing, exhibiting and maintaining collections of valuable materials.

3) Select and edit documents for publication and display, applying knowledge of subject, literary expression, and presentation techniques.

4) Prepare archival records, such as document descriptions, to allow easy access to information.

5) Preserve records, documents, and objects, copying records to film, videotape, audiotape, disk, or computer formats as necessary.

6) Research and record the origins and historical significance of archival materials.

7) Establish and administer policy guidelines concerning public access and use of materials.

8) Coordinate educational and public outreach programs, such as tours, workshops, lectures, and classes.

9) Organize archival records and develop classification systems to facilitate access to archival materials.

10) Create and maintain accessible, retrievable computer archives and databases, incorporating current advances in electric information storage technology.

11) Provide reference services and assistance for users needing archival materials.

12) Specialize in an area of history or technology, researching topics or items relevant to collections to determine what should be retained or acquired.

25-4012.00 - Curators

Administer affairs of museum and conduct research programs. Direct instructional, research, and public service activities of institution.

Tasks

1) Provide information from the institution's holdings to other curators and to the public.

2) Plan and organize the acquisition, storage, and exhibition of collections and related materials, including the selection of exhibition themes and designs.

3) Conduct or organize tours, workshops, and instructional sessions to acquaint individuals with an institution's facilities and materials.

4) Negotiate and authorize purchase, sale, exchange, or loan of collections.

5) Inspect premises to assess the need for repairs and to ensure that climate and pest-control issues are addressed.

6) Attend meetings, conventions, and civic events to promote use of institution's services, to seek financing, and to maintain community alliances.

7) Plan and conduct special research projects in area of interest or expertise.

8) Schedule events, and organize details including refreshment, entertainment, decorations, and the collection of any fees.

9) Develop and maintain an institution's registration, cataloging, and basic record-keeping systems, using computer databases.

10) Confer with the board of directors to formulate and interpret policies, to determine budget requirements, and to plan overall operations.

11) Write and review grant proposals, journal articles, institutional reports, and publicity materials.

12) Study, examine, and test acquisitions to authenticate their origin, composition, history, and to assess their current value.

13) Arrange insurance coverage for objects on loan or for special exhibits, and recommend changes in coverage for the entire collection.

14) Establish specifications for reproductions and oversee their manufacture, or select items from commercially available replica sources.

Knowledge	Knowledge Definitions
English Language	Knowledge of the structure and content of the English language including the meaning and spelling of words, rules of composition, and grammar.
Clerical	Knowledge of administrative and clerical procedures and systems such as word processing, managing files and records, stenography and transcription, designing forms, and other office procedures and terminology.
Computers and Electronics	Knowledge of circuit boards, processors, chips, electronic equipment, and computer hardware and software, including applications and programming.
Education and Training	Knowledge of principles and methods for curriculum and training design, teaching and instruction for individuals and groups, and the measurement of training effects.
Customer and Personal Service	Knowledge of principles and processes for providing customer and personal services. This includes customer needs assessment, meeting quality standards for services, and evaluation of customer satisfaction.
Administration and Management	Knowledge of business and management principles involved in strategic planning, resource allocation, human resources modeling, leadership technique, production methods, and coordination of people and resources.
History and Archeology	Knowledge of historical events and their causes, indicators, and effects on civilizations and cultures.
Communications and Media	Knowledge of media production, communication, and dissemination techniques and methods. This includes alternative ways to inform and entertain via written, oral, and visual media.
Fine Arts	Knowledge of the theory and techniques required to compose, produce, and perform works of music, dance, visual arts, drama, and sculpture.
Public Safety and Security	Knowledge of relevant equipment, policies, procedures, and strategies to promote effective local, state, or national security operations for the protection of people, data, property, and institutions.
Law and Government	Knowledge of laws, legal codes, court procedures, precedents, government regulations, executive orders, agency rules, and the democratic political process.
Personnel and Human Resources	Knowledge of principles and procedures for personnel recruitment, selection, training, compensation and benefits, labor relations and negotiation, and personnel information systems.
Philosophy and Theology	Knowledge of different philosophical systems and religions. This includes their basic principles, values, ethics, ways of thinking, customs, practices, and their impact on human culture.
Sociology and Anthropology	Knowledge of group behavior and dynamics, societal trends and influences, human migrations, ethnicity, cultures and their history and origins.
Economics and Accounting	Knowledge of economic and accounting principles and practices, the financial markets, banking and the analysis and reporting of financial data.
Geography	Knowledge of principles and methods for describing the features of land, sea, and air masses, including their physical characteristics, locations, interrelationships, and distribution of plant, animal, and human life.
Design	Knowledge of design techniques, tools, and principles involved in production of precision technical plans, blueprints, drawings, and models.
Mathematics	Knowledge of arithmetic, algebra, geometry, calculus, statistics, and their applications.
Chemistry	Knowledge of the chemical composition, structure, and properties of substances and of the chemical processes and transformations that they undergo. This includes uses of chemicals and their interactions, danger signs, production techniques, and disposal methods.
Mechanical	Knowledge of machines and tools, including their designs, uses, repair, and maintenance.
Psychology	Knowledge of human behavior and performance; individual differences in ability, personality, and interests; learning and motivation; psychological research methods; and the assessment and treatment of behavioral and affective disorders.
Telecommunications	Knowledge of transmission, broadcasting, switching, control, and operation of telecommunications systems.
Production and Processing	Knowledge of raw materials, production processes, quality control, costs, and other techniques for maximizing the effective manufacture and distribution of goods.

Sales and Marketing	Knowledge of principles and methods for showing, promoting, and selling products or services. This includes marketing strategy and tactics, product demonstration, sales techniques, and sales control systems.
Transportation	Knowledge of principles and methods for moving people or goods by air, rail, sea, or road, including the relative costs and benefits.
Building and Construction	Knowledge of materials, methods, and the tools involved in the construction or repair of houses, buildings, or other structures such as highways and roads.
Physics	Knowledge and prediction of physical principles, laws, their interrelationships, and applications to understanding fluid, material, and atmospheric dynamics, and mechanical, electrical, atomic and sub-atomic structures and processes.
Engineering and Technology	Knowledge of the practical application of engineering science and technology. This includes applying principles, techniques, procedures, and equipment to the design and production of various goods and services.
Medicine and Dentistry	Knowledge of the information and techniques needed to diagnose and treat human injuries, diseases, and deformities. This includes symptoms, treatment alternatives, drug properties and interactions, and preventive health-care measures.
Therapy and Counseling	Knowledge of principles, methods, and procedures for diagnosis, treatment, and rehabilitation of physical and mental dysfunctions, and for career counseling and guidance.
Foreign Language	Knowledge of the structure and content of a foreign (non-English) language including the meaning and spelling of words, rules of composition and grammar, and pronunciation.
Biology	Knowledge of plant and animal organisms, their tissues, cells, functions, interdependencies, and interactions with each other and the environment.
Food Production	Knowledge of techniques and equipment for planting, growing, and harvesting food products (both plant and animal) for consumption, including storage/handling techniques.

Skills	Skills Definitions
Active Listening	Giving full attention to what other people are saying, taking time to understand the points being made, asking questions as appropriate, and not interrupting at inappropriate times.
Reading Comprehension	Understanding written sentences and paragraphs in work related documents.
Writing	Communicating effectively in writing as appropriate for the needs of the audience.
Speaking	Talking to others to convey information effectively.
Critical Thinking	Using logic and reasoning to identify the strengths and weaknesses of alternative solutions, conclusions or approaches to problems.
Time Management	Managing one's own time and the time of others.
Active Learning	Understanding the implications of new information for both current and future problem-solving and decision-making.
Instructing	Teaching others how to do something.
Monitoring	Monitoring/Assessing performance of yourself, other individuals, or organizations to make improvements or take corrective action.
Coordination	Adjusting actions in relation to others' actions.
Judgment and Decision Making	Considering the relative costs and benefits of potential actions to choose the most appropriate one.
Management of Personnel Resources	Motivating, developing, and directing people as they work, identifying the best people for the job.
Learning Strategies	Selecting and using training/instructional methods and procedures appropriate for the situation when learning or teaching new things.
Social Perceptiveness	Being aware of others' reactions and understanding why they react as they do.
Persuasion	Persuading others to change their minds or behavior.
Negotiation	Bringing others together and trying to reconcile differences.
Service Orientation	Actively looking for ways to help people.
Management of Financial Resources	Determining how money will be spent to get the work done, and accounting for these expenditures.
Management of Material Resources	Obtaining and seeing to the appropriate use of equipment, facilities, and materials needed to do certain work.
Complex Problem Solving	Identifying complex problems and reviewing related information to develop and evaluate options and implement solutions.
Mathematics	Using mathematics to solve problems.
Equipment Selection	Determining the kind of tools and equipment needed to do a job.

Installation	Installing equipment, machines, wiring, or programs to meet specifications.
Quality Control Analysis	Conducting tests and inspections of products, services, or processes to evaluate quality or performance.
Operations Analysis	Analyzing needs and product requirements to create a design.
Systems Evaluation	Identifying measures or indicators of system performance and the actions needed to improve or correct performance, relative to the goals of the system.
Technology Design	Generating or adapting equipment and technology to serve user needs.
Equipment Maintenance	Performing routine maintenance on equipment and determining when and what kind of maintenance is needed.
Troubleshooting	Determining causes of operating errors and deciding what to do about it.
Operation and Control	Controlling operations of equipment or systems.
Repairing	Repairing machines or systems using the needed tools.
Science	Using scientific rules and methods to solve problems.
Systems Analysis	Determining how a system should work and how changes in conditions, operations, and the environment will affect outcomes.
Operation Monitoring	Watching gauges, dials, or other indicators to make sure a machine is working properly.
Programming	Writing computer programs for various purposes.

Ability	Ability Definitions
Speech Clarity	The ability to speak clearly so others can understand you.
Near Vision	The ability to see details at close range (within a few feet of the observer).
Information Ordering	The ability to arrange things or actions in a certain order or pattern according to a specific rule or set of rules (e.g., patterns of numbers, letters, words, pictures, mathematical operations).
Deductive Reasoning	The ability to apply general rules to specific problems to produce answers that make sense.
Speech Recognition	The ability to identify and understand the speech of another person.
Oral Comprehension	The ability to listen to and understand information and ideas presented through spoken words and sentences.
Written Comprehension	The ability to read and understand information and ideas presented in writing.
Inductive Reasoning	The ability to combine pieces of information to form general rules or conclusions (includes finding a relationship among seemingly unrelated events).
Category Flexibility	The ability to generate or use different sets of rules for combining or grouping things in different ways.
Written Expression	The ability to communicate information and ideas in writing so others will understand.
Far Vision	The ability to see details at a distance.
Oral Expression	The ability to communicate information and ideas in speaking so others will understand.
Originality	The ability to come up with unusual or clever ideas about a given topic or situation, or to develop creative ways to solve a problem.
Visual Color Discrimination	The ability to match or detect differences between colors, including shades of color and brightness.
Problem Sensitivity	The ability to tell when something is wrong or is likely to go wrong. It does not involve solving the problem, only recognizing there is a problem.
Fluency of Ideas	The ability to come up with a number of ideas about a topic (the number of ideas is important, not their quality, correctness, or creativity).
Selective Attention	The ability to concentrate on a task over a period of time without being distracted.
Visualization	The ability to imagine how something will look after it is moved around or when its parts are moved or rearranged.
Flexibility of Closure	The ability to identify or detect a known pattern (a figure, object, word, or sound) that is hidden in other distracting material.
Perceptual Speed	The ability to quickly and accurately compare similarities and differences among sets of letters, numbers, objects, pictures, or patterns. The things to be compared may be presented at the same time or one after the other. This ability also includes comparing a presented object with a remembered object.
Number Facility	The ability to add, subtract, multiply, or divide quickly and correctly.
Arm-Hand Steadiness	The ability to keep your hand and arm steady while moving your arm or while holding your arm and hand in one position.

Mathematical Reasoning	The ability to choose the right mathematical methods or formulas to solve a problem.
Finger Dexterity	The ability to make precisely coordinated movements of the fingers of one or both hands to grasp, manipulate, or assemble very small objects.
Static Strength	The ability to exert maximum muscle force to lift, push, pull, or carry objects.
Time Sharing	The ability to shift back and forth between two or more activities or sources of information (such as speech, sounds, touch, or other sources).
Speed of Closure	The ability to quickly make sense of, combine, and organize information into meaningful patterns.
Memorization	The ability to remember information such as words, numbers, pictures, and procedures.
Auditory Attention	The ability to focus on a single source of sound in the presence of other distracting sounds.
Manual Dexterity	The ability to quickly move your hand, your hand together with your arm, or your two hands to grasp, manipulate, or assemble objects.
Depth Perception	The ability to judge which of several objects is closer or farther away from you, or to judge the distance between you and an object.
Extent Flexibility	The ability to bend, stretch, twist, or reach with your body, arms, and/or legs.
Trunk Strength	The ability to use your abdominal and lower back muscles to support part of the body repeatedly or continuously over time without 'giving out' or fatiguing.
Multilimb Coordination	The ability to coordinate two or more limbs (for example, two arms, two legs, or one leg and one arm) while sitting, standing, or lying down. It does not involve performing the activities while the whole body is in motion.
Stamina	The ability to exert yourself physically over long periods of time without getting winded or out of breath.
Control Precision	The ability to quickly and repeatedly adjust the controls of a machine or a vehicle to exact positions.
Gross Body Coordination	The ability to coordinate the movement of your arms, legs, and torso together when the whole body is in motion.
Hearing Sensitivity	The ability to detect or tell the differences between sounds that vary in pitch and loudness.
Gross Body Equilibrium	The ability to keep or regain your body balance or stay upright when in an unstable position.
Dynamic Strength	The ability to exert muscle force repeatedly or continuously over time. This involves muscular endurance and resistance to muscle fatigue.
Spatial Orientation	The ability to know your location in relation to the environment or to know where other objects are in relation to you.
Speed of Limb Movement	The ability to quickly move the arms and legs.
Wrist-Finger Speed	The ability to make fast, simple, repeated movements of the fingers, hands, and wrists.
Dynamic Flexibility	The ability to quickly and repeatedly bend, stretch, twist, or reach out with your body, arms, and/or legs.
Night Vision	The ability to see under low light conditions.
Glare Sensitivity	The ability to see objects in the presence of glare or bright lighting.
Sound Localization	The ability to tell the direction from which a sound originated.
Explosive Strength	The ability to use short bursts of muscle force to propel oneself (as in jumping or sprinting), or to throw an object.
Peripheral Vision	The ability to see objects or movement of objects to one's side when the eyes are looking ahead.
Rate Control	The ability to time your movements or the movement of a piece of equipment in anticipation of changes in the speed and/or direction of a moving object or scene.
Reaction Time	The ability to quickly respond (with the hand, finger, or foot) to a signal (sound, light, picture) when it appears.
Response Orientation	The ability to choose quickly between two or more movements in response to two or more different signals (lights, sounds, pictures). It includes the speed with which the correct response is started with the hand, foot, or other body part.

Work_Activity	Work_Activity Definitions
Organizing, Planning, and Prioritizing Work	Developing specific goals and plans to prioritize, organize, and accomplish your work.
Thinking Creatively	Developing, designing, or creating new applications, ideas, relationships, systems, or products, including artistic contributions.

Identifying Objects, Actions, and Events	Identifying information by categorizing, estimating, recognizing differences or similarities, and detecting changes in circumstances or events.
Communicating with Supervisors, Peers, or Subordin	Providing information to supervisors, co-workers, and subordinates by telephone, in written form, e-mail, or in person.
Scheduling Work and Activities	Scheduling events, programs, and activities, as well as the work of others.
Judging the Qualities of Things, Services, or Peop	Assessing the value, importance, or quality of things or people.
Documenting/Recording Information	Entering, transcribing, recording, storing, or maintaining information in written or electronic/magnetic form.
Making Decisions and Solving Problems	Analyzing information and evaluating results to choose the best solution and solve problems.
Handling and Moving Objects	Using hands and arms in handling, installing, positioning, and moving materials, and manipulating things.
Getting Information	Observing, receiving, and otherwise obtaining information from all relevant sources.
Monitor Processes, Materials, or Surroundings	Monitoring and reviewing information from materials, events, or the environment, to detect or assess problems.
Performing for or Working Directly with the Public	Performing for people or dealing directly with the public. This includes serving customers in restaurants and stores, and receiving clients or guests.
Communicating with Persons Outside Organization	Communicating with people outside the organization, representing the organization to customers, the public, government, and other external sources. This information can be exchanged in person, in writing, or by telephone or e-mail.
Establishing and Maintaining Interpersonal Relatio	Developing constructive and cooperative working relationships with others, and maintaining them over time.
Developing Objectives and Strategies	Establishing long-range objectives and specifying the strategies and actions to achieve them.
Performing General Physical Activities	Performing physical activities that require considerable use of your arms and legs and moving your whole body, such as climbing, lifting, balancing, walking, stooping, and handling of materials.
Interacting With Computers	Using computers and computer systems (including hardware and software) to program, write software, set up functions, enter data, or process information.
Updating and Using Relevant Knowledge	Keeping up-to-date technically and applying new knowledge to your job.
Coordinating the Work and Activities of Others	Getting members of a group to work together to accomplish tasks.
Inspecting Equipment, Structures, or Material	Inspecting equipment, structures, or materials to identify the cause of errors or other problems or defects.
Interpreting the Meaning of Information for Others	Translating or explaining what information means and how it can be used.
Training and Teaching Others	Identifying the educational needs of others, developing formal educational or training programs or classes, and teaching or instructing others.
Performing Administrative Activities	Performing day-to-day administrative tasks such as maintaining information files and processing paperwork.
Coaching and Developing Others	Identifying the developmental needs of others and coaching, mentoring, or otherwise helping others to improve their knowledge or skills.
Developing and Building Teams	Encouraging and building mutual trust, respect, and cooperation among team members.
Monitoring and Controlling Resources	Monitoring and controlling resources and overseeing the spending of money.
Selling or Influencing Others	Convincing others to buy merchandise/goods or to otherwise change their minds or actions.
Processing Information	Compiling, coding, categorizing, calculating, tabulating, auditing, or verifying information or data.
Guiding, Directing, and Motivating Subordinates	Providing guidance and direction to subordinates, including setting performance standards and monitoring performance.
Resolving Conflicts and Negotiating with Others	Handling complaints, settling disputes, and resolving grievances and conflicts, or otherwise negotiating with others.
Estimating the Quantifiable Characteristics of Pro	Estimating sizes, distances, and quantities; or determining time, costs, resources, or materials needed to perform a work activity.
Analyzing Data or Information	Identifying the underlying principles, reasons, or facts of information by breaking down information or data into separate parts.
Assisting and Caring for Others	Providing personal assistance, medical attention, emotional support, or other personal care to others such as coworkers, customers, or patients.

Drafting, Laying Out, and Specifying Technical Dev	Providing documentation, detailed instructions, drawings, or specifications to tell others about how devices, parts, equipment, or structures are to be fabricated, constructed, assembled, modified, maintained, or used.
Evaluating Information to Determine Compliance wit	Using relevant information and individual judgment to determine whether events or processes comply with laws, regulations, or standards.
Provide Consultation and Advice to Others	Providing guidance and expert advice to management or other groups on technical, systems-, or process-related topics.
Staffing Organizational Units	Recruiting, interviewing, selecting, hiring, and promoting employees in an organization.
Operating Vehicles, Mechanized Devices, or Equipme	Running, maneuvering, navigating, or driving vehicles or mechanized equipment, such as forklifts, passenger vehicles, aircraft, or water craft.
Repairing and Maintaining Mechanical Equipment	Servicing, repairing, adjusting, and testing machines, devices, moving parts, and equipment that operate primarily on the basis of mechanical (not electronic) principles.
Repairing and Maintaining Electronic Equipment	Servicing, repairing, calibrating, regulating, fine-tuning, or testing machines, devices, and equipment that operate primarily on the basis of electrical or electronic (not mechanical) principles.
Controlling Machines and Processes	Using either control mechanisms or direct physical activity to operate machines or processes (not including computers or vehicles).

Work_Context / Work_Context Definitions

Work_Context	Work_Context Definitions
Face-to-Face Discussions	How often do you have to have face-to-face discussions with individuals or teams in this job?
Freedom to Make Decisions	How much decision making freedom, without supervision, does the job offer?
Telephone	How often do you have telephone conversations in this job?
Structured versus Unstructured Work	To what extent is this job structured for the worker, rather than allowing the worker to determine tasks, priorities, and goals?
Contact With Others	How much does this job require the worker to be in contact with others (face-to-face, by telephone, or otherwise) in order to perform it?
Electronic Mail	How often do you use electronic mail in this job?
Letters and Memos	How often does the job require written letters and memos?
Importance of Being Exact or Accurate	How important is being very exact or highly accurate in performing this job?
Indoors, Environmentally Controlled	How often does this job require working indoors in environmentally controlled conditions?
Physical Proximity	To what extent does this job require the worker to perform job tasks in close physical proximity to other people?
Spend Time Sitting	How much does this job require sitting?
Coordinate or Lead Others	How important is it to coordinate or lead others in accomplishing work activities in this job?
Work With Work Group or Team	How important is it to work with others in a group or team in this job?
Spend Time Standing	How much does this job require standing?
Impact of Decisions on Co-workers or Company Resul	How do the decisions an employee makes impact the results of co-workers, clients or the company?
Public Speaking	How often do you have to perform public speaking in this job?
Frequency of Decision Making	How frequently is the worker required to make decisions that affect other people, the financial resources, and/or the image and reputation of the organization?
Time Pressure	How often does this job require the worker to meet strict deadlines?
Deal With External Customers	How important is it to work with external customers or the public in this job?
Spend Time Using Your Hands to Handle, Control, or	How much does this job require using your hands to handle, control, or feel objects, tools or controls?
Responsibility for Outcomes and Results	How responsible is the worker for work outcomes and results of other workers?
Indoors, Not Environmentally Controlled	How often does this job require working indoors in non-controlled environmental conditions (e.g., warehouse without heat)?
Level of Competition	To what extent does this job require the worker to compete or to be aware of competitive pressures?
Spend Time Walking and Running	How much does this job require walking and running?
Outdoors, Exposed to Weather	How often does this job require working outdoors, exposed to all weather conditions?
Responsible for Others' Health and Safety	How much responsibility is there for the health and safety of others in this job?

Spend Time Making Repetitive Motions	How much does this job require making repetitive motions?
Sounds, Noise Levels Are Distracting or Uncomforta	How often does this job require working exposed to sounds and noise levels that are distracting or uncomfortable?
Deal With Unpleasant or Angry People	How frequently does the worker have to deal with unpleasant, angry, or discourteous individuals as part of the job requirements?
Exposed to Contaminants	How often does this job require working exposed to contaminants (such as pollutants, gases, dust or odors)?
Importance of Repeating Same Tasks	How important is repeating the same physical activities (e.g., key entry) or mental activities (e.g., checking entries in a ledger) over and over, without stopping, to performing this job?
Consequence of Error	How serious would the result usually be if the worker made a mistake that was not readily correctable?
Spend Time Kneeling, Crouching, Stooping, or Crawl	How much does this job require kneeling, crouching, stooping or crawling?
Cramped Work Space, Awkward Positions	How often does this job require working in cramped work spaces that requires getting into awkward positions?
Frequency of Conflict Situations	How often are there conflict situations the employee has to face in this job?
Spend Time Bending or Twisting the Body	How much does this job require bending or twisting your body?
Spend Time Climbing Ladders, Scaffolds, or Poles	How much does this job require climbing ladders, scaffolds, or poles?
Wear Common Protective or Safety Equipment such as	How much does this job require wearing common protective or safety equipment such as safety shoes, glasses, gloves, hard hats or live jackets?
Extremely Bright or Inadequate Lighting	How often does this job require working in extremely bright or inadequate lighting conditions?
In an Enclosed Vehicle or Equipment	How often does this job require working in a closed vehicle or equipment (e.g., car)?
Very Hot or Cold Temperatures	How often does this job require working in very hot (above 90 F degrees) or very cold (below 32 F degrees) temperatures?
Exposed to Minor Burns, Cuts, Bites, or Stings	How often does this job require exposure to minor burns, cuts, bites, or stings?
Outdoors, Under Cover	How often does this job require working outdoors, under cover (e.g., structure with roof but no walls)?
Exposed to High Places	How often does this job require exposure to high places?
Spend Time Keeping or Regaining Balance	How much does this job require keeping or regaining your balance?
Exposed to Hazardous Equipment	How often does this job require exposure to hazardous equipment?
Exposed to Hazardous Conditions	How often does this job require exposure to hazardous conditions?
Degree of Automation	How automated is the job?
In an Open Vehicle or Equipment	How often does this job require working in an open vehicle or equipment (e.g., tractor)?
Wear Specialized Protective or Safety Equipment su	How much does this job require wearing specialized protective or safety equipment such as breathing apparatus, safety harness, full protection suits, or radiation protection?
Deal With Physically Aggressive People	How frequently does this job require the worker to deal with physical aggression of violent individuals?
Exposed to Disease or Infections	How often does this job require exposure to disease/infections?
Pace Determined by Speed of Equipment	How important is it to this job that the pace is determined by the speed of equipment or machinery? (This does not refer to keeping busy at all times on this job.)
Exposed to Radiation	How often does this job require exposure to radiation?
Exposed to Whole Body Vibration	How often does this job require exposure to whole body vibration (e.g., operate a jackhammer)?

Job Zone Component	Job Zone Component Definitions
Title	Job Zone Four: Considerable Preparation Needed
Overall Experience	A minimum of two to four years of work-related skill, knowledge, or experience is needed for these occupations. For example, an accountant must complete four years of college and work for several years in accounting to be considered qualified.
Job Training	Employees in these occupations usually need several years of work-related experience, on-the-job training, and/or vocational training.

Job Zone Examples	Many of these occupations involve coordinating, supervising, managing, or training others. Examples include accountants, chefs and head cooks, computer programmers, historians, pharmacists, and police detectives.
SVP Range	(7.0 to < 8.0)
Education	Most of these occupations require a four - year bachelor's degree, but some do not.

Work_Styles	Work_Styles Definitions
Attention to Detail	Job requires being careful about detail and thorough in completing work tasks.
Dependability	Job requires being reliable, responsible, and dependable, and fulfilling obligations.
Independence	Job requires developing one's own ways of doing things, guiding oneself with little or no supervision, and depending on oneself to get things done.
Initiative	Job requires a willingness to take on responsibilities and challenges.
Integrity	Job requires being honest and ethical.
Cooperation	Job requires being pleasant with others on the job and displaying a good-natured, cooperative attitude.
Innovation	Job requires creativity and alternative thinking to develop new ideas for and answers to work-related problems.
Analytical Thinking	Job requires analyzing information and using logic to address work-related issues and problems.
Self Control	Job requires maintaining composure, keeping emotions in check, controlling anger, and avoiding aggressive behavior, even in very difficult situations.
Achievement/Effort	Job requires establishing and maintaining personally challenging achievement goals and exerting effort toward mastering tasks.
Adaptability/Flexibility	Job requires being open to change (positive or negative) and to considerable variety in the workplace.
Leadership	Job requires a willingness to lead, take charge, and offer opinions and direction.
Persistence	Job requires persistence in the face of obstacles.
Concern for Others	Job requires being sensitive to others' needs and feelings and being understanding and helpful on the job.
Stress Tolerance	Job requires accepting criticism and dealing calmly and effectively with high stress situations.
Social Orientation	Job requires preferring to work with others rather than alone, and being personally connected with others on the job.

25-4013.00 - Museum Technicians and Conservators

Prepare specimens, such as fossils, skeletal parts, lace, and textiles, for museum collection and exhibits. May restore documents or install, arrange, and exhibit materials.

Tasks

1) Coordinate exhibit installations, assisting with design, constructing displays, dioramas, display cases, and models, and ensuring the availability of necessary materials.

2) Determine whether objects need repair and choose the safest and most effective method of repair.

3) Supervise and work with volunteers.

4) Clean objects, such as paper, textiles, wood, metal, glass, rock, pottery, and furniture, using cleansers, solvents, soap solutions, and polishes.

5) Prepare artifacts for storage and shipping.

6) Present public programs and tours.

7) Notify superior when restoration of artifacts requires outside experts.

8) Repair, restore and reassemble artifacts, designing and fabricating missing or broken parts, to restore them to their original appearance and prevent deterioration.

9) Direct and supervise curatorial and technical staff in the handling, mounting, care, and storage of art objects.

10) Recommend preservation procedures, such as control of temperature and humidity, to curatorial and building staff.

11) Perform tests and examinations to establish storage and conservation requirements, policies, and procedures.

12) Classify and assign registration numbers to artifacts, and supervise inventory control.

13) Plan and conduct research to develop and improve methods of restoring and preserving specimens.

14) Preserve or direct preservation of objects, using plaster, resin, sealants, hardeners, and shellac.

15) Specialize in particular materials or types of object, such as documents and books, paintings, decorative arts, textiles, metals, or architectural materials.

16) Perform on-site field work which may involve interviewing people, inspecting and identifying artifacts, note-taking, viewing sites and collections, and repainting exhibition spaces.

17) Estimate cost of restoration work.

18) Prepare reports on the operation of conservation laboratories, documenting the condition of artifacts, treatment options, and the methods of preservation and repair used.

19) Build, repair, and install wooden steps, scaffolds, and walkways to gain access to or permit improved view of exhibited equipment.

20) Study object documentation or conduct standard chemical and physical tests to ascertain the object's age, composition, original appearance, need for treatment or restoration, and appropriate preservation method.

21) Construct skeletal mounts of fossils, replicas of archaeological artifacts, or duplicate specimens, using a variety of materials and hand tools.

22) Cut and weld metal sections in reconstruction or renovation of exterior structural sections and accessories of exhibits.

Knowledge	Knowledge Definitions
English Language	Knowledge of the structure and content of the English language including the meaning and spelling of words, rules of composition, and grammar.
Design	Knowledge of design techniques, tools, and principles involved in production of precision technical plans, blueprints, drawings, and models.
History and Archeology	Knowledge of historical events and their causes, indicators, and effects on civilizations and cultures.
Administration and Management	Knowledge of business and management principles involved in strategic planning, resource allocation, human resources modeling, leadership technique, production methods, and coordination of people and resources.
Customer and Personal Service	Knowledge of principles and processes for providing customer and personal services. This includes customer needs assessment, meeting quality standards for services, and evaluation of customer satisfaction.
Education and Training	Knowledge of principles and methods for curriculum and training design, teaching and instruction for individuals and groups, and the measurement of training effects.
Mathematics	Knowledge of arithmetic, algebra, geometry, calculus, statistics, and their applications.
Clerical	Knowledge of administrative and clerical procedures and systems such as word processing, managing files and records, stenography and transcription, designing forms, and other office procedures and terminology.
Fine Arts	Knowledge of the theory and techniques required to compose, produce, and perform works of music, dance, visual arts, drama, and sculpture.
Computers and Electronics	Knowledge of circuit boards, processors, chips, electronic equipment, and computer hardware and software, including applications and programming.
Mechanical	Knowledge of machines and tools, including their designs, uses, repair, and maintenance.
Sociology and Anthropology	Knowledge of group behavior and dynamics, societal trends and influences, human migrations, ethnicity, cultures and their history and origins.
Production and Processing	Knowledge of raw materials, production processes, quality control, costs, and other techniques for maximizing the effective manufacture and distribution of goods.
Building and Construction	Knowledge of materials, methods, and the tools involved in the construction or repair of houses, buildings, or other structures such as highways and roads.
Personnel and Human Resources	Knowledge of principles and procedures for personnel recruitment, selection, training, compensation and benefits, labor relations and negotiation, and personnel information systems.

Communications and Media	Knowledge of media production, communication, and dissemination techniques and methods. This includes alternative ways to inform and entertain via written, oral, and visual media.
Economics and Accounting	Knowledge of economic and accounting principles and practices, the financial markets, banking and the analysis and reporting of financial data.
Public Safety and Security	Knowledge of relevant equipment, policies, procedures, and strategies to promote effective local, state, or national security operations for the protection of people, data, property, and institutions.
Engineering and Technology	Knowledge of the practical application of engineering science and technology. This includes applying principles, techniques, procedures, and equipment to the design and production of various goods and services.
Geography	Knowledge of principles and methods for describing the features of land, sea, and air masses, including their physical characteristics, locations, interrelationships, and distribution of plant, animal, and human life.
Psychology	Knowledge of human behavior and performance; individual differences in ability, personality, and interests; learning and motivation; psychological research methods; and the assessment and treatment of behavioral and affective disorders.
Philosophy and Theology	Knowledge of different philosophical systems and religions. This includes their basic principles, values, ethics, ways of thinking, customs, practices, and their impact on human culture.
Chemistry	Knowledge of the chemical composition, structure, and properties of substances and of the chemical processes and transformations that they undergo. This includes uses of chemicals and their interactions, danger signs, production techniques, and disposal methods.
Law and Government	Knowledge of laws, legal codes, court procedures, precedents, government regulations, executive orders, agency rules, and the democratic political process.
Transportation	Knowledge of principles and methods for moving people or goods by air, rail, sea, or road, including the relative costs and benefits.
Physics	Knowledge and prediction of physical principles, laws, their interrelationships, and applications to understanding fluid, material, and atmospheric dynamics, and mechanical, electrical, atomic and sub- atomic structures and processes.
Sales and Marketing	Knowledge of principles and methods for showing, promoting, and selling products or services. This includes marketing strategy and tactics, product demonstration, sales techniques, and sales control systems.
Telecommunications	Knowledge of transmission, broadcasting, switching, control, and operation of telecommunications systems.
Foreign Language	Knowledge of the structure and content of a foreign (non-English) language including the meaning and spelling of words, rules of composition and grammar, and pronunciation.
Medicine and Dentistry	Knowledge of the information and techniques needed to diagnose and treat human injuries, diseases, and deformities. This includes symptoms, treatment alternatives, drug properties and interactions, and preventive health-care measures.
Biology	Knowledge of plant and animal organisms, their tissues, cells, functions, interdependencies, and interactions with each other and the environment.
Therapy and Counseling	Knowledge of principles, methods, and procedures for diagnosis, treatment, and rehabilitation of physical and mental dysfunctions, and for career counseling and guidance.
Food Production	Knowledge of techniques and equipment for planting, growing, and harvesting food products (both plant and animal) for consumption, including storage/handling techniques.

Skills	Skills Definitions
Critical Thinking	Using logic and reasoning to identify the strengths and weaknesses of alternative solutions, conclusions or approaches to problems.
Active Listening	Giving full attention to what other people are saying, taking time to understand the points being made, asking questions as appropriate, and not interrupting at inappropriate times.
Judgment and Decision Making	Considering the relative costs and benefits of potential actions to choose the most appropriate one.
Reading Comprehension	Understanding written sentences and paragraphs in work related documents.
Time Management	Managing one's own time and the time of others.

Active Learning	Understanding the implications of new information for both current and future problem-solving and decision-making.
Equipment Selection	Determining the kind of tools and equipment needed to do a job.
Complex Problem Solving	Identifying complex problems and reviewing related information to develop and evaluate options and implement solutions.
Management of Material Resources	Obtaining and seeing to the appropriate use of equipment, facilities, and materials needed to do certain work.
Coordination	Adjusting actions in relation to others' actions.
Installation	Installing equipment, machines, wiring, or programs to meet specifications.
Operations Analysis	Analyzing needs and product requirements to create a design.
Speaking	Talking to others to convey information effectively.
Learning Strategies	Selecting and using training/instructional methods and procedures appropriate for the situation when learning or teaching new things.
Repairing	Repairing machines or systems using the needed tools.
Monitoring	Monitoring/Assessing performance of yourself, other individuals, or organizations to make improvements or take corrective action.
Persuasion	Persuading others to change their minds or behavior.
Instructing	Teaching others how to do something.
Writing	Communicating effectively in writing as appropriate for the needs of the audience.
Equipment Maintenance	Performing routine maintenance on equipment and determining when and what kind of maintenance is needed.
Troubleshooting	Determining causes of operating errors and deciding what to do about it.
Mathematics	Using mathematics to solve problems.
Service Orientation	Actively looking for ways to help people.
Science	Using scientific rules and methods to solve problems.
Technology Design	Generating or adapting equipment and technology to serve user needs.
Negotiation	Bringing others together and trying to reconcile differences.
Social Perceptiveness	Being aware of others' reactions and understanding why they react as they do.
Management of Financial Resources	Determining how money will be spent to get the work done, and accounting for these expenditures.
Operation Monitoring	Watching gauges, dials, or other indicators to make sure a machine is working properly.
Quality Control Analysis	Conducting tests and inspections of products, services, or processes to evaluate quality or performance.
Management of Personnel Resources	Motivating, developing, and directing people as they work, identifying the best people for the job.
Operation and Control	Controlling operations of equipment or systems.
Systems Evaluation	Identifying measures or indicators of system performance and the actions needed to improve or correct performance, relative to the goals of the system.
Programming	Writing computer programs for various purposes.
Systems Analysis	Determining how a system should work and how changes in conditions, operations, and the environment will affect outcomes.

Ability	Ability Definitions
Near Vision	The ability to see details at close range (within a few feet of the observer).
Problem Sensitivity	The ability to tell when something is wrong or is likely to go wrong. It does not involve solving the problem, only recognizing there is a problem.
Information Ordering	The ability to arrange things or actions in a certain order or pattern according to a specific rule or set of rules (e.g., patterns of numbers, letters, words, pictures, mathematical operations).
Deductive Reasoning	The ability to apply general rules to specific problems to produce answers that make sense.
Oral Expression	The ability to communicate information and ideas in speaking so others will understand.
Visualization	The ability to imagine how something will look after it is moved around or when its parts are moved or rearranged.
Oral Comprehension	The ability to listen to and understand information and ideas presented through spoken words and sentences.
Inductive Reasoning	The ability to combine pieces of information to form general rules or conclusions (includes finding a relationship among seemingly unrelated events).
Speech Clarity	The ability to speak clearly so others can understand you.
Written Expression	The ability to communicate information and ideas in writing so others will understand.

Speech Recognition	The ability to identify and understand the speech of another person.
Written Comprehension	The ability to read and understand information and ideas presented in writing.
Category Flexibility	The ability to generate or use different sets of rules for combining or grouping things in different ways.
Fluency of Ideas	The ability to come up with a number of ideas about a topic (the number of ideas is important, not their quality, correctness, or creativity).
Originality	The ability to come up with unusual or clever ideas about a given topic or situation, or to develop creative ways to solve a problem.
Finger Dexterity	The ability to make precisely coordinated movements of the fingers of one or both hands to grasp, manipulate, or assemble very small objects.
Arm-Hand Steadiness	The ability to keep your hand and arm steady while moving your arm or while holding your arm and hand in one position.
Manual Dexterity	The ability to quickly move your hand, your hand together with your arm, or your two hands to grasp, manipulate, or assemble objects.
Mathematical Reasoning	The ability to choose the right mathematical methods or formulas to solve a problem.
Trunk Strength	The ability to use your abdominal and lower back muscles to support part of the body repeatedly or continuously over time without 'giving out' or fatiguing.
Selective Attention	The ability to concentrate on a task over a period of time without being distracted.
Static Strength	The ability to exert maximum muscle force to lift, push, pull, or carry objects.
Visual Color Discrimination	The ability to match or detect differences between colors, including shades of color and brightness.
Far Vision	The ability to see details at a distance.
Time Sharing	The ability to shift back and forth between two or more activities or sources of information (such as speech, sounds, touch, or other sources).
Multilimb Coordination	The ability to coordinate two or more limbs (for example, two arms, two legs, or one leg and one arm) while sitting, standing, or lying down. It does not involve performing the activities while the whole body is in motion.
Flexibility of Closure	The ability to identify or detect a known pattern (a figure, object, word, or sound) that is hidden in other distracting material.
Perceptual Speed	The ability to quickly and accurately compare similarities and differences among sets of letters, numbers, objects, pictures, or patterns. The things to be compared may be presented at the same time or one after the other. This ability also includes comparing a presented object with a remembered object.
Memorization	The ability to remember information such as words, numbers, pictures, and procedures.
Control Precision	The ability to quickly and repeatedly adjust the controls of a machine or a vehicle to exact positions.
Auditory Attention	The ability to focus on a single source of sound in the presence of other distracting sounds.
Dynamic Strength	The ability to exert muscle force repeatedly or continuously over time. This involves muscular endurance and resistance to muscle fatigue.
Stamina	The ability to exert yourself physically over long periods of time without getting winded or out of breath.
Extent Flexibility	The ability to bend, stretch, twist, or reach with your body, arms, and/or legs.
Gross Body Coordination	The ability to coordinate the movement of your arms, legs, and torso together when the whole body is in motion.
Wrist-Finger Speed	The ability to make fast, simple, repeated movements of the fingers, hands, and wrists.
Speed of Closure	The ability to quickly make sense of, combine, and organize information into meaningful patterns.
Number Facility	The ability to add, subtract, multiply, or divide quickly and correctly.
Depth Perception	The ability to judge which of several objects is closer or farther away from you, or to judge the distance between you and an object.
Gross Body Equilibrium	The ability to keep or regain your body balance or stay upright when in an unstable position.
Hearing Sensitivity	The ability to detect or tell the differences between sounds that vary in pitch and loudness.
Speed of Limb Movement	The ability to quickly move the arms and legs.
Reaction Time	The ability to quickly respond (with the hand, finger, or foot) to a signal (sound, light, picture) when it appears.

Rate Control	The ability to time your movements or the movement of a piece of equipment in anticipation of changes in the speed and/or direction of a moving object or scene.
Response Orientation	The ability to choose quickly between two or more movements in response to two or more different signals (lights, sounds, pictures). It includes the speed with which the correct response is started with the hand, foot, or other body part.
Spatial Orientation	The ability to know your location in relation to the environment or to know where other objects are in relation to you.
Night Vision	The ability to see under low light conditions.
Dynamic Flexibility	The ability to quickly and repeatedly bend, stretch, twist, or reach out with your body, arms, and/or legs.
Explosive Strength	The ability to use short bursts of muscle force to propel oneself (as in jumping or sprinting), or to throw an object.
Glare Sensitivity	The ability to see objects in the presence of glare or bright lighting.
Sound Localization	The ability to tell the direction from which a sound originated.
Peripheral Vision	The ability to see objects or movement of objects to one's side when the eyes are looking ahead.

Work_Activity	Work_Activity Definitions
Identifying Objects, Actions, and Events	Identifying information by categorizing, estimating, recognizing differences or similarities, and detecting changes in circumstances or events.
Getting Information	Observing, receiving, and otherwise obtaining information from all relevant sources.
Handling and Moving Objects	Using hands and arms in handling, installing, positioning, and moving materials, and manipulating things.
Documenting/Recording Information	Entering, transcribing, recording, storing, or maintaining information in written or electronic/magnetic form.
Making Decisions and Solving Problems	Analyzing information and evaluating results to choose the best solution and solve problems.
Updating and Using Relevant Knowledge	Keeping up-to-date technically and applying new knowledge to your job.
Organizing, Planning, and Prioritizing Work	Developing specific goals and plans to prioritize, organize, and accomplish your work.
Communicating with Supervisors, Peers, or Subordin	Providing information to supervisors, co-workers, and subordinates by telephone, in written form, e-mail, or in person.
Monitor Processes, Materials, or Surroundings	Monitoring and reviewing information from materials, events, or the environment, to detect or assess problems.
Performing General Physical Activities	Performing physical activities that require considerable use of your arms and legs and moving your whole body, such as climbing, lifting, balancing, walking, stooping, and handling of materials.
Judging the Qualities of Things, Services, or Peop	Assessing the value, importance, or quality of things or people.
Thinking Creatively	Developing, designing, or creating new applications, ideas, relationships, systems, or products, including artistic contributions.
Establishing and Maintaining Interpersonal Relatio	Developing constructive and cooperative working relationships with others, and maintaining them over time.
Estimating the Quantifiable Characteristics of Pro	Estimating sizes, distances, and quantities; or determining time, costs, resources, or materials needed to perform a work activity.
Processing Information	Compiling, coding, categorizing, calculating, tabulating, auditing, or verifying information or data.
Interacting With Computers	Using computers and computer systems (including hardware and software) to program, write software, set up functions, enter data, or process information.
Communicating with Persons Outside Organization	Communicating with people outside the organization, representing the organization to customers, the public, government, and other external sources. This information can be exchanged in person, in writing, or by telephone or e-mail.
Evaluating Information to Determine Compliance wit	Using relevant information and individual judgment to determine whether events or processes comply with laws, regulations, or standards.
Analyzing Data or Information	Identifying the underlying principles, reasons, or facts of information by breaking down information or data into separate parts.
Inspecting Equipment, Structures, or Material	Inspecting equipment, structures, or materials to identify the cause of errors or other problems or defects.
Controlling Machines and Processes	Using either control mechanisms or direct physical activity to operate machines or processes (not including computers or vehicles).

Scheduling Work and Activities	Scheduling events, programs, and activities, as well as the work of others.
Developing Objectives and Strategies	Establishing long-range objectives and specifying the strategies and actions to achieve them.
Interpreting the Meaning of Information for Others	Translating or explaining what information means and how it can be used.
Training and Teaching Others	Identifying the educational needs of others, developing formal educational or training programs or classes, and teaching or instructing others.
Performing for or Working Directly with the Public	Performing for people or dealing directly with the public. This includes serving customers in restaurants and stores, and receiving clients or guests.
Developing and Building Teams	Encouraging and building mutual trust, respect, and cooperation among team members.
Coordinating the Work and Activities of Others	Getting members of a group to work together to accomplish tasks.
Coaching and Developing Others	Identifying the developmental needs of others and coaching, mentoring, or otherwise helping others to improve their knowledge or skills.
Monitoring and Controlling Resources	Monitoring and controlling resources and overseeing the spending of money.
Guiding, Directing, and Motivating Subordinates	Providing guidance and direction to subordinates, including setting performance standards and monitoring performance.
Provide Consultation and Advice to Others	Providing guidance and expert advice to management or other groups on technical, systems-, or process-related topics.
Drafting, Laying Out, and Specifying Technical Dev	Providing documentation, detailed instructions, drawings, or specifications to tell others about how devices, parts, equipment, or structures are to be fabricated, constructed, assembled, modified, maintained, or used.
Performing Administrative Activities	Performing day-to-day administrative tasks such as maintaining information files and processing paperwork.
Operating Vehicles, Mechanized Devices, or Equipme	Running, maneuvering, navigating, or driving vehicles or mechanized equipment, such as forklifts, passenger vehicles, aircraft, or water craft.
Resolving Conflicts and Negotiating with Others	Handling complaints, settling disputes, and resolving grievances and conflicts, or otherwise negotiating with others.
Assisting and Caring for Others	Providing personal assistance, medical attention, emotional support, or other personal care to others such as coworkers, customers, or patients.
Repairing and Maintaining Mechanical Equipment	Servicing, repairing, adjusting, and testing machines, devices, moving parts, and equipment that operate primarily on the basis of mechanical (not electronic) principles.
Selling or Influencing Others	Convincing others to buy merchandise/goods or to otherwise change their minds or actions.
Staffing Organizational Units	Recruiting, interviewing, selecting, hiring, and promoting employees in an organization.
Repairing and Maintaining Electronic Equipment	Servicing, repairing, calibrating, regulating, fine-tuning, or testing machines, devices, and equipment that operate primarily on the basis of electrical or electronic (not mechanical) principles.

Work_Context	Work_Context Definitions
Face-to-Face Discussions	How often do you have to have face-to-face discussions with individuals or teams in this job?
Indoors, Environmentally Controlled	How often does this job require working indoors in environmentally controlled conditions?
Telephone	How often do you have telephone conversations in this job?
Structured versus Unstructured Work	To what extent is this job structured for the worker, rather than allowing the worker to determine tasks, priorities, and goals?
Freedom to Make Decisions	How much decision making freedom, without supervision, does the job offer?
Work With Work Group or Team	How important is it to work with others in a group or team in this job?
Importance of Being Exact or Accurate	How important is being very exact or highly accurate in performing this job?
Contact With Others	How much does this job require the worker to be in contact with others (face-to-face, by telephone, or otherwise) in order to perform it?
Spend Time Using Your Hands to Handle, Control, or	How much does this job require using your hands to handle, control, or feel objects, tools or controls?
Letters and Memos	How often does the job require written letters and memos?
Spend Time Standing	How much does this job require standing?
Electronic Mail	How often do you use electronic mail in this job?
Physical Proximity	To what extent does this job require the worker to perform job tasks in close physical proximity to other people?

Impact of Decisions on Co-workers or Company Resul	How do the decisions an employee makes impact the results of co-workers, clients or the company?
Deal With External Customers	How important is it to work with external customers or the public in this job?
Consequence of Error	How serious would the result usually be if the worker made a mistake that was not readily correctable?
Importance of Repeating Same Tasks	How important is repeating the same physical activities (e.g., key entry) or mental activities (e.g., checking entries in a ledger) over and over, without stopping, to performing this job?
Responsible for Others' Health and Safety	How much responsibility is there for the health and safety of others in this job?
Spend Time Sitting	How much does this job require sitting?
Sounds, Noise Levels Are Distracting or Uncomforta	How often does this job require working exposed to sounds and noise levels that are distracting or uncomfortable?
Frequency of Decision Making	How frequently is the worker required to make decisions that affect other people, the financial resources, and/or the image and reputation of the organization?
Coordinate or Lead Others	How important is it to coordinate or lead others in accomplishing work activities in this job?
Exposed to Contaminants	How often does this job require working exposed to contaminants (such as pollutants, gases, dust or odors)?
Time Pressure	How often does this job require the worker to meet strict deadlines?
Indoors, Not Environmentally Controlled	How often does this job require working indoors in non-controlled environmental conditions (e.g., warehouse without heat)?
Responsibility for Outcomes and Results	How responsible is the worker for work outcomes and results of other workers?
Frequency of Conflict Situations	How often are there conflict situations the employee has to face in this job?
Outdoors, Exposed to Weather	How often does this job require working outdoors, exposed to all weather conditions?
Cramped Work Space, Awkward Positions	How often does this job require working in cramped work spaces that requires getting into awkward positions?
Spend Time Walking and Running	How much does this job require walking and running?
Exposed to Hazardous Equipment	How often does this job require exposure to hazardous equipment?
Spend Time Bending or Twisting the Body	How much does this job require bending or twisting your body?
Spend Time Making Repetitive Motions	How much does this job require making repetitive motions?
Spend Time Kneeling, Crouching, Stooping, or Crawl	How much does this job require kneeling, crouching, stooping or crawling?
Wear Common Protective or Safety Equipment such as	How much does this job require wearing common protective or safety equipment such as safety shoes, glasses, gloves, hard hats or life jackets?
In an Enclosed Vehicle or Equipment	How often does this job require working in a closed vehicle or equipment (e.g., car)?
Outdoors, Under Cover	How often does this job require working outdoors, under cover (e.g., structure with roof but no walls)?
Deal With Unpleasant or Angry People	How frequently does the worker have to deal with unpleasant, angry, or discourteous individuals as part of the job requirements?
Exposed to Hazardous Conditions	How often does this job require exposure to hazardous conditions?
Exposed to Minor Burns, Cuts, Bites, or Stings	How often does this job require exposure to minor burns, cuts, bites, or stings?
Spend Time Climbing Ladders, Scaffolds, or Poles	How much does this job require climbing ladders, scaffolds, or poles?
Public Speaking	How often do you have to perform public speaking in this job?
Level of Competition	To what extent does this job require the worker to compete or to be aware of competitive pressures?
Exposed to High Places	How often does this job require exposure to high places?
Very Hot or Cold Temperatures	How often does this job require working in very hot (above 90 F degrees) or very cold (below 32 F degrees) temperatures?
Wear Specialized Protective or Safety Equipment su	How much does this job require wearing specialized protective or safety equipment such as breathing apparatus, safety harness, full protection suits, or radiation protection?
Degree of Automation	How automated is the job?
Spend Time Keeping or Regaining Balance	How much does this job require keeping or regaining your balance?
Extremely Bright or Inadequate Lighting	How often does this job require working in extremely bright or inadequate lighting conditions?

Pace Determined by Speed of Equipment	How important is it to this job that the pace is determined by the speed of equipment or machinery? (This does not refer to keeping busy at all times on this job.)
Exposed to Radiation	How often does this job require exposure to radiation?
In an Open Vehicle or Equipment	How often does this job require working in an open vehicle or equipment (e.g., tractor)?
Deal With Physically Aggressive People	How frequently does this job require the worker to deal with physical aggression of violent individuals?
Exposed to Disease or Infections	How often does this job require exposure to disease/infections?
Exposed to Whole Body Vibration	How often does this job require exposure to whole body vibration (e.g., operate a jackhammer)?

Job Zone Component	Job Zone Component Definitions
Title	Job Zone Three: Medium Preparation Needed
Overall Experience	Previous work-related skill, knowledge, or experience is required for these occupations. For example, an electrician must have completed three or four years of apprenticeship or several years of vocational training, and often must have passed a licensing exam, in order to perform the job.
Job Training	Employees in these occupations usually need one or two years of training involving both on-the-job experience and informal training with experienced workers.
Job Zone Examples	These occupations usually involve using communication and organizational skills to coordinate, supervise, manage, or train others to accomplish goals. Examples include dental assistants, electricians, fish and game wardens, legal secretaries, personnel recruiters, and recreation workers.
SVP Range	(6.0 to < 7.0)
Education	Most occupations in this zone require training in vocational schools, related on-the-job experience, or an associate's degree. Some may require a bachelor's degree.

Work_Styles	Work_Styles Definitions
Attention to Detail	Job requires being careful about detail and thorough in completing work tasks.
Dependability	Job requires being reliable, responsible, and dependable, and fulfilling obligations.
Cooperation	Job requires being pleasant with others on the job and displaying a good-natured, cooperative attitude.
Integrity	Job requires being honest and ethical.
Self Control	Job requires maintaining composure, keeping emotions in check, controlling anger, and avoiding aggressive behavior, even in very difficult situations.
Concern for Others	Job requires being sensitive to others' needs and feelings and being understanding and helpful on the job.
Adaptability/Flexibility	Job requires being open to change (positive or negative) and to considerable variety in the workplace.
Independence	Job requires developing one's own ways of doing things, guiding oneself with little or no supervision, and depending on oneself to get things done.
Leadership	Job requires a willingness to lead, take charge, and offer opinions and direction.
Analytical Thinking	Job requires analyzing information and using logic to address work-related issues and problems.
Initiative	Job requires a willingness to take on responsibilities and challenges.
Innovation	Job requires creativity and alternative thinking to develop new ideas for and answers to work-related problems.
Persistence	Job requires persistence in the face of obstacles.
Stress Tolerance	Job requires accepting criticism and dealing calmly and effectively with high stress situations.
Achievement/Effort	Job requires establishing and maintaining personally challenging achievement goals and exerting effort toward mastering tasks.
Social Orientation	Job requires preferring to work with others rather than alone, and being personally connected with others on the job.

25-4021.00 - Librarians

Administer libraries and perform related library services. Work in a variety of settings, including public libraries, schools, colleges and universities, museums, corporations, government agencies, law firms, non-profit organizations, and healthcare providers. Tasks may include selecting, acquiring, cataloguing, classifying, circulating, and maintaining library materials; and furnishing reference, bibliographical, and readers' advisory services. May perform in-depth, strategic research, and synthesize, analyze, edit, and filter information. May set up or work with databases and information systems to catalogue and access information.

Tasks

1) Explain use of library facilities, resources, equipment, and services, and provide information about library policies.

2) Analyze patrons' requests to determine needed information, and assist in furnishing or locating that information.

3) Search standard reference materials, including on-line sources and the Internet, in order to answer patrons' reference questions.

4) Teach library patrons to search for information using databases.

5) Evaluate materials to determine outdated or unused items to be discarded.

6) Review and evaluate resource material, such as book reviews and catalogs, in order to select and order print, audiovisual, and electronic resources.

7) Respond to customer complaints, taking action as necessary.

8) Develop library policies and procedures.

9) Compile lists of books, periodicals, articles, and audiovisual materials on particular subjects.

10) Direct and train library staff in duties such as receiving, shelving, researching, cataloging, and equipment use.

11) Organize collections of books, publications, documents, audiovisual aids, and other reference materials for convenient access.

12) Develop information access aids such as indexes and annotated bibliographies, web pages, electronic pathfinders, and on-line tutorials.

13) Assemble and arrange display materials.

14) Keep records of circulation and materials.

15) Plan and deliver client-centered programs and services such as special services for corporate clients, storytelling for children, newsletters, or programs for special groups.

16) Supervise budgeting, planning, and personnel activities.

17) Check books in and out of the library.

18) Code, classify, and catalog books, publications, films, audiovisual aids, and other library materials based on subject matter or standard library classification systems.

19) Arrange for interlibrary loans of materials not available in a particular library.

20) Write proposals for research or project grants.

21) Collect and organize books, pamphlets, manuscripts, and other materials in specific fields, such as rare books, genealogy, or music.

22) Confer with teachers, parents, and community organizations to develop, plan, and conduct programs in reading, viewing, and communication skills.

23) Design information storage and retrieval systems, and develop procedures for collecting, organizing, interpreting, and classifying information.

24) Provide input into the architectural planning of library facilities.

25) Compile lists of overdue materials, and notify borrowers that their materials are overdue.

26) Perform public relations work for the library, such as giving televised book reviews and community talks.

27) Negotiate contracts for library services, materials, and equipment.

28) Develop and index databases that provide information for library users.

29) Plan and participate in fundraising drives.

Knowledge

Knowledge	Knowledge Definitions
Customer and Personal Service	Knowledge of principles and processes for providing customer and personal services. This includes customer needs assessment, meeting quality standards for services, and evaluation of customer satisfaction.
English Language	Knowledge of the structure and content of the English language including the meaning and spelling of words, rules of composition, and grammar.
Administration and Management	Knowledge of business and management principles involved in strategic planning, resource allocation, human resources modeling, leadership technique, production methods, and coordination of people and resources.
Education and Training	Knowledge of principles and methods for curriculum and training design, teaching and instruction for individuals and groups, and the measurement of training effects.
Computers and Electronics	Knowledge of circuit boards, processors, chips, electronic equipment, and computer hardware and software, including applications and programming.
Clerical	Knowledge of administrative and clerical procedures and systems such as word processing, managing files and records, stenography and transcription, designing forms, and other office procedures and terminology.
Personnel and Human Resources	Knowledge of principles and procedures for personnel recruitment, selection, training, compensation and benefits, labor relations and negotiation, and personnel information systems.
Communications and Media	Knowledge of media production, communication, and dissemination techniques and methods. This includes alternative ways to inform and entertain via written, oral, and visual media.
Psychology	Knowledge of human behavior and performance; individual differences in ability, personality, and interests; learning and motivation; psychological research methods; and the assessment and treatment of behavioral and affective disorders.
Economics and Accounting	Knowledge of economic and accounting principles and practices, the financial markets, banking and the analysis and reporting of financial data.
Mathematics	Knowledge of arithmetic, algebra, geometry, calculus, statistics, and their applications.
Sociology and Anthropology	Knowledge of group behavior and dynamics, societal trends and influences, human migrations, ethnicity, cultures and their history and origins.
Law and Government	Knowledge of laws, legal codes, court procedures, precedents, government regulations, executive orders, agency rules, and the democratic political process.
Geography	Knowledge of principles and methods for describing the features of land, sea, and air masses, including their physical characteristics, locations, interrelationships, and distribution of plant, animal, and human life.
Telecommunications	Knowledge of transmission, broadcasting, switching, control, and operation of telecommunications systems.
Sales and Marketing	Knowledge of principles and methods for showing, promoting, and selling products or services. This includes marketing strategy and tactics, product demonstration, sales techniques, and sales control systems.
Public Safety and Security	Knowledge of relevant equipment, policies, procedures, and strategies to promote effective local, state, or national security operations for the protection of people, data, property, and institutions.
History and Archeology	Knowledge of historical events and their causes, indicators, and effects on civilizations and cultures.
Philosophy and Theology	Knowledge of different philosophical systems and religions. This includes their basic principles, values, ethics, ways of thinking, customs, practices, and their impact on human culture.
Production and Processing	Knowledge of raw materials, production processes, quality control, costs, and other techniques for maximizing the effective manufacture and distribution of goods.
Therapy and Counseling	Knowledge of principles, methods, and procedures for diagnosis, treatment, and rehabilitation of physical and mental dysfunctions, and for career counseling and guidance.
Mechanical	Knowledge of machines and tools, including their designs, uses, repair, and maintenance.
Fine Arts	Knowledge of the theory and techniques required to compose, produce, and perform works of music, dance, visual arts, drama, and sculpture.
Foreign Language	Knowledge of the structure and content of a foreign (non-English) language including the meaning and spelling of words, rules of composition and grammar, and pronunciation.
Design	Knowledge of design techniques, tools, and principles involved in production of precision technical plans, blueprints, drawings, and models.
Transportation	Knowledge of principles and methods for moving people or goods by air, rail, sea, or road, including the relative costs and benefits.

Chemistry	Knowledge of the chemical composition, structure, and properties of substances and of the chemical processes and transformations that they undergo. This includes uses of chemicals and their interactions, danger signs, production techniques, and disposal methods.
Medicine and Dentistry	Knowledge of the information and techniques needed to diagnose and treat human injuries, diseases, and deformities. This includes symptoms, treatment alternatives, drug properties and interactions, and preventive health-care measures.
Engineering and Technology	Knowledge of the practical application of engineering science and technology. This includes applying principles, techniques, procedures, and equipment to the design and production of various goods and services.
Biology	Knowledge of plant and animal organisms, their tissues, cells, functions, interdependencies, and interactions with each other and the environment.
Physics	Knowledge and prediction of physical principles, laws, their interrelationships, and applications to understanding fluid, material, and atmospheric dynamics, and mechanical, electrical, atomic and sub- atomic structures and processes.
Building and Construction	Knowledge of materials, methods, and the tools involved in the construction or repair of houses, buildings, or other structures such as highways and roads.
Food Production	Knowledge of techniques and equipment for planting, growing, and harvesting food products (both plant and animal) for consumption, including storage/handling techniques.

Skills	Skills Definitions
Reading Comprehension	Understanding written sentences and paragraphs in work related documents.
Active Listening	Giving full attention to what other people are saying, taking time to understand the points being made, asking questions as appropriate, and not interrupting at inappropriate times.
Active Learning	Understanding the implications of new information for both current and future problem-solving and decision-making.
Learning Strategies	Selecting and using training/instructional methods and procedures appropriate for the situation when learning or teaching new things.
Instructing	Teaching others how to do something.
Speaking	Talking to others to convey information effectively.
Service Orientation	Actively looking for ways to help people.
Critical Thinking	Using logic and reasoning to identify the strengths and weaknesses of alternative solutions, conclusions or approaches to problems.
Writing	Communicating effectively in writing as appropriate for the needs of the audience.
Monitoring	Monitoring/Assessing performance of yourself, other individuals, or organizations to make improvements or take corrective action.
Time Management	Managing one's own time and the time of others.
Social Perceptiveness	Being aware of others' reactions and understanding why they react as they do.
Coordination	Adjusting actions in relation to others' actions.
Persuasion	Persuading others to change their minds or behavior.
Complex Problem Solving	Identifying complex problems and reviewing related information to develop and evaluate options and implement solutions.
Equipment Selection	Determining the kind of tools and equipment needed to do a job.
Judgment and Decision Making	Considering the relative costs and benefits of potential actions to choose the most appropriate one.
Management of Financial Resources	Determining how money will be spent to get the work done, and accounting for these expenditures.
Management of Material Resources	Obtaining and seeing to the appropriate use of equipment, facilities, and materials needed to do certain work.
Management of Personnel Resources	Motivating, developing, and directing people as they work, identifying the best people for the job.
Negotiation	Bringing others together and trying to reconcile differences.
Systems Evaluation	Identifying measures or indicators of system performance and the actions needed to improve or correct performance, relative to the goals of the system.
Operations Analysis	Analyzing needs and product requirements to create a design.
Mathematics	Using mathematics to solve problems.
Systems Analysis	Determining how a system should work and how changes in conditions, operations, and the environment will affect outcomes.

Troubleshooting	Determining causes of operating errors and deciding what to do about it.
Quality Control Analysis	Conducting tests and inspections of products, services, or processes to evaluate quality or performance.
Operation and Control	Controlling operations of equipment or systems.
Technology Design	Generating or adapting equipment and technology to serve user needs.
Science	Using scientific rules and methods to solve problems.
Equipment Maintenance	Performing routine maintenance on equipment and determining when and what kind of maintenance is needed.
Installation	Installing equipment, machines, wiring, or programs to meet specifications.
Repairing	Repairing machines or systems using the needed tools.
Operation Monitoring	Watching gauges, dials, or other indicators to make sure a machine is working properly.
Programming	Writing computer programs for various purposes.

Ability	Ability Definitions
Written Comprehension	The ability to read and understand information and ideas presented in writing.
Oral Comprehension	The ability to listen to and understand information and ideas presented through spoken words and sentences.
Information Ordering	The ability to arrange things or actions in a certain order or pattern according to a specific rule or set of rules (e.g., patterns of numbers, letters, words, pictures, mathematical operations).
Near Vision	The ability to see details at close range (within a few feet of the observer).
Oral Expression	The ability to communicate information and ideas in speaking so others will understand.
Inductive Reasoning	The ability to combine pieces of information to form general rules or conclusions (includes finding a relationship among seemingly unrelated events).
Category Flexibility	The ability to generate or use different sets of rules for combining or grouping things in different ways.
Written Expression	The ability to communicate information and ideas in writing so others will understand.
Speech Recognition	The ability to identify and understand the speech of another person.
Speech Clarity	The ability to speak clearly so others can understand you.
Flexibility of Closure	The ability to identify or detect a known pattern (a figure, object, word, or sound) that is hidden in other distracting material.
Deductive Reasoning	The ability to apply general rules to specific problems to produce answers that make sense.
Problem Sensitivity	The ability to tell when something is wrong or is likely to go wrong. It does not involve solving the problem, only recognizing there is a problem.
Far Vision	The ability to see details at a distance.
Fluency of Ideas	The ability to come up with a number of ideas about a topic (the number of ideas is important, not their quality, correctness, or creativity).
Selective Attention	The ability to concentrate on a task over a period of time without being distracted.
Memorization	The ability to remember information such as words, numbers, pictures, and procedures.
Originality	The ability to come up with unusual or clever ideas about a given topic or situation, or to develop creative ways to solve a problem.
Finger Dexterity	The ability to make precisely coordinated movements of the fingers of one or both hands to grasp, manipulate, or assemble very small objects.
Speed of Closure	The ability to quickly make sense of, combine, and organize information into meaningful patterns.
Number Facility	The ability to add, subtract, multiply, or divide quickly and correctly.
Mathematical Reasoning	The ability to choose the right mathematical methods or formulas to solve a problem.
Time Sharing	The ability to shift back and forth between two or more activities or sources of information (such as speech, sounds, touch, or other sources).
Perceptual Speed	The ability to quickly and accurately compare similarities and differences among sets of letters, numbers, objects, pictures, or patterns. The things to be compared may be presented at the same time or one after the other. This ability also includes comparing a presented object with a remembered object.
Visual Color Discrimination	The ability to match or detect differences between colors, including shades of color and brightness.

Arm-Hand Steadiness	The ability to keep your hand and arm steady while moving your arm or while holding your arm and hand in one position.
Visualization	The ability to imagine how something will look after it is moved around or when its parts are moved or rearranged.
Manual Dexterity	The ability to quickly move your hand, your hand together with your arm, or your two hands to grasp, manipulate, or assemble objects.
Multilimb Coordination	The ability to coordinate two or more limbs (for example, two arms, two legs, or one leg and one arm) while sitting, standing, or lying down. It does not involve performing the activities while the whole body is in motion.
Trunk Strength	The ability to use your abdominal and lower back muscles to support part of the body repeatedly or continuously over time without 'giving out' or fatiguing.
Static Strength	The ability to exert maximum muscle force to lift, push, pull, or carry objects.
Auditory Attention	The ability to focus on a single source of sound in the presence of other distracting sounds.
Hearing Sensitivity	The ability to detect or tell the differences between sounds that vary in pitch and loudness.
Control Precision	The ability to quickly and repeatedly adjust the controls of a machine or a vehicle to exact positions.
Spatial Orientation	The ability to know your location in relation to the environment or to know where other objects are in relation to you.
Depth Perception	The ability to judge which of several objects is closer or farther away from you, or to judge the distance between you and an object.
Wrist-Finger Speed	The ability to make fast, simple, repeated movements of the fingers, hands, and wrists.
Extent Flexibility	The ability to bend, stretch, twist, or reach with your body, arms, and/or legs.
Gross Body Equilibrium	The ability to keep or regain your body balance or stay upright when in an unstable position.
Sound Localization	The ability to tell the direction from which a sound originated.
Response Orientation	The ability to choose quickly between two or more movements in response to two or more different signals (lights, sounds, pictures). It includes the speed with which the correct response is started with the hand, foot, or other body part.
Gross Body Coordination	The ability to coordinate the movement of your arms, legs, and torso together when the whole body is in motion.
Glare Sensitivity	The ability to see objects in the presence of glare or bright lighting.
Dynamic Strength	The ability to exert muscle force repeatedly or continuously over time. This involves muscular endurance and resistance to muscle fatigue.
Speed of Limb Movement	The ability to quickly move the arms and legs.
Night Vision	The ability to see under low light conditions.
Dynamic Flexibility	The ability to quickly and repeatedly bend, stretch, twist, or reach out with your body, arms, and/or legs.
Stamina	The ability to exert yourself physically over long periods of time without getting winded or out of breath.
Explosive Strength	The ability to use short bursts of muscle force to propel oneself (as in jumping or sprinting), or to throw an object.
Rate Control	The ability to time your movements or the movement of a piece of equipment in anticipation of changes in the speed and/or direction of a moving object or scene.
Peripheral Vision	The ability to see objects or movement of objects to one's side when the eyes are looking ahead.
Reaction Time	The ability to quickly respond (with the hand, finger, or foot) to a signal (sound, light, picture) when it appears.

Work_Activity	Work_Activity Definitions
Getting Information	Observing, receiving, and otherwise obtaining information from all relevant sources.
Updating and Using Relevant Knowledge	Keeping up-to-date technically and applying new knowledge to your job.
Interacting With Computers	Using computers and computer systems (including hardware and software) to program, write software, set up functions, enter data, or process information.
Communicating with Supervisors, Peers, or Subordin	Providing information to supervisors, co-workers, and subordinates by telephone, in written form, e-mail, or in person.
Establishing and Maintaining Interpersonal Relatio	Developing constructive and cooperative working relationships with others, and maintaining them over time.

Training and Teaching Others	Identifying the educational needs of others, developing formal educational or training programs or classes, and teaching or instructing others.
Performing for or Working Directly with the Public	Performing for people or dealing directly with the public. This includes serving customers in restaurants and stores, and receiving clients or guests.
Processing Information	Compiling, coding, categorizing, calculating, tabulating, auditing, or verifying information or data.
Identifying Objects, Actions, and Events	Identifying information by categorizing, estimating, recognizing differences or similarities, and detecting changes in circumstances or events.
Making Decisions and Solving Problems	Analyzing information and evaluating results to choose the best solution and solve problems.
Interpreting the Meaning of Information for Others	Translating or explaining what information means and how it can be used.
Organizing, Planning, and Prioritizing Work	Developing specific goals and plans to prioritize, organize, and accomplish your work.
Analyzing Data or Information	Identifying the underlying principles, reasons, or facts of information by breaking down information or data into separate parts.
Monitor Processes, Materials, or Surroundings	Monitoring and reviewing information from materials, events, or the environment, to detect or assess problems.
Performing Administrative Activities	Performing day-to-day administrative tasks such as maintaining information files and processing paperwork.
Communicating with Persons Outside Organization	Communicating with people outside the organization, representing the organization to customers, the public, government, and other external sources. This information can be exchanged in person, in writing, or by telephone or e-mail.
Monitoring and Controlling Resources	Monitoring and controlling resources and overseeing the spending of money.
Judging the Qualities of Things, Services, or Peop	Assessing the value, importance, or quality of things or people.
Thinking Creatively	Developing, designing, or creating new applications, ideas, relationships, systems, or products, including artistic contributions.
Coaching and Developing Others	Identifying the developmental needs of others and coaching, mentoring, or otherwise helping others to improve their knowledge or skills.
Scheduling Work and Activities	Scheduling events, programs, and activities, as well as the work of others.
Coordinating the Work and Activities of Others	Getting members of a group to work together to accomplish tasks.
Documenting/Recording Information	Entering, transcribing, recording, storing, or maintaining information in written or electronic/magnetic form.
Developing Objectives and Strategies	Establishing long-range objectives and specifying the strategies and actions to achieve them.
Guiding, Directing, and Motivating Subordinates	Providing guidance and direction to subordinates, including setting performance standards and monitoring performance.
Assisting and Caring for Others	Providing personal assistance, medical attention, emotional support, or other personal care to others such as coworkers, customers, or patients.
Handling and Moving Objects	Using hands and arms in handling, installing, positioning, and moving materials, and manipulating things.
Developing and Building Teams	Encouraging and building mutual trust, respect, and cooperation among team members.
Provide Consultation and Advice to Others	Providing guidance and expert advice to management or other groups on technical, systems-, or process-related topics.
Evaluating Information to Determine Compliance wit	Using relevant information and individual judgment to determine whether events or processes comply with laws, regulations, or standards.
Inspecting Equipment, Structures, or Material	Inspecting equipment, structures, or materials to identify the cause of errors or other problems or defects.
Resolving Conflicts and Negotiating with Others	Handling complaints, settling disputes, and resolving grievances and conflicts, or otherwise negotiating with others.
Estimating the Quantifiable Characteristics of Pro	Estimating sizes, distances, and quantities; or determining time, costs, resources, or materials needed to perform a work activity.
Performing General Physical Activities	Performing physical activities that require considerable use of your arms and legs and moving your whole body, such as climbing, lifting, balancing, walking, stooping, and handling of materials.
Selling or Influencing Others	Convincing others to buy merchandise/goods or to otherwise change their minds or actions.
Repairing and Maintaining Electronic Equipment	Servicing, repairing, calibrating, regulating, fine-tuning, or testing machines, devices, and equipment that operate primarily on the basis of electrical or electronic (not mechanical) principles.

403

Staffing Organizational Units	Recruiting, interviewing, selecting, hiring, and promoting employees in an organization.
Controlling Machines and Processes	Using either control mechanisms or direct physical activity to operate machines or processes (not including computers or vehicles).
Repairing and Maintaining Mechanical Equipment	Servicing, repairing, adjusting, and testing machines, devices, moving parts, and equipment that operate primarily on the basis of mechanical (not electronic) principles.
Drafting, Laying Out, and Specifying Technical Dev	Providing documentation, detailed instructions, drawings, or specifications to tell others about how devices, parts, equipment, or structures are to be fabricated, constructed, assembled, modified, maintained, or used.
Operating Vehicles, Mechanized Devices, or Equipme	Running, maneuvering, navigating, or driving vehicles or mechanized equipment, such as forklifts, passenger vehicles, aircraft, or water craft.

Work_Context	Work_Context Definitions
Face-to-Face Discussions	How often do you have to have face-to-face discussions with individuals or teams in this job?
Electronic Mail	How often do you use electronic mail in this job?
Telephone	How often do you have telephone conversations in this job?
Contact With Others	How much does this job require the worker to be in contact with others (face-to-face, by telephone, or otherwise) in order to perform it?
Structured versus Unstructured Work	To what extent is this job structured for the worker, rather than allowing the worker to determine tasks, priorities, and goals?
Indoors, Environmentally Controlled	How often does this job require working indoors in environmentally controlled conditions?
Freedom to Make Decisions	How much decision making freedom, without supervision, does the job offer?
Work With Work Group or Team	How important is it to work with others in a group or team in this job?
Importance of Being Exact or Accurate	How important is being very exact or highly accurate in performing this job?
Deal With External Customers	How important is it to work with external customers or the public in this job?
Coordinate or Lead Others	How important is it to coordinate or lead others in accomplishing work activities in this job?
Degree of Automation	How automated is the job?
Letters and Memos	How often does the job require written letters and memos?
Physical Proximity	To what extent does this job require the worker to perform job tasks in close physical proximity to other people?
Importance of Repeating Same Tasks	How important is repeating the same physical activities (e.g., key entry) or mental activities (e.g., checking entries in a ledger) over and over, without stopping, to performing this job?
Spend Time Using Your Hands to Handle, Control, or	How much does this job require using your hands to handle, control, or feel objects, tools or controls?
Responsibility for Outcomes and Results	How responsible is the worker for work outcomes and results of other workers?
Spend Time Sitting	How much does this job require sitting?
Frequency of Decision Making	How frequently is the worker required to make decisions that affect other people, the financial resources, and/or the image and reputation of the organization?
Time Pressure	How often does this job require the worker to meet strict deadlines?
Impact of Decisions on Co-workers or Company Resul	How do the decisions an employee makes impact the results of co-workers, clients or the company?
Spend Time Making Repetitive Motions	How much does this job require making repetitive motions?
Deal With Unpleasant or Angry People	How frequently does the worker have to deal with unpleasant, angry, or discourteous individuals as part of the job requirements?
Public Speaking	How often do you have to perform public speaking in this job?
Frequency of Conflict Situations	How often are there conflict situations the employee has to face in this job?
Spend Time Standing	How much does this job require standing?
Responsible for Others' Health and Safety	How much responsibility is there for the health and safety of others in this job?
Sounds, Noise Levels Are Distracting or Uncomforta	How often does this job require working exposed to sounds and noise levels that are distracting or uncomfortable?
Spend Time Walking and Running	How much does this job require walking and running?
Level of Competition	To what extent does this job require the worker to compete or to be aware of competitive pressures?

Spend Time Bending or Twisting the Body	How much does this job require bending or twisting your body?
Exposed to Contaminants	How often does this job require working exposed to contaminants (such as pollutants, gases, dust or odors)?
Deal With Physically Aggressive People	How frequently does this job require the worker to deal with physical aggression of violent individuals?
Spend Time Kneeling, Crouching, Stooping, or Crawl	How much does this job require kneeling, crouching, stooping or crawling?
Exposed to Disease or Infections	How often does this job require exposure to disease/infections?
Consequence of Error	How serious would the result usually be if the worker made a mistake that was not readily correctable?
Cramped Work Space, Awkward Positions	How often does this job require working in cramped work spaces that requires getting into awkward positions?
Indoors, Not Environmentally Controlled	How often does this job require working indoors in non-controlled environmental conditions (e.g., warehouse without heat)?
In an Enclosed Vehicle or Equipment	How often does this job require working in a closed vehicle or equipment (e.g., car)?
Pace Determined by Speed of Equipment	How important is it to this job that the pace is determined by the speed of equipment or machinery? (This does not refer to keeping busy at all times on this job.)
Exposed to Minor Burns, Cuts, Bites, or Stings	How often does this job require exposure to minor burns, cuts, bites, or stings?
Spend Time Keeping or Regaining Balance	How much does this job require keeping or regaining your balance?
Very Hot or Cold Temperatures	How often does this job require working in very hot (above 90 F degrees) or very cold (below 32 F degrees) temperatures?
Spend Time Climbing Ladders, Scaffolds, or Poles	How much does this job require climbing ladders, scaffolds, or poles?
Extremely Bright or Inadequate Lighting	How often does this job require working in extremely bright or inadequate lighting conditions?
Outdoors, Under Cover	How often does this job require working outdoors, under cover (e.g., structure with roof but no walls)?
Exposed to High Places	How often does this job require exposure to high places?
Wear Common Protective or Safety Equipment such as	How much does this job require wearing common protective or safety equipment such as safety shoes, glasses, gloves, hard hats or live jackets?
Exposed to Hazardous Conditions	How often does this job require exposure to hazardous conditions?
Outdoors, Exposed to Weather	How often does this job require working outdoors, exposed to all weather conditions?
Exposed to Whole Body Vibration	How often does this job require exposure to whole body vibration (e.g., operate a jackhammer)?
Exposed to Radiation	How often does this job require exposure to radiation?
In an Open Vehicle or Equipment	How often does this job require working in an open vehicle or equipment (e.g., tractor)?
Exposed to Hazardous Equipment	How often does this job require exposure to hazardous equipment?
Wear Specialized Protective or Safety Equipment su	How much does this job require wearing specialized protective or safety equipment such as breathing apparatus, safety harness, full protection suits, or radiation protection?

Job Zone Component	Job Zone Component Definitions
Title	Job Zone Five: Extensive Preparation Needed
Overall Experience	Extensive skill, knowledge, and experience are needed for these occupations. Many require more than five years of experience. For example, surgeons must complete four years of college and an additional five to seven years of specialized medical training to be able to do their job.
Job Training	Employees may need some on-the-job training, but most of these occupations assume that the person will already have the required skills, knowledge, work-related experience, and/or training.
Job Zone Examples	These occupations often involve coordinating, training, supervising, or managing the activities of others to accomplish goals. Very advanced communication and organizational skills are required. Examples include athletic trainers, lawyers, managing editors, phyicists, social psychologists, and surgeons. (8.0 and above)
SVP Range	A bachelor's degree is the minimum formal education required for these occupations.
Education	However, many also require graduate school. For example, they may require a master's degree, and some require a Ph.D., M.D., or J.D. (law degree).

Work_Styles	Work_Styles Definitions
Cooperation	Job requires being pleasant with others on the job and displaying a good-natured. cooperative attitude.
Dependability	Job requires being reliable, responsible, and dependable, and fulfilling obligations.
Attention to Detail	Job requires being careful about detail and thorough in completing work tasks.
Adaptability/Flexibility	Job requires being open to change (positive or negative) and to considerable variety in the workplace.
Integrity	Job requires being honest and ethical.
Self Control	Job requires maintaining composure, keeping emotions in check, controlling anger, and avoiding aggressive behavior, even in very difficult situations.
Concern for Others	Job requires being sensitive to others' needs and feelings and being understanding and helpful on the job.
Initiative	Job requires a willingness to take on responsibilities and challenges.
Achievement/Effort	Job requires establishing and maintaining personally challenging achievement goals and exerting effort toward mastering tasks.
Independence	Job requires developing one's own ways of doing things, guiding oneself with little or no supervision, and depending on oneself to get things done.
Social Orientation	Job requires preferring to work with others rather than alone, and being personally connected with others on the job.
Leadership	Job requires a willingness to lead, take charge, and offer opinions and direction.
Persistence	Job requires persistence in the face of obstacles.
Stress Tolerance	Job requires accepting criticism and dealing calmly and effectively with high stress situations.
Innovation	Job requires creativity and alternative thinking to develop new ideas for and answers to work-related problems.
Analytical Thinking	Job requires analyzing information and using logic to address work-related issues and problems.

25-4031.00 - Library Technicians

Assist librarians by helping readers in the use of library catalogs, databases, and indexes to locate books and other materials; and by answering questions that require only brief consultation of standard reference. Compile records; sort and shelve books; remove or repair damaged books; register patrons; check materials in and out of the circulation process. Replace materials in shelving area (stacks) or files. Includes bookmobile drivers who operate bookmobiles or light trucks that pull trailers to specific locations on a predetermined schedule and assist with providing services in mobile libraries.

Tasks

1) Guide patrons in finding and using library resources, including reference materials, audiovisual equipment, computers, and electronic resources.

2) Provide assistance to teachers and students by locating materials and helping to complete special projects.

3) Conduct reference searches, using printed materials and in-house and online databases.

4) Sort books, publications, and other items according to procedure and return them to shelves, files, or other designated storage areas.

5) Reserve, circulate, renew, and discharge books and other materials.

6) Deliver and retrieve items throughout the library by hand or using pushcart.

7) Train other staff, volunteers and/or student assistants, and schedule and supervise their work.

8) Take actions to halt disruption of library activities by problem patrons.

9) Enter and update patrons' records on computers.

10) Compile and maintain records relating to circulation, materials, and equipment.

11) Verify bibliographic data for materials, including author, title, publisher, publication date, and edition.

12) Process print and non-print library materials to prepare them for inclusion in library collections.

13) Organize and maintain periodicals and reference materials.

14) Repair damaged books.

15) Process interlibrary loans for patrons.

16) Collect fines, and respond to complaints about fines.

17) Prepare order slips for materials to be acquired, checking prices and figuring costs.

18) Send out notices about lost or overdue books.

19) Issue identification cards to borrowers.

20) Design posters and special displays to promote use of library facilities or specific reading programs at libraries.

21) Prepare volumes for binding.

22) Retrieve information from central databases for storage in a library's computer.

23) Operate and maintain audiovisual equipment such as projectors, tape recorders, and videocassette recorders.

24) Conduct children's programs and other specialized programs such as library tours.

25) Review subject matter of materials to be classified, and select classification numbers and headings according to classification systems.

26) Design, customize, and maintain databases, web pages, and local area networks.

27) Compose explanatory summaries of contents of books and other reference materials.

28) File catalog cards according to system used.

29) Compile bibliographies and prepare abstracts on subjects of interest to particular organizations or groups.

30) Collaborate with archivists to arrange for the safe storage of historical records and documents.

Knowledge	Knowledge Definitions
Clerical	Knowledge of administrative and clerical procedures and systems such as word processing, managing files and records. stenography and transcription, designing forms, and other office procedures and terminology.
Computers and Electronics	Knowledge of circuit boards, processors, chips, electronic equipment, and computer hardware and software, including applications and programming.
Customer and Personal Service	Knowledge of principles and processes for providing customer and personal services. This includes customer needs assessment, meeting quality standards for services, and evaluation of customer satisfaction.
English Language	Knowledge of the structure and content of the English language including the meaning and spelling of words, rules of composition, and grammar.
Education and Training	Knowledge of principles and methods for curriculum and training design, teaching and instruction for individuals and groups, and the measurement of training effects.
Administration and Management	Knowledge of business and management principles involved in strategic planning, resource allocation, human resources modeling, leadership technique, production methods, and coordination of people and resources.
Personnel and Human Resources	Knowledge of principles and procedures for personnel recruitment, selection, training, compensation and benefits, labor relations and negotiation, and personnel information systems.
Public Safety and Security	Knowledge of relevant equipment, policies, procedures, and strategies to promote effective local, state, or national security operations for the protection of people, data, property, and institutions.
Mathematics	Knowledge of arithmetic, algebra, geometry, calculus, statistics, and their applications.
Psychology	Knowledge of human behavior and performance; individual differences in ability, personality, and interests; learning and motivation; psychological research methods; and the assessment and treatment of behavioral and affective disorders.
Communications and Media	Knowledge of media production, communication, and dissemination techniques and methods. This includes alternative ways to inform and entertain via written, oral, and visual media.
History and Archeology	Knowledge of historical events and their causes, indicators, and effects on civilizations and cultures.
Economics and Accounting	Knowledge of economic and accounting principles and practices, the financial markets, banking and the analysis and reporting of financial data.
Sociology and Anthropology	Knowledge of group behavior and dynamics, societal trends and influences, human migrations, ethnicity, cultures and their history and origins.

Geography	Knowledge of principles and methods for describing the features of land, sea, and air masses, including their physical characteristics, locations, interrelationships, and distribution of plant, animal, and human life.
Foreign Language	Knowledge of the structure and content of a foreign (non-English) language including the meaning and spelling of words, rules of composition and grammar, and pronunciation.
Engineering and Technology	Knowledge of the practical application of engineering science and technology. This includes applying principles, techniques, procedures, and equipment to the design and production of various goods and services.
Law and Government	Knowledge of laws, legal codes, court procedures, precedents, government regulations, executive orders, agency rules, and the democratic political process.
Philosophy and Theology	Knowledge of different philosophical systems and religions. This includes their basic principles, values, ethics, ways of thinking, customs, practices, and their impact on human culture.
Transportation	Knowledge of principles and methods for moving people or goods by air, rail, sea, or road, including the relative costs and benefits.
Medicine and Dentistry	Knowledge of the information and techniques needed to diagnose and treat human injuries, diseases, and deformities. This includes symptoms, treatment alternatives, drug properties and interactions, and preventive health-care measures.
Mechanical	Knowledge of machines and tools, including their designs, uses, repair, and maintenance.
Sales and Marketing	Knowledge of principles and methods for showing, promoting, and selling products or services. This includes marketing strategy and tactics, product demonstration, sales techniques, and sales control systems.
Therapy and Counseling	Knowledge of principles, methods, and procedures for diagnosis, treatment, and rehabilitation of physical and mental dysfunctions, and for career counseling and guidance.
Production and Processing	Knowledge of raw materials, production processes, quality control, costs, and other techniques for maximizing the effective manufacture and distribution of goods.
Telecommunications	Knowledge of transmission, broadcasting, switching, control, and operation of telecommunications systems.
Fine Arts	Knowledge of the theory and techniques required to compose, produce, and perform works of music, dance, visual arts, drama, and sculpture.
Design	Knowledge of design techniques, tools, and principles involved in production of precision technical plans, blueprints, drawings, and models.
Biology	Knowledge of plant and animal organisms, their tissues, cells, functions, interdependencies, and interactions with each other and the environment.
Chemistry	Knowledge of the chemical composition, structure, and properties of substances and of the chemical processes and transformations that they undergo. This includes uses of chemicals and their interactions, danger signs, production techniques, and disposal methods.
Building and Construction	Knowledge of materials, methods, and the tools involved in the construction or repair of houses, buildings, or other structures such as highways and roads.
Physics	Knowledge and prediction of physical principles, laws, their interrelationships, and applications to understanding fluid, material, and atmospheric dynamics, and mechanical, electrical, atomic and sub- atomic structures and processes.
Food Production	Knowledge of techniques and equipment for planting, growing, and harvesting food products (both plant and animal) for consumption, including storage/handling techniques.

Skills	Skills Definitions
Active Listening	Giving full attention to what other people are saying, taking time to understand the points being made, asking questions as appropriate, and not interrupting at inappropriate times.
Reading Comprehension	Understanding written sentences and paragraphs in work related documents.
Service Orientation	Actively looking for ways to help people.
Speaking	Talking to others to convey information effectively.
Social Perceptiveness	Being aware of others' reactions and understanding why they react as they do.
Instructing	Teaching others how to do something.
Time Management	Managing one's own time and the time of others.
Coordination	Adjusting actions in relation to others' actions.

Active Learning	Understanding the implications of new information for both current and future problem-solving and decision-making.
Critical Thinking	Using logic and reasoning to identify the strengths and weaknesses of alternative solutions, conclusions or approaches to problems.
Learning Strategies	Selecting and using training/instructional methods and procedures appropriate for the situation when learning or teaching new things.
Writing	Communicating effectively in writing as appropriate for the needs of the audience.
Monitoring	Monitoring/Assessing performance of yourself, other individuals, or organizations to make improvements or take corrective action.
Judgment and Decision Making	Considering the relative costs and benefits of potential actions to choose the most appropriate one.
Equipment Selection	Determining the kind of tools and equipment needed to do a job.
Negotiation	Bringing others together and trying to reconcile differences.
Management of Personnel Resources	Motivating, developing, and directing people as they work, identifying the best people for the job.
Complex Problem Solving	Identifying complex problems and reviewing related information to develop and evaluate options and implement solutions.
Persuasion	Persuading others to change their minds or behavior.
Troubleshooting	Determining causes of operating errors and deciding what to do about it.
Technology Design	Generating or adapting equipment and technology to serve user needs.
Mathematics	Using mathematics to solve problems.
Management of Material Resources	Obtaining and seeing to the appropriate use of equipment, facilities, and materials needed to do certain work.
Quality Control Analysis	Conducting tests and inspections of products, services, or processes to evaluate quality or performance.
Operations Analysis	Analyzing needs and product requirements to create a design.
Operation and Control	Controlling operations of equipment or systems.
Equipment Maintenance	Performing routine maintenance on equipment and determining when and what kind of maintenance is needed.
Systems Evaluation	Identifying measures or indicators of system performance and the actions needed to improve or correct performance, relative to the goals of the system.
Repairing	Repairing machines or systems using the needed tools.
Systems Analysis	Determining how a system should work and how changes in conditions, operations, and the environment will affect outcomes.
Management of Financial Resources	Determining how money will be spent to get the work done, and accounting for these expenditures.
Installation	Installing equipment, machines, wiring, or programs to meet specifications.
Operation Monitoring	Watching gauges, dials, or other indicators to make sure a machine is working properly.
Programming	Writing computer programs for various purposes.
Science	Using scientific rules and methods to solve problems.

Ability	Ability Definitions
Written Comprehension	The ability to read and understand information and ideas presented in writing.
Oral Comprehension	The ability to listen to and understand information and ideas presented through spoken words and sentences.
Oral Expression	The ability to communicate information and ideas in speaking so others will understand.
Information Ordering	The ability to arrange things or actions in a certain order or pattern according to a specific rule or set of rules (e.g., patterns of numbers, letters, words, pictures, mathematical operations).
Category Flexibility	The ability to generate or use different sets of rules for combining or grouping things in different ways.
Near Vision	The ability to see details at close range (within a few feet of the observer).
Written Expression	The ability to communicate information and ideas in writing so others will understand.
Deductive Reasoning	The ability to apply general rules to specific problems to produce answers that make sense.
Inductive Reasoning	The ability to combine pieces of information to form general rules or conclusions (includes finding a relationship among seemingly unrelated events).
Speech Clarity	The ability to speak clearly so others can understand you.
Speech Recognition	The ability to identify and understand the speech of another person.

Selective Attention	The ability to concentrate on a task over a period of time without being distracted.
Problem Sensitivity	The ability to tell when something is wrong or is likely to go wrong. It does not involve solving the problem, only recognizing there is a problem.
Fluency of Ideas	The ability to come up with a number of ideas about a topic (the number of ideas is important, not their quality, correctness, or creativity).
Finger Dexterity	The ability to make precisely coordinated movements of the fingers of one or both hands to grasp, manipulate, or assemble very small objects.
Flexibility of Closure	The ability to identify or detect a known pattern (a figure, object, word, or sound) that is hidden in other distracting material.
Memorization	The ability to remember information such as words, numbers, pictures, and procedures.
Originality	The ability to come up with unusual or clever ideas about a given topic or situation, or to develop creative ways to solve a problem.
Arm-Hand Steadiness	The ability to keep your hand and arm steady while moving your arm or while holding your arm and hand in one position.
Mathematical Reasoning	The ability to choose the right mathematical methods or formulas to solve a problem.
Time Sharing	The ability to shift back and forth between two or more activities or sources of information (such as speech, sounds, touch, or other sources).
Perceptual Speed	The ability to quickly and accurately compare similarities and differences among sets of letters, numbers, objects, pictures, or patterns. The things to be compared may be presented at the same time or one after the other. This ability also includes comparing a presented object with a remembered object.
Number Facility	The ability to add, subtract, multiply, or divide quickly and correctly.
Manual Dexterity	The ability to quickly move your hand, your hand together with your arm, or your two hands to grasp, manipulate, or assemble objects.
Far Vision	The ability to see details at a distance.
Static Strength	The ability to exert maximum muscle force to lift, push, pull, or carry objects.
Visual Color Discrimination	The ability to match or detect differences between colors, including shades of color and brightness.
Speed of Closure	The ability to quickly make sense of, combine, and organize information into meaningful patterns.
Visualization	The ability to imagine how something will look after it is moved around or when its parts are moved or rearranged.
Multilimb Coordination	The ability to coordinate two or more limbs (for example, two arms, two legs, or one leg and one arm) while sitting, standing, or lying down. It does not involve performing the activities while the whole body is in motion.
Gross Body Equilibrium	The ability to keep or regain your body balance or stay upright when in an unstable position.
Extent Flexibility	The ability to bend, stretch, twist, or reach with your body, arms, and/or legs.
Dynamic Strength	The ability to exert muscle force repeatedly or continuously over time. This involves muscular endurance and resistance to muscle fatigue.
Trunk Strength	The ability to use your abdominal and lower back muscles to support part of the body repeatedly or continuously over time without 'giving out' or fatiguing.
Control Precision	The ability to quickly and repeatedly adjust the controls of a machine or a vehicle to exact positions.
Gross Body Coordination	The ability to coordinate the movement of your arms, legs, and torso together when the whole body is in motion.
Spatial Orientation	The ability to know your location in relation to the environment or to know where other objects are in relation to you.
Stamina	The ability to exert yourself physically over long periods of time without getting winded or out of breath.
Hearing Sensitivity	The ability to detect or tell the differences between sounds that vary in pitch and loudness.
Depth Perception	The ability to judge which of several objects is closer or farther away from you, or to judge the distance between you and an object.
Sound Localization	The ability to tell the direction from which a sound originated.
Auditory Attention	The ability to focus on a single source of sound in the presence of other distracting sounds.
Wrist-Finger Speed	The ability to make fast, simple, repeated movements of the fingers, hands, and wrists.
Dynamic Flexibility	The ability to quickly and repeatedly bend, stretch, twist, or reach out with your body, arms, and/or legs.
Night Vision	The ability to see under low light conditions.
Peripheral Vision	The ability to see objects or movement of objects to one's side when the eyes are looking ahead.
Response Orientation	The ability to choose quickly between two or more movements in response to two or more different signals (lights, sounds, pictures). It includes the speed with which the correct response is started with the hand, foot, or other body part.
Speed of Limb Movement	The ability to quickly move the arms and legs.
Glare Sensitivity	The ability to see objects in the presence of glare or bright lighting.
Reaction Time	The ability to quickly respond (with the hand, finger, or foot) to a signal (sound, light, picture) when it appears.
Explosive Strength	The ability to use short bursts of muscle force to propel oneself (as in jumping or sprinting), or to throw an object.
Rate Control	The ability to time your movements or the movement of a piece of equipment in anticipation of changes in the speed and/or direction of a moving object or scene.

Work_Activity	Work_Activity Definitions
Interacting With Computers	Using computers and computer systems (including hardware and software) to program, write software, set up functions, enter data, or process information.
Establishing and Maintaining Interpersonal Relatio	Developing constructive and cooperative working relationships with others, and maintaining them over time.
Processing Information	Compiling, coding, categorizing, calculating, tabulating, auditing, or verifying information or data.
Communicating with Supervisors, Peers, or Subordin	Providing information to supervisors, co-workers, and subordinates by telephone, in written form, e-mail, or in person.
Performing for or Working Directly with the Public	Performing for people or dealing directly with the public. This includes serving customers in restaurants and stores, and receiving clients or guests.
Documenting/Recording Information	Entering, transcribing, recording, storing, or maintaining information in written or electronic/magnetic form.
Handling and Moving Objects	Using hands and arms in handling, installing, positioning, and moving materials, and manipulating things.
Identifying Objects, Actions, and Events	Identifying information by categorizing, estimating, recognizing differences or similarities, and detecting changes in circumstances or events.
Getting Information	Observing, receiving, and otherwise obtaining information from all relevant sources.
Training and Teaching Others	Identifying the educational needs of others, developing formal educational or training programs or classes, and teaching or instructing others.
Updating and Using Relevant Knowledge	Keeping up-to-date technically and applying new knowledge to your job.
Making Decisions and Solving Problems	Analyzing information and evaluating results to choose the best solution and solve problems.
Organizing, Planning, and Prioritizing Work	Developing specific goals and plans to prioritize, organize, and accomplish your work.
Communicating with Persons Outside Organization	Communicating with people outside the organization, representing the organization to customers, the public, government, and other external sources. This information can be exchanged in person, in writing, or by telephone or e-mail.
Performing General Physical Activities	Performing physical activities that require considerable use of your arms and legs and moving your whole body, such as climbing, lifting, balancing, walking, stooping, and handling of materials.
Interpreting the Meaning of Information for Others	Translating or explaining what information means and how it can be used.
Resolving Conflicts and Negotiating with Others	Handling complaints, settling disputes, and resolving grievances and conflicts, or otherwise negotiating with others.
Scheduling Work and Activities	Scheduling events, programs, and activities, as well as the work of others.
Thinking Creatively	Developing, designing, or creating new applications, ideas, relationships, systems, or products, including artistic contributions.
Assisting and Caring for Others	Providing personal assistance, medical attention, emotional support, or other personal care to others such as coworkers, customers, or patients.
Monitor Processes, Materials, or Surroundings	Monitoring and reviewing information from materials, events, or the environment, to detect or assess problems.

Developing Objectives and Strategies	Establishing long-range objectives and specifying the strategies and actions to achieve them.
Judging the Qualities of Things, Services, or Peop	Assessing the value, importance, or quality of things or people.
Performing Administrative Activities	Performing day-to-day administrative tasks such as maintaining information files and processing paperwork.
Analyzing Data or Information	Identifying the underlying principles, reasons, or facts of information by breaking down information or data into separate parts.
Coordinating the Work and Activities of Others	Getting members of a group to work together to accomplish tasks.
Guiding, Directing, and Motivating Subordinates	Providing guidance and direction to subordinates, including setting performance standards and monitoring performance.
Developing and Building Teams	Encouraging and building mutual trust, respect, and cooperation among team members.
Coaching and Developing Others	Identifying the developmental needs of others and coaching, mentoring, or otherwise helping others to improve their knowledge or skills.
Evaluating Information to Determine Compliance wit	Using relevant information and individual judgment to determine whether events or processes comply with laws, regulations, or standards.
Estimating the Quantifiable Characteristics of Pro	Estimating sizes, distances, and quantities; or determining time, costs, resources, or materials needed to perform a work activity.
Inspecting Equipment, Structures, or Material	Inspecting equipment, structures, or materials to identify the cause of errors or other problems or defects.
Staffing Organizational Units	Recruiting, interviewing, selecting, hiring, and promoting employees in an organization.
Monitoring and Controlling Resources	Monitoring and controlling resources and overseeing the spending of money.
Provide Consultation and Advice to Others	Providing guidance and expert advice to management or other groups on technical, systems-, or process-related topics.
Controlling Machines and Processes	Using either control mechanisms or direct physical activity to operate machines or processes (not including computers or vehicles).
Selling or Influencing Others	Convincing others to buy merchandise/goods or to otherwise change their minds or actions.
Repairing and Maintaining Electronic Equipment	Servicing, repairing, calibrating, regulating, fine-tuning, or testing machines, devices, and equipment that operate primarily on the basis of electrical or electronic (not mechanical) principles.
Drafting, Laying Out, and Specifying Technical Dev	Providing documentation, detailed instructions, drawings, or specifications to tell others about how devices, parts, equipment, or structures are to be fabricated, constructed, assembled, modified, maintained, or used.
Repairing and Maintaining Mechanical Equipment	Servicing, repairing, adjusting, and testing machines, devices, moving parts, and equipment that operate primarily on the basis of mechanical (not electronic) principles.
Operating Vehicles, Mechanized Devices, or Equipme	Running, maneuvering, navigating, or driving vehicles or mechanized equipment, such as forklifts, passenger vehicles, aircraft, or water craft.

Work_Context

Work_Context Definitions

Telephone	How often do you have telephone conversations in this job?
Face-to-Face Discussions	How often do you have to have face-to-face discussions with individuals or teams in this job?
Electronic Mail	How often do you use electronic mail in this job?
Indoors, Environmentally Controlled	How often does this job require working indoors in environmentally controlled conditions?
Contact With Others	How much does this job require the worker to be in contact with others (face-to-face, by telephone, or otherwise) in order to perform it?
Freedom to Make Decisions	How much decision making freedom, without supervision, does the job offer?
Structured versus Unstructured Work	To what extent is this job structured for the worker, rather than allowing the worker to determine tasks, priorities, and goals?
Importance of Being Exact or Accurate	How important is being very exact or highly accurate in performing this job?
Spend Time Using Your Hands to Handle, Control, or	How much does this job require using your hands to handle, control, or feel objects, tools or controls?
Work With Work Group or Team	How important is it to work with others in a group or team in this job?
Importance of Repeating Same Tasks	How important is repeating the same physical activities (e.g., key entry) or mental activities (e.g., checking entries in a ledger) over and over, without stopping, to performing this job?
Spend Time Sitting	How much does this job require sitting?

Frequency of Decision Making	How frequently is the worker required to make decisions that affect other people, the financial resources, and/or the image and reputation of the organization?
Deal With External Customers	How important is it to work with external customers or the public in this job?
Letters and Memos	How often does the job require written letters and memos?
Impact of Decisions on Co-workers or Company Resul	How do the decisions an employee makes impact the results of co-workers, clients or the company?
Time Pressure	How often does this job require the worker to meet strict deadlines?
Degree of Automation	How automated is the job?
Spend Time Making Repetitive Motions	How much does this job require making repetitive motions?
Frequency of Conflict Situations	How often are there conflict situations the employee has to face in this job?
Responsibility for Outcomes and Results	How responsible is the worker for work outcomes and results of other workers?
Deal With Unpleasant or Angry People	How frequently does the worker have to deal with unpleasant, angry, or discourteous individuals as part of the job requirements?
Physical Proximity	To what extent does this job require the worker to perform job tasks in close physical proximity to other people?
Exposed to Contaminants	How often does this job require working exposed to contaminants (such as pollutants, gases, dust or odors)?
Coordinate or Lead Others	How important is it to coordinate or lead others in accomplishing work activities in this job?
Spend Time Standing	How much does this job require standing?
Sounds, Noise Levels Are Distracting or Uncomforta	How often does this job require working exposed to sounds and noise levels that are distracting or uncomfortable?
Spend Time Walking and Running	How much does this job require walking and running?
Public Speaking	How often do you have to perform public speaking in this job?
Responsible for Others' Health and Safety	How much responsibility is there for the health and safety of others in this job?
Spend Time Bending or Twisting the Body	How much does this job require bending or twisting your body?
Cramped Work Space, Awkward Positions	How often does this job require working in cramped work spaces that requires getting into awkward positions?
Level of Competition	To what extent does this job require the worker to compete or to be aware of competitive pressures?
Spend Time Kneeling, Crouching, Stooping, or Crawl	How much does this job require kneeling, crouching, stooping or crawling?
Exposed to Disease or Infections	How often does this job require exposure to disease/infections?
Consequence of Error	How serious would the result usually be if the worker made a mistake that was not readily correctable?
Deal With Physically Aggressive People	How frequently does this job require the worker to deal with physical aggression of violent individuals?
In an Enclosed Vehicle or Equipment	How often does this job require working in a closed vehicle or equipment (e.g., car)?
Outdoors, Under Cover	How often does this job require working outdoors, under cover (e.g., structure with roof but no walls)?
Outdoors, Exposed to Weather	How often does this job require working outdoors, exposed to all weather conditions?
Very Hot or Cold Temperatures	How often does this job require working in very hot (above 90 F degrees) or very cold (below 32 F degrees) temperatures?
Exposed to Minor Burns, Cuts, Bites, or Stings	How often does this job require exposure to minor burns, cuts, bites, or stings?
Indoors, Not Environmentally Controlled	How often does this job require working indoors in non-controlled environmental conditions (e.g., warehouse without heat)?
Pace Determined by Speed of Equipment	How important is it to this job that the pace is determined by the speed of equipment or machinery? (This does not refer to keeping busy at all times on this job.)
Extremely Bright or Inadequate Lighting	How often does this job require working in extremely bright or inadequate lighting conditions?
Wear Common Protective or Safety Equipment such as	How much does this job require wearing common protective or safety equipment such as safety shoes, glasses, gloves, hard hats or live jackets?
Spend Time Keeping or Regaining Balance	How much does this job require keeping or regaining your balance?
In an Open Vehicle or Equipment	How often does this job require working in an open vehicle or equipment (e.g., tractor)?
Exposed to Hazardous Conditions	How often does this job require exposure to hazardous conditions?

Wear Specialized Protective or Safety Equipment su	How much does this job require wearing specialized protective or safety equipment such as breathing apparatus, safety harness, full protection suits, or radiation protection?
Exposed to High Places	How often does this job require exposure to high places?
Spend Time Climbing Ladders, Scaffolds, or Poles	How much does this job require climbing ladders, scaffolds, or poles?
Exposed to Hazardous Equipment	How often does this job require exposure to hazardous equipment?
Exposed to Radiation	How often does this job require exposure to radiation?
Exposed to Whole Body Vibration	How often does this job require exposure to whole body vibration (e.g., operate a jackhammer)?

Job Zone Component	Job Zone Component Definitions
Title	Job Zone Three: Medium Preparation Needed
Overall Experience	Previous work-related skill, knowledge, or experience is required for these occupations. For example, an electrician must have completed three or four years of apprenticeship or several years of vocational training, and often must have passed a licensing exam, in order to perform the job.
Job Training	Employees in these occupations usually need one or two years of training involving both on-the-job experience and informal training with experienced workers.
Job Zone Examples	These occupations usually involve using communication and organizational skills to coordinate, supervise, manage, or train others to accomplish goals. Examples include dental assistants, electricians, fish and game wardens, legal secretaries, personnel recruiters, and recreation workers.
SVP Range	(6.0 to < 7.0)
Education	Most occupations in this zone require training in vocational schools, related on-the-job experience, or an associate's degree. Some may require a bachelor's degree.

Work_Styles	Work_Styles Definitions
Dependability	Job requires being reliable, responsible, and dependable, and fulfilling obligations.
Cooperation	Job requires being pleasant with others on the job and displaying a good-natured, cooperative attitude.
Integrity	Job requires being honest and ethical.
Independence	Job requires developing one's own ways of doing things, guiding oneself with little or no supervision, and depending on oneself to get things done.
Attention to Detail	Job requires being careful about detail and thorough in completing work tasks.
Concern for Others	Job requires being sensitive to others' needs and feelings and being understanding and helpful on the job.
Initiative	Job requires a willingness to take on responsibilities and challenges.
Self Control	Job requires maintaining composure, keeping emotions in check, controlling anger, and avoiding aggressive behavior, even in very difficult situations.
Leadership	Job requires a willingness to lead, take charge, and offer opinions and direction.
Stress Tolerance	Job requires accepting criticism and dealing calmly and effectively with high stress situations.
Social Orientation	Job requires preferring to work with others rather than alone, and being personally connected with others on the job.
Adaptability/Flexibility	Job requires being open to change (positive or negative) and to considerable variety in the workplace.
Innovation	Job requires creativity and alternative thinking to develop new ideas for and answers to work-related problems.
Achievement/Effort	Job requires establishing and maintaining personally challenging achievement goals and exerting effort toward mastering tasks.
Analytical Thinking	Job requires analyzing information and using logic to address work-related issues and problems.
Persistence	Job requires persistence in the face of obstacles.

25-9011.00 - Audio-Visual Collections Specialists

Prepare, plan, and operate audio-visual teaching aids for use in education. May record, catalogue, and file audio-visual materials.

Tasks

1) Instruct users in the selection, use, and design of audiovisual materials, and assist them in the preparation of instructional materials and the rehearsal of presentations.

2) Attend conventions and conferences, read trade journals, and communicate with industry insiders in order to keep abreast of industry developments.

3) Maintain hardware and software, including computers, scanners, color copiers, and color laser printers.

4) Perform simple maintenance tasks such as cleaning monitors and lenses and changing batteries and light bulbs.

5) Develop manuals, texts, workbooks, or related materials for use in conjunction with production materials.

6) Offer presentations and workshops on the role of multimedia in effective presentations.

7) Confer with teachers in order to select course materials and to determine which training aids are best suited to particular grade levels.

8) Produce rough and finished graphics and graphic designs.

9) Narrate presentations and productions.

10) Locate and secure settings, properties, effects, and other production necessities.

11) Plan and prepare audiovisual teaching aids and methods for use in school systems.

12) Determine formats, approaches, content, levels, and mediums necessary to meet production objectives effectively and within budgetary constraints.

13) Acquire, catalog, and maintain collections of audiovisual material such as films, video- and audio-tapes, photographs, and software programs.

14) Develop preproduction ideas and incorporate them into outlines, scripts, story boards, and graphics.

15) Direct and coordinate activities of assistants and other personnel during production.

16) Construct and position properties, sets, lighting equipment, and other equipment.

Knowledge	Knowledge Definitions
Computers and Electronics	Knowledge of circuit boards, processors, chips, electronic equipment, and computer hardware and software, including applications and programming.
Education and Training	Knowledge of principles and methods for curriculum and training design, teaching and instruction for individuals and groups, and the measurement of training effects.
Communications and Media	Knowledge of media production, communication, and dissemination techniques and methods. This includes alternative ways to inform and entertain via written, oral, and visual media.
Customer and Personal Service	Knowledge of principles and processes for providing customer and personal services. This includes customer needs assessment, meeting quality standards for services, and evaluation of customer satisfaction.
English Language	Knowledge of the structure and content of the English language including the meaning and spelling of words, rules of composition, and grammar.
Telecommunications	Knowledge of transmission, broadcasting, switching, control, and operation of telecommunications systems.
Mathematics	Knowledge of arithmetic, algebra, geometry, calculus, statistics, and their applications.
Administration and Management	Knowledge of business and management principles involved in strategic planning, resource allocation, human resources modeling, leadership technique, production methods, and coordination of people and resources.
Clerical	Knowledge of administrative and clerical procedures and systems such as word processing, managing files and records, stenography and transcription, designing forms, and other office procedures and terminology.
Design	Knowledge of design techniques, tools, and principles involved in production of precision technical plans, blueprints, drawings, and models.
Psychology	Knowledge of human behavior and performance; individual differences in ability, personality, and interests; learning and motivation; psychological research methods; and the assessment and treatment of behavioral and affective disorders.
Law and Government	Knowledge of laws, legal codes, court procedures, precedents, government regulations, executive orders, agency rules, and the democratic political process.

Personnel and Human Resources	Knowledge of principles and procedures for personnel recruitment, selection, training, compensation and benefits, labor relations and negotiation, and personnel information systems.
Public Safety and Security	Knowledge of relevant equipment, policies, procedures, and strategies to promote effective local, state, or national security operations for the protection of people, data, property, and institutions.
Production and Processing	Knowledge of raw materials, production processes, quality control, costs, and other techniques for maximizing the effective manufacture and distribution of goods.
Mechanical	Knowledge of machines and tools, including their designs, uses, repair, and maintenance.
Sales and Marketing	Knowledge of principles and methods for showing, promoting, and selling products or services. This includes marketing strategy and tactics, product demonstration, sales techniques, and sales control systems.
Transportation	Knowledge of principles and methods for moving people or goods by air, rail, sea, or road, including the relative costs and benefits.
History and Archeology	Knowledge of historical events and their causes, indicators, and effects on civilizations and cultures.
Sociology and Anthropology	Knowledge of group behavior and dynamics, societal trends and influences, human migrations, ethnicity, cultures and their history and origins.
Engineering and Technology	Knowledge of the practical application of engineering science and technology. This includes applying principles, techniques, procedures, and equipment to the design and production of various goods and services.
Economics and Accounting	Knowledge of economic and accounting principles and practices, the financial markets, banking and the analysis and reporting of financial data.
Medicine and Dentistry	Knowledge of the information and techniques needed to diagnose and treat human injuries, diseases, and deformities. This includes symptoms, treatment alternatives, drug properties and interactions, and preventive health-care measures.
Geography	Knowledge of principles and methods for describing the features of land, sea, and air masses, including their physical characteristics, locations, interrelationships, and distribution of plant, animal, and human life.
Fine Arts	Knowledge of the theory and techniques required to compose, produce, and perform works of music, dance, visual arts, drama, and sculpture.
Philosophy and Theology	Knowledge of different philosophical systems and religions. This includes their basic principles, values, ethics, ways of thinking, customs, practices, and their impact on human culture.
Therapy and Counseling	Knowledge of principles, methods, and procedures for diagnosis, treatment, and rehabilitation of physical and mental dysfunctions, and for career counseling and guidance.
Building and Construction	Knowledge of materials, methods, and the tools involved in the construction or repair of houses, buildings, or other structures such as highways and roads.
Biology	Knowledge of plant and animal organisms, their tissues, cells, functions, interdependencies, and interactions with each other and the environment.
Physics	Knowledge and prediction of physical principles, laws, their interrelationships, and applications to understanding fluid, material, and atmospheric dynamics, and mechanical, electrical, atomic and sub-atomic structures and processes.
Chemistry	Knowledge of the chemical composition, structure, and properties of substances and of the chemical processes and transformations that they undergo. This includes uses of chemicals and their interactions, danger signs, production techniques, and disposal methods.
Foreign Language	Knowledge of the structure and content of a foreign (non-English) language including the meaning and spelling of words, rules of composition and grammar, and pronunciation.
Food Production	Knowledge of techniques and equipment for planting, growing, and harvesting food products (both plant and animal) for consumption, including storage/handling techniques.

Skills	**Skills Definitions**
Active Listening	Giving full attention to what other people are saying, taking time to understand the points being made, asking questions as appropriate, and not interrupting at inappropriate times.

Active Learning	Understanding the implications of new information for both current and future problem-solving and decision-making.
Instructing	Teaching others how to do something.
Equipment Selection	Determining the kind of tools and equipment needed to do a job.
Troubleshooting	Determining causes of operating errors and deciding what to do about it.
Speaking	Talking to others to convey information effectively.
Reading Comprehension	Understanding written sentences and paragraphs in work related documents.
Learning Strategies	Selecting and using training/instructional methods and procedures appropriate for the situation when learning or teaching new things.
Writing	Communicating effectively in writing as appropriate for the needs of the audience.
Operations Analysis	Analyzing needs and product requirements to create a design.
Complex Problem Solving	Identifying complex problems and reviewing related information to develop and evaluate options and implement solutions.
Critical Thinking	Using logic and reasoning to identify the strengths and weaknesses of alternative solutions, conclusions or approaches to problems.
Technology Design	Generating or adapting equipment and technology to serve user needs.
Coordination	Adjusting actions in relation to others' actions.
Monitoring	Monitoring/Assessing performance of yourself, other individuals, or organizations to make improvements or take corrective action.
Time Management	Managing one's own time and the time of others.
Installation	Installing equipment, machines, wiring, or programs to meet specifications.
Equipment Maintenance	Performing routine maintenance on equipment and determining when and what kind of maintenance is needed.
Judgment and Decision Making	Considering the relative costs and benefits of potential actions to choose the most appropriate one.
Repairing	Repairing machines or systems using the needed tools.
Service Orientation	Actively looking for ways to help people.
Persuasion	Persuading others to change their minds or behavior.
Social Perceptiveness	Being aware of others' reactions and understanding why they react as they do.
Operation and Control	Controlling operations of equipment or systems.
Systems Analysis	Determining how a system should work and how changes in conditions, operations, and the environment will affect outcomes.
Management of Material Resources	Obtaining and seeing to the appropriate use of equipment, facilities, and materials needed to do certain work.
Mathematics	Using mathematics to solve problems.
Negotiation	Bringing others together and trying to reconcile differences.
Quality Control Analysis	Conducting tests and inspections of products, services, or processes to evaluate quality or performance.
Systems Evaluation	Identifying measures or indicators of system performance and the actions needed to improve or correct performance, relative to the goals of the system.
Management of Personnel Resources	Motivating, developing, and directing people as they work, identifying the best people for the job.
Science	Using scientific rules and methods to solve problems.
Programming	Writing computer programs for various purposes.
Management of Financial Resources	Determining how money will be spent to get the work done, and accounting for these expenditures.
Operation Monitoring	Watching gauges, dials, or other indicators to make sure a machine is working properly.

Ability	**Ability Definitions**
Oral Expression	The ability to communicate information and ideas in speaking so others will understand.
Problem Sensitivity	The ability to tell when something is wrong or is likely to go wrong. It does not involve solving the problem, only recognizing there is a problem.
Oral Comprehension	The ability to listen to and understand information and ideas presented through spoken words and sentences.
Inductive Reasoning	The ability to combine pieces of information to form general rules or conclusions (includes finding a relationship among seemingly unrelated events).
Deductive Reasoning	The ability to apply general rules to specific problems to produce answers that make sense.
Speech Clarity	The ability to speak clearly so others can understand you.

Near Vision	The ability to see details at close range (within a few feet of the observer).
Written Comprehension	The ability to read and understand information and ideas presented in writing.
Category Flexibility	The ability to generate or use different sets of rules for combining or grouping things in different ways.
Written Expression	The ability to communicate information and ideas in writing so others will understand.
Information Ordering	The ability to arrange things or actions in a certain order or pattern according to a specific rule or set of rules (e.g., patterns of numbers, letters, words, pictures, mathematical operations).
Fluency of Ideas	The ability to come up with a number of ideas about a topic (the number of ideas is important, not their quality, correctness, or creativity).
Far Vision	The ability to see details at a distance.
Visualization	The ability to imagine how something will look after it is moved around or when its parts are moved or rearranged.
Speech Recognition	The ability to identify and understand the speech of another person.
Selective Attention	The ability to concentrate on a task over a period of time without being distracted.
Originality	The ability to come up with unusual or clever ideas about a given topic or situation, or to develop creative ways to solve a problem.
Control Precision	The ability to quickly and repeatedly adjust the controls of a machine or a vehicle to exact positions.
Manual Dexterity	The ability to quickly move your hand, your hand together with your arm, or your two hands to grasp, manipulate, or assemble objects.
Arm-Hand Steadiness	The ability to keep your hand and arm steady while moving your arm or while holding your arm and hand in one position.
Visual Color Discrimination	The ability to match or detect differences between colors, including shades of color and brightness.
Finger Dexterity	The ability to make precisely coordinated movements of the fingers of one or both hands to grasp, manipulate, or assemble very small objects.
Trunk Strength	The ability to use your abdominal and lower back muscles to support part of the body repeatedly or continuously over time without 'giving out' or fatiguing.
Time Sharing	The ability to shift back and forth between two or more activities or sources of information (such as speech, sounds, touch, or other sources).
Memorization	The ability to remember information such as words, numbers, pictures, and procedures.
Perceptual Speed	The ability to quickly and accurately compare similarities and differences among sets of letters, numbers, objects, pictures, or patterns. The things to be compared may be presented at the same time or one after the other. This ability also includes comparing a presented object with a remembered object.
Multilimb Coordination	The ability to coordinate two or more limbs (for example, two arms, two legs, or one leg and one arm) while sitting, standing, or lying down. It does not involve performing the activities while the whole body is in motion.
Static Strength	The ability to exert maximum muscle force to lift, push, pull, or carry objects.
Flexibility of Closure	The ability to identify or detect a known pattern (a figure, object, word, or sound) that is hidden in other distracting material.
Hearing Sensitivity	The ability to detect or tell the differences between sounds that vary in pitch and loudness.
Mathematical Reasoning	The ability to choose the right mathematical methods or formulas to solve a problem.
Speed of Closure	The ability to quickly make sense of, combine, and organize information into meaningful patterns.
Depth Perception	The ability to judge which of several objects is closer or farther away from you, or to judge the distance between you and an object.
Gross Body Coordination	The ability to coordinate the movement of your arms, legs, and torso together when the whole body is in motion.
Extent Flexibility	The ability to bend, stretch, twist, or reach with your body, arms, and/or legs.
Auditory Attention	The ability to focus on a single source of sound in the presence of other distracting sounds.
Number Facility	The ability to add, subtract, multiply, or divide quickly and correctly.
Wrist-Finger Speed	The ability to make fast, simple, repeated movements of the fingers, hands, and wrists.
Night Vision	The ability to see under low light conditions.

Response Orientation	The ability to choose quickly between two or more movements in response to two or more different signals (lights, sounds, pictures). It includes the speed with which the correct response is started with the hand, foot, or other body part.
Spatial Orientation	The ability to know your location in relation to the environment or to know where other objects are in relation to you.
Rate Control	The ability to time your movements or the movement of a piece of equipment in anticipation of changes in the speed and/or direction of a moving object or scene.
Reaction Time	The ability to quickly respond (with the hand, finger, or foot) to a signal (sound, light, picture) when it appears.
Glare Sensitivity	The ability to see objects in the presence of glare or bright lighting.
Dynamic Strength	The ability to exert muscle force repeatedly or continuously over time. This involves muscular endurance and resistance to muscle fatigue.
Stamina	The ability to exert yourself physically over long periods of time without getting winded or out of breath.
Speed of Limb Movement	The ability to quickly move the arms and legs.
Peripheral Vision	The ability to see objects or movement of objects to one's side when the eyes are looking ahead.
Sound Localization	The ability to tell the direction from which a sound originated.
Gross Body Equilibrium	The ability to keep or regain your body balance or stay upright when in an unstable position.
Dynamic Flexibility	The ability to quickly and repeatedly bend, stretch, twist, or reach out with your body, arms, and/or legs.
Explosive Strength	The ability to use short bursts of muscle force to propel oneself (as in jumping or sprinting), or to throw an object.

Work_Activity	Work_Activity Definitions
Interacting With Computers	Using computers and computer systems (including hardware and software) to program, write software, set up functions, enter data, or process information.
Making Decisions and Solving Problems	Analyzing information and evaluating results to choose the best solution and solve problems.
Updating and Using Relevant Knowledge	Keeping up-to-date technically and applying new knowledge to your job.
Identifying Objects, Actions, and Events	Identifying information by categorizing, estimating, recognizing differences or similarities, and detecting changes in circumstances or events.
Thinking Creatively	Developing, designing, or creating new applications, ideas, relationships, systems, or products, including artistic contributions.
Getting Information	Observing, receiving, and otherwise obtaining information from all relevant sources.
Scheduling Work and Activities	Scheduling events, programs, and activities, as well as the work of others.
Establishing and Maintaining Interpersonal Relatio	Developing constructive and cooperative working relationships with others, and maintaining them over time.
Organizing, Planning, and Prioritizing Work	Developing specific goals and plans to prioritize, organize, and accomplish your work.
Communicating with Persons Outside Organization	Communicating with people outside the organization, representing the organization to customers, the public, government, and other external sources. This information can be exchanged in person, in writing, or by telephone or e-mail.
Processing Information	Compiling, coding, categorizing, calculating, tabulating, auditing, or verifying information or data.
Communicating with Supervisors, Peers, or Subordin	Providing information to supervisors, co-workers, and subordinates by telephone, in written form, e-mail, or in person.
Documenting/Recording Information	Entering, transcribing, recording, storing, or maintaining information in written or electronic/magnetic form.
Training and Teaching Others	Identifying the educational needs of others, developing formal educational or training programs or classes, and teaching or instructing others.
Developing Objectives and Strategies	Establishing long-range objectives and specifying the strategies and actions to achieve them.
Controlling Machines and Processes	Using either control mechanisms or direct physical activity to operate machines or processes (not including computers or vehicles).
Judging the Qualities of Things, Services, or Peop	Assessing the value, importance, or quality of things or people.
Monitor Processes, Materials, or Surroundings	Monitoring and reviewing information from materials, events, or the environment, to detect or assess problems.

Repairing and Maintaining Electronic Equipment	Servicing, repairing. calibrating, regulating, fine-tuning, or testing machines. devices, and equipment that operate primarily on the basis of electrical or electronic (not mechanical) principles.
Analyzing Data or Information	Identifying the underlying principles, reasons, or facts of information by breaking down information or data into separate parts.
Performing for or Working Directly with the Public	Performing for people or dealing directly with the public. This includes serving customers in restaurants and stores, and receiving clients or guests.
Evaluating Information to Determine Compliance wit	Using relevant information and individual judgment to determine whether events or processes comply with laws, regulations, or standards.
Handling and Moving Objects	Using hands and arms in handling, installing, positioning, and moving materials, and manipulating things.
Coordinating the Work and Activities of Others	Getting members of a group to work together to accomplish tasks.
Resolving Conflicts and Negotiating with Others	Handling complaints, settling disputes, and resolving grievances and conflicts, or otherwise negotiating with others.
Guiding, Directing, and Motivating Subordinates	Providing guidance and direction to subordinates, including setting performance standards and monitoring performance.
Interpreting the Meaning of Information for Others	Translating or explaining what information means and how it can be used.
Inspecting Equipment, Structures, or Material	Inspecting equipment, structures, or materials to identify the cause of errors or other problems or defects.
Provide Consultation and Advice to Others	Providing guidance and expert advice to management or other groups on technical, systems-, or process-related topics.
Performing Administrative Activities	Performing day-to-day administrative tasks such as maintaining information files and processing paperwork.
Coaching and Developing Others	Identifying the developmental needs of others and coaching, mentoring, or otherwise helping others to improve their knowledge or skills.
Monitoring and Controlling Resources	Monitoring and controlling resources and overseeing the spending of money.
Developing and Building Teams	Encouraging and building mutual trust, respect, and cooperation among team members.
Drafting, Laying Out, and Specifying Technical Dev	Providing documentation, detailed instructions, drawings, or specifications to tell others about how devices, parts, equipment, or structures are to be fabricated, constructed, assembled, modified, maintained, or used.
Estimating the Quantifiable Characteristics of Pro	Estimating sizes, distances, and quantities; or determining time, costs, resources, or materials needed to perform a work activity.
Assisting and Caring for Others	Providing personal assistance, medical attention, emotional support, or other personal care to others such as coworkers, customers, or patients.
Repairing and Maintaining Mechanical Equipment	Servicing, repairing, adjusting, and testing machines, devices, moving parts, and equipment that operate primarily on the basis of mechanical (not electronic) principles.
Selling or Influencing Others	Convincing others to buy merchandise/goods or to otherwise change their minds or actions.
Performing General Physical Activities	Performing physical activities that require considerable use of your arms and legs and moving your whole body, such as climbing, lifting, balancing, walking, stooping, and handling of materials.
Operating Vehicles, Mechanized Devices, or Equipme	Running, maneuvering, navigating, or driving vehicles or mechanized equipment, such as forklifts, passenger vehicles, aircraft, or water craft.
Staffing Organizational Units	Recruiting, interviewing, selecting, hiring, and promoting employees in an organization.

Work_Context	Work_Context Definitions
Face-to-Face Discussions	How often do you have to have face-to-face discussions with individuals or teams in this job?
Telephone	How often do you have telephone conversations in this job?
Electronic Mail	How often do you use electronic mail in this job?
Indoors, Environmentally Controlled	How often does this job require working indoors in environmentally controlled conditions?
Contact With Others	How much does this job require the worker to be in contact with others (face-to-face, by telephone, or otherwise) in order to perform it?
Freedom to Make Decisions	How much decision making freedom, without supervision, does the job offer?
Structured versus Unstructured Work	To what extent is this job structured for the worker, rather than allowing the worker to determine tasks, priorities, and goals?
Work With Work Group or Team	How important is it to work with others in a group or team in this job?

Impact of Decisions on Co-workers or Company Resul	How do the decisions an employee makes impact the results of co-workers, clients or the company?
Coordinate or Lead Others	How important is it to coordinate or lead others in accomplishing work activities in this job?
Spend Time Sitting	How much does this job require sitting?
Physical Proximity	To what extent does this job require the worker to perform job tasks in close physical proximity to other people?
Importance of Being Exact or Accurate	How important is being very exact or highly accurate in performing this job?
Time Pressure	How often does this job require the worker to meet strict deadlines?
Frequency of Decision Making	How frequently is the worker required to make decisions that affect other people, the financial resources, and/or the image and reputation of the organization?
Spend Time Using Your Hands to Handle, Control, or	How much does this job require using your hands to handle, control, or feel objects, tools or controls?
Public Speaking	How often do you have to perform public speaking in this job?
Letters and Memos	How often does the job require written letters and memos?
Importance of Repeating Same Tasks	How important is repeating the same physical activities (e.g., key entry) or mental activities (e.g., checking entries in a ledger) over and over, without stopping, to performing this job?
Deal With External Customers	How important is it to work with external customers or the public in this job?
Responsibility for Outcomes and Results	How responsible is the worker for work outcomes and results of other workers?
Frequency of Conflict Situations	How often are there conflict situations the employee has to face in this job?
Spend Time Standing	How much does this job require standing?
Deal With Unpleasant or Angry People	How frequently does the worker have to deal with unpleasant, angry, or discourteous individuals as part of the job requirements?
Sounds, Noise Levels Are Distracting or Uncomforta	How often does this job require working exposed to sounds and noise levels that are distracting or uncomfortable?
Indoors, Not Environmentally Controlled	How often does this job require working indoors in non-controlled environmental conditions (e.g., warehouse without heat)?
Level of Competition	To what extent does this job require the worker to compete or to be aware of competitive pressures?
Very Hot or Cold Temperatures	How often does this job require working in very hot (above 90 F degrees) or very cold (below 32 F degrees) temperatures?
Spend Time Making Repetitive Motions	How much does this job require making repetitive motions?
Spend Time Walking and Running	How much does this job require walking and running?
Degree of Automation	How automated is the job?
Extremely Bright or Inadequate Lighting	How often does this job require working in extremely bright or inadequate lighting conditions?
In an Enclosed Vehicle or Equipment	How often does this job require working in a closed vehicle or equipment (e.g., car)?
Outdoors, Exposed to Weather	How often does this job require working outdoors, exposed to all weather conditions?
Cramped Work Space, Awkward Positions	How often does this job require working in cramped work spaces that requires getting into awkward positions?
Spend Time Kneeling, Crouching, Stooping, or Crawl	How much does this job require kneeling, crouching, stooping or crawling?
Responsible for Others' Health and Safety	How much responsibility is there for the health and safety of others in this job?
Spend Time Bending or Twisting the Body	How much does this job require bending or twisting your body?
Consequence of Error	How serious would the result usually be if the worker made a mistake that was not readily correctable?
Exposed to Contaminants	How often does this job require working exposed to contaminants (such as pollutants, gases, dust or odors)?
Spend Time Climbing Ladders, Scaffolds, or Poles	How much does this job require climbing ladders, scaffolds, or poles?
Exposed to Disease or Infections	How often does this job require exposure to disease/infections?
Exposed to Minor Burns, Cuts, Bites, or Stings	How often does this job require exposure to minor burns, cuts, bites, or stings?
Outdoors, Under Cover	How often does this job require working outdoors, under cover (e.g., structure with roof but no walls)?
Spend Time Keeping or Regaining Balance	How much does this job require keeping or regaining your balance?
Exposed to High Places	How often does this job require exposure to high places?

Wear Common Protective or Safety Equipment such as	How much does this job require wearing common protective or safety equipment such as safety shoes, glasses, gloves, hard hats or live jackets?
Deal With Physically Aggressive People	How frequently does this job require the worker to deal with physical aggression of violent individuals?
Pace Determined by Speed of Equipment	How important is it to this job that the pace is determined by the speed of equipment or machinery? (This does not refer to keeping busy at all times on this job.)
Exposed to Hazardous Equipment	How often does this job require exposure to hazardous equipment?
Exposed to Hazardous Conditions	How often does this job require exposure to hazardous conditions?
Exposed to Radiation	How often does this job require exposure to radiation?
Wear Specialized Protective or Safety Equipment su	How much does this job require wearing specialized protective or safety equipment such as breathing apparatus, safety harness, full protection suits, or radiation protection?
Exposed to Whole Body Vibration	How often does this job require exposure to whole body vibration (e.g., operate a jackhammer)?
In an Open Vehicle or Equipment	How often does this job require working in an open vehicle or equipment (e.g., tractor)?

Job Zone Component	Job Zone Component Definitions
Title	Job Zone Five: Extensive Preparation Needed
	Extensive skill, knowledge, and experience are needed for these occupations. Many require more than five years of experience.
Overall Experience	For example, surgeons must complete four years of college and an additional five to seven years of specialized medical training to be able to do their job.
Job Training	Employees may need some on-the-job training, but most of these occupations assume that the person will already have the required skills, knowledge, work-related experience, and/or training.
Job Zone Examples	These occupations often involve coordinating, training, supervising, or managing the activities of others to accomplish goals. Very advanced communication and organizational skills are required. Examples include athletic trainers, lawyers, managing editors, phyicists, social psychologists, and surgeons.
SVP Range	(8.0 and above)
Education	A bachelor's degree is the minimum formal education required for these occupations. However, many also require graduate school. For example, they may require a master's degree, and some require a Ph.D., M.D., or J.D. (law degree).

Work_Styles	Work_Styles Definitions
Cooperation	Job requires being pleasant with others on the job and displaying a good-natured, cooperative attitude.
Dependability	Job requires being reliable, responsible, and dependable, and fulfilling obligations.
Initiative	Job requires a willingness to take on responsibilities and challenges.
Attention to Detail	Job requires being careful about detail and thorough in completing work tasks.
Persistence	Job requires persistence in the face of obstacles.
Concern for Others	Job requires being sensitive to others' needs and feelings and being understanding and helpful on the job.
Adaptability/Flexibility	Job requires being open to change (positive or negative) and to considerable variety in the workplace.
Stress Tolerance	Job requires accepting criticism and dealing calmly and effectively with high stress situations.
Achievement/Effort	Job requires establishing and maintaining personally challenging achievement goals and exerting effort toward mastering tasks.
Analytical Thinking	Job requires analyzing information and using logic to address work-related issues and problems.
Integrity	Job requires being honest and ethical.
Innovation	Job requires creativity and alternative thinking to develop new ideas for and answers to work-related problems.
Leadership	Job requires a willingness to lead, take charge, and offer opinions and direction.
Independence	Job requires developing one's own ways of doing things, guiding oneself with little or no supervision, and depending on oneself to get things done.
Self Control	Job requires maintaining composure, keeping emotions in check, controlling anger, and avoiding aggressive behavior, even in very difficult situations.

Social Orientation	Job requires preferring to work with others rather than alone, and being personally connected with others on the job.

25-9041.00 - Teacher Assistants

Perform duties that are instructional in nature or deliver direct services to students or parents. Serve in a position for which a teacher or another professional has ultimate responsibility for the design and implementation of educational programs and services.

Tasks

1) Discuss assigned duties with classroom teachers in order to coordinate instructional efforts.

2) Assist in bus loading and unloading.

3) Take class attendance, and maintain attendance records.

4) Provide extra assistance to students with special needs, such as non-English-speaking students or those with physical and mental disabilities.

5) Monitor classroom viewing of live or recorded courses transmitted by communication satellites.

6) Plan, prepare, and develop various teaching aids such as bibliographies, charts, and graphs.

7) Assist librarians in school libraries.

8) Supervise students in classrooms, halls, cafeterias, school yards, and gymnasiums, or on field trips.

9) Prepare lesson outlines and plans in assigned subject areas, and submit outlines to teachers for review.

10) Type, file, and duplicate materials.

11) Tutor and assist children individually or in small groups in order to help them master assignments and to reinforce learning concepts presented by teachers.

12) Distribute teaching materials such as textbooks, workbooks, papers, and pencils to students.

13) Conduct demonstrations to teach such skills as sports, dancing, and handicrafts.

14) Use computers, audiovisual aids, and other equipment and materials to supplement presentations.

15) Organize and supervise games and other recreational activities to promote physical, mental, and social development.

16) Provide disabled students with assistive devices, supportive technology, and assistance accessing facilities such as restrooms.

17) Maintain computers in classrooms and laboratories, and assist students with hardware and software use.

18) Participate in teacher-parent conferences regarding students' progress or problems.

19) Operate and maintain audiovisual equipment.

20) Prepare lesson materials, bulletin board displays, exhibits, equipment, and demonstrations.

21) Laminate teaching materials to increase their durability under repeated use.

22) Collect money from students for school-related projects.

23) Carry out therapeutic regimens such as behavior modification and personal development programs, under the supervision of special education instructors, psychologists, or speech-language pathologists.

24) Attend staff meetings, and serve on committees as required.

25) Observe students' performance, and record relevant data to assess progress.

26) Instruct and monitor students in the use and care of equipment and materials, in order to prevent injuries and damage.

27) Requisition and stock teaching materials and supplies.

28) Enforce administration policies and rules governing students.

29) Present subject matter to students under the direction and guidance of teachers, using lectures, discussions, or supervised role-playing methods.

30) Grade homework and tests, and compute and record results, using answer sheets or electronic marking devices.

31) Organize and label materials, and display students' work in a manner appropriate for their eye levels and perceptual skills.

413

27-1011.00 - Art Directors

Formulate design concepts and presentation approaches, and direct workers engaged in art work, layout design, and copy writing for visual communications media, such as magazines, books, newspapers, and packaging.

Tasks

1) Confer with creative, art, copy-writing, or production department heads to discuss client requirements and presentation concepts, and to coordinate creative activities.

2) Create custom illustrations or other graphic elements.

3) Review and approve proofs of printed copy and art and copy materials developed by staff members.

4) Review illustrative material to determine if it conforms to standards and specifications.

5) Present final layouts to clients for approval.

6) Work with creative directors to develop design solutions.

7) Confer with clients to determine objectives, budget, background information, and presentation approaches, styles, and techniques.

8) Mark up, paste, and complete layouts, and write typography instructions to prepare materials for typesetting or printing.

9) Hire, train and direct staff members who develop design concepts into art layouts or who prepare layouts for printing.

10) Manage own accounts and projects, working within budget and scheduling requirements.

11) Attend photo shoots and printing sessions to ensure that the products needed are obtained.

12) Negotiate with printers and estimators to determine what services will be performed.

13) Prepare detailed storyboards showing sequence and timing of story development for television production.

14) Conceptualize and help design interfaces for multimedia games, products and devices.

Knowledge	Knowledge Definitions
Design	Knowledge of design techniques, tools, and principles involved in production of precision technical plans, blueprints, drawings, and models.
Administration and Management	Knowledge of business and management principles involved in strategic planning, resource allocation, human resources modeling, leadership technique, production methods, and coordination of people and resources.
Computers and Electronics	Knowledge of circuit boards, processors, chips, electronic equipment, and computer hardware and software, including applications and programming.
Customer and Personal Service	Knowledge of principles and processes for providing customer and personal services. This includes customer needs assessment, meeting quality standards for services, and evaluation of customer satisfaction.
Production and Processing	Knowledge of raw materials, production processes, quality control, costs, and other techniques for maximizing the effective manufacture and distribution of goods.
Communications and Media	Knowledge of media production, communication, and dissemination techniques and methods. This includes alternative ways to inform and entertain via written, oral, and visual media.
Fine Arts	Knowledge of the theory and techniques required to compose, produce, and perform works of music, dance, visual arts, drama, and sculpture.
English Language	Knowledge of the structure and content of the English language including the meaning and spelling of words, rules of composition, and grammar.
Sales and Marketing	Knowledge of principles and methods for showing, promoting, and selling products or services. This includes marketing strategy and tactics, product demonstration, sales techniques, and sales control systems.
Education and Training	Knowledge of principles and methods for curriculum and training design, teaching and instruction for individuals and groups, and the measurement of training effects.
Engineering and Technology	Knowledge of the practical application of engineering science and technology. This includes applying principles, techniques, procedures, and equipment to the design and production of various goods and services.

Personnel and Human Resources	Knowledge of principles and procedures for personnel recruitment, selection, training, compensation and benefits, labor relations and negotiation, and personnel information systems.
Psychology	Knowledge of human behavior and performance; individual differences in ability, personality, and interests; learning and motivation; psychological research methods; and the assessment and treatment of behavioral and affective disorders.
Telecommunications	Knowledge of transmission, broadcasting, switching, control, and operation of telecommunications systems.
Mathematics	Knowledge of arithmetic, algebra, geometry, calculus, statistics, and their applications.
Clerical	Knowledge of administrative and clerical procedures and systems such as word processing, managing files and records, stenography and transcription, designing forms, and other office procedures and terminology.
Geography	Knowledge of principles and methods for describing the features of land, sea, and air masses, including their physical characteristics, locations, interrelationships, and distribution of plant, animal, and human life.
Sociology and Anthropology	Knowledge of group behavior and dynamics, societal trends and influences, human migrations, ethnicity, cultures and their history and origins.
Mechanical	Knowledge of machines and tools, including their designs, uses, repair, and maintenance.
History and Archeology	Knowledge of historical events and their causes, indicators, and effects on civilizations and cultures.
Economics and Accounting	Knowledge of economic and accounting principles and practices, the financial markets, banking and the analysis and reporting of financial data.
Law and Government	Knowledge of laws, legal codes, court procedures, precedents, government regulations, executive orders, agency rules, and the democratic political process.
Foreign Language	Knowledge of the structure and content of a foreign (non-English) language including the meaning and spelling of words, rules of composition and grammar, and pronunciation.
Therapy and Counseling	Knowledge of principles, methods, and procedures for diagnosis, treatment, and rehabilitation of physical and mental dysfunctions, and for career counseling and guidance.
Public Safety and Security	Knowledge of relevant equipment, policies, procedures, and strategies to promote effective local, state, or national security operations for the protection of people, data, property, and institutions.
Philosophy and Theology	Knowledge of different philosophical systems and religions. This includes their basic principles, values, ethics, ways of thinking, customs, practices, and their impact on human culture.
Transportation	Knowledge of principles and methods for moving people or goods by air, rail, sea, or road, including the relative costs and benefits.
Building and Construction	Knowledge of materials, methods, and the tools involved in the construction or repair of houses, buildings, or other structures such as highways and roads.
Physics	Knowledge and prediction of physical principles, laws, their interrelationships, and applications to understanding fluid, material, and atmospheric dynamics, and mechanical, electrical, atomic and sub-atomic structures and processes.
Chemistry	Knowledge of the chemical composition, structure, and properties of substances and of the chemical processes and transformations that they undergo. This includes uses of chemicals and their interactions, danger signs, production techniques, and disposal methods.
Food Production	Knowledge of techniques and equipment for planting, growing, and harvesting food products (both plant and animal) for consumption, including storage/handling techniques.
Biology	Knowledge of plant and animal organisms, their tissues, cells, functions, interdependencies, and interactions with each other and the environment.
Medicine and Dentistry	Knowledge of the information and techniques needed to diagnose and treat human injuries, diseases, and deformities. This includes symptoms, treatment alternatives, drug properties and interactions, and preventive health-care measures.

Skills	Skills Definitions
Active Listening	Giving full attention to what other people are saying, taking time to understand the points being made, asking questions as appropriate, and not interrupting at inappropriate times.

Time Management	Managing one's own time and the time of others.
Reading Comprehension	Understanding written sentences and paragraphs in work related documents.
Critical Thinking	Using logic and reasoning to identify the strengths and weaknesses of alternative solutions, conclusions or approaches to problems.
Coordination	Adjusting actions in relation to others' actions.
Speaking	Talking to others to convey information effectively.
Judgment and Decision Making	Considering the relative costs and benefits of potential actions to choose the most appropriate one.
Active Learning	Understanding the implications of new information for both current and future problem-solving and decision-making.
Negotiation	Bringing others together and trying to reconcile differences.
Persuasion	Persuading others to change their minds or behavior.
Complex Problem Solving	Identifying complex problems and reviewing related information to develop and evaluate options and implement solutions.
Instructing	Teaching others how to do something.
Operations Analysis	Analyzing needs and product requirements to create a design.
Equipment Selection	Determining the kind of tools and equipment needed to do a job.
Writing	Communicating effectively in writing as appropriate for the needs of the audience.
Social Perceptiveness	Being aware of others' reactions and understanding why they react as they do.
Learning Strategies	Selecting and using training/instructional methods and procedures appropriate for the situation when learning or teaching new things.
Monitoring	Monitoring/Assessing performance of yourself, other individuals, or organizations to make improvements or take corrective action.
Management of Financial Resources	Determining how money will be spent to get the work done, and accounting for these expenditures.
Mathematics	Using mathematics to solve problems.
Management of Personnel Resources	Motivating, developing, and directing people as they work, identifying the best people for the job.
Service Orientation	Actively looking for ways to help people.
Quality Control Analysis	Conducting tests and inspections of products, services, or processes to evaluate quality or performance.
Management of Material Resources	Obtaining and seeing to the appropriate use of equipment, facilities, and materials needed to do certain work.
Systems Evaluation	Identifying measures or indicators of system performance and the actions needed to improve or correct performance, relative to the goals of the system.
Technology Design	Generating or adapting equipment and technology to serve user needs.
Troubleshooting	Determining causes of operating errors and deciding what to do about it.
Operation and Control	Controlling operations of equipment or systems.
Equipment Maintenance	Performing routine maintenance on equipment and determining when and what kind of maintenance is needed.
Installation	Installing equipment, machines, wiring, or programs to meet specifications.
Science	Using scientific rules and methods to solve problems.
Systems Analysis	Determining how a system should work and how changes in conditions, operations, and the environment will affect outcomes.
Operation Monitoring	Watching gauges, dials, or other indicators to make sure a machine is working properly.
Repairing	Repairing machines or systems using the needed tools.
Programming	Writing computer programs for various purposes.

Ability	Ability Definitions
Originality	The ability to come up with unusual or clever ideas about a given topic or situation, or to develop creative ways to solve a problem.
Fluency of Ideas	The ability to come up with a number of ideas about a topic (the number of ideas is important, not their quality, correctness, or creativity).
Oral Comprehension	The ability to listen to and understand information and ideas presented through spoken words and sentences.
Oral Expression	The ability to communicate information and ideas in speaking so others will understand.
Near Vision	The ability to see details at close range (within a few feet of the observer).
Written Comprehension	The ability to read and understand information and ideas presented in writing.

Problem Sensitivity	The ability to tell when something is wrong or is likely to go wrong. It does not involve solving the problem, only recognizing there is a problem.
Information Ordering	The ability to arrange things or actions in a certain order or pattern according to a specific rule or set of rules (e.g., patterns of numbers, letters, words, pictures, mathematical operations).
Speech Clarity	The ability to speak clearly so others can understand you.
Inductive Reasoning	The ability to combine pieces of information to form general rules or conclusions (includes finding a relationship among seemingly unrelated events).
Visualization	The ability to imagine how something will look after it is moved around or when its parts are moved or rearranged.
Written Expression	The ability to communicate information and ideas in writing so others will understand.
Deductive Reasoning	The ability to apply general rules to specific problems to produce answers that make sense.
Speech Recognition	The ability to identify and understand the speech of another person.
Visual Color Discrimination	The ability to match or detect differences between colors, including shades of color and brightness.
Category Flexibility	The ability to generate or use different sets of rules for combining or grouping things in different ways.
Selective Attention	The ability to concentrate on a task over a period of time without being distracted.
Far Vision	The ability to see details at a distance.
Speed of Closure	The ability to quickly make sense of, combine, and organize information into meaningful patterns.
Time Sharing	The ability to shift back and forth between two or more activities or sources of information (such as speech, sounds, touch, or other sources).
Flexibility of Closure	The ability to identify or detect a known pattern (a figure, object, word, or sound) that is hidden in other distracting material.
Mathematical Reasoning	The ability to choose the right mathematical methods or formulas to solve a problem.
Finger Dexterity	The ability to make precisely coordinated movements of the fingers of one or both hands to grasp, manipulate, or assemble very small objects.
Perceptual Speed	The ability to quickly and accurately compare similarities and differences among sets of letters, numbers, objects, pictures, or patterns. The things to be compared may be presented at the same time or one after the other. This ability also includes comparing a presented object with a remembered object.
Memorization	The ability to remember information such as words, numbers, pictures, and procedures.
Arm-Hand Steadiness	The ability to keep your hand and arm steady while moving your arm or while holding your arm and hand in one position.
Number Facility	The ability to add, subtract, multiply, or divide quickly and correctly.
Manual Dexterity	The ability to quickly move your hand, your hand together with your arm, or your two hands to grasp, manipulate, or assemble objects.
Auditory Attention	The ability to focus on a single source of sound in the presence of other distracting sounds.
Depth Perception	The ability to judge which of several objects is closer or farther away from you, or to judge the distance between you and an object.
Control Precision	The ability to quickly and repeatedly adjust the controls of a machine or a vehicle to exact positions.
Hearing Sensitivity	The ability to detect or tell the differences between sounds that vary in pitch and loudness.
Multilimb Coordination	The ability to coordinate two or more limbs (for example, two arms, two legs, or one leg and one arm) while sitting, standing, or lying down. It does not involve performing the activities while the whole body is in motion.
Trunk Strength	The ability to use your abdominal and lower back muscles to support part of the body repeatedly or continuously over time without 'giving out' or fatiguing.
Wrist-Finger Speed	The ability to make fast, simple, repeated movements of the fingers, hands, and wrists.
Extent Flexibility	The ability to bend, stretch, twist, or reach with your body, arms, and/or legs.
Reaction Time	The ability to quickly respond (with the hand, finger, or foot) to a signal (sound, light, picture) when it appears.
Speed of Limb Movement	The ability to quickly move the arms and legs.
Static Strength	The ability to exert maximum muscle force to lift, push, pull, or carry objects.

Explosive Strength	The ability to use short bursts of muscle force to propel oneself (as in jumping or sprinting). or to throw an object.
Stamina	The ability to exert yourself physically over long periods of time without getting winded or out of breath.
Gross Body Coordination	The ability to coordinate the movement of your arms, legs, and torso together when the whole body is in motion.
Response Orientation	The ability to choose quickly between two or more movements in response to two or more different signals (lights, sounds, pictures). It includes the speed with which the correct response is started with the hand, foot, or other body part.
Dynamic Flexibility	The ability to quickly and repeatedly bend, stretch, twist, or reach out with your body, arms, and/or legs.
Gross Body Equilibrium	The ability to keep or regain your body balance or stay upright when in an unstable position.
Spatial Orientation	The ability to know your location in relation to the environment or to know where other objects are in relation to you.
Rate Control	The ability to time your movements or the movement of a piece of equipment in anticipation of changes in the speed and/or direction of a moving object or scene.
Night Vision	The ability to see under low light conditions.
Peripheral Vision	The ability to see objects or movement of objects to one's side when the eyes are looking ahead.
Sound Localization	The ability to tell the direction from which a sound originated.
Dynamic Strength	The ability to exert muscle force repeatedly or continuously over time. This involves muscular endurance and resistance to muscle fatigue.
Glare Sensitivity	The ability to see objects in the presence of glare or bright lighting.

Work_Activity	**Work_Activity Definitions**
Thinking Creatively	Developing, designing, or creating new applications, ideas, relationships, systems, or products, including artistic contributions.
Interacting With Computers	Using computers and computer systems (including hardware and software) to program, write software, set up functions, enter data, or process information.
Making Decisions and Solving Problems	Analyzing information and evaluating results to choose the best solution and solve problems.
Communicating with Supervisors, Peers, or Subordin	Providing information to supervisors, co-workers, and subordinates by telephone, in written form, e-mail, or in person.
Updating and Using Relevant Knowledge	Keeping up-to-date technically and applying new knowledge to your job.
Getting Information	Observing, receiving, and otherwise obtaining information from all relevant sources.
Establishing and Maintaining Interpersonal Relatio	Developing constructive and cooperative working relationships with others, and maintaining them over time.
Organizing, Planning, and Prioritizing Work	Developing specific goals and plans to prioritize, organize, and accomplish your work.
Interpreting the Meaning of Information for Others	Translating or explaining what information means and how it can be used.
Guiding, Directing, and Motivating Subordinates	Providing guidance and direction to subordinates, including setting performance standards and monitoring performance.
Provide Consultation and Advice to Others	Providing guidance and expert advice to management or other groups on technical, systems-, or process-related topics.
Coordinating the Work and Activities of Others	Getting members of a group to work together to accomplish tasks.
Identifying Objects, Actions, and Events	Identifying information by categorizing, estimating, recognizing differences or similarities, and detecting changes in circumstances or events.
Communicating with Persons Outside Organization	Communicating with people outside the organization, representing the organization to customers, the public, government, and other external sources. This information can be exchanged in person, in writing, or by telephone or e-mail.
Judging the Qualities of Things, Services, or Peop	Assessing the value, importance, or quality of things or people.
Scheduling Work and Activities	Scheduling events, programs, and activities, as well as the work of others.
Developing Objectives and Strategies	Establishing long-range objectives and specifying the strategies and actions to achieve them.
Estimating the Quantifiable Characteristics of Pro	Estimating sizes, distances, and quantities; or determining time, costs, resources, or materials needed to perform a work activity.
Analyzing Data or Information	Identifying the underlying principles, reasons, or facts of information by breaking down information or data into separate parts.

Documenting/Recording Information	Entering. transcribing, recording, storing, or maintaining information in written or electronic/magnetic form.
Performing Administrative Activities	Performing day-to-day administrative tasks such as maintaining information files and processing paperwork.
Processing Information	Compiling, coding, categorizing, calculating, tabulating, auditing, or verifying information or data.
Training and Teaching Others	Identifying the educational needs of others, developing formal educational or training programs or classes, and teaching or instructing others.
Monitoring and Controlling Resources	Monitoring and controlling resources and overseeing the spending of money.
Resolving Conflicts and Negotiating with Others	Handling complaints, settling disputes, and resolving grievances and conflicts, or otherwise negotiating with others.
Coaching and Developing Others	Identifying the developmental needs of others and coaching, mentoring, or otherwise helping others to improve their knowledge or skills.
Selling or Influencing Others	Convincing others to buy merchandise/goods or to otherwise change their minds or actions.
Evaluating Information to Determine Compliance wit	Using relevant information and individual judgment to determine whether events or processes comply with laws, regulations, or standards.
Assisting and Caring for Others	Providing personal assistance, medical attention, emotional support, or other personal care to others such as coworkers, customers, or patients.
Developing and Building Teams	Encouraging and building mutual trust, respect, and cooperation among team members.
Monitor Processes, Materials, or Surroundings	Monitoring and reviewing information from materials, events, or the environment, to detect or assess problems.
Performing for or Working Directly with the Public	Performing for people or dealing directly with the public. This includes serving customers in restaurants and stores, and receiving clients or guests.
Repairing and Maintaining Mechanical Equipment	Servicing, repairing, adjusting, and testing machines, devices, moving parts, and equipment that operate primarily on the basis of mechanical (not electronic) principles.
Repairing and Maintaining Electronic Equipment	Servicing, repairing, calibrating, regulating, fine-tuning, or testing machines, devices, and equipment that operate primarily on the basis of electrical or electronic (not mechanical) principles.
Controlling Machines and Processes	Using either control mechanisms or direct physical activity to operate machines or processes (not including computers or vehicles).
Performing General Physical Activities	Performing physical activities that require considerable use of your arms and legs and moving your whole body, such as climbing, lifting, balancing, walking, stooping, and handling of materials.
Handling and Moving Objects	Using hands and arms in handling, installing, positioning, and moving materials, and manipulating things.
Inspecting Equipment, Structures, or Material	Inspecting equipment, structures, or materials to identify the cause of errors or other problems or defects.
Drafting, Laying Out, and Specifying Technical Dev	Providing documentation, detailed instructions, drawings, or specifications to tell others about how devices, parts, equipment, or structures are to be fabricated, constructed, assembled, modified, maintained, or used.
Staffing Organizational Units	Recruiting, interviewing, selecting, hiring, and promoting employees in an organization.
Operating Vehicles, Mechanized Devices, or Equipme	Running, maneuvering, navigating, or driving vehicles or mechanized equipment, such as forklifts, passenger vehicles, aircraft, or water craft.

Work_Context	**Work_Context Definitions**
Telephone	How often do you have telephone conversations in this job?
Electronic Mail	How often do you use electronic mail in this job?
Face-to-Face Discussions	How often do you have to have face-to-face discussions with individuals or teams in this job?
Contact With Others	How much does this job require the worker to be in contact with others (face-to-face, by telephone, or otherwise) in order to perform it?
Indoors, Environmentally Controlled	How often does this job require working indoors in environmentally controlled conditions?
Work With Work Group or Team	How important is it to work with others in a group or team in this job?
Time Pressure	How often does this job require the worker to meet strict deadlines?
Freedom to Make Decisions	How much decision making freedom, without supervision, does the job offer?

Importance of Being Exact or Accurate	How important is being very exact or highly accurate in performing this job?
Coordinate or Lead Others	How important is it to coordinate or lead others in accomplishing work activities in this job?
Spend Time Sitting	How much does this job require sitting?
Structured versus Unstructured Work	To what extent is this job structured for the worker, rather than allowing the worker to determine tasks, priorities, and goals?
Responsibility for Outcomes and Results	How responsible is the worker for work outcomes and results of other workers?
Deal With External Customers	How important is it to work with external customers or the public in this job?
Frequency of Decision Making	How frequently is the worker required to make decisions that affect other people, the financial resources, and/or the image and reputation of the organization?
Impact of Decisions on Co-workers or Company Resul	How do the decisions an employee makes impact the results of co-workers, clients or the company?
Frequency of Conflict Situations	How often are there conflict situations the employee has to face in this job?
Spend Time Making Repetitive Motions	How much does this job require making repetitive motions?
Spend Time Using Your Hands to Handle, Control, or	How much does this job require using your hands to handle, control, or feel objects, tools or controls?
Physical Proximity	To what extent does this job require the worker to perform job tasks in close physical proximity to other people?
Deal With Unpleasant or Angry People	How frequently does the worker have to deal with unpleasant, angry, or discourteous individuals as part of the job requirements?
Letters and Memos	How often does the job require written letters and memos?
Level of Competition	To what extent does this job require the worker to compete or to be aware of competitive pressures?
Sounds, Noise Levels Are Distracting or Uncomforta	How often does this job require working exposed to sounds and noise levels that are distracting or uncomfortable?
Consequence of Error	How serious would the result usually be if the worker made a mistake that was not readily correctable?
Public Speaking	How often do you have to perform public speaking in this job?
Importance of Repeating Same Tasks	How important is repeating the same physical activities (e.g., key entry) or mental activities (e.g., checking entries in a ledger) over and over, without stopping, to performing this job?
Degree of Automation	How automated is the job?
Responsible for Others' Health and Safety	How much responsibility is there for the health and safety of others in this job?
Spend Time Standing	How much does this job require standing?
Spend Time Walking and Running	How much does this job require walking and running?
Pace Determined by Speed of Equipment	How important is it to this job that the pace is determined by the speed of equipment or machinery? (This does not refer to keeping busy at all times on this job.)
Exposed to Contaminants	How often does this job require working exposed to contaminants (such as pollutants, gases, dust or odors)?
Extremely Bright or Inadequate Lighting	How often does this job require working in extremely bright or inadequate lighting conditions?
In an Enclosed Vehicle or Equipment	How often does this job require working in a closed vehicle or equipment (e.g., car)?
Exposed to Hazardous Conditions	How often does this job require exposure to hazardous conditions?
Spend Time Bending or Twisting the Body	How much does this job require bending or twisting your body?
Outdoors, Exposed to Weather	How often does this job require working outdoors, exposed to all weather conditions?
Indoors, Not Environmentally Controlled	How often does this job require working indoors in non-controlled environmental conditions (e.g., warehouse without heat)?
Spend Time Kneeling, Crouching, Stooping, or Crawl	How much does this job require kneeling, crouching, stooping or crawling?
Cramped Work Space, Awkward Positions	How often does this job require working in cramped work spaces that requires getting into awkward positions?
Spend Time Climbing Ladders, Scaffolds, or Poles	How much does this job require climbing ladders, scaffolds, or poles?
Outdoors, Under Cover	How often does this job require working outdoors, under cover (e.g., structure with roof but no walls)?
Wear Common Protective or Safety Equipment such as	How much does this job require wearing common protective or safety equipment such as safety shoes, glasses, gloves, hard hats or live jackets?

Exposed to Minor Burns, Cuts, Bites, or Stings	How often does this job require exposure to minor burns, cuts, bites, or stings?
Spend Time Keeping or Regaining Balance	How much does this job require keeping or regaining your balance?
Very Hot or Cold Temperatures	How often does this job require working in very hot (above 90 F degrees) or very cold (below 32 F degrees) temperatures?
Exposed to Disease or Infections	How often does this job require exposure to disease/infections?
Exposed to High Places	How often does this job require exposure to high places?
Exposed to Hazardous Equipment	How often does this job require exposure to hazardous equipment?
In an Open Vehicle or Equipment	How often does this job require working in an open vehicle or equipment (e.g., tractor)?
Wear Specialized Protective or Safety Equipment su	How much does this job require wearing specialized protective or safety equipment such as breathing apparatus, safety harness, full protection suits, or radiation protection?
Exposed to Whole Body Vibration	How often does this job require exposure to whole body vibration (e.g., operate a jackhammer)?
Deal With Physically Aggressive People	How frequently does this job require the worker to deal with physical aggression of violent individuals?
Exposed to Radiation	How often does this job require exposure to radiation?

Job Zone Component	Job Zone Component Definitions
Title	Job Zone Four: Considerable Preparation Needed
Overall Experience	A minimum of two to four years of work-related skill, knowledge, or experience is needed for these occupations. For example, an accountant must complete four years of college and work for several years in accounting to be considered qualified.
Job Training	Employees in these occupations usually need several years of work-related experience, on-the-job training, and/or vocational training.
Job Zone Examples	Many of these occupations involve coordinating, supervising, managing, or training others. Examples include accountants, chefs and head cooks, computer programmers, historians, pharmacists, and police detectives.
SVP Range	(7.0 to < 8.0)
Education	Most of these occupations require a four - year bachelor's degree, but some do not.

Work_Styles	Work_Styles Definitions
Dependability	Job requires being reliable, responsible, and dependable, and fulfilling obligations.
Attention to Detail	Job requires being careful about detail and thorough in completing work tasks.
Adaptability/Flexibility	Job requires being open to change (positive or negative) and to considerable variety in the workplace.
Integrity	Job requires being honest and ethical.
Achievement/Effort	Job requires establishing and maintaining personally challenging achievement goals and exerting effort toward mastering tasks.
Stress Tolerance	Job requires accepting criticism and dealing calmly and effectively with high stress situations.
Cooperation	Job requires being pleasant with others on the job and displaying a good-natured, cooperative attitude.
Initiative	Job requires a willingness to take on responsibilities and challenges.
Innovation	Job requires creativity and alternative thinking to develop new ideas for and answers to work-related problems.
Leadership	Job requires a willingness to lead, take charge, and offer opinions and direction.
Persistence	Job requires persistence in the face of obstacles.
Analytical Thinking	Job requires analyzing information and using logic to address work-related issues and problems.
Concern for Others	Job requires being sensitive to others' needs and feelings and being understanding and helpful on the job.
Self Control	Job requires maintaining composure, keeping emotions in check, controlling anger, and avoiding aggressive behavior, even in very difficult situations.
Independence	Job requires developing one's own ways of doing things, guiding oneself with little or no supervision, and depending on oneself to get things done.
Social Orientation	Job requires preferring to work with others rather than alone, and being personally connected with others on the job.

27-1013.00 - Fine Artists, Including Painters, Sculptors, and Illustrators

Create original artwork using any of a wide variety of mediums and techniques, such as painting and sculpture.

Tasks

1) Model substances such as clay or wax, using fingers and small hand tools to form objects.

2) Shade and fill in sketch outlines and backgrounds, using a variety of media such as water colors, markers, and transparent washes, labeling designated colors when necessary.

3) Study styles, techniques, colors, textures, and materials used in works undergoing restoration to ensure consistency during the restoration process.

4) Trace drawings onto clear acetate for painting or coloring, or trace them with ink to make final copies.

5) Alter, modify, or retouch photographs to update likenesses so that photographs can be used in criminal investigations.

6) Classify and code components of images to help identify suspects, using established systems; search police photograph records to locate any existing photographs of suspects.

7) Cut, bend, laminate, arrange, and fasten individual or mixed raw and manufactured materials and products to form works of art.

8) Collaborate with writers who create ideas, stories, or captions that are combined with artists' work.

9) Prepare line drawings conforming to descriptions of suspects or crime scene details, presenting drawings to witnesses or victims for approval and completion of composite sketches.

10) Interview crime victims or witnesses to obtain descriptive information about suspects, as well as objects such as jewelry or weapons.

11) Provide photographs, sketches, and/or expert testimony on identification for criminal trials.

12) Show crime victims and witnesses photographs depicting different facial features, head shapes, and hair types so that those best representing suspects may be selected for use in composites.

13) Sketch courtroom scenes for media broadcast or publication.

14) Confer with clients, editors, writers, art directors, and other interested parties regarding the nature and content of artwork to be produced.

15) Create finished art work as decoration, or to elucidate or substitute for spoken or written messages.

16) Prepare graphic design material for uses such as departmental training sessions, public safety programs, and recruitment efforts.

17) Brush or spray protective or decorative finishes on completed background panels, informational legends, exhibit accessories, or finished paintings.

18) Develop project budgets for approval, estimating time lines and material costs.

19) Apply solvents and cleaning agents to clean surfaces of paintings, and to remove accretions, discolorations, and deteriorated varnish.

20) Use materials such as pens and ink, watercolors, charcoal, oil, or computer software to create artwork.

21) Study different techniques to learn how to apply them to artistic endeavors.

22) Submit preliminary or finished artwork or project plans to clients for approval, incorporating changes as necessary.

23) Maintain portfolios of artistic work to demonstrate styles, interests, and abilities.

24) Monitor events, trends, and other circumstances, research specific subject areas, attend art exhibitions, and read art publications in order to develop ideas and keep current on art world activities.

25) Render drawings, illustrations, and sketches of buildings, manufactured products, or models, working from sketches, blueprints, memory, models, or reference materials.

26) Create graphics, illustrations, and three-dimensional models to be used in research or in teaching, such as in demonstrating anatomy, pathology, or surgical procedures.

27) Perform two- and three-dimensional facial reconstructions, using drawings, enlarged photographs, clay, and tissue markers.

28) Integrate and develop visual elements, such as line, space, mass, color, and perspective, in order to produce desired effects such as the illustration of ideas, emotions, or moods.

29) Draw sketches of crime scenes, depicting such details as locations of doors and windows and exact positions of pieces of evidence.

30) Consult with criminal justice specialists, hypnotists, psychics, and medical doctors to obtain information needed to render likenesses of suspects and victims.

31) Create and prepare sketches and model drawings of cartoon characters, providing details from memory, live models, manufactured products, or reference materials.

32) Gather relevant information about unidentified human remains, including photographs, bones, hair, and any other artifacts, for use in facial reconstructions.

33) Create age-progression drawings to show what individuals might look like after a certain number of years, using photographs of individuals, knowledge of the aging process, and computer software.

34) Create sculptures, statues, and other three-dimensional artwork by using abrasives and tools to shape, carve, and fabricate materials such as clay, stone, wood, or metal.

35) Create sketches, profiles, or likenesses of posed subjects or photographs, using any combination of freehand drawing, mechanical assembly kits, and computer imaging.

36) Collaborate with engineers, mechanics, and other technical experts as necessary to build and install creations.

37) Render sequential drawings that can be turned into animated films or advertisements.

38) Examine and test paintings in need of restoration or cleaning to determine techniques and materials to be used.

27-1022.00 - Fashion Designers

Design clothing and accessories. Create original garments or design garments that follow well established fashion trends. May develop the line of color and kinds of materials.

Tasks

1) Sew together sections of material to form mockups or samples of garments or articles, using sewing equipment.

2) Direct and coordinate workers involved in drawing and cutting patterns and constructing samples or finished garments.

3) Develop a group of products and/or accessories, and market them through venues such as boutiques or mail-order catalogs.

4) Determine prices for styles.

5) Confer with sales and management executives or with clients in order to discuss design ideas.

6) Collaborate with other designers to coordinate special products and designs.

7) Test fabrics or oversee testing so that garment care labels can be created.

8) Adapt other designers' ideas for the mass market.

9) Research the styles and periods of clothing needed for film or theatrical productions.

10) Design custom clothing and accessories for individuals, retailers, or theatrical, television, or film productions.

11) Examine sample garments on and off models; then modify designs to achieve desired effects.

12) Visit textile showrooms to keep up-to-date on the latest fabrics.

13) Select materials and production techniques to be used for products.

14) Sketch rough and detailed drawings of apparel or accessories, and write specifications such as color schemes, construction, material types, and accessory requirements.

15) Purchase new or used clothing and accessory items as needed to complete designs.

16) Draw patterns for articles designed; then cut patterns, and cut material according to patterns, using measuring instruments and scissors.

17) Read scripts and consult directors and other production staff in order to develop design concepts and plan productions.

18) Attend fashion shows and review garment magazines and manuals in order to gather information about fashion trends and consumer preferences.

19) Identify target markets for designs, looking at factors such as age, gender, and socioeconomic status.

27-1023.00 - Floral Designers

Design, cut, and arrange live, dried, or artificial flowers and foliage.

Tasks

1) Select flora and foliage for arrangements, working with numerous combinations to synthesize and develop new creations.

2) Unpack stock as it comes into the shop.

3) Plan arrangement according to client's requirements, utilizing knowledge of design and properties of materials, or select appropriate standard design pattern.

4) Water plants, and cut, condition, and clean flowers and foliage for storage.

5) Create and change in-store and window displays, designs, and looks to enhance a shop's image.

6) Perform general cleaning duties in the store to ensure the shop is clean and tidy.

7) Order and purchase flowers and supplies from wholesalers and growers.

8) Perform office and retail service duties such as keeping financial records, serving customers, answering telephones, selling giftware items and receiving payment.

9) Decorate or supervise the decoration of buildings, halls, churches, or other facilities for parties, weddings and other occasions.

10) Conduct classes or demonstrations, or train other workers.

11) Grow flowers for use in arrangements or for sale in shop.

12) Confer with clients regarding price and type of arrangement desired and the date, time, and place of delivery.

13) Trim material and arrange bouquets, wreaths, terrariums, and other items using trimmers, shapers, wire, pins, floral tape, foam, and other materials.

14) Inform customers about the care, maintenance, and handling of various flowers and foliage, indoor plants, and other items.

Knowledge	Knowledge Definitions
Customer and Personal Service	Knowledge of principles and processes for providing customer and personal services. This includes customer needs assessment, meeting quality standards for services, and evaluation of customer satisfaction.
English Language	Knowledge of the structure and content of the English language including the meaning and spelling of words, rules of composition, and grammar.
Sales and Marketing	Knowledge of principles and methods for showing, promoting, and selling products or services. This includes marketing strategy and tactics, product demonstration, sales techniques, and sales control systems.
Administration and Management	Knowledge of business and management principles involved in strategic planning, resource allocation, human resources modeling, leadership technique, production methods, and coordination of people and resources.
Design	Knowledge of design techniques, tools, and principles involved in production of precision technical plans, blueprints, drawings, and models.
Production and Processing	Knowledge of raw materials, production processes, quality control, costs, and other techniques for maximizing the effective manufacture and distribution of goods.
Mathematics	Knowledge of arithmetic, algebra, geometry, calculus, statistics, and their applications.
Education and Training	Knowledge of principles and methods for curriculum and training design, teaching and instruction for individuals and groups, and the measurement of training effects.
Personnel and Human Resources	Knowledge of principles and procedures for personnel recruitment, selection, training, compensation and benefits, labor relations and negotiation, and personnel information systems.
Fine Arts	Knowledge of the theory and techniques required to compose, produce, and perform works of music, dance, visual arts, drama, and sculpture.
Clerical	Knowledge of administrative and clerical procedures and systems such as word processing, managing files and records, stenography and transcription, designing forms, and other office procedures and terminology.
Computers and Electronics	Knowledge of circuit boards, processors, chips, electronic equipment, and computer hardware and software, including applications and programming.
Telecommunications	Knowledge of transmission, broadcasting, switching, control, and operation of telecommunications systems.
Public Safety and Security	Knowledge of relevant equipment, policies, procedures, and strategies to promote effective local, state, or national security operations for the protection of people, data, property, and institutions.
Communications and Media	Knowledge of media production, communication, and dissemination techniques and methods. This includes alternative ways to inform and entertain via written, oral, and visual media.
Psychology	Knowledge of human behavior and performance; individual differences in ability, personality, and interests; learning and motivation; psychological research methods; and the assessment and treatment of behavioral and affective disorders.
Economics and Accounting	Knowledge of economic and accounting principles and practices, the financial markets, banking and the analysis and reporting of financial data.
Biology	Knowledge of plant and animal organisms, their tissues, cells, functions, interdependencies, and interactions with each other and the environment.
Transportation	Knowledge of principles and methods for moving people or goods by air, rail, sea, or road, including the relative costs and benefits.
Mechanical	Knowledge of machines and tools, including their designs, uses, repair, and maintenance.
Chemistry	Knowledge of the chemical composition, structure, and properties of substances and of the chemical processes and transformations that they undergo. This includes uses of chemicals and their interactions, danger signs, production techniques, and disposal methods.
Food Production	Knowledge of techniques and equipment for planting, growing, and harvesting food products (both plant and animal) for consumption, including storage/handling techniques.
Geography	Knowledge of principles and methods for describing the features of land, sea, and air masses, including their physical characteristics, locations, interrelationships, and distribution of plant, animal, and human life.
Engineering and Technology	Knowledge of the practical application of engineering science and technology. This includes applying principles, techniques, procedures, and equipment to the design and production of various goods and services.
Law and Government	Knowledge of laws, legal codes, court procedures, precedents, government regulations, executive orders, agency rules, and the democratic political process.
Philosophy and Theology	Knowledge of different philosophical systems and religions. This includes their basic principles, values, ethics, ways of thinking, customs, practices, and their impact on human culture.
Physics	Knowledge and prediction of physical principles, laws, their interrelationships, and applications to understanding fluid, material, and atmospheric dynamics, and mechanical, electrical, atomic and sub-atomic structures and processes.
Sociology and Anthropology	Knowledge of group behavior and dynamics, societal trends and influences, human migrations, ethnicity, cultures and their history and origins.
Building and Construction	Knowledge of materials, methods, and the tools involved in the construction or repair of houses, buildings, or other structures such as highways and roads.
Therapy and Counseling	Knowledge of principles, methods, and procedures for diagnosis, treatment, and rehabilitation of physical and mental dysfunctions, and for career counseling and guidance.
History and Archeology	Knowledge of historical events and their causes, indicators, and effects on civilizations and cultures.
Foreign Language	Knowledge of the structure and content of a foreign (non-English) language including the meaning and spelling of words, rules of composition and grammar, and pronunciation.
Medicine and Dentistry	Knowledge of the information and techniques needed to diagnose and treat human injuries, diseases, and deformities. This includes symptoms, treatment alternatives, drug properties and interactions, and preventive health-care measures.

Skills	Skills Definitions
Active Listening	Giving full attention to what other people are saying, taking time to understand the points being made, asking questions as appropriate, and not interrupting at inappropriate times.
Speaking	Talking to others to convey information effectively.
Reading Comprehension	Understanding written sentences and paragraphs in work related documents.
Social Perceptiveness	Being aware of others' reactions and understanding why they react as they do.
Service Orientation	Actively looking for ways to help people.
Time Management	Managing one's own time and the time of others.
Instructing	Teaching others how to do something.
Learning Strategies	Selecting and using training/instructional methods and procedures appropriate for the situation when learning or teaching new things.
Coordination	Adjusting actions in relation to others' actions.
Active Learning	Understanding the implications of new information for both current and future problem-solving and decision-making.
Writing	Communicating effectively in writing as appropriate for the needs of the audience.
Critical Thinking	Using logic and reasoning to identify the strengths and weaknesses of alternative solutions, conclusions or approaches to problems.
Management of Financial Resources	Determining how money will be spent to get the work done, and accounting for these expenditures.
Judgment and Decision Making	Considering the relative costs and benefits of potential actions to choose the most appropriate one.
Management of Material Resources	Obtaining and seeing to the appropriate use of equipment, facilities, and materials needed to do certain work.
Mathematics	Using mathematics to solve problems.
Management of Personnel Resources	Motivating, developing, and directing people as they work, identifying the best people for the job.
Operations Analysis	Analyzing needs and product requirements to create a design.
Monitoring	Monitoring/Assessing performance of yourself, other individuals, or organizations to make improvements or take corrective action.
Equipment Selection	Determining the kind of tools and equipment needed to do a job.
Persuasion	Persuading others to change their minds or behavior.
Negotiation	Bringing others together and trying to reconcile differences.
Quality Control Analysis	Conducting tests and inspections of products, services, or processes to evaluate quality or performance.
Systems Evaluation	Identifying measures or indicators of system performance and the actions needed to improve or correct performance, relative to the goals of the system.
Complex Problem Solving	Identifying complex problems and reviewing related information to develop and evaluate options and implement solutions.
Operation and Control	Controlling operations of equipment or systems.
Troubleshooting	Determining causes of operating errors and deciding what to do about it.
Technology Design	Generating or adapting equipment and technology to serve user needs.
Systems Analysis	Determining how a system should work and how changes in conditions, operations, and the environment will affect outcomes.
Equipment Maintenance	Performing routine maintenance on equipment and determining when and what kind of maintenance is needed.
Operation Monitoring	Watching gauges, dials, or other indicators to make sure a machine is working properly.
Repairing	Repairing machines or systems using the needed tools.
Installation	Installing equipment, machines, wiring, or programs to meet specifications.
Science	Using scientific rules and methods to solve problems.
Programming	Writing computer programs for various purposes.

Ability	Ability Definitions
Oral Comprehension	The ability to listen to and understand information and ideas presented through spoken words and sentences.
Oral Expression	The ability to communicate information and ideas in speaking so others will understand.
Speech Clarity	The ability to speak clearly so others can understand you.
Originality	The ability to come up with unusual or clever ideas about a given topic or situation, or to develop creative ways to solve a problem.

Visualization	The ability to imagine how something will look after it is moved around or when its parts are moved or rearranged.
Category Flexibility	The ability to generate or use different sets of rules for combining or grouping things in different ways.
Near Vision	The ability to see details at close range (within a few feet of the observer).
Visual Color Discrimination	The ability to match or detect differences between colors, including shades of color and brightness.
Information Ordering	The ability to arrange things or actions in a certain order or pattern according to a specific rule or set of rules (e.g., patterns of numbers, letters, words, pictures, mathematical operations).
Speech Recognition	The ability to identify and understand the speech of another person.
Trunk Strength	The ability to use your abdominal and lower back muscles to support part of the body repeatedly or continuously over time without 'giving out' or fatiguing.
Fluency of Ideas	The ability to come up with a number of ideas about a topic (the number of ideas is important, not their quality, correctness, or creativity).
Manual Dexterity	The ability to quickly move your hand, your hand together with your arm, or your two hands to grasp, manipulate, or assemble objects.
Deductive Reasoning	The ability to apply general rules to specific problems to produce answers that make sense.
Arm-Hand Steadiness	The ability to keep your hand and arm steady while moving your arm or while holding your arm and hand in one position.
Inductive Reasoning	The ability to combine pieces of information to form general rules or conclusions (includes finding a relationship among seemingly unrelated events).
Problem Sensitivity	The ability to tell when something is wrong or is likely to go wrong. It does not involve solving the problem, only recognizing there is a problem.
Written Comprehension	The ability to read and understand information and ideas presented in writing.
Written Expression	The ability to communicate information and ideas in writing so others will understand.
Far Vision	The ability to see details at a distance.
Finger Dexterity	The ability to make precisely coordinated movements of the fingers of one or both hands to grasp, manipulate, or assemble very small objects.
Multilimb Coordination	The ability to coordinate two or more limbs (for example, two arms, two legs, or one leg and one arm) while sitting, standing, or lying down. It does not involve performing the activities while the whole body is in motion.
Selective Attention	The ability to concentrate on a task over a period of time without being distracted.
Mathematical Reasoning	The ability to choose the right mathematical methods or formulas to solve a problem.
Time Sharing	The ability to shift back and forth between two or more activities or sources of information (such as speech, sounds, touch, or other sources).
Depth Perception	The ability to judge which of several objects is closer or farther away from you, or to judge the distance between you and an object.
Perceptual Speed	The ability to quickly and accurately compare similarities and differences among sets of letters, numbers, objects, pictures, or patterns. The things to be compared may be presented at the same time or one after the other. This ability also includes comparing a presented object with a remembered object.
Control Precision	The ability to quickly and repeatedly adjust the controls of a machine or a vehicle to exact positions.
Memorization	The ability to remember information such as words, numbers, pictures, and procedures.
Static Strength	The ability to exert maximum muscle force to lift, push, pull, or carry objects.
Speed of Closure	The ability to quickly make sense of, combine, and organize information into meaningful patterns.
Gross Body Coordination	The ability to coordinate the movement of your arms, legs, and torso together when the whole body is in motion.
Stamina	The ability to exert yourself physically over long periods of time without getting winded or out of breath.
Dynamic Strength	The ability to exert muscle force repeatedly or continuously over time. This involves muscular endurance and resistance to muscle fatigue.
Number Facility	The ability to add, subtract, multiply, or divide quickly and correctly.

Flexibility of Closure	The ability to identify or detect a known pattern (a figure, object, word, or sound) that is hidden in other distracting material.
Spatial Orientation	The ability to know your location in relation to the environment or to know where other objects are in relation to you.
Extent Flexibility	The ability to bend, stretch, twist, or reach with your body, arms, and/or legs.
Wrist-Finger Speed	The ability to make fast, simple, repeated movements of the fingers, hands, and wrists.
Peripheral Vision	The ability to see objects or movement of objects to one's side when the eyes are looking ahead.
Auditory Attention	The ability to focus on a single source of sound in the presence of other distracting sounds.
Gross Body Equilibrium	The ability to keep or regain your body balance or stay upright when in an unstable position.
Response Orientation	The ability to choose quickly between two or more movements in response to two or more different signals (lights, sounds, pictures). It includes the speed with which the correct response is started with the hand, foot, or other body part.
Sound Localization	The ability to tell the direction from which a sound originated.
Glare Sensitivity	The ability to see objects in the presence of glare or bright lighting.
Rate Control	The ability to time your movements or the movement of a piece of equipment in anticipation of changes in the speed and/or direction of a moving object or scene.
Night Vision	The ability to see under low light conditions.
Speed of Limb Movement	The ability to quickly move the arms and legs.
Reaction Time	The ability to quickly respond (with the hand, finger, or foot) to a signal (sound, light, picture) when it appears.
Hearing Sensitivity	The ability to detect or tell the differences between sounds that vary in pitch and loudness.
Dynamic Flexibility	The ability to quickly and repeatedly bend, stretch, twist, or reach out with your body, arms, and/or legs.
Explosive Strength	The ability to use short bursts of muscle force to propel oneself (as in jumping or sprinting), or to throw an object.

Work_Activity	**Work_Activity Definitions**
Organizing, Planning, and Prioritizing Work	Developing specific goals and plans to prioritize, organize, and accomplish your work.
Getting Information	Observing, receiving, and otherwise obtaining information from all relevant sources.
Thinking Creatively	Developing, designing, or creating new applications, ideas, relationships, systems, or products, including artistic contributions.
Identifying Objects, Actions, and Events	Identifying information by categorizing, estimating, recognizing differences or similarities, and detecting changes in circumstances or events.
Performing for or Working Directly with the Public	Performing for people or dealing directly with the public. This includes serving customers in restaurants and stores, and receiving clients or guests.
Selling or Influencing Others	Convincing others to buy merchandise/goods or to otherwise change their minds or actions.
Scheduling Work and Activities	Scheduling events, programs, and activities, as well as the work of others.
Processing Information	Compiling, coding, categorizing, calculating, tabulating, auditing, or verifying information or data.
Judging the Qualities of Things, Services, or Peop	Assessing the value, importance, or quality of things or people.
Monitor Processes, Materials, or Surroundings	Monitoring and reviewing information from materials, events, or the environment, to detect or assess problems.
Handling and Moving Objects	Using hands and arms in handling, installing, positioning, and moving materials, and manipulating things.
Updating and Using Relevant Knowledge	Keeping up-to-date technically and applying new knowledge to your job.
Inspecting Equipment, Structures, or Material	Inspecting equipment, structures, or materials to identify the cause of errors or other problems or defects.
Establishing and Maintaining Interpersonal Relatio	Developing constructive and cooperative working relationships with others, and maintaining them over time.
Communicating with Supervisors, Peers, or Subordin	Providing information to supervisors, co-workers, and subordinates by telephone, in written form, e-mail, or in person.
Performing General Physical Activities	Performing physical activities that require considerable use of your arms and legs and moving your whole body, such as climbing, lifting, balancing, walking, stooping, and handling of materials.

Estimating the Quantifiable Characteristics of Pro	Estimating sizes, distances, and quantities; or determining time, costs, resources, or materials needed to perform a work activity.
Developing Objectives and Strategies	Establishing long-range objectives and specifying the strategies and actions to achieve them.
Making Decisions and Solving Problems	Analyzing information and evaluating results to choose the best solution and solve problems.
Communicating with Persons Outside Organization	Communicating with people outside the organization, representing the organization to customers, the public, government, and other external sources. This information can be exchanged in person, in writing, or by telephone or e-mail.
Operating Vehicles, Mechanized Devices, or Equipme	Running, maneuvering, navigating, or driving vehicles or mechanized equipment, such as forklifts, passenger vehicles, aircraft, or water craft.
Evaluating Information to Determine Compliance wit	Using relevant information and individual judgment to determine whether events or processes comply with laws, regulations, or standards.
Developing and Building Teams	Encouraging and building mutual trust, respect, and cooperation among team members.
Documenting/Recording Information	Entering, transcribing, recording, storing, or maintaining information in written or electronic/magnetic form.
Coaching and Developing Others	Identifying the developmental needs of others and coaching, mentoring, or otherwise helping others to improve their knowledge or skills.
Resolving Conflicts and Negotiating with Others	Handling complaints, settling disputes, and resolving grievances and conflicts, or otherwise negotiating with others.
Provide Consultation and Advice to Others	Providing guidance and expert advice to management or other groups on technical, systems-, or process-related topics.
Performing Administrative Activities	Performing day-to-day administrative tasks such as maintaining information files and processing paperwork.
Assisting and Caring for Others	Providing personal assistance, medical attention, emotional support, or other personal care to others such as coworkers, customers, or patients.
Coordinating the Work and Activities of Others	Getting members of a group to work together to accomplish tasks.
Monitoring and Controlling Resources	Monitoring and controlling resources and overseeing the spending of money.
Interpreting the Meaning of Information for Others	Translating or explaining what information means and how it can be used.
Drafting, Laying Out, and Specifying Technical Dev	Providing documentation, detailed instructions, drawings, or specifications to tell others about how devices, parts, equipment, or structures are to be fabricated, constructed, assembled, modified, maintained, or used.
Controlling Machines and Processes	Using either control mechanisms or direct physical activity to operate machines or processes (not including computers or vehicles).
Staffing Organizational Units	Recruiting, interviewing, selecting, hiring, and promoting employees in an organization.
Guiding, Directing, and Motivating Subordinates	Providing guidance and direction to subordinates, including setting performance standards and monitoring performance.
Interacting With Computers	Using computers and computer systems (including hardware and software) to program, write software, set up functions, enter data, or process information.
Training and Teaching Others	Identifying the educational needs of others, developing formal educational or training programs or classes, and teaching or instructing others.
Analyzing Data or Information	Identifying the underlying principles, reasons, or facts of information by breaking down information or data into separate parts.
Repairing and Maintaining Electronic Equipment	Servicing, repairing, calibrating, regulating, fine-tuning, or testing machines, devices, and equipment that operate primarily on the basis of electrical or electronic (not mechanical) principles.
Repairing and Maintaining Mechanical Equipment	Servicing, repairing, adjusting, and testing machines, devices, moving parts, and equipment that operate primarily on the basis of mechanical (not electronic) principles.

Work_Context	**Work_Context Definitions**
Telephone	How often do you have telephone conversations in this job?
Contact With Others	How much does this job require the worker to be in contact with others (face-to-face, by telephone, or otherwise) in order to perform it?
Spend Time Using Your Hands to Handle, Control, or	How much does this job require using your hands to handle, control, or feel objects, tools or controls?
Face-to-Face Discussions	How often do you have to have face-to-face discussions with individuals or teams in this job?

Spend Time Standing	How much does this job require standing?
Time Pressure	How often does this job require the worker to meet strict deadlines?
Impact of Decisions on Co-workers or Company Resul	How do the decisions an employee makes impact the results of co-workers, clients or the company?
Freedom to Make Decisions	How much decision making freedom, without supervision, does the job offer?
Structured versus Unstructured Work	To what extent is this job structured for the worker, rather than allowing the worker to determine tasks, priorities, and goals?
Work With Work Group or Team	How important is it to work with others in a group or team in this job?
Frequency of Decision Making	How frequently is the worker required to make decisions that affect other people, the financial resources, and/or the image and reputation of the organization?
Deal With External Customers	How important is it to work with external customers or the public in this job?
Spend Time Making Repetitive Motions	How much does this job require making repetitive motions?
Physical Proximity	To what extent does this job require the worker to perform job tasks in close physical proximity to other people?
Coordinate or Lead Others	How important is it to coordinate or lead others in accomplishing work activities in this job?
Indoors, Environmentally Controlled	How often does this job require working indoors in environmentally controlled conditions?
In an Enclosed Vehicle or Equipment	How often does this job require working in a closed vehicle or equipment (e.g., car)?
Level of Competition	To what extent does this job require the worker to compete or to be aware of competitive pressures?
Responsibility for Outcomes and Results	How responsible is the worker for work outcomes and results of other workers?
Importance of Being Exact or Accurate	How important is being very exact or highly accurate in performing this job?
Deal With Unpleasant or Angry People	How frequently does the worker have to deal with unpleasant, angry, or discourteous individuals as part of the job requirements?
Importance of Repeating Same Tasks	How important is repeating the same physical activities (e.g., key entry) or mental activities (e.g., checking entries in a ledger) over and over, without stopping, to performing this job?
Exposed to Minor Burns, Cuts, Bites, or Stings	How often does this job require exposure to minor burns, cuts, bites, or stings?
Letters and Memos	How often does the job require written letters and memos?
Responsible for Others' Health and Safety	How much responsibility is there for the health and safety of others in this job?
Frequency of Conflict Situations	How often are there conflict situations the employee has to face in this job?
Consequence of Error	How serious would the result usually be if the worker made a mistake that was not readily correctable?
Spend Time Bending or Twisting the Body	How much does this job require bending or twisting your body?
Electronic Mail	How often do you use electronic mail in this job?
Spend Time Walking and Running	How much does this job require walking and running?
Outdoors, Exposed to Weather	How often does this job require working outdoors, exposed to all weather conditions?
Degree of Automation	How automated is the job?
Cramped Work Space, Awkward Positions	How often does this job require working in cramped work spaces that requires getting into awkward positions?
Indoors, Not Environmentally Controlled	How often does this job require working indoors in non-controlled environmental conditions (e.g., warehouse without heat)?
Exposed to Contaminants	How often does this job require working exposed to contaminants (such as pollutants, gases, dust or odors)?
Spend Time Kneeling, Crouching, Stooping, or Crawl	How much does this job require kneeling, crouching, stooping or crawling?
Outdoors, Under Cover	How often does this job require working outdoors, under cover (e.g., structure with roof but no walls)?
Very Hot or Cold Temperatures	How often does this job require working in very hot (above 90 F degrees) or very cold (below 32 F degrees) temperatures?
Sounds, Noise Levels Are Distracting or Uncomforta	How often does this job require working exposed to sounds and noise levels that are distracting or uncomfortable?
Spend Time Sitting	How much does this job require sitting?
Pace Determined by Speed of Equipment	How important is it to this job that the pace is determined by the speed of equipment or machinery? (This does not refer to keeping busy at all times on this job.)
Exposed to Hazardous Equipment	How often does this job require exposure to hazardous equipment?

Wear Common Protective or Safety Equipment such as	How much does this job require wearing common protective or safety equipment such as safety shoes, glasses, gloves, hard hats or live jackets?
Exposed to Hazardous Conditions	How often does this job require exposure to hazardous conditions?
Public Speaking	How often do you have to perform public speaking in this job?
Spend Time Keeping or Regaining Balance	How much does this job require keeping or regaining your balance?
Exposed to High Places	How often does this job require exposure to high places?
Exposed to Disease or Infections	How often does this job require exposure to disease/infections?
Spend Time Climbing Ladders, Scaffolds, or Poles	How much does this job require climbing ladders, scaffolds, or poles?
Extremely Bright or Inadequate Lighting	How often does this job require working in extremely bright or inadequate lighting conditions?
Exposed to Radiation	How often does this job require exposure to radiation?
Deal With Physically Aggressive People	How frequently does this job require the worker to deal with physical aggression of violent individuals?
Wear Specialized Protective or Safety Equipment su	How much does this job require wearing specialized protective or safety equipment such as breathing apparatus, safety harness, full protection suits, or radiation protection?
Exposed to Whole Body Vibration	How often does this job require exposure to whole body vibration (e.g., operate a jackhammer)?
In an Open Vehicle or Equipment	How often does this job require working in an open vehicle or equipment (e.g., tractor)?

Job Zone Component	Job Zone Component Definitions
Title	Job Zone Two: Some Preparation Needed
Overall Experience	Some previous work-related skill, knowledge, or experience may be helpful in these occupations, but usually is not needed. For example, a drywall installer might benefit from experience installing drywall, but an inexperienced person could still learn to be an installer with little difficulty.
Job Training	Employees in these occupations need anywhere from a few months to one year of working with experienced employees.
Job Zone Examples	These occupations often involve using your knowledge and skills to help others. Examples include drywall installers, fire inspectors, flight attendants, pharmacy technicians, salespersons (retail), and tellers.
SVP Range	(4.0 to < 6.0)
Education	These occupations usually require a high school diploma and may require some vocational training or job-related course work. In some cases, an associate's or bachelor's degree could be needed.

Work_Styles	Work_Styles Definitions
Attention to Detail	Job requires being careful about detail and thorough in completing work tasks.
Cooperation	Job requires being pleasant with others on the job and displaying a good-natured, cooperative attitude.
Dependability	Job requires being reliable, responsible, and dependable, and fulfilling obligations.
Self Control	Job requires maintaining composure, keeping emotions in check, controlling anger, and avoiding aggressive behavior, even in very difficult situations.
Integrity	Job requires being honest and ethical.
Innovation	Job requires creativity and alternative thinking to develop new ideas for and answers to work-related problems.
Stress Tolerance	Job requires accepting criticism and dealing calmly and effectively with high stress situations.
Concern for Others	Job requires being sensitive to others' needs and feelings and being understanding and helpful on the job.
Independence	Job requires developing one's own ways of doing things, guiding oneself with little or no supervision, and depending on oneself to get things done.
Initiative	Job requires a willingness to take on responsibilities and challenges.
Social Orientation	Job requires preferring to work with others rather than alone, and being personally connected with others on the job.
Adaptability/Flexibility	Job requires being open to change (positive or negative) and to considerable variety in the workplace.
Leadership	Job requires a willingness to lead, take charge, and offer opinions and direction.

Analytical Thinking	Job requires analyzing information and using logic to address work-related issues and problems.
Achievement/Effort	Job requires establishing and maintaining personally challenging achievement goals and exerting effort toward mastering tasks.
Persistence	Job requires persistence in the face of obstacles.

27-1024.00 - Graphic Designers

Design or create graphics to meet specific commercial or promotional needs, such as packaging, displays, or logos. May use a variety of mediums to achieve artistic or decorative effects.

Tasks

1) Determine size and arrangement of illustrative material and copy, and select style and size of type.

2) Create designs, concepts, and sample layouts based on knowledge of layout principles and esthetic design concepts.

3) Develop graphics and layouts for product illustrations, company logos, and Internet websites.

4) Use computer software to generate new images.

5) Draw and print charts, graphs, illustrations, and other artwork, using computer.

6) Mark up, paste, and assemble final layouts to prepare layouts for printer.

7) Review final layouts and suggest improvements as needed.

8) Confer with clients to discuss and determine layout design.

9) Prepare illustrations or rough sketches of material, discussing them with clients and/or supervisors and making necessary changes.

10) Study illustrations and photographs to plan presentation of materials, products, or services.

11) Prepare notes and instructions for workers who assemble and prepare final layouts for printing.

12) Produce still and animated graphics for on-air and taped portions of television news broadcasts, using electronic video equipment.

13) Develop negatives and prints to produce layout photographs, using negative and print developing equipment and tools.

14) Photograph layouts, using camera, to make layout prints for supervisors or clients.

Knowledge	Knowledge Definitions
Computers and Electronics	Knowledge of circuit boards, processors, chips, electronic equipment, and computer hardware and software, including applications and programming.
English Language	Knowledge of the structure and content of the English language including the meaning and spelling of words, rules of composition, and grammar.
Communications and Media	Knowledge of media production, communication, and dissemination techniques and methods. This includes alternative ways to inform and entertain via written, oral, and visual media.
Design	Knowledge of design techniques, tools, and principles involved in production of precision technical plans, blueprints, drawings, and models.
Customer and Personal Service	Knowledge of principles and processes for providing customer and personal services. This includes customer needs assessment, meeting quality standards for services, and evaluation of customer satisfaction.
Sales and Marketing	Knowledge of principles and methods for showing, promoting, and selling products or services. This includes marketing strategy and tactics, product demonstration, sales techniques, and sales control systems.
Fine Arts	Knowledge of the theory and techniques required to compose, produce, and perform works of music, dance, visual arts, drama, and sculpture.
Mathematics	Knowledge of arithmetic, algebra, geometry, calculus, statistics, and their applications.
Production and Processing	Knowledge of raw materials, production processes, quality control, costs, and other techniques for maximizing the effective manufacture and distribution of goods.
Psychology	Knowledge of human behavior and performance; individual differences in ability, personality, and interests; learning and motivation; psychological research methods; and the assessment and treatment of behavioral and affective disorders.
Engineering and Technology	Knowledge of the practical application of engineering science and technology. This includes applying principles, techniques, procedures, and equipment to the design and production of various goods and services.
Clerical	Knowledge of administrative and clerical procedures and systems such as word processing, managing files and records, stenography and transcription, designing forms, and other office procedures and terminology.
Sociology and Anthropology	Knowledge of group behavior and dynamics, societal trends and influences, human migrations, ethnicity, cultures and their history and origins.
Administration and Management	Knowledge of business and management principles involved in strategic planning, resource allocation, human resources modeling, leadership technique, production methods, and coordination of people and resources.
Geography	Knowledge of principles and methods for describing the features of land, sea, and air masses, including their physical characteristics, locations, interrelationships, and distribution of plant, animal, and human life.
Personnel and Human Resources	Knowledge of principles and procedures for personnel recruitment, selection, training, compensation and benefits, labor relations and negotiation, and personnel information systems.
Mechanical	Knowledge of machines and tools, including their designs, uses, repair, and maintenance.
Education and Training	Knowledge of principles and methods for curriculum and training design, teaching and instruction for individuals and groups, and the measurement of training effects.
Economics and Accounting	Knowledge of economic and accounting principles and practices, the financial markets, banking and the analysis and reporting of financial data.
Philosophy and Theology	Knowledge of different philosophical systems and religions. This includes their basic principles, values, ethics, ways of thinking, customs, practices, and their impact on human culture.
Telecommunications	Knowledge of transmission, broadcasting, switching, control, and operation of telecommunications systems.
Law and Government	Knowledge of laws, legal codes, court procedures, precedents, government regulations, executive orders, agency rules, and the democratic political process.
History and Archeology	Knowledge of historical events and their causes, indicators, and effects on civilizations and cultures.
Physics	Knowledge and prediction of physical principles, laws, their interrelationships, and applications to understanding fluid, material, and atmospheric dynamics, and mechanical, electrical, atomic and sub- atomic structures and processes.
Public Safety and Security	Knowledge of relevant equipment, policies, procedures, and strategies to promote effective local, state, or national security operations for the protection of people, data, property, and institutions.
Foreign Language	Knowledge of the structure and content of a foreign (non-English) language including the meaning and spelling of words, rules of composition and grammar, and pronunciation.
Building and Construction	Knowledge of materials, methods, and the tools involved in the construction or repair of houses, buildings, or other structures such as highways and roads.
Transportation	Knowledge of principles and methods for moving people or goods by air, rail, sea, or road, including the relative costs and benefits.
Medicine and Dentistry	Knowledge of the information and techniques needed to diagnose and treat human injuries, diseases, and deformities. This includes symptoms, treatment alternatives, drug properties and interactions, and preventive health-care measures.
Chemistry	Knowledge of the chemical composition, structure, and properties of substances and of the chemical processes and transformations that they undergo. This includes uses of chemicals and their interactions, danger signs, production techniques, and disposal methods.
Therapy and Counseling	Knowledge of principles, methods, and procedures for diagnosis, treatment, and rehabilitation of physical and mental dysfunctions, and for career counseling and guidance.
Biology	Knowledge of plant and animal organisms, their tissues, cells, functions, interdependencies, and interactions with each other and the environment.

Food Production	Knowledge of techniques and equipment for planting, growing, and harvesting food products (both plant and animal) for consumption, including storage/handling techniques.

Skills	Skills Definitions
Time Management	Managing one's own time and the time of others.
Coordination	Adjusting actions in relation to others' actions.
Active Listening	Giving full attention to what other people are saying, taking time to understand the points being made, asking questions as appropriate, and not interrupting at inappropriate times.
Judgment and Decision Making	Considering the relative costs and benefits of potential actions to choose the most appropriate one.
Active Learning	Understanding the implications of new information for both current and future problem-solving and decision-making.
Critical Thinking	Using logic and reasoning to identify the strengths and weaknesses of alternative solutions, conclusions or approaches to problems.
Complex Problem Solving	Identifying complex problems and reviewing related information to develop and evaluate options and implement solutions.
Reading Comprehension	Understanding written sentences and paragraphs in work related documents.
Monitoring	Monitoring/Assessing performance of yourself, other individuals, or organizations to make improvements or take corrective action.
Social Perceptiveness	Being aware of others' reactions and understanding why they react as they do.
Troubleshooting	Determining causes of operating errors and deciding what to do about it.
Learning Strategies	Selecting and using training/instructional methods and procedures appropriate for the situation when learning or teaching new things.
Persuasion	Persuading others to change their minds or behavior.
Speaking	Talking to others to convey information effectively.
Operations Analysis	Analyzing needs and product requirements to create a design.
Equipment Selection	Determining the kind of tools and equipment needed to do a job.
Instructing	Teaching others how to do something.
Writing	Communicating effectively in writing as appropriate for the needs of the audience.
Quality Control Analysis	Conducting tests and inspections of products, services, or processes to evaluate quality or performance.
Service Orientation	Actively looking for ways to help people.
Operation and Control	Controlling operations of equipment or systems.
Equipment Maintenance	Performing routine maintenance on equipment and determining when and what kind of maintenance is needed.
Technology Design	Generating or adapting equipment and technology to serve user needs.
Negotiation	Bringing others together and trying to reconcile differences.
Systems Evaluation	Identifying measures or indicators of system performance and the actions needed to improve or correct performance, relative to the goals of the system.
Mathematics	Using mathematics to solve problems.
Management of Material Resources	Obtaining and seeing to the appropriate use of equipment, facilities, and materials needed to do certain work.
Installation	Installing equipment, machines, wiring, or programs to meet specifications.
Management of Personnel Resources	Motivating, developing, and directing people as they work, identifying the best people for the job.
Management of Financial Resources	Determining how money will be spent to get the work done, and accounting for these expenditures.
Systems Analysis	Determining how a system should work and how changes in conditions, operations, and the environment will affect outcomes.
Operation Monitoring	Watching gauges, dials, or other indicators to make sure a machine is working properly.
Repairing	Repairing machines or systems using the needed tools.
Science	Using scientific rules and methods to solve problems.
Programming	Writing computer programs for various purposes.

Ability	Ability Definitions
Originality	The ability to come up with unusual or clever ideas about a given topic or situation, or to develop creative ways to solve a problem.
Near Vision	The ability to see details at close range (within a few feet of the observer).
Fluency of Ideas	The ability to come up with a number of ideas about a topic (the number of ideas is important, not their quality, correctness, or creativity).
Visualization	The ability to imagine how something will look after it is moved around or when its parts are moved or rearranged.
Speech Recognition	The ability to identify and understand the speech of another person.
Oral Comprehension	The ability to listen to and understand information and ideas presented through spoken words and sentences.
Speech Clarity	The ability to speak clearly so others can understand you.
Inductive Reasoning	The ability to combine pieces of information to form general rules or conclusions (includes finding a relationship among seemingly unrelated events).
Oral Expression	The ability to communicate information and ideas in speaking so others will understand.
Information Ordering	The ability to arrange things or actions in a certain order or pattern according to a specific rule or set of rules (e.g., patterns of numbers, letters, words, pictures, mathematical operations).
Category Flexibility	The ability to generate or use different sets of rules for combining or grouping things in different ways.
Visual Color Discrimination	The ability to match or detect differences between colors, including shades of color and brightness.
Selective Attention	The ability to concentrate on a task over a period of time without being distracted.
Written Comprehension	The ability to read and understand information and ideas presented in writing.
Finger Dexterity	The ability to make precisely coordinated movements of the fingers of one or both hands to grasp, manipulate, or assemble very small objects.
Problem Sensitivity	The ability to tell when something is wrong or is likely to go wrong. It does not involve solving the problem, only recognizing there is a problem.
Deductive Reasoning	The ability to apply general rules to specific problems to produce answers that make sense.
Arm-Hand Steadiness	The ability to keep your hand and arm steady while moving your arm or while holding your arm and hand in one position.
Written Expression	The ability to communicate information and ideas in writing so others will understand.
Manual Dexterity	The ability to quickly move your hand, your hand together with your arm, or your two hands to grasp, manipulate, or assemble objects.
Far Vision	The ability to see details at a distance.
Speed of Closure	The ability to quickly make sense of, combine, and organize information into meaningful patterns.
Perceptual Speed	The ability to quickly and accurately compare similarities and differences among sets of letters, numbers, objects, pictures, or patterns. The things to be compared may be presented at the same time or one after the other. This ability also includes comparing a presented object with a remembered object.
Flexibility of Closure	The ability to identify or detect a known pattern (a figure, object, word, or sound) that is hidden in other distracting material.
Control Precision	The ability to quickly and repeatedly adjust the controls of a machine or a vehicle to exact positions.
Time Sharing	The ability to shift back and forth between two or more activities or sources of information (such as speech, sounds, touch, or other sources).
Memorization	The ability to remember information such as words, numbers, pictures, and procedures.
Auditory Attention	The ability to focus on a single source of sound in the presence of other distracting sounds.
Wrist-Finger Speed	The ability to make fast, simple, repeated movements of the fingers, hands, and wrists.
Mathematical Reasoning	The ability to choose the right mathematical methods or formulas to solve a problem.
Hearing Sensitivity	The ability to detect or tell the differences between sounds that vary in pitch and loudness.
Trunk Strength	The ability to use your abdominal and lower back muscles to support part of the body repeatedly or continuously over time without 'giving out' or fatiguing.
Multilimb Coordination	The ability to coordinate two or more limbs (for example, two arms, two legs, or one leg and one arm) while sitting, standing, or lying down. It does not involve performing the activities while the whole body is in motion.
Depth Perception	The ability to judge which of several objects is closer or farther away from you, or to judge the distance between you and an object.

Number Facility	The ability to add, subtract, multiply, or divide quickly and correctly.
Dynamic Flexibility	The ability to quickly and repeatedly bend, stretch, twist, or reach out with your body, arms, and/or legs.
Extent Flexibility	The ability to bend, stretch, twist, or reach with your body, arms, and/or legs.
Stamina	The ability to exert yourself physically over long periods of time without getting winded or out of breath.
Dynamic Strength	The ability to exert muscle force repeatedly or continuously over time. This involves muscular endurance and resistance to muscle fatigue.
Explosive Strength	The ability to use short bursts of muscle force to propel oneself (as in jumping or sprinting), or to throw an object.
Static Strength	The ability to exert maximum muscle force to lift, push, pull, or carry objects.
Speed of Limb Movement	The ability to quickly move the arms and legs.
Gross Body Coordination	The ability to coordinate the movement of your arms, legs, and torso together when the whole body is in motion.
Reaction Time	The ability to quickly respond (with the hand, finger, or foot) to a signal (sound, light, picture) when it appears.
Spatial Orientation	The ability to know your location in relation to the environment or to know where other objects are in relation to you.
Glare Sensitivity	The ability to see objects in the presence of glare or bright lighting.
Sound Localization	The ability to tell the direction from which a sound originated.
Night Vision	The ability to see under low light conditions.
Peripheral Vision	The ability to see objects or movement of objects to one's side when the eyes are looking ahead.
Response Orientation	The ability to choose quickly between two or more movements in response to two or more different signals (lights, sounds, pictures). It includes the speed with which the correct response is started with the hand, foot, or other body part.
Rate Control	The ability to time your movements or the movement of a piece of equipment in anticipation of changes in the speed and/or direction of a moving object or scene.
Gross Body Equilibrium	The ability to keep or regain your body balance or stay upright when in an unstable position.

Work_Activity	Work_Activity Definitions
Thinking Creatively	Developing, designing, or creating new applications, ideas, relationships, systems, or products, including artistic contributions.
Interacting With Computers	Using computers and computer systems (including hardware and software) to program, write software, set up functions, enter data, or process information.
Getting Information	Observing, receiving, and otherwise obtaining information from all relevant sources.
Making Decisions and Solving Problems	Analyzing information and evaluating results to choose the best solution and solve problems.
Updating and Using Relevant Knowledge	Keeping up-to-date technically and applying new knowledge to your job.
Establishing and Maintaining Interpersonal Relatio	Developing constructive and cooperative working relationships with others, and maintaining them over time.
Communicating with Supervisors, Peers, or Subordin	Providing information to supervisors, co-workers, and subordinates by telephone, in written form, e-mail, or in person.
Organizing, Planning, and Prioritizing Work	Developing specific goals and plans to prioritize, organize, and accomplish your work.
Communicating with Persons Outside Organization	Communicating with people outside the organization, representing the organization to customers, the public, government, and other external sources. This information can be exchanged in person, in writing, or by telephone or e-mail.
Identifying Objects, Actions, and Events	Identifying information by categorizing, estimating, recognizing differences or similarities, and detecting changes in circumstances or events.
Scheduling Work and Activities	Scheduling events, programs, and activities, as well as the work of others.
Drafting, Laying Out, and Specifying Technical Dev	Providing documentation, detailed instructions, drawings, or specifications to tell others about how devices, parts, equipment, or structures are to be fabricated, constructed, assembled, modified, maintained, or used.
Selling or Influencing Others	Convincing others to buy merchandise/goods or to otherwise change their minds or actions.
Documenting/Recording Information	Entering, transcribing, recording, storing, or maintaining information in written or electronic/magnetic form.

Resolving Conflicts and Negotiating with Others	Handling complaints, settling disputes, and resolving grievances and conflicts, or otherwise negotiating with others.
Interpreting the Meaning of Information for Others	Translating or explaining what information means and how it can be used.
Estimating the Quantifiable Characteristics of Pro	Estimating sizes, distances, and quantities; or determining time, costs, resources, or materials needed to perform a work activity.
Judging the Qualities of Things, Services, or Peop	Assessing the value, importance, or quality of things or people.
Performing Administrative Activities	Performing day-to-day administrative tasks such as maintaining information files and processing paperwork.
Controlling Machines and Processes	Using either control mechanisms or direct physical activity to operate machines or processes (not including computers or vehicles).
Inspecting Equipment, Structures, or Material	Inspecting equipment, structures, or materials to identify the cause of errors or other problems or defects.
Provide Consultation and Advice to Others	Providing guidance and expert advice to management or other groups on technical, systems-, or process-related topics.
Performing for or Working Directly with the Public	Performing for people or dealing directly with the public. This includes serving customers in restaurants and stores, and receiving clients or guests.
Processing Information	Compiling, coding, categorizing, calculating, tabulating, auditing, or verifying information or data.
Repairing and Maintaining Electronic Equipment	Servicing, repairing, calibrating, regulating, fine-tuning, or testing machines, devices, and equipment that operate primarily on the basis of electrical or electronic (not mechanical) principles.
Monitor Processes, Materials, or Surroundings	Monitoring and reviewing information from materials, events, or the environment, to detect or assess problems.
Handling and Moving Objects	Using hands and arms in handling, installing, positioning, and moving materials, and manipulating things.
Performing General Physical Activities	Performing physical activities that require considerable use of your arms and legs and moving your whole body, such as climbing, lifting, balancing, walking, stooping, and handling of materials.
Evaluating Information to Determine Compliance wit	Using relevant information and individual judgment to determine whether events or processes comply with laws, regulations, or standards.
Developing Objectives and Strategies	Establishing long-range objectives and specifying the strategies and actions to achieve them.
Monitoring and Controlling Resources	Monitoring and controlling resources and overseeing the spending of money.
Coordinating the Work and Activities of Others	Getting members of a group to work together to accomplish tasks.
Assisting and Caring for Others	Providing personal assistance, medical attention, emotional support, or other personal care to others such as coworkers, customers, or patients.
Operating Vehicles, Mechanized Devices, or Equipme	Running, maneuvering, navigating, or driving vehicles or mechanized equipment, such as forklifts, passenger vehicles, aircraft, or water craft.
Analyzing Data or Information	Identifying the underlying principles, reasons, or facts of information by breaking down information or data into separate parts.
Developing and Building Teams	Encouraging and building mutual trust, respect, and cooperation among team members.
Training and Teaching Others	Identifying the educational needs of others, developing formal educational or training programs or classes, and teaching or instructing others.
Coaching and Developing Others	Identifying the developmental needs of others and coaching, mentoring, or otherwise helping others to improve their knowledge or skills.
Repairing and Maintaining Mechanical Equipment	Servicing, repairing, adjusting, and testing machines, devices, moving parts, and equipment that operate primarily on the basis of mechanical (not electronic) principles.
Guiding, Directing, and Motivating Subordinates	Providing guidance and direction to subordinates, including setting performance standards and monitoring performance.
Staffing Organizational Units	Recruiting, interviewing, selecting, hiring, and promoting employees in an organization.

Work_Context	Work_Context Definitions
Electronic Mail	How often do you use electronic mail in this job?
Spend Time Sitting	How much does this job require sitting?
Face-to-Face Discussions	How often do you have to have face-to-face discussions with individuals or teams in this job?
Importance of Being Exact or Accurate	How important is being very exact or highly accurate in performing this job?

Contact With Others	How much does this job require the worker to be in contact with others (face-to-face, by telephone, or otherwise) in order to perform it?
Time Pressure	How often does this job require the worker to meet strict deadlines?
Indoors, Environmentally Controlled	How often does this job require working indoors in environmentally controlled conditions?
Work With Work Group or Team	How important is it to work with others in a group or team in this job?
Structured versus Unstructured Work	To what extent is this job structured for the worker, rather than allowing the worker to determine tasks, priorities, and goals?
Freedom to Make Decisions	How much decision making freedom, without supervision, does the job offer?
Spend Time Making Repetitive Motions	How much does this job require making repetitive motions?
Telephone	How often do you have telephone conversations in this job?
Importance of Repeating Same Tasks	How important is repeating the same physical activities (e.g., key entry) or mental activities (e.g., checking entries in a ledger) over and over, without stopping, to performing this job?
Spend Time Using Your Hands to Handle, Control, or	How much does this job require using your hands to handle, control, or feel objects, tools or controls?
Frequency of Decision Making	How frequently is the worker required to make decisions that affect other people, the financial resources, and/or the image and reputation of the organization?
Impact of Decisions on Co-workers or Company Resul	How do the decisions an employee makes impact the results of co-workers, clients or the company?
Letters and Memos	How often does the job require written letters and memos?
Coordinate or Lead Others	How important is it to coordinate or lead others in accomplishing work activities in this job?
Physical Proximity	To what extent does this job require the worker to perform job tasks in close physical proximity to other people?
Frequency of Conflict Situations	How often are there conflict situations the employee has to face in this job?
Responsibility for Outcomes and Results	How responsible is the worker for work outcomes and results of other workers?
Degree of Automation	How automated is the job?
Sounds, Noise Levels Are Distracting or Uncomforta	How often does this job require working exposed to sounds and noise levels that are distracting or uncomfortable?
Consequence of Error	How serious would the result usually be if the worker made a mistake that was not readily correctable?
Deal With External Customers	How important is it to work with external customers or the public in this job?
Level of Competition	To what extent does this job require the worker to compete or to be aware of competitive pressures?
Deal With Unpleasant or Angry People	How frequently does the worker have to deal with unpleasant, angry, or discourteous individuals as part of the job requirements?
Pace Determined by Speed of Equipment	How important is it to this job that the pace is determined by the speed of equipment or machinery? (This does not refer to keeping busy at all times on this job.)
Exposed to Contaminants	How often does this job require working exposed to contaminants (such as pollutants, gases, dust or odors)?
Responsible for Others' Health and Safety	How much responsibility is there for the health and safety of others in this job?
Spend Time Walking and Running	How much does this job require walking and running?
Public Speaking	How often do you have to perform public speaking in this job?
Spend Time Standing	How much does this job require standing?
Very Hot or Cold Temperatures	How often does this job require working in very hot (above 90 F degrees) or very cold (below 32 F degrees) temperatures?
Cramped Work Space, Awkward Positions	How often does this job require working in cramped work spaces that requires getting into awkward positions?
Spend Time Bending or Twisting the Body	How much does this job require bending or twisting your body?
In an Enclosed Vehicle or Equipment	How often does this job require working in a closed vehicle or equipment (e.g., car)?
Extremely Bright or Inadequate Lighting	How often does this job require working in extremely bright or inadequate lighting conditions?
Spend Time Kneeling, Crouching, Stooping, or Crawl	How much does this job require kneeling, crouching, stooping or crawling?
Deal With Physically Aggressive People	How frequently does this job require the worker to deal with physical aggression of violent individuals?
Wear Common Protective or Safety Equipment such as	How much does this job require wearing common protective or safety equipment such as safety shoes, glasses, gloves, hard hats or live jackets?

Exposed to Hazardous Equipment	How often does this job require exposure to hazardous equipment?
Exposed to Minor Burns, Cuts, Bites, or Stings	How often does this job require exposure to minor burns, cuts, bites, or stings?
Indoors, Not Environmentally Controlled	How often does this job require working indoors in non-controlled environmental conditions (e.g., warehouse without heat)?
Outdoors, Exposed to Weather	How often does this job require working outdoors, exposed to all weather conditions?
Exposed to Hazardous Conditions	How often does this job require exposure to hazardous conditions?
Outdoors, Under Cover	How often does this job require working outdoors, under cover (e.g., structure with roof but no walls)?
Spend Time Climbing Ladders, Scaffolds, or Poles	How much does this job require climbing ladders, scaffolds, or poles?
Spend Time Keeping or Regaining Balance	How much does this job require keeping or regaining your balance?
In an Open Vehicle or Equipment	How often does this job require working in an open vehicle or equipment (e.g., tractor)?
Exposed to High Places	How often does this job require exposure to high places?
Wear Specialized Protective or Safety Equipment su	How much does this job require wearing specialized protective or safety equipment such as breathing apparatus, safety harness, full protection suits, or radiation protection?
Exposed to Disease or Infections	How often does this job require exposure to disease/infections?
Exposed to Radiation	How often does this job require exposure to radiation?
Exposed to Whole Body Vibration	How often does this job require exposure to whole body vibration (e.g., operate a jackhammer)?

Job Zone Component	Job Zone Component Definitions
Title	Job Zone Four: Considerable Preparation Needed
Overall Experience	A minimum of two to four years of work-related skill, knowledge, or experience is needed for these occupations. For example, an accountant must complete four years of college and work for several years in accounting to be considered qualified.
Job Training	Employees in these occupations usually need several years of work-related experience, on-the-job training, and/or vocational training.
Job Zone Examples	Many of these occupations involve coordinating, supervising, managing, or training others. Examples include accountants, chefs and head cooks, computer programmers, historians, pharmacists, and police detectives.
SVP Range	(7.0 to < 8.0)
Education	Most of these occupations require a four - year bachelor's degree, but some do not.

Work_Styles	Work_Styles Definitions
Attention to Detail	Job requires being careful about detail and thorough in completing work tasks.
Dependability	Job requires being reliable, responsible, and dependable, and fulfilling obligations.
Cooperation	Job requires being pleasant with others on the job and displaying a good-natured, cooperative attitude.
Innovation	Job requires creativity and alternative thinking to develop new ideas for and answers to work-related problems.
Adaptability/Flexibility	Job requires being open to change (positive or negative) and to considerable variety in the workplace.
Stress Tolerance	Job requires accepting criticism and dealing calmly and effectively with high stress situations.
Analytical Thinking	Job requires analyzing information and using logic to address work-related issues and problems.
Achievement/Effort	Job requires establishing and maintaining personally challenging achievement goals and exerting effort toward mastering tasks.
Persistence	Job requires persistence in the face of obstacles.
Independence	Job requires developing one's own ways of doing things, guiding oneself with little or no supervision, and depending on oneself to get things done.
Initiative	Job requires a willingness to take on responsibilities and challenges.
Self Control	Job requires maintaining composure, keeping emotions in check, controlling anger, and avoiding aggressive behavior, even in very difficult situations.

Concern for Others	Job requires being sensitive to others' needs and feelings and being understanding and helpful on the job.
Integrity	Job requires being honest and ethical.
Leadership	Job requires a willingness to lead, take charge, and offer opinions and direction.
Social Orientation	Job requires preferring to work with others rather than alone, and being personally connected with others on the job.

27-1025.00 - Interior Designers

Plan, design, and furnish interiors of residential, commercial, or industrial buildings. Formulate design which is practical, aesthetic, and conducive to intended purposes, such as raising productivity, selling merchandise, or improving life style. May specialize in a particular field, style, or phase of interior design.

Tasks

1) Render design ideas in form of paste-ups or drawings.

2) Select or design, and purchase furnishings, art works, and accessories.

3) Subcontract fabrication, installation, and arrangement of carpeting, fixtures, accessories, draperies, paint and wall coverings, art work, furniture, and related items.

4) Formulate environmental plan to be practical, esthetic, and conducive to intended purposes, such as raising productivity or selling merchandise.

5) Plan and design interior environments for boats, planes, buses, trains, and other enclosed spaces.

6) Confer with client to determine factors affecting planning interior environments, such as budget, architectural preferences, and purpose and function.

7) Advise client on interior design factors, such as space planning, layout and utilization of furnishings and equipment, and color coordination.

Knowledge	Knowledge Definitions
Customer and Personal Service	Knowledge of principles and processes for providing customer and personal services. This includes customer needs assessment, meeting quality standards for services, and evaluation of customer satisfaction.
Design	Knowledge of design techniques, tools, and principles involved in production of precision technical plans, blueprints, drawings, and models.
Administration and Management	Knowledge of business and management principles involved in strategic planning, resource allocation, human resources modeling, leadership technique, production methods, and coordination of people and resources.
Sales and Marketing	Knowledge of principles and methods for showing, promoting, and selling products or services. This includes marketing strategy and tactics, product demonstration, sales techniques, and sales control systems.
English Language	Knowledge of the structure and content of the English language including the meaning and spelling of words, rules of composition, and grammar.
Clerical	Knowledge of administrative and clerical procedures and systems such as word processing, managing files and records, stenography and transcription, designing forms, and other office procedures and terminology.
Computers and Electronics	Knowledge of circuit boards, processors, chips, electronic equipment, and computer hardware and software, including applications and programming.
Building and Construction	Knowledge of materials, methods, and the tools involved in the construction or repair of houses, buildings, or other structures such as highways and roads.
Mathematics	Knowledge of arithmetic, algebra, geometry, calculus, statistics, and their applications.
Production and Processing	Knowledge of raw materials, production processes, quality control, costs, and other techniques for maximizing the effective manufacture and distribution of goods.
Economics and Accounting	Knowledge of economic and accounting principles and practices, the financial markets, banking and the analysis and reporting of financial data.
Education and Training	Knowledge of principles and methods for curriculum and training design, teaching and instruction for individuals and groups, and the measurement of training effects.

Personnel and Human Resources	Knowledge of principles and procedures for personnel recruitment, selection, training, compensation and benefits, labor relations and negotiation, and personnel information systems.
Public Safety and Security	Knowledge of relevant equipment, policies, procedures, and strategies to promote effective local, state, or national security operations for the protection of people, data, property, and institutions.
Psychology	Knowledge of human behavior and performance; individual differences in ability, personality, and interests; learning and motivation; psychological research methods; and the assessment and treatment of behavioral and affective disorders.
Law and Government	Knowledge of laws, legal codes, court procedures, precedents, government regulations, executive orders, agency rules, and the democratic political process.
Fine Arts	Knowledge of the theory and techniques required to compose, produce, and perform works of music, dance, visual arts, drama, and sculpture.
Communications and Media	Knowledge of media production, communication, and dissemination techniques and methods. This includes alternative ways to inform and entertain via written, oral, and visual media.
Engineering and Technology	Knowledge of the practical application of engineering science and technology. This includes applying principles, techniques, procedures, and equipment to the design and production of various goods and services.
Mechanical	Knowledge of machines and tools, including their designs, uses, repair, and maintenance.
Sociology and Anthropology	Knowledge of group behavior and dynamics, societal trends and influences, human migrations, ethnicity, cultures and their history and origins.
Transportation	Knowledge of principles and methods for moving people or goods by air, rail, sea, or road, including the relative costs and benefits.
History and Archeology	Knowledge of historical events and their causes, indicators, and effects on civilizations and cultures.
Telecommunications	Knowledge of transmission, broadcasting, switching, control, and operation of telecommunications systems.
Philosophy and Theology	Knowledge of different philosophical systems and religions. This includes their basic principles, values, ethics, ways of thinking, customs, practices, and their impact on human culture.
Geography	Knowledge of principles and methods for describing the features of land, sea, and air masses, including their physical characteristics, locations, interrelationships, and distribution of plant, animal, and human life.
Foreign Language	Knowledge of the structure and content of a foreign (non-English) language including the meaning and spelling of words, rules of composition and grammar, and pronunciation.
Therapy and Counseling	Knowledge of principles, methods, and procedures for diagnosis, treatment, and rehabilitation of physical and mental dysfunctions, and for career counseling and guidance.
Chemistry	Knowledge of the chemical composition, structure, and properties of substances and of the chemical processes and transformations that they undergo. This includes uses of chemicals and their interactions, danger signs, production techniques, and disposal methods.
Physics	Knowledge and prediction of physical principles, laws, their interrelationships, and applications to understanding fluid, material, and atmospheric dynamics, and mechanical, electrical, atomic and sub-atomic structures and processes.
Biology	Knowledge of plant and animal organisms, their tissues, cells, functions, interdependencies, and interactions with each other and the environment.
Medicine and Dentistry	Knowledge of the information and techniques needed to diagnose and treat human injuries, diseases, and deformities. This includes symptoms, treatment alternatives, drug properties and interactions, and preventive health-care measures.
Food Production	Knowledge of techniques and equipment for planting, growing, and harvesting food products (both plant and animal) for consumption, including storage/handling techniques.

Skills	Skills Definitions
Active Listening	Giving full attention to what other people are saying, taking time to understand the points being made, asking questions as appropriate, and not interrupting at inappropriate times.

Reading Comprehension	Understanding written sentences and paragraphs in work related documents.
Management of Financial Resources	Determining how money will be spent to get the work done, and accounting for these expenditures.
Speaking	Talking to others to convey information effectively.
Writing	Communicating effectively in writing as appropriate for the needs of the audience.
Persuasion	Persuading others to change their minds or behavior.
Time Management	Managing one's own time and the time of others.
Mathematics	Using mathematics to solve problems.
Active Learning	Understanding the implications of new information for both current and future problem-solving and decision-making.
Installation	Installing equipment, machines, wiring, or programs to meet specifications.
Complex Problem Solving	Identifying complex problems and reviewing related information to develop and evaluate options and implement solutions.
Critical Thinking	Using logic and reasoning to identify the strengths and weaknesses of alternative solutions, conclusions or approaches to problems.
Service Orientation	Actively looking for ways to help people.
Operations Analysis	Analyzing needs and product requirements to create a design.
Social Perceptiveness	Being aware of others' reactions and understanding why they react as they do.
Coordination	Adjusting actions in relation to others' actions.
Troubleshooting	Determining causes of operating errors and deciding what to do about it.
Equipment Selection	Determining the kind of tools and equipment needed to do a job.
Judgment and Decision Making	Considering the relative costs and benefits of potential actions to choose the most appropriate one.
Learning Strategies	Selecting and using training/instructional methods and procedures appropriate for the situation when learning or teaching new things.
Monitoring	Monitoring/Assessing performance of yourself, other individuals, or organizations to make improvements or take corrective action.
Instructing	Teaching others how to do something.
Negotiation	Bringing others together and trying to reconcile differences.
Technology Design	Generating or adapting equipment and technology to serve user needs.
Systems Evaluation	Identifying measures or indicators of system performance and the actions needed to improve or correct performance, relative to the goals of the system.
Management of Material Resources	Obtaining and seeing to the appropriate use of equipment, facilities, and materials needed to do certain work.
Science	Using scientific rules and methods to solve problems.
Operation and Control	Controlling operations of equipment or systems.
Management of Personnel Resources	Motivating, developing, and directing people as they work, identifying the best people for the job.
Repairing	Repairing machines or systems using the needed tools.
Quality Control Analysis	Conducting tests and inspections of products, services, or processes to evaluate quality or performance.
Operation Monitoring	Watching gauges, dials, or other indicators to make sure a machine is working properly.
Systems Analysis	Determining how a system should work and how changes in conditions, operations, and the environment will affect outcomes.
Equipment Maintenance	Performing routine maintenance on equipment and determining when and what kind of maintenance is needed.
Programming	Writing computer programs for various purposes.

Ability	Ability Definitions
Originality	The ability to come up with unusual or clever ideas about a given topic or situation, or to develop creative ways to solve a problem.
Visualization	The ability to imagine how something will look after it is moved around or when its parts are moved or rearranged.
Oral Expression	The ability to communicate information and ideas in speaking so others will understand.
Oral Comprehension	The ability to listen to and understand information and ideas presented through spoken words and sentences.
Fluency of Ideas	The ability to come up with a number of ideas about a topic (the number of ideas is important, not their quality, correctness, or creativity).
Speech Clarity	The ability to speak clearly so others can understand you.

Deductive Reasoning	The ability to apply general rules to specific problems to produce answers that make sense.
Speech Recognition	The ability to identify and understand the speech of another person.
Visual Color Discrimination	The ability to match or detect differences between colors, including shades of color and brightness.
Inductive Reasoning	The ability to combine pieces of information to form general rules or conclusions (includes finding a relationship among seemingly unrelated events).
Problem Sensitivity	The ability to tell when something is wrong or is likely to go wrong. It does not involve solving the problem, only recognizing there is a problem.
Information Ordering	The ability to arrange things or actions in a certain order or pattern according to a specific rule or set of rules (e.g., patterns of numbers, letters, words, pictures, mathematical operations).
Category Flexibility	The ability to generate or use different sets of rules for combining or grouping things in different ways.
Near Vision	The ability to see details at close range (within a few feet of the observer).
Written Comprehension	The ability to read and understand information and ideas presented in writing.
Written Expression	The ability to communicate information and ideas in writing so others will understand.
Far Vision	The ability to see details at a distance.
Mathematical Reasoning	The ability to choose the right mathematical methods or formulas to solve a problem.
Flexibility of Closure	The ability to identify or detect a known pattern (a figure, object, word, or sound) that is hidden in other distracting material.
Selective Attention	The ability to concentrate on a task over a period of time without being distracted.
Time Sharing	The ability to shift back and forth between two or more activities or sources of information (such as speech, sounds, touch, or other sources).
Speed of Closure	The ability to quickly make sense of, combine, and organize information into meaningful patterns.
Depth Perception	The ability to judge which of several objects is closer or farther away from you, or to judge the distance between you and an object.
Spatial Orientation	The ability to know your location in relation to the environment or to know where other objects are in relation to you.
Perceptual Speed	The ability to quickly and accurately compare similarities and differences among sets of letters, numbers, objects, pictures, or patterns. The things to be compared may be presented at the same time or one after the other. This ability also includes comparing a presented object with a remembered object.
Memorization	The ability to remember information such as words, numbers, pictures, and procedures.
Arm-Hand Steadiness	The ability to keep your hand and arm steady while moving your arm or while holding your arm and hand in one position.
Multilimb Coordination	The ability to coordinate two or more limbs (for example, two arms, two legs, or one leg and one arm) while sitting, standing, or lying down. It does not involve performing the activities while the whole body is in motion.
Number Facility	The ability to add, subtract, multiply, or divide quickly and correctly.
Manual Dexterity	The ability to quickly move your hand, your hand together with your arm, or your two hands to grasp, manipulate, or assemble objects.
Finger Dexterity	The ability to make precisely coordinated movements of the fingers of one or both hands to grasp, manipulate, or assemble very small objects.
Static Strength	The ability to exert maximum muscle force to lift, push, pull, or carry objects.
Control Precision	The ability to quickly and repeatedly adjust the controls of a machine or a vehicle to exact positions.
Dynamic Strength	The ability to exert muscle force repeatedly or continuously over time. This involves muscular endurance and resistance to muscle fatigue.
Trunk Strength	The ability to use your abdominal and lower back muscles to support part of the body repeatedly or continuously over time without 'giving out' or fatiguing.
Stamina	The ability to exert yourself physically over long periods of time without getting winded or out of breath.
Extent Flexibility	The ability to bend, stretch, twist, or reach with your body, arms, and/or legs.
Auditory Attention	The ability to focus on a single source of sound in the presence of other distracting sounds.

Gross Body Equilibrium	The ability to keep or regain your body balance or stay upright when in an unstable position.
Gross Body Coordination	The ability to coordinate the movement of your arms, legs, and torso together when the whole body is in motion.
Wrist-Finger Speed	The ability to make fast, simple, repeated movements of the fingers, hands, and wrists.
Hearing Sensitivity	The ability to detect or tell the differences between sounds that vary in pitch and loudness.
Dynamic Flexibility	The ability to quickly and repeatedly bend, stretch, twist, or reach out with your body, arms, and/or legs.
Night Vision	The ability to see under low light conditions.
Glare Sensitivity	The ability to see objects in the presence of glare or bright lighting.
Response Orientation	The ability to choose quickly between two or more movements in response to two or more different signals (lights, sounds, pictures). It includes the speed with which the correct response is started with the hand, foot, or other body part.
Rate Control	The ability to time your movements or the movement of a piece of equipment in anticipation of changes in the speed and/or direction of a moving object or scene.
Explosive Strength	The ability to use short bursts of muscle force to propel oneself (as in jumping or sprinting), or to throw an object.
Sound Localization	The ability to tell the direction from which a sound originated.
Peripheral Vision	The ability to see objects or movement of objects to one's side when the eyes are looking ahead.
Reaction Time	The ability to quickly respond (with the hand, finger, or foot) to a signal (sound, light, picture) when it appears.
Speed of Limb Movement	The ability to quickly move the arms and legs.

Work_Activity	Work_Activity Definitions
Thinking Creatively	Developing, designing, or creating new applications, ideas, relationships, systems, or products, including artistic contributions.
Interacting With Computers	Using computers and computer systems (including hardware and software) to program, write software, set up functions, enter data, or process information.
Communicating with Supervisors, Peers, or Subordin	Providing information to supervisors, co-workers, and subordinates by telephone, in written form, e-mail, or in person.
Getting Information	Observing, receiving, and otherwise obtaining information from all relevant sources.
Selling or Influencing Others	Convincing others to buy merchandise/goods or to otherwise change their minds or actions.
Making Decisions and Solving Problems	Analyzing information and evaluating results to choose the best solution and solve problems.
Estimating the Quantifiable Characteristics of Pro	Estimating sizes, distances, and quantities; or determining time, costs, resources, or materials needed to perform a work activity.
Drafting, Laying Out, and Specifying Technical Dev	Providing documentation, detailed instructions, drawings, or specifications to tell others about how devices, parts, equipment, or structures are to be fabricated, constructed, assembled, modified, maintained, or used.
Organizing, Planning, and Prioritizing Work	Developing specific goals and plans to prioritize, organize, and accomplish your work.
Performing for or Working Directly with the Public	Performing for people or dealing directly with the public. This includes serving customers in restaurants and stores, and receiving clients or guests.
Coordinating the Work and Activities of Others	Getting members of a group to work together to accomplish tasks.
Updating and Using Relevant Knowledge	Keeping up-to-date technically and applying new knowledge to your job.
Inspecting Equipment, Structures, or Material	Inspecting equipment, structures, or materials to identify the cause of errors or other problems or defects.
Establishing and Maintaining Interpersonal Relatio	Developing constructive and cooperative working relationships with others, and maintaining them over time.
Scheduling Work and Activities	Scheduling events, programs, and activities, as well as the work of others.
Processing Information	Compiling, coding, categorizing, calculating, tabulating, auditing, or verifying information or data.
Monitor Processes, Materials, or Surroundings	Monitoring and reviewing information from materials, events, or the environment, to detect or assess problems.
Documenting/Recording Information	Entering, transcribing, recording, storing, or maintaining information in written or electronic/magnetic form.

Communicating with Persons Outside Organization	Communicating with people outside the organization, representing the organization to customers, the public, government, and other external sources. This information can be exchanged in person, in writing, or by telephone or e-mail.
Developing and Building Teams	Encouraging and building mutual trust, respect, and cooperation among team members.
Interpreting the Meaning of Information for Others	Translating or explaining what information means and how it can be used.
Judging the Qualities of Things, Services, or Peop	Assessing the value, importance, or quality of things or people.
Evaluating Information to Determine Compliance wit	Using relevant information and individual judgment to determine whether events or processes comply with laws, regulations, or standards.
Analyzing Data or Information	Identifying the underlying principles, reasons, or facts of information by breaking down information or data into separate parts.
Identifying Objects, Actions, and Events	Identifying information by categorizing, estimating, recognizing differences or similarities, and detecting changes in circumstances or events.
Resolving Conflicts and Negotiating with Others	Handling complaints, settling disputes, and resolving grievances and conflicts, or otherwise negotiating with others.
Coaching and Developing Others	Identifying the developmental needs of others and coaching, mentoring, or otherwise helping others to improve their knowledge or skills.
Developing Objectives and Strategies	Establishing long-range objectives and specifying the strategies and actions to achieve them.
Performing Administrative Activities	Performing day-to-day administrative tasks such as maintaining information files and processing paperwork.
Handling and Moving Objects	Using hands and arms in handling, installing, positioning, and moving materials, and manipulating things.
Performing General Physical Activities	Performing physical activities that require considerable use of your arms and legs and moving your whole body, such as climbing, lifting, balancing, walking, stooping, and handling of materials.
Provide Consultation and Advice to Others	Providing guidance and expert advice to management or other groups on technical, systems-, or process-related topics.
Guiding, Directing, and Motivating Subordinates	Providing guidance and direction to subordinates, including setting performance standards and monitoring performance.
Staffing Organizational Units	Recruiting, interviewing, selecting, hiring, and promoting employees in an organization.
Monitoring and Controlling Resources	Monitoring and controlling resources and overseeing the spending of money.
Training and Teaching Others	Identifying the educational needs of others, developing formal educational or training programs or classes, and teaching or instructing others.
Assisting and Caring for Others	Providing personal assistance, medical attention, emotional support, or other personal care to others such as coworkers, customers, or patients.
Controlling Machines and Processes	Using either control mechanisms or direct physical activity to operate machines or processes (not including computers or vehicles).
Repairing and Maintaining Electronic Equipment	Servicing, repairing, calibrating, regulating, fine-tuning, or testing machines, devices, and equipment that operate primarily on the basis of electrical or electronic (not mechanical) principles.
Repairing and Maintaining Mechanical Equipment	Servicing, repairing, adjusting, and testing machines, devices, moving parts, and equipment that operate primarily on the basis of mechanical (not electronic) principles.
Operating Vehicles, Mechanized Devices, or Equipme	Running, maneuvering, navigating, or driving vehicles or mechanized equipment, such as forklifts, passenger vehicles, aircraft, or water craft.

Work_Context	Work_Context Definitions
Face-to-Face Discussions	How often do you have to have face-to-face discussions with individuals or teams in this job?
Telephone	How often do you have telephone conversations in this job?
Impact of Decisions on Co-workers or Company Resul	How do the decisions an employee makes impact the results of co-workers, clients or the company?
Contact With Others	How much does this job require the worker to be in contact with others (face-to-face, by telephone, or otherwise) in order to perform it?
Freedom to Make Decisions	How much decision making freedom, without supervision, does the job offer?
Structured versus Unstructured Work	To what extent is this job structured for the worker, rather than allowing the worker to determine tasks, priorities, and goals?

Importance of Being Exact or Accurate	How important is being very exact or highly accurate in performing this job?
Frequency of Decision Making	How frequently is the worker required to make decisions that affect other people, the financial resources, and/or the image and reputation of the organization?
Work With Work Group or Team	How important is it to work with others in a group or team in this job?
Deal With External Customers	How important is it to work with external customers or the public in this job?
Letters and Memos	How often does the job require written letters and memos?
Indoors, Environmentally Controlled	How often does this job require working indoors in environmentally controlled conditions?
Level of Competition	To what extent does this job require the worker to compete or to be aware of competitive pressures?
Spend Time Sitting	How much does this job require sitting?
Coordinate or Lead Others	How important is it to coordinate or lead others in accomplishing work activities in this job?
Electronic Mail	How often do you use electronic mail in this job?
Time Pressure	How often does this job require the worker to meet strict deadlines?
Physical Proximity	To what extent does this job require the worker to perform job tasks in close physical proximity to other people?
Responsibility for Outcomes and Results	How responsible is the worker for work outcomes and results of other workers?
Deal With Unpleasant or Angry People	How frequently does the worker have to deal with unpleasant, angry, or discourteous individuals as part of the job requirements?
In an Enclosed Vehicle or Equipment	How often does this job require working in a closed vehicle or equipment (e.g., car)?
Frequency of Conflict Situations	How often are there conflict situations the employee has to face in this job?
Spend Time Using Your Hands to Handle, Control, or	How much does this job require using your hands to handle, control, or feel objects, tools or controls?
Responsible for Others' Health and Safety	How much responsibility is there for the health and safety of others in this job?
Consequence of Error	How serious would the result usually be if the worker made a mistake that was not readily correctable?
Public Speaking	How often do you have to perform public speaking in this job?
Spend Time Standing	How much does this job require standing?
Degree of Automation	How automated is the job?
Spend Time Making Repetitive Motions	How much does this job require making repetitive motions?
Indoors, Not Environmentally Controlled	How often does this job require working indoors in non-controlled environmental conditions (e.g., warehouse without heat)?
Spend Time Walking and Running	How much does this job require walking and running?
Outdoors, Exposed to Weather	How often does this job require working outdoors, exposed to all weather conditions?
Importance of Repeating Same Tasks	How important is repeating the same physical activities (e.g., key entry) or mental activities (e.g., checking entries in a ledger) over and over, without stopping, to performing this job?
Sounds, Noise Levels Are Distracting or Uncomfortabl	How often does this job require working exposed to sounds and noise levels that are distracting or uncomfortable?
Cramped Work Space, Awkward Positions	How often does this job require working in cramped work spaces that requires getting into awkward positions?
Extremely Bright or Inadequate Lighting	How often does this job require working in extremely bright or inadequate lighting conditions?
Spend Time Climbing Ladders, Scaffolds, or Poles	How much does this job require climbing ladders, scaffolds, or poles?
Spend Time Bending or Twisting the Body	How much does this job require bending or twisting your body?
Spend Time Kneeling, Crouching, Stooping, or Crawl	How much does this job require kneeling, crouching, stooping, or crawling?
Exposed to Contaminants	How often does this job require working exposed to contaminants (such as pollutants, gases, dust or odors)?
Outdoors, Under Cover	How often does this job require working outdoors, under cover (e.g., structure with roof but no walls)?
Wear Common Protective or Safety Equipment such as	How much does this job require wearing common protective or safety equipment such as safety shoes, glasses, gloves, hard hats or life jackets?
Exposed to High Places	How often does this job require exposure to high places?
Deal With Physically Aggressive People	How frequently does this job require the worker to deal with physical aggression of violent individuals?
Exposed to Hazardous	How often does this job require exposure to hazardous

Exposed to Minor Burns. Cuts. Bites, or Stings	How often does this job require exposure to minor burns. cuts. bites, or stings?
Spend Time Keeping or Regaining Balance	How much does this job require keeping or regaining your balance?
Pace Determined by Speed of Equipment	How important is it to this job that the pace is determined by the speed of equipment or machinery? (This does not refer to keeping busy at all times on this job.)
Very Hot or Cold Temperatures	How often does this job require working in very hot (above 90 F degrees) or very cold (below 32 F degrees) temperatures?
Exposed to Radiation	How often does this job require exposure to radiation?
Exposed to Hazardous Conditions	How often does this job require exposure to hazardous conditions?
Wear Specialized Protective or Safety Equipment su	How much does this job require wearing specialized protective or safety equipment such as breathing apparatus, safety harness. full protection suits, or radiation protection?
Exposed to Disease or Infections	How often does this job require exposure to disease/infections?
Exposed to Whole Body Vibration	How often does this job require exposure to whole body vibration (e.g., operate a jackhammer)?
In an Open Vehicle or Equipment	How often does this job require working in an open vehicle or equipment (e.g., tractor)?

Job Zone Component	Job Zone Component Definitions
Title	Job Zone Three: Medium Preparation Needed
Overall Experience	Previous work-related skill, knowledge, or experience is required for these occupations. For example, an electrician must have completed three or four years of apprenticeship or several years of vocational training, and often must have passed a licensing exam, in order to perform the job.
Job Training	Employees in these occupations usually need one or two years of training involving both on-the-job experience and informal training with experienced workers.
Job Zone Examples	These occupations usually involve using communication and organizational skills to coordinate, supervise, manage, or train others to accomplish goals. Examples include dental assistants, electricians, fish and game wardens, legal secretaries, personnel recruiters, and recreation workers.
SVP Range	(6.0 to < 7.0)
Education	Most occupations in this zone require training in vocational schools, related on-the-job experience, or an associate's degree. Some may require a bachelor's degree.

Work_Styles	Work_Styles Definitions
Attention to Detail	Job requires being careful about detail and thorough in completing work tasks.
Dependability	Job requires being reliable, responsible, and dependable, and fulfilling obligations.
Innovation	Job requires creativity and alternative thinking to develop new ideas for and answers to work-related problems.
Integrity	Job requires being honest and ethical.
Independence	Job requires developing one's own ways of doing things, guiding oneself with little or no supervision, and depending on oneself to get things done.
Cooperation	Job requires being pleasant with others on the job and displaying a good-natured, cooperative attitude.
Self Control	Job requires maintaining composure, keeping emotions in check, controlling anger, and avoiding aggressive behavior, even in very difficult situations.
Initiative	Job requires a willingness to take on responsibilities and challenges.
Adaptability/Flexibility	Job requires being open to change (positive or negative) and to considerable variety in the workplace.
Achievement/Effort	Job requires establishing and maintaining personally challenging achievement goals and exerting effort toward mastering tasks.
Concern for Others	Job requires being sensitive to others' needs and feelings and being understanding and helpful on the job.
Leadership	Job requires a willingness to lead, take charge, and offer opinions and direction.
Stress Tolerance	Job requires accepting criticism and dealing calmly and effectively with high stress situations.
Persistence	Job requires persistence in the face of obstacles.
Analytical Thinking	Job requires analyzing information and using logic to address work-related issues and problems.

Social Orientation	Job requires preferring to work with others rather than alone, and being personally connected with others on the job.

27-1026.00 - Merchandise Displayers and Window Trimmers

Plan and erect commercial displays, such as those in windows and interiors of retail stores and at trade exhibitions.

Tasks

1) Change or rotate window displays, interior display areas, and signage to reflect changes in inventory or promotion.

2) Attend training sessions and corporate planning meetings to obtain new ideas for product launches.

3) Develop ideas or plans for merchandise displays or window decorations.

4) Place prices and descriptive signs on backdrops, fixtures, merchandise, or floor.

5) Cut out designs on cardboard, hardboard, and plywood, according to motif of event.

6) Construct or assemble displays and display components from fabric, glass, paper, and plastic, using hand tools and woodworking power tools, according to specifications.

7) Collaborate with others to obtain products and other display items.

8) Create and enhance mannequin faces by mixing and applying paint and attaching measured eyelash strips, using artist's brush, airbrush, pins, ruler, and scissors.

9) Dress mannequins for displays.

10) Take photographs of displays and signage.

11) Maintain props and mannequins, inspecting them for imperfections and applying preservative coatings as necessary.

12) Install decorations such as flags, banners, festive lights, and bunting on or in building, street, exhibit hall, or booth.

13) Select themes, lighting, colors, and props to be used.

14) Store, pack, and maintain records of props and display items.

15) Plan and erect commercial displays to entice and appeal to customers.

16) Consult with advertising and sales staff to determine type of merchandise to be featured and time and place for each display.

17) Use computers to produce signage.

18) Arrange properties, furniture, merchandise, backdrops, and other accessories, as shown in prepared sketches.

19) Obtain plans from display designers or display managers, and discuss their implementation with clients or supervisors.

20) Prepare sketches, floor plans or models of proposed displays.

21) Install booths, exhibits, displays, carpets, and drapes, as guided by floor plan of building and specifications.

27-1027.00 - Set and Exhibit Designers

Design special exhibits and movie, television, and theater sets. May study scripts, confer with directors, and conduct research to determine appropriate architectural styles.

Tasks

1) Estimate set- or exhibit-related costs including materials, construction, and rental of props or locations.

2) Design and build scale models of set designs, or miniature sets used in filming backgrounds or special effects.

3) Coordinate the transportation of sets that are built off-site, and coordinate their setup at the site of use.

4) Collaborate with those in charge of lighting and sound so that those production aspects can be coordinated with set designs or exhibit layouts.

5) Attend rehearsals and production meetings in order to obtain and share information related to sets.

6) Assign staff to complete design ideas and prepare sketches, illustrations, and detailed drawings of sets, or graphics and animation.

7) Provide supportive materials for exhibits and displays, such as press kits and advertising, posters, brochures, catalogues, and invitations and publicity notices.

8) Acquire, or arrange for acquisition of, specimens or graphics required to complete exhibits.

9) Design and produce displays and materials that can be used to decorate windows, interior displays, or event locations such as streets and fairgrounds.

10) Incorporate security systems into exhibit layouts.

11) Arrange for outside contractors to construct exhibit structures.

12) Confer with clients and staff in order to gather information about exhibit space, proposed themes and content, timelines, budgets, materials, and/or promotion requirements.

13) Select set props such as furniture, pictures, lamps, and rugs.

14) Coordinate the removal of sets, props, and exhibits after productions or events are complete.

15) Submit plans for approval, and adapt plans to serve intended purposes, or to conform to budget or fabrication restrictions.

16) Develop set designs based on evaluation of scripts, budgets, research information, and available locations.

17) Direct and coordinate construction, erection, or decoration activities in order to ensure that sets or exhibits meet design, budget, and schedule requirements.

18) Examine objects to be included in exhibits in order to plan where and how to display them.

19) Inspect installed exhibits for conformance to specifications, and satisfactory operation of special effects components.

20) Observe sets during rehearsals in order to ensure that set elements do not interfere with performance aspects such as cast movement and camera angles.

21) Prepare preliminary renderings of proposed exhibits, including detailed construction, layout, and material specifications, and diagrams relating to aspects such as special effects and/or lighting.

22) Plan for location-specific issues such as space limitations, traffic flow patterns, and safety concerns.

23) Select and purchase lumber and hardware necessary for set construction.

24) Prepare rough drafts and scale working drawings of sets, including floor plans, scenery, and properties to be constructed.

25) Read scripts in order to determine location, set, and design requirements.

26) Confer with conservators in order to determine how to handle an exhibit's environmental aspects, such as lighting, temperature, and humidity, so that objects will be protected and exhibits will be enhanced.

27-2011.00 - Actors

Play parts in stage, television, radio, video, or motion picture productions for entertainment, information, or instruction. Interpret serious or comic role by speech, gesture, and body movement to entertain or inform audience. May dance and sing.

Tasks

1) Construct puppets and ventriloquist dummies, and sew accessory clothing, using hand tools and machines.

2) Attend auditions and casting calls in order to audition for roles.

3) Read from scripts or books to narrate action or to inform or entertain audiences, utilizing few or no stage props.

4) Portray and interpret roles, using speech, gestures, and body movements in order to entertain, inform, or instruct radio, film, television, or live audiences.

5) Sing and/or dance during dramatic or comedic performances.

6) Prepare and perform action stunts for motion picture, television, or stage productions.

7) Introduce performances and performers in order to stimulate excitement and coordinate smooth transition of acts during events.

8) Study and rehearse roles from scripts in order to interpret, learn and memorize lines, stunts, and cues as directed.

9) Learn about characters in scripts and their relationships to each other in order to develop

role interpretations.

10) Tell jokes, perform comic dances, songs and skits, impersonate mannerisms and voices of others, contort face, and use other devices to amuse audiences.

11) Write original or adapted material for dramas, comedies, puppet shows, narration, or other performances.

12) Promote productions using means such as interviews about plays or movies.

13) Manipulate strings, wires, rods, or fingers to animate puppets or dummies in synchronization with talking, singing, or recorded programs.

14) Perform original and stock tricks of illusion to entertain and mystify audiences, occasionally including audience members as participants.

15) Perform humorous and serious interpretations of emotions, actions, and situations, using body movements, facial expressions, and gestures.

16) Collaborate with other actors as part of an ensemble.

17) Dress in comical clown costumes and makeup, and perform comedy routines to entertain audiences.

18) Work with other crewmembers responsible for lighting, costumes, makeup, and props.

27-2012.01 - Producers

Plan and coordinate various aspects of radio, television, stage, or motion picture production, such as selecting script, coordinating writing, directing and editing, and arranging financing.

Tasks

1) Conduct meetings with staff to discuss production progress and to ensure production objectives are attained.

2) Compose and edit scripts, or provide screenwriters with story outlines from which scripts can be written.

3) Coordinate the activities of writers, directors, managers, and other personnel throughout the production process.

4) Perform management activities such as budgeting, scheduling, planning, and marketing.

5) Resolve personnel problems that arise during the production process by acting as liaisons between dissenting parties when necessary.

6) Determine production size, content, and budget, establishing details such as production schedules and management policies.

7) Produce shows for special occasions, such as holidays or testimonials.

8) Review film, recordings, or rehearsals to ensure conformance to production and broadcast standards.

9) Plan and coordinate the production of musical recordings, selecting music and directing performers.

10) Hire directors, principal cast members, and key production staff members.

11) Write and submit proposals to bid on contracts for projects.

12) Obtain and distribute costumes, props, music, and studio equipment needed to complete productions.

13) Perform administrative duties such as preparing operational reports, distributing rehearsal call sheets and script copies, and arranging for rehearsal quarters.

14) Obtain rights to scripts, or to such items as existing video footage.

15) Negotiate contracts with artistic personnel, often in accordance with collective bargaining agreements.

16) Arrange financing for productions.

17) Maintain knowledge of minimum wages and working conditions established by unions and/or associations of actors and technicians.

18) Select plays, scripts, books, or ideas to be produced.

19) Develop marketing plans for finished products, collaborating with sales associates to supervise product distribution.

20) Negotiate with parties including independent producers, and the distributors and broadcasters who will be handling completed productions.

21) Edit and write news stories from information collected by reporters.

22) Determine and direct the content of radio programming.

23) Repay investors when completed projects begin to generate revenue.

Knowledge	Knowledge Definitions
English Language	Knowledge of the structure and content of the English language including the meaning and spelling of words, rules of composition, and grammar.
Communications and Media	Knowledge of media production, communication, and dissemination techniques and methods. This includes alternative ways to inform and entertain via written, oral, and visual media.
Administration and Management	Knowledge of business and management principles involved in strategic planning, resource allocation, human resources modeling, leadership technique, production methods, and coordination of people and resources.
Customer and Personal Service	Knowledge of principles and processes for providing customer and personal services. This includes customer needs assessment, meeting quality standards for services, and evaluation of customer satisfaction.
Personnel and Human Resources	Knowledge of principles and procedures for personnel recruitment, selection, training, compensation and benefits, labor relations and negotiation, and personnel information systems.
Sales and Marketing	Knowledge of principles and methods for showing, promoting, and selling products or services. This includes marketing strategy and tactics, product demonstration, sales techniques, and sales control systems.
Psychology	Knowledge of human behavior and performance; individual differences in ability, personality, and interests; learning and motivation; psychological research methods; and the assessment and treatment of behavioral and affective disorders.
Clerical	Knowledge of administrative and clerical procedures and systems such as word processing, managing files and records, stenography and transcription, designing forms, and other office procedures and terminology.
Telecommunications	Knowledge of transmission, broadcasting, switching, control, and operation of telecommunications systems.
Production and Processing	Knowledge of raw materials, production processes, quality control, costs, and other techniques for maximizing the effective manufacture and distribution of goods.
Mathematics	Knowledge of arithmetic, algebra, geometry, calculus, statistics, and their applications.
Fine Arts	Knowledge of the theory and techniques required to compose, produce, and perform works of music, dance, visual arts, drama, and sculpture.
Computers and Electronics	Knowledge of circuit boards, processors, chips, electronic equipment, and computer hardware and software, including applications and programming.
Education and Training	Knowledge of principles and methods for curriculum and training design, teaching and instruction for individuals and groups, and the measurement of training effects.
Economics and Accounting	Knowledge of economic and accounting principles and practices, the financial markets, banking and the analysis and reporting of financial data.
Sociology and Anthropology	Knowledge of group behavior and dynamics, societal trends and influences, human migrations, ethnicity, cultures and their history and origins.
Public Safety and Security	Knowledge of relevant equipment, policies, procedures, and strategies to promote effective local, state, or national security operations for the protection of people, data, property, and institutions.
Transportation	Knowledge of principles and methods for moving people or goods by air, rail, sea, or road, including the relative costs and benefits.
Law and Government	Knowledge of laws, legal codes, court procedures, precedents, government regulations, executive orders, agency rules, and the democratic political process.
Geography	Knowledge of principles and methods for describing the features of land, sea, and air masses, including their physical characteristics, locations, interrelationships, and distribution of plant, animal, and human life.
History and Archeology	Knowledge of historical events and their causes, indicators, and effects on civilizations and cultures.
Engineering and Technology	Knowledge of the practical application of engineering science and technology. This includes applying principles, techniques, procedures, and equipment to the design and production of various goods and services.
Design	Knowledge of design techniques, tools, and principles involved in production of precision technical plans, blueprints, drawings, and models.

Foreign Language	Knowledge of the structure and content of a foreign (non-English) language including the meaning and spelling of words, rules of composition and grammar, and pronunciation.
Philosophy and Theology	Knowledge of different philosophical systems and religions. This includes their basic principles, values, ethics, ways of thinking, customs, practices, and their impact on human culture.
Mechanical	Knowledge of machines and tools, including their designs, uses, repair, and maintenance.
Building and Construction	Knowledge of materials, methods, and the tools involved in the construction or repair of houses, buildings, or other structures such as highways and roads.
Physics	Knowledge and prediction of physical principles, laws, their interrelationships, and applications to understanding fluid, material, and atmospheric dynamics, and mechanical, electrical, atomic and sub- atomic structures and processes.
Therapy and Counseling	Knowledge of principles, methods, and procedures for diagnosis, treatment, and rehabilitation of physical and mental dysfunctions, and for career counseling and guidance.
Medicine and Dentistry	Knowledge of the information and techniques needed to diagnose and treat human injuries, diseases, and deformities. This includes symptoms, treatment alternatives, drug properties and interactions, and preventive health-care measures.
Food Production	Knowledge of techniques and equipment for planting, growing, and harvesting food products (both plant and animal) for consumption, including storage/handling techniques.
Biology	Knowledge of plant and animal organisms, their tissues, cells, functions, interdependencies, and interactions with each other and the environment.
Chemistry	Knowledge of the chemical composition, structure, and properties of substances and of the chemical processes and transformations that they undergo. This includes uses of chemicals and their interactions, danger signs, production techniques, and disposal methods.

Skills	**Skills Definitions**
Active Listening	Giving full attention to what other people are saying, taking time to understand the points being made, asking questions as appropriate, and not interrupting at inappropriate times.
Time Management	Managing one's own time and the time of others.
Reading Comprehension	Understanding written sentences and paragraphs in work related documents.
Writing	Communicating effectively in writing as appropriate for the needs of the audience.
Speaking	Talking to others to convey information effectively.
Judgment and Decision Making	Considering the relative costs and benefits of potential actions to choose the most appropriate one.
Coordination	Adjusting actions in relation to others' actions.
Critical Thinking	Using logic and reasoning to identify the strengths and weaknesses of alternative solutions, conclusions or approaches to problems.
Monitoring	Monitoring/Assessing performance of yourself, other individuals, or organizations to make improvements or take corrective action.
Social Perceptiveness	Being aware of others' reactions and understanding why they react as they do.
Active Learning	Understanding the implications of new information for both current and future problem-solving and decision-making.
Learning Strategies	Selecting and using training/instructional methods and procedures appropriate for the situation when learning or teaching new things.
Instructing	Teaching others how to do something.
Management of Personnel Resources	Motivating, developing, and directing people as they work, identifying the best people for the job.
Persuasion	Persuading others to change their minds or behavior.
Service Orientation	Actively looking for ways to help people.
Equipment Selection	Determining the kind of tools and equipment needed to do a job.
Management of Financial Resources	Determining how money will be spent to get the work done, and accounting for these expenditures.
Negotiation	Bringing others together and trying to reconcile differences.
Complex Problem Solving	Identifying complex problems and reviewing related information to develop and evaluate options and implement solutions.
Management of Material Resources	Obtaining and seeing to the appropriate use of equipment, facilities, and materials needed to do certain work.
Operations Analysis	Analyzing needs and product requirements to create a design.

Troubleshooting	Determining causes of operating errors and deciding what to do about it.
Systems Evaluation	Identifying measures or indicators of system performance and the actions needed to improve or correct performance, relative to the goals of the system.
Mathematics	Using mathematics to solve problems.
Operation and Control	Controlling operations of equipment or systems.
Operation Monitoring	Watching gauges, dials, or other indicators to make sure a machine is working properly.
Installation	Installing equipment, machines, wiring, or programs to meet specifications.
Quality Control Analysis	Conducting tests and inspections of products, services, or processes to evaluate quality or performance.
Technology Design	Generating or adapting equipment and technology to serve user needs.
Systems Analysis	Determining how a system should work and how changes in conditions, operations, and the environment will affect outcomes.
Equipment Maintenance	Performing routine maintenance on equipment and determining when and what kind of maintenance is needed.
Repairing	Repairing machines or systems using the needed tools.
Science	Using scientific rules and methods to solve problems.
Programming	Writing computer programs for various purposes.

Ability	**Ability Definitions**
Problem Sensitivity	The ability to tell when something is wrong or is likely to go wrong. It does not involve solving the problem, only recognizing there is a problem.
Oral Comprehension	The ability to listen to and understand information and ideas presented through spoken words and sentences.
Oral Expression	The ability to communicate information and ideas in speaking so others will understand.
Speech Recognition	The ability to identify and understand the speech of another person.
Written Comprehension	The ability to read and understand information and ideas presented in writing.
Speech Clarity	The ability to speak clearly so others can understand you.
Near Vision	The ability to see details at close range (within a few feet of the observer).
Inductive Reasoning	The ability to combine pieces of information to form general rules or conclusions (includes finding a relationship among seemingly unrelated events).
Deductive Reasoning	The ability to apply general rules to specific problems to produce answers that make sense.
Originality	The ability to come up with unusual or clever ideas about a given topic or situation, or to develop creative ways to solve a problem.
Written Expression	The ability to communicate information and ideas in writing so others will understand.
Fluency of Ideas	The ability to come up with a number of ideas about a topic (the number of ideas is important, not their quality, correctness, or creativity).
Information Ordering	The ability to arrange things or actions in a certain order or pattern according to a specific rule or set of rules (e.g., patterns of numbers, letters, words, pictures, mathematical operations).
Selective Attention	The ability to concentrate on a task over a period of time without being distracted.
Number Facility	The ability to add, subtract, multiply, or divide quickly and correctly.
Far Vision	The ability to see details at a distance.
Time Sharing	The ability to shift back and forth between two or more activities or sources of information (such as speech, sounds, touch, or other sources).
Visualization	The ability to imagine how something will look after it is moved around or when its parts are moved or rearranged.
Hearing Sensitivity	The ability to detect or tell the differences between sounds that vary in pitch and loudness.
Category Flexibility	The ability to generate or use different sets of rules for combining or grouping things in different ways.
Mathematical Reasoning	The ability to choose the right mathematical methods or formulas to solve a problem.
Auditory Attention	The ability to focus on a single source of sound in the presence of other distracting sounds.

Perceptual Speed	The ability to quickly and accurately compare similarities and differences among sets of letters, numbers, objects, pictures, or patterns. The things to be compared may be presented at the same time or one after the other. This ability also includes comparing a presented object with a remembered object.
Speed of Closure	The ability to quickly make sense of, combine, and organize information into meaningful patterns.
Flexibility of Closure	The ability to identify or detect a known pattern (a figure, object, word, or sound) that is hidden in other distracting material.
Visual Color Discrimination	The ability to match or detect differences between colors, including shades of color and brightness.
Memorization	The ability to remember information such as words, numbers, pictures, and procedures.
Depth Perception	The ability to judge which of several objects is closer or farther away from you, or to judge the distance between you and an object.
Finger Dexterity	The ability to make precisely coordinated movements of the fingers of one or both hands to grasp, manipulate, or assemble very small objects.
Arm-Hand Steadiness	The ability to keep your hand and arm steady while moving your arm or while holding your arm and hand in one position.
Control Precision	The ability to quickly and repeatedly adjust the controls of a machine or a vehicle to exact positions.
Trunk Strength	The ability to use your abdominal and lower back muscles to support part of the body repeatedly or continuously over time without 'giving out' or fatiguing.
Glare Sensitivity	The ability to see objects in the presence of glare or bright lighting.
Reaction Time	The ability to quickly respond (with the hand, finger, or foot) to a signal (sound, light, picture) when it appears.
Rate Control	The ability to time your movements or the movement of a piece of equipment in anticipation of changes in the speed and/or direction of a moving object or scene.
Response Orientation	The ability to choose quickly between two or more movements in response to two or more different signals (lights, sounds, pictures). It includes the speed with which the correct response is started with the hand, foot, or other body part.
Multilimb Coordination	The ability to coordinate two or more limbs (for example, two arms, two legs, or one leg and one arm) while sitting, standing, or lying down. It does not involve performing the activities while the whole body is in motion.
Wrist-Finger Speed	The ability to make fast, simple, repeated movements of the fingers, hands, and wrists.
Manual Dexterity	The ability to quickly move your hand, your hand together with your arm, or your two hands to grasp, manipulate, or assemble objects.
Sound Localization	The ability to tell the direction from which a sound originated.
Stamina	The ability to exert yourself physically over long periods of time without getting winded or out of breath.
Explosive Strength	The ability to use short bursts of muscle force to propel oneself (as in jumping or sprinting), or to throw an object.
Static Strength	The ability to exert maximum muscle force to lift, push, pull, or carry objects.
Spatial Orientation	The ability to know your location in relation to the environment or to know where other objects are in relation to you.
Dynamic Strength	The ability to exert muscle force repeatedly or continuously over time. This involves muscular endurance and resistance to muscle fatigue.
Dynamic Flexibility	The ability to quickly and repeatedly bend, stretch, twist, or reach out with your body, arms, and/or legs.
Gross Body Coordination	The ability to coordinate the movement of your arms, legs, and torso together when the whole body is in motion.
Gross Body Equilibrium	The ability to keep or regain your body balance or stay upright when in an unstable position.
Night Vision	The ability to see under low light conditions.
Peripheral Vision	The ability to see objects or movement of objects to one's side when the eyes are looking ahead.
Speed of Limb Movement	The ability to quickly move the arms and legs.
Extent Flexibility	The ability to bend, stretch, twist, or reach with your body, arms, and/or legs.

Work_Activity	Work_Activity Definitions
Getting Information	Observing, receiving, and otherwise obtaining information from all relevant sources.
Establishing and Maintaining Interpersonal Relatio	Developing constructive and cooperative working relationships with others, and maintaining them over time.
Interacting With Computers	Using computers and computer systems (including hardware and software) to program, write software, set up functions, enter data, or process information.
Communicating with Persons Outside Organization	Communicating with people outside the organization, representing the organization to customers, the public, government, and other external sources. This information can be exchanged in person, in writing, or by telephone or e-mail.
Making Decisions and Solving Problems	Analyzing information and evaluating results to choose the best solution and solve problems.
Thinking Creatively	Developing, designing, or creating new applications, ideas, relationships, systems, or products, including artistic contributions.
Communicating with Supervisors, Peers, or Subordin	Providing information to supervisors, co-workers, and subordinates by telephone, in written form, e-mail, or in person.
Identifying Objects, Actions, and Events	Identifying information by categorizing, estimating, recognizing differences or similarities, and detecting changes in circumstances or events.
Updating and Using Relevant Knowledge	Keeping up-to-date technically and applying new knowledge to your job.
Organizing, Planning, and Prioritizing Work	Developing specific goals and plans to prioritize, organize, and accomplish your work.
Scheduling Work and Activities	Scheduling events, programs, and activities, as well as the work of others.
Performing for or Working Directly with the Public	Performing for people or dealing directly with the public. This includes serving customers in restaurants and stores, and receiving clients or guests.
Monitor Processes, Materials, or Surroundings	Monitoring and reviewing information from materials, events, or the environment, to detect or assess problems.
Judging the Qualities of Things, Services, or Peop	Assessing the value, importance, or quality of things or people.
Documenting/Recording Information	Entering, transcribing, recording, storing, or maintaining information in written or electronic/magnetic form.
Resolving Conflicts and Negotiating with Others	Handling complaints, settling disputes, and resolving grievances and conflicts, or otherwise negotiating with others.
Developing and Building Teams	Encouraging and building mutual trust, respect, and cooperation among team members.
Estimating the Quantifiable Characteristics of Pro	Estimating sizes, distances, and quantities; or determining time, costs, resources, or materials needed to perform a work activity.
Coordinating the Work and Activities of Others	Getting members of a group to work together to accomplish tasks.
Guiding, Directing, and Motivating Subordinates	Providing guidance and direction to subordinates, including setting performance standards and monitoring performance.
Selling or Influencing Others	Convincing others to buy merchandise/goods or to otherwise change their minds or actions.
Monitoring and Controlling Resources	Monitoring and controlling resources and overseeing the spending of money.
Interpreting the Meaning of Information for Others	Translating or explaining what information means and how it can be used.
Developing Objectives and Strategies	Establishing long-range objectives and specifying the strategies and actions to achieve them.
Inspecting Equipment, Structures, or Material	Inspecting equipment, structures, or materials to identify the cause of errors or other problems or defects.
Evaluating Information to Determine Compliance wit	Using relevant information and individual judgment to determine whether events or processes comply with laws, regulations, or standards.
Processing Information	Compiling, coding, categorizing, calculating, tabulating, auditing, or verifying information or data.
Analyzing Data or Information	Identifying the underlying principles, reasons, or facts of information by breaking down information or data into separate parts.
Performing Administrative Activities	Performing day-to-day administrative tasks such as maintaining information files and processing paperwork.
Provide Consultation and Advice to Others	Providing guidance and expert advice to management or other groups on technical, systems-, or process-related topics.
Coaching and Developing Others	Identifying the developmental needs of others and coaching, mentoring, or otherwise helping others to improve their knowledge or skills.
Staffing Organizational Units	Recruiting, interviewing, selecting, hiring, and promoting employees in an organization.
Controlling Machines and Processes	Using either control mechanisms or direct physical activity to operate machines or processes (not including computers or vehicles).

Training and Teaching Others	Identifying the educational needs of others, developing formal educational or training programs or classes, and teaching or instructing others.
Assisting and Caring for Others	Providing personal assistance, medical attention, emotional support, or other personal care to others such as coworkers, customers, or patients.
Operating Vehicles, Mechanized Devices, or Equipme	Running, maneuvering, navigating, or driving vehicles or mechanized equipment, such as forklifts, passenger vehicles, aircraft, or water craft.
Performing General Physical Activities	Performing physical activities that require considerable use of your arms and legs and moving your whole body, such as climbing, lifting, balancing, walking, stooping, and handling of materials.
Handling and Moving Objects	Using hands and arms in handling, installing, positioning, and moving materials, and manipulating things.
Repairing and Maintaining Electronic Equipment	Servicing, repairing, calibrating, regulating, fine-tuning, or testing machines, devices, and equipment that operate primarily on the basis of electrical or electronic (not mechanical) principles.
Drafting, Laying Out, and Specifying Technical Dev	Providing documentation, detailed instructions, drawings, or specifications to tell others about how devices, parts, equipment, or structures are to be fabricated, constructed, assembled, modified, maintained, or used.
Repairing and Maintaining Mechanical Equipment	Servicing, repairing, adjusting, and testing machines, devices, moving parts, and equipment that operate primarily on the basis of mechanical (not electronic) principles.

Work_Context	Work_Context Definitions
Telephone	How often do you have telephone conversations in this job?
Electronic Mail	How often do you use electronic mail in this job?
Work With Work Group or Team	How important is it to work with others in a group or team in this job?
Face-to-Face Discussions	How often do you have to have face-to-face discussions with individuals or teams in this job?
Importance of Being Exact or Accurate	How important is being very exact or highly accurate in performing this job?
Impact of Decisions on Co-workers or Company Resul	How do the decisions an employee makes impact the results of co-workers, clients or the company?
Structured versus Unstructured Work	To what extent is this job structured for the worker, rather than allowing the worker to determine tasks, priorities, and goals?
Time Pressure	How often does this job require the worker to meet strict deadlines?
Freedom to Make Decisions	How much decision making freedom, without supervision, does the job offer?
Responsibility for Outcomes and Results	How responsible is the worker for work outcomes and results of other workers?
Frequency of Decision Making	How frequently is the worker required to make decisions that affect other people, the financial resources, and/or the image and reputation of the organization?
Coordinate or Lead Others	How important is it to coordinate or lead others in accomplishing work activities in this job?
Indoors, Environmentally Controlled	How often does this job require working indoors in environmentally controlled conditions?
Contact With Others	How much does this job require the worker to be in contact with others (face-to-face, by telephone, or otherwise) in order to perform it?
Level of Competition	To what extent does this job require the worker to compete or to be aware of competitive pressures?
Deal With External Customers	How important is it to work with external customers or the public in this job?
Spend Time Sitting	How much does this job require sitting?
Consequence of Error	How serious would the result usually be if the worker made a mistake that was not readily correctable?
Importance of Repeating Same Tasks	How important is repeating the same physical activities (e.g., key entry) or mental activities (e.g., checking entries in a ledger) over and over, without stopping, to performing this job?
Letters and Memos	How often does the job require written letters and memos?
Physical Proximity	To what extent does this job require the worker to perform job tasks in close physical proximity to other people?
Frequency of Conflict Situations	How often are there conflict situations the employee has to face in this job?
In an Enclosed Vehicle or Equipment	How often does this job require working in a closed vehicle or equipment (e.g., car)?
Spend Time Using Your Hands to Handle, Control, or	How much does this job require using your hands to handle, control, or feel objects, tools or controls?

Deal With Unpleasant or Angry People	How frequently does the worker have to deal with unpleasant, angry, or discourteous individuals as part of the job requirements?
Responsible for Others' Health and Safety	How much responsibility is there for the health and safety of others in this job?
Sounds, Noise Levels Are Distracting or Uncomforta	How often does this job require working exposed to sounds and noise levels that are distracting or uncomfortable?
Outdoors, Exposed to Weather	How often does this job require working outdoors, exposed to all weather conditions?
Extremely Bright or Inadequate Lighting	How often does this job require working in extremely bright or inadequate lighting conditions?
Spend Time Making Repetitive Motions	How much does this job require making repetitive motions?
Spend Time Standing	How much does this job require standing?
Public Speaking	How often do you have to perform public speaking in this job?
Spend Time Walking and Running	How much does this job require walking and running?
Indoors, Not Environmentally Controlled	How often does this job require working indoors in non-controlled environmental conditions (e.g., warehouse without heat)?
Very Hot or Cold Temperatures	How often does this job require working in very hot (above 90 F degrees) or very cold (below 32 F degrees) temperatures?
Exposed to Contaminants	How often does this job require working exposed to contaminants (such as pollutants, gases, dust or odors)?
Outdoors, Under Cover	How often does this job require working outdoors, under cover (e.g., structure with roof but no walls)?
Pace Determined by Speed of Equipment	How important is it to this job that the pace is determined by the speed of equipment or machinery? (This does not refer to keeping busy at all times on this job.)
Cramped Work Space, Awkward Positions	How often does this job require working in cramped work spaces that requires getting into awkward positions?
Degree of Automation	How automated is the job?
Spend Time Bending or Twisting the Body	How much does this job require bending or twisting your body?
Deal With Physically Aggressive People	How frequently does this job require the worker to deal with physical aggression of violent individuals?
Exposed to Hazardous Equipment	How often does this job require exposure to hazardous equipment?
Spend Time Kneeling, Crouching, Stooping, or Crawl	How much does this job require kneeling, crouching, stooping or crawling?
Exposed to High Places	How often does this job require exposure to high places?
Exposed to Minor Burns, Cuts, Bites, or Stings	How often does this job require exposure to minor burns, cuts, bites, or stings?
Spend Time Climbing Ladders, Scaffolds, or Poles	How much does this job require climbing ladders, scaffolds, or poles?
Spend Time Keeping or Regaining Balance	How much does this job require keeping or regaining your balance?
Exposed to Hazardous Conditions	How often does this job require exposure to hazardous conditions?
Wear Common Protective or Safety Equipment such as	How much does this job require wearing common protective or safety equipment such as safety shoes, glasses, gloves, hard hats or live jackets?
Exposed to Disease or Infections	How often does this job require exposure to disease/infections?
In an Open Vehicle or Equipment	How often does this job require working in an open vehicle or equipment (e.g., tractor)?
Wear Specialized Protective or Safety Equipment su	How much does this job require wearing specialized protective or safety equipment such as breathing apparatus, safety harness, full protection suits, or radiation protection?
Exposed to Whole Body Vibration	How often does this job require exposure to whole body vibration (e.g., operate a jackhammer)?
Exposed to Radiation	How often does this job require exposure to radiation?

Job Zone Component	Job Zone Component Definitions
Title	Job Zone Four: Considerable Preparation Needed
Overall Experience	A minimum of two to four years of work-related skill, knowledge, or experience is needed for these occupations. For example, an accountant must complete four years of college and work for several years in accounting to be considered qualified.
Job Training	Employees in these occupations usually need several years of work-related experience, on-the-job training, and/or vocational training.

	Many of these occupations involve coordinating, supervising, managing, or training others. Examples include accountants, chefs and head cooks, computer programmers, historians, pharmacists, and police detectives.
Job Zone Examples	
SVP Range	(7.0 to < 8.0)
Education	Most of these occupations require a four - year bachelor's degree, but some do not.

Work_Styles	Work_Styles Definitions
Attention to Detail	Job requires being careful about detail and thorough in completing work tasks.
Persistence	Job requires persistence in the face of obstacles.
Adaptability/Flexibility	Job requires being open to change (positive or negative) and to considerable variety in the workplace.
Dependability	Job requires being reliable, responsible, and dependable, and fulfilling obligations.
Stress Tolerance	Job requires accepting criticism and dealing calmly and effectively with high stress situations.
Initiative	Job requires a willingness to take on responsibilities and challenges.
Integrity	Job requires being honest and ethical.
Leadership	Job requires a willingness to lead, take charge, and offer opinions and direction.
Achievement/Effort	Job requires establishing and maintaining personally challenging achievement goals and exerting effort toward mastering tasks.
Self Control	Job requires maintaining composure, keeping emotions in check, controlling anger, and avoiding aggressive behavior, even in very difficult situations.
Independence	Job requires developing one's own ways of doing things, guiding oneself with little or no supervision, and depending on oneself to get things done.
Cooperation	Job requires being pleasant with others on the job and displaying a good-natured, cooperative attitude.
Social Orientation	Job requires preferring to work with others rather than alone, and being personally connected with others on the job.
Analytical Thinking	Job requires analyzing information and using logic to address work-related issues and problems.
Innovation	Job requires creativity and alternative thinking to develop new ideas for and answers to work-related problems.
Concern for Others	Job requires being sensitive to others' needs and feelings and being understanding and helpful on the job.

27-2012.02 - Directors- Stage, Motion Pictures, Television, and Radio

Interpret script, conduct rehearsals, and direct activities of cast and technical crew for stage, motion pictures, television, or radio programs.

Tasks

1) Plan details such as framing, composition, camera movement, sound, and actor movement for each shot or scene.

2) Confer with technical directors, managers, crew members, and writers to discuss details of production, such as photography, script, music, sets, and costumes.

3) Cut and edit film or tape in order to integrate component parts into desired sequences.

4) Study and research scripts in order to determine how they should be directed.

5) Direct live broadcasts, films and recordings, or non-broadcast programming for public entertainment or education.

6) Identify and approve equipment and elements required for productions, such as scenery, lights, props, costumes, choreography, and music.

7) Collaborate with film and sound editors during the post-production process as films are edited and soundtracks are added.

8) Choose settings and locations for films and determine how scenes will be shot in these settings.

9) Communicate to actors the approach, characterization, and movement needed for each scene in such a way that rehearsals and takes are minimized.

10) Compile scripts, program notes, and other material related to productions.

11) Establish pace of programs and sequences of scenes according to time requirements and cast and set accessibility.

12) Interpret stage-set diagrams to determine stage layouts, and supervise placement of equipment and scenery.

13) Review film daily in order to check on work in progress and to plan for future filming.

14) Consult with writers, producers, and/or actors about script changes, or workshop scripts, through rehearsal with writers and actors to create final drafts.

15) Collaborate with producers in order to hire crewmembers such as art directors, cinematographers, and costumer designers.

16) Confer with stage managers in order to arrange schedules for rehearsals, costume fittings, and sound/light development.

17) Perform producers' duties such as securing financial backing, establishing and administering budgets, and recruiting cast and crew.

18) Create and approve storyboards in conjunction with art directors.

19) Hold auditions for parts and/or negotiate contracts with actors determined suitable for specific roles, working in conjunction with producers.

20) Select plays or scripts for production, and determine how material should be interpreted and performed.

21) Compile cue words and phrases, and cue announcers, cast members, and technicians during performances.

22) Promote and market productions by giving interviews, participating in talk shows, and making other public appearances.

23) Introduce plays, and meet with audiences after shows in order to explain how the play was interpreted.

Knowledge	Knowledge Definitions
Communications and Media	Knowledge of media production, communication, and dissemination techniques and methods. This includes alternative ways to inform and entertain via written, oral, and visual media.
Telecommunications	Knowledge of transmission, broadcasting, switching, control, and operation of telecommunications systems.
Computers and Electronics	Knowledge of circuit boards, processors, chips, electronic equipment, and computer hardware and software, including applications and programming.
Administration and Management	Knowledge of business and management principles involved in strategic planning, resource allocation, human resources modeling, leadership technique, production methods, and coordination of people and resources.
English Language	Knowledge of the structure and content of the English language including the meaning and spelling of words, rules of composition, and grammar.
Education and Training	Knowledge of principles and methods for curriculum and training design, teaching and instruction for individuals and groups, and the measurement of training effects.
Mathematics	Knowledge of arithmetic, algebra, geometry, calculus, statistics, and their applications.
Engineering and Technology	Knowledge of the practical application of engineering science and technology. This includes applying principles, techniques, procedures, and equipment to the design and production of various goods and services.
Clerical	Knowledge of administrative and clerical procedures and systems such as word processing, managing files and records, stenography and transcription, designing forms, and other office procedures and terminology.
Law and Government	Knowledge of laws, legal codes, court procedures, precedents, government regulations, executive orders, agency rules, and the democratic political process.
Geography	Knowledge of principles and methods for describing the features of land, sea, and air masses, including their physical characteristics, locations, interrelationships, and distribution of plant, animal, and human life.
Production and Processing	Knowledge of raw materials, production processes, quality control, costs, and other techniques for maximizing the effective manufacture and distribution of goods.
Fine Arts	Knowledge of the theory and techniques required to compose, produce, and perform works of music, dance, visual arts, drama, and sculpture.
Personnel and Human Resources	Knowledge of principles and procedures for personnel recruitment, selection, training, compensation and benefits, labor relations and negotiation, and personnel information systems.

Customer and Personal Service	Knowledge of principles and processes for providing customer and personal services. This includes customer needs assessment, meeting quality standards for services, and evaluation of customer satisfaction.
Psychology	Knowledge of human behavior and performance; individual differences in ability, personality, and interests; learning and motivation; psychological research methods; and the assessment and treatment of behavioral and affective disorders.
Public Safety and Security	Knowledge of relevant equipment, policies, procedures, and strategies to promote effective local, state, or national security operations for the protection of people, data, property, and institutions.
Sales and Marketing	Knowledge of principles and methods for showing, promoting, and selling products or services. This includes marketing strategy and tactics, product demonstration, sales techniques, and sales control systems.
Design	Knowledge of design techniques, tools, and principles involved in production of precision technical plans, blueprints, drawings, and models.
Mechanical	Knowledge of machines and tools, including their designs, uses, repair, and maintenance.
History and Archeology	Knowledge of historical events and their causes, indicators, and effects on civilizations and cultures.
Economics and Accounting	Knowledge of economic and accounting principles and practices, the financial markets, banking and the analysis and reporting of financial data.
Philosophy and Theology	Knowledge of different philosophical systems and religions. This includes their basic principles, values, ethics, ways of thinking, customs, practices, and their impact on human culture.
Transportation	Knowledge of principles and methods for moving people or goods by air, rail, sea, or road, including the relative costs and benefits.
Sociology and Anthropology	Knowledge of group behavior and dynamics, societal trends and influences, human migrations, ethnicity, cultures and their history and origins.
Therapy and Counseling	Knowledge of principles, methods, and procedures for diagnosis, treatment, and rehabilitation of physical and mental dysfunctions, and for career counseling and guidance.
Foreign Language	Knowledge of the structure and content of a foreign (non-English) language including the meaning and spelling of words, rules of composition and grammar, and pronunciation.
Building and Construction	Knowledge of materials, methods, and the tools involved in the construction or repair of houses, buildings, or other structures such as highways and roads.
Physics	Knowledge and prediction of physical principles, laws, their interrelationships, and applications to understanding fluid, material, and atmospheric dynamics, and mechanical, electrical, atomic and sub- atomic structures and processes.
Biology	Knowledge of plant and animal organisms, their tissues, cells, functions, interdependencies, and interactions with each other and the environment.
Chemistry	Knowledge of the chemical composition, structure, and properties of substances and of the chemical processes and transformations that they undergo. This includes uses of chemicals and their interactions, danger signs, production techniques, and disposal methods.
Medicine and Dentistry	Knowledge of the information and techniques needed to diagnose and treat human injuries, diseases, and deformities. This includes symptoms, treatment alternatives, drug properties and interactions, and preventive health-care measures.
Food Production	Knowledge of techniques and equipment for planting, growing, and harvesting food products (both plant and animal) for consumption, including storage/handling techniques.

Skills	Skills Definitions
Reading Comprehension	Understanding written sentences and paragraphs in work related documents.
Active Listening	Giving full attention to what other people are saying, taking time to understand the points being made, asking questions as appropriate, and not interrupting at inappropriate times.
Judgment and Decision Making	Considering the relative costs and benefits of potential actions to choose the most appropriate one.
Critical Thinking	Using logic and reasoning to identify the strengths and weaknesses of alternative solutions, conclusions or approaches to problems.
Time Management	Managing one's own time and the time of others.

Speaking	Talking to others to convey information effectively.
Management of Personnel Resources	Motivating, developing, and directing people as they work, identifying the best people for the job.
Writing	Communicating effectively in writing as appropriate for the needs of the audience.
Active Learning	Understanding the implications of new information for both current and future problem-solving and decision-making.
Equipment Selection	Determining the kind of tools and equipment needed to do a job.
Coordination	Adjusting actions in relation to others' actions.
Operations Analysis	Analyzing needs and product requirements to create a design.
Social Perceptiveness	Being aware of others' reactions and understanding why they react as they do.
Troubleshooting	Determining causes of operating errors and deciding what to do about it.
Monitoring	Monitoring/Assessing performance of yourself, other individuals, or organizations to make improvements or take corrective action.
Persuasion	Persuading others to change their minds or behavior.
Negotiation	Bringing others together and trying to reconcile differences.
Complex Problem Solving	Identifying complex problems and reviewing related information to develop and evaluate options and implement solutions.
Management of Financial Resources	Determining how money will be spent to get the work done, and accounting for these expenditures.
Learning Strategies	Selecting and using training/instructional methods and procedures appropriate for the situation when learning or teaching new things.
Service Orientation	Actively looking for ways to help people.
Instructing	Teaching others how to do something.
Technology Design	Generating or adapting equipment and technology to serve user needs.
Management of Material Resources	Obtaining and seeing to the appropriate use of equipment, facilities, and materials needed to do certain work.
Systems Analysis	Determining how a system should work and how changes in conditions, operations, and the environment will affect outcomes.
Operation and Control	Controlling operations of equipment or systems.
Mathematics	Using mathematics to solve problems.
Systems Evaluation	Identifying measures or indicators of system performance and the actions needed to improve or correct performance, relative to the goals of the system.
Quality Control Analysis	Conducting tests and inspections of products, services, or processes to evaluate quality or performance.
Operation Monitoring	Watching gauges, dials, or other indicators to make sure a machine is working properly.
Equipment Maintenance	Performing routine maintenance on equipment and determining when and what kind of maintenance is needed.
Science	Using scientific rules and methods to solve problems.
Programming	Writing computer programs for various purposes.
Installation	Installing equipment, machines, wiring, or programs to meet specifications.
Repairing	Repairing machines or systems using the needed tools.

Ability	Ability Definitions
Oral Comprehension	The ability to listen to and understand information and ideas presented through spoken words and sentences.
Oral Expression	The ability to communicate information and ideas in speaking so others will understand.
Originality	The ability to come up with unusual or clever ideas about a given topic or situation, or to develop creative ways to solve a problem.
Speech Recognition	The ability to identify and understand the speech of another person.
Written Comprehension	The ability to read and understand information and ideas presented in writing.
Speech Clarity	The ability to speak clearly so others can understand you.
Problem Sensitivity	The ability to tell when something is wrong or is likely to go wrong. It does not involve solving the problem, only recognizing there is a problem.
Inductive Reasoning	The ability to combine pieces of information to form general rules or conclusions (includes finding a relationship among seemingly unrelated events).
Written Expression	The ability to communicate information and ideas in writing so others will understand.

Fluency of Ideas	The ability to come up with a number of ideas about a topic (the number of ideas is important, not their quality, correctness, or creativity).
Deductive Reasoning	The ability to apply general rules to specific problems to produce answers that make sense.
Far Vision	The ability to see details at a distance.
Near Vision	The ability to see details at close range (within a few feet of the observer).
Information Ordering	The ability to arrange things or actions in a certain order or pattern according to a specific rule or set of rules (e.g., patterns of numbers, letters, words, pictures, mathematical operations).
Visualization	The ability to imagine how something will look after it is moved around or when its parts are moved or rearranged.
Category Flexibility	The ability to generate or use different sets of rules for combining or grouping things in different ways.
Time Sharing	The ability to shift back and forth between two or more activities or sources of information (such as speech, sounds, touch, or other sources).
Number Facility	The ability to add, subtract, multiply, or divide quickly and correctly.
Selective Attention	The ability to concentrate on a task over a period of time without being distracted.
Mathematical Reasoning	The ability to choose the right mathematical methods or formulas to solve a problem.
Visual Color Discrimination	The ability to match or detect differences between colors, including shades of color and brightness.
Hearing Sensitivity	The ability to detect or tell the differences between sounds that vary in pitch and loudness.
Speed of Closure	The ability to quickly make sense of, combine, and organize information into meaningful patterns.
Flexibility of Closure	The ability to identify or detect a known pattern (a figure, object, word, or sound) that is hidden in other distracting material.
Memorization	The ability to remember information such as words, numbers, pictures, and procedures.
Depth Perception	The ability to judge which of several objects is closer or farther away from you, or to judge the distance between you and an object.
Auditory Attention	The ability to focus on a single source of sound in the presence of other distracting sounds.
Perceptual Speed	The ability to quickly and accurately compare similarities and differences among sets of letters, numbers, objects, pictures, or patterns. The things to be compared may be presented at the same time or one after the other. This ability also includes comparing a presented object with a remembered object.
Arm-Hand Steadiness	The ability to keep your hand and arm steady while moving your arm or while holding your arm and hand in one position.
Finger Dexterity	The ability to make precisely coordinated movements of the fingers of one or both hands to grasp, manipulate, or assemble very small objects.
Reaction Time	The ability to quickly respond (with the hand, finger, or foot) to a signal (sound, light, picture) when it appears.
Control Precision	The ability to quickly and repeatedly adjust the controls of a machine or a vehicle to exact positions.
Rate Control	The ability to time your movements or the movement of a piece of equipment in anticipation of changes in the speed and/or direction of a moving object or scene.
Manual Dexterity	The ability to quickly move your hand, your hand together with your arm, or your two hands to grasp, manipulate, or assemble objects.
Multilimb Coordination	The ability to coordinate two or more limbs (for example, two arms, two legs, or one leg and one arm) while sitting, standing, or lying down. It does not involve performing the activities while the whole body is in motion.
Response Orientation	The ability to choose quickly between two or more movements in response to two or more different signals (lights, sounds, pictures). It includes the speed with which the correct response is started with the hand, foot, or other body part.
Trunk Strength	The ability to use your abdominal and lower back muscles to support part of the body repeatedly or continuously over time without 'giving out' or fatiguing.
Wrist-Finger Speed	The ability to make fast, simple, repeated movements of the fingers, hands, and wrists.
Static Strength	The ability to exert maximum muscle force to lift, push, pull, or carry objects.
Stamina	The ability to exert yourself physically over long periods of time without getting winded or out of breath.

Extent Flexibility	The ability to bend, stretch, twist, or reach with your body, arms, and/or legs.
Gross Body Coordination	The ability to coordinate the movement of your arms, legs, and torso together when the whole body is in motion.
Gross Body Equilibrium	The ability to keep or regain your body balance or stay upright when in an unstable position.
Dynamic Strength	The ability to exert muscle force repeatedly or continuously over time. This involves muscular endurance and resistance to muscle fatigue.
Spatial Orientation	The ability to know your location in relation to the environment or to know where other objects are in relation to you.
Sound Localization	The ability to tell the direction from which a sound originated.
Peripheral Vision	The ability to see objects or movement of objects to one's side when the eyes are looking ahead.
Night Vision	The ability to see under low light conditions.
Glare Sensitivity	The ability to see objects in the presence of glare or bright lighting.
Speed of Limb Movement	The ability to quickly move the arms and legs.
Explosive Strength	The ability to use short bursts of muscle force to propel oneself (as in jumping or sprinting), or to throw an object.
Dynamic Flexibility	The ability to quickly and repeatedly bend, stretch, twist, or reach out with your body, arms, and/or legs.

Work_Activity	Work_Activity Definitions
Making Decisions and Solving Problems	Analyzing information and evaluating results to choose the best solution and solve problems.
Thinking Creatively	Developing, designing, or creating new applications, ideas, relationships, systems, or products, including artistic contributions.
Establishing and Maintaining Interpersonal Relatio	Developing constructive and cooperative working relationships with others, and maintaining them over time.
Getting Information	Observing, receiving, and otherwise obtaining information from all relevant sources.
Identifying Objects, Actions, and Events	Identifying information by categorizing, estimating, recognizing differences or similarities, and detecting changes in circumstances or events.
Monitor Processes, Materials, or Surroundings	Monitoring and reviewing information from materials, events, or the environment, to detect or assess problems.
Interacting With Computers	Using computers and computer systems (including hardware and software) to program, write software, set up functions, enter data, or process information.
Developing and Building Teams	Encouraging and building mutual trust, respect, and cooperation among team members.
Communicating with Supervisors, Peers, or Subordin	Providing information to supervisors, co-workers, and subordinates by telephone, in written form, e-mail, or in person.
Organizing, Planning, and Prioritizing Work	Developing specific goals and plans to prioritize, organize, and accomplish your work.
Processing Information	Compiling, coding, categorizing, calculating, tabulating, auditing, or verifying information or data.
Communicating with Persons Outside Organization	Communicating with people outside the organization, representing the organization to customers, the public, government, and other external sources. This information can be exchanged in person, in writing, or by telephone or e-mail.
Coordinating the Work and Activities of Others	Getting members of a group to work together to accomplish tasks.
Estimating the Quantifiable Characteristics of Pro	Estimating sizes, distances, and quantities; or determining time, costs, resources, or materials needed to perform a work activity.
Judging the Qualities of Things, Services, or Peop	Assessing the value, importance, or quality of things or people.
Scheduling Work and Activities	Scheduling events, programs, and activities, as well as the work of others.
Guiding, Directing, and Motivating Subordinates	Providing guidance and direction to subordinates, including setting performance standards and monitoring performance.
Updating and Using Relevant Knowledge	Keeping up-to-date technically and applying new knowledge to your job.
Training and Teaching Others	Identifying the educational needs of others, developing formal educational or training programs or classes, and teaching or instructing others.
Documenting/Recording Information	Entering, transcribing, recording, storing, or maintaining information in written or electronic/magnetic form.
Developing Objectives and Strategies	Establishing long-range objectives and specifying the strategies and actions to achieve them.

Analyzing Data or Information	Identifying the underlying principles, reasons, or facts of information by breaking down information or data into separate parts.
Interpreting the Meaning of Information for Others	Translating or explaining what information means and how it can be used.
Resolving Conflicts and Negotiating with Others	Handling complaints, settling disputes, and resolving grievances and conflicts, or otherwise negotiating with others.
Coaching and Developing Others	Identifying the developmental needs of others and coaching, mentoring, or otherwise helping others to improve their knowledge or skills.
Provide Consultation and Advice to Others	Providing guidance and expert advice to management or other groups on technical, systems-, or process-related topics.
Controlling Machines and Processes	Using either control mechanisms or direct physical activity to operate machines or processes (not including computers or vehicles).
Monitoring and Controlling Resources	Monitoring and controlling resources and overseeing the spending of money.
Selling or Influencing Others	Convincing others to buy merchandise/goods or to otherwise change their minds or actions.
Evaluating Information to Determine Compliance wit	Using relevant information and individual judgment to determine whether events or processes comply with laws, regulations, or standards.
Staffing Organizational Units	Recruiting, interviewing, selecting, hiring, and promoting employees in an organization.
Performing General Physical Activities	Performing physical activities that require considerable use of your arms and legs and moving your whole body, such as climbing, lifting, balancing, walking, stooping, and handling of materials.
Inspecting Equipment, Structures, or Material	Inspecting equipment, structures, or materials to identify the cause of errors or other problems or defects.
Drafting, Laying Out, and Specifying Technical Dev	Providing documentation, detailed instructions, drawings, or specifications to tell others about how devices, parts, equipment, or structures are to be fabricated, constructed, assembled, modified, maintained, or used.
Performing Administrative Activities	Performing day-to-day administrative tasks such as maintaining information files and processing paperwork.
Handling and Moving Objects	Using hands and arms in handling, installing, positioning, and moving materials, and manipulating things.
Performing for or Working Directly with the Public	Performing for people or dealing directly with the public. This includes serving customers in restaurants and stores, and receiving clients or guests.
Assisting and Caring for Others	Providing personal assistance, medical attention, emotional support, or other personal care to others such as coworkers, customers, or patients.
Operating Vehicles, Mechanized Devices, or Equipme	Running, maneuvering, navigating, or driving vehicles or mechanized equipment, such as forklifts, passenger vehicles, aircraft, or water craft.
Repairing and Maintaining Electronic Equipment	Servicing, repairing, calibrating, regulating, fine-tuning, or testing machines, devices, and equipment that operate primarily on the basis of electrical or electronic (not mechanical) principles.
Repairing and Maintaining Mechanical Equipment	Servicing, repairing, adjusting, and testing machines, devices, moving parts, and equipment that operate primarily on the basis of mechanical (not electronic) principles.

Work_Context   Work_Context Definitions

Face-to-Face Discussions	How often do you have to have face-to-face discussions with individuals or teams in this job?
Indoors, Environmentally Controlled	How often does this job require working indoors in environmentally controlled conditions?
Electronic Mail	How often do you use electronic mail in this job?
Contact With Others	How much does this job require the worker to be in contact with others (face-to-face, by telephone, or otherwise) in order to perform it?
Work With Work Group or Team	How important is it to work with others in a group or team in this job?
Importance of Being Exact or Accurate	How important is being very exact or highly accurate in performing this job?
Telephone	How often do you have telephone conversations in this job?
Coordinate or Lead Others	How important is it to coordinate or lead others in accomplishing work activities in this job?
Time Pressure	How often does this job require the worker to meet strict deadlines?
Freedom to Make Decisions	How much decision making freedom, without supervision, does the job offer?
Responsibility for Outcomes and Results	How responsible is the worker for work outcomes and results of other workers?

Structured versus Unstructured Work	To what extent is this job structured for the worker, rather than allowing the worker to determine tasks, priorities, and goals?
Frequency of Decision Making	How frequently is the worker required to make decisions that affect other people, the financial resources, and/or the image and reputation of the organization?
Impact of Decisions on Co-workers or Company Resul	How do the decisions an employee makes impact the results of co-workers, clients or the company?
Spend Time Using Your Hands to Handle, Control, or	How much does this job require using your hands to handle, control, or feel objects, tools or controls?
Letters and Memos	How often does the job require written letters and memos?
Level of Competition	To what extent does this job require the worker to compete or to be aware of competitive pressures?
Physical Proximity	To what extent does this job require the worker to perform job tasks in close physical proximity to other people?
Deal With External Customers	How important is it to work with external customers or the public in this job?
Spend Time Sitting	How much does this job require sitting?
Frequency of Conflict Situations	How often are there conflict situations the employee has to face in this job?
Responsible for Others' Health and Safety	How much responsibility is there for the health and safety of others in this job?
Sounds, Noise Levels Are Distracting or Uncomforta	How often does this job require working exposed to sounds and noise levels that are distracting or uncomfortable?
In an Enclosed Vehicle or Equipment	How often does this job require working in a closed vehicle or equipment (e.g., car)?
Consequence of Error	How serious would the result usually be if the worker made a mistake that was not readily correctable?
Outdoors, Exposed to Weather	How often does this job require working outdoors, exposed to all weather conditions?
Deal With Unpleasant or Angry People	How frequently does the worker have to deal with unpleasant, angry, or discourteous individuals as part of the job requirements?
Spend Time Making Repetitive Motions	How much does this job require making repetitive motions?
Importance of Repeating Same Tasks	How important is repeating the same physical activities (e.g., key entry) or mental activities (e.g., checking entries in a ledger) over and over, without stopping, to performing this job?
Indoors, Not Environmentally Controlled	How often does this job require working indoors in non-controlled environmental conditions (e.g., warehouse without heat)?
Degree of Automation	How automated is the job?
Spend Time Standing	How much does this job require standing?
Outdoors, Under Cover	How often does this job require working outdoors, under cover (e.g., structure with roof but no walls)?
Very Hot or Cold Temperatures	How often does this job require working in very hot (above 90 F degrees) or very cold (below 32 F degrees) temperatures?
Public Speaking	How often do you have to perform public speaking in this job?
Extremely Bright or Inadequate Lighting	How often does this job require working in extremely bright or inadequate lighting conditions?
Exposed to High Places	How often does this job require exposure to high places?
Spend Time Walking and Running	How much does this job require walking and running?
Exposed to Hazardous Conditions	How often does this job require exposure to hazardous conditions?
Spend Time Climbing Ladders, Scaffolds, or Poles	How much does this job require climbing ladders, scaffolds, or poles?
Pace Determined by Speed of Equipment	How important is it to this job that the pace is determined by the speed of equipment or machinery? (This does not refer to keeping busy at all times on this job.)
Spend Time Bending or Twisting the Body	How much does this job require bending or twisting your body?
Cramped Work Space, Awkward Positions	How often does this job require working in cramped work spaces that requires getting into awkward positions?
Exposed to Hazardous Equipment	How often does this job require exposure to hazardous equipment?
Spend Time Kneeling, Crouching, Stooping, or Crawl	How much does this job require kneeling, crouching, stooping or crawling?
Exposed to Minor Burns, Cuts, Bites, or Stings	How often does this job require exposure to minor burns, cuts, bites, or stings?
Spend Time Keeping or Regaining Balance	How much does this job require keeping or regaining your balance?
Exposed to Contaminants	How often does this job require working exposed to contaminants (such as pollutants, gases, dust or odors)?

Deal With Physically Aggressive People	How frequently does this job require the worker to deal with physical aggression of violent individuals?
In an Open Vehicle or Equipment	How often does this job require working in an open vehicle or equipment (e.g., tractor)?
Wear Common Protective or Safety Equipment such as	How much does this job require wearing common protective or safety equipment such as safety shoes, glasses, gloves, hard hats or live jackets?
Exposed to Radiation	How often does this job require exposure to radiation?
Wear Specialized Protective or Safety Equipment su	How much does this job require wearing specialized protective or safety equipment such as breathing apparatus, safety harness, full protection suits, or radiation protection?
Exposed to Whole Body Vibration	How often does this job require exposure to whole body vibration (e.g., operate a jackhammer)?
Exposed to Disease or Infections	How often does this job require exposure to disease/infections?

Job Zone Component	Job Zone Component Definitions
Title	Job Zone Four: Considerable Preparation Needed
Overall Experience	A minimum of two to four years of work-related skill, knowledge, or experience is needed for these occupations. For example, an accountant must complete four years of college and work for several years in accounting to be considered qualified.
Job Training	Employees in these occupations usually need several years of work-related experience, on-the-job training, and/or vocational training.
Job Zone Examples	Many of these occupations involve coordinating, supervising, managing, or training others. Examples include accountants, chefs and head cooks, computer programmers, historians, pharmacists, and police detectives.
SVP Range	(7.0 to < 8.0)
Education	Most of these occupations require a four - year bachelor's degree, but some do not.

Work_Styles	Work_Styles Definitions
Stress Tolerance	Job requires accepting criticism and dealing calmly and effectively with high stress situations.
Attention to Detail	Job requires being careful about detail and thorough in completing work tasks.
Dependability	Job requires being reliable, responsible, and dependable, and fulfilling obligations.
Leadership	Job requires a willingness to lead, take charge, and offer opinions and direction.
Achievement/Effort	Job requires establishing and maintaining personally challenging achievement goals and exerting effort toward mastering tasks.
Adaptability/Flexibility	Job requires being open to change (positive or negative) and to considerable variety in the workplace.
Cooperation	Job requires being pleasant with others on the job and displaying a good-natured, cooperative attitude.
Initiative	Job requires a willingness to take on responsibilities and challenges.
Persistence	Job requires persistence in the face of obstacles.
Self Control	Job requires maintaining composure, keeping emotions in check, controlling anger, and avoiding aggressive behavior, even in very difficult situations.
Concern for Others	Job requires being sensitive to others' needs and feelings and being understanding and helpful on the job.
Social Orientation	Job requires preferring to work with others rather than alone, and being personally connected with others on the job.
Innovation	Job requires creativity and alternative thinking to develop new ideas for and answers to work-related problems.
Integrity	Job requires being honest and ethical.
Analytical Thinking	Job requires analyzing information and using logic to address work-related issues and problems.
Independence	Job requires developing one's own ways of doing things, guiding oneself with little or no supervision, and depending on oneself to get things done.

27-2012.03 - Program Directors

Direct and coordinate activities of personnel engaged in preparation of radio or television

station program schedules and programs, such as sports or news.

Tasks

1) Coordinate activities between departments, such as news and programming.

2) Confer with directors and production staff to discuss issues such as production and casting problems, budgets, policies, and news coverage.

3) Prepare copy and edit tape so that material is ready for broadcasting.

4) Check completed program logs for accuracy and conformance with FCC rules and regulations, and resolve program log inaccuracies.

5) Monitor and review programming in order to ensure that schedules are met, guidelines are adhered to, and performances are of adequate quality.

6) Direct and coordinate activities of personnel engaged in broadcast news, sports, or programming.

7) Develop promotions for current programs and specials.

8) Evaluate new and existing programming for suitability and in order to assess the need for changes, using information such as audience surveys and feedback.

9) Perform personnel duties such as hiring staff and evaluating work performance.

10) Cue announcers, actors, performers, and guests.

11) Conduct interviews for broadcasts.

12) Select, acquire, and maintain programs, music, films, and other needed materials, and obtain legal clearances for their use as necessary.

13) Review information about programs and schedules in order to ensure accuracy and provide such information to local media outlets as necessary.

14) Establish work schedules and assign work to staff members.

15) Direct setup of remote facilities and install or cancel programs at remote stations.

16) Read news, read and/or record public service and promotional announcements, and otherwise participate as a member of an on-air shift as required.

17) Operate and maintain on-air and production audio equipment.

18) Develop ideas for programs and features that a station could produce.

19) Develop budgets for programming and broadcasting activities, and monitor expenditures to ensure that they remain within budgetary limits.

20) Plan and schedule programming and event coverage based on broadcast length, time availability, and other factors such as community needs, ratings data, and viewer demographics.

21) Participate in the planning and execution of fundraising activities.

22) Monitor network transmissions for advisories concerning daily program schedules, program content, special feeds, and/or program changes.

27-2012.04 - Talent Directors

Audition and interview performers to select most appropriate talent for parts in stage, television, radio, or motion picture productions.

Tasks

1) Maintain talent files that include information such as performers' specialties, past performances, and availability.

2) Locate performers or extras for crowd and background scenes, and stand-ins or photo doubles for actors, by direct contact or through agents.

3) Audition and interview performers in order to match their attributes to specific roles or to increase the pool of available acting talent.

4) Hire and supervise workers who help locate people with specified attributes and talents.

5) Select performers for roles or submit lists of suitable performers to producers or directors for final selection.

6) Review performer information such as photos, resumes, voice tapes, videos, and union membership, in order to decide whom to audition for parts.

7) Read scripts and confer with producers in order to determine the types and numbers of performers required for a given production.

8) Serve as liaisons between directors, actors, and agents.

9) Prepare actors for auditions by providing scripts and information about roles and casting requirements.

10) Arrange for and/or design screen tests or auditions for prospective performers.

11) Negotiate contract agreements with performers, with agents, or between performers and agents or production companies.

12) Attend or view productions in order to maintain knowledge of available actors.

27-2012.05 - Technical Directors/Managers

Coordinate activities of technical departments, such as taping, editing, engineering, and maintenance, to produce radio or television programs.

Tasks

1) Monitor broadcasts in order to ensure that programs conform to station or network policies and regulations.

2) Supervise and assign duties to workers engaged in technical control and production of radio and television programs.

3) Operate equipment to produce programs or broadcast live programs from remote locations.

4) Train workers in use of equipment such as switchers, cameras, monitors, microphones, and lights.

5) Test equipment in order to ensure proper operation.

6) Confer with operations directors in order to formulate and maintain fair and attainable technical policies for programs.

7) Schedule use of studio and editing facilities for producers and engineering and maintenance staff.

8) Switch between video sources in a studio or on multi-camera remotes, using equipment such as switchers, video slide projectors, and video effects generators.

9) Direct technical aspects of newscasts and other productions, checking and switching between video sources, and taking responsibility for the on-air product, including camera shots and graphics.

10) Observe pictures through monitors, and direct camera and video staff concerning shading and composition.

11) Discuss filter options, lens choices, and the visual effects of objects being filmed with photography directors and video operators.

12) Set up and execute video transitions and special effects such as fades, dissolves, cuts, keys, and supers, using computers to manipulate pictures as necessary.

13) Collaborate with promotions directors to produce on-air station promotions.

14) Follow instructions from production managers and directors during productions, such as commands for camera cuts, effects, graphics, and takes.

Knowledge	Knowledge Definitions
Communications and Media	Knowledge of media production, communication, and dissemination techniques and methods. This includes alternative ways to inform and entertain via written, oral, and visual media.
English Language	Knowledge of the structure and content of the English language including the meaning and spelling of words, rules of composition, and grammar.
Computers and Electronics	Knowledge of circuit boards, processors, chips, electronic equipment, and computer hardware and software, including applications and programming.
Administration and Management	Knowledge of business and management principles involved in strategic planning, resource allocation, human resources modeling, leadership technique, production methods, and coordination of people and resources.
Telecommunications	Knowledge of transmission, broadcasting, switching, control, and operation of telecommunications systems.
Customer and Personal Service	Knowledge of principles and processes for providing customer and personal services. This includes customer needs assessment, meeting quality standards for services, and evaluation of customer satisfaction.
Sales and Marketing	Knowledge of principles and methods for showing, promoting, and selling products or services. This includes marketing strategy and tactics, product demonstration, sales techniques, and sales control systems.

Engineering and Technology	Knowledge of the practical application of engineering science and technology. This includes applying principles, techniques, procedures, and equipment to the design and production of various goods and services.
Mathematics	Knowledge of arithmetic, algebra, geometry, calculus, statistics, and their applications.
Law and Government	Knowledge of laws, legal codes, court procedures, precedents, government regulations, executive orders, agency rules, and the democratic political process.
Clerical	Knowledge of administrative and clerical procedures and systems such as word processing, managing files and records, stenography and transcription, designing forms, and other office procedures and terminology.
Personnel and Human Resources	Knowledge of principles and procedures for personnel recruitment, selection, training, compensation and benefits, labor relations and negotiation, and personnel information systems.
Production and Processing	Knowledge of raw materials, production processes, quality control, costs, and other techniques for maximizing the effective manufacture and distribution of goods.
Economics and Accounting	Knowledge of economic and accounting principles and practices, the financial markets, banking and the analysis and reporting of financial data.
Sociology and Anthropology	Knowledge of group behavior and dynamics, societal trends and influences, human migrations, ethnicity, cultures and their history and origins.
Education and Training	Knowledge of principles and methods for curriculum and training design, teaching and instruction for individuals and groups, and the measurement of training effects.
Psychology	Knowledge of human behavior and performance; individual differences in ability, personality, and interests; learning and motivation; psychological research methods; and the assessment and treatment of behavioral and affective disorders.
Philosophy and Theology	Knowledge of different philosophical systems and religions. This includes their basic principles, values, ethics, ways of thinking, customs, practices, and their impact on human culture.
Geography	Knowledge of principles and methods for describing the features of land, sea, and air masses, including their physical characteristics, locations, interrelationships, and distribution of plant, animal, and human life.
Public Safety and Security	Knowledge of relevant equipment, policies, procedures, and strategies to promote effective local, state, or national security operations for the protection of people, data, property, and institutions.
Fine Arts	Knowledge of the theory and techniques required to compose, produce, and perform works of music, dance, visual arts, drama, and sculpture.
Design	Knowledge of design techniques, tools, and principles involved in production of precision technical plans, blueprints, drawings, and models.
Mechanical	Knowledge of machines and tools, including their designs, uses, repair, and maintenance.
Foreign Language	Knowledge of the structure and content of a foreign (non-English) language including the meaning and spelling of words, rules of composition and grammar, and pronunciation.
History and Archeology	Knowledge of historical events and their causes, indicators, and effects on civilizations and cultures.
Physics	Knowledge and prediction of physical principles, laws, their interrelationships, and applications to understanding fluid, material, and atmospheric dynamics, and mechanical, electrical, atomic and sub- atomic structures and processes.
Building and Construction	Knowledge of materials, methods, and the tools involved in the construction or repair of houses, buildings, or other structures such as highways and roads.
Therapy and Counseling	Knowledge of principles, methods, and procedures for diagnosis, treatment, and rehabilitation of physical and mental dysfunctions, and for career counseling and guidance.
Chemistry	Knowledge of the chemical composition, structure, and properties of substances and of the chemical processes and transformations that they undergo. This includes uses of chemicals and their interactions, danger signs, production techniques, and disposal methods.
Transportation	Knowledge of principles and methods for moving people or goods by air, rail, sea, or road, including the relative costs and benefits.

441

Medicine and Dentistry	Knowledge of the information and techniques needed to diagnose and treat human injuries, diseases, and deformities. This includes symptoms, treatment alternatives, drug properties and interactions, and preventive health-care measures.
Food Production	Knowledge of techniques and equipment for planting, growing, and harvesting food products (both plant and animal) for consumption, including storage/handling techniques.
Biology	Knowledge of plant and animal organisms, their tissues, cells, functions, interdependencies, and interactions with each other and the environment.

Skills	**Skills Definitions**
Monitoring	Monitoring/Assessing performance of yourself, other individuals, or organizations to make improvements or take corrective action.
Operation and Control	Controlling operations of equipment or systems.
Time Management	Managing one's own time and the time of others.
Active Listening	Giving full attention to what other people are saying, taking time to understand the points being made, asking questions as appropriate, and not interrupting at inappropriate times.
Critical Thinking	Using logic and reasoning to identify the strengths and weaknesses of alternative solutions, conclusions or approaches to problems.
Speaking	Talking to others to convey information effectively.
Coordination	Adjusting actions in relation to others' actions.
Troubleshooting	Determining causes of operating errors and deciding what to do about it.
Active Learning	Understanding the implications of new information for both current and future problem-solving and decision-making.
Reading Comprehension	Understanding written sentences and paragraphs in work related documents.
Instructing	Teaching others how to do something.
Equipment Maintenance	Performing routine maintenance on equipment and determining when and what kind of maintenance is needed.
Management of Personnel Resources	Motivating, developing, and directing people as they work, identifying the best people for the job.
Equipment Selection	Determining the kind of tools and equipment needed to do a job.
Technology Design	Generating or adapting equipment and technology to serve user needs.
Social Perceptiveness	Being aware of others' reactions and understanding why they react as they do.
Complex Problem Solving	Identifying complex problems and reviewing related information to develop and evaluate options and implement solutions.
Operation Monitoring	Watching gauges, dials, or other indicators to make sure a machine is working properly.
Learning Strategies	Selecting and using training/instructional methods and procedures appropriate for the situation when learning or teaching new things.
Systems Analysis	Determining how a system should work and how changes in conditions, operations, and the environment will affect outcomes.
Judgment and Decision Making	Considering the relative costs and benefits of potential actions to choose the most appropriate one.
Repairing	Repairing machines or systems using the needed tools.
Writing	Communicating effectively in writing as appropriate for the needs of the audience.
Installation	Installing equipment, machines, wiring, or programs to meet specifications.
Operations Analysis	Analyzing needs and product requirements to create a design.
Mathematics	Using mathematics to solve problems.
Negotiation	Bringing others together and trying to reconcile differences.
Service Orientation	Actively looking for ways to help people.
Management of Material Resources	Obtaining and seeing to the appropriate use of equipment, facilities, and materials needed to do certain work.
Systems Evaluation	Identifying measures or indicators of system performance and the actions needed to improve or correct performance, relative to the goals of the system.
Persuasion	Persuading others to change their minds or behavior.
Quality Control Analysis	Conducting tests and inspections of products, services, or processes to evaluate quality or performance.
Management of Financial Resources	Determining how money will be spent to get the work done, and accounting for these expenditures.
Science	Using scientific rules and methods to solve problems.
Programming	Writing computer programs for various purposes.

Ability	**Ability Definitions**
Oral Comprehension	The ability to listen to and understand information and ideas presented through spoken words and sentences.
Oral Expression	The ability to communicate information and ideas in speaking so others will understand.
Problem Sensitivity	The ability to tell when something is wrong or is likely to go wrong. It does not involve solving the problem, only recognizing there is a problem.
Deductive Reasoning	The ability to apply general rules to specific problems to produce answers that make sense.
Inductive Reasoning	The ability to combine pieces of information to form general rules or conclusions (includes finding a relationship among seemingly unrelated events).
Speech Clarity	The ability to speak clearly so others can understand you.
Speech Recognition	The ability to identify and understand the speech of another person.
Information Ordering	The ability to arrange things or actions in a certain order or pattern according to a specific rule or set of rules (e.g., patterns of numbers, letters, words, pictures, mathematical operations).
Selective Attention	The ability to concentrate on a task over a period of time without being distracted.
Near Vision	The ability to see details at close range (within a few feet of the observer).
Written Comprehension	The ability to read and understand information and ideas presented in writing.
Written Expression	The ability to communicate information and ideas in writing so others will understand.
Fluency of Ideas	The ability to come up with a number of ideas about a topic (the number of ideas is important, not their quality, correctness, or creativity).
Originality	The ability to come up with unusual or clever ideas about a given topic or situation, or to develop creative ways to solve a problem.
Visualization	The ability to imagine how something will look after it is moved around or when its parts are moved or rearranged.
Category Flexibility	The ability to generate or use different sets of rules for combining or grouping things in different ways.
Visual Color Discrimination	The ability to match or detect differences between colors, including shades of color and brightness.
Perceptual Speed	The ability to quickly and accurately compare similarities and differences among sets of letters, numbers, objects, pictures, or patterns. The things to be compared may be presented at the same time or one after the other. This ability also includes comparing a presented object with a remembered object.
Auditory Attention	The ability to focus on a single source of sound in the presence of other distracting sounds.
Far Vision	The ability to see details at a distance.
Time Sharing	The ability to shift back and forth between two or more activities or sources of information (such as speech, sounds, touch, or other sources).
Control Precision	The ability to quickly and repeatedly adjust the controls of a machine or a vehicle to exact positions.
Flexibility of Closure	The ability to identify or detect a known pattern (a figure, object, word, or sound) that is hidden in other distracting material.
Hearing Sensitivity	The ability to detect or tell the differences between sounds that vary in pitch and loudness.
Arm-Hand Steadiness	The ability to keep your hand and arm steady while moving your arm or while holding your arm and hand in one position.
Finger Dexterity	The ability to make precisely coordinated movements of the fingers of one or both hands to grasp, manipulate, or assemble very small objects.
Depth Perception	The ability to judge which of several objects is closer or farther away from you, or to judge the distance between you and an object.
Speed of Closure	The ability to quickly make sense of, combine, and organize information into meaningful patterns.
Memorization	The ability to remember information such as words, numbers, pictures, and procedures.
Number Facility	The ability to add, subtract, multiply, or divide quickly and correctly.
Reaction Time	The ability to quickly respond (with the hand, finger, or foot) to a signal (sound, light, picture) when it appears.
Rate Control	The ability to time your movements or the movement of a piece of equipment in anticipation of changes in the speed and/or direction of a moving object or scene.

Response Orientation	The ability to choose quickly between two or more movements in response to two or more different signals (lights, sounds, pictures). It includes the speed with which the correct response is started with the hand, foot, or other body part.
Manual Dexterity	The ability to quickly move your hand, your hand together with your arm, or your two hands to grasp, manipulate, or assemble objects.
Multilimb Coordination	The ability to coordinate two or more limbs (for example, two arms, two legs, or one leg and one arm) while sitting, standing, or lying down. It does not involve performing the activities while the whole body is in motion.
Mathematical Reasoning	The ability to choose the right mathematical methods or formulas to solve a problem.
Wrist-Finger Speed	The ability to make fast, simple, repeated movements of the fingers, hands, and wrists.
Sound Localization	The ability to tell the direction from which a sound originated.
Trunk Strength	The ability to use your abdominal and lower back muscles to support part of the body repeatedly or continuously over time without 'giving out' or fatiguing.
Spatial Orientation	The ability to know your location in relation to the environment or to know where other objects are in relation to you.
Gross Body Coordination	The ability to coordinate the movement of your arms, legs, and torso together when the whole body is in motion.
Peripheral Vision	The ability to see objects or movement of objects to one's side when the eyes are looking ahead.
Night Vision	The ability to see under low light conditions.
Dynamic Strength	The ability to exert muscle force repeatedly or continuously over time. This involves muscular endurance and resistance to muscle fatigue.
Speed of Limb Movement	The ability to quickly move the arms and legs.
Explosive Strength	The ability to use short bursts of muscle force to propel oneself (as in jumping or sprinting), or to throw an object.
Glare Sensitivity	The ability to see objects in the presence of glare or bright lighting.
Stamina	The ability to exert yourself physically over long periods of time without getting winded or out of breath.
Extent Flexibility	The ability to bend, stretch, twist, or reach with your body, arms, and/or legs.
Dynamic Flexibility	The ability to quickly and repeatedly bend, stretch, twist, or reach out with your body, arms, and/or legs.
Gross Body Equilibrium	The ability to keep or regain your body balance or stay upright when in an unstable position.
Static Strength	The ability to exert maximum muscle force to lift, push, pull, or carry objects.

Work_Activity	Work_Activity Definitions
Making Decisions and Solving Problems	Analyzing information and evaluating results to choose the best solution and solve problems.
Getting Information	Observing, receiving, and otherwise obtaining information from all relevant sources.
Communicating with Supervisors, Peers, or Subordin	Providing information to supervisors, co-workers, and subordinates by telephone, in written form, e-mail, or in person.
Establishing and Maintaining Interpersonal Relatio	Developing constructive and cooperative working relationships with others, and maintaining them over time.
Coordinating the Work and Activities of Others	Getting members of a group to work together to accomplish tasks.
Guiding, Directing, and Motivating Subordinates	Providing guidance and direction to subordinates, including setting performance standards and monitoring performance.
Organizing, Planning, and Prioritizing Work	Developing specific goals and plans to prioritize, organize, and accomplish your work.
Inspecting Equipment, Structures, or Material	Inspecting equipment, structures, or materials to identify the cause of errors or other problems or defects.
Monitor Processes, Materials, or Surroundings	Monitoring and reviewing information from materials, events, or the environment, to detect or assess problems.
Developing and Building Teams	Encouraging and building mutual trust, respect, and cooperation among team members.
Developing Objectives and Strategies	Establishing long-range objectives and specifying the strategies and actions to achieve them.
Documenting/Recording Information	Entering, transcribing, recording, storing, or maintaining information in written or electronic/magnetic form.
Monitoring and Controlling Resources	Monitoring and controlling resources and overseeing the spending of money.

Estimating the Quantifiable Characteristics of Pro	Estimating sizes, distances, and quantities; or determining time, costs, resources, or materials needed to perform a work activity.
Updating and Using Relevant Knowledge	Keeping up-to-date technically and applying new knowledge to your job.
Thinking Creatively	Developing, designing, or creating new applications, ideas, relationships, systems, or products, including artistic contributions.
Interpreting the Meaning of Information for Others	Translating or explaining what information means and how it can be used.
Identifying Objects, Actions, and Events	Identifying information by categorizing, estimating, recognizing differences or similarities, and detecting changes in circumstances or events.
Performing Administrative Activities	Performing day-to-day administrative tasks such as maintaining information files and processing paperwork.
Drafting, Laying Out, and Specifying Technical Dev	Providing documentation, detailed instructions, drawings, or specifications to tell others about how devices, parts, equipment, or structures are to be fabricated, constructed, assembled, modified, maintained, or used.
Communicating with Persons Outside Organization	Communicating with people outside the organization, representing the organization to customers, the public, government, and other external sources. This information can be exchanged in person, in writing, or by telephone or e-mail.
Coaching and Developing Others	Identifying the developmental needs of others and coaching, mentoring, or otherwise helping others to improve their knowledge or skills.
Performing for or Working Directly with the Public	Performing for people or dealing directly with the public. This includes serving customers in restaurants and stores, and receiving clients or guests.
Interacting With Computers	Using computers and computer systems (including hardware and software) to program, write software, set up functions, enter data, or process information.
Scheduling Work and Activities	Scheduling events, programs, and activities, as well as the work of others.
Provide Consultation and Advice to Others	Providing guidance and expert advice to management or other groups on technical, systems-, or process-related topics.
Assisting and Caring for Others	Providing personal assistance, medical attention, emotional support, or other personal care to others such as coworkers, customers, or patients.
Training and Teaching Others	Identifying the educational needs of others, developing formal educational or training programs or classes, and teaching or instructing others.
Judging the Qualities of Things, Services, or Peop	Assessing the value, importance, or quality of things or people.
Analyzing Data or Information	Identifying the underlying principles, reasons, or facts of information by breaking down information or data into separate parts.
Resolving Conflicts and Negotiating with Others	Handling complaints, settling disputes, and resolving grievances and conflicts, or otherwise negotiating with others.
Staffing Organizational Units	Recruiting, interviewing, selecting, hiring, and promoting employees in an organization.
Evaluating Information to Determine Compliance wit	Using relevant information and individual judgment to determine whether events or processes comply with laws, regulations, or standards.
Controlling Machines and Processes	Using either control mechanisms or direct physical activity to operate machines or processes (not including computers or vehicles).
Repairing and Maintaining Electronic Equipment	Servicing, repairing, calibrating, regulating, fine-tuning, or testing machines, devices, and equipment that operate primarily on the basis of electrical or electronic (not mechanical) principles.
Processing Information	Compiling, coding, categorizing, calculating, tabulating, auditing, or verifying information or data.
Repairing and Maintaining Mechanical Equipment	Servicing, repairing, adjusting, and testing machines, devices, moving parts, and equipment that operate primarily on the basis of mechanical (not electronic) principles.
Performing General Physical Activities	Performing physical activities that require considerable use of your arms and legs and moving your whole body, such as climbing, lifting, balancing, walking, stooping, and handling of materials.
Handling and Moving Objects	Using hands and arms in handling, installing, positioning, and moving materials, and manipulating things.
Selling or Influencing Others	Convincing others to buy merchandise/goods or to otherwise change their minds or actions.
Operating Vehicles, Mechanized Devices, or Equipme	Running, maneuvering, navigating, or driving vehicles or mechanized equipment, such as forklifts, passenger vehicles, aircraft, or water craft.

Work_Context	Work_Context Definitions
Telephone	How often do you have telephone conversations in this job?
Indoors, Environmentally Controlled	How often does this job require working indoors in environmentally controlled conditions?
Face-to-Face Discussions	How often do you have to have face-to-face discussions with individuals or teams in this job?
Importance of Being Exact or Accurate	How important is being very exact or highly accurate in performing this job?
Freedom to Make Decisions	How much decision making freedom, without supervision, does the job offer?
Structured versus Unstructured Work	To what extent is this job structured for the worker, rather than allowing the worker to determine tasks, priorities, and goals?
Impact of Decisions on Co-workers or Company Resul	How do the decisions an employee makes impact the results of co-workers, clients or the company?
Frequency of Decision Making	How frequently is the worker required to make decisions that affect other people, the financial resources, and/or the image and reputation of the organization?
Time Pressure	How often does this job require the worker to meet strict deadlines?
Responsibility for Outcomes and Results	How responsible is the worker for work outcomes and results of other workers?
Electronic Mail	How often do you use electronic mail in this job?
Contact With Others	How much does this job require the worker to be in contact with others (face-to-face, by telephone, or otherwise) in order to perform it?
Spend Time Sitting	How much does this job require sitting?
Work With Work Group or Team	How important is it to work with others in a group or team in this job?
Coordinate or Lead Others	How important is it to coordinate or lead others in accomplishing work activities in this job?
Letters and Memos	How often does the job require written letters and memos?
Spend Time Using Your Hands to Handle, Control, or	How much does this job require using your hands to handle, control, or feel objects, tools or controls?
Responsible for Others' Health and Safety	How much responsibility is there for the health and safety of others in this job?
Sounds, Noise Levels Are Distracting or Uncomforta	How often does this job require working exposed to sounds and noise levels that are distracting or uncomfortable?
Deal With External Customers	How important is it to work with external customers or the public in this job?
Frequency of Conflict Situations	How often are there conflict situations the employee has to face in this job?
Deal With Unpleasant or Angry People	How frequently does the worker have to deal with unpleasant, angry, or discourteous individuals as part of the job requirements?
Physical Proximity	To what extent does this job require the worker to perform job tasks in close physical proximity to other people?
Importance of Repeating Same Tasks	How important is repeating the same physical activities (e.g., key entry) or mental activities (e.g., checking entries in a ledger) over and over, without stopping, to performing this job?
Level of Competition	To what extent does this job require the worker to compete or to be aware of competitive pressures?
In an Enclosed Vehicle or Equipment	How often does this job require working in a closed vehicle or equipment (e.g., car)?
Outdoors, Exposed to Weather	How often does this job require working outdoors, exposed to all weather conditions?
Public Speaking	How often do you have to perform public speaking in this job?
Spend Time Making Repetitive Motions	How much does this job require making repetitive motions?
Indoors, Not Environmentally Controlled	How often does this job require working indoors in non-controlled environmental conditions (e.g., warehouse without heat)?
Degree of Automation	How automated is the job?
Consequence of Error	How serious would the result usually be if the worker made a mistake that was not readily correctable?
Extremely Bright or Inadequate Lighting	How often does this job require working in extremely bright or inadequate lighting conditions?
Very Hot or Cold Temperatures	How often does this job require working in very hot (above 90 F degrees) or very cold (below 32 F degrees) temperatures?
Spend Time Standing	How much does this job require standing?
Exposed to High Places	How often does this job require exposure to high places?
Exposed to Hazardous Conditions	How often does this job require exposure to hazardous conditions?
Outdoors, Under Cover	How often does this job require working outdoors, under cover (e.g., structure with roof but no walls)?

Spend Time Walking and Running	How much does this job require walking and running?
Spend Time Kneeling, Crouching, Stooping, or Crawl	How much does this job require kneeling. crouching, stooping, or crawling?
Deal With Physically Aggressive People	How frequently does this job require the worker to deal with physical aggression of violent individuals?
Cramped Work Space, Awkward Positions	How often does this job require working in cramped work spaces that requires getting into awkward positions?
Spend Time Bending or Twisting the Body	How much does this job require bending or twisting your body?
Spend Time Climbing Ladders, Scaffolds, or Poles	How much does this job require climbing ladders, scaffolds, or poles?
Exposed to Radiation	How often does this job require exposure to radiation?
Pace Determined by Speed of Equipment	How important is it to this job that the pace is determined by the speed of equipment or machinery? (This does not refer to keeping busy at all times on this job.)
Exposed to Minor Burns, Cuts, Bites, or Stings	How often does this job require exposure to minor burns, cuts, bites, or stings?
Wear Common Protective or Safety Equipment such as	How much does this job require wearing common protective or safety equipment such as safety shoes, glasses, gloves, hard hats or live jackets?
Exposed to Contaminants	How often does this job require working exposed to contaminants (such as pollutants, gases, dust or odors)?
Spend Time Keeping or Regaining Balance	How much does this job require keeping or regaining your balance?
Exposed to Hazardous Equipment	How often does this job require exposure to hazardous equipment?
In an Open Vehicle or Equipment	How often does this job require working in an open vehicle or equipment (e.g., tractor)?
Exposed to Disease or Infections	How often does this job require exposure to disease/infections?
Wear Specialized Protective or Safety Equipment su	How much does this job require wearing specialized protective or safety equipment such as breathing apparatus, safety harness, full protection suits, or radiation protection?
Exposed to Whole Body Vibration	How often does this job require exposure to whole body vibration (e.g., operate a jackhammer)?

Job Zone Component	Job Zone Component Definitions
Title	Job Zone Three: Medium Preparation Needed
Overall Experience	Previous work-related skill, knowledge, or experience is required for these occupations. For example, an electrician must have completed three or four years of apprenticeship or several years of vocational training, and often must have passed a licensing exam, in order to perform the job.
Job Training	Employees in these occupations usually need one or two years of training involving both on-the-job experience and informal training with experienced workers.
Job Zone Examples	These occupations usually involve using communication and organizational skills to coordinate, supervise, manage, or train others to accomplish goals. Examples include dental assistants, electricians, fish and game wardens, legal secretaries, personnel recruiters, and recreation workers.
SVP Range	(6.0 to < 7.0)
Education	Most occupations in this zone require training in vocational schools, related on-the-job experience, or an associate's degree. Some may require a bachelor's degree.

Work_Styles	Work_Styles Definitions
Dependability	Job requires being reliable, responsible, and dependable, and fulfilling obligations.
Initiative	Job requires a willingness to take on responsibilities and challenges.
Adaptability/Flexibility	Job requires being open to change (positive or negative) and to considerable variety in the workplace.
Cooperation	Job requires being pleasant with others on the job and displaying a good-natured, cooperative attitude.
Achievement/Effort	Job requires establishing and maintaining personally challenging achievement goals and exerting effort toward mastering tasks.
Attention to Detail	Job requires being careful about detail and thorough in completing work tasks.
Innovation	Job requires creativity and alternative thinking to develop new ideas for and answers to work-related problems.

Leadership	Job requires a willingness to lead, take charge, and offer opinions and direction.
Self Control	Job requires maintaining composure, keeping emotions in check, controlling anger, and avoiding aggressive behavior, even in very difficult situations.
Persistence	Job requires persistence in the face of obstacles.
Integrity	Job requires being honest and ethical.
Independence	Job requires developing one's own ways of doing things, guiding oneself with little or no supervision, and depending on oneself to get things done.
Stress Tolerance	Job requires accepting criticism and dealing calmly and effectively with high stress situations.
Social Orientation	Job requires preferring to work with others rather than alone, and being personally connected with others on the job.
Analytical Thinking	Job requires analyzing information and using logic to address work-related issues and problems.
Concern for Others	Job requires being sensitive to others' needs and feelings and being understanding and helpful on the job.

27-2021.00 - Athletes and Sports Competitors

Compete in athletic events.

Tasks

1) Assess performance following athletic competition, identifying strengths and weaknesses, and making adjustments to improve future performance.

2) Represent teams or professional sports clubs, performing such activities as meeting with members of the media, making speeches, or participating in charity events.

3) Exercise and practice under the direction of athletic trainers or professional coaches, in order to develop skills, improve physical condition, and prepare for competitions.

4) Maintain equipment used in a particular sport.

5) Participate in athletic events and competitive sports, according to established rules and regulations.

6) Lead teams by serving as captains.

7) Attend scheduled practice and training sessions.

8) Receive instructions from coaches and other sports staff prior to events, and discuss their performance afterwards.

27-2022.00 - Coaches and Scouts

Instruct or coach groups or individuals in the fundamentals of sports. Demonstrate techniques and methods of participation. May evaluate athletes' strengths and weaknesses as possible recruits or to improve the athletes' technique to prepare them for competition. Those required to hold teaching degrees should be reported in the appropriate teaching category.

Tasks

1) Plan, organize, and conduct practice sessions.

2) Keep abreast of changing rules, techniques, technologies, and philosophies relevant to their sport.

3) Adjust coaching techniques based on the strengths and weaknesses of athletes.

4) Instruct individuals or groups in sports rules, game strategies, and performance principles such as specific ways of moving the body, hands, and/or feet in order to achieve desired results.

5) Evaluate athletes' skills, and review performance records, in order to determine their fitness and potential in a particular area of athletics.

6) Plan strategies and choose team members for individual games and/or sports seasons.

7) Explain and enforce safety rules and regulations.

8) Keep records of athlete, team, and opposing team performance.

9) Plan and direct physical conditioning programs that will enable athletes to achieve maximum performance.

10) Analyze the strengths and weaknesses of opposing teams in order to develop game strategies.

11) Arrange and conduct sports-related activities such as training camps, skill-improvement courses, clinics, and/or pre-season try-outs.

12) Select, acquire, store, and issue equipment and other materials as necessary.

13) Perform activities that support a team or a specific sport, such as meeting with media representatives and appearing at fundraising events.

14) Monitor athletes' use of equipment in order to ensure safe and proper use.

15) Develop and arrange competition schedules and programs.

16) File scouting reports that detail player assessments, provide recommendations on athlete recruitment, and identify locations and individuals to be targeted for future recruitment efforts.

17) Identify and recruit potential athletes, arranging and offering incentives such as athletic scholarships.

18) Explain and demonstrate the use of sports and training equipment, such as trampolines or weights.

19) Serve as organizer, leader, instructor, or referee for outdoor and indoor games, such as volleyball, football, and soccer.

20) Negotiate with professional athletes or their representatives in order to obtain services and arrange contracts.

Knowledge	Knowledge Definitions
Education and Training	Knowledge of principles and methods for curriculum and training design, teaching and instruction for individuals and groups, and the measurement of training effects.
Psychology	Knowledge of human behavior and performance; individual differences in ability, personality, and interests; learning and motivation; psychological research methods; and the assessment and treatment of behavioral and affective disorders.
Customer and Personal Service	Knowledge of principles and processes for providing customer and personal services. This includes customer needs assessment, meeting quality standards for services, and evaluation of customer satisfaction.
Administration and Management	Knowledge of business and management principles involved in strategic planning, resource allocation, human resources modeling, leadership technique, production methods, and coordination of people and resources.
English Language	Knowledge of the structure and content of the English language including the meaning and spelling of words, rules of composition, and grammar.
Sales and Marketing	Knowledge of principles and methods for showing, promoting, and selling products or services. This includes marketing strategy and tactics, product demonstration, sales techniques, and sales control systems.
Personnel and Human Resources	Knowledge of principles and procedures for personnel recruitment, selection, training, compensation and benefits, labor relations and negotiation, and personnel information systems.
Clerical	Knowledge of administrative and clerical procedures and systems such as word processing, managing files and records, stenography and transcription, designing forms, and other office procedures and terminology.
Therapy and Counseling	Knowledge of principles, methods, and procedures for diagnosis, treatment, and rehabilitation of physical and mental dysfunctions, and for career counseling and guidance.
Sociology and Anthropology	Knowledge of group behavior and dynamics, societal trends and influences, human migrations, ethnicity, cultures and their history and origins.
Computers and Electronics	Knowledge of circuit boards, processors, chips, electronic equipment, and computer hardware and software, including applications and programming.
Communications and Media	Knowledge of media production, communication, and dissemination techniques and methods. This includes alternative ways to inform and entertain via written, oral, and visual media.
Transportation	Knowledge of principles and methods for moving people or goods by air, rail, sea, or road, including the relative costs and benefits.
Public Safety and Security	Knowledge of relevant equipment, policies, procedures, and strategies to promote effective local, state, or national security operations for the protection of people, data, property, and institutions.
Mathematics	Knowledge of arithmetic, algebra, geometry, calculus, statistics, and their applications.

Economics and Accounting	Knowledge of economic and accounting principles and practices, the financial markets, banking and the analysis and reporting of financial data.
Telecommunications	Knowledge of transmission, broadcasting, switching, control, and operation of telecommunications systems.
Law and Government	Knowledge of laws, legal codes, court procedures, precedents, government regulations, executive orders, agency rules, and the democratic political process.
Medicine and Dentistry	Knowledge of the information and techniques needed to diagnose and treat human injuries, diseases, and deformities. This includes symptoms, treatment alternatives, drug properties and interactions, and preventive health-care measures.
Philosophy and Theology	Knowledge of different philosophical systems and religions. This includes their basic principles, values, ethics, ways of thinking, customs, practices, and their impact on human culture.
Geography	Knowledge of principles and methods for describing the features of land, sea, and air masses, including their physical characteristics, locations, interrelationships, and distribution of plant, animal, and human life.
Production and Processing	Knowledge of raw materials, production processes, quality control, costs, and other techniques for maximizing the effective manufacture and distribution of goods.
Design	Knowledge of design techniques, tools, and principles involved in production of precision technical plans, blueprints, drawings, and models.
Biology	Knowledge of plant and animal organisms, their tissues, cells, functions, interdependencies, and interactions with each other and the environment.
Foreign Language	Knowledge of the structure and content of a foreign (non-English) language including the meaning and spelling of words, rules of composition and grammar, and pronunciation.
Physics	Knowledge and prediction of physical principles, laws, their interrelationships, and applications to understanding fluid, material, and atmospheric dynamics, and mechanical, electrical, atomic and sub- atomic structures and processes.
Mechanical	Knowledge of machines and tools, including their designs, uses, repair, and maintenance.
History and Archeology	Knowledge of historical events and their causes, indicators, and effects on civilizations and cultures.
Engineering and Technology	Knowledge of the practical application of engineering science and technology. This includes applying principles, techniques, procedures, and equipment to the design and production of various goods and services.
Fine Arts	Knowledge of the theory and techniques required to compose, produce, and perform works of music, dance, visual arts, drama, and sculpture.
Building and Construction	Knowledge of materials, methods, and the tools involved in the construction or repair of houses, buildings, or other structures such as highways and roads.
Chemistry	Knowledge of the chemical composition, structure, and properties of substances and of the chemical processes and transformations that they undergo. This includes uses of chemicals and their interactions, danger signs, production techniques, and disposal methods.
Food Production	Knowledge of techniques and equipment for planting, growing, and harvesting food products (both plant and animal) for consumption, including storage/handling techniques.

Skills	Skills Definitions
Instructing	Teaching others how to do something.
Speaking	Talking to others to convey information effectively.
Time Management	Managing one's own time and the time of others.
Active Listening	Giving full attention to what other people are saying, taking time to understand the points being made, asking questions as appropriate, and not interrupting at inappropriate times.
Social Perceptiveness	Being aware of others' reactions and understanding why they react as they do.
Coordination	Adjusting actions in relation to others' actions.
Monitoring	Monitoring/Assessing performance of yourself, other individuals, or organizations to make improvements or take corrective action.
Active Learning	Understanding the implications of new information for both current and future problem-solving and decision-making.
Learning Strategies	Selecting and using training/instructional methods and procedures appropriate for the situation when learning or teaching new things.

Critical Thinking	Using logic and reasoning to identify the strengths and weaknesses of alternative solutions, conclusions, or approaches to problems.
Persuasion	Persuading others to change their minds or behavior.
Judgment and Decision Making	Considering the relative costs and benefits of potential actions to choose the most appropriate one.
Management of Personnel Resources	Motivating, developing, and directing people as they work, identifying the best people for the job.
Negotiation	Bringing others together and trying to reconcile differences.
Reading Comprehension	Understanding written sentences and paragraphs in work related documents.
Writing	Communicating effectively in writing as appropriate for the needs of the audience.
Equipment Selection	Determining the kind of tools and equipment needed to do a job.
Service Orientation	Actively looking for ways to help people.
Complex Problem Solving	Identifying complex problems and reviewing related information to develop and evaluate options and implement solutions.
Management of Financial Resources	Determining how money will be spent to get the work done, and accounting for these expenditures.
Operations Analysis	Analyzing needs and product requirements to create a design.
Management of Material Resources	Obtaining and seeing to the appropriate use of equipment, facilities, and materials needed to do certain work.
Mathematics	Using mathematics to solve problems.
Science	Using scientific rules and methods to solve problems.
Systems Evaluation	Identifying measures or indicators of system performance and the actions needed to improve or correct performance, relative to the goals of the system.
Equipment Maintenance	Performing routine maintenance on equipment and determining when and what kind of maintenance is needed.
Systems Analysis	Determining how a system should work and how changes in conditions, operations, and the environment will affect outcomes.
Troubleshooting	Determining causes of operating errors and deciding what to do about it.
Technology Design	Generating or adapting equipment and technology to serve user needs.
Quality Control Analysis	Conducting tests and inspections of products, services, or processes to evaluate quality or performance.
Installation	Installing equipment, machines, wiring, or programs to meet specifications.
Operation and Control	Controlling operations of equipment or systems.
Repairing	Repairing machines or systems using the needed tools.
Operation Monitoring	Watching gauges, dials, or other indicators to make sure a machine is working properly.
Programming	Writing computer programs for various purposes.

Ability	Ability Definitions
Oral Expression	The ability to communicate information and ideas in speaking so others will understand.
Speech Clarity	The ability to speak clearly so others can understand you.
Deductive Reasoning	The ability to apply general rules to specific problems to produce answers that make sense.
Inductive Reasoning	The ability to combine pieces of information to form general rules or conclusions (includes finding a relationship among seemingly unrelated events).
Problem Sensitivity	The ability to tell when something is wrong or is likely to go wrong. It does not involve solving the problem, only recognizing there is a problem.
Oral Comprehension	The ability to listen to and understand information and ideas presented through spoken words and sentences.
Speech Recognition	The ability to identify and understand the speech of another person.
Fluency of Ideas	The ability to come up with a number of ideas about a topic (the number of ideas is important, not their quality, correctness, or creativity).
Written Expression	The ability to communicate information and ideas in writing so others will understand.
Originality	The ability to come up with unusual or clever ideas about a given topic or situation, or to develop creative ways to solve a problem.
Near Vision	The ability to see details at close range (within a few feet of the observer).
Category Flexibility	The ability to generate or use different sets of rules for combining or grouping things in different ways.

Visualization	The ability to imagine how something will look after it is moved around or when its parts are moved or rearranged.
Information Ordering	The ability to arrange things or actions in a certain order or pattern according to a specific rule or set of rules (e.g., patterns of numbers, letters, words, pictures, mathematical operations).
Written Comprehension	The ability to read and understand information and ideas presented in writing.
Selective Attention	The ability to concentrate on a task over a period of time without being distracted.
Memorization	The ability to remember information such as words, numbers, pictures, and procedures.
Time Sharing	The ability to shift back and forth between two or more activities or sources of information (such as speech, sounds, touch, or other sources).
Far Vision	The ability to see details at a distance.
Flexibility of Closure	The ability to identify or detect a known pattern (a figure, object, word, or sound) that is hidden in other distracting material.
Multilimb Coordination	The ability to coordinate two or more limbs (for example, two arms, two legs, or one leg and one arm) while sitting, standing, or lying down. It does not involve performing the activities while the whole body is in motion.
Trunk Strength	The ability to use your abdominal and lower back muscles to support part of the body repeatedly or continuously over time without 'giving out' or fatiguing.
Speed of Closure	The ability to quickly make sense of, combine, and organize information into meaningful patterns.
Static Strength	The ability to exert maximum muscle force to lift, push, pull, or carry objects.
Arm-Hand Steadiness	The ability to keep your hand and arm steady while moving your arm or while holding your arm and hand in one position.
Depth Perception	The ability to judge which of several objects is closer or farther away from you, or to judge the distance between you and an object.
Manual Dexterity	The ability to quickly move your hand, your hand together with your arm, or your two hands to grasp, manipulate, or assemble objects.
Auditory Attention	The ability to focus on a single source of sound in the presence of other distracting sounds.
Visual Color Discrimination	The ability to match or detect differences between colors, including shades of color and brightness.
Hearing Sensitivity	The ability to detect or tell the differences between sounds that vary in pitch and loudness.
Stamina	The ability to exert yourself physically over long periods of time without getting winded or out of breath.
Perceptual Speed	The ability to quickly and accurately compare similarities and differences among sets of letters, numbers, objects, pictures, or patterns. The things to be compared may be presented at the same time or one after the other. This ability also includes comparing a presented object with a remembered object.
Dynamic Strength	The ability to exert muscle force repeatedly or continuously over time. This involves muscular endurance and resistance to muscle fatigue.
Gross Body Coordination	The ability to coordinate the movement of your arms, legs, and torso together when the whole body is in motion.
Number Facility	The ability to add, subtract, multiply, or divide quickly and correctly.
Gross Body Equilibrium	The ability to keep or regain your body balance or stay upright when in an unstable position.
Mathematical Reasoning	The ability to choose the right mathematical methods or formulas to solve a problem.
Control Precision	The ability to quickly and repeatedly adjust the controls of a machine or a vehicle to exact positions.
Finger Dexterity	The ability to make precisely coordinated movements of the fingers of one or both hands to grasp, manipulate, or assemble very small objects.
Extent Flexibility	The ability to bend, stretch, twist, or reach with your body, arms, and/or legs.
Spatial Orientation	The ability to know your location in relation to the environment or to know where other objects are in relation to you.
Peripheral Vision	The ability to see objects or movement of objects to one's side when the eyes are looking ahead.
Explosive Strength	The ability to use short bursts of muscle force to propel oneself (as in jumping or sprinting), or to throw an object.
Speed of Limb Movement	The ability to quickly move the arms and legs.
Glare Sensitivity	The ability to see objects in the presence of glare or bright lighting.
Night Vision	The ability to see under low light conditions.

Dynamic Flexibility	The ability to quickly and repeatedly bend, stretch, twist, or reach out with your body, arms, and/or legs.
Reaction Time	The ability to quickly respond (with the hand, finger, or foot) to a signal (sound, light, picture) when it appears.
Rate Control	The ability to time your movements or the movement of a piece of equipment in anticipation of changes in the speed and/or direction of a moving object or scene.
Sound Localization	The ability to tell the direction from which a sound originated.
Response Orientation	The ability to choose quickly between two or more movements in response to two or more different signals (lights, sounds, pictures). It includes the speed with which the correct response is started with the hand, foot, or other body part.
Wrist-Finger Speed	The ability to make fast, simple, repeated movements of the fingers, hands, and wrists.

Work_Activity	Work_Activity Definitions
Coaching and Developing Others	Identifying the developmental needs of others and coaching, mentoring, or otherwise helping others to improve their knowledge or skills.
Coordinating the Work and Activities of Others	Getting members of a group to work together to accomplish tasks.
Developing and Building Teams	Encouraging and building mutual trust, respect, and cooperation among team members.
Guiding, Directing, and Motivating Subordinates	Providing guidance and direction to subordinates, including setting performance standards and monitoring performance.
Establishing and Maintaining Interpersonal Relatio	Developing constructive and cooperative working relationships with others, and maintaining them over time.
Making Decisions and Solving Problems	Analyzing information and evaluating results to choose the best solution and solve problems.
Training and Teaching Others	Identifying the educational needs of others, developing formal educational or training programs or classes, and teaching or instructing others.
Communicating with Supervisors, Peers, or Subordin	Providing information to supervisors, co-workers, and subordinates by telephone, in written form, e-mail, or in person.
Performing General Physical Activities	Performing physical activities that require considerable use of your arms and legs and moving your whole body, such as climbing, lifting, balancing, walking, stooping, and handling of materials.
Communicating with Persons Outside Organization	Communicating with people outside the organization, representing the organization to customers, the public, government, and other external sources. This information can be exchanged in person, in writing, or by telephone or e-mail.
Scheduling Work and Activities	Scheduling events, programs, and activities, as well as the work of others.
Resolving Conflicts and Negotiating with Others	Handling complaints, settling disputes, and resolving grievances and conflicts, or otherwise negotiating with others.
Assisting and Caring for Others	Providing personal assistance, medical attention, emotional support, or other personal care to others such as coworkers, customers, or patients.
Developing Objectives and Strategies	Establishing long-range objectives and specifying the strategies and actions to achieve them.
Performing for or Working Directly with the Public	Performing for people or dealing directly with the public. This includes serving customers in restaurants and stores, and receiving clients or guests.
Judging the Qualities of Things, Services, or Peop	Assessing the value, importance, or quality of things or people.
Staffing Organizational Units	Recruiting, interviewing, selecting, hiring, and promoting employees in an organization.
Getting Information	Observing, receiving, and otherwise obtaining information from all relevant sources.
Selling or Influencing Others	Convincing others to buy merchandise/goods or to otherwise change their minds or actions.
Organizing, Planning, and Prioritizing Work	Developing specific goals and plans to prioritize, organize, and accomplish your work.
Performing Administrative Activities	Performing day-to-day administrative tasks such as maintaining information files and processing paperwork.
Thinking Creatively	Developing, designing, or creating new applications, ideas, relationships, systems, or products, including artistic contributions.
Updating and Using Relevant Knowledge	Keeping up-to-date technically and applying new knowledge to your job.
Provide Consultation and Advice to Others	Providing guidance and expert advice to management or other groups on technical, systems-, or process-related topics.

Identifying Objects, Actions, and Events	Identifying information by categorizing, estimating, recognizing differences or similarities, and detecting changes in circumstances or events.
Interpreting the Meaning of Information for Others	Translating or explaining what information means and how it can be used.
Monitoring and Controlling Resources	Monitoring and controlling resources and overseeing the spending of money.
Documenting/Recording Information	Entering, transcribing, recording, storing, or maintaining information in written or electronic/magnetic form.
Processing Information	Compiling, coding, categorizing, calculating, tabulating, auditing, or verifying information or data.
Evaluating Information to Determine Compliance wit	Using relevant information and individual judgment to determine whether events or processes comply with laws, regulations, or standards.
Analyzing Data or Information	Identifying the underlying principles, reasons, or facts of information by breaking down information or data into separate parts.
Handling and Moving Objects	Using hands and arms in handling, installing, positioning, and moving materials, and manipulating things.
Monitor Processes, Materials, or Surroundings	Monitoring and reviewing information from materials, events, or the environment, to detect or assess problems.
Inspecting Equipment, Structures, or Material	Inspecting equipment, structures, or materials to identify the cause of errors or other problems or defects.
Interacting With Computers	Using computers and computer systems (including hardware and software) to program, write software, set up functions, enter data, or process information.
Estimating the Quantifiable Characteristics of Pro	Estimating sizes, distances, and quantities; or determining time, costs, resources, or materials needed to perform a work activity.
Operating Vehicles, Mechanized Devices, or Equipme	Running, maneuvering, navigating, or driving vehicles or mechanized equipment, such as forklifts, passenger vehicles, aircraft, or water craft.
Controlling Machines and Processes	Using either control mechanisms or direct physical activity to operate machines or processes (not including computers or vehicles).
Drafting, Laying Out, and Specifying Technical Dev	Providing documentation, detailed instructions, drawings, or specifications to tell others about how devices, parts, equipment, or structures are to be fabricated, constructed, assembled, modified, maintained, or used.
Repairing and Maintaining Mechanical Equipment	Servicing, repairing, adjusting, and testing machines, devices, moving parts, and equipment that operate primarily on the basis of mechanical (not electronic) principles.
Repairing and Maintaining Electronic Equipment	Servicing, repairing, calibrating, regulating, fine-tuning, or testing machines, devices, and equipment that operate primarily on the basis of electrical or electronic (not mechanical) principles.

Work_Context	Work_Context Definitions
Contact With Others	How much does this job require the worker to be in contact with others (face-to-face, by telephone, or otherwise) in order to perform it?
Face-to-Face Discussions	How often do you have to have face-to-face discussions with individuals or teams in this job?
Telephone	How often do you have telephone conversations in this job?
Electronic Mail	How often do you use electronic mail in this job?
Work With Work Group or Team	How important is it to work with others in a group or team in this job?
Level of Competition	To what extent does this job require the worker to compete or to be aware of competitive pressures?
Structured versus Unstructured Work	To what extent is this job structured for the worker, rather than allowing the worker to determine tasks, priorities, and goals?
Freedom to Make Decisions	How much decision making freedom, without supervision, does the job offer?
Impact of Decisions on Co-workers or Company Resul	How do the decisions an employee makes impact the results of co-workers, clients or the company?
Frequency of Decision Making	How frequently is the worker required to make decisions that affect other people, the financial resources, and/or the image and reputation of the organization?
Coordinate or Lead Others	How important is it to coordinate or lead others in accomplishing work activities in this job?
Responsibility for Outcomes and Results	How responsible is the worker for work outcomes and results of other workers?
Deal With External Customers	How important is it to work with external customers or the public in this job?

Physical Proximity	To what extent does this job require the worker to perform job tasks in close physical proximity to other people?
Time Pressure	How often does this job require the worker to meet strict deadlines?
Letters and Memos	How often does the job require written letters and memos?
Responsible for Others' Health and Safety	How much responsibility is there for the health and safety of others in this job?
Frequency of Conflict Situations	How often are there conflict situations the employee has to face in this job?
Public Speaking	How often do you have to perform public speaking in this job?
Indoors, Environmentally Controlled	How often does this job require working indoors in environmentally controlled conditions?
Spend Time Standing	How much does this job require standing?
Importance of Being Exact or Accurate	How important is being very exact or highly accurate in performing this job?
Outdoors, Exposed to Weather	How often does this job require working outdoors, exposed to all weather conditions?
Deal With Unpleasant or Angry People	How frequently does the worker have to deal with unpleasant, angry, or discourteous individuals as part of the job requirements?
Sounds, Noise Levels Are Distracting or Uncomforta	How often does this job require working exposed to sounds and noise levels that are distracting or uncomfortable?
Spend Time Walking and Running	How much does this job require walking and running?
Importance of Repeating Same Tasks	How important is repeating the same physical activities (e.g., key entry) or mental activities (e.g., checking entries in a ledger) over and over, without stopping, to performing this job?
In an Enclosed Vehicle or Equipment	How often does this job require working in a closed vehicle or equipment (e.g., car)?
Indoors, Not Environmentally Controlled	How often does this job require working indoors in non-controlled environmental conditions (e.g., warehouse without heat)?
Very Hot or Cold Temperatures	How often does this job require working in very hot (above 90 F degrees) or very cold (below 32 F degrees) temperatures?
Spend Time Sitting	How much does this job require sitting?
Consequence of Error	How serious would the result usually be if the worker made a mistake that was not readily correctable?
Spend Time Making Repetitive Motions	How much does this job require making repetitive motions?
Spend Time Bending or Twisting the Body	How much does this job require bending or twisting your body?
Extremely Bright or Inadequate Lighting	How often does this job require working in extremely bright or inadequate lighting conditions?
Exposed to Contaminants	How often does this job require working exposed to contaminants (such as pollutants, gases, dust or odors)?
Spend Time Using Your Hands to Handle, Control, or	How much does this job require using your hands to handle, control, or feel objects, tools or controls?
Exposed to Minor Burns, Cuts, Bites, or Stings	How often does this job require exposure to minor burns, cuts, bites, or stings?
Deal With Physically Aggressive People	How frequently does this job require the worker to deal with physical aggression of violent individuals?
Cramped Work Space, Awkward Positions	How often does this job require working in cramped work spaces that requires getting into awkward positions?
Outdoors, Under Cover	How often does this job require working outdoors, under cover (e.g., structure with roof but no walls)?
Degree of Automation	How automated is the job?
Spend Time Kneeling, Crouching, Stooping, or Crawl	How much does this job require kneeling, crouching, stooping or crawling?
Spend Time Keeping or Regaining Balance	How much does this job require keeping or regaining your balance?
Exposed to Disease or Infections	How often does this job require exposure to disease/infections?
Exposed to Hazardous Conditions	How often does this job require exposure to hazardous conditions?
In an Open Vehicle or Equipment	How often does this job require working in an open vehicle or equipment (e.g., tractor)?
Exposed to Hazardous Equipment	How often does this job require exposure to hazardous equipment?
Exposed to High Places	How often does this job require exposure to high places?
Pace Determined by Speed of Equipment	How important is it to this job that the pace is determined by the speed of equipment or machinery? (This does not refer to keeping busy at all times on this job.)
Wear Common Protective or Safety Equipment such as	How much does this job require wearing common protective or safety equipment such as safety shoes, glasses, gloves, hard hats or life jackets?

Exposed to Whole Body Vibration	How often does this job require exposure to whole body vibration (e.g., operate a jackhammer)?
Wear Specialized Protective or Safety Equipment su	How much does this job require wearing specialized protective or safety equipment such as breathing apparatus, safety harness, full protection suits, or radiation protection?
Exposed to Radiation	How often does this job require exposure to radiation?
Spend Time Climbing Ladders, Scaffolds, or Poles	How much does this job require climbing ladders, scaffolds, or poles?

Job Zone Component	Job Zone Component Definitions
Title	Job Zone Five: Extensive Preparation Needed
Overall Experience	Extensive skill, knowledge, and experience are needed for these occupations. Many require more than five years of experience. For example, surgeons must complete four years of college and an additional five to seven years of specialized medical training to be able to do their job.
Job Training	Employees may need some on-the-job training, but most of these occupations assume that the person will already have the required skills, knowledge, work-related experience, and/or training.
Job Zone Examples	These occupations often involve coordinating, training, supervising, or managing the activities of others to accomplish goals. Very advanced communication and organizational skills are required. Examples include athletic trainers, lawyers, managing editors, physicists, social psychologists, and surgeons.
SVP Range	(8.0 and above)
Education	A bachelor's degree is the minimum formal education required for these occupations. However, many also require graduate school. For example, they may require a master's degree, and some require a Ph.D., M.D., or J.D. (law degree).

Work_Styles	Work_Styles Definitions
Leadership	Job requires a willingness to lead, take charge, and offer opinions and direction.
Dependability	Job requires being reliable, responsible, and dependable, and fulfilling obligations.
Integrity	Job requires being honest and ethical.
Persistence	Job requires persistence in the face of obstacles.
Initiative	Job requires a willingness to take on responsibilities and challenges.
Adaptability/Flexibility	Job requires being open to change (positive or negative) and to considerable variety in the workplace.
Cooperation	Job requires being pleasant with others on the job and displaying a good-natured, cooperative attitude.
Stress Tolerance	Job requires accepting criticism and dealing calmly and effectively with high stress situations.
Concern for Others	Job requires being sensitive to others' needs and feelings and being understanding and helpful on the job.
Achievement/Effort	Job requires establishing and maintaining personally challenging achievement goals and exerting effort toward mastering tasks.
Attention to Detail	Job requires being careful about detail and thorough in completing work tasks.
Social Orientation	Job requires preferring to work with others rather than alone, and being personally connected with others on the job.
Self Control	Job requires maintaining composure, keeping emotions in check, controlling anger, and avoiding aggressive behavior, even in very difficult situations.
Independence	Job requires developing one's own ways of doing things, guiding oneself with little or no supervision, and depending on oneself to get things done.
Innovation	Job requires creativity and alternative thinking to develop new ideas for and answers to work-related problems.
Analytical Thinking	Job requires analyzing information and using logic to address work-related issues and problems.

27-2023.00 - Umpires, Referees, and Other Sports Officials

Officiate at competitive athletic or sporting events. Detect infractions of rules and decide penalties according to established regulations.

Tasks

1) Inspect sporting equipment and/or examine participants in order to ensure compliance with event and safety regulations.

2) Report to regulating organizations regarding sporting activities, complaints made, and actions taken or needed such as fines or other disciplinary actions.

3) Teach and explain the rules and regulations governing a specific sport.

4) Direct participants to assigned areas such as starting blocks or penalty areas.

5) Keep track of event times, including race times and elapsed time during game segments, starting or stopping play when necessary.

6) Verify scoring calculations before competition winners are announced.

7) Start races and competitions.

8) Judge performances in sporting competitions in order to award points, impose scoring penalties, and determine results.

9) Research and study players and teams in order to anticipate issues that might arise in future engagements.

10) Verify credentials of participants in sporting events, and make other qualifying determinations such as starting order or handicap number.

11) Compile scores and other athletic records.

12) Confer with other sporting officials, coaches, players, and facility managers in order to provide information, coordinate activities, and discuss problems.

13) Signal participants or other officials to make them aware of infractions or to otherwise regulate play or competition.

14) Officiate at sporting events, games, or competitions, to maintain standards of play and to ensure that game rules are observed.

Knowledge	Knowledge Definitions
Psychology	Knowledge of human behavior and performance; individual differences in ability, personality, and interests; learning and motivation; psychological research methods; and the assessment and treatment of behavioral and affective disorders.
Customer and Personal Service	Knowledge of principles and processes for providing customer and personal services. This includes customer needs assessment, meeting quality standards for services, and evaluation of customer satisfaction.
English Language	Knowledge of the structure and content of the English language including the meaning and spelling of words, rules of composition, and grammar.
Sociology and Anthropology	Knowledge of group behavior and dynamics, societal trends and influences, human migrations, ethnicity, cultures and their history and origins.
Administration and Management	Knowledge of business and management principles involved in strategic planning, resource allocation, human resources modeling, leadership technique, production methods, and coordination of people and resources.
Education and Training	Knowledge of principles and methods for curriculum and training design, teaching and instruction for individuals and groups, and the measurement of training effects.
Public Safety and Security	Knowledge of relevant equipment, policies, procedures, and strategies to promote effective local, state, or national security operations for the protection of people, data, property, and institutions.
Personnel and Human Resources	Knowledge of principles and procedures for personnel recruitment, selection, training, compensation and benefits, labor relations and negotiation, and personnel information systems.
Communications and Media	Knowledge of media production, communication, and dissemination techniques and methods. This includes alternative ways to inform and entertain via written, oral, and visual media.
Computers and Electronics	Knowledge of circuit boards, processors, chips, electronic equipment, and computer hardware and software, including applications and programming.
Transportation	Knowledge of principles and methods for moving people or goods by air, rail, sea, or road, including the relative costs and benefits.
Clerical	Knowledge of administrative and clerical procedures and systems such as word processing, managing files and records, stenography and transcription, designing forms, and other office procedures and terminology.
Mathematics	Knowledge of arithmetic, algebra, geometry, calculus, statistics, and their applications.

Law and Government	Knowledge of laws, legal codes, court procedures, precedents, government regulations, executive orders, agency rules, and the democratic political process.
Telecommunications	Knowledge of transmission, broadcasting, switching, control, and operation of telecommunications systems.
Therapy and Counseling	Knowledge of principles, methods, and procedures for diagnosis, treatment, and rehabilitation of physical and mental dysfunctions, and for career counseling and guidance.
Sales and Marketing	Knowledge of principles and methods for showing, promoting, and selling products or services. This includes marketing strategy and tactics, product demonstration, sales techniques, and sales control systems.
Philosophy and Theology	Knowledge of different philosophical systems and religions. This includes their basic principles, values, ethics, ways of thinking, customs, practices, and their impact on human culture.
Medicine and Dentistry	Knowledge of the information and techniques needed to diagnose and treat human injuries, diseases, and deformities. This includes symptoms, treatment alternatives, drug properties and interactions, and preventive health-care measures.
Economics and Accounting	Knowledge of economic and accounting principles and practices, the financial markets, banking and the analysis and reporting of financial data.
Foreign Language	Knowledge of the structure and content of a foreign (non-English) language including the meaning and spelling of words, rules of composition and grammar, and pronunciation.
Geography	Knowledge of principles and methods for describing the features of land, sea, and air masses, including their physical characteristics, locations, interrelationships, and distribution of plant, animal, and human life.
Physics	Knowledge and prediction of physical principles, laws, their interrelationships, and applications to understanding fluid, material, and atmospheric dynamics, and mechanical, electrical, atomic and sub- atomic structures and processes.
Biology	Knowledge of plant and animal organisms, their tissues, cells, functions, interdependencies, and interactions with each other and the environment.
History and Archeology	Knowledge of historical events and their causes, indicators, and effects on civilizations and cultures.
Fine Arts	Knowledge of the theory and techniques required to compose, produce, and perform works of music, dance, visual arts, drama, and sculpture.
Production and Processing	Knowledge of raw materials, production processes, quality control, costs, and other techniques for maximizing the effective manufacture and distribution of goods.
Engineering and Technology	Knowledge of the practical application of engineering science and technology. This includes applying principles, techniques, procedures, and equipment to the design and production of various goods and services.
Mechanical	Knowledge of machines and tools, including their designs, uses, repair, and maintenance.
Building and Construction	Knowledge of materials, methods, and the tools involved in the construction or repair of houses, buildings, or other structures such as highways and roads.
Design	Knowledge of design techniques, tools, and principles involved in production of precision technical plans, blueprints, drawings, and models.
Food Production	Knowledge of techniques and equipment for planting, growing, and harvesting food products (both plant and animal) for consumption, including storage/handling techniques.
Chemistry	Knowledge of the chemical composition, structure, and properties of substances and of the chemical processes and transformations that they undergo. This includes uses of chemicals and their interactions, danger signs, production techniques, and disposal methods.

Skills	Skills Definitions
Judgment and Decision Making	Considering the relative costs and benefits of potential actions to choose the most appropriate one.
Social Perceptiveness	Being aware of others' reactions and understanding why they react as they do.
Active Listening	Giving full attention to what other people are saying, taking time to understand the points being made, asking questions as appropriate, and not interrupting at inappropriate times.
Persuasion	Persuading others to change their minds or behavior.
Coordination	Adjusting actions in relation to others' actions.
Speaking	Talking to others to convey information effectively.

Monitoring	Monitoring/Assessing performance of yourself, other individuals, or organizations to make improvements or take corrective action.
Reading Comprehension	Understanding written sentences and paragraphs in work related documents.
Active Learning	Understanding the implications of new information for both current and future problem-solving and decision-making.
Critical Thinking	Using logic and reasoning to identify the strengths and weaknesses of alternative solutions, conclusions or approaches to problems.
Negotiation	Bringing others together and trying to reconcile differences.
Learning Strategies	Selecting and using training/instructional methods and procedures appropriate for the situation when learning or teaching new things.
Time Management	Managing one's own time and the time of others.
Instructing	Teaching others how to do something.
Complex Problem Solving	Identifying complex problems and reviewing related information to develop and evaluate options and implement solutions.
Management of Personnel Resources	Motivating, developing, and directing people as they work, identifying the best people for the job.
Service Orientation	Actively looking for ways to help people.
Writing	Communicating effectively in writing as appropriate for the needs of the audience.
Quality Control Analysis	Conducting tests and inspections of products, services, or processes to evaluate quality or performance.
Systems Evaluation	Identifying measures or indicators of system performance and the actions needed to improve or correct performance, relative to the goals of the system.
Equipment Selection	Determining the kind of tools and equipment needed to do a job.
Operations Analysis	Analyzing needs and product requirements to create a design.
Mathematics	Using mathematics to solve problems.
Systems Analysis	Determining how a system should work and how changes in conditions, operations, and the environment will affect outcomes.
Troubleshooting	Determining causes of operating errors and deciding what to do about it.
Management of Financial Resources	Determining how money will be spent to get the work done, and accounting for these expenditures.
Management of Material Resources	Obtaining and seeing to the appropriate use of equipment, facilities, and materials needed to do certain work.
Technology Design	Generating or adapting equipment and technology to serve user needs.
Operation and Control	Controlling operations of equipment or systems.
Equipment Maintenance	Performing routine maintenance on equipment and determining when and what kind of maintenance is needed.
Science	Using scientific rules and methods to solve problems.
Repairing	Repairing machines or systems using the needed tools.
Programming	Writing computer programs for various purposes.
Operation Monitoring	Watching gauges, dials, or other indicators to make sure a machine is working properly.
Installation	Installing equipment, machines, wiring, or programs to meet specifications.

Ability	Ability Definitions
Problem Sensitivity	The ability to tell when something is wrong or is likely to go wrong. It does not involve solving the problem, only recognizing there is a problem.
Oral Expression	The ability to communicate information and ideas in speaking so others will understand.
Speech Clarity	The ability to speak clearly so others can understand you.
Oral Comprehension	The ability to listen to and understand information and ideas presented through spoken words and sentences.
Speech Recognition	The ability to identify and understand the speech of another person.
Trunk Strength	The ability to use your abdominal and lower back muscles to support part of the body repeatedly or continuously over time without 'giving out' or fatiguing.
Far Vision	The ability to see details at a distance.
Stamina	The ability to exert yourself physically over long periods of time without getting winded or out of breath.
Near Vision	The ability to see details at close range (within a few feet of the observer).
Information Ordering	The ability to arrange things or actions in a certain order or pattern according to a specific rule or set of rules (e.g., patterns of numbers, letters, words, pictures, mathematical operations).

Deductive Reasoning	The ability to apply general rules to specific problems to produce answers that make sense.
Selective Attention	The ability to concentrate on a task over a period of time without being distracted.
Speed of Limb Movement	The ability to quickly move the arms and legs.
Inductive Reasoning	The ability to combine pieces of information to form general rules or conclusions (includes finding a relationship among seemingly unrelated events).
Written Comprehension	The ability to read and understand information and ideas presented in writing.
Perceptual Speed	The ability to quickly and accurately compare similarities and differences among sets of letters, numbers, objects, pictures, or patterns. The things to be compared may be presented at the same time or one after the other. This ability also includes comparing a presented object with a remembered object.
Multilimb Coordination	The ability to coordinate two or more limbs (for example, two arms, two legs, or one leg and one arm) while sitting, standing, or lying down. It does not involve performing the activities while the whole body is in motion.
Gross Body Coordination	The ability to coordinate the movement of your arms, legs, and torso together when the whole body is in motion.
Flexibility of Closure	The ability to identify or detect a known pattern (a figure, object, word, or sound) that is hidden in other distracting material.
Category Flexibility	The ability to generate or use different sets of rules for combining or grouping things in different ways.
Gross Body Equilibrium	The ability to keep or regain your body balance or stay upright when in an unstable position.
Dynamic Strength	The ability to exert muscle force repeatedly or continuously over time. This involves muscular endurance and resistance to muscle fatigue.
Written Expression	The ability to communicate information and ideas in writing so others will understand.
Static Strength	The ability to exert maximum muscle force to lift, push, pull, or carry objects.
Extent Flexibility	The ability to bend, stretch, twist, or reach with your body, arms, and/or legs.
Reaction Time	The ability to quickly respond (with the hand, finger, or foot) to a signal (sound, light, picture) when it appears.
Time Sharing	The ability to shift back and forth between two or more activities or sources of information (such as speech, sounds, touch, or other sources).
Speed of Closure	The ability to quickly make sense of, combine, and organize information into meaningful patterns.
Auditory Attention	The ability to focus on a single source of sound in the presence of other distracting sounds.
Visual Color Discrimination	The ability to match or detect differences between colors, including shades of color and brightness.
Depth Perception	The ability to judge which of several objects is closer or farther away from you, or to judge the distance between you and an object.
Hearing Sensitivity	The ability to detect or tell the differences between sounds that vary in pitch and loudness.
Originality	The ability to come up with unusual or clever ideas about a given topic or situation, or to develop creative ways to solve a problem.
Fluency of Ideas	The ability to come up with a number of ideas about a topic (the number of ideas is important, not their quality, correctness, or creativity).
Arm-Hand Steadiness	The ability to keep your hand and arm steady while moving your arm or while holding your arm and hand in one position.
Number Facility	The ability to add, subtract, multiply, or divide quickly and correctly.
Response Orientation	The ability to choose quickly between two or more movements in response to two or more different signals (lights, sounds, pictures). It includes the speed with which the correct response is started with the hand, foot, or other body part.
Memorization	The ability to remember information such as words, numbers, pictures, and procedures.
Visualization	The ability to imagine how something will look after it is moved around or when its parts are moved or rearranged.
Explosive Strength	The ability to use short bursts of muscle force to propel oneself (as in jumping or sprinting), or to throw an object.
Mathematical Reasoning	The ability to choose the right mathematical methods or formulas to solve a problem.
Finger Dexterity	The ability to make precisely coordinated movements of the fingers of one or both hands to grasp, manipulate, or assemble very small objects.

Peripheral Vision	The ability to see objects or movement of objects to one's side when the eyes are looking ahead.
Glare Sensitivity	The ability to see objects in the presence of glare or bright lighting.
Spatial Orientation	The ability to know your location in relation to the environment or to know where other objects are in relation to you.
Manual Dexterity	The ability to quickly move your hand, your hand together with your arm, or your two hands to grasp, manipulate, or assemble objects.
Rate Control	The ability to time your movements or the movement of a piece of equipment in anticipation of changes in the speed and/or direction of a moving object or scene.
Sound Localization	The ability to tell the direction from which a sound originated.
Wrist-Finger Speed	The ability to make fast, simple, repeated movements of the fingers, hands, and wrists.
Night Vision	The ability to see under low light conditions.
Dynamic Flexibility	The ability to quickly and repeatedly bend, stretch, twist, or reach out with your body, arms, and/or legs.
Control Precision	The ability to quickly and repeatedly adjust the controls of a machine or a vehicle to exact positions.

Work_Activity	Work_Activity Definitions
Resolving Conflicts and Negotiating with Others	Handling complaints, settling disputes, and resolving grievances and conflicts, or otherwise negotiating with others.
Performing General Physical Activities	Performing physical activities that require considerable use of your arms and legs and moving your whole body, such as climbing, lifting, balancing, walking, stooping, and handling of materials.
Making Decisions and Solving Problems	Analyzing information and evaluating results to choose the best solution and solve problems.
Establishing and Maintaining Interpersonal Relatio	Developing constructive and cooperative working relationships with others, and maintaining them over time.
Evaluating Information to Determine Compliance wit	Using relevant information and individual judgment to determine whether events or processes comply with laws, regulations, or standards.
Getting Information	Observing, receiving, and otherwise obtaining information from all relevant sources.
Developing and Building Teams	Encouraging and building mutual trust, respect, and cooperation among team members.
Updating and Using Relevant Knowledge	Keeping up-to-date technically and applying new knowledge to your job.
Communicating with Supervisors, Peers, or Subordin	Providing information to supervisors, co-workers, and subordinates by telephone, in written form, e-mail, or in person.
Coaching and Developing Others	Identifying the developmental needs of others and coaching, mentoring, or otherwise helping others to improve their knowledge or skills.
Training and Teaching Others	Identifying the educational needs of others, developing formal educational or training programs or classes, and teaching or instructing others.
Identifying Objects, Actions, and Events	Identifying information by categorizing, estimating, recognizing differences or similarities, and detecting changes in circumstances or events.
Performing for or Working Directly with the Public	Performing for people or dealing directly with the public. This includes serving customers in restaurants and stores, and receiving clients or guests.
Guiding, Directing, and Motivating Subordinates	Providing guidance and direction to subordinates, including setting performance standards and monitoring performance.
Communicating with Persons Outside Organization	Communicating with people outside the organization, representing the organization to customers, the public, government, and other external sources. This information can be exchanged in person, in writing, or by telephone or e-mail.
Selling or Influencing Others	Convincing others to buy merchandise/goods or to otherwise change their minds or actions.
Coordinating the Work and Activities of Others	Getting members of a group to work together to accomplish tasks.
Interpreting the Meaning of Information for Others	Translating or explaining what information means and how it can be used.
Scheduling Work and Activities	Scheduling events, programs, and activities, as well as the work of others.
Organizing, Planning, and Prioritizing Work	Developing specific goals and plans to prioritize, organize, and accomplish your work.
Documenting/Recording Information	Entering, transcribing, recording, storing, or maintaining information in written or electronic/magnetic form.
Provide Consultation and Advice to Others	Providing guidance and expert advice to management or other groups on technical, systems-, or process-related topics.

Judging the Qualities of Things, Services, or Peop	Assessing the value, importance, or quality of things or people.
Performing Administrative Activities	Performing day-to-day administrative tasks such as maintaining information files and processing paperwork.
Inspecting Equipment, Structures, or Material	Inspecting equipment, structures, or materials to identify the cause of errors or other problems or defects.
Thinking Creatively	Developing, designing, or creating new applications, ideas, relationships, systems, or products, including artistic contributions.
Processing Information	Compiling, coding, categorizing, calculating, tabulating, auditing, or verifying information or data.
Assisting and Caring for Others	Providing personal assistance, medical attention, emotional support, or other personal care to others such as coworkers, customers, or patients.
Analyzing Data or Information	Identifying the underlying principles, reasons, or facts of information by breaking down information or data into separate parts.
Monitor Processes, Materials, or Surroundings	Monitoring and reviewing information from materials, events, or the environment, to detect or assess problems.
Developing Objectives and Strategies	Establishing long-range objectives and specifying the strategies and actions to achieve them.
Staffing Organizational Units	Recruiting, interviewing, selecting, hiring, and promoting employees in an organization.
Interacting With Computers	Using computers and computer systems (including hardware and software) to program, write software, set up functions, enter data, or process information.
Handling and Moving Objects	Using hands and arms in handling, installing, positioning, and moving materials, and manipulating things.
Estimating the Quantifiable Characteristics of Pro	Estimating sizes, distances, and quantities; or determining time, costs, resources, or materials needed to perform a work activity.
Monitoring and Controlling Resources	Monitoring and controlling resources and overseeing the spending of money.
Controlling Machines and Processes	Using either control mechanisms or direct physical activity to operate machines or processes (not including computers or vehicles).
Operating Vehicles, Mechanized Devices, or Equipme	Running, maneuvering, navigating, or driving vehicles or mechanized equipment, such as forklifts, passenger vehicles, aircraft, or water craft.
Drafting, Laying Out, and Specifying Technical Dev	Providing documentation, detailed instructions, drawings, or specifications to tell others about how devices, parts, equipment, or structures are to be fabricated, constructed, assembled, modified, maintained, or used.
Repairing and Maintaining Electronic Equipment	Servicing, repairing, calibrating, regulating, fine-tuning, or testing machines, devices, and equipment that operate primarily on the basis of electrical or electronic (not mechanical) principles.
Repairing and Maintaining Mechanical Equipment	Servicing, repairing, adjusting, and testing machines, devices, moving parts, and equipment that operate primarily on the basis of mechanical (not electronic) principles.

Work_Context	Work_Context Definitions
Spend Time Standing	How much does this job require standing?
Importance of Being Exact or Accurate	How important is being very exact or highly accurate in performing this job?
Frequency of Conflict Situations	How often are there conflict situations the employee has to face in this job?
Work With Work Group or Team	How important is it to work with others in a group or team in this job?
Deal With Unpleasant or Angry People	How frequently does the worker have to deal with unpleasant, angry, or discourteous individuals as part of the job requirements?
Freedom to Make Decisions	How much decision making freedom, without supervision, does the job offer?
Contact With Others	How much does this job require the worker to be in contact with others (face-to-face, by telephone, or otherwise) in order to perform it?
Spend Time Walking and Running	How much does this job require walking and running?
Level of Competition	To what extent does this job require the worker to compete or to be aware of competitive pressures?
Face-to-Face Discussions	How often do you have to have face-to-face discussions with individuals or teams in this job?
Physical Proximity	To what extent does this job require the worker to perform job tasks in close physical proximity to other people?

Sounds, Noise Levels Are Distracting or Uncomforta	How often does this job require working exposed to sounds and noise levels that are distracting or uncomfortable?
Telephone	How often do you have telephone conversations in this job?
Time Pressure	How often does this job require the worker to meet strict deadlines?
Deal With External Customers	How important is it to work with external customers or the public in this job?
Impact of Decisions on Co-workers or Company Resul	How do the decisions an employee makes impact the results of co-workers, clients or the company?
Frequency of Decision Making	How frequently is the worker required to make decisions that affect other people, the financial resources, and/or the image and reputation of the organization?
Spend Time Making Repetitive Motions	How much does this job require making repetitive motions?
Importance of Repeating Same Tasks	How important is repeating the same physical activities (e.g., key entry) or mental activities (e.g., checking entries in a ledger) over and over, without stopping, to performing this job?
Structured versus Unstructured Work	To what extent is this job structured for the worker, rather than allowing the worker to determine tasks, priorities, and goals?
Electronic Mail	How often do you use electronic mail in this job?
Outdoors, Exposed to Weather	How often does this job require working outdoors, exposed to all weather conditions?
Deal With Physically Aggressive People	How frequently does this job require the worker to deal with physical aggression of violent individuals?
Consequence of Error	How serious would the result usually be if the worker made a mistake that was not readily correctable?
Coordinate or Lead Others	How important is it to coordinate or lead others in accomplishing work activities in this job?
Indoors, Environmentally Controlled	How often does this job require working indoors in environmentally controlled conditions?
Very Hot or Cold Temperatures	How often does this job require working in very hot (above 90 F degrees) or very cold (below 32 F degrees) temperatures?
Responsible for Others' Health and Safety	How much responsibility is there for the health and safety of others in this job?
Indoors, Not Environmentally Controlled	How often does this job require working indoors in non-controlled environmental conditions (e.g., warehouse without heat)?
Letters and Memos	How often does the job require written letters and memos?
Spend Time Keeping or Regaining Balance	How much does this job require keeping or regaining your balance?
Extremely Bright or Inadequate Lighting	How often does this job require working in extremely bright or inadequate lighting conditions?
Responsibility for Outcomes and Results	How responsible is the worker for work outcomes and results of other workers?
Spend Time Bending or Twisting the Body	How much does this job require bending or twisting your body?
Wear Common Protective or Safety Equipment such as	How much does this job require wearing common protective or safety equipment such as safety shoes, glasses, gloves, hard hats or live jackets?
Spend Time Using Your Hands to Handle, Control, or	How much does this job require using your hands to handle, control, or feel objects, tools or controls?
Public Speaking	How often do you have to perform public speaking in this job?
Exposed to Minor Burns, Cuts, Bites, or Stings	How often does this job require exposure to minor burns, cuts, bites, or stings?
Wear Specialized Protective or Safety Equipment su	How much does this job require wearing specialized protective or safety equipment such as breathing apparatus, safety harness, full protection suits, or radiation protection?
Exposed to Disease or Infections	How often does this job require exposure to disease/infections?
Spend Time Kneeling, Crouching, Stooping, or Crawl	How much does this job require kneeling, crouching, stooping, or crawling?
Exposed to Contaminants	How often does this job require working exposed to contaminants (such as pollutants, gases, dust or odors)?
Outdoors, Under Cover	How often does this job require working outdoors, under cover (e.g., structure with roof but no walls)?
Cramped Work Space, Awkward Positions	How often does this job require working in cramped work spaces that requires getting into awkward positions?
Pace Determined by Speed of Equipment	How important is it to this job that the pace is determined by the speed of equipment or machinery? (This does not refer to keeping busy at all times on this job.)
Exposed to Hazardous Conditions	How often does this job require exposure to hazardous conditions?
In an Enclosed Vehicle or Equipment	How often does this job require working in a closed vehicle or equipment (e.g., car)?

| Job Zone Component | | |

Exposed to Hazardous Equipment — How often does this job require exposure to hazardous equipment?

Degree of Automation — How automated is the job?

Exposed to Radiation — How often does this job require exposure to radiation?

Spend Time Sitting — How much does this job require sitting?

Exposed to Whole Body Vibration — How often does this job require exposure to whole body vibration (e.g., operate a jackhammer)?

Spend Time Climbing Ladders, Scaffolds, or Poles — How much does this job require climbing ladders, scaffolds, or poles?

Exposed to High Places — How often does this job require exposure to high places?

In an Open Vehicle or Equipment — How often does this job require working in an open vehicle or equipment (e.g., tractor)?

Job Zone Component	Job Zone Component Definitions
Title	Job Zone Two: Some Preparation Needed
Overall Experience	Some previous work-related skill, knowledge, or experience may be helpful in these occupations, but usually is not needed. For example, a drywall installer might benefit from experience installing drywall, but an inexperienced person could still learn to be an installer with little difficulty.
Job Training	Employees in these occupations need anywhere from a few months to one year of working with experienced employees.
Job Zone Examples	These occupations often involve using your knowledge and skills to help others. Examples include drywall installers, fire inspectors, flight attendants, pharmacy technicians, salespersons (retail), and tellers.
SVP Range	(4.0 to < 6.0)
Education	These occupations usually require a high school diploma and may require some vocational training or job-related course work. In some cases, an associate's or bachelor's degree could be needed.

Work_Styles	Work_Styles Definitions
Integrity	Job requires being honest and ethical.
Stress Tolerance	Job requires accepting criticism and dealing calmly and effectively with high stress situations.
Self Control	Job requires maintaining composure, keeping emotions in check, controlling anger, and avoiding aggressive behavior, even in very difficult situations.
Dependability	Job requires being reliable, responsible, and dependable, and fulfilling obligations.
Persistence	Job requires persistence in the face of obstacles.
Achievement/Effort	Job requires establishing and maintaining personally challenging achievement goals and exerting effort toward mastering tasks.
Cooperation	Job requires being pleasant with others on the job and displaying a good-natured, cooperative attitude.
Adaptability/Flexibility	Job requires being open to change (positive or negative) and to considerable variety in the workplace.
Attention to Detail	Job requires being careful about detail and thorough in completing work tasks.
Leadership	Job requires a willingness to lead, take charge, and offer opinions and direction.
Initiative	Job requires a willingness to take on responsibilities and challenges.
Social Orientation	Job requires preferring to work with others rather than alone, and being personally connected with others on the job.
Independence	Job requires developing one's own ways of doing things, guiding oneself with little or no supervision, and depending on oneself to get things done.
Concern for Others	Job requires being sensitive to others' needs and feelings and being understanding and helpful on the job.
Analytical Thinking	Job requires analyzing information and using logic to address work-related issues and problems.
Innovation	Job requires creativity and alternative thinking to develop new ideas for and answers to work-related problems.

27-2031.00 - Dancers

Perform dances. May also sing or act.

Tasks

1) Audition for dance roles or for membership in dance companies.

2) Develop self-understanding of physical capabilities and limitations, and choose dance styles accordingly.

3) Attend costume fittings, photography sessions, and makeup calls associated with dance performances.

4) Collaborate with choreographers in order to refine or modify dance steps.

5) Coordinate dancing with that of partners or dance ensembles.

6) Study and practice dance moves required in roles.

7) Train, exercise, and attend dance classes to maintain high levels of technical proficiency, physical ability, and physical fitness.

8) Devise and choreograph dance for self or others.

9) Teach dance students.

10) Monitor the field of dance to remain aware of current trends and innovations.

11) Harmonize body movements to rhythm of musical accompaniment.

12) Perform classical, modern, or acrobatic dances in productions, expressing stories, rhythm, and sound with their bodies.

27-2041.01 - Music Directors

Direct and conduct instrumental or vocal performances by musical groups, such as orchestras or choirs.

Tasks

1) Coordinate and organize tours, or hire touring companies to arrange concert dates, venues, accommodations, and transportation for longer tours.

2) Confer with clergy to select music for church services.

3) Perform administrative tasks such as applying for grants, developing budgets, negotiating contracts, and designing and printing programs and other promotional materials.

4) Plan and implement fund-raising and promotional activities.

5) Engage services of composers to write scores.

6) Conduct guest soloists in addition to ensemble members.

7) Assign and review staff work in such areas as scoring, arranging, and copying music, and vocal coaching.

8) Plan and schedule rehearsals and performances, and arrange details such as locations, accompanists, and instrumentalists.

9) Transcribe musical compositions and melodic lines to adapt them to a particular group, or to create a particular musical style.

10) Meet with soloists and concertmasters to discuss and prepare for performances.

11) Consider such factors as ensemble size and abilities, availability of scores, and the need for musical variety, in order to select music to be performed.

12) Study scores to learn the music in detail, and to develop interpretations.

13) Audition and select performers for musical presentations.

14) Position members within groups to obtain balance among instrumental or vocal sections.

15) Meet with composers to discuss interpretations of their work.

16) Use gestures to shape the music being played, communicating desired tempo, phrasing, tone, color, pitch, volume, and other performance aspects.

17) Direct groups at rehearsals and live or recorded performances in order to achieve desired effects such as tonal and harmonic balance dynamics, rhythm, and tempo.

27-2042.01 - Singers

Sing songs on stage, radio, television, or motion pictures.

Tasks

1) Memorize musical selections and routines, or sing following printed text, musical notation, or customer instructions.

2) Observe choral leaders or prompters for cues or directions in vocal presentation.

3) Perform before live audiences, or in television, radio, or movie productions.

4) Compose songs and/or create vocal arrangements.

5) Sing as a soloist or as a member of a vocal group.

6) Learn acting, dancing, and other skills required for dramatic singing roles.

7) Practice singing exercises and study with vocal coaches, in order to develop their voices and skills and to rehearse for upcoming roles.

8) Interpret or modify music, applying knowledge of harmony, melody, rhythm, and voice production to individualize presentations and maintain audience interest.

9) Sing a cappella or with musical accompaniment.

10) Make or participate in recordings.

11) Research particular roles to find out more about a character, or the time and place in which a piece is set.

12) Seek out and learn new music that is suitable for live performance and/or recording.

27-2042.02 - Musicians, Instrumental

Play one or more musical instruments in recital, in accompaniment, or as members of an orchestra, band, or other musical group.

Tasks

1) Provide the musical background for live shows such as ballets, operas, musical theatre, and cabarets.

2) Teach music for specific instruments.

3) Specialize in playing a specific family of instruments and/or a particular type of music.

4) Make or participate in recordings in music studios.

5) Improvise music during performances.

6) Practice musical instrument performances, individually or in rehearsal with other musicians, to master individual pieces of music and to maintain and improve skills.

7) Play musical instruments as soloists, or as members or guest artists of musical groups such as orchestras, ensembles, or bands.

8) Play from memory or by following scores.

9) Perform before live audiences.

10) Direct bands or orchestras.

11) Promote their own or their group's music by participating in media interviews and other activities.

12) Audition for orchestras, bands, or other musical groups.

13) Compose original music such as popular songs, symphonies, or sonatas.

14) Transpose music to alternate keys, or to fit individual styles or purposes.

27-3011.00 - Radio and Television Announcers

Talk on radio or television. May interview guests, act as master of ceremonies, read news flashes, identify station by giving call letters, or announce song title and artist.

Tasks

1) Identify stations, and introduce or close shows, using memorized or read scripts, and/or ad-libs.

2) Interview show guests about their lives, their work, or topics of current interest.

3) Make promotional appearances at public or private events in order to represent their employers.

4) Prepare and deliver news, sports, and/or weather reports, gathering and rewriting material so that it will convey required information and fit specific time slots.

5) Read news flashes to inform audiences of important events.

6) Host civic, charitable, or promotional events that are broadcast over television or radio.

7) Discuss various topics over the telephone with viewers or listeners.

8) Comment on music and other matters, such as weather or traffic conditions.

9) Select program content, in conjunction with producers and assistants, based on factors such as program specialties, audience tastes, or requests from the public.

10) Announce musical selections, station breaks, commercials, or public service information, and accept requests from listening audience.

11) Operate control consoles.

12) Attend press conferences in order to gather information for broadcast.

13) Provide commentary and conduct interviews during sporting events, parades, conventions, and other events.

14) Moderate panels or discussion shows on topics such as current affairs, art, or education.

15) Locate guests to appear on talk or interview shows.

16) Record commercials for later broadcast.

17) Keep daily program logs to provide information on all elements aired during broadcast, such as musical selections and station promotions.

18) Coordinate games, contests, or other on-air competitions, performing such duties as asking questions and awarding prizes.

19) Describe or demonstrate products that viewers may purchase through specific shows or in stores.

20) Give network cues permitting selected stations to receive programs.

Knowledge	Knowledge Definitions
Communications and Media	Knowledge of media production, communication, and dissemination techniques and methods. This includes alternative ways to inform and entertain via written, oral, and visual media.
English Language	Knowledge of the structure and content of the English language including the meaning and spelling of words, rules of composition, and grammar.
Telecommunications	Knowledge of transmission, broadcasting, switching, control, and operation of telecommunications systems.
Computers and Electronics	Knowledge of circuit boards, processors, chips, electronic equipment, and computer hardware and software, including applications and programming.
Customer and Personal Service	Knowledge of principles and processes for providing customer and personal services. This includes customer needs assessment, meeting quality standards for services, and evaluation of customer satisfaction.
Administration and Management	Knowledge of business and management principles involved in strategic planning, resource allocation, human resources modeling, leadership technique, production methods, and coordination of people and resources.
Sales and Marketing	Knowledge of principles and methods for showing, promoting, and selling products or services. This includes marketing strategy and tactics, product demonstration, sales techniques, and sales control systems.
Education and Training	Knowledge of principles and methods for curriculum and training design, teaching and instruction for individuals and groups, and the measurement of training effects.
Psychology	Knowledge of human behavior and performance; individual differences in ability, personality, and interests; learning and motivation; psychological research methods; and the assessment and treatment of behavioral and affective disorders.
Clerical	Knowledge of administrative and clerical procedures and systems such as word processing, managing files and records, stenography and transcription, designing forms, and other office procedures and terminology.
Fine Arts	Knowledge of the theory and techniques required to compose, produce, and perform works of music, dance, visual arts, drama, and sculpture.

Geography	Knowledge of principles and methods for describing the features of land, sea, and air masses, including their physical characteristics, locations, interrelationships, and distribution of plant, animal, and human life.
Law and Government	Knowledge of laws, legal codes, court procedures, precedents, government regulations, executive orders, agency rules, and the democratic political process.
History and Archeology	Knowledge of historical events and their causes, indicators, and effects on civilizations and cultures.
Mathematics	Knowledge of arithmetic, algebra, geometry, calculus, statistics, and their applications.
Public Safety and Security	Knowledge of relevant equipment, policies, procedures, and strategies to promote effective local, state, or national security operations for the protection of people, data, property, and institutions.
Engineering and Technology	Knowledge of the practical application of engineering science and technology. This includes applying principles, techniques, procedures, and equipment to the design and production of various goods and services.
Sociology and Anthropology	Knowledge of group behavior and dynamics, societal trends and influences, human migrations, ethnicity, cultures and their history and origins.
Personnel and Human Resources	Knowledge of principles and procedures for personnel recruitment, selection, training, compensation and benefits, labor relations and negotiation, and personnel information systems.
Production and Processing	Knowledge of raw materials, production processes, quality control, costs, and other techniques for maximizing the effective manufacture and distribution of goods.
Mechanical	Knowledge of machines and tools, including their designs, uses, repair, and maintenance.
Foreign Language	Knowledge of the structure and content of a foreign (non-English) language including the meaning and spelling of words, rules of composition and grammar, and pronunciation.
Economics and Accounting	Knowledge of economic and accounting principles and practices, the financial markets, banking and the analysis and reporting of financial data.
Philosophy and Theology	Knowledge of different philosophical systems and religions. This includes their basic principles, values, ethics, ways of thinking, customs, practices, and their impact on human culture.
Transportation	Knowledge of principles and methods for moving people or goods by air, rail, sea, or road, including the relative costs and benefits.
Design	Knowledge of design techniques, tools, and principles involved in production of precision technical plans, blueprints, drawings, and models.
Therapy and Counseling	Knowledge of principles, methods, and procedures for diagnosis, treatment, and rehabilitation of physical and mental dysfunctions, and for career counseling and guidance.
Physics	Knowledge and prediction of physical principles, laws, their interrelationships, and applications to understanding fluid, material, and atmospheric dynamics, and mechanical, electrical, atomic and sub- atomic structures and processes.
Building and Construction	Knowledge of materials, methods, and the tools involved in the construction or repair of houses, buildings, or other structures such as highways and roads.
Biology	Knowledge of plant and animal organisms, their tissues, cells, functions, interdependencies, and interactions with each other and the environment.
Chemistry	Knowledge of the chemical composition, structure, and properties of substances and of the chemical processes and transformations that they undergo. This includes uses of chemicals and their interactions, danger signs, production techniques, and disposal methods.
Medicine and Dentistry	Knowledge of the information and techniques needed to diagnose and treat human injuries, diseases, and deformities. This includes symptoms, treatment alternatives, drug properties and interactions, and preventive health-care measures.
Food Production	Knowledge of techniques and equipment for planting, growing, and harvesting food products (both plant and animal) for consumption, including storage/handling techniques.

Skills	Skills Definitions
Speaking	Talking to others to convey information effectively.
Reading Comprehension	Understanding written sentences and paragraphs in work related documents.

Time Management	Managing one's own time and the time of others.
Active Listening	Giving full attention to what other people are saying, taking time to understand the points being made, asking questions as appropriate, and not interrupting at inappropriate times.
Social Perceptiveness	Being aware of others' reactions and understanding why they react as they do.
Writing	Communicating effectively in writing as appropriate for the needs of the audience.
Critical Thinking	Using logic and reasoning to identify the strengths and weaknesses of alternative solutions, conclusions or approaches to problems.
Active Learning	Understanding the implications of new information for both current and future problem-solving and decision-making.
Monitoring	Monitoring/Assessing performance of yourself, other individuals, or organizations to make improvements or take corrective action.
Coordination	Adjusting actions in relation to others' actions.
Judgment and Decision Making	Considering the relative costs and benefits of potential actions to choose the most appropriate one.
Learning Strategies	Selecting and using training/instructional methods and procedures appropriate for the situation when learning or teaching new things.
Instructing	Teaching others how to do something.
Persuasion	Persuading others to change their minds or behavior.
Service Orientation	Actively looking for ways to help people.
Negotiation	Bringing others together and trying to reconcile differences.
Equipment Selection	Determining the kind of tools and equipment needed to do a job.
Management of Personnel Resources	Motivating, developing, and directing people as they work, identifying the best people for the job.
Complex Problem Solving	Identifying complex problems and reviewing related information to develop and evaluate options and implement solutions.
Operation and Control	Controlling operations of equipment or systems.
Operation Monitoring	Watching gauges, dials, or other indicators to make sure a machine is working properly.
Troubleshooting	Determining causes of operating errors and deciding what to do about it.
Quality Control Analysis	Conducting tests and inspections of products, services, or processes to evaluate quality or performance.
Operations Analysis	Analyzing needs and product requirements to create a design.
Mathematics	Using mathematics to solve problems.
Management of Material Resources	Obtaining and seeing to the appropriate use of equipment, facilities, and materials needed to do certain work.
Management of Financial Resources	Determining how money will be spent to get the work done, and accounting for these expenditures.
Technology Design	Generating or adapting equipment and technology to serve user needs.
Systems Evaluation	Identifying measures or indicators of system performance and the actions needed to improve or correct performance, relative to the goals of the system.
Equipment Maintenance	Performing routine maintenance on equipment and determining when and what kind of maintenance is needed.
Installation	Installing equipment, machines, wiring, or programs to meet specifications.
Science	Using scientific rules and methods to solve problems.
Systems Analysis	Determining how a system should work and how changes in conditions, operations, and the environment will affect outcomes.
Repairing	Repairing machines or systems using the needed tools.
Programming	Writing computer programs for various purposes.

Ability	Ability Definitions
Oral Expression	The ability to communicate information and ideas in speaking so others will understand.
Speech Clarity	The ability to speak clearly so others can understand you.
Oral Comprehension	The ability to listen to and understand information and ideas presented through spoken words and sentences.
Written Comprehension	The ability to read and understand information and ideas presented in writing.
Speech Recognition	The ability to identify and understand the speech of another person.
Written Expression	The ability to communicate information and ideas in writing so others will understand.
Originality	The ability to come up with unusual or clever ideas about a given topic or situation, or to develop creative ways to solve a problem.

Information Ordering	The ability to arrange things or actions in a certain order or pattern according to a specific rule or set of rules (e.g., patterns of numbers, letters, words, pictures, mathematical operations).
Near Vision	The ability to see details at close range (within a few feet of the observer).
Inductive Reasoning	The ability to combine pieces of information to form general rules or conclusions (includes finding a relationship among seemingly unrelated events).
Problem Sensitivity	The ability to tell when something is wrong or is likely to go wrong. It does not involve solving the problem, only recognizing there is a problem.
Deductive Reasoning	The ability to apply general rules to specific problems to produce answers that make sense.
Fluency of Ideas	The ability to come up with a number of ideas about a topic (the number of ideas is important, not their quality, correctness, or creativity).
Memorization	The ability to remember information such as words, numbers, pictures, and procedures.
Selective Attention	The ability to concentrate on a task over a period of time without being distracted.
Category Flexibility	The ability to generate or use different sets of rules for combining or grouping things in different ways.
Speed of Closure	The ability to quickly make sense of, combine, and organize information into meaningful patterns.
Time Sharing	The ability to shift back and forth between two or more activities or sources of information (such as speech, sounds, touch, or other sources).
Far Vision	The ability to see details at a distance.
Auditory Attention	The ability to focus on a single source of sound in the presence of other distracting sounds.
Control Precision	The ability to quickly and repeatedly adjust the controls of a machine or a vehicle to exact positions.
Reaction Time	The ability to quickly respond (with the hand, finger, or foot) to a signal (sound, light, picture) when it appears.
Trunk Strength	The ability to use your abdominal and lower back muscles to support part of the body repeatedly or continuously over time without 'giving out' or fatiguing.
Flexibility of Closure	The ability to identify or detect a known pattern (a figure, object, word, or sound) that is hidden in other distracting material.
Finger Dexterity	The ability to make precisely coordinated movements of the fingers of one or both hands to grasp, manipulate, or assemble very small objects.
Perceptual Speed	The ability to quickly and accurately compare similarities and differences among sets of letters, numbers, objects, pictures, or patterns. The things to be compared may be presented at the same time or one after the other. This ability also includes comparing a presented object with a remembered object.
Visual Color Discrimination	The ability to match or detect differences between colors, including shades of color and brightness.
Arm-Hand Steadiness	The ability to keep your hand and arm steady while moving your arm or while holding your arm and hand in one position.
Manual Dexterity	The ability to quickly move your hand, your hand together with your arm, or your two hands to grasp, manipulate, or assemble objects.
Rate Control	The ability to time your movements or the movement of a piece of equipment in anticipation of changes in the speed and/or direction of a moving object or scene.
Number Facility	The ability to add, subtract, multiply, or divide quickly and correctly.
Hearing Sensitivity	The ability to detect or tell the differences between sounds that vary in pitch and loudness.
Visualization	The ability to imagine how something will look after it is moved around or when its parts are moved or rearranged.
Mathematical Reasoning	The ability to choose the right mathematical methods or formulas to solve a problem.
Response Orientation	The ability to choose quickly between two or more movements in response to two or more different signals (lights, sounds, pictures). It includes the speed with which the correct response is started with the hand, foot, or other body part.
Multilimb Coordination	The ability to coordinate two or more limbs (for example, two arms, two legs, or one leg and one arm) while sitting, standing, or lying down. It does not involve performing the activities while the whole body is in motion.
Wrist-Finger Speed	The ability to make fast, simple, repeated movements of the fingers, hands, and wrists.
Sound Localization	The ability to tell the direction from which a sound originated.

Depth Perception	The ability to judge which of several objects is closer or farther away from you, or to judge the distance between you and an object.
Gross Body Equilibrium	The ability to keep or regain your body balance or stay upright when in an unstable position.
Peripheral Vision	The ability to see objects or movement of objects to one's side when the eyes are looking ahead.
Explosive Strength	The ability to use short bursts of muscle force to propel oneself (as in jumping or sprinting), or to throw an object.
Stamina	The ability to exert yourself physically over long periods of time without getting winded or out of breath.
Extent Flexibility	The ability to bend, stretch, twist, or reach with your body, arms, and/or legs.
Gross Body Coordination	The ability to coordinate the movement of your arms, legs, and torso together when the whole body is in motion.
Static Strength	The ability to exert maximum muscle force to lift, push, pull, or carry objects.
Speed of Limb Movement	The ability to quickly move the arms and legs.
Night Vision	The ability to see under low light conditions.
Dynamic Strength	The ability to exert muscle force repeatedly or continuously over time. This involves muscular endurance and resistance to muscle fatigue.
Glare Sensitivity	The ability to see objects in the presence of glare or bright lighting.
Spatial Orientation	The ability to know your location in relation to the environment or to know where other objects are in relation to you.
Dynamic Flexibility	The ability to quickly and repeatedly bend, stretch, twist, or reach out with your body, arms, and/or legs.

Work_Activity	Work_Activity Definitions
Thinking Creatively	Developing, designing, or creating new applications, ideas, relationships, systems, or products, including artistic contributions.
Getting Information	Observing, receiving, and otherwise obtaining information from all relevant sources.
Communicating with Persons Outside Organization	Communicating with people outside the organization, representing the organization to customers, the public, government, and other external sources. This information can be exchanged in person, in writing, or by telephone or e-mail.
Performing for or Working Directly with the Public	Performing for people or dealing directly with the public. This includes serving customers in restaurants and stores, and receiving clients or guests.
Identifying Objects, Actions, and Events	Identifying information by categorizing, estimating, recognizing differences or similarities, and detecting changes in circumstances or events.
Communicating with Supervisors, Peers, or Subordin	Providing information to supervisors, co-workers, and subordinates by telephone, in written form, e-mail, or in person.
Interacting With Computers	Using computers and computer systems (including hardware and software) to program, write software, set up functions, enter data, or process information.
Updating and Using Relevant Knowledge	Keeping up-to-date technically and applying new knowledge to your job.
Establishing and Maintaining Interpersonal Relatio	Developing constructive and cooperative working relationships with others, and maintaining them over time.
Interpreting the Meaning of Information for Others	Translating or explaining what information means and how it can be used.
Processing Information	Compiling, coding, categorizing, calculating, tabulating, auditing, or verifying information or data.
Analyzing Data or Information	Identifying the underlying principles, reasons, or facts of information by breaking down information or data into separate parts.
Documenting/Recording Information	Entering, transcribing, recording, storing, or maintaining information in written or electronic/magnetic form.
Making Decisions and Solving Problems	Analyzing information and evaluating results to choose the best solution and solve problems.
Organizing, Planning, and Prioritizing Work	Developing specific goals and plans to prioritize, organize, and accomplish your work.
Monitor Processes, Materials, or Surroundings	Monitoring and reviewing information from materials, events, or the environment, to detect or assess problems.
Judging the Qualities of Things, Services, or Peop	Assessing the value, importance, or quality of things or people.
Scheduling Work and Activities	Scheduling events, programs, and activities, as well as the work of others.

Developing Objectives and Strategies	Establishing long-range objectives and specifying the strategies and actions to achieve them.
Selling or Influencing Others	Convincing others to buy merchandise/goods or to otherwise change their minds or actions.
Training and Teaching Others	Identifying the educational needs of others, developing formal educational or training programs or classes, and teaching or instructing others.
Coordinating the Work and Activities of Others	Getting members of a group to work together to accomplish tasks.
Developing and Building Teams	Encouraging and building mutual trust, respect, and cooperation among team members.
Resolving Conflicts and Negotiating with Others	Handling complaints, settling disputes, and resolving grievances and conflicts, or otherwise negotiating with others.
Estimating the Quantifiable Characteristics of Pro	Estimating sizes, distances, and quantities; or determining time, costs, resources, or materials needed to perform a work activity.
Evaluating Information to Determine Compliance wit	Using relevant information and individual judgment to determine whether events or processes comply with laws, regulations, or standards.
Guiding, Directing, and Motivating Subordinates	Providing guidance and direction to subordinates, including setting performance standards and monitoring performance.
Controlling Machines and Processes	Using either control mechanisms or direct physical activity to operate machines or processes (not including computers or vehicles).
Coaching and Developing Others	Identifying the developmental needs of others and coaching, mentoring, or otherwise helping others to improve their knowledge or skills.
Provide Consultation and Advice to Others	Providing guidance and expert advice to management or other groups on technical, systems-, or process-related topics.
Performing Administrative Activities	Performing day-to-day administrative tasks such as maintaining information files and processing paperwork.
Inspecting Equipment, Structures, or Material	Inspecting equipment, structures, or materials to identify the cause of errors or other problems or defects.
Monitoring and Controlling Resources	Monitoring and controlling resources and overseeing the spending of money.
Assisting and Caring for Others	Providing personal assistance, medical attention, emotional support, or other personal care to others such as coworkers, customers, or patients.
Repairing and Maintaining Electronic Equipment	Servicing, repairing, calibrating, regulating, fine-tuning, or testing machines, devices, and equipment that operate primarily on the basis of electrical or electronic (not mechanical) principles.
Performing General Physical Activities	Performing physical activities that require considerable use of your arms and legs and moving your whole body, such as climbing, lifting, balancing, walking, stooping, and handling of materials.
Handling and Moving Objects	Using hands and arms in handling, installing, positioning, and moving materials, and manipulating things.
Staffing Organizational Units	Recruiting, interviewing, selecting, hiring, and promoting employees in an organization.
Operating Vehicles, Mechanized Devices, or Equipme	Running, maneuvering, navigating, or driving vehicles or mechanized equipment, such as forklifts, passenger vehicles, aircraft, or water craft.
Repairing and Maintaining Mechanical Equipment	Servicing, repairing, adjusting, and testing machines, devices, moving parts, and equipment that operate primarily on the basis of mechanical (not electronic) principles.
Drafting, Laying Out, and Specifying Technical Dev	Providing documentation, detailed instructions, drawings, or specifications to tell others about how devices, parts, equipment, or structures are to be fabricated, constructed, assembled, modified, maintained, or used.

Work_Context	Work_Context Definitions
Telephone	How often do you have telephone conversations in this job?
Indoors, Environmentally Controlled	How often does this job require working indoors in environmentally controlled conditions?
Time Pressure	How often does this job require the worker to meet strict deadlines?
Frequency of Decision Making	How frequently is the worker required to make decisions that affect other people, the financial resources, and/or the image and reputation of the organization?
Contact With Others	How much does this job require the worker to be in contact with others (face-to-face, by telephone, or otherwise) in order to perform it?
Freedom to Make Decisions	How much decision making freedom, without supervision, does the job offer?
Face-to-Face Discussions	How often do you have to have face-to-face discussions with individuals or teams in this job?

Structured versus Unstructured Work	To what extent is this job structured for the worker, rather than allowing the worker to determine tasks, priorities, and goals?
Importance of Being Exact or Accurate	How important is being very exact or highly accurate in performing this job?
Public Speaking	How often do you have to perform public speaking in this job?
Work With Work Group or Team	How important is it to work with others in a group or team in this job?
Electronic Mail	How often do you use electronic mail in this job?
Impact of Decisions on Co-workers or Company Resul	How do the decisions an employee makes impact the results of co-workers, clients or the company?
Deal With External Customers	How important is it to work with external customers or the public in this job?
Spend Time Sitting	How much does this job require sitting?
Letters and Memos	How often does the job require written letters and memos?
Level of Competition	To what extent does this job require the worker to compete or to be aware of competitive pressures?
Spend Time Using Your Hands to Handle, Control, or	How much does this job require using your hands to handle, control, or feel objects, tools or controls?
Coordinate or Lead Others	How important is it to coordinate or lead others in accomplishing work activities in this job?
Frequency of Conflict Situations	How often are there conflict situations the employee has to face in this job?
Physical Proximity	To what extent does this job require the worker to perform job tasks in close physical proximity to other people?
Importance of Repeating Same Tasks	How important is repeating the same physical activities (e.g., key entry) or mental activities (e.g., checking entries in a ledger) over and over, without stopping, to performing this job?
Responsibility for Outcomes and Results	How responsible is the worker for work outcomes and results of other workers?
Deal With Unpleasant or Angry People	How frequently does the worker have to deal with unpleasant, angry, or discourteous individuals as part of the job requirements?
Consequence of Error	How serious would the result usually be if the worker made a mistake that was not readily correctable?
Pace Determined by Speed of Equipment	How important is it to this job that the pace is determined by the speed of equipment or machinery? (This does not refer to keeping busy at all times on this job.)
Spend Time Making Repetitive Motions	How much does this job require making repetitive motions?
Sounds, Noise Levels Are Distracting or Uncomforta	How often does this job require working exposed to sounds and noise levels that are distracting or uncomfortable?
Degree of Automation	How automated is the job?
Spend Time Standing	How much does this job require standing?
Responsible for Others' Health and Safety	How much responsibility is there for the health and safety of others in this job?
Extremely Bright or Inadequate Lighting	How often does this job require working in extremely bright or inadequate lighting conditions?
In an Enclosed Vehicle or Equipment	How often does this job require working in a closed vehicle or equipment (e.g., car)?
Outdoors, Exposed to Weather	How often does this job require working outdoors, exposed to all weather conditions?
Indoors, Not Environmentally Controlled	How often does this job require working indoors in non-controlled environmental conditions (e.g., warehouse without heat)?
Spend Time Walking and Running	How much does this job require walking and running?
Very Hot or Cold Temperatures	How often does this job require working in very hot (above 90 F degrees) or very cold (below 32 F degrees) temperatures?
Cramped Work Space, Awkward Positions	How often does this job require working in cramped work spaces that requires getting into awkward positions?
Exposed to Minor Burns, Cuts, Bites, or Stings	How often does this job require exposure to minor burns, cuts, bites, or stings?
Spend Time Bending or Twisting the Body	How much does this job require bending or twisting your body?
Exposed to Contaminants	How often does this job require working exposed to contaminants (such as pollutants, gases, dust or odors)?
Outdoors, Under Cover	How often does this job require working outdoors, under cover (e.g., structure with roof but no walls)?
Deal With Physically Aggressive People	How frequently does this job require the worker to deal with physical aggression of violent individuals?
Spend Time Kneeling, Crouching, Stooping, or Crawl	How much does this job require kneeling, crouching, stooping or crawling?
Exposed to Radiation	How often does this job require exposure to radiation?
Exposed to Hazardous Equipment	How often does this job require exposure to hazardous equipment?

Exposed to Disease or Infections	How often does this job require exposure to disease/infections?
Exposed to Hazardous Conditions	How often does this job require exposure to hazardous conditions?
Spend Time Keeping or Regaining Balance	How much does this job require keeping or regaining your balance?
Wear Specialized Protective or Safety Equipment su	How much does this job require wearing specialized protective or safety equipment such as breathing apparatus, safety harness, full protection suits, or radiation protection?
Spend Time Climbing Ladders, Scaffolds, or Poles	How much does this job require climbing ladders, scaffolds, or poles?
Exposed to High Places	How often does this job require exposure to high places?
In an Open Vehicle or Equipment	How often does this job require working in an open vehicle or equipment (e.g., tractor)?
Wear Common Protective or Safety Equipment such as	How much does this job require wearing common protective or safety equipment such as safety shoes, glasses, gloves, hard hats or life jackets?
Exposed to Whole Body Vibration	How often does this job require exposure to whole body vibration (e.g., operate a jackhammer)?

Job Zone Component	Job Zone Component Definitions
Title	Job Zone Three: Medium Preparation Needed
Overall Experience	Previous work-related skill, knowledge, or experience is required for these occupations. For example, an electrician must have completed three or four years of apprenticeship or several years of vocational training, and often must have passed a licensing exam, in order to perform the job.
Job Training	Employees in these occupations usually need one or two years of training involving both on-the-job experience and informal training with experienced workers.
Job Zone Examples	These occupations usually involve using communication and organizational skills to coordinate, supervise, manage, or train others to accomplish goals. Examples include dental assistants, electricians, fish and game wardens, legal secretaries, personnel recruiters, and recreation workers.
SVP Range	(6.0 to < 7.0)
Education	Most occupations in this zone require training in vocational schools, related on-the-job experience, or an associate's degree. Some may require a bachelor's degree.

Work_Styles	Work_Styles Definitions
Dependability	Job requires being reliable, responsible, and dependable, and fulfilling obligations.
Integrity	Job requires being honest and ethical.
Stress Tolerance	Job requires accepting criticism and dealing calmly and effectively with high stress situations.
Initiative	Job requires a willingness to take on responsibilities and challenges.
Self Control	Job requires maintaining composure, keeping emotions in check, controlling anger, and avoiding aggressive behavior, even in very difficult situations.
Cooperation	Job requires being pleasant with others on the job and displaying a good-natured, cooperative attitude.
Attention to Detail	Job requires being careful about detail and thorough in completing work tasks.
Adaptability/Flexibility	Job requires being open to change (positive or negative) and to considerable variety in the workplace.
Independence	Job requires developing one's own ways of doing things, guiding oneself with little or no supervision, and depending on oneself to get things done.
Innovation	Job requires creativity and alternative thinking to develop new ideas for and answers to work-related problems.
Persistence	Job requires persistence in the face of obstacles.
Achievement/Effort	Job requires establishing and maintaining personally challenging achievement goals and exerting effort toward mastering tasks.
Social Orientation	Job requires preferring to work with others rather than alone, and being personally connected with others on the job.
Concern for Others	Job requires being sensitive to others' needs and feelings and being understanding and helpful on the job.
Leadership	Job requires a willingness to lead, take charge, and offer opinions and direction.
Analytical Thinking	Job requires analyzing information and using logic to address work-related issues and problems.

27-3012.00 - Public Address System and Other Announcers

Make announcements over loud speaker at sporting or other public events. May act as master of ceremonies or disc jockey at weddings, parties, clubs, or other gathering places.

Tasks

1) Announce programs and player substitutions or other changes to patrons.

2) Provide running commentaries of event activities, such as play-by-play descriptions, or explanations of official decisions.

3) Instruct and calm crowds during emergencies.

4) Greet attendees and serve as masters of ceremonies at banquets, store openings, and other events.

5) Read prepared scripts describing acts or tricks presented during performances.

6) Organize team information, such as statistics and tournament records, in order to ensure accessibility for use during events.

7) Preview any music intended to be broadcast over the public address system.

8) Review and announce crowd control procedures before the beginning of each event.

9) Study the layout of an event venue in order to be able to give accurate directions in the event of an emergency.

10) Meet with event directors in order to review schedules and exchange information about details, such as national anthem performers and starting lineups.

11) Improvise commentary on items of interest, such as background and history of an event or past records of participants.

12) Furnish information concerning plays to scoreboard operators.

13) Learn to pronounce the names of players, coaches, institutional personnel, officials, and other individuals involved in an event.

27-3021.00 - Broadcast News Analysts

Analyze, interpret, and broadcast news received from various sources.

Tasks

1) Present news stories, and introduce in-depth videotaped segments or live transmissions from on-the-scene reporters.

2) Analyze and interpret news and information received from various sources in order to be able to broadcast the information.

3) Edit news material to ensure that it fits within available time or space.

4) Examine news items of local, national, and international significance in order to determine topics to address, or obtain assignments from editorial staff members.

5) Gather information and develop perspectives about news subjects through research, interviews, observation, and experience.

6) Select material most pertinent to presentation, and organize this material into appropriate formats.

7) Write commentaries, columns, or scripts, using computers.

27-3022.00 - Reporters and Correspondents

Collect and analyze facts about newsworthy events by interview, investigation, or observation. Report and write stories for newspaper, news magazine, radio, or television.

Tasks

1) Determine a story's emphasis, length, and format, and organize material accordingly.

2) Arrange interviews with people who can provide information about a particular story.

3) Research and analyze background information related to stories in order to be able to provide complete and accurate information.

4) Check reference materials such as books, news files, and public records in order to obtain relevant facts.

5) Investigate breaking news developments such as disasters, crimes, and human interest stories.

6) Revise work in order to meet editorial approval or to fit time or space requirements.

7) Receive assignments or evaluate leads and tips in order to develop story ideas.

8) Gather information about events through research, interviews, experience, and attendance at political, news, sports, artistic, social, and other functions.

9) Discuss issues with editors in order to establish priorities and positions.

10) Report and write news stories for publication or broadcast, describing the background and details of events.

11) Research and report on specialized fields such as medicine, science and technology, politics, foreign affairs, sports, arts, consumer affairs, business, religion, crime, or education.

12) Review copy and correct errors in content, grammar, and punctuation, following prescribed editorial style and formatting guidelines.

13) Photograph or videotape news events, or request that a photographer be assigned to provide such coverage.

14) Develop ideas and material for columns or commentaries by analyzing and interpreting news, current issues, and personal experiences.

15) Transmit news stories or reporting information from remote locations, using equipment such as satellite phones, telephones, fax machines, or modems.

16) Write columns, editorials, commentaries, or reviews that interpret events or offer opinions.

17) Conduct taped or filmed interviews or narratives.

18) Present live or recorded commentary via broadcast media.

19) Write reviews of literary, musical, and other artwork based on knowledge, judgment, and experience.

20) Edit or assist in editing videos for broadcast.

Knowledge	Knowledge Definitions
English Language	Knowledge of the structure and content of the English language including the meaning and spelling of words, rules of composition, and grammar.
Communications and Media	Knowledge of media production, communication, and dissemination techniques and methods. This includes alternative ways to inform and entertain via written, oral, and visual media.
Customer and Personal Service	Knowledge of principles and processes for providing customer and personal services. This includes customer needs assessment, meeting quality standards for services, and evaluation of customer satisfaction.
Administration and Management	Knowledge of business and management principles involved in strategic planning, resource allocation, human resources modeling, leadership technique, production methods, and coordination of people and resources.
Computers and Electronics	Knowledge of circuit boards, processors, chips, electronic equipment, and computer hardware and software, including applications and programming.
Clerical	Knowledge of administrative and clerical procedures and systems such as word processing, managing files and records, stenography and transcription, designing forms, and other office procedures and terminology.
Law and Government	Knowledge of laws, legal codes, court procedures, precedents, government regulations, executive orders, agency rules, and the democratic political process.
Telecommunications	Knowledge of transmission, broadcasting, switching, control, and operation of telecommunications systems.
Education and Training	Knowledge of principles and methods for curriculum and training design, teaching and instruction for individuals and groups, and the measurement of training effects.
Geography	Knowledge of principles and methods for describing the features of land, sea, and air masses, including their physical characteristics, locations, interrelationships, and distribution of plant, animal, and human life.
Public Safety and Security	Knowledge of relevant equipment, policies, procedures, and strategies to promote effective local, state, or national security operations for the protection of people, data, property, and institutions.

Sociology and Anthropology	Knowledge of group behavior and dynamics, societal trends and influences, human migrations, ethnicity, cultures and their history and origins.
Mathematics	Knowledge of arithmetic, algebra, geometry, calculus, statistics, and their applications.
Psychology	Knowledge of human behavior and performance; individual differences in ability, personality, and interests; learning and motivation; psychological research methods; and the assessment and treatment of behavioral and affective disorders.
History and Archeology	Knowledge of historical events and their causes, indicators, and effects on civilizations and cultures.
Sales and Marketing	Knowledge of principles and methods for showing, promoting, and selling products or services. This includes marketing strategy and tactics, product demonstration, sales techniques, and sales control systems.
Personnel and Human Resources	Knowledge of principles and procedures for personnel recruitment, selection, training, compensation and benefits, labor relations and negotiation, and personnel information systems.
Transportation	Knowledge of principles and methods for moving people or goods by air, rail, sea, or road, including the relative costs and benefits.
Economics and Accounting	Knowledge of economic and accounting principles and practices, the financial markets, banking and the analysis and reporting of financial data.
Fine Arts	Knowledge of the theory and techniques required to compose, produce, and perform works of music, dance, visual arts, drama, and sculpture.
Production and Processing	Knowledge of raw materials, production processes, quality control, costs, and other techniques for maximizing the effective manufacture and distribution of goods.
Philosophy and Theology	Knowledge of different philosophical systems and religions. This includes their basic principles, values, ethics, ways of thinking, customs, practices, and their impact on human culture.
Design	Knowledge of design techniques, tools, and principles involved in production of precision technical plans, blueprints, drawings, and models.
Engineering and Technology	Knowledge of the practical application of engineering science and technology. This includes applying principles, techniques, procedures, and equipment to the design and production of various goods and services.
Therapy and Counseling	Knowledge of principles, methods, and procedures for diagnosis, treatment, and rehabilitation of physical and mental dysfunctions, and for career counseling and guidance.
Foreign Language	Knowledge of the structure and content of a foreign (non-English) language including the meaning and spelling of words, rules of composition and grammar, and pronunciation
Medicine and Dentistry	Knowledge of the information and techniques needed to diagnose and treat human injuries, diseases, and deformities. This includes symptoms, treatment alternatives, drug properties and interactions, and preventive health-care measures.
Mechanical	Knowledge of machines and tools, including their designs, uses, repair, and maintenance.
Biology	Knowledge of plant and animal organisms, their tissues, cells, functions, interdependencies, and interactions with each other and the environment.
Physics	Knowledge and prediction of physical principles, laws, their interrelationships, and applications to understanding fluid, material, and atmospheric dynamics, and mechanical, electrical, atomic and sub- atomic structures and processes.
Building and Construction	Knowledge of materials, methods, and the tools involved in the construction or repair of houses, buildings, or other structures such as highways and roads.
Food Production	Knowledge of techniques and equipment for planting, growing, and harvesting food products (both plant and animal) for consumption, including storage/handling techniques.
Chemistry	Knowledge of the chemical composition, structure, and properties of substances and of the chemical processes and transformations that they undergo. This includes uses of chemicals and their interactions, danger signs, production techniques, and disposal methods.

Skills	Skills Definitions
Writing	Communicating effectively in writing as appropriate for the needs of the audience.

Skill	Definition
Active Listening	Giving full attention to what other people are saying, taking time to understand the points being made, asking questions as appropriate, and not interrupting at inappropriate times.
Reading Comprehension	Understanding written sentences and paragraphs in work related documents.
Time Management	Managing one's own time and the time of others.
Critical Thinking	Using logic and reasoning to identify the strengths and weaknesses of alternative solutions, conclusions or approaches to problems.
Speaking	Talking to others to convey information effectively.
Active Learning	Understanding the implications of new information for both current and future problem-solving and decision-making.
Social Perceptiveness	Being aware of others' reactions and understanding why they react as they do.
Judgment and Decision Making	Considering the relative costs and benefits of potential actions to choose the most appropriate one.
Coordination	Adjusting actions in relation to others' actions.
Monitoring	Monitoring/Assessing performance of yourself, other individuals, or organizations to make improvements or take corrective action.
Persuasion	Persuading others to change their minds or behavior.
Complex Problem Solving	Identifying complex problems and reviewing related information to develop and evaluate options and implement solutions.
Learning Strategies	Selecting and using training/instructional methods and procedures appropriate for the situation when learning or teaching new things.
Instructing	Teaching others how to do something.
Mathematics	Using mathematics to solve problems.
Negotiation	Bringing others together and trying to reconcile differences.
Service Orientation	Actively looking for ways to help people.
Quality Control Analysis	Conducting tests and inspections of products, services, or processes to evaluate quality or performance.
Systems Analysis	Determining how a system should work and how changes in conditions, operations, and the environment will affect outcomes.
Operations Analysis	Analyzing needs and product requirements to create a design.
Management of Personnel Resources	Motivating, developing, and directing people as they work, identifying the best people for the job.
Systems Evaluation	Identifying measures or indicators of system performance and the actions needed to improve or correct performance, relative to the goals of the system.
Science	Using scientific rules and methods to solve problems.
Equipment Selection	Determining the kind of tools and equipment needed to do a job.
Troubleshooting	Determining causes of operating errors and deciding what to do about it.
Operation and Control	Controlling operations of equipment or systems.
Management of Financial Resources	Determining how money will be spent to get the work done, and accounting for these expenditures.
Management of Material Resources	Obtaining and seeing to the appropriate use of equipment, facilities, and materials needed to do certain work.
Equipment Maintenance	Performing routine maintenance on equipment and determining when and what kind of maintenance is needed.
Technology Design	Generating or adapting equipment and technology to serve user needs.
Operation Monitoring	Watching gauges, dials, or other indicators to make sure a machine is working properly.
Programming	Writing computer programs for various purposes.
Repairing	Repairing machines or systems using the needed tools.
Installation	Installing equipment, machines, wiring, or programs to meet specifications.

Ability	Ability Definitions
Oral Comprehension	The ability to listen to and understand information and ideas presented through spoken words and sentences.
Written Comprehension	The ability to read and understand information and ideas presented in writing.
Written Expression	The ability to communicate information and ideas in writing so others will understand.
Oral Expression	The ability to communicate information and ideas in speaking so others will understand.
Speech Clarity	The ability to speak clearly so others can understand you.
Speech Recognition	The ability to identify and understand the speech of another person.

Ability	Definition
Inductive Reasoning	The ability to combine pieces of information to form general rules or conclusions (includes finding a relationship among seemingly unrelated events).
Problem Sensitivity	The ability to tell when something is wrong or is likely to go wrong. It does not involve solving the problem, only recognizing there is a problem.
Near Vision	The ability to see details at close range (within a few feet of the observer).
Originality	The ability to come up with unusual or clever ideas about a given topic or situation, or to develop creative ways to solve a problem.
Information Ordering	The ability to arrange things or actions in a certain order or pattern according to a specific rule or set of rules (e.g., patterns of numbers, letters, words, pictures, mathematical operations).
Deductive Reasoning	The ability to apply general rules to specific problems to produce answers that make sense.
Fluency of Ideas	The ability to come up with a number of ideas about a topic (the number of ideas is important, not their quality, correctness, or creativity).
Selective Attention	The ability to concentrate on a task over a period of time without being distracted.
Category Flexibility	The ability to generate or use different sets of rules for combining or grouping things in different ways.
Speed of Closure	The ability to quickly make sense of, combine, and organize information into meaningful patterns.
Flexibility of Closure	The ability to identify or detect a known pattern (a figure, object, word, or sound) that is hidden in other distracting material.
Memorization	The ability to remember information such as words, numbers, pictures, and procedures.
Time Sharing	The ability to shift back and forth between two or more activities or sources of information (such as speech, sounds, touch, or other sources).
Far Vision	The ability to see details at a distance.
Auditory Attention	The ability to focus on a single source of sound in the presence of other distracting sounds.
Perceptual Speed	The ability to quickly and accurately compare similarities and differences among sets of letters, numbers, objects, pictures, or patterns. The things to be compared may be presented at the same time or one after the other. This ability also includes comparing a presented object with a remembered object.
Finger Dexterity	The ability to make precisely coordinated movements of the fingers of one or both hands to grasp, manipulate, or assemble very small objects.
Trunk Strength	The ability to use your abdominal and lower back muscles to support part of the body repeatedly or continuously over time without 'giving out' or fatiguing.
Visualization	The ability to imagine how something will look after it is moved around or when its parts are moved or rearranged.
Control Precision	The ability to quickly and repeatedly adjust the controls of a machine or a vehicle to exact positions.
Visual Color Discrimination	The ability to match or detect differences between colors, including shades of color and brightness.
Depth Perception	The ability to judge which of several objects is closer or farther away from you, or to judge the distance between you and an object.
Manual Dexterity	The ability to quickly move your hand, your hand together with your arm, or your two hands to grasp, manipulate, or assemble objects.
Number Facility	The ability to add, subtract, multiply, or divide quickly and correctly.
Multilimb Coordination	The ability to coordinate two or more limbs (for example, two arms, two legs, or one leg and one arm) while sitting, standing, or lying down. It does not involve performing the activities while the whole body is in motion.
Mathematical Reasoning	The ability to choose the right mathematical methods or formulas to solve a problem.
Arm-Hand Steadiness	The ability to keep your hand and arm steady while moving your arm or while holding your arm and hand in one position.
Hearing Sensitivity	The ability to detect or tell the differences between sounds that vary in pitch and loudness.
Rate Control	The ability to time your movements or the movement of a piece of equipment in anticipation of changes in the speed and/or direction of a moving object or scene.
Reaction Time	The ability to quickly respond (with the hand, finger, or foot) to a signal (sound, light, picture) when it appears.
Wrist-Finger Speed	The ability to make fast, simple, repeated movements of the fingers, hands, and wrists.

Glare Sensitivity	The ability to see objects in the presence of glare or bright lighting.
Extent Flexibility	The ability to bend, stretch, twist, or reach with your body, arms, and/or legs.
Night Vision	The ability to see under low light conditions.
Gross Body Coordination	The ability to coordinate the movement of your arms, legs, and torso together when the whole body is in motion.
Sound Localization	The ability to tell the direction from which a sound originated.
Gross Body Equilibrium	The ability to keep or regain your body balance or stay upright when in an unstable position.
Static Strength	The ability to exert maximum muscle force to lift, push, pull, or carry objects.
Speed of Limb Movement	The ability to quickly move the arms and legs.
Dynamic Strength	The ability to exert muscle force repeatedly or continuously over time. This involves muscular endurance and resistance to muscle fatigue.
Stamina	The ability to exert yourself physically over long periods of time without getting winded or out of breath.
Dynamic Flexibility	The ability to quickly and repeatedly bend, stretch, twist, or reach out with your body, arms, and/or legs.
Spatial Orientation	The ability to know your location in relation to the environment or to know where other objects are in relation to you.
Response Orientation	The ability to choose quickly between two or more movements in response to two or more different signals (lights, sounds, pictures). It includes the speed with which the correct response is started with the hand, foot, or other body part.
Explosive Strength	The ability to use short bursts of muscle force to propel oneself (as in jumping or sprinting), or to throw an object.
Peripheral Vision	The ability to see objects or movement of objects to one's side when the eyes are looking ahead.

Work_Activity	Work_Activity Definitions
Getting Information	Observing, receiving, and otherwise obtaining information from all relevant sources.
Communicating with Persons Outside Organization	Communicating with people outside the organization, representing the organization to customers, the public, government, and other external sources. This information can be exchanged in person, in writing, or by telephone or e-mail.
Interpreting the Meaning of Information for Others	Translating or explaining what information means and how it can be used.
Thinking Creatively	Developing, designing, or creating new applications, ideas, relationships, systems, or products, including artistic contributions.
Interacting With Computers	Using computers and computer systems (including hardware and software) to program, write software, set up functions, enter data, or process information.
Identifying Objects, Actions, and Events	Identifying information by categorizing, estimating, recognizing differences or similarities, and detecting changes in circumstances or events.
Establishing and Maintaining Interpersonal Relatio	Developing constructive and cooperative working relationships with others, and maintaining them over time.
Performing for or Working Directly with the Public	Performing for people or dealing directly with the public. This includes serving customers in restaurants and stores, and receiving clients or guests.
Documenting/Recording Information	Entering, transcribing, recording, storing, or maintaining information in written or electronic/magnetic form.
Processing Information	Compiling, coding, categorizing, calculating, tabulating, auditing, or verifying information or data.
Updating and Using Relevant Knowledge	Keeping up-to-date technically and applying new knowledge to your job.
Communicating with Supervisors, Peers, or Subordin	Providing information to supervisors, co-workers, and subordinates by telephone, in written form, e-mail, or in person.
Organizing, Planning, and Prioritizing Work	Developing specific goals and plans to prioritize, organize, and accomplish your work.
Analyzing Data or Information	Identifying the underlying principles, reasons, or facts of information by breaking down information or data into separate parts.
Making Decisions and Solving Problems	Analyzing information and evaluating results to choose the best solution and solve problems.
Scheduling Work and Activities	Scheduling events, programs, and activities, as well as the work of others.
Judging the Qualities of Things, Services, or Peop	Assessing the value, importance, or quality of things or people.

Monitor Processes, Materials, or Surroundings	Monitoring and reviewing information from materials, events, or the environment, to detect or assess problems.
Evaluating Information to Determine Compliance wit	Using relevant information and individual judgment to determine whether events or processes comply with laws, regulations, or standards.
Developing Objectives and Strategies	Establishing long-range objectives and specifying the strategies and actions to achieve them.
Selling or Influencing Others	Convincing others to buy merchandise/goods or to otherwise change their minds or actions.
Resolving Conflicts and Negotiating with Others	Handling complaints, settling disputes, and resolving grievances and conflicts, or otherwise negotiating with others.
Estimating the Quantifiable Characteristics of Pro	Estimating sizes, distances, and quantities; or determining time, costs, resources, or materials needed to perform a work activity.
Coordinating the Work and Activities of Others	Getting members of a group to work together to accomplish tasks.
Assisting and Caring for Others	Providing personal assistance, medical attention, emotional support, or other personal care to others such as coworkers, customers, or patients.
Developing and Building Teams	Encouraging and building mutual trust, respect, and cooperation among team members.
Provide Consultation and Advice to Others	Providing guidance and expert advice to management or other groups on technical, systems-, or process-related topics.
Performing Administrative Activities	Performing day-to-day administrative tasks such as maintaining information files and processing paperwork.
Coaching and Developing Others	Identifying the developmental needs of others and coaching, mentoring, or otherwise helping others to improve their knowledge or skills.
Guiding, Directing, and Motivating Subordinates	Providing guidance and direction to subordinates, including setting performance standards and monitoring performance.
Inspecting Equipment, Structures, or Material	Inspecting equipment, structures, or materials to identify the cause of errors or other problems or defects.
Performing General Physical Activities	Performing physical activities that require considerable use of your arms and legs and moving your whole body, such as climbing, lifting, balancing, walking, stooping, and handling of materials.
Training and Teaching Others	Identifying the educational needs of others, developing formal educational or training programs or classes, and teaching or instructing others.
Operating Vehicles, Mechanized Devices, or Equipme	Running, maneuvering, navigating, or driving vehicles or mechanized equipment, such as forklifts, passenger vehicles, aircraft, or water craft.
Controlling Machines and Processes	Using either control mechanisms or direct physical activity to operate machines or processes (not including computers or vehicles).
Monitoring and Controlling Resources	Monitoring and controlling resources and overseeing the spending of money.
Handling and Moving Objects	Using hands and arms in handling, installing, positioning, and moving materials, and manipulating things.
Repairing and Maintaining Electronic Equipment	Servicing, repairing, calibrating, regulating, fine-tuning, or testing machines, devices, and equipment that operate primarily on the basis of electrical or electronic (not mechanical) principles.
Repairing and Maintaining Mechanical Equipment	Servicing, repairing, adjusting, and testing machines, devices, moving parts, and equipment that operate primarily on the basis of mechanical (not electronic) principles.
Staffing Organizational Units	Recruiting, interviewing, selecting, hiring, and promoting employees in an organization.
Drafting, Laying Out, and Specifying Technical Dev	Providing documentation, detailed instructions, drawings, or specifications to tell others about how devices, parts, equipment, or structures are to be fabricated, constructed, assembled, modified, maintained, or used.

Work_Context	Work_Context Definitions
Telephone	How often do you have telephone conversations in this job?
Contact With Others	How much does this job require the worker to be in contact with others (face-to-face, by telephone, or otherwise) in order to perform it?
Electronic Mail	How often do you use electronic mail in this job?
Face-to-Face Discussions	How often do you have to have face-to-face discussions with individuals or teams in this job?
Importance of Being Exact or Accurate	How important is being very exact or highly accurate in performing this job?
Time Pressure	How often does this job require the worker to meet strict deadlines?

Work With Work Group or Team	How important is it to work with others in a group or team in this job?
Frequency of Decision Making	How frequently is the worker required to make decisions that affect other people, the financial resources, and/or the image and reputation of the organization?
Indoors, Environmentally Controlled	How often does this job require working indoors in environmentally controlled conditions?
Freedom to Make Decisions	How much decision making freedom, without supervision, does the job offer?
Impact of Decisions on Co-workers or Company Resul	How do the decisions an employee makes impact the results of co-workers, clients or the company?
Structured versus Unstructured Work	To what extent is this job structured for the worker, rather than allowing the worker to determine tasks, priorities, and goals?
Deal With External Customers	How important is it to work with external customers or the public in this job?
Level of Competition	To what extent does this job require the worker to compete or to be aware of competitive pressures?
Physical Proximity	To what extent does this job require the worker to perform job tasks in close physical proximity to other people?
Letters and Memos	How often does the job require written letters and memos?
Sounds, Noise Levels Are Distracting or Uncomforta	How often does this job require working exposed to sounds and noise levels that are distracting or uncomfortable?
Coordinate or Lead Others	How important is it to coordinate or lead others in accomplishing work activities in this job?
In an Enclosed Vehicle or Equipment	How often does this job require working in a closed vehicle or equipment (e.g., car)?
Spend Time Sitting	How much does this job require sitting?
Consequence of Error	How serious would the result usually be if the worker made a mistake that was not readily correctable?
Outdoors, Exposed to Weather	How often does this job require working outdoors, exposed to all weather conditions?
Deal With Unpleasant or Angry People	How frequently does the worker have to deal with unpleasant, angry, or discourteous individuals as part of the job requirements?
Frequency of Conflict Situations	How often are there conflict situations the employee has to face in this job?
Responsibility for Outcomes and Results	How responsible is the worker for work outcomes and results of other workers?
Public Speaking	How often do you have to perform public speaking in this job?
Spend Time Using Your Hands to Handle, Control, or	How much does this job require using your hands to handle, control, or feel objects, tools or controls?
Importance of Repeating Same Tasks	How important is repeating the same physical activities (e.g., key entry) or mental activities (e.g., checking entries in a ledger) over and over, without stopping, to performing this job?
Spend Time Making Repetitive Motions	How much does this job require making repetitive motions?
Spend Time Standing	How much does this job require standing?
Degree of Automation	How automated is the job?
Indoors, Not Environmentally Controlled	How often does this job require working indoors in non-controlled environmental conditions (e.g., warehouse without heat)?
Very Hot or Cold Temperatures	How often does this job require working in very hot (above 90 F degrees) or very cold (below 32 F degrees) temperatures?
Spend Time Walking and Running	How much does this job require walking and running?
Outdoors, Under Cover	How often does this job require working outdoors, under cover (e.g., structure with roof but no walls)?
Extremely Bright or Inadequate Lighting	How often does this job require working in extremely bright or inadequate lighting conditions?
Exposed to Contaminants	How often does this job require working exposed to contaminants (such as pollutants, gases, dust or odors)?
Exposed to Hazardous Equipment	How often does this job require exposure to hazardous equipment?
Responsible for Others' Health and Safety	How much responsibility is there for the health and safety of others in this job?
Cramped Work Space, Awkward Positions	How often does this job require working in cramped work spaces that requires getting into awkward positions?
Deal With Physically Aggressive People	How frequently does this job require the worker to deal with physical aggression of violent individuals?
Spend Time Bending or Twisting the Body	How much does this job require bending or twisting your body?
Exposed to Minor Burns, Cuts, Bites, or Stings	How often does this job require exposure to minor burns, cuts, bites, or stings?
Spend Time Kneeling, Crouching, Stooping, or Crawl	How much does this job require kneeling, crouching, stooping, or crawling?

Exposed to High Places	How often does this job require exposure to high places?
Pace Determined by Speed of Equipment	How important is it to this job that the pace is determined by the speed of equipment or machinery? (This does not refer to keeping busy at all times on this job.)
Exposed to Hazardous Conditions	How often does this job require exposure to hazardous conditions?
Exposed to Disease or Infections	How often does this job require exposure to disease/infections?
Spend Time Keeping or Regaining Balance	How much does this job require keeping or regaining your balance?
Wear Common Protective or Safety Equipment such as	How much does this job require wearing common protective or safety equipment such as safety shoes, glasses, gloves, hard hats or life jackets?
In an Open Vehicle or Equipment	How often does this job require working in an open vehicle or equipment (e.g., tractor)?
Spend Time Climbing Ladders, Scaffolds, or Poles	How much does this job require climbing ladders, scaffolds, or poles?
Exposed to Radiation	How often does this job require exposure to radiation?
Wear Specialized Protective or Safety Equipment su	How much does this job require wearing specialized protective or safety equipment such as breathing apparatus, safety harness, full protection suits, or radiation protection?
Exposed to Whole Body Vibration	How often does this job require exposure to whole body vibration (e.g., operate a jackhammer)?

Job Zone Component	Job Zone Component Definitions
Title	Job Zone Four: Considerable Preparation Needed
Overall Experience	A minimum of two to four years of work-related skill, knowledge, or experience is needed for these occupations. For example, an accountant must complete four years of college and work for several years in accounting to be considered qualified.
Job Training	Employees in these occupations usually need several years of work-related experience, on-the-job training, and/or vocational training.
Job Zone Examples	Many of these occupations involve coordinating, supervising, managing, or training others. Examples include accountants, chefs and head cooks, computer programmers, historians, pharmacists, and police detectives.
SVP Range	(7.0 to < 8.0)
Education	Most of these occupations require a four - year bachelor's degree, but some do not.

Work_Styles	Work_Styles Definitions
Attention to Detail	Job requires being careful about detail and thorough in completing work tasks.
Initiative	Job requires a willingness to take on responsibilities and challenges.
Persistence	Job requires persistence in the face of obstacles.
Dependability	Job requires being reliable, responsible, and dependable, and fulfilling obligations.
Integrity	Job requires being honest and ethical.
Stress Tolerance	Job requires accepting criticism and dealing calmly and effectively with high stress situations.
Independence	Job requires developing one's own ways of doing things, guiding oneself with little or no supervision, and depending on oneself to get things done.
Achievement/Effort	Job requires establishing and maintaining personally challenging achievement goals and exerting effort toward mastering tasks.
Adaptability/Flexibility	Job requires being open to change (positive or negative) and to considerable variety in the workplace.
Self Control	Job requires maintaining composure, keeping emotions in check, controlling anger, and avoiding aggressive behavior, even in very difficult situations.
Cooperation	Job requires being pleasant with others on the job and displaying a good-natured, cooperative attitude.
Analytical Thinking	Job requires analyzing information and using logic to address work-related issues and problems.
Innovation	Job requires creativity and alternative thinking to develop new ideas for and answers to work-related problems.
Leadership	Job requires a willingness to lead, take charge, and offer opinions and direction.
Concern for Others	Job requires being sensitive to others' needs and feelings and being understanding and helpful on the job.

Social Orientation	Job requires preferring to work with others rather than alone, and being personally connected with others on the job.

27-3031.00 - Public Relations Specialists

Engage in promoting or creating good will for individuals, groups, or organizations by writing or selecting favorable publicity material and releasing it through various communications media. May prepare and arrange displays, and make speeches.

Tasks

1) Establish and maintain cooperative relationships with representatives of community, consumer, employee, and public interest groups.

2) Consult with advertising agencies or staff to arrange promotional campaigns in all types of media for products, organizations, or individuals.

3) Respond to requests for information from the media or designate another appropriate spokesperson or information source.

4) Confer with production and support personnel to produce or coordinate production of advertisements and promotions.

5) Prepare or edit organizational publications for internal and external audiences, including employee newsletters and stockholders' reports.

6) Arrange public appearances, lectures, contests, or exhibits for clients to increase product and service awareness and to promote goodwill.

7) Plan and direct development and communication of informational programs to maintain favorable public and stockholder perceptions of an organization's accomplishments and agenda.

8) Confer with other managers to identify trends and key group interests and concerns or to provide advice on business decisions.

9) Prepare and deliver speeches to further public relations objectives.

10) Coach client representatives in effective communication with the public and with employees.

11) Plan and conduct market and public opinion research to test products or determine potential for product success, communicating results to client or management.

12) Purchase advertising space and time as required to promote client's product or agenda.

Knowledge	Knowledge Definitions
English Language	Knowledge of the structure and content of the English language including the meaning and spelling of words, rules of composition, and grammar.
Communications and Media	Knowledge of media production, communication, and dissemination techniques and methods. This includes alternative ways to inform and entertain via written, oral, and visual media.
Sales and Marketing	Knowledge of principles and methods for showing, promoting, and selling products or services. This includes marketing strategy and tactics, product demonstration, sales techniques, and sales control systems.
Customer and Personal Service	Knowledge of principles and processes for providing customer and personal services. This includes customer needs assessment, meeting quality standards for services, and evaluation of customer satisfaction.
Administration and Management	Knowledge of business and management principles involved in strategic planning, resource allocation, human resources modeling, leadership technique, production methods, and coordination of people and resources.
Psychology	Knowledge of human behavior and performance; individual differences in ability, personality, and interests; learning and motivation; psychological research methods; and the assessment and treatment of behavioral and affective disorders.
Computers and Electronics	Knowledge of circuit boards, processors, chips, electronic equipment, and computer hardware and software, including applications and programming.
Education and Training	Knowledge of principles and methods for curriculum and training design, teaching and instruction for individuals and groups, and the measurement of training effects.
Clerical	Knowledge of administrative and clerical procedures and systems such as word processing, managing files and records, stenography and transcription, designing forms, and other office procedures and terminology.
Telecommunications	Knowledge of transmission, broadcasting, switching, control, and operation of telecommunications systems.
Personnel and Human Resources	Knowledge of principles and procedures for personnel recruitment, selection, training, compensation and benefits, labor relations and negotiation, and personnel information systems.
Mathematics	Knowledge of arithmetic, algebra, geometry, calculus, statistics, and their applications.
Sociology and Anthropology	Knowledge of group behavior and dynamics, societal trends and influences, human migrations, ethnicity, cultures and their history and origins.
Economics and Accounting	Knowledge of economic and accounting principles and practices, the financial markets, banking and the analysis and reporting of financial data.
Medicine and Dentistry	Knowledge of the information and techniques needed to diagnose and treat human injuries, diseases, and deformities. This includes symptoms, treatment alternatives, drug properties and interactions, and preventive health-care measures.
Public Safety and Security	Knowledge of relevant equipment, policies, procedures, and strategies to promote effective local, state, or national security operations for the protection of people, data, property, and institutions.
Law and Government	Knowledge of laws, legal codes, court procedures, precedents, government regulations, executive orders, agency rules, and the democratic political process.
Therapy and Counseling	Knowledge of principles, methods, and procedures for diagnosis, treatment, and rehabilitation of physical and mental dysfunctions, and for career counseling and guidance.
Design	Knowledge of design techniques, tools, and principles involved in production of precision technical plans, blueprints, drawings, and models.
Transportation	Knowledge of principles and methods for moving people or goods by air, rail, sea, or road, including the relative costs and benefits.
Geography	Knowledge of principles and methods for describing the features of land, sea, and air masses, including their physical characteristics, locations, interrelationships, and distribution of plant, animal, and human life.
History and Archeology	Knowledge of historical events and their causes, indicators, and effects on civilizations and cultures.
Biology	Knowledge of plant and animal organisms, their tissues, cells, functions, interdependencies, and interactions with each other and the environment.
Philosophy and Theology	Knowledge of different philosophical systems and religions. This includes their basic principles, values, ethics, ways of thinking, customs, practices, and their impact on human culture.
Production and Processing	Knowledge of raw materials, production processes, quality control, costs, and other techniques for maximizing the effective manufacture and distribution of goods.
Foreign Language	Knowledge of the structure and content of a foreign (non-English) language including the meaning and spelling of words, rules of composition and grammar, and pronunciation.
Mechanical	Knowledge of machines and tools, including their designs, uses, repair, and maintenance.
Engineering and Technology	Knowledge of the practical application of engineering science and technology. This includes applying principles, techniques, procedures, and equipment to the design and production of various goods and services.
Fine Arts	Knowledge of the theory and techniques required to compose, produce, and perform works of music, dance, visual arts, drama, and sculpture.
Chemistry	Knowledge of the chemical composition, structure, and properties of substances and of the chemical processes and transformations that they undergo. This includes uses of chemicals and their interactions, danger signs, production techniques, and disposal methods.
Physics	Knowledge and prediction of physical principles, laws, their interrelationships, and applications to understanding fluid, material, and atmospheric dynamics, and mechanical, electrical, atomic and sub-atomic structures and processes.
Building and Construction	Knowledge of materials, methods, and the tools involved in the construction or repair of houses, buildings, or other structures such as highways and roads.
Food Production	Knowledge of techniques and equipment for planting, growing, and harvesting food products (both plant and animal) for consumption, including storage/handling techniques.

Skills	Skills Definitions
Writing	Communicating effectively in writing as appropriate for the needs of the audience.
Critical Thinking	Using logic and reasoning to identify the strengths and weaknesses of alternative solutions, conclusions or approaches to problems.
Reading Comprehension	Understanding written sentences and paragraphs in work related documents.
Active Listening	Giving full attention to what other people are saying, taking time to understand the points being made, asking questions as appropriate, and not interrupting at inappropriate times.
Speaking	Talking to others to convey information effectively.
Judgment and Decision Making	Considering the relative costs and benefits of potential actions to choose the most appropriate one.
Time Management	Managing one's own time and the time of others.
Persuasion	Persuading others to change their minds or behavior.
Social Perceptiveness	Being aware of others' reactions and understanding why they react as they do.
Coordination	Adjusting actions in relation to others' actions.
Active Learning	Understanding the implications of new information for both current and future problem-solving and decision-making.
Service Orientation	Actively looking for ways to help people.
Monitoring	Monitoring/Assessing performance of yourself, other individuals, or organizations to make improvements or take corrective action.
Complex Problem Solving	Identifying complex problems and reviewing related information to develop and evaluate options and implement solutions.
Learning Strategies	Selecting and using training/instructional methods and procedures appropriate for the situation when learning or teaching new things.
Negotiation	Bringing others together and trying to reconcile differences.
Management of Financial Resources	Determining how money will be spent to get the work done, and accounting for these expenditures.
Instructing	Teaching others how to do something.
Operations Analysis	Analyzing needs and product requirements to create a design.
Equipment Selection	Determining the kind of tools and equipment needed to do a job.
Management of Personnel Resources	Motivating, developing, and directing people as they work, identifying the best people for the job.
Management of Material Resources	Obtaining and seeing to the appropriate use of equipment, facilities, and materials needed to do certain work.
Quality Control Analysis	Conducting tests and inspections of products, services, or processes to evaluate quality or performance.
Mathematics	Using mathematics to solve problems.
Systems Evaluation	Identifying measures or indicators of system performance and the actions needed to improve or correct performance, relative to the goals of the system.
Troubleshooting	Determining causes of operating errors and deciding what to do about it.
Systems Analysis	Determining how a system should work and how changes in conditions, operations, and the environment will affect outcomes.
Installation	Installing equipment, machines, wiring, or programs to meet specifications.
Technology Design	Generating or adapting equipment and technology to serve user needs.
Science	Using scientific rules and methods to solve problems.
Equipment Maintenance	Performing routine maintenance on equipment and determining when and what kind of maintenance is needed.
Programming	Writing computer programs for various purposes.
Operation and Control	Controlling operations of equipment or systems.
Repairing	Repairing machines or systems using the needed tools.
Operation Monitoring	Watching gauges, dials, or other indicators to make sure a machine is working properly.

Ability	Ability Definitions
Oral Expression	The ability to communicate information and ideas in speaking so others will understand.
Oral Comprehension	The ability to listen to and understand information and ideas presented through spoken words and sentences.
Written Expression	The ability to communicate information and ideas in writing so others will understand.
Speech Clarity	The ability to speak clearly so others can understand you.

Problem Sensitivity	The ability to tell when something is wrong or is likely to go wrong. It does not involve solving the problem, only recognizing there is a problem.
Written Comprehension	The ability to read and understand information and ideas presented in writing.
Originality	The ability to come up with unusual or clever ideas about a given topic or situation, or to develop creative ways to solve a problem.
Speech Recognition	The ability to identify and understand the speech of another person.
Inductive Reasoning	The ability to combine pieces of information to form general rules or conclusions (includes finding a relationship among seemingly unrelated events).
Fluency of Ideas	The ability to come up with a number of ideas about a topic (the number of ideas is important, not their quality, correctness, or creativity).
Near Vision	The ability to see details at close range (within a few feet of the observer).
Deductive Reasoning	The ability to apply general rules to specific problems to produce answers that make sense.
Information Ordering	The ability to arrange things or actions in a certain order or pattern according to a specific rule or set of rules (e.g., patterns of numbers, letters, words, pictures, mathematical operations).
Selective Attention	The ability to concentrate on a task over a period of time without being distracted.
Visualization	The ability to imagine how something will look after it is moved around or when its parts are moved or rearranged.
Memorization	The ability to remember information such as words, numbers, pictures, and procedures.
Time Sharing	The ability to shift back and forth between two or more activities or sources of information (such as speech, sounds, touch, or other sources).
Category Flexibility	The ability to generate or use different sets of rules for combining or grouping things in different ways.
Flexibility of Closure	The ability to identify or detect a known pattern (a figure, object, word, or sound) that is hidden in other distracting material.
Perceptual Speed	The ability to quickly and accurately compare similarities and differences among sets of letters, numbers, objects, pictures, or patterns. The things to be compared may be presented at the same time or one after the other. This ability also includes comparing a presented object with a remembered object.
Mathematical Reasoning	The ability to choose the right mathematical methods or formulas to solve a problem.
Speed of Closure	The ability to quickly make sense of, combine, and organize information into meaningful patterns.
Visual Color Discrimination	The ability to match or detect differences between colors, including shades of color and brightness.
Far Vision	The ability to see details at a distance.
Depth Perception	The ability to judge which of several objects is closer or farther away from you, or to judge the distance between you and an object.
Wrist-Finger Speed	The ability to make fast, simple, repeated movements of the fingers, hands, and wrists.
Number Facility	The ability to add, subtract, multiply, or divide quickly and correctly.
Auditory Attention	The ability to focus on a single source of sound in the presence of other distracting sounds.
Multilimb Coordination	The ability to coordinate two or more limbs (for example, two arms, two legs, or one leg and one arm) while sitting, standing, or lying down. It does not involve performing the activities while the whole body is in motion.
Finger Dexterity	The ability to make precisely coordinated movements of the fingers of one or both hands to grasp, manipulate, or assemble very small objects.
Hearing Sensitivity	The ability to detect or tell the differences between sounds that vary in pitch and loudness.
Extent Flexibility	The ability to bend, stretch, twist, or reach with your body, arms, and/or legs.
Manual Dexterity	The ability to quickly move your hand, your hand together with your arm, or your two hands to grasp, manipulate, or assemble objects.
Dynamic Strength	The ability to exert muscle force repeatedly or continuously over time. This involves muscular endurance and resistance to muscle fatigue.
Explosive Strength	The ability to use short bursts of muscle force to propel oneself (as in jumping or sprinting), or to throw an object.

Trunk Strength	The ability to use your abdominal and lower back muscles to support part of the body repeatedly or continuously over time without 'giving out' or fatiguing.
Static Strength	The ability to exert maximum muscle force to lift, push, pull, or carry objects.
Stamina	The ability to exert yourself physically over long periods of time without getting winded or out of breath.
Speed of Limb Movement	The ability to quickly move the arms and legs.
Rate Control	The ability to time your movements or the movement of a piece of equipment in anticipation of changes in the speed and/or direction of a moving object or scene.
Response Orientation	The ability to choose quickly between two or more movements in response to two or more different signals (lights, sounds, pictures). It includes the speed with which the correct response is started with the hand, foot, or other body part.
Dynamic Flexibility	The ability to quickly and repeatedly bend, stretch, twist, or reach out with your body, arms, and/or legs.
Spatial Orientation	The ability to know your location in relation to the environment or to know where other objects are in relation to you.
Control Precision	The ability to quickly and repeatedly adjust the controls of a machine or a vehicle to exact positions.
Gross Body Equilibrium	The ability to keep or regain your body balance or stay upright when in an unstable position.
Gross Body Coordination	The ability to coordinate the movement of your arms, legs, and torso together when the whole body is in motion.
Night Vision	The ability to see under low light conditions.
Peripheral Vision	The ability to see objects or movement of objects to one's side when the eyes are looking ahead.
Sound Localization	The ability to tell the direction from which a sound originated.
Glare Sensitivity	The ability to see objects in the presence of glare or bright lighting.
Arm-Hand Steadiness	The ability to keep your hand and arm steady while moving your arm or while holding your arm and hand in one position.
Reaction Time	The ability to quickly respond (with the hand, finger, or foot) to a signal (sound, light, picture) when it appears.

Work_Activity	Work_Activity Definitions
Communicating with Persons Outside Organization	Communicating with people outside the organization, representing the organization to customers, the public, government, and other external sources. This information can be exchanged in person, in writing, or by telephone or e-mail.
Getting Information	Observing, receiving, and otherwise obtaining information from all relevant sources.
Thinking Creatively	Developing, designing, or creating new applications, ideas, relationships, systems, or products, including artistic contributions.
Communicating with Supervisors, Peers, or Subordin	Providing information to supervisors, co-workers, and subordinates by telephone, in written form, e-mail, or in person.
Organizing, Planning, and Prioritizing Work	Developing specific goals and plans to prioritize, organize, and accomplish your work.
Interacting With Computers	Using computers and computer systems (including hardware and software) to program, write software, set up functions, enter data, or process information.
Establishing and Maintaining Interpersonal Relatio	Developing constructive and cooperative working relationships with others, and maintaining them over time.
Making Decisions and Solving Problems	Analyzing information and evaluating results to choose the best solution and solve problems.
Updating and Using Relevant Knowledge	Keeping up-to-date technically and applying new knowledge to your job.
Scheduling Work and Activities	Scheduling events, programs, and activities, as well as the work of others.
Selling or Influencing Others	Convincing others to buy merchandise/goods or to otherwise change their minds or actions.
Developing Objectives and Strategies	Establishing long-range objectives and specifying the strategies and actions to achieve them.
Identifying Objects, Actions, and Events	Identifying information by categorizing, estimating, recognizing differences or similarities, and detecting changes in circumstances or events.
Processing Information	Compiling, coding, categorizing, calculating, tabulating, auditing, or verifying information or data.
Performing Administrative Activities	Performing day-to-day administrative tasks such as maintaining information files and processing paperwork.
Analyzing Data or Information	Identifying the underlying principles, reasons, or facts of information by breaking down information or data into separate parts.

Documenting Recording Information	Entering, transcribing, recording, storing, or maintaining information in written or electronic magnetic form.
Developing and Building Teams	Encouraging and building mutual trust, respect, and cooperation among team members.
Judging the Qualities of Things, Services, or Peop	Assessing the value, importance, or quality of things or people.
Performing for or Working Directly with the Public	Performing for people or dealing directly with the public. This includes serving customers in restaurants and stores, and receiving clients or guests.
Coordinating the Work and Activities of Others	Getting members of a group to work together to accomplish tasks.
Interpreting the Meaning of Information for Others	Translating or explaining what information means and how it can be used.
Resolving Conflicts and Negotiating with Others	Handling complaints, settling disputes, and resolving grievances and conflicts, or otherwise negotiating with others.
Provide Consultation and Advice to Others	Providing guidance and expert advice to management or other groups on technical, systems-, or process-related topics.
Estimating the Quantifiable Characteristics of Pro	Estimating sizes, distances, and quantities; or determining time, costs, resources, or materials needed to perform a work activity.
Monitoring and Controlling Resources	Monitoring and controlling resources and overseeing the spending of money.
Monitor Processes, Materials, or Surroundings	Monitoring and reviewing information from materials, events, or the environment, to detect or assess problems.
Coaching and Developing Others	Identifying the developmental needs of others and coaching, mentoring, or otherwise helping others to improve their knowledge or skills.
Guiding, Directing, and Motivating Subordinates	Providing guidance and direction to subordinates, including setting performance standards and monitoring performance.
Training and Teaching Others	Identifying the educational needs of others, developing formal educational or training programs or classes, and teaching or instructing others.
Evaluating Information to Determine Compliance wit	Using relevant information and individual judgment to determine whether events or processes comply with laws, regulations, or standards.
Assisting and Caring for Others	Providing personal assistance, medical attention, emotional support, or other personal care to others such as coworkers, customers, or patients.
Staffing Organizational Units	Recruiting, interviewing, selecting, hiring, and promoting employees in an organization.
Controlling Machines and Processes	Using either control mechanisms or direct physical activity to operate machines or processes (not including computers or vehicles).
Handling and Moving Objects	Using hands and arms in handling, installing, positioning, and moving materials, and manipulating things.
Performing General Physical Activities	Performing physical activities that require considerable use of your arms and legs and moving your whole body, such as climbing, lifting, balancing, walking, stooping, and handling of materials.
Inspecting Equipment, Structures, or Material	Inspecting equipment, structures, or materials to identify the cause of errors or other problems or defects.
Repairing and Maintaining Mechanical Equipment	Servicing, repairing, adjusting, and testing machines, devices, moving parts, and equipment that operate primarily on the basis of mechanical (not electronic) principles.
Repairing and Maintaining Electronic Equipment	Servicing, repairing, calibrating, regulating, fine-tuning, or testing machines, devices, and equipment that operate primarily on the basis of electrical or electronic (not mechanical) principles.
Drafting, Laying Out, and Specifying Technical Dev	Providing documentation, detailed instructions, drawings, or specifications to tell others about how devices, parts, equipment, or structures are to be fabricated, constructed, assembled, modified, maintained, or used.
Operating Vehicles, Mechanized Devices, or Equipme	Running, maneuvering, navigating, or driving vehicles or mechanized equipment, such as forklifts, passenger vehicles, aircraft, or water craft.

Work_Context	Work_Context Definitions
Electronic Mail	How often do you use electronic mail in this job?
Telephone	How often do you have telephone conversations in this job?
Contact With Others	How much does this job require the worker to be in contact with others (face-to-face, by telephone, or otherwise) in order to perform it?
Face-to-Face Discussions	How often do you have to have face-to-face discussions with individuals or teams in this job?

Frequency of Decision Making	How frequently is the worker required to make decisions that affect other people, the financial resources, and/or the image and reputation of the organization?
Letters and Memos	How often does the job require written letters and memos?
Impact of Decisions on Co-workers or Company Resul	How do the decisions an employee makes impact the results of co-workers, clients or the company?
Importance of Being Exact or Accurate	How important is being very exact or highly accurate in performing this job?
Spend Time Sitting	How much does this job require sitting?
Time Pressure	How often does this job require the worker to meet strict deadlines?
Work With Work Group or Team	How important is it to work with others in a group or team in this job?
Deal With External Customers	How important is it to work with external customers or the public in this job?
Structured versus Unstructured Work	To what extent is this job structured for the worker, rather than allowing the worker to determine tasks, priorities, and goals?
Freedom to Make Decisions	How much decision making freedom, without supervision, does the job offer?
Coordinate or Lead Others	How important is it to coordinate or lead others in accomplishing work activities in this job?
Level of Competition	To what extent does this job require the worker to compete or to be aware of competitive pressures?
Responsibility for Outcomes and Results	How responsible is the worker for work outcomes and results of other workers?
Indoors, Environmentally Controlled	How often does this job require working indoors in environmentally controlled conditions?
Frequency of Conflict Situations	How often are there conflict situations the employee has to face in this job?
Deal With Unpleasant or Angry People	How frequently does the worker have to deal with unpleasant, angry, or discourteous individuals as part of the job requirements?
Physical Proximity	To what extent does this job require the worker to perform job tasks in close physical proximity to other people?
Public Speaking	How often do you have to perform public speaking in this job?
Spend Time Making Repetitive Motions	How much does this job require making repetitive motions?
Importance of Repeating Same Tasks	How important is repeating the same physical activities (e.g., key entry) or mental activities (e.g., checking entries in a ledger) over and over, without stopping, to performing this job?
Consequence of Error	How serious would the result usually be if the worker made a mistake that was not readily correctable?
Degree of Automation	How automated is the job?
Responsible for Others' Health and Safety	How much responsibility is there for the health and safety of others in this job?
Spend Time Standing	How much does this job require standing?
In an Enclosed Vehicle or Equipment	How often does this job require working in a closed vehicle or equipment (e.g., car)?
Outdoors, Exposed to Weather	How often does this job require working outdoors, exposed to all weather conditions?
Spend Time Walking and Running	How much does this job require walking and running?
Sounds, Noise Levels Are Distracting or Uncomforta	How often does this job require working exposed to sounds and noise levels that are distracting or uncomfortable?
Spend Time Using Your Hands to Handle, Control, or	How much does this job require using your hands to handle, control, or feel objects, tools or controls?
Outdoors, Under Cover	How often does this job require working outdoors, under cover (e.g., structure with roof but no walls)?
Indoors, Not Environmentally Controlled	How often does this job require working indoors in non-controlled environmental conditions (e.g., warehouse without heat)?
Spend Time Bending or Twisting the Body	How much does this job require bending or twisting your body?
Very Hot or Cold Temperatures	How often does this job require working in very hot (above 90 F degrees) or very cold (below 32 F degrees) temperatures?
Extremely Bright or Inadequate Lighting	How often does this job require working in extremely bright or inadequate lighting conditions?
Exposed to Disease or Infections	How often does this job require exposure to disease/infections?
Exposed to Contaminants	How often does this job require working exposed to contaminants (such as pollutants, gases, dust or odors)?
Exposed to Hazardous Equipment	How often does this job require exposure to hazardous equipment?
Spend Time Kneeling, Crouching, Stooping, or Crawl	How much does this job require kneeling, crouching, stooping, or crawling?

Spend Time Keeping or Regaining Balance	How much does this job require keeping or regaining your balance?
Cramped Work Space, Awkward Positions	How often does this job require working in cramped work spaces that requires getting into awkward positions?
Deal With Physically Aggressive People	How frequently does this job require the worker to deal with physical aggression of violent individuals?
Wear Common Protective or Safety Equipment such as	How much does this job require wearing common protective or safety equipment such as safety shoes, glasses, gloves, hard hats or life jackets?
Spend Time Climbing Ladders, Scaffolds, or Poles	How much does this job require climbing ladders, scaffolds, or poles?
Exposed to High Places	How often does this job require exposure to high places?
Exposed to Minor Burns, Cuts, Bites, or Stings	How often does this job require exposure to minor burns, cuts, bites, or stings?
Pace Determined by Speed of Equipment	How important is it to this job that the pace is determined by the speed of equipment or machinery? (This does not refer to keeping busy at all times on this job.)
Exposed to Whole Body Vibration	How often does this job require exposure to whole body vibration (e.g., operate a jackhammer)?
In an Open Vehicle or Equipment	How often does this job require working in an open vehicle or equipment (e.g., tractor)?
Wear Specialized Protective or Safety Equipment su	How much does this job require wearing specialized protective or safety equipment such as breathing apparatus, safety harness, full protection suits, or radiation protection?
Exposed to Radiation	How often does this job require exposure to radiation?
Exposed to Hazardous Conditions	How often does this job require exposure to hazardous conditions?

Job Zone Component	Job Zone Component Definitions
Title	Job Zone Four: Considerable Preparation Needed
Overall Experience	A minimum of two to four years of work-related skill, knowledge, or experience is needed for these occupations. For example, an accountant must complete four years of college and work for several years in accounting to be considered qualified.
Job Training	Employees in these occupations usually need several years of work-related experience, on-the-job training, and/or vocational training.
Job Zone Examples	Many of these occupations involve coordinating, supervising, managing, or training others. Examples include accountants, chefs and head cooks, computer programmers, historians, pharmacists, and police detectives.
SVP Range	(7.0 to < 8.0)
Education	Most of these occupations require a four - year bachelor's degree, but some do not.

Work_Styles	Work_Styles Definitions
Attention to Detail	Job requires being careful about detail and thorough in completing work tasks.
Dependability	Job requires being reliable, responsible, and dependable, and fulfilling obligations.
Cooperation	Job requires being pleasant with others on the job and displaying a good-natured, cooperative attitude.
Initiative	Job requires a willingness to take on responsibilities and challenges.
Self Control	Job requires maintaining composure, keeping emotions in check, controlling anger, and avoiding aggressive behavior, even in very difficult situations.
Leadership	Job requires a willingness to lead, take charge, and offer opinions and direction.
Integrity	Job requires being honest and ethical.
Concern for Others	Job requires being sensitive to others' needs and feelings and being understanding and helpful on the job.
Persistence	Job requires persistence in the face of obstacles.
Social Orientation	Job requires preferring to work with others rather than alone, and being personally connected with others on the job.
Adaptability/Flexibility	Job requires being open to change (positive or negative) and to considerable variety in the workplace.
Stress Tolerance	Job requires accepting criticism and dealing calmly and effectively with high stress situations.
Achievement/Effort	Job requires establishing and maintaining personally challenging achievement goals and exerting effort toward mastering tasks.

Independence	Job requires developing one's own ways of doing things, guiding oneself with little or no supervision, and depending on oneself to get things done.
Innovation	Job requires creativity and alternative thinking to develop new ideas for and answers to work-related problems.
Analytical Thinking	Job requires analyzing information and using logic to address work-related issues and problems.

27-3041.00 - Editors

Perform variety of editorial duties, such as laying out, indexing, and revising content of written materials, in preparation for final publication.

Tasks

1) Prepare, rewrite and edit copy to improve readability, or supervise others who do this work.

2) Verify facts, dates, and statistics, using standard reference sources.

3) Read, evaluate and edit manuscripts or other materials submitted for publication and confer with authors regarding changes in content, style or organization, or publication.

4) Develop story or content ideas, considering reader or audience appeal.

5) Meet frequently with artists, typesetters, layout personnel, marketing directors, and production managers to discuss projects and resolve problems.

6) Plan the contents of publications according to the publication's style, editorial policy, and publishing requirements.

7) Oversee publication production, including artwork, layout, computer typesetting, and printing, ensuring adherence to deadlines and budget requirements.

8) Confer with management and editorial staff members regarding placement and emphasis of developing news stories.

9) Review and approve proofs submitted by composing room prior to publication production.

10) Allocate print space for story text, photos, and illustrations according to space parameters and copy significance, using knowledge of layout principles.

11) Assign topics, events and stories to individual writers or reporters for coverage.

12) Monitor news-gathering operations to ensure utilization of all news sources, such as press releases, telephone contacts, radio, television, wire services, and other reporters.

13) Supervise and coordinate work of reporters and other editors.

14) Select local, state, national, and international news items received from wire services, based on assessment of items' significance and interest value.

15) Interview and hire writers and reporters or negotiate contracts, royalties, and payments for authors or freelancers.

16) Arrange for copyright permissions.

17) Make manuscript acceptance or revision recommendations to the publisher.

18) Read material to determine index items and arrange them alphabetically or topically, indicating page or chapter location.

19) Direct the policies and departments of newspapers, magazines and other publishing establishments.

Knowledge

Knowledge	Knowledge Definitions
English Language	Knowledge of the structure and content of the English language including the meaning and spelling of words, rules of composition, and grammar.
Communications and Media	Knowledge of media production, communication, and dissemination techniques and methods. This includes alternative ways to inform and entertain via written, oral, and visual media.
Customer and Personal Service	Knowledge of principles and processes for providing customer and personal services. This includes customer needs assessment, meeting quality standards for services, and evaluation of customer satisfaction.
Law and Government	Knowledge of laws, legal codes, court procedures, precedents, government regulations, executive orders, agency rules, and the democratic political process.
Computers and Electronics	Knowledge of circuit boards, processors, chips, electronic equipment, and computer hardware and software, including applications and programming.
Administration and Management	Knowledge of business and management principles involved in strategic planning, resource allocation, human resources modeling, leadership technique, production methods, and coordination of people and resources.
Clerical	Knowledge of administrative and clerical procedures and systems such as word processing, managing files and records, stenography and transcription, designing forms, and other office procedures and terminology.
Education and Training	Knowledge of principles and methods for curriculum and training design, teaching and instruction for individuals and groups, and the measurement of training effects.
Sales and Marketing	Knowledge of principles and methods for showing, promoting, and selling products or services. This includes marketing strategy and tactics, product demonstration, sales techniques, and sales control systems.
Mathematics	Knowledge of arithmetic, algebra, geometry, calculus, statistics, and their applications.
Personnel and Human Resources	Knowledge of principles and procedures for personnel recruitment, selection, training, compensation and benefits, labor relations and negotiation, and personnel information systems.
Psychology	Knowledge of human behavior and performance; individual differences in ability, personality, and interests; learning and motivation; psychological research methods; and the assessment and treatment of behavioral and affective disorders.
Geography	Knowledge of principles and methods for describing the features of land, sea, and air masses, including their physical characteristics, locations, interrelationships, and distribution of plant, animal, and human life.
History and Archeology	Knowledge of historical events and their causes, indicators, and effects on civilizations and cultures.
Production and Processing	Knowledge of raw materials, production processes, quality control, costs, and other techniques for maximizing the effective manufacture and distribution of goods.
Sociology and Anthropology	Knowledge of group behavior and dynamics, societal trends and influences, human migrations, ethnicity, cultures and their history and origins.
Economics and Accounting	Knowledge of economic and accounting principles and practices, the financial markets, banking and the analysis and reporting of financial data.
Fine Arts	Knowledge of the theory and techniques required to compose, produce, and perform works of music, dance, visual arts, drama, and sculpture.
Design	Knowledge of design techniques, tools, and principles involved in production of precision technical plans, blueprints, drawings, and models.
Public Safety and Security	Knowledge of relevant equipment, policies, procedures, and strategies to promote effective local, state, or national security operations for the protection of people, data, property, and institutions.
Philosophy and Theology	Knowledge of different philosophical systems and religions. This includes their basic principles, values, ethics, ways of thinking, customs, practices, and their impact on human culture.
Telecommunications	Knowledge of transmission, broadcasting, switching, control, and operation of telecommunications systems.
Transportation	Knowledge of principles and methods for moving people or goods by air, rail, sea, or road, including the relative costs and benefits.
Therapy and Counseling	Knowledge of principles, methods, and procedures for diagnosis, treatment, and rehabilitation of physical and mental dysfunctions, and for career counseling and guidance.
Foreign Language	Knowledge of the structure and content of a foreign (non-English) language including the meaning and spelling of words, rules of composition and grammar, and pronunciation.
Engineering and Technology	Knowledge of the practical application of engineering science and technology. This includes applying principles, techniques, procedures, and equipment to the design and production of various goods and services.
Mechanical	Knowledge of machines and tools, including their designs, uses, repair, and maintenance.
Medicine and Dentistry	Knowledge of the information and techniques needed to diagnose and treat human injuries, diseases, and deformities. This includes symptoms, treatment alternatives, drug properties and interactions, and preventive health-care measures.

Physics	Knowledge and prediction of physical principles, laws, their interrelationships, and applications to understanding fluid, material, and atmospheric dynamics, and mechanical, electrical, atomic and sub-atomic structures and processes.
Biology	Knowledge of plant and animal organisms, their tissues, cells, functions, interdependencies, and interactions with each other and the environment.
Building and Construction	Knowledge of materials, methods, and the tools involved in the construction or repair of houses, buildings, or other structures such as highways and roads.
Chemistry	Knowledge of the chemical composition, structure, and properties of substances and of the chemical processes and transformations that they undergo. This includes uses of chemicals and their interactions, danger signs, production techniques, and disposal methods.
Food Production	Knowledge of techniques and equipment for planting, growing, and harvesting food products (both plant and animal) for consumption, including storage/handling techniques.

Skills	**Skills Definitions**
Reading Comprehension	Understanding written sentences and paragraphs in work related documents.
Writing	Communicating effectively in writing as appropriate for the needs of the audience.
Active Listening	Giving full attention to what other people are saying, taking time to understand the points being made, asking questions as appropriate, and not interrupting at inappropriate times.
Critical Thinking	Using logic and reasoning to identify the strengths and weaknesses of alternative solutions, conclusions or approaches to problems.
Time Management	Managing one's own time and the time of others.
Judgment and Decision Making	Considering the relative costs and benefits of potential actions to choose the most appropriate one.
Active Learning	Understanding the implications of new information for both current and future problem-solving and decision-making.
Coordination	Adjusting actions in relation to others' actions.
Speaking	Talking to others to convey information effectively.
Monitoring	Monitoring/Assessing performance of yourself, other individuals, or organizations to make improvements or take corrective action.
Social Perceptiveness	Being aware of others' reactions and understanding why they react as they do.
Learning Strategies	Selecting and using training/instructional methods and procedures appropriate for the situation when learning or teaching new things.
Persuasion	Persuading others to change their minds or behavior.
Quality Control Analysis	Conducting tests and inspections of products, services, or processes to evaluate quality or performance.
Complex Problem Solving	Identifying complex problems and reviewing related information to develop and evaluate options and implement solutions.
Management of Financial Resources	Determining how money will be spent to get the work done, and accounting for these expenditures.
Negotiation	Bringing others together and trying to reconcile differences.
Mathematics	Using mathematics to solve problems.
Service Orientation	Actively looking for ways to help people.
Instructing	Teaching others how to do something.
Management of Personnel Resources	Motivating, developing, and directing people as they work, identifying the best people for the job.
Operations Analysis	Analyzing needs and product requirements to create a design.
Troubleshooting	Determining causes of operating errors and deciding what to do about it.
Equipment Selection	Determining the kind of tools and equipment needed to do a job.
Operation and Control	Controlling operations of equipment or systems.
Systems Evaluation	Identifying measures or indicators of system performance and the actions needed to improve or correct performance, relative to the goals of the system.
Technology Design	Generating or adapting equipment and technology to serve user needs.
Systems Analysis	Determining how a system should work and how changes in conditions, operations, and the environment will affect outcomes.
Equipment Maintenance	Performing routine maintenance on equipment and determining when and what kind of maintenance is needed.
Management of Material Resources	Obtaining and seeing to the appropriate use of equipment, facilities, and materials needed to do certain work.

Operation Monitoring	Watching gauges, dials, or other indicators to make sure a machine is working properly.
Installation	Installing equipment, machines, wiring, or programs to meet specifications.
Science	Using scientific rules and methods to solve problems.
Programming	Writing computer programs for various purposes.
Repairing	Repairing machines or systems using the needed tools.

Ability	**Ability Definitions**
Written Comprehension	The ability to read and understand information and ideas presented in writing.
Written Expression	The ability to communicate information and ideas in writing so others will understand.
Oral Expression	The ability to communicate information and ideas in speaking so others will understand.
Problem Sensitivity	The ability to tell when something is wrong or is likely to go wrong. It does not involve solving the problem, only recognizing there is a problem.
Oral Comprehension	The ability to listen to and understand information and ideas presented through spoken words and sentences.
Speech Clarity	The ability to speak clearly so others can understand you.
Near Vision	The ability to see details at close range (within a few feet of the observer).
Deductive Reasoning	The ability to apply general rules to specific problems to produce answers that make sense.
Originality	The ability to come up with unusual or clever ideas about a given topic or situation, or to develop creative ways to solve a problem.
Speech Recognition	The ability to identify and understand the speech of another person.
Fluency of Ideas	The ability to come up with a number of ideas about a topic (the number of ideas is important, not their quality, correctness, or creativity).
Information Ordering	The ability to arrange things or actions in a certain order or pattern according to a specific rule or set of rules (e.g., patterns of numbers, letters, words, pictures, mathematical operations).
Inductive Reasoning	The ability to combine pieces of information to form general rules or conclusions (includes finding a relationship among seemingly unrelated events).
Visualization	The ability to imagine how something will look after it is moved around or when its parts are moved or rearranged.
Category Flexibility	The ability to generate or use different sets of rules for combining or grouping things in different ways.
Selective Attention	The ability to concentrate on a task over a period of time without being distracted.
Memorization	The ability to remember information such as words, numbers, pictures, and procedures.
Time Sharing	The ability to shift back and forth between two or more activities or sources of information (such as speech, sounds, touch, or other sources).
Perceptual Speed	The ability to quickly and accurately compare similarities and differences among sets of letters, numbers, objects, pictures, or patterns. The things to be compared may be presented at the same time or one after the other. This ability also includes comparing a presented object with a remembered object.
Speed of Closure	The ability to quickly make sense of, combine, and organize information into meaningful patterns.
Flexibility of Closure	The ability to identify or detect a known pattern (a figure, object, word, or sound) that is hidden in other distracting material.
Auditory Attention	The ability to focus on a single source of sound in the presence of other distracting sounds.
Visual Color Discrimination	The ability to match or detect differences between colors, including shades of color and brightness.
Mathematical Reasoning	The ability to choose the right mathematical methods or formulas to solve a problem.
Far Vision	The ability to see details at a distance.
Number Facility	The ability to add, subtract, multiply, or divide quickly and correctly.
Manual Dexterity	The ability to quickly move your hand, your hand together with your arm, or your two hands to grasp, manipulate, or assemble objects.
Finger Dexterity	The ability to make precisely coordinated movements of the fingers of one or both hands to grasp, manipulate, or assemble very small objects.
Arm-Hand Steadiness	The ability to keep your hand and arm steady while moving your arm or while holding your arm and hand in one position.

Hearing Sensitivity	The ability to detect or tell the differences between sounds that vary in pitch and loudness.
Depth Perception	The ability to judge which of several objects is closer or farther away from you, or to judge the distance between you and an object.
Control Precision	The ability to quickly and repeatedly adjust the controls of a machine or a vehicle to exact positions.
Trunk Strength	The ability to use your abdominal and lower back muscles to support part of the body repeatedly or continuously over time without 'giving out' or fatiguing.
Gross Body Coordination	The ability to coordinate the movement of your arms, legs, and torso together when the whole body is in motion.
Speed of Limb Movement	The ability to quickly move the arms and legs.
Wrist-Finger Speed	The ability to make fast, simple, repeated movements of the fingers, hands, and wrists.
Dynamic Flexibility	The ability to quickly and repeatedly bend, stretch, twist, or reach out with your body, arms, and/or legs.
Glare Sensitivity	The ability to see objects in the presence of glare or bright lighting.
Night Vision	The ability to see under low light conditions.
Dynamic Strength	The ability to exert muscle force repeatedly or continuously over time. This involves muscular endurance and resistance to muscle fatigue.
Stamina	The ability to exert yourself physically over long periods of time without getting winded or out of breath.
Sound Localization	The ability to tell the direction from which a sound originated.
Extent Flexibility	The ability to bend, stretch, twist, or reach with your body, arms, and/or legs.
Explosive Strength	The ability to use short bursts of muscle force to propel oneself (as in jumping or sprinting), or to throw an object.
Reaction Time	The ability to quickly respond (with the hand, finger, or foot) to a signal (sound, light, picture) when it appears.
Spatial Orientation	The ability to know your location in relation to the environment or to know where other objects are in relation to you.
Rate Control	The ability to time your movements or the movement of a piece of equipment in anticipation of changes in the speed and/or direction of a moving object or scene.
Peripheral Vision	The ability to see objects or movement of objects to one's side when the eyes are looking ahead.
Response Orientation	The ability to choose quickly between two or more movements in response to two or more different signals (lights, sounds, pictures). It includes the speed with which the correct response is started with the hand, foot, or other body part.
Multilimb Coordination	The ability to coordinate two or more limbs (for example, two arms, two legs, or one leg and one arm) while sitting, standing, or lying down. It does not involve performing the activities while the whole body is in motion.
Static Strength	The ability to exert maximum muscle force to lift, push, pull, or carry objects.
Gross Body Equilibrium	The ability to keep or regain your body balance or stay upright when in an unstable position.

Work_Activity	Work_Activity Definitions
Interacting With Computers	Using computers and computer systems (including hardware and software) to program, write software, set up functions, enter data, or process information.
Getting Information	Observing, receiving, and otherwise obtaining information from all relevant sources.
Making Decisions and Solving Problems	Analyzing information and evaluating results to choose the best solution and solve problems.
Communicating with Supervisors, Peers, or Subordin	Providing information to supervisors, co-workers, and subordinates by telephone, in written form, e-mail, or in person.
Organizing, Planning, and Prioritizing Work	Developing specific goals and plans to prioritize, organize, and accomplish your work.
Thinking Creatively	Developing, designing, or creating new applications, ideas, relationships, systems, or products, including artistic contributions.
Identifying Objects, Actions, and Events	Identifying information by categorizing, estimating, recognizing differences or similarities, and detecting changes in circumstances or events.
Interpreting the Meaning of Information for Others	Translating or explaining what information means and how it can be used.
Establishing and Maintaining Interpersonal Relatio	Developing constructive and cooperative working relationships with others, and maintaining them over time.

Documenting/Recording Information	Entering, transcribing, recording, storing, or maintaining information in written or electronic/magnetic form.
Updating and Using Relevant Knowledge	Keeping up-to-date technically and applying new knowledge to your job.
Communicating with Persons Outside Organization	Communicating with people outside the organization, representing the organization to customers, the public, government, and other external sources. This information can be exchanged in person, in writing, or by telephone or e-mail.
Processing Information	Compiling, coding, categorizing, calculating, tabulating, auditing, or verifying information or data.
Evaluating Information to Determine Compliance wit	Using relevant information and individual judgment to determine whether events or processes comply with laws, regulations, or standards.
Analyzing Data or Information	Identifying the underlying principles, reasons, or facts of information by breaking down information or data into separate parts.
Coordinating the Work and Activities of Others	Getting members of a group to work together to accomplish tasks.
Judging the Qualities of Things, Services, or Peop	Assessing the value, importance, or quality of things or people.
Performing Administrative Activities	Performing day-to-day administrative tasks such as maintaining information files and processing paperwork.
Scheduling Work and Activities	Scheduling events, programs, and activities, as well as the work of others.
Performing for or Working Directly with the Public	Performing for people or dealing directly with the public. This includes serving customers in restaurants and stores, and receiving clients or guests.
Monitor Processes, Materials, or Surroundings	Monitoring and reviewing information from materials, events, or the environment, to detect or assess problems.
Developing Objectives and Strategies	Establishing long-range objectives and specifying the strategies and actions to achieve them.
Developing and Building Teams	Encouraging and building mutual trust, respect, and cooperation among team members.
Estimating the Quantifiable Characteristics of Pro	Estimating sizes, distances, and quantities; or determining time, costs, resources, or materials needed to perform a work activity.
Resolving Conflicts and Negotiating with Others	Handling complaints, settling disputes, and resolving grievances and conflicts, or otherwise negotiating with others.
Provide Consultation and Advice to Others	Providing guidance and expert advice to management or other groups on technical, systems-, or process-related topics.
Coaching and Developing Others	Identifying the developmental needs of others and coaching, mentoring, or otherwise helping others to improve their knowledge or skills.
Guiding, Directing, and Motivating Subordinates	Providing guidance and direction to subordinates, including setting performance standards and monitoring performance.
Training and Teaching Others	Identifying the educational needs of others, developing formal educational or training programs or classes, and teaching or instructing others.
Monitoring and Controlling Resources	Monitoring and controlling resources and overseeing the spending of money.
Assisting and Caring for Others	Providing personal assistance, medical attention, emotional support, or other personal care to others such as coworkers, customers, or patients.
Selling or Influencing Others	Convincing others to buy merchandise/goods or to otherwise change their minds or actions.
Controlling Machines and Processes	Using either control mechanisms or direct physical activity to operate machines or processes (not including computers or vehicles).
Staffing Organizational Units	Recruiting, interviewing, selecting, hiring, and promoting employees in an organization.
Inspecting Equipment, Structures, or Material	Inspecting equipment, structures, or materials to identify the cause of errors or other problems or defects.
Operating Vehicles, Mechanized Devices, or Equipme	Running, maneuvering, navigating, or driving vehicles or mechanized equipment, such as forklifts, passenger vehicles, aircraft, or water craft.
Handling and Moving Objects	Using hands and arms in handling, installing, positioning, and moving materials, and manipulating things.
Performing General Physical Activities	Performing physical activities that require considerable use of your arms and legs and moving your whole body, such as climbing, lifting, balancing, walking, stooping, and handling of materials.
Repairing and Maintaining Electronic Equipment	Servicing, repairing, calibrating, regulating, fine-tuning, or testing machines, devices, and equipment that operate primarily on the basis of electrical or electronic (not mechanical) principles.

Drafting, Laying Out, and Specifying Technical Dev	Providing documentation, detailed instructions, drawings, or specifications to tell others about how devices, parts, equipment, or structures are to be fabricated, constructed, assembled, modified, maintained, or used.
Repairing and Maintaining Mechanical Equipment	Servicing, repairing, adjusting, and testing machines, devices, moving parts, and equipment that operate primarily on the basis of mechanical (not electronic) principles.

Work_Context	Work_Context Definitions
Face-to-Face Discussions	How often do you have to have face-to-face discussions with individuals or teams in this job?
Telephone	How often do you have telephone conversations in this job?
Time Pressure	How often does this job require the worker to meet strict deadlines?
Importance of Being Exact or Accurate	How important is being very exact or highly accurate in performing this job?
Freedom to Make Decisions	How much decision making freedom, without supervision, does the job offer?
Spend Time Sitting	How much does this job require sitting?
Frequency of Decision Making	How frequently is the worker required to make decisions that affect other people, the financial resources, and/or the image and reputation of the organization?
Electronic Mail	How often do you use electronic mail in this job?
Work With Work Group or Team	How important is it to work with others in a group or team in this job?
Impact of Decisions on Co-workers or Company Resul	How do the decisions an employee makes impact the results of co-workers, clients or the company?
Contact With Others	How much does this job require the worker to be in contact with others (face-to-face, by telephone, or otherwise) in order to perform it?
Indoors, Environmentally Controlled	How often does this job require working indoors in environmentally controlled conditions?
Structured versus Unstructured Work	To what extent is this job structured for the worker, rather than allowing the worker to determine tasks, priorities, and goals?
Letters and Memos	How often does the job require written letters and memos?
Coordinate or Lead Others	How important is it to coordinate or lead others in accomplishing work activities in this job?
Importance of Repeating Same Tasks	How important is repeating the same physical activities (e.g., key entry) or mental activities (e.g., checking entries in a ledger) over and over, without stopping, to performing this job?
Spend Time Using Your Hands to Handle, Control, or	How much does this job require using your hands to handle, control, or feel objects, tools or controls?
Spend Time Making Repetitive Motions	How much does this job require making repetitive motions?
Deal With External Customers	How important is it to work with external customers or the public in this job?
Frequency of Conflict Situations	How often are there conflict situations the employee has to face in this job?
Responsibility for Outcomes and Results	How responsible is the worker for work outcomes and results of other workers?
Level of Competition	To what extent does this job require the worker to compete or to be aware of competitive pressures?
Physical Proximity	To what extent does this job require the worker to perform job tasks in close physical proximity to other people?
Deal With Unpleasant or Angry People	How frequently does the worker have to deal with unpleasant, angry, or discourteous individuals as part of the job requirements?
Consequence of Error	How serious would the result usually be if the worker made a mistake that was not readily correctable?
Degree of Automation	How automated is the job?
Sounds, Noise Levels Are Distracting or Uncomforta	How often does this job require working exposed to sounds and noise levels that are distracting or uncomfortable?
Public Speaking	How often do you have to perform public speaking in this job?
Responsible for Others' Health and Safety	How much responsibility is there for the health and safety of others in this job?
Exposed to Contaminants	How often does this job require working exposed to contaminants (such as pollutants, gases, dust or odors)?
Spend Time Standing	How much does this job require standing?
In an Enclosed Vehicle or Equipment	How often does this job require working in a closed vehicle or equipment (e.g., car)?
Outdoors, Exposed to Weather	How often does this job require working outdoors, exposed to all weather conditions?
Spend Time Walking and Running	How much does this job require walking and running?

Indoors, Not Environmentally Controlled	How often does this job require working indoors in non-controlled environmental conditions (e.g., warehouse without heat)?
Outdoors, Under Cover	How often does this job require working outdoors, under cover (e.g., structure with roof but no walls)?
Extremely Bright or Inadequate Lighting	How often does this job require working in extremely bright or inadequate lighting conditions?
Spend Time Bending or Twisting the Body	How much does this job require bending or twisting your body?
Exposed to Minor Burns, Cuts, Bites, or Stings	How often does this job require exposure to minor burns, cuts, bites, or stings?
Pace Determined by Speed of Equipment	How important is it to this job that the pace is determined by the speed of equipment or machinery? (This does not refer to keeping busy at all times on this job.)
Very Hot or Cold Temperatures	How often does this job require working in very hot (above 90 F degrees) or very cold (below 32 F degrees) temperatures?
Cramped Work Space, Awkward Positions	How often does this job require working in cramped work spaces that requires getting into awkward positions?
Deal With Physically Aggressive People	How frequently does this job require the worker to deal with physical aggression of violent individuals?
Exposed to Hazardous Equipment	How often does this job require exposure to hazardous equipment?
Exposed to Disease or Infections	How often does this job require exposure to disease/infections?
Exposed to High Places	How often does this job require exposure to high places?
Exposed to Hazardous Conditions	How often does this job require exposure to hazardous conditions?
Exposed to Radiation	How often does this job require exposure to radiation?
Spend Time Kneeling, Crouching, Stooping, or Crawl	How much does this job require kneeling, crouching, stooping or crawling?
Spend Time Keeping or Regaining Balance	How much does this job require keeping or regaining your balance?
Wear Common Protective or Safety Equipment such as	How much does this job require wearing common protective or safety equipment such as safety shoes, glasses, gloves, hard hats or life jackets?
Spend Time Climbing Ladders, Scaffolds, or Poles	How much does this job require climbing ladders, scaffolds, or poles?
In an Open Vehicle or Equipment	How often does this job require working in an open vehicle or equipment (e.g., tractor)?
Wear Specialized Protective or Safety Equipment su	How much does this job require wearing specialized protective or safety equipment such as breathing apparatus, safety harness, full protection suits, or radiation protection?
Exposed to Whole Body Vibration	How often does this job require exposure to whole body vibration (e.g., operate a jackhammer)?

Job Zone Component	Job Zone Component Definitions
Title	Job Zone Four: Considerable Preparation Needed
Overall Experience	A minimum of two to four years of work-related skill, knowledge, or experience is needed for these occupations. For example, an accountant must complete four years of college and work for several years in accounting to be considered qualified.
Job Training	Employees in these occupations usually need several years of work-related experience, on-the-job training, and/or vocational training.
Job Zone Examples	Many of these occupations involve coordinating, supervising, managing, or training others. Examples include accountants, chefs and head cooks, computer programmers, historians, pharmacists, and police detectives.
SVP Range	(7.0 to < 8.0)
Education	Most of these occupations require a four - year bachelor's degree, but some do not.

Work_Styles	Work_Styles Definitions
Attention to Detail	Job requires being careful about detail and thorough in completing work tasks.
Dependability	Job requires being reliable, responsible, and dependable, and fulfilling obligations.
Stress Tolerance	Job requires accepting criticism and dealing calmly and effectively with high stress situations.
Integrity	Job requires being honest and ethical.
Initiative	Job requires a willingness to take on responsibilities and challenges.

Adaptability/Flexibility	Job requires being open to change (positive or negative) and to considerable variety in the workplace.
Persistence	Job requires persistence in the face of obstacles.
Self Control	Job requires maintaining composure, keeping emotions in check, controlling anger, and avoiding aggressive behavior, even in very difficult situations.
Independence	Job requires developing one's own ways of doing things, guiding oneself with little or no supervision, and depending on oneself to get things done.
Achievement/Effort	Job requires establishing and maintaining personally challenging achievement goals and exerting effort toward mastering tasks.
Cooperation	Job requires being pleasant with others on the job and displaying a good-natured, cooperative attitude.
Leadership	Job requires a willingness to lead, take charge, and offer opinions and direction.
Analytical Thinking	Job requires analyzing information and using logic to address work-related issues and problems.
Innovation	Job requires creativity and alternative thinking to develop new ideas for and answers to work-related problems.
Concern for Others	Job requires being sensitive to others' needs and feelings and being understanding and helpful on the job.
Social Orientation	Job requires preferring to work with others rather than alone, and being personally connected with others on the job.

27-3042.00 - Technical Writers

Write technical materials, such as equipment manuals, appendices, or operating and maintenance instructions. May assist in layout work.

Tasks

1) Edit, standardize, or make changes to material prepared by other writers or establishment personnel.

2) Review published materials and recommend revisions or changes in scope, format, content, and methods of reproduction and binding.

3) Select photographs, drawings, sketches, diagrams, and charts to illustrate material.

4) Assist in laying out material for publication.

5) Interview production and engineering personnel and read journals and other material to become familiar with product technologies and production methods.

6) Analyze developments in specific field to determine need for revisions in previously published materials and development of new material.

7) Confer with customer representatives, vendors, plant executives, or publisher to establish technical specifications and to determine subject material to be developed for publication.

8) Observe production, developmental, and experimental activities to determine operating procedure and detail.

9) Study drawings, specifications, mockups, and product samples to integrate and delineate technology, operating procedure, and production sequence and detail.

10) Arrange for typing, duplication, and distribution of material.

11) Review manufacturer's and trade catalogs, drawings and other data relative to operation, maintenance, and service of equipment.

12) Draw sketches to illustrate specified materials or assembly sequence.

13) Organize material and complete writing assignment according to set standards regarding order, clarity, conciseness, style, and terminology.

Knowledge	Knowledge Definitions
English Language	Knowledge of the structure and content of the English language including the meaning and spelling of words, rules of composition, and grammar.
Computers and Electronics	Knowledge of circuit boards, processors, chips, electronic equipment, and computer hardware and software, including applications and programming.
Communications and Media	Knowledge of media production, communication, and dissemination techniques and methods. This includes alternative ways to inform and entertain via written, oral, and visual media.
Education and Training	Knowledge of principles and methods for curriculum and training design, teaching and instruction for individuals and groups, and the measurement of training effects.
Engineering and Technology	Knowledge of the practical application of engineering science and technology. This includes applying principles, techniques, procedures, and equipment to the design and production of various goods and services.
Sales and Marketing	Knowledge of principles and methods for showing, promoting, and selling products or services. This includes marketing strategy and tactics, product demonstration, sales techniques, and sales control systems.
Clerical	Knowledge of administrative and clerical procedures and systems such as word processing, managing files and records, stenography and transcription, designing forms, and other office procedures and terminology.
Design	Knowledge of design techniques, tools, and principles involved in production of precision technical plans, blueprints, drawings, and models.
Mathematics	Knowledge of arithmetic, algebra, geometry, calculus, statistics, and their applications.
Administration and Management	Knowledge of business and management principles involved in strategic planning, resource allocation, human resources modeling, leadership technique, production methods, and coordination of people and resources.
Telecommunications	Knowledge of transmission, broadcasting, switching, control, and operation of telecommunications systems.
Customer and Personal Service	Knowledge of principles and processes for providing customer and personal services. This includes customer needs assessment, meeting quality standards for services, and evaluation of customer satisfaction.
Law and Government	Knowledge of laws, legal codes, court procedures, precedents, government regulations, executive orders, agency rules, and the democratic political process.
Public Safety and Security	Knowledge of relevant equipment, policies, procedures, and strategies to promote effective local, state, or national security operations for the protection of people, data, property, and institutions.
Psychology	Knowledge of human behavior and performance; individual differences in ability, personality, and interests; learning and motivation; psychological research methods; and the assessment and treatment of behavioral and affective disorders.
Production and Processing	Knowledge of raw materials, production processes, quality control, costs, and other techniques for maximizing the effective manufacture and distribution of goods.
Mechanical	Knowledge of machines and tools, including their designs, uses, repair, and maintenance.
Geography	Knowledge of principles and methods for describing the features of land, sea, and air masses, including their physical characteristics, locations, interrelationships, and distribution of plant, animal, and human life.
Sociology and Anthropology	Knowledge of group behavior and dynamics, societal trends and influences, human migrations, ethnicity, cultures and their history and origins.
Physics	Knowledge and prediction of physical principles, laws, their interrelationships, and applications to understanding fluid, material, and atmospheric dynamics, and mechanical, electrical, atomic and sub-atomic structures and processes.
Personnel and Human Resources	Knowledge of principles and procedures for personnel recruitment, selection, training, compensation and benefits, labor relations and negotiation, and personnel information systems.
Economics and Accounting	Knowledge of economic and accounting principles and practices, the financial markets, banking and the analysis and reporting of financial data.
Chemistry	Knowledge of the chemical composition, structure, and properties of substances and of the chemical processes and transformations that they undergo. This includes uses of chemicals and their interactions, danger signs, production techniques, and disposal methods.
Transportation	Knowledge of principles and methods for moving people or goods by air, rail, sea, or road, including the relative costs and benefits.
Fine Arts	Knowledge of the theory and techniques required to compose, produce, and perform works of music, dance, visual arts, drama, and sculpture.

Philosophy and Theology	Knowledge of different philosophical systems and religions. This includes their basic principles, values, ethics, ways of thinking, customs, practices, and their impact on human culture.
Building and Construction	Knowledge of materials, methods, and the tools involved in the construction or repair of houses, buildings, or other structures such as highways and roads.
Therapy and Counseling	Knowledge of principles, methods, and procedures for diagnosis, treatment, and rehabilitation of physical and mental dysfunctions, and for career counseling and guidance.
Medicine and Dentistry	Knowledge of the information and techniques needed to diagnose and treat human injuries, diseases, and deformities. This includes symptoms, treatment alternatives, drug properties and interactions, and preventive health-care measures.
Food Production	Knowledge of techniques and equipment for planting, growing, and harvesting food products (both plant and animal) for consumption, including storage/handling techniques.
Foreign Language	Knowledge of the structure and content of a foreign (non-English) language including the meaning and spelling of words, rules of composition and grammar, and pronunciation.
Biology	Knowledge of plant and animal organisms, their tissues, cells, functions, interdependencies, and interactions with each other and the environment.
History and Archeology	Knowledge of historical events and their causes, indicators, and effects on civilizations and cultures.

Skills	Skills Definitions
Reading Comprehension	Understanding written sentences and paragraphs in work related documents.
Writing	Communicating effectively in writing as appropriate for the needs of the audience.
Time Management	Managing one's own time and the time of others.
Active Learning	Understanding the implications of new information for both current and future problem-solving and decision-making.
Active Listening	Giving full attention to what other people are saying, taking time to understand the points being made, asking questions as appropriate, and not interrupting at inappropriate times.
Learning Strategies	Selecting and using training/instructional methods and procedures appropriate for the situation when learning or teaching new things.
Critical Thinking	Using logic and reasoning to identify the strengths and weaknesses of alternative solutions, conclusions or approaches to problems.
Complex Problem Solving	Identifying complex problems and reviewing related information to develop and evaluate options and implement solutions.
Judgment and Decision Making	Considering the relative costs and benefits of potential actions to choose the most appropriate one.
Speaking	Talking to others to convey information effectively.
Coordination	Adjusting actions in relation to others' actions.
Instructing	Teaching others how to do something.
Social Perceptiveness	Being aware of others' reactions and understanding why they react as they do.
Service Orientation	Actively looking for ways to help people.
Monitoring	Monitoring/Assessing performance of yourself, other individuals, or organizations to make improvements or take corrective action.
Operations Analysis	Analyzing needs and product requirements to create a design.
Equipment Selection	Determining the kind of tools and equipment needed to do a job.
Quality Control Analysis	Conducting tests and inspections of products, services, or processes to evaluate quality or performance.
Technology Design	Generating or adapting equipment and technology to serve user needs.
Systems Evaluation	Identifying measures or indicators of system performance and the actions needed to improve or correct performance, relative to the goals of the system.
Management of Material Resources	Obtaining and seeing to the appropriate use of equipment, facilities, and materials needed to do certain work.
Persuasion	Persuading others to change their minds or behavior.
Troubleshooting	Determining causes of operating errors and deciding what to do about it.
Installation	Installing equipment, machines, wiring, or programs to meet specifications.
Management of Personnel Resources	Motivating, developing, and directing people as they work, identifying the best people for the job.
Mathematics	Using mathematics to solve problems.

Negotiation	Bringing others together and trying to reconcile differences.
Science	Using scientific rules and methods to solve problems.
Systems Analysis	Determining how a system should work and how changes in conditions, operations, and the environment will affect outcomes.
Management of Financial Resources	Determining how money will be spent to get the work done, and accounting for these expenditures.
Equipment Maintenance	Performing routine maintenance on equipment and determining when and what kind of maintenance is needed.
Operation and Control	Controlling operations of equipment or systems.
Repairing	Repairing machines or systems using the needed tools.
Programming	Writing computer programs for various purposes.
Operation Monitoring	Watching gauges, dials, or other indicators to make sure a machine is working properly.

Ability	Ability Definitions
Written Comprehension	The ability to read and understand information and ideas presented in writing.
Written Expression	The ability to communicate information and ideas in writing so others will understand.
Near Vision	The ability to see details at close range (within a few feet of the observer).
Oral Comprehension	The ability to listen to and understand information and ideas presented through spoken words and sentences.
Oral Expression	The ability to communicate information and ideas in speaking so others will understand.
Information Ordering	The ability to arrange things or actions in a certain order or pattern according to a specific rule or set of rules (e.g., patterns of numbers, letters, words, pictures, mathematical operations).
Deductive Reasoning	The ability to apply general rules to specific problems to produce answers that make sense.
Problem Sensitivity	The ability to tell when something is wrong or is likely to go wrong. It does not involve solving the problem, only recognizing there is a problem.
Originality	The ability to come up with unusual or clever ideas about a given topic or situation, or to develop creative ways to solve a problem.
Speech Clarity	The ability to speak clearly so others can understand you.
Fluency of Ideas	The ability to come up with a number of ideas about a topic (the number of ideas is important, not their quality, correctness, or creativity).
Inductive Reasoning	The ability to combine pieces of information to form general rules or conclusions (includes finding a relationship among seemingly unrelated events).
Visualization	The ability to imagine how something will look after it is moved around or when its parts are moved or rearranged.
Speech Recognition	The ability to identify and understand the speech of another person.
Category Flexibility	The ability to generate or use different sets of rules for combining or grouping things in different ways.
Selective Attention	The ability to concentrate on a task over a period of time without being distracted.
Flexibility of Closure	The ability to identify or detect a known pattern (a figure, object, word, or sound) that is hidden in other distracting material.
Far Vision	The ability to see details at a distance.
Perceptual Speed	The ability to quickly and accurately compare similarities and differences among sets of letters, numbers, objects, pictures, or patterns. The things to be compared may be presented at the same time or one after the other. This ability also includes comparing a presented object with a remembered object.
Time Sharing	The ability to shift back and forth between two or more activities or sources of information (such as speech, sounds, touch, or other sources).
Auditory Attention	The ability to focus on a single source of sound in the presence of other distracting sounds.
Manual Dexterity	The ability to quickly move your hand, your hand together with your arm, or your two hands to grasp, manipulate, or assemble objects.
Speed of Closure	The ability to quickly make sense of, combine, and organize information into meaningful patterns.
Visual Color Discrimination	The ability to match or detect differences between colors, including shades of color and brightness.
Arm-Hand Steadiness	The ability to keep your hand and arm steady while moving your arm or while holding your arm and hand in one position.

Finger Dexterity	The ability to make precisely coordinated movements of the fingers of one or both hands to grasp, manipulate, or assemble very small objects.
Memorization	The ability to remember information such as words, numbers, pictures, and procedures.
Wrist-Finger Speed	The ability to make fast, simple, repeated movements of the fingers, hands, and wrists.
Number Facility	The ability to add, subtract, multiply, or divide quickly and correctly.
Mathematical Reasoning	The ability to choose the right mathematical methods or formulas to solve a problem.
Control Precision	The ability to quickly and repeatedly adjust the controls of a machine or a vehicle to exact positions.
Hearing Sensitivity	The ability to detect or tell the differences between sounds that vary in pitch and loudness.
Spatial Orientation	The ability to know your location in relation to the environment or to know where other objects are in relation to you.
Depth Perception	The ability to judge which of several objects is closer or farther away from you, or to judge the distance between you and an object.
Dynamic Flexibility	The ability to quickly and repeatedly bend, stretch, twist, or reach out with your body, arms, and/or legs.
Trunk Strength	The ability to use your abdominal and lower back muscles to support part of the body repeatedly or continuously over time without 'giving out' or fatiguing.
Speed of Limb Movement	The ability to quickly move the arms and legs.
Extent Flexibility	The ability to bend, stretch, twist, or reach with your body, arms, and/or legs.
Gross Body Coordination	The ability to coordinate the movement of your arms, legs, and torso together when the whole body is in motion.
Gross Body Equilibrium	The ability to keep or regain your body balance or stay upright when in an unstable position.
Static Strength	The ability to exert maximum muscle force to lift, push, pull, or carry objects.
Dynamic Strength	The ability to exert muscle force repeatedly or continuously over time. This involves muscular endurance and resistance to muscle fatigue.
Reaction Time	The ability to quickly respond (with the hand, finger, or foot) to a signal (sound, light, picture) when it appears.
Rate Control	The ability to time your movements or the movement of a piece of equipment in anticipation of changes in the speed and/or direction of a moving object or scene.
Night Vision	The ability to see under low light conditions.
Sound Localization	The ability to tell the direction from which a sound originated.
Explosive Strength	The ability to use short bursts of muscle force to propel oneself (as in jumping or sprinting), or to throw an object.
Peripheral Vision	The ability to see objects or movement of objects to one's side when the eyes are looking ahead.
Multilimb Coordination	The ability to coordinate two or more limbs (for example, two arms, two legs, or one leg and one arm) while sitting, standing, or lying down. It does not involve performing the activities while the whole body is in motion.
Glare Sensitivity	The ability to see objects in the presence of glare or bright lighting.
Response Orientation	The ability to choose quickly between two or more movements in response to two or more different signals (lights, sounds, pictures). It includes the speed with which the correct response is started with the hand, foot, or other body part.
Stamina	The ability to exert yourself physically over long periods of time without getting winded or out of breath.

Work_Activity	Work_Activity Definitions
Getting Information	Observing, receiving, and otherwise obtaining information from all relevant sources.
Interacting With Computers	Using computers and computer systems (including hardware and software) to program, write software, set up functions, enter data, or process information.
Documenting/Recording Information	Entering, transcribing, recording, storing, or maintaining information in written or electronic/magnetic form.
Communicating with Supervisors, Peers, or Subordin	Providing information to supervisors, co-workers, and subordinates by telephone, in written form, e-mail, or in person.
Updating and Using Relevant Knowledge	Keeping up-to-date technically and applying new knowledge to your job.
Evaluating Information to Determine Compliance wit	Using relevant information and individual judgment to determine whether events or processes comply with laws, regulations, or standards.

Thinking Creatively	Developing, designing, or creating new applications, ideas, relationships, systems, or products, including artistic contributions.
Identifying Objects, Actions, and Events	Identifying information by categorizing, estimating, recognizing differences or similarities, and detecting changes in circumstances or events.
Establishing and Maintaining Interpersonal Relatio	Developing constructive and cooperative working relationships with others, and maintaining them over time.
Organizing, Planning, and Prioritizing Work	Developing specific goals and plans to prioritize, organize, and accomplish your work.
Processing Information	Compiling, coding, categorizing, calculating, tabulating, auditing, or verifying information or data.
Interpreting the Meaning of Information for Others	Translating or explaining what information means and how it can be used.
Making Decisions and Solving Problems	Analyzing information and evaluating results to choose the best solution and solve problems.
Communicating with Persons Outside Organization	Communicating with people outside the organization, representing the organization to customers, the public, government, and other external sources. This information can be exchanged in person, in writing, or by telephone or e-mail.
Performing Administrative Activities	Performing day-to-day administrative tasks such as maintaining information files and processing paperwork.
Analyzing Data or Information	Identifying the underlying principles, reasons, or facts of information by breaking down information or data into separate parts.
Developing and Building Teams	Encouraging and building mutual trust, respect, and cooperation among team members.
Coordinating the Work and Activities of Others	Getting members of a group to work together to accomplish tasks.
Monitor Processes, Materials, or Surroundings	Monitoring and reviewing information from materials, events, or the environment, to detect or assess problems.
Inspecting Equipment, Structures, or Material	Inspecting equipment, structures, or materials to identify the cause of errors or other problems or defects.
Estimating the Quantifiable Characteristics of Pro	Estimating sizes, distances, and quantities; or determining time, costs, resources, or materials needed to perform a work activity.
Drafting, Laying Out, and Specifying Technical Dev	Providing documentation, detailed instructions, drawings, or specifications to tell others about how devices, parts, equipment, or structures are to be fabricated, constructed, assembled, modified, maintained, or used.
Scheduling Work and Activities	Scheduling events, programs, and activities, as well as the work of others.
Judging the Qualities of Things, Services, or Peop	Assessing the value, importance, or quality of things or people.
Developing Objectives and Strategies	Establishing long-range objectives and specifying the strategies and actions to achieve them.
Training and Teaching Others	Identifying the educational needs of others, developing formal educational or training programs or classes, and teaching or instructing others.
Resolving Conflicts and Negotiating with Others	Handling complaints, settling disputes, and resolving grievances and conflicts, or otherwise negotiating with others.
Provide Consultation and Advice to Others	Providing guidance and expert advice to management or other groups on technical, systems-, or process-related topics.
Handling and Moving Objects	Using hands and arms in handling, installing, positioning, and moving materials, and manipulating things.
Assisting and Caring for Others	Providing personal assistance, medical attention, emotional support, or other personal care to others such as coworkers, customers, or patients.
Selling or Influencing Others	Convincing others to buy merchandise/goods or to otherwise change their minds or actions.
Guiding, Directing, and Motivating Subordinates	Providing guidance and direction to subordinates, including setting performance standards and monitoring performance.
Coaching and Developing Others	Identifying the developmental needs of others and coaching, mentoring, or otherwise helping others to improve their knowledge or skills.
Repairing and Maintaining Electronic Equipment	Servicing, repairing, calibrating, regulating, fine-tuning, or testing machines, devices, and equipment that operate primarily on the basis of electrical or electronic (not mechanical) principles.
Performing General Physical Activities	Performing physical activities that require considerable use of your arms and legs and moving your whole body, such as climbing, lifting, balancing, walking, stooping, and handling of materials.
Controlling Machines and Processes	Using either control mechanisms or direct physical activity to operate machines or processes (not including computers or vehicles).

Repairing and Maintaining Mechanical Equipment	Servicing, repairing, adjusting, and testing machines, devices, moving parts, and equipment that operate primarily on the basis of mechanical (not electronic) principles.
Monitoring and Controlling Resources	Monitoring and controlling resources and overseeing the spending of money.
Performing for or Working Directly with the Public	Performing for people or dealing directly with the public. This includes serving customers in restaurants and stores, and receiving clients or guests.
Staffing Organizational Units	Recruiting, interviewing, selecting, hiring, and promoting employees in an organization.
Operating Vehicles, Mechanized Devices, or Equipme	Running, maneuvering, navigating, or driving vehicles or mechanized equipment, such as forklifts, passenger vehicles, aircraft, or water craft.

Work_Context / Work_Context Definitions

Telephone	How often do you have telephone conversations in this job?
Electronic Mail	How often do you use electronic mail in this job?
Face-to-Face Discussions	How often do you have to have face-to-face discussions with individuals or teams in this job?
Spend Time Sitting	How much does this job require sitting?
Freedom to Make Decisions	How much decision making freedom, without supervision, does the job offer?
Importance of Being Exact or Accurate	How important is being very exact or highly accurate in performing this job?
Indoors, Environmentally Controlled	How often does this job require working indoors in environmentally controlled conditions?
Coordinate or Lead Others	How important is it to coordinate or lead others in accomplishing work activities in this job?
Contact With Others	How much does this job require the worker to be in contact with others (face-to-face, by telephone, or otherwise) in order to perform it?
Work With Work Group or Team	How important is it to work with others in a group or team in this job?
Structured versus Unstructured Work	To what extent is this job structured for the worker, rather than allowing the worker to determine tasks, priorities, and goals?
Spend Time Making Repetitive Motions	How much does this job require making repetitive motions?
Importance of Repeating Same Tasks	How important is repeating the same physical activities (e.g., key entry) or mental activities (e.g., checking entries in a ledger) over and over, without stopping, to performing this job?
Spend Time Using Your Hands to Handle, Control, or	How much does this job require using your hands to handle, control, or feel objects, tools or controls?
Time Pressure	How often does this job require the worker to meet strict deadlines?
Impact of Decisions on Co-workers or Company Resul	How do the decisions an employee makes impact the results of co-workers, clients or the company?
Letters and Memos	How often does the job require written letters and memos?
Frequency of Decision Making	How frequently is the worker required to make decisions that affect other people, the financial resources, and/or the image and reputation of the organization?
Consequence of Error	How serious would the result usually be if the worker made a mistake that was not readily correctable?
Responsibility for Outcomes and Results	How responsible is the worker for work outcomes and results of other workers?
Sounds, Noise Levels Are Distracting or Uncomforta	How often does this job require working exposed to sounds and noise levels that are distracting or uncomfortable?
Physical Proximity	To what extent does this job require the worker to perform job tasks in close physical proximity to other people?
Frequency of Conflict Situations	How often are there conflict situations the employee has to face in this job?
Deal With External Customers	How important is it to work with external customers or the public in this job?
Deal With Unpleasant or Angry People	How frequently does the worker have to deal with unpleasant, angry, or discourteous individuals as part of the job requirements?
Level of Competition	To what extent does this job require the worker to compete or to be aware of competitive pressures?
Public Speaking	How often do you have to perform public speaking in this job?
Degree of Automation	How automated is the job?
Extremely Bright or Inadequate Lighting	How often does this job require working in extremely bright or inadequate lighting conditions?
Spend Time Standing	How much does this job require standing?
Wear Common Protective or Safety Equipment such as	How much does this job require wearing common protective or safety equipment such as safety shoes, glasses, gloves, hard hats or life jackets?
Spend Time Walking and Running	How much does this job require walking and running?
Responsible for Others' Health and Safety	How much responsibility is there for the health and safety of others in this job?
Spend Time Kneeling, Crouching, Stooping, or Crawl	How much does this job require kneeling, crouching, stooping or crawling?
Pace Determined by Speed of Equipment	How important is it to this job that the pace is determined by the speed of equipment or machinery? (This does not refer to keeping busy at all times on this job.)
In an Enclosed Vehicle or Equipment	How often does this job require working in a closed vehicle or equipment (e.g., car)?
Cramped Work Space, Awkward Positions	How often does this job require working in cramped work spaces that requires getting into awkward positions?
Exposed to Minor Burns, Cuts, Bites, or Stings	How often does this job require exposure to minor burns, cuts, bites, or stings?
Indoors, Not Environmentally Controlled	How often does this job require working indoors in non-controlled environmental conditions (e.g., warehouse without heat)?
Spend Time Bending or Twisting the Body	How much does this job require bending or twisting your body?
Deal With Physically Aggressive People	How frequently does this job require the worker to deal with physical aggression of violent individuals?
Exposed to Contaminants	How often does this job require working exposed to contaminants (such as pollutants, gases, dust or odors)?
Very Hot or Cold Temperatures	How often does this job require working in very hot (above 90 F degrees) or very cold (below 32 F degrees) temperatures?
Outdoors, Exposed to Weather	How often does this job require working outdoors, exposed to all weather conditions?
Outdoors, Under Cover	How often does this job require working outdoors, under cover (e.g., structure with roof but no walls)?
Exposed to Hazardous Equipment	How often does this job require exposure to hazardous equipment?
Exposed to Hazardous Conditions	How often does this job require exposure to hazardous conditions?
Wear Specialized Protective or Safety Equipment su	How much does this job require wearing specialized protective or safety equipment such as breathing apparatus, safety harness, full protection suits, or radiation protection?
Exposed to Disease or Infections	How often does this job require exposure to disease/infections?
Exposed to High Places	How often does this job require exposure to high places?
Exposed to Radiation	How often does this job require exposure to radiation?
Exposed to Whole Body Vibration	How often does this job require exposure to whole body vibration (e.g., operate a jackhammer)?
Spend Time Climbing Ladders, Scaffolds, or Poles	How much does this job require climbing ladders, scaffolds, or poles?
Spend Time Keeping or Regaining Balance	How much does this job require keeping or regaining your balance?
In an Open Vehicle or Equipment	How often does this job require working in an open vehicle or equipment (e.g., tractor)?

Job Zone Component / Job Zone Component Definitions

Title	Job Zone Four: Considerable Preparation Needed
Overall Experience	A minimum of two to four years of work-related skill, knowledge, or experience is needed for these occupations. For example, an accountant must complete four years of college and work for several years in accounting to be considered qualified.
Job Training	Employees in these occupations usually need several years of work-related experience, on-the-job training, and/or vocational training.
Job Zone Examples	Many of these occupations involve coordinating, supervising, managing, or training others. Examples include accountants, chefs and head cooks, computer programmers, historians, pharmacists, and police detectives.
SVP Range	(7.0 to < 8.0)
Education	Most of these occupations require a four-year bachelor's degree, but some do not.

Work_Styles / Work_Styles Definitions

Adaptability/Flexibility	Job requires being open to change (positive or negative) and to considerable variety in the workplace.
Attention to Detail	Job requires being careful about detail and thorough in completing work tasks.

Cooperation	Job requires being pleasant with others on the job and displaying a good-natured, cooperative attitude.
Persistence	Job requires persistence in the face of obstacles.
Dependability	Job requires being reliable, responsible, and dependable, and fulfilling obligations.
Stress Tolerance	Job requires accepting criticism and dealing calmly and effectively with high stress situations.
Innovation	Job requires creativity and alternative thinking to develop new ideas for and answers to work-related problems.
Analytical Thinking	Job requires analyzing information and using logic to address work-related issues and problems.
Independence	Job requires developing one's own ways of doing things, guiding oneself with little or no supervision, and depending on oneself to get things done.
Initiative	Job requires a willingness to take on responsibilities and challenges.
Achievement/Effort	Job requires establishing and maintaining personally challenging achievement goals and exerting effort toward mastering tasks.
Integrity	Job requires being honest and ethical.
Self Control	Job requires maintaining composure, keeping emotions in check, controlling anger, and avoiding aggressive behavior, even in very difficult situations.
Concern for Others	Job requires being sensitive to others' needs and feelings and being understanding and helpful on the job.
Leadership	Job requires a willingness to lead, take charge, and offer opinions and direction.
Social Orientation	Job requires preferring to work with others rather than alone, and being personally connected with others on the job.

27-3043.04 - Copy Writers

Write advertising copy for use by publication or broadcast media to promote sale of goods and services.

Tasks

1) Present drafts and ideas to clients.

2) Vary language and tone of messages based on product and medium.

3) Discuss with the client the product, advertising themes and methods, and any changes that should be made in advertising copy.

4) Write advertising copy for use by publication, broadcast or internet media to promote the sale of goods and services.

5) Consult with sales, media and marketing representatives to obtain information on product or service and discuss style and length of advertising copy.

6) Review advertising trends, consumer surveys, and other data regarding marketing of goods and services to determine the best way to promote products.

7) Write to customers in their terms and on their level so that the advertiser's sales message is more readily received.

8) Write articles, bulletins, sales letters, speeches, and other related informative, marketing and promotional material.

9) Invent names for products and write the slogans that appear on packaging, brochures and other promotional material.

10) Conduct research and interviews to determine which of a product's selling features should be promoted.

11) Develop advertising campaigns for a wide range of clients, working with an advertising agency's creative director and art director to determine the best way to present advertising information.

Knowledge	Knowledge Definitions
English Language	Knowledge of the structure and content of the English language including the meaning and spelling of words, rules of composition, and grammar.
Communications and Media	Knowledge of media production, communication, and dissemination techniques and methods. This includes alternative ways to inform and entertain via written, oral, and visual media.
Sales and Marketing	Knowledge of principles and methods for showing, promoting, and selling products or services. This includes marketing strategy and tactics, product demonstration, sales techniques, and sales control systems.
Computers and Electronics	Knowledge of circuit boards, processors, chips, electronic equipment, and computer hardware and software, including applications and programming.
Psychology	Knowledge of human behavior and performance; individual differences in ability, personality, and interests, learning and motivation; psychological research methods; and the assessment and treatment of behavioral and affective disorders.
Clerical	Knowledge of administrative and clerical procedures and systems such as word processing, managing files and records, stenography and transcription, designing forms, and other office procedures and terminology.
Sociology and Anthropology	Knowledge of group behavior and dynamics, societal trends and influences, human migrations, ethnicity, cultures and their history and origins.
Customer and Personal Service	Knowledge of principles and processes for providing customer and personal services. This includes customer needs assessment, meeting quality standards for services, and evaluation of customer satisfaction.
Design	Knowledge of design techniques, tools, and principles involved in production of precision technical plans, blueprints, drawings, and models.
Law and Government	Knowledge of laws, legal codes, court procedures, precedents, government regulations, executive orders, agency rules, and the democratic political process.
Administration and Management	Knowledge of business and management principles involved in strategic planning, resource allocation, human resources modeling, leadership technique, production methods, and coordination of people and resources.
Fine Arts	Knowledge of the theory and techniques required to compose, produce, and perform works of music, dance, visual arts, drama, and sculpture.
Telecommunications	Knowledge of transmission, broadcasting, switching, control, and operation of telecommunications systems.
Foreign Language	Knowledge of the structure and content of a foreign (non-English) language including the meaning and spelling of words, rules of composition and grammar, and pronunciation.
Education and Training	Knowledge of principles and methods for curriculum and training design, teaching and instruction for individuals and groups, and the measurement of training effects.
History and Archeology	Knowledge of historical events and their causes, indicators, and effects on civilizations and cultures.
Philosophy and Theology	Knowledge of different philosophical systems and religions. This includes their basic principles, values, ethics, ways of thinking, customs, practices, and their impact on human culture.
Geography	Knowledge of principles and methods for describing the features of land, sea, and air masses, including their physical characteristics, locations, interrelationships, and distribution of plant, animal, and human life.
Mathematics	Knowledge of arithmetic, algebra, geometry, calculus, statistics, and their applications.
Personnel and Human Resources	Knowledge of principles and procedures for personnel recruitment, selection, training, compensation and benefits, labor relations and negotiation, and personnel information systems.
Engineering and Technology	Knowledge of the practical application of engineering science and technology. This includes applying principles, techniques, procedures, and equipment to the design and production of various goods and services.
Economics and Accounting	Knowledge of economic and accounting principles and practices, the financial markets, banking and the analysis and reporting of financial data.
Production and Processing	Knowledge of raw materials, production processes, quality control, costs, and other techniques for maximizing the effective manufacture and distribution of goods.
Public Safety and Security	Knowledge of relevant equipment, policies, procedures, and strategies to promote effective local, state, or national security operations for the protection of people, data, property, and institutions.
Therapy and Counseling	Knowledge of principles, methods, and procedures for diagnosis, treatment, and rehabilitation of physical and mental dysfunctions, and for career counseling and guidance.

Medicine and Dentistry	Knowledge of the information and techniques needed to diagnose and treat human injuries, diseases, and deformities. This includes symptoms, treatment alternatives, drug properties and interactions, and preventive health-care measures.
Mechanical	Knowledge of machines and tools, including their designs, uses, repair, and maintenance.
Transportation	Knowledge of principles and methods for moving people or goods by air, rail, sea, or road, including the relative costs and benefits.
Chemistry	Knowledge of the chemical composition, structure, and properties of substances and of the chemical processes and transformations that they undergo. This includes uses of chemicals and their interactions, danger signs, production techniques, and disposal methods.
Building and Construction	Knowledge of materials, methods, and the tools involved in the construction or repair of houses, buildings, or other structures such as highways and roads.
Biology	Knowledge of plant and animal organisms, their tissues, cells, functions, interdependencies, and interactions with each other and the environment.
Physics	Knowledge and prediction of physical principles, laws, their interrelationships, and applications to understanding fluid, material, and atmospheric dynamics, and mechanical, electrical, atomic and sub-atomic structures and processes.
Food Production	Knowledge of techniques and equipment for planting, growing, and harvesting food products (both plant and animal) for consumption, including storage/handling techniques.

Skills	Skills Definitions
Active Listening	Giving full attention to what other people are saying, taking time to understand the points being made, asking questions as appropriate, and not interrupting at inappropriate times.
Critical Thinking	Using logic and reasoning to identify the strengths and weaknesses of alternative solutions, conclusions or approaches to problems.
Time Management	Managing one's own time and the time of others.
Writing	Communicating effectively in writing as appropriate for the needs of the audience.
Reading Comprehension	Understanding written sentences and paragraphs in work related documents.
Speaking	Talking to others to convey information effectively.
Active Learning	Understanding the implications of new information for both current and future problem-solving and decision-making.
Persuasion	Persuading others to change their minds or behavior.
Coordination	Adjusting actions in relation to others' actions.
Equipment Selection	Determining the kind of tools and equipment needed to do a job.
Monitoring	Monitoring/Assessing performance of yourself, other individuals, or organizations to make improvements or take corrective action.
Complex Problem Solving	Identifying complex problems and reviewing related information to develop and evaluate options and implement solutions.
Judgment and Decision Making	Considering the relative costs and benefits of potential actions to choose the most appropriate one.
Instructing	Teaching others how to do something.
Learning Strategies	Selecting and using training/instructional methods and procedures appropriate for the situation when learning or teaching new things.
Negotiation	Bringing others together and trying to reconcile differences.
Social Perceptiveness	Being aware of others' reactions and understanding why they react as they do.
Technology Design	Generating or adapting equipment and technology to serve user needs.
Service Orientation	Actively looking for ways to help people.
Quality Control Analysis	Conducting tests and inspections of products, services, or processes to evaluate quality or performance.
Operations Analysis	Analyzing needs and product requirements to create a design.
Management of Personnel Resources	Motivating, developing, and directing people as they work, identifying the best people for the job.
Troubleshooting	Determining causes of operating errors and deciding what to do about it.
Management of Financial Resources	Determining how money will be spent to get the work done, and accounting for these expenditures.
Management of Material Resources	Obtaining and seeing to the appropriate use of equipment, facilities, and materials needed to do certain work.
Mathematics	Using mathematics to solve problems.

Operation and Control	Controlling operations of equipment or systems.
Equipment Maintenance	Performing routine maintenance on equipment and determining when and what kind of maintenance is needed.
Systems Evaluation	Identifying measures or indicators of system performance and the actions needed to improve or correct performance, relative to the goals of the system.
Installation	Installing equipment, machines, wiring, or programs to meet specifications.
Operation Monitoring	Watching gauges, dials, or other indicators to make sure a machine is working properly.
Programming	Writing computer programs for various purposes.
Systems Analysis	Determining how a system should work and how changes in conditions, operations, and the environment will affect outcomes.
Repairing	Repairing machines or systems using the needed tools.
Science	Using scientific rules and methods to solve problems.

Ability	Ability Definitions
Written Expression	The ability to communicate information and ideas in writing so others will understand.
Originality	The ability to come up with unusual or clever ideas about a given topic or situation, or to develop creative ways to solve a problem.
Written Comprehension	The ability to read and understand information and ideas presented in writing.
Oral Expression	The ability to communicate information and ideas in speaking so others will understand.
Oral Comprehension	The ability to listen to and understand information and ideas presented through spoken words and sentences.
Near Vision	The ability to see details at close range (within a few feet of the observer).
Fluency of Ideas	The ability to come up with a number of ideas about a topic (the number of ideas is important, not their quality, correctness, or creativity).
Speech Clarity	The ability to speak clearly so others can understand you.
Speech Recognition	The ability to identify and understand the speech of another person.
Problem Sensitivity	The ability to tell when something is wrong or is likely to go wrong. It does not involve solving the problem, only recognizing there is a problem.
Inductive Reasoning	The ability to combine pieces of information to form general rules or conclusions (includes finding a relationship among seemingly unrelated events).
Category Flexibility	The ability to generate or use different sets of rules for combining or grouping things in different ways.
Deductive Reasoning	The ability to apply general rules to specific problems to produce answers that make sense.
Visualization	The ability to imagine how something will look after it is moved around or when its parts are moved or rearranged.
Information Ordering	The ability to arrange things or actions in a certain order or pattern according to a specific rule or set of rules (e.g., patterns of numbers, letters, words, pictures, mathematical operations).
Selective Attention	The ability to concentrate on a task over a period of time without being distracted.
Time Sharing	The ability to shift back and forth between two or more activities or sources of information (such as speech, sounds, touch, or other sources).
Flexibility of Closure	The ability to identify or detect a known pattern (a figure, object, word, or sound) that is hidden in other distracting material.
Speed of Closure	The ability to quickly make sense of, combine, and organize information into meaningful patterns.
Memorization	The ability to remember information such as words, numbers, pictures, and procedures.
Perceptual Speed	The ability to quickly and accurately compare similarities and differences among sets of letters, numbers, objects, pictures, or patterns. The things to be compared may be presented at the same time or one after the other. This ability also includes comparing a presented object with a remembered object.
Arm-Hand Steadiness	The ability to keep your hand and arm steady while moving your arm or while holding your arm and hand in one position.
Manual Dexterity	The ability to quickly move your hand, your hand together with your arm, or your two hands to grasp, manipulate, or assemble objects.
Control Precision	The ability to quickly and repeatedly adjust the controls of a machine or a vehicle to exact positions.

Finger Dexterity	The ability to make precisely coordinated movements of the fingers of one or both hands to grasp, manipulate, or assemble very small objects.
Far Vision	The ability to see details at a distance.
Visual Color Discrimination	The ability to match or detect differences between colors, including shades of color and brightness.
Depth Perception	The ability to judge which of several objects is closer or farther away from you, or to judge the distance between you and an object.
Multilimb Coordination	The ability to coordinate two or more limbs (for example, two arms, two legs, or one leg and one arm) while sitting, standing, or lying down. It does not involve performing the activities while the whole body is in motion.
Extent Flexibility	The ability to bend, stretch, twist, or reach with your body, arms, and/or legs.
Trunk Strength	The ability to use your abdominal and lower back muscles to support part of the body repeatedly or continuously over time without 'giving out' or fatiguing.
Number Facility	The ability to add, subtract, multiply, or divide quickly and correctly.
Hearing Sensitivity	The ability to detect or tell the differences between sounds that vary in pitch and loudness.
Mathematical Reasoning	The ability to choose the right mathematical methods or formulas to solve a problem.
Response Orientation	The ability to choose quickly between two or more movements in response to two or more different signals (lights, sounds, pictures). It includes the speed with which the correct response is started with the hand, foot, or other body part.
Auditory Attention	The ability to focus on a single source of sound in the presence of other distracting sounds.
Wrist-Finger Speed	The ability to make fast, simple, repeated movements of the fingers, hands, and wrists.
Stamina	The ability to exert yourself physically over long periods of time without getting winded or out of breath.
Dynamic Flexibility	The ability to quickly and repeatedly bend, stretch, twist, or reach out with your body, arms, and/or legs.
Reaction Time	The ability to quickly respond (with the hand, finger, or foot) to a signal (sound, light, picture) when it appears.
Dynamic Strength	The ability to exert muscle force repeatedly or continuously over time. This involves muscular endurance and resistance to muscle fatigue.
Explosive Strength	The ability to use short bursts of muscle force to propel oneself (as in jumping or sprinting), or to throw an object.
Static Strength	The ability to exert maximum muscle force to lift, push, pull, or carry objects.
Spatial Orientation	The ability to know your location in relation to the environment or to know where other objects are in relation to you.
Gross Body Coordination	The ability to coordinate the movement of your arms, legs, and torso together when the whole body is in motion.
Peripheral Vision	The ability to see objects or movement of objects to one's side when the eyes are looking ahead.
Night Vision	The ability to see under low light conditions.
Glare Sensitivity	The ability to see objects in the presence of glare or bright lighting.
Sound Localization	The ability to tell the direction from which a sound originated.
Speed of Limb Movement	The ability to quickly move the arms and legs.
Gross Body Equilibrium	The ability to keep or regain your body balance or stay upright when in an unstable position.
Rate Control	The ability to time your movements or the movement of a piece of equipment in anticipation of changes in the speed and/or direction of a moving object or scene.

Work_Activity	**Work_Activity Definitions**
Thinking Creatively	Developing, designing, or creating new applications, ideas, relationships, systems, or products, including artistic contributions.
Communicating with Persons Outside Organization	Communicating with people outside the organization, representing the organization to customers, the public, government, and other external sources. This information can be exchanged in person, in writing, or by telephone or e-mail.
Interacting With Computers	Using computers and computer systems (including hardware and software) to program, write software, set up functions, enter data, or process information.
Getting Information	Observing, receiving, and otherwise obtaining information from all relevant sources.

Establishing and Maintaining Interpersonal Relatio	Developing constructive and cooperative working relationships with others, and maintaining them over time.
Selling or Influencing Others	Convincing others to buy merchandise/goods or to otherwise change their minds or actions.
Communicating with Supervisors, Peers, or Subordin	Providing information to supervisors, co-workers, and subordinates by telephone, in written form, e-mail, or in person.
Organizing, Planning, and Prioritizing Work	Developing specific goals and plans to prioritize, organize, and accomplish your work.
Making Decisions and Solving Problems	Analyzing information and evaluating results to choose the best solution and solve problems.
Updating and Using Relevant Knowledge	Keeping up-to-date technically and applying new knowledge to your job.
Identifying Objects, Actions, and Events	Identifying information by categorizing, estimating, recognizing differences or similarities, and detecting changes in circumstances or events.
Interpreting the Meaning of Information for Others	Translating or explaining what information means and how it can be used.
Developing Objectives and Strategies	Establishing long-range objectives and specifying the strategies and actions to achieve them.
Processing Information	Compiling, coding, categorizing, calculating, tabulating, auditing, or verifying information or data.
Performing for or Working Directly with the Public	Performing for people or dealing directly with the public. This includes serving customers in restaurants and stores, and receiving clients or guests.
Resolving Conflicts and Negotiating with Others	Handling complaints, settling disputes, and resolving grievances and conflicts, or otherwise negotiating with others.
Performing Administrative Activities	Performing day-to-day administrative tasks such as maintaining information files and processing paperwork.
Judging the Qualities of Things, Services, or Peop	Assessing the value, importance, or quality of things or people.
Monitor Processes, Materials, or Surroundings	Monitoring and reviewing information from materials, events, or the environment, to detect or assess problems.
Provide Consultation and Advice to Others	Providing guidance and expert advice to management or other groups on technical, systems-, or process-related topics.
Analyzing Data or Information	Identifying the underlying principles, reasons, or facts of information by breaking down information or data into separate parts.
Coordinating the Work and Activities of Others	Getting members of a group to work together to accomplish tasks.
Scheduling Work and Activities	Scheduling events, programs, and activities, as well as the work of others.
Estimating the Quantifiable Characteristics of Pro	Estimating sizes, distances, and quantities; or determining time, costs, resources, or materials needed to perform a work activity.
Documenting/Recording Information	Entering, transcribing, recording, storing, or maintaining information in written or electronic/magnetic form.
Developing and Building Teams	Encouraging and building mutual trust, respect, and cooperation among team members.
Guiding, Directing, and Motivating Subordinates	Providing guidance and direction to subordinates, including setting performance standards and monitoring performance.
Coaching and Developing Others	Identifying the developmental needs of others and coaching, mentoring, or otherwise helping others to improve their knowledge or skills.
Evaluating Information to Determine Compliance wit	Using relevant information and individual judgment to determine whether events or processes comply with laws, regulations, or standards.
Training and Teaching Others	Identifying the educational needs of others, developing formal educational or training programs or classes, and teaching or instructing others.
Monitoring and Controlling Resources	Monitoring and controlling resources and overseeing the spending of money.
Inspecting Equipment, Structures, or Material	Inspecting equipment, structures, or materials to identify the cause of errors or other problems or defects.
Assisting and Caring for Others	Providing personal assistance, medical attention, emotional support, or other personal care to others such as coworkers, customers, or patients.
Staffing Organizational Units	Recruiting, interviewing, selecting, hiring, and promoting employees in an organization.
Performing General Physical Activities	Performing physical activities that require considerable use of your arms and legs and moving your whole body, such as climbing, lifting, balancing, walking, stooping, and handling of materials.

477

Drafting, Laying Out, and Specifying Technical Dev	Providing documentation, detailed instructions, drawings, or specifications to tell others about how devices, parts, equipment, or structures are to be fabricated, constructed, assembled, modified, maintained, or used.
Operating Vehicles, Mechanized Devices, or Equipme	Running, maneuvering, navigating, or driving vehicles or mechanized equipment, such as forklifts, passenger vehicles, aircraft, or water craft.
Handling and Moving Objects	Using hands and arms in handling, installing, positioning, and moving materials, and manipulating things.
Controlling Machines and Processes	Using either control mechanisms or direct physical activity to operate machines or processes (not including computers or vehicles).
Repairing and Maintaining Mechanical Equipment	Servicing, repairing, adjusting, and testing machines, devices, moving parts, and equipment that operate primarily on the basis of mechanical (not electronic) principles.
Repairing and Maintaining Electronic Equipment	Servicing, repairing, calibrating, regulating, fine-tuning, or testing machines, devices, and equipment that operate primarily on the basis of electrical or electronic (not mechanical) principles.

Work_Context	Work_Context Definitions
Face-to-Face Discussions	How often do you have to have face-to-face discussions with individuals or teams in this job?
Telephone	How often do you have telephone conversations in this job?
Work With Work Group or Team	How important is it to work with others in a group or team in this job?
Electronic Mail	How often do you use electronic mail in this job?
Indoors, Environmentally Controlled	How often does this job require working indoors in environmentally controlled conditions?
Time Pressure	How often does this job require the worker to meet strict deadlines?
Contact With Others	How much does this job require the worker to be in contact with others (face-to-face, by telephone, or otherwise) in order to perform it?
Freedom to Make Decisions	How much decision making freedom, without supervision, does the job offer?
Importance of Being Exact or Accurate	How important is being very exact or highly accurate in performing this job?
Spend Time Sitting	How much does this job require sitting?
Structured versus Unstructured Work	To what extent is this job structured for the worker, rather than allowing the worker to determine tasks, priorities, and goals?
Deal With External Customers	How important is it to work with external customers or the public in this job?
Impact of Decisions on Co-workers or Company Resul	How do the decisions an employee makes impact the results of co-workers, clients or the company?
Spend Time Using Your Hands to Handle, Control, or	How much does this job require using your hands to handle, control, or feel objects, tools or controls?
Importance of Repeating Same Tasks	How important is repeating the same physical activities (e.g., key entry) or mental activities (e.g., checking entries in a ledger) over and over, without stopping, to performing this job?
Frequency of Decision Making	How frequently is the worker required to make decisions that affect other people, the financial resources, and/or the image and reputation of the organization?
Coordinate or Lead Others	How important is it to coordinate or lead others in accomplishing work activities in this job?
Spend Time Making Repetitive Motions	How much does this job require making repetitive motions?
Frequency of Conflict Situations	How often are there conflict situations the employee has to face in this job?
Letters and Memos	How often does the job require written letters and memos?
Exposed to Contaminants	How often does this job require working exposed to contaminants (such as pollutants, gases, dust or odors)?
Physical Proximity	To what extent does this job require the worker to perform job tasks in close physical proximity to other people?
Responsibility for Outcomes and Results	How responsible is the worker for work outcomes and results of other workers?
Deal With Unpleasant or Angry People	How frequently does the worker have to deal with unpleasant, angry, or discourteous individuals as part of the job requirements?
Level of Competition	To what extent does this job require the worker to compete or to be aware of competitive pressures?
Sounds, Noise Levels Are Distracting or Uncomforta	How often does this job require working exposed to sounds and noise levels that are distracting or uncomfortable?
In an Enclosed Vehicle or Equipment	How often does this job require working in a closed vehicle or equipment (e.g., car)?

Consequence of Error	How serious would the result usually be if the worker made a mistake that was not readily correctable?
Extremely Bright or Inadequate Lighting	How often does this job require working in extremely bright or inadequate lighting conditions?
Spend Time Standing	How much does this job require standing?
Degree of Automation	How automated is the job?
Outdoors, Exposed to Weather	How often does this job require working outdoors, exposed to all weather conditions?
Public Speaking	How often do you have to perform public speaking in this job?
Responsible for Others' Health and Safety	How much responsibility is there for the health and safety of others in this job?
Spend Time Walking and Running	How much does this job require walking and running?
Spend Time Bending or Twisting the Body	How much does this job require bending or twisting your body?
Indoors, Not Environmentally Controlled	How often does this job require working indoors in non-controlled environmental conditions (e.g., warehouse without heat)?
Outdoors, Under Cover	How often does this job require working outdoors, under cover (e.g., structure with roof but no walls)?
Very Hot or Cold Temperatures	How often does this job require working in very hot (above 90 F degrees) or very cold (below 32 F degrees) temperatures?
Exposed to Minor Burns, Cuts, Bites, or Stings	How often does this job require exposure to minor burns, cuts, bites, or stings?
Cramped Work Space, Awkward Positions	How often does this job require working in cramped work spaces that requires getting into awkward positions?
Deal With Physically Aggressive People	How frequently does this job require the worker to deal with physical aggression of violent individuals?
Pace Determined by Speed of Equipment	How important is it to this job that the pace is determined by the speed of equipment or machinery? (This does not refer to keeping busy at all times on this job.)
Spend Time Kneeling, Crouching, Stooping, or Crawl	How much does this job require kneeling, crouching, stooping or crawling?
Exposed to High Places	How often does this job require exposure to high places?
Exposed to Radiation	How often does this job require exposure to radiation?
Wear Specialized Protective or Safety Equipment su	How much does this job require wearing specialized protective or safety equipment such as breathing apparatus, safety harness, full protection suits, or radiation protection?
In an Open Vehicle or Equipment	How often does this job require working in an open vehicle or equipment (e.g., tractor)?
Exposed to Whole Body Vibration	How often does this job require exposure to whole body vibration (e.g., operate a jackhammer)?
Exposed to Hazardous Conditions	How often does this job require exposure to hazardous conditions?
Exposed to Hazardous Equipment	How often does this job require exposure to hazardous equipment?
Spend Time Keeping or Regaining Balance	How much does this job require keeping or regaining your balance?
Wear Common Protective or Safety Equipment such as	How much does this job require wearing common protective or safety equipment such as safety shoes, glasses, gloves, hard hats or live jackets?
Spend Time Climbing Ladders, Scaffolds, or Poles	How much does this job require climbing ladders, scaffolds, or poles?
Exposed to Disease or Infections	How often does this job require exposure to disease/infections?

Job Zone Component	Job Zone Component Definitions
Title	Job Zone Four: Considerable Preparation Needed
Overall Experience	A minimum of two to four years of work-related skill, knowledge, or experience is needed for these occupations. For example, an accountant must complete four years of college and work for several years in accounting to be considered qualified.
Job Training	Employees in these occupations usually need several years of work-related experience, on-the-job training, and/or vocational training.
Job Zone Examples	Many of these occupations involve coordinating, supervising, managing, or training others. Examples include accountants, chefs and head cooks, computer programmers, historians, pharmacists, and police detectives.
SVP Range	(7.0 to < 8.0)
Education	Most of these occupations require a four - year bachelor's degree, but some do not.

Work_Styles	Work_Styles Definitions
Dependability	Job requires being reliable, responsible, and dependable, and fulfilling obligations.
Persistence	Job requires persistence in the face of obstacles.
Attention to Detail	Job requires being careful about detail and thorough in completing work tasks.
Initiative	Job requires a willingness to take on responsibilities and challenges.
Cooperation	Job requires being pleasant with others on the job and displaying a good-natured, cooperative attitude.
Achievement/Effort	Job requires establishing and maintaining personally challenging achievement goals and exerting effort toward mastering tasks.
Stress Tolerance	Job requires accepting criticism and dealing calmly and effectively with high stress situations.
Independence	Job requires developing one's own ways of doing things, guiding oneself with little or no supervision, and depending on oneself to get things done.
Innovation	Job requires creativity and alternative thinking to develop new ideas for and answers to work-related problems.
Adaptability/Flexibility	Job requires being open to change (positive or negative) and to considerable variety in the workplace.
Social Orientation	Job requires preferring to work with others rather than alone, and being personally connected with others on the job.
Self Control	Job requires maintaining composure, keeping emotions in check, controlling anger, and avoiding aggressive behavior, even in very difficult situations.
Integrity	Job requires being honest and ethical.
Concern for Others	Job requires being sensitive to others' needs and feelings and being understanding and helpful on the job.
Analytical Thinking	Job requires analyzing information and using logic to address work-related issues and problems.
Leadership	Job requires a willingness to lead, take charge, and offer opinions and direction.

27-3091.00 - Interpreters and Translators

Translate or interpret written, oral, or sign language text into another language for others.

Tasks

1) Follow ethical codes that protect the confidentiality of information.

2) Educate students, parents, staff, and teachers about the roles and functions of educational interpreters.

3) Adapt software and accompanying technical documents to another language and culture.

4) Train and supervise other translators/interpreters.

5) Read written materials such as legal documents, scientific works, or news reports, and rewrite material into specified languages.

6) Identify and resolve conflicts related to the meanings of words, concepts, practices, or behaviors.

7) Travel with or guide tourists who speak another language.

8) Adapt translations to students' cognitive and grade levels, collaborating with educational team members as necessary.

9) Translate messages simultaneously or consecutively into specified languages, orally or by using hand signs, maintaining message content, context, and style as much as possible.

10) Compile terminology and information to be used in translations, including technical terms such as those for legal or medical material.

11) Refer to reference materials such as dictionaries, lexicons, encyclopedias, and computerized terminology banks as needed to ensure translation accuracy.

12) Discuss translation requirements with clients, and determine any fees to be charged for services provided.

13) Listen to speakers' statements in order to determine meanings and to prepare translations, using electronic listening systems as necessary.

14) Compile information about the content and context of information to be translated, as well as details of the groups for whom translation or interpretation is being performed.

15) Check original texts or confer with authors to ensure that translations retain the content, meaning, and feeling of the original material.

16) Proofread, edit, and revise translated materials.

27-4011.00 - Audio and Video Equipment Technicians

Set up or set up and operate audio and video equipment including microphones, sound speakers, video screens, projectors, video monitors, recording equipment, connecting wires and cables, sound and mixing boards, and related electronic equipment for concerts, sports events, meetings and conventions, presentations, and news conferences. May also set up and operate associated spotlights and other custom lighting systems.

Tasks

1) Perform minor repairs and routine cleaning of audio and video equipment.

2) Design layouts of audio and video equipment, and perform upgrades and maintenance.

3) Mix and regulate sound inputs and feeds, or coordinate audio feeds with television pictures.

4) Install, adjust, and operate electronic equipment used to record, edit, and transmit radio and television programs, cable programs, and motion pictures.

5) Monitor incoming and outgoing pictures and sound feeds to ensure quality, and notify directors of any possible problems.

6) Record and edit audio material such as movie soundtracks, using audio recording and editing equipment.

7) Compress, digitize, duplicate, and store audio and video data.

8) Maintain inventories of audio and video tapes and related supplies.

9) Control the lights and sound of events, such as live concerts, before and after performances, and during intermissions.

10) Switch sources of video input from one camera or studio to another, from film to live programming, or from network to local programming.

11) Obtain, set up, and load videotapes for scheduled productions or broadcasts.

12) Edit videotapes by erasing and removing portions of programs and adding video and/or sound as required.

13) Construct and position properties, sets, lighting equipment, and other equipment.

14) Direct and coordinate activities of assistants and other personnel during production.

15) Diagnose and resolve media system problems in classrooms.

16) Plan and develop pre-production ideas into outlines, scripts, story boards, and graphics, using own ideas or specifications of assignments.

17) Locate and secure settings, properties, effects, and other production necessities.

18) Meet with directors and senior members of camera crews to discuss assignments and determine filming sequences, camera movements, and picture composition.

19) Inform users of audio and videotaping service policies and procedures.

20) Determine formats, approaches, content, levels, and mediums to effectively meet objectives within budgetary constraints, utilizing research, knowledge, and training.

21) Develop manuals, texts, workbooks, or related materials for use in conjunction with production materials or for training.

22) Conduct training sessions on selection, use, and design of audiovisual materials and on operation of presentation equipment.

23) Organize and maintain compliance, license, and warranty information related to audio and video facilities.

24) Perform narration of productions, or present announcements.

25) Produce rough and finished graphics and graphic designs.

26) Obtain and preview musical performance programs prior to events in order to become familiar with the order and approximate times of pieces.

Knowledge	Knowledge Definitions
Computers and Electronics	Knowledge of circuit boards, processors, chips, electronic equipment, and computer hardware and software, including applications and programming.
Engineering and Technology	Knowledge of the practical application of engineering science and technology. This includes applying principles, techniques, procedures, and equipment to the design and production of various goods and services.

Telecommunications	Knowledge of transmission, broadcasting, switching, control, and operation of telecommunications systems.
Communications and Media	Knowledge of media production, communication, and dissemination techniques and methods. This includes alternative ways to inform and entertain via written, oral, and visual media.
Customer and Personal Service	Knowledge of principles and processes for providing customer and personal services. This includes customer needs assessment, meeting quality standards for services, and evaluation of customer satisfaction.
English Language	Knowledge of the structure and content of the English language including the meaning and spelling of words, rules of composition, and grammar.
Education and Training	Knowledge of principles and methods for curriculum and training design, teaching and instruction for individuals and groups, and the measurement of training effects.
Mechanical	Knowledge of machines and tools, including their designs, uses, repair, and maintenance.
Mathematics	Knowledge of arithmetic, algebra, geometry, calculus, statistics, and their applications.
Design	Knowledge of design techniques, tools, and principles involved in production of precision technical plans, blueprints, drawings, and models.
Clerical	Knowledge of administrative and clerical procedures and systems such as word processing, managing files and records, stenography and transcription, designing forms, and other office procedures and terminology.
Fine Arts	Knowledge of the theory and techniques required to compose, produce, and perform works of music, dance, visual arts, drama, and sculpture.
Physics	Knowledge and prediction of physical principles, laws, their interrelationships, and applications to understanding fluid, material, and atmospheric dynamics, and mechanical, electrical, atomic and sub-atomic structures and processes.
Transportation	Knowledge of principles and methods for moving people or goods by air, rail, sea, or road, including the relative costs and benefits.
Production and Processing	Knowledge of raw materials, production processes, quality control, costs, and other techniques for maximizing the effective manufacture and distribution of goods.
Administration and Management	Knowledge of business and management principles involved in strategic planning, resource allocation, human resources modeling, leadership technique, production methods, and coordination of people and resources.
Geography	Knowledge of principles and methods for describing the features of land, sea, and air masses, including their physical characteristics, locations, interrelationships, and distribution of plant, animal, and human life.
Public Safety and Security	Knowledge of relevant equipment, policies, procedures, and strategies to promote effective local, state, or national security operations for the protection of people, data, property, and institutions.
Building and Construction	Knowledge of materials, methods, and the tools involved in the construction or repair of houses, buildings, or other structures such as highways and roads.
Psychology	Knowledge of human behavior and performance; individual differences in ability, personality, and interests; learning and motivation; psychological research methods; and the assessment and treatment of behavioral and affective disorders.
Personnel and Human Resources	Knowledge of principles and procedures for personnel recruitment, selection, training, compensation and benefits, labor relations and negotiation, and personnel information systems.
Law and Government	Knowledge of laws, legal codes, court procedures, precedents, government regulations, executive orders, agency rules, and the democratic political process.
Economics and Accounting	Knowledge of economic and accounting principles and practices, the financial markets, banking and the analysis and reporting of financial data.
Chemistry	Knowledge of the chemical composition, structure, and properties of substances and of the chemical processes and transformations that they undergo. This includes uses of chemicals and their interactions, danger signs, production techniques, and disposal methods.
Sales and Marketing	Knowledge of principles and methods for showing, promoting, and selling products or services. This includes marketing strategy and tactics, product demonstration, sales techniques, and sales control systems.
Sociology and Anthropology	Knowledge of group behavior and dynamics, societal trends and influences, human migrations, ethnicity, cultures and their history and origins.
Medicine and Dentistry	Knowledge of the information and techniques needed to diagnose and treat human injuries, diseases, and deformities. This includes symptoms, treatment alternatives, drug properties and interactions, and preventive health-care measures.
Foreign Language	Knowledge of the structure and content of a foreign (non-English) language including the meaning and spelling of words, rules of composition and grammar, and pronunciation.
Therapy and Counseling	Knowledge of principles, methods, and procedures for diagnosis, treatment, and rehabilitation of physical and mental dysfunctions, and for career counseling and guidance.
History and Archeology	Knowledge of historical events and their causes, indicators, and effects on civilizations and cultures.
Philosophy and Theology	Knowledge of different philosophical systems and religions. This includes their basic principles, values, ethics, ways of thinking, customs, practices, and their impact on human culture.
Biology	Knowledge of plant and animal organisms, their tissues, cells, functions, interdependencies, and interactions with each other and the environment.
Food Production	Knowledge of techniques and equipment for planting, growing, and harvesting food products (both plant and animal) for consumption, including storage/handling techniques.

Skills	Skills Definitions
Active Listening	Giving full attention to what other people are saying, taking time to understand the points being made, asking questions as appropriate, and not interrupting at inappropriate times.
Critical Thinking	Using logic and reasoning to identify the strengths and weaknesses of alternative solutions, conclusions or approaches to problems.
Troubleshooting	Determining causes of operating errors and deciding what to do about it.
Reading Comprehension	Understanding written sentences and paragraphs in work related documents.
Operation and Control	Controlling operations of equipment or systems.
Equipment Maintenance	Performing routine maintenance on equipment and determining when and what kind of maintenance is needed.
Active Learning	Understanding the implications of new information for both current and future problem-solving and decision-making.
Time Management	Managing one's own time and the time of others.
Speaking	Talking to others to convey information effectively.
Judgment and Decision Making	Considering the relative costs and benefits of potential actions to choose the most appropriate one.
Equipment Selection	Determining the kind of tools and equipment needed to do a job.
Writing	Communicating effectively in writing as appropriate for the needs of the audience.
Operation Monitoring	Watching gauges, dials, or other indicators to make sure a machine is working properly.
Learning Strategies	Selecting and using training/instructional methods and procedures appropriate for the situation when learning or teaching new things.
Instructing	Teaching others how to do something.
Complex Problem Solving	Identifying complex problems and reviewing related information to develop and evaluate options and implement solutions.
Service Orientation	Actively looking for ways to help people.
Coordination	Adjusting actions in relation to others' actions.
Installation	Installing equipment, machines, wiring, or programs to meet specifications.
Technology Design	Generating or adapting equipment and technology to serve user needs.
Monitoring	Monitoring/Assessing performance of yourself, other individuals, or organizations to make improvements or take corrective action.
Social Perceptiveness	Being aware of others' reactions and understanding why they react as they do.
Repairing	Repairing machines or systems using the needed tools.
Quality Control Analysis	Conducting tests and inspections of products, services, or processes to evaluate quality or performance.
Mathematics	Using mathematics to solve problems.
Systems Analysis	Determining how a system should work and how changes in conditions, operations, and the environment will affect outcomes.

Management of Material Resources	Obtaining and seeing to the appropriate use of equipment, facilities, and materials needed to do certain work.
Persuasion	Persuading others to change their minds or behavior.
Operations Analysis	Analyzing needs and product requirements to create a design.
Negotiation	Bringing others together and trying to reconcile differences.
Systems Evaluation	Identifying measures or indicators of system performance and the actions needed to improve or correct performance, relative to the goals of the system.
Management of Personnel Resources	Motivating, developing, and directing people as they work, identifying the best people for the job.
Management of Financial Resources	Determining how money will be spent to get the work done, and accounting for these expenditures.
Science	Using scientific rules and methods to solve problems.
Programming	Writing computer programs for various purposes.

Ability	Ability Definitions
Problem Sensitivity	The ability to tell when something is wrong or is likely to go wrong. It does not involve solving the problem, only recognizing there is a problem.
Information Ordering	The ability to arrange things or actions in a certain order or pattern according to a specific rule or set of rules (e.g., patterns of numbers, letters, words, pictures, mathematical operations).
Oral Comprehension	The ability to listen to and understand information and ideas presented through spoken words and sentences.
Inductive Reasoning	The ability to combine pieces of information to form general rules or conclusions (includes finding a relationship among seemingly unrelated events).
Deductive Reasoning	The ability to apply general rules to specific problems to produce answers that make sense.
Written Comprehension	The ability to read and understand information and ideas presented in writing.
Speech Recognition	The ability to identify and understand the speech of another person.
Selective Attention	The ability to concentrate on a task over a period of time without being distracted.
Near Vision	The ability to see details at close range (within a few feet of the observer).
Control Precision	The ability to quickly and repeatedly adjust the controls of a machine or a vehicle to exact positions.
Hearing Sensitivity	The ability to detect or tell the differences between sounds that vary in pitch and loudness.
Oral Expression	The ability to communicate information and ideas in speaking so others will understand.
Finger Dexterity	The ability to make precisely coordinated movements of the fingers of one or both hands to grasp, manipulate, or assemble very small objects.
Arm-Hand Steadiness	The ability to keep your hand and arm steady while moving your arm or while holding your arm and hand in one position.
Visual Color Discrimination	The ability to match or detect differences between colors, including shades of color and brightness.
Category Flexibility	The ability to generate or use different sets of rules for combining or grouping things in different ways.
Fluency of Ideas	The ability to come up with a number of ideas about a topic (the number of ideas is important, not their quality, correctness, or creativity).
Visualization	The ability to imagine how something will look after it is moved around or when its parts are moved or rearranged.
Speech Clarity	The ability to speak clearly so others can understand you.
Far Vision	The ability to see details at a distance.
Auditory Attention	The ability to focus on a single source of sound in the presence of other distracting sounds.
Speed of Closure	The ability to quickly make sense of, combine, and organize information into meaningful patterns.
Manual Dexterity	The ability to quickly move your hand, your hand together with your arm, or your two hands to grasp, manipulate, or assemble objects.
Flexibility of Closure	The ability to identify or detect a known pattern (a figure, object, word, or sound) that is hidden in other distracting material.
Perceptual Speed	The ability to quickly and accurately compare similarities and differences among sets of letters, numbers, objects, pictures, or patterns. The things to be compared may be presented at the same time or one after the other. This ability also includes comparing a presented object with a remembered object.
Time Sharing	The ability to shift back and forth between two or more activities or sources of information (such as speech, sounds, touch, or other sources).

Written Expression	The ability to communicate information and ideas in writing so others will understand.
Originality	The ability to come up with unusual or clever ideas about a given topic or situation, or to develop creative ways to solve a problem.
Memorization	The ability to remember information such as words, numbers, pictures, and procedures.
Reaction Time	The ability to quickly respond (with the hand, finger, or foot) to a signal (sound, light, picture) when it appears.
Multilimb Coordination	The ability to coordinate two or more limbs (for example, two arms, two legs, or one leg and one arm) while sitting, standing, or lying down. It does not involve performing the activities while the whole body is in motion.
Response Orientation	The ability to choose quickly between two or more movements in response to two or more different signals (lights, sounds, pictures). It includes the speed with which the correct response is started with the hand, foot, or other body part.
Sound Localization	The ability to tell the direction from which a sound originated.
Depth Perception	The ability to judge which of several objects is closer or farther away from you, or to judge the distance between you and an object.
Static Strength	The ability to exert maximum muscle force to lift, push, pull, or carry objects.
Mathematical Reasoning	The ability to choose the right mathematical methods or formulas to solve a problem.
Glare Sensitivity	The ability to see objects in the presence of glare or bright lighting.
Rate Control	The ability to time your movements or the movement of a piece of equipment in anticipation of changes in the speed and/or direction of a moving object or scene.
Number Facility	The ability to add, subtract, multiply, or divide quickly and correctly.
Trunk Strength	The ability to use your abdominal and lower back muscles to support part of the body repeatedly or continuously over time without 'giving out' or fatiguing.
Extent Flexibility	The ability to bend, stretch, twist, or reach with your body, arms, and/or legs.
Gross Body Coordination	The ability to coordinate the movement of your arms, legs, and torso together when the whole body is in motion.
Gross Body Equilibrium	The ability to keep or regain your body balance or stay upright when in an unstable position.
Speed of Limb Movement	The ability to quickly move the arms and legs.
Wrist-Finger Speed	The ability to make fast, simple, repeated movements of the fingers, hands, and wrists.
Peripheral Vision	The ability to see objects or movement of objects to one's side when the eyes are looking ahead.
Night Vision	The ability to see under low light conditions.
Stamina	The ability to exert yourself physically over long periods of time without getting winded or out of breath.
Spatial Orientation	The ability to know your location in relation to the environment or to know where other objects are in relation to you.
Dynamic Strength	The ability to exert muscle force repeatedly or continuously over time. This involves muscular endurance and resistance to muscle fatigue.
Explosive Strength	The ability to use short bursts of muscle force to propel oneself (as in jumping or sprinting), or to throw an object.
Dynamic Flexibility	The ability to quickly and repeatedly bend, stretch, twist, or reach out with your body, arms, and/or legs.

Work_Activity	Work_Activity Definitions
Interacting With Computers	Using computers and computer systems (including hardware and software) to program, write software, set up functions, enter data, or process information.
Updating and Using Relevant Knowledge	Keeping up-to-date technically and applying new knowledge to your job.
Getting Information	Observing, receiving, and otherwise obtaining information from all relevant sources.
Communicating with Supervisors, Peers, or Subordin	Providing information to supervisors, co-workers, and subordinates by telephone, in written form, e-mail, or in person.
Repairing and Maintaining Electronic Equipment	Servicing, repairing, calibrating, regulating, fine-tuning, or testing machines, devices, and equipment that operate primarily on the basis of electrical or electronic (not mechanical) principles.
Evaluating Information to Determine Compliance wit	Using relevant information and individual judgment to determine whether events or processes comply with laws, regulations, or standards.

Inspecting Equipment. Structures, or Material	Inspecting equipment, structures, or materials to identify the cause of errors or other problems or defects.
Organizing, Planning, and Prioritizing Work	Developing specific goals and plans to prioritize, organize, and accomplish your work.
Making Decisions and Solving Problems	Analyzing information and evaluating results to choose the best solution and solve problems.
Thinking Creatively	Developing, designing, or creating new applications, ideas, relationships, systems, or products, including artistic contributions.
Documenting/Recording Information	Entering, transcribing, recording, storing, or maintaining information in written or electronic/magnetic form.
Identifying Objects, Actions, and Events	Identifying information by categorizing, estimating, recognizing differences or similarities, and detecting changes in circumstances or events.
Scheduling Work and Activities	Scheduling events, programs, and activities, as well as the work of others.
Monitor Processes, Materials, or Surroundings	Monitoring and reviewing information from materials, events, or the environment, to detect or assess problems.
Controlling Machines and Processes	Using either control mechanisms or direct physical activity to operate machines or processes (not including computers or vehicles).
Judging the Qualities of Things, Services, or Peop	Assessing the value, importance, or quality of things or people.
Analyzing Data or Information	Identifying the underlying principles, reasons, or facts of information by breaking down information or data into separate parts.
Repairing and Maintaining Mechanical Equipment	Servicing, repairing, adjusting, and testing machines, devices, moving parts, and equipment that operate primarily on the basis of mechanical (not electronic) principles.
Processing Information	Compiling, coding, categorizing, calculating, tabulating, auditing, or verifying information or data.
Handling and Moving Objects	Using hands and arms in handling, installing, positioning, and moving materials, and manipulating things.
Communicating with Persons Outside Organization	Communicating with people outside the organization, representing the organization to customers, the public, government, and other external sources. This information can be exchanged in person, in writing, or by telephone or e-mail.
Training and Teaching Others	Identifying the educational needs of others, developing formal educational or training programs or classes, and teaching or instructing others.
Establishing and Maintaining Interpersonal Relatio	Developing constructive and cooperative working relationships with others, and maintaining them over time.
Developing Objectives and Strategies	Establishing long-range objectives and specifying the strategies and actions to achieve them.
Performing Administrative Activities	Performing day-to-day administrative tasks such as maintaining information files and processing paperwork.
Monitoring and Controlling Resources	Monitoring and controlling resources and overseeing the spending of money.
Performing General Physical Activities	Performing physical activities that require considerable use of your arms and legs and moving your whole body, such as climbing, lifting, balancing, walking, stooping, and handling of materials.
Coaching and Developing Others	Identifying the developmental needs of others and coaching, mentoring, or otherwise helping others to improve their knowledge or skills.
Estimating the Quantifiable Characteristics of Pro	Estimating sizes, distances, and quantities; or determining time, costs, resources, or materials needed to perform a work activity.
Drafting, Laying Out, and Specifying Technical Dev	Providing documentation, detailed instructions, drawings, or specifications to tell others about how devices, parts, equipment, or structures are to be fabricated, constructed, assembled, modified, maintained, or used.
Interpreting the Meaning of Information for Others	Translating or explaining what information means and how it can be used.
Coordinating the Work and Activities of Others	Getting members of a group to work together to accomplish tasks.
Performing for or Working Directly with the Public	Performing for people or dealing directly with the public. This includes serving customers in restaurants and stores, and receiving clients or guests.
Resolving Conflicts and Negotiating with Others	Handling complaints, settling disputes, and resolving grievances and conflicts, or otherwise negotiating with others.
Guiding, Directing, and Motivating Subordinates	Providing guidance and direction to subordinates, including setting performance standards and monitoring performance.
Developing and Building Teams	Encouraging and building mutual trust, respect, and cooperation among team members.

Provide Consultation and Advice to Others	Providing guidance and expert advice to management or other groups on technical, systems-, or process-related topics.
Assisting and Caring for Others	Providing personal assistance, medical attention, emotional support, or other personal care to others such as coworkers, customers, or patients.
Operating Vehicles, Mechanized Devices, or Equipme	Running, maneuvering, navigating, or driving vehicles or mechanized equipment, such as forklifts, passenger vehicles, aircraft, or water craft.
Selling or Influencing Others	Convincing others to buy merchandise/goods or to otherwise change their minds or actions.
Staffing Organizational Units	Recruiting, interviewing, selecting, hiring, and promoting employees in an organization.

Work_Context	Work_Context Definitions
Telephone	How often do you have telephone conversations in this job?
Time Pressure	How often does this job require the worker to meet strict deadlines?
Face-to-Face Discussions	How often do you have to have face-to-face discussions with individuals or teams in this job?
Electronic Mail	How often do you use electronic mail in this job?
Freedom to Make Decisions	How much decision making freedom, without supervision, does the job offer?
Indoors, Environmentally Controlled	How often does this job require working indoors in environmentally controlled conditions?
Contact With Others	How much does this job require the worker to be in contact with others (face-to-face, by telephone, or otherwise) in order to perform it?
Structured versus Unstructured Work	To what extent is this job structured for the worker, rather than allowing the worker to determine tasks, priorities, and goals?
Work With Work Group or Team	How important is it to work with others in a group or team in this job?
Impact of Decisions on Co-workers or Company Resul	How do the decisions an employee makes impact the results of co-workers, clients or the company?
Coordinate or Lead Others	How important is it to coordinate or lead others in accomplishing work activities in this job?
Responsibility for Outcomes and Results	How responsible is the worker for work outcomes and results of other workers?
Letters and Memos	How often does the job require written letters and memos?
Frequency of Decision Making	How frequently is the worker required to make decisions that affect other people, the financial resources, and/or the image and reputation of the organization?
Importance of Being Exact or Accurate	How important is being very exact or highly accurate in performing this job?
Spend Time Using Your Hands to Handle, Control, or	How much does this job require using your hands to handle, control, or feel objects, tools or controls?
Importance of Repeating Same Tasks	How important is repeating the same physical activities (e.g., key entry) or mental activities (e.g., checking entries in a ledger) over and over, without stopping, to performing this job?
Frequency of Conflict Situations	How often are there conflict situations the employee has to face in this job?
Physical Proximity	To what extent does this job require the worker to perform job tasks in close physical proximity to other people?
Deal With External Customers	How important is it to work with external customers or the public in this job?
Responsible for Others' Health and Safety	How much responsibility is there for the health and safety of others in this job?
Deal With Unpleasant or Angry People	How frequently does the worker have to deal with unpleasant, angry, or discourteous individuals as part of the job requirements?
Spend Time Standing	How much does this job require standing?
Spend Time Sitting	How much does this job require sitting?
Sounds, Noise Levels Are Distracting or Uncomforta	How often does this job require working exposed to sounds and noise levels that are distracting or uncomfortable?
Level of Competition	To what extent does this job require the worker to compete or to be aware of competitive pressures?
Cramped Work Space, Awkward Positions	How often does this job require working in cramped work spaces that requires getting into awkward positions?
Exposed to High Places	How often does this job require exposure to high places?
Extremely Bright or Inadequate Lighting	How often does this job require working in extremely bright or inadequate lighting conditions?
Spend Time Making Repetitive Motions	How much does this job require making repetitive motions?
Outdoors, Exposed to Weather	How often does this job require working outdoors, exposed to all weather conditions?

Spend Time Walking and Running	How much does this job require walking and running?
Degree of Automation	How automated is the job?
Exposed to Contaminants	How often does this job require working exposed to contaminants (such as pollutants, gases, dust or odors)?
Consequence of Error	How serious would the result usually be if the worker made a mistake that was not readily correctable?
Indoors, Not Environmentally Controlled	How often does this job require working indoors in non-controlled environmental conditions (e.g., warehouse without heat)?
Spend Time Bending or Twisting the Body	How much does this job require bending or twisting your body?
Public Speaking	How often do you have to perform public speaking in this job?
Spend Time Kneeling, Crouching, Stooping, or Crawl	How much does this job require kneeling, crouching, stooping or crawling?
Pace Determined by Speed of Equipment	How important is it to this job that the pace is determined by the speed of equipment or machinery? (This does not refer to keeping busy at all times on this job.)
Exposed to Minor Burns, Cuts, Bites, or Stings	How often does this job require exposure to minor burns, cuts, bites, or stings?
Exposed to Hazardous Conditions	How often does this job require exposure to hazardous conditions?
Very Hot or Cold Temperatures	How often does this job require working in very hot (above 90 F degrees) or very cold (below 32 F degrees) temperatures?
In an Enclosed Vehicle or Equipment	How often does this job require working in a closed vehicle or equipment (e.g., car)?
Wear Common Protective or Safety Equipment such as	How much does this job require wearing common protective or safety equipment such as safety shoes, glasses, gloves, hard hats or life jackets?
Outdoors, Under Cover	How often does this job require working outdoors, under cover (e.g., structure with roof but no walls)?
Exposed to Hazardous Equipment	How often does this job require exposure to hazardous equipment?
Spend Time Climbing Ladders, Scaffolds, or Poles	How much does this job require climbing ladders, scaffolds, or poles?
Spend Time Keeping or Regaining Balance	How much does this job require keeping or regaining your balance?
Exposed to Radiation	How often does this job require exposure to radiation?
Deal With Physically Aggressive People	How frequently does this job require the worker to deal with physical aggression of violent individuals?
Exposed to Whole Body Vibration	How often does this job require exposure to whole body vibration (e.g., operate a jackhammer)?
Wear Specialized Protective or Safety Equipment su	How much does this job require wearing specialized protective or safety equipment such as breathing apparatus, safety harness, full protection suits, or radiation protection?
Exposed to Disease or Infections	How often does this job require exposure to disease/infections?
In an Open Vehicle or Equipment	How often does this job require working in an open vehicle or equipment (e.g., tractor)?

Job Zone Component	Job Zone Component Definitions
Title	Job Zone Three: Medium Preparation Needed
Overall Experience	Previous work-related skill, knowledge, or experience is required for these occupations. For example, an electrician must have completed three or four years of apprenticeship or several years of vocational training, and often must have passed a licensing exam, in order to perform the job.
Job Training	Employees in these occupations usually need one or two years of training involving both on-the-job experience and informal training with experienced workers.
Job Zone Examples	These occupations usually involve using communication and organizational skills to coordinate, supervise, manage, or train others to accomplish goals. Examples include dental assistants, electricians, fish and game wardens, legal secretaries, personnel recruiters, and recreation workers.
SVP Range	(6.0 to < 7.0)
Education	Most occupations in this zone require training in vocational schools, related on-the-job experience, or an associate's degree. Some may require a bachelor's degree.

Work_Styles	Work_Styles Definitions
Attention to Detail	Job requires being careful about detail and thorough in completing work tasks.

Independence	Job requires developing one's own ways of doing things, guiding oneself with little or no supervision, and depending on oneself to get things done.
Dependability	Job requires being reliable, responsible, and dependable, and fulfilling obligations.
Cooperation	Job requires being pleasant with others on the job and displaying a good-natured, cooperative attitude.
Integrity	Job requires being honest and ethical.
Adaptability/Flexibility	Job requires being open to change (positive or negative) and to considerable variety in the workplace.
Analytical Thinking	Job requires analyzing information and using logic to address work-related issues and problems.
Innovation	Job requires creativity and alternative thinking to develop new ideas for and answers to work-related problems.
Achievement/Effort	Job requires establishing and maintaining personally challenging achievement goals and exerting effort toward mastering tasks.
Stress Tolerance	Job requires accepting criticism and dealing calmly and effectively with high stress situations.
Concern for Others	Job requires being sensitive to others' needs and feelings and being understanding and helpful on the job.
Persistence	Job requires persistence in the face of obstacles.
Initiative	Job requires a willingness to take on responsibilities and challenges.
Self Control	Job requires maintaining composure, keeping emotions in check, controlling anger, and avoiding aggressive behavior, even in very difficult situations.
Leadership	Job requires a willingness to lead, take charge, and offer opinions and direction.
Social Orientation	Job requires preferring to work with others rather than alone, and being personally connected with others on the job.

27-4012.00 - Broadcast Technicians

Set up, operate, and maintain the electronic equipment used to transmit radio and television programs. Control audio equipment to regulate volume level and quality of sound during radio and television broadcasts. Operate radio transmitter to broadcast radio and television programs.

Tasks

1) Monitor strength, clarity, and reliability of incoming and outgoing signals, and adjust equipment as necessary to maintain quality broadcasts.

2) Observe monitors and converse with station personnel in order to determine audio and video levels and to ascertain that programs are airing.

3) Control audio equipment in order to regulate the volume and sound quality during radio and television broadcasts.

4) Regulate the fidelity, brightness, and contrast of video transmissions, using video console control panels.

5) Preview scheduled programs to ensure that signals are functioning and programs are ready for transmission.

6) Record sound onto tape or film for radio or television, checking its quality and making adjustments where necessary.

7) Select sources from which programming will be received, or through which programming will be transmitted.

8) Instruct trainees in how to use television production equipment, how to film events, and how to copy/edit graphics or sound onto videotape.

9) Maintain programming logs, as required by station management and the Federal Communications Commission.

10) Substitute programs in cases where signals fail.

11) Perform preventive and minor equipment maintenance, using hand tools.

12) Organize recording sessions, and prepare areas such as radio booths and television stations for recording.

13) Align antennae with receiving dishes in order to obtain the clearest signal for transmission of broadcasts from field locations.

14) Edit broadcast material electronically, using computers.

15) Schedule programming, and/or read television programming logs in order to determine which programs are to be recorded or aired.

16) Determine the number, type, and approximate location of microphones needed for best sound recording or transmission quality, and position them appropriately.

17) Give technical directions to other personnel during filming.

18) Design and modify equipment to employer specifications.

19) Set up and operate portable field transmission equipment outside the studio.

20) Discuss production requirements with clients.

21) Prepare reports outlining past and future programs, including content.

22) Produce educational and training films and videotapes by performing activities such as selecting equipment and preparing scripts.

Knowledge	Knowledge Definitions
Telecommunications	Knowledge of transmission, broadcasting, switching, control, and operation of telecommunications systems.
Communications and Media	Knowledge of media production, communication, and dissemination techniques and methods. This includes alternative ways to inform and entertain via written, oral, and visual media.
Computers and Electronics	Knowledge of circuit boards, processors, chips, electronic equipment, and computer hardware and software, including applications and programming.
English Language	Knowledge of the structure and content of the English language including the meaning and spelling of words, rules of composition, and grammar.
Engineering and Technology	Knowledge of the practical application of engineering science and technology. This includes applying principles, techniques, procedures, and equipment to the design and production of various goods and services.
Education and Training	Knowledge of principles and methods for curriculum and training design, teaching and instruction for individuals and groups, and the measurement of training effects.
Mechanical	Knowledge of machines and tools, including their designs, uses, repair, and maintenance.
Production and Processing	Knowledge of raw materials, production processes, quality control, costs, and other techniques for maximizing the effective manufacture and distribution of goods.
Mathematics	Knowledge of arithmetic, algebra, geometry, calculus, statistics, and their applications.
Administration and Management	Knowledge of business and management principles involved in strategic planning, resource allocation, human resources modeling, leadership technique, production methods, and coordination of people and resources.
Public Safety and Security	Knowledge of relevant equipment, policies, procedures, and strategies to promote effective local, state, or national security operations for the protection of people, data, property, and institutions.
Customer and Personal Service	Knowledge of principles and processes for providing customer and personal services. This includes customer needs assessment, meeting quality standards for services, and evaluation of customer satisfaction.
Design	Knowledge of design techniques, tools, and principles involved in production of precision technical plans, blueprints, drawings, and models.
Clerical	Knowledge of administrative and clerical procedures and systems such as word processing, managing files and records, stenography and transcription, designing forms, and other office procedures and terminology.
Law and Government	Knowledge of laws, legal codes, court procedures, precedents, government regulations, executive orders, agency rules, and the democratic political process.
Personnel and Human Resources	Knowledge of principles and procedures for personnel recruitment, selection, training, compensation and benefits, labor relations and negotiation, and personnel information systems.
Transportation	Knowledge of principles and methods for moving people or goods by air, rail, sea, or road, including the relative costs and benefits.
Physics	Knowledge and prediction of physical principles, laws, their interrelationships, and applications to understanding fluid, material, and atmospheric dynamics, and mechanical, electrical, atomic and sub-atomic structures and processes.
Economics and Accounting	Knowledge of economic and accounting principles and practices, the financial markets, banking and the analysis and reporting of financial data.

Geography	Knowledge of principles and methods for describing the features of land, sea, and air masses, including their physical characteristics, locations, interrelationships, and distribution of plant, animal, and human life.
Fine Arts	Knowledge of the theory and techniques required to compose, produce, and perform works of music, dance, visual arts, drama, and sculpture.
Sales and Marketing	Knowledge of principles and methods for showing, promoting, and selling products or services. This includes marketing strategy and tactics, product demonstration, sales techniques, and sales control systems.
Building and Construction	Knowledge of materials, methods, and the tools involved in the construction or repair of houses, buildings, or other structures such as highways and roads.
Psychology	Knowledge of human behavior and performance; individual differences in ability, personality, and interests; learning and motivation; psychological research methods; and the assessment and treatment of behavioral and affective disorders.
Foreign Language	Knowledge of the structure and content of a foreign (non-English) language including the meaning and spelling of words, rules of composition and grammar, and pronunciation.
Chemistry	Knowledge of the chemical composition, structure, and properties of substances and of the chemical processes and transformations that they undergo. This includes uses of chemicals and their interactions, danger signs, production techniques, and disposal methods.
Sociology and Anthropology	Knowledge of group behavior and dynamics, societal trends and influences, human migrations, ethnicity, cultures and their history and origins.
Philosophy and Theology	Knowledge of different philosophical systems and religions. This includes their basic principles, values, ethics, ways of thinking, customs, practices, and their impact on human culture.
History and Archeology	Knowledge of historical events and their causes, indicators, and effects on civilizations and cultures.
Medicine and Dentistry	Knowledge of the information and techniques needed to diagnose and treat human injuries, diseases, and deformities. This includes symptoms, treatment alternatives, drug properties and interactions, and preventive health-care measures.
Therapy and Counseling	Knowledge of principles, methods, and procedures for diagnosis, treatment, and rehabilitation of physical and mental dysfunctions, and for career counseling and guidance.
Biology	Knowledge of plant and animal organisms, their tissues, cells, functions, interdependencies, and interactions with each other and the environment.
Food Production	Knowledge of techniques and equipment for planting, growing, and harvesting food products (both plant and animal) for consumption, including storage/handling techniques.

Skills	Skills Definitions
Operation Monitoring	Watching gauges, dials, or other indicators to make sure a machine is working properly.
Reading Comprehension	Understanding written sentences and paragraphs in work related documents.
Operation and Control	Controlling operations of equipment or systems.
Troubleshooting	Determining causes of operating errors and deciding what to do about it.
Active Listening	Giving full attention to what other people are saying, taking time to understand the points being made, asking questions as appropriate, and not interrupting at inappropriate times.
Active Learning	Understanding the implications of new information for both current and future problem-solving and decision-making.
Critical Thinking	Using logic and reasoning to identify the strengths and weaknesses of alternative solutions, conclusions or approaches to problems.
Coordination	Adjusting actions in relation to others' actions.
Judgment and Decision Making	Considering the relative costs and benefits of potential actions to choose the most appropriate one.
Monitoring	Monitoring/Assessing performance of yourself, other individuals, or organizations to make improvements or take corrective action.
Time Management	Managing one's own time and the time of others.
Learning Strategies	Selecting and using training/instructional methods and procedures appropriate for the situation when learning or teaching new things.
Instructing	Teaching others how to do something.

Complex Problem Solving	Identifying complex problems and reviewing related information to develop and evaluate options and implement solutions.
Equipment Selection	Determining the kind of tools and equipment needed to do a job.
Speaking	Talking to others to convey information effectively.
Equipment Maintenance	Performing routine maintenance on equipment and determining when and what kind of maintenance is needed.
Writing	Communicating effectively in writing as appropriate for the needs of the audience.
Quality Control Analysis	Conducting tests and inspections of products, services, or processes to evaluate quality or performance.
Mathematics	Using mathematics to solve problems.
Installation	Installing equipment, machines, wiring, or programs to meet specifications.
Technology Design	Generating or adapting equipment and technology to serve user needs.
Operations Analysis	Analyzing needs and product requirements to create a design.
Repairing	Repairing machines or systems using the needed tools.
Service Orientation	Actively looking for ways to help people.
Social Perceptiveness	Being aware of others' reactions and understanding why they react as they do.
Systems Analysis	Determining how a system should work and how changes in conditions, operations, and the environment will affect outcomes.
Systems Evaluation	Identifying measures or indicators of system performance and the actions needed to improve or correct performance, relative to the goals of the system.
Science	Using scientific rules and methods to solve problems.
Management of Material Resources	Obtaining and seeing to the appropriate use of equipment, facilities, and materials needed to do certain work.
Persuasion	Persuading others to change their minds or behavior.
Negotiation	Bringing others together and trying to reconcile differences.
Management of Personnel Resources	Motivating, developing, and directing people as they work, identifying the best people for the job.
Programming	Writing computer programs for various purposes.
Management of Financial Resources	Determining how money will be spent to get the work done, and accounting for these expenditures.

Ability — Ability Definitions

Problem Sensitivity	The ability to tell when something is wrong or is likely to go wrong. It does not involve solving the problem, only recognizing there is a problem.
Oral Comprehension	The ability to listen to and understand information and ideas presented through spoken words and sentences.
Hearing Sensitivity	The ability to detect or tell the differences between sounds that vary in pitch and loudness.
Visual Color Discrimination	The ability to match or detect differences between colors, including shades of color and brightness.
Near Vision	The ability to see details at close range (within a few feet of the observer).
Speech Recognition	The ability to identify and understand the speech of another person.
Selective Attention	The ability to concentrate on a task over a period of time without being distracted.
Finger Dexterity	The ability to make precisely coordinated movements of the fingers of one or both hands to grasp, manipulate, or assemble very small objects.
Control Precision	The ability to quickly and repeatedly adjust the controls of a machine or a vehicle to exact positions.
Written Comprehension	The ability to read and understand information and ideas presented in writing.
Deductive Reasoning	The ability to apply general rules to specific problems to produce answers that make sense.
Flexibility of Closure	The ability to identify or detect a known pattern (a figure, object, word, or sound) that is hidden in other distracting material.
Inductive Reasoning	The ability to combine pieces of information to form general rules or conclusions (includes finding a relationship among seemingly unrelated events).
Auditory Attention	The ability to focus on a single source of sound in the presence of other distracting sounds.
Oral Expression	The ability to communicate information and ideas in speaking so others will understand.
Information Ordering	The ability to arrange things or actions in a certain order or pattern according to a specific rule or set of rules (e.g., patterns of numbers, letters, words, pictures, mathematical operations).

Perceptual Speed	The ability to quickly and accurately compare similarities and differences among sets of letters, numbers, objects, pictures, or patterns. The things to be compared may be presented at the same time or one after the other. This ability also includes comparing a presented object with a remembered object.
Speech Clarity	The ability to speak clearly so others can understand you.
Far Vision	The ability to see details at a distance.
Visualization	The ability to imagine how something will look after it is moved around or when its parts are moved or rearranged.
Manual Dexterity	The ability to quickly move your hand, your hand together with your arm, or your two hands to grasp, manipulate, or assemble objects.
Written Expression	The ability to communicate information and ideas in writing so others will understand.
Arm-Hand Steadiness	The ability to keep your hand and arm steady while moving your arm or while holding your arm and hand in one position.
Category Flexibility	The ability to generate or use different sets of rules for combining or grouping things in different ways.
Depth Perception	The ability to judge which of several objects is closer or farther away from you, or to judge the distance between you and an object.
Response Orientation	The ability to choose quickly between two or more movements in response to two or more different signals (lights, sounds, pictures). It includes the speed with which the correct response is started with the hand, foot, or other body part.
Fluency of Ideas	The ability to come up with a number of ideas about a topic (the number of ideas is important, not their quality, correctness, or creativity).
Time Sharing	The ability to shift back and forth between two or more activities or sources of information (such as speech, sounds, touch, or other sources).
Originality	The ability to come up with unusual or clever ideas about a given topic or situation, or to develop creative ways to solve a problem.
Memorization	The ability to remember information such as words, numbers, pictures, and procedures.
Speed of Closure	The ability to quickly make sense of, combine, and organize information into meaningful patterns.
Reaction Time	The ability to quickly respond (with the hand, finger, or foot) to a signal (sound, light, picture) when it appears.
Rate Control	The ability to time your movements or the movement of a piece of equipment in anticipation of changes in the speed and/or direction of a moving object or scene.
Multilimb Coordination	The ability to coordinate two or more limbs (for example, two arms, two legs, or one leg and one arm) while sitting, standing, or lying down. It does not involve performing the activities while the whole body is in motion.
Static Strength	The ability to exert maximum muscle force to lift, push, pull, or carry objects.
Number Facility	The ability to add, subtract, multiply, or divide quickly and correctly.
Wrist-Finger Speed	The ability to make fast, simple, repeated movements of the fingers, hands, and wrists.
Mathematical Reasoning	The ability to choose the right mathematical methods or formulas to solve a problem.
Sound Localization	The ability to tell the direction from which a sound originated.
Glare Sensitivity	The ability to see objects in the presence of glare or bright lighting.
Dynamic Strength	The ability to exert muscle force repeatedly or continuously over time. This involves muscular endurance and resistance to muscle fatigue.
Explosive Strength	The ability to use short bursts of muscle force to propel oneself (as in jumping or sprinting), or to throw an object.
Speed of Limb Movement	The ability to quickly move the arms and legs.
Spatial Orientation	The ability to know your location in relation to the environment or to know where other objects are in relation to you.
Gross Body Coordination	The ability to coordinate the movement of your arms, legs, and torso together when the whole body is in motion.
Trunk Strength	The ability to use your abdominal and lower back muscles to support part of the body repeatedly or continuously over time without 'giving out' or fatiguing.
Dynamic Flexibility	The ability to quickly and repeatedly bend, stretch, twist, or reach out with your body, arms, and/or legs.
Stamina	The ability to exert yourself physically over long periods of time without getting winded or out of breath.
Peripheral Vision	The ability to see objects or movement of objects to one's side when the eyes are looking ahead.

Extent Flexibility	The ability to bend, stretch, twist, or reach with your body, arms, and/or legs.
Night Vision	The ability to see under low light conditions.
Gross Body Equilibrium	The ability to keep or regain your body balance or stay upright when in an unstable position.

Work_Activity	Work_Activity Definitions
Interacting With Computers	Using computers and computer systems (including hardware and software) to program, write software, set up functions, enter data, or process information.
Identifying Objects, Actions, and Events	Identifying information by categorizing, estimating, recognizing differences or similarities, and detecting changes in circumstances or events.
Making Decisions and Solving Problems	Analyzing information and evaluating results to choose the best solution and solve problems.
Getting Information	Observing, receiving, and otherwise obtaining information from all relevant sources.
Monitor Processes, Materials, or Surroundings	Monitoring and reviewing information from materials, events, or the environment, to detect or assess problems.
Updating and Using Relevant Knowledge	Keeping up-to-date technically and applying new knowledge to your job.
Communicating with Supervisors, Peers, or Subordin	Providing information to supervisors, co-workers, and subordinates by telephone, in written form, e-mail, or in person.
Documenting/Recording Information	Entering, transcribing, recording, storing, or maintaining information in written or electronic/magnetic form.
Controlling Machines and Processes	Using either control mechanisms or direct physical activity to operate machines or processes (not including computers or vehicles).
Establishing and Maintaining Interpersonal Relatio	Developing constructive and cooperative working relationships with others, and maintaining them over time.
Inspecting Equipment, Structures, or Material	Inspecting equipment, structures, or materials to identify the cause of errors or other problems or defects.
Organizing, Planning, and Prioritizing Work	Developing specific goals and plans to prioritize, organize, and accomplish your work.
Evaluating Information to Determine Compliance wit	Using relevant information and individual judgment to determine whether events or processes comply with laws, regulations, or standards.
Repairing and Maintaining Electronic Equipment	Servicing, repairing, calibrating, regulating, fine-tuning, or testing machines, devices, and equipment that operate primarily on the basis of electrical or electronic (not mechanical) principles.
Processing Information	Compiling, coding, categorizing, calculating, tabulating, auditing, or verifying information or data.
Analyzing Data or Information	Identifying the underlying principles, reasons, or facts of information by breaking down information or data into separate parts.
Thinking Creatively	Developing, designing, or creating new applications, ideas, relationships, systems, or products, including artistic contributions.
Training and Teaching Others	Identifying the educational needs of others, developing formal educational or training programs or classes, and teaching or instructing others.
Coordinating the Work and Activities of Others	Getting members of a group to work together to accomplish tasks.
Judging the Qualities of Things, Services, or Peop	Assessing the value, importance, or quality of things or people.
Estimating the Quantifiable Characteristics of Pro	Estimating sizes, distances, and quantities; or determining time, costs, resources, or materials needed to perform a work activity.
Scheduling Work and Activities	Scheduling events, programs, and activities, as well as the work of others.
Handling and Moving Objects	Using hands and arms in handling, installing, positioning, and moving materials, and manipulating things.
Guiding, Directing, and Motivating Subordinates	Providing guidance and direction to subordinates, including setting performance standards and monitoring performance.
Coaching and Developing Others	Identifying the developmental needs of others and coaching, mentoring, or otherwise helping others to improve their knowledge or skills.
Repairing and Maintaining Mechanical Equipment	Servicing, repairing, adjusting, and testing machines, devices, moving parts, and equipment that operate primarily on the basis of mechanical (not electronic) principles.

Communicating with Persons Outside Organization	Communicating with people outside the organization, representing the organization to customers, the public, government, and other external sources. This information can be exchanged in person, in writing, or by telephone or e-mail.
Interpreting the Meaning of Information for Others	Translating or explaining what information means and how it can be used.
Developing Objectives and Strategies	Establishing long-range objectives and specifying the strategies and actions to achieve them.
Resolving Conflicts and Negotiating with Others	Handling complaints, settling disputes, and resolving grievances and conflicts, or otherwise negotiating with others.
Provide Consultation and Advice to Others	Providing guidance and expert advice to management or other groups on technical, systems-, or process-related topics.
Performing Administrative Activities	Performing day-to-day administrative tasks such as maintaining information files and processing paperwork.
Operating Vehicles, Mechanized Devices, or Equipme	Running, maneuvering, navigating, or driving vehicles or mechanized equipment, such as forklifts, passenger vehicles, aircraft, or water craft.
Developing and Building Teams	Encouraging and building mutual trust, respect, and cooperation among team members.
Performing General Physical Activities	Performing physical activities that require considerable use of your arms and legs and moving your whole body, such as climbing, lifting, balancing, walking, stooping, and handling of materials.
Assisting and Caring for Others	Providing personal assistance, medical attention, emotional support, or other personal care to others such as coworkers, customers, or patients.
Drafting, Laying Out, and Specifying Technical Dev	Providing documentation, detailed instructions, drawings, or specifications to tell others about how devices, parts, equipment, or structures are to be fabricated, constructed, assembled, modified, maintained, or used.
Monitoring and Controlling Resources	Monitoring and controlling resources and overseeing the spending of money.
Performing for or Working Directly with the Public	Performing for people or dealing directly with the public. This includes serving customers in restaurants and stores, and receiving clients or guests.
Selling or Influencing Others	Convincing others to buy merchandise/goods or to otherwise change their minds or actions.
Staffing Organizational Units	Recruiting, interviewing, selecting, hiring, and promoting employees in an organization.

Work_Context	Work_Context Definitions
Indoors, Environmentally Controlled	How often does this job require working indoors in environmentally controlled conditions?
Face-to-Face Discussions	How often do you have to have face-to-face discussions with individuals or teams in this job?
Importance of Being Exact or Accurate	How important is being very exact or highly accurate in performing this job?
Telephone	How often do you have telephone conversations in this job?
Time Pressure	How often does this job require the worker to meet strict deadlines?
Electronic Mail	How often do you use electronic mail in this job?
Contact With Others	How much does this job require the worker to be in contact with others (face-to-face, by telephone, or otherwise) in order to perform it?
Work With Work Group or Team	How important is it to work with others in a group or team in this job?
Freedom to Make Decisions	How much decision making freedom, without supervision, does the job offer?
Frequency of Decision Making	How frequently is the worker required to make decisions that affect other people, the financial resources, and/or the image and reputation of the organization?
Spend Time Sitting	How much does this job require sitting?
Impact of Decisions on Co-workers or Company Resul	How do the decisions an employee makes impact the results of co-workers, clients or the company?
Spend Time Using Your Hands to Handle, Control, or	How much does this job require using your hands to handle, control, or feel objects, tools or controls?
Structured versus Unstructured Work	To what extent is this job structured for the worker, rather than allowing the worker to determine tasks, priorities, and goals?
Importance of Repeating Same Tasks	How important is repeating the same physical activities (e.g., key entry) or mental activities (e.g., checking entries in a ledger) over and over, without stopping, to performing this job?
Physical Proximity	To what extent does this job require the worker to perform job tasks in close physical proximity to other people?
Sounds, Noise Levels Are Distracting or Uncomforta	How often does this job require working exposed to sounds and noise levels that are distracting or uncomfortable?

Letters and Memos	How often does the job require written letters and memos?
Coordinate or Lead Others	How important is it to coordinate or lead others in accomplishing work activities in this job?
Responsibility for Outcomes and Results	How responsible is the worker for work outcomes and results of other workers?
Consequence of Error	How serious would the result usually be if the worker made a mistake that was not readily correctable?
Pace Determined by Speed of Equipment	How important is it to this job that the pace is determined by the speed of equipment or machinery? (This does not refer to keeping busy at all times on this job.)
Frequency of Conflict Situations	How often are there conflict situations the employee has to face in this job?
Spend Time Making Repetitive Motions	How much does this job require making repetitive motions?
Deal With Unpleasant or Angry People	How frequently does the worker have to deal with unpleasant, angry, or discourteous individuals as part of the job requirements?
Level of Competition	To what extent does this job require the worker to compete or to be aware of competitive pressures?
Degree of Automation	How automated is the job?
Deal With External Customers	How important is it to work with external customers or the public in this job?
Spend Time Standing	How much does this job require standing?
Responsible for Others' Health and Safety	How much responsibility is there for the health and safety of others in this job?
In an Enclosed Vehicle or Equipment	How often does this job require working in a closed vehicle or equipment (e.g., car)?
Extremely Bright or Inadequate Lighting	How often does this job require working in extremely bright or inadequate lighting conditions?
Outdoors, Exposed to Weather	How often does this job require working outdoors, exposed to all weather conditions?
Exposed to Contaminants	How often does this job require working exposed to contaminants (such as pollutants, gases, dust or odors)?
Indoors, Not Environmentally Controlled	How often does this job require working indoors in non-controlled environmental conditions (e.g., warehouse without heat)?
Cramped Work Space, Awkward Positions	How often does this job require working in cramped work spaces that requires getting into awkward positions?
Exposed to Hazardous Conditions	How often does this job require exposure to hazardous conditions?
Spend Time Walking and Running	How much does this job require walking and running?
Very Hot or Cold Temperatures	How often does this job require working in very hot (above 90 F degrees) or very cold (below 32 F degrees) temperatures?
Outdoors, Under Cover	How often does this job require working outdoors, under cover (e.g., structure with roof but no walls)?
Spend Time Bending or Twisting the Body	How much does this job require bending or twisting your body?
Exposed to Radiation	How often does this job require exposure to radiation?
Exposed to Hazardous Equipment	How often does this job require exposure to hazardous equipment?
Exposed to High Places	How often does this job require exposure to high places?
Exposed to Minor Burns, Cuts, Bites, or Stings	How often does this job require exposure to minor burns, cuts, bites, or stings?
Spend Time Kneeling, Crouching, Stooping, or Crawl	How much does this job require kneeling, crouching, stooping, or crawling?
Public Speaking	How often do you have to perform public speaking in this job?
Spend Time Climbing Ladders, Scaffolds, or Poles	How much does this job require climbing ladders, scaffolds, or poles?
Wear Common Protective or Safety Equipment such as	How much does this job require wearing common protective or safety equipment such as safety shoes, glasses, gloves, hard hats or life jackets?
In an Open Vehicle or Equipment	How often does this job require working in an open vehicle or equipment (e.g., tractor)?
Spend Time Keeping or Regaining Balance	How much does this job require keeping or regaining your balance?
Deal With Physically Aggressive People	How frequently does this job require the worker to deal with physical aggression of violent individuals?
Wear Specialized Protective or Safety Equipment su	How much does this job require wearing specialized protective or safety equipment such as breathing apparatus, safety harness, full protection suits, or radiation protection?
Exposed to Disease or Infections	How often does this job require exposure to disease/infections?
Exposed to Whole Body Vibration	How often does this job require exposure to whole body vibration (e.g., operate a jackhammer)?

Job Zone Component	Job Zone Component Definitions
Title	Job Zone Three: Medium Preparation Needed
Overall Experience	Previous work-related skill, knowledge, or experience is required for these occupations. For example, an electrician must have completed three or four years of apprenticeship or several years of vocational training, and often must have passed a licensing exam, in order to perform the job.
Job Training	Employees in these occupations usually need one or two years of training involving both on-the-job experience and informal training with experienced workers.
Job Zone Examples	These occupations usually involve using communication and organizational skills to coordinate, supervise, manage, or train others to accomplish goals. Examples include dental assistants, electricians, fish and game wardens, legal secretaries, personnel recruiters, and recreation workers.
SVP Range	(6.0 to < 7.0)
Education	Most occupations in this zone require training in vocational schools, related on-the-job experience, or an associate's degree. Some may require a bachelor's degree.

Work_Styles	Work_Styles Definitions
Attention to Detail	Job requires being careful about detail and thorough in completing work tasks.
Dependability	Job requires being reliable, responsible, and dependable, and fulfilling obligations.
Adaptability/Flexibility	Job requires being open to change (positive or negative) and to considerable variety in the workplace.
Cooperation	Job requires being pleasant with others on the job and displaying a good-natured, cooperative attitude.
Stress Tolerance	Job requires accepting criticism and dealing calmly and effectively with high stress situations.
Independence	Job requires developing one's own ways of doing things, guiding oneself with little or no supervision, and depending on oneself to get things done.
Integrity	Job requires being honest and ethical.
Self Control	Job requires maintaining composure, keeping emotions in check, controlling anger, and avoiding aggressive behavior, even in very difficult situations.
Analytical Thinking	Job requires analyzing information and using logic to address work-related issues and problems.
Initiative	Job requires a willingness to take on responsibilities and challenges.
Achievement/Effort	Job requires establishing and maintaining personally challenging achievement goals and exerting effort toward mastering tasks.
Persistence	Job requires persistence in the face of obstacles.
Innovation	Job requires creativity and alternative thinking to develop new ideas for and answers to work-related problems.
Concern for Others	Job requires being sensitive to others' needs and feelings and being understanding and helpful on the job.
Leadership	Job requires a willingness to lead, take charge, and offer opinions and direction.
Social Orientation	Job requires preferring to work with others rather than alone, and being personally connected with others on the job.

27-4013.00 - Radio Operators

Receive and transmit communications using radiotelegraph or radiotelephone equipment in accordance with government regulations. May repair equipment.

Tasks

1) Set up antennas and mobile communication units during military field exercises.

2) Examine and operate new equipment prior to installation in order to ensure that it performs properly.

3) Repair radio equipment as necessary, using electronic testing equipment, hand tools, and power tools.

4) Review applicable regulations regarding radio communications, and report violations.

5) Coordinate radio-related aspects of locating and contacting airplanes and ships that are

missing or in distress.

6) Send, receive, and interpret coded messages.

7) Communicate with receiving operators in order to exchange transmission instructions.

8) Operate sound-recording equipment in order to record signals and preserve broadcasts for purposes such as analysis by intelligence personnel.

9) Broadcast weather reports and warnings.

10) Monitor emergency frequencies in order to detect distress calls and respond by dispatching emergency equipment.

11) Conduct periodic equipment inspections and routine tests in order to ensure that operations standards are met.

12) Maintain station logs of messages transmitted and received for activities such as flight testing and fire locations.

13) Operate radio equipment in order to communicate with ships, aircraft, mining crews, offshore oil rigs, logging camps and other remote operations.

14) Determine and obtain bearings of sources from which signals originate, using direction-finding procedures and equipment.

27-4014.00 - Sound Engineering Technicians

Operate machines and equipment to record, synchronize, mix, or reproduce music, voices, or sound effects in sporting arenas, theater productions, recording studios, or movie and video productions.

Tasks

1) Separate instruments, vocals, and other sounds, then combine sounds later during the mixing or post-production stage.

2) Reproduce and duplicate sound recordings from original recording media, using sound editing and duplication equipment.

3) Regulate volume level and sound quality during recording sessions, using control consoles.

4) Record speech, music, and other sounds on recording media, using recording equipment.

5) Mix and edit voices, music, and taped sound effects for live performances and for prerecorded events, using sound mixing boards.

6) Keep logs of recordings.

7) Report equipment problems, and ensure that required repairs are made.

8) Prepare for recording sessions by performing activities such as selecting and setting up microphones.

9) Create musical instrument digital interface programs for music projects, commercials or film post-production.

10) Set up, test, and adjust recording equipment for recording sessions and live performances; tear down equipment after event completion.

11) Confer with producers, performers, and others in order to determine and achieve the desired sound for a production such as a musical recording or a film.

27-4021.00 - Photographers

Photograph persons, subjects, merchandise, or other commercial products. May develop negatives and produce finished prints.

Tasks

1) Develop and print exposed film, using chemicals, touchup tools, and developing and printing equipment, or send film to photofinishing laboratories for processing.

2) Use traditional or digital cameras, along with a variety of equipment such as tripods, filters, and flash attachments.

3) Perform maintenance tasks necessary to keep equipment working properly.

4) Produce computer-readable, digital images from film, using flatbed scanners and photofinishing laboratories.

5) Scan photographs into computers for editing, storage, and electronic transmission.

6) Set up, mount, or install photographic equipment and cameras.

7) Develop visual aids and charts for use in lectures or to present evidence in court.

8) Employ a variety of specialized photographic materials and techniques, including infrared and ultraviolet films, macro-photography, photogrammetry and sensitometry.

9) Select and assemble equipment and required background properties, according to subjects, materials, and conditions.

10) License the use of their photographs through stock photo agencies.

11) Enhance, retouch, and resize photographs and negatives, using airbrushing and other techniques.

12) Load and unload film.

13) Photograph subject material to illustrate or record scientific/medical data or phenomena, using knowledge of scientific procedures and photographic technology and techniques.

14) Create artificial light, using flashes and reflectors.

15) Use specialized equipment such as electron microscopes for producing photographs of microscopic items, assisting as necessary in the preparation of specimens to be photographed.

16) Set up photographic exhibitions for the purpose of displaying and selling their work.

17) Sell camera equipment and film to the public.

18) Take pictures of individuals, families, and small groups, either in studio or on location.

19) Adjust apertures, shutter speeds, and camera focus based on a combination of factors such as lighting, field depth, subject motion, film type, and film speed.

20) Test equipment prior to use to ensure that it is in good working order.

21) Estimate or measure light levels, distances, and numbers of exposures needed, using measuring devices and formulas.

22) Determine desired images and picture composition; and select and adjust subjects, equipment, and lighting to achieve desired effects.

23) Review sets of photographs to select the best work.

24) Manipulate and enhance scanned or digital images to create desired effects, using computers and specialized software.

25) Engage in research to develop new photographic procedures and materials.

26) Mount, frame, laminate, and/or lacquer finished photographs.

27) Direct activities of workers who are setting up photographic equipment.

28) Consult with clients or advertising staff, and study assignments to determine project goals, locations, and equipment needs.

29) Photograph legal evidence at crime scenes, in hospitals, or in forensic laboratories.

27-4031.00 - Camera Operators, Television, Video, and Motion Picture

Operate television, video, or motion picture camera to photograph images or scenes for various purposes, such as TV broadcasts, advertising, video production, or motion pictures.

Tasks

1) Operate zoom lenses, changing images according to specifications and rehearsal instructions.

2) Operate television or motion picture cameras to record scenes for television broadcasts, advertising, or motion pictures.

3) Adjust positions and controls of cameras, printers, and related equipment in order to change focus, exposure, and lighting.

4) Gather and edit raw footage on location to send to television affiliates for broadcast, using electronic news-gathering or film-production equipment.

5) Observe sets or locations for potential problems and to determine filming and lighting requirements.

6) Test, clean, and maintain equipment to ensure proper working condition.

7) Compose and frame each shot, applying the technical aspects of light, lenses, film, filters, and camera settings in order to achieve the effects sought by directors.

8) Instruct camera operators regarding camera setups, angles, distances, movement, and variables and cues for starting and stopping filming.

9) Confer with directors, sound and lighting technicians, electricians, and other crew members to discuss assignments and determine filming sequences, desired effects, camera movements, and lighting requirements.

10) Select and assemble cameras, accessories, equipment, and film stock to be used during filming, using knowledge of filming techniques, requirements, and computations.

11) Read and analyze work orders and specifications to determine locations of subject material, work procedures, sequences of operations, and machine setups.

12) Set up cameras, optical printers, and related equipment to produce photographs and special effects.

13) View films to resolve problems of exposure control, subject and camera movement, changes in subject distance, and related variables.

14) Label and record contents of exposed film, and note details on report forms.

15) Read charts and compute ratios to determine variables such as lighting, shutter angles, filter factors, and camera distances.

16) Receive raw film stock, and maintain film inventories.

17) Prepare slates that describe the scenes being filmed.

18) Reload camera magazines with fresh raw film stock.

19) Download exposed film for shipment to processing labs.

Knowledge	Knowledge Definitions
Computers and Electronics	Knowledge of circuit boards, processors, chips, electronic equipment, and computer hardware and software, including applications and programming.
Communications and Media	Knowledge of media production, communication, and dissemination techniques and methods. This includes alternative ways to inform and entertain via written, oral, and visual media.
English Language	Knowledge of the structure and content of the English language including the meaning and spelling of words, rules of composition, and grammar.
Customer and Personal Service	Knowledge of principles and processes for providing customer and personal services. This includes customer needs assessment, meeting quality standards for services, and evaluation of customer satisfaction.
Telecommunications	Knowledge of transmission, broadcasting, switching, control, and operation of telecommunications systems.
Administration and Management	Knowledge of business and management principles involved in strategic planning, resource allocation, human resources modeling, leadership technique, production methods, and coordination of people and resources.
Engineering and Technology	Knowledge of the practical application of engineering science and technology. This includes applying principles, techniques, procedures, and equipment to the design and production of various goods and services.
Education and Training	Knowledge of principles and methods for curriculum and training design, teaching and instruction for individuals and groups, and the measurement of training effects.
Clerical	Knowledge of administrative and clerical procedures and systems such as word processing, managing files and records, stenography and transcription, designing forms, and other office procedures and terminology.
Production and Processing	Knowledge of raw materials, production processes, quality control, costs, and other techniques for maximizing the effective manufacture and distribution of goods.
Sales and Marketing	Knowledge of principles and methods for showing, promoting, and selling products or services. This includes marketing strategy and tactics, product demonstration, sales techniques, and sales control systems.
Psychology	Knowledge of human behavior and performance; individual differences in ability, personality, and interests; learning and motivation; psychological research methods; and the assessment and treatment of behavioral and affective disorders.
Fine Arts	Knowledge of the theory and techniques required to compose, produce, and perform works of music, dance, visual arts, drama, and sculpture.
Public Safety and Security	Knowledge of relevant equipment, policies, procedures, and strategies to promote effective local, state, or national security operations for the protection of people, data, property, and institutions.
Foreign Language	Knowledge of the structure and content of a foreign (non-English) language including the meaning and spelling of words, rules of composition and grammar, and pronunciation.
Mathematics	Knowledge of arithmetic, algebra, geometry, calculus, statistics, and their applications.
Personnel and Human Resources	Knowledge of principles and procedures for personnel recruitment, selection, training, compensation and benefits, labor relations and negotiation, and personnel information systems.
Mechanical	Knowledge of machines and tools, including their designs, uses, repair, and maintenance.
Medicine and Dentistry	Knowledge of the information and techniques needed to diagnose and treat human injuries, diseases and deformities. This includes symptoms, treatment alternatives, drug properties and interactions, and preventive health-care measures.
Transportation	Knowledge of principles and methods for moving people or goods by air, rail, sea, or road, including the relative costs and benefits.
Therapy and Counseling	Knowledge of principles, methods, and procedures for diagnosis, treatment, and rehabilitation of physical and mental dysfunctions, and for career counseling and guidance.
Economics and Accounting	Knowledge of economic and accounting principles and practices, the financial markets, banking and the analysis and reporting of financial data.
Chemistry	Knowledge of the chemical composition, structure, and properties of substances and of the chemical processes and transformations that they undergo. This includes uses of chemicals and their interactions, danger signs, production techniques, and disposal methods.
Law and Government	Knowledge of laws, legal codes, court procedures, precedents, government regulations, executive orders, agency rules, and the democratic political process.
Biology	Knowledge of plant and animal organisms, their tissues, cells, functions, interdependencies, and interactions with each other and the environment.
Sociology and Anthropology	Knowledge of group behavior and dynamics, societal trends and influences, human migrations, ethnicity, cultures and their history and origins.
Geography	Knowledge of principles and methods for describing the features of land, sea, and air masses, including their physical characteristics, locations, interrelationships, and distribution of plant, animal, and human life.
Design	Knowledge of design techniques, tools, and principles involved in production of precision technical plans, blueprints, drawings, and models.
Philosophy and Theology	Knowledge of different philosophical systems and religions. This includes their basic principles, values, ethics, ways of thinking, customs, practices, and their impact on human culture.
Physics	Knowledge and prediction of physical principles, laws, their interrelationships, and applications to understanding fluid, material, and atmospheric dynamics, and mechanical, electrical, atomic and sub-atomic structures and processes.
History and Archeology	Knowledge of historical events and their causes, indicators, and effects on civilizations and cultures.
Building and Construction	Knowledge of materials, methods, and the tools involved in the construction or repair of houses, buildings, or other structures such as highways and roads.
Food Production	Knowledge of techniques and equipment for planting, growing, and harvesting food products (both plant and animal) for consumption, including storage/handling techniques.

Skills	Skills Definitions
Active Listening	Giving full attention to what other people are saying, taking time to understand the points being made, asking questions as appropriate, and not interrupting at inappropriate times.
Time Management	Managing one's own time and the time of others.
Operation and Control	Controlling operations of equipment or systems.
Coordination	Adjusting actions in relation to others' actions.
Speaking	Talking to others to convey information effectively.
Reading Comprehension	Understanding written sentences and paragraphs in work related documents.
Critical Thinking	Using logic and reasoning to identify the strengths and weaknesses of alternative solutions, conclusions or approaches to problems.
Operation Monitoring	Watching gauges, dials, or other indicators to make sure a machine is working properly.
Social Perceptiveness	Being aware of others' reactions and understanding why they react as they do.
Equipment Selection	Determining the kind of tools and equipment needed to do a job.

Troubleshooting	Determining causes of operating errors and deciding what to do about it.
Judgment and Decision Making	Considering the relative costs and benefits of potential actions to choose the most appropriate one.
Active Learning	Understanding the implications of new information for both current and future problem-solving and decision-making.
Equipment Maintenance	Performing routine maintenance on equipment and determining when and what kind of maintenance is needed.
Writing	Communicating effectively in writing as appropriate for the needs of the audience.
Monitoring	Monitoring/Assessing performance of yourself, other individuals, or organizations to make improvements or take corrective action.
Learning Strategies	Selecting and using training/instructional methods and procedures appropriate for the situation when learning or teaching new things.
Instructing	Teaching others how to do something.
Service Orientation	Actively looking for ways to help people.
Persuasion	Persuading others to change their minds or behavior.
Complex Problem Solving	Identifying complex problems and reviewing related information to develop and evaluate options and implement solutions.
Negotiation	Bringing others together and trying to reconcile differences.
Operations Analysis	Analyzing needs and product requirements to create a design.
Technology Design	Generating or adapting equipment and technology to serve user needs.
Quality Control Analysis	Conducting tests and inspections of products, services, or processes to evaluate quality or performance.
Management of Material Resources	Obtaining and seeing to the appropriate use of equipment, facilities, and materials needed to do certain work.
Management of Personnel Resources	Motivating, developing, and directing people as they work, identifying the best people for the job.
Installation	Installing equipment, machines, wiring, or programs to meet specifications.
Systems Analysis	Determining how a system should work and how changes in conditions, operations, and the environment will affect outcomes.
Repairing	Repairing machines or systems using the needed tools.
Management of Financial Resources	Determining how money will be spent to get the work done, and accounting for these expenditures.
Mathematics	Using mathematics to solve problems.
Systems Evaluation	Identifying measures or indicators of system performance and the actions needed to improve or correct performance, relative to the goals of the system.
Science	Using scientific rules and methods to solve problems.
Programming	Writing computer programs for various purposes.

Ability	**Ability Definitions**
Problem Sensitivity	The ability to tell when something is wrong or is likely to go wrong. It does not involve solving the problem, only recognizing there is a problem.
Near Vision	The ability to see details at close range (within a few feet of the observer).
Oral Comprehension	The ability to listen to and understand information and ideas presented through spoken words and sentences.
Arm-Hand Steadiness	The ability to keep your hand and arm steady while moving your arm or while holding your arm and hand in one position.
Deductive Reasoning	The ability to apply general rules to specific problems to produce answers that make sense.
Visualization	The ability to imagine how something will look after it is moved around or when its parts are moved or rearranged.
Far Vision	The ability to see details at a distance.
Speech Recognition	The ability to identify and understand the speech of another person.
Selective Attention	The ability to concentrate on a task over a period of time without being distracted.
Originality	The ability to come up with unusual or clever ideas about a given topic or situation, or to develop creative ways to solve a problem.
Oral Expression	The ability to communicate information and ideas in speaking so others will understand.
Control Precision	The ability to quickly and repeatedly adjust the controls of a machine or a vehicle to exact positions.

Perceptual Speed	The ability to quickly and accurately compare similarities and differences among sets of letters, numbers, objects, pictures, or patterns. The things to be compared may be presented at the same time or one after the other. This ability also includes comparing a presented object with a remembered object.
Finger Dexterity	The ability to make precisely coordinated movements of the fingers of one or both hands to grasp, manipulate, or assemble very small objects.
Visual Color Discrimination	The ability to match or detect differences between colors, including shades of color and brightness.
Speech Clarity	The ability to speak clearly so others can understand you.
Manual Dexterity	The ability to quickly move your hand, your hand together with your arm, or your two hands to grasp, manipulate, or assemble objects.
Information Ordering	The ability to arrange things or actions in a certain order or pattern according to a specific rule or set of rules (e.g., patterns of numbers, letters, words, pictures, mathematical operations).
Inductive Reasoning	The ability to combine pieces of information to form general rules or conclusions (includes finding a relationship among seemingly unrelated events).
Depth Perception	The ability to judge which of several objects is closer or farther away from you, or to judge the distance between you and an object.
Written Comprehension	The ability to read and understand information and ideas presented in writing.
Static Strength	The ability to exert maximum muscle force to lift, push, pull, or carry objects.
Flexibility of Closure	The ability to identify or detect a known pattern (a figure, object, word, or sound) that is hidden in other distracting material.
Category Flexibility	The ability to generate or use different sets of rules for combining or grouping things in different ways.
Fluency of Ideas	The ability to come up with a number of ideas about a topic (the number of ideas is important, not their quality, correctness, or creativity).
Written Expression	The ability to communicate information and ideas in writing so others will understand.
Reaction Time	The ability to quickly respond (with the hand, finger, or foot) to a signal (sound, light, picture) when it appears.
Rate Control	The ability to time your movements or the movement of a piece of equipment in anticipation of changes in the speed and/or direction of a moving object or scene.
Hearing Sensitivity	The ability to detect or tell the differences between sounds that vary in pitch and loudness.
Memorization	The ability to remember information such as words, numbers, pictures, and procedures.
Auditory Attention	The ability to focus on a single source of sound in the presence of other distracting sounds.
Extent Flexibility	The ability to bend, stretch, twist, or reach with your body, arms, and/or legs.
Response Orientation	The ability to choose quickly between two or more movements in response to two or more different signals (lights, sounds, pictures). It includes the speed with which the correct response is started with the hand, foot, or other body part.
Multilimb Coordination	The ability to coordinate two or more limbs (for example, two arms, two legs, or one leg and one arm) while sitting, standing, or lying down. It does not involve performing the activities while the whole body is in motion.
Time Sharing	The ability to shift back and forth between two or more activities or sources of information (such as speech, sounds, touch, or other sources).
Speed of Closure	The ability to quickly make sense of, combine, and organize information into meaningful patterns.
Glare Sensitivity	The ability to see objects in the presence of glare or bright lighting.
Mathematical Reasoning	The ability to choose the right mathematical methods or formulas to solve a problem.
Number Facility	The ability to add, subtract, multiply, or divide quickly and correctly.
Spatial Orientation	The ability to know your location in relation to the environment or to know where other objects are in relation to you.
Trunk Strength	The ability to use your abdominal and lower back muscles to support part of the body repeatedly or continuously over time without 'giving out' or fatiguing.
Sound Localization	The ability to tell the direction from which a sound originated.
Wrist-Finger Speed	The ability to make fast, simple, repeated movements of the fingers, hands, and wrists.

Gross Body Coordination	The ability to coordinate the movement of your arms, legs, and torso together when the whole body is in motion.
Stamina	The ability to exert yourself physically over long periods of time without getting winded or out of breath.
Gross Body Equilibrium	The ability to keep or regain your body balance or stay upright when in an unstable position.
Speed of Limb Movement	The ability to quickly move the arms and legs.
Peripheral Vision	The ability to see objects or movement of objects to one's side when the eyes are looking ahead.
Night Vision	The ability to see under low light conditions.
Dynamic Strength	The ability to exert muscle force repeatedly or continuously over time. This involves muscular endurance and resistance to muscle fatigue.
Dynamic Flexibility	The ability to quickly and repeatedly bend, stretch, twist, or reach out with your body, arms, and/or legs.
Explosive Strength	The ability to use short bursts of muscle force to propel oneself (as in jumping or sprinting), or to throw an object.

Work_Activity	Work_Activity Definitions
Thinking Creatively	Developing, designing, or creating new applications, ideas, relationships, systems, or products, including artistic contributions.
Getting Information	Observing, receiving, and otherwise obtaining information from all relevant sources.
Communicating with Supervisors, Peers, or Subordin	Providing information to supervisors, co-workers, and subordinates by telephone, in written form, e-mail, or in person.
Updating and Using Relevant Knowledge	Keeping up-to-date technically and applying new knowledge to your job.
Identifying Objects, Actions, and Events	Identifying information by categorizing, estimating, recognizing differences or similarities, and detecting changes in circumstances or events.
Performing for or Working Directly with the Public	Performing for people or dealing directly with the public. This includes serving customers in restaurants and stores, and receiving clients or guests.
Making Decisions and Solving Problems	Analyzing information and evaluating results to choose the best solution and solve problems.
Communicating with Persons Outside Organization	Communicating with people outside the organization, representing the organization to customers, the public, government, and other external sources. This information can be exchanged in person, in writing, or by telephone or e-mail.
Establishing and Maintaining Interpersonal Relatio	Developing constructive and cooperative working relationships with others, and maintaining them over time.
Handling and Moving Objects	Using hands and arms in handling, installing, positioning, and moving materials, and manipulating things.
Performing General Physical Activities	Performing physical activities that require considerable use of your arms and legs and moving your whole body, such as climbing, lifting, balancing, walking, stooping, and handling of materials.
Controlling Machines and Processes	Using either control mechanisms or direct physical activity to operate machines or processes (not including computers or vehicles).
Interacting With Computers	Using computers and computer systems (including hardware and software) to program, write software, set up functions, enter data, or process information.
Inspecting Equipment, Structures, or Material	Inspecting equipment, structures, or materials to identify the cause of errors or other problems or defects.
Organizing, Planning, and Prioritizing Work	Developing specific goals and plans to prioritize, organize, and accomplish your work.
Monitor Processes, Materials, or Surroundings	Monitoring and reviewing information from materials, events, or the environment, to detect or assess problems.
Operating Vehicles, Mechanized Devices, or Equipme	Running, maneuvering, navigating, or driving vehicles or mechanized equipment, such as forklifts, passenger vehicles, aircraft, or water craft.
Documenting/Recording Information	Entering, transcribing, recording, storing, or maintaining information in written or electronic/magnetic form.
Interpreting the Meaning of Information for Others	Translating or explaining what information means and how it can be used.
Judging the Qualities of Things, Services, or Peop	Assessing the value, importance, or quality of things or people.
Repairing and Maintaining Electronic Equipment	Servicing, repairing, calibrating, regulating, fine-tuning, or testing machines, devices, and equipment that operate primarily on the basis of electrical or electronic (not mechanical) principles.

Processing Information	Compiling, coding, categorizing, calculating, tabulating, auditing, or verifying information or data.
Scheduling Work and Activities	Scheduling events, programs, and activities, as well as the work of others.
Coordinating the Work and Activities of Others	Getting members of a group to work together to accomplish tasks.
Estimating the Quantifiable Characteristics of Pro	Estimating sizes, distances, and quantities; or determining time, costs, resources, or materials needed to perform a work activity.
Developing and Building Teams	Encouraging and building mutual trust, respect, and cooperation among team members.
Analyzing Data or Information	Identifying the underlying principles, reasons, or facts of information by breaking down information or data into separate parts.
Training and Teaching Others	Identifying the educational needs of others, developing formal educational or training programs or classes, and teaching or instructing others.
Evaluating Information to Determine Compliance wit	Using relevant information and individual judgment to determine whether events or processes comply with laws, regulations, or standards.
Resolving Conflicts and Negotiating with Others	Handling complaints, settling disputes, and resolving grievances and conflicts, or otherwise negotiating with others.
Repairing and Maintaining Mechanical Equipment	Servicing, repairing, adjusting, and testing machines, devices, moving parts, and equipment that operate primarily on the basis of mechanical (not electronic) principles.
Developing Objectives and Strategies	Establishing long-range objectives and specifying the strategies and actions to achieve them.
Coaching and Developing Others	Identifying the developmental needs of others and coaching, mentoring, or otherwise helping others to improve their knowledge or skills.
Assisting and Caring for Others	Providing personal assistance, medical attention, emotional support, or other personal care to others such as coworkers, customers, or patients.
Guiding, Directing, and Motivating Subordinates	Providing guidance and direction to subordinates, including setting performance standards and monitoring performance.
Provide Consultation and Advice to Others	Providing guidance and expert advice to management or other groups on technical, systems-, or process-related topics.
Selling or Influencing Others	Convincing others to buy merchandise/goods or to otherwise change their minds or actions.
Performing Administrative Activities	Performing day-to-day administrative tasks such as maintaining information files and processing paperwork.
Drafting, Laying Out, and Specifying Technical Dev	Providing documentation, detailed instructions, drawings, or specifications to tell others about how devices, parts, equipment, or structures are to be fabricated, constructed, assembled, modified, maintained, or used.
Monitoring and Controlling Resources	Monitoring and controlling resources and overseeing the spending of money.
Staffing Organizational Units	Recruiting, interviewing, selecting, hiring, and promoting employees in an organization.

Work_Context	Work_Context Definitions
Face-to-Face Discussions	How often do you have to have face-to-face discussions with individuals or teams in this job?
Indoors, Environmentally Controlled	How often does this job require working indoors in environmentally controlled conditions?
Contact With Others	How much does this job require the worker to be in contact with others (face-to-face, by telephone, or otherwise) in order to perform it?
Work With Work Group or Team	How important is it to work with others in a group or team in this job?
Time Pressure	How often does this job require the worker to meet strict deadlines?
Freedom to Make Decisions	How much decision making freedom, without supervision, does the job offer?
Importance of Being Exact or Accurate	How important is being very exact or highly accurate in performing this job?
Telephone	How often do you have telephone conversations in this job?
Structured versus Unstructured Work	To what extent is this job structured for the worker, rather than allowing the worker to determine tasks, priorities, and goals?
Spend Time Using Your Hands to Handle, Control, or	How much does this job require using your hands to handle, control, or feel objects, tools or controls?
Frequency of Decision Making	How frequently is the worker required to make decisions that affect other people, the financial resources, and/or the image and reputation of the organization?
Electronic Mail	How often do you use electronic mail in this job?

Deal With External Customers	How important is it to work with external customers or the public in this job?
Impact of Decisions on Co-workers or Company Resul	How do the decisions an employee makes impact the results of co-workers, clients or the company?
Coordinate or Lead Others	How important is it to coordinate or lead others in accomplishing work activities in this job?
Physical Proximity	To what extent does this job require the worker to perform job tasks in close physical proximity to other people?
Responsibility for Outcomes and Results	How responsible is the worker for work outcomes and results of other workers?
Spend Time Standing	How much does this job require standing?
Outdoors, Exposed to Weather	How often does this job require working outdoors, exposed to all weather conditions?
Level of Competition	To what extent does this job require the worker to compete or to be aware of competitive pressures?
In an Enclosed Vehicle or Equipment	How often does this job require working in a closed vehicle or equipment (e.g., car)?
Consequence of Error	How serious would the result usually be if the worker made a mistake that was not readily correctable?
Importance of Repeating Same Tasks	How important is repeating the same physical activities (e.g., key entry) or mental activities (e.g., checking entries in a ledger) over and over, without stopping, to performing this job?
Extremely Bright or Inadequate Lighting	How often does this job require working in extremely bright or inadequate lighting conditions?
Letters and Memos	How often does the job require written letters and memos?
Deal With Unpleasant or Angry People	How frequently does the worker have to deal with unpleasant, angry, or discourteous individuals as part of the job requirements?
Frequency of Conflict Situations	How often are there conflict situations the employee has to face in this job?
Spend Time Making Repetitive Motions	How much does this job require making repetitive motions?
Responsible for Others' Health and Safety	How much responsibility is there for the health and safety of others in this job?
Sounds, Noise Levels Are Distracting or Uncomforta	How often does this job require working exposed to sounds and noise levels that are distracting or uncomfortable?
Cramped Work Space, Awkward Positions	How often does this job require working in cramped work spaces that requires getting into awkward positions?
Spend Time Sitting	How much does this job require sitting?
Outdoors, Under Cover	How often does this job require working outdoors, under cover (e.g., structure with roof but no walls)?
Spend Time Bending or Twisting the Body	How much does this job require bending or twisting your body?
Indoors, Not Environmentally Controlled	How often does this job require working indoors in non-controlled environmental conditions (e.g., warehouse without heat)?
Spend Time Walking and Running	How much does this job require walking and running?
Very Hot or Cold Temperatures	How often does this job require working in very hot (above 90 F degrees) or very cold (below 32 F degrees) temperatures?
Pace Determined by Speed of Equipment	How important is it to this job that the pace is determined by the speed of equipment or machinery? (This does not refer to keeping busy at all times on this job.)
Exposed to Contaminants	How often does this job require working exposed to contaminants (such as pollutants, gases, dust or odors)?
Public Speaking	How often do you have to perform public speaking in this job?
Spend Time Kneeling, Crouching, Stooping, or Crawl	How much does this job require kneeling, crouching, stooping or crawling?
Spend Time Keeping or Regaining Balance	How much does this job require keeping or regaining your balance?
Exposed to High Places	How often does this job require exposure to high places?
Degree of Automation	How automated is the job?
Exposed to Hazardous Equipment	How often does this job require exposure to hazardous equipment?
In an Open Vehicle or Equipment	How often does this job require working in an open vehicle or equipment (e.g., tractor)?
Exposed to Minor Burns, Cuts, Bites, or Stings	How often does this job require exposure to minor burns, cuts, bites, or stings?
Deal With Physically Aggressive People	How frequently does this job require the worker to deal with physical aggression of violent individuals?
Exposed to Hazardous Conditions	How often does this job require exposure to hazardous conditions?
Wear Common Protective or Safety Equipment such as	How much does this job require wearing common protective or safety equipment such as safety shoes, glasses, gloves, hard hats or live jackets?

Spend Time Climbing Ladders, Scaffolds, or Poles	How much does this job require climbing ladders, scaffolds, or poles?
Wear Specialized Protective or Safety Equipment su	How much does this job require wearing specialized protective or safety equipment such as breathing apparatus, safety harness, full protection suits, or radiation protection?
Exposed to Radiation	How often does this job require exposure to radiation?
Exposed to Disease or Infections	How often does this job require exposure to disease/infections?
Exposed to Whole Body Vibration	How often does this job require exposure to whole body vibration (e.g., operate a jackhammer)?

Job Zone Component	Job Zone Component Definitions
Title	Job Zone Three: Medium Preparation Needed
Overall Experience	Previous work-related skill, knowledge, or experience is required for these occupations. For example, an electrician must have completed three or four years of apprenticeship or several years of vocational training, and often must have passed a licensing exam, in order to perform the job.
Job Training	Employees in these occupations usually need one or two years of training involving both on-the-job experience and informal training with experienced workers.
Job Zone Examples	These occupations usually involve using communication and organizational skills to coordinate, supervise, manage, or train others to accomplish goals. Examples include dental assistants, electricians, fish and game wardens, legal secretaries, personnel recruiters, and recreation workers.
SVP Range	(6.0 to < 7.0)
Education	Most occupations in this zone require training in vocational schools, related on-the-job experience, or an associate's degree. Some may require a bachelor's degree.

Work_Styles	Work_Styles Definitions
Dependability	Job requires being reliable, responsible, and dependable, and fulfilling obligations.
Attention to Detail	Job requires being careful about detail and thorough in completing work tasks.
Initiative	Job requires a willingness to take on responsibilities and challenges.
Stress Tolerance	Job requires accepting criticism and dealing calmly and effectively with high stress situations.
Adaptability/Flexibility	Job requires being open to change (positive or negative) and to considerable variety in the workplace.
Independence	Job requires developing one's own ways of doing things, guiding oneself with little or no supervision, and depending on oneself to get things done.
Innovation	Job requires creativity and alternative thinking to develop new ideas for and answers to work-related problems.
Persistence	Job requires persistence in the face of obstacles.
Cooperation	Job requires being pleasant with others on the job and displaying a good-natured, cooperative attitude.
Integrity	Job requires being honest and ethical.
Achievement/Effort	Job requires establishing and maintaining personally challenging achievement goals and exerting effort toward mastering tasks.
Leadership	Job requires a willingness to lead, take charge, and offer opinions and direction.
Analytical Thinking	Job requires analyzing information and using logic to address work-related issues and problems.
Self Control	Job requires maintaining composure, keeping emotions in check, controlling anger, and avoiding aggressive behavior, even in very difficult situations.
Social Orientation	Job requires preferring to work with others rather than alone, and being personally connected with others on the job.
Concern for Others	Job requires being sensitive to others' needs and feelings and being understanding and helpful on the job.

27-4032.00 - Film and Video Editors

Edit motion picture soundtracks, film, and video.

Tasks

1) Set up and operate computer editing systems, electronic titling systems, video switching equipment, and digital video effects units in order to produce a final product.

2) Mark frames where a particular shot or piece of sound is to begin or end.

3) Review assembled films or edited videotapes on screens or monitors in order to determine if corrections are necessary.

4) Verify key numbers and time codes on materials.

5) Cut shot sequences to different angles at specific points in scenes, making each individual cut as fluid and seamless as possible.

6) Select and combine the most effective shots of each scene in order to form a logical and smoothly running story.

7) Review footage sequence by sequence in order to become familiar with it before assembling it into a final product.

8) Organize and string together raw footage into a continuous whole according to scripts and/or the instructions of directors and producers.

9) Program computerized graphic effects.

10) Record needed sounds, or obtain them from sound effects libraries.

11) Determine the specific audio and visual effects and music necessary to complete films.

12) Study scripts to become familiar with production concepts and requirements.

13) Confer with producers and directors concerning layout or editing approaches needed to increase dramatic or entertainment value of productions.

14) Piece sounds together to develop film soundtracks.

15) Trim film segments to specified lengths, and reassemble segments in sequences that present stories with maximum effect.

16) Collaborate with music editors to select appropriate passages of music and develop production scores.

17) Supervise and coordinate activities of workers engaged in film editing, assembling, and recording activities.

18) Conduct film screenings for directors and members of production staffs.

19) Manipulate plot, score, sound, and graphics to make the parts into a continuous whole, working closely with people in audio, visual, music, optical and/or special effects departments.

20) Discuss the sound requirements of pictures with sound effects editors.

21) Develop post-production models for films.

22) Estimate how long audiences watching comedies will laugh at each gag line or situation, in order to space scenes appropriately.

Knowledge	Knowledge Definitions
Communications and Media	Knowledge of media production, communication, and dissemination techniques and methods. This includes alternative ways to inform and entertain via written, oral, and visual media.
Computers and Electronics	Knowledge of circuit boards, processors, chips, electronic equipment, and computer hardware and software, including applications and programming.
English Language	Knowledge of the structure and content of the English language including the meaning and spelling of words, rules of composition, and grammar.
Design	Knowledge of design techniques, tools, and principles involved in production of precision technical plans, blueprints, drawings, and models.
Fine Arts	Knowledge of the theory and techniques required to compose, produce, and perform works of music, dance, visual arts, drama, and sculpture.
Education and Training	Knowledge of principles and methods for curriculum and training design, teaching and instruction for individuals and groups, and the measurement of training effects.
Customer and Personal Service	Knowledge of principles and processes for providing customer and personal services. This includes customer needs assessment, meeting quality standards for services, and evaluation of customer satisfaction.
Production and Processing	Knowledge of raw materials, production processes, quality control, costs, and other techniques for maximizing the effective manufacture and distribution of goods.
Telecommunications	Knowledge of transmission, broadcasting, switching, control, and operation of telecommunications systems.
Sales and Marketing	Knowledge of principles and methods for showing, promoting, and selling products or services. This includes marketing strategy and tactics, product demonstration, sales techniques, and sales control systems.
Clerical	Knowledge of administrative and clerical procedures and systems such as word processing, managing files and records, stenography and transcription, designing forms, and other office procedures and terminology.
Psychology	Knowledge of human behavior and performance; individual differences in ability, personality, and interests; learning and motivation; psychological research methods; and the assessment and treatment of behavioral and affective disorders.
Mathematics	Knowledge of arithmetic, algebra, geometry, calculus, statistics, and their applications.
Administration and Management	Knowledge of business and management principles involved in strategic planning, resource allocation, human resources modeling, leadership technique, production methods, and coordination of people and resources.
Philosophy and Theology	Knowledge of different philosophical systems and religions. This includes their basic principles, values, ethics, ways of thinking, customs, practices, and their impact on human culture.
Law and Government	Knowledge of laws, legal codes, court procedures, precedents, government regulations, executive orders, agency rules, and the democratic political process.
Engineering and Technology	Knowledge of the practical application of engineering science and technology. This includes applying principles, techniques, procedures, and equipment to the design and production of various goods and services.
Economics and Accounting	Knowledge of economic and accounting principles and practices, the financial markets, banking and the analysis and reporting of financial data.
Foreign Language	Knowledge of the structure and content of a foreign (non-English) language including the meaning and spelling of words, rules of composition and grammar, and pronunciation.
Personnel and Human Resources	Knowledge of principles and procedures for personnel recruitment, selection, training, compensation and benefits, labor relations and negotiation, and personnel information systems.
Mechanical	Knowledge of machines and tools, including their designs, uses, repair, and maintenance.
Chemistry	Knowledge of the chemical composition, structure, and properties of substances and of the chemical processes and transformations that they undergo. This includes uses of chemicals and their interactions, danger signs, production techniques, and disposal methods.
Geography	Knowledge of principles and methods for describing the features of land, sea, and air masses, including their physical characteristics, locations, interrelationships, and distribution of plant, animal, and human life.
Public Safety and Security	Knowledge of relevant equipment, policies, procedures, and strategies to promote effective local, state, or national security operations for the protection of people, data, property, and institutions.
Physics	Knowledge and prediction of physical principles, laws, their interrelationships, and applications to understanding fluid, material, and atmospheric dynamics, and mechanical, electrical, atomic and sub-atomic structures and processes.
Sociology and Anthropology	Knowledge of group behavior and dynamics, societal trends and influences, human migrations, ethnicity, cultures and their history and origins.
Transportation	Knowledge of principles and methods for moving people or goods by air, rail, sea, or road, including the relative costs and benefits.
History and Archeology	Knowledge of historical events and their causes, indicators, and effects on civilizations and cultures.
Therapy and Counseling	Knowledge of principles, methods, and procedures for diagnosis, treatment, and rehabilitation of physical and mental dysfunctions, and for career counseling and guidance.
Medicine and Dentistry	Knowledge of the information and techniques needed to diagnose and treat human injuries, diseases, and deformities. This includes symptoms, treatment alternatives, drug properties and interactions, and preventive health-care measures.
Building and Construction	Knowledge of materials, methods, and the tools involved in the construction or repair of houses, buildings, or other structures such as highways and roads.

Food Production	Knowledge of techniques and equipment for planting, growing, and harvesting food products (both plant and animal) for consumption, including storage/handling techniques.
Biology	Knowledge of plant and animal organisms, their tissues, cells, functions, interdependencies, and interactions with each other and the environment.

Skills	Skills Definitions
Active Listening	Giving full attention to what other people are saying, taking time to understand the points being made, asking questions as appropriate, and not interrupting at inappropriate times.
Active Learning	Understanding the implications of new information for both current and future problem-solving and decision-making.
Coordination	Adjusting actions in relation to others' actions.
Troubleshooting	Determining causes of operating errors and deciding what to do about it.
Equipment Selection	Determining the kind of tools and equipment needed to do a job.
Time Management	Managing one's own time and the time of others.
Speaking	Talking to others to convey information effectively.
Operation and Control	Controlling operations of equipment or systems.
Monitoring	Monitoring/Assessing performance of yourself, other individuals, or organizations to make improvements or take corrective action.
Judgment and Decision Making	Considering the relative costs and benefits of potential actions to choose the most appropriate one.
Critical Thinking	Using logic and reasoning to identify the strengths and weaknesses of alternative solutions, conclusions or approaches to problems.
Learning Strategies	Selecting and using training/instructional methods and procedures appropriate for the situation when learning or teaching new things.
Reading Comprehension	Understanding written sentences and paragraphs in work related documents.
Social Perceptiveness	Being aware of others' reactions and understanding why they react as they do.
Persuasion	Persuading others to change their minds or behavior.
Equipment Maintenance	Performing routine maintenance on equipment and determining when and what kind of maintenance is needed.
Complex Problem Solving	Identifying complex problems and reviewing related information to develop and evaluate options and implement solutions.
Operation Monitoring	Watching gauges, dials, or other indicators to make sure a machine is working properly.
Instructing	Teaching others how to do something.
Operations Analysis	Analyzing needs and product requirements to create a design.
Writing	Communicating effectively in writing as appropriate for the needs of the audience.
Negotiation	Bringing others together and trying to reconcile differences.
Installation	Installing equipment, machines, wiring, or programs to meet specifications.
Service Orientation	Actively looking for ways to help people.
Management of Financial Resources	Determining how money will be spent to get the work done, and accounting for these expenditures.
Technology Design	Generating or adapting equipment and technology to serve user needs.
Quality Control Analysis	Conducting tests and inspections of products, services, or processes to evaluate quality or performance.
Management of Material Resources	Obtaining and seeing to the appropriate use of equipment, facilities, and materials needed to do certain work.
Mathematics	Using mathematics to solve problems.
Repairing	Repairing machines or systems using the needed tools.
Management of Personnel Resources	Motivating, developing, and directing people as they work, identifying the best people for the job.
Systems Analysis	Determining how a system should work and how changes in conditions, operations, and the environment will affect outcomes.
Systems Evaluation	Identifying measures or indicators of system performance and the actions needed to improve or correct performance, relative to the goals of the system.
Programming	Writing computer programs for various purposes.
Science	Using scientific rules and methods to solve problems.

Ability	Ability Definitions
Near Vision	The ability to see details at close range (within a few feet of the observer).

Information Ordering	The ability to arrange things or actions in a certain order or pattern according to a specific rule or set of rules (e.g., patterns of numbers, letters, words, pictures, mathematical operations).
Oral Expression	The ability to communicate information and ideas in speaking so others will understand.
Originality	The ability to come up with unusual or clever ideas about a given topic or situation, or to develop creative ways to solve a problem.
Written Comprehension	The ability to read and understand information and ideas presented in writing.
Speech Recognition	The ability to identify and understand the speech of another person.
Problem Sensitivity	The ability to tell when something is wrong or is likely to go wrong. It does not involve solving the problem, only recognizing there is a problem.
Deductive Reasoning	The ability to apply general rules to specific problems to produce answers that make sense.
Oral Comprehension	The ability to listen to and understand information and ideas presented through spoken words and sentences.
Visualization	The ability to imagine how something will look after it is moved around or when its parts are moved or rearranged.
Fluency of Ideas	The ability to come up with a number of ideas about a topic (the number of ideas is important, not their quality, correctness, or creativity).
Selective Attention	The ability to concentrate on a task over a period of time without being distracted.
Inductive Reasoning	The ability to combine pieces of information to form general rules or conclusions (includes finding a relationship among seemingly unrelated events).
Category Flexibility	The ability to generate or use different sets of rules for combining or grouping things in different ways.
Written Expression	The ability to communicate information and ideas in writing so others will understand.
Speech Clarity	The ability to speak clearly so others can understand you.
Finger Dexterity	The ability to make precisely coordinated movements of the fingers of one or both hands to grasp, manipulate, or assemble very small objects.
Hearing Sensitivity	The ability to detect or tell the differences between sounds that vary in pitch and loudness.
Arm-Hand Steadiness	The ability to keep your hand and arm steady while moving your arm or while holding your arm and hand in one position.
Far Vision	The ability to see details at a distance.
Visual Color Discrimination	The ability to match or detect differences between colors, including shades of color and brightness.
Manual Dexterity	The ability to quickly move your hand, your hand together with your arm, or your two hands to grasp, manipulate, or assemble objects.
Memorization	The ability to remember information such as words, numbers, pictures, and procedures.
Flexibility of Closure	The ability to identify or detect a known pattern (a figure, object, word, or sound) that is hidden in other distracting material.
Speed of Closure	The ability to quickly make sense of, combine, and organize information into meaningful patterns.
Auditory Attention	The ability to focus on a single source of sound in the presence of other distracting sounds.
Perceptual Speed	The ability to quickly and accurately compare similarities and differences among sets of letters, numbers, objects, pictures, or patterns. The things to be compared may be presented at the same time or one after the other. This ability also includes comparing a presented object with a remembered object.
Time Sharing	The ability to shift back and forth between two or more activities or sources of information (such as speech, sounds, touch, or other sources).
Control Precision	The ability to quickly and repeatedly adjust the controls of a machine or a vehicle to exact positions.
Mathematical Reasoning	The ability to choose the right mathematical methods or formulas to solve a problem.
Number Facility	The ability to add, subtract, multiply, or divide quickly and correctly.
Depth Perception	The ability to judge which of several objects is closer or farther away from you, or to judge the distance between you and an object.
Reaction Time	The ability to quickly respond (with the hand, finger, or foot) to a signal (sound, light, picture) when it appears.
Rate Control	The ability to time your movements or the movement of a piece of equipment in anticipation of changes in the speed and/or direction of a moving object or scene.

Response Orientation	The ability to choose quickly between two or more movements in response to two or more different signals (lights, sounds, pictures). It includes the speed with which the correct response is started with the hand, foot, or other body part.
Multilimb Coordination	The ability to coordinate two or more limbs (for example, two arms, two legs, or one leg and one arm) while sitting, standing, or lying down. It does not involve performing the activities while the whole body is in motion.
Static Strength	The ability to exert maximum muscle force to lift, push, pull, or carry objects.
Trunk Strength	The ability to use your abdominal and lower back muscles to support part of the body repeatedly or continuously over time without 'giving out' or fatiguing.
Wrist-Finger Speed	The ability to make fast, simple, repeated movements of the fingers, hands, and wrists.
Dynamic Strength	The ability to exert muscle force repeatedly or continuously over time. This involves muscular endurance and resistance to muscle fatigue.
Stamina	The ability to exert yourself physically over long periods of time without getting winded or out of breath.
Gross Body Coordination	The ability to coordinate the movement of your arms, legs, and torso together when the whole body is in motion.
Gross Body Equilibrium	The ability to keep or regain your body balance or stay upright when in an unstable position.
Extent Flexibility	The ability to bend, stretch, twist, or reach with your body, arms, and/or legs.
Sound Localization	The ability to tell the direction from which a sound originated.
Glare Sensitivity	The ability to see objects in the presence of glare or bright lighting.
Dynamic Flexibility	The ability to quickly and repeatedly bend, stretch, twist, or reach out with your body, arms, and legs.
Speed of Limb Movement	The ability to quickly move the arms and legs.
Peripheral Vision	The ability to see objects or movement of objects to one's side when the eyes are looking ahead.
Night Vision	The ability to see under low light conditions.
Spatial Orientation	The ability to know your location in relation to the environment or to know where other objects are in relation to you.
Explosive Strength	The ability to use short bursts of muscle force to propel oneself (as in jumping or sprinting), or to throw an object.

Work_Activity	Work_Activity Definitions
Interacting With Computers	Using computers and computer systems (including hardware and software) to program, write software, set up functions, enter data, or process information.
Thinking Creatively	Developing, designing, or creating new applications, ideas, relationships, systems, or products, including artistic contributions.
Making Decisions and Solving Problems	Analyzing information and evaluating results to choose the best solution and solve problems.
Identifying Objects, Actions, and Events	Identifying information by categorizing, estimating, recognizing differences or similarities, and detecting changes in circumstances or events.
Organizing, Planning, and Prioritizing Work	Developing specific goals and plans to prioritize, organize, and accomplish your work.
Communicating with Supervisors, Peers, or Subordin	Providing information to supervisors, co-workers, and subordinates by telephone, in written form, e-mail, or in person.
Getting Information	Observing, receiving, and otherwise obtaining information from all relevant sources.
Performing for or Working Directly with the Public	Performing for people or dealing directly with the public. This includes serving customers in restaurants and stores, and receiving clients or guests.
Documenting/Recording Information	Entering, transcribing, recording, storing, or maintaining information in written or electronic/magnetic form.
Updating and Using Relevant Knowledge	Keeping up-to-date technically and applying new knowledge to your job.
Monitor Processes, Materials, or Surroundings	Monitoring and reviewing information from materials, events, or the environment, to detect or assess problems.
Communicating with Persons Outside Organization	Communicating with people outside the organization, representing the organization to customers, the public, government, and other external sources. This information can be exchanged in person, in writing, or by telephone or e-mail.
Controlling Machines and Processes	Using either control mechanisms or direct physical activity to operate machines or processes (not including computers or vehicles).

Monitoring and Controlling Resources	Monitoring and controlling resources and overseeing the spending of money.
Coordinating the Work and Activities of Others	Getting members of a group to work together to accomplish tasks.
Inspecting Equipment, Structures, or Material	Inspecting equipment, structures, or materials to identify the cause of errors or other problems or defects.
Establishing and Maintaining Interpersonal Relatio	Developing constructive and cooperative working relationships with others, and maintaining them over time.
Processing Information	Compiling, coding, categorizing, calculating, tabulating, auditing, or verifying information or data.
Analyzing Data or Information	Identifying the underlying principles, reasons, or facts of information by breaking down information or data into separate parts.
Scheduling Work and Activities	Scheduling events, programs, and activities, as well as the work of others.
Estimating the Quantifiable Characteristics of Pro	Estimating sizes, distances, and quantities; or determining time, costs, resources, or materials needed to perform a work activity.
Evaluating Information to Determine Compliance wit	Using relevant information and individual judgment to determine whether events or processes comply with laws, regulations, or standards.
Selling or Influencing Others	Convincing others to buy merchandise/goods or to otherwise change their minds or actions.
Judging the Qualities of Things, Services, or Peop	Assessing the value, importance, or quality of things or people.
Provide Consultation and Advice to Others	Providing guidance and expert advice to management or other groups on technical, systems-, or process-related topics.
Developing Objectives and Strategies	Establishing long-range objectives and specifying the strategies and actions to achieve them.
Performing General Physical Activities	Performing physical activities that require considerable use of your arms and legs and moving your whole body, such as climbing, lifting, balancing, walking, stooping, and handling of materials.
Interpreting the Meaning of Information for Others	Translating or explaining what information means and how it can be used.
Training and Teaching Others	Identifying the educational needs of others, developing formal educational or training programs or classes, and teaching or instructing others.
Performing Administrative Activities	Performing day-to-day administrative tasks such as maintaining information files and processing paperwork.
Handling and Moving Objects	Using hands and arms in handling, installing, positioning, and moving materials, and manipulating things.
Resolving Conflicts and Negotiating with Others	Handling complaints, settling disputes, and resolving grievances and conflicts, or otherwise negotiating with others.
Guiding, Directing, and Motivating Subordinates	Providing guidance and direction to subordinates, including setting performance standards and monitoring performance.
Assisting and Caring for Others	Providing personal assistance, medical attention, emotional support, or other personal care to others such as coworkers, customers, or patients.
Coaching and Developing Others	Identifying the developmental needs of others and coaching, mentoring, or otherwise helping others to improve their knowledge or skills.
Repairing and Maintaining Electronic Equipment	Servicing, repairing, calibrating, regulating, fine-tuning, or testing machines, devices, and equipment that operate primarily on the basis of electrical or electronic (not mechanical) principles.
Developing and Building Teams	Encouraging and building mutual trust, respect, and cooperation among team members.
Repairing and Maintaining Mechanical Equipment	Servicing, repairing, adjusting, and testing machines, devices, moving parts, and equipment that operate primarily on the basis of mechanical (not electronic) principles.
Drafting, Laying Out, and Specifying Technical Dev	Providing documentation, detailed instructions, drawings, or specifications to tell others about how devices, parts, equipment, or structures are to be fabricated, constructed, assembled, modified, maintained, or used.
Operating Vehicles, Mechanized Devices, or Equipme	Running, maneuvering, navigating, or driving vehicles or mechanized equipment, such as forklifts, passenger vehicles, aircraft, or water craft.
Staffing Organizational Units	Recruiting, interviewing, selecting, hiring, and promoting employees in an organization.

Work_Context	Work_Context Definitions
Indoors, Environmentally Controlled	How often does this job require working indoors in environmentally controlled conditions?

495

Spend Time Using Your Hands to Handle, Control, or	How much does this job require using your hands to handle, control, or feel objects, tools or controls?
Face-to-Face Discussions	How often do you have to have face-to-face discussions with individuals or teams in this job?
Spend Time Sitting	How much does this job require sitting?
Work With Work Group or Team	How important is it to work with others in a group or team in this job?
Electronic Mail	How often do you use electronic mail in this job?
Freedom to Make Decisions	How much decision making freedom, without supervision, does the job offer?
Structured versus Unstructured Work	To what extent is this job structured for the worker, rather than allowing the worker to determine tasks, priorities, and goals?
Importance of Being Exact or Accurate	How important is being very exact or highly accurate in performing this job?
Time Pressure	How often does this job require the worker to meet strict deadlines?
Telephone	How often do you have telephone conversations in this job?
Spend Time Making Repetitive Motions	How much does this job require making repetitive motions?
Contact With Others	How much does this job require the worker to be in contact with others (face-to-face, by telephone, or otherwise) in order to perform it?
Frequency of Decision Making	How frequently is the worker required to make decisions that affect other people, the financial resources, and/or the image and reputation of the organization?
Impact of Decisions on Co-workers or Company Resul	How do the decisions an employee makes impact the results of co-workers, clients or the company?
Coordinate or Lead Others	How important is it to coordinate or lead others in accomplishing work activities in this job?
Consequence of Error	How serious would the result usually be if the worker made a mistake that was not readily correctable?
Physical Proximity	To what extent does this job require the worker to perform job tasks in close physical proximity to other people?
Responsibility for Outcomes and Results	How responsible is the worker for work outcomes and results of other workers?
Importance of Repeating Same Tasks	How important is repeating the same physical activities (e.g., key entry) or mental activities (e.g., checking entries in a ledger) over and over, without stopping, to performing this job?
Letters and Memos	How often does the job require written letters and memos?
Level of Competition	To what extent does this job require the worker to compete or to be aware of competitive pressures?
Frequency of Conflict Situations	How often are there conflict situations the employee has to face in this job?
Deal With External Customers	How important is it to work with external customers or the public in this job?
Pace Determined by Speed of Equipment	How important is it to this job that the pace is determined by the speed of equipment or machinery? (This does not refer to keeping busy at all times on this job.)
Responsible for Others' Health and Safety	How much responsibility is there for the health and safety of others in this job?
Sounds, Noise Levels Are Distracting or Uncomforta	How often does this job require working exposed to sounds and noise levels that are distracting or uncomfortable?
Degree of Automation	How automated is the job?
Deal With Unpleasant or Angry People	How frequently does the worker have to deal with unpleasant, angry, or discourteous individuals as part of the job requirements?
Spend Time Bending or Twisting the Body	How much does this job require bending or twisting your body?
Spend Time Standing	How much does this job require standing?
Cramped Work Space, Awkward Positions	How often does this job require working in cramped work spaces that requires getting into awkward positions?
Exposed to Contaminants	How often does this job require working exposed to contaminants (such as pollutants, gases, dust or odors)?
Spend Time Walking and Running	How much does this job require walking and running?
Outdoors, Exposed to Weather	How often does this job require working outdoors, exposed to all weather conditions?
Extremely Bright or Inadequate Lighting	How often does this job require working in extremely bright or inadequate lighting conditions?
In an Enclosed Vehicle or Equipment	How often does this job require working in a closed vehicle or equipment (e.g., car)?
Outdoors, Under Cover	How often does this job require working outdoors, under cover (e.g., structure with roof but no walls)?
Spend Time Kneeling, Crouching, Stooping, or Crawl	How much does this job require kneeling, crouching, stooping, or crawling?

Indoors, Not Environmentally Controlled	How often does this job require working indoors in non-controlled environmental conditions (e.g., warehouse without heat)?
Public Speaking	How often do you have to perform public speaking in this job?
Exposed to Hazardous Equipment	How often does this job require exposure to hazardous equipment?
Very Hot or Cold Temperatures	How often does this job require working in very hot (above 90 F degrees) or very cold (below 32 F degrees) temperatures?
In an Open Vehicle or Equipment	How often does this job require working in an open vehicle or equipment (e.g., tractor)?
Exposed to High Places	How often does this job require exposure to high places?
Exposed to Minor Burns, Cuts, Bites, or Stings	How often does this job require exposure to minor burns, cuts, bites, or stings?
Spend Time Climbing Ladders, Scaffolds, or Poles	How much does this job require climbing ladders, scaffolds, or poles?
Spend Time Keeping or Regaining Balance	How much does this job require keeping or regaining your balance?
Exposed to Whole Body Vibration	How often does this job require exposure to whole body vibration (e.g., operate a jackhammer)?
Wear Common Protective or Safety Equipment such as	How much does this job require wearing common protective or safety equipment such as safety shoes, glasses, gloves, hard hats or life jackets?
Exposed to Hazardous Conditions	How often does this job require exposure to hazardous conditions?
Wear Specialized Protective or Safety Equipment su	How much does this job require wearing specialized protective or safety equipment such as breathing apparatus, safety harness, full protection suits, or radiation protection?
Deal With Physically Aggressive People	How frequently does this job require the worker to deal with physical aggression of violent individuals?
Exposed to Radiation	How often does this job require exposure to radiation?
Exposed to Disease or Infections	How often does this job require exposure to disease/infections?

Job Zone Component	Job Zone Component Definitions
Title	Job Zone Three: Medium Preparation Needed
Overall Experience	Previous work-related skill, knowledge, or experience is required for these occupations. For example, an electrician must have completed three or four years of apprenticeship or several years of vocational training, and often must have passed a licensing exam, in order to perform the job.
Job Training	Employees in these occupations usually need one or two years of training involving both on-the-job experience and informal training with experienced workers.
Job Zone Examples	These occupations usually involve using communication and organizational skills to coordinate, supervise, manage, or train others to accomplish goals. Examples include dental assistants, electricians, fish and game wardens, legal secretaries, personnel recruiters, and recreation workers.
SVP Range	(6.0 to < 7.0)
Education	Most occupations in this zone require training in vocational schools, related on-the-job experience, or an associate's degree. Some may require a bachelor's degree.

Work_Styles	Work_Styles Definitions
Dependability	Job requires being reliable, responsible, and dependable, and fulfilling obligations.
Attention to Detail	Job requires being careful about detail and thorough in completing work tasks.
Independence	Job requires developing one's own ways of doing things, guiding oneself with little or no supervision, and depending on oneself to get things done.
Stress Tolerance	Job requires accepting criticism and dealing calmly and effectively with high stress situations.
Adaptability/Flexibility	Job requires being open to change (positive or negative) and to considerable variety in the workplace.
Persistence	Job requires persistence in the face of obstacles.
Initiative	Job requires a willingness to take on responsibilities and challenges.
Achievement/Effort	Job requires establishing and maintaining personally challenging achievement goals and exerting effort toward mastering tasks.
Self Control	Job requires maintaining composure, keeping emotions in check, controlling anger, and avoiding aggressive behavior, even in very difficult situations.

Cooperation	Job requires being pleasant with others on the job and displaying a good-natured, cooperative attitude.
Innovation	Job requires creativity and alternative thinking to develop new ideas for and answers to work-related problems.
Integrity	Job requires being honest and ethical.
Leadership	Job requires a willingness to lead, take charge, and offer opinions and direction.
Analytical Thinking	Job requires analyzing information and using logic to address work-related issues and problems.
Concern for Others	Job requires being sensitive to others' needs and feelings and being understanding and helpful on the job.
Social Orientation	Job requires preferring to work with others rather than alone, and being personally connected with others on the job.

29-1022.00 - Oral and Maxillofacial Surgeons

Perform surgery on mouth, jaws, and related head and neck structure to execute difficult and multiple extractions of teeth, to remove tumors and other abnormal growths, to correct abnormal jaw relations by mandibular or maxillary revision, to prepare mouth for insertion of dental prosthesis, or to treat fractured jaws.

Tasks

1) Treat infections of the oral cavity, salivary glands, jaws, and neck.

2) Perform surgery to prepare the mouth for dental implants, and to aid in the regeneration of deficient bone and gum tissues.

3) Treat problems affecting the oral mucosa such as mouth ulcers and infections.

4) Administer general and local anesthetics.

5) Remove tumors and other abnormal growths of the oral and facial regions, using surgical instruments.

6) Remove impacted, damaged, and non-restorable teeth.

7) Restore form and function by moving skin, bone, nerves, and other tissues from other parts of the body in order to reconstruct the jaws and face.

8) Evaluate the position of the wisdom teeth in order to determine whether problems exist currently or might occur in the future.

9) Perform minor cosmetic procedures such as chin and cheek-bone enhancements, and minor facial rejuvenation procedures including the use of Botox and laser technology.

10) Perform surgery on the mouth and jaws in order to treat conditions such as cleft lip and palate and jaw growth problems.

11) Treat snoring problems, using laser surgery.

12) Collaborate with other professionals such as restorative dentists and orthodontists in order to plan treatment.

29-1023.00 - Orthodontists

Examine, diagnose, and treat dental malocclusions and oral cavity anomalies. Design and fabricate appliances to realign teeth and jaws to produce and maintain normal function and to improve appearance.

Tasks

1) Study diagnostic records such as medical/dental histories, plaster models of the teeth, photos of a patient's face and teeth, and X-rays in order to develop patient treatment plans.

2) Provide patients with proposed treatment plans and cost estimates.

3) Fit dental appliances in patients' mouths in order to alter the position and relationship of teeth and jaws, and to realign teeth.

4) Instruct dental officers and technical assistants in orthodontic procedures and techniques.

5) Design and fabricate appliances, such as space maintainers, retainers, and labial and lingual arch wires.

6) Prepare diagnostic and treatment records.

7) Adjust dental appliances periodically in order to produce and maintain normal function.

8) Diagnose teeth and jaw or other dental-facial abnormalities.

9) Coordinate orthodontic services with other dental and medical services.

29-1024.00 - Prosthodontists

Construct oral prostheses to replace missing teeth and other oral structures to correct natural and acquired deformation of mouth and jaws, to restore and maintain oral function, such as chewing and speaking, and to improve appearance.

Tasks

1) Measure and take impressions of patients' jaws and teeth in order to determine the shape and size of dental prostheses, using face bows, dental articulators, recording devices, and other materials.

2) Use bonding technology on the surface of the teeth in order to change tooth shape or to close gaps.

3) Treat facial pain and jaw joint problems.

4) Restore function and aesthetics to traumatic injury victims, or to individuals with diseases or birth defects.

5) Design and fabricate dental prostheses, or supervise dental technicians and laboratory bench workers who construct the devices.

6) Fit prostheses to patients, making any necessary adjustments and modifications.

7) Place veneers onto teeth in order to conceal defects.

8) Collaborate with general dentists, specialists, and other health professionals in order to develop solutions to dental and oral health concerns.

9) Bleach discolored teeth in order to brighten and whiten them.

10) Replace missing teeth and associated oral structures with permanent fixtures, such as crowns and bridges, or removable fixtures, such as dentures.

29-1031.00 - Dietitians and Nutritionists

Plan and conduct food service or nutritional programs to assist in the promotion of health and control of disease. May supervise activities of a department providing quantity food services, counsel individuals, or conduct nutritional research.

Tasks

1) Assess nutritional needs, diet restrictions and current health plans to develop and implement dietary-care plans and provide nutritional counseling.

2) Counsel individuals and groups on basic rules of good nutrition, healthy eating habits, and nutrition monitoring to improve their quality of life.

3) Consult with physicians and health care personnel to determine nutritional needs and diet restrictions of patient or client.

4) Develop curriculum and prepare manuals, visual aids, course outlines, and other materials used in teaching.

5) Inspect meals served for conformance to prescribed diets and standards of palatability and appearance.

6) Develop policies for food service or nutritional programs to assist in health promotion and disease control.

7) Coordinate recipe development and standardization and develop new menus for independent food service operations.

8) Monitor food service operations to ensure conformance to nutritional, safety, sanitation and quality standards.

9) Coordinate diet counseling services.

10) Test new food products and equipment.

11) Plan and conduct training programs in dietetics, nutrition, and institutional management and administration for medical students, health-care personnel and the general public.

12) Manage quantity food service departments or clinical and community nutrition services.

13) Organize, develop, analyze, test, and prepare special meals such as low-fat, low-cholesterol and chemical-free meals.

14) Advise food service managers and organizations on sanitation, safety procedures, menu development, budgeting, and planning to assist with the establishment, operation, and

evaluation of food service facilities and nutrition programs.

15) Purchase food in accordance with health and safety codes.

16) Select, train and supervise workers who plan, prepare and serve meals.

17) Prepare and administer budgets for food, equipment and supplies.

18) Plan, conduct, and evaluate dietary, nutritional, and epidemiological research.

19) Make recommendations regarding public policy, such as nutrition labeling, food fortification, and nutrition standards for school programs.

20) Plan and prepare grant proposals to request program funding.

21) Write research reports and other publications to document and communicate research findings.

22) Confer with design, building, and equipment personnel to plan for construction and remodeling of food service units.

Knowledge	Knowledge Definitions
Education and Training	Knowledge of principles and methods for curriculum and training design, teaching and instruction for individuals and groups, and the measurement of training effects.
Customer and Personal Service	Knowledge of principles and processes for providing customer and personal services. This includes customer needs assessment, meeting quality standards for services, and evaluation of customer satisfaction.
English Language	Knowledge of the structure and content of the English language including the meaning and spelling of words, rules of composition, and grammar.
Medicine and Dentistry	Knowledge of the information and techniques needed to diagnose and treat human injuries, diseases, and deformities. This includes symptoms, treatment alternatives, drug properties and interactions, and preventive health-care measures.
Psychology	Knowledge of human behavior and performance; individual differences in ability, personality, and interests; learning and motivation; psychological research methods; and the assessment and treatment of behavioral and affective disorders.
Therapy and Counseling	Knowledge of principles, methods, and procedures for diagnosis, treatment, and rehabilitation of physical and mental dysfunctions, and for career counseling and guidance.
Mathematics	Knowledge of arithmetic, algebra, geometry, calculus, statistics, and their applications.
Food Production	Knowledge of techniques and equipment for planting, growing, and harvesting food products (both plant and animal) for consumption, including storage/handling techniques.
Sociology and Anthropology	Knowledge of group behavior and dynamics, societal trends and influences, human migrations, ethnicity, cultures and their history and origins.
Computers and Electronics	Knowledge of circuit boards, processors, chips, electronic equipment, and computer hardware and software, including applications and programming.
Chemistry	Knowledge of the chemical composition, structure, and properties of substances and of the chemical processes and transformations that they undergo. This includes uses of chemicals and their interactions, danger signs, production techniques, and disposal methods.
Administration and Management	Knowledge of business and management principles involved in strategic planning, resource allocation, human resources modeling, leadership technique, production methods, and coordination of people and resources.
Clerical	Knowledge of administrative and clerical procedures and systems such as word processing, managing files and records, stenography and transcription, designing forms, and other office procedures and terminology.
Biology	Knowledge of plant and animal organisms, their tissues, cells, functions, interdependencies, and interactions with each other and the environment.
Communications and Media	Knowledge of media production, communication, and dissemination techniques and methods. This includes alternative ways to inform and entertain via written, oral, and visual media.
Law and Government	Knowledge of laws, legal codes, court procedures, precedents, government regulations, executive orders, agency rules, and the democratic political process.
Public Safety and Security	Knowledge of relevant equipment, policies, procedures, and strategies to promote effective local, state, or national security operations for the protection of people, data, property, and institutions.

Personnel and Human Resources	Knowledge of principles and procedures for personnel recruitment, selection, training, compensation and benefits, labor relations and negotiation, and personnel information systems.
Economics and Accounting	Knowledge of economic and accounting principles and practices, the financial markets, banking and the analysis and reporting of financial data.
Telecommunications	Knowledge of transmission, broadcasting, switching, control, and operation of telecommunications systems.
Philosophy and Theology	Knowledge of different philosophical systems and religions. This includes their basic principles, values, ethics, ways of thinking, customs, practices, and their impact on human culture.
Transportation	Knowledge of principles and methods for moving people or goods by air, rail, sea, or road, including the relative costs and benefits.
Sales and Marketing	Knowledge of principles and methods for showing, promoting, and selling products or services. This includes marketing strategy and tactics, product demonstration, sales techniques, and sales control systems.
Foreign Language	Knowledge of the structure and content of a foreign (non-English) language including the meaning and spelling of words, rules of composition and grammar, and pronunciation.
Production and Processing	Knowledge of raw materials, production processes, quality control, costs, and other techniques for maximizing the effective manufacture and distribution of goods.
Engineering and Technology	Knowledge of the practical application of engineering science and technology. This includes applying principles, techniques, procedures, and equipment to the design and production of various goods and services.
Fine Arts	Knowledge of the theory and techniques required to compose, produce, and perform works of music, dance, visual arts, drama, and sculpture.
History and Archeology	Knowledge of historical events and their causes, indicators, and effects on civilizations and cultures.
Geography	Knowledge of principles and methods for describing the features of land, sea, and air masses, including their physical characteristics, locations, interrelationships, and distribution of plant, animal, and human life.
Mechanical	Knowledge of machines and tools, including their designs, uses, repair, and maintenance.
Physics	Knowledge and prediction of physical principles, laws, their interrelationships, and applications to understanding fluid, material, and atmospheric dynamics, and mechanical, electrical, atomic and sub-atomic structures and processes.
Design	Knowledge of design techniques, tools, and principles involved in production of precision technical plans, blueprints, drawings, and models.
Building and Construction	Knowledge of materials, methods, and the tools involved in the construction or repair of houses, buildings, or other structures such as highways and roads.

Skills	Skills Definitions
Active Listening	Giving full attention to what other people are saying, taking time to understand the points being made, asking questions as appropriate, and not interrupting at inappropriate times.
Reading Comprehension	Understanding written sentences and paragraphs in work related documents.
Instructing	Teaching others how to do something.
Speaking	Talking to others to convey information effectively.
Writing	Communicating effectively in writing as appropriate for the needs of the audience.
Time Management	Managing one's own time and the time of others.
Critical Thinking	Using logic and reasoning to identify the strengths and weaknesses of alternative solutions, conclusions or approaches to problems.
Active Learning	Understanding the implications of new information for both current and future problem-solving and decision-making.
Judgment and Decision Making	Considering the relative costs and benefits of potential actions to choose the most appropriate one.
Social Perceptiveness	Being aware of others' reactions and understanding why they react as they do.
Service Orientation	Actively looking for ways to help people.
Science	Using scientific rules and methods to solve problems.
Coordination	Adjusting actions in relation to others' actions.

Learning Strategies	Selecting and using training/instructional methods and procedures appropriate for the situation when learning or teaching new things.
Monitoring	Monitoring/Assessing performance of yourself, other individuals, or organizations to make improvements or take corrective action.
Complex Problem Solving	Identifying complex problems and reviewing related information to develop and evaluate options and implement solutions.
Persuasion	Persuading others to change their minds or behavior.
Mathematics	Using mathematics to solve problems.
Quality Control Analysis	Conducting tests and inspections of products, services, or processes to evaluate quality or performance.
Negotiation	Bringing others together and trying to reconcile differences.
Management of Personnel Resources	Motivating, developing, and directing people as they work, identifying the best people for the job.
Systems Evaluation	Identifying measures or indicators of system performance and the actions needed to improve or correct performance, relative to the goals of the system.
Systems Analysis	Determining how a system should work and how changes in conditions, operations, and the environment will affect outcomes.
Troubleshooting	Determining causes of operating errors and deciding what to do about it.
Management of Financial Resources	Determining how money will be spent to get the work done, and accounting for these expenditures.
Equipment Selection	Determining the kind of tools and equipment needed to do a job.
Management of Material Resources	Obtaining and seeing to the appropriate use of equipment, facilities, and materials needed to do certain work.
Operations Analysis	Analyzing needs and product requirements to create a design.
Operation Monitoring	Watching gauges, dials, or other indicators to make sure a machine is working properly.
Equipment Maintenance	Performing routine maintenance on equipment and determining when and what kind of maintenance is needed.
Operation and Control	Controlling operations of equipment or systems.
Repairing	Repairing machines or systems using the needed tools.
Installation	Installing equipment, machines, wiring, or programs to meet specifications.
Technology Design	Generating or adapting equipment and technology to serve user needs.
Programming	Writing computer programs for various purposes.

Ability	**Ability Definitions**
Written Comprehension	The ability to read and understand information and ideas presented in writing.
Oral Expression	The ability to communicate information and ideas in speaking so others will understand.
Problem Sensitivity	The ability to tell when something is wrong or is likely to go wrong. It does not involve solving the problem, only recognizing there is a problem.
Oral Comprehension	The ability to listen to and understand information and ideas presented through spoken words and sentences.
Speech Clarity	The ability to speak clearly so others can understand you.
Inductive Reasoning	The ability to combine pieces of information to form general rules or conclusions (includes finding a relationship among seemingly unrelated events).
Deductive Reasoning	The ability to apply general rules to specific problems to produce answers that make sense.
Near Vision	The ability to see details at close range (within a few feet of the observer).
Written Expression	The ability to communicate information and ideas in writing so others will understand.
Speech Recognition	The ability to identify and understand the speech of another person.
Category Flexibility	The ability to generate or use different sets of rules for combining or grouping things in different ways.
Fluency of Ideas	The ability to come up with a number of ideas about a topic (the number of ideas is important, not their quality, correctness, or creativity).
Information Ordering	The ability to arrange things or actions in a certain order or pattern according to a specific rule or set of rules (e.g., patterns of numbers, letters, words, pictures, mathematical operations).
Originality	The ability to come up with unusual or clever ideas about a given topic or situation, or to develop creative ways to solve a problem.

Selective Attention	The ability to concentrate on a task over a period of time without being distracted.
Flexibility of Closure	The ability to identify or detect a known pattern (a figure, object, word, or sound) that is hidden in other distracting material.
Mathematical Reasoning	The ability to choose the right mathematical methods or formulas to solve a problem.
Visual Color Discrimination	The ability to match or detect differences between colors, including shades of color and brightness.
Perceptual Speed	The ability to quickly and accurately compare similarities and differences among sets of letters, numbers, objects, pictures, or patterns. The things to be compared may be presented at the same time or one after the other. This ability also includes comparing a presented object with a remembered object.
Memorization	The ability to remember information such as words, numbers, pictures, and procedures.
Far Vision	The ability to see details at a distance.
Time Sharing	The ability to shift back and forth between two or more activities or sources of information (such as speech, sounds, touch, or other sources).
Speed of Closure	The ability to quickly make sense of, combine, and organize information into meaningful patterns.
Number Facility	The ability to add, subtract, multiply, or divide quickly and correctly.
Visualization	The ability to imagine how something will look after it is moved around or when its parts are moved or rearranged.
Finger Dexterity	The ability to make precisely coordinated movements of the fingers of one or both hands to grasp, manipulate, or assemble very small objects.
Trunk Strength	The ability to use your abdominal and lower back muscles to support part of the body repeatedly or continuously over time without 'giving out' or fatiguing.
Auditory Attention	The ability to focus on a single source of sound in the presence of other distracting sounds.
Hearing Sensitivity	The ability to detect or tell the differences between sounds that vary in pitch and loudness.
Wrist-Finger Speed	The ability to make fast, simple, repeated movements of the fingers, hands, and wrists.
Speed of Limb Movement	The ability to quickly move the arms and legs.
Gross Body Equilibrium	The ability to keep or regain your body balance or stay upright when in an unstable position.
Gross Body Coordination	The ability to coordinate the movement of your arms, legs, and torso together when the whole body is in motion.
Dynamic Flexibility	The ability to quickly and repeatedly bend, stretch, twist, or reach out with your body, arms, and/or legs.
Extent Flexibility	The ability to bend, stretch, twist, or reach with your body, arms, and/or legs.
Stamina	The ability to exert yourself physically over long periods of time without getting winded or out of breath.
Depth Perception	The ability to judge which of several objects is closer or farther away from you, or to judge the distance between you and an object.
Dynamic Strength	The ability to exert muscle force repeatedly or continuously over time. This involves muscular endurance and resistance to muscle fatigue.
Explosive Strength	The ability to use short bursts of muscle force to propel oneself (as in jumping or sprinting), or to throw an object.
Static Strength	The ability to exert maximum muscle force to lift, push, pull, or carry objects.
Arm-Hand Steadiness	The ability to keep your hand and arm steady while moving your arm or while holding your arm and hand in one position.
Rate Control	The ability to time your movements or the movement of a piece of equipment in anticipation of changes in the speed and/or direction of a moving object or scene.
Night Vision	The ability to see under low light conditions.
Reaction Time	The ability to quickly respond (with the hand, finger, or foot) to a signal (sound, light, picture) when it appears.
Spatial Orientation	The ability to know your location in relation to the environment or to know where other objects are in relation to you.
Manual Dexterity	The ability to quickly move your hand, your hand together with your arm, or your two hands to grasp, manipulate, or assemble objects.
Control Precision	The ability to quickly and repeatedly adjust the controls of a machine or a vehicle to exact positions.
Glare Sensitivity	The ability to see objects in the presence of glare or bright lighting.
Peripheral Vision	The ability to see objects or movement of objects to one's side when the eyes are looking ahead.

Multilimb Coordination	The ability to coordinate two or more limbs (for example, two arms, two legs, or one leg and one arm) while sitting, standing, or lying down. It does not involve performing the activities while the whole body is in motion.
Response Orientation	The ability to choose quickly between two or more movements in response to two or more different signals (lights, sounds, pictures). It includes the speed with which the correct response is started with the hand, foot, or other body part.
Sound Localization	The ability to tell the direction from which a sound originated.

Work_Activity	Work_Activity Definitions
Interpreting the Meaning of Information for Others	Translating or explaining what information means and how it can be used.
Documenting/Recording Information	Entering, transcribing, recording, storing, or maintaining information in written or electronic/magnetic form.
Analyzing Data or Information	Identifying the underlying principles, reasons, or facts of information by breaking down information or data into separate parts.
Updating and Using Relevant Knowledge	Keeping up-to-date technically and applying new knowledge to your job.
Getting Information	Observing, receiving, and otherwise obtaining information from all relevant sources.
Communicating with Supervisors, Peers, or Subordin	Providing information to supervisors, co-workers, and subordinates by telephone, in written form, e-mail, or in person.
Making Decisions and Solving Problems	Analyzing information and evaluating results to choose the best solution and solve problems.
Interacting With Computers	Using computers and computer systems (including hardware and software) to program, write software, set up functions, enter data, or process information.
Assisting and Caring for Others	Providing personal assistance, medical attention, emotional support, or other personal care to others such as coworkers, customers, or patients.
Identifying Objects, Actions, and Events	Identifying information by categorizing, estimating, recognizing differences or similarities, and detecting changes in circumstances or events.
Organizing, Planning, and Prioritizing Work	Developing specific goals and plans to prioritize, organize, and accomplish your work.
Processing Information	Compiling, coding, categorizing, calculating, tabulating, auditing, or verifying information or data.
Provide Consultation and Advice to Others	Providing guidance and expert advice to management or other groups on technical, systems-, or process-related topics.
Training and Teaching Others	Identifying the educational needs of others, developing formal educational or training programs or classes, and teaching or instructing others.
Judging the Qualities of Things, Services, or Peop	Assessing the value, importance, or quality of things or people.
Establishing and Maintaining Interpersonal Relatio	Developing constructive and cooperative working relationships with others, and maintaining them over time.
Selling or Influencing Others	Convincing others to buy merchandise/goods or to otherwise change their minds or actions.
Developing and Building Teams	Encouraging and building mutual trust, respect, and cooperation among team members.
Monitor Processes, Materials, or Surroundings	Monitoring and reviewing information from materials, events, or the environment, to detect or assess problems.
Evaluating Information to Determine Compliance wit	Using relevant information and individual judgment to determine whether events or processes comply with laws, regulations, or standards.
Thinking Creatively	Developing, designing, or creating new applications, ideas, relationships, systems, or products, including artistic contributions.
Communicating with Persons Outside Organization	Communicating with people outside the organization, representing the organization to customers, the public, government, and other external sources. This information can be exchanged in person, in writing, or by telephone or e-mail.
Performing for or Working Directly with the Public	Performing for people or dealing directly with the public. This includes serving customers in restaurants and stores, and receiving clients or guests.
Coordinating the Work and Activities of Others	Getting members of a group to work together to accomplish tasks.
Monitoring and Controlling Resources	Monitoring and controlling resources and overseeing the spending of money.
Performing Administrative Activities	Performing day-to-day administrative tasks such as maintaining information files and processing paperwork.

Developing Objectives and Strategies	Establishing long-range objectives and specifying the strategies and actions to achieve them.
Coaching and Developing Others	Identifying the developmental needs of others and coaching, mentoring, or otherwise helping others to improve their knowledge or skills.
Scheduling Work and Activities	Scheduling events, programs, and activities, as well as the work of others.
Guiding, Directing, and Motivating Subordinates	Providing guidance and direction to subordinates, including setting performance standards and monitoring performance.
Estimating the Quantifiable Characteristics of Pro	Estimating sizes, distances, and quantities; or determining time, costs, resources, or materials needed to perform a work activity.
Inspecting Equipment, Structures, or Material	Inspecting equipment, structures, or materials to identify the cause of errors or other problems or defects.
Resolving Conflicts and Negotiating with Others	Handling complaints, settling disputes, and resolving grievances and conflicts, or otherwise negotiating with others.
Performing General Physical Activities	Performing physical activities that require considerable use of your arms and legs and moving your whole body, such as climbing, lifting, balancing, walking, stooping, and handling of materials.
Staffing Organizational Units	Recruiting, interviewing, selecting, hiring, and promoting employees in an organization.
Handling and Moving Objects	Using hands and arms in handling, installing, positioning, and moving materials, and manipulating things.
Controlling Machines and Processes	Using either control mechanisms or direct physical activity to operate machines or processes (not including computers or vehicles).
Operating Vehicles, Mechanized Devices, or Equipme	Running, maneuvering, navigating, or driving vehicles or mechanized equipment, such as forklifts, passenger vehicles, aircraft, or water craft.
Repairing and Maintaining Mechanical Equipment	Servicing, repairing, adjusting, and testing machines, devices, moving parts, and equipment that operate primarily on the basis of mechanical (not electronic) principles.
Repairing and Maintaining Electronic Equipment	Servicing, repairing, calibrating, regulating, fine-tuning, or testing machines, devices, and equipment that operate primarily on the basis of electrical or electronic (not mechanical) principles.
Drafting, Laying Out, and Specifying Technical Dev	Providing documentation, detailed instructions, drawings, or specifications to tell others about how devices, parts, equipment, or structures are to be fabricated, constructed, assembled, modified, maintained, or used.

Work_Context	Work_Context Definitions
Freedom to Make Decisions	How much decision making freedom, without supervision, does the job offer?
Structured versus Unstructured Work	To what extent is this job structured for the worker, rather than allowing the worker to determine tasks, priorities, and goals?
Frequency of Decision Making	How frequently is the worker required to make decisions that affect other people, the financial resources, and/or the image and reputation of the organization?
Face-to-Face Discussions	How often do you have to have face-to-face discussions with individuals or teams in this job?
Contact With Others	How much does this job require the worker to be in contact with others (face-to-face, by telephone, or otherwise) in order to perform it?
Impact of Decisions on Co-workers or Company Resul	How do the decisions an employee makes impact the results of co-workers, clients or the company?
Telephone	How often do you have telephone conversations in this job?
Indoors, Environmentally Controlled	How often does this job require working indoors in environmentally controlled conditions?
Spend Time Sitting	How much does this job require sitting?
Work With Work Group or Team	How important is it to work with others in a group or team in this job?
Time Pressure	How often does this job require the worker to meet strict deadlines?
Importance of Being Exact or Accurate	How important is being very exact or highly accurate in performing this job?
Spend Time Standing	How much does this job require standing?
Physical Proximity	To what extent does this job require the worker to perform job tasks in close physical proximity to other people?
Wear Common Protective or Safety Equipment such as	How much does this job require wearing common protective or safety equipment such as safety shoes, glasses, gloves, hard hats or life jackets?
Deal With External Customers	How important is it to work with external customers or the public in this job?
Letters and Memos	How often does the job require written letters and memos?

Deal With Unpleasant or Angry People	How frequently does the worker have to deal with unpleasant, angry, or discourteous individuals as part of the job requirements?
Coordinate or Lead Others	How important is it to coordinate or lead others in accomplishing work activities in this job?
Electronic Mail	How often do you use electronic mail in this job?
Frequency of Conflict Situations	How often are there conflict situations the employee has to face in this job?
Responsibility for Outcomes and Results	How responsible is the worker for work outcomes and results of other workers?
Spend Time Walking and Running	How much does this job require walking and running?
Exposed to Disease or Infections	How often does this job require exposure to disease/infections?
Indoors, Not Environmentally Controlled	How often does this job require working indoors in non-controlled environmental conditions (e.g., warehouse without heat)?
Responsible for Others' Health and Safety	How much responsibility is there for the health and safety of others in this job?
In an Enclosed Vehicle or Equipment	How often does this job require working in a closed vehicle or equipment (e.g., car)?
Sounds, Noise Levels Are Distracting or Uncomfortable	How often does this job require working exposed to sounds and noise levels that are distracting or uncomfortable?
Level of Competition	To what extent does this job require the worker to compete or to be aware of competitive pressures?
Exposed to Minor Burns, Cuts, Bites, or Stings	How often does this job require exposure to minor burns, cuts, bites, or stings?
Deal With Physically Aggressive People	How frequently does this job require the worker to deal with physical aggression of violent individuals?
Spend Time Making Repetitive Motions	How much does this job require making repetitive motions?
Very Hot or Cold Temperatures	How often does this job require working in very hot (above 90 F degrees) or very cold (below 32 F degrees) temperatures?
Public Speaking	How often do you have to perform public speaking in this job?
Importance of Repeating Same Tasks	How important is repeating the same physical activities (e.g., key entry) or mental activities (e.g., checking entries in a ledger) over and over, without stopping, to performing this job?
Exposed to Contaminants	How often does this job require working exposed to contaminants (such as pollutants, gases, dust or odors)?
Consequence of Error	How serious would the result usually be if the worker made a mistake that was not readily correctable?
Spend Time Using Your Hands to Handle, Control, or	How much does this job require using your hands to handle, control, or feel objects, tools or controls?
Spend Time Kneeling, Crouching, Stooping, or Crawl	How much does this job require kneeling, crouching, stooping or crawling?
Spend Time Bending or Twisting the Body	How much does this job require bending or twisting your body?
Outdoors, Exposed to Weather	How often does this job require working outdoors, exposed to all weather conditions?
Cramped Work Space, Awkward Positions	How often does this job require working in cramped work spaces that requires getting into awkward positions?
Degree of Automation	How automated is the job?
Exposed to Hazardous Conditions	How often does this job require exposure to hazardous conditions?
Extremely Bright or Inadequate Lighting	How often does this job require working in extremely bright or inadequate lighting conditions?
Wear Specialized Protective or Safety Equipment su	How much does this job require wearing specialized protective or safety equipment such as breathing apparatus, safety harness, full protection suits, or radiation protection?
Exposed to Radiation	How often does this job require exposure to radiation?
Exposed to Hazardous Equipment	How often does this job require exposure to hazardous equipment?
Pace Determined by Speed of Equipment	How important is it to this job that the pace is determined by the speed of equipment or machinery? (This does not refer to keeping busy at all times on this job.)
In an Open Vehicle or Equipment	How often does this job require working in an open vehicle or equipment (e.g., tractor)?
Exposed to Whole Body Vibration	How often does this job require exposure to whole body vibration (e.g., operate a jackhammer)?
Outdoors, Under Cover	How often does this job require working outdoors, under cover (e.g., structure with roof but no walls)?
Spend Time Keeping or Regaining Balance	How much does this job require keeping or regaining your balance?
Exposed to High Places	How often does this job require exposure to high places?

Spend Time Climbing Ladders, Scaffolds, or Poles	How much does this job require climbing ladders, scaffolds, or poles?

Job Zone Component	Job Zone Component Definitions
Title	Job Zone Five: Extensive Preparation Needed
Overall Experience	Extensive skill, knowledge, and experience are needed for these occupations. Many require more than five years of experience. For example, surgeons must complete four years of college and an additional five to seven years of specialized medical training to be able to do their job.
Job Training	Employees may need some on-the-job training, but most of these occupations assume that the person will already have the required skills, knowledge, work-related experience, and/or training.
Job Zone Examples	These occupations often involve coordinating, training, supervising, or managing the activities of others to accomplish goals. Very advanced communication and organizational skills are required. Examples include athletic trainers, lawyers, managing editors, phyicists, social psychologists, and surgeons.
SVP Range	(8.0 and above)
Education	A bachelor's degree is the minimum formal education required for these occupations. However, many also require graduate school. For example, they may require a master's degree, and some require a Ph.D., M.D., or J.D. (law degree).

Work_Styles	Work_Styles Definitions
Integrity	Job requires being honest and ethical.
Concern for Others	Job requires being sensitive to others' needs and feelings and being understanding and helpful on the job.
Dependability	Job requires being reliable, responsible, and dependable, and fulfilling obligations.
Cooperation	Job requires being pleasant with others on the job and displaying a good-natured, cooperative attitude.
Independence	Job requires developing one's own ways of doing things, guiding oneself with little or no supervision, and depending on oneself to get things done.
Attention to Detail	Job requires being careful about detail and thorough in completing work tasks.
Self Control	Job requires maintaining composure, keeping emotions in check, controlling anger, and avoiding aggressive behavior, even in very difficult situations.
Adaptability/Flexibility	Job requires being open to change (positive or negative) and to considerable variety in the workplace.
Achievement/Effort	Job requires establishing and maintaining personally challenging achievement goals and exerting effort toward mastering tasks.
Initiative	Job requires a willingness to take on responsibilities and challenges.
Social Orientation	Job requires preferring to work with others rather than alone, and being personally connected with others on the job.
Stress Tolerance	Job requires accepting criticism and dealing calmly and effectively with high stress situations.
Persistence	Job requires persistence in the face of obstacles.
Analytical Thinking	Job requires analyzing information and using logic to address work-related issues and problems.
Leadership	Job requires a willingness to lead, take charge, and offer opinions and direction.
Innovation	Job requires creativity and alternative thinking to develop new ideas for and answers to work-related problems.

29-1041.00 - Optometrists

Diagnose, manage, and treat conditions and diseases of the human eye and visual system. Examine eyes and visual system, diagnose problems or impairments, prescribe corrective lenses, and provide treatment. May prescribe therapeutic drugs to treat specific eye conditions.

Tasks

1) Analyze test results and develop a treatment plan.

2) Prescribe medications to treat eye diseases if state laws permit.

3) Prescribe therapeutic procedures to correct or conserve vision.

4) Provide patients undergoing eye surgeries, such as cataract and laser vision correction, with pre- and post-operative care.

5) Remove foreign bodies from the eye.

6) Provide vision therapy and low vision rehabilitation.

7) Consult with and refer patients to ophthalmologist or other health care practitioner if additional medical treatment is determined necessary.

8) Educate and counsel patients on contact lens care, visual hygiene, lighting arrangements and safety factors.

9) Examine eyes, using observation, instruments and pharmaceutical agents, to determine visual acuity and perception, focus and coordination and to diagnose diseases and other abnormalities such as glaucoma or color blindness.

Knowledge	Knowledge Definitions
Medicine and Dentistry	Knowledge of the information and techniques needed to diagnose and treat human injuries, diseases, and deformities. This includes symptoms, treatment alternatives, drug properties and interactions, and preventive health-care measures.
Customer and Personal Service	Knowledge of principles and processes for providing customer and personal services. This includes customer needs assessment, meeting quality standards for services, and evaluation of customer satisfaction.
English Language	Knowledge of the structure and content of the English language including the meaning and spelling of words, rules of composition, and grammar.
Biology	Knowledge of plant and animal organisms, their tissues, cells, functions, interdependencies, and interactions with each other and the environment.
Mathematics	Knowledge of arithmetic, algebra, geometry, calculus, statistics, and their applications.
Economics and Accounting	Knowledge of economic and accounting principles and practices, the financial markets, banking and the analysis and reporting of financial data.
Administration and Management	Knowledge of business and management principles involved in strategic planning, resource allocation, human resources modeling, leadership technique, production methods, and coordination of people and resources.
Psychology	Knowledge of human behavior and performance; individual differences in ability, personality, and interests; learning and motivation; psychological research methods; and the assessment and treatment of behavioral and affective disorders.
Sales and Marketing	Knowledge of principles and methods for showing, promoting, and selling products or services. This includes marketing strategy and tactics, product demonstration, sales techniques, and sales control systems.
Personnel and Human Resources	Knowledge of principles and procedures for personnel recruitment, selection, training, compensation and benefits, labor relations and negotiation, and personnel information systems.
Clerical	Knowledge of administrative and clerical procedures and systems such as word processing, managing files and records, stenography and transcription, designing forms, and other office procedures and terminology.
Education and Training	Knowledge of principles and methods for curriculum and training design, teaching and instruction for individuals and groups, and the measurement of training effects.
Chemistry	Knowledge of the chemical composition, structure, and properties of substances and of the chemical processes and transformations that they undergo. This includes uses of chemicals and their interactions, danger signs, production techniques, and disposal methods.
Production and Processing	Knowledge of raw materials, production processes, quality control, costs, and other techniques for maximizing the effective manufacture and distribution of goods.
Physics	Knowledge and prediction of physical principles, laws, their interrelationships, and applications to understanding fluid, material, and atmospheric dynamics, and mechanical, electrical, atomic and sub-atomic structures and processes.
Therapy and Counseling	Knowledge of principles, methods, and procedures for diagnosis, treatment, and rehabilitation of physical and mental dysfunctions, and for career counseling and guidance.

Computers and Electronics	Knowledge of circuit boards, processors, chips, electronic equipment, and computer hardware and software, including applications and programming.
Law and Government	Knowledge of laws, legal codes, court procedures, precedents, government regulations, executive orders, agency rules, and the democratic political process.
Engineering and Technology	Knowledge of the practical application of engineering science and technology. This includes applying principles, techniques, procedures, and equipment to the design and production of various goods and services.
Sociology and Anthropology	Knowledge of group behavior and dynamics, societal trends and influences, human migrations, ethnicity, cultures and their history and origins.
Telecommunications	Knowledge of transmission, broadcasting, switching, control, and operation of telecommunications systems.
Communications and Media	Knowledge of media production, communication, and dissemination techniques and methods. This includes alternative ways to inform and entertain via written, oral, and visual media.
Foreign Language	Knowledge of the structure and content of a foreign (non-English) language including the meaning and spelling of words, rules of composition and grammar, and pronunciation.
Public Safety and Security	Knowledge of relevant equipment, policies, procedures, and strategies to promote effective local, state, or national security operations for the protection of people, data, property, and institutions.
Design	Knowledge of design techniques, tools, and principles involved in production of precision technical plans, blueprints, drawings, and models.
Mechanical	Knowledge of machines and tools, including their designs, uses, repair, and maintenance.
Transportation	Knowledge of principles and methods for moving people or goods by air, rail, sea, or road, including the relative costs and benefits.
Philosophy and Theology	Knowledge of different philosophical systems and religions. This includes their basic principles, values, ethics, ways of thinking, customs, practices, and their impact on human culture.
Geography	Knowledge of principles and methods for describing the features of land, sea, and air masses, including their physical characteristics, locations, interrelationships, and distribution of plant, animal, and human life.
History and Archeology	Knowledge of historical events and their causes, indicators, and effects on civilizations and cultures.
Building and Construction	Knowledge of materials, methods, and the tools involved in the construction or repair of houses, buildings, or other structures such as highways and roads.
Fine Arts	Knowledge of the theory and techniques required to compose, produce, and perform works of music, dance, visual arts, drama, and sculpture.
Food Production	Knowledge of techniques and equipment for planting, growing, and harvesting food products (both plant and animal) for consumption, including storage/handling techniques.

Skills	Skills Definitions
Active Listening	Giving full attention to what other people are saying, taking time to understand the points being made, asking questions as appropriate, and not interrupting at inappropriate times.
Reading Comprehension	Understanding written sentences and paragraphs in work related documents.
Judgment and Decision Making	Considering the relative costs and benefits of potential actions to choose the most appropriate one.
Critical Thinking	Using logic and reasoning to identify the strengths and weaknesses of alternative solutions, conclusions or approaches to problems.
Science	Using scientific rules and methods to solve problems.
Service Orientation	Actively looking for ways to help people.
Speaking	Talking to others to convey information effectively.
Complex Problem Solving	Identifying complex problems and reviewing related information to develop and evaluate options and implement solutions.
Instructing	Teaching others how to do something.
Mathematics	Using mathematics to solve problems.
Active Learning	Understanding the implications of new information for both current and future problem-solving and decision-making.
Coordination	Adjusting actions in relation to others' actions.
Persuasion	Persuading others to change their minds or behavior.

Social Perceptiveness	Being aware of others' reactions and understanding why they react as they do.
Time Management	Managing one's own time and the time of others.
Equipment Selection	Determining the kind of tools and equipment needed to do a job.
Management of Personnel Resources	Motivating, developing, and directing people as they work, identifying the best people for the job.
Writing	Communicating effectively in writing as appropriate for the needs of the audience.
Learning Strategies	Selecting and using training/instructional methods and procedures appropriate for the situation when learning or teaching new things.
Monitoring	Monitoring/Assessing performance of yourself, other individuals, or organizations to make improvements or take corrective action.
Troubleshooting	Determining causes of operating errors and deciding what to do about it.
Quality Control Analysis	Conducting tests and inspections of products, services, or processes to evaluate quality or performance.
Negotiation	Bringing others together and trying to reconcile differences.
Operation and Control	Controlling operations of equipment or systems.
Operation Monitoring	Watching gauges, dials, or other indicators to make sure a machine is working properly.
Systems Evaluation	Identifying measures or indicators of system performance and the actions needed to improve or correct performance, relative to the goals of the system.
Management of Material Resources	Obtaining and seeing to the appropriate use of equipment, facilities, and materials needed to do certain work.
Operations Analysis	Analyzing needs and product requirements to create a design.
Management of Financial Resources	Determining how money will be spent to get the work done, and accounting for these expenditures.
Equipment Maintenance	Performing routine maintenance on equipment and determining when and what kind of maintenance is needed.
Technology Design	Generating or adapting equipment and technology to serve user needs.
Installation	Installing equipment, machines, wiring, or programs to meet specifications.
Systems Analysis	Determining how a system should work and how changes in conditions, operations, and the environment will affect outcomes.
Repairing	Repairing machines or systems using the needed tools.
Programming	Writing computer programs for various purposes.

Ability	**Ability Definitions**
Oral Expression	The ability to communicate information and ideas in speaking so others will understand.
Problem Sensitivity	The ability to tell when something is wrong or is likely to go wrong. It does not involve solving the problem, only recognizing there is a problem.
Arm-Hand Steadiness	The ability to keep your hand and arm steady while moving your arm or while holding your arm and hand in one position.
Oral Comprehension	The ability to listen to and understand information and ideas presented through spoken words and sentences.
Near Vision	The ability to see details at close range (within a few feet of the observer).
Inductive Reasoning	The ability to combine pieces of information to form general rules or conclusions (includes finding a relationship among seemingly unrelated events).
Speech Recognition	The ability to identify and understand the speech of another person.
Speech Clarity	The ability to speak clearly so others can understand you.
Manual Dexterity	The ability to quickly move your hand, your hand together with your arm, or your two hands to grasp, manipulate, or assemble objects.
Finger Dexterity	The ability to make precisely coordinated movements of the fingers of one or both hands to grasp, manipulate, or assemble very small objects.
Written Comprehension	The ability to read and understand information and ideas presented in writing.
Deductive Reasoning	The ability to apply general rules to specific problems to produce answers that make sense.
Control Precision	The ability to quickly and repeatedly adjust the controls of a machine or a vehicle to exact positions.
Flexibility of Closure	The ability to identify or detect a known pattern (a figure, object, word, or sound) that is hidden in other distracting material.

Written Expression	The ability to communicate information and ideas in writing so others will understand.
Information Ordering	The ability to arrange things or actions in a certain order or pattern according to a specific rule or set of rules (e.g., patterns of numbers, letters, words, pictures, mathematical operations).
Visual Color Discrimination	The ability to match or detect differences between colors, including shades of color and brightness.
Speed of Closure	The ability to quickly make sense of, combine, and organize information into meaningful patterns.
Multilimb Coordination	The ability to coordinate two or more limbs (for example, two arms, two legs, or one leg and one arm) while sitting, standing, or lying down. It does not involve performing the activities while the whole body is in motion.
Category Flexibility	The ability to generate or use different sets of rules for combining or grouping things in different ways.
Selective Attention	The ability to concentrate on a task over a period of time without being distracted.
Far Vision	The ability to see details at a distance.
Depth Perception	The ability to judge which of several objects is closer or farther away from you, or to judge the distance between you and an object.
Originality	The ability to come up with unusual or clever ideas about a given topic or situation, or to develop creative ways to solve a problem.
Perceptual Speed	The ability to quickly and accurately compare similarities and differences among sets of letters, numbers, objects, pictures, or patterns. The things to be compared may be presented at the same time or one after the other. This ability also includes comparing a presented object with a remembered object.
Visualization	The ability to imagine how something will look after it is moved around or when its parts are moved or rearranged.
Memorization	The ability to remember information such as words, numbers, pictures, and procedures.
Number Facility	The ability to add, subtract, multiply, or divide quickly and correctly.
Trunk Strength	The ability to use your abdominal and lower back muscles to support part of the body repeatedly or continuously over time without 'giving out' or fatiguing.
Time Sharing	The ability to shift back and forth between two or more activities or sources of information (such as speech, sounds, touch, or other sources).
Mathematical Reasoning	The ability to choose the right mathematical methods or formulas to solve a problem.
Fluency of Ideas	The ability to come up with a number of ideas about a topic (the number of ideas is important, not their quality, correctness, or creativity).
Wrist-Finger Speed	The ability to make fast, simple, repeated movements of the fingers, hands, and wrists.
Rate Control	The ability to time your movements or the movement of a piece of equipment in anticipation of changes in the speed and/or direction of a moving object or scene.
Reaction Time	The ability to quickly respond (with the hand, finger, or foot) to a signal (sound, light, picture) when it appears.
Response Orientation	The ability to choose quickly between two or more movements in response to two or more different signals (lights, sounds, pictures). It includes the speed with which the correct response is started with the hand, foot, or other body part.
Spatial Orientation	The ability to know your location in relation to the environment or to know where other objects are in relation to you.
Auditory Attention	The ability to focus on a single source of sound in the presence of other distracting sounds.
Hearing Sensitivity	The ability to detect or tell the differences between sounds that vary in pitch and loudness.
Night Vision	The ability to see under low light conditions.
Extent Flexibility	The ability to bend, stretch, twist, or reach with your body, arms, and/or legs.
Static Strength	The ability to exert maximum muscle force to lift, push, pull, or carry objects.
Sound Localization	The ability to tell the direction from which a sound originated.
Glare Sensitivity	The ability to see objects in the presence of glare or bright lighting.
Peripheral Vision	The ability to see objects or movement of objects to one's side when the eyes are looking ahead.
Stamina	The ability to exert yourself physically over long periods of time without getting winded or out of breath.
Dynamic Strength	The ability to exert muscle force repeatedly or continuously over time. This involves muscular endurance and resistance to muscle fatigue.

Explosive Strength	The ability to use short bursts of muscle force to propel oneself (as in jumping or sprinting), or to throw an object.
Gross Body Coordination	The ability to coordinate the movement of your arms, legs, and torso together when the whole body is in motion.
Gross Body Equilibrium	The ability to keep or regain your body balance or stay upright when in an unstable position.
Speed of Limb Movement	The ability to quickly move the arms and legs.
Dynamic Flexibility	The ability to quickly and repeatedly bend, stretch, twist, or reach out with your body, arms, and/or legs.

Work_Activity	Work_Activity Definitions
Making Decisions and Solving Problems	Analyzing information and evaluating results to choose the best solution and solve problems.
Performing for or Working Directly with the Public	Performing for people or dealing directly with the public. This includes serving customers in restaurants and stores, and receiving clients or guests.
Updating and Using Relevant Knowledge	Keeping up-to-date technically and applying new knowledge to your job.
Establishing and Maintaining Interpersonal Relatio	Developing constructive and cooperative working relationships with others, and maintaining them over time.
Processing Information	Compiling, coding, categorizing, calculating, tabulating, auditing, or verifying information or data.
Evaluating Information to Determine Compliance wit	Using relevant information and individual judgment to determine whether events or processes comply with laws, regulations, or standards.
Organizing, Planning, and Prioritizing Work	Developing specific goals and plans to prioritize, organize, and accomplish your work.
Assisting and Caring for Others	Providing personal assistance, medical attention, emotional support, or other personal care to others such as coworkers, customers, or patients.
Getting Information	Observing, receiving, and otherwise obtaining information from all relevant sources.
Scheduling Work and Activities	Scheduling events, programs, and activities, as well as the work of others.
Communicating with Supervisors, Peers, or Subordin	Providing information to supervisors, co-workers, and subordinates by telephone, in written form, e-mail, or in person.
Resolving Conflicts and Negotiating with Others	Handling complaints, settling disputes, and resolving grievances and conflicts, or otherwise negotiating with others.
Selling or Influencing Others	Convincing others to buy merchandise/goods or to otherwise change their minds or actions.
Training and Teaching Others	Identifying the educational needs of others, developing formal educational or training programs or classes, and teaching or instructing others.
Interpreting the Meaning of Information for Others	Translating or explaining what information means and how it can be used.
Documenting/Recording Information	Entering, transcribing, recording, storing, or maintaining information in written or electronic/magnetic form.
Provide Consultation and Advice to Others	Providing guidance and expert advice to management or other groups on technical, systems-, or process-related topics.
Performing Administrative Activities	Performing day-to-day administrative tasks such as maintaining information files and processing paperwork.
Identifying Objects, Actions, and Events	Identifying information by categorizing, estimating, recognizing differences or similarities, and detecting changes in circumstances or events.
Handling and Moving Objects	Using hands and arms in handling, installing, positioning, and moving materials, and manipulating things.
Analyzing Data or Information	Identifying the underlying principles, reasons, or facts of information by breaking down information or data into separate parts.
Interacting With Computers	Using computers and computer systems (including hardware and software) to program, write software, set up functions, enter data, or process information.
Coaching and Developing Others	Identifying the developmental needs of others and coaching, mentoring, or otherwise helping others to improve their knowledge or skills.
Judging the Qualities of Things, Services, or Peop	Assessing the value, importance, or quality of things or people.
Guiding, Directing, and Motivating Subordinates	Providing guidance and direction to subordinates, including setting performance standards and monitoring performance.
Monitor Processes, Materials, or Surroundings	Monitoring and reviewing information from materials, events, or the environment, to detect or assess problems.
Controlling Machines and Processes	Using either control mechanisms or direct physical activity to operate machines or processes (not including computers or vehicles).

Thinking Creatively	Developing, designing, or creating new applications, ideas, relationships, systems, or products, including artistic contributions.
Coordinating the Work and Activities of Others	Getting members of a group to work together to accomplish tasks.
Developing and Building Teams	Encouraging and building mutual trust, respect, and cooperation among team members.
Developing Objectives and Strategies	Establishing long-range objectives and specifying the strategies and actions to achieve them.
Inspecting Equipment, Structures, or Material	Inspecting equipment, structures, or materials to identify the cause of errors or other problems or defects.
Staffing Organizational Units	Recruiting, interviewing, selecting, hiring, and promoting employees in an organization.
Estimating the Quantifiable Characteristics of Pro	Estimating sizes, distances, and quantities; or determining time, costs, resources, or materials needed to perform a work activity.
Monitoring and Controlling Resources	Monitoring and controlling resources and overseeing the spending of money.
Communicating with Persons Outside Organization	Communicating with people outside the organization, representing the organization to customers, the public, government, and other external sources. This information can be exchanged in person, in writing, or by telephone or e-mail.
Performing General Physical Activities	Performing physical activities that require considerable use of your arms and legs and moving your whole body, such as climbing, lifting, balancing, walking, stooping, and handling of materials.
Repairing and Maintaining Electronic Equipment	Servicing, repairing, calibrating, regulating, fine-tuning, or testing machines, devices, and equipment that operate primarily on the basis of electrical or electronic (not mechanical) principles.
Repairing and Maintaining Mechanical Equipment	Servicing, repairing, adjusting, and testing machines, devices, moving parts, and equipment that operate primarily on the basis of mechanical (not electronic) principles.
Operating Vehicles, Mechanized Devices, or Equipme	Running, maneuvering, navigating, or driving vehicles or mechanized equipment, such as forklifts, passenger vehicles, aircraft, or water craft.
Drafting, Laying Out, and Specifying Technical Dev	Providing documentation, detailed instructions, drawings, or specifications to tell others about how devices, parts, equipment, or structures are to be fabricated, constructed, assembled, modified, maintained, or used.

Work_Context	Work_Context Definitions
Freedom to Make Decisions	How much decision making freedom, without supervision, does the job offer?
Face-to-Face Discussions	How often do you have to have face-to-face discussions with individuals or teams in this job?
Physical Proximity	To what extent does this job require the worker to perform job tasks in close physical proximity to other people?
Contact With Others	How much does this job require the worker to be in contact with others (face-to-face, by telephone, or otherwise) in order to perform it?
Indoors, Environmentally Controlled	How often does this job require working indoors in environmentally controlled conditions?
Structured versus Unstructured Work	To what extent is this job structured for the worker, rather than allowing the worker to determine tasks, priorities, and goals?
Deal With External Customers	How important is it to work with external customers or the public in this job?
Telephone	How often do you have telephone conversations in this job?
Importance of Being Exact or Accurate	How important is being very exact or highly accurate in performing this job?
Frequency of Decision Making	How frequently is the worker required to make decisions that affect other people, the financial resources, and/or the image and reputation of the organization?
Impact of Decisions on Co-workers or Company Resul	How do the decisions an employee makes impact the results of co-workers, clients or the company?
Work With Work Group or Team	How important is it to work with others in a group or team in this job?
Exposed to Disease or Infections	How often does this job require exposure to disease/infections?
Spend Time Using Your Hands to Handle, Control, or	How much does this job require using your hands to handle, control, or feel objects, tools or controls?
Time Pressure	How often does this job require the worker to meet strict deadlines?
Responsibility for Outcomes and Results	How responsible is the worker for work outcomes and results of other workers?

Letters and Memos	How often does the job require written letters and memos?
Responsible for Others' Health and Safety	How much responsibility is there for the health and safety of others in this job?
Level of Competition	To what extent does this job require the worker to compete or to be aware of competitive pressures?
Spend Time Making Repetitive Motions	How much does this job require making repetitive motions?
Consequence of Error	How serious would the result usually be if the worker made a mistake that was not readily correctable?
Coordinate or Lead Others	How important is it to coordinate or lead others in accomplishing work activities in this job?
Frequency of Conflict Situations	How often are there conflict situations the employee has to face in this job?
Spend Time Sitting	How much does this job require sitting?
Deal With Unpleasant or Angry People	How frequently does the worker have to deal with unpleasant, angry, or discourteous individuals as part of the job requirements?
Spend Time Standing	How much does this job require standing?
Electronic Mail	How often do you use electronic mail in this job?
Importance of Repeating Same Tasks	How important is repeating the same physical activities (e.g., key entry) or mental activities (e.g., checking entries in a ledger) over and over, without stopping, to performing this job?
Degree of Automation	How automated is the job?
Spend Time Bending or Twisting the Body	How much does this job require bending or twisting your body?
Wear Common Protective or Safety Equipment such as	How much does this job require wearing common protective or safety equipment such as safety shoes, glasses, gloves, hard hats or life jackets?
Spend Time Walking and Running	How much does this job require walking and running?
Exposed to Contaminants	How often does this job require working exposed to contaminants (such as pollutants, gases, dust or odors)?
Public Speaking	How often do you have to perform public speaking in this job?
Deal With Physically Aggressive People	How frequently does this job require the worker to deal with physical aggression of violent individuals?
Extremely Bright or Inadequate Lighting	How often does this job require working in extremely bright or inadequate lighting conditions?
Sounds, Noise Levels Are Distracting or Uncomforta	How often does this job require working exposed to sounds and noise levels that are distracting or uncomfortable?
Exposed to Minor Burns, Cuts, Bites, or Stings	How often does this job require exposure to minor burns, cuts, bites, or stings?
Exposed to Hazardous Conditions	How often does this job require exposure to hazardous conditions?
Cramped Work Space, Awkward Positions	How often does this job require working in cramped work spaces that requires getting into awkward positions?
Spend Time Kneeling, Crouching, Stooping, or Crawl	How much does this job require kneeling, crouching, stooping or crawling?
Wear Specialized Protective or Safety Equipment su	How much does this job require wearing specialized protective or safety equipment such as breathing apparatus, safety harness, full protection suits, or radiation protection?
Spend Time Keeping or Regaining Balance	How much does this job require keeping or regaining your balance?
Pace Determined by Speed of Equipment	How important is it to this job that the pace is determined by the speed of equipment or machinery? (This does not refer to keeping busy at all times on this job.)
Spend Time Climbing Ladders, Scaffolds, or Poles	How much does this job require climbing ladders, scaffolds, or poles?
Indoors, Not Environmentally Controlled	How often does this job require working indoors in non-controlled environmental conditions (e.g., warehouse without heat)?
Very Hot or Cold Temperatures	How often does this job require working in very hot (above 90 F degrees) or very cold (below 32 F degrees) temperatures?
In an Enclosed Vehicle or Equipment	How often does this job require working in a closed vehicle or equipment (e.g., car)?
Outdoors, Exposed to Weather	How often does this job require working outdoors, exposed to all weather conditions?
Exposed to High Places	How often does this job require exposure to high places?
Exposed to Radiation	How often does this job require exposure to radiation?
Exposed to Whole Body Vibration	How often does this job require exposure to whole body vibration (e.g., operate a jackhammer)?
In an Open Vehicle or Equipment	How often does this job require working in an open vehicle or equipment (e.g., tractor)?
Outdoors, Under Cover	How often does this job require working outdoors, under cover (e.g., structure with roof but no walls)?
Exposed to Hazardous Equipment	How often does this job require exposure to hazardous equipment?

Job Zone Component	Job Zone Component Definitions
Title	Job Zone Five: Extensive Preparation Needed
Overall Experience	Extensive skill, knowledge, and experience are needed for these occupations. Many require more than five years of experience. For example, surgeons must complete four years of college and an additional five to seven years of specialized medical training to be able to do their job.
Job Training	Employees may need some on-the-job training, but most of these occupations assume that the person will already have the required skills, knowledge, work-related experience, and/or training.
Job Zone Examples	These occupations often involve coordinating, training, supervising, or managing the activities of others to accomplish goals. Very advanced communication and organizational skills are required. Examples include athletic trainers, lawyers, managing editors, physicists, social psychologists, and surgeons.
SVP Range	(8.0 and above)
Education	A bachelor's degree is the minimum formal education required for these occupations. However, many also require graduate school. For example, they may require a master's degree, and some require a Ph.D., M.D., or J.D. (law degree).

Work_Styles	Work_Styles Definitions
Attention to Detail	Job requires being careful about detail and thorough in completing work tasks.
Concern for Others	Job requires being sensitive to others' needs and feelings and being understanding and helpful on the job.
Integrity	Job requires being honest and ethical.
Dependability	Job requires being reliable, responsible, and dependable, and fulfilling obligations.
Cooperation	Job requires being pleasant with others on the job and displaying a good-natured, cooperative attitude.
Self Control	Job requires maintaining composure, keeping emotions in check, controlling anger, and avoiding aggressive behavior, even in very difficult situations.
Analytical Thinking	Job requires analyzing information and using logic to address work-related issues and problems.
Stress Tolerance	Job requires accepting criticism and dealing calmly and effectively with high stress situations.
Adaptability/Flexibility	Job requires being open to change (positive or negative) and to considerable variety in the workplace.
Initiative	Job requires a willingness to take on responsibilities and challenges.
Independence	Job requires developing one's own ways of doing things, guiding oneself with little or no supervision, and depending on oneself to get things done.
Achievement/Effort	Job requires establishing and maintaining personally challenging achievement goals and exerting effort toward mastering tasks.
Persistence	Job requires persistence in the face of obstacles.
Leadership	Job requires a willingness to lead, take charge, and offer opinions and direction.
Social Orientation	Job requires preferring to work with others rather than alone, and being personally connected with others on the job.
Innovation	Job requires creativity and alternative thinking to develop new ideas for and answers to work-related problems.

29-1051.00 - Pharmacists

Compound and dispense medications following prescriptions issued by physicians, dentists, or other authorized medical practitioners.

Tasks

1) Compound and dispense medications as prescribed by doctors and dentists, by calculating, weighing, measuring, and mixing ingredients, or oversee these activities.

2) Maintain records, such as pharmacy files, patient profiles, charge system files, inventories, control records for radioactive nuclei, and registries of poisons, narcotics, and controlled drugs.

3) Review prescriptions to assure accuracy, to ascertain the needed ingredients, and to evaluate their suitability.

4) Advise customers on the selection of medication brands, medical equipment and health-care supplies.

5) Analyze prescribing trends to monitor patient compliance and to prevent excessive usage or harmful interactions.

6) Order and purchase pharmaceutical supplies, medical supplies, and drugs, maintaining stock and storing and handling it properly.

7) Refer patients to other health professionals and agencies when appropriate.

8) Collaborate with other health care professionals to plan, monitor, review, and evaluate the quality and effectiveness of drugs and drug regimens, providing advice on drug applications and characteristics.

9) Offer health promotion and prevention activities, for example, training people to use devices such as blood pressure or diabetes monitors.

10) Provide specialized services to help patients manage conditions such as diabetes, asthma, smoking cessation, or high blood pressure.

11) Manage pharmacy operations, hiring and supervising staff, performing administrative duties, and buying and selling non-pharmaceutical merchandise.

12) Plan, implement, and maintain procedures for mixing, packaging, and labeling pharmaceuticals, according to policy and legal requirements, to ensure quality, security, and proper disposal.

13) Teach pharmacy students serving as interns in preparation for their graduation or licensure.

14) Assess the identity, strength and purity of medications.

15) Prepare sterile solutions and infusions for use in surgical procedures, emergency rooms, or patients' homes.

16) Work in hospitals, clinics, or for HMOs, dispensing prescriptions, serving as a medical team consultants, or specializing in specific drug therapy areas such as oncology or nuclear pharmacotherapy.

17) Publish educational information for other pharmacists, doctors, and/or patients.

18) Assay radiopharmaceuticals, verify rates of disintegration, and calculate the volume required to produce the desired results, to ensure proper dosages.

Knowledge	Knowledge Definitions
Customer and Personal Service	Knowledge of principles and processes for providing customer and personal services. This includes customer needs assessment, meeting quality standards for services, and evaluation of customer satisfaction.
Medicine and Dentistry	Knowledge of the information and techniques needed to diagnose and treat human injuries, diseases, and deformities. This includes symptoms, treatment alternatives, drug properties and interactions, and preventive health-care measures.
Mathematics	Knowledge of arithmetic, algebra, geometry, calculus, statistics, and their applications.
Chemistry	Knowledge of the chemical composition, structure, and properties of substances and of the chemical processes and transformations that they undergo. This includes uses of chemicals and their interactions, danger signs, production techniques, and disposal methods.
English Language	Knowledge of the structure and content of the English language including the meaning and spelling of words, rules of composition, and grammar.
Computers and Electronics	Knowledge of circuit boards, processors, chips, electronic equipment, and computer hardware and software, including applications and programming.
Administration and Management	Knowledge of business and management principles involved in strategic planning, resource allocation, human resources modeling, leadership technique, production methods, and coordination of people and resources.
Psychology	Knowledge of human behavior and performance; individual differences in ability, personality, and interests; learning and motivation; psychological research methods; and the assessment and treatment of behavioral and affective disorders.
Education and Training	Knowledge of principles and methods for curriculum and training design, teaching and instruction for individuals and groups, and the measurement of training effects.
Biology	Knowledge of plant and animal organisms, their tissues, cells, functions, interdependencies, and interactions with each other and the environment.
Law and Government	Knowledge of laws, legal codes, court procedures, precedents, government regulations, executive orders, agency rules, and the democratic political process.
Therapy and Counseling	Knowledge of principles, methods, and procedures for diagnosis, treatment, and rehabilitation of physical and mental dysfunctions, and for career counseling and guidance.
Clerical	Knowledge of administrative and clerical procedures and systems such as word processing, managing files and records, stenography and transcription, designing forms, and other office procedures and terminology.
Communications and Media	Knowledge of media production, communication, and dissemination techniques and methods. This includes alternative ways to inform and entertain via written, oral, and visual media.
Telecommunications	Knowledge of transmission, broadcasting, switching, control, and operation of telecommunications systems.
Sales and Marketing	Knowledge of principles and methods for showing, promoting, and selling products or services. This includes marketing strategy and tactics, product demonstration, sales techniques, and sales control systems.
Production and Processing	Knowledge of raw materials, production processes, quality control, costs, and other techniques for maximizing the effective manufacture and distribution of goods.
Personnel and Human Resources	Knowledge of principles and procedures for personnel recruitment, selection, training, compensation and benefits, labor relations and negotiation, and personnel information systems.
Physics	Knowledge and prediction of physical principles, laws, their interrelationships, and applications to understanding fluid, material, and atmospheric dynamics, and mechanical, electrical, atomic and sub-atomic structures and processes.
Economics and Accounting	Knowledge of economic and accounting principles and practices, the financial markets, banking and the analysis and reporting of financial data.
Public Safety and Security	Knowledge of relevant equipment, policies, procedures, and strategies to promote effective local, state, or national security operations for the protection of people, data, property, and institutions.
Sociology and Anthropology	Knowledge of group behavior and dynamics, societal trends and influences, human migrations, ethnicity, cultures and their history and origins.
Foreign Language	Knowledge of the structure and content of a foreign (non-English) language including the meaning and spelling of words, rules of composition and grammar, and pronunciation.
Transportation	Knowledge of principles and methods for moving people or goods by air, rail, sea, or road, including the relative costs and benefits.
Engineering and Technology	Knowledge of the practical application of engineering science and technology. This includes applying principles, techniques, procedures, and equipment to the design and production of various goods and services.
Design	Knowledge of design techniques, tools, and principles involved in production of precision technical plans, blueprints, drawings, and models.
Philosophy and Theology	Knowledge of different philosophical systems and religions. This includes their basic principles, values, ethics, ways of thinking, customs, practices, and their impact on human culture.
Mechanical	Knowledge of machines and tools, including their designs, uses, repair, and maintenance.
Building and Construction	Knowledge of materials, methods, and the tools involved in the construction or repair of houses, buildings, or other structures such as highways and roads.
Geography	Knowledge of principles and methods for describing the features of land, sea, and air masses, including their physical characteristics, locations, interrelationships, and distribution of plant, animal, and human life.
Fine Arts	Knowledge of the theory and techniques required to compose, produce, and perform works of music, dance, visual arts, drama, and sculpture.
History and Archeology	Knowledge of historical events and their causes, indicators, and effects on civilizations and cultures.
Food Production	Knowledge of techniques and equipment for planting, growing, and harvesting food products (both plant and animal) for consumption, including storage/handling techniques.

Skills	Skills Definitions
Active Listening	Giving full attention to what other people are saying, taking time to understand the points being made, asking questions as appropriate, and not interrupting at inappropriate times.
Speaking	Talking to others to convey information effectively.
Reading Comprehension	Understanding written sentences and paragraphs in work related documents.
Mathematics	Using mathematics to solve problems.
Science	Using scientific rules and methods to solve problems.
Critical Thinking	Using logic and reasoning to identify the strengths and weaknesses of alternative solutions, conclusions or approaches to problems.
Writing	Communicating effectively in writing as appropriate for the needs of the audience.
Instructing	Teaching others how to do something.
Social Perceptiveness	Being aware of others' reactions and understanding why they react as they do.
Active Learning	Understanding the implications of new information for both current and future problem-solving and decision-making.
Coordination	Adjusting actions in relation to others' actions.
Persuasion	Persuading others to change their minds or behavior.
Service Orientation	Actively looking for ways to help people.
Learning Strategies	Selecting and using training/instructional methods and procedures appropriate for the situation when learning or teaching new things.
Monitoring	Monitoring/Assessing performance of yourself, other individuals, or organizations to make improvements or take corrective action.
Complex Problem Solving	Identifying complex problems and reviewing related information to develop and evaluate options and implement solutions.
Time Management	Managing one's own time and the time of others.
Negotiation	Bringing others together and trying to reconcile differences.
Judgment and Decision Making	Considering the relative costs and benefits of potential actions to choose the most appropriate one.
Management of Personnel Resources	Motivating, developing, and directing people as they work, identifying the best people for the job.
Operation and Control	Controlling operations of equipment or systems.
Troubleshooting	Determining causes of operating errors and deciding what to do about it.
Quality Control Analysis	Conducting tests and inspections of products, services, or processes to evaluate quality or performance.
Management of Financial Resources	Determining how money will be spent to get the work done, and accounting for these expenditures.
Operations Analysis	Analyzing needs and product requirements to create a design.
Equipment Selection	Determining the kind of tools and equipment needed to do a job.
Repairing	Repairing machines or systems using the needed tools.
Systems Evaluation	Identifying measures or indicators of system performance and the actions needed to improve or correct performance, relative to the goals of the system.
Management of Material Resources	Obtaining and seeing to the appropriate use of equipment, facilities, and materials needed to do certain work.
Operation Monitoring	Watching gauges, dials, or other indicators to make sure a machine is working properly.
Equipment Maintenance	Performing routine maintenance on equipment and determining when and what kind of maintenance is needed.
Technology Design	Generating or adapting equipment and technology to serve user needs.
Programming	Writing computer programs for various purposes.
Installation	Installing equipment, machines, wiring, or programs to meet specifications.
Systems Analysis	Determining how a system should work and how changes in conditions, operations, and the environment will affect outcomes.

Ability	Ability Definitions
Oral Expression	The ability to communicate information and ideas in speaking so others will understand.
Problem Sensitivity	The ability to tell when something is wrong or is likely to go wrong. It does not involve solving the problem, only recognizing there is a problem.
Speech Clarity	The ability to speak clearly so others can understand you.
Oral Comprehension	The ability to listen to and understand information and ideas presented through spoken words and sentences.

Written Comprehension	The ability to read and understand information and ideas presented in writing.
Near Vision	The ability to see details at close range (within a few feet of the observer).
Deductive Reasoning	The ability to apply general rules to specific problems to produce answers that make sense.
Speech Recognition	The ability to identify and understand the speech of another person.
Information Ordering	The ability to arrange things or actions in a certain order or pattern according to a specific rule or set of rules (e.g., patterns of numbers, letters, words, pictures, mathematical operations).
Inductive Reasoning	The ability to combine pieces of information to form general rules or conclusions (includes finding a relationship among seemingly unrelated events).
Category Flexibility	The ability to generate or use different sets of rules for combining or grouping things in different ways.
Selective Attention	The ability to concentrate on a task over a period of time without being distracted.
Written Expression	The ability to communicate information and ideas in writing so others will understand.
Time Sharing	The ability to shift back and forth between two or more activities or sources of information (such as speech, sounds, touch, or other sources).
Visual Color Discrimination	The ability to match or detect differences between colors, including shades of color and brightness.
Perceptual Speed	The ability to quickly and accurately compare similarities and differences among sets of letters, numbers, objects, pictures, or patterns. The things to be compared may be presented at the same time or one after the other. This ability also includes comparing a presented object with a remembered object.
Mathematical Reasoning	The ability to choose the right mathematical methods or formulas to solve a problem.
Flexibility of Closure	The ability to identify or detect a known pattern (a figure, object, word, or sound) that is hidden in other distracting material.
Trunk Strength	The ability to use your abdominal and lower back muscles to support part of the body repeatedly or continuously over time without 'giving out' or fatiguing.
Arm-Hand Steadiness	The ability to keep your hand and arm steady while moving your arm or while holding your arm and hand in one position.
Number Facility	The ability to add, subtract, multiply, or divide quickly and correctly.
Memorization	The ability to remember information such as words, numbers, pictures, and procedures.
Speed of Closure	The ability to quickly make sense of, combine, and organize information into meaningful patterns.
Finger Dexterity	The ability to make precisely coordinated movements of the fingers of one or both hands to grasp, manipulate, or assemble very small objects.
Originality	The ability to come up with unusual or clever ideas about a given topic or situation, or to develop creative ways to solve a problem.
Manual Dexterity	The ability to quickly move your hand, your hand together with your arm, or your two hands to grasp, manipulate, or assemble objects.
Fluency of Ideas	The ability to come up with a number of ideas about a topic (the number of ideas is important, not their quality, correctness, or creativity).
Control Precision	The ability to quickly and repeatedly adjust the controls of a machine or a vehicle to exact positions.
Depth Perception	The ability to judge which of several objects is closer or farther away from you, or to judge the distance between you and an object.
Stamina	The ability to exert yourself physically over long periods of time without getting winded or out of breath.
Auditory Attention	The ability to focus on a single source of sound in the presence of other distracting sounds.
Gross Body Coordination	The ability to coordinate the movement of your arms, legs, and torso together when the whole body is in motion.
Far Vision	The ability to see details at a distance.
Speed of Limb Movement	The ability to quickly move the arms and legs.
Visualization	The ability to imagine how something will look after it is moved around or when its parts are moved or rearranged.
Multilimb Coordination	The ability to coordinate two or more limbs (for example, two arms, two legs, or one leg and one arm) while sitting, standing, or lying down. It does not involve performing the activities while the whole body is in motion.

Extent Flexibility	The ability to bend, stretch, twist, or reach with your body, arms, and/or legs.
Hearing Sensitivity	The ability to detect or tell the differences between sounds that vary in pitch and loudness.
Wrist-Finger Speed	The ability to make fast, simple, repeated movements of the fingers, hands, and wrists.
Reaction Time	The ability to quickly respond (with the hand, finger, or foot) to a signal (sound, light, picture) when it appears.
Response Orientation	The ability to choose quickly between two or more movements in response to two or more different signals (lights, sounds, pictures). It includes the speed with which the correct response is started with the hand, foot, or other body part.
Spatial Orientation	The ability to know your location in relation to the environment or to know where other objects are in relation to you.
Static Strength	The ability to exert maximum muscle force to lift, push, pull, or carry objects.
Rate Control	The ability to time your movements or the movement of a piece of equipment in anticipation of changes in the speed and/or direction of a moving object or scene.
Peripheral Vision	The ability to see objects or movement of objects to one's side when the eyes are looking ahead.
Glare Sensitivity	The ability to see objects in the presence of glare or bright lighting.
Gross Body Equilibrium	The ability to keep or regain your body balance or stay upright when in an unstable position.
Dynamic Flexibility	The ability to quickly and repeatedly bend, stretch, twist, or reach out with your body, arms, and/or legs.
Sound Localization	The ability to tell the direction from which a sound originated.
Dynamic Strength	The ability to exert muscle force repeatedly or continuously over time. This involves muscular endurance and resistance to muscle fatigue.
Explosive Strength	The ability to use short bursts of muscle force to propel oneself (as in jumping or sprinting), or to throw an object.
Night Vision	The ability to see under low light conditions.

Work_Activity	Work_Activity Definitions
Getting Information	Observing, receiving, and otherwise obtaining information from all relevant sources.
Interacting With Computers	Using computers and computer systems (including hardware and software) to program, write software, set up functions, enter data, or process information.
Updating and Using Relevant Knowledge	Keeping up-to-date technically and applying new knowledge to your job.
Making Decisions and Solving Problems	Analyzing information and evaluating results to choose the best solution and solve problems.
Establishing and Maintaining Interpersonal Relatio	Developing constructive and cooperative working relationships with others, and maintaining them over time.
Performing for or Working Directly with the Public	Performing for people or dealing directly with the public. This includes serving customers in restaurants and stores, and receiving clients or guests.
Organizing, Planning, and Prioritizing Work	Developing specific goals and plans to prioritize, organize, and accomplish your work.
Processing Information	Compiling, coding, categorizing, calculating, tabulating, auditing, or verifying information or data.
Monitor Processes, Materials, or Surroundings	Monitoring and reviewing information from materials, events, or the environment, to detect or assess problems.
Judging the Qualities of Things, Services, or Peop	Assessing the value, importance, or quality of things or people.
Identifying Objects, Actions, and Events	Identifying information by categorizing, estimating, recognizing differences or similarities, and detecting changes in circumstances or events.
Analyzing Data or Information	Identifying the underlying principles, reasons, or facts of information by breaking down information or data into separate parts.
Evaluating Information to Determine Compliance wit	Using relevant information and individual judgment to determine whether events or processes comply with laws, regulations, or standards.
Documenting/Recording Information	Entering, transcribing, recording, storing, or maintaining information in written or electronic/magnetic form.
Assisting and Caring for Others	Providing personal assistance, medical attention, emotional support, or other personal care to others such as coworkers, customers, or patients.
Communicating with Supervisors, Peers, or Subordin	Providing information to supervisors, co-workers, and subordinates by telephone, in written form, e-mail, or in person.

Interpreting the Meaning of Information for Others	Translating or explaining what information means and how it can be used.
Training and Teaching Others	Identifying the educational needs of others, developing formal educational or training programs or classes, and teaching or instructing others.
Performing Administrative Activities	Performing day-to-day administrative tasks such as maintaining information files and processing paperwork.
Inspecting Equipment, Structures, or Material	Inspecting equipment, structures, or materials to identify the cause of errors or other problems or defects.
Provide Consultation and Advice to Others	Providing guidance and expert advice to management or other groups on technical, systems-, or process-related topics.
Resolving Conflicts and Negotiating with Others	Handling complaints, settling disputes, and resolving grievances and conflicts, or otherwise negotiating with others.
Coordinating the Work and Activities of Others	Getting members of a group to work together to accomplish tasks.
Scheduling Work and Activities	Scheduling events, programs, and activities, as well as the work of others.
Guiding, Directing, and Motivating Subordinates	Providing guidance and direction to subordinates, including setting performance standards and monitoring performance.
Monitoring and Controlling Resources	Monitoring and controlling resources and overseeing the spending of money.
Developing Objectives and Strategies	Establishing long-range objectives and specifying the strategies and actions to achieve them.
Developing and Building Teams	Encouraging and building mutual trust, respect, and cooperation among team members.
Communicating with Persons Outside Organization	Communicating with people outside the organization, representing the organization to customers, the public, government, and other external sources. This information can be exchanged in person, in writing, or by telephone or e-mail.
Coaching and Developing Others	Identifying the developmental needs of others and coaching, mentoring, or otherwise helping others to improve their knowledge or skills.
Thinking Creatively	Developing, designing, or creating new applications, ideas, relationships, systems, or products, including artistic contributions.
Staffing Organizational Units	Recruiting, interviewing, selecting, hiring, and promoting employees in an organization.
Estimating the Quantifiable Characteristics of Pro	Estimating sizes, distances, and quantities; or determining time, costs, resources, or materials needed to perform a work activity.
Controlling Machines and Processes	Using either control mechanisms or direct physical activity to operate machines or processes (not including computers or vehicles).
Selling or Influencing Others	Convincing others to buy merchandise/goods or to otherwise change their minds or actions.
Handling and Moving Objects	Using hands and arms in handling, installing, positioning, and moving materials, and manipulating things.
Performing General Physical Activities	Performing physical activities that require considerable use of your arms and legs and moving your whole body, such as climbing, lifting, balancing, walking, stooping, and handling of materials.
Repairing and Maintaining Electronic Equipment	Servicing, repairing, calibrating, regulating, fine-tuning, or testing machines, devices, and equipment that operate primarily on the basis of electrical or electronic (not mechanical) principles.
Repairing and Maintaining Mechanical Equipment	Servicing, repairing, adjusting, and testing machines, devices, moving parts, and equipment that operate primarily on the basis of mechanical (not electronic) principles.
Drafting, Laying Out, and Specifying Technical Dev	Providing documentation, detailed instructions, drawings, or specifications to tell others about how devices, parts, equipment, or structures are to be fabricated, constructed, assembled, modified, maintained, or used.
Operating Vehicles, Mechanized Devices, or Equipme	Running, maneuvering, navigating, or driving vehicles or mechanized equipment, such as forklifts, passenger vehicles, aircraft, or water craft.

Work_Context	Work_Context Definitions
Importance of Being Exact or Accurate	How important is being very exact or highly accurate in performing this job?
Telephone	How often do you have telephone conversations in this job?
Indoors, Environmentally Controlled	How often does this job require working indoors in environmentally controlled conditions?
Contact With Others	How much does this job require the worker to be in contact with others (face-to-face, by telephone, or otherwise) in order to perform it?
Consequence of Error	How serious would the result usually be if the worker made a mistake that was not readily correctable?

Face-to-Face Discussions	How often do you have to have face-to-face discussions with individuals or teams in this job?
Importance of Repeating Same Tasks	How important is repeating the same physical activities (e.g., key entry) or mental activities (e.g., checking entries in a ledger) over and over, without stopping, to performing this job?
Frequency of Decision Making	How frequently is the worker required to make decisions that affect other people, the financial resources, and/or the image and reputation of the organization?
Freedom to Make Decisions	How much decision making freedom, without supervision, does the job offer?
Spend Time Standing	How much does this job require standing?
Deal With External Customers	How important is it to work with external customers or the public in this job?
Impact of Decisions on Co-workers or Company Resul	How do the decisions an employee makes impact the results of co-workers, clients or the company?
Physical Proximity	To what extent does this job require the worker to perform job tasks in close physical proximity to other people?
Time Pressure	How often does this job require the worker to meet strict deadlines?
Responsibility for Outcomes and Results	How responsible is the worker for work outcomes and results of other workers?
Spend Time Making Repetitive Motions	How much does this job require making repetitive motions?
Exposed to Disease or Infections	How often does this job require exposure to disease/infections?
Structured versus Unstructured Work	To what extent is this job structured for the worker, rather than allowing the worker to determine tasks, priorities, and goals?
Work With Work Group or Team	How important is it to work with others in a group or team in this job?
Deal With Unpleasant or Angry People	How frequently does the worker have to deal with unpleasant, angry, or discourteous individuals as part of the job requirements?
Level of Competition	To what extent does this job require the worker to compete or to be aware of competitive pressures?
Responsible for Others' Health and Safety	How much responsibility is there for the health and safety of others in this job?
Letters and Memos	How often does the job require written letters and memos?
Coordinate or Lead Others	How important is it to coordinate or lead others in accomplishing work activities in this job?
Spend Time Using Your Hands to Handle, Control, or	How much does this job require using your hands to handle, control, or feel objects, tools or controls?
Degree of Automation	How automated is the job?
Sounds, Noise Levels Are Distracting or Uncomforta	How often does this job require working exposed to sounds and noise levels that are distracting or uncomfortable?
Spend Time Walking and Running	How much does this job require walking and running?
Frequency of Conflict Situations	How often are there conflict situations the employee has to face in this job?
Electronic Mail	How often do you use electronic mail in this job?
Spend Time Sitting	How much does this job require sitting?
Spend Time Bending or Twisting the Body	How much does this job require bending or twisting your body?
Cramped Work Space, Awkward Positions	How often does this job require working in cramped work spaces that requires getting into awkward positions?
Exposed to Contaminants	How often does this job require working exposed to contaminants (such as pollutants, gases, dust or odors)?
Exposed to Minor Burns, Cuts, Bites, or Stings	How often does this job require exposure to minor burns, cuts, bites, or stings?
Wear Specialized Protective or Safety Equipment su	How much does this job require wearing specialized protective or safety equipment such as breathing apparatus, safety harness, full protection suits, or radiation protection?
Wear Common Protective or Safety Equipment such as	How much does this job require wearing common protective or safety equipment such as safety shoes, glasses, gloves, hard hats or live jackets?
Spend Time Kneeling, Crouching, Stooping, or Crawl	How much does this job require kneeling, crouching, stooping or crawling?
Extremely Bright or Inadequate Lighting	How often does this job require working in extremely bright or inadequate lighting conditions?
Exposed to Hazardous Conditions	How often does this job require exposure to hazardous conditions?
Pace Determined by Speed of Equipment	How important is it to this job that the pace is determined by the speed of equipment or machinery? (This does not refer to keeping busy at all times on this job.)
Public Speaking	How often do you have to perform public speaking in this job?

Spend Time Climbing Ladders, Scaffolds, or Poles	How much does this job require climbing ladders, scaffolds, or poles?
Deal With Physically Aggressive People	How frequently does this job require the worker to deal with physical aggression of violent individuals?
In an Enclosed Vehicle or Equipment	How often does this job require working in a closed vehicle or equipment (e.g., car)?
Spend Time Keeping or Regaining Balance	How much does this job require keeping or regaining your balance?
Exposed to Radiation	How often does this job require exposure to radiation?
Outdoors, Exposed to Weather	How often does this job require working outdoors, exposed to all weather conditions?
Exposed to Hazardous Equipment	How often does this job require exposure to hazardous equipment?
Exposed to High Places	How often does this job require exposure to high places?
Indoors, Not Environmentally Controlled	How often does this job require working indoors in non-controlled environmental conditions (e.g., warehouse without heat)?
Exposed to Whole Body Vibration	How often does this job require exposure to whole body vibration (e.g., operate a jackhammer)?
Outdoors, Under Cover	How often does this job require working outdoors, under cover (e.g., structure with roof but no walls)?
Very Hot or Cold Temperatures	How often does this job require working in very hot (above 90 F degrees) or very cold (below 32 F degrees) temperatures?
In an Open Vehicle or Equipment	How often does this job require working in an open vehicle or equipment (e.g., tractor)?

Job Zone Component	Job Zone Component Definitions
Title	Job Zone Five: Extensive Preparation Needed
	Extensive skill, knowledge, and experience are needed for these occupations. Many require more than five years of experience.
Overall Experience	For example, surgeons must complete four years of college and an additional five to seven years of specialized medical training to be able to do their job.
Job Training	Employees may need some on-the-job training, but most of these occupations assume that the person will already have the required skills, knowledge, work-related experience, and/or training.
Job Zone Examples	These occupations often involve coordinating, training, supervising, or managing the activities of others to accomplish goals. Very advanced communication and organizational skills are required. Examples include athletic trainers, lawyers, managing editors, phyicists, social psychologists, and surgeons.
SVP Range	(8.0 and above)
Education	A bachelor's degree is the minimum formal education required for these occupations. However, many also require graduate school. For example, they may require a master's degree, and some require a Ph.D., M.D., or J.D. (law degree).

Work_Styles	Work_Styles Definitions
Attention to Detail	Job requires being careful about detail and thorough in completing work tasks.
Dependability	Job requires being reliable, responsible, and dependable, and fulfilling obligations.
Integrity	Job requires being honest and ethical.
Stress Tolerance	Job requires accepting criticism and dealing calmly and effectively with high stress situations.
Concern for Others	Job requires being sensitive to others' needs and feelings and being understanding and helpful on the job.
Cooperation	Job requires being pleasant with others on the job and displaying a good-natured, cooperative attitude.
Independence	Job requires developing one's own ways of doing things, guiding oneself with little or no supervision, and depending on oneself to get things done.
Analytical Thinking	Job requires analyzing information and using logic to address work-related issues and problems.
Self Control	Job requires maintaining composure, keeping emotions in check, controlling anger, and avoiding aggressive behavior, even in very difficult situations.
Adaptability/Flexibility	Job requires being open to change (positive or negative) and to considerable variety in the workplace.
Persistence	Job requires persistence in the face of obstacles.
Initiative	Job requires a willingness to take on responsibilities and challenges.

Social Orientation	Job requires preferring to work with others rather than alone, and being personally connected with others on the job.
Achievement/Effort	Job requires establishing and maintaining personally challenging achievement goals and exerting effort toward mastering tasks.
Leadership	Job requires a willingness to lead, take charge, and offer opinions and direction.
Innovation	Job requires creativity and alternative thinking to develop new ideas for and answers to work-related problems.

29-1061.00 - Anesthesiologists

Administer anesthetics during surgery or other medical procedures.

Tasks

1) Provide medical care and consultation in many settings, prescribing medication and treatment and referring patients for surgery.

2) Order laboratory tests, x-rays and other diagnostic procedures.

3) Position patient on operating table to maximize patient comfort and surgical accessibility.

4) Inform students and staff of types and methods of anesthesia administration, signs of complications, and emergency methods to counteract reactions.

5) Provide and maintain life support and airway management, and help prepare patients for emergency surgery.

6) Schedule and maintain use of surgical suite, including operating, wash-up, waiting rooms and anesthetic and sterilizing equipment.

7) Coordinate administration of anesthetics with surgeons during operation.

8) Instruct individuals and groups on ways to preserve health and prevent disease.

9) Coordinate and direct work of nurses, medical technicians and other health care providers.

10) Administer anesthetic or sedation during medical procedures, using local, intravenous, spinal or caudal methods.

11) Record type and amount of anesthesia and patient condition throughout procedure.

12) Monitor patient before, during, and after anesthesia and counteract adverse reactions or complications.

13) Manage anesthesiological services, coordinating them with other medical activities and formulating plans and procedures.

14) Decide when patients have recovered or stabilized enough to be sent to another room or ward or to be sent home following outpatient surgery.

15) Confer with other medical professionals to determine type and method of anesthetic or sedation to render patient insensible to pain.

16) Conduct medical research to aid in controlling and curing disease, to investigate new medications, and to develop and test new medical techniques.

17) Diagnose illnesses, using examinations, tests and reports.

29-1062.00 - Family and General Practitioners

Diagnose, treat, and help prevent diseases and injuries that commonly occur in the general population.

Tasks

1) Plan, implement, or administer health programs or standards in hospital, business, or community for information, prevention, or treatment of injury or illness.

2) Conduct research to study anatomy and develop or test medications, treatments, or procedures to prevent or control disease or injury.

3) Coordinate work with nurses, social workers, rehabilitation therapists, pharmacists, psychologists and other health care providers.

4) Explain procedures and discuss test results or prescribed treatments with patients.

5) Collect, record, and maintain patient information, such as medical history, reports, and examination results.

6) Monitor the patients' conditions and progress and re-evaluate treatments as necessary.

7) Prescribe or administer treatment, therapy, medication, vaccination, and other specialized medical care to treat or prevent illness, disease, or injury.

8) Refer patients to medical specialists or other practitioners when necessary.

9) Advise patients and community members concerning diet, activity, hygiene, and disease prevention.

10) Deliver babies.

11) Direct and coordinate activities of nurses, students, assistants, specialists, therapists, and other medical staff.

12) Order, perform and interpret tests, and analyze records, reports and examination information to diagnose patients' condition.

13) Prepare reports for government or management of birth, death, and disease statistics, workforce evaluations, or medical status of individuals.

29-1063.00 - Internists, General

Diagnose and provide non-surgical treatment of diseases and injuries of internal organ systems. Provide care mainly for adults who have a wide range of problems associated with the internal organs.

Tasks

1) Collect, record, and maintain patient information, such as medical history, reports, and examination results.

2) Explain procedures and discuss test results or prescribed treatments with patients.

3) Immunize patients to protect them from preventable diseases.

4) Manage and treat common health problems, such as infections, influenza and pneumonia, as well as serious, chronic, and complex illnesses, in adolescents, adults, and the elderly.

5) Monitor patients' conditions and progress and re-evaluate treatments as necessary.

6) Provide and manage long-term, comprehensive medical care, including diagnosis and non-surgical treatment of diseases, for adult patients in an office or hospital.

7) Refer patient to medical specialist or other practitioner when necessary.

8) Prescribe or administer medication, therapy, and other specialized medical care to treat or prevent illness, disease, or injury.

9) Plan, implement, or administer health programs in hospitals, businesses, or communities for prevention and treatment of injuries or illnesses.

10) Advise patients and community members concerning diet, activity, hygiene, and disease prevention.

11) Direct and coordinate activities of nurses, students, assistants, specialists, therapists, and other medical staff.

12) Prepare government or organizational reports on birth, death, and disease statistics, workforce evaluations, or the medical status of individuals.

13) Provide consulting services to other doctors caring for patients with special or difficult problems.

14) Operate on patients to remove, repair, or improve functioning of diseased or injured body parts and systems.

15) Conduct research to develop or test medications, treatments, or procedures to prevent or control disease or injury.

16) Make diagnoses when different illnesses occur together or in situations where the diagnosis may be obscure.

17) Treat internal disorders, such as hypertension, heart disease, diabetes, and problems of the lung, brain, kidney, and gastrointestinal tract.

18) Advise surgeon of a patient's risk status and recommend appropriate intervention to minimize risk.

29-1064.00 - Obstetricians and Gynecologists

Diagnose, treat, and help prevent diseases of women, especially those affecting the reproductive system and the process of childbirth.

Tasks

1) Refer patient to medical specialist or other practitioner when necessary.

2) Perform cesarean sections or other surgical procedures as needed to preserve patients' health and deliver babies safely.

3) Monitor patients' condition and progress and re-evaluate treatments as necessary.

4) Prescribe or administer therapy, medication, and other specialized medical care to treat or prevent illness, disease, or injury.

5) Collect, record, and maintain patient information, such as medical histories, reports, and examination results.

6) Analyze records, reports, test results, or examination information to diagnose medical condition of patient.

7) Consult with, or provide consulting services to, other physicians.

8) Conduct research to develop or test medications, treatments, or procedures to prevent or control disease or injury.

9) Direct and coordinate activities of nurses, students, assistants, specialists, therapists, and other medical staff.

10) Advise patients and community members concerning diet, activity, hygiene, and disease prevention.

11) Treat diseases of female organs.

12) Care for and treat women during prenatal, natal and post-natal periods.

13) Prepare government and organizational reports on birth, death, and disease statistics, workforce evaluations, or the medical status of individuals.

14) Explain procedures and discuss test results or prescribed treatments with patients.

29-1065.00 - Pediatricians, General

Diagnose, treat, and help prevent children's diseases and injuries.

Tasks

1) Conduct research to study anatomy and develop or test medications, treatments, or procedures to prevent, or control disease or injury.

2) Collect, record, and maintain patient information, such as medical history, reports, and examination results.

3) Examine children regularly to assess their growth and development.

4) Plan and execute medical care programs to aid in the mental and physical growth and development of children and adolescents.

5) Examine patients or order, perform and interpret diagnostic tests to obtain information on medical condition and determine diagnosis.

6) Treat children who have minor illnesses, acute and chronic health problems, and growth and development concerns.

7) Monitor patients' condition and progress and re-evaluate treatments as necessary.

8) Prepare reports for government or management of birth, death, and disease statistics, workforce evaluations, or medical status of individuals.

9) Explain procedures and discuss test results or prescribed treatments with patients and parents or guardians.

10) Plan, implement, or administer health programs or standards in hospital, business, or community for information, prevention, or treatment of injury or illness.

11) Direct and coordinate activities of nurses, students, assistants, specialists, therapists, and other medical staff.

12) Refer patient to medical specialist or other practitioner when necessary.

13) Prescribe or administer treatment, therapy, medication, vaccination, and other specialized medical care to treat or prevent illness, disease, or injury in infants and children.

14) Advise patients, parents or guardians and community members concerning diet, activity, hygiene, and disease prevention.

15) Provide consulting services to other physicians.

29-1066.00 - Psychiatrists

Diagnose, treat, and help prevent disorders of the mind.

Tasks

1) Prescribe, direct, and administer psychotherapeutic treatments or medications to treat mental, emotional, or behavioral disorders.

2) Analyze and evaluate patient data and test or examination findings to diagnose nature and extent of mental disorder.

3) Advise and inform guardians, relatives, and significant others of patients' conditions and treatment.

4) Gather and maintain patient information and records, including social and medical history obtained from patients, relatives, and other professionals.

5) Design individualized care plans, using a variety of treatments.

6) Review and evaluate treatment procedures and outcomes of other psychiatrists and medical professionals.

7) Examine or conduct laboratory or diagnostic tests on patient to provide information on general physical condition and mental disorder.

8) Teach, conduct research, and publish findings to increase understanding of mental, emotional, and behavioral states and disorders.

9) Prepare and submit case reports and summaries to government and mental health agencies.

10) Counsel outpatients and other patients during office visits.

11) Serve on committees to promote and maintain community mental health services and delivery systems.

Knowledge	Knowledge Definitions
Medicine and Dentistry	Knowledge of the information and techniques needed to diagnose and treat human injuries, diseases, and deformities. This includes symptoms, treatment alternatives, drug properties and interactions, and preventive health-care measures.
Therapy and Counseling	Knowledge of principles, methods, and procedures for diagnosis, treatment, and rehabilitation of physical and mental dysfunctions, and for career counseling and guidance.
Psychology	Knowledge of human behavior and performance; individual differences in ability, personality, and interests; learning and motivation; psychological research methods; and the assessment and treatment of behavioral and affective disorders.
English Language	Knowledge of the structure and content of the English language including the meaning and spelling of words, rules of composition, and grammar.
Biology	Knowledge of plant and animal organisms, their tissues, cells, functions, interdependencies, and interactions with each other and the environment.
Education and Training	Knowledge of principles and methods for curriculum and training design, teaching and instruction for individuals and groups, and the measurement of training effects.
Customer and Personal Service	Knowledge of principles and processes for providing customer and personal services. This includes customer needs assessment, meeting quality standards for services, and evaluation of customer satisfaction.
Sociology and Anthropology	Knowledge of group behavior and dynamics, societal trends and influences, human migrations, ethnicity, cultures and their history and origins.
Chemistry	Knowledge of the chemical composition, structure, and properties of substances and of the chemical processes and transformations that they undergo. This includes uses of chemicals and their interactions, danger signs, production techniques, and disposal methods.
Philosophy and Theology	Knowledge of different philosophical systems and religions. This includes their basic principles, values, ethics, ways of thinking, customs, practices, and their impact on human culture.
Mathematics	Knowledge of arithmetic, algebra, geometry, calculus, statistics, and their applications.
Law and Government	Knowledge of laws, legal codes, court procedures, precedents, government regulations, executive orders, agency rules, and the democratic political process.
Public Safety and Security	Knowledge of relevant equipment, policies, procedures, and strategies to promote effective local, state, or national security operations for the protection of people, data, property, and institutions.

Administration and Management	Knowledge of business and management principles involved in strategic planning, resource allocation, human resources modeling, leadership technique, production methods, and coordination of people and resources.
Personnel and Human Resources	Knowledge of principles and procedures for personnel recruitment, selection, training, compensation and benefits, labor relations and negotiation, and personnel information systems.
Computers and Electronics	Knowledge of circuit boards, processors, chips, electronic equipment, and computer hardware and software, including applications and programming.
Communications and Media	Knowledge of media production, communication, and dissemination techniques and methods. This includes alternative ways to inform and entertain via written, oral, and visual media.
Clerical	Knowledge of administrative and clerical procedures and systems such as word processing, managing files and records, stenography and transcription, designing forms, and other office procedures and terminology.
Foreign Language	Knowledge of the structure and content of a foreign (non-English) language including the meaning and spelling of words, rules of composition and grammar, and pronunciation.
Production and Processing	Knowledge of raw materials, production processes, quality control, costs, and other techniques for maximizing the effective manufacture and distribution of goods.
Economics and Accounting	Knowledge of economic and accounting principles and practices, the financial markets, banking and the analysis and reporting of financial data.
Sales and Marketing	Knowledge of principles and methods for showing, promoting, and selling products or services. This includes marketing strategy and tactics, product demonstration, sales techniques, and sales control systems.
Physics	Knowledge and prediction of physical principles, laws, their interrelationships, and applications to understanding fluid, material, and atmospheric dynamics, and mechanical, electrical, atomic and sub- atomic structures and processes.
History and Archeology	Knowledge of historical events and their causes, indicators, and effects on civilizations and cultures.
Geography	Knowledge of principles and methods for describing the features of land, sea, and air masses, including their physical characteristics, locations, interrelationships, and distribution of plant, animal, and human life.
Telecommunications	Knowledge of transmission, broadcasting, switching, control, and operation of telecommunications systems.
Fine Arts	Knowledge of the theory and techniques required to compose, produce, and perform works of music, dance, visual arts, drama, and sculpture.
Transportation	Knowledge of principles and methods for moving people or goods by air, rail, sea, or road, including the relative costs and benefits.
Engineering and Technology	Knowledge of the practical application of engineering science and technology. This includes applying principles, techniques, procedures, and equipment to the design and production of various goods and services.
Mechanical	Knowledge of machines and tools, including their designs, uses, repair, and maintenance.
Food Production	Knowledge of techniques and equipment for planting, growing, and harvesting food products (both plant and animal) for consumption, including storage/handling techniques.
Design	Knowledge of design techniques, tools, and principles involved in production of precision technical plans, blueprints, drawings, and models.
Building and Construction	Knowledge of materials, methods, and the tools involved in the construction or repair of houses, buildings, or other structures such as highways and roads.

Skills	Skills Definitions
Active Listening	Giving full attention to what other people are saying, taking time to understand the points being made, asking questions as appropriate, and not interrupting at inappropriate times.
Critical Thinking	Using logic and reasoning to identify the strengths and weaknesses of alternative solutions, conclusions or approaches to problems.
Active Learning	Understanding the implications of new information for both current and future problem-solving and decision-making.
Social Perceptiveness	Being aware of others' reactions and understanding why they react as they do.

Complex Problem Solving	Identifying complex problems and reviewing related information to develop and evaluate options and implement solutions.
Judgment and Decision Making	Considering the relative costs and benefits of potential actions to choose the most appropriate one.
Time Management	Managing one's own time and the time of others.
Persuasion	Persuading others to change their minds or behavior.
Speaking	Talking to others to convey information effectively.
Reading Comprehension	Understanding written sentences and paragraphs in work related documents.
Writing	Communicating effectively in writing as appropriate for the needs of the audience.
Monitoring	Monitoring/Assessing performance of yourself, other individuals, or organizations to make improvements or take corrective action.
Service Orientation	Actively looking for ways to help people.
Coordination	Adjusting actions in relation to others' actions.
Science	Using scientific rules and methods to solve problems.
Learning Strategies	Selecting and using training/instructional methods and procedures appropriate for the situation when learning or teaching new things.
Negotiation	Bringing others together and trying to reconcile differences.
Instructing	Teaching others how to do something
Systems Evaluation	Identifying measures or indicators of system performance and the actions needed to improve or correct performance, relative to the goals of the system.
Systems Analysis	Determining how a system should work and how changes in conditions, operations, and the environment will affect outcomes.
Quality Control Analysis	Conducting tests and inspections of products, services, or processes to evaluate quality or performance.
Management of Personnel Resources	Motivating, developing, and directing people as they work, identifying the best people for the job.
Operations Analysis	Analyzing needs and product requirements to create a design.
Management of Financial Resources	Determining how money will be spent to get the work done, and accounting for these expenditures.
Troubleshooting	Determining causes of operating errors and deciding what to do about it.
Equipment Selection	Determining the kind of tools and equipment needed to do a job.
Management of Material Resources	Obtaining and seeing to the appropriate use of equipment, facilities, and materials needed to do certain work.
Mathematics	Using mathematics to solve problems.
Equipment Maintenance	Performing routine maintenance on equipment and determining when and what kind of maintenance is needed.
Operation and Control	Controlling operations of equipment or systems.
Technology Design	Generating or adapting equipment and technology to serve user needs.
Repairing	Repairing machines or systems using the needed tools.
Operation Monitoring	Watching gauges, dials, or other indicators to make sure a machine is working properly.
Installation	Installing equipment, machines, wiring, or programs to meet specifications.
Programming	Writing computer programs for various purposes.

Ability	Ability Definitions
Oral Expression	The ability to communicate information and ideas in speaking so others will understand.
Oral Comprehension	The ability to listen to and understand information and ideas presented through spoken words and sentences.
Problem Sensitivity	The ability to tell when something is wrong or is likely to go wrong. It does not involve solving the problem, only recognizing there is a problem.
Inductive Reasoning	The ability to combine pieces of information to form general rules or conclusions (includes finding a relationship among seemingly unrelated events).
Deductive Reasoning	The ability to apply general rules to specific problems to produce answers that make sense.
Written Comprehension	The ability to read and understand information and ideas presented in writing.
Speech Clarity	The ability to speak clearly so others can understand you.
Speech Recognition	The ability to identify and understand the speech of another person.
Written Expression	The ability to communicate information and ideas in writing so others will understand.
Near Vision	The ability to see details at close range (within a few feet of the observer).

Information Ordering	The ability to arrange things or actions in a certain order or pattern according to a specific rule or set of rules (e.g., patterns of numbers, letters, words, pictures, mathematical operations).
Selective Attention	The ability to concentrate on a task over a period of time without being distracted.
Category Flexibility	The ability to generate or use different sets of rules for combining or grouping things in different ways.
Flexibility of Closure	The ability to identify or detect a known pattern (a figure, object, word, or sound) that is hidden in other distracting material.
Fluency of Ideas	The ability to come up with a number of ideas about a topic (the number of ideas is important, not their quality, correctness, or creativity).
Originality	The ability to come up with unusual or clever ideas about a given topic or situation, or to develop creative ways to solve a problem.
Memorization	The ability to remember information such as words, numbers, pictures, and procedures.
Time Sharing	The ability to shift back and forth between two or more activities or sources of information (such as speech, sounds, touch, or other sources).
Mathematical Reasoning	The ability to choose the right mathematical methods or formulas to solve a problem.
Perceptual Speed	The ability to quickly and accurately compare similarities and differences among sets of letters, numbers, objects, pictures, or patterns. The things to be compared may be presented at the same time or one after the other. This ability also includes comparing a presented object with a remembered object.
Speed of Closure	The ability to quickly make sense of, combine, and organize information into meaningful patterns.
Auditory Attention	The ability to focus on a single source of sound in the presence of other distracting sounds.
Static Strength	The ability to exert maximum muscle force to lift, push, pull, or carry objects.
Extent Flexibility	The ability to bend, stretch, twist, or reach with your body, arms, and/or legs.
Response Orientation	The ability to choose quickly between two or more movements in response to two or more different signals (lights, sounds, pictures). It includes the speed with which the correct response is started with the hand, foot, or other body part.
Far Vision	The ability to see details at a distance.
Gross Body Coordination	The ability to coordinate the movement of your arms, legs, and torso together when the whole body is in motion.
Trunk Strength	The ability to use your abdominal and lower back muscles to support part of the body repeatedly or continuously over time without 'giving out' or fatiguing.
Stamina	The ability to exert yourself physically over long periods of time without getting winded or out of breath.
Visualization	The ability to imagine how something will look after it is moved around or when its parts are moved or rearranged.
Reaction Time	The ability to quickly respond (with the hand, finger, or foot) to a signal (sound, light, picture) when it appears.
Visual Color Discrimination	The ability to match or detect differences between colors, including shades of color and brightness.
Explosive Strength	The ability to use short bursts of muscle force to propel oneself (as in jumping or sprinting), or to throw an object.
Number Facility	The ability to add, subtract, multiply, or divide quickly and correctly.
Gross Body Equilibrium	The ability to keep or regain your body balance or stay upright when in an unstable position.
Finger Dexterity	The ability to make precisely coordinated movements of the fingers of one or both hands to grasp, manipulate, or assemble very small objects.
Speed of Limb Movement	The ability to quickly move the arms and legs.
Depth Perception	The ability to judge which of several objects is closer or farther away from you, or to judge the distance between you and an object.
Control Precision	The ability to quickly and repeatedly adjust the controls of a machine or a vehicle to exact positions.
Arm-Hand Steadiness	The ability to keep your hand and arm steady while moving your arm or while holding your arm and hand in one position.
Manual Dexterity	The ability to quickly move your hand, your hand together with your arm, or your two hands to grasp, manipulate, or assemble objects.
Hearing Sensitivity	The ability to detect or tell the differences between sounds that vary in pitch and loudness.
Multilimb Coordination	The ability to coordinate two or more limbs (for example, two arms, two legs, or one leg and one arm) while sitting, standing, or lying down. It does not involve performing the activities while the whole body is in motion.
Peripheral Vision	The ability to see objects or movement of objects to one's side when the eyes are looking ahead.
Dynamic Strength	The ability to exert muscle force repeatedly or continuously over time. This involves muscular endurance and resistance to muscle fatigue.
Sound Localization	The ability to tell the direction from which a sound originated.
Rate Control	The ability to time your movements or the movement of a piece of equipment in anticipation of changes in the speed and/or direction of a moving object or scene.
Dynamic Flexibility	The ability to quickly and repeatedly bend, stretch, twist, or reach out with your body, arms, and/or legs.
Wrist-Finger Speed	The ability to make fast, simple, repeated movements of the fingers, hands, and wrists.
Night Vision	The ability to see under low light conditions.
Spatial Orientation	The ability to know your location in relation to the environment or to know where other objects are in relation to you.
Glare Sensitivity	The ability to see objects in the presence of glare or bright lighting.

Work_Activity	Work_Activity Definitions
Getting Information	Observing, receiving, and otherwise obtaining information from all relevant sources.
Establishing and Maintaining Interpersonal Relatio	Developing constructive and cooperative working relationships with others, and maintaining them over time.
Making Decisions and Solving Problems	Analyzing information and evaluating results to choose the best solution and solve problems.
Assisting and Caring for Others	Providing personal assistance, medical attention, emotional support, or other personal care to others such as coworkers, customers, or patients.
Documenting/Recording Information	Entering, transcribing, recording, storing, or maintaining information in written or electronic/magnetic form.
Updating and Using Relevant Knowledge	Keeping up-to-date technically and applying new knowledge to your job.
Communicating with Supervisors, Peers, or Subordin	Providing information to supervisors, co-workers, and subordinates by telephone, in written form, e-mail, or in person.
Interpreting the Meaning of Information for Others	Translating or explaining what information means and how it can be used.
Analyzing Data or Information	Identifying the underlying principles, reasons, or facts of information by breaking down information or data into separate parts.
Identifying Objects, Actions, and Events	Identifying information by categorizing, estimating, recognizing differences or similarities, and detecting changes in circumstances or events.
Resolving Conflicts and Negotiating with Others	Handling complaints, settling disputes, and resolving grievances and conflicts, or otherwise negotiating with others.
Judging the Qualities of Things, Services, or Peop	Assessing the value, importance, or quality of things or people.
Evaluating Information to Determine Compliance wit	Using relevant information and individual judgment to determine whether events or processes comply with laws, regulations, or standards.
Training and Teaching Others	Identifying the educational needs of others, developing formal educational or training programs or classes, and teaching or instructing others.
Developing Objectives and Strategies	Establishing long-range objectives and specifying the strategies and actions to achieve them.
Developing and Building Teams	Encouraging and building mutual trust, respect, and cooperation among team members.
Provide Consultation and Advice to Others	Providing guidance and expert advice to management or other groups on technical, systems-, or process-related topics.
Organizing, Planning, and Prioritizing Work	Developing specific goals and plans to prioritize, organize, and accomplish your work.
Thinking Creatively	Developing, designing, or creating new applications, ideas, relationships, systems, or products, including artistic contributions.
Coordinating the Work and Activities of Others	Getting members of a group to work together to accomplish tasks.
Processing Information	Compiling, coding, categorizing, calculating, tabulating, auditing, or verifying information or data.
Monitor Processes, Materials, or Surroundings	Monitoring and reviewing information from materials, events, or the environment, to detect or assess problems.

Coaching and Developing Others	Identifying the developmental needs of others and coaching, mentoring, or otherwise helping others to improve their knowledge or skills.
Guiding, Directing, and Motivating Subordinates	Providing guidance and direction to subordinates, including setting performance standards and monitoring performance.
Communicating with Persons Outside Organization	Communicating with people outside the organization, representing the organization to customers, the public, government, and other external sources. This information can be exchanged in person, in writing, or by telephone or e-mail.
Interacting With Computers	Using computers and computer systems (including hardware and software) to program, write software, set up functions, enter data, or process information.
Estimating the Quantifiable Characteristics of Pro	Estimating sizes, distances, and quantities; or determining time, costs, resources, or materials needed to perform a work activity.
Performing for or Working Directly with the Public	Performing for people or dealing directly with the public. This includes serving customers in restaurants and stores, and receiving clients or guests.
Performing Administrative Activities	Performing day-to-day administrative tasks such as maintaining information files and processing paperwork.
Scheduling Work and Activities	Scheduling events, programs, and activities, as well as the work of others.
Staffing Organizational Units	Recruiting, interviewing, selecting, hiring, and promoting employees in an organization.
Selling or Influencing Others	Convincing others to buy merchandise/goods or to otherwise change their minds or actions.
Performing General Physical Activities	Performing physical activities that require considerable use of your arms and legs and moving your whole body, such as climbing, lifting, balancing, walking, stooping, and handling of materials.
Monitoring and Controlling Resources	Monitoring and controlling resources and overseeing the spending of money.
Inspecting Equipment, Structures, or Material	Inspecting equipment, structures, or materials to identify the cause of errors or other problems or defects.
Handling and Moving Objects	Using hands and arms in handling, installing, positioning, and moving materials, and manipulating things.
Operating Vehicles, Mechanized Devices, or Equipme	Running, maneuvering, navigating, or driving vehicles or mechanized equipment, such as forklifts, passenger vehicles, aircraft, or water craft.
Controlling Machines and Processes	Using either control mechanisms or direct physical activity to operate machines or processes (not including computers or vehicles).
Drafting, Laying Out, and Specifying Technical Dev	Providing documentation, detailed instructions, drawings, or specifications to tell others about how devices, parts, equipment, or structures are to be fabricated, constructed, assembled, modified, maintained, or used.
Repairing and Maintaining Electronic Equipment	Servicing, repairing, calibrating, regulating, fine-tuning, or testing machines, devices, and equipment that operate primarily on the basis of electrical or electronic (not mechanical) principles.
Repairing and Maintaining Mechanical Equipment	Servicing, repairing, adjusting, and testing machines, devices, moving parts, and equipment that operate primarily on the basis of mechanical (not electronic) principles.

Work_Context — Work_Context Definitions

Face-to-Face Discussions	How often do you have to have face-to-face discussions with individuals or teams in this job?
Freedom to Make Decisions	How much decision making freedom, without supervision, does the job offer?
Frequency of Decision Making	How frequently is the worker required to make decisions that affect other people, the financial resources, and/or the image and reputation of the organization?
Telephone	How often do you have telephone conversations in this job?
Impact of Decisions on Co-workers or Company Resul	How do the decisions an employee makes impact the results of co-workers, clients or the company?
Contact With Others	How much does this job require the worker to be in contact with others (face-to-face, by telephone, or otherwise) in order to perform it?
Indoors, Environmentally Controlled	How often does this job require working indoors in environmentally controlled conditions?
Work With Work Group or Team	How important is it to work with others in a group or team in this job?
Consequence of Error	How serious would the result usually be if the worker made a mistake that was not readily correctable?
Importance of Being Exact or Accurate	How important is being very exact or highly accurate in performing this job?

Electronic Mail	How often do you use electronic mail in this job?
Structured versus Unstructured Work	To what extent is this job structured for the worker, rather than allowing the worker to determine tasks, priorities, and goals?
Spend Time Sitting	How much does this job require sitting?
Deal With External Customers	How important is it to work with external customers or the public in this job?
Physical Proximity	To what extent does this job require the worker to perform job tasks in close physical proximity to other people?
Time Pressure	How often does this job require the worker to meet strict deadlines?
Deal With Unpleasant or Angry People	How frequently does the worker have to deal with unpleasant, angry, or discourteous individuals as part of the job requirements?
Coordinate or Lead Others	How important is it to coordinate or lead others in accomplishing work activities in this job?
Exposed to Disease or Infections	How often does this job require exposure to disease/infections?
Letters and Memos	How often does the job require written letters and memos?
Frequency of Conflict Situations	How often are there conflict situations the employee has to face in this job?
Deal With Physically Aggressive People	How frequently does this job require the worker to deal with physical aggression of violent individuals?
Responsibility for Outcomes and Results	How responsible is the worker for work outcomes and results of other workers?
Level of Competition	To what extent does this job require the worker to compete or to be aware of competitive pressures?
Responsible for Others' Health and Safety	How much responsibility is there for the health and safety of others in this job?
Sounds, Noise Levels Are Distracting or Uncomforta	How often does this job require working exposed to sounds and noise levels that are distracting or uncomfortable?
Spend Time Standing	How much does this job require standing?
Public Speaking	How often do you have to perform public speaking in this job?
Importance of Repeating Same Tasks	How important is repeating the same physical activities (e.g., key entry) or mental activities (e.g., checking entries in a ledger) over and over, without stopping, to performing this job?
Exposed to Contaminants	How often does this job require working exposed to contaminants (such as pollutants, gases, dust or odors)?
Spend Time Walking and Running	How much does this job require walking and running?
In an Enclosed Vehicle or Equipment	How often does this job require working in a closed vehicle or equipment (e.g., car)?
Spend Time Making Repetitive Motions	How much does this job require making repetitive motions?
Indoors, Not Environmentally Controlled	How often does this job require working indoors in non-controlled environmental conditions (e.g., warehouse without heat)?
Spend Time Using Your Hands to Handle, Control, or	How much does this job require using your hands to handle, control, or feel objects, tools or controls?
Degree of Automation	How automated is the job?
Spend Time Keeping or Regaining Balance	How much does this job require keeping or regaining your balance?
Exposed to Minor Burns, Cuts, Bites, or Stings	How often does this job require exposure to minor burns, cuts, bites, or stings?
Wear Common Protective or Safety Equipment such as	How much does this job require wearing common protective or safety equipment such as safety shoes, glasses, gloves, hard hats or live jackets?
Exposed to Hazardous Equipment	How often does this job require exposure to hazardous equipment?
Spend Time Bending or Twisting the Body	How much does this job require bending or twisting your body?
Exposed to Hazardous Conditions	How often does this job require exposure to hazardous conditions?
Outdoors, Exposed to Weather	How often does this job require working outdoors, exposed to all weather conditions?
Outdoors, Under Cover	How often does this job require working outdoors, under cover (e.g., structure with roof but no walls)?
Extremely Bright or Inadequate Lighting	How often does this job require working in extremely bright or inadequate lighting conditions?
Cramped Work Space, Awkward Positions	How often does this job require working in cramped work spaces that requires getting into awkward positions?
Spend Time Kneeling, Crouching, Stooping, or Crawl	How much does this job require kneeling, crouching, stooping or crawling?
Very Hot or Cold Temperatures	How often does this job require working in very hot (above 90 F degrees) or very cold (below 32 F degrees) temperatures?

Pace Determined by Speed of Equipment	How important is it to this job that the pace is determined by the speed of equipment or machinery? (This does not refer to keeping busy at all times on this job.)
Spend Time Climbing Ladders, Scaffolds, or Poles	How much does this job require climbing ladders, scaffolds, or poles?
In an Open Vehicle or Equipment	How often does this job require working in an open vehicle or equipment (e.g., tractor)?
Exposed to Whole Body Vibration	How often does this job require exposure to whole body vibration (e.g., operate a jackhammer)?
Exposed to High Places	How often does this job require exposure to high places?
Wear Specialized Protective or Safety Equipment su	How much does this job require wearing specialized protective or safety equipment such as breathing apparatus, safety harness, full protection suits, or radiation protection?
Exposed to Radiation	How often does this job require exposure to radiation?

Job Zone Component	Job Zone Component Definitions
Title	Job Zone Five: Extensive Preparation Needed
Overall Experience	Extensive skill, knowledge, and experience are needed for these occupations. Many require more than five years of experience. For example, surgeons must complete four years of college and an additional five to seven years of specialized medical training to be able to do their job.
Job Training	Employees may need some on-the-job training, but most of these occupations assume that the person will already have the required skills, knowledge, work-related experience, and/or training.
Job Zone Examples	These occupations often involve coordinating, training, supervising, or managing the activities of others to accomplish goals. Very advanced communication and organizational skills are required. Examples include athletic trainers, lawyers, managing editors, physicists, social psychologists, and surgeons.
SVP Range	(8.0 and above)
Education	A bachelor's degree is the minimum formal education required for these occupations. However, many also require graduate school. For example, they may require a master's degree, and some require a Ph.D., M.D., or J.D. (law degree).

Work_Styles	Work_Styles Definitions
Concern for Others	Job requires being sensitive to others' needs and feelings and being understanding and helpful on the job.
Integrity	Job requires being honest and ethical.
Self Control	Job requires maintaining composure, keeping emotions in check, controlling anger, and avoiding aggressive behavior, even in very difficult situations.
Attention to Detail	Job requires being careful about detail and thorough in completing work tasks.
Dependability	Job requires being reliable, responsible, and dependable, and fulfilling obligations.
Stress Tolerance	Job requires accepting criticism and dealing calmly and effectively with high stress situations.
Cooperation	Job requires being pleasant with others on the job and displaying a good-natured, cooperative attitude.
Social Orientation	Job requires preferring to work with others rather than alone, and being personally connected with others on the job.
Achievement/Effort	Job requires establishing and maintaining personally challenging achievement goals and exerting effort toward mastering tasks.
Independence	Job requires developing one's own ways of doing things, guiding oneself with little or no supervision, and depending on oneself to get things done.
Adaptability/Flexibility	Job requires being open to change (positive or negative) and to considerable variety in the workplace.
Analytical Thinking	Job requires analyzing information and using logic to address work-related issues and problems.
Persistence	Job requires persistence in the face of obstacles.
Initiative	Job requires a willingness to take on responsibilities and challenges.
Leadership	Job requires a willingness to lead, take charge, and offer opinions and direction.
Innovation	Job requires creativity and alternative thinking to develop new ideas for and answers to work-related problems.

29-1067.00 - Surgeons

Treat diseases, injuries, and deformities by invasive methods, such as manual manipulation or by using instruments and appliances.

Tasks

1) Follow established surgical techniques during the operation.

2) Analyze patient's medical history, medication allergies, physical condition, and examination results to verify operation's necessity and to determine best procedure.

3) Refer patient to medical specialist or other practitioners when necessary.

4) Conduct research to develop and test surgical techniques that can improve operating procedures and outcomes.

5) Manage surgery services, including planning, scheduling and coordination, determination of procedures, and procurement of supplies and equipment.

6) Provide consultation and surgical assistance to other physicians and surgeons.

7) Diagnose bodily disorders and orthopedic conditions and provide treatments, such as medicines and surgeries, in clinics, hospital wards, and operating rooms.

8) Examine patient to provide information on medical condition and surgical risk.

9) Examine instruments, equipment, and operating room to ensure sterility.

10) Operate on patients to correct deformities, repair injuries, prevent and treat diseases, or improve or restore patients' functions.

11) Prescribe preoperative and postoperative treatments and procedures, such as sedatives, diets, antibiotics, and preparation and treatment of the patient's operative area.

12) Direct and coordinate activities of nurses, assistants, specialists, residents and other medical staff.

29-1071.00 - Physician Assistants

Provide healthcare services typically performed by a physician, under the supervision of a physician. Conduct complete physicals, provide treatment, and counsel patients. May, in some cases, prescribe medication. Must graduate from an accredited educational program for physician assistants.

Tasks

1) Prescribe therapy or medication with physician approval.

2) Obtain, compile and record patient medical data, including health history, progress notes and results of physical examination.

3) Interpret diagnostic test results for deviations from normal.

4) Make tentative diagnoses and decisions about management and treatment of patients.

5) Instruct and counsel patients about prescribed therapeutic regimens, normal growth and development, family planning, emotional problems of daily living, and health maintenance.

6) Provide physicians with assistance during surgery or complicated medical procedures.

7) Visit and observe patients on hospital rounds or house calls, updating charts, ordering therapy, and reporting back to physician.

8) Supervise and coordinate activities of technicians and technical assistants.

9) Order medical and laboratory supplies and equipment.

10) Examine patients to obtain information about their physical condition.

11) Administer or order diagnostic tests, such as x-ray, electrocardiogram, and laboratory tests.

Knowledge	Knowledge Definitions
Medicine and Dentistry	Knowledge of the information and techniques needed to diagnose and treat human injuries, diseases, and deformities. This includes symptoms, treatment alternatives, drug properties and interactions, and preventive health-care measures.
Biology	Knowledge of plant and animal organisms, their tissues, cells, functions, interdependencies, and interactions with each other and the environment.

515

Psychology	Knowledge of human behavior and performance; individual differences in ability, personality, and interests; learning and motivation; psychological research methods; and the assessment and treatment of behavioral and affective disorders.
Therapy and Counseling	Knowledge of principles, methods, and procedures for diagnosis, treatment, and rehabilitation of physical and mental dysfunctions, and for career counseling and guidance.
Customer and Personal Service	Knowledge of principles and processes for providing customer and personal services. This includes customer needs assessment, meeting quality standards for services, and evaluation of customer satisfaction.
English Language	Knowledge of the structure and content of the English language including the meaning and spelling of words, rules of composition, and grammar.
Chemistry	Knowledge of the chemical composition, structure, and properties of substances and of the chemical processes and transformations that they undergo. This includes uses of chemicals and their interactions, danger signs, production techniques, and disposal methods.
Mathematics	Knowledge of arithmetic, algebra, geometry, calculus, statistics, and their applications.
Public Safety and Security	Knowledge of relevant equipment, policies, procedures, and strategies to promote effective local, state, or national security operations for the protection of people, data, property, and institutions.
Education and Training	Knowledge of principles and methods for curriculum and training design, teaching and instruction for individuals and groups, and the measurement of training effects.
Law and Government	Knowledge of laws, legal codes, court procedures, precedents, government regulations, executive orders, agency rules, and the democratic political process.
Administration and Management	Knowledge of business and management principles involved in strategic planning, resource allocation, human resources modeling, leadership technique, production methods, and coordination of people and resources.
Philosophy and Theology	Knowledge of different philosophical systems and religions. This includes their basic principles, values, ethics, ways of thinking, customs, practices, and their impact on human culture.
Sociology and Anthropology	Knowledge of group behavior and dynamics, societal trends and influences, human migrations, ethnicity, cultures and their history and origins.
Computers and Electronics	Knowledge of circuit boards, processors, chips, electronic equipment, and computer hardware and software, including applications and programming.
Communications and Media	Knowledge of media production, communication, and dissemination techniques and methods. This includes alternative ways to inform and entertain via written, oral, and visual media.
Personnel and Human Resources	Knowledge of principles and procedures for personnel recruitment, selection, training, compensation and benefits, labor relations and negotiation, and personnel information systems.
Physics	Knowledge and prediction of physical principles, laws, their interrelationships, and applications to understanding fluid, material, and atmospheric dynamics, and mechanical, electrical, atomic and sub-atomic structures and processes.
Clerical	Knowledge of administrative and clerical procedures and systems such as word processing, managing files and records, stenography and transcription, designing forms, and other office procedures and terminology.
Telecommunications	Knowledge of transmission, broadcasting, switching, control, and operation of telecommunications systems.
Foreign Language	Knowledge of the structure and content of a foreign (non-English) language including the meaning and spelling of words, rules of composition and grammar, and pronunciation.
Transportation	Knowledge of principles and methods for moving people or goods by air, rail, sea, or road, including the relative costs and benefits.
Geography	Knowledge of principles and methods for describing the features of land, sea, and air masses, including their physical characteristics, locations, interrelationships, and distribution of plant, animal, and human life.
Sales and Marketing	Knowledge of principles and methods for showing, promoting, and selling products or services. This includes marketing strategy and tactics, product demonstration, sales techniques, and sales control systems.

Food Production	Knowledge of techniques and equipment for planting, growing, and harvesting food products (both plant and animal) for consumption, including storage/handling techniques.
Economics and Accounting	Knowledge of economic and accounting principles and practices, the financial markets, banking and the analysis and reporting of financial data.
Mechanical	Knowledge of machines and tools, including their designs, uses, repair, and maintenance.
History and Archeology	Knowledge of historical events and their causes, indicators, and effects on civilizations and cultures.
Engineering and Technology	Knowledge of the practical application of engineering science and technology. This includes applying principles, techniques, procedures, and equipment to the design and production of various goods and services.
Production and Processing	Knowledge of raw materials, production processes, quality control, costs, and other techniques for maximizing the effective manufacture and distribution of goods.
Design	Knowledge of design techniques, tools, and principles involved in production of precision technical plans, blueprints, drawings, and models.
Fine Arts	Knowledge of the theory and techniques required to compose, produce, and perform works of music, dance, visual arts, drama, and sculpture.
Building and Construction	Knowledge of materials, methods, and the tools involved in the construction or repair of houses, buildings, or other structures such as highways and roads.

Skills	Skills Definitions
Active Listening	Giving full attention to what other people are saying, taking time to understand the points being made, asking questions as appropriate, and not interrupting at inappropriate times.
Active Learning	Understanding the implications of new information for both current and future problem-solving and decision-making.
Speaking	Talking to others to convey information effectively.
Reading Comprehension	Understanding written sentences and paragraphs in work related documents.
Critical Thinking	Using logic and reasoning to identify the strengths and weaknesses of alternative solutions, conclusions or approaches to problems.
Writing	Communicating effectively in writing as appropriate for the needs of the audience.
Coordination	Adjusting actions in relation to others' actions.
Time Management	Managing one's own time and the time of others.
Judgment and Decision Making	Considering the relative costs and benefits of potential actions to choose the most appropriate one.
Science	Using scientific rules and methods to solve problems.
Social Perceptiveness	Being aware of others' reactions and understanding why they react as they do.
Complex Problem Solving	Identifying complex problems and reviewing related information to develop and evaluate options and implement solutions.
Instructing	Teaching others how to do something.
Learning Strategies	Selecting and using training/instructional methods and procedures appropriate for the situation when learning or teaching new things.
Service Orientation	Actively looking for ways to help people.
Persuasion	Persuading others to change their minds or behavior.
Mathematics	Using mathematics to solve problems.
Monitoring	Monitoring/Assessing performance of yourself, other individuals, or organizations to make improvements or take corrective action.
Equipment Selection	Determining the kind of tools and equipment needed to do a job.
Negotiation	Bringing others together and trying to reconcile differences.
Operations Analysis	Analyzing needs and product requirements to create a design.
Technology Design	Generating or adapting equipment and technology to serve user needs.
Troubleshooting	Determining causes of operating errors and deciding what to do about it.
Management of Personnel Resources	Motivating, developing, and directing people as they work, identifying the best people for the job.
Management of Material Resources	Obtaining and seeing to the appropriate use of equipment, facilities, and materials needed to do certain work.
Equipment Maintenance	Performing routine maintenance on equipment and determining when and what kind of maintenance is needed.
Operation and Control	Controlling operations of equipment or systems.

Installation	Installing equipment, machines, wiring, or programs to meet specifications.
Management of Financial Resources	Determining how money will be spent to get the work done, and accounting for these expenditures.
Quality Control Analysis	Conducting tests and inspections of products, services, or processes to evaluate quality or performance.
Operation Monitoring	Watching gauges, dials, or other indicators to make sure a machine is working properly.
Systems Analysis	Determining how a system should work and how changes in conditions, operations, and the environment will affect outcomes.
Systems Evaluation	Identifying measures or indicators of system performance and the actions needed to improve or correct performance, relative to the goals of the system.
Repairing	Repairing machines or systems using the needed tools.
Programming	Writing computer programs for various purposes.

Ability	Ability Definitions
Problem Sensitivity	The ability to tell when something is wrong or is likely to go wrong. It does not involve solving the problem, only recognizing there is a problem.
Oral Expression	The ability to communicate information and ideas in speaking so others will understand.
Oral Comprehension	The ability to listen to and understand information and ideas presented through spoken words and sentences.
Inductive Reasoning	The ability to combine pieces of information to form general rules or conclusions (includes finding a relationship among seemingly unrelated events).
Speech Clarity	The ability to speak clearly so others can understand you.
Deductive Reasoning	The ability to apply general rules to specific problems to produce answers that make sense.
Written Comprehension	The ability to read and understand information and ideas presented in writing.
Near Vision	The ability to see details at close range (within a few feet of the observer).
Written Expression	The ability to communicate information and ideas in writing so others will understand.
Speech Recognition	The ability to identify and understand the speech of another person.
Information Ordering	The ability to arrange things or actions in a certain order or pattern according to a specific rule or set of rules (e.g., patterns of numbers, letters, words, pictures, mathematical operations).
Speed of Closure	The ability to quickly make sense of, combine, and organize information into meaningful patterns.
Flexibility of Closure	The ability to identify or detect a known pattern (a figure, object, word, or sound) that is hidden in other distracting material.
Category Flexibility	The ability to generate or use different sets of rules for combining or grouping things in different ways.
Fluency of Ideas	The ability to come up with a number of ideas about a topic (the number of ideas is important, not their quality, correctness, or creativity).
Trunk Strength	The ability to use your abdominal and lower back muscles to support part of the body repeatedly or continuously over time without 'giving out' or fatiguing.
Selective Attention	The ability to concentrate on a task over a period of time without being distracted.
Time Sharing	The ability to shift back and forth between two or more activities or sources of information (such as speech, sounds, touch, or other sources).
Perceptual Speed	The ability to quickly and accurately compare similarities and differences among sets of letters, numbers, objects, pictures, or patterns. The things to be compared may be presented at the same time or one after the other. This ability also includes comparing a presented object with a remembered object.
Arm-Hand Steadiness	The ability to keep your hand and arm steady while moving your arm or while holding your arm and hand in one position.
Originality	The ability to come up with unusual or clever ideas about a given topic or situation, or to develop creative ways to solve a problem.
Finger Dexterity	The ability to make precisely coordinated movements of the fingers of one or both hands to grasp, manipulate, or assemble very small objects.
Visualization	The ability to imagine how something will look after it is moved around or when its parts are moved or rearranged.
Mathematical Reasoning	The ability to choose the right mathematical methods or formulas to solve a problem.

Manual Dexterity	The ability to quickly move your hand, your hand together with your arm, or your two hands to grasp, manipulate, or assemble objects.
Memorization	The ability to remember information such as words, numbers, pictures, and procedures.
Stamina	The ability to exert yourself physically over long periods of time without getting winded or out of breath.
Number Facility	The ability to add, subtract, multiply, or divide quickly and correctly.
Multilimb Coordination	The ability to coordinate two or more limbs (for example, two arms, two legs, or one leg and one arm) while sitting, standing, or lying down. It does not involve performing the activities while the whole body is in motion.
Far Vision	The ability to see details at a distance.
Gross Body Coordination	The ability to coordinate the movement of your arms, legs, and torso together when the whole body is in motion.
Control Precision	The ability to quickly and repeatedly adjust the controls of a machine or a vehicle to exact positions.
Extent Flexibility	The ability to bend, stretch, twist, or reach with your body, arms, and/or legs.
Hearing Sensitivity	The ability to detect or tell the differences between sounds that vary in pitch and loudness.
Visual Color Discrimination	The ability to match or detect differences between colors, including shades of color and brightness.
Speed of Limb Movement	The ability to quickly move the arms and legs.
Auditory Attention	The ability to focus on a single source of sound in the presence of other distracting sounds.
Static Strength	The ability to exert maximum muscle force to lift, push, pull, or carry objects.
Depth Perception	The ability to judge which of several objects is closer or farther away from you, or to judge the distance between you and an object.
Dynamic Strength	The ability to exert muscle force repeatedly or continuously over time. This involves muscular endurance and resistance to muscle fatigue.
Wrist-Finger Speed	The ability to make fast, simple, repeated movements of the fingers, hands, and wrists.
Gross Body Equilibrium	The ability to keep or regain your body balance or stay upright when in an unstable position.
Response Orientation	The ability to choose quickly between two or more movements in response to two or more different signals (lights, sounds, pictures). It includes the speed with which the correct response is started with the hand, foot, or other body part.
Glare Sensitivity	The ability to see objects in the presence of glare or bright lighting.
Explosive Strength	The ability to use short bursts of muscle force to propel oneself (as in jumping or sprinting), or to throw an object.
Dynamic Flexibility	The ability to quickly and repeatedly bend, stretch, twist, or reach out with your body, arms, and/or legs.
Rate Control	The ability to time your movements or the movement of a piece of equipment in anticipation of changes in the speed and/or direction of a moving object or scene.
Spatial Orientation	The ability to know your location in relation to the environment or to know where other objects are in relation to you.
Night Vision	The ability to see under low light conditions.
Peripheral Vision	The ability to see objects or movement of objects to one's side when the eyes are looking ahead.
Sound Localization	The ability to tell the direction from which a sound originated.
Reaction Time	The ability to quickly respond (with the hand, finger, or foot) to a signal (sound, light, picture) when it appears.

Work_Activity	Work_Activity Definitions
Assisting and Caring for Others	Providing personal assistance, medical attention, emotional support, or other personal care to others such as coworkers, customers, or patients.
Making Decisions and Solving Problems	Analyzing information and evaluating results to choose the best solution and solve problems.
Communicating with Supervisors, Peers, or Subordin	Providing information to supervisors, co-workers, and subordinates by telephone, in written form, e-mail, or in person.
Documenting/Recording Information	Entering, transcribing, recording, storing, or maintaining information in written or electronic/magnetic form.
Performing for or Working Directly with the Public	Performing for people or dealing directly with the public. This includes serving customers in restaurants and stores, and receiving clients or guests.
Getting Information	Observing, receiving, and otherwise obtaining information from all relevant sources.

Establishing and Maintaining Interpersonal Relatio	Developing constructive and cooperative working relationships with others, and maintaining them over time.
Updating and Using Relevant Knowledge	Keeping up-to-date technically and applying new knowledge to your job.
Interpreting the Meaning of Information for Others	Translating or explaining what information means and how it can be used.
Provide Consultation and Advice to Others	Providing guidance and expert advice to management or other groups on technical, systems-, or process-related topics.
Identifying Objects, Actions, and Events	Identifying information by categorizing, estimating, recognizing differences or similarities, and detecting changes in circumstances or events.
Processing Information	Compiling, coding, categorizing, calculating, tabulating, auditing, or verifying information or data.
Analyzing Data or Information	Identifying the underlying principles, reasons, or facts of information by breaking down information or data into separate parts.
Organizing, Planning, and Prioritizing Work	Developing specific goals and plans to prioritize, organize, and accomplish your work.
Monitor Processes, Materials, or Surroundings	Monitoring and reviewing information from materials, events, or the environment, to detect or assess problems.
Training and Teaching Others	Identifying the educational needs of others, developing formal educational or training programs or classes, and teaching or instructing others.
Communicating with Persons Outside Organization	Communicating with people outside the organization, representing the organization to customers, the public, government, and other external sources. This information can be exchanged in person, in writing, or by telephone or e-mail.
Coordinating the Work and Activities of Others	Getting members of a group to work together to accomplish tasks.
Interacting With Computers	Using computers and computer systems (including hardware and software) to program, write software, set up functions, enter data, or process information.
Performing General Physical Activities	Performing physical activities that require considerable use of your arms and legs and moving your whole body, such as climbing, lifting, balancing, walking, stooping, and handling of materials.
Developing Objectives and Strategies	Establishing long-range objectives and specifying the strategies and actions to achieve them.
Developing and Building Teams	Encouraging and building mutual trust, respect, and cooperation among team members.
Evaluating Information to Determine Compliance wit	Using relevant information and individual judgment to determine whether events or processes comply with laws, regulations, or standards.
Resolving Conflicts and Negotiating with Others	Handling complaints, settling disputes, and resolving grievances and conflicts, or otherwise negotiating with others.
Thinking Creatively	Developing, designing, or creating new applications, ideas, relationships, systems, or products, including artistic contributions.
Estimating the Quantifiable Characteristics of Pro	Estimating sizes, distances, and quantities; or determining time, costs, resources, or materials needed to perform a work activity.
Judging the Qualities of Things, Services, or Peop	Assessing the value, importance, or quality of things or people.
Inspecting Equipment, Structures, or Material	Inspecting equipment, structures, or materials to identify the cause of errors or other problems or defects.
Guiding, Directing, and Motivating Subordinates	Providing guidance and direction to subordinates, including setting performance standards and monitoring performance.
Scheduling Work and Activities	Scheduling events, programs, and activities, as well as the work of others.
Monitoring and Controlling Resources	Monitoring and controlling resources and overseeing the spending of money.
Coaching and Developing Others	Identifying the developmental needs of others and coaching, mentoring, or otherwise helping others to improve their knowledge or skills.
Performing Administrative Activities	Performing day-to-day administrative tasks such as maintaining information files and processing paperwork.
Handling and Moving Objects	Using hands and arms in handling, installing, positioning, and moving materials, and manipulating things.
Controlling Machines and Processes	Using either control mechanisms or direct physical activity to operate machines or processes (not including computers or vehicles).
Selling or Influencing Others	Convincing others to buy merchandise/goods or to otherwise change their minds or actions.
Staffing Organizational Units	Recruiting, interviewing, selecting, hiring, and promoting employees in an organization.

Operating Vehicles, Mechanized Devices, or Equipme	Running, maneuvering, navigating, or driving vehicles or mechanized equipment, such as forklifts, passenger vehicles, aircraft, or water craft.
Repairing and Maintaining Electronic Equipment	Servicing, repairing, calibrating, regulating, fine-tuning, or testing machines, devices, and equipment that operate primarily on the basis of electrical or electronic (not mechanical) principles.
Drafting, Laying Out, and Specifying Technical Dev	Providing documentation, detailed instructions, drawings, or specifications to tell others about how devices, parts, equipment, or structures are to be fabricated, constructed, assembled, modified, maintained, or used.
Repairing and Maintaining Mechanical Equipment	Servicing, repairing, adjusting, and testing machines, devices, moving parts, and equipment that operate primarily on the basis of mechanical (not electronic) principles.

Work_Context	Work_Context Definitions
Telephone	How often do you have telephone conversations in this job?
Indoors, Environmentally Controlled	How often does this job require working indoors in environmentally controlled conditions?
Exposed to Disease or Infections	How often does this job require exposure to disease/infections?
Face-to-Face Discussions	How often do you have to have face-to-face discussions with individuals or teams in this job?
Importance of Being Exact or Accurate	How important is being very exact or highly accurate in performing this job?
Contact With Others	How much does this job require the worker to be in contact with others (face-to-face, by telephone, or otherwise) in order to perform it?
Impact of Decisions on Co-workers or Company Resul	How do the decisions an employee makes impact the results of co-workers, clients or the company?
Deal With External Customers	How important is it to work with external customers or the public in this job?
Consequence of Error	How serious would the result usually be if the worker made a mistake that was not readily correctable?
Physical Proximity	To what extent does this job require the worker to perform job tasks in close physical proximity to other people?
Work With Work Group or Team	How important is it to work with others in a group or team in this job?
Structured versus Unstructured Work	To what extent is this job structured for the worker, rather than allowing the worker to determine tasks, priorities, and goals?
Wear Common Protective or Safety Equipment such as	How much does this job require wearing common protective or safety equipment such as safety shoes, glasses, gloves, hard hats or live jackets?
Frequency of Decision Making	How frequently is the worker required to make decisions that affect other people, the financial resources, and/or the image and reputation of the organization?
Letters and Memos	How often does the job require written letters and memos?
Freedom to Make Decisions	How much decision making freedom, without supervision, does the job offer?
Coordinate or Lead Others	How important is it to coordinate or lead others in accomplishing work activities in this job?
Time Pressure	How often does this job require the worker to meet strict deadlines?
Spend Time Standing	How much does this job require standing?
Deal With Unpleasant or Angry People	How frequently does the worker have to deal with unpleasant, angry, or discourteous individuals as part of the job requirements?
Responsible for Others' Health and Safety	How much responsibility is there for the health and safety of others in this job?
Frequency of Conflict Situations	How often are there conflict situations the employee has to face in this job?
Level of Competition	To what extent does this job require the worker to compete or to be aware of competitive pressures?
Electronic Mail	How often do you use electronic mail in this job?
Responsibility for Outcomes and Results	How responsible is the worker for work outcomes and results of other workers?
Spend Time Using Your Hands to Handle, Control, or	How much does this job require using your hands to handle, control, or feel objects, tools or controls?
Spend Time Walking and Running	How much does this job require walking and running?
Importance of Repeating Same Tasks	How important is repeating the same physical activities (e.g., key entry) or mental activities (e.g., checking entries in a ledger) over and over, without stopping, to performing this job?
Spend Time Sitting	How much does this job require sitting?
Public Speaking	How often do you have to perform public speaking in this job?

Exposed to Radiation	How often does this job require exposure to radiation?
Spend Time Making Repetitive Motions	How much does this job require making repetitive motions?
Cramped Work Space, Awkward Positions	How often does this job require working in cramped work spaces that requires getting into awkward positions?
Exposed to Contaminants	How often does this job require working exposed to contaminants (such as pollutants, gases, dust or odors)?
Wear Specialized Protective or Safety Equipment su	How much does this job require wearing specialized protective or safety equipment such as breathing apparatus, safety harness, full protection suits, or radiation protection?
Exposed to Minor Burns, Cuts, Bites, or Stings	How often does this job require exposure to minor burns, cuts, bites, or stings?
Exposed to Hazardous Conditions	How often does this job require exposure to hazardous conditions?
Degree of Automation	How automated is the job?
Spend Time Bending or Twisting the Body	How much does this job require bending or twisting your body?
Sounds, Noise Levels Are Distracting or Uncomforta	How often does this job require working exposed to sounds and noise levels that are distracting or uncomfortable?
In an Enclosed Vehicle or Equipment	How often does this job require working in a closed vehicle or equipment (e.g., car)?
Deal With Physically Aggressive People	How frequently does this job require the worker to deal with physical aggression of violent individuals?
Spend Time Keeping or Regaining Balance	How much does this job require keeping or regaining your balance?
Spend Time Kneeling, Crouching, Stooping, or Crawl	How much does this job require kneeling, crouching, stooping, or crawling?
Extremely Bright or Inadequate Lighting	How often does this job require working in extremely bright or inadequate lighting conditions?
Exposed to Hazardous Equipment	How often does this job require exposure to hazardous equipment?
Very Hot or Cold Temperatures	How often does this job require working in very hot (above 90 F degrees) or very cold (below 32 F degrees) temperatures?
Indoors, Not Environmentally Controlled	How often does this job require working indoors in non-controlled environmental conditions (e.g., warehouse without heat)?
Outdoors, Exposed to Weather	How often does this job require working outdoors, exposed to all weather conditions?
Pace Determined by Speed of Equipment	How important is it to this job that the pace is determined by the speed of equipment or machinery? (This does not refer to keeping busy at all times on this job.)
Spend Time Climbing Ladders, Scaffolds, or Poles	How much does this job require climbing ladders, scaffolds, or poles?
Exposed to High Places	How often does this job require exposure to high places?
In an Open Vehicle or Equipment	How often does this job require working in an open vehicle or equipment (e.g., tractor)?
Outdoors, Under Cover	How often does this job require working outdoors, under cover (e.g., structure with roof but no walls)?
Exposed to Whole Body Vibration	How often does this job require exposure to whole body vibration (e.g., operate a jackhammer)?

Job Zone Component	Job Zone Component Definitions
Title	Job Zone Four: Considerable Preparation Needed
Overall Experience	A minimum of two to four years of work-related skill, knowledge, or experience is needed for these occupations. For example, an accountant must complete four years of college and work for several years in accounting to be considered qualified.
Job Training	Employees in these occupations usually need several years of work-related experience, on-the-job training, and/or vocational training.
Job Zone Examples	Many of these occupations involve coordinating, supervising, managing, or training others. Examples include accountants, chefs and head cooks, computer programmers, historians, pharmacists, and police detectives.
SVP Range	(7.0 to < 8.0)
Education	Most of these occupations require a four - year bachelor's degree, but some do not.

Work_Styles	Work_Styles Definitions
Concern for Others	Job requires being sensitive to others' needs and feelings and being understanding and helpful on the job.
Attention to Detail	Job requires being careful about detail and thorough in completing work tasks.
Cooperation	Job requires being pleasant with others on the job and displaying a good-natured, cooperative attitude.
Stress Tolerance	Job requires accepting criticism and dealing calmly and effectively with high stress situations.
Integrity	Job requires being honest and ethical.
Self Control	Job requires maintaining composure, keeping emotions in check, controlling anger, and avoiding aggressive behavior, even in very difficult situations.
Dependability	Job requires being reliable, responsible, and dependable, and fulfilling obligations.
Adaptability/Flexibility	Job requires being open to change (positive or negative) and to considerable variety in the workplace.
Persistence	Job requires persistence in the face of obstacles.
Initiative	Job requires a willingness to take on responsibilities and challenges.
Social Orientation	Job requires preferring to work with others rather than alone, and being personally connected with others on the job.
Achievement/Effort	Job requires establishing and maintaining personally challenging achievement goals and exerting effort toward mastering tasks.
Independence	Job requires developing one's own ways of doing things, guiding oneself with little or no supervision, and depending on oneself to get things done.
Leadership	Job requires a willingness to lead, take charge, and offer opinions and direction.
Analytical Thinking	Job requires analyzing information and using logic to address work-related issues and problems.
Innovation	Job requires creativity and alternative thinking to develop new ideas for and answers to work-related problems.

29-1081.00 - Podiatrists

Diagnose and treat diseases and deformities of the human foot.

Tasks

1) Perform administrative duties such as hiring employees, ordering supplies, and keeping records.

2) Educate the public about the benefits of foot care through techniques such as speaking engagements, advertising, and other forums.

3) Treat bone, muscle, and joint disorders affecting the feet.

4) Advise patients about treatments and foot care techniques necessary for prevention of future problems.

5) Treat conditions such as corns, calluses, ingrown nails, tumors, shortened tendons, bunions, cysts, and abscesses by surgical methods.

6) Diagnose diseases and deformities of the foot using medical histories, physical examinations, x-rays, and laboratory test results.

7) Prescribe medications, corrective devices, physical therapy, or surgery.

8) Refer patients to physicians when symptoms indicative of systemic disorders, such as arthritis or diabetes, are observed in feet and legs.

9) Correct deformities by means of plaster casts and strapping.

10) Treat deformities using mechanical methods, such as whirlpool or paraffin baths, and electrical methods, such as short wave and low voltage currents.

29-1111.00 - Registered Nurses

Assess patient health problems and needs, develop and implement nursing care plans, and maintain medical records. Administer nursing care to ill, injured, convalescent, or disabled patients. May advise patients on health maintenance and disease prevention or provide case management. Licensing or registration required. Includes advance practice nurses such as: nurse practitioners, clinical nurse specialists, certified nurse midwives, and certified registered nurse anesthetists. Advanced practice nursing is practiced by RNs who have specialized formal, post-basic education and who function in highly autonomous and specialized roles.

Tasks

1) Record patients' medical information and vital signs.

2) Monitor, record and report symptoms and changes in patients' conditions.

3) Consult and coordinate with health care team members to assess, plan, implement and evaluate patient care plans.

4) Prepare patients for, and assist with, examinations and treatments.

5) Monitor all aspects of patient care, including diet and physical activity.

6) Modify patient treatment plans as indicated by patients' responses and conditions.

7) Direct and supervise less skilled nursing/health care personnel, or supervise a particular unit on one shift.

8) Assess the needs of individuals, families and/or communities, including assessment of individuals' home and/or work environments to identify potential health or safety problems.

9) Prepare rooms, sterile instruments, equipment and supplies, and ensure that stock of supplies is maintained.

10) Instruct individuals, families and other groups on topics such as health education, disease prevention and childbirth, and develop health improvement programs.

11) Observe nurses and visit patients to ensure that proper nursing care is provided.

12) Order, interpret, and evaluate diagnostic tests to identify and assess patient's condition.

13) Conduct specified laboratory tests.

14) Provide health care, first aid, immunizations and assistance in convalescence and rehabilitation in locations such as schools, hospitals, and industry.

15) Refer students or patients to specialized health resources or community agencies furnishing assistance.

16) Consult with institutions or associations regarding issues and concerns relevant to the practice and profession of nursing.

17) Prescribe or recommend drugs, medical devices or other forms of treatment, such as physical therapy, inhalation therapy, or related therapeutic procedures.

18) Provide or arrange for training/instruction of auxiliary personnel or students.

19) Administer local, inhalation, intravenous, and other anesthetics.

20) Work with individuals, groups, and families to plan and implement programs designed to improve the overall health of communities.

21) Engage in research activities related to nursing.

22) Direct and coordinate infection control programs, advising and consulting with specified personnel about necessary precautions.

23) Perform administrative and managerial functions, such as taking responsibility for a unit's staff, budget, planning, and long-range goals.

24) Inform physician of patient's condition during anesthesia.

25) Hand items to surgeons during operations.

26) Perform physical examinations, make tentative diagnoses, and treat patients en route to hospitals or at disaster site triage centers.

27) Deliver infants and provide prenatal and postpartum care and treatment under obstetrician's supervision.

Knowledge	Knowledge Definitions
Medicine and Dentistry	Knowledge of the information and techniques needed to diagnose and treat human injuries, diseases, and deformities. This includes symptoms, treatment alternatives, drug properties and interactions, and preventive health-care measures.
Psychology	Knowledge of human behavior and performance; individual differences in ability, personality, and interests; learning and motivation; psychological research methods; and the assessment and treatment of behavioral and affective disorders.
Customer and Personal Service	Knowledge of principles and processes for providing customer and personal services. This includes customer needs assessment, meeting quality standards for services, and evaluation of customer satisfaction.
English Language	Knowledge of the structure and content of the English language including the meaning and spelling of words, rules of composition, and grammar.
Biology	Knowledge of plant and animal organisms, their tissues, cells, functions, interdependencies, and interactions with each other and the environment.
Therapy and Counseling	Knowledge of principles, methods, and procedures for diagnosis, treatment, and rehabilitation of physical and mental dysfunctions, and for career counseling and guidance.
Mathematics	Knowledge of arithmetic, algebra, geometry, calculus, statistics, and their applications.
Education and Training	Knowledge of principles and methods for curriculum and training design, teaching and instruction for individuals and groups, and the measurement of training effects.
Sociology and Anthropology	Knowledge of group behavior and dynamics, societal trends and influences, human migrations, ethnicity, cultures and their history and origins.
Public Safety and Security	Knowledge of relevant equipment, policies, procedures, and strategies to promote effective local, state, or national security operations for the protection of people, data, property, and institutions.
Chemistry	Knowledge of the chemical composition, structure, and properties of substances and of the chemical processes and transformations that they undergo. This includes uses of chemicals and their interactions, danger signs, production techniques, and disposal methods.
Law and Government	Knowledge of laws, legal codes, court procedures, precedents, government regulations, executive orders, agency rules, and the democratic political process.
Philosophy and Theology	Knowledge of different philosophical systems and religions. This includes their basic principles, values, ethics, ways of thinking, customs, practices, and their impact on human culture.
Personnel and Human Resources	Knowledge of principles and procedures for personnel recruitment, selection, training, compensation and benefits, labor relations and negotiation, and personnel information systems.
Administration and Management	Knowledge of business and management principles involved in strategic planning, resource allocation, human resources modeling, leadership technique, production methods, and coordination of people and resources.
Computers and Electronics	Knowledge of circuit boards, processors, chips, electronic equipment, and computer hardware and software, including applications and programming.
Clerical	Knowledge of administrative and clerical procedures and systems such as word processing, managing files and records, stenography and transcription, designing forms, and other office procedures and terminology.
Communications and Media	Knowledge of media production, communication, and dissemination techniques and methods. This includes alternative ways to inform and entertain via written, oral, and visual media.
Mechanical	Knowledge of machines and tools, including their designs, uses, repair, and maintenance.
Telecommunications	Knowledge of transmission, broadcasting, switching, control, and operation of telecommunications systems.
Physics	Knowledge and prediction of physical principles, laws, their interrelationships, and applications to understanding fluid, material, and atmospheric dynamics, and mechanical, electrical, atomic and sub-atomic structures and processes.
Foreign Language	Knowledge of the structure and content of a foreign (non-English) language including the meaning and spelling of words, rules of composition and grammar, and pronunciation.
Production and Processing	Knowledge of raw materials, production processes, quality control, costs, and other techniques for maximizing the effective manufacture and distribution of goods.
Transportation	Knowledge of principles and methods for moving people or goods by air, rail, sea, or road, including the relative costs and benefits.
Sales and Marketing	Knowledge of principles and methods for showing, promoting, and selling products or services. This includes marketing strategy and tactics, product demonstration, sales techniques, and sales control systems.
Engineering and Technology	Knowledge of the practical application of engineering science and technology. This includes applying principles, techniques, procedures, and equipment to the design and production of various goods and services.
Economics and Accounting	Knowledge of economic and accounting principles and practices, the financial markets, banking and the analysis and reporting of financial data.
Geography	Knowledge of principles and methods for describing the features of land, sea, and air masses, including their physical characteristics, locations, interrelationships, and distribution of plant, animal, and human life.

Design	Knowledge of design techniques, tools, and principles involved in production of precision technical plans, blueprints, drawings, and models.
History and Archeology	Knowledge of historical events and their causes, indicators, and effects on civilizations and cultures.
Food Production	Knowledge of techniques and equipment for planting, growing, and harvesting food products (both plant and animal) for consumption, including storage/handling techniques.
Fine Arts	Knowledge of the theory and techniques required to compose, produce, and perform works of music, dance, visual arts, drama, and sculpture.
Building and Construction	Knowledge of materials, methods, and the tools involved in the construction or repair of houses, buildings, or other structures such as highways and roads.

Skills — Skills Definitions

Skills	Skills Definitions
Active Listening	Giving full attention to what other people are saying, taking time to understand the points being made, asking questions as appropriate, and not interrupting at inappropriate times.
Reading Comprehension	Understanding written sentences and paragraphs in work related documents.
Critical Thinking	Using logic and reasoning to identify the strengths and weaknesses of alternative solutions, conclusions or approaches to problems.
Instructing	Teaching others how to do something.
Speaking	Talking to others to convey information effectively.
Time Management	Managing one's own time and the time of others.
Service Orientation	Actively looking for ways to help people.
Monitoring	Monitoring/Assessing performance of yourself, other individuals, or organizations to make improvements or take corrective action.
Social Perceptiveness	Being aware of others' reactions and understanding why they react as they do.
Writing	Communicating effectively in writing as appropriate for the needs of the audience.
Active Learning	Understanding the implications of new information for both current and future problem-solving and decision-making.
Coordination	Adjusting actions in relation to others' actions.
Judgment and Decision Making	Considering the relative costs and benefits of potential actions to choose the most appropriate one.
Science	Using scientific rules and methods to solve problems.
Learning Strategies	Selecting and using training/instructional methods and procedures appropriate for the situation when learning or teaching new things.
Complex Problem Solving	Identifying complex problems and reviewing related information to develop and evaluate options and implement solutions.
Mathematics	Using mathematics to solve problems.
Persuasion	Persuading others to change their minds or behavior.
Negotiation	Bringing others together and trying to reconcile differences.
Operation Monitoring	Watching gauges, dials, or other indicators to make sure a machine is working properly.
Equipment Selection	Determining the kind of tools and equipment needed to do a job.
Management of Personnel Resources	Motivating, developing, and directing people as they work, identifying the best people for the job.
Troubleshooting	Determining causes of operating errors and deciding what to do about it.
Quality Control Analysis	Conducting tests and inspections of products, services, or processes to evaluate quality or performance.
Technology Design	Generating or adapting equipment and technology to serve user needs.
Operation and Control	Controlling operations of equipment or systems.
Operations Analysis	Analyzing needs and product requirements to create a design.
Systems Evaluation	Identifying measures or indicators of system performance and the actions needed to improve or correct performance, relative to the goals of the system.
Systems Analysis	Determining how a system should work and how changes in conditions, operations, and the environment will affect outcomes.
Management of Material Resources	Obtaining and seeing to the appropriate use of equipment, facilities, and materials needed to do certain work.
Equipment Maintenance	Performing routine maintenance on equipment and determining when and what kind of maintenance is needed.
Management of Financial Resources	Determining how money will be spent to get the work done, and accounting for these expenditures.

Installation	Installing equipment, machines, wiring, or programs to meet specifications.
Repairing	Repairing machines or systems using the needed tools.
Programming	Writing computer programs for various purposes.

Ability — Ability Definitions

Ability	Ability Definitions
Problem Sensitivity	The ability to tell when something is wrong or is likely to go wrong. It does not involve solving the problem, only recognizing there is a problem.
Oral Expression	The ability to communicate information and ideas in speaking so others will understand.
Oral Comprehension	The ability to listen to and understand information and ideas presented through spoken words and sentences.
Inductive Reasoning	The ability to combine pieces of information to form general rules or conclusions (includes finding a relationship among seemingly unrelated events).
Speech Clarity	The ability to speak clearly so others can understand you.
Speech Recognition	The ability to identify and understand the speech of another person.
Deductive Reasoning	The ability to apply general rules to specific problems to produce answers that make sense.
Written Expression	The ability to communicate information and ideas in writing so others will understand.
Written Comprehension	The ability to read and understand information and ideas presented in writing.
Near Vision	The ability to see details at close range (within a few feet of the observer).
Information Ordering	The ability to arrange things or actions in a certain order or pattern according to a specific rule or set of rules (e.g., patterns of numbers, letters, words, pictures, mathematical operations).
Selective Attention	The ability to concentrate on a task over a period of time without being distracted.
Trunk Strength	The ability to use your abdominal and lower back muscles to support part of the body repeatedly or continuously over time without 'giving out' or fatiguing.
Flexibility of Closure	The ability to identify or detect a known pattern (a figure, object, word, or sound) that is hidden in other distracting material.
Time Sharing	The ability to shift back and forth between two or more activities or sources of information (such as speech, sounds, touch, or other sources).
Manual Dexterity	The ability to quickly move your hand, your hand together with your arm, or your two hands to grasp, manipulate, or assemble objects.
Category Flexibility	The ability to generate or use different sets of rules for combining or grouping things in different ways.
Speed of Closure	The ability to quickly make sense of, combine, and organize information into meaningful patterns.
Arm-Hand Steadiness	The ability to keep your hand and arm steady while moving your arm or while holding your arm and hand in one position.
Extent Flexibility	The ability to bend, stretch, twist, or reach with your body, arms, and/or legs.
Perceptual Speed	The ability to quickly and accurately compare similarities and differences among sets of letters, numbers, objects, pictures, or patterns. The things to be compared may be presented at the same time or one after the other. This ability also includes comparing a presented object with a remembered object.
Memorization	The ability to remember information such as words, numbers, pictures, and procedures.
Stamina	The ability to exert yourself physically over long periods of time without getting winded or out of breath.
Gross Body Coordination	The ability to coordinate the movement of your arms, legs, and torso together when the whole body is in motion.
Fluency of Ideas	The ability to come up with a number of ideas about a topic (the number of ideas is important, not their quality, correctness, or creativity).
Auditory Attention	The ability to focus on a single source of sound in the presence of other distracting sounds.
Finger Dexterity	The ability to make precisely coordinated movements of the fingers of one or both hands to grasp, manipulate, or assemble very small objects.
Static Strength	The ability to exert maximum muscle force to lift, push, pull, or carry objects.
Originality	The ability to come up with unusual or clever ideas about a given topic or situation, or to develop creative ways to solve a problem.

Control Precision	The ability to quickly and repeatedly adjust the controls of a machine or a vehicle to exact positions.
Multilimb Coordination	The ability to coordinate two or more limbs (for example, two arms, two legs, or one leg and one arm) while sitting, standing, or lying down. It does not involve performing the activities while the whole body is in motion.
Depth Perception	The ability to judge which of several objects is closer or farther away from you, or to judge the distance between you and an object.
Visual Color Discrimination	The ability to match or detect differences between colors, including shades of color and brightness.
Far Vision	The ability to see details at a distance.
Hearing Sensitivity	The ability to detect or tell the differences between sounds that vary in pitch and loudness.
Reaction Time	The ability to quickly respond (with the hand, finger, or foot) to a signal (sound, light, picture) when it appears.
Response Orientation	The ability to choose quickly between two or more movements in response to two or more different signals (lights, sounds, pictures). It includes the speed with which the correct response is started with the hand, foot, or other body part.
Mathematical Reasoning	The ability to choose the right mathematical methods or formulas to solve a problem.
Speed of Limb Movement	The ability to quickly move the arms and legs.
Visualization	The ability to imagine how something will look after it is moved around or when its parts are moved or rearranged.
Dynamic Strength	The ability to exert muscle force repeatedly or continuously over time. This involves muscular endurance and resistance to muscle fatigue.
Number Facility	The ability to add, subtract, multiply, or divide quickly and correctly.
Gross Body Equilibrium	The ability to keep or regain your body balance or stay upright when in an unstable position.
Explosive Strength	The ability to use short bursts of muscle force to propel oneself (as in jumping or sprinting), or to throw an object.
Spatial Orientation	The ability to know your location in relation to the environment or to know where other objects are in relation to you.
Wrist-Finger Speed	The ability to make fast, simple, repeated movements of the fingers, hands, and wrists.
Rate Control	The ability to time your movements or the movement of a piece of equipment in anticipation of changes in the speed and/or direction of a moving object or scene.
Dynamic Flexibility	The ability to quickly and repeatedly bend, stretch, twist, or reach out with your body, arms, and/or legs.
Peripheral Vision	The ability to see objects or movement of objects to one's side when the eyes are looking ahead.
Sound Localization	The ability to tell the direction from which a sound originated.
Night Vision	The ability to see under low light conditions.
Glare Sensitivity	The ability to see objects in the presence of glare or bright lighting.

Work_Activity	Work_Activity Definitions
Assisting and Caring for Others	Providing personal assistance, medical attention, emotional support, or other personal care to others such as coworkers, customers, or patients.
Documenting/Recording Information	Entering, transcribing, recording, storing, or maintaining information in written or electronic/magnetic form.
Getting Information	Observing, receiving, and otherwise obtaining information from all relevant sources.
Updating and Using Relevant Knowledge	Keeping up-to-date technically and applying new knowledge to your job.
Organizing, Planning, and Prioritizing Work	Developing specific goals and plans to prioritize, organize, and accomplish your work.
Identifying Objects, Actions, and Events	Identifying information by categorizing, estimating, recognizing differences or similarities, and detecting changes in circumstances or events.
Making Decisions and Solving Problems	Analyzing information and evaluating results to choose the best solution and solve problems.
Performing for or Working Directly with the Public	Performing for people or dealing directly with the public. This includes serving customers in restaurants and stores, and receiving clients or guests.
Communicating with Supervisors, Peers, or Subordin	Providing information to supervisors, co-workers, and subordinates by telephone, in written form, e-mail, or in person.
Establishing and Maintaining Interpersonal Relatio	Developing constructive and cooperative working relationships with others, and maintaining them over time.

Monitor Processes, Materials, or Surroundings	Monitoring and reviewing information from materials, events, or the environment, to detect or assess problems.
Interpreting the Meaning of Information for Others	Translating or explaining what information means and how it can be used.
Training and Teaching Others	Identifying the educational needs of others, developing formal educational or training programs or classes, and teaching or instructing others.
Developing and Building Teams	Encouraging and building mutual trust, respect, and cooperation among team members.
Coordinating the Work and Activities of Others	Getting members of a group to work together to accomplish tasks.
Processing Information	Compiling, coding, categorizing, calculating, tabulating, auditing, or verifying information or data.
Performing General Physical Activities	Performing physical activities that require considerable use of your arms and legs and moving your whole body, such as climbing, lifting, balancing, walking, stooping, and handling of materials.
Evaluating Information to Determine Compliance wit	Using relevant information and individual judgment to determine whether events or processes comply with laws, regulations, or standards.
Coaching and Developing Others	Identifying the developmental needs of others and coaching, mentoring, or otherwise helping others to improve their knowledge or skills.
Resolving Conflicts and Negotiating with Others	Handling complaints, settling disputes, and resolving grievances and conflicts, or otherwise negotiating with others.
Analyzing Data or Information	Identifying the underlying principles, reasons, or facts of information by breaking down information or data into separate parts.
Communicating with Persons Outside Organization	Communicating with people outside the organization, representing the organization to customers, the public, government, and other external sources. This information can be exchanged in person, in writing, or by telephone or e-mail.
Judging the Qualities of Things, Services, or Peop	Assessing the value, importance, or quality of things or people.
Interacting With Computers	Using computers and computer systems (including hardware and software) to program, write software, set up functions, enter data, or process information.
Handling and Moving Objects	Using hands and arms in handling, installing, positioning, and moving materials, and manipulating things.
Inspecting Equipment, Structures, or Material	Inspecting equipment, structures, or materials to identify the cause of errors or other problems or defects.
Provide Consultation and Advice to Others	Providing guidance and expert advice to management or other groups on technical, systems-, or process-related topics.
Guiding, Directing, and Motivating Subordinates	Providing guidance and direction to subordinates, including setting performance standards and monitoring performance.
Thinking Creatively	Developing, designing, or creating new applications, ideas, relationships, systems, or products, including artistic contributions.
Developing Objectives and Strategies	Establishing long-range objectives and specifying the strategies and actions to achieve them.
Estimating the Quantifiable Characteristics of Pro	Estimating sizes, distances, and quantities; or determining time, costs, resources, or materials needed to perform a work activity.
Scheduling Work and Activities	Scheduling events, programs, and activities, as well as the work of others.
Performing Administrative Activities	Performing day-to-day administrative tasks such as maintaining information files and processing paperwork.
Controlling Machines and Processes	Using either control mechanisms or direct physical activity to operate machines or processes (not including computers or vehicles).
Monitoring and Controlling Resources	Monitoring and controlling resources and overseeing the spending of money.
Selling or Influencing Others	Convincing others to buy merchandise/goods or to otherwise change their minds or actions.
Staffing Organizational Units	Recruiting, interviewing, selecting, hiring, and promoting employees in an organization.
Operating Vehicles, Mechanized Devices, or Equipme	Running, maneuvering, navigating, or driving vehicles or mechanized equipment, such as forklifts, passenger vehicles, aircraft, or water craft.
Repairing and Maintaining Electronic Equipment	Servicing, repairing, calibrating, regulating, fine-tuning, or testing machines, devices, and equipment that operate primarily on the basis of electrical or electronic (not mechanical) principles.
Repairing and Maintaining Mechanical Equipment	Servicing, repairing, adjusting, and testing machines, devices, moving parts, and equipment that operate primarily on the basis of mechanical (not electronic) principles.

Drafting, Laying Out, and Specifying Technical Dev	Providing documentation, detailed instructions, drawings, or specifications to tell others about how devices, parts, equipment, or structures are to be fabricated, constructed, assembled, modified, maintained, or used.

Work_Context	Work_Context Definitions
Telephone	How often do you have telephone conversations in this job?
Contact With Others	How much does this job require the worker to be in contact with others (face-to-face, by telephone, or otherwise) in order to perform it?
Face-to-Face Discussions	How often do you have to have face-to-face discussions with individuals or teams in this job?
Exposed to Disease or Infections	How often does this job require exposure to disease/infections?
Physical Proximity	To what extent does this job require the worker to perform job tasks in close physical proximity to other people?
Work With Work Group or Team	How important is it to work with others in a group or team in this job?
Frequency of Decision Making	How frequently is the worker required to make decisions that affect other people, the financial resources, and/or the image and reputation of the organization?
Importance of Being Exact or Accurate	How important is being very exact or highly accurate in performing this job?
Indoors, Environmentally Controlled	How often does this job require working indoors in environmentally controlled conditions?
Impact of Decisions on Co-workers or Company Resul	How do the decisions an employee makes impact the results of co-workers, clients or the company?
Consequence of Error	How serious would the result usually be if the worker made a mistake that was not readily correctable?
Deal With External Customers	How important is it to work with external customers or the public in this job?
Wear Common Protective or Safety Equipment such as	How much does this job require wearing common protective or safety equipment such as safety shoes, glasses, gloves, hard hats or life jackets?
Structured versus Unstructured Work	To what extent is this job structured for the worker, rather than allowing the worker to determine tasks, priorities, and goals?
Freedom to Make Decisions	How much decision making freedom, without supervision, does the job offer?
Time Pressure	How often does this job require the worker to meet strict deadlines?
Coordinate or Lead Others	How important is it to coordinate or lead others in accomplishing work activities in this job?
Deal With Unpleasant or Angry People	How frequently does the worker have to deal with unpleasant, angry, or discourteous individuals as part of the job requirements?
Responsible for Others' Health and Safety	How much responsibility is there for the health and safety of others in this job?
Spend Time Standing	How much does this job require standing?
Spend Time Using Your Hands to Handle, Control, or	How much does this job require using your hands to handle, control, or feel objects, tools or controls?
Importance of Repeating Same Tasks	How important is repeating the same physical activities (e.g., key entry) or mental activities (e.g., checking entries in a ledger) over and over, without stopping, to performing this job?
Exposed to Contaminants	How often does this job require working exposed to contaminants (such as pollutants, gases, dust or odors)?
Frequency of Conflict Situations	How often are there conflict situations the employee has to face in this job?
Responsibility for Outcomes and Results	How responsible is the worker for work outcomes and results of other workers?
Sounds, Noise Levels Are Distracting or Uncomforta	How often does this job require working exposed to sounds and noise levels that are distracting or uncomfortable?
Letters and Memos	How often does the job require written letters and memos?
Spend Time Walking and Running	How much does this job require walking and running?
Cramped Work Space, Awkward Positions	How often does this job require working in cramped work spaces that requires getting into awkward positions?
Electronic Mail	How often do you use electronic mail in this job?
Spend Time Bending or Twisting the Body	How much does this job require bending or twisting your body?
Exposed to Minor Burns, Cuts, Bites, or Stings	How often does this job require exposure to minor burns, cuts, bites, or stings?
Level of Competition	To what extent does this job require the worker to compete or to be aware of competitive pressures?
Exposed to Radiation	How often does this job require exposure to radiation?

Exposed to Hazardous Conditions	How often does this job require exposure to hazardous conditions?
Deal With Physically Aggressive People	How frequently does this job require the worker to deal with physical aggression of violent individuals?
Spend Time Making Repetitive Motions	How much does this job require making repetitive motions?
Spend Time Sitting	How much does this job require sitting?
Wear Specialized Protective or Safety Equipment su	How much does this job require wearing specialized protective or safety equipment such as breathing apparatus, safety harness, full protection suits, or radiation protection?
Extremely Bright or Inadequate Lighting	How often does this job require working in extremely bright or inadequate lighting conditions?
Spend Time Kneeling, Crouching, Stooping, or Crawl	How much does this job require kneeling, crouching, stooping, or crawling?
Public Speaking	How often do you have to perform public speaking in this job?
Degree of Automation	How automated is the job?
Indoors, Not Environmentally Controlled	How often does this job require working indoors in non-controlled environmental conditions (e.g., warehouse without heat)?
In an Enclosed Vehicle or Equipment	How often does this job require working in a closed vehicle or equipment (e.g., car)?
Spend Time Keeping or Regaining Balance	How much does this job require keeping or regaining your balance?
Exposed to Hazardous Equipment	How often does this job require exposure to hazardous equipment?
Very Hot or Cold Temperatures	How often does this job require working in very hot (above 90 F degrees) or very cold (below 32 F degrees) temperatures?
Pace Determined by Speed of Equipment	How important is it to this job that the pace is determined by the speed of equipment or machinery? (This does not refer to keeping busy at all times on this job.)
Outdoors, Exposed to Weather	How often does this job require working outdoors, exposed to all weather conditions?
Outdoors, Under Cover	How often does this job require working outdoors, under cover (e.g., structure with roof but no walls)?
Exposed to Whole Body Vibration	How often does this job require exposure to whole body vibration (e.g., operate a jackhammer)?
Exposed to High Places	How often does this job require exposure to high places?
Spend Time Climbing Ladders, Scaffolds, or Poles	How much does this job require climbing ladders, scaffolds, or poles?
In an Open Vehicle or Equipment	How often does this job require working in an open vehicle or equipment (e.g., tractor)?

Job Zone Component	Job Zone Component Definitions
Title	Job Zone Three: Medium Preparation Needed
Overall Experience	Previous work-related skill, knowledge, or experience is required for these occupations. For example, an electrician must have completed three or four years of apprenticeship or several years of vocational training, and often must have passed a licensing exam, in order to perform the job.
Job Training	Employees in these occupations usually need one or two years of training involving both on-the-job experience and informal training with experienced workers.
Job Zone Examples	These occupations usually involve using communication and organizational skills to coordinate, supervise, manage, or train others to accomplish goals. Examples include dental assistants, electricians, fish and game wardens, legal secretaries, personnel recruiters, and recreation workers.
SVP Range	(6.0 to < 7.0)
Education	Most occupations in this zone require training in vocational schools, related on-the-job experience, or an associate's degree. Some may require a bachelor's degree.

Work_Styles	Work_Styles Definitions
Integrity	Job requires being honest and ethical.
Dependability	Job requires being reliable, responsible, and dependable, and fulfilling obligations.
Self Control	Job requires maintaining composure, keeping emotions in check, controlling anger, and avoiding aggressive behavior, even in very difficult situations.
Concern for Others	Job requires being sensitive to others' needs and feelings and being understanding and helpful on the job.
Cooperation	Job requires being pleasant with others on the job and displaying a good-natured, cooperative attitude.

Adaptability/Flexibility	Job requires being open to change (positive or negative) and to considerable variety in the workplace.
Attention to Detail	Job requires being careful about detail and thorough in completing work tasks.
Stress Tolerance	Job requires accepting criticism and dealing calmly and effectively with high stress situations.
Initiative	Job requires a willingness to take on responsibilities and challenges.
Independence	Job requires developing one's own ways of doing things, guiding oneself with little or no supervision, and depending on oneself to get things done.
Social Orientation	Job requires preferring to work with others rather than alone, and being personally connected with others on the job.
Analytical Thinking	Job requires analyzing information and using logic to address work-related issues and problems.
Achievement/Effort	Job requires establishing and maintaining personally challenging achievement goals and exerting effort toward mastering tasks.
Leadership	Job requires a willingness to lead, take charge, and offer opinions and direction.
Persistence	Job requires persistence in the face of obstacles.
Innovation	Job requires creativity and alternative thinking to develop new ideas for and answers to work-related problems.

29-1121.00 - Audiologists

Assess and treat persons with hearing and related disorders. May fit hearing aids and provide auditory training. May perform research related to hearing problems.

Tasks

1) Educate and supervise audiology students and health care personnel.

2) Work with multi-disciplinary teams to assess and rehabilitate recipients of implanted hearing devices.

3) Recommend assistive devices according to clients' needs or nature of impairments.

4) Measure noise levels in workplaces and conduct hearing protection programs in industry, schools, and communities.

5) Participate in conferences or training to update or share knowledge of new hearing or speech disorder treatment methods or technologies.

6) Develop and supervise hearing screening programs.

7) Advise educators or other medical staff on speech or hearing topics.

8) Fit and tune cochlear implants, providing rehabilitation for adjustment to listening with implant amplification systems.

9) Plan and conduct treatment programs for clients' hearing or speech problems, consulting with physicians, nurses, psychologists, and other health care personnel as necessary.

10) Instruct clients, parents, teachers, or employers in how to avoid behavior patterns that lead to miscommunication.

11) Refer clients to additional medical or educational services if needed.

12) Counsel and instruct clients in techniques to improve hearing or speech impairment, including sign language or lip-reading.

13) Monitor clients' progress and discharge them from treatment when goals have been attained.

14) Maintain client records at all stages, including initial evaluation and discharge.

15) Fit and dispense assistive devices, such as hearing aids.

16) Examine and clean patients' ear canals.

17) Evaluate hearing and speech/language disorders to determine diagnoses and courses of treatment.

18) Conduct or direct research on hearing or speech topics and report findings to help in the development of procedures, technology, or treatments.

29-1122.00 - Occupational Therapists

Assess, plan, organize, and participate in rehabilitative programs that help restore vocational, homemaking, and daily living skills, as well as general independence, to disabled persons.

Tasks

1) Plan, organize, and conduct occupational therapy programs in hospital, institutional, or community settings to help rehabilitate those impaired because of illness, injury or psychological or developmental problems.

2) Provide training and supervision in therapy techniques and objectives for students and nurses and other medical staff.

3) Lay out materials such as puzzles, scissors and eating utensils for use in therapy, and clean and repair these tools after therapy sessions.

4) Develop and participate in health promotion programs, group activities, or discussions to promote client health, facilitate social adjustment, alleviate stress, and prevent physical or mental disability.

5) Plan and implement programs and social activities to help patients learn work and school skills and adjust to handicaps.

6) Help clients improve decision making, abstract reasoning, memory, sequencing, coordination and perceptual skills, using computer programs.

7) Advise on health risks in the workplace and on health-related transition to retirement.

8) Conduct research in occupational therapy.

9) Provide patients with assistance in locating and holding jobs.

10) Recommend changes in patients' work or living environments, consistent with their needs and capabilities.

11) Design and create, or requisition, special supplies and equipment, such as splints, braces and computer-aided adaptive equipment.

12) Evaluate patients' progress and prepare reports that detail progress.

13) Complete and maintain necessary records.

14) Consult with rehabilitation team to select activity programs and coordinate occupational therapy with other therapeutic activities.

15) Test and evaluate patients' physical and mental abilities and analyze medical data to determine realistic rehabilitation goals for patients.

Knowledge	Knowledge Definitions
Therapy and Counseling	Knowledge of principles, methods, and procedures for diagnosis, treatment, and rehabilitation of physical and mental dysfunctions, and for career counseling and guidance.
Psychology	Knowledge of human behavior and performance; individual differences in ability, personality, and interests; learning and motivation; psychological research methods; and the assessment and treatment of behavioral and affective disorders.
Customer and Personal Service	Knowledge of principles and processes for providing customer and personal services. This includes customer needs assessment, meeting quality standards for services, and evaluation of customer satisfaction.
English Language	Knowledge of the structure and content of the English language including the meaning and spelling of words, rules of composition, and grammar.
Education and Training	Knowledge of principles and methods for curriculum and training design, teaching and instruction for individuals and groups, and the measurement of training effects.
Medicine and Dentistry	Knowledge of the information and techniques needed to diagnose and treat human injuries, diseases, and deformities. This includes symptoms, treatment alternatives, drug properties and interactions, and preventive health-care measures.
Biology	Knowledge of plant and animal organisms, their tissues, cells, functions, interdependencies, and interactions with each other and the environment.
Sociology and Anthropology	Knowledge of group behavior and dynamics, societal trends and influences, human migrations, ethnicity, cultures and their history and origins.
Public Safety and Security	Knowledge of relevant equipment, policies, procedures, and strategies to promote effective local, state, or national security operations for the protection of people, data, property, and institutions.
Computers and Electronics	Knowledge of circuit boards, processors, chips, electronic equipment, and computer hardware and software, including applications and programming.
Administration and Management	Knowledge of business and management principles involved in strategic planning, resource allocation, human resources modeling, leadership technique, production methods, and coordination of people and resources.

Clerical	Knowledge of administrative and clerical procedures and systems such as word processing, managing files and records, stenography and transcription, designing forms, and other office procedures and terminology.
Sales and Marketing	Knowledge of principles and methods for showing, promoting, and selling products or services. This includes marketing strategy and tactics, product demonstration, sales techniques, and sales control systems.
Communications and Media	Knowledge of media production, communication, and dissemination techniques and methods. This includes alternative ways to inform and entertain via written, oral, and visual media.
Physics	Knowledge and prediction of physical principles, laws, their interrelationships, and applications to understanding fluid, material, and atmospheric dynamics, and mechanical, electrical, atomic and sub- atomic structures and processes.
Law and Government	Knowledge of laws, legal codes, court procedures, precedents, government regulations, executive orders, agency rules, and the democratic political process.
Personnel and Human Resources	Knowledge of principles and procedures for personnel recruitment, selection, training, compensation and benefits, labor relations and negotiation, and personnel information systems.
Telecommunications	Knowledge of transmission, broadcasting, switching, control, and operation of telecommunications systems.
Mathematics	Knowledge of arithmetic, algebra, geometry, calculus, statistics, and their applications.
Philosophy and Theology	Knowledge of different philosophical systems and religions. This includes their basic principles, values, ethics, ways of thinking, customs, practices, and their impact on human culture.
Engineering and Technology	Knowledge of the practical application of engineering science and technology. This includes applying principles, techniques, procedures, and equipment to the design and production of various goods and services.
Chemistry	Knowledge of the chemical composition, structure, and properties of substances and of the chemical processes and transformations that they undergo. This includes uses of chemicals and their interactions, danger signs, production techniques, and disposal methods.
Foreign Language	Knowledge of the structure and content of a foreign (non-English) language including the meaning and spelling of words, rules of composition and grammar, and pronunciation.
Design	Knowledge of design techniques, tools, and principles involved in production of precision technical plans, blueprints, drawings, and models.
Transportation	Knowledge of principles and methods for moving people or goods by air, rail, sea, or road, including the relative costs and benefits.
Mechanical	Knowledge of machines and tools, including their designs, uses, repair, and maintenance.
Production and Processing	Knowledge of raw materials, production processes, quality control, costs, and other techniques for maximizing the effective manufacture and distribution of goods.
Economics and Accounting	Knowledge of economic and accounting principles and practices, the financial markets, banking and the analysis and reporting of financial data.
Geography	Knowledge of principles and methods for describing the features of land, sea, and air masses, including their physical characteristics, locations, interrelationships, and distribution of plant, animal, and human life.
Building and Construction	Knowledge of materials, methods, and the tools involved in the construction or repair of houses, buildings, or other structures such as highways and roads.
History and Archeology	Knowledge of historical events and their causes, indicators, and effects on civilizations and cultures.
Fine Arts	Knowledge of the theory and techniques required to compose, produce, and perform works of music, dance, visual arts, drama, and sculpture.
Food Production	Knowledge of techniques and equipment for planting, growing, and harvesting food products (both plant and animal) for consumption, including storage/handling techniques.

Skills	**Skills Definitions**
Active Listening	Giving full attention to what other people are saying, taking time to understand the points being made, asking questions as appropriate, and not interrupting at inappropriate times.

Reading Comprehension	Understanding written sentences and paragraphs in work related documents.
Service Orientation	Actively looking for ways to help people.
Writing	Communicating effectively in writing as appropriate for the needs of the audience.
Speaking	Talking to others to convey information effectively.
Instructing	Teaching others how to do something.
Social Perceptiveness	Being aware of others' reactions and understanding why they react as they do.
Time Management	Managing one's own time and the time of others.
Critical Thinking	Using logic and reasoning to identify the strengths and weaknesses of alternative solutions, conclusions or approaches to problems.
Active Learning	Understanding the implications of new information for both current and future problem-solving and decision-making.
Coordination	Adjusting actions in relation to others' actions.
Learning Strategies	Selecting and using training/instructional methods and procedures appropriate for the situation when learning or teaching new things.
Monitoring	Monitoring/Assessing performance of yourself, other individuals, or organizations to make improvements or take corrective action.
Science	Using scientific rules and methods to solve problems.
Complex Problem Solving	Identifying complex problems and reviewing related information to develop and evaluate options and implement solutions.
Judgment and Decision Making	Considering the relative costs and benefits of potential actions to choose the most appropriate one.
Persuasion	Persuading others to change their minds or behavior.
Equipment Selection	Determining the kind of tools and equipment needed to do a job.
Technology Design	Generating or adapting equipment and technology to serve user needs.
Negotiation	Bringing others together and trying to reconcile differences.
Management of Personnel Resources	Motivating, developing, and directing people as they work, identifying the best people for the job.
Quality Control Analysis	Conducting tests and inspections of products, services, or processes to evaluate quality or performance.
Mathematics	Using mathematics to solve problems.
Troubleshooting	Determining causes of operating errors and deciding what to do about it.
Management of Material Resources	Obtaining and seeing to the appropriate use of equipment, facilities, and materials needed to do certain work.
Management of Financial Resources	Determining how money will be spent to get the work done, and accounting for these expenditures.
Operations Analysis	Analyzing needs and product requirements to create a design.
Systems Evaluation	Identifying measures or indicators of system performance and the actions needed to improve or correct performance, relative to the goals of the system.
Operation and Control	Controlling operations of equipment or systems.
Equipment Maintenance	Performing routine maintenance on equipment and determining when and what kind of maintenance is needed.
Repairing	Repairing machines or systems using the needed tools.
Systems Analysis	Determining how a system should work and how changes in conditions, operations, and the environment will affect outcomes.
Operation Monitoring	Watching gauges, dials, or other indicators to make sure a machine is working properly.
Installation	Installing equipment, machines, wiring, or programs to meet specifications.
Programming	Writing computer programs for various purposes.

Ability	**Ability Definitions**
Oral Comprehension	The ability to listen to and understand information and ideas presented through spoken words and sentences.
Oral Expression	The ability to communicate information and ideas in speaking so others will understand.
Written Expression	The ability to communicate information and ideas in writing so others will understand.
Problem Sensitivity	The ability to tell when something is wrong or is likely to go wrong. It does not involve solving the problem, only recognizing there is a problem.
Information Ordering	The ability to arrange things or actions in a certain order or pattern according to a specific rule or set of rules (e.g., patterns of numbers, letters, words, pictures, mathematical operations).

Ability	Definition
Inductive Reasoning	The ability to combine pieces of information to form general rules or conclusions (includes finding a relationship among seemingly unrelated events).
Deductive Reasoning	The ability to apply general rules to specific problems to produce answers that make sense.
Speech Recognition	The ability to identify and understand the speech of another person.
Speech Clarity	The ability to speak clearly so others can understand you.
Written Comprehension	The ability to read and understand information and ideas presented in writing.
Near Vision	The ability to see details at close range (within a few feet of the observer).
Category Flexibility	The ability to generate or use different sets of rules for combining or grouping things in different ways.
Time Sharing	The ability to shift back and forth between two or more activities or sources of information (such as speech, sounds, touch, or other sources).
Originality	The ability to come up with unusual or clever ideas about a given topic or situation, or to develop creative ways to solve a problem.
Finger Dexterity	The ability to make precisely coordinated movements of the fingers of one or both hands to grasp, manipulate, or assemble very small objects.
Fluency of Ideas	The ability to come up with a number of ideas about a topic (the number of ideas is important, not their quality, correctness, or creativity).
Selective Attention	The ability to concentrate on a task over a period of time without being distracted.
Flexibility of Closure	The ability to identify or detect a known pattern (a figure, object, word, or sound) that is hidden in other distracting material.
Speed of Closure	The ability to quickly make sense of, combine, and organize information into meaningful patterns.
Trunk Strength	The ability to use your abdominal and lower back muscles to support part of the body repeatedly or continuously over time without 'giving out' or fatiguing.
Far Vision	The ability to see details at a distance.
Multilimb Coordination	The ability to coordinate two or more limbs (for example, two arms, two legs, or one leg and one arm) while sitting, standing, or lying down. It does not involve performing the activities while the whole body is in motion.
Perceptual Speed	The ability to quickly and accurately compare similarities and differences among sets of letters, numbers, objects, pictures, or patterns. The things to be compared may be presented at the same time or one after the other. This ability also includes comparing a presented object with a remembered object.
Visualization	The ability to imagine how something will look after it is moved around or when its parts are moved or rearranged.
Memorization	The ability to remember information such as words, numbers, pictures, and procedures.
Manual Dexterity	The ability to quickly move your hand, your hand together with your arm, or your two hands to grasp, manipulate, or assemble objects.
Arm-Hand Steadiness	The ability to keep your hand and arm steady while moving your arm or while holding your arm and hand in one position.
Extent Flexibility	The ability to bend, stretch, twist, or reach with your body, arms, and/or legs.
Visual Color Discrimination	The ability to match or detect differences between colors, including shades of color and brightness.
Mathematical Reasoning	The ability to choose the right mathematical methods or formulas to solve a problem.
Static Strength	The ability to exert maximum muscle force to lift, push, pull, or carry objects.
Stamina	The ability to exert yourself physically over long periods of time without getting winded or out of breath.
Gross Body Coordination	The ability to coordinate the movement of your arms, legs, and torso together when the whole body is in motion.
Number Facility	The ability to add, subtract, multiply, or divide quickly and correctly.
Auditory Attention	The ability to focus on a single source of sound in the presence of other distracting sounds.
Hearing Sensitivity	The ability to detect or tell the differences between sounds that vary in pitch and loudness.
Depth Perception	The ability to judge which of several objects is closer or farther away from you, or to judge the distance between you and an object.
Dynamic Strength	The ability to exert muscle force repeatedly or continuously over time. This involves muscular endurance and resistance to muscle fatigue.
Control Precision	The ability to quickly and repeatedly adjust the controls of a machine or a vehicle to exact positions.
Gross Body Equilibrium	The ability to keep or regain your body balance or stay upright when in an unstable position.
Spatial Orientation	The ability to know your location in relation to the environment or to know where other objects are in relation to you.
Glare Sensitivity	The ability to see objects in the presence of glare or bright lighting.
Night Vision	The ability to see under low light conditions.
Sound Localization	The ability to tell the direction from which a sound originated.
Explosive Strength	The ability to use short bursts of muscle force to propel oneself (as in jumping or sprinting), or to throw an object.
Speed of Limb Movement	The ability to quickly move the arms and legs.
Peripheral Vision	The ability to see objects or movement of objects to one's side when the eyes are looking ahead.
Reaction Time	The ability to quickly respond (with the hand, finger, or foot) to a signal (sound, light, picture) when it appears.
Rate Control	The ability to time your movements or the movement of a piece of equipment in anticipation of changes in the speed and/or direction of a moving object or scene.
Response Orientation	The ability to choose quickly between two or more movements in response to two or more different signals (lights, sounds, pictures). It includes the speed with which the correct response is started with the hand, foot, or other body part.
Dynamic Flexibility	The ability to quickly and repeatedly bend, stretch, twist, or reach out with your body, arms, and/or legs.
Wrist-Finger Speed	The ability to make fast, simple, repeated movements of the fingers, hands, and wrists.

Work_Activity	Work_Activity Definitions
Getting Information	Observing, receiving, and otherwise obtaining information from all relevant sources.
Establishing and Maintaining Interpersonal Relatio	Developing constructive and cooperative working relationships with others, and maintaining them over time.
Documenting/Recording Information	Entering, transcribing, recording, storing, or maintaining information in written or electronic/magnetic form.
Assisting and Caring for Others	Providing personal assistance, medical attention, emotional support, or other personal care to others such as coworkers, customers, or patients.
Developing Objectives and Strategies	Establishing long-range objectives and specifying the strategies and actions to achieve them.
Performing General Physical Activities	Performing physical activities that require considerable use of your arms and legs and moving your whole body, such as climbing, lifting, balancing, walking, stooping, and handling of materials.
Training and Teaching Others	Identifying the educational needs of others, developing formal educational or training programs or classes, and teaching or instructing others.
Making Decisions and Solving Problems	Analyzing information and evaluating results to choose the best solution and solve problems.
Communicating with Supervisors, Peers, or Subordin	Providing information to supervisors, co-workers, and subordinates by telephone, in written form, e-mail, or in person.
Updating and Using Relevant Knowledge	Keeping up-to-date technically and applying new knowledge to your job.
Organizing, Planning, and Prioritizing Work	Developing specific goals and plans to prioritize, organize, and accomplish your work.
Developing and Building Teams	Encouraging and building mutual trust, respect, and cooperation among team members.
Monitor Processes, Materials, or Surroundings	Monitoring and reviewing information from materials, events, or the environment, to detect or assess problems.
Coaching and Developing Others	Identifying the developmental needs of others and coaching, mentoring, or otherwise helping others to improve their knowledge or skills.
Interpreting the Meaning of Information for Others	Translating or explaining what information means and how it can be used.
Identifying Objects, Actions, and Events	Identifying information by categorizing, estimating, recognizing differences or similarities, and detecting changes in circumstances or events.
Performing for or Working Directly with the Public	Performing for people or dealing directly with the public. This includes serving customers in restaurants and stores, and receiving clients or guests.

Handling and Moving Objects	Using hands and arms in handling, installing, positioning, and moving materials, and manipulating things.
Analyzing Data or Information	Identifying the underlying principles, reasons, or facts of information by breaking down information or data into separate parts.
Thinking Creatively	Developing, designing, or creating new applications, ideas, relationships, systems, or products, including artistic contributions.
Evaluating Information to Determine Compliance wit	Using relevant information and individual judgment to determine whether events or processes comply with laws, regulations, or standards.
Resolving Conflicts and Negotiating with Others	Handling complaints, settling disputes, and resolving grievances and conflicts, or otherwise negotiating with others.
Judging the Qualities of Things, Services, or Peop	Assessing the value, importance, or quality of things or people.
Coordinating the Work and Activities of Others	Getting members of a group to work together to accomplish tasks.
Inspecting Equipment, Structures, or Material	Inspecting equipment, structures, or materials to identify the cause of errors or other problems or defects.
Provide Consultation and Advice to Others	Providing guidance and expert advice to management or other groups on technical, systems-, or process-related topics.
Communicating with Persons Outside Organization	Communicating with people outside the organization, representing the organization to customers, the public, government, and other external sources. This information can be exchanged in person, in writing, or by telephone or e-mail.
Performing Administrative Activities	Performing day-to-day administrative tasks such as maintaining information files and processing paperwork.
Guiding, Directing, and Motivating Subordinates	Providing guidance and direction to subordinates, including setting performance standards and monitoring performance.
Estimating the Quantifiable Characteristics of Pro	Estimating sizes, distances, and quantities; or determining time, costs, resources, or materials needed to perform a work activity.
Scheduling Work and Activities	Scheduling events, programs, and activities, as well as the work of others.
Processing Information	Compiling, coding, categorizing, calculating, tabulating, auditing, or verifying information or data.
Interacting With Computers	Using computers and computer systems (including hardware and software) to program, write software, set up functions, enter data, or process information.
Staffing Organizational Units	Recruiting, interviewing, selecting, hiring, and promoting employees in an organization.
Controlling Machines and Processes	Using either control mechanisms or direct physical activity to operate machines or processes (not including computers or vehicles).
Monitoring and Controlling Resources	Monitoring and controlling resources and overseeing the spending of money.
Selling or Influencing Others	Convincing others to buy merchandise/goods or to otherwise change their minds or actions.
Operating Vehicles, Mechanized Devices, or Equipme	Running, maneuvering, navigating, or driving vehicles or mechanized equipment, such as forklifts, passenger vehicles, aircraft, or water craft.
Repairing and Maintaining Mechanical Equipment	Servicing, repairing, adjusting, and testing machines, devices, moving parts, and equipment that operate primarily on the basis of mechanical (not electronic) principles.
Drafting, Laying Out, and Specifying Technical Dev	Providing documentation, detailed instructions, drawings, or specifications to tell others about how devices, parts, equipment, or structures are to be fabricated, constructed, assembled, modified, maintained, or used.
Repairing and Maintaining Electronic Equipment	Servicing, repairing, calibrating, regulating, fine-tuning, or testing machines, devices, and equipment that operate primarily on the basis of electrical or electronic (not mechanical) principles.

Work_Context	**Work_Context Definitions**
Face-to-Face Discussions	How often do you have to have face-to-face discussions with individuals or teams in this job?
Contact With Others	How much does this job require the worker to be in contact with others (face-to-face, by telephone, or otherwise) in order to perform it?
Structured versus Unstructured Work	To what extent is this job structured for the worker, rather than allowing the worker to determine tasks, priorities, and goals?
Freedom to Make Decisions	How much decision making freedom, without supervision, does the job offer?
Physical Proximity	To what extent does this job require the worker to perform job tasks in close physical proximity to other people?

Frequency of Decision Making	How frequently is the worker required to make decisions that affect other people, the financial resources, and/or the image and reputation of the organization?
Work With Work Group or Team	How important is it to work with others in a group or team in this job?
Telephone	How often do you have telephone conversations in this job?
Indoors, Environmentally Controlled	How often does this job require working indoors in environmentally controlled conditions?
Letters and Memos	How often does the job require written letters and memos?
Exposed to Disease or Infections	How often does this job require exposure to disease/infections?
Time Pressure	How often does this job require the worker to meet strict deadlines?
Coordinate or Lead Others	How important is it to coordinate or lead others in accomplishing work activities in this job?
Impact of Decisions on Co-workers or Company Resul	How do the decisions an employee makes impact the results of co-workers, clients or the company?
Importance of Being Exact or Accurate	How important is being very exact or highly accurate in performing this job?
Deal With External Customers	How important is it to work with external customers or the public in this job?
Spend Time Standing	How much does this job require standing?
Deal With Unpleasant or Angry People	How frequently does the worker have to deal with unpleasant, angry, or discourteous individuals as part of the job requirements?
Responsible for Others' Health and Safety	How much responsibility is there for the health and safety of others in this job?
Wear Common Protective or Safety Equipment such as	How much does this job require wearing common protective or safety equipment such as safety shoes, glasses, gloves, hard hats or live jackets?
Level of Competition	To what extent does this job require the worker to compete or to be aware of competitive pressures?
Frequency of Conflict Situations	How often are there conflict situations the employee has to face in this job?
Spend Time Using Your Hands to Handle, Control, or	How much does this job require using your hands to handle, control, or feel objects, tools or controls?
Consequence of Error	How serious would the result usually be if the worker made a mistake that was not readily correctable?
Spend Time Sitting	How much does this job require sitting?
Responsibility for Outcomes and Results	How responsible is the worker for work outcomes and results of other workers?
Spend Time Walking and Running	How much does this job require walking and running?
Sounds, Noise Levels Are Distracting or Uncomforta	How often does this job require working exposed to sounds and noise levels that are distracting or uncomfortable?
In an Enclosed Vehicle or Equipment	How often does this job require working in a closed vehicle or equipment (e.g., car)?
Spend Time Bending or Twisting the Body	How much does this job require bending or twisting your body?
Electronic Mail	How often do you use electronic mail in this job?
Exposed to Contaminants	How often does this job require working exposed to contaminants (such as pollutants, gases, dust or odors)?
Cramped Work Space, Awkward Positions	How often does this job require working in cramped work spaces that requires getting into awkward positions?
Spend Time Kneeling, Crouching, Stooping, or Crawl	How much does this job require kneeling, crouching, stooping or crawling?
Deal With Physically Aggressive People	How frequently does this job require the worker to deal with physical aggression of violent individuals?
Spend Time Making Repetitive Motions	How much does this job require making repetitive motions?
Importance of Repeating Same Tasks	How important is repeating the same physical activities (e.g., key entry) or mental activities (e.g., checking entries in a ledger) over and over, without stopping, to performing this job?
Public Speaking	How often do you have to perform public speaking in this job?
Exposed to Minor Burns, Cuts, Bites, or Stings	How often does this job require exposure to minor burns, cuts, bites, or stings?
Degree of Automation	How automated is the job?
Spend Time Keeping or Regaining Balance	How much does this job require keeping or regaining your balance?
Indoors, Not Environmentally Controlled	How often does this job require working indoors in non-controlled environmental conditions (e.g., warehouse without heat)?
Wear Specialized Protective or Safety Equipment su	How often does this job require wearing specialized protective or safety equipment such as breathing apparatus, safety harness, full protection suits, or radiation protection?

Outdoors, Exposed to Weather	How often does this job require working outdoors, exposed to all weather conditions?
Extremely Bright or Inadequate Lighting	How often does this job require working in extremely bright or inadequate lighting conditions?
Very Hot or Cold Temperatures	How often does this job require working in very hot (above 90 F degrees) or very cold (below 32 F degrees) temperatures?
Spend Time Climbing Ladders, Scaffolds, or Poles	How much does this job require climbing ladders, scaffolds, or poles?
Exposed to Radiation	How often does this job require exposure to radiation?
Exposed to Hazardous Equipment	How often does this job require exposure to hazardous equipment?
Outdoors, Under Cover	How often does this job require working outdoors, under cover (e.g., structure with roof but no walls)?
Exposed to Hazardous Conditions	How often does this job require exposure to hazardous conditions?
Exposed to High Places	How often does this job require exposure to high places?
Pace Determined by Speed of Equipment	How important is it to this job that the pace is determined by the speed of equipment or machinery? (This does not refer to keeping busy at all times on this job.)
Exposed to Whole Body Vibration	How often does this job require exposure to whole body vibration (e.g., operate a jackhammer)?
In an Open Vehicle or Equipment	How often does this job require working in an open vehicle or equipment (e.g., tractor)?

Job Zone Component	Job Zone Component Definitions
Title	Job Zone Four: Considerable Preparation Needed
Overall Experience	A minimum of two to four years of work-related skill, knowledge, or experience is needed for these occupations. For example, an accountant must complete four years of college and work for several years in accounting to be considered qualified.
Job Training	Employees in these occupations usually need several years of work-related experience, on-the-job training, and/or vocational training.
Job Zone Examples	Many of these occupations involve coordinating, supervising, managing, or training others. Examples include accountants, chefs and head cooks, computer programmers, historians, pharmacists, and police detectives.
SVP Range	(7.0 to < 8.0)
Education	Most of these occupations require a four - year bachelor's degree, but some do not.

Work_Styles	Work_Styles Definitions
Concern for Others	Job requires being sensitive to others' needs and feelings and being understanding and helpful on the job.
Adaptability/Flexibility	Job requires being open to change (positive or negative) and to considerable variety in the workplace.
Integrity	Job requires being honest and ethical.
Cooperation	Job requires being pleasant with others on the job and displaying a good-natured, cooperative attitude.
Dependability	Job requires being reliable, responsible, and dependable, and fulfilling obligations.
Self Control	Job requires maintaining composure, keeping emotions in check, controlling anger, and avoiding aggressive behavior, even in very difficult situations.
Stress Tolerance	Job requires accepting criticism and dealing calmly and effectively with high stress situations.
Social Orientation	Job requires preferring to work with others rather than alone, and being personally connected with others on the job.
Innovation	Job requires creativity and alternative thinking to develop new ideas for and answers to work-related problems.
Attention to Detail	Job requires being careful about detail and thorough in completing work tasks.
Initiative	Job requires a willingness to take on responsibilities and challenges.
Persistence	Job requires persistence in the face of obstacles.
Independence	Job requires developing one's own ways of doing things, guiding oneself with little or no supervision, and depending on oneself to get things done.
Analytical Thinking	Job requires analyzing information and using logic to address work-related issues and problems.
Achievement/Effort	Job requires establishing and maintaining personally challenging achievement goals and exerting effort toward mastering tasks.

Leadership	Job requires a willingness to lead, take charge, and offer opinions and direction.

29-1123.00 - Physical Therapists

Assess, plan, organize, and participate in rehabilitative programs that improve mobility, relieve pain, increase strength, and decrease or prevent deformity of patients suffering from disease or injury.

Tasks

1) Refer clients to community resources and services.

2) Provide information to the patient about the proposed intervention, its material risks and expected benefits and any reasonable alternatives.

3) Inform the patient when diagnosis reveals findings outside their scope and refer to an appropriate practitioner.

4) Teach physical therapy students as well as those in other health professions.

5) Direct and supervise supportive personnel, assessing their competence, delegating specific tasks to them and establishing channels of communication.

6) Evaluate, fit, and adjust prosthetic and orthotic devices and recommend modification to orthotist.

7) Obtain patients' informed consent to proposed interventions.

8) Direct group rehabilitation activities.

9) Conduct and support research and apply research findings to practice.

10) Participate in community and community agency activities and help to formulate public policy.

11) Construct, maintain and repair medical supportive devices.

12) Instruct patient and family in treatment procedures to be continued at home.

13) Perform and document an initial exam, evaluating the data to identify problems and determine a diagnosis prior to intervention.

14) Evaluate effects of treatment at various stages and adjust treatments to achieve maximum benefit.

15) Administer manual exercises, massage and/or traction to help relieve pain, increase the patient's strength, and decrease or prevent deformity and crippling.

16) Provide educational information about physical therapy and physical therapists, injury prevention, ergonomics and ways to promote health.

17) Plan, prepare and carry out individually designed programs of physical treatment to maintain, improve or restore physical functioning, alleviate pain and prevent physical dysfunction in patients.

18) Discharge patient from physical therapy when goals or projected outcomes have been attained and provide for appropriate followup care or referrals.

19) Test and measure patient's strength, motor development and function, sensory perception, functional capacity, and respiratory and circulatory efficiency and record data.

20) Record prognosis, treatment, response, and progress in patient's chart or enter information into computer.

21) Review physician's referral and patient's medical records to help determine diagnosis and physical therapy treatment required.

22) Confer with the patient, medical practitioners and appropriate others to plan, implement and assess the intervention program.

23) Identify and document goals, anticipated progress and plans for reevaluation.

Knowledge	Knowledge Definitions
Medicine and Dentistry	Knowledge of the information and techniques needed to diagnose and treat human injuries, diseases, and deformities. This includes symptoms, treatment alternatives, drug properties and interactions, and preventive health-care measures.
Therapy and Counseling	Knowledge of principles, methods, and procedures for diagnosis, treatment, and rehabilitation of physical and mental dysfunctions, and for career counseling and guidance.

Customer and Personal Service	Knowledge of principles and processes for providing customer and personal services. This includes customer needs assessment, meeting quality standards for services, and evaluation of customer satisfaction.
Education and Training	Knowledge of principles and methods for curriculum and training design, teaching and instruction for individuals and groups, and the measurement of training effects.
Biology	Knowledge of plant and animal organisms, their tissues, cells, functions, interdependencies, and interactions with each other and the environment.
Psychology	Knowledge of human behavior and performance; individual differences in ability, personality, and interests; learning and motivation; psychological research methods; and the assessment and treatment of behavioral and affective disorders.
English Language	Knowledge of the structure and content of the English language including the meaning and spelling of words, rules of composition, and grammar.
Sociology and Anthropology	Knowledge of group behavior and dynamics, societal trends and influences, human migrations, ethnicity, cultures and their history and origins.
Physics	Knowledge and prediction of physical principles, laws, their interrelationships, and applications to understanding fluid, material, and atmospheric dynamics, and mechanical, electrical, atomic and sub- atomic structures and processes.
Communications and Media	Knowledge of media production, communication, and dissemination techniques and methods. This includes alternative ways to inform and entertain via written, oral, and visual media.
Law and Government	Knowledge of laws, legal codes, court procedures, precedents, government regulations, executive orders, agency rules, and the democratic political process.
Administration and Management	Knowledge of business and management principles involved in strategic planning, resource allocation, human resources modeling, leadership technique, production methods, and coordination of people and resources.
Computers and Electronics	Knowledge of circuit boards, processors, chips, electronic equipment, and computer hardware and software, including applications and programming.
Public Safety and Security	Knowledge of relevant equipment, policies, procedures, and strategies to promote effective local, state, or national security operations for the protection of people, data, property, and institutions.
Chemistry	Knowledge of the chemical composition, structure, and properties of substances and of the chemical processes and transformations that they undergo. This includes uses of chemicals and their interactions, danger signs, production techniques, and disposal methods.
Mathematics	Knowledge of arithmetic, algebra, geometry, calculus, statistics, and their applications.
Personnel and Human Resources	Knowledge of principles and procedures for personnel recruitment, selection, training, compensation and benefits, labor relations and negotiation, and personnel information systems.
Telecommunications	Knowledge of transmission, broadcasting, switching, control, and operation of telecommunications systems.
Clerical	Knowledge of administrative and clerical procedures and systems such as word processing, managing files and records, stenography and transcription, designing forms, and other office procedures and terminology.
Foreign Language	Knowledge of the structure and content of a foreign (non-English) language including the meaning and spelling of words, rules of composition and grammar, and pronunciation.
Sales and Marketing	Knowledge of principles and methods for showing, promoting, and selling products or services. This includes marketing strategy and tactics, product demonstration, sales techniques, and sales control systems.
Mechanical	Knowledge of machines and tools, including their designs, uses, repair, and maintenance.
Philosophy and Theology	Knowledge of different philosophical systems and religions. This includes their basic principles, values, ethics, ways of thinking, customs, practices, and their impact on human culture.
Transportation	Knowledge of principles and methods for moving people or goods by air, rail, sea, or road, including the relative costs and benefits.
Economics and Accounting	Knowledge of economic and accounting principles and practices, the financial markets, banking and the analysis and reporting of financial data.

Engineering and Technology	Knowledge of the practical application of engineering science and technology. This includes applying principles, techniques, procedures, and equipment to the design and production of various goods and services.
Geography	Knowledge of principles and methods for describing the features of land, sea, and air masses, including their physical characteristics, locations, interrelationships, and distribution of plant, animal, and human life.
Production and Processing	Knowledge of raw materials, production processes, quality control, costs, and other techniques for maximizing the effective manufacture and distribution of goods.
Design	Knowledge of design techniques, tools, and principles involved in production of precision technical plans, blueprints, drawings, and models.
Fine Arts	Knowledge of the theory and techniques required to compose, produce, and perform works of music, dance, visual arts, drama, and sculpture.
History and Archeology	Knowledge of historical events and their causes, indicators, and effects on civilizations and cultures.
Building and Construction	Knowledge of materials, methods, and the tools involved in the construction or repair of houses, buildings, or other structures such as highways and roads.
Food Production	Knowledge of techniques and equipment for planting, growing, and harvesting food products (both plant and animal) for consumption, including storage/handling techniques.

Skills	Skills Definitions
Active Listening	Giving full attention to what other people are saying, taking time to understand the points being made, asking questions as appropriate, and not interrupting at inappropriate times.
Instructing	Teaching others how to do something.
Time Management	Managing one's own time and the time of others.
Speaking	Talking to others to convey information effectively.
Critical Thinking	Using logic and reasoning to identify the strengths and weaknesses of alternative solutions, conclusions or approaches to problems.
Learning Strategies	Selecting and using training/instructional methods and procedures appropriate for the situation when learning or teaching new things.
Science	Using scientific rules and methods to solve problems.
Active Learning	Understanding the implications of new information for both current and future problem-solving and decision-making.
Monitoring	Monitoring/Assessing performance of yourself, other individuals, or organizations to make improvements or take corrective action.
Reading Comprehension	Understanding written sentences and paragraphs in work related documents.
Service Orientation	Actively looking for ways to help people.
Writing	Communicating effectively in writing as appropriate for the needs of the audience.
Judgment and Decision Making	Considering the relative costs and benefits of potential actions to choose the most appropriate one.
Complex Problem Solving	Identifying complex problems and reviewing related information to develop and evaluate options and implement solutions.
Coordination	Adjusting actions in relation to others' actions.
Social Perceptiveness	Being aware of others' reactions and understanding why they react as they do.
Equipment Selection	Determining the kind of tools and equipment needed to do a job.
Persuasion	Persuading others to change their minds or behavior.
Management of Personnel Resources	Motivating, developing, and directing people as they work, identifying the best people for the job.
Negotiation	Bringing others together and trying to reconcile differences.
Quality Control Analysis	Conducting tests and inspections of products, services, or processes to evaluate quality or performance.
Troubleshooting	Determining causes of operating errors and deciding what to do about it.
Technology Design	Generating or adapting equipment and technology to serve user needs.
Operations Analysis	Analyzing needs and product requirements to create a design.
Operation and Control	Controlling operations of equipment or systems.
Mathematics	Using mathematics to solve problems.
Operation Monitoring	Watching gauges, dials, or other indicators to make sure a machine is working properly.
Management of Financial Resources	Determining how money will be spent to get the work done, and accounting for these expenditures.

Management of Material Resources	Obtaining and seeing to the appropriate use of equipment. facilities, and materials needed to do certain work.
Equipment Maintenance	Performing routine maintenance on equipment and determining when and what kind of maintenance is needed.
Systems Evaluation	Identifying measures or indicators of system performance and the actions needed to improve or correct performance, relative to the goals of the system.
Repairing	Repairing machines or systems using the needed tools.
Systems Analysis	Determining how a system should work and how changes in conditions, operations, and the environment will affect outcomes.
Installation	Installing equipment, machines, wiring, or programs to meet specifications.
Programming	Writing computer programs for various purposes.

Ability	Ability Definitions
Oral Expression	The ability to communicate information and ideas in speaking so others will understand.
Oral Comprehension	The ability to listen to and understand information and ideas presented through spoken words and sentences.
Problem Sensitivity	The ability to tell when something is wrong or is likely to go wrong. It does not involve solving the problem, only recognizing there is a problem.
Inductive Reasoning	The ability to combine pieces of information to form general rules or conclusions (includes finding a relationship among seemingly unrelated events).
Written Comprehension	The ability to read and understand information and ideas presented in writing.
Written Expression	The ability to communicate information and ideas in writing so others will understand.
Deductive Reasoning	The ability to apply general rules to specific problems to produce answers that make sense.
Trunk Strength	The ability to use your abdominal and lower back muscles to support part of the body repeatedly or continuously over time without 'giving out' or fatiguing.
Speech Clarity	The ability to speak clearly so others can understand you.
Information Ordering	The ability to arrange things or actions in a certain order or pattern according to a specific rule or set of rules (e.g., patterns of numbers, letters, words, pictures, mathematical operations).
Finger Dexterity	The ability to make precisely coordinated movements of the fingers of one or both hands to grasp, manipulate, or assemble very small objects.
Near Vision	The ability to see details at close range (within a few feet of the observer).
Speech Recognition	The ability to identify and understand the speech of another person.
Static Strength	The ability to exert maximum muscle force to lift, push, pull, or carry objects.
Multilimb Coordination	The ability to coordinate two or more limbs (for example, two arms, two legs, or one leg and one arm) while sitting, standing, or lying down. It does not involve performing the activities while the whole body is in motion.
Manual Dexterity	The ability to quickly move your hand, your hand together with your arm, or your two hands to grasp, manipulate, or assemble objects.
Category Flexibility	The ability to generate or use different sets of rules for combining or grouping things in different ways.
Arm-Hand Steadiness	The ability to keep your hand and arm steady while moving your arm or while holding your arm and hand in one position.
Stamina	The ability to exert yourself physically over long periods of time without getting winded or out of breath.
Selective Attention	The ability to concentrate on a task over a period of time without being distracted.
Speed of Closure	The ability to quickly make sense of, combine, and organize information into meaningful patterns.
Dynamic Strength	The ability to exert muscle force repeatedly or continuously over time. This involves muscular endurance and resistance to muscle fatigue.
Time Sharing	The ability to shift back and forth between two or more activities or sources of information (such as speech, sounds, touch, or other sources).
Extent Flexibility	The ability to bend, stretch, twist, or reach with your body, arms, and/or legs
Flexibility of Closure	The ability to identify or detect a known pattern (a figure, object, word, or sound) that is hidden in other distracting material.

Perceptual Speed	The ability to quickly and accurately compare similarities and differences among sets of letters, numbers, objects, pictures, or patterns. The things to be compared may be presented at the same time or one after the other. This ability also includes comparing a presented object with a remembered object.
Gross Body Coordination	The ability to coordinate the movement of your arms, legs, and torso together when the whole body is in motion.
Originality	The ability to come up with unusual or clever ideas about a given topic or situation, or to develop creative ways to solve a problem.
Fluency of Ideas	The ability to come up with a number of ideas about a topic (the number of ideas is important, not their quality, correctness, or creativity).
Far Vision	The ability to see details at a distance.
Memorization	The ability to remember information such as words, numbers, pictures, and procedures.
Control Precision	The ability to quickly and repeatedly adjust the controls of a machine or a vehicle to exact positions.
Speed of Limb Movement	The ability to quickly move the arms and legs.
Gross Body Equilibrium	The ability to keep or regain your body balance or stay upright when in an unstable position.
Depth Perception	The ability to judge which of several objects is closer or farther away from you, or to judge the distance between you and an object.
Auditory Attention	The ability to focus on a single source of sound in the presence of other distracting sounds.
Mathematical Reasoning	The ability to choose the right mathematical methods or formulas to solve a problem.
Visualization	The ability to imagine how something will look after it is moved around or when its parts are moved or rearranged.
Hearing Sensitivity	The ability to detect or tell the differences between sounds that vary in pitch and loudness.
Visual Color Discrimination	The ability to match or detect differences between colors, including shades of color and brightness.
Number Facility	The ability to add, subtract, multiply, or divide quickly and correctly.
Wrist-Finger Speed	The ability to make fast, simple, repeated movements of the fingers, hands, and wrists.
Rate Control	The ability to time your movements or the movement of a piece of equipment in anticipation of changes in the speed and/or direction of a moving object or scene.
Dynamic Flexibility	The ability to quickly and repeatedly bend, stretch, twist, or reach out with your body, arms, and/or legs.
Response Orientation	The ability to choose quickly between two or more movements in response to two or more different signals (lights, sounds, pictures). It includes the speed with which the correct response is started with the hand, foot, or other body part.
Reaction Time	The ability to quickly respond (with the hand, finger, or foot) to a signal (sound, light, picture) when it appears.
Spatial Orientation	The ability to know your location in relation to the environment or to know where other objects are in relation to you.
Night Vision	The ability to see under low light conditions.
Peripheral Vision	The ability to see objects or movement of objects to one's side when the eyes are looking ahead.
Explosive Strength	The ability to use short bursts of muscle force to propel oneself (as in jumping or sprinting), or to throw an object.
Sound Localization	The ability to tell the direction from which a sound originated.
Glare Sensitivity	The ability to see objects in the presence of glare or bright lighting.

Work_Activity	Work_Activity Definitions
Assisting and Caring for Others	Providing personal assistance, medical attention, emotional support, or other personal care to others such as coworkers, customers, or patients.
Getting Information	Observing, receiving, and otherwise obtaining information from all relevant sources.
Establishing and Maintaining Interpersonal Relatio	Developing constructive and cooperative working relationships with others, and maintaining them over time.
Making Decisions and Solving Problems	Analyzing information and evaluating results to choose the best solution and solve problems.
Identifying Objects, Actions, and Events	Identifying information by categorizing, estimating, recognizing differences or similarities, and detecting changes in circumstances or events.
Communicating with Supervisors, Peers, or Subordin	Providing information to supervisors, co-workers, and subordinates by telephone, in written form, e-mail, or in person.

Updating and Using Relevant Knowledge	Keeping up-to-date technically and applying new knowledge to your job.
Analyzing Data or Information	Identifying the underlying principles, reasons, or facts of information by breaking down information or data into separate parts.
Organizing, Planning, and Prioritizing Work	Developing specific goals and plans to prioritize, organize, and accomplish your work.
Performing General Physical Activities	Performing physical activities that require considerable use of your arms and legs and moving your whole body, such as climbing, lifting, balancing, walking, stooping, and handling of materials.
Documenting/Recording Information	Entering, transcribing, recording, storing, or maintaining information in written or electronic/magnetic form.
Monitor Processes, Materials, or Surroundings	Monitoring and reviewing information from materials, events, or the environment, to detect or assess problems.
Handling and Moving Objects	Using hands and arms in handling, installing, positioning, and moving materials, and manipulating things.
Developing Objectives and Strategies	Establishing long-range objectives and specifying the strategies and actions to achieve them.
Judging the Qualities of Things, Services, or Peop	Assessing the value, importance, or quality of things or people.
Performing for or Working Directly with the Public	Performing for people or dealing directly with the public. This includes serving customers in restaurants and stores, and receiving clients or guests.
Developing and Building Teams	Encouraging and building mutual trust, respect, and cooperation among team members.
Evaluating Information to Determine Compliance wit	Using relevant information and individual judgment to determine whether events or processes comply with laws, regulations, or standards.
Interpreting the Meaning of Information for Others	Translating or explaining what information means and how it can be used.
Estimating the Quantifiable Characteristics of Pro	Estimating sizes, distances, and quantities; or determining time, costs, resources, or materials needed to perform a work activity.
Scheduling Work and Activities	Scheduling events, programs, and activities, as well as the work of others.
Coordinating the Work and Activities of Others	Getting members of a group to work together to accomplish tasks.
Guiding, Directing, and Motivating Subordinates	Providing guidance and direction to subordinates, including setting performance standards and monitoring performance.
Processing Information	Compiling, coding, categorizing, calculating, tabulating, auditing, or verifying information or data.
Resolving Conflicts and Negotiating with Others	Handling complaints, settling disputes, and resolving grievances and conflicts, or otherwise negotiating with others.
Thinking Creatively	Developing, designing, or creating new applications, ideas, relationships, systems, or products, including artistic contributions.
Provide Consultation and Advice to Others	Providing guidance and expert advice to management or other groups on technical, systems-, or process-related topics.
Training and Teaching Others	Identifying the educational needs of others, developing formal educational or training programs or classes, and teaching or instructing others.
Communicating with Persons Outside Organization	Communicating with people outside the organization, representing the organization to customers, the public, government, and other external sources. This information can be exchanged in person, in writing, or by telephone or e-mail.
Performing Administrative Activities	Performing day-to-day administrative tasks such as maintaining information files and processing paperwork.
Inspecting Equipment, Structures, or Material	Inspecting equipment, structures, or materials to identify the cause of errors or other problems or defects.
Coaching and Developing Others	Identifying the developmental needs of others and coaching, mentoring, or otherwise helping others to improve their knowledge or skills.
Interacting With Computers	Using computers and computer systems (including hardware and software) to program, write software, set up functions, enter data, or process information.
Controlling Machines and Processes	Using either control mechanisms or direct physical activity to operate machines or processes (not including computers or vehicles).
Monitoring and Controlling Resources	Monitoring and controlling resources and overseeing the spending of money.
Selling or Influencing Others	Convincing others to buy merchandise/goods or to otherwise change their minds or actions.
Staffing Organizational Units	Recruiting, interviewing, selecting, hiring, and promoting employees in an organization.

Operating Vehicles, Mechanized Devices, or Equipme	Running, maneuvering, navigating, or driving vehicles or mechanized equipment, such as forklifts, passenger vehicles, aircraft, or water craft.
Drafting, Laying Out, and Specifying Technical Dev	Providing documentation, detailed instructions, drawings, or specifications to tell others about how devices, parts, equipment, or structures are to be fabricated, constructed, assembled, modified, maintained, or used.
Repairing and Maintaining Mechanical Equipment	Servicing, repairing, adjusting, and testing machines, devices, moving parts, and equipment that operate primarily on the basis of mechanical (not electronic) principles.
Repairing and Maintaining Electronic Equipment	Servicing, repairing, calibrating, regulating, fine-tuning, or testing machines, devices, and equipment that operate primarily on the basis of electrical or electronic (not mechanical) principles.

Work_Context	Work_Context Definitions
Indoors, Environmentally Controlled	How often does this job require working indoors in environmentally controlled conditions?
Contact With Others	How much does this job require the worker to be in contact with others (face-to-face, by telephone, or otherwise) in order to perform it?
Physical Proximity	To what extent does this job require the worker to perform job tasks in close physical proximity to other people?
Face-to-Face Discussions	How often do you have to have face-to-face discussions with individuals or teams in this job?
Telephone	How often do you have telephone conversations in this job?
Structured versus Unstructured Work	To what extent is this job structured for the worker, rather than allowing the worker to determine tasks, priorities, and goals?
Freedom to Make Decisions	How much decision making freedom, without supervision, does the job offer?
Frequency of Decision Making	How frequently is the worker required to make decisions that affect other people, the financial resources, and/or the image and reputation of the organization?
Work With Work Group or Team	How important is it to work with others in a group or team in this job?
Spend Time Standing	How much does this job require standing?
Exposed to Disease or Infections	How often does this job require exposure to disease/infections?
Impact of Decisions on Co-workers or Company Resul	How do the decisions an employee makes impact the results of co-workers, clients or the company?
Coordinate or Lead Others	How important is it to coordinate or lead others in accomplishing work activities in this job?
Importance of Being Exact or Accurate	How important is being very exact or highly accurate in performing this job?
Deal With External Customers	How important is it to work with external customers or the public in this job?
Letters and Memos	How often does the job require written letters and memos?
Responsible for Others' Health and Safety	How much responsibility is there for the health and safety of others in this job?
Level of Competition	To what extent does this job require the worker to compete or to be aware of competitive pressures?
Wear Common Protective or Safety Equipment such as	How much does this job require wearing common protective or safety equipment such as safety shoes, glasses, gloves, hard hats or live jackets?
Time Pressure	How often does this job require the worker to meet strict deadlines?
Consequence of Error	How serious would the result usually be if the worker made a mistake that was not readily correctable?
Spend Time Bending or Twisting the Body	How much does this job require bending or twisting your body?
Deal With Unpleasant or Angry People	How frequently does the worker have to deal with unpleasant, angry, or discourteous individuals as part of the job requirements?
Exposed to Contaminants	How often does this job require working exposed to contaminants (such as pollutants, gases, dust or odors)?
Spend Time Walking and Running	How much does this job require walking and running?
Cramped Work Space, Awkward Positions	How often does this job require working in cramped work spaces that requires getting into awkward positions?
Responsibility for Outcomes and Results	How responsible is the worker for work outcomes and results of other workers?
Frequency of Conflict Situations	How often are there conflict situations the employee has to face in this job?
Importance of Repeating Same Tasks	How important is repeating the same physical activities (e.g., key entry) or mental activities (e.g., checking entries in a ledger) over and over, without stopping, to performing this job?

Spend Time Using Your Hands to Handle, Control, or	How much does this job require using your hands to handle, control, or feel objects, tools or controls?
Spend Time Kneeling, Crouching, Stooping, or Crawl	How much does this job require kneeling, crouching, stooping or crawling?
Spend Time Keeping or Regaining Balance	How much does this job require keeping or regaining your balance?
Spend Time Making Repetitive Motions	How much does this job require making repetitive motions?
Sounds, Noise Levels Are Distracting or Uncomforta	How often does this job require working exposed to sounds and noise levels that are distracting or uncomfortable?
Wear Specialized Protective or Safety Equipment su	How much does this job require wearing specialized protective or safety equipment such as breathing apparatus, safety harness, full protection suits, or radiation protection?
In an Enclosed Vehicle or Equipment	How often does this job require working in a closed vehicle or equipment (e.g., car)?
Electronic Mail	How often do you use electronic mail in this job?
Spend Time Sitting	How much does this job require sitting?
Exposed to Minor Burns, Cuts, Bites, or Stings	How often does this job require exposure to minor burns, cuts, bites, or stings?
Public Speaking	How often do you have to perform public speaking in this job?
Indoors, Not Environmentally Controlled	How often does this job require working indoors in non-controlled environmental conditions (e.g., warehouse without heat)?
Extremely Bright or Inadequate Lighting	How often does this job require working in extremely bright or inadequate lighting conditions?
Deal With Physically Aggressive People	How frequently does this job require the worker to deal with physical aggression of violent individuals?
Degree of Automation	How automated is the job?
Exposed to Hazardous Conditions	How often does this job require exposure to hazardous conditions?
Very Hot or Cold Temperatures	How often does this job require working in very hot (above 90 F degrees) or very cold (below 32 F degrees) temperatures?
Exposed to Radiation	How often does this job require exposure to radiation?
Exposed to Hazardous Equipment	How often does this job require exposure to hazardous equipment?
Outdoors, Exposed to Weather	How often does this job require working outdoors, exposed to all weather conditions?
Outdoors, Under Cover	How often does this job require working outdoors, under cover (e.g., structure with roof but no walls)?
Pace Determined by Speed of Equipment	How important is it to this job that the pace is determined by the speed of equipment or machinery? (This does not refer to keeping busy at all times on this job.)
Exposed to High Places	How often does this job require exposure to high places?
In an Open Vehicle or Equipment	How often does this job require working in an open vehicle or equipment (e.g., tractor)?
Spend Time Climbing Ladders, Scaffolds, or Poles	How much does this job require climbing ladders, scaffolds, or poles?
Exposed to Whole Body Vibration	How often does this job require exposure to whole body vibration (e.g., operate a jackhammer)?

Job Zone Component	Job Zone Component Definitions
Title	Job Zone Five: Extensive Preparation Needed
Overall Experience	Extensive skill, knowledge, and experience are needed for these occupations. Many require more than five years of experience. For example, surgeons must complete four years of college and an additional five to seven years of specialized medical training to be able to do their job.
Job Training	Employees may need some on-the-job training, but most of these occupations assume that the person will already have the required skills, knowledge, work-related experience, and/or training.
Job Zone Examples	These occupations often involve coordinating, training, supervising, or managing the activities of others to accomplish goals. Very advanced communication and organizational skills are required. Examples include athletic trainers, lawyers, managing editors, phyicists, social psychologists, and surgeons.
SVP Range	(8.0 and above)
Education	A bachelor's degree is the minimum formal education required for these occupations. However, many also require graduate school. For example, they may require a master's degree, and some require a Ph.D., M.D., or J.D. (law degree).

Work_Styles	Work_Styles Definitions

Concern for Others	Job requires being sensitive to others' needs and feelings and being understanding and helpful on the job.
Integrity	Job requires being honest and ethical.
Dependability	Job requires being reliable, responsible, and dependable, and fulfilling obligations.
Cooperation	Job requires being pleasant with others on the job and displaying a good-natured, cooperative attitude.
Self Control	Job requires maintaining composure, keeping emotions in check, controlling anger, and avoiding aggressive behavior, even in very difficult situations.
Independence	Job requires developing one's own ways of doing things, guiding oneself with little or no supervision, and depending on oneself to get things done.
Social Orientation	Job requires preferring to work with others rather than alone, and being personally connected with others on the job.
Adaptability/Flexibility	Job requires being open to change (positive or negative) and to considerable variety in the workplace.
Initiative	Job requires a willingness to take on responsibilities and challenges.
Leadership	Job requires a willingness to lead, take charge, and offer opinions and direction.
Attention to Detail	Job requires being careful about detail and thorough in completing work tasks.
Stress Tolerance	Job requires accepting criticism and dealing calmly and effectively with high stress situations.
Achievement/Effort	Job requires establishing and maintaining personally challenging achievement goals and exerting effort toward mastering tasks.
Analytical Thinking	Job requires analyzing information and using logic to address work-related issues and problems.
Persistence	Job requires persistence in the face of obstacles.
Innovation	Job requires creativity and alternative thinking to develop new ideas for and answers to work-related problems.

29-1124.00 - Radiation Therapists

Provide radiation therapy to patients as prescribed by a radiologist according to established practices and standards. Duties may include reviewing prescription and diagnosis; acting as liaison with physician and supportive care personnel; preparing equipment, such as immobilization, treatment, and protection devices; and maintaining records, reports, and files. May assist in dosimetry procedures and tumor localization.

Tasks

1) Conduct most treatment sessions independently, in accordance with the long-term treatment plan and under the general direction of the patient's physician.

2) Check radiation therapy equipment to ensure proper operation.

3) Prepare and construct equipment, such as immobilization, treatment, and protection devices.

4) Educate, prepare and reas   ents and their families by answering questions, providing physical assista   , and   inforcing physicians' advice regarding treatment reactions and post-treatment care.

5) Enter data into computer and set controls to operate and adjust equipment and regulate dosage.

6) Calculate actual treatment dosages delivered during each session.

7) Act as liaison with physicist and supportive care personnel.

8) Train and supervise student or subordinate radiotherapy technologists.

9) Help physicians, radiation oncologists and clinical physicists to prepare physical and technical aspects of radiation treatment plans, using information about patient condition and anatomy.

10) Provide assistance to other health-care personnel during dosimetry procedures and tumor localization.

11) Implement appropriate follow-up care plans.

12) Assist in the preparation of sealed radioactive materials, such as cobalt, radium, cesium and isotopes, for use in radiation treatments.

13) Store, sterilize, or prepare the special applicators containing the radioactive substance implanted by the physician.

14) Observe and reassure patients during treatment and report unusual reactions to physician

or turn equipment off if unexpected adverse reactions occur.

15) Follow principles of radiation protection for patient, self, and others.

16) Review prescription, diagnosis, patient chart, and identification.

17) Photograph treated area of patient and process film.

18) Position patients for treatment with accuracy according to prescription.

19) Administer prescribed doses of radiation to specific body parts, using radiation therapy equipment according to established practices and standards.

20) Maintain records, reports and files as required, including such information as radiation dosages, equipment settings and patients' reactions.

Knowledge	Knowledge Definitions
Customer and Personal Service	Knowledge of principles and processes for providing customer and personal services. This includes customer needs assessment, meeting quality standards for services, and evaluation of customer satisfaction.
Medicine and Dentistry	Knowledge of the information and techniques needed to diagnose and treat human injuries, diseases, and deformities. This includes symptoms, treatment alternatives, drug properties and interactions, and preventive health-care measures.
Mathematics	Knowledge of arithmetic, algebra, geometry, calculus, statistics, and their applications.
English Language	Knowledge of the structure and content of the English language including the meaning and spelling of words, rules of composition, and grammar.
Psychology	Knowledge of human behavior and performance; individual differences in ability, personality, and interests; learning and motivation; psychological research methods; and the assessment and treatment of behavioral and affective disorders.
Biology	Knowledge of plant and animal organisms, their tissues, cells, functions, interdependencies, and interactions with each other and the environment.
Physics	Knowledge and prediction of physical principles, laws, their interrelationships, and applications to understanding fluid, material, and atmospheric dynamics, and mechanical, electrical, atomic and sub- atomic structures and processes.
Education and Training	Knowledge of principles and methods for curriculum and training design, teaching and instruction for individuals and groups, and the measurement of training effects.
Computers and Electronics	Knowledge of circuit boards, processors, chips, electronic equipment, and computer hardware and software, including applications and programming.
Therapy and Counseling	Knowledge of principles, methods, and procedures for diagnosis, treatment, and rehabilitation of physical and mental dysfunctions, and for career counseling and guidance.
Mechanical	Knowledge of machines and tools, including their designs, uses, repair, and maintenance.
Public Safety and Security	Knowledge of relevant equipment, policies, procedures, and strategies to promote effective local, state, or national security operations for the protection of people, data, property, and institutions.
Engineering and Technology	Knowledge of the practical application of engineering science and technology. This includes applying principles, techniques, procedures, and equipment to the design and production of various goods and services.
Administration and Management	Knowledge of business and management principles involved in strategic planning, resource allocation, human resources modeling, leadership technique, production methods, and coordination of people and resources.
Clerical	Knowledge of administrative and clerical procedures and systems such as word processing, managing files and records, stenography and transcription, designing forms, and other office procedures and terminology.
Sociology and Anthropology	Knowledge of group behavior and dynamics, societal trends and influences, human migrations, ethnicity, cultures and their history and origins.
Personnel and Human Resources	Knowledge of principles and procedures for personnel recruitment, selection, training, compensation and benefits, labor relations and negotiation, and personnel information systems.
Chemistry	Knowledge of the chemical composition, structure, and properties of substances and of the chemical processes and transformations that they undergo. This includes uses of chemicals and their interactions, danger signs, production techniques, and disposal methods.

Law and Government	Knowledge of laws, legal codes, court procedures, precedents, government regulations, executive orders, agency rules, and the democratic political process.
Telecommunications	Knowledge of transmission, broadcasting, switching, control, and operation of telecommunications systems.
Design	Knowledge of design techniques, tools, and principles involved in production of precision technical plans, blueprints, drawings, and models.
Production and Processing	Knowledge of raw materials, production processes, quality control, costs, and other techniques for maximizing the effective manufacture and distribution of goods.
Foreign Language	Knowledge of the structure and content of a foreign (non-English) language including the meaning and spelling of words, rules of composition and grammar, and pronunciation.
Philosophy and Theology	Knowledge of different philosophical systems and religions. This includes their basic principles, values, ethics, ways of thinking, customs, practices, and their impact on human culture.
Communications and Media	Knowledge of media production, communication, and dissemination techniques and methods. This includes alternative ways to inform and entertain via written, oral, and visual media.
History and Archeology	Knowledge of historical events and their causes, indicators, and effects on civilizations and cultures.
Economics and Accounting	Knowledge of economic and accounting principles and practices, the financial markets, banking and the analysis and reporting of financial data.
Transportation	Knowledge of principles and methods for moving people or goods by air, rail, sea, or road, including the relative costs and benefits.
Sales and Marketing	Knowledge of principles and methods for showing, promoting, and selling products or services. This includes marketing strategy and tactics, product demonstration, sales techniques, and sales control systems.
Geography	Knowledge of principles and methods for describing the features of land, sea, and air masses, including their physical characteristics, locations, interrelationships, and distribution of plant, animal, and human life.
Building and Construction	Knowledge of materials, methods, and the tools involved in the construction or repair of houses, buildings, or other structures such as highways and roads.
Fine Arts	Knowledge of the theory and techniques required to compose, produce, and perform works of music, dance, visual arts, drama, and sculpture.
Food Production	Knowledge of techniques and equipment for planting, growing, and harvesting food products (both plant and animal) for consumption, including storage/handling techniques.

Skills	Skills Definitions
Operation Monitoring	Watching gauges, dials, or other indicators to make sure a machine is working properly.
Time Management	Managing one's own time and the time of others.
Operation and Control	Controlling operations of equipment or systems.
Active Listening	Giving full attention to what other people are saying, taking time to understand the points being made, asking questions as appropriate, and not interrupting at inappropriate times.
Speaking	Talking to others to convey information effectively.
Instructing	Teaching others how to do something.
Critical Thinking	Using logic and reasoning to identify the strengths and weaknesses of alternative solutions, conclusions or approaches to problems.
Service Orientation	Actively looking for ways to help people.
Social Perceptiveness	Being aware of others' reactions and understanding why they react as they do.
Reading Comprehension	Understanding written sentences and paragraphs in work related documents.
Technology Design	Generating or adapting equipment and technology to serve user needs.
Coordination	Adjusting actions in relation to others' actions.
Science	Using scientific rules and methods to solve problems.
Complex Problem Solving	Identifying complex problems and reviewing related information to develop and evaluate options and implement solutions.
Mathematics	Using mathematics to solve problems.
Active Learning	Understanding the implications of new information for both current and future problem-solving and decision-making.

Equipment Selection	Determining the kind of tools and equipment needed to do a job.
Quality Control Analysis	Conducting tests and inspections of products, services, or processes to evaluate quality or performance.
Writing	Communicating effectively in writing as appropriate for the needs of the audience.
Management of Personnel Resources	Motivating, developing, and directing people as they work, identifying the best people for the job.
Learning Strategies	Selecting and using training/instructional methods and procedures appropriate for the situation when learning or teaching new things.
Monitoring	Monitoring/Assessing performance of yourself, other individuals, or organizations to make improvements or take corrective action.
Troubleshooting	Determining causes of operating errors and deciding what to do about it.
Operations Analysis	Analyzing needs and product requirements to create a design.
Equipment Maintenance	Performing routine maintenance on equipment and determining when and what kind of maintenance is needed.
Judgment and Decision Making	Considering the relative costs and benefits of potential actions to choose the most appropriate one.
Negotiation	Bringing others together and trying to reconcile differences.
Management of Material Resources	Obtaining and seeing to the appropriate use of equipment, facilities, and materials needed to do certain work.
Systems Evaluation	Identifying measures or indicators of system performance and the actions needed to improve or correct performance, relative to the goals of the system.
Persuasion	Persuading others to change their minds or behavior.
Installation	Installing equipment, machines, wiring, or programs to meet specifications.
Repairing	Repairing machines or systems using the needed tools.
Systems Analysis	Determining how a system should work and how changes in conditions, operations, and the environment will affect outcomes.
Management of Financial Resources	Determining how money will be spent to get the work done, and accounting for these expenditures.
Programming	Writing computer programs for various purposes.

Ability	Ability Definitions
Problem Sensitivity	The ability to tell when something is wrong or is likely to go wrong. It does not involve solving the problem, only recognizing there is a problem.
Near Vision	The ability to see details at close range (within a few feet of the observer).
Oral Comprehension	The ability to listen to and understand information and ideas presented through spoken words and sentences.
Written Comprehension	The ability to read and understand information and ideas presented in writing.
Speech Clarity	The ability to speak clearly so others can understand you.
Oral Expression	The ability to communicate information and ideas in speaking so others will understand.
Deductive Reasoning	The ability to apply general rules to specific problems to produce answers that make sense.
Information Ordering	The ability to arrange things or actions in a certain order or pattern according to a specific rule or set of rules (e.g., patterns of numbers, letters, words, pictures, mathematical operations).
Inductive Reasoning	The ability to combine pieces of information to form general rules or conclusions (includes finding a relationship among seemingly unrelated events).
Written Expression	The ability to communicate information and ideas in writing so others will understand.
Speech Recognition	The ability to identify and understand the speech of another person.
Number Facility	The ability to add, subtract, multiply, or divide quickly and correctly.
Mathematical Reasoning	The ability to choose the right mathematical methods or formulas to solve a problem.
Perceptual Speed	The ability to quickly and accurately compare similarities and differences among sets of letters, numbers, objects, pictures, or patterns. The things to be compared may be presented at the same time or one after the other. This ability also includes comparing a presented object with a remembered object.
Control Precision	The ability to quickly and repeatedly adjust the controls of a machine or a vehicle to exact positions.
Selective Attention	The ability to concentrate on a task over a period of time without being distracted.

Time Sharing	The ability to shift back and forth between two or more activities or sources of information (such as speech, sounds, touch, or other sources).
Arm-Hand Steadiness	The ability to keep your hand and arm steady while moving your arm or while holding your arm and hand in one position.
Category Flexibility	The ability to generate or use different sets of rules for combining or grouping things in different ways.
Visual Color Discrimination	The ability to match or detect differences between colors, including shades of color and brightness.
Flexibility of Closure	The ability to identify or detect a known pattern (a figure, object, word, or sound) that is hidden in other distracting material.
Finger Dexterity	The ability to make precisely coordinated movements of the fingers of one or both hands to grasp, manipulate, or assemble very small objects.
Memorization	The ability to remember information such as words, numbers, pictures, and procedures.
Manual Dexterity	The ability to quickly move your hand, your hand together with your arm, or your two hands to grasp, manipulate, or assemble objects.
Hearing Sensitivity	The ability to detect or tell the differences between sounds that vary in pitch and loudness.
Visualization	The ability to imagine how something will look after it is moved around or when its parts are moved or rearranged.
Reaction Time	The ability to quickly respond (with the hand, finger, or foot) to a signal (sound, light, picture) when it appears.
Speed of Closure	The ability to quickly make sense of, combine, and organize information into meaningful patterns.
Originality	The ability to come up with unusual or clever ideas about a given topic or situation, or to develop creative ways to solve a problem.
Response Orientation	The ability to choose quickly between two or more movements in response to two or more different signals (lights, sounds, pictures). It includes the speed with which the correct response is started with the hand, foot, or other body part.
Fluency of Ideas	The ability to come up with a number of ideas about a topic (the number of ideas is important, not their quality, correctness, or creativity).
Far Vision	The ability to see details at a distance.
Trunk Strength	The ability to use your abdominal and lower back muscles to support part of the body repeatedly or continuously over time without 'giving out' or fatiguing.
Depth Perception	The ability to judge which of several objects is closer or farther away from you, or to judge the distance between you and an object.
Auditory Attention	The ability to focus on a single source of sound in the presence of other distracting sounds.
Extent Flexibility	The ability to bend, stretch, twist, or reach with your body, arms, and/or legs.
Multilimb Coordination	The ability to coordinate two or more limbs (for example, two arms, two legs, or one leg and one arm) while sitting, standing, or lying down. It does not involve performing the activities while the whole body is in motion.
Wrist-Finger Speed	The ability to make fast, simple, repeated movements of the fingers, hands, and wrists.
Stamina	The ability to exert yourself physically over long periods of time without getting winded or out of breath.
Rate Control	The ability to time your movements or the movement of a piece of equipment in anticipation of changes in the speed and/or direction of a moving object or scene.
Speed of Limb Movement	The ability to quickly move the arms and legs.
Static Strength	The ability to exert maximum muscle force to lift, push, pull, or carry objects.
Dynamic Strength	The ability to exert muscle force repeatedly or continuously over time. This involves muscular endurance and resistance to muscle fatigue.
Gross Body Coordination	The ability to coordinate the movement of your arms, legs, and torso together when the whole body is in motion.
Spatial Orientation	The ability to know your location in relation to the environment or to know where other objects are in relation to you.
Sound Localization	The ability to tell the direction from which a sound originated.
Glare Sensitivity	The ability to see objects in the presence of glare or bright lighting.
Peripheral Vision	The ability to see objects or movement of objects to one's side when the eyes are looking ahead.
Night Vision	The ability to see under low light conditions.
Gross Body Equilibrium	The ability to keep or regain your body balance or stay upright when in an unstable position.

| Dynamic Flexibility | The ability to quickly and repeatedly bend. stretch, twist, or reach out with your body, arms, and/or legs. |
| Explosive Strength | The ability to use short bursts of muscle force to propel oneself (as in jumping or sprinting), or to throw an object. |

Work_Activity	Work_Activity Definitions
Monitor Processes, Materials, or Surroundings	Monitoring and reviewing information from materials, events, or the environment, to detect or assess problems.
Processing Information	Compiling, coding, categorizing, calculating, tabulating, auditing, or verifying information or data.
Documenting/Recording Information	Entering, transcribing, recording, storing, or maintaining information in written or electronic/magnetic form.
Interacting With Computers	Using computers and computer systems (including hardware and software) to program, write software, set up functions, enter data, or process information.
Updating and Using Relevant Knowledge	Keeping up-to-date technically and applying new knowledge to your job.
Getting Information	Observing, receiving, and otherwise obtaining information from all relevant sources.
Assisting and Caring for Others	Providing personal assistance, medical attention, emotional support, or other personal care to others such as coworkers, customers, or patients.
Inspecting Equipment, Structures, or Material	Inspecting equipment, structures, or materials to identify the cause of errors or other problems or defects.
Communicating with Supervisors, Peers, or Subordin	Providing information to supervisors, co-workers, and subordinates by telephone, in written form, e-mail, or in person.
Evaluating Information to Determine Compliance wit	Using relevant information and individual judgment to determine whether events or processes comply with laws, regulations, or standards.
Identifying Objects, Actions, and Events	Identifying information by categorizing, estimating, recognizing differences or similarities, and detecting changes in circumstances or events.
Establishing and Maintaining Interpersonal Relatio	Developing constructive and cooperative working relationships with others, and maintaining them over time.
Estimating the Quantifiable Characteristics of Pro	Estimating sizes, distances, and quantities; or determining time, costs, resources, or materials needed to perform a work activity.
Performing for or Working Directly with the Public	Performing for people or dealing directly with the public. This includes serving customers in restaurants and stores, and receiving clients or guests.
Making Decisions and Solving Problems	Analyzing information and evaluating results to choose the best solution and solve problems.
Controlling Machines and Processes	Using either control mechanisms or direct physical activity to operate machines or processes (not including computers or vehicles).
Training and Teaching Others	Identifying the educational needs of others, developing formal educational or training programs or classes, and teaching or instructing others.
Judging the Qualities of Things, Services, or Peop	Assessing the value, importance, or quality of things or people.
Coaching and Developing Others	Identifying the developmental needs of others and coaching, mentoring, or otherwise helping others to improve their knowledge or skills.
Organizing, Planning, and Prioritizing Work	Developing specific goals and plans to prioritize, organize, and accomplish your work.
Performing General Physical Activities	Performing physical activities that require considerable use of your arms and legs and moving your whole body, such as climbing, lifting, balancing, walking, stooping, and handling of materials.
Interpreting the Meaning of Information for Others	Translating or explaining what information means and how it can be used.
Guiding, Directing, and Motivating Subordinates	Providing guidance and direction to subordinates, including setting performance standards and monitoring performance.
Analyzing Data or Information	Identifying the underlying principles, reasons, or facts of information by breaking down information or data into separate parts.
Resolving Conflicts and Negotiating with Others	Handling complaints, settling disputes, and resolving grievances and conflicts, or otherwise negotiating with others.
Coordinating the Work and Activities of Others	Getting members of a group to work together to accomplish tasks.
Scheduling Work and Activities	Scheduling events, programs, and activities, as well as the work of others.

Thinking Creatively	Developing, designing, or creating new applications, ideas, relationships, systems, or products, including artistic contributions.
Communicating with Persons Outside Organization	Communicating with people outside the organization, representing the organization to customers, the public, government, and other external sources. This information can be exchanged in person, in writing, or by telephone or e-mail.
Handling and Moving Objects	Using hands and arms in handling, installing, positioning, and moving materials, and manipulating things.
Developing and Building Teams	Encouraging and building mutual trust, respect, and cooperation among team members.
Developing Objectives and Strategies	Establishing long-range objectives and specifying the strategies and actions to achieve them.
Provide Consultation and Advice to Others	Providing guidance and expert advice to management or other groups on technical, systems-, or process-related topics.
Operating Vehicles, Mechanized Devices, or Equipme	Running, maneuvering, navigating, or driving vehicles or mechanized equipment, such as forklifts, passenger vehicles, aircraft, or water craft.
Repairing and Maintaining Electronic Equipment	Servicing, repairing, calibrating, regulating, fine-tuning, or testing machines, devices, and equipment that operate primarily on the basis of electrical or electronic (not mechanical) principles.
Repairing and Maintaining Mechanical Equipment	Servicing, repairing, adjusting, and testing machines, devices, moving parts, and equipment that operate primarily on the basis of mechanical (not electronic) principles.
Performing Administrative Activities	Performing day-to-day administrative tasks such as maintaining information files and processing paperwork.
Selling or Influencing Others	Convincing others to buy merchandise/goods or to otherwise change their minds or actions.
Monitoring and Controlling Resources	Monitoring and controlling resources and overseeing the spending of money.
Staffing Organizational Units	Recruiting, interviewing, selecting, hiring, and promoting employees in an organization.
Drafting, Laying Out, and Specifying Technical Dev	Providing documentation, detailed instructions, drawings, or specifications to tell others about how devices, parts, equipment, or structures are to be fabricated, constructed, assembled, modified, maintained, or used.

Work_Context	Work_Context Definitions
Importance of Being Exact or Accurate	How important is being very exact or highly accurate in performing this job?
Face-to-Face Discussions	How often do you have to have face-to-face discussions with individuals or teams in this job?
Contact With Others	How much does this job require the worker to be in contact with others (face-to-face, by telephone, or otherwise) in order to perform it?
Work With Work Group or Team	How important is it to work with others in a group or team in this job?
Telephone	How often do you have telephone conversations in this job?
Importance of Repeating Same Tasks	How important is repeating the same physical activities (e.g., key entry) or mental activities (e.g., checking entries in a ledger) over and over, without stopping, to performing this job?
Exposed to Disease or Infections	How often does this job require exposure to disease/infections?
Indoors, Environmentally Controlled	How often does this job require working indoors in environmentally controlled conditions?
Physical Proximity	To what extent does this job require the worker to perform job tasks in close physical proximity to other people?
Spend Time Using Your Hands to Handle, Control, or	How much does this job require using your hands to handle, control, or feel objects, tools or controls?
Deal With External Customers	How important is it to work with external customers or the public in this job?
Structured versus Unstructured Work	To what extent is this job structured for the worker, rather than allowing the worker to determine tasks, priorities, and goals?
Spend Time Standing	How much does this job require standing?
Coordinate or Lead Others	How important is it to coordinate or lead others in accomplishing work activities in this job?
Time Pressure	How often does this job require the worker to meet strict deadlines?
Frequency of Decision Making	How frequently is the worker required to make decisions that affect other people, the financial resources, and/or the image and reputation of the organization?
Spend Time Walking and Running	How much does this job require walking and running?
Consequence of Error	How serious would the result usually be if the worker made a mistake that was not readily correctable?

Freedom to Make Decisions	How much decision making freedom, without supervision, does the job offer?
Impact of Decisions on Co-workers or Company Resul	How do the decisions an employee makes impact the results of co-workers, clients or the company?
Spend Time Making Repetitive Motions	How much does this job require making repetitive motions?
Exposed to Radiation	How often does this job require exposure to radiation?
Responsible for Others' Health and Safety	How much responsibility is there for the health and safety of others in this job?
Deal With Unpleasant or Angry People	How frequently does the worker have to deal with unpleasant, angry, or discourteous individuals as part of the job requirements?
Frequency of Conflict Situations	How often are there conflict situations the employee has to face in this job?
Responsibility for Outcomes and Results	How responsible is the worker for work outcomes and results of other workers?
Spend Time Bending or Twisting the Body	How much does this job require bending or twisting your body?
Level of Competition	To what extent does this job require the worker to compete or to be aware of competitive pressures?
Pace Determined by Speed of Equipment	How important is it to this job that the pace is determined by the speed of equipment or machinery? (This does not refer to keeping busy at all times on this job.)
Electronic Mail	How often do you use electronic mail in this job?
Letters and Memos	How often does the job require written letters and memos?
Wear Common Protective or Safety Equipment such as	How much does this job require wearing common protective or safety equipment such as safety shoes, glasses, gloves, hard hats or live jackets?
Sounds, Noise Levels Are Distracting or Uncomforta	How often does this job require working exposed to sounds and noise levels that are distracting or uncomfortable?
Wear Specialized Protective or Safety Equipment su	How much does this job require wearing specialized protective or safety equipment such as breathing apparatus, safety harness, full protection suits, or radiation protection?
Degree of Automation	How automated is the job?
Exposed to Hazardous Equipment	How often does this job require exposure to hazardous equipment?
Exposed to Contaminants	How often does this job require working exposed to contaminants (such as pollutants, gases, dust or odors)?
Exposed to Minor Burns, Cuts, Bites, or Stings	How often does this job require exposure to minor burns, cuts, bites, or stings?
Exposed to Hazardous Conditions	How often does this job require exposure to hazardous conditions?
Public Speaking	How often do you have to perform public speaking in this job?
Spend Time Kneeling, Crouching, Stooping, or Crawl	How much does this job require kneeling, crouching, stooping or crawling?
Extremely Bright or Inadequate Lighting	How often does this job require working in extremely bright or inadequate lighting conditions?
Spend Time Sitting	How much does this job require sitting?
Cramped Work Space, Awkward Positions	How often does this job require working in cramped work spaces that requires getting into awkward positions?
Deal With Physically Aggressive People	How frequently does this job require the worker to deal with physical aggression of violent individuals?
Spend Time Keeping or Regaining Balance	How much does this job require keeping or regaining your balance?
Exposed to Whole Body Vibration	How often does this job require exposure to whole body vibration (e.g., operate a jackhammer)?
Indoors, Not Environmentally Controlled	How often does this job require working indoors in non-controlled environmental conditions (e.g., warehouse without heat)?
Spend Time Climbing Ladders, Scaffolds, or Poles	How much does this job require climbing ladders, scaffolds, or poles?
Very Hot or Cold Temperatures	How often does this job require working in very hot (above 90 F degrees) or very cold (below 32 F degrees) temperatures?
In an Open Vehicle or Equipment	How often does this job require working in an open vehicle or equipment (e.g., tractor)?
Outdoors, Under Cover	How often does this job require working outdoors, under cover (e.g., structure with roof but no walls)?
In an Enclosed Vehicle or Equipment	How often does this job require working in a closed vehicle or equipment (e.g., car)?
Exposed to High Places	How often does this job require exposure to high places?
Outdoors, Exposed to Weather	How often does this job require working outdoors, exposed to all weather conditions?

Job Zone Component	Job Zone Component Definitions
Title	Job Zone Three: Medium Preparation Needed
Overall Experience	Previous work-related skill, knowledge, or experience is required for these occupations. For example, an electrician must have completed three or four years of apprenticeship or several years of vocational training, and often must have passed a licensing exam, in order to perform the job.
Job Training	Employees in these occupations usually need one or two years of training involving both on-the-job experience and informal training with experienced workers.
Job Zone Examples	These occupations usually involve using communication and organizational skills to coordinate, supervise, manage, or train others to accomplish goals. Examples include dental assistants, electricians, fish and game wardens, legal secretaries, personnel recruiters, and recreation workers.
SVP Range	(6.0 to < 7.0)
Education	Most occupations in this zone require training in vocational schools, related on-the-job experience, or an associate's degree. Some may require a bachelor's degree.

Work_Styles	Work_Styles Definitions
Integrity	Job requires being honest and ethical.
Attention to Detail	Job requires being careful about detail and thorough in completing work tasks.
Concern for Others	Job requires being sensitive to others' needs and feelings and being understanding and helpful on the job.
Dependability	Job requires being reliable, responsible, and dependable, and fulfilling obligations.
Cooperation	Job requires being pleasant with others on the job and displaying a good-natured, cooperative attitude.
Social Orientation	Job requires preferring to work with others rather than alone, and being personally connected with others on the job.
Self Control	Job requires maintaining composure, keeping emotions in check, controlling anger, and avoiding aggressive behavior, even in very difficult situations.
Achievement/Effort	Job requires establishing and maintaining personally challenging achievement goals and exerting effort toward mastering tasks.
Stress Tolerance	Job requires accepting criticism and dealing calmly and effectively with high stress situations.
Adaptability/Flexibility	Job requires being open to change (positive or negative) and to considerable variety in the workplace.
Initiative	Job requires a willingness to take on responsibilities and challenges.
Analytical Thinking	Job requires analyzing information and using logic to address work-related issues and problems.
Independence	Job requires developing one's own ways of doing things, guiding oneself with little or no supervision, and depending on oneself to get things done.
Persistence	Job requires persistence in the face of obstacles.
Leadership	Job requires a willingness to lead, take charge, and offer opinions and direction.
Innovation	Job requires creativity and alternative thinking to develop new ideas for and answers to work-related problems.

29-1125.00 - Recreational Therapists

Plan, direct, or coordinate medically-approved recreation programs for patients in hospitals, nursing homes, or other institutions. Activities include sports, trips, dramatics, social activities, and arts and crafts. May assess a patient condition and recommend appropriate recreational activity.

Tasks

1) Instruct patient in activities and techniques, such as sports, dance, music, art or relaxation techniques, designed to meet their specific physical or psychological needs.

2) Develop treatment plan to meet needs of patient, based on needs assessment, patient interests and objectives of therapy.

3) Confer with members of treatment team to plan and evaluate therapy programs.

4) Prepare and submit reports and charts to treatment team to reflect patients' reactions and

evidence of progress or regression.

5) Plan, organize, direct and participate in treatment programs and activities to facilitate patients' rehabilitation, help them integrate into the community and prevent further medical problems.

6) Conduct therapy sessions to improve patients' mental and physical well-being.

7) Obtain information from medical records, medical staff, family members and the patients themselves to assess patients' capabilities, needs and interests.

8) Observe, analyze, and record patients' participation, reactions, and progress during treatment sessions, modifying treatment programs as needed.

9) Counsel and encourage patients to develop leisure activities.

Knowledge	Knowledge Definitions
Psychology	Knowledge of human behavior and performance; individual differences in ability, personality, and interests; learning and motivation; psychological research methods; and the assessment and treatment of behavioral and affective disorders.
Therapy and Counseling	Knowledge of principles, methods, and procedures for diagnosis, treatment, and rehabilitation of physical and mental dysfunctions, and for career counseling and guidance.
Customer and Personal Service	Knowledge of principles and processes for providing customer and personal services. This includes customer needs assessment, meeting quality standards for services, and evaluation of customer satisfaction.
Sociology and Anthropology	Knowledge of group behavior and dynamics, societal trends and influences, human migrations, ethnicity, cultures and their history and origins.
Education and Training	Knowledge of principles and methods for curriculum and training design, teaching and instruction for individuals and groups, and the measurement of training effects.
English Language	Knowledge of the structure and content of the English language including the meaning and spelling of words, rules of composition, and grammar.
Fine Arts	Knowledge of the theory and techniques required to compose, produce, and perform works of music, dance, visual arts, drama, and sculpture.
Medicine and Dentistry	Knowledge of the information and techniques needed to diagnose and treat human injuries, diseases, and deformities. This includes symptoms, treatment alternatives, drug properties and interactions, and preventive health-care measures.
Public Safety and Security	Knowledge of relevant equipment, policies, procedures, and strategies to promote effective local, state, or national security operations for the protection of people, data, property, and institutions.
Administration and Management	Knowledge of business and management principles involved in strategic planning, resource allocation, human resources modeling, leadership technique, production methods, and coordination of people and resources.
Transportation	Knowledge of principles and methods for moving people or goods by air, rail, sea, or road, including the relative costs and benefits.
Law and Government	Knowledge of laws, legal codes, court procedures, precedents, government regulations, executive orders, agency rules, and the democratic political process.
Communications and Media	Knowledge of media production, communication, and dissemination techniques and methods. This includes alternative ways to inform and entertain via written, oral, and visual media.
Mathematics	Knowledge of arithmetic, algebra, geometry, calculus, statistics, and their applications.
Philosophy and Theology	Knowledge of different philosophical systems and religions. This includes their basic principles, values, ethics, ways of thinking, customs, practices, and their impact on human culture.
Clerical	Knowledge of administrative and clerical procedures and systems such as word processing, managing files and records, stenography and transcription, designing forms, and other office procedures and terminology.
Computers and Electronics	Knowledge of circuit boards, processors, chips, electronic equipment, and computer hardware and software, including applications and programming.
Personnel and Human Resources	Knowledge of principles and procedures for personnel recruitment, selection, training, compensation and benefits, labor relations and negotiation, and personnel information systems.

Biology	Knowledge of plant and animal organisms, their tissues, cells, functions, interdependencies, and interactions with each other and the environment.
Telecommunications	Knowledge of transmission, broadcasting, switching, control, and operation of telecommunications systems.
Food Production	Knowledge of techniques and equipment for planting, growing, and harvesting food products (both plant and animal) for consumption, including storage/handling techniques.
Geography	Knowledge of principles and methods for describing the features of land, sea, and air masses, including their physical characteristics, locations, interrelationships, and distribution of plant, animal, and human life.
History and Archeology	Knowledge of historical events and their causes, indicators, and effects on civilizations and cultures.
Economics and Accounting	Knowledge of economic and accounting principles and practices, the financial markets, banking and the analysis and reporting of financial data.
Sales and Marketing	Knowledge of principles and methods for showing, promoting, and selling products or services. This includes marketing strategy and tactics, product demonstration, sales techniques, and sales-control systems.
Physics	Knowledge and prediction of physical principles, laws, their interrelationships, and applications to understanding fluid, material, and atmospheric dynamics, and mechanical, electrical, atomic and sub-atomic structures and processes.
Production and Processing	Knowledge of raw materials, production processes, quality control, costs, and other techniques for maximizing the effective manufacture and distribution of goods.
Foreign Language	Knowledge of the structure and content of a foreign (non-English) language including the meaning and spelling of words, rules of composition and grammar, and pronunciation.
Mechanical	Knowledge of machines and tools, including their designs, uses, repair, and maintenance.
Design	Knowledge of design techniques, tools, and principles involved in production of precision technical plans, blueprints, drawings, and models.
Chemistry	Knowledge of the chemical composition, structure, and properties of substances and of the chemical processes and transformations that they undergo. This includes uses of chemicals and their interactions, danger signs, production techniques, and disposal methods.
Building and Construction	Knowledge of materials, methods, and the tools involved in the construction or repair of houses, buildings, or other structures such as highways and roads.
Engineering and Technology	Knowledge of the practical application of engineering science and technology. This includes applying principles, techniques, procedures, and equipment to the design and production of various goods and services.

Skills	Skills Definitions
Social Perceptiveness	Being aware of others' reactions and understanding why they react as they do.
Active Listening	Giving full attention to what other people are saying, taking time to understand the points being made, asking questions as appropriate, and not interrupting at inappropriate times.
Writing	Communicating effectively in writing as appropriate for the needs of the audience.
Speaking	Talking to others to convey information effectively.
Reading Comprehension	Understanding written sentences and paragraphs in work related documents.
Monitoring	Monitoring/Assessing performance of yourself, other individuals, or organizations to make improvements or take corrective action.
Service Orientation	Actively looking for ways to help people.
Coordination	Adjusting actions in relation to others' actions.
Time Management	Managing one's own time and the time of others.
Learning Strategies	Selecting and using training/instructional methods and procedures appropriate for the situation when learning or teaching new things.
Persuasion	Persuading others to change their minds or behavior.
Instructing	Teaching others how to do something.
Critical Thinking	Using logic and reasoning to identify the strengths and weaknesses of alternative solutions, conclusions or approaches to problems.
Active Learning	Understanding the implications of new information for both current and future problem-solving and decision-making.

Judgment and Decision Making	Considering the relative costs and benefits of potential actions to choose the most appropriate one.
Negotiation	Bringing others together and trying to reconcile differences.
Complex Problem Solving	Identifying complex problems and reviewing related information to develop and evaluate options and implement solutions.
Management of Personnel Resources	Motivating, developing, and directing people as they work, identifying the best people for the job.
Management of Financial Resources	Determining how money will be spent to get the work done, and accounting for these expenditures.
Systems Evaluation	Identifying measures or indicators of system performance and the actions needed to improve or correct performance, relative to the goals of the system.
Equipment Selection	Determining the kind of tools and equipment needed to do a job.
Operations Analysis	Analyzing needs and product requirements to create a design.
Management of Material Resources	Obtaining and seeing to the appropriate use of equipment, facilities, and materials needed to do certain work.
Quality Control Analysis	Conducting tests and inspections of products, services, or processes to evaluate quality or performance.
Technology Design	Generating or adapting equipment and technology to serve user needs.
Mathematics	Using mathematics to solve problems.
Systems Analysis	Determining how a system should work and how changes in conditions, operations, and the environment will affect outcomes.
Troubleshooting	Determining causes of operating errors and deciding what to do about it.
Operation and Control	Controlling operations of equipment or systems.
Science	Using scientific rules and methods to solve problems.
Repairing	Repairing machines or systems using the needed tools.
Equipment Maintenance	Performing routine maintenance on equipment and determining when and what kind of maintenance is needed.
Operation Monitoring	Watching gauges, dials, or other indicators to make sure a machine is working properly.
Programming	Writing computer programs for various purposes.
Installation	Installing equipment, machines, wiring, or programs to meet specifications.

Ability	Ability Definitions
Oral Expression	The ability to communicate information and ideas in speaking so others will understand.
Oral Comprehension	The ability to listen to and understand information and ideas presented through spoken words and sentences.
Inductive Reasoning	The ability to combine pieces of information to form general rules or conclusions (includes finding a relationship among seemingly unrelated events).
Problem Sensitivity	The ability to tell when something is wrong or is likely to go wrong. It does not involve solving the problem, only recognizing there is a problem.
Speech Clarity	The ability to speak clearly so others can understand you.
Near Vision	The ability to see details at close range (within a few feet of the observer).
Originality	The ability to come up with unusual or clever ideas about a given topic or situation, or to develop creative ways to solve a problem.
Written Expression	The ability to communicate information and ideas in writing so others will understand.
Deductive Reasoning	The ability to apply general rules to specific problems to produce answers that make sense.
Written Comprehension	The ability to read and understand information and ideas presented in writing.
Speech Recognition	The ability to identify and understand the speech of another person.
Information Ordering	The ability to arrange things or actions in a certain order or pattern according to a specific rule or set of rules (e.g., patterns of numbers, letters, words, pictures, mathematical operations).
Fluency of Ideas	The ability to come up with a number of ideas about a topic (the number of ideas is important, not their quality, correctness, or creativity).
Selective Attention	The ability to concentrate on a task over a period of time without being distracted.
Time Sharing	The ability to shift back and forth between two or more activities or sources of information (such as speech, sounds, touch, or other sources).
Gross Body Coordination	The ability to coordinate the movement of your arms, legs, and torso together when the whole body is in motion.

Flexibility of Closure	The ability to identify or detect a known pattern (a figure, object, word, or sound) that is hidden in other distracting material.
Stamina	The ability to exert yourself physically over long periods of time without getting winded or out of breath.
Static Strength	The ability to exert maximum muscle force to lift, push, pull, or carry objects.
Category Flexibility	The ability to generate or use different sets of rules for combining or grouping things in different ways.
Trunk Strength	The ability to use your abdominal and lower back muscles to support part of the body repeatedly or continuously over time without 'giving out' or fatiguing.
Multilimb Coordination	The ability to coordinate two or more limbs (for example, two arms, two legs, or one leg and one arm) while sitting, standing, or lying down. It does not involve performing the activities while the whole body is in motion.
Far Vision	The ability to see details at a distance.
Finger Dexterity	The ability to make precisely coordinated movements of the fingers of one or both hands to grasp, manipulate, or assemble very small objects.
Visualization	The ability to imagine how something will look after it is moved around or when its parts are moved or rearranged.
Reaction Time	The ability to quickly respond (with the hand, finger, or foot) to a signal (sound, light, picture) when it appears.
Manual Dexterity	The ability to quickly move your hand, your hand together with your arm, or your two hands to grasp, manipulate, or assemble objects.
Gross Body Equilibrium	The ability to keep or regain your body balance or stay upright when in an unstable position.
Memorization	The ability to remember information such as words, numbers, pictures, and procedures.
Auditory Attention	The ability to focus on a single source of sound in the presence of other distracting sounds.
Dynamic Strength	The ability to exert muscle force repeatedly or continuously over time. This involves muscular endurance and resistance to muscle fatigue.
Speed of Closure	The ability to quickly make sense of, combine, and organize information into meaningful patterns.
Arm-Hand Steadiness	The ability to keep your hand and arm steady while moving your arm or while holding your arm and hand in one position.
Response Orientation	The ability to choose quickly between two or more movements in response to two or more different signals (lights, sounds, pictures). It includes the speed with which the correct response is started with the hand, foot, or other body part.
Extent Flexibility	The ability to bend, stretch, twist, or reach with your body, arms, and/or legs.
Speed of Limb Movement	The ability to quickly move the arms and legs.
Perceptual Speed	The ability to quickly and accurately compare similarities and differences among sets of letters, numbers, objects, pictures, or patterns. The things to be compared may be presented at the same time or one after the other. This ability also includes comparing a presented object with a remembered object.
Depth Perception	The ability to judge which of several objects is closer or farther away from you, or to judge the distance between you and an object.
Explosive Strength	The ability to use short bursts of muscle force to propel oneself (as in jumping or sprinting), or to throw an object.
Control Precision	The ability to quickly and repeatedly adjust the controls of a machine or a vehicle to exact positions.
Hearing Sensitivity	The ability to detect or tell the differences between sounds that vary in pitch and loudness.
Number Facility	The ability to add, subtract, multiply, or divide quickly and correctly.
Visual Color Discrimination	The ability to match or detect differences between colors, including shades of color and brightness.
Mathematical Reasoning	The ability to choose the right mathematical methods or formulas to solve a problem.
Glare Sensitivity	The ability to see objects in the presence of glare or bright lighting.
Dynamic Flexibility	The ability to quickly and repeatedly bend, stretch, twist, or reach out with your body, arms, and/or legs.
Rate Control	The ability to time your movements or the movement of a piece of equipment in anticipation of changes in the speed and/or direction of a moving object or scene.
Wrist-Finger Speed	The ability to make fast, simple, repeated movements of the fingers, hands, and wrists.
Peripheral Vision	The ability to see objects or movement of objects to one's side when the eyes are looking ahead.

Night Vision	The ability to see under low light conditions.
Spatial Orientation	The ability to know your location in relation to the environment or to know where other objects are in relation to you.
Sound Localization	The ability to tell the direction from which a sound originated.

Work_Activity | Work_Activity Definitions

Assisting and Caring for Others	Providing personal assistance, medical attention, emotional support, or other personal care to others such as coworkers, customers, or patients.
Scheduling Work and Activities	Scheduling events, programs, and activities, as well as the work of others.
Getting Information	Observing, receiving, and otherwise obtaining information from all relevant sources.
Thinking Creatively	Developing, designing, or creating new applications, ideas, relationships, systems, or products, including artistic contributions.
Monitor Processes, Materials, or Surroundings	Monitoring and reviewing information from materials, events, or the environment, to detect or assess problems.
Organizing, Planning, and Prioritizing Work	Developing specific goals and plans to prioritize, organize, and accomplish your work.
Identifying Objects, Actions, and Events	Identifying information by categorizing, estimating, recognizing differences or similarities, and detecting changes in circumstances or events.
Communicating with Supervisors, Peers, or Subordin	Providing information to supervisors, co-workers, and subordinates by telephone, in written form, e-mail, or in person.
Making Decisions and Solving Problems	Analyzing information and evaluating results to choose the best solution and solve problems.
Documenting/Recording Information	Entering, transcribing, recording, storing, or maintaining information in written or electronic/magnetic form.
Performing General Physical Activities	Performing physical activities that require considerable use of your arms and legs and moving your whole body, such as climbing, lifting, balancing, walking, stooping, and handling of materials.
Establishing and Maintaining Interpersonal Relatio	Developing constructive and cooperative working relationships with others, and maintaining them over time.
Evaluating Information to Determine Compliance wit	Using relevant information and individual judgment to determine whether events or processes comply with laws, regulations, or standards.
Updating and Using Relevant Knowledge	Keeping up-to-date technically and applying new knowledge to your job.
Inspecting Equipment, Structures, or Material	Inspecting equipment, structures, or materials to identify the cause of errors or other problems or defects.
Coordinating the Work and Activities of Others	Getting members of a group to work together to accomplish tasks.
Judging the Qualities of Things, Services, or Peop	Assessing the value, importance, or quality of things or people.
Communicating with Persons Outside Organization	Communicating with people outside the organization, representing the organization to customers, the public, government, and other external sources. This information can be exchanged in person, in writing, or by telephone or e-mail.
Monitoring and Controlling Resources	Monitoring and controlling resources and overseeing the spending of money.
Interacting With Computers	Using computers and computer systems (including hardware and software) to program, write software, set up functions, enter data, or process information.
Processing Information	Compiling, coding, categorizing, calculating, tabulating, auditing, or verifying information or data.
Performing Administrative Activities	Performing day-to-day administrative tasks such as maintaining information files and processing paperwork.
Developing and Building Teams	Encouraging and building mutual trust, respect, and cooperation among team members.
Resolving Conflicts and Negotiating with Others	Handling complaints, settling disputes, and resolving grievances and conflicts, or otherwise negotiating with others.
Training and Teaching Others	Identifying the educational needs of others, developing formal educational or training programs or classes, and teaching or instructing others.
Analyzing Data or Information	Identifying the underlying principles, reasons, or facts of information by breaking down information or data into separate parts.
Estimating the Quantifiable Characteristics of Pro	Estimating sizes, distances, and quantities; or determining time, costs, resources, or materials needed to perform a work activity.
Developing Objectives and Strategies	Establishing long-range objectives and specifying the strategies and actions to achieve them.

Coaching and Developing Others	Identifying the developmental needs of others and coaching, mentoring, or otherwise helping others to improve their knowledge or skills.
Handling and Moving Objects	Using hands and arms in handling, installing, positioning, and moving materials, and manipulating things.
Guiding, Directing, and Motivating Subordinates	Providing guidance and direction to subordinates, including setting performance standards and monitoring performance.
Interpreting the Meaning of Information for Others	Translating or explaining what information means and how it can be used.
Provide Consultation and Advice to Others	Providing guidance and expert advice to management or other groups on technical, systems-, or process-related topics.
Operating Vehicles, Mechanized Devices, or Equipme	Running, maneuvering, navigating, or driving vehicles or mechanized equipment, such as forklifts, passenger vehicles, aircraft, or water craft.
Performing for or Working Directly with the Public	Performing for people or dealing directly with the public. This includes serving customers in restaurants and stores, and receiving clients or guests.
Selling or Influencing Others	Convincing others to buy merchandise/goods or to otherwise change their minds or actions.
Staffing Organizational Units	Recruiting, interviewing, selecting, hiring, and promoting employees in an organization.
Controlling Machines and Processes	Using either control mechanisms or direct physical activity to operate machines or processes (not including computers or vehicles).
Drafting, Laying Out, and Specifying Technical Dev	Providing documentation, detailed instructions, drawings, or specifications to tell others about how devices, parts, equipment, or structures are to be fabricated, constructed, assembled, modified, maintained, or used.
Repairing and Maintaining Electronic Equipment	Servicing, repairing, calibrating, regulating, fine-tuning, or testing machines, devices, and equipment that operate primarily on the basis of electrical or electronic (not mechanical) principles.
Repairing and Maintaining Mechanical Equipment	Servicing, repairing, adjusting, and testing machines, devices, moving parts, and equipment that operate primarily on the basis of mechanical (not electronic) principles.

Work_Context | Work_Context Definitions

Face-to-Face Discussions	How often do you have to have face-to-face discussions with individuals or teams in this job?
Work With Work Group or Team	How important is it to work with others in a group or team in this job?
Contact With Others	How much does this job require the worker to be in contact with others (face-to-face, by telephone, or otherwise) in order to perform it?
Physical Proximity	To what extent does this job require the worker to perform job tasks in close physical proximity to other people?
Deal With Physically Aggressive People	How frequently does this job require the worker to deal with physical aggression of violent individuals?
Structured versus Unstructured Work	To what extent is this job structured for the worker, rather than allowing the worker to determine tasks, priorities, and goals?
Freedom to Make Decisions	How much decision making freedom, without supervision, does the job offer?
Telephone	How often do you have telephone conversations in this job?
Exposed to Disease or Infections	How often does this job require exposure to disease/infections?
Time Pressure	How often does this job require the worker to meet strict deadlines?
Coordinate or Lead Others	How important is it to coordinate or lead others in accomplishing work activities in this job?
Frequency of Decision Making	How frequently is the worker required to make decisions that affect other people, the financial resources, and/or the image and reputation of the organization?
Electronic Mail	How often do you use electronic mail in this job?
Responsible for Others' Health and Safety	How much responsibility is there for the health and safety of others in this job?
Deal With Unpleasant or Angry People	How frequently does the worker have to deal with unpleasant, angry, or discourteous individuals as part of the job requirements?
Impact of Decisions on Co-workers or Company Resul	How do the decisions an employee makes impact the results of co-workers, clients or the company?
Importance of Being Exact or Accurate	How important is being very exact or highly accurate in performing this job?
Frequency of Conflict Situations	How often are there conflict situations the employee has to face in this job?
Deal With External Customers	How important is it to work with external customers or the public in this job?

Spend Time Standing	How much does this job require standing?
Indoors, Environmentally Controlled	How often does this job require working indoors in environmentally controlled conditions?
Letters and Memos	How often does the job require written letters and memos?
Consequence of Error	How serious would the result usually be if the worker made a mistake that was not readily correctable?
Importance of Repeating Same Tasks	How important is repeating the same physical activities (e.g., key entry) or mental activities (e.g., checking entries in a ledger) over and over, without stopping, to performing this job?
Sounds, Noise Levels Are Distracting or Uncomfortable	How often does this job require working exposed to sounds and noise levels that are distracting or uncomfortable?
Exposed to Contaminants	How often does this job require working exposed to contaminants (such as pollutants, gases, dust or odors)?
In an Enclosed Vehicle or Equipment	How often does this job require working in a closed vehicle or equipment (e.g., car)?
Public Speaking	How often do you have to perform public speaking in this job?
Outdoors, Exposed to Weather	How often does this job require working outdoors, exposed to all weather conditions?
Spend Time Walking and Running	How much does this job require walking and running?
Exposed to Minor Burns, Cuts, Bites, or Stings	How often does this job require exposure to minor burns, cuts, bites, or stings?
Responsibility for Outcomes and Results	How responsible is the worker for work outcomes and results of other workers?
Level of Competition	To what extent does this job require the worker to compete or to be aware of competitive pressures?
Degree of Automation	How automated is the job?
Spend Time Bending or Twisting the Body	How much does this job require bending or twisting your body?
Wear Common Protective or Safety Equipment such as	How much does this job require wearing common protective or safety equipment such as safety shoes, glasses, gloves, hard hats or life jackets?
Spend Time Making Repetitive Motions	How much does this job require making repetitive motions?
Spend Time Sitting	How much does this job require sitting?
Spend Time Using Your Hands to Handle, Control, or	How much does this job require using your hands to handle, control, or feel objects, tools or controls?
Extremely Bright or Inadequate Lighting	How often does this job require working in extremely bright or inadequate lighting conditions?
Very Hot or Cold Temperatures	How often does this job require working in very hot (above 90 F degrees) or very cold (below 32 F degrees) temperatures?
Cramped Work Space, Awkward Positions	How often does this job require working in cramped work spaces that requires getting into awkward positions?
Exposed to Hazardous Conditions	How often does this job require exposure to hazardous conditions?
Indoors, Not Environmentally Controlled	How often does this job require working indoors in non-controlled environmental conditions (e.g., warehouse without heat)?
Spend Time Kneeling, Crouching, Stooping, or Crawl	How much does this job require kneeling, crouching, stooping, or crawling?
Spend Time Keeping or Regaining Balance	How much does this job require keeping or regaining your balance?
Outdoors, Under Cover	How often does this job require working outdoors, under cover (e.g., structure with roof but no walls)?
In an Open Vehicle or Equipment	How often does this job require working in an open vehicle or equipment (e.g., tractor)?
Spend Time Climbing Ladders, Scaffolds, or Poles	How much does this job require climbing ladders, scaffolds, or poles?
Exposed to Radiation	How often does this job require exposure to radiation?
Wear Specialized Protective or Safety Equipment su	How much does this job require wearing specialized protective or safety equipment such as breathing apparatus, safety harness, full protection suits, or radiation protection?
Pace Determined by Speed of Equipment	How important is it to this job that the pace is determined by the speed of equipment or machinery? (This does not refer to keeping busy at all times on this job.)
Exposed to High Places	How often does this job require exposure to high places?
Exposed to Hazardous Equipment	How often does this job require exposure to hazardous equipment?
Exposed to Whole Body Vibration	How often does this job require exposure to whole body vibration (e.g., operate a jackhammer)?

Job Zone Component	Job Zone Component Definitions
Title	Job Zone Four: Considerable Preparation Needed

Overall Experience	A minimum of two to four years of work-related skill, knowledge, or experience is needed for these occupations. For example, an accountant must complete four years of college and work for several years in accounting to be considered qualified.
Job Training	Employees in these occupations usually need several years of work-related experience, on-the-job training, and/or vocational training.
Job Zone Examples	Many of these occupations involve coordinating, supervising, managing, or training others. Examples include accountants, chefs and head cooks, computer programmers, historians, pharmacists, and police detectives.
SVP Range	(7.0 to < 8.0)
Education	Most of these occupations require a four - year bachelor's degree, but some do not.

Work_Styles	Work_Styles Definitions
Concern for Others	Job requires being sensitive to others' needs and feelings and being understanding and helpful on the job.
Self Control	Job requires maintaining composure, keeping emotions in check, controlling anger, and avoiding aggressive behavior, even in very difficult situations.
Cooperation	Job requires being pleasant with others on the job and displaying a good-natured, cooperative attitude.
Integrity	Job requires being honest and ethical.
Dependability	Job requires being reliable, responsible, and dependable, and fulfilling obligations.
Adaptability/Flexibility	Job requires being open to change (positive or negative) and to considerable variety in the workplace.
Social Orientation	Job requires preferring to work with others rather than alone, and being personally connected with others on the job.
Innovation	Job requires creativity and alternative thinking to develop new ideas for and answers to work-related problems.
Stress Tolerance	Job requires accepting criticism and dealing calmly and effectively with high stress situations.
Leadership	Job requires a willingness to lead, take charge, and offer opinions and direction.
Attention to Detail	Job requires being careful about detail and thorough in completing work tasks.
Initiative	Job requires a willingness to take on responsibilities and challenges.
Independence	Job requires developing one's own ways of doing things, guiding oneself with little or no supervision, and depending on oneself to get things done.
Achievement/Effort	Job requires establishing and maintaining personally challenging achievement goals and exerting effort toward mastering tasks.
Persistence	Job requires persistence in the face of obstacles.
Analytical Thinking	Job requires analyzing information and using logic to address work-related issues and problems.

29-1126.00 - Respiratory Therapists

Assess, treat, and care for patients with breathing disorders. Assume primary responsibility for all respiratory care modalities, including the supervision of respiratory therapy technicians. Initiate and conduct therapeutic procedures; maintain patient records; and select, assemble, check, and operate equipment.

Tasks

1) Enforce safety rules and ensure careful adherence to physicians' orders.

2) Determine requirements for treatment, such as type, method and duration of therapy, precautions to be taken, and medication and dosages, compatible with physicians' orders.

3) Work as part of a team of physicians, nurses and other health care professionals to manage patient care.

4) Set up and operate devices such as mechanical ventilators, therapeutic gas administration apparatus, environmental control systems, and aerosol generators, following specified parameters of treatment.

5) Provide emergency care, including artificial respiration, external cardiac massage and assistance with cardiopulmonary resuscitation.

6) Teach, train, supervise, and utilize the assistance of students, respiratory therapy

technicians, and assistants.

7) Inspect, clean, test and maintain respiratory therapy equipment to ensure equipment is functioning safely and efficiently, ordering repairs when necessary.

8) Monitor patient's physiological responses to therapy, such as vital signs, arterial blood gases, and blood chemistry changes, and consult with physician if adverse reactions occur.

9) Perform bronchopulmonary drainage and assist or instruct patients in performance of breathing exercises.

10) Read prescription, measure arterial blood gases, and review patient information to assess patient condition.

11) Conduct tests, such as electrocardiograms, stress testing, and lung capacity tests, to evaluate patients' cardiopulmonary functions.

12) Relay blood analysis results to a physician.

13) Make emergency visits to resolve equipment problems.

14) Use a variety of testing techniques to assist doctors in cardiac and pulmonary research and to diagnose disorders.

15) Perform pulmonary function and adjust equipment to obtain optimum results in therapy.

16) Maintain charts that contain patients' pertinent identification and therapy information.

17) Educate patients and their families about their conditions and teach appropriate disease management techniques, such as breathing exercises and the use of medications and respiratory equipment.

18) Explain treatment procedures to patients to gain cooperation and allay fears.

Knowledge	Knowledge Definitions
Medicine and Dentistry	Knowledge of the information and techniques needed to diagnose and treat human injuries, diseases, and deformities. This includes symptoms, treatment alternatives, drug properties and interactions, and preventive health-care measures.
Customer and Personal Service	Knowledge of principles and processes for providing customer and personal services. This includes customer needs assessment, meeting quality standards for services, and evaluation of customer satisfaction.
Psychology	Knowledge of human behavior and performance; individual differences in ability, personality, and interests; learning and motivation; psychological research methods; and the assessment and treatment of behavioral and affective disorders.
Education and Training	Knowledge of principles and methods for curriculum and training design, teaching and instruction for individuals and groups, and the measurement of training effects.
English Language	Knowledge of the structure and content of the English language including the meaning and spelling of words, rules of composition, and grammar.
Chemistry	Knowledge of the chemical composition, structure, and properties of substances and of the chemical processes and transformations that they undergo. This includes uses of chemicals and their interactions, danger signs, production techniques, and disposal methods.
Biology	Knowledge of plant and animal organisms, their tissues, cells, functions, interdependencies, and interactions with each other and the environment.
Mechanical	Knowledge of machines and tools, including their designs, uses, repair, and maintenance.
Mathematics	Knowledge of arithmetic, algebra, geometry, calculus, statistics, and their applications.
Physics	Knowledge and prediction of physical principles, laws, their interrelationships, and applications to understanding fluid, material, and atmospheric dynamics, and mechanical, electrical, atomic and sub- atomic structures and processes.
Computers and Electronics	Knowledge of circuit boards, processors, chips, electronic equipment, and computer hardware and software, including applications and programming.
Clerical	Knowledge of administrative and clerical procedures and systems such as word processing, managing files and records, stenography and transcription, designing forms, and other office procedures and terminology.
Therapy and Counseling	Knowledge of principles, methods, and procedures for diagnosis, treatment, and rehabilitation of physical and mental dysfunctions, and for career counseling and guidance.
Personnel and Human Resources	Knowledge of principles and procedures for personnel recruitment, selection, training, compensation and benefits, labor relations and negotiation, and personnel information systems.
Administration and Management	Knowledge of business and management principles involved in strategic planning, resource allocation, human resources modeling, leadership technique, production methods, and coordination of people and resources.
Law and Government	Knowledge of laws, legal codes, court procedures, precedents, government regulations, executive orders, agency rules, and the democratic political process.
Public Safety and Security	Knowledge of relevant equipment, policies, procedures, and strategies to promote effective local, state, or national security operations for the protection of people, data, property, and institutions.
Engineering and Technology	Knowledge of the practical application of engineering science and technology. This includes applying principles, techniques, procedures, and equipment to the design and production of various goods and services.
Philosophy and Theology	Knowledge of different philosophical systems and religions. This includes their basic principles, values, ethics, ways of thinking, customs, practices, and their impact on human culture.
Communications and Media	Knowledge of media production, communication, and dissemination techniques and methods. This includes alternative ways to inform and entertain via written, oral, and visual media.
Sociology and Anthropology	Knowledge of group behavior and dynamics, societal trends and influences, human migrations, ethnicity, cultures and their history and origins.
Telecommunications	Knowledge of transmission, broadcasting, switching, control, and operation of telecommunications systems.
Production and Processing	Knowledge of raw materials, production processes, quality control, costs, and other techniques for maximizing the effective manufacture and distribution of goods.
Foreign Language	Knowledge of the structure and content of a foreign (non-English) language including the meaning and spelling of words, rules of composition and grammar, and pronunciation.
Sales and Marketing	Knowledge of principles and methods for showing, promoting, and selling products or services. This includes marketing strategy and tactics, product demonstration, sales techniques, and sales control systems.
Transportation	Knowledge of principles and methods for moving people or goods by air, rail, sea, or road, including the relative costs and benefits.
History and Archeology	Knowledge of historical events and their causes, indicators, and effects on civilizations and cultures.
Economics and Accounting	Knowledge of economic and accounting principles and practices, the financial markets, banking and the analysis and reporting of financial data.
Geography	Knowledge of principles and methods for describing the features of land, sea, and air masses, including their physical characteristics, locations, interrelationships, and distribution of plant, animal, and human life.
Design	Knowledge of design techniques, tools, and principles involved in production of precision technical plans, blueprints, drawings, and models.
Building and Construction	Knowledge of materials, methods, and the tools involved in the construction or repair of houses, buildings, or other structures such as highways and roads.
Food Production	Knowledge of techniques and equipment for planting, growing, and harvesting food products (both plant and animal) for consumption, including storage/handling techniques.
Fine Arts	Knowledge of the theory and techniques required to compose, produce, and perform works of music, dance, visual arts, drama, and sculpture.

Skills	Skills Definitions
Active Listening	Giving full attention to what other people are saying, taking time to understand the points being made, asking questions as appropriate, and not interrupting at inappropriate times.
Instructing	Teaching others how to do something.
Reading Comprehension	Understanding written sentences and paragraphs in work related documents.
Critical Thinking	Using logic and reasoning to identify the strengths and weaknesses of alternative solutions, conclusions or approaches to problems.
Monitoring	Monitoring/Assessing performance of yourself, other individuals, or organizations to make improvements or take corrective action.
Time Management	Managing one's own time and the time of others.

Speaking	Talking to others to convey information effectively.
Operation Monitoring	Watching gauges, dials, or other indicators to make sure a machine is working properly.
Active Learning	Understanding the implications of new information for both current and future problem-solving and decision-making.
Troubleshooting	Determining causes of operating errors and deciding what to do about it.
Writing	Communicating effectively in writing as appropriate for the needs of the audience.
Service Orientation	Actively looking for ways to help people.
Science	Using scientific rules and methods to solve problems.
Mathematics	Using mathematics to solve problems.
Complex Problem Solving	Identifying complex problems and reviewing related information to develop and evaluate options and implement solutions.
Learning Strategies	Selecting and using training/instructional methods and procedures appropriate for the situation when learning or teaching new things.
Coordination	Adjusting actions in relation to others' actions.
Quality Control Analysis	Conducting tests and inspections of products, services, or processes to evaluate quality or performance.
Judgment and Decision Making	Considering the relative costs and benefits of potential actions to choose the most appropriate one.
Social Perceptiveness	Being aware of others' reactions and understanding why they react as they do.
Persuasion	Persuading others to change their minds or behavior.
Equipment Selection	Determining the kind of tools and equipment needed to do a job.
Equipment Maintenance	Performing routine maintenance on equipment and determining when and what kind of maintenance is needed.
Operation and Control	Controlling operations of equipment or systems.
Negotiation	Bringing others together and trying to reconcile differences.
Repairing	Repairing machines or systems using the needed tools.
Management of Material Resources	Obtaining and seeing to the appropriate use of equipment, facilities, and materials needed to do certain work.
Systems Evaluation	Identifying measures or indicators of system performance and the actions needed to improve or correct performance, relative to the goals of the system.
Systems Analysis	Determining how a system should work and how changes in conditions, operations, and the environment will affect outcomes.
Management of Personnel Resources	Motivating, developing, and directing people as they work, identifying the best people for the job.
Technology Design	Generating or adapting equipment and technology to serve user needs.
Installation	Installing equipment, machines, wiring, or programs to meet specifications.
Operations Analysis	Analyzing needs and product requirements to create a design.
Management of Financial Resources	Determining how money will be spent to get the work done, and accounting for these expenditures.
Programming	Writing computer programs for various purposes.

Ability	Ability Definitions
Oral Expression	The ability to communicate information and ideas in speaking so others will understand.
Oral Comprehension	The ability to listen to and understand information and ideas presented through spoken words and sentences.
Problem Sensitivity	The ability to tell when something is wrong or is likely to go wrong. It does not involve solving the problem, only recognizing there is a problem.
Speech Clarity	The ability to speak clearly so others can understand you.
Speech Recognition	The ability to identify and understand the speech of another person.
Written Comprehension	The ability to read and understand information and ideas presented in writing.
Inductive Reasoning	The ability to combine pieces of information to form general rules or conclusions (includes finding a relationship among seemingly unrelated events).
Information Ordering	The ability to arrange things or actions in a certain order or pattern according to a specific rule or set of rules (e.g., patterns of numbers, letters, words, pictures, mathematical operations).
Near Vision	The ability to see details at close range (within a few feet of the observer).
Deductive Reasoning	The ability to apply general rules to specific problems to produce answers that make sense.

Finger Dexterity	The ability to make precisely coordinated movements of the fingers of one or both hands to grasp, manipulate, or assemble very small objects.
Speed of Closure	The ability to quickly make sense of, combine, and organize information into meaningful patterns.
Selective Attention	The ability to concentrate on a task over a period of time without being distracted.
Flexibility of Closure	The ability to identify or detect a known pattern (a figure, object, word, or sound) that is hidden in other distracting material.
Control Precision	The ability to quickly and repeatedly adjust the controls of a machine or a vehicle to exact positions.
Category Flexibility	The ability to generate or use different sets of rules for combining or grouping things in different ways.
Manual Dexterity	The ability to quickly move your hand, your hand together with your arm, or your two hands to grasp, manipulate, or assemble objects.
Arm-Hand Steadiness	The ability to keep your hand and arm steady while moving your arm or while holding your arm and hand in one position.
Trunk Strength	The ability to use your abdominal and lower back muscles to support part of the body repeatedly or continuously over time without 'giving out' or fatiguing.
Perceptual Speed	The ability to quickly and accurately compare similarities and differences among sets of letters, numbers, objects, pictures, or patterns. The things to be compared may be presented at the same time or one after the other. This ability also includes comparing a presented object with a remembered object.
Written Expression	The ability to communicate information and ideas in writing so others will understand.
Multilimb Coordination	The ability to coordinate two or more limbs (for example, two arms, two legs, or one leg and one arm) while sitting, standing, or lying down. It does not involve performing the activities while the whole body is in motion.
Hearing Sensitivity	The ability to detect or tell the differences between sounds that vary in pitch and loudness.
Memorization	The ability to remember information such as words, numbers, pictures, and procedures.
Time Sharing	The ability to shift back and forth between two or more activities or sources of information (such as speech, sounds, touch, or other sources).
Auditory Attention	The ability to focus on a single source of sound in the presence of other distracting sounds.
Visual Color Discrimination	The ability to match or detect differences between colors, including shades of color and brightness.
Response Orientation	The ability to choose quickly between two or more movements in response to two or more different signals (lights, sounds, pictures). It includes the speed with which the correct response is started with the hand, foot, or other body part.
Originality	The ability to come up with unusual or clever ideas about a given topic or situation, or to develop creative ways to solve a problem.
Static Strength	The ability to exert maximum muscle force to lift, push, pull, or carry objects.
Far Vision	The ability to see details at a distance.
Reaction Time	The ability to quickly respond (with the hand, finger, or foot) to a signal (sound, light, picture) when it appears.
Fluency of Ideas	The ability to come up with a number of ideas about a topic (the number of ideas is important, not their quality, correctness, or creativity).
Dynamic Strength	The ability to exert muscle force repeatedly or continuously over time. This involves muscular endurance and resistance to muscle fatigue.
Visualization	The ability to imagine how something will look after it is moved around or when its parts are moved or rearranged.
Depth Perception	The ability to judge which of several objects is closer or farther away from you, or to judge the distance between you and an object.
Gross Body Coordination	The ability to coordinate the movement of your arms, legs, and torso together when the whole body is in motion.
Rate Control	The ability to time your movements or the movement of a piece of equipment in anticipation of changes in the speed and/or direction of a moving object or scene.
Stamina	The ability to exert yourself physically over long periods of time without getting winded or out of breath.
Number Facility	The ability to add, subtract, multiply, or divide quickly and correctly.
Wrist-Finger Speed	The ability to make fast, simple, repeated movements of the fingers, hands, and wrists.

Extent Flexibility	The ability to bend, stretch, twist, or reach with your body, arms, and/or legs.
Speed of Limb Movement	The ability to quickly move the arms and legs.
Mathematical Reasoning	The ability to choose the right mathematical methods or formulas to solve a problem.
Gross Body Equilibrium	The ability to keep or regain your body balance or stay upright when in an unstable position.
Spatial Orientation	The ability to know your location in relation to the environment or to know where other objects are in relation to you.
Sound Localization	The ability to tell the direction from which a sound originated.
Dynamic Flexibility	The ability to quickly and repeatedly bend, stretch, twist, or reach out with your body, arms, and/or legs.
Peripheral Vision	The ability to see objects or movement of objects to one's side when the eyes are looking ahead.
Explosive Strength	The ability to use short bursts of muscle force to propel oneself (as in jumping or sprinting), or to throw an object.
Glare Sensitivity	The ability to see objects in the presence of glare or bright lighting.
Night Vision	The ability to see under low light conditions.

Work_Activity	Work_Activity Definitions
Assisting and Caring for Others	Providing personal assistance, medical attention, emotional support, or other personal care to others such as coworkers, customers, or patients.
Documenting/Recording Information	Entering, transcribing, recording, storing, or maintaining information in written or electronic/magnetic form.
Communicating with Supervisors, Peers, or Subordin	Providing information to supervisors, co-workers, and subordinates by telephone, in written form, e-mail, or in person.
Getting Information	Observing, receiving, and otherwise obtaining information from all relevant sources.
Organizing, Planning, and Prioritizing Work	Developing specific goals and plans to prioritize, organize, and accomplish your work.
Identifying Objects, Actions, and Events	Identifying information by categorizing, estimating, recognizing differences or similarities, and detecting changes in circumstances or events.
Making Decisions and Solving Problems	Analyzing information and evaluating results to choose the best solution and solve problems.
Monitor Processes, Materials, or Surroundings	Monitoring and reviewing information from materials, events, or the environment, to detect or assess problems.
Updating and Using Relevant Knowledge	Keeping up-to-date technically and applying new knowledge to your job.
Establishing and Maintaining Interpersonal Relatio	Developing constructive and cooperative working relationships with others, and maintaining them over time.
Training and Teaching Others	Identifying the educational needs of others, developing formal educational or training programs or classes, and teaching or instructing others.
Communicating with Persons Outside Organization	Communicating with people outside the organization, representing the organization to customers, the public, government, and other external sources. This information can be exchanged in person, in writing, or by telephone or e-mail.
Inspecting Equipment, Structures, or Material	Inspecting equipment, structures, or materials to identify the cause of errors or other problems or defects.
Interacting With Computers	Using computers and computer systems (including hardware and software) to program, write software, set up functions, enter data, or process information.
Analyzing Data or Information	Identifying the underlying principles, reasons, or facts of information by breaking down information or data into separate parts.
Developing and Building Teams	Encouraging and building mutual trust, respect, and cooperation among team members.
Evaluating Information to Determine Compliance wit	Using relevant information and individual judgment to determine whether events or processes comply with laws, regulations, or standards.
Performing for or Working Directly with the Public	Performing for people or dealing directly with the public. This includes serving customers in restaurants and stores, and receiving clients or guests.
Processing Information	Compiling, coding, categorizing, calculating, tabulating, auditing, or verifying information or data.
Interpreting the Meaning of Information for Others	Translating or explaining what information means and how it can be used.
Controlling Machines and Processes	Using either control mechanisms or direct physical activity to operate machines or processes (not including computers or vehicles).

Coordinating the Work and Activities of Others	Getting members of a group to work together to accomplish tasks.
Judging the Qualities of Things, Services, or Peop	Assessing the value, importance, or quality of things or people.
Guiding, Directing, and Motivating Subordinates	Providing guidance and direction to subordinates, including setting performance standards and monitoring performance.
Resolving Conflicts and Negotiating with Others	Handling complaints, settling disputes, and resolving grievances and conflicts, or otherwise negotiating with others.
Scheduling Work and Activities	Scheduling events, programs, and activities, as well as the work of others.
Performing General Physical Activities	Performing physical activities that require considerable use of your arms and legs and moving your whole body, such as climbing, lifting, balancing, walking, stooping, and handling of materials.
Coaching and Developing Others	Identifying the developmental needs of others and coaching, mentoring, or otherwise helping others to improve their knowledge or skills.
Handling and Moving Objects	Using hands and arms in handling, installing, positioning, and moving materials, and manipulating things.
Developing Objectives and Strategies	Establishing long-range objectives and specifying the strategies and actions to achieve them.
Thinking Creatively	Developing, designing, or creating new applications, ideas, relationships, systems, or products, including artistic contributions.
Provide Consultation and Advice to Others	Providing guidance and expert advice to management or other groups on technical, systems-, or process-related topics.
Estimating the Quantifiable Characteristics of Pro	Estimating sizes, distances, and quantities; or determining time, costs, resources, or materials needed to perform a work activity.
Repairing and Maintaining Electronic Equipment	Servicing, repairing, calibrating, regulating, fine-tuning, or testing machines, devices, and equipment that operate primarily on the basis of electrical or electronic (not mechanical) principles.
Performing Administrative Activities	Performing day-to-day administrative tasks such as maintaining information files and processing paperwork.
Operating Vehicles, Mechanized Devices, or Equipme	Running, maneuvering, navigating, or driving vehicles or mechanized equipment, such as forklifts, passenger vehicles, aircraft, or water craft.
Selling or Influencing Others	Convincing others to buy merchandise/goods or to otherwise change their minds or actions.
Staffing Organizational Units	Recruiting, interviewing, selecting, hiring, and promoting employees in an organization.
Drafting, Laying Out, and Specifying Technical Dev	Providing documentation, detailed instructions, drawings, or specifications to tell others about how devices, parts, equipment, or structures are to be fabricated, constructed, assembled, modified, maintained, or used.
Repairing and Maintaining Mechanical Equipment	Servicing, repairing, adjusting, and testing machines, devices, moving parts, and equipment that operate primarily on the basis of mechanical (not electronic) principles.
Monitoring and Controlling Resources	Monitoring and controlling resources and overseeing the spending of money.

Work_Context	Work_Context Definitions
Face-to-Face Discussions	How often do you have to have face-to-face discussions with individuals or teams in this job?
Contact With Others	How much does this job require the worker to be in contact with others (face-to-face, by telephone, or otherwise) in order to perform it?
Indoors, Environmentally Controlled	How often does this job require working indoors in environmentally controlled conditions?
Physical Proximity	To what extent does this job require the worker to perform job tasks in close physical proximity to other people?
Exposed to Disease or Infections	How often does this job require exposure to disease/infections?
Telephone	How often do you have telephone conversations in this job?
Work With Work Group or Team	How important is it to work with others in a group or team in this job?
Wear Common Protective or Safety Equipment such as	How much does this job require wearing common protective or safety equipment such as safety shoes, glasses, gloves, hard hats or life jackets?
Impact of Decisions on Co-workers or Company Resul	How do the decisions an employee makes impact the results of co-workers, clients or the company?
Structured versus Unstructured Work	To what extent is this job structured for the worker, rather than allowing the worker to determine tasks, priorities, and goals?
Freedom to Make Decisions	How much decision making freedom, without supervision, does the job offer?

Importance of Being Exact or Accurate	How important is being very exact or highly accurate in performing this job?	Indoors, Not Environmentally Controlled	How often does this job require working indoors in non-controlled environmental conditions (e.g., warehouse without heat)?
Deal With Unpleasant or Angry People	How frequently does the worker have to deal with unpleasant, angry, or discourteous individuals as part of the job requirements?	Extremely Bright or Inadequate Lighting	How often does this job require working in extremely bright or inadequate lighting conditions?
Spend Time Standing	How much does this job require standing?	Spend Time Climbing Ladders, Scaffolds, or Poles	How much does this job require climbing ladders, scaffolds, or poles?
Consequence of Error	How serious would the result usually be if the worker made a mistake that was not readily correctable?	In an Open Vehicle or Equipment	How often does this job require working in an open vehicle or equipment (e.g., tractor)?
Frequency of Decision Making	How frequently is the worker required to make decisions that affect other people, the financial resources, and/or the image and reputation of the organization?	Exposed to High Places	How often does this job require exposure to high places?

Job Zone Component	Job Zone Component Definitions

Deal With External Customers	How important is it to work with external customers or the public in this job?
Responsibility for Outcomes and Results	How responsible is the worker for work outcomes and results of other workers?
Coordinate or Lead Others	How important is it to coordinate or lead others in accomplishing work activities in this job?
Frequency of Conflict Situations	How often are there conflict situations the employee has to face in this job?
Spend Time Making Repetitive Motions	How much does this job require making repetitive motions?
Spend Time Using Your Hands to Handle, Control, or	How much does this job require using your hands to handle, control, or feel objects, tools or controls?
Spend Time Walking and Running	How much does this job require walking and running?
Letters and Memos	How often does the job require written letters and memos?
Spend Time Sitting	How much does this job require sitting?
Level of Competition	To what extent does this job require the worker to compete or to be aware of competitive pressures?
Electronic Mail	How often do you use electronic mail in this job?
Exposed to Radiation	How often does this job require exposure to radiation?
Time Pressure	How often does this job require the worker to meet strict deadlines?
Responsible for Others' Health and Safety	How much responsibility is there for the health and safety of others in this job?
Exposed to Hazardous Conditions	How often does this job require exposure to hazardous conditions?
Exposed to Minor Burns, Cuts, Bites, or Stings	How often does this job require exposure to minor burns, cuts, bites, or stings?
Importance of Repeating Same Tasks	How important is repeating the same physical activities (e.g., key entry) or mental activities (e.g., checking entries in a ledger) over and over, without stopping, to performing this job?
Sounds, Noise Levels Are Distracting or Uncomforta	How often does this job require working exposed to sounds and noise levels that are distracting or uncomfortable?
Cramped Work Space, Awkward Positions	How often does this job require working in cramped work spaces that requires getting into awkward positions?
Wear Specialized Protective or Safety Equipment su	How much does this job require wearing specialized protective or safety equipment such as breathing apparatus, safety harness, full protection suits, or radiation protection?
Exposed to Contaminants	How often does this job require working exposed to contaminants (such as pollutants, gases, dust or odors)?
Degree of Automation	How automated is the job?
Deal With Physically Aggressive People	How frequently does this job require the worker to deal with physical aggression of violent individuals?
Spend Time Bending or Twisting the Body	How much does this job require bending or twisting your body?
Spend Time Kneeling, Crouching, Stooping, or Crawl	How much does this job require kneeling, crouching, stooping, or crawling?
Pace Determined by Speed of Equipment	How important is it to this job that the pace is determined by the speed of equipment or machinery? (This does not refer to keeping busy at all times on this job.)
Public Speaking	How often do you have to perform public speaking in this job?
Outdoors, Exposed to Weather	How often does this job require working outdoors, exposed to all weather conditions?
Spend Time Keeping or Regaining Balance	How much does this job require keeping or regaining your balance?
Outdoors, Under Cover	How often does this job require working outdoors, under cover (e.g., structure with roof but no walls)?
In an Enclosed Vehicle or Equipment	How often does this job require working in a closed vehicle or equipment (e.g., car)?
Exposed to Hazardous Equipment	How often does this job require exposure to hazardous equipment?
Exposed to Whole Body Vibration	How often does this job require exposure to whole body vibration (e.g., operate a jackhammer)?
Very Hot or Cold Temperatures	How often does this job require working in very hot (above 90 F degrees) or very cold (below 32 F degrees) temperatures?

Job Zone Component	Job Zone Component Definitions
Title	Job Zone Three: Medium Preparation Needed
Overall Experience	Previous work-related skill, knowledge, or experience is required for these occupations. For example, an electrician must have completed three or four years of apprenticeship or several years of vocational training, and often must have passed a licensing exam, in order to perform the job.
Job Training	Employees in these occupations usually need one or two years of training involving both on-the-job experience and informal training with experienced workers.
Job Zone Examples	These occupations usually involve using communication and organizational skills to coordinate, supervise, manage, or train others to accomplish goals. Examples include dental assistants, electricians, fish and game wardens, legal secretaries, personnel recruiters, and recreation workers.
SVP Range	(6.0 to < 7.0)
Education	Most occupations in this zone require training in vocational schools, related on-the-job experience, or an associate's degree. Some may require a bachelor's degree.

Work_Styles	Work_Styles Definitions
Dependability	Job requires being reliable, responsible, and dependable, and fulfilling obligations.
Self Control	Job requires maintaining composure, keeping emotions in check, controlling anger, and avoiding aggressive behavior, even in very difficult situations.
Integrity	Job requires being honest and ethical.
Concern for Others	Job requires being sensitive to others' needs and feelings and being understanding and helpful on the job.
Attention to Detail	Job requires being careful about detail and thorough in completing work tasks.
Cooperation	Job requires being pleasant with others on the job and displaying a good-natured, cooperative attitude.
Stress Tolerance	Job requires accepting criticism and dealing calmly and effectively with high stress situations.
Analytical Thinking	Job requires analyzing information and using logic to address work-related issues and problems.
Independence	Job requires developing one's own ways of doing things, guiding oneself with little or no supervision, and depending on oneself to get things done.
Adaptability/Flexibility	Job requires being open to change (positive or negative) and to considerable variety in the workplace.
Achievement/Effort	Job requires establishing and maintaining personally challenging achievement goals and exerting effort toward mastering tasks.
Persistence	Job requires persistence in the face of obstacles.
Social Orientation	Job requires preferring to work with others rather than alone, and being personally connected with others on the job.
Initiative	Job requires a willingness to take on responsibilities and challenges.
Leadership	Job requires a willingness to lead, take charge, and offer opinions and direction.
Innovation	Job requires creativity and alternative thinking to develop new ideas for and answers to work-related problems.

29-1127.00 - Speech-Language Pathologists

Assess and treat persons with speech, language, voice, and fluency disorders. May select alternative communication systems and teach their use. May perform research related to speech and language problems.

Tasks

1) Monitor patients' progress and adjust treatments accordingly.

2) Consult with and advise educators or medical staff on speech or hearing topics such as communication strategies and speech and language stimulation.

3) Refer clients to additional medical or educational services if needed.

4) Instruct clients in techniques for more effective communication, including sign language, lip reading, and voice improvement.

5) Develop and implement treatment plans for problems such as stuttering, delayed language, swallowing disorders, and inappropriate pitch or harsh voice problems, based on own assessments and recommendations of physicians, psychologists, and social workers.

6) Teach clients to control or strengthen tongue, jaw, face muscles, and breathing mechanisms.

7) Administer hearing or speech/language evaluations, tests, or examinations to patients to collect information on type and degree of impairments, using written and oral tests and special instruments.

8) Participate in conferences or training, or publish research results, to share knowledge of new hearing or speech disorder treatment methods or technologies.

9) Instruct patients and family members in strategies to cope with or avoid communication-related misunderstandings.

10) Develop individual or group programs in schools to deal with speech or language problems.

11) Develop speech exercise programs to reduce disabilities.

12) Conduct lessons and direct educational or therapeutic games to assist teachers dealing with speech problems.

13) Design, develop, and employ alternative diagnostic or communication devices and strategies.

14) Use computer applications to identify and assist with communication disabilities.

15) Communicate with non-speaking students, using sign language or computer technology.

16) Provide communication instruction to dialect speakers or students with limited English proficiency.

17) Conduct or direct research on speech or hearing topics, and report findings for use in developing procedures, technologies, or treatments.

18) Record information on the initial evaluation, treatment, progress, and discharge of clients.

Knowledge	Knowledge Definitions
English Language	Knowledge of the structure and content of the English language including the meaning and spelling of words, rules of composition, and grammar.
Therapy and Counseling	Knowledge of principles, methods, and procedures for diagnosis, treatment, and rehabilitation of physical and mental dysfunctions, and for career counseling and guidance.
Education and Training	Knowledge of principles and methods for curriculum and training design, teaching and instruction for individuals and groups, and the measurement of training effects.
Psychology	Knowledge of human behavior and performance; individual differences in ability, personality, and interests; learning and motivation; psychological research methods; and the assessment and treatment of behavioral and affective disorders.
Customer and Personal Service	Knowledge of principles and processes for providing customer and personal services. This includes customer needs assessment, meeting quality standards for services, and evaluation of customer satisfaction.
Clerical	Knowledge of administrative and clerical procedures and systems such as word processing, managing files and records, stenography and transcription, designing forms, and other office procedures and terminology.
Medicine and Dentistry	Knowledge of the information and techniques needed to diagnose and treat human injuries, diseases, and deformities. This includes symptoms, treatment alternatives, drug properties and interactions, and preventive health-care measures.
Sociology and Anthropology	Knowledge of group behavior and dynamics, societal trends and influences, human migrations, ethnicity, cultures and their history and origins.
Computers and Electronics	Knowledge of circuit boards, processors, chips, electronic equipment, and computer hardware and software, including applications and programming.
Law and Government	Knowledge of laws, legal codes, court procedures, precedents, government regulations, executive orders, agency rules, and the democratic political process.
Communications and Media	Knowledge of media production, communication, and dissemination techniques and methods. This includes alternative ways to inform and entertain via written, oral, and visual media.
Mathematics	Knowledge of arithmetic, algebra, geometry, calculus, statistics, and their applications.
Philosophy and Theology	Knowledge of different philosophical systems and religions. This includes their basic principles, values, ethics, ways of thinking, customs, practices, and their impact on human culture.
Administration and Management	Knowledge of business and management principles involved in strategic planning, resource allocation, human resources modeling, leadership technique, production methods, and coordination of people and resources.
Public Safety and Security	Knowledge of relevant equipment, policies, procedures, and strategies to promote effective local, state, or national security operations for the protection of people, data, property, and institutions.
Biology	Knowledge of plant and animal organisms, their tissues, cells, functions, interdependencies, and interactions with each other and the environment.
History and Archeology	Knowledge of historical events and their causes, indicators, and effects on civilizations and cultures.
Geography	Knowledge of principles and methods for describing the features of land, sea, and air masses, including their physical characteristics, locations, interrelationships, and distribution of plant, animal, and human life.
Foreign Language	Knowledge of the structure and content of a foreign (non-English) language including the meaning and spelling of words, rules of composition and grammar, and pronunciation.
Telecommunications	Knowledge of transmission, broadcasting, switching, control, and operation of telecommunications systems.
Sales and Marketing	Knowledge of principles and methods for showing, promoting, and selling products or services. This includes marketing strategy and tactics, product demonstration, sales techniques, and sales control systems.
Fine Arts	Knowledge of the theory and techniques required to compose, produce, and perform works of music, dance, visual arts, drama, and sculpture.
Mechanical	Knowledge of machines and tools, including their designs, uses, repair, and maintenance.
Personnel and Human Resources	Knowledge of principles and procedures for personnel recruitment, selection, training, compensation and benefits, labor relations and negotiation, and personnel information systems.
Transportation	Knowledge of principles and methods for moving people or goods by air, rail, sea, or road, including the relative costs and benefits.
Engineering and Technology	Knowledge of the practical application of engineering science and technology. This includes applying principles, techniques, procedures, and equipment to the design and production of various goods and services.
Chemistry	Knowledge of the chemical composition, structure, and properties of substances and of the chemical processes and transformations that they undergo. This includes uses of chemicals and their interactions, danger signs, production techniques, and disposal methods.
Production and Processing	Knowledge of raw materials, production processes, quality control, costs, and other techniques for maximizing the effective manufacture and distribution of goods.
Design	Knowledge of design techniques, tools, and principles involved in production of precision technical plans, blueprints, drawings, and models.
Physics	Knowledge and prediction of physical principles, laws, their interrelationships, and applications to understanding fluid, material, and atmospheric dynamics, and mechanical, electrical, atomic and sub-atomic structures and processes.
Economics and Accounting	Knowledge of economic and accounting principles and practices, the financial markets, banking and the analysis and reporting of financial data.
Building and Construction	Knowledge of materials, methods, and the tools involved in the construction or repair of houses, buildings, or other structures such as highways and roads.
Food Production	Knowledge of techniques and equipment for planting, growing, and harvesting food products (both plant and animal) for consumption, including storage/handling techniques.

Skills	Skills Definitions
Instructing	Teaching others how to do something.
Speaking	Talking to others to convey information effectively.
Reading Comprehension	Understanding written sentences and paragraphs in work related documents.
Active Listening	Giving full attention to what other people are saying, taking time to understand the points being made, asking questions as appropriate, and not interrupting at inappropriate times.
Time Management	Managing one's own time and the time of others.
Learning Strategies	Selecting and using training/instructional methods and procedures appropriate for the situation when learning or teaching new things.
Active Learning	Understanding the implications of new information for both current and future problem-solving and decision-making.
Critical Thinking	Using logic and reasoning to identify the strengths and weaknesses of alternative solutions, conclusions or approaches to problems.
Writing	Communicating effectively in writing as appropriate for the needs of the audience.
Monitoring	Monitoring/Assessing performance of yourself, other individuals, or organizations to make improvements or take corrective action.
Coordination	Adjusting actions in relation to others' actions.
Service Orientation	Actively looking for ways to help people.
Social Perceptiveness	Being aware of others' reactions and understanding why they react as they do.
Complex Problem Solving	Identifying complex problems and reviewing related information to develop and evaluate options and implement solutions.
Judgment and Decision Making	Considering the relative costs and benefits of potential actions to choose the most appropriate one.
Persuasion	Persuading others to change their minds or behavior.
Negotiation	Bringing others together and trying to reconcile differences.
Equipment Selection	Determining the kind of tools and equipment needed to do a job.
Mathematics	Using mathematics to solve problems.
Science	Using scientific rules and methods to solve problems.
Operations Analysis	Analyzing needs and product requirements to create a design.
Management of Material Resources	Obtaining and seeing to the appropriate use of equipment, facilities, and materials needed to do certain work.
Technology Design	Generating or adapting equipment and technology to serve user needs.
Systems Evaluation	Identifying measures or indicators of system performance and the actions needed to improve or correct performance, relative to the goals of the system.
Troubleshooting	Determining causes of operating errors and deciding what to do about it.
Management of Personnel Resources	Motivating, developing, and directing people as they work, identifying the best people for the job.
Systems Analysis	Determining how a system should work and how changes in conditions, operations, and the environment will affect outcomes.
Quality Control Analysis	Conducting tests and inspections of products, services, or processes to evaluate quality or performance.
Operation and Control	Controlling operations of equipment or systems.
Management of Financial Resources	Determining how money will be spent to get the work done, and accounting for these expenditures.
Operation Monitoring	Watching gauges, dials, or other indicators to make sure a machine is working properly.
Equipment Maintenance	Performing routine maintenance on equipment and determining when and what kind of maintenance is needed.
Installation	Installing equipment, machines, wiring, or programs to meet specifications.
Repairing	Repairing machines or systems using the needed tools.
Programming	Writing computer programs for various purposes.

Ability	Ability Definitions
Speech Recognition	The ability to identify and understand the speech of another person.
Oral Comprehension	The ability to listen to and understand information and ideas presented through spoken words and sentences.
Oral Expression	The ability to communicate information and ideas in speaking so others will understand.
Problem Sensitivity	The ability to tell when something is wrong or is likely to go wrong. It does not involve solving the problem, only recognizing there is a problem.

Hearing Sensitivity	The ability to detect or tell the differences between sounds that vary in pitch and loudness.
Speech Clarity	The ability to speak clearly so others can understand you.
Written Comprehension	The ability to read and understand information and ideas presented in writing.
Deductive Reasoning	The ability to apply general rules to specific problems to produce answers that make sense.
Inductive Reasoning	The ability to combine pieces of information to form general rules or conclusions (includes finding a relationship among seemingly unrelated events).
Flexibility of Closure	The ability to identify or detect a known pattern (a figure, object, word, or sound) that is hidden in other distracting material.
Near Vision	The ability to see details at close range (within a few feet of the observer).
Written Expression	The ability to communicate information and ideas in writing so others will understand.
Selective Attention	The ability to concentrate on a task over a period of time without being distracted.
Originality	The ability to come up with unusual or clever ideas about a given topic or situation, or to develop creative ways to solve a problem.
Auditory Attention	The ability to focus on a single source of sound in the presence of other distracting sounds.
Information Ordering	The ability to arrange things or actions in a certain order or pattern according to a specific rule or set of rules (e.g., patterns of numbers, letters, words, pictures, mathematical operations).
Fluency of Ideas	The ability to come up with a number of ideas about a topic (the number of ideas is important, not their quality, correctness, or creativity).
Far Vision	The ability to see details at a distance.
Category Flexibility	The ability to generate or use different sets of rules for combining or grouping things in different ways.
Perceptual Speed	The ability to quickly and accurately compare similarities and differences among sets of letters, numbers, objects, pictures, or patterns. The things to be compared may be presented at the same time or one after the other. This ability also includes comparing a presented object with a remembered object.
Speed of Closure	The ability to quickly make sense of, combine, and organize information into meaningful patterns.
Finger Dexterity	The ability to make precisely coordinated movements of the fingers of one or both hands to grasp, manipulate, or assemble very small objects.
Time Sharing	The ability to shift back and forth between two or more activities or sources of information (such as speech, sounds, touch, or other sources).
Visualization	The ability to imagine how something will look after it is moved around or when its parts are moved or rearranged.
Memorization	The ability to remember information such as words, numbers, pictures, and procedures.
Mathematical Reasoning	The ability to choose the right mathematical methods or formulas to solve a problem.
Number Facility	The ability to add, subtract, multiply, or divide quickly and correctly.
Visual Color Discrimination	The ability to match or detect differences between colors, including shades of color and brightness.
Depth Perception	The ability to judge which of several objects is closer or farther away from you, or to judge the distance between you and an object.
Multilimb Coordination	The ability to coordinate two or more limbs (for example, two arms, two legs, or one leg and one arm) while sitting, standing, or lying down. It does not involve performing the activities while the whole body is in motion.
Trunk Strength	The ability to use your abdominal and lower back muscles to support part of the body repeatedly or continuously over time without 'giving out' or fatiguing.
Wrist-Finger Speed	The ability to make fast, simple, repeated movements of the fingers, hands, and wrists.
Sound Localization	The ability to tell the direction from which a sound originated.
Arm-Hand Steadiness	The ability to keep your hand and arm steady while moving your arm or while holding your arm and hand in one position.
Control Precision	The ability to quickly and repeatedly adjust the controls of a machine or a vehicle to exact positions.
Manual Dexterity	The ability to quickly move your hand, your hand together with your arm, or your two hands to grasp, manipulate, or assemble objects.

Response Orientation	The ability to choose quickly between two or more movements in response to two or more different signals (lights, sounds, pictures). It includes the speed with which the correct response is started with the hand, foot, or other body part.
Gross Body Coordination	The ability to coordinate the movement of your arms, legs, and torso together when the whole body is in motion.
Peripheral Vision	The ability to see objects or movement of objects to one's side when the eyes are looking ahead.
Speed of Limb Movement	The ability to quickly move the arms and legs.
Spatial Orientation	The ability to know your location in relation to the environment or to know where other objects are in relation to you.
Static Strength	The ability to exert maximum muscle force to lift, push, pull, or carry objects.
Reaction Time	The ability to quickly respond (with the hand, finger, or foot) to a signal (sound, light, picture) when it appears.
Dynamic Flexibility	The ability to quickly and repeatedly bend, stretch, twist, or reach out with your body, arms, and/or legs.
Extent Flexibility	The ability to bend, stretch, twist, or reach with your body, arms, and/or legs.
Stamina	The ability to exert yourself physically over long periods of time without getting winded or out of breath.
Rate Control	The ability to time your movements or the movement of a piece of equipment in anticipation of changes in the speed and/or direction of a moving object or scene.
Gross Body Equilibrium	The ability to keep or regain your body balance or stay upright when in an unstable position.
Glare Sensitivity	The ability to see objects in the presence of glare or bright lighting.
Dynamic Strength	The ability to exert muscle force repeatedly or continuously over time. This involves muscular endurance and resistance to muscle fatigue.
Night Vision	The ability to see under low light conditions.
Explosive Strength	The ability to use short bursts of muscle force to propel oneself (as in jumping or sprinting), or to throw an object.

Work_Activity	Work_Activity Definitions
Making Decisions and Solving Problems	Analyzing information and evaluating results to choose the best solution and solve problems.
Developing Objectives and Strategies	Establishing long-range objectives and specifying the strategies and actions to achieve them.
Getting Information	Observing, receiving, and otherwise obtaining information from all relevant sources.
Organizing, Planning, and Prioritizing Work	Developing specific goals and plans to prioritize, organize, and accomplish your work.
Establishing and Maintaining Interpersonal Relatio	Developing constructive and cooperative working relationships with others, and maintaining them over time.
Communicating with Supervisors, Peers, or Subordin	Providing information to supervisors, co-workers, and subordinates by telephone, in written form, e-mail, or in person.
Evaluating Information to Determine Compliance wit	Using relevant information and individual judgment to determine whether events or processes comply with laws, regulations, or standards.
Updating and Using Relevant Knowledge	Keeping up-to-date technically and applying new knowledge to your job.
Analyzing Data or Information	Identifying the underlying principles, reasons, or facts of information by breaking down information or data into separate parts.
Processing Information	Compiling, coding, categorizing, calculating, tabulating, auditing, or verifying information or data.
Thinking Creatively	Developing, designing, or creating new applications, ideas, relationships, systems, or products, including artistic contributions.
Documenting/Recording Information	Entering, transcribing, recording, storing, or maintaining information in written or electronic/magnetic form.
Interpreting the Meaning of Information for Others	Translating or explaining what information means and how it can be used.
Identifying Objects, Actions, and Events	Identifying information by categorizing, estimating, recognizing differences or similarities, and detecting changes in circumstances or events.
Interacting With Computers	Using computers and computer systems (including hardware and software) to program, write software, set up functions, enter data, or process information.
Performing Administrative Activities	Performing day-to-day administrative tasks such as maintaining information files and processing paperwork.
Scheduling Work and Activities	Scheduling events, programs, and activities, as well as the work of others.

Assisting and Caring for Others	Providing personal assistance, medical attention, emotional support, or other personal care to others such as coworkers, customers, or patients.
Monitor Processes, Materials, or Surroundings	Monitoring and reviewing information from materials, events, or the environment, to detect or assess problems.
Coaching and Developing Others	Identifying the developmental needs of others and coaching, mentoring, or otherwise helping others to improve their knowledge or skills.
Training and Teaching Others	Identifying the educational needs of others, developing formal educational or training programs or classes, and teaching or instructing others.
Performing for or Working Directly with the Public	Performing for people or dealing directly with the public. This includes serving customers in restaurants and stores, and receiving clients or guests.
Developing and Building Teams	Encouraging and building mutual trust, respect, and cooperation among team members.
Judging the Qualities of Things, Services, or Peop	Assessing the value, importance, or quality of things or people.
Provide Consultation and Advice to Others	Providing guidance and expert advice to management or other groups on technical, systems-, or process-related topics.
Communicating with Persons Outside Organization	Communicating with people outside the organization, representing the organization to customers, the public, government, and other external sources. This information can be exchanged in person, in writing, or by telephone or e-mail.
Coordinating the Work and Activities of Others	Getting members of a group to work together to accomplish tasks.
Resolving Conflicts and Negotiating with Others	Handling complaints, settling disputes, and resolving grievances and conflicts, or otherwise negotiating with others.
Estimating the Quantifiable Characteristics of Pro	Estimating sizes, distances, and quantities; or determining time, costs, resources, or materials needed to perform a work activity.
Inspecting Equipment, Structures, or Material	Inspecting equipment, structures, or materials to identify the cause of errors or other problems or defects.
Handling and Moving Objects	Using hands and arms in handling, installing, positioning, and moving materials, and manipulating things.
Selling or Influencing Others	Convincing others to buy merchandise/goods or to otherwise change their minds or actions.
Guiding, Directing, and Motivating Subordinates	Providing guidance and direction to subordinates, including setting performance standards and monitoring performance.
Performing General Physical Activities	Performing physical activities that require considerable use of your arms and legs and moving your whole body, such as climbing, lifting, balancing, walking, stooping, and handling of materials.
Monitoring and Controlling Resources	Monitoring and controlling resources and overseeing the spending of money.
Drafting, Laying Out, and Specifying Technical Dev	Providing documentation, detailed instructions, drawings, or specifications to tell others about how devices, parts, equipment, or structures are to be fabricated, constructed, assembled, modified, maintained, or used.
Controlling Machines and Processes	Using either control mechanisms or direct physical activity to operate machines or processes (not including computers or vehicles).
Repairing and Maintaining Mechanical Equipment	Servicing, repairing, adjusting, and testing machines, devices, moving parts, and equipment that operate primarily on the basis of mechanical (not electronic) principles.
Operating Vehicles, Mechanized Devices, or Equipme	Running, maneuvering, navigating, or driving vehicles or mechanized equipment, such as forklifts, passenger vehicles, aircraft, or water craft.
Repairing and Maintaining Electronic Equipment	Servicing, repairing, calibrating, regulating, fine-tuning, or testing machines, devices, and equipment that operate primarily on the basis of electrical or electronic (not mechanical) principles.
Staffing Organizational Units	Recruiting, interviewing, selecting, hiring, and promoting employees in an organization.

Work_Context	Work_Context Definitions
Face-to-Face Discussions	How often do you have to have face-to-face discussions with individuals or teams in this job?
Contact With Others	How much does this job require the worker to be in contact with others (face-to-face, by telephone, or otherwise) in order to perform it?
Structured versus Unstructured Work	To what extent is this job structured for the worker, rather than allowing the worker to determine tasks, priorities, and goals?
Work With Work Group or Team	How important is it to work with others in a group or team in this job?

Freedom to Make Decisions	How much decision making freedom, without supervision, does the job offer?
Frequency of Decision Making	How frequently is the worker required to make decisions that affect other people, the financial resources, and/or the image and reputation of the organization?
Telephone	How often do you have telephone conversations in this job?
Impact of Decisions on Co-workers or Company Resul	How do the decisions an employee makes impact the results of co-workers, clients or the company?
Physical Proximity	To what extent does this job require the worker to perform job tasks in close physical proximity to other people?
Indoors, Environmentally Controlled	How often does this job require working indoors in environmentally controlled conditions?
Time Pressure	How often does this job require the worker to meet strict deadlines?
Importance of Being Exact or Accurate	How important is being very exact or highly accurate in performing this job?
Letters and Memos	How often does the job require written letters and memos?
Spend Time Sitting	How much does this job require sitting?
Electronic Mail	How often do you use electronic mail in this job?
Deal With External Customers	How important is it to work with external customers or the public in this job?
Exposed to Disease or Infections	How often does this job require exposure to disease/infections?
Coordinate or Lead Others	How important is it to coordinate or lead others in accomplishing work activities in this job?
Sounds, Noise Levels Are Distracting or Uncomforta	How often does this job require working exposed to sounds and noise levels that are distracting or uncomfortable?
Level of Competition	To what extent does this job require the worker to compete or to be aware of competitive pressures?
Importance of Repeating Same Tasks	How important is repeating the same physical activities (e.g., key entry) or mental activities (e.g., checking entries in a ledger) over and over, without stopping, to performing this job?
Frequency of Conflict Situations	How often are there conflict situations the employee has to face in this job?
Consequence of Error	How serious would the result usually be if the worker made a mistake that was not readily correctable?
Deal With Unpleasant or Angry People	How frequently does the worker have to deal with unpleasant, angry, or discourteous individuals as part of the job requirements?
Spend Time Standing	How much does this job require standing?
Indoors, Not Environmentally Controlled	How often does this job require working indoors in non-controlled environmental conditions (e.g., warehouse without heat)?
Public Speaking	How often do you have to perform public speaking in this job?
In an Enclosed Vehicle or Equipment	How often does this job require working in a closed vehicle or equipment (e.g., car)?
Responsible for Others' Health and Safety	How much responsibility is there for the health and safety of others in this job?
Exposed to Contaminants	How often does this job require working exposed to contaminants (such as pollutants, gases, dust or odors)?
Spend Time Walking and Running	How much does this job require walking and running?
Responsibility for Outcomes and Results	How responsible is the worker for work outcomes and results of other workers?
Wear Common Protective or Safety Equipment such as	How much does this job require wearing common protective or safety equipment such as safety shoes, glasses, gloves, hard hats or life jackets?
Very Hot or Cold Temperatures	How often does this job require working in very hot (above 90 F degrees) or very cold (below 32 F degrees) temperatures?
Spend Time Kneeling, Crouching, Stooping, or Crawl	How much does this job require kneeling, crouching, stooping or crawling?
Spend Time Using Your Hands to Handle, Control, or	How much does this job require using your hands to handle, control, or feel objects, tools or controls?
Spend Time Making Repetitive Motions	How much does this job require making repetitive motions?
Deal With Physically Aggressive People	How frequently does this job require the worker to deal with physical aggression of violent individuals?
Degree of Automation	How automated is the job?
Outdoors, Exposed to Weather	How often does this job require working outdoors, exposed to all weather conditions?
Cramped Work Space, Awkward Positions	How often does this job require working in cramped work spaces that requires getting into awkward positions?
Exposed to Minor Burns, Cuts, Bites, or Stings	How often does this job require exposure to minor burns, cuts, bites, or stings?

Spend Time Bending or Twisting the Body	How much does this job require bending or twisting your body?
Wear Specialized Protective or Safety Equipment su	How much does this job require wearing specialized protective or safety equipment such as breathing apparatus, safety harness, full protection suits, or radiation protection?
Exposed to Radiation	How often does this job require exposure to radiation?
Extremely Bright or Inadequate Lighting	How often does this job require working in extremely bright or inadequate lighting conditions?
Outdoors, Under Cover	How often does this job require working outdoors, under cover (e.g., structure with roof but no walls)?
Exposed to Hazardous Conditions	How often does this job require exposure to hazardous conditions?
Spend Time Keeping or Regaining Balance	How much does this job require keeping or regaining your balance?
Exposed to Hazardous Equipment	How often does this job require exposure to hazardous equipment?
Pace Determined by Speed of Equipment	How important is it to this job that the pace is determined by the speed of equipment or machinery? (This does not refer to keeping busy at all times on this job.)
Exposed to Whole Body Vibration	How often does this job require exposure to whole body vibration (e.g., operate a jackhammer)?
Exposed to High Places	How often does this job require exposure to high places?
Spend Time Climbing Ladders, Scaffolds, or Poles	How much does this job require climbing ladders, scaffolds, or poles?
In an Open Vehicle or Equipment	How often does this job require working in an open vehicle or equipment (e.g., tractor)?

Job Zone Component	Job Zone Component Definitions
Title	Job Zone Five: Extensive Preparation Needed
Overall Experience	Extensive skill, knowledge, and experience are needed for these occupations. Many require more than five years of experience. For example, surgeons must complete four years of college and an additional five to seven years of specialized medical training to be able to do their job.
Job Training	Employees may need some on-the-job training, but most of these occupations assume that the person will already have the required skills, knowledge, work-related experience, and/or training.
Job Zone Examples	These occupations often involve coordinating, training, supervising, or managing the activities of others to accomplish goals. Very advanced communication and organizational skills are required. Examples include athletic trainers, lawyers, managing editors, physicists, social psychologists, and surgeons.
SVP Range	(8.0 and above)
Education	A bachelor's degree is the minimum formal education required for these occupations. However, many also require graduate school. For example, they may require a master's degree, and some require a Ph.D., M.D., or J.D. (law degree).

Work_Styles	Work_Styles Definitions
Integrity	Job requires being honest and ethical.
Cooperation	Job requires being pleasant with others on the job and displaying a good-natured, cooperative attitude.
Dependability	Job requires being reliable, responsible, and dependable, and fulfilling obligations.
Concern for Others	Job requires being sensitive to others' needs and feelings and being understanding and helpful on the job.
Independence	Job requires developing one's own ways of doing things, guiding oneself with little or no supervision, and depending on oneself to get things done.
Attention to Detail	Job requires being careful about detail and thorough in completing work tasks.
Self Control	Job requires maintaining composure, keeping emotions in check, controlling anger, and avoiding aggressive behavior, even in very difficult situations.
Social Orientation	Job requires preferring to work with others rather than alone, and being personally connected with others on the job.
Adaptability/Flexibility	Job requires being open to change (positive or negative) and to considerable variety in the workplace.
Initiative	Job requires a willingness to take on responsibilities and challenges.
Analytical Thinking	Job requires analyzing information and using logic to address work-related issues and problems.

Stress Tolerance	Job requires accepting criticism and dealing calmly and effectively with high stress situations.
Persistence	Job requires persistence in the face of obstacles.
Achievement/Effort	Job requires establishing and maintaining personally challenging achievement goals and exerting effort toward mastering tasks.
Innovation	Job requires creativity and alternative thinking to develop new ideas for and answers to work-related problems.
Leadership	Job requires a willingness to lead, take charge, and offer opinions and direction.

29-1131.00 - Veterinarians

Diagnose and treat diseases and dysfunctions of animals. May engage in a particular function, such as research and development, consultation, administration, technical writing, sale or production of commercial products, or rendering of technical services to commercial firms or other organizations. Includes veterinarians who inspect livestock.

Tasks

1) Collect body tissue, feces, blood, urine, or other body fluids for examination and analysis.

2) Euthanize animals.

3) Inoculate animals against various diseases such as rabies and distemper.

4) Operate diagnostic equipment such as radiographic and ultrasound equipment, and interpret the resulting images.

5) Conduct postmortem studies and analyses to determine the causes of animals' deaths.

6) Educate the public about diseases that can be spread from animals to humans.

7) Train and supervise workers who handle and care for animals.

8) Establish and conduct quarantine and testing procedures that prevent the spread of diseases to other animals or to humans, and that comply with applicable government regulations.

9) Provide care to a wide range of animals or specialize in a particular species, such as horses or exotic birds.

10) Perform administrative duties such as scheduling appointments, accepting payments from clients, and maintaining business records.

11) Plan and execute animal nutrition and reproduction programs.

12) Specialize in a particular type of treatment such as dentistry, pathology, nutrition, surgery, microbiology, or internal medicine.

13) Direct the overall operations of animal hospitals, clinics, or mobile services to farms.

14) Inspect and test horses, sheep, poultry, and other animals to detect the presence of communicable diseases.

15) Determine the effects of drug therapies, antibiotics, or new surgical techniques by testing them on animals.

16) Inspect animal housing facilities to determine their cleanliness and adequacy.

17) Drive mobile clinic vans to farms so that health problems can be treated and/or prevented.

18) Research diseases to which animals could be susceptible.

19) Advise animal owners regarding sanitary measures, feeding, and general care necessary to promote health of animals.

20) Examine animals to detect and determine the nature of diseases or injuries.

Knowledge

Knowledge	Knowledge Definitions
Biology	Knowledge of plant and animal organisms, their tissues, cells, functions, interdependencies, and interactions with each other and the environment.
Medicine and Dentistry	Knowledge of the information and techniques needed to diagnose and treat human injuries, diseases, and deformities. This includes symptoms, treatment alternatives, drug properties and interactions, and preventive health-care measures.
Customer and Personal Service	Knowledge of principles and processes for providing customer and personal services. This includes customer needs assessment, meeting quality standards for services, and evaluation of customer satisfaction.
English Language	Knowledge of the structure and content of the English language including the meaning and spelling of words, rules of composition, and grammar.
Mathematics	Knowledge of arithmetic, algebra, geometry, calculus, statistics, and their applications.
Chemistry	Knowledge of the chemical composition, structure, and properties of substances and of the chemical processes and transformations that they undergo. This includes uses of chemicals and their interactions, danger signs, production techniques, and disposal methods.
Education and Training	Knowledge of principles and methods for curriculum and training design, teaching and instruction for individuals and groups, and the measurement of training effects.
Administration and Management	Knowledge of business and management principles involved in strategic planning, resource allocation, human resources modeling, leadership technique, production methods, and coordination of people and resources.
Sales and Marketing	Knowledge of principles and methods for showing, promoting, and selling products or services. This includes marketing strategy and tactics, product demonstration, sales techniques, and sales control systems.
Psychology	Knowledge of human behavior and performance; individual differences in ability, personality, and interests; learning and motivation; psychological research methods; and the assessment and treatment of behavioral and affective disorders.
Therapy and Counseling	Knowledge of principles, methods, and procedures for diagnosis, treatment, and rehabilitation of physical and mental dysfunctions, and for career counseling and guidance.
Computers and Electronics	Knowledge of circuit boards, processors, chips, electronic equipment, and computer hardware and software, including applications and programming.
Personnel and Human Resources	Knowledge of principles and procedures for personnel recruitment, selection, training, compensation and benefits, labor relations and negotiation, and personnel information systems.
Law and Government	Knowledge of laws, legal codes, court procedures, precedents, government regulations, executive orders, agency rules, and the democratic political process.
Public Safety and Security	Knowledge of relevant equipment, policies, procedures, and strategies to promote effective local, state, or national security operations for the protection of people, data, property, and institutions.
Communications and Media	Knowledge of media production, communication, and dissemination techniques and methods. This includes alternative ways to inform and entertain via written, oral, and visual media.
Economics and Accounting	Knowledge of economic and accounting principles and practices, the financial markets, banking and the analysis and reporting of financial data.
Physics	Knowledge and prediction of physical principles, laws, their interrelationships, and applications to understanding fluid, material, and atmospheric dynamics, and mechanical, electrical, atomic and sub- atomic structures and processes.
Clerical	Knowledge of administrative and clerical procedures and systems such as word processing, managing files and records, stenography and transcription, designing forms, and other office procedures and terminology.
Mechanical	Knowledge of machines and tools, including their designs, uses, repair, and maintenance.
Transportation	Knowledge of principles and methods for moving people or goods by air, rail, sea, or road, including the relative costs and benefits.
Engineering and Technology	Knowledge of the practical application of engineering science and technology. This includes applying principles, techniques, procedures, and equipment to the design and production of various goods and services.
Food Production	Knowledge of techniques and equipment for planting, growing, and harvesting food products (both plant and animal) for consumption, including storage/handling techniques.
Production and Processing	Knowledge of raw materials, production processes, quality control, costs, and other techniques for maximizing the effective manufacture and distribution of goods.
Geography	Knowledge of principles and methods for describing the features of land, sea, and air masses, including their physical characteristics, locations, interrelationships, and distribution of plant, animal, and human life.
Telecommunications	Knowledge of transmission, broadcasting, switching, control, and operation of telecommunications systems.
Sociology and Anthropology	Knowledge of group behavior and dynamics, societal trends and influences, human migrations, ethnicity, cultures and their history and origins.

Philosophy and Theology	Knowledge of different philosophical systems and religions. This includes their basic principles, values, ethics, ways of thinking, customs, practices, and their impact on human culture.
Foreign Language	Knowledge of the structure and content of a foreign (non-English) language including the meaning and spelling of words, rules of composition and grammar, and pronunciation.
Design	Knowledge of design techniques, tools, and principles involved in production of precision technical plans, blueprints, drawings, and models.
Building and Construction	Knowledge of materials, methods, and the tools involved in the construction or repair of houses, buildings, or other structures such as highways and roads.
History and Archeology	Knowledge of historical events and their causes, indicators, and effects on civilizations and cultures.
Fine Arts	Knowledge of the theory and techniques required to compose, produce, and perform works of music, dance, visual arts, drama, and sculpture.

Skills — Skills Definitions

Active Listening	Giving full attention to what other people are saying, taking time to understand the points being made, asking questions as appropriate, and not interrupting at inappropriate times.
Reading Comprehension	Understanding written sentences and paragraphs in work related documents.
Critical Thinking	Using logic and reasoning to identify the strengths and weaknesses of alternative solutions, conclusions or approaches to problems.
Complex Problem Solving	Identifying complex problems and reviewing related information to develop and evaluate options and implement solutions.
Speaking	Talking to others to convey information effectively.
Science	Using scientific rules and methods to solve problems.
Time Management	Managing one's own time and the time of others.
Judgment and Decision Making	Considering the relative costs and benefits of potential actions to choose the most appropriate one.
Active Learning	Understanding the implications of new information for both current and future problem-solving and decision-making.
Mathematics	Using mathematics to solve problems.
Instructing	Teaching others how to do something.
Monitoring	Monitoring/Assessing performance of yourself, other individuals, or organizations to make improvements or take corrective action.
Writing	Communicating effectively in writing as appropriate for the needs of the audience.
Equipment Selection	Determining the kind of tools and equipment needed to do a job.
Service Orientation	Actively looking for ways to help people.
Learning Strategies	Selecting and using training/instructional methods and procedures appropriate for the situation when learning or teaching new things.
Coordination	Adjusting actions in relation to others' actions.
Management of Financial Resources	Determining how money will be spent to get the work done, and accounting for these expenditures.
Social Perceptiveness	Being aware of others' reactions and understanding why they react as they do.
Management of Personnel Resources	Motivating, developing, and directing people as they work, identifying the best people for the job.
Troubleshooting	Determining causes of operating errors and deciding what to do about it.
Persuasion	Persuading others to change their minds or behavior.
Operation Monitoring	Watching gauges, dials, or other indicators to make sure a machine is working properly.
Management of Material Resources	Obtaining and seeing to the appropriate use of equipment, facilities, and materials needed to do certain work.
Negotiation	Bringing others together and trying to reconcile differences.
Operation and Control	Controlling operations of equipment or systems.
Equipment Maintenance	Performing routine maintenance on equipment and determining when and what kind of maintenance is needed.
Technology Design	Generating or adapting equipment and technology to serve user needs.
Operations Analysis	Analyzing needs and product requirements to create a design.
Quality Control Analysis	Conducting tests and inspections of products, services, or processes to evaluate quality or performance.
Systems Evaluation	Identifying measures or indicators of system performance and the actions needed to improve or correct performance, relative to the goals of the system.
Systems Analysis	Determining how a system should work and how changes in conditions, operations, and the environment will affect outcomes.
Repairing	Repairing machines or systems using the needed tools.
Installation	Installing equipment, machines, wiring, or programs to meet specifications.
Programming	Writing computer programs for various purposes.

Ability — Ability Definitions

Oral Comprehension	The ability to listen to and understand information and ideas presented through spoken words and sentences.
Inductive Reasoning	The ability to combine pieces of information to form general rules or conclusions (includes finding a relationship among seemingly unrelated events).
Problem Sensitivity	The ability to tell when something is wrong or is likely to go wrong. It does not involve solving the problem, only recognizing there is a problem.
Oral Expression	The ability to communicate information and ideas in speaking so others will understand.
Speech Clarity	The ability to speak clearly so others can understand you.
Speech Recognition	The ability to identify and understand the speech of another person.
Written Comprehension	The ability to read and understand information and ideas presented in writing.
Deductive Reasoning	The ability to apply general rules to specific problems to produce answers that make sense.
Near Vision	The ability to see details at close range (within a few feet of the observer).
Information Ordering	The ability to arrange things or actions in a certain order or pattern according to a specific rule or set of rules (e.g., patterns of numbers, letters, words, pictures, mathematical operations).
Finger Dexterity	The ability to make precisely coordinated movements of the fingers of one or both hands to grasp, manipulate, or assemble very small objects.
Selective Attention	The ability to concentrate on a task over a period of time without being distracted.
Manual Dexterity	The ability to quickly move your hand, your hand together with your arm, or your two hands to grasp, manipulate, or assemble objects.
Written Expression	The ability to communicate information and ideas in writing so others will understand.
Category Flexibility	The ability to generate or use different sets of rules for combining or grouping things in different ways.
Arm-Hand Steadiness	The ability to keep your hand and arm steady while moving your arm or while holding your arm and hand in one position.
Visual Color Discrimination	The ability to match or detect differences between colors, including shades of color and brightness.
Originality	The ability to come up with unusual or clever ideas about a given topic or situation, or to develop creative ways to solve a problem.
Perceptual Speed	The ability to quickly and accurately compare similarities and differences among sets of letters, numbers, objects, pictures, or patterns. The things to be compared may be presented at the same time or one after the other. This ability also includes comparing a presented object with a remembered object.
Flexibility of Closure	The ability to identify or detect a known pattern (a figure, object, word, or sound) that is hidden in other distracting material.
Far Vision	The ability to see details at a distance.
Time Sharing	The ability to shift back and forth between two or more activities or sources of information (such as speech, sounds, touch, or other sources).
Fluency of Ideas	The ability to come up with a number of ideas about a topic (the number of ideas is important, not their quality, correctness, or creativity).
Speed of Closure	The ability to quickly make sense of, combine, and organize information into meaningful patterns.
Number Facility	The ability to add, subtract, multiply, or divide quickly and correctly.
Mathematical Reasoning	The ability to choose the right mathematical methods or formulas to solve a problem.
Extent Flexibility	The ability to bend, stretch, twist, or reach with your body, arms, and/or legs.
Auditory Attention	The ability to focus on a single source of sound in the presence of other distracting sounds.
Hearing Sensitivity	The ability to detect or tell the differences between sounds that vary in pitch and loudness.

Multilimb Coordination	The ability to coordinate two or more limbs (for example, two arms, two legs, or one leg and one arm) while sitting, standing, or lying down. It does not involve performing the activities while the whole body is in motion.
Visualization	The ability to imagine how something will look after it is moved around or when its parts are moved or rearranged.
Control Precision	The ability to quickly and repeatedly adjust the controls of a machine or a vehicle to exact positions.
Static Strength	The ability to exert maximum muscle force to lift, push, pull, or carry objects.
Depth Perception	The ability to judge which of several objects is closer or farther away from you, or to judge the distance between you and an object.
Trunk Strength	The ability to use your abdominal and lower back muscles to support part of the body repeatedly or continuously over time without 'giving out' or fatiguing.
Memorization	The ability to remember information such as words, numbers, pictures, and procedures.
Reaction Time	The ability to quickly respond (with the hand, finger, or foot) to a signal (sound, light, picture) when it appears.
Response Orientation	The ability to choose quickly between two or more movements in response to two or more different signals (lights, sounds, pictures). It includes the speed with which the correct response is started with the hand, foot, or other body part.
Stamina	The ability to exert yourself physically over long periods of time without getting winded or out of breath.
Gross Body Coordination	The ability to coordinate the movement of your arms, legs, and torso together when the whole body is in motion.
Wrist-Finger Speed	The ability to make fast, simple, repeated movements of the fingers, hands, and wrists.
Rate Control	The ability to time your movements or the movement of a piece of equipment in anticipation of changes in the speed and/or direction of a moving object or scene.
Gross Body Equilibrium	The ability to keep or regain your body balance or stay upright when in an unstable position.
Speed of Limb Movement	The ability to quickly move the arms and legs.
Dynamic Strength	The ability to exert muscle force repeatedly or continuously over time. This involves muscular endurance and resistance to muscle fatigue.
Sound Localization	The ability to tell the direction from which a sound originated.
Peripheral Vision	The ability to see objects or movement of objects to one's side when the eyes are looking ahead.
Explosive Strength	The ability to use short bursts of muscle force to propel oneself (as in jumping or sprinting), or to throw an object.
Spatial Orientation	The ability to know your location in relation to the environment or to know where other objects are in relation to you.
Glare Sensitivity	The ability to see objects in the presence of glare or bright lighting.
Night Vision	The ability to see under low light conditions.
Dynamic Flexibility	The ability to quickly and repeatedly bend, stretch, twist, or reach out with your body, arms, and/or legs.

Work_Activity	Work_Activity Definitions
Updating and Using Relevant Knowledge	Keeping up-to-date technically and applying new knowledge to your job.
Making Decisions and Solving Problems	Analyzing information and evaluating results to choose the best solution and solve problems.
Getting Information	Observing, receiving, and otherwise obtaining information from all relevant sources.
Identifying Objects, Actions, and Events	Identifying information by categorizing, estimating, recognizing differences or similarities, and detecting changes in circumstances or events.
Performing for or Working Directly with the Public	Performing for people or dealing directly with the public. This includes serving customers in restaurants and stores, and receiving clients or guests.
Documenting/Recording Information	Entering, transcribing, recording, storing, or maintaining information in written or electronic/magnetic form.
Assisting and Caring for Others	Providing personal assistance, medical attention, emotional support, or other personal care to others such as coworkers, customers, or patients.
Analyzing Data or Information	Identifying the underlying principles, reasons, or facts of information by breaking down information or data into separate parts.
Monitor Processes, Materials, or Surroundings	Monitoring and reviewing information from materials, events, or the environment, to detect or assess problems.

Establishing and Maintaining Interpersonal Relatio	Developing constructive and cooperative working relationships with others, and maintaining them over time.
Communicating with Persons Outside Organization	Communicating with people outside the organization, representing the organization to customers, the public, government, and other external sources. This information can be exchanged in person, in writing, or by telephone or e-mail.
Interpreting the Meaning of Information for Others	Translating or explaining what information means and how it can be used.
Organizing, Planning, and Prioritizing Work	Developing specific goals and plans to prioritize, organize, and accomplish your work.
Processing Information	Compiling, coding, categorizing, calculating, tabulating, auditing, or verifying information or data.
Communicating with Supervisors, Peers, or Subordin	Providing information to supervisors, co-workers, and subordinates by telephone, in written form, e-mail, or in person.
Developing and Building Teams	Encouraging and building mutual trust, respect, and cooperation among team members.
Selling or Influencing Others	Convincing others to buy merchandise/goods or to otherwise change their minds or actions.
Handling and Moving Objects	Using hands and arms in handling, installing, positioning, and moving materials, and manipulating things.
Guiding, Directing, and Motivating Subordinates	Providing guidance and direction to subordinates, including setting performance standards and monitoring performance.
Inspecting Equipment, Structures, or Material	Inspecting equipment, structures, or materials to identify the cause of errors or other problems or defects.
Performing General Physical Activities	Performing physical activities that require considerable use of your arms and legs and moving your whole body, such as climbing, lifting, balancing, walking, stooping, and handling of materials.
Estimating the Quantifiable Characteristics of Pro	Estimating sizes, distances, and quantities; or determining time, costs, resources, or materials needed to perform a work activity.
Coordinating the Work and Activities of Others	Getting members of a group to work together to accomplish tasks.
Provide Consultation and Advice to Others	Providing guidance and expert advice to management or other groups on technical, systems-, or process-related topics.
Training and Teaching Others	Identifying the educational needs of others, developing formal educational or training programs or classes, and teaching or instructing others.
Judging the Qualities of Things, Services, or Peop	Assessing the value, importance, or quality of things or people.
Evaluating Information to Determine Compliance wit	Using relevant information and individual judgment to determine whether events or processes comply with laws, regulations, or standards.
Scheduling Work and Activities	Scheduling events, programs, and activities, as well as the work of others.
Developing Objectives and Strategies	Establishing long-range objectives and specifying the strategies and actions to achieve them.
Resolving Conflicts and Negotiating with Others	Handling complaints, settling disputes, and resolving grievances and conflicts, or otherwise negotiating with others.
Performing Administrative Activities	Performing day-to-day administrative tasks such as maintaining information files and processing paperwork.
Thinking Creatively	Developing, designing, or creating new applications, ideas, relationships, systems, or products, including artistic contributions.
Coaching and Developing Others	Identifying the developmental needs of others and coaching, mentoring, or otherwise helping others to improve their knowledge or skills.
Controlling Machines and Processes	Using either control mechanisms or direct physical activity to operate machines or processes (not including computers or vehicles).
Monitoring and Controlling Resources	Monitoring and controlling resources and overseeing the spending of money.
Interacting With Computers	Using computers and computer systems (including hardware and software) to program, write software, set up functions, enter data, or process information.
Staffing Organizational Units	Recruiting, interviewing, selecting, hiring, and promoting employees in an organization.
Repairing and Maintaining Mechanical Equipment	Servicing, repairing, adjusting, and testing machines, devices, moving parts, and equipment that operate primarily on the basis of mechanical (not electronic) principles.
Repairing and Maintaining Electronic Equipment	Servicing, repairing, calibrating, regulating, fine-tuning, or testing machines, devices, and equipment that operate primarily on the basis of electrical or electronic (not mechanical) principles.

Operating Vehicles, Mechanized Devices, or Equipme	Running, maneuvering, navigating, or driving vehicles or mechanized equipment, such as forklifts, passenger vehicles, aircraft, or water craft.
Drafting, Laying Out, and Specifying Technical Dev	Providing documentation, detailed instructions, drawings, or specifications to tell others about how devices, parts, equipment, or structures are to be fabricated, constructed, assembled, modified, maintained, or used.

Work_Context	Work_Context Definitions
Telephone	How often do you have telephone conversations in this job?
Face-to-Face Discussions	How often do you have to have face-to-face discussions with individuals or teams in this job?
Freedom to Make Decisions	How much decision making freedom, without supervision, does the job offer?
Contact With Others	How much does this job require the worker to be in contact with others (face-to-face, by telephone, or otherwise) in order to perform it?
Frequency of Decision Making	How frequently is the worker required to make decisions that affect other people, the financial resources, and/or the image and reputation of the organization?
Impact of Decisions on Co-workers or Company Resul	How do the decisions an employee makes impact the results of co-workers, clients or the company?
Work With Work Group or Team	How important is it to work with others in a group or team in this job?
Structured versus Unstructured Work	To what extent is this job structured for the worker, rather than allowing the worker to determine tasks, priorities, and goals?
Deal With External Customers	How important is it to work with external customers or the public in this job?
Exposed to Contaminants	How often does this job require working exposed to contaminants (such as pollutants, gases, dust or odors)?
Exposed to Disease or Infections	How often does this job require exposure to disease/infections?
Indoors, Environmentally Controlled	How often does this job require working indoors in environmentally controlled conditions?
Physical Proximity	To what extent does this job require the worker to perform job tasks in close physical proximity to other people?
Spend Time Using Your Hands to Handle, Control, or	How much does this job require using your hands to handle, control, or feel objects, tools or controls?
Coordinate or Lead Others	How important is it to coordinate or lead others in accomplishing work activities in this job?
Responsible for Others' Health and Safety	How much responsibility is there for the health and safety of others in this job?
Importance of Being Exact or Accurate	How important is being very exact or highly accurate in performing this job?
Consequence of Error	How serious would the result usually be if the worker made a mistake that was not readily correctable?
Responsibility for Outcomes and Results	How responsible is the worker for work outcomes and results of other workers?
Spend Time Standing	How much does this job require standing?
Sounds, Noise Levels Are Distracting or Uncomforta	How often does this job require working exposed to sounds and noise levels that are distracting or uncomfortable?
Exposed to Radiation	How often does this job require exposure to radiation?
Time Pressure	How often does this job require the worker to meet strict deadlines?
Exposed to Minor Burns, Cuts, Bites, or Stings	How often does this job require exposure to minor burns, cuts, bites, or stings?
Letters and Memos	How often does the job require written letters and memos?
Frequency of Conflict Situations	How often are there conflict situations the employee has to face in this job?
Wear Common Protective or Safety Equipment such as	How much does this job require wearing common protective or safety equipment such as safety shoes, glasses, gloves, hard hats or life jackets?
Deal With Unpleasant or Angry People	How frequently does the worker have to deal with unpleasant, angry, or discourteous individuals as part of the job requirements?
Wear Specialized Protective or Safety Equipment su	How much does this job require wearing specialized protective or safety equipment such as breathing apparatus, safety harness, full protection suits, or radiation protection?
Importance of Repeating Same Tasks	How important is repeating the same physical activities (e.g., key entry) or mental activities (e.g., checking entries in a ledger) over and over, without stopping, to performing this job?
Exposed to Hazardous Conditions	How often does this job require exposure to hazardous conditions?
Cramped Work Space, Awkward Positions	How often does this job require working in cramped work spaces that requires getting into awkward positions?

Level of Competition	To what extent does this job require the worker to compete or to be aware of competitive pressures?
Spend Time Bending or Twisting the Body	How much does this job require bending or twisting your body?
Spend Time Walking and Running	How much does this job require walking and running?
Spend Time Making Repetitive Motions	How much does this job require making repetitive motions?
Extremely Bright or Inadequate Lighting	How often does this job require working in extremely bright or inadequate lighting conditions?
Spend Time Kneeling, Crouching, Stooping, or Crawl	How much does this job require kneeling, crouching, stooping or crawling?
Electronic Mail	How often do you use electronic mail in this job?
In an Enclosed Vehicle or Equipment	How often does this job require working in a closed vehicle or equipment (e.g., car)?
Outdoors, Exposed to Weather	How often does this job require working outdoors, exposed to all weather conditions?
Outdoors, Under Cover	How often does this job require working outdoors, under cover (e.g., structure with roof but no walls)?
Public Speaking	How often do you have to perform public speaking in this job?
Spend Time Sitting	How much does this job require sitting?
Exposed to Hazardous Equipment	How often does this job require exposure to hazardous equipment?
Indoors, Not Environmentally Controlled	How often does this job require working indoors in non-controlled environmental conditions (e.g., warehouse without heat)?
Very Hot or Cold Temperatures	How often does this job require working in very hot (above 90 F degrees) or very cold (below 32 F degrees) temperatures?
Degree of Automation	How automated is the job?
Spend Time Keeping or Regaining Balance	How much does this job require keeping or regaining your balance?
In an Open Vehicle or Equipment	How often does this job require working in an open vehicle or equipment (e.g., tractor)?
Deal With Physically Aggressive People	How frequently does this job require the worker to deal with physical aggression of violent individuals?
Pace Determined by Speed of Equipment	How important is it to this job that the pace is determined by the speed of equipment or machinery? (This does not refer to keeping busy at all times on this job.)
Exposed to High Places	How often does this job require exposure to high places?
Exposed to Whole Body Vibration	How often does this job require exposure to whole body vibration (e.g., operate a jackhammer)?
Spend Time Climbing Ladders, Scaffolds, or Poles	How much does this job require climbing ladders, scaffolds, or poles?

Job Zone Component	Job Zone Component Definitions
Title	Job Zone Five: Extensive Preparation Needed Extensive skill, knowledge, and experience are needed for these occupations. Many require more than five years of experience.
Overall Experience	For example, surgeons must complete four years of college and an additional five to seven years of specialized medical training to be able to do their job.
Job Training	Employees may need some on-the-job training, but most of these occupations assume that the person will already have the required skills, knowledge, work-related experience, and/or training.
Job Zone Examples	These occupations often involve coordinating, training, supervising, or managing the activities of others to accomplish goals. Very advanced communication and organizational skills are required. Examples include athletic trainers, lawyers, managing editors, phyicists, social psychologists, and surgeons.
SVP Range	(8.0 and above)
Education	A bachelor's degree is the minimum formal education required for these occupations. However, many also require graduate school. For example, they may require a master's degree, and some require a Ph.D., M.D., or J.D. (law degree).

Work_Styles	Work_Styles Definitions
Integrity	Job requires being honest and ethical.
Attention to Detail	Job requires being careful about detail and thorough in completing work tasks.
Dependability	Job requires being reliable, responsible, and dependable, and fulfilling obligations.

Concern for Others	Job requires being sensitive to others' needs and feelings and being understanding and helpful on the job.
Cooperation	Job requires being pleasant with others on the job and displaying a good-natured, cooperative attitude.
Stress Tolerance	Job requires accepting criticism and dealing calmly and effectively with high stress situations.
Self Control	Job requires maintaining composure, keeping emotions in check, controlling anger, and avoiding aggressive behavior, even in very difficult situations.
Persistence	Job requires persistence in the face of obstacles.
Initiative	Job requires a willingness to take on responsibilities and challenges.
Analytical Thinking	Job requires analyzing information and using logic to address work-related issues and problems.
Achievement/Effort	Job requires establishing and maintaining personally challenging achievement goals and exerting effort toward mastering tasks.
Social Orientation	Job requires preferring to work with others rather than alone, and being personally connected with others on the job.
Leadership	Job requires a willingness to lead, take charge, and offer opinions and direction.
Adaptability/Flexibility	Job requires being open to change (positive or negative) and to considerable variety in the workplace.
Independence	Job requires developing one's own ways of doing things, guiding oneself with little or no supervision, and depending on oneself to get things done.
Innovation	Job requires creativity and alternative thinking to develop new ideas for and answers to work-related problems.

29-2011.00 - Medical and Clinical Laboratory Technologists

Perform complex medical laboratory tests for diagnosis, treatment, and prevention of disease. May train or supervise staff.

Tasks

1) Operate, calibrate and maintain equipment used in quantitative and qualitative analysis, such as spectrophotometers, calorimeters, flame photometers, and computer-controlled analyzers.

2) Conduct chemical analysis of body fluids, including blood, urine, and spinal fluid, to determine presence of normal and abnormal components.

3) Enter data from analysis of medical tests and clinical results into computer for storage.

4) Analyze laboratory findings to check the accuracy of the results.

5) Provide technical information about test results to physicians, family members and researchers.

6) Analyze samples of biological material for chemical content or reaction.

7) Supervise, train, and direct lab assistants, medical and clinical laboratory technicians and technologists, and other medical laboratory workers engaged in laboratory testing.

8) Develop, standardize, evaluate, and modify procedures, techniques and tests used in the analysis of specimens and in medical laboratory experiments.

9) Establish and monitor programs to ensure the accuracy of laboratory results.

10) Cultivate, isolate, and assist in identifying microbial organisms, and perform various tests on these microorganisms.

11) Study blood samples to determine the number of cells and their morphology, as well as the blood group, type and compatibility for transfusion purposes, using microscopic technique.

12) Obtain, cut, stain, and mount biological material on slides for microscopic study and diagnosis, following standard laboratory procedures.

13) Select and prepare specimen and media for cell culture, using aseptic technique and knowledge of medium components and cell requirements.

14) Harvest cell cultures at optimum time based on knowledge of cell cycle differences and culture conditions.

15) Conduct medical research under direction of microbiologist or biochemist.

Knowledge	Knowledge Definitions
Chemistry	Knowledge of the chemical composition, structure, and properties of substances and of the chemical processes and transformations that they undergo. This includes uses of chemicals and their interactions, danger signs, production techniques, and disposal methods.
Biology	Knowledge of plant and animal organisms, their tissues, cells, functions, interdependencies, and interactions with each other and the environment.
English Language	Knowledge of the structure and content of the English language including the meaning and spelling of words, rules of composition, and grammar.
Computers and Electronics	Knowledge of circuit boards, processors, chips, electronic equipment, and computer hardware and software, including applications and programming.
Public Safety and Security	Knowledge of relevant equipment, policies, procedures, and strategies to promote effective local, state, or national security operations for the protection of people, data, property, and institutions.
Mathematics	Knowledge of arithmetic, algebra, geometry, calculus, statistics, and their applications.
Customer and Personal Service	Knowledge of principles and processes for providing customer and personal services. This includes customer needs assessment, meeting quality standards for services, and evaluation of customer satisfaction.
Education and Training	Knowledge of principles and methods for curriculum and training design, teaching and instruction for individuals and groups, and the measurement of training effects.
Mechanical	Knowledge of machines and tools, including their designs, uses, repair, and maintenance.
Medicine and Dentistry	Knowledge of the information and techniques needed to diagnose and treat human injuries, diseases, and deformities. This includes symptoms, treatment alternatives, drug properties and interactions, and preventive health-care measures.
Design	Knowledge of design techniques, tools, and principles involved in production of precision technical plans, blueprints, drawings, and models.
Clerical	Knowledge of administrative and clerical procedures and systems such as word processing, managing files and records, stenography and transcription, designing forms, and other office procedures and terminology.
Engineering and Technology	Knowledge of the practical application of engineering science and technology. This includes applying principles, techniques, procedures, and equipment to the design and production of various goods and services.
Psychology	Knowledge of human behavior and performance; individual differences in ability, personality, and interests; learning and motivation; psychological research methods; and the assessment and treatment of behavioral and affective disorders.
Communications and Media	Knowledge of media production, communication, and dissemination techniques and methods. This includes alternative ways to inform and entertain via written, oral, and visual media.
Telecommunications	Knowledge of transmission, broadcasting, switching, control, and operation of telecommunications systems.
Physics	Knowledge and prediction of physical principles, laws, their interrelationships, and applications to understanding fluid, material, and atmospheric dynamics, and mechanical, electrical, atomic and sub-atomic structures and processes.
Personnel and Human Resources	Knowledge of principles and procedures for personnel recruitment, selection, training, compensation and benefits, labor relations and negotiation, and personnel information systems.
Production and Processing	Knowledge of raw materials, production processes, quality control, costs, and other techniques for maximizing the effective manufacture and distribution of goods.
Administration and Management	Knowledge of business and management principles involved in strategic planning, resource allocation, human resources modeling, leadership technique, production methods, and coordination of people and resources.
Law and Government	Knowledge of laws, legal codes, court procedures, precedents, government regulations, executive orders, agency rules, and the democratic political process.
Sociology and Anthropology	Knowledge of group behavior and dynamics, societal trends and influences, human migrations, ethnicity, cultures and their history and origins.

Economics and Accounting	Knowledge of economic and accounting principles and practices, the financial markets, banking and the analysis and reporting of financial data.
Transportation	Knowledge of principles and methods for moving people or goods by air, rail, sea, or road, including the relative costs and benefits.
Therapy and Counseling	Knowledge of principles, methods, and procedures for diagnosis, treatment, and rehabilitation of physical and mental dysfunctions, and for career counseling and guidance.
Sales and Marketing	Knowledge of principles and methods for showing, promoting, and selling products or services. This includes marketing strategy and tactics, product demonstration, sales techniques, and sales control systems.
Geography	Knowledge of principles and methods for describing the features of land, sea, and air masses, including their physical characteristics, locations, interrelationships, and distribution of plant, animal, and human life.
Foreign Language	Knowledge of the structure and content of a foreign (non-English) language including the meaning and spelling of words, rules of composition and grammar, and pronunciation.
Philosophy and Theology	Knowledge of different philosophical systems and religions. This includes their basic principles, values, ethics, ways of thinking, customs, practices, and their impact on human culture.
Fine Arts	Knowledge of the theory and techniques required to compose, produce, and perform works of music, dance, visual arts, drama, and sculpture.
History and Archeology	Knowledge of historical events and their causes, indicators, and effects on civilizations and cultures.
Food Production	Knowledge of techniques and equipment for planting, growing, and harvesting food products (both plant and animal) for consumption, including storage/handling techniques.
Building and Construction	Knowledge of materials, methods, and the tools involved in the construction or repair of houses, buildings, or other structures such as highways and roads.

Skills   Skills Definitions

Quality Control Analysis	Conducting tests and inspections of products, services, or processes to evaluate quality or performance.
Equipment Maintenance	Performing routine maintenance on equipment and determining when and what kind of maintenance is needed.
Reading Comprehension	Understanding written sentences and paragraphs in work related documents.
Troubleshooting	Determining causes of operating errors and deciding what to do about it.
Operation and Control	Controlling operations of equipment or systems.
Operation Monitoring	Watching gauges, dials, or other indicators to make sure a machine is working properly.
Science	Using scientific rules and methods to solve problems.
Critical Thinking	Using logic and reasoning to identify the strengths and weaknesses of alternative solutions, conclusions or approaches to problems.
Active Listening	Giving full attention to what other people are saying, taking time to understand the points being made, asking questions as appropriate, and not interrupting at inappropriate times.
Complex Problem Solving	Identifying complex problems and reviewing related information to develop and evaluate options and implement solutions.
Active Learning	Understanding the implications of new information for both current and future problem-solving and decision-making.
Time Management	Managing one's own time and the time of others.
Monitoring	Monitoring/Assessing performance of yourself, other individuals, or organizations to make improvements or take corrective action.
Instructing	Teaching others how to do something.
Mathematics	Using mathematics to solve problems.
Equipment Selection	Determining the kind of tools and equipment needed to do a job.
Judgment and Decision Making	Considering the relative costs and benefits of potential actions to choose the most appropriate one.
Learning Strategies	Selecting and using training/instructional methods and procedures appropriate for the situation when learning or teaching new things.
Speaking	Talking to others to convey information effectively.
Coordination	Adjusting actions in relation to others' actions.
Repairing	Repairing machines or systems using the needed tools.

Writing	Communicating effectively in writing as appropriate for the needs of the audience.
Service Orientation	Actively looking for ways to help people.
Social Perceptiveness	Being aware of others' reactions and understanding why they react as they do.
Systems Analysis	Determining how a system should work and how changes in conditions, operations, and the environment will affect outcomes.
Operations Analysis	Analyzing needs and product requirements to create a design.
Systems Evaluation	Identifying measures or indicators of system performance and the actions needed to improve or correct performance, relative to the goals of the system.
Management of Personnel Resources	Motivating, developing, and directing people as they work, identifying the best people for the job.
Management of Material Resources	Obtaining and seeing to the appropriate use of equipment, facilities, and materials needed to do certain work.
Technology Design	Generating or adapting equipment and technology to serve user needs.
Negotiation	Bringing others together and trying to reconcile differences.
Installation	Installing equipment, machines, wiring, or programs to meet specifications.
Persuasion	Persuading others to change their minds or behavior.
Management of Financial Resources	Determining how money will be spent to get the work done, and accounting for these expenditures.
Programming	Writing computer programs for various purposes.

Ability   Ability Definitions

Near Vision	The ability to see details at close range (within a few feet of the observer).
Problem Sensitivity	The ability to tell when something is wrong or is likely to go wrong. It does not involve solving the problem, only recognizing there is a problem.
Inductive Reasoning	The ability to combine pieces of information to form general rules or conclusions (includes finding a relationship among seemingly unrelated events).
Written Comprehension	The ability to read and understand information and ideas presented in writing.
Oral Expression	The ability to communicate information and ideas in speaking so others will understand.
Deductive Reasoning	The ability to apply general rules to specific problems to produce answers that make sense.
Information Ordering	The ability to arrange things or actions in a certain order or pattern according to a specific rule or set of rules (e.g., patterns of numbers, letters, words, pictures, mathematical operations).
Flexibility of Closure	The ability to identify or detect a known pattern (a figure, object, word, or sound) that is hidden in other distracting material.
Category Flexibility	The ability to generate or use different sets of rules for combining or grouping things in different ways.
Oral Comprehension	The ability to listen to and understand information and ideas presented through spoken words and sentences.
Finger Dexterity	The ability to make precisely coordinated movements of the fingers of one or both hands to grasp, manipulate, or assemble very small objects.
Visual Color Discrimination	The ability to match or detect differences between colors, including shades of color and brightness.
Perceptual Speed	The ability to quickly and accurately compare similarities and differences among sets of letters, numbers, objects, pictures, or patterns. The things to be compared may be presented at the same time or one after the other. This ability also includes comparing a presented object with a remembered object.
Speech Clarity	The ability to speak clearly so others can understand you.
Arm-Hand Steadiness	The ability to keep your hand and arm steady while moving your arm or while holding your arm and hand in one position.
Selective Attention	The ability to concentrate on a task over a period of time without being distracted.
Written Expression	The ability to communicate information and ideas in writing so others will understand.
Speech Recognition	The ability to identify and understand the speech of another person.
Memorization	The ability to remember information such as words, numbers, pictures, and procedures.
Fluency of Ideas	The ability to come up with a number of ideas about a topic (the number of ideas is important, not their quality, correctness, or creativity).
Speed of Closure	The ability to quickly make sense of, combine, and organize information into meaningful patterns.

Mathematical Reasoning	The ability to choose the right mathematical methods or formulas to solve a problem.
Number Facility	The ability to add, subtract, multiply, or divide quickly and correctly.
Visualization	The ability to imagine how something will look after it is moved around or when its parts are moved or rearranged.
Originality	The ability to come up with unusual or clever ideas about a given topic or situation, or to develop creative ways to solve a problem.
Control Precision	The ability to quickly and repeatedly adjust the controls of a machine or a vehicle to exact positions.
Far Vision	The ability to see details at a distance.
Hearing Sensitivity	The ability to detect or tell the differences between sounds that vary in pitch and loudness.
Manual Dexterity	The ability to quickly move your hand, your hand together with your arm, or your two hands to grasp, manipulate, or assemble objects.
Depth Perception	The ability to judge which of several objects is closer or farther away from you, or to judge the distance between you and an object.
Multilimb Coordination	The ability to coordinate two or more limbs (for example, two arms, two legs, or one leg and one arm) while sitting, standing, or lying down. It does not involve performing the activities while the whole body is in motion.
Time Sharing	The ability to shift back and forth between two or more activities or sources of information (such as speech, sounds, touch, or other sources).
Trunk Strength	The ability to use your abdominal and lower back muscles to support part of the body repeatedly or continuously over time without 'giving out' or fatiguing.
Rate Control	The ability to time your movements or the movement of a piece of equipment in anticipation of changes in the speed and/or direction of a moving object or scene.
Auditory Attention	The ability to focus on a single source of sound in the presence of other distracting sounds.
Wrist-Finger Speed	The ability to make fast, simple, repeated movements of the fingers, hands, and wrists.
Stamina	The ability to exert yourself physically over long periods of time without getting winded or out of breath.
Reaction Time	The ability to quickly respond (with the hand, finger, or foot) to a signal (sound, light, picture) when it appears.
Static Strength	The ability to exert maximum muscle force to lift, push, pull, or carry objects.
Response Orientation	The ability to choose quickly between two or more movements in response to two or more different signals (lights, sounds, pictures). It includes the speed with which the correct response is started with the hand, foot, or other body part.
Speed of Limb Movement	The ability to quickly move the arms and legs.
Gross Body Coordination	The ability to coordinate the movement of your arms, legs, and torso together when the whole body is in motion.
Extent Flexibility	The ability to bend, stretch, twist, or reach with your body, arms, and/or legs.
Dynamic Strength	The ability to exert muscle force repeatedly or continuously over time. This involves muscular endurance and resistance to muscle fatigue.
Gross Body Equilibrium	The ability to keep or regain your body balance or stay upright when in an unstable position.
Night Vision	The ability to see under low light conditions.
Glare Sensitivity	The ability to see objects in the presence of glare or bright lighting.
Peripheral Vision	The ability to see objects or movement of objects to one's side when the eyes are looking ahead.
Spatial Orientation	The ability to know your location in relation to the environment or to know where other objects are in relation to you.
Dynamic Flexibility	The ability to quickly and repeatedly bend, stretch, twist, or reach out with your body, arms, and/or legs.
Sound Localization	The ability to tell the direction from which a sound originated.
Explosive Strength	The ability to use short bursts of muscle force to propel oneself (as in jumping or sprinting), or to throw an object.

Work_Activity	Work_Activity Definitions
Making Decisions and Solving Problems	Analyzing information and evaluating results to choose the best solution and solve problems.
Identifying Objects, Actions, and Events	Identifying information by categorizing, estimating, recognizing differences or similarities, and detecting changes in circumstances or events.

Documenting/Recording Information	Entering, transcribing, recording, storing, or maintaining information in written or electronic/magnetic form.
Evaluating Information to Determine Compliance wit	Using relevant information and individual judgment to determine whether events or processes comply with laws, regulations, or standards.
Organizing, Planning, and Prioritizing Work	Developing specific goals and plans to prioritize, organize, and accomplish your work.
Processing Information	Compiling, coding, categorizing, calculating, tabulating, auditing, or verifying information or data.
Getting Information	Observing, receiving, and otherwise obtaining information from all relevant sources.
Updating and Using Relevant Knowledge	Keeping up-to-date technically and applying new knowledge to your job.
Inspecting Equipment, Structures, or Material	Inspecting equipment, structures, or materials to identify the cause of errors or other problems or defects.
Establishing and Maintaining Interpersonal Relatio	Developing constructive and cooperative working relationships with others, and maintaining them over time.
Communicating with Supervisors, Peers, or Subordin	Providing information to supervisors, co-workers, and subordinates by telephone, in written form, e-mail, or in person.
Interacting With Computers	Using computers and computer systems (including hardware and software) to program, write software, set up functions, enter data, or process information.
Monitor Processes, Materials, or Surroundings	Monitoring and reviewing information from materials, events, or the environment, to detect or assess problems.
Judging the Qualities of Things, Services, or Peop	Assessing the value, importance, or quality of things or people.
Analyzing Data or Information	Identifying the underlying principles, reasons, or facts of information by breaking down information or data into separate parts.
Controlling Machines and Processes	Using either control mechanisms or direct physical activity to operate machines or processes (not including computers or vehicles).
Estimating the Quantifiable Characteristics of Pro	Estimating sizes, distances, and quantities; or determining time, costs, resources, or materials needed to perform a work activity.
Coordinating the Work and Activities of Others	Getting members of a group to work together to accomplish tasks.
Repairing and Maintaining Electronic Equipment	Servicing, repairing, calibrating, regulating, fine-tuning, or testing machines, devices, and equipment that operate primarily on the basis of electrical or electronic (not mechanical) principles.
Handling and Moving Objects	Using hands and arms in handling, installing, positioning, and moving materials, and manipulating things.
Interpreting the Meaning of Information for Others	Translating or explaining what information means and how it can be used.
Communicating with Persons Outside Organization	Communicating with people outside the organization, representing the organization to customers, the public, government, and other external sources. This information can be exchanged in person, in writing, or by telephone or e-mail.
Performing for or Working Directly with the Public	Performing for people or dealing directly with the public. This includes serving customers in restaurants and stores, and receiving clients or guests.
Guiding, Directing, and Motivating Subordinates	Providing guidance and direction to subordinates, including setting performance standards and monitoring performance.
Repairing and Maintaining Mechanical Equipment	Servicing, repairing, adjusting, and testing machines, devices, moving parts, and equipment that operate primarily on the basis of mechanical (not electronic) principles.
Developing and Building Teams	Encouraging and building mutual trust, respect, and cooperation among team members.
Performing General Physical Activities	Performing physical activities that require considerable use of your arms and legs and moving your whole body, such as climbing, lifting, balancing, walking, stooping, and handling of materials.
Training and Teaching Others	Identifying the educational needs of others, developing formal educational or training programs or classes, and teaching or instructing others.
Assisting and Caring for Others	Providing personal assistance, medical attention, emotional support, or other personal care to others such as coworkers, customers, or patients.
Performing Administrative Activities	Performing day-to-day administrative tasks such as maintaining information files and processing paperwork
Coaching and Developing Others	Identifying the developmental needs of others and coaching, mentoring, or otherwise helping others to improve their knowledge or skills.

Resolving Conflicts and Negotiating with Others	Handling complaints, settling disputes, and resolving grievances and conflicts, or otherwise negotiating with others.
Thinking Creatively	Developing, designing, or creating new applications, ideas, relationships, systems, or products, including artistic contributions.
Provide Consultation and Advice to Others	Providing guidance and expert advice to management or other groups on technical, systems-, or process-related topics.
Developing Objectives and Strategies	Establishing long-range objectives and specifying the strategies and actions to achieve them.
Monitoring and Controlling Resources	Monitoring and controlling resources and overseeing the spending of money.
Drafting, Laying Out, and Specifying Technical Dev	Providing documentation, detailed instructions, drawings, or specifications to tell others about how devices, parts, equipment, or structures are to be fabricated, constructed, assembled, modified, maintained, or used.
Scheduling Work and Activities	Scheduling events, programs, and activities, as well as the work of others.
Selling or Influencing Others	Convincing others to buy merchandise/goods or to otherwise change their minds or actions.
Staffing Organizational Units	Recruiting, interviewing, selecting, hiring, and promoting employees in an organization.
Operating Vehicles, Mechanized Devices, or Equipme	Running, maneuvering, navigating, or driving vehicles or mechanized equipment, such as forklifts, passenger vehicles, aircraft, or water craft.

Work_Context	**Work_Context Definitions**
Face-to-Face Discussions	How often do you have to have face-to-face discussions with individuals or teams in this job?
Exposed to Disease or Infections	How often does this job require exposure to disease/infections?
Time Pressure	How often does this job require the worker to meet strict deadlines?
Importance of Being Exact or Accurate	How important is being very exact or highly accurate in performing this job?
Telephone	How often do you have telephone conversations in this job?
Wear Common Protective or Safety Equipment such as	How much does this job require wearing common protective or safety equipment such as safety shoes, glasses, gloves, hard hats or life jackets?
Indoors, Environmentally Controlled	How often does this job require working indoors in environmentally controlled conditions?
Work With Work Group or Team	How important is it to work with others in a group or team in this job?
Contact With Others	How much does this job require the worker to be in contact with others (face-to-face, by telephone, or otherwise) in order to perform it?
Importance of Repeating Same Tasks	How important is repeating the same physical activities (e.g., key entry) or mental activities (e.g., checking entries in a ledger) over and over, without stopping, to performing this job?
Frequency of Decision Making	How frequently is the worker required to make decisions that affect other people, the financial resources, and/or the image and reputation of the organization?
Freedom to Make Decisions	How much decision making freedom, without supervision, does the job offer?
Electronic Mail	How often do you use electronic mail in this job?
Impact of Decisions on Co-workers or Company Resul	How do the decisions an employee makes impact the results of co-workers, clients or the company?
Exposed to Contaminants	How often does this job require working exposed to contaminants (such as pollutants, gases, dust or odors)?
Coordinate or Lead Others	How important is it to coordinate or lead others in accomplishing work activities in this job?
Spend Time Making Repetitive Motions	How much does this job require making repetitive motions?
Consequence of Error	How serious would the result usually be if the worker made a mistake that was not readily correctable?
Spend Time Using Your Hands to Handle, Control, or	How much does this job require using your hands to handle, control, or feel objects, tools or controls?
Structured versus Unstructured Work	To what extent is this job structured for the worker, rather than allowing the worker to determine tasks, priorities, and goals?
Exposed to Hazardous Conditions	How often does this job require exposure to hazardous conditions?
Deal With External Customers	How important is it to work with external customers or the public in this job?
Responsibility for Outcomes and Results	How responsible is the worker for work outcomes and results of other workers?

Physical Proximity	To what extent does this job require the worker to perform job tasks in close physical proximity to other people?
Degree of Automation	How automated is the job?
Letters and Memos	How often does the job require written letters and memos?
Responsible for Others' Health and Safety	How much responsibility is there for the health and safety of others in this job?
Sounds, Noise Levels Are Distracting or Uncomforta	How often does this job require working exposed to sounds and noise levels that are distracting or uncomfortable?
Deal With Unpleasant or Angry People	How frequently does the worker have to deal with unpleasant, angry, or discourteous individuals as part of the job requirements?
Pace Determined by Speed of Equipment	How important is it to this job that the pace is determined by the speed of equipment or machinery? (This does not refer to keeping busy at all times on this job.)
Spend Time Standing	How much does this job require standing?
Frequency of Conflict Situations	How often are there conflict situations the employee has to face in this job?
Exposed to Hazardous Equipment	How often does this job require exposure to hazardous equipment?
Spend Time Sitting	How much does this job require sitting?
Spend Time Walking and Running	How much does this job require walking and running?
Exposed to Minor Burns, Cuts, Bites, or Stings	How often does this job require exposure to minor burns, cuts, bites, or stings?
Spend Time Bending or Twisting the Body	How much does this job require bending or twisting your body?
Level of Competition	To what extent does this job require the worker to compete or to be aware of competitive pressures?
Cramped Work Space, Awkward Positions	How often does this job require working in cramped work spaces that requires getting into awkward positions?
Wear Specialized Protective or Safety Equipment su	How much does this job require wearing specialized protective or safety equipment such as breathing apparatus, safety harness, full protection suits, or radiation protection?
Deal With Physically Aggressive People	How frequently does this job require the worker to deal with physical aggression of violent individuals?
Exposed to Radiation	How often does this job require exposure to radiation?
Public Speaking	How often do you have to perform public speaking in this job?
Spend Time Kneeling, Crouching, Stooping, or Crawl	How much does this job require kneeling, crouching, stooping, or crawling?
In an Enclosed Vehicle or Equipment	How often does this job require working in a closed vehicle or equipment (e.g., car)?
Very Hot or Cold Temperatures	How often does this job require working in very hot (above 90 F degrees) or very cold (below 32 F degrees) temperatures?
Extremely Bright or Inadequate Lighting	How often does this job require working in extremely bright or inadequate lighting conditions?
Spend Time Keeping or Regaining Balance	How much does this job require keeping or regaining your balance?
Exposed to High Places	How often does this job require exposure to high places?
Indoors, Not Environmentally Controlled	How often does this job require working indoors in non-controlled environmental conditions (e.g., warehouse without heat)?
Exposed to Whole Body Vibration	How often does this job require exposure to whole body vibration (e.g., operate a jackhammer)?
Outdoors, Under Cover	How often does this job require working outdoors, under cover (e.g., structure with roof but no walls)?
Spend Time Climbing Ladders, Scaffolds, or Poles	How much does this job require climbing ladders, scaffolds, or poles?
In an Open Vehicle or Equipment	How often does this job require working in an open vehicle or equipment (e.g., tractor)?
Outdoors, Exposed to Weather	How often does this job require working outdoors, exposed to all weather conditions?

Job Zone Component	**Job Zone Component Definitions**
Title	Job Zone Four: Considerable Preparation Needed
Overall Experience	A minimum of two to four years of work-related skill, knowledge, or experience is needed for these occupations. For example, an accountant must complete four years of college and work for several years in accounting to be considered qualified.
Job Training	Employees in these occupations usually need several years of work-related experience, on-the-job training, and/or vocational training.

Job Zone Examples	Many of these occupations involve coordinating, supervising, managing, or training others. Examples include accountants, chefs and head cooks, computer programmers, historians, pharmacists, and police detectives.
SVP Range	(7.0 to < 8.0)
Education	Most of these occupations require a four - year bachelor's degree, but some do not.

Work_Styles	Work_Styles Definitions
Attention to Detail	Job requires being careful about detail and thorough in completing work tasks.
Analytical Thinking	Job requires analyzing information and using logic to address work-related issues and problems.
Independence	Job requires developing one's own ways of doing things, guiding oneself with little or no supervision, and depending on oneself to get things done.
Initiative	Job requires a willingness to take on responsibilities and challenges.
Achievement/Effort	Job requires establishing and maintaining personally challenging achievement goals and exerting effort toward mastering tasks.
Persistence	Job requires persistence in the face of obstacles.
Dependability	Job requires being reliable, responsible, and dependable, and fulfilling obligations.
Stress Tolerance	Job requires accepting criticism and dealing calmly and effectively with high stress situations.
Integrity	Job requires being honest and ethical.
Adaptability/Flexibility	Job requires being open to change (positive or negative) and to considerable variety in the workplace.
Innovation	Job requires creativity and alternative thinking to develop new ideas for and answers to work-related problems.
Cooperation	Job requires being pleasant with others on the job and displaying a good-natured, cooperative attitude.
Concern for Others	Job requires being sensitive to others' needs and feelings and being understanding and helpful on the job.
Self Control	Job requires maintaining composure, keeping emotions in check, controlling anger, and avoiding aggressive behavior, even in very difficult situations.
Social Orientation	Job requires preferring to work with others rather than alone, and being personally connected with others on the job.
Leadership	Job requires a willingness to lead, take charge, and offer opinions and direction.

29-2012.00 - Medical and Clinical Laboratory Technicians

Perform routine medical laboratory tests for the diagnosis, treatment, and prevention of disease. May work under the supervision of a medical technologist.

Tasks

1) Analyze and record test data to issue reports that use charts, graphs and narratives.

2) Analyze the results of tests and experiments to ensure conformity to specifications, using special mechanical and electrical devices.

3) Conduct chemical analyses of body fluids, such as blood and urine, using microscope or automatic analyzer to detect abnormalities or diseases, and enter findings into computer.

4) Collect blood or tissue samples from patients, observing principles of asepsis to obtain blood sample.

5) Supervise and instruct other technicians and laboratory assistants.

6) Obtain specimens, cultivating, isolating and identifying microorganisms for analysis.

7) Prepare standard volumetric solutions and reagents to be combined with samples, following standardized formulas or experimental procedures.

8) Conduct blood tests for transfusion purposes and perform blood counts.

9) Consult with a pathologist to determine a final diagnosis when abnormal cells are found.

10) Examine cells stained with dye to locate abnormalities.

11) Test raw materials, processes and finished products to determine quality and quantity of materials or characteristics of a substance.

12) Prepare vaccines and serums by standard laboratory methods, testing for virus inactivity and sterility.

13) Cut, stain and mount tissue samples for examination by pathologists.

14) Inoculate fertilized eggs, broths, or other bacteriological media with organisms.

15) Perform medical research to further control and cure disease.

Knowledge	Knowledge Definitions
Customer and Personal Service	Knowledge of principles and processes for providing customer and personal services. This includes customer needs assessment, meeting quality standards for services, and evaluation of customer satisfaction.
Clerical	Knowledge of administrative and clerical procedures and systems such as word processing, managing files and records, stenography and transcription, designing forms, and other office procedures and terminology.
Medicine and Dentistry	Knowledge of the information and techniques needed to diagnose and treat human injuries, diseases, and deformities. This includes symptoms, treatment alternatives, drug properties and interactions, and preventive health-care measures.
Education and Training	Knowledge of principles and methods for curriculum and training design, teaching and instruction for individuals and groups, and the measurement of training effects.
Therapy and Counseling	Knowledge of principles, methods, and procedures for diagnosis, treatment, and rehabilitation of physical and mental dysfunctions, and for career counseling and guidance.
Public Safety and Security	Knowledge of relevant equipment, policies, procedures, and strategies to promote effective local, state, or national security operations for the protection of people, data, property, and institutions.
Biology	Knowledge of plant and animal organisms, their tissues, cells, functions, interdependencies, and interactions with each other and the environment.
Administration and Management	Knowledge of business and management principles involved in strategic planning, resource allocation, human resources modeling, leadership technique, production methods, and coordination of people and resources.
Computers and Electronics	Knowledge of circuit boards, processors, chips, electronic equipment, and computer hardware and software, including applications and programming.
Chemistry	Knowledge of the chemical composition, structure, and properties of substances and of the chemical processes and transformations that they undergo. This includes uses of chemicals and their interactions, danger signs, production techniques, and disposal methods.
Mathematics	Knowledge of arithmetic, algebra, geometry, calculus, statistics, and their applications.
Personnel and Human Resources	Knowledge of principles and procedures for personnel recruitment, selection, training, compensation and benefits, labor relations and negotiation, and personnel information systems.
English Language	Knowledge of the structure and content of the English language including the meaning and spelling of words, rules of composition, and grammar.
Sales and Marketing	Knowledge of principles and methods for showing, promoting, and selling products or services. This includes marketing strategy and tactics, product demonstration, sales techniques, and sales control systems.
Economics and Accounting	Knowledge of economic and accounting principles and practices, the financial markets, banking and the analysis and reporting of financial data.
Psychology	Knowledge of human behavior and performance; individual differences in ability, personality, and interests; learning and motivation; psychological research methods; and the assessment and treatment of behavioral and affective disorders.
Production and Processing	Knowledge of raw materials, production processes, quality control, costs, and other techniques for maximizing the effective manufacture and distribution of goods.
Sociology and Anthropology	Knowledge of group behavior and dynamics, societal trends and influences, human migrations, ethnicity, cultures and their history and origins.
Engineering and Technology	Knowledge of the practical application of engineering science and technology. This includes applying principles, techniques, procedures, and equipment to the design and production of various goods and services.
Mechanical	Knowledge of machines and tools, including their designs, uses, repair, and maintenance.

Physics	Knowledge and prediction of physical principles, laws, their interrelationships, and applications to understanding fluid, material, and atmospheric dynamics, and mechanical, electrical, atomic and sub- atomic structures and processes.
Communications and Media	Knowledge of media production, communication, and dissemination techniques and methods. This includes alternative ways to inform and entertain via written, oral, and visual media.
Philosophy and Theology	Knowledge of different philosophical systems and religions. This includes their basic principles, values, ethics, ways of thinking, customs, practices, and their impact on human culture.
Telecommunications	Knowledge of transmission, broadcasting, switching, control, and operation of telecommunications systems.
Foreign Language	Knowledge of the structure and content of a foreign (non-English) language including the meaning and spelling of words, rules of composition and grammar, and pronunciation.
Law and Government	Knowledge of laws, legal codes, court procedures, precedents, government regulations, executive orders, agency rules, and the democratic political process.
Transportation	Knowledge of principles and methods for moving people or goods by air, rail, sea, or road, including the relative costs and benefits.
Design	Knowledge of design techniques, tools, and principles involved in production of precision technical plans, blueprints, drawings, and models.
Geography	Knowledge of principles and methods for describing the features of land, sea, and air masses, including their physical characteristics, locations, interrelationships, and distribution of plant, animal, and human life.
Building and Construction	Knowledge of materials, methods, and the tools involved in the construction or repair of houses, buildings, or other structures such as highways and roads.
History and Archeology	Knowledge of historical events and their causes, indicators, and effects on civilizations and cultures.
Food Production	Knowledge of techniques and equipment for planting, growing, and harvesting food products (both plant and animal) for consumption, including storage/handling techniques.
Fine Arts	Knowledge of the theory and techniques required to compose, produce, and perform works of music, dance, visual arts, drama, and sculpture.

Skills	Skills Definitions
Reading Comprehension	Understanding written sentences and paragraphs in work related documents.
Active Listening	Giving full attention to what other people are saying, taking time to understand the points being made, asking questions as appropriate, and not interrupting at inappropriate times.
Speaking	Talking to others to convey information effectively.
Science	Using scientific rules and methods to solve problems.
Equipment Maintenance	Performing routine maintenance on equipment and determining when and what kind of maintenance is needed.
Time Management	Managing one's own time and the time of others.
Instructing	Teaching others how to do something.
Monitoring	Monitoring/Assessing performance of yourself, other individuals, or organizations to make improvements or take corrective action.
Judgment and Decision Making	Considering the relative costs and benefits of potential actions to choose the most appropriate one.
Active Learning	Understanding the implications of new information for both current and future problem-solving and decision-making.
Troubleshooting	Determining causes of operating errors and deciding what to do about it.
Critical Thinking	Using logic and reasoning to identify the strengths and weaknesses of alternative solutions, conclusions or approaches to problems.
Writing	Communicating effectively in writing as appropriate for the needs of the audience.
Quality Control Analysis	Conducting tests and inspections of products, services, or processes to evaluate quality or performance.
Operation Monitoring	Watching gauges, dials, or other indicators to make sure a machine is working properly.
Coordination	Adjusting actions in relation to others' actions.
Learning Strategies	Selecting and using training/instructional methods and procedures appropriate for the situation when learning or teaching new things.
Mathematics	Using mathematics to solve problems.

Service Orientation	Actively looking for ways to help people.
Social Perceptiveness	Being aware of others' reactions and understanding why they react as they do.
Operation and Control	Controlling operations of equipment or systems.
Equipment Selection	Determining the kind of tools and equipment needed to do a job.
Complex Problem Solving	Identifying complex problems and reviewing related information to develop and evaluate options and implement solutions.
Negotiation	Bringing others together and trying to reconcile differences.
Installation	Installing equipment, machines, wiring, or programs to meet specifications.
Management of Material Resources	Obtaining and seeing to the appropriate use of equipment, facilities, and materials needed to do certain work.
Repairing	Repairing machines or systems using the needed tools.
Persuasion	Persuading others to change their minds or behavior.
Systems Analysis	Determining how a system should work and how changes in conditions, operations, and the environment will affect outcomes.
Systems Evaluation	Identifying measures or indicators of system performance and the actions needed to improve or correct performance, relative to the goals of the system.
Operations Analysis	Analyzing needs and product requirements to create a design.
Management of Personnel Resources	Motivating, developing, and directing people as they work, identifying the best people for the job.
Technology Design	Generating or adapting equipment and technology to serve user needs.
Management of Financial Resources	Determining how money will be spent to get the work done, and accounting for these expenditures.
Programming	Writing computer programs for various purposes.

Ability	Ability Definitions
Near Vision	The ability to see details at close range (within a few feet of the observer).
Inductive Reasoning	The ability to combine pieces of information to form general rules or conclusions (includes finding a relationship among seemingly unrelated events).
Deductive Reasoning	The ability to apply general rules to specific problems to produce answers that make sense.
Oral Comprehension	The ability to listen to and understand information and ideas presented through spoken words and sentences.
Problem Sensitivity	The ability to tell when something is wrong or is likely to go wrong. It does not involve solving the problem, only recognizing there is a problem.
Arm-Hand Steadiness	The ability to keep your hand and arm steady while moving your arm or while holding your arm and hand in one position.
Written Comprehension	The ability to read and understand information and ideas presented in writing.
Visual Color Discrimination	The ability to match or detect differences between colors, including shades of color and brightness.
Information Ordering	The ability to arrange things or actions in a certain order or pattern according to a specific rule or set of rules (e.g., patterns of numbers, letters, words, pictures, mathematical operations).
Flexibility of Closure	The ability to identify or detect a known pattern (a figure, object, word, or sound) that is hidden in other distracting material.
Oral Expression	The ability to communicate information and ideas in speaking so others will understand.
Finger Dexterity	The ability to make precisely coordinated movements of the fingers of one or both hands to grasp, manipulate, or assemble very small objects.
Speech Clarity	The ability to speak clearly so others can understand you.
Written Expression	The ability to communicate information and ideas in writing so others will understand.
Category Flexibility	The ability to generate or use different sets of rules for combining or grouping things in different ways.
Control Precision	The ability to quickly and repeatedly adjust the controls of a machine or a vehicle to exact positions.
Perceptual Speed	The ability to quickly and accurately compare similarities and differences among sets of letters, numbers, objects, pictures, or patterns. The things to be compared may be presented at the same time or one after the other. This ability also includes comparing a presented object with a remembered object.
Mathematical Reasoning	The ability to choose the right mathematical methods or formulas to solve a problem.
Speech Recognition	The ability to identify and understand the speech of another person.

Selective Attention	The ability to concentrate on a task over a period of time without being distracted.
Far Vision	The ability to see details at a distance.
Memorization	The ability to remember information such as words, numbers, pictures, and procedures.
Number Facility	The ability to add, subtract, multiply, or divide quickly and correctly.
Fluency of Ideas	The ability to come up with a number of ideas about a topic (the number of ideas is important, not their quality, correctness, or creativity).
Speed of Closure	The ability to quickly make sense of, combine, and organize information into meaningful patterns.
Depth Perception	The ability to judge which of several objects is closer or farther away from you, or to judge the distance between you and an object.
Visualization	The ability to imagine how something will look after it is moved around or when its parts are moved or rearranged.
Rate Control	The ability to time your movements or the movement of a piece of equipment in anticipation of changes in the speed and/or direction of a moving object or scene.
Originality	The ability to come up with unusual or clever ideas about a given topic or situation, or to develop creative ways to solve a problem.
Manual Dexterity	The ability to quickly move your hand, your hand together with your arm, or your two hands to grasp, manipulate, or assemble objects.
Trunk Strength	The ability to use your abdominal and lower back muscles to support part of the body repeatedly or continuously over time without 'giving out' or fatiguing.
Hearing Sensitivity	The ability to detect or tell the differences between sounds that vary in pitch and loudness.
Time Sharing	The ability to shift back and forth between two or more activities or sources of information (such as speech, sounds, touch, or other sources).
Multilimb Coordination	The ability to coordinate two or more limbs (for example, two arms, two legs, or one leg and one arm) while sitting, standing, or lying down. It does not involve performing the activities while the whole body is in motion.
Auditory Attention	The ability to focus on a single source of sound in the presence of other distracting sounds.
Reaction Time	The ability to quickly respond (with the hand, finger, or foot) to a signal (sound, light, picture) when it appears.
Response Orientation	The ability to choose quickly between two or more movements in response to two or more different signals (lights, sounds, pictures). It includes the speed with which the correct response is started with the hand, foot, or other body part.
Static Strength	The ability to exert maximum muscle force to lift, push, pull, or carry objects.
Wrist-Finger Speed	The ability to make fast, simple, repeated movements of the fingers, hands, and wrists.
Stamina	The ability to exert yourself physically over long periods of time without getting winded or out of breath.
Gross Body Coordination	The ability to coordinate the movement of your arms, legs, and torso together when the whole body is in motion.
Speed of Limb Movement	The ability to quickly move the arms and legs.
Extent Flexibility	The ability to bend, stretch, twist, or reach with your body, arms, and/or legs.
Peripheral Vision	The ability to see objects or movement of objects to one's side when the eyes are looking ahead.
Night Vision	The ability to see under low light conditions.
Gross Body Equilibrium	The ability to keep or regain your body balance or stay upright when in an unstable position.
Glare Sensitivity	The ability to see objects in the presence of glare or bright lighting.
Dynamic Flexibility	The ability to quickly and repeatedly bend, stretch, twist, or reach out with your body, arms, and/or legs.
Spatial Orientation	The ability to know your location in relation to the environment or to know where other objects are in relation to you.
Sound Localization	The ability to tell the direction from which a sound originated.
Dynamic Strength	The ability to exert muscle force repeatedly or continuously over time. This involves muscular endurance and resistance to muscle fatigue.
Explosive Strength	The ability to use short bursts of muscle force to propel oneself (as in jumping or sprinting), or to throw an object.

Work_Activity	Work_Activity Definitions
Documenting/Recording Information	Entering, transcribing, recording, storing, or maintaining information in written or electronic/magnetic form.
Getting Information	Observing, receiving, and otherwise obtaining information from all relevant sources.
Updating and Using Relevant Knowledge	Keeping up-to-date technically and applying new knowledge to your job.
Inspecting Equipment, Structures, or Material	Inspecting equipment, structures, or materials to identify the cause of errors or other problems or defects.
Evaluating Information to Determine Compliance wit	Using relevant information and individual judgment to determine whether events or processes comply with laws, regulations, or standards.
Interacting With Computers	Using computers and computer systems (including hardware and software) to program, write software, set up functions, enter data, or process information.
Communicating with Supervisors, Peers, or Subordin	Providing information to supervisors, co-workers, and subordinates by telephone, in written form, e-mail, or in person.
Processing Information	Compiling, coding, categorizing, calculating, tabulating, auditing, or verifying information or data.
Organizing, Planning, and Prioritizing Work	Developing specific goals and plans to prioritize, organize, and accomplish your work.
Analyzing Data or Information	Identifying the underlying principles, reasons, or facts of information by breaking down information or data into separate parts.
Controlling Machines and Processes	Using either control mechanisms or direct physical activity to operate machines or processes (not including computers or vehicles).
Identifying Objects, Actions, and Events	Identifying information by categorizing, estimating, recognizing differences or similarities, and detecting changes in circumstances or events.
Making Decisions and Solving Problems	Analyzing information and evaluating results to choose the best solution and solve problems.
Estimating the Quantifiable Characteristics of Pro	Estimating sizes, distances, and quantities; or determining time, costs, resources, or materials needed to perform a work activity.
Repairing and Maintaining Mechanical Equipment	Servicing, repairing, adjusting, and testing machines, devices, moving parts, and equipment that operate primarily on the basis of mechanical (not electronic) principles.
Assisting and Caring for Others	Providing personal assistance, medical attention, emotional support, or other personal care to others such as coworkers, customers, or patients.
Performing for or Working Directly with the Public	Performing for people or dealing directly with the public. This includes serving customers in restaurants and stores, and receiving clients or guests.
Establishing and Maintaining Interpersonal Relatio	Developing constructive and cooperative working relationships with others, and maintaining them over time.
Scheduling Work and Activities	Scheduling events, programs, and activities, as well as the work of others.
Monitor Processes, Materials, or Surroundings	Monitoring and reviewing information from materials, events, or the environment, to detect or assess problems.
Communicating with Persons Outside Organization	Communicating with people outside the organization, representing the organization to customers, the public, government, and other external sources. This information can be exchanged in person, in writing, or by telephone or e-mail.
Interpreting the Meaning of Information for Others	Translating or explaining what information means and how it can be used.
Handling and Moving Objects	Using hands and arms in handling, installing, positioning, and moving materials, and manipulating things.
Judging the Qualities of Things, Services, or Peop	Assessing the value, importance, or quality of things or people.
Performing General Physical Activities	Performing physical activities that require considerable use of your arms and legs and moving your whole body, such as climbing, lifting, balancing, walking, stooping, and handling of materials.
Resolving Conflicts and Negotiating with Others	Handling complaints, settling disputes, and resolving grievances and conflicts, or otherwise negotiating with others.
Training and Teaching Others	Identifying the educational needs of others, developing formal educational or training programs or classes, and teaching or instructing others.
Performing Administrative Activities	Performing day-to-day administrative tasks such as maintaining information files and processing paperwork.
Developing and Building Teams	Encouraging and building mutual trust, respect, and cooperation among team members.

Repairing and Maintaining Electronic Equipment	Servicing, repairing, calibrating, regulating, fine-tuning, or testing machines, devices, and equipment that operate primarily on the basis of electrical or electronic (not mechanical) principles.
Thinking Creatively	Developing, designing, or creating new applications, ideas, relationships, systems, or products, including artistic contributions.
Monitoring and Controlling Resources	Monitoring and controlling resources and overseeing the spending of money.
Coordinating the Work and Activities of Others	Getting members of a group to work together to accomplish tasks.
Coaching and Developing Others	Identifying the developmental needs of others and coaching, mentoring, or otherwise helping others to improve their knowledge or skills.
Developing Objectives and Strategies	Establishing long-range objectives and specifying the strategies and actions to achieve them.
Provide Consultation and Advice to Others	Providing guidance and expert advice to management or other groups on technical, systems-, or process-related topics.
Drafting, Laying Out, and Specifying Technical Dev	Providing documentation, detailed instructions, drawings, or specifications to tell others about how devices, parts, equipment, or structures are to be fabricated, constructed, assembled, modified, maintained, or used.
Operating Vehicles, Mechanized Devices, or Equipme	Running, maneuvering, navigating, or driving vehicles or mechanized equipment, such as forklifts, passenger vehicles, aircraft, or water craft.
Staffing Organizational Units	Recruiting, interviewing, selecting, hiring, and promoting employees in an organization.
Guiding, Directing, and Motivating Subordinates	Providing guidance and direction to subordinates, including setting performance standards and monitoring performance.
Selling or Influencing Others	Convincing others to buy merchandise/goods or to otherwise change their minds or actions.

Work_Context	**Work_Context Definitions**
Indoors, Environmentally Controlled	How often does this job require working indoors in environmentally controlled conditions?
Telephone	How often do you have telephone conversations in this job?
Face-to-Face Discussions	How often do you have to have face-to-face discussions with individuals or teams in this job?
Contact With Others	How much does this job require the worker to be in contact with others (face-to-face, by telephone, or otherwise) in order to perform it?
Importance of Being Exact or Accurate	How important is being very exact or highly accurate in performing this job?
Exposed to Disease or Infections	How often does this job require exposure to disease/infections?
Wear Common Protective or Safety Equipment such as	How much does this job require wearing common protective or safety equipment such as safety shoes, glasses, gloves, hard hats or live jackets?
Consequence of Error	How serious would the result usually be if the worker made a mistake that was not readily correctable?
Work With Work Group or Team	How important is it to work with others in a group or team in this job?
Spend Time Standing	How much does this job require standing?
Structured versus Unstructured Work	To what extent is this job structured for the worker, rather than allowing the worker to determine tasks, priorities, and goals?
Impact of Decisions on Co-workers or Company Resul	How do the decisions an employee makes impact the results of co-workers, clients and the company?
Freedom to Make Decisions	How much decision making freedom, without supervision, does the job offer?
Frequency of Decision Making	How frequently is the worker required to make decisions that affect other people, the financial resources, and/or the image and reputation of the organization?
Spend Time Using Your Hands to Handle, Control, or	How much does this job require using your hands to handle, control, or feel objects, tools or controls?
Physical Proximity	To what extent does this job require the worker to perform job tasks in close physical proximity to other people?
Responsible for Others' Health and Safety	How much responsibility is there for the health and safety of others in this job?
Letters and Memos	How often does the job require written letters and memos?
Importance of Repeating Same Tasks	How important is repeating the same physical activities (e.g., key entry) or mental activities (e.g., checking entries in a ledger) over and over, without stopping, to performing this job?
Electronic Mail	How often do you use electronic mail in this job?
Deal With External Customers	How important is it to work with external customers or the public in this job?

Deal With Unpleasant or Angry People	How frequently does the worker have to deal with unpleasant, angry, or discourteous individuals as part of the job requirements?
Spend Time Walking and Running	How much does this job require walking and running?
Level of Competition	To what extent does this job require the worker to compete or to be aware of competitive pressures?
Degree of Automation	How automated is the job?
Coordinate or Lead Others	How important is it to coordinate or lead others in accomplishing work activities in this job?
Time Pressure	How often does this job require the worker to meet strict deadlines?
Exposed to Contaminants	How often does this job require working exposed to contaminants (such as pollutants, gases, dust or odors)?
Exposed to Hazardous Conditions	How often does this job require exposure to hazardous conditions?
Frequency of Conflict Situations	How often are there conflict situations the employee has to face in this job?
Pace Determined by Speed of Equipment	How important is it to this job that the pace is determined by the speed of equipment or machinery? (This does not refer to keeping busy at all times on this job.)
Exposed to Minor Burns, Cuts, Bites, or Stings	How often does this job require exposure to minor burns, cuts, bites, or stings?
Spend Time Making Repetitive Motions	How much does this job require making repetitive motions?
Responsibility for Outcomes and Results	How responsible is the worker for work outcomes and results of other workers?
Deal With Physically Aggressive People	How frequently does this job require the worker to deal with physical aggression of violent individuals?
Spend Time Bending or Twisting the Body	How much does this job require bending or twisting your body?
Sounds, Noise Levels Are Distracting or Uncomforta	How often does this job require working exposed to sounds and noise levels that are distracting or uncomfortable?
Spend Time Sitting	How much does this job require sitting?
Cramped Work Space, Awkward Positions	How often does this job require working in cramped work spaces that requires getting into awkward positions?
Spend Time Kneeling, Crouching, Stooping, or Crawl	How much does this job require kneeling, crouching, stooping or crawling?
Wear Specialized Protective or Safety Equipment su	How much does this job require wearing specialized protective or safety equipment such as breathing apparatus, safety harness, full protection suits, or radiation protection?
Exposed to Radiation	How often does this job require exposure to radiation?
Public Speaking	How often do you have to perform public speaking in this job?
Spend Time Keeping or Regaining Balance	How much does this job require keeping or regaining your balance?
Extremely Bright or Inadequate Lighting	How often does this job require working in extremely bright or inadequate lighting conditions?
Exposed to Hazardous Equipment	How often does this job require exposure to hazardous equipment?
Very Hot or Cold Temperatures	How often does this job require working in very hot (above 90 F degrees) or very cold (below 32 F degrees) temperatures?
Indoors, Not Environmentally Controlled	How often does this job require working indoors in non-controlled environmental conditions (e.g., warehouse without heat)?
Spend Time Climbing Ladders, Scaffolds, or Poles	How much does this job require climbing ladders, scaffolds, or poles?
Outdoors, Exposed to Weather	How often does this job require working outdoors, exposed to all weather conditions?
In an Enclosed Vehicle or Equipment	How often does this job require working in a closed vehicle or equipment (e.g., car)?
Exposed to Whole Body Vibration	How often does this job require exposure to whole body vibration (e.g., operate a jackhammer)?
Exposed to High Places	How often does this job require exposure to high places?
Outdoors, Under Cover	How often does this job require working outdoors, under cover (e.g., structure with roof but no walls)?
In an Open Vehicle or Equipment	How often does this job require working in an open vehicle or equipment (e.g., tractor)?

Job Zone Component	**Job Zone Component Definitions**
Title	Job Zone Two: Some Preparation Needed

Overall Experience	Some previous work-related skill, knowledge, or experience may be helpful in these occupations, but usually is not needed. For example, a drywall installer might benefit from experience installing drywall, but an inexperienced person could still learn to be an installer with little difficulty.
Job Training	Employees in these occupations need anywhere from a few months to one year of working with experienced employees.
Job Zone Examples	These occupations often involve using your knowledge and skills to help others. Examples include drywall installers, fire inspectors, flight attendants, pharmacy technicians, salespersons (retail), and tellers.
SVP Range	(4.0 to < 6.0)
Education	These occupations usually require a high school diploma and may require some vocational training or job-related course work. In some cases, an associate's or bachelor's degree could be needed.

Work_Styles	Work_Styles Definitions
Integrity	Job requires being honest and ethical.
Attention to Detail	Job requires being careful about detail and thorough in completing work tasks.
Dependability	Job requires being reliable, responsible, and dependable, and fulfilling obligations.
Concern for Others	Job requires being sensitive to others' needs and feelings and being understanding and helpful on the job.
Stress Tolerance	Job requires accepting criticism and dealing calmly and effectively with high stress situations.
Cooperation	Job requires being pleasant with others on the job and displaying a good-natured, cooperative attitude.
Self Control	Job requires maintaining composure, keeping emotions in check, controlling anger, and avoiding aggressive behavior, even in very difficult situations.
Independence	Job requires developing one's own ways of doing things, guiding oneself with little or no supervision, and depending on oneself to get things done.
Initiative	Job requires a willingness to take on responsibilities and challenges.
Leadership	Job requires a willingness to lead, take charge, and offer opinions and direction.
Adaptability/Flexibility	Job requires being open to change (positive or negative) and to considerable variety in the workplace.
Persistence	Job requires persistence in the face of obstacles.
Analytical Thinking	Job requires analyzing information and using logic to address work-related issues and problems.
Social Orientation	Job requires preferring to work with others rather than alone, and being personally connected with others on the job.
Innovation	Job requires creativity and alternative thinking to develop new ideas for and answers to work-related problems.
Achievement/Effort	Job requires establishing and maintaining personally challenging achievement goals and exerting effort toward mastering tasks.

29-2021.00 - Dental Hygienists

Clean teeth and examine oral areas, head, and neck for signs of oral disease. May educate patients on oral hygiene, take and develop X-rays, or apply fluoride or sealants.

Tasks

1) Provide clinical services and health education to improve and maintain oral health of school children.

2) Feel lymph nodes under patient's chin to detect swelling or tenderness that could indicate presence of oral cancer.

3) Examine gums, using probes, to locate periodontal recessed gums and signs of gum disease.

4) Chart conditions of decay and disease for diagnosis and treatment by dentist.

5) Feel and visually examine gums for sores and signs of disease.

6) Remove excess cement from coronal surfaces of teeth.

7) Make impressions for study casts.

8) Administer local anesthetic agents.

9) Remove sutures and dressings.

10) Conduct dental health clinics for community groups to augment services of dentist.

11) Place and remove rubber dams, matrices, and temporary restorations.

12) Place, carve, and finish amalgam restorations.

13) Apply fluorides and other cavity preventing agents to arrest dental decay.

14) Clean calcareous deposits, accretions, and stains from teeth and beneath margins of gums, using dental instruments.

Knowledge	Knowledge Definitions
Medicine and Dentistry	Knowledge of the information and techniques needed to diagnose and treat human injuries, diseases, and deformities. This includes symptoms, treatment alternatives, drug properties and interactions, and preventive health-care measures.
Customer and Personal Service	Knowledge of principles and processes for providing customer and personal services. This includes customer needs assessment, meeting quality standards for services, and evaluation of customer satisfaction.
Biology	Knowledge of plant and animal organisms, their tissues, cells, functions, interdependencies, and interactions with each other and the environment.
Education and Training	Knowledge of principles and methods for curriculum and training design, teaching and instruction for individuals and groups, and the measurement of training effects.
English Language	Knowledge of the structure and content of the English language including the meaning and spelling of words, rules of composition, and grammar.
Psychology	Knowledge of human behavior and performance; individual differences in ability, personality, and interests; learning and motivation; psychological research methods; and the assessment and treatment of behavioral and affective disorders.
Sales and Marketing	Knowledge of principles and methods for showing, promoting, and selling products or services. This includes marketing strategy and tactics, product demonstration, sales techniques, and sales control systems.
Public Safety and Security	Knowledge of relevant equipment, policies, procedures, and strategies to promote effective local, state, or national security operations for the protection of people, data, property, and institutions.
Production and Processing	Knowledge of raw materials, production processes, quality control, costs, and other techniques for maximizing the effective manufacture and distribution of goods.
Law and Government	Knowledge of laws, legal codes, court procedures, precedents, government regulations, executive orders, agency rules, and the democratic political process.
Chemistry	Knowledge of the chemical composition, structure, and properties of substances and of the chemical processes and transformations that they undergo. This includes uses of chemicals and their interactions, danger signs, production techniques, and disposal methods.
Therapy and Counseling	Knowledge of principles, methods, and procedures for diagnosis, treatment, and rehabilitation of physical and mental dysfunctions, and for career counseling and guidance.
Computers and Electronics	Knowledge of circuit boards, processors, chips, electronic equipment, and computer hardware and software, including applications and programming.
Clerical	Knowledge of administrative and clerical procedures and systems such as word processing, managing files and records, stenography and transcription, designing forms, and other office procedures and terminology.
Administration and Management	Knowledge of business and management principles involved in strategic planning, resource allocation, human resources modeling, leadership technique, production methods, and coordination of people and resources.
Personnel and Human Resources	Knowledge of principles and procedures for personnel recruitment, selection, training, compensation and benefits, labor relations and negotiation, and personnel information systems.
Sociology and Anthropology	Knowledge of group behavior and dynamics, societal trends and influences, human migrations, ethnicity, cultures and their history and origins.
Mechanical	Knowledge of machines and tools, including their designs, uses, repair, and maintenance.

Communications and Media	Knowledge of media production, communication, and dissemination techniques and methods. This includes alternative ways to inform and entertain via written, oral, and visual media.
Mathematics	Knowledge of arithmetic, algebra, geometry, calculus, statistics, and their applications.
Philosophy and Theology	Knowledge of different philosophical systems and religions. This includes their basic principles, values, ethics, ways of thinking, customs, practices, and their impact on human culture.
Engineering and Technology	Knowledge of the practical application of engineering science and technology. This includes applying principles, techniques, procedures, and equipment to the design and production of various goods and services.
Economics and Accounting	Knowledge of economic and accounting principles and practices, the financial markets, banking and the analysis and reporting of financial data.
Telecommunications	Knowledge of transmission, broadcasting, switching, control, and operation of telecommunications systems.
Physics	Knowledge and prediction of physical principles, laws, their interrelationships, and applications to understanding fluid, material, and atmospheric dynamics, and mechanical, electrical, atomic and sub- atomic structures and processes.
History and Archeology	Knowledge of historical events and their causes, indicators, and effects on civilizations and cultures.
Building and Construction	Knowledge of materials, methods, and the tools involved in the construction or repair of houses, buildings, or other structures such as highways and roads.
Design	Knowledge of design techniques, tools, and principles involved in production of precision technical plans, blueprints, drawings, and models.
Foreign Language	Knowledge of the structure and content of a foreign (non-English) language including the meaning and spelling of words, rules of composition and grammar, and pronunciation.
Transportation	Knowledge of principles and methods for moving people or goods by air, rail, sea, or road, including the relative costs and benefits.
Fine Arts	Knowledge of the theory and techniques required to compose, produce, and perform works of music, dance, visual arts, drama, and sculpture.
Food Production	Knowledge of techniques and equipment for planting, growing, and harvesting food products (both plant and animal) for consumption, including storage/handling techniques.
Geography	Knowledge of principles and methods for describing the features of land, sea, and air masses, including their physical characteristics, locations, interrelationships, and distribution of plant, animal, and human life.

Skills	**Skills Definitions**
Active Listening	Giving full attention to what other people are saying, taking time to understand the points being made, asking questions as appropriate, and not interrupting at inappropriate times.
Speaking	Talking to others to convey information effectively.
Reading Comprehension	Understanding written sentences and paragraphs in work related documents.
Active Learning	Understanding the implications of new information for both current and future problem-solving and decision-making.
Time Management	Managing one's own time and the time of others.
Social Perceptiveness	Being aware of others' reactions and understanding why they react as they do.
Critical Thinking	Using logic and reasoning to identify the strengths and weaknesses of alternative solutions, conclusions or approaches to problems.
Coordination	Adjusting actions in relation to others' actions.
Instructing	Teaching others how to do something.
Writing	Communicating effectively in writing as appropriate for the needs of the audience.
Equipment Selection	Determining the kind of tools and equipment needed to do a job.
Science	Using scientific rules and methods to solve problems.
Learning Strategies	Selecting and using training/instructional methods and procedures appropriate for the situation when learning or teaching new things.
Persuasion	Persuading others to change their minds or behavior.
Service Orientation	Actively looking for ways to help people.
Judgment and Decision Making	Considering the relative costs and benefits of potential actions to choose the most appropriate one.

Monitoring	Monitoring/Assessing performance of yourself, other individuals, or organizations to make improvements or take corrective action.
Complex Problem Solving	Identifying complex problems and reviewing related information to develop and evaluate options and implement solutions.
Equipment Maintenance	Performing routine maintenance on equipment and determining when and what kind of maintenance is needed.
Troubleshooting	Determining causes of operating errors and deciding what to do about it.
Negotiation	Bringing others together and trying to reconcile differences.
Operation and Control	Controlling operations of equipment or systems.
Operation Monitoring	Watching gauges, dials, or other indicators to make sure a machine is working properly.
Mathematics	Using mathematics to solve problems.
Operations Analysis	Analyzing needs and product requirements to create a design.
Management of Material Resources	Obtaining and seeing to the appropriate use of equipment, facilities, and materials needed to do certain work.
Quality Control Analysis	Conducting tests and inspections of products, services, or processes to evaluate quality or performance.
Technology Design	Generating or adapting equipment and technology to serve user needs.
Systems Evaluation	Identifying measures or indicators of system performance and the actions needed to improve or correct performance, relative to the goals of the system.
Installation	Installing equipment, machines, wiring, or programs to meet specifications.
Management of Personnel Resources	Motivating, developing, and directing people as they work, identifying the best people for the job.
Repairing	Repairing machines or systems using the needed tools.
Management of Financial Resources	Determining how money will be spent to get the work done, and accounting for these expenditures.
Systems Analysis	Determining how a system should work and how changes in conditions, operations, and the environment will affect outcomes.
Programming	Writing computer programs for various purposes.

Ability	**Ability Definitions**
Near Vision	The ability to see details at close range (within a few feet of the observer).
Finger Dexterity	The ability to make precisely coordinated movements of the fingers of one or both hands to grasp, manipulate, or assemble very small objects.
Manual Dexterity	The ability to quickly move your hand, your hand together with your arm, or your two hands to grasp, manipulate, or assemble objects.
Problem Sensitivity	The ability to tell when something is wrong or is likely to go wrong. It does not involve solving the problem, only recognizing there is a problem.
Arm-Hand Steadiness	The ability to keep your hand and arm steady while moving your arm or while holding your arm and hand in one position.
Control Precision	The ability to quickly and repeatedly adjust the controls of a machine or a vehicle to exact positions.
Oral Expression	The ability to communicate information and ideas in speaking so others will understand.
Speech Clarity	The ability to speak clearly so others can understand you.
Selective Attention	The ability to concentrate on a task over a period of time without being distracted.
Inductive Reasoning	The ability to combine pieces of information to form general rules or conclusions (includes finding a relationship among seemingly unrelated events).
Oral Comprehension	The ability to listen to and understand information and ideas presented through spoken words and sentences.
Deductive Reasoning	The ability to apply general rules to specific problems to produce answers that make sense.
Extent Flexibility	The ability to bend, stretch, twist, or reach with your body, arms, and/or legs.
Multilimb Coordination	The ability to coordinate two or more limbs (for example, two arms, two legs, or one leg and one arm) while sitting, standing, or lying down. It does not involve performing the activities while the whole body is in motion.
Visual Color Discrimination	The ability to match or detect differences between colors, including shades of color and brightness.
Information Ordering	The ability to arrange things or actions in a certain order or pattern according to a specific rule or set of rules (e.g., patterns of numbers, letters, words, pictures, mathematical operations).

Written Comprehension	The ability to read and understand information and ideas presented in writing.
Speech Recognition	The ability to identify and understand the speech of another person.
Flexibility of Closure	The ability to identify or detect a known pattern (a figure, object, word, or sound) that is hidden in other distracting material.
Category Flexibility	The ability to generate or use different sets of rules for combining or grouping things in different ways.
Written Expression	The ability to communicate information and ideas in writing so others will understand.
Trunk Strength	The ability to use your abdominal and lower back muscles to support part of the body repeatedly or continuously over time without 'giving out' or fatiguing.
Speed of Closure	The ability to quickly make sense of, combine, and organize information into meaningful patterns.
Time Sharing	The ability to shift back and forth between two or more activities or sources of information (such as speech, sounds, touch, or other sources).
Memorization	The ability to remember information such as words, numbers, pictures, and procedures.
Depth Perception	The ability to judge which of several objects is closer or farther away from you, or to judge the distance between you and an object.
Perceptual Speed	The ability to quickly and accurately compare similarities and differences among sets of letters, numbers, objects, pictures, or patterns. The things to be compared may be presented at the same time or one after the other. This ability also includes comparing a presented object with a remembered object.
Far Vision	The ability to see details at a distance.
Originality	The ability to come up with unusual or clever ideas about a given topic or situation, or to develop creative ways to solve a problem.
Hearing Sensitivity	The ability to detect or tell the differences between sounds that vary in pitch and loudness.
Visualization	The ability to imagine how something will look after it is moved around or when its parts are moved or rearranged.
Fluency of Ideas	The ability to come up with a number of ideas about a topic (the number of ideas is important, not their quality, correctness, or creativity).
Static Strength	The ability to exert maximum muscle force to lift, push, pull, or carry objects.
Dynamic Strength	The ability to exert muscle force repeatedly or continuously over time. This involves muscular endurance and resistance to muscle fatigue.
Stamina	The ability to exert yourself physically over long periods of time without getting winded or out of breath.
Response Orientation	The ability to choose quickly between two or more movements in response to two or more different signals (lights, sounds, pictures). It includes the speed with which the correct response is started with the hand, foot, or other body part.
Auditory Attention	The ability to focus on a single source of sound in the presence of other distracting sounds.
Wrist-Finger Speed	The ability to make fast, simple, repeated movements of the fingers, hands, and wrists.
Rate Control	The ability to time your movements or the movement of a piece of equipment in anticipation of changes in the speed and/or direction of a moving object or scene.
Reaction Time	The ability to quickly respond (with the hand, finger, or foot) to a signal (sound, light, picture) when it appears.
Gross Body Coordination	The ability to coordinate the movement of your arms, legs, and torso together when the whole body is in motion.
Gross Body Equilibrium	The ability to keep or regain your body balance or stay upright when in an unstable position.
Dynamic Flexibility	The ability to quickly and repeatedly bend, stretch, twist, or reach out with your body, arms, and/or legs.
Spatial Orientation	The ability to know your location in relation to the environment or to know where other objects are in relation to you.
Mathematical Reasoning	The ability to choose the right mathematical methods or formulas to solve a problem.
Speed of Limb Movement	The ability to quickly move the arms and legs.
Glare Sensitivity	The ability to see objects in the presence of glare or bright lighting.
Number Facility	The ability to add, subtract, multiply, or divide quickly and correctly.
Sound Localization	The ability to tell the direction from which a sound originated.
Peripheral Vision	The ability to see objects or movement of objects to one's side when the eyes are looking ahead.

Night Vision	The ability to see under low light conditions.
Explosive Strength	The ability to use short bursts of muscle force to propel oneself (as in jumping or sprinting), or to throw an object.

Work_Activity	Work_Activity Definitions
Assisting and Caring for Others	Providing personal assistance, medical attention, emotional support, or other personal care to others such as coworkers, customers, or patients.
Getting Information	Observing, receiving, and otherwise obtaining information from all relevant sources.
Updating and Using Relevant Knowledge	Keeping up-to-date technically and applying new knowledge to your job.
Identifying Objects, Actions, and Events	Identifying information by categorizing, estimating, recognizing differences or similarities, and detecting changes in circumstances or events.
Performing for or Working Directly with the Public	Performing for people or dealing directly with the public. This includes serving customers in restaurants and stores, and receiving clients or guests.
Establishing and Maintaining Interpersonal Relatio	Developing constructive and cooperative working relationships with others, and maintaining them over time.
Interpreting the Meaning of Information for Others	Translating or explaining what information means and how it can be used.
Documenting/Recording Information	Entering, transcribing, recording, storing, or maintaining information in written or electronic/magnetic form.
Making Decisions and Solving Problems	Analyzing information and evaluating results to choose the best solution and solve problems.
Communicating with Supervisors, Peers, or Subordin	Providing information to supervisors, co-workers, and subordinates by telephone, in written form, e-mail, or in person.
Judging the Qualities of Things, Services, or Peop	Assessing the value, importance, or quality of things or people.
Organizing, Planning, and Prioritizing Work	Developing specific goals and plans to prioritize, organize, and accomplish your work.
Coaching and Developing Others	Identifying the developmental needs of others and coaching, mentoring, or otherwise helping others to improve their knowledge or skills.
Performing Administrative Activities	Performing day-to-day administrative tasks such as maintaining information files and processing paperwork.
Coordinating the Work and Activities of Others	Getting members of a group to work together to accomplish tasks.
Training and Teaching Others	Identifying the educational needs of others, developing formal educational or training programs or classes, and teaching or instructing others.
Developing and Building Teams	Encouraging and building mutual trust, respect, and cooperation among team members.
Monitor Processes, Materials, or Surroundings	Monitoring and reviewing information from materials, events, or the environment, to detect or assess problems.
Handling and Moving Objects	Using hands and arms in handling, installing, positioning, and moving materials, and manipulating things.
Selling or Influencing Others	Convincing others to buy merchandise/goods or to otherwise change their minds or actions.
Inspecting Equipment, Structures, or Material	Inspecting equipment, structures, or materials to identify the cause of errors or other problems or defects.
Scheduling Work and Activities	Scheduling events, programs, and activities, as well as the work of others.
Communicating with Persons Outside Organization	Communicating with people outside the organization, representing the organization to customers, the public, government, and other external sources. This information can be exchanged in person, in writing, or by telephone or e-mail.
Interacting With Computers	Using computers and computer systems (including hardware and software) to program, write software, set up functions, enter data, or process information.
Evaluating Information to Determine Compliance wit	Using relevant information and individual judgment to determine whether events or processes comply with laws, regulations, or standards.
Analyzing Data or Information	Identifying the underlying principles, reasons, or facts of information by breaking down information or data into separate parts.
Performing General Physical Activities	Performing physical activities that require considerable use of your arms and legs and moving your whole body, such as climbing, lifting, balancing, walking, stooping, and handling of materials.
Processing Information	Compiling, coding, categorizing, calculating, tabulating, auditing, or verifying information or data.

Guiding, Directing, and Motivating Subordinates	Providing guidance and direction to subordinates, including setting performance standards and monitoring performance.
Resolving Conflicts and Negotiating with Others	Handling complaints, settling disputes, and resolving grievances and conflicts, or otherwise negotiating with others.
Developing Objectives and Strategies	Establishing long-range objectives and specifying the strategies and actions to achieve them.
Provide Consultation and Advice to Others	Providing guidance and expert advice to management or other groups on technical, systems-, or process-related topics.
Controlling Machines and Processes	Using either control mechanisms or direct physical activity to operate machines or processes (not including computers or vehicles).
Estimating the Quantifiable Characteristics of Pro	Estimating sizes, distances, and quantities; or determining time, costs, resources, or materials needed to perform a work activity.
Thinking Creatively	Developing, designing, or creating new applications, ideas, relationships, systems, or products, including artistic contributions.
Repairing and Maintaining Electronic Equipment	Servicing, repairing, calibrating, regulating, fine-tuning, or testing machines, devices, and equipment that operate primarily on the basis of electrical or electronic (not mechanical) principles.
Repairing and Maintaining Mechanical Equipment	Servicing, repairing, adjusting, and testing machines, devices, moving parts, and equipment that operate primarily on the basis of mechanical (not electronic) principles.
Monitoring and Controlling Resources	Monitoring and controlling resources and overseeing the spending of money.
Staffing Organizational Units	Recruiting, interviewing, selecting, hiring, and promoting employees in an organization.
Drafting, Laying Out, and Specifying Technical Dev	Providing documentation, detailed instructions, drawings, or specifications to tell others about how devices, parts, equipment, or structures are to be fabricated, constructed, assembled, modified, maintained, or used.
Operating Vehicles, Mechanized Devices, or Equipme	Running, maneuvering, navigating, or driving vehicles or mechanized equipment, such as forklifts, passenger vehicles, aircraft, or water craft.

Work_Context	**Work_Context Definitions**
Wear Common Protective or Safety Equipment such as	How much does this job require wearing common protective or safety equipment such as safety shoes, glasses, gloves, hard hats or life jackets?
Spend Time Using Your Hands to Handle, Control, or	How much does this job require using your hands to handle, control, or feel objects, tools or controls?
Contact With Others	How much does this job require the worker to be in contact with others (face-to-face, by telephone, or otherwise) in order to perform it?
Physical Proximity	To what extent does this job require the worker to perform job tasks in close physical proximity to other people?
Work With Work Group or Team	How important is it to work with others in a group or team in this job?
Spend Time Sitting	How much does this job require sitting?
Spend Time Making Repetitive Motions	How much does this job require making repetitive motions?
Exposed to Disease or Infections	How often does this job require exposure to disease/infections?
Importance of Being Exact or Accurate	How important is being very exact or highly accurate in performing this job?
Frequency of Decision Making	How frequently is the worker required to make decisions that affect other people, the financial resources, and/or the image and reputation of the organization?
Impact of Decisions on Co-workers or Company Resul	How do the decisions an employee makes impact the results of co-workers, clients or the company?
Face-to-Face Discussions	How often do you have to have face-to-face discussions with individuals or teams in this job?
Structured versus Unstructured Work	To what extent is this job structured for the worker, rather than allowing the worker to determine tasks, priorities, and goals?
Freedom to Make Decisions	How much decision making freedom, without supervision, does the job offer?
Deal With External Customers	How important is it to work with external customers or the public in this job?
Telephone	How often do you have telephone conversations in this job?
Indoors, Environmentally Controlled	How often does this job require working indoors in environmentally controlled conditions?
Exposed to Radiation	How often does this job require exposure to radiation?
Spend Time Bending or Twisting the Body	How much does this job require bending or twisting your body?
Importance of Repeating Same Tasks	How important is repeating the same physical activities (e.g., key entry) or mental activities (e.g., checking entries in a ledger) over and over, without stopping, to performing this job?
Responsible for Others' Health and Safety	How much responsibility is there for the health and safety of others in this job?
Exposed to Contaminants	How often does this job require working exposed to contaminants (such as pollutants, gases, dust or odors)?
Consequence of Error	How serious would the result usually be if the worker made a mistake that was not readily correctable?
Letters and Memos	How often does the job require written letters and memos?
Coordinate or Lead Others	How important is it to coordinate or lead others in accomplishing work activities in this job?
Exposed to Hazardous Conditions	How often does this job require exposure to hazardous conditions?
Deal With Unpleasant or Angry People	How frequently does the worker have to deal with unpleasant, angry, or discourteous individuals as part of the job requirements?
Time Pressure	How often does this job require the worker to meet strict deadlines?
Frequency of Conflict Situations	How often are there conflict situations the employee has to face in this job?
Level of Competition	To what extent does this job require the worker to compete or to be aware of competitive pressures?
Sounds, Noise Levels Are Distracting or Uncomforta	How often does this job require working exposed to sounds and noise levels that are distracting or uncomfortable?
Spend Time Standing	How much does this job require standing?
Responsibility for Outcomes and Results	How responsible is the worker for work outcomes and results of other workers?
Exposed to Minor Burns, Cuts, Bites, or Stings	How often does this job require exposure to minor burns, cuts, bites, or stings?
Cramped Work Space, Awkward Positions	How often does this job require working in cramped work spaces that requires getting into awkward positions?
Degree of Automation	How automated is the job?
Wear Specialized Protective or Safety Equipment su	How much does this job require wearing specialized protective or safety equipment such as breathing apparatus, safety harness, full protection suits, or radiation protection?
Spend Time Walking and Running	How much does this job require walking and running?
Exposed to Hazardous Equipment	How often does this job require exposure to hazardous equipment?
Indoors, Not Environmentally Controlled	How often does this job require working indoors in non-controlled environmental conditions (e.g., warehouse without heat)?
Pace Determined by Speed of Equipment	How important is it to this job that the pace is determined by the speed of equipment or machinery? (This does not refer to keeping busy at all times on this job.)
Public Speaking	How often do you have to perform public speaking in this job?
Spend Time Keeping or Regaining Balance	How much does this job require keeping or regaining your balance?
Spend Time Kneeling, Crouching, Stooping, or Crawl	How much does this job require kneeling, crouching, stooping or crawling?
Electronic Mail	How often do you use electronic mail in this job?
Deal With Physically Aggressive People	How frequently does this job require the worker to deal with physical aggression of violent individuals?
Extremely Bright or Inadequate Lighting	How often does this job require working in extremely bright or inadequate lighting conditions?
Very Hot or Cold Temperatures	How often does this job require working in very hot (above 90 F degrees) or very cold (below 32 F degrees) temperatures?
Outdoors, Under Cover	How often does this job require working outdoors, under cover (e.g., structure with roof but no walls)?
In an Open Vehicle or Equipment	How often does this job require working in an open vehicle or equipment (e.g., tractor)?
In an Enclosed Vehicle or Equipment	How often does this job require working in a closed vehicle or equipment (e.g., car)?
Exposed to Whole Body Vibration	How often does this job require exposure to whole body vibration (e.g., operate a jackhammer)?
Exposed to High Places	How often does this job require exposure to high places?
Spend Time Climbing Ladders, Scaffolds, or Poles	How much does this job require climbing ladders, scaffolds, or poles?
Outdoors, Exposed to Weather	How often does this job require working outdoors, exposed to all weather conditions?

Job Zone Component	**Job Zone Component Definitions**
Title	Job Zone Three: Medium Preparation Needed

564

Overall Experience	Previous work-related skill, knowledge, or experience is required for these occupations. For example, an electrician must have completed three or four years of apprenticeship or several years of vocational training, and often must have passed a licensing exam, in order to perform the job.
Job Training	Employees in these occupations usually need one or two years of training involving both on-the-job experience and informal training with experienced workers.
Job Zone Examples	These occupations usually involve using communication and organizational skills to coordinate, supervise, manage, or train others to accomplish goals. Examples include dental assistants, electricians, fish and game wardens, legal secretaries, personnel recruiters, and recreation workers.
SVP Range	(6.0 to < 7.0)
Education	Most occupations in this zone require training in vocational schools, related on-the-job experience, or an associate's degree. Some may require a bachelor's degree.

Work_Styles	Work_Styles Definitions
Dependability	Job requires being reliable, responsible, and dependable, and fulfilling obligations.
Cooperation	Job requires being pleasant with others on the job and displaying a good-natured, cooperative attitude.
Attention to Detail	Job requires being careful about detail and thorough in completing work tasks.
Concern for Others	Job requires being sensitive to others' needs and feelings and being understanding and helpful on the job.
Independence	Job requires developing one's own ways of doing things, guiding oneself with little or no supervision, and depending on oneself to get things done.
Integrity	Job requires being honest and ethical.
Self Control	Job requires maintaining composure, keeping emotions in check, controlling anger, and avoiding aggressive behavior, even in very difficult situations.
Stress Tolerance	Job requires accepting criticism and dealing calmly and effectively with high stress situations.
Initiative	Job requires a willingness to take on responsibilities and challenges.
Achievement/Effort	Job requires establishing and maintaining personally challenging achievement goals and exerting effort toward mastering tasks.
Social Orientation	Job requires preferring to work with others rather than alone, and being personally connected with others on the job.
Adaptability/Flexibility	Job requires being open to change (positive or negative) and to considerable variety in the workplace.
Persistence	Job requires persistence in the face of obstacles.
Analytical Thinking	Job requires analyzing information and using logic to address work-related issues and problems.
Innovation	Job requires creativity and alternative thinking to develop new ideas for and answers to work-related problems.
Leadership	Job requires a willingness to lead, take charge, and offer opinions and direction.

29-2031.00 - Cardiovascular Technologists and Technicians

Conduct tests on pulmonary or cardiovascular systems of patients for diagnostic purposes. May conduct or assist in electrocardiograms, cardiac catheterizations, pulmonary-functions, lung capacity, and similar tests.

Tasks

1) Prepare and position patients for testing.

2) Monitor patients' comfort and safety during tests, alerting physicians to abnormalities or changes in patient responses.

3) Monitor patients' blood pressure and heart rate using electrocardiogram (EKG) equipment during diagnostic and therapeutic procedures in order to notify the physician if something appears wrong.

4) Obtain and record patient identification, medical history and test results.

5) Attach electrodes to the patients' chests, arms, and legs, connect electrodes to leads from the electrocardiogram (EKG) machine, and operate the EKG machine to obtain a reading.

6) Adjust equipment and controls according to physicians' orders or established protocol.

7) Conduct electrocardiogram, phonocardiogram, echocardiogram, stress testing, and other cardiovascular tests to record patients' cardiac activity, using specialized electronic test equipment, recording devices, and laboratory instruments.

8) Check, test, and maintain cardiology equipment, making minor repairs when necessary, to ensure proper operation.

9) Prepare reports of diagnostic procedures for interpretation by physician.

10) Supervise and train other cardiology technologists and students.

11) Observe gauges, recorder, and video screens of data analysis system during imaging of cardiovascular system.

12) Assess cardiac physiology and calculate valve areas from blood flow velocity measurements.

13) Compare measurements of heart wall thickness and chamber sizes to standard norms to identify abnormalities.

14) Observe ultrasound display screen and listen to signals to record vascular information such as blood pressure, limb volume changes, oxygen saturation and cerebral circulation.

15) Operate diagnostic imaging equipment to produce contrast enhanced radiographs of heart and cardiovascular system.

16) Assist physicians in diagnosis and treatment of cardiac and peripheral vascular treatments, for example, assisting with balloon angioplasties to treat blood vessel blockages.

17) Inject contrast medium into patients' blood vessels.

18) Activate fluoroscope and camera to produce images used to guide catheter through cardiovascular system.

19) Conduct tests of pulmonary system, using spirometer and other respiratory testing equipment.

20) Enter factors such as amount and quality of radiation beam, and filming sequence, into computer.

Knowledge	Knowledge Definitions
Customer and Personal Service	Knowledge of principles and processes for providing customer and personal services. This includes customer needs assessment, meeting quality standards for services, and evaluation of customer satisfaction.
Medicine and Dentistry	Knowledge of the information and techniques needed to diagnose and treat human injuries, diseases, and deformities. This includes symptoms, treatment alternatives, drug properties and interactions, and preventive health-care measures.
English Language	Knowledge of the structure and content of the English language including the meaning and spelling of words, rules of composition, and grammar.
Mathematics	Knowledge of arithmetic, algebra, geometry, calculus, statistics, and their applications.
Education and Training	Knowledge of principles and methods for curriculum and training design, teaching and instruction for individuals and groups, and the measurement of training effects.
Computers and Electronics	Knowledge of circuit boards, processors, chips, electronic equipment, and computer hardware and software, including applications and programming.
Psychology	Knowledge of human behavior and performance; individual differences in ability, personality, and interests; learning and motivation; psychological research methods; and the assessment and treatment of behavioral and affective disorders.
Physics	Knowledge and prediction of physical principles, laws, their interrelationships, and applications to understanding fluid, material, and atmospheric dynamics, and mechanical, electrical, atomic and sub-atomic structures and processes.
Clerical	Knowledge of administrative and clerical procedures and systems such as word processing, managing files and records, stenography and transcription, designing forms, and other office procedures and terminology.
Biology	Knowledge of plant and animal organisms, their tissues, cells, functions, interdependencies, and interactions with each other and the environment.
Public Safety and Security	Knowledge of relevant equipment, policies, procedures, and strategies to promote effective local, state, or national security operations for the protection of people, data, property, and institutions.
Therapy and Counseling	Knowledge of principles, methods, and procedures for diagnosis, treatment, and rehabilitation of physical and mental dysfunctions, and for career counseling and guidance.

Administration and Management	Knowledge of business and management principles involved in strategic planning, resource allocation, human resources modeling, leadership technique, production methods, and coordination of people and resources.
Chemistry	Knowledge of the chemical composition, structure, and properties of substances and of the chemical processes and transformations that they undergo. This includes uses of chemicals and their interactions, danger signs, production techniques, and disposal methods.
Engineering and Technology	Knowledge of the practical application of engineering science and technology. This includes applying principles, techniques, procedures, and equipment to the design and production of various goods and services.
Law and Government	Knowledge of laws, legal codes, court procedures, precedents, government regulations, executive orders, agency rules, and the democratic political process.
Personnel and Human Resources	Knowledge of principles and procedures for personnel recruitment, selection, training, compensation and benefits, labor relations and negotiation, and personnel information systems.
Sociology and Anthropology	Knowledge of group behavior and dynamics, societal trends and influences, human migrations, ethnicity, cultures and their history and origins.
Foreign Language	Knowledge of the structure and content of a foreign (non-English) language including the meaning and spelling of words, rules of composition and grammar, and pronunciation.
Communications and Media	Knowledge of media production, communication, and dissemination techniques and methods. This includes alternative ways to inform and entertain via written, oral, and visual media.
Telecommunications	Knowledge of transmission, broadcasting, switching, control, and operation of telecommunications systems.
Mechanical	Knowledge of machines and tools, including their designs, uses, repair, and maintenance.
Production and Processing	Knowledge of raw materials, production processes, quality control, costs, and other techniques for maximizing the effective manufacture and distribution of goods.
Philosophy and Theology	Knowledge of different philosophical systems and religions. This includes their basic principles, values, ethics, ways of thinking, customs, practices, and their impact on human culture.
Design	Knowledge of design techniques, tools, and principles involved in production of precision technical plans, blueprints, drawings, and models.
Economics and Accounting	Knowledge of economic and accounting principles and practices, the financial markets, banking and the analysis and reporting of financial data.
Transportation	Knowledge of principles and methods for moving people or goods by air, rail, sea, or road, including the relative costs and benefits.
Sales and Marketing	Knowledge of principles and methods for showing, promoting, and selling products or services. This includes marketing strategy and tactics, product demonstration, sales techniques, and sales control systems.
Geography	Knowledge of principles and methods for describing the features of land, sea, and air masses, including their physical characteristics, locations, interrelationships, and distribution of plant, animal, and human life.
Fine Arts	Knowledge of the theory and techniques required to compose, produce, and perform works of music, dance, visual arts, drama, and sculpture.
History and Archeology	Knowledge of historical events and their causes, indicators, and effects on civilizations and cultures.
Building and Construction	Knowledge of materials, methods, and the tools involved in the construction or repair of houses, buildings, or other structures such as highways and roads.
Food Production	Knowledge of techniques and equipment for planting, growing, and harvesting food products (both plant and animal) for consumption, including storage/handling techniques.

Skills	Skills Definitions
Active Listening	Giving full attention to what other people are saying, taking time to understand the points being made, asking questions as appropriate, and not interrupting at inappropriate times.
Reading Comprehension	Understanding written sentences and paragraphs in work related documents.
Instructing	Teaching others how to do something.

Speaking	Talking to others to convey information effectively.
Active Learning	Understanding the implications of new information for both current and future problem-solving and decision-making.
Critical Thinking	Using logic and reasoning to identify the strengths and weaknesses of alternative solutions, conclusions or approaches to problems.
Time Management	Managing one's own time and the time of others.
Service Orientation	Actively looking for ways to help people.
Equipment Selection	Determining the kind of tools and equipment needed to do a job.
Learning Strategies	Selecting and using training/instructional methods and procedures appropriate for the situation when learning or teaching new things.
Coordination	Adjusting actions in relation to others' actions.
Writing	Communicating effectively in writing as appropriate for the needs of the audience.
Monitoring	Monitoring/Assessing performance of yourself, other individuals, or organizations to make improvements or take corrective action.
Social Perceptiveness	Being aware of others' reactions and understanding why they react as they do.
Operation Monitoring	Watching gauges, dials, or other indicators to make sure a machine is working properly.
Complex Problem Solving	Identifying complex problems and reviewing related information to develop and evaluate options and implement solutions.
Judgment and Decision Making	Considering the relative costs and benefits of potential actions to choose the most appropriate one.
Operation and Control	Controlling operations of equipment or systems.
Troubleshooting	Determining causes of operating errors and deciding what to do about it.
Equipment Maintenance	Performing routine maintenance on equipment and determining when and what kind of maintenance is needed.
Quality Control Analysis	Conducting tests and inspections of products, services, or processes to evaluate quality or performance.
Mathematics	Using mathematics to solve problems.
Science	Using scientific rules and methods to solve problems.
Management of Material Resources	Obtaining and seeing to the appropriate use of equipment, facilities, and materials needed to do certain work.
Management of Personnel Resources	Motivating, developing, and directing people as they work, identifying the best people for the job.
Negotiation	Bringing others together and trying to reconcile differences.
Persuasion	Persuading others to change their minds or behavior.
Systems Analysis	Determining how a system should work and how changes in conditions, operations, and the environment will affect outcomes.
Systems Evaluation	Identifying measures or indicators of system performance and the actions needed to improve or correct performance, relative to the goals of the system.
Technology Design	Generating or adapting equipment and technology to serve user needs.
Operations Analysis	Analyzing needs and product requirements to create a design.
Repairing	Repairing machines or systems using the needed tools.
Installation	Installing equipment, machines, wiring, or programs to meet specifications.
Management of Financial Resources	Determining how money will be spent to get the work done, and accounting for these expenditures.
Programming	Writing computer programs for various purposes.

Ability	Ability Definitions
Problem Sensitivity	The ability to tell when something is wrong or is likely to go wrong. It does not involve solving the problem, only recognizing there is a problem.
Oral Comprehension	The ability to listen to and understand information and ideas presented through spoken words and sentences.
Oral Expression	The ability to communicate information and ideas in speaking so others will understand.
Near Vision	The ability to see details at close range (within a few feet of the observer).
Speech Clarity	The ability to speak clearly so others can understand you.
Speech Recognition	The ability to identify and understand the speech of another person.
Deductive Reasoning	The ability to apply general rules to specific problems to produce answers that make sense.
Inductive Reasoning	The ability to combine pieces of information to form general rules or conclusions (includes finding a relationship among seemingly unrelated events).

Information Ordering	The ability to arrange things or actions in a certain order or pattern according to a specific rule or set of rules (e.g., patterns of numbers, letters, words, pictures, mathematical operations).
Perceptual Speed	The ability to quickly and accurately compare similarities and differences among sets of letters, numbers, objects, pictures, or patterns. The things to be compared may be presented at the same time or one after the other. This ability also includes comparing a presented object with a remembered object.
Written Comprehension	The ability to read and understand information and ideas presented in writing.
Selective Attention	The ability to concentrate on a task over a period of time without being distracted.
Written Expression	The ability to communicate information and ideas in writing so others will understand.
Category Flexibility	The ability to generate or use different sets of rules for combining or grouping things in different ways.
Flexibility of Closure	The ability to identify or detect a known pattern (a figure, object, word, or sound) that is hidden in other distracting material.
Finger Dexterity	The ability to make precisely coordinated movements of the fingers of one or both hands to grasp, manipulate, or assemble very small objects.
Time Sharing	The ability to shift back and forth between two or more activities or sources of information (such as speech, sounds, touch, or other sources).
Visual Color Discrimination	The ability to match or detect differences between colors, including shades of color and brightness.
Originality	The ability to come up with unusual or clever ideas about a given topic or situation, or to develop creative ways to solve a problem.
Far Vision	The ability to see details at a distance.
Fluency of Ideas	The ability to come up with a number of ideas about a topic (the number of ideas is important, not their quality, correctness, or creativity).
Control Precision	The ability to quickly and repeatedly adjust the controls of a machine or a vehicle to exact positions.
Hearing Sensitivity	The ability to detect or tell the differences between sounds that vary in pitch and loudness.
Arm-Hand Steadiness	The ability to keep your hand and arm steady while moving your arm or while holding your arm and hand in one position.
Visualization	The ability to imagine how something will look after it is moved around or when its parts are moved or rearranged.
Memorization	The ability to remember information such as words, numbers, pictures, and procedures.
Speed of Closure	The ability to quickly make sense of, combine, and organize information into meaningful patterns.
Depth Perception	The ability to judge which of several objects is closer or farther away from you, or to judge the distance between you and an object.
Auditory Attention	The ability to focus on a single source of sound in the presence of other distracting sounds.
Multilimb Coordination	The ability to coordinate two or more limbs (for example, two arms, two legs, or one leg and one arm) while sitting, standing, or lying down. It does not involve performing the activities while the whole body is in motion.
Manual Dexterity	The ability to quickly move your hand, your hand together with your arm, or your two hands to grasp, manipulate, or assemble objects.
Mathematical Reasoning	The ability to choose the right mathematical methods or formulas to solve a problem.
Number Facility	The ability to add, subtract, multiply, or divide quickly and correctly.
Reaction Time	The ability to quickly respond (with the hand, finger, or foot) to a signal (sound, light, picture) when it appears.
Response Orientation	The ability to choose quickly between two or more movements in response to two or more different signals (lights, sounds, pictures). It includes the speed with which the correct response is started with the hand, foot, or other body part.
Static Strength	The ability to exert maximum muscle force to lift, push, pull, or carry objects.
Stamina	The ability to exert yourself physically over long periods of time without getting winded or out of breath.
Gross Body Coordination	The ability to coordinate the movement of your arms, legs, and torso together when the whole body is in motion.
Extent Flexibility	The ability to bend, stretch, twist, or reach with your body, arms, and/or legs.

Trunk Strength	The ability to use your abdominal and lower back muscles to support part of the body repeatedly or continuously over time without 'giving out' or fatiguing.
Speed of Limb Movement	The ability to quickly move the arms and legs.
Gross Body Equilibrium	The ability to keep or regain your body balance or stay upright when in an unstable position.
Dynamic Strength	The ability to exert muscle force repeatedly or continuously over time. This involves muscular endurance and resistance to muscle fatigue.
Wrist-Finger Speed	The ability to make fast, simple, repeated movements of the fingers, hands, and wrists.
Rate Control	The ability to time your movements or the movement of a piece of equipment in anticipation of changes in the speed and/or direction of a moving object or scene.
Explosive Strength	The ability to use short bursts of muscle force to propel oneself (as in jumping or sprinting), or to throw an object.
Night Vision	The ability to see under low light conditions.
Peripheral Vision	The ability to see objects or movement of objects to one's side when the eyes are looking ahead.
Sound Localization	The ability to tell the direction from which a sound originated.
Spatial Orientation	The ability to know your location in relation to the environment or to know where other objects are in relation to you.
Dynamic Flexibility	The ability to quickly and repeatedly bend, stretch, twist, or reach out with your body, arms, and/or legs.
Glare Sensitivity	The ability to see objects in the presence of glare or bright lighting.

Work_Activity	Work_Activity Definitions
Assisting and Caring for Others	Providing personal assistance, medical attention, emotional support, or other personal care to others such as coworkers, customers, or patients.
Updating and Using Relevant Knowledge	Keeping up-to-date technically and applying new knowledge to your job.
Communicating with Supervisors, Peers, or Subordin	Providing information to supervisors, co-workers, and subordinates by telephone, in written form, e-mail, or in person.
Making Decisions and Solving Problems	Analyzing information and evaluating results to choose the best solution and solve problems.
Interacting With Computers	Using computers and computer systems (including hardware and software) to program, write software, set up functions, enter data, or process information.
Getting Information	Observing, receiving, and otherwise obtaining information from all relevant sources.
Inspecting Equipment, Structures, or Material	Inspecting equipment, structures, or materials to identify the cause of errors or other problems or defects.
Identifying Objects, Actions, and Events	Identifying information by categorizing, estimating, recognizing differences or similarities, and detecting changes in circumstances or events.
Documenting/Recording Information	Entering, transcribing, recording, storing, or maintaining information in written or electronic/magnetic form.
Monitor Processes, Materials, or Surroundings	Monitoring and reviewing information from materials, events, or the environment, to detect or assess problems.
Evaluating Information to Determine Compliance wit	Using relevant information and individual judgment to determine whether events or processes comply with laws, regulations, or standards.
Organizing, Planning, and Prioritizing Work	Developing specific goals and plans to prioritize, organize, and accomplish your work.
Establishing and Maintaining Interpersonal Relatio	Developing constructive and cooperative working relationships with others, and maintaining them over time.
Interpreting the Meaning of Information for Others	Translating or explaining what information means and how it can be used.
Processing Information	Compiling, coding, categorizing, calculating, tabulating, auditing, or verifying information or data.
Training and Teaching Others	Identifying the educational needs of others, developing formal educational or training programs or classes, and teaching or instructing others.
Performing for or Working Directly with the Public	Performing for people or dealing directly with the public. This includes serving customers in restaurants and stores, and receiving clients or guests.
Coordinating the Work and Activities of Others	Getting members of a group to work together to accomplish tasks.
Developing and Building Teams	Encouraging and building mutual trust, respect, and cooperation among team members.

Controlling Machines and Processes	Using either control mechanisms or direct physical activity to operate machines or processes (not including computers or vehicles).
Performing General Physical Activities	Performing physical activities that require considerable use of your arms and legs and moving your whole body, such as climbing, lifting, balancing, walking, stooping, and handling of materials.
Judging the Qualities of Things, Services, or Peop	Assessing the value, importance, or quality of things or people.
Analyzing Data or Information	Identifying the underlying principles, reasons, or facts of information by breaking down information or data into separate parts.
Handling and Moving Objects	Using hands and arms in handling, installing, positioning, and moving materials, and manipulating things.
Estimating the Quantifiable Characteristics of Pro	Estimating sizes, distances, and quantities; or determining time, costs, resources, or materials needed to perform a work activity.
Guiding, Directing, and Motivating Subordinates	Providing guidance and direction to subordinates, including setting performance standards and monitoring performance.
Coaching and Developing Others	Identifying the developmental needs of others and coaching, mentoring, or otherwise helping others to improve their knowledge or skills.
Performing Administrative Activities	Performing day-to-day administrative tasks such as maintaining information files and processing paperwork.
Resolving Conflicts and Negotiating with Others	Handling complaints, settling disputes, and resolving grievances and conflicts, or otherwise negotiating with others.
Communicating with Persons Outside Organization	Communicating with people outside the organization, representing the organization to customers, the public, government, and other external sources. This information can be exchanged in person, in writing, or by telephone or e-mail.
Scheduling Work and Activities	Scheduling events, programs, and activities, as well as the work of others.
Developing Objectives and Strategies	Establishing long-range objectives and specifying the strategies and actions to achieve them.
Thinking Creatively	Developing, designing, or creating new applications, ideas, relationships, systems, or products, including artistic contributions.
Provide Consultation and Advice to Others	Providing guidance and expert advice to management or other groups on technical, systems-, or process-related topics.
Repairing and Maintaining Electronic Equipment	Servicing, repairing, calibrating, regulating, fine-tuning, or testing machines, devices, and equipment that operate primarily on the basis of electrical or electronic (not mechanical) principles.
Monitoring and Controlling Resources	Monitoring and controlling resources and overseeing the spending of money.
Staffing Organizational Units	Recruiting, interviewing, selecting, hiring, and promoting employees in an organization.
Selling or Influencing Others	Convincing others to buy merchandise/goods or to otherwise change their minds or actions.
Repairing and Maintaining Mechanical Equipment	Servicing, repairing, adjusting, and testing machines, devices, moving parts, and equipment that operate primarily on the basis of mechanical (not electronic) principles.
Operating Vehicles, Mechanized Devices, or Equipme	Running, maneuvering, navigating, or driving vehicles or mechanized equipment, such as forklifts, passenger vehicles, aircraft, or water craft.
Drafting, Laying Out, and Specifying Technical Dev	Providing documentation, detailed instructions, drawings, or specifications to tell others about how devices, parts, equipment, or structures are to be fabricated, constructed, assembled, modified, maintained, or used.

Work_Context	Work_Context Definitions
Physical Proximity	To what extent does this job require the worker to perform job tasks in close physical proximity to other people?
Exposed to Disease or Infections	How often does this job require exposure to disease/infections?
Indoors, Environmentally Controlled	How often does this job require working indoors in environmentally controlled conditions?
Contact With Others	How much does this job require the worker to be in contact with others (face-to-face, by telephone, or otherwise) in order to perform it?
Importance of Being Exact or Accurate	How important is being very exact or highly accurate in performing this job?
Telephone	How often do you have telephone conversations in this job?
Work With Work Group or Team	How important is it to work with others in a group or team in this job?
Face-to-Face Discussions	How often do you have to have face-to-face discussions with individuals or teams in this job?

Deal With External Customers	How important is it to work with external customers or the public in this job?
Exposed to Radiation	How often does this job require exposure to radiation?
Spend Time Using Your Hands to Handle, Control, or	How much does this job require using your hands to handle, control, or feel objects, tools or controls?
Freedom to Make Decisions	How much decision making freedom, without supervision, does the job offer?
Importance of Repeating Same Tasks	How important is repeating the same physical activities (e.g., key entry) or mental activities (e.g., checking entries in a ledger) over and over, without stopping, to performing this job?
Impact of Decisions on Co-workers or Company Resul	How do the decisions an employee makes impact the results of co-workers, clients or the company?
Structured versus Unstructured Work	To what extent is this job structured for the worker, rather than allowing the worker to determine tasks, priorities, and goals?
Frequency of Decision Making	How frequently is the worker required to make decisions that affect other people, the financial resources, and/or the image and reputation of the organization?
Coordinate or Lead Others	How important is it to coordinate or lead others in accomplishing work activities in this job?
Responsible for Others' Health and Safety	How much responsibility is there for the health and safety of others in this job?
Consequence of Error	How serious would the result usually be if the worker made a mistake that was not readily correctable?
Spend Time Standing	How much does this job require standing?
Wear Common Protective or Safety Equipment such as	How much does this job require wearing common protective or safety equipment such as safety shoes, glasses, gloves, hard hats or live jackets?
Spend Time Walking and Running	How much does this job require walking and running?
Responsibility for Outcomes and Results	How responsible is the worker for work outcomes and results of other workers?
Time Pressure	How often does this job require the worker to meet strict deadlines?
Spend Time Making Repetitive Motions	How much does this job require making repetitive motions?
Deal With Unpleasant or Angry People	How frequently does the worker have to deal with unpleasant, angry, or discourteous individuals as part of the job requirements?
Exposed to Contaminants	How often does this job require working exposed to contaminants (such as pollutants, gases, dust or odors)?
Electronic Mail	How often do you use electronic mail in this job?
Wear Specialized Protective or Safety Equipment su	How much does this job require wearing specialized protective or safety equipment such as breathing apparatus, safety harness, full protection suits, or radiation protection?
Spend Time Bending or Twisting the Body	How much does this job require bending or twisting your body?
Level of Competition	To what extent does this job require the worker to compete or to be aware of competitive pressures?
Letters and Memos	How often does the job require written letters and memos?
Frequency of Conflict Situations	How often are there conflict situations the employee has to face in this job?
Exposed to Hazardous Conditions	How often does this job require exposure to hazardous conditions?
Degree of Automation	How automated is the job?
Spend Time Sitting	How much does this job require sitting?
Sounds, Noise Levels Are Distracting or Uncomforta	How often does this job require working exposed to sounds and noise levels that are distracting or uncomfortable?
Pace Determined by Speed of Equipment	How important is it to this job that the pace is determined by the speed of equipment or machinery? (This does not refer to keeping busy at all times on this job.)
Cramped Work Space, Awkward Positions	How often does this job require working in cramped work spaces that requires getting into awkward positions?
Deal With Physically Aggressive People	How frequently does this job require the worker to deal with physical aggression of violent individuals?
Public Speaking	How often do you have to perform public speaking in this job?
Extremely Bright or Inadequate Lighting	How often does this job require working in extremely bright or inadequate lighting conditions?
Spend Time Kneeling, Crouching, Stooping, or Crawl	How much does this job require kneeling, crouching, stooping or crawling?
Exposed to Minor Burns, Cuts, Bites, or Stings	How often does this job require exposure to minor burns, cuts, bites, or stings?
Exposed to Hazardous Equipment	How often does this job require exposure to hazardous equipment?
Spend Time Keeping or Regaining Balance	How much does this job require keeping or regaining your balance?

Very Hot or Cold Temperatures	How often does this job require working in very hot (above 90 F degrees) or very cold (below 32 F degrees) temperatures?
Indoors, Not Environmentally Controlled	How often does this job require working indoors in non-controlled environmental conditions (e.g., warehouse without heat)?
Outdoors, Under Cover	How often does this job require working outdoors, under cover (e.g., structure with roof but no walls)?
Exposed to Whole Body Vibration	How often does this job require exposure to whole body vibration (e.g., operate a jackhammer)?
Outdoors, Exposed to Weather	How often does this job require working outdoors, exposed to all weather conditions?
In an Enclosed Vehicle or Equipment	How often does this job require working in a closed vehicle or equipment (e.g., car)?
Exposed to High Places	How often does this job require exposure to high places?
Spend Time Climbing Ladders, Scaffolds, or Poles	How much does this job require climbing ladders, scaffolds, or poles?
In an Open Vehicle or Equipment	How often does this job require working in an open vehicle or equipment (e.g., tractor)?

Job Zone Component	Job Zone Component Definitions
Title	Job Zone Three: Medium Preparation Needed
Overall Experience	Previous work-related skill, knowledge, or experience is required for these occupations. For example, an electrician must have completed three or four years of apprenticeship or several years of vocational training, and often must have passed a licensing exam, in order to perform the job.
Job Training	Employees in these occupations usually need one or two years of training involving both on-the-job experience and informal training with experienced workers.
Job Zone Examples	These occupations usually involve using communication and organizational skills to coordinate, supervise, manage, or train others to accomplish goals. Examples include dental assistants, electricians,fish and game wardens, legal secretaries, personnel recruiters, and recreation workers.
SVP Range	(6.0 to < 7.0)
Education	Most occupations in this zone require training in vocational schools, related on-the-job experience, or an associate's degree. Some may require a bachelor's degree.

Work_Styles	Work_Styles Definitions
Attention to Detail	Job requires being careful about detail and thorough in completing work tasks.
Dependability	Job requires being reliable, responsible, and dependable, and fulfilling obligations.
Integrity	Job requires being honest and ethical.
Self Control	Job requires maintaining composure, keeping emotions in check, controlling anger, and avoiding aggressive behavior, even in very difficult situations.
Stress Tolerance	Job requires accepting criticism and dealing calmly and effectively with high stress situations.
Concern for Others	Job requires being sensitive to others' needs and feelings and being understanding and helpful on the job.
Cooperation	Job requires being pleasant with others on the job and displaying a good-natured, cooperative attitude.
Adaptability/Flexibility	Job requires being open to change (positive or negative) and to considerable variety in the workplace.
Initiative	Job requires a willingness to take on responsibilities and challenges.
Independence	Job requires developing one's own ways of doing things, guiding oneself with little or no supervision, and depending on oneself to get things done.
Achievement/Effort	Job requires establishing and maintaining personally challenging achievement goals and exerting effort toward mastering tasks.
Analytical Thinking	Job requires analyzing information and using logic to address work-related issues and problems.
Persistence	Job requires persistence in the face of obstacles.
Leadership	Job requires a willingness to lead, take charge, and offer opinions and direction.
Innovation	Job requires creativity and alternative thinking to develop new ideas for and answers to work-related problems.
Social Orientation	Job requires preferring to work with others rather than alone, and being personally connected with others on the job.

29-2032.00 - Diagnostic Medical Sonographers

Produce ultrasonic recordings of internal organs for use by physicians.

Tasks

1) Obtain and record accurate patient history, including prior test results and information from physical examinations.

2) Coordinate work with physicians and other health-care team members, including providing assistance during invasive procedures.

3) Record and store suitable images, using camera unit connected to the ultrasound equipment.

4) Maintain stock and supplies, preparing supplies for special examinations and ordering supplies when necessary.

5) Process and code film from procedures and complete appropriate documentation.

6) Maintain records that include patient information, sonographs and interpretations, files of correspondence, publications and regulations, and quality assurance records (e.g., pathology, biopsy, post-operative reports).

7) Perform clerical duties such as scheduling exams and special procedures, keeping records and archiving computerized images.

8) Supervise and train students and other medical sonographers.

9) Perform legal and ethical duties including preparing safety and accident reports, obtaining written consent from patient to perform invasive procedures, and reporting symptoms of abuse and neglect.

10) Load and unload film cassettes used to record images from procedures.

11) Perform medical procedures such as administering oxygen, inserting and removing airways, taking vital signs, and giving emergency treatment such as first aid or cardiopulmonary resuscitation.

12) Observe screen during scan to ensure that image produced is satisfactory for diagnostic purposes, making adjustments to equipment as required.

13) Operate ultrasound equipment to produce and record images of the motion, shape and composition of blood, organs, tissues and bodily masses such as fluid accumulations.

14) Provide sonogram and oral or written summary of technical findings to physician for use in medical diagnosis.

15) Observe and care for patients throughout examinations to ensure their safety and comfort.

16) Prepare patient for exam by explaining procedure, transferring them to ultrasound table, scrubbing skin and applying gel, and positioning them properly.

17) Determine whether scope of exam should be extended, based on findings.

18) Decide which images to include, looking for differences between healthy and pathological areas.

19) Select appropriate equipment settings and adjust patient positions to obtain the best sites and angles.

Knowledge	Knowledge Definitions
Medicine and Dentistry	Knowledge of the information and techniques needed to diagnose and treat human injuries, diseases, and deformities. This includes symptoms, treatment alternatives, drug properties and interactions, and preventive health-care measures.
English Language	Knowledge of the structure and content of the English language including the meaning and spelling of words, rules of composition, and grammar.
Customer and Personal Service	Knowledge of principles and processes for providing customer and personal services. This includes customer needs assessment, meeting quality standards for services, and evaluation of customer satisfaction.
Education and Training	Knowledge of principles and methods for curriculum and training design, teaching and instruction for individuals and groups, and the measurement of training effects.
Biology	Knowledge of plant and animal organisms, their tissues, cells, functions, interdependencies, and interactions with each other and the environment.
Physics	Knowledge and prediction of physical principles, laws, their interrelationships, and applications to understanding fluid, material, and atmospheric dynamics, and mechanical, electrical, atomic and sub- atomic structures and processes.

Clerical	Knowledge of administrative and clerical procedures and systems such as word processing, managing files and records, stenography and transcription, designing forms, and other office procedures and terminology.
Computers and Electronics	Knowledge of circuit boards, processors, chips, electronic equipment, and computer hardware and software, including applications and programming.
Mathematics	Knowledge of arithmetic, algebra, geometry, calculus, statistics, and their applications.
Therapy and Counseling	Knowledge of principles, methods, and procedures for diagnosis, treatment, and rehabilitation of physical and mental dysfunctions, and for career counseling and guidance.
Administration and Management	Knowledge of business and management principles involved in strategic planning, resource allocation, human resources modeling, leadership technique, production methods, and coordination of people and resources.
Psychology	Knowledge of human behavior and performance; individual differences in ability, personality, and interests; learning and motivation; psychological research methods; and the assessment and treatment of behavioral and affective disorders.
Personnel and Human Resources	Knowledge of principles and procedures for personnel recruitment, selection, training, compensation and benefits, labor relations and negotiation, and personnel information systems.
Engineering and Technology	Knowledge of the practical application of engineering science and technology. This includes applying principles, techniques, procedures, and equipment to the design and production of various goods and services.
Chemistry	Knowledge of the chemical composition, structure, and properties of substances and of the chemical processes and transformations that they undergo. This includes uses of chemicals and their interactions, danger signs, production techniques, and disposal methods.
Communications and Media	Knowledge of media production, communication, and dissemination techniques and methods. This includes alternative ways to inform and entertain via written, oral, and visual media.
Public Safety and Security	Knowledge of relevant equipment, policies, procedures, and strategies to promote effective local, state, or national security operations for the protection of people, data, property, and institutions.
Law and Government	Knowledge of laws, legal codes, court procedures, precedents, government regulations, executive orders, agency rules, and the democratic political process.
Telecommunications	Knowledge of transmission, broadcasting, switching, control, and operation of telecommunications systems.
Mechanical	Knowledge of machines and tools, including their designs, uses, repair, and maintenance.
Philosophy and Theology	Knowledge of different philosophical systems and religions. This includes their basic principles, values, ethics, ways of thinking, customs, practices, and their impact on human culture.
Sociology and Anthropology	Knowledge of group behavior and dynamics, societal trends and influences, human migrations, ethnicity, cultures and their history and origins.
Foreign Language	Knowledge of the structure and content of a foreign (non-English) language including the meaning and spelling of words, rules of composition and grammar, and pronunciation.
Design	Knowledge of design techniques, tools, and principles involved in production of precision technical plans, blueprints, drawings, and models.
Production and Processing	Knowledge of raw materials, production processes, quality control, costs, and other techniques for maximizing the effective manufacture and distribution of goods.
Sales and Marketing	Knowledge of principles and methods for showing, promoting, and selling products or services. This includes marketing strategy and tactics, product demonstration, sales techniques, and sales control systems.
Economics and Accounting	Knowledge of economic and accounting principles and practices, the financial markets, banking and the analysis and reporting of financial data.
Transportation	Knowledge of principles and methods for moving people or goods by air, rail, sea, or road, including the relative costs and benefits.
Building and Construction	Knowledge of materials, methods, and the tools involved in the construction or repair of houses, buildings, or other structures such as highways and roads.

History and Archeology	Knowledge of historical events and their causes, indicators, and effects on civilizations and cultures.
Geography	Knowledge of principles and methods for describing the features of land, sea, and air masses, including their physical characteristics, locations, interrelationships, and distribution of plant, animal, and human life.
Fine Arts	Knowledge of the theory and techniques required to compose, produce, and perform works of music, dance, visual arts, drama, and sculpture.
Food Production	Knowledge of techniques and equipment for planting, growing, and harvesting food products (both plant and animal) for consumption, including storage/handling techniques.

Skills	Skills Definitions
Active Listening	Giving full attention to what other people are saying, taking time to understand the points being made, asking questions as appropriate, and not interrupting at inappropriate times.
Reading Comprehension	Understanding written sentences and paragraphs in work related documents.
Social Perceptiveness	Being aware of others' reactions and understanding why they react as they do.
Speaking	Talking to others to convey information effectively.
Critical Thinking	Using logic and reasoning to identify the strengths and weaknesses of alternative solutions, conclusions or approaches to problems.
Active Learning	Understanding the implications of new information for both current and future problem-solving and decision-making.
Learning Strategies	Selecting and using training/instructional methods and procedures appropriate for the situation when learning or teaching new things.
Instructing	Teaching others how to do something.
Coordination	Adjusting actions in relation to others' actions.
Service Orientation	Actively looking for ways to help people.
Writing	Communicating effectively in writing as appropriate for the needs of the audience.
Operation and Control	Controlling operations of equipment or systems.
Science	Using scientific rules and methods to solve problems.
Time Management	Managing one's own time and the time of others.
Monitoring	Monitoring/Assessing performance of yourself, other individuals, or organizations to make improvements or take corrective action.
Judgment and Decision Making	Considering the relative costs and benefits of potential actions to choose the most appropriate one.
Equipment Selection	Determining the kind of tools and equipment needed to do a job.
Mathematics	Using mathematics to solve problems.
Quality Control Analysis	Conducting tests and inspections of products, services, or processes to evaluate quality or performance.
Troubleshooting	Determining causes of operating errors and deciding what to do about it.
Management of Material Resources	Obtaining and seeing to the appropriate use of equipment, facilities, and materials needed to do certain work.
Equipment Maintenance	Performing routine maintenance on equipment and determining when and what kind of maintenance is needed.
Operation Monitoring	Watching gauges, dials, or other indicators to make sure a machine is working properly.
Complex Problem Solving	Identifying complex problems and reviewing related information to develop and evaluate options and implement solutions.
Systems Evaluation	Identifying measures or indicators of system performance and the actions needed to improve or correct performance, relative to the goals of the system.
Systems Analysis	Determining how a system should work and how changes in conditions, operations, and the environment will affect outcomes.
Management of Personnel Resources	Motivating, developing, and directing people as they work, identifying the best people for the job.
Persuasion	Persuading others to change their minds or behavior.
Technology Design	Generating or adapting equipment and technology to serve user needs.
Operations Analysis	Analyzing needs and product requirements to create a design.
Negotiation	Bringing others together and trying to reconcile differences.
Installation	Installing equipment, machines, wiring, or programs to meet specifications.
Management of Financial Resources	Determining how money will be spent to get the work done, and accounting for these expenditures.
Repairing	Repairing machines or systems using the needed tools.

Programming	Writing computer programs for various purposes.

Ability	Ability Definitions
Oral Expression	The ability to communicate information and ideas in speaking so others will understand.
Problem Sensitivity	The ability to tell when something is wrong or is likely to go wrong. It does not involve solving the problem, only recognizing there is a problem.
Oral Comprehension	The ability to listen to and understand information and ideas presented through spoken words and sentences.
Written Expression	The ability to communicate information and ideas in writing so others will understand.
Speech Recognition	The ability to identify and understand the speech of another person.
Near Vision	The ability to see details at close range (within a few feet of the observer).
Speech Clarity	The ability to speak clearly so others can understand you.
Inductive Reasoning	The ability to combine pieces of information to form general rules or conclusions (includes finding a relationship among seemingly unrelated events).
Control Precision	The ability to quickly and repeatedly adjust the controls of a machine or a vehicle to exact positions.
Perceptual Speed	The ability to quickly and accurately compare similarities and differences among sets of letters, numbers, objects, pictures, or patterns. The things to be compared may be presented at the same time or one after the other. This ability also includes comparing a presented object with a remembered object.
Written Comprehension	The ability to read and understand information and ideas presented in writing.
Deductive Reasoning	The ability to apply general rules to specific problems to produce answers that make sense.
Flexibility of Closure	The ability to identify or detect a known pattern (a figure, object, word, or sound) that is hidden in other distracting material.
Finger Dexterity	The ability to make precisely coordinated movements of the fingers of one or both hands to grasp, manipulate, or assemble very small objects.
Arm-Hand Steadiness	The ability to keep your hand and arm steady while moving your arm or while holding your arm and hand in one position.
Manual Dexterity	The ability to quickly move your hand, your hand together with your arm, or your two hands to grasp, manipulate, or assemble objects.
Speed of Closure	The ability to quickly make sense of, combine, and organize information into meaningful patterns.
Extent Flexibility	The ability to bend, stretch, twist, or reach with your body, arms, and/or legs.
Information Ordering	The ability to arrange things or actions in a certain order or pattern according to a specific rule or set of rules (e.g., patterns of numbers, letters, words, pictures, mathematical operations).
Multilimb Coordination	The ability to coordinate two or more limbs (for example, two arms, two legs, or one leg and one arm) while sitting, standing, or lying down. It does not involve performing the activities while the whole body is in motion.
Selective Attention	The ability to concentrate on a task over a period of time without being distracted.
Response Orientation	The ability to choose quickly between two or more movements in response to two or more different signals (lights, sounds, pictures). It includes the speed with which the correct response is started with the hand, foot, or other body part.
Category Flexibility	The ability to generate or use different sets of rules for combining or grouping things in different ways.
Visual Color Discrimination	The ability to match or detect differences between colors, including shades of color and brightness.
Time Sharing	The ability to shift back and forth between two or more activities or sources of information (such as speech, sounds, touch, or other sources).
Depth Perception	The ability to judge which of several objects is closer or farther away from you, or to judge the distance between you and an object.
Visualization	The ability to imagine how something will look after it is moved around or when its parts are moved or rearranged.
Wrist-Finger Speed	The ability to make fast, simple, repeated movements of the fingers, hands, and wrists.
Reaction Time	The ability to quickly respond (with the hand, finger, or foot) to a signal (sound, light, picture) when it appears.
Far Vision	The ability to see details at a distance.

Trunk Strength	The ability to use your abdominal and lower back muscles to support part of the body repeatedly or continuously over time without 'giving out' or fatiguing.
Static Strength	The ability to exert maximum muscle force to lift, push, pull, or carry objects.
Fluency of Ideas	The ability to come up with a number of ideas about a topic (the number of ideas is important, not their quality, correctness, or creativity).
Originality	The ability to come up with unusual or clever ideas about a given topic or situation, or to develop creative ways to solve a problem.
Hearing Sensitivity	The ability to detect or tell the differences between sounds that vary in pitch and loudness.
Auditory Attention	The ability to focus on a single source of sound in the presence of other distracting sounds.
Rate Control	The ability to time your movements or the movement of a piece of equipment in anticipation of changes in the speed and/or direction of a moving object or scene.
Mathematical Reasoning	The ability to choose the right mathematical methods or formulas to solve a problem.
Stamina	The ability to exert yourself physically over long periods of time without getting winded or out of breath.
Gross Body Coordination	The ability to coordinate the movement of your arms, legs, and torso together when the whole body is in motion.
Memorization	The ability to remember information such as words, numbers, pictures, and procedures.
Speed of Limb Movement	The ability to quickly move the arms and legs.
Gross Body Equilibrium	The ability to keep or regain your body balance or stay upright when in an unstable position.
Dynamic Strength	The ability to exert muscle force repeatedly or continuously over time. This involves muscular endurance and resistance to muscle fatigue.
Explosive Strength	The ability to use short bursts of muscle force to propel oneself (as in jumping or sprinting), or to throw an object.
Number Facility	The ability to add, subtract, multiply, or divide quickly and correctly.
Spatial Orientation	The ability to know your location in relation to the environment or to know where other objects are in relation to you.
Peripheral Vision	The ability to see objects or movement of objects to one's side when the eyes are looking ahead.
Dynamic Flexibility	The ability to quickly and repeatedly bend, stretch, twist, or reach out with your body, arms, and/or legs.
Sound Localization	The ability to tell the direction from which a sound originated.
Night Vision	The ability to see under low light conditions.
Glare Sensitivity	The ability to see objects in the presence of glare or bright lighting.

Work_Activity	Work_Activity Definitions
Assisting and Caring for Others	Providing personal assistance, medical attention, emotional support, or other personal care to others such as coworkers, customers, or patients.
Documenting/Recording Information	Entering, transcribing, recording, storing, or maintaining information in written or electronic/magnetic form.
Getting Information	Observing, receiving, and otherwise obtaining information from all relevant sources.
Identifying Objects, Actions, and Events	Identifying information by categorizing, estimating, recognizing differences or similarities, and detecting changes in circumstances or events.
Establishing and Maintaining Interpersonal Relatio	Developing constructive and cooperative working relationships with others, and maintaining them over time.
Communicating with Supervisors, Peers, or Subordin	Providing information to supervisors, co-workers, and subordinates by telephone, in written form, e-mail, or in person.
Interacting With Computers	Using computers and computer systems (including hardware and software) to program, write software, set up functions, enter data, or process information.
Controlling Machines and Processes	Using either control mechanisms or direct physical activity to operate machines or processes (not including computers or vehicles).
Making Decisions and Solving Problems	Analyzing information and evaluating results to choose the best solution and solve problems.
Resolving Conflicts and Negotiating with Others	Handling complaints, settling disputes, and resolving grievances and conflicts, or otherwise negotiating with others.
Interpreting the Meaning of Information for Others	Translating or explaining what information means and how it can be used.

Monitor Processes, Materials, or Surroundings	Monitoring and reviewing information from materials, events, or the environment, to detect or assess problems.
Performing for or Working Directly with the Public	Performing for people or dealing directly with the public. This includes serving customers in restaurants and stores, and receiving clients or guests.
Handling and Moving Objects	Using hands and arms in handling, installing, positioning, and moving materials, and manipulating things.
Organizing, Planning, and Prioritizing Work	Developing specific goals and plans to prioritize, organize, and accomplish your work.
Updating and Using Relevant Knowledge	Keeping up-to-date technically and applying new knowledge to your job.
Estimating the Quantifiable Characteristics of Pro	Estimating sizes, distances, and quantities; or determining time, costs, resources, or materials needed to perform a work activity.
Performing General Physical Activities	Performing physical activities that require considerable use of your arms and legs and moving your whole body, such as climbing, lifting, balancing, walking, stooping, and handling of materials.
Analyzing Data or Information	Identifying the underlying principles, reasons, or facts of information by breaking down information or data into separate parts.
Evaluating Information to Determine Compliance wit	Using relevant information and individual judgment to determine whether events or processes comply with laws, regulations, or standards.
Inspecting Equipment, Structures, or Material	Inspecting equipment, structures, or materials to identify the cause of errors or other problems or defects.
Training and Teaching Others	Identifying the educational needs of others, developing formal educational or training programs or classes, and teaching or instructing others.
Communicating with Persons Outside Organization	Communicating with people outside the organization, representing the organization to customers, the public, government, and other external sources. This information can be exchanged in person, in writing, or by telephone or e-mail.
Coordinating the Work and Activities of Others	Getting members of a group to work together to accomplish tasks.
Developing and Building Teams	Encouraging and building mutual trust, respect, and cooperation among team members.
Performing Administrative Activities	Performing day-to-day administrative tasks such as maintaining information files and processing paperwork.
Judging the Qualities of Things, Services, or Peop	Assessing the value, importance, or quality of things or people.
Scheduling Work and Activities	Scheduling events, programs, and activities, as well as the work of others.
Processing Information	Compiling, coding, categorizing, calculating, tabulating, auditing, or verifying information or data.
Thinking Creatively	Developing, designing, or creating new applications, ideas, relationships, systems, or products, including artistic contributions.
Repairing and Maintaining Mechanical Equipment	Servicing, repairing, adjusting, and testing machines, devices, moving parts, and equipment that operate primarily on the basis of mechanical (not electronic) principles.
Coaching and Developing Others	Identifying the developmental needs of others and coaching, mentoring, or otherwise helping others to improve their knowledge or skills.
Guiding, Directing, and Motivating Subordinates	Providing guidance and direction to subordinates, including setting performance standards and monitoring performance.
Developing Objectives and Strategies	Establishing long-range objectives and specifying the strategies and actions to achieve them.
Provide Consultation and Advice to Others	Providing guidance and expert advice to management or other groups on technical, systems-, or process-related topics.
Repairing and Maintaining Electronic Equipment	Servicing, repairing, calibrating, regulating, fine-tuning, or testing machines, devices, and equipment that operate primarily on the basis of electrical or electronic (not mechanical) principles.
Monitoring and Controlling Resources	Monitoring and controlling resources and overseeing the spending of money.
Staffing Organizational Units	Recruiting, interviewing, selecting, hiring, and promoting employees in an organization.
Operating Vehicles, Mechanized Devices, or Equipme	Running, maneuvering, navigating, or driving vehicles or mechanized equipment, such as forklifts, passenger vehicles, aircraft, or water craft.
Drafting, Laying Out, and Specifying Technical Dev	Providing documentation, detailed instructions, drawings, or specifications to tell others about how devices, parts, equipment, or structures are to be fabricated, constructed, assembled, modified, maintained, or used.
Selling or Influencing Others	Convincing others to buy merchandise/goods or to otherwise change their minds or actions.

Work_Context	Work_Context Definitions
Spend Time Using Your Hands to Handle, Control, or	How much does this job require using your hands to handle, control, or feel objects, tools or controls?
Importance of Being Exact or Accurate	How important is being very exact or highly accurate in performing this job?
Contact With Others	How much does this job require the worker to be in contact with others (face-to-face, by telephone, or otherwise) in order to perform it?
Exposed to Disease or Infections	How often does this job require exposure to disease/infections?
Indoors, Environmentally Controlled	How often does this job require working indoors in environmentally controlled conditions?
Face-to-Face Discussions	How often do you have to have face-to-face discussions with individuals or teams in this job?
Physical Proximity	To what extent does this job require the worker to perform job tasks in close physical proximity to other people?
Telephone	How often do you have telephone conversations in this job?
Spend Time Making Repetitive Motions	How much does this job require making repetitive motions?
Frequency of Decision Making	How frequently is the worker required to make decisions that affect other people, the financial resources, and/or the image and reputation of the organization?
Work With Work Group or Team	How important is it to work with others in a group or team in this job?
Time Pressure	How often does this job require the worker to meet strict deadlines?
Structured versus Unstructured Work	To what extent is this job structured for the worker, rather than allowing the worker to determine tasks, priorities, and goals?
Impact of Decisions on Co-workers or Company Resul	How do the decisions an employee makes impact the results of co-workers, clients or the company?
Freedom to Make Decisions	How much decision making freedom, without supervision, does the job offer?
Deal With External Customers	How important is it to work with external customers or the public in this job?
Importance of Repeating Same Tasks	How important is repeating the same physical activities (e.g., key entry) or mental activities (e.g., checking entries in a ledger) over and over, without stopping, to performing this job?
Deal With Unpleasant or Angry People	How frequently does the worker have to deal with unpleasant, angry, or discourteous individuals as part of the job requirements?
Spend Time Bending or Twisting the Body	How much does this job require bending or twisting your body?
Responsible for Others' Health and Safety	How much responsibility is there for the health and safety of others in this job?
Level of Competition	To what extent does this job require the worker to compete or to be aware of competitive pressures?
Cramped Work Space, Awkward Positions	How often does this job require working in cramped work spaces that requires getting into awkward positions?
Consequence of Error	How serious would the result usually be if the worker made a mistake that was not readily correctable?
Spend Time Sitting	How much does this job require sitting?
Sounds, Noise Levels Are Distracting or Uncomforta	How often does this job require working exposed to sounds and noise levels that are distracting or uncomfortable?
Wear Common Protective or Safety Equipment such as	How much does this job require wearing common protective or safety equipment such as safety shoes, glasses, gloves, hard hats or live jackets?
Coordinate or Lead Others	How important is it to coordinate or lead others in accomplishing work activities in this job?
Exposed to Contaminants	How often does this job require working exposed to contaminants (such as pollutants, gases, dust or odors)?
Responsibility for Outcomes and Results	How responsible is the worker for work outcomes and results of other workers?
Spend Time Standing	How much does this job require standing?
Frequency of Conflict Situations	How often are there conflict situations the employee has to face in this job?
Spend Time Walking and Running	How much does this job require walking and running?
Deal With Physically Aggressive People	How frequently does this job require the worker to deal with physical aggression of violent individuals?
Exposed to Hazardous Conditions	How often does this job require exposure to hazardous conditions?
Letters and Memos	How often does the job require written letters and memos?
Extremely Bright or Inadequate Lighting	How often does this job require working in extremely bright or inadequate lighting conditions?

Exposed to Radiation	How often does this job require exposure to radiation?
Pace Determined by Speed of Equipment	How important is it to this job that the pace is determined by the speed of equipment or machinery? (This does not refer to keeping busy at all times on this job.)
Wear Specialized Protective or Safety Equipment su	How much does this job require wearing specialized protective or safety equipment such as breathing apparatus, safety harness, full protection suits, or radiation protection?
Electronic Mail	How often do you use electronic mail in this job?
Degree of Automation	How automated is the job?
Spend Time Keeping or Regaining Balance	How much does this job require keeping or regaining your balance?
Public Speaking	How often do you have to perform public speaking in this job?
Spend Time Kneeling, Crouching, Stooping, or Crawl	How much does this job require kneeling, crouching, stooping or crawling?
In an Enclosed Vehicle or Equipment	How often does this job require working in a closed vehicle or equipment (e.g., car)?
Exposed to Minor Burns, Cuts, Bites, or Stings	How often does this job require exposure to minor burns, cuts, bites, or stings?
Exposed to Hazardous Equipment	How often does this job require exposure to hazardous equipment?
Very Hot or Cold Temperatures	How often does this job require working in very hot (above 90 F degrees) or very cold (below 32 F degrees) temperatures?
Spend Time Climbing Ladders, Scaffolds, or Poles	How much does this job require climbing ladders, scaffolds, or poles?
Indoors, Not Environmentally Controlled	How often does this job require working indoors in non-controlled environmental conditions (e.g., warehouse without heat)?
Exposed to Whole Body Vibration	How often does this job require exposure to whole body vibration (e.g., operate a jackhammer)?
Outdoors, Exposed to Weather	How often does this job require working outdoors, exposed to all weather conditions?
Outdoors, Under Cover	How often does this job require working outdoors, under cover (e.g., structure with roof but no walls)?
In an Open Vehicle or Equipment	How often does this job require working in an open vehicle or equipment (e.g., tractor)?
Exposed to High Places	How often does this job require exposure to high places?

Job Zone Component	Job Zone Component Definitions
Title	Job Zone Three: Medium Preparation Needed
Overall Experience	Previous work-related skill, knowledge, or experience is required for these occupations. For example, an electrician must have completed three or four years of apprenticeship or several years of vocational training, and often must have passed a licensing exam, in order to perform the job.
Job Training	Employees in these occupations usually need one or two years of training involving both on-the-job experience and informal training with experienced workers.
Job Zone Examples	These occupations usually involve using communication and organizational skills to coordinate, supervise, manage, or train others to accomplish goals. Examples include dental assistants, electricians, fish and game wardens, legal secretaries, personnel recruiters, and recreation workers.
SVP Range	(6.0 to < 7.0)
Education	Most occupations in this zone require training in vocational schools, related on-the-job experience, or an associate's degree. Some may require a bachelor's degree.

Work_Styles	Work_Styles Definitions
Attention to Detail	Job requires being careful about detail and thorough in completing work tasks.
Integrity	Job requires being honest and ethical.
Concern for Others	Job requires being sensitive to others' needs and feelings and being understanding and helpful on the job.
Dependability	Job requires being reliable, responsible, and dependable, and fulfilling obligations.
Self Control	Job requires maintaining composure, keeping emotions in check, controlling anger, and avoiding aggressive behavior, even in very difficult situations.
Analytical Thinking	Job requires analyzing information and using logic to address work-related issues and problems.
Independence	Job requires developing one's own ways of doing things, guiding oneself with little or no supervision, and depending on oneself to get things done.

Cooperation	Job requires being pleasant with others on the job and displaying a good-natured, cooperative attitude.
Initiative	Job requires a willingness to take on responsibilities and challenges.
Persistence	Job requires persistence in the face of obstacles.
Stress Tolerance	Job requires accepting criticism and dealing calmly and effectively with high stress situations.
Adaptability/Flexibility	Job requires being open to change (positive or negative) and to considerable variety in the workplace.
Achievement/Effort	Job requires establishing and maintaining personally challenging achievement goals and exerting effort toward mastering tasks.
Social Orientation	Job requires preferring to work with others rather than alone, and being personally connected with others on the job.
Innovation	Job requires creativity and alternative thinking to develop new ideas for and answers to work-related problems.
Leadership	Job requires a willingness to lead, take charge, and offer opinions and direction.

29-2033.00 - Nuclear Medicine Technologists

Prepare, administer, and measure radioactive isotopes in therapeutic, diagnostic, and tracer studies utilizing a variety of radioisotope equipment. Prepare stock solutions of radioactive materials and calculate doses to be administered by radiologists. Subject patients to radiation. Execute blood volume, red cell survival, and fat absorption studies following standard laboratory techniques.

Tasks

1) Administer radiopharmaceuticals or radiation to patients to detect or treat diseases, using radioisotope equipment, under direction of physician.

2) Produce a computer-generated or film image for interpretation by a physician.

3) Process cardiac function studies, using computer.

4) Maintain and calibrate radioisotope and laboratory equipment.

5) Calculate, measure and record radiation dosage or radiopharmaceuticals received, used and disposed, using computer and following physician's prescription.

6) Record and process results of procedures.

7) Prepare stock radiopharmaceuticals, adhering to safety standards that minimize radiation exposure to workers and patients.

8) Measure glandular activity, blood volume, red cell survival, and radioactivity of patient, using scanners, Geiger counters, scintillometers, and other laboratory equipment.

9) Train and supervise student or subordinate nuclear medicine technologists.

10) Gather information on patients' illnesses and medical history to guide the choice of diagnostic procedures for therapy.

11) Add radioactive substances to biological specimens, such as blood, urine and feces, to determine therapeutic drug or hormone levels.

12) Develop treatment procedures for nuclear medicine treatment programs.

13) Position radiation fields, radiation beams, and patient to allow for most effective treatment of patient's disease, using computer.

14) Detect and map radiopharmaceuticals in patients' bodies, using a camera to produce photographic or computer images.

15) Explain test procedures and safety precautions to patients and provide them with assistance during test procedures.

Knowledge	Knowledge Definitions
Customer and Personal Service	Knowledge of principles and processes for providing customer and personal services. This includes customer needs assessment, meeting quality standards for services, and evaluation of customer satisfaction.
Medicine and Dentistry	Knowledge of the information and techniques needed to diagnose and treat human injuries, diseases, and deformities. This includes symptoms, treatment alternatives, drug properties and interactions, and preventive health-care measures.
Physics	Knowledge and prediction of physical principles, laws, their interrelationships, and applications to understanding fluid, material, and atmospheric dynamics, and mechanical, electrical, atomic and sub-atomic structures and processes.

English Language	Knowledge of the structure and content of the English language including the meaning and spelling of words, rules of composition, and grammar.
Computers and Electronics	Knowledge of circuit boards, processors, chips, electronic equipment, and computer hardware and software, including applications and programming.
Biology	Knowledge of plant and animal organisms, their tissues, cells, functions, interdependencies, and interactions with each other and the environment.
Mathematics	Knowledge of arithmetic, algebra, geometry, calculus, statistics, and their applications.
Chemistry	Knowledge of the chemical composition, structure, and properties of substances and of the chemical processes and transformations that they undergo. This includes uses of chemicals and their interactions, danger signs, production techniques, and disposal methods.
Public Safety and Security	Knowledge of relevant equipment, policies, procedures, and strategies to promote effective local, state, or national security operations for the protection of people, data, property, and institutions.
Clerical	Knowledge of administrative and clerical procedures and systems such as word processing, managing files and records, stenography and transcription, designing forms, and other office procedures and terminology.
Education and Training	Knowledge of principles and methods for curriculum and training design, teaching and instruction for individuals and groups, and the measurement of training effects.
Psychology	Knowledge of human behavior and performance; individual differences in ability, personality, and interests; learning and motivation; psychological research methods; and the assessment and treatment of behavioral and affective disorders.
Law and Government	Knowledge of laws, legal codes, court procedures, precedents, government regulations, executive orders, agency rules, and the democratic political process.
Administration and Management	Knowledge of business and management principles involved in strategic planning, resource allocation, human resources modeling, leadership technique, production methods, and coordination of people and resources.
Engineering and Technology	Knowledge of the practical application of engineering science and technology. This includes applying principles, techniques, procedures, and equipment to the design and production of various goods and services.
Mechanical	Knowledge of machines and tools, including their designs, uses, repair, and maintenance.
Production and Processing	Knowledge of raw materials, production processes, quality control, costs, and other techniques for maximizing the effective manufacture and distribution of goods.
Communications and Media	Knowledge of media production, communication, and dissemination techniques and methods. This includes alternative ways to inform and entertain via written, oral, and visual media.
Therapy and Counseling	Knowledge of principles, methods, and procedures for diagnosis, treatment, and rehabilitation of physical and mental dysfunctions, and for career counseling and guidance.
Personnel and Human Resources	Knowledge of principles and procedures for personnel recruitment, selection, training, compensation and benefits, labor relations and negotiation, and personnel information systems.
Telecommunications	Knowledge of transmission, broadcasting, switching, control, and operation of telecommunications systems.
Sociology and Anthropology	Knowledge of group behavior and dynamics, societal trends and influences, human migrations, ethnicity, cultures and their history and origins.
Foreign Language	Knowledge of the structure and content of a foreign (non-English) language including the meaning and spelling of words, rules of composition and grammar, and pronunciation.
Transportation	Knowledge of principles and methods for moving people or goods by air, rail, sea, or road, including the relative costs and benefits.
Philosophy and Theology	Knowledge of different philosophical systems and religions. This includes their basic principles, values, ethics, ways of thinking, customs, practices, and their impact on human culture.
Economics and Accounting	Knowledge of economic and accounting principles and practices, the financial markets, banking and the analysis and reporting of financial data.

Design	Knowledge of design techniques, tools, and principles involved in production of precision technical plans, blueprints, drawings, and models.
Sales and Marketing	Knowledge of principles and methods for showing, promoting, and selling products or services. This includes marketing strategy and tactics, product demonstration, sales techniques, and sales control systems.
Geography	Knowledge of principles and methods for describing the features of land, sea, and air masses, including their physical characteristics, locations, interrelationships, and distribution of plant, animal, and human life.
Building and Construction	Knowledge of materials, methods, and the tools involved in the construction or repair of houses, buildings, or other structures such as highways and roads.
Food Production	Knowledge of techniques and equipment for planting, growing, and harvesting food products (both plant and animal) for consumption, including storage/handling techniques.
History and Archeology	Knowledge of historical events and their causes, indicators, and effects on civilizations and cultures.
Fine Arts	Knowledge of the theory and techniques required to compose, produce, and perform works of music, dance, visual arts, drama, and sculpture.

Skills	Skills Definitions
Active Listening	Giving full attention to what other people are saying, taking time to understand the points being made, asking questions as appropriate, and not interrupting at inappropriate times.
Reading Comprehension	Understanding written sentences and paragraphs in work related documents.
Active Learning	Understanding the implications of new information for both current and future problem-solving and decision-making.
Speaking	Talking to others to convey information effectively.
Time Management	Managing one's own time and the time of others.
Critical Thinking	Using logic and reasoning to identify the strengths and weaknesses of alternative solutions, conclusions or approaches to problems.
Science	Using scientific rules and methods to solve problems.
Social Perceptiveness	Being aware of others' reactions and understanding why they react as they do.
Coordination	Adjusting actions in relation to others' actions.
Instructing	Teaching others how to do something.
Monitoring	Monitoring/Assessing performance of yourself, other individuals, or organizations to make improvements or take corrective action.
Operation Monitoring	Watching gauges, dials, or other indicators to make sure a machine is working properly.
Learning Strategies	Selecting and using training/instructional methods and procedures appropriate for the situation when learning or teaching new things.
Writing	Communicating effectively in writing as appropriate for the needs of the audience.
Quality Control Analysis	Conducting tests and inspections of products, services, or processes to evaluate quality or performance.
Operation and Control	Controlling operations of equipment or systems.
Mathematics	Using mathematics to solve problems.
Service Orientation	Actively looking for ways to help people.
Troubleshooting	Determining causes of operating errors and deciding what to do about it.
Equipment Selection	Determining the kind of tools and equipment needed to do a job.
Judgment and Decision Making	Considering the relative costs and benefits of potential actions to choose the most appropriate one.
Complex Problem Solving	Identifying complex problems and reviewing related information to develop and evaluate options and implement solutions.
Equipment Maintenance	Performing routine maintenance on equipment and determining when and what kind of maintenance is needed.
Persuasion	Persuading others to change their minds or behavior.
Operations Analysis	Analyzing needs and product requirements to create a design.
Negotiation	Bringing others together and trying to reconcile differences.
Technology Design	Generating or adapting equipment and technology to serve user needs.
Systems Evaluation	Identifying measures or indicators of system performance and the actions needed to improve or correct performance, relative to the goals of the system.
Management of Material Resources	Obtaining and seeing to the appropriate use of equipment, facilities, and materials needed to do certain work.

Systems Analysis	Determining how a system should work and how changes in conditions, operations, and the environment will affect outcomes.
Management of Personnel Resources	Motivating, developing, and directing people as they work, identifying the best people for the job.
Management of Financial Resources	Determining how money will be spent to get the work done, and accounting for these expenditures.
Repairing	Repairing machines or systems using the needed tools.
Installation	Installing equipment, machines, wiring, or programs to meet specifications.
Programming	Writing computer programs for various purposes.

Ability	Ability Definitions
Problem Sensitivity	The ability to tell when something is wrong or is likely to go wrong. It does not involve solving the problem, only recognizing there is a problem.
Oral Comprehension	The ability to listen to and understand information and ideas presented through spoken words and sentences.
Deductive Reasoning	The ability to apply general rules to specific problems to produce answers that make sense.
Written Comprehension	The ability to read and understand information and ideas presented in writing.
Oral Expression	The ability to communicate information and ideas in speaking so others will understand.
Near Vision	The ability to see details at close range (within a few feet of the observer).
Inductive Reasoning	The ability to combine pieces of information to form general rules or conclusions (includes finding a relationship among seemingly unrelated events).
Information Ordering	The ability to arrange things or actions in a certain order or pattern according to a specific rule or set of rules (e.g., patterns of numbers, letters, words, pictures, mathematical operations).
Speech Clarity	The ability to speak clearly so others can understand you.
Speech Recognition	The ability to identify and understand the speech of another person.
Arm-Hand Steadiness	The ability to keep your hand and arm steady while moving your arm or while holding your arm and hand in one position.
Category Flexibility	The ability to generate or use different sets of rules for combining or grouping things in different ways.
Finger Dexterity	The ability to make precisely coordinated movements of the fingers of one or both hands to grasp, manipulate, or assemble very small objects.
Selective Attention	The ability to concentrate on a task over a period of time without being distracted.
Perceptual Speed	The ability to quickly and accurately compare similarities and differences among sets of letters, numbers, objects, pictures, or patterns. The things to be compared may be presented at the same time or one after the other. This ability also includes comparing a presented object with a remembered object.
Mathematical Reasoning	The ability to choose the right mathematical methods or formulas to solve a problem.
Flexibility of Closure	The ability to identify or detect a known pattern (a figure, object, word, or sound) that is hidden in other distracting material.
Written Expression	The ability to communicate information and ideas in writing so others will understand.
Manual Dexterity	The ability to quickly move your hand, your hand together with your arm, or your two hands to grasp, manipulate, or assemble objects.
Number Facility	The ability to add, subtract, multiply, or divide quickly and correctly.
Control Precision	The ability to quickly and repeatedly adjust the controls of a machine or a vehicle to exact positions.
Hearing Sensitivity	The ability to detect or tell the differences between sounds that vary in pitch and loudness.
Visualization	The ability to imagine how something will look after it is moved around or when its parts are moved or rearranged.
Time Sharing	The ability to shift back and forth between two or more activities or sources of information (such as speech, sounds, touch, or other sources).
Depth Perception	The ability to judge which of several objects is closer or farther away from you, or to judge the distance between you and an object.
Visual Color Discrimination	The ability to match or detect differences between colors, including shades of color and brightness.
Auditory Attention	The ability to focus on a single source of sound in the presence of other distracting sounds.

Originality	The ability to come up with unusual or clever ideas about a given topic or situation, or to develop creative ways to solve a problem.
Far Vision	The ability to see details at a distance.
Multilimb Coordination	The ability to coordinate two or more limbs (for example, two arms, two legs, or one leg and one arm) while sitting, standing, or lying down. It does not involve performing the activities while the whole body is in motion.
Speed of Closure	The ability to quickly make sense of, combine, and organize information into meaningful patterns.
Memorization	The ability to remember information such as words, numbers, pictures, and procedures.
Response Orientation	The ability to choose quickly between two or more movements in response to two or more different signals (lights, sounds, pictures). It includes the speed with which the correct response is started with the hand, foot, or other body part.
Fluency of Ideas	The ability to come up with a number of ideas about a topic (the number of ideas is important, not their quality, correctness, or creativity).
Reaction Time	The ability to quickly respond (with the hand, finger, or foot) to a signal (sound, light, picture) when it appears.
Static Strength	The ability to exert maximum muscle force to lift, push, pull, or carry objects.
Trunk Strength	The ability to use your abdominal and lower back muscles to support part of the body repeatedly or continuously over time without 'giving out' or fatiguing.
Rate Control	The ability to time your movements or the movement of a piece of equipment in anticipation of changes in the speed and/or direction of a moving object or scene.
Gross Body Coordination	The ability to coordinate the movement of your arms, legs, and torso together when the whole body is in motion.
Stamina	The ability to exert yourself physically over long periods of time without getting winded or out of breath.
Wrist-Finger Speed	The ability to make fast, simple, repeated movements of the fingers, hands, and wrists.
Extent Flexibility	The ability to bend, stretch, twist, or reach with your body, arms, and/or legs.
Speed of Limb Movement	The ability to quickly move the arms and legs.
Sound Localization	The ability to tell the direction from which a sound originated.
Spatial Orientation	The ability to know your location in relation to the environment or to know where other objects are in relation to you.
Peripheral Vision	The ability to see objects or movement of objects to one's side when the eyes are looking ahead.
Glare Sensitivity	The ability to see objects in the presence of glare or bright lighting.
Dynamic Strength	The ability to exert muscle force repeatedly or continuously over time. This involves muscular endurance and resistance to muscle fatigue.
Gross Body Equilibrium	The ability to keep or regain your body balance or stay upright when in an unstable position.
Night Vision	The ability to see under low light conditions.
Explosive Strength	The ability to use short bursts of muscle force to propel oneself (as in jumping or sprinting), or to throw an object.
Dynamic Flexibility	The ability to quickly and repeatedly bend, stretch, twist, or reach out with your body, arms, and/or legs.

Work_Activity	Work_Activity Definitions
Assisting and Caring for Others	Providing personal assistance, medical attention, emotional support, or other personal care to others such as coworkers, customers, or patients.
Interacting With Computers	Using computers and computer systems (including hardware and software) to program, write software, set up functions, enter data, or process information.
Documenting/Recording Information	Entering, transcribing, recording, storing, or maintaining information in written or electronic/magnetic form.
Performing for or Working Directly with the Public	Performing for people or dealing directly with the public. This includes serving customers in restaurants and stores, and receiving clients or guests.
Inspecting Equipment, Structures, or Material	Inspecting equipment, structures, or materials to identify the cause of errors or other problems or defects.
Evaluating Information to Determine Compliance wit	Using relevant information and individual judgment to determine whether events or processes comply with laws, regulations, or standards.
Updating and Using Relevant Knowledge	Keeping up-to-date technically and applying new knowledge to your job.

Communicating with Supervisors, Peers, or Subordin	Providing information to supervisors, co-workers, and subordinates by telephone, in written form, e-mail, or in person.
Getting Information	Observing, receiving, and otherwise obtaining information from all relevant sources.
Establishing and Maintaining Interpersonal Relatio	Developing constructive and cooperative working relationships with others, and maintaining them over time.
Monitor Processes, Materials, or Surroundings	Monitoring and reviewing information from materials, events, or the environment, to detect or assess problems.
Identifying Objects, Actions, and Events	Identifying information by categorizing, estimating, recognizing differences or similarities, and detecting changes in circumstances or events.
Making Decisions and Solving Problems	Analyzing information and evaluating results to choose the best solution and solve problems.
Organizing, Planning, and Prioritizing Work	Developing specific goals and plans to prioritize, organize, and accomplish your work.
Controlling Machines and Processes	Using either control mechanisms or direct physical activity to operate machines or processes (not including computers or vehicles).
Processing Information	Compiling, coding, categorizing, calculating, tabulating, auditing, or verifying information or data.
Scheduling Work and Activities	Scheduling events, programs, and activities, as well as the work of others.
Handling and Moving Objects	Using hands and arms in handling, installing, positioning, and moving materials, and manipulating things.
Judging the Qualities of Things, Services, or Peop	Assessing the value, importance, or quality of things or people.
Analyzing Data or Information	Identifying the underlying principles, reasons, or facts of information by breaking down information or data into separate parts.
Communicating with Persons Outside Organization	Communicating with people outside the organization, representing the organization to customers, the public, government, and other external sources. This information can be exchanged in person, in writing, or by telephone or e-mail.
Performing General Physical Activities	Performing physical activities that require considerable use of your arms and legs and moving your whole body, such as climbing, lifting, balancing, walking, stooping, and handling of materials.
Training and Teaching Others	Identifying the educational needs of others, developing formal educational or training programs or classes, and teaching or instructing others.
Coordinating the Work and Activities of Others	Getting members of a group to work together to accomplish tasks.
Estimating the Quantifiable Characteristics of Pro	Estimating sizes, distances, and quantities; or determining time, costs, resources, or materials needed to perform a work activity.
Interpreting the Meaning of Information for Others	Translating or explaining what information means and how it can be used.
Resolving Conflicts and Negotiating with Others	Handling complaints, settling disputes, and resolving grievances and conflicts, or otherwise negotiating with others.
Thinking Creatively	Developing, designing, or creating new applications, ideas, relationships, systems, or products, including artistic contributions.
Performing Administrative Activities	Performing day-to-day administrative tasks such as maintaining information files and processing paperwork.
Developing and Building Teams	Encouraging and building mutual trust, respect, and cooperation among team members.
Repairing and Maintaining Electronic Equipment	Servicing, repairing, calibrating, regulating, fine-tuning, or testing machines, devices, and equipment that operate primarily on the basis of electrical or electronic (not mechanical) principles.
Guiding, Directing, and Motivating Subordinates	Providing guidance and direction to subordinates, including setting performance standards and monitoring performance.
Developing Objectives and Strategies	Establishing long-range objectives and specifying the strategies and actions to achieve them.
Coaching and Developing Others	Identifying the developmental needs of others and coaching, mentoring, or otherwise helping others to improve their knowledge or skills.
Operating Vehicles, Mechanized Devices, or Equipme	Running, maneuvering, navigating, or driving vehicles or mechanized equipment, such as forklifts, passenger vehicles, aircraft, or water craft.
Repairing and Maintaining Mechanical Equipment	Servicing, repairing, adjusting, and testing machines, devices, moving parts, and equipment that operate primarily on the basis of mechanical (not electronic) principles.
Monitoring and Controlling Resources	Monitoring and controlling resources and overseeing the spending of money.
Provide Consultation and Advice to Others	Providing guidance and expert advice to management or other groups on technical, systems-, or process-related topics.
Selling or Influencing Others	Convincing others to buy merchandise/goods or to otherwise change their minds or actions.
Staffing Organizational Units	Recruiting, interviewing, selecting, hiring, and promoting employees in an organization.
Drafting, Laying Out, and Specifying Technical Dev	Providing documentation, detailed instructions, drawings, or specifications to tell others about how devices, parts, equipment, or structures are to be fabricated, constructed, assembled, modified, maintained, or used.

Work_Context	Work_Context Definitions
Exposed to Radiation	How often does this job require exposure to radiation?
Indoors, Environmentally Controlled	How often does this job require working indoors in environmentally controlled conditions?
Telephone	How often do you have telephone conversations in this job?
Exposed to Disease or Infections	How often does this job require exposure to disease/infections?
Contact With Others	How much does this job require the worker to be in contact with others (face-to-face, by telephone, or otherwise) in order to perform it?
Face-to-Face Discussions	How often do you have to have face-to-face discussions with individuals or teams in this job?
Importance of Being Exact or Accurate	How important is being very exact or highly accurate in performing this job?
Wear Common Protective or Safety Equipment such as	How much does this job require wearing common protective or safety equipment such as safety shoes, glasses, gloves, hard hats or live jackets?
Physical Proximity	To what extent does this job require the worker to perform job tasks in close physical proximity to other people?
Freedom to Make Decisions	How much decision making freedom, without supervision, does the job offer?
Work With Work Group or Team	How important is it to work with others in a group or team in this job?
Deal With External Customers	How important is it to work with external customers or the public in this job?
Impact of Decisions on Co-workers or Company Resul	How do the decisions an employee makes impact the results of co-workers, clients or the company?
Frequency of Decision Making	How frequently is the worker required to make decisions that affect other people, the financial resources, and/or the image and reputation of the organization?
Spend Time Using Your Hands to Handle, Control, or	How much does this job require using your hands to handle, control, or feel objects, tools or controls?
Structured versus Unstructured Work	To what extent is this job structured for the worker, rather than allowing the worker to determine tasks, priorities, and goals?
Responsible for Others' Health and Safety	How much responsibility is there for the health and safety of others in this job?
Consequence of Error	How serious would the result usually be if the worker made a mistake that was not readily correctable?
Time Pressure	How often does this job require the worker to meet strict deadlines?
Importance of Repeating Same Tasks	How important is repeating the same physical activities (e.g., key entry) or mental activities (e.g., checking entries in a ledger) over and over, without stopping, to performing this job?
Coordinate or Lead Others	How important is it to coordinate or lead others in accomplishing work activities in this job?
Deal With Unpleasant or Angry People	How frequently does the worker have to deal with unpleasant, angry, or discourteous individuals as part of the job requirements?
Exposed to Contaminants	How often does this job require working exposed to contaminants (such as pollutants, gases, dust or odors)?
Spend Time Standing	How much does this job require standing?
Frequency of Conflict Situations	How often are there conflict situations the employee has to face in this job?
Wear Specialized Protective or Safety Equipment su	How much does this job require wearing specialized protective or safety equipment such as breathing apparatus, safety harness, full protection suits, or radiation protection?
Level of Competition	To what extent does this job require the worker to compete or to be aware of competitive pressures?
Responsibility for Outcomes and Results	How responsible is the worker for work outcomes and results of other workers?
Electronic Mail	How often do you use electronic mail in this job?
Degree of Automation	How automated is the job?
Spend Time Walking and Running	How much does this job require walking and running?

Letters and Memos	How often does the job require written letters and memos?
Spend Time Sitting	How much does this job require sitting?
Spend Time Making Repetitive Motions	How much does this job require making repetitive motions?
Pace Determined by Speed of Equipment	How important is it to this job that the pace is determined by the speed of equipment or machinery? (This does not refer to keeping busy at all times on this job.)
Exposed to Hazardous Conditions	How often does this job require exposure to hazardous conditions?
Spend Time Bending or Twisting the Body	How much does this job require bending or twisting your body?
Exposed to Hazardous Equipment	How often does this job require exposure to hazardous equipment?
Sounds, Noise Levels Are Distracting or Uncomforta	How often does this job require working exposed to sounds and noise levels that are distracting or uncomfortable?
Deal With Physically Aggressive People	How frequently does this job require the worker to deal with physical aggression of violent individuals?
Cramped Work Space, Awkward Positions	How often does this job require working in cramped work spaces that requires getting into awkward positions?
Spend Time Kneeling, Crouching, Stooping, or Crawl	How much does this job require kneeling, crouching, stooping or crawling?
Extremely Bright or Inadequate Lighting	How often does this job require working in extremely bright or inadequate lighting conditions?
Exposed to Minor Burns, Cuts, Bites, or Stings	How often does this job require exposure to minor burns, cuts, bites, or stings?
Spend Time Keeping or Regaining Balance	How much does this job require keeping or regaining your balance?
Public Speaking	How often do you have to perform public speaking in this job?
Very Hot or Cold Temperatures	How often does this job require working in very hot (above 90 F degrees) or very cold (below 32 F degrees) temperatures?
In an Enclosed Vehicle or Equipment	How often does this job require working in a closed vehicle or equipment (e.g., car)?
Indoors, Not Environmentally Controlled	How often does this job require working indoors in non-controlled environmental conditions (e.g., warehouse without heat)?
Outdoors, Under Cover	How often does this job require working outdoors, under cover (e.g., structure with roof but no walls)?
Exposed to Whole Body Vibration	How often does this job require exposure to whole body vibration (e.g., operate a jackhammer)?
Outdoors, Exposed to Weather	How often does this job require working outdoors, exposed to all weather conditions?
Exposed to High Places	How often does this job require exposure to high places?
In an Open Vehicle or Equipment	How often does this job require working in an open vehicle or equipment (e.g., tractor)?
Spend Time Climbing Ladders, Scaffolds, or Poles	How much does this job require climbing ladders, scaffolds, or poles?

Job Zone Component	Job Zone Component Definitions
Title	Job Zone Three: Medium Preparation Needed
Overall Experience	Previous work-related skill, knowledge, or experience is required for these occupations. For example, an electrician must have completed three or four years of apprenticeship or several years of vocational training, and often must have passed a licensing exam, in order to perform the job.
Job Training	Employees in these occupations usually need one or two years of training involving both on-the-job experience and informal training with experienced workers.
Job Zone Examples	These occupations usually involve using communication and organizational skills to coordinate, supervise, manage, or train others to accomplish goals. Examples include dental assistants, electricians, fish and game wardens, legal secretaries, personnel recruiters, and recreation workers.
SVP Range	(6.0 to < 7.0)
Education	Most occupations in this zone require training in vocational schools, related on-the-job experience, or an associate's degree. Some may require a bachelor's degree.

Work_Styles	Work_Styles Definitions
Concern for Others	Job requires being sensitive to others' needs and feelings and being understanding and helpful on the job.
Attention to Detail	Job requires being careful about detail and thorough in completing work tasks.
Cooperation	Job requires being pleasant with others on the job and displaying a good-natured, cooperative attitude.
Integrity	Job requires being honest and ethical.
Dependability	Job requires being reliable, responsible, and dependable, and fulfilling obligations.
Self Control	Job requires maintaining composure, keeping emotions in check, controlling anger, and avoiding aggressive behavior, even in very difficult situations.
Independence	Job requires developing one's own ways of doing things, guiding oneself with little or no supervision, and depending on oneself to get things done.
Stress Tolerance	Job requires accepting criticism and dealing calmly and effectively with high stress situations.
Initiative	Job requires a willingness to take on responsibilities and challenges.
Adaptability/Flexibility	Job requires being open to change (positive or negative) and to considerable variety in the workplace.
Social Orientation	Job requires preferring to work with others rather than alone, and being personally connected with others on the job.
Leadership	Job requires a willingness to lead, take charge, and offer opinions and direction.
Analytical Thinking	Job requires analyzing information and using logic to address work-related issues and problems.
Persistence	Job requires persistence in the face of obstacles.
Achievement/Effort	Job requires establishing and maintaining personally challenging achievement goals and exerting effort toward mastering tasks.
Innovation	Job requires creativity and alternative thinking to develop new ideas for and answers to work-related problems.

29-2034.01 - Radiologic Technologists

Take X-rays and CAT scans or administer nonradioactive materials into patient's blood stream for diagnostic purposes. Includes technologists who specialize in other modalities, such as computed tomography, ultrasound, and magnetic resonance.

Tasks

1) Set up examination rooms, ensuring that all necessary equipment is ready.

2) Review and evaluate developed x-rays, video tape, or computer generated information to determine if images are satisfactory for diagnostic purposes.

3) Position and immobilize patient on examining table.

4) Monitor patients' conditions and reactions, reporting abnormal signs to physician.

5) Take thorough and accurate patient medical histories.

6) Use radiation safety measures and protection devices to comply with government regulations and to ensure safety of patients and staff.

7) Explain procedures and observe patients to ensure safety and comfort during scan.

8) Position imaging equipment and adjust controls to set exposure time and distance, according to specification of examination.

9) Monitor video display of area being scanned and adjust density or contrast to improve picture quality.

10) Operate or oversee operation of radiologic and magnetic imaging equipment to produce images of the body for diagnostic purposes.

11) Key commands and data into computer to document and specify scan sequences, adjust transmitters and receivers, or photograph certain images.

12) Remove and process film.

13) Prepare and administer oral or injected contrast media to patients.

14) Provide assistance with such tasks as dressing and changing to seriously ill, injured, or disabled patients.

15) Demonstrate new equipment, procedures, and techniques to staff, and provide technical assistance.

16) Record, process and maintain patient data and treatment records, and prepare reports.

17) Measure thickness of section to be radiographed, using instruments similar to measuring tapes.

18) Assign duties to radiologic staff to maintain patient flows and achieve production goals.

19) Perform scheduled maintenance and minor emergency repairs on radiographic equipment.

20) Collaborate with other medical team members, such as physicians and nurses, to conduct angiography or special vascular procedures.

21) Operate fluoroscope to aid physician to view and guide wire or catheter through blood vessels to area of interest.

22) Perform administrative duties such as developing departmental operating budget, coordinating purchases of supplies and equipment and preparing work schedules.

23) Move ultrasound scanner over patient's body and watch pattern produced on video screen.

Knowledge	Knowledge Definitions
Customer and Personal Service	Knowledge of principles and processes for providing customer and personal services. This includes customer needs assessment, meeting quality standards for services, and evaluation of customer satisfaction.
Medicine and Dentistry	Knowledge of the information and techniques needed to diagnose and treat human injuries, diseases, and deformities. This includes symptoms, treatment alternatives, drug properties and interactions, and preventive health-care measures.
Physics	Knowledge and prediction of physical principles, laws, their interrelationships, and applications to understanding fluid, material, and atmospheric dynamics, and mechanical, electrical, atomic and sub-atomic structures and processes.
Psychology	Knowledge of human behavior and performance; individual differences in ability, personality, and interests; learning and motivation; psychological research methods; and the assessment and treatment of behavioral and affective disorders.
English Language	Knowledge of the structure and content of the English language including the meaning and spelling of words, rules of composition, and grammar.
Computers and Electronics	Knowledge of circuit boards, processors, chips, electronic equipment, and computer hardware and software, including applications and programming.
Mathematics	Knowledge of arithmetic, algebra, geometry, calculus, statistics, and their applications.
Biology	Knowledge of plant and animal organisms, their tissues, cells, functions, interdependencies, and interactions with each other and the environment.
Chemistry	Knowledge of the chemical composition, structure, and properties of substances and of the chemical processes and transformations that they undergo. This includes uses of chemicals and their interactions, danger signs, production techniques, and disposal methods.
Public Safety and Security	Knowledge of relevant equipment, policies, procedures, and strategies to promote effective local, state, or national security operations for the protection of people, data, property, and institutions.
Clerical	Knowledge of administrative and clerical procedures and systems such as word processing, managing files and records, stenography and transcription, designing forms, and other office procedures and terminology.
Education and Training	Knowledge of principles and methods for curriculum and training design, teaching and instruction for individuals and groups, and the measurement of training effects.
Administration and Management	Knowledge of business and management principles involved in strategic planning, resource allocation, human resources modeling, leadership technique, production methods, and coordination of people and resources.
Mechanical	Knowledge of machines and tools, including their designs, uses, repair, and maintenance.
Engineering and Technology	Knowledge of the practical application of engineering science and technology. This includes applying principles, techniques, procedures, and equipment to the design and production of various goods and services.
Therapy and Counseling	Knowledge of principles, methods, and procedures for diagnosis, treatment, and rehabilitation of physical and mental dysfunctions, and for career counseling and guidance.
Foreign Language	Knowledge of the structure and content of a foreign (non-English) language including the meaning and spelling of words, rules of composition and grammar, and pronunciation.
Personnel and Human Resources	Knowledge of principles and procedures for personnel recruitment, selection, training, compensation and benefits, labor relations and negotiation, and personnel information systems.
Production and Processing	Knowledge of raw materials, production processes, quality control, costs, and other techniques for maximizing the effective manufacture and distribution of goods.
Sociology and Anthropology	Knowledge of group behavior and dynamics, societal trends and influences, human migrations, ethnicity, cultures and their history and origins.
Law and Government	Knowledge of laws, legal codes, court procedures, precedents, government regulations, executive orders, agency rules, and the democratic political process.
Communications and Media	Knowledge of media production, communication, and dissemination techniques and methods. This includes alternative ways to inform and entertain via written, oral, and visual media.
Telecommunications	Knowledge of transmission, broadcasting, switching, control, and operation of telecommunications systems.
Economics and Accounting	Knowledge of economic and accounting principles and practices, the financial markets, banking and the analysis and reporting of financial data.
Sales and Marketing	Knowledge of principles and methods for showing, promoting, and selling products or services. This includes marketing strategy and tactics, product demonstration, sales techniques, and sales control systems.
Design	Knowledge of design techniques, tools, and principles involved in production of precision technical plans, blueprints, drawings, and models.
Philosophy and Theology	Knowledge of different philosophical systems and religions. This includes their basic principles, values, ethics, ways of thinking, customs, practices, and their impact on human culture.
Transportation	Knowledge of principles and methods for moving people or goods by air, rail, sea, or road, including the relative costs and benefits.
History and Archeology	Knowledge of historical events and their causes, indicators, and effects on civilizations and cultures.
Geography	Knowledge of principles and methods for describing the features of land, sea, and air masses, including their physical characteristics, locations, interrelationships, and distribution of plant, animal, and human life.
Fine Arts	Knowledge of the theory and techniques required to compose, produce, and perform works of music, dance, visual arts, drama, and sculpture.
Building and Construction	Knowledge of materials, methods, and the tools involved in the construction or repair of houses, buildings, or other structures such as highways and roads.
Food Production	Knowledge of techniques and equipment for planting, growing, and harvesting food products (both plant and animal) for consumption, including storage/handling techniques.

Skills	Skills Definitions
Active Listening	Giving full attention to what other people are saying, taking time to understand the points being made, asking questions as appropriate, and not interrupting at inappropriate times.
Speaking	Talking to others to convey information effectively.
Reading Comprehension	Understanding written sentences and paragraphs in work related documents.
Time Management	Managing one's own time and the time of others.
Critical Thinking	Using logic and reasoning to identify the strengths and weaknesses of alternative solutions, conclusions or approaches to problems.
Instructing	Teaching others how to do something.
Coordination	Adjusting actions in relation to others' actions.
Social Perceptiveness	Being aware of others' reactions and understanding why they react as they do.
Monitoring	Monitoring/Assessing performance of yourself, other individuals, or organizations to make improvements or take corrective action.
Active Learning	Understanding the implications of new information for both current and future problem-solving and decision-making.
Service Orientation	Actively looking for ways to help people.
Learning Strategies	Selecting and using training/instructional methods and procedures appropriate for the situation when learning or teaching new things.
Operation Monitoring	Watching gauges, dials, or other indicators to make sure a machine is working properly.
Troubleshooting	Determining causes of operating errors and deciding what to do about it.
Writing	Communicating effectively in writing as appropriate for the needs of the audience.
Quality Control Analysis	Conducting tests and inspections of products, services, or processes to evaluate quality or performance.

Mathematics	Using mathematics to solve problems.
Operation and Control	Controlling operations of equipment or systems.
Equipment Selection	Determining the kind of tools and equipment needed to do a job.
Science	Using scientific rules and methods to solve problems.
Systems Evaluation	Identifying measures or indicators of system performance and the actions needed to improve or correct performance, relative to the goals of the system.
Equipment Maintenance	Performing routine maintenance on equipment and determining when and what kind of maintenance is needed.
Persuasion	Persuading others to change their minds or behavior.
Judgment and Decision Making	Considering the relative costs and benefits of potential actions to choose the most appropriate one.
Complex Problem Solving	Identifying complex problems and reviewing related information to develop and evaluate options and implement solutions.
Negotiation	Bringing others together and trying to reconcile differences.
Systems Analysis	Determining how a system should work and how changes in conditions, operations, and the environment will affect outcomes.
Management of Personnel Resources	Motivating, developing, and directing people as they work, identifying the best people for the job.
Management of Material Resources	Obtaining and seeing to the appropriate use of equipment, facilities, and materials needed to do certain work.
Operations Analysis	Analyzing needs and product requirements to create a design.
Technology Design	Generating or adapting equipment and technology to serve user needs.
Repairing	Repairing machines or systems using the needed tools.
Programming	Writing computer programs for various purposes.
Installation	Installing equipment, machines, wiring, or programs to meet specifications.
Management of Financial Resources	Determining how money will be spent to get the work done, and accounting for these expenditures.

Ability — Ability Definitions

Near Vision	The ability to see details at close range (within a few feet of the observer).
Oral Comprehension	The ability to listen to and understand information and ideas presented through spoken words and sentences.
Oral Expression	The ability to communicate information and ideas in speaking so others will understand.
Problem Sensitivity	The ability to tell when something is wrong or is likely to go wrong. It does not involve solving the problem, only recognizing there is a problem.
Inductive Reasoning	The ability to combine pieces of information to form general rules or conclusions (includes finding a relationship among seemingly unrelated events).
Control Precision	The ability to quickly and repeatedly adjust the controls of a machine or a vehicle to exact positions.
Speech Clarity	The ability to speak clearly so others can understand you.
Speech Recognition	The ability to identify and understand the speech of another person.
Deductive Reasoning	The ability to apply general rules to specific problems to produce answers that make sense.
Written Expression	The ability to communicate information and ideas in writing so others will understand.
Flexibility of Closure	The ability to identify or detect a known pattern (a figure, object, word, or sound) that is hidden in other distracting material.
Finger Dexterity	The ability to make precisely coordinated movements of the fingers of one or both hands to grasp, manipulate, or assemble very small objects.
Arm-Hand Steadiness	The ability to keep your hand and arm steady while moving your arm or while holding your arm and hand in one position.
Written Comprehension	The ability to read and understand information and ideas presented in writing.
Information Ordering	The ability to arrange things or actions in a certain order or pattern according to a specific rule or set of rules (e.g., patterns of numbers, letters, words, pictures, mathematical operations).
Multilimb Coordination	The ability to coordinate two or more limbs (for example, two arms, two legs, or one leg and one arm) while sitting, standing, or lying down. It does not involve performing the activities while the whole body is in motion.
Manual Dexterity	The ability to quickly move your hand, your hand together with your arm, or your two hands to grasp, manipulate, or assemble objects.
Far Vision	The ability to see details at a distance.

Perceptual Speed	The ability to quickly and accurately compare similarities and differences among sets of letters, numbers, objects, pictures, or patterns. The things to be compared may be presented at the same time or one after the other. This ability also includes comparing a presented object with a remembered object.
Selective Attention	The ability to concentrate on a task over a period of time without being distracted.
Speed of Closure	The ability to quickly make sense of, combine, and organize information into meaningful patterns.
Visual Color Discrimination	The ability to match or detect differences between colors, including shades of color and brightness.
Depth Perception	The ability to judge which of several objects is closer or farther away from you, or to judge the distance between you and an object.
Time Sharing	The ability to shift back and forth between two or more activities or sources of information (such as speech, sounds, touch, or other sources).
Category Flexibility	The ability to generate or use different sets of rules for combining or grouping things in different ways.
Visualization	The ability to imagine how something will look after it is moved around or when its parts are moved or rearranged.
Originality	The ability to come up with unusual or clever ideas about a given topic or situation, or to develop creative ways to solve a problem.
Rate Control	The ability to time your movements or the movement of a piece of equipment in anticipation of changes in the speed and/or direction of a moving object or scene.
Mathematical Reasoning	The ability to choose the right mathematical methods or formulas to solve a problem.
Fluency of Ideas	The ability to come up with a number of ideas about a topic (the number of ideas is important, not their quality, correctness, or creativity).
Memorization	The ability to remember information such as words, numbers, pictures, and procedures.
Reaction Time	The ability to quickly respond (with the hand, finger, or foot) to a signal (sound, light, picture) when it appears.
Hearing Sensitivity	The ability to detect or tell the differences between sounds that vary in pitch and loudness.
Extent Flexibility	The ability to bend, stretch, twist, or reach with your body, arms, and/or legs.
Trunk Strength	The ability to use your abdominal and lower back muscles to support part of the body repeatedly or continuously over time without 'giving out' or fatiguing.
Auditory Attention	The ability to focus on a single source of sound in the presence of other distracting sounds.
Static Strength	The ability to exert maximum muscle force to lift, push, pull, or carry objects.
Stamina	The ability to exert yourself physically over long periods of time without getting winded or out of breath.
Number Facility	The ability to add, subtract, multiply, or divide quickly and correctly.
Response Orientation	The ability to choose quickly between two or more movements in response to two or more different signals (lights, sounds, pictures). It includes the speed with which the correct response is started with the hand, foot, or other body part.
Gross Body Coordination	The ability to coordinate the movement of your arms, legs, and torso together when the whole body is in motion.
Wrist-Finger Speed	The ability to make fast, simple, repeated movements of the fingers, hands, and wrists.
Dynamic Strength	The ability to exert muscle force repeatedly or continuously over time. This involves muscular endurance and resistance to muscle fatigue.
Gross Body Equilibrium	The ability to keep or regain your body balance or stay upright when in an unstable position.
Speed of Limb Movement	The ability to quickly move the arms and legs.
Spatial Orientation	The ability to know your location in relation to the environment or to know where other objects are in relation to you.
Peripheral Vision	The ability to see objects or movement of objects to one's side when the eyes are looking ahead.
Night Vision	The ability to see under low light conditions.
Explosive Strength	The ability to use short bursts of muscle force to propel oneself (as in jumping or sprinting), or to throw an object.
Sound Localization	The ability to tell the direction from which a sound originated.
Dynamic Flexibility	The ability to quickly and repeatedly bend, stretch, twist, or reach out with your body, arms, and/or legs.
Glare Sensitivity	The ability to see objects in the presence of glare or bright lighting.

Work_Activity	Work_Activity Definitions
Assisting and Caring for Others	Providing personal assistance. medical attention. emotional support. or other personal care to others such as coworkers. customers. or patients.
Performing for or Working Directly with the Public	Performing for people or dealing directly with the public. This includes serving customers in restaurants and stores. and receiving clients or guests.
Documenting/Recording Information	Entering. transcribing. recording. storing. or maintaining information in written or electronic/magnetic form.
Communicating with Supervisors, Peers, or Subordin	Providing information to supervisors. co-workers. and subordinates by telephone. in written form. e-mail. or in person.
Interacting With Computers	Using computers and computer systems (including hardware and software) to program. write software. set up functions. enter data, or process information.
Handling and Moving Objects	Using hands and arms in handling. installing. positioning. and moving materials. and manipulating things.
Identifying Objects, Actions, and Events	Identifying information by categorizing. estimating. recognizing differences or similarities. and detecting changes in circumstances or events.
Getting Information	Observing. receiving. and otherwise obtaining information from all relevant sources.
Establishing and Maintaining Interpersonal Relatio	Developing constructive and cooperative working relationships with others. and maintaining them over time.
Performing General Physical Activities	Performing physical activities that require considerable use of your arms and legs and moving your whole body. such as climbing. lifting. balancing. walking. stooping. and handling of materials.
Updating and Using Relevant Knowledge	Keeping up-to-date technically and applying new knowledge to your job.
Controlling Machines and Processes	Using either control mechanisms or direct physical activity to operate machines or processes (not including computers or vehicles).
Making Decisions and Solving Problems	Analyzing information and evaluating results to choose the best solution and solve problems.
Inspecting Equipment, Structures, or Material	Inspecting equipment, structures, or materials to identify the cause of errors or other problems or defects.
Monitor Processes, Materials, or Surroundings	Monitoring and reviewing information from materials, events, or the environment, to detect or assess problems.
Coaching and Developing Others	Identifying the developmental needs of others and coaching, mentoring, or otherwise helping others to improve their knowledge or skills.
Training and Teaching Others	Identifying the educational needs of others, developing formal educational or training programs or classes. and teaching or instructing others.
Processing Information	Compiling, coding, categorizing, calculating, tabulating, auditing, or verifying information or data.
Organizing, Planning, and Prioritizing Work	Developing specific goals and plans to prioritize, organize, and accomplish your work.
Evaluating Information to Determine Compliance wit	Using relevant information and individual judgment to determine whether events or processes comply with laws, regulations, or standards.
Interpreting the Meaning of Information for Others	Translating or explaining what information means and how it can be used.
Thinking Creatively	Developing, designing, or creating new applications, ideas, relationships, systems, or products, including artistic contributions.
Developing and Building Teams	Encouraging and building mutual trust, respect, and cooperation among team members.
Estimating the Quantifiable Characteristics of Pro	Estimating sizes, distances, and quantities; or determining time, costs, resources, or materials needed to perform a work activity.
Coordinating the Work and Activities of Others	Getting members of a group to work together to accomplish tasks.
Resolving Conflicts and Negotiating with Others	Handling complaints, settling disputes, and resolving grievances and conflicts, or otherwise negotiating with others.
Communicating with Persons Outside Organization	Communicating with people outside the organization, representing the organization to customers, the public, government, and other external sources. This information can be exchanged in person, in writing, or by telephone or e-mail.
Repairing and Maintaining Electronic Equipment	Servicing, repairing, calibrating, regulating, fine-tuning, or testing machines, devices, and equipment that operate primarily on the basis of electrical or electronic (not mechanical) principles.
Analyzing Data or Information	Identifying the underlying principles, reasons, or facts of information by breaking down information or data into separate parts.
Developing Objectives and Strategies	Establishing long-range objectives and specifying the strategies and actions to achieve them.
Judging the Qualities of Things, Services, or Peop	Assessing the value, importance, or quality of things or people.
Performing Administrative Activities	Performing day-to-day administrative tasks such as maintaining information files and processing paperwork.
Scheduling Work and Activities	Scheduling events. programs. and activities, as well as the work of others.
Operating Vehicles, Mechanized Devices, or Equipme	Running, maneuvering, navigating, or driving vehicles or mechanized equipment, such as forklifts, passenger vehicles. aircraft, or water craft.
Guiding, Directing, and Motivating Subordinates	Providing guidance and direction to subordinates, including setting performance standards and monitoring performance.
Provide Consultation and Advice to Others	Providing guidance and expert advice to management or other groups on technical, systems-, or process-related topics.
Selling or Influencing Others	Convincing others to buy merchandise/goods or to otherwise change their minds or actions.
Drafting, Laying Out, and Specifying Technical Dev	Providing documentation, detailed instructions, drawings, or specifications to tell others about how devices, parts, equipment, or structures are to be fabricated, constructed, assembled, modified, maintained, or used.
Repairing and Maintaining Mechanical Equipment	Servicing, repairing, adjusting, and testing machines, devices. moving parts, and equipment that operate primarily on the basis of mechanical (not electronic) principles.
Monitoring and Controlling Resources	Monitoring and controlling resources and overseeing the spending of money.
Staffing Organizational Units	Recruiting, interviewing, selecting, hiring, and promoting employees in an organization.

Work_Context	Work_Context Definitions
Exposed to Disease or Infections	How often does this job require exposure to disease/infections?
Telephone	How often do you have telephone conversations in this job?
Indoors, Environmentally Controlled	How often does this job require working indoors in environmentally controlled conditions?
Face-to-Face Discussions	How often do you have to have face-to-face discussions with individuals or teams in this job?
Contact With Others	How much does this job require the worker to be in contact with others (face-to-face, by telephone, or otherwise) in order to perform it?
Deal With External Customers	How important is it to work with external customers or the public in this job?
Work With Work Group or Team	How important is it to work with others in a group or team in this job?
Freedom to Make Decisions	How much decision making freedom, without supervision, does the job offer?
Importance of Being Exact or Accurate	How important is being very exact or highly accurate in performing this job?
Impact of Decisions on Co-workers or Company Resul	How do the decisions an employee makes impact the results of co-workers, clients or the company?
Frequency of Decision Making	How frequently is the worker required to make decisions that affect other people, the financial resources, and/or the image and reputation of the organization?
Physical Proximity	To what extent does this job require the worker to perform job tasks in close physical proximity to other people?
Importance of Repeating Same Tasks	How important is repeating the same physical activities (e.g., key entry) or mental activities (e.g., checking entries in a ledger) over and over, without stopping, to performing this job?
Spend Time Using Your Hands to Handle, Control, or	How much does this job require using your hands to handle. control, or feel objects, tools or controls?
Structured versus Unstructured Work	To what extent is this job structured for the worker, rather than allowing the worker to determine tasks, priorities, and goals?
Responsible for Others' Health and Safety	How much responsibility is there for the health and safety of others in this job?
Deal With Unpleasant or Angry People	How frequently does the worker have to deal with unpleasant. angry, or discourteous individuals as part of the job requirements?
Coordinate or Lead Others	How important is it to coordinate or lead others in accomplishing work activities in this job?
Consequence of Error	How serious would the result usually be if the worker made a mistake that was not readily correctable?
Spend Time Standing	How much does this job require standing?

Spend Time Making Repetitive Motions	How much does this job require making repetitive motions?
Spend Time Walking and Running	How much does this job require walking and running?
Exposed to Contaminants	How often does this job require working exposed to contaminants (such as pollutants, gases, dust or odors)?
Time Pressure	How often does this job require the worker to meet strict deadlines?
Exposed to Radiation	How often does this job require exposure to radiation?
Sounds, Noise Levels Are Distracting or Uncomforta	How often does this job require working exposed to sounds and noise levels that are distracting or uncomfortable?
Wear Specialized Protective or Safety Equipment su	How much does this job require wearing specialized protective or safety equipment such as breathing apparatus, safety harness, full protection suits, or radiation protection?
Cramped Work Space, Awkward Positions	How often does this job require working in cramped work spaces that requires getting into awkward positions?
Frequency of Conflict Situations	How often are there conflict situations the employee has to face in this job?
Responsibility for Outcomes and Results	How responsible is the worker for work outcomes and results of other workers?
Letters and Memos	How often does the job require written letters and memos?
Spend Time Sitting	How much does this job require sitting?
Degree of Automation	How automated is the job?
Pace Determined by Speed of Equipment	How important is it to this job that the pace is determined by the speed of equipment or machinery? (This does not refer to keeping busy at all times on this job.)
Level of Competition	To what extent does this job require the worker to compete or to be aware of competitive pressures?
Spend Time Bending or Twisting the Body	How much does this job require bending or twisting your body?
Electronic Mail	How often do you use electronic mail in this job?
Wear Common Protective or Safety Equipment such as	How much does this job require wearing common protective or safety equipment such as safety shoes, glasses, gloves, hard hats or live jackets?
Deal With Physically Aggressive People	How frequently does this job require the worker to deal with physical aggression of violent individuals?
Exposed to Hazardous Conditions	How often does this job require exposure to hazardous conditions?
Outdoors, Exposed to Weather	How often does this job require working outdoors, exposed to all weather conditions?
Spend Time Kneeling, Crouching, Stooping, or Crawl	How much does this job require kneeling, crouching, stooping, or crawling?
Extremely Bright or Inadequate Lighting	How often does this job require working in extremely bright or inadequate lighting conditions?
Indoors, Not Environmentally Controlled	How often does this job require working indoors in non-controlled environmental conditions (e.g., warehouse without heat)?
Exposed to Hazardous Equipment	How often does this job require exposure to hazardous equipment?
Very Hot or Cold Temperatures	How often does this job require working in very hot (above 90 F degrees) or very cold (below 32 F degrees) temperatures?
Exposed to Minor Burns, Cuts, Bites, or Stings	How often does this job require exposure to minor burns, cuts, bites, or stings?
In an Enclosed Vehicle or Equipment	How often does this job require working in a closed vehicle or equipment (e.g., car)?
Outdoors, Under Cover	How often does this job require working outdoors, under cover (e.g., structure with roof but no walls)?
Public Speaking	How often do you have to perform public speaking in this job?
Spend Time Keeping or Regaining Balance	How much does this job require keeping or regaining your balance?
Exposed to Whole Body Vibration	How often does this job require exposure to whole body vibration (e.g., operate a jackhammer)?
Spend Time Climbing Ladders, Scaffolds, or Poles	How much does this job require climbing ladders, scaffolds, or poles?
Exposed to High Places	How often does this job require exposure to high places?
In an Open Vehicle or Equipment	How often does this job require working in an open vehicle or equipment (e.g., tractor)?

Job Zone Component	Job Zone Component Definitions
Title	Job Zone Three: Medium Preparation Needed

Overall Experience	Previous work-related skill, knowledge, or experience is required for these occupations. For example, an electrician must have completed three or four years of apprenticeship or several years of vocational training, and often must have passed a licensing exam, in order to perform the job.
Job Training	Employees in these occupations usually need one or two years of training involving both on-the-job experience and informal training with experienced workers.
Job Zone Examples	These occupations usually involve using communication and organizational skills to coordinate, supervise, manage, or train others to accomplish goals. Examples include dental assistants, electricians, fish and game wardens, legal secretaries, personnel recruiters, and recreation workers.
SVP Range	(6.0 to < 7.0)
Education	Most occupations in this zone require training in vocational schools, related on-the-job experience, or an associate's degree. Some may require a bachelor's degree.

Work_Styles	Work_Styles Definitions
Dependability	Job requires being reliable, responsible, and dependable, and fulfilling obligations.
Attention to Detail	Job requires being careful about detail and thorough in completing work tasks.
Integrity	Job requires being honest and ethical.
Cooperation	Job requires being pleasant with others on the job and displaying a good-natured, cooperative attitude.
Self Control	Job requires maintaining composure, keeping emotions in check, controlling anger, and avoiding aggressive behavior, even in very difficult situations.
Concern for Others	Job requires being sensitive to others' needs and feelings and being understanding and helpful on the job.
Initiative	Job requires a willingness to take on responsibilities and challenges.
Stress Tolerance	Job requires accepting criticism and dealing calmly and effectively with high stress situations.
Adaptability/Flexibility	Job requires being open to change (positive or negative) and to considerable variety in the workplace.
Persistence	Job requires persistence in the face of obstacles.
Social Orientation	Job requires preferring to work with others rather than alone, and being personally connected with others on the job.
Independence	Job requires developing one's own ways of doing things, guiding oneself with little or no supervision, and depending on oneself to get things done.
Innovation	Job requires creativity and alternative thinking to develop new ideas for and answers to work-related problems.
Analytical Thinking	Job requires analyzing information and using logic to address work-related issues and problems.
Achievement/Effort	Job requires establishing and maintaining personally challenging achievement goals and exerting effort toward mastering tasks.
Leadership	Job requires a willingness to lead, take charge, and offer opinions and direction.

29-2034.02 - Radiologic Technicians

Maintain and use equipment and supplies necessary to demonstrate portions the human body on X-ray film or fluoroscopic screen for diagnostic purposes.

Tasks

1) Position x-ray equipment and adjust controls to set exposure factors, such as time and distance.

2) Process exposed radiographs using film processors or computer generated methods.

3) Provide students and other technologists with suggestions of additional views, alternate positioning or improved techniques to ensure the images produced are of the highest quality.

4) Maintain records of patients examined, examinations performed, views taken, and technical factors used.

5) Assist with on-the-job training of new employees and students, and provide input to supervisors regarding training performance.

6) Provide assistance to physicians or other technologists in the performance of more complex procedures.

7) Maintain a current file of examination protocols.

8) Coordinate work of other technicians or technologists when procedures require more than one person.

9) Assure that sterile supplies, contrast materials, catheters, and other required equipment are present and in working order, requisitioning materials as necessary.

10) Perform procedures such as linear tomography, mammography, sonograms, joint and cyst aspirations, routine contrast studies, routine fluoroscopy and examinations of the head, trunk, and extremities under supervision of physician.

11) Prepare contast material, radiopharmaceuticals and anesthetic or antispasmodic drugs under the direction of a radiologist.

12) Provide assistance in radiopharmaceutical administration, monitoring patients' vital signs and notifying the radiologist of any relevant changes.

13) Operate mobile x-ray equipment in operating room, emergency room, or at patient's bedside.

14) Operate digital picture archiving communications systems.

15) Determine patients' x-ray needs by reading requests or instructions from physicians.

16) Explain procedures to patients to reduce anxieties and obtain cooperation.

17) Monitor equipment operation and report malfunctioning equipment to supervisor.

18) Make exposures necessary for the requested procedures, rejecting and repeating work that does not meet established standards.

19) Position patient on examining table and set up and adjust equipment to obtain optimum view of specific body area as requested by physician.

20) Use beam-restrictive devices and patient-shielding techniques to minimize radiation exposure to patient and staff.

Knowledge / Knowledge Definitions

English Language — Knowledge of the structure and content of the English language including the meaning and spelling of words, rules of composition, and grammar.

Customer and Personal Service — Knowledge of principles and processes for providing customer and personal services. This includes customer needs assessment, meeting quality standards for services, and evaluation of customer satisfaction.

Clerical — Knowledge of administrative and clerical procedures and systems such as word processing, managing files and records, stenography and transcription, designing forms, and other office procedures and terminology.

Psychology — Knowledge of human behavior and performance; individual differences in ability, personality, and interests; learning and motivation; psychological research methods; and the assessment and treatment of behavioral and affective disorders.

Medicine and Dentistry — Knowledge of the information and techniques needed to diagnose and treat human injuries, diseases, and deformities. This includes symptoms, treatment alternatives, drug properties and interactions, and preventive health-care measures.

Mathematics — Knowledge of arithmetic, algebra, geometry, calculus, statistics, and their applications.

Physics — Knowledge and prediction of physical principles, laws, their interrelationships, and applications to understanding fluid, material, and atmospheric dynamics, and mechanical, electrical, atomic and sub-atomic structures and processes.

Public Safety and Security — Knowledge of relevant equipment, policies, procedures, and strategies to promote effective local, state, or national security operations for the protection of people, data, property, and institutions.

Education and Training — Knowledge of principles and methods for curriculum and training design, teaching and instruction for individuals and groups, and the measurement of training effects.

Biology — Knowledge of plant and animal organisms, their tissues, cells, functions, interdependencies, and interactions with each other and the environment.

Personnel and Human Resources — Knowledge of principles and procedures for personnel recruitment, selection, training, compensation and benefits, labor relations and negotiation, and personnel information systems.

Chemistry — Knowledge of the chemical composition, structure, and properties of substances and of the chemical processes and transformations that they undergo. This includes uses of chemicals and their interactions, danger signs, production techniques, and disposal methods.

Computers and Electronics — Knowledge of circuit boards, processors, chips, electronic equipment, and computer hardware and software, including applications and programming.

Production and Processing — Knowledge of raw materials, production processes, quality control, costs, and other techniques for maximizing the effective manufacture and distribution of goods.

Mechanical — Knowledge of machines and tools, including their designs, uses, repair, and maintenance.

Telecommunications — Knowledge of transmission, broadcasting, switching, control, and operation of telecommunications systems.

Law and Government — Knowledge of laws, legal codes, court procedures, precedents, government regulations, executive orders, agency rules, and the democratic political process.

Engineering and Technology — Knowledge of the practical application of engineering science and technology. This includes applying principles, techniques, procedures, and equipment to the design and production of various goods and services.

Administration and Management — Knowledge of business and management principles involved in strategic planning, resource allocation, human resources modeling, leadership technique, production methods, and coordination of people and resources.

Therapy and Counseling — Knowledge of principles, methods, and procedures for diagnosis, treatment, and rehabilitation of physical and mental dysfunctions, and for career counseling and guidance.

Communications and Media — Knowledge of media production, communication, and dissemination techniques and methods. This includes alternative ways to inform and entertain via written, oral, and visual media.

Transportation — Knowledge of principles and methods for moving people or goods by air, rail, sea, or road, including the relative costs and benefits.

Sales and Marketing — Knowledge of principles and methods for showing, promoting, and selling products or services. This includes marketing strategy and tactics, product demonstration, sales techniques, and sales control systems.

Foreign Language — Knowledge of the structure and content of a foreign (non-English) language including the meaning and spelling of words, rules of composition and grammar, and pronunciation.

Philosophy and Theology — Knowledge of different philosophical systems and religions. This includes their basic principles, values, ethics, ways of thinking, customs, practices, and their impact on human culture.

Design — Knowledge of design techniques, tools, and principles involved in production of precision technical plans, blueprints, drawings, and models.

Sociology and Anthropology — Knowledge of group behavior and dynamics, societal trends and influences, human migrations, ethnicity, cultures and their history and origins.

History and Archeology — Knowledge of historical events and their causes, indicators, and effects on civilizations and cultures.

Economics and Accounting — Knowledge of economic and accounting principles and practices, the financial markets, banking and the analysis and reporting of financial data.

Building and Construction — Knowledge of materials, methods, and the tools involved in the construction or repair of houses, buildings, or other structures such as highways and roads.

Geography — Knowledge of principles and methods for describing the features of land, sea, and air masses, including their physical characteristics, locations, interrelationships, and distribution of plant, animal, and human life.

Fine Arts — Knowledge of the theory and techniques required to compose, produce, and perform works of music, dance, visual arts, drama, and sculpture.

Food Production — Knowledge of techniques and equipment for planting, growing, and harvesting food products (both plant and animal) for consumption, including storage/handling techniques.

Skills / Skills Definitions

Active Listening — Giving full attention to what other people are saying, taking time to understand the points being made, asking questions as appropriate, and not interrupting at inappropriate times.

Reading Comprehension — Understanding written sentences and paragraphs in work related documents.

Speaking — Talking to others to convey information effectively.

Critical Thinking — Using logic and reasoning to identify the strengths and weaknesses of alternative solutions, conclusions or approaches to problems.

Writing	Communicating effectively in writing as appropriate for the needs of the audience.
Instructing	Teaching others how to do something.
Service Orientation	Actively looking for ways to help people.
Learning Strategies	Selecting and using training/instructional methods and procedures appropriate for the situation when learning or teaching new things.
Active Learning	Understanding the implications of new information for both current and future problem-solving and decision-making.
Coordination	Adjusting actions in relation to others' actions.
Science	Using scientific rules and methods to solve problems.
Operation Monitoring	Watching gauges, dials, or other indicators to make sure a machine is working properly.
Social Perceptiveness	Being aware of others' reactions and understanding why they react as they do.
Time Management	Managing one's own time and the time of others.
Troubleshooting	Determining causes of operating errors and deciding what to do about it.
Monitoring	Monitoring/Assessing performance of yourself, other individuals, or organizations to make improvements or take corrective action.
Equipment Selection	Determining the kind of tools and equipment needed to do a job.
Complex Problem Solving	Identifying complex problems and reviewing related information to develop and evaluate options and implement solutions.
Operation and Control	Controlling operations of equipment or systems.
Mathematics	Using mathematics to solve problems.
Judgment and Decision Making	Considering the relative costs and benefits of potential actions to choose the most appropriate one.
Persuasion	Persuading others to change their minds or behavior.
Equipment Maintenance	Performing routine maintenance on equipment and determining when and what kind of maintenance is needed.
Negotiation	Bringing others together and trying to reconcile differences.
Quality Control Analysis	Conducting tests and inspections of products, services, or processes to evaluate quality or performance.
Operations Analysis	Analyzing needs and product requirements to create a design.
Systems Evaluation	Identifying measures or indicators of system performance and the actions needed to improve or correct performance, relative to the goals of the system.
Technology Design	Generating or adapting equipment and technology to serve user needs.
Management of Personnel Resources	Motivating, developing, and directing people as they work, identifying the best people for the job.
Management of Material Resources	Obtaining and seeing to the appropriate use of equipment, facilities, and materials needed to do certain work.
Systems Analysis	Determining how a system should work and how changes in conditions, operations, and the environment will affect outcomes.
Management of Financial Resources	Determining how money will be spent to get the work done, and accounting for these expenditures.
Installation	Installing equipment, machines, wiring, or programs to meet specifications.
Programming	Writing computer programs for various purposes.
Repairing	Repairing machines or systems using the needed tools.

Ability	Ability Definitions
Problem Sensitivity	The ability to tell when something is wrong or is likely to go wrong. It does not involve solving the problem, only recognizing there is a problem.
Oral Comprehension	The ability to listen to and understand information and ideas presented through spoken words and sentences.
Control Precision	The ability to quickly and repeatedly adjust the controls of a machine or a vehicle to exact positions.
Written Comprehension	The ability to read and understand information and ideas presented in writing.
Oral Expression	The ability to communicate information and ideas in speaking so others will understand.
Speech Clarity	The ability to speak clearly so others can understand you.
Speech Recognition	The ability to identify and understand the speech of another person.
Arm-Hand Steadiness	The ability to keep your hand and arm steady while moving your arm or while holding your arm and hand in one position.
Information Ordering	The ability to arrange things or actions in a certain order or pattern according to a specific rule or set of rules (e.g., patterns of numbers, letters, words, pictures, mathematical operations).

Near Vision	The ability to see details at close range (within a few feet of the observer).
Deductive Reasoning	The ability to apply general rules to specific problems to produce answers that make sense.
Manual Dexterity	The ability to quickly move your hand, your hand together with your arm, or your two hands to grasp, manipulate, or assemble objects.
Extent Flexibility	The ability to bend, stretch, twist, or reach with your body, arms, and/or legs.
Selective Attention	The ability to concentrate on a task over a period of time without being distracted.
Written Expression	The ability to communicate information and ideas in writing so others will understand.
Multilimb Coordination	The ability to coordinate two or more limbs (for example, two arms, two legs, or one leg and one arm) while sitting, standing, or lying down. It does not involve performing the activities while the whole body is in motion.
Inductive Reasoning	The ability to combine pieces of information to form general rules or conclusions (includes finding a relationship among seemingly unrelated events).
Time Sharing	The ability to shift back and forth between two or more activities or sources of information (such as speech, sounds, touch, or other sources).
Visualization	The ability to imagine how something will look after it is moved around or when its parts are moved or rearranged.
Finger Dexterity	The ability to make precisely coordinated movements of the fingers of one or both hands to grasp, manipulate, or assemble very small objects.
Flexibility of Closure	The ability to identify or detect a known pattern (a figure, object, word, or sound) that is hidden in other distracting material.
Trunk Strength	The ability to use your abdominal and lower back muscles to support part of the body repeatedly or continuously over time without 'giving out' or fatiguing.
Gross Body Coordination	The ability to coordinate the movement of your arms, legs, and torso together when the whole body is in motion.
Stamina	The ability to exert yourself physically over long periods of time without getting winded or out of breath.
Perceptual Speed	The ability to quickly and accurately compare similarities and differences among sets of letters, numbers, objects, pictures, or patterns. The things to be compared may be presented at the same time or one after the other. This ability also includes comparing a presented object with a remembered object.
Static Strength	The ability to exert maximum muscle force to lift, push, pull, or carry objects.
Reaction Time	The ability to quickly respond (with the hand, finger, or foot) to a signal (sound, light, picture) when it appears.
Depth Perception	The ability to judge which of several objects is closer or farther away from you, or to judge the distance between you and an object.
Category Flexibility	The ability to generate or use different sets of rules for combining or grouping things in different ways.
Originality	The ability to come up with unusual or clever ideas about a given topic or situation, or to develop creative ways to solve a problem.
Dynamic Strength	The ability to exert muscle force repeatedly or continuously over time. This involves muscular endurance and resistance to muscle fatigue.
Memorization	The ability to remember information such as words, numbers, pictures, and procedures.
Speed of Closure	The ability to quickly make sense of, combine, and organize information into meaningful patterns.
Fluency of Ideas	The ability to come up with a number of ideas about a topic (the number of ideas is important, not their quality, correctness, or creativity).
Response Orientation	The ability to choose quickly between two or more movements in response to two or more different signals (lights, sounds, pictures). It includes the speed with which the correct response is started with the hand, foot, or other body part.
Far Vision	The ability to see details at a distance.
Visual Color Discrimination	The ability to match or detect differences between colors, including shades of color and brightness.
Speed of Limb Movement	The ability to quickly move the arms and legs.
Number Facility	The ability to add, subtract, multiply, or divide quickly and correctly.
Glare Sensitivity	The ability to see objects in the presence of glare or bright lighting.

Hearing Sensitivity	The ability to detect or tell the differences between sounds that vary in pitch and loudness.
Gross Body Equilibrium	The ability to keep or regain your body balance or stay upright when in an unstable position.
Explosive Strength	The ability to use short bursts of muscle force to propel oneself (as in jumping or sprinting), or to throw an object.
Mathematical Reasoning	The ability to choose the right mathematical methods or formulas to solve a problem.
Wrist-Finger Speed	The ability to make fast, simple, repeated movements of the fingers, hands, and wrists.
Spatial Orientation	The ability to know your location in relation to the environment or to know where other objects are in relation to you.
Auditory Attention	The ability to focus on a single source of sound in the presence of other distracting sounds.
Rate Control	The ability to time your movements or the movement of a piece of equipment in anticipation of changes in the speed and/or direction of a moving object or scene.
Dynamic Flexibility	The ability to quickly and repeatedly bend, stretch, twist, or reach out with your body, arms, and/or legs.
Sound Localization	The ability to tell the direction from which a sound originated.
Peripheral Vision	The ability to see objects or movement of objects to one's side when the eyes are looking ahead.
Night Vision	The ability to see under low light conditions.

Work_Activity	Work_Activity Definitions
Assisting and Caring for Others	Providing personal assistance, medical attention, emotional support, or other personal care to others such as coworkers, customers, or patients.
Getting Information	Observing, receiving, and otherwise obtaining information from all relevant sources.
Updating and Using Relevant Knowledge	Keeping up-to-date technically and applying new knowledge to your job.
Performing for or Working Directly with the Public	Performing for people or dealing directly with the public. This includes serving customers in restaurants and stores, and receiving clients or guests.
Performing General Physical Activities	Performing physical activities that require considerable use of your arms and legs and moving your whole body, such as climbing, lifting, balancing, walking, stooping, and handling of materials.
Establishing and Maintaining Interpersonal Relatio	Developing constructive and cooperative working relationships with others, and maintaining them over time.
Making Decisions and Solving Problems	Analyzing information and evaluating results to choose the best solution and solve problems.
Handling and Moving Objects	Using hands and arms in handling, installing, positioning, and moving materials, and manipulating things.
Monitor Processes, Materials, or Surroundings	Monitoring and reviewing information from materials, events, or the environment, to detect or assess problems.
Communicating with Supervisors, Peers, or Subordin	Providing information to supervisors, co-workers, and subordinates by telephone, in written form, e-mail, or in person.
Controlling Machines and Processes	Using either control mechanisms or direct physical activity to operate machines or processes (not including computers or vehicles).
Evaluating Information to Determine Compliance wit	Using relevant information and individual judgment to determine whether events or processes comply with laws, regulations, or standards.
Interacting With Computers	Using computers and computer systems (including hardware and software) to program, write software, set up functions, enter data, or process information.
Inspecting Equipment, Structures, or Material	Inspecting equipment, structures, or materials to identify the cause of errors or other problems or defects.
Developing and Building Teams	Encouraging and building mutual trust, respect, and cooperation among team members.
Interpreting the Meaning of Information for Others	Translating or explaining what information means and how it can be used.
Processing Information	Compiling, coding, categorizing, calculating, tabulating, auditing, or verifying information or data.
Documenting/Recording Information	Entering, transcribing, recording, storing, or maintaining information in written or electronic/magnetic form.
Communicating with Persons Outside Organization	Communicating with people outside the organization, representing the organization to customers, the public, government, and other external sources. This information can be exchanged in person, in writing, or by telephone or e-mail.

Identifying Objects, Actions, and Events	Identifying information by categorizing, estimating, recognizing differences or similarities, and detecting changes in circumstances or events.
Judging the Qualities of Things, Services, or Peop	Assessing the value, importance, or quality of things or people.
Analyzing Data or Information	Identifying the underlying principles, reasons, or facts of information by breaking down information or data into separate parts.
Thinking Creatively	Developing, designing, or creating new applications, ideas, relationships, systems, or products, including artistic contributions.
Organizing, Planning, and Prioritizing Work	Developing specific goals and plans to prioritize, organize, and accomplish your work.
Estimating the Quantifiable Characteristics of Pro	Estimating sizes, distances, and quantities; or determining time, costs, resources, or materials needed to perform a work activity.
Performing Administrative Activities	Performing day-to-day administrative tasks such as maintaining information files and processing paperwork.
Coaching and Developing Others	Identifying the developmental needs of others and coaching, mentoring, or otherwise helping others to improve their knowledge or skills.
Developing Objectives and Strategies	Establishing long-range objectives and specifying the strategies and actions to achieve them.
Resolving Conflicts and Negotiating with Others	Handling complaints, settling disputes, and resolving grievances and conflicts, or otherwise negotiating with others.
Coordinating the Work and Activities of Others	Getting members of a group to work together to accomplish tasks.
Selling or Influencing Others	Convincing others to buy merchandise/goods or to otherwise change their minds or actions.
Training and Teaching Others	Identifying the educational needs of others, developing formal educational or training programs or classes, and teaching or instructing others.
Scheduling Work and Activities	Scheduling events, programs, and activities, as well as the work of others.
Operating Vehicles, Mechanized Devices, or Equipme	Running, maneuvering, navigating, or driving vehicles or mechanized equipment, such as forklifts, passenger vehicles, aircraft, or water craft.
Repairing and Maintaining Electronic Equipment	Servicing, repairing, calibrating, regulating, fine-tuning, or testing machines, devices, and equipment that operate primarily on the basis of electrical or electronic (not mechanical) principles.
Provide Consultation and Advice to Others	Providing guidance and expert advice to management or other groups on technical, systems-, or process-related topics.
Repairing and Maintaining Mechanical Equipment	Servicing, repairing, adjusting, and testing machines, devices, moving parts, and equipment that operate primarily on the basis of mechanical (not electronic) principles.
Guiding, Directing, and Motivating Subordinates	Providing guidance and direction to subordinates, including setting performance standards and monitoring performance.
Drafting, Laying Out, and Specifying Technical Dev	Providing documentation, detailed instructions, drawings, or specifications to tell others about how devices, parts, equipment, or structures are to be fabricated, constructed, assembled, modified, maintained, or used.
Monitoring and Controlling Resources	Monitoring and controlling resources and overseeing the spending of money.
Staffing Organizational Units	Recruiting, interviewing, selecting, hiring, and promoting employees in an organization.

Work_Context	Work_Context Definitions
Telephone	How often do you have telephone conversations in this job?
Contact With Others	How much does this job require the worker to be in contact with others (face-to-face, by telephone, or otherwise) in order to perform it?
Indoors, Environmentally Controlled	How often does this job require working indoors in environmentally controlled conditions?
Exposed to Disease or Infections	How often does this job require exposure to disease/infections?
Work With Work Group or Team	How important is it to work with others in a group or team in this job?
Importance of Being Exact or Accurate	How important is being very exact or highly accurate in performing this job?
Frequency of Decision Making	How frequently is the worker required to make decisions that affect other people, the financial resources, and/or the image and reputation of the organization?
Face-to-Face Discussions	How often do you have to have face-to-face discussions with individuals or teams in this job?

Spend Time Using Your Hands to Handle, Control, or	How much does this job require using your hands to handle, control, or feel objects, tools or controls?
Freedom to Make Decisions	How much decision making freedom, without supervision, does the job offer?
Physical Proximity	To what extent does this job require the worker to perform job tasks in close physical proximity to other people?
Spend Time Standing	How much does this job require standing?
Exposed to Radiation	How often does this job require exposure to radiation?
Deal With External Customers	How important is it to work with external customers or the public in this job?
Impact of Decisions on Co-workers or Company Resul	How do the decisions an employee makes impact the results of co-workers, clients or the company?
Spend Time Walking and Running	How much does this job require walking and running?
Spend Time Bending or Twisting the Body	How much does this job require bending or twisting your body?
Wear Specialized Protective or Safety Equipment su	How much does this job require wearing specialized protective or safety equipment such as breathing apparatus, safety harness, full protection suits, or radiation protection?
Responsible for Others' Health and Safety	How much responsibility is there for the health and safety of others in this job?
Structured versus Unstructured Work	To what extent is this job structured for the worker, rather than allowing the worker to determine tasks, priorities, and goals?
Spend Time Making Repetitive Motions	How much does this job require making repetitive motions?
Coordinate or Lead Others	How important is it to coordinate or lead others in accomplishing work activities in this job?
Importance of Repeating Same Tasks	How important is repeating the same physical activities (e.g., key entry) or mental activities (e.g., checking entries in a ledger) over and over, without stopping, to performing this job?
Deal With Unpleasant or Angry People	How frequently does the worker have to deal with unpleasant, angry, or discourteous individuals as part of the job requirements?
Time Pressure	How often does this job require the worker to meet strict deadlines?
Exposed to Contaminants	How often does this job require working exposed to contaminants (such as pollutants, gases, dust or odors)?
Consequence of Error	How serious would the result usually be if the worker made a mistake that was not readily correctable?
Wear Common Protective or Safety Equipment such as	How much does this job require wearing common protective or safety equipment such as safety shoes, glasses, gloves, hard hats or live jackets?
Frequency of Conflict Situations	How often are there conflict situations the employee has to face in this job?
Degree of Automation	How automated is the job?
Exposed to Hazardous Conditions	How often does this job require exposure to hazardous conditions?
Deal With Physically Aggressive People	How frequently does this job require the worker to deal with physical aggression of violent individuals?
Letters and Memos	How often does the job require written letters and memos?
Responsibility for Outcomes and Results	How responsible is the worker for work outcomes and results of other workers?
Extremely Bright or Inadequate Lighting	How often does this job require working in extremely bright or inadequate lighting conditions?
Spend Time Kneeling, Crouching, Stooping, or Crawl	How much does this job require kneeling, crouching, stooping or crawling?
Level of Competition	To what extent does this job require the worker to compete or to be aware of competitive pressures?
Exposed to Hazardous Equipment	How often does this job require exposure to hazardous equipment?
Cramped Work Space, Awkward Positions	How often does this job require working in cramped work spaces that requires getting into awkward positions?
Electronic Mail	How often do you use electronic mail in this job?
Sounds, Noise Levels Are Distracting or Uncomforta	How often does this job require working exposed to sounds and noise levels that are distracting or uncomfortable?
Spend Time Keeping or Regaining Balance	How much does this job require keeping or regaining your balance?
Spend Time Sitting	How much does this job require sitting?
Exposed to Minor Burns, Cuts, Bites, or Stings	How often does this job require exposure to minor burns, cuts, bites, or stings?
Pace Determined by Speed of Equipment	How important is it to this job that the pace is determined by the speed of equipment or machinery? (This does not refer to keeping busy at all times in this job.)
Very Hot or Cold Temperatures	How often does this job require working in very hot (above 90 F degrees) or very cold (below 32 F degrees) temperatures?

Public Speaking	How often do you have to perform public speaking in this job?
In an Enclosed Vehicle or Equipment	How often does this job require working in a closed vehicle or equipment (e.g., car)?
Indoors, Not Environmentally Controlled	How often does this job require working indoors in non-controlled environmental conditions (e.g., warehouse without heat)?
Outdoors, Exposed to Weather	How often does this job require working outdoors, exposed to all weather conditions?
Outdoors, Under Cover	How often does this job require working outdoors, under cover (e.g., structure with roof but no walls)?
Exposed to Whole Body Vibration	How often does this job require exposure to whole body vibration (e.g., operate a jackhammer)?
In an Open Vehicle or Equipment	How often does this job require working in an open vehicle or equipment (e.g., tractor)?
Exposed to High Places	How often does this job require exposure to high places?
Spend Time Climbing Ladders, Scaffolds, or Poles	How much does this job require climbing ladders, scaffolds, or poles?

Job Zone Component	Job Zone Component Definitions
Title	Job Zone Three: Medium Preparation Needed
Overall Experience	Previous work-related skill, knowledge, or experience is required for these occupations. For example, an electrician must have completed three or four years of apprenticeship or several years of vocational training, and often must have passed a licensing exam, in order to perform the job.
Job Training	Employees in these occupations usually need one or two years of training involving both on-the-job experience and informal training with experienced workers.
Job Zone Examples	These occupations usually involve using communication and organizational skills to coordinate, supervise, manage, or train others to accomplish goals. Examples include dental assistants, electricians, fish and game wardens, legal secretaries, personnel recruiters, and recreation workers.
SVP Range	(6.0 to < 7.0)
Education	Most occupations in this zone require training in vocational schools, related on-the-job experience, or an associate's degree. Some may require a bachelor's degree.

Work_Styles	Work_Styles Definitions
Dependability	Job requires being reliable, responsible, and dependable, and fulfilling obligations.
Attention to Detail	Job requires being careful about detail and thorough in completing work tasks.
Integrity	Job requires being honest and ethical.
Self Control	Job requires maintaining composure, keeping emotions in check, controlling anger, and avoiding aggressive behavior, even in very difficult situations.
Concern for Others	Job requires being sensitive to others' needs and feelings and being understanding and helpful on the job.
Initiative	Job requires a willingness to take on responsibilities and challenges.
Persistence	Job requires persistence in the face of obstacles.
Stress Tolerance	Job requires accepting criticism and dealing calmly and effectively with high stress situations.
Cooperation	Job requires being pleasant with others on the job and displaying a good-natured, cooperative attitude.
Adaptability/Flexibility	Job requires being open to change (positive or negative) and to considerable variety in the workplace.
Independence	Job requires developing one's own ways of doing things, guiding oneself with little or no supervision, and depending on oneself to get things done.
Social Orientation	Job requires preferring to work with others rather than alone, and being personally connected with others on the job.
Innovation	Job requires creativity and alternative thinking to develop new ideas for and answers to work-related problems.
Achievement/Effort	Job requires establishing and maintaining personally challenging achievement goals and exerting effort toward mastering tasks.
Leadership	Job requires a willingness to lead, take charge, and offer opinions and direction.
Analytical Thinking	Job requires analyzing information and using logic to address work-related issues and problems.

29-2041.00 - Emergency Medical Technicians and Paramedics

Assess injuries. administer emergency medical care. and extricate trapped individuals. Transport injured or sick persons to medical facilities.

Tasks

1) Coordinate work with other emergency medical team members and police and fire department personnel.

2) Maintain vehicles and medical and communication equipment, and replenish first-aid equipment and supplies.

3) Operate equipment such as EKGs, external defibrillators and bag-valve mask resuscitators in advanced life-support environments.

4) Communicate with dispatchers and treatment center personnel to provide information about situation, to arrange reception of victims, and to receive instructions for further treatment.

5) Coordinate with treatment center personnel to obtain patients' vital statistics and medical history, to determine the circumstances of the emergency, and to administer emergency treatment.

6) Observe, record, and report to physician the patient's condition or injury, the treatment provided, and reactions to drugs and treatment.

7) Administer drugs, orally or by injection, and perform intravenous procedures under a physician's direction.

8) Perform emergency diagnostic and treatment procedures, such as stomach suction, airway management and heart monitoring, during ambulance ride.

9) Decontaminate ambulance interior following treatment of patient with infectious disease and report case to proper authorities.

10) Drive mobile intensive care unit to specified location, following instructions from emergency medical dispatcher.

11) Assess nature and extent of illness or injury to establish and prioritize medical procedures.

12) Comfort and reassure patients.

13) Administer first-aid treatment and life-support care to sick or injured persons in prehospital setting.

Knowledge	Knowledge Definitions
Customer and Personal Service	Knowledge of principles and processes for providing customer and personal services. This includes customer needs assessment, meeting quality standards for services, and evaluation of customer satisfaction.
Medicine and Dentistry	Knowledge of the information and techniques needed to diagnose and treat human injuries, diseases, and deformities. This includes symptoms, treatment alternatives, drug properties and interactions, and preventive health-care measures.
Public Safety and Security	Knowledge of relevant equipment, policies, procedures, and strategies to promote effective local, state, or national security operations for the protection of people, data, property, and institutions.
Education and Training	Knowledge of principles and methods for curriculum and training design, teaching and instruction for individuals and groups, and the measurement of training effects.
Chemistry	Knowledge of the chemical composition, structure, and properties of substances and of the chemical processes and transformations that they undergo. This includes uses of chemicals and their interactions, danger signs, production techniques, and disposal methods.
Mathematics	Knowledge of arithmetic, algebra, geometry, calculus, statistics, and their applications.
English Language	Knowledge of the structure and content of the English language including the meaning and spelling of words, rules of composition, and grammar.
Psychology	Knowledge of human behavior and performance; individual differences in ability, personality, and interests; learning and motivation; psychological research methods; and the assessment and treatment of behavioral and affective disorders.
Administration and Management	Knowledge of business and management principles involved in strategic planning, resource allocation, human resources modeling, leadership technique, production methods, and coordination of people and resources.
Biology	Knowledge of plant and animal organisms, their tissues, cells, functions, interdependencies, and interactions with each other and the environment.
Personnel and Human Resources	Knowledge of principles and procedures for personnel recruitment, selection, training, compensation and benefits, labor relations and negotiation, and personnel information systems.
Law and Government	Knowledge of laws, legal codes, court procedures, precedents, government regulations, executive orders, agency rules, and the democratic political process.
Transportation	Knowledge of principles and methods for moving people or goods by air, rail, sea, or road, including the relative costs and benefits.
Mechanical	Knowledge of machines and tools, including their designs, uses, repair, and maintenance.
Therapy and Counseling	Knowledge of principles, methods, and procedures for diagnosis, treatment, and rehabilitation of physical and mental dysfunctions, and for career counseling and guidance.
Physics	Knowledge and prediction of physical principles, laws, their interrelationships, and applications to understanding fluid, material, and atmospheric dynamics, and mechanical, electrical, atomic and sub- atomic structures and processes.
Telecommunications	Knowledge of transmission, broadcasting, switching, control, and operation of telecommunications systems.
Communications and Media	Knowledge of media production, communication, and dissemination techniques and methods. This includes alternative ways to inform and entertain via written, oral, and visual media.
Computers and Electronics	Knowledge of circuit boards, processors, chips, electronic equipment, and computer hardware and software, including applications and programming.
Building and Construction	Knowledge of materials, methods, and the tools involved in the construction or repair of houses, buildings, or other structures such as highways and roads.
Clerical	Knowledge of administrative and clerical procedures and systems such as word processing, managing files and records, stenography and transcription, designing forms, and other office procedures and terminology.
Geography	Knowledge of principles and methods for describing the features of land, sea, and air masses, including their physical characteristics, locations, interrelationships, and distribution of plant, animal, and human life.
Engineering and Technology	Knowledge of the practical application of engineering science and technology. This includes applying principles, techniques, procedures, and equipment to the design and production of various goods and services.
Sociology and Anthropology	Knowledge of group behavior and dynamics, societal trends and influences, human migrations, ethnicity, cultures and their history and origins.
Foreign Language	Knowledge of the structure and content of a foreign (non-English) language including the meaning and spelling of words, rules of composition and grammar, and pronunciation.
Economics and Accounting	Knowledge of economic and accounting principles and practices, the financial markets, banking and the analysis and reporting of financial data.
Philosophy and Theology	Knowledge of different philosophical systems and religions. This includes their basic principles, values, ethics, ways of thinking, customs, practices, and their impact on human culture.
Production and Processing	Knowledge of raw materials, production processes, quality control, costs, and other techniques for maximizing the effective manufacture and distribution of goods.
Design	Knowledge of design techniques, tools, and principles involved in production of precision technical plans, blueprints, drawings, and models.
Sales and Marketing	Knowledge of principles and methods for showing, promoting, and selling products or services. This includes marketing strategy and tactics, product demonstration, sales techniques, and sales control systems.
History and Archeology	Knowledge of historical events and their causes, indicators, and effects on civilizations and cultures.
Food Production	Knowledge of techniques and equipment for planting, growing, and harvesting food products (both plant and animal) for consumption, including storage/handling techniques.
Fine Arts	Knowledge of the theory and techniques required to compose, produce, and perform works of music, dance, visual arts, drama, and sculpture.

Skills	Skills Definitions
Active Listening	Giving full attention to what other people are saying, taking time to understand the points being made, asking questions as appropriate, and not interrupting at inappropriate times.
Critical Thinking	Using logic and reasoning to identify the strengths and weaknesses of alternative solutions, conclusions or approaches to problems.
Speaking	Talking to others to convey information effectively.
Coordination	Adjusting actions in relation to others' actions.
Equipment Maintenance	Performing routine maintenance on equipment and determining when and what kind of maintenance is needed.
Reading Comprehension	Understanding written sentences and paragraphs in work related documents.
Writing	Communicating effectively in writing as appropriate for the needs of the audience.
Learning Strategies	Selecting and using training/instructional methods and procedures appropriate for the situation when learning or teaching new things.
Active Learning	Understanding the implications of new information for both current and future problem-solving and decision-making.
Instructing	Teaching others how to do something.
Social Perceptiveness	Being aware of others' reactions and understanding why they react as they do.
Monitoring	Monitoring/Assessing performance of yourself, other individuals, or organizations to make improvements or take corrective action.
Service Orientation	Actively looking for ways to help people.
Judgment and Decision Making	Considering the relative costs and benefits of potential actions to choose the most appropriate one.
Complex Problem Solving	Identifying complex problems and reviewing related information to develop and evaluate options and implement solutions.
Equipment Selection	Determining the kind of tools and equipment needed to do a job.
Mathematics	Using mathematics to solve problems.
Time Management	Managing one's own time and the time of others.
Troubleshooting	Determining causes of operating errors and deciding what to do about it.
Negotiation	Bringing others together and trying to reconcile differences.
Persuasion	Persuading others to change their minds or behavior.
Operation and Control	Controlling operations of equipment or systems.
Management of Personnel Resources	Motivating, developing, and directing people as they work, identifying the best people for the job.
Operation Monitoring	Watching gauges, dials, or other indicators to make sure a machine is working properly.
Quality Control Analysis	Conducting tests and inspections of products, services, or processes to evaluate quality or performance.
Science	Using scientific rules and methods to solve problems.
Management of Material Resources	Obtaining and seeing to the appropriate use of equipment, facilities, and materials needed to do certain work.
Operations Analysis	Analyzing needs and product requirements to create a design.
Repairing	Repairing machines or systems using the needed tools.
Technology Design	Generating or adapting equipment and technology to serve user needs.
Systems Analysis	Determining how a system should work and how changes in conditions, operations, and the environment will affect outcomes.
Systems Evaluation	Identifying measures or indicators of system performance and the actions needed to improve or correct performance, relative to the goals of the system.
Installation	Installing equipment, machines, wiring, or programs to meet specifications.
Management of Financial Resources	Determining how money will be spent to get the work done, and accounting for these expenditures.
Programming	Writing computer programs for various purposes.

Ability	Ability Definitions
Oral Comprehension	The ability to listen to and understand information and ideas presented through spoken words and sentences.
Oral Expression	The ability to communicate information and ideas in speaking so others will understand.
Problem Sensitivity	The ability to tell when something is wrong or is likely to go wrong. It does not involve solving the problem, only recognizing there is a problem.
Deductive Reasoning	The ability to apply general rules to specific problems to produce answers that make sense.
Inductive Reasoning	The ability to combine pieces of information to form general rules or conclusions (includes finding a relationship among seemingly unrelated events).
Static Strength	The ability to exert maximum muscle force to lift, push, pull, or carry objects.
Response Orientation	The ability to choose quickly between two or more movements in response to two or more different signals (lights, sounds, pictures). It includes the speed with which the correct response is started with the hand, foot, or other body part.
Extent Flexibility	The ability to bend, stretch, twist, or reach with your body, arms, and/or legs.
Arm-Hand Steadiness	The ability to keep your hand and arm steady while moving your arm or while holding your arm and hand in one position.
Information Ordering	The ability to arrange things or actions in a certain order or pattern according to a specific rule or set of rules (e.g., patterns of numbers, letters, words, pictures, mathematical operations).
Manual Dexterity	The ability to quickly move your hand, your hand together with your arm, or your two hands to grasp, manipulate, or assemble objects.
Control Precision	The ability to quickly and repeatedly adjust the controls of a machine or a vehicle to exact positions.
Reaction Time	The ability to quickly respond (with the hand, finger, or foot) to a signal (sound, light, picture) when it appears.
Near Vision	The ability to see details at close range (within a few feet of the observer).
Far Vision	The ability to see details at a distance.
Glare Sensitivity	The ability to see objects in the presence of glare or bright lighting.
Time Sharing	The ability to shift back and forth between two or more activities or sources of information (such as speech, sounds, touch, or other sources).
Speech Clarity	The ability to speak clearly so others can understand you.
Speech Recognition	The ability to identify and understand the speech of another person.
Speed of Closure	The ability to quickly make sense of, combine, and organize information into meaningful patterns.
Multilimb Coordination	The ability to coordinate two or more limbs (for example, two arms, two legs, or one leg and one arm) while sitting, standing, or lying down. It does not involve performing the activities while the whole body is in motion.
Perceptual Speed	The ability to quickly and accurately compare similarities and differences among sets of letters, numbers, objects, pictures, or patterns. The things to be compared may be presented at the same time or one after the other. This ability also includes comparing a presented object with a remembered object.
Selective Attention	The ability to concentrate on a task over a period of time without being distracted.
Gross Body Coordination	The ability to coordinate the movement of your arms, legs, and torso together when the whole body is in motion.
Stamina	The ability to exert yourself physically over long periods of time without getting winded or out of breath.
Written Expression	The ability to communicate information and ideas in writing so others will understand.
Finger Dexterity	The ability to make precisely coordinated movements of the fingers of one or both hands to grasp, manipulate, or assemble very small objects.
Flexibility of Closure	The ability to identify or detect a known pattern (a figure, object, word, or sound) that is hidden in other distracting material.
Spatial Orientation	The ability to know your location in relation to the environment or to know where other objects are in relation to you.
Depth Perception	The ability to judge which of several objects is closer or farther away from you, or to judge the distance between you and an object.
Rate Control	The ability to time your movements or the movement of a piece of equipment in anticipation of changes in the speed and/or direction of a moving object or scene.
Category Flexibility	The ability to generate or use different sets of rules for combining or grouping things in different ways.
Trunk Strength	The ability to use your abdominal and lower back muscles to support part of the body repeatedly or continuously over time without 'giving out' or fatiguing.
Hearing Sensitivity	The ability to detect or tell the differences between sounds that vary in pitch and loudness.
Written Comprehension	The ability to read and understand information and ideas presented in writing.
Speed of Limb Movement	The ability to quickly move the arms and legs.

Auditory Attention	The ability to focus on a single source of sound in the presence of other distracting sounds.
Visualization	The ability to imagine how something will look after it is moved around or when its parts are moved or rearranged.
Visual Color Discrimination	The ability to match or detect differences between colors, including shades of color and brightness.
Gross Body Equilibrium	The ability to keep or regain your body balance or stay upright when in an unstable position.
Memorization	The ability to remember information such as words, numbers, pictures, and procedures.
Night Vision	The ability to see under low light conditions.
Explosive Strength	The ability to use short bursts of muscle force to propel oneself (as in jumping or sprinting), or to throw an object.
Originality	The ability to come up with unusual or clever ideas about a given topic or situation, or to develop creative ways to solve a problem.
Peripheral Vision	The ability to see objects or movement of objects to one's side when the eyes are looking ahead.
Dynamic Strength	The ability to exert muscle force repeatedly or continuously over time. This involves muscular endurance and resistance to muscle fatigue.
Fluency of Ideas	The ability to come up with a number of ideas about a topic (the number of ideas is important, not their quality, correctness, or creativity).
Wrist-Finger Speed	The ability to make fast, simple, repeated movements of the fingers, hands, and wrists.
Sound Localization	The ability to tell the direction from which a sound originated.
Mathematical Reasoning	The ability to choose the right mathematical methods or formulas to solve a problem.
Number Facility	The ability to add, subtract, multiply, or divide quickly and correctly.
Dynamic Flexibility	The ability to quickly and repeatedly bend, stretch, twist, or reach out with your body, arms, and/or legs.

Work_Activity	Work_Activity Definitions
Making Decisions and Solving Problems	Analyzing information and evaluating results to choose the best solution and solve problems.
Assisting and Caring for Others	Providing personal assistance, medical attention, emotional support, or other personal care to others such as coworkers, customers, or patients.
Getting Information	Observing, receiving, and otherwise obtaining information from all relevant sources.
Operating Vehicles, Mechanized Devices, or Equipme	Running, maneuvering, navigating, or driving vehicles or mechanized equipment, such as forklifts, passenger vehicles, aircraft, or water craft.
Performing General Physical Activities	Performing physical activities that require considerable use of your arms and legs and moving your whole body, such as climbing, lifting, balancing, walking, stooping, and handling of materials.
Documenting/Recording Information	Entering, transcribing, recording, storing, or maintaining information in written or electronic/magnetic form.
Performing for or Working Directly with the Public	Performing for people or dealing directly with the public. This includes serving customers in restaurants and stores, and receiving clients or guests.
Communicating with Supervisors, Peers, or Subordin	Providing information to supervisors, co-workers, and subordinates by telephone, in written form, e-mail, or in person.
Identifying Objects, Actions, and Events	Identifying information by categorizing, estimating, recognizing differences or similarities, and detecting changes in circumstances or events.
Updating and Using Relevant Knowledge	Keeping up-to-date technically and applying new knowledge to your job.
Inspecting Equipment, Structures, or Material	Inspecting equipment, structures, or materials to identify the cause of errors or other problems or defects.
Processing Information	Compiling, coding, categorizing, calculating, tabulating, auditing, or verifying information or data.
Training and Teaching Others	Identifying the educational needs of others, developing formal educational or training programs or classes, and teaching or instructing others.
Handling and Moving Objects	Using hands and arms in handling, installing, positioning, and moving materials, and manipulating things.
Establishing and Maintaining Interpersonal Relatio	Developing constructive and cooperative working relationships with others, and maintaining them over time.

Communicating with Persons Outside Organization	Communicating with people outside the organization, representing the organization to customers, the public, government, and other external sources. This information can be exchanged in person, in writing, or by telephone or e-mail.
Monitor Processes, Materials, or Surroundings	Monitoring and reviewing information from materials, events, or the environment, to detect or assess problems.
Developing and Building Teams	Encouraging and building mutual trust, respect, and cooperation among team members.
Coaching and Developing Others	Identifying the developmental needs of others and coaching, mentoring, or otherwise helping others to improve their knowledge or skills.
Judging the Qualities of Things, Services, or Peop	Assessing the value, importance, or quality of things or people.
Guiding, Directing, and Motivating Subordinates	Providing guidance and direction to subordinates, including setting performance standards and monitoring performance.
Organizing, Planning, and Prioritizing Work	Developing specific goals and plans to prioritize, organize, and accomplish your work.
Analyzing Data or Information	Identifying the underlying principles, reasons, or facts of information by breaking down information or data into separate parts.
Evaluating Information to Determine Compliance wit	Using relevant information and individual judgment to determine whether events or processes comply with laws, regulations, or standards.
Resolving Conflicts and Negotiating with Others	Handling complaints, settling disputes, and resolving grievances and conflicts, or otherwise negotiating with others.
Thinking Creatively	Developing, designing, or creating new applications, ideas, relationships, systems, or products, including artistic contributions.
Coordinating the Work and Activities of Others	Getting members of a group to work together to accomplish tasks.
Estimating the Quantifiable Characteristics of Pro	Estimating sizes, distances, and quantities; or determining time, costs, resources, or materials needed to perform a work activity.
Scheduling Work and Activities	Scheduling events, programs, and activities, as well as the work of others.
Provide Consultation and Advice to Others	Providing guidance and expert advice to management or other groups on technical, systems-, or process-related topics.
Controlling Machines and Processes	Using either control mechanisms or direct physical activity to operate machines or processes (not including computers or vehicles).
Interpreting the Meaning of Information for Others	Translating or explaining what information means and how it can be used.
Performing Administrative Activities	Performing day-to-day administrative tasks such as maintaining information files and processing paperwork.
Interacting With Computers	Using computers and computer systems (including hardware and software) to program, write software, set up functions, enter data, or process information.
Developing Objectives and Strategies	Establishing long-range objectives and specifying the strategies and actions to achieve them.
Repairing and Maintaining Mechanical Equipment	Servicing, repairing, adjusting, and testing machines, devices, moving parts, and equipment that operate primarily on the basis of mechanical (not electronic) principles.
Monitoring and Controlling Resources	Monitoring and controlling resources and overseeing the spending of money.
Selling or Influencing Others	Convincing others to buy merchandise/goods or to otherwise change their minds or actions.
Repairing and Maintaining Electronic Equipment	Servicing, repairing, calibrating, regulating, fine-tuning, or testing machines, devices, and equipment that operate primarily on the basis of electrical or electronic (not mechanical) principles.
Staffing Organizational Units	Recruiting, interviewing, selecting, hiring, and promoting employees in an organization.
Drafting, Laying Out, and Specifying Technical Dev	Providing documentation, detailed instructions, drawings, or specifications to tell others about how devices, parts, equipment, or structures are to be fabricated, constructed, assembled, modified, maintained, or used.

Work_Context	Work_Context Definitions
Face-to-Face Discussions	How often do you have to have face-to-face discussions with individuals or teams in this job?
Physical Proximity	To what extent does this job require the worker to perform job tasks in close physical proximity to other people?
Exposed to Disease or Infections	How often does this job require exposure to disease/infections?
Work With Work Group or Team	How important is it to work with others in a group or team in this job?

Contact With Others	How much does this job require the worker to be in contact with others (face-to-face, by telephone, or otherwise) in order to perform it?
Deal With External Customers	How important is it to work with external customers or the public in this job?
Frequency of Decision Making	How frequently is the worker required to make decisions that affect other people, the financial resources, and/or the image and reputation of the organization?
Extremely Bright or Inadequate Lighting	How often does this job require working in extremely bright or inadequate lighting conditions?
Impact of Decisions on Co-workers or Company Resul	How do the decisions an employee makes impact the results of co-workers, clients or the company?
Outdoors, Exposed to Weather	How often does this job require working outdoors, exposed to all weather conditions?
Sounds, Noise Levels Are Distracting or Uncomforta	How often does this job require working exposed to sounds and noise levels that are distracting or uncomfortable?
Importance of Being Exact or Accurate	How important is being very exact or highly accurate in performing this job?
Consequence of Error	How serious would the result usually be if the worker made a mistake that was not readily correctable?
In an Enclosed Vehicle or Equipment	How often does this job require working in a closed vehicle or equipment (e.g., car)?
Telephone	How often do you have telephone conversations in this job?
Wear Common Protective or Safety Equipment such as	How much does this job require wearing common protective or safety equipment such as safety shoes, glasses, gloves, hard hats or life jackets?
Responsible for Others' Health and Safety	How much responsibility is there for the health and safety of others in this job?
Cramped Work Space, Awkward Positions	How often does this job require working in cramped work spaces that requires getting into awkward positions?
Coordinate or Lead Others	How important is it to coordinate or lead others in accomplishing work activities in this job?
Exposed to Contaminants	How often does this job require working exposed to contaminants (such as pollutants, gases, dust or odors)?
Very Hot or Cold Temperatures	How often does this job require working in very hot (above 90 F degrees) or very cold (below 32 F degrees) temperatures?
Exposed to Hazardous Equipment	How often does this job require exposure to hazardous equipment?
Deal With Unpleasant or Angry People	How frequently does the worker have to deal with unpleasant, angry, or discourteous individuals as part of the job requirements?
Exposed to Minor Burns, Cuts, Bites, or Stings	How often does this job require exposure to minor burns, cuts, bites, or stings?
Freedom to Make Decisions	How much decision making freedom, without supervision, does the job offer?
Responsibility for Outcomes and Results	How responsible is the worker for work outcomes and results of other workers?
Time Pressure	How often does this job require the worker to meet strict deadlines?
Spend Time Using Your Hands to Handle, Control, or	How much does this job require using your hands to handle, control, or feel objects, tools or controls?
Deal With Physically Aggressive People	How frequently does this job require the worker to deal with physical aggression of violent individuals?
Structured versus Unstructured Work	To what extent is this job structured for the worker, rather than allowing the worker to determine tasks, priorities, and goals?
Importance of Repeating Same Tasks	How important is repeating the same physical activities (e.g., key entry) or mental activities (e.g., checking entries in a ledger) over and over, without stopping, to performing this job?
Indoors, Environmentally Controlled	How often does this job require working indoors in environmentally controlled conditions?
Frequency of Conflict Situations	How often are there conflict situations the employee has to face in this job?
Exposed to Hazardous Conditions	How often does this job require exposure to hazardous conditions?
Spend Time Walking and Running	How much does this job require walking and running?
Spend Time Making Repetitive Motions	How much does this job require making repetitive motions?
Indoors, Not Environmentally Controlled	How often does this job require working indoors in non-controlled environmental conditions (e.g., warehouse without heat)?
Spend Time Standing	How much does this job require standing?
Letters and Memos	How often does the job require written letters and memos?
Spend Time Bending or Twisting the Body	How much does this job require bending or twisting your body?

Spend Time Kneeling, Crouching, Stooping, or Crawl	How much does this job require kneeling, crouching, stooping or crawling?
Wear Specialized Protective or Safety Equipment su	How much does this job require wearing specialized protective or safety equipment such as breathing apparatus, safety harness, full protection suits, or radiation protection?
Level of Competition	To what extent does this job require the worker to compete or to be aware of competitive pressures?
Exposed to High Places	How often does this job require exposure to high places?
Spend Time Sitting	How much does this job require sitting?
In an Open Vehicle or Equipment	How often does this job require working in an open vehicle or equipment (e.g., tractor)?
Spend Time Keeping or Regaining Balance	How much does this job require keeping or regaining your balance?
Pace Determined by Speed of Equipment	How important is it to this job that the pace is determined by the speed of equipment or machinery? (This does not refer to keeping busy at all times on this job.)
Outdoors, Under Cover	How often does this job require working outdoors, under cover (e.g., structure with roof but no walls)?
Public Speaking	How often do you have to perform public speaking in this job?
Degree of Automation	How automated is the job?
Exposed to Radiation	How often does this job require exposure to radiation?
Spend Time Climbing Ladders, Scaffolds, or Poles	How much does this job require climbing ladders, scaffolds, or poles?
Electronic Mail	How often do you use electronic mail in this job?
Exposed to Whole Body Vibration	How often does this job require exposure to whole body vibration (e.g., operate a jackhammer)?

Job Zone Component	Job Zone Component Definitions
Title	Job Zone Two: Some Preparation Needed
Overall Experience	Some previous work-related skill, knowledge, or experience may be helpful in these occupations, but usually is not needed. For example, a drywall installer might benefit from experience installing drywall, but an inexperienced person could still learn to be an installer with little difficulty.
Job Training	Employees in these occupations need anywhere from a few months to one year of working with experienced employees.
Job Zone Examples	These occupations often involve using your knowledge and skills to help others. Examples include drywall installers, fire inspectors, flight attendants, pharmacy technicians, salespersons (retail), and tellers.
SVP Range	(4.0 to < 6.0)
Education	These occupations usually require a high school diploma and may require some vocational training or job-related course work. In some cases, an associate's or bachelor's degree could be needed.

Work_Styles	Work_Styles Definitions
Stress Tolerance	Job requires accepting criticism and dealing calmly and effectively with high stress situations.
Dependability	Job requires being reliable, responsible, and dependable, and fulfilling obligations.
Attention to Detail	Job requires being careful about detail and thorough in completing work tasks.
Self Control	Job requires maintaining composure, keeping emotions in check, controlling anger, and avoiding aggressive behavior, even in very difficult situations.
Adaptability/Flexibility	Job requires being open to change (positive or negative) and to considerable variety in the workplace.
Integrity	Job requires being honest and ethical.
Concern for Others	Job requires being sensitive to others' needs and feelings and being understanding and helpful on the job.
Cooperation	Job requires being pleasant with others on the job and displaying a good-natured, cooperative attitude.
Initiative	Job requires a willingness to take on responsibilities and challenges.
Social Orientation	Job requires preferring to work with others rather than alone, and being personally connected with others on the job.
Persistence	Job requires persistence in the face of obstacles.
Analytical Thinking	Job requires analyzing information and using logic to address work-related issues and problems.
Innovation	Job requires creativity and alternative thinking to develop new ideas for and answers to work-related problems.

Leadership	Job requires a willingness to lead, take charge, and offer opinions and direction.
Achievement/Effort	Job requires establishing and maintaining personally challenging achievement goals and exerting effort toward mastering tasks.
Independence	Job requires developing one's own ways of doing things, guiding oneself with little or no supervision, and depending on oneself to get things done.

29-2051.00 - Dietetic Technicians

Assist dietitians in the provision of food service and nutritional programs. Under the supervision of dietitians, may plan and produce meals based on established guidelines, teach principles of food and nutrition, or counsel individuals.

Tasks

1) Analyze menus and recipes, standardize recipes and test new products.

2) Prepare a major meal, following recipes and determining group food quantities.

3) Obtain and evaluate dietary histories of individuals to plan nutritional programs.

4) Plan menus and diets or guide individuals and families in food selection, preparation, and menu planning, based upon nutritional needs and established guidelines.

5) Supervise food production and service, or assist dietitians and nutritionists in food service supervision and planning.

6) Provide dietitians with assistance researching food, nutrition and food service systems.

7) Deliver speeches on diet, nutrition and health to promote healthy eating habits and illness prevention and treatment.

8) Determine food and beverage costs and assist in implementing cost control procedures.

9) Develop job specifications, job descriptions, and work schedules.

10) Select, schedule, and conduct orientation and in-service education programs.

11) Refer patients to other relevant services to provide continuity of care.

Knowledge	Knowledge Definitions
English Language	Knowledge of the structure and content of the English language including the meaning and spelling of words, rules of composition, and grammar.
Food Production	Knowledge of techniques and equipment for planting, growing, and harvesting food products (both plant and animal) for consumption, including storage/handling techniques.
Customer and Personal Service	Knowledge of principles and processes for providing customer and personal services. This includes customer needs assessment, meeting quality standards for services, and evaluation of customer satisfaction.
Clerical	Knowledge of administrative and clerical procedures and systems such as word processing, managing files and records, stenography and transcription, designing forms, and other office procedures and terminology.
Public Safety and Security	Knowledge of relevant equipment, policies, procedures, and strategies to promote effective local, state, or national security operations for the protection of people, data, property, and institutions.
Mathematics	Knowledge of arithmetic, algebra, geometry, calculus, statistics, and their applications.
Education and Training	Knowledge of principles and methods for curriculum and training design, teaching and instruction for individuals and groups, and the measurement of training effects.
Production and Processing	Knowledge of raw materials, production processes, quality control, costs, and other techniques for maximizing the effective manufacture and distribution of goods.
Medicine and Dentistry	Knowledge of the information and techniques needed to diagnose and treat human injuries, diseases, and deformities. This includes symptoms, treatment alternatives, drug properties and interactions, and preventive health-care measures.
Computers and Electronics	Knowledge of circuit boards, processors, chips, electronic equipment, and computer hardware and software, including applications and programming.
Biology	Knowledge of plant and animal organisms, their tissues, cells, functions, interdependencies, and interactions with each other and the environment.
Therapy and Counseling	Knowledge of principles, methods, and procedures for diagnosis, treatment, and rehabilitation of physical and mental dysfunctions, and for career counseling and guidance.
Psychology	Knowledge of human behavior and performance; individual differences in ability, personality, and interests; learning and motivation; psychological research methods; and the assessment and treatment of behavioral and affective disorders.
Administration and Management	Knowledge of business and management principles involved in strategic planning, resource allocation, human resources modeling, leadership technique, production methods, and coordination of people and resources.
Personnel and Human Resources	Knowledge of principles and procedures for personnel recruitment, selection, training, compensation and benefits, labor relations and negotiation, and personnel information systems.
Law and Government	Knowledge of laws, legal codes, court procedures, precedents, government regulations, executive orders, agency rules, and the democratic political process.
Mechanical	Knowledge of machines and tools, including their designs, uses, repair, and maintenance.
Chemistry	Knowledge of the chemical composition, structure, and properties of substances and of the chemical processes and transformations that they undergo. This includes uses of chemicals and their interactions, danger signs, production techniques, and disposal methods.
Telecommunications	Knowledge of transmission, broadcasting, switching, control, and operation of telecommunications systems.
Communications and Media	Knowledge of media production, communication, and dissemination techniques and methods. This includes alternative ways to inform and entertain via written, oral, and visual media.
Economics and Accounting	Knowledge of economic and accounting principles and practices, the financial markets, banking and the analysis and reporting of financial data.
Geography	Knowledge of principles and methods for describing the features of land, sea, and air masses, including their physical characteristics, locations, interrelationships, and distribution of plant, animal, and human life.
Sociology and Anthropology	Knowledge of group behavior and dynamics, societal trends and influences, human migrations, ethnicity, cultures and their history and origins.
Philosophy and Theology	Knowledge of different philosophical systems and religions. This includes their basic principles, values, ethics, ways of thinking, customs, practices, and their impact on human culture.
Transportation	Knowledge of principles and methods for moving people or goods by air, rail, sea, or road, including the relative costs and benefits.
Design	Knowledge of design techniques, tools, and principles involved in production of precision technical plans, blueprints, drawings, and models.
Sales and Marketing	Knowledge of principles and methods for showing, promoting, and selling products or services. This includes marketing strategy and tactics, product demonstration, sales techniques, and sales control systems.
Physics	Knowledge and prediction of physical principles, laws, their interrelationships, and applications to understanding fluid, material, and atmospheric dynamics, and mechanical, electrical, atomic and sub-atomic structures and processes.
Foreign Language	Knowledge of the structure and content of a foreign (non-English) language including the meaning and spelling of words, rules of composition and grammar, and pronunciation.
Fine Arts	Knowledge of the theory and techniques required to compose, produce, and perform works of music, dance, visual arts, drama, and sculpture.
Engineering and Technology	Knowledge of the practical application of engineering science and technology. This includes applying principles, techniques, procedures, and equipment to the design and production of various goods and services.
History and Archeology	Knowledge of historical events and their causes, indicators, and effects on civilizations and cultures.
Building and Construction	Knowledge of materials, methods, and the tools involved in the construction or repair of houses, buildings, or other structures such as highways and roads.

Skills	Skills Definitions
Active Listening	Giving full attention to what other people are saying, taking time to understand the points being made, asking questions as appropriate, and not interrupting at inappropriate times.
Reading Comprehension	Understanding written sentences and paragraphs in work related documents.
Social Perceptiveness	Being aware of others' reactions and understanding why they react as they do.
Writing	Communicating effectively in writing as appropriate for the needs of the audience.
Service Orientation	Actively looking for ways to help people.
Instructing	Teaching others how to do something.
Active Learning	Understanding the implications of new information for both current and future problem-solving and decision-making.
Learning Strategies	Selecting and using training/instructional methods and procedures appropriate for the situation when learning or teaching new things.
Critical Thinking	Using logic and reasoning to identify the strengths and weaknesses of alternative solutions, conclusions or approaches to problems.
Speaking	Talking to others to convey information effectively.
Time Management	Managing one's own time and the time of others.
Negotiation	Bringing others together and trying to reconcile differences.
Management of Personnel Resources	Motivating, developing, and directing people as they work, identifying the best people for the job.
Mathematics	Using mathematics to solve problems.
Monitoring	Monitoring/Assessing performance of yourself, other individuals, or organizations to make improvements or take corrective action.
Judgment and Decision Making	Considering the relative costs and benefits of potential actions to choose the most appropriate one.
Coordination	Adjusting actions in relation to others' actions.
Complex Problem Solving	Identifying complex problems and reviewing related information to develop and evaluate options and implement solutions.
Operation Monitoring	Watching gauges, dials, or other indicators to make sure a machine is working properly.
Equipment Selection	Determining the kind of tools and equipment needed to do a job.
Systems Analysis	Determining how a system should work and how changes in conditions, operations, and the environment will affect outcomes.
Systems Evaluation	Identifying measures or indicators of system performance and the actions needed to improve or correct performance, relative to the goals of the system.
Persuasion	Persuading others to change their minds or behavior.
Troubleshooting	Determining causes of operating errors and deciding what to do about it.
Operations Analysis	Analyzing needs and product requirements to create a design.
Operation and Control	Controlling operations of equipment or systems.
Equipment Maintenance	Performing routine maintenance on equipment and determining when and what kind of maintenance is needed.
Quality Control Analysis	Conducting tests and inspections of products, services, or processes to evaluate quality or performance.
Management of Financial Resources	Determining how money will be spent to get the work done, and accounting for these expenditures.
Technology Design	Generating or adapting equipment and technology to serve user needs.
Repairing	Repairing machines or systems using the needed tools.
Management of Material Resources	Obtaining and seeing to the appropriate use of equipment, facilities, and materials needed to do certain work.
Installation	Installing equipment, machines, wiring, or programs to meet specifications.
Science	Using scientific rules and methods to solve problems.
Programming	Writing computer programs for various purposes.

Ability	Ability Definitions
Oral Expression	The ability to communicate information and ideas in speaking so others will understand.
Oral Comprehension	The ability to listen to and understand information and ideas presented through spoken words and sentences.
Speech Clarity	The ability to speak clearly so others can understand you.
Problem Sensitivity	The ability to tell when something is wrong or is likely to go wrong. It does not involve solving the problem, only recognizing there is a problem.

Speech Recognition	The ability to identify and understand the speech of another person.
Near Vision	The ability to see details at close range (within a few feet of the observer).
Information Ordering	The ability to arrange things or actions in a certain order or pattern according to a specific rule or set of rules (e.g., patterns of numbers, letters, words, pictures, mathematical operations).
Written Comprehension	The ability to read and understand information and ideas presented in writing.
Deductive Reasoning	The ability to apply general rules to specific problems to produce answers that make sense.
Fluency of Ideas	The ability to come up with a number of ideas about a topic (the number of ideas is important, not their quality, correctness, or creativity).
Written Expression	The ability to communicate information and ideas in writing so others will understand.
Inductive Reasoning	The ability to combine pieces of information to form general rules or conclusions (includes finding a relationship among seemingly unrelated events).
Category Flexibility	The ability to generate or use different sets of rules for combining or grouping things in different ways.
Originality	The ability to come up with unusual or clever ideas about a given topic or situation, or to develop creative ways to solve a problem.
Selective Attention	The ability to concentrate on a task over a period of time without being distracted.
Arm-Hand Steadiness	The ability to keep your hand and arm steady while moving your arm or while holding your arm and hand in one position.
Stamina	The ability to exert yourself physically over long periods of time without getting winded or out of breath.
Trunk Strength	The ability to use your abdominal and lower back muscles to support part of the body repeatedly or continuously over time without 'giving out' or fatiguing.
Mathematical Reasoning	The ability to choose the right mathematical methods or formulas to solve a problem.
Time Sharing	The ability to shift back and forth between two or more activities or sources of information (such as speech, sounds, touch, or other sources).
Speed of Limb Movement	The ability to quickly move the arms and legs.
Extent Flexibility	The ability to bend, stretch, twist, or reach with your body, arms, and/or legs.
Manual Dexterity	The ability to quickly move your hand, your hand together with your arm, or your two hands to grasp, manipulate, or assemble objects.
Flexibility of Closure	The ability to identify or detect a known pattern (a figure, object, word, or sound) that is hidden in other distracting material.
Gross Body Coordination	The ability to coordinate the movement of your arms, legs, and torso together when the whole body is in motion.
Memorization	The ability to remember information such as words, numbers, pictures, and procedures.
Auditory Attention	The ability to focus on a single source of sound in the presence of other distracting sounds.
Far Vision	The ability to see details at a distance.
Static Strength	The ability to exert maximum muscle force to lift, push, pull, or carry objects.
Perceptual Speed	The ability to quickly and accurately compare similarities and differences among sets of letters, numbers, objects, pictures, or patterns. The things to be compared may be presented at the same time or one after the other. This ability also includes comparing a presented object with a remembered object.
Number Facility	The ability to add, subtract, multiply, or divide quickly and correctly.
Multilimb Coordination	The ability to coordinate two or more limbs (for example, two arms, two legs, or one leg and one arm) while sitting, standing, or lying down. It does not involve performing the activities while the whole body is in motion.
Response Orientation	The ability to choose quickly between two or more movements in response to two or more different signals (lights, sounds, pictures). It includes the speed with which the correct response is started with the hand, foot, or other body part.
Explosive Strength	The ability to use short bursts of muscle force to propel oneself (as in jumping or sprinting), or to throw an object.
Visualization	The ability to imagine how something will look after it is moved around or when its parts are moved or rearranged.
Speed of Closure	The ability to quickly make sense of, combine, and organize information into meaningful patterns.

591

Finger Dexterity	The ability to make precisely coordinated movements of the fingers of one or both hands to grasp, manipulate, or assemble very small objects.
Reaction Time	The ability to quickly respond (with the hand, finger, or foot) to a signal (sound, light, picture) when it appears.
Dynamic Strength	The ability to exert muscle force repeatedly or continuously over time. This involves muscular endurance and resistance to muscle fatigue.
Control Precision	The ability to quickly and repeatedly adjust the controls of a machine or a vehicle to exact positions.
Visual Color Discrimination	The ability to match or detect differences between colors, including shades of color and brightness.
Wrist-Finger Speed	The ability to make fast, simple, repeated movements of the fingers, hands, and wrists.
Gross Body Equilibrium	The ability to keep or regain your body balance or stay upright when in an unstable position.
Hearing Sensitivity	The ability to detect or tell the differences between sounds that vary in pitch and loudness.
Rate Control	The ability to time your movements or the movement of a piece of equipment in anticipation of changes in the speed and/or direction of a moving object or scene.
Depth Perception	The ability to judge which of several objects is closer or farther away from you, or to judge the distance between you and an object.
Night Vision	The ability to see under low light conditions.
Spatial Orientation	The ability to know your location in relation to the environment or to know where other objects are in relation to you.
Glare Sensitivity	The ability to see objects in the presence of glare or bright lighting.
Peripheral Vision	The ability to see objects or movement of objects to one's side when the eyes are looking ahead.
Sound Localization	The ability to tell the direction from which a sound originated.
Dynamic Flexibility	The ability to quickly and repeatedly bend, stretch, twist, or reach out with your body, arms, and/or legs.

Work_Activity	Work_Activity Definitions
Assisting and Caring for Others	Providing personal assistance, medical attention, emotional support, or other personal care to others such as coworkers, customers, or patients.
Establishing and Maintaining Interpersonal Relatio	Developing constructive and cooperative working relationships with others, and maintaining them over time.
Communicating with Supervisors, Peers, or Subordin	Providing information to supervisors, co-workers, and subordinates by telephone, in written form, e-mail, or in person.
Getting Information	Observing, receiving, and otherwise obtaining information from all relevant sources.
Making Decisions and Solving Problems	Analyzing information and evaluating results to choose the best solution and solve problems.
Identifying Objects, Actions, and Events	Identifying information by categorizing, estimating, recognizing differences or similarities, and detecting changes in circumstances or events.
Coaching and Developing Others	Identifying the developmental needs of others and coaching, mentoring, or otherwise helping others to improve their knowledge or skills.
Performing General Physical Activities	Performing physical activities that require considerable use of your arms and legs and moving your whole body, such as climbing, lifting, balancing, walking, stooping, and handling of materials.
Handling and Moving Objects	Using hands and arms in handling, installing, positioning, and moving materials, and manipulating things.
Training and Teaching Others	Identifying the educational needs of others, developing formal educational or training programs or classes, and teaching or instructing others.
Resolving Conflicts and Negotiating with Others	Handling complaints, settling disputes, and resolving grievances and conflicts, or otherwise negotiating with others.
Coordinating the Work and Activities of Others	Getting members of a group to work together to accomplish tasks.
Updating and Using Relevant Knowledge	Keeping up-to-date technically and applying new knowledge to your job.
Organizing, Planning, and Prioritizing Work	Developing specific goals and plans to prioritize, organize, and accomplish your work.
Developing and Building Teams	Encouraging and building mutual trust, respect, and cooperation among team members.
Inspecting Equipment, Structures, or Material	Inspecting equipment, structures, or materials to identify the cause of errors or other problems or defects.

Controlling Machines and Processes	Using either control mechanisms or direct physical activity to operate machines or processes (not including computers or vehicles).
Evaluating Information to Determine Compliance wit	Using relevant information and individual judgment to determine whether events or processes comply with laws, regulations, or standards.
Processing Information	Compiling, coding, categorizing, calculating, tabulating, auditing, or verifying information or data.
Guiding, Directing, and Motivating Subordinates	Providing guidance and direction to subordinates, including setting performance standards and monitoring performance.
Performing for or Working Directly with the Public	Performing for people or dealing directly with the public. This includes serving customers in restaurants and stores, and receiving clients or guests.
Thinking Creatively	Developing, designing, or creating new applications, ideas, relationships, systems, or products, including artistic contributions.
Provide Consultation and Advice to Others	Providing guidance and expert advice to management or other groups on technical, systems-, or process-related topics.
Monitoring and Controlling Resources	Monitoring and controlling resources and overseeing the spending of money.
Performing Administrative Activities	Performing day-to-day administrative tasks such as maintaining information files and processing paperwork.
Documenting/Recording Information	Entering, transcribing, recording, storing, or maintaining information in written or electronic/magnetic form.
Staffing Organizational Units	Recruiting, interviewing, selecting, hiring, and promoting employees in an organization.
Judging the Qualities of Things, Services, or Peop	Assessing the value, importance, or quality of things or people.
Monitor Processes, Materials, or Surroundings	Monitoring and reviewing information from materials, events, or the environment, to detect or assess problems.
Estimating the Quantifiable Characteristics of Pro	Estimating sizes, distances, and quantities; or determining time, costs, resources, or materials needed to perform a work activity.
Communicating with Persons Outside Organization	Communicating with people outside the organization, representing the organization to customers, the public, government, and other external sources. This information can be exchanged in person, in writing, or by telephone or e-mail.
Developing Objectives and Strategies	Establishing long-range objectives and specifying the strategies and actions to achieve them.
Scheduling Work and Activities	Scheduling events, programs, and activities, as well as the work of others.
Interpreting the Meaning of Information for Others	Translating or explaining what information means and how it can be used.
Analyzing Data or Information	Identifying the underlying principles, reasons, or facts of information by breaking down information or data into separate parts.
Repairing and Maintaining Mechanical Equipment	Servicing, repairing, adjusting, and testing machines, devices, moving parts, and equipment that operate primarily on the basis of mechanical (not electronic) principles.
Repairing and Maintaining Electronic Equipment	Servicing, repairing, calibrating, regulating, fine-tuning, or testing machines, devices, or equipment that operate primarily on the basis of electrical or electronic (not mechanical) principles.
Interacting With Computers	Using computers and computer systems (including hardware and software) to program, write software, set up functions, enter data, or process information.
Operating Vehicles, Mechanized Devices, or Equipme	Running, maneuvering, navigating, or driving vehicles or mechanized equipment, such as forklifts, passenger vehicles, aircraft, or water craft.
Selling or Influencing Others	Convincing others to buy merchandise/goods or to otherwise change their minds or actions.
Drafting, Laying Out, and Specifying Technical Dev	Providing documentation, detailed instructions, drawings, or specifications to tell others about how devices, parts, equipment, or structures are to be fabricated, constructed, assembled, modified, maintained, or used.

Work_Context	Work_Context Definitions
Time Pressure	How often does this job require the worker to meet strict deadlines?
Work With Work Group or Team	How important is it to work with others in a group or team in this job?
Face-to-Face Discussions	How often do you have to have face-to-face discussions with individuals or teams in this job?
Contact With Others	How much does this job require the worker to be in contact with others (face-to-face, by telephone, or otherwise) in order to perform it?

Indoors, Environmentally Controlled	How often does this job require working indoors in environmentally controlled conditions?
Physical Proximity	To what extent does this job require the worker to perform job tasks in close physical proximity to other people?
Frequency of Decision Making	How frequently is the worker required to make decisions that affect other people, the financial resources, and/or the image and reputation of the organization?
Spend Time Standing	How much does this job require standing?
Responsible for Others' Health and Safety	How much responsibility is there for the health and safety of others in this job?
Exposed to Disease or Infections	How often does this job require exposure to disease/infections?
Freedom to Make Decisions	How much decision making freedom, without supervision, does the job offer?
Exposed to Minor Burns, Cuts, Bites, or Stings	How often does this job require exposure to minor burns, cuts, bites, or stings?
Frequency of Conflict Situations	How often are there conflict situations the employee has to face in this job?
Responsibility for Outcomes and Results	How responsible is the worker for work outcomes and results of other workers?
Importance of Being Exact or Accurate	How important is being very exact or highly accurate in performing this job?
Coordinate or Lead Others	How important is it to coordinate or lead others in accomplishing work activities in this job?
Structured versus Unstructured Work	To what extent is this job structured for the worker, rather than allowing the worker to determine tasks, priorities, and goals?
Telephone	How often do you have telephone conversations in this job?
Deal With Unpleasant or Angry People	How frequently does the worker have to deal with unpleasant, angry, or discourteous individuals as part of the job requirements?
Spend Time Walking and Running	How much does this job require walking and running?
Spend Time Making Repetitive Motions	How much does this job require making repetitive motions?
Sounds, Noise Levels Are Distracting or Uncomfortable	How often does this job require working exposed to sounds and noise levels that are distracting or uncomfortable?
Importance of Repeating Same Tasks	How important is repeating the same physical activities (e.g., key entry) or mental activities (e.g., checking entries in a ledger) over and over, without stopping, to performing this job?
Letters and Memos	How often does the job require written letters and memos?
Spend Time Bending or Twisting the Body	How much does this job require bending or twisting your body?
Impact of Decisions on Co-workers or Company Resul	How do the decisions an employee makes impact the results of co-workers, clients or the company?
Deal With External Customers	How important is it to work with external customers or the public in this job?
Cramped Work Space, Awkward Positions	How often does this job require working in cramped work spaces that requires getting into awkward positions?
Wear Common Protective or Safety Equipment such as	How much does this job require wearing common protective or safety equipment such as safety shoes, glasses, gloves, hard hats or life jackets?
Spend Time Using Your Hands to Handle, Control, or	How much does this job require using your hands to handle, control, or feel objects, tools or controls?
Deal With Physically Aggressive People	How frequently does this job require the worker to deal with physical aggression of violent individuals?
Level of Competition	To what extent does this job require the worker to compete or to be aware of competitive pressures?
Exposed to Hazardous Conditions	How often does this job require exposure to hazardous conditions?
Spend Time Sitting	How much does this job require sitting?
Degree of Automation	How automated is the job?
Exposed to Hazardous Equipment	How often does this job require exposure to hazardous equipment?
Exposed to Contaminants	How often does this job require working exposed to contaminants (such as pollutants, gases, dust or odors)?
Consequence of Error	How serious would the result usually be if the worker made a mistake that was not readily correctable?
Spend Time Kneeling, Crouching, Stooping, or Crawl	How much does this job require kneeling, crouching, stooping or crawling?
Indoors, Not Environmentally Controlled	How often does this job require working indoors in non-controlled environmental conditions (e.g., warehouse without heat)?
Extremely Bright or Inadequate Lighting	How often does this job require working in extremely bright or inadequate lighting conditions?
Public Speaking	How often do you have to perform public speaking in this job?

Outdoors, Exposed to Weather	How often does this job require working outdoors, exposed to all weather conditions?
Very Hot or Cold Temperatures	How often does this job require working in very hot (above 90 F degrees) or very cold (below 32 F degrees) temperatures?
Pace Determined by Speed of Equipment	How important is it to this job that the pace is determined by the speed of equipment or machinery? (This does not refer to keeping busy at all times on this job.)
Electronic Mail	How often do you use electronic mail in this job?
Outdoors, Under Cover	How often does this job require working outdoors, under cover (e.g., structure with roof but no walls)?
Spend Time Keeping or Regaining Balance	How much does this job require keeping or regaining your balance?
In an Enclosed Vehicle or Equipment	How often does this job require working in a closed vehicle or equipment (e.g., car)?
Wear Specialized Protective or Safety Equipment su	How often does this job require wearing specialized protective or safety equipment such as breathing apparatus, safety harness, full protection suits, or radiation protection?
In an Open Vehicle or Equipment	How often does this job require working in an open vehicle or equipment (e.g., tractor)?
Exposed to Radiation	How often does this job require exposure to radiation?
Spend Time Climbing Ladders, Scaffolds, or Poles	How much does this job require climbing ladders, scaffolds, or poles?
Exposed to High Places	How often does this job require exposure to high places?
Exposed to Whole Body Vibration	How often does this job require exposure to whole body vibration (e.g., operate a jackhammer)?

Job Zone Component	Job Zone Component Definitions
Title	Job Zone Three: Medium Preparation Needed
Overall Experience	Previous work-related skill, knowledge, or experience is required for these occupations. For example, an electrician must have completed three or four years of apprenticeship or several years of vocational training, and often must have passed a licensing exam, in order to perform the job.
Job Training	Employees in these occupations usually need one or two years of training involving both on-the-job experience and informal training with experienced workers.
Job Zone Examples	These occupations usually involve using communication and organizational skills to coordinate, supervise, manage, or train others to accomplish goals. Examples include dental assistants, electricians, fish and game wardens, legal secretaries, personnel recruiters, and recreation workers.
SVP Range	(6.0 to < 7.0)
Education	Most occupations in this zone require training in vocational schools, related on-the-job experience, or an associate's degree. Some may require a bachelor's degree.

Work_Styles	Work_Styles Definitions
Dependability	Job requires being reliable, responsible, and dependable, and fulfilling obligations.
Integrity	Job requires being honest and ethical.
Cooperation	Job requires being pleasant with others on the job and displaying a good-natured, cooperative attitude.
Concern for Others	Job requires being sensitive to others' needs and feelings and being understanding and helpful on the job.
Self Control	Job requires maintaining composure, keeping emotions in check, controlling anger, and avoiding aggressive behavior, even in very difficult situations.
Adaptability/Flexibility	Job requires being open to change (positive or negative) and to considerable variety in the workplace.
Attention to Detail	Job requires being careful about detail and thorough in completing work tasks.
Independence	Job requires developing one's own ways of doing things, guiding oneself with little or no supervision, and depending on oneself to get things done.
Stress Tolerance	Job requires accepting criticism and dealing calmly and effectively with high stress situations.
Social Orientation	Job requires preferring to work with others rather than alone, and being personally connected with others on the job.
Innovation	Job requires creativity and alternative thinking to develop new ideas for and answers to work-related problems.
Analytical Thinking	Job requires analyzing information and using logic to address work-related issues and problems.
Initiative	Job requires a willingness to take on responsibilities and challenges.

Persistence	Job requires persistence in the face of obstacles.
Achievement/Effort	Job requires establishing and maintaining personally challenging achievement goals and exerting effort toward mastering tasks.
Leadership	Job requires a willingness to lead, take charge, and offer opinions and direction.

29-2052.00 - Pharmacy Technicians

Prepare medications under the direction of a pharmacist. May measure, mix, count out, label, and record amounts and dosages of medications.

Tasks

1) Assist customers by answering simple questions, locating items or referring them to the pharmacist for medication information.

2) Receive and store incoming supplies, verify quantities against invoices, and inform supervisors of stock needs and shortages.

3) Fill bottles with prescribed medications and type and affix labels.

4) Receive written prescription or refill requests and verify that information is complete and accurate.

5) Clean, and help maintain, equipment and work areas, and sterilize glassware according to prescribed methods.

6) Order, label, and count stock of medications, chemicals, and supplies, and enter inventory data into computer.

7) Maintain proper storage and security conditions for drugs.

8) Establish and maintain patient profiles, including lists of medications taken by individual patients.

9) Price and file prescriptions that have been filled.

10) Operate cash registers to accept payment from customers.

11) Mix pharmaceutical preparations according to written prescriptions.

12) Prepare and process medical insurance claim forms and records.

13) Deliver medications and pharmaceutical supplies to patients, nursing stations or surgery.

14) Price stock and mark items for sale.

15) Maintain and merchandise home health-care products and services.

16) Add measured drugs or nutrients to intravenous solutions under sterile conditions to prepare intravenous (IV) packs under pharmacist supervision.

17) Supply and monitor robotic machines that dispense medicine into containers, and label the containers.

18) Compute charges for medication and equipment dispensed to hospital patients, and enter data in computer.

19) Transfer medication from vials to the appropriate number of sterile, disposable syringes, using aseptic techniques.

Knowledge	Knowledge Definitions
English Language	Knowledge of the structure and content of the English language including the meaning and spelling of words, rules of composition, and grammar.
Customer and Personal Service	Knowledge of principles and processes for providing customer and personal services. This includes customer needs assessment, meeting quality standards for services, and evaluation of customer satisfaction.
Mathematics	Knowledge of arithmetic, algebra, geometry, calculus, statistics, and their applications.
Medicine and Dentistry	Knowledge of the information and techniques needed to diagnose and treat human injuries, diseases, and deformities. This includes symptoms, treatment alternatives, drug properties and interactions, and preventive health-care measures.
Clerical	Knowledge of administrative and clerical procedures and systems such as word processing, managing files and records, stenography and transcription, designing forms, and other office procedures and terminology.
Chemistry	Knowledge of the chemical composition, structure, and properties of substances and of the chemical processes and transformations that they undergo. This includes uses of chemicals and their interactions, danger signs, production techniques, and disposal methods.
Education and Training	Knowledge of principles and methods for curriculum and training design, teaching and instruction for individuals and groups, and the measurement of training effects.
Computers and Electronics	Knowledge of circuit boards, processors, chips, electronic equipment, and computer hardware and software, including applications and programming.
Law and Government	Knowledge of laws, legal codes, court procedures, precedents, government regulations, executive orders, agency rules, and the democratic political process.
Therapy and Counseling	Knowledge of principles, methods, and procedures for diagnosis, treatment, and rehabilitation of physical and mental dysfunctions, and for career counseling and guidance.
Psychology	Knowledge of human behavior and performance; individual differences in ability, personality, and interests; learning and motivation; psychological research methods; and the assessment and treatment of behavioral and affective disorders.
Telecommunications	Knowledge of transmission, broadcasting, switching, control, and operation of telecommunications systems.
Production and Processing	Knowledge of raw materials, production processes, quality control, costs, and other techniques for maximizing the effective manufacture and distribution of goods.
Sales and Marketing	Knowledge of principles and methods for showing, promoting, and selling products or services. This includes marketing strategy and tactics, product demonstration, sales techniques, and sales control systems.
Administration and Management	Knowledge of business and management principles involved in strategic planning, resource allocation, human resources modeling, leadership technique, production methods, and coordination of people and resources.
Public Safety and Security	Knowledge of relevant equipment, policies, procedures, and strategies to promote effective local, state, or national security operations for the protection of people, data, property, and institutions.
Personnel and Human Resources	Knowledge of principles and procedures for personnel recruitment, selection, training, compensation and benefits, labor relations and negotiation, and personnel information systems.
Foreign Language	Knowledge of the structure and content of a foreign (non-English) language including the meaning and spelling of words, rules of composition and grammar, and pronunciation.
Sociology and Anthropology	Knowledge of group behavior and dynamics, societal trends and influences, human migrations, ethnicity, cultures and their history and origins.
Communications and Media	Knowledge of media production, communication, and dissemination techniques and methods. This includes alternative ways to inform and entertain via written, oral, and visual media.
Economics and Accounting	Knowledge of economic and accounting principles and practices, the financial markets, banking and the analysis and reporting of financial data.
Biology	Knowledge of plant and animal organisms, their tissues, cells, functions, interdependencies, and interactions with each other and the environment.
Physics	Knowledge and prediction of physical principles, laws, their interrelationships, and applications to understanding fluid, material, and atmospheric dynamics, and mechanical, electrical, atomic and sub- atomic structures and processes.
Philosophy and Theology	Knowledge of different philosophical systems and religions. This includes their basic principles, values, ethics, ways of thinking, customs, practices, and their impact on human culture.
Engineering and Technology	Knowledge of the practical application of engineering science and technology. This includes applying principles, techniques, procedures, and equipment to the design and production of various goods and services.
Food Production	Knowledge of techniques and equipment for planting, growing, and harvesting food products (both plant and animal) for consumption, including storage/handling techniques.
Transportation	Knowledge of principles and methods for moving people or goods by air, rail, sea, or road, including the relative costs and benefits.
Mechanical	Knowledge of machines and tools, including their designs, uses, repair, and maintenance.

Design	Knowledge of design techniques, tools, and principles involved in production of precision technical plans, blueprints, drawings, and models.
Fine Arts	Knowledge of the theory and techniques required to compose, produce, and perform works of music, dance, visual arts, drama, and sculpture.
Geography	Knowledge of principles and methods for describing the features of land, sea, and air masses, including their physical characteristics, locations, interrelationships, and distribution of plant, animal, and human life.
History and Archeology	Knowledge of historical events and their causes, indicators, and effects on civilizations and cultures.
Building and Construction	Knowledge of materials, methods, and the tools involved in the construction or repair of houses, buildings, or other structures such as highways and roads.

Skills

Skills	Skills Definitions
Active Listening	Giving full attention to what other people are saying, taking time to understand the points being made, asking questions as appropriate, and not interrupting at inappropriate times.
Speaking	Talking to others to convey information effectively.
Active Learning	Understanding the implications of new information for both current and future problem-solving and decision-making.
Service Orientation	Actively looking for ways to help people.
Instructing	Teaching others how to do something.
Reading Comprehension	Understanding written sentences and paragraphs in work related documents.
Mathematics	Using mathematics to solve problems.
Time Management	Managing one's own time and the time of others.
Learning Strategies	Selecting and using training/instructional methods and procedures appropriate for the situation when learning or teaching new things.
Writing	Communicating effectively in writing as appropriate for the needs of the audience.
Coordination	Adjusting actions in relation to others' actions.
Monitoring	Monitoring/Assessing performance of yourself, other individuals, or organizations to make improvements or take corrective action.
Critical Thinking	Using logic and reasoning to identify the strengths and weaknesses of alternative solutions, conclusions or approaches to problems.
Social Perceptiveness	Being aware of others' reactions and understanding why they react as they do.
Complex Problem Solving	Identifying complex problems and reviewing related information to develop and evaluate options and implement solutions.
Judgment and Decision Making	Considering the relative costs and benefits of potential actions to choose the most appropriate one.
Troubleshooting	Determining causes of operating errors and deciding what to do about it.
Science	Using scientific rules and methods to solve problems.
Persuasion	Persuading others to change their minds or behavior.
Technology Design	Generating or adapting equipment and technology to serve user needs.
Management of Personnel Resources	Motivating, developing, and directing people as they work, identifying the best people for the job.
Quality Control Analysis	Conducting tests and inspections of products, services, or processes to evaluate quality or performance.
Operation and Control	Controlling operations of equipment or systems.
Systems Analysis	Determining how a system should work and how changes in conditions, operations, and the environment will affect outcomes.
Repairing	Repairing machines or systems using the needed tools.
Installation	Installing equipment, machines, wiring, or programs to meet specifications.
Equipment Selection	Determining the kind of tools and equipment needed to do a job.
Operation Monitoring	Watching gauges, dials, or other indicators to make sure a machine is working properly.
Negotiation	Bringing others together and trying to reconcile differences.
Equipment Maintenance	Performing routine maintenance on equipment and determining when and what kind of maintenance is needed.
Operations Analysis	Analyzing needs and product requirements to create a design.
Management of Material Resources	Obtaining and seeing to the appropriate use of equipment, facilities, and materials needed to do certain work.

Systems Evaluation	Identifying measures or indicators of system performance and the actions needed to improve or correct performance, relative to the goals of the system.
Programming	Writing computer programs for various purposes.
Management of Financial Resources	Determining how money will be spent to get the work done, and accounting for these expenditures.

Ability

Ability	Ability Definitions
Oral Expression	The ability to communicate information and ideas in speaking so others will understand.
Problem Sensitivity	The ability to tell when something is wrong or is likely to go wrong. It does not involve solving the problem, only recognizing there is a problem.
Oral Comprehension	The ability to listen to and understand information and ideas presented through spoken words and sentences.
Near Vision	The ability to see details at close range (within a few feet of the observer).
Speech Clarity	The ability to speak clearly so others can understand you.
Speech Recognition	The ability to identify and understand the speech of another person.
Information Ordering	The ability to arrange things or actions in a certain order or pattern according to a specific rule or set of rules (e.g., patterns of numbers, letters, words, pictures, mathematical operations).
Deductive Reasoning	The ability to apply general rules to specific problems to produce answers that make sense.
Written Comprehension	The ability to read and understand information and ideas presented in writing.
Selective Attention	The ability to concentrate on a task over a period of time without being distracted.
Manual Dexterity	The ability to quickly move your hand, your hand together with your arm, or your two hands to grasp, manipulate, or assemble objects.
Category Flexibility	The ability to generate or use different sets of rules for combining or grouping things in different ways.
Arm-Hand Steadiness	The ability to keep your hand and arm steady while moving your arm or while holding your arm and hand in one position.
Written Expression	The ability to communicate information and ideas in writing so others will understand.
Trunk Strength	The ability to use your abdominal and lower back muscles to support part of the body repeatedly or continuously over time without 'giving out' or fatiguing.
Finger Dexterity	The ability to make precisely coordinated movements of the fingers of one or both hands to grasp, manipulate, or assemble very small objects.
Inductive Reasoning	The ability to combine pieces of information to form general rules or conclusions (includes finding a relationship among seemingly unrelated events).
Mathematical Reasoning	The ability to choose the right mathematical methods or formulas to solve a problem.
Extent Flexibility	The ability to bend, stretch, twist, or reach with your body, arms, and/or legs.
Time Sharing	The ability to shift back and forth between two or more activities or sources of information (such as speech, sounds, touch, or other sources).
Flexibility of Closure	The ability to identify or detect a known pattern (a figure, object, word, or sound) that is hidden in other distracting material.
Number Facility	The ability to add, subtract, multiply, or divide quickly and correctly.
Memorization	The ability to remember information such as words, numbers, pictures, and procedures.
Visual Color Discrimination	The ability to match or detect differences between colors, including shades of color and brightness.
Stamina	The ability to exert yourself physically over long periods of time without getting winded or out of breath.
Perceptual Speed	The ability to quickly and accurately compare similarities and differences among sets of letters, numbers, objects, pictures, or patterns. The things to be compared may be presented at the same time or one after the other. This ability also includes comparing a presented object with a remembered object.
Control Precision	The ability to quickly and repeatedly adjust the controls of a machine or a vehicle to exact positions.
Multilimb Coordination	The ability to coordinate two or more limbs (for example, two arms, two legs, or one leg and one arm) while sitting, standing, or lying down. It does not involve performing the activities while the whole body is in motion.

Speed of Closure	The ability to quickly make sense of, combine, and organize information into meaningful patterns.
Visualization	The ability to imagine how something will look after it is moved around or when its parts are moved or rearranged.
Gross Body Coordination	The ability to coordinate the movement of your arms, legs, and torso together when the whole body is in motion.
Static Strength	The ability to exert maximum muscle force to lift, push, pull, or carry objects.
Auditory Attention	The ability to focus on a single source of sound in the presence of other distracting sounds.
Fluency of Ideas	The ability to come up with a number of ideas about a topic (the number of ideas is important, not their quality, correctness, or creativity).
Speed of Limb Movement	The ability to quickly move the arms and legs.
Far Vision	The ability to see details at a distance.
Depth Perception	The ability to judge which of several objects is closer or farther away from you, or to judge the distance between you and an object.
Wrist-Finger Speed	The ability to make fast, simple, repeated movements of the fingers, hands, and wrists.
Hearing Sensitivity	The ability to detect or tell the differences between sounds that vary in pitch and loudness.
Response Orientation	The ability to choose quickly between two or more movements in response to two or more different signals (lights, sounds, pictures). It includes the speed with which the correct response is started with the hand, foot, or other body part.
Originality	The ability to come up with unusual or clever ideas about a given topic or situation, or to develop creative ways to solve a problem.
Gross Body Equilibrium	The ability to keep or regain your body balance or stay upright when in an unstable position.
Explosive Strength	The ability to use short bursts of muscle force to propel oneself (as in jumping or sprinting), or to throw an object.
Reaction Time	The ability to quickly respond (with the hand, finger, or foot) to a signal (sound, light, picture) when it appears.
Sound Localization	The ability to tell the direction from which a sound originated.
Peripheral Vision	The ability to see objects or movement of objects to one's side when the eyes are looking ahead.
Dynamic Flexibility	The ability to quickly and repeatedly bend, stretch, twist, or reach out with your body, arms, and/or legs.
Glare Sensitivity	The ability to see objects in the presence of glare or bright lighting.
Dynamic Strength	The ability to exert muscle force repeatedly or continuously over time. This involves muscular endurance and resistance to muscle fatigue.
Rate Control	The ability to time your movements or the movement of a piece of equipment in anticipation of changes in the speed and/or direction of a moving object or scene.
Spatial Orientation	The ability to know your location in relation to the environment or to know where other objects are in relation to you.
Night Vision	The ability to see under low light conditions.

Work_Activity	Work_Activity Definitions
Interacting With Computers	Using computers and computer systems (including hardware and software) to program, write software, set up functions, enter data, or process information.
Getting Information	Observing, receiving, and otherwise obtaining information from all relevant sources.
Performing for or Working Directly with the Public	Performing for people or dealing directly with the public. This includes serving customers in restaurants and stores, and receiving clients or guests.
Establishing and Maintaining Interpersonal Relatio	Developing constructive and cooperative working relationships with others, and maintaining them over time.
Communicating with Supervisors, Peers, or Subordin	Providing information to supervisors, co-workers, and subordinates by telephone, in written form, e-mail, or in person.
Processing Information	Compiling, coding, categorizing, calculating, tabulating, auditing, or verifying information or data.
Making Decisions and Solving Problems	Analyzing information and evaluating results to choose the best solution and solve problems.
Identifying Objects, Actions, and Events	Identifying information by categorizing, estimating, recognizing differences or similarities, and detecting changes in circumstances or events.
Documenting/Recording Information	Entering, transcribing, recording, storing, or maintaining information in written or electronic/magnetic form.

Handling and Moving Objects	Using hands and arms in handling, installing, positioning, and moving materials, and manipulating things.
Interpreting the Meaning of Information for Others	Translating or explaining what information means and how it can be used.
Organizing, Planning, and Prioritizing Work	Developing specific goals and plans to prioritize, organize, and accomplish your work.
Evaluating Information to Determine Compliance wit	Using relevant information and individual judgment to determine whether events or processes comply with laws, regulations, or standards.
Inspecting Equipment, Structures, or Material	Inspecting equipment, structures, or materials to identify the cause of errors or other problems or defects.
Communicating with Persons Outside Organization	Communicating with people outside the organization, representing the organization to customers, the public, government, and other external sources. This information can be exchanged in person, in writing, or by telephone or e-mail.
Estimating the Quantifiable Characteristics of Pro	Estimating sizes, distances, and quantities; or determining time, costs, resources, or materials needed to perform a work activity.
Updating and Using Relevant Knowledge	Keeping up-to-date technically and applying new knowledge to your job.
Monitor Processes, Materials, or Surroundings	Monitoring and reviewing information from materials, events, or the environment, to detect or assess problems.
Coordinating the Work and Activities of Others	Getting members of a group to work together to accomplish tasks.
Training and Teaching Others	Identifying the educational needs of others, developing formal educational or training programs or classes, and teaching or instructing others.
Performing General Physical Activities	Performing physical activities that require considerable use of your arms and legs and moving your whole body, such as climbing, lifting, balancing, walking, stooping, and handling of materials.
Assisting and Caring for Others	Providing personal assistance, medical attention, emotional support, or other personal care to others such as coworkers, customers, or patients.
Judging the Qualities of Things, Services, or Peop	Assessing the value, importance, or quality of things or people.
Performing Administrative Activities	Performing day-to-day administrative tasks such as maintaining information files and processing paperwork.
Analyzing Data or Information	Identifying the underlying principles, reasons, or facts of information by breaking down information or data into separate parts.
Resolving Conflicts and Negotiating with Others	Handling complaints, settling disputes, and resolving grievances and conflicts, or otherwise negotiating with others.
Provide Consultation and Advice to Others	Providing guidance and expert advice to management or other groups on technical, systems-, or process-related topics.
Guiding, Directing, and Motivating Subordinates	Providing guidance and direction to subordinates, including setting performance standards and monitoring performance.
Developing and Building Teams	Encouraging and building mutual trust, respect, and cooperation among team members.
Coaching and Developing Others	Identifying the developmental needs of others and coaching, mentoring, or otherwise helping others to improve their knowledge or skills.
Selling or Influencing Others	Convincing others to buy merchandise/goods or to otherwise their minds or actions.
Thinking Creatively	Developing, designing, or creating new applications, ideas, relationships, systems, or products, including artistic contributions.
Developing Objectives and Strategies	Establishing long-range objectives and specifying the strategies and actions to achieve them.
Controlling Machines and Processes	Using either control mechanisms or direct physical activity to operate machines or processes (not including computers or vehicles).
Drafting, Laying Out, and Specifying Technical Dev	Providing documentation, detailed instructions, drawings, or specifications to tell others about how devices, parts, equipment, or structures are to be fabricated, constructed, assembled, modified, maintained, or used.
Repairing and Maintaining Electronic Equipment	Servicing, repairing, calibrating, regulating, fine-tuning, or testing machines, devices, and equipment that operate primarily on the basis of electrical or electronic (not mechanical) principles.
Repairing and Maintaining Mechanical Equipment	Servicing, repairing, adjusting, and testing machines, devices, moving parts, and equipment that operate primarily on the basis of mechanical (not electronic) principles.
Monitoring and Controlling Resources	Monitoring and controlling resources and overseeing the spending of money.
Scheduling Work and Activities	Scheduling events, programs, and activities, as well as the work of others.

| Operating Vehicles. Mechanized Devices. or Equipme | Running. maneuvering. navigating. or driving vehicles or mechanized equipment, such as forklifts. passenger vehicles. aircraft. or water craft. |
| Staffing Organizational Units | Recruiting. interviewing. selecting. hiring. and promoting employees in an organization. |

Work_Context	Work_Context Definitions
Telephone	How often do you have telephone conversations in this job?
Contact With Others	How much does this job require the worker to be in contact with others (face-to-face, by telephone, or otherwise) in order to perform it?
Importance of Being Exact or Accurate	How important is being very exact or highly accurate in performing this job?
Face-to-Face Discussions	How often do you have to have face-to-face discussions with individuals or teams in this job?
Spend Time Standing	How much does this job require standing?
Work With Work Group or Team	How important is it to work with others in a group or team in this job?
Importance of Repeating Same Tasks	How important is repeating the same physical activities (e.g., key entry) or mental activities (e.g.. checking entries in a ledger) over and over, without stopping. to performing this job?
Physical Proximity	To what extent does this job require the worker to perform job tasks in close physical proximity to other people?
Spend Time Using Your Hands to Handle, Control, or	How much does this job require using your hands to handle, control. or feel objects, tools or controls?
Spend Time Making Repetitive Motions	How much does this job require making repetitive motions?
Indoors, Environmentally Controlled	How often does this job require working indoors in environmentally controlled conditions?
Deal With Unpleasant or Angry People	How frequently does the worker have to deal with unpleasant, angry. or discourteous individuals as part of the job requirements?
Deal With External Customers	How important is it to work with external customers or the public in this job?
Time Pressure	How often does this job require the worker to meet strict deadlines?
Structured versus Unstructured Work	To what extent is this job structured for the worker, rather than allowing the worker to determine tasks, priorities, and goals?
Coordinate or Lead Others	How important is it to coordinate or lead others in accomplishing work activities in this job?
Freedom to Make Decisions	How much decision making freedom, without supervision, does the job offer?
Impact of Decisions on Co-workers or Company Resul	How do the decisions an employee makes impact the results of co-workers, clients or the company?
Level of Competition	To what extent does this job require the worker to compete or to be aware of competitive pressures?
Frequency of Decision Making	How frequently is the worker required to make decisions that affect other people, the financial resources, and/or the image and reputation of the organization?
Responsibility for Outcomes and Results	How responsible is the worker for work outcomes and results of other workers?
Degree of Automation	How automated is the job?
Consequence of Error	How serious would the result usually be if the worker made a mistake that was not readily correctable?
Frequency of Conflict Situations	How often are there conflict situations the employee has to face in this job?
Spend Time Bending or Twisting the Body	How much does this job require bending or twisting your body?
Letters and Memos	How often does the job require written letters and memos?
Sounds, Noise Levels Are Distracting or Uncomforta	How often does this job require working exposed to sounds and noise levels that are distracting or uncomfortable?
Spend Time Walking and Running	How much does this job require walking and running?
Public Speaking	How often do you have to perform public speaking in this job?
Exposed to Disease or Infections	How often does this job require exposure to disease/infections?
Pace Determined by Speed of Equipment	How important is it to this job that the pace is determined by the speed of equipment or machinery? (This does not refer to keeping busy at all times on this job.)
Electronic Mail	How often do you use electronic mail in this job?
Responsible for Others' Health and Safety	How much responsibility is there for the health and safety of others in this job?
Exposed to Minor Burns, Cuts, Bites, or Stings	How often does this job require exposure to minor burns, cuts, bites, or stings?

Exposed to Contaminants	How often does this job require working exposed to contaminants (such as pollutants. gases. dust or odors)?
Spend Time Kneeling. Crouching. Stooping. or Crawl	How much does this job require kneeling. crouching. stooping or crawling?
Extremely Bright or Inadequate Lighting	How often does this job require working in extremely bright or inadequate lighting conditions?
Deal With Physically Aggressive People	How frequently does this job require the worker to deal with physical aggression of violent individuals?
Spend Time Sitting	How much does this job require sitting?
Very Hot or Cold Temperatures	How often does this job require working in very hot (above 90 F degrees) or very cold (below 32 F degrees) temperatures?
Wear Common Protective or Safety Equipment such as	How much does this job require wearing common protective or safety equipment such as safety shoes. glasses. gloves. hard hats or live jackets?
Cramped Work Space, Awkward Positions	How often does this job require working in cramped work spaces that requires getting into awkward positions?
Exposed to Hazardous Conditions	How often does this job require exposure to hazardous conditions?
Spend Time Keeping or Regaining Balance	How much does this job require keeping or regaining your balance?
In an Enclosed Vehicle or Equipment	How often does this job require working in a closed vehicle or equipment (e.g.. car)?
Wear Specialized Protective or Safety Equipment su	How much does this job require wearing specialized protective or safety equipment such as breathing apparatus. safety harness, full protection suits, or radiation protection?
Indoors, Not Environmentally Controlled	How often does this job require working indoors in non-controlled environmental conditions (e.g.. warehouse without heat)?
Exposed to Hazardous Equipment	How often does this job require exposure to hazardous equipment?
Exposed to Whole Body Vibration	How often does this job require exposure to whole body vibration (e.g.. operate a jackhammer)?
In an Open Vehicle or Equipment	How often does this job require working in an open vehicle or equipment (e.g.. tractor)?
Exposed to Radiation	How often does this job require exposure to radiation?
Spend Time Climbing Ladders, Scaffolds, or Poles	How much does this job require climbing ladders. scaffolds, or poles?
Outdoors, Exposed to Weather	How often does this job require working outdoors. exposed to all weather conditions?
Outdoors, Under Cover	How often does this job require working outdoors, under cover (e.g., structure with roof but no walls)?
Exposed to High Places	How often does this job require exposure to high places?

Job Zone Component	Job Zone Component Definitions
Title	Job Zone Two: Some Preparation Needed
Overall Experience	Some previous work-related skill, knowledge, or experience may be helpful in these occupations, but usually is not needed. For example, a drywall installer might benefit from experience installing drywall, but an inexperienced person could still learn to be an installer with little difficulty.
Job Training	Employees in these occupations need anywhere from a few months to one year of working with experienced employees.
Job Zone Examples	These occupations often involve using your knowledge and skills to help others. Examples include drywall installers, fire inspectors, flight attendants, pharmacy technicians, salespersons (retail), and tellers.
SVP Range	(4.0 to < 6.0)
Education	These occupations usually require a high school diploma and may require some vocational training or job-related course work. In some cases, an associate's or bachelor's degree could be needed.

Work_Styles	Work_Styles Definitions
Attention to Detail	Job requires being careful about detail and thorough in completing work tasks.
Dependability	Job requires being reliable, responsible. and dependable. and fulfilling obligations.
Cooperation	Job requires being pleasant with others on the job and displaying a good-natured, cooperative attitude.
Integrity	Job requires being honest and ethical.
Self Control	Job requires maintaining composure, keeping emotions in check, controlling anger, and avoiding aggressive behavior, even in very difficult situations.

597

Concern for Others	Job requires being sensitive to others' needs and feelings and being understanding and helpful on the job.
Social Orientation	Job requires preferring to work with others rather than alone, and being personally connected with others on the job.
Stress Tolerance	Job requires accepting criticism and dealing calmly and effectively with high stress situations.
Initiative	Job requires a willingness to take on responsibilities and challenges.
Adaptability/Flexibility	Job requires being open to change (positive or negative) and to considerable variety in the workplace.
Independence	Job requires developing one's own ways of doing things, guiding oneself with little or no supervision, and depending on oneself to get things done.
Analytical Thinking	Job requires analyzing information and using logic to address work-related issues and problems.
Achievement/Effort	Job requires establishing and maintaining personally challenging achievement goals and exerting effort toward mastering tasks.
Leadership	Job requires a willingness to lead, take charge, and offer opinions and direction.
Persistence	Job requires persistence in the face of obstacles.
Innovation	Job requires creativity and alternative thinking to develop new ideas for and answers to work-related problems.

29-2054.00 - Respiratory Therapy Technicians

Provide specific, well defined respiratory care procedures under the direction of respiratory therapists and physicians.

Tasks

1) Administer breathing and oxygen procedures such as intermittent positive pressure breathing treatments, ultrasonic nebulizer treatments and incentive spirometer treatments.

2) Follow and enforce safety rules applying to equipment.

3) Perform diagnostic procedures to assess the severity of respiratory dysfunction in patients.

4) Clean, sterilize, check and maintain respiratory therapy equipment.

5) Teach patients how to use respiratory equipment at home.

6) Use ventilators and various oxygen devices and aerosol and breathing treatments in the provision of respiratory therapy.

7) Interview and examine patients to collect clinical data.

8) Prepare and test devices such as mechanical ventilators, therapeutic gas administration apparatus, environmental control systems, aerosol generators and EKG machines.

9) Monitor patients during treatment and report any unusual reactions to the respiratory therapist.

10) Provide respiratory care involving the application of well-defined therapeutic techniques under the supervision of a respiratory therapist and a physician.

11) Teach or oversee other workers who provide respiratory care services.

12) Recommend and review bedside procedures, x-rays, and laboratory tests.

13) Keep records of patients' therapy, completing all necessary forms.

14) Explain treatment procedures to patients.

15) Set equipment controls to regulate the flow of oxygen, gases, mists, or aerosols.

16) Assess patients' response to treatments and modify treatments according to protocol if necessary.

17) Read and evaluate physicians' orders and patients' chart information to determine patients' condition and treatment protocols.

Knowledge	Knowledge Definitions
Medicine and Dentistry	Knowledge of the information and techniques needed to diagnose and treat human injuries, diseases, and deformities. This includes symptoms, treatment alternatives, drug properties and interactions, and preventive health-care measures.
Customer and Personal Service	Knowledge of principles and processes for providing customer and personal services. This includes customer needs assessment, meeting quality standards for services, and evaluation of customer satisfaction.
Chemistry	Knowledge of the chemical composition, structure, and properties of substances and of the chemical processes and transformations that they undergo. This includes uses of chemicals and their interactions, danger signs, production techniques, and disposal methods.
Psychology	Knowledge of human behavior and performance; individual differences in ability, personality, and interests; learning and motivation; psychological research methods; and the assessment and treatment of behavioral and affective disorders.
English Language	Knowledge of the structure and content of the English language including the meaning and spelling of words, rules of composition, and grammar.
Mathematics	Knowledge of arithmetic, algebra, geometry, calculus, statistics, and their applications.
Education and Training	Knowledge of principles and methods for curriculum and training design, teaching and instruction for individuals and groups, and the measurement of training effects.
Biology	Knowledge of plant and animal organisms, their tissues, cells, functions, interdependencies, and interactions with each other and the environment.
Public Safety and Security	Knowledge of relevant equipment, policies, procedures, and strategies to promote effective local, state, or national security operations for the protection of people, data, property, and institutions.
Physics	Knowledge and prediction of physical principles, laws, their interrelationships, and applications to understanding fluid, material, and atmospheric dynamics, and mechanical, electrical, atomic and sub-atomic structures and processes.
Computers and Electronics	Knowledge of circuit boards, processors, chips, electronic equipment, and computer hardware and software, including applications and programming.
Mechanical	Knowledge of machines and tools, including their designs, uses, repair, and maintenance.
Therapy and Counseling	Knowledge of principles, methods, and procedures for diagnosis, treatment, and rehabilitation of physical and mental dysfunctions, and for career counseling and guidance.
Law and Government	Knowledge of laws, legal codes, court procedures, precedents, government regulations, executive orders, agency rules, and the democratic political process.
Clerical	Knowledge of administrative and clerical procedures and systems such as word processing, managing files and records, stenography and transcription, designing forms, and other office procedures and terminology.
Administration and Management	Knowledge of business and management principles involved in strategic planning, resource allocation, human resources modeling, leadership technique, production methods, and coordination of people and resources.
Engineering and Technology	Knowledge of the practical application of engineering science and technology. This includes applying principles, techniques, procedures, and equipment to the design and production of various goods and services.
Sociology and Anthropology	Knowledge of group behavior and dynamics, societal trends and influences, human migrations, ethnicity, cultures and their history and origins.
Philosophy and Theology	Knowledge of different philosophical systems and religions. This includes their basic principles, values, ethics, ways of thinking, customs, practices, and their impact on human culture.
Personnel and Human Resources	Knowledge of principles and procedures for personnel recruitment, selection, training, compensation and benefits, labor relations and negotiation, and personnel information systems.
Economics and Accounting	Knowledge of economic and accounting principles and practices, the financial markets, banking and the analysis and reporting of financial data.
Foreign Language	Knowledge of the structure and content of a foreign (non-English) language including the meaning and spelling of words, rules of composition and grammar, and pronunciation.
Communications and Media	Knowledge of media production, communication, and dissemination techniques and methods. This includes alternative ways to inform and entertain via written, oral, and visual media.
Production and Processing	Knowledge of raw materials, production processes, quality control, costs, and other techniques for maximizing the effective manufacture and distribution of goods.
Telecommunications	Knowledge of transmission, broadcasting, switching, control, and operation of telecommunications systems.

Sales and Marketing	Knowledge of principles and methods for showing, promoting, and selling products or services. This includes marketing strategy and tactics, product demonstration, sales techniques, and sales control systems.
Geography	Knowledge of principles and methods for describing the features of land, sea, and air masses, including their physical characteristics, locations, interrelationships, and distribution of plant, animal, and human life.
Design	Knowledge of design techniques, tools, and principles involved in production of precision technical plans, blueprints, drawings, and models.
History and Archeology	Knowledge of historical events and their causes, indicators, and effects on civilizations and cultures.
Transportation	Knowledge of principles and methods for moving people or goods by air, rail, sea, or road, including the relative costs and benefits.
Food Production	Knowledge of techniques and equipment for planting, growing, and harvesting food products (both plant and animal) for consumption, including storage/handling techniques.
Building and Construction	Knowledge of materials, methods, and the tools involved in the construction or repair of houses, buildings, or other structures such as highways and roads.
Fine Arts	Knowledge of the theory and techniques required to compose, produce, and perform works of music, dance, visual arts, drama, and sculpture.

Skills — Skills Definitions

Time Management	Managing one's own time and the time of others.
Critical Thinking	Using logic and reasoning to identify the strengths and weaknesses of alternative solutions, conclusions or approaches to problems.
Reading Comprehension	Understanding written sentences and paragraphs in work related documents.
Troubleshooting	Determining causes of operating errors and deciding what to do about it.
Active Listening	Giving full attention to what other people are saying, taking time to understand the points being made, asking questions as appropriate, and not interrupting at inappropriate times.
Instructing	Teaching others how to do something.
Operation Monitoring	Watching gauges, dials, or other indicators to make sure a machine is working properly.
Judgment and Decision Making	Considering the relative costs and benefits of potential actions to choose the most appropriate one.
Speaking	Talking to others to convey information effectively.
Service Orientation	Actively looking for ways to help people.
Operation and Control	Controlling operations of equipment or systems.
Active Learning	Understanding the implications of new information for both current and future problem-solving and decision-making.
Equipment Maintenance	Performing routine maintenance on equipment and determining when and what kind of maintenance is needed.
Monitoring	Monitoring/Assessing performance of yourself, other individuals, or organizations to make improvements or take corrective action.
Learning Strategies	Selecting and using training/instructional methods and procedures appropriate for the situation when learning or teaching new things.
Equipment Selection	Determining the kind of tools and equipment needed to do a job.
Writing	Communicating effectively in writing as appropriate for the needs of the audience.
Science	Using scientific rules and methods to solve problems.
Mathematics	Using mathematics to solve problems.
Quality Control Analysis	Conducting tests and inspections of products, services, or processes to evaluate quality or performance.
Social Perceptiveness	Being aware of others' reactions and understanding why they react as they do.
Management of Material Resources	Obtaining and seeing to the appropriate use of equipment, facilities, and materials needed to do certain work.
Complex Problem Solving	Identifying complex problems and reviewing related information to develop and evaluate options and implement solutions.
Management of Personnel Resources	Motivating, developing, and directing people as they work, identifying the best people for the job.
Persuasion	Persuading others to change their minds or behavior.
Technology Design	Generating or adapting equipment and technology to serve user needs.
Coordination	Adjusting actions in relation to others' actions.

Operations Analysis	Analyzing needs and product requirements to create a design.
Systems Analysis	Determining how a system should work and how changes in conditions, operations, and the environment will affect outcomes.
Systems Evaluation	Identifying measures or indicators of system performance and the actions needed to improve or correct performance, relative to the goals of the system.
Negotiation	Bringing others together and trying to reconcile differences.
Repairing	Repairing machines or systems using the needed tools.
Installation	Installing equipment, machines, wiring, or programs to meet specifications.
Management of Financial Resources	Determining how money will be spent to get the work done, and accounting for these expenditures.
Programming	Writing computer programs for various purposes.

Ability — Ability Definitions

Oral Expression	The ability to communicate information and ideas in speaking so others will understand.
Problem Sensitivity	The ability to tell when something is wrong or is likely to go wrong. It does not involve solving the problem, only recognizing there is a problem.
Oral Comprehension	The ability to listen to and understand information and ideas presented through spoken words and sentences.
Written Comprehension	The ability to read and understand information and ideas presented in writing.
Speech Clarity	The ability to speak clearly so others can understand you.
Near Vision	The ability to see details at close range (within a few feet of the observer).
Information Ordering	The ability to arrange things or actions in a certain order or pattern according to a specific rule or set of rules (e.g., patterns of numbers, letters, words, pictures, mathematical operations).
Speech Recognition	The ability to identify and understand the speech of another person.
Inductive Reasoning	The ability to combine pieces of information to form general rules or conclusions (includes finding a relationship among seemingly unrelated events).
Deductive Reasoning	The ability to apply general rules to specific problems to produce answers that make sense.
Written Expression	The ability to communicate information and ideas in writing so others will understand.
Category Flexibility	The ability to generate or use different sets of rules for combining or grouping things in different ways.
Control Precision	The ability to quickly and repeatedly adjust the controls of a machine or a vehicle to exact positions.
Flexibility of Closure	The ability to identify or detect a known pattern (a figure, object, word, or sound) that is hidden in other distracting material.
Finger Dexterity	The ability to make precisely coordinated movements of the fingers of one or both hands to grasp, manipulate, or assemble very small objects.
Selective Attention	The ability to concentrate on a task over a period of time without being distracted.
Perceptual Speed	The ability to quickly and accurately compare similarities and differences among sets of letters, numbers, objects, pictures, or patterns. The things to be compared may be presented at the same time or one after the other. This ability also includes comparing a presented object with a remembered object.
Originality	The ability to come up with unusual or clever ideas about a given topic or situation, or to develop creative ways to solve a problem.
Time Sharing	The ability to shift back and forth between two or more activities or sources of information (such as speech, sounds, touch, or other sources).
Arm-Hand Steadiness	The ability to keep your hand and arm steady while moving your arm or while holding your arm and hand in one position.
Extent Flexibility	The ability to bend, stretch, twist, or reach with your body, arms, and/or legs.
Trunk Strength	The ability to use your abdominal and lower back muscles to support part of the body repeatedly or continuously over time without 'giving out' or fatiguing.
Fluency of Ideas	The ability to come up with a number of ideas about a topic (the number of ideas is important, not their quality, correctness, or creativity).
Auditory Attention	The ability to focus on a single source of sound in the presence of other distracting sounds.
Speed of Closure	The ability to quickly make sense of, combine, and organize information into meaningful patterns.

599

Multilimb Coordination	The ability to coordinate two or more limbs (for example, two arms, two legs, or one leg and one arm) while sitting, standing, or lying down. It does not involve performing the activities while the whole body is in motion.
Manual Dexterity	The ability to quickly move your hand, your hand together with your arm, or your two hands to grasp, manipulate, or assemble objects.
Hearing Sensitivity	The ability to detect or tell the differences between sounds that vary in pitch and loudness.
Memorization	The ability to remember information such as words, numbers, pictures, and procedures.
Stamina	The ability to exert yourself physically over long periods of time without getting winded or out of breath.
Static Strength	The ability to exert maximum muscle force to lift, push, pull, or carry objects.
Gross Body Coordination	The ability to coordinate the movement of your arms, legs, and torso together when the whole body is in motion.
Visual Color Discrimination	The ability to match or detect differences between colors, including shades of color and brightness.
Speed of Limb Movement	The ability to quickly move the arms and legs.
Response Orientation	The ability to choose quickly between two or more movements in response to two or more different signals (lights, sounds, pictures). It includes the speed with which the correct response is started with the hand, foot, or other body part.
Visualization	The ability to imagine how something will look after it is moved around or when its parts are moved or rearranged.
Reaction Time	The ability to quickly respond (with the hand, finger, or foot) to a signal (sound, light, picture) when it appears.
Depth Perception	The ability to judge which of several objects is closer or farther away from you, or to judge the distance between you and an object.
Far Vision	The ability to see details at a distance.
Mathematical Reasoning	The ability to choose the right mathematical methods or formulas to solve a problem.
Number Facility	The ability to add, subtract, multiply, or divide quickly and correctly.
Rate Control	The ability to time your movements or the movement of a piece of equipment in anticipation of changes in the speed and/or direction of a moving object or scene.
Wrist-Finger Speed	The ability to make fast, simple, repeated movements of the fingers, hands, and wrists.
Gross Body Equilibrium	The ability to keep or regain your body balance or stay upright when in an unstable position.
Dynamic Strength	The ability to exert muscle force repeatedly or continuously over time. This involves muscular endurance and resistance to muscle fatigue.
Explosive Strength	The ability to use short bursts of muscle force to propel oneself (as in jumping or sprinting), or to throw an object.
Spatial Orientation	The ability to know your location in relation to the environment or to know where other objects are in relation to you.
Sound Localization	The ability to tell the direction from which a sound originated.
Glare Sensitivity	The ability to see objects in the presence of glare or bright lighting.
Peripheral Vision	The ability to see objects or movement of objects to one's side when the eyes are looking ahead.
Night Vision	The ability to see under low light conditions.
Dynamic Flexibility	The ability to quickly and repeatedly bend, stretch, twist, or reach out with your body, arms, and/or legs.

Work_Activity	Work_Activity Definitions
Assisting and Caring for Others	Providing personal assistance, medical attention, emotional support, or other personal care to others such as coworkers, customers, or patients.
Inspecting Equipment, Structures, or Material	Inspecting equipment, structures, or materials to identify the cause of errors or other problems or defects.
Performing for or Working Directly with the Public	Performing for people or dealing directly with the public. This includes serving customers in restaurants and stores, and receiving clients or guests.
Communicating with Supervisors, Peers, or Subordin	Providing information to supervisors, co-workers, and subordinates by telephone, in written form, e-mail, or in person.
Identifying Objects, Actions, and Events	Identifying information by categorizing, estimating, recognizing differences or similarities, and detecting changes in circumstances or events.
Making Decisions and Solving Problems	Analyzing information and evaluating results to choose the best solution and solve problems.

Getting Information	Observing, receiving, and otherwise obtaining information from all relevant sources.
Updating and Using Relevant Knowledge	Keeping up-to-date technically and applying new knowledge to your job.
Establishing and Maintaining Interpersonal Relatio	Developing constructive and cooperative working relationships with others, and maintaining them over time.
Organizing, Planning, and Prioritizing Work	Developing specific goals and plans to prioritize, organize, and accomplish your work.
Evaluating Information to Determine Compliance wit	Using relevant information and individual judgment to determine whether events or processes comply with laws, regulations, or standards.
Interpreting the Meaning of Information for Others	Translating or explaining what information means and how it can be used.
Controlling Machines and Processes	Using either control mechanisms or direct physical activity to operate machines or processes (not including computers or vehicles).
Training and Teaching Others	Identifying the educational needs of others, developing formal educational or training programs or classes, and teaching or instructing others.
Documenting/Recording Information	Entering, transcribing, recording, storing, or maintaining information in written or electronic/magnetic form.
Processing Information	Compiling, coding, categorizing, calculating, tabulating, auditing, or verifying information or data.
Developing Objectives and Strategies	Establishing long-range objectives and specifying the strategies and actions to achieve them.
Monitor Processes, Materials, or Surroundings	Monitoring and reviewing information from materials, events, or the environment, to detect or assess problems.
Judging the Qualities of Things, Services, or Peop	Assessing the value, importance, or quality of things or people.
Coordinating the Work and Activities of Others	Getting members of a group to work together to accomplish tasks.
Thinking Creatively	Developing, designing, or creating new applications, ideas, relationships, systems, or products, including artistic contributions.
Provide Consultation and Advice to Others	Providing guidance and expert advice to management or other groups on technical, systems-, or process-related topics.
Developing and Building Teams	Encouraging and building mutual trust, respect, and cooperation among team members.
Analyzing Data or Information	Identifying the underlying principles, reasons, or facts of information by breaking down information or data into separate parts.
Performing General Physical Activities	Performing physical activities that require considerable use of your arms and legs and moving your whole body, such as climbing, lifting, balancing, walking, stooping, and handling of materials.
Communicating with Persons Outside Organization	Communicating with people outside the organization, representing the organization to customers, the public, government, and other external sources. This information can be exchanged in person, in writing, or by telephone or e-mail.
Guiding, Directing, and Motivating Subordinates	Providing guidance and direction to subordinates, including setting performance standards and monitoring performance.
Interacting With Computers	Using computers and computer systems (including hardware and software) to program, write software, set up functions, enter data, or process information.
Selling or Influencing Others	Convincing others to buy merchandise/goods or to otherwise change their minds or actions.
Handling and Moving Objects	Using hands and arms in handling, installing, positioning, and moving materials, and manipulating things.
Resolving Conflicts and Negotiating with Others	Handling complaints, settling disputes, and resolving grievances and conflicts, or otherwise negotiating with others.
Scheduling Work and Activities	Scheduling events, programs, and activities, as well as the work of others.
Estimating the Quantifiable Characteristics of Pro	Estimating sizes, distances, and quantities; or determining time, costs, resources, or materials needed to perform a work activity.
Performing Administrative Activities	Performing day-to-day administrative tasks such as maintaining information files and processing paperwork.
Coaching and Developing Others	Identifying the developmental needs of others and coaching, mentoring, or otherwise helping others to improve their knowledge or skills.
Repairing and Maintaining Electronic Equipment	Servicing, repairing, calibrating, regulating, fine-tuning, or testing machines, devices, and equipment that operate primarily on the basis of electrical or electronic (not mechanical) principles.
Staffing Organizational Units	Recruiting, interviewing, selecting, hiring, and promoting employees in an organization.

Monitoring and Controlling Resources	Monitoring and controlling resources and overseeing the spending of money.
Repairing and Maintaining Mechanical Equipment	Servicing, repairing, adjusting, and testing machines, devices, moving parts, and equipment that operate primarily on the basis of mechanical (not electronic) principles.
Drafting, Laying Out, and Specifying Technical Dev	Providing documentation, detailed instructions, drawings, or specifications to tell others about how devices, parts, equipment, or structures are to be fabricated, constructed, assembled, modified, maintained, or used.
Operating Vehicles, Mechanized Devices, or Equipme	Running, maneuvering, navigating, or driving vehicles or mechanized equipment, such as forklifts, passenger vehicles, aircraft, or water craft.

Work_Context	Work_Context Definitions
Contact With Others	How much does this job require the worker to be in contact with others (face-to-face, by telephone, or otherwise) in order to perform it?
Indoors, Environmentally Controlled	How often does this job require working indoors in environmentally controlled conditions?
Face-to-Face Discussions	How often do you have to have face-to-face discussions with individuals or teams in this job?
Exposed to Disease or Infections	How often does this job require exposure to disease/infections?
Telephone	How often do you have telephone conversations in this job?
Structured versus Unstructured Work	To what extent is this job structured for the worker, rather than allowing the worker to determine tasks, priorities, and goals?
Physical Proximity	To what extent does this job require the worker to perform job tasks in close physical proximity to other people?
Consequence of Error	How serious would the result usually be if the worker made a mistake that was not readily correctable?
Work With Work Group or Team	How important is it to work with others in a group or team in this job?
Frequency of Decision Making	How frequently is the worker required to make decisions that affect other people, the financial resources, and/or the image and reputation of the organization?
Freedom to Make Decisions	How much decision making freedom, without supervision, does the job offer?
Spend Time Using Your Hands to Handle, Control, or	How much does this job require using your hands to handle, control, or feel objects, tools or controls?
Exposed to Contaminants	How often does this job require working exposed to contaminants (such as pollutants, gases, dust or odors)?
Wear Common Protective or Safety Equipment such as	How much does this job require wearing common protective or safety equipment such as safety shoes, glasses, gloves, hard hats or life jackets?
Deal With Unpleasant or Angry People	How frequently does the worker have to deal with unpleasant, angry, or discourteous individuals as part of the job requirements?
Importance of Being Exact or Accurate	How important is being very exact or highly accurate in performing this job?
Spend Time Walking and Running	How much does this job require walking and running?
Spend Time Standing	How much does this job require standing?
Time Pressure	How often does this job require the worker to meet strict deadlines?
Impact of Decisions on Co-workers or Company Resul	How do the decisions an employee makes impact the results of co-workers, clients or the company?
Responsible for Others' Health and Safety	How much responsibility is there for the health and safety of others in this job?
Sounds, Noise Levels Are Distracting or Uncomforta	How often does this job require working exposed to sounds and noise levels that are distracting or uncomfortable?
Cramped Work Space, Awkward Positions	How often does this job require working in cramped work spaces that requires getting into awkward positions?
Exposed to Radiation	How often does this job require exposure to radiation?
Deal With External Customers	How important is it to work with external customers or the public in this job?
Responsibility for Outcomes and Results	How responsible is the worker for work outcomes and results of other workers?
Importance of Repeating Same Tasks	How important is repeating the same physical activities (e.g., key entry) or mental activities (e.g., checking entries in a ledger) over and over, without stopping, to performing this job?
Coordinate or Lead Others	How important is it to coordinate or lead others in accomplishing work activities in this job?
Spend Time Making Repetitive Motions	How much does this job require making repetitive motions?
Frequency of Conflict Situations	How often are there conflict situations the employee has to face in this job?
Spend Time Bending or Twisting the Body	How much does this job require bending or twisting your body?
Level of Competition	To what extent does this job require the worker to compete or to be aware of competitive pressures?
Letters and Memos	How often does the job require written letters and memos?
Deal With Physically Aggressive People	How frequently does this job require the worker to deal with physical aggression of violent individuals?
Spend Time Kneeling, Crouching, Stooping, or Crawl	How much does this job require kneeling, crouching, stooping or crawling?
Spend Time Sitting	How much does this job require sitting?
Wear Specialized Protective or Safety Equipment su	How much does this job require wearing specialized protective or safety equipment such as breathing apparatus, safety harness, full protection suits, or radiation protection?
Extremely Bright or Inadequate Lighting	How often does this job require working in extremely bright or inadequate lighting conditions?
Electronic Mail	How often do you use electronic mail in this job?
Public Speaking	How often do you have to perform public speaking in this job?
Exposed to Hazardous Conditions	How often does this job require exposure to hazardous conditions?
Exposed to Minor Burns, Cuts, Bites, or Stings	How often does this job require exposure to minor burns, cuts, bites, or stings?
Degree of Automation	How automated is the job?
Spend Time Keeping or Regaining Balance	How much does this job require keeping or regaining your balance?
Pace Determined by Speed of Equipment	How important is it to this job that the pace is determined by the speed of equipment or machinery? (This does not refer to keeping busy at all times on this job.)
In an Enclosed Vehicle or Equipment	How often does this job require working in a closed vehicle or equipment (e.g., car)?
Exposed to Hazardous Equipment	How often does this job require exposure to hazardous equipment?
Indoors, Not Environmentally Controlled	How often does this job require working indoors in non-controlled environmental conditions (e.g., warehouse without heat)?
Outdoors, Exposed to Weather	How often does this job require working outdoors, exposed to all weather conditions?
Very Hot or Cold Temperatures	How often does this job require working in very hot (above 90 F degrees) or very cold (below 32 F degrees) temperatures?
In an Open Vehicle or Equipment	How often does this job require working in an open vehicle or equipment (e.g., tractor)?
Outdoors, Under Cover	How often does this job require working outdoors, under cover (e.g., structure with roof but no walls)?
Spend Time Climbing Ladders, Scaffolds, or Poles	How much does this job require climbing ladders, scaffolds, or poles?
Exposed to High Places	How often does this job require exposure to high places?
Exposed to Whole Body Vibration	How often does this job require exposure to whole body vibration (e.g., operate a jackhammer)?

Job Zone Component	Job Zone Component Definitions
Title	Job Zone Three: Medium Preparation Needed
Overall Experience	Previous work-related skill, knowledge, or experience is required for these occupations. For example, an electrician must have completed three or four years of apprenticeship or several years of vocational training, and often must have passed a licensing exam, in order to perform the job.
Job Training	Employees in these occupations usually need one or two years of training involving both on-the-job experience and informal training with experienced workers.
Job Zone Examples	These occupations usually involve using communication and organizational skills to coordinate, supervise, manage, or train others to accomplish goals. Examples include dental assistants, electricians, fish and game wardens, legal secretaries, personnel recruiters, and recreation workers.
SVP Range	(6.0 to < 7.0)
Education	Most occupations in this zone require training in vocational schools, related on-the-job experience, or an associate's degree. Some may require a bachelor's degree.

Work_Styles	Work_Styles Definitions
Dependability	Job requires being reliable, responsible, and dependable, and fulfilling obligations.

601

Integrity	Job requires being honest and ethical.	
Attention to Detail	Job requires being careful about detail and thorough in completing work tasks.	
Concern for Others	Job requires being sensitive to others' needs and feelings and being understanding and helpful on the job.	
Cooperation	Job requires being pleasant with others on the job and displaying a good-natured, cooperative attitude.	
Self Control	Job requires maintaining composure, keeping emotions in check, controlling anger, and avoiding aggressive behavior, even in very difficult situations.	
Stress Tolerance	Job requires accepting criticism and dealing calmly and effectively with high stress situations.	
Independence	Job requires developing one's own ways of doing things, guiding oneself with little or no supervision, and depending on oneself to get things done.	
Adaptability/Flexibility	Job requires being open to change (positive or negative) and to considerable variety in the workplace.	
Social Orientation	Job requires preferring to work with others rather than alone, and being personally connected with others on the job.	
Initiative	Job requires a willingness to take on responsibilities and challenges.	
Achievement/Effort	Job requires establishing and maintaining personally challenging achievement goals and exerting effort toward mastering tasks.	
Analytical Thinking	Job requires analyzing information and using logic to address work-related issues and problems.	
Persistence	Job requires persistence in the face of obstacles.	
Leadership	Job requires a willingness to lead, take charge, and offer opinions and direction.	
Innovation	Job requires creativity and alternative thinking to develop new ideas for and answers to work-related problems.	

29-2055.00 - Surgical Technologists

Assist in operations, under the supervision of surgeons, registered nurses, or other surgical personnel. May help set up operating room, prepare and transport patients for surgery, adjust lights and equipment, pass instruments and other supplies to surgeons and surgeon's assistants, hold retractors, cut sutures, and help count sponges, needles, supplies, and instruments.

Tasks

1) Provide technical assistance to surgeons, surgical nurses and anesthesiologists.

2) Operate, assemble, adjust, or monitor sterilizers, lights, suction machines, and diagnostic equipment to ensure proper operation.

3) Scrub arms and hands and assist the surgical team to scrub and put on gloves, masks, and surgical clothing.

4) Count sponges, needles, and instruments before and after operation.

5) Wash and sterilize equipment using germicides and sterilizers.

6) Position patients on the operating table and cover them with sterile surgical drapes to prevent exposure.

7) Monitor and continually assess operating room conditions, including patient and surgical team needs.

8) Clean and restock the operating room, placing equipment and supplies and arranging instruments according to instruction.

9) Prepare, care for and dispose of tissue specimens taken for laboratory analysis.

10) Observe patients' vital signs to assess physical condition.

11) Maintain supply of fluids, such as plasma, saline, blood and glucose, for use during operations.

12) Maintain files and records of surgical procedures.

13) Hand instruments and supplies to surgeons and surgeons' assistants, hold retractors and cut sutures, and perform other tasks as directed by surgeon during operation.

Knowledge	Knowledge Definitions
Medicine and Dentistry	Knowledge of the information and techniques needed to diagnose and treat human injuries, diseases, and deformities. This includes symptoms, treatment alternatives, drug properties and interactions, and preventive health-care measures.
Customer and Personal Service	Knowledge of principles and processes for providing customer and personal services. This includes customer needs assessment, meeting quality standards for services, and evaluation of customer satisfaction.
English Language	Knowledge of the structure and content of the English language including the meaning and spelling of words, rules of composition, and grammar.
Education and Training	Knowledge of principles and methods for curriculum and training design, teaching and instruction for individuals and groups, and the measurement of training effects.
Chemistry	Knowledge of the chemical composition, structure, and properties of substances and of the chemical processes and transformations that they undergo. This includes uses of chemicals and their interactions, danger signs, production techniques, and disposal methods.
Psychology	Knowledge of human behavior and performance; individual differences in ability, personality, and interests; learning and motivation; psychological research methods; and the assessment and treatment of behavioral and affective disorders.
Biology	Knowledge of plant and animal organisms, their tissues, cells, functions, interdependencies, and interactions with each other and the environment.
Law and Government	Knowledge of laws, legal codes, court procedures, precedents, government regulations, executive orders, agency rules, and the democratic political process.
Public Safety and Security	Knowledge of relevant equipment, policies, procedures, and strategies to promote effective local, state, or national security operations for the protection of people, data, property, and institutions.
Mathematics	Knowledge of arithmetic, algebra, geometry, calculus, statistics, and their applications.
Mechanical	Knowledge of machines and tools, including their designs, uses, repair, and maintenance.
Philosophy and Theology	Knowledge of different philosophical systems and religions. This includes their basic principles, values, ethics, ways of thinking, customs, practices, and their impact on human culture.
Therapy and Counseling	Knowledge of principles, methods, and procedures for diagnosis, treatment, and rehabilitation of physical and mental dysfunctions, and for career counseling and guidance.
Computers and Electronics	Knowledge of circuit boards, processors, chips, electronic equipment, and computer hardware and software, including applications and programming.
Engineering and Technology	Knowledge of the practical application of engineering science and technology. This includes applying principles, techniques, procedures, and equipment to the design and production of various goods and services.
Production and Processing	Knowledge of raw materials, production processes, quality control, costs, and other techniques for maximizing the effective manufacture and distribution of goods.
Personnel and Human Resources	Knowledge of principles and procedures for personnel recruitment, selection, training, compensation and benefits, labor relations and negotiation, and personnel information systems.
Clerical	Knowledge of administrative and clerical procedures and systems such as word processing, managing files and records, stenography and transcription, designing forms, and other office procedures and terminology.
Transportation	Knowledge of principles and methods for moving people or goods by air, rail, sea, or road, including the relative costs and benefits.
Administration and Management	Knowledge of business and management principles involved in strategic planning, resource allocation, human resources modeling, leadership technique, production methods, and coordination of people and resources.
Communications and Media	Knowledge of media production, communication, and dissemination techniques and methods. This includes alternative ways to inform and entertain via written, oral, and visual media.
Telecommunications	Knowledge of transmission, broadcasting, switching, control, and operation of telecommunications systems.
Sociology and Anthropology	Knowledge of group behavior and dynamics, societal trends and influences, human migrations, ethnicity, cultures and their history and origins.
Design	Knowledge of design techniques, tools, and principles involved in production of precision technical plans, blueprints, drawings, and models.

Physics	Knowledge and prediction of physical principles, laws, their interrelationships, and applications to understanding fluid, material, and atmospheric dynamics, and mechanical, electrical, atomic and sub-atomic structures and processes.
Foreign Language	Knowledge of the structure and content of a foreign (non-English) language including the meaning and spelling of words, rules of composition and grammar, and pronunciation.
Economics and Accounting	Knowledge of economic and accounting principles and practices, the financial markets, banking and the analysis and reporting of financial data.
Sales and Marketing	Knowledge of principles and methods for showing, promoting, and selling products or services. This includes marketing strategy and tactics, product demonstration, sales techniques, and sales control systems.
Building and Construction	Knowledge of materials, methods, and the tools involved in the construction or repair of houses, buildings, or other structures such as highways and roads.
Food Production	Knowledge of techniques and equipment for planting, growing, and harvesting food products (both plant and animal) for consumption, including storage/handling techniques.
Geography	Knowledge of principles and methods for describing the features of land, sea, and air masses, including their physical characteristics, locations, interrelationships, and distribution of plant, animal, and human life.
Fine Arts	Knowledge of the theory and techniques required to compose, produce, and perform works of music, dance, visual arts, drama, and sculpture.
History and Archeology	Knowledge of historical events and their causes, indicators, and effects on civilizations and cultures.

Skills — Skills Definitions

Active Listening	Giving full attention to what other people are saying, taking time to understand the points being made, asking questions as appropriate, and not interrupting at inappropriate times.
Active Learning	Understanding the implications of new information for both current and future problem-solving and decision-making.
Critical Thinking	Using logic and reasoning to identify the strengths and weaknesses of alternative solutions, conclusions or approaches to problems.
Equipment Selection	Determining the kind of tools and equipment needed to do a job.
Coordination	Adjusting actions in relation to others' actions.
Speaking	Talking to others to convey information effectively.
Instructing	Teaching others how to do something.
Learning Strategies	Selecting and using training/instructional methods and procedures appropriate for the situation when learning or teaching new things.
Monitoring	Monitoring/Assessing performance of yourself, other individuals, or organizations to make improvements or take corrective action.
Troubleshooting	Determining causes of operating errors and deciding what to do about it.
Reading Comprehension	Understanding written sentences and paragraphs in work related documents.
Time Management	Managing one's own time and the time of others.
Science	Using scientific rules and methods to solve problems.
Service Orientation	Actively looking for ways to help people.
Judgment and Decision Making	Considering the relative costs and benefits of potential actions to choose the most appropriate one.
Operation Monitoring	Watching gauges, dials, or other indicators to make sure a machine is working properly.
Quality Control Analysis	Conducting tests and inspections of products, services, or processes to evaluate quality or performance.
Social Perceptiveness	Being aware of others' reactions and understanding why they react as they do.
Mathematics	Using mathematics to solve problems.
Writing	Communicating effectively in writing as appropriate for the needs of the audience.
Complex Problem Solving	Identifying complex problems and reviewing related information to develop and evaluate options and implement solutions.
Operation and Control	Controlling operations of equipment or systems.
Operations Analysis	Analyzing needs and product requirements to create a design.
Technology Design	Generating or adapting equipment and technology to serve user needs.
Management of Material Resources	Obtaining and seeing to the appropriate use of equipment, facilities, and materials needed to do certain work.
Negotiation	Bringing others together and trying to reconcile differences.
Equipment Maintenance	Performing routine maintenance on equipment and determining when and what kind of maintenance is needed.
Persuasion	Persuading others to change their minds or behavior.
Installation	Installing equipment, machines, wiring, or programs to meet specifications.
Management of Personnel Resources	Motivating, developing, and directing people as they work, identifying the best people for the job.
Systems Evaluation	Identifying measures or indicators of system performance and the actions needed to improve or correct performance, relative to the goals of the system.
Systems Analysis	Determining how a system should work and how changes in conditions, operations, and the environment will affect outcomes.
Repairing	Repairing machines or systems using the needed tools.
Management of Financial Resources	Determining how money will be spent to get the work done, and accounting for these expenditures.
Programming	Writing computer programs for various purposes.

Ability — Ability Definitions

Oral Comprehension	The ability to listen to and understand information and ideas presented through spoken words and sentences.
Problem Sensitivity	The ability to tell when something is wrong or is likely to go wrong. It does not involve solving the problem, only recognizing there is a problem.
Oral Expression	The ability to communicate information and ideas in speaking so others will understand.
Arm-Hand Steadiness	The ability to keep your hand and arm steady while moving your arm or while holding your arm and hand in one position.
Near Vision	The ability to see details at close range (within a few feet of the observer).
Speech Recognition	The ability to identify and understand the speech of another person.
Speech Clarity	The ability to speak clearly so others can understand you.
Manual Dexterity	The ability to quickly move your hand, your hand together with your arm, or your two hands to grasp, manipulate, or assemble objects.
Inductive Reasoning	The ability to combine pieces of information to form general rules or conclusions (includes finding a relationship among seemingly unrelated events).
Finger Dexterity	The ability to make precisely coordinated movements of the fingers of one or both hands to grasp, manipulate, or assemble very small objects.
Deductive Reasoning	The ability to apply general rules to specific problems to produce answers that make sense.
Information Ordering	The ability to arrange things or actions in a certain order or pattern according to a specific rule or set of rules (e.g., patterns of numbers, letters, words, pictures, mathematical operations).
Multilimb Coordination	The ability to coordinate two or more limbs (for example, two arms, two legs, or one leg and one arm) while sitting, standing, or lying down. It does not involve performing the activities while the whole body is in motion.
Selective Attention	The ability to concentrate on a task over a period of time without being distracted.
Control Precision	The ability to quickly and repeatedly adjust the controls of a machine or a vehicle to exact positions.
Time Sharing	The ability to shift back and forth between two or more activities or sources of information (such as speech, sounds, touch, or other sources).
Trunk Strength	The ability to use your abdominal and lower back muscles to support part of the body repeatedly or continuously over time without 'giving out' or fatiguing.
Written Comprehension	The ability to read and understand information and ideas presented in writing.
Written Expression	The ability to communicate information and ideas in writing so others will understand.
Perceptual Speed	The ability to quickly and accurately compare similarities and differences among sets of letters, numbers, objects, pictures, or patterns. The things to be compared may be presented at the same time or one after the other. This ability also includes comparing a presented object with a remembered object.
Static Strength	The ability to exert maximum muscle force to lift, push, pull, or carry objects.
Flexibility of Closure	The ability to identify or detect a known pattern (a figure, object, word, or sound) that is hidden in other distracting material.

Depth Perception	The ability to judge which of several objects is closer or farther away from you, or to judge the distance between you and an object.
Speed of Closure	The ability to quickly make sense of, combine, and organize information into meaningful patterns.
Visual Color Discrimination	The ability to match or detect differences between colors, including shades of color and brightness.
Reaction Time	The ability to quickly respond (with the hand, finger, or foot) to a signal (sound, light, picture) when it appears.
Memorization	The ability to remember information such as words, numbers, pictures, and procedures.
Auditory Attention	The ability to focus on a single source of sound in the presence of other distracting sounds.
Spatial Orientation	The ability to know your location in relation to the environment or to know where other objects are in relation to you.
Extent Flexibility	The ability to bend, stretch, twist, or reach with your body, arms, and/or legs.
Response Orientation	The ability to choose quickly between two or more movements in response to two or more different signals (lights, sounds, pictures). It includes the speed with which the correct response is started with the hand, foot, or other body part.
Number Facility	The ability to add, subtract, multiply, or divide quickly and correctly.
Hearing Sensitivity	The ability to detect or tell the differences between sounds that vary in pitch and loudness.
Stamina	The ability to exert yourself physically over long periods of time without getting winded or out of breath.
Gross Body Coordination	The ability to coordinate the movement of your arms, legs, and torso together when the whole body is in motion.
Category Flexibility	The ability to generate or use different sets of rules for combining or grouping things in different ways.
Far Vision	The ability to see details at a distance.
Speed of Limb Movement	The ability to quickly move the arms and legs.
Mathematical Reasoning	The ability to choose the right mathematical methods or formulas to solve a problem.
Peripheral Vision	The ability to see objects or movement of objects to one's side when the eyes are looking ahead.
Rate Control	The ability to time your movements or the movement of a piece of equipment in anticipation of changes in the speed and/or direction of a moving object or scene.
Originality	The ability to come up with unusual or clever ideas about a given topic or situation, or to develop creative ways to solve a problem.
Dynamic Strength	The ability to exert muscle force repeatedly or continuously over time. This involves muscular endurance and resistance to muscle fatigue.
Fluency of Ideas	The ability to come up with a number of ideas about a topic (the number of ideas is important, not their quality, correctness, or creativity).
Visualization	The ability to imagine how something will look after it is moved around or when its parts are moved or rearranged.
Sound Localization	The ability to tell the direction from which a sound originated.
Dynamic Flexibility	The ability to quickly and repeatedly bend, stretch, twist, or reach out with your body, arms, and/or legs.
Wrist-Finger Speed	The ability to make fast, simple, repeated movements of the fingers, hands, and wrists.
Gross Body Equilibrium	The ability to keep or regain your body balance or stay upright when in an unstable position.
Glare Sensitivity	The ability to see objects in the presence of glare or bright lighting.
Night Vision	The ability to see under low light conditions.
Explosive Strength	The ability to use short bursts of muscle force to propel oneself (as in jumping or sprinting), or to throw an object.

Work_Activity	Work_Activity Definitions
Assisting and Caring for Others	Providing personal assistance, medical attention, emotional support, or other personal care to others such as coworkers, customers, or patients.
Getting Information	Observing, receiving, and otherwise obtaining information from all relevant sources.
Inspecting Equipment, Structures, or Material	Inspecting equipment, structures, or materials to identify the cause of errors or other problems or defects.
Performing General Physical Activities	Performing physical activities that require considerable use of your arms and legs and moving your whole body, such as climbing, lifting, balancing, walking, stooping, and handling of materials.

Identifying Objects, Actions, and Events	Identifying information by categorizing, estimating, recognizing differences or similarities, and detecting changes in circumstances or events.
Handling and Moving Objects	Using hands and arms in handling, installing, positioning, and moving materials, and manipulating things.
Updating and Using Relevant Knowledge	Keeping up-to-date technically and applying new knowledge to your job.
Communicating with Supervisors, Peers, or Subordin	Providing information to supervisors, co-workers, and subordinates by telephone, in written form, e-mail, or in person.
Training and Teaching Others	Identifying the educational needs of others, developing formal educational or training programs or classes, and teaching or instructing others.
Establishing and Maintaining Interpersonal Relatio	Developing constructive and cooperative working relationships with others, and maintaining them over time.
Monitor Processes, Materials, or Surroundings	Monitoring and reviewing information from materials, events, or the environment, to detect or assess problems.
Organizing, Planning, and Prioritizing Work	Developing specific goals and plans to prioritize, organize, and accomplish your work.
Making Decisions and Solving Problems	Analyzing information and evaluating results to choose the best solution and solve problems.
Developing and Building Teams	Encouraging and building mutual trust, respect, and cooperation among team members.
Interpreting the Meaning of Information for Others	Translating or explaining what information means and how it can be used.
Evaluating Information to Determine Compliance wit	Using relevant information and individual judgment to determine whether events or processes comply with laws, regulations, or standards.
Developing Objectives and Strategies	Establishing long-range objectives and specifying the strategies and actions to achieve them.
Coaching and Developing Others	Identifying the developmental needs of others and coaching, mentoring, or otherwise helping others to improve their knowledge or skills.
Judging the Qualities of Things, Services, or Peop	Assessing the value, importance, or quality of things or people.
Estimating the Quantifiable Characteristics of Pro	Estimating sizes, distances, and quantities; or determining time, costs, resources, or materials needed to perform a work activity.
Documenting/Recording Information	Entering, transcribing, recording, storing, or maintaining information in written or electronic/magnetic form.
Performing for or Working Directly with the Public	Performing for people or dealing directly with the public. This includes serving customers in restaurants and stores, and receiving clients or guests.
Guiding, Directing, and Motivating Subordinates	Providing guidance and direction to subordinates, including setting performance standards and monitoring performance.
Coordinating the Work and Activities of Others	Getting members of a group to work together to accomplish tasks.
Thinking Creatively	Developing, designing, or creating new applications, ideas, relationships, systems, or products, including artistic contributions.
Resolving Conflicts and Negotiating with Others	Handling complaints, settling disputes, and resolving grievances and conflicts, or otherwise negotiating with others.
Processing Information	Compiling, coding, categorizing, calculating, tabulating, auditing, or verifying information or data.
Repairing and Maintaining Mechanical Equipment	Servicing, repairing, adjusting, and testing machines, devices, moving parts, and equipment that operate primarily on the basis of mechanical (not electronic) principles.
Communicating with Persons Outside Organization	Communicating with people outside the organization, representing the organization to customers, the public, government, and other external sources. This information can be exchanged in person, in writing, or by telephone or e-mail.
Repairing and Maintaining Electronic Equipment	Servicing, repairing, calibrating, regulating, fine-tuning, or testing machines, devices, and equipment that operate primarily on the basis of electrical or electronic (not mechanical) principles.
Controlling Machines and Processes	Using either control mechanisms or direct physical activity to operate machines or processes (not including computers or vehicles).
Provide Consultation and Advice to Others	Providing guidance and expert advice to management or other groups on technical, systems-, or process-related topics.
Analyzing Data or Information	Identifying the underlying principles, reasons, or facts of information by breaking down information or data into separate parts.
Monitoring and Controlling Resources	Monitoring and controlling resources and overseeing the spending of money.

Scheduling Work and Activities	Scheduling events, programs, and activities, as well as the work of others.
Selling or Influencing Others	Convincing others to buy merchandise/goods or to otherwise change their minds or actions.
Drafting, Laying Out, and Specifying Technical Dev	Providing documentation, detailed instructions, drawings, or specifications to tell others about how devices, parts, equipment, or structures are to be fabricated, constructed, assembled, modified, maintained, or used.
Interacting With Computers	Using computers and computer systems (including hardware and software) to program, write software, set up functions, enter data, or process information.
Performing Administrative Activities	Performing day-to-day administrative tasks such as maintaining information files and processing paperwork.
Staffing Organizational Units	Recruiting, interviewing, selecting, hiring, and promoting employees in an organization.
Operating Vehicles, Mechanized Devices, or Equipme	Running, maneuvering, navigating, or driving vehicles or mechanized equipment, such as forklifts, passenger vehicles, aircraft, or water craft.

Work_Context	Work_Context Definitions
Indoors, Environmentally Controlled	How often does this job require working indoors in environmentally controlled conditions?
Physical Proximity	To what extent does this job require the worker to perform job tasks in close physical proximity to other people?
Wear Common Protective or Safety Equipment such as	How much does this job require wearing common protective or safety equipment such as safety shoes, glasses, gloves, hard hats or live jackets?
Contact With Others	How much does this job require the worker to be in contact with others (face-to-face, by telephone, or otherwise) in order to perform it?
Spend Time Standing	How much does this job require standing?
Exposed to Disease or Infections	How often does this job require exposure to disease/infections?
Face-to-Face Discussions	How often do you have to have face-to-face discussions with individuals or teams in this job?
Importance of Being Exact or Accurate	How important is being very exact or highly accurate in performing this job?
Spend Time Using Your Hands to Handle, Control, or	How much does this job require using your hands to handle, control, or feel objects, tools or controls?
Work With Work Group or Team	How important is it to work with others in a group or team in this job?
Consequence of Error	How serious would the result usually be if the worker made a mistake that was not readily correctable?
Responsible for Others' Health and Safety	How much responsibility is there for the health and safety of others in this job?
Impact of Decisions on Co-workers or Company Resul	How do the decisions an employee makes impact the results of co-workers, clients or the company?
Wear Specialized Protective or Safety Equipment su	How much does this job require wearing specialized protective or safety equipment such as breathing apparatus, safety harness, full protection suits, or radiation protection?
Telephone	How often do you have telephone conversations in this job?
Exposed to Contaminants	How often does this job require working exposed to contaminants (such as pollutants, gases, dust or odors)?
Frequency of Decision Making	How frequently is the worker required to make decisions that affect other people, the financial resources, and/or the image and reputation of the organization?
Structured versus Unstructured Work	To what extent is this job structured for the worker, rather than allowing the worker to determine tasks, priorities, and goals?
Coordinate or Lead Others	How important is it to coordinate or lead others in accomplishing work activities in this job?
Exposed to Hazardous Conditions	How often does this job require exposure to hazardous conditions?
Responsibility for Outcomes and Results	How responsible is the worker for work outcomes and results of other workers?
Exposed to Radiation	How often does this job require exposure to radiation?
Freedom to Make Decisions	How much decision making freedom, without supervision, does the job offer?
Spend Time Making Repetitive Motions	How much does this job require making repetitive motions?
Exposed to Hazardous Equipment	How often does this job require exposure to hazardous equipment?
Deal With Unpleasant or Angry People	How frequently does the worker have to deal with unpleasant, angry, or discourteous individuals as part of the job requirements?

Deal With External Customers	How important is it to work with external customers or the public in this job?
Cramped Work Space, Awkward Positions	How often does this job require working in cramped work spaces that requires getting into awkward positions?
Spend Time Bending or Twisting the Body	How much does this job require bending or twisting your body?
Sounds, Noise Levels Are Distracting or Uncomforta	How often does this job require working exposed to sounds and noise levels that are distracting or uncomfortable?
Time Pressure	How often does this job require the worker to meet strict deadlines?
Frequency of Conflict Situations	How often are there conflict situations the employee has to face in this job?
Importance of Repeating Same Tasks	How important is repeating the same physical activities (e.g., key entry) or mental activities (e.g., checking entries in a ledger) over and over, without stopping, to performing this job?
Letters and Memos	How often does the job require written letters and memos?
Exposed to Minor Burns, Cuts, Bites, or Stings	How often does this job require exposure to minor burns, cuts, bites, or stings?
Extremely Bright or Inadequate Lighting	How often does this job require working in extremely bright or inadequate lighting conditions?
Spend Time Walking and Running	How much does this job require walking and running?
Pace Determined by Speed of Equipment	How important is it to this job that the pace is determined by the speed of equipment or machinery? (This does not refer to keeping busy at all times on this job.)
Level of Competition	To what extent does this job require the worker to compete or to be aware of competitive pressures?
Electronic Mail	How often do you use electronic mail in this job?
Degree of Automation	How automated is the job?
Deal With Physically Aggressive People	How frequently does this job require the worker to deal with physical aggression of violent individuals?
Spend Time Kneeling, Crouching, Stooping, or Crawl	How much does this job require kneeling, crouching, stooping or crawling?
Spend Time Sitting	How much does this job require sitting?
Very Hot or Cold Temperatures	How often does this job require working in very hot (above 90 F degrees) or very cold (below 32 F degrees) temperatures?
Public Speaking	How often do you have to perform public speaking in this job?
Spend Time Keeping or Regaining Balance	How much does this job require keeping or regaining your balance?
Exposed to Whole Body Vibration	How often does this job require exposure to whole body vibration (e.g., operate a jackhammer)?
In an Enclosed Vehicle or Equipment	How often does this job require working in a closed vehicle or equipment (e.g., car)?
Indoors, Not Environmentally Controlled	How often does this job require working indoors in non-controlled environmental conditions (e.g., warehouse without heat)?
Outdoors, Exposed to Weather	How often does this job require working outdoors, exposed to all weather conditions?
Exposed to High Places	How often does this job require exposure to high places?
Outdoors, Under Cover	How often does this job require working outdoors, under cover (e.g., structure with roof but no walls)?
Spend Time Climbing Ladders, Scaffolds, or Poles	How much does this job require climbing ladders, scaffolds, or poles?
In an Open Vehicle or Equipment	How often does this job require working in an open vehicle or equipment (e.g., tractor)?

Job Zone Component	Job Zone Component Definitions
Title	Job Zone Three: Medium Preparation Needed
Overall Experience	Previous work-related skill, knowledge, or experience is required for these occupations. For example, an electrician must have completed three or four years of apprenticeship or several years of vocational training, and often must have passed a licensing exam, in order to perform the job.
Job Training	Employees in these occupations usually need one or two years of training involving both on-the-job experience and informal training with experienced workers.
Job Zone Examples	These occupations usually involve using communication and organizational skills to coordinate, supervise, manage, or train others to accomplish goals. Examples include dental assistants, electricians, fish and game wardens, legal secretaries, personnel recruiters, and recreation workers.
SVP Range	(6.0 to < 7.0)

Education	Most occupations in this zone require training in vocational schools, related on-the-job experience, or an associate's degree. Some may require a bachelor's degree.

Work_Styles	Work_Styles Definitions
Attention to Detail	Job requires being careful about detail and thorough in completing work tasks.
Dependability	Job requires being reliable, responsible, and dependable, and fulfilling obligations.
Stress Tolerance	Job requires accepting criticism and dealing calmly and effectively with high stress situations.
Self Control	Job requires maintaining composure, keeping emotions in check, controlling anger, and avoiding aggressive behavior, even in very difficult situations.
Cooperation	Job requires being pleasant with others on the job and displaying a good-natured, cooperative attitude.
Concern for Others	Job requires being sensitive to others' needs and feelings and being understanding and helpful on the job.
Social Orientation	Job requires preferring to work with others rather than alone, and being personally connected with others on the job.
Adaptability/Flexibility	Job requires being open to change (positive or negative) and to considerable variety in the workplace.
Integrity	Job requires being honest and ethical.
Persistence	Job requires persistence in the face of obstacles.
Initiative	Job requires a willingness to take on responsibilities and challenges.
Achievement/Effort	Job requires establishing and maintaining personally challenging achievement goals and exerting effort toward mastering tasks.
Independence	Job requires developing one's own ways of doing things, guiding oneself with little or no supervision, and depending on oneself to get things done.
Analytical Thinking	Job requires analyzing information and using logic to address work-related issues and problems.
Leadership	Job requires a willingness to lead, take charge, and offer opinions and direction.
Innovation	Job requires creativity and alternative thinking to develop new ideas for and answers to work-related problems.

29-2056.00 - Veterinary Technologists and Technicians

Perform medical tests in a laboratory environment for use in the treatment and diagnosis of diseases in animals. Prepare vaccines and serums for prevention of diseases. Prepare tissue samples, take blood samples, and execute laboratory tests, such as urinalysis and blood counts. Clean and sterilize instruments and materials and maintain equipment and machines.

Tasks

1) Collect, prepare, and label samples for laboratory testing, culture, or microscopic examination.

2) Provide assistance with animal euthanasia and the disposal of remains.

3) Prepare animals for surgery, performing such tasks as shaving surgical areas.

4) Care for and monitor the condition of animals recovering from surgery.

5) Take animals into treatment areas, and assist with physical examinations by performing such duties as obtaining temperature, pulse, and respiration data.

6) Clean and sterilize instruments, equipment, and materials.

7) Take and develop diagnostic radiographs, using x-ray equipment.

8) Fill prescriptions, measuring medications and labeling containers.

9) Clean kennels, animal holding areas, surgery suites, examination rooms, and animal loading/unloading facilities to control the spread of disease.

10) Perform laboratory tests on blood, urine, and feces, such as urinalyses and blood counts, to assist in the diagnosis and treatment of animal health problems.

11) Provide information and counseling regarding issues such as animal health care, behavior problems, and nutrition.

12) Observe the behavior and condition of animals, and monitor their clinical symptoms.

13) Provide veterinarians with the correct equipment and instruments, as needed.

14) Prepare treatment rooms for surgery.

15) Maintain instruments, equipment, and machinery to ensure proper working condition.

16) Administer anesthesia to animals, under the direction of a veterinarian, and monitor animals' responses to anesthetics so that dosages can be adjusted.

17) Give enemas and perform catheterizations, ear flushes, intravenous feedings, and gavages.

18) Administer emergency first aid, such as performing emergency resuscitation or other life saving procedures.

19) Bathe animals, clip nails or claws, and brush and cut animals' hair.

20) Perform dental work such as cleaning, polishing, and extracting teeth.

21) Maintain laboratory, research, and treatment records, as well as inventories of pharmaceuticals, equipment, and supplies.

22) Dress and suture wounds, and apply splints and other protective devices.

23) Perform a variety of office, clerical, and accounting duties, such as reception, billing, bookkeeping, and/or selling products.

24) Conduct specialized procedures such as animal branding or tattooing, and hoof trimming.

Knowledge	Knowledge Definitions
Customer and Personal Service	Knowledge of principles and processes for providing customer and personal services. This includes customer needs assessment, meeting quality standards for services, and evaluation of customer satisfaction.
Biology	Knowledge of plant and animal organisms, their tissues, cells, functions, interdependencies, and interactions with each other and the environment.
Mathematics	Knowledge of arithmetic, algebra, geometry, calculus, statistics, and their applications.
English Language	Knowledge of the structure and content of the English language including the meaning and spelling of words, rules of composition, and grammar.
Medicine and Dentistry	Knowledge of the information and techniques needed to diagnose and treat human injuries, diseases, and deformities. This includes symptoms, treatment alternatives, drug properties and interactions, and preventive health-care measures.
Clerical	Knowledge of administrative and clerical procedures and systems such as word processing, managing files and records, stenography and transcription, designing forms, and other office procedures and terminology.
Chemistry	Knowledge of the chemical composition, structure, and properties of substances and of the chemical processes and transformations that they undergo. This includes uses of chemicals and their interactions, danger signs, production techniques, and disposal methods.
Education and Training	Knowledge of principles and methods for curriculum and training design, teaching and instruction for individuals and groups, and the measurement of training effects.
Sales and Marketing	Knowledge of principles and methods for showing, promoting, and selling products or services. This includes marketing strategy and tactics, product demonstration, sales techniques, and sales control systems.
Administration and Management	Knowledge of business and management principles involved in strategic planning, resource allocation, human resources modeling, leadership technique, production methods, and coordination of people and resources.
Mechanical	Knowledge of machines and tools, including their designs, uses, repair, and maintenance.
Psychology	Knowledge of human behavior and performance; individual differences in ability, personality, and interests; learning and motivation; psychological research methods; and the assessment and treatment of behavioral and affective disorders.
Therapy and Counseling	Knowledge of principles, methods, and procedures for diagnosis, treatment, and rehabilitation of physical and mental dysfunctions, and for career counseling and guidance.
Computers and Electronics	Knowledge of circuit boards, processors, chips, electronic equipment, and computer hardware and software, including applications and programming.
Public Safety and Security	Knowledge of relevant equipment, policies, procedures, and strategies to promote effective local, state, or national security operations for the protection of people, data, property, and institutions.
Law and Government	Knowledge of laws, legal codes, court procedures, precedents, government regulations, executive orders, agency rules, and the democratic political process.

Personnel and Human Resources	Knowledge of principles and procedures for personnel recruitment, selection, training, compensation and benefits, labor relations and negotiation, and personnel information systems.
Communications and Media	Knowledge of media production, communication, and dissemination techniques and methods. This includes alternative ways to inform and entertain via written, oral, and visual media.
Engineering and Technology	Knowledge of the practical application of engineering science and technology. This includes applying principles, techniques, procedures, and equipment to the design and production of various goods and services.
Physics	Knowledge and prediction of physical principles, laws, their interrelationships, and applications to understanding fluid, material, and atmospheric dynamics, and mechanical, electrical, atomic and sub-atomic structures and processes.
Production and Processing	Knowledge of raw materials, production processes, quality control, costs, and other techniques for maximizing the effective manufacture and distribution of goods.
Economics and Accounting	Knowledge of economic and accounting principles and practices, the financial markets, banking and the analysis and reporting of financial data.
Transportation	Knowledge of principles and methods for moving people or goods by air, rail, sea, or road, including the relative costs and benefits.
Sociology and Anthropology	Knowledge of group behavior and dynamics, societal trends and influences, human migrations, ethnicity, cultures and their history and origins.
Telecommunications	Knowledge of transmission, broadcasting, switching, control, and operation of telecommunications systems.
Foreign Language	Knowledge of the structure and content of a foreign (non-English) language including the meaning and spelling of words, rules of composition and grammar, and pronunciation.
Food Production	Knowledge of techniques and equipment for planting, growing, and harvesting food products (both plant and animal) for consumption, including storage/handling techniques.
Geography	Knowledge of principles and methods for describing the features of land, sea, and air masses, including their physical characteristics, locations, interrelationships, and distribution of plant, animal, and human life.
Design	Knowledge of design techniques, tools, and principles involved in production of precision technical plans, blueprints, drawings, and models.
Philosophy and Theology	Knowledge of different philosophical systems and religions. This includes their basic principles, values, ethics, ways of thinking, customs, practices, and their impact on human culture.
Building and Construction	Knowledge of materials, methods, and the tools involved in the construction or repair of houses, buildings, or other structures such as highways and roads.
History and Archeology	Knowledge of historical events and their causes, indicators, and effects on civilizations and cultures.
Fine Arts	Knowledge of the theory and techniques required to compose, produce, and perform works of music, dance, visual arts, drama, and sculpture.

Skills	Skills Definitions
Active Listening	Giving full attention to what other people are saying, taking time to understand the points being made, asking questions as appropriate, and not interrupting at inappropriate times.
Reading Comprehension	Understanding written sentences and paragraphs in work related documents.
Speaking	Talking to others to convey information effectively.
Critical Thinking	Using logic and reasoning to identify the strengths and weaknesses of alternative solutions, conclusions or approaches to problems.
Active Learning	Understanding the implications of new information for both current and future problem-solving and decision-making.
Mathematics	Using mathematics to solve problems.
Instructing	Teaching others how to do something.
Learning Strategies	Selecting and using training/instructional methods and procedures appropriate for the situation when learning or teaching new things.
Science	Using scientific rules and methods to solve problems.
Time Management	Managing one's own time and the time of others.
Coordination	Adjusting actions in relation to others' actions.

Writing	Communicating effectively in writing as appropriate for the needs of the audience.
Operation Monitoring	Watching gauges, dials, or other indicators to make sure a machine is working properly.
Social Perceptiveness	Being aware of others' reactions and understanding why they react as they do.
Equipment Selection	Determining the kind of tools and equipment needed to do a job.
Service Orientation	Actively looking for ways to help people.
Monitoring	Monitoring/Assessing performance of yourself, other individuals, or organizations to make improvements or take corrective action.
Equipment Maintenance	Performing routine maintenance on equipment and determining when and what kind of maintenance is needed.
Operation and Control	Controlling operations of equipment or systems.
Complex Problem Solving	Identifying complex problems and reviewing related information to develop and evaluate options and implement solutions.
Troubleshooting	Determining causes of operating errors and deciding what to do about it.
Judgment and Decision Making	Considering the relative costs and benefits of potential actions to choose the most appropriate one.
Management of Personnel Resources	Motivating, developing, and directing people as they work, identifying the best people for the job.
Quality Control Analysis	Conducting tests and inspections of products, services, or processes to evaluate quality or performance.
Negotiation	Bringing others together and trying to reconcile differences.
Management of Material Resources	Obtaining and seeing to the appropriate use of equipment, facilities, and materials needed to do certain work.
Technology Design	Generating or adapting equipment and technology to serve user needs.
Operations Analysis	Analyzing needs and product requirements to create a design.
Persuasion	Persuading others to change their minds or behavior.
Systems Analysis	Determining how a system should work and how changes in conditions, operations, and the environment will affect outcomes.
Systems Evaluation	Identifying measures or indicators of system performance and the actions needed to improve or correct performance, relative to the goals of the system.
Repairing	Repairing machines or systems using the needed tools.
Installation	Installing equipment, machines, wiring, or programs to meet specifications.
Management of Financial Resources	Determining how money will be spent to get the work done, and accounting for these expenditures.
Programming	Writing computer programs for various purposes.

Ability	Ability Definitions
Problem Sensitivity	The ability to tell when something is wrong or is likely to go wrong. It does not involve solving the problem, only recognizing there is a problem.
Oral Expression	The ability to communicate information and ideas in speaking so others will understand.
Oral Comprehension	The ability to listen to and understand information and ideas presented through spoken words and sentences.
Near Vision	The ability to see details at close range (within a few feet of the observer).
Deductive Reasoning	The ability to apply general rules to specific problems to produce answers that make sense.
Information Ordering	The ability to arrange things or actions in a certain order or pattern according to a specific rule or set of rules (e.g., patterns of numbers, letters, words, pictures, mathematical operations).
Inductive Reasoning	The ability to combine pieces of information to form general rules or conclusions (includes finding a relationship among seemingly unrelated events).
Arm-Hand Steadiness	The ability to keep your hand and arm steady while moving your arm or while holding your arm and hand in one position.
Speech Recognition	The ability to identify and understand the speech of another person.
Written Comprehension	The ability to read and understand information and ideas presented in writing.
Selective Attention	The ability to concentrate on a task over a period of time without being distracted.
Speech Clarity	The ability to speak clearly so others can understand you.
Manual Dexterity	The ability to quickly move your hand, your hand together with your arm, or your two hands to grasp, manipulate, or assemble objects.

Finger Dexterity	The ability to make precisely coordinated movements of the fingers of one or both hands to grasp, manipulate, or assemble very small objects.
Category Flexibility	The ability to generate or use different sets of rules for combining or grouping things in different ways.
Written Expression	The ability to communicate information and ideas in writing so others will understand.
Flexibility of Closure	The ability to identify or detect a known pattern (a figure, object, word, or sound) that is hidden in other distracting material.
Originality	The ability to come up with unusual or clever ideas about a given topic or situation, or to develop creative ways to solve a problem.
Memorization	The ability to remember information such as words, numbers, pictures, and procedures.
Control Precision	The ability to quickly and repeatedly adjust the controls of a machine or a vehicle to exact positions.
Speed of Closure	The ability to quickly make sense of, combine, and organize information into meaningful patterns.
Time Sharing	The ability to shift back and forth between two or more activities or sources of information (such as speech, sounds, touch, or other sources).
Mathematical Reasoning	The ability to choose the right mathematical methods or formulas to solve a problem.
Trunk Strength	The ability to use your abdominal and lower back muscles to support part of the body repeatedly or continuously over time without 'giving out' or fatiguing.
Static Strength	The ability to exert maximum muscle force to lift, push, pull, or carry objects.
Perceptual Speed	The ability to quickly and accurately compare similarities and differences among sets of letters, numbers, objects, pictures, or patterns. The things to be compared may be presented at the same time or one after the other. This ability also includes comparing a presented object with a remembered object.
Multilimb Coordination	The ability to coordinate two or more limbs (for example, two arms, two legs, or one leg and one arm) while sitting, standing, or lying down. It does not involve performing the activities while the whole body is in motion.
Extent Flexibility	The ability to bend, stretch, twist, or reach with your body, arms, and/or legs.
Fluency of Ideas	The ability to come up with a number of ideas about a topic (the number of ideas is important, not their quality, correctness, or creativity).
Auditory Attention	The ability to focus on a single source of sound in the presence of other distracting sounds.
Number Facility	The ability to add, subtract, multiply, or divide quickly and correctly.
Visualization	The ability to imagine how something will look after it is moved around or when its parts are moved or rearranged.
Hearing Sensitivity	The ability to detect or tell the differences between sounds that vary in pitch and loudness.
Gross Body Coordination	The ability to coordinate the movement of your arms, legs, and torso together when the whole body is in motion.
Depth Perception	The ability to judge which of several objects is closer or farther away from you, or to judge the distance between you and an object.
Stamina	The ability to exert yourself physically over long periods of time without getting winded or out of breath.
Speed of Limb Movement	The ability to quickly move the arms and legs.
Response Orientation	The ability to choose quickly between two or more movements in response to two or more different signals (lights, sounds, pictures). It includes the speed with which the correct response is started with the hand, foot, or other body part.
Far Vision	The ability to see details at a distance.
Visual Color Discrimination	The ability to match or detect differences between colors, including shades of color and brightness.
Reaction Time	The ability to quickly respond (with the hand, finger, or foot) to a signal (sound, light, picture) when it appears.
Dynamic Strength	The ability to exert muscle force repeatedly or continuously over time. This involves muscular endurance and resistance to muscle fatigue.
Wrist-Finger Speed	The ability to make fast, simple, repeated movements of the fingers, hands, and wrists.
Gross Body Equilibrium	The ability to keep or regain your body balance or stay upright when in an unstable position.
Rate Control	The ability to time your movements or the movement of a piece of equipment in anticipation of changes in the speed and/or direction of a moving object or scene.

Sound Localization	The ability to tell the direction from which a sound originated.
Glare Sensitivity	The ability to see objects in the presence of glare or bright lighting.
Night Vision	The ability to see under low light conditions.
Explosive Strength	The ability to use short bursts of muscle force to propel oneself (as in jumping or sprinting), or to throw an object.
Dynamic Flexibility	The ability to quickly and repeatedly bend, stretch, twist, or reach out with your body, arms, and/or legs.
Peripheral Vision	The ability to see objects or movement of objects to one's side when the eyes are looking ahead.
Spatial Orientation	The ability to know your location in relation to the environment or to know where other objects are in relation to you.

Work_Activity	Work_Activity Definitions
Performing General Physical Activities	Performing physical activities that require considerable use of your arms and legs and moving your whole body, such as climbing, lifting, balancing, walking, stooping, and handling of materials.
Getting Information	Observing, receiving, and otherwise obtaining information from all relevant sources.
Communicating with Supervisors, Peers, or Subordin	Providing information to supervisors, co-workers, and subordinates by telephone, in written form, e-mail, or in person.
Documenting/Recording Information	Entering, transcribing, recording, storing, or maintaining information in written or electronic/magnetic form.
Identifying Objects, Actions, and Events	Identifying information by categorizing, estimating, recognizing differences or similarities, and detecting changes in circumstances or events.
Updating and Using Relevant Knowledge	Keeping up-to-date technically and applying new knowledge to your job.
Monitor Processes, Materials, or Surroundings	Monitoring and reviewing information from materials, events, or the environment, to detect or assess problems.
Handling and Moving Objects	Using hands and arms in handling, installing, positioning, and moving materials, and manipulating things.
Making Decisions and Solving Problems	Analyzing information and evaluating results to choose the best solution and solve problems.
Organizing, Planning, and Prioritizing Work	Developing specific goals and plans to prioritize, organize, and accomplish your work.
Assisting and Caring for Others	Providing personal assistance, medical attention, emotional support, or other personal care to others such as coworkers, customers, or patients.
Performing for or Working Directly with the Public	Performing for people or dealing directly with the public. This includes serving customers in restaurants and stores, and receiving clients or guests.
Inspecting Equipment, Structures, or Material	Inspecting equipment, structures, or materials to identify the cause of errors or other problems or defects.
Interacting With Computers	Using computers and computer systems (including hardware and software) to program, write software, set up functions, enter data, or process information.
Processing Information	Compiling, coding, categorizing, calculating, tabulating, auditing, or verifying information or data.
Establishing and Maintaining Interpersonal Relatio	Developing constructive and cooperative working relationships with others, and maintaining them over time.
Evaluating Information to Determine Compliance wit	Using relevant information and individual judgment to determine whether events or processes comply with laws, regulations, or standards.
Judging the Qualities of Things, Services, or Peop	Assessing the value, importance, or quality of things or people.
Analyzing Data or Information	Identifying the underlying principles, reasons, or facts of information by breaking down information or data into separate parts.
Communicating with Persons Outside Organization	Communicating with people outside the organization, representing the organization to customers, the public, government, and other external sources. This information can be exchanged in person, in writing, or by telephone or e-mail.
Training and Teaching Others	Identifying the educational needs of others, developing formal educational or training programs or classes, and teaching or instructing others.
Interpreting the Meaning of Information for Others	Translating or explaining what information means and how it can be used.
Performing Administrative Activities	Performing day-to-day administrative tasks such as maintaining information files and processing paperwork.
Estimating the Quantifiable Characteristics of Pro	Estimating sizes, distances, and quantities; or determining time, costs, resources, or materials needed to perform a work activity.

Developing and Building Teams	Encouraging and building mutual trust, respect, and cooperation among team members.
Coordinating the Work and Activities of Others	Getting members of a group to work together to accomplish tasks.
Scheduling Work and Activities	Scheduling events, programs, and activities, as well as the work of others.
Guiding, Directing, and Motivating Subordinates	Providing guidance and direction to subordinates, including setting performance standards and monitoring performance.
Resolving Conflicts and Negotiating with Others	Handling complaints, settling disputes, and resolving grievances and conflicts, or otherwise negotiating with others.
Thinking Creatively	Developing, designing, or creating new applications, ideas, relationships, systems, or products, including artistic contributions.
Developing Objectives and Strategies	Establishing long-range objectives and specifying the strategies and actions to achieve them.
Coaching and Developing Others	Identifying the developmental needs of others and coaching, mentoring, or otherwise helping others to improve their knowledge or skills.
Controlling Machines and Processes	Using either control mechanisms or direct physical activity to operate machines or processes (not including computers or vehicles).
Selling or Influencing Others	Convincing others to buy merchandise/goods or to otherwise change their minds or actions.
Provide Consultation and Advice to Others	Providing guidance and expert advice to management or other groups on technical, systems-, or process-related topics.
Repairing and Maintaining Mechanical Equipment	Servicing, repairing, adjusting, and testing machines, devices, moving parts, and equipment that operate primarily on the basis of mechanical (not electronic) principles.
Staffing Organizational Units	Recruiting, interviewing, selecting, hiring, and promoting employees in an organization.
Monitoring and Controlling Resources	Monitoring and controlling resources and overseeing the spending of money.
Repairing and Maintaining Electronic Equipment	Servicing, repairing, calibrating, regulating, fine-tuning, or testing machines, devices, and equipment that operate primarily on the basis of electrical or electronic (not mechanical) principles.
Operating Vehicles, Mechanized Devices, or Equipme	Running, maneuvering, navigating, or driving vehicles or mechanized equipment, such as forklifts, passenger vehicles, aircraft, or water craft.
Drafting, Laying Out, and Specifying Technical Dev	Providing documentation, detailed instructions, drawings, or specifications to tell others about how devices, parts, equipment, or structures are to be fabricated, constructed, assembled, modified, maintained, or used.

Work_Context

Work_Context	Work_Context Definitions
Contact With Others	How much does this job require the worker to be in contact with others (face-to-face, by telephone, or otherwise) in order to perform it?
Telephone	How often do you have telephone conversations in this job?
Work With Work Group or Team	How important is it to work with others in a group or team in this job?
Indoors, Environmentally Controlled	How often does this job require working indoors in environmentally controlled conditions?
Face-to-Face Discussions	How often do you have to have face-to-face discussions with individuals or teams in this job?
Physical Proximity	To what extent does this job require the worker to perform job tasks in close physical proximity to other people?
Spend Time Standing	How much does this job require standing?
Consequence of Error	How serious would the result usually be if the worker made a mistake that was not readily correctable?
Deal With External Customers	How important is it to work with external customers or the public in this job?
Exposed to Disease or Infections	How often does this job require exposure to disease/infections?
Importance of Being Exact or Accurate	How important is being very exact or highly accurate in performing this job?
Exposed to Contaminants	How often does this job require working exposed to contaminants (such as pollutants, gases, dust or odors)?
Exposed to Minor Burns, Cuts, Bites, or Stings	How often does this job require exposure to minor burns, cuts, bites, or stings?
Frequency of Decision Making	How frequently is the worker required to make decisions that affect other people, the financial resources, and/or the image and reputation of the organization?
Structured versus Unstructured Work	To what extent is this job structured for the worker, rather than allowing the worker to determine tasks, priorities, and goals?
Freedom to Make Decisions	How much decision making freedom, without supervision, does the job offer?

Exposed to Radiation	How often does this job require exposure to radiation?
Coordinate or Lead Others	How important is it to coordinate or lead others in accomplishing work activities in this job?
Impact of Decisions on Co-workers or Company Resul	How do the decisions an employee makes impact the results of co-workers, clients or the company?
Sounds, Noise Levels Are Distracting or Uncomforta	How often does this job require working exposed to sounds and noise levels that are distracting or uncomfortable?
Deal With Unpleasant or Angry People	How frequently does the worker have to deal with unpleasant, angry, or discourteous individuals as part of the job requirements?
Responsible for Others' Health and Safety	How much responsibility is there for the health and safety of others in this job?
Spend Time Using Your Hands to Handle, Control, or	How much does this job require using your hands to handle, control, or feel objects, tools or controls?
Wear Specialized Protective or Safety Equipment su	How much does this job require wearing specialized protective or safety equipment such as breathing apparatus, safety harness, full protection suits, or radiation protection?
Frequency of Conflict Situations	How often are there conflict situations the employee has to face in this job?
Importance of Repeating Same Tasks	How important is repeating the same physical activities (e.g., key entry) or mental activities (e.g., checking entries in a ledger) over and over, without stopping, to performing this job?
Time Pressure	How often does this job require the worker to meet strict deadlines?
Cramped Work Space, Awkward Positions	How often does this job require working in cramped work spaces that requires getting into awkward positions?
Spend Time Walking and Running	How much does this job require walking and running?
Letters and Memos	How often does the job require written letters and memos?
Wear Common Protective or Safety Equipment such as	How much does this job require wearing common protective or safety equipment such as safety shoes, glasses, gloves, hard hats or live jackets?
Responsibility for Outcomes and Results	How responsible is the worker for work outcomes and results of other workers?
Exposed to Hazardous Conditions	How often does this job require exposure to hazardous conditions?
Outdoors, Exposed to Weather	How often does this job require working outdoors, exposed to all weather conditions?
Spend Time Bending or Twisting the Body	How much does this job require bending or twisting your body?
Spend Time Kneeling, Crouching, Stooping, or Crawl	How much does this job require kneeling, crouching, stooping or crawling?
Spend Time Making Repetitive Motions	How much does this job require making repetitive motions?
Level of Competition	To what extent does this job require the worker to compete or to be aware of competitive pressures?
Degree of Automation	How automated is the job?
Spend Time Sitting	How much does this job require sitting?
Indoors, Not Environmentally Controlled	How often does this job require working indoors in non-controlled environmental conditions (e.g., warehouse without heat)?
Electronic Mail	How often do you use electronic mail in this job?
Public Speaking	How often do you have to perform public speaking in this job?
Very Hot or Cold Temperatures	How often does this job require working in very hot (above 90 F degrees) or very cold (below 32 F degrees) temperatures?
Spend Time Keeping or Regaining Balance	How much does this job require keeping or regaining your balance?
In an Enclosed Vehicle or Equipment	How often does this job require working in a closed vehicle or equipment (e.g., car)?
Extremely Bright or Inadequate Lighting	How often does this job require working in extremely bright or inadequate lighting conditions?
Outdoors, Under Cover	How often does this job require working outdoors, under cover (e.g., structure with roof but no walls)?
Pace Determined by Speed of Equipment	How important is it to this job that the pace is determined by the speed of equipment or machinery? (This does not refer to keeping busy at all times on this job.)
Exposed to Hazardous Equipment	How often does this job require exposure to hazardous equipment?
Deal With Physically Aggressive People	How frequently does this job require the worker to deal with physical aggression of violent individuals?
In an Open Vehicle or Equipment	How often does this job require working in an open vehicle or equipment (e.g., tractor)?
Exposed to High Places	How often does this job require exposure to high places?

Spend Time Climbing Ladders, Scaffolds, or Poles	How much does this job require climbing ladders, scaffolds, or poles?
Exposed to Whole Body Vibration	How often does this job require exposure to whole body vibration (e.g., operate a jackhammer)?

Job Zone Component	Job Zone Component Definitions
Title	Job Zone Three: Medium Preparation Needed
Overall Experience	Previous work-related skill, knowledge, or experience is required for these occupations. For example, an electrician must have completed three or four years of apprenticeship or several years of vocational training, and often must have passed a licensing exam, in order to perform the job.
Job Training	Employees in these occupations usually need one or two years of training involving both on-the-job experience and informal training with experienced workers.
Job Zone Examples	These occupations usually involve using communication and organizational skills to coordinate, supervise, manage, or train others to accomplish goals. Examples include dental assistants, electricians, fish and game wardens, legal secretaries, personnel recruiters, and recreation workers.
SVP Range	(6.0 to < 7.0)
Education	Most occupations in this zone require training in vocational schools, related on-the-job experience, or an associate's degree. Some may require a bachelor's degree.

Work_Styles	Work_Styles Definitions
Dependability	Job requires being reliable, responsible, and dependable, and fulfilling obligations.
Integrity	Job requires being honest and ethical.
Attention to Detail	Job requires being careful about detail and thorough in completing work tasks.
Stress Tolerance	Job requires accepting criticism and dealing calmly and effectively with high stress situations.
Self Control	Job requires maintaining composure, keeping emotions in check, controlling anger, and avoiding aggressive behavior, even in very difficult situations.
Cooperation	Job requires being pleasant with others on the job and displaying a good-natured, cooperative attitude.
Initiative	Job requires a willingness to take on responsibilities and challenges.
Concern for Others	Job requires being sensitive to others' needs and feelings and being understanding and helpful on the job.
Adaptability/Flexibility	Job requires being open to change (positive or negative) and to considerable variety in the workplace.
Persistence	Job requires persistence in the face of obstacles.
Social Orientation	Job requires preferring to work with others rather than alone, and being personally connected with others on the job.
Achievement/Effort	Job requires establishing and maintaining personally challenging achievement goals and exerting effort toward mastering tasks.
Independence	Job requires developing one's own ways of doing things, guiding oneself with little or no supervision, and depending on oneself to get things done.
Leadership	Job requires a willingness to lead, take charge, and offer opinions and direction.
Innovation	Job requires creativity and alternative thinking to develop new ideas for and answers to work-related problems.
Analytical Thinking	Job requires analyzing information and using logic to address work-related issues and problems.

29-2061.00 - Licensed Practical and Licensed Vocational Nurses

Care for ill, injured, convalescent, or disabled persons in hospitals, nursing homes, clinics, private homes, group homes, and similar institutions. May work under the supervision of a registered nurse. Licensing required.

Tasks

1) Measure and record patients' vital signs, such as height, weight, temperature, blood pressure, pulse and respiration.

2) Answer patients' calls and determine how to assist them.

3) Prepare patients for examinations, tests and treatments and explain procedures.

4) Provide basic patient care and treatments, such as taking temperatures and blood pressure, dressing wounds, treating bedsores, giving enemas, douches, alcohol rubs, and massages, or performing catheterizations.

5) Apply compresses, ice bags, and hot water bottles.

6) Evaluate nursing intervention outcomes, conferring with other health-care team members as necessary.

7) Work as part of a health care team to assess patient needs, plan and modify care and implement interventions.

8) Supervise nurses' aides and assistants.

9) Assemble and use equipment such as catheters, tracheotomy tubes, and oxygen suppliers.

10) Help patients with bathing, dressing, personal hygiene, moving in bed, and standing and walking.

11) Record food and fluid intake and output.

12) Collect samples such as blood, urine and sputum from patients, and perform routine laboratory tests on samples.

13) Inventory and requisition supplies and instruments.

14) Prepare food trays and examine them for conformance to prescribed diet.

15) Clean rooms and make beds.

16) Set up equipment and prepare medical treatment rooms.

17) Wash and dress bodies of deceased persons.

18) Make appointments, keep records and perform other clerical duties in doctors' offices and clinics.

19) Sterilize equipment and supplies, using germicides, sterilizer, or autoclave.

20) Assist in delivery, care, and feeding of infants.

21) Provide medical treatment and personal care to patients in private home settings, such as cooking, keeping rooms orderly, seeing that patients are comfortable and in good spirits, and instructing family members in simple nursing tasks.

22) Observe patients, charting and reporting changes in patients' conditions, such as adverse reactions to medication or treatment, and taking any necessary action.

Knowledge	Knowledge Definitions
English Language	Knowledge of the structure and content of the English language including the meaning and spelling of words, rules of composition, and grammar.
Medicine and Dentistry	Knowledge of the information and techniques needed to diagnose and treat human injuries, diseases, and deformities. This includes symptoms, treatment alternatives, drug properties and interactions, and preventive health-care measures.
Customer and Personal Service	Knowledge of principles and processes for providing customer and personal services. This includes customer needs assessment, meeting quality standards for services, and evaluation of customer satisfaction.
Therapy and Counseling	Knowledge of principles, methods, and procedures for diagnosis, treatment, and rehabilitation of physical and mental dysfunctions, and for career counseling and guidance.
Education and Training	Knowledge of principles and methods for curriculum and training design, teaching and instruction for individuals and groups, and the measurement of training effects.
Psychology	Knowledge of human behavior and performance; individual differences in ability, personality, and interests; learning and motivation; psychological research methods; and the assessment and treatment of behavioral and affective disorders.
Mathematics	Knowledge of arithmetic, algebra, geometry, calculus, statistics, and their applications.
Public Safety and Security	Knowledge of relevant equipment, policies, procedures, and strategies to promote effective local, state, or national security operations for the protection of people, data, property, and institutions.
Administration and Management	Knowledge of business and management principles involved in strategic planning, resource allocation, human resources modeling, leadership technique, production methods, and coordination of people and resources.

Chemistry — Knowledge of the chemical composition, structure, and properties of substances and of the chemical processes and transformations that they undergo. This includes uses of chemicals and their interactions, danger signs, production techniques, and disposal methods.

Personnel and Human Resources — Knowledge of principles and procedures for personnel recruitment, selection, training, compensation and benefits, labor relations and negotiation, and personnel information systems.

Sociology and Anthropology — Knowledge of group behavior and dynamics, societal trends and influences, human migrations, ethnicity, cultures and their history and origins.

Biology — Knowledge of plant and animal organisms, their tissues, cells, functions, interdependencies, and interactions with each other and the environment.

Law and Government — Knowledge of laws, legal codes, court procedures, precedents, government regulations, executive orders, agency rules, and the democratic political process.

Telecommunications — Knowledge of transmission, broadcasting, switching, control, and operation of telecommunications systems.

Clerical — Knowledge of administrative and clerical procedures and systems such as word processing, managing files and records, stenography and transcription, designing forms, and other office procedures and terminology.

Transportation — Knowledge of principles and methods for moving people or goods by air, rail, sea, or road, including the relative costs and benefits.

Philosophy and Theology — Knowledge of different philosophical systems and religions. This includes their basic principles, values, ethics, ways of thinking, customs, practices, and their impact on human culture.

Communications and Media — Knowledge of media production, communication, and dissemination techniques and methods. This includes alternative ways to inform and entertain via written, oral, and visual media.

Foreign Language — Knowledge of the structure and content of a foreign (non-English) language including the meaning and spelling of words, rules of composition and grammar, and pronunciation.

Computers and Electronics — Knowledge of circuit boards, processors, chips, electronic equipment, and computer hardware and software, including applications and programming.

Production and Processing — Knowledge of raw materials, production processes, quality control, costs, and other techniques for maximizing the effective manufacture and distribution of goods.

Mechanical — Knowledge of machines and tools, including their designs, uses, repair, and maintenance.

Food Production — Knowledge of techniques and equipment for planting, growing, and harvesting food products (both plant and animal) for consumption, including storage/handling techniques.

Physics — Knowledge and prediction of physical principles, laws, their interrelationships, and applications to understanding fluid, material, and atmospheric dynamics, and mechanical, electrical, atomic and sub- atomic structures and processes.

Engineering and Technology — Knowledge of the practical application of engineering science and technology. This includes applying principles, techniques, procedures, and equipment to the design and production of various goods and services.

History and Archeology — Knowledge of historical events and their causes, indicators, and effects on civilizations and cultures.

Geography — Knowledge of principles and methods for describing the features of land, sea, and air masses, including their physical characteristics, locations, interrelationships, and distribution of plant, animal, and human life.

Economics and Accounting — Knowledge of economic and accounting principles and practices, the financial markets, banking and the analysis and reporting of financial data.

Sales and Marketing — Knowledge of principles and methods for showing, promoting, and selling products or services. This includes marketing strategy and tactics, product demonstration, sales techniques, and sales control systems.

Fine Arts — Knowledge of the theory and techniques required to compose, produce, and perform works of music, dance, visual arts, drama, and sculpture.

Design — Knowledge of design techniques, tools, and principles involved in production of precision technical plans, blueprints, drawings, and models.

Building and Construction — Knowledge of materials, methods, and the tools involved in the construction or repair of houses, buildings, or other structures such as highways and roads.

Skills	Skills Definitions
Active Listening	Giving full attention to what other people are saying, taking time to understand the points being made, asking questions as appropriate, and not interrupting at inappropriate times.
Reading Comprehension	Understanding written sentences and paragraphs in work related documents.
Time Management	Managing one's own time and the time of others.
Writing	Communicating effectively in writing as appropriate for the needs of the audience.
Monitoring	Monitoring/Assessing performance of yourself, other individuals, or organizations to make improvements or take corrective action.
Critical Thinking	Using logic and reasoning to identify the strengths and weaknesses of alternative solutions, conclusions or approaches to problems.
Speaking	Talking to others to convey information effectively.
Service Orientation	Actively looking for ways to help people.
Judgment and Decision Making	Considering the relative costs and benefits of potential actions to choose the most appropriate one.
Active Learning	Understanding the implications of new information for both current and future problem-solving and decision-making.
Instructing	Teaching others how to do something.
Learning Strategies	Selecting and using training/instructional methods and procedures appropriate for the situation when learning or teaching new things.
Complex Problem Solving	Identifying complex problems and reviewing related information to develop and evaluate options and implement solutions.
Coordination	Adjusting actions in relation to others' actions.
Troubleshooting	Determining causes of operating errors and deciding what to do about it.
Science	Using scientific rules and methods to solve problems.
Social Perceptiveness	Being aware of others' reactions and understanding why they react as they do.
Operation Monitoring	Watching gauges, dials, or other indicators to make sure a machine is working properly.
Mathematics	Using mathematics to solve problems.
Management of Personnel Resources	Motivating, developing, and directing people as they work, identifying the best people for the job.
Equipment Maintenance	Performing routine maintenance on equipment and determining when and what kind of maintenance is needed.
Persuasion	Persuading others to change their minds or behavior.
Repairing	Repairing machines or systems using the needed tools.
Equipment Selection	Determining the kind of tools and equipment needed to do a job.
Operation and Control	Controlling operations of equipment or systems.
Systems Evaluation	Identifying measures or indicators of system performance and the actions needed to improve or correct performance, relative to the goals of the system.
Systems Analysis	Determining how a system should work and how changes in conditions, operations, and the environment will affect outcomes.
Management of Material Resources	Obtaining and seeing to the appropriate use of equipment, facilities, and materials needed to do certain work.
Quality Control Analysis	Conducting tests and inspections of products, services, or processes to evaluate quality or performance.
Technology Design	Generating or adapting equipment and technology to serve user needs.
Negotiation	Bringing others together and trying to reconcile differences.
Installation	Installing equipment, machines, wiring, or programs to meet specifications.
Operations Analysis	Analyzing needs and product requirements to create a design.
Management of Financial Resources	Determining how money will be spent to get the work done, and accounting for these expenditures.
Programming	Writing computer programs for various purposes.

Ability	Ability Definitions
Oral Comprehension	The ability to listen to and understand information and ideas presented through spoken words and sentences.
Problem Sensitivity	The ability to tell when something is wrong or is likely to go wrong. It does not involve solving the problem, only recognizing there is a problem.

Oral Expression	The ability to communicate information and ideas in speaking so others will understand.
Deductive Reasoning	The ability to apply general rules to specific problems to produce answers that make sense.
Inductive Reasoning	The ability to combine pieces of information to form general rules or conclusions (includes finding a relationship among seemingly unrelated events).
Information Ordering	The ability to arrange things or actions in a certain order or pattern according to a specific rule or set of rules (e.g., patterns of numbers, letters, words, pictures, mathematical operations).
Written Expression	The ability to communicate information and ideas in writing so others will understand.
Speech Clarity	The ability to speak clearly so others can understand you.
Near Vision	The ability to see details at close range (within a few feet of the observer).
Speech Recognition	The ability to identify and understand the speech of another person.
Written Comprehension	The ability to read and understand information and ideas presented in writing.
Time Sharing	The ability to shift back and forth between two or more activities or sources of information (such as speech, sounds, touch, or other sources).
Selective Attention	The ability to concentrate on a task over a period of time without being distracted.
Finger Dexterity	The ability to make precisely coordinated movements of the fingers of one or both hands to grasp, manipulate, or assemble very small objects.
Category Flexibility	The ability to generate or use different sets of rules for combining or grouping things in different ways.
Speed of Closure	The ability to quickly make sense of, combine, and organize information into meaningful patterns.
Perceptual Speed	The ability to quickly and accurately compare similarities and differences among sets of letters, numbers, objects, pictures, or patterns. The things to be compared may be presented at the same time or one after the other. This ability also includes comparing a presented object with a remembered object.
Arm-Hand Steadiness	The ability to keep your hand and arm steady while moving your arm or while holding your arm and hand in one position.
Flexibility of Closure	The ability to identify or detect a known pattern (a figure, object, word, or sound) that is hidden in other distracting material.
Memorization	The ability to remember information such as words, numbers, pictures, and procedures.
Originality	The ability to come up with unusual or clever ideas about a given topic or situation, or to develop creative ways to solve a problem.
Manual Dexterity	The ability to quickly move your hand, your hand together with your arm, or your two hands to grasp, manipulate, or assemble objects.
Hearing Sensitivity	The ability to detect or tell the differences between sounds that vary in pitch and loudness.
Gross Body Coordination	The ability to coordinate the movement of your arms, legs, and torso together when the whole body is in motion.
Far Vision	The ability to see details at a distance.
Stamina	The ability to exert yourself physically over long periods of time without getting winded or out of breath.
Visual Color Discrimination	The ability to match or detect differences between colors, including shades of color and brightness.
Number Facility	The ability to add, subtract, multiply, or divide quickly and correctly.
Trunk Strength	The ability to use your abdominal and lower back muscles to support part of the body repeatedly or continuously over time without 'giving out' or fatiguing.
Mathematical Reasoning	The ability to choose the right mathematical methods or formulas to solve a problem.
Auditory Attention	The ability to focus on a single source of sound in the presence of other distracting sounds.
Depth Perception	The ability to judge which of several objects is closer or farther away from you, or to judge the distance between you and an object.
Extent Flexibility	The ability to bend, stretch, twist, or reach with your body, arms, and/or legs.
Fluency of Ideas	The ability to come up with a number of ideas about a topic (the number of ideas is important, not their quality, correctness, or creativity).
Static Strength	The ability to exert maximum muscle force to lift, push, pull, or carry objects.

Multilimb Coordination	The ability to coordinate two or more limbs (for example, two arms, two legs, or one leg and one arm) while sitting, standing, or lying down. It does not involve performing the activities while the whole body is in motion.
Speed of Limb Movement	The ability to quickly move the arms and legs.
Control Precision	The ability to quickly and repeatedly adjust the controls of a machine or a vehicle to exact positions.
Visualization	The ability to imagine how something will look after it is moved around or when its parts are moved or rearranged.
Reaction Time	The ability to quickly respond (with the hand, finger, or foot) to a signal (sound, light, picture) when it appears.
Dynamic Strength	The ability to exert muscle force repeatedly or continuously over time. This involves muscular endurance and resistance to muscle fatigue.
Response Orientation	The ability to choose quickly between two or more movements in response to two or more different signals (lights, sounds, pictures). It includes the speed with which the correct response is started with the hand, foot, or other body part.
Gross Body Equilibrium	The ability to keep or regain your body balance or stay upright when in an unstable position.
Rate Control	The ability to time your movements or the movement of a piece of equipment in anticipation of changes in the speed and/or direction of a moving object or scene.
Sound Localization	The ability to tell the direction from which a sound originated.
Peripheral Vision	The ability to see objects or movement of objects to one's side when the eyes are looking ahead.
Night Vision	The ability to see under low light conditions.
Glare Sensitivity	The ability to see objects in the presence of glare or bright lighting.
Spatial Orientation	The ability to know your location in relation to the environment or to know where other objects are in relation to you.
Dynamic Flexibility	The ability to quickly and repeatedly bend, stretch, twist, or reach out with your body, arms, and/or legs.
Explosive Strength	The ability to use short bursts of muscle force to propel oneself (as in jumping or sprinting), or to throw an object.
Wrist-Finger Speed	The ability to make fast, simple, repeated movements of the fingers, hands, and wrists.

Work_Activity	Work_Activity Definitions
Documenting/Recording Information	Entering, transcribing, recording, storing, or maintaining information in written or electronic/magnetic form.
Assisting and Caring for Others	Providing personal assistance, medical attention, emotional support, or other personal care to others such as coworkers, customers, or patients.
Making Decisions and Solving Problems	Analyzing information and evaluating results to choose the best solution and solve problems.
Updating and Using Relevant Knowledge	Keeping up-to-date technically and applying new knowledge to your job.
Organizing, Planning, and Prioritizing Work	Developing specific goals and plans to prioritize, organize, and accomplish your work.
Getting Information	Observing, receiving, and otherwise obtaining information from all relevant sources.
Communicating with Supervisors, Peers, or Subordin	Providing information to supervisors, co-workers, and subordinates by telephone, in written form, e-mail, or in person.
Monitor Processes, Materials, or Surroundings	Monitoring and reviewing information from materials, events, or the environment, to detect or assess problems.
Evaluating Information to Determine Compliance wit	Using relevant information and individual judgment to determine whether events or processes comply with laws, regulations, or standards.
Identifying Objects, Actions, and Events	Identifying information by categorizing, estimating, recognizing differences or similarities, and detecting changes in circumstances or events.
Interpreting the Meaning of Information for Others	Translating or explaining what information means and how it can be used.
Establishing and Maintaining Interpersonal Relatio	Developing constructive and cooperative working relationships with others, and maintaining them over time.
Training and Teaching Others	Identifying the educational needs of others, developing formal educational or training programs or classes, and teaching or instructing others.
Scheduling Work and Activities	Scheduling events, programs, and activities, as well as the work of others.
Judging the Qualities of Things, Services, or Peop	Assessing the value, importance, or quality of things or people.

Developing and Building Teams	Encouraging and building mutual trust, respect, and cooperation among team members.
Performing Administrative Activities	Performing day-to-day administrative tasks such as maintaining information files and processing paperwork.
Performing for or Working Directly with the Public	Performing for people or dealing directly with the public. This includes serving customers in restaurants and stores, and receiving clients or guests.
Performing General Physical Activities	Performing physical activities that require considerable use of your arms and legs and moving your whole body, such as climbing, lifting, balancing, walking, stooping, and handling of materials.
Repairing and Maintaining Electronic Equipment	Servicing, repairing, calibrating, regulating, fine-tuning, or testing machines, devices, and equipment that operate primarily on the basis of electrical or electronic (not mechanical) principles.
Estimating the Quantifiable Characteristics of Pro	Estimating sizes, distances, and quantities; or determining time, costs, resources, or materials needed to perform a work activity.
Resolving Conflicts and Negotiating with Others	Handling complaints, settling disputes, and resolving grievances and conflicts, or otherwise negotiating with others.
Developing Objectives and Strategies	Establishing long-range objectives and specifying the strategies and actions to achieve them.
Inspecting Equipment, Structures, or Material	Inspecting equipment, structures, or materials to identify the cause of errors or other problems or defects.
Processing Information	Compiling, coding, categorizing, calculating, tabulating, auditing, or verifying information or data.
Analyzing Data or Information	Identifying the underlying principles, reasons, or facts of information by breaking down information or data into separate parts.
Provide Consultation and Advice to Others	Providing guidance and expert advice to management or other groups on technical, systems-, or process-related topics.
Communicating with Persons Outside Organization	Communicating with people outside the organization, representing the organization to customers, the public, government, and other external sources. This information can be exchanged in person, in writing, or by telephone or e-mail.
Coordinating the Work and Activities of Others	Getting members of a group to work together to accomplish tasks.
Coaching and Developing Others	Identifying the developmental needs of others and coaching, mentoring, or otherwise helping others to improve their knowledge or skills.
Interacting With Computers	Using computers and computer systems (including hardware and software) to program, write software, set up functions, enter data, or process information.
Handling and Moving Objects	Using hands and arms in handling, installing, positioning, and moving materials, and manipulating things.
Guiding, Directing, and Motivating Subordinates	Providing guidance and direction to subordinates, including setting performance standards and monitoring performance.
Thinking Creatively	Developing, designing, or creating new applications, ideas, relationships, systems, or products, including artistic contributions.
Controlling Machines and Processes	Using either control mechanisms or direct physical activity to operate machines or processes (not including computers or vehicles).
Repairing and Maintaining Mechanical Equipment	Servicing, repairing, adjusting, and testing machines, devices, moving parts, and equipment that operate primarily on the basis of mechanical (not electronic) principles.
Staffing Organizational Units	Recruiting, interviewing, selecting, hiring, and promoting employees in an organization.
Selling or Influencing Others	Convincing others to buy merchandise/goods or to otherwise change their minds or actions.
Monitoring and Controlling Resources	Monitoring and controlling resources and overseeing the spending of money.
Operating Vehicles, Mechanized Devices, or Equipme	Running, maneuvering, navigating, or driving vehicles or mechanized equipment, such as forklifts, passenger vehicles, aircraft, or water craft.
Drafting, Laying Out, and Specifying Technical Dev	Providing documentation, detailed instructions, drawings, or specifications to tell others about how devices, parts, equipment, or structures are to be fabricated, constructed, assembled, modified, maintained, or used.

Work_Context	**Work_Context Definitions**
Telephone	How often do you have telephone conversations in this job?
Contact With Others	How much does this job require the worker to be in contact with others (face-to-face, by telephone, or otherwise) in order to perform it?
Face-to-Face Discussions	How often do you have to have face-to-face discussions with individuals or teams in this job?

Structured versus Unstructured Work	To what extent is this job structured for the worker, rather than allowing the worker to determine tasks, priorities, and goals?
Work With Work Group or Team	How important is it to work with others in a group or team in this job?
Coordinate or Lead Others	How important is it to coordinate or lead others in accomplishing work activities in this job?
Deal With External Customers	How important is it to work with external customers or the public in this job?
Exposed to Disease or Infections	How often does this job require exposure to disease/infections?
Importance of Being Exact or Accurate	How important is being very exact or highly accurate in performing this job?
Time Pressure	How often does this job require the worker to meet strict deadlines?
Impact of Decisions on Co-workers or Company Resul	How do the decisions an employee makes impact the results of co-workers, clients or the company?
Frequency of Decision Making	How frequently is the worker required to make decisions that affect other people, the financial resources, and/or the image and reputation of the organization?
Indoors, Environmentally Controlled	How often does this job require working indoors in environmentally controlled conditions?
Freedom to Make Decisions	How much decision making freedom, without supervision, does the job offer?
Consequence of Error	How serious would the result usually be if the worker made a mistake that was not readily correctable?
Physical Proximity	To what extent does this job require the worker to perform job tasks in close physical proximity to other people?
Deal With Unpleasant or Angry People	How frequently does the worker have to deal with unpleasant, angry, or discourteous individuals as part of the job requirements?
Responsibility for Outcomes and Results	How responsible is the worker for work outcomes and results of other workers?
Responsible for Others' Health and Safety	How much responsibility is there for the health and safety of others in this job?
Frequency of Conflict Situations	How often are there conflict situations the employee has to face in this job?
Letters and Memos	How often does the job require written letters and memos?
Importance of Repeating Same Tasks	How important is repeating the same physical activities (e.g., key entry) or mental activities (e.g., checking entries in a ledger) over and over, without stopping, to performing this job?
Spend Time Walking and Running	How much does this job require walking and running?
Spend Time Standing	How much does this job require standing?
Wear Common Protective or Safety Equipment such as	How much does this job require wearing common protective or safety equipment such as safety shoes, glasses, gloves, hard hats or live jackets?
Electronic Mail	How often do you use electronic mail in this job?
Level of Competition	To what extent does this job require the worker to compete or to be aware of competitive pressures?
Sounds, Noise Levels Are Distracting or Uncomforta	How often does this job require working exposed to sounds and noise levels that are distracting or uncomfortable?
Spend Time Sitting	How much does this job require sitting?
Deal With Physically Aggressive People	How frequently does this job require the worker to deal with physical aggression of violent individuals?
Spend Time Bending or Twisting the Body	How much does this job require bending or twisting your body?
Public Speaking	How often do you have to perform public speaking in this job?
In an Enclosed Vehicle or Equipment	How often does this job require working in a closed vehicle or equipment (e.g., car)?
Spend Time Making Repetitive Motions	How much does this job require making repetitive motions?
Spend Time Using Your Hands to Handle, Control, or	How much does this job require using your hands to handle, control, or feel objects, tools or controls?
Degree of Automation	How automated is the job?
Exposed to Contaminants	How often does this job require working exposed to contaminants (such as pollutants, gases, dust or odors)?
Spend Time Kneeling, Crouching, Stooping, or Crawl	How much does this job require kneeling, crouching, stooping or crawling?
Cramped Work Space, Awkward Positions	How often does this job require working in cramped work spaces that requires getting into awkward positions?
Spend Time Keeping or Regaining Balance	How much does this job require keeping or regaining your balance?
Wear Specialized Protective or Safety Equipment su	How much does this job require wearing specialized protective or safety equipment such as breathing apparatus, safety harness, full protection suits, or radiation protection?

Exposed to Hazardous Conditions	How often does this job require exposure to hazardous conditions?
Indoors, Not Environmentally Controlled	How often does this job require working indoors in non-controlled environmental conditions (e.g., warehouse without heat)?
Exposed to Minor Burns, Cuts, Bites, or Stings	How often does this job require exposure to minor burns, cuts, bites, or stings?
Very Hot or Cold Temperatures	How often does this job require working in very hot (above 90 F degrees) or very cold (below 32 F degrees) temperatures?
Extremely Bright or Inadequate Lighting	How often does this job require working in extremely bright or inadequate lighting conditions?
Exposed to Radiation	How often does this job require exposure to radiation?
Outdoors, Under Cover	How often does this job require working outdoors, under cover (e.g., structure with roof but no walls)?
Pace Determined by Speed of Equipment	How important is it to this job that the pace is determined by the speed of equipment or machinery? (This does not refer to keeping busy at all times on this job.)
Outdoors, Exposed to Weather	How often does this job require working outdoors, exposed to all weather conditions?
In an Open Vehicle or Equipment	How often does this job require working in an open vehicle or equipment (e.g., tractor)?
Exposed to High Places	How often does this job require exposure to high places?
Exposed to Whole Body Vibration	How often does this job require exposure to whole body vibration (e.g., operate a jackhammer)?
Exposed to Hazardous Equipment	How often does this job require exposure to hazardous equipment?
Spend Time Climbing Ladders, Scaffolds, or Poles	How much does this job require climbing ladders, scaffolds, or poles?

Job Zone Component	Job Zone Component Definitions
Title	Job Zone Three: Medium Preparation Needed
Overall Experience	Previous work-related skill, knowledge, or experience is required for these occupations. For example, an electrician must have completed three or four years of apprenticeship or several years of vocational training, and often must have passed a licensing exam, in order to perform the job.
Job Training	Employees in these occupations usually need one or two years of training involving both on-the-job experience and informal training with experienced workers.
Job Zone Examples	These occupations usually involve using communication and organizational skills to coordinate, supervise, manage, or train others to accomplish goals. Examples include dental assistants, electricians, fish and game wardens, legal secretaries, personnel recruiters, and recreation workers.
SVP Range	(6.0 to < 7.0)
Education	Most occupations in this zone require training in vocational schools, related on-the-job experience, or an associate's degree. Some may require a bachelor's degree.

Work_Styles	Work_Styles Definitions
Concern for Others	Job requires being sensitive to others' needs and feelings and being understanding and helpful on the job.
Stress Tolerance	Job requires accepting criticism and dealing calmly and effectively with high stress situations.
Dependability	Job requires being reliable, responsible, and dependable, and fulfilling obligations.
Attention to Detail	Job requires being careful about detail and thorough in completing work tasks.
Self Control	Job requires maintaining composure, keeping emotions in check, controlling anger, and avoiding aggressive behavior, even in very difficult situations.
Cooperation	Job requires being pleasant with others on the job and displaying a good-natured, cooperative attitude.
Integrity	Job requires being honest and ethical.
Adaptability/Flexibility	Job requires being open to change (positive or negative) and to considerable variety in the workplace.
Leadership	Job requires a willingness to lead, take charge, and offer opinions and direction.
Achievement/Effort	Job requires establishing and maintaining personally challenging achievement goals and exerting effort toward mastering tasks.
Initiative	Job requires a willingness to take on responsibilities and challenges.

Social Orientation	Job requires preferring to work with others rather than alone, and being personally connected with others on the job.
Persistence	Job requires persistence in the face of obstacles.
Analytical Thinking	Job requires analyzing information and using logic to address work-related issues and problems.
Independence	Job requires developing one's own ways of doing things, guiding oneself with little or no supervision, and depending on oneself to get things done.
Innovation	Job requires creativity and alternative thinking to develop new ideas for and answers to work-related problems.

29-2071.00 - Medical Records and Health Information Technicians

Compile, process, and maintain medical records of hospital and clinic patients in a manner consistent with medical, administrative, ethical, legal, and regulatory requirements of the health care system. Process, maintain, compile, and report patient information for health requirements and standards.

Tasks

1) Release information to persons and agencies according to regulations.

2) Review records for completeness, accuracy and compliance with regulations.

3) Plan, develop, maintain and operate a variety of health record indexes and storage and retrieval systems to collect, classify, store and analyze information.

4) Compile and maintain patients' medical records to document condition and treatment and to provide data for research or cost control and care improvement efforts.

5) Process patient admission and discharge documents.

6) Enter data, such as demographic characteristics, history and extent of disease, diagnostic procedures and treatment into computer.

7) Train medical records staff.

8) Manage the department and supervise clerical workers, directing and controlling activities of personnel in the medical records department.

9) Resolve/clarify codes and diagnoses with conflicting, missing, or unclear information by consulting with doctors or others to get additional information and by participating in the coding team's regular meetings.

10) Identify, compile, abstract and code patient data, using standard classification systems.

11) Process and prepare business and government forms.

12) Transcribe medical reports.

13) Develop in-service educational materials.

14) Assign the patient to one of several hundred diagnosis-related groups, or DRGs, using appropriate computer software.

15) Consult classification manuals to locate information about disease processes.

16) Prepare statistical reports, narrative reports and graphic presentations of information such as tumor registry data for use by hospital staff, researchers, and other users.

17) Post medical insurance billings.

18) Compile medical care and census data for statistical reports on diseases treated, surgery performed, and use of hospital beds.

19) Contact discharged patients, their families, and physicians to maintain registry with follow-up information, such as quality of life and length of survival of cancer patients.

Knowledge	Knowledge Definitions
Clerical	Knowledge of administrative and clerical procedures and systems such as word processing, managing files and records, stenography and transcription, designing forms, and other office procedures and terminology.
Customer and Personal Service	Knowledge of principles and processes for providing customer and personal services. This includes customer needs assessment, meeting quality standards for services, and evaluation of customer satisfaction.
English Language	Knowledge of the structure and content of the English language including the meaning and spelling of words, rules of composition, and grammar.

Computers and Electronics	Knowledge of circuit boards, processors, chips, electronic equipment, and computer hardware and software, including applications and programming.
Administration and Management	Knowledge of business and management principles involved in strategic planning, resource allocation, human resources modeling, leadership technique, production methods, and coordination of people and resources.
Foreign Language	Knowledge of the structure and content of a foreign (non-English) language including the meaning and spelling of words, rules of composition and grammar, and pronunciation.
Mathematics	Knowledge of arithmetic, algebra, geometry, calculus, statistics, and their applications.
Personnel and Human Resources	Knowledge of principles and procedures for personnel recruitment, selection, training, compensation and benefits, labor relations and negotiation, and personnel information systems.
Telecommunications	Knowledge of transmission, broadcasting, switching, control, and operation of telecommunications systems.
Education and Training	Knowledge of principles and methods for curriculum and training design, teaching and instruction for individuals and groups, and the measurement of training effects.
Medicine and Dentistry	Knowledge of the information and techniques needed to diagnose and treat human injuries, diseases, and deformities. This includes symptoms, treatment alternatives, drug properties and interactions, and preventive health-care measures.
Public Safety and Security	Knowledge of relevant equipment, policies, procedures, and strategies to promote effective local, state, or national security operations for the protection of people, data, property, and institutions.
Communications and Media	Knowledge of media production, communication, and dissemination techniques and methods. This includes alternative ways to inform and entertain via written, oral, and visual media.
Law and Government	Knowledge of laws, legal codes, court procedures, precedents, government regulations, executive orders, agency rules, and the democratic political process.
Sales and Marketing	Knowledge of principles and methods for showing, promoting, and selling products or services. This includes marketing strategy and tactics, product demonstration, sales techniques, and sales control systems.
Philosophy and Theology	Knowledge of different philosophical systems and religions. This includes their basic principles, values, ethics, ways of thinking, customs, practices, and their impact on human culture.
Psychology	Knowledge of human behavior and performance; individual differences in ability, personality, and interests; learning and motivation; psychological research methods; and the assessment and treatment of behavioral and affective disorders.
Economics and Accounting	Knowledge of economic and accounting principles and practices, the financial markets, banking and the analysis and reporting of financial data.
Production and Processing	Knowledge of raw materials, production processes, quality control, costs, and other techniques for maximizing the effective manufacture and distribution of goods.
Biology	Knowledge of plant and animal organisms, their tissues, cells, functions, interdependencies, and interactions with each other and the environment.
Therapy and Counseling	Knowledge of principles, methods, and procedures for diagnosis, treatment, and rehabilitation of physical and mental dysfunctions, and for career counseling and guidance.
Transportation	Knowledge of principles and methods for moving people or goods by air, rail, sea, or road, including the relative costs and benefits.
Sociology and Anthropology	Knowledge of group behavior and dynamics, societal trends and influences, human migrations, ethnicity, cultures and their history and origins.
Geography	Knowledge of principles and methods for describing the features of land, sea, and air masses, including their physical characteristics, locations, interrelationships, and distribution of plant, animal, and human life.
Mechanical	Knowledge of machines and tools, including their designs, uses, repair, and maintenance.
Engineering and Technology	Knowledge of the practical application of engineering science and technology. This includes applying principles, techniques, procedures, and equipment to the design and production of various goods and services.
Design	Knowledge of design techniques, tools, and principles involved in production of precision technical plans, blueprints, drawings, and models.
Physics	Knowledge and prediction of physical principles, laws, their interrelationships, and applications to understanding fluid, material, and atmospheric dynamics, and mechanical, electrical, atomic and sub-atomic structures and processes.
Chemistry	Knowledge of the chemical composition, structure, and properties of substances and of the chemical processes and transformations that they undergo. This includes uses of chemicals and their interactions, danger signs, production techniques, and disposal methods.
History and Archeology	Knowledge of historical events and their causes, indicators, and effects on civilizations and cultures.
Building and Construction	Knowledge of materials, methods, and the tools involved in the construction or repair of houses, buildings, or other structures such as highways and roads.
Fine Arts	Knowledge of the theory and techniques required to compose, produce, and perform works of music, dance, visual arts, drama, and sculpture.
Food Production	Knowledge of techniques and equipment for planting, growing, and harvesting food products (both plant and animal) for consumption, including storage/handling techniques.

Skills	Skills Definitions
Active Listening	Giving full attention to what other people are saying, taking time to understand the points being made, asking questions as appropriate, and not interrupting at inappropriate times.
Reading Comprehension	Understanding written sentences and paragraphs in work related documents.
Time Management	Managing one's own time and the time of others.
Speaking	Talking to others to convey information effectively.
Writing	Communicating effectively in writing as appropriate for the needs of the audience.
Instructing	Teaching others how to do something.
Active Learning	Understanding the implications of new information for both current and future problem-solving and decision-making.
Critical Thinking	Using logic and reasoning to identify the strengths and weaknesses of alternative solutions, conclusions or approaches to problems.
Social Perceptiveness	Being aware of others' reactions and understanding why they react as they do.
Judgment and Decision Making	Considering the relative costs and benefits of potential actions to choose the most appropriate one.
Learning Strategies	Selecting and using training/instructional methods and procedures appropriate for the situation when learning or teaching new things.
Service Orientation	Actively looking for ways to help people.
Monitoring	Monitoring/Assessing performance of yourself, other individuals, or organizations to make improvements or take corrective action.
Systems Evaluation	Identifying measures or indicators of system performance and the actions needed to improve or correct performance, relative to the goals of the system.
Complex Problem Solving	Identifying complex problems and reviewing related information to develop and evaluate options and implement solutions.
Quality Control Analysis	Conducting tests and inspections of products, services, or processes to evaluate quality or performance.
Coordination	Adjusting actions in relation to others' actions.
Negotiation	Bringing others together and trying to reconcile differences.
Operation and Control	Controlling operations of equipment or systems.
Equipment Selection	Determining the kind of tools and equipment needed to do a job.
Management of Personnel Resources	Motivating, developing, and directing people as they work, identifying the best people for the job.
Troubleshooting	Determining causes of operating errors and deciding what to do about it.
Systems Analysis	Determining how a system should work and how changes in conditions, operations, and the environment will affect outcomes.
Persuasion	Persuading others to change their minds or behavior.
Operations Analysis	Analyzing needs and product requirements to create a design.
Management of Material Resources	Obtaining and seeing to the appropriate use of equipment, facilities, and materials needed to do certain work.
Mathematics	Using mathematics to solve problems.

Management of Financial Resources	Determining how money will be spent to get the work done, and accounting for these expenditures.
Operation Monitoring	Watching gauges, dials, or other indicators to make sure a machine is working properly.
Science	Using scientific rules and methods to solve problems.
Equipment Maintenance	Performing routine maintenance on equipment and determining when and what kind of maintenance is needed.
Programming	Writing computer programs for various purposes.
Installation	Installing equipment, machines, wiring, or programs to meet specifications.
Technology Design	Generating or adapting equipment and technology to serve user needs.
Repairing	Repairing machines or systems using the needed tools.

Ability	Ability Definitions
Oral Comprehension	The ability to listen to and understand information and ideas presented through spoken words and sentences.
Written Comprehension	The ability to read and understand information and ideas presented in writing.
Information Ordering	The ability to arrange things or actions in a certain order or pattern according to a specific rule or set of rules (e.g., patterns of numbers, letters, words, pictures, mathematical operations).
Oral Expression	The ability to communicate information and ideas in speaking so others will understand.
Near Vision	The ability to see details at close range (within a few feet of the observer).
Speech Clarity	The ability to speak clearly so others can understand you.
Speech Recognition	The ability to identify and understand the speech of another person.
Category Flexibility	The ability to generate or use different sets of rules for combining or grouping things in different ways.
Written Expression	The ability to communicate information and ideas in writing so others will understand.
Problem Sensitivity	The ability to tell when something is wrong or is likely to go wrong. It does not involve solving the problem, only recognizing there is a problem.
Selective Attention	The ability to concentrate on a task over a period of time without being distracted.
Deductive Reasoning	The ability to apply general rules to specific problems to produce answers that make sense.
Inductive Reasoning	The ability to combine pieces of information to form general rules or conclusions (includes finding a relationship among seemingly unrelated events).
Finger Dexterity	The ability to make precisely coordinated movements of the fingers of one or both hands to grasp, manipulate, or assemble very small objects.
Perceptual Speed	The ability to quickly and accurately compare similarities and differences among sets of letters, numbers, objects, pictures, or patterns. The things to be compared may be presented at the same time or one after the other. This ability also includes comparing a presented object with a remembered object.
Flexibility of Closure	The ability to identify or detect a known pattern (a figure, object, word, or sound) that is hidden in other distracting material.
Manual Dexterity	The ability to quickly move your hand, your hand together with your arm, or your two hands to grasp, manipulate, or assemble objects.
Originality	The ability to come up with unusual or clever ideas about a given topic or situation, or to develop creative ways to solve a problem.
Memorization	The ability to remember information such as words, numbers, pictures, and procedures.
Auditory Attention	The ability to focus on a single source of sound in the presence of other distracting sounds.
Time Sharing	The ability to shift back and forth between two or more activities or sources of information (such as speech, sounds, touch, or other sources).
Static Strength	The ability to exert maximum muscle force to lift, push, pull, or carry objects.
Number Facility	The ability to add, subtract, multiply, or divide quickly and correctly.
Speed of Closure	The ability to quickly make sense of, combine, and organize information into meaningful patterns.
Mathematical Reasoning	The ability to choose the right mathematical methods or formulas to solve a problem.
Arm-Hand Steadiness	The ability to keep your hand and arm steady while moving your arm or while holding your arm and hand in one position.

Trunk Strength	The ability to use your abdominal and lower back muscles to support part of the body repeatedly or continuously over time without 'giving out' or fatiguing.
Multilimb Coordination	The ability to coordinate two or more limbs (for example, two arms, two legs, or one leg and one arm) while sitting, standing, or lying down. It does not involve performing the activities while the whole body is in motion.
Fluency of Ideas	The ability to come up with a number of ideas about a topic (the number of ideas is important, not their quality, correctness, or creativity).
Visual Color Discrimination	The ability to match or detect differences between colors, including shades of color and brightness.
Wrist-Finger Speed	The ability to make fast, simple, repeated movements of the fingers, hands, and wrists.
Visualization	The ability to imagine how something will look after it is moved around or when its parts are moved or rearranged.
Far Vision	The ability to see details at a distance.
Gross Body Coordination	The ability to coordinate the movement of your arms, legs, and torso together when the whole body is in motion.
Extent Flexibility	The ability to bend, stretch, twist, or reach with your body, arms, and/or legs.
Dynamic Strength	The ability to exert muscle force repeatedly or continuously over time. This involves muscular endurance and resistance to muscle fatigue.
Control Precision	The ability to quickly and repeatedly adjust the controls of a machine or a vehicle to exact positions.
Hearing Sensitivity	The ability to detect or tell the differences between sounds that vary in pitch and loudness.
Gross Body Equilibrium	The ability to keep or regain your body balance or stay upright when in an unstable position.
Stamina	The ability to exert yourself physically over long periods of time without getting winded or out of breath.
Sound Localization	The ability to tell the direction from which a sound originated.
Reaction Time	The ability to quickly respond (with the hand, finger, or foot) to a signal (sound, light, picture) when it appears.
Peripheral Vision	The ability to see objects or movement of objects to one's side when the eyes are looking ahead.
Dynamic Flexibility	The ability to quickly and repeatedly bend, stretch, twist, or reach out with your body, arms, and/or legs.
Explosive Strength	The ability to use short bursts of muscle force to propel oneself (as in jumping or sprinting), or to throw an object.
Night Vision	The ability to see under low light conditions.
Depth Perception	The ability to judge which of several objects is closer or farther away from you, or to judge the distance between you and an object.
Glare Sensitivity	The ability to see objects in the presence of glare or bright lighting.
Rate Control	The ability to time your movements or the movement of a piece of equipment in anticipation of changes in the speed and/or direction of a moving object or scene.
Response Orientation	The ability to choose quickly between two or more movements in response to two or more different signals (lights, sounds, pictures). It includes the speed with which the correct response is started with the hand, foot, or other body part.
Spatial Orientation	The ability to know your location in relation to the environment or to know where other objects are in relation to you.
Speed of Limb Movement	The ability to quickly move the arms and legs.

Work_Activity	Work_Activity Definitions
Getting Information	Observing, receiving, and otherwise obtaining information from all relevant sources.
Interacting With Computers	Using computers and computer systems (including hardware and software) to program, write software, set up functions, enter data, or process information.
Communicating with Supervisors, Peers, or Subordin	Providing information to supervisors, co-workers, and subordinates by telephone, in written form, e-mail, or in person.
Performing Administrative Activities	Performing day-to-day administrative tasks such as maintaining information files and processing paperwork.
Updating and Using Relevant Knowledge	Keeping up-to-date technically and applying new knowledge to your job.
Evaluating Information to Determine Compliance wit	Using relevant information and individual judgment to determine whether events or processes comply with laws, regulations, or standards.
Documenting/Recording Information	Entering, transcribing, recording, storing, or maintaining information in written or electronic/magnetic form.

Establishing and Maintaining Interpersonal Relatio	Developing constructive and cooperative working relationships with others, and maintaining them over time.
Handling and Moving Objects	Using hands and arms in handling, installing, positioning, and moving materials, and manipulating things.
Organizing, Planning, and Prioritizing Work	Developing specific goals and plans to prioritize, organize, and accomplish your work.
Processing Information	Compiling, coding, categorizing, calculating, tabulating, auditing, or verifying information or data.
Interpreting the Meaning of Information for Others	Translating or explaining what information means and how it can be used.
Making Decisions and Solving Problems	Analyzing information and evaluating results to choose the best solution and solve problems.
Performing General Physical Activities	Performing physical activities that require considerable use of your arms and legs and moving your whole body, such as climbing, lifting, balancing, walking, stooping, and handling of materials.
Identifying Objects, Actions, and Events	Identifying information by categorizing, estimating, recognizing differences or similarities, and detecting changes in circumstances or events.
Communicating with Persons Outside Organization	Communicating with people outside the organization, representing the organization to customers, the public, government, and other external sources. This information can be exchanged in person, in writing, or by telephone or e-mail.
Training and Teaching Others	Identifying the educational needs of others, developing formal educational or training programs or classes, and teaching or instructing others.
Coordinating the Work and Activities of Others	Getting members of a group to work together to accomplish tasks.
Analyzing Data or Information	Identifying the underlying principles, reasons, or facts of information by breaking down information or data into separate parts.
Monitor Processes, Materials, or Surroundings	Monitoring and reviewing information from materials, events, or the environment, to detect or assess problems.
Provide Consultation and Advice to Others	Providing guidance and expert advice to management or other groups on technical, systems-, or process-related topics.
Assisting and Caring for Others	Providing personal assistance, medical attention, emotional support, or other personal care to others such as coworkers, customers, or patients.
Coaching and Developing Others	Identifying the developmental needs of others and coaching, mentoring, or otherwise helping others to improve their knowledge or skills.
Performing for or Working Directly with the Public	Performing for people or dealing directly with the public. This includes serving customers in restaurants and stores, and receiving clients or guests.
Thinking Creatively	Developing, designing, or creating new applications, ideas, relationships, systems, or products, including artistic contributions.
Guiding, Directing, and Motivating Subordinates	Providing guidance and direction to subordinates, including setting performance standards and monitoring performance.
Developing Objectives and Strategies	Establishing long-range objectives and specifying the strategies and actions to achieve them.
Scheduling Work and Activities	Scheduling events, programs, and activities, as well as the work of others.
Developing and Building Teams	Encouraging and building mutual trust, respect, and cooperation among team members.
Inspecting Equipment, Structures, or Material	Inspecting equipment, structures, or materials to identify the cause of errors or other problems or defects.
Estimating the Quantifiable Characteristics of Pro	Estimating sizes, distances, and quantities; or determining time, costs, resources, or materials needed to perform a work activity.
Resolving Conflicts and Negotiating with Others	Handling complaints, settling disputes, and resolving grievances and conflicts, or otherwise negotiating with others.
Judging the Qualities of Things, Services, or Peop	Assessing the value, importance, or quality of things or people.
Controlling Machines and Processes	Using either control mechanisms or direct physical activity to operate machines or processes (not including computers or vehicles).
Repairing and Maintaining Electronic Equipment	Servicing, repairing, calibrating, regulating, fine-tuning, or testing machines, devices, and equipment that operate primarily on the basis of electrical or electronic (not mechanical) principles.
Selling or Influencing Others	Convincing others to buy merchandise/goods or to otherwise change their minds or actions.
Monitoring and Controlling Resources	Monitoring and controlling resources and overseeing the spending of money.

Staffing Organizational Units	Recruiting, interviewing, selecting, hiring, and promoting employees in an organization.
Repairing and Maintaining Mechanical Equipment	Servicing, repairing, adjusting, and testing machines, devices, moving parts, and equipment that operate primarily on the basis of mechanical (not electronic) principles.
Drafting, Laying Out, and Specifying Technical Dev	Providing documentation, detailed instructions, drawings, or specifications to tell others about how devices, parts, equipment, or structures are to be fabricated, constructed, assembled, modified, maintained, or used.
Operating Vehicles, Mechanized Devices, or Equipme	Running, maneuvering, navigating, or driving vehicles or mechanized equipment, such as forklifts, passenger vehicles, aircraft, or water craft.

Work_Context	Work_Context Definitions
Telephone	How often do you have telephone conversations in this job?
Face-to-Face Discussions	How often do you have to have face-to-face discussions with individuals or teams in this job?
Contact With Others	How often does this job require the worker to be in contact with others (face-to-face, by telephone, or otherwise) in order to perform it?
Importance of Being Exact or Accurate	How important is being very exact or highly accurate in performing this job?
Indoors, Environmentally Controlled	How often does this job require working indoors in environmentally controlled conditions?
Letters and Memos	How often does the job require written letters and memos?
Importance of Repeating Same Tasks	How important is repeating the same physical activities (e.g., key entry) or mental activities (e.g., checking entries in a ledger) over and over, without stopping, to performing this job?
Freedom to Make Decisions	How much decision making freedom, without supervision, does the job offer?
Structured versus Unstructured Work	To what extent is this job structured for the worker, rather than allowing the worker to determine tasks, priorities, and goals?
Physical Proximity	To what extent does this job require the worker to perform job tasks in close physical proximity to other people?
Work With Work Group or Team	How important is it to work with others in a group or team in this job?
Spend Time Sitting	How much does this job require sitting?
Frequency of Decision Making	How frequently is the worker required to make decisions that affect other people, the financial resources, and/or the image and reputation of the organization?
Time Pressure	How often does this job require the worker to meet strict deadlines?
Impact of Decisions on Co-workers or Company Resul	How do the decisions an employee makes impact the results of co-workers, clients or the company?
Deal With External Customers	How important is it to work with external customers or the public in this job?
Coordinate or Lead Others	How important is it to coordinate or lead others in accomplishing work activities in this job?
Spend Time Making Repetitive Motions	How much does this job require making repetitive motions?
Spend Time Using Your Hands to Handle, Control, or	How much does this job require using your hands to handle, control, or feel objects, tools or controls?
Sounds, Noise Levels Are Distracting or Uncomforta	How often does this job require working exposed to sounds and noise levels that are distracting or uncomfortable?
Frequency of Conflict Situations	How often are there conflict situations the employee has to face in this job?
Degree of Automation	How automated is the job?
Responsibility for Outcomes and Results	How responsible is the worker for work outcomes and results of other workers?
Deal With Unpleasant or Angry People	How frequently does the worker have to deal with unpleasant, angry, or discourteous individuals as part of the job requirements?
Electronic Mail	How often do you use electronic mail in this job?
Level of Competition	To what extent does this job require the worker to compete or to be aware of competitive pressures?
Exposed to Contaminants	How often does this job require working exposed to contaminants (such as pollutants, gases, dust or odors)?
Pace Determined by Speed of Equipment	How important is it to this job that the pace is determined by the speed of equipment or machinery? (This does not refer to keeping busy at all times on this job.)
Cramped Work Space, Awkward Positions	How often does this job require working in cramped work spaces that requires getting into awkward positions?
Spend Time Bending or Twisting the Body	How much does this job require bending or twisting your body?
Spend Time Standing	How much does this job require standing?

Exposed to Disease or Infections	How often does this job require exposure to disease/infections?
Spend Time Walking and Running	How much does this job require walking and running?
Consequence of Error	How serious would the result usually be if the worker made a mistake that was not readily correctable?
Responsible for Others' Health and Safety	How much responsibility is there for the health and safety of others in this job?
Spend Time Kneeling. Crouching, Stooping, or Crawl	How much does this job require kneeling, crouching, stooping or crawling?
Exposed to Minor Burns. Cuts, Bites, or Stings	How often does this job require exposure to minor burns, cuts, bites, or stings?
Extremely Bright or Inadequate Lighting	How often does this job require working in extremely bright or inadequate lighting conditions?
Wear Common Protective or Safety Equipment such as	How much does this job require wearing common protective or safety equipment such as safety shoes, glasses, gloves, hard hats or live jackets?
Spend Time Keeping or Regaining Balance	How much does this job require keeping or regaining your balance?
Public Speaking	How often do you have to perform public speaking in this job?
Deal With Physically Aggressive People	How frequently does this job require the worker to deal with physical aggression of violent individuals?
Very Hot or Cold Temperatures	How often does this job require working in very hot (above 90 F degrees) or very cold (below 32 F degrees) temperatures?
Exposed to Hazardous Conditions	How often does this job require exposure to hazardous conditions?
Spend Time Climbing Ladders, Scaffolds, or Poles	How much does this job require climbing ladders, scaffolds, or poles?
Exposed to Radiation	How often does this job require exposure to radiation?
Outdoors, Under Cover	How often does this job require working outdoors, under cover (e.g., structure with roof but no walls)?
In an Enclosed Vehicle or Equipment	How often does this job require working in a closed vehicle or equipment (e.g., car)?
In an Open Vehicle or Equipment	How often does this job require working in an open vehicle or equipment (e.g., tractor)?
Indoors, Not Environmentally Controlled	How often does this job require working indoors in non-controlled environmental conditions (e.g., warehouse without heat)?
Wear Specialized Protective or Safety Equipment su	How much does this job require wearing specialized protective or safety equipment such as breathing apparatus, safety harness, full protection suits, or radiation protection?
Exposed to Whole Body Vibration	How often does this job require exposure to whole body vibration (e.g., operate a jackhammer)?
Exposed to High Places	How often does this job require exposure to high places?
Exposed to Hazardous Equipment	How often does this job require exposure to hazardous equipment?
Outdoors, Exposed to Weather	How often does this job require working outdoors, exposed to all weather conditions?

Job Zone Component	Job Zone Component Definitions
Title	Job Zone Three: Medium Preparation Needed
Overall Experience	Previous work-related skill, knowledge, or experience is required for these occupations. For example, an electrician must have completed three or four years of apprenticeship or several years of vocational training, and often must have passed a licensing exam, in order to perform the job.
Job Training	Employees in these occupations usually need one or two years of training involving both on-the-job experience and informal training with experienced workers.
Job Zone Examples	These occupations usually involve using communication and organizational skills to coordinate, supervise, manage, or train others to accomplish goals. Examples include dental assistants, electricians, fish and game wardens, legal secretaries, personnel recruiters, and recreation workers.
SVP Range	(6.0 to < 7.0)
Education	Most occupations in this zone require training in vocational schools, related on-the-job experience, or an associate's degree. Some may require a bachelor's degree.

Work_Styles	Work_Styles Definitions
Cooperation	Job requires being pleasant with others on the job and displaying a good-natured, cooperative attitude.

Stress Tolerance	Job requires accepting criticism and dealing calmly and effectively with high stress situations.
Integrity	Job requires being honest and ethical.
Dependability	Job requires being reliable, responsible, and dependable, and fulfilling obligations.
Attention to Detail	Job requires being careful about detail and thorough in completing work tasks.
Concern for Others	Job requires being sensitive to others' needs and feelings and being understanding and helpful on the job.
Independence	Job requires developing one's own ways of doing things, guiding oneself with little or no supervision, and depending on oneself to get things done.
Adaptability/Flexibility	Job requires being open to change (positive or negative) and to considerable variety in the workplace.
Initiative	Job requires a willingness to take on responsibilities and challenges.
Self Control	Job requires maintaining composure, keeping emotions in check, controlling anger, and avoiding aggressive behavior, even in very difficult situations.
Persistence	Job requires persistence in the face of obstacles.
Achievement/Effort	Job requires establishing and maintaining personally challenging achievement goals and exerting effort toward mastering tasks.
Analytical Thinking	Job requires analyzing information and using logic to address work-related issues and problems.
Innovation	Job requires creativity and alternative thinking to develop new ideas for and answers to work-related problems.
Social Orientation	Job requires preferring to work with others rather than alone, and being personally connected with others on the job.
Leadership	Job requires a willingness to lead, take charge, and offer opinions and direction.

29-2081.00 - Opticians, Dispensing

Design, measure, fit, and adapt lenses and frames for client according to written optical prescription or specification. Assist client with selecting frames. Measure customer for size of eyeglasses and coordinate frames with facial and eye measurements and optical prescription. Prepare work order for optical laboratory containing instructions for grinding and mounting lenses in frames. Verify exactness of finished lens spectacles. Adjust frame and lens position to fit client. May shape or reshape frames.

Tasks

1) Obtain a customer's previous record, or verify a prescription with the examining optometrist or ophthalmologist.

2) Repair damaged frames.

3) Determine clients' current lens prescriptions, when necessary, using lensometers or lens analyzers and clients' eyeglasses.

4) Prepare work orders and instructions for grinding lenses and fabricating eyeglasses.

5) Evaluate prescriptions in conjunction with clients' vocational and avocational visual requirements.

6) Verify that finished lenses are ground to specifications.

7) Show customers how to insert, remove, and care for their contact lenses.

8) Fabricate lenses to meet prescription specifications.

9) Assemble eyeglasses by cutting and edging lenses, then fitting the lenses into frames.

10) Grind lens edges, or apply coatings to lenses.

11) Supervise the training of student opticians.

12) Maintain records of customer prescriptions, work orders, and payments.

13) Recommend specific lenses, lens coatings, and frames to suit client needs.

14) Heat, shape, or bend plastic or metal frames in order to adjust eyeglasses to fit clients, using pliers and hands.

15) Measure clients' bridge and eye size, temple length, vertex distance, pupillary distance, and optical centers of eyes, using measuring devices.

16) Perform administrative duties such as tracking inventory and sales, submitting patient insurance information, and performing simple bookkeeping.

17) Sell goods such as contact lenses, spectacles, sunglasses, and other goods related to eyes in general.

18) Instruct clients in how to wear and care for eyeglasses.

19) Assist clients in selecting frames according to style and color, and ensure that frames are coordinated with facial and eye measurements and optical prescriptions.

Knowledge	Knowledge Definitions
Customer and Personal Service	Knowledge of principles and processes for providing customer and personal services. This includes customer needs assessment, meeting quality standards for services, and evaluation of customer satisfaction.
Sales and Marketing	Knowledge of principles and methods for showing, promoting, and selling products or services. This includes marketing strategy and tactics, product demonstration, sales techniques, and sales control systems.
English Language	Knowledge of the structure and content of the English language including the meaning and spelling of words, rules of composition, and grammar.
Mathematics	Knowledge of arithmetic, algebra, geometry, calculus, statistics, and their applications.
Clerical	Knowledge of administrative and clerical procedures and systems such as word processing, managing files and records, stenography and transcription, designing forms, and other office procedures and terminology.
Administration and Management	Knowledge of business and management principles involved in strategic planning, resource allocation, human resources modeling, leadership technique, production methods, and coordination of people and resources.
Production and Processing	Knowledge of raw materials, production processes, quality control, costs, and other techniques for maximizing the effective manufacture and distribution of goods.
Education and Training	Knowledge of principles and methods for curriculum and training design, teaching and instruction for individuals and groups, and the measurement of training effects.
Computers and Electronics	Knowledge of circuit boards, processors, chips, electronic equipment, and computer hardware and software, including applications and programming.
Personnel and Human Resources	Knowledge of principles and procedures for personnel recruitment, selection, training, compensation and benefits, labor relations and negotiation, and personnel information systems.
Mechanical	Knowledge of machines and tools, including their designs, uses, repair, and maintenance.
Psychology	Knowledge of human behavior and performance; individual differences in ability, personality, and interests; learning and motivation; psychological research methods; and the assessment and treatment of behavioral and affective disorders.
Economics and Accounting	Knowledge of economic and accounting principles and practices, the financial markets, banking and the analysis and reporting of financial data.
Law and Government	Knowledge of laws, legal codes, court procedures, precedents, government regulations, executive orders, agency rules, and the democratic political process.
Design	Knowledge of design techniques, tools, and principles involved in production of precision technical plans, blueprints, drawings, and models.
Engineering and Technology	Knowledge of the practical application of engineering science and technology. This includes applying principles, techniques, procedures, and equipment to the design and production of various goods and services.
Communications and Media	Knowledge of media production, communication, and dissemination techniques and methods. This includes alternative ways to inform and entertain via written, oral, and visual media.
Telecommunications	Knowledge of transmission, broadcasting, switching, control, and operation of telecommunications systems.
Chemistry	Knowledge of the chemical composition, structure, and properties of substances and of the chemical processes and transformations that they undergo. This includes uses of chemicals and their interactions, danger signs, production techniques, and disposal methods.
Medicine and Dentistry	Knowledge of the information and techniques needed to diagnose and treat human injuries, diseases, and deformities. This includes symptoms, treatment alternatives, drug properties and interactions, and preventive health-care measures.
Sociology and Anthropology	Knowledge of group behavior and dynamics, societal trends and influences, human migrations, ethnicity, cultures and their history and origins.
Public Safety and Security	Knowledge of relevant equipment, policies, procedures, and strategies to promote effective local, state, or national security operations for the protection of people, data, property, and institutions.
Transportation	Knowledge of principles and methods for moving people or goods by air, rail, sea, or road, including the relative costs and benefits.
Physics	Knowledge and prediction of physical principles, laws, their interrelationships, and applications to understanding fluid, material, atomic and mechanical, electrical, atomic and sub-atomic structures and processes.
Therapy and Counseling	Knowledge of principles, methods, and procedures for diagnosis, treatment, and rehabilitation of physical and mental dysfunctions, and for career counseling and guidance.
Fine Arts	Knowledge of the theory and techniques required to compose, produce, and perform works of music, dance, visual arts, drama, and sculpture.
Philosophy and Theology	Knowledge of different philosophical systems and religions. This includes their basic principles, values, ethics, ways of thinking, customs, practices, and their impact on human culture.
Foreign Language	Knowledge of the structure and content of a foreign (non-English) language including the meaning and spelling of words, rules of composition and grammar, and pronunciation.
Geography	Knowledge of principles and methods for describing the features of land, sea, and air masses, including their physical characteristics, locations, interrelationships, and distribution of plant, animal, and human life.
Biology	Knowledge of plant and animal organisms, their tissues, cells, functions, interdependencies, and interactions with each other and the environment.
Building and Construction	Knowledge of materials, methods, and the tools involved in the construction or repair of houses, buildings, or other structures such as highways and roads.
History and Archeology	Knowledge of historical events and their causes, indicators, and effects on civilizations and cultures.
Food Production	Knowledge of techniques and equipment for planting, growing, and harvesting food products (both plant and animal) for consumption, including storage/handling techniques.

Skills	Skills Definitions
Active Listening	Giving full attention to what other people are saying, taking time to understand the points being made, asking questions as appropriate, and not interrupting at inappropriate times.
Speaking	Talking to others to convey information effectively.
Service Orientation	Actively looking for ways to help people.
Reading Comprehension	Understanding written sentences and paragraphs in work related documents.
Mathematics	Using mathematics to solve problems.
Critical Thinking	Using logic and reasoning to identify the strengths and weaknesses of alternative solutions, conclusions or approaches to problems.
Writing	Communicating effectively in writing as appropriate for the needs of the audience.
Instructing	Teaching others how to do something.
Active Learning	Understanding the implications of new information for both current and future problem-solving and decision-making.
Social Perceptiveness	Being aware of others' reactions and understanding why they react as they do.
Equipment Selection	Determining the kind of tools and equipment needed to do a job.
Time Management	Managing one's own time and the time of others.
Judgment and Decision Making	Considering the relative costs and benefits of potential actions to choose the most appropriate one.
Persuasion	Persuading others to change their minds or behavior.
Coordination	Adjusting actions in relation to others' actions.
Learning Strategies	Selecting and using training/instructional methods and procedures appropriate for the situation when learning or teaching new things.
Negotiation	Bringing others together and trying to reconcile differences.
Quality Control Analysis	Conducting tests and inspections of products, services, or processes to evaluate quality or performance.
Monitoring	Monitoring/Assessing performance of yourself, other individuals, or organizations to make improvements or take corrective action.
Troubleshooting	Determining causes of operating errors and deciding what to do about it.

Repairing	Repairing machines or systems using the needed tools.
Management of Financial Resources	Determining how money will be spent to get the work done, and accounting for these expenditures.
Management of Personnel Resources	Motivating, developing, and directing people as they work, identifying the best people for the job.
Complex Problem Solving	Identifying complex problems and reviewing related information to develop and evaluate options and implement solutions.
Technology Design	Generating or adapting equipment and technology to serve user needs.
Science	Using scientific rules and methods to solve problems.
Operation and Control	Controlling operations of equipment or systems.
Systems Evaluation	Identifying measures or indicators of system performance and the actions needed to improve or correct performance, relative to the goals of the system.
Equipment Maintenance	Performing routine maintenance on equipment and determining when and what kind of maintenance is needed.
Management of Material Resources	Obtaining and seeing to the appropriate use of equipment, facilities, and materials needed to do certain work.
Operations Analysis	Analyzing needs and product requirements to create a design.
Operation Monitoring	Watching gauges, dials, or other indicators to make sure a machine is working properly.
Installation	Installing equipment, machines, wiring, or programs to meet specifications.
Systems Analysis	Determining how a system should work and how changes in conditions, operations, and the environment will affect outcomes.
Programming	Writing computer programs for various purposes.

Ability	**Ability Definitions**
Oral Comprehension	The ability to listen to and understand information and ideas presented through spoken words and sentences.
Oral Expression	The ability to communicate information and ideas in speaking so others will understand.
Near Vision	The ability to see details at close range (within a few feet of the observer).
Written Comprehension	The ability to read and understand information and ideas presented in writing.
Problem Sensitivity	The ability to tell when something is wrong or is likely to go wrong. It does not involve solving the problem, only recognizing there is a problem.
Finger Dexterity	The ability to make precisely coordinated movements of the fingers of one or both hands to grasp, manipulate, or assemble very small objects.
Inductive Reasoning	The ability to combine pieces of information to form general rules or conclusions (includes finding a relationship among seemingly unrelated events).
Written Expression	The ability to communicate information and ideas in writing so others will understand.
Speech Clarity	The ability to speak clearly so others can understand you.
Arm-Hand Steadiness	The ability to keep your hand and arm steady while moving your arm or while holding your arm and hand in one position.
Speech Recognition	The ability to identify and understand the speech of another person.
Deductive Reasoning	The ability to apply general rules to specific problems to produce answers that make sense.
Manual Dexterity	The ability to quickly move your hand, your hand together with your arm, or your two hands to grasp, manipulate, or assemble objects.
Information Ordering	The ability to arrange things or actions in a certain order or pattern according to a specific rule or set of rules (e.g., patterns of numbers, letters, words, pictures, mathematical operations).
Originality	The ability to come up with unusual or clever ideas about a given topic or situation, or to develop creative ways to solve a problem.
Category Flexibility	The ability to generate or use different sets of rules for combining or grouping things in different ways.
Mathematical Reasoning	The ability to choose the right mathematical methods or formulas to solve a problem.
Fluency of Ideas	The ability to come up with a number of ideas about a topic (the number of ideas is important, not their quality, correctness, or creativity).
Visualization	The ability to imagine how something will look after it is moved around or when its parts are moved or rearranged.
Flexibility of Closure	The ability to identify or detect a known pattern (a figure, object, word, or sound) that is hidden in other distracting material.

Selective Attention	The ability to concentrate on a task over a period of time without being distracted.
Perceptual Speed	The ability to quickly and accurately compare similarities and differences among sets of letters, numbers, objects, pictures, or patterns. The things to be compared may be presented at the same time or one after the other. This ability also includes comparing a presented object with a remembered object.
Control Precision	The ability to quickly and repeatedly adjust the controls of a machine or a vehicle to exact positions.
Number Facility	The ability to add, subtract, multiply, or divide quickly and correctly.
Far Vision	The ability to see details at a distance.
Memorization	The ability to remember information such as words, numbers, pictures, and procedures.
Visual Color Discrimination	The ability to match or detect differences between colors, including shades of color and brightness.
Time Sharing	The ability to shift back and forth between two or more activities or sources of information (such as speech, sounds, touch, or other sources).
Multilimb Coordination	The ability to coordinate two or more limbs (for example, two arms, two legs, or one leg and one arm) while sitting, standing, or lying down. It does not involve performing the activities while the whole body is in motion.
Wrist-Finger Speed	The ability to make fast, simple, repeated movements of the fingers, hands, and wrists.
Static Strength	The ability to exert maximum muscle force to lift, push, pull, or carry objects.
Speed of Closure	The ability to quickly make sense of, combine, and organize information into meaningful patterns.
Trunk Strength	The ability to use your abdominal and lower back muscles to support part of the body repeatedly or continuously over time without 'giving out' or fatiguing.
Auditory Attention	The ability to focus on a single source of sound in the presence of other distracting sounds.
Response Orientation	The ability to choose quickly between two or more movements in response to two or more different signals (lights, sounds, pictures). It includes the speed with which the correct response is started with the hand, foot, or other body part.
Rate Control	The ability to time your movements or the movement of a piece of equipment in anticipation of changes in the speed and/or direction of a moving object or scene.
Hearing Sensitivity	The ability to detect or tell the differences between sounds that vary in pitch and loudness.
Depth Perception	The ability to judge which of several objects is closer or farther away from you, or to judge the distance between you and an object.
Reaction Time	The ability to quickly respond (with the hand, finger, or foot) to a signal (sound, light, picture) when it appears.
Speed of Limb Movement	The ability to quickly move the arms and legs.
Spatial Orientation	The ability to know your location in relation to the environment or to know where other objects are in relation to you.
Explosive Strength	The ability to use short bursts of muscle force to propel oneself (as in jumping or sprinting), or to throw an object.
Stamina	The ability to exert yourself physically over long periods of time without getting winded or out of breath.
Extent Flexibility	The ability to bend, stretch, twist, or reach with your body, arms, and/or legs.
Dynamic Flexibility	The ability to quickly and repeatedly bend, stretch, twist, or reach out with your body, arms, and/or legs.
Gross Body Equilibrium	The ability to keep or regain your body balance or stay upright when in an unstable position.
Night Vision	The ability to see under low light conditions.
Peripheral Vision	The ability to see objects or movement of objects to one's side when the eyes are looking ahead.
Dynamic Strength	The ability to exert muscle force repeatedly or continuously over time. This involves muscular endurance and resistance to muscle fatigue.
Sound Localization	The ability to tell the direction from which a sound originated.
Glare Sensitivity	The ability to see objects in the presence of glare or bright lighting.
Gross Body Coordination	The ability to coordinate the movement of your arms, legs, and torso together when the whole body is in motion.

Work_Activity	**Work_Activity Definitions**
Getting Information	Observing, receiving, and otherwise obtaining information from all relevant sources.

Performing for or Working Directly with the Public	Performing for people or dealing directly with the public. This includes serving customers in restaurants and stores, and receiving clients or guests.
Making Decisions and Solving Problems	Analyzing information and evaluating results to choose the best solution and solve problems.
Communicating with Supervisors, Peers, or Subordin	Providing information to supervisors, co-workers, and subordinates by telephone, in written form, e-mail, or in person.
Selling or Influencing Others	Convincing others to buy merchandise/goods or to otherwise change their minds or actions.
Assisting and Caring for Others	Providing personal assistance, medical attention, emotional support, or other personal care to others such as coworkers, customers, or patients.
Documenting/Recording Information	Entering, transcribing, recording, storing, or maintaining information in written or electronic/magnetic form.
Updating and Using Relevant Knowledge	Keeping up-to-date technically and applying new knowledge to your job.
Resolving Conflicts and Negotiating with Others	Handling complaints, settling disputes, and resolving grievances and conflicts, or otherwise negotiating with others.
Performing Administrative Activities	Performing day-to-day administrative tasks such as maintaining information files and processing paperwork.
Interpreting the Meaning of Information for Others	Translating or explaining what information means and how it can be used.
Establishing and Maintaining Interpersonal Relatio	Developing constructive and cooperative working relationships with others, and maintaining them over time.
Processing Information	Compiling, coding, categorizing, calculating, tabulating, auditing, or verifying information or data.
Identifying Objects, Actions, and Events	Identifying information by categorizing, estimating, recognizing differences or similarities, and detecting changes in circumstances or events.
Inspecting Equipment, Structures, or Material	Inspecting equipment, structures, or materials to identify the cause of errors or other problems or defects.
Evaluating Information to Determine Compliance wit	Using relevant information and individual judgment to determine whether events or processes comply with laws, regulations, or standards.
Coordinating the Work and Activities of Others	Getting members of a group to work together to accomplish tasks.
Judging the Qualities of Things, Services, or Peop	Assessing the value, importance, or quality of things or people.
Developing and Building Teams	Encouraging and building mutual trust, respect, and cooperation among team members.
Organizing, Planning, and Prioritizing Work	Developing specific goals and plans to prioritize, organize, and accomplish your work.
Communicating with Persons Outside Organization	Communicating with people outside the organization, representing the organization to customers, the public, government, and other external sources. This information can be exchanged in person, in writing, or by telephone or e-mail.
Coaching and Developing Others	Identifying the developmental needs of others and coaching, mentoring, or otherwise helping others to improve their knowledge or skills.
Estimating the Quantifiable Characteristics of Pro	Estimating sizes, distances, and quantities; or determining time, costs, resources, or materials needed to perform a work activity.
Interacting With Computers	Using computers and computer systems (including hardware and software) to program, write software, set up functions, enter data, or process information.
Monitor Processes, Materials, or Surroundings	Monitoring and reviewing information from materials, events, or the environment, to detect or assess problems.
Guiding, Directing, and Motivating Subordinates	Providing guidance and direction to subordinates, including setting performance standards and monitoring performance.
Training and Teaching Others	Identifying the educational needs of others, developing formal educational or training programs or classes, and teaching or instructing others.
Monitoring and Controlling Resources	Monitoring and controlling resources and overseeing the spending of money.
Handling and Moving Objects	Using hands and arms in handling, installing, positioning, and moving materials, and manipulating things.
Scheduling Work and Activities	Scheduling events, programs, and activities, as well as the work of others.
Controlling Machines and Processes	Using either control mechanisms or direct physical activity to operate machines or processes (not including computers or vehicles).
Developing Objectives and Strategies	Establishing long-range objectives and specifying the strategies and actions to achieve them.
Analyzing Data or Information	Identifying the underlying principles, reasons, or facts of information by breaking down information or data into separate parts.
Thinking Creatively	Developing, designing, or creating new applications, ideas, relationships, systems, or products, including artistic contributions.
Repairing and Maintaining Mechanical Equipment	Servicing, repairing, adjusting, and testing machines, devices, moving parts, and equipment that operate primarily on the basis of mechanical (not electronic) principles.
Staffing Organizational Units	Recruiting, interviewing, selecting, hiring, and promoting employees in an organization.
Repairing and Maintaining Electronic Equipment	Servicing, repairing, calibrating, regulating, fine-tuning, or testing machines, devices, and equipment that operate primarily on the basis of electrical or electronic (not mechanical) principles.
Provide Consultation and Advice to Others	Providing guidance and expert advice to management or other groups on technical, systems-, or process-related topics.
Drafting, Laying Out, and Specifying Technical Dev	Providing documentation, detailed instructions, drawings, or specifications to tell others about how devices, parts, equipment, or structures are to be fabricated, constructed, assembled, modified, maintained, or used.
Performing General Physical Activities	Performing physical activities that require considerable use of your arms and legs and moving your whole body, such as climbing, lifting, balancing, walking, stooping, and handling of materials.
Operating Vehicles, Mechanized Devices, or Equipme	Running, maneuvering, navigating, or driving vehicles or mechanized equipment, such as forklifts, passenger vehicles, aircraft, or water craft.

Work_Context	Work_Context Definitions
Telephone	How often do you have telephone conversations in this job?
Contact With Others	How much does this job require the worker to be in contact with others (face-to-face, by telephone, or otherwise) in order to perform it?
Freedom to Make Decisions	How much decision making freedom, without supervision, does the job offer?
Importance of Being Exact or Accurate	How important is being very exact or highly accurate in performing this job?
Deal With External Customers	How important is it to work with external customers or the public in this job?
Physical Proximity	To what extent does this job require the worker to perform job tasks in close physical proximity to other people?
Face-to-Face Discussions	How often do you have to have face-to-face discussions with individuals or teams in this job?
Structured versus Unstructured Work	To what extent is this job structured for the worker, rather than allowing the worker to determine tasks, priorities, and goals?
Frequency of Decision Making	How frequently is the worker required to make decisions that affect other people, the financial resources, and/or the image and reputation of the organization?
Indoors, Environmentally Controlled	How often does this job require working indoors in environmentally controlled conditions?
Impact of Decisions on Co-workers or Company Resul	How do the decisions an employee makes impact the results of co-workers, clients or the company?
Work With Work Group or Team	How important is it to work with others in a group or team in this job?
Spend Time Using Your Hands to Handle, Control, or	How much does this job require using your hands to handle, control, or feel objects, tools or controls?
Time Pressure	How often does this job require the worker to meet strict deadlines?
Letters and Memos	How often does the job require written letters and memos?
Importance of Repeating Same Tasks	How important is repeating the same physical activities (e.g., key entry) or mental activities (e.g., checking entries in a ledger) over and over, without stopping, to performing this job?
Deal With Unpleasant or Angry People	How frequently does the worker have to deal with unpleasant, angry, or discourteous individuals as part of the job requirements?
Spend Time Standing	How much does this job require standing?
Level of Competition	To what extent does this job require the worker to compete or to be aware of competitive pressures?
Responsibility for Outcomes and Results	How responsible is the worker for work outcomes and results of other workers?
Coordinate or Lead Others	How important is it to coordinate or lead others in accomplishing work activities in this job?
Degree of Automation	How automated is the job?
Spend Time Sitting	How much does this job require sitting?

Frequency of Conflict Situations	How often are there conflict situations the employee has to face in this job?
Spend Time Making Repetitive Motions	How much does this job require making repetitive motions?
Responsible for Others' Health and Safety	How much responsibility is there for the health and safety of others in this job?
Exposed to Minor Burns, Cuts, Bites, or Stings	How often does this job require exposure to minor burns, cuts, bites, or stings?
Consequence of Error	How serious would the result usually be if the worker made a mistake that was not readily correctable?
Spend Time Walking and Running	How much does this job require walking and running?
Exposed to Disease or Infections	How often does this job require exposure to disease/infections?
Exposed to Contaminants	How often does this job require working exposed to contaminants (such as pollutants, gases, dust or odors)?
Public Speaking	How often do you have to perform public speaking in this job?
Pace Determined by Speed of Equipment	How important is it to this job that the pace is determined by the speed of equipment or machinery? (This does not refer to keeping busy at all times on this job.)
Spend Time Bending or Twisting the Body	How much does this job require bending or twisting your body?
Deal With Physically Aggressive People	How frequently does this job require the worker to deal with physical aggression of violent individuals?
Spend Time Kneeling, Crouching, Stooping, or Crawl	How much does this job require kneeling, crouching, stooping or crawling?
Exposed to Hazardous Equipment	How often does this job require exposure to hazardous equipment?
Wear Common Protective or Safety Equipment such as	How much does this job require wearing common protective or safety equipment such as safety shoes, glasses, gloves, hard hats or life jackets?
Sounds, Noise Levels Are Distracting or Uncomforta	How often does this job require working exposed to sounds and noise levels that are distracting or uncomfortable?
Very Hot or Cold Temperatures	How often does this job require working in very hot (above 90 F degrees) or very cold (below 32 F degrees) temperatures?
Electronic Mail	How often do you use electronic mail in this job?
Extremely Bright or Inadequate Lighting	How often does this job require working in extremely bright or inadequate lighting conditions?
In an Enclosed Vehicle or Equipment	How often does this job require working in a closed vehicle or equipment (e.g., car)?
Cramped Work Space, Awkward Positions	How often does this job require working in cramped work spaces that requires getting into awkward positions?
Exposed to Hazardous Conditions	How often does this job require exposure to hazardous conditions?
Indoors, Not Environmentally Controlled	How often does this job require working indoors in non-controlled environmental conditions (e.g., warehouse without heat)?
Outdoors, Exposed to Weather	How often does this job require working outdoors, exposed to all weather conditions?
Outdoors, Under Cover	How often does this job require working outdoors, under cover (e.g., structure with roof but no walls)?
Exposed to Whole Body Vibration	How often does this job require exposure to whole body vibration (e.g., operate a jackhammer)?
In an Open Vehicle or Equipment	How often does this job require working in an open vehicle or equipment (e.g., tractor)?
Spend Time Climbing Ladders, Scaffolds, or Poles	How much does this job require climbing ladders, scaffolds, or poles?
Exposed to Radiation	How often does this job require exposure to radiation?
Exposed to High Places	How often does this job require exposure to high places?
Spend Time Keeping or Regaining Balance	How much does this job require keeping or regaining your balance?
Wear Specialized Protective or Safety Equipment su	How much does this job require wearing specialized protective or safety equipment such as breathing apparatus, safety harness, full protection suits, or radiation protection?

29-2081.00

Job Zone Component	Job Zone Component Definitions
Title	Job Zone Three: Medium Preparation Needed
Overall Experience	Previous work-related skill, knowledge, or experience is required for these occupations. For example, an electrician must have completed three or four years of apprenticeship or several years of vocational training, and often must have passed a licensing exam, in order to perform the job.
Job Training	Employees in these occupations usually need one or two years of training involving both on-the-job experience and informal training with experienced workers.
Job Zone Examples	These occupations usually involve using communication and organizational skills to coordinate, supervise, manage, or train others to accomplish goals. Examples include dental assistants, electricians, fish and game wardens, legal secretaries, personnel recruiters, and recreation workers.
SVP Range	(6.0 to < 7.0)
Education	Most occupations in this zone require training in vocational schools, related on-the-job experience, or an associate's degree. Some may require a bachelor's degree.

Work_Styles	Work_Styles Definitions
Attention to Detail	Job requires being careful about detail and thorough in completing work tasks.
Dependability	Job requires being reliable, responsible, and dependable, and fulfilling obligations.
Integrity	Job requires being honest and ethical.
Independence	Job requires developing one's own ways of doing things, guiding oneself with little or no supervision, and depending on oneself to get things done.
Self Control	Job requires maintaining composure, keeping emotions in check, controlling anger, and avoiding aggressive behavior, even in very difficult situations.
Concern for Others	Job requires being sensitive to others' needs and feelings and being understanding and helpful on the job.
Cooperation	Job requires being pleasant with others on the job and displaying a good-natured, cooperative attitude.
Stress Tolerance	Job requires accepting criticism and dealing calmly and effectively with high stress situations.
Initiative	Job requires a willingness to take on responsibilities and challenges.
Adaptability/Flexibility	Job requires being open to change (positive or negative) and to considerable variety in the workplace.
Social Orientation	Job requires preferring to work with others rather than alone, and being personally connected with others on the job.
Achievement/Effort	Job requires establishing and maintaining personally challenging achievement goals and exerting effort toward mastering tasks.
Leadership	Job requires a willingness to lead, take charge, and offer opinions and direction.
Innovation	Job requires creativity and alternative thinking to develop new ideas for and answers to work-related problems.
Analytical Thinking	Job requires analyzing information and using logic to address work-related issues and problems.
Persistence	Job requires persistence in the face of obstacles.

29-2091.00 - Orthotists and Prosthetists

Assist patients with disabling conditions of limbs and spine or with partial or total absence of limb by fitting and preparing orthopedic braces or prostheses.

Tasks

1) Repair, rebuild, and modify prosthetic and orthopedic appliances.

2) Select materials and components to be used, based on device design.

3) Maintain patients' records.

4) Publish research findings, and present them at conferences and seminars.

5) Research new ways to construct and use orthopedic and prosthetic devices.

6) Show and explain orthopedic and prosthetic appliances to healthcare workers.

7) Fit, test, and evaluate devices on patients, and make adjustments for proper fit, function, and comfort.

8) Update skills and knowledge by attending conferences and seminars.

9) Train and supervise orthopedic and prosthetic assistants and technicians, and other support staff.

10) Design orthopedic and prosthetic devices, based on physicians' prescriptions, and examination and measurement of patients.

11) Construct and fabricate appliances or supervise others who are constructing the appliances.

12) Confer with physicians in order to formulate specifications and prescriptions for orthopedic and/or prosthetic devices.

13) Make and modify plaster casts of areas that will be fitted with prostheses or orthoses, for use in the device construction process.

14) Instruct patients in the use and care of orthoses and prostheses.

29-9091.00 - Athletic Trainers

Evaluate, advise, and treat athletes to assist recovery from injury, avoid injury, or maintain peak physical fitness.

Tasks

1) Massage body parts in order to relieve soreness, strains, and bruises.

2) Plan and implement comprehensive athletic injury and illness prevention programs.

3) Conduct an initial assessment of an athlete's injury or illness in order to provide emergency or continued care, and to determine whether they should be referred to physicians for definitive diagnosis and treatment.

4) Recommend special diets in order to improve athletes' health, increase their stamina, and/or alter their weight.

5) Develop training programs and routines designed to improve athletic performance.

6) Collaborate with physicians in order to develop and implement comprehensive rehabilitation programs for athletic injuries.

7) Care for athletic injuries using physical therapy equipment, techniques, and medication.

8) Apply protective or injury preventive devices such as tape, bandages, or braces to body parts such as ankles, fingers, or wrists.

9) Perform team-support duties such as running errands, maintaining equipment, and stocking supplies.

10) Instruct coaches, athletes, parents, medical personnel, and community members in the care and prevention of athletic injuries.

11) Assess and report the progress of recovering athletes to coaches and physicians.

12) Travel with athletic teams in order to be available at sporting events.

13) Inspect playing fields in order to locate any items that could injure players.

14) Accompany injured athletes to hospitals.

15) Evaluate athletes' readiness to play, and provide participation clearances when necessary and warranted.

16) Confer with coaches in order to select protective equipment.

17) Conduct research and provide instruction on subject matter related to athletic training or sports medicine.

18) Lead stretching exercises for team members prior to games and practices.

Knowledge	Knowledge Definitions
Medicine and Dentistry	Knowledge of the information and techniques needed to diagnose and treat human injuries, diseases, and deformities. This includes symptoms, treatment alternatives, drug properties and interactions, and preventive health-care measures.
Customer and Personal Service	Knowledge of principles and processes for providing customer and personal services. This includes customer needs assessment, meeting quality standards for services, and evaluation of customer satisfaction.
Therapy and Counseling	Knowledge of principles, methods, and procedures for diagnosis, treatment, and rehabilitation of physical and mental dysfunctions, and for career counseling and guidance.
Clerical	Knowledge of administrative and clerical procedures and systems such as word processing, managing files and records, stenography and transcription, designing forms, and other office procedures and terminology.
Biology	Knowledge of plant and animal organisms, their tissues, cells, functions, interdependencies, and interactions with each other and the environment.
Psychology	Knowledge of human behavior and performance; individual differences in ability, personality, and interests; learning and motivation; psychological research methods; and the assessment and treatment of behavioral and affective disorders.
Administration and Management	Knowledge of business and management principles involved in strategic planning, resource allocation, human resources modeling, leadership technique, production methods, and coordination of people and resources.
English Language	Knowledge of the structure and content of the English language including the meaning and spelling of words, rules of composition, and grammar.
Education and Training	Knowledge of principles and methods for curriculum and training design, teaching and instruction for individuals and groups, and the measurement of training effects.
Physics	Knowledge and prediction of physical principles, laws, their interrelationships, and applications to understanding fluid, material, and atmospheric dynamics, and mechanical, electrical, atomic and sub- atomic structures and processes.
Personnel and Human Resources	Knowledge of principles and procedures for personnel recruitment, selection, training, compensation and benefits, labor relations and negotiation, and personnel information systems.
Chemistry	Knowledge of the chemical composition, structure, and properties of substances and of the chemical processes and transformations that they undergo. This includes uses of chemicals and their interactions, danger signs, production techniques, and disposal methods.
Sociology and Anthropology	Knowledge of group behavior and dynamics, societal trends and influences, human migrations, ethnicity, cultures and their history and origins.
Public Safety and Security	Knowledge of relevant equipment, policies, procedures, and strategies to promote effective local, state, or national security operations for the protection of people, data, property, and institutions.
Mathematics	Knowledge of arithmetic, algebra, geometry, calculus, statistics, and their applications.
Law and Government	Knowledge of laws, legal codes, court procedures, precedents, government regulations, executive orders, agency rules, and the democratic political process.
Communications and Media	Knowledge of media production, communication, and dissemination techniques and methods. This includes alternative ways to inform and entertain via written, oral, and visual media.
Computers and Electronics	Knowledge of circuit boards, processors, chips, electronic equipment, and computer hardware and software, including applications and programming.
Economics and Accounting	Knowledge of economic and accounting principles and practices, the financial markets, banking and the analysis and reporting of financial data.
Engineering and Technology	Knowledge of the practical application of engineering science and technology. This includes applying principles, techniques, procedures, and equipment to the design and production of various goods and services.
Telecommunications	Knowledge of transmission, broadcasting, switching, control, and operation of telecommunications systems.
Design	Knowledge of design techniques, tools, and principles involved in production of precision technical plans, blueprints, drawings, and models.
Mechanical	Knowledge of machines and tools, including their designs, uses, repair, and maintenance.
Transportation	Knowledge of principles and methods for moving people or goods by air, rail, sea, or road, including the relative costs and benefits.
Sales and Marketing	Knowledge of principles and methods for showing, promoting, and selling products or services. This includes marketing strategy and tactics, product demonstration, sales techniques, and sales control systems.
Foreign Language	Knowledge of the structure and content of a foreign (non-English) language including the meaning and spelling of words, rules of composition and grammar, and pronunciation.
Philosophy and Theology	Knowledge of different philosophical systems and religions. This includes their basic principles, values, ethics, ways of thinking, customs, practices, and their impact on human culture.
Production and Processing	Knowledge of raw materials, production processes, quality control, costs, and other techniques for maximizing the effective manufacture and distribution of goods.
Building and Construction	Knowledge of materials, methods, and the tools involved in the construction or repair of houses, buildings, or other structures such as highways and roads.
History and Archeology	Knowledge of historical events and their causes, indicators, and effects on civilizations and cultures.

Fine Arts	Knowledge of the theory and techniques required to compose, produce, and perform works of music, dance, visual arts, drama, and sculpture.
•	Knowledge of principles and methods for describing the features of land, sea, and air masses, including their physical
Geography	characteristics, locations, interrelationships, and distribution of plant, animal, and human life.
Food Production	Knowledge of techniques and equipment for planting, growing, and harvesting food products (both plant and animal) for consumption, including storage/handling techniques.

Skills	Skills Definitions
Active Listening	Giving full attention to what other people are saying, taking time to understand the points being made, asking questions as appropriate, and not interrupting at inappropriate times.
Time Management	Managing one's own time and the time of others.
Reading Comprehension	Understanding written sentences and paragraphs in work related documents.
Critical Thinking	Using logic and reasoning to identify the strengths and weaknesses of alternative solutions, conclusions or approaches to problems.
Coordination	Adjusting actions in relation to others' actions.
Instructing	Teaching others how to do something.
Speaking	Talking to others to convey information effectively.
Active Learning	Understanding the implications of new information for both current and future problem-solving and decision-making.
Science	Using scientific rules and methods to solve problems.
Monitoring	Monitoring/Assessing performance of yourself, other individuals, or organizations to make improvements or take corrective action.
Learning Strategies	Selecting and using training/instructional methods and procedures appropriate for the situation when learning or teaching new things.
Equipment Selection	Determining the kind of tools and equipment needed to do a job.
Social Perceptiveness	Being aware of others' reactions and understanding why they react as they do.
Writing	Communicating effectively in writing as appropriate for the needs of the audience.
Judgment and Decision Making	Considering the relative costs and benefits of potential actions to choose the most appropriate one.
Complex Problem Solving	Identifying complex problems and reviewing related information to develop and evaluate options and implement solutions.
Service Orientation	Actively looking for ways to help people.
Persuasion	Persuading others to change their minds or behavior.
Management of Material Resources	Obtaining and seeing to the appropriate use of equipment, facilities, and materials needed to do certain work.
Management of Personnel Resources	Motivating, developing, and directing people as they work, identifying the best people for the job.
Negotiation	Bringing others together and trying to reconcile differences.
Equipment Maintenance	Performing routine maintenance on equipment and determining when and what kind of maintenance is needed.
Operations Analysis	Analyzing needs and product requirements to create a design.
Troubleshooting	Determining causes of operating errors and deciding what to do about it.
Management of Financial Resources	Determining how money will be spent to get the work done, and accounting for these expenditures.
Mathematics	Using mathematics to solve problems.
Technology Design	Generating or adapting equipment and technology to serve user needs.
Systems Evaluation	Identifying measures or indicators of system performance and the actions needed to improve or correct performance, relative to the goals of the system.
Systems Analysis	Determining how a system should work and how changes in conditions, operations, and the environment will affect outcomes.
Quality Control Analysis	Conducting tests and inspections of products, services, or processes to evaluate quality or performance.
Operation and Control	Controlling operations of equipment or systems.
Operation Monitoring	Watching gauges, dials, or other indicators to make sure a machine is working properly.
Repairing	Repairing machines or systems using the needed tools.
Installation	Installing equipment, machines, wiring, or programs to meet specifications.
Programming	Writing computer programs for various purposes.

Ability	Ability Definitions
Problem Sensitivity	The ability to tell when something is wrong or is likely to go wrong. It does not involve solving the problem, only recognizing there is a problem.
Oral Expression	The ability to communicate information and ideas in speaking so others will understand.
Oral Comprehension	The ability to listen to and understand information and ideas presented through spoken words and sentences.
Inductive Reasoning	The ability to combine pieces of information to form general rules or conclusions (includes finding a relationship among seemingly unrelated events).
Speech Clarity	The ability to speak clearly so others can understand you.
Information Ordering	The ability to arrange things or actions in a certain order or pattern according to a specific rule or set of rules (e.g., patterns of numbers, letters, words, pictures, mathematical operations).
Written Comprehension	The ability to read and understand information and ideas presented in writing.
Deductive Reasoning	The ability to apply general rules to specific problems to produce answers that make sense.
Speech Recognition	The ability to identify and understand the speech of another person.
Written Expression	The ability to communicate information and ideas in writing so others will understand.
Near Vision	The ability to see details at close range (within a few feet of the observer).
Trunk Strength	The ability to use your abdominal and lower back muscles to support part of the body repeatedly or continuously over time without 'giving out' or fatiguing.
Category Flexibility	The ability to generate or use different sets of rules for combining or grouping things in different ways.
Fluency of Ideas	The ability to come up with a number of ideas about a topic (the number of ideas is important, not their quality, correctness, or creativity).
Extent Flexibility	The ability to bend, stretch, twist, or reach with your body, arms, and/or legs.
Manual Dexterity	The ability to quickly move your hand, your hand together with your arm, or your two hands to grasp, manipulate, or assemble objects.
Originality	The ability to come up with unusual or clever ideas about a given topic or situation, or to develop creative ways to solve a problem.
Multilimb Coordination	The ability to coordinate two or more limbs (for example, two arms, two legs, or one leg and one arm) while sitting, standing, or lying down. It does not involve performing the activities while the whole body is in motion.
Gross Body Coordination	The ability to coordinate the movement of your arms, legs, and torso together when the whole body is in motion.
Speed of Closure	The ability to quickly make sense of, combine, and organize information into meaningful patterns.
Static Strength	The ability to exert maximum muscle force to lift, push, pull, or carry objects.
Stamina	The ability to exert yourself physically over long periods of time without getting winded or out of breath.
Selective Attention	The ability to concentrate on a task over a period of time without being distracted.
Flexibility of Closure	The ability to identify or detect a known pattern (a figure, object, word, or sound) that is hidden in other distracting material.
Arm-Hand Steadiness	The ability to keep your hand and arm steady while moving your arm or while holding your arm and hand in one position.
Control Precision	The ability to quickly and repeatedly adjust the controls of a machine or a vehicle to exact positions.
Dynamic Strength	The ability to exert muscle force repeatedly or continuously over time. This involves muscular endurance and resistance to muscle fatigue.
Far Vision	The ability to see details at a distance.
Time Sharing	The ability to shift back and forth between two or more activities or sources of information (such as speech, sounds, touch, or other sources).
Visualization	The ability to imagine how something will look after it is moved around or when its parts are moved or rearranged.
Perceptual Speed	The ability to quickly and accurately compare similarities and differences among sets of letters, numbers, objects, pictures, or patterns. The things to be compared may be presented at the same time or one after the other. This ability also includes comparing a presented object with a remembered object.

Finger Dexterity	The ability to make precisely coordinated movements of the fingers of one or both hands to grasp, manipulate, or assemble very small objects.
Auditory Attention	The ability to focus on a single source of sound in the presence of other distracting sounds.
Memorization	The ability to remember information such as words, numbers, pictures, and procedures.
Speed of Limb Movement	The ability to quickly move the arms and legs.
Depth Perception	The ability to judge which of several objects is closer or farther away from you, or to judge the distance between you and an object.
Number Facility	The ability to add, subtract, multiply, or divide quickly and correctly.
Visual Color Discrimination	The ability to match or detect differences between colors, including shades of color and brightness.
Dynamic Flexibility	The ability to quickly and repeatedly bend, stretch, twist, or reach out with your body, arms, and/or legs.
Gross Body Equilibrium	The ability to keep or regain your body balance or stay upright when in an unstable position.
Mathematical Reasoning	The ability to choose the right mathematical methods or formulas to solve a problem.
Wrist-Finger Speed	The ability to make fast, simple, repeated movements of the fingers, hands, and wrists.
Explosive Strength	The ability to use short bursts of muscle force to propel oneself (as in jumping or sprinting), or to throw an object.
Reaction Time	The ability to quickly respond (with the hand, finger, or foot) to a signal (sound, light, picture) when it appears.
Rate Control	The ability to time your movements or the movement of a piece of equipment in anticipation of changes in the speed and/or direction of a moving object or scene.
Response Orientation	The ability to choose quickly between two or more movements in response to two or more different signals (lights, sounds, pictures). It includes the speed with which the correct response is started with the hand, foot, or other body part.
Hearing Sensitivity	The ability to detect or tell the differences between sounds that vary in pitch and loudness.
Spatial Orientation	The ability to know your location in relation to the environment or to know where other objects are in relation to you.
Glare Sensitivity	The ability to see objects in the presence of glare or bright lighting.
Peripheral Vision	The ability to see objects or movement of objects to one's side when the eyes are looking ahead.
Night Vision	The ability to see under low light conditions.
Sound Localization	The ability to tell the direction from which a sound originated.

Work_Activity	Work_Activity Definitions
Assisting and Caring for Others	Providing personal assistance, medical attention, emotional support, or other personal care to others such as coworkers, customers, or patients.
Making Decisions and Solving Problems	Analyzing information and evaluating results to choose the best solution and solve problems.
Updating and Using Relevant Knowledge	Keeping up-to-date technically and applying new knowledge to your job.
Establishing and Maintaining Interpersonal Relatio	Developing constructive and cooperative working relationships with others, and maintaining them over time.
Identifying Objects, Actions, and Events	Identifying information by categorizing, estimating, recognizing differences or similarities, and detecting changes in circumstances or events.
Communicating with Supervisors, Peers, or Subordin	Providing information to supervisors, co-workers, and subordinates by telephone, in written form, e-mail, or in person.
Getting Information	Observing, receiving, and otherwise obtaining information from all relevant sources.
Training and Teaching Others	Identifying the educational needs of others, developing formal educational or training programs or classes, and teaching or instructing others.
Evaluating Information to Determine Compliance wit	Using relevant information and individual judgment to determine whether events or processes comply with laws, regulations, or standards.
Interpreting the Meaning of Information for Others	Translating or explaining what information means and how it can be used.
Documenting/Recording Information	Entering, transcribing, recording, storing, or maintaining information in written or electronic/magnetic form.
Coaching and Developing Others	Identifying the developmental needs of others and coaching, mentoring, or otherwise helping others to improve their knowledge or skills.

Scheduling Work and Activities	Scheduling events, programs, and activities, as well as the work of others.
Analyzing Data or Information	Identifying the underlying principles, reasons, or facts of information by breaking down information or data into separate parts.
Monitor Processes, Materials, or Surroundings	Monitoring and reviewing information from materials, events, or the environment, to detect or assess problems.
Organizing, Planning, and Prioritizing Work	Developing specific goals and plans to prioritize, organize, and accomplish your work.
Coordinating the Work and Activities of Others	Getting members of a group to work together to accomplish tasks.
Guiding, Directing, and Motivating Subordinates	Providing guidance and direction to subordinates, including setting performance standards and monitoring performance.
Inspecting Equipment, Structures, or Material	Inspecting equipment, structures, or materials to identify the cause of errors or other problems or defects.
Thinking Creatively	Developing, designing, or creating new applications, ideas, relationships, systems, or products, including artistic contributions.
Developing and Building Teams	Encouraging and building mutual trust, respect, and cooperation among team members.
Communicating with Persons Outside Organization	Communicating with people outside the organization, representing the organization to customers, the public, government, and other external sources. This information can be exchanged in person, in writing, or by telephone or e-mail.
Resolving Conflicts and Negotiating with Others	Handling complaints, settling disputes, and resolving grievances and conflicts, or otherwise negotiating with others.
Performing Administrative Activities	Performing day-to-day administrative tasks such as maintaining information files and processing paperwork.
Performing General Physical Activities	Performing physical activities that require considerable use of your arms and legs and moving your whole body, such as climbing, lifting, balancing, walking, stooping, and handling of materials.
Handling and Moving Objects	Using hands and arms in handling, installing, positioning, and moving materials, and manipulating things.
Provide Consultation and Advice to Others	Providing guidance and expert advice to management or other groups on technical, systems-, or process-related topics.
Processing Information	Compiling, coding, categorizing, calculating, tabulating, auditing, or verifying information or data.
Developing Objectives and Strategies	Establishing long-range objectives and specifying the strategies and actions to achieve them.
Interacting With Computers	Using computers and computer systems (including hardware and software) to program, write software, set up functions, enter data, or process information.
Estimating the Quantifiable Characteristics of Pro	Estimating sizes, distances, and quantities; or determining time, costs, resources, or materials needed to perform a work activity.
Judging the Qualities of Things, Services, or Peop	Assessing the value, importance, or quality of things or people.
Monitoring and Controlling Resources	Monitoring and controlling resources and overseeing the spending of money.
Performing for or Working Directly with the Public	Performing for people or dealing directly with the public. This includes serving customers in restaurants and stores, and receiving clients or guests.
Controlling Machines and Processes	Using either control mechanisms or direct physical activity to operate machines or processes (not including computers or vehicles).
Staffing Organizational Units	Recruiting, interviewing, selecting, hiring, and promoting employees in an organization.
Operating Vehicles, Mechanized Devices, or Equipme	Running, maneuvering, navigating, or driving vehicles or mechanized equipment, such as forklifts, passenger vehicles, aircraft, or water craft.
Selling or Influencing Others	Convincing others to buy merchandise/goods or to otherwise change their minds or actions.
Drafting, Laying Out, and Specifying Technical Dev	Providing documentation, detailed instructions, drawings, or specifications to tell others about how devices, parts, equipment, or structures are to be fabricated, constructed, assembled, modified, maintained, or used.
Repairing and Maintaining Mechanical Equipment	Servicing, repairing, adjusting, and testing machines, devices, moving parts, and equipment that operate primarily on the basis of mechanical (not electronic) principles.
Repairing and Maintaining Electronic Equipment	Servicing, repairing, calibrating, regulating, fine-tuning, or testing machines, devices, and equipment that operate primarily on the basis of electrical or electronic (not mechanical) principles.

Work_Context	Work_Context Definitions
Contact With Others	How much does this job require the worker to be in contact with others (face-to-face, by telephone, or otherwise) in order to perform it?
Telephone	How often do you have telephone conversations in this job?
Physical Proximity	To what extent does this job require the worker to perform job tasks in close physical proximity to other people?
Face-to-Face Discussions	How often do you have to have face-to-face discussions with individuals or teams in this job?
Indoors, Environmentally Controlled	How often does this job require working indoors in environmentally controlled conditions?
Electronic Mail	How often do you use electronic mail in this job?
Structured versus Unstructured Work	To what extent is this job structured for the worker, rather than allowing the worker to determine tasks, priorities, and goals?
Freedom to Make Decisions	How much decision making freedom, without supervision, does the job offer?
Work With Work Group or Team	How important is it to work with others in a group or team in this job?
Responsible for Others' Health and Safety	How much responsibility is there for the health and safety of others in this job?
Importance of Being Exact or Accurate	How important is being very exact or highly accurate in performing this job?
Outdoors, Exposed to Weather	How often does this job require working outdoors, exposed to all weather conditions?
Frequency of Decision Making	How frequently is the worker required to make decisions that affect other people, the financial resources, and/or the image and reputation of the organization?
Coordinate or Lead Others	How important is it to coordinate or lead others in accomplishing work activities in this job?
Exposed to Disease or Infections	How often does this job require exposure to disease/infections?
Letters and Memos	How often does the job require written letters and memos?
Impact of Decisions on Co-workers or Company Resul	How do the decisions an employee makes impact the results of co-workers, clients or the company?
Frequency of Conflict Situations	How often are there conflict situations the employee has to face in this job?
Time Pressure	How often does this job require the worker to meet strict deadlines?
Spend Time Standing	How much does this job require standing?
Responsibility for Outcomes and Results	How responsible is the worker for work outcomes and results of other workers?
Deal With Unpleasant or Angry People	How frequently does the worker have to deal with unpleasant, angry, or discourteous individuals as part of the job requirements?
Consequence of Error	How serious would the result usually be if the worker made a mistake that was not readily correctable?
Exposed to Contaminants	How often does this job require working exposed to contaminants (such as pollutants, gases, dust or odors)?
Deal With External Customers	How important is it to work with external customers or the public in this job?
Very Hot or Cold Temperatures	How often does this job require working in very hot (above 90 F degrees) or very cold (below 32 F degrees) temperatures?
Spend Time Bending or Twisting the Body	How much does this job require bending or twisting your body?
Spend Time Walking and Running	How much does this job require walking and running?
Importance of Repeating Same Tasks	How important is repeating the same physical activities (e.g., key entry) or mental activities (e.g., checking entries in a ledger) over and over, without stopping, to performing this job?
Wear Common Protective or Safety Equipment such as	How much does this job require wearing common protective or safety equipment such as safety shoes, glasses, gloves, hard hats or live jackets?
Level of Competition	To what extent does this job require the worker to compete or to be aware of competitive pressures?
Sounds, Noise Levels Are Distracting or Uncomforta	How often does this job require working exposed to sounds and noise levels that are distracting or uncomfortable?
Exposed to Minor Burns, Cuts, Bites, or Stings	How often does this job require exposure to minor burns, cuts, bites, or stings?
Public Speaking	How often do you have to perform public speaking in this job?
Spend Time Making Repetitive Motions	How much does this job require making repetitive motions?
Indoors, Not Environmentally Controlled	How often does this job require working indoors in non-controlled environmental conditions (e.g., warehouse without heat)?
Spend Time Using Your Hands to Handle, Control, or	How much does this job require using your hands to handle, control, or feel objects, tools or controls?
Spend Time Kneeling, Crouching, Stooping, or Crawl	How much does this job require kneeling, crouching, stooping, or crawling?
Outdoors, Under Cover	How often does this job require working outdoors, under cover (e.g., structure with roof but no walls)?
In an Open Vehicle or Equipment	How often does this job require working in an open vehicle or equipment (e.g., tractor)?
Extremely Bright or Inadequate Lighting	How often does this job require working in extremely bright or inadequate lighting conditions?
Spend Time Sitting	How much does this job require sitting?
Cramped Work Space, Awkward Positions	How often does this job require working in cramped work spaces that requires getting into awkward positions?
Deal With Physically Aggressive People	How frequently does this job require the worker to deal with physical aggression of violent individuals?
In an Enclosed Vehicle or Equipment	How often does this job require working in a closed vehicle or equipment (e.g., car)?
Spend Time Keeping or Regaining Balance	How much does this job require keeping or regaining your balance?
Exposed to Hazardous Conditions	How often does this job require exposure to hazardous conditions?
Degree of Automation	How automated is the job?
Wear Specialized Protective or Safety Equipment su	How much does this job require wearing specialized protective or safety equipment such as breathing apparatus, safety harness, full protection suits, or radiation protection?
Exposed to Hazardous Equipment	How often does this job require exposure to hazardous equipment?
Exposed to Radiation	How often does this job require exposure to radiation?
Exposed to High Places	How often does this job require exposure to high places?
Spend Time Climbing Ladders, Scaffolds, or Poles	How much does this job require climbing ladders, scaffolds, or poles?
Exposed to Whole Body Vibration	How often does this job require exposure to whole body vibration (e.g., operate a jackhammer)?
Pace Determined by Speed of Equipment	How important is it to this job that the pace is determined by the speed of equipment or machinery? (This does not refer to keeping busy at all times on this job.)

Job Zone Component	Job Zone Component Definitions
Title	Job Zone Five: Extensive Preparation Needed
Overall Experience	Extensive skill, knowledge, and experience are needed for these occupations. Many require more than five years of experience. For example, surgeons must complete four years of college and an additional five to seven years of specialized medical training to be able to do their job.
Job Training	Employees may need some on-the-job training, but most of these occupations assume that the person will already have the required skills, knowledge, work-related experience, and/or training.
Job Zone Examples	These occupations often involve coordinating, training, supervising, or managing the activities of others to accomplish goals. Very advanced communication and organizational skills are required. Examples include athletic trainers, lawyers, managing editors, phyicists, social psychologists, and surgeons.
SVP Range	(8.0 and above)
Education	A bachelor's degree is the minimum formal education required for these occupations. However, many also require graduate school. For example, they may require a master's degree, and some require a Ph.D., M.D., or J.D. (law degree).

Work_Styles	Work_Styles Definitions
Concern for Others	Job requires being sensitive to others' needs and feelings and being understanding and helpful on the job.
Dependability	Job requires being reliable, responsible, and dependable, and fulfilling obligations.
Adaptability/Flexibility	Job requires being open to change (positive or negative) and to considerable variety in the workplace.
Cooperation	Job requires being pleasant with others on the job and displaying a good-natured, cooperative attitude.
Attention to Detail	Job requires being careful about detail and thorough in completing work tasks.
Initiative	Job requires a willingness to take on responsibilities and challenges.

Integrity	Job requires being honest and ethical.
Social Orientation	Job requires preferring to work with others rather than alone, and being personally connected with others on the job.
Analytical Thinking	Job requires analyzing information and using logic to address work-related issues and problems.
Stress Tolerance	Job requires accepting criticism and dealing calmly and effectively with high stress situations.
Leadership	Job requires a willingness to lead, take charge, and offer opinions and direction.
Self Control	Job requires maintaining composure, keeping emotions in check, controlling anger, and avoiding aggressive behavior, even in very difficult situations.
Persistence	Job requires persistence in the face of obstacles.
Independence	Job requires developing one's own ways of doing things, guiding oneself with little or no supervision, and depending on oneself to get things done.
Innovation	Job requires creativity and alternative thinking to develop new ideas for and answers to work-related problems.
Achievement/Effort	Job requires establishing and maintaining personally challenging achievement goals and exerting effort toward mastering tasks.

31-1011.00 - Home Health Aides

Provide routine, personal healthcare, such as bathing, dressing, or grooming, to elderly, convalescent, or disabled persons in the home of patients or in a residential care facility.

Tasks

1) Entertain, converse with, or read aloud to patients to keep them mentally healthy and alert.

2) Maintain records of patient care, condition, progress, and problems in order to report and discuss observations with a supervisor or case manager.

3) Plan, purchase, prepare, and serve meals to patients and other family members, according to prescribed diets.

4) Change bed linens, wash and iron patients' laundry, and clean patients' quarters.

5) Accompany clients to doctors' offices and on other trips outside the home, providing transportation, assistance and companionship.

6) Perform a variety of duties as requested by client, such as obtaining household supplies and running errands.

7) Check patients' pulse, temperature and respiration.

8) Provide patients and families with emotional support and instruction in areas such as infant care, preparing healthy meals, independent living, and adaptation to disability or illness.

9) Direct patients in simple prescribed exercises and in the use of braces or artificial limbs.

10) Change dressings.

11) Administer prescribed oral medications under written direction of physician or as directed by home care nurse and aide.

12) Massage patients and apply preparations and treatments, such as liniment, alcohol rubs, and heat-lamp stimulation.

13) Care for children who are disabled or who have sick or disabled parents.

Knowledge	Knowledge Definitions
Customer and Personal Service	Knowledge of principles and processes for providing customer and personal services. This includes customer needs assessment, meeting quality standards for services, and evaluation of customer satisfaction.
English Language	Knowledge of the structure and content of the English language including the meaning and spelling of words, rules of composition, and grammar.
Medicine and Dentistry	Knowledge of the information and techniques needed to diagnose and treat human injuries, diseases, and deformities. This includes symptoms, treatment alternatives, drug properties and interactions, and preventive health-care measures.
Public Safety and Security	Knowledge of relevant equipment, policies, procedures, and strategies to promote effective local, state, or national security operations for the protection of people, data, property, and institutions.
Therapy and Counseling	Knowledge of principles, methods, and procedures for diagnosis, treatment, and rehabilitation of physical and mental dysfunctions, and for career counseling and guidance.
Education and Training	Knowledge of principles and methods for curriculum and training design, teaching and instruction for individuals and groups, and the measurement of training effects.
Psychology	Knowledge of human behavior and performance; individual differences in ability, personality, and interests; learning and motivation; psychological research methods; and the assessment and treatment of behavioral and affective disorders.
Mathematics	Knowledge of arithmetic, algebra, geometry, calculus, statistics, and their applications.
Administration and Management	Knowledge of business and management principles involved in strategic planning, resource allocation, human resources modeling, leadership technique, production methods, and coordination of people and resources.
Law and Government	Knowledge of laws, legal codes, court procedures, precedents, government regulations, executive orders, agency rules, and the democratic political process.
Personnel and Human Resources	Knowledge of principles and procedures for personnel recruitment, selection, training, compensation and benefits, labor relations and negotiation, and personnel information systems.
Telecommunications	Knowledge of transmission, broadcasting, switching, control, and operation of telecommunications systems.
Food Production	Knowledge of techniques and equipment for planting, growing, and harvesting food products (both plant and animal) for consumption, including storage/handling techniques.
Communications and Media	Knowledge of media production, communication, and dissemination techniques and methods. This includes alternative ways to inform and entertain via written, oral, and visual media.
Clerical	Knowledge of administrative and clerical procedures and systems such as word processing, managing files and records, stenography and transcription, designing forms, and other office procedures and terminology.
Transportation	Knowledge of principles and methods for moving people or goods by air, rail, sea, or road, including the relative costs and benefits.
Sociology and Anthropology	Knowledge of group behavior and dynamics, societal trends and influences, human migrations, ethnicity, cultures and their history and origins.
Mechanical	Knowledge of machines and tools, including their designs, uses, repair, and maintenance.
Chemistry	Knowledge of the chemical composition, structure, and properties of substances and of the chemical processes and transformations that they undergo. This includes uses of chemicals and their interactions, danger signs, production techniques, and disposal methods.
Philosophy and Theology	Knowledge of different philosophical systems and religions. This includes their basic principles, values, ethics, ways of thinking, customs, practices, and their impact on human culture.
Biology	Knowledge of plant and animal organisms, their tissues, cells, functions, interdependencies, and interactions with each other and the environment.
Computers and Electronics	Knowledge of circuit boards, processors, chips, electronic equipment, and computer hardware and software, including applications and programming.
Foreign Language	Knowledge of the structure and content of a foreign (non-English) language including the meaning and spelling of words, rules of composition and grammar, and pronunciation.
Geography	Knowledge of principles and methods for describing the features of land, sea, and air masses, including their physical characteristics, locations, interrelationships, and distribution of plant, animal, and human life.
Engineering and Technology	Knowledge of the practical application of engineering science and technology. This includes applying principles, techniques, procedures, and equipment to the design and production of various goods and services.
Building and Construction	Knowledge of materials, methods, and the tools involved in the construction or repair of houses, buildings, or other structures such as highways and roads.
Sales and Marketing	Knowledge of principles and methods for showing, promoting, and selling products or services. This includes marketing strategy and tactics, product demonstration, sales techniques, and sales control systems.

Design	Knowledge of design techniques, tools, and principles involved in production of precision technical plans, blueprints, drawings, and models.
Fine Arts	Knowledge of the theory and techniques required to compose, produce, and perform works of music, dance, visual arts, drama, and sculpture.
Economics and Accounting	Knowledge of economic and accounting principles and practices, the financial markets, banking and the analysis and reporting of financial data.
Production and Processing	Knowledge of raw materials, production processes, quality control, costs, and other techniques for maximizing the effective manufacture and distribution of goods.
History and Archeology	Knowledge of historical events and their causes, indicators, and effects on civilizations and cultures.
Physics	Knowledge and prediction of physical principles, laws, their interrelationships, and applications to understanding fluid, material, and atmospheric dynamics, and mechanical, electrical, atomic and sub- atomic structures and processes.

Skills	Skills Definitions
Active Listening	Giving full attention to what other people are saying, taking time to understand the points being made, asking questions as appropriate, and not interrupting at inappropriate times.
Reading Comprehension	Understanding written sentences and paragraphs in work related documents.
Writing	Communicating effectively in writing as appropriate for the needs of the audience.
Coordination	Adjusting actions in relation to others' actions.
Service Orientation	Actively looking for ways to help people.
Social Perceptiveness	Being aware of others' reactions and understanding why they react as they do.
Monitoring	Monitoring/Assessing performance of yourself, other individuals, or organizations to make improvements or take corrective action.
Instructing	Teaching others how to do something.
Speaking	Talking to others to convey information effectively.
Critical Thinking	Using logic and reasoning to identify the strengths and weaknesses of alternative solutions, conclusions or approaches to problems.
Time Management	Managing one's own time and the time of others.
Active Learning	Understanding the implications of new information for both current and future problem-solving and decision-making.
Learning Strategies	Selecting and using training/instructional methods and procedures appropriate for the situation when learning or teaching new things.
Persuasion	Persuading others to change their minds or behavior.
Negotiation	Bringing others together and trying to reconcile differences.
Complex Problem Solving	Identifying complex problems and reviewing related information to develop and evaluate options and implement solutions.
Judgment and Decision Making	Considering the relative costs and benefits of potential actions to choose the most appropriate one.
Equipment Selection	Determining the kind of tools and equipment needed to do a job.
Troubleshooting	Determining causes of operating errors and deciding what to do about it.
Mathematics	Using mathematics to solve problems.
Operation and Control	Controlling operations of equipment or systems.
Science	Using scientific rules and methods to solve problems.
Operation Monitoring	Watching gauges, dials, or other indicators to make sure a machine is working properly.
Management of Material Resources	Obtaining and seeing to the appropriate use of equipment, facilities, and materials needed to do certain work.
Operations Analysis	Analyzing needs and product requirements to create a design.
Technology Design	Generating or adapting equipment and technology to serve user needs.
Quality Control Analysis	Conducting tests and inspections of products, services, or processes to evaluate quality or performance.
Equipment Maintenance	Performing routine maintenance on equipment and determining when and what kind of maintenance is needed.
Management of Personnel Resources	Motivating, developing, and directing people as they work, identifying the best people for the job.
Systems Evaluation	Identifying measures or indicators of system performance and the actions needed to improve or correct performance, relative to the goals of the system.
Programming	Writing computer programs for various purposes.

Installation	Installing equipment, machines, wiring, or programs to meet specifications.
Management of Financial Resources	Determining how money will be spent to get the work done, and accounting for these expenditures.
Systems Analysis	Determining how a system should work and how changes in conditions, operations, and the environment will affect outcomes.
Repairing	Repairing machines or systems using the needed tools.

Ability	Ability Definitions
Speech Recognition	The ability to identify and understand the speech of another person.
Problem Sensitivity	The ability to tell when something is wrong or is likely to go wrong. It does not involve solving the problem, only recognizing there is a problem.
Oral Comprehension	The ability to listen to and understand information and ideas presented through spoken words and sentences.
Oral Expression	The ability to communicate information and ideas in speaking so others will understand.
Speech Clarity	The ability to speak clearly so others can understand you.
Near Vision	The ability to see details at close range (within a few feet of the observer).
Written Comprehension	The ability to read and understand information and ideas presented in writing.
Information Ordering	The ability to arrange things or actions in a certain order or pattern according to a specific rule or set of rules (e.g., patterns of numbers, letters, words, pictures, mathematical operations).
Static Strength	The ability to exert maximum muscle force to lift, push, pull, or carry objects.
Inductive Reasoning	The ability to combine pieces of information to form general rules or conclusions (includes finding a relationship among seemingly unrelated events).
Written Expression	The ability to communicate information and ideas in writing so others will understand.
Arm-Hand Steadiness	The ability to keep your hand and arm steady while moving your arm or while holding your arm and hand in one position.
Deductive Reasoning	The ability to apply general rules to specific problems to produce answers that make sense.
Far Vision	The ability to see details at a distance.
Stamina	The ability to exert yourself physically over long periods of time without getting winded or out of breath.
Flexibility of Closure	The ability to identify or detect a known pattern (a figure, object, word, or sound) that is hidden in other distracting material.
Perceptual Speed	The ability to quickly and accurately compare similarities and differences among sets of letters, numbers, objects, pictures, or patterns. The things to be compared may be presented at the same time or one after the other. This ability also includes comparing a presented object with a remembered object.
Originality	The ability to come up with unusual or clever ideas about a given topic or situation, or to develop creative ways to solve a problem.
Visual Color Discrimination	The ability to match or detect differences between colors, including shades of color and brightness.
Multilimb Coordination	The ability to coordinate two or more limbs (for example, two arms, two legs, or one leg and one arm) while sitting, standing, or lying down. It does not involve performing the activities while the whole body is in motion.
Selective Attention	The ability to concentrate on a task over a period of time without being distracted.
Time Sharing	The ability to shift back and forth between two or more activities or sources of information (such as speech, sounds, touch, or other sources).
Category Flexibility	The ability to generate or use different sets of rules for combining or grouping things in different ways.
Trunk Strength	The ability to use your abdominal and lower back muscles to support part of the body repeatedly or continuously over time without 'giving out' or fatiguing.
Finger Dexterity	The ability to make precisely coordinated movements of the fingers of one or both hands to grasp, manipulate, or assemble very small objects.
Manual Dexterity	The ability to quickly move your hand, your hand together with your arm, or your two hands to grasp, manipulate, or assemble objects.
Depth Perception	The ability to judge which of several objects is closer or farther away from you, or to judge the distance between you and an object.

Speed of Closure	The ability to quickly make sense of, combine, and organize information into meaningful patterns.
Hearing Sensitivity	The ability to detect or tell the differences between sounds that vary in pitch and loudness.
Gross Body Coordination	The ability to coordinate the movement of your arms, legs, and torso together when the whole body is in motion.
Fluency of Ideas	The ability to come up with a number of ideas about a topic (the number of ideas is important, not their quality, correctness, or creativity).
Control Precision	The ability to quickly and repeatedly adjust the controls of a machine or a vehicle to exact positions.
Auditory Attention	The ability to focus on a single source of sound in the presence of other distracting sounds.
Extent Flexibility	The ability to bend, stretch, twist, or reach with your body, arms, and/or legs.
Gross Body Equilibrium	The ability to keep or regain your body balance or stay upright when in an unstable position.
Dynamic Strength	The ability to exert muscle force repeatedly or continuously over time. This involves muscular endurance and resistance to muscle fatigue.
Spatial Orientation	The ability to know your location in relation to the environment or to know where other objects are in relation to you.
Reaction Time	The ability to quickly respond (with the hand, finger, or foot) to a signal (sound, light, picture) when it appears.
Visualization	The ability to imagine how something will look after it is moved around or when its parts are moved or rearranged.
Response Orientation	The ability to choose quickly between two or more movements in response to two or more different signals (lights, sounds, pictures). It includes the speed with which the correct response is started with the hand, foot, or other body part.
Memorization	The ability to remember information such as words, numbers, pictures, and procedures.
Explosive Strength	The ability to use short bursts of muscle force to propel oneself (as in jumping or sprinting), or to throw an object.
Speed of Limb Movement	The ability to quickly move the arms and legs.
Rate Control	The ability to time your movements or the movement of a piece of equipment in anticipation of changes in the speed and/or direction of a moving object or scene.
Sound Localization	The ability to tell the direction from which a sound originated.
Peripheral Vision	The ability to see objects or movement of objects to one's side when the eyes are looking ahead.
Glare Sensitivity	The ability to see objects in the presence of glare or bright lighting.
Number Facility	The ability to add, subtract, multiply, or divide quickly and correctly.
Mathematical Reasoning	The ability to choose the right mathematical methods or formulas to solve a problem.
Night Vision	The ability to see under low light conditions.
Dynamic Flexibility	The ability to quickly and repeatedly bend, stretch, twist, or reach out with your body, arms, and/or legs.
Wrist-Finger Speed	The ability to make fast, simple, repeated movements of the fingers, hands, and wrists.

Work_Activity	Work_Activity Definitions
Assisting and Caring for Others	Providing personal assistance, medical attention, emotional support, or other personal care to others such as coworkers, customers, or patients.
Getting Information	Observing, receiving, and otherwise obtaining information from all relevant sources.
Communicating with Supervisors, Peers, or Subordin	Providing information to supervisors, co-workers, and subordinates by telephone, in written form, e-mail, or in person.
Identifying Objects, Actions, and Events	Identifying information by categorizing, estimating, recognizing differences or similarities, and detecting changes in circumstances or events.
Monitor Processes, Materials, or Surroundings	Monitoring and reviewing information from materials, events, or the environment, to detect or assess problems.
Establishing and Maintaining Interpersonal Relatio	Developing constructive and cooperative working relationships with others, and maintaining them over time.
Resolving Conflicts and Negotiating with Others	Handling complaints, settling disputes, and resolving grievances and conflicts, or otherwise negotiating with others.
Making Decisions and Solving Problems	Analyzing information and evaluating results to choose the best solution and solve problems.
Organizing, Planning, and Prioritizing Work	Developing specific goals and plans to prioritize, organize, and accomplish your work.

Documenting/Recording Information	Entering, transcribing, recording, storing, or maintaining information in written or electronic/magnetic form.
Coaching and Developing Others	Identifying the developmental needs of others and coaching, mentoring, or otherwise helping others to improve their knowledge or skills.
Thinking Creatively	Developing, designing, or creating new applications, ideas, relationships, systems, or products, including artistic contributions.
Inspecting Equipment, Structures, or Material	Inspecting equipment, structures, or materials to identify the cause of errors or other problems or defects.
Interpreting the Meaning of Information for Others	Translating or explaining what information means and how it can be used.
Performing for or Working Directly with the Public	Performing for people or dealing directly with the public. This includes serving customers in restaurants and stores, and receiving clients or guests.
Handling and Moving Objects	Using hands and arms in handling, installing, positioning, and moving materials, and manipulating things.
Updating and Using Relevant Knowledge	Keeping up-to-date technically and applying new knowledge to your job.
Operating Vehicles, Mechanized Devices, or Equipme	Running, maneuvering, navigating, or driving vehicles or mechanized equipment, such as forklifts, passenger vehicles, aircraft, or water craft.
Performing General Physical Activities	Performing physical activities that require considerable use of your arms and legs and moving your whole body, such as climbing, lifting, balancing, walking, stooping, and handling of materials.
Evaluating Information to Determine Compliance wit	Using relevant information and individual judgment to determine whether events or processes comply with laws, regulations, or standards.
Processing Information	Compiling, coding, categorizing, calculating, tabulating, auditing, or verifying information or data.
Developing Objectives and Strategies	Establishing long-range objectives and specifying the strategies and actions to achieve them.
Performing Administrative Activities	Performing day-to-day administrative tasks such as maintaining information files and processing paperwork.
Judging the Qualities of Things, Services, or Peop	Assessing the value, importance, or quality of things or people.
Scheduling Work and Activities	Scheduling events, programs, and activities, as well as the work of others.
Training and Teaching Others	Identifying the educational needs of others, developing formal educational or training programs or classes, and teaching or instructing others.
Communicating with Persons Outside Organization	Communicating with people outside the organization, representing the organization to customers, the public, government, and other external sources. This information can be exchanged in person, in writing, or by telephone or e-mail.
Developing and Building Teams	Encouraging and building mutual trust, respect, and cooperation among team members.
Coordinating the Work and Activities of Others	Getting members of a group to work together to accomplish tasks.
Monitoring and Controlling Resources	Monitoring and controlling resources and overseeing the spending of money.
Selling or Influencing Others	Convincing others to buy merchandise/goods or to otherwise change their minds or actions.
Analyzing Data or Information	Identifying the underlying principles, reasons, or facts of information by breaking down information or data into separate parts.
Controlling Machines and Processes	Using either control mechanisms or direct physical activity to operate machines or processes (not including computers or vehicles).
Estimating the Quantifiable Characteristics of Pro	Estimating sizes, distances, and quantities; or determining time, costs, resources, or materials needed to perform a work activity.
Provide Consultation and Advice to Others	Providing guidance and expert advice to management or other groups on technical, systems-, or process-related topics.
Guiding, Directing, and Motivating Subordinates	Providing guidance and direction to subordinates, including setting performance standards and monitoring performance.
Drafting, Laying Out, and Specifying Technical Dev	Providing documentation, detailed instructions, drawings, or specifications to tell others about how devices, parts, equipment, or structures are to be fabricated, constructed, assembled, modified, maintained, and used.
Repairing and Maintaining Electronic Equipment	Servicing, repairing, calibrating, regulating, fine-tuning, or testing machines, devices, and equipment that operate primarily on the basis of electrical or electronic (not mechanical) principles.
Interacting With Computers	Using computers and computer systems (including hardware and software) to program, write software, set up functions, enter data, or process information.

629

Repairing and Maintaining Mechanical Equipment	Servicing, repairing, adjusting, and testing machines, devices, moving parts, and equipment that operate primarily on the basis' of mechanical (not electronic) principles.
Staffing Organizational Units	Recruiting, interviewing, selecting, hiring, and promoting employees in an organization.

Work_Context	Work_Context Definitions
Physical Proximity	To what extent does this job require the worker to perform job tasks in close physical proximity to other people?
Contact With Others	How much does this job require the worker to be in contact with others (face-to-face, by telephone, or otherwise) in order to perform it?
Face-to-Face Discussions	How often do you have to have face-to-face discussions with individuals or teams in this job?
Telephone	How often do you have telephone conversations in this job?
Spend Time Standing	How much does this job require standing?
Frequency of Decision Making	How frequently is the worker required to make decisions that affect other people, the financial resources, and/or the image and reputation of the organization?
Wear Common Protective or Safety Equipment such as	How much does this job require wearing common protective or safety equipment such as safety shoes, glasses, gloves, hard hats or life jackets?
Importance of Being Exact or Accurate	How important is being very exact or highly accurate in performing this job?
Freedom to Make Decisions	How much decision making freedom, without supervision, does the job offer?
Exposed to Disease or Infections	How often does this job require exposure to disease/infections?
Work With Work Group or Team	How important is it to work with others in a group or team in this job?
Indoors, Environmentally Controlled	How often does this job require working indoors in environmentally controlled conditions?
Spend Time Walking and Running	How much does this job require walking and running?
Time Pressure	How often does this job require the worker to meet strict deadlines?
Letters and Memos	How often does the job require written letters and memos?
Impact of Decisions on Co-workers or Company Resul	How do the decisions an employee makes impact the results of co-workers, clients or the company?
Structured versus Unstructured Work	To what extent is this job structured for the worker, rather than allowing the worker to determine tasks, priorities, and goals?
Consequence of Error	How serious would the result usually be if the worker made a mistake that was not readily correctable?
Deal With Unpleasant or Angry People	How frequently does the worker have to deal with unpleasant, angry, or discourteous individuals as part of the job requirements?
In an Enclosed Vehicle or Equipment	How often does this job require working in a closed vehicle or equipment (e.g., car)?
Spend Time Making Repetitive Motions	How much does this job require making repetitive motions?
Frequency of Conflict Situations	How often are there conflict situations the employee has to face in this job?
Exposed to Contaminants	How often does this job require working exposed to contaminants (such as pollutants, gases, dust or odors)?
Importance of Repeating Same Tasks	How important is repeating the same physical activities (e.g., key entry) or mental activities (e.g., checking entries in a ledger) over and over, without stopping, to performing this job?
Deal With External Customers	How important is it to work with external customers or the public in this job?
Exposed to Minor Burns, Cuts, Bites, or Stings	How often does this job require exposure to minor burns, cuts, bites, or stings?
Deal With Physically Aggressive People	How frequently does this job require the worker to deal with physical aggression of violent individuals?
Indoors, Not Environmentally Controlled	How often does this job require working indoors in non-controlled environmental conditions (e.g., warehouse without heat)?
Coordinate or Lead Others	How important is it to coordinate or lead others in accomplishing work activities in this job?
Spend Time Bending or Twisting the Body	How much does this job require bending or twisting your body?
Spend Time Using Your Hands to Handle, Control, or	How much does this job require using your hands to handle, control, or feel objects, tools or controls?
Outdoors, Exposed to Weather	How often does this job require working outdoors, exposed to all weather conditions?
Degree of Automation	How automated is the job?

Responsibility for Outcomes and Results	How responsible is the worker for work outcomes and results of other workers?
Level of Competition	To what extent does this job require the worker to compete or to be aware of competitive pressures?
Spend Time Kneeling, Crouching, Stooping, or Crawl	How much does this job require kneeling, crouching, stooping or crawling?
Responsible for Others' Health and Safety	How much responsibility is there for the health and safety of others in this job?
Sounds, Noise Levels Are Distracting or Uncomforta	How often does this job require working exposed to sounds and noise levels that are distracting or uncomfortable?
Spend Time Sitting	How much does this job require sitting?
Extremely Bright or Inadequate Lighting	How often does this job require working in extremely bright or inadequate lighting conditions?
Outdoors, Under Cover	How often does this job require working outdoors, under cover (e.g., structure with roof but no walls)?
Spend Time Keeping or Regaining Balance	How much does this job require keeping or regaining your balance?
Very Hot or Cold Temperatures	How often does this job require working in very hot (above 90 F degrees) or very cold (below 32 F degrees) temperatures?
Cramped Work Space, Awkward Positions	How often does this job require working in cramped work spaces that requires getting into awkward positions?
Wear Specialized Protective or Safety Equipment su	How much does this job require wearing specialized protective or safety equipment such as breathing apparatus, safety harness, full protection suits, or radiation protection?
Electronic Mail	How often do you use electronic mail in this job?
Pace Determined by Speed of Equipment	How important is it to this job that the pace is determined by the speed of equipment or machinery? (This does not refer to keeping busy at all times on this job.)
Public Speaking	How often do you have to perform public speaking in this job?
Exposed to Hazardous Conditions	How often does this job require exposure to hazardous conditions?
Exposed to Whole Body Vibration	How often does this job require exposure to whole body vibration (e.g., operate a jackhammer)?
Spend Time Climbing Ladders, Scaffolds, or Poles	How much does this job require climbing ladders, scaffolds, or poles?
Exposed to Hazardous Equipment	How often does this job require exposure to hazardous equipment?
In an Open Vehicle or Equipment	How often does this job require working in an open vehicle or equipment (e.g., tractor)?
Exposed to Radiation	How often does this job require exposure to radiation?
Exposed to High Places	How often does this job require exposure to high places?

Job Zone Component	Job Zone Component Definitions
Title	Job Zone Two: Some Preparation Needed
	Some previous work-related skill, knowledge, or experience may be helpful in these occupations, but usually is not needed.
Overall Experience	For example, a drywall installer might benefit from experience installing drywall, but an inexperienced person could still learn to be an installer with little difficulty.
Job Training	Employees in these occupations need anywhere from a few months to one year of working with experienced employees.
Job Zone Examples	These occupations often involve using your knowledge and skills to help others. Examples include drywall installers, fire inspectors, flight attendants, pharmacy technicians, salespersons (retail), and tellers.
SVP Range	(4.0 to < 6.0)
Education	These occupations usually require a high school diploma and may require some vocational training or job-related course work. In some cases, an associate's or bachelor's degree could be needed.

Work_Styles	Work_Styles Definitions
Dependability	Job requires being reliable, responsible, and dependable, and fulfilling obligations.
Adaptability/Flexibility	Job requires being open to change (positive or negative) and to considerable variety in the workplace.
Integrity	Job requires being honest and ethical.
Stress Tolerance	Job requires accepting criticism and dealing calmly and effectively with high stress situations.
Attention to Detail	Job requires being careful about detail and thorough in completing work tasks.

Self Control	Job requires maintaining composure, keeping emotions in check, controlling anger, and avoiding aggressive behavior, even in very difficult situations.
Concern for Others	Job requires being sensitive to others' needs and feelings and being understanding and helpful on the job.
Cooperation	Job requires being pleasant with others on the job and displaying a good-natured, cooperative attitude.
Independence	Job requires developing one's own ways of doing things, guiding oneself with little or no supervision, and depending on oneself to get things done.
Achievement/Effort	Job requires establishing and maintaining personally challenging achievement goals and exerting effort toward mastering tasks.
Initiative	Job requires a willingness to take on responsibilities and challenges.
Leadership	Job requires a willingness to lead, take charge, and offer opinions and direction.
Social Orientation	Job requires preferring to work with others rather than alone, and being personally connected with others on the job.
Persistence	Job requires persistence in the face of obstacles.
Analytical Thinking	Job requires analyzing information and using logic to address work-related issues and problems.
Innovation	Job requires creativity and alternative thinking to develop new ideas for and answers to work-related problems.

31-1012.00 - Nursing Aides, Orderlies, and Attendants

Provide basic patient care under direction of nursing staff. Perform duties, such as feed, bathe, dress, groom, or move patients, or change linens.

Tasks

1) Provide patients with help walking, exercising, and moving in and out of bed.

2) Observe patients' conditions, measuring and recording food and liquid intake and output and vital signs, and report changes to professional staff.

3) Feed patients who are unable to feed themselves.

4) Answer patients' call signals.

5) Prepare, serve, and collect food trays.

6) Turn and re-position bedridden patients, alone or with assistance, to prevent bedsores.

7) Answer phones and direct visitors.

8) Bathe, groom, shave, dress, and/or drape patients to prepare them for surgery, treatment, or examination.

9) Provide patient care by supplying and emptying bed pans, applying dressings and supervising exercise routines.

10) Transport patients to treatment units, using a wheelchair or stretcher.

11) Collect specimens such as urine, feces, or sputum.

12) Deliver messages, documents and specimens.

13) Administer medications and treatments, such as catheterizations, suppositories, irrigations, enemas, massages, and douches, as directed by a physician or nurse.

14) Restrain patients if necessary.

15) Explain medical instructions to patients and family members.

16) Perform clerical duties such as processing documents and scheduling appointments.

17) Work as part of a medical team that examines and treats clinic outpatients.

18) Maintain inventory by storing, preparing, sterilizing, and issuing supplies such as dressing packs and treatment trays.

19) Set up equipment such as oxygen tents, portable x-ray machines, and overhead irrigation bottles.

Knowledge	Knowledge Definitions
Customer and Personal Service	Knowledge of principles and processes for providing customer and personal services. This includes customer needs assessment, meeting quality standards for services, and evaluation of customer satisfaction.
English Language	Knowledge of the structure and content of the English language including the meaning and spelling of words, rules of composition, and grammar.
Education and Training	Knowledge of principles and methods for curriculum and training design, teaching and instruction for individuals and groups, and the measurement of training effects.
Medicine and Dentistry	Knowledge of the information and techniques needed to diagnose and treat human injuries, diseases, and deformities. This includes symptoms, treatment alternatives, drug properties and interactions, and preventive health-care measures.
Public Safety and Security	Knowledge of relevant equipment, policies, procedures, and strategies to promote effective local, state, or national security operations for the protection of people, data, property, and institutions.
Psychology	Knowledge of human behavior and performance; individual differences in ability, personality, and interests; learning and motivation; psychological research methods; and the assessment and treatment of behavioral and affective disorders.
Clerical	Knowledge of administrative and clerical procedures and systems such as word processing, managing files and records, stenography and transcription, designing forms, and other office procedures and terminology.
Chemistry	Knowledge of the chemical composition, structure, and properties of substances and of the chemical processes and transformations that they undergo. This includes uses of chemicals and their interactions, danger signs, production techniques, and disposal methods.
Administration and Management	Knowledge of business and management principles involved in strategic planning, resource allocation, human resources modeling, leadership technique, production methods, and coordination of people and resources.
Biology	Knowledge of plant and animal organisms, their tissues, cells, functions, interdependencies, and interactions with each other and the environment.
Mechanical	Knowledge of machines and tools, including their designs, uses, repair, and maintenance.
Transportation	Knowledge of principles and methods for moving people or goods by air, rail, sea, or road, including the relative costs and benefits.
Telecommunications	Knowledge of transmission, broadcasting, switching, control, and operation of telecommunications systems.
Physics	Knowledge and prediction of physical principles, laws, their interrelationships, and applications to understanding fluid, material, and atmospheric dynamics, and mechanical, electrical, atomic and sub-atomic structures and processes.
Law and Government	Knowledge of laws, legal codes, court procedures, precedents, government regulations, executive orders, agency rules, and the democratic political process.
Foreign Language	Knowledge of the structure and content of a foreign (non-English) language including the meaning and spelling of words, rules of composition and grammar, and pronunciation.
Communications and Media	Knowledge of media production, communication, and dissemination techniques and methods. This includes alternative ways to inform and entertain via written, oral, and visual media.
Therapy and Counseling	Knowledge of principles, methods, and procedures for diagnosis, treatment, and rehabilitation of physical and mental dysfunctions, and for career counseling and guidance.
Mathematics	Knowledge of arithmetic, algebra, geometry, calculus, statistics, and their applications.
Personnel and Human Resources	Knowledge of principles and procedures for personnel recruitment, selection, training, compensation and benefits, labor relations and negotiation, and personnel information systems.
Computers and Electronics	Knowledge of circuit boards, processors, chips, electronic equipment, and computer hardware and software, including applications and programming.
Sales and Marketing	Knowledge of principles and methods for showing, promoting, and selling products or services. This includes marketing strategy and tactics, product demonstration, sales techniques, and sales control systems.
Engineering and Technology	Knowledge of the practical application of engineering science and technology. This includes applying principles, techniques, procedures, and equipment to the design and production of various goods and services.
Production and Processing	Knowledge of raw materials, production processes, quality control, costs, and other techniques for maximizing the effective manufacture and distribution of goods.

Building and Construction	Knowledge of materials, methods, and the tools involved in the construction or repair of houses, buildings, or other structures such as highways and roads.
Food Production	Knowledge of techniques and equipment for planting, growing, and harvesting food products (both plant and animal) for consumption, including storage/handling techniques.
Economics and Accounting	Knowledge of economic and accounting principles and practices, the financial markets, banking and the analysis and reporting of financial data.
Sociology and Anthropology	Knowledge of group behavior and dynamics, societal trends and influences, human migrations, ethnicity, cultures and their history and origins.
History and Archeology	Knowledge of historical events and their causes, indicators, and effects on civilizations and cultures.
Design	Knowledge of design techniques, tools, and principles involved in production of precision technical plans, blueprints, drawings, and models.
Philosophy and Theology	Knowledge of different philosophical systems and religions. This includes their basic principles, values, ethics, ways of thinking, customs, practices, and their impact on human culture.
Geography	Knowledge of principles and methods for describing the features of land, sea, and air masses, including their physical characteristics, locations, interrelationships, and distribution of plant, animal, and human life.
Fine Arts	Knowledge of the theory and techniques required to compose, produce, and perform works of music, dance, visual arts, drama, and sculpture.

Skills / Skills Definitions

Active Listening	Giving full attention to what other people are saying, taking time to understand the points being made, asking questions as appropriate, and not interrupting at inappropriate times.
Instructing	Teaching others how to do something.
Speaking	Talking to others to convey information effectively.
Time Management	Managing one's own time and the time of others.
Coordination	Adjusting actions in relation to others' actions.
Service Orientation	Actively looking for ways to help people.
Monitoring	Monitoring/Assessing performance of yourself, other individuals, or organizations to make improvements or take corrective action.
Social Perceptiveness	Being aware of others' reactions and understanding why they react as they do.
Reading Comprehension	Understanding written sentences and paragraphs in work related documents.
Critical Thinking	Using logic and reasoning to identify the strengths and weaknesses of alternative solutions, conclusions or approaches to problems.
Writing	Communicating effectively in writing as appropriate for the needs of the audience.
Judgment and Decision Making	Considering the relative costs and benefits of potential actions to choose the most appropriate one.
Active Learning	Understanding the implications of new information for both current and future problem-solving and decision-making.
Persuasion	Persuading others to change their minds or behavior.
Learning Strategies	Selecting and using training/instructional methods and procedures appropriate for the situation when learning or teaching new things.
Complex Problem Solving	Identifying complex problems and reviewing related information to develop and evaluate options and implement solutions.
Operation Monitoring	Watching gauges, dials, or other indicators to make sure a machine is working properly.
Equipment Selection	Determining the kind of tools and equipment needed to do a job.
Negotiation	Bringing others together and trying to reconcile differences.
Troubleshooting	Determining causes of operating errors and deciding what to do about it.
Operation and Control	Controlling operations of equipment or systems.
Management of Personnel Resources	Motivating, developing, and directing people as they work, identifying the best people for the job.
Systems Analysis	Determining how a system should work and how changes in conditions, operations, and the environment will affect outcomes.
Mathematics	Using mathematics to solve problems.

Systems Evaluation	Identifying measures or indicators of system performance and the actions needed to improve or correct performance, relative to the goals of the system.
Quality Control Analysis	Conducting tests and inspections of products, services, or processes to evaluate quality or performance.
Management of Material Resources	Obtaining and seeing to the appropriate use of equipment, facilities, and materials needed to do certain work.
Technology Design	Generating or adapting equipment and technology to serve user needs.
Science	Using scientific rules and methods to solve problems.
Equipment Maintenance	Performing routine maintenance on equipment and determining when and what kind of maintenance is needed.
Management of Financial Resources	Determining how money will be spent to get the work done, and accounting for these expenditures.
Operations Analysis	Analyzing needs and product requirements to create a design.
Installation	Installing equipment, machines, wiring, or programs to meet specifications.
Repairing	Repairing machines or systems using the needed tools.
Programming	Writing computer programs for various purposes.

Ability / Ability Definitions

Problem Sensitivity	The ability to tell when something is wrong or is likely to go wrong. It does not involve solving the problem, only recognizing there is a problem.
Oral Comprehension	The ability to listen to and understand information and ideas presented through spoken words and sentences.
Oral Expression	The ability to communicate information and ideas in speaking so others will understand.
Speech Clarity	The ability to speak clearly so others can understand you.
Near Vision	The ability to see details at close range (within a few feet of the observer).
Speech Recognition	The ability to identify and understand the speech of another person.
Static Strength	The ability to exert maximum muscle force to lift, push, pull, or carry objects.
Written Comprehension	The ability to read and understand information and ideas presented in writing.
Arm-Hand Steadiness	The ability to keep your hand and arm steady while moving your arm or while holding your arm and hand in one position.
Deductive Reasoning	The ability to apply general rules to specific problems to produce answers that make sense.
Inductive Reasoning	The ability to combine pieces of information to form general rules or conclusions (includes finding a relationship among seemingly unrelated events).
Trunk Strength	The ability to use your abdominal and lower back muscles to support part of the body repeatedly or continuously over time without 'giving out' or fatiguing.
Extent Flexibility	The ability to bend, stretch, twist, or reach with your body, arms, and/or legs.
Information Ordering	The ability to arrange things or actions in a certain order or pattern according to a specific rule or set of rules (e.g., patterns of numbers, letters, words, pictures, mathematical operations).
Flexibility of Closure	The ability to identify or detect a known pattern (a figure, object, word, or sound) that is hidden in other distracting material.
Selective Attention	The ability to concentrate on a task over a period of time without being distracted.
Manual Dexterity	The ability to quickly move your hand, your hand together with your arm, or your two hands to grasp, manipulate, or assemble objects.
Far Vision	The ability to see details at a distance.
Stamina	The ability to exert yourself physically over long periods of time without getting winded or out of breath.
Finger Dexterity	The ability to make precisely coordinated movements of the fingers of one or both hands to grasp, manipulate, or assemble very small objects.
Gross Body Coordination	The ability to coordinate the movement of your arms, legs, and torso together when the whole body is in motion.
Perceptual Speed	The ability to quickly and accurately compare similarities and differences among sets of letters, numbers, objects, pictures, or patterns. The things to be compared may be presented at the same time or one after the other. This ability also includes comparing a presented object with a remembered object.
Written Expression	The ability to communicate information and ideas in writing so others will understand.
Hearing Sensitivity	The ability to detect or tell the differences between sounds that vary in pitch and loudness.

Visual Color Discrimination	The ability to match or detect differences between colors, including shades of color and brightness.
Category Flexibility	The ability to generate or use different sets of rules for combining or grouping things in different ways.
Time Sharing	The ability to shift back and forth between two or more activities or sources of information (such as speech, sounds, touch, or other sources).
Speed of Closure	The ability to quickly make sense of, combine, and organize information into meaningful patterns.
Multilimb Coordination	The ability to coordinate two or more limbs (for example, two arms, two legs, or one leg and one arm) while sitting, standing, or lying down. It does not involve performing the activities while the whole body is in motion.
Reaction Time	The ability to quickly respond (with the hand, finger, or foot) to a signal (sound, light, picture) when it appears.
Auditory Attention	The ability to focus on a single source of sound in the presence of other distracting sounds.
Originality	The ability to come up with unusual or clever ideas about a given topic or situation, or to develop creative ways to solve a problem.
Memorization	The ability to remember information such as words, numbers, pictures, and procedures.
Dynamic Strength	The ability to exert muscle force repeatedly or continuously over time. This involves muscular endurance and resistance to muscle fatigue.
Visualization	The ability to imagine how something will look after it is moved around or when its parts are moved or rearranged.
Response Orientation	The ability to choose quickly between two or more movements in response to two or more different signals (lights, sounds, pictures). It includes the speed with which the correct response is started with the hand, foot, or other body part.
Number Facility	The ability to add, subtract, multiply, or divide quickly and correctly.
Fluency of Ideas	The ability to come up with a number of ideas about a topic (the number of ideas is important, not their quality, correctness, or creativity).
Depth Perception	The ability to judge which of several objects is closer or farther away from you, or to judge the distance between you and an object.
Gross Body Equilibrium	The ability to keep or regain your body balance or stay upright when in an unstable position.
Control Precision	The ability to quickly and repeatedly adjust the controls of a machine or a vehicle to exact positions.
Mathematical Reasoning	The ability to choose the right mathematical methods or formulas to solve a problem.
Speed of Limb Movement	The ability to quickly move the arms and legs.
Explosive Strength	The ability to use short bursts of muscle force to propel oneself (as in jumping or sprinting), or to throw an object.
Peripheral Vision	The ability to see objects or movement of objects to one's side when the eyes are looking ahead.
Wrist-Finger Speed	The ability to make fast, simple, repeated movements of the fingers, hands, and wrists.
Spatial Orientation	The ability to know your location in relation to the environment or to know where other objects are in relation to you.
Dynamic Flexibility	The ability to quickly and repeatedly bend, stretch, twist, or reach out with your body, arms, and/or legs.
Sound Localization	The ability to tell the direction from which a sound originated.
Rate Control	The ability to time your movements or the movement of a piece of equipment in anticipation of changes in the speed and/or direction of a moving object or scene.
Night Vision	The ability to see under low light conditions.
Glare Sensitivity	The ability to see objects in the presence of glare or bright lighting.

Work_Activity	Work_Activity Definitions
Assisting and Caring for Others	Providing personal assistance, medical attention, emotional support, or other personal care to others such as coworkers, customers, or patients.
Performing General Physical Activities	Performing physical activities that require considerable use of your arms and legs and moving your whole body, such as climbing, lifting, balancing, walking, stooping, and handling of materials.
Getting Information	Observing, receiving, and otherwise obtaining information from all relevant sources.
Identifying Objects, Actions, and Events	Identifying information by categorizing, estimating, recognizing differences or similarities, and detecting changes in circumstances or events.

Monitor Processes, Materials, or Surroundings	Monitoring and reviewing information from materials, events, or the environment, to detect or assess problems.
Documenting/Recording Information	Entering, transcribing, recording, storing, or maintaining information in written or electronic/magnetic form.
Establishing and Maintaining Interpersonal Relatio	Developing constructive and cooperative working relationships with others, and maintaining them over time.
Organizing, Planning, and Prioritizing Work	Developing specific goals and plans to prioritize, organize, and accomplish your work.
Coordinating the Work and Activities of Others	Getting members of a group to work together to accomplish tasks.
Thinking Creatively	Developing, designing, or creating new applications, ideas, relationships, systems, or products, including artistic contributions.
Training and Teaching Others	Identifying the educational needs of others, developing formal educational or training programs or classes, and teaching or instructing others.
Communicating with Supervisors, Peers, or Subordin	Providing information to supervisors, co-workers, and subordinates by telephone, in written form, e-mail, or in person.
Inspecting Equipment, Structures, or Material	Inspecting equipment, structures, or materials to identify the cause of errors or other problems or defects.
Developing and Building Teams	Encouraging and building mutual trust, respect, and cooperation among team members.
Handling and Moving Objects	Using hands and arms in handling, installing, positioning, and moving materials, and manipulating things.
Judging the Qualities of Things, Services, or Peop	Assessing the value, importance, or quality of things or people.
Processing Information	Compiling, coding, categorizing, calculating, tabulating, auditing, or verifying information or data.
Evaluating Information to Determine Compliance wit	Using relevant information and individual judgment to determine whether events or processes comply with laws, regulations, or standards.
Resolving Conflicts and Negotiating with Others	Handling complaints, settling disputes, and resolving grievances and conflicts, or otherwise negotiating with others.
Performing for or Working Directly with the Public	Performing for people or dealing directly with the public. This includes serving customers in restaurants and stores, and receiving clients or guests.
Guiding, Directing, and Motivating Subordinates	Providing guidance and direction to subordinates, including setting performance standards and monitoring performance.
Scheduling Work and Activities	Scheduling events, programs, and activities, as well as the work of others.
Making Decisions and Solving Problems	Analyzing information and evaluating results to choose the best solution and solve problems.
Performing Administrative Activities	Performing day-to-day administrative tasks such as maintaining information files and processing paperwork.
Interpreting the Meaning of Information for Others	Translating or explaining what information means and how it can be used.
Coaching and Developing Others	Identifying the developmental needs of others and coaching, mentoring, or otherwise helping others to improve their knowledge or skills.
Interacting With Computers	Using computers and computer systems (including hardware and software) to program, write software, set up functions, enter data, or process information.
Updating and Using Relevant Knowledge	Keeping up-to-date technically and applying new knowledge to your job.
Selling or Influencing Others	Convincing others to buy merchandise/goods or to otherwise change their minds or actions.
Provide Consultation and Advice to Others	Providing guidance and expert advice to management or other groups on technical, systems-, or process-related topics.
Monitoring and Controlling Resources	Monitoring and controlling resources and overseeing the spending of money.
Controlling Machines and Processes	Using either control mechanisms or direct physical activity to operate machines or processes (not including computers or vehicles).
Estimating the Quantifiable Characteristics of Pro	Estimating sizes, distances, and quantities; or determining time, costs, resources, or materials needed to perform a work activity.
Communicating with Persons Outside Organization	Communicating with people outside the organization, representing the organization to customers, the public, government, and other external sources. This information can be exchanged in person, in writing, or by telephone or e-mail.
Staffing Organizational Units	Recruiting, interviewing, selecting, hiring, and promoting employees in an organization.
Operating Vehicles, Mechanized Devices, or Equipme	Running, maneuvering, navigating, or driving vehicles or mechanized equipment, such as forklifts, passenger vehicles, aircraft, or water craft.

Analyzing Data or Information	Identifying the underlying principles, reasons, or facts of information by breaking down information or data into separate parts.
Developing Objectives and Strategies	Establishing long-range objectives and specifying the strategies and actions to achieve them.
Repairing and Maintaining Mechanical Equipment	Servicing, repairing, adjusting, and testing machines, devices, moving parts, and equipment that operate primarily on the basis of mechanical (not electronic) principles.
Repairing and Maintaining Electronic Equipment	Servicing, repairing, calibrating, regulating, fine-tuning, or testing machines, devices, and equipment that operate primarily on the basis of electrical or electronic (not mechanical) principles.
Drafting, Laying Out, and Specifying Technical Dev	Providing documentation, detailed instructions, drawings, or specifications to tell others about how devices, parts, equipment, or structures are to be fabricated, constructed, assembled, modified, maintained, or used.

Work_Context	Work_Context Definitions
Work With Work Group or Team	How important is it to work with others in a group or team in this job?
Physical Proximity	To what extent does this job require the worker to perform job tasks in close physical proximity to other people?
Exposed to Disease or Infections	How often does this job require exposure to disease/infections?
Indoors, Environmentally Controlled	How often does this job require working indoors in environmentally controlled conditions?
Contact With Others	How much does this job require the worker to be in contact with others (face-to-face, by telephone, or otherwise) in order to perform it?
Face-to-Face Discussions	How often do you have to have face-to-face discussions with individuals or teams in this job?
Spend Time Walking and Running	How much does this job require walking and running?
Wear Common Protective or Safety Equipment such as	How much does this job require wearing common protective or safety equipment such as safety shoes, glasses, gloves, hard hats or live jackets?
Importance of Being Exact or Accurate	How important is being very exact or highly accurate in performing this job?
Spend Time Standing	How much does this job require standing?
Responsible for Others' Health and Safety	How much responsibility is there for the health and safety of others in this job?
Structured versus Unstructured Work	To what extent is this job structured for the worker, rather than allowing the worker to determine tasks, priorities, and goals?
Deal With Unpleasant or Angry People	How frequently does the worker have to deal with unpleasant, angry, or discourteous individuals as part of the job requirements?
Spend Time Using Your Hands to Handle, Control, or	How much does this job require using your hands to handle, control, or feel objects, tools or controls?
Frequency of Decision Making	How frequently is the worker required to make decisions that affect other people, the financial resources, and/or the image and reputation of the organization?
Consequence of Error	How serious would the result usually be if the worker made a mistake that was not readily correctable?
Freedom to Make Decisions	How much decision making freedom, without supervision, does the job offer?
Telephone	How often do you have telephone conversations in this job?
Time Pressure	How often does this job require the worker to meet strict deadlines?
Deal With External Customers	How important is it to work with external customers or the public in this job?
Responsibility for Outcomes and Results	How responsible is the worker for work outcomes and results of other workers?
Importance of Repeating Same Tasks	How important is repeating the same physical activities (e.g., key entry) or mental activities (e.g., checking entries in a ledger) over and over, without stopping, to performing this job?
Coordinate or Lead Others	How important is it to coordinate or lead others in accomplishing work activities in this job?
Spend Time Bending or Twisting the Body	How much does this job require bending or twisting your body?
Impact of Decisions on Co-workers or Company Resul	How do the decisions an employee makes impact the results of co-workers, clients or the company?
Sounds, Noise Levels Are Distracting or Uncomforta	How often does this job require working exposed to sounds and noise levels that are distracting or uncomfortable?
Level of Competition	To what extent does this job require the worker to compete or to be aware of competitive pressures?

Deal With Physically Aggressive People	How frequently does this job require the worker to deal with physical aggression of violent individuals?
Spend Time Making Repetitive Motions	How much does this job require making repetitive motions?
Exposed to Contaminants	How often does this job require working exposed to contaminants (such as pollutants, gases, dust or odors)?
Spend Time Kneeling, Crouching, Stooping, or Crawl	How much does this job require kneeling, crouching, stooping or crawling?
Frequency of Conflict Situations	How often are there conflict situations the employee has to face in this job?
Letters and Memos	How often does the job require written letters and memos?
Spend Time Sitting	How much does this job require sitting?
Exposed to Minor Burns, Cuts, Bites, or Stings	How often does this job require exposure to minor burns, cuts, bites, or stings?
Degree of Automation	How automated is the job?
Public Speaking	How often do you have to perform public speaking in this job?
Spend Time Keeping or Regaining Balance	How much does this job require keeping or regaining your balance?
Cramped Work Space, Awkward Positions	How often does this job require working in cramped work spaces that requires getting into awkward positions?
Wear Specialized Protective or Safety Equipment su	How much does this job require wearing specialized protective or safety equipment such as breathing apparatus, safety harness, full protection suits, or radiation protection?
Pace Determined by Speed of Equipment	How important is it to this job that the pace is determined by the speed of equipment or machinery? (This does not refer to keeping busy at all times on this job.)
Exposed to Hazardous Conditions	How often does this job require exposure to hazardous conditions?
Outdoors, Exposed to Weather	How often does this job require working outdoors, exposed to all weather conditions?
In an Enclosed Vehicle or Equipment	How often does this job require working in a closed vehicle or equipment (e.g., car)?
Very Hot or Cold Temperatures	How often does this job require working in very hot (above 90 F degrees) or very cold (below 32 F degrees) temperatures?
Extremely Bright or Inadequate Lighting	How often does this job require working in extremely bright or inadequate lighting conditions?
Electronic Mail	How often do you use electronic mail in this job?
Indoors, Not Environmentally Controlled	How often does this job require working indoors in non-controlled environmental conditions (e.g., warehouse without heat)?
Outdoors, Under Cover	How often does this job require working outdoors, under cover (e.g., structure with roof but no walls)?
Exposed to Radiation	How often does this job require exposure to radiation?
Exposed to Hazardous Equipment	How often does this job require exposure to hazardous equipment?
Exposed to Whole Body Vibration	How often does this job require exposure to whole body vibration (e.g., operate a jackhammer)?
Exposed to High Places	How often does this job require exposure to high places?
In an Open Vehicle or Equipment	How often does this job require working in an open vehicle or equipment (e.g., tractor)?
Spend Time Climbing Ladders, Scaffolds, or Poles	How much does this job require climbing ladders, scaffolds, or poles?

Job Zone Component	Job Zone Component Definitions
Title	Job Zone Two: Some Preparation Needed
Overall Experience	Some previous work-related skill, knowledge, or experience may be helpful in these occupations, but usually is not needed. For example, a drywall installer might benefit from experience installing drywall, but an inexperienced person could still learn to be an installer with little difficulty.
Job Training	Employees in these occupations need anywhere from a few months to one year of working with experienced employees.
Job Zone Examples	These occupations often involve using your knowledge and skills to help others. Examples include drywall installers, fire inspectors, flight attendants, pharmacy technicians, salespersons (retail), and tellers.
SVP Range	(4.0 to < 6.0)
Education	These occupations usually require a high school diploma and may require some vocational training or job-related course work. In some cases, an associate's or bachelor's degree could be needed.

634

Work_Styles	Work_Styles Definitions
Concern for Others	Job requires being sensitive to others' needs and feelings and being understanding and helpful on the job.
Integrity	Job requires being honest and ethical.
Cooperation	Job requires being pleasant with others on the job and displaying a good-natured, cooperative attitude.
Dependability	Job requires being reliable, responsible, and dependable, and fulfilling obligations.
Self Control	Job requires maintaining composure, keeping emotions in check, controlling anger, and avoiding aggressive behavior, even in very difficult situations.
Stress Tolerance	Job requires accepting criticism and dealing calmly and effectively with high stress situations.
Adaptability/Flexibility	Job requires being open to change (positive or negative) and to considerable variety in the workplace.
Social Orientation	Job requires preferring to work with others rather than alone, and being personally connected with others on the job.
Attention to Detail	Job requires being careful about detail and thorough in completing work tasks.
Initiative	Job requires a willingness to take on responsibilities and challenges.
Innovation	Job requires creativity and alternative thinking to develop new ideas for and answers to work-related problems.
Analytical Thinking	Job requires analyzing information and using logic to address work-related issues and problems.
Leadership	Job requires a willingness to lead, take charge, and offer opinions and direction.
Independence	Job requires developing one's own ways of doing things, guiding oneself with little or no supervision, and depending on oneself to get things done.
Persistence	Job requires persistence in the face of obstacles.
Achievement/Effort	Job requires establishing and maintaining personally challenging achievement goals and exerting effort toward mastering tasks.

31-1013.00 - Psychiatric Aides

Assist mentally impaired or emotionally disturbed patients, working under direction of nursing and medical staff.

Tasks

1) Organize, supervise, and encourage patient participation in social, educational, and recreational activities.

2) Participate in recreational activities with patients, including card games, sports, or television viewing.

3) Accompany patients to and from wards for medical and dental treatments, shopping trips, and religious and recreational events.

4) Provide patients with assistance in bathing, dressing, and grooming, demonstrating these skills as necessary.

5) Work as part of a team that may include psychiatrists, psychologists, psychiatric nurses and social workers.

6) Maintain patients' restrictions to assigned areas.

7) Restrain or aid patients as necessary to prevent injury.

8) Record and maintain records of patient condition and activity, including vital signs, eating habits, and behavior.

9) Aid patients in becoming accustomed to hospital routine.

10) Serve meals, and feed patients needing assistance or persuasion.

11) Interview patients upon admission and record information.

12) Clean and disinfect rooms and furnishings to maintain a safe and orderly environment.

13) Perform nursing duties such as administering medications, measuring vital signs, collecting specimens and drawing blood samples.

14) Provide mentally impaired or emotionally disturbed patients with routine physical, emotional, psychological or rehabilitation care under the direction of nursing and medical staff.

Knowledge	Knowledge Definitions
Psychology	Knowledge of human behavior and performance; individual differences in ability, personality, and interests; learning and motivation; psychological research methods; and the assessment and treatment of behavioral and affective disorders.
Therapy and Counseling	Knowledge of principles, methods, and procedures for diagnosis, treatment, and rehabilitation of physical and mental dysfunctions, and for career counseling and guidance.
English Language	Knowledge of the structure and content of the English language including the meaning and spelling of words, rules of composition, and grammar.
Public Safety and Security	Knowledge of relevant equipment, policies, procedures, and strategies to promote effective local, state, or national security operations for the protection of people, data, property, and institutions.
Customer and Personal Service	Knowledge of principles and processes for providing customer and personal services. This includes customer needs assessment, meeting quality standards for services, and evaluation of customer satisfaction.
Education and Training	Knowledge of principles and methods for curriculum and training design, teaching and instruction for individuals and groups, and the measurement of training effects.
Sociology and Anthropology	Knowledge of group behavior and dynamics, societal trends and influences, human migrations, ethnicity, cultures and their history and origins.
Medicine and Dentistry	Knowledge of the information and techniques needed to diagnose and treat human injuries, diseases, and deformities. This includes symptoms, treatment alternatives, drug properties and interactions, and preventive health-care measures.
Philosophy and Theology	Knowledge of different philosophical systems and religions. This includes their basic principles, values, ethics, ways of thinking, customs, practices, and their impact on human culture.
Administration and Management	Knowledge of business and management principles involved in strategic planning, resource allocation, human resources modeling, leadership technique, production methods, and coordination of people and resources.
Law and Government	Knowledge of laws, legal codes, court procedures, precedents, government regulations, executive orders, agency rules, and the democratic political process.
Computers and Electronics	Knowledge of circuit boards, processors, chips, electronic equipment, and computer hardware and software, including applications and programming.
Personnel and Human Resources	Knowledge of principles and procedures for personnel recruitment, selection, training, compensation and benefits, labor relations and negotiation, and personnel information systems.
Mathematics	Knowledge of arithmetic, algebra, geometry, calculus, statistics, and their applications.
Telecommunications	Knowledge of transmission, broadcasting, switching, control, and operation of telecommunications systems.
Communications and Media	Knowledge of media production, communication, and dissemination techniques and methods. This includes alternative ways to inform and entertain via written, oral, and visual media.
Clerical	Knowledge of administrative and clerical procedures and systems such as word processing, managing files and records, stenography and transcription, designing forms, and other office procedures and terminology.
Transportation	Knowledge of principles and methods for moving people or goods by air, rail, sea, or road, including the relative costs and benefits.
Geography	Knowledge of principles and methods for describing the features of land, sea, and air masses, including their physical characteristics, locations, interrelationships, and distribution of plant, animal, and human life.
Food Production	Knowledge of techniques and equipment for planting, growing, and harvesting food products (both plant and animal) for consumption, including storage/handling techniques.
Mechanical	Knowledge of machines and tools, including their designs, uses, repair, and maintenance.
Biology	Knowledge of plant and animal organisms, their tissues, cells, functions, interdependencies, and interactions with each other and the environment.
Foreign Language	Knowledge of the structure and content of a foreign (non-English) language including the meaning and spelling of words, rules of composition and grammar, and pronunciation.

Chemistry	Knowledge of the chemical composition, structure, and properties of substances and of the chemical processes and transformations that they undergo. This includes uses of chemicals and their interactions, danger signs, production techniques, and disposal methods.
Production and Processing	Knowledge of raw materials, production processes, quality control, costs, and other techniques for maximizing the effective manufacture and distribution of goods.
Engineering and Technology	Knowledge of the practical application of engineering science and technology. This includes applying principles, techniques, procedures, and equipment to the design and production of various goods and services.
Building and Construction	Knowledge of materials, methods, and the tools involved in the construction or repair of houses, buildings, or other structures such as highways and roads.
Sales and Marketing	Knowledge of principles and methods for showing, promoting, and selling products or services. This includes marketing strategy and tactics, product demonstration, sales techniques, and sales control systems.
History and Archeology	Knowledge of historical events and their causes, indicators, and effects on civilizations and cultures.
Design	Knowledge of design techniques, tools, and principles involved in production of precision technical plans, blueprints, drawings, and models.
Economics and Accounting	Knowledge of economic and accounting principles and practices, the financial markets, banking and the analysis and reporting of financial data.
Fine Arts	Knowledge of the theory and techniques required to compose, produce, and perform works of music, dance, visual arts, drama, and sculpture.
Physics	Knowledge and prediction of physical principles, laws, their interrelationships, and applications to understanding fluid, material, and atmospheric dynamics, and mechanical, electrical, atomic and sub- atomic structures and processes.

Skills	Skills Definitions
Social Perceptiveness	Being aware of others' reactions and understanding why they react as they do.
Active Listening	Giving full attention to what other people are saying, taking time to understand the points being made, asking questions as appropriate, and not interrupting at inappropriate times.
Service Orientation	Actively looking for ways to help people.
Writing	Communicating effectively in writing as appropriate for the needs of the audience.
Persuasion	Persuading others to change their minds or behavior.
Reading Comprehension	Understanding written sentences and paragraphs in work related documents.
Speaking	Talking to others to convey information effectively.
Coordination	Adjusting actions in relation to others' actions.
Critical Thinking	Using logic and reasoning to identify the strengths and weaknesses of alternative solutions, conclusions or approaches to problems.
Instructing	Teaching others how to do something.
Active Learning	Understanding the implications of new information for both current and future problem-solving and decision-making.
Learning Strategies	Selecting and using training/instructional methods and procedures appropriate for the situation when learning or teaching new things.
Negotiation	Bringing others together and trying to reconcile differences.
Judgment and Decision Making	Considering the relative costs and benefits of potential actions to choose the most appropriate one.
Monitoring	Monitoring/Assessing performance of yourself, other individuals, or organizations to make improvements or take corrective action.
Time Management	Managing one's own time and the time of others.
Complex Problem Solving	Identifying complex problems and reviewing related information to develop and evaluate options and implement solutions.
Equipment Selection	Determining the kind of tools and equipment needed to do a job.
Management of Personnel Resources	Motivating, developing, and directing people as they work, identifying the best people for the job.
Troubleshooting	Determining causes of operating errors and deciding what to do about it.
Science	Using scientific rules and methods to solve problems.
Mathematics	Using mathematics to solve problems.
Operations Analysis	Analyzing needs and product requirements to create a design.

Management of Material Resources	Obtaining and seeing to the appropriate use of equipment, facilities, and materials needed to do certain work.
Systems Evaluation	Identifying measures or indicators of system performance and the actions needed to improve or correct performance, relative to the goals of the system.
Operation and Control	Controlling operations of equipment or systems.
Systems Analysis	Determining how a system should work and how changes in conditions, operations, and the environment will affect outcomes.
Technology Design	Generating or adapting equipment and technology to serve user needs.
Quality Control Analysis	Conducting tests and inspections of products, services, or processes to evaluate quality or performance.
Management of Financial Resources	Determining how money will be spent to get the work done, and accounting for these expenditures.
Installation	Installing equipment, machines, wiring, or programs to meet specifications.
Operation Monitoring	Watching gauges, dials, or other indicators to make sure a machine is working properly.
Equipment Maintenance	Performing routine maintenance on equipment and determining when and what kind of maintenance is needed.
Repairing	Repairing machines or systems using the needed tools.
Programming	Writing computer programs for various purposes.

Ability	Ability Definitions
Oral Expression	The ability to communicate information and ideas in speaking so others will understand.
Problem Sensitivity	The ability to tell when something is wrong or is likely to go wrong. It does not involve solving the problem, only recognizing there is a problem.
Oral Comprehension	The ability to listen to and understand information and ideas presented through spoken words and sentences.
Speech Clarity	The ability to speak clearly so others can understand you.
Speech Recognition	The ability to identify and understand the speech of another person.
Inductive Reasoning	The ability to combine pieces of information to form general rules or conclusions (includes finding a relationship among seemingly unrelated events).
Written Comprehension	The ability to read and understand information and ideas presented in writing.
Near Vision	The ability to see details at close range (within a few feet of the observer).
Information Ordering	The ability to arrange things or actions in a certain order or pattern according to a specific rule or set of rules (e.g., patterns of numbers, letters, words, pictures, mathematical operations).
Deductive Reasoning	The ability to apply general rules to specific problems to produce answers that make sense.
Written Expression	The ability to communicate information and ideas in writing so others will understand.
Selective Attention	The ability to concentrate on a task over a period of time without being distracted.
Arm-Hand Steadiness	The ability to keep your hand and arm steady while moving your arm or while holding your arm and hand in one position.
Time Sharing	The ability to shift back and forth between two or more activities or sources of information (such as speech, sounds, touch, or other sources).
Speed of Closure	The ability to quickly make sense of, combine, and organize information into meaningful patterns.
Static Strength	The ability to exert maximum muscle force to lift, push, pull, or carry objects.
Multilimb Coordination	The ability to coordinate two or more limbs (for example, two arms, two legs, or one leg and one arm) while sitting, standing, or lying down. It does not involve performing the activities while the whole body is in motion.
Trunk Strength	The ability to use your abdominal and lower back muscles to support part of the body repeatedly or continuously over time without 'giving out' or fatiguing.
Memorization	The ability to remember information such as words, numbers, pictures, and procedures.
Flexibility of Closure	The ability to identify or detect a known pattern (a figure, object, word, or sound) that is hidden in other distracting material.
Auditory Attention	The ability to focus on a single source of sound in the presence of other distracting sounds.
Far Vision	The ability to see details at a distance.

636

Originality	The ability to come up with unusual or clever ideas about a given topic or situation, or to develop creative ways to solve a problem.
Perceptual Speed	The ability to quickly and accurately compare similarities and differences among sets of letters, numbers, objects, pictures, or patterns. The things to be compared may be presented at the same time or one after the other. This ability also includes comparing a presented object with a remembered object.
Extent Flexibility	The ability to bend, stretch, twist, or reach with your body, arms, and/or legs.
Response Orientation	The ability to choose quickly between two or more movements in response to two or more different signals (lights, sounds, pictures). It includes the speed with which the correct response is started with the hand, foot, or other body part.
Fluency of Ideas	The ability to come up with a number of ideas about a topic (the number of ideas is important, not their quality, correctness, or creativity).
Category Flexibility	The ability to generate or use different sets of rules for combining or grouping things in different ways.
Reaction Time	The ability to quickly respond (with the hand, finger, or foot) to a signal (sound, light, picture) when it appears.
Depth Perception	The ability to judge which of several objects is closer or farther away from you, or to judge the distance between you and an object.
Manual Dexterity	The ability to quickly move your hand, your hand together with your arm, or your two hands to grasp, manipulate, or assemble objects.
Gross Body Coordination	The ability to coordinate the movement of your arms, legs, and torso together when the whole body is in motion.
Stamina	The ability to exert yourself physically over long periods of time without getting winded or out of breath.
Peripheral Vision	The ability to see objects or movement of objects to one's side when the eyes are looking ahead.
Speed of Limb Movement	The ability to quickly move the arms and legs.
Dynamic Strength	The ability to exert muscle force repeatedly or continuously over time. This involves muscular endurance and resistance to muscle fatigue.
Finger Dexterity	The ability to make precisely coordinated movements of the fingers of one or both hands to grasp, manipulate, or assemble very small objects.
Explosive Strength	The ability to use short bursts of muscle force to propel oneself (as in jumping or sprinting), or to throw an object.
Control Precision	The ability to quickly and repeatedly adjust the controls of a machine or a vehicle to exact positions.
Gross Body Equilibrium	The ability to keep or regain your body balance or stay upright when in an unstable position.
Hearing Sensitivity	The ability to detect or tell the differences between sounds that vary in pitch and loudness.
Spatial Orientation	The ability to know your location in relation to the environment or to know where other objects are in relation to you.
Number Facility	The ability to add, subtract, multiply, or divide quickly and correctly.
Visual Color Discrimination	The ability to match or detect differences between colors, including shades of color and brightness.
Mathematical Reasoning	The ability to choose the right mathematical methods or formulas to solve a problem.
Rate Control	The ability to time your movements or the movement of a piece of equipment in anticipation of changes in the speed and/or direction of a moving object or scene.
Night Vision	The ability to see under low light conditions.
Wrist-Finger Speed	The ability to make fast, simple, repeated movements of the fingers, hands, and wrists.
Glare Sensitivity	The ability to see objects in the presence of glare or bright lighting.
Sound Localization	The ability to tell the direction from which a sound originated.
Visualization	The ability to imagine how something will look after it is moved around or when its parts are moved or rearranged.
Dynamic Flexibility	The ability to quickly and repeatedly bend, stretch, twist, or reach out with your body, arms, and/or legs.

Work_Activity	Work_Activity Definitions
Assisting and Caring for Others	Providing personal assistance, medical attention, emotional support, or other personal care to others such as coworkers, customers, or patients.
Communicating with Supervisors, Peers, or Subordin	Providing information to supervisors, co-workers, and subordinates by telephone, in written form, e-mail, or in person.
Documenting/Recording Information	Entering, transcribing, recording, storing, or maintaining information in written or electronic/magnetic form.
Getting Information	Observing, receiving, and otherwise obtaining information from all relevant sources.
Establishing and Maintaining Interpersonal Relatio	Developing constructive and cooperative working relationships with others, and maintaining them over time.
Making Decisions and Solving Problems	Analyzing information and evaluating results to choose the best solution and solve problems.
Identifying Objects, Actions, and Events	Identifying information by categorizing, estimating, recognizing differences or similarities, and detecting changes in circumstances or events.
Monitor Processes, Materials, or Surroundings	Monitoring and reviewing information from materials, events, or the environment, to detect or assess problems.
Resolving Conflicts and Negotiating with Others	Handling complaints, settling disputes, and resolving grievances and conflicts, or otherwise negotiating with others.
Developing and Building Teams	Encouraging and building mutual trust, respect, and cooperation among team members.
Coordinating the Work and Activities of Others	Getting members of a group to work together to accomplish tasks.
Coaching and Developing Others	Identifying the developmental needs of others and coaching, mentoring, or otherwise helping others to improve their knowledge or skills.
Evaluating Information to Determine Compliance wit	Using relevant information and individual judgment to determine whether events or processes comply with laws, regulations, or standards.
Performing General Physical Activities	Performing physical activities that require considerable use of your arms and legs and moving your whole body, such as climbing, lifting, balancing, walking, stooping, and handling of materials.
Operating Vehicles, Mechanized Devices, or Equipme	Running, maneuvering, navigating, or driving vehicles or mechanized equipment, such as forklifts, passenger vehicles, aircraft, or water craft.
Training and Teaching Others	Identifying the educational needs of others, developing formal educational or training programs or classes, and teaching or instructing others.
Judging the Qualities of Things, Services, or Peop	Assessing the value, importance, or quality of things or people.
Performing for or Working Directly with the Public	Performing for people or dealing directly with the public. This includes serving customers in restaurants and stores, and receiving clients or guests.
Updating and Using Relevant Knowledge	Keeping up-to-date technically and applying new knowledge to your job.
Selling or Influencing Others	Convincing others to buy merchandise/goods or to otherwise change their minds or actions.
Inspecting Equipment, Structures, or Material	Inspecting equipment, structures, or materials to identify the cause of errors or other problems or defects.
Performing Administrative Activities	Performing day-to-day administrative tasks such as maintaining information files and processing paperwork.
Scheduling Work and Activities	Scheduling events, programs, and activities, as well as the work of others.
Organizing, Planning, and Prioritizing Work	Developing specific goals and plans to prioritize, organize, and accomplish your work.
Processing Information	Compiling, coding, categorizing, calculating, tabulating, auditing, or verifying information or data.
Guiding, Directing, and Motivating Subordinates	Providing guidance and direction to subordinates, including setting performance standards and monitoring performance.
Thinking Creatively	Developing, designing, or creating new applications, ideas, relationships, systems, or products, including artistic contributions.
Monitoring and Controlling Resources	Monitoring and controlling resources and overseeing the spending of money.
Developing Objectives and Strategies	Establishing long-range objectives and specifying the strategies and actions to achieve them.
Handling and Moving Objects	Using hands and arms in handling, installing, positioning, and moving materials, and manipulating things.
Interpreting the Meaning of Information for Others	Translating or explaining what information means and how it can be used.
Communicating with Persons Outside Organization	Communicating with people outside the organization, representing the organization to customers, the public, government, and other external sources. This information can be exchanged in person, in writing, or by telephone or e-mail.
Interacting With Computers	Using computers and computer systems (including hardware and software) to program, write software, set up functions, enter data, or process information.
Provide Consultation and Advice to Others	Providing guidance and expert advice to management or other groups on technical, systems-, or process-related topics.

Staffing Organizational Units	Recruiting, interviewing, selecting, hiring, and promoting employees in an organization.
Analyzing Data or Information	Identifying the underlying principles, reasons, or facts of information by breaking down information or data into separate parts.
Estimating the Quantifiable Characteristics of Pro	Estimating sizes, distances, and quantities; or determining time, costs, resources, or materials needed to perform a work activity.
Repairing and Maintaining Electronic Equipment	Servicing, repairing, calibrating, regulating, fine-tuning, or testing machines, devices, and equipment that operate primarily on the basis of electrical or electronic (not mechanical) principles.
Controlling Machines and Processes	Using either control mechanisms or direct physical activity to operate machines or processes (not including computers or vehicles).
Drafting, Laying Out, and Specifying Technical Dev	Providing documentation, detailed instructions, drawings, or specifications to tell others about how devices, parts, equipment, or structures are to be fabricated, constructed, assembled, modified, maintained, or used.
Repairing and Maintaining Mechanical Equipment	Servicing, repairing, adjusting, and testing machines, devices, moving parts, and equipment that operate primarily on the basis of mechanical (not electronic) principles.

Work_Context	Work_Context Definitions
Deal With Unpleasant or Angry People	How frequently does the worker have to deal with unpleasant, angry, or discourteous individuals as part of the job requirements?
Responsible for Others' Health and Safety	How much responsibility is there for the health and safety of others in this job?
Work With Work Group or Team	How important is it to work with others in a group or team in this job?
Telephone	How often do you have telephone conversations in this job?
Frequency of Conflict Situations	How often are there conflict situations the employee has to face in this job?
Contact With Others	How much does this job require the worker to be in contact with others (face-to-face, by telephone, or otherwise) in order to perform it?
Physical Proximity	To what extent does this job require the worker to perform job tasks in close physical proximity to other people?
Face-to-Face Discussions	How often do you have to have face-to-face discussions with individuals or teams in this job?
Freedom to Make Decisions	How much decision making freedom, without supervision, does the job offer?
Indoors, Environmentally Controlled	How often does this job require working indoors in environmentally controlled conditions?
Deal With Physically Aggressive People	How frequently does this job require the worker to deal with physical aggression of violent individuals?
Sounds, Noise Levels Are Distracting or Uncomforta	How often does this job require working exposed to sounds and noise levels that are distracting or uncomfortable?
Exposed to Disease or Infections	How often does this job require exposure to disease/infections?
Letters and Memos	How often does the job require written letters and memos?
Structured versus Unstructured Work	To what extent is this job structured for the worker, rather than allowing the worker to determine tasks, priorities, and goals?
Spend Time Standing	How much does this job require standing?
Time Pressure	How often does this job require the worker to meet strict deadlines?
Importance of Being Exact or Accurate	How important is being very exact or highly accurate in performing this job?
Consequence of Error	How serious would the result usually be if the worker made a mistake that was not readily correctable?
Impact of Decisions on Co-workers or Company Resul	How do the decisions an employee makes impact the results of co-workers, clients or the company?
Spend Time Walking and Running	How much does this job require walking and running?
Responsibility for Outcomes and Results	How responsible is the worker for work outcomes and results of other workers?
Coordinate or Lead Others	How important is it to coordinate or lead others in accomplishing work activities in this job?
Importance of Repeating Same Tasks	How important is repeating the same physical activities (e.g., key entry) or mental activities (e.g., checking entries in a ledger) over and over, without stopping, to performing this job?
Deal With External Customers	How important is it to work with external customers or the public in this job?

Wear Common Protective or Safety Equipment such as	How much does this job require wearing common protective or safety equipment such as safety shoes, glasses, gloves, hard hats or life jackets?
Frequency of Decision Making	How frequently is the worker required to make decisions that affect other people, the financial resources, and/or the image and reputation of the organization?
Exposed to Minor Burns, Cuts, Bites, or Stings	How often does this job require exposure to minor burns, cuts, bites, or stings?
Spend Time Sitting	How much does this job require sitting?
Outdoors, Exposed to Weather	How often does this job require working outdoors, exposed to all weather conditions?
Exposed to Contaminants	How often does this job require working exposed to contaminants (such as pollutants, gases, dust or odors)?
Public Speaking	How often do you have to perform public speaking in this job?
Cramped Work Space, Awkward Positions	How often does this job require working in cramped work spaces that requires getting into awkward positions?
Electronic Mail	How often do you use electronic mail in this job?
Spend Time Bending or Twisting the Body	How much does this job require bending or twisting your body?
In an Enclosed Vehicle or Equipment	How often does this job require working in a closed vehicle or equipment (e.g., car)?
Level of Competition	To what extent does this job require the worker to compete or to be aware of competitive pressures?
Spend Time Making Repetitive Motions	How much does this job require making repetitive motions?
Spend Time Kneeling, Crouching, Stooping, or Crawl	How much does this job require kneeling, crouching, stooping or crawling?
Spend Time Using Your Hands to Handle, Control, or	How much does this job require using your hands to handle, control, or feel objects, tools or controls?
Degree of Automation	How automated is the job?
Very Hot or Cold Temperatures	How often does this job require working in very hot (above 90 F degrees) or very cold (below 32 F degrees) temperatures?
Outdoors, Under Cover	How often does this job require working outdoors, under cover (e.g., structure with roof but no walls)?
Extremely Bright or Inadequate Lighting	How often does this job require working in extremely bright or inadequate lighting conditions?
Spend Time Keeping or Regaining Balance	How much does this job require keeping or regaining your balance?
Indoors, Not Environmentally Controlled	How often does this job require working indoors in non-controlled environmental conditions (e.g., warehouse without heat)?
Exposed to High Places	How often does this job require exposure to high places?
Wear Specialized Protective or Safety Equipment su	How much does this job require wearing specialized protective or safety equipment such as breathing apparatus, safety harness, full protection suits, or radiation protection?
Exposed to Hazardous Conditions	How often does this job require exposure to hazardous conditions?
Spend Time Climbing Ladders, Scaffolds, or Poles	How much does this job require climbing ladders, scaffolds, or poles?
Exposed to Radiation	How often does this job require exposure to radiation?
Pace Determined by Speed of Equipment	How important is it to this job that the pace is determined by the speed of equipment or machinery? (This does not refer to keeping busy at all times on this job.)
Exposed to Hazardous Equipment	How often does this job require exposure to hazardous equipment?
In an Open Vehicle or Equipment	How often does this job require working in an open vehicle or equipment (e.g., tractor)?
Exposed to Whole Body Vibration	How often does this job require exposure to whole body vibration (e.g., operate a jackhammer)?

Job Zone Component	Job Zone Component Definitions
Title	Job Zone Two: Some Preparation Needed
Overall Experience	Some previous work-related skill, knowledge, or experience may be helpful in these occupations, but usually is not needed. For example, a drywall installer might benefit from experience installing drywall, but an inexperienced person could still learn to be an installer with little difficulty.
Job Training	Employees in these occupations need anywhere from a few months to one year of working with experienced employees.
Job Zone Examples	These occupations often involve using your knowledge and skills to help others. Examples include drywall installers, fire inspectors, flight attendants, pharmacy technicians, salespersons (retail), and tellers.

638

SVP Range	(4.0 to 6.0)
Education	These occupations usually require a high school diploma and may require some vocational training or job-related course work. In some cases, an associate's or bachelor's degree could be needed.

Work_Styles	Work_Styles Definitions
Self Control	Job requires maintaining composure, keeping emotions in check, controlling anger, and avoiding aggressive behavior, even in very difficult situations.
Concern for Others	Job requires being sensitive to others' needs and feelings and being understanding and helpful on the job.
Stress Tolerance	Job requires accepting criticism and dealing calmly and effectively with high stress situations.
Integrity	Job requires being honest and ethical.
Dependability	Job requires being reliable, responsible, and dependable, and fulfilling obligations.
Adaptability/Flexibility	Job requires being open to change (positive or negative) and to considerable variety in the workplace.
Cooperation	Job requires being pleasant with others on the job and displaying a good-natured, cooperative attitude.
Attention to Detail	Job requires being careful about detail and thorough in completing work tasks.
Social Orientation	Job requires preferring to work with others rather than alone, and being personally connected with others on the job.
Independence	Job requires developing one's own ways of doing things, guiding oneself with little or no supervision, and depending on oneself to get things done.
Leadership	Job requires a willingness to lead, take charge, and offer opinions and direction.
Initiative	Job requires a willingness to take on responsibilities and challenges.
Innovation	Job requires creativity and alternative thinking to develop new ideas for and answers to work-related problems.
Persistence	Job requires persistence in the face of obstacles.
Analytical Thinking	Job requires analyzing information and using logic to address work-related issues and problems.
Achievement/Effort	Job requires establishing and maintaining personally challenging achievement goals and exerting effort toward mastering tasks.

31-2011.00 - Occupational Therapist Assistants

Assist occupational therapists in providing occupational therapy treatments and procedures. May, in accordance with State laws, assist in development of treatment plans, carry out routine functions, direct activity programs, and document the progress of treatments. Generally requires formal training.

Tasks

1) Implement, or assist occupational therapists with implementing, treatment plans designed to help clients function independently.

2) Select therapy activities to fit patients' needs and capabilities.

3) Transport patients to and from the occupational therapy work area.

4) Instruct, or assist in instructing, patients and families in home programs, basic living skills, and the care and use of adaptive equipment.

5) Demonstrate therapy techniques, such as manual and creative arts, and games.

6) Assemble, clean, and maintain equipment and materials for patient use.

7) Alter treatment programs to obtain better results if treatment is not having the intended effect.

8) Work under the direction of occupational therapists to plan, implement and administer educational, vocational, and recreational programs that restore and enhance performance in individuals with functional impairments.

9) Evaluate the daily living skills and capacities of physically, developmentally or emotionally disabled clients.

10) Design, fabricate, and repair assistive devices and make adaptive changes to equipment and environments.

11) Order any needed educational or treatment supplies.

12) Aid patients in dressing and grooming themselves.

13) Perform clerical duties such as scheduling appointments, collecting data, and documenting health insurance billings.

14) Assist educational specialists or clinical psychologists in administering situational or diagnostic tests to measure client's abilities or progress.

15) Monitor patients' performance in therapy activities, providing encouragement.

16) Maintain and promote a positive attitude toward clients and their treatment programs.

17) Report to supervisors, verbally or in writing, on patients' progress, attitudes and behavior.

18) Observe and record patients' progress, attitudes, and behavior, and maintain this information in client records.

Knowledge	Knowledge Definitions
Psychology	Knowledge of human behavior and performance; individual differences in ability, personality, and interests; learning and motivation; psychological research methods; and the assessment and treatment of behavioral and affective disorders.
Therapy and Counseling	Knowledge of principles, methods, and procedures for diagnosis, treatment, and rehabilitation of physical and mental dysfunctions, and for career counseling and guidance.
Customer and Personal Service	Knowledge of principles and processes for providing customer and personal services. This includes customer needs assessment, meeting quality standards for services, and evaluation of customer satisfaction.
English Language	Knowledge of the structure and content of the English language including the meaning and spelling of words, rules of composition, and grammar.
Sociology and Anthropology	Knowledge of group behavior and dynamics, societal trends and influences, human migrations, ethnicity, cultures and their history and origins.
Medicine and Dentistry	Knowledge of the information and techniques needed to diagnose and treat human injuries, diseases, and deformities. This includes symptoms, treatment alternatives, drug properties and interactions, and preventive health-care measures.
Education and Training	Knowledge of principles and methods for curriculum and training design, teaching and instruction for individuals and groups, and the measurement of training effects.
Philosophy and Theology	Knowledge of different philosophical systems and religions. This includes their basic principles, values, ethics, ways of thinking, customs, practices, and their impact on human culture.
Clerical	Knowledge of administrative and clerical procedures and systems such as word processing, managing files and records, stenography and transcription, designing forms, and other office procedures and terminology.
Administration and Management	Knowledge of business and management principles involved in strategic planning, resource allocation, human resources modeling, leadership technique, production methods, and coordination of people and resources.
Law and Government	Knowledge of laws, legal codes, court procedures, precedents, government regulations, executive orders, agency rules, and the democratic political process.
Public Safety and Security	Knowledge of relevant equipment, policies, procedures, and strategies to promote effective local, state, or national security operations for the protection of people, data, property, and institutions.
Mathematics	Knowledge of arithmetic, algebra, geometry, calculus, statistics, and their applications.
Biology	Knowledge of plant and animal organisms, their tissues, cells, functions, interdependencies, and interactions with each other and the environment.
Personnel and Human Resources	Knowledge of principles and procedures for personnel recruitment, selection, training, compensation and benefits, labor relations and negotiation, and personnel information systems.
Computers and Electronics	Knowledge of circuit boards, processors, chips, electronic equipment, and computer hardware and software, including applications and programming.
Chemistry	Knowledge of the chemical composition, structure, and properties of substances and of the chemical processes and transformations that they undergo. This includes uses of chemicals and their interactions, danger signs, production techniques, and disposal methods.

Sales and Marketing	Knowledge of principles and methods for showing, promoting, and selling products or services. This includes marketing strategy and tactics, product demonstration, sales techniques, and sales control systems.
Communications and Media	Knowledge of media production, communication, and dissemination techniques and methods. This includes alternative ways to inform and entertain via written, oral, and visual media.
Engineering and Technology	Knowledge of the practical application of engineering science and technology. This includes applying principles, techniques, procedures, and equipment to the design and production of various goods and services.
Foreign Language	Knowledge of the structure and content of a foreign (non-English) language including the meaning and spelling of words, rules of composition and grammar, and pronunciation.
Transportation	Knowledge of principles and methods for moving people or goods by air, rail, sea, or road, including the relative costs and benefits.
Telecommunications	Knowledge of transmission, broadcasting, switching, control, and operation of telecommunications systems.
Production and Processing	Knowledge of raw materials, production processes, quality control, costs, and other techniques for maximizing the effective manufacture and distribution of goods.
Mechanical	Knowledge of machines and tools, including their designs, uses, repair, and maintenance.
Economics and Accounting	Knowledge of economic and accounting principles and practices, the financial markets, banking and the analysis and reporting of financial data.
Physics	Knowledge and prediction of physical principles, laws, their interrelationships, and applications to understanding fluid, material, and atmospheric dynamics, and mechanical, electrical, atomic and sub-atomic structures and processes.
Design	Knowledge of design techniques, tools, and principles involved in production of precision technical plans, blueprints, drawings, and models.
Food Production	Knowledge of techniques and equipment for planting, growing, and harvesting food products (both plant and animal) for consumption, including storage/handling techniques.
Geography	Knowledge of principles and methods for describing the features of land, sea, and air masses, including their physical characteristics, locations, interrelationships, and distribution of plant, animal, and human life.
Fine Arts	Knowledge of the theory and techniques required to compose, produce, and perform works of music, dance, visual arts, drama, and sculpture.
Building and Construction	Knowledge of materials, methods, and the tools involved in the construction or repair of houses, buildings, or other structures such as highways and roads.
History and Archeology	Knowledge of historical events and their causes, indicators, and effects on civilizations and cultures.

Skills	Skills Definitions
Active Listening	Giving full attention to what other people are saying, taking time to understand the points being made, asking questions as appropriate, and not interrupting at inappropriate times.
Time Management	Managing one's own time and the time of others.
Instructing	Teaching others how to do something.
Speaking	Talking to others to convey information effectively.
Social Perceptiveness	Being aware of others' reactions and understanding why they react as they do.
Critical Thinking	Using logic and reasoning to identify the strengths and weaknesses of alternative solutions, conclusions or approaches to problems.
Learning Strategies	Selecting and using training/instructional methods and procedures appropriate for the situation when learning or teaching new things.
Reading Comprehension	Understanding written sentences and paragraphs in work related documents.
Writing	Communicating effectively in writing as appropriate for the needs of the audience.
Monitoring	Monitoring/Assessing performance of yourself, other individuals, or organizations to make improvements or take corrective action.
Service Orientation	Actively looking for ways to help people.
Active Learning	Understanding the implications of new information for both current and future problem-solving and decision-making.

Judgment and Decision Making	Considering the relative costs and benefits of potential actions to choose the most appropriate one.
Complex Problem Solving	Identifying complex problems and reviewing related information to develop and evaluate options and implement solutions.
Persuasion	Persuading others to change their minds or behavior.
Coordination	Adjusting actions in relation to others' actions.
Equipment Selection	Determining the kind of tools and equipment needed to do a job.
Operations Analysis	Analyzing needs and product requirements to create a design.
Systems Evaluation	Identifying measures or indicators of system performance and the actions needed to improve or correct performance, relative to the goals of the system.
Science	Using scientific rules and methods to solve problems.
Negotiation	Bringing others together and trying to reconcile differences.
Management of Personnel Resources	Motivating, developing, and directing people as they work, identifying the best people for the job.
Technology Design	Generating or adapting equipment and technology to serve user needs.
Mathematics	Using mathematics to solve problems.
Troubleshooting	Determining causes of operating errors and deciding what to do about it.
Equipment Maintenance	Performing routine maintenance on equipment and determining when and what kind of maintenance is needed.
Systems Analysis	Determining how a system should work and how changes in conditions, operations, and the environment will affect outcomes.
Management of Material Resources	Obtaining and seeing to the appropriate use of equipment, facilities, and materials needed to do certain work.
Quality Control Analysis	Conducting tests and inspections of products, services, or processes to evaluate quality or performance.
Operation Monitoring	Watching gauges, dials, or other indicators to make sure a machine is working properly.
Operation and Control	Controlling operations of equipment or systems.
Repairing	Repairing machines or systems using the needed tools.
Installation	Installing equipment, machines, wiring, or programs to meet specifications.
Management of Financial Resources	Determining how money will be spent to get the work done, and accounting for these expenditures.
Programming	Writing computer programs for various purposes.

Ability	Ability Definitions
Problem Sensitivity	The ability to tell when something is wrong or is likely to go wrong. It does not involve solving the problem, only recognizing there is a problem.
Oral Comprehension	The ability to listen to and understand information and ideas presented through spoken words and sentences.
Speech Recognition	The ability to identify and understand the speech of another person.
Speech Clarity	The ability to speak clearly so others can understand you.
Oral Expression	The ability to communicate information and ideas in speaking so others will understand.
Written Comprehension	The ability to read and understand information and ideas presented in writing.
Information Ordering	The ability to arrange things or actions in a certain order or pattern according to a specific rule or set of rules (e.g., patterns of numbers, letters, words, pictures, mathematical operations).
Near Vision	The ability to see details at close range (within a few feet of the observer).
Deductive Reasoning	The ability to apply general rules to specific problems to produce answers that make sense.
Selective Attention	The ability to concentrate on a task over a period of time without being distracted.
Written Expression	The ability to communicate information and ideas in writing so others will understand.
Fluency of Ideas	The ability to come up with a number of ideas about a topic (the number of ideas is important, not their quality, correctness, or creativity).
Stamina	The ability to exert yourself physically over long periods of time without getting winded or out of breath.
Category Flexibility	The ability to generate or use different sets of rules for combining or grouping things in different ways.
Perceptual Speed	The ability to quickly and accurately compare similarities and differences among sets of letters, numbers, objects, pictures, or patterns. The things to be compared may be presented at the same time or one after the other. This ability also includes comparing a presented object with a remembered object.

Trunk Strength	The ability to use your abdominal and lower back muscles to support part of the body repeatedly or continuously over time without 'giving out' or fatiguing.
Inductive Reasoning	The ability to combine pieces of information to form general rules or conclusions (includes finding a relationship among seemingly unrelated events).
Originality	The ability to come up with unusual or clever ideas about a given topic or situation, or to develop creative ways to solve a problem.
Static Strength	The ability to exert maximum muscle force to lift, push, pull, or carry objects.
Finger Dexterity	The ability to make precisely coordinated movements of the fingers of one or both hands to grasp, manipulate, or assemble very small objects.
Far Vision	The ability to see details at a distance.
Arm-Hand Steadiness	The ability to keep your hand and arm steady while moving your arm or while holding your arm and hand in one position.
Manual Dexterity	The ability to quickly move your hand, your hand together with your arm, or your two hands to grasp, manipulate, or assemble objects.
Time Sharing	The ability to shift back and forth between two or more activities or sources of information (such as speech, sounds, touch, or other sources).
Speed of Closure	The ability to quickly make sense of, combine, and organize information into meaningful patterns.
Extent Flexibility	The ability to bend, stretch, twist, or reach with your body, arms, and/or legs.
Flexibility of Closure	The ability to identify or detect a known pattern (a figure, object, word, or sound) that is hidden in other distracting material.
Visualization	The ability to imagine how something will look after it is moved around or when its parts are moved or rearranged.
Auditory Attention	The ability to focus on a single source of sound in the presence of other distracting sounds.
Number Facility	The ability to add, subtract, multiply, or divide quickly and correctly.
Gross Body Coordination	The ability to coordinate the movement of your arms, legs, and torso together when the whole body is in motion.
Control Precision	The ability to quickly and repeatedly adjust the controls of a machine or a vehicle to exact positions.
Visual Color Discrimination	The ability to match or detect differences between colors, including shades of color and brightness.
Multilimb Coordination	The ability to coordinate two or more limbs (for example, two arms, two legs, or one leg and one arm) while sitting, standing, or lying down. It does not involve performing the activities while the whole body is in motion.
Memorization	The ability to remember information such as words, numbers, pictures, and procedures.
Hearing Sensitivity	The ability to detect or tell the differences between sounds that vary in pitch and loudness.
Reaction Time	The ability to quickly respond (with the hand, finger, or foot) to a signal (sound, light, picture) when it appears.
Response Orientation	The ability to choose quickly between two or more movements in response to two or more different signals (lights, sounds, pictures). It includes the speed with which the correct response is started with the hand, foot, or other body part.
Dynamic Strength	The ability to exert muscle force repeatedly or continuously over time. This involves muscular endurance and resistance to muscle fatigue.
Speed of Limb Movement	The ability to quickly move the arms and legs.
Mathematical Reasoning	The ability to choose the right mathematical methods or formulas to solve a problem.
Depth Perception	The ability to judge which of several objects is closer or farther away from you, or to judge the distance between you and an object.
Sound Localization	The ability to tell the direction from which a sound originated.
Gross Body Equilibrium	The ability to keep or regain your body balance or stay upright when in an unstable position.
Glare Sensitivity	The ability to see objects in the presence of glare or bright lighting.
Spatial Orientation	The ability to know your location in relation to the environment or to know where other objects are in relation to you.
Peripheral Vision	The ability to see objects or movement of objects to one's side when the eyes are looking ahead.
Explosive Strength	The ability to use short bursts of muscle force to propel oneself (as in jumping or sprinting), or to throw an object.
Night Vision	The ability to see under low light conditions.

Rate Control	The ability to time your movements or the movement of a piece of equipment in anticipation of changes in the speed and/or direction of a moving object or scene.
Wrist-Finger Speed	The ability to make fast, simple, repeated movements of the fingers, hands, and wrists.
Dynamic Flexibility	The ability to quickly and repeatedly bend, stretch, twist, or reach out with your body, arms, and/or legs.

Work_Activity	Work_Activity Definitions
Assisting and Caring for Others	Providing personal assistance, medical attention, emotional support, or other personal care to others such as coworkers, customers, or patients.
Making Decisions and Solving Problems	Analyzing information and evaluating results to choose the best solution and solve problems.
Communicating with Supervisors, Peers, or Subordin	Providing information to supervisors, co-workers, and subordinates by telephone, in written form, e-mail, or in person.
Getting Information	Observing, receiving, and otherwise obtaining information from all relevant sources.
Establishing and Maintaining Interpersonal Relatio	Developing constructive and cooperative working relationships with others, and maintaining them over time.
Evaluating Information to Determine Compliance wit	Using relevant information and individual judgment to determine whether events or processes comply with laws, regulations, or standards.
Documenting/Recording Information	Entering, transcribing, recording, storing, or maintaining information in written or electronic/magnetic form.
Organizing, Planning, and Prioritizing Work	Developing specific goals and plans to prioritize, organize, and accomplish your work.
Identifying Objects, Actions, and Events	Identifying information by categorizing, estimating, recognizing differences or similarities, and detecting changes in circumstances or events.
Scheduling Work and Activities	Scheduling events, programs, and activities, as well as the work of others.
Resolving Conflicts and Negotiating with Others	Handling complaints, settling disputes, and resolving grievances and conflicts, or otherwise negotiating with others.
Monitor Processes, Materials, or Surroundings	Monitoring and reviewing information from materials, events, or the environment, to detect or assess problems.
Thinking Creatively	Developing, designing, or creating new applications, ideas, relationships, systems, or products, including artistic contributions.
Performing General Physical Activities	Performing physical activities that require considerable use of your arms and legs and moving your whole body, such as climbing, lifting, balancing, walking, stooping, and handling of materials.
Developing and Building Teams	Encouraging and building mutual trust, respect, and cooperation among team members.
Coordinating the Work and Activities of Others	Getting members of a group to work together to accomplish tasks.
Processing Information	Compiling, coding, categorizing, calculating, tabulating, auditing, or verifying information or data.
Interpreting the Meaning of Information for Others	Translating or explaining what information means and how it can be used.
Performing for or Working Directly with the Public	Performing for people or dealing directly with the public. This includes serving customers in restaurants and stores, and receiving clients or guests.
Updating and Using Relevant Knowledge	Keeping up-to-date technically and applying new knowledge to your job.
Operating Vehicles, Mechanized Devices, or Equipme	Running, maneuvering, navigating, or driving vehicles or mechanized equipment, such as forklifts, passenger vehicles, aircraft, or water craft.
Communicating with Persons Outside Organization	Communicating with people outside the organization, representing the organization to customers, the public, government, and other external sources. This information can be exchanged in person, in writing, or by telephone or e-mail.
Estimating the Quantifiable Characteristics of Pro	Estimating sizes, distances, and quantities; or determining time, costs, resources, or materials needed to perform a work activity.
Judging the Qualities of Things, Services, or Peop	Assessing the value, importance, or quality of things or people.
Guiding, Directing, and Motivating Subordinates	Providing guidance and direction to subordinates, including setting performance standards and monitoring performance.
Analyzing Data or Information	Identifying the underlying principles, reasons, or facts of information by breaking down information or data into separate parts.

Interacting With Computers	Using computers and computer systems (including hardware and software) to program, write software, set up functions, enter data, or process information.
Monitoring and Controlling Resources	Monitoring and controlling resources and overseeing the spending of money.
Inspecting Equipment, Structures, or Material	Inspecting equipment, structures, or materials to identify the cause of errors or other problems or defects.
Handling and Moving Objects	Using hands and arms in handling, installing, positioning, and moving materials, and manipulating things.
Developing Objectives and Strategies	Establishing long-range objectives and specifying the strategies and actions to achieve them.
Provide Consultation and Advice to Others	Providing guidance and expert advice to management or other groups on technical, systems-, or process-related topics.
Training and Teaching Others	Identifying the educational needs of others, developing formal educational or training programs or classes, and teaching or instructing others.
Performing Administrative Activities	Performing day-to-day administrative tasks such as maintaining information files and processing paperwork.
Coaching and Developing Others	Identifying the developmental needs of others and coaching, mentoring, or otherwise helping others to improve their knowledge or skills.
Controlling Machines and Processes	Using either control mechanisms or direct physical activity to operate machines or processes (not including computers or vehicles).
Selling or Influencing Others	Convincing others to buy merchandise/goods or to otherwise change their minds or actions.
Staffing Organizational Units	Recruiting, interviewing, selecting, hiring, and promoting employees in an organization.
Repairing and Maintaining Electronic Equipment	Servicing, repairing, calibrating, regulating, fine-tuning, or testing machines, devices, and equipment that operate primarily on the basis of electrical or electronic (not mechanical) principles.
Repairing and Maintaining Mechanical Equipment	Servicing, repairing, adjusting, and testing machines, devices, moving parts, and equipment that operate primarily on the basis of mechanical (not electronic) principles.
Drafting, Laying Out, and Specifying Technical Dev	Providing documentation, detailed instructions, drawings, or specifications to tell others about how devices, parts, equipment, or structures are to be fabricated, constructed, assembled, modified, maintained, or used.

Work_Context	Work_Context Definitions
Face-to-Face Discussions	How often do you have to have face-to-face discussions with individuals or teams in this job?
Physical Proximity	To what extent does this job require the worker to perform job tasks in close physical proximity to other people?
Contact With Others	How much does this job require the worker to be in contact with others (face-to-face, by telephone, or otherwise) in order to perform it?
Exposed to Disease or Infections	How often does this job require exposure to disease/infections?
Work With Work Group or Team	How important is it to work with others in a group or team in this job?
Time Pressure	How often does this job require the worker to meet strict deadlines?
Frequency of Decision Making	How frequently is the worker required to make decisions that affect other people, the financial resources, and/or the image and reputation of the organization?
Importance of Being Exact or Accurate	How important is being very exact or highly accurate in performing this job?
Coordinate or Lead Others	How important is it to coordinate or lead others in accomplishing work activities in this job?
Telephone	How often do you have telephone conversations in this job?
Spend Time Standing	How much does this job require standing?
Indoors, Environmentally Controlled	How often does this job require working indoors in environmentally controlled conditions?
Spend Time Using Your Hands to Handle, Control, or	How much does this job require using your hands to handle, control, or feel objects, tools or controls?
Deal With Unpleasant or Angry People	How frequently does the worker have to deal with unpleasant, angry, or discourteous individuals as part of the job requirements?
Impact of Decisions on Co-workers or Company Resul	How do the decisions an employee makes impact the results of co-workers, clients or the company?
Freedom to Make Decisions	How much decision making freedom, without supervision, does the job offer?

Wear Common Protective or Safety Equipment such as	How much does this job require wearing common protective or safety equipment such as safety shoes, glasses, gloves, hard hats or live jackets?
Structured versus Unstructured Work	To what extent is this job structured for the worker, rather than allowing the worker to determine tasks, priorities, and goals?
Spend Time Walking and Running	How much does this job require walking and running?
Letters and Memos	How often does the job require written letters and memos?
Frequency of Conflict Situations	How often are there conflict situations the employee has to face in this job?
Responsible for Others' Health and Safety	How much responsibility is there for the health and safety of others in this job?
Spend Time Bending or Twisting the Body	How much does this job require bending or twisting your body?
Importance of Repeating Same Tasks	How important is repeating the same physical activities (e.g., key entry) or mental activities (e.g., checking entries in a ledger) over and over, without stopping, to performing this job?
Spend Time Kneeling, Crouching, Stooping, or Crawl	How much does this job require kneeling, crouching, stooping or crawling?
Consequence of Error	How serious would the result usually be if the worker made a mistake that was not readily correctable?
Electronic Mail	How often do you use electronic mail in this job?
Exposed to Contaminants	How often does this job require working exposed to contaminants (such as pollutants, gases, dust or odors)?
Cramped Work Space, Awkward Positions	How often does this job require working in cramped work spaces that requires getting into awkward positions?
Spend Time Making Repetitive Motions	How much does this job require making repetitive motions?
Deal With External Customers	How important is it to work with external customers or the public in this job?
Public Speaking	How often do you have to perform public speaking in this job?
Deal With Physically Aggressive People	How frequently does this job require the worker to deal with physical aggression of violent individuals?
Sounds, Noise Levels Are Distracting or Uncomforta	How often does this job require working exposed to sounds and noise levels that are distracting or uncomfortable?
Level of Competition	To what extent does this job require the worker to compete or to be aware of competitive pressures?
Very Hot or Cold Temperatures	How often does this job require working in very hot (above 90 F degrees) or very cold (below 32 F degrees) temperatures?
Spend Time Keeping or Regaining Balance	How much does this job require keeping or regaining your balance?
Extremely Bright or Inadequate Lighting	How often does this job require working in extremely bright or inadequate lighting conditions?
Wear Specialized Protective or Safety Equipment su	How much does this job require wearing specialized protective or safety equipment such as breathing apparatus, safety harness, full protection suits, or radiation protection?
Indoors, Not Environmentally Controlled	How often does this job require working indoors in non-controlled environmental conditions (e.g., warehouse without heat)?
Responsibility for Outcomes and Results	How responsible is the worker for work outcomes and results of other workers?
Spend Time Sitting	How much does this job require sitting?
In an Enclosed Vehicle or Equipment	How often does this job require working in a closed vehicle or equipment (e.g., car)?
Exposed to Minor Burns, Cuts, Bites, or Stings	How often does this job require exposure to minor burns, cuts, bites, or stings?
Outdoors, Exposed to Weather	How often does this job require working outdoors, exposed to all weather conditions?
Exposed to Hazardous Conditions	How often does this job require exposure to hazardous conditions?
Exposed to Hazardous Equipment	How often does this job require exposure to hazardous equipment?
Pace Determined by Speed of Equipment	How important is it to this job that the pace is determined by the speed of equipment or machinery? (This does not refer to keeping busy at all times on this job.)
Degree of Automation	How automated is the job?
Outdoors, Under Cover	How often does this job require working outdoors, under cover (e.g., structure with roof but no walls)?
Exposed to Radiation	How often does this job require exposure to radiation?
Spend Time Climbing Ladders, Scaffolds, or Poles	How much does this job require climbing ladders, scaffolds, or poles?
Exposed to Whole Body Vibration	How often does this job require exposure to whole body vibration (e.g., operate a jackhammer)?
In an Open Vehicle or Equipment	How often does this job require working in an open vehicle or equipment (e.g., tractor)?
Exposed to High Places	How often does this job require exposure to high places?

Job Zone Component	Job Zone Component Definitions
Title	Job Zone Three: Medium Preparation Needed
Overall Experience	Previous work-related skill, knowledge, or experience is required for these occupations. For example, an electrician must have completed three or four years of apprenticeship or several years of vocational training, and often must have passed a licensing exam, in order to perform the job.
Job Training	Employees in these occupations usually need one or two years of training involving both on-the-job experience and informal training with experienced workers.
Job Zone Examples	These occupations usually involve using communication and organizational skills to coordinate, supervise, manage, or train others to accomplish goals. Examples include dental assistants, electricians, fish and game wardens, legal secretaries, personnel recruiters, and recreation workers.
SVP Range	(6.0 to < 7.0)
Education	Most occupations in this zone require training in vocational schools, related on-the-job experience, or an associate's degree. Some may require a bachelor's degree.

Work_Styles	Work_Styles Definitions
Cooperation	Job requires being pleasant with others on the job and displaying a good-natured, cooperative attitude.
Integrity	Job requires being honest and ethical.
Dependability	Job requires being reliable, responsible, and dependable, and fulfilling obligations.
Adaptability/Flexibility	Job requires being open to change (positive or negative) and to considerable variety in the workplace.
Concern for Others	Job requires being sensitive to others' needs and feelings and being understanding and helpful on the job.
Stress Tolerance	Job requires accepting criticism and dealing calmly and effectively with high stress situations.
Self Control	Job requires maintaining composure, keeping emotions in check, controlling anger, and avoiding aggressive behavior, even in very difficult situations.
Attention to Detail	Job requires being careful about detail and thorough in completing work tasks.
Independence	Job requires developing one's own ways of doing things, guiding oneself with little or no supervision, and depending on oneself to get things done.
Social Orientation	Job requires preferring to work with others rather than alone, and being personally connected with others on the job.
Innovation	Job requires creativity and alternative thinking to develop new ideas for and answers to work-related problems.
Initiative	Job requires a willingness to take on responsibilities and challenges.
Analytical Thinking	Job requires analyzing information and using logic to address work-related issues and problems.
Persistence	Job requires persistence in the face of obstacles.
Achievement/Effort	Job requires establishing and maintaining personally challenging achievement goals and exerting effort toward mastering tasks.
Leadership	Job requires a willingness to lead, take charge, and offer opinions and direction.

31-2012.00 - Occupational Therapist Aides

Under close supervision of an occupational therapist or occupational therapy assistant, perform only delegated, selected, or routine tasks in specific situations. These duties include preparing patient and treatment room.

Tasks

1) Assist occupational therapists in planning, implementing, and administering therapy programs to restore, reinforce, and enhance performance, using selected activities and special equipment.

2) Adjust and repair assistive devices and make adaptive changes to other equipment and to environments.

3) Assist educational specialists or clinical psychologists in administering situational or

diagnostic tests to measure client's abilities or progress.

4) Accompany patients on outings, providing transportation when necessary.

5) Supervise patients in choosing and completing work details or arts and crafts projects.

6) Encourage patients and attend to their physical needs to facilitate the attainment of therapeutic goals.

7) Observe patients' attendance, progress, attitudes, and accomplishments, and record and maintain information in client records.

8) Transport patients to and from the occupational therapy work area.

9) Manage intra-departmental infection control and equipment security.

10) Perform clerical, administrative and secretarial duties such as answering phones, restocking and ordering supplies, filling out paperwork and scheduling appointments.

11) Prepare and maintain work area, materials, and equipment, and maintain inventory of treatment and educational supplies.

12) Report to supervisors or therapists, verbally or in writing, on patients' progress, attitudes, attendance and accomplishments.

13) Instruct patients and families in work, social, and living skills, the care and use of adaptive equipment and other skills to facilitate home and work adjustment to disability.

14) Demonstrate therapy techniques, such as manual and creative arts, and games.

31-2021.00 - Physical Therapist Assistants

Assist physical therapists in providing physical therapy treatments and procedures. May, in accordance with State laws, assist in the development of treatment plans, carry out routine functions, document the progress of treatment, and modify specific treatments in accordance with patient status and within the scope of treatment plans established by a physical therapist. Generally requires formal training.

Tasks

1) Secure patients into or onto therapy equipment.

2) Confer with physical therapy staff and others to discuss and evaluate patient information for planning, modifying, and coordinating treatment.

3) Assist patients to dress, undress, and put on and remove supportive devices, such as braces, splints, and slings.

4) Measure patients' range-of-joint motion, body parts, and vital signs to determine effects of treatments or for patient evaluations.

5) Train patients in the use of orthopedic braces, prostheses, and supportive devices.

6) Perform clerical duties, such as taking inventory, ordering supplies, answering telephone, taking messages, and filling out forms.

7) Monitor operation of equipment and record use of equipment and administration of treatment.

8) Fit patients for orthopedic braces, prostheses, and supportive devices, such as crutches.

9) Administer traction to relieve neck and back pain, using intermittent and static traction equipment.

10) Transport patients to and from treatment areas, lifting and transferring them according to positioning requirements.

11) Perform postural drainage, percussions and vibrations, and teach deep breathing exercises to treat respiratory conditions.

12) Prepare treatment areas and electrotherapy equipment for use by physiotherapists.

13) Observe patients during treatments to compile and evaluate data on patients' responses and progress, and report to physical therapist.

14) Instruct, motivate, safeguard and assist patients as they practice exercises and functional activities.

15) Administer active and passive manual therapeutic exercises, therapeutic massage, and heat, light, sound, water, and electrical modality treatments, such as ultrasound.

Knowledge	Knowledge Definitions
Therapy and Counseling	Knowledge of principles, methods, and procedures for diagnosis, treatment, and rehabilitation of physical and mental dysfunctions, and for career counseling and guidance.

English Language	Knowledge of the structure and content of the English language including the meaning and spelling of words, rules of composition, and grammar.
Education and Training	Knowledge of principles and methods for curriculum and training design, teaching and instruction for individuals and groups, and the measurement of training effects.
Customer and Personal Service	Knowledge of principles and processes for providing customer and personal services. This includes customer needs assessment, meeting quality standards for services, and evaluation of customer satisfaction.
Medicine and Dentistry	Knowledge of the information and techniques needed to diagnose and treat human injuries, diseases, and deformities. This includes symptoms, treatment alternatives, drug properties and interactions, and preventive health-care measures.
Psychology	Knowledge of human behavior and performance; individual differences in ability, personality, and interests; learning and motivation; psychological research methods; and the assessment and treatment of behavioral and affective disorders.
Public Safety and Security	Knowledge of relevant equipment, policies, procedures, and strategies to promote effective local, state, or national security operations for the protection of people, data, property, and institutions.
Biology	Knowledge of plant and animal organisms, their tissues, cells, functions, interdependencies, and interactions with each other and the environment.
Sociology and Anthropology	Knowledge of group behavior and dynamics, societal trends and influences, human migrations, ethnicity, cultures and their history and origins.
Law and Government	Knowledge of laws, legal codes, court procedures, precedents, government regulations, executive orders, agency rules, and the democratic political process.
Philosophy and Theology	Knowledge of different philosophical systems and religions. This includes their basic principles, values, ethics, ways of thinking, customs, practices, and their impact on human culture.
Communications and Media	Knowledge of media production, communication, and dissemination techniques and methods. This includes alternative ways to inform and entertain via written, oral, and visual media.
Administration and Management	Knowledge of business and management principles involved in strategic planning, resource allocation, human resources modeling, leadership technique, production methods, and coordination of people and resources.
Foreign Language	Knowledge of the structure and content of a foreign (non-English) language including the meaning and spelling of words, rules of composition and grammar, and pronunciation.
Computers and Electronics	Knowledge of circuit boards, processors, chips, electronic equipment, and computer hardware and software, including applications and programming.
Clerical	Knowledge of administrative and clerical procedures and systems such as word processing, managing files and records, stenography and transcription, designing forms, and other office procedures and terminology.
Chemistry	Knowledge of the chemical composition, structure, and properties of substances and of the chemical processes and transformations that they undergo. This includes uses of chemicals and their interactions, danger signs, production techniques, and disposal methods.
Physics	Knowledge and prediction of physical principles, laws, their interrelationships, and applications to understanding fluid, material, and atmospheric dynamics, and mechanical, electrical, atomic and sub- atomic structures and processes.
Mathematics	Knowledge of arithmetic, algebra, geometry, calculus, statistics, and their applications.
Mechanical	Knowledge of machines and tools, including their designs, uses, repair, and maintenance.
Telecommunications	Knowledge of transmission, broadcasting, switching, control, and operation of telecommunications systems.
Engineering and Technology	Knowledge of the practical application of engineering science and technology. This includes applying principles, techniques, procedures, and equipment to the design and production of various goods and services.
Sales and Marketing	Knowledge of principles and methods for showing, promoting, and selling products or services. This includes marketing strategy and tactics, product demonstration, sales techniques, and sales control systems.

Transportation	Knowledge of principles and methods for moving people or goods by air, rail, sea, or road, including the relative costs and benefits.
Personnel and Human Resources	Knowledge of principles and procedures for personnel recruitment, selection, training, compensation and benefits, labor relations and negotiation, and personnel information systems.
Geography	Knowledge of principles and methods for describing the features of land, sea, and air masses, including their physical characteristics, locations, interrelationships, and distribution of plant, animal, and human life.
History and Archeology	Knowledge of historical events and their causes, indicators, and effects on civilizations and cultures.
Production and Processing	Knowledge of raw materials, production processes, quality control, costs, and other techniques for maximizing the effective manufacture and distribution of goods.
Design	Knowledge of design techniques, tools, and principles involved in production of precision technical plans, blueprints, drawings, and models.
Economics and Accounting	Knowledge of economic and accounting principles and practices, the financial markets, banking and the analysis and reporting of financial data.
Building and Construction	Knowledge of materials, methods, and the tools involved in the construction or repair of houses, buildings, or other structures such as highways and roads.
Fine Arts	Knowledge of the theory and techniques required to compose, produce, and perform works of music, dance, visual arts, drama, and sculpture.
Food Production	Knowledge of techniques and equipment for planting, growing, and harvesting food products (both plant and animal) for consumption, including storage/handling techniques.

Skills	Skills Definitions
Active Listening	Giving full attention to what other people are saying, taking time to understand the points being made, asking questions as appropriate, and not interrupting at inappropriate times.
Reading Comprehension	Understanding written sentences and paragraphs in work related documents.
Time Management	Managing one's own time and the time of others.
Instructing	Teaching others how to do something.
Writing	Communicating effectively in writing as appropriate for the needs of the audience.
Critical Thinking	Using logic and reasoning to identify the strengths and weaknesses of alternative solutions, conclusions or approaches to problems.
Speaking	Talking to others to convey information effectively.
Social Perceptiveness	Being aware of others' reactions and understanding why they react as they do.
Service Orientation	Actively looking for ways to help people.
Active Learning	Understanding the implications of new information for both current and future problem-solving and decision-making.
Monitoring	Monitoring/Assessing performance of yourself, other individuals, or organizations to make improvements or take corrective action.
Learning Strategies	Selecting and using training/instructional methods and procedures appropriate for the situation when learning or teaching new things.
Coordination	Adjusting actions in relation to others' actions.
Judgment and Decision Making	Considering the relative costs and benefits of potential actions to choose the most appropriate one.
Equipment Selection	Determining the kind of tools and equipment needed to do a job.
Science	Using scientific rules and methods to solve problems.
Persuasion	Persuading others to change their minds or behavior.
Complex Problem Solving	Identifying complex problems and reviewing related information to develop and evaluate options and implement solutions.
Operation Monitoring	Watching gauges, dials, or other indicators to make sure a machine is working properly.
Technology Design	Generating or adapting equipment and technology to serve user needs.
Management of Material Resources	Obtaining and seeing to the appropriate use of equipment, facilities, and materials needed to do certain work.
Operation and Control	Controlling operations of equipment or systems.
Negotiation	Bringing others together and trying to reconcile differences.
Mathematics	Using mathematics to solve problems.

Troubleshooting	Determining causes of operating errors and deciding what to do about it.
Equipment Maintenance	Performing routine maintenance on equipment and determining when and what kind of maintenance is needed.
Quality Control Analysis	Conducting tests and inspections of products, services, or processes to evaluate quality or performance.
Operations Analysis	Analyzing needs and product requirements to create a design.
Management of Personnel Resources	Motivating, developing, and directing people as they work, identifying the best people for the job.
Systems Evaluation	Identifying measures or indicators of system performance and the actions needed to improve or correct performance, relative to the goals of the system.
Systems Analysis	Determining how a system should work and how changes in conditions, operations, and the environment will affect outcomes.
Installation	Installing equipment, machines, wiring, or programs to meet specifications.
Management of Financial Resources	Determining how money will be spent to get the work done, and accounting for these expenditures.
Repairing	Repairing machines or systems using the needed tools.
Programming	Writing computer programs for various purposes.

Ability	Ability Definitions
Oral Comprehension	The ability to listen to and understand information and ideas presented through spoken words and sentences.
Oral Expression	The ability to communicate information and ideas in speaking so others will understand.
Speech Clarity	The ability to speak clearly so others can understand you.
Problem Sensitivity	The ability to tell when something is wrong or is likely to go wrong. It does not involve solving the problem, only recognizing there is a problem.
Speech Recognition	The ability to identify and understand the speech of another person.
Static Strength	The ability to exert maximum muscle force to lift, push, pull, or carry objects.
Extent Flexibility	The ability to bend, stretch, twist, or reach with your body, arms, and/or legs.
Deductive Reasoning	The ability to apply general rules to specific problems to produce answers that make sense.
Information Ordering	The ability to arrange things or actions in a certain order or pattern according to a specific rule or set of rules (e.g., patterns of numbers, letters, words, pictures, mathematical operations).
Written Comprehension	The ability to read and understand information and ideas presented in writing.
Near Vision	The ability to see details at close range (within a few feet of the observer).
Gross Body Coordination	The ability to coordinate the movement of your arms, legs, and torso together when the whole body is in motion.
Multilimb Coordination	The ability to coordinate two or more limbs (for example, two arms, two legs, or one leg and one arm) while sitting, standing, or lying down. It does not involve performing the activities while the whole body is in motion.
Trunk Strength	The ability to use your abdominal and lower back muscles to support part of the body repeatedly or continuously over time without 'giving out' or fatiguing.
Inductive Reasoning	The ability to combine pieces of information to form general rules or conclusions (includes finding a relationship among seemingly unrelated events).
Written Expression	The ability to communicate information and ideas in writing so others will understand.
Selective Attention	The ability to concentrate on a task over a period of time without being distracted.
Dynamic Strength	The ability to exert muscle force repeatedly or continuously over time. This involves muscular endurance and resistance to muscle fatigue.
Arm-Hand Steadiness	The ability to keep your hand and arm steady while moving your arm or while holding your arm and hand in one position.
Manual Dexterity	The ability to quickly move your hand, your hand together with your arm, or your two hands to grasp, manipulate, or assemble objects.
Stamina	The ability to exert yourself physically over long periods of time without getting winded or out of breath.
Time Sharing	The ability to shift back and forth between two or more activities or sources of information (such as speech, sounds, touch, or other sources).
Category Flexibility	The ability to generate or use different sets of rules for combining or grouping things in different ways.

Gross Body Equilibrium	The ability to keep or regain your body balance or stay upright when in an unstable position.
Finger Dexterity	The ability to make precisely coordinated movements of the fingers of one or both hands to grasp, manipulate, or assemble very small objects.
Speed of Limb Movement	The ability to quickly move the arms and legs.
Originality	The ability to come up with unusual or clever ideas about a given topic or situation, or to develop creative ways to solve a problem.
Flexibility of Closure	The ability to identify or detect a known pattern (a figure, object, word, or sound) that is hidden in other distracting material.
Visualization	The ability to imagine how something will look after it is moved around or when its parts are moved or rearranged.
Memorization	The ability to remember information such as words, numbers, pictures, and procedures.
Fluency of Ideas	The ability to come up with a number of ideas about a topic (the number of ideas is important, not their quality, correctness, or creativity).
Far Vision	The ability to see details at a distance.
Perceptual Speed	The ability to quickly and accurately compare similarities and differences among sets of letters, numbers, objects, pictures, or patterns. The things to be compared may be presented at the same time or one after the other. This ability also includes comparing a presented object with a remembered object.
Auditory Attention	The ability to focus on a single source of sound in the presence of other distracting sounds.
Control Precision	The ability to quickly and repeatedly adjust the controls of a machine or a vehicle to exact positions.
Speed of Closure	The ability to quickly make sense of, combine, and organize information into meaningful patterns.
Depth Perception	The ability to judge which of several objects is closer or farther away from you, or to judge the distance between you and an object.
Spatial Orientation	The ability to know your location in relation to the environment or to know where other objects are in relation to you.
Dynamic Flexibility	The ability to quickly and repeatedly bend, stretch, twist, or reach out with your body, arms, and/or legs.
Number Facility	The ability to add, subtract, multiply, or divide quickly and correctly.
Mathematical Reasoning	The ability to choose the right mathematical methods or formulas to solve a problem.
Rate Control	The ability to time your movements or the movement of a piece of equipment in anticipation of changes in the speed and/or direction of a moving object or scene.
Visual Color Discrimination	The ability to match or detect differences between colors, including shades of color and brightness.
Reaction Time	The ability to quickly respond (with the hand, finger, or foot) to a signal (sound, light, picture) when it appears.
Hearing Sensitivity	The ability to detect or tell the differences between sounds that vary in pitch and loudness.
Response Orientation	The ability to choose quickly between two or more movements in response to two or more different signals (lights, sounds, pictures). It includes the speed with which the correct response is started with the hand, foot, or other body part.
Explosive Strength	The ability to use short bursts of muscle force to propel oneself (as in jumping or sprinting), or to throw an object.
Wrist-Finger Speed	The ability to make fast, simple, repeated movements of the fingers, hands, and wrists.
Sound Localization	The ability to tell the direction from which a sound originated.
Peripheral Vision	The ability to see objects or movement of objects to one's side when the eyes are looking ahead.
Night Vision	The ability to see under low light conditions.
Glare Sensitivity	The ability to see objects in the presence of glare or bright lighting.

Work_Activity	Work_Activity Definitions
Assisting and Caring for Others	Providing personal assistance, medical attention, emotional support, or other personal care to others such as coworkers, customers, or patients.
Performing General Physical Activities	Performing physical activities that require considerable use of your arms and legs and moving your whole body, such as climbing, lifting, balancing, walking, stooping, and handling of materials.
Getting Information	Observing, receiving, and otherwise obtaining information from all relevant sources.

Performing for or Working Directly with the Public — Performing for people or dealing directly with the public. This includes serving customers in restaurants and stores, and receiving clients or guests.

Documenting/Recording Information — Entering, transcribing, recording, storing, or maintaining information in written or electronic/magnetic form.

Communicating with Supervisors, Peers, or Subordin — Providing information to supervisors, co-workers, and subordinates by telephone, in written form, e-mail, or in person.

Updating and Using Relevant Knowledge — Keeping up-to-date technically and applying new knowledge to your job.

Making Decisions and Solving Problems — Analyzing information and evaluating results to choose the best solution and solve problems.

Identifying Objects, Actions, and Events — Identifying information by categorizing, estimating, recognizing differences or similarities, and detecting changes in circumstances or events.

Monitor Processes, Materials, or Surroundings — Monitoring and reviewing information from materials, events, or the environment, to detect or assess problems.

Establishing and Maintaining Interpersonal Relatio — Developing constructive and cooperative working relationships with others, and maintaining them over time.

Handling and Moving Objects — Using hands and arms in handling, installing, positioning, and moving materials, and manipulating things.

Organizing, Planning, and Prioritizing Work — Developing specific goals and plans to prioritize, organize, and accomplish your work.

Scheduling Work and Activities — Scheduling events, programs, and activities, as well as the work of others.

Evaluating Information to Determine Compliance wit — Using relevant information and individual judgment to determine whether events or processes comply with laws, regulations, or standards.

Interpreting the Meaning of Information for Others — Translating or explaining what information means and how it can be used.

Communicating with Persons Outside Organization — Communicating with people outside the organization, representing the organization to customers, the public, government, and other external sources. This information can be exchanged in person, in writing, or by telephone or e-mail.

Developing and Building Teams — Encouraging and building mutual trust, respect, and cooperation among team members.

Training and Teaching Others — Identifying the educational needs of others, developing formal educational or training programs or classes, and teaching or instructing others.

Thinking Creatively — Developing, designing, or creating new applications, ideas, relationships, systems, or products, including artistic contributions.

Coordinating the Work and Activities of Others — Getting members of a group to work together to accomplish tasks.

Judging the Qualities of Things, Services, or Peop — Assessing the value, importance, or quality of things or people.

Developing Objectives and Strategies — Establishing long-range objectives and specifying the strategies and actions to achieve them.

Analyzing Data or Information — Identifying the underlying principles, reasons, or facts of information by breaking down information or data into separate parts.

Processing Information — Compiling, coding, categorizing, calculating, tabulating, auditing, or verifying information or data.

Guiding, Directing, and Motivating Subordinates — Providing guidance and direction to subordinates, including setting performance standards and monitoring performance.

Inspecting Equipment, Structures, or Material — Inspecting equipment, structures, or materials to identify the cause of errors or other problems or defects.

Resolving Conflicts and Negotiating with Others — Handling complaints, settling disputes, and resolving grievances and conflicts, or otherwise negotiating with others.

Coaching and Developing Others — Identifying the developmental needs of others and coaching, mentoring, or otherwise helping others to improve their knowledge or skills.

Interacting With Computers — Using computers and computer systems (including hardware and software) to program, write software, set up functions, enter data, or process information.

Performing Administrative Activities — Performing day-to-day administrative tasks such as maintaining information files and processing paperwork.

Controlling Machines and Processes — Using either control mechanisms or direct physical activity to operate machines or processes (not including computers or vehicles).

Provide Consultation and Advice to Others — Providing guidance and expert advice to management or other groups on technical, systems-, or process-related topics.

Estimating the Quantifiable Characteristics of Pro — Estimating sizes, distances, and quantities; or determining time, costs, resources, or materials needed to perform a work activity.

Selling or Influencing Others — Convincing others to buy merchandise/goods or to otherwise change their minds or actions.

Drafting, Laying Out, and Specifying Technical Dev — Providing documentation, detailed instructions, drawings, or specifications to tell others about how devices, parts, equipment, or structures are to be fabricated, constructed, assembled, modified, maintained, or used.

Repairing and Maintaining Mechanical Equipment — Servicing, repairing, adjusting, and testing machines, devices, moving parts, and equipment that operate primarily on the basis of mechanical (not electronic) principles.

Staffing Organizational Units — Recruiting, interviewing, selecting, hiring, and promoting employees in an organization.

Repairing and Maintaining Electronic Equipment — Servicing, repairing, calibrating, regulating, fine-tuning, or testing machines, devices, and equipment that operate primarily on the basis of electrical or electronic (not mechanical) principles.

Monitoring and Controlling Resources — Monitoring and controlling resources and overseeing the spending of money.

Operating Vehicles, Mechanized Devices, or Equipme — Running, maneuvering, navigating, or driving vehicles or mechanized equipment, such as forklifts, passenger vehicles, aircraft, or water craft.

Work_Context — Work_Context Definitions

Contact With Others — How much does this job require the worker to be in contact with others (face-to-face, by telephone, or otherwise) in order to perform it?

Face-to-Face Discussions — How often do you have to have face-to-face discussions with individuals or teams in this job?

Physical Proximity — To what extent does this job require the worker to perform job tasks in close physical proximity to other people?

Indoors, Environmentally Controlled — How often does this job require working indoors in environmentally controlled conditions?

Work With Work Group or Team — How important is it to work with others in a group or team in this job?

Frequency of Decision Making — How frequently is the worker required to make decisions that affect other people, the financial resources, and/or the image and reputation of the organization?

Structured versus Unstructured Work — To what extent is this job structured for the worker, rather than allowing the worker to determine tasks, priorities, and goals?

Telephone — How often do you have telephone conversations in this job?

Impact of Decisions on Co-workers or Company Resul — How do the decisions an employee makes impact the results of co-workers, clients or the company?

Freedom to Make Decisions — How much decision making freedom, without supervision, does the job offer?

Time Pressure — How often does this job require the worker to meet strict deadlines?

Importance of Being Exact or Accurate — How important is being very exact or highly accurate in performing this job?

Exposed to Disease or Infections — How often does this job require exposure to disease/infections?

Letters and Memos — How often does the job require written letters and memos?

Coordinate or Lead Others — How important is it to coordinate or lead others in accomplishing work activities in this job?

Spend Time Standing — How much does this job require standing?

Spend Time Using Your Hands to Handle, Control, or — How much does this job require using your hands to handle, control, or feel objects, tools or controls?

Spend Time Walking and Running — How much does this job require walking and running?

Responsibility for Outcomes and Results — How responsible is the worker for work outcomes and results of other workers?

Deal With Unpleasant or Angry People — How frequently does the worker have to deal with unpleasant, angry, or discourteous individuals as part of the job requirements?

Spend Time Bending or Twisting the Body — How much does this job require bending or twisting your body?

Deal With External Customers — How important is it to work with external customers or the public in this job?

Responsible for Others' Health and Safety — How much responsibility is there for the health and safety of others in this job?

Consequence of Error — How serious would the result usually be if the worker made a mistake that was not readily correctable?

Frequency of Conflict Situations — How often are there conflict situations the employee has to face in this job?

Spend Time Making Repetitive Motions — How much does this job require making repetitive motions?

Spend Time Kneeling, Crouching, Stooping, or Crawl	How much does this job require kneeling, crouching, stooping or crawling?
Level of Competition	To what extent does this job require the worker to compete or to be aware of competitive pressures?
Cramped Work Space, Awkward Positions	How often does this job require working in cramped work spaces that requires getting into awkward positions?
Spend Time Keeping or Regaining Balance	How much does this job require keeping or regaining your balance?
Sounds, Noise Levels Are Distracting or Uncomforta	How often does this job require working exposed to sounds and noise levels that are distracting or uncomfortable?
Importance of Repeating Same Tasks	How important is repeating the same physical activities (e.g., key entry) or mental activities (e.g., checking entries in a ledger) over and over, without stopping, to performing this job?
Exposed to Contaminants	How often does this job require working exposed to contaminants (such as pollutants, gases, dust or odors)?
Spend Time Sitting	How much does this job require sitting?
Wear Common Protective or Safety Equipment such as	How much does this job require wearing common protective or safety equipment such as safety shoes, glasses, gloves, hard hats or live jackets?
Deal With Physically Aggressive People	How frequently does this job require the worker to deal with physical aggression of violent individuals?
Exposed to Minor Burns, Cuts, Bites, or Stings	How often does this job require exposure to minor burns, cuts, bites, or stings?
Electronic Mail	How often do you use electronic mail in this job?
Public Speaking	How often do you have to perform public speaking in this job?
Extremely Bright or Inadequate Lighting	How often does this job require working in extremely bright or inadequate lighting conditions?
In an Enclosed Vehicle or Equipment	How often does this job require working in a closed vehicle or equipment (e.g., car)?
Very Hot or Cold Temperatures	How often does this job require working in very hot (above 90 F degrees) or very cold (below 32 F degrees) temperatures?
Exposed to Hazardous Conditions	How often does this job require exposure to hazardous conditions?
Indoors, Not Environmentally Controlled	How often does this job require working indoors in non-controlled environmental conditions (e.g., warehouse without heat)?
Outdoors, Under Cover	How often does this job require working outdoors, under cover (e.g., structure with roof but no walls)?
Degree of Automation	How automated is the job?
Pace Determined by Speed of Equipment	How important is it to this job that the pace is determined by the speed of equipment or machinery? (This does not refer to keeping busy at all times on this job.)
Outdoors, Exposed to Weather	How often does this job require working outdoors, exposed to all weather conditions?
Wear Specialized Protective or Safety Equipment su	How much does this job require wearing specialized protective or safety equipment such as breathing apparatus, safety harness, full protection suits, or radiation protection?
Exposed to Radiation	How often does this job require exposure to radiation?
Exposed to Hazardous Equipment	How often does this job require exposure to hazardous equipment?
Spend Time Climbing Ladders, Scaffolds, or Poles	How much does this job require climbing ladders, scaffolds, or poles?
Exposed to Whole Body Vibration	How often does this job require exposure to whole body vibration (e.g., operate a jackhammer)?
In an Open Vehicle or Equipment	How often does this job require working in an open vehicle or equipment (e.g., tractor)?
Exposed to High Places	How often does this job require exposure to high places?

Job Zone Component	Job Zone Component Definitions
Title	Job Zone Three: Medium Preparation Needed
Overall Experience	Previous work-related skill, knowledge, or experience is required for these occupations. For example, an electrician must have completed three or four years of apprenticeship or several years of vocational training, and often must have passed a licensing exam, in order to perform the job.
Job Training	Employees in these occupations usually need one or two years of training involving both on-the-job experience and informal training with experienced workers.
Job Zone Examples	These occupations usually involve using communication and organizational skills to coordinate, supervise, manage, or train others to accomplish goals. Examples include dental assistants, electricians, fish and game wardens, legal secretaries, personnel recruiters, and recreation workers.
SVP Range	(6.0 to < 7.0)

Education	Most occupations in this zone require training in vocational schools, related on-the-job experience, or an associate's degree. Some may require a bachelor's degree.

Work_Styles	Work_Styles Definitions
Integrity	Job requires being honest and ethical.
Dependability	Job requires being reliable, responsible, and dependable, and fulfilling obligations.
Concern for Others	Job requires being sensitive to others' needs and feelings and being understanding and helpful on the job.
Cooperation	Job requires being pleasant with others on the job and displaying a good-natured, cooperative attitude.
Independence	Job requires developing one's own ways of doing things, guiding oneself with little or no supervision, and depending on oneself to get things done.
Self Control	Job requires maintaining composure, keeping emotions in check, controlling anger, and avoiding aggressive behavior, even in very difficult situations.
Adaptability/Flexibility	Job requires being open to change (positive or negative) and to considerable variety in the workplace.
Attention to Detail	Job requires being careful about detail and thorough in completing work tasks.
Social Orientation	Job requires preferring to work with others rather than alone, and being personally connected with others on the job.
Initiative	Job requires a willingness to take on responsibilities and challenges.
Stress Tolerance	Job requires accepting criticism and dealing calmly and effectively with high stress situations.
Innovation	Job requires creativity and alternative thinking to develop new ideas for and answers to work-related problems.
Analytical Thinking	Job requires analyzing information and using logic to address work-related issues and problems.
Leadership	Job requires a willingness to lead, take charge, and offer opinions and direction.
Achievement/Effort	Job requires establishing and maintaining personally challenging achievement goals and exerting effort toward mastering tasks.
Persistence	Job requires persistence in the face of obstacles.

31-2022.00 - Physical Therapist Aides

Under close supervision of a physical therapist or physical therapy assistant, perform only delegated, selected, or routine tasks in specific situations. These duties include preparing the patient and the treatment area.

Tasks

1) Clean and organize work area and disinfect equipment after treatment.

2) Instruct, motivate, safeguard and assist patients practicing exercises and functional activities, under direction of medical staff.

3) Arrange treatment supplies to keep them in order.

4) Assist patients to dress, undress, and put on and remove supportive devices, such as braces, splints, and slings.

5) Change linens, such as bed sheets and pillow cases.

6) Perform clerical duties, such as taking inventory, ordering supplies, answering telephone, taking messages, and filling out forms.

7) Secure patients into or onto therapy equipment.

8) Maintain equipment and furniture to keep it in good working condition, including performing the assembly and disassembly of equipment and accessories.

9) Observe patients during treatment to compile and evaluate data on patients' responses and progress, and report to physical therapist.

10) Confer with physical therapy staff and others to discuss and evaluate patient information for planning, modifying, and coordinating treatment.

11) Administer active and passive manual therapeutic exercises, therapeutic massage, and heat, light, sound, water, and electrical modality treatments, such as ultrasound.

12) Record treatment given and equipment used.

13) Train patients to use orthopedic braces, prostheses and supportive devices.

14) Measure patient's range-of-joint motion, body parts, and vital signs to determine effects of treatments or for patient evaluations.

15) Participate in patient care tasks, such as assisting with passing food trays and feeding residents, and bathing residents on bed rest.

16) Administer traction to relieve neck and back pain, using intermittent and static traction equipment.

17) Fit patients for orthopedic braces, prostheses, and supportive devices, adjusting fit as needed.

Knowledge	Knowledge Definitions
Customer and Personal Service	Knowledge of principles and processes for providing customer and personal services. This includes customer needs assessment, meeting quality standards for services, and evaluation of customer satisfaction.
Therapy and Counseling	Knowledge of principles, methods, and procedures for diagnosis, treatment, and rehabilitation of physical and mental dysfunctions, and for career counseling and guidance.
Psychology	Knowledge of human behavior and performance; individual differences in ability, personality, and interests; learning and motivation; psychological research methods; and the assessment and treatment of behavioral and affective disorders.
English Language	Knowledge of the structure and content of the English language including the meaning and spelling of words, rules of composition, and grammar.
Medicine and Dentistry	Knowledge of the information and techniques needed to diagnose and treat human injuries, diseases, and deformities. This includes symptoms, treatment alternatives, drug properties and interactions, and preventive health-care measures.
Education and Training	Knowledge of principles and methods for curriculum and training design, teaching and instruction for individuals and groups, and the measurement of training effects.
Clerical	Knowledge of administrative and clerical procedures and systems such as word processing, managing files and records, stenography and transcription, designing forms, and other office procedures and terminology.
Public Safety and Security	Knowledge of relevant equipment, policies, procedures, and strategies to promote effective local, state, or national security operations for the protection of people, data, property, and institutions.
Administration and Management	Knowledge of business and management principles involved in strategic planning, resource allocation, human resources modeling, leadership technique, production methods, and coordination of people and resources.
Personnel and Human Resources	Knowledge of principles and procedures for personnel recruitment, selection, training, compensation and benefits, labor relations and negotiation, and personnel information systems.
Law and Government	Knowledge of laws, legal codes, court procedures, precedents, government regulations, executive orders, agency rules, and the democratic political process.
Mathematics	Knowledge of arithmetic, algebra, geometry, calculus, statistics, and their applications.
Communications and Media	Knowledge of media production, communication, and dissemination techniques and methods. This includes alternative ways to inform and entertain via written, oral, and visual media.
Computers and Electronics	Knowledge of circuit boards, processors, chips, electronic equipment, and computer hardware and software, including applications and programming.
Telecommunications	Knowledge of transmission, broadcasting, switching, control, and operation of telecommunications systems.
Philosophy and Theology	Knowledge of different philosophical systems and religions. This includes their basic principles, values, ethics, ways of thinking, customs, practices, and their impact on human culture.
Foreign Language	Knowledge of the structure and content of a foreign (non-English) language including the meaning and spelling of words, rules of composition and grammar, and pronunciation.
Economics and Accounting	Knowledge of economic and accounting principles and practices, the financial markets, banking and the analysis and reporting of financial data.
Sociology and Anthropology	Knowledge of group behavior and dynamics, societal trends and influences, human migrations, ethnicity, cultures and their history and origins.

Production and Processing	Knowledge of raw materials, production processes, quality control, costs, and other techniques for maximizing the effective manufacture and distribution of goods.
Mechanical	Knowledge of machines and tools, including their designs, uses, repair, and maintenance.
Transportation	Knowledge of principles and methods for moving people or goods by air, rail, sea, or road, including the relative costs and benefits.
Sales and Marketing	Knowledge of principles and methods for showing, promoting, and selling products or services. This includes marketing strategy and tactics, product demonstration, sales techniques, and sales control systems.
Chemistry	Knowledge of the chemical composition, structure, and properties of substances and of the chemical processes and transformations that they undergo. This includes uses of chemicals and their interactions, danger signs, production techniques, and disposal methods.
Physics	Knowledge and prediction of physical principles, laws, their interrelationships, and applications to understanding fluid, material, and atmospheric dynamics, and mechanical, electrical, atomic and sub-atomic structures and processes.
Biology	Knowledge of plant and animal organisms, their tissues, cells, functions, interdependencies, and interactions with each other and the environment.
History and Archeology	Knowledge of historical events and their causes, indicators, and effects on civilizations and cultures.
Engineering and Technology	Knowledge of the practical application of engineering science and technology. This includes applying principles, techniques, procedures, and equipment to the design and production of various goods and services.
Fine Arts	Knowledge of the theory and techniques required to compose, produce, and perform works of music, dance, visual arts, drama, and sculpture.
Building and Construction	Knowledge of materials, methods, and the tools involved in the construction or repair of houses, buildings, or other structures such as highways and roads.
Geography	Knowledge of principles and methods for describing the features of land, sea, and air masses, including their physical characteristics, locations, interrelationships, and distribution of plant, animal, and human life.
Food Production	Knowledge of techniques and equipment for planting, growing, and harvesting food products (both plant and animal) for consumption, including storage/handling techniques.
Design	Knowledge of design techniques, tools, and principles involved in production of precision technical plans, blueprints, drawings, and models.

Skills	Skills Definitions
Service Orientation	Actively looking for ways to help people.
Active Listening	Giving full attention to what other people are saying, taking time to understand the points being made, asking questions as appropriate, and not interrupting at inappropriate times.
Time Management	Managing one's own time and the time of others.
Monitoring	Monitoring/Assessing performance of yourself, other individuals, or organizations to make improvements or take corrective action.
Social Perceptiveness	Being aware of others' reactions and understanding why they react as they do.
Learning Strategies	Selecting and using training/instructional methods and procedures appropriate for the situation when learning or teaching new things.
Speaking	Talking to others to convey information effectively.
Reading Comprehension	Understanding written sentences and paragraphs in work related documents.
Active Learning	Understanding the implications of new information for both current and future problem-solving and decision-making.
Coordination	Adjusting actions in relation to others' actions.
Critical Thinking	Using logic and reasoning to identify the strengths and weaknesses of alternative solutions, conclusions or approaches to problems.
Operation Monitoring	Watching gauges, dials, or other indicators to make sure a machine is working properly.
Writing	Communicating effectively in writing as appropriate for the needs of the audience.
Persuasion	Persuading others to change their minds or behavior.
Instructing	Teaching others how to do something.

Equipment Maintenance	Performing routine maintenance on equipment and determining when and what kind of maintenance is needed.
Negotiation	Bringing others together and trying to reconcile differences.
Troubleshooting	Determining causes of operating errors and deciding what to do about it.
Equipment Selection	Determining the kind of tools and equipment needed to do a job.
Judgment and Decision Making	Considering the relative costs and benefits of potential actions to choose the most appropriate one.
Technology Design	Generating or adapting equipment and technology to serve user needs.
Mathematics	Using mathematics to solve problems.
Complex Problem Solving	Identifying complex problems and reviewing related information to develop and evaluate options and implement solutions.
Operation and Control	Controlling operations of equipment or systems.
Management of Material Resources	Obtaining and seeing to the appropriate use of equipment, facilities, and materials needed to do certain work.
Repairing	Repairing machines or systems using the needed tools.
Science	Using scientific rules and methods to solve problems.
Systems Evaluation	Identifying measures or indicators of system performance and the actions needed to improve or correct performance, relative to the goals of the system.
Systems Analysis	Determining how a system should work and how changes in conditions, operations, and the environment will affect outcomes.
Quality Control Analysis	Conducting tests and inspections of products, services, or processes to evaluate quality or performance.
Operations Analysis	Analyzing needs and product requirements to create a design.
Installation	Installing equipment, machines, wiring, or programs to meet specifications.
Management of Personnel Resources	Motivating, developing, and directing people as they work, identifying the best people for the job.
Management of Financial Resources	Determining how money will be spent to get the work done, and accounting for these expenditures.
Programming	Writing computer programs for various purposes.

Ability	Ability Definitions
Oral Comprehension	The ability to listen to and understand information and ideas presented through spoken words and sentences.
Speech Recognition	The ability to identify and understand the speech of another person.
Problem Sensitivity	The ability to tell when something is wrong or is likely to go wrong. It does not involve solving the problem, only recognizing there is a problem.
Speech Clarity	The ability to speak clearly so others can understand you.
Oral Expression	The ability to communicate information and ideas in speaking so others will understand.
Information Ordering	The ability to arrange things or actions in a certain order or pattern according to a specific rule or set of rules (e.g., patterns of numbers, letters, words, pictures, mathematical operations).
Near Vision	The ability to see details at close range (within a few feet of the observer).
Deductive Reasoning	The ability to apply general rules to specific problems to produce answers that make sense.
Written Comprehension	The ability to read and understand information and ideas presented in writing.
Category Flexibility	The ability to generate or use different sets of rules for combining or grouping things in different ways.
Inductive Reasoning	The ability to combine pieces of information to form general rules or conclusions (includes finding a relationship among seemingly unrelated events).
Perceptual Speed	The ability to quickly and accurately compare similarities and differences among sets of letters, numbers, objects, pictures, or patterns. The things to be compared may be presented at the same time or one after the other. This ability also includes comparing a presented object with a remembered object.
Trunk Strength	The ability to use your abdominal and lower back muscles to support part of the body repeatedly or continuously over time without 'giving out' or fatiguing.
Selective Attention	The ability to concentrate on a task over a period of time without being distracted.
Finger Dexterity	The ability to make precisely coordinated movements of the fingers of one or both hands to grasp, manipulate, or assemble very small objects.
Arm-Hand Steadiness	The ability to keep your hand and arm steady while moving your arm or while holding your arm and hand in one position.

Flexibility of Closure	The ability to identify or detect a known pattern (a figure, object, word, or sound) that is hidden in other distracting material.
Far Vision	The ability to see details at a distance.
Written Expression	The ability to communicate information and ideas in writing so others will understand.
Extent Flexibility	The ability to bend, stretch, twist, or reach with your body, arms, and/or legs.
Manual Dexterity	The ability to quickly move your hand, your hand together with your arm, or your two hands to grasp, manipulate, or assemble objects.
Auditory Attention	The ability to focus on a single source of sound in the presence of other distracting sounds.
Visualization	The ability to imagine how something will look after it is moved around or when its parts are moved or rearranged.
Static Strength	The ability to exert maximum muscle force to lift, push, pull, or carry objects.
Visual Color Discrimination	The ability to match or detect differences between colors, including shades of color and brightness.
Time Sharing	The ability to shift back and forth between two or more activities or sources of information (such as speech, sounds, touch, or other sources).
Control Precision	The ability to quickly and repeatedly adjust the controls of a machine or a vehicle to exact positions.
Depth Perception	The ability to judge which of several objects is closer or farther away from you, or to judge the distance between you and an object.
Hearing Sensitivity	The ability to detect or tell the differences between sounds that vary in pitch and loudness.
Stamina	The ability to exert yourself physically over long periods of time without getting winded or out of breath.
Multilimb Coordination	The ability to coordinate two or more limbs (for example, two arms, two legs, or one leg and one arm) while sitting, standing, or lying down. It does not involve performing the activities while the whole body is in motion.
Number Facility	The ability to add, subtract, multiply, or divide quickly and correctly.
Fluency of Ideas	The ability to come up with a number of ideas about a topic (the number of ideas is important, not their quality, correctness, or creativity).
Gross Body Coordination	The ability to coordinate the movement of your arms, legs, and torso together when the whole body is in motion.
Originality	The ability to come up with unusual or clever ideas about a given topic or situation, or to develop creative ways to solve a problem.
Dynamic Strength	The ability to exert muscle force repeatedly or continuously over time. This involves muscular endurance and resistance to muscle fatigue.
Speed of Closure	The ability to quickly make sense of, combine, and organize information into meaningful patterns.
Mathematical Reasoning	The ability to choose the right mathematical methods or formulas to solve a problem.
Memorization	The ability to remember information such as words, numbers, pictures, and procedures.
Reaction Time	The ability to quickly respond (with the hand, finger, or foot) to a signal (sound, light, picture) when it appears.
Wrist-Finger Speed	The ability to make fast, simple, repeated movements of the fingers, hands, and wrists.
Rate Control	The ability to time your movements or the movement of a piece of equipment in anticipation of changes in the speed and/or direction of a moving object or scene.
Response Orientation	The ability to choose quickly between two or more movements in response to two or more different signals (lights, sounds, pictures). It includes the speed with which the correct response is started with the hand, foot, or other body part.
Gross Body Equilibrium	The ability to keep or regain your body balance or stay upright when in an unstable position.
Speed of Limb Movement	The ability to quickly move the arms and legs.
Spatial Orientation	The ability to know your location in relation to the environment or to know where other objects are in relation to you.
Dynamic Flexibility	The ability to quickly and repeatedly bend, stretch, twist, or reach out with your body, arms, and/or legs.
Explosive Strength	The ability to use short bursts of muscle force to propel oneself (as in jumping or sprinting), or to throw an object.
Peripheral Vision	The ability to see objects or movement of objects to one's side when the eyes are looking ahead.
Sound Localization	The ability to tell the direction from which a sound originated.

Glare Sensitivity	The ability to see objects in the presence of glare or bright lighting.
Night Vision	The ability to see under low light conditions.

Work_Activity	Work_Activity Definitions
Assisting and Caring for Others	Providing personal assistance, medical attention, emotional support, or other personal care to others such as coworkers, customers, or patients.
Performing General Physical Activities	Performing physical activities that require considerable use of your arms and legs and moving your whole body, such as climbing, lifting, balancing, walking, stooping, and handling of materials.
Getting Information	Observing, receiving, and otherwise obtaining information from all relevant sources.
Documenting/Recording Information	Entering, transcribing, recording, storing, or maintaining information in written or electronic/magnetic form.
Communicating with Supervisors, Peers, or Subordin	Providing information to supervisors, co-workers, and subordinates by telephone, in written form, e-mail, or in person.
Monitor Processes, Materials, or Surroundings	Monitoring and reviewing information from materials, events, or the environment, to detect or assess problems.
Evaluating Information to Determine Compliance wit	Using relevant information and individual judgment to determine whether events or processes comply with laws, regulations, or standards.
Establishing and Maintaining Interpersonal Relatio	Developing constructive and cooperative working relationships with others, and maintaining them over time.
Inspecting Equipment, Structures, or Material	Inspecting equipment, structures, or materials to identify the cause of errors or other problems or defects.
Identifying Objects, Actions, and Events	Identifying information by categorizing, estimating, recognizing differences or similarities, and detecting changes in circumstances or events.
Handling and Moving Objects	Using hands and arms in handling, installing, positioning, and moving materials, and manipulating things.
Organizing, Planning, and Prioritizing Work	Developing specific goals and plans to prioritize, organize, and accomplish your work.
Performing for or Working Directly with the Public	Performing for people or dealing directly with the public. This includes serving customers in restaurants and stores, and receiving clients or guests.
Updating and Using Relevant Knowledge	Keeping up-to-date technically and applying new knowledge to your job.
Making Decisions and Solving Problems	Analyzing information and evaluating results to choose the best solution and solve problems.
Judging the Qualities of Things, Services, or Peop	Assessing the value, importance, or quality of things or people.
Interpreting the Meaning of Information for Others	Translating or explaining what information means and how it can be used.
Processing Information	Compiling, coding, categorizing, calculating, tabulating, auditing, or verifying information or data.
Coordinating the Work and Activities of Others	Getting members of a group to work together to accomplish tasks.
Training and Teaching Others	Identifying the educational needs of others, developing formal educational or training programs or classes, and teaching or instructing others.
Resolving Conflicts and Negotiating with Others	Handling complaints, settling disputes, and resolving grievances and conflicts, or otherwise negotiating with others.
Analyzing Data or Information	Identifying the underlying principles, reasons, or facts of information by breaking down information or data into separate parts.
Developing and Building Teams	Encouraging and building mutual trust, respect, and cooperation among team members.
Controlling Machines and Processes	Using either control mechanisms or direct physical activity to operate machines or processes (not including computers or vehicles).
Scheduling Work and Activities	Scheduling events, programs, and activities, as well as the work of others.
Estimating the Quantifiable Characteristics of Pro	Estimating sizes, distances, and quantities; or determining time, costs, resources, or materials needed to perform a work activity.
Coaching and Developing Others	Identifying the developmental needs of others and coaching, mentoring, or otherwise helping others to improve their knowledge or skills.
Thinking Creatively	Developing, designing, or creating new applications, ideas, relationships, systems, or products, including artistic contributions.

Communicating with Persons Outside Organization	Communicating with people outside the organization, representing the organization to customers, the public, government, and other external sources. This information can be exchanged in person, in writing, or by telephone or e-mail.
Developing Objectives and Strategies	Establishing long-range objectives and specifying the strategies and actions to achieve them.
Guiding, Directing, and Motivating Subordinates	Providing guidance and direction to subordinates, including setting performance standards and monitoring performance.
Provide Consultation and Advice to Others	Providing guidance and expert advice to management or other groups on technical, systems-, or process-related topics.
Performing Administrative Activities	Performing day-to-day administrative tasks such as maintaining information files and processing paperwork.
Monitoring and Controlling Resources	Monitoring and controlling resources and overseeing the spending of money.
Selling or Influencing Others	Convincing others to buy merchandise/goods or to otherwise change their minds or actions.
Interacting With Computers	Using computers and computer systems (including hardware and software) to program, write software, set up functions, enter data, or process information.
Operating Vehicles, Mechanized Devices, or Equipme	Running, maneuvering, navigating, or driving vehicles or mechanized equipment, such as forklifts, passenger vehicles, aircraft, or water craft.
Repairing and Maintaining Mechanical Equipment	Servicing, repairing, adjusting, and testing machines, devices, moving parts, and equipment that operate primarily on the basis of mechanical (not electronic) principles.
Staffing Organizational Units	Recruiting, interviewing, selecting, hiring, and promoting employees in an organization.
Drafting, Laying Out, and Specifying Technical Dev	Providing documentation, detailed instructions, drawings, or specifications to tell others about how devices, parts, equipment, or structures are to be fabricated, constructed, assembled, modified, or used.
Repairing and Maintaining Electronic Equipment	Servicing, repairing, calibrating, regulating, fine-tuning, or testing machines, devices, and equipment that operate primarily on the basis of electrical or electronic (not mechanical) principles.

Work_Context	Work_Context Definitions
Contact With Others	How much does this job require the worker to be in contact with others (face-to-face, by telephone, or otherwise) in order to perform it?
Physical Proximity	To what extent does this job require the worker to perform job tasks in close physical proximity to other people?
Work With Work Group or Team	How important is it to work with others in a group or team in this job?
Face-to-Face Discussions	How often do you have to have face-to-face discussions with individuals or teams in this job?
Telephone	How often do you have telephone conversations in this job?
Exposed to Disease or Infections	How often does this job require exposure to disease/infections?
Indoors, Environmentally Controlled	How often does this job require working indoors in environmentally controlled conditions?
Importance of Being Exact or Accurate	How important is being very exact or highly accurate in performing this job?
Deal With External Customers	How important is it to work with external customers or the public in this job?
Coordinate or Lead Others	How important is it to coordinate or lead others in accomplishing work activities in this job?
Spend Time Standing	How much does this job require standing?
Freedom to Make Decisions	How much decision making freedom, without supervision, does the job offer?
Structured versus Unstructured Work	To what extent is this job structured for the worker, rather than allowing the worker to determine tasks, priorities, and goals?
Time Pressure	How often does this job require the worker to meet strict deadlines?
Letters and Memos	How often does the job require written letters and memos?
Impact of Decisions on Co-workers or Company Resul	How do the decisions an employee makes impact the results of co-workers, clients or the company?
Spend Time Walking and Running	How much does this job require walking and running?
Frequency of Decision Making	How frequently is the worker required to make decisions that affect other people, the financial resources, and/or the image and reputation of the organization?
Responsible for Others' Health and Safety	How much responsibility is there for the health and safety of others in this job?

Deal With Unpleasant or Angry People	How frequently does the worker have to deal with unpleasant, angry, or discourteous individuals as part of the job requirements?
Spend Time Using Your Hands to Handle, Control, or	How much does this job require using your hands to handle, control, or feel objects, tools or controls?
Responsibility for Outcomes and Results	How responsible is the worker for work outcomes and results of other workers?
Spend Time Making Repetitive Motions	How much does this job require making repetitive motions?
Consequence of Error	How serious would the result usually be if the worker made a mistake that was not readily correctable?
Spend Time Bending or Twisting the Body	How much does this job require bending or twisting your body?
Cramped Work Space, Awkward Positions	How often does this job require working in cramped work spaces that requires getting into awkward positions?
Wear Common Protective or Safety Equipment such as	How much does this job require wearing common protective or safety equipment such as safety shoes, glasses, gloves, hard hats or life jackets?
Frequency of Conflict Situations	How often are there conflict situations the employee has to face in this job?
Importance of Repeating Same Tasks	How important is repeating the same physical activities (e.g., key entry) or mental activities (e.g., checking entries in a ledger) over and over, without stopping, to performing this job?
Exposed to Contaminants	How often does this job require working exposed to contaminants (such as pollutants, gases, dust or odors)?
Sounds, Noise Levels Are Distracting or Uncomforta	How often does this job require working exposed to sounds and noise levels that are distracting or uncomfortable?
Level of Competition	To what extent does this job require the worker to compete or to be aware of competitive pressures?
Spend Time Kneeling, Crouching, Stooping, or Crawl	How much does this job require kneeling, crouching, stooping or crawling?
Deal With Physically Aggressive People	How frequently does this job require the worker to deal with physical aggression of violent individuals?
Spend Time Sitting	How much does this job require sitting?
Electronic Mail	How often do you use electronic mail in this job?
Spend Time Keeping or Regaining Balance	How much does this job require keeping or regaining your balance?
Degree of Automation	How automated is the job?
Public Speaking	How often do you have to perform public speaking in this job?
Wear Specialized Protective or Safety Equipment su	How much does this job require wearing specialized protective or safety equipment such as breathing apparatus, safety harness, full protection suits, or radiation protection?
Exposed to Hazardous Conditions	How often does this job require exposure to hazardous conditions?
Very Hot or Cold Temperatures	How often does this job require working in very hot (above 90 F degrees) or very cold (below 32 F degrees) temperatures?
Exposed to Minor Burns, Cuts, Bites, or Stings	How often does this job require exposure to minor burns, cuts, bites, or stings?
Outdoors, Exposed to Weather	How often does this job require working outdoors, exposed to all weather conditions?
Extremely Bright or Inadequate Lighting	How often does this job require working in extremely bright or inadequate lighting conditions?
Pace Determined by Speed of Equipment	How important is it to this job that the pace is determined by the speed of equipment or machinery? (This does not refer to keeping busy at all times on this job.)
In an Enclosed Vehicle or Equipment	How often does this job require working in a closed vehicle or equipment (e.g., car)?
Indoors, Not Environmentally Controlled	How often does this job require working indoors in non-controlled environmental conditions (e.g., warehouse without heat)?
Outdoors, Under Cover	How often does this job require working outdoors, under cover (e.g., structure with roof but no walls)?
In an Open Vehicle or Equipment	How often does this job require working in an open vehicle or equipment (e.g., tractor)?
Exposed to Hazardous Equipment	How often does this job require exposure to hazardous equipment?
Spend Time Climbing Ladders, Scaffolds, or Poles	How much does this job require climbing ladders, scaffolds, or poles?
Exposed to High Places	How often does this job require exposure to high places?
Exposed to Radiation	How often does this job require exposure to radiation?
Exposed to Whole Body Vibration	How often does this job require exposure to whole body vibration (e.g., operate a jackhammer)?

Job Zone Component	Job Zone Component Definitions
Title	Job Zone Two: Some Preparation Needed
	Some previous work-related skill, knowledge, or experience may be helpful in these occupations, but usually is not needed.
Overall Experience	For example, a drywall installer might benefit from experience installing drywall, but an inexperienced person could still learn to be an installer with little difficulty.
Job Training	Employees in these occupations need anywhere from a few months to one year of working with experienced employees. These occupations often involve using your knowledge and skills to help others. Examples include drywall installers, fire inspectors, flight attendants, pharmacy technicians, salespersons (retail), and tellers.
Job Zone Examples	
SVP Range	(4.0 to < 6.0)
	These occupations usually require a high school diploma and may require some vocational training or job-related course work. In some cases, an associate's or bachelor's degree could be needed.
Education	

Work_Styles	Work_Styles Definitions
Self Control	Job requires maintaining composure, keeping emotions in check, controlling anger, and avoiding aggressive behavior, even in very difficult situations.
Dependability	Job requires being reliable, responsible, and dependable, and fulfilling obligations.
Cooperation	Job requires being pleasant with others on the job and displaying a good-natured, cooperative attitude.
Concern for Others	Job requires being sensitive to others' needs and feelings and being understanding and helpful on the job.
Social Orientation	Job requires preferring to work with others rather than alone, and being personally connected with others on the job.
Stress Tolerance	Job requires accepting criticism and dealing calmly and effectively with high stress situations.
Integrity	Job requires being honest and ethical.
Adaptability/Flexibility	Job requires being open to change (positive or negative) and to considerable variety in the workplace.
Independence	Job requires developing one's own ways of doing things, guiding oneself with little or no supervision, and depending on oneself to get things done.
Attention to Detail	Job requires being careful about detail and thorough in completing work tasks.
Initiative	Job requires a willingness to take on responsibilities and challenges.
Persistence	Job requires persistence in the face of obstacles.
Leadership	Job requires a willingness to lead, take charge, and offer opinions and direction.
Innovation	Job requires creativity and alternative thinking to develop new ideas for and answers to work-related problems.
Achievement/Effort	Job requires establishing and maintaining personally challenging achievement goals and exerting effort toward mastering tasks.
Analytical Thinking	Job requires analyzing information and using logic to address work-related issues and problems.

31-9011.00 - Massage Therapists

Massage customers for hygienic or remedial purposes.

Tasks

1) Use complementary aids, such as infrared lamps, wet compresses, ice, and whirlpool baths in order to promote clients' recovery, relaxation and well-being.

2) Treat clients in own offices, or travel to clients' offices and homes.

3) Consult with other health care professionals such as physiotherapists, chiropractors, physicians and psychologists in order to develop treatment plans for clients.

4) Prepare and blend oils, and apply the blends to clients' skin.

5) Confer with clients about their medical histories and any problems with stress and/or pain in order to determine whether massage would be helpful.

6) Assess clients' soft tissue condition, joint quality and function, muscle strength, and range of motion.

7) Provide clients with guidance and information about techniques for postural improvement, and stretching, strengthening, relaxation and rehabilitative exercises.

8) Apply finger and hand pressure to specific points of the body.

9) Massage and knead the muscles and soft tissues of the human body in order to provide courses of treatment for medical conditions and injuries or wellness maintenance.

10) Develop and propose client treatment plans that specify which types of massage are to be used.

11) Refer clients to other types of therapists when necessary.

31-9091.00 - Dental Assistants

Assist dentist, set up patient and equipment, and keep records.

Tasks

1) Expose dental diagnostic x-rays.

2) Assist dentist in management of medical and dental emergencies.

3) Instruct patients in oral hygiene and plaque control programs.

4) Make preliminary impressions for study casts and occlusal registrations for mounting study casts.

5) Record treatment information in patient records.

6) Pour, trim, and polish study casts.

7) Clean and polish removable appliances.

8) Take and record medical and dental histories and vital signs of patients.

9) Schedule appointments, prepare bills and receive payment for dental services, complete insurance forms, and maintain records, manually or using computer.

10) Apply protective coating of fluoride to teeth.

11) Fabricate temporary restorations and custom impressions from preliminary impressions.

12) Clean teeth, using dental instruments.

13) Prepare patient, sterilize and disinfect instruments, set up instrument trays, prepare materials, and assist dentist during dental procedures.

Knowledge	Knowledge Definitions
Medicine and Dentistry	Knowledge of the information and techniques needed to diagnose and treat human injuries, diseases, and deformities. This includes symptoms, treatment alternatives, drug properties and interactions, and preventive health-care measures.
Customer and Personal Service	Knowledge of principles and processes for providing customer and personal services. This includes customer needs assessment, meeting quality standards for services, and evaluation of customer satisfaction.
English Language	Knowledge of the structure and content of the English language including the meaning and spelling of words, rules of composition, and grammar.
Clerical	Knowledge of administrative and clerical procedures and systems such as word processing, managing files and records, stenography and transcription, designing forms, and other office procedures and terminology.
Chemistry	Knowledge of the chemical composition, structure, and properties of substances and of the chemical processes and transformations that they undergo. This includes uses of chemicals and their interactions, danger signs, production techniques, and disposal methods.
Computers and Electronics	Knowledge of circuit boards, processors, chips, electronic equipment, and computer hardware and software, including applications and programming.
Psychology	Knowledge of human behavior and performance; individual differences in ability, personality, and interests; learning and motivation; psychological research methods; and the assessment and treatment of behavioral and affective disorders.
Public Safety and Security	Knowledge of relevant equipment, policies, procedures, and strategies to promote effective local, state, or national security operations for the protection of people, data, property, and institutions.
Mechanical	Knowledge of machines and tools, including their designs, uses, repair, and maintenance.
Communications and Media	Knowledge of media production, communication, and dissemination techniques and methods. This includes alternative ways to inform and entertain via written, oral, and visual media.
Administration and Management	Knowledge of business and management principles involved in strategic planning, resource allocation, human resources modeling, leadership technique, production methods, and coordination of people and resources.
Production and Processing	Knowledge of raw materials, production processes, quality control, costs, and other techniques for maximizing the effective manufacture and distribution of goods.
Economics and Accounting	Knowledge of economic and accounting principles and practices, the financial markets, banking and the analysis and reporting of financial data.
Education and Training	Knowledge of principles and methods for curriculum and training design, teaching and instruction for individuals and groups, and the measurement of training effects.
Law and Government	Knowledge of laws, legal codes, court procedures, precedents, government regulations, executive orders, agency rules, and the democratic political process.
Biology	Knowledge of plant and animal organisms, their tissues, cells, functions, interdependencies, and interactions with each other and the environment.
Sales and Marketing	Knowledge of principles and methods for showing, promoting, and selling products or services. This includes marketing strategy and tactics, product demonstration, sales techniques, and sales control systems.
Engineering and Technology	Knowledge of the practical application of engineering science and technology. This includes applying principles, techniques, procedures, and equipment to the design and production of various goods and services.
Mathematics	Knowledge of arithmetic, algebra, geometry, calculus, statistics, and their applications.
Design	Knowledge of design techniques, tools, and principles involved in production of precision technical plans, blueprints, drawings, and models.
Foreign Language	Knowledge of the structure and content of a foreign (non-English) language including the meaning and spelling of words, rules of composition and grammar, and pronunciation.
Sociology and Anthropology	Knowledge of group behavior and dynamics, societal trends and influences, human migrations, ethnicity, cultures and their history and origins.
Philosophy and Theology	Knowledge of different philosophical systems and religions. This includes their basic principles, values, ethics, ways of thinking, customs, practices, and their impact on human culture.
Telecommunications	Knowledge of transmission, broadcasting, switching, control, and operation of telecommunications systems.
Personnel and Human Resources	Knowledge of principles and procedures for personnel recruitment, selection, training, compensation and benefits, labor relations and negotiation, and personnel information systems.
Therapy and Counseling	Knowledge of principles, methods, and procedures for diagnosis, treatment, and rehabilitation of physical and mental dysfunctions, and for career counseling and guidance.
Transportation	Knowledge of principles and methods for moving people or goods by air, rail, sea, or road, including the relative costs and benefits.
Physics	Knowledge and prediction of physical principles, laws, their interrelationships, and applications to understanding fluid, material, and atmospheric dynamics, and mechanical, electrical, atomic and sub- atomic structures and processes.
History and Archeology	Knowledge of historical events and their causes, indicators, and effects on civilizations and cultures.
Geography	Knowledge of principles and methods for describing the features of land, sea, and air masses, including their physical characteristics, locations, interrelationships, and distribution of plant, animal, and human life.
Building and Construction	Knowledge of materials, methods, and the tools involved in the construction or repair of houses, buildings, or other structures such as highways and roads.
Fine Arts	Knowledge of the theory and techniques required to compose, produce, and perform works of music, dance, visual arts, drama, and sculpture.
Food Production	Knowledge of techniques and equipment for planting, growing, and harvesting food products (both plant and animal) for consumption, including storage/handling techniques.

Skills	Skills Definitions
Active Listening	Giving full attention to what other people are saying, taking time to understand the points being made, asking questions as appropriate, and not interrupting at inappropriate times.
Reading Comprehension	Understanding written sentences and paragraphs in work related documents.
Speaking	Talking to others to convey information effectively.
Coordination	Adjusting actions in relation to others' actions.
Social Perceptiveness	Being aware of others' reactions and understanding why they react as they do.
Equipment Maintenance	Performing routine maintenance on equipment and determining when and what kind of maintenance is needed.
Active Learning	Understanding the implications of new information for both current and future problem-solving and decision-making.
Time Management	Managing one's own time and the time of others.
Instructing	Teaching others how to do something.
Equipment Selection	Determining the kind of tools and equipment needed to do a job.
Writing	Communicating effectively in writing as appropriate for the needs of the audience.
Learning Strategies	Selecting and using training/instructional methods and procedures appropriate for the situation when learning or teaching new things.
Management of Material Resources	Obtaining and seeing to the appropriate use of equipment, facilities, and materials needed to do certain work.
Troubleshooting	Determining causes of operating errors and deciding what to do about it.
Monitoring	Monitoring/Assessing performance of yourself, other individuals, or organizations to make improvements or take corrective action.
Service Orientation	Actively looking for ways to help people.
Judgment and Decision Making	Considering the relative costs and benefits of potential actions to choose the most appropriate one.
Critical Thinking	Using logic and reasoning to identify the strengths and weaknesses of alternative solutions, conclusions or approaches to problems.
Operation and Control	Controlling operations of equipment or systems.
Persuasion	Persuading others to change their minds or behavior.
Operation Monitoring	Watching gauges, dials, or other indicators to make sure a machine is working properly.
Complex Problem Solving	Identifying complex problems and reviewing related information to develop and evaluate options and implement solutions.
Repairing	Repairing machines or systems using the needed tools.
Operations Analysis	Analyzing needs and product requirements to create a design.
Installation	Installing equipment, machines, wiring, or programs to meet specifications.
Quality Control Analysis	Conducting tests and inspections of products, services, or processes to evaluate quality or performance.
Science	Using scientific rules and methods to solve problems.
Technology Design	Generating or adapting equipment and technology to serve user needs.
Negotiation	Bringing others together and trying to reconcile differences.
Mathematics	Using mathematics to solve problems.
Management of Personnel Resources	Motivating, developing, and directing people as they work, identifying the best people for the job.
Management of Financial Resources	Determining how money will be spent to get the work done, and accounting for these expenditures.
Systems Analysis	Determining how a system should work and how changes in conditions, operations, and the environment will affect outcomes.
Systems Evaluation	Identifying measures or indicators of system performance and the actions needed to improve or correct performance, relative to the goals of the system.
Programming	Writing computer programs for various purposes.

Ability	Ability Definitions
Oral Expression	The ability to communicate information and ideas in speaking so others will understand.
Oral Comprehension	The ability to listen to and understand information and ideas presented through spoken words and sentences.
Near Vision	The ability to see details at close range (within a few feet of the observer).
Written Expression	The ability to communicate information and ideas in writing so others will understand.
Information Ordering	The ability to arrange things or actions in a certain order or pattern according to a specific rule or set of rules (e.g., patterns of numbers, letters, words, pictures, mathematical operations).
Speech Clarity	The ability to speak clearly so others can understand you.
Arm-Hand Steadiness	The ability to keep your hand and arm steady while moving your arm or while holding your arm and hand in one position.
Speech Recognition	The ability to identify and understand the speech of another person.
Finger Dexterity	The ability to make precisely coordinated movements of the fingers of one or both hands to grasp, manipulate, or assemble very small objects.
Selective Attention	The ability to concentrate on a task over a period of time without being distracted.
Problem Sensitivity	The ability to tell when something is wrong or is likely to go wrong. It does not involve solving the problem, only recognizing there is a problem.
Written Comprehension	The ability to read and understand information and ideas presented in writing.
Flexibility of Closure	The ability to identify or detect a known pattern (a figure, object, word, or sound) that is hidden in other distracting material.
Manual Dexterity	The ability to quickly move your hand, your hand together with your arm, or your two hands to grasp, manipulate, or assemble objects.
Time Sharing	The ability to shift back and forth between two or more activities or sources of information (such as speech, sounds, touch, or other sources).
Control Precision	The ability to quickly and repeatedly adjust the controls of a machine or a vehicle to exact positions.
Category Flexibility	The ability to generate or use different sets of rules for combining or grouping things in different ways.
Deductive Reasoning	The ability to apply general rules to specific problems to produce answers that make sense.
Inductive Reasoning	The ability to combine pieces of information to form general rules or conclusions (includes finding a relationship among seemingly unrelated events).
Memorization	The ability to remember information such as words, numbers, pictures, and procedures.
Extent Flexibility	The ability to bend, stretch, twist, or reach with your body, arms, and/or legs.
Far Vision	The ability to see details at a distance.
Multilimb Coordination	The ability to coordinate two or more limbs (for example, two arms, two legs, or one leg and one arm) while sitting, standing, or lying down. It does not involve performing the activities while the whole body is in motion.
Trunk Strength	The ability to use your abdominal and lower back muscles to support part of the body repeatedly or continuously over time without 'giving out' or fatiguing.
Perceptual Speed	The ability to quickly and accurately compare similarities and differences among sets of letters, numbers, objects, pictures, or patterns. The things to be compared may be presented at the same time or one after the other. This ability also includes comparing a presented object with a remembered object.
Depth Perception	The ability to judge which of several objects is closer or farther away from you, or to judge the distance between you and an object.
Visual Color Discrimination	The ability to match or detect differences between colors, including shades of color and brightness.
Auditory Attention	The ability to focus on a single source of sound in the presence of other distracting sounds.
Visualization	The ability to imagine how something will look after it is moved around or when its parts are moved or rearranged.
Mathematical Reasoning	The ability to choose the right mathematical methods or formulas to solve a problem.
Speed of Closure	The ability to quickly make sense of, combine, and organize information into meaningful patterns.
Originality	The ability to come up with unusual or clever ideas about a given topic or situation, or to develop creative ways to solve a problem.
Number Facility	The ability to add, subtract, multiply, or divide quickly and correctly.
Hearing Sensitivity	The ability to detect or tell the differences between sounds that vary in pitch and loudness.
Fluency of Ideas	The ability to come up with a number of ideas about a topic (the number of ideas is important, not their quality, correctness, or creativity).

653

Rate Control	The ability to time your movements or the movement of a piece of equipment in anticipation of changes in the speed and/or direction of a moving object or scene.
Wrist-Finger Speed	The ability to make fast, simple, repeated movements of the fingers, hands, and wrists.
Static Strength	The ability to exert maximum muscle force to lift, push, pull, or carry objects.
Response Orientation	The ability to choose quickly between two or more movements in response to two or more different signals (lights, sounds, pictures). It includes the speed with which the correct response is started with the hand, foot, or other body part.
Stamina	The ability to exert yourself physically over long periods of time without getting winded or out of breath.
Glare Sensitivity	The ability to see objects in the presence of glare or bright lighting.
Gross Body Coordination	The ability to coordinate the movement of your arms, legs, and torso together when the whole body is in motion.
Dynamic Strength	The ability to exert muscle force repeatedly or continuously over time. This involves muscular endurance and resistance to muscle fatigue.
Reaction Time	The ability to quickly respond (with the hand, finger, or foot) to a signal (sound, light, picture) when it appears.
Speed of Limb Movement	The ability to quickly move the arms and legs.
Gross Body Equilibrium	The ability to keep or regain your body balance or stay upright when in an unstable position.
Dynamic Flexibility	The ability to quickly and repeatedly bend, stretch, twist, or reach out with your body, arms, and/or legs.
Explosive Strength	The ability to use short bursts of muscle force to propel oneself (as in jumping or sprinting), or to throw an object.
Peripheral Vision	The ability to see objects or movement of objects to one's side when the eyes are looking ahead.
Night Vision	The ability to see under low light conditions.
Sound Localization	The ability to tell the direction from which a sound originated.
Spatial Orientation	The ability to know your location in relation to the environment or to know where other objects are in relation to you.

Work_Activity	**Work_Activity Definitions**
Assisting and Caring for Others	Providing personal assistance, medical attention, emotional support, or other personal care to others such as coworkers, customers, or patients.
Communicating with Supervisors, Peers, or Subordin	Providing information to supervisors, co-workers, and subordinates by telephone, in written form, e-mail, or in person.
Documenting/Recording Information	Entering, transcribing, recording, storing, or maintaining information in written or electronic/magnetic form.
Developing and Building Teams	Encouraging and building mutual trust, respect, and cooperation among team members.
Getting Information	Observing, receiving, and otherwise obtaining information from all relevant sources.
Training and Teaching Others	Identifying the educational needs of others, developing formal educational or training programs or classes, and teaching or instructing others.
Performing for or Working Directly with the Public	Performing for people or dealing directly with the public. This includes serving customers in restaurants and stores, and receiving clients or guests.
Coordinating the Work and Activities of Others	Getting members of a group to work together to accomplish tasks.
Identifying Objects, Actions, and Events	Identifying information by categorizing, estimating, recognizing differences or similarities, and detecting changes in circumstances or events.
Interpreting the Meaning of Information for Others	Translating or explaining what information means and how it can be used.
Processing Information	Compiling, coding, categorizing, calculating, tabulating, auditing, or verifying information or data.
Monitor Processes, Materials, or Surroundings	Monitoring and reviewing information from materials, events, or the environment, to detect or assess problems.
Organizing, Planning, and Prioritizing Work	Developing specific goals and plans to prioritize, organize, and accomplish your work.
Communicating with Persons Outside Organization	Communicating with people outside the organization, representing the organization to customers, the public, government, and other external sources. This information can be exchanged in person, in writing, or by telephone or e-mail.
Resolving Conflicts and Negotiating with Others	Handling complaints, settling disputes, and resolving grievances and conflicts, or otherwise negotiating with others.
Performing Administrative Activities	Performing day-to-day administrative tasks such as maintaining information files and processing paperwork.

Updating and Using Relevant Knowledge	Keeping up-to-date technically and applying new knowledge to your job.
Handling and Moving Objects	Using hands and arms in handling, installing, positioning, and moving materials, and manipulating things.
Inspecting Equipment, Structures, or Material	Inspecting equipment, structures, or materials to identify the cause of errors or other problems or defects.
Establishing and Maintaining Interpersonal Relatio	Developing constructive and cooperative working relationships with others, and maintaining them over time.
Making Decisions and Solving Problems	Analyzing information and evaluating results to choose the best solution and solve problems.
Evaluating Information to Determine Compliance wit	Using relevant information and individual judgment to determine whether events or processes comply with laws, regulations, or standards.
Provide Consultation and Advice to Others	Providing guidance and expert advice to management or other groups on technical, systems-, or process-related topics.
Scheduling Work and Activities	Scheduling events, programs, and activities, as well as the work of others.
Interacting With Computers	Using computers and computer systems (including hardware and software) to program, write software, set up functions, enter data, or process information.
Guiding, Directing, and Motivating Subordinates	Providing guidance and direction to subordinates, including setting performance standards and monitoring performance.
Judging the Qualities of Things, Services, or Peop	Assessing the value, importance, or quality of things or people.
Thinking Creatively	Developing, designing, or creating new applications, ideas, relationships, systems, or products, including artistic contributions.
Controlling Machines and Processes	Using either control mechanisms or direct physical activity to operate machines or processes (not including computers or vehicles).
Estimating the Quantifiable Characteristics of Pro	Estimating sizes, distances, and quantities; or determining time, costs, resources, or materials needed to perform a work activity.
Coaching and Developing Others	Identifying the developmental needs of others and coaching, mentoring, or otherwise helping others to improve their knowledge or skills.
Selling or Influencing Others	Convincing others to buy merchandise/goods or to otherwise change their minds or actions.
Analyzing Data or Information	Identifying the underlying principles, reasons, or facts of information by breaking down information or data into separate parts.
Performing General Physical Activities	Performing physical activities that require considerable use of your arms and legs and moving your whole body, such as climbing, lifting, balancing, walking, stooping, and handling of materials.
Monitoring and Controlling Resources	Monitoring and controlling resources and overseeing the spending of money.
Developing Objectives and Strategies	Establishing long-range objectives and specifying the strategies and actions to achieve them.
Staffing Organizational Units	Recruiting, interviewing, selecting, hiring, and promoting employees in an organization.
Repairing and Maintaining Electronic Equipment	Servicing, repairing, calibrating, regulating, fine-tuning, or testing machines, devices, and equipment that operate primarily on the basis of electrical or electronic (not mechanical) principles.
Repairing and Maintaining Mechanical Equipment	Servicing, repairing, adjusting, and testing machines, devices, moving parts, and equipment that operate primarily on the basis of mechanical (not electronic) principles.
Drafting, Laying Out, and Specifying Technical Dev	Providing documentation, detailed instructions, drawings, or specifications to tell others about how devices, parts, equipment, or structures are to be fabricated, constructed, assembled, modified, maintained, or used.
Operating Vehicles, Mechanized Devices, or Equipme	Running, maneuvering, navigating, or driving vehicles or mechanized equipment, such as forklifts, passenger vehicles, aircraft, or water craft.

Work_Context	**Work_Context Definitions**
Contact With Others	How much does this job require the worker to be in contact with others (face-to-face, by telephone, or otherwise) in order to perform it?
Physical Proximity	To what extent does this job require the worker to perform job tasks in close physical proximity to other people?
Wear Common Protective or Safety Equipment such as	How much does this job require wearing common protective or safety equipment such as safety shoes, glasses, gloves, hard hats or live jackets?

Spend Time Using Your Hands to Handle, Control, or	How much does this job require using your hands to handle, control, or feel objects, tools or controls?
Indoors, Environmentally Controlled	How often does this job require working indoors in environmentally controlled conditions?
Exposed to Disease or Infections	How often does this job require exposure to disease/infections?
Work With Work Group or Team	How important is it to work with others in a group or team in this job?
Face-to-Face Discussions	How often do you have to have face-to-face discussions with individuals or teams in this job?
Importance of Being Exact or Accurate	How important is being very exact or highly accurate in performing this job?
Spend Time Making Repetitive Motions	How much does this job require making repetitive motions?
Telephone	How often do you have telephone conversations in this job?
Frequency of Decision Making	How frequently is the worker required to make decisions that affect other people, the financial resources, and/or the image and reputation of the organization?
Exposed to Contaminants	How often does this job require working exposed to contaminants (such as pollutants, gases, dust or odors)?
Deal With External Customers	How important is it to work with external customers or the public in this job?
Structured versus Unstructured Work	To what extent is this job structured for the worker, rather than allowing the worker to determine tasks, priorities, and goals?
Responsible for Others' Health and Safety	How much responsibility is there for the health and safety of others in this job?
Time Pressure	How often does this job require the worker to meet strict deadlines?
Spend Time Bending or Twisting the Body	How much does this job require bending or twisting your body?
Freedom to Make Decisions	How much decision making freedom, without supervision, does the job offer?
Impact of Decisions on Co-workers or Company Resul	How do the decisions an employee makes impact the results of co-workers, clients or the company?
Exposed to Radiation	How often does this job require exposure to radiation?
Spend Time Sitting	How much does this job require sitting?
Importance of Repeating Same Tasks	How important is repeating the same physical activities (e.g., key entry) or mental activities (e.g., checking entries in a ledger) over and over, without stopping, to performing this job?
Sounds, Noise Levels Are Distracting or Uncomforta	How often does this job require working exposed to sounds and noise levels that are distracting or uncomfortable?
Spend Time Standing	How much does this job require standing?
Coordinate or Lead Others	How important is it to coordinate or lead others in accomplishing work activities in this job?
Deal With Unpleasant or Angry People	How frequently does the worker have to deal with unpleasant, angry, or discourteous individuals as part of the job requirements?
Cramped Work Space, Awkward Positions	How often does this job require working in cramped work spaces that requires getting into awkward positions?
Level of Competition	To what extent does this job require the worker to compete or to be aware of competitive pressures?
Spend Time Walking and Running	How much does this job require walking and running?
Extremely Bright or Inadequate Lighting	How often does this job require working in extremely bright or inadequate lighting conditions?
Frequency of Conflict Situations	How often are there conflict situations the employee has to face in this job?
Responsibility for Outcomes and Results	How responsible is the worker for work outcomes and results of other workers?
Letters and Memos	How often does the job require written letters and memos?
Exposed to Minor Burns, Cuts, Bites, or Stings	How often does this job require exposure to minor burns, cuts, bites, or stings?
Exposed to Hazardous Conditions	How often does this job require exposure to hazardous conditions?
Degree of Automation	How automated is the job?
Consequence of Error	How serious would the result usually be if the worker made a mistake that was not readily correctable?
Exposed to Hazardous Equipment	How often does this job require exposure to hazardous equipment?
Spend Time Keeping or Regaining Balance	How much does this job require keeping or regaining your balance?
Spend Time Kneeling, Crouching, Stooping, or Crawl	How much does this job require kneeling, crouching, stooping or crawling?
Deal With Physically Aggressive People	How frequently does this job require the worker to deal with physical aggression of violent individuals?

Very Hot or Cold Temperatures	How often does this job require working in very hot (above 90 F degrees) or very cold (below 32 F degrees) temperatures?
Pace Determined by Speed of Equipment	How important is it to this job that the pace is determined by the speed of equipment or machinery? (This does not refer to keeping busy at all times on this job.)
Public Speaking	How often do you have to perform public speaking in this job?
Wear Specialized Protective or Safety Equipment su	How much does this job require wearing specialized protective or safety equipment such as breathing apparatus, safety harness, full protection suits, or radiation protection?
Spend Time Climbing Ladders, Scaffolds, or Poles	How much does this job require climbing ladders, scaffolds, or poles?
Electronic Mail	How often do you use electronic mail in this job?
Exposed to High Places	How often does this job require exposure to high places?
In an Enclosed Vehicle or Equipment	How often does this job require working in a closed vehicle or equipment (e.g., car)?
In an Open Vehicle or Equipment	How often does this job require working in an open vehicle or equipment (e.g., tractor)?
Outdoors, Under Cover	How often does this job require working outdoors, under cover (e.g., structure with roof but no walls)?
Outdoors, Exposed to Weather	How often does this job require working outdoors, exposed to all weather conditions?
Indoors, Not Environmentally Controlled	How often does this job require working indoors in non-controlled environmental conditions (e.g., warehouse without heat)?
Exposed to Whole Body Vibration	How often does this job require exposure to whole body vibration (e.g., operate a jackhammer)?

Job Zone Component	Job Zone Component Definitions
Title	Job Zone Two: Some Preparation Needed
Overall Experience	Some previous work-related skill, knowledge, or experience may be helpful in these occupations, but usually is not needed. For example, a drywall installer might benefit from experience installing drywall, but an inexperienced person could still learn to be an installer with little difficulty.
Job Training	Employees in these occupations need anywhere from a few months to one year of working with experienced employees. These occupations often involve using your knowledge and skills to help others. Examples include drywall installers, fire inspectors, flight attendants, pharmacy technicians, salespersons (retail), and tellers.
Job Zone Examples	
SVP Range	(4.0 to < 6.0)
Education	These occupations usually require a high school diploma and may require some vocational training or job-related course work. In some cases, an associate's or bachelor's degree could be needed.

Work_Styles	Work_Styles Definitions
Attention to Detail	Job requires being careful about detail and thorough in completing work tasks.
Dependability	Job requires being reliable, responsible, and dependable, and fulfilling obligations.
Self Control	Job requires maintaining composure, keeping emotions in check, controlling anger, and avoiding aggressive behavior, even in very difficult situations.
Cooperation	Job requires being pleasant with others on the job and displaying a good-natured, cooperative attitude.
Social Orientation	Job requires preferring to work with others rather than alone, and being personally connected with others on the job.
Concern for Others	Job requires being sensitive to others' needs and feelings and being understanding and helpful on the job.
Integrity	Job requires being honest and ethical.
Initiative	Job requires a willingness to take on responsibilities and challenges.
Adaptability/Flexibility	Job requires being open to change (positive or negative) and to considerable variety in the workplace.
Stress Tolerance	Job requires accepting criticism and dealing calmly and effectively with high stress situations.
Independence	Job requires developing one's own ways of doing things, guiding oneself with little or no supervision, and depending on oneself to get things done.
Leadership	Job requires a willingness to lead, take charge, and offer opinions and direction.

Achievement/Effort	Job requires establishing and maintaining personally challenging achievement goals and exerting effort toward mastering tasks.
Persistence	Job requires persistence in the face of obstacles.
Innovation	Job requires creativity and alternative thinking to develop new ideas for and answers to work-related problems.
Analytical Thinking	Job requires analyzing information and using logic to address work-related issues and problems.

31-9092.00 - Medical Assistants

Perform administrative and certain clinical duties under the direction of physician. Administrative duties may include scheduling appointments, maintaining medical records, billing, and coding for insurance purposes. Clinical duties may include taking and recording vital signs and medical histories, preparing patients for examination, drawing blood, and administering medications as directed by physician.

Tasks

1) Help physicians examine and treat patients, handing them instruments and materials or performing such tasks as giving injections and removing sutures.

2) Clean and sterilize instruments and dispose of contaminated supplies.

3) Show patients to examination rooms and prepare them for the physician.

4) Prepare treatment rooms for patient examinations, keeping the rooms neat and clean.

5) Record patients' medical history, vital statistics and information such as test results in medical records.

6) Perform general office duties such as answering telephones, taking dictation and completing insurance forms.

7) Contact medical facilities or departments to schedule patients for tests and/or admission.

8) Schedule appointments for patients.

9) Interview patients to obtain medical information and measure their vital signs, weight, and height.

10) Inventory and order medical, lab, and office supplies and equipment.

11) Greet and log in patients arriving at office or clinic.

12) Authorize drug refills and provide prescription information to pharmacies.

13) Collect blood, tissue or other laboratory specimens, log the specimens, and prepare them for testing.

14) Prepare and administer medications as directed by a physician.

15) Change dressings on wounds.

16) Operate x-ray, electrocardiogram (EKG), and other equipment to administer routine diagnostic tests.

17) Set up medical laboratory equipment.

18) Perform routine laboratory tests and sample analyses.

19) Keep financial records and perform other bookkeeping duties, such as handling credit and collections and mailing monthly statements to patients.

20) Give physiotherapy treatments, such as diathermy, galvanics, and hydrotherapy.

Knowledge	Knowledge Definitions
English Language	Knowledge of the structure and content of the English language including the meaning and spelling of words, rules of composition, and grammar.
Customer and Personal Service	Knowledge of principles and processes for providing customer and personal services. This includes customer needs assessment, meeting quality standards for services, and evaluation of customer satisfaction.
Medicine and Dentistry	Knowledge of the information and techniques needed to diagnose and treat human injuries, diseases, and deformities. This includes symptoms, treatment alternatives, drug properties and interactions, and preventive health-care measures.
Clerical	Knowledge of administrative and clerical procedures and systems such as word processing, managing files and records, stenography and transcription, designing forms, and other office procedures and terminology.
Therapy and Counseling	Knowledge of principles, methods, and procedures for diagnosis, treatment, and rehabilitation of physical and mental dysfunctions, and for career counseling and guidance.
Mathematics	Knowledge of arithmetic, algebra, geometry, calculus, statistics, and their applications.
Education and Training	Knowledge of principles and methods for curriculum and training design, teaching and instruction for individuals and groups, and the measurement of training effects.
Administration and Management	Knowledge of business and management principles involved in strategic planning, resource allocation, human resources modeling, leadership technique, production methods, and coordination of people and resources.
Public Safety and Security	Knowledge of relevant equipment, policies, procedures, and strategies to promote effective local, state, or national security operations for the protection of people, data, property, and institutions.
Psychology	Knowledge of human behavior and performance; individual differences in ability, personality, and interests; learning and motivation; psychological research methods; and the assessment and treatment of behavioral and affective disorders.
Telecommunications	Knowledge of transmission, broadcasting, switching, control, and operation of telecommunications systems.
Chemistry	Knowledge of the chemical composition, structure, and properties of substances and of the chemical processes and transformations that they undergo. This includes uses of chemicals and their interactions, danger signs, production techniques, and disposal methods.
Computers and Electronics	Knowledge of circuit boards, processors, chips, electronic equipment, and computer hardware and software, including applications and programming.
Biology	Knowledge of plant and animal organisms, their tissues, cells, functions, interdependencies, and interactions with each other and the environment.
Personnel and Human Resources	Knowledge of principles and procedures for personnel recruitment, selection, training, compensation and benefits, labor relations and negotiation, and personnel information systems.
Sales and Marketing	Knowledge of principles and methods for showing, promoting, and selling products or services. This includes marketing strategy and tactics, product demonstration, sales techniques, and sales control systems.
Law and Government	Knowledge of laws, legal codes, court procedures, precedents, government regulations, executive orders, agency rules, and the democratic political process.
Transportation	Knowledge of principles and methods for moving people or goods by air, rail, sea, or road, including the relative costs and benefits.
Economics and Accounting	Knowledge of economic and accounting principles and practices, the financial markets, banking and the analysis and reporting of financial data.
Foreign Language	Knowledge of the structure and content of a foreign (non-English) language including the meaning and spelling of words, rules of composition and grammar, and pronunciation.
Physics	Knowledge and prediction of physical principles, laws, their interrelationships, and applications to understanding fluid, material, and atmospheric dynamics, and mechanical, electrical, atomic and sub-atomic structures and processes.
Communications and Media	Knowledge of media production, communication, and dissemination techniques and methods. This includes alternative ways to inform and entertain via written, oral, and visual media.
Production and Processing	Knowledge of raw materials, production processes, quality control, costs, and other techniques for maximizing the effective manufacture and distribution of goods.
Engineering and Technology	Knowledge of the practical application of engineering science and technology. This includes applying principles, techniques, procedures, and equipment to the design and production of various goods and services.
Sociology and Anthropology	Knowledge of group behavior and dynamics, societal trends and influences, human migrations, ethnicity, cultures and their history and origins.
Geography	Knowledge of principles and methods for describing the features of land, sea, and air masses, including their physical characteristics, locations, interrelationships, and distribution of plant, animal, and human life.

Philosophy and Theology	Knowledge of different philosophical systems and religions. This includes their basic principles, values, ethics, ways of thinking, customs, practices, and their impact on human culture.
Mechanical	Knowledge of machines and tools, including their designs, uses, repair, and maintenance.
Design	Knowledge of design techniques, tools, and principles involved in production of precision technical plans, blueprints, drawings, and models.
Fine Arts	Knowledge of the theory and techniques required to compose, produce, and perform works of music, dance, visual arts, drama, and sculpture.
Building and Construction	Knowledge of materials, methods, and the tools involved in the construction or repair of houses, buildings, or other structures such as highways and roads.
Food Production	Knowledge of techniques and equipment for planting, growing, and harvesting food products (both plant and animal) for consumption, including storage/handling techniques.
History and Archeology	Knowledge of historical events and their causes, indicators, and effects on civilizations and cultures.

Skills	Skills Definitions
Active Listening	Giving full attention to what other people are saying, taking time to understand the points being made, asking questions as appropriate, and not interrupting at inappropriate times.
Speaking	Talking to others to convey information effectively.
Social Perceptiveness	Being aware of others' reactions and understanding why they react as they do.
Instructing	Teaching others how to do something.
Reading Comprehension	Understanding written sentences and paragraphs in work related documents.
Active Learning	Understanding the implications of new information for both current and future problem-solving and decision-making.
Service Orientation	Actively looking for ways to help people.
Time Management	Managing one's own time and the time of others.
Learning Strategies	Selecting and using training/instructional methods and procedures appropriate for the situation when learning or teaching new things.
Writing	Communicating effectively in writing as appropriate for the needs of the audience.
Monitoring	Monitoring/Assessing performance of yourself, other individuals, or organizations to make improvements or take corrective action.
Coordination	Adjusting actions in relation to others' actions.
Critical Thinking	Using logic and reasoning to identify the strengths and weaknesses of alternative solutions, conclusions or approaches to problems.
Troubleshooting	Determining causes of operating errors and deciding what to do about it.
Mathematics	Using mathematics to solve problems.
Operation Monitoring	Watching gauges, dials, or other indicators to make sure a machine is working properly.
Operation and Control	Controlling operations of equipment or systems.
Judgment and Decision Making	Considering the relative costs and benefits of potential actions to choose the most appropriate one.
Science	Using scientific rules and methods to solve problems.
Complex Problem Solving	Identifying complex problems and reviewing related information to develop and evaluate options and implement solutions.
Equipment Selection	Determining the kind of tools and equipment needed to do a job.
Negotiation	Bringing others together and trying to reconcile differences.
Persuasion	Persuading others to change their minds or behavior.
Quality Control Analysis	Conducting tests and inspections of products, services, or processes to evaluate quality or performance.
Equipment Maintenance	Performing routine maintenance on equipment and determining when and what kind of maintenance is needed.
Systems Analysis	Determining how a system should work and how changes in conditions, operations, and the environment will affect outcomes.
Systems Evaluation	Identifying measures or indicators of system performance and the actions needed to improve or correct performance, relative to the goals of the system.
Technology Design	Generating or adapting equipment and technology to serve user needs.
Operations Analysis	Analyzing needs and product requirements to create a design.

Management of Material Resources	Obtaining and seeing to the appropriate use of equipment, facilities, and materials needed to do certain work.
Management of Personnel Resources	Motivating, developing, and directing people as they work, identifying the best people for the job.
Installation	Installing equipment, machines, wiring, or programs to meet specifications.
Management of Financial Resources	Determining how money will be spent to get the work done, and accounting for these expenditures.
Repairing	Repairing machines or systems using the needed tools.
Programming	Writing computer programs for various purposes.

Ability	Ability Definitions
Oral Comprehension	The ability to listen to and understand information and ideas presented through spoken words and sentences.
Oral Expression	The ability to communicate information and ideas in speaking so others will understand.
Speech Clarity	The ability to speak clearly so others can understand you.
Near Vision	The ability to see details at close range (within a few feet of the observer).
Problem Sensitivity	The ability to tell when something is wrong or is likely to go wrong. It does not involve solving the problem, only recognizing there is a problem.
Information Ordering	The ability to arrange things or actions in a certain order or pattern according to a specific rule or set of rules (e.g., patterns of numbers, letters, words, pictures, mathematical operations).
Speech Recognition	The ability to identify and understand the speech of another person.
Written Comprehension	The ability to read and understand information and ideas presented in writing.
Written Expression	The ability to communicate information and ideas in writing so others will understand.
Deductive Reasoning	The ability to apply general rules to specific problems to produce answers that make sense.
Arm-Hand Steadiness	The ability to keep your hand and arm steady while moving your arm or while holding your arm and hand in one position.
Time Sharing	The ability to shift back and forth between two or more activities or sources of information (such as speech, sounds, touch, or other sources).
Trunk Strength	The ability to use your abdominal and lower back muscles to support part of the body repeatedly or continuously over time without 'giving out' or fatiguing.
Selective Attention	The ability to concentrate on a task over a period of time without being distracted.
Inductive Reasoning	The ability to combine pieces of information to form general rules or conclusions (includes finding a relationship among seemingly unrelated events).
Manual Dexterity	The ability to quickly move your hand, your hand together with your arm, or your two hands to grasp, manipulate, or assemble objects.
Memorization	The ability to remember information such as words, numbers, pictures, and procedures.
Multilimb Coordination	The ability to coordinate two or more limbs (for example, two arms, two legs, or one leg and one arm) while sitting, standing, or lying down. It does not involve performing the activities while the whole body is in motion.
Category Flexibility	The ability to generate or use different sets of rules for combining or grouping things in different ways.
Control Precision	The ability to quickly and repeatedly adjust the controls of a machine or a vehicle to exact positions.
Finger Dexterity	The ability to make precisely coordinated movements of the fingers of one or both hands to grasp, manipulate, or assemble very small objects.
Gross Body Coordination	The ability to coordinate the movement of your arms, legs, and torso together when the whole body is in motion.
Originality	The ability to come up with unusual or clever ideas about a given topic or situation, or to develop creative ways to solve a problem.
Extent Flexibility	The ability to bend, stretch, twist, or reach with your body, arms, and/or legs.
Visual Color Discrimination	The ability to match or detect differences between colors, including shades of color and brightness.
Static Strength	The ability to exert maximum muscle force to lift, push, pull, or carry objects.

Perceptual Speed	The ability to quickly and accurately compare similarities and differences among sets of letters, numbers, objects, pictures, or patterns. The things to be compared may be presented at the same time or one after the other. This ability also includes comparing a presented object with a remembered object.
Auditory Attention	The ability to focus on a single source of sound in the presence of other distracting sounds.
Depth Perception	The ability to judge which of several objects is closer or farther away from you, or to judge the distance between you and an object.
Stamina	The ability to exert yourself physically over long periods of time without getting winded or out of breath.
Visualization	The ability to imagine how something will look after it is moved around or when its parts are moved or rearranged.
Speed of Closure	The ability to quickly make sense of, combine, and organize information into meaningful patterns.
Fluency of Ideas	The ability to come up with a number of ideas about a topic (the number of ideas is important, not their quality, correctness, or creativity).
Far Vision	The ability to see details at a distance.
Flexibility of Closure	The ability to identify or detect a known pattern (a figure, object, word, or sound) that is hidden in other distracting material.
Mathematical Reasoning	The ability to choose the right mathematical methods or formulas to solve a problem.
Number Facility	The ability to add, subtract, multiply, or divide quickly and correctly.
Spatial Orientation	The ability to know your location in relation to the environment or to know where other objects are in relation to you.
Speed of Limb Movement	The ability to quickly move the arms and legs.
Hearing Sensitivity	The ability to detect or tell the differences between sounds that vary in pitch and loudness.
Dynamic Strength	The ability to exert muscle force repeatedly or continuously over time. This involves muscular endurance and resistance to muscle fatigue.
Reaction Time	The ability to quickly respond (with the hand, finger, or foot) to a signal (sound, light, picture) when it appears.
Response Orientation	The ability to choose quickly between two or more movements in response to two or more different signals (lights, sounds, pictures). It includes the speed with which the correct response is started with the hand, foot, or other body part.
Wrist-Finger Speed	The ability to make fast, simple, repeated movements of the fingers, hands, and wrists.
Gross Body Equilibrium	The ability to keep or regain your body balance or stay upright when in an unstable position.
Sound Localization	The ability to tell the direction from which a sound originated.
Glare Sensitivity	The ability to see objects in the presence of glare or bright lighting.
Night Vision	The ability to see under low light conditions.
Dynamic Flexibility	The ability to quickly and repeatedly bend, stretch, twist, or reach out with your body, arms, and/or legs.
Rate Control	The ability to time your movements or the movement of a piece of equipment in anticipation of changes in the speed and/or direction of a moving object or scene.
Explosive Strength	The ability to use short bursts of muscle force to propel oneself (as in jumping or sprinting), or to throw an object.
Peripheral Vision	The ability to see objects or movement of objects to one's side when the eyes are looking ahead.

Work_Activity	**Work_Activity Definitions**
Assisting and Caring for Others	Providing personal assistance, medical attention, emotional support, or other personal care to others such as coworkers, customers, or patients.
Getting Information	Observing, receiving, and otherwise obtaining information from all relevant sources.
Updating and Using Relevant Knowledge	Keeping up-to-date technically and applying new knowledge to your job.
Communicating with Supervisors, Peers, or Subordin	Providing information to supervisors, co-workers, and subordinates by telephone, in written form, e-mail, or in person.
Identifying Objects, Actions, and Events	Identifying information by categorizing, estimating, recognizing differences or similarities, and detecting changes in circumstances or events.
Evaluating Information to Determine Compliance wit	Using relevant information and individual judgment to determine whether events or processes comply with laws, regulations, or standards.

Establishing and Maintaining Interpersonal Relatio	Developing constructive and cooperative working relationships with others, and maintaining them over time.
Making Decisions and Solving Problems	Analyzing information and evaluating results to choose the best solution and solve problems.
Interpreting the Meaning of Information for Others	Translating or explaining what information means and how it can be used.
Documenting/Recording Information	Entering, transcribing, recording, storing, or maintaining information in written or electronic/magnetic form.
Organizing, Planning, and Prioritizing Work	Developing specific goals and plans to prioritize, organize, and accomplish your work.
Judging the Qualities of Things, Services, or Peop	Assessing the value, importance, or quality of things or people.
Performing General Physical Activities	Performing physical activities that require considerable use of your arms and legs and moving your whole body, such as climbing, lifting, balancing, walking, stooping, and handling of materials.
Performing for or Working Directly with the Public	Performing for people or dealing directly with the public. This includes serving customers in restaurants and stores, and receiving clients or guests.
Inspecting Equipment, Structures, or Material	Inspecting equipment, structures, or materials to identify the cause of errors or other problems or defects.
Processing Information	Compiling, coding, categorizing, calculating, tabulating, auditing, or verifying information or data.
Performing Administrative Activities	Performing day-to-day administrative tasks such as maintaining information files and processing paperwork.
Training and Teaching Others	Identifying the educational needs of others, developing formal educational or training programs or classes, and teaching or instructing others.
Analyzing Data or Information	Identifying the underlying principles, reasons, or facts of information by breaking down information or data into separate parts.
Monitor Processes, Materials, or Surroundings	Monitoring and reviewing information from materials, events, or the environment, to detect or assess problems.
Developing and Building Teams	Encouraging and building mutual trust, respect, and cooperation among team members.
Communicating with Persons Outside Organization	Communicating with people outside the organization, representing the organization to customers, the public, government, and other external sources. This information can be exchanged in person, in writing, or by telephone or e-mail.
Resolving Conflicts and Negotiating with Others	Handling complaints, settling disputes, and resolving grievances and conflicts, or otherwise negotiating with others.
Estimating the Quantifiable Characteristics of Pro	Estimating sizes, distances, and quantities; or determining time, costs, resources, or materials needed to perform a work activity.
Coaching and Developing Others	Identifying the developmental needs of others and coaching, mentoring, or otherwise helping others to improve their knowledge or skills.
Interacting With Computers	Using computers and computer systems (including hardware and software) to program, write software, set up functions, enter data, or process information.
Handling and Moving Objects	Using hands and arms in handling, installing, positioning, and moving materials, and manipulating things.
Scheduling Work and Activities	Scheduling events, programs, and activities, as well as the work of others.
Coordinating the Work and Activities of Others	Getting members of a group to work together to accomplish tasks.
Thinking Creatively	Developing, designing, or creating new applications, ideas, relationships, systems, or products, including artistic contributions.
Guiding, Directing, and Motivating Subordinates	Providing guidance and direction to subordinates, including setting performance standards and monitoring performance.
Provide Consultation and Advice to Others	Providing guidance and expert advice to management or other groups on technical, systems-, or process-related topics.
Developing Objectives and Strategies	Establishing long-range objectives and specifying the strategies and actions to achieve them.
Controlling Machines and Processes	Using either control mechanisms or direct physical activity to operate machines or processes (not including computers or vehicles).
Repairing and Maintaining Electronic Equipment	Servicing, repairing, calibrating, regulating, fine-tuning, or testing machines, devices, and equipment that operate primarily on the basis of electrical or electronic (not mechanical) principles.
Monitoring and Controlling Resources	Monitoring and controlling resources and overseeing the spending of money.
Selling or Influencing Others	Convincing others to buy merchandise/goods or to otherwise change their minds or actions.

Operating Vehicles, Mechanized Devices, or Equipme	Running, maneuvering, navigating, or driving vehicles or mechanized equipment, such as forklifts, passenger vehicles, aircraft, or water craft.
Repairing and Maintaining Mechanical Equipment	Servicing, repairing, adjusting, and testing machines, devices, moving parts, and equipment that operate primarily on the basis of mechanical (not electronic) principles.
Drafting, Laying Out, and Specifying Technical Dev	Providing documentation, detailed instructions, drawings, or specifications to tell others about how devices, parts, equipment, or structures are to be fabricated, constructed, assembled, modified, maintained, or used.
Staffing Organizational Units	Recruiting, interviewing, selecting, hiring, and promoting employees in an organization.

Work_Context	Work_Context Definitions
Indoors, Environmentally Controlled	How often does this job require working indoors in environmentally controlled conditions?
Physical Proximity	To what extent does this job require the worker to perform job tasks in close physical proximity to other people?
Telephone	How often do you have telephone conversations in this job?
Contact With Others	How much does this job require the worker to be in contact with others (face-to-face, by telephone, or otherwise) in order to perform it?
Work With Work Group or Team	How important is it to work with others in a group or team in this job?
Exposed to Disease or Infections	How often does this job require exposure to disease/infections?
Importance of Being Exact or Accurate	How important is being very exact or highly accurate in performing this job?
Deal With External Customers	How important is it to work with external customers or the public in this job?
Face-to-Face Discussions	How often do you have to have face-to-face discussions with individuals or teams in this job?
Wear Common Protective or Safety Equipment such as	How much does this job require wearing common protective or safety equipment such as safety shoes, glasses, gloves, hard hats or life jackets?
Deal With Unpleasant or Angry People	How frequently does the worker have to deal with unpleasant, angry, or discourteous individuals as part of the job requirements?
Structured versus Unstructured Work	To what extent is this job structured for the worker, rather than allowing the worker to determine tasks, priorities, and goals?
Responsible for Others' Health and Safety	How much responsibility is there for the health and safety of others in this job?
Spend Time Standing	How much does this job require standing?
Frequency of Decision Making	How frequently is the worker required to make decisions that affect other people, the financial resources, and/or the image and reputation of the organization?
Freedom to Make Decisions	How much decision making freedom, without supervision, does the job offer?
Coordinate or Lead Others	How important is it to coordinate or lead others in accomplishing work activities in this job?
Letters and Memos	How often does the job require written letters and memos?
Impact of Decisions on Co-workers or Company Resul	How do the decisions an employee makes impact the results of co-workers, clients or the company?
Frequency of Conflict Situations	How often are there conflict situations the employee has to face in this job?
Spend Time Using Your Hands to Handle, Control, or	How much does this job require using your hands to handle, control, or feel objects, tools or controls?
Time Pressure	How often does this job require the worker to meet strict deadlines?
Spend Time Walking and Running	How much does this job require walking and running?
Importance of Repeating Same Tasks	How important is repeating the same physical activities (e.g., key entry) or mental activities (e.g., checking entries in a ledger) over and over, without stopping, to performing this job?
Responsibility for Outcomes and Results	How responsible is the worker for work outcomes and results of other workers?
Consequence of Error	How serious would the result usually be if the worker made a mistake that was not readily correctable?
Spend Time Making Repetitive Motions	How much does this job require making repetitive motions?
Sounds, Noise Levels Are Distracting or Uncomforta	How often does this job require working exposed to sounds and noise levels that are distracting or uncomfortable?
Electronic Mail	How often do you use electronic mail in this job?
Level of Competition	To what extent does this job require the worker to compete or to be aware of competitive pressures?

Exposed to Contaminants	How often does this job require working exposed to contaminants (such as pollutants, gases, dust or odors)?
Spend Time Sitting	How much does this job require sitting?
Spend Time Kneeling, Crouching, Stooping, or Crawl	How much does this job require kneeling, crouching, stooping or crawling?
Cramped Work Space, Awkward Positions	How often does this job require working in cramped work spaces that requires getting into awkward positions?
Exposed to Minor Burns, Cuts, Bites, or Stings	How often does this job require exposure to minor burns, cuts, bites, or stings?
Deal With Physically Aggressive People	How frequently does this job require the worker to deal with physical aggression of violent individuals?
Degree of Automation	How automated is the job?
Spend Time Bending or Twisting the Body	How much does this job require bending or twisting your body?
Spend Time Keeping or Regaining Balance	How much does this job require keeping or regaining your balance?
Public Speaking	How often do you have to perform public speaking in this job?
Exposed to Hazardous Conditions	How often does this job require exposure to hazardous conditions?
Extremely Bright or Inadequate Lighting	How often does this job require working in extremely bright or inadequate lighting conditions?
Wear Specialized Protective or Safety Equipment su	How much does this job require wearing specialized protective or safety equipment such as breathing apparatus, safety harness, full protection suits, or radiation protection?
Exposed to Radiation	How often does this job require exposure to radiation?
Exposed to High Places	How often does this job require exposure to high places?
Very Hot or Cold Temperatures	How often does this job require working in very hot (above 90 F degrees) or very cold (below 32 F degrees) temperatures?
Pace Determined by Speed of Equipment	How important is it to this job that the pace is determined by the speed of equipment or machinery? (This does not refer to keeping busy at all times on this job.)
In an Enclosed Vehicle or Equipment	How often does this job require working in a closed vehicle or equipment (e.g., car)?
Outdoors, Exposed to Weather	How often does this job require working outdoors, exposed to all weather conditions?
Indoors, Not Environmentally Controlled	How often does this job require working indoors in non-controlled environmental conditions (e.g., warehouse without heat)?
In an Open Vehicle or Equipment	How often does this job require working in an open vehicle or equipment (e.g., tractor)?
Outdoors, Under Cover	How often does this job require working outdoors, under cover (e.g., structure with roof but no walls)?
Exposed to Whole Body Vibration	How often does this job require exposure to whole body vibration (e.g., operate a jackhammer)?
Spend Time Climbing Ladders, Scaffolds, or Poles	How much does this job require climbing ladders, scaffolds, or poles?
Exposed to Hazardous Equipment	How often does this job require exposure to hazardous equipment?

Job Zone Component	Job Zone Component Definitions
Title	Job Zone Three: Medium Preparation Needed
Overall Experience	Previous work-related skill, knowledge, or experience is required for these occupations. For example, an electrician must have completed three or four years of apprenticeship or several years of vocational training, and often must have passed a licensing exam, in order to perform the job.
Job Training	Employees in these occupations usually need one or two years of training involving both on-the-job experience and informal training with experienced workers.
Job Zone Examples	These occupations usually involve using communication and organizational skills to coordinate, supervise, manage, or train others to accomplish goals. Examples include dental assistants, electricians, fish and game wardens, legal secretaries, personnel recruiters, and recreation workers.
SVP Range	(6.0 to < 7.0)
Education	Most occupations in this zone require training in vocational schools, related on-the-job experience, or an associate's degree. Some may require a bachelor's degree.

Work_Styles	Work_Styles Definitions
Concern for Others	Job requires being sensitive to others' needs and feelings and being understanding and helpful on the job.
Integrity	Job requires being honest and ethical.

Self Control	Job requires maintaining composure, keeping emotions in check, controlling anger, and avoiding aggressive behavior, even in very difficult situations.
Cooperation	Job requires being pleasant with others on the job and displaying a good-natured, cooperative attitude.
Attention to Detail	Job requires being careful about detail and thorough in completing work tasks.
Social Orientation	Job requires preferring to work with others rather than alone, and being personally connected with others on the job.
Dependability	Job requires being reliable, responsible, and dependable, and fulfilling obligations.
Initiative	Job requires a willingness to take on responsibilities and challenges.
Persistence	Job requires persistence in the face of obstacles.
Adaptability/Flexibility	Job requires being open to change (positive or negative) and to considerable variety in the workplace.
Leadership	Job requires a willingness to lead, take charge, and offer opinions and direction.
Achievement/Effort	Job requires establishing and maintaining personally challenging achievement goals and exerting effort toward mastering tasks.
Stress Tolerance	Job requires accepting criticism and dealing calmly and effectively with high stress situations.
Independence	Job requires developing one's own ways of doing things, guiding oneself with little or no supervision, and depending on oneself to get things done.
Innovation	Job requires creativity and alternative thinking to develop new ideas for and answers to work-related problems.
Analytical Thinking	Job requires analyzing information and using logic to address work-related issues and problems.

31-9093.00 - Medical Equipment Preparers

Prepare, sterilize, install, or clean laboratory or healthcare equipment. May perform routine laboratory tasks and operate or inspect equipment.

Tasks

1) Report defective equipment to appropriate supervisors or staff.

2) Record sterilizer test results.

3) Operate and maintain steam autoclaves, keeping records of loads completed, items in loads, and maintenance procedures performed.

4) Attend hospital in-service programs related to areas of work specialization.

5) Check sterile supplies to ensure that they are not outdated.

6) Organize and assemble routine and specialty surgical instrument trays and other sterilized supplies, filling special requests as needed.

7) Examine equipment to detect leaks, worn or loose parts, or other indications of disrepair.

8) Start equipment and observe gauges and equipment operation, in order to detect malfunctions and to ensure equipment is operating to prescribed standards.

9) Maintain records of inventory and equipment usage.

10) Disinfect and sterilize equipment such as respirators, hospital beds, and oxygen and dialysis equipment, using sterilizers, aerators, and washers.

11) Purge wastes from equipment by connecting equipment to water sources and flushing water through systems.

12) Deliver equipment to specified hospital locations or to patients' residences.

13) Assist hospital staff with patient care duties such as providing transportation and setting up traction.

14) Install and set up medical equipment using hand tools.

Knowledge	Knowledge Definitions
English Language	Knowledge of the structure and content of the English language including the meaning and spelling of words, rules of composition, and grammar.
Customer and Personal Service	Knowledge of principles and processes for providing customer and personal services. This includes customer needs assessment, meeting quality standards for services, and evaluation of customer satisfaction.
Administration and Management	Knowledge of business and management principles involved in strategic planning, resource allocation, human resources modeling, leadership technique, production methods, and coordination of people and resources.
Production and Processing	Knowledge of raw materials, production processes, quality control, costs, and other techniques for maximizing the effective manufacture and distribution of goods.
Education and Training	Knowledge of principles and methods for curriculum and training design, teaching and instruction for individuals and groups, and the measurement of training effects.
Chemistry	Knowledge of the chemical composition, structure, and properties of substances and of the chemical processes and transformations that they undergo. This includes uses of chemicals and their interactions, danger signs, production techniques, and disposal methods.
Public Safety and Security	Knowledge of relevant equipment, policies, procedures, and strategies to promote effective local, state, or national security operations for the protection of people, data, property, and institutions.
Medicine and Dentistry	Knowledge of the information and techniques needed to diagnose and treat human injuries, diseases, and deformities. This includes symptoms, treatment alternatives, drug properties and interactions, and preventive health-care measures.
Mathematics	Knowledge of arithmetic, algebra, geometry, calculus, statistics, and their applications.
Communications and Media	Knowledge of media production, communication, and dissemination techniques and methods. This includes alternative ways to inform and entertain via written, oral, and visual media.
Clerical	Knowledge of administrative and clerical procedures and systems such as word processing, managing files and records, stenography and transcription, designing forms, and other office procedures and terminology.
Biology	Knowledge of plant and animal organisms, their tissues, cells, functions, interdependencies, and interactions with each other and the environment.
Mechanical	Knowledge of machines and tools, including their designs, uses, repair, and maintenance.
Computers and Electronics	Knowledge of circuit boards, processors, chips, electronic equipment, and computer hardware and software, including applications and programming.
Personnel and Human Resources	Knowledge of principles and procedures for personnel recruitment, selection, training, compensation and benefits, labor relations and negotiation, and personnel information systems.
Telecommunications	Knowledge of transmission, broadcasting, switching, control, and operation of telecommunications systems.
Transportation	Knowledge of principles and methods for moving people or goods by air, rail, sea, or road, including the relative costs and benefits.
Psychology	Knowledge of human behavior and performance; individual differences in ability, personality, and interests; learning and motivation; psychological research methods; and the assessment and treatment of behavioral and affective disorders.
Engineering and Technology	Knowledge of the practical application of engineering science and technology. This includes applying principles, techniques, procedures, and equipment to the design and production of various goods and services.
Law and Government	Knowledge of laws, legal codes, court procedures, precedents, government regulations, executive orders, agency rules, and the democratic political process.
Physics	Knowledge and prediction of physical principles, laws, their interrelationships, and applications to understanding fluid, material, and atmospheric dynamics, and mechanical, electrical, atomic and sub-atomic structures and processes.
Economics and Accounting	Knowledge of economic and accounting principles and practices, the financial markets, banking and the analysis and reporting of financial data.
Design	Knowledge of design techniques, tools, and principles involved in production of precision technical plans, blueprints, drawings, and models.
Foreign Language	Knowledge of the structure and content of a foreign (non-English) language including the meaning and spelling of words, rules of composition and grammar, and pronunciation.
Philosophy and Theology	Knowledge of different philosophical systems and religions. This includes their basic principles, values, ethics, ways of thinking, customs, practices, and their impact on human culture.

Sociology and Anthropology	Knowledge of group behavior and dynamics, societal trends and influences, human migrations, ethnicity, cultures and their history and origins.
History and Archeology	Knowledge of historical events and their causes, indicators, and effects on civilizations and cultures.
Therapy and Counseling	Knowledge of principles, methods, and procedures for diagnosis, treatment, and rehabilitation of physical and mental dysfunctions, and for career counseling and guidance.
Sales and Marketing	Knowledge of principles and methods for showing, promoting, and selling products or services. This includes marketing strategy and tactics, product demonstration, sales techniques, and sales control systems.
Building and Construction	Knowledge of materials, methods, and the tools involved in the construction or repair of houses, buildings, or other structures such as highways and roads.
Food Production	Knowledge of techniques and equipment for planting, growing, and harvesting food products (both plant and animal) for consumption, including storage/handling techniques.
Fine Arts	Knowledge of the theory and techniques required to compose, produce, and perform works of music, dance, visual arts, drama, and sculpture.
Geography	Knowledge of principles and methods for describing the features of land, sea, and air masses, including their physical characteristics, locations, interrelationships, and distribution of plant, animal, and human life.

Skills	Skills Definitions
Operation Monitoring	Watching gauges, dials, or other indicators to make sure a machine is working properly.
Active Listening	Giving full attention to what other people are saying, taking time to understand the points being made, asking questions as appropriate, and not interrupting at inappropriate times.
Reading Comprehension	Understanding written sentences and paragraphs in work related documents.
Instructing	Teaching others how to do something.
Speaking	Talking to others to convey information effectively.
Active Learning	Understanding the implications of new information for both current and future problem-solving and decision-making.
Learning Strategies	Selecting and using training/instructional methods and procedures appropriate for the situation when learning or teaching new things.
Monitoring	Monitoring/Assessing performance of yourself, other individuals, or organizations to make improvements or take corrective action.
Quality Control Analysis	Conducting tests and inspections of products, services, or processes to evaluate quality or performance.
Service Orientation	Actively looking for ways to help people.
Critical Thinking	Using logic and reasoning to identify the strengths and weaknesses of alternative solutions, conclusions or approaches to problems.
Operation and Control	Controlling operations of equipment or systems.
Complex Problem Solving	Identifying complex problems and reviewing related information to develop and evaluate options and implement solutions.
Writing	Communicating effectively in writing as appropriate for the needs of the audience.
Equipment Selection	Determining the kind of tools and equipment needed to do a job.
Coordination	Adjusting actions in relation to others' actions.
Time Management	Managing one's own time and the time of others.
Equipment Maintenance	Performing routine maintenance on equipment and determining when and what kind of maintenance is needed.
Social Perceptiveness	Being aware of others' reactions and understanding why they react as they do.
Management of Material Resources	Obtaining and seeing to the appropriate use of equipment, facilities, and materials needed to do certain work.
Management of Personnel Resources	Motivating, developing, and directing people as they work, identifying the best people for the job.
Judgment and Decision Making	Considering the relative costs and benefits of potential actions to choose the most appropriate one.
Troubleshooting	Determining causes of operating errors and deciding what to do about it.
Management of Financial Resources	Determining how money will be spent to get the work done, and accounting for these expenditures.
Mathematics	Using mathematics to solve problems.
Science	Using scientific rules and methods to solve problems.

Systems Analysis	Determining how a system should work and how changes in conditions, operations, and the environment will affect outcomes.
Systems Evaluation	Identifying measures or indicators of system performance and the actions needed to improve or correct performance, relative to the goals of the system.
Operations Analysis	Analyzing needs and product requirements to create a design.
Technology Design	Generating or adapting equipment and technology to serve user needs.
Repairing	Repairing machines or systems using the needed tools.
Negotiation	Bringing others together and trying to reconcile differences.
Persuasion	Persuading others to change their minds or behavior.
Installation	Installing equipment, machines, wiring, or programs to meet specifications.
Programming	Writing computer programs for various purposes.

Ability	Ability Definitions
Problem Sensitivity	The ability to tell when something is wrong or is likely to go wrong. It does not involve solving the problem, only recognizing there is a problem.
Near Vision	The ability to see details at close range (within a few feet of the observer).
Oral Comprehension	The ability to listen to and understand information and ideas presented through spoken words and sentences.
Information Ordering	The ability to arrange things or actions in a certain order or pattern according to a specific rule or set of rules (e.g., patterns of numbers, letters, words, pictures, mathematical operations).
Written Expression	The ability to communicate information and ideas in writing so others will understand.
Deductive Reasoning	The ability to apply general rules to specific problems to produce answers that make sense.
Inductive Reasoning	The ability to combine pieces of information to form general rules or conclusions (includes finding a relationship among seemingly unrelated events).
Oral Expression	The ability to communicate information and ideas in speaking so others will understand.
Speech Recognition	The ability to identify and understand the speech of another person.
Manual Dexterity	The ability to quickly move your hand, your hand together with your arm, or your two hands to grasp, manipulate, or assemble objects.
Arm-Hand Steadiness	The ability to keep your hand and arm steady while moving your arm or while holding your arm and hand in one position.
Written Comprehension	The ability to read and understand information and ideas presented in writing.
Speech Clarity	The ability to speak clearly so others can understand you.
Category Flexibility	The ability to generate or use different sets of rules for combining or grouping things in different ways.
Trunk Strength	The ability to use your abdominal and lower back muscles to support part of the body repeatedly or continuously over time without 'giving out' or fatiguing.
Selective Attention	The ability to concentrate on a task over a period of time without being distracted.
Perceptual Speed	The ability to quickly and accurately compare similarities and differences among sets of letters, numbers, objects, pictures, or patterns. The things to be compared may be presented at the same time or one after the other. This ability also includes comparing a presented object with a remembered object.
Control Precision	The ability to quickly and repeatedly adjust the controls of a machine or a vehicle to exact positions.
Flexibility of Closure	The ability to identify or detect a known pattern (a figure, object, word, or sound) that is hidden in other distracting material.
Finger Dexterity	The ability to make precisely coordinated movements of the fingers of one or both hands to grasp, manipulate, or assemble very small objects.
Static Strength	The ability to exert maximum muscle force to lift, push, pull, or carry objects.
Visualization	The ability to imagine how something will look after it is moved around or when its parts are moved or rearranged.
Extent Flexibility	The ability to bend, stretch, twist, or reach with your body, arms, and/or legs.
Rate Control	The ability to time your movements or the movement of a piece of equipment in anticipation of changes in the speed and/or direction of a moving object or scene.
Auditory Attention	The ability to focus on a single source of sound in the presence of other distracting sounds.

Multilimb Coordination	The ability to coordinate two or more limbs (for example, two arms, two legs, or one leg and one arm) while sitting, standing, or lying down. It does not involve performing the activities while the whole body is in motion.
Far Vision	The ability to see details at a distance.
Mathematical Reasoning	The ability to choose the right mathematical methods or formulas to solve a problem.
Number Facility	The ability to add, subtract, multiply, or divide quickly and correctly.
Stamina	The ability to exert yourself physically over long periods of time without getting winded or out of breath.
Gross Body Coordination	The ability to coordinate the movement of your arms, legs, and torso together when the whole body is in motion.
Fluency of Ideas	The ability to come up with a number of ideas about a topic (the number of ideas is important, not their quality, correctness, or creativity).
Originality	The ability to come up with unusual or clever ideas about a given topic or situation, or to develop creative ways to solve a problem.
Hearing Sensitivity	The ability to detect or tell the differences between sounds that vary in pitch and loudness.
Depth Perception	The ability to judge which of several objects is closer or farther away from you, or to judge the distance between you and an object.
Visual Color Discrimination	The ability to match or detect differences between colors, including shades of color and brightness.
Memorization	The ability to remember information such as words, numbers, pictures, and procedures.
Reaction Time	The ability to quickly respond (with the hand, finger, or foot) to a signal (sound, light, picture) when it appears.
Wrist-Finger Speed	The ability to make fast, simple, repeated movements of the fingers, hands, and wrists.
Dynamic Strength	The ability to exert muscle force repeatedly or continuously over time. This involves muscular endurance and resistance to muscle fatigue.
Time Sharing	The ability to shift back and forth between two or more activities or sources of information (such as speech, sounds, touch, or other sources).
Speed of Closure	The ability to quickly make sense of, combine, and organize information into meaningful patterns.
Response Orientation	The ability to choose quickly between two or more movements in response to two or more different signals (lights, sounds, pictures). It includes the speed with which the correct response is started with the hand, foot, or other body part.
Speed of Limb Movement	The ability to quickly move the arms and legs.
Gross Body Equilibrium	The ability to keep or regain your body balance or stay upright when in an unstable position.
Glare Sensitivity	The ability to see objects in the presence of glare or bright lighting.
Explosive Strength	The ability to use short bursts of muscle force to propel oneself (as in jumping or sprinting), or to throw an object.
Sound Localization	The ability to tell the direction from which a sound originated.
Spatial Orientation	The ability to know your location in relation to the environment or to know where other objects are in relation to you.
Peripheral Vision	The ability to see objects or movement of objects to one's side when the eyes are looking ahead.
Night Vision	The ability to see under low light conditions.
Dynamic Flexibility	The ability to quickly and repeatedly bend, stretch, twist, and reach out with your body, arms, and/or legs.

Work_Activity	Work_Activity Definitions
Inspecting Equipment, Structures, or Material	Inspecting equipment, structures, or materials to identify the cause of errors or other problems or defects.
Monitor Processes, Materials, or Surroundings	Monitoring and reviewing information from materials, events, or the environment, to detect or assess problems.
Handling and Moving Objects	Using hands and arms in handling, installing, positioning, and moving materials, and manipulating things
Updating and Using Relevant Knowledge	Keeping up-to-date technically and applying new knowledge to your job.
Documenting/Recording Information	Entering, transcribing, recording, storing, or maintaining information in written or electronic/magnetic form.
Controlling Machines and Processes	Using either control mechanisms or direct physical activity to operate machines or processes (not including computers or vehicles).

Evaluating Information to Determine Compliance wit	Using relevant information and individual judgment to determine whether events or processes comply with laws, regulations, or standards.
Performing General Physical Activities	Performing physical activities that require considerable use of your arms and legs and moving your whole body, such as climbing, lifting, balancing, walking, stooping, and handling of materials.
Communicating with Supervisors, Peers, or Subordin	Providing information to supervisors, co-workers, and subordinates by telephone, in written form, e-mail, or in person.
Identifying Objects, Actions, and Events	Identifying information by categorizing, estimating, recognizing differences or similarities, and detecting changes in circumstances or events.
Getting Information	Observing, receiving, and otherwise obtaining information from all relevant sources.
Making Decisions and Solving Problems	Analyzing information and evaluating results to choose the best solution and solve problems.
Assisting and Caring for Others	Providing personal assistance, medical attention, emotional support, or other personal care to others such as coworkers, customers, or patients.
Training and Teaching Others	Identifying the educational needs of others, developing formal educational or training programs or classes, and teaching or instructing others.
Establishing and Maintaining Interpersonal Relatio	Developing constructive and cooperative working relationships with others, and maintaining them over time.
Organizing, Planning, and Prioritizing Work	Developing specific goals and plans to prioritize, organize, and accomplish your work.
Processing Information	Compiling, coding, categorizing, calculating, tabulating, auditing, or verifying information or data.
Judging the Qualities of Things, Services, or Peop	Assessing the value, importance, or quality of things or people.
Interpreting the Meaning of Information for Others	Translating or explaining what information means and how it can be used.
Analyzing Data or Information	Identifying the underlying principles, reasons, or facts of information by breaking down information or data into separate parts.
Repairing and Maintaining Mechanical Equipment	Servicing, repairing, adjusting, and testing machines, devices, moving parts, and equipment that operate primarily on the basis of mechanical (not electronic) principles.
Thinking Creatively	Developing, designing, or creating new applications, ideas, relationships, systems, or products, including artistic contributions.
Developing and Building Teams	Encouraging and building mutual trust, respect, and cooperation among team members.
Estimating the Quantifiable Characteristics of Pro	Estimating sizes, distances, and quantities; or determining time, costs, resources, or materials needed to perform a work activity.
Interacting With Computers	Using computers and computer systems (including hardware and software) to program, write software, set up functions, enter data, or process information.
Coordinating the Work and Activities of Others	Getting members of a group to work together to accomplish tasks.
Performing Administrative Activities	Performing day-to-day administrative tasks such as maintaining information files and processing paperwork.
Developing Objectives and Strategies	Establishing long-range objectives and specifying the strategies and actions to achieve them.
Monitoring and Controlling Resources	Monitoring and controlling resources and overseeing the spending of money.
Scheduling Work and Activities	Scheduling events, programs, and activities, as well as the work of others.
Coaching and Developing Others	Identifying the developmental needs of others and coaching, mentoring, or otherwise helping others to improve their knowledge or skills.
Drafting, Laying Out, and Specifying Technical Dev	Providing documentation, detailed instructions, drawings, or specifications to tell others about how devices, parts, equipment, or structures are to be fabricated, constructed, assembled, modified, maintained, or used.
Provide Consultation and Advice to Others	Providing guidance and expert advice to management or other groups on technical, systems-, or process-related topics.
Guiding, Directing, and Motivating Subordinates	Providing guidance and direction to subordinates, including setting performance standards and monitoring performance.
Resolving Conflicts and Negotiating with Others	Handling complaints, settling disputes, and resolving grievances and conflicts, or otherwise negotiating with others.
Repairing and Maintaining Electronic Equipment	Servicing, repairing, calibrating, regulating, fine-tuning, or testing machines, devices, and equipment that operate primarily on the basis of electrical or electronic (not mechanical) principles.

Communicating with Persons Outside Organization — Communicating with people outside the organization, representing the organization to customers, the public, government, and other external sources. This information can be exchanged in person, in writing, or by telephone or e-mail.

Performing for or Working Directly with the Public — Performing for people or dealing directly with the public. This includes serving customers in restaurants and stores, and receiving clients or guests.

Staffing Organizational Units — Recruiting, interviewing, selecting, hiring, and promoting employees in an organization.

Operating Vehicles, Mechanized Devices, or Equipme — Running, maneuvering, navigating, or driving vehicles or mechanized equipment, such as forklifts, passenger vehicles, aircraft, or water craft.

Selling or Influencing Others — Convincing others to buy merchandise/goods or to otherwise change their minds or actions.

Work_Context	Work_Context Definitions
Indoors, Environmentally Controlled	How often does this job require working indoors in environmentally controlled conditions?
Exposed to Disease or Infections	How often does this job require exposure to disease/infections?
Importance of Being Exact or Accurate	How important is being very exact or highly accurate in performing this job?
Contact With Others	How much does this job require the worker to be in contact with others (face-to-face, by telephone, or otherwise) in order to perform it?
Face-to-Face Discussions	How often do you have to have face-to-face discussions with individuals or teams in this job?
Spend Time Using Your Hands to Handle, Control, or	How much does this job require using your hands to handle, control, or feel objects, tools or controls?
Wear Common Protective or Safety Equipment such as	How much does this job require wearing common protective or safety equipment such as safety shoes, glasses, gloves, hard hats or life jackets?
Spend Time Standing	How much does this job require standing?
Telephone	How often do you have telephone conversations in this job?
Work With Work Group or Team	How important is it to work with others in a group or team in this job?
Physical Proximity	To what extent does this job require the worker to perform job tasks in close physical proximity to other people?
Structured versus Unstructured Work	To what extent is this job structured for the worker, rather than allowing the worker to determine tasks, priorities, and goals?
Freedom to Make Decisions	How much decision making freedom, without supervision, does the job offer?
Exposed to Contaminants	How often does this job require working exposed to contaminants (such as pollutants, gases, dust or odors)?
Time Pressure	How often does this job require the worker to meet strict deadlines?
Spend Time Making Repetitive Motions	How much does this job require making repetitive motions?
Consequence of Error	How serious would the result usually be if the worker made a mistake that was not readily correctable?
Responsible for Others' Health and Safety	How much responsibility is there for the health and safety of others in this job?
Exposed to Minor Burns, Cuts, Bites, or Stings	How often does this job require exposure to minor burns, cuts, bites, or stings?
Spend Time Walking and Running	How much does this job require walking and running?
Importance of Repeating Same Tasks	How important is repeating the same physical activities (e.g., key entry) or mental activities (e.g., checking entries in a ledger) over and over, without stopping, to performing this job?
Coordinate or Lead Others	How important is it to coordinate or lead others in accomplishing work activities in this job?
Pace Determined by Speed of Equipment	How important is it to this job that the pace is determined by the speed of equipment or machinery? (This does not refer to keeping busy at all times on this job.)
Spend Time Bending or Twisting the Body	How much does this job require bending or twisting your body?
Deal With Unpleasant or Angry People	How frequently does the worker have to deal with unpleasant, angry, or discourteous individuals as part of the job requirements?
Deal With External Customers	How important is it to work with external customers or the public in this job?
Sounds, Noise Levels Are Distracting or Uncomforta	How often does this job require working exposed to sounds and noise levels that are distracting or uncomfortable?
Frequency of Decision Making	How frequently is the worker required to make decisions that affect other people, the financial resources, and/or the image and reputation of the organization?

Responsibility for Outcomes and Results	How responsible is the worker for work outcomes and results of other workers?
Impact of Decisions on Co-workers or Company Resul	How do the decisions an employee makes impact the results of co-workers, clients or the company?
Exposed to Hazardous Conditions	How often does this job require exposure to hazardous conditions?
Wear Specialized Protective or Safety Equipment su	How much does this job require wearing specialized protective or safety equipment such as breathing apparatus, safety harness, full protection suits, or radiation protection?
Degree of Automation	How automated is the job?
Frequency of Conflict Situations	How often are there conflict situations the employee has to face in this job?
Letters and Memos	How often does the job require written letters and memos?
Level of Competition	To what extent does this job require the worker to compete or to be aware of competitive pressures?
Very Hot or Cold Temperatures	How often does this job require working in very hot (above 90 F degrees) or very cold (below 32 F degrees) temperatures?
Electronic Mail	How often do you use electronic mail in this job?
Cramped Work Space, Awkward Positions	How often does this job require working in cramped work spaces that requires getting into awkward positions?
Spend Time Kneeling, Crouching, Stooping, or Crawl	How much does this job require kneeling, crouching, stooping, or crawling?
Spend Time Keeping or Regaining Balance	How much does this job require keeping or regaining your balance?
Spend Time Sitting	How much does this job require sitting?
Exposed to Hazardous Equipment	How often does this job require exposure to hazardous equipment?
Extremely Bright or Inadequate Lighting	How often does this job require working in extremely bright or inadequate lighting conditions?
Public Speaking	How often do you have to perform public speaking in this job?
Deal With Physically Aggressive People	How frequently does this job require the worker to deal with physical aggression of violent individuals?
Exposed to Radiation	How often does this job require exposure to radiation?
Indoors, Not Environmentally Controlled	How often does this job require working indoors in non-controlled environmental conditions (e.g., warehouse without heat)?
Exposed to Whole Body Vibration	How often does this job require exposure to whole body vibration (e.g., operate a jackhammer)?
Outdoors, Under Cover	How often does this job require working outdoors, under cover (e.g., structure with roof but no walls)?
Outdoors, Exposed to Weather	How often does this job require working outdoors, exposed to all weather conditions?
Spend Time Climbing Ladders, Scaffolds, or Poles	How much does this job require climbing ladders, scaffolds, or poles?
Exposed to High Places	How often does this job require exposure to high places?
In an Enclosed Vehicle or Equipment	How often does this job require working in a closed vehicle or equipment (e.g., car)?
In an Open Vehicle or Equipment	How often does this job require working in an open vehicle or equipment (e.g., tractor)?

Job Zone Component	Job Zone Component Definitions
Title	Job Zone Two: Some Preparation Needed
Overall Experience	Some previous work-related skill, knowledge, or experience may be helpful in these occupations, but usually is not needed. For example, a drywall installer might benefit from experience installing drywall, but an inexperienced person could still learn to be an installer with little difficulty.
Job Training	Employees in these occupations need anywhere from a few months to one year of working with experienced employees. These occupations often involve using your knowledge and skills to help others.
Job Zone Examples	Examples include drywall installers, fire inspectors, flight attendants, pharmacy technicians, salespersons (retail), and tellers.
SVP Range	(4.0 to < 6.0)
Education	These occupations usually require a high school diploma and may require some vocational training or job-related course work. In some cases, an associate's or bachelor's degree could be needed.

Work_Styles	Work_Styles Definitions
Attention to Detail	Job requires being careful about detail and thorough in completing work tasks.

Cooperation	Job requires being pleasant with others on the job and displaying a good-natured, cooperative attitude.
Dependability	Job requires being reliable, responsible, and dependable, and fulfilling obligations.
Integrity	Job requires being honest and ethical.
Stress Tolerance	Job requires accepting criticism and dealing calmly and effectively with high stress situations.
Independence	Job requires developing one's own ways of doing things, guiding oneself with little or no supervision, and depending on oneself to get things done.
Achievement/Effort	Job requires establishing and maintaining personally challenging achievement goals and exerting effort toward mastering tasks.
Self Control	Job requires maintaining composure, keeping emotions in check, controlling anger, and avoiding aggressive behavior, even in very difficult situations.
Initiative	Job requires a willingness to take on responsibilities and challenges.
Concern for Others	Job requires being sensitive to others' needs and feelings and being understanding and helpful on the job.
Adaptability/Flexibility	Job requires being open to change (positive or negative) and to considerable variety in the workplace.
Leadership	Job requires a willingness to lead, take charge, and offer opinions and direction.
Social Orientation	Job requires preferring to work with others rather than alone, and being personally connected with others on the job.
Analytical Thinking	Job requires analyzing information and using logic to address work-related issues and problems.
Persistence	Job requires persistence in the face of obstacles.
Innovation	Job requires creativity and alternative thinking to develop new ideas for and answers to work-related problems.

31-9094.00 - Medical Transcriptionists

Use transcribing machines with headset and foot pedal to listen to recordings by physicians and other healthcare professionals dictating a variety of medical reports, such as emergency room visits, diagnostic imaging studies, operations, chart reviews, and final summaries. Transcribe dictated reports and translate medical jargon and abbreviations into their expanded forms. Edit as necessary and return reports in either printed or electronic form to the dictator for review and signature, or correction.

Tasks

1) Review and edit transcribed reports or dictated material for spelling, grammar, clarity, consistency, and proper medical terminology.

2) Take dictation using either shorthand or a stenotype machine, or using headsets and transcribing machines; then convert dictated materials or rough notes to written form.

3) Identify mistakes in reports, and check with doctors to obtain the correct information.

4) Answer inquiries concerning the progress of medical cases, within the limits of confidentiality laws.

5) Return dictated reports in printed or electronic form for physicians' review, signature, and corrections, and for inclusion in patients' medical records.

6) Produce medical reports, correspondence, records, patient-care information, statistics, medical research, and administrative material.

7) Perform data entry and data retrieval services, providing data for inclusion in medical records and for transmission to physicians.

8) Distinguish between homonyms, and recognize inconsistencies and mistakes in medical terms, referring to dictionaries, drug references, and other sources on anatomy, physiology, and medicine.

9) Decide which information should be included or excluded in reports.

10) Transcribe dictation for a variety of medical reports such as patient histories, physical examinations, emergency room visits, operations, chart reviews, consultation, and/or discharge summaries.

11) Receive and screen telephone calls and visitors.

12) Receive patients, schedule appointments, and maintain patient records.

13) Set up and maintain medical files and databases, including records such as x-ray, lab, and procedure reports, medical histories, diagnostic workups, admission and discharge summaries, and clinical resumes.

14) Perform a variety of clerical and office tasks, such as handling incoming and outgoing mail, completing and submitting insurance claims, typing, filing, and operating office machines.

31-9095.00 - Pharmacy Aides

Record drugs delivered to the pharmacy, store incoming merchandise, and inform the supervisor of stock needs. May operate cash register and accept prescriptions for filling.

Tasks

1) Greet customers and help them locate merchandise.

2) Accept prescriptions for filling, gathering and processing necessary information.

3) Perform clerical tasks such as filing, compiling and maintaining prescription records, and composing letters.

4) Unpack, sort, count and label incoming merchandise, including items requiring special handling or refrigeration.

5) Restock storage areas, replenishing items on shelves.

6) Operate cash register to process cash and credit sales.

7) Receive, store and inventory pharmaceutical supplies, notifying pharmacist when levels are low.

8) Prepare prescription labels by typing and/or operating a computer and printer.

9) Prepare solid and liquid dosage medications for dispensing into bottles and unit dose packaging.

10) Compound, package and label pharmaceutical products under direction of pharmacist.

11) Provide customers with information about the uses and effects of drugs.

12) Calculate anticipated drug usage for a prescribed period.

13) Process medical insurance claims, posting bill amounts and calculating co-payments.

14) Prepare, maintain and record records of inventories, receipts, purchases and deliveries, using a variety of computer screen formats.

15) Deliver medication to treatment areas, living units, residences and clinics, using various means of transportation.

16) Operate capsule and tablet counting machine that automatically distributes a certain number of capsules or tablets into smaller containers.

17) Answer telephone inquiries, referring callers to pharmacist when necessary.

Knowledge	Knowledge Definitions
Customer and Personal Service	Knowledge of principles and processes for providing customer and personal services. This includes customer needs assessment, meeting quality standards for services, and evaluation of customer satisfaction.
Mathematics	Knowledge of arithmetic, algebra, geometry, calculus, statistics, and their applications.
English Language	Knowledge of the structure and content of the English language including the meaning and spelling of words, rules of composition, and grammar.
Medicine and Dentistry	Knowledge of the information and techniques needed to diagnose and treat human injuries, diseases, and deformities. This includes symptoms, treatment alternatives, drug properties and interactions, and preventive health-care measures.
Clerical	Knowledge of administrative and clerical procedures and systems such as word processing, managing files and records, stenography and transcription, designing forms, and other office procedures and terminology.
Computers and Electronics	Knowledge of circuit boards, processors, chips, electronic equipment, and computer hardware and software, including applications and programming.
Administration and Management	Knowledge of business and management principles involved in strategic planning, resource allocation, human resources modeling, leadership technique, production methods, and coordination of people and resources.
Telecommunications	Knowledge of transmission, broadcasting, switching, control, and operation of telecommunications systems.

Chemistry	Knowledge of the chemical composition, structure, and properties of substances and of the chemical processes and transformations that they undergo. This includes uses of chemicals and their interactions, danger signs, production techniques, and disposal methods.
Law and Government	Knowledge of laws, legal codes, court procedures, precedents, government regulations, executive orders, agency rules, and the democratic political process.
Production and Processing	Knowledge of raw materials, production processes, quality control, costs, and other techniques for maximizing the effective manufacture and distribution of goods.
Personnel and Human Resources	Knowledge of principles and procedures for personnel recruitment, selection, training, compensation and benefits, labor relations and negotiation, and personnel information systems.
Public Safety and Security	Knowledge of relevant equipment, policies, procedures, and strategies to promote effective local, state, or national security operations for the protection of people, data, property, and institutions.
Economics and Accounting	Knowledge of economic and accounting principles and practices, the financial markets, banking and the analysis and reporting of financial data.
Education and Training	Knowledge of principles and methods for curriculum and training design, teaching and instruction for individuals and groups, and the measurement of training effects.
Psychology	Knowledge of human behavior and performance; individual differences in ability, personality, and interests; learning and motivation; psychological research methods; and the assessment and treatment of behavioral and affective disorders.
Communications and Media	Knowledge of media production, communication, and dissemination techniques and methods. This includes alternative ways to inform and entertain via written, oral, and visual media.
Therapy and Counseling	Knowledge of principles, methods, and procedures for diagnosis, treatment, and rehabilitation of physical and mental dysfunctions, and for career counseling and guidance.
Sales and Marketing	Knowledge of principles and methods for showing, promoting, and selling products or services. This includes marketing strategy and tactics, product demonstration, sales techniques, and sales control systems.
Foreign Language	Knowledge of the structure and content of a foreign (non-English) language including the meaning and spelling of words, rules of composition and grammar, and pronunciation.
Physics	Knowledge and prediction of physical principles, laws, their interrelationships, and applications to understanding fluid, material, and atmospheric dynamics, and mechanical, electrical, atomic and sub- atomic structures and processes.
Biology	Knowledge of plant and animal organisms, their tissues, cells, functions, interdependencies, and interactions with each other and the environment.
Sociology and Anthropology	Knowledge of group behavior and dynamics, societal trends and influences, human migrations, ethnicity, cultures and their history and origins.
Engineering and Technology	Knowledge of the practical application of engineering science and technology. This includes applying principles, techniques, procedures, and equipment to the design and production of various goods and services.
Philosophy and Theology	Knowledge of different philosophical systems and religions. This includes their basic principles, values, ethics, ways of thinking, customs, practices, and their impact on human culture.
Transportation	Knowledge of principles and methods for moving people or goods by air, rail, sea, or road, including the relative costs and benefits.
Mechanical	Knowledge of machines and tools, including their designs, uses, repair, and maintenance.
Food Production	Knowledge of techniques and equipment for planting, growing, and harvesting food products (both plant and animal) for consumption, including storage/handling techniques.
Geography	Knowledge of principles and methods for describing the features of land, sea, and air masses, including their physical characteristics, locations, interrelationships, and distribution of plant, animal, and human life.
Building and Construction	Knowledge of materials, methods, and the tools involved in the construction or repair of houses, buildings, or other structures such as highways and roads.

Design	Knowledge of design techniques, tools, and principles involved in production of precision technical plans, blueprints, drawings, and models.
History and Archeology	Knowledge of historical events and their causes, indicators, and effects on civilizations and cultures.
Fine Arts	Knowledge of the theory and techniques required to compose, produce, and perform works of music, dance, visual arts, drama, and sculpture.

Skills	Skills Definitions
Reading Comprehension	Understanding written sentences and paragraphs in work related documents.
Active Listening	Giving full attention to what other people are saying, taking time to understand the points being made, asking questions as appropriate, and not interrupting at inappropriate times.
Service Orientation	Actively looking for ways to help people.
Speaking	Talking to others to convey information effectively.
Active Learning	Understanding the implications of new information for both current and future problem-solving and decision-making.
Time Management	Managing one's own time and the time of others.
Learning Strategies	Selecting and using training/instructional methods and procedures appropriate for the situation when learning or teaching new things.
Critical Thinking	Using logic and reasoning to identify the strengths and weaknesses of alternative solutions, conclusions or approaches to problems.
Judgment and Decision Making	Considering the relative costs and benefits of potential actions to choose the most appropriate one.
Mathematics	Using mathematics to solve problems.
Social Perceptiveness	Being aware of others' reactions and understanding why they react as they do.
Coordination	Adjusting actions in relation to others' actions.
Writing	Communicating effectively in writing as appropriate for the needs of the audience.
Instructing	Teaching others how to do something.
Monitoring	Monitoring/Assessing performance of yourself, other individuals, or organizations to make improvements or take corrective action.
Complex Problem Solving	Identifying complex problems and reviewing related information to develop and evaluate options and implement solutions.
Negotiation	Bringing others together and trying to reconcile differences.
Operation and Control	Controlling operations of equipment or systems.
Systems Evaluation	Identifying measures or indicators of system performance and the actions needed to improve or correct performance, relative to the goals of the system.
Management of Personnel Resources	Motivating, developing, and directing people as they work, identifying the best people for the job.
Troubleshooting	Determining causes of operating errors and deciding what to do about it.
Equipment Maintenance	Performing routine maintenance on equipment and determining when and what kind of maintenance is needed.
Operation Monitoring	Watching gauges, dials, or other indicators to make sure a machine is working properly.
Persuasion	Persuading others to change their minds or behavior.
Equipment Selection	Determining the kind of tools and equipment needed to do a job.
Management of Material Resources	Obtaining and seeing to the appropriate use of equipment, facilities, and materials needed to do certain work.
Science	Using scientific rules and methods to solve problems.
Repairing	Repairing machines or systems using the needed tools.
Technology Design	Generating or adapting equipment and technology to serve user needs.
Operations Analysis	Analyzing needs and product requirements to create a design.
Quality Control Analysis	Conducting tests and inspections of products, services, or processes to evaluate quality or performance.
Installation	Installing equipment, machines, wiring, or programs to meet specifications.
Systems Analysis	Determining how a system should work and how changes in conditions, operations, and the environment will affect outcomes.
Management of Financial Resources	Determining how money will be spent to get the work done, and accounting for these expenditures.
Programming	Writing computer programs for various purposes.

Ability	Ability Definitions
Oral Expression	The ability to communicate information and ideas in speaking so others will understand.
Oral Comprehension	The ability to listen to and understand information and ideas presented through spoken words and sentences.
Speech Clarity	The ability to speak clearly so others can understand you.
Speech Recognition	The ability to identify and understand the speech of another person.
Written Comprehension	The ability to read and understand information and ideas presented in writing.
Problem Sensitivity	The ability to tell when something is wrong or is likely to go wrong. It does not involve solving the problem, only recognizing there is a problem.
Near Vision	The ability to see details at close range (within a few feet of the observer).
Information Ordering	The ability to arrange things or actions in a certain order or pattern according to a specific rule or set of rules (e.g., patterns of numbers, letters, words, pictures, mathematical operations).
Deductive Reasoning	The ability to apply general rules to specific problems to produce answers that make sense.
Written Expression	The ability to communicate information and ideas in writing so others will understand.
Mathematical Reasoning	The ability to choose the right mathematical methods or formulas to solve a problem.
Selective Attention	The ability to concentrate on a task over a period of time without being distracted.
Trunk Strength	The ability to use your abdominal and lower back muscles to support part of the body repeatedly or continuously over time without 'giving out' or fatiguing.
Arm-Hand Steadiness	The ability to keep your hand and arm steady while moving your arm or while holding your arm and hand in one position.
Inductive Reasoning	The ability to combine pieces of information to form general rules or conclusions (includes finding a relationship among seemingly unrelated events).
Category Flexibility	The ability to generate or use different sets of rules for combining or grouping things in different ways.
Time Sharing	The ability to shift back and forth between two or more activities or sources of information (such as speech, sounds, touch, or other sources).
Manual Dexterity	The ability to quickly move your hand, your hand together with your arm, or your two hands to grasp, manipulate, or assemble objects.
Memorization	The ability to remember information such as words, numbers, pictures, and procedures.
Extent Flexibility	The ability to bend, stretch, twist, or reach with your body, arms, and/or legs.
Finger Dexterity	The ability to make precisely coordinated movements of the fingers of one or both hands to grasp, manipulate, or assemble very small objects.
Multilimb Coordination	The ability to coordinate two or more limbs (for example, two arms, two legs, or one leg and one arm) while sitting, standing, or lying down. It does not involve performing the activities while the whole body is in motion.
Stamina	The ability to exert yourself physically over long periods of time without getting winded or out of breath.
Perceptual Speed	The ability to quickly and accurately compare similarities and differences among sets of letters, numbers, objects, pictures, or patterns. The things to be compared may be presented at the same time or one after the other. This ability also includes comparing a presented object with a remembered object.
Number Facility	The ability to add, subtract, multiply, or divide quickly and correctly.
Gross Body Coordination	The ability to coordinate the movement of your arms, legs, and torso together when the whole body is in motion.
Static Strength	The ability to exert maximum muscle force to lift, push, pull, or carry objects.
Visual Color Discrimination	The ability to match or detect differences between colors, including shades of color and brightness.
Flexibility of Closure	The ability to identify or detect a known pattern (a figure, object, word, or sound) that is hidden in other distracting material.
Fluency of Ideas	The ability to come up with a number of ideas about a topic (the number of ideas is important, not their quality, correctness, or creativity).
Depth Perception	The ability to judge which of several objects is closer or farther away from you, or to judge the distance between you and an object.
Speed of Closure	The ability to quickly make sense of, combine, and organize information into meaningful patterns.
Speed of Limb Movement	The ability to quickly move the arms and legs.
Control Precision	The ability to quickly and repeatedly adjust the controls of a machine or a vehicle to exact positions.
Visualization	The ability to imagine how something will look after it is moved around or when its parts are moved or rearranged.
Auditory Attention	The ability to focus on a single source of sound in the presence of other distracting sounds.
Far Vision	The ability to see details at a distance.
Spatial Orientation	The ability to know your location in relation to the environment or to know where other objects are in relation to you.
Response Orientation	The ability to choose quickly between two or more movements in response to two or more different signals (lights, sounds, pictures). It includes the speed with which the correct response is started with the hand, foot, or other body part.
Gross Body Equilibrium	The ability to keep or regain your body balance or stay upright when in an unstable position.
Wrist-Finger Speed	The ability to make fast, simple, repeated movements of the fingers, hands, and wrists.
Originality	The ability to come up with unusual or clever ideas about a given topic or situation, or to develop creative ways to solve a problem.
Dynamic Strength	The ability to exert muscle force repeatedly or continuously over time. This involves muscular endurance and resistance to muscle fatigue.
Hearing Sensitivity	The ability to detect or tell the differences between sounds that vary in pitch and loudness.
Explosive Strength	The ability to use short bursts of muscle force to propel oneself (as in jumping or sprinting), or to throw an object.
Reaction Time	The ability to quickly respond (with the hand, finger, or foot) to a signal (sound, light, picture) when it appears.
Dynamic Flexibility	The ability to quickly and repeatedly bend, stretch, twist, or reach out with your body, arms, and/or legs.
Peripheral Vision	The ability to see objects or movement of objects to one's side when the eyes are looking ahead.
Sound Localization	The ability to tell the direction from which a sound originated.
Rate Control	The ability to time your movements or the movement of a piece of equipment in anticipation of changes in the speed and/or direction of a moving object or scene.
Night Vision	The ability to see under low light conditions.
Glare Sensitivity	The ability to see objects in the presence of glare or bright lighting.

Work_Activity	Work_Activity Definitions
Getting Information	Observing, receiving, and otherwise obtaining information from all relevant sources.
Establishing and Maintaining Interpersonal Relatio	Developing constructive and cooperative working relationships with others, and maintaining them over time.
Interacting With Computers	Using computers and computer systems (including hardware and software) to program, write software, set up functions, enter data, or process information.
Performing for or Working Directly with the Public	Performing for people or dealing directly with the public. This includes serving customers in restaurants and stores, and receiving clients or guests.
Updating and Using Relevant Knowledge	Keeping up-to-date technically and applying new knowledge to your job.
Communicating with Supervisors, Peers, or Subordin	Providing information to supervisors, co-workers, and subordinates by telephone, in written form, e-mail, or in person.
Processing Information	Compiling, coding, categorizing, calculating, tabulating, auditing, or verifying information or data.
Assisting and Caring for Others	Providing personal assistance, medical attention, emotional support, or other personal care to others such as coworkers, customers, or patients.
Identifying Objects, Actions and Events	Identifying information by categorizing, estimating, recognizing differences or similarities, and detecting changes in circumstances or events.
Resolving Conflicts and Negotiating with Others	Handling complaints, settling disputes, and resolving grievances and conflicts, or otherwise negotiating with others.
Making Decisions and Solving Problems	Analyzing information and evaluating results to choose the best solution and solve problems.
Coordinating the Work and Activities of Others	Getting members of a group to work together to accomplish tasks.
Documenting/Recording Information	Entering, transcribing, recording, storing, or maintaining information in written or electronic/magnetic form.

Organizing. Planning. and Prioritizing Work	Developing specific goals and plans to prioritize. organize. and accomplish your work.
Judging the Qualities of Things. Services. or Peop	Assessing the value. importance. or quality of things or people.
Evaluating Information to Determine Compliance wit	Using relevant information and individual judgment to determine whether events or processes comply with laws. regulations. or standards.
Developing and Building Teams	Encouraging and building mutual trust. respect. and cooperation among team members.
Monitor Processes, Materials. or Surroundings	Monitoring and reviewing information from materials. events. or the environment. to detect or assess problems.
Performing General Physical Activities	Performing physical activities that require considerable use of your arms and legs and moving your whole body. such as climbing. lifting. balancing. walking. stooping. and handling of materials.
Performing Administrative Activities	Performing day-to-day administrative tasks such as maintaining information files and processing paperwork.
Handling and Moving Objects	Using hands and arms in handling. installing. positioning. and moving materials. and manipulating things.
Estimating the Quantifiable Characteristics of Pro	Estimating sizes. distances. and quantities; or determining time. costs, resources. or materials needed to perform a work activity.
Interpreting the Meaning of Information for Others	Translating or explaining what information means and how it can be used.
Selling or Influencing Others	Convincing others to buy merchandise/goods or to otherwise change their minds or actions.
Coaching and Developing Others	Identifying the developmental needs of others and coaching. mentoring. or otherwise helping others to improve their knowledge or skills.
Training and Teaching Others	Identifying the educational needs of others. developing formal educational or training programs or classes. and teaching or instructing others.
Communicating with Persons Outside Organization	Communicating with people outside the organization. representing the organization to customers. the public. government. and other external sources. This information can be exchanged in person. in writing. or by telephone or e-mail.
Inspecting Equipment, Structures, or Material	Inspecting equipment. structures. or materials to identify the cause of errors or other problems or defects.
Guiding, Directing, and Motivating Subordinates	Providing guidance and direction to subordinates, including setting performance standards and monitoring performance.
Analyzing Data or Information	Identifying the underlying principles, reasons, or facts of information by breaking down information or data into separate parts.
Scheduling Work and Activities	Scheduling events, programs, and activities, as well as the work of others.
Thinking Creatively	Developing, designing, or creating new applications, ideas, relationships, systems, or products, including artistic contributions.
Controlling Machines and Processes	Using either control mechanisms or direct physical activity to operate machines or processes (not including computers or vehicles).
Developing Objectives and Strategies	Establishing long-range objectives and specifying the strategies and actions to achieve them.
Staffing Organizational Units	Recruiting, interviewing, selecting, hiring, and promoting employees in an organization.
Monitoring and Controlling Resources	Monitoring and controlling resources and overseeing the spending of money.
Provide Consultation and Advice to Others	Providing guidance and expert advice to management or other groups on technical. systems-. or process-related topics.
Repairing and Maintaining Electronic Equipment	Servicing, repairing, calibrating, regulating, fine-tuning, or testing machines, devices, and equipment that operate primarily on the basis of electrical or electronic (not mechanical) principles.
Operating Vehicles, Mechanized Devices, or Equipme	Running, maneuvering, navigating, or driving vehicles or mechanized equipment, such as forklifts, passenger vehicles, aircraft, or water craft.
Repairing and Maintaining Mechanical Equipment	Servicing, repairing, adjusting, and testing machines, devices, moving parts, and equipment that operate primarily on the basis of mechanical (not electronic) principles.
Drafting, Laying Out, and Specifying Technical Dev	Providing documentation, detailed instructions, drawings, or specifications to tell others about how devices, parts, equipment, or structures are to be fabricated, constructed, assembled, modified, maintained, or used.

Work_Context	Work_Context Definitions
Telephone	How often do you have telephone conversations in this job?
Contact With Others	How much does this job require the worker to be in contact with others (face-to-face, by telephone, or otherwise) in order to perform it?
Spend Time Standing	How much does this job require standing?
Face-to-Face Discussions	How often do you have to have face-to-face discussions with individuals or teams in this job?
Importance of Being Exact or Accurate	How important is being very exact or highly accurate in performing this job?
Deal With External Customers	How important is it to work with external customers or the public in this job?
Indoors, Environmentally Controlled	How often does this job require working indoors in environmentally controlled conditions?
Physical Proximity	To what extent does this job require the worker to perform job tasks in close physical proximity to other people?
Deal With Unpleasant or Angry People	How frequently does the worker have to deal with unpleasant. angry. or discourteous individuals as part of the job requirements?
Work With Work Group or Team	How important is it to work with others in a group or team in this job?
Exposed to Disease or Infections	How often does this job require exposure to disease/infections?
Frequency of Decision Making	How frequently is the worker required to make decisions that affect other people, the financial resources, and/or the image and reputation of the organization?
Spend Time Making Repetitive Motions	How much does this job require making repetitive motions?
Impact of Decisions on Co-workers or Company Resul	How do the decisions an employee makes impact the results of co-workers, clients or the company?
Spend Time Using Your Hands to Handle, Control, or	How much does this job require using your hands to handle, control, or feel objects, tools or controls?
Time Pressure	How often does this job require the worker to meet strict deadlines?
Importance of Repeating Same Tasks	How important is repeating the same physical activities (e.g., key entry) or mental activities (e.g., checking entries in a ledger) over and over, without stopping, to performing this job?
Consequence of Error	How serious would the result usually be if the worker made a mistake that was not readily correctable?
Spend Time Walking and Running	How much does this job require walking and running?
Structured versus Unstructured Work	To what extent is this job structured for the worker, rather than allowing the worker to determine tasks, priorities, and goals?
Coordinate or Lead Others	How important is it to coordinate or lead others in accomplishing work activities in this job?
Freedom to Make Decisions	How much decision making freedom, without supervision, does the job offer?
Responsible for Others' Health and Safety	How much responsibility is there for the health and safety of others in this job?
Electronic Mail	How often do you use electronic mail in this job?
Frequency of Conflict Situations	How often are there conflict situations the employee has to face in this job?
Responsibility for Outcomes and Results	How responsible is the worker for work outcomes and results of other workers?
Degree of Automation	How automated is the job?
Level of Competition	To what extent does this job require the worker to compete or to be aware of competitive pressures?
Sounds, Noise Levels Are Distracting or Uncomforta	How often does this job require working exposed to sounds and noise levels that are distracting or uncomfortable?
Letters and Memos	How often does the job require written letters and memos?
Pace Determined by Speed of Equipment	How important is it to this job that the pace is determined by the speed of equipment or machinery? (This does not refer to keeping busy at all times on this job.)
Spend Time Kneeling, Crouching, Stooping, or Crawl	How much does this job require kneeling, crouching, stooping or crawling?
Exposed to Contaminants	How often does this job require working exposed to contaminants (such as pollutants, gases, dust or odors)?
Spend Time Bending or Twisting the Body	How much does this job require bending or twisting your body?
Deal With Physically Aggressive People	How frequently does this job require the worker to deal with physical aggression of violent individuals?
In an Enclosed Vehicle or Equipment	How often does this job require working in a closed vehicle or equipment (e.g., car)?
Spend Time Sitting	How much does this job require sitting?

Extremely Bright or Inadequate Lighting	How often does this job require working in extremely bright or inadequate lighting conditions?
Spend Time Keeping or Regaining Balance	How much does this job require keeping or regaining your balance?
Exposed to Hazardous Conditions	How often does this job require exposure to hazardous conditions?
Exposed to High Places	How often does this job require exposure to high places?
Exposed to Minor Burns, Cuts, Bites, or Stings	How often does this job require exposure to minor burns, cuts, bites, or stings?
Spend Time Climbing Ladders, Scaffolds, or Poles	How much does this job require climbing ladders, scaffolds, or poles?
Cramped Work Space, Awkward Positions	How often does this job require working in cramped work spaces that requires getting into awkward positions?
Wear Common Protective or Safety Equipment such as	How much does this job require wearing common protective or safety equipment such as safety shoes, glasses, gloves, hard hats or life jackets?
Public Speaking	How often do you have to perform public speaking in this job?
Very Hot or Cold Temperatures	How often does this job require working in very hot (above 90 F degrees) or very cold (below 32 F degrees) temperatures?
Exposed to Whole Body Vibration	How often does this job require exposure to whole body vibration (e.g., operate a jackhammer)?
Outdoors, Under Cover	How often does this job require working outdoors, under cover (e.g., structure with roof but no walls)?
Exposed to Hazardous Equipment	How often does this job require exposure to hazardous equipment?
In an Open Vehicle or Equipment	How often does this job require working in an open vehicle or equipment (e.g., tractor)?
Outdoors, Exposed to Weather	How often does this job require working outdoors, exposed to all weather conditions?
Wear Specialized Protective or Safety Equipment su	How much does this job require wearing specialized protective or safety equipment such as breathing apparatus, safety harness, full protection suits, or radiation protection?
Indoors, Not Environmentally Controlled	How often does this job require working indoors in non-controlled environmental conditions (e.g., warehouse without heat)?
Exposed to Radiation	How often does this job require exposure to radiation?

Job Zone Component	Job Zone Component Definitions
Title	Job Zone Two: Some Preparation Needed
Overall Experience	Some previous work-related skill, knowledge, or experience may be helpful in these occupations, but usually is not needed. For example, a drywall installer might benefit from experience installing drywall, but an inexperienced person could still learn to be an installer with little difficulty.
Job Training	Employees in these occupations need anywhere from a few months to one year of working with experienced employees.
Job Zone Examples	These occupations often involve using your knowledge and skills to help others. Examples include drywall installers, fire inspectors, flight attendants, pharmacy technicians, salespersons (retail), and tellers.
SVP Range	(4.0 to < 6.0)
Education	These occupations usually require a high school diploma and may require some vocational training or job-related course work. In some cases, an associate's or bachelor's degree could be needed.

Work_Styles	Work_Styles Definitions
Integrity	Job requires being honest and ethical.
Dependability	Job requires being reliable, responsible, and dependable, and fulfilling obligations.
Cooperation	Job requires being pleasant with others on the job and displaying a good-natured, cooperative attitude.
Self Control	Job requires maintaining composure, keeping emotions in check, controlling anger, and avoiding aggressive behavior, even in very difficult situations.
Concern for Others	Job requires being sensitive to others' needs and feelings and being understanding and helpful on the job.
Attention to Detail	Job requires being careful about detail and thorough in completing work tasks.
Initiative	Job requires a willingness to take on responsibilities and challenges.
Social Orientation	Job requires preferring to work with others rather than alone, and being personally connected with others on the job.

Stress Tolerance	Job requires accepting criticism and dealing calmly and effectively with high stress situations.
Adaptability/Flexibility	Job requires being open to change (positive or negative) and to considerable variety in the workplace.
Achievement/Effort	Job requires establishing and maintaining personally challenging achievement goals and exerting effort toward mastering tasks.
Leadership	Job requires a willingness to lead, take charge, and offer opinions and direction.
Persistence	Job requires persistence in the face of obstacles.
Independence	Job requires developing one's own ways of doing things, guiding oneself with little or no supervision, and depending on oneself to get things done.
Innovation	Job requires creativity and alternative thinking to develop new ideas for and answers to work-related problems.
Analytical Thinking	Job requires analyzing information and using logic to address work-related issues and problems.

31-9096.00 - Veterinary Assistants and Laboratory Animal Caretakers

Feed, water, and examine pets and other nonfarm animals for signs of illness, disease, or injury in laboratories and animal hospitals and clinics. Clean and disinfect cages and work areas, and sterilize laboratory and surgical equipment. May provide routine post-operative care, administer medication orally or topically, or prepare samples for laboratory examination under the supervision of veterinary or laboratory animal technologists or technicians, veterinarians, or scientists.

Tasks

1) Exercise animals, and provide them with companionship.

2) Monitor animals' recovering from surgery and notify veterinarians of any unusual changes or symptoms.

3) Prepare feed for animals according to specific instructions such as diet lists and schedules.

4) Assist veterinarians in examining animals to determine the nature of illnesses or injuries.

5) Clean, maintain, and sterilize instruments and equipment.

6) Provide assistance with euthanasia of animals and disposal of corpses.

7) Collect laboratory specimens such as blood, urine, and feces for testing.

8) Prepare examination or treatment rooms by stocking them with appropriate supplies.

9) Fill medication prescriptions.

10) Examine animals to detect behavioral changes or clinical symptoms that could indicate illness or injury.

11) Perform hygiene-related duties such as clipping animals' claws, and cleaning and polishing teeth.

12) Administer medication, immunizations, and blood plasma to animals as prescribed by veterinarians.

13) Prepare surgical equipment, and pass instruments and materials to veterinarians during surgical procedures.

14) Dust, spray, or bathe animals to control insect pests.

15) Perform routine laboratory tests or diagnostic tests such as taking and developing x-rays.

16) Provide emergency first aid to sick or injured animals.

17) Record information relating to animal genealogy, feeding schedules, appearance, behavior, and breeding.

18) Perform enemas, catheterization, ear flushes, intravenous feedings, and gavages.

19) Educate and advise clients on animal health care, nutrition, and behavior problems.

20) Administer anesthetics during surgery and monitor the effects on animals.

21) Perform office reception duties such as scheduling appointments and helping customers.

22) Sell pet food and supplies to customers.

23) Groom, trim, or clip animals' coats.

24) Write reports, maintain research information, and perform clerical duties.

25) Perform accounting duties, including bookkeeping, billing customers for services, and maintaining inventories.

26) Assist professional personnel with research projects in commercial, public health, or research laboratories.

27) Hold or restrain animals during veterinary procedures.

Knowledge	Knowledge Definitions
Customer and Personal Service	Knowledge of principles and processes for providing customer and personal services. This includes customer needs assessment, meeting quality standards for services, and evaluation of customer satisfaction.
Clerical	Knowledge of administrative and clerical procedures and systems such as word processing, managing files and records, stenography and transcription, designing forms, and other office procedures and terminology.
Biology	Knowledge of plant and animal organisms, their tissues, cells, functions, interdependencies, and interactions with each other and the environment.
English Language	Knowledge of the structure and content of the English language including the meaning and spelling of words, rules of composition, and grammar.
Mathematics	Knowledge of arithmetic, algebra, geometry, calculus, statistics, and their applications.
Medicine and Dentistry	Knowledge of the information and techniques needed to diagnose and treat human injuries, diseases, and deformities. This includes symptoms, treatment alternatives, drug properties and interactions, and preventive health-care measures.
Chemistry	Knowledge of the chemical composition, structure, and properties of substances and of the chemical processes and transformations that they undergo. This includes uses of chemicals and their interactions, danger signs, production techniques, and disposal methods.
Administration and Management	Knowledge of business and management principles involved in strategic planning, resource allocation, human resources modeling, leadership technique, production methods, and coordination of people and resources.
Computers and Electronics	Knowledge of circuit boards, processors, chips, electronic equipment, and computer hardware and software, including applications and programming.
Public Safety and Security	Knowledge of relevant equipment, policies, procedures, and strategies to promote effective local, state, or national security operations for the protection of people, data, property, and institutions.
Sales and Marketing	Knowledge of principles and methods for showing, promoting, and selling products or services. This includes marketing strategy and tactics, product demonstration, sales techniques, and sales control systems.
Education and Training	Knowledge of principles and methods for curriculum and training design, teaching and instruction for individuals and groups, and the measurement of training effects.
Personnel and Human Resources	Knowledge of principles and procedures for personnel recruitment, selection, training, compensation and benefits, labor relations and negotiation, and personnel information systems.
Psychology	Knowledge of human behavior and performance; individual differences in ability, personality, and interests; learning and motivation; psychological research methods; and the assessment and treatment of behavioral and affective disorders.
Production and Processing	Knowledge of raw materials, production processes, quality control, costs, and other techniques for maximizing the effective manufacture and distribution of goods.
Economics and Accounting	Knowledge of economic and accounting principles and practices, the financial markets, banking and the analysis and reporting of financial data.
Mechanical	Knowledge of machines and tools, including their designs, uses, repair, and maintenance.
Telecommunications	Knowledge of transmission, broadcasting, switching, control, and operation of telecommunications systems.
Law and Government	Knowledge of laws, legal codes, court procedures, precedents, government regulations, executive orders, agency rules, and the democratic political process.
Therapy and Counseling	Knowledge of principles, methods, and procedures for diagnosis, treatment, and rehabilitation of physical and mental dysfunctions, and for career counseling and guidance.
Communications and Media	Knowledge of media production, communication, and dissemination techniques and methods. This includes alternative ways to inform and entertain via written, oral, and visual media.
Physics	Knowledge and prediction of physical principles, laws, their interrelationships, and applications to understanding fluid, material, and atmospheric dynamics, and mechanical, electrical, atomic and sub-atomic structures and processes.
Engineering and Technology	Knowledge of the practical application of engineering science and technology. This includes applying principles, techniques, procedures, and equipment to the design and production of various goods and services.
Food Production	Knowledge of techniques and equipment for planting, growing, and harvesting food products (both plant and animal) for consumption, including storage/handling techniques.
Sociology and Anthropology	Knowledge of group behavior and dynamics, societal trends and influences, human migrations, ethnicity, cultures and their history and origins.
Transportation	Knowledge of principles and methods for moving people or goods by air, rail, sea, or road, including the relative costs and benefits.
Foreign Language	Knowledge of the structure and content of a foreign (non-English) language including the meaning and spelling of words, rules of composition and grammar, and pronunciation.
Design	Knowledge of design techniques, tools, and principles involved in production of precision technical plans, blueprints, drawings, and models.
Geography	Knowledge of principles and methods for describing the features of land, sea, and air masses, including their physical characteristics, locations, interrelationships, and distribution of plant, animal, and human life.
History and Archeology	Knowledge of historical events and their causes, indicators, and effects on civilizations and cultures.
Building and Construction	Knowledge of materials, methods, and the tools involved in the construction or repair of houses, buildings, or other structures such as highways and roads.
Philosophy and Theology	Knowledge of different philosophical systems and religions. This includes their basic principles, values, ethics, ways of thinking, customs, practices, and their impact on human culture.
Fine Arts	Knowledge of the theory and techniques required to compose, produce, and perform works of music, dance, visual arts, drama, and sculpture.

Skills	Skills Definitions
Active Listening	Giving full attention to what other people are saying, taking time to understand the points being made, asking questions as appropriate, and not interrupting at inappropriate times.
Reading Comprehension	Understanding written sentences and paragraphs in work related documents.
Speaking	Talking to others to convey information effectively.
Active Learning	Understanding the implications of new information for both current and future problem-solving and decision-making.
Instructing	Teaching others how to do something.
Learning Strategies	Selecting and using training/instructional methods and procedures appropriate for the situation when learning or teaching new things.
Time Management	Managing one's own time and the time of others.
Service Orientation	Actively looking for ways to help people.
Critical Thinking	Using logic and reasoning to identify the strengths and weaknesses of alternative solutions, conclusions or approaches to problems.
Writing	Communicating effectively in writing as appropriate for the needs of the audience.
Mathematics	Using mathematics to solve problems.
Social Perceptiveness	Being aware of others' reactions and understanding why they react as they do.
Monitoring	Monitoring/Assessing performance of yourself, other individuals, or organizations to make improvements or take corrective action.
Coordination	Adjusting actions in relation to others' actions.
Operation Monitoring	Watching gauges, dials, or other indicators to make sure a machine is working properly.
Judgment and Decision Making	Considering the relative costs and benefits of potential actions to choose the most appropriate one.
Science	Using scientific rules and methods to solve problems.
Troubleshooting	Determining causes of operating errors and deciding what to do about it.
Complex Problem Solving	Identifying complex problems and reviewing related information to develop and evaluate options and implement solutions.

Operation and Control	Controlling operations of equipment or systems.
Equipment Maintenance	Performing routine maintenance on equipment and determining when and what kind of maintenance is needed.
Negotiation	Bringing others together and trying to reconcile differences.
Equipment Selection	Determining the kind of tools and equipment needed to do a job.
Persuasion	Persuading others to change their minds or behavior.
Management of Personnel Resources	Motivating, developing, and directing people as they work, identifying the best people for the job.
Repairing	Repairing machines or systems using the needed tools.
Management of Material Resources	Obtaining and seeing to the appropriate use of equipment, facilities, and materials needed to do certain work.
Systems Evaluation	Identifying measures or indicators of system performance and the actions needed to improve or correct performance, relative to the goals of the system.
Operations Analysis	Analyzing needs and product requirements to create a design.
Quality Control Analysis	Conducting tests and inspections of products, services, or processes to evaluate quality or performance.
Technology Design	Generating or adapting equipment and technology to serve user needs.
Installation	Installing equipment, machines, wiring, or programs to meet specifications.
Systems Analysis	Determining how a system should work and how changes in conditions, operations, and the environment will affect outcomes.
Management of Financial Resources	Determining how money will be spent to get the work done, and accounting for these expenditures.
Programming	Writing computer programs for various purposes.

Ability	Ability Definitions
Problem Sensitivity	The ability to tell when something is wrong or is likely to go wrong. It does not involve solving the problem, only recognizing there is a problem.
Oral Comprehension	The ability to listen to and understand information and ideas presented through spoken words and sentences.
Oral Expression	The ability to communicate information and ideas in speaking so others will understand.
Speech Clarity	The ability to speak clearly so others can understand you.
Near Vision	The ability to see details at close range (within a few feet of the observer).
Speech Recognition	The ability to identify and understand the speech of another person.
Inductive Reasoning	The ability to combine pieces of information to form general rules or conclusions (includes finding a relationship among seemingly unrelated events).
Extent Flexibility	The ability to bend, stretch, twist, or reach with your body, arms, and/or legs.
Static Strength	The ability to exert maximum muscle force to lift, push, pull, or carry objects.
Manual Dexterity	The ability to quickly move your hand, your hand together with your arm, or your two hands to grasp, manipulate, or assemble objects.
Deductive Reasoning	The ability to apply general rules to specific problems to produce answers that make sense.
Written Comprehension	The ability to read and understand information and ideas presented in writing.
Arm-Hand Steadiness	The ability to keep your hand and arm steady while moving your arm or while holding your arm and hand in one position.
Information Ordering	The ability to arrange things or actions in a certain order or pattern according to a specific rule or set of rules (e.g., patterns of numbers, letters, words, pictures, mathematical operations).
Multilimb Coordination	The ability to coordinate two or more limbs (for example, two arms, two legs, or one leg and one arm) while sitting, standing, or lying down. It does not involve performing the activities while the whole body is in motion.
Written Expression	The ability to communicate information and ideas in writing so others will understand.
Trunk Strength	The ability to use your abdominal and lower back muscles to support part of the body repeatedly or continuously over time without 'giving out' or fatiguing.
Stamina	The ability to exert yourself physically over long periods of time without getting winded or out of breath.
Gross Body Coordination	The ability to coordinate the movement of your arms, legs, and torso together when the whole body is in motion.
Control Precision	The ability to quickly and repeatedly adjust the controls of a machine or a vehicle to exact positions.

Speed of Closure	The ability to quickly make sense of, combine, and organize information into meaningful patterns.
Finger Dexterity	The ability to make precisely coordinated movements of the fingers of one or both hands to grasp, manipulate, or assemble very small objects.
Flexibility of Closure	The ability to identify or detect a known pattern (a figure, object, word, or sound) that is hidden in other distracting material.
Selective Attention	The ability to concentrate on a task over a period of time without being distracted.
Category Flexibility	The ability to generate or use different sets of rules for combining or grouping things in different ways.
Dynamic Strength	The ability to exert muscle force repeatedly or continuously over time. This involves muscular endurance and resistance to muscle fatigue.
Perceptual Speed	The ability to quickly and accurately compare similarities and differences among sets of letters, numbers, objects, pictures, or patterns. The things to be compared may be presented at the same time or one after the other. This ability also includes comparing a presented object with a remembered object.
Fluency of Ideas	The ability to come up with a number of ideas about a topic (the number of ideas is important, not their quality, correctness, or creativity).
Speed of Limb Movement	The ability to quickly move the arms and legs.
Memorization	The ability to remember information such as words, numbers, pictures, and procedures.
Auditory Attention	The ability to focus on a single source of sound in the presence of other distracting sounds.
Time Sharing	The ability to shift back and forth between two or more activities or sources of information (such as speech, sounds, touch, or other sources).
Gross Body Equilibrium	The ability to keep or regain your body balance or stay upright when in an unstable position.
Mathematical Reasoning	The ability to choose the right mathematical methods or formulas to solve a problem.
Visual Color Discrimination	The ability to match or detect differences between colors, including shades of color and brightness.
Far Vision	The ability to see details at a distance.
Glare Sensitivity	The ability to see objects in the presence of glare or bright lighting.
Originality	The ability to come up with unusual or clever ideas about a given topic or situation, or to develop creative ways to solve a problem.
Number Facility	The ability to add, subtract, multiply, or divide quickly and correctly.
Reaction Time	The ability to quickly respond (with the hand, finger, or foot) to a signal (sound, light, picture) when it appears.
Response Orientation	The ability to choose quickly between two or more movements in response to two or more different signals (lights, sounds, pictures). It includes the speed with which the correct response is started with the hand, foot, or other body part.
Depth Perception	The ability to judge which of several objects is closer or farther away from you, or to judge the distance between you and an object.
Visualization	The ability to imagine how something will look after it is moved around or when its parts are moved or rearranged.
Hearing Sensitivity	The ability to detect or tell the differences between sounds that vary in pitch and loudness.
Wrist-Finger Speed	The ability to make fast, simple, repeated movements of the fingers, hands, and wrists.
Rate Control	The ability to time your movements or the movement of a piece of equipment in anticipation of changes in the speed and/or direction of a moving object or scene.
Dynamic Flexibility	The ability to quickly and repeatedly bend, stretch, twist, or reach out with your body, arms, and/or legs.
Sound Localization	The ability to tell the direction from which a sound originated.
Spatial Orientation	The ability to know your location in relation to the environment or to know where other objects are in relation to you.
Peripheral Vision	The ability to see objects or movement of objects to one's side when the eyes are looking ahead.
Explosive Strength	The ability to use short bursts of muscle force to propel oneself (as in jumping or sprinting), or to throw an object.
Night Vision	The ability to see under low light conditions.

Work_Activity	Work_Activity Definitions
Assisting and Caring for Others	Providing personal assistance, medical attention, emotional support, or other personal care to others such as coworkers, customers, or patients.
Performing General Physical Activities	Performing physical activities that require considerable use of your arms and legs and moving your whole body, such as climbing, lifting, balancing, walking, stooping, and handling of materials.
Getting Information	Observing, receiving, and otherwise obtaining information from all relevant sources.
Handling and Moving Objects	Using hands and arms in handling, installing, positioning, and moving materials, and manipulating things.
Communicating with Supervisors, Peers, or Subordin	Providing information to supervisors, co-workers, and subordinates by telephone, in written form, e-mail, or in person.
Identifying Objects, Actions, and Events	Identifying information by categorizing, estimating, recognizing differences or similarities, and detecting changes in circumstances or events.
Documenting/Recording Information	Entering, transcribing, recording, storing, or maintaining information in written or electronic/magnetic form.
Establishing and Maintaining Interpersonal Relatio	Developing constructive and cooperative working relationships with others, and maintaining them over time.
Monitor Processes, Materials, or Surroundings	Monitoring and reviewing information from materials, events, or the environment, to detect or assess problems.
Inspecting Equipment, Structures, or Material	Inspecting equipment, structures, or materials to identify the cause of errors or other problems or defects.
Updating and Using Relevant Knowledge	Keeping up-to-date technically and applying new knowledge to your job.
Performing for or Working Directly with the Public	Performing for people or dealing directly with the public. This includes serving customers in restaurants and stores, and receiving clients or guests.
Organizing, Planning, and Prioritizing Work	Developing specific goals and plans to prioritize, organize, and accomplish your work.
Communicating with Persons Outside Organization	Communicating with people outside the organization, representing the organization to customers, the public, government, and other external sources. This information can be exchanged in person, in writing, or by telephone or e-mail.
Making Decisions and Solving Problems	Analyzing information and evaluating results to choose the best solution and solve problems.
Processing Information	Compiling, coding, categorizing, calculating, tabulating, auditing, or verifying information or data.
Interpreting the Meaning of Information for Others	Translating or explaining what information means and how it can be used.
Coordinating the Work and Activities of Others	Getting members of a group to work together to accomplish tasks.
Interacting With Computers	Using computers and computer systems (including hardware and software) to program, write software, set up functions, enter data, or process information.
Developing and Building Teams	Encouraging and building mutual trust, respect, and cooperation among team members.
Performing Administrative Activities	Performing day-to-day administrative tasks such as maintaining information files and processing paperwork.
Judging the Qualities of Things, Services, or Peop	Assessing the value, importance, or quality of things or people.
Training and Teaching Others	Identifying the educational needs of others, developing formal educational or training programs or classes, and teaching or instructing others.
Resolving Conflicts and Negotiating with Others	Handling complaints, settling disputes, and resolving grievances and conflicts, or otherwise negotiating with others.
Controlling Machines and Processes	Using either control mechanisms or direct physical activity to operate machines or processes (not including computers or vehicles).
Coaching and Developing Others	Identifying the developmental needs of others and coaching, mentoring, or otherwise helping others to improve their knowledge or skills.
Estimating the Quantifiable Characteristics of Pro	Estimating sizes, distances, and quantities; or determining time, costs, resources, or materials needed to perform a work activity.
Selling or Influencing Others	Convincing others to buy merchandise/goods or to otherwise change their minds or actions.
Evaluating Information to Determine Compliance wit	Using relevant information and individual judgment to determine whether events or processes comply with laws, regulations, or standards.
Analyzing Data or Information	Identifying the underlying principles, reasons, or facts of information by breaking down information or data into separate parts.
Scheduling Work and Activities	Scheduling events, programs, and activities, as well as the work of others.
Guiding, Directing, and Motivating Subordinates	Providing guidance and direction to subordinates, including setting performance standards and monitoring performance.
Thinking Creatively	Developing, designing, or creating new applications, ideas, relationships, systems, or products, including artistic contributions.
Provide Consultation and Advice to Others	Providing guidance and expert advice to management or other groups on technical, systems-, or process-related topics.
Repairing and Maintaining Electronic Equipment	Servicing, repairing, calibrating, regulating, fine-tuning, or testing machines, devices, and equipment that operate primarily on the basis of electrical or electronic (not mechanical) principles.
Repairing and Maintaining Mechanical Equipment	Servicing, repairing, adjusting, and testing machines, devices, moving parts, and equipment that operate primarily on the basis of mechanical (not electronic) principles.
Monitoring and Controlling Resources	Monitoring and controlling resources and overseeing the spending of money.
Developing Objectives and Strategies	Establishing long-range objectives and specifying the strategies and actions to achieve them.
Drafting, Laying Out, and Specifying Technical Dev	Providing documentation, detailed instructions, drawings, or specifications to tell others about how devices, parts, equipment, or structures are to be fabricated, constructed, assembled, modified, maintained, or used.
Operating Vehicles, Mechanized Devices, or Equipme	Running, maneuvering, navigating, or driving vehicles or mechanized equipment, such as forklifts, passenger vehicles, aircraft, or water craft.
Staffing Organizational Units	Recruiting, interviewing, selecting, hiring, and promoting employees in an organization.

Work_Context	Work_Context Definitions
Face-to-Face Discussions	How often do you have to have face-to-face discussions with individuals or teams in this job?
Indoors, Environmentally Controlled	How often does this job require working indoors in environmentally controlled conditions?
Work With Work Group or Team	How important is it to work with others in a group or team in this job?
Importance of Being Exact or Accurate	How important is being very exact or highly accurate in performing this job?
Telephone	How often do you have telephone conversations in this job?
Spend Time Standing	How much does this job require standing?
Exposed to Minor Burns, Cuts, Bites, or Stings	How often does this job require exposure to minor burns, cuts, bites, or stings?
Contact With Others	How much does this job require the worker to be in contact with others (face-to-face, by telephone, or otherwise) in order to perform it?
Spend Time Using Your Hands to Handle, Control, or	How much does this job require using your hands to handle, control, or feel objects, tools or controls?
Exposed to Disease or Infections	How often does this job require exposure to disease/infections?
Impact of Decisions on Co-workers or Company Resul	How do the decisions an employee makes impact the results of co-workers, clients or the company?
Spend Time Walking and Running	How much does this job require walking and running?
Frequency of Decision Making	How frequently is the worker required to make decisions that affect other people, the financial resources, and/or the image and reputation of the organization?
Exposed to Contaminants	How often does this job require working exposed to contaminants (such as pollutants, gases, dust or odors)?
Consequence of Error	How serious would the result usually be if the worker made a mistake that was not readily correctable?
Importance of Repeating Same Tasks	How important is repeating the same physical activities (e.g., key entry) or mental activities (e.g., checking entries in a ledger) over and over, without stopping, to performing this job?
Exposed to Radiation	How often does this job require exposure to radiation?
Time Pressure	How often does this job require the worker to meet strict deadlines?
Spend Time Bending or Twisting the Body	How much does this job require bending or twisting your body?
Spend Time Kneeling, Crouching, Stooping, or Crawl	How much does this job require kneeling, crouching, stooping or crawling?

671

Frequency of Conflict Situations	How often are there conflict situations the employee has to face in this job?
Spend Time Making Repetitive Motions	How much does this job require making repetitive motions?
Letters and Memos	How often does the job require written letters and memos?
Wear Specialized Protective or Safety Equipment su	How much does this job require wearing specialized protective or safety equipment such as breathing apparatus, safety harness, full protection suits, or radiation protection?
Outdoors, Exposed to Weather	How often does this job require working outdoors, exposed to all weather conditions?
Wear Common Protective or Safety Equipment such as	How much does this job require wearing common protective or safety equipment such as safety shoes, glasses, gloves, hard hats or life jackets?
Structured versus Unstructured Work	To what extent is this job structured for the worker, rather than allowing the worker to determine tasks, priorities, and goals?
Cramped Work Space, Awkward Positions	How often does this job require working in cramped work spaces that requires getting into awkward positions?
Exposed to Hazardous Conditions	How often does this job require exposure to hazardous conditions?
Deal With External Customers	How important is it to work with external customers or the public in this job?
Freedom to Make Decisions	How much decision making freedom, without supervision, does the job offer?
Physical Proximity	To what extent does this job require the worker to perform job tasks in close physical proximity to other people?
Indoors, Not Environmentally Controlled	How often does this job require working indoors in non-controlled environmental conditions (e.g., warehouse without heat)?
Responsible for Others' Health and Safety	How much responsibility is there for the health and safety of others in this job?
Very Hot or Cold Temperatures	How often does this job require working in very hot (above 90 F degrees) or very cold (below 32 F degrees) temperatures?
Outdoors, Under Cover	How often does this job require working outdoors, under cover (e.g., structure with roof but no walls)?
Exposed to Hazardous Equipment	How often does this job require exposure to hazardous equipment?
Extremely Bright or Inadequate Lighting	How often does this job require working in extremely bright or inadequate lighting conditions?
In an Enclosed Vehicle or Equipment	How often does this job require working in a closed vehicle or equipment (e.g., car)?
Sounds, Noise Levels Are Distracting or Uncomforta	How often does this job require working exposed to sounds and noise levels that are distracting or uncomfortable?
In an Open Vehicle or Equipment	How often does this job require working in an open vehicle or equipment (e.g., tractor)?
Coordinate or Lead Others	How important is it to coordinate or lead others in accomplishing work activities in this job?
Deal With Unpleasant or Angry People	How frequently does the worker have to deal with unpleasant, angry, or discourteous individuals as part of the job requirements?
Level of Competition	To what extent does this job require the worker to compete or to be aware of competitive pressures?
Exposed to High Places	How often does this job require exposure to high places?
Degree of Automation	How automated is the job?
Responsibility for Outcomes and Results	How responsible is the worker for work outcomes and results of other workers?
Spend Time Sitting	How much does this job require sitting?
Spend Time Keeping or Regaining Balance	How much does this job require keeping or regaining your balance?
Exposed to Whole Body Vibration	How often does this job require exposure to whole body vibration (e.g., operate a jackhammer)?
Spend Time Climbing Ladders, Scaffolds, or Poles	How much does this job require climbing ladders, scaffolds, or poles?
Public Speaking	How often do you have to perform public speaking in this job?
Electronic Mail	How often do you use electronic mail in this job?
Deal With Physically Aggressive People	How frequently does this job require the worker to deal with physical aggression of violent individuals?
Pace Determined by Speed of Equipment	How important is it to this job that the pace is determined by the speed of equipment or machinery? (This does not refer to keeping busy at all times on this job.)

Job Zone Component

Title	Job Zone Two: Some Preparation Needed
Overall Experience	Some previous work-related skill, knowledge, or experience may be helpful in these occupations, but usually is not needed. For example, a drywall installer might benefit from experience installing drywall, but an inexperienced person could still learn to be an installer with little difficulty.
Job Training	Employees in these occupations need anywhere from a few months to one year of working with experienced employees. These occupations often involve using your knowledge and skills to help others. Examples include drywall installers, fire inspectors, flight attendants, pharmacy technicians, salespersons (retail), and tellers.
Job Zone Examples	
SVP Range	(4.0 to < 6.0)
Education	These occupations usually require a high school diploma and may require some vocational training or job-related course work. In some cases, an associate's or bachelor's degree could be needed.

Work_Styles

Work_Styles	Work_Styles Definitions
Dependability	Job requires being reliable, responsible, and dependable, and fulfilling obligations.
Cooperation	Job requires being pleasant with others on the job and displaying a good-natured, cooperative attitude.
Stress Tolerance	Job requires accepting criticism and dealing calmly and effectively with high stress situations.
Attention to Detail	Job requires being careful about detail and thorough in completing work tasks.
Integrity	Job requires being honest and ethical.
Self Control	Job requires maintaining composure, keeping emotions in check, controlling anger, and avoiding aggressive behavior, even in very difficult situations.
Concern for Others	Job requires being sensitive to others' needs and feelings and being understanding and helpful on the job.
Initiative	Job requires a willingness to take on responsibilities and challenges.
Adaptability/Flexibility	Job requires being open to change (positive or negative) and to considerable variety in the workplace.
Independence	Job requires developing one's own ways of doing things, guiding oneself with little or no supervision, and depending on oneself to get things done.
Persistence	Job requires persistence in the face of obstacles.
Achievement/Effort	Job requires establishing and maintaining personally challenging achievement goals and exerting effort toward mastering tasks.
Social Orientation	Job requires preferring to work with others rather than alone, and being personally connected with others on the job.
Leadership	Job requires a willingness to lead, take charge, and offer opinions and direction.
Analytical Thinking	Job requires analyzing information and using logic to address work-related issues and problems.
Innovation	Job requires creativity and alternative thinking to develop new ideas for and answers to work-related problems.

33-1011.00 - First-Line Supervisors/Managers of Correctional Officers

Supervise and coordinate activities of correctional officers and jailers.

Tasks

1) Set up employee work schedules.

2) Examine incoming and outgoing mail to ensure conformance with regulations.

3) Convey correctional officers' and inmates' complaints to superiors.

4) Rate behavior of inmates, promoting acceptable attitudes and behaviors to those with low ratings.

5) Carry injured offenders or employees to safety, and provide emergency first aid when necessary.

6) Supervise activities such as searches, shakedowns, riot control, and institutional tours.

7) Take, receive, and check periodic inmate counts.

8) Instruct employees, and provide on-the-job training.

9) Monitor behavior of subordinates to ensure alert, courteous, and professional behavior toward inmates, parolees, fellow employees, visitors, and the public.

10) Supervise and direct the work of correctional officers to ensure the safe custody, discipline, and welfare of inmates.

11) Respond to emergencies such as escapes.

12) Restrain, secure, and control offenders, using chemical agents, firearms, and other weapons of force as necessary.

13) Complete administrative paperwork, and supervise the preparation and maintenance of records, forms, and reports.

14) Develop work and security procedures.

15) Supervise and perform searches of inmates and their quarters to locate contraband items.

16) Maintain knowledge of, comply with, and enforce all institutional policies, rules, procedures, and regulations.

17) Read and review offender information to identify issues that require special attention.

18) Supervise and provide security for offenders performing tasks such as construction, maintenance, laundry, food service, and other industrial or agricultural operations.

19) Maintain order, discipline, and security within assigned areas in accordance with relevant rules, regulations, policies, and laws.

20) Transfer and transport offenders on foot, or by driving vehicles such as trailers, vans, and buses.

21) Resolve problems between inmates.

33-1012.00 - First-Line Supervisors/Managers of Police and Detectives

Supervise and coordinate activities of members of police force.

Tasks

1) Inspect facilities, supplies, vehicles, and equipment to ensure conformance to standards.

2) Prepare work schedules and assign duties to subordinates.

3) Investigate and resolve personnel problems within organization and charges of misconduct against staff.

4) Train staff in proper police work procedures.

5) Maintain logs, prepare reports, and direct the preparation, handling, and maintenance of departmental records.

6) Cooperate with court personnel and officials from other law enforcement agencies and testify in court as necessary.

7) Discipline staff for violation of department rules and regulations.

8) Supervise and coordinate the investigation of criminal cases, offering guidance and expertise to investigators, and ensuring that procedures are conducted in accordance with laws and regulations.

9) Monitor and evaluate the job performance of subordinates, and authorize promotions and transfers.

10) Develop, implement and revise departmental policies and procedures.

11) Review contents of written orders to ensure adherence to legal requirements.

12) Requisition and issue equipment and supplies.

13) Meet with civic, educational, and community groups to develop community programs and events, and to discuss law enforcement subjects.

14) Conduct raids and order detention of witnesses and suspects for questioning.

15) Direct collection, preparation, and handling of evidence and personal property of prisoners.

16) Prepare news releases and respond to police correspondence.

17) Prepare budgets and manage expenditures of department funds.

18) Direct release or transfer of prisoners.

19) Inform personnel of changes in regulations and policies, implications of new or amended laws, and new techniques of police work.

Knowledge	Knowledge Definitions
Law and Government	Knowledge of laws, legal codes, court procedures, precedents, government regulations, executive orders, agency rules, and the democratic political process.
Public Safety and Security	Knowledge of relevant equipment, policies, procedures, and strategies to promote effective local, state, or national security operations for the protection of people, data, property, and institutions.
English Language	Knowledge of the structure and content of the English language including the meaning and spelling of words, rules of composition, and grammar.
Education and Training	Knowledge of principles and methods for curriculum and training design, teaching and instruction for individuals and groups, and the measurement of training effects.
Administration and Management	Knowledge of business and management principles involved in strategic planning, resource allocation, human resources modeling, leadership technique, production methods, and coordination of people and resources.
Psychology	Knowledge of human behavior and performance; individual differences in ability, personality, and interests; learning and motivation; psychological research methods; and the assessment and treatment of behavioral and affective disorders.
Customer and Personal Service	Knowledge of principles and processes for providing customer and personal services. This includes customer needs assessment, meeting quality standards for services, and evaluation of customer satisfaction.
Personnel and Human Resources	Knowledge of principles and procedures for personnel recruitment, selection, training, compensation and benefits, labor relations and negotiation, and personnel information systems.
Telecommunications	Knowledge of transmission, broadcasting, switching, control, and operation of telecommunications systems.
Computers and Electronics	Knowledge of circuit boards, processors, chips, electronic equipment, and computer hardware and software, including applications and programming.
Communications and Media	Knowledge of media production, communication, and dissemination techniques and methods. This includes alternative ways to inform and entertain via written, oral, and visual media.
Clerical	Knowledge of administrative and clerical procedures and systems such as word processing, managing files and records, stenography and transcription, designing forms, and other office procedures and terminology.
Sociology and Anthropology	Knowledge of group behavior and dynamics, societal trends and influences, human migrations, ethnicity, cultures and their history and origins.
Therapy and Counseling	Knowledge of principles, methods, and procedures for diagnosis, treatment, and rehabilitation of physical and mental dysfunctions, and for career counseling and guidance.
Mathematics	Knowledge of arithmetic, algebra, geometry, calculus, statistics, and their applications.
Geography	Knowledge of principles and methods for describing the features of land, sea, and air masses, including their physical characteristics, locations, interrelationships, and distribution of plant, animal, and human life.
Transportation	Knowledge of principles and methods for moving people or goods by air, rail, sea, or road, including the relative costs and benefits.
Philosophy and Theology	Knowledge of different philosophical systems and religions. This includes their basic principles, values, ethics, ways of thinking, customs, practices, and their impact on human culture.
Medicine and Dentistry	Knowledge of the information and techniques needed to diagnose and treat human injuries, diseases, and deformities. This includes symptoms, treatment alternatives, drug properties and interactions, and preventive health-care measures.
Physics	Knowledge and prediction of physical principles, laws, their interrelationships, and applications to understanding fluid, material, and atmospheric dynamics, and mechanical, electrical, atomic and sub-atomic structures and processes.
Foreign Language	Knowledge of the structure and content of a foreign (non-English) language including the meaning and spelling of words, rules of composition and grammar, and pronunciation.
Economics and Accounting	Knowledge of economic and accounting principles and practices, the financial markets, banking and the analysis and reporting of financial data.
History and Archeology	Knowledge of historical events and their causes, indicators, and effects on civilizations and cultures.

Chemistry	Knowledge of the chemical composition, structure, and properties of substances and of the chemical processes and transformations that they undergo. This includes uses of chemicals and their interactions, danger signs, production techniques, and disposal methods.
Mechanical	Knowledge of machines and tools, including their designs, uses, repair, and maintenance.
Sales and Marketing	Knowledge of principles and methods for showing, promoting, and selling products or services. This includes marketing strategy and tactics, product demonstration, sales techniques, and sales control systems.
Biology	Knowledge of plant and animal organisms, their tissues, cells, functions, interdependencies, and interactions with each other and the environment.
Production and Processing	Knowledge of raw materials, production processes, quality control, costs, and other techniques for maximizing the effective manufacture and distribution of goods.
Engineering and Technology	Knowledge of the practical application of engineering science and technology. This includes applying principles, techniques, procedures, and equipment to the design and production of various goods and services.
Design	Knowledge of design techniques, tools, and principles involved in production of precision technical plans, blueprints, drawings, and models.
Building and Construction	Knowledge of materials, methods, and the tools involved in the construction or repair of houses, buildings, or other structures such as highways and roads.
Fine Arts	Knowledge of the theory and techniques required to compose, produce, and perform works of music, dance, visual arts, drama, and sculpture.
Food Production	Knowledge of techniques and equipment for planting, growing, and harvesting food products (both plant and animal) for consumption, including storage/handling techniques.

Skills	Skills Definitions
Judgment and Decision Making	Considering the relative costs and benefits of potential actions to choose the most appropriate one.
Active Listening	Giving full attention to what other people are saying, taking time to understand the points being made, asking questions as appropriate, and not interrupting at inappropriate times.
Management of Personnel Resources	Motivating, developing, and directing people as they work, identifying the best people for the job.
Critical Thinking	Using logic and reasoning to identify the strengths and weaknesses of alternative solutions, conclusions or approaches to problems.
Speaking	Talking to others to convey information effectively.
Writing	Communicating effectively in writing as appropriate for the needs of the audience.
Reading Comprehension	Understanding written sentences and paragraphs in work related documents.
Time Management	Managing one's own time and the time of others.
Coordination	Adjusting actions in relation to others' actions.
Negotiation	Bringing others together and trying to reconcile differences.
Persuasion	Persuading others to change their minds or behavior.
Social Perceptiveness	Being aware of others' reactions and understanding why they react as they do.
Active Learning	Understanding the implications of new information for both current and future problem-solving and decision-making.
Instructing	Teaching others how to do something.
Monitoring	Monitoring/Assessing performance of yourself, other individuals, or organizations to make improvements or take corrective action.
Service Orientation	Actively looking for ways to help people.
Learning Strategies	Selecting and using training/instructional methods and procedures appropriate for the situation when learning or teaching new things.
Complex Problem Solving	Identifying complex problems and reviewing related information to develop and evaluate options and implement solutions.
Equipment Selection	Determining the kind of tools and equipment needed to do a job.
Systems Evaluation	Identifying measures or indicators of system performance and the actions needed to improve or correct performance, relative to the goals of the system.
Management of Material Resources	Obtaining and seeing to the appropriate use of equipment, facilities, and materials needed to do certain work.

Equipment Maintenance	Performing routine maintenance on equipment and determining when and what kind of maintenance is needed.
Operations Analysis	Analyzing needs and product requirements to create a design.
Troubleshooting	Determining causes of operating errors and deciding what to do about it.
Quality Control Analysis	Conducting tests and inspections of products, services, or processes to evaluate quality or performance.
Operation and Control	Controlling operations of equipment or systems.
Management of Financial Resources	Determining how money will be spent to get the work done, and accounting for these expenditures.
Mathematics	Using mathematics to solve problems.
Systems Analysis	Determining how a system should work and how changes in conditions, operations, and the environment will affect outcomes.
Technology Design	Generating or adapting equipment and technology to serve user needs.
Science	Using scientific rules and methods to solve problems.
Operation Monitoring	Watching gauges, dials, or other indicators to make sure a machine is working properly.
Installation	Installing equipment, machines, wiring, or programs to meet specifications.
Repairing	Repairing machines or systems using the needed tools.
Programming	Writing computer programs for various purposes.

Ability	Ability Definitions
Oral Expression	The ability to communicate information and ideas in speaking so others will understand.
Inductive Reasoning	The ability to combine pieces of information to form general rules or conclusions (includes finding a relationship among seemingly unrelated events).
Problem Sensitivity	The ability to tell when something is wrong or is likely to go wrong. It does not involve solving the problem, only recognizing there is a problem.
Oral Comprehension	The ability to listen to and understand information and ideas presented through spoken words and sentences.
Deductive Reasoning	The ability to apply general rules to specific problems to produce answers that make sense.
Speech Clarity	The ability to speak clearly so others can understand you.
Written Comprehension	The ability to read and understand information and ideas presented in writing.
Speech Recognition	The ability to identify and understand the speech of another person.
Information Ordering	The ability to arrange things or actions in a certain order or pattern according to a specific rule or set of rules (e.g., patterns of numbers, letters, words, pictures, mathematical operations).
Written Expression	The ability to communicate information and ideas in writing so others will understand.
Near Vision	The ability to see details at close range (within a few feet of the observer).
Time Sharing	The ability to shift back and forth between two or more activities or sources of information (such as speech, sounds, touch, or other sources).
Reaction Time	The ability to quickly respond (with the hand, finger, or foot) to a signal (sound, light, picture) when it appears.
Selective Attention	The ability to concentrate on a task over a period of time without being distracted.
Far Vision	The ability to see details at a distance.
Flexibility of Closure	The ability to identify or detect a known pattern (a figure, object, word, or sound) that is hidden in other distracting material.
Category Flexibility	The ability to generate or use different sets of rules for combining or grouping things in different ways.
Multilimb Coordination	The ability to coordinate two or more limbs (for example, two arms, two legs, or one leg and one arm) while sitting, standing, or lying down. It does not involve performing the activities while the whole body is in motion.
Speed of Closure	The ability to quickly make sense of, combine, and organize information into meaningful patterns.
Control Precision	The ability to quickly and repeatedly adjust the controls of a machine or a vehicle to exact positions.
Memorization	The ability to remember information such as words, numbers, pictures, and procedures.
Fluency of Ideas	The ability to come up with a number of ideas about a topic (the number of ideas is important, not their quality, correctness, or creativity).

Response Orientation	The ability to choose quickly between two or more movements in response to two or more different signals (lights, sounds, pictures). It includes the speed with which the correct response is started with the hand, foot, or other body part.
Depth Perception	The ability to judge which of several objects is closer or farther away from you, or to judge the distance between you and an object.
Perceptual Speed	The ability to quickly and accurately compare similarities and differences among sets of letters, numbers, objects, pictures, or patterns. The things to be compared may be presented at the same time or one after the other. This ability also includes comparing a presented object with a remembered object.
Spatial Orientation	The ability to know your location in relation to the environment or to know where other objects are in relation to you.
Arm-Hand Steadiness	The ability to keep your hand and arm steady while moving your arm or while holding your arm and hand in one position.
Originality	The ability to come up with unusual or clever ideas about a given topic or situation, or to develop creative ways to solve a problem.
Stamina	The ability to exert yourself physically over long periods of time without getting winded or out of breath.
Manual Dexterity	The ability to quickly move your hand, your hand together with your arm, or your two hands to grasp, manipulate, or assemble objects.
Finger Dexterity	The ability to make precisely coordinated movements of the fingers of one or both hands to grasp, manipulate, or assemble very small objects.
Rate Control	The ability to time your movements or the movement of a piece of equipment in anticipation of changes in the speed and/or direction of a moving object or scene.
Glare Sensitivity	The ability to see objects in the presence of glare or bright lighting.
Visual Color Discrimination	The ability to match or detect differences between colors, including shades of color and brightness.
Static Strength	The ability to exert maximum muscle force to lift, push, pull, or carry objects.
Visualization	The ability to imagine how something will look after it is moved around or when its parts are moved or rearranged.
Trunk Strength	The ability to use your abdominal and lower back muscles to support part of the body repeatedly or continuously over time without 'giving out' or fatiguing.
Auditory Attention	The ability to focus on a single source of sound in the presence of other distracting sounds.
Hearing Sensitivity	The ability to detect or tell the differences between sounds that vary in pitch and loudness.
Gross Body Coordination	The ability to coordinate the movement of your arms, legs, and torso together when the whole body is in motion.
Night Vision	The ability to see under low light conditions.
Mathematical Reasoning	The ability to choose the right mathematical methods or formulas to solve a problem.
Peripheral Vision	The ability to see objects or movement of objects to one's side when the eyes are looking ahead.
Extent Flexibility	The ability to bend, stretch, twist, or reach with your body, arms, and/or legs.
Number Facility	The ability to add, subtract, multiply, or divide quickly and correctly.
Speed of Limb Movement	The ability to quickly move the arms and legs.
Sound Localization	The ability to tell the direction from which a sound originated.
Gross Body Equilibrium	The ability to keep or regain your body balance or stay upright when in an unstable position.
Explosive Strength	The ability to use short bursts of muscle force to propel oneself (as in jumping or sprinting), or to throw an object.
Dynamic Strength	The ability to exert muscle force repeatedly or continuously over time. This involves muscular endurance and resistance to muscle fatigue.
Wrist-Finger Speed	The ability to make fast, simple, repeated movements of the fingers, hands, and wrists.
Dynamic Flexibility	The ability to quickly and repeatedly bend, stretch, twist, or reach out with your body, arms, and/or legs.

Work_Activity	Work_Activity Definitions
Making Decisions and Solving Problems	Analyzing information and evaluating results to choose the best solution and solve problems.
Communicating with Supervisors, Peers, or Subordin	Providing information to supervisors, co-workers, and subordinates by telephone, in written form, e-mail, or in person.
Performing for or Working Directly with the Public	Performing for people or dealing directly with the public. This includes serving customers in restaurants and stores, and receiving clients or guests.
Operating Vehicles, Mechanized Devices, or Equipme	Running, maneuvering, navigating, or driving vehicles or mechanized equipment, such as forklifts, passenger vehicles, aircraft, or water craft.
Guiding, Directing, and Motivating Subordinates	Providing guidance and direction to subordinates, including setting performance standards and monitoring performance.
Resolving Conflicts and Negotiating with Others	Handling complaints, settling disputes, and resolving grievances and conflicts, or otherwise negotiating with others.
Documenting/Recording Information	Entering, transcribing, recording, storing, or maintaining information in written or electronic/magnetic form.
Getting Information	Observing, receiving, and otherwise obtaining information from all relevant sources.
Training and Teaching Others	Identifying the educational needs of others, developing formal educational or training programs or classes, and teaching or instructing others.
Coaching and Developing Others	Identifying the developmental needs of others and coaching, mentoring, or otherwise helping others to improve their knowledge or skills.
Updating and Using Relevant Knowledge	Keeping up-to-date technically and applying new knowledge to your job.
Communicating with Persons Outside Organization	Communicating with people outside the organization, representing the organization to customers, the public, government, and other external sources. This information can be exchanged in person, in writing, or by telephone or e-mail.
Identifying Objects, Actions, and Events	Identifying information by categorizing, estimating, recognizing differences or similarities, and detecting changes in circumstances or events.
Coordinating the Work and Activities of Others	Getting members of a group to work together to accomplish tasks.
Establishing and Maintaining Interpersonal Relatio	Developing constructive and cooperative working relationships with others, and maintaining them over time.
Assisting and Caring for Others	Providing personal assistance, medical attention, emotional support, or other personal care to others such as coworkers, customers, or patients.
Evaluating Information to Determine Compliance wit	Using relevant information and individual judgment to determine whether events or processes comply with laws, regulations, or standards.
Scheduling Work and Activities	Scheduling events, programs, and activities, as well as the work of others.
Performing General Physical Activities	Performing physical activities that require considerable use of your arms and legs and moving your whole body, such as climbing, lifting, balancing, walking, stooping, and handling of materials.
Organizing, Planning, and Prioritizing Work	Developing specific goals and plans to prioritize, organize, and accomplish your work.
Performing Administrative Activities	Performing day-to-day administrative tasks such as maintaining information files and processing paperwork.
Monitor Processes, Materials, or Surroundings	Monitoring and reviewing information from materials, events, or the environment, to detect or assess problems.
Interacting With Computers	Using computers and computer systems (including hardware and software) to program, write software, set up functions, enter data, or process information.
Developing and Building Teams	Encouraging and building mutual trust, respect, and cooperation among team members.
Processing Information	Compiling, coding, categorizing, calculating, tabulating, auditing, or verifying information or data.
Analyzing Data or Information	Identifying the underlying principles, reasons, or facts of information by breaking down information or data into separate parts.
Interpreting the Meaning of Information for Others	Translating or explaining what information means and how it can be used.
Judging the Qualities of Things, Services, or Peop	Assessing the value, importance, or quality of things or people.
Thinking Creatively	Developing, designing, or creating new applications, ideas, relationships, systems, or products, including artistic contributions.
Developing Objectives and Strategies	Establishing long-range objectives and specifying the strategies and actions to achieve them.
Provide Consultation and Advice to Others	Providing guidance and expert advice to management or other groups on technical, systems-, or process-related topics.
Staffing Organizational Units	Recruiting, interviewing, selecting, hiring, and promoting employees in an organization.

Estimating the Quantifiable Characteristics of Pro	Estimating sizes. distances. and quantities: or determining time, costs. resources. or materials needed to perform a work activity.
Handling and Moving Objects	Using hands and arms in handling. installing. positioning, and moving materials, and manipulating things.
Inspecting Equipment. Structures. or Material	Inspecting equipment, structures. or materials to identify the cause of errors or other problems or defects.
Monitoring and Controlling Resources	Monitoring and controlling resources and overseeing the spending of money.
Controlling Machines and Processes	Using either control mechanisms or direct physical activity to operate machines or processes (not including computers or vehicles).
Selling or Influencing Others	Convincing others to buy merchandise/goods or to otherwise change their minds or actions.
Repairing and Maintaining Mechanical Equipment	Servicing. repairing. adjusting. and testing machines. devices, moving parts. and equipment that operate primarily on the basis of mechanical (not electronic) principles.
Repairing and Maintaining Electronic Equipment	Servicing. repairing. calibrating. regulating. fine-tuning, or testing machines. devices. and equipment that operate primarily on the basis of electrical or electronic (not mechanical) principles.
Drafting, Laying Out, and Specifying Technical Dev	Providing documentation, detailed instructions, drawings. or specifications to tell others about how devices. parts. equipment. or structures are to be fabricated, constructed, assembled. modified, maintained. or used.

Work_Context	Work_Context Definitions
Telephone	How often do you have telephone conversations in this job?
In an Enclosed Vehicle or Equipment	How often does this job require working in a closed vehicle or equipment (e.g.. car)?
Face-to-Face Discussions	How often do you have to have face-to-face discussions with individuals or teams in this job?
Frequency of Decision Making	How frequently is the worker required to make decisions that affect other people, the financial resources, and/or the image and reputation of the organization?
Outdoors, Exposed to Weather	How often does this job require working outdoors, exposed to all weather conditions?
Deal With External Customers	How important is it to work with external customers or the public in this job?
Importance of Being Exact or Accurate	How important is being very exact or highly accurate in performing this job?
Impact of Decisions on Co-workers or Company Resul	How do the decisions an employee makes impact the results of co-workers, clients or the company?
Contact With Others	How much does this job require the worker to be in contact with others (face-to-face, by telephone, or otherwise) in order to perform it?
Responsible for Others' Health and Safety	How much responsibility is there for the health and safety of others in this job?
Work With Work Group or Team	How important is it to work with others in a group or team in this job?
Frequency of Conflict Situations	How often are there conflict situations the employee has to face in this job?
Responsibility for Outcomes and Results	How responsible is the worker for work outcomes and results of other workers?
Freedom to Make Decisions	How much decision making freedom, without supervision, does the job offer?
Consequence of Error	How serious would the result usually be if the worker made a mistake that was not readily correctable?
Deal With Unpleasant or Angry People	How frequently does the worker have to deal with unpleasant, angry. or discourteous individuals as part of the job requirements?
Coordinate or Lead Others	How important is it to coordinate or lead others in accomplishing work activities in this job?
Very Hot or Cold Temperatures	How often does this job require working in very hot (above 90 F degrees) or very cold (below 32 F degrees) temperatures?
Physical Proximity	To what extent does this job require the worker to perform job tasks in close physical proximity to other people?
Electronic Mail	How often do you use electronic mail in this job?
Indoors, Environmentally Controlled	How often does this job require working indoors in environmentally controlled conditions?
Structured versus Unstructured Work	To what extent is this job structured for the worker, rather than allowing the worker to determine tasks, priorities, and goals?
Exposed to Hazardous Equipment	How often does this job require exposure to hazardous equipment?
Deal With Physically Aggressive People	How frequently does this job require the worker to deal with physical aggression of violent individuals?

Time Pressure	How often does this job require the worker to meet strict deadlines?
Extremely Bright or Inadequate Lighting	How often does this job require working in extremely bright or inadequate lighting conditions?
Letters and Memos	How often does the job require written letters and memos?
Wear Common Protective or Safety Equipment such as	How much does this job require wearing common protective or safety equipment such as safety shoes. glasses. gloves. hard hats or live jackets?
Spend Time Sitting	How much does this job require sitting?
Importance of Repeating Same Tasks	How important is repeating the same physical activities (e.g.. key entry) or mental activities (e.g.. checking entries in a ledger) over and over, without stopping. to performing this job?
Exposed to Disease or Infections	How often does this job require exposure to disease/infections?
Exposed to Contaminants	How often does this job require working exposed to contaminants (such as pollutants. gases. dust or odors)?
Exposed to Minor Burns, Cuts. Bites. or Stings	How often does this job require exposure to minor burns. cuts. bites. or stings?
Sounds, Noise Levels Are Distracting or Uncomforta	How often does this job require working exposed to sounds and noise levels that are distracting or uncomfortable?
Public Speaking	How often do you have to perform public speaking in this job?
Spend Time Using Your Hands to Handle. Control. or	How much does this job require using your hands to handle. control. or feel objects. tools or controls?
Level of Competition	To what extent does this job require the worker to compete or to be aware of competitive pressures?
Exposed to Hazardous Conditions	How often does this job require exposure to hazardous conditions?
Indoors, Not Environmentally Controlled	How often does this job require working indoors in non-controlled environmental conditions (e.g.. warehouse without heat)?
Cramped Work Space, Awkward Positions	How often does this job require working in cramped work spaces that requires getting into awkward positions?
Degree of Automation	How automated is the job?
Spend Time Standing	How much does this job require standing?
Wear Specialized Protective or Safety Equipment su	How much does this job require wearing specialized protective or safety equipment such as breathing apparatus, safety harness, full protection suits, or radiation protection?
Spend Time Making Repetitive Motions	How much does this job require making repetitive motions?
Spend Time Walking and Running	How much does this job require walking and running?
Outdoors, Under Cover	How often does this job require working outdoors, under cover (e.g., structure with roof but no walls)?
Spend Time Bending or Twisting the Body	How much does this job require bending or twisting your body?
In an Open Vehicle or Equipment	How often does this job require working in an open vehicle or equipment (e.g., tractor)?
Spend Time Keeping or Regaining Balance	How much does this job require keeping or regaining your balance?
Exposed to High Places	How often does this job require exposure to high places?
Spend Time Kneeling, Crouching, Stooping, or Crawl	How much does this job require kneeling, crouching, stooping, or crawling?
Pace Determined by Speed of Equipment	How important is it to this job that the pace is determined by the speed of equipment or machinery? (This does not refer to keeping busy at all times on this job.)
Exposed to Radiation	How often does this job require exposure to radiation?
Spend Time Climbing Ladders. Scaffolds, or Poles	How much does this job require climbing ladders. scaffolds, or poles?
Exposed to Whole Body Vibration	How often does this job require exposure to whole body vibration (e.g.. operate a jackhammer)?

Job Zone Component	Job Zone Component Definitions
Title	Job Zone Four: Considerable Preparation Needed A minimum of two to four years of work-related skill, knowledge, or experience is needed for these occupations. For
Overall Experience	example. an accountant must complete four years of college and work for several years in accounting to be considered qualified.
Job Training	Employees in these occupations usually need several years of work-related experience, on-the-job training, and/or vocational training.

Job Zone Examples	Many of these occupations involve coordinating, supervising, managing, or training others. Examples include accountants, chefs and head cooks, computer programmers, historians, pharmacists, and police detectives.
SVP Range	(7.0 to < 8.0)
Education	Most of these occupations require a four - year bachelor's degree, but some do not.

Work_Styles	Work_Styles Definitions
Integrity	Job requires being honest and ethical.
Stress Tolerance	Job requires accepting criticism and dealing calmly and effectively with high stress situations.
Dependability	Job requires being reliable, responsible, and dependable, and fulfilling obligations.
Self Control	Job requires maintaining composure, keeping emotions in check, controlling anger, and avoiding aggressive behavior, even in very difficult situations.
Leadership	Job requires a willingness to lead, take charge, and offer opinions and direction.
Adaptability/Flexibility	Job requires being open to change (positive or negative) and to considerable variety in the workplace.
Attention to Detail	Job requires being careful about detail and thorough in completing work tasks.
Initiative	Job requires a willingness to take on responsibilities and challenges.
Cooperation	Job requires being pleasant with others on the job and displaying a good-natured, cooperative attitude.
Independence	Job requires developing one's own ways of doing things, guiding oneself with little or no supervision, and depending on oneself to get things done.
Analytical Thinking	Job requires analyzing information and using logic to address work-related issues and problems.
Concern for Others	Job requires being sensitive to others' needs and feelings and being understanding and helpful on the job.
Persistence	Job requires persistence in the face of obstacles.
Innovation	Job requires creativity and alternative thinking to develop new ideas for and answers to work-related problems.
Social Orientation	Job requires preferring to work with others rather than alone, and being personally connected with others on the job.
Achievement/Effort	Job requires establishing and maintaining personally challenging achievement goals and exerting effort toward mastering tasks.

33-1021.01 - Municipal Fire Fighting and Prevention Supervisors

Supervise fire fighters who control and extinguish municipal fires, protect life and property, and conduct rescue efforts.

Tasks

1) Direct firefighters in station maintenance duties, and participate in these duties.

2) Provide emergency medical services as required, and perform light to heavy rescue functions at emergencies.

3) Evaluate the performance of assigned firefighting personnel.

4) Instruct and drill fire department personnel in assigned duties, including firefighting, medical care, hazardous materials response, fire prevention, and related subjects.

5) Prepare activity reports listing fire call locations, actions taken, fire types and probable causes, damage estimates, and situation dispositions.

6) Assess nature and extent of fire, condition of building, danger to adjacent buildings, and water supply status in order to determine crew or company requirements.

7) Compile and maintain equipment and personnel records, including accident reports.

8) Maintain required maps and records.

9) Evaluate fire station procedures in order to ensure efficiency and enforcement of departmental regulations.

10) Recommend personnel actions related to disciplinary procedures, performance, leaves of absence, and grievances.

11) Attend in-service training classes to remain current in knowledge of codes, laws, ordinances, and regulations.

12) Direct the training of firefighters, assigning of instructors to training classes, and providing of supervisors with reports on training progress and status.

13) Write and submit proposals for repair, modification, or replacement of firefighting equipment.

14) Direct investigation of cases of suspected arson, hazards, and false alarms and submit reports outlining findings.

15) Identify corrective actions needed to bring properties into compliance with applicable fire codes and ordinances and conduct follow-up inspections to see if corrective actions have been taken.

16) Coordinate the distribution of fire prevention promotional materials.

17) Supervise and participate in the inspection of properties in order to ensure that they are in compliance with applicable fire codes, ordinances, laws, regulations, and standards.

18) Inspect and test new and existing fire protection systems, fire detection systems, and fire safety equipment in order to ensure that they are operating properly.

19) Develop or review building fire exit plans.

20) Conduct fire drills for building occupants and report on the outcomes of such drills.

21) Document efforts taken to bring property owners into compliance with laws, codes, regulations, ordinances, and standards.

22) Present and interpret fire prevention and fire code information to citizens' groups, organizations, contractors, engineers, and developers.

23) Participate in creating fire safety guidelines and evacuation schemes for non-residential buildings.

24) Recommend to proper authorities possible fire code revisions, additions, and deletions.

25) Oversee review of new building plans to ensure compliance with laws, ordinances, and administrative rules for public fire safety.

26) Report and issue citations for fire code violations found during inspections, testifying in court about violations when required to do so.

27) Study and interpret fire safety codes to establish procedures for issuing permits regulating storage or use of hazardous or flammable substances.

Knowledge	Knowledge Definitions
Public Safety and Security	Knowledge of relevant equipment, policies, procedures, and strategies to promote effective local, state, or national security operations for the protection of people, data, property, and institutions.
Education and Training	Knowledge of principles and methods for curriculum and training design, teaching and instruction for individuals and groups, and the measurement of training effects.
Building and Construction	Knowledge of materials, methods, and the tools involved in the construction or repair of houses, buildings, or other structures such as highways and roads.
Customer and Personal Service	Knowledge of principles and processes for providing customer and personal services. This includes customer needs assessment, meeting quality standards for services, and evaluation of customer satisfaction.
Mechanical	Knowledge of machines and tools, including their designs, uses, repair, and maintenance.
English Language	Knowledge of the structure and content of the English language including the meaning and spelling of words, rules of composition, and grammar.
Administration and Management	Knowledge of business and management principles involved in strategic planning, resource allocation, human resources modeling, leadership technique, production methods, and coordination of people and resources.
Medicine and Dentistry	Knowledge of the information and techniques needed to diagnose and treat human injuries, diseases, and deformities. This includes symptoms, treatment alternatives, drug properties and interactions, and preventive health-care measures.
Law and Government	Knowledge of laws, legal codes, court procedures, precedents, government regulations, executive orders, agency rules, and the democratic political process.
Personnel and Human Resources	Knowledge of principles and procedures for personnel recruitment, selection, training, compensation and benefits, labor relations and negotiation, and personnel information systems.
Telecommunications	Knowledge of transmission, broadcasting, switching, control, and operation of telecommunications systems.

Chemistry	Knowledge of the chemical composition, structure, and properties of substances and of the chemical processes and transformations that they undergo. This includes uses of chemicals and their interactions, danger signs, production techniques, and disposal methods.
Psychology	Knowledge of human behavior and performance; individual differences in ability, personality, and interests; learning and motivation; psychological research methods; and the assessment and treatment of behavioral and affective disorders.
Clerical	Knowledge of administrative and clerical procedures and systems such as word processing, managing files and records, stenography and transcription, designing forms, and other office procedures and terminology.
Communications and Media	Knowledge of media production, communication, and dissemination techniques and methods. This includes alternative ways to inform and entertain via written, oral, and visual media.
Computers and Electronics	Knowledge of circuit boards, processors, chips, electronic equipment, and computer hardware and software, including applications and programming.
Physics	Knowledge and prediction of physical principles, laws, their interrelationships, and applications to understanding fluid, material, and atmospheric dynamics, and mechanical, electrical, atomic and sub-atomic structures and processes.
Mathematics	Knowledge of arithmetic, algebra, geometry, calculus, statistics, and their applications.
Transportation	Knowledge of principles and methods for moving people or goods by air, rail, sea, or road, including the relative costs and benefits.
Engineering and Technology	Knowledge of the practical application of engineering science and technology. This includes applying principles, techniques, procedures, and equipment to the design and production of various goods and services.
Therapy and Counseling	Knowledge of principles, methods, and procedures for diagnosis, treatment, and rehabilitation of physical and mental dysfunctions, and for career counseling and guidance.
Design	Knowledge of design techniques, tools, and principles involved in production of precision technical plans, blueprints, drawings, and models.
Geography	Knowledge of principles and methods for describing the features of land, sea, and air masses, including their physical characteristics, locations, interrelationships, and distribution of plant, animal, and human life.
Economics and Accounting	Knowledge of economic and accounting principles and practices, the financial markets, banking and the analysis and reporting of financial data.
Biology	Knowledge of plant and animal organisms, their tissues, cells, functions, interdependencies, and interactions with each other and the environment.
Sociology and Anthropology	Knowledge of group behavior and dynamics, societal trends and influences, human migrations, ethnicity, cultures and their history and origins.
Foreign Language	Knowledge of the structure and content of a foreign (non-English) language including the meaning and spelling of words, rules of composition and grammar, and pronunciation.
Production and Processing	Knowledge of raw materials, production processes, quality control, costs, and other techniques for maximizing the effective manufacture and distribution of goods.
Philosophy and Theology	Knowledge of different philosophical systems and religions. This includes their basic principles, values, ethics, ways of thinking, customs, practices, and their impact on human culture.
Sales and Marketing	Knowledge of principles and methods for showing, promoting, and selling products or services. This includes marketing strategy and tactics, product demonstration, sales techniques, and sales control systems.
History and Archeology	Knowledge of historical events and their causes, indicators, and effects on civilizations and cultures.
Food Production	Knowledge of techniques and equipment for planting, growing, and harvesting food products (both plant and animal) for consumption, including storage/handling techniques.
Fine Arts	Knowledge of the theory and techniques required to compose, produce, and perform works of music, dance, visual arts, drama, and sculpture.

Skills	**Skills Definitions**

Active Listening	Giving full attention to what other people are saying, taking time to understand the points being made, asking questions as appropriate, and not interrupting at inappropriate times.
Service Orientation	Actively looking for ways to help people.
Coordination	Adjusting actions in relation to others' actions.
Instructing	Teaching others how to do something.
Critical Thinking	Using logic and reasoning to identify the strengths and weaknesses of alternative solutions, conclusions or approaches to problems.
Judgment and Decision Making	Considering the relative costs and benefits of potential actions to choose the most appropriate one.
Equipment Maintenance	Performing routine maintenance on equipment and determining when and what kind of maintenance is needed.
Equipment Selection	Determining the kind of tools and equipment needed to do a job.
Reading Comprehension	Understanding written sentences and paragraphs in work related documents.
Speaking	Talking to others to convey information effectively.
Management of Personnel Resources	Motivating, developing, and directing people as they work, identifying the best people for the job.
Learning Strategies	Selecting and using training/instructional methods and procedures appropriate for the situation when learning or teaching new things.
Active Learning	Understanding the implications of new information for both current and future problem-solving and decision-making.
Complex Problem Solving	Identifying complex problems and reviewing related information to develop and evaluate options and implement solutions.
Monitoring	Monitoring/Assessing performance of yourself, other individuals, or organizations to make improvements or take corrective action.
Operation Monitoring	Watching gauges, dials, or other indicators to make sure a machine is working properly.
Time Management	Managing one's own time and the time of others.
Writing	Communicating effectively in writing as appropriate for the needs of the audience.
Social Perceptiveness	Being aware of others' reactions and understanding why they react as they do.
Operation and Control	Controlling operations of equipment or systems.
Troubleshooting	Determining causes of operating errors and deciding what to do about it.
Management of Material Resources	Obtaining and seeing to the appropriate use of equipment, facilities, and materials needed to do certain work.
Mathematics	Using mathematics to solve problems.
Negotiation	Bringing others together and trying to reconcile differences.
Persuasion	Persuading others to change their minds or behavior.
Science	Using scientific rules and methods to solve problems.
Operations Analysis	Analyzing needs and product requirements to create a design.
Technology Design	Generating or adapting equipment and technology to serve user needs.
Management of Financial Resources	Determining how money will be spent to get the work done, and accounting for these expenditures.
Installation	Installing equipment, machines, wiring, or programs to meet specifications.
Quality Control Analysis	Conducting tests and inspections of products, services, or processes to evaluate quality or performance.
Systems Evaluation	Identifying measures or indicators of system performance and the actions needed to improve or correct performance, relative to the goals of the system.
Repairing	Repairing machines or systems using the needed tools.
Systems Analysis	Determining how a system should work and how changes in conditions, operations, and the environment will affect outcomes.
Programming	Writing computer programs for various purposes.

Ability	**Ability Definitions**
Oral Expression	The ability to communicate information and ideas in speaking so others will understand.
Problem Sensitivity	The ability to tell when something is wrong or is likely to go wrong. It does not involve solving the problem, only recognizing there is a problem.
Speech Clarity	The ability to speak clearly so others can understand you.
Inductive Reasoning	The ability to combine pieces of information to form general rules or conclusions (includes finding a relationship among seemingly unrelated events).
Oral Comprehension	The ability to listen to and understand information and ideas presented through spoken words and sentences.

Deductive Reasoning	The ability to apply general rules to specific problems to produce answers that make sense.
Written Expression	The ability to communicate information and ideas in writing so others will understand.
Speech Recognition	The ability to identify and understand the speech of another person.
Information Ordering	The ability to arrange things or actions in a certain order or pattern according to a specific rule or set of rules (e.g., patterns of numbers, letters, words, pictures, mathematical operations).
Near Vision	The ability to see details at close range (within a few feet of the observer).
Selective Attention	The ability to concentrate on a task over a period of time without being distracted.
Written Comprehension	The ability to read and understand information and ideas presented in writing.
Fluency of Ideas	The ability to come up with a number of ideas about a topic (the number of ideas is important, not their quality, correctness, or creativity).
Speed of Closure	The ability to quickly make sense of, combine, and organize information into meaningful patterns.
Far Vision	The ability to see details at a distance.
Flexibility of Closure	The ability to identify or detect a known pattern (a figure, object, word, or sound) that is hidden in other distracting material.
Category Flexibility	The ability to generate or use different sets of rules for combining or grouping things in different ways.
Time Sharing	The ability to shift back and forth between two or more activities or sources of information (such as speech, sounds, touch, or other sources).
Originality	The ability to come up with unusual or clever ideas about a given topic or situation, or to develop creative ways to solve a problem.
Reaction Time	The ability to quickly respond (with the hand, finger, or foot) to a signal (sound, light, picture) when it appears.
Multilimb Coordination	The ability to coordinate two or more limbs (for example, two arms, two legs, or one leg and one arm) while sitting, standing, or lying down. It does not involve performing the activities while the whole body is in motion.
Depth Perception	The ability to judge which of several objects is closer or farther away from you, or to judge the distance between you and an object.
Memorization	The ability to remember information such as words, numbers, pictures, and procedures.
Static Strength	The ability to exert maximum muscle force to lift, push, pull, or carry objects.
Control Precision	The ability to quickly and repeatedly adjust the controls of a machine or a vehicle to exact positions.
Manual Dexterity	The ability to quickly move your hand, your hand together with your arm, or your two hands to grasp, manipulate, or assemble objects.
Spatial Orientation	The ability to know your location in relation to the environment or to know where other objects are in relation to you.
Gross Body Coordination	The ability to coordinate the movement of your arms, legs, and torso together when the whole body is in motion.
Stamina	The ability to exert yourself physically over long periods of time without getting winded or out of breath.
Auditory Attention	The ability to focus on a single source of sound in the presence of other distracting sounds.
Perceptual Speed	The ability to quickly and accurately compare similarities and differences among sets of letters, numbers, objects, pictures, or patterns. The things to be compared may be presented at the same time or one after the other. This ability also includes comparing a presented object with a remembered object.
Visual Color Discrimination	The ability to match or detect differences between colors, including shades of color and brightness.
Arm-Hand Steadiness	The ability to keep your hand and arm steady while moving your arm or while holding your arm and hand in one position.
Extent Flexibility	The ability to bend, stretch, twist, or reach with your body, arms, and/or legs.
Dynamic Strength	The ability to exert muscle force repeatedly or continuously over time. This involves muscular endurance and resistance to muscle fatigue.
Gross Body Equilibrium	The ability to keep or regain your body balance or stay upright when in an unstable position.
Response Orientation	The ability to choose quickly between two or more movements in response to two or more different signals (lights, sounds, pictures). It includes the speed with which the correct response is started with the hand, foot, or other body part.

Trunk Strength	The ability to use your abdominal and lower back muscles to support part of the body repeatedly or continuously over time without 'giving out' or fatiguing.
Visualization	The ability to imagine how something will look after it is moved around or when its parts are moved or rearranged.
Hearing Sensitivity	The ability to detect or tell the differences between sounds that vary in pitch and loudness.
Finger Dexterity	The ability to make precisely coordinated movements of the fingers of one or both hands to grasp, manipulate, or assemble very small objects.
Sound Localization	The ability to tell the direction from which a sound originated.
Mathematical Reasoning	The ability to choose the right mathematical methods or formulas to solve a problem.
Glare Sensitivity	The ability to see objects in the presence of glare or bright lighting.
Explosive Strength	The ability to use short bursts of muscle force to propel oneself (as in jumping or sprinting), or to throw an object.
Speed of Limb Movement	The ability to quickly move the arms and legs.
Number Facility	The ability to add, subtract, multiply, or divide quickly and correctly.
Night Vision	The ability to see under low light conditions.
Peripheral Vision	The ability to see objects or movement of objects to one's side when the eyes are looking ahead.
Rate Control	The ability to time your movements or the movement of a piece of equipment in anticipation of changes in the speed and/or direction of a moving object or scene.
Wrist-Finger Speed	The ability to make fast, simple, repeated movements of the fingers, hands, and wrists.
Dynamic Flexibility	The ability to quickly and repeatedly bend, stretch, twist, or reach out with your body, arms, and/or legs.

Work_Activity	Work_Activity Definitions
Making Decisions and Solving Problems	Analyzing information and evaluating results to choose the best solution and solve problems.
Assisting and Caring for Others	Providing personal assistance, medical attention, emotional support, or other personal care to others such as coworkers, customers, or patients.
Identifying Objects, Actions, and Events	Identifying information by categorizing, estimating, recognizing differences or similarities, and detecting changes in circumstances or events.
Getting Information	Observing, receiving, and otherwise obtaining information from all relevant sources.
Performing for or Working Directly with the Public	Performing for people or dealing directly with the public. This includes serving customers in restaurants and stores, and receiving clients or guests.
Performing General Physical Activities	Performing physical activities that require considerable use of your arms and legs and moving your whole body, such as climbing, lifting, balancing, walking, stooping, and handling of materials.
Communicating with Supervisors, Peers, or Subordin	Providing information to supervisors, co-workers, and subordinates by telephone, in written form, e-mail, or in person.
Inspecting Equipment, Structures, or Material	Inspecting equipment, structures, or materials to identify the cause of errors or other problems or defects.
Coordinating the Work and Activities of Others	Getting members of a group to work together to accomplish tasks.
Documenting/Recording Information	Entering, transcribing, recording, storing, or maintaining information in written or electronic/magnetic form.
Monitor Processes, Materials, or Surroundings	Monitoring and reviewing information from materials, events, or the environment, to detect or assess problems.
Training and Teaching Others	Identifying the educational needs of others, developing formal educational or training programs or classes, and teaching or instructing others.
Operating Vehicles, Mechanized Devices, or Equipme	Running, maneuvering, navigating, or driving vehicles or mechanized equipment, such as forklifts, passenger vehicles, aircraft, or water craft.
Resolving Conflicts and Negotiating with Others	Handling complaints, settling disputes, and resolving grievances and conflicts, or otherwise negotiating with others.
Guiding, Directing, and Motivating Subordinates	Providing guidance and direction to subordinates, including setting performance standards and monitoring performance.
Developing and Building Teams	Encouraging and building mutual trust, respect, and cooperation among team members.
Establishing and Maintaining Interpersonal Relatio	Developing constructive and cooperative working relationships with others, and maintaining them over time.

Handling and Moving Objects	Using hands and arms in handling, installing, positioning, and moving materials, and manipulating things.
Updating and Using Relevant Knowledge	Keeping up-to-date technically and applying new knowledge to your job.
Developing Objectives and Strategies	Establishing long-range objectives and specifying the strategies and actions to achieve them.
Communicating with Persons Outside Organization	Communicating with people outside the organization, representing the organization to customers, the public, government, and other external sources. This information can be exchanged in person, in writing, or by telephone or e-mail.
Evaluating Information to Determine Compliance wit	Using relevant information and individual judgment to determine whether events or processes comply with laws, regulations, or standards.
Organizing, Planning, and Prioritizing Work	Developing specific goals and plans to prioritize, organize, and accomplish your work.
Coaching and Developing Others	Identifying the developmental needs of others and coaching, mentoring, or otherwise helping others to improve their knowledge or skills.
Scheduling Work and Activities	Scheduling events, programs, and activities, as well as the work of others.
Judging the Qualities of Things, Services, or Peop	Assessing the value, importance, or quality of things or people.
Processing Information	Compiling, coding, categorizing, calculating, tabulating, auditing, or verifying information or data.
Controlling Machines and Processes	Using either control mechanisms or direct physical activity to operate machines or processes (not including computers or vehicles).
Estimating the Quantifiable Characteristics of Pro	Estimating sizes, distances, and quantities; or determining time, costs, resources, or materials needed to perform a work activity.
Performing Administrative Activities	Performing day-to-day administrative tasks such as maintaining information files and processing paperwork.
Interpreting the Meaning of Information for Others	Translating or explaining what information means and how it can be used.
Thinking Creatively	Developing, designing, or creating new applications, ideas, relationships, systems, or products, including artistic contributions.
Provide Consultation and Advice to Others	Providing guidance and expert advice to management or other groups on technical, systems-, or process-related topics.
Interacting With Computers	Using computers and computer systems (including hardware and software) to program, write software, set up functions, enter data, or process information.
Analyzing Data or Information	Identifying the underlying principles, reasons, or facts of information by breaking down information or data into separate parts.
Repairing and Maintaining Mechanical Equipment	Servicing, repairing, adjusting, and testing machines, devices, moving parts, and equipment that operate primarily on the basis of mechanical (not electronic) principles.
Monitoring and Controlling Resources	Monitoring and controlling resources and overseeing the spending of money.
Staffing Organizational Units	Recruiting, interviewing, selecting, hiring, and promoting employees in an organization.
Selling or Influencing Others	Convincing others to buy merchandise/goods or to otherwise change their minds or actions.
Drafting, Laying Out, and Specifying Technical Dev	Providing documentation, detailed instructions, drawings, or specifications to tell others about how devices, parts, equipment, or structures are to be fabricated, constructed, assembled, modified, maintained, or used.
Repairing and Maintaining Electronic Equipment	Servicing, repairing, calibrating, regulating, fine-tuning, or testing machines, devices, and equipment that operate primarily on the basis of electrical or electronic (not mechanical) principles.

Work_Context	Work_Context Definitions
Face-to-Face Discussions	How often do you have to have face-to-face discussions with individuals or teams in this job?
Work With Work Group or Team	How important is it to work with others in a group or team in this job?
Responsible for Others' Health and Safety	How much responsibility is there for the health and safety of others in this job?
Telephone	How often do you have telephone conversations in this job?
Deal With External Customers	How important is it to work with external customers or the public in this job?
Freedom to Make Decisions	How much decision making freedom, without supervision, does the job offer?

Contact With Others	How much does this job require the worker to be in contact with others (face-to-face, by telephone, or otherwise) in order to perform it?
Impact of Decisions on Co-workers or Company Resul	How do the decisions an employee makes impact the results of co-workers, clients or the company?
Physical Proximity	To what extent does this job require the worker to perform job tasks in close physical proximity to other people?
Responsibility for Outcomes and Results	How responsible is the worker for work outcomes and results of other workers?
Frequency of Decision Making	How frequently is the worker required to make decisions that affect other people, the financial resources, and/or the image and reputation of the organization?
Wear Common Protective or Safety Equipment such as	How much does this job require wearing common protective or safety equipment such as safety shoes, glasses, gloves, hard hats or live jackets?
Outdoors, Exposed to Weather	How often does this job require working outdoors, exposed to all weather conditions?
In an Enclosed Vehicle or Equipment	How often does this job require working in a closed vehicle or equipment (e.g., car)?
Sounds, Noise Levels Are Distracting or Uncomforta	How often does this job require working exposed to sounds and noise levels that are distracting or uncomfortable?
Coordinate or Lead Others	How important is it to coordinate or lead others in accomplishing work activities in this job?
Indoors, Environmentally Controlled	How often does this job require working indoors in environmentally controlled conditions?
Importance of Being Exact or Accurate	How important is being very exact or highly accurate in performing this job?
Structured versus Unstructured Work	To what extent is this job structured for the worker, rather than allowing the worker to determine tasks, priorities, and goals?
Wear Specialized Protective or Safety Equipment su	How much does this job require wearing specialized protective or safety equipment such as breathing apparatus, safety harness, full protection suits, or radiation protection?
Exposed to Hazardous Equipment	How often does this job require exposure to hazardous equipment?
Exposed to Contaminants	How often does this job require working exposed to contaminants (such as pollutants, gases, dust or odors)?
Consequence of Error	How serious would the result usually be if the worker made a mistake that was not readily correctable?
Indoors, Not Environmentally Controlled	How often does this job require working indoors in non-controlled environmental conditions (e.g., warehouse without heat)?
Letters and Memos	How often does the job require written letters and memos?
Spend Time Using Your Hands to Handle, Control, or	How much does this job require using your hands to handle, control, or feel objects, tools or controls?
Exposed to Disease or Infections	How often does this job require exposure to disease/infections?
Exposed to Hazardous Conditions	How often does this job require exposure to hazardous conditions?
Electronic Mail	How often do you use electronic mail in this job?
Very Hot or Cold Temperatures	How often does this job require working in very hot (above 90 F degrees) or very cold (below 32 F degrees) temperatures?
Frequency of Conflict Situations	How often are there conflict situations the employee has to face in this job?
Exposed to Minor Burns, Cuts, Bites, or Stings	How often does this job require exposure to minor burns, cuts, bites, or stings?
Time Pressure	How often does this job require the worker to meet strict deadlines?
Extremely Bright or Inadequate Lighting	How often does this job require working in extremely bright or inadequate lighting conditions?
Importance of Repeating Same Tasks	How important is repeating the same physical activities (e.g., key entry) or mental activities (e.g., checking entries in a ledger) over and over, without stopping, to performing this job?
Spend Time Standing	How much does this job require standing?
Exposed to High Places	How often does this job require exposure to high places?
Cramped Work Space, Awkward Positions	How often does this job require working in cramped work spaces that requires getting into awkward positions?
Deal With Unpleasant or Angry People	How frequently does the worker have to deal with unpleasant, angry, or discourteous individuals as part of the job requirements?
Spend Time Bending or Twisting the Body	How much does this job require bending or twisting your body?
Public Speaking	How often do you have to perform public speaking in this job?
Level of Competition	To what extent does this job require the worker to compete or to be aware of competitive pressures?
Spend Time Walking and Running	How much does this job require walking and running?

Outdoors, Under Cover	How often does this job require working outdoors, under cover (e.g., structure with roof but no walls)?
In an Open Vehicle or Equipment	How often does this job require working in an open vehicle or equipment (e.g., tractor)?
Spend Time Making Repetitive Motions	How much does this job require making repetitive motions?
Deal With Physically Aggressive People	How frequently does this job require the worker to deal with physical aggression of violent individuals?
Spend Time Sitting	How much does this job require sitting?
Spend Time Kneeling, Crouching, Stooping, or Crawl	How much does this job require kneeling, crouching, stooping or crawling?
Spend Time Climbing Ladders, Scaffolds, or Poles	How much does this job require climbing ladders, scaffolds, or poles?
Spend Time Keeping or Regaining Balance	How much does this job require keeping or regaining your balance?
Degree of Automation	How automated is the job?
Exposed to Whole Body Vibration	How often does this job require exposure to whole body vibration (e.g., operate a jackhammer)?
Pace Determined by Speed of Equipment	How important is it to this job that the pace is determined by the speed of equipment or machinery? (This does not refer to keeping busy at all times on this job.)
Exposed to Radiation	How often does this job require exposure to radiation?

Job Zone Component	Job Zone Component Definitions
Title	Job Zone Three: Medium Preparation Needed
Overall Experience	Previous work-related skill, knowledge, or experience is required for these occupations. For example, an electrician must have completed three or four years of apprenticeship or several years of vocational training, and often must have passed a licensing exam, in order to perform the job.
Job Training	Employees in these occupations usually need one or two years of training involving both on-the-job experience and informal training with experienced workers.
Job Zone Examples	These occupations usually involve using communication and organizational skills to coordinate, supervise, manage, or train others to accomplish goals. Examples include dental assistants, electricians, fish and game wardens, legal secretaries, personnel recruiters, and recreation workers.
SVP Range	(6.0 to < 7.0)
Education	Most occupations in this zone require training in vocational schools, related on-the-job experience, or an associate's degree. Some may require a bachelor's degree.

Work_Styles	Work_Styles Definitions
Leadership	Job requires a willingness to lead, take charge, and offer opinions and direction.
Dependability	Job requires being reliable, responsible, and dependable, and fulfilling obligations.
Stress Tolerance	Job requires accepting criticism and dealing calmly and effectively with high stress situations.
Integrity	Job requires being honest and ethical.
Self Control	Job requires maintaining composure, keeping emotions in check, controlling anger, and avoiding aggressive behavior, even in very difficult situations.
Concern for Others	Job requires being sensitive to others' needs and feelings and being understanding and helpful on the job.
Adaptability/Flexibility	Job requires being open to change (positive or negative) and to considerable variety in the workplace.
Persistence	Job requires persistence in the face of obstacles.
Cooperation	Job requires being pleasant with others on the job and displaying a good-natured, cooperative attitude.
Initiative	Job requires a willingness to take on responsibilities and challenges.
Attention to Detail	Job requires being careful about detail and thorough in completing work tasks.
Social Orientation	Job requires preferring to work with others rather than alone, and being personally connected with others on the job.
Achievement/Effort	Job requires establishing and maintaining personally challenging achievement goals and exerting effort toward mastering tasks.
Analytical Thinking	Job requires analyzing information and using logic to address work-related issues and problems.

Innovation	Job requires creativity and alternative thinking to develop new ideas for and answers to work-related problems.
Independence	Job requires developing one's own ways of doing things, guiding oneself with little or no supervision, and depending on oneself to get things done.

33-1021.02 - Forest Fire Fighting and Prevention Supervisors

Supervise fire fighters who control and suppress fires in forests or vacant public land.

Tasks

1) Direct the loading of fire suppression equipment into aircraft and the parachuting of equipment to crews on the ground.

2) Parachute to major fire locations in order to direct fire containment and suppression activities.

3) Evaluate size, location, and condition of forest fires in order to request and dispatch crews and position equipment so fires can be contained safely and effectively.

4) Schedule employee work assignments, and set work priorities.

5) Maintain fire suppression equipment in good condition, checking equipment periodically in order to ensure that it is ready for use.

6) Observe fires and crews from air to determine fire-fighting force requirements and to note changing conditions that will affect fire-fighting efforts.

7) Operate wildland fire engines and hoselays.

8) Review and evaluate employee performance.

9) Recruit and hire forest fire-fighting personnel.

10) Direct investigations of suspected arsons in wildfires, working closely with other investigating agencies.

11) Monitor prescribed burns to ensure that they are conducted safely and effectively.

12) Direct and supervise prescribed burn projects, and prepare post-burn reports analyzing burn conditions and results.

13) Perform administrative duties such as compiling and maintaining records, completing forms, preparing reports, and composing correspondence.

14) Serve as working leader of an engine-, hand-, helicopter-, or prescribed fire crew of three or more firefighters.

15) Regulate open burning by issuing burning permits, inspecting problem sites, issuing citations for violations of laws and ordinances, and educating the public in proper burning practices.

16) Inspect all stations, uniforms, equipment, and recreation areas in order to ensure compliance with safety standards, taking corrective action as necessary.

17) Train workers in such skills as parachute jumping, fire suppression, aerial observation, and radio communication, both in the classroom and on the job.

18) Investigate special fire issues such as railroad fire problems, right-of-way burning, and slash disposal problems.

19) Communicate fire details to superiors, subordinates, and interagency dispatch centers, using two-way radios.

20) Monitor fire suppression expenditures in order to ensure that they are necessary and reasonable.

21) Lead work crews in the maintenance of structures and access roads in forest areas.

22) Educate the public about forest fire prevention by participating in activities such as exhibits and presentations, and by distributing promotional materials.

23) Appraise damage caused by fires in order to prepare damage reports.

24) Recommend equipment modifications or new equipment purchases.

25) Identify staff training and development needs in order to ensure that appropriate training can be arranged.

26) Drive crew carriers in order to transport firefighters to fire sites.

33-2011.01 - Municipal Fire Fighters

Control and extinguish municipal fires, protect life and property and conduct rescue efforts.

681

Tasks

1) Clean and maintain fire stations and fire fighting equipment and apparatus.

2) Participate in courses, seminars and conferences, and study fire science literature, in order to learn firefighting techniques.

3) Lay hose lines and connect them to water supplies.

4) Drive and operate fire fighting vehicles and equipment.

5) Dress with equipment such as fire resistant clothing and breathing apparatus.

6) Participate in fire drills and demonstrations of fire fighting techniques.

7) Select and attach hose nozzles, depending on fire type, and direct streams of water or chemicals onto fires.

8) Operate pumps connected to high-pressure hoses.

9) Salvage property by removing broken glass, pumping out water, and ventilating buildings to remove smoke.

10) Assess fires and situations and report conditions to superiors in order to receive instructions, using two-way radios.

11) Rescue victims from burning buildings and accident sites.

12) Protect property from water and smoke using waterproof salvage covers, smoke ejectors, and deodorants.

13) Inform and educate the public on fire prevention.

14) Position and climb ladders in order to gain access to upper levels of buildings, or to rescue individuals from burning structures.

15) Take action to contain hazardous chemicals that might catch fire, leak, or spill.

16) Move toward the source of a fire using knowledge of types of fires, construction design, building materials, and physical layout of properties.

17) Participate in physical training activities in order to maintain a high level of physical fitness.

18) Search burning buildings to locate fire victims.

19) Create openings in buildings for ventilation or entrance, using axes, chisels, crowbars, electric saws, or core cutters.

20) Establish firelines to prevent unauthorized persons from entering areas near fires.

21) Administer first aid and cardiopulmonary resuscitation to injured persons.

22) Inspect buildings for fire hazards and compliance with fire prevention ordinances, testing and checking smoke alarms and fire suppression equipment as necessary.

23) Collaborate with police to respond to accidents, disasters, and arson investigation calls.

24) Inspect fire sites after flames have been extinguished in order to ensure that there is no further danger.

25) Prepare written reports that detail specifics of fire incidents.

26) Spray foam onto runways, extinguish fires, and rescue aircraft crew and passengers in air-crash emergencies.

Knowledge	Knowledge Definitions
Customer and Personal Service	Knowledge of principles and processes for providing customer and personal services. This includes customer needs assessment, meeting quality standards for services, and evaluation of customer satisfaction.
Public Safety and Security	Knowledge of relevant equipment, policies, procedures, and strategies to promote effective local, state, or national security operations for the protection of people, data, property, and institutions.
Mechanical	Knowledge of machines and tools, including their designs, uses, repair, and maintenance.
Medicine and Dentistry	Knowledge of the information and techniques needed to diagnose and treat human injuries, diseases, and deformities. This includes symptoms, treatment alternatives, drug properties and interactions, and preventive health-care measures.
Chemistry	Knowledge of the chemical composition, structure, and properties of substances and of the chemical processes and transformations that they undergo. This includes uses of chemicals and their interactions, danger signs, production techniques, and disposal methods.
Building and Construction	Knowledge of materials, methods, and the tools involved in the construction or repair of houses, buildings, or other structures such as highways and roads.
English Language	Knowledge of the structure and content of the English language including the meaning and spelling of words, rules of composition, and grammar.
Physics	Knowledge and prediction of physical principles, laws, their interrelationships, and applications to understanding fluid, material, and atmospheric dynamics, and mechanical, electrical, atomic and sub-atomic structures and processes.
Law and Government	Knowledge of laws, legal codes, court procedures, precedents, government regulations, executive orders, agency rules, and the democratic political process.
Mathematics	Knowledge of arithmetic, algebra, geometry, calculus, statistics, and their applications.
Psychology	Knowledge of human behavior and performance; individual differences in ability, personality, and interests; learning and motivation; psychological research methods; and the assessment and treatment of behavioral and affective disorders.
Transportation	Knowledge of principles and methods for moving people or goods by air, rail, sea, or road, including the relative costs and benefits.
Administration and Management	Knowledge of business and management principles involved in strategic planning, resource allocation, human resources modeling, leadership technique, production methods, and coordination of people and resources.
Education and Training	Knowledge of principles and methods for curriculum and training design, teaching and instruction for individuals and groups, and the measurement of training effects.
Telecommunications	Knowledge of transmission, broadcasting, switching, control, and operation of telecommunications systems.
Engineering and Technology	Knowledge of the practical application of engineering science and technology. This includes applying principles, techniques, procedures, and equipment to the design and production of various goods and services.
Personnel and Human Resources	Knowledge of principles and procedures for personnel recruitment, selection, training, compensation and benefits, labor relations and negotiation, and personnel information systems.
Therapy and Counseling	Knowledge of principles, methods, and procedures for diagnosis, treatment, and rehabilitation of physical and mental dysfunctions, and for career counseling and guidance.
Computers and Electronics	Knowledge of circuit boards, processors, chips, electronic equipment, and computer hardware and software, including applications and programming.
Design	Knowledge of design techniques, tools, and principles involved in production of precision technical plans, blueprints, drawings, and models.
Geography	Knowledge of principles and methods for describing the features of land, sea, and air masses, including their physical characteristics, locations, interrelationships, and distribution of plant, animal, and human life.
Clerical	Knowledge of administrative and clerical procedures and systems such as word processing, managing files and records, stenography and transcription, designing forms, and other office procedures and terminology.
Biology	Knowledge of plant and animal organisms, their tissues, cells, functions, interdependencies, and interactions with each other and the environment.
Philosophy and Theology	Knowledge of different philosophical systems and religions. This includes their basic principles, values, ethics, ways of thinking, customs, practices, and their impact on human culture.
Sociology and Anthropology	Knowledge of group behavior and dynamics, societal trends and influences, human migrations, ethnicity, cultures and their history and origins.
Communications and Media	Knowledge of media production, communication, and dissemination techniques and methods. This includes alternative ways to inform and entertain via written, oral, and visual media.
Foreign Language	Knowledge of the structure and content of a foreign (non-English) language including the meaning and spelling of words, rules of composition and grammar, and pronunciation.
Sales and Marketing	Knowledge of principles and methods for showing, promoting, and selling products or services. This includes marketing strategy and tactics, product demonstration, sales techniques, and sales control systems.
History and Archeology	Knowledge of historical events and their causes, indicators, and effects on civilizations and cultures.

Production and Processing	Knowledge of raw materials, production processes, quality control, costs, and other techniques for maximizing the effective manufacture and distribution of goods.
Economics and Accounting	Knowledge of economic and accounting principles and practices, the financial markets, banking and the analysis and reporting of financial data.
Food Production	Knowledge of techniques and equipment for planting, growing, and harvesting food products (both plant and animal) for consumption, including storage/handling techniques.
Fine Arts	Knowledge of the theory and techniques required to compose, produce, and perform works of music, dance, visual arts, drama, and sculpture.

Skills	Skills Definitions
Active Listening	Giving full attention to what other people are saying, taking time to understand the points being made, asking questions as appropriate, and not interrupting at inappropriate times.
Coordination	Adjusting actions in relation to others' actions.
Equipment Selection	Determining the kind of tools and equipment needed to do a job.
Critical Thinking	Using logic and reasoning to identify the strengths and weaknesses of alternative solutions, conclusions or approaches to problems.
Equipment Maintenance	Performing routine maintenance on equipment and determining when and what kind of maintenance is needed.
Reading Comprehension	Understanding written sentences and paragraphs in work related documents.
Service Orientation	Actively looking for ways to help people.
Speaking	Talking to others to convey information effectively.
Instructing	Teaching others how to do something.
Complex Problem Solving	Identifying complex problems and reviewing related information to develop and evaluate options and implement solutions.
Social Perceptiveness	Being aware of others' reactions and understanding why they react as they do.
Active Learning	Understanding the implications of new information for both current and future problem-solving and decision-making.
Monitoring	Monitoring/Assessing performance of yourself, other individuals, or organizations to make improvements or take corrective action.
Judgment and Decision Making	Considering the relative costs and benefits of potential actions to choose the most appropriate one.
Learning Strategies	Selecting and using training/instructional methods and procedures appropriate for the situation when learning or teaching new things.
Operation Monitoring	Watching gauges, dials, or other indicators to make sure a machine is working properly.
Writing	Communicating effectively in writing as appropriate for the needs of the audience.
Mathematics	Using mathematics to solve problems.
Science	Using scientific rules and methods to solve problems.
Troubleshooting	Determining causes of operating errors and deciding what to do about it.
Technology Design	Generating or adapting equipment and technology to serve user needs.
Operation and Control	Controlling operations of equipment or systems.
Time Management	Managing one's own time and the time of others.
Negotiation	Bringing others together and trying to reconcile differences.
Repairing	Repairing machines or systems using the needed tools.
Management of Material Resources	Obtaining and seeing to the appropriate use of equipment, facilities, and materials needed to do certain work.
Persuasion	Persuading others to change their minds or behavior.
Operations Analysis	Analyzing needs and product requirements to create a design.
Quality Control Analysis	Conducting tests and inspections of products, services, or processes to evaluate quality or performance.
Management of Personnel Resources	Motivating, developing, and directing people as they work, identifying the best people for the job.
Installation	Installing equipment, machines, wiring, or programs to meet specifications.
Systems Evaluation	Identifying measures or indicators of system performance and the actions needed to improve or correct performance, relative to the goals of the system.
Systems Analysis	Determining how a system should work and how changes in conditions, operations, and the environment will affect outcomes.
Management of Financial Resources	Determining how money will be spent to get the work done, and accounting for these expenditures.

Programming	Writing computer programs for various purposes.

Ability	Ability Definitions
Problem Sensitivity	The ability to tell when something is wrong or is likely to go wrong. It does not involve solving the problem, only recognizing there is a problem.
Deductive Reasoning	The ability to apply general rules to specific problems to produce answers that make sense.
Static Strength	The ability to exert maximum muscle force to lift, push, pull, or carry objects.
Flexibility of Closure	The ability to identify or detect a known pattern (a figure, object, word, or sound) that is hidden in other distracting material.
Spatial Orientation	The ability to know your location in relation to the environment or to know where other objects are in relation to you.
Multilimb Coordination	The ability to coordinate two or more limbs (for example, two arms, two legs, or one leg and one arm) while sitting, standing, or lying down. It does not involve performing the activities while the whole body is in motion.
Oral Expression	The ability to communicate information and ideas in speaking so others will understand.
Speed of Closure	The ability to quickly make sense of, combine, and organize information into meaningful patterns.
Oral Comprehension	The ability to listen to and understand information and ideas presented through spoken words and sentences.
Inductive Reasoning	The ability to combine pieces of information to form general rules or conclusions (includes finding a relationship among seemingly unrelated events).
Manual Dexterity	The ability to quickly move your hand, your hand together with your arm, or your two hands to grasp, manipulate, or assemble objects.
Information Ordering	The ability to arrange things or actions in a certain order or pattern according to a specific rule or set of rules (e.g., patterns of numbers, letters, words, pictures, mathematical operations).
Trunk Strength	The ability to use your abdominal and lower back muscles to support part of the body repeatedly or continuously over time without 'giving out' or fatiguing.
Gross Body Coordination	The ability to coordinate the movement of your arms, legs, and torso together when the whole body is in motion.
Stamina	The ability to exert yourself physically over long periods of time without getting winded or out of breath.
Dynamic Strength	The ability to exert muscle force repeatedly or continuously over time. This involves muscular endurance and resistance to muscle fatigue.
Speech Recognition	The ability to identify and understand the speech of another person.
Far Vision	The ability to see details at a distance.
Control Precision	The ability to quickly and repeatedly adjust the controls of a machine or a vehicle to exact positions.
Selective Attention	The ability to concentrate on a task over a period of time without being distracted.
Speech Clarity	The ability to speak clearly so others can understand you.
Near Vision	The ability to see details at close range (within a few feet of the observer).
Depth Perception	The ability to judge which of several objects is closer or farther away from you, or to judge the distance between you and an object.
Speed of Limb Movement	The ability to quickly move the arms and legs.
Explosive Strength	The ability to use short bursts of muscle force to propel oneself (as in jumping or sprinting), or to throw an object.
Extent Flexibility	The ability to bend, stretch, twist, or reach with your body, arms, and/or legs.
Arm-Hand Steadiness	The ability to keep your hand and arm steady while moving your arm or while holding your arm and hand in one position.
Gross Body Equilibrium	The ability to keep or regain your body balance or stay upright when in an unstable position.
Reaction Time	The ability to quickly respond (with the hand, finger, or foot) to a signal (sound, light, picture) when it appears.
Auditory Attention	The ability to focus on a single source of sound in the presence of other distracting sounds.
Perceptual Speed	The ability to quickly and accurately compare similarities and differences among sets of letters, numbers, objects, pictures, or patterns. The things to be compared may be presented at the same time or one after the other. This ability also includes comparing a presented object with a remembered object.
Written Comprehension	The ability to read and understand information and ideas presented in writing.

Response Orientation	The ability to choose quickly between two or more movements in response to two or more different signals (lights, sounds, pictures). It includes the speed with which the correct response is started with the hand, foot, or other body part.
Category Flexibility	The ability to generate or use different sets of rules for combining or grouping things in different ways.
Time Sharing	The ability to shift back and forth between two or more activities or sources of information (such as speech, sounds, touch, or other sources).
Peripheral Vision	The ability to see objects or movement of objects to one's side when the eyes are looking ahead.
Written Expression	The ability to communicate information and ideas in writing so others will understand.
Glare Sensitivity	The ability to see objects in the presence of glare or bright lighting.
Night Vision	The ability to see under low light conditions.
Memorization	The ability to remember information such as words, numbers, pictures, and procedures.
Visualization	The ability to imagine how something will look after it is moved around or when its parts are moved or rearranged.
Rate Control	The ability to time your movements or the movement of a piece of equipment in anticipation of changes in the speed and/or direction of a moving object or scene.
Sound Localization	The ability to tell the direction from which a sound originated.
Fluency of Ideas	The ability to come up with a number of ideas about a topic (the number of ideas is important, not their quality, correctness, or creativity).
Visual Color Discrimination	The ability to match or detect differences between colors, including shades of color and brightness.
Originality	The ability to come up with unusual or clever ideas about a given topic or situation, or to develop creative ways to solve a problem.
Hearing Sensitivity	The ability to detect or tell the differences between sounds that vary in pitch and loudness.
Finger Dexterity	The ability to make precisely coordinated movements of the fingers of one or both hands to grasp, manipulate, or assemble very small objects.
Wrist-Finger Speed	The ability to make fast, simple, repeated movements of the fingers, hands, and wrists.
Dynamic Flexibility	The ability to quickly and repeatedly bend, stretch, twist, or reach out with your body, arms, and/or legs.
Number Facility	The ability to add, subtract, multiply, or divide quickly and correctly.
Mathematical Reasoning	The ability to choose the right mathematical methods or formulas to solve a problem.

Work_Activity	Work_Activity Definitions
Inspecting Equipment, Structures, or Material	Inspecting equipment, structures, or materials to identify the cause of errors or other problems or defects.
Identifying Objects, Actions, and Events	Identifying information by categorizing, estimating, recognizing differences or similarities, and detecting changes in circumstances or events.
Getting Information	Observing, receiving, and otherwise obtaining information from all relevant sources.
Communicating with Supervisors, Peers, or Subordin	Providing information to supervisors, co-workers, and subordinates by telephone, in written form, e-mail, or in person.
Operating Vehicles, Mechanized Devices, or Equipme	Running, maneuvering, navigating, or driving vehicles or mechanized equipment, such as forklifts, passenger vehicles, aircraft, or water craft.
Monitor Processes, Materials, or Surroundings	Monitoring and reviewing information from materials, events, or the environment, to detect or assess problems.
Making Decisions and Solving Problems	Analyzing information and evaluating results to choose the best solution and solve problems.
Performing General Physical Activities	Performing physical activities that require considerable use of your arms and legs and moving your whole body, such as climbing, lifting, balancing, walking, stooping, and handling of materials.
Handling and Moving Objects	Using hands and arms in handling, installing, positioning, and moving materials, and manipulating things.
Updating and Using Relevant Knowledge	Keeping up-to-date technically and applying new knowledge to your job.
Establishing and Maintaining Interpersonal Relatio	Developing constructive and cooperative working relationships with others, and maintaining them over time.

Evaluating Information to Determine Compliance wit	Using relevant information and individual judgment to determine whether events or processes comply with laws, regulations, or standards.
Performing for or Working Directly with the Public	Performing for people or dealing directly with the public. This includes serving customers in restaurants and stores, and receiving clients or guests.
Developing Objectives and Strategies	Establishing long-range objectives and specifying the strategies and actions to achieve them.
Assisting and Caring for Others	Providing personal assistance, medical attention, emotional support, or other personal care to others such as coworkers, customers, or patients.
Thinking Creatively	Developing, designing, or creating new applications, ideas, relationships, systems, or products, including artistic contributions.
Processing Information	Compiling, coding, categorizing, calculating, tabulating, auditing, or verifying information or data.
Documenting/Recording Information	Entering, transcribing, recording, storing, or maintaining information in written or electronic/magnetic form.
Judging the Qualities of Things, Services, or Peop	Assessing the value, importance, or quality of things or people.
Communicating with Persons Outside Organization	Communicating with people outside the organization, representing the organization to customers, the public, government, and other external sources. This information can be exchanged in person, in writing, or by telephone or e-mail.
Training and Teaching Others	Identifying the educational needs of others, developing formal educational or training programs or classes, and teaching or instructing others.
Developing and Building Teams	Encouraging and building mutual trust, respect, and cooperation among team members.
Controlling Machines and Processes	Using either control mechanisms or direct physical activity to operate machines or processes (not including computers or vehicles).
Repairing and Maintaining Mechanical Equipment	Servicing, repairing, adjusting, and testing machines, devices, moving parts, and equipment that operate primarily on the basis of mechanical (not electronic) principles.
Estimating the Quantifiable Characteristics of Pro	Estimating sizes, distances, and quantities; or determining time, costs, resources, or materials needed to perform a work activity.
Scheduling Work and Activities	Scheduling events, programs, and activities, as well as the work of others.
Organizing, Planning, and Prioritizing Work	Developing specific goals and plans to prioritize, organize, and accomplish your work.
Analyzing Data or Information	Identifying the underlying principles, reasons, or facts of information by breaking down information or data into separate parts.
Interpreting the Meaning of Information for Others	Translating or explaining what information means and how it can be used.
Coordinating the Work and Activities of Others	Getting members of a group to work together to accomplish tasks.
Interacting With Computers	Using computers and computer systems (including hardware and software) to program, write software, set up functions, enter data, or process information.
Resolving Conflicts and Negotiating with Others	Handling complaints, settling disputes, and resolving grievances and conflicts, or otherwise negotiating with others.
Guiding, Directing, and Motivating Subordinates	Providing guidance and direction to subordinates, including setting performance standards and monitoring performance.
Coaching and Developing Others	Identifying the developmental needs of others and coaching, mentoring, or otherwise helping others to improve their knowledge or skills.
Monitoring and Controlling Resources	Monitoring and controlling resources and overseeing the spending of money.
Provide Consultation and Advice to Others	Providing guidance and expert advice to management or other groups on technical, systems-, or process-related topics.
Repairing and Maintaining Electronic Equipment	Servicing, repairing, calibrating, regulating, fine-tuning, or testing machines, devices, and equipment that operate primarily on the basis of electrical or electronic (not mechanical) principles.
Staffing Organizational Units	Recruiting, interviewing, selecting, hiring, and promoting employees in an organization.
Drafting, Laying Out, and Specifying Technical Dev	Providing documentation, detailed instructions, drawings, or specifications to tell others about how devices, parts, equipment, or structures are to be fabricated, constructed, assembled, modified, maintained, or used.
Selling or Influencing Others	Convincing others to buy merchandise/goods or to otherwise change their minds or actions.
Performing Administrative Activities	Performing day-to-day administrative tasks such as maintaining information files and processing paperwork.

Work_Context	Work_Context Definitions
Physical Proximity	To what extent does this job require the worker to perform job tasks in close physical proximity to other people?
Deal With External Customers	How important is it to work with external customers or the public in this job?
Responsible for Others' Health and Safety	How much responsibility is there for the health and safety of others in this job?
Outdoors, Exposed to Weather	How often does this job require working outdoors, exposed to all weather conditions?
Work With Work Group or Team	How important is it to work with others in a group or team in this job?
Telephone	How often do you have telephone conversations in this job?
Face-to-Face Discussions	How often do you have to have face-to-face discussions with individuals or teams in this job?
Frequency of Decision Making	How frequently is the worker required to make decisions that affect other people, the financial resources, and/or the image and reputation of the organization?
In an Enclosed Vehicle or Equipment	How often does this job require working in a closed vehicle or equipment (e.g., car)?
Impact of Decisions on Co-workers or Company Resul	How do the decisions an employee makes impact the results of co-workers, clients or the company?
Contact With Others	How much does this job require the worker to be in contact with others (face-to-face, by telephone, or otherwise) in order to perform it?
Wear Common Protective or Safety Equipment such as	How much does this job require wearing common protective or safety equipment such as safety shoes, glasses, gloves, hard hats or life jackets?
Exposed to Hazardous Equipment	How often does this job require exposure to hazardous equipment?
Exposed to Contaminants	How often does this job require working exposed to contaminants (such as pollutants, gases, dust or odors)?
Indoors, Not Environmentally Controlled	How often does this job require working indoors in non-controlled environmental conditions (e.g., warehouse without heat)?
Sounds, Noise Levels Are Distracting or Uncomforta	How often does this job require working exposed to sounds and noise levels that are distracting or uncomfortable?
Wear Specialized Protective or Safety Equipment su	How much does this job require wearing specialized protective or safety equipment such as breathing apparatus, safety harness, full protection suits, or radiation protection?
Exposed to Disease or Infections	How often does this job require exposure to disease/infections?
Coordinate or Lead Others	How important is it to coordinate or lead others in accomplishing work activities in this job?
Importance of Being Exact or Accurate	How important is being very exact or highly accurate in performing this job?
Indoors, Environmentally Controlled	How often does this job require working indoors in environmentally controlled conditions?
Exposed to Hazardous Conditions	How often does this job require exposure to hazardous conditions?
Very Hot or Cold Temperatures	How often does this job require working in very hot (above 90 F degrees) or very cold (below 32 F degrees) temperatures?
Freedom to Make Decisions	How much decision making freedom, without supervision, does the job offer?
Letters and Memos	How often does the job require written letters and memos?
Structured versus Unstructured Work	To what extent is this job structured for the worker, rather than allowing the worker to determine tasks, priorities, and goals?
Consequence of Error	How serious would the result usually be if the worker made a mistake that was not readily correctable?
Responsibility for Outcomes and Results	How responsible is the worker for work outcomes and results of other workers?
Deal With Unpleasant or Angry People	How frequently does the worker have to deal with unpleasant, angry, or discourteous individuals as part of the job requirements?
Spend Time Standing	How much does this job require standing?
Exposed to High Places	How often does this job require exposure to high places?
Importance of Repeating Same Tasks	How important is repeating the same physical activities (e.g., key entry) or mental activities (e.g., checking entries in a ledger) over and over, without stopping, to performing this job?
Cramped Work Space, Awkward Positions	How often does this job require working in cramped work spaces that requires getting into awkward positions?
Level of Competition	To what extent does this job require the worker to compete or to be aware of competitive pressures?
Frequency of Conflict Situations	How often are there conflict situations the employee has to face in this job?

Spend Time Using Your Hands to Handle, Control, or	How much does this job require using your hands to handle, control, or feel objects, tools or controls?
Exposed to Minor Burns, Cuts, Bites, or Stings	How often does this job require exposure to minor burns, cuts, bites, or stings?
Spend Time Bending or Twisting the Body	How much does this job require bending or twisting your body?
Extremely Bright or Inadequate Lighting	How often does this job require working in extremely bright or inadequate lighting conditions?
Public Speaking	How often do you have to perform public speaking in this job?
Outdoors, Under Cover	How often does this job require working outdoors, under cover (e.g., structure with roof but no walls)?
In an Open Vehicle or Equipment	How often does this job require working in an open vehicle or equipment (e.g., tractor)?
Time Pressure	How often does this job require the worker to meet strict deadlines?
Deal With Physically Aggressive People	How frequently does this job require the worker to deal with physical aggression of violent individuals?
Electronic Mail	How often do you use electronic mail in this job?
Spend Time Walking and Running	How much does this job require walking and running?
Spend Time Climbing Ladders, Scaffolds, or Poles	How much does this job require climbing ladders, scaffolds, or poles?
Spend Time Sitting	How much does this job require sitting?
Spend Time Kneeling, Crouching, Stooping, or Crawl	How much does this job require kneeling, crouching, stooping or crawling?
Spend Time Making Repetitive Motions	How much does this job require making repetitive motions?
Pace Determined by Speed of Equipment	How important is it to this job that the pace is determined by the speed of equipment or machinery? (This does not refer to keeping busy at all times on this job.)
Spend Time Keeping or Regaining Balance	How much does this job require keeping or regaining your balance?
Exposed to Whole Body Vibration	How often does this job require exposure to whole body vibration (e.g., operate a jackhammer)?
Degree of Automation	How automated is the job?
Exposed to Radiation	How often does this job require exposure to radiation?

Job Zone Component	Job Zone Component Definitions
Title	Job Zone Three: Medium Preparation Needed
Overall Experience	Previous work-related skill, knowledge, or experience is required for these occupations. For example, an electrician must have completed three or four years of apprenticeship or several years of vocational training, and often must have passed a licensing exam, in order to perform the job.
Job Training	Employees in these occupations usually need one or two years of training involving both on-the-job experience and informal training with experienced workers.
Job Zone Examples	These occupations usually involve using communication and organizational skills to coordinate, supervise, manage, or train others to accomplish goals. Examples include dental assistants, electricians, fish and game wardens, legal secretaries, personnel recruiters, and recreation workers.
SVP Range	(6.0 to < 7.0)
Education	Most occupations in this zone require training in vocational schools, related on-the-job experience, or an associate's degree. Some may require a bachelor's degree.

Work_Styles	Work_Styles Definitions
Dependability	Job requires being reliable, responsible, and dependable, and fulfilling obligations.
Cooperation	Job requires being pleasant with others on the job and displaying a good-natured, cooperative attitude.
Attention to Detail	Job requires being careful about detail and thorough in completing work tasks.
Self Control	Job requires maintaining composure, keeping emotions in check, controlling anger, and avoiding aggressive behavior, even in very difficult situations.
Stress Tolerance	Job requires accepting criticism and dealing calmly and effectively with high stress situations.
Initiative	Job requires a willingness to take on responsibilities and challenges.

685

Concern for Others	Job requires being sensitive to others' needs and feelings and being understanding and helpful on the job.
Analytical Thinking	Job requires analyzing information and using logic to address work-related issues and problems.
Social Orientation	Job requires preferring to work with others rather than alone, and being personally connected with others on the job.
Persistence	Job requires persistence in the face of obstacles.
Adaptability/Flexibility	Job requires being open to change (positive or negative) and to considerable variety in the workplace.
Achievement/Effort	Job requires establishing and maintaining personally challenging achievement goals and exerting effort toward mastering tasks.
Integrity	Job requires being honest and ethical.
Innovation	Job requires creativity and alternative thinking to develop new ideas for and answers to work-related problems.
Leadership	Job requires a willingness to lead, take charge, and offer opinions and direction.
Independence	Job requires developing one's own ways of doing things, guiding oneself with little or no supervision, and depending on oneself to get things done.

33-2011.02 - Forest Fire Fighters

Control and suppress fires in forests or vacant public land.

Tasks

1) Fell trees, cut and clear brush, and dig trenches in order to create firelines, using axes, chainsaws or shovels.

2) Maintain fire equipment and firehouse living quarters.

3) Collaborate with other firefighters as a member of a firefighting crew.

4) Participate in physical training in order to maintain high levels of physical fitness.

5) Establish water supplies, connect hoses, and direct water onto fires.

6) Take action to contain any hazardous chemicals that could catch fire, leak, or spill.

7) Participate in fire prevention and inspection programs.

8) Maintain contact with fire dispatchers at all times in order to notify them of the need for additional firefighters and supplies, or to detail any difficulties encountered.

9) Perform forest maintenance and improvement tasks such as cutting brush, planting trees, building trails and marking timber.

10) Inform and educate the public about fire prevention.

11) Operate pumps connected to high-pressure hoses.

12) Transport personnel and cargo to and from fire areas.

13) Organize fire caches, positioning equipment for the most effective response.

14) Rescue fire victims, and administer emergency medical aid.

15) Orient self in relation to fire, using compass and map, and collect supplies and equipment dropped by parachute.

16) Test and maintain tools, equipment, jump gear and parachutes in order to ensure readiness for fire suppression activities.

17) Observe forest areas from fire lookout towers in order to spot potential problems.

18) Drop weighted paper streamers from aircraft to determine the speed and direction of the wind at fire sites.

19) Serve as fully trained lead helicopter crewmember and as helispot manager.

20) Patrol burned areas after fires to locate and eliminate hot spots that may restart fires.

21) Extinguish flames and embers to suppress fires, using shovels, or engine- or hand-driven water or chemical pumps.

Knowledge	Knowledge Definitions
Mechanical	Knowledge of machines and tools, including their designs, uses, repair, and maintenance.
Geography	Knowledge of principles and methods for describing the features of land, sea, and air masses, including their physical characteristics, locations, interrelationships, and distribution of plant, animal, and human life.
Education and Training	Knowledge of principles and methods for curriculum and training design, teaching and instruction for individuals and groups, and the measurement of training effects.
Customer and Personal Service	Knowledge of principles and processes for providing customer and personal services. This includes customer needs assessment, meeting quality standards for services, and evaluation of customer satisfaction.
Psychology	Knowledge of human behavior and performance; individual differences in ability, personality, and interests; learning and motivation; psychological research methods; and the assessment and treatment of behavioral and affective disorders.
English Language	Knowledge of the structure and content of the English language including the meaning and spelling of words, rules of composition, and grammar.
Personnel and Human Resources	Knowledge of principles and procedures for personnel recruitment, selection, training, compensation and benefits, labor relations and negotiation, and personnel information systems.
Administration and Management	Knowledge of business and management principles involved in strategic planning, resource allocation, human resources modeling, leadership technique, production methods, and coordination of people and resources.
Public Safety and Security	Knowledge of relevant equipment, policies, procedures, and strategies to promote effective local, state, or national security operations for the protection of people, data, property, and institutions.
Law and Government	Knowledge of laws, legal codes, court procedures, precedents, government regulations, executive orders, agency rules, and the democratic political process.
Design	Knowledge of design techniques, tools, and principles involved in production of precision technical plans, blueprints, drawings, and models.
Sociology and Anthropology	Knowledge of group behavior and dynamics, societal trends and influences, human migrations, ethnicity, cultures and their history and origins.
Telecommunications	Knowledge of transmission, broadcasting, switching, control, and operation of telecommunications systems.
Mathematics	Knowledge of arithmetic, algebra, geometry, calculus, statistics, and their applications.
Communications and Media	Knowledge of media production, communication, and dissemination techniques and methods. This includes alternative ways to inform and entertain via written, oral, and visual media.
Transportation	Knowledge of principles and methods for moving people or goods by air, rail, sea, or road, including the relative costs and benefits.
Medicine and Dentistry	Knowledge of the information and techniques needed to diagnose and treat human injuries, diseases, and deformities. This includes symptoms, treatment alternatives, drug properties and interactions, and preventive health-care measures.
Building and Construction	Knowledge of materials, methods, and the tools involved in the construction or repair of houses, buildings, or other structures such as highways and roads.
Clerical	Knowledge of administrative and clerical procedures and systems such as word processing, managing files and records, stenography and transcription, designing forms, and other office procedures and terminology.
Engineering and Technology	Knowledge of the practical application of engineering science and technology. This includes applying principles, techniques, procedures, and equipment to the design and production of various goods and services.
Physics	Knowledge and prediction of physical principles, laws, their interrelationships, and applications to understanding fluid, material, and atmospheric dynamics, and mechanical, electrical, atomic and sub- atomic structures and processes.
Biology	Knowledge of plant and animal organisms, their tissues, cells, functions, interdependencies, and interactions with each other and the environment.
Computers and Electronics	Knowledge of circuit boards, processors, chips, electronic equipment, and computer hardware and software, including applications and programming.
History and Archeology	Knowledge of historical events and their causes, indicators, and effects on civilizations and cultures.
Chemistry	Knowledge of the chemical composition, structure, and properties of substances and of the chemical processes and transformations that they undergo. This includes uses of chemicals and their interactions, danger signs, production techniques, and disposal methods.

Therapy and Counseling	Knowledge of principles, methods, and procedures for diagnosis, treatment, and rehabilitation of physical and mental dysfunctions, and for career counseling and guidance.
Economics and Accounting	Knowledge of economic and accounting principles and practices, the financial markets, banking and the analysis and reporting of financial data.
Production and Processing	Knowledge of raw materials, production processes, quality control, costs, and other techniques for maximizing the effective manufacture and distribution of goods.
Foreign Language	Knowledge of the structure and content of a foreign (non-English) language including the meaning and spelling of words, rules of composition and grammar, and pronunciation.
Philosophy and Theology	Knowledge of different philosophical systems and religions. This includes their basic principles, values, ethics, ways of thinking, customs, practices, and their impact on human culture.
Sales and Marketing	Knowledge of principles and methods for showing, promoting, and selling products or services. This includes marketing strategy and tactics, product demonstration, sales techniques, and sales control systems.
Food Production	Knowledge of techniques and equipment for planting, growing, and harvesting food products (both plant and animal) for consumption, including storage/handling techniques.
Fine Arts	Knowledge of the theory and techniques required to compose, produce, and perform works of music, dance, visual arts, drama, and sculpture.

Skills	Skills Definitions
Equipment Maintenance	Performing routine maintenance on equipment and determining when and what kind of maintenance is needed.
Active Listening	Giving full attention to what other people are saying, taking time to understand the points being made, asking questions as appropriate, and not interrupting at inappropriate times.
Judgment and Decision Making	Considering the relative costs and benefits of potential actions to choose the most appropriate one.
Service Orientation	Actively looking for ways to help people.
Equipment Selection	Determining the kind of tools and equipment needed to do a job.
Coordination	Adjusting actions in relation to others' actions.
Instructing	Teaching others how to do something.
Operation Monitoring	Watching gauges, dials, or other indicators to make sure a machine is working properly.
Complex Problem Solving	Identifying complex problems and reviewing related information to develop and evaluate options and implement solutions.
Operation and Control	Controlling operations of equipment or systems.
Management of Personnel Resources	Motivating, developing, and directing people as they work, identifying the best people for the job.
Active Learning	Understanding the implications of new information for both current and future problem-solving and decision-making.
Reading Comprehension	Understanding written sentences and paragraphs in work related documents.
Critical Thinking	Using logic and reasoning to identify the strengths and weaknesses of alternative solutions, conclusions or approaches to problems.
Monitoring	Monitoring/Assessing performance of yourself, other individuals, or organizations to make improvements or take corrective action.
Learning Strategies	Selecting and using training/instructional methods and procedures appropriate for the situation when learning or teaching new things.
Speaking	Talking to others to convey information effectively.
Time Management	Managing one's own time and the time of others.
Troubleshooting	Determining causes of operating errors and deciding what to do about it.
Writing	Communicating effectively in writing as appropriate for the needs of the audience.
Social Perceptiveness	Being aware of others' reactions and understanding why they react as they do.
Operations Analysis	Analyzing needs and product requirements to create a design.
Repairing	Repairing machines or systems using the needed tools.
Management of Material Resources	Obtaining and seeing to the appropriate use of equipment, facilities, and materials needed to do certain work.
Quality Control Analysis	Conducting tests and inspections of products, services, or processes to evaluate quality or performance.

Systems Analysis	Determining how a system should work and how changes in conditions, operations, and the environment will affect outcomes.
Management of Financial Resources	Determining how money will be spent to get the work done, and accounting for these expenditures.
Persuasion	Persuading others to change their minds or behavior.
Mathematics	Using mathematics to solve problems.
Systems Evaluation	Identifying measures or indicators of system performance and the actions needed to improve or correct performance, relative to the goals of the system.
Negotiation	Bringing others together and trying to reconcile differences.
Science	Using scientific rules and methods to solve problems.
Technology Design	Generating or adapting equipment and technology to serve user needs.
Installation	Installing equipment, machines, wiring, or programs to meet specifications.
Programming	Writing computer programs for various purposes.

Ability	Ability Definitions
Problem Sensitivity	The ability to tell when something is wrong or is likely to go wrong. It does not involve solving the problem, only recognizing there is a problem.
Oral Comprehension	The ability to listen to and understand information and ideas presented through spoken words and sentences.
Oral Expression	The ability to communicate information and ideas in speaking so others will understand.
Speech Clarity	The ability to speak clearly so others can understand you.
Deductive Reasoning	The ability to apply general rules to specific problems to produce answers that make sense.
Inductive Reasoning	The ability to combine pieces of information to form general rules or conclusions (includes finding a relationship among seemingly unrelated events).
Speech Recognition	The ability to identify and understand the speech of another person.
Stamina	The ability to exert yourself physically over long periods of time without getting winded or out of breath.
Speed of Limb Movement	The ability to quickly move the arms and legs.
Static Strength	The ability to exert maximum muscle force to lift, push, pull, or carry objects.
Trunk Strength	The ability to use your abdominal and lower back muscles to support part of the body repeatedly or continuously over time without 'giving out' or fatiguing.
Selective Attention	The ability to concentrate on a task over a period of time without being distracted.
Speed of Closure	The ability to quickly make sense of, combine, and organize information into meaningful patterns.
Near Vision	The ability to see details at close range (within a few feet of the observer).
Manual Dexterity	The ability to quickly move your hand, your hand together with your arm, or your two hands to grasp, manipulate, or assemble objects.
Far Vision	The ability to see details at a distance.
Dynamic Strength	The ability to exert muscle force repeatedly or continuously over time. This involves muscular endurance and resistance to muscle fatigue.
Control Precision	The ability to quickly and repeatedly adjust the controls of a machine or a vehicle to exact positions.
Information Ordering	The ability to arrange things or actions in a certain order or pattern according to a specific rule or set of rules (e.g., patterns of numbers, letters, words, pictures, mathematical operations).
Flexibility of Closure	The ability to identify or detect a known pattern (a figure, object, word, or sound) that is hidden in other distracting material.
Arm-Hand Steadiness	The ability to keep your hand and arm steady while moving your arm or while holding your arm and hand in one position.
Multilimb Coordination	The ability to coordinate two or more limbs (for example, two arms, two legs, or one leg and one arm) while sitting, standing, or lying down. It does not involve performing the activities while the whole body is in motion.
Gross Body Coordination	The ability to coordinate the movement of your arms, legs, and torso together when the whole body is in motion.
Depth Perception	The ability to judge which of several objects is closer or farther away from you, or to judge the distance between you and an object.
Time Sharing	The ability to shift back and forth between two or more activities or sources of information (such as speech, sounds, touch, or other sources).

687

Extent Flexibility	The ability to bend, stretch, twist, or reach with your body, arms, and/or legs.
Written Comprehension	The ability to read and understand information and ideas presented in writing.
Reaction Time	The ability to quickly respond (with the hand, finger, or foot) to a signal (sound, light, picture) when it appears.
Spatial Orientation	The ability to know your location in relation to the environment or to know where other objects are in relation to you.
Auditory Attention	The ability to focus on a single source of sound in the presence of other distracting sounds.
Gross Body Equilibrium	The ability to keep or regain your body balance or stay upright when in an unstable position.
Visualization	The ability to imagine how something will look after it is moved around or when its parts are moved or rearranged.
Fluency of Ideas	The ability to come up with a number of ideas about a topic (the number of ideas is important, not their quality, correctness, or creativity).
Written Expression	The ability to communicate information and ideas in writing so others will understand.
Perceptual Speed	The ability to quickly and accurately compare similarities and differences among sets of letters, numbers, objects, pictures, or patterns. The things to be compared may be presented at the same time or one after the other. This ability also includes comparing a presented object with a remembered object.
Category Flexibility	The ability to generate or use different sets of rules for combining or grouping things in different ways.
Response Orientation	The ability to choose quickly between two or more movements in response to two or more different signals (lights, sounds, pictures). It includes the speed with which the correct response is started with the hand, foot, or other body part.
Memorization	The ability to remember information such as words, numbers, pictures, and procedures.
Glare Sensitivity	The ability to see objects in the presence of glare or bright lighting.
Originality	The ability to come up with unusual or clever ideas about a given topic or situation, or to develop creative ways to solve a problem.
Rate Control	The ability to time your movements or the movement of a piece of equipment in anticipation of changes in the speed and/or direction of a moving object or scene.
Finger Dexterity	The ability to make precisely coordinated movements of the fingers of one or both hands to grasp, manipulate, or assemble very small objects.
Visual Color Discrimination	The ability to match or detect differences between colors, including shades of color and brightness.
Peripheral Vision	The ability to see objects or movement of objects to one's side when the eyes are looking ahead.
Hearing Sensitivity	The ability to detect or tell the differences between sounds that vary in pitch and loudness.
Night Vision	The ability to see under low light conditions.
Number Facility	The ability to add, subtract, multiply, or divide quickly and correctly.
Explosive Strength	The ability to use short bursts of muscle force to propel oneself (as in jumping or sprinting), or to throw an object.
Mathematical Reasoning	The ability to choose the right mathematical methods or formulas to solve a problem.
Sound Localization	The ability to tell the direction from which a sound originated.
Dynamic Flexibility	The ability to quickly and repeatedly bend, stretch, twist, or reach out with your body, arms, and/or legs.
Wrist-Finger Speed	The ability to make fast, simple, repeated movements of the fingers, hands, and wrists.

Work_Activity	Work_Activity Definitions
Performing General Physical Activities	Performing physical activities that require considerable use of your arms and legs and moving your whole body, such as climbing, lifting, balancing, walking, stooping, and handling of materials.
Inspecting Equipment, Structures, or Material	Inspecting equipment, structures, or materials to identify the cause of errors or other problems or defects.
Communicating with Supervisors, Peers, or Subordin	Providing information to supervisors, co-workers, and subordinates by telephone, in written form, e-mail, or in person.
Operating Vehicles, Mechanized Devices, or Equipme	Running, maneuvering, navigating, or driving vehicles or mechanized equipment, such as forklifts, passenger vehicles, aircraft, or water craft.
Making Decisions and Solving Problems	Analyzing information and evaluating results to choose the best solution and solve problems.

Monitor Processes, Materials, or Surroundings	Monitoring and reviewing information from materials, events, or the environment, to detect or assess problems.
Getting Information	Observing, receiving, and otherwise obtaining information from all relevant sources.
Handling and Moving Objects	Using hands and arms in handling, installing, positioning, and moving materials, and manipulating things.
Controlling Machines and Processes	Using either control mechanisms or direct physical activity to operate machines or processes (not including computers or vehicles).
Coaching and Developing Others	Identifying the developmental needs of others and coaching, mentoring, or otherwise helping others to improve their knowledge or skills.
Identifying Objects, Actions, and Events	Identifying information by categorizing, estimating, recognizing differences or similarities, and detecting changes in circumstances or events.
Establishing and Maintaining Interpersonal Relatio	Developing constructive and cooperative working relationships with others, and maintaining them over time.
Repairing and Maintaining Mechanical Equipment	Servicing, repairing, adjusting, and testing machines, devices, moving parts, and equipment that operate primarily on the basis of mechanical (not electronic) principles.
Guiding, Directing, and Motivating Subordinates	Providing guidance and direction to subordinates, including setting performance standards and monitoring performance.
Judging the Qualities of Things, Services, or Peop	Assessing the value, importance, or quality of things or people.
Assisting and Caring for Others	Providing personal assistance, medical attention, emotional support, or other personal care to others such as coworkers, customers, or patients.
Training and Teaching Others	Identifying the educational needs of others, developing formal educational or training programs or classes, and teaching or instructing others.
Developing Objectives and Strategies	Establishing long-range objectives and specifying the strategies and actions to achieve them.
Interpreting the Meaning of Information for Others	Translating or explaining what information means and how it can be used.
Coordinating the Work and Activities of Others	Getting members of a group to work together to accomplish tasks.
Updating and Using Relevant Knowledge	Keeping up-to-date technically and applying new knowledge to your job.
Performing for or Working Directly with the Public	Performing for people or dealing directly with the public. This includes serving customers in restaurants and stores, and receiving clients or guests.
Communicating with Persons Outside Organization	Communicating with people outside the organization, representing the organization to customers, the public, government, and other external sources. This information can be exchanged in person, in writing, or by telephone or e-mail.
Organizing, Planning, and Prioritizing Work	Developing specific goals and plans to prioritize, organize, and accomplish your work.
Developing and Building Teams	Encouraging and building mutual trust, respect, and cooperation among team members.
Estimating the Quantifiable Characteristics of Pro	Estimating sizes, distances, and quantities; or determining time, costs, resources, or materials needed to perform a work activity.
Documenting/Recording Information	Entering, transcribing, recording, storing, or maintaining information in written or electronic/magnetic form.
Analyzing Data or Information	Identifying the underlying principles, reasons, or facts of information by breaking down information or data into separate parts.
Provide Consultation and Advice to Others	Providing guidance and expert advice to management or other groups on technical, systems-, or process-related topics.
Staffing Organizational Units	Recruiting, interviewing, selecting, hiring, and promoting employees in an organization.
Monitoring and Controlling Resources	Monitoring and controlling resources and overseeing the spending of money.
Resolving Conflicts and Negotiating with Others	Handling complaints, settling disputes, and resolving grievances and conflicts, or otherwise negotiating with others.
Evaluating Information to Determine Compliance wit	Using relevant information and individual judgment to determine whether events or processes comply with laws, regulations, or standards.
Drafting, Laying Out, and Specifying Technical Dev	Providing documentation, detailed instructions, drawings, or specifications to tell others about how devices, parts, equipment, or structures are to be fabricated, constructed, assembled, modified, maintained, or used.
Thinking Creatively	Developing, designing, or creating new applications, ideas, relationships, systems, or products, including artistic contributions.

Performing Administrative Activities	Performing day-to-day administrative tasks such as maintaining information files and processing paperwork.
Processing Information	Compiling, coding, categorizing, calculating, tabulating, auditing, or verifying information or data.
Scheduling Work and Activities	Scheduling events, programs, and activities, as well as the work of others.
Interacting With Computers	Using computers and computer systems (including hardware and software) to program, write software, set up functions, enter data, or process information.
Repairing and Maintaining Electronic Equipment	Servicing, repairing, calibrating, regulating, fine-tuning, or testing machines, devices, and equipment that operate primarily on the basis of electrical or electronic (not mechanical) principles.
Selling or Influencing Others	Convincing others to buy merchandise/goods or to otherwise change their minds or actions.

Work_Context	Work_Context Definitions
Wear Common Protective or Safety Equipment such as	How much does this job require wearing common protective or safety equipment such as safety shoes, glasses, gloves, hard hats or life jackets?
Outdoors, Exposed to Weather	How often does this job require working outdoors, exposed to all weather conditions?
Contact With Others	How much does this job require the worker to be in contact with others (face-to-face, by telephone, or otherwise) in order to perform it?
Face-to-Face Discussions	How often do you have to have face-to-face discussions with individuals or teams in this job?
Work With Work Group or Team	How important is it to work with others in a group or team in this job?
Exposed to Minor Burns, Cuts, Bites, or Stings	How often does this job require exposure to minor burns, cuts, bites, or stings?
Telephone	How often do you have telephone conversations in this job?
Exposed to Contaminants	How often does this job require working exposed to contaminants (such as pollutants, gases, dust or odors)?
In an Enclosed Vehicle or Equipment	How often does this job require working in a closed vehicle or equipment (e.g., car)?
Very Hot or Cold Temperatures	How often does this job require working in very hot (above 90 F degrees) or very cold (below 32 F degrees) temperatures?
Consequence of Error	How serious would the result usually be if the worker made a mistake that was not readily correctable?
Impact of Decisions on Co-workers or Company Resul	How do the decisions an employee makes impact the results of co-workers, clients or the company?
Exposed to Hazardous Conditions	How often does this job require exposure to hazardous conditions?
Frequency of Decision Making	How frequently is the worker required to make decisions that affect other people, the financial resources, and/or the image and reputation of the organization?
Spend Time Using Your Hands to Handle, Control, or	How much does this job require using your hands to handle, control, or feel objects, tools or controls?
Spend Time Walking and Running	How much does this job require walking and running?
Exposed to Hazardous Equipment	How often does this job require exposure to hazardous equipment?
Responsible for Others' Health and Safety	How much responsibility is there for the health and safety of others in this job?
Spend Time Standing	How much does this job require standing?
Freedom to Make Decisions	How much decision making freedom, without supervision, does the job offer?
Indoors, Not Environmentally Controlled	How often does this job require working indoors in non-controlled environmental conditions (e.g., warehouse without heat)?
Cramped Work Space, Awkward Positions	How often does this job require working in cramped work spaces that requires getting into awkward positions?
Spend Time Bending or Twisting the Body	How much does this job require bending or twisting your body?
Extremely Bright or Inadequate Lighting	How often does this job require working in extremely bright or inadequate lighting conditions?
Responsibility for Outcomes and Results	How responsible is the worker for work outcomes and results of other workers?
Physical Proximity	To what extent does this job require the worker to perform job tasks in close physical proximity to other people?
Coordinate or Lead Others	How important is it to coordinate or lead others in accomplishing work activities in this job?
Sounds, Noise Levels Are Distracting or Uncomforta	How often does this job require working exposed to sounds and noise levels that are distracting or uncomfortable?

Importance of Repeating Same Tasks	How important is repeating the same physical activities (e.g., key entry) or mental activities (e.g., checking entries in a ledger) over and over, without stopping, to performing this job?
Deal With External Customers	How important is it to work with external customers or the public in this job?
Deal With Unpleasant or Angry People	How frequently does the worker have to deal with unpleasant, angry, or discourteous individuals as part of the job requirements?
Frequency of Conflict Situations	How often are there conflict situations the employee has to face in this job?
Importance of Being Exact or Accurate	How important is being very exact or highly accurate in performing this job?
Level of Competition	To what extent does this job require the worker to compete or to be aware of competitive pressures?
Structured versus Unstructured Work	To what extent is this job structured for the worker, rather than allowing the worker to determine tasks, priorities, and goals?
Public Speaking	How often do you have to perform public speaking in this job?
Spend Time Keeping or Regaining Balance	How much does this job require keeping or regaining your balance?
Wear Specialized Protective or Safety Equipment su	How much does this job require wearing specialized protective or safety equipment such as breathing apparatus, safety harness, full protection suits, or radiation protection?
Time Pressure	How often does this job require the worker to meet strict deadlines?
Outdoors, Under Cover	How often does this job require working outdoors, under cover (e.g., structure with roof but no walls)?
Spend Time Kneeling, Crouching, Stooping, or Crawl	How much does this job require kneeling, crouching, stooping, or crawling?
Spend Time Making Repetitive Motions	How much does this job require making repetitive motions?
Electronic Mail	How often do you use electronic mail in this job?
Exposed to Whole Body Vibration	How often does this job require exposure to whole body vibration (e.g., operate a jackhammer)?
Exposed to High Places	How often does this job require exposure to high places?
Letters and Memos	How often does the job require written letters and memos?
Indoors, Environmentally Controlled	How often does this job require working indoors in environmentally controlled conditions?
Spend Time Sitting	How much does this job require sitting?
In an Open Vehicle or Equipment	How often does this job require working in an open vehicle or equipment (e.g., tractor)?
Spend Time Climbing Ladders, Scaffolds, or Poles	How much does this job require climbing ladders, scaffolds, or poles?
Degree of Automation	How automated is the job?
Exposed to Disease or Infections	How often does this job require exposure to disease/infections?
Deal With Physically Aggressive People	How frequently does this job require the worker to deal with physical aggression of violent individuals?
Pace Determined by Speed of Equipment	How important is it to this job that the pace is determined by the speed of equipment or machinery? (This does not refer to keeping busy at all times on this job.)
Exposed to Radiation	How often does this job require exposure to radiation?

Job Zone Component	Job Zone Component Definitions
Title	Job Zone Two: Some Preparation Needed
Overall Experience	Some previous work-related skill, knowledge, or experience may be helpful in these occupations, but usually is not needed. For example, a drywall installer might benefit from experience installing drywall, but an inexperienced person could still learn to be an installer with little difficulty.
Job Training	Employees in these occupations need anywhere from a few months to one year of working with experienced employees.
Job Zone Examples	These occupations often involve using your knowledge and skills to help others. Examples include drywall installers, fire inspectors, flight attendants, pharmacy technicians, salespersons (retail), and tellers.
SVP Range	(4.0 to < 6.0)
Education	These occupations usually require a high school diploma and may require some vocational training or job-related course work. In some cases, an associate's or bachelor's degree could be needed.

Work_Styles	Work_Styles Definitions

689

Dependability	Job requires being reliable, responsible, and dependable, and fulfilling obligations.
Attention to Detail	Job requires being careful about detail and thorough in completing work tasks.
Cooperation	Job requires being pleasant with others on the job and displaying a good-natured, cooperative attitude.
Stress Tolerance	Job requires accepting criticism and dealing calmly and effectively with high stress situations.
Self Control	Job requires maintaining composure, keeping emotions in check, controlling anger, and avoiding aggressive behavior, even in very difficult situations.
Integrity	Job requires being honest and ethical.
Leadership	Job requires a willingness to lead, take charge, and offer opinions and direction.
Adaptability/Flexibility	Job requires being open to change (positive or negative) and to considerable variety in the workplace.
Initiative	Job requires a willingness to take on responsibilities and challenges.
Concern for Others	Job requires being sensitive to others' needs and feelings and being understanding and helpful on the job.
Social Orientation	Job requires preferring to work with others rather than alone, and being personally connected with others on the job.
Persistence	Job requires persistence in the face of obstacles.
Achievement/Effort	Job requires establishing and maintaining personally challenging achievement goals and exerting effort toward mastering tasks.
Analytical Thinking	Job requires analyzing information and using logic to address work-related issues and problems.
Independence	Job requires developing one's own ways of doing things, guiding oneself with little or no supervision, and depending on oneself to get things done.
Innovation	Job requires creativity and alternative thinking to develop new ideas for and answers to work-related problems.

33-2021.01 - Fire Inspectors

Inspect buildings and equipment to detect fire hazards and enforce state and local regulations.

Tasks

1) Identify corrective actions necessary to bring properties into compliance with applicable fire codes, laws, regulations, and standards, and explain these measures to property owners or their representatives.

2) Write detailed reports of fire inspections performed, fire code violations observed, and corrective recommendations offered.

3) Inspect buildings to locate hazardous conditions and fire code violations such as accumulations of combustible material, electrical wiring problems, and inadequate or non-functional fire exits.

4) Attend training classes in order to maintain current knowledge of fire prevention, safety, and firefighting procedures.

5) Inspect and test fire protection and/or fire detection systems to verify that such systems are installed in accordance with appropriate laws, codes, ordinances, regulations, and standards.

6) Conduct fire exit drills to monitor and evaluate evacuation procedures.

7) Present and explain fire code requirements and fire prevention information to architects, contractors, attorneys, engineers, developers, fire service personnel, and the general public.

8) Inspect properties that store, handle, and use hazardous materials to ensure compliance with laws, codes, and regulations, and issue hazardous materials permits to facilities found in compliance.

9) Develop or review fire exit plans.

10) Conduct inspections and acceptance testing of newly installed fire protection systems.

11) Recommend changes to fire prevention, inspection, and fire code endorsement procedures.

12) Review blueprints and plans for new or remodeled buildings in order to ensure the structures meet fire safety codes.

13) Inspect liquefied petroleum installations, storage containers, and transportation and delivery systems for compliance with fire laws.

14) Search for clues as to the cause of a fire, once the fire is completely extinguished.

15) Testify in court regarding fire code and fire safety issues.

16) Develop and coordinate fire prevention programs such as false alarm billing, fire inspection reporting, and hazardous materials management.

17) Investigate causes of fires, collecting and preparing evidence and presenting it in court when necessary.

18) Supervise staff, training them, planning their work, and evaluating their performance.

19) Issue permits for public assemblies.

20) Serve court appearance summonses and/or condemnation notices on parties responsible for violations of fire codes, laws, and ordinances.

21) Arrange for the replacement of defective fire fighting equipment and for repair of fire alarm and sprinkler systems, making minor repairs such as servicing fire extinguishers when feasible.

22) Collect fees for permits and licenses.

Knowledge	Knowledge Definitions
Public Safety and Security	Knowledge of relevant equipment, policies, procedures, and strategies to promote effective local, state, or national security operations for the protection of people, data, property, and institutions.
Building and Construction	Knowledge of materials, methods, and the tools involved in the construction or repair of houses, buildings, or other structures such as highways and roads.
Customer and Personal Service	Knowledge of principles and processes for providing customer and personal services. This includes customer needs assessment, meeting quality standards for services, and evaluation of customer satisfaction.
Law and Government	Knowledge of laws, legal codes, court procedures, precedents, government regulations, executive orders, agency rules, and the democratic political process.
English Language	Knowledge of the structure and content of the English language including the meaning and spelling of words, rules of composition, and grammar.
Education and Training	Knowledge of principles and methods for curriculum and training design, teaching and instruction for individuals and groups, and the measurement of training effects.
Design	Knowledge of design techniques, tools, and principles involved in production of precision technical plans, blueprints, drawings, and models.
Administration and Management	Knowledge of business and management principles involved in strategic planning, resource allocation, human resources modeling, leadership technique, production methods, and coordination of people and resources.
Mechanical	Knowledge of machines and tools, including their designs, uses, repair, and maintenance.
Chemistry	Knowledge of the chemical composition, structure, and properties of substances and of the chemical processes and transformations that they undergo. This includes uses of chemicals and their interactions, danger signs, production techniques, and disposal methods.
Computers and Electronics	Knowledge of circuit boards, processors, chips, electronic equipment, and computer hardware and software, including applications and programming.
Clerical	Knowledge of administrative and clerical procedures and systems such as word processing, managing files and records, stenography and transcription, designing forms, and other office procedures and terminology.
Engineering and Technology	Knowledge of the practical application of engineering science and technology. This includes applying principles, techniques, procedures, and equipment to the design and production of various goods and services.
Mathematics	Knowledge of arithmetic, algebra, geometry, calculus, statistics, and their applications.
Physics	Knowledge and prediction of physical principles, laws, their interrelationships, and applications to understanding fluid, material, and atmospheric dynamics, and mechanical, electrical, atomic and sub- atomic structures and processes.
Communications and Media	Knowledge of media production, communication, and dissemination techniques and methods. This includes alternative ways to inform and entertain via written, oral, and visual media.
Psychology	Knowledge of human behavior and performance; individual differences in ability, personality, and interests; learning and motivation; psychological research methods; and the assessment and treatment of behavioral and affective disorders.

Medicine and Dentistry	Knowledge of the information and techniques needed to diagnose and treat human injuries, diseases, and deformities. This includes symptoms, treatment alternatives, drug properties and interactions, and preventive health-care measures.
Personnel and Human Resources	Knowledge of principles and procedures for personnel recruitment, selection, training, compensation and benefits, labor relations and negotiation, and personnel information systems.
Telecommunications	Knowledge of transmission, broadcasting, switching, control, and operation of telecommunications systems.
Transportation	Knowledge of principles and methods for moving people or goods by air, rail, sea, or road, including the relative costs and benefits.
Geography	Knowledge of principles and methods for describing the features of land, sea, and air masses, including their physical characteristics, locations, interrelationships, and distribution of plant, animal, and human life.
Sociology and Anthropology	Knowledge of group behavior and dynamics, societal trends and influences, human migrations, ethnicity, cultures and their history and origins.
Therapy and Counseling	Knowledge of principles, methods, and procedures for diagnosis, treatment, and rehabilitation of physical and mental dysfunctions, and for career counseling and guidance.
Sales and Marketing	Knowledge of principles and methods for showing, promoting, and selling products or services. This includes marketing strategy and tactics, product demonstration, sales techniques, and sales control systems.
Biology	Knowledge of plant and animal organisms, their tissues, cells, functions, interdependencies, and interactions with each other and the environment.
Production and Processing	Knowledge of raw materials, production processes, quality control, costs, and other techniques for maximizing the effective manufacture and distribution of goods.
Philosophy and Theology	Knowledge of different philosophical systems and religions. This includes their basic principles, values, ethics, ways of thinking, customs, practices, and their impact on human culture.
Economics and Accounting	Knowledge of economic and accounting principles and practices, the financial markets, banking and the analysis and reporting of financial data.
History and Archeology	Knowledge of historical events and their causes, indicators, and effects on civilizations and cultures.
Foreign Language	Knowledge of the structure and content of a foreign (non-English) language including the meaning and spelling of words, rules of composition and grammar, and pronunciation.
Food Production	Knowledge of techniques and equipment for planting, growing, and harvesting food products (both plant and animal) for consumption, including storage/handling techniques.
Fine Arts	Knowledge of the theory and techniques required to compose, produce, and perform works of music, dance, visual arts, drama, and sculpture.

Skills	Skills Definitions
Active Listening	Giving full attention to what other people are saying, taking time to understand the points being made, asking questions as appropriate, and not interrupting at inappropriate times.
Reading Comprehension	Understanding written sentences and paragraphs in work related documents.
Writing	Communicating effectively in writing as appropriate for the needs of the audience.
Time Management	Managing one's own time and the time of others.
Speaking	Talking to others to convey information effectively.
Critical Thinking	Using logic and reasoning to identify the strengths and weaknesses of alternative solutions, conclusions or approaches to problems.
Active Learning	Understanding the implications of new information for both current and future problem-solving and decision-making.
Instructing	Teaching others how to do something.
Service Orientation	Actively looking for ways to help people.
Coordination	Adjusting actions in relation to others' actions.
Social Perceptiveness	Being aware of others' reactions and understanding why they react as they do.
Complex Problem Solving	Identifying complex problems and reviewing related information to develop and evaluate options and implement solutions.

Learning Strategies	Selecting and using training/instructional methods and procedures appropriate for the situation when learning or teaching new things.
Persuasion	Persuading others to change their minds or behavior.
Judgment and Decision Making	Considering the relative costs and benefits of potential actions to choose the most appropriate one.
Monitoring	Monitoring/Assessing performance of yourself, other individuals, or organizations to make improvements or take corrective action.
Negotiation	Bringing others together and trying to reconcile differences.
Science	Using scientific rules and methods to solve problems.
Quality Control Analysis	Conducting tests and inspections of products, services, or processes to evaluate quality or performance.
Mathematics	Using mathematics to solve problems.
Operation Monitoring	Watching gauges, dials, or other indicators to make sure a machine is working properly.
Operations Analysis	Analyzing needs and product requirements to create a design.
Troubleshooting	Determining causes of operating errors and deciding what to do about it.
Equipment Selection	Determining the kind of tools and equipment needed to do a job.
Systems Analysis	Determining how a system should work and how changes in conditions, operations, and the environment will affect outcomes.
Operation and Control	Controlling operations of equipment or systems.
Technology Design	Generating or adapting equipment and technology to serve user needs.
Equipment Maintenance	Performing routine maintenance on equipment and determining when and what kind of maintenance is needed.
Systems Evaluation	Identifying measures or indicators of system performance and the actions needed to improve or correct performance, relative to the goals of the system.
Management of Personnel Resources	Motivating, developing, and directing people as they work, identifying the best people for the job.
Management of Material Resources	Obtaining and seeing to the appropriate use of equipment, facilities, and materials needed to do certain work.
Installation	Installing equipment, machines, wiring, or programs to meet specifications.
Management of Financial Resources	Determining how money will be spent to get the work done, and accounting for these expenditures.
Programming	Writing computer programs for various purposes.
Repairing	Repairing machines or systems using the needed tools.

Ability	Ability Definitions
Problem Sensitivity	The ability to tell when something is wrong or is likely to go wrong. It does not involve solving the problem, only recognizing there is a problem.
Oral Expression	The ability to communicate information and ideas in speaking so others will understand.
Oral Comprehension	The ability to listen to and understand information and ideas presented through spoken words and sentences.
Inductive Reasoning	The ability to combine pieces of information to form general rules or conclusions (includes finding a relationship among seemingly unrelated events).
Near Vision	The ability to see details at close range (within a few feet of the observer).
Speech Clarity	The ability to speak clearly so others can understand you.
Written Expression	The ability to communicate information and ideas in writing so others will understand.
Deductive Reasoning	The ability to apply general rules to specific problems to produce answers that make sense.
Written Comprehension	The ability to read and understand information and ideas presented in writing.
Speech Recognition	The ability to identify and understand the speech of another person.
Information Ordering	The ability to arrange things or actions in a certain order or pattern according to a specific rule or set of rules (e.g., patterns of numbers, letters, words, pictures, mathematical operations).
Flexibility of Closure	The ability to identify or detect a known pattern (a figure, object, word, or sound) that is hidden in other distracting material.
Selective Attention	The ability to concentrate on a task over a period of time without being distracted.
Category Flexibility	The ability to generate or use different sets of rules for combining or grouping things in different ways.
Far Vision	The ability to see details at a distance.

Perceptual Speed	The ability to quickly and accurately compare similarities and differences among sets of letters, numbers, objects, pictures, or patterns. The things to be compared may be presented at the same time or one after the other. This ability also includes comparing a presented object with a remembered object.
Visualization	The ability to imagine how something will look after it is moved around or when its parts are moved or rearranged.
Auditory Attention	The ability to focus on a single source of sound in the presence of other distracting sounds.
Fluency of Ideas	The ability to come up with a number of ideas about a topic (the number of ideas is important, not their quality, correctness, or creativity).
Depth Perception	The ability to judge which of several objects is closer or farther away from you, or to judge the distance between you and an object.
Reaction Time	The ability to quickly respond (with the hand, finger, or foot) to a signal (sound, light, picture) when it appears.
Control Precision	The ability to quickly and repeatedly adjust the controls of a machine or a vehicle to exact positions.
Extent Flexibility	The ability to bend, stretch, twist, or reach with your body, arms, and/or legs.
Multilimb Coordination	The ability to coordinate two or more limbs (for example, two arms, two legs, or one leg and one arm) while sitting, standing, or lying down. It does not involve performing the activities while the whole body is in motion.
Memorization	The ability to remember information such as words, numbers, pictures, and procedures.
Spatial Orientation	The ability to know your location in relation to the environment or to know where other objects are in relation to you.
Visual Color Discrimination	The ability to match or detect differences between colors, including shades of color and brightness.
Arm-Hand Steadiness	The ability to keep your hand and arm steady while moving your arm or while holding your arm and hand in one position.
Time Sharing	The ability to shift back and forth between two or more activities or sources of information (such as speech, sounds, touch, or other sources).
Originality	The ability to come up with unusual or clever ideas about a given topic or situation, or to develop creative ways to solve a problem.
Manual Dexterity	The ability to quickly move your hand, your hand together with your arm, or your two hands to grasp, manipulate, or assemble objects.
Glare Sensitivity	The ability to see objects in the presence of glare or bright lighting.
Gross Body Coordination	The ability to coordinate the movement of your arms, legs, and torso together when the whole body is in motion.
Speed of Closure	The ability to quickly make sense of, combine, and organize information into meaningful patterns.
Gross Body Equilibrium	The ability to keep or regain your body balance or stay upright when in an unstable position.
Trunk Strength	The ability to use your abdominal and lower back muscles to support part of the body repeatedly or continuously over time without 'giving out' or fatiguing.
Finger Dexterity	The ability to make precisely coordinated movements of the fingers of one or both hands to grasp, manipulate, or assemble very small objects.
Hearing Sensitivity	The ability to detect or tell the differences between sounds that vary in pitch and loudness.
Static Strength	The ability to exert maximum muscle force to lift, push, pull, or carry objects.
Stamina	The ability to exert yourself physically over long periods of time without getting winded or out of breath.
Number Facility	The ability to add, subtract, multiply, or divide quickly and correctly.
Mathematical Reasoning	The ability to choose the right mathematical methods or formulas to solve a problem.
Dynamic Strength	The ability to exert muscle force repeatedly or continuously over time. This involves muscular endurance and resistance to muscle fatigue.
Speed of Limb Movement	The ability to quickly move the arms and legs.
Peripheral Vision	The ability to see objects or movement of objects to one's side when the eyes are looking ahead.
Night Vision	The ability to see under low light conditions.
Response Orientation	The ability to choose quickly between two or more movements in response to two or more different signals (lights, sounds, pictures). It includes the speed with which the correct response is started with the hand, foot, or other body part.

Wrist-Finger Speed	The ability to make fast, simple, repeated movements of the fingers, hands, and wrists.
Sound Localization	The ability to tell the direction from which a sound originated.
Rate Control	The ability to time your movements or the movement of a piece of equipment in anticipation of changes in the speed and/or direction of a moving object or scene.
Dynamic Flexibility	The ability to quickly and repeatedly bend, stretch, twist, or reach out with your body, arms, and/or legs.
Explosive Strength	The ability to use short bursts of muscle force to propel oneself (as in jumping or sprinting), or to throw an object.

Work_Activity	Work_Activity Definitions
Inspecting Equipment, Structures, or Material	Inspecting equipment, structures, or materials to identify the cause of errors or other problems or defects.
Performing for or Working Directly with the Public	Performing for people or dealing directly with the public. This includes serving customers in restaurants and stores, and receiving clients or guests.
Getting Information	Observing, receiving, and otherwise obtaining information from all relevant sources.
Documenting/Recording Information	Entering, transcribing, recording, storing, or maintaining information in written or electronic/magnetic form.
Evaluating Information to Determine Compliance wit	Using relevant information and individual judgment to determine whether events or processes comply with laws, regulations, or standards.
Identifying Objects, Actions, and Events	Identifying information by categorizing, estimating, recognizing differences or similarities, and detecting changes in circumstances or events.
Updating and Using Relevant Knowledge	Keeping up-to-date technically and applying new knowledge to your job.
Communicating with Persons Outside Organization	Communicating with people outside the organization, representing the organization to customers, the public, government, and other external sources. This information can be exchanged in person, in writing, or by telephone or e-mail.
Communicating with Supervisors, Peers, or Subordin	Providing information to supervisors, co-workers, and subordinates by telephone, in written form, e-mail, or in person.
Establishing and Maintaining Interpersonal Relatio	Developing constructive and cooperative working relationships with others, and maintaining them over time.
Making Decisions and Solving Problems	Analyzing information and evaluating results to choose the best solution and solve problems.
Processing Information	Compiling, coding, categorizing, calculating, tabulating, auditing, or verifying information or data.
Operating Vehicles, Mechanized Devices, or Equipme	Running, maneuvering, navigating, or driving vehicles or mechanized equipment, such as forklifts, passenger vehicles, aircraft, or water craft.
Organizing, Planning, and Prioritizing Work	Developing specific goals and plans to prioritize, organize, and accomplish your work.
Monitor Processes, Materials, or Surroundings	Monitoring and reviewing information from materials, events, or the environment, to detect or assess problems.
Resolving Conflicts and Negotiating with Others	Handling complaints, settling disputes, and resolving grievances and conflicts, or otherwise negotiating with others.
Judging the Qualities of Things, Services, or Peop	...ing the value, importance, or quality of things or people.
Interacting With Computers	Using computers and computer systems (including hardware and software) to program, write software, set up functions, enter data, or process information.
Performing Administrative Activities	Performing day-to-day administrative tasks such as maintaining information files and processing paperwork.
Analyzing Data or Information	Identifying the underlying principles, reasons, or facts of information by breaking down information or data into separate parts.
Interpreting the Meaning of Information for Others	Translating or explaining what information means and how it can be used.
Scheduling Work and Activities	Scheduling events, programs, and activities, as well as the work of others.
Developing Objectives and Strategies	Establishing long-range objectives and specifying the strategies and actions to achieve them.
Training and Teaching Others	Identifying the educational needs of others, developing formal educational or training programs or classes, and teaching or instructing others.
Performing General Physical Activities	Performing physical activities that require considerable use of your arms and legs and moving your whole body, such as climbing, lifting, balancing, walking, stooping, and handling of materials.

Provide Consultation and Advice to Others	Providing guidance and expert advice to management or other groups on technical, systems-, or process-related topics.
Assisting and Caring for Others	Providing personal assistance, medical attention, emotional support, or other personal care to others such as coworkers, customers, or patients.
Thinking Creatively	Developing, designing, or creating new applications, ideas, relationships, systems, or products, including artistic contributions.
Selling or Influencing Others	Convincing others to buy merchandise/goods or to otherwise change their minds or actions.
Estimating the Quantifiable Characteristics of Pro	Estimating sizes, distances, and quantities; or determining time, costs, resources, or materials needed to perform a work activity.
Coaching and Developing Others	Identifying the developmental needs of others and coaching, mentoring, or otherwise helping others to improve their knowledge or skills.
Developing and Building Teams	Encouraging and building mutual trust, respect, and cooperation among team members.
Coordinating the Work and Activities of Others	Getting members of a group to work together to accomplish tasks.
Monitoring and Controlling Resources	Monitoring and controlling resources and overseeing the spending of money.
Guiding, Directing, and Motivating Subordinates	Providing guidance and direction to subordinates, including setting performance standards and monitoring performance.
Handling and Moving Objects	Using hands and arms in handling, installing, positioning, and moving materials, and manipulating things.
Controlling Machines and Processes	Using either control mechanisms or direct physical activity to operate machines or processes (not including computers or vehicles).
Drafting, Laying Out, and Specifying Technical Dev	Providing documentation, detailed instructions, drawings, or specifications to tell others about how devices, parts, equipment, or structures are to be fabricated, constructed, assembled, modified, maintained, or used.
Staffing Organizational Units	Recruiting, interviewing, selecting, hiring, and promoting employees in an organization.
Repairing and Maintaining Mechanical Equipment	Servicing, repairing, adjusting, and testing machines, devices, moving parts, and equipment that operate primarily on the basis of mechanical (not electronic) principles.
Repairing and Maintaining Electronic Equipment	Servicing, repairing, calibrating, regulating, fine-tuning, or testing machines, devices, and equipment that operate primarily on the basis of electrical or electronic (not mechanical) principles.

Work_Context	**Work_Context Definitions**
Deal With External Customers	How important is it to work with external customers or the public in this job?
In an Enclosed Vehicle or Equipment	How often does this job require working in a closed vehicle or equipment (e.g., car)?
Contact With Others	How much does this job require the worker to be in contact with others (face-to-face, by telephone, or otherwise) in order to perform it?
Face-to-Face Discussions	How often do you have to have face-to-face discussions with individuals or teams in this job?
Telephone	How often do you have telephone conversations in this job?
Work With Work Group or Team	How important is it to work with others in a group or team in this job?
Outdoors, Exposed to Weather	How often does this job require working outdoors, exposed to all weather conditions?
Freedom to Make Decisions	How much decision making freedom, without supervision, does the job offer?
Structured versus Unstructured Work	To what extent is this job structured for the worker, rather than allowing the worker to determine tasks, priorities, and goals?
Frequency of Decision Making	How frequently is the worker required to make decisions that affect other people, the financial resources, and/or the image and reputation of the organization?
Impact of Decisions on Co-workers or Company Resul	How do the decisions an employee makes impact the results of co-workers, clients or the company?
Importance of Being Exact or Accurate	How important is being very exact or highly accurate in performing this job?
Sounds, Noise Levels Are Distracting or Uncomforta	How often does this job require working exposed to sounds and noise levels that are distracting or uncomfortable?
Letters and Memos	How often does the job require written letters and memos?
Wear Common Protective or Safety Equipment such as	How much does this job require wearing common protective or safety equipment such as safety shoes, glasses, gloves, hard hats or live jackets?

Coordinate or Lead Others	How important is it to coordinate or lead others in accomplishing work activities in this job?
Electronic Mail	How often do you use electronic mail in this job?
Physical Proximity	To what extent does this job require the worker to perform job tasks in close physical proximity to other people?
Responsible for Others' Health and Safety	How much responsibility is there for the health and safety of others in this job?
Extremely Bright or Inadequate Lighting	How often does this job require working in extremely bright or inadequate lighting conditions?
Indoors, Environmentally Controlled	How often does this job require working indoors in environmentally controlled conditions?
Frequency of Conflict Situations	How often are there conflict situations the employee has to face in this job?
Very Hot or Cold Temperatures	How often does this job require working in very hot (above 90 F degrees) or very cold (below 32 F degrees) temperatures?
Exposed to Hazardous Equipment	How often does this job require exposure to hazardous equipment?
Time Pressure	How often does this job require the worker to meet strict deadlines?
Exposed to Contaminants	How often does this job require working exposed to contaminants (such as pollutants, gases, dust or odors)?
Deal With Unpleasant or Angry People	How frequently does the worker have to deal with unpleasant, angry, or discourteous individuals as part of the job requirements?
Indoors, Not Environmentally Controlled	How often does this job require working indoors in non-controlled environmental conditions (e.g., warehouse without heat)?
Consequence of Error	How serious would the result usually be if the worker made a mistake that was not readily correctable?
Exposed to Hazardous Conditions	How often does this job require exposure to hazardous conditions?
Responsibility for Outcomes and Results	How responsible is the worker for work outcomes and results of other workers?
Exposed to High Places	How often does this job require exposure to high places?
Importance of Repeating Same Tasks	How important is repeating the same physical activities (e.g., key entry) or mental activities (e.g., checking entries in a ledger) over and over, without stopping, to performing this job?
Exposed to Disease or Infections	How often does this job require exposure to disease/infections?
Exposed to Minor Burns, Cuts, Bites, or Stings	How often does this job require exposure to minor burns, cuts, bites, or stings?
Spend Time Standing	How much does this job require standing?
Cramped Work Space, Awkward Positions	How often does this job require working in cramped work spaces that requires getting into awkward positions?
Wear Specialized Protective or Safety Equipment su	How much does this job require wearing specialized protective or safety equipment such as breathing apparatus, safety harness, full protection suits, or radiation protection?
Spend Time Using Your Hands to Handle, Control, or	How much does this job require using your hands to handle, control, or feel objects, tools or controls?
Spend Time Walking and Running	How much does this job require walking and running?
Spend Time Sitting	How much does this job require sitting?
Outdoors, Under Cover	How often does this job require working outdoors, under cover (e.g., structure with roof but no walls)?
Spend Time Bending or Twisting the Body	How much does this job require bending or twisting your body?
Public Speaking	How often do you have to perform public speaking in this job?
Level of Competition	To what extent does this job require the worker to compete or to be aware of competitive pressures?
Degree of Automation	How automated is the job?
Spend Time Kneeling, Crouching, Stooping, or Crawl	How much does this job require kneeling, crouching, stooping or crawling?
Spend Time Making Repetitive Motions	How much does this job require making repetitive motions?
Deal With Physically Aggressive People	How frequently does this job require the worker to deal with physical aggression of violent individuals?
In an Open Vehicle or Equipment	How often does this job require working in an open vehicle or equipment (e.g., tractor)?
Spend Time Keeping or Regaining Balance	How much does this job require keeping or regaining your balance?
Spend Time Climbing Ladders, Scaffolds, or Poles	How much does this job require climbing ladders, scaffolds, or poles?
Pace Determined by Speed of Equipment	How important is it to this job that the pace is determined by the speed of equipment or machinery? (This does not refer to keeping busy at all times on this job.)

Exposed to Whole Body Vibration	How often does this job require exposure to whole body vibration (e.g., operate a jackhammer)?
Exposed to Radiation	How often does this job require exposure to radiation?

Job Zone Component	Job Zone Component Definitions
Title	Job Zone Three: Medium Preparation Needed
Overall Experience	Previous work-related skill, knowledge, or experience is required for these occupations. For example, an electrician must have completed three or four years of apprenticeship or several years of vocational training, and often must have passed a licensing exam, in order to perform the job.
Job Training	Employees in these occupations usually need one or two years of training involving both on-the-job experience and informal training with experienced workers.
Job Zone Examples	These occupations usually involve using communication and organizational skills to coordinate, supervise, manage, or train others to accomplish goals. Examples include dental assistants, electricians, fish and game wardens, legal secretaries, personnel recruiters, and recreation workers.
SVP Range	(6.0 to < 7.0)
Education	Most occupations in this zone require training in vocational schools, related on-the-job experience, or an associate's degree. Some may require a bachelor's degree.

Work_Styles	Work_Styles Definitions
Integrity	Job requires being honest and ethical.
Dependability	Job requires being reliable, responsible, and dependable, and fulfilling obligations.
Attention to Detail	Job requires being careful about detail and thorough in completing work tasks.
Cooperation	Job requires being pleasant with others on the job and displaying a good-natured, cooperative attitude.
Self Control	Job requires maintaining composure, keeping emotions in check, controlling anger, and avoiding aggressive behavior, even in very difficult situations.
Stress Tolerance	Job requires accepting criticism and dealing calmly and effectively with high stress situations.
Independence	Job requires developing one's own ways of doing things, guiding oneself with little or no supervision, and depending on oneself to get things done.
Analytical Thinking	Job requires analyzing information and using logic to address work-related issues and problems.
Adaptability/Flexibility	Job requires being open to change (positive or negative) and to considerable variety in the workplace.
Initiative	Job requires a willingness to take on responsibilities and challenges.
Persistence	Job requires persistence in the face of obstacles.
Concern for Others	Job requires being sensitive to others' needs and feelings and being understanding and helpful on the job.
Achievement/Effort	Job requires establishing and maintaining personally challenging achievement goals and exerting effort toward mastering tasks.
Leadership	Job requires a willingness to lead, take charge, and offer opinions and direction.
Innovation	Job requires creativity and alternative thinking to develop new ideas for and answers to work-related problems.
Social Orientation	Job requires preferring to work with others rather than alone, and being personally connected with others on the job.

33-2022.00 - Forest Fire Inspectors and Prevention Specialists

Enforce fire regulations and inspect for forest fire hazards. Report forest fires and weather conditions.

Tasks

1) Inspect camp sites to ensure that campers are in compliance with forest use regulations.

2) Extinguish smaller fires with portable extinguishers, shovels, and axes.

3) Estimate sizes and characteristics of fires, and report findings to base camps by radio or telephone.

4) Inspect forest tracts and logging areas for fire hazards such as accumulated wastes or mishandling of combustibles, and recommend appropriate fire prevention measures.

5) Compile and report meteorological data, such as temperature, relative humidity, wind direction and velocity, and types of cloud formations.

6) Administer regulations regarding sanitation, fire prevention, violation corrections, and related forest regulations.

7) Maintain records and logbooks.

8) Restrict public access and recreational use of forest lands during critical fire seasons.

9) Direct maintenance and repair of firefighting equipment, or requisition new equipment.

10) Patrol assigned areas, looking for forest fires, hazardous conditions, and weather phenomena.

11) Relay messages about emergencies, accidents, locations of crew and personnel, and fire hazard conditions.

12) Direct crews working on firelines during forest fires.

13) Locate forest fires on area maps, using azimuth sighters and known landmarks.

33-3011.00 - Bailiffs

Maintain order in courts of law.

Tasks

1) Announce entrance of judge.

2) Check courtroom for security and cleanliness and assure availability of sundry supplies for use of judge.

3) Stop people from entering courtroom while judge charges jury.

4) Provide jury escort to restaurant and other areas outside of courtroom to prevent jury contact with public.

5) Report need for police or medical assistance to sheriff's office.

6) Guard lodging of sequestered jury.

7) Collect and retain unauthorized firearms from persons entering courtroom.

8) Enforce courtroom rules of behavior and warn persons not to smoke or disturb court procedure.

Knowledge	Knowledge Definitions
Public Safety and Security	Knowledge of relevant equipment, policies, procedures, and strategies to promote effective local, state, or national security operations for the protection of people, data, property, and institutions.
Law and Government	Knowledge of laws, legal codes, court procedures, precedents, government regulations, executive orders, agency rules, and the democratic political process.
Customer and Personal Service	Knowledge of principles and processes for providing customer and personal services. This includes customer needs assessment, meeting quality standards for services, and evaluation of customer satisfaction.
English Language	Knowledge of the structure and content of the English language including the meaning and spelling of words, rules of composition, and grammar.
Education and Training	Knowledge of principles and methods for curriculum and training design, teaching and instruction for individuals and groups, and the measurement of training effects.
Administration and Management	Knowledge of business and management principles involved in strategic planning, resource allocation, human resources modeling, leadership technique, production methods, and coordination of people and resources.
Psychology	Knowledge of human behavior and performance; individual differences in ability, personality, and interests; learning and motivation; psychological research methods; and the assessment and treatment of behavioral and affective disorders.
Telecommunications	Knowledge of transmission, broadcasting, switching, control, and operation of telecommunications systems.
Sociology and Anthropology	Knowledge of group behavior and dynamics, societal trends and influences, human migrations, ethnicity, cultures and their history and origins.

Clerical	Knowledge of administrative and clerical procedures and systems such as word processing, managing files and records, stenography and transcription, designing forms, and other office procedures and terminology.
Medicine and Dentistry	Knowledge of the information and techniques needed to diagnose and treat human injuries, diseases, and deformities. This includes symptoms, treatment alternatives, drug properties and interactions, and preventive health-care measures.
Personnel and Human Resources	Knowledge of principles and procedures for personnel recruitment, selection, training, compensation and benefits, labor relations and negotiation, and personnel information systems.
Communications and Media	Knowledge of media production, communication, and dissemination techniques and methods. This includes alternative ways to inform and entertain via written, oral, and visual media.
Computers and Electronics	Knowledge of circuit boards, processors, chips, electronic equipment, and computer hardware and software, including applications and programming.
Foreign Language	Knowledge of the structure and content of a foreign (non-English) language including the meaning and spelling of words, rules of composition and grammar, and pronunciation.
Philosophy and Theology	Knowledge of different philosophical systems and religions. This includes their basic principles, values, ethics, ways of thinking, customs, practices, and their impact on human culture.
Mathematics	Knowledge of arithmetic, algebra, geometry, calculus, statistics, and their applications.
Transportation	Knowledge of principles and methods for moving people or goods by air, rail, sea, or road, including the relative costs and benefits.
Therapy and Counseling	Knowledge of principles, methods, and procedures for diagnosis, treatment, and rehabilitation of physical and mental dysfunctions, and for career counseling and guidance.
Economics and Accounting	Knowledge of economic and accounting principles and practices, the financial markets, banking and the analysis and reporting of financial data.
Geography	Knowledge of principles and methods for describing the features of land, sea, and air masses, including their physical characteristics, locations, interrelationships, and distribution of plant, animal, and human life.
Mechanical	Knowledge of machines and tools, including their designs, uses, repair, and maintenance.
Building and Construction	Knowledge of materials, methods, and the tools involved in the construction or repair of houses, buildings, or other structures such as highways and roads.
Production and Processing	Knowledge of raw materials, production processes, quality control, costs, and other techniques for maximizing the effective manufacture and distribution of goods.
Design	Knowledge of design techniques, tools, and principles involved in production of precision technical plans, blueprints, drawings, and models.
Engineering and Technology	Knowledge of the practical application of engineering science and technology. This includes applying principles, techniques, procedures, and equipment to the design and production of various goods and services.
History and Archeology	Knowledge of historical events and their causes, indicators, and effects on civilizations and cultures.
Food Production	Knowledge of techniques and equipment for planting, growing, and harvesting food products (both plant and animal) for consumption, including storage/handling techniques.
Sales and Marketing	Knowledge of principles and methods for showing, promoting, and selling products or services. This includes marketing strategy and tactics, product demonstration, sales techniques, and sales control systems.
Chemistry	Knowledge of the chemical composition, structure, and properties of substances and of the chemical processes and transformations that they undergo. This includes uses of chemicals and their interactions, danger signs, production techniques, and disposal methods.
Physics	Knowledge and prediction of physical principles, laws, their interrelationships, and applications to understanding fluid, material, and atmospheric dynamics, and mechanical, electrical, atomic and sub-atomic structures and processes.
Biology	Knowledge of plant and animal organisms, their tissues, cells, functions, interdependencies, and interactions with each other and the environment.
Fine Arts	Knowledge of the theory and techniques required to compose, produce, and perform works of music, dance, visual arts, drama, and sculpture.

Skills	Skills Definitions
Active Listening	Giving full attention to what other people are saying, taking time to understand the points being made, asking questions as appropriate, and not interrupting at inappropriate times.
Speaking	Talking to others to convey information effectively.
Reading Comprehension	Understanding written sentences and paragraphs in work related documents.
Social Perceptiveness	Being aware of others' reactions and understanding why they react as they do.
Critical Thinking	Using logic and reasoning to identify the strengths and weaknesses of alternative solutions, conclusions or approaches to problems.
Monitoring	Monitoring/Assessing performance of yourself, other individuals, or organizations to make improvements or take corrective action.
Learning Strategies	Selecting and using training/instructional methods and procedures appropriate for the situation when learning or teaching new things.
Active Learning	Understanding the implications of new information for both current and future problem-solving and decision-making.
Time Management	Managing one's own time and the time of others.
Writing	Communicating effectively in writing as appropriate for the needs of the audience.
Persuasion	Persuading others to change their minds or behavior.
Service Orientation	Actively looking for ways to help people.
Negotiation	Bringing others together and trying to reconcile differences.
Equipment Selection	Determining the kind of tools and equipment needed to do a job.
Instructing	Teaching others how to do something.
Coordination	Adjusting actions in relation to others' actions.
Judgment and Decision Making	Considering the relative costs and benefits of potential actions to choose the most appropriate one.
Management of Personnel Resources	Motivating, developing, and directing people as they work, identifying the best people for the job.
Operations Analysis	Analyzing needs and product requirements to create a design.
Complex Problem Solving	Identifying complex problems and reviewing related information to develop and evaluate options and implement solutions.
Quality Control Analysis	Conducting tests and inspections of products, services, or processes to evaluate quality or performance.
Mathematics	Using mathematics to solve problems.
Systems Evaluation	Identifying measures or indicators of system performance and the actions needed to improve or correct performance, relative to the goals of the system.
Operation and Control	Controlling operations of equipment or systems.
Troubleshooting	Determining causes of operating errors and deciding what to do about it.
Management of Material Resources	Obtaining and seeing to the appropriate use of equipment, facilities, and materials needed to do certain work.
Operation Monitoring	Watching gauges, dials, or other indicators to make sure a machine is working properly.
Equipment Maintenance	Performing routine maintenance on equipment and determining when and what kind of maintenance is needed.
Technology Design	Generating or adapting equipment and technology to serve user needs.
Systems Analysis	Determining how a system should work and how changes in conditions, operations, and the environment will affect outcomes.
Programming	Writing computer programs for various purposes.
Repairing	Repairing machines or systems using the needed tools.
Science	Using scientific rules and methods to solve problems.
Installation	Installing equipment, machines, wiring, or programs to meet specifications.
Management of Financial Resources	Determining how money will be spent to get the work done, and accounting for these expenditures.

Ability	Ability Definitions
Oral Expression	The ability to communicate information and ideas in speaking so others will understand.
Selective Attention	The ability to concentrate on a task over a period of time without being distracted.

Problem Sensitivity	The ability to tell when something is wrong or is likely to go wrong. It does not involve solving the problem, only recognizing there is a problem.
Speech Clarity	The ability to speak clearly so others can understand you.
Oral Comprehension	The ability to listen to and understand information and ideas presented through spoken words and sentences.
Speech Recognition	The ability to identify and understand the speech of another person.
Gross Body Coordination	The ability to coordinate the movement of your arms, legs, and torso together when the whole body is in motion.
Far Vision	The ability to see details at a distance.
Near Vision	The ability to see details at close range (within a few feet of the observer).
Static Strength	The ability to exert maximum muscle force to lift, push, pull, or carry objects.
Deductive Reasoning	The ability to apply general rules to specific problems to produce answers that make sense.
Inductive Reasoning	The ability to combine pieces of information to form general rules or conclusions (includes finding a relationship among seemingly unrelated events).
Information Ordering	The ability to arrange things or actions in a certain order or pattern according to a specific rule or set of rules (e.g., patterns of numbers, letters, words, pictures, mathematical operations).
Reaction Time	The ability to quickly respond (with the hand, finger, or foot) to a signal (sound, light, picture) when it appears.
Written Expression	The ability to communicate information and ideas in writing so others will understand.
Written Comprehension	The ability to read and understand information and ideas presented in writing.
Response Orientation	The ability to choose quickly between two or more movements in response to two or more different signals (lights, sounds, pictures). It includes the speed with which the correct response is started with the hand, foot, or other body part.
Time Sharing	The ability to shift back and forth between two or more activities or sources of information (such as speech, sounds, touch, or other sources).
Trunk Strength	The ability to use your abdominal and lower back muscles to support part of the body repeatedly or continuously over time without 'giving out' or fatiguing.
Speed of Closure	The ability to quickly make sense of, combine, and organize information into meaningful patterns.
Stamina	The ability to exert yourself physically over long periods of time without getting winded or out of breath.
Flexibility of Closure	The ability to identify or detect a known pattern (a figure, object, word, or sound) that is hidden in other distracting material.
Explosive Strength	The ability to use short bursts of muscle force to propel oneself (as in jumping or sprinting), or to throw an object.
Speed of Limb Movement	The ability to quickly move the arms and legs.
Multilimb Coordination	The ability to coordinate two or more limbs (for example, two arms, two legs, or one leg and one arm) while sitting, standing, or lying down. It does not involve performing the activities while the whole body is in motion.
Gross Body Equilibrium	The ability to keep or regain your body balance or stay upright when in an unstable position.
Memorization	The ability to remember information such as words, numbers, pictures, and procedures.
Perceptual Speed	The ability to quickly and accurately compare similarities and differences among sets of letters, numbers, objects, pictures, or patterns. The things to be compared may be presented at the same time or one after the other. This ability also includes comparing a presented object with a remembered object.
Category Flexibility	The ability to generate or use different sets of rules for combining or grouping things in different ways.
Auditory Attention	The ability to focus on a single source of sound in the presence of other distracting sounds.
Arm-Hand Steadiness	The ability to keep your hand and arm steady while moving your arm or while holding your arm and hand in one position.
Dynamic Strength	The ability to exert muscle force repeatedly or continuously over time. This involves muscular endurance and resistance to muscle fatigue.
Extent Flexibility	The ability to bend, stretch, twist, or reach with your body, arms, and/or legs.
Depth Perception	The ability to judge which of several objects is closer or farther away from you, or to judge the distance between you and an object.
Peripheral Vision	The ability to see objects or movement of objects to one's side when the eyes are looking ahead.

Hearing Sensitivity	The ability to detect or tell the differences between sounds that vary in pitch and loudness.
Manual Dexterity	The ability to quickly move your hand, your hand together with your arm, or your two hands to grasp, manipulate, or assemble objects.
Spatial Orientation	The ability to know your location in relation to the environment or to know where other objects are in relation to you.
Fluency of Ideas	The ability to come up with a number of ideas about a topic (the number of ideas is important, not their quality, correctness, or creativity).
Originality	The ability to come up with unusual or clever ideas about a given topic or situation, or to develop creative ways to solve a problem.
Visual Color Discrimination	The ability to match or detect differences between colors, including shades of color and brightness.
Finger Dexterity	The ability to make precisely coordinated movements of the fingers of one or both hands to grasp, manipulate, or assemble very small objects.
Number Facility	The ability to add, subtract, multiply, or divide quickly and correctly.
Mathematical Reasoning	The ability to choose the right mathematical methods or formulas to solve a problem.
Visualization	The ability to imagine how something will look after it is moved around or when its parts are moved or rearranged.
Rate Control	The ability to time your movements or the movement of a piece of equipment in anticipation of changes in the speed and/or direction of a moving object or scene.
Wrist-Finger Speed	The ability to make fast, simple, repeated movements of the fingers, hands, and wrists.
Control Precision	The ability to quickly and repeatedly adjust the controls of a machine or a vehicle to exact positions.
Glare Sensitivity	The ability to see objects in the presence of glare or bright lighting.
Night Vision	The ability to see under low light conditions.
Dynamic Flexibility	The ability to quickly and repeatedly bend, stretch, twist, or reach out with your body, arms, and/or legs.
Sound Localization	The ability to tell the direction from which a sound originated.

Work_Activity	Work_Activity Definitions
Identifying Objects, Actions, and Events	Identifying information by categorizing, estimating, recognizing differences or similarities, and detecting changes in circumstances or events.
Monitor Processes, Materials, or Surroundings	Monitoring and reviewing information from materials, events, or the environment, to detect or assess problems.
Performing for or Working Directly with the Public	Performing for people or dealing directly with the public. This includes serving customers in restaurants and stores, and receiving clients or guests.
Getting Information	Observing, receiving, and otherwise obtaining information from all relevant sources.
Communicating with Persons Outside Organization	Communicating with people outside the organization, representing the organization to customers, the public, government, and other external sources. This information can be exchanged in person, in writing, or by telephone or e-mail.
Resolving Conflicts and Negotiating with Others	Handling complaints, settling disputes, and resolving grievances and conflicts, or otherwise negotiating with others.
Making Decisions and Solving Problems	Analyzing information and evaluating results to choose the best solution and solve problems.
Establishing and Maintaining Interpersonal Relatio	Developing constructive and cooperative working relationships with others, and maintaining them over time.
Performing Administrative Activities	Performing day-to-day administrative tasks such as maintaining information files and processing paperwork.
Processing Information	Compiling, coding, categorizing, calculating, tabulating, auditing, or verifying information or data.
Communicating with Supervisors, Peers, or Subordin	Providing information to supervisors, co-workers, and subordinates by telephone, in written form, e-mail, or in person.
Documenting/Recording Information	Entering, transcribing, recording, storing, or maintaining information in written or electronic/magnetic form.
Performing General Physical Activities	Performing physical activities that require considerable use of your arms and legs and moving your whole body, such as climbing, lifting, balancing, walking, stooping, and handling of materials.
Assisting and Caring for Others	Providing personal assistance, medical attention, emotional support, or other personal care to others such as coworkers, customers, or patients.

Judging the Qualities of Things. Services. or Peop	Assessing the value. importance. or quality of things or people.
Inspecting Equipment. Structures. or Material	Inspecting equipment. structures. or materials to identify the cause of errors or other problems or defects.
Interacting With Computers	Using computers and computer systems (including hardware and software) to program. write software. set up functions. enter data. or process information.
Analyzing Data or Information	Identifying the underlying principles, reasons. or facts of information by breaking down information or data into separate parts.
Evaluating Information to Determine Compliance wit	Using relevant information and individual judgment to determine whether events or processes comply with laws. regulations. or standards.
Updating and Using Relevant Knowledge	Keeping up-to-date technically and applying new knowledge to your job.
Developing and Building Teams	Encouraging and building mutual trust. respect. and cooperation among team members.
Coordinating the Work and Activities of Others	Getting members of a group to work together to accomplish tasks.
Training and Teaching Others	Identifying the educational needs of others. developing formal educational or training programs or classes. and teaching or instructing others.
Handling and Moving Objects	Using hands and arms in handling. installing. positioning, and moving materials, and manipulating things.
Scheduling Work and Activities	Scheduling events. programs. and activities, as well as the work of others.
Guiding, Directing, and Motivating Subordinates	Providing guidance and direction to subordinates, including setting performance standards and monitoring performance.
Interpreting the Meaning of Information for Others	Translating or explaining what information means and how it can be used.
Developing Objectives and Strategies	Establishing long-range objectives and specifying the strategies and actions to achieve them.
Organizing, Planning, and Prioritizing Work	Developing specific goals and plans to prioritize. organize. and accomplish your work.
Estimating the Quantifiable Characteristics of Pro	Estimating sizes, distances, and quantities; or determining time, costs, resources, or materials needed to perform a work activity.
Thinking Creatively	Developing. designing, or creating new applications, ideas, relationships, systems, or products, including artistic contributions.
Coaching and Developing Others	Identifying the developmental needs of others and coaching, mentoring, or otherwise helping others to improve their knowledge or skills.
Repairing and Maintaining Electronic Equipment	Servicing, repairing, calibrating, regulating, fine-tuning, or testing machines, devices, and equipment that operate primarily on the basis of electrical or electronic (not mechanical) principles.
Staffing Organizational Units	Recruiting, interviewing, selecting, hiring, and promoting employees in an organization.
Monitoring and Controlling Resources	Monitoring and controlling resources and overseeing the spending of money.
Operating Vehicles, Mechanized Devices, or Equipme	Running, maneuvering, navigating, or driving vehicles or mechanized equipment, such as forklifts, passenger vehicles, aircraft, or water craft.
Provide Consultation and Advice to Others	Providing guidance and expert advice to management or other groups on technical, systems-, or process-related topics.
Selling or Influencing Others	Convincing others to buy merchandise/goods or to otherwise change their minds or actions.
Controlling Machines and Processes	Using either control mechanisms or direct physical activity to operate machines or processes (not including computers or vehicles).
Repairing and Maintaining Mechanical Equipment	Servicing, repairing, adjusting, and testing machines. devices. moving parts, and equipment that operate primarily on the basis of mechanical (not electronic) principles.
Drafting, Laying Out, and Specifying Technical Dev	Providing documentation, detailed instructions, drawings. or specifications to tell others about how devices. parts. equipment, or structures are to be fabricated. constructed. assembled, modified, maintained, or used.

Work_Context	**Work_Context Definitions**
Contact With Others	How much does this job require the worker to be in contact with others (face-to-face, by telephone, or otherwise) in order to perform it?
Indoors, Environmentally Controlled	How often does this job require working indoors in environmentally controlled conditions?
Face-to-Face Discussions	How often do you have to have face-to-face discussions with individuals or teams in this job?

Telephone	How often do you have telephone conversations in this job?
Physical Proximity	To what extent does this job require the worker to perform job tasks in close physical proximity to other people?
Deal With Unpleasant or Angry People	How frequently does the worker have to deal with unpleasant. angry. or discourteous individuals as part of the job requirements?
Freedom to Make Decisions	How much decision making freedom, without supervision, does the job offer?
Time Pressure	How often does this job require the worker to meet strict deadlines?
Responsible for Others' Health and Safety	How much responsibility is there for the health and safety of others in this job?
Importance of Being Exact or Accurate	How important is being very exact or highly accurate in performing this job?
Deal With External Customers	How important is it to work with external customers or the public in this job?
Work With Work Group or Team	How important is it to work with others in a group or team in this job?
Exposed to Contaminants	How often does this job require working exposed to contaminants (such as pollutants, gases, dust or odors)?
Deal With Physically Aggressive People	How frequently does this job require the worker to deal with physical aggression of violent individuals?
Public Speaking	How often do you have to perform public speaking in this job?
Exposed to Disease or Infections	How often does this job require exposure to disease/infections?
Frequency of Conflict Situations	How often are there conflict situations the employee has to face in this job?
Frequency of Decision Making	How frequently is the worker required to make decisions that affect other people, the financial resources, and/or the image and reputation of the organization?
Importance of Repeating Same Tasks	How important is repeating the same physical activities (e.g., key entry) or mental activities (e.g., checking entries in a ledger) over and over, without stopping, to performing this job?
Spend Time Sitting	How much does this job require sitting?
Coordinate or Lead Others	How important is it to coordinate or lead others in accomplishing work activities in this job?
Structured versus Unstructured Work	To what extent is this job structured for the worker, rather than allowing the worker to determine tasks, priorities, and goals?
Outdoors, Exposed to Weather	How often does this job require working outdoors, exposed to all weather conditions?
Spend Time Standing	How much does this job require standing?
Impact of Decisions on Co-workers or Company Resul	How do the decisions an employee makes impact the results of co-workers, clients or the company?
Consequence of Error	How serious would the result usually be if the worker made a mistake that was not readily correctable?
Level of Competition	To what extent does this job require the worker to compete or to be aware of competitive pressures?
Wear Common Protective or Safety Equipment such as	How much does this job require wearing common protective or safety equipment such as safety shoes, glasses, gloves, hard hats or live jackets?
Spend Time Walking and Running	How much does this job require walking and running?
Sounds, Noise Levels Are Distracting or Uncomforta	How often does this job require working exposed to sounds and noise levels that are distracting or uncomfortable?
Indoors, Not Environmentally Controlled	How often does this job require working indoors in non-controlled environmental conditions (e.g., warehouse without heat)?
Letters and Memos	How often does the job require written letters and memos?
Cramped Work Space. Awkward Positions	How often does this job require working in cramped work spaces that requires getting into awkward positions?
Responsibility for Outcomes and Results	How responsible is the worker for work outcomes and results of other workers?
Spend Time Making Repetitive Motions	How much does this job require making repetitive motions?
Very Hot or Cold Temperatures	How often does this job require working in very hot (above 90 F degrees) or very cold (below 32 F degrees) temperatures?
Wear Specialized Protective or Safety Equipment su	How much does this job require wearing specialized protective or safety equipment such as breathing apparatus, safety harness, full protection suits, or radiation protection?
Spend Time Using Your Hands to Handle, Control, or	How much does this job require using your hands to handle, control, or feel objects, tools or controls?
Spend Time Bending or Twisting the Body	How much does this job require bending or twisting your body?
Outdoors, Under Cover	How often does this job require working outdoors, under cover (e.g., structure with roof but no walls)?

Extremely Bright or Inadequate Lighting	How often does this job require working in extremely bright or inadequate lighting conditions?
Exposed to Radiation	How often does this job require exposure to radiation?
Electronic Mail	How often do you use electronic mail in this job?
In an Enclosed Vehicle or Equipment	How often does this job require working in a closed vehicle or equipment (e.g., car)?
Exposed to Hazardous Equipment	How often does this job require exposure to hazardous equipment?
Spend Time Keeping or Regaining Balance	How much does this job require keeping or regaining your balance?
Exposed to Minor Burns, Cuts, Bites, or Stings	How often does this job require exposure to minor burns, cuts, bites, or stings?
Pace Determined by Speed of Equipment	How important is it to this job that the pace is determined by the speed of equipment or machinery? (This does not refer to keeping busy at all times on this job.)
Degree of Automation	How automated is the job?
Exposed to Hazardous Conditions	How often does this job require exposure to hazardous conditions?
Spend Time Kneeling, Crouching, Stooping, or Crawl	How much does this job require kneeling, crouching, stooping, or crawling?
Exposed to High Places	How often does this job require exposure to high places?
Exposed to Whole Body Vibration	How often does this job require exposure to whole body vibration (e.g., operate a jackhammer)?
In an Open Vehicle or Equipment	How often does this job require working in an open vehicle or equipment (e.g., tractor)?
Spend Time Climbing Ladders, Scaffolds, or Poles	How much does this job require climbing ladders, scaffolds, or poles?

Job Zone Component	Job Zone Component Definitions
Title	Job Zone Two: Some Preparation Needed
Overall Experience	Some previous work-related skill, knowledge, or experience may be helpful in these occupations, but usually is not needed. For example, a drywall installer might benefit from experience installing drywall, but an inexperienced person could still learn to be an installer with little difficulty.
Job Training	Employees in these occupations need anywhere from a few months to one year of working with experienced employees. These occupations often involve using your knowledge and skills to help others.
Job Zone Examples	Examples include drywall installers, fire inspectors, flight attendants, pharmacy technicians, salespersons (retail), and tellers.
SVP Range	(4.0 to < 6.0)
Education	These occupations usually require a high school diploma and may require some vocational training or job-related course work. In some cases, an associate's or bachelor's degree could be needed.

Work_Styles	Work_Styles Definitions
Integrity	Job requires being honest and ethical.
Stress Tolerance	Job requires accepting criticism and dealing calmly and effectively with high stress situations.
Self Control	Job requires maintaining composure, keeping emotions in check, controlling anger, and avoiding aggressive behavior, even in very difficult situations.
Attention to Detail	Job requires being careful about detail and thorough in completing work tasks.
Adaptability/Flexibility	Job requires being open to change (positive or negative) and to considerable variety in the workplace.
Dependability	Job requires being reliable, responsible, and dependable, and fulfilling obligations.
Concern for Others	Job requires being sensitive to others' needs and feelings and being understanding and helpful on the job.
Cooperation	Job requires being pleasant with others on the job and displaying a good-natured, cooperative attitude.
Initiative	Job requires a willingness to take on responsibilities and challenges.
Leadership	Job requires a willingness to lead, take charge, and offer opinions and direction.
Social Orientation	Job requires preferring to work with others rather than alone, and being personally connected with others on the job.
Persistence	Job requires persistence in the face of obstacles.

Achievement/Effort	Job requires establishing and maintaining personally challenging achievement goals and exerting effort toward mastering tasks.
Independence	Job requires developing one's own ways of doing things, guiding oneself with little or no supervision, and depending on oneself to get things done.
Analytical Thinking	Job requires analyzing information and using logic to address work-related issues and problems.
Innovation	Job requires creativity and alternative thinking to develop new ideas for and answers to work-related problems.

33-3012.00 - Correctional Officers and Jailers

Guard inmates in penal or rehabilitative institution in accordance with established regulations and procedures. May guard prisoners in transit between jail, courtroom, prison, or other point. Includes deputy sheriffs and police who spend the majority of their time guarding prisoners in correctional institutions.

Tasks

1) Search prisoners, cells, and vehicles for weapons, valuables, or drugs.

2) Record information, such as prisoner identification, charges, and incidences of inmate disturbance.

3) Take prisoners into custody and escort to locations within and outside of facility, such as visiting room, courtroom, or airport.

4) Provide to supervisors oral and written reports of the quality and quantity of work performed by inmates, inmate disturbances and rule violations, and unusual occurrences.

5) Use weapons, handcuffs, and physical force to maintain discipline and order among prisoners.

6) Inspect conditions of locks, window bars, grills, doors, and gates at correctional facilities, in order to ensure that they will prevent escapes.

7) Conduct fire, safety, and sanitation inspections.

8) Assign duties to inmates, providing instructions as needed.

9) Drive passenger vehicles and trucks used to transport inmates to other institutions, courtrooms, hospitals, and work sites.

10) Issue clothing, tools, and other authorized items to inmates.

11) Guard facility entrances in order to screen visitors.

12) Serve meals and distribute commissary items to prisoners.

13) Inspect mail for the presence of contraband.

14) Arrange daily schedules for prisoners including library visits, work assignments, family visits, and counseling appointments.

15) Search for and recapture escapees.

16) Investigate crimes that have occurred within an institution, or assist police in their investigations of crimes and inmates.

17) Supervise and coordinate work of other correctional service officers.

18) Maintain records of prisoners' identification and charges.

19) Sponsor inmate recreational activities such as newspapers and self-help groups.

20) Monitor conduct of prisoners, according to established policies, regulations, and procedures, in order to prevent escape or violence.

Knowledge	Knowledge Definitions
Public Safety and Security	Knowledge of relevant equipment, policies, procedures, and strategies to promote effective local, state, or national security operations for the protection of people, data, property, and institutions.
Psychology	Knowledge of human behavior and performance; individual differences in ability, personality, and interests; learning and motivation; psychological research methods; and the assessment and treatment of behavioral and affective disorders.
Law and Government	Knowledge of laws, legal codes, court procedures, precedents, government regulations, executive orders, agency rules, and the democratic political process.
English Language	Knowledge of the structure and content of the English language including the meaning and spelling of words, rules of composition, and grammar.

Administration and Management	Knowledge of business and management principles involved in strategic planning, resource allocation, human resources modeling, leadership technique, production methods, and coordination of people and resources.
Education and Training	Knowledge of principles and methods for curriculum and training design, teaching and instruction for individuals and groups, and the measurement of training effects.
Sociology and Anthropology	Knowledge of group behavior and dynamics, societal trends and influences, human migrations, ethnicity, cultures and their history and origins.
Personnel and Human Resources	Knowledge of principles and procedures for personnel recruitment, selection, training, compensation and benefits, labor relations and negotiation, and personnel information systems.
Clerical	Knowledge of administrative and clerical procedures and systems such as word processing, managing files and records, stenography and transcription, designing forms, and other office procedures and terminology.
Transportation	Knowledge of principles and methods for moving people or goods by air, rail, sea, or road, including the relative costs and benefits.
Telecommunications	Knowledge of transmission, broadcasting, switching, control, and operation of telecommunications systems.
Customer and Personal Service	Knowledge of principles and processes for providing customer and personal services. This includes customer needs assessment, meeting quality standards for services, and evaluation of customer satisfaction.
Mathematics	Knowledge of arithmetic, algebra, geometry, calculus, statistics, and their applications.
Computers and Electronics	Knowledge of circuit boards, processors, chips, electronic equipment, and computer hardware and software, including applications and programming.
Therapy and Counseling	Knowledge of principles, methods, and procedures for diagnosis, treatment, and rehabilitation of physical and mental dysfunctions, and for career counseling and guidance.
Philosophy and Theology	Knowledge of different philosophical systems and religions. This includes their basic principles, values, ethics, ways of thinking, customs, practices, and their impact on human culture.
Communications and Media	Knowledge of media production, communication, and dissemination techniques and methods. This includes alternative ways to inform and entertain via written, oral, and visual media.
Medicine and Dentistry	Knowledge of the information and techniques needed to diagnose and treat human injuries, diseases, and deformities. This includes symptoms, treatment alternatives, drug properties and interactions, and preventive health-care measures.
Foreign Language	Knowledge of the structure and content of a foreign (non-English) language including the meaning and spelling of words, rules of composition and grammar, and pronunciation.
Mechanical	Knowledge of machines and tools, including their designs, uses, repair, and maintenance.
Engineering and Technology	Knowledge of the practical application of engineering science and technology. This includes applying principles, techniques, procedures, and equipment to the design and production of various goods and services.
Economics and Accounting	Knowledge of economic and accounting principles and practices, the financial markets, banking and the analysis and reporting of financial data.
Chemistry	Knowledge of the chemical composition, structure, and properties of substances and of the chemical processes and transformations that they undergo. This includes uses of chemicals and their interactions, danger signs, production techniques, and disposal methods.
History and Archeology	Knowledge of historical events and their causes, indicators, and effects on civilizations and cultures.
Geography	Knowledge of principles and methods for describing the features of land, sea, and air masses, including their physical characteristics, locations, interrelationships, and distribution of plant, animal, and human life.
Building and Construction	Knowledge of materials, methods, and the tools involved in the construction or repair of houses, buildings, or other structures such as highways and roads.
Food Production	Knowledge of techniques and equipment for planting, growing, and harvesting food products (both plant and animal) for consumption, including storage/handling techniques.
Design	Knowledge of design techniques, tools, and principles involved in production of precision technical plans, blueprints, drawings, and models.
Production and Processing	Knowledge of raw materials, production processes, quality control, costs, and other techniques for maximizing the effective manufacture and distribution of goods.
Biology	Knowledge of plant and animal organisms, their tissues, cells, functions, interdependencies, and interactions with each other and the environment.
Physics	Knowledge and prediction of physical principles, laws, their interrelationships, and applications to understanding fluid, material, and atmospheric dynamics, and mechanical, electrical, atomic and sub-atomic structures and processes.
Sales and Marketing	Knowledge of principles and methods for showing, promoting, and selling products or services. This includes marketing strategy and tactics, product demonstration, sales techniques, and sales control systems.
Fine Arts	Knowledge of the theory and techniques required to compose, produce, and perform works of music, dance, visual arts, drama, and sculpture.

Skills	Skills Definitions
Active Listening	Giving full attention to what other people are saying, taking time to understand the points being made, asking questions as appropriate, and not interrupting at inappropriate times.
Social Perceptiveness	Being aware of others' reactions and understanding why they react as they do.
Speaking	Talking to others to convey information effectively.
Writing	Communicating effectively in writing as appropriate for the needs of the audience.
Monitoring	Monitoring/Assessing performance of yourself, other individuals, or organizations to make improvements or take corrective action.
Critical Thinking	Using logic and reasoning to identify the strengths and weaknesses of alternative solutions, conclusions or approaches to problems.
Reading Comprehension	Understanding written sentences and paragraphs in work related documents.
Coordination	Adjusting actions in relation to others' actions.
Persuasion	Persuading others to change their minds or behavior.
Instructing	Teaching others how to do something.
Judgment and Decision Making	Considering the relative costs and benefits of potential actions to choose the most appropriate one.
Active Learning	Understanding the implications of new information for both current and future problem-solving and decision-making.
Negotiation	Bringing others together and trying to reconcile differences.
Time Management	Managing one's own time and the time of others.
Learning Strategies	Selecting and using training/instructional methods and procedures appropriate for the situation when learning or teaching new things.
Complex Problem Solving	Identifying complex problems and reviewing related information to develop and evaluate options and implement solutions.
Service Orientation	Actively looking for ways to help people.
Management of Personnel Resources	Motivating, developing, and directing people as they work, identifying the best people for the job.
Mathematics	Using mathematics to solve problems.
Operation and Control	Controlling operations of equipment or systems.
Equipment Maintenance	Performing routine maintenance on equipment and determining when and what kind of maintenance is needed.
Management of Material Resources	Obtaining and seeing to the appropriate use of equipment, facilities, and materials needed to do certain work.
Equipment Selection	Determining the kind of tools and equipment needed to do a job.
Troubleshooting	Determining causes of operating errors and deciding what to do about it.
Operations Analysis	Analyzing needs and product requirements to create a design.
Repairing	Repairing machines or systems using the needed tools.
Quality Control Analysis	Conducting tests and inspections of products, services, or processes to evaluate quality or performance.
Systems Evaluation	Identifying measures or indicators of system performance and the actions needed to improve or correct performance, relative to the goals of the system.
Systems Analysis	Determining how a system should work and how changes in conditions, operations, and the environment will affect outcomes.

Operation Monitoring	Watching gauges, dials, or other indicators to make sure a machine is working properly.
Technology Design	Generating or adapting equipment and technology to serve user needs.
Installation	Installing equipment, machines, wiring, or programs to meet specifications.
Management of Financial Resources	Determining how money will be spent to get the work done, and accounting for these expenditures.
Science	Using scientific rules and methods to solve problems.
Programming	Writing computer programs for various purposes.

Ability	Ability Definitions
Problem Sensitivity	The ability to tell when something is wrong or is likely to go wrong. It does not involve solving the problem, only recognizing there is a problem.
Oral Expression	The ability to communicate information and ideas in speaking so others will understand.
Oral Comprehension	The ability to listen to and understand information and ideas presented through spoken words and sentences.
Near Vision	The ability to see details at close range (within a few feet of the observer).
Speech Clarity	The ability to speak clearly so others can understand you.
Far Vision	The ability to see details at a distance.
Selective Attention	The ability to concentrate on a task over a period of time without being distracted.
Information Ordering	The ability to arrange things or actions in a certain order or pattern according to a specific rule or set of rules (e.g., patterns of numbers, letters, words, pictures, mathematical operations).
Flexibility of Closure	The ability to identify or detect a known pattern (a figure, object, word, or sound) that is hidden in other distracting material.
Deductive Reasoning	The ability to apply general rules to specific problems to produce answers that make sense.
Inductive Reasoning	The ability to combine pieces of information to form general rules or conclusions (includes finding a relationship among seemingly unrelated events).
Speech Recognition	The ability to identify and understand the speech of another person.
Written Expression	The ability to communicate information and ideas in writing so others will understand.
Reaction Time	The ability to quickly respond (with the hand, finger, or foot) to a signal (sound, light, picture) when it appears.
Perceptual Speed	The ability to quickly and accurately compare similarities and differences among sets of letters, numbers, objects, pictures, or patterns. The things to be compared may be presented at the same time or one after the other. This ability also includes comparing a presented object with a remembered object.
Speed of Closure	The ability to quickly make sense of, combine, and organize information into meaningful patterns.
Static Strength	The ability to exert maximum muscle force to lift, push, pull, or carry objects.
Written Comprehension	The ability to read and understand information and ideas presented in writing.
Time Sharing	The ability to shift back and forth between two or more activities or sources of information (such as speech, sounds, touch, or other sources).
Response Orientation	The ability to choose quickly between two or more movements in response to two or more different signals (lights, sounds, pictures). It includes the speed with which the correct response is started with the hand, foot, or other body part.
Auditory Attention	The ability to focus on a single source of sound in the presence of other distracting sounds.
Stamina	The ability to exert yourself physically over long periods of time without getting winded or out of breath.
Category Flexibility	The ability to generate or use different sets of rules for combining or grouping things in different ways.
Explosive Strength	The ability to use short bursts of muscle force to propel oneself (as in jumping or sprinting), or to throw an object.
Fluency of Ideas	The ability to come up with a number of ideas about a topic (the number of ideas is important, not their quality, correctness, or creativity).
Gross Body Coordination	The ability to coordinate the movement of your arms, legs, and torso together when the whole body is in motion.
Finger Dexterity	The ability to make precisely coordinated movements of the fingers of one or both hands to grasp, manipulate, or assemble very small objects.

Depth Perception	The ability to judge which of several objects is closer or farther away from you, or to judge the distance between you and an object.
Multilimb Coordination	The ability to coordinate two or more limbs (for example, two arms, two legs, or one leg and one arm) while sitting, standing, or lying down. It does not involve performing the activities while the whole body is in motion.
Originality	The ability to come up with unusual or clever ideas about a given topic or situation, or to develop creative ways to solve a problem.
Arm-Hand Steadiness	The ability to keep your hand and arm steady while moving your arm or while holding your arm and hand in one position.
Hearing Sensitivity	The ability to detect or tell the differences between sounds that vary in pitch and loudness.
Trunk Strength	The ability to use your abdominal and lower back muscles to support part of the body repeatedly or continuously over time without 'giving out' or fatiguing.
Extent Flexibility	The ability to bend, stretch, twist, or reach with your body, arms, and/or legs.
Manual Dexterity	The ability to quickly move your hand, your hand together with your arm, or your two hands to grasp, manipulate, or assemble objects.
Visualization	The ability to imagine how something will look after it is moved around or when its parts are moved or rearranged.
Visual Color Discrimination	The ability to match or detect differences between colors, including shades of color and brightness.
Memorization	The ability to remember information such as words, numbers, pictures, and procedures.
Speed of Limb Movement	The ability to quickly move the arms and legs.
Spatial Orientation	The ability to know your location in relation to the environment or to know where other objects are in relation to you.
Gross Body Equilibrium	The ability to keep or regain your body balance or stay upright when in an unstable position.
Control Precision	The ability to quickly and repeatedly adjust the controls of a machine or a vehicle to exact positions.
Peripheral Vision	The ability to see objects or movement of objects to one's side when the eyes are looking ahead.
Dynamic Strength	The ability to exert muscle force repeatedly or continuously over time. This involves muscular endurance and resistance to muscle fatigue.
Number Facility	The ability to add, subtract, multiply, or divide quickly and correctly.
Glare Sensitivity	The ability to see objects in the presence of glare or bright lighting.
Sound Localization	The ability to tell the direction from which a sound originated.
Night Vision	The ability to see under low light conditions.
Mathematical Reasoning	The ability to choose the right mathematical methods or formulas to solve a problem.
Rate Control	The ability to time your movements or the movement of a piece of equipment in anticipation of changes in the speed and/or direction of a moving object or scene.
Dynamic Flexibility	The ability to quickly and repeatedly bend, stretch, twist, or reach out with your body, arms, and/or legs.
Wrist-Finger Speed	The ability to make fast, simple, repeated movements of the fingers, hands, and wrists.

Work_Activity	Work_Activity Definitions
Communicating with Supervisors, Peers, or Subordin	Providing information to supervisors, co-workers, and subordinates by telephone, in written form, e-mail, or in person.
Getting Information	Observing, receiving, and otherwise obtaining information from all relevant sources.
Documenting/Recording Information	Entering, transcribing, recording, storing, or maintaining information in written or electronic/magnetic form.
Identifying Objects, Actions, and Events	Identifying information by categorizing, estimating, recognizing differences or similarities, and detecting changes in circumstances or events.
Making Decisions and Solving Problems	Analyzing information and evaluating results to choose the best solution and solve problems.
Resolving Conflicts and Negotiating with Others	Handling complaints, settling disputes, and resolving grievances and conflicts, or otherwise negotiating with others.
Monitor Processes, Materials, or Surroundings	Monitoring and reviewing information from materials, events, or the environment, to detect or assess problems.
Evaluating Information to Determine Compliance wit	Using relevant information and individual judgment to determine whether events or processes comply with laws, regulations, or standards.

Establishing and Maintaining Interpersonal Relatio	Developing constructive and cooperative working relationships with others, and maintaining them over time.
Inspecting Equipment, Structures, or Material	Inspecting equipment, structures, or materials to identify the cause of errors or other problems or defects.
Updating and Using Relevant Knowledge	Keeping up-to-date technically and applying new knowledge to your job.
Performing General Physical Activities	Performing physical activities that require considerable use of your arms and legs and moving your whole body, such as climbing, lifting, balancing, walking, stooping, and handling of materials.
Assisting and Caring for Others	Providing personal assistance, medical attention, emotional support, or other personal care to others such as coworkers, customers, or patients.
Training and Teaching Others	Identifying the educational needs of others, developing formal educational or training programs or classes, and teaching or instructing others.
Developing and Building Teams	Encouraging and building mutual trust, respect, and cooperation among team members.
Processing Information	Compiling, coding, categorizing, calculating, tabulating, auditing, or verifying information or data.
Judging the Qualities of Things, Services, or Peop	Assessing the value, importance, or quality of things or people.
Guiding, Directing, and Motivating Subordinates	Providing guidance and direction to subordinates, including setting performance standards and monitoring performance.
Interpreting the Meaning of Information for Others	Translating or explaining what information means and how it can be used.
Coordinating the Work and Activities of Others	Getting members of a group to work together to accomplish tasks.
Performing Administrative Activities	Performing day-to-day administrative tasks such as maintaining information files and processing paperwork.
Organizing, Planning, and Prioritizing Work	Developing specific goals and plans to prioritize, organize, and accomplish your work.
Interacting With Computers	Using computers and computer systems (including hardware and software) to program, write software, set up functions, enter data, or process information.
Communicating with Persons Outside Organization	Communicating with people outside the organization, representing the organization to customers, the public, government, and other external sources. This information can be exchanged in person, in writing, or by telephone or e-mail.
Coaching and Developing Others	Identifying the developmental needs of others and coaching, mentoring, or otherwise helping others to improve their knowledge or skills.
Operating Vehicles, Mechanized Devices, or Equipme	Running, maneuvering, navigating, or driving vehicles or mechanized equipment, such as forklifts, passenger vehicles, aircraft, or water craft.
Performing for or Working Directly with the Public	Performing for people or dealing directly with the public. This includes serving customers in restaurants and stores, and receiving clients or guests.
Scheduling Work and Activities	Scheduling events, programs, and activities, as well as the work of others.
Thinking Creatively	Developing, designing, or creating new applications, ideas, relationships, systems, or products, including artistic contributions.
Analyzing Data or Information	Identifying the underlying principles, reasons, or facts of information by breaking down information or data into separate parts.
Developing Objectives and Strategies	Establishing long-range objectives and specifying the strategies and actions to achieve them.
Provide Consultation and Advice to Others	Providing guidance and expert advice to management or other groups on technical, systems-, or process-related topics.
Estimating the Quantifiable Characteristics of Pro	Estimating sizes, distances, and quantities; or determining time, costs, resources, or materials needed to perform a work activity.
Handling and Moving Objects	Using hands and arms in handling, installing, positioning, and moving materials, and manipulating things.
Monitoring and Controlling Resources	Monitoring and controlling resources and overseeing the spending of money.
Staffing Organizational Units	Recruiting, interviewing, selecting, hiring, and promoting employees in an organization.
Selling or Influencing Others	Convincing others to buy merchandise/goods or to otherwise change their minds or actions.
Controlling Machines and Processes	Using either control mechanisms or direct physical activity to operate machines or processes (not including computers or vehicles).
Repairing and Maintaining Mechanical Equipment	Servicing, repairing, adjusting, and testing machines, devices, moving parts, and equipment that operate primarily on the basis of mechanical (not electronic) principles.
Repairing and Maintaining Electronic Equipment	Servicing, repairing, calibrating, regulating, fine-tuning, or testing machines, devices, and equipment that operate primarily on the basis of electrical or electronic (not mechanical) principles.
Drafting, Laying Out, and Specifying Technical Dev	Providing documentation, detailed instructions, drawings, or specifications to tell others about how devices, parts, equipment, or structures are to be fabricated, constructed, assembled, modified, maintained, or used.

Work_Context	Work_Context Definitions
Face-to-Face Discussions	How often do you have to have face-to-face discussions with individuals or teams in this job?
Telephone	How often do you have telephone conversations in this job?
Contact With Others	How much does this job require the worker to be in contact with others (face-to-face, by telephone, or otherwise) in order to perform it?
Deal With Unpleasant or Angry People	How frequently does the worker have to deal with unpleasant, angry, or discourteous individuals as part of the job requirements?
Work With Work Group or Team	How important is it to work with others in a group or team in this job?
Exposed to Disease or Infections	How often does this job require exposure to disease/infections?
Deal With Physically Aggressive People	How frequently does this job require the worker to deal with physical aggression of violent individuals?
Responsible for Others' Health and Safety	How much responsibility is there for the health and safety of others in this job?
Frequency of Conflict Situations	How often are there conflict situations the employee has to face in this job?
Importance of Being Exact or Accurate	How important is being very exact or highly accurate in performing this job?
Physical Proximity	To what extent does this job require the worker to perform job tasks in close physical proximity to other people?
Importance of Repeating Same Tasks	How important is repeating the same physical activities (e.g., key entry) or mental activities (e.g., checking entries in a ledger) over and over, without stopping, to performing this job?
Letters and Memos	How often does the job require written letters and memos?
Frequency of Decision Making	How frequently is the worker required to make decisions that affect other people, the financial resources, and/or the image and reputation of the organization?
Indoors, Environmentally Controlled	How often does this job require working indoors in environmentally controlled conditions?
Sounds, Noise Levels Are Distracting or Uncomforta	How often does this job require working exposed to sounds and noise levels that are distracting or uncomfortable?
Freedom to Make Decisions	How much decision making freedom, without supervision, does the job offer?
Coordinate or Lead Others	How important is it to coordinate or lead others in accomplishing work activities in this job?
Consequence of Error	How serious would the result usually be if the worker made a mistake that was not readily correctable?
Impact of Decisions on Co-workers or Company Resul	How do the decisions an employee makes impact the results of co-workers, clients or the company?
Time Pressure	How often does this job require the worker to meet strict deadlines?
Deal With External Customers	How important is it to work with external customers or the public in this job?
Responsibility for Outcomes and Results	How responsible is the worker for work outcomes and results of other workers?
Exposed to Contaminants	How often does this job require working exposed to contaminants (such as pollutants, gases, dust or odors)?
Structured versus Unstructured Work	To what extent is this job structured for the worker, rather than allowing the worker to determine tasks, priorities, and goals?
Spend Time Standing	How much does this job require standing?
Outdoors, Exposed to Weather	How often does this job require working outdoors, exposed to all weather conditions?
Spend Time Walking and Running	How much does this job require walking and running?
Wear Common Protective or Safety Equipment such as	How much does this job require wearing common protective or safety equipment such as safety shoes, glasses, gloves, hard hats or life jackets?
Spend Time Using Your Hands to Handle, Control, or	How much does this job require using your hands to handle, control, or feel objects, tools or controls?
Very Hot or Cold Temperatures	How often does this job require working in very hot (above 90 F degrees) or very cold (below 32 F degrees) temperatures?

701

Spend Time Making Repetitive Motions — How much does this job require making repetitive motions?

In an Enclosed Vehicle or Equipment — How often does this job require working in a closed vehicle or equipment (e.g., car)?

Public Speaking — How often do you have to perform public speaking in this job?

Indoors, Not Environmentally Controlled — How often does this job require working indoors in non-controlled environmental conditions (e.g., warehouse without heat)?

Level of Competition — To what extent does this job require the worker to compete or to be aware of competitive pressures?

Electronic Mail — How often do you use electronic mail in this job?

Spend Time Sitting — How much does this job require sitting?

Extremely Bright or Inadequate Lighting — How often does this job require working in extremely bright or inadequate lighting conditions?

Exposed to Minor Burns, Cuts, Bites, or Stings — How often does this job require exposure to minor burns, cuts, bites, or stings?

Exposed to High Places — How often does this job require exposure to high places?

Spend Time Bending or Twisting the Body — How much does this job require bending or twisting your body?

Outdoors, Under Cover — How often does this job require working outdoors, under cover (e.g., structure with roof but no walls)?

Cramped Work Space, Awkward Positions — How often does this job require working in cramped work spaces that requires getting into awkward positions?

Spend Time Kneeling, Crouching, Stooping, or Crawl — How much does this job require kneeling, crouching, stooping, or crawling?

Wear Specialized Protective or Safety Equipment su — How much does this job require wearing specialized protective or safety equipment such as breathing apparatus, safety harness, full protection suits, or radiation protection?

Degree of Automation — How automated is the job?

Exposed to Hazardous Conditions — How often does this job require exposure to hazardous conditions?

Spend Time Keeping or Regaining Balance — How much does this job require keeping or regaining your balance?

Exposed to Hazardous Equipment — How often does this job require exposure to hazardous equipment?

Spend Time Climbing Ladders, Scaffolds, or Poles — How much does this job require climbing ladders, scaffolds, or poles?

Exposed to Radiation — How often does this job require exposure to radiation?

Pace Determined by Speed of Equipment — How important is it to this job that the pace is determined by the speed of equipment or machinery? (This does not refer to keeping busy at all times on this job.)

In an Open Vehicle or Equipment — How often does this job require working in an open vehicle or equipment (e.g., tractor)?

Exposed to Whole Body Vibration — How often does this job require exposure to whole body vibration (e.g., operate a jackhammer)?

Job Zone Component	Job Zone Component Definitions
Title	Job Zone Three: Medium Preparation Needed
Overall Experience	Previous work-related skill, knowledge, or experience is required for these occupations. For example, an electrician must have completed three or four years of apprenticeship or several years of vocational training, and often must have passed a licensing exam, in order to perform the job.
Job Training	Employees in these occupations usually need one or two years of training involving both on-the-job experience and informal training with experienced workers.
Job Zone Examples	These occupations usually involve using communication and organizational skills to coordinate, supervise, manage, or train others to accomplish goals. Examples include dental assistants, electricians, fish and game wardens, legal secretaries, personnel recruiters, and recreation workers.
SVP Range	(6.0 to < 7.0)
Education	Most occupations in this zone require training in vocational schools, related on-the-job experience, or an associate's degree. Some may require a bachelor's degree.

Work_Styles	Work_Styles Definitions
Self Control	Job requires maintaining composure, keeping emotions in check, controlling anger, and avoiding aggressive behavior, even in very difficult situations.
Dependability	Job requires being reliable, responsible, and dependable, and fulfilling obligations.
Integrity	Job requires being honest and ethical.
Stress Tolerance	Job requires accepting criticism and dealing calmly and effectively with high stress situations.
Attention to Detail	Job requires being careful about detail and thorough in completing work tasks.
Cooperation	Job requires being pleasant with others on the job and displaying a good-natured, cooperative attitude.
Adaptability/Flexibility	Job requires being open to change (positive or negative) and to considerable variety in the workplace.
Concern for Others	Job requires being sensitive to others' needs and feelings and being understanding and helpful on the job.
Leadership	Job requires a willingness to lead, take charge, and offer opinions and direction.
Initiative	Job requires a willingness to take on responsibilities and challenges.
Social Orientation	Job requires preferring to work with others rather than alone, and being personally connected with others on the job.
Independence	Job requires developing one's own ways of doing things, guiding oneself with little or no supervision, and depending on oneself to get things done.
Persistence	Job requires persistence in the face of obstacles.
Analytical Thinking	Job requires analyzing information and using logic to address work-related issues and problems.
Achievement/Effort	Job requires establishing and maintaining personally challenging achievement goals and exerting effort toward mastering tasks.
Innovation	Job requires creativity and alternative thinking to develop new ideas for and answers to work-related problems.

33-3021.01 - Police Detectives

Conduct investigations to prevent crimes or solve criminal cases.

Tasks

1) Analyze completed police reports to determine what additional information and investigative work is needed.

2) Provide testimony as a witness in court.

3) Prepare and serve search and arrest warrants.

4) Obtain evidence from suspects.

5) Maintain surveillance of establishments to obtain identifying information on suspects.

6) Obtain facts or statements from complainants, witnesses, and accused persons and record interviews, using recording device.

7) Record progress of investigation, maintain informational files on suspects, and submit reports to commanding officer or magistrate to authorize warrants.

8) Prepare charges or responses to charges, or information for court cases, according to formalized procedures.

9) Notify command of situation and request assistance.

10) Participate or assist in raids and arrests.

11) Question individuals or observe persons and establishments to confirm information given to patrol officers.

12) Block or rope off scene and check perimeter to ensure that entire scene is secured.

13) Note relevant details upon arrival at scene, such as time of day and weather conditions.

14) Coordinate with outside agencies and serve on interagency task forces to combat specific types of crime.

15) Provide information to lab personnel concerning the source of an item of evidence and tests to be performed.

16) Obtain summary of incident from officer in charge at crime scene, taking care to avoid disturbing evidence.

17) Examine crime scenes to obtain clues and evidence, such as loose hairs, fibers, clothing, or weapons.

18) Note, mark, and photograph location of objects found, such as footprints, tire tracks, bullets and bloodstains, and take measurements of the scene.

19) Organize scene search, assigning specific tasks and areas of search to individual officers and obtaining adequate lighting as necessary.

20) Notify, or request notification of, medical examiner or district attorney representative.

21) Preserve, process, and analyze items of evidence obtained from crime scenes and suspects, placing them in proper containers and destroying evidence no longer needed.

22) Schedule polygraph tests for consenting parties and record results of test interpretations for presentation with findings.

23) Take photographs from all angles of relevant parts of a crime scene, including entrance and exit routes and streets and intersections.

24) Monitor conditions of victims who are unconscious so that arrangements can be made to take statements if consciousness is regained.

25) Secure persons at scene, keeping witnesses from conversing or leaving the scene before investigators arrive.

26) Summon medical help for injured individuals and alert medical personnel to take statements from them.

27) Videotape scenes where possible, including collection of evidence, examination of victim at scene, and defendants and witnesses.

28) Secure deceased body and obtain evidence from it, preventing bystanders from tampering with it prior to medical examiner's arrival.

29) Check victims for signs of life, such as breathing and pulse.

30) Observe and photograph narcotic purchase transactions to compile evidence and protect undercover investigators.

Knowledge	Knowledge Definitions
Law and Government	Knowledge of laws, legal codes, court procedures, precedents, government regulations, executive orders, agency rules, and the democratic political process.
Public Safety and Security	Knowledge of relevant equipment, policies, procedures, and strategies to promote effective local, state, or national security operations for the protection of people, data, property, and institutions.
English Language	Knowledge of the structure and content of the English language including the meaning and spelling of words, rules of composition, and grammar.
Psychology	Knowledge of human behavior and performance; individual differences in ability, personality, and interests; learning and motivation; psychological research methods; and the assessment and treatment of behavioral and affective disorders.
Administration and Management	Knowledge of business and management principles involved in strategic planning, resource allocation, human resources modeling, leadership technique, production methods, and coordination of people and resources.
Education and Training	Knowledge of principles and methods for curriculum and training design, teaching and instruction for individuals and groups, and the measurement of training effects.
Customer and Personal Service	Knowledge of principles and processes for providing customer and personal services. This includes customer needs assessment, meeting quality standards for services, and evaluation of customer satisfaction.
Computers and Electronics	Knowledge of circuit boards, processors, chips, electronic equipment, and computer hardware and software, including applications and programming.
Communications and Media	Knowledge of media production, communication, and dissemination techniques and methods. This includes alternative ways to inform and entertain via written, oral, and visual media.
Telecommunications	Knowledge of transmission, broadcasting, switching, control, and operation of telecommunications systems.
Clerical	Knowledge of administrative and clerical procedures and systems such as word processing, managing files and records, stenography and transcription, designing forms, and other office procedures and terminology.
Therapy and Counseling	Knowledge of principles, methods, and procedures for diagnosis, treatment, and rehabilitation of physical and mental dysfunctions, and for career counseling and guidance.
Sociology and Anthropology	Knowledge of group behavior and dynamics, societal trends and influences, human migrations, ethnicity, cultures and their history and origins.
Transportation	Knowledge of principles and methods for moving people or goods by air, rail, sea, or road, including the relative costs and benefits.
Personnel and Human Resources	Knowledge of principles and procedures for personnel recruitment, selection, training, compensation and benefits, labor relations and negotiation, and personnel information systems.
Mathematics	Knowledge of arithmetic, algebra, geometry, calculus, statistics, and their applications.
Philosophy and Theology	Knowledge of different philosophical systems and religions. This includes their basic principles, values, ethics, ways of thinking, customs, practices, and their impact on human culture.
Foreign Language	Knowledge of the structure and content of a foreign (non-English) language including the meaning and spelling of words, rules of composition and grammar, and pronunciation.
Geography	Knowledge of principles and methods for describing the features of land, sea, and air masses, including their physical characteristics, locations, interrelationships, and distribution of plant, animal, and human life.
Medicine and Dentistry	Knowledge of the information and techniques needed to diagnose and treat human injuries, diseases, and deformities. This includes symptoms, treatment alternatives, drug properties and interactions, and preventive health-care measures.
Engineering and Technology	Knowledge of the practical application of engineering science and technology. This includes applying principles, techniques, procedures, and equipment to the design and production of various goods and services.
Economics and Accounting	Knowledge of economic and accounting principles and practices, the financial markets, banking and the analysis and reporting of financial data.
Design	Knowledge of design techniques, tools, and principles involved in production of precision technical plans, blueprints, drawings, and models.
Chemistry	Knowledge of the chemical composition, structure, and properties of substances and of the chemical processes and transformations that they undergo. This includes uses of chemicals and their interactions, danger signs, production techniques, and disposal methods.
Production and Processing	Knowledge of raw materials, production processes, quality control, costs, and other techniques for maximizing the effective manufacture and distribution of goods.
Biology	Knowledge of plant and animal organisms, their tissues, cells, functions, interdependencies, and interactions with each other and the environment.
Mechanical	Knowledge of machines and tools, including their designs, uses, repair, and maintenance.
Physics	Knowledge and prediction of physical principles, laws, their interrelationships, and applications to understanding fluid, material, and atmospheric dynamics, and mechanical, electrical, atomic and sub-atomic structures and processes.
History and Archeology	Knowledge of historical events and their causes, indicators, and effects on civilizations and cultures.
Building and Construction	Knowledge of materials, methods, and the tools involved in the construction or repair of houses, buildings, or other structures such as highways and roads.
Sales and Marketing	Knowledge of principles and methods for showing, promoting, and selling products or services. This includes marketing strategy and tactics, product demonstration, sales techniques, and sales control systems.
Fine Arts	Knowledge of the theory and techniques required to compose, produce, and perform works of music, dance, visual arts, drama, and sculpture.
Food Production	Knowledge of techniques and equipment for planting, growing, and harvesting food products (both plant and animal) for consumption, including storage/handling techniques.

Skills	Skills Definitions
Active Listening	Giving full attention to what other people are saying, taking time to understand the points being made, asking questions as appropriate, and not interrupting at inappropriate times.
Writing	Communicating effectively in writing as appropriate for the needs of the audience.
Reading Comprehension	Understanding written sentences and paragraphs in work related documents.
Critical Thinking	Using logic and reasoning to identify the strengths and weaknesses of alternative solutions, conclusions or approaches to problems.
Speaking	Talking to others to convey information effectively.
Coordination	Adjusting actions in relation to others' actions.
Active Learning	Understanding the implications of new information for both current and future problem-solving and decision-making.
Social Perceptiveness	Being aware of others' reactions and understanding why they react as they do.

Persuasion	Persuading others to change their minds or behavior.
Time Management	Managing one's own time and the time of others.
Judgment and Decision Making	Considering the relative costs and benefits of potential actions to choose the most appropriate one.
Negotiation	Bringing others together and trying to reconcile differences.
Learning Strategies	Selecting and using training/instructional methods and procedures appropriate for the situation when learning or teaching new things.
Complex Problem Solving	Identifying complex problems and reviewing related information to develop and evaluate options and implement solutions.
Service Orientation	Actively looking for ways to help people.
Instructing	Teaching others how to do something.
Monitoring	Monitoring/Assessing performance of yourself, other individuals, or organizations to make improvements or take corrective action.
Equipment Selection	Determining the kind of tools and equipment needed to do a job.
Science	Using scientific rules and methods to solve problems.
Management of Personnel Resources	Motivating, developing, and directing people as they work, identifying the best people for the job.
Mathematics	Using mathematics to solve problems.
Equipment Maintenance	Performing routine maintenance on equipment and determining when and what kind of maintenance is needed.
Operations Analysis	Analyzing needs and product requirements to create a design.
Troubleshooting	Determining causes of operating errors and deciding what to do about it.
Technology Design	Generating or adapting equipment and technology to serve user needs.
Management of Material Resources	Obtaining and seeing to the appropriate use of equipment, facilities, and materials needed to do certain work.
Systems Evaluation	Identifying measures or indicators of system performance and the actions needed to improve or correct performance, relative to the goals of the system.
Management of Financial Resources	Determining how money will be spent to get the work done, and accounting for these expenditures.
Systems Analysis	Determining how a system should work and how changes in conditions, operations, and the environment will affect outcomes.
Operation and Control	Controlling operations of equipment or systems.
Quality Control Analysis	Conducting tests and inspections of products, services, or processes to evaluate quality or performance.
Operation Monitoring	Watching gauges, dials, or other indicators to make sure a machine is working properly.
Repairing	Repairing machines or systems using the needed tools.
Installation	Installing equipment, machines, wiring, or programs to meet specifications.
Programming	Writing computer programs for various purposes.

Ability	Ability Definitions
Inductive Reasoning	The ability to combine pieces of information to form general rules or conclusions (includes finding a relationship among seemingly unrelated events).
Oral Comprehension	The ability to listen to and understand information and ideas presented through spoken words and sentences.
Oral Expression	The ability to communicate information and ideas in speaking so others will understand.
Speech Recognition	The ability to identify and understand the speech of another person.
Near Vision	The ability to see details at close range (within a few feet of the observer).
Information Ordering	The ability to arrange things or actions in a certain order or pattern according to a specific rule or set of rules (e.g., patterns of numbers, letters, words, pictures, mathematical operations).
Problem Sensitivity	The ability to tell when something is wrong or is likely to go wrong. It does not involve solving the problem, only recognizing there is a problem.
Flexibility of Closure	The ability to identify or detect a known pattern (a figure, object, word, or sound) that is hidden in other distracting material.
Deductive Reasoning	The ability to apply general rules to specific problems to produce answers that make sense.
Speech Clarity	The ability to speak clearly so others can understand you.
Written Comprehension	The ability to read and understand information and ideas presented in writing.
Speed of Closure	The ability to quickly make sense of, combine, and organize information into meaningful patterns.

Written Expression	The ability to communicate information and ideas in writing so others will understand.
Far Vision	The ability to see details at a distance.
Selective Attention	The ability to concentrate on a task over a period of time without being distracted.
Originality	The ability to come up with unusual or clever ideas about a given topic or situation, or to develop creative ways to solve a problem.
Multilimb Coordination	The ability to coordinate two or more limbs (for example, two arms, two legs, or one leg and one arm) while sitting, standing, or lying down. It does not involve performing the activities while the whole body is in motion.
Fluency of Ideas	The ability to come up with a number of ideas about a topic (the number of ideas is important, not their quality, correctness, or creativity).
Time Sharing	The ability to shift back and forth between two or more activities or sources of information (such as speech, sounds, touch, or other sources).
Category Flexibility	The ability to generate or use different sets of rules for combining or grouping things in different ways.
Depth Perception	The ability to judge which of several objects is closer or farther away from you, or to judge the distance between you and an object.
Memorization	The ability to remember information such as words, numbers, pictures, and procedures.
Control Precision	The ability to quickly and repeatedly adjust the controls of a machine or a vehicle to exact positions.
Visualization	The ability to imagine how something will look after it is moved around or when its parts are moved or rearranged.
Perceptual Speed	The ability to quickly and accurately compare similarities and differences among sets of letters, numbers, objects, pictures, or patterns. The things to be compared may be presented at the same time or one after the other. This ability also includes comparing a presented object with a remembered object.
Finger Dexterity	The ability to make precisely coordinated movements of the fingers of one or both hands to grasp, manipulate, or assemble very small objects.
Arm-Hand Steadiness	The ability to keep your hand and arm steady while moving your arm or while holding your arm and hand in one position.
Reaction Time	The ability to quickly respond (with the hand, finger, or foot) to a signal (sound, light, picture) when it appears.
Visual Color Discrimination	The ability to match or detect differences between colors, including shades of color and brightness.
Response Orientation	The ability to choose quickly between two or more movements in response to two or more different signals (lights, sounds, pictures). It includes the speed with which the correct response is started with the hand, foot, or other body part.
Manual Dexterity	The ability to quickly move your hand, your hand together with your arm, or your two hands to grasp, manipulate, or assemble objects.
Auditory Attention	The ability to focus on a single source of sound in the presence of other distracting sounds.
Static Strength	The ability to exert maximum muscle force to lift, push, pull, or carry objects.
Stamina	The ability to exert yourself physically over long periods of time without getting winded or out of breath.
Gross Body Coordination	The ability to coordinate the movement of your arms, legs, and torso together when the whole body is in motion.
Spatial Orientation	The ability to know your location in relation to the environment or to know where other objects are in relation to you.
Rate Control	The ability to time your movements or the movement of a piece of equipment in anticipation of changes in the speed and/or direction of a moving object or scene.
Extent Flexibility	The ability to bend, stretch, twist, or reach with your body, arms, and/or legs.
Dynamic Strength	The ability to exert muscle force repeatedly or continuously over time. This involves muscular endurance and resistance to muscle fatigue.
Explosive Strength	The ability to use short bursts of muscle force to propel oneself (as in jumping or sprinting), or to throw an object.
Trunk Strength	The ability to use your abdominal and lower back muscles to support part of the body repeatedly or continuously over time without 'giving out' or fatiguing.
Speed of Limb Movement	The ability to quickly move the arms and legs.
Night Vision	The ability to see under low light conditions.
Peripheral Vision	The ability to see objects or movement of objects to one's side when the eyes are looking ahead.

Glare Sensitivity	The ability to see objects in the presence of glare or bright lighting.
Number Facility	The ability to add, subtract, multiply, or divide quickly and correctly.
Sound Localization	The ability to tell the direction from which a sound originated.
Mathematical Reasoning	The ability to choose the right mathematical methods or formulas to solve a problem.
Gross Body Equilibrium	The ability to keep or regain your body balance or stay upright when in an unstable position.
Hearing Sensitivity	The ability to detect or tell the differences between sounds that vary in pitch and loudness.
Wrist-Finger Speed	The ability to make fast, simple, repeated movements of the fingers, hands, and wrists.
Dynamic Flexibility	The ability to quickly and repeatedly bend, stretch, twist, or reach out with your body, arms, and/or legs.

Work_Activity	Work_Activity Definitions
Getting Information	Observing, receiving, and otherwise obtaining information from all relevant sources.
Identifying Objects, Actions, and Events	Identifying information by categorizing, estimating, recognizing differences or similarities, and detecting changes in circumstances or events.
Documenting/Recording Information	Entering, transcribing, recording, storing, or maintaining information in written or electronic/magnetic form.
Making Decisions and Solving Problems	Analyzing information and evaluating results to choose the best solution and solve problems.
Performing for or Working Directly with the Public	Performing for people or dealing directly with the public. This includes serving customers in restaurants and stores, and receiving clients or guests.
Updating and Using Relevant Knowledge	Keeping up-to-date technically and applying new knowledge to your job.
Communicating with Supervisors, Peers, or Subordin	Providing information to supervisors, co-workers, and subordinates by telephone, in written form, e-mail, or in person.
Processing Information	Compiling, coding, categorizing, calculating, tabulating, auditing, or verifying information or data.
Organizing, Planning, and Prioritizing Work	Developing specific goals and plans to prioritize, organize, and accomplish your work.
Interacting With Computers	Using computers and computer systems (including hardware and software) to program, write software, set up functions, enter data, or process information.
Communicating with Persons Outside Organization	Communicating with people outside the organization, representing the organization to customers, the public, government, and other external sources. This information can be exchanged in person, in writing, or by telephone or e-mail.
Analyzing Data or Information	Identifying the underlying principles, reasons, or facts of information by breaking down information or data into separate parts.
Establishing and Maintaining Interpersonal Relatio	Developing constructive and cooperative working relationships with others, and maintaining them over time.
Operating Vehicles, Mechanized Devices, or Equipme	Running, maneuvering, navigating, or driving vehicles or mechanized equipment, such as forklifts, passenger vehicles, aircraft, or water craft.
Evaluating Information to Determine Compliance wit	Using relevant information and individual judgment to determine whether events or processes comply with laws, regulations, or standards.
Performing General Physical Activities	Performing physical activities that require considerable use of your arms and legs and moving your whole body, such as climbing, lifting, balancing, walking, stooping, and handling of materials.
Monitor Processes, Materials, or Surroundings	Monitoring and reviewing information from materials, events, or the environment, to detect or assess problems.
Resolving Conflicts and Negotiating with Others	Handling complaints, settling disputes, and resolving grievances and conflicts, or otherwise negotiating with others.
Assisting and Caring for Others	Providing personal assistance, medical attention, emotional support, or other personal care to others such as coworkers, customers, or patients.
Training and Teaching Others	Identifying the educational needs of others, developing formal educational or training programs or classes, and teaching or instructing others.
Thinking Creatively	Developing, designing, or creating new applications, ideas, relationships, systems, or products, including artistic contributions.
Developing Objectives and Strategies	Establishing long-range objectives and specifying the strategies and actions to achieve them.

Interpreting the Meaning of Information for Others	Translating or explaining what information means and how it can be used.
Judging the Qualities of Things, Services, or Peop	Assessing the value, importance, or quality of things or people.
Scheduling Work and Activities	Scheduling events, programs, and activities, as well as the work of others.
Coordinating the Work and Activities of Others	Getting members of a group to work together to accomplish tasks.
Performing Administrative Activities	Performing day-to-day administrative tasks such as maintaining information files and processing paperwork.
Provide Consultation and Advice to Others	Providing guidance and expert advice to management or other groups on technical, systems-, or process-related topics.
Developing and Building Teams	Encouraging and building mutual trust, respect, and cooperation among team members.
Guiding, Directing, and Motivating Subordinates	Providing guidance and direction to subordinates, including setting performance standards and monitoring performance.
Inspecting Equipment, Structures, or Material	Inspecting equipment, structures, or materials to identify the cause of errors or other problems or defects.
Coaching and Developing Others	Identifying the developmental needs of others and coaching, mentoring, or otherwise helping others to improve their knowledge or skills.
Estimating the Quantifiable Characteristics of Pro	Estimating sizes, distances, and quantities; or determining time, costs, resources, or materials needed to perform a work activity.
Handling and Moving Objects	Using hands and arms in handling, installing, positioning, and moving materials, and manipulating things.
Monitoring and Controlling Resources	Monitoring and controlling resources and overseeing the spending of money.
Selling or Influencing Others	Convincing others to buy merchandise/goods or to otherwise change their minds or actions.
Controlling Machines and Processes	Using either control mechanisms or direct physical activity to operate machines or processes (not including computers or vehicles).
Staffing Organizational Units	Recruiting, interviewing, selecting, hiring, and promoting employees in an organization.
Repairing and Maintaining Electronic Equipment	Servicing, repairing, calibrating, regulating, fine-tuning, or testing machines, devices, and equipment that operate primarily on the basis of electrical or electronic (not mechanical) principles.
Drafting, Laying Out, and Specifying Technical Dev	Providing documentation, detailed instructions, drawings, or specifications to tell others about how devices, parts, equipment, or structures are to be fabricated, constructed, assembled, modified, maintained, or used.
Repairing and Maintaining Mechanical Equipment	Servicing, repairing, adjusting, and testing machines, devices, moving parts, and equipment that operate primarily on the basis of mechanical (not electronic) principles.

Work_Context	Work_Context Definitions
Telephone	How often do you have telephone conversations in this job?
In an Enclosed Vehicle or Equipment	How often does this job require working in a closed vehicle or equipment (e.g., car)?
Face-to-Face Discussions	How often do you have to have face-to-face discussions with individuals or teams in this job?
Contact With Others	How much does this job require the worker to be in contact with others (face-to-face, by telephone, or otherwise) in order to perform it?
Impact of Decisions on Co-workers or Company Resul	How do the decisions an employee makes impact the results of co-workers, clients or the company?
Freedom to Make Decisions	How much decision making freedom, without supervision, does the job offer?
Indoors, Environmentally Controlled	How often does this job require working indoors in environmentally controlled conditions?
Structured versus Unstructured Work	To what extent is this job structured for the worker, rather than allowing the worker to determine tasks, priorities, and goals?
Deal With External Customers	How important is it to work with external customers or the public in this job?
Importance of Being Exact or Accurate	How important is being very exact or highly accurate in performing this job?
Deal With Unpleasant or Angry People	How frequently does the worker have to deal with unpleasant, angry, or discourteous individuals as part of the job requirements?
Work With Work Group or Team	How important is it to work with others in a group or team in this job?
Letters and Memos	How often does the job require written letters and memos?

Frequency of Decision Making	How frequently is the worker required to make decisions that affect other people, the financial resources, and/or the image and reputation of the organization?
Consequence of Error	How serious would the result usually be if the worker made a mistake that was not readily correctable?
Outdoors, Exposed to Weather	How often does this job require working outdoors, exposed to all weather conditions?
Frequency of Conflict Situations	How often are there conflict situations the employee has to face in this job?
Coordinate or Lead Others	How important is it to coordinate or lead others in accomplishing work activities in this job?
Physical Proximity	To what extent does this job require the worker to perform job tasks in close physical proximity to other people?
Indoors, Not Environmentally Controlled	How often does this job require working indoors in non-controlled environmental conditions (e.g., warehouse without heat)?
Responsible for Others' Health and Safety	How much responsibility is there for the health and safety of others in this job?
Deal With Physically Aggressive People	How frequently does this job require the worker to deal with physical aggression of violent individuals?
Very Hot or Cold Temperatures	How often does this job require working in very hot (above 90 F degrees) or very cold (below 32 F degrees) temperatures?
Spend Time Sitting	How much does this job require sitting?
Time Pressure	How often does this job require the worker to meet strict deadlines?
Electronic Mail	How often do you use electronic mail in this job?
Importance of Repeating Same Tasks	How important is repeating the same physical activities (e.g., key entry) or mental activities (e.g., checking entries in a ledger) over and over, without stopping, to performing this job?
Level of Competition	To what extent does this job require the worker to compete or to be aware of competitive pressures?
Outdoors, Under Cover	How often does this job require working outdoors, under cover (e.g., structure with roof but no walls)?
Extremely Bright or Inadequate Lighting	How often does this job require working in extremely bright or inadequate lighting conditions?
Exposed to Hazardous Equipment	How often does this job require exposure to hazardous equipment?
Sounds, Noise Levels Are Distracting or Uncomforta	How often does this job require working exposed to sounds and noise levels that are distracting or uncomfortable?
Exposed to Contaminants	How often does this job require working exposed to contaminants (such as pollutants, gases, dust or odors)?
Exposed to Disease or Infections	How often does this job require exposure to disease/infections?
Responsibility for Outcomes and Results	How responsible is the worker for work outcomes and results of other workers?
Wear Common Protective or Safety Equipment such as	How much does this job require wearing common protective or safety equipment such as safety shoes, glasses, gloves, hard hats or life jackets?
Spend Time Standing	How much does this job require standing?
Public Speaking	How often do you have to perform public speaking in this job?
Degree of Automation	How automated is the job?
Spend Time Using Your Hands to Handle, Control, or	How much does this job require using your hands to handle, control, or feel objects, tools or controls?
Spend Time Walking and Running	How much does this job require walking and running?
Exposed to Hazardous Conditions	How often does this job require exposure to hazardous conditions?
Spend Time Making Repetitive Motions	How much does this job require making repetitive motions?
Spend Time Bending or Twisting the Body	How much does this job require bending or twisting your body?
Wear Specialized Protective or Safety Equipment su	How much does this job require wearing specialized protective or safety equipment such as breathing apparatus, safety harness, full protection suits, or radiation protection?
Exposed to Minor Burns, Cuts, Bites, or Stings	How often does this job require exposure to minor burns, cuts, bites, or stings?
Cramped Work Space, Awkward Positions	How often does this job require working in cramped work spaces that requires getting into awkward positions?
Spend Time Kneeling, Crouching, Stooping, or Crawl	How much does this job require kneeling, crouching, stooping or crawling?
Exposed to High Places	How often does this job require exposure to high places?
Spend Time Keeping or Regaining Balance	How much does this job require keeping or regaining your balance?
Pace Determined by Speed of Equipment	How important is it to this job that the pace is determined by the speed of equipment or machinery? (This does not refer to keeping busy at all times on this job.)

Spend Time Climbing Ladders, Scaffolds, or Poles	How much does this job require climbing ladders, scaffolds, or poles?
In an Open Vehicle or Equipment	How often does this job require working in an open vehicle or equipment (e.g., tractor)?
Exposed to Radiation	How often does this job require exposure to radiation?
Exposed to Whole Body Vibration	How often does this job require exposure to whole body vibration (e.g., operate a jackhammer)?

Job Zone Component	Job Zone Component Definitions
Title	Job Zone Four: Considerable Preparation Needed
Overall Experience	A minimum of two to four years of work-related skill, knowledge, or experience is needed for these occupations. For example, an accountant must complete four years of college and work for several years in accounting to be considered qualified.
Job Training	Employees in these occupations usually need several years of work-related experience, on-the-job training, and/or vocational training.
Job Zone Examples	Many of these occupations involve coordinating, supervising, managing, or training others. Examples include accountants, chefs and head cooks, computer programmers, historians, pharmacists, and police detectives.
SVP Range	(7.0 to < 8.0)
Education	Most of these occupations require a four - year bachelor's degree, but some do not.

Work_Styles	Work_Styles Definitions
Integrity	Job requires being honest and ethical.
Self Control	Job requires maintaining composure, keeping emotions in check, controlling anger, and avoiding aggressive behavior, even in very difficult situations.
Dependability	Job requires being reliable, responsible, and dependable, and fulfilling obligations.
Attention to Detail	Job requires being careful about detail and thorough in completing work tasks.
Stress Tolerance	Job requires accepting criticism and dealing calmly and effectively with high stress situations.
Initiative	Job requires a willingness to take on responsibilities and challenges.
Adaptability/Flexibility	Job requires being open to change (positive or negative) and to considerable variety in the workplace.
Cooperation	Job requires being pleasant with others on the job and displaying a good-natured, cooperative attitude.
Persistence	Job requires persistence in the face of obstacles.
Analytical Thinking	Job requires analyzing information and using logic to address work-related issues and problems.
Independence	Job requires developing one's own ways of doing things, guiding oneself with little or no supervision, and depending on oneself to get things done.
Concern for Others	Job requires being sensitive to others' needs and feelings and being understanding and helpful on the job.
Leadership	Job requires a willingness to lead, take charge, and offer opinions and direction.
Achievement/Effort	Job requires establishing and maintaining personally challenging achievement goals and exerting effort toward mastering tasks.
Innovation	Job requires creativity and alternative thinking to develop new ideas for and answers to work-related problems.
Social Orientation	Job requires preferring to work with others rather than alone, and being personally connected with others on the job.

33-3021.02 - Police Identification and Records Officers

Collect evidence at crime scene, classify and identify fingerprints, and photograph evidence for use in criminal and civil cases.

Tasks

1) Package, store and retrieve evidence.

2) Dust selected areas of crime scene and lift latent fingerprints, adhering to proper

preservation procedures.

3) Photograph crime or accident scenes for evidence records.

4) Look for trace evidence, such as fingerprints, hairs, fibers, or shoe impressions, using alternative light sources when necessary.

5) Analyze and process evidence at crime scenes and in the laboratory, wearing protective equipment and using powders and chemicals.

6) Submit evidence to supervisors.

7) Serve as technical advisor and coordinate with other law enforcement workers to exchange information on crime scene collection activities.

8) Perform emergency work during off-hours.

9) Identify, classify, and file fingerprints, using systems such as the Henry Classification system.

10) Process film and prints from crime or accident scenes.

Knowledge	Knowledge Definitions
Law and Government	Knowledge of laws, legal codes, court procedures, precedents, government regulations, executive orders, agency rules, and the democratic political process.
Public Safety and Security	Knowledge of relevant equipment, policies, procedures, and strategies to promote effective local, state, or national security operations for the protection of people, data, property, and institutions.
English Language	Knowledge of the structure and content of the English language including the meaning and spelling of words, rules of composition, and grammar.
Customer and Personal Service	Knowledge of principles and processes for providing customer and personal services. This includes customer needs assessment, meeting quality standards for services, and evaluation of customer satisfaction.
Telecommunications	Knowledge of transmission, broadcasting, switching, control, and operation of telecommunications systems.
Clerical	Knowledge of administrative and clerical procedures and systems such as word processing, managing files and records, stenography and transcription, designing forms, and other office procedures and terminology.
Education and Training	Knowledge of principles and methods for curriculum and training design, teaching and instruction for individuals and groups, and the measurement of training effects.
Computers and Electronics	Knowledge of circuit boards, processors, chips, electronic equipment, and computer hardware and software, including applications and programming.
Mathematics	Knowledge of arithmetic, algebra, geometry, calculus, statistics, and their applications.
Psychology	Knowledge of human behavior and performance; individual differences in ability, personality, and interests; learning and motivation; psychological research methods; and the assessment and treatment of behavioral and affective disorders.
Administration and Management	Knowledge of business and management principles involved in strategic planning, resource allocation, human resources modeling, leadership technique, production methods, and coordination of people and resources.
Transportation	Knowledge of principles and methods for moving people or goods by air, rail, sea, or road, including the relative costs and benefits.
Communications and Media	Knowledge of media production, communication, and dissemination techniques and methods. This includes alternative ways to inform and entertain via written, oral, and visual media.
Chemistry	Knowledge of the chemical composition, structure, and properties of substances and of the chemical processes and transformations that they undergo. This includes uses of chemicals and their interactions, danger signs, production techniques, and disposal methods.
Personnel and Human Resources	Knowledge of principles and procedures for personnel recruitment, selection, training, compensation and benefits, labor relations and negotiation, and personnel information systems.
Sociology and Anthropology	Knowledge of group behavior and dynamics, societal trends and influences, human migrations, ethnicity, cultures and their history and origins.
Medicine and Dentistry	Knowledge of the information and techniques needed to diagnose and treat human injuries, diseases, and deformities. This includes symptoms, treatment alternatives, drug properties and interactions, and preventive health-care measures.
Design	Knowledge of design techniques, tools, and principles involved in production of precision technical plans, blueprints, drawings, and models.
Physics	Knowledge and prediction of physical principles, laws, their interrelationships, and applications to understanding fluid, material, and atmospheric dynamics, and mechanical, electrical, atomic and sub- atomic structures and processes.
Geography	Knowledge of principles and methods for describing the features of land, sea, and air masses, including their physical characteristics, locations, interrelationships, and distribution of plant, animal, and human life.
Therapy and Counseling	Knowledge of principles, methods, and procedures for diagnosis, treatment, and rehabilitation of physical and mental dysfunctions, and for career counseling and guidance.
Mechanical	Knowledge of machines and tools, including their designs, uses, repair, and maintenance.
Biology	Knowledge of plant and animal organisms, their tissues, cells, functions, interdependencies, and interactions with each other and the environment.
Foreign Language	Knowledge of the structure and content of a foreign (non-English) language including the meaning and spelling of words, rules of composition and grammar, and pronunciation.
Engineering and Technology	Knowledge of the practical application of engineering science and technology. This includes applying principles, techniques, procedures, and equipment to the design and production of various goods and services.
Philosophy and Theology	Knowledge of different philosophical systems and religions. This includes their basic principles, values, ethics, ways of thinking, customs, practices, and their impact on human culture.
Economics and Accounting	Knowledge of economic and accounting principles and practices, the financial markets, banking and the analysis and reporting of financial data.
History and Archeology	Knowledge of historical events and their causes, indicators, and effects on civilizations and cultures.
Production and Processing	Knowledge of raw materials, production processes, quality control, costs, and other techniques for maximizing the effective manufacture and distribution of goods.
Building and Construction	Knowledge of materials, methods, and the tools involved in the construction or repair of houses, buildings, or other structures such as highways and roads.
Sales and Marketing	Knowledge of principles and methods for showing, promoting, and selling products or services. This includes marketing strategy and tactics, product demonstration, sales techniques, and sales control systems.
Fine Arts	Knowledge of the theory and techniques required to compose, produce, and perform works of music, dance, visual arts, drama, and sculpture.
Food Production	Knowledge of techniques and equipment for planting, growing, and harvesting food products (both plant and animal) for consumption, including storage/handling techniques.

Skills	Skills Definitions
Active Listening	Giving full attention to what other people are saying, taking time to understand the points being made, asking questions as appropriate, and not interrupting at inappropriate times
Speaking	Talking to others to convey information effectively.
Writing	Communicating effectively in writing as appropriate for the needs of the audience.
Judgment and Decision Making	Considering the relative costs and benefits of potential actions to choose the most appropriate one.
Critical Thinking	Using logic and reasoning to identify the strengths and weaknesses of alternative solutions, conclusions or approaches to problems.
Reading Comprehension	Understanding written sentences and paragraphs in work related documents.
Negotiation	Bringing others together and trying to reconcile differences.
Social Perceptiveness	Being aware of others' reactions and understanding why they react as they do.
Time Management	Managing one's own time and the time of others.
Coordination	Adjusting actions in relation to others' actions.
Active Learning	Understanding the implications of new information for both current and future problem-solving and decision-making.
Persuasion	Persuading others to change their minds or behavior.
Complex Problem Solving	Identifying complex problems and reviewing related information to develop and evaluate options and implement solutions.

Service Orientation	Actively looking for ways to help people.
Learning Strategies	Selecting and using training/instructional methods and procedures appropriate for the situation when learning or teaching new things.
Monitoring	Monitoring/Assessing performance of yourself, other individuals, or organizations to make improvements or take corrective action.
Equipment Selection	Determining the kind of tools and equipment needed to do a job.
Instructing	Teaching others how to do something.
Science	Using scientific rules and methods to solve problems.
Technology Design	Generating or adapting equipment and technology to serve user needs.
Management of Personnel Resources	Motivating, developing, and directing people as they work, identifying the best people for the job.
Mathematics	Using mathematics to solve problems.
Operation and Control	Controlling operations of equipment or systems.
Equipment Maintenance	Performing routine maintenance on equipment and determining when and what kind of maintenance is needed.
Operations Analysis	Analyzing needs and product requirements to create a design.
Quality Control Analysis	Conducting tests and inspections of products, services, or processes to evaluate quality or performance.
Troubleshooting	Determining causes of operating errors and deciding what to do about it.
Installation	Installing equipment, machines, wiring, or programs to meet specifications.
Management of Material Resources	Obtaining and seeing to the appropriate use of equipment, facilities, and materials needed to do certain work.
Operation Monitoring	Watching gauges, dials, or other indicators to make sure a machine is working properly.
Management of Financial Resources	Determining how money will be spent to get the work done, and accounting for these expenditures.
Systems Evaluation	Identifying measures or indicators of system performance and the actions needed to improve or correct performance, relative to the goals of the system.
Systems Analysis	Determining how a system should work and how changes in conditions, operations, and the environment will affect outcomes.
Programming	Writing computer programs for various purposes.
Repairing	Repairing machines or systems using the needed tools.

Ability	Ability Definitions
Inductive Reasoning	The ability to combine pieces of information to form general rules or conclusions (includes finding a relationship among seemingly unrelated events).
Oral Expression	The ability to communicate information and ideas in speaking so others will understand.
Flexibility of Closure	The ability to identify or detect a known pattern (a figure, object, word, or sound) that is hidden in other distracting material.
Near Vision	The ability to see details at close range (within a few feet of the observer).
Oral Comprehension	The ability to listen to and understand information and ideas presented through spoken words and sentences.
Deductive Reasoning	The ability to apply general rules to specific problems to produce answers that make sense.
Information Ordering	The ability to arrange things or actions in a certain order or pattern according to a specific rule or set of rules (e.g., patterns of numbers, letters, words, pictures, mathematical operations).
Written Comprehension	The ability to read and understand information and ideas presented in writing.
Problem Sensitivity	The ability to tell when something is wrong or is likely to go wrong. It does not involve solving the problem, only recognizing there is a problem.
Speech Clarity	The ability to speak clearly so others can understand you.
Speech Recognition	The ability to identify and understand the speech of another person.
Far Vision	The ability to see details at a distance.
Arm-Hand Steadiness	The ability to keep your hand and arm steady while moving your arm or while holding your arm and hand in one position.
Category Flexibility	The ability to generate or use different sets of rules for combining or grouping things in different ways.
Speed of Closure	The ability to quickly make sense of, combine, and organize information into meaningful patterns.
Visual Color Discrimination	The ability to match or detect differences between colors, including shades of color and brightness.

Perceptual Speed	The ability to quickly and accurately compare similarities and differences among sets of letters, numbers, objects, pictures, or patterns. The things to be compared may be presented at the same time or one after the other. This ability also includes comparing a presented object with a remembered object.
Selective Attention	The ability to concentrate on a task over a period of time without being distracted.
Written Expression	The ability to communicate information and ideas in writing so others will understand.
Finger Dexterity	The ability to make precisely coordinated movements of the fingers of one or both hands to grasp, manipulate, or assemble very small objects.
Fluency of Ideas	The ability to come up with a number of ideas about a topic (the number of ideas is important, not their quality, correctness, or creativity).
Control Precision	The ability to quickly and repeatedly adjust the controls of a machine or a vehicle to exact positions.
Time Sharing	The ability to shift back and forth between two or more activities or sources of information (such as speech, sounds, touch, or other sources).
Glare Sensitivity	The ability to see objects in the presence of glare or bright lighting.
Originality	The ability to come up with unusual or clever ideas about a given topic or situation, or to develop creative ways to solve a problem.
Depth Perception	The ability to judge which of several objects is closer or farther away from you, or to judge the distance between you and an object.
Manual Dexterity	The ability to quickly move your hand, your hand together with your arm, or your two hands to grasp, manipulate, or assemble objects.
Visualization	The ability to imagine how something will look after it is moved around or when its parts are moved or rearranged.
Multilimb Coordination	The ability to coordinate two or more limbs (for example, two arms, two legs, or one leg and one arm) while sitting, standing, or lying down. It does not involve performing the activities while the whole body is in motion.
Extent Flexibility	The ability to bend, stretch, twist, or reach with your body, arms, and/or legs.
Auditory Attention	The ability to focus on a single source of sound in the presence of other distracting sounds.
Spatial Orientation	The ability to know your location in relation to the environment or to know where other objects are in relation to you.
Memorization	The ability to remember information such as words, numbers, pictures, and procedures.
Night Vision	The ability to see under low light conditions.
Gross Body Coordination	The ability to coordinate the movement of your arms, legs, and torso together when the whole body is in motion.
Reaction Time	The ability to quickly respond (with the hand, finger, or foot) to a signal (sound, light, picture) when it appears.
Trunk Strength	The ability to use your abdominal and lower back muscles to support part of the body repeatedly or continuously over time without 'giving out' or fatiguing.
Static Strength	The ability to exert maximum muscle force to lift, push, pull, or carry objects.
Hearing Sensitivity	The ability to detect or tell the differences between sounds that vary in pitch and loudness.
Stamina	The ability to exert yourself physically over long periods of time without getting winded or out of breath.
Response Orientation	The ability to choose quickly between two or more movements in response to two or more different signals (lights, sounds, pictures). It includes the speed with which the correct response is started with the hand, foot, or other body part.
Number Facility	The ability to add, subtract, multiply, or divide quickly and correctly.
Mathematical Reasoning	The ability to choose the right mathematical methods or formulas to solve a problem.
Speed of Limb Movement	The ability to quickly move the arms and legs.
Gross Body Equilibrium	The ability to keep or regain your body balance or stay upright when in an unstable position.
Peripheral Vision	The ability to see objects or movement of objects to one's side when the eyes are looking ahead.
Rate Control	The ability to time your movements or the movement of a piece of equipment in anticipation of changes in the speed and/or direction of a moving object or scene.
Wrist-Finger Speed	The ability to make fast, simple, repeated movements of the fingers, hands, and wrists.
Sound Localization	The ability to tell the direction from which a sound originated.

Explosive Strength	The ability to use short bursts of muscle force to propel oneself (as in jumping or sprinting), or to throw an object.
Dynamic Strength	The ability to exert muscle force repeatedly or continuously over time. This involves muscular endurance and resistance to muscle fatigue.
Dynamic Flexibility	The ability to quickly and repeatedly bend, stretch, twist, or reach out with your body, arms, and/or legs.

Work_Activity	**Work_Activity Definitions**
Getting Information	Observing, receiving, and otherwise obtaining information from all relevant sources.
Identifying Objects, Actions, and Events	Identifying information by categorizing, estimating, recognizing differences or similarities, and detecting changes in circumstances or events.
Evaluating Information to Determine Compliance wit	Using relevant information and individual judgment to determine whether events or processes comply with laws, regulations, or standards.
Communicating with Supervisors, Peers, or Subordin	Providing information to supervisors, co-workers, and subordinates by telephone, in written form, e-mail, or in person.
Making Decisions and Solving Problems	Analyzing information and evaluating results to choose the best solution and solve problems.
Performing for or Working Directly with the Public	Performing for people or dealing directly with the public. This includes serving customers in restaurants and stores, and receiving clients or guests.
Updating and Using Relevant Knowledge	Keeping up-to-date technically and applying new knowledge to your job.
Monitor Processes, Materials, or Surroundings	Monitoring and reviewing information from materials, events, or the environment, to detect or assess problems.
Documenting/Recording Information	Entering, transcribing, recording, storing, or maintaining information in written or electronic/magnetic form.
Processing Information	Compiling, coding, categorizing, calculating, tabulating, auditing, or verifying information or data.
Analyzing Data or Information	Identifying the underlying principles, reasons, or facts of information by breaking down information or data into separate parts.
Establishing and Maintaining Interpersonal Relatio	Developing constructive and cooperative working relationships with others, and maintaining them over time.
Interpreting the Meaning of Information for Others	Translating or explaining what information means and how it can be used.
Communicating with Persons Outside Organization	Communicating with people outside the organization, representing the organization to customers, the public, government, and other external sources. This information can be exchanged in person, in writing, or by telephone or e-mail.
Organizing, Planning, and Prioritizing Work	Developing specific goals and plans to prioritize, organize, and accomplish your work.
Operating Vehicles, Mechanized Devices, or Equipme	Running, maneuvering, navigating, or driving vehicles or mechanized equipment, such as forklifts, passenger vehicles, aircraft, or water craft.
Judging the Qualities of Things, Services, or Peop	Assessing the value, importance, or quality of things or people.
Performing Administrative Activities	Performing day-to-day administrative tasks such as maintaining information files and processing paperwork.
Resolving Conflicts and Negotiating with Others	Handling complaints, settling disputes, and resolving grievances and conflicts, or otherwise negotiating with others.
Thinking Creatively	Developing, designing, or creating new applications, ideas, relationships, systems, or products, including artistic contributions.
Inspecting Equipment, Structures, or Material	Inspecting equipment, structures, or materials to identify the cause of errors or other problems or defects.
Interacting With Computers	Using computers and computer systems (including hardware and software) to program, write software, set up functions, enter data, or process information.
Handling and Moving Objects	Using hands and arms in handling, installing, positioning, and moving materials, and manipulating things.
Coaching and Developing Others	Identifying the developmental needs of others and coaching, mentoring, or otherwise helping others to improve their knowledge or skills.
Performing General Physical Activities	Performing physical activities that require considerable use of your arms and legs and moving your whole body, such as climbing, lifting, balancing, walking, stooping, and handling of materials.
Coordinating the Work and Activities of Others	Getting members of a group to work together to accomplish tasks.

Developing Objectives and Strategies	Establishing long-range objectives and specifying the strategies and actions to achieve them.
Developing and Building Teams	Encouraging and building mutual trust, respect, and cooperation among team members.
Training and Teaching Others	Identifying the educational needs of others, developing formal educational or training programs or classes, and teaching or instructing others.
Estimating the Quantifiable Characteristics of Pro	Estimating sizes, distances, and quantities; or determining time, costs, resources, or materials needed to perform a work activity.
Assisting and Caring for Others	Providing personal assistance, medical attention, emotional support, or other personal care to others such as coworkers, customers, or patients.
Scheduling Work and Activities	Scheduling events, programs, and activities, as well as the work of others.
Provide Consultation and Advice to Others	Providing guidance and expert advice to management or other groups on technical, systems-, or process-related topics.
Guiding, Directing, and Motivating Subordinates	Providing guidance and direction to subordinates, including setting performance standards and monitoring performance.
Controlling Machines and Processes	Using either control mechanisms or direct physical activity to operate machines or processes (not including computers or vehicles).
Selling or Influencing Others	Convincing others to buy merchandise/goods or to otherwise change their minds or actions.
Monitoring and Controlling Resources	Monitoring and controlling resources and overseeing the spending of money.
Staffing Organizational Units	Recruiting, interviewing, selecting, hiring, and promoting employees in an organization.
Drafting, Laying Out, and Specifying Technical Dev	Providing documentation, detailed instructions, drawings, or specifications to tell others about how devices, parts, equipment, or structures are to be fabricated, constructed, assembled, modified, maintained, or used.
Repairing and Maintaining Electronic Equipment	Servicing, repairing, calibrating, regulating, fine-tuning, or testing machines, devices, and equipment that operate primarily on the basis of electrical or electronic (not mechanical) principles.
Repairing and Maintaining Mechanical Equipment	Servicing, repairing, adjusting, and testing machines, devices, moving parts, and equipment that operate primarily on the basis of mechanical (not electronic) principles.

Work_Context	**Work_Context Definitions**
Telephone	How often do you have telephone conversations in this job?
Face-to-Face Discussions	How often do you have to have face-to-face discussions with individuals or teams in this job?
Importance of Being Exact or Accurate	How important is being very exact or highly accurate in performing this job?
In an Enclosed Vehicle or Equipment	How often does this job require working in a closed vehicle or equipment (e.g., car)?
Freedom to Make Decisions	How much decision making freedom, without supervision, does the job offer?
Contact With Others	How much does this job require the worker to be in contact with others (face-to-face, by telephone, or otherwise) in order to perform it?
Letters and Memos	How often does the job require written letters and memos?
Frequency of Decision Making	How frequently is the worker required to make decisions that affect other people, the financial resources, and/or the image and reputation of the organization?
Outdoors, Exposed to Weather	How often does this job require working outdoors, exposed to all weather conditions?
Impact of Decisions on Co-workers or Company Resul	How do the decisions an employee makes impact the results of co-workers, clients or the company?
Deal With Unpleasant or Angry People	How frequently does the worker have to deal with unpleasant, angry, or discourteous individuals as part of the job requirements?
Indoors, Environmentally Controlled	How often does this job require working indoors in environmentally controlled conditions?
Structured versus Unstructured Work	To what extent is this job structured for the worker, rather than allowing the worker to determine tasks, priorities, and goals?
Work With Work Group or Team	How important is it to work with others in a group or team in this job?
Time Pressure	How often does this job require the worker to meet strict deadlines?
Deal With External Customers	How important is it to work with external customers or the public in this job?
Physical Proximity	To what extent does this job require the worker to perform job tasks in close physical proximity to other people?

Consequence of Error	How serious would the result usually be if the worker made a mistake that was not readily correctable?
Sounds, Noise Levels Are Distracting or Uncomforta	How often does this job require working exposed to sounds and noise levels that are distracting or uncomfortable?
Very Hot or Cold Temperatures	How often does this job require working in very hot (above 90 F degrees) or very cold (below 32 F degrees) temperatures?
Exposed to Contaminants	How often does this job require working exposed to contaminants (such as pollutants, gases, dust or odors)?
Spend Time Using Your Hands to Handle, Control, or	How much does this job require using your hands to handle, control, or feel objects, tools or controls?
Extremely Bright or Inadequate Lighting	How often does this job require working in extremely bright or inadequate lighting conditions?
Coordinate or Lead Others	How important is it to coordinate or lead others in accomplishing work activities in this job?
Responsibility for Outcomes and Results	How responsible is the worker for work outcomes and results of other workers?
Frequency of Conflict Situations	How often are there conflict situations the employee has to face in this job?
Electronic Mail	How often do you use electronic mail in this job?
Spend Time Sitting	How much does this job require sitting?
Wear Common Protective or Safety Equipment such as	How much does this job require wearing common protective or safety equipment such as safety shoes, glasses, gloves, hard hats or life jackets?
Importance of Repeating Same Tasks	How important is repeating the same physical activities (e.g., key entry) or mental activities (e.g., checking entries in a ledger) over and over, without stopping, to performing this job?
Deal With Physically Aggressive People	How frequently does this job require the worker to deal with physical aggression of violent individuals?
Indoors, Not Environmentally Controlled	How often does this job require working indoors in non-controlled environmental conditions (e.g., warehouse without heat)?
Responsible for Others' Health and Safety	How much responsibility is there for the health and safety of others in this job?
Cramped Work Space, Awkward Positions	How often does this job require working in cramped work spaces that requires getting into awkward positions?
Exposed to Disease or Infections	How often does this job require exposure to disease/infections?
Spend Time Making Repetitive Motions	How much does this job require making repetitive motions?
Exposed to Minor Burns, Cuts, Bites, or Stings	How often does this job require exposure to minor burns, cuts, bites, or stings?
Spend Time Standing	How much does this job require standing?
Outdoors, Under Cover	How often does this job require working outdoors, under cover (e.g., structure with roof but no walls)?
Spend Time Bending or Twisting the Body	How much does this job require bending or twisting your body?
Exposed to Hazardous Conditions	How often does this job require exposure to hazardous conditions?
Spend Time Walking and Running	How much does this job require walking and running?
Public Speaking	How often do you have to perform public speaking in this job?
Degree of Automation	How automated is the job?
Exposed to Hazardous Equipment	How often does this job require exposure to hazardous equipment?
Level of Competition	To what extent does this job require the worker to compete or to be aware of competitive pressures?
Spend Time Kneeling, Crouching, Stooping, or Crawl	How much does this job require kneeling, crouching, stooping, or crawling?
Wear Specialized Protective or Safety Equipment su	How much does this job require wearing specialized protective or safety equipment such as breathing apparatus, safety harness, full protection suits, or radiation protection?
Pace Determined by Speed of Equipment	How important is it to this job that the pace is determined by the speed of equipment or machinery? (This does not refer to keeping busy at all times on this job.)
Exposed to High Places	How often does this job require exposure to high places?
Spend Time Keeping or Regaining Balance	How much does this job require keeping or regaining your balance?
Spend Time Climbing Ladders, Scaffolds, or Poles	How much does this job require climbing ladders, scaffolds, or poles?
Exposed to Radiation	How often does this job require exposure to radiation?
Exposed to Whole Body Vibration	How often does this job require exposure to whole body vibration (e.g., operate a jackhammer)?
In an Open Vehicle or Equipment	How often does this job require working in an open vehicle or equipment (e.g., tractor)?

Job Zone Component	Job Zone Component Definitions
Title	Job Zone Three: Medium Preparation Needed
Overall Experience	Previous work-related skill, knowledge, or experience is required for these occupations. For example, an electrician must have completed three or four years of apprenticeship or several years of vocational training, and often must have passed a licensing exam, in order to perform the job.
Job Training	Employees in these occupations usually need one or two years of training involving both on-the-job experience and informal training with experienced workers.
Job Zone Examples	These occupations usually involve using communication and organizational skills to coordinate, supervise, manage, or train others to accomplish goals. Examples include dental assistants, electricians, fish and game wardens, legal secretaries, personnel recruiters, and recreation workers.
SVP Range	(6.0 to < 7.0)
Education	Most occupations in this zone require training in vocational schools, related on-the-job experience, or an associate's degree. Some may require a bachelor's degree.

Work_Styles	Work_Styles Definitions
Integrity	Job requires being honest and ethical.
Dependability	Job requires being reliable, responsible, and dependable, and fulfilling obligations.
Attention to Detail	Job requires being careful about detail and thorough in completing work tasks.
Stress Tolerance	Job requires accepting criticism and dealing calmly and effectively with high stress situations.
Adaptability/Flexibility	Job requires being open to change (positive or negative) and to considerable variety in the workplace.
Cooperation	Job requires being pleasant with others on the job and displaying a good-natured, cooperative attitude.
Self Control	Job requires maintaining composure, keeping emotions in check, controlling anger, and avoiding aggressive behavior, even in very difficult situations.
Independence	Job requires developing one's own ways of doing things, guiding oneself with little or no supervision, and depending on oneself to get things done.
Initiative	Job requires a willingness to take on responsibilities and challenges.
Concern for Others	Job requires being sensitive to others' needs and feelings and being understanding and helpful on the job.
Persistence	Job requires persistence in the face of obstacles.
Leadership	Job requires a willingness to lead, take charge, and offer opinions and direction.
Achievement/Effort	Job requires establishing and maintaining personally challenging achievement goals and exerting effort toward mastering tasks.
Analytical Thinking	Job requires analyzing information and using logic to address work-related issues and problems.
Innovation	Job requires creativity and alternative thinking to develop new ideas for and answers to work-related problems.
Social Orientation	Job requires preferring to work with others rather than alone, and being personally connected with others on the job.

33-3021.03 - Criminal Investigators and Special Agents

Investigate alleged or suspected criminal violations of Federal, state, or local laws to determine if evidence is sufficient to recommend prosecution.

Tasks

1) Obtain and use search and arrest warrants.

2) Obtain and verify evidence by interviewing and observing suspects and witnesses, or by analyzing records.

3) Perform undercover assignments and maintain surveillance, including monitoring authorized wiretaps.

4) Prepare reports that detail investigation findings.

5) Analyze evidence in laboratories, or in the field.

6) Collaborate with other authorities on activities such as surveillance, transcription and

research.

7) Collaborate with other offices and agencies in order to exchange information and coordinate activities.

8) Examine records in order to locate links in chains of evidence or information.

9) Develop relationships with informants in order to obtain information related to cases.

10) Provide protection for individuals such as government leaders, political candidates and visiting foreign dignitaries.

11) Identify case issues and evidence needed, based on analysis of charges, complaints, or allegations of law violations.

12) Testify before grand juries concerning criminal activity investigations.

13) Investigate organized crime, public corruption, financial crime, copyright infringement, civil rights violations, bank robbery, extortion, kidnapping, and other violations of federal or state statutes.

14) Manage security programs designed to protect personnel, facilities, and information.

15) Record evidence and documents, using equipment such as cameras and photocopy machines.

16) Determine scope, timing, and direction of investigations.

17) Administer counter-terrorism and counter-narcotics reward programs.

18) Issue security clearances.

19) Train foreign civilian police.

20) Compare crime scene fingerprints with those from suspects or fingerprint files to identify perpetrators, using computers.

21) Serve subpoenas or other official papers.

22) Search for and collect evidence such as fingerprints, using investigative equipment.

33-3021.05 - Immigration and Customs Inspectors

Investigate and inspect persons, common carriers, goods, and merchandise, arriving in or departing from the United States or between states to detect violations of immigration and customs laws and regulations.

Tasks

1) Institute civil and criminal prosecutions, and cooperate with other law enforcement agencies in the investigation and prosecution of those in violation of immigration or customs laws.

2) Locate and seize contraband, undeclared merchandise, and vehicles, aircraft, or boats that contain such merchandise.

3) Testify regarding decisions at immigration appeals or in federal court.

4) Record and report job-related activities, findings, transactions, violations, discrepancies, and decisions.

5) Inspect cargo, baggage, and personal articles entering or leaving U.S. for compliance with revenue laws and U.S. Customs Service regulations.

6) Examine immigration applications, visas, and passports, and interview persons in order to determine eligibility for admission, residence, and travel in U.S.

7) Detain persons found to be in violation of customs or immigration laws, and arrange for legal action such as deportation.

8) Investigate applications for duty refunds, and petition for remission or mitigation of penalties when warranted.

9) Collect samples of merchandise for examination, appraisal, or testing.

10) Determine duty and taxes to be paid on goods.

33-3041.00 - Parking Enforcement Workers

Patrol assigned area, such as public parking lot or section of city to issue tickets to overtime parking violators and illegally parked vehicles.

Tasks

1) Observe and report hazardous conditions such as missing traffic signals or signs, and street markings that need to be repainted.

2) Locate lost, stolen, and counterfeit parking permits, and take necessary enforcement action.

3) Maintain assigned equipment and supplies such as handheld citation computers, citation books, rain gear, tire-marking chalk, and street cones.

4) Maintain close communications with dispatching personnel, using two-way radios or cell phones.

5) Investigate and answer complaints regarding contested parking citations, determining their validity and routing them appropriately.

6) Provide information to the public regarding parking regulations and facilities, and the location of streets, buildings and points of interest.

7) Write warnings and citations for illegally parked vehicles.

8) Respond to and make radio dispatch calls regarding parking violations and complaints.

9) Perform simple vehicle maintenance procedures such as checking oil and gas, and report mechanical problems to supervisors.

10) Remove handbills within patrol areas.

11) Collect coins deposited in meters.

12) Identify vehicles in violation of parking codes, checking with dispatchers when necessary to confirm identities or to determine whether vehicles need to be booted or towed.

13) Appear in court at hearings regarding contested traffic citations.

14) Prepare and maintain required records, including logs of parking enforcement activities, and records of contested citations.

15) Perform traffic control duties such as setting up barricades and temporary signs, placing bags on parking meters to limit their use, or directing traffic.

16) Patrol an assigned area by vehicle or on foot to ensure public compliance with existing parking ordinance.

17) Mark tires of parked vehicles with chalk and record time of marking, and return at regular intervals to ensure that parking time limits are not exceeded.

18) Make arrangements for illegally parked or abandoned vehicles to be towed, and direct tow-truck drivers to the correct vehicles.

19) Assign and review the work of subordinates.

20) Train new or temporary staff.

21) Provide assistance to motorists needing help with problems, such as flat tires, keys locked in cars, or dead batteries.

22) Deliver money to be used as change at attended parking facilities.

23) Wind parking meter clocks.

33-3051.01 - Police Patrol Officers

Patrol assigned area to enforce laws and ordinances, regulate traffic, control crowds, prevent crime, and arrest violators.

Tasks

1) Monitor, note, report, and investigate suspicious persons and situations, safety hazards, and unusual or illegal activity in patrol area.

2) Issue citations or warnings to violators of motor vehicle ordinances.

3) Testify in court to present evidence or act as witness in traffic and criminal cases.

4) Review facts of incidents to determine if criminal act or statute violations were involved.

5) Monitor traffic to ensure motorists observe traffic regulations and exhibit safe driving procedures.

6) Direct traffic flow and reroute traffic in case of emergencies.

7) Photograph or draw diagrams of crime or accident scenes and interview principals and eyewitnesses.

8) Investigate traffic accidents and other accidents to determine causes and to determine if a crime has been committed.

9) Provide road information to assist motorists.

10) Render aid to accident victims and other persons requiring first aid for physical injuries.

11) Patrol specific area on foot, horseback, or motorized conveyance, responding promptly to calls for assistance.

12) Inform citizens of community services and recommend options to facilitate longer-term problem resolution.

13) Relay complaint and emergency-request information to appropriate agency dispatchers.

14) Evaluate complaint and emergency-request information to determine response requirements.

15) Act as official escorts, such as when leading funeral processions or firefighters.

16) Inspect public establishments to ensure compliance with rules and regulations.

17) Process prisoners, and prepare and maintain records of prisoner bookings and prisoner status during booking and pre-trial process.

18) Provide for public safety by maintaining order, responding to emergencies, protecting people and property, enforcing motor vehicle and criminal laws, and promoting good community relations.

19) Identify, pursue, and arrest suspects and perpetrators of criminal acts.

Knowledge	Knowledge Definitions
Law and Government	Knowledge of laws, legal codes, court procedures, precedents, government regulations, executive orders, agency rules, and the democratic political process.
Public Safety and Security	Knowledge of relevant equipment, policies, procedures, and strategies to promote effective local, state, or national security operations for the protection of people, data, property, and institutions.
English Language	Knowledge of the structure and content of the English language including the meaning and spelling of words, rules of composition, and grammar.
Customer and Personal Service	Knowledge of principles and processes for providing customer and personal services. This includes customer needs assessment, meeting quality standards for services, and evaluation of customer satisfaction.
Psychology	Knowledge of human behavior and performance; individual differences in ability, personality, and interests; learning and motivation; psychological research methods; and the assessment and treatment of behavioral and affective disorders.
Education and Training	Knowledge of principles and methods for curriculum and training design, teaching and instruction for individuals and groups, and the measurement of training effects.
Administration and Management	Knowledge of business and management principles involved in strategic planning, resource allocation, human resources modeling, leadership technique, production methods, and coordination of people and resources.
Telecommunications	Knowledge of transmission, broadcasting, switching, control, and operation of telecommunications systems.
Transportation	Knowledge of principles and methods for moving people or goods by air, rail, sea, or road, including the relative costs and benefits.
Clerical	Knowledge of administrative and clerical procedures and systems such as word processing, managing files and records, stenography and transcription, designing forms, and other office procedures and terminology.
Sociology and Anthropology	Knowledge of group behavior and dynamics, societal trends and influences, human migrations, ethnicity, cultures and their history and origins.
Computers and Electronics	Knowledge of circuit boards, processors, chips, electronic equipment, and computer hardware and software, including applications and programming.
Mathematics	Knowledge of arithmetic, algebra, geometry, calculus, statistics, and their applications.
Geography	Knowledge of principles and methods for describing the features of land, sea, and air masses, including their physical characteristics, locations, interrelationships, and distribution of plant, animal, and human life.
Therapy and Counseling	Knowledge of principles, methods, and procedures for diagnosis, treatment, and rehabilitation of physical and mental dysfunctions, and for career counseling and guidance.
Communications and Media	Knowledge of media production, communication, and dissemination techniques and methods. This includes alternative ways to inform and entertain via written, oral, and visual media.
Personnel and Human Resources	Knowledge of principles and procedures for personnel recruitment, selection, training, compensation and benefits, labor relations and negotiation, and personnel information systems.
Philosophy and Theology	Knowledge of different philosophical systems and religions. This includes their basic principles, values, ethics, ways of thinking, customs, practices, and their impact on human culture.
Foreign Language	Knowledge of the structure and content of a foreign (non-English) language including the meaning and spelling of words, rules of composition and grammar, and pronunciation.
Medicine and Dentistry	Knowledge of the information and techniques needed to diagnose and treat human injuries, diseases, and deformities. This includes symptoms, treatment alternatives, drug properties and interactions, and preventive health-care measures.
Chemistry	Knowledge of the chemical composition, structure, and properties of substances and of the chemical processes and transformations that they undergo. This includes uses of chemicals and their interactions, danger signs, production techniques, and disposal methods.
Physics	Knowledge and prediction of physical principles, laws, their interrelationships, and applications to understanding fluid, material, and atmospheric dynamics, and mechanical, electrical, atomic and sub-atomic structures and processes.
History and Archeology	Knowledge of historical events and their causes, indicators, and effects on civilizations and cultures.
Economics and Accounting	Knowledge of economic and accounting principles and practices, the financial markets, banking and the analysis and reporting of financial data.
Mechanical	Knowledge of machines and tools, including their designs, uses, repair, and maintenance.
Biology	Knowledge of plant and animal organisms, their tissues, cells, functions, interdependencies, and interactions with each other and the environment.
Design	Knowledge of design techniques, tools, and principles involved in production of precision technical plans, blueprints, drawings, and models.
Building and Construction	Knowledge of materials, methods, and the tools involved in the construction or repair of houses, buildings, or other structures such as highways and roads.
Engineering and Technology	Knowledge of the practical application of engineering science and technology. This includes applying principles, techniques, procedures, and equipment to the design and production of various goods and services.
Production and Processing	Knowledge of raw materials, production processes, quality control, costs, and other techniques for maximizing the effective manufacture and distribution of goods.
Sales and Marketing	Knowledge of principles and methods for showing, promoting, and selling products or services. This includes marketing strategy and tactics, product demonstration, sales techniques, and sales control systems.
Fine Arts	Knowledge of the theory and techniques required to compose, produce, and perform works of music, dance, visual arts, drama, and sculpture.
Food Production	Knowledge of techniques and equipment for planting, growing, and harvesting food products (both plant and animal) for consumption, including storage/handling techniques.

Skills	Skills Definitions
Judgment and Decision Making	Considering the relative costs and benefits of potential actions to choose the most appropriate one.
Active Listening	Giving full attention to what other people are saying, taking time to understand the points being made, asking questions as appropriate, and not interrupting at inappropriate times.
Critical Thinking	Using logic and reasoning to identify the strengths and weaknesses of alternative solutions, conclusions or approaches to problems.
Writing	Communicating effectively in writing as appropriate for the needs of the audience.
Speaking	Talking to others to convey information effectively.
Reading Comprehension	Understanding written sentences and paragraphs in work related documents.
Social Perceptiveness	Being aware of others' reactions and understanding why they react as they do.
Negotiation	Bringing others together and trying to reconcile differences.
Persuasion	Persuading others to change their minds or behavior.

Active Learning	Understanding the implications of new information for both current and future problem-solving and decision-making.
Coordination	Adjusting actions in relation to others' actions.
Complex Problem Solving	Identifying complex problems and reviewing related information to develop and evaluate options and implement solutions.
Service Orientation	Actively looking for ways to help people.
Time Management	Managing one's own time and the time of others.
Learning Strategies	Selecting and using training/instructional methods and procedures appropriate for the situation when learning or teaching new things.
Instructing	Teaching others how to do something.
Monitoring	Monitoring/Assessing performance of yourself, other individuals, or organizations to make improvements or take corrective action.
Equipment Selection	Determining the kind of tools and equipment needed to do a job.
Equipment Maintenance	Performing routine maintenance on equipment and determining when and what kind of maintenance is needed.
Management of Personnel Resources	Motivating, developing, and directing people as they work, identifying the best people for the job.
Troubleshooting	Determining causes of operating errors and deciding what to do about it.
Operations Analysis	Analyzing needs and product requirements to create a design.
Operation and Control	Controlling operations of equipment or systems.
Mathematics	Using mathematics to solve problems.
Operation Monitoring	Watching gauges, dials, or other indicators to make sure a machine is working properly.
Technology Design	Generating or adapting equipment and technology to serve user needs.
Quality Control Analysis	Conducting tests and inspections of products, services, or processes to evaluate quality or performance.
Science	Using scientific rules and methods to solve problems.
Systems Evaluation	Identifying measures or indicators of system performance and the actions needed to improve or correct performance, relative to the goals of the system.
Management of Material Resources	Obtaining and seeing to the appropriate use of equipment, facilities, and materials needed to do certain work.
Systems Analysis	Determining how a system should work and how changes in conditions, operations, and the environment will affect outcomes.
Repairing	Repairing machines or systems using the needed tools.
Installation	Installing equipment, machines, wiring, or programs to meet specifications.
Management of Financial Resources	Determining how money will be spent to get the work done, and accounting for these expenditures.
Programming	Writing computer programs for various purposes.

Ability	Ability Definitions
Inductive Reasoning	The ability to combine pieces of information to form general rules or conclusions (includes finding a relationship among seemingly unrelated events).
Oral Comprehension	The ability to listen to and understand information and ideas presented through spoken words and sentences.
Oral Expression	The ability to communicate information and ideas in speaking so others will understand.
Near Vision	The ability to see details at close range (within a few feet of the observer).
Speech Recognition	The ability to identify and understand the speech of another person.
Far Vision	The ability to see details at a distance.
Problem Sensitivity	The ability to tell when something is wrong or is likely to go wrong. It does not involve solving the problem, only recognizing there is a problem.
Deductive Reasoning	The ability to apply general rules to specific problems to produce answers that make sense.
Speech Clarity	The ability to speak clearly so others can understand you.
Reaction Time	The ability to quickly respond (with the hand, finger, or foot) to a signal (sound, light, picture) when it appears.
Flexibility of Closure	The ability to identify or detect a known pattern (a figure, object, word, or sound) that is hidden in other distracting material.
Response Orientation	The ability to choose quickly between two or more movements in response to two or more different signals (lights, sounds, pictures). It includes the speed with which the correct response is started with the hand, foot, or other body part.

Speed of Closure	The ability to quickly make sense of, combine, and organize information into meaningful patterns.
Time Sharing	The ability to shift back and forth between two or more activities or sources of information (such as speech, sounds, touch, or other sources).
Selective Attention	The ability to concentrate on a task over a period of time without being distracted.
Multilimb Coordination	The ability to coordinate two or more limbs (for example, two arms, two legs, or one leg and one arm) while sitting, standing, or lying down. It does not involve performing the activities while the whole body is in motion.
Control Precision	The ability to quickly and repeatedly adjust the controls of a machine or a vehicle to exact positions.
Written Comprehension	The ability to read and understand information and ideas presented in writing.
Rate Control	The ability to time your movements or the movement of a piece of equipment in anticipation of changes in the speed and/or direction of a moving object or scene.
Information Ordering	The ability to arrange things or actions in a certain order or pattern according to a specific rule or set of rules (e.g., patterns of numbers, letters, words, pictures, mathematical operations).
Written Expression	The ability to communicate information and ideas in writing so others will understand.
Perceptual Speed	The ability to quickly and accurately compare similarities and differences among sets of letters, numbers, objects, pictures, or patterns. The things to be compared may be presented at the same time or one after the other. This ability also includes comparing a presented object with a remembered object.
Spatial Orientation	The ability to know your location in relation to the environment or to know where other objects are in relation to you.
Speed of Limb Movement	The ability to quickly move the arms and legs.
Category Flexibility	The ability to generate or use different sets of rules for combining or grouping things in different ways.
Depth Perception	The ability to judge which of several objects is closer or farther away from you, or to judge the distance between you and an object.
Static Strength	The ability to exert maximum muscle force to lift, push, pull, or carry objects.
Night Vision	The ability to see under low light conditions.
Stamina	The ability to exert yourself physically over long periods of time without getting winded or out of breath.
Peripheral Vision	The ability to see objects or movement of objects to one's side when the eyes are looking ahead.
Gross Body Equilibrium	The ability to keep or regain your body balance or stay upright when in an unstable position.
Arm-Hand Steadiness	The ability to keep your hand and arm steady while moving your arm or while holding your arm and hand in one position.
Gross Body Coordination	The ability to coordinate the movement of your arms, legs, and torso together when the whole body is in motion.
Explosive Strength	The ability to use short bursts of muscle force to propel oneself (as in jumping or sprinting), or to throw an object.
Visualization	The ability to imagine how something will look after it is moved around or when its parts are moved or rearranged.
Finger Dexterity	The ability to make precisely coordinated movements of the fingers of one or both hands to grasp, manipulate, or assemble very small objects.
Glare Sensitivity	The ability to see objects in the presence of glare or bright lighting.
Manual Dexterity	The ability to quickly move your hand, your hand together with your arm, or your two hands to grasp, manipulate, or assemble objects.
Memorization	The ability to remember information such as words, numbers, pictures, and procedures.
Auditory Attention	The ability to focus on a single source of sound in the presence of other distracting sounds.
Originality	The ability to come up with unusual or clever ideas about a given topic or situation, or to develop creative ways to solve a problem.
Fluency of Ideas	The ability to come up with a number of ideas about a topic (the number of ideas is important, not their quality, correctness, or creativity).
Visual Color Discrimination	The ability to match or detect differences between colors, including shades of color and brightness.
Sound Localization	The ability to tell the direction from which a sound originated.
Extent Flexibility	The ability to bend, stretch, twist, or reach with your body, arms, and/or legs.
Hearing Sensitivity	The ability to detect or tell the differences between sounds that vary in pitch and loudness.

Dynamic Strength	The ability to exert muscle force repeatedly or continuously over time. This involves muscular endurance and resistance to muscle fatigue.
Trunk Strength	The ability to use your abdominal and lower back muscles to support part of the body repeatedly or continuously over time without 'giving out' or fatiguing.
Mathematical Reasoning	The ability to choose the right mathematical methods or formulas to solve a problem.
Number Facility	The ability to add, subtract, multiply, or divide quickly and correctly.
Wrist-Finger Speed	The ability to make fast, simple, repeated movements of the fingers, hands, and wrists.
Dynamic Flexibility	The ability to quickly and repeatedly bend, stretch, twist, or reach out with your body, arms, and/or legs.

Work_Activity	Work_Activity Definitions
Getting Information	Observing, receiving, and otherwise obtaining information from all relevant sources.
Performing for or Working Directly with the Public	Performing for people or dealing directly with the public. This includes serving customers in restaurants and stores, and receiving clients or guests.
Operating Vehicles, Mechanized Devices, or Equipme	Running, maneuvering, navigating, or driving vehicles or mechanized equipment, such as forklifts, passenger vehicles, aircraft, or water craft.
Resolving Conflicts and Negotiating with Others	Handling complaints, settling disputes, and resolving grievances and conflicts, or otherwise negotiating with others.
Identifying Objects, Actions, and Events	Identifying information by categorizing, estimating, recognizing differences or similarities, and detecting changes in circumstances or events.
Making Decisions and Solving Problems	Analyzing information and evaluating results to choose the best solution and solve problems.
Communicating with Supervisors, Peers, or Subordin	Providing information to supervisors, co-workers, and subordinates by telephone, in written form, e-mail, or in person.
Communicating with Persons Outside Organization	Communicating with people outside the organization, representing the organization to customers, the public, government, and other external sources. This information can be exchanged in person, in writing, or by telephone or e-mail.
Evaluating Information to Determine Compliance wit	Using relevant information and individual judgment to determine whether events or processes comply with laws, regulations, or standards.
Documenting/Recording Information	Entering, transcribing, recording, storing, or maintaining information in written or electronic/magnetic form.
Monitor Processes, Materials, or Surroundings	Monitoring and reviewing information from materials, events, or the environment, to detect or assess problems.
Performing General Physical Activities	Performing physical activities that require considerable use of your arms and legs and moving your whole body, such as climbing, lifting, balancing, walking, stooping, and handling of materials.
Establishing and Maintaining Interpersonal Relatio	Developing constructive and cooperative working relationships with others, and maintaining them over time.
Assisting and Caring for Others	Providing personal assistance, medical attention, emotional support, or other personal care to others such as coworkers, customers, or patients.
Updating and Using Relevant Knowledge	Keeping up-to-date technically and applying new knowledge to your job.
Analyzing Data or Information	Identifying the underlying principles, reasons, or facts of information by breaking down information or data into separate parts.
Training and Teaching Others	Identifying the educational needs of others, developing formal educational or training programs or classes, and teaching or instructing others.
Processing Information	Compiling, coding, categorizing, calculating, tabulating, auditing, or verifying information or data.
Inspecting Equipment, Structures, or Material	Inspecting equipment, structures, or materials to identify the cause of errors or other problems or defects.
Interacting With Computers	Using computers and computer systems (including hardware and software) to program, write software, set up functions, enter data, or process information.
Judging the Qualities of Things, Services, or Peop	Assessing the value, importance, or quality of things or people.
Interpreting the Meaning of Information for Others	Translating or explaining what information means and how it can be used.
Organizing, Planning, and Prioritizing Work	Developing specific goals and plans to prioritize, organize, and accomplish your work.

Performing Administrative Activities	Performing day-to-day administrative tasks such as maintaining information files and processing paperwork.
Thinking Creatively	Developing, designing, or creating new applications, ideas, relationships, systems, or products, including artistic contributions.
Developing and Building Teams	Encouraging and building mutual trust, respect, and cooperation among team members.
Coaching and Developing Others	Identifying the developmental needs of others and coaching, mentoring, or otherwise helping others to improve their knowledge or skills.
Handling and Moving Objects	Using hands and arms in handling, installing, positioning, and moving materials, and manipulating things.
Scheduling Work and Activities	Scheduling events, programs, and activities, as well as the work of others.
Guiding, Directing, and Motivating Subordinates	Providing guidance and direction to subordinates, including setting performance standards and monitoring performance.
Estimating the Quantifiable Characteristics of Pro	Estimating sizes, distances, and quantities; or determining time, costs, resources, or materials needed to perform a work activity.
Coordinating the Work and Activities of Others	Getting members of a group to work together to accomplish tasks.
Selling or Influencing Others	Convincing others to buy merchandise/goods or to otherwise change their minds or actions.
Developing Objectives and Strategies	Establishing long-range objectives and specifying the strategies and actions to achieve them.
Provide Consultation and Advice to Others	Providing guidance and expert advice to management or other groups on technical, systems-, or process-related topics.
Controlling Machines and Processes	Using either control mechanisms or direct physical activity to operate machines or processes (not including computers or vehicles).
Monitoring and Controlling Resources	Monitoring and controlling resources and overseeing the spending of money.
Staffing Organizational Units	Recruiting, interviewing, selecting, hiring, and promoting employees in an organization.
Repairing and Maintaining Electronic Equipment	Servicing, repairing, calibrating, regulating, fine-tuning, or testing machines, devices, and equipment that operate primarily on the basis of electrical or electronic (not mechanical) principles.
Drafting, Laying Out, and Specifying Technical Dev	Providing documentation, detailed instructions, drawings, or specifications to tell others about how devices, parts, equipment, or structures are to be fabricated, constructed, assembled, modified, maintained, or used.
Repairing and Maintaining Mechanical Equipment	Servicing, repairing, adjusting, and testing machines, devices, moving parts, and equipment that operate primarily on the basis of mechanical (not electronic) principles.

Work_Context	Work_Context Definitions
In an Enclosed Vehicle or Equipment	How often does this job require working in a closed vehicle or equipment (e.g., car)?
Face-to-Face Discussions	How often do you have to have face-to-face discussions with individuals or teams in this job?
Deal With External Customers	How important is it to work with external customers or the public in this job?
Contact With Others	How much does this job require the worker to be in contact with others (face-to-face, by telephone, or otherwise) in order to perform it?
Freedom to Make Decisions	How much decision making freedom, without supervision, does the job offer?
Frequency of Decision Making	How frequently is the worker required to make decisions that affect other people, the financial resources, and/or the image and reputation of the organization?
Frequency of Conflict Situations	How often are there conflict situations the employee has to face in this job?
Deal With Unpleasant or Angry People	How frequently does the worker have to deal with unpleasant, angry, or discourteous individuals as part of the job requirements?
Work With Work Group or Team	How important is it to work with others in a group or team in this job?
Outdoors, Exposed to Weather	How often does this job require working outdoors, exposed to all weather conditions?
Impact of Decisions on Co-workers or Company Resul	How do the decisions an employee makes impact the results of co-workers, clients or the company?
Importance of Being Exact or Accurate	How important is being very exact or highly accurate in performing this job?
Structured versus Unstructured Work	To what extent is this job structured for the worker, rather than allowing the worker to determine tasks, priorities, and goals?

714

Telephone	How often do you have telephone conversations in this job?
Exposed to Contaminants	How often does this job require working exposed to contaminants (such as pollutants, gases, dust or odors)?
Letters and Memos	How often does the job require written letters and memos?
Exposed to Hazardous Equipment	How often does this job require exposure to hazardous equipment?
Consequence of Error	How serious would the result usually be if the worker made a mistake that was not readily correctable?
Physical Proximity	To what extent does this job require the worker to perform job tasks in close physical proximity to other people?
Wear Common Protective or Safety Equipment such as	How much does this job require wearing common protective or safety equipment such as safety shoes, glasses, gloves, hard hats or life jackets?
Responsible for Others' Health and Safety	How much responsibility is there for the health and safety of others in this job?
Sounds, Noise Levels Are Distracting or Uncomforta	How often does this job require working exposed to sounds and noise levels that are distracting or uncomfortable?
Deal With Physically Aggressive People	How frequently does this job require the worker to deal with physical aggression of violent individuals?
Coordinate or Lead Others	How important is it to coordinate or lead others in accomplishing work activities in this job?
Spend Time Using Your Hands to Handle, Control, or	How much does this job require using your hands to handle, control, or feel objects, tools or controls?
Time Pressure	How often does this job require the worker to meet strict deadlines?
Very Hot or Cold Temperatures	How often does this job require working in very hot (above 90 F degrees) or very cold (below 32 F degrees) temperatures?
Importance of Repeating Same Tasks	How important is repeating the same physical activities (e.g., key entry) or mental activities (e.g., checking entries in a ledger) over and over, without stopping, to performing this job?
Exposed to Disease or Infections	How often does this job require exposure to disease/infections?
Electronic Mail	How often do you use electronic mail in this job?
Extremely Bright or Inadequate Lighting	How often does this job require working in extremely bright or inadequate lighting conditions?
Wear Specialized Protective or Safety Equipment su	How much does this job require wearing specialized protective or safety equipment such as breathing apparatus, safety harness, full protection suits, or radiation protection?
Spend Time Sitting	How much does this job require sitting?
Level of Competition	To what extent does this job require the worker to compete or to be aware of competitive pressures?
Exposed to Hazardous Conditions	How often does this job require exposure to hazardous conditions?
Responsibility for Outcomes and Results	How responsible is the worker for work outcomes and results of other workers?
Spend Time Making Repetitive Motions	How much does this job require making repetitive motions?
Spend Time Standing	How much does this job require standing?
Exposed to Minor Burns, Cuts, Bites, or Stings	How often does this job require exposure to minor burns, cuts, bites, or stings?
Indoors, Not Environmentally Controlled	How often does this job require working indoors in non-controlled environmental conditions (e.g., warehouse without heat)?
Indoors, Environmentally Controlled	How often does this job require working indoors in environmentally controlled conditions?
Public Speaking	How often do you have to perform public speaking in this job?
Degree of Automation	How automated is the job?
Spend Time Walking and Running	How much does this job require walking and running?
Spend Time Bending or Twisting the Body	How much does this job require bending or twisting your body?
Outdoors, Under Cover	How often does this job require working outdoors, under cover (e.g., structure with roof but no walls)?
Cramped Work Space, Awkward Positions	How often does this job require working in cramped work spaces that requires getting into awkward positions?
Exposed to High Places	How often does this job require exposure to high places?
Spend Time Keeping or Regaining Balance	How much does this job require keeping or regaining your balance?
Spend Time Kneeling, Crouching, Stooping, or Crawl	How much does this job require kneeling, crouching, stooping or crawling?
Spend Time Climbing Ladders, Scaffolds, or Poles	How much does this job require climbing ladders, scaffolds, or poles?
Exposed to Radiation	How often does this job require exposure to radiation?

Pace Determined by Speed of Equipment	How important is it to this job that the pace is determined by the speed of equipment or machinery? (This does not refer to keeping busy at all times on this job.)
In an Open Vehicle or Equipment	How often does this job require working in an open vehicle or equipment (e.g., tractor)?
Exposed to Whole Body Vibration	How often does this job require exposure to whole body vibration (e.g., operate a jackhammer)?

Job Zone Component	Job Zone Component Definitions
Title	Job Zone Three: Medium Preparation Needed
Overall Experience	Previous work-related skill, knowledge, or experience is required for these occupations. For example, an electrician must have completed three or four years of apprenticeship or several years of vocational training, and often must have passed a licensing exam, in order to perform the job.
Job Training	Employees in these occupations usually need one or two years of training involving both on-the-job experience and informal training with experienced workers.
Job Zone Examples	These occupations usually involve using communication and organizational skills to coordinate, supervise, manage, or train others to accomplish goals. Examples include dental assistants, electricians, fish and game wardens, legal secretaries, personnel recruiters, and recreation workers.
SVP Range	(6.0 to < 7.0)
Education	Most occupations in this zone require training in vocational schools, related on-the-job experience, or an associate's degree. Some may require a bachelor's degree.

Work_Styles	Work_Styles Definitions
Self Control	Job requires maintaining composure, keeping emotions in check, controlling anger, and avoiding aggressive behavior, even in very difficult situations.
Integrity	Job requires being honest and ethical.
Stress Tolerance	Job requires accepting criticism and dealing calmly and effectively with high stress situations.
Attention to Detail	Job requires being careful about detail and thorough in completing work tasks.
Dependability	Job requires being reliable, responsible, and dependable, and fulfilling obligations.
Concern for Others	Job requires being sensitive to others' needs and feelings and being understanding and helpful on the job.
Initiative	Job requires a willingness to take on responsibilities and challenges.
Independence	Job requires developing one's own ways of doing things, guiding oneself with little or no supervision, and depending on oneself to get things done.
Cooperation	Job requires being pleasant with others on the job and displaying a good-natured, cooperative attitude.
Adaptability/Flexibility	Job requires being open to change (positive or negative) and to considerable variety in the workplace.
Leadership	Job requires a willingness to lead, take charge, and offer opinions and direction.
Persistence	Job requires persistence in the face of obstacles.
Analytical Thinking	Job requires analyzing information and using logic to address work-related issues and problems.
Social Orientation	Job requires preferring to work with others rather than alone, and being personally connected with others on the job.
Achievement/Effort	Job requires establishing and maintaining personally challenging achievement goals and exerting effort toward mastering tasks.
Innovation	Job requires creativity and alternative thinking to develop new ideas for and answers to work-related problems.

33-3051.03 - Sheriffs and Deputy Sheriffs

Enforce law and order in rural or unincorporated districts or serve legal processes of courts. May patrol courthouse, guard court or grand jury, or escort defendants.

Tasks

1) Serve statements of claims, subpoenas, summonses, jury summonses, orders to pay

alimony, and other court orders.

2) Verify that the proper legal charges have been made against law offenders.

3) Take control of accident scenes to maintain traffic flow, to assist accident victims, and to investigate causes.

4) Locate and confiscate real or personal property, as directed by court order.

5) Manage jail operations, and tend to jail inmates.

6) Investigate illegal or suspicious activities.

7) Question individuals entering secured areas to determine their business, directing and rerouting individuals as necessary.

8) Transport or escort prisoners and defendants en route to courtrooms, prisons or jails, attorneys' offices, or medical facilities.

9) Drive vehicles or patrol specific areas to detect law violators, issue citations, and make arrests.

10) Execute arrest warrants, locating and taking persons into custody.

11) Record daily activities, and submit logs and other related reports and paperwork to appropriate authorities.

12) Place people in protective custody.

13) Notify patrol units to take violators into custody or to provide needed assistance or medical aid.

33-3052.00 - Transit and Railroad Police

Protect and police railroad and transit property, employees, or passengers.

Tasks

1) Investigate or direct investigations of freight theft, suspicious damage or loss of passengers' valuables, and other crimes on railroad property.

2) Interview neighbors, associates, and former employers of job applicants in order to verify personal references and to obtain work history data.

3) Prepare reports documenting investigation activities and results.

4) Patrol railroad yards, cars, stations, and other facilities in order to protect company property and shipments, and to maintain order.

5) Direct security activities at derailments, fires, floods, and strikes involving railroad property.

6) Record and verify seal numbers from boxcars containing frequently pilfered items, such as cigarettes and liquor, in order to detect tampering.

7) Apprehend or remove trespassers or thieves from railroad property, or coordinate with law enforcement agencies in apprehensions and removals.

8) Plan and implement special safety and preventive programs, such as fire and accident prevention.

9) Seal empty boxcars by twisting nails in door hasps, using nail twisters.

10) Examine credentials of unauthorized persons attempting to enter secured areas.

33-9011.00 - Animal Control Workers

Handle animals for the purpose of investigations of mistreatment, or control of abandoned, dangerous, or unattended animals.

Tasks

1) Examine animal licenses, and inspect establishments housing animals for compliance with laws.

2) Organize the adoption of unclaimed animals.

3) Educate the public about animal welfare, and animal control laws and regulations.

4) Contact animal owners to inform them that their pets are at animal holding facilities.

5) Answer inquiries from the public concerning animal control operations.

6) Clean facilities and equipment such as dog pens and animal control trucks.

7) Capture and remove stray, uncontrolled, or abused animals from undesirable conditions,

using nets, nooses, or tranquilizer darts as necessary.

8) Issue warnings or citations in connection with animal-related offenses, or contact police to report violations and request arrests.

9) Train police officers in dog handling and training techniques for tracking, crowd control, and narcotics and bomb detection.

10) Remove captured animals from animal-control service vehicles and place animals in shelter cages or other enclosures.

11) Euthanize rabid, unclaimed, or severely injured animals.

12) Supply animals with food, water, and personal care.

13) Write reports of activities, and maintain files of impoundments and dispositions of animals.

14) Prepare for prosecutions related to animal treatment, and give evidence in court.

15) Investigate reports of animal attacks or animal cruelty, interviewing witnesses, collecting evidence, and writing reports.

33-9021.00 - Private Detectives and Investigators

Detect occurrences of unlawful acts or infractions of rules in private establishment, or seek, examine, and compile information for client.

Tasks

1) Write reports and case summaries to document investigations.

2) Warn troublemakers causing problems on establishment premises, and eject them from premises when necessary.

3) Alert appropriate personnel to suspects' locations.

4) Count cash, and review transactions, sales checks, and register tapes in order to verify amounts and to identify shortages.

5) Expose fraudulent insurance claims or stolen funds.

6) Testify at hearings and court trials to present evidence.

7) Obtain and analyze information on suspects, crimes, and disturbances in order to solve cases, to identify criminal activity, and to gather information for court cases.

8) Investigate companies' financial standings or locate funds stolen by embezzlers, using accounting skills.

9) Conduct private investigations on a paid basis.

10) Confer with establishment officials, security departments, police, or postal officials to identify problems, provide information, and receive instructions.

11) Perform undercover operations such as evaluating the performance and honesty of employees by posing as customers or employees.

12) Search computer databases, credit reports, public records, tax and legal filings, and other resources in order to locate persons or to compile information for investigations.

13) Apprehend suspects and release them to law enforcement authorities or security personnel.

14) Monitor industrial or commercial properties to enforce conformance to establishment rules, and to protect people or property.

15) Observe and document activities of individuals in order to detect unlawful acts or to obtain evidence for cases, using binoculars and still or video cameras.

16) Question persons to obtain evidence for cases of divorce, child custody, or missing persons, or information about individuals' character or financial status.

33-9031.00 - Gaming Surveillance Officers and Gaming Investigators

Act as oversight and security agent for management and customers. Observe casino or casino hotel operation for irregular activities such as cheating or theft by either employees or patrons. May utilize one-way mirrors above the casino floor, cashier's cage, and from desk. Use of audio/video equipment is also common to observe operation of the business. Usually required to provide verbal and written reports of all violations and suspicious behavior to supervisor.

Tasks

1) Act as oversight and security agents for management and customers.

2) Supervise and train surveillance observers.

3) Monitor establishment activities to ensure adherence to all state gaming regulations and company policies and procedures.

4) Observe casino or casino hotel operations for irregular activities such as cheating or theft by employees or patrons, using audio/video equipment and one-way mirrors.

Knowledge	Knowledge Definitions
Public Safety and Security	Knowledge of relevant equipment, policies, procedures, and strategies to promote effective local, state, or national security operations for the protection of people, data, property, and institutions.
English Language	Knowledge of the structure and content of the English language including the meaning and spelling of words, rules of composition, and grammar.
Computers and Electronics	Knowledge of circuit boards, processors, chips, electronic equipment, and computer hardware and software, including applications and programming.
Clerical	Knowledge of administrative and clerical procedures and systems such as word processing, managing files and records, stenography and transcription, designing forms, and other office procedures and terminology.
Education and Training	Knowledge of principles and methods for curriculum and training design, teaching and instruction for individuals and groups, and the measurement of training effects.
Mathematics	Knowledge of arithmetic, algebra, geometry, calculus, statistics, and their applications.
Administration and Management	Knowledge of business and management principles involved in strategic planning, resource allocation, human resources modeling, leadership technique, production methods, and coordination of people and resources.
Law and Government	Knowledge of laws, legal codes, court procedures, precedents, government regulations, executive orders, agency rules, and the democratic political process.
Telecommunications	Knowledge of transmission, broadcasting, switching, control, and operation of telecommunications systems.
Psychology	Knowledge of human behavior and performance; individual differences in ability, personality, and interests; learning and motivation; psychological research methods; and the assessment and treatment of behavioral and affective disorders.
Customer and Personal Service	Knowledge of principles and processes for providing customer and personal services. This includes customer needs assessment, meeting quality standards for services, and evaluation of customer satisfaction.
Economics and Accounting	Knowledge of economic and accounting principles and practices, the financial markets, banking and the analysis and reporting of financial data.
Engineering and Technology	Knowledge of the practical application of engineering science and technology. This includes applying principles, techniques, procedures, and equipment to the design and production of various goods and services.
Communications and Media	Knowledge of media production, communication, and dissemination techniques and methods. This includes alternative ways to inform and entertain via written, oral, and visual media.
Personnel and Human Resources	Knowledge of principles and procedures for personnel recruitment, selection, training, compensation and benefits, labor relations and negotiation, and personnel information systems.
Mechanical	Knowledge of machines and tools, including their designs, uses, repair, and maintenance.
Sociology and Anthropology	Knowledge of group behavior and dynamics, societal trends and influences, human migrations, ethnicity, cultures and their history and origins.
Medicine and Dentistry	Knowledge of the information and techniques needed to diagnose and treat human injuries, diseases, and deformities. This includes symptoms, treatment alternatives, drug properties and interactions, and preventive health-care measures.
Building and Construction	Knowledge of materials, methods, and the tools involved in the construction or repair of houses, buildings, or other structures such as highways and roads.
Philosophy and Theology	Knowledge of different philosophical systems and religions. This includes their basic principles, values, ethics, ways of thinking, customs, practices, and their impact on human culture.
Transportation	Knowledge of principles and methods for moving people or goods by air, rail, sea, or road, including the relative costs and benefits.
Production and Processing	Knowledge of raw materials, production processes, quality control, costs, and other techniques for maximizing the effective manufacture and distribution of goods.
Therapy and Counseling	Knowledge of principles, methods, and procedures for diagnosis, treatment, and rehabilitation of physical and mental dysfunctions, and for career counseling and guidance.
Food Production	Knowledge of techniques and equipment for planting, growing, and harvesting food products (both plant and animal) for consumption, including storage/handling techniques.
Foreign Language	Knowledge of the structure and content of a foreign (non-English) language including the meaning and spelling of words, rules of composition and grammar, and pronunciation.
Sales and Marketing	Knowledge of principles and methods for showing, promoting, and selling products or services. This includes marketing strategy and tactics, product demonstration, sales techniques, and sales control systems.
Geography	Knowledge of principles and methods for describing the features of land, sea, and air masses, including their physical characteristics, locations, interrelationships, and distribution of plant, animal, and human life.
History and Archeology	Knowledge of historical events and their causes, indicators, and effects on civilizations and cultures.
Fine Arts	Knowledge of the theory and techniques required to compose, produce, and perform works of music, dance, visual arts, drama, and sculpture.
Physics	Knowledge and prediction of physical principles, laws, their interrelationships, and applications to understanding fluid, material, and atmospheric dynamics, and mechanical, electrical, atomic and sub- atomic structures and processes.
Design	Knowledge of design techniques, tools, and principles involved in production of precision technical plans, blueprints, drawings, and models.
Chemistry	Knowledge of the chemical composition, structure, and properties of substances and of the chemical processes and transformations that they undergo. This includes uses of chemicals and their interactions, danger signs, production techniques, and disposal methods.
Biology	Knowledge of plant and animal organisms, their tissues, cells, functions, interdependencies, and interactions with each other and the environment.

Skills	Skills Definitions
Active Listening	Giving full attention to what other people are saying, taking time to understand the points being made, asking questions as appropriate, and not interrupting at inappropriate times.
Critical Thinking	Using logic and reasoning to identify the strengths and weaknesses of alternative solutions, conclusions or approaches to problems.
Writing	Communicating effectively in writing as appropriate for the needs of the audience.
Instructing	Teaching others how to do something.
Reading Comprehension	Understanding written sentences and paragraphs in work related documents.
Learning Strategies	Selecting and using training/instructional methods and procedures appropriate for the situation when learning or teaching new things.
Speaking	Talking to others to convey information effectively.
Judgment and Decision Making	Considering the relative costs and benefits of potential actions to choose the most appropriate one.
Monitoring	Monitoring/Assessing performance of yourself, other individuals, or organizations to make improvements or take corrective action.
Service Orientation	Actively looking for ways to help people.
Social Perceptiveness	Being aware of others' reactions and understanding why they react as they do.
Time Management	Managing one's own time and the time of others.
Coordination	Adjusting actions in relation to others' actions.
Complex Problem Solving	Identifying complex problems and reviewing related information to develop and evaluate options and implement solutions.
Active Learning	Understanding the implications of new information for both current and future problem-solving and decision-making.
Mathematics	Using mathematics to solve problems.
Negotiation	Bringing others together and trying to reconcile differences.

Management of Personnel Resources	Motivating, developing, and directing people as they work, identifying the best people for the job.
Equipment Selection	Determining the kind of tools and equipment needed to do a job.
Persuasion	Persuading others to change their minds or behavior.
Operation and Control	Controlling operations of equipment or systems.
Systems Evaluation	Identifying measures or indicators of system performance and the actions needed to improve or correct performance, relative to the goals of the system.
Equipment Maintenance	Performing routine maintenance on equipment and determining when and what kind of maintenance is needed.
Operations Analysis	Analyzing needs and product requirements to create a design.
Management of Material Resources	Obtaining and seeing to the appropriate use of equipment, facilities, and materials needed to do certain work.
Operation Monitoring	Watching gauges, dials, or other indicators to make sure a machine is working properly.
Quality Control Analysis	Conducting tests and inspections of products, services, or processes to evaluate quality or performance.
Installation	Installing equipment, machines, wiring, or programs to meet specifications.
Troubleshooting	Determining causes of operating errors and deciding what to do about it.
Technology Design	Generating or adapting equipment and technology to serve user needs.
Systems Analysis	Determining how a system should work and how changes in conditions, operations, and the environment will affect outcomes.
Repairing	Repairing machines or systems using the needed tools.
Programming	Writing computer programs for various purposes.
Science	Using scientific rules and methods to solve problems.
Management of Financial Resources	Determining how money will be spent to get the work done, and accounting for these expenditures.

Ability	Ability Definitions
Problem Sensitivity	The ability to tell when something is wrong or is likely to go wrong. It does not involve solving the problem, only recognizing there is a problem.
Oral Expression	The ability to communicate information and ideas in speaking so others will understand.
Selective Attention	The ability to concentrate on a task over a period of time without being distracted.
Written Expression	The ability to communicate information and ideas in writing so others will understand.
Inductive Reasoning	The ability to combine pieces of information to form general rules or conclusions (includes finding a relationship among seemingly unrelated events).
Near Vision	The ability to see details at close range (within a few feet of the observer).
Oral Comprehension	The ability to listen to and understand information and ideas presented through spoken words and sentences.
Far Vision	The ability to see details at a distance.
Deductive Reasoning	The ability to apply general rules to specific problems to produce answers that make sense.
Written Comprehension	The ability to read and understand information and ideas presented in writing.
Speech Clarity	The ability to speak clearly so others can understand you.
Perceptual Speed	The ability to quickly and accurately compare similarities and differences among sets of letters, numbers, objects, pictures, or patterns. The things to be compared may be presented at the same time or one after the other. This ability also includes comparing a presented object with a remembered object.
Speed of Closure	The ability to quickly make sense of, combine, and organize information into meaningful patterns.
Flexibility of Closure	The ability to identify or detect a known pattern (a figure, object, word, or sound) that is hidden in other distracting material.
Speech Recognition	The ability to identify and understand the speech of another person.
Time Sharing	The ability to shift back and forth between two or more activities or sources of information (such as speech, sounds, touch, or other sources).
Information Ordering	The ability to arrange things or actions in a certain order or pattern according to a specific rule or set of rules (e.g., patterns of numbers, letters, words, pictures, mathematical operations).
Memorization	The ability to remember information such as words, numbers, pictures, and procedures

Originality	The ability to come up with unusual or clever ideas about a given topic or situation, or to develop creative ways to solve a problem.
Category Flexibility	The ability to generate or use different sets of rules for combining or grouping things in different ways.
Fluency of Ideas	The ability to come up with a number of ideas about a topic (the number of ideas is important, not their quality, correctness, or creativity).
Auditory Attention	The ability to focus on a single source of sound in the presence of other distracting sounds.
Stamina	The ability to exert yourself physically over long periods of time without getting winded or out of breath.
Visualization	The ability to imagine how something will look after it is moved around or when its parts are moved or rearranged.
Manual Dexterity	The ability to quickly move your hand, your hand together with your arm, or your two hands to grasp, manipulate, or assemble objects.
Control Precision	The ability to quickly and repeatedly adjust the controls of a machine or a vehicle to exact positions.
Static Strength	The ability to exert maximum muscle force to lift, push, pull, or carry objects.
Gross Body Coordination	The ability to coordinate the movement of your arms, legs, and torso together when the whole body is in motion.
Reaction Time	The ability to quickly respond (with the hand, finger, or foot) to a signal (sound, light, picture) when it appears.
Trunk Strength	The ability to use your abdominal and lower back muscles to support part of the body repeatedly or continuously over time without 'giving out' or fatiguing.
Response Orientation	The ability to choose quickly between two or more movements in response to two or more different signals (lights, sounds, pictures). It includes the speed with which the correct response is started with the hand, foot, or other body part.
Number Facility	The ability to add, subtract, multiply, or divide quickly and correctly.
Visual Color Discrimination	The ability to match or detect differences between colors, including shades of color and brightness.
Speed of Limb Movement	The ability to quickly move the arms and legs.
Finger Dexterity	The ability to make precisely coordinated movements of the fingers of one or both hands to grasp, manipulate, or assemble very small objects.
Explosive Strength	The ability to use short bursts of muscle force to propel oneself (as in jumping or sprinting), or to throw an object.
Hearing Sensitivity	The ability to detect or tell the differences between sounds that vary in pitch and loudness.
Arm-Hand Steadiness	The ability to keep your hand and arm steady while moving your arm or while holding your arm and hand in one position.
Peripheral Vision	The ability to see objects or movement of objects to one's side when the eyes are looking ahead.
Gross Body Equilibrium	The ability to keep or regain your body balance or stay upright when in an unstable position.
Mathematical Reasoning	The ability to choose the right mathematical methods or formulas to solve a problem.
Extent Flexibility	The ability to bend, stretch, twist, or reach with your body, arms, and/or legs.
Multilimb Coordination	The ability to coordinate two or more limbs (for example, two arms, two legs, or one leg and one arm) while sitting, standing, or lying down. It does not involve performing the activities while the whole body is in motion.
Sound Localization	The ability to tell the direction from which a sound originated.
Depth Perception	The ability to judge which of several objects is closer or farther away from you, or to judge the distance between you and an object.
Spatial Orientation	The ability to know your location in relation to the environment or to know where other objects are in relation to you.
Wrist-Finger Speed	The ability to make fast, simple, repeated movements of the fingers, hands, and wrists.
Dynamic Strength	The ability to exert muscle force repeatedly or continuously over time. This involves muscular endurance and resistance to muscle fatigue.
Night Vision	The ability to see under low light conditions.
Rate Control	The ability to time your movements or the movement of a piece of equipment in anticipation of changes in the speed and/or direction of a moving object or scene.
Glare Sensitivity	The ability to see objects in the presence of glare or bright lighting.
Dynamic Flexibility	The ability to quickly and repeatedly bend, stretch, twist, or reach out with your body, arms, and/or legs.

Work_Activity	Work_Activity Definitions
Getting Information	Observing, receiving, and otherwise obtaining information from all relevant sources.
Monitor Processes, Materials, or Surroundings	Monitoring and reviewing information from materials, events, or the environment, to detect or assess problems.
Identifying Objects, Actions, and Events	Identifying information by categorizing, estimating, recognizing differences or similarities, and detecting changes in circumstances or events.
Documenting/Recording Information	Entering, transcribing, recording, storing, or maintaining information in written or electronic/magnetic form.
Evaluating Information to Determine Compliance wit	Using relevant information and individual judgment to determine whether events or processes comply with laws, regulations, or standards.
Communicating with Supervisors, Peers, or Subordin	Providing information to supervisors, co-workers, and subordinates by telephone, in written form, e-mail, or in person.
Making Decisions and Solving Problems	Analyzing information and evaluating results to choose the best solution and solve problems.
Inspecting Equipment, Structures, or Material	Inspecting equipment, structures, or materials to identify the cause of errors or other problems or defects.
Updating and Using Relevant Knowledge	Keeping up-to-date technically and applying new knowledge to your job.
Processing Information	Compiling, coding, categorizing, calculating, tabulating, auditing, or verifying information or data.
Analyzing Data or Information	Identifying the underlying principles, reasons, or facts of information by breaking down information or data into separate parts.
Monitoring and Controlling Resources	Monitoring and controlling resources and overseeing the spending of money.
Training and Teaching Others	Identifying the educational needs of others, developing formal educational or training programs or classes, and teaching or instructing others.
Interacting With Computers	Using computers and computer systems (including hardware and software) to program, write software, set up functions, enter data, or process information.
Organizing, Planning, and Prioritizing Work	Developing specific goals and plans to prioritize, organize, and accomplish your work.
Judging the Qualities of Things, Services, or Peop	Assessing the value, importance, or quality of things or people.
Performing Administrative Activities	Performing day-to-day administrative tasks such as maintaining information files and processing paperwork.
Coordinating the Work and Activities of Others	Getting members of a group to work together to accomplish tasks.
Developing and Building Teams	Encouraging and building mutual trust, respect, and cooperation among team members.
Repairing and Maintaining Electronic Equipment	Servicing, repairing, calibrating, regulating, fine-tuning, or testing machines, devices, and equipment that operate primarily on the basis of electrical or electronic (not mechanical) principles.
Handling and Moving Objects	Using hands and arms in handling, installing, positioning, and moving materials, and manipulating things.
Resolving Conflicts and Negotiating with Others	Handling complaints, settling disputes, and resolving grievances and conflicts, or otherwise negotiating with others.
Guiding, Directing, and Motivating Subordinates	Providing guidance and direction to subordinates, including setting performance standards and monitoring performance.
Coaching and Developing Others	Identifying the developmental needs of others and coaching, mentoring, or otherwise helping others to improve their knowledge or skills.
Estimating the Quantifiable Characteristics of Pro	Estimating sizes, distances, and quantities; or determining time, costs, resources, or materials needed to perform a work activity.
Performing General Physical Activities	Performing physical activities that require considerable use of your arms and legs and moving your whole body, such as climbing, lifting, balancing, walking, stooping, and handling of materials.
Provide Consultation and Advice to Others	Providing guidance and expert advice to management or other groups on technical, systems-, or process-related topics.
Controlling Machines and Processes	Using either control mechanisms or direct physical activity to operate machines or processes (not including computers or vehicles).
Scheduling Work and Activities	Scheduling events, programs, and activities, as well as the work of others.
Thinking Creatively	Developing, designing, or creating new applications, ideas, relationships, systems, or products, including artistic contributions.
Assisting and Caring for Others	Providing personal assistance, medical attention, emotional support, or other personal care to others such as co-workers, customers, or patients.
Developing Objectives and Strategies	Establishing long-range objectives and specifying the strategies and actions to achieve them.
Establishing and Maintaining Interpersonal Relatio	Developing constructive and cooperative working relationships with others, and maintaining them over time.
Communicating with Persons Outside Organization	Communicating with people outside the organization, representing the organization to customers, the public, government, and other external sources. This information can be exchanged in person, in writing, or by telephone or e-mail.
Interpreting the Meaning of Information for Others	Translating or explaining what information means and how it can be used.
Performing for or Working Directly with the Public	Performing for people or dealing directly with the public. This includes serving customers in restaurants and stores, and receiving clients or guests.
Repairing and Maintaining Mechanical Equipment	Servicing, repairing, adjusting, and testing machines, devices, moving parts, and equipment that operate primarily on the basis of mechanical (not electronic) principles.
Drafting, Laying Out, and Specifying Technical Dev	Providing documentation, detailed instructions, drawings, or specifications to tell others about how devices, parts, equipment, or structures are to be fabricated, constructed, assembled, modified, maintained, or used.
Operating Vehicles, Mechanized Devices, or Equipme	Running, maneuvering, navigating, or driving vehicles or mechanized equipment, such as forklifts, passenger vehicles, aircraft, or water craft.
Selling or Influencing Others	Convincing others to buy merchandise/goods or to otherwise change their minds or actions.
Staffing Organizational Units	Recruiting, interviewing, selecting, hiring, and promoting employees in an organization.

Work_Context	Work_Context Definitions
Contact With Others	How much does this job require the worker to be in contact with others (face-to-face, by telephone, or otherwise) in order to perform it?
Indoors, Environmentally Controlled	How often does this job require working indoors in environmentally controlled conditions?
Work With Work Group or Team	How important is it to work with others in a group or team in this job?
Importance of Being Exact or Accurate	How important is being very exact or highly accurate in performing this job?
Letters and Memos	How often does the job require written letters and memos?
Importance of Repeating Same Tasks	How important is repeating the same physical activities (e.g., key entry) or mental activities (e.g., checking entries in a ledger) over and over, without stopping, to performing this job?
Coordinate or Lead Others	How important is it to coordinate or lead others in accomplishing work activities in this job?
Freedom to Make Decisions	How much decision making freedom, without supervision, does the job offer?
Impact of Decisions on Co-workers or Company Resul	How do the decisions an employee makes impact the results of co-workers, clients or the company?
Face-to-Face Discussions	How often do you have to have face-to-face discussions with individuals or teams in this job?
Frequency of Decision Making	How frequently is the worker required to make decisions that affect other people, the financial resources, and/or the image and reputation of the organization?
Spend Time Making Repetitive Motions	How much does this job require making repetitive motions?
Frequency of Conflict Situations	How often are there conflict situations the employee has to face in this job?
Telephone	How often do you have telephone conversations in this job?
Time Pressure	How often does this job require the worker to meet strict deadlines?
Physical Proximity	To what extent does this job require the worker to perform job tasks in close physical proximity to other people?
Structured versus Unstructured Work	To what extent is this job structured for the worker, rather than allowing the worker to determine tasks, priorities, and goals?
Responsible for Others' Health and Safety	How much responsibility is there for the health and safety of others in this job?
Responsibility for Outcomes and Results	How responsible is the worker for work outcomes and results of other workers?
Spend Time Sitting	How much does this job require sitting?
Deal With Unpleasant or Angry People	How frequently does the worker have to deal with unpleasant, angry, or discourteous individuals as part of the job requirements?

719

Spend Time Using Your Hands to Handle, Control, or	How much does this job require using your hands to handle, control, or feel objects, tools or controls?
Exposed to Contaminants	How often does this job require working exposed to contaminants (such as pollutants, gases, dust or odors)?
Deal With External Customers	How important is it to work with external customers or the public in this job?
Degree of Automation	How automated is the job?
Sounds, Noise Levels Are Distracting or Uncomforta	How often does this job require working exposed to sounds and noise levels that are distracting or uncomfortable?
Level of Competition	To what extent does this job require the worker to compete or to be aware of competitive pressures?
Spend Time Standing	How much does this job require standing?
Deal With Physically Aggressive People	How frequently does this job require the worker to deal with physical aggression of violent individuals?
Consequence of Error	How serious would the result usually be if the worker made a mistake that was not readily correctable?
Spend Time Walking and Running	How much does this job require walking and running?
Electronic Mail	How often do you use electronic mail in this job?
Extremely Bright or Inadequate Lighting	How often does this job require working in extremely bright or inadequate lighting conditions?
Cramped Work Space, Awkward Positions	How often does this job require working in cramped work spaces that requires getting into awkward positions?
Spend Time Bending or Twisting the Body	How much does this job require bending or twisting your body?
Exposed to Hazardous Conditions	How often does this job require exposure to hazardous conditions?
In an Enclosed Vehicle or Equipment	How often does this job require working in a closed vehicle or equipment (e.g., car)?
Outdoors, Exposed to Weather	How often does this job require working outdoors, exposed to all weather conditions?
Very Hot or Cold Temperatures	How often does this job require working in very hot (above 90 F degrees) or very cold (below 32 F degrees) temperatures?
Spend Time Kneeling, Crouching, Stooping, or Crawl	How much does this job require kneeling, crouching, stooping or crawling?
Outdoors, Under Cover	How often does this job require working outdoors, under cover (e.g., structure with roof but no walls)?
Exposed to Disease or Infections	How often does this job require exposure to disease/infections?
Indoors, Not Environmentally Controlled	How often does this job require working indoors in non-controlled environmental conditions (e.g., warehouse without heat)?
Wear Common Protective or Safety Equipment such as	How much does this job require wearing common protective or safety equipment such as safety shoes, glasses, gloves, hard hats or life jackets?
Pace Determined by Speed of Equipment	How important is it to this job that the pace is determined by the speed of equipment or machinery? (This does not refer to keeping busy at all times on this job.)
Public Speaking	How often do you have to perform public speaking in this job?
Exposed to Hazardous Equipment	How often does this job require exposure to hazardous equipment?
Exposed to Minor Burns, Cuts, Bites, or Stings	How often does this job require exposure to minor burns, cuts, bites, or stings?
Wear Specialized Protective or Safety Equipment su	How much does this job require wearing specialized protective or safety equipment such as breathing apparatus, safety harness, full protection suits, or radiation protection?
In an Open Vehicle or Equipment	How often does this job require working in an open vehicle or equipment (e.g., tractor)?
Spend Time Keeping or Regaining Balance	How much does this job require keeping or regaining your balance?
Exposed to High Places	How often does this job require exposure to high places?
Spend Time Climbing Ladders, Scaffolds, or Poles	How much does this job require climbing ladders, scaffolds, or poles?
Exposed to Radiation	How often does this job require exposure to radiation?
Exposed to Whole Body Vibration	How often does this job require exposure to whole body vibration (e.g., operate a jackhammer)?

Job Zone Component	Job Zone Component Definitions
Title	Job Zone Two: Some Preparation Needed
	Some previous work-related skill, knowledge, or experience may be helpful in these occupations, but usually is not needed.
Overall Experience	For example, a drywall installer might benefit from experience installing drywall, but an inexperienced person could still learn to be an installer with little difficulty.

Job Training	Employees in these occupations need anywhere from a few months to one year of working with experienced employees. These occupations often involve using your knowledge and skills to help others.
Job Zone Examples	Examples include drywall installers, fire inspectors, flight attendants, pharmacy technicians, salespersons (retail), and tellers.
SVP Range	(4.0 to < 6.0)
Education	These occupations usually require a high school diploma and may require some vocational training or job-related course work. In some cases, an associate's or bachelor's degree could be needed.

Work_Styles	Work_Styles Definitions
Attention to Detail	Job requires being careful about detail and thorough in completing work tasks.
Integrity	Job requires being honest and ethical.
Dependability	Job requires being reliable, responsible, and dependable, and fulfilling obligations.
Cooperation	Job requires being pleasant with others on the job and displaying a good-natured, cooperative attitude.
Self Control	Job requires maintaining composure, keeping emotions in check, controlling anger, and avoiding aggressive behavior, even in very difficult situations.
Adaptability/Flexibility	Job requires being open to change (positive or negative) and to considerable variety in the workplace.
Initiative	Job requires a willingness to take on responsibilities and challenges.
Independence	Job requires developing one's own ways of doing things, guiding oneself with little or no supervision, and depending on oneself to get things done.
Stress Tolerance	Job requires accepting criticism and dealing calmly and effectively with high stress situations.
Analytical Thinking	Job requires analyzing information and using logic to address work-related issues and problems.
Leadership	Job requires a willingness to lead, take charge, and offer opinions and direction.
Persistence	Job requires persistence in the face of obstacles.
Achievement/Effort	Job requires establishing and maintaining personally challenging achievement goals and exerting effort toward mastering tasks.
Innovation	Job requires creativity and alternative thinking to develop new ideas for and answers to work-related problems.
Concern for Others	Job requires being sensitive to others' needs and feelings and being understanding and helpful on the job.
Social Orientation	Job requires preferring to work with others rather than alone, and being personally connected with others on the job.

33-9032.00 - Security Guards

Guard, patrol, or monitor premises to prevent theft, violence, or infractions of rules.

Tasks

1) Call police or fire departments in cases of emergency, such as fire or presence of unauthorized persons.

2) Circulate among visitors, patrons, and employees to preserve order and protect property.

3) Patrol industrial and commercial premises to prevent and detect signs of intrusion and ensure security of doors, windows, and gates.

4) Answer alarms and investigate disturbances.

5) Warn persons of rule infractions or violations, and apprehend or evict violators from premises, using force when necessary.

6) Monitor and authorize entrance and departure of employees, visitors, and other persons to guard against theft and maintain security of premises.

7) Answer telephone calls to take messages, answer questions, and provide information during non- business hours or when switchboard is closed.

8) Inspect and adjust security systems, equipment, and machinery to ensure operational use and to detect evidence of tampering.

9) Operate detecting devices to screen individuals and prevent passage of prohibited articles into restricted areas.

10) Escort or drive motor vehicle to transport individuals to specified locations and to provide personal protection.

11) Monitor and adjust controls that regulate building systems, such as air conditioning, furnace, or boiler.

12) Drive and guard armored vehicle to transport money and valuables to prevent theft and ensure safe delivery.

Knowledge	Knowledge Definitions
Public Safety and Security	Knowledge of relevant equipment, policies, procedures, and strategies to promote effective local, state, or national security operations for the protection of people, data, property, and institutions.
Customer and Personal Service	Knowledge of principles and processes for providing customer and personal services. This includes customer needs assessment, meeting quality standards for services, and evaluation of customer satisfaction.
English Language	Knowledge of the structure and content of the English language including the meaning and spelling of words, rules of composition, and grammar.
Law and Government	Knowledge of laws, legal codes, court procedures, precedents, government regulations, executive orders, agency rules, and the democratic political process.
Clerical	Knowledge of administrative and clerical procedures and systems such as word processing, managing files and records, stenography and transcription, designing forms, and other office procedures and terminology.
Administration and Management	Knowledge of business and management principles involved in strategic planning, resource allocation, human resources modeling, leadership technique, production methods, and coordination of people and resources.
Education and Training	Knowledge of principles and methods for curriculum and training design, teaching and instruction for individuals and groups, and the measurement of training effects.
Telecommunications	Knowledge of transmission, broadcasting, switching, control, and operation of telecommunications systems.
Computers and Electronics	Knowledge of circuit boards, processors, chips, electronic equipment, and computer hardware and software, including applications and programming.
Transportation	Knowledge of principles and methods for moving people or goods by air, rail, sea, or road, including the relative costs and benefits.
Communications and Media	Knowledge of media production, communication, and dissemination techniques and methods. This includes alternative ways to inform and entertain via written, oral, and visual media.
Personnel and Human Resources	Knowledge of principles and procedures for personnel recruitment, selection, training, compensation and benefits, labor relations and negotiation, and personnel information systems.
Economics and Accounting	Knowledge of economic and accounting principles and practices, the financial markets, banking and the analysis and reporting of financial data.
Psychology	Knowledge of human behavior and performance; individual differences in ability, personality, and interests; learning and motivation; psychological research methods; and the assessment and treatment of behavioral and affective disorders.
Mathematics	Knowledge of arithmetic, algebra, geometry, calculus, statistics, and their applications.
Geography	Knowledge of principles and methods for describing the features of land, sea, and air masses, including their physical characteristics, locations, interrelationships, and distribution of plant, animal, and human life.
Therapy and Counseling	Knowledge of principles, methods, and procedures for diagnosis, treatment, and rehabilitation of physical and mental dysfunctions, and for career counseling and guidance.
Foreign Language	Knowledge of the structure and content of a foreign (non-English) language including the meaning and spelling of words, rules of composition and grammar, and pronunciation.
Medicine and Dentistry	Knowledge of the information and techniques needed to diagnose and treat human injuries, diseases, and deformities. This includes symptoms, treatment alternatives, drug properties and interactions, and preventive health-care measures.
Production and Processing	Knowledge of raw materials, production processes, quality control, costs, and other techniques for maximizing the effective manufacture and distribution of goods.
Mechanical	Knowledge of machines and tools, including their designs, uses, repair, and maintenance.
Building and Construction	Knowledge of materials, methods, and the tools involved in the construction or repair of houses, buildings, or other structures such as highways and roads.
Sales and Marketing	Knowledge of principles and methods for showing, promoting, and selling products or services. This includes marketing strategy and tactics, product demonstration, sales techniques, and sales control systems.
Sociology and Anthropology	Knowledge of group behavior and dynamics, societal trends and influences, human migrations, ethnicity, cultures and their history and origins.
Physics	Knowledge and prediction of physical principles, laws, their interrelationships, and applications to understanding fluid, material, and atmospheric dynamics, and mechanical, electrical, atomic and sub- atomic structures and processes.
Chemistry	Knowledge of the chemical composition, structure, and properties of substances and of the chemical processes and transformations that they undergo. This includes uses of chemicals and their interactions, danger signs, production techniques, and disposal methods.
Philosophy and Theology	Knowledge of different philosophical systems and religions. This includes their basic principles, values, ethics, ways of thinking, customs, practices, and their impact on human culture.
History and Archeology	Knowledge of historical events and their causes, indicators, and effects on civilizations and cultures.
Engineering and Technology	Knowledge of the practical application of engineering science and technology. This includes applying principles, techniques, procedures, and equipment to the design and production of various goods and services.
Biology	Knowledge of plant and animal organisms, their tissues, cells, functions, interdependencies, and interactions with each other and the environment.
Food Production	Knowledge of techniques and equipment for planting, growing, and harvesting food products (both plant and animal) for consumption, including storage/handling techniques.
Design	Knowledge of design techniques, tools, and principles involved in production of precision technical plans, blueprints, drawings, and models.
Fine Arts	Knowledge of the theory and techniques required to compose, produce, and perform works of music, dance, visual arts, drama, and sculpture.

Skills	Skills Definitions
Reading Comprehension	Understanding written sentences and paragraphs in work related documents.
Active Listening	Giving full attention to what other people are saying, taking time to understand the points being made, asking questions as appropriate, and not interrupting at inappropriate times.
Social Perceptiveness	Being aware of others' reactions and understanding why they react as they do.
Speaking	Talking to others to convey information effectively.
Monitoring	Monitoring/Assessing performance of yourself, other individuals, or organizations to make improvements or take corrective action.
Writing	Communicating effectively in writing as appropriate for the needs of the audience.
Critical Thinking	Using logic and reasoning to identify the strengths and weaknesses of alternative solutions, conclusions or approaches to problems.
Time Management	Managing one's own time and the time of others.
Coordination	Adjusting actions in relation to others' actions.
Judgment and Decision Making	Considering the relative costs and benefits of potential actions to choose the most appropriate one.
Active Learning	Understanding the implications of new information for both current and future problem-solving and decision-making.
Instructing	Teaching others how to do something.
Negotiation	Bringing others together and trying to reconcile differences.
Complex Problem Solving	Identifying complex problems and reviewing related information to develop and evaluate options and implement solutions.
Learning Strategies	Selecting and using training/instructional methods and procedures appropriate for the situation when learning or teaching new things.
Management of Personnel Resources	Motivating, developing, and directing people as they work, identifying the best people for the job.
Service Orientation	Actively looking for ways to help people.

Equipment Selection	Determining the kind of tools and equipment needed to do a job.
Operation Monitoring	Watching gauges, dials, or other indicators to make sure a machine is working properly.
Persuasion	Persuading others to change their minds or behavior.
Equipment Maintenance	Performing routine maintenance on equipment and determining when and what kind of maintenance is needed.
Management of Material Resources	Obtaining and seeing to the appropriate use of equipment, facilities, and materials needed to do certain work.
Systems Evaluation	Identifying measures or indicators of system performance and the actions needed to improve or correct performance, relative to the goals of the system.
Troubleshooting	Determining causes of operating errors and deciding what to do about it.
Mathematics	Using mathematics to solve problems.
Operations Analysis	Analyzing needs and product requirements to create a design.
Quality Control Analysis	Conducting tests and inspections of products, services, or processes to evaluate quality or performance.
Operation and Control	Controlling operations of equipment or systems.
Installation	Installing equipment, machines, wiring, or programs to meet specifications.
Technology Design	Generating or adapting equipment and technology to serve user needs.
Management of Financial Resources	Determining how money will be spent to get the work done, and accounting for these expenditures.
Repairing	Repairing machines or systems using the needed tools.
Systems Analysis	Determining how a system should work and how changes in conditions, operations, and the environment will affect outcomes.
Science	Using scientific rules and methods to solve problems.
Programming	Writing computer programs for various purposes.

Ability	Ability Definitions
Problem Sensitivity	The ability to tell when something is wrong or is likely to go wrong. It does not involve solving the problem, only recognizing there is a problem.
Selective Attention	The ability to concentrate on a task over a period of time without being distracted.
Inductive Reasoning	The ability to combine pieces of information to form general rules or conclusions (includes finding a relationship among seemingly unrelated events).
Near Vision	The ability to see details at close range (within a few feet of the observer).
Far Vision	The ability to see details at a distance.
Deductive Reasoning	The ability to apply general rules to specific problems to produce answers that make sense.
Oral Expression	The ability to communicate information and ideas in speaking so others will understand.
Oral Comprehension	The ability to listen to and understand information and ideas presented through spoken words and sentences.
Hearing Sensitivity	The ability to detect or tell the differences between sounds that vary in pitch and loudness.
Flexibility of Closure	The ability to identify or detect a known pattern (a figure, object, word, or sound) that is hidden in other distracting material.
Written Expression	The ability to communicate information and ideas in writing so others will understand.
Information Ordering	The ability to arrange things or actions in a certain order or pattern according to a specific rule or set of rules (e.g., patterns of numbers, letters, words, pictures, mathematical operations).
Speech Clarity	The ability to speak clearly so others can understand you.
Perceptual Speed	The ability to quickly and accurately compare similarities and differences among sets of letters, numbers, objects, pictures, or patterns. The things to be compared may be presented at the same time or one after the other. This ability also includes comparing a presented object with a remembered object.
Speech Recognition	The ability to identify and understand the speech of another person.
Time Sharing	The ability to shift back and forth between two or more activities or sources of information (such as speech, sounds, touch, or other sources).
Speed of Closure	The ability to quickly make sense of, combine, and organize information into meaningful patterns.
Written Comprehension	The ability to read and understand information and ideas presented in writing.

Originality	The ability to come up with unusual or clever ideas about a given topic or situation, or to develop creative ways to solve a problem.
Auditory Attention	The ability to focus on a single source of sound in the presence of other distracting sounds.
Category Flexibility	The ability to generate or use different sets of rules for combining or grouping things in different ways.
Fluency of Ideas	The ability to come up with a number of ideas about a topic (the number of ideas is important, not their quality, correctness, or creativity).
Visual Color Discrimination	The ability to match or detect differences between colors, including shades of color and brightness.
Response Orientation	The ability to choose quickly between two or more movements in response to two or more different signals (lights, sounds, pictures). It includes the speed with which the correct response is started with the hand, foot, or other body part.
Finger Dexterity	The ability to make precisely coordinated movements of the fingers of one or both hands to grasp, manipulate, or assemble very small objects.
Depth Perception	The ability to judge which of several objects is closer or farther away from you, or to judge the distance between you and an object.
Stamina	The ability to exert yourself physically over long periods of time without getting winded or out of breath.
Gross Body Coordination	The ability to coordinate the movement of your arms, legs, and torso together when the whole body is in motion.
Static Strength	The ability to exert maximum muscle force to lift, push, pull, or carry objects.
Memorization	The ability to remember information such as words, numbers, pictures, and procedures.
Reaction Time	The ability to quickly respond (with the hand, finger, or foot) to a signal (sound, light, picture) when it appears.
Trunk Strength	The ability to use your abdominal and lower back muscles to support part of the body repeatedly or continuously over time without 'giving out' or fatiguing.
Arm-Hand Steadiness	The ability to keep your hand and arm steady while moving your arm or while holding your arm and hand in one position.
Multilimb Coordination	The ability to coordinate two or more limbs (for example, two arms, two legs, or one leg and one arm) while sitting, standing, or lying down. It does not involve performing the activities while the whole body is in motion.
Visualization	The ability to imagine how something will look after it is moved around or when its parts are moved or rearranged.
Sound Localization	The ability to tell the direction from which a sound originated.
Spatial Orientation	The ability to know your location in relation to the environment or to know where other objects are in relation to you.
Explosive Strength	The ability to use short bursts of muscle force to propel oneself (as in jumping or sprinting), or to throw an object.
Glare Sensitivity	The ability to see objects in the presence of glare or bright lighting.
Peripheral Vision	The ability to see objects or movement of objects to one's side when the eyes are looking ahead.
Speed of Limb Movement	The ability to quickly move the arms and legs.
Night Vision	The ability to see under low light conditions.
Extent Flexibility	The ability to bend, stretch, twist, or reach with your body, arms, and/or legs.
Dynamic Strength	The ability to exert muscle force repeatedly or continuously over time. This involves muscular endurance and resistance to muscle fatigue.
Number Facility	The ability to add, subtract, multiply, or divide quickly and correctly.
Gross Body Equilibrium	The ability to keep or regain your body balance or stay upright when in an unstable position.
Mathematical Reasoning	The ability to choose the right mathematical methods or formulas to solve a problem.
Manual Dexterity	The ability to quickly move your hand, your hand together with your arm, or your two hands to grasp, manipulate, or assemble objects.
Control Precision	The ability to quickly and repeatedly adjust the controls of a machine or a vehicle to exact positions.
Wrist-Finger Speed	The ability to make fast, simple, repeated movements of the fingers, hands, and wrists.
Rate Control	The ability to time your movements or the movement of a piece of equipment in anticipation of changes in the speed and/or direction of a moving object or scene.
Dynamic Flexibility	The ability to quickly and repeatedly bend, stretch, twist, or reach out with your body, arms, and/or legs.

Work_Activity	Work_Activity Definitions
Making Decisions and Solving Problems	Analyzing information and evaluating results to choose the best solution and solve problems.
Documenting/Recording Information	Entering, transcribing, recording, storing, or maintaining information in written or electronic/magnetic form.
Getting Information	Observing, receiving, and otherwise obtaining information from all relevant sources.
Monitor Processes, Materials, or Surroundings	Monitoring and reviewing information from materials, events, or the environment, to detect or assess problems.
Identifying Objects, Actions, and Events	Identifying information by categorizing, estimating, recognizing differences or similarities, and detecting changes in circumstances or events.
Communicating with Supervisors, Peers, or Subordin	Providing information to supervisors, co-workers, and subordinates by telephone, in written form, e-mail, or in person.
Resolving Conflicts and Negotiating with Others	Handling complaints, settling disputes, and resolving grievances and conflicts, or otherwise negotiating with others.
Performing for or Working Directly with the Public	Performing for people or dealing directly with the public. This includes serving customers in restaurants and stores, and receiving clients or guests.
Inspecting Equipment, Structures, or Material	Inspecting equipment, structures, or materials to identify the cause of errors or other problems or defects.
Establishing and Maintaining Interpersonal Relatio	Developing constructive and cooperative working relationships with others, and maintaining them over time.
Interpreting the Meaning of Information for Others	Translating or explaining what information means and how it can be used.
Communicating with Persons Outside Organization	Communicating with people outside the organization, representing the organization to customers, the public, government, and other external sources. This information can be exchanged in person, in writing, or by telephone or e-mail.
Performing General Physical Activities	Performing physical activities that require considerable use of your arms and legs and moving your whole body, such as climbing, lifting, balancing, walking, stooping, and handling of materials.
Updating and Using Relevant Knowledge	Keeping up-to-date technically and applying new knowledge to your job.
Organizing, Planning, and Prioritizing Work	Developing specific goals and plans to prioritize, organize, and accomplish your work.
Processing Information	Compiling, coding, categorizing, calculating, tabulating, auditing, or verifying information or data.
Evaluating Information to Determine Compliance wit	Using relevant information and individual judgment to determine whether events or processes comply with laws, regulations, or standards.
Assisting and Caring for Others	Providing personal assistance, medical attention, emotional support, or other personal care to others such as coworkers, customers, or patients.
Training and Teaching Others	Identifying the educational needs of others, developing formal educational or training programs or classes, and teaching or instructing others.
Scheduling Work and Activities	Scheduling events, programs, and activities, as well as the work of others.
Developing Objectives and Strategies	Establishing long-range objectives and specifying the strategies and actions to achieve them.
Performing Administrative Activities	Performing day-to-day administrative tasks such as maintaining information files and processing paperwork.
Coordinating the Work and Activities of Others	Getting members of a group to work together to accomplish tasks.
Developing and Building Teams	Encouraging and building mutual trust, respect, and cooperation among team members.
Monitoring and Controlling Resources	Monitoring and controlling resources and overseeing the spending of money.
Estimating the Quantifiable Characteristics of Pro	Estimating sizes, distances, and quantities; or determining time, costs, resources, or materials needed to perform a work activity.
Thinking Creatively	Developing, designing, or creating new applications, ideas, relationships, systems, or products, including artistic contributions.
Guiding, Directing, and Motivating Subordinates	Providing guidance and direction to subordinates, including setting performance standards and monitoring performance.
Judging the Qualities of Things, Services, or Peop	Assessing the value, importance, or quality of things or people.
Provide Consultation and Advice to Others	Providing guidance and expert advice to management or other groups on technical, systems-, or process-related topics.
Coaching and Developing Others	Identifying the developmental needs of others and coaching, mentoring, or otherwise helping others to improve their knowledge or skills.
Staffing Organizational Units	Recruiting, interviewing, selecting, hiring, and promoting employees in an organization.
Analyzing Data or Information	Identifying the underlying principles, reasons, or facts of information by breaking down information or data into separate parts.
Operating Vehicles, Mechanized Devices, or Equipme	Running, maneuvering, navigating, or driving vehicles or mechanized equipment, such as forklifts, passenger vehicles, aircraft, or water craft.
Interacting With Computers	Using computers and computer systems (including hardware and software) to program, write software, set up functions, enter data, or process information.
Handling and Moving Objects	Using hands and arms in handling, installing, positioning, and moving materials, and manipulating things.
Selling or Influencing Others	Convincing others to buy merchandise/goods or to otherwise change their minds or actions.
Controlling Machines and Processes	Using either control mechanisms or direct physical activity to operate machines or processes (not including computers or vehicles).
Repairing and Maintaining Electronic Equipment	Servicing, repairing, calibrating, regulating, fine-tuning, or testing machines, devices, and equipment that operate primarily on the basis of electrical or electronic (not mechanical) principles.
Repairing and Maintaining Mechanical Equipment	Servicing, repairing, adjusting, and testing machines, devices, moving parts, and equipment that operate primarily on the basis of mechanical (not electronic) principles.
Drafting, Laying Out, and Specifying Technical Dev	Providing documentation, detailed instructions, drawings, or specifications to tell others about how devices, parts, equipment, or structures are to be fabricated, constructed, assembled, modified, maintained, or used.

Work_Context	Work_Context Definitions
Telephone	How often do you have telephone conversations in this job?
Contact With Others	How much does this job require the worker to be in contact with others (face-to-face, by telephone, or otherwise) in order to perform it?
Face-to-Face Discussions	How often do you have to have face-to-face discussions with individuals or teams in this job?
Frequency of Decision Making	How frequently is the worker required to make decisions that affect other people, the financial resources, and/or the image and reputation of the organization?
Work With Work Group or Team	How important is it to work with others in a group or team in this job?
Importance of Being Exact or Accurate	How important is being very exact or highly accurate in performing this job?
Impact of Decisions on Co-workers or Company Resul	How do the decisions an employee makes impact the results of co-workers, clients or the company?
Freedom to Make Decisions	How much decision making freedom, without supervision, does the job offer?
Structured versus Unstructured Work	To what extent is this job structured for the worker, rather than allowing the worker to determine tasks, priorities, and goals?
Physical Proximity	To what extent does this job require the worker to perform job tasks in close physical proximity to other people?
Deal With External Customers	How important is it to work with external customers or the public in this job?
Importance of Repeating Same Tasks	How important is repeating the same physical activities (e.g., key entry) or mental activities (e.g., checking entries in a ledger) over and over, without stopping, to performing this job?
Responsible for Others' Health and Safety	How much responsibility is there for the health and safety of others in this job?
Deal With Unpleasant or Angry People	How frequently does the worker have to deal with unpleasant, angry, or discourteous individuals as part of the job requirements?
Outdoors, Exposed to Weather	How often does this job require working outdoors, exposed to all weather conditions?
Sounds, Noise Levels Are Distracting or Uncomforta	How often does this job require working exposed to sounds and noise levels that are distracting or uncomfortable?
Indoors, Environmentally Controlled	How often does this job require working indoors in environmentally controlled conditions?
Coordinate or Lead Others	How important is it to coordinate or lead others in accomplishing work activities in this job?
Spend Time Sitting	How much does this job require sitting?
Time Pressure	How often does this job require the worker to meet strict deadlines?

Spend Time Standing	How much does this job require standing?	
Letters and Memos	How often does the job require written letters and memos?	
Frequency of Conflict Situations	How often are there conflict situations the employee has to face in this job?	
Very Hot or Cold Temperatures	How often does this job require working in very hot (above 90 F degrees) or very cold (below 32 F degrees) temperatures?	
Responsibility for Outcomes and Results	How responsible is the worker for work outcomes and results of other workers?	
Extremely Bright or Inadequate Lighting	How often does this job require working in extremely bright or inadequate lighting conditions?	
Spend Time Walking and Running	How much does this job require walking and running?	
Consequence of Error	How serious would the result usually be if the worker made a mistake that was not readily correctable?	
Indoors, Not Environmentally Controlled	How often does this job require working indoors in non-controlled environmental conditions (e.g., warehouse without heat)?	
Deal With Physically Aggressive People	How frequently does this job require the worker to deal with physical aggression of violent individuals?	
In an Enclosed Vehicle or Equipment	How often does this job require working in a closed vehicle or equipment (e.g., car)?	
Level of Competition	To what extent does this job require the worker to compete or to be aware of competitive pressures?	
Spend Time Using Your Hands to Handle, Control, or	How much does this job require using your hands to handle, control, or feel objects, tools or controls?	
Exposed to Contaminants	How often does this job require working exposed to contaminants (such as pollutants, gases, dust or odors)?	
Spend Time Making Repetitive Motions	How much does this job require making repetitive motions?	
Outdoors, Under Cover	How often does this job require working outdoors, under cover (e.g., structure with roof but no walls)?	
Exposed to Minor Burns, Cuts, Bites, or Stings	How often does this job require exposure to minor burns, cuts, bites, or stings?	
Wear Common Protective or Safety Equipment such as	How much does this job require wearing common protective or safety equipment such as safety shoes, glasses, gloves, hard hats or life jackets?	
Degree of Automation	How automated is the job?	
Electronic Mail	How often do you use electronic mail in this job?	
Spend Time Bending or Twisting the Body	How much does this job require bending or twisting your body?	
Cramped Work Space, Awkward Positions	How often does this job require working in cramped work spaces that requires getting into awkward positions?	
Exposed to Hazardous Conditions	How often does this job require exposure to hazardous conditions?	
Spend Time Kneeling, Crouching, Stooping, or Crawl	How much does this job require kneeling, crouching, stooping or crawling?	
Exposed to High Places	How often does this job require exposure to high places?	
Public Speaking	How often do you have to perform public speaking in this job?	
Exposed to Whole Body Vibration	How often does this job require exposure to whole body vibration (e.g., operate a jackhammer)?	
Exposed to Hazardous Equipment	How often does this job require exposure to hazardous equipment?	
Spend Time Keeping or Regaining Balance	How much does this job require keeping or regaining your balance?	
Exposed to Disease or Infections	How often does this job require exposure to disease/infections?	
Spend Time Climbing Ladders, Scaffolds, or Poles	How much does this job require climbing ladders, scaffolds, or poles?	
Pace Determined by Speed of Equipment	How important is it to this job that the pace is determined by the speed of equipment or machinery? (This does not refer to keeping busy at all times on this job.)	
Wear Specialized Protective or Safety Equipment su	How much does this job require wearing specialized protective or safety equipment such as breathing apparatus, safety harness, full protection suits, or radiation protection?	
In an Open Vehicle or Equipment	How often does this job require working in an open vehicle or equipment (e.g., tractor)?	
Exposed to Radiation	How often does this job require exposure to radiation?	

Job Zone Component	Job Zone Component Definitions
Title	Job Zone Two: Some Preparation Needed
Overall Experience	Some previous work-related skill, knowledge, or experience may be helpful in these occupations, but usually is not needed. For example, a drywall installer might benefit from experience installing drywall, but an inexperienced person could still learn to be an installer with little difficulty.
Job Training	Employees in these occupations need anywhere from a few months to one year of working with experienced employees.
Job Zone Examples	These occupations often involve using your knowledge and skills to help others. Examples include drywall installers, fire inspectors, flight attendants, pharmacy technicians, salespersons (retail), and tellers.
SVP Range	(4.0 to 6.0)
Education	These occupations usually require a high school diploma and may require some vocational training or job-related course work. In some cases, an associate's or bachelor's degree could be needed.

Work_Styles	Work_Styles Definitions
Attention to Detail	Job requires being careful about detail and thorough in completing work tasks.
Integrity	Job requires being honest and ethical.
Cooperation	Job requires being pleasant with others on the job and displaying a good-natured, cooperative attitude.
Dependability	Job requires being reliable, responsible, and dependable, and fulfilling obligations.
Stress Tolerance	Job requires accepting criticism and dealing calmly and effectively with high stress situations.
Self Control	Job requires maintaining composure, keeping emotions in check, controlling anger, and avoiding aggressive behavior, even in very difficult situations.
Concern for Others	Job requires being sensitive to others' needs and feelings and being understanding and helpful on the job.
Leadership	Job requires a willingness to lead, take charge, and offer opinions and direction.
Adaptability/Flexibility	Job requires being open to change (positive or negative) and to considerable variety in the workplace.
Initiative	Job requires a willingness to take on responsibilities and challenges.
Independence	Job requires developing one's own ways of doing things, guiding oneself with little or no supervision, and depending on oneself to get things done.
Social Orientation	Job requires preferring to work with others rather than alone, and being personally connected with others on the job.
Persistence	Job requires persistence in the face of obstacles.
Achievement/Effort	Job requires establishing and maintaining personally challenging achievement goals and exerting effort toward mastering tasks.
Innovation	Job requires creativity and alternative thinking to develop new ideas for and answers to work-related problems.
Analytical Thinking	Job requires analyzing information and using logic to address work-related issues and problems.

33-9091.00 - Crossing Guards

Guide or control vehicular or pedestrian traffic at such places as streets, schools, railroad crossings, or construction sites.

Tasks

1) Record license numbers of vehicles disregarding traffic signals, and report infractions to appropriate authorities.

2) Monitor traffic flow to locate safe gaps through which pedestrians can cross streets.

3) Activate railroad warning signal lights, lower crossing gates until trains pass, and raise gates when crossings are clear.

4) Report unsafe behavior of children to school officials.

5) Discuss traffic routing plans and control point locations with superiors.

6) Stop speeding vehicles to warn drivers of traffic laws.

7) Direct or escort pedestrians across streets, stopping traffic as necessary.

8) Guide or control vehicular or pedestrian traffic at such places as street and railroad crossings and construction sites.

9) Communicate traffic and crossing rules and other information to students and adults.

10) Direct traffic movement or warn of hazards, using signs, flags, lanterns, and hand signals.

11) Inform drivers of detour routes through construction sites.

12) Learn the location and purpose of street traffic signs within assigned patrol areas.

35-1011.00 - Chefs and Head Cooks

Direct the preparation, seasoning, and cooking of salads, soups, fish, meats, vegetables, desserts, or other foods. May plan and price menu items, order supplies, and keep records and accounts. May participate in cooking.

Tasks

1) Arrange for equipment purchases and repairs.

2) Estimate amounts and costs of required supplies, such as food and ingredients.

3) Supervise and coordinate activities of cooks and workers engaged in food preparation.

4) Collaborate with other personnel to plan and develop recipes and menus, taking into account such factors as seasonal availability of ingredients and the likely number of customers.

5) Check the quality of raw and cooked food products to ensure that standards are met.

6) Demonstrate new cooking techniques and equipment to staff.

7) Coordinate planning, budgeting, and purchasing for all the food operations within establishments such as clubs, hotels, or restaurant chains.

8) Plan, direct, and supervise the food preparation and cooking activities of multiple kitchens or restaurants in an establishment such as a restaurant chain, hospital, or hotel.

9) Prepare and cook foods of all types, either on a regular basis or for special guests or functions.

10) Meet with sales representatives in order to negotiate prices and order supplies.

11) Check the quantity and quality of received products.

12) Analyze recipes to assign prices to menu items, based on food, labor, and overhead costs.

13) Recruit and hire staff, including cooks and other kitchen workers.

14) Order or requisition food and other supplies needed to ensure efficient operation.

15) Monitor sanitation practices to ensure that employees follow standards and regulations.

16) Instruct cooks and other workers in the preparation, cooking, garnishing, and presentation of food.

17) Inspect supplies, equipment, and work areas to ensure conformance to established standards.

18) Determine production schedules and staff requirements necessary to ensure timely delivery of services.

19) Record production and operational data on specified forms.

20) Meet with customers to discuss menus for special occasions such as weddings, parties, and banquets.

35-1012.00 - First-Line Supervisors/Managers of Food Preparation and Serving Workers

Supervise workers engaged in preparing and serving food.

Tasks

1) Inspect supplies, equipment, and work areas in order to ensure efficient service and conformance to standards.

2) Resolve customer complaints regarding food service.

3) Observe and evaluate workers and work procedures in order to ensure quality standards and service.

4) Assign duties, responsibilities, and work stations to employees in accordance with work requirements.

5) Control inventories of food, equipment, smallware, and liquor, and report shortages to designated personnel.

6) Specify food portions and courses, production and time sequences, and workstation and equipment arrangements.

7) Recommend measures for improving work procedures and worker performance in order to increase service quality and enhance job safety.

8) Compile and balance cash receipts at the end of the day or shift.

9) Estimate ingredients and supplies required to prepare a recipe.

10) Analyze operational problems, such as theft and wastage, and establish procedures to alleviate these problems.

11) Perform personnel actions such as hiring and firing staff, consulting with other managers as necessary.

12) Forecast staff, equipment, and supply requirements based on a master menu.

13) Record production and operational data on specified forms.

14) Collaborate with other personnel in order to plan menus, serving arrangements, and related details.

15) Develop equipment maintenance schedules and arrange for repairs.

16) Purchase or requisition supplies and equipment needed to ensure quality and timely delivery of services.

17) Evaluate new products for usefulness and suitability.

18) Present bills and accept payments.

19) Greet and seat guests, and present menus and wine lists.

20) Perform serving duties such as carving meat, preparing flambe dishes, or serving wine and liquor.

21) Develop departmental objectives, budgets, policies, procedures, and strategies.

22) Schedule parties and take reservations.

23) Supervise and check the assembly of regular and special diet trays and the delivery of food trolleys to hospital patients.

Knowledge	Knowledge Definitions
Customer and Personal Service	Knowledge of principles and processes for providing customer and personal services. This includes customer needs assessment, meeting quality standards for services, and evaluation of customer satisfaction.
Administration and Management	Knowledge of business and management principles involved in strategic planning, resource allocation, human resources modeling, leadership technique, production methods, and coordination of people and resources.
Production and Processing	Knowledge of raw materials, production processes, quality control, costs, and other techniques for maximizing the effective manufacture and distribution of goods.
Food Production	Knowledge of techniques and equipment for planting, growing, and harvesting food products (both plant and animal) for consumption, including storage/handling techniques.
Personnel and Human Resources	Knowledge of principles and procedures for personnel recruitment, selection, training, compensation and benefits, labor relations and negotiation, and personnel information systems.
Sales and Marketing	Knowledge of principles and methods for showing, promoting, and selling products or services. This includes marketing strategy and tactics, product demonstration, sales techniques, and sales control systems.
Education and Training	Knowledge of principles and methods for curriculum and training design, teaching and instruction for individuals and groups, and the measurement of training effects.
Clerical	Knowledge of administrative and clerical procedures and systems such as word processing, managing files and records, stenography and transcription, designing forms, and other office procedures and terminology.
Economics and Accounting	Knowledge of economic and accounting principles and practices, the financial markets, banking and the analysis and reporting of financial data.
English Language	Knowledge of the structure and content of the English language including the meaning and spelling of words, rules of composition, and grammar.
Mathematics	Knowledge of arithmetic, algebra, geometry, calculus, statistics, and their applications.
Public Safety and Security	Knowledge of relevant equipment, policies, procedures, and strategies to promote effective local, state, or national security operations for the protection of people, data, property, and institutions.

Psychology	Knowledge of human behavior and performance: individual differences in ability. personality. and interests: learning and motivation; psychological research methods; and the assessment and treatment of behavioral and affective disorders.
Computers and Electronics	Knowledge of circuit boards. processors. chips. electronic equipment. and computer hardware and software. including applications and programming.
Chemistry	Knowledge of the chemical composition, structure, and properties of substances and of the chemical processes and transformations that they undergo. This includes uses of chemicals and their interactions. danger signs. production techniques. and disposal methods.
Law and Government	Knowledge of laws. legal codes. court procedures. precedents. government regulations. executive orders. agency rules. and the democratic political process.
Communications and Media	Knowledge of media production. communication. and dissemination techniques and methods. This includes alternative ways to inform and entertain via written, oral, and visual media.
Foreign Language	Knowledge of the structure and content of a foreign (non-English) language including the meaning and spelling of words. rules of composition and grammar. and pronunciation.
Mechanical	Knowledge of machines and tools. including their designs. uses, repair, and maintenance.
Telecommunications	Knowledge of transmission, broadcasting. switching, control. and operation of telecommunications systems.
Therapy and Counseling	Knowledge of principles, methods, and procedures for diagnosis, treatment, and rehabilitation of physical and mental dysfunctions. and for career counseling and guidance.
Design	Knowledge of design techniques, tools, and principles involved in production of precision technical plans. blueprints. drawings. and models.
Engineering and Technology	Knowledge of the practical application of engineering science and technology. This includes applying principles, techniques. procedures. and equipment to the design and production of various goods and services.
Sociology and Anthropology	Knowledge of group behavior and dynamics, societal trends and influences, human migrations, ethnicity, cultures and their history and origins.
Medicine and Dentistry	Knowledge of the information and techniques needed to diagnose and treat human injuries, diseases, and deformities. This includes symptoms, treatment alternatives, drug properties and interactions, and preventive health-care measures.
Philosophy and Theology	Knowledge of different philosophical systems and religions. This includes their basic principles, values, ethics, ways of thinking, customs, practices, and their impact on human culture.
Biology	Knowledge of plant and animal organisms, their tissues, cells, functions, interdependencies, and interactions with each other and the environment.
Physics	Knowledge and prediction of physical principles, laws, their interrelationships, and applications to understanding fluid, material, and atmospheric dynamics, and mechanical, electrical, atomic and sub-atomic structures and processes.
Geography	Knowledge of principles and methods for describing the features of land, sea, and air masses, including their physical characteristics, locations, interrelationships, and distribution of plant, animal, and human life.
Transportation	Knowledge of principles and methods for moving people or goods by air, rail, sea, or road, including the relative costs and benefits.
Building and Construction	Knowledge of materials, methods, and the tools involved in the construction or repair of houses, buildings, or other structures such as highways and roads.
Fine Arts	Knowledge of the theory and techniques required to compose, produce, and perform works of music, dance, visual arts, drama, and sculpture.
History and Archeology	Knowledge of historical events and their causes, indicators, and effects on civilizations and cultures.

Skills	Skills Definitions
Speaking	Talking to others to convey information effectively.
Active Listening	Giving full attention to what other people are saying. taking time to understand the points being made. asking questions as appropriate. and not interrupting at inappropriate times.
Time Management	Managing one's own time and the time of others.

Reading Comprehension	Understanding written sentences and paragraphs in work related documents.
Instructing	Teaching others how to do something.
Monitoring	Monitoring/Assessing performance of yourself, other individuals. or organizations to make improvements or take corrective action.
Mathematics	Using mathematics to solve problems.
Service Orientation	Actively looking for ways to help people.
Social Perceptiveness	Being aware of others' reactions and understanding why they react as they do.
Management of Personnel Resources	Motivating, developing, and directing people as they work. identifying the best people for the job.
Learning Strategies	Selecting and using training/instructional methods and procedures appropriate for the situation when learning or teaching new things.
Critical Thinking	Using logic and reasoning to identify the strengths and weaknesses of alternative solutions. conclusions or approaches to problems.
Active Learning	Understanding the implications of new information for both current and future problem-solving and decision-making.
Judgment and Decision Making	Considering the relative costs and benefits of potential actions to choose the most appropriate one.
Coordination	Adjusting actions in relation to others' actions.
Equipment Maintenance	Performing routine maintenance on equipment and determining when and what kind of maintenance is needed.
Quality Control Analysis	Conducting tests and inspections of products, services, or processes to evaluate quality or performance.
Writing	Communicating effectively in writing as appropriate for the needs of the audience.
Operation Monitoring	Watching gauges, dials, or other indicators to make sure a machine is working properly.
Management of Financial Resources	Determining how money will be spent to get the work done, and accounting for these expenditures.
Troubleshooting	Determining causes of operating errors and deciding what to do about it.
Negotiation	Bringing others together and trying to reconcile differences.
Management of Material Resources	Obtaining and seeing to the appropriate use of equipment, facilities, and materials needed to do certain work.
Persuasion	Persuading others to change their minds or behavior.
Equipment Selection	Determining the kind of tools and equipment needed to do a job.
Complex Problem Solving	Identifying complex problems and reviewing related information to develop and evaluate options and implement solutions.
Repairing	Repairing machines or systems using the needed tools.
Operations Analysis	Analyzing needs and product requirements to create a design.
Operation and Control	Controlling operations of equipment or systems.
Systems Evaluation	Identifying measures or indicators of system performance and the actions needed to improve or correct performance, relative to the goals of the system.
Systems Analysis	Determining how a system should work and how changes in conditions, operations, and the environment will affect outcomes.
Science	Using scientific rules and methods to solve problems.
Technology Design	Generating or adapting equipment and technology to serve user needs.
Installation	Installing equipment, machines, wiring, or programs to meet specifications.
Programming	Writing computer programs for various purposes.

Ability	Ability Definitions
Oral Expression	The ability to communicate information and ideas in speaking so others will understand.
Oral Comprehension	The ability to listen to and understand information and ideas presented through spoken words and sentences.
Speech Clarity	The ability to speak clearly so others can understand you.
Problem Sensitivity	The ability to tell when something is wrong or is likely to go wrong. It does not involve solving the problem. only recognizing there is a problem.
Speech Recognition	The ability to identify and understand the speech of another person.
Information Ordering	The ability to arrange things or actions in a certain order or pattern according to a specific rule or set of rules (e.g., patterns of numbers, letters, words, pictures, mathematical operations).
Deductive Reasoning	The ability to apply general rules to specific problems to produce answers that make sense.

Near Vision	The ability to see details at close range (within a few feet of the observer).
Inductive Reasoning	The ability to combine pieces of information to form general rules or conclusions (includes finding a relationship among seemingly unrelated events).
Time Sharing	The ability to shift back and forth between two or more activities or sources of information (such as speech, sounds, touch, or other sources).
Category Flexibility	The ability to generate or use different sets of rules for combining or grouping things in different ways.
Written Comprehension	The ability to read and understand information and ideas presented in writing.
Selective Attention	The ability to concentrate on a task over a period of time without being distracted.
Trunk Strength	The ability to use your abdominal and lower back muscles to support part of the body repeatedly or continuously over time without 'giving out' or fatiguing.
Written Expression	The ability to communicate information and ideas in writing so others will understand.
Manual Dexterity	The ability to quickly move your hand, your hand together with your arm, or your two hands to grasp, manipulate, or assemble objects.
Arm-Hand Steadiness	The ability to keep your hand and arm steady while moving your arm or while holding your arm and hand in one position.
Fluency of Ideas	The ability to come up with a number of ideas about a topic (the number of ideas is important, not their quality, correctness, or creativity).
Stamina	The ability to exert yourself physically over long periods of time without getting winded or out of breath.
Memorization	The ability to remember information such as words, numbers, pictures, and procedures.
Gross Body Coordination	The ability to coordinate the movement of your arms, legs, and torso together when the whole body is in motion.
Mathematical Reasoning	The ability to choose the right mathematical methods or formulas to solve a problem.
Originality	The ability to come up with unusual or clever ideas about a given topic or situation, or to develop creative ways to solve a problem.
Speed of Closure	The ability to quickly make sense of, combine, and organize information into meaningful patterns.
Number Facility	The ability to add, subtract, multiply, or divide quickly and correctly.
Extent Flexibility	The ability to bend, stretch, twist, or reach with your body, arms, and/or legs.
Perceptual Speed	The ability to quickly and accurately compare similarities and differences among sets of letters, numbers, objects, pictures, or patterns. The things to be compared may be presented at the same time or one after the other. This ability also includes comparing a presented object with a remembered object.
Visualization	The ability to imagine how something will look after it is moved around or when its parts are moved or rearranged.
Flexibility of Closure	The ability to identify or detect a known pattern (a figure, object, word, or sound) that is hidden in other distracting material.
Far Vision	The ability to see details at a distance.
Multilimb Coordination	The ability to coordinate two or more limbs (for example, two arms, two legs, or one leg and one arm) while sitting, standing, or lying down. It does not involve performing the activities while the whole body is in motion.
Static Strength	The ability to exert maximum muscle force to lift, push, pull, or carry objects.
Auditory Attention	The ability to focus on a single source of sound in the presence of other distracting sounds.
Speed of Limb Movement	The ability to quickly move the arms and legs.
Control Precision	The ability to quickly and repeatedly adjust the controls of a machine or a vehicle to exact positions.
Finger Dexterity	The ability to make precisely coordinated movements of the fingers of one or both hands to grasp, manipulate, or assemble very small objects.
Visual Color Discrimination	The ability to match or detect differences between colors, including shades of color and brightness.
Dynamic Strength	The ability to exert muscle force repeatedly or continuously over time. This involves muscular endurance and resistance to muscle fatigue.
Wrist-Finger Speed	The ability to make fast, simple, repeated movements of the fingers, hands, and wrists.

Depth Perception	The ability to judge which of several objects is closer or farther away from you, or to judge the distance between you and an object.
Response Orientation	The ability to choose quickly between two or more movements in response to two or more different signals (lights, sounds, pictures). It includes the speed with which the correct response is started with the hand, foot, or other body part.
Gross Body Equilibrium	The ability to keep or regain your body balance or stay upright when in an unstable position.
Reaction Time	The ability to quickly respond (with the hand, finger, or foot) to a signal (sound, light, picture) when it appears.
Rate Control	The ability to time your movements or the movement of a piece of equipment in anticipation of changes in the speed and/or direction of a moving object or scene.
Hearing Sensitivity	The ability to detect or tell the differences between sounds that vary in pitch and loudness.
Explosive Strength	The ability to use short bursts of muscle force to propel oneself (as in jumping or sprinting), or to throw an object.
Night Vision	The ability to see under low light conditions.
Peripheral Vision	The ability to see objects or movement of objects to one's side when the eyes are looking ahead.
Glare Sensitivity	The ability to see objects in the presence of glare or bright lighting.
Sound Localization	The ability to tell the direction from which a sound originated.
Spatial Orientation	The ability to know your location in relation to the environment or to know where other objects are in relation to you.
Dynamic Flexibility	The ability to quickly and repeatedly bend, stretch, twist, or reach out with your body, arms, and/or legs.

Work_Activity	Work_Activity Definitions
Performing for or Working Directly with the Public	Performing for people or dealing directly with the public. This includes serving customers in restaurants and stores, and receiving clients or guests.
Identifying Objects, Actions, and Events	Identifying information by categorizing, estimating, recognizing differences or similarities, and detecting changes in circumstances or events.
Getting Information	Observing, receiving, and otherwise obtaining information from all relevant sources.
Making Decisions and Solving Problems	Analyzing information and evaluating results to choose the best solution and solve problems.
Communicating with Supervisors, Peers, or Subordin	Providing information to supervisors, co-workers, and subordinates by telephone, in written form, e-mail, or in person.
Establishing and Maintaining Interpersonal Relatio	Developing constructive and cooperative working relationships with others, and maintaining them over time.
Training and Teaching Others	Identifying the educational needs of others, developing formal educational or training programs or classes, and teaching or instructing others.
Evaluating Information to Determine Compliance wit	Using relevant information and individual judgment to determine whether events or processes comply with laws, regulations, or standards.
Resolving Conflicts and Negotiating with Others	Handling complaints, settling disputes, and resolving grievances and conflicts, or otherwise negotiating with others.
Selling or Influencing Others	Convincing others to buy merchandise/goods or to otherwise change their minds or actions.
Monitor Processes, Materials, or Surroundings	Monitoring and reviewing information from materials, events, or the environment, to detect or assess problems.
Guiding, Directing, and Motivating Subordinates	Providing guidance and direction to subordinates, including setting performance standards and monitoring performance.
Performing Administrative Activities	Performing day-to-day administrative tasks such as maintaining information files and processing paperwork.
Handling and Moving Objects	Using hands and arms in handling, installing, positioning, and moving materials, and manipulating things.
Coordinating the Work and Activities of Others	Getting members of a group to work together to accomplish tasks.
Performing General Physical Activities	Performing physical activities that require considerable use of your arms and legs and moving your whole body, such as climbing, lifting, balancing, walking, stooping, and handling of materials.
Inspecting Equipment, Structures, or Material	Inspecting equipment, structures, or materials to identify the cause of errors or other problems or defects.
Interacting With Computers	Using computers and computer systems (including hardware and software) to program, write software, set up functions, enter data, or process information.

Judging the Qualities of Things, Services, or Peop	Assessing the value, importance, or quality of things or people.
Communicating with Persons Outside Organization	Communicating with people outside the organization, representing the organization to customers, the public, government, and other external sources. This information can be exchanged in person, in writing, or by telephone or e-mail.
Coaching and Developing Others	Identifying the developmental needs of others and coaching, mentoring, or otherwise helping others to improve their knowledge or skills.
Developing and Building Teams	Encouraging and building mutual trust, respect, and cooperation among team members.
Organizing, Planning, and Prioritizing Work	Developing specific goals and plans to prioritize, organize, and accomplish your work.
Processing Information	Compiling, coding, categorizing, calculating, tabulating, auditing, or verifying information or data.
Documenting/Recording Information	Entering, transcribing, recording, storing, or maintaining information in written or electronic/magnetic form.
Estimating the Quantifiable Characteristics of Pro	Estimating sizes, distances, and quantities; or determining time, costs, resources, or materials needed to perform a work activity.
Controlling Machines and Processes	Using either control mechanisms or direct physical activity to operate machines or processes (not including computers or vehicles).
Updating and Using Relevant Knowledge	Keeping up-to-date technically and applying new knowledge to your job.
Scheduling Work and Activities	Scheduling events, programs, and activities, as well as the work of others.
Monitoring and Controlling Resources	Monitoring and controlling resources and overseeing the spending of money.
Interpreting the Meaning of Information for Others	Translating or explaining what information means and how it can be used.
Thinking Creatively	Developing, designing, or creating new applications, ideas, relationships, systems, or products, including artistic contributions.
Provide Consultation and Advice to Others	Providing guidance and expert advice to management or other groups on technical, systems-, or process-related topics.
Staffing Organizational Units	Recruiting, interviewing, selecting, hiring, and promoting employees in an organization.
Developing Objectives and Strategies	Establishing long-range objectives and specifying the strategies and actions to achieve them.
Assisting and Caring for Others	Providing personal assistance, medical attention, emotional support, or other personal care to others such as coworkers, customers, or patients.
Analyzing Data or Information	Identifying the underlying principles, reasons, or facts of information by breaking down information or data into separate parts.
Operating Vehicles, Mechanized Devices, or Equipme	Running, maneuvering, navigating, or driving vehicles or mechanized equipment, such as forklifts, passenger vehicles, aircraft, or water craft.
Repairing and Maintaining Mechanical Equipment	Servicing, repairing, adjusting, and testing machines, devices, moving parts, and equipment that operate primarily on the basis of mechanical (not electronic) principles.
Repairing and Maintaining Electronic Equipment	Servicing, repairing, calibrating, regulating, fine-tuning, or testing machines, devices, and equipment that operate primarily on the basis of electrical or electronic (not mechanical) principles.
Drafting, Laying Out, and Specifying Technical Dev	Providing documentation, detailed instructions, drawings, or specifications to tell others about how devices, parts, equipment, or structures are to be fabricated, constructed, assembled, modified, maintained, or used.

Work_Context	Work_Context Definitions
Face-to-Face Discussions	How often do you have to have face-to-face discussions with individuals or teams in this job?
Contact With Others	How much does this job require the worker to be in contact with others (face-to-face, by telephone, or otherwise) in order to perform it?
Telephone	How often do you have telephone conversations in this job?
Work With Work Group or Team	How important is it to work with others in a group or team in this job?
Indoors, Environmentally Controlled	How often does this job require working indoors in environmentally controlled conditions?
Spend Time Standing	How much does this job require standing?
Physical Proximity	To what extent does this job require the worker to perform job tasks in close physical proximity to other people?
Responsible for Others' Health and Safety	How much responsibility is there for the health and safety of others in this job?

Freedom to Make Decisions	How much decision making freedom, without supervision, does the job offer?
Frequency of Decision Making	How frequently is the worker required to make decisions that affect other people, the financial resources, and/or the image and reputation of the organization?
Responsibility for Outcomes and Results	How responsible is the worker for work outcomes and results of other workers?
Coordinate or Lead Others	How important is it to coordinate or lead others in accomplishing work activities in this job?
Structured versus Unstructured Work	To what extent is this job structured for the worker, rather than allowing the worker to determine tasks, priorities, and goals?
Impact of Decisions on Co-workers or Company Resul	How do the decisions an employee makes impact the results of co-workers, clients or the company?
Spend Time Walking and Running	How much does this job require walking and running?
Frequency of Conflict Situations	How often are there conflict situations the employee has to face in this job?
Deal With Unpleasant or Angry People	How frequently does the worker have to deal with unpleasant, angry, or discourteous individuals as part of the job requirements?
Deal With External Customers	How important is it to work with external customers or the public in this job?
Spend Time Making Repetitive Motions	How much does this job require making repetitive motions?
Importance of Being Exact or Accurate	How important is being very exact or highly accurate in performing this job?
Spend Time Using Your Hands to Handle, Control, or	How much does this job require using your hands to handle, control, or feel objects, tools or controls?
Time Pressure	How often does this job require the worker to meet strict deadlines?
Exposed to Minor Burns, Cuts, Bites, or Stings	How often does this job require exposure to minor burns, cuts, bites, or stings?
Importance of Repeating Same Tasks	How important is repeating the same physical activities (e.g., key entry) or mental activities (e.g., checking entries in a ledger) over and over, without stopping, to performing this job?
Sounds, Noise Levels Are Distracting or Uncomforta	How often does this job require working exposed to sounds and noise levels that are distracting or uncomfortable?
Very Hot or Cold Temperatures	How often does this job require working in very hot (above 90 F degrees) or very cold (below 32 F degrees) temperatures?
Wear Common Protective or Safety Equipment such as	How much does this job require wearing common protective or safety equipment such as safety shoes, glasses, gloves, hard hats or live jackets?
Consequence of Error	How serious would the result usually be if the worker made a mistake that was not readily correctable?
Level of Competition	To what extent does this job require the worker to compete or to be aware of competitive pressures?
Letters and Memos	How often does the job require written letters and memos?
Spend Time Bending or Twisting the Body	How much does this job require bending or twisting your body?
Exposed to Contaminants	How often does this job require working exposed to contaminants (such as pollutants, gases, dust or odors)?
Public Speaking	How often do you have to perform public speaking in this job?
Deal With Physically Aggressive People	How frequently does this job require the worker to deal with physical aggression of violent individuals?
Indoors, Not Environmentally Controlled	How often does this job require working indoors in non-controlled environmental conditions (e.g., warehouse without heat)?
Electronic Mail	How often do you use electronic mail in this job?
Degree of Automation	How automated is the job?
Exposed to Disease or Infections	How often does this job require exposure to disease/infections?
Pace Determined by Speed of Equipment	How important is it to this job that the pace is determined by the speed of equipment or machinery? (This does not refer to keeping busy at all times on this job.)
Exposed to Hazardous Equipment	How often does this job require exposure to hazardous equipment?
Exposed to Hazardous Conditions	How often does this job require exposure to hazardous conditions?
Extremely Bright or Inadequate Lighting	How often does this job require working in extremely bright or inadequate lighting conditions?
Spend Time Sitting	How much does this job require sitting?
Spend Time Keeping or Regaining Balance	How much does this job require keeping or regaining your balance?
Outdoors, Exposed to Weather	How often does this job require working outdoors, exposed to all weather conditions?

In an Enclosed Vehicle or Equipment	How often does this job require working in a closed vehicle or equipment (e.g., car)?
Spend Time Kneeling. Crouching. Stooping. or Crawl	How much does this job require kneeling. crouching. stooping or crawling?
Cramped Work Space. Awkward Positions	How often does this job require working in cramped work spaces that requires getting into awkward positions?
Exposed to High Places	How often does this job require exposure to high places?
Outdoors. Under Cover	How often does this job require working outdoors. under cover (e.g., structure with roof but no walls)?
Wear Specialized Protective or Safety Equipment su	How much does this job require wearing specialized protective or safety equipment such as breathing apparatus. safety harness. full protection suits, or radiation protection?
Exposed to Radiation	How often does this job require exposure to radiation?
In an Open Vehicle or Equipment	How often does this job require working in an open vehicle or equipment (e.g., tractor)?
Spend Time Climbing Ladders. Scaffolds. or Poles	How much does this job require climbing ladders. scaffolds. or poles?
Exposed to Whole Body Vibration	How often does this job require exposure to whole body vibration (e.g., operate a jackhammer)?

Job Zone Component	Job Zone Component Definitions
Title	Job Zone Two: Some Preparation Needed
	Some previous work-related skill, knowledge. or experience may be helpful in these occupations. but usually is not needed.
Overall Experience	For example, a drywall installer might benefit from experience installing drywall, but an inexperienced person could still learn to be an installer with little difficulty.
Job Training	Employees in these occupations need anywhere from a few months to one year of working with experienced employees. These occupations often involve using your knowledge and skills to help others. Examples include drywall installers. fire inspectors, flight attendants, pharmacy technicians.
Job Zone Examples	salespersons (retail), and tellers.
SVP Range	(4.0 to < 6.0)
Education	These occupations usually require a high school diploma and may require some vocational training or job-related course work. In some cases, an associate's or bachelor's degree could be needed.

Work_Styles	Work_Styles Definitions
Dependability	Job requires being reliable, responsible. and dependable, and fulfilling obligations.
Cooperation	Job requires being pleasant with others on the job and displaying a good-natured, cooperative attitude.
Self Control	Job requires maintaining composure, keeping emotions in check, controlling anger, and avoiding aggressive behavior, even in very difficult situations.
Leadership	Job requires a willingness to lead, take charge, and offer opinions and direction.
Stress Tolerance	Job requires accepting criticism and dealing calmly and effectively with high stress situations.
Integrity	Job requires being honest and ethical.
Initiative	Job requires a willingness to take on responsibilities and challenges.
Attention to Detail	Job requires being careful about detail and thorough in completing work tasks.
Adaptability/Flexibility	Job requires being open to change (positive or negative) and to considerable variety in the workplace.
Concern for Others	Job requires being sensitive to others' needs and feelings and being understanding and helpful on the job.
Social Orientation	Job requires preferring to work with others rather than alone, and being personally connected with others on the job.
Independence	Job requires developing one's own ways of doing things, guiding oneself with little or no supervision, and depending on oneself to get things done.
Persistence	Job requires persistence in the face of obstacles.
Achievement/Effort	Job requires establishing and maintaining personally challenging achievement goals and exerting effort toward mastering tasks.
Analytical Thinking	Job requires analyzing information and using logic to address work-related issues and problems.
Innovation	Job requires creativity and alternative thinking to develop new ideas for and answers to work-related problems.

35-2012.00 - Cooks, Institution and Cafeteria

Prepare and cook large quantities of food for institutions. such as schools. hospitals. or cafeterias.

Tasks

1) Cook foodstuffs according to menus. special dietary or nutritional restrictions. and numbers of portions to be served.

2) Clean. cut. and cook meat. fish. and poultry.

3) Clean and inspect galley equipment. kitchen appliances. and work areas in order to ensure cleanliness and functional operation.

4) Take inventory of supplies and equipment.

5) Wash pots, pans, dishes, utensils. and other cooking equipment.

6) Train new employees.

7) Plan menus that are varied, nutritionally balanced. and appetizing. taking advantage of foods in season and local availability.

8) Apportion and serve food to facility residents. employees, or patrons.

9) Direct activities of one or more workers who assist in preparing and serving meals.

10) Bake breads. rolls, and other pastries.

11) Determine meal prices based on calculations of ingredient prices.

12) Compile and maintain records of food use and expenditures.

13) Monitor menus and spending in order to ensure that meals are prepared economically.

14) Monitor use of government food commodities to ensure that proper procedures are followed.

35-2014.00 - Cooks, Restaurant

Prepare, season, and cook soups. meats. vegetables. desserts, or other foodstuffs in restaurants. May order supplies, keep records and accounts, price items on menu, or plan menu.

Tasks

1) Season and cook food according to recipes or personal judgment and experience.

2) Portion, arrange, and garnish food, and serve food to waiters or patrons.

3) Observe and test foods to determine if they have been cooked sufficiently, using methods such as tasting, smelling, or piercing them with utensils.

4) Weigh, measure, and mix ingredients according to recipes or personal judgment, using various kitchen utensils and equipment.

5) Regulate temperature of ovens, broilers, grills, and roasters.

6) Substitute for or assist other cooks during emergencies or rush periods.

7) Wash, peel, cut, and seed fruits and vegetables to prepare them for consumption.

8) Inspect food preparation and serving areas to ensure observance of safe, sanitary food-handling practices.

9) Bake, roast, broil, and steam meats. fish, vegetables, and other foods.

10) Carve and trim meats such as beef, veal, ham, pork, and lamb for hot or cold service, or for sandwiches.

11) Estimate expected food consumption); then requisition or purchase supplies, or procure food from storage.

12) Coordinate and supervise work of kitchen staff.

13) Consult with supervisory staff to plan menus, taking into consideration factors such as costs and special event needs.

14) Butcher and dress animals, fowl, or shellfish, or cut and bone meat prior to cooking.

15) Bake breads, rolls, cakes, and pastries.

16) Prepare relishes and hors d'oeuvres.

17) Plan and price menu items.

18) Keep records and accounts.

Knowledge	Knowledge Definitions
Food Production	Knowledge of techniques and equipment for planting, growing, and harvesting food products (both plant and animal) for consumption, including storage/handling techniques.
Customer and Personal Service	Knowledge of principles and processes for providing customer and personal services. This includes customer needs assessment, meeting quality standards for services, and evaluation of customer satisfaction.
Production and Processing	Knowledge of raw materials, production processes, quality control, costs, and other techniques for maximizing the effective manufacture and distribution of goods.
Administration and Management	Knowledge of business and management principles involved in strategic planning, resource allocation, human resources modeling, leadership technique, production methods, and coordination of people and resources.
English Language	Knowledge of the structure and content of the English language including the meaning and spelling of words, rules of composition, and grammar.
Education and Training	Knowledge of principles and methods for curriculum and training design, teaching and instruction for individuals and groups, and the measurement of training effects.
Mathematics	Knowledge of arithmetic, algebra, geometry, calculus, statistics, and their applications.
Public Safety and Security	Knowledge of relevant equipment, policies, procedures, and strategies to promote effective local, state, or national security operations for the protection of people, data, property, and institutions.
Chemistry	Knowledge of the chemical composition, structure, and properties of substances and of the chemical processes and transformations that they undergo. This includes uses of chemicals and their interactions, danger signs, production techniques, and disposal methods.
Sales and Marketing	Knowledge of principles and methods for showing, promoting, and selling products or services. This includes marketing strategy and tactics, product demonstration, sales techniques, and sales control systems.
Foreign Language	Knowledge of the structure and content of a foreign (non-English) language including the meaning and spelling of words, rules of composition and grammar, and pronunciation.
Personnel and Human Resources	Knowledge of principles and procedures for personnel recruitment, selection, training, compensation and benefits, labor relations and negotiation, and personnel information systems.
Mechanical	Knowledge of machines and tools, including their designs, uses, repair, and maintenance.
Law and Government	Knowledge of laws, legal codes, court procedures, precedents, government regulations, executive orders, agency rules, and the democratic political process.
Transportation	Knowledge of principles and methods for moving people or goods by air, rail, sea, or road, including the relative costs and benefits.
Computers and Electronics	Knowledge of circuit boards, processors, chips, electronic equipment, and computer hardware and software, including applications and programming.
Clerical	Knowledge of administrative and clerical procedures and systems such as word processing, managing files and records, stenography and transcription, designing forms, and other office procedures and terminology.
Psychology	Knowledge of human behavior and performance; individual differences in ability, personality, and interests; learning and motivation; psychological research methods; and the assessment and treatment of behavioral and affective disorders.
Economics and Accounting	Knowledge of economic and accounting principles and practices, the financial markets, banking and the analysis and reporting of financial data.
Design	Knowledge of design techniques, tools, and principles involved in production of precision technical plans, blueprints, drawings, and models.
Communications and Media	Knowledge of media production, communication, and dissemination techniques and methods. This includes alternative ways to inform and entertain via written, oral, and visual media.
Engineering and Technology	Knowledge of the practical application of engineering science and technology. This includes applying principles, techniques, procedures, and equipment to the design and production of various goods and services.
Geography	Knowledge of principles and methods for describing the features of land, sea, and air masses, including their physical characteristics, locations, interrelationships, and distribution of plant, animal, and human life.
Telecommunications	Knowledge of transmission, broadcasting, switching, control, and operation of telecommunications systems.
Medicine and Dentistry	Knowledge of the information and techniques needed to diagnose and treat human injuries, diseases, and deformities. This includes symptoms, treatment alternatives, drug properties and interactions, and preventive health-care measures.
Biology	Knowledge of plant and animal organisms, their tissues, cells, functions, interdependencies, and interactions with each other and the environment.
Physics	Knowledge and prediction of physical principles, laws, their interrelationships, and applications to understanding fluid, material, and atmospheric dynamics, and mechanical, electrical, atomic and sub-atomic structures and processes.
Building and Construction	Knowledge of materials, methods, and the tools involved in the construction or repair of houses, buildings, or other structures such as highways and roads.
Therapy and Counseling	Knowledge of principles, methods, and procedures for diagnosis, treatment, and rehabilitation of physical and mental dysfunctions, and for career counseling and guidance.
History and Archeology	Knowledge of historical events and their causes, indicators, and effects on civilizations and cultures.
Sociology and Anthropology	Knowledge of group behavior and dynamics, societal trends and influences, human migrations, ethnicity, cultures and their history and origins.
Philosophy and Theology	Knowledge of different philosophical systems and religions. This includes their basic principles, values, ethics, ways of thinking, customs, practices, and their impact on human culture.
Fine Arts	Knowledge of the theory and techniques required to compose, produce, and perform works of music, dance, visual arts, drama, and sculpture.

Skills	Skills Definitions
Active Listening	Giving full attention to what other people are saying, taking time to understand the points being made, asking questions as appropriate, and not interrupting at inappropriate times.
Reading Comprehension	Understanding written sentences and paragraphs in work related documents.
Speaking	Talking to others to convey information effectively.
Active Learning	Understanding the implications of new information for both current and future problem-solving and decision-making.
Instructing	Teaching others how to do something.
Learning Strategies	Selecting and using training/instructional methods and procedures appropriate for the situation when learning or teaching new things.
Social Perceptiveness	Being aware of others' reactions and understanding why they react as they do.
Coordination	Adjusting actions in relation to others' actions.
Time Management	Managing one's own time and the time of others.
Critical Thinking	Using logic and reasoning to identify the strengths and weaknesses of alternative solutions, conclusions or approaches to problems.
Equipment Selection	Determining the kind of tools and equipment needed to do a job.
Judgment and Decision Making	Considering the relative costs and benefits of potential actions to choose the most appropriate one.
Service Orientation	Actively looking for ways to help people.
Mathematics	Using mathematics to solve problems.
Management of Personnel Resources	Motivating, developing, and directing people as they work, identifying the best people for the job.
Equipment Maintenance	Performing routine maintenance on equipment and determining when and what kind of maintenance is needed.
Monitoring	Monitoring/Assessing performance of yourself, other individuals, or organizations to make improvements or take corrective action.
Negotiation	Bringing others together and trying to reconcile differences.
Quality Control Analysis	Conducting tests and inspections of products, services, or processes to evaluate quality or performance.
Troubleshooting	Determining causes of operating errors and deciding what to do about it.
Repairing	Repairing machines or systems using the needed tools.

Systems Evaluation	Identifying measures or indicators of system performance and the actions needed to improve or correct performance, relative to the goals of the system.
Complex Problem Solving	Identifying complex problems and reviewing related information to develop and evaluate options and implement solutions.
Management of Material Resources	Obtaining and seeing to the appropriate use of equipment, facilities, and materials needed to do certain work.
Operation Monitoring	Watching gauges, dials, or other indicators to make sure a machine is working properly.
Operation and Control	Controlling operations of equipment or systems.
Writing	Communicating effectively in writing as appropriate for the needs of the audience.
Persuasion	Persuading others to change their minds or behavior.
Systems Analysis	Determining how a system should work and how changes in conditions, operations, and the environment will affect outcomes.
Operations Analysis	Analyzing needs and product requirements to create a design.
Management of Financial Resources	Determining how money will be spent to get the work done, and accounting for these expenditures.
Installation	Installing equipment, machines, wiring, or programs to meet specifications.
Technology Design	Generating or adapting equipment and technology to serve user needs.
Science	Using scientific rules and methods to solve problems.
Programming	Writing computer programs for various purposes.

Ability / **Ability Definitions**

Problem Sensitivity	The ability to tell when something is wrong or is likely to go wrong. It does not involve solving the problem, only recognizing there is a problem.
Near Vision	The ability to see details at close range (within a few feet of the observer).
Time Sharing	The ability to shift back and forth between two or more activities or sources of information (such as speech, sounds, touch, or other sources).
Information Ordering	The ability to arrange things or actions in a certain order or pattern according to a specific rule or set of rules (e.g., patterns of numbers, letters, words, pictures, mathematical operations).
Manual Dexterity	The ability to quickly move your hand, your hand together with your arm, or your two hands to grasp, manipulate, or assemble objects.
Oral Comprehension	The ability to listen to and understand information and ideas presented through spoken words and sentences.
Oral Expression	The ability to communicate information and ideas in speaking so others will understand.
Speech Clarity	The ability to speak clearly so others can understand you.
Speech Recognition	The ability to identify and understand the speech of another person.
Deductive Reasoning	The ability to apply general rules to specific problems to produce answers that make sense.
Inductive Reasoning	The ability to combine pieces of information to form general rules or conclusions (includes finding a relationship among seemingly unrelated events).
Multilimb Coordination	The ability to coordinate two or more limbs (for example, two arms, two legs, or one leg and one arm) while sitting, standing, or lying down. It does not involve performing the activities while the whole body is in motion.
Selective Attention	The ability to concentrate on a task over a period of time without being distracted.
Wrist-Finger Speed	The ability to make fast, simple, repeated movements of the fingers, hands, and wrists.
Arm-Hand Steadiness	The ability to keep your hand and arm steady while moving your arm or while holding your arm and hand in one position.
Perceptual Speed	The ability to quickly and accurately compare similarities and differences among sets of letters, numbers, objects, pictures, or patterns. The things to be compared may be presented at the same time or one after the other. This ability also includes comparing a presented object with a remembered object.
Category Flexibility	The ability to generate or use different sets of rules for combining or grouping things in different ways.
Originality	The ability to come up with unusual or clever ideas about a given topic or situation, or to develop creative ways to solve a problem.
Written Comprehension	The ability to read and understand information and ideas presented in writing.

Mathematical Reasoning	The ability to choose the right mathematical methods or formulas to solve a problem.
Memorization	The ability to remember information such as words, numbers, pictures, and procedures.
Trunk Strength	The ability to use your abdominal and lower back muscles to support part of the body repeatedly or continuously over time without 'giving out' or fatiguing.
Control Precision	The ability to quickly and repeatedly adjust the controls of a machine or a vehicle to exact positions.
Extent Flexibility	The ability to bend, stretch, twist, or reach with your body, arms, and/or legs.
Visualization	The ability to imagine how something will look after it is moved around or when its parts are moved or rearranged.
Written Expression	The ability to communicate information and ideas in writing so others will understand.
Fluency of Ideas	The ability to come up with a number of ideas about a topic (the number of ideas is important, not their quality, correctness, or creativity).
Number Facility	The ability to add, subtract, multiply, or divide quickly and correctly.
Speed of Limb Movement	The ability to quickly move the arms and legs.
Speed of Closure	The ability to quickly make sense of, combine, and organize information into meaningful patterns.
Gross Body Coordination	The ability to coordinate the movement of your arms, legs, and torso together when the whole body is in motion.
Dynamic Strength	The ability to exert muscle force repeatedly or continuously over time. This involves muscular endurance and resistance to muscle fatigue.
Spatial Orientation	The ability to know your location in relation to the environment or to know where other objects are in relation to you.
Reaction Time	The ability to quickly respond (with the hand, finger, or foot) to a signal (sound, light, picture) when it appears.
Depth Perception	The ability to judge which of several objects is closer or farther away from you, or to judge the distance between you and an object.
Visual Color Discrimination	The ability to match or detect differences between colors, including shades of color and brightness.
Auditory Attention	The ability to focus on a single source of sound in the presence of other distracting sounds.
Flexibility of Closure	The ability to identify or detect a known pattern (a figure, object, word, or sound) that is hidden in other distracting material.
Stamina	The ability to exert yourself physically over long periods of time without getting winded or out of breath.
Static Strength	The ability to exert maximum muscle force to lift, push, pull, or carry objects.
Finger Dexterity	The ability to make precisely coordinated movements of the fingers of one or both hands to grasp, manipulate, or assemble very small objects.
Response Orientation	The ability to choose quickly between two or more movements in response to two or more different signals (lights, sounds, pictures). It includes the speed with which the correct response is started with the hand, foot, or other body part.
Hearing Sensitivity	The ability to detect or tell the differences between sounds that vary in pitch and loudness.
Dynamic Flexibility	The ability to quickly and repeatedly bend, stretch, twist, or reach out with your body, arms, and/or legs.
Peripheral Vision	The ability to see objects or movement of objects to one's side when the eyes are looking ahead.
Rate Control	The ability to time your movements or the movement of a piece of equipment in anticipation of changes in the speed and/or direction of a moving object or scene.
Far Vision	The ability to see details at a distance.
Gross Body Equilibrium	The ability to keep or regain your body balance or stay upright when in an unstable position.
Explosive Strength	The ability to use short bursts of muscle force to propel oneself (as in jumping or sprinting), or to throw an object.
Sound Localization	The ability to tell the direction from which a sound originated.
Glare Sensitivity	The ability to see objects in the presence of glare or bright lighting.
Night Vision	The ability to see under low light conditions.

Work_Activity / **Work_Activity Definitions**

Getting Information	Observing, receiving, and otherwise obtaining information from all relevant sources.

Monitor Processes, Materials, or Surroundings	Monitoring and reviewing information from materials, events, or the environment, to detect or assess problems.
Inspecting Equipment, Structures, or Material	Inspecting equipment, structures, or materials to identify the cause of errors or other problems or defects.
Identifying Objects, Actions, and Events	Identifying information by categorizing, estimating, recognizing differences or similarities, and detecting changes in circumstances or events.
Handling and Moving Objects	Using hands and arms in handling, installing, positioning, and moving materials, and manipulating things.
Training and Teaching Others	Identifying the educational needs of others, developing formal educational or training programs or classes, and teaching or instructing others.
Communicating with Supervisors, Peers, or Subordin	Providing information to supervisors, co-workers, and subordinates by telephone, in written form, e-mail, or in person.
Making Decisions and Solving Problems	Analyzing information and evaluating results to choose the best solution and solve problems.
Performing General Physical Activities	Performing physical activities that require considerable use of your arms and legs and moving your whole body, such as climbing, lifting, balancing, walking, stooping, and handling of materials.
Judging the Qualities of Things, Services, or Peop	Assessing the value, importance, or quality of things or people.
Coordinating the Work and Activities of Others	Getting members of a group to work together to accomplish tasks.
Organizing, Planning, and Prioritizing Work	Developing specific goals and plans to prioritize, organize, and accomplish your work.
Evaluating Information to Determine Compliance wit	Using relevant information and individual judgment to determine whether events or processes comply with laws, regulations, or standards.
Processing Information	Compiling, coding, categorizing, calculating, tabulating, auditing, or verifying information or data.
Estimating the Quantifiable Characteristics of Pro	Estimating sizes, distances, and quantities; or determining time, costs, resources, or materials needed to perform a work activity.
Monitoring and Controlling Resources	Monitoring and controlling resources and overseeing the spending of money.
Coaching and Developing Others	Identifying the developmental needs of others and coaching, mentoring, or otherwise helping others to improve their knowledge or skills.
Controlling Machines and Processes	Using either control mechanisms or direct physical activity to operate machines or processes (not including computers or vehicles).
Resolving Conflicts and Negotiating with Others	Handling complaints, settling disputes, and resolving grievances and conflicts, or otherwise negotiating with others.
Establishing and Maintaining Interpersonal Relatio	Developing constructive and cooperative working relationships with others, and maintaining them over time.
Updating and Using Relevant Knowledge	Keeping up-to-date technically and applying new knowledge to your job.
Developing and Building Teams	Encouraging and building mutual trust, respect, and cooperation among team members.
Performing for or Working Directly with the Public	Performing for people or dealing directly with the public. This includes serving customers in restaurants and stores, and receiving clients or guests.
Guiding, Directing, and Motivating Subordinates	Providing guidance and direction to subordinates, including setting performance standards and monitoring performance.
Interpreting the Meaning of Information for Others	Translating or explaining what information means and how it can be used.
Scheduling Work and Activities	Scheduling events, programs, and activities, as well as the work of others.
Thinking Creatively	Developing, designing, or creating new applications, ideas, relationships, systems, or products, including artistic contributions.
Provide Consultation and Advice to Others	Providing guidance and expert advice to management or other groups on technical, systems-, or process-related topics.
Selling or Influencing Others	Convincing others to buy merchandise/goods or to otherwise change their minds or actions.
Documenting/Recording Information	Entering, transcribing, recording, storing, or maintaining information in written or electronic/magnetic form.
Assisting and Caring for Others	Providing personal assistance, medical attention, emotional support, or other personal care to others such as coworkers, customers, or patients.
Analyzing Data or Information	Identifying the underlying principles, reasons, or facts of information by breaking down information or data into separate parts.

Repairing and Maintaining Mechanical Equipment	Servicing, repairing, adjusting, and testing machines, devices, moving parts, and equipment that operate primarily on the basis of mechanical (not electronic) principles.
Communicating with Persons Outside Organization	Communicating with people outside the organization, representing the organization to customers, the public, government, and other external sources. This information can be exchanged in person, in writing, or by telephone or e-mail.
Developing Objectives and Strategies	Establishing long-range objectives and specifying the strategies and actions to achieve them.
Staffing Organizational Units	Recruiting, interviewing, selecting, hiring, and promoting employees in an organization.
Performing Administrative Activities	Performing day-to-day administrative tasks such as maintaining information files and processing paperwork.
Repairing and Maintaining Electronic Equipment	Servicing, repairing, calibrating, regulating, fine-tuning, or testing machines, devices, and equipment that operate primarily on the basis of electrical or electronic (not mechanical) principles.
Operating Vehicles, Mechanized Devices, or Equipme	Running, maneuvering, navigating, or driving vehicles or mechanized equipment, such as forklifts, passenger vehicles, aircraft, or water craft.
Interacting With Computers	Using computers and computer systems (including hardware and software) to program, write software, set up functions, enter data, or process information.
Drafting, Laying Out, and Specifying Technical Dev	Providing documentation, detailed instructions, drawings, or specifications to tell others about how devices, parts, equipment, or structures are to be fabricated, constructed, assembled, modified, maintained, or used.

Work_Context	Work_Context Definitions
Spend Time Standing	How much does this job require standing?
Face-to-Face Discussions	How often do you have to have face-to-face discussions with individuals or teams in this job?
Exposed to Minor Burns, Cuts, Bites, or Stings	How often does this job require exposure to minor burns, cuts, bites, or stings?
Contact With Others	How much does this job require the worker to be in contact with others (face-to-face, by telephone, or otherwise) in order to perform it?
Work With Work Group or Team	How important is it to work with others in a group or team in this job?
Spend Time Using Your Hands to Handle, Control, or	How much does this job require using your hands to handle, control, or feel objects, tools or controls?
Spend Time Making Repetitive Motions	How much does this job require making repetitive motions?
Physical Proximity	To what extent does this job require the worker to perform job tasks in close physical proximity to other people?
Indoors, Environmentally Controlled	How often does this job require working indoors in environmentally controlled conditions?
Very Hot or Cold Temperatures	How often does this job require working in very hot (above 90 F degrees) or very cold (below 32 F degrees) temperatures?
Freedom to Make Decisions	How much decision making freedom, without supervision, does the job offer?
Frequency of Decision Making	How frequently is the worker required to make decisions that affect other people, the financial resources, and/or the image and reputation of the organization?
Spend Time Walking and Running	How much does this job require walking and running?
Wear Common Protective or Safety Equipment such as	How much does this job require wearing common protective or safety equipment such as safety shoes, glasses, gloves, hard hats or live jackets?
Coordinate or Lead Others	How important is it to coordinate or lead others in accomplishing work activities in this job?
Time Pressure	How often does this job require the worker to meet strict deadlines?
Structured versus Unstructured Work	To what extent is this job structured for the worker, rather than allowing the worker to determine tasks, priorities, and goals?
Responsibility for Outcomes and Results	How responsible is the worker for work outcomes and results of other workers?
Impact of Decisions on Co-workers or Company Resul	How do the decisions an employee makes impact the results of co-workers, clients or the company?
Importance of Being Exact or Accurate	How important is being very exact or highly accurate in performing this job?
Responsible for Others' Health and Safety	How much responsibility is there for the health and safety of others in this job?

Deal With Unpleasant or Angry People	How frequently does the worker have to deal with unpleasant, angry, or discourteous individuals as part of the job requirements?
Frequency of Conflict Situations	How often are there conflict situations the employee has to face in this job?
Sounds, Noise Levels Are Distracting or Uncomforta	How often does this job require working exposed to sounds and noise levels that are distracting or uncomfortable?
Spend Time Bending or Twisting the Body	How much does this job require bending or twisting your body?
Importance of Repeating Same Tasks	How important is repeating the same physical activities (e.g., key entry) or mental activities (e.g., checking entries in a ledger) over and over, without stopping, to performing this job?
Exposed to Contaminants	How often does this job require working exposed to contaminants (such as pollutants, gases, dust or odors)?
Level of Competition	To what extent does this job require the worker to compete or to be aware of competitive pressures?
Deal With External Customers	How important is it to work with external customers or the public in this job?
Telephone	How often do you have telephone conversations in this job?
Letters and Memos	How often does the job require written letters and memos?
Exposed to Hazardous Equipment	How often does this job require exposure to hazardous equipment?
Spend Time Kneeling, Crouching, Stooping, or Crawl	How much does this job require kneeling, crouching, stooping or crawling?
Exposed to Hazardous Conditions	How often does this job require exposure to hazardous conditions?
Pace Determined by Speed of Equipment	How important is it to this job that the pace is determined by the speed of equipment or machinery? (This does not refer to keeping busy at all times on this job.)
Extremely Bright or Inadequate Lighting	How often does this job require working in extremely bright or inadequate lighting conditions?
Consequence of Error	How serious would the result usually be if the worker made a mistake that was not readily correctable?
Cramped Work Space, Awkward Positions	How often does this job require working in cramped work spaces that requires getting into awkward positions?
Public Speaking	How often do you have to perform public speaking in this job?
Indoors, Not Environmentally Controlled	How often does this job require working indoors in non-controlled environmental conditions (e.g., warehouse without heat)?
Spend Time Keeping or Regaining Balance	How much does this job require keeping or regaining your balance?
Degree of Automation	How automated is the job?
Deal With Physically Aggressive People	How frequently does this job require the worker to deal with physical aggression of violent individuals?
Exposed to Disease or Infections	How often does this job require exposure to disease/infections?
Wear Specialized Protective or Safety Equipment su	How much does this job require wearing specialized protective or safety equipment such as breathing apparatus, safety harness, full protection suits, or radiation protection?
Outdoors, Exposed to Weather	How often does this job require working outdoors, exposed to all weather conditions?
Electronic Mail	How often do you use electronic mail in this job?
Spend Time Sitting	How much does this job require sitting?
Spend Time Climbing Ladders, Scaffolds, or Poles	How much does this job require climbing ladders, scaffolds, or poles?
Exposed to High Places	How often does this job require exposure to high places?
In an Open Vehicle or Equipment	How often does this job require working in an open vehicle or equipment (e.g., tractor)?
Outdoors, Under Cover	How often does this job require working outdoors, under cover (e.g., structure with roof but no walls)?
Exposed to Whole Body Vibration	How often does this job require exposure to whole body vibration (e.g., operate a jackhammer)?
In an Enclosed Vehicle or Equipment	How often does this job require working in a closed vehicle or equipment (e.g., car)?
Exposed to Radiation	How often does this job require exposure to radiation?

Job Zone Component	Job Zone Component Definitions
Title	Job Zone Two: Some Preparation Needed
Overall Experience	Some previous work-related skill, knowledge, or experience may be helpful in these occupations, but usually is not needed. For example, a drywall installer might benefit from experience installing drywall, but an inexperienced person could still learn to be an installer with little difficulty.

Job Training	Employees in these occupations need anywhere from a few months to one year of working with experienced employees. These occupations often involve using your knowledge and skills to help others. Examples include drywall installers, fire inspectors, flight attendants, pharmacy technicians, salespersons (retail), and tellers.
Job Zone Examples	
SVP Range	(4.0 to 6.0)
Education	These occupations usually require a high school diploma and may require some vocational training or job-related course work. In some cases, an associate's or bachelor's degree could be needed.

Work_Styles	Work_Styles Definitions
Dependability	Job requires being reliable, responsible, and dependable, and fulfilling obligations.
Attention to Detail	Job requires being careful about detail and thorough in completing work tasks.
Cooperation	Job requires being pleasant with others on the job and displaying a good-natured, cooperative attitude.
Self Control	Job requires maintaining composure, keeping emotions in check, controlling anger, and avoiding aggressive behavior, even in very difficult situations.
Stress Tolerance	Job requires accepting criticism and dealing calmly and effectively with high stress situations.
Initiative	Job requires a willingness to take on responsibilities and challenges.
Achievement/Effort	Job requires establishing and maintaining personally challenging achievement goals and exerting effort toward mastering tasks.
Persistence	Job requires persistence in the face of obstacles.
Integrity	Job requires being honest and ethical.
Concern for Others	Job requires being sensitive to others' needs and feelings and being understanding and helpful on the job.
Social Orientation	Job requires preferring to work with others rather than alone, and being personally connected with others on the job.
Adaptability/Flexibility	Job requires being open to change (positive or negative) and to considerable variety in the workplace.
Leadership	Job requires a willingness to lead, take charge, and offer opinions and direction.
Independence	Job requires developing one's own ways of doing things, guiding oneself with little or no supervision, and depending on oneself to get things done.
Innovation	Job requires creativity and alternative thinking to develop new ideas for and answers to work-related problems.
Analytical Thinking	Job requires analyzing information and using logic to address work-related issues and problems.

35-2015.00 - Cooks, Short Order

Prepare and cook to order a variety of foods that require only a short preparation time. May take orders from customers and serve patrons at counters or tables.

Tasks

1) Grill and garnish hamburgers or other meats such as steaks and chops.

2) Plan work on orders so that items served together are finished at the same time.

3) Grill, cook, and fry foods such as french fries, eggs, and pancakes.

4) Order supplies and stock them on shelves.

5) Complete orders from steam tables, placing food on plates and serving customers at tables or counters.

6) Take orders from customers and cook foods requiring short preparation times, according to customer requirements.

7) Accept payments, and make change or write charge slips as necessary.

8) Clean food preparation equipment, work areas, and counters or tables.

Knowledge	Knowledge Definitions
Customer and Personal Service	Knowledge of principles and processes for providing customer and personal services. This includes customer needs assessment, meeting quality standards for services, and evaluation of customer satisfaction.
Food Production	Knowledge of techniques and equipment for planting, growing, and harvesting food products (both plant and animal) for consumption, including storage/handling techniques.
Production and Processing	Knowledge of raw materials, production processes, quality control, costs, and other techniques for maximizing the effective manufacture and distribution of goods.
English Language	Knowledge of the structure and content of the English language including the meaning and spelling of words, rules of composition, and grammar.
Education and Training	Knowledge of principles and methods for curriculum and training design, teaching and instruction for individuals and groups, and the measurement of training effects.
Mathematics	Knowledge of arithmetic, algebra, geometry, calculus, statistics, and their applications.
Administration and Management	Knowledge of business and management principles involved in strategic planning, resource allocation, human resources modeling, leadership technique, production methods, and coordination of people and resources.
Public Safety and Security	Knowledge of relevant equipment, policies, procedures, and strategies to promote effective local, state, or national security operations for the protection of people, data, property, and institutions.
Mechanical	Knowledge of machines and tools, including their designs, uses, repair, and maintenance.
Personnel and Human Resources	Knowledge of principles and procedures for personnel recruitment, selection, training, compensation and benefits, labor relations and negotiation, and personnel information systems.
Sales and Marketing	Knowledge of principles and methods for showing, promoting, and selling products or services. This includes marketing strategy and tactics, product demonstration, sales techniques, and sales control systems.
Psychology	Knowledge of human behavior and performance; individual differences in ability, personality, and interests; learning and motivation; psychological research methods; and the assessment and treatment of behavioral and affective disorders.
Foreign Language	Knowledge of the structure and content of a foreign (non-English) language including the meaning and spelling of words, rules of composition and grammar, and pronunciation.
Transportation	Knowledge of principles and methods for moving people or goods by air, rail, sea, or road, including the relative costs and benefits.
Chemistry	Knowledge of the chemical composition, structure, and properties of substances and of the chemical processes and transformations that they undergo. This includes uses of chemicals and their interactions, danger signs, production techniques, and disposal methods.
Geography	Knowledge of principles and methods for describing the features of land, sea, and air masses, including their physical characteristics, locations, interrelationships, and distribution of plant, animal, and human life.
Economics and Accounting	Knowledge of economic and accounting principles and practices, the financial markets, banking and the analysis and reporting of financial data.
Law and Government	Knowledge of laws, legal codes, court procedures, precedents, government regulations, executive orders, agency rules, and the democratic political process.
Communications and Media	Knowledge of media production, communication, and dissemination techniques and methods. This includes alternative ways to inform and entertain via written, oral, and visual media.
Telecommunications	Knowledge of transmission, broadcasting, switching, control, and operation of telecommunications systems.
Medicine and Dentistry	Knowledge of the information and techniques needed to diagnose and treat human injuries, diseases, and deformities. This includes symptoms, treatment alternatives, drug properties and interactions, and preventive health-care measures.
Biology	Knowledge of plant and animal organisms, their tissues, cells, functions, interdependencies, and interactions with each other and the environment.
Sociology and Anthropology	Knowledge of group behavior and dynamics, societal trends and influences, human migrations, ethnicity, cultures and their history and origins.
Therapy and Counseling	Knowledge of principles, methods, and procedures for diagnosis, treatment, and rehabilitation of physical and mental dysfunctions, and for career counseling and guidance.
Engineering and Technology	Knowledge of the practical application of engineering science and technology. This includes applying principles, techniques, procedures, and equipment to the design and production of various goods and services.
Clerical	Knowledge of administrative and clerical procedures and systems such as word processing, managing files and records, stenography and transcription, designing forms, and other office procedures and terminology.
Computers and Electronics	Knowledge of circuit boards, processors, chips, electronic equipment, and computer hardware and software, including applications and programming.
Physics	Knowledge and prediction of physical principles, laws, their interrelationships, and applications to understanding fluid, material, and atmospheric dynamics, and mechanical, electrical, atomic and sub-atomic structures and processes.
Design	Knowledge of design techniques, tools, and principles involved in production of precision technical plans, blueprints, drawings, and models.
History and Archeology	Knowledge of historical events and their causes, indicators, and effects on civilizations and cultures.
Building and Construction	Knowledge of materials, methods, and the tools involved in the construction or repair of houses, buildings, or other structures such as highways and roads.
Philosophy and Theology	Knowledge of different philosophical systems and religions. This includes their basic principles, values, ethics, ways of thinking, customs, practices, and their impact on human culture.
Fine Arts	Knowledge of the theory and techniques required to compose, produce, and perform works of music, dance, visual arts, drama, and sculpture.

Skills	Skills Definitions
Coordination	Adjusting actions in relation to others' actions.
Active Listening	Giving full attention to what other people are saying, taking time to understand the points being made, asking questions as appropriate, and not interrupting at inappropriate times.
Time Management	Managing one's own time and the time of others.
Judgment and Decision Making	Considering the relative costs and benefits of potential actions to choose the most appropriate one.
Service Orientation	Actively looking for ways to help people.
Instructing	Teaching others how to do something.
Learning Strategies	Selecting and using training/instructional methods and procedures appropriate for the situation when learning or teaching new things.
Troubleshooting	Determining causes of operating errors and deciding what to do about it.
Active Learning	Understanding the implications of new information for both current and future problem-solving and decision-making.
Speaking	Talking to others to convey information effectively.
Monitoring	Monitoring/Assessing performance of yourself, other individuals, or organizations to make improvements or take corrective action.
Mathematics	Using mathematics to solve problems.
Reading Comprehension	Understanding written sentences and paragraphs in work related documents.
Management of Personnel Resources	Motivating, developing, and directing people as they work, identifying the best people for the job.
Critical Thinking	Using logic and reasoning to identify the strengths and weaknesses of alternative solutions, conclusions or approaches to problems.
Equipment Selection	Determining the kind of tools and equipment needed to do a job.
Operation and Control	Controlling operations of equipment or systems.
Operation Monitoring	Watching gauges, dials, or other indicators to make sure a machine is working properly.
Social Perceptiveness	Being aware of others' reactions and understanding why they react as they do.
Quality Control Analysis	Conducting tests and inspections of products, services, or processes to evaluate quality or performance.

Complex Problem Solving	Identifying complex problems and reviewing related information to develop and evaluate options and implement solutions.
Equipment Maintenance	Performing routine maintenance on equipment and determining when and what kind of maintenance is needed.
Management of Material Resources	Obtaining and seeing to the appropriate use of equipment, facilities, and materials needed to do certain work.
Writing	Communicating effectively in writing as appropriate for the needs of the audience.
Systems Evaluation	Identifying measures or indicators of system performance and the actions needed to improve or correct performance, relative to the goals of the system.
Systems Analysis	Determining how a system should work and how changes in conditions, operations, and the environment will affect outcomes.
Science	Using scientific rules and methods to solve problems.
Operations Analysis	Analyzing needs and product requirements to create a design.
Management of Financial Resources	Determining how money will be spent to get the work done, and accounting for these expenditures.
Negotiation	Bringing others together and trying to reconcile differences.
Repairing	Repairing machines or systems using the needed tools.
Persuasion	Persuading others to change their minds or behavior.
Installation	Installing equipment, machines, wiring, or programs to meet specifications.
Technology Design	Generating or adapting equipment and technology to serve user needs.
Programming	Writing computer programs for various purposes.

Ability	Ability Definitions
Oral Comprehension	The ability to listen to and understand information and ideas presented through spoken words and sentences.
Speech Recognition	The ability to identify and understand the speech of another person.
Speech Clarity	The ability to speak clearly so others can understand you.
Information Ordering	The ability to arrange things or actions in a certain order or pattern according to a specific rule or set of rules (e.g., patterns of numbers, letters, words, pictures, mathematical operations).
Arm-Hand Steadiness	The ability to keep your hand and arm steady while moving your arm or while holding your arm and hand in one position.
Selective Attention	The ability to concentrate on a task over a period of time without being distracted.
Near Vision	The ability to see details at close range (within a few feet of the observer).
Manual Dexterity	The ability to quickly move your hand, your hand together with your arm, or your two hands to grasp, manipulate, or assemble objects.
Oral Expression	The ability to communicate information and ideas in speaking so others will understand.
Time Sharing	The ability to shift back and forth between two or more activities or sources of information (such as speech, sounds, touch, or other sources).
Problem Sensitivity	The ability to tell when something is wrong or is likely to go wrong. It does not involve solving the problem, only recognizing there is a problem.
Deductive Reasoning	The ability to apply general rules to specific problems to produce answers that make sense.
Multilimb Coordination	The ability to coordinate two or more limbs (for example, two arms, two legs, or one leg and one arm) while sitting, standing, or lying down. It does not involve performing the activities while the whole body is in motion.
Trunk Strength	The ability to use your abdominal and lower back muscles to support part of the body repeatedly or continuously over time without 'giving out' or fatiguing.
Wrist-Finger Speed	The ability to make fast, simple, repeated movements of the fingers, hands, and wrists.
Category Flexibility	The ability to generate or use different sets of rules for combining or grouping things in different ways.
Written Comprehension	The ability to read and understand information and ideas presented in writing.
Visual Color Discrimination	The ability to match or detect differences between colors, including shades of color and brightness.
Finger Dexterity	The ability to make precisely coordinated movements of the fingers of one or both hands to grasp, manipulate, or assemble very small objects.
Control Precision	The ability to quickly and repeatedly adjust the controls of a machine or a vehicle to exact positions.

Reaction Time	The ability to quickly respond (with the hand, finger, or foot) to a signal (sound, light, picture) when it appears.
Static Strength	The ability to exert maximum muscle force to lift, push, pull, or carry objects.
Inductive Reasoning	The ability to combine pieces of information to form general rules or conclusions (includes finding a relationship among seemingly unrelated events).
Flexibility of Closure	The ability to identify or detect a known pattern (a figure, object, word, or sound) that is hidden in other distracting material.
Stamina	The ability to exert yourself physically over long periods of time without getting winded or out of breath.
Perceptual Speed	The ability to quickly and accurately compare similarities and differences among sets of letters, numbers, objects, pictures, or patterns. The things to be compared may be presented at the same time or one after the other. This ability also includes comparing a presented object with a remembered object.
Visualization	The ability to imagine how something will look after it is moved around or when its parts are moved or rearranged.
Auditory Attention	The ability to focus on a single source of sound in the presence of other distracting sounds.
Written Expression	The ability to communicate information and ideas in writing so others will understand.
Extent Flexibility	The ability to bend, stretch, twist, or reach with your body, arms, and/or legs.
Memorization	The ability to remember information such as words, numbers, pictures, and procedures.
Far Vision	The ability to see details at a distance.
Hearing Sensitivity	The ability to detect or tell the differences between sounds that vary in pitch and loudness.
Number Facility	The ability to add, subtract, multiply, or divide quickly and correctly.
Speed of Closure	The ability to quickly make sense of, combine, and organize information into meaningful patterns.
Response Orientation	The ability to choose quickly between two or more movements in response to two or more different signals (lights, sounds, pictures). It includes the speed with which the correct response is started with the hand, foot, or other body part.
Fluency of Ideas	The ability to come up with a number of ideas about a topic (the number of ideas is important, not their quality, correctness, or creativity).
Dynamic Strength	The ability to exert muscle force repeatedly or continuously over time. This involves muscular endurance and resistance to muscle fatigue.
Gross Body Coordination	The ability to coordinate the movement of your arms, legs, and torso together when the whole body is in motion.
Originality	The ability to come up with unusual or clever ideas about a given topic or situation, or to develop creative ways to solve a problem.
Depth Perception	The ability to judge which of several objects is closer or farther away from you, or to judge the distance between you and an object.
Mathematical Reasoning	The ability to choose the right mathematical methods or formulas to solve a problem.
Gross Body Equilibrium	The ability to keep or regain your body balance or stay upright when in an unstable position.
Rate Control	The ability to time your movements or the movement of a piece of equipment in anticipation of changes in the speed and/or direction of a moving object or scene.
Spatial Orientation	The ability to know your location in relation to the environment or to know where other objects are in relation to you.
Dynamic Flexibility	The ability to quickly and repeatedly bend, stretch, twist, or reach out with your body, arms, and/or legs.
Speed of Limb Movement	The ability to quickly move the arms and legs.
Sound Localization	The ability to tell the direction from which a sound originated.
Peripheral Vision	The ability to see objects or movement of objects to one's side when the eyes are looking ahead.
Night Vision	The ability to see under low light conditions.
Explosive Strength	The ability to use short bursts of muscle force to propel oneself (as in jumping or sprinting), or to throw an object.
Glare Sensitivity	The ability to see objects in the presence of glare or bright lighting.

Work_Activity	Work_Activity Definitions
Getting Information	Observing, receiving, and otherwise obtaining information from all relevant sources.

Performing for or Working Directly with the Public	Performing for people or dealing directly with the public. This includes serving customers in restaurants and stores, and receiving clients or guests.
Performing General Physical Activities	Performing physical activities that require considerable use of your arms and legs and moving your whole body, such as climbing, lifting, balancing, walking, stooping, and handling of materials.
Monitor Processes, Materials, or Surroundings	Monitoring and reviewing information from materials, events, or the environment, to detect or assess problems.
Establishing and Maintaining Interpersonal Relatio	Developing constructive and cooperative working relationships with others, and maintaining them over time.
Communicating with Supervisors, Peers, or Subordin	Providing information to supervisors, co-workers, and subordinates by telephone, in written form, e-mail, or in person.
Assisting and Caring for Others	Providing personal assistance, medical attention, emotional support, or other personal care to others such as coworkers, customers, or patients.
Handling and Moving Objects	Using hands and arms in handling, installing, positioning, and moving materials, and manipulating things.
Identifying Objects, Actions, and Events	Identifying information by categorizing, estimating, recognizing differences or similarities, and detecting changes in circumstances or events.
Controlling Machines and Processes	Using either control mechanisms or direct physical activity to operate machines or processes (not including computers or vehicles).
Making Decisions and Solving Problems	Analyzing information and evaluating results to choose the best solution and solve problems.
Judging the Qualities of Things, Services, or Peop	Assessing the value, importance, or quality of things or people.
Organizing, Planning, and Prioritizing Work	Developing specific goals and plans to prioritize, organize, and accomplish your work.
Coordinating the Work and Activities of Others	Getting members of a group to work together to accomplish tasks.
Selling or Influencing Others	Convincing others to buy merchandise/goods or to otherwise change their minds or actions.
Training and Teaching Others	Identifying the educational needs of others, developing formal educational or training programs or classes, and teaching or instructing others.
Inspecting Equipment, Structures, or Material	Inspecting equipment, structures, or materials to identify the cause of errors or other problems or defects.
Resolving Conflicts and Negotiating with Others	Handling complaints, settling disputes, and resolving grievances and conflicts, or otherwise negotiating with others.
Developing and Building Teams	Encouraging and building mutual trust, respect, and cooperation among team members.
Updating and Using Relevant Knowledge	Keeping up-to-date technically and applying new knowledge to your job.
Coaching and Developing Others	Identifying the developmental needs of others and coaching, mentoring, or otherwise helping others to improve their knowledge or skills.
Guiding, Directing, and Motivating Subordinates	Providing guidance and direction to subordinates, including setting performance standards and monitoring performance.
Estimating the Quantifiable Characteristics of Pro	Estimating sizes, distances, and quantities; or determining time, costs, resources, or materials needed to perform a work activity.
Interpreting the Meaning of Information for Others	Translating or explaining what information means and how it can be used.
Thinking Creatively	Developing, designing, or creating new applications, ideas, relationships, systems, or products, including artistic contributions.
Monitoring and Controlling Resources	Monitoring and controlling resources and overseeing the spending of money.
Provide Consultation and Advice to Others	Providing guidance and expert advice to management or other groups on technical, systems-, or process-related topics.
Communicating with Persons Outside Organization	Communicating with people outside the organization, representing the organization to customers, the public, government, and other external sources. This information can be exchanged in person, in writing, or by telephone or e-mail.
Scheduling Work and Activities	Scheduling events, programs, and activities, as well as the work of others.
Evaluating Information to Determine Compliance wit	Using relevant information and individual judgment to determine whether events or processes comply with laws, regulations, or standards.
Documenting/Recording Information	Entering, transcribing, recording, storing, or maintaining information in written or electronic/magnetic form.

Analyzing Data or Information	Identifying the underlying principles, reasons, or facts of information by breaking down information or data into separate parts.
Operating Vehicles, Mechanized Devices, or Equipme	Running, maneuvering, navigating, or driving vehicles or mechanized equipment, such as forklifts, passenger vehicles, aircraft, or water craft.
Repairing and Maintaining Mechanical Equipment	Servicing, repairing, adjusting, and testing machines, devices, moving parts, and equipment that operate primarily on the basis of mechanical (not electronic) principles.
Developing Objectives and Strategies	Establishing long-range objectives and specifying the strategies and actions to achieve them.
Staffing Organizational Units	Recruiting, interviewing, selecting, hiring, and promoting employees in an organization.
Processing Information	Compiling, coding, categorizing, calculating, tabulating, auditing, or verifying information or data.
Performing Administrative Activities	Performing day-to-day administrative tasks such as maintaining information files and processing paperwork.
Repairing and Maintaining Electronic Equipment	Servicing, repairing, calibrating, regulating, fine-tuning, or testing machines, devices, and equipment that operate primarily on the basis of electrical or electronic (not mechanical) principles.
Interacting With Computers	Using computers and computer systems (including hardware and software) to program, write software, set up functions, enter data, or process information.
Drafting, Laying Out, and Specifying Technical Dev	Providing documentation, detailed instructions, drawings, or specifications to tell others about how devices, parts, equipment, or structures are to be fabricated, constructed, assembled, modified, maintained, or used.

Work_Context	Work_Context Definitions
Spend Time Standing	How much does this job require standing?
Indoors, Environmentally Controlled	How often does this job require working indoors in environmentally controlled conditions?
Face-to-Face Discussions	How often do you have to have face-to-face discussions with individuals or teams in this job?
Contact With Others	How much does this job require the worker to be in contact with others (face-to-face, by telephone, or otherwise) in order to perform it?
Spend Time Using Your Hands to Handle, Control, or	How much does this job require using your hands to handle, control, or feel objects, tools or controls?
Physical Proximity	To what extent does this job require the worker to perform job tasks in close physical proximity to other people?
Very Hot or Cold Temperatures	How often does this job require working in very hot (above 90 F degrees) or very cold (below 32 F degrees) temperatures?
Freedom to Make Decisions	How much decision making freedom, without supervision, does the job offer?
Work With Work Group or Team	How important is it to work with others in a group or team in this job?
Exposed to Minor Burns, Cuts, Bites, or Stings	How often does this job require exposure to minor burns, cuts, bites, or stings?
Spend Time Making Repetitive Motions	How much does this job require making repetitive motions?
Importance of Being Exact or Accurate	How important is being very exact or highly accurate in performing this job?
Structured versus Unstructured Work	To what extent is this job structured for the worker, rather than allowing the worker to determine tasks, priorities, and goals?
Time Pressure	How often does this job require the worker to meet strict deadlines?
Responsibility for Outcomes and Results	How responsible is the worker for work outcomes and results of other workers?
Frequency of Decision Making	How frequently is the worker required to make decisions that affect other people, the financial resources, and/or the image and reputation of the organization?
Responsible for Others' Health and Safety	How much responsibility is there for the health and safety of others in this job?
Spend Time Walking and Running	How much does this job require walking and running?
Spend Time Bending or Twisting the Body	How much does this job require bending or twisting your body?
Impact of Decisions on Co-workers or Company Resul	How do the decisions an employee makes impact the results of co-workers, clients or the company?
Telephone	How often do you have telephone conversations in this job?
Wear Common Protective or Safety Equipment such as	How much does this job require wearing common protective or safety equipment such as safety shoes, glasses, gloves, hard hats or life jackets?

Level of Competition	To what extent does this job require the worker to compete or to be aware of competitive pressures?
Importance of Repeating Same Tasks	How important is repeating the same physical activities (e.g., key entry) or mental activities (e.g., checking entries in a ledger) over and over, without stopping, to performing this job?
Coordinate or Lead Others	How important is it to coordinate or lead others in accomplishing work activities in this job?
Deal With External Customers	How important is it to work with external customers or the public in this job?
Sounds, Noise Levels Are Distracting or Uncomforta	How often does this job require working exposed to sounds and noise levels that are distracting or uncomfortable?
Frequency of Conflict Situations	How often are there conflict situations the employee has to face in this job?
Exposed to Contaminants	How often does this job require working exposed to contaminants (such as pollutants, gases, dust or odors)?
Extremely Bright or Inadequate Lighting	How often does this job require working in extremely bright or inadequate lighting conditions?
Degree of Automation	How automated is the job?
Outdoors, Under Cover	How often does this job require working outdoors, under cover (e.g., structure with roof but no walls)?
Public Speaking	How often do you have to perform public speaking in this job?
Deal With Unpleasant or Angry People	How frequently does the worker have to deal with unpleasant, angry, or discourteous individuals as part of the job requirements?
Wear Specialized Protective or Safety Equipment su	How much does this job require wearing specialized protective or safety equipment such as breathing apparatus, safety harness, full protection suits, or radiation protection?
Consequence of Error	How serious would the result usually be if the worker made a mistake that was not readily correctable?
Pace Determined by Speed of Equipment	How important is it to this job that the pace is determined by the speed of equipment or machinery? (This does not refer to keeping busy at all times on this job.)
Letters and Memos	How often does the job require written letters and memos?
Indoors, Not Environmentally Controlled	How often does this job require working indoors in non-controlled environmental conditions (e.g., warehouse without heat)?
Cramped Work Space, Awkward Positions	How often does this job require working in cramped work spaces that requires getting into awkward positions?
Outdoors, Exposed to Weather	How often does this job require working outdoors, exposed to all weather conditions?
Exposed to Hazardous Conditions	How often does this job require exposure to hazardous conditions?
Spend Time Sitting	How much does this job require sitting?
In an Open Vehicle or Equipment	How often does this job require working in an open vehicle or equipment (e.g., tractor)?
Exposed to Whole Body Vibration	How often does this job require exposure to whole body vibration (e.g., operate a jackhammer)?
Spend Time Kneeling, Crouching, Stooping, or Crawl	How much does this job require kneeling, crouching, stooping or crawling?
Electronic Mail	How often do you use electronic mail in this job?
Deal With Physically Aggressive People	How frequently does this job require the worker to deal with physical aggression of violent individuals?
Exposed to Hazardous Equipment	How often does this job require exposure to hazardous equipment?
Exposed to Disease or Infections	How often does this job require exposure to disease/infections?
In an Enclosed Vehicle or Equipment	How often does this job require working in a closed vehicle or equipment (e.g., car)?
Spend Time Keeping or Regaining Balance	How much does this job require keeping or regaining your balance?
Exposed to High Places	How often does this job require exposure to high places?
Spend Time Climbing Ladders, Scaffolds, or Poles	How much does this job require climbing ladders, scaffolds, or poles?
Exposed to Radiation	How often does this job require exposure to radiation?

Job Zone Component	Job Zone Component Definitions
Title	Job Zone One: Little or No Preparation Needed
Overall Experience	No previous work-related skill, knowledge, or experience is needed for these occupations. For example, a person can become a general office clerk even if he/she has never worked in an office before.
Job Training	Employees in these occupations need anywhere from a few days to a few months of training. Usually, an experienced worker could show you how to do the job.
Job Zone Examples	These occupations involve following instructions and helping others. Examples include bus drivers, forest and conservation workers, general office clerks, home health aides, and waiters/waitresses.
SVP Range	(Below 4.0)
Education	These occupations may require a high school diploma or GED certificate. Some may require a formal training course to obtain a license.

Work_Styles	Work_Styles Definitions
Dependability	Job requires being reliable, responsible, and dependable, and fulfilling obligations.
Attention to Detail	Job requires being careful about detail and thorough in completing work tasks.
Integrity	Job requires being honest and ethical.
Stress Tolerance	Job requires accepting criticism and dealing calmly and effectively with high stress situations.
Cooperation	Job requires being pleasant with others on the job and displaying a good-natured, cooperative attitude.
Initiative	Job requires a willingness to take on responsibilities and challenges.
Self Control	Job requires maintaining composure, keeping emotions in check, controlling anger, and avoiding aggressive behavior, even in very difficult situations.
Adaptability/Flexibility	Job requires being open to change (positive or negative) and to considerable variety in the workplace.
Concern for Others	Job requires being sensitive to others' needs and feelings and being understanding and helpful on the job.
Persistence	Job requires persistence in the face of obstacles.
Independence	Job requires developing one's own ways of doing things, guiding oneself with little or no supervision, and depending on oneself to get things done.
Achievement/Effort	Job requires establishing and maintaining personally challenging achievement goals and exerting effort toward mastering tasks.
Social Orientation	Job requires preferring to work with others rather than alone, and being personally connected with others on the job.
Leadership	Job requires a willingness to lead, take charge, and offer opinions and direction.
Innovation	Job requires creativity and alternative thinking to develop new ideas for and answers to work-related problems.
Analytical Thinking	Job requires analyzing information and using logic to address work-related issues and problems.

35-2021.00 - Food Preparation Workers

Perform a variety of food preparation duties other than cooking, such as preparing cold foods and shellfish, slicing meat, and brewing coffee or tea.

Tasks

1) Store food in designated containers and storage areas to prevent spoilage.

2) Inform supervisors when supplies are getting low or equipment is not working properly.

3) Carry food supplies, equipment, and utensils to and from storage and work areas.

4) Portion and wrap the food, or place it directly on plates for service to patrons.

5) Wash, peel and/or cut various foods to prepare for cooking or serving.

6) Remove trash and clean kitchen garbage containers.

7) Prepare a variety of foods according to customers' orders or supervisors' instructions, following approved procedures.

8) Weigh or measure ingredients.

9) Receive and store food supplies, equipment, and utensils in refrigerators, cupboards, and other storage areas.

10) Assist cooks and kitchen staff with various tasks as needed, and provide cooks with needed items.

11) Use manual and/or electric appliances to clean, peel, slice, and trim foods.

12) Package take-out foods and/or serve food to customers.

13) Prepare and serve a variety of beverages such as coffee, tea, and soft drinks.

14) Place food trays over food warmers for immediate service, or store them in refrigerated storage cabinets.

15) Scrape leftovers from dishes into garbage containers.

16) Stock cupboards and refrigerators, and tend salad bars and buffet meals.

17) Stir and strain soups and sauces.

18) Make special dressings and sauces as condiments for sandwiches.

19) Keep records of the quantities of food used.

20) Mix ingredients for green salads, molded fruit salads, vegetable salads, and pasta salads.

21) Work on assembly lines adding cutlery, napkins, food, and other items to trays in hospitals, cafeterias, airline kitchens, and similar establishments.

22) Load dishes, glasses, and tableware into dishwashing machines.

23) Cut, slice and/or grind meat, poultry, and seafood to prepare for cooking.

24) Distribute food to waiters and waitresses to serve to customers.

25) Butcher and clean fowl, fish, poultry, and shellfish to prepare for cooking or serving.

26) Distribute menus to hospital patients, collect diet sheets, and deliver food trays and snacks to nursing units or directly to patients.

Knowledge	Knowledge Definitions
Customer and Personal Service	Knowledge of principles and processes for providing customer and personal services. This includes customer needs assessment, meeting quality standards for services, and evaluation of customer satisfaction.
Food Production	Knowledge of techniques and equipment for planting, growing, and harvesting food products (both plant and animal) for consumption, including storage/handling techniques.
Mathematics	Knowledge of arithmetic, algebra, geometry, calculus, statistics, and their applications.
English Language	Knowledge of the structure and content of the English language including the meaning and spelling of words, rules of composition, and grammar.
Administration and Management	Knowledge of business and management principles involved in strategic planning, resource allocation, human resources modeling, leadership technique, production methods, and coordination of people and resources.
Production and Processing	Knowledge of raw materials, production processes, quality control, costs, and other techniques for maximizing the effective manufacture and distribution of goods.
Public Safety and Security	Knowledge of relevant equipment, policies, procedures, and strategies to promote effective local, state, or national security operations for the protection of people, data, property, and institutions.
Sales and Marketing	Knowledge of principles and methods for showing, promoting, and selling products or services. This includes marketing strategy and tactics, product demonstration, sales techniques, and sales control systems.
Education and Training	Knowledge of principles and methods for curriculum and training design, teaching and instruction for individuals and groups, and the measurement of training effects.
Personnel and Human Resources	Knowledge of principles and procedures for personnel recruitment, selection, training, compensation and benefits, labor relations and negotiation, and personnel information systems.
Clerical	Knowledge of administrative and clerical procedures and systems such as word processing, managing files and records, stenography and transcription, designing forms, and other office procedures and terminology.
Computers and Electronics	Knowledge of circuit boards, processors, chips, electronic equipment, and computer hardware and software, including applications and programming.
Transportation	Knowledge of principles and methods for moving people or goods by air, rail, sea, or road, including the relative costs and benefits.
Economics and Accounting	Knowledge of economic and accounting principles and practices, the financial markets, banking and the analysis and reporting of financial data.
Psychology	Knowledge of human behavior and performance; individual differences in ability, personality, and interests; learning and motivation; psychological research methods; and the assessment and treatment of behavioral and affective disorders.
Law and Government	Knowledge of laws, legal codes, court procedures, precedents, government regulations, executive orders, agency rules, and the democratic political process.
Mechanical	Knowledge of machines and tools, including their designs, uses, repair, and maintenance.
Chemistry	Knowledge of the chemical composition, structure, and properties of substances and of the chemical processes and transformations that they undergo. This includes uses of chemicals and their interactions, danger signs, production techniques, and disposal methods.
Telecommunications	Knowledge of transmission, broadcasting, switching, control, and operation of telecommunications systems.
Communications and Media	Knowledge of media production, communication, and dissemination techniques and methods. This includes alternative ways to inform and entertain via written, oral, and visual media.
Engineering and Technology	Knowledge of the practical application of engineering science and technology. This includes applying principles, techniques, procedures, and equipment to the design and production of various goods and services.
Foreign Language	Knowledge of the structure and content of a foreign (non-English) language including the meaning and spelling of words, rules of composition and grammar, and pronunciation.
Design	Knowledge of design techniques, tools, and principles involved in production of precision technical plans, blueprints, drawings, and models.
Medicine and Dentistry	Knowledge of the information and techniques needed to diagnose and treat human injuries, diseases, and deformities. This includes symptoms, treatment alternatives, drug properties and interactions, and preventive health-care measures.
Philosophy and Theology	Knowledge of different philosophical systems and religions. This includes their basic principles, values, ethics, ways of thinking, customs, practices, and their impact on human culture.
Building and Construction	Knowledge of materials, methods, and the tools involved in the construction or repair of houses, buildings, or other structures such as highways and roads.
Therapy and Counseling	Knowledge of principles, methods, and procedures for diagnosis, treatment, and rehabilitation of physical and mental dysfunctions, and for career counseling and guidance.
Geography	Knowledge of principles and methods for describing the features of land, sea, and air masses, including their physical characteristics, locations, interrelationships, and distribution of plant, animal, and human life.
Sociology and Anthropology	Knowledge of group behavior and dynamics, societal trends and influences, human migrations, ethnicity, cultures and their history and origins.
Biology	Knowledge of plant and animal organisms, their tissues, cells, functions, interdependencies, and interactions with each other and the environment.
Physics	Knowledge and prediction of physical principles, laws, their interrelationships, and applications to understanding fluid, material, and atmospheric dynamics, and mechanical, electrical, atomic and sub- atomic structures and processes.
History and Archeology	Knowledge of historical events and their causes, indicators, and effects on civilizations and cultures.
Fine Arts	Knowledge of the theory and techniques required to compose, produce, and perform works of music, dance, visual arts, drama, and sculpture.

Skills	Skills Definitions
Active Listening	Giving full attention to what other people are saying, taking time to understand the points being made, asking questions as appropriate, and not interrupting at inappropriate times.
Reading Comprehension	Understanding written sentences and paragraphs in work related documents.
Instructing	Teaching others how to do something.
Speaking	Talking to others to convey information effectively.
Learning Strategies	Selecting and using training/instructional methods and procedures appropriate for the situation when learning or teaching new things.
Service Orientation	Actively looking for ways to help people.
Social Perceptiveness	Being aware of others' reactions and understanding why they react as they do.
Coordination	Adjusting actions in relation to others' actions.
Mathematics	Using mathematics to solve problems.
Critical Thinking	Using logic and reasoning to identify the strengths and weaknesses of alternative solutions, conclusions or approaches to problems.

Active Learning	Understanding the implications of new information for both current and future problem-solving and decision-making.
Management of Personnel Resources	Motivating, developing, and directing people as they work, identifying the best people for the job.
Monitoring	Monitoring/Assessing performance of yourself, other individuals, or organizations to make improvements or take corrective action.
Persuasion	Persuading others to change their minds or behavior.
Judgment and Decision Making	Considering the relative costs and benefits of potential actions to choose the most appropriate one.
Time Management	Managing one's own time and the time of others.
Writing	Communicating effectively in writing as appropriate for the needs of the audience.
Complex Problem Solving	Identifying complex problems and reviewing related information to develop and evaluate options and implement solutions.
Quality Control Analysis	Conducting tests and inspections of products, services, or processes to evaluate quality or performance.
Equipment Selection	Determining the kind of tools and equipment needed to do a job.
Negotiation	Bringing others together and trying to reconcile differences.
Equipment Maintenance	Performing routine maintenance on equipment and determining when and what kind of maintenance is needed.
Operation Monitoring	Watching gauges, dials, or other indicators to make sure a machine is working properly.
Troubleshooting	Determining causes of operating errors and deciding what to do about it.
Systems Analysis	Determining how a system should work and how changes in conditions, operations, and the environment will affect outcomes.
Management of Financial Resources	Determining how money will be spent to get the work done, and accounting for these expenditures.
Systems Evaluation	Identifying measures or indicators of system performance and the actions needed to improve or correct performance, relative to the goals of the system.
Operation and Control	Controlling operations of equipment or systems.
Repairing	Repairing machines or systems using the needed tools.
Operations Analysis	Analyzing needs and product requirements to create a design.
Management of Material Resources	Obtaining and seeing to the appropriate use of equipment, facilities, and materials needed to do certain work.
Technology Design	Generating or adapting equipment and technology to serve user needs.
Installation	Installing equipment, machines, wiring, or programs to meet specifications.
Science	Using scientific rules and methods to solve problems.
Programming	Writing computer programs for various purposes.

Ability — Ability Definitions

Ability	Ability Definitions
Oral Comprehension	The ability to listen to and understand information and ideas presented through spoken words and sentences.
Arm-Hand Steadiness	The ability to keep your hand and arm steady while moving your arm or while holding your arm and hand in one position.
Manual Dexterity	The ability to quickly move your hand, your hand together with your arm, or your two hands to grasp, manipulate, or assemble objects.
Speech Recognition	The ability to identify and understand the speech of another person.
Near Vision	The ability to see details at close range (within a few feet of the observer).
Deductive Reasoning	The ability to apply general rules to specific problems to produce answers that make sense.
Information Ordering	The ability to arrange things or actions in a certain order or pattern according to a specific rule or set of rules (e.g., patterns of numbers, letters, words, pictures, mathematical operations).
Oral Expression	The ability to communicate information and ideas in speaking so others will understand.
Problem Sensitivity	The ability to tell when something is wrong or is likely to go wrong. It does not involve solving the problem, only recognizing there is a problem.
Static Strength	The ability to exert maximum muscle force to lift, push, pull, or carry objects.
Trunk Strength	The ability to use your abdominal and lower back muscles to support part of the body repeatedly or continuously over time without 'giving out' or fatiguing.
Speech Clarity	The ability to speak clearly so others can understand you.
Extent Flexibility	The ability to bend, stretch, twist, or reach with your body, arms, and/or legs.

Inductive Reasoning	The ability to combine pieces of information to form general rules or conclusions (includes finding a relationship among seemingly unrelated events).
Visual Color Discrimination	The ability to match or detect differences between colors, including shades of color and brightness.
Flexibility of Closure	The ability to identify or detect a known pattern (a figure, object, word, or sound) that is hidden in other distracting material.
Category Flexibility	The ability to generate or use different sets of rules for combining or grouping things in different ways.
Visualization	The ability to imagine how something will look after it is moved around or when its parts are moved or rearranged.
Selective Attention	The ability to concentrate on a task over a period of time without being distracted.
Wrist-Finger Speed	The ability to make fast, simple, repeated movements of the fingers, hands, and wrists.
Stamina	The ability to exert yourself physically over long periods of time without getting winded or out of breath.
Perceptual Speed	The ability to quickly and accurately compare similarities and differences among sets of letters, numbers, objects, pictures, or patterns. The things to be compared may be presented at the same time or one after the other. This ability also includes comparing a presented object with a remembered object.
Finger Dexterity	The ability to make precisely coordinated movements of the fingers of one or both hands to grasp, manipulate, or assemble very small objects.
Number Facility	The ability to add, subtract, multiply, or divide quickly and correctly.
Time Sharing	The ability to shift back and forth between two or more activities or sources of information (such as speech, sounds, touch, or other sources).
Control Precision	The ability to quickly and repeatedly adjust the controls of a machine or a vehicle to exact positions.
Multilimb Coordination	The ability to coordinate two or more limbs (for example, two arms, two legs, or one leg and one arm) while sitting, standing, or lying down. It does not involve performing the activities while the whole body is in motion.
Memorization	The ability to remember information such as words, numbers, pictures, and procedures.
Written Expression	The ability to communicate information and ideas in writing so others will understand.
Written Comprehension	The ability to read and understand information and ideas presented in writing.
Fluency of Ideas	The ability to come up with a number of ideas about a topic (the number of ideas is important, not their quality, correctness, or creativity).
Originality	The ability to come up with unusual or clever ideas about a given topic or situation, or to develop creative ways to solve a problem.
Speed of Limb Movement	The ability to quickly move the arms and legs.
Auditory Attention	The ability to focus on a single source of sound in the presence of other distracting sounds.
Hearing Sensitivity	The ability to detect or tell the differences between sounds that vary in pitch and loudness.
Gross Body Coordination	The ability to coordinate the movement of your arms, legs, and torso together when the whole body is in motion.
Depth Perception	The ability to judge which of several objects is closer or farther away from you, or to judge the distance between you and an object.
Far Vision	The ability to see details at a distance.
Dynamic Strength	The ability to exert muscle force repeatedly or continuously over time. This involves muscular endurance and resistance to muscle fatigue.
Speed of Closure	The ability to quickly make sense of, combine, and organize information into meaningful patterns.
Reaction Time	The ability to quickly respond (with the hand, finger, or foot) to a signal (sound, light, picture) when it appears.
Mathematical Reasoning	The ability to choose the right mathematical methods or formulas to solve a problem.
Response Orientation	The ability to choose quickly between two or more movements in response to two or more different signals (lights, sounds, pictures). It includes the speed with which the correct response is started with the hand, foot, or other body part.
Gross Body Equilibrium	The ability to keep or regain your body balance or stay upright when in an unstable position.
Rate Control	The ability to time your movements or the movement of a piece of equipment in anticipation of changes in the speed and/or direction of a moving object or scene.

Dynamic Flexibility	The ability to quickly and repeatedly bend. stretch. twist, or reach out with your body. arms. and/or legs.
Sound Localization	The ability to tell the direction from which a sound originated.
Spatial Orientation	The ability to know your location in relation to the environment or to know where other objects are in relation to you.
Peripheral Vision	The ability to see objects or movement of objects to one's side when the eyes are looking ahead.
Explosive Strength	The ability to use short bursts of muscle force to propel oneself (as in jumping or sprinting), or to throw an object.
Glare Sensitivity	The ability to see objects in the presence of glare or bright lighting.
Night Vision	The ability to see under low light conditions.

Work_Activity	Work_Activity Definitions
Communicating with Supervisors, Peers, or Subordin	Providing information to supervisors, co-workers. and subordinates by telephone, in written form, e-mail. or in person.
Performing General Physical Activities	Performing physical activities that require considerable use of your arms and legs and moving your whole body, such as climbing, lifting. balancing. walking, stooping, and handling of materials.
Establishing and Maintaining Interpersonal Relatio	Developing constructive and cooperative working relationships with others, and maintaining them over time.
Performing for or Working Directly with the Public	Performing for people or dealing directly with the public. This includes serving customers in restaurants and stores. and receiving clients or guests.
Getting Information	Observing. receiving, and otherwise obtaining information from all relevant sources.
Identifying Objects, Actions, and Events	Identifying information by categorizing, estimating. recognizing differences or similarities. and detecting changes in circumstances or events.
Evaluating Information to Determine Compliance wit	Using relevant information and individual judgment to determine whether events or processes comply with laws, regulations, or standards.
Handling and Moving Objects	Using hands and arms in handling, installing, positioning, and moving materials, and manipulating things.
Coordinating the Work and Activities of Others	Getting members of a group to work together to accomplish tasks.
Organizing, Planning, and Prioritizing Work	Developing specific goals and plans to prioritize. organize, and accomplish your work.
Estimating the Quantifiable Characteristics of Pro	Estimating sizes, distances, and quantities; or determining time, costs, resources, or materials needed to perform a work activity.
Assisting and Caring for Others	Providing personal assistance, medical attention, emotional support, or other personal care to others such as coworkers, customers, or patients.
Judging the Qualities of Things, Services, or Peop	Assessing the value, importance, or quality of things or people.
Monitor Processes, Materials, or Surroundings	Monitoring and reviewing information from materials, events, or the environment, to detect or assess problems.
Selling or Influencing Others	Convincing others to buy merchandise/goods or to otherwise change their minds or actions.
Resolving Conflicts and Negotiating with Others	Handling complaints, settling disputes, and resolving grievances and conflicts, or otherwise negotiating with others.
Communicating with Persons Outside Organization	Communicating with people outside the organization. representing the organization to customers, the public, government, and other external sources. This information can be exchanged in person, in writing, or by telephone or e-mail.
Making Decisions and Solving Problems	Analyzing information and evaluating results to choose the best solution and solve problems.
Training and Teaching Others	Identifying the educational needs of others, developing formal educational or training programs or classes, and teaching or instructing others.
Inspecting Equipment, Structures, or Material	Inspecting equipment, structures, or materials to identify the cause of errors or other problems or defects.
Controlling Machines and Processes	Using either control mechanisms or direct physical activity to operate machines or processes (not including computers or vehicles).
Updating and Using Relevant Knowledge	Keeping up-to-date technically and applying new knowledge to your job.
Processing Information	Compiling, coding, categorizing. calculating, tabulating. auditing, or verifying information or data.
Developing and Building Teams	Encouraging and building mutual trust, respect, and cooperation among team members.

Guiding. Directing, and Motivating Subordinates	Providing guidance and direction to subordinates, including setting performance standards and monitoring performance.
Monitoring and Controlling Resources	Monitoring and controlling resources and overseeing the spending of money.
Documenting/Recording Information	Entering, transcribing, recording, storing, or maintaining information in written or electronic/magnetic form.
Coaching and Developing Others	Identifying the developmental needs of others and coaching. mentoring, or otherwise helping others to improve their knowledge or skills.
Thinking Creatively	Developing, designing, or creating new applications, ideas, relationships, systems, or products, including artistic contributions.
Developing Objectives and Strategies	Establishing long-range objectives and specifying the strategies and actions to achieve them.
Scheduling Work and Activities	Scheduling events, programs, and activities, as well as the work of others.
Interacting With Computers	Using computers and computer systems (including hardware and software) to program, write software, set up functions, enter data, or process information.
Provide Consultation and Advice to Others	Providing guidance and expert advice to management or other groups on technical, systems-, or process-related topics.
Interpreting the Meaning of Information for Others	Translating or explaining what information means and how it can be used.
Analyzing Data or Information	Identifying the underlying principles, reasons, or facts of information by breaking down information or data into separate parts.
Performing Administrative Activities	Performing day-to-day administrative tasks such as maintaining information files and processing paperwork.
Staffing Organizational Units	Recruiting, interviewing, selecting, hiring, and promoting employees in an organization.
Drafting, Laying Out, and Specifying Technical Dev	Providing documentation, detailed instructions, drawings, or specifications to tell others about how devices, parts, equipment, or structures are to be fabricated, constructed, assembled, modified, maintained, or used.
Repairing and Maintaining Electronic Equipment	Servicing, repairing, calibrating, regulating, fine-tuning, or testing machines, devices, and equipment that operate primarily on the basis of electrical or electronic (not mechanical) principles.
Repairing and Maintaining Mechanical Equipment	Servicing, repairing, adjusting, and testing machines, devices. moving parts, and equipment that operate primarily on the basis of mechanical (not electronic) principles.
Operating Vehicles, Mechanized Devices, or Equipme	Running, maneuvering, navigating, or driving vehicles or mechanized equipment, such as forklifts, passenger vehicles, aircraft, or water craft.

Work_Context	Work_Context Definitions
Spend Time Standing	How much does this job require standing?
Contact With Others	How much does this job require the worker to be in contact with others (face-to-face, by telephone, or otherwise) in order to perform it?
Face-to-Face Discussions	How often do you have to have face-to-face discussions with individuals or teams in this job?
Work With Work Group or Team	How important is it to work with others in a group or team in this job?
Spend Time Walking and Running	How much does this job require walking and running?
Spend Time Using Your Hands to Handle, Control, or	How much does this job require using your hands to handle, control, or feel objects, tools or controls?
Indoors, Environmentally Controlled	How often does this job require working indoors in environmentally controlled conditions?
Physical Proximity	To what extent does this job require the worker to perform job tasks in close physical proximity to other people?
Wear Common Protective or Safety Equipment such as	How much does this job require wearing common protective or safety equipment such as safety shoes, glasses, gloves, hard hats or live jackets?
Spend Time Making Repetitive Motions	How much does this job require making repetitive motions?
Time Pressure	How often does this job require the worker to meet strict deadlines?
Freedom to Make Decisions	How much decision making freedom, without supervision, does the job offer?
Exposed to Minor Burns, Cuts, Bites. or Stings	How often does this job require exposure to minor burns, cuts, bites, or stings?
Structured versus Unstructured Work	To what extent is this job structured for the worker, rather than allowing the worker to determine tasks, priorities, and goals?

Importance of Being Exact or Accurate	How important is being very exact or highly accurate in performing this job?
Deal With External Customers	How important is it to work with external customers or the public in this job?
Telephone	How often do you have telephone conversations in this job?
Deal With Unpleasant or Angry People	How frequently does the worker have to deal with unpleasant, angry, or discourteous individuals as part of the job requirements?
Responsible for Others' Health and Safety	How much responsibility is there for the health and safety of others in this job?
Coordinate or Lead Others	How important is it to coordinate or lead others in accomplishing work activities in this job?
Spend Time Bending or Twisting the Body	How much does this job require bending or twisting your body?
Very Hot or Cold Temperatures	How often does this job require working in very hot (above 90 F degrees) or very cold (below 32 F degrees) temperatures?
Impact of Decisions on Co-workers or Company Resul	How do the decisions an employee makes impact the results of co-workers, clients or the company?
Frequency of Decision Making	How frequently is the worker required to make decisions that affect other people, the financial resources, and/or the image and reputation of the organization?
Importance of Repeating Same Tasks	How important is repeating the same physical activities (e.g., key entry) or mental activities (e.g., checking entries in a ledger) over and over, without stopping, to performing this job?
Responsibility for Outcomes and Results	How responsible is the worker for work outcomes and results of other workers?
Sounds, Noise Levels Are Distracting or Uncomforta	How often does this job require working exposed to sounds and noise levels that are distracting or uncomfortable?
Pace Determined by Speed of Equipment	How important is it to this job that the pace is determined by the speed of equipment or machinery? (This does not refer to keeping busy at all times on this job.)
Frequency of Conflict Situations	How often are there conflict situations the employee has to face in this job?
Level of Competition	To what extent does this job require the worker to compete or to be aware of competitive pressures?
Exposed to Contaminants	How often does this job require working exposed to contaminants (such as pollutants, gases, dust or odors)?
Consequence of Error	How serious would the result usually be if the worker made a mistake that was not readily correctable?
Spend Time Kneeling, Crouching, Stooping, or Crawl	How much does this job require kneeling, crouching, stooping, or crawling?
Extremely Bright or Inadequate Lighting	How often does this job require working in extremely bright or inadequate lighting conditions?
Exposed to Disease or Infections	How often does this job require exposure to disease/infections?
Letters and Memos	How often does the job require written letters and memos?
Degree of Automation	How automated is the job?
Spend Time Keeping or Regaining Balance	How much does this job require keeping or regaining your balance?
Cramped Work Space, Awkward Positions	How often does this job require working in cramped work spaces that requires getting into awkward positions?
Outdoors, Exposed to Weather	How often does this job require working outdoors, exposed to all weather conditions?
Indoors, Not Environmentally Controlled	How often does this job require working indoors in non-controlled environmental conditions (e.g., warehouse without heat)?
Spend Time Sitting	How much does this job require sitting?
Exposed to Hazardous Equipment	How often does this job require exposure to hazardous equipment?
Deal With Physically Aggressive People	How frequently does this job require the worker to deal with physical aggression of violent individuals?
Public Speaking	How often do you have to perform public speaking in this job?
Wear Specialized Protective or Safety Equipment su	How much does this job require wearing specialized protective or safety equipment such as breathing apparatus, safety harness, full protection suits, or radiation protection?
Exposed to Radiation	How often does this job require exposure to radiation?
Outdoors, Under Cover	How often does this job require working outdoors, under cover (e.g., structure with roof but no walls)?
Exposed to Hazardous Conditions	How often does this job require exposure to hazardous conditions?
Exposed to High Places	How often does this job require exposure to high places?
Electronic Mail	How often do you use electronic mail in this job?
In an Enclosed Vehicle or Equipment	How often does this job require working in a closed vehicle or equipment (e.g., car)?

Spend Time Climbing Ladders, Scaffolds, or Poles	How much does this job require climbing ladders, scaffolds, or poles?
In an Open Vehicle or Equipment	How often does this job require working in an open vehicle or equipment (e.g., tractor)?
Exposed to Whole Body Vibration	How often does this job require exposure to whole body vibration (e.g., operate a jackhammer)?

Job Zone Component	Job Zone Component Definitions
Title	Job Zone One: Little or No Preparation Needed
Overall Experience	No previous work-related skill, knowledge, or experience is needed for these occupations. For example, a person can become a general office clerk even if he/she has never worked in an office before.
Job Training	Employees in these occupations need anywhere from a few days to a few months of training. Usually, an experienced worker could show you how to do the job.
Job Zone Examples	These occupations involve following instructions and helping others. Examples include bus drivers, forest and conservation workers, general office clerks, home health aides, and waiters/waitresses.
SVP Range	(Below 4.0)
Education	These occupations may require a high school diploma or GED certificate. Some may require a formal training course to obtain a license.

Work_Styles	Work_Styles Definitions
Dependability	Job requires being reliable, responsible, and dependable, and fulfilling obligations.
Self Control	Job requires maintaining composure, keeping emotions in check, controlling anger, and avoiding aggressive behavior, even in very difficult situations.
Cooperation	Job requires being pleasant with others on the job and displaying a good-natured, cooperative attitude.
Integrity	Job requires being honest and ethical.
Independence	Job requires developing one's own ways of doing things, guiding oneself with little or no supervision, and depending on oneself to get things done.
Attention to Detail	Job requires being careful about detail and thorough in completing work tasks.
Initiative	Job requires a willingness to take on responsibilities and challenges.
Adaptability/Flexibility	Job requires being open to change (positive or negative) and to considerable variety in the workplace.
Concern for Others	Job requires being sensitive to others' needs and feelings and being understanding and helpful on the job.
Stress Tolerance	Job requires accepting criticism and dealing calmly and effectively with high stress situations.
Social Orientation	Job requires preferring to work with others rather than alone, and being personally connected with others on the job.
Leadership	Job requires a willingness to lead, take charge, and offer opinions and direction.
Achievement/Effort	Job requires establishing and maintaining personally challenging achievement goals and exerting effort toward mastering tasks.
Persistence	Job requires persistence in the face of obstacles.
Innovation	Job requires creativity and alternative thinking to develop new ideas for and answers to work-related problems.
Analytical Thinking	Job requires analyzing information and using logic to address work-related issues and problems.

35-3011.00 - Bartenders

Mix and serve drinks to patrons, directly or through waitstaff.

Tasks

1) Clean glasses, utensils, and bar equipment.

2) Attempt to limit problems and liability related to customers' excessive drinking by taking steps such as persuading customers to stop drinking, or ordering taxis or other transportation for intoxicated patrons.

3) Collect money for drinks served.

4) Check identification of customers in order to verify age requirements for purchase of alcohol.

5) Serve wine, and bottled or draft beer.

6) Mix ingredients, such as liquor, soda, water, sugar, and bitters, in order to prepare cocktails and other drinks.

7) Slice and pit fruit for garnishing drinks.

8) Arrange bottles and glasses to make attractive displays.

9) Serve snacks or food items to customers seated at the bar.

10) Ask customers who become loud and obnoxious to leave, or physically remove them.

11) Balance cash receipts.

12) Order or requisition liquors and supplies.

13) Create drink recipes.

14) Plan, organize, and control the operations of a cocktail lounge or bar.

15) Supervise the work of bar staff and other bartenders.

16) Prepare appetizers, such as pickles, cheese, and cold meats.

17) Plan bar menus.

18) Clean bars, work areas, and tables.

Knowledge	Knowledge Definitions
Customer and Personal Service	Knowledge of principles and processes for providing customer and personal services. This includes customer needs assessment, meeting quality standards for services, and evaluation of customer satisfaction.
Psychology	Knowledge of human behavior and performance; individual differences in ability, personality, and interests; learning and motivation; psychological research methods; and the assessment and treatment of behavioral and affective disorders.
Mathematics	Knowledge of arithmetic, algebra, geometry, calculus, statistics, and their applications.
Sales and Marketing	Knowledge of principles and methods for showing, promoting, and selling products or services. This includes marketing strategy and tactics, product demonstration, sales techniques, and sales control systems.
English Language	Knowledge of the structure and content of the English language including the meaning and spelling of words, rules of composition, and grammar.
Administration and Management	Knowledge of business and management principles involved in strategic planning, resource allocation, human resources modeling, leadership technique, production methods, and coordination of people and resources.
Food Production	Knowledge of techniques and equipment for planting, growing, and harvesting food products (both plant and animal) for consumption, including storage/handling techniques.
Production and Processing	Knowledge of raw materials, production processes, quality control, costs, and other techniques for maximizing the effective manufacture and distribution of goods.
Law and Government	Knowledge of laws, legal codes, court procedures, precedents, government regulations, executive orders, agency rules, and the democratic political process.
Education and Training	Knowledge of principles and methods for curriculum and training design, teaching and instruction for individuals and groups, and the measurement of training effects.
Public Safety and Security	Knowledge of relevant equipment, policies, procedures, and strategies to promote effective local, state, or national security operations for the protection of people, data, property, and institutions.
Computers and Electronics	Knowledge of circuit boards, processors, chips, electronic equipment, and computer hardware and software, including applications and programming.
Sociology and Anthropology	Knowledge of group behavior and dynamics, societal trends and influences, human migrations, ethnicity, cultures and their history and origins.
Economics and Accounting	Knowledge of economic and accounting principles and practices, the financial markets, banking and the analysis and reporting of financial data.
Personnel and Human Resources	Knowledge of principles and procedures for personnel recruitment, selection, training, compensation and benefits, labor relations and negotiation, and personnel information systems.
Clerical	Knowledge of administrative and clerical procedures and systems such as word processing, managing files and records, stenography and transcription, designing forms, and other office procedures and terminology.
Foreign Language	Knowledge of the structure and content of a foreign (non-English) language including the meaning and spelling of words, rules of composition and grammar, and pronunciation.
Philosophy and Theology	Knowledge of different philosophical systems and religions. This includes their basic principles, values, ethics, ways of thinking, customs, practices, and their impact on human culture.
Mechanical	Knowledge of machines and tools, including their designs, uses, repair, and maintenance.
Geography	Knowledge of principles and methods for describing the features of land, sea, and air masses, including their physical characteristics, locations, interrelationships, and distribution of plant, animal, and human life.
Communications and Media	Knowledge of media production, communication, and dissemination techniques and methods. This includes alternative ways to inform and entertain via written, oral, and visual media.
Medicine and Dentistry	Knowledge of the information and techniques needed to diagnose and treat human injuries, diseases, and deformities. This includes symptoms, treatment alternatives, drug properties and interactions, and preventive health-care measures.
Telecommunications	Knowledge of transmission, broadcasting, switching, control, and operation of telecommunications systems.
Transportation	Knowledge of principles and methods for moving people or goods by air, rail, sea, or road, including the relative costs and benefits.
Therapy and Counseling	Knowledge of principles, methods, and procedures for diagnosis, treatment, and rehabilitation of physical and mental dysfunctions, and for career counseling and guidance.
Chemistry	Knowledge of the chemical composition, structure, and properties of substances and of the chemical processes and transformations that they undergo. This includes uses of chemicals and their interactions, danger signs, production techniques, and disposal methods.
History and Archeology	Knowledge of historical events and their causes, indicators, and effects on civilizations and cultures.
Design	Knowledge of design techniques, tools, and principles involved in production of precision technical plans, blueprints, drawings, and models.
Fine Arts	Knowledge of the theory and techniques required to compose, produce, and perform works of music, dance, visual arts, drama, and sculpture.
Engineering and Technology	Knowledge of the practical application of engineering science and technology. This includes applying principles, techniques, procedures, and equipment to the design and production of various goods and services.
Building and Construction	Knowledge of materials, methods, and the tools involved in the construction or repair of houses, buildings, or other structures such as highways and roads.
Biology	Knowledge of plant and animal organisms, their tissues, cells, functions, interdependencies, and interactions with each other and the environment.
Physics	Knowledge and prediction of physical principles, laws, their interrelationships, and applications to understanding fluid, material, and atmospheric dynamics, and mechanical, electrical, atomic and sub- atomic structures and processes.

Skills	Skills Definitions
Active Listening	Giving full attention to what other people are saying, taking time to understand the points being made, asking questions as appropriate, and not interrupting at inappropriate times.
Speaking	Talking to others to convey information effectively.
Social Perceptiveness	Being aware of others' reactions and understanding why they react as they do.
Mathematics	Using mathematics to solve problems.
Service Orientation	Actively looking for ways to help people.
Critical Thinking	Using logic and reasoning to identify the strengths and weaknesses of alternative solutions, conclusions or approaches to problems.
Reading Comprehension	Understanding written sentences and paragraphs in work related documents.

Learning Strategies	Selecting and using training/instructional methods and procedures appropriate for the situation when learning or teaching new things.
Coordination	Adjusting actions in relation to others' actions.
Judgment and Decision Making	Considering the relative costs and benefits of potential actions to choose the most appropriate one.
Active Learning	Understanding the implications of new information for both current and future problem-solving and decision-making.
Monitoring	Monitoring/Assessing performance of yourself, other individuals, or organizations to make improvements or take corrective action.
Persuasion	Persuading others to change their minds or behavior.
Instructing	Teaching others how to do something.
Negotiation	Bringing others together and trying to reconcile differences.
Time Management	Managing one's own time and the time of others.
Writing	Communicating effectively in writing as appropriate for the needs of the audience.
Equipment Selection	Determining the kind of tools and equipment needed to do a job.
Equipment Maintenance	Performing routine maintenance on equipment and determining when and what kind of maintenance is needed.
Complex Problem Solving	Identifying complex problems and reviewing related information to develop and evaluate options and implement solutions.
Troubleshooting	Determining causes of operating errors and deciding what to do about it.
Management of Material Resources	Obtaining and seeing to the appropriate use of equipment, facilities, and materials needed to do certain work.
Management of Personnel Resources	Motivating, developing, and directing people as they work, identifying the best people for the job.
Quality Control Analysis	Conducting tests and inspections of products, services, or processes to evaluate quality or performance.
Systems Evaluation	Identifying measures or indicators of system performance and the actions needed to improve or correct performance, relative to the goals of the system.
Management of Financial Resources	Determining how money will be spent to get the work done, and accounting for these expenditures.
Operation and Control	Controlling operations of equipment or systems.
Repairing	Repairing machines or systems using the needed tools.
Operation Monitoring	Watching gauges, dials, or other indicators to make sure a machine is working properly.
Operations Analysis	Analyzing needs and product requirements to create a design.
Installation	Installing equipment, machines, wiring, or programs to meet specifications.
Systems Analysis	Determining how a system should work and how changes in conditions, operations, and the environment will affect outcomes.
Science	Using scientific rules and methods to solve problems.
Technology Design	Generating or adapting equipment and technology to serve user needs.
Programming	Writing computer programs for various purposes.

Ability	Ability Definitions
Oral Comprehension	The ability to listen to and understand information and ideas presented through spoken words and sentences.
Oral Expression	The ability to communicate information and ideas in speaking so others will understand.
Problem Sensitivity	The ability to tell when something is wrong or is likely to go wrong. It does not involve solving the problem, only recognizing there is a problem.
Speech Recognition	The ability to identify and understand the speech of another person.
Speech Clarity	The ability to speak clearly so others can understand you.
Near Vision	The ability to see details at close range (within a few feet of the observer).
Information Ordering	The ability to arrange things or actions in a certain order or pattern according to a specific rule or set of rules (e.g., patterns of numbers, letters, words, pictures, mathematical operations).
Trunk Strength	The ability to use your abdominal and lower back muscles to support part of the body repeatedly or continuously over time without 'giving out' or fatiguing.
Memorization	The ability to remember information such as words, numbers, pictures, and procedures.
Manual Dexterity	The ability to quickly move your hand, your hand together with your arm, or your two hands to grasp, manipulate, or assemble objects.

Arm-Hand Steadiness	The ability to keep your hand and arm steady while moving your arm or while holding your arm and hand in one position.
Originality	The ability to come up with unusual or clever ideas about a given topic or situation, or to develop creative ways to solve a problem.
Fluency of Ideas	The ability to come up with a number of ideas about a topic (the number of ideas is important, not their quality, correctness, or creativity).
Deductive Reasoning	The ability to apply general rules to specific problems to produce answers that make sense.
Number Facility	The ability to add, subtract, multiply, or divide quickly and correctly.
Stamina	The ability to exert yourself physically over long periods of time without getting winded or out of breath.
Written Comprehension	The ability to read and understand information and ideas presented in writing.
Category Flexibility	The ability to generate or use different sets of rules for combining or grouping things in different ways.
Selective Attention	The ability to concentrate on a task over a period of time without being distracted.
Time Sharing	The ability to shift back and forth between two or more activities or sources of information (such as speech, sounds, touch, or other sources).
Inductive Reasoning	The ability to combine pieces of information to form general rules or conclusions (includes finding a relationship among seemingly unrelated events).
Static Strength	The ability to exert maximum muscle force to lift, push, pull, or carry objects.
Gross Body Coordination	The ability to coordinate the movement of your arms, legs, and torso together when the whole body is in motion.
Multilimb Coordination	The ability to coordinate two or more limbs (for example, two arms, two legs, or one leg and one arm) while sitting, standing, or lying down. It does not involve performing the activities while the whole body is in motion.
Speed of Closure	The ability to quickly make sense of, combine, and organize information into meaningful patterns.
Mathematical Reasoning	The ability to choose the right mathematical methods or formulas to solve a problem.
Extent Flexibility	The ability to bend, stretch, twist, or reach with your body, arms, and/or legs.
Written Expression	The ability to communicate information and ideas in writing so others will understand.
Auditory Attention	The ability to focus on a single source of sound in the presence of other distracting sounds.
Perceptual Speed	The ability to quickly and accurately compare similarities and differences among sets of letters, numbers, objects, pictures, or patterns. The things to be compared may be presented at the same time or one after the other. This ability also includes comparing a presented object with a remembered object.
Finger Dexterity	The ability to make precisely coordinated movements of the fingers of one or both hands to grasp, manipulate, or assemble very small objects.
Visualization	The ability to imagine how something will look after it is moved around or when its parts are moved or rearranged.
Speed of Limb Movement	The ability to quickly move the arms and legs.
Depth Perception	The ability to judge which of several objects is closer or farther away from you, or to judge the distance between you and an object.
Flexibility of Closure	The ability to identify or detect a known pattern (a figure, object, word, or sound) that is hidden in other distracting material.
Far Vision	The ability to see details at a distance.
Control Precision	The ability to quickly and repeatedly adjust the controls of a machine or a vehicle to exact positions.
Visual Color Discrimination	The ability to match or detect differences between colors, including shades of color and brightness.
Dynamic Strength	The ability to exert muscle force repeatedly or continuously over time. This involves muscular endurance and resistance to muscle fatigue.
Wrist-Finger Speed	The ability to make fast, simple, repeated movements of the fingers, hands, and wrists.
Dynamic Flexibility	The ability to quickly and repeatedly bend, stretch, twist, or reach out with your body, arms, and/or legs.
Spatial Orientation	The ability to know your location in relation to the environment or to know where other objects are in relation to you.
Reaction Time	The ability to quickly respond (with the hand, finger, or foot) to a signal (sound, light, picture) when it appears.

Response Orientation	The ability to choose quickly between two or more movements in response to two or more different signals (lights, sounds, pictures). It includes the speed with which the correct response is started with the hand, foot, or other body part.
Hearing Sensitivity	The ability to detect or tell the differences between sounds that vary in pitch and loudness.
Peripheral Vision	The ability to see objects or movement of objects to one's side when the eyes are looking ahead.
Night Vision	The ability to see under low light conditions.
Gross Body Equilibrium	The ability to keep or regain your body balance or stay upright when in an unstable position.
Explosive Strength	The ability to use short bursts of muscle force to propel oneself (as in jumping or sprinting), or to throw an object.
Rate Control	The ability to time your movements or the movement of a piece of equipment in anticipation of changes in the speed and/or direction of a moving object or scene.
Sound Localization	The ability to tell the direction from which a sound originated.
Glare Sensitivity	The ability to see objects in the presence of glare or bright lighting.

Work_Activity	Work_Activity Definitions
Performing for or Working Directly with the Public	Performing for people or dealing directly with the public. This includes serving customers in restaurants and stores, and receiving clients or guests.
Communicating with Persons Outside Organization	Communicating with people outside the organization, representing the organization to customers, the public, government, and other external sources. This information can be exchanged in person, in writing, or by telephone or e-mail.
Establishing and Maintaining Interpersonal Relatio	Developing constructive and cooperative working relationships with others, and maintaining them over time.
Identifying Objects, Actions, and Events	Identifying information by categorizing, estimating, recognizing differences or similarities, and detecting changes in circumstances or events.
Communicating with Supervisors, Peers, or Subordin	Providing information to supervisors, co-workers, and subordinates by telephone, in written form, e-mail, or in person.
Judging the Qualities of Things, Services, or Peop	Assessing the value, importance, or quality of things or people.
Getting Information	Observing, receiving, and otherwise obtaining information from all relevant sources.
Selling or Influencing Others	Convincing others to buy merchandise/goods or to otherwise change their minds or actions.
Performing General Physical Activities	Performing physical activities that require considerable use of your arms and legs and moving your whole body, such as climbing, lifting, balancing, walking, stooping, and handling of materials.
Monitor Processes, Materials, or Surroundings	Monitoring and reviewing information from materials, events, or the environment, to detect or assess problems.
Resolving Conflicts and Negotiating with Others	Handling complaints, settling disputes, and resolving grievances and conflicts, or otherwise negotiating with others.
Making Decisions and Solving Problems	Analyzing information and evaluating results to choose the best solution and solve problems.
Evaluating Information to Determine Compliance wit	Using relevant information and individual judgment to determine whether events or processes comply with laws, regulations, or standards.
Handling and Moving Objects	Using hands and arms in handling, installing, positioning, and moving materials, and manipulating things.
Inspecting Equipment, Structures, or Material	Inspecting equipment, structures, or materials to identify the cause of errors or other problems or defects.
Assisting and Caring for Others	Providing personal assistance, medical attention, emotional support, or other personal care to others such as coworkers, customers, or patients.
Updating and Using Relevant Knowledge	Keeping up-to-date technically and applying new knowledge to your job.
Training and Teaching Others	Identifying the educational needs of others, developing formal educational or training programs or classes, and teaching or instructing others.
Estimating the Quantifiable Characteristics of Pro	Estimating sizes, distances, and quantities; or determining time, costs, resources, or materials needed to perform a work activity.
Scheduling Work and Activities	Scheduling events, programs, and activities, as well as the work of others.
Developing and Building Teams	Encouraging and building mutual trust, respect, and cooperation among team members.

Organizing, Planning, and Prioritizing Work	Developing specific goals and plans to prioritize, organize, and accomplish your work.
Thinking Creatively	Developing, designing, or creating new applications, ideas, relationships, systems, or products, including artistic contributions.
Controlling Machines and Processes	Using either control mechanisms or direct physical activity to operate machines or processes (not including computers or vehicles).
Guiding, Directing, and Motivating Subordinates	Providing guidance and direction to subordinates, including setting performance standards and monitoring performance.
Coaching and Developing Others	Identifying the developmental needs of others and coaching, mentoring, or otherwise helping others to improve their knowledge or skills.
Processing Information	Compiling, coding, categorizing, calculating, tabulating, auditing, or verifying information or data.
Performing Administrative Activities	Performing day-to-day administrative tasks such as maintaining information files and processing paperwork.
Coordinating the Work and Activities of Others	Getting members of a group to work together to accomplish tasks.
Documenting/Recording Information	Entering, transcribing, recording, storing, or maintaining information in written or electronic/magnetic form.
Provide Consultation and Advice to Others	Providing guidance and expert advice to management or other groups on technical, systems-, or process-related topics.
Developing Objectives and Strategies	Establishing long-range objectives and specifying the strategies and actions to achieve them.
Interacting With Computers	Using computers and computer systems (including hardware and software) to program, write software, set up functions, enter data, or process information.
Analyzing Data or Information	Identifying the underlying principles, reasons, or facts of information by breaking down information or data into separate parts.
Monitoring and Controlling Resources	Monitoring and controlling resources and overseeing the spending of money.
Interpreting the Meaning of Information for Others	Translating or explaining what information means and how it can be used.
Staffing Organizational Units	Recruiting, interviewing, selecting, hiring, and promoting employees in an organization.
Repairing and Maintaining Mechanical Equipment	Servicing, repairing, adjusting, and testing machines, devices, moving parts, and equipment that operate primarily on the basis of mechanical (not electronic) principles.
Repairing and Maintaining Electronic Equipment	Servicing, repairing, calibrating, regulating, fine-tuning, or testing machines, devices, and equipment that operate primarily on the basis of electrical or electronic (not mechanical) principles.
Operating Vehicles, Mechanized Devices, or Equipme	Running, maneuvering, navigating, or driving vehicles or mechanized equipment, such as forklifts, passenger vehicles, aircraft, or water craft.
Drafting, Laying Out, and Specifying Technical Dev	Providing documentation, detailed instructions, drawings, or specifications to tell others about how devices, parts, equipment, or structures are to be fabricated, constructed, assembled, modified, maintained, or used.

Work_Context	Work_Context Definitions
Contact With Others	How much does this job require the worker to be in contact with others (face-to-face, by telephone, or otherwise) in order to perform it?
Spend Time Standing	How much does this job require standing?
Face-to-Face Discussions	How often do you have to have face-to-face discussions with individuals or teams in this job?
Physical Proximity	To what extent does this job require the worker to perform job tasks in close physical proximity to other people?
Spend Time Walking and Running	How much does this job require walking and running?
Freedom to Make Decisions	How much decision making freedom, without supervision, does the job offer?
Indoors, Environmentally Controlled	How often does this job require working indoors in environmentally controlled conditions?
Telephone	How often do you have telephone conversations in this job?
Deal With External Customers	How important is it to work with external customers or the public in this job?
Structured versus Unstructured Work	To what extent is this job structured for the worker, rather than allowing the worker to determine tasks, priorities, and goals?
Work With Work Group or Team	How important is it to work with others in a group or team in this job?
Frequency of Decision Making	How frequently is the worker required to make decisions that affect other people, the financial resources, and/or the image and reputation of the organization?

Deal With Unpleasant or Angry People	How frequently does the worker have to deal with unpleasant. angry. or discourteous individuals as part of the job requirements?
Spend Time Using Your Hands to Handle, Control. or	How much does this job require using your hands to handle. control. or feel objects. tools or controls?
Importance of Being Exact or Accurate	How important is being very exact or highly accurate in performing this job?
Spend Time Making Repetitive Motions	How much does this job require making repetitive motions?
Impact of Decisions on Co-workers or Company Resul	How do the decisions an employee makes impact the results of co-workers. clients or the company?
Frequency of Conflict Situations	How often are there conflict situations the employee has to face in this job?
Sounds, Noise Levels Are Distracting or Uncomforta	How often does this job require working exposed to sounds and noise levels that are distracting or uncomfortable?
Coordinate or Lead Others	How important is it to coordinate or lead others in accomplishing work activities in this job?
Responsible for Others' Health and Safety	How much responsibility is there for the health and safety of others in this job?
Spend Time Bending or Twisting the Body	How much does this job require bending or twisting your body?
Importance of Repeating Same Tasks	How important is repeating the same physical activities (e.g.. key entry) or mental activities (e.g., checking entries in a ledger) over and over. without stopping, to performing this job?
Responsibility for Outcomes and Results	How responsible is the worker for work outcomes and results of other workers?
Level of Competition	To what extent does this job require the worker to compete or to be aware of competitive pressures?
Exposed to Minor Burns, Cuts. Bites, or Stings	How often does this job require exposure to minor burns, cuts. bites, or stings?
Exposed to Contaminants	How often does this job require working exposed to contaminants (such as pollutants, gases, dust or odors)?
Deal With Physically Aggressive People	How frequently does this job require the worker to deal with physical aggression of violent individuals?
Extremely Bright or Inadequate Lighting	How often does this job require working in extremely bright or inadequate lighting conditions?
Spend Time Keeping or Regaining Balance	How much does this job require keeping or regaining your balance?
Cramped Work Space, Awkward Positions	How often does this job require working in cramped work spaces that requires getting into awkward positions?
Time Pressure	How often does this job require the worker to meet strict deadlines?
Spend Time Kneeling, Crouching, Stooping, or Crawl	How much does this job require kneeling, crouching, stooping or crawling?
Letters and Memos	How often does the job require written letters and memos?
Public Speaking	How often do you have to perform public speaking in this job?
Degree of Automation	How automated is the job?
Consequence of Error	How serious would the result usually be if the worker made a mistake that was not readily correctable?
Outdoors, Exposed to Weather	How often does this job require working outdoors, exposed to all weather conditions?
Exposed to Disease or Infections	How often does this job require exposure to disease/infections?
Outdoors, Under Cover	How often does this job require working outdoors, under cover (e.g., structure with roof but no walls)?
Spend Time Sitting	How much does this job require sitting?
Wear Common Protective or Safety Equipment such as	How much does this job require wearing common protective or safety equipment such as safety shoes, glasses, gloves, hard hats or live jackets?
Pace Determined by Speed of Equipment	How important is it to this job that the pace is determined by the speed of equipment or machinery? (This does not refer to keeping busy at all times on this job.)
Very Hot or Cold Temperatures	How often does this job require working in very hot (above 90 F degrees) or very cold (below 32 F degrees) temperatures?
Indoors, Not Environmentally Controlled	How often does this job require working indoors in non-controlled environmental conditions (e.g., warehouse without heat)?
Exposed to Hazardous Conditions	How often does this job require exposure to hazardous conditions?
Electronic Mail	How often do you use electronic mail in this job?
Exposed to Whole Body Vibration	How often does this job require exposure to whole body vibration (e.g., operate a jackhammer)?
Exposed to High Places	How often does this job require exposure to high places?
In an Enclosed Vehicle or Equipment	How often does this job require working in a closed vehicle or equipment (e.g.. car)?
Exposed to Radiation	How often does this job require exposure to radiation?
Exposed to Hazardous Equipment	How often does this job require exposure to hazardous equipment?
Spend Time Climbing Ladders. Scaffolds. or Poles	How much does this job require climbing ladders. scaffolds. or poles?
In an Open Vehicle or Equipment	How often does this job require working in an open vehicle or equipment (e.g., tractor)?
Wear Specialized Protective or Safety Equipment su	How much does this job require wearing specialized protective or safety equipment such as breathing apparatus, safety harness. full protection suits, or radiation protection?

Job Zone Component	Job Zone Component Definitions
Title	Job Zone Two: Some Preparation Needed
Overall Experience	Some previous work-related skill, knowledge, or experience may be helpful in these occupations, but usually is not needed. For example, a drywall installer might benefit from experience installing drywall, but an inexperienced person could still learn to be an installer with little difficulty.
Job Training	Employees in these occupations need anywhere from a few months to one year of working with experienced employees.
Job Zone Examples	These occupations often involve using your knowledge and skills to help others. Examples include drywall installers, fire inspectors, flight attendants, pharmacy technicians, salespersons (retail), and tellers.
SVP Range	(4.0 to < 6.0)
Education	These occupations usually require a high school diploma and may require some vocational training or job-related course work. In some cases, an associate's or bachelor's degree could be needed.

Work_Styles	Work_Styles Definitions
Self Control	Job requires maintaining composure, keeping emotions in check, controlling anger, and avoiding aggressive behavior, even in very difficult situations.
Cooperation	Job requires being pleasant with others on the job and displaying a good-natured, cooperative attitude.
Integrity	Job requires being honest and ethical.
Stress Tolerance	Job requires accepting criticism and dealing calmly and effectively with high stress situations.
Dependability	Job requires being reliable, responsible, and dependable, and fulfilling obligations.
Social Orientation	Job requires preferring to work with others rather than alone, and being personally connected with others on the job.
Concern for Others	Job requires being sensitive to others' needs and feelings and being understanding and helpful on the job.
Attention to Detail	Job requires being careful about detail and thorough in completing work tasks.
Adaptability/Flexibility	Job requires being open to change (positive or negative) and to considerable variety in the workplace.
Independence	Job requires developing one's own ways of doing things, guiding oneself with little or no supervision, and depending on oneself to get things done.
Initiative	Job requires a willingness to take on responsibilities and challenges.
Leadership	Job requires a willingness to lead, take charge, and offer opinions and direction.
Achievement/Effort	Job requires establishing and maintaining personally challenging achievement goals and exerting effort toward mastering tasks.
Analytical Thinking	Job requires analyzing information and using logic to address work-related issues and problems.
Persistence	Job requires persistence in the face of obstacles.
Innovation	Job requires creativity and alternative thinking to develop new ideas for and answers to work-related problems.

35-3021.00 - Combined Food Preparation and Serving Workers, Including Fast Food

Perform duties which combine both food preparation and food service.

Tasks

1) Select food items from serving or storage areas and place them in dishes, on serving trays, or in takeout bags.

2) Collect and return dirty dishes to the kitchen for washing.

3) Notify kitchen personnel of shortages or special orders.

4) Accept payment from customers, and make change as necessary.

5) Serve customers in eating places that specialize in fast service and inexpensive carry-out food.

6) Request and record customer orders, and compute bills using cash registers, multicounting machines, or pencil and paper.

7) Prepare simple foods and beverages such as sandwiches, salads, and coffee.

8) Wash dishes, glassware, and silverware after meals.

9) Cook or re-heat food items such as french fries.

10) Prepare and serve cold drinks, or frozen milk drinks or desserts, using drink-dispensing, milkshake, or frozen custard machines.

11) Distribute food to servers.

12) Relay food orders to cooks.

13) Pack food, dishes, utensils, tablecloths, and accessories for transportation from catering or food preparation establishments to locations designated by customers.

14) Arrange tables and decorations according to instructions.

15) Provide caterers with assistance in food preparation or service.

16) Serve food and beverages to guests at banquets or other social functions.

Knowledge	Knowledge Definitions
Customer and Personal Service	Knowledge of principles and processes for providing customer and personal services. This includes customer needs assessment, meeting quality standards for services, and evaluation of customer satisfaction.
Food Production	Knowledge of techniques and equipment for planting, growing, and harvesting food products (both plant and animal) for consumption, including storage/handling techniques.
Sales and Marketing	Knowledge of principles and methods for showing, promoting, and selling products or services. This includes marketing strategy and tactics, product demonstration, sales techniques, and sales control systems.
Mathematics	Knowledge of arithmetic, algebra, geometry, calculus, statistics, and their applications.
Administration and Management	Knowledge of business and management principles involved in strategic planning, resource allocation, human resources modeling, leadership technique, production methods, and coordination of people and resources.
Production and Processing	Knowledge of raw materials, production processes, quality control, costs, and other techniques for maximizing the effective manufacture and distribution of goods.
Public Safety and Security	Knowledge of relevant equipment, policies, procedures, and strategies to promote effective local, state, or national security operations for the protection of people, data, property, and institutions.
English Language	Knowledge of the structure and content of the English language including the meaning and spelling of words, rules of composition, and grammar.
Economics and Accounting	Knowledge of economic and accounting principles and practices, the financial markets, banking and the analysis and reporting of financial data.
Education and Training	Knowledge of principles and methods for curriculum and training design, teaching and instruction for individuals and groups, and the measurement of training effects.
Personnel and Human Resources	Knowledge of principles and procedures for personnel recruitment, selection, training, compensation and benefits, labor relations and negotiation, and personnel information systems.
Psychology	Knowledge of human behavior and performance; individual differences in ability, personality, and interests; learning and motivation; psychological research methods; and the assessment and treatment of behavioral and affective disorders.
Law and Government	Knowledge of laws, legal codes, court procedures, precedents, government regulations, executive orders, agency rules, and the democratic political process.
Chemistry	Knowledge of the chemical composition, structure, and properties of substances and of the chemical processes and transformations that they undergo. This includes uses of chemicals and their interactions, danger signs, production techniques, and disposal methods.
Sociology and Anthropology	Knowledge of group behavior and dynamics, societal trends and influences, human migrations, ethnicity, cultures and their history and origins.
Mechanical	Knowledge of machines and tools, including their designs, uses, repair, and maintenance.
Computers and Electronics	Knowledge of circuit boards, processors, chips, electronic equipment, and computer hardware and software, including applications and programming.
Clerical	Knowledge of administrative and clerical procedures and systems such as word processing, managing files and records, stenography and transcription, designing forms, and other office procedures and terminology.
Communications and Media	Knowledge of media production, communication, and dissemination techniques and methods. This includes alternative ways to inform and entertain via written, oral, and visual media.
Transportation	Knowledge of principles and methods for moving people or goods by air, rail, sea, or road, including the relative costs and benefits.
Telecommunications	Knowledge of transmission, broadcasting, switching, control, and operation of telecommunications systems.
Foreign Language	Knowledge of the structure and content of a foreign (non-English) language including the meaning and spelling of words, rules of composition and grammar, and pronunciation.
Engineering and Technology	Knowledge of the practical application of engineering science and technology. This includes applying principles, techniques, procedures, and equipment to the design and production of various goods and services.
Geography	Knowledge of principles and methods for describing the features of land, sea, and air masses, including their physical characteristics, locations, interrelationships, and distribution of plant, animal, and human life.
Medicine and Dentistry	Knowledge of the information and techniques needed to diagnose and treat human injuries, diseases, and deformities. This includes symptoms, treatment alternatives, drug properties and interactions, and preventive health-care measures.
Design	Knowledge of design techniques, tools, and principles involved in production of precision technical plans, blueprints, drawings, and models.
Biology	Knowledge of plant and animal organisms, their tissues, cells, functions, interdependencies, and interactions with each other and the environment.
Physics	Knowledge and prediction of physical principles, laws, their interrelationships, and applications to understanding fluid, material, and atmospheric dynamics, and mechanical, electrical, atomic and sub- atomic structures and processes.
Philosophy and Theology	Knowledge of different philosophical systems and religions. This includes their basic principles, values, ethics, ways of thinking, customs, practices, and their impact on human culture.
Building and Construction	Knowledge of materials, methods, and the tools involved in the construction or repair of houses, buildings, or other structures such as highways and roads.
History and Archeology	Knowledge of historical events and their causes, indicators, and effects on civilizations and cultures.
Therapy and Counseling	Knowledge of principles, methods, and procedures for diagnosis, treatment, and rehabilitation of physical and mental dysfunctions, and for career counseling and guidance.
Fine Arts	Knowledge of the theory and techniques required to compose, produce, and perform works of music, dance, visual arts, drama, and sculpture.

Skills	Skills Definitions
Active Listening	Giving full attention to what other people are saying, taking time to understand the points being made, asking questions as appropriate, and not interrupting at inappropriate times.
Speaking	Talking to others to convey information effectively.
Instructing	Teaching others how to do something.
Mathematics	Using mathematics to solve problems.
Social Perceptiveness	Being aware of others' reactions and understanding why they react as they do.
Service Orientation	Actively looking for ways to help people.

Learning Strategies	Selecting and using training/instructional methods and procedures appropriate for the situation when learning or teaching new things.
Time Management	Managing one's own time and the time of others.
Reading Comprehension	Understanding written sentences and paragraphs in work related documents.
Coordination	Adjusting actions in relation to others' actions.
Monitoring	Monitoring/Assessing performance of yourself, other individuals, or organizations to make improvements or take corrective action.
Management of Personnel Resources	Motivating, developing, and directing people as they work, identifying the best people for the job.
Active Learning	Understanding the implications of new information for both current and future problem-solving and decision-making.
Critical Thinking	Using logic and reasoning to identify the strengths and weaknesses of alternative solutions, conclusions or approaches to problems.
Management of Material Resources	Obtaining and seeing to the appropriate use of equipment, facilities, and materials needed to do certain work.
Writing	Communicating effectively in writing as appropriate for the needs of the audience.
Negotiation	Bringing others together and trying to reconcile differences.
Judgment and Decision Making	Considering the relative costs and benefits of potential actions to choose the most appropriate one.
Persuasion	Persuading others to change their minds or behavior.
Systems Evaluation	Identifying measures or indicators of system performance and the actions needed to improve or correct performance, relative to the goals of the system.
Management of Financial Resources	Determining how money will be spent to get the work done, and accounting for these expenditures.
Systems Analysis	Determining how a system should work and how changes in conditions, operations, and the environment will affect outcomes.
Equipment Maintenance	Performing routine maintenance on equipment and determining when and what kind of maintenance is needed.
Troubleshooting	Determining causes of operating errors and deciding what to do about it.
Complex Problem Solving	Identifying complex problems and reviewing related information to develop and evaluate options and implement solutions.
Equipment Selection	Determining the kind of tools and equipment needed to do a job.
Operation and Control	Controlling operations of equipment or systems.
Quality Control Analysis	Conducting tests and inspections of products, services, or processes to evaluate quality or performance.
Operation Monitoring	Watching gauges, dials, or other indicators to make sure a machine is working properly.
Repairing	Repairing machines or systems using the needed tools.
Technology Design	Generating or adapting equipment and technology to serve user needs.
Operations Analysis	Analyzing needs and product requirements to create a design.
Installation	Installing equipment, machines, wiring, or programs to meet specifications.
Science	Using scientific rules and methods to solve problems.
Programming	Writing computer programs for various purposes.

Ability	Ability Definitions
Oral Comprehension	The ability to listen to and understand information and ideas presented through spoken words and sentences.
Speech Clarity	The ability to speak clearly so others can understand you.
Oral Expression	The ability to communicate information and ideas in speaking so others will understand.
Trunk Strength	The ability to use your abdominal and lower back muscles to support part of the body repeatedly or continuously over time without 'giving out' or fatiguing.
Problem Sensitivity	The ability to tell when something is wrong or is likely to go wrong. It does not involve solving the problem, only recognizing there is a problem.
Near Vision	The ability to see details at close range (within a few feet of the observer).
Speech Recognition	The ability to identify and understand the speech of another person.
Information Ordering	The ability to arrange things or actions in a certain order or pattern according to a specific rule or set of rules (e.g., patterns of numbers, letters, words, pictures, mathematical operations).

Manual Dexterity	The ability to quickly move your hand, your hand together with your arm, or your two hands to grasp, manipulate, or assemble objects.
Deductive Reasoning	The ability to apply general rules to specific problems to produce answers that make sense.
Selective Attention	The ability to concentrate on a task over a period of time without being distracted.
Stamina	The ability to exert yourself physically over long periods of time without getting winded or out of breath.
Gross Body Coordination	The ability to coordinate the movement of your arms, legs, and torso together when the whole body is in motion.
Arm-Hand Steadiness	The ability to keep your hand and arm steady while moving your arm or while holding your arm and hand in one position.
Number Facility	The ability to add, subtract, multiply, or divide quickly and correctly.
Mathematical Reasoning	The ability to choose the right mathematical methods or formulas to solve a problem.
Multilimb Coordination	The ability to coordinate two or more limbs (for example, two arms, two legs, or one leg and one arm) while sitting, standing, or lying down. It does not involve performing the activities while the whole body is in motion.
Written Expression	The ability to communicate information and ideas in writing so others will understand.
Inductive Reasoning	The ability to combine pieces of information to form general rules or conclusions (includes finding a relationship among seemingly unrelated events).
Static Strength	The ability to exert maximum muscle force to lift, push, pull, or carry objects.
Extent Flexibility	The ability to bend, stretch, twist, or reach with your body, arms, and/or legs.
Time Sharing	The ability to shift back and forth between two or more activities or sources of information (such as speech, sounds, touch, or other sources).
Written Comprehension	The ability to read and understand information and ideas presented in writing.
Auditory Attention	The ability to focus on a single source of sound in the presence of other distracting sounds.
Control Precision	The ability to quickly and repeatedly adjust the controls of a machine or a vehicle to exact positions.
Memorization	The ability to remember information such as words, numbers, pictures, and procedures.
Category Flexibility	The ability to generate or use different sets of rules for combining or grouping things in different ways.
Far Vision	The ability to see details at a distance.
Speed of Limb Movement	The ability to quickly move the arms and legs.
Depth Perception	The ability to judge which of several objects is closer or farther away from you, or to judge the distance between you and an object.
Dynamic Strength	The ability to exert muscle force repeatedly or continuously over time. This involves muscular endurance and resistance to muscle fatigue.
Visualization	The ability to imagine how something will look after it is moved around or when its parts are moved or rearranged.
Finger Dexterity	The ability to make precisely coordinated movements of the fingers of one or both hands to grasp, manipulate, or assemble very small objects.
Reaction Time	The ability to quickly respond (with the hand, finger, or foot) to a signal (sound, light, picture) when it appears.
Spatial Orientation	The ability to know your location in relation to the environment or to know where other objects are in relation to you.
Speed of Closure	The ability to quickly make sense of, combine, and organize information into meaningful patterns.
Wrist-Finger Speed	The ability to make fast, simple, repeated movements of the fingers, hands, and wrists.
Flexibility of Closure	The ability to identify or detect a known pattern (a figure, object, word, or sound) that is hidden in other distracting material.
Perceptual Speed	The ability to quickly and accurately compare similarities and differences among sets of letters, numbers, objects, pictures, or patterns. The things to be compared may be presented at the same time or one after the other. This ability also includes comparing a presented object with a remembered object.
Fluency of Ideas	The ability to come up with a number of ideas about a topic (the number of ideas is important, not their quality, correctness, or creativity).
Hearing Sensitivity	The ability to detect or tell the differences between sounds that vary in pitch and loudness.

Originality	The ability to come up with unusual or clever ideas about a given topic or situation, or to develop creative ways to solve a problem.
Visual Color Discrimination	The ability to match or detect differences between colors, including shades of color and brightness.
Response Orientation	The ability to choose quickly between two or more movements in response to two or more different signals (lights, sounds, pictures). It includes the speed with which the correct response is started with the hand, foot, or other body part.
Rate Control	The ability to time your movements or the movement of a piece of equipment in anticipation of changes in the speed and/or direction of a moving object or scene.
Sound Localization	The ability to tell the direction from which a sound originated.
Peripheral Vision	The ability to see objects or movement of objects to one's side when the eyes are looking ahead.
Gross Body Equilibrium	The ability to keep or regain your body balance or stay upright when in an unstable position.
Dynamic Flexibility	The ability to quickly and repeatedly bend, stretch, twist, or reach out with your body, arms, and/or legs.
Night Vision	The ability to see under low light conditions.
Explosive Strength	The ability to use short bursts of muscle force to propel oneself (as in jumping or sprinting), or to throw an object.
Glare Sensitivity	The ability to see objects in the presence of glare or bright lighting.

Work_Activity	**Work_Activity Definitions**
Performing for or Working Directly with the Public	Performing for people or dealing directly with the public. This includes serving customers in restaurants and stores, and receiving clients or guests.
Getting Information	Observing, receiving, and otherwise obtaining information from all relevant sources.
Identifying Objects, Actions, and Events	Identifying information by categorizing, estimating, recognizing differences or similarities, and detecting changes in circumstances or events.
Coordinating the Work and Activities of Others	Getting members of a group to work together to accomplish tasks.
Establishing and Maintaining Interpersonal Relatio	Developing constructive and cooperative working relationships with others, and maintaining them over time.
Selling or Influencing Others	Convincing others to buy merchandise/goods or to otherwise change their minds or actions.
Performing General Physical Activities	Performing physical activities that require considerable use of your arms and legs and moving your whole body, such as climbing, lifting, balancing, walking, stooping, and handling of materials.
Monitor Processes, Materials, or Surroundings	Monitoring and reviewing information from materials, events, or the environment, to detect or assess problems.
Communicating with Supervisors, Peers, or Subordin	Providing information to supervisors, co-workers, and subordinates by telephone, in written form, e-mail, or in person.
Handling and Moving Objects	Using hands and arms in handling, installing, positioning, and moving materials, and manipulating things.
Judging the Qualities of Things, Services, or Peop	Assessing the value, importance, or quality of things or people.
Resolving Conflicts and Negotiating with Others	Handling complaints, settling disputes, and resolving grievances and conflicts, or otherwise negotiating with others.
Inspecting Equipment, Structures, or Material	Inspecting equipment, structures, or materials to identify the cause of errors or other problems or defects.
Communicating with Persons Outside Organization	Communicating with people outside the organization, representing the organization to customers, the public, government, and other external sources. This information can be exchanged in person, in writing, or by telephone or e-mail.
Evaluating Information to Determine Compliance wit	Using relevant information and individual judgment to determine whether events or processes comply with laws, regulations, or standards.
Making Decisions and Solving Problems	Analyzing information and evaluating results to choose the best solution and solve problems.
Coaching and Developing Others	Identifying the developmental needs of others and coaching, mentoring, or otherwise helping others to improve their knowledge or skills.
Estimating the Quantifiable Characteristics of Pro	Estimating sizes, distances, and quantities; or determining time, costs, resources, or materials needed to perform a work activity.
Controlling Machines and Processes	Using either control mechanisms or direct physical activity to operate machines or processes (not including computers or vehicles).

Organizing, Planning, and Prioritizing Work	Developing specific goals and plans to prioritize, organize, and accomplish your work.
Assisting and Caring for Others	Providing personal assistance, medical attention, emotional support, or other personal care to others such as coworkers, customers, or patients.
Documenting/Recording Information	Entering, transcribing, recording, storing, or maintaining information in written or electronic/magnetic form.
Training and Teaching Others	Identifying the educational needs of others, developing formal educational or training programs or classes, and teaching or instructing others.
Interpreting the Meaning of Information for Others	Translating or explaining what information means and how it can be used.
Developing and Building Teams	Encouraging and building mutual trust, respect, and cooperation among team members.
Processing Information	Compiling, coding, categorizing, calculating, tabulating, auditing, or verifying information or data.
Guiding, Directing, and Motivating Subordinates	Providing guidance and direction to subordinates, including setting performance standards and monitoring performance.
Performing Administrative Activities	Performing day-to-day administrative tasks such as maintaining information files and processing paperwork.
Updating and Using Relevant Knowledge	Keeping up-to-date technically and applying new knowledge to your job.
Scheduling Work and Activities	Scheduling events, programs, and activities, as well as the work of others.
Monitoring and Controlling Resources	Monitoring and controlling resources and overseeing the spending of money.
Provide Consultation and Advice to Others	Providing guidance and expert advice to management or other groups on technical, systems-, or process-related topics.
Thinking Creatively	Developing, designing, or creating new applications, ideas, relationships, systems, or products, including artistic contributions.
Analyzing Data or Information	Identifying the underlying principles, reasons, or facts of information by breaking down information or data into separate parts.
Repairing and Maintaining Mechanical Equipment	Servicing, repairing, adjusting, and testing machines, devices, moving parts, and equipment that operate primarily on the basis of mechanical (not electronic) principles.
Interacting With Computers	Using computers and computer systems (including hardware and software) to program, write software, set up functions, enter data, or process information.
Staffing Organizational Units	Recruiting, interviewing, selecting, hiring, and promoting employees in an organization.
Developing Objectives and Strategies	Establishing long-range objectives and specifying the strategies and actions to achieve them.
Repairing and Maintaining Electronic Equipment	Servicing, repairing, calibrating, regulating, fine-tuning, or testing machines, devices, and equipment that operate primarily on the basis of electrical or electronic (not mechanical) principles.
Drafting, Laying Out, and Specifying Technical Dev	Providing documentation, detailed instructions, drawings, or specifications to tell others about how devices, parts, equipment, or structures are to be fabricated, constructed, assembled, modified, maintained, or used.
Operating Vehicles, Mechanized Devices, or Equipme	Running, maneuvering, navigating, or driving vehicles or mechanized equipment, such as forklifts, passenger vehicles, aircraft, or water craft.

Work_Context	**Work_Context Definitions**
Contact With Others	How much does this job require the worker to be in contact with others (face-to-face, by telephone, or otherwise) in order to perform it?
Spend Time Standing	How much does this job require standing?
Work With Work Group or Team	How important is it to work with others in a group or team in this job?
Indoors, Environmentally Controlled	How often does this job require working indoors in environmentally controlled conditions?
Physical Proximity	To what extent does this job require the worker to perform job tasks in close physical proximity to other people?
Spend Time Walking and Running	How much does this job require walking and running?
Spend Time Making Repetitive Motions	How much does this job require making repetitive motions?
Spend Time Using Your Hands to Handle, Control, or	How much does this job require using your hands to handle, control, or feel objects, tools or controls?
Face-to-Face Discussions	How often do you have to have face-to-face discussions with individuals or teams in this job?

Deal With Unpleasant or Angry People	How frequently does the worker have to deal with unpleasant, angry, or discourteous individuals as part of the job requirements?
Structured versus Unstructured Work	To what extent is this job structured for the worker, rather than allowing the worker to determine tasks, priorities, and goals?
Impact of Decisions on Co-workers or Company Resul	How do the decisions an employee makes impact the results of co-workers, clients or the company?
Importance of Being Exact or Accurate	How important is being very exact or highly accurate in performing this job?
Frequency of Decision Making	How frequently is the worker required to make decisions that affect other people, the financial resources, and/or the image and reputation of the organization?
Freedom to Make Decisions	How much decision making freedom, without supervision, does the job offer?
Exposed to Minor Burns, Cuts, Bites, or Stings	How often does this job require exposure to minor burns, cuts, bites, or stings?
Deal With External Customers	How important is it to work with external customers or the public in this job?
Responsible for Others' Health and Safety	How much responsibility is there for the health and safety of others in this job?
Telephone	How often do you have telephone conversations in this job?
Time Pressure	How often does this job require the worker to meet strict deadlines?
Coordinate or Lead Others	How important is it to coordinate or lead others in accomplishing work activities in this job?
Importance of Repeating Same Tasks	How important is repeating the same physical activities (e.g., key entry) or mental activities (e.g., checking entries in a ledger) over and over, without stopping, to performing this job?
Frequency of Conflict Situations	How often are there conflict situations the employee has to face in this job?
Responsibility for Outcomes and Results	How responsible is the worker for work outcomes and results of other workers?
Spend Time Bending or Twisting the Body	How much does this job require bending or twisting your body?
Wear Common Protective or Safety Equipment such as	How much does this job require wearing common protective or safety equipment such as safety shoes, glasses, gloves, hard hats or life jackets?
Level of Competition	To what extent does this job require the worker to compete or to be aware of competitive pressures?
Sounds, Noise Levels Are Distracting or Uncomforta	How often does this job require working exposed to sounds and noise levels that are distracting or uncomfortable?
Very Hot or Cold Temperatures	How often does this job require working in very hot (above 90 F degrees) or very cold (below 32 F degrees) temperatures?
Consequence of Error	How serious would the result usually be if the worker made a mistake that was not readily correctable?
Spend Time Kneeling, Crouching, Stooping, or Crawl	How much does this job require kneeling, crouching, stooping or crawling?
Exposed to Contaminants	How often does this job require working exposed to contaminants (such as pollutants, gases, dust or odors)?
Letters and Memos	How often does the job require written letters and memos?
Cramped Work Space, Awkward Positions	How often does this job require working in cramped work spaces that requires getting into awkward positions?
Pace Determined by Speed of Equipment	How important is it to this job that the pace is determined by the speed of equipment or machinery? (This does not refer to keeping busy at all times on this job.)
Degree of Automation	How automated is the job?
Spend Time Keeping or Regaining Balance	How much does this job require keeping or regaining your balance?
Extremely Bright or Inadequate Lighting	How often does this job require working in extremely bright or inadequate lighting conditions?
Deal With Physically Aggressive People	How frequently does this job require the worker to deal with physical aggression of violent individuals?
Spend Time Sitting	How much does this job require sitting?
Exposed to Hazardous Equipment	How often does this job require exposure to hazardous equipment?
Indoors, Not Environmentally Controlled	How often does this job require working indoors in non-controlled environmental conditions (e.g., warehouse without heat)?
Outdoors, Exposed to Weather	How often does this job require working outdoors, exposed to all weather conditions?
Wear Specialized Protective or Safety Equipment su	How much does this job require wearing specialized protective or safety equipment such as breathing apparatus, safety harness, full protection suits, or radiation protection?
Exposed to Radiation	How often does this job require exposure to radiation?
Exposed to Disease or Infections	How often does this job require exposure to disease/infections?

Exposed to Hazardous Conditions	How often does this job require exposure to hazardous conditions?
Outdoors, Under Cover	How often does this job require working outdoors, under cover (e.g., structure with roof but no walls)?
Public Speaking	How often do you have to perform public speaking in this job?
Spend Time Climbing Ladders, Scaffolds, or Poles	How much does this job require climbing ladders, scaffolds, or poles?
Exposed to High Places	How often does this job require exposure to high places?
Electronic Mail	How often do you use electronic mail in this job?
In an Enclosed Vehicle or Equipment	How often does this job require working in a closed vehicle or equipment (e.g., car)?
Exposed to Whole Body Vibration	How often does this job require exposure to whole body vibration (e.g., operate a jackhammer)?
In an Open Vehicle or Equipment	How often does this job require working in an open vehicle or equipment (e.g., tractor)?

Job Zone Component	Job Zone Component Definitions
Title	Job Zone One: Little or No Preparation Needed
Overall Experience	No previous work-related skill, knowledge, or experience is needed for these occupations. For example, a person can become a general office clerk even if he/she has never worked in an office before.
Job Training	Employees in these occupations need anywhere from a few days to a few months of training. Usually, an experienced worker could show you how to do the job.
Job Zone Examples	These occupations involve following instructions and helping others. Examples include bus drivers, forest and conservation workers, general office clerks, home health aides, and waiters/waitresses.
SVP Range	(Below 4.0)
Education	These occupations may require a high school diploma or GED certificate. Some may require a formal training course to obtain a license.

Work_Styles	Work_Styles Definitions
Dependability	Job requires being reliable, responsible, and dependable, and fulfilling obligations.
Cooperation	Job requires being pleasant with others on the job and displaying a good-natured, cooperative attitude.
Integrity	Job requires being honest and ethical.
Stress Tolerance	Job requires accepting criticism and dealing calmly and effectively with high stress situations.
Self Control	Job requires maintaining composure, keeping emotions in check, controlling anger, and avoiding aggressive behavior, even in very difficult situations.
Attention to Detail	Job requires being careful about detail and thorough in completing work tasks.
Adaptability/Flexibility	Job requires being open to change (positive or negative) and to considerable variety in the workplace.
Initiative	Job requires a willingness to take on responsibilities and challenges.
Social Orientation	Job requires preferring to work with others rather than alone, and being personally connected with others on the job.
Independence	Job requires developing one's own ways of doing things, guiding oneself with little or no supervision, and depending on oneself to get things done.
Leadership	Job requires a willingness to lead, take charge, and offer opinions and direction.
Concern for Others	Job requires being sensitive to others' needs and feelings and being understanding and helpful on the job.
Persistence	Job requires persistence in the face of obstacles.
Achievement/Effort	Job requires establishing and maintaining personally challenging achievement goals and exerting effort toward mastering tasks.
Innovation	Job requires creativity and alternative thinking to develop new ideas for and answers to work-related problems.
Analytical Thinking	Job requires analyzing information and using logic to address work-related issues and problems.

35-3022.00 - Counter Attendants, Cafeteria, Food Concession, and Coffee Shop

Serve food to diners at counter or from a steam table.

Tasks

1) Wrap menu item such as sandwiches, hot entrees, and desserts for serving or for takeout.

2) Serve food, beverages, or desserts to customers in such settings as take-out counters of restaurants or lunchrooms, business or industrial establishments, hotel rooms, and cars.

3) Replenish foods at serving stations.

4) Prepare food such as sandwiches, salads, and ice cream dishes, using standard formulas or following directions.

5) Take customers' orders and write ordered items on tickets, giving ticket stubs to customers when needed to identify filled orders.

6) Prepare bills for food, using cash registers, calculators, or adding machines); and accept payment and make change.

7) Add relishes and garnishes to food orders, according to instructions.

8) Set up dining areas for meals and clear them following meals.

9) Serve salads, vegetables, meat, breads, and cocktails); ladle soups and sauces); portion desserts); and fill beverage cups and glasses.

10) Balance receipts and payments in cash registers.

11) Brew coffee and tea, and fill containers with requested beverages.

12) Order items needed to replenish supplies.

13) Deliver orders to kitchens, and pick up and serve food when it is ready.

14) Carve meat.

15) Arrange reservations for patrons of dining establishments.

Knowledge	Knowledge Definitions
Customer and Personal Service	Knowledge of principles and processes for providing customer and personal services. This includes customer needs assessment, meeting quality standards for services, and evaluation of customer satisfaction.
Food Production	Knowledge of techniques and equipment for planting, growing, and harvesting food products (both plant and animal) for consumption, including storage/handling techniques.
Mathematics	Knowledge of arithmetic, algebra, geometry, calculus, statistics, and their applications.
Sales and Marketing	Knowledge of principles and methods for showing, promoting, and selling products or services. This includes marketing strategy and tactics, product demonstration, sales techniques, and sales control systems.
Administration and Management	Knowledge of business and management principles involved in strategic planning, resource allocation, human resources modeling, leadership technique, production methods, and coordination of people and resources.
English Language	Knowledge of the structure and content of the English language including the meaning and spelling of words, rules of composition, and grammar.
Public Safety and Security	Knowledge of relevant equipment, policies, procedures, and strategies to promote effective local, state, or national security operations for the protection of people, data, property, and institutions.
Education and Training	Knowledge of principles and methods for curriculum and training design, teaching and instruction for individuals and groups, and the measurement of training effects.
Personnel and Human Resources	Knowledge of principles and procedures for personnel recruitment, selection, training, compensation and benefits, labor relations and negotiation, and personnel information systems.
Economics and Accounting	Knowledge of economic and accounting principles and practices, the financial markets, banking and the analysis and reporting of financial data.
Production and Processing	Knowledge of raw materials, production processes, quality control, costs, and other techniques for maximizing the effective manufacture and distribution of goods.
Clerical	Knowledge of administrative and clerical procedures and systems such as word processing, managing files and records, stenography and transcription, designing forms, and other office procedures and terminology.
Psychology	Knowledge of human behavior and performance; individual differences in ability, personality, and interests; learning and motivation; psychological research methods; and the assessment and treatment of behavioral and affective disorders.
Transportation	Knowledge of principles and methods for moving people or goods by air, rail, sea, or road, including the relative costs and benefits.
Chemistry	Knowledge of the chemical composition, structure, and properties of substances and of the chemical processes and transformations that they undergo. This includes uses of chemicals and their interactions, danger signs, production techniques, and disposal methods.
Mechanical	Knowledge of machines and tools, including their designs, uses, repair, and maintenance.
Law and Government	Knowledge of laws, legal codes, court procedures, precedents, government regulations, executive orders, agency rules, and the democratic political process.
Medicine and Dentistry	Knowledge of the information and techniques needed to diagnose and treat human injuries, diseases, and deformities. This includes symptoms, treatment alternatives, drug properties and interactions, and preventive health-care measures.
Communications and Media	Knowledge of media production, communication, and dissemination techniques and methods. This includes alternative ways to inform and entertain via written, oral, and visual media.
Computers and Electronics	Knowledge of circuit boards, processors, chips, electronic equipment, and computer hardware and software, including applications and programming.
Telecommunications	Knowledge of transmission, broadcasting, switching, control, and operation of telecommunications systems.
Sociology and Anthropology	Knowledge of group behavior and dynamics, societal trends and influences, human migrations, ethnicity, cultures and their history and origins.
Engineering and Technology	Knowledge of the practical application of engineering science and technology. This includes applying principles, techniques, procedures, and equipment to the design and production of various goods and services.
Foreign Language	Knowledge of the structure and content of a foreign (non-English) language including the meaning and spelling of words, rules of composition and grammar, and pronunciation.
Philosophy and Theology	Knowledge of different philosophical systems and religions. This includes their basic principles, values, ethics, ways of thinking, customs, practices, and their impact on human culture.
History and Archeology	Knowledge of historical events and their causes, indicators, and effects on civilizations and cultures.
Physics	Knowledge and prediction of physical principles, laws, their interrelationships, and applications to understanding fluid, material, and atmospheric dynamics, and mechanical, electrical, atomic and sub-atomic structures and processes.
Therapy and Counseling	Knowledge of principles, methods, and procedures for diagnosis, treatment, and rehabilitation of physical and mental dysfunctions, and for career counseling and guidance.
Geography	Knowledge of principles and methods for describing the features of land, sea, and air masses, including their physical characteristics, locations, interrelationships, and distribution of plant, animal, and human life.
Design	Knowledge of design techniques, tools, and principles involved in production of precision technical plans, blueprints, drawings, and models.
Fine Arts	Knowledge of the theory and techniques required to compose, produce, and perform works of music, dance, visual arts, drama, and sculpture.
Building and Construction	Knowledge of materials, methods, and the tools involved in the construction or repair of houses, buildings, or other structures such as highways and roads.
Biology	Knowledge of plant and animal organisms, their tissues, cells, functions, interdependencies, and interactions with each other and the environment.

Skills	Skills Definitions
Speaking	Talking to others to convey information effectively.
Instructing	Teaching others how to do something.

750

Active Listening	Giving full attention to what other people are saying, taking time to understand the points being made, asking questions as appropriate, and not interrupting at inappropriate times.
Reading Comprehension	Understanding written sentences and paragraphs in work related documents.
Social Perceptiveness	Being aware of others' reactions and understanding why they react as they do.
Service Orientation	Actively looking for ways to help people.
Writing	Communicating effectively in writing as appropriate for the needs of the audience.
Time Management	Managing one's own time and the time of others.
Coordination	Adjusting actions in relation to others' actions.
Mathematics	Using mathematics to solve problems.
Learning Strategies	Selecting and using training/instructional methods and procedures appropriate for the situation when learning or teaching new things.
Management of Personnel Resources	Motivating, developing, and directing people as they work, identifying the best people for the job.
Troubleshooting	Determining causes of operating errors and deciding what to do about it.
Persuasion	Persuading others to change their minds or behavior.
Judgment and Decision Making	Considering the relative costs and benefits of potential actions to choose the most appropriate one.
Negotiation	Bringing others together and trying to reconcile differences.
Operation Monitoring	Watching gauges, dials, or other indicators to make sure a machine is working properly.
Active Learning	Understanding the implications of new information for both current and future problem-solving and decision-making.
Complex Problem Solving	Identifying complex problems and reviewing related information to develop and evaluate options and implement solutions.
Critical Thinking	Using logic and reasoning to identify the strengths and weaknesses of alternative solutions, conclusions or approaches to problems.
Monitoring	Monitoring/Assessing performance of yourself, other individuals, or organizations to make improvements or take corrective action.
Equipment Maintenance	Performing routine maintenance on equipment and determining when and what kind of maintenance is needed.
Installation	Installing equipment, machines, wiring, or programs to meet specifications.
Repairing	Repairing machines or systems using the needed tools.
Equipment Selection	Determining the kind of tools and equipment needed to do a job.
Systems Analysis	Determining how a system should work and how changes in conditions, operations, and the environment will affect outcomes.
Technology Design	Generating or adapting equipment and technology to serve user needs.
Quality Control Analysis	Conducting tests and inspections of products, services, or processes to evaluate quality or performance.
Systems Evaluation	Identifying measures or indicators of system performance and the actions needed to improve or correct performance, relative to the goals of the system.
Management of Material Resources	Obtaining and seeing to the appropriate use of equipment, facilities, and materials needed to do certain work.
Operation and Control	Controlling operations of equipment or systems.
Science	Using scientific rules and methods to solve problems.
Management of Financial Resources	Determining how money will be spent to get the work done, and accounting for these expenditures.
Operations Analysis	Analyzing needs and product requirements to create a design.
Programming	Writing computer programs for various purposes.

Ability	**Ability Definitions**
Oral Comprehension	The ability to listen to and understand information and ideas presented through spoken words and sentences.
Speech Recognition	The ability to identify and understand the speech of another person.
Oral Expression	The ability to communicate information and ideas in speaking so others will understand.
Speech Clarity	The ability to speak clearly so others can understand you.
Trunk Strength	The ability to use your abdominal and lower back muscles to support part of the body repeatedly or continuously over time without 'giving out' or fatiguing.
Deductive Reasoning	The ability to apply general rules to specific problems to produce answers that make sense.

Information Ordering	The ability to arrange things or actions in a certain order or pattern according to a specific rule or set of rules (e.g., patterns of numbers, letters, words, pictures, mathematical operations).
Problem Sensitivity	The ability to tell when something is wrong or is likely to go wrong. It does not involve solving the problem, only recognizing there is a problem.
Near Vision	The ability to see details at close range (within a few feet of the observer).
Written Expression	The ability to communicate information and ideas in writing so others will understand.
Stamina	The ability to exert yourself physically over long periods of time without getting winded or out of breath.
Inductive Reasoning	The ability to combine pieces of information to form general rules or conclusions (includes finding a relationship among seemingly unrelated events).
Gross Body Coordination	The ability to coordinate the movement of your arms, legs, and torso together when the whole body is in motion.
Manual Dexterity	The ability to quickly move your hand, your hand together with your arm, or your two hands to grasp, manipulate, or assemble objects.
Time Sharing	The ability to shift back and forth between two or more activities or sources of information (such as speech, sounds, touch, or other sources).
Written Comprehension	The ability to read and understand information and ideas presented in writing.
Extent Flexibility	The ability to bend, stretch, twist, or reach with your body, arms, and/or legs.
Selective Attention	The ability to concentrate on a task over a period of time without being distracted.
Arm-Hand Steadiness	The ability to keep your hand and arm steady while moving your arm or while holding your arm and hand in one position.
Multilimb Coordination	The ability to coordinate two or more limbs (for example, two arms, two legs, or one leg and one arm) while sitting, standing, or lying down. It does not involve performing the activities while the whole body is in motion.
Number Facility	The ability to add, subtract, multiply, or divide quickly and correctly.
Speed of Limb Movement	The ability to quickly move the arms and legs.
Static Strength	The ability to exert maximum muscle force to lift, push, pull, or carry objects.
Memorization	The ability to remember information such as words, numbers, pictures, and procedures.
Category Flexibility	The ability to generate or use different sets of rules for combining or grouping things in different ways.
Auditory Attention	The ability to focus on a single source of sound in the presence of other distracting sounds.
Visualization	The ability to imagine how something will look after it is moved around or when its parts are moved or rearranged.
Mathematical Reasoning	The ability to choose the right mathematical methods or formulas to solve a problem.
Far Vision	The ability to see details at a distance.
Wrist-Finger Speed	The ability to make fast, simple, repeated movements of the fingers, hands, and wrists.
Gross Body Equilibrium	The ability to keep or regain your body balance or stay upright when in an unstable position.
Fluency of Ideas	The ability to come up with a number of ideas about a topic (the number of ideas is important, not their quality, correctness, or creativity).
Depth Perception	The ability to judge which of several objects is closer or farther away from you, or to judge the distance between you and an object.
Finger Dexterity	The ability to make precisely coordinated movements of the fingers of one or both hands to grasp, manipulate, or assemble very small objects.
Spatial Orientation	The ability to know your location in relation to the environment or to know where other objects are in relation to you.
Perceptual Speed	The ability to quickly and accurately compare similarities and differences among sets of letters, numbers, objects, pictures, or patterns. The things to be compared may be presented at the same time or one after the other. This ability also includes comparing a presented object with a remembered object.
Response Orientation	The ability to choose quickly between two or more movements in response to two or more different signals (lights, sounds, pictures). It includes the speed with which the correct response is started with the hand, foot, or other body part.
Control Precision	The ability to quickly and repeatedly adjust the controls of a machine or a vehicle to exact positions.

Dynamic Strength	The ability to exert muscle force repeatedly or continuously over time. This involves muscular endurance and resistance to muscle fatigue.
Hearing Sensitivity	The ability to detect or tell the differences between sounds that vary in pitch and loudness.
Visual Color Discrimination	The ability to match or detect differences between colors, including shades of color and brightness.
Originality	The ability to come up with unusual or clever ideas about a given topic or situation, or to develop creative ways to solve a problem.
Flexibility of Closure	The ability to identify or detect a known pattern (a figure, object, word, or sound) that is hidden in other distracting material.
Reaction Time	The ability to quickly respond (with the hand, finger, or foot) to a signal (sound, light, picture) when it appears.
Peripheral Vision	The ability to see objects or movement of objects to one's side when the eyes are looking ahead.
Speed of Closure	The ability to quickly make sense of, combine, and organize information into meaningful patterns.
Explosive Strength	The ability to use short bursts of muscle force to propel oneself (as in jumping or sprinting), or to throw an object.
Glare Sensitivity	The ability to see objects in the presence of glare or bright lighting.
Rate Control	The ability to time your movements or the movement of a piece of equipment in anticipation of changes in the speed and/or direction of a moving object or scene.
Dynamic Flexibility	The ability to quickly and repeatedly bend, stretch, twist, or reach out with your body, arms, and/or legs.
Sound Localization	The ability to tell the direction from which a sound originated.
Night Vision	The ability to see under low light conditions.

Work_Activity	**Work_Activity Definitions**
Performing for or Working Directly with the Public	Performing for people or dealing directly with the public. This includes serving customers in restaurants and stores, and receiving clients or guests.
Identifying Objects, Actions, and Events	Identifying information by categorizing, estimating, recognizing differences or similarities, and detecting changes in circumstances or events.
Communicating with Supervisors, Peers, or Subordin	Providing information to supervisors, co-workers, and subordinates by telephone, in written form, e-mail, or in person.
Handling and Moving Objects	Using hands and arms in handling, installing, positioning, and moving materials, and manipulating things.
Making Decisions and Solving Problems	Analyzing information and evaluating results to choose the best solution and solve problems.
Training and Teaching Others	Identifying the educational needs of others, developing formal educational or training programs or classes, and teaching or instructing others.
Selling or Influencing Others	Convincing others to buy merchandise/goods or to otherwise change their minds or actions.
Developing and Building Teams	Encouraging and building mutual trust, respect, and cooperation among team members.
Establishing and Maintaining Interpersonal Relatio	Developing constructive and cooperative working relationships with others, and maintaining them over time.
Assisting and Caring for Others	Providing personal assistance, medical attention, emotional support, or other personal care to others such as coworkers, customers, or patients.
Coordinating the Work and Activities of Others	Getting members of a group to work together to accomplish tasks.
Thinking Creatively	Developing, designing, or creating new applications, ideas, relationships, systems, or products, including artistic contributions.
Getting Information	Observing, receiving, and otherwise obtaining information from all relevant sources.
Performing General Physical Activities	Performing physical activities that require considerable use of your arms and legs and moving your whole body, such as climbing, lifting, balancing, walking, stooping, and handling of materials.
Provide Consultation and Advice to Others	Providing guidance and expert advice to management or other groups on technical, systems-, or process-related topics.
Resolving Conflicts and Negotiating with Others	Handling complaints, settling disputes, and resolving grievances and conflicts, or otherwise negotiating with others.
Controlling Machines and Processes	Using either control mechanisms or direct physical activity to operate machines or processes (not including computers or vehicles).

Judging the Qualities of Things, Services, or Peop	Assessing the value, importance, or quality of things or people.
Inspecting Equipment, Structures, or Material	Inspecting equipment, structures, or materials to identify the cause of errors or other problems or defects.
Organizing, Planning, and Prioritizing Work	Developing specific goals and plans to prioritize, organize, and accomplish your work.
Documenting/Recording Information	Entering, transcribing, recording, storing, or maintaining information in written or electronic/magnetic form.
Guiding, Directing, and Motivating Subordinates	Providing guidance and direction to subordinates, including setting performance standards and monitoring performance.
Evaluating Information to Determine Compliance wit	Using relevant information and individual judgment to determine whether events or processes comply with laws, regulations, or standards.
Monitor Processes, Materials, or Surroundings	Monitoring and reviewing information from materials, events, or the environment, to detect or assess problems.
Updating and Using Relevant Knowledge	Keeping up-to-date technically and applying new knowledge to your job.
Coaching and Developing Others	Identifying the developmental needs of others and coaching, mentoring, or otherwise helping others to improve their knowledge or skills.
Analyzing Data or Information	Identifying the underlying principles, reasons, or facts of information by breaking down information or data into separate parts.
Processing Information	Compiling, coding, categorizing, calculating, tabulating, auditing, or verifying information or data.
Monitoring and Controlling Resources	Monitoring and controlling resources and overseeing the spending of money.
Staffing Organizational Units	Recruiting, interviewing, selecting, hiring, and promoting employees in an organization.
Scheduling Work and Activities	Scheduling events, programs, and activities, as well as the work of others.
Interacting With Computers	Using computers and computer systems (including hardware and software) to program, write software, set up functions, enter data, or process information.
Developing Objectives and Strategies	Establishing long-range objectives and specifying the strategies and actions to achieve them.
Estimating the Quantifiable Characteristics of Pro	Estimating sizes, distances, and quantities; or determining time, costs, resources, or materials needed to perform a work activity.
Performing Administrative Activities	Performing day-to-day administrative tasks such as maintaining information files and processing paperwork.
Repairing and Maintaining Mechanical Equipment	Servicing, repairing, adjusting, and testing machines, devices, moving parts, and equipment that operate primarily on the basis of mechanical (not electronic) principles.
Communicating with Persons Outside Organization	Communicating with people outside the organization, representing the organization to customers, the public, government, and other external sources. This information can be exchanged in person, in writing, or by telephone or e-mail.
Repairing and Maintaining Electronic Equipment	Servicing, repairing, calibrating, regulating, fine-tuning, or testing machines, devices, and equipment that operate primarily on the basis of electrical or electronic (not mechanical) principles.
Interpreting the Meaning of Information for Others	Translating or explaining what information means and how it can be used.
Operating Vehicles, Mechanized Devices, or Equipme	Running, maneuvering, navigating, or driving vehicles or mechanized equipment, such as forklifts, passenger vehicles, aircraft, or water craft.
Drafting, Laying Out, and Specifying Technical Dev	Providing documentation, detailed instructions, drawings, or specifications to tell others about how devices, parts, equipment, or structures are to be fabricated, constructed, assembled, modified, maintained, or used.

Work_Context	**Work_Context Definitions**
Spend Time Standing	How much does this job require standing?
Face-to-Face Discussions	How often do you have to have face-to-face discussions with individuals or teams in this job?
Contact With Others	How much does this job require the worker to be in contact with others (face-to-face, by telephone, or otherwise) in order to perform it?
Telephone	How often do you have telephone conversations in this job?
Work With Work Group or Team	How important is it to work with others in a group or team in this job?
Physical Proximity	To what extent does this job require the worker to perform job tasks in close physical proximity to other people?
Deal With External Customers	How important is it to work with external customers or the public in this job?

Indoors, Environmentally Controlled	How often does this job require working indoors in environmentally controlled conditions?
Coordinate or Lead Others	How important is it to coordinate or lead others in accomplishing work activities in this job?
Spend Time Walking and Running	How much does this job require walking and running?
Frequency of Decision Making	How frequently is the worker required to make decisions that affect other people, the financial resources, and/or the image and reputation of the organization?
Structured versus Unstructured Work	To what extent is this job structured for the worker, rather than allowing the worker to determine tasks, priorities, and goals?
Responsibility for Outcomes and Results	How responsible is the worker for work outcomes and results of other workers?
Importance of Being Exact or Accurate	How important is being very exact or highly accurate in performing this job?
Freedom to Make Decisions	How much decision making freedom, without supervision, does the job offer?
Spend Time Using Your Hands to Handle, Control, or	How much does this job require using your hands to handle, control, or feel objects, tools or controls?
Impact of Decisions on Co-workers or Company Resul	How do the decisions an employee makes impact the results of co-workers, clients or the company?
Responsible for Others' Health and Safety	How much responsibility is there for the health and safety of others in this job?
Spend Time Making Repetitive Motions	How much does this job require making repetitive motions?
Sounds, Noise Levels Are Distracting or Uncomforta	How often does this job require working exposed to sounds and noise levels that are distracting or uncomfortable?
Exposed to Minor Burns, Cuts, Bites, or Stings	How often does this job require exposure to minor burns, cuts, bites, or stings?
Frequency of Conflict Situations	How often are there conflict situations the employee has to face in this job?
Spend Time Bending or Twisting the Body	How much does this job require bending or twisting your body?
Deal With Unpleasant or Angry People	How frequently does the worker have to deal with unpleasant, angry, or discourteous individuals as part of the job requirements?
Time Pressure	How often does this job require the worker to meet strict deadlines?
Public Speaking	How often do you have to perform public speaking in this job?
Letters and Memos	How often does the job require written letters and memos?
Importance of Repeating Same Tasks	How important is repeating the same physical activities (e.g., key entry) or mental activities (e.g., checking entries in a ledger) over and over, without stopping, to performing this job?
Very Hot or Cold Temperatures	How often does this job require working in very hot (above 90 F degrees) or very cold (below 32 F degrees) temperatures?
Degree of Automation	How automated is the job?
Level of Competition	To what extent does this job require the worker to compete or to be aware of competitive pressures?
Wear Common Protective or Safety Equipment such as	How much does this job require wearing common protective or safety equipment such as safety shoes, glasses, gloves, hard hats or live jackets?
Consequence of Error	How serious would the result usually be if the worker made a mistake that was not readily correctable?
Spend Time Kneeling, Crouching, Stooping, or Crawl	How much does this job require kneeling, crouching, stooping or crawling?
Spend Time Keeping or Regaining Balance	How much does this job require keeping or regaining your balance?
Outdoors, Exposed to Weather	How often does this job require working outdoors, exposed to all weather conditions?
Extremely Bright or Inadequate Lighting	How often does this job require working in extremely bright or inadequate lighting conditions?
Pace Determined by Speed of Equipment	How important is it to this job that the pace is determined by the speed of equipment or machinery? (This does not refer to keeping busy at all times on this job.)
Exposed to Hazardous Equipment	How often does this job require exposure to hazardous equipment?
Exposed to Contaminants	How often does this job require working exposed to contaminants (such as pollutants, gases, dust or odors)?
Electronic Mail	How often do you use electronic mail in this job?
Cramped Work Space, Awkward Positions	How often does this job require working in cramped work spaces that requires getting into awkward positions?
Exposed to Radiation	How often does this job require exposure to radiation?
Exposed to Disease or Infections	How often does this job require exposure to disease/infections?

Indoors, Not Environmentally Controlled	How often does this job require working indoors in non-controlled environmental conditions (e.g., warehouse without heat)?
Exposed to Hazardous Conditions	How often does this job require exposure to hazardous conditions?
In an Enclosed Vehicle or Equipment	How often does this job require working in a closed vehicle or equipment (e.g., car)?
Spend Time Sitting	How much does this job require sitting?
Deal With Physically Aggressive People	How frequently does this job require the worker to deal with physical aggression of violent individuals?
Exposed to High Places	How often does this job require exposure to high places?
Wear Specialized Protective or Safety Equipment su	How much does this job require wearing specialized protective or safety equipment such as breathing apparatus, safety harness, full protection suits, or radiation protection?
Spend Time Climbing Ladders, Scaffolds, or Poles	How much does this job require climbing ladders, scaffolds, or poles?
In an Open Vehicle or Equipment	How often does this job require working in an open vehicle or equipment (e.g., tractor)?
Exposed to Whole Body Vibration	How often does this job require exposure to whole body vibration (e.g., operate a jackhammer)?
Outdoors, Under Cover	How often does this job require working outdoors, under cover (e.g., structure with roof but no walls)?

Job Zone Component	Job Zone Component Definitions
Title	Job Zone One: Little or No Preparation Needed
Overall Experience	No previous work-related skill, knowledge, or experience is needed for these occupations. For example, a person can become a general office clerk even if he/she has never worked in an office before.
Job Training	Employees in these occupations need anywhere from a few days to a few months of training. Usually, an experienced worker could show you how to do the job.
Job Zone Examples	These occupations involve following instructions and helping others. Examples include bus drivers, forest and conservation workers, general office clerks, home health aides, and waiters/waitresses.
SVP Range	(Below 4.0)
Education	These occupations may require a high school diploma or GED certificate. Some may require a formal training course to obtain a license.

Work_Styles	Work_Styles Definitions
Dependability	Job requires being reliable, responsible, and dependable, and fulfilling obligations.
Attention to Detail	Job requires being careful about detail and thorough in completing work tasks.
Concern for Others	Job requires being sensitive to others' needs and feelings and being understanding and helpful on the job.
Cooperation	Job requires being pleasant with others on the job and displaying a good-natured, cooperative attitude.
Self Control	Job requires maintaining composure, keeping emotions in check, controlling anger, and avoiding aggressive behavior, even in very difficult situations.
Stress Tolerance	Job requires accepting criticism and dealing calmly and effectively with high stress situations.
Integrity	Job requires being honest and ethical.
Adaptability/Flexibility	Job requires being open to change (positive or negative) and to considerable variety in the workplace.
Social Orientation	Job requires preferring to work with others rather than alone, and being personally connected with others on the job.
Independence	Job requires developing one's own ways of doing things, guiding oneself with little or no supervision, and depending on oneself to get things done.
Innovation	Job requires creativity and alternative thinking to develop new ideas for and answers to work-related problems.
Initiative	Job requires a willingness to take on responsibilities and challenges.
Analytical Thinking	Job requires analyzing information and using logic to address work-related issues and problems.
Leadership	Job requires a willingness to lead, take charge, and offer opinions and direction.
Achievement/Effort	Job requires establishing and maintaining personally challenging achievement goals and exerting effort toward mastering tasks.

Persistence　　　　　Job requires persistence in the face of obstacles.

35-3031.00 - Waiters and Waitresses

Take orders and serve food and beverages to patrons at tables in dining establishment.

Tasks

1) Remove dishes and glasses from tables or counters, and take them to kitchen for cleaning.

2) Stock service areas with supplies such as coffee, food, tableware, and linens.

3) Clean tables and/or counters after patrons have finished dining.

4) Fill salt, pepper, sugar, cream, condiment, and napkin containers.

5) Take orders from patrons for food or beverages.

6) Write patrons' food orders on order slips, memorize orders, or enter orders into computers for transmittal to kitchen staff.

7) Explain how various menu items are prepared, describing ingredients and cooking methods.

8) Present menus to patrons and answer questions about menu items, making recommendations upon request.

9) Perform food preparation duties such as preparing salads, appetizers, and cold dishes, portioning desserts, and brewing coffee.

10) Inform customers of daily specials.

11) Collect payments from customers.

12) Serve food and/or beverages to patrons); prepare and serve specialty dishes at tables as required.

13) Prepare checks that itemize and total meal costs and sales taxes.

14) Escort customers to their tables.

15) Prepare tables for meals, including setting up items such as linens, silverware, and glassware.

16) Prepare hot, cold, and mixed drinks for patrons, and chill bottles of wine.

17) Garnish and decorate dishes in preparation for serving.

18) Describe and recommend wines to customers.

19) Check patrons' identification in order to ensure that they meet minimum age requirements for consumption of alcoholic beverages.

20) Bring wine selections to tables with appropriate glasses, and pour the wines for customers.

Knowledge	Knowledge Definitions
Customer and Personal Service	Knowledge of principles and processes for providing customer and personal services. This includes customer needs assessment, meeting quality standards for services, and evaluation of customer satisfaction.
English Language	Knowledge of the structure and content of the English language including the meaning and spelling of words, rules of composition, and grammar.
Sales and Marketing	Knowledge of principles and methods for showing, promoting, and selling products or services. This includes marketing strategy and tactics, product demonstration, sales techniques, and sales control systems.
Food Production	Knowledge of techniques and equipment for planting, growing, and harvesting food products (both plant and animal) for consumption, including storage/handling techniques.
Mathematics	Knowledge of arithmetic, algebra, geometry, calculus, statistics, and their applications.
Administration and Management	Knowledge of business and management principles involved in strategic planning, resource allocation, human resources modeling, leadership technique, production methods, and coordination of people and resources.
Education and Training	Knowledge of principles and methods for curriculum and training design, teaching and instruction for individuals and groups, and the measurement of training effects.
Psychology	Knowledge of human behavior and performance; individual differences in ability, personality, and interests; learning and motivation; psychological research methods; and the assessment and treatment of behavioral and affective disorders.

Production and Processing	Knowledge of raw materials, production processes, quality control, costs, and other techniques for maximizing the effective manufacture and distribution of goods.
Public Safety and Security	Knowledge of relevant equipment, policies, procedures, and strategies to promote effective local, state, or national security operations for the protection of people, data, property, and institutions.
Personnel and Human Resources	Knowledge of principles and procedures for personnel recruitment, selection, training, compensation and benefits, labor relations and negotiation, and personnel information systems.
Law and Government	Knowledge of laws, legal codes, court procedures, precedents, government regulations, executive orders, agency rules, and the democratic political process.
Clerical	Knowledge of administrative and clerical procedures and systems such as word processing, managing files and records, stenography and transcription, designing forms, and other office procedures and terminology.
Computers and Electronics	Knowledge of circuit boards, processors, chips, electronic equipment, and computer hardware and software, including applications and programming.
Communications and Media	Knowledge of media production, communication, and dissemination techniques and methods. This includes alternative ways to inform and entertain via written, oral, and visual media.
Economics and Accounting	Knowledge of economic and accounting principles and practices, the financial markets, banking and the analysis and reporting of financial data.
Sociology and Anthropology	Knowledge of group behavior and dynamics, societal trends and influences, human migrations, ethnicity, cultures and their history and origins.
Foreign Language	Knowledge of the structure and content of a foreign (non-English) language including the meaning and spelling of words, rules of composition and grammar, and pronunciation.
Chemistry	Knowledge of the chemical composition, structure, and properties of substances and of the chemical processes and transformations that they undergo. This includes uses of chemicals and their interactions, danger signs, production techniques, and disposal methods.
Medicine and Dentistry	Knowledge of the information and techniques needed to diagnose and treat human injuries, diseases, and deformities. This includes symptoms, treatment alternatives, drug properties and interactions, and preventive health-care measures.
Transportation	Knowledge of principles and methods for moving people or goods by air, rail, sea, or road, including the relative costs and benefits.
Therapy and Counseling	Knowledge of principles, methods, and procedures for diagnosis, treatment, and rehabilitation of physical and mental dysfunctions, and for career counseling and guidance.
Philosophy and Theology	Knowledge of different philosophical systems and religions. This includes their basic principles, values, ethics, ways of thinking, customs, practices, and their impact on human culture.
Mechanical	Knowledge of machines and tools, including their designs, uses, repair, and maintenance.
Telecommunications	Knowledge of transmission, broadcasting, switching, control, and operation of telecommunications systems.
Geography	Knowledge of principles and methods for describing the features of land, sea, and air masses, including their physical characteristics, locations, interrelationships, and distribution of plant, animal, and human life.
Biology	Knowledge of plant and animal organisms, their tissues, cells, functions, interdependencies, and interactions with each other and the environment.
History and Archeology	Knowledge of historical events and their causes, indicators, and effects on civilizations and cultures.
Design	Knowledge of design techniques, tools, and principles involved in production of precision technical plans, blueprints, drawings, and models.
Physics	Knowledge and prediction of physical principles, laws, their interrelationships, and applications to understanding fluid, material, and atmospheric dynamics, and mechanical, electrical, atomic and sub-atomic structures and processes.
Fine Arts	Knowledge of the theory and techniques required to compose, produce, and perform works of music, dance, visual arts, drama, and sculpture.

Engineering and Technology	Knowledge of the practical application of engineering science and technology. This includes applying principles, techniques, procedures, and equipment to the design and production of various goods and services.
Building and Construction	Knowledge of materials, methods, and the tools involved in the construction or repair of houses, buildings, or other structures such as highways and roads.

Skills	Skills Definitions
Speaking	Talking to others to convey information effectively.
Active Listening	Giving full attention to what other people are saying, taking time to understand the points being made, asking questions as appropriate, and not interrupting at inappropriate times.
Service Orientation	Actively looking for ways to help people.
Social Perceptiveness	Being aware of others' reactions and understanding why they react as they do.
Coordination	Adjusting actions in relation to others' actions.
Reading Comprehension	Understanding written sentences and paragraphs in work related documents.
Instructing	Teaching others how to do something.
Learning Strategies	Selecting and using training/instructional methods and procedures appropriate for the situation when learning or teaching new things.
Time Management	Managing one's own time and the time of others.
Critical Thinking	Using logic and reasoning to identify the strengths and weaknesses of alternative solutions, conclusions or approaches to problems.
Active Learning	Understanding the implications of new information for both current and future problem-solving and decision-making.
Writing	Communicating effectively in writing as appropriate for the needs of the audience.
Mathematics	Using mathematics to solve problems.
Persuasion	Persuading others to change their minds or behavior.
Negotiation	Bringing others together and trying to reconcile differences.
Judgment and Decision Making	Considering the relative costs and benefits of potential actions to choose the most appropriate one.
Monitoring	Monitoring/Assessing performance of yourself, other individuals, or organizations to make improvements or take corrective action.
Management of Personnel Resources	Motivating, developing, and directing people as they work, identifying the best people for the job.
Complex Problem Solving	Identifying complex problems and reviewing related information to develop and evaluate options and implement solutions.
Systems Evaluation	Identifying measures or indicators of system performance and the actions needed to improve or correct performance, relative to the goals of the system.
Quality Control Analysis	Conducting tests and inspections of products, services, or processes to evaluate quality or performance.
Operations Analysis	Analyzing needs and product requirements to create a design.
Equipment Selection	Determining the kind of tools and equipment needed to do a job.
Troubleshooting	Determining causes of operating errors and deciding what to do about it.
Systems Analysis	Determining how a system should work and how changes in conditions, operations, and the environment will affect outcomes.
Equipment Maintenance	Performing routine maintenance on equipment and determining when and what kind of maintenance is needed.
Management of Material Resources	Obtaining and seeing to the appropriate use of equipment, facilities, and materials needed to do certain work.
Operation and Control	Controlling operations of equipment or systems.
Operation Monitoring	Watching gauges, dials, or other indicators to make sure a machine is working properly.
Management of Financial Resources	Determining how money will be spent to get the work done, and accounting for these expenditures.
Repairing	Repairing machines or systems using the needed tools.
Technology Design	Generating or adapting equipment and technology to serve user needs.
Science	Using scientific rules and methods to solve problems.
Installation	Installing equipment, machines, wiring, or programs to meet specifications.
Programming	Writing computer programs for various purposes.

Ability	Ability Definitions
Oral Comprehension	The ability to listen to and understand information and ideas presented through spoken words and sentences.
Oral Expression	The ability to communicate information and ideas in speaking so others will understand.
Speech Clarity	The ability to speak clearly so others can understand you.
Speech Recognition	The ability to identify and understand the speech of another person.
Trunk Strength	The ability to use your abdominal and lower back muscles to support part of the body repeatedly or continuously over time without 'giving out' or fatiguing.
Gross Body Coordination	The ability to coordinate the movement of your arms, legs, and torso together when the whole body is in motion.
Information Ordering	The ability to arrange things or actions in a certain order or pattern according to a specific rule or set of rules (e.g., patterns of numbers, letters, words, pictures, mathematical operations).
Problem Sensitivity	The ability to tell when something is wrong or is likely to go wrong. It does not involve solving the problem, only recognizing there is a problem.
Arm-Hand Steadiness	The ability to keep your hand and arm steady while moving your arm or while holding your arm and hand in one position.
Deductive Reasoning	The ability to apply general rules to specific problems to produce answers that make sense.
Stamina	The ability to exert yourself physically over long periods of time without getting winded or out of breath.
Near Vision	The ability to see details at close range (within a few feet of the observer).
Selective Attention	The ability to concentrate on a task over a period of time without being distracted.
Time Sharing	The ability to shift back and forth between two or more activities or sources of information (such as speech, sounds, touch, or other sources).
Extent Flexibility	The ability to bend, stretch, twist, or reach with your body, arms, and/or legs.
Manual Dexterity	The ability to quickly move your hand, your hand together with your arm, or your two hands to grasp, manipulate, or assemble objects.
Memorization	The ability to remember information such as words, numbers, pictures, and procedures.
Written Expression	The ability to communicate information and ideas in writing so others will understand.
Number Facility	The ability to add, subtract, multiply, or divide quickly and correctly.
Speed of Limb Movement	The ability to quickly move the arms and legs.
Written Comprehension	The ability to read and understand information and ideas presented in writing.
Mathematical Reasoning	The ability to choose the right mathematical methods or formulas to solve a problem.
Category Flexibility	The ability to generate or use different sets of rules for combining or grouping things in different ways.
Inductive Reasoning	The ability to combine pieces of information to form general rules or conclusions (includes finding a relationship among seemingly unrelated events).
Static Strength	The ability to exert maximum muscle force to lift, push, pull, or carry objects.
Multilimb Coordination	The ability to coordinate two or more limbs (for example, two arms, two legs, or one leg and one arm) while sitting, standing, or lying down. It does not involve performing the activities while the whole body is in motion.
Fluency of Ideas	The ability to come up with a number of ideas about a topic (the number of ideas is important, not their quality, correctness, or creativity).
Auditory Attention	The ability to focus on a single source of sound in the presence of other distracting sounds.
Originality	The ability to come up with unusual or clever ideas about a given topic or situation, or to develop creative ways to solve a problem.
Visualization	The ability to imagine how something will look after it is moved around or when its parts are moved or rearranged.
Dynamic Strength	The ability to exert muscle force repeatedly or continuously over time. This involves muscular endurance and resistance to muscle fatigue.
Far Vision	The ability to see details at a distance.
Speed of Closure	The ability to quickly make sense of, combine, and organize information into meaningful patterns.

Finger Dexterity	The ability to make precisely coordinated movements of the fingers of one or both hands to grasp, manipulate, or assemble very small objects.
Depth Perception	The ability to judge which of several objects is closer or farther away from you, or to judge the distance between you and an object.
Wrist-Finger Speed	The ability to make fast, simple, repeated movements of the fingers, hands, and wrists.
Control Precision	The ability to quickly and repeatedly adjust the controls of a machine or a vehicle to exact positions.
Perceptual Speed	The ability to quickly and accurately compare similarities and differences among sets of letters, numbers, objects, pictures, or patterns. The things to be compared may be presented at the same time or one after the other. This ability also includes comparing a presented object with a remembered object.
Spatial Orientation	The ability to know your location in relation to the environment or to know where other objects are in relation to you.
Visual Color Discrimination	The ability to match or detect differences between colors, including shades of color and brightness.
Dynamic Flexibility	The ability to quickly and repeatedly bend, stretch, twist, or reach out with your body, arms, and/or legs.
Gross Body Equilibrium	The ability to keep or regain your body balance or stay upright when in an unstable position.
Peripheral Vision	The ability to see objects or movement of objects to one's side when the eyes are looking ahead.
Hearing Sensitivity	The ability to detect or tell the differences between sounds that vary in pitch and loudness.
Flexibility of Closure	The ability to identify or detect a known pattern (a figure, object, word, or sound) that is hidden in other distracting material.
Response Orientation	The ability to choose quickly between two or more movements in response to two or more different signals (lights, sounds, pictures). It includes the speed with which the correct response is started with the hand, foot, or other body part.
Glare Sensitivity	The ability to see objects in the presence of glare or bright lighting.
Sound Localization	The ability to tell the direction from which a sound originated.
Reaction Time	The ability to quickly respond (with the hand, finger, or foot) to a signal (sound, light, picture) when it appears.
Explosive Strength	The ability to use short bursts of muscle force to propel oneself (as in jumping or sprinting), or to throw an object.
Night Vision	The ability to see under low light conditions.
Rate Control	The ability to time your movements or the movement of a piece of equipment in anticipation of changes in the speed and/or direction of a moving object or scene.

Work_Activity	Work_Activity Definitions
Performing for or Working Directly with the Public	Performing for people or dealing directly with the public. This includes serving customers in restaurants and stores, and receiving clients or guests.
Establishing and Maintaining Interpersonal Relatio	Developing constructive and cooperative working relationships with others, and maintaining them over time.
Communicating with Supervisors, Peers, or Subordin	Providing information to supervisors, co-workers, and subordinates by telephone, in written form, e-mail, or in person.
Handling and Moving Objects	Using hands and arms in handling, installing, positioning, and moving materials, and manipulating things.
Identifying Objects, Actions, and Events	Identifying information by categorizing, estimating, recognizing differences or similarities, and detecting changes in circumstances or events.
Getting Information	Observing, receiving, and otherwise obtaining information from all relevant sources.
Judging the Qualities of Things, Services, or Peop	Assessing the value, importance, or quality of things or people.
Performing General Physical Activities	Performing physical activities that require considerable use of your arms and legs and moving your whole body, such as climbing, lifting, balancing, walking, stooping, and handling of materials.
Making Decisions and Solving Problems	Analyzing information and evaluating results to choose the best solution and solve problems.
Assisting and Caring for Others	Providing personal assistance, medical attention, emotional support, or other personal care to others such as coworkers, customers, or patients.
Monitor Processes, Materials, or Surroundings	Monitoring and reviewing information from materials, events, or the environment, to detect or assess problems.

Training and Teaching Others	Identifying the educational needs of others, developing formal educational or training programs or classes, and teaching or instructing others.
Coordinating the Work and Activities of Others	Getting members of a group to work together to accomplish tasks.
Organizing, Planning, and Prioritizing Work	Developing specific goals and plans to prioritize, organize, and accomplish your work.
Selling or Influencing Others	Convincing others to buy merchandise/goods or to otherwise change their minds or actions.
Inspecting Equipment, Structures, or Material	Inspecting equipment, structures, or materials to identify the cause of errors or other problems or defects.
Resolving Conflicts and Negotiating with Others	Handling complaints, settling disputes, and resolving grievances and conflicts, or otherwise negotiating with others.
Processing Information	Compiling, coding, categorizing, calculating, tabulating, auditing, or verifying information or data.
Communicating with Persons Outside Organization	Communicating with people outside the organization, representing the organization to customers, the public, government, and other external sources. This information can be exchanged in person, in writing, or by telephone or e-mail.
Interacting With Computers	Using computers and computer systems (including hardware and software) to program, write software, set up functions, enter data, or process information.
Evaluating Information to Determine Compliance wit	Using relevant information and individual judgment to determine whether events or processes comply with laws, regulations, or standards.
Coaching and Developing Others	Identifying the developmental needs of others and coaching, mentoring, or otherwise helping others to improve their knowledge or skills.
Interpreting the Meaning of Information for Others	Translating or explaining what information means and how it can be used.
Documenting/Recording Information	Entering, transcribing, recording, storing, or maintaining information in written or electronic/magnetic form.
Updating and Using Relevant Knowledge	Keeping up-to-date technically and applying new knowledge to your job.
Estimating the Quantifiable Characteristics of Pro	Estimating sizes, distances, and quantities; or determining time, costs, resources, or materials needed to perform a work activity.
Thinking Creatively	Developing, designing, or creating new applications, ideas, relationships, systems, or products, including artistic contributions.
Scheduling Work and Activities	Scheduling events, programs, and activities, as well as the work of others.
Developing and Building Teams	Encouraging and building mutual trust, respect, and cooperation among team members.
Guiding, Directing, and Motivating Subordinates	Providing guidance and direction to subordinates, including setting performance standards and monitoring performance.
Analyzing Data or Information	Identifying the underlying principles, reasons, or facts of information by breaking down information or data into separate parts.
Monitoring and Controlling Resources	Monitoring and controlling resources and overseeing the spending of money.
Controlling Machines and Processes	Using either control mechanisms or direct physical activity to operate machines or processes (not including computers or vehicles).
Developing Objectives and Strategies	E____ing long-range objectives and specifying the strategies a____s to achieve them.
Provide Consultation and Advice to Others	Providing guidance and expert advice to management or other groups on technical, systems-, or process-related topics.
Performing Administrative Activities	Performing day-to-day administrative tasks such as maintaining information files and processing paperwork.
Staffing Organizational Units	Recruiting, interviewing, selecting, hiring, and promoting employees in an organization.
Operating Vehicles, Mechanized Devices, or Equipme	Running, maneuvering, navigating, or driving vehicles or mechanized equipment, such as forklifts, passenger vehicles, aircraft, or water craft.
Repairing and Maintaining Mechanical Equipment	Servicing, repairing, adjusting, and testing machines, devices, moving parts, and equipment that operate primarily on the basis of mechanical (not electronic) principles.
Repairing and Maintaining Electronic Equipment	Servicing, repairing, calibrating, regulating, fine-tuning, or testing machines, devices, and equipment that operate primarily on the basis of electrical or electronic (not mechanical) principles.
Drafting, Laying Out, and Specifying Technical Dev	Providing documentation, detailed instructions, drawings, or specifications to tell others about how devices, parts, equipment, or structures are to be fabricated, constructed, assembled, modified, maintained, or used.

Work_Context	Work_Context Definitions
Spend Time Standing	How much does this job require standing?
Contact With Others	How much does this job require the worker to be in contact with others (face-to-face, by telephone, or otherwise) in order to perform it?
Face-to-Face Discussions	How often do you have to have face-to-face discussions with individuals or teams in this job?
Spend Time Walking and Running	How much does this job require walking and running?
Work With Work Group or Team	How important is it to work with others in a group or team in this job?
Physical Proximity	To what extent does this job require the worker to perform job tasks in close physical proximity to other people?
Deal With External Customers	How important is it to work with external customers or the public in this job?
Telephone	How often do you have telephone conversations in this job?
Spend Time Using Your Hands to Handle, Control, or	How much does this job require using your hands to handle, control, or feel objects, tools or controls?
Importance of Being Exact or Accurate	How important is being very exact or highly accurate in performing this job?
Deal With Unpleasant or Angry People	How frequently does the worker have to deal with unpleasant, angry, or discourteous individuals as part of the job requirements?
Frequency of Decision Making	How frequently is the worker required to make decisions that affect other people, the financial resources, and/or the image and reputation of the organization?
Indoors, Environmentally Controlled	How often does this job require working indoors in environmentally controlled conditions?
Spend Time Making Repetitive Motions	How much does this job require making repetitive motions?
Impact of Decisions on Co-workers or Company Resul	How do the decisions an employee makes impact the results of co-workers, clients or the company?
Coordinate or Lead Others	How important is it to coordinate or lead others in accomplishing work activities in this job?
Responsible for Others' Health and Safety	How much responsibility is there for the health and safety of others in this job?
Structured versus Unstructured Work	To what extent is this job structured for the worker, rather than allowing the worker to determine tasks, priorities, and goals?
Responsibility for Outcomes and Results	How responsible is the worker for work outcomes and results of other workers?
Frequency of Conflict Situations	How often are there conflict situations the employee has to face in this job?
Freedom to Make Decisions	How much decision making freedom, without supervision, does the job offer?
Exposed to Minor Burns, Cuts, Bites, or Stings	How often does this job require exposure to minor burns, cuts, bites, or stings?
Importance of Repeating Same Tasks	How important is repeating the same physical activities (e.g., key entry) or mental activities (e.g., checking entries in a ledger) over and over, without stopping, to performing this job?
Level of Competition	To what extent does this job require the worker to compete or to be aware of competitive pressures?
Spend Time Bending or Twisting the Body	How much does this job require bending or twisting your body?
Public Speaking	How often do you have to perform public speaking in this job?
Sounds, Noise Levels Are Distracting or Uncomforta	How often does this job require working exposed to sounds and noise levels that are distracting or uncomfortable?
Time Pressure	How often does this job require the worker to meet strict deadlines?
Very Hot or Cold Temperatures	How often does this job require working in very hot (above 90 F degrees) or very cold (below 32 F degrees) temperatures?
Degree of Automation	How automated is the job?
Spend Time Keeping or Regaining Balance	How much does this job require keeping or regaining your balance?
Letters and Memos	How often does the job require written letters and memos?
Wear Common Protective or Safety Equipment such as	How much does this job require wearing common protective or safety equipment such as safety shoes, glasses, gloves, hard hats or life jackets?
Cramped Work Space, Awkward Positions	How often does this job require working in cramped work spaces that requires getting into awkward positions?
Consequence of Error	How serious would the result usually be if the worker made a mistake that was not readily correctable?
Spend Time Kneeling, Crouching, Stooping, or Crawl	How much does this job require kneeling, crouching, stooping, or crawling?

Exposed to Contaminants	How often does this job require working exposed to contaminants (such as pollutants, gases, dust or odors)?
Exposed to Disease or Infections	How often does this job require exposure to disease/infections?
Deal With Physically Aggressive People	How frequently does this job require the worker to deal with physical aggression of violent individuals?
Extremely Bright or Inadequate Lighting	How often does this job require working in extremely bright or inadequate lighting conditions?
Indoors, Not Environmentally Controlled	How often does this job require working indoors in non-controlled environmental conditions (e.g., warehouse without heat)?
Outdoors, Exposed to Weather	How often does this job require working outdoors, exposed to all weather conditions?
Pace Determined by Speed of Equipment	How important is it to this job that the pace is determined by the speed of equipment or machinery? (This does not refer to keeping busy at all times on this job.)
Spend Time Sitting	How much does this job require sitting?
In an Enclosed Vehicle or Equipment	How often does this job require working in a closed vehicle or equipment (e.g., car)?
Outdoors, Under Cover	How often does this job require working outdoors, under cover (e.g., structure with roof but no walls)?
Exposed to Hazardous Equipment	How often does this job require exposure to hazardous equipment?
Exposed to Hazardous Conditions	How often does this job require exposure to hazardous conditions?
Exposed to High Places	How often does this job require exposure to high places?
Electronic Mail	How often do you use electronic mail in this job?
Spend Time Climbing Ladders, Scaffolds, or Poles	How much does this job require climbing ladders, scaffolds, or poles?
Wear Specialized Protective or Safety Equipment su	How much does this job require wearing specialized protective or safety equipment such as breathing apparatus, safety harness, full protection suits, or radiation protection?
In an Open Vehicle or Equipment	How often does this job require working in an open vehicle or equipment (e.g., tractor)?
Exposed to Radiation	How often does this job require exposure to radiation?
Exposed to Whole Body Vibration	How often does this job require exposure to whole body vibration (e.g., operate a jackhammer)?

Job Zone Component	Job Zone Component Definitions
Title	Job Zone One: Little or No Preparation Needed
Overall Experience	No previous work-related skill, knowledge, or experience is needed for these occupations. For example, a person can become a general office clerk even if he/she has never worked in an office before.
Job Training	Employees in these occupations need anywhere from a few days to a few months of training. Usually, an experienced worker could show you how to do the job.
Job Zone Examples	These occupations involve following instructions and helping others. Examples include bus drivers, forest and conservation workers, general office clerks, home health aides, and waiters/waitresses.
SVP Range	(Below 4.0)
Education	These occupations may require a high school diploma or GED certificate. Some may require a formal training course to obtain a license.

Work_Styles	Work_Styles Definitions
Self Control	Job requires maintaining composure, keeping emotions in check, controlling anger, and avoiding aggressive behavior, even in very difficult situations.
Dependability	Job requires being reliable, responsible, and dependable, and fulfilling obligations.
Stress Tolerance	Job requires accepting criticism and dealing calmly and effectively with high stress situations.
Cooperation	Job requires being pleasant with others on the job and displaying a good-natured, cooperative attitude.
Integrity	Job requires being honest and ethical.
Concern for Others	Job requires being sensitive to others' needs and feelings and being understanding and helpful on the job.
Social Orientation	Job requires preferring to work with others rather than alone, and being personally connected with others on the job.
Attention to Detail	Job requires being careful about detail and thorough in completing work tasks.

Adaptability/Flexibility	Job requires being open to change (positive or negative) and to considerable variety in the workplace.
Initiative	Job requires a willingness to take on responsibilities and challenges.
Independence	Job requires developing one's own ways of doing things, guiding oneself with little or no supervision, and depending on oneself to get things done.
Persistence	Job requires persistence in the face of obstacles.
Leadership	Job requires a willingness to lead, take charge, and offer opinions and direction.
Achievement/Effort	Job requires establishing and maintaining personally challenging achievement goals and exerting effort toward mastering tasks.
Innovation	Job requires creativity and alternative thinking to develop new ideas for and answers to work-related problems.
Analytical Thinking	Job requires analyzing information and using logic to address work-related issues and problems.

35-3041.00 - Food Servers, Nonrestaurant

Serve food to patrons outside of a restaurant environment, such as in hotels, hospital rooms, or cars.

Tasks

1) Remove trays and stack dishes for return to kitchen after meals are finished.

2) Place food servings on plates and trays according to orders or instructions.

3) Total checks, present them to customers, and accept payment for services.

4) Examine trays to ensure that they contain required items.

5) Load trays with accessories such as eating utensils, napkins, and condiments.

6) Prepare food items such as sandwiches, salads, soups, and beverages.

7) Carry food, silverware, and/or linen on trays, or use carts to carry trays.

8) Stock service stations with items such as ice, napkins, and straws.

9) Monitor food preparation and serving techniques to ensure that proper procedures are followed.

10) Take food orders and relay orders to kitchens or serving counters so they can be filled.

11) Clean and sterilize dishes, kitchen utensils, equipment, and facilities.

12) Monitor food distribution, ensuring that meals are delivered to the correct recipients and that guidelines such as those for special diets are followed.

13) Determine where patients or patrons would like to eat their meals and help them get situated.

35-9011.00 - Dining Room and Cafeteria Attendants and Bartender Helpers

Facilitate food service. Clean tables, carry dirty dishes, replace soiled table linens; set tables; replenish supply of clean linens, silverware, glassware, and dishes; supply service bar with food, and serve water, butter, and coffee to patrons.

Tasks

1) Fill beverage and ice dispensers.

2) Carry food, dishes, trays, and silverware from kitchens and supply departments to serving counters.

3) Slice and pit fruit used to garnish drinks.

4) Carry linens to and from laundry areas.

5) Scrape and stack dirty dishes, and carry dishes and other tableware to kitchens for cleaning.

6) Stock refrigerating units with wines and bottled beer, and replace empty beer kegs.

7) Clean up spilled food, drink and broken dishes, and remove empty bottles and trash.

8) Maintain adequate supplies of items such as clean linens, silverware, glassware, dishes, and trays.

9) Perform serving, cleaning, and stocking duties in establishments such as cafeterias or dining rooms in order to facilitate customer service.

10) Garnish foods, and position them on tables to make them visible and accessible.

11) Set tables with clean linens, condiments, and other supplies.

12) Wash glasses and other serving equipment at bars.

13) Serve food to customers when waiters and waitresses need assistance.

14) Stock vending machines with food.

15) Replenish supplies of food and equipment at steam tables and service bars.

16) Wipe tables and seats with dampened cloths, and replace dirty tablecloths.

17) Mix and prepare flavors for mixed drinks.

18) Locate items requested by customers.

19) Carry trays from food counters to tables for cafeteria patrons.

20) Clean and polish counters, shelves, walls, furniture, and equipment in food service areas and other areas of restaurants, and mop and vacuum floors.

21) Serve ice water, coffee, rolls, and butter to patrons.

22) Stock cabinets and serving areas with condiments, and refill condiment containers as necessary.

35-9021.00 - Dishwashers

Clean dishes, kitchen, food preparation equipment, or utensils.

Tasks

1) Wash dishes, glassware, flatware, pots, and/or pans using dishwashers or by hand.

2) Receive and store supplies.

3) Transfer supplies and equipment between storage and work areas, by hand or using hand trucks.

4) Stock supplies such as food and utensils in serving stations, cupboards, refrigerators, and salad bars.

5) Set up banquet tables.

6) Sort and remove trash, placing it in designated pickup areas.

7) Maintain kitchen work areas, equipment, and utensils in clean and orderly condition.

8) Clean garbage cans with water or steam.

9) Sweep and scrub floors.

10) Prepare and package individual place settings.

11) Load or unload trucks that deliver or pick up food and supplies.

12) Place clean dishes, utensils, and cooking equipment in storage areas.

35-9031.00 - Hosts and Hostesses, Restaurant, Lounge, and Coffee Shop

Welcome patrons, seat them at tables or in lounge, and help ensure quality of facilities and service.

Tasks

1) Provide guests with menus.

2) Assign patrons to tables suitable for their needs.

3) Maintain contact with kitchen staff, management, serving staff, and customers to ensure that dining details are handled properly and customers' concerns are addressed.

4) Inspect dining and serving areas to ensure cleanliness and proper setup.

5) Speak with patrons to ensure satisfaction with food and service, and to respond to complaints.

6) Direct patrons to coatrooms and waiting areas such as lounges.

7) Inform patrons of establishment specialties and features.

8) Receive and record patrons' dining reservations.

9) Operate cash registers to accept payments for food and beverages.

10) Supervise and coordinate activities of dining room staff to ensure that patrons receive prompt and courteous service.

11) Confer with other staff to help plan establishments' menus.

12) Order or requisition supplies and equipment for tables and serving stations.

13) Perform marketing and advertising services.

14) Plan parties or other special events and services.

15) Hire, train, and supervise food and beverage service staff.

16) Prepare cash receipts after establishments close, and make bank deposits.

17) Prepare staff work schedules.

Knowledge	Knowledge Definitions
Customer and Personal Service	Knowledge of principles and processes for providing customer and personal services. This includes customer needs assessment, meeting quality standards for services, and evaluation of customer satisfaction.
English Language	Knowledge of the structure and content of the English language including the meaning and spelling of words, rules of composition, and grammar.
Administration and Management	Knowledge of business and management principles involved in strategic planning, resource allocation, human resources modeling, leadership technique, production methods, and coordination of people and resources.
Mathematics	Knowledge of arithmetic, algebra, geometry, calculus, statistics, and their applications.
Food Production	Knowledge of techniques and equipment for planting, growing, and harvesting food products (both plant and animal) for consumption, including storage/handling techniques.
Public Safety and Security	Knowledge of relevant equipment, policies, procedures, and strategies to promote effective local, state, or national security operations for the protection of people, data, property, and institutions.
Sales and Marketing	Knowledge of principles and methods for showing, promoting, and selling products or services. This includes marketing strategy and tactics, product demonstration, sales techniques, and sales control systems.
Computers and Electronics	Knowledge of circuit boards, processors, chips, electronic equipment, and computer hardware and software, including applications and programming.
Psychology	Knowledge of human behavior and performance; individual differences in ability, personality, and interests; learning and motivation; psychological research methods; and the assessment and treatment of behavioral and affective disorders.
Education and Training	Knowledge of principles and methods for curriculum and training design, teaching and instruction for individuals and groups, and the measurement of training effects.
Foreign Language	Knowledge of the structure and content of a foreign (non-English) language including the meaning and spelling of words, rules of composition and grammar, and pronunciation.
Personnel and Human Resources	Knowledge of principles and procedures for personnel recruitment, selection, training, compensation and benefits, labor relations and negotiation, and personnel information systems.
Production and Processing	Knowledge of raw materials, production processes, quality control, costs, and other techniques for maximizing the effective manufacture and distribution of goods.
Economics and Accounting	Knowledge of economic and accounting principles and practices, the financial markets, banking and the analysis and reporting of financial data.
Sociology and Anthropology	Knowledge of group behavior and dynamics, societal trends and influences, human migrations, ethnicity, cultures and their history and origins.
Communications and Media	Knowledge of media production, communication, and dissemination techniques and methods. This includes alternative ways to inform and entertain via written, oral, and visual media.
Medicine and Dentistry	Knowledge of the information and techniques needed to diagnose and treat human injuries, diseases, and deformities. This includes symptoms, treatment alternatives, drug properties and interactions, and preventive health-care measures.
Telecommunications	Knowledge of transmission, broadcasting, switching, control, and operation of telecommunications systems.
Transportation	Knowledge of principles and methods for moving people or goods by air, rail, sea, or road, including the relative costs and benefits.

Law and Government	Knowledge of laws, legal codes, court procedures, precedents, government regulations, executive orders, agency rules, and the democratic political process.
Geography	Knowledge of principles and methods for describing the features of land, sea, and air masses, including their physical characteristics, locations, interrelationships, and distribution of plant, animal, and human life.
Clerical	Knowledge of administrative and clerical procedures and systems such as word processing, managing files and records, stenography and transcription, designing forms, and other office procedures and terminology.
Mechanical	Knowledge of machines and tools, including their designs, uses, repair, and maintenance.
Engineering and Technology	Knowledge of the practical application of engineering science and technology. This includes applying principles, techniques, procedures, and equipment to the design and production of various goods and services.
Design	Knowledge of design techniques, tools, and principles involved in production of precision technical plans, blueprints, drawings, and models.
Therapy and Counseling	Knowledge of principles, methods, and procedures for diagnosis, treatment, and rehabilitation of physical and mental dysfunctions, and for career counseling and guidance.
Chemistry	Knowledge of the chemical composition, structure, and properties of substances and of the chemical processes and transformations that they undergo. This includes uses of chemicals and their interactions, danger signs, production techniques, and disposal methods.
Physics	Knowledge and prediction of physical principles, laws, their interrelationships, and applications to understanding fluid, material, and atmospheric dynamics, and mechanical, electrical, atomic and sub-atomic structures and processes.
Biology	Knowledge of plant and animal organisms, their tissues, cells, functions, interdependencies, and interactions with each other and the environment.
Philosophy and Theology	Knowledge of different philosophical systems and religions. This includes their basic principles, values, ethics, ways of thinking, customs, practices, and their impact on human culture.
Building and Construction	Knowledge of materials, methods, and the tools involved in the construction or repair of houses, buildings, or other structures such as highways and roads.
Fine Arts	Knowledge of the theory and techniques required to compose, produce, and perform works of music, dance, visual arts, drama, and sculpture.
History and Archeology	Knowledge of historical events and their causes, indicators, and effects on civilizations and cultures.

Skills	Skills Definitions
Active Listening	Giving full attention to what other people are saying, taking time to understand the points being made, asking questions as appropriate, and not interrupting at inappropriate times.
Speaking	Talking to others to convey information effectively.
Social Perceptiveness	Being aware of others' reactions and understanding why they react as they do.
Service Orientation	Actively looking for ways to help people.
Instructing	Teaching others how to do something.
Reading Comprehension	Understanding written sentences and paragraphs in work related documents.
Persuasion	Persuading others to change their minds or behavior.
Coordination	Adjusting actions in relation to others' actions.
Mathematics	Using mathematics to solve problems.
Learning Strategies	Selecting and using training/instructional methods and procedures appropriate for the situation when learning or teaching new things.
Critical Thinking	Using logic and reasoning to identify the strengths and weaknesses of alternative solutions, conclusions or approaches to problems.
Active Learning	Understanding the implications of new information for both current and future problem-solving and decision-making.
Time Management	Managing one's own time and the time of others.
Monitoring	Monitoring/Assessing performance of yourself, other individuals, or organizations to make improvements or take corrective action.
Writing	Communicating effectively in writing as appropriate for the needs of the audience.
Negotiation	Bringing others together and trying to reconcile differences.
Judgment and Decision Making	Considering the relative costs and benefits of potential actions to choose the most appropriate one.

Management of Personnel Resources	Motivating, developing, and directing people as they work, identifying the best people for the job.
Complex Problem Solving	Identifying complex problems and reviewing related information to develop and evaluate options and implement solutions.
Operation and Control	Controlling operations of equipment or systems.
Troubleshooting	Determining causes of operating errors and deciding what to do about it.
Systems Analysis	Determining how a system should work and how changes in conditions, operations, and the environment will affect outcomes.
Systems Evaluation	Identifying measures or indicators of system performance and the actions needed to improve or correct performance, relative to the goals of the system.
Quality Control Analysis	Conducting tests and inspections of products, services, or processes to evaluate quality or performance.
Operations Analysis	Analyzing needs and product requirements to create a design.
Equipment Maintenance	Performing routine maintenance on equipment and determining when and what kind of maintenance is needed.
Equipment Selection	Determining the kind of tools and equipment needed to do a job.
Operation Monitoring	Watching gauges, dials, or other indicators to make sure a machine is working properly.
Management of Financial Resources	Determining how money will be spent to get the work done, and accounting for these expenditures.
Management of Material Resources	Obtaining and seeing to the appropriate use of equipment, facilities, and materials needed to do certain work.
Technology Design	Generating or adapting equipment and technology to serve user needs.
Science	Using scientific rules and methods to solve problems.
Installation	Installing equipment, machines, wiring, or programs to meet specifications.
Repairing	Repairing machines or systems using the needed tools.
Programming	Writing computer programs for various purposes.

Ability	**Ability Definitions**
Oral Comprehension	The ability to listen to and understand information and ideas presented through spoken words and sentences.
Oral Expression	The ability to communicate information and ideas in speaking so others will understand.
Speech Clarity	The ability to speak clearly so others can understand you.
Speech Recognition	The ability to identify and understand the speech of another person.
Problem Sensitivity	The ability to tell when something is wrong or is likely to go wrong. It does not involve solving the problem, only recognizing there is a problem.
Trunk Strength	The ability to use your abdominal and lower back muscles to support part of the body repeatedly or continuously over time without 'giving out' or fatiguing.
Near Vision	The ability to see details at close range (within a few feet of the observer).
Deductive Reasoning	The ability to apply general rules to specific problems to produce answers that make sense.
Information Ordering	The ability to arrange things or actions in a certain order or pattern according to a specific rule or set of rules (e.g., patterns of numbers, letters, words, pictures, mathematical operations).
Inductive Reasoning	The ability to combine pieces of information to form general rules or conclusions (includes finding a relationship among seemingly unrelated events).
Written Comprehension	The ability to read and understand information and ideas presented in writing.
Category Flexibility	The ability to generate or use different sets of rules for combining or grouping things in different ways.
Written Expression	The ability to communicate information and ideas in writing so others will understand.
Time Sharing	The ability to shift back and forth between two or more activities or sources of information (such as speech, sounds, touch, or other sources).
Far Vision	The ability to see details at a distance.
Selective Attention	The ability to concentrate on a task over a period of time without being distracted.
Stamina	The ability to exert yourself physically over long periods of time without getting winded or out of breath.
Memorization	The ability to remember information such as words, numbers, pictures, and procedures.
Gross Body Coordination	The ability to coordinate the movement of your arms, legs, and torso together when the whole body is in motion.

Number Facility	The ability to add, subtract, multiply, or divide quickly and correctly.
Originality	The ability to come up with unusual or clever ideas about a given topic or situation, or to develop creative ways to solve a problem.
Multilimb Coordination	The ability to coordinate two or more limbs (for example, two arms, two legs, or one leg and one arm) while sitting, standing, or lying down. It does not involve performing the activities while the whole body is in motion.
Arm-Hand Steadiness	The ability to keep your hand and arm steady while moving your arm or while holding your arm and hand in one position.
Auditory Attention	The ability to focus on a single source of sound in the presence of other distracting sounds.
Speed of Limb Movement	The ability to quickly move the arms and legs.
Mathematical Reasoning	The ability to choose the right mathematical methods or formulas to solve a problem.
Perceptual Speed	The ability to quickly and accurately compare similarities and differences among sets of letters, numbers, objects, pictures, or patterns. The things to be compared may be presented at the same time or one after the other. This ability also includes comparing a presented object with a remembered object.
Manual Dexterity	The ability to quickly move your hand, your hand together with your arm, or your two hands to grasp, manipulate, or assemble objects.
Visualization	The ability to imagine how something will look after it is moved around or when its parts are moved or rearranged.
Flexibility of Closure	The ability to identify or detect a known pattern (a figure, object, word, or sound) that is hidden in other distracting material.
Fluency of Ideas	The ability to come up with a number of ideas about a topic (the number of ideas is important, not their quality, correctness, or creativity).
Spatial Orientation	The ability to know your location in relation to the environment or to know where other objects are in relation to you.
Speed of Closure	The ability to quickly make sense of, combine, and organize information into meaningful patterns.
Static Strength	The ability to exert maximum muscle force to lift, push, pull, or carry objects.
Dynamic Strength	The ability to exert muscle force repeatedly or continuously over time. This involves muscular endurance and resistance to muscle fatigue.
Extent Flexibility	The ability to bend, stretch, twist, or reach with your body, arms, and/or legs.
Response Orientation	The ability to choose quickly between two or more movements in response to two or more different signals (lights, sounds, pictures). It includes the speed with which the correct response is started with the hand, foot, or other body part.
Hearing Sensitivity	The ability to detect or tell the differences between sounds that vary in pitch and loudness.
Finger Dexterity	The ability to make precisely coordinated movements of the fingers of one or both hands to grasp, manipulate, or assemble very small objects.
Sound Localization	The ability to tell the direction from which a sound originated.
Wrist-Finger Speed	The ability to make fast, simple, repeated movements of the fingers, hands, and wrists.
Visual Color Discrimination	The ability to match or detect differences between colors, including shades of color and brightness.
Depth Perception	The ability to judge which of several objects is closer or farther away from you, or to judge the distance between you and an object.
Gross Body Equilibrium	The ability to keep or regain your body balance or stay upright when in an unstable position.
Dynamic Flexibility	The ability to quickly and repeatedly bend, stretch, twist, or reach out with your body, arms, and/or legs.
Rate Control	The ability to time your movements or the movement of a piece of equipment in anticipation of changes in the speed and/or direction of a moving object or scene.
Explosive Strength	The ability to use short bursts of muscle force to propel oneself (as in jumping or sprinting), or to throw an object.
Peripheral Vision	The ability to see objects or movement of objects to one's side when the eyes are looking ahead.
Reaction Time	The ability to quickly respond (with the hand, finger, or foot) to a signal (sound, light, picture) when it appears.
Glare Sensitivity	The ability to see objects in the presence of glare or bright lighting.
Night Vision	The ability to see under low light conditions.
Control Precision	The ability to quickly and repeatedly adjust the controls of a machine or a vehicle to exact positions.

Work_Activity	Work_Activity Definitions
Performing for or Working Directly with the Public	Performing for people or dealing directly with the public. This includes serving customers in restaurants and stores, and receiving clients or guests.
Communicating with Supervisors, Peers, or Subordin	Providing information to supervisors, co-workers, and subordinates by telephone, in written form, e-mail, or in person.
Establishing and Maintaining Interpersonal Relatio	Developing constructive and cooperative working relationships with others, and maintaining them over time.
Getting Information	Observing, receiving, and otherwise obtaining information from all relevant sources.
Resolving Conflicts and Negotiating with Others	Handling complaints, settling disputes, and resolving grievances and conflicts, or otherwise negotiating with others.
Identifying Objects, Actions, and Events	Identifying information by categorizing, estimating, recognizing differences or similarities, and detecting changes in circumstances or events.
Performing General Physical Activities	Performing physical activities that require considerable use of your arms and legs and moving your whole body, such as climbing, lifting, balancing, walking, stooping, and handling of materials.
Making Decisions and Solving Problems	Analyzing information and evaluating results to choose the best solution and solve problems.
Organizing, Planning, and Prioritizing Work	Developing specific goals and plans to prioritize, organize, and accomplish your work.
Assisting and Caring for Others	Providing personal assistance, medical attention, emotional support, or other personal care to others such as coworkers, customers, or patients.
Processing Information	Compiling, coding, categorizing, calculating, tabulating, auditing, or verifying information or data.
Judging the Qualities of Things, Services, or Peop	Assessing the value, importance, or quality of things or people.
Communicating with Persons Outside Organization	Communicating with people outside the organization, representing the organization to customers, the public, government, and other external sources. This information can be exchanged in person, in writing, or by telephone or e-mail.
Coordinating the Work and Activities of Others	Getting members of a group to work together to accomplish tasks.
Monitor Processes, Materials, or Surroundings	Monitoring and reviewing information from materials, events, or the environment, to detect or assess problems.
Scheduling Work and Activities	Scheduling events, programs, and activities, as well as the work of others.
Handling and Moving Objects	Using hands and arms in handling, installing, positioning, and moving materials, and manipulating things.
Training and Teaching Others	Identifying the educational needs of others, developing formal educational or training programs or classes, and teaching or instructing others.
Documenting/Recording Information	Entering, transcribing, recording, storing, or maintaining information in written or electronic/magnetic form.
Developing and Building Teams	Encouraging and building mutual trust, respect, and cooperation among team members.
Interpreting the Meaning of Information for Others	Translating or explaining what information means and how it can be used.
Selling or Influencing Others	Convincing others to buy merchandise/goods or to otherwise change their minds or actions.
Interacting With Computers	Using computers and computer systems (including hardware and software) to program, write software, set up functions, enter data, or process information.
Estimating the Quantifiable Characteristics of Pro	Estimating sizes, distances, and quantities; or determining time, costs, resources, or materials needed to perform a work activity.
Evaluating Information to Determine Compliance wit	Using relevant information and individual judgment to determine whether events or processes comply with laws, regulations, or standards.
Analyzing Data or Information	Identifying the underlying principles, reasons, or facts of information by breaking down information or data into separate parts.
Developing Objectives and Strategies	Establishing long-range objectives and specifying the strategies and actions to achieve them.
Inspecting Equipment, Structures, or Material	Inspecting equipment, structures, or materials to identify the cause of errors or other problems or defects.
Updating and Using Relevant Knowledge	Keeping up-to-date technically and applying new knowledge to your job.
Thinking Creatively	Developing, designing, or creating new applications, ideas, relationships, systems, or products, including artistic contributions.

Coaching and Developing Others	Identifying the developmental needs of others and coaching, mentoring, or otherwise helping others to improve their knowledge or skills.
Performing Administrative Activities	Performing day-to-day administrative tasks such as maintaining information files and processing paperwork.
Guiding, Directing, and Motivating Subordinates	Providing guidance and direction to subordinates, including setting performance standards and monitoring performance.
Controlling Machines and Processes	Using either control mechanisms or direct physical activity to operate machines or processes (not including computers or vehicles).
Provide Consultation and Advice to Others	Providing guidance and expert advice to management or other groups on technical, systems-, or process-related topics.
Monitoring and Controlling Resources	Monitoring and controlling resources and overseeing the spending of money.
Staffing Organizational Units	Recruiting, interviewing, selecting, hiring, and promoting employees in an organization.
Drafting, Laying Out, and Specifying Technical Dev	Providing documentation, detailed instructions, drawings, or specifications to tell others about how devices, parts, equipment, or structures are to be fabricated, constructed, assembled, modified, maintained, or used.
Operating Vehicles, Mechanized Devices, or Equipme	Running, maneuvering, navigating, or driving vehicles or mechanized equipment, such as forklifts, passenger vehicles, aircraft, or water craft.
Repairing and Maintaining Mechanical Equipment	Servicing, repairing, adjusting, and testing machines, devices, moving parts, and equipment that operate primarily on the basis of mechanical (not electronic) principles.
Repairing and Maintaining Electronic Equipment	Servicing, repairing, calibrating, regulating, fine-tuning, or testing machines, devices, and equipment that operate primarily on the basis of electrical or electronic (not mechanical) principles.

Work_Context	Work_Context Definitions
Contact With Others	How much does this job require the worker to be in contact with others (face-to-face, by telephone, or otherwise) in order to perform it?
Spend Time Standing	How much does this job require standing?
Face-to-Face Discussions	How often do you have to have face-to-face discussions with individuals or teams in this job?
Indoors, Environmentally Controlled	How often does this job require working indoors in environmentally controlled conditions?
Physical Proximity	To what extent does this job require the worker to perform job tasks in close physical proximity to other people?
Deal With External Customers	How important is it to work with external customers or the public in this job?
Work With Work Group or Team	How important is it to work with others in a group or team in this job?
Telephone	How often do you have telephone conversations in this job?
Spend Time Walking and Running	How much does this job require walking and running?
Deal With Unpleasant or Angry People	How frequently does the worker have to deal with unpleasant, angry, or discourteous individuals as part of the job requirements?
Coordinate or Lead Others	How important is it to coordinate or lead others in accomplishing work activities in this job?
Structured versus Unstructured Work	To what extent is this job structured for the worker, rather than allowing the worker to determine tasks, priorities, and goals?
Freedom to Make Decisions	How much decision making freedom, without supervision, does the job offer?
Frequency of Conflict Situations	How often are there conflict situations the employee has to face in this job?
Importance of Being Exact or Accurate	How important is being very exact or highly accurate in performing this job?
Frequency of Decision Making	How frequently is the worker required to make decisions that affect other people, the financial resources, and/or the image and reputation of the organization?
Impact of Decisions on Co-workers or Company Resul	How do the decisions an employee makes impact the results of co-workers, clients or the company?
Responsibility for Outcomes and Results	How responsible is the worker for work outcomes and results of other workers?
Responsible for Others' Health and Safety	How much responsibility is there for the health and safety of others in this job?
Importance of Repeating Same Tasks	How important is repeating the same physical activities (e.g., key entry) or mental activities (e.g., checking entries in a ledger) over and over, without stopping, to performing this job?
Sounds, Noise Levels Are Distracting or Uncomforta	How often does this job require working exposed to sounds and noise levels that are distracting or uncomfortable?
Spend Time Making Repetitive Motions	How much does this job require making repetitive motions?

Level of Competition	To what extent does this job require the worker to compete or to be aware of competitive pressures?
Spend Time Using Your Hands to Handle, Control, or	How much does this job require using your hands to handle, control, or feel objects, tools or controls?
Public Speaking	How often do you have to perform public speaking in this job?
Exposed to Minor Burns, Cuts, Bites, or Stings	How often does this job require exposure to minor burns, cuts, bites, or stings?
Time Pressure	How often does this job require the worker to meet strict deadlines?
Spend Time Bending or Twisting the Body	How much does this job require bending or twisting your body?
Degree of Automation	How automated is the job?
Wear Common Protective or Safety Equipment such as	How much does this job require wearing common protective or safety equipment such as safety shoes, glasses, gloves, hard hats or live jackets?
Consequence of Error	How serious would the result usually be if the worker made a mistake that was not readily correctable?
Letters and Memos	How often does the job require written letters and memos?
Spend Time Kneeling, Crouching, Stooping, or Crawl	How much does this job require kneeling, crouching, stooping, or crawling?
Cramped Work Space, Awkward Positions	How often does this job require working in cramped work spaces that requires getting into awkward positions?
Very Hot or Cold Temperatures	How often does this job require working in very hot (above 90 F degrees) or very cold (below 32 F degrees) temperatures?
Deal With Physically Aggressive People	How frequently does this job require the worker to deal with physical aggression of violent individuals?
Exposed to Contaminants	How often does this job require working exposed to contaminants (such as pollutants, gases, dust or odors)?
Spend Time Keeping or Regaining Balance	How much does this job require keeping or regaining your balance?
Exposed to Hazardous Conditions	How often does this job require exposure to hazardous conditions?
Spend Time Sitting	How much does this job require sitting?
Pace Determined by Speed of Equipment	How important is it to this job that the pace is determined by the speed of equipment or machinery? (This does not refer to keeping busy at all times on this job.)
Exposed to Disease or Infections	How often does this job require exposure to disease/infections?
Extremely Bright or Inadequate Lighting	How often does this job require working in extremely bright or inadequate lighting conditions?
Outdoors, Under Cover	How often does this job require working outdoors, under cover (e.g., structure with roof but no walls)?
Electronic Mail	How often do you use electronic mail in this job?
Outdoors, Exposed to Weather	How often does this job require working outdoors, exposed to all weather conditions?
Exposed to Hazardous Equipment	How often does this job require exposure to hazardous equipment?
In an Enclosed Vehicle or Equipment	How often does this job require working in a closed vehicle or equipment (e.g., car)?
Spend Time Climbing Ladders, Scaffolds, or Poles	How much does this job require climbing ladders, scaffolds, or poles?
Exposed to High Places	How often does this job require exposure to high places?
Exposed to Whole Body Vibration	How often does this job require exposure to whole body vibration (e.g., operate a jackhammer)?
Indoors, Not Environmentally Controlled	How often does this job require working indoors in non-controlled environmental conditions (e.g., warehouse without heat)?
Wear Specialized Protective or Safety Equipment su	How much does this job require wearing specialized protective or safety equipment such as breathing apparatus, safety harness, full protection suits, or radiation protection?
Exposed to Radiation	How often does this job require exposure to radiation?
In an Open Vehicle or Equipment	How often does this job require working in an open vehicle or equipment (e.g., tractor)?

Job Zone Component	Job Zone Component Definitions
Title	Job Zone One: Little or No Preparation Needed
Overall Experience	No previous work-related skill, knowledge, or experience is needed for these occupations. For example, a person can become a general office clerk even if he/she has never worked in an office before.
Job Training	Employees in these occupations need anywhere from a few days to a few months of training. Usually, an experienced worker could show you how to do the job.

Job Zone Examples	These occupations involve following instructions and helping others. Examples include bus drivers, forest and conservation workers, general office clerks, home health aides, and waiters/waitresses.
SVP Range	(Below 4.0)
Education	These occupations may require a high school diploma or GED certificate. Some may require a formal training course to obtain a license.

Work_Styles	Work_Styles Definitions
Stress Tolerance	Job requires accepting criticism and dealing calmly and effectively with high stress situations.
Cooperation	Job requires being pleasant with others on the job and displaying a good-natured, cooperative attitude.
Dependability	Job requires being reliable, responsible, and dependable, and fulfilling obligations.
Self Control	Job requires maintaining composure, keeping emotions in check, controlling anger, and avoiding aggressive behavior, even in very difficult situations.
Social Orientation	Job requires preferring to work with others rather than alone, and being personally connected with others on the job.
Concern for Others	Job requires being sensitive to others' needs and feelings and being understanding and helpful on the job.
Integrity	Job requires being honest and ethical.
Attention to Detail	Job requires being careful about detail and thorough in completing work tasks.
Independence	Job requires developing one's own ways of doing things, guiding oneself with little or no supervision, and depending on oneself to get things done.
Adaptability/Flexibility	Job requires being open to change (positive or negative) and to considerable variety in the workplace.
Initiative	Job requires a willingness to take on responsibilities and challenges.
Leadership	Job requires a willingness to lead, take charge, and offer opinions and direction.
Persistence	Job requires persistence in the face of obstacles.
Achievement/Effort	Job requires establishing and maintaining personally challenging achievement goals and exerting effort toward mastering tasks.
Innovation	Job requires creativity and alternative thinking to develop new ideas for and answers to work-related problems.
Analytical Thinking	Job requires analyzing information and using logic to address work-related issues and problems.

37-1011.00 - First-Line Supervisors/Managers of Housekeeping and Janitorial Workers

Supervise work activities of cleaning personnel in hotels, hospitals, offices, and other establishments.

Tasks

1) Instruct staff in work policies and procedures, and the use and maintenance of equipment.

2) Inspect work performed to ensure that it meets specifications and established standards.

3) Direct activities for stopping the spread of infections in facilities such as hospitals.

4) Establish and implement operational standards and procedures for the departments they supervise.

5) Forecast necessary levels of staffing and stock at different times, in order to facilitate effective scheduling and ordering.

6) Perform financial tasks such as estimating costs, and preparing and managing budgets.

7) Prepare activity and personnel reports, and reports containing information such as occupancy, hours worked, facility usage, work performed, and departmental expenses.

8) Recommend or arrange for additional services such as painting, repair work, renovations, and the replacement of furnishings and equipment.

9) Maintain required records of work hours, budgets, payrolls, and other information.

10) Plan and prepare employee work schedules.

11) Recommend changes that could improve service and increase operational efficiency.

12) Screen job applicants, and hire new employees.

13) Select the most suitable cleaning materials for different types of linens, furniture, flooring, and surfaces.

14) Perform or assist with cleaning duties as necessary.

15) Issue supplies and equipment to workers.

16) Investigate complaints about service and equipment, and take corrective action.

17) Inventory stock to ensure that supplies and equipment are available in adequate amounts.

18) Inspect and evaluate the physical condition of facilities in order to determine the type of work required.

19) Confer with staff in order to resolve performance and personnel problems, and to discuss company policies.

20) Evaluate employee performance, and recommend personnel actions such as promotions, transfers, and dismissals.

21) Supervise in-house services such as laundries, maintenance and repair, dry cleaning, and/or valet services.

22) Coordinate activities with other departments to ensure that services are provided in an efficient and timely manner.

23) Select and order or purchase new equipment, supplies, and furnishings.

24) Advise managers, desk clerks, or admitting personnel of rooms ready for occupancy.

37-1012.00 - First-Line Supervisors/Managers of Landscaping, Lawn Service, and Groundskeeping Workers

Plan, organize, direct, or coordinate activities of workers engaged in landscaping or groundskeeping activities, such as planting and maintaining ornamental trees, shrubs, flowers, and lawns, and applying fertilizers, pesticides, and other chemicals, according to contract specifications. May also coordinate activities of workers engaged in terracing hillsides, building retaining walls, constructing pathways, installing patios, and similar activities in following a landscape design plan. Work may involve reviewing contracts to ascertain service, machine, and work force requirements; answering inquiries from potential customers regarding methods, material, and price ranges; and preparing estimates according to labor, material, and machine costs.

Tasks

1) Review contracts or work assignments to determine service, machine, and workforce requirements for jobs.

2) Tour grounds such as parks, botanical gardens, cemeteries, or golf courses to inspect conditions of plants and soil.

3) Design and supervise the installation of sprinkler systems, calculating water pressure, and valve and pipe coverage needs.

4) Recommend changes in working conditions or equipment use, in order to increase crew efficiency.

5) Prepare service estimates based on labor, material, and machine costs, and maintain budgets for individual projects.

6) Prepare and maintain required records such as work activity and personnel reports.

7) Plant and maintain vegetation through activities such as mulching, fertilizing, watering, mowing, and pruning.

8) Perform administrative duties such as authorizing leaves and processing time sheets.

9) Maintain required records such as personnel information and project records.

10) Identify diseases and pests affecting landscaping, and order appropriate treatments.

11) Inventory supplies of tools, equipment, and materials to ensure that sufficient supplies are available and items are in usable condition.

12) Inspect completed work to ensure conformance to specifications, standards, and contract requirements.

13) Direct activities of workers who perform duties such as landscaping, cultivating lawns, or pruning trees and shrubs.

14) Confer with other supervisors to coordinate work activities with those of other departments or units.

15) Direct or perform mixing and application of fertilizers, insecticides, herbicides, and fungicides.

16) Establish and enforce operating procedures and work standards that will ensure adequate performance and personnel safety.

17) Negotiate with customers regarding fees for landscaping, lawn service, or

37-1012.00 - First-Line Supervisors/Managers of Landscaping, Lawn

groundskeeping work.

18) Perform personnel-related activities such as hiring workers, evaluating staff performance, and taking disciplinary actions when performance problems occur.

19) Order the performance of corrective work when problems occur, and recommend procedural changes to avoid such problems.

20) Direct and assist workers engaged in the maintenance and repair of equipment such as power tools and motorized equipment.

21) Confer with managers and landscape architects to develop plans and schedules for landscaping maintenance and improvement.

22) Answer inquiries from current or prospective customers regarding methods, materials, and price ranges.

23) Train workers in tasks such as transplanting and pruning trees and shrubs, finishing cement, using equipment, and caring for turf.

24) Provide workers with assistance in performing duties as necessary to meet deadlines.

25) Monitor project activities to ensure that instructions are followed, deadlines are met, and schedules are maintained.

26) Install and maintain landscaped areas, performing tasks such as removing snow, pouring cement curbs, and repairing sidewalks.

27) Investigate work-related complaints in order to verify problems, and to determine responses.

37-2011.00 - Janitors and Cleaners, Except Maids and Housekeeping Cleaners

Keep buildings in clean and orderly condition. Perform heavy cleaning duties, such as cleaning floors, shampooing rugs, washing walls and glass, and removing rubbish. Duties may include tending furnace and boiler, performing routine maintenance activities, notifying management of need for repairs, and cleaning snow or debris from sidewalk.

Tasks

1) Clean windows, glass partitions, and mirrors, using soapy water or other cleaners, sponges, and squeegees.

2) Clean and polish furniture and fixtures.

3) Follow procedures for the use of chemical cleaners and power equipment, in order to prevent damage to floors and fixtures.

4) Clean laboratory equipment, such as glassware and metal instruments, using solvents, brushes, rags, and power cleaning equipment.

5) Gather and empty trash.

6) Service, clean, and supply restrooms.

7) Spray insecticides and fumigants to prevent insect and rodent infestation.

8) Set up, arrange, and remove decorations, tables, chairs, ladders, and scaffolding to prepare facilities for events such as banquets and meetings.

9) Requisition supplies and equipment needed for cleaning and maintenance duties.

10) Notify managers concerning the need for major repairs or additions to building operating systems.

11) Move heavy furniture, equipment, and supplies, either manually or by using hand trucks.

12) Clean building floors by sweeping, mopping, scrubbing, or vacuuming them.

13) Remove snow from sidewalks, driveways, and parking areas, using snowplows, snow blowers, and snow shovels, and spread snow melting chemicals.

14) Clean chimneys, flues, and connecting pipes, using power and hand tools.

15) Clean and restore building interiors damaged by fire, smoke, or water, using commercial cleaning equipment.

16) Strip, seal, finish, and polish floors.

17) Steam-clean or shampoo carpets.

18) Mix water and detergents or acids in containers to prepare cleaning solutions, according to specifications.

19) Make adjustments and minor repairs to heating, cooling, ventilating, plumbing, and electrical systems.

20) Mow and trim lawns and shrubbery, using mowers and hand and power trimmers, and clear debris from grounds.

21) Dust furniture. walls. machines. and equipment.

22) Monitor building security and safety by performing such tasks as locking doors after operating hours and checking electrical appliance use to ensure that hazards are not created.

37-2012.00 - Maids and Housekeeping Cleaners

Perform any combination of light cleaning duties to maintain private households or commercial establishments. such as hotels, restaurants. and hospitals. in a clean and orderly manner. Duties include making beds, replenishing linens, cleaning rooms and halls, and vacuuming.

Tasks

1) Assign duties to other staff and give instructions regarding work methods and routines.

2) Answer telephones and doorbells.

3) Deliver television sets. ironing boards, baby cribs, and rollaway beds to guests' rooms.

4) Wash windows, walls. ceilings. and woodwork, waxing and polishing as necessary.

5) Take care of pets by grooming, exercising, and/or feeding them.

6) Prepare rooms for meetings. and arrange decorations. media equipment, and furniture for social or business functions.

7) Plan menus, and cook and serve meals and refreshments following employer's instructions or own methods.

8) Observe precautions required to protect hotel and guest property, and report damage, theft, and found articles to supervisors.

9) Polish silver accessories and metalwork such as fixtures and fittings.

10) Move and arrange furniture, and turn mattresses.

11) Sort clothing and other articles, load washing machines, and iron and fold dried items.

12) Disinfect equipment and supplies, using germicides or steam-operated sterilizers.

13) Clean rugs, carpets, upholstered furniture, and/or draperies, using vacuum cleaners and/or shampooers.

14) Request repair services and wait for repair workers to arrive.

15) Replace light bulbs.

16) Sort, count, and mark clean linens, and store them in linen closets.

17) Remove debris from driveways, garages, and swimming pool areas.

18) Keep storage areas and carts well-stocked, clean, and tidy.

19) Dust and polish furniture and equipment.

20) Hang draperies, and dust window blinds.

21) Wash dishes and clean kitchens, cooking utensils, and silverware.

22) Clean rooms, hallways, lobbies, lounges, restrooms, corridors, elevators, stairways, locker rooms and other work areas so that health standards are met.

23) Empty wastebaskets, empty and clean ashtrays, and transport other trash and waste to disposal areas.

24) Care for children and/or elderly persons by overseeing their activities, providing companionship, and assisting them with dressing, bathing, eating, and other needs.

25) Carry linens, towels, toilet items, and cleaning supplies, using wheeled carts.

26) Purchase or order groceries and household supplies to keep kitchens stocked, and record expenditures.

27) Sweep, scrub, wax, and/or polish floors, using brooms, mops, and/or powered scrubbing and waxing machines.

28) Replenish supplies such as drinking glasses, linens, writing supplies, and bathroom items.

37-2021.00 - Pest Control Workers

Spray or release chemical solutions or toxic gases and set traps to kill pests and vermin, such as mice, termites, and roaches, that infest buildings and surrounding areas.

Tasks

1) Position and fasten edges of tarpaulins over building and tape vents to ensure air-tight environment and check for leaks.

2) Post warning signs and lock building doors to secure area to be fumigated.

3) Record work activities performed.

4) Clean and remove blockages from infested areas to facilitate spraying procedure and provide drainage. using broom, mop, shovel, and rake.

5) Dig up and burn, or spray weeds with herbicides.

6) Measure area dimensions requiring treatment, using rule, calculate fumigant requirements, and estimate cost for service.

7) Spray or dust chemical solutions, powders, or gases into rooms, onto clothing, furnishings or wood, and over marshlands, ditches, and catch-basins.

8) Direct and/or assist other workers in treatment and extermination processes to eliminate and control rodents, insects, and weeds.

9) Study preliminary reports and diagrams of infested area and determine treatment type required to eliminate and prevent recurrence of infestation.

10) Cut or bore openings in building or surrounding concrete, access infested areas, insert nozzle, and inject pesticide to impregnate ground.

11) Inspect premises to identify infestation source and extent of damage to property, wall and roof porosity, and access to infested locations.

12) Set mechanical traps and place poisonous paste or bait in sewers, burrows, and ditches.

13) Clean work site after completion of job.

37-3011.00 - Landscaping and Groundskeeping Workers

Landscape or maintain grounds of property using hand or power tools or equipment. Workers typically perform a variety of tasks, which may include any combination of the following: sod laying, mowing, trimming, planting, watering, fertilizing, digging, raking, sprinkler installation, and installation of mortarless segmental concrete masonry wall units.

Tasks

1) Haul or spread topsoil, and spread straw over seeded soil to hold soil in place.

2) Plan and cultivate lawns and gardens.

3) Maintain irrigation systems, including winterizing the systems and starting them up in spring.

4) Rake, mulch, and compost leaves.

5) Attach wires from planted trees to support stakes.

6) Use irrigation methods to adjust the amount of water consumption and to prevent waste.

7) Use hand tools such as shovels, rakes, pruning saws, saws, hedge and brush trimmers, and axes.

8) Plant seeds, bulbs, foliage, flowering plants, grass, ground covers, trees, and shrubs, and apply mulch for protection, using gardening tools.

9) Build forms, and mix and pour cement to form garden borders.

10) Install rock gardens, ponds, decks. drainage systems, irrigation systems, retaining walls, fences, planters, and/or playground equipment.

11) Mow and edge lawns, using power mowers and edgers.

12) Follow planned landscaping designs to determine where to lay sod, sow grass, or plant flowers and foliage.

13) Gather and remove litter.

14) Water lawns, trees, and plants, using portable sprinkler systems, hoses, or watering cans.

15) Shovel snow from walks, driveways, and parking lots, and spread salt in those areas.

16) Advise customers on plant selection and care.

17) Care for artificial turf fields, periodically removing the turf and replacing cushioning pads, and vacuuming and disinfecting the turf after use to prevent the growth of harmful bacteria.

18) Care for natural turf fields, making sure the underlying soil has the required composition to allow proper drainage and to support the grasses used on the fields.

19) Mark design boundaries, and paint natural and artificial turf fields with team logos and names before events.

20) Operate powered equipment such as mowers, tractors, twin-axle vehicles, snow blowers, chain-saws, electric clippers, sod cutters, and pruning saws.

21) Decorate gardens with stones and plants.

22) Trim and pick flowers, and clean flower beds.

23) Mix and spray or spread fertilizers, herbicides, or insecticides onto grass, shrubs, and trees, using hand or automatic sprayers or spreaders.

24) Care for established lawns by mulching, aerating, weeding, grubbing and removing thatch, and trimming and edging around flower beds, walks, and walls.

25) Provide proper upkeep of sidewalks, driveways, parking lots, fountains, planters, burial sites, and other grounds features.

26) Maintain and repair tools, equipment, and structures such as buildings, greenhouses, fences, and benches, using hand and power tools.

39-1011.00 - Gaming Supervisors

Supervise gaming operations and personnel in an assigned area. Circulate among tables and observe operations. Ensure that stations and games are covered for each shift. May explain and interpret operating rules of house to patrons. May plan and organize activities and create friendly atmosphere for guests in hotels/casinos. May adjust service complaints.

Tasks

1) Report customer-related incidents occurring in gaming areas to supervisors.

2) Explain and interpret house rules, such as game rules and betting limits, for patrons.

3) Greet customers and ask about the quality of service they are receiving.

4) Maintain familiarity with the games at a facility, and with strategies and tricks used by cheaters at such games.

5) Observe gamblers' behavior for signs of cheating such as marking, switching, or counting cards; notify security staff of suspected cheating.

6) Perform paperwork required for monetary transactions.

7) Evaluate workers' performance and prepare written performance evaluations.

8) Monitor stations and games, and move dealers from game to game to ensure adequate staffing.

9) Establish and maintain banks and table limits for each game.

10) Monitor patrons for signs of compulsive gambling, offering assistance if necessary.

11) Supervise the distribution of complimentary meals, hotel rooms, discounts, and other items given to players based on length of play and amount bet.

12) Determine how many gaming tables to open each day and schedule staff accordingly.

13) Record, issue receipts for, and pay off bets.

14) Provide fire protection and first-aid assistance when necessary.

15) Interview, hire, and train workers.

16) Monitor and verify the counting, wrapping, weighing, and distribution of currency and coins.

17) Direct workers compiling summary sheets for each race or event to record amounts wagered and amounts to be paid to winners.

18) Establish policies on types of gambling offered, odds, and extension of credit.

19) Review operational expenses, budget estimates, betting accounts, and collection reports for accuracy.

20) Resolve customer and employee complaints.

Knowledge	Knowledge Definitions
Customer and Personal Service	Knowledge of principles and processes for providing customer and personal services. This includes customer needs assessment, meeting quality standards for services, and evaluation of customer satisfaction.
Mathematics	Knowledge of arithmetic, algebra, geometry, calculus, statistics, and their applications.
Administration and Management	Knowledge of business and management principles involved in strategic planning, resource allocation, human resources modeling, leadership technique, production methods, and coordination of people and resources.
Education and Training	Knowledge of principles and methods for curriculum and training design, teaching and instruction for individuals and groups, and the measurement of training effects.
Public Safety and Security	Knowledge of relevant equipment, policies, procedures, and strategies to promote effective local, state, or national security operations for the protection of people, data, property, and institutions.
Law and Government	Knowledge of laws, legal codes, court procedures, precedents, government regulations, executive orders, agency rules, and the democratic political process.
Psychology	Knowledge of human behavior and performance; individual differences in ability, personality, and interests; learning and motivation; psychological research methods; and the assessment and treatment of behavioral and affective disorders.
English Language	Knowledge of the structure and content of the English language including the meaning and spelling of words, rules of composition, and grammar.
Personnel and Human Resources	Knowledge of principles and procedures for personnel recruitment, selection, training, compensation and benefits, labor relations and negotiation, and personnel information systems.
Clerical	Knowledge of administrative and clerical procedures and systems such as word processing, managing files and records, stenography and transcription, designing forms, and other office procedures and terminology.
Sales and Marketing	Knowledge of principles and methods for showing, promoting, and selling products or services. This includes marketing strategy and tactics, product demonstration, sales techniques, and sales control systems.
Computers and Electronics	Knowledge of circuit boards, processors, chips, electronic equipment, and computer hardware and software, including applications and programming.
Economics and Accounting	Knowledge of economic and accounting principles and practices, the financial markets, banking and the analysis and reporting of financial data.
Production and Processing	Knowledge of raw materials, production processes, quality control, costs, and other techniques for maximizing the effective manufacture and distribution of goods.
Sociology and Anthropology	Knowledge of group behavior and dynamics, societal trends and influences, human migrations, ethnicity, cultures and their history and origins.
Therapy and Counseling	Knowledge of principles, methods, and procedures for diagnosis, treatment, and rehabilitation of physical and mental dysfunctions, and for career counseling and guidance.
Mechanical	Knowledge of machines and tools, including their designs, uses, repair, and maintenance.
Communications and Media	Knowledge of media production, communication, and dissemination techniques and methods. This includes alternative ways to inform and entertain via written, oral, and visual media.
Transportation	Knowledge of principles and methods for moving people or goods by air, rail, sea, or road, including the relative costs and benefits.
Engineering and Technology	Knowledge of the practical application of engineering science and technology. This includes applying principles, techniques, procedures, and equipment to the design and production of various goods and services.
Philosophy and Theology	Knowledge of different philosophical systems and religions. This includes their basic principles, values, ethics, ways of thinking, customs, practices, and their impact on human culture.
Telecommunications	Knowledge of transmission, broadcasting, switching, control, and operation of telecommunications systems.
Food Production	Knowledge of techniques and equipment for planting, growing, and harvesting food products (both plant and animal) for consumption, including storage/handling techniques.
Foreign Language	Knowledge of the structure and content of a foreign (non-English) language including the meaning and spelling of words, rules of composition and grammar, and pronunciation.
Building and Construction	Knowledge of materials, methods, and the tools involved in the construction or repair of houses, buildings, or other structures such as highways and roads.
Physics	Knowledge and prediction of physical principles, laws, their interrelationships, and applications to understanding fluid, material, and atmospheric dynamics, and mechanical, electrical, atomic and sub-atomic structures and processes.

Medicine and Dentistry	Knowledge of the information and techniques needed to diagnose and treat human injuries, diseases, and deformities. This includes symptoms, treatment alternatives, drug properties and interactions, and preventive health-care measures.
History and Archeology	Knowledge of historical events and their causes, indicators, and effects on civilizations and cultures.
Geography	Knowledge of principles and methods for describing the features of land, sea, and air masses, including their physical characteristics, locations, interrelationships, and distribution of plant, animal, and human life.
Design	Knowledge of design techniques, tools, and principles involved in production of precision technical plans, blueprints, drawings, and models.
Chemistry	Knowledge of the chemical composition, structure, and properties of substances and of the chemical processes and transformations that they undergo. This includes uses of chemicals and their interactions, danger signs, production techniques, and disposal methods.
Fine Arts	Knowledge of the theory and techniques required to compose, produce, and perform works of music, dance, visual arts, drama, and sculpture.
Biology	Knowledge of plant and animal organisms, their tissues, cells, functions, interdependencies, and interactions with each other and the environment.

Skills	Skills Definitions
Mathematics	Using mathematics to solve problems.
Instructing	Teaching others how to do something.
Active Listening	Giving full attention to what other people are saying, taking time to understand the points being made, asking questions as appropriate, and not interrupting at inappropriate times.
Service Orientation	Actively looking for ways to help people.
Speaking	Talking to others to convey information effectively.
Monitoring	Monitoring/Assessing performance of yourself, other individuals, or organizations to make improvements or take corrective action.
Social Perceptiveness	Being aware of others' reactions and understanding why they react as they do.
Judgment and Decision Making	Considering the relative costs and benefits of potential actions to choose the most appropriate one.
Critical Thinking	Using logic and reasoning to identify the strengths and weaknesses of alternative solutions, conclusions or approaches to problems.
Management of Personnel Resources	Motivating, developing, and directing people as they work, identifying the best people for the job.
Time Management	Managing one's own time and the time of others.
Active Learning	Understanding the implications of new information for both current and future problem-solving and decision-making.
Coordination	Adjusting actions in relation to others' actions.
Learning Strategies	Selecting and using training/instructional methods and procedures appropriate for the situation when learning or teaching new things.
Reading Comprehension	Understanding written sentences and paragraphs in work related documents.
Persuasion	Persuading others to change their minds or behavior.
Complex Problem Solving	Identifying complex problems and reviewing related information to develop and evaluate options and implement solutions.
Writing	Communicating effectively in writing as appropriate for the needs of the audience.
Negotiation	Bringing others together and trying to reconcile differences.
Operation Monitoring	Watching gauges, dials, or other indicators to make sure a machine is working properly.
Management of Financial Resources	Determining how money will be spent to get the work done, and accounting for these expenditures.
Operation and Control	Controlling operations of equipment or systems.
Equipment Selection	Determining the kind of tools and equipment needed to do a job.
Systems Evaluation	Identifying measures or indicators of system performance and the actions needed to improve or correct performance, relative to the goals of the system.
Operations Analysis	Analyzing needs and product requirements to create a design.
Systems Analysis	Determining how a system should work and how changes in conditions, operations, and the environment will affect outcomes.
Troubleshooting	Determining causes of operating errors and deciding what to do about it.

Equipment Maintenance	Performing routine maintenance on equipment and determining when and what kind of maintenance is needed.
Repairing	Repairing machines or systems using the needed tools.
Quality Control Analysis	Conducting tests and inspections of products, services, or processes to evaluate quality or performance.
Installation	Installing equipment, machines, wiring, or programs to meet specifications.
Technology Design	Generating or adapting equipment and technology to serve user needs.
Management of Material Resources	Obtaining and seeing to the appropriate use of equipment, facilities, and materials needed to do certain work.
Science	Using scientific rules and methods to solve problems.
Programming	Writing computer programs for various purposes.

Ability	Ability Definitions
Problem Sensitivity	The ability to tell when something is wrong or is likely to go wrong. It does not involve solving the problem, only recognizing there is a problem.
Oral Expression	The ability to communicate information and ideas in speaking so others will understand.
Inductive Reasoning	The ability to combine pieces of information to form general rules or conclusions (includes finding a relationship among seemingly unrelated events).
Oral Comprehension	The ability to listen to and understand information and ideas presented through spoken words and sentences.
Near Vision	The ability to see details at close range (within a few feet of the observer).
Deductive Reasoning	The ability to apply general rules to specific problems to produce answers that make sense.
Speech Recognition	The ability to identify and understand the speech of another person.
Speech Clarity	The ability to speak clearly so others can understand you.
Information Ordering	The ability to arrange things or actions in a certain order or pattern according to a specific rule or set of rules (e.g., patterns of numbers, letters, words, pictures, mathematical operations).
Written Comprehension	The ability to read and understand information and ideas presented in writing.
Selective Attention	The ability to concentrate on a task over a period of time without being distracted.
Speed of Closure	The ability to quickly make sense of, combine, and organize information into meaningful patterns.
Written Expression	The ability to communicate information and ideas in writing so others will understand.
Flexibility of Closure	The ability to identify or detect a known pattern (a figure, object, word, or sound) that is hidden in other distracting material.
Perceptual Speed	The ability to quickly and accurately compare similarities and differences among sets of letters, numbers, objects, pictures, or patterns. The things to be compared may be presented at the same time or one after the other. This ability also includes comparing a presented object with a remembered object.
Time Sharing	The ability to shift back and forth between two or more activities or sources of information (such as speech, sounds, touch, or other sources).
Category Flexibility	The ability to generate or use different sets of rules for combining or grouping things in different ways.
Far Vision	The ability to see details at a distance.
Originality	The ability to come up with unusual or clever ideas about a given topic or situation, or to develop creative ways to solve a problem.
Fluency of Ideas	The ability to come up with a number of ideas about a topic (the number of ideas is important, not their quality, correctness, or creativity).
Trunk Strength	The ability to use your abdominal and lower back muscles to support part of the body repeatedly or continuously over time without 'giving out' or fatiguing.
Number Facility	The ability to add, subtract, multiply, or divide quickly and correctly.
Memorization	The ability to remember information such as words, numbers, pictures, and procedures.
Mathematical Reasoning	The ability to choose the right mathematical methods or formulas to solve a problem.
Auditory Attention	The ability to focus on a single source of sound in the presence of other distracting sounds.
Visualization	The ability to imagine how something will look after it is moved around or when its parts are moved or rearranged.

Stamina	The ability to exert yourself physically over long periods of time without getting winded or out of breath.
Gross Body Coordination	The ability to coordinate the movement of your arms, legs, and torso together when the whole body is in motion.
Visual Color Discrimination	The ability to match or detect differences between colors, including shades of color and brightness.
Static Strength	The ability to exert maximum muscle force to lift, push, pull, or carry objects.
Explosive Strength	The ability to use short bursts of muscle force to propel oneself (as in jumping or sprinting), or to throw an object.
Glare Sensitivity	The ability to see objects in the presence of glare or bright lighting.
Reaction Time	The ability to quickly respond (with the hand, finger, or foot) to a signal (sound, light, picture) when it appears.
Finger Dexterity	The ability to make precisely coordinated movements of the fingers of one or both hands to grasp, manipulate, or assemble very small objects.
Speed of Limb Movement	The ability to quickly move the arms and legs.
Hearing Sensitivity	The ability to detect or tell the differences between sounds that vary in pitch and loudness.
Gross Body Equilibrium	The ability to keep or regain your body balance or stay upright when in an unstable position.
Response Orientation	The ability to choose quickly between two or more movements in response to two or more different signals (lights, sounds, pictures). It includes the speed with which the correct response is started with the hand, foot, or other body part.
Multilimb Coordination	The ability to coordinate two or more limbs (for example, two arms, two legs, or one leg and one arm) while sitting, standing, or lying down. It does not involve performing the activities while the whole body is in motion.
Dynamic Strength	The ability to exert muscle force repeatedly or continuously over time. This involves muscular endurance and resistance to muscle fatigue.
Arm-Hand Steadiness	The ability to keep your hand and arm steady while moving your arm or while holding your arm and hand in one position.
Manual Dexterity	The ability to quickly move your hand, your hand together with your arm, or your two hands to grasp, manipulate, or assemble objects.
Depth Perception	The ability to judge which of several objects is closer or farther away from you, or to judge the distance between you and an object.
Peripheral Vision	The ability to see objects or movement of objects to one's side when the eyes are looking ahead.
Extent Flexibility	The ability to bend, stretch, twist, or reach with your body, arms, and/or legs.
Night Vision	The ability to see under low light conditions.
Wrist-Finger Speed	The ability to make fast, simple, repeated movements of the fingers, hands, and wrists.
Sound Localization	The ability to tell the direction from which a sound originated.
Spatial Orientation	The ability to know your location in relation to the environment or to know where other objects are in relation to you.
Control Precision	The ability to quickly and repeatedly adjust the controls of a machine or a vehicle to exact positions.
Rate Control	The ability to time your movements or the movement of a piece of equipment in anticipation of changes in the speed and/or direction of a moving object or scene.
Dynamic Flexibility	The ability to quickly and repeatedly bend, stretch, twist, or reach out with your body, arms, and/or legs.

Work_Activity

Work_Activity	Work_Activity Definitions
Communicating with Supervisors, Peers, or Subordin	Providing information to supervisors, co-workers, and subordinates by telephone, in written form, e-mail, or in person.
Performing for or Working Directly with the Public	Performing for people or dealing directly with the public. This includes serving customers in restaurants and stores, and receiving clients or guests.
Guiding, Directing, and Motivating Subordinates	Providing guidance and direction to subordinates, including setting performance standards and monitoring performance.
Resolving Conflicts and Negotiating with Others	Handling complaints, settling disputes, and resolving grievances and conflicts, or otherwise negotiating with others.
Making Decisions and Solving Problems	Analyzing information and evaluating results to choose the best solution and solve problems.
Evaluating Information to Determine Compliance wit	Using relevant information and individual judgment to determine whether events or processes comply with laws, regulations, or standards.
Coaching and Developing Others	Identifying the developmental needs of others and coaching, mentoring, or otherwise helping others to improve their knowledge or skills.
Establishing and Maintaining Interpersonal Relatio	Developing constructive and cooperative working relationships with others, and maintaining them over time.
Training and Teaching Others	Identifying the educational needs of others, developing formal educational or training programs or classes, and teaching or instructing others.
Documenting/Recording Information	Entering, transcribing, recording, storing, or maintaining information in written or electronic/magnetic form.
Getting Information	Observing, receiving, and otherwise obtaining information from all relevant sources.
Judging the Qualities of Things, Services, or Peop	Assessing the value, importance, or quality of things or people.
Processing Information	Compiling, coding, categorizing, calculating, tabulating, auditing, or verifying information or data.
Communicating with Persons Outside Organization	Communicating with people outside the organization, representing the organization to customers, the public, government, and other external sources. This information can be exchanged in person, in writing, or by telephone or e-mail.
Monitor Processes, Materials, or Surroundings	Monitoring and reviewing information from materials, events, or the environment, to detect or assess problems.
Identifying Objects, Actions, and Events	Identifying information by categorizing, estimating, recognizing differences or similarities, and detecting changes in circumstances or events.
Performing Administrative Activities	Performing day-to-day administrative tasks such as maintaining information files and processing paperwork.
Developing and Building Teams	Encouraging and building mutual trust, respect, and cooperation among team members.
Coordinating the Work and Activities of Others	Getting members of a group to work together to accomplish tasks.
Interacting With Computers	Using computers and computer systems (including hardware and software) to program, write software, set up functions, enter data, or process information.
Updating and Using Relevant Knowledge	Keeping up-to-date technically and applying new knowledge to your job.
Interpreting the Meaning of Information for Others	Translating or explaining what information means and how it can be used.
Organizing, Planning, and Prioritizing Work	Developing specific goals and plans to prioritize, organize, and accomplish your work.
Assisting and Caring for Others	Providing personal assistance, medical attention, emotional support, or other personal care to others such as coworkers, customers, or patients.
Thinking Creatively	Developing, designing, or creating new applications, ideas, relationships, systems, or products, including artistic contributions.
Developing Objectives and Strategies	Establishing long-range objectives and specifying the strategies and actions to achieve them.
Inspecting Equipment, Structures, or Material	Inspecting equipment, structures, or materials to identify the cause of errors or other problems or defects.
Scheduling Work and Activities	Scheduling events, programs, and activities, as well as the work of others.
Staffing Organizational Units	Recruiting, interviewing, selecting, hiring, and promoting employees in an organization.
Provide Consultation and Advice to Others	Providing guidance and expert advice to management or other groups on technical, systems-, or process-related topics.
Monitoring and Controlling Resources	Monitoring and controlling resources and overseeing the spending of money.
Analyzing Data or Information	Identifying the underlying principles, reasons, or facts of information by breaking down information or data into separate parts.
Performing General Physical Activities	Performing physical activities that require considerable use of your arms and legs and moving your whole body, such as climbing, lifting, balancing, walking, stooping, and handling of materials.
Estimating the Quantifiable Characteristics of Pro	Estimating sizes, distances, and quantities; or determining time, costs, resources, or materials needed to perform a work activity.
Selling or Influencing Others	Convincing others to buy merchandise/goods or to otherwise change their minds or actions.
Handling and Moving Objects	Using hands and arms in handling, installing, positioning, and moving materials, and manipulating things.
Controlling Machines and Processes	Using either control mechanisms or direct physical activity to operate machines or processes (not including computers or vehicles).

Repairing and Maintaining Electronic Equipment	Servicing, repairing, calibrating, regulating, fine-tuning, or testing machines, devices, and equipment that operate primarily on the basis of electrical or electronic (not mechanical) principles.
Repairing and Maintaining Mechanical Equipment	Servicing, repairing, adjusting, and testing machines, devices, moving parts, and equipment that operate primarily on the basis of mechanical (not electronic) principles.
Drafting, Laying Out, and Specifying Technical Dev	Providing documentation, detailed instructions, drawings, or specifications to tell others about how devices, parts, equipment, or structures are to be fabricated, constructed, assembled, modified, maintained, or used.
Operating Vehicles, Mechanized Devices, or Equipme	Running, maneuvering, navigating, or driving vehicles or mechanized equipment, such as forklifts, passenger vehicles, aircraft, or water craft.

Work_Context	Work_Context Definitions
Contact With Others	How much does this job require the worker to be in contact with others (face-to-face, by telephone, or otherwise) in order to perform it?
Indoors, Environmentally Controlled	How often does this job require working indoors in environmentally controlled conditions?
Frequency of Decision Making	How frequently is the worker required to make decisions that affect other people, the financial resources, and/or the image and reputation of the organization?
Face-to-Face Discussions	How often do you have to have face-to-face discussions with individuals or teams in this job?
Deal With External Customers	How important is it to work with external customers or the public in this job?
Frequency of Conflict Situations	How often are there conflict situations the employee has to face in this job?
Freedom to Make Decisions	How much decision making freedom, without supervision, does the job offer?
Work With Work Group or Team	How important is it to work with others in a group or team in this job?
Spend Time Standing	How much does this job require standing?
Deal With Unpleasant or Angry People	How frequently does the worker have to deal with unpleasant, angry, or discourteous individuals as part of the job requirements?
Telephone	How often do you have telephone conversations in this job?
Impact of Decisions on Co-workers or Company Resul	How do the decisions an employee makes impact the results of co-workers, clients or the company?
Importance of Being Exact or Accurate	How important is being very exact or highly accurate in performing this job?
Responsibility for Outcomes and Results	How responsible is the worker for work outcomes and results of other workers?
Physical Proximity	To what extent does this job require the worker to perform job tasks in close physical proximity to other people?
Sounds, Noise Levels Are Distracting or Uncomforta	How often does this job require working exposed to sounds and noise levels that are distracting or uncomfortable?
Structured versus Unstructured Work	To what extent is this job structured for the worker, rather than allowing the worker to determine tasks, priorities, and goals?
Coordinate or Lead Others	How important is it to coordinate or lead others in accomplishing work activities in this job?
Importance of Repeating Same Tasks	How important is repeating the same physical activities (e.g., key entry) or mental activities (e.g., checking entries in a ledger) over and over, without stopping, to performing this job?
Exposed to Contaminants	How often does this job require working exposed to contaminants (such as pollutants, gases, dust or odors)?
Spend Time Walking and Running	How much does this job require walking and running?
Letters and Memos	How often does the job require written letters and memos?
Level of Competition	To what extent does this job require the worker to compete or to be aware of competitive pressures?
Responsible for Others' Health and Safety	How much responsibility is there for the health and safety of others in this job?
Consequence of Error	How serious would the result usually be if the worker made a mistake that was not readily correctable?
Time Pressure	How often does this job require the worker to meet strict deadlines?
Extremely Bright or Inadequate Lighting	How often does this job require working in extremely bright or inadequate lighting conditions?
Public Speaking	How often do you have to perform public speaking in this job?
Spend Time Making Repetitive Motions	How much does this job require making repetitive motions?
Deal With Physically Aggressive People	How frequently does this job require the worker to deal with physical aggression of violent individuals?

Spend Time Using Your Hands to Handle, Control, or	How much does this job require using your hands to handle, control, or feel objects, tools or controls?
Electronic Mail	How often do you use electronic mail in this job?
Spend Time Bending or Twisting the Body	How much does this job require bending or twisting your body?
Exposed to Disease or Infections	How often does this job require exposure to disease/infections?
Cramped Work Space, Awkward Positions	How often does this job require working in cramped work spaces that requires getting into awkward positions?
Spend Time Sitting	How much does this job require sitting?
Degree of Automation	How automated is the job?
Exposed to Minor Burns, Cuts, Bites, or Stings	How often does this job require exposure to minor burns, cuts, bites, or stings?
Indoors, Not Environmentally Controlled	How often does this job require working indoors in non-controlled environmental conditions (e.g., warehouse without heat)?
Very Hot or Cold Temperatures	How often does this job require working in very hot (above 90 F degrees) or very cold (below 32 F degrees) temperatures?
Spend Time Keeping or Regaining Balance	How much does this job require keeping or regaining your balance?
Spend Time Kneeling, Crouching, Stooping, or Crawl	How much does this job require kneeling, crouching, stooping, or crawling?
Pace Determined by Speed of Equipment	How important is it to this job that the pace is determined by the speed of equipment or machinery? (This does not refer to keeping busy at all times on this job.)
Spend Time Climbing Ladders, Scaffolds, or Poles	How much does this job require climbing ladders, scaffolds, or poles?
Exposed to Whole Body Vibration	How often does this job require exposure to whole body vibration (e.g., operate a jackhammer)?
Exposed to Hazardous Equipment	How often does this job require exposure to hazardous equipment?
Exposed to Hazardous Conditions	How often does this job require exposure to hazardous conditions?
Outdoors, Exposed to Weather	How often does this job require working outdoors, exposed to all weather conditions?
Outdoors, Under Cover	How often does this job require working outdoors, under cover (e.g., structure with roof but no walls)?
Exposed to High Places	How often does this job require exposure to high places?
In an Enclosed Vehicle or Equipment	How often does this job require working in a closed vehicle or equipment (e.g., car)?
In an Open Vehicle or Equipment	How often does this job require working in an open vehicle or equipment (e.g., tractor)?
Exposed to Radiation	How often does this job require exposure to radiation?
Wear Common Protective or Safety Equipment such as	How much does this job require wearing common protective or safety equipment such as safety shoes, glasses, gloves, hard hats or live jackets?
Wear Specialized Protective or Safety Equipment su	How much does this job require wearing specialized protective or safety equipment such as breathing apparatus, safety harness, full protection suits, or radiation protection?

Job Zone Component	Job Zone Component Definitions
Title	Job Zone Two: Some Preparation Needed
Overall Experience	Some previous work-related skill, knowledge, or experience may be helpful in these occupations, but usually is not needed. For example, a drywall installer might benefit from experience installing drywall, but an inexperienced person could still learn to be an installer with little difficulty.
Job Training	Employees in these occupations need anywhere from a few months to one year of working with experienced employees.
Job Zone Examples	These occupations often involve using your knowledge and skills to help others. Examples include drywall installers, fire inspectors, flight attendants, pharmacy technicians, salespersons (retail), and tellers.
SVP Range	(4.0 to < 6.0)
Education	These occupations usually require a high school diploma and may require some vocational training or job-related course work. In some cases, an associate's or bachelor's degree could be needed.

768

Work_Styles	Work_Styles Definitions
Self Control	Job requires maintaining composure, keeping emotions in check, controlling anger, and avoiding aggressive behavior, even in very difficult situations.
Integrity	Job requires being honest and ethical.
Stress Tolerance	Job requires accepting criticism and dealing calmly and effectively with high stress situations.
Dependability	Job requires being reliable, responsible, and dependable, and fulfilling obligations.
Cooperation	Job requires being pleasant with others on the job and displaying a good-natured, cooperative attitude.
Adaptability/Flexibility	Job requires being open to change (positive or negative) and to considerable variety in the workplace.
Attention to Detail	Job requires being careful about detail and thorough in completing work tasks.
Leadership	Job requires a willingness to lead, take charge, and offer opinions and direction.
Social Orientation	Job requires preferring to work with others rather than alone, and being personally connected with others on the job.
Concern for Others	Job requires being sensitive to others' needs and feelings and being understanding and helpful on the job.
Initiative	Job requires a willingness to take on responsibilities and challenges.
Persistence	Job requires persistence in the face of obstacles.
Analytical Thinking	Job requires analyzing information and using logic to address work-related issues and problems.
Independence	Job requires developing one's own ways of doing things, guiding oneself with little or no supervision, and depending on oneself to get things done.
Achievement/Effort	Job requires establishing and maintaining personally challenging achievement goals and exerting effort toward mastering tasks.
Innovation	Job requires creativity and alternative thinking to develop new ideas for and answers to work-related problems.

39-1012.00 - Slot Key Persons

Coordinate/supervise functions of slot department workers to provide service to patrons. Handle and settle complaints of players. Verify and payoff jackpots. Reset slot machines after payoffs. Make minor repairs or adjustments to slot machines. Recommend removal of slot machines for repair. Report hazards and enforces safety rules.

Tasks

1) Monitor payment of hand-delivered jackpots to ensure promptness.

2) Reset slot machines after payoffs.

3) Perform minor repairs or make adjustments to slot machines, resolving problems such as machine tilts and coin jams.

4) Respond to and resolve patrons' complaints.

5) Exchange currency for customers, converting currency into requested combinations of bills and coins.

6) Record the specifics of malfunctioning machines and document malfunctions needing repair.

7) Attach out of order signs to malfunctioning machines, and notify technicians when machines need to be repaired or removed.

8) Monitor functioning of slot machine coin dispensers and fill coin hoppers when necessary.

9) Enforce safety rules, and report or remove safety hazards as well as guests who are underage, intoxicated, disruptive, or cheating.

10) Coordinate and oversee the work of slot department workers, including change runners and slot technicians.

11) Answer patrons' questions about gaming machine functions and payouts.

Knowledge	Knowledge Definitions
Customer and Personal Service	Knowledge of principles and processes for providing customer and personal services. This includes customer needs assessment, meeting quality standards for services, and evaluation of customer satisfaction.
Mathematics	Knowledge of arithmetic, algebra, geometry, calculus, statistics, and their applications.
Administration and Management	Knowledge of business and management principles involved in strategic planning, resource allocation, human resources modeling, leadership technique, production methods, and coordination of people and resources.
Public Safety and Security	Knowledge of relevant equipment, policies, procedures, and strategies to promote effective local, state, or national security operations for the protection of people, data, property, and institutions.
English Language	Knowledge of the structure and content of the English language including the meaning and spelling of words, rules of composition, and grammar.
Education and Training	Knowledge of principles and methods for curriculum and training design, teaching and instruction for individuals and groups, and the measurement of training effects.
Mechanical	Knowledge of machines and tools, including their designs, uses, repair, and maintenance.
Computers and Electronics	Knowledge of circuit boards, processors, chips, electronic equipment, and computer hardware and software, including applications and programming.
Economics and Accounting	Knowledge of economic and accounting principles and practices, the financial markets, banking and the analysis and reporting of financial data.
Sales and Marketing	Knowledge of principles and methods for showing, promoting, and selling products or services. This includes marketing strategy and tactics, product demonstration, sales techniques, and sales control systems.
Personnel and Human Resources	Knowledge of principles and procedures for personnel recruitment, selection, training, compensation and benefits, labor relations and negotiation, and personnel information systems.
Clerical	Knowledge of administrative and clerical procedures and systems such as word processing, managing files and records, stenography and transcription, designing forms, and other office procedures and terminology.
Production and Processing	Knowledge of raw materials, production processes, quality control, costs, and other techniques for maximizing the effective manufacture and distribution of goods.
Psychology	Knowledge of human behavior and performance; individual differences in ability, personality, and interests; learning and motivation; psychological research methods; and the assessment and treatment of behavioral and affective disorders.
Communications and Media	Knowledge of media production, communication, and dissemination techniques and methods. This includes alternative ways to inform and entertain via written, oral, and visual media.
Foreign Language	Knowledge of the structure and content of a foreign (non-English) language including the meaning and spelling of words, rules of composition and grammar, and pronunciation.
Law and Government	Knowledge of laws, legal codes, court procedures, precedents, government regulations, executive orders, agency rules, and the democratic political process.
Sociology and Anthropology	Knowledge of group behavior and dynamics, societal trends and influences, human migrations, ethnicity, cultures and their history and origins.
Telecommunications	Knowledge of transmission, broadcasting, switching, control, and operation of telecommunications systems.
Engineering and Technology	Knowledge of the practical application of engineering science and technology. This includes applying principles, techniques, procedures, and equipment to the design and production of various goods and services.
Design	Knowledge of design techniques, tools, and principles involved in production of precision technical plans, blueprints, drawings, and models.
Philosophy and Theology	Knowledge of different philosophical systems and religions. This includes their basic principles, values, ethics, ways of thinking, customs, practices, and their impact on human culture.
Therapy and Counseling	Knowledge of principles, methods, and procedures for diagnosis, treatment, and rehabilitation of physical and mental dysfunctions, and for career counseling and guidance.
Geography	Knowledge of principles and methods for describing the features of land, sea, and air masses, including their physical characteristics, locations, interrelationships, and distribution of plant, animal, and human life.
History and Archeology	Knowledge of historical events and their causes, indicators, and effects on civilizations and cultures.

Building and Construction	Knowledge of materials, methods, and the tools involved in the construction or repair of houses, buildings, or other structures such as highways and roads.
Transportation	Knowledge of principles and methods for moving people or goods by air, rail, sea, or road, including the relative costs and benefits.
Food Production	Knowledge of techniques and equipment for planting, growing, and harvesting food products (both plant and animal) for consumption, including storage/handling techniques.
Fine Arts	Knowledge of the theory and techniques required to compose, produce, and perform works of music, dance, visual arts, drama, and sculpture.
Physics	Knowledge and prediction of physical principles, laws, their interrelationships, and applications to understanding fluid, material, and atmospheric dynamics, and mechanical, electrical, atomic and sub- atomic structures and processes.
Medicine and Dentistry	Knowledge of the information and techniques needed to diagnose and treat human injuries, diseases, and deformities. This includes symptoms, treatment alternatives, drug properties and interactions, and preventive health-care measures.
Chemistry	Knowledge of the chemical composition, structure, and properties of substances and of the chemical processes and transformations that they undergo. This includes uses of chemicals and their interactions, danger signs, production techniques, and disposal methods.
Biology	Knowledge of plant and animal organisms, their tissues, cells, functions, interdependencies, and interactions with each other and the environment.

Skills   Skills Definitions

Active Listening	Giving full attention to what other people are saying, taking time to understand the points being made, asking questions as appropriate, and not interrupting at inappropriate times.
Mathematics	Using mathematics to solve problems.
Speaking	Talking to others to convey information effectively.
Active Learning	Understanding the implications of new information for both current and future problem-solving and decision-making.
Social Perceptiveness	Being aware of others' reactions and understanding why they react as they do.
Critical Thinking	Using logic and reasoning to identify the strengths and weaknesses of alternative solutions, conclusions or approaches to problems.
Service Orientation	Actively looking for ways to help people.
Instructing	Teaching others how to do something.
Monitoring	Monitoring/Assessing performance of yourself, other individuals, or organizations to make improvements or take corrective action.
Learning Strategies	Selecting and using training/instructional methods and procedures appropriate for the situation when learning or teaching new things.
Writing	Communicating effectively in writing as appropriate for the needs of the audience.
Reading Comprehension	Understanding written sentences and paragraphs in work related documents.
Time Management	Managing one's own time and the time of others.
Coordination	Adjusting actions in relation to others' actions.
Management of Personnel Resources	Motivating, developing, and directing people as they work, identifying the best people for the job.
Judgment and Decision Making	Considering the relative costs and benefits of potential actions to choose the most appropriate one.
Negotiation	Bringing others together and trying to reconcile differences.
Complex Problem Solving	Identifying complex problems and reviewing related information to develop and evaluate options and implement solutions.
Repairing	Repairing machines or systems using the needed tools.
Troubleshooting	Determining causes of operating errors and deciding what to do about it.
Operation Monitoring	Watching gauges, dials, or other indicators to make sure a machine is working properly.
Persuasion	Persuading others to change their minds or behavior.
Equipment Maintenance	Performing routine maintenance on equipment and determining when and what kind of maintenance is needed.
Management of Material Resources	Obtaining and seeing to the appropriate use of equipment, facilities, and materials needed to do certain work.
Operation and Control	Controlling operations of equipment or systems.

Systems Evaluation	Identifying measures or indicators of system performance and the actions needed to improve or correct performance, relative to the goals of the system.
Equipment Selection	Determining the kind of tools and equipment needed to do a job.
Installation	Installing equipment, machines, wiring, or programs to meet specifications.
Systems Analysis	Determining how a system should work and how changes in conditions, operations, and the environment will affect outcomes.
Management of Financial Resources	Determining how money will be spent to get the work done, and accounting for these expenditures.
Technology Design	Generating or adapting equipment and technology to serve user needs.
Operations Analysis	Analyzing needs and product requirements to create a design.
Quality Control Analysis	Conducting tests and inspections of products, services, or processes to evaluate quality or performance.
Science	Using scientific rules and methods to solve problems.
Programming	Writing computer programs for various purposes.

Ability   Ability Definitions

Oral Expression	The ability to communicate information and ideas in speaking so others will understand.
Oral Comprehension	The ability to listen to and understand information and ideas presented through spoken words and sentences.
Problem Sensitivity	The ability to tell when something is wrong or is likely to go wrong. It does not involve solving the problem, only recognizing there is a problem.
Near Vision	The ability to see details at close range (within a few feet of the observer).
Speech Recognition	The ability to identify and understand the speech of another person.
Trunk Strength	The ability to use your abdominal and lower back muscles to support part of the body repeatedly or continuously over time without 'giving out' or fatiguing.
Deductive Reasoning	The ability to apply general rules to specific problems to produce answers that make sense.
Speech Clarity	The ability to speak clearly so others can understand you.
Selective Attention	The ability to concentrate on a task over a period of time without being distracted.
Information Ordering	The ability to arrange things or actions in a certain order or pattern according to a specific rule or set of rules (e.g., patterns of numbers, letters, words, pictures, mathematical operations).
Inductive Reasoning	The ability to combine pieces of information to form general rules or conclusions (includes finding a relationship among seemingly unrelated events).
Written Expression	The ability to communicate information and ideas in writing so others will understand.
Written Comprehension	The ability to read and understand information and ideas presented in writing.
Mathematical Reasoning	The ability to choose the right mathematical methods or formulas to solve a problem.
Manual Dexterity	The ability to quickly move your hand, your hand together with your arm, or your two hands to grasp, manipulate, or assemble objects.
Auditory Attention	The ability to focus on a single source of sound in the presence of other distracting sounds.
Category Flexibility	The ability to generate or use different sets of rules for combining or grouping things in different ways.
Perceptual Speed	The ability to quickly and accurately compare similarities and differences among sets of letters, numbers, objects, pictures, or patterns. The things to be compared may be presented at the same time or one after the other. This ability also includes comparing a presented object with a remembered object.
Extent Flexibility	The ability to bend, stretch, twist, or reach with your body, arms, and/or legs.
Arm-Hand Steadiness	The ability to keep your hand and arm steady while moving your arm or while holding your arm and hand in one position.
Finger Dexterity	The ability to make precisely coordinated movements of the fingers of one or both hands to grasp, manipulate, or assemble very small objects.
Stamina	The ability to exert yourself physically over long periods of time without getting winded or out of breath.
Number Facility	The ability to add, subtract, multiply, or divide quickly and correctly.
Far Vision	The ability to see details at a distance.

Time Sharing	The ability to shift back and forth between two or more activities or sources of information (such as speech, sounds, touch, or other sources).
Control Precision	The ability to quickly and repeatedly adjust the controls of a machine or a vehicle to exact positions.
Flexibility of Closure	The ability to identify or detect a known pattern (a figure, object, word, or sound) that is hidden in other distracting material.
Static Strength	The ability to exert maximum muscle force to lift, push, pull, or carry objects.
Fluency of Ideas	The ability to come up with a number of ideas about a topic (the number of ideas is important, not their quality, correctness, or creativity).
Originality	The ability to come up with unusual or clever ideas about a given topic or situation, or to develop creative ways to solve a problem.
Gross Body Coordination	The ability to coordinate the movement of your arms, legs, and torso together when the whole body is in motion.
Multilimb Coordination	The ability to coordinate two or more limbs (for example, two arms, two legs, or one leg and one arm) while sitting, standing, or lying down. It does not involve performing the activities while the whole body is in motion.
Visual Color Discrimination	The ability to match or detect differences between colors, including shades of color and brightness.
Visualization	The ability to imagine how something will look after it is moved around or when its parts are moved or rearranged.
Memorization	The ability to remember information such as words, numbers, pictures, and procedures.
Hearing Sensitivity	The ability to detect or tell the differences between sounds that vary in pitch and loudness.
Rate Control	The ability to time your movements or the movement of a piece of equipment in anticipation of changes in the speed and/or direction of a moving object or scene.
Speed of Closure	The ability to quickly make sense of, combine, and organize information into meaningful patterns.
Reaction Time	The ability to quickly respond (with the hand, finger, or foot) to a signal (sound, light, picture) when it appears.
Glare Sensitivity	The ability to see objects in the presence of glare or bright lighting.
Depth Perception	The ability to judge which of several objects is closer or farther away from you, or to judge the distance between you and an object.
Dynamic Strength	The ability to exert muscle force repeatedly or continuously over time. This involves muscular endurance and resistance to muscle fatigue.
Response Orientation	The ability to choose quickly between two or more movements in response to two or more different signals (lights, sounds, pictures). It includes the speed with which the correct response is started with the hand, foot, or other body part.
Sound Localization	The ability to tell the direction from which a sound originated.
Speed of Limb Movement	The ability to quickly move the arms and legs.
Gross Body Equilibrium	The ability to keep or regain your body balance or stay upright when in an unstable position.
Wrist-Finger Speed	The ability to make fast, simple, repeated movements of the fingers, hands, and wrists.
Night Vision	The ability to see under low light conditions.
Peripheral Vision	The ability to see objects or movement of objects to one's side when the eyes are looking ahead.
Dynamic Flexibility	The ability to quickly and repeatedly bend, stretch, twist, or reach out with your body, arms, and/or legs.
Spatial Orientation	The ability to know your location in relation to the environment or to know where other objects are in relation to you.
Explosive Strength	The ability to use short bursts of muscle force to propel oneself (as in jumping or sprinting), or to throw an object.

Work_Activity	Work_Activity Definitions
Getting Information	Observing, receiving, and otherwise obtaining information from all relevant sources.
Making Decisions and Solving Problems	Analyzing information and evaluating results to choose the best solution and solve problems.
Evaluating Information to Determine Compliance wit	Using relevant information and individual judgment to determine whether events or processes comply with laws, regulations, or standards.
Communicating with Supervisors, Peers, or Subordin	Providing information to supervisors, co-workers, and subordinates by telephone, in written form, e-mail, or in person.

Handling and Moving Objects	Using hands and arms in handling, installing, positioning, and moving materials, and manipulating things.
Identifying Objects, Actions, and Events	Identifying information by categorizing, estimating, recognizing differences or similarities, and detecting changes in circumstances or events.
Performing General Physical Activities	Performing physical activities that require considerable use of your arms and legs and moving your whole body, such as climbing, lifting, balancing, walking, stooping, and handling of materials.
Performing for or Working Directly with the Public	Performing for people or dealing directly with the public. This includes serving customers in restaurants and stores, and receiving clients or guests.
Processing Information	Compiling, coding, categorizing, calculating, tabulating, auditing, or verifying information or data.
Monitor Processes, Materials, or Surroundings	Monitoring and reviewing information from materials, events, or the environment, to detect or assess problems.
Documenting/Recording Information	Entering, transcribing, recording, storing, or maintaining information in written or electronic/magnetic form.
Establishing and Maintaining Interpersonal Relatio	Developing constructive and cooperative working relationships with others, and maintaining them over time.
Judging the Qualities of Things, Services, or Peop	Assessing the value, importance, or quality of things or people.
Inspecting Equipment, Structures, or Material	Inspecting equipment, structures, or materials to identify the cause of errors or other problems or defects.
Interacting With Computers	Using computers and computer systems (including hardware and software) to program, write software, set up functions, enter data, or process information.
Resolving Conflicts and Negotiating with Others	Handling complaints, settling disputes, and resolving grievances and conflicts, or otherwise negotiating with others.
Assisting and Caring for Others	Providing personal assistance, medical attention, emotional support, or other personal care to others such as coworkers, customers, or patients.
Developing and Building Teams	Encouraging and building mutual trust, respect, and cooperation among team members.
Organizing, Planning, and Prioritizing Work	Developing specific goals and plans to prioritize, organize, and accomplish your work.
Updating and Using Relevant Knowledge	Keeping up-to-date technically and applying new knowledge to your job.
Coordinating the Work and Activities of Others	Getting members of a group to work together to accomplish tasks.
Repairing and Maintaining Electronic Equipment	Servicing, repairing, calibrating, regulating, fine-tuning, or testing machines, devices, and equipment that operate primarily on the basis of electrical or electronic (not mechanical) principles.
Guiding, Directing, and Motivating Subordinates	Providing guidance and direction to subordinates, including setting performance standards and monitoring performance.
Scheduling Work and Activities	Scheduling events, programs, and activities, as well as the work of others.
Thinking Creatively	Developing, designing, or creating new applications, ideas, relationships, systems, or products, including artistic contributions.
Coaching and Developing Others	Identifying the developmental needs of others and coaching, mentoring, or otherwise helping others to improve their knowledge or skills.
Training and Teaching Others	Identifying the educational needs of others, developing formal educational or training programs or classes, and teaching or instructing others.
Interpreting the Meaning of Information for Others	Translating or explaining what information means and how it can be used.
Estimating the Quantifiable Characteristics of Pro	Estimating sizes, distances, and quantities; or determining time, costs, resources, or materials needed to perform a work activity.
Controlling Machines and Processes	Using either control mechanisms or direct physical activity to operate machines or processes (not including computers or vehicles).
Analyzing Data or Information	Identifying the underlying principles, reasons, or facts of information by breaking down information or data into separate parts.
Developing Objectives and Strategies	Establishing long-range objectives and specifying the strategies and actions to achieve them.
Repairing and Maintaining Mechanical Equipment	Servicing, repairing, adjusting, and testing machines, devices, moving parts, and equipment that operate primarily on the basis of mechanical (not electronic) principles.

Communicating with Persons Outside Organization	Communicating with people outside the organization, representing the organization to customers, the public, government, and other external sources. This information can be exchanged in person, in writing, or by telephone or e-mail.
Selling or Influencing Others	Convincing others to buy merchandise/goods or to otherwise change their minds or actions.
Provide Consultation and Advice to Others	Providing guidance and expert advice to management or other groups on technical, systems-, or process-related topics.
Staffing Organizational Units	Recruiting, interviewing, selecting, hiring, and promoting employees in an organization.
Monitoring and Controlling Resources	Monitoring and controlling resources and overseeing the spending of money.
Performing Administrative Activities	Performing day-to-day administrative tasks such as maintaining information files and processing paperwork.
Drafting, Laying Out, and Specifying Technical Dev	Providing documentation, detailed instructions, drawings, or specifications to tell others about how devices, parts, equipment, or structures are to be fabricated, constructed, assembled, modified, maintained, or used.
Operating Vehicles, Mechanized Devices, or Equipme	Running, maneuvering, navigating, or driving vehicles or mechanized equipment, such as forklifts, passenger vehicles, aircraft, or water craft.

Work_Context	Work_Context Definitions
Indoors, Environmentally Controlled	How often does this job require working indoors in environmentally controlled conditions?
Work With Work Group or Team	How important is it to work with others in a group or team in this job?
Contact With Others	How much does this job require the worker to be in contact with others (face-to-face, by telephone, or otherwise) in order to perform it?
Frequency of Decision Making	How frequently is the worker required to make decisions that affect other people, the financial resources, and/or the image and reputation of the organization?
Physical Proximity	To what extent does this job require the worker to perform job tasks in close physical proximity to other people?
Importance of Being Exact or Accurate	How important is being very exact or highly accurate in performing this job?
Face-to-Face Discussions	How often do you have to have face-to-face discussions with individuals or teams in this job?
Spend Time Standing	How much does this job require standing?
Deal With Unpleasant or Angry People	How frequently does the worker have to deal with unpleasant, angry, or discourteous individuals as part of the job requirements?
Spend Time Walking and Running	How much does this job require walking and running?
Frequency of Conflict Situations	How often are there conflict situations the employee has to face in this job?
Sounds, Noise Levels Are Distracting or Uncomforta	How often does this job require working exposed to sounds and noise levels that are distracting or uncomfortable?
Impact of Decisions on Co-workers or Company Resul	How do the decisions an employee makes impact the results of co-workers, clients or the company?
Level of Competition	To what extent does this job require the worker to compete or to be aware of competitive pressures?
Deal With External Customers	How important is it to work with external customers or the public in this job?
Importance of Repeating Same Tasks	How important is repeating the same physical activities (e.g., key entry) or mental activities (e.g., checking entries in a ledger) over and over, without stopping, to performing this job?
Coordinate or Lead Others	How important is it to coordinate or lead others in accomplishing work activities in this job?
Structured versus Unstructured Work	To what extent is this job structured for the worker, rather than allowing the worker to determine tasks, priorities, and goals?
Spend Time Using Your Hands to Handle, Control, or	How much does this job require using your hands to handle, control, or feel objects, tools or controls?
Exposed to Contaminants	How often does this job require working exposed to contaminants (such as pollutants, gases, dust or odors)?
Cramped Work Space, Awkward Positions	How often does this job require working in cramped work spaces that requires getting into awkward positions?
Time Pressure	How often does this job require the worker to meet strict deadlines?
Consequence of Error	How serious would the result usually be if the worker made a mistake that was not readily correctable?
Spend Time Bending or Twisting the Body	How much does this job require bending or twisting your body?

Freedom to Make Decisions	How much decision making freedom, without supervision, does the job offer?
Letters and Memos	How often does the job require written letters and memos?
Spend Time Making Repetitive Motions	How much does this job require making repetitive motions?
Responsible for Others' Health and Safety	How much responsibility is there for the health and safety of others in this job?
Responsibility for Outcomes and Results	How responsible is the worker for work outcomes and results of other workers?
Telephone	How often do you have telephone conversations in this job?
Extremely Bright or Inadequate Lighting	How often does this job require working in extremely bright or inadequate lighting conditions?
Exposed to Minor Burns, Cuts, Bites, or Stings	How often does this job require exposure to minor burns, cuts, bites, or stings?
Public Speaking	How often do you have to perform public speaking in this job?
Degree of Automation	How automated is the job?
Pace Determined by Speed of Equipment	How important is it to this job that the pace is determined by the speed of equipment or machinery? (This does not refer to keeping busy at all times on this job.)
Deal With Physically Aggressive People	How frequently does this job require the worker to deal with physical aggression of violent individuals?
Exposed to Disease or Infections	How often does this job require exposure to disease/infections?
Spend Time Kneeling, Crouching, Stooping, or Crawl	How much does this job require kneeling, crouching, stooping or crawling?
Electronic Mail	How often do you use electronic mail in this job?
Spend Time Sitting	How much does this job require sitting?
Spend Time Keeping or Regaining Balance	How much does this job require keeping or regaining your balance?
Very Hot or Cold Temperatures	How often does this job require working in very hot (above 90 F degrees) or very cold (below 32 F degrees) temperatures?
Indoors, Not Environmentally Controlled	How often does this job require working indoors in non-controlled environmental conditions (e.g., warehouse without heat)?
Exposed to Hazardous Conditions	How often does this job require exposure to hazardous conditions?
Exposed to Hazardous Equipment	How often does this job require exposure to hazardous equipment?
Outdoors, Under Cover	How often does this job require working outdoors, under cover (e.g., structure with roof but no walls)?
Exposed to Whole Body Vibration	How often does this job require exposure to whole body vibration (e.g., operate a jackhammer)?
Outdoors, Exposed to Weather	How often does this job require working outdoors, exposed to all weather conditions?
Exposed to High Places	How often does this job require exposure to high places?
Exposed to Radiation	How often does this job require exposure to radiation?
Wear Common Protective or Safety Equipment such as	How much does this job require wearing common protective or safety equipment such as safety shoes, glasses, gloves, hard hats or live jackets?
Spend Time Climbing Ladders, Scaffolds, or Poles	How much does this job require climbing ladders, scaffolds, or poles?
In an Enclosed Vehicle or Equipment	How often does this job require working in a closed vehicle or equipment (e.g., car)?
Wear Specialized Protective or Safety Equipment su	How much does this job require wearing specialized protective or safety equipment such as breathing apparatus, safety harness, full protection suits, or radiation protection?
In an Open Vehicle or Equipment	How often does this job require working in an open vehicle or equipment (e.g., tractor)?

Job Zone Component	Job Zone Component Definitions
Title	Job Zone Two: Some Preparation Needed
Overall Experience	Some previous work-related skill, knowledge, or experience may be helpful in these occupations, but usually is not needed. For example, a drywall installer might benefit from experience installing drywall, but an inexperienced person could still learn to be an installer with little difficulty.
Job Training	Employees in these occupations need anywhere from a few months to one year of working with experienced employees.
Job Zone Examples	These occupations often involve using your knowledge and skills to help others. Examples include drywall installers, fire inspectors, flight attendants, pharmacy technicians, salespersons (retail), and tellers.
SVP Range	(4.0 to < 6.0)

Education	These occupations usually require a high school diploma and may require some vocational training or job-related course work. In some cases, an associate's or bachelor's degree could be needed.

Work_Styles	Work_Styles Definitions
Cooperation	Job requires being pleasant with others on the job and displaying a good-natured, cooperative attitude.
Integrity	Job requires being honest and ethical.
Concern for Others	Job requires being sensitive to others' needs and feelings and being understanding and helpful on the job.
Self Control	Job requires maintaining composure, keeping emotions in check, controlling anger, and avoiding aggressive behavior, even in very difficult situations.
Stress Tolerance	Job requires accepting criticism and dealing calmly and effectively with high stress situations.
Social Orientation	Job requires preferring to work with others rather than alone, and being personally connected with others on the job.
Dependability	Job requires being reliable, responsible, and dependable, and fulfilling obligations.
Attention to Detail	Job requires being careful about detail and thorough in completing work tasks.
Adaptability/Flexibility	Job requires being open to change (positive or negative) and to considerable variety in the workplace.
Independence	Job requires developing one's own ways of doing things, guiding oneself with little or no supervision, and depending on oneself to get things done.
Analytical Thinking	Job requires analyzing information and using logic to address work-related issues and problems.
Initiative	Job requires a willingness to take on responsibilities and challenges.
Leadership	Job requires a willingness to lead, take charge, and offer opinions and direction.
Achievement/Effort	Job requires establishing and maintaining personally challenging achievement goals and exerting effort toward mastering tasks.
Innovation	Job requires creativity and alternative thinking to develop new ideas for and answers to work-related problems.
Persistence	Job requires persistence in the face of obstacles.

39-1021.00 - First-Line Supervisors/Managers of Personal Service Workers

Supervise and coordinate activities of personal service workers, such as supervisors of flight attendants, hairdressers, or caddies.

Tasks

1) Take disciplinary action to address performance problems.

2) Participate in continuing education to stay abreast of industry trends and developments.

3) Furnish customers with information on events and activities.

4) Recruit and hire staff members.

5) Train workers in proper operational procedures and functions, and explain company policies.

6) Inform workers about interests and special needs of specific groups.

7) Direct marketing, advertising, and other customer recruitment efforts.

8) Assign work schedules, following work requirements, to ensure quality and timely delivery of service.

9) Requisition necessary supplies, equipment, and services.

10) Analyze and record personnel and operational data, and write related activity reports.

11) Resolve customer complaints regarding worker performance and services rendered.

12) Inspect work areas and operating equipment to ensure conformance to established standards in areas such as cleanliness and maintenance.

13) Direct and coordinate the activities of workers such as flight attendants, hotel staff, or hair stylists.

14) Collaborate with staff members to plan and develop programs of events, schedules of activities, or menus.

15) Apply customer/guest feedback to service improvement efforts.

16) Observe and evaluate workers' appearance and performance to ensure quality service and compliance with specifications.

39-2011.00 - Animal Trainers

Train animals for riding, harness, security, performance, or obedience, or assisting persons with disabilities. Accustom animals to human voice and contact; and condition animals to respond to commands. Train animals according to prescribed standards for show or competition. May train animals to carry pack loads or work as part of pack team.

Tasks

1) Conduct training programs in order to develop and maintain desired animal behaviors for competition, entertainment, obedience, security, riding and related areas.

2) Administer prescribed medications to animals.

3) Use oral, spur, rein, and/or hand commands in order to condition horses to carry riders or to pull horse-drawn equipment.

4) Retrain horses to break bad habits, such as kicking, bolting, and resisting bridling and grooming.

5) Talk to and interact with animals in order to familiarize them to human voices and contact.

6) Evaluate animals in order to determine their temperaments, abilities, and aptitude for training.

7) Organize and conduct animal shows.

8) Cue or signal animals during performances.

9) Instruct jockeys in handling specific horses during races.

10) Feed and exercise animals, and provide other general care such as cleaning and maintaining holding and performance areas.

11) Arrange for mating of stallions and mares, and assist mares during foaling.

12) Observe animals' physical conditions in order to detect illness or unhealthy conditions requiring medical care.

13) Train dogs in human-assistance or property protection duties.

14) Train horses or other equines for riding, harness, show, racing, or other work, using knowledge of breed characteristics, training methods, performance standards, and the peculiarities of each animal.

15) Advise animal owners regarding the purchase of specific animals.

16) Keep records documenting animal health, diet, and behavior.

17) Place tack or harnesses on horses in order to accustom horses to the feel of equipment.

39-3011.00 - Gaming Dealers

Operate table games. Stand or sit behind table and operate games of chance by dispensing the appropriate number of cards or blocks to players, or operating other gaming equipment. Compare the house's hand against players' hands and payoff or collect players' money or chips.

Tasks

1) Conduct gambling games such as dice, roulette, cards, or keno, following all applicable rules and regulations.

2) Inspect cards and equipment to be used in games to ensure that they are in good condition.

3) Answer questions about game rules and casino policies.

4) Stand behind a gaming table and deal the appropriate number of cards to each player.

5) Deal cards to house hands, and compare these with players' hands to determine winners, as in black jack.

6) Exchange paper currency for playing chips or coin money.

7) Open and close cash floats and game tables.

8) Compute amounts of players' wins or losses, or scan winning tickets presented by patrons to calculate the amount of money won.

9) Refer patrons to gaming cashiers to collect winnings.

10) Apply rule variations to card games such as poker, in which players bet on the value of their hands.

11) Start and control games and gaming equipment, and announce winning numbers or colors.

12) Receive, verify, and record patrons' cash wagers.

13) Work as part of a team of dealers in games such as baccarat or craps.

14) Train new dealers.

15) Seat patrons at gaming tables.

16) Monitor gambling tables and supervise staff.

17) Participate in games for gambling establishments in order to provide the minimum complement of players at a table.

18) Prepare collection reports for submission to supervisors.

19) Check to ensure that all players have placed bets before play begins.

Knowledge	Knowledge Definitions
Mathematics	Knowledge of arithmetic, algebra, geometry, calculus, statistics, and their applications.
Customer and Personal Service	Knowledge of principles and processes for providing customer and personal services. This includes customer needs assessment, meeting quality standards for services, and evaluation of customer satisfaction.
Psychology	Knowledge of human behavior and performance; individual differences in ability, personality, and interests; learning and motivation; psychological research methods; and the assessment and treatment of behavioral and affective disorders.
Education and Training	Knowledge of principles and methods for curriculum and training design, teaching and instruction for individuals and groups, and the measurement of training effects.
Administration and Management	Knowledge of business and management principles involved in strategic planning, resource allocation, human resources modeling, leadership technique, production methods, and coordination of people and resources.
English Language	Knowledge of the structure and content of the English language including the meaning and spelling of words, rules of composition, and grammar.
Sales and Marketing	Knowledge of principles and methods for showing, promoting, and selling products or services. This includes marketing strategy and tactics, product demonstration, sales techniques, and sales control systems.
Law and Government	Knowledge of laws, legal codes, court procedures, precedents, government regulations, executive orders, agency rules, and the democratic political process.
Public Safety and Security	Knowledge of relevant equipment, policies, procedures, and strategies to promote effective local, state, or national security operations for the protection of people, data, property, and institutions.
Personnel and Human Resources	Knowledge of principles and procedures for personnel recruitment, selection, training, compensation and benefits, labor relations and negotiation, and personnel information systems.
Sociology and Anthropology	Knowledge of group behavior and dynamics, societal trends and influences, human migrations, ethnicity, cultures and their history and origins.
Economics and Accounting	Knowledge of economic and accounting principles and practices, the financial markets, banking and the analysis and reporting of financial data.
Computers and Electronics	Knowledge of circuit boards, processors, chips, electronic equipment, and computer hardware and software, including applications and programming.
Production and Processing	Knowledge of raw materials, production processes, quality control, costs, and other techniques for maximizing the effective manufacture and distribution of goods.
Communications and Media	Knowledge of media production, communication, and dissemination techniques and methods. This includes alternative ways to inform and entertain via written, oral, and visual media.
Therapy and Counseling	Knowledge of principles, methods, and procedures for diagnosis, treatment, and rehabilitation of physical and mental dysfunctions, and for career counseling and guidance.
Clerical	Knowledge of administrative and clerical procedures and systems such as word processing, managing files and records, stenography and transcription, designing forms, and other office procedures and terminology.
Geography	Knowledge of principles and methods for describing the features of land, sea, and air masses, including their physical characteristics, locations, interrelationships, and distribution of plant, animal, and human life.
Transportation	Knowledge of principles and methods for moving people or goods by air, rail, sea, or road, including the relative costs and benefits.
Building and Construction	Knowledge of materials, methods, and the tools involved in the construction or repair of houses, buildings, or other structures such as highways and roads.
Foreign Language	Knowledge of the structure and content of a foreign (non-English) language including the meaning and spelling of words, rules of composition and grammar, and pronunciation.
Biology	Knowledge of plant and animal organisms, their tissues, cells, functions, interdependencies, and interactions with each other and the environment.
Food Production	Knowledge of techniques and equipment for planting, growing, and harvesting food products (both plant and animal) for consumption, including storage/handling techniques.
Engineering and Technology	Knowledge of the practical application of engineering science and technology. This includes applying principles, techniques, procedures, and equipment to the design and production of various goods and services.
Design	Knowledge of design techniques, tools, and principles involved in production of precision technical plans, blueprints, drawings, and models.
Chemistry	Knowledge of the chemical composition, structure, and properties of substances and of the chemical processes and transformations that they undergo. This includes uses of chemicals and their interactions, danger signs, production techniques, and disposal methods.
Mechanical	Knowledge of machines and tools, including their designs, uses, repair, and maintenance.
Medicine and Dentistry	Knowledge of the information and techniques needed to diagnose and treat human injuries, diseases, and deformities. This includes symptoms, treatment alternatives, drug properties and interactions, and preventive health-care measures.
Physics	Knowledge and prediction of physical principles, laws, their interrelationships, and applications to understanding fluid, material, and atmospheric dynamics, and mechanical, electrical, atomic and sub-atomic structures and processes.
History and Archeology	Knowledge of historical events and their causes, indicators, and effects on civilizations and cultures.
Telecommunications	Knowledge of transmission, broadcasting, switching, control, and operation of telecommunications systems.
Fine Arts	Knowledge of the theory and techniques required to compose, produce, and perform works of music, dance, visual arts, drama, and sculpture.
Philosophy and Theology	Knowledge of different philosophical systems and religions. This includes their basic principles, values, ethics, ways of thinking, customs, practices, and their impact on human culture.

Skills	Skills Definitions
Mathematics	Using mathematics to solve problems.
Speaking	Talking to others to convey information effectively.
Active Listening	Giving full attention to what other people are saying, taking time to understand the points being made, asking questions as appropriate, and not interrupting at inappropriate times.
Service Orientation	Actively looking for ways to help people.
Social Perceptiveness	Being aware of others' reactions and understanding why they react as they do.
Monitoring	Monitoring/Assessing performance of yourself, other individuals, or organizations to make improvements or take corrective action.
Learning Strategies	Selecting and using training/instructional methods and procedures appropriate for the situation when learning or teaching new things.
Coordination	Adjusting actions in relation to others' actions.
Reading Comprehension	Understanding written sentences and paragraphs in work related documents.
Time Management	Managing one's own time and the time of others.
Active Learning	Understanding the implications of new information for both current and future problem-solving and decision-making.
Critical Thinking	Using logic and reasoning to identify the strengths and weaknesses of alternative solutions, conclusions or approaches to problems.

Instructing	Teaching others how to do something.
Persuasion	Persuading others to change their minds or behavior.
Judgment and Decision Making	Considering the relative costs and benefits of potential actions to choose the most appropriate one.
Negotiation	Bringing others together and trying to reconcile differences.
Writing	Communicating effectively in writing as appropriate for the needs of the audience.
Complex Problem Solving	Identifying complex problems and reviewing related information to develop and evaluate options and implement solutions.
Quality Control Analysis	Conducting tests and inspections of products, services, or processes to evaluate quality or performance.
Management of Material Resources	Obtaining and seeing to the appropriate use of equipment, facilities, and materials needed to do certain work.
Equipment Selection	Determining the kind of tools and equipment needed to do a job.
Management of Personnel Resources	Motivating, developing, and directing people as they work, identifying the best people for the job.
Operation and Control	Controlling operations of equipment or systems.
Troubleshooting	Determining causes of operating errors and deciding what to do about it.
Equipment Maintenance	Performing routine maintenance on equipment and determining when and what kind of maintenance is needed.
Operations Analysis	Analyzing needs and product requirements to create a design.
Technology Design	Generating or adapting equipment and technology to serve user needs.
Repairing	Repairing machines or systems using the needed tools.
Systems Evaluation	Identifying measures or indicators of system performance and the actions needed to improve or correct performance, relative to the goals of the system.
Installation	Installing equipment, machines, wiring, or programs to meet specifications.
Systems Analysis	Determining how a system should work and how changes in conditions, operations, and the environment will affect outcomes.
Management of Financial Resources	Determining how money will be spent to get the work done, and accounting for these expenditures.
Programming	Writing computer programs for various purposes.
Science	Using scientific rules and methods to solve problems.
Operation Monitoring	Watching gauges, dials, or other indicators to make sure a machine is working properly.

Ability	Ability Definitions
Oral Expression	The ability to communicate information and ideas in speaking so others will understand.
Problem Sensitivity	The ability to tell when something is wrong or is likely to go wrong. It does not involve solving the problem, only recognizing there is a problem.
Speech Clarity	The ability to speak clearly so others can understand you.
Oral Comprehension	The ability to listen to and understand information and ideas presented through spoken words and sentences.
Speech Recognition	The ability to identify and understand the speech of another person.
Near Vision	The ability to see details at close range (within a few feet of the observer).
Manual Dexterity	The ability to quickly move your hand, your hand together with your arm, or your two hands to grasp, manipulate, or assemble objects.
Selective Attention	The ability to concentrate on a task over a period of time without being distracted.
Category Flexibility	The ability to generate or use different sets of rules for combining or grouping things in different ways.
Deductive Reasoning	The ability to apply general rules to specific problems to produce answers that make sense.
Perceptual Speed	The ability to quickly and accurately compare similarities and differences among sets of letters, numbers, objects, pictures, or patterns. The things to be compared may be presented at the same time or one after the other. This ability also includes comparing a presented object with a remembered object.
Information Ordering	The ability to arrange things or actions in a certain order or pattern according to a specific rule or set of rules (e.g., patterns of numbers, letters, words, pictures, mathematical operations).
Inductive Reasoning	The ability to combine pieces of information to form general rules or conclusions (includes finding a relationship among seemingly unrelated events).

Finger Dexterity	The ability to make precisely coordinated movements of the fingers of one or both hands to grasp, manipulate, or assemble very small objects.
Arm-Hand Steadiness	The ability to keep your hand and arm steady while moving your arm or while holding your arm and hand in one position.
Time Sharing	The ability to shift back and forth between two or more activities or sources of information (such as speech, sounds, touch, or other sources).
Visual Color Discrimination	The ability to match or detect differences between colors, including shades of color and brightness.
Trunk Strength	The ability to use your abdominal and lower back muscles to support part of the body repeatedly or continuously over time without 'giving out' or fatiguing.
Written Comprehension	The ability to read and understand information and ideas presented in writing.
Speed of Closure	The ability to quickly make sense of, combine, and organize information into meaningful patterns.
Written Expression	The ability to communicate information and ideas in writing so others will understand.
Flexibility of Closure	The ability to identify or detect a known pattern (a figure, object, word, or sound) that is hidden in other distracting material.
Far Vision	The ability to see details at a distance.
Originality	The ability to come up with unusual or clever ideas about a given topic or situation, or to develop creative ways to solve a problem.
Number Facility	The ability to add, subtract, multiply, or divide quickly and correctly.
Auditory Attention	The ability to focus on a single source of sound in the presence of other distracting sounds.
Fluency of Ideas	The ability to come up with a number of ideas about a topic (the number of ideas is important, not their quality, correctness, or creativity).
Hearing Sensitivity	The ability to detect or tell the differences between sounds that vary in pitch and loudness.
Mathematical Reasoning	The ability to choose the right mathematical methods or formulas to solve a problem.
Extent Flexibility	The ability to bend, stretch, twist, or reach with your body, arms, and/or legs.
Multilimb Coordination	The ability to coordinate two or more limbs (for example, two arms, two legs, or one leg and one arm) while sitting, standing, or lying down. It does not involve performing the activities while the whole body is in motion.
Visualization	The ability to imagine how something will look after it is moved around or when its parts are moved or rearranged.
Control Precision	The ability to quickly and repeatedly adjust the controls of a machine or a vehicle to exact positions.
Stamina	The ability to exert yourself physically over long periods of time without getting winded or out of breath.
Static Strength	The ability to exert maximum muscle force to lift, push, pull, or carry objects.
Dynamic Strength	The ability to exert muscle force repeatedly or continuously over time. This involves muscular endurance and resistance to muscle fatigue.
Depth Perception	The ability to judge which of several objects is closer or farther away from you, or to judge the distance between you and an object.
Gross Body Coordination	The ability to coordinate the movement of your arms, legs, and torso together when the whole body is in motion.
Memorization	The ability to remember information such as words, numbers, pictures, and procedures.
Gross Body Equilibrium	The ability to keep or regain your body balance or stay upright when in an unstable position.
Wrist-Finger Speed	The ability to make fast, simple, repeated movements of the fingers, hands, and wrists.
Night Vision	The ability to see under low light conditions.
Sound Localization	The ability to tell the direction from which a sound originated.
Dynamic Flexibility	The ability to quickly and repeatedly bend, stretch, twist, or reach out with your body, arms, and/or legs.
Explosive Strength	The ability to use short bursts of muscle force to propel oneself (as in jumping or sprinting), or to throw an object.
Speed of Limb Movement	The ability to quickly move the arms and legs.
Reaction Time	The ability to quickly respond (with the hand, finger, or foot) to a signal (sound, light, picture) when it appears.
Rate Control	The ability to time your movements or the movement of a piece of equipment in anticipation of changes in the speed and/or direction of a moving object or scene.

Response Orientation	The ability to choose quickly between two or more movements in response to two or more different signals (lights, sounds, pictures). It includes the speed with which the correct response is started with the hand, foot, or other body part.
Peripheral Vision	The ability to see objects or movement of objects to one's side when the eyes are looking ahead.
Glare Sensitivity	The ability to see objects in the presence of glare or bright lighting.
Spatial Orientation	The ability to know your location in relation to the environment or to know where other objects are in relation to you.

Work_Activity	Work_Activity Definitions
Performing for or Working Directly with the Public	Performing for people or dealing directly with the public. This includes serving customers in restaurants and stores, and receiving clients or guests.
Communicating with Supervisors, Peers, or Subordin	Providing information to supervisors, co-workers, and subordinates by telephone, in written form, e-mail, or in person.
Identifying Objects, Actions, and Events	Identifying information by categorizing, estimating, recognizing differences or similarities, and detecting changes in circumstances or events.
Getting Information	Observing, receiving, and otherwise obtaining information from all relevant sources.
Handling and Moving Objects	Using hands and arms in handling, installing, positioning, and moving materials, and manipulating things.
Monitor Processes, Materials, or Surroundings	Monitoring and reviewing information from materials, events, or the environment, to detect or assess problems.
Updating and Using Relevant Knowledge	Keeping up-to-date technically and applying new knowledge to your job.
Judging the Qualities of Things, Services, or Peop	Assessing the value, importance, or quality of things or people.
Assisting and Caring for Others	Providing personal assistance, medical attention, emotional support, or other personal care to others such as coworkers, customers, or patients.
Communicating with Persons Outside Organization	Communicating with people outside the organization, representing the organization to customers, the public, government, and other external sources. This information can be exchanged in person, in writing, or by telephone or e-mail.
Inspecting Equipment, Structures, or Material	Inspecting equipment, structures, or materials to identify the cause of errors or other problems or defects.
Establishing and Maintaining Interpersonal Relatio	Developing constructive and cooperative working relationships with others, and maintaining them over time.
Performing General Physical Activities	Performing physical activities that require considerable use of your arms and legs and moving your whole body, such as climbing, lifting, balancing, walking, stooping, and handling of materials.
Making Decisions and Solving Problems	Analyzing information and evaluating results to choose the best solution and solve problems.
Developing and Building Teams	Encouraging and building mutual trust, respect, and cooperation among team members.
Evaluating Information to Determine Compliance wit	Using relevant information and individual judgment to determine whether events or processes comply with laws, regulations, or standards.
Coordinating the Work and Activities of Others	Getting members of a group to work together to accomplish tasks.
Selling or Influencing Others	Convincing others to buy merchandise/goods or to otherwise change their minds or actions.
Thinking Creatively	Developing, designing, or creating new applications, ideas, relationships, systems, or products, including artistic contributions.
Resolving Conflicts and Negotiating with Others	Handling complaints, settling disputes, and resolving grievances and conflicts, or otherwise negotiating with others.
Processing Information	Compiling, coding, categorizing, calculating, tabulating, auditing, or verifying information or data.
Organizing, Planning, and Prioritizing Work	Developing specific goals and plans to prioritize, organize, and accomplish your work.
Interpreting the Meaning of Information for Others	Translating or explaining what information means and how it can be used.
Estimating the Quantifiable Characteristics of Pro	Estimating sizes, distances, and quantities; or determining time, costs, resources, or materials needed to perform a work activity.
Training and Teaching Others	Identifying the educational needs of others, developing formal educational or training programs or classes, and teaching or instructing others.

Scheduling Work and Activities	Scheduling events, programs, and activities, as well as the work of others.
Developing Objectives and Strategies	Establishing long-range objectives and specifying the strategies and actions to achieve them.
Analyzing Data or Information	Identifying the underlying principles, reasons, or facts of information by breaking down information or data into separate parts.
Monitoring and Controlling Resources	Monitoring and controlling resources and overseeing the spending of money.
Coaching and Developing Others	Identifying the developmental needs of others and coaching, mentoring, or otherwise helping others to improve their knowledge or skills.
Guiding, Directing, and Motivating Subordinates	Providing guidance and direction to subordinates, including setting performance standards and monitoring performance.
Provide Consultation and Advice to Others	Providing guidance and expert advice to management or other groups on technical, systems-, or process-related topics.
Controlling Machines and Processes	Using either control mechanisms or direct physical activity to operate machines or processes (not including computers or vehicles).
Documenting/Recording Information	Entering, transcribing, recording, storing, or maintaining information in written or electronic/magnetic form.
Performing Administrative Activities	Performing day-to-day administrative tasks such as maintaining information files and processing paperwork.
Interacting With Computers	Using computers and computer systems (including hardware and software) to program, write software, set up functions, enter data, or process information.
Staffing Organizational Units	Recruiting, interviewing, selecting, hiring, and promoting employees in an organization.
Repairing and Maintaining Mechanical Equipment	Servicing, repairing, adjusting, and testing machines, devices, moving parts, and equipment that operate primarily on the basis of mechanical (not electronic) principles.
Repairing and Maintaining Electronic Equipment	Servicing, repairing, calibrating, regulating, fine-tuning, or testing machines, devices, and equipment that operate primarily on the basis of electrical or electronic (not mechanical) principles.
Drafting, Laying Out, and Specifying Technical Dev	Providing documentation, detailed instructions, drawings, or specifications to tell others about how devices, parts, equipment, or structures are to be fabricated, constructed, assembled, modified, maintained, or used.
Operating Vehicles, Mechanized Devices, or Equipme	Running, maneuvering, navigating, or driving vehicles or mechanized equipment, such as forklifts, passenger vehicles, aircraft, or water craft.

Work_Context	Work_Context Definitions
Spend Time Making Repetitive Motions	How much does this job require making repetitive motions?
Importance of Being Exact or Accurate	How important is being very exact or highly accurate in performing this job?
Spend Time Standing	How much does this job require standing?
Face-to-Face Discussions	How often do you have to have face-to-face discussions with individuals or teams in this job?
Contact With Others	How much does this job require the worker to be in contact with others (face-to-face, by telephone, or otherwise) in order to perform it?
Deal With External Customers	How important is it to work with external customers or the public in this job?
Deal With Unpleasant or Angry People	How frequently does the worker have to deal with unpleasant, angry, or discourteous individuals as part of the job requirements?
Sounds, Noise Levels Are Distracting or Uncomforta	How often does this job require working exposed to sounds and noise levels that are distracting or uncomfortable?
Spend Time Using Your Hands to Handle, Control, or	How much does this job require using your hands to handle, control, or feel objects, tools or controls?
Physical Proximity	To what extent does this job require the worker to perform job tasks in close physical proximity to other people?
Work With Work Group or Team	How important is it to work with others in a group or team in this job?
Indoors, Environmentally Controlled	How often does this job require working indoors in environmentally controlled conditions?
Frequency of Conflict Situations	How often are there conflict situations the employee has to face in this job?
Importance of Repeating Same Tasks	How important is repeating the same physical activities (e.g., key entry) or mental activities (e.g., checking entries in a ledger) over and over, without stopping, to performing this job?
Level of Competition	To what extent does this job require the worker to compete or to be aware of competitive pressures?

Spend Time Bending or Twisting the Body	How much does this job require bending or twisting your body?
Frequency of Decision Making	How frequently is the worker required to make decisions that affect other people, the financial resources, and/or the image and reputation of the organization?
Public Speaking	How often do you have to perform public speaking in this job?
Impact of Decisions on Co-workers or Company Resul	How do the decisions an employee makes impact the results of co-workers, clients or the company?
Coordinate or Lead Others	How important is it to coordinate or lead others in accomplishing work activities in this job?
Structured versus Unstructured Work	To what extent is this job structured for the worker, rather than allowing the worker to determine tasks, priorities, and goals?
Responsible for Others' Health and Safety	How much responsibility is there for the health and safety of others in this job?
Exposed to Disease or Infections	How often does this job require exposure to disease/infections?
Consequence of Error	How serious would the result usually be if the worker made a mistake that was not readily correctable?
Responsibility for Outcomes and Results	How responsible is the worker for work outcomes and results of other workers?
Exposed to Contaminants	How often does this job require working exposed to contaminants (such as pollutants, gases, dust or odors)?
Deal With Physically Aggressive People	How frequently does this job require the worker to deal with physical aggression of violent individuals?
Degree of Automation	How automated is the job?
Freedom to Make Decisions	How much decision making freedom, without supervision, does the job offer?
Extremely Bright or Inadequate Lighting	How often does this job require working in extremely bright or inadequate lighting conditions?
Spend Time Sitting	How much does this job require sitting?
Spend Time Kneeling, Crouching, Stooping, or Crawl	How much does this job require kneeling, crouching, stooping or crawling?
Spend Time Walking and Running	How much does this job require walking and running?
Letters and Memos	How often does the job require written letters and memos?
Indoors, Not Environmentally Controlled	How often does this job require working indoors in non-controlled environmental conditions (e.g., warehouse without heat)?
Spend Time Keeping or Regaining Balance	How much does this job require keeping or regaining your balance?
Cramped Work Space, Awkward Positions	How often does this job require working in cramped work spaces that requires getting into awkward positions?
Time Pressure	How often does this job require the worker to meet strict deadlines?
Pace Determined by Speed of Equipment	How important is it to this job that the pace is determined by the speed of equipment or machinery? (This does not refer to keeping busy at all times on this job.)
Wear Common Protective or Safety Equipment such as	How much does this job require wearing common protective or safety equipment such as safety shoes, glasses, gloves, hard hats or live jackets?
Telephone	How often do you have telephone conversations in this job?
Exposed to Hazardous Equipment	How often does this job require exposure to hazardous equipment?
Very Hot or Cold Temperatures	How often does this job require working in very hot (above 90 F degrees) or very cold (below 32 F degrees) temperatures?
Electronic Mail	How often do you use electronic mail in this job?
Exposed to Whole Body Vibration	How often does this job require exposure to whole body vibration (e.g., operate a jackhammer)?
Exposed to Minor Burns, Cuts, Bites, or Stings	How often does this job require exposure to minor burns, cuts, bites, or stings?
Exposed to High Places	How often does this job require exposure to high places?
Exposed to Hazardous Conditions	How often does this job require exposure to hazardous conditions?
Outdoors, Exposed to Weather	How often does this job require working outdoors, exposed to all weather conditions?
Exposed to Radiation	How often does this job require exposure to radiation?
Wear Specialized Protective or Safety Equipment su	How much does this job require wearing specialized protective or safety equipment such as breathing apparatus, safety harness, full protection suits, or radiation protection?
Outdoors, Under Cover	How often does this job require working outdoors, under cover (e.g., structure with roof but no walls)?
Spend Time Climbing Ladders, Scaffolds, or Poles	How much does this job require climbing ladders, scaffolds, or poles?
In an Open Vehicle or Equipment	How often does this job require working in an open vehicle or equipment (e.g., tractor)?
In an Enclosed Vehicle or Equipment	How often does this job require working in a closed vehicle or equipment (e.g., car)?

Job Zone Component	Job Zone Component Definitions
Title	Job Zone Two: Some Preparation Needed
Overall Experience	Some previous work-related skill, knowledge, or experience may be helpful in these occupations, but usually is not needed. For example, a drywall installer might benefit from experience installing drywall, but an inexperienced person could still learn to be an installer with little difficulty.
Job Training	Employees in these occupations need anywhere from a few months to one year of working with experienced employees.
Job Zone Examples	These occupations often involve using your knowledge and skills to help others. Examples include drywall installers, fire inspectors, flight attendants, pharmacy technicians, salespersons (retail), and tellers.
SVP Range	(4.0 to < 6.0)
Education	These occupations usually require a high school diploma and may require some vocational training or job-related course work. In some cases, an associate's or bachelor's degree could be needed.

Work_Styles	Work_Styles Definitions
Integrity	Job requires being honest and ethical.
Self Control	Job requires maintaining composure, keeping emotions in check, controlling anger, and avoiding aggressive behavior, even in very difficult situations.
Attention to Detail	Job requires being careful about detail and thorough in completing work tasks.
Cooperation	Job requires being pleasant with others on the job and displaying a good-natured, cooperative attitude.
Stress Tolerance	Job requires accepting criticism and dealing calmly and effectively with high stress situations.
Dependability	Job requires being reliable, responsible, and dependable, and fulfilling obligations.
Concern for Others	Job requires being sensitive to others' needs and feelings and being understanding and helpful on the job.
Adaptability/Flexibility	Job requires being open to change (positive or negative) and to considerable variety in the workplace.
Social Orientation	Job requires preferring to work with others rather than alone, and being personally connected with others on the job.
Achievement/Effort	Job requires establishing and maintaining personally challenging achievement goals and exerting effort toward mastering tasks.
Persistence	Job requires persistence in the face of obstacles.
Initiative	Job requires a willingness to take on responsibilities and challenges.
Leadership	Job requires a willingness to lead, take charge, and offer opinions and direction.
Analytical Thinking	Job requires analyzing information and using logic to address work-related issues and problems.
Independence	Job requires developing one's own ways of doing things, guiding oneself with little or no supervision, and depending on oneself to get things done.
Innovation	Job requires creativity and alternative thinking to develop new ideas for and answers to work-related problems.

39-3012.00 - Gaming and Sports Book Writers and Runners

Assist in the operation of games such as keno and bingo. Scan winning tickets presented by patrons, calculate amount of winnings and pay patrons. May operate keno and bingo equipment. May start gaming equipment that randomly selects numbers. May announce number selected until total numbers specified for each game are selected. May pick up tickets from players, collect bets, receive, verify and record patrons' cash wages.

Tasks

1) Collect bets in the form of cash or chips, verifying and recording amounts.

2) Answer questions about game rules and casino policies.

3) Check to ensure that all players have placed their bets before play begins.

4) Exchange paper currency for playing chips or coins.

5) Sell food, beverages, and tobacco to players.

6) Prepare collection reports for submission to supervisors.

7) Supervise staff and games, and mediate disputes.

8) Start gaming equipment that randomly selects numbered balls, and announce winning numbers and colors.

9) Collect cards or tickets from players.

10) Take the house percentage from each pot.

11) Record the number of tickets cashed and the amount paid out after each race or event.

12) Push dice to shooters and retrieve thrown dice.

13) Pay off or move bets as established by game rules and procedures.

14) Operate games in which players bet that a ball will come to rest in a particular slot on a rotating wheel, performing actions such as spinning the wheel and releasing the ball.

15) Open and close cash floats and game tables.

16) Inspect cards and equipment to be used in games to ensure they are in proper condition.

17) Compare the house hand with players' hands in order to determine the winner.

18) Compute and verify amounts won and lost, then pay out winnings or refer patrons to workers such as gaming cashiers so that winnings can be collected.

19) Participate in games for gambling establishments in order to provide the minimum complement of players at a table.

20) Conduct gambling tables or games, such as dice, roulette, cards, or keno, and ensure that game rules are followed.

21) Seat patrons at gaming tables.

39-3021.00 - Motion Picture Projectionists

Set up and operate motion picture projection and related sound reproduction equipment.

Tasks

1) Prepare film inspection reports, attendance sheets, and log books.

2) Observe projector operation in order to anticipate need to transfer operations from one projector to another.

3) Start projectors and open shutters to project images onto screens.

4) Install and connect auxiliary equipment, such as microphones, amplifiers, disc playback machines, and lights.

5) Perform minor repairs such as replacing worn sprockets, or notify maintenance personnel of the need for major repairs.

6) Perform regular maintenance tasks such as rotating or replacing xenon bulbs, cleaning lenses, lubricating machinery, and keeping electrical contacts clean and tight.

7) Monitor operations to ensure that standards for sound and image projection quality are met.

8) Set up and adjust picture projectors and screens to achieve proper size, illumination, and focus of images, and proper volume and tone of sound.

9) Project motion pictures onto back screens for inclusion in scenes within film or stage productions.

10) Insert film into top magazine reel, or thread film through a series of sprockets and guide rollers, attaching the end to a take-up reel.

11) Remove full take-up reels and run film through rewinding machines to rewind projected films so they may be shown again.

12) Open and close facilities according to rules and schedules.

13) Splice and rewind film onto reels automatically, or by hand, to repair faulty or broken sections of film.

14) Coordinate equipment operation with presentation of supplemental material, such as music, oral commentaries, or sound effects.

15) Inspect movie films to ensure that they are complete and in good condition.

16) Set up and inspect curtain and screen controls.

17) Operate special-effects equipment, such as stereopticons, to project pictures onto screens.

18) Inspect projection equipment prior to operation in order to ensure proper working order.

19) Operate equipment in order to show films in a number of theaters simultaneously.

20) Remove film splicing in order to prepare films for shipment after showings, and return films to their sources.

39-3092.00 - Costume Attendants

Select, fit, and take care of costumes for cast members, and aid entertainers.

Tasks

1) Provide managers with budget recommendations, and take responsibility for budgetary line items related to costumes, storage, and makeup needs.

2) Arrange costumes in order of use to facilitate quick-change procedures for performances.

3) Purchase, rent, or requisition costumes and other wardrobe necessities.

4) Recommend vendors and monitor their work.

5) Assign lockers to employees, and maintain locker rooms, dressing rooms, wig rooms, and costume storage and laundry areas.

6) Design and construct costumes or send them to tailors for construction, major repairs, or alterations.

7) Check the appearance of costumes on-stage and under lights in order to determine whether desired effects are being achieved.

8) Direct the work of wardrobe crews during dress rehearsals and performances.

9) Collaborate with production designers, costume designers, and other production staff in order to discuss and execute costume design details.

10) Create worksheets for dressing lists, show notes, and costume checks.

11) Distribute costumes and related equipment, and keep records of item status.

12) Study books, pictures, and examples of period clothing in order to determine styles worn during specific periods in history.

13) Inventory stock in order to determine types and conditions of available costuming.

14) Care for non-clothing items such as flags, table skirts, and draperies.

15) Examine costume fit on cast members, and sketch or write notes for alterations.

16) Provide assistance to cast members in wearing costumes, or assign cast dressers to assist specific cast members with costume changes.

17) Return borrowed or rented items when productions are complete and return other items to storage.

18) Review scripts or other production information in order to determine a story's locale and period, as well as the number of characters and required costumes.

19) Monitor, maintain, and secure inventories of costumes, wigs, and makeup, providing keys or access to assigned directors, costume designers, and wardrobe mistresses/masters.

20) Participate in the hiring, training, scheduling, and supervision of alteration workers.

39-3093.00 - Locker Room, Coatroom, and Dressing Room Attendants

Provide personal items to patrons or customers in locker rooms, dressing rooms, or coatrooms.

Tasks

1) Check supplies to ensure adequate availability, and order new supplies when necessary.

2) Answer customer inquiries; and explain cost, availability, policies, and procedures of facilities.

3) Assign dressing room facilities, locker space, or clothing containers to patrons of athletic or bathing establishments.

4) Maintain inventories of clothing or uniforms, accessories, equipment, and/or linens.

5) Maintain a lost-and-found collection.

6) Store personal possessions for patrons, issue claim checks for articles stored, and return articles on receipt of checks.

7) Activate emergency action plans and administer first aid, as necessary.

8) Collect soiled linen or clothing for laundering.

9) Provide towels and sheets to clients in public baths, steam rooms, and restrooms.

10) Report and document safety hazards, potentially hazardous conditions, and unsafe practices and procedures.

11) Monitor patrons' facility use in order to ensure that rules and regulations are followed, and safety and order are maintained.

12) Stencil identifying information on equipment.

13) Issue gym clothes, uniforms, towels, athletic equipment, and special athletic apparel.

14) Clean and polish footwear, using brushes, sponges, cleaning fluid, polishes, waxes, liquid or sole dressing, and daubers.

15) Provide assistance to patrons by performing duties such as opening doors and carrying bags.

16) Procure beverages, food, and other items as requested.

17) Set up various apparatus or athletic equipment.

18) Operate washing machines and dryers in order to clean soiled apparel and towels.

19) Operate controls that regulate temperatures or room environments.

20) Attend to needs of athletic teams in clubhouses.

21) Provide or arrange for services such as clothes pressing, cleaning, and repair.

Knowledge	Knowledge Definitions
Customer and Personal Service	Knowledge of principles and processes for providing customer and personal services. This includes customer needs assessment, meeting quality standards for services, and evaluation of customer satisfaction.
Mathematics	Knowledge of arithmetic, algebra, geometry, calculus, statistics, and their applications.
English Language	Knowledge of the structure and content of the English language including the meaning and spelling of words, rules of composition, and grammar.
Education and Training	Knowledge of principles and methods for curriculum and training design, teaching and instruction for individuals and groups, and the measurement of training effects.
Sales and Marketing	Knowledge of principles and methods for showing, promoting, and selling products or services. This includes marketing strategy and tactics, product demonstration, sales techniques, and sales control systems.
Administration and Management	Knowledge of business and management principles involved in strategic planning, resource allocation, human resources modeling, leadership technique, production methods, and coordination of people and resources.
Computers and Electronics	Knowledge of circuit boards, processors, chips, electronic equipment, and computer hardware and software, including applications and programming.
Personnel and Human Resources	Knowledge of principles and procedures for personnel recruitment, selection, training, compensation and benefits, labor relations and negotiation, and personnel information systems.
Communications and Media	Knowledge of media production, communication, and dissemination techniques and methods. This includes alternative ways to inform and entertain via written, oral, and visual media.
Psychology	Knowledge of human behavior and performance; individual differences in ability, personality, and interests; learning and motivation; psychological research methods; and the assessment and treatment of behavioral and affective disorders.
Public Safety and Security	Knowledge of relevant equipment, policies, procedures, and strategies to promote effective local, state, or national security operations for the protection of people, data, property, and institutions.
Transportation	Knowledge of principles and methods for moving people or goods by air, rail, sea, or road, including the relative costs and benefits.
Clerical	Knowledge of administrative and clerical procedures and systems such as word processing, managing files and records, stenography and transcription, designing forms, and other office procedures and terminology.
Chemistry	Knowledge of the chemical composition, structure, and properties of substances and of the chemical processes and transformations that they undergo. This includes uses of chemicals and their interactions, danger signs, production techniques, and disposal methods.
Economics and Accounting	Knowledge of economic and accounting principles and practices, the financial markets, banking and the analysis and reporting of financial data.
Foreign Language	Knowledge of the structure and content of a foreign (non-English) language including the meaning and spelling of words, rules of composition and grammar, and pronunciation.
Telecommunications	Knowledge of transmission, broadcasting, switching, control, and operation of telecommunications systems.
Mechanical	Knowledge of machines and tools, including their designs, uses, repair, and maintenance.
Medicine and Dentistry	Knowledge of the information and techniques needed to diagnose and treat human injuries, diseases, and deformities. This includes symptoms, treatment alternatives, drug properties and interactions, and preventive health-care measures.
Therapy and Counseling	Knowledge of principles, methods, and procedures for diagnosis, treatment, and rehabilitation of physical and mental dysfunctions, and for career counseling and guidance.
Engineering and Technology	Knowledge of the practical application of engineering science and technology. This includes applying principles, techniques, procedures, and equipment to the design and production of various goods and services.
Production and Processing	Knowledge of raw materials, production processes, quality control, costs, and other techniques for maximizing the effective manufacture and distribution of goods.
Design	Knowledge of design techniques, tools, and principles involved in production of precision technical plans, blueprints, drawings, and models.
Physics	Knowledge and prediction of physical principles, laws, their interrelationships, and applications to understanding fluid, material, and atmospheric dynamics, and mechanical, electrical, atomic and sub-atomic structures and processes.
Sociology and Anthropology	Knowledge of group behavior and dynamics, societal trends and influences, human migrations, ethnicity, cultures and their history and origins.
Law and Government	Knowledge of laws, legal codes, court procedures, precedents, government regulations, executive orders, agency rules, and the democratic political process.
Philosophy and Theology	Knowledge of different philosophical systems and religions. This includes their basic principles, values, ethics, ways of thinking, customs, practices, and their impact on human culture.
Geography	Knowledge of principles and methods for describing the features of land, sea, and air masses, including their physical characteristics, locations, interrelationships, and distribution of plant, animal, and human life.
Food Production	Knowledge of techniques and equipment for planting, growing, and harvesting food products (both plant and animal) for consumption, including storage/handling techniques.
Building and Construction	Knowledge of materials, methods, and the tools involved in the construction or repair of houses, buildings, or other structures such as highways and roads.
Fine Arts	Knowledge of the theory and techniques required to compose, produce, and perform works of music, dance, visual arts, drama, and sculpture.
Biology	Knowledge of plant and animal organisms, their tissues, cells, functions, interdependencies, and interactions with each other and the environment.
History and Archeology	Knowledge of historical events and their causes, indicators, and effects on civilizations and cultures.

Skills	Skills Definitions
Active Listening	Giving full attention to what other people are saying, taking time to understand the points being made, asking questions as appropriate, and not interrupting at inappropriate times.
Speaking	Talking to others to convey information effectively.
Service Orientation	Actively looking for ways to help people.
Reading Comprehension	Understanding written sentences and paragraphs in work related documents.
Social Perceptiveness	Being aware of others' reactions and understanding why they react as they do.

Critical Thinking	Using logic and reasoning to identify the strengths and weaknesses of alternative solutions, conclusions or approaches to problems.
Writing	Communicating effectively in writing as appropriate for the needs of the audience.
Instructing	Teaching others how to do something.
Negotiation	Bringing others together and trying to reconcile differences.
Time Management	Managing one's own time and the time of others.
Learning Strategies	Selecting and using training/instructional methods and procedures appropriate for the situation when learning or teaching new things.
Persuasion	Persuading others to change their minds or behavior.
Active Learning	Understanding the implications of new information for both current and future problem-solving and decision-making.
Monitoring	Monitoring/Assessing performance of yourself, other individuals, or organizations to make improvements or take corrective action.
Mathematics	Using mathematics to solve problems.
Coordination	Adjusting actions in relation to others' actions.
Judgment and Decision Making	Considering the relative costs and benefits of potential actions to choose the most appropriate one.
Equipment Selection	Determining the kind of tools and equipment needed to do a job.
Complex Problem Solving	Identifying complex problems and reviewing related information to develop and evaluate options and implement solutions.
Quality Control Analysis	Conducting tests and inspections of products, services, or processes to evaluate quality or performance.
Operations Analysis	Analyzing needs and product requirements to create a design.
Equipment Maintenance	Performing routine maintenance on equipment and determining when and what kind of maintenance is needed.
Management of Material Resources	Obtaining and seeing to the appropriate use of equipment, facilities, and materials needed to do certain work.
Systems Evaluation	Identifying measures or indicators of system performance and the actions needed to improve or correct performance, relative to the goals of the system.
Operation and Control	Controlling operations of equipment or systems.
Management of Personnel Resources	Motivating, developing, and directing people as they work, identifying the best people for the job.
Operation Monitoring	Watching gauges, dials, or other indicators to make sure a machine is working properly.
Repairing	Repairing machines or systems using the needed tools.
Science	Using scientific rules and methods to solve problems.
Systems Analysis	Determining how a system should work and how changes in conditions, operations, and the environment will affect outcomes.
Troubleshooting	Determining causes of operating errors and deciding what to do about it.
Management of Financial Resources	Determining how money will be spent to get the work done, and accounting for these expenditures.
Installation	Installing equipment, machines, wiring, or programs to meet specifications.
Technology Design	Generating or adapting equipment and technology to serve user needs.
Programming	Writing computer programs for various purposes.

Ability	**Ability Definitions**
Oral Comprehension	The ability to listen to and understand information and ideas presented through spoken words and sentences.
Oral Expression	The ability to communicate information and ideas in speaking so others will understand.
Speech Clarity	The ability to speak clearly so others can understand you.
Speech Recognition	The ability to identify and understand the speech of another person.
Problem Sensitivity	The ability to tell when something is wrong or is likely to go wrong. It does not involve solving the problem, only recognizing there is a problem.
Information Ordering	The ability to arrange things or actions in a certain order or pattern according to a specific rule or set of rules (e.g., patterns of numbers, letters, words, pictures, mathematical operations).
Trunk Strength	The ability to use your abdominal and lower back muscles to support part of the body repeatedly or continuously over time without 'giving out' or fatiguing.
Near Vision	The ability to see details at close range (within a few feet of the observer).

Inductive Reasoning	The ability to combine pieces of information to form general rules or conclusions (includes finding a relationship among seemingly unrelated events).
Written Comprehension	The ability to read and understand information and ideas presented in writing.
Deductive Reasoning	The ability to apply general rules to specific problems to produce answers that make sense.
Written Expression	The ability to communicate information and ideas in writing so others will understand.
Extent Flexibility	The ability to bend, stretch, twist, or reach with your body, arms, and/or legs.
Selective Attention	The ability to concentrate on a task over a period of time without being distracted.
Stamina	The ability to exert yourself physically over long periods of time without getting winded or out of breath.
Category Flexibility	The ability to generate or use different sets of rules for combining or grouping things in different ways.
Far Vision	The ability to see details at a distance.
Manual Dexterity	The ability to quickly move your hand, your hand together with your arm, or your two hands to grasp, manipulate, or assemble objects.
Visual Color Discrimination	The ability to match or detect differences between colors, including shades of color and brightness.
Control Precision	The ability to quickly and repeatedly adjust the controls of a machine or a vehicle to exact positions.
Gross Body Coordination	The ability to coordinate the movement of your arms, legs, and torso together when the whole body is in motion.
Memorization	The ability to remember information such as words, numbers, pictures, and procedures.
Time Sharing	The ability to shift back and forth between two or more activities or sources of information (such as speech, sounds, touch, or other sources).
Static Strength	The ability to exert maximum muscle force to lift, push, pull, or carry objects.
Fluency of Ideas	The ability to come up with a number of ideas about a topic (the number of ideas is important, not their quality, correctness, or creativity).
Speed of Limb Movement	The ability to quickly move the arms and legs.
Finger Dexterity	The ability to make precisely coordinated movements of the fingers of one or both hands to grasp, manipulate, or assemble very small objects.
Perceptual Speed	The ability to quickly and accurately compare similarities and differences among sets of letters, numbers, objects, pictures, or patterns. The things to be compared may be presented at the same time or one after the other. This ability also includes comparing a presented object with a remembered object.
Multilimb Coordination	The ability to coordinate two or more limbs (for example, two arms, two legs, or one leg and one arm) while sitting, standing, or lying down. It does not involve performing the activities while the whole body is in motion.
Flexibility of Closure	The ability to identify or detect a known pattern (a figure, object, word, or sound) that is hidden in other distracting material.
Gross Body Equilibrium	The ability to keep or regain your body balance or stay upright when in an unstable position.
Number Facility	The ability to add, subtract, multiply, or divide quickly and correctly.
Auditory Attention	The ability to focus on a single source of sound in the presence of other distracting sounds.
Arm-Hand Steadiness	The ability to keep your hand and arm steady while moving your arm or while holding your arm and hand in one position.
Visualization	The ability to imagine how something will look after it is moved around or when its parts are moved or rearranged.
Originality	The ability to come up with unusual or clever ideas about a given topic or situation, or to develop creative ways to solve a problem.
Mathematical Reasoning	The ability to choose the right mathematical methods or formulas to solve a problem.
Speed of Closure	The ability to quickly make sense of, combine, and organize information into meaningful patterns.
Wrist-Finger Speed	The ability to make fast, simple, repeated movements of the fingers, hands, and wrists.
Response Orientation	The ability to choose quickly between two or more movements in response to two or more different signals (lights, sounds, pictures). It includes the speed with which the correct response is started with the hand, foot, or other body part.
Dynamic Flexibility	The ability to quickly and repeatedly bend, stretch, twist, or reach out with your body, arms, and/or legs.

Spatial Orientation	The ability to know your location in relation to the environment or to know where other objects are in relation to you.
Hearing Sensitivity	The ability to detect or tell the differences between sounds that vary in pitch and loudness.
Glare Sensitivity	The ability to see objects in the presence of glare or bright lighting.
Sound Localization	The ability to tell the direction from which a sound originated.
Rate Control	The ability to time your movements or the movement of a piece of equipment in anticipation of changes in the speed and/or direction of a moving object or scene.
Reaction Time	The ability to quickly respond (with the hand, finger, or foot) to a signal (sound, light, picture) when it appears.
Dynamic Strength	The ability to exert muscle force repeatedly or continuously over time. This involves muscular endurance and resistance to muscle fatigue.
Depth Perception	The ability to judge which of several objects is closer or farther away from you, or to judge the distance between you and an object.
Peripheral Vision	The ability to see objects or movement of objects to one's side when the eyes are looking ahead.
Night Vision	The ability to see under low light conditions.
Explosive Strength	The ability to use short bursts of muscle force to propel oneself (as in jumping or sprinting), or to throw an object.

Work_Activity	Work_Activity Definitions
Establishing and Maintaining Interpersonal Relatio	Developing constructive and cooperative working relationships with others, and maintaining them over time.
Monitor Processes, Materials, or Surroundings	Monitoring and reviewing information from materials, events, or the environment, to detect or assess problems.
Getting Information	Observing, receiving, and otherwise obtaining information from all relevant sources.
Identifying Objects, Actions, and Events	Identifying information by categorizing, estimating, recognizing differences or similarities, and detecting changes in circumstances or events.
Training and Teaching Others	Identifying the educational needs of others, developing formal educational or training programs or classes, and teaching or instructing others.
Resolving Conflicts and Negotiating with Others	Handling complaints, settling disputes, and resolving grievances and conflicts, or otherwise negotiating with others.
Performing for or Working Directly with the Public	Performing for people or dealing directly with the public. This includes serving customers in restaurants and stores, and receiving clients or guests.
Coordinating the Work and Activities of Others	Getting members of a group to work together to accomplish tasks.
Communicating with Supervisors, Peers, or Subordin	Providing information to supervisors, co-workers, and subordinates by telephone, in written form, e-mail, or in person.
Selling or Influencing Others	Convincing others to buy merchandise/goods or to otherwise change their minds or actions.
Staffing Organizational Units	Recruiting, interviewing, selecting, hiring, and promoting employees in an organization.
Coaching and Developing Others	Identifying the developmental needs of others and coaching, mentoring, or otherwise helping others to improve their knowledge or skills.
Handling and Moving Objects	Using hands and arms in handling, installing, positioning, and moving materials, and manipulating things.
Judging the Qualities of Things, Services, or Peop	Assessing the value, importance, or quality of things or people.
Organizing, Planning, and Prioritizing Work	Developing specific goals and plans to prioritize, organize, and accomplish your work.
Performing General Physical Activities	Performing physical activities that require considerable use of your arms and legs and moving your whole body, such as climbing, lifting, balancing, walking, stooping, and handling of materials.
Making Decisions and Solving Problems	Analyzing information and evaluating results to choose the best solution and solve problems.
Inspecting Equipment, Structures, or Material	Inspecting equipment, structures, or materials to identify the cause of errors or other problems or defects.
Estimating the Quantifiable Characteristics of Pro	Estimating sizes, distances, and quantities; or determining time, costs, resources, or materials needed to perform a work activity.
Evaluating Information to Determine Compliance wit	Using relevant information and individual judgment to determine whether events or processes comply with laws, regulations, or standards.

Scheduling Work and Activities	Scheduling events, programs, and activities, as well as the work of others.
Updating and Using Relevant Knowledge	Keeping up-to-date technically and applying new knowledge to your job.
Interpreting the Meaning of Information for Others	Translating or explaining what information means and how it can be used.
Thinking Creatively	Developing, designing, or creating new applications, ideas, relationships, systems, or products, including artistic contributions.
Monitoring and Controlling Resources	Monitoring and controlling resources and overseeing the spending of money.
Assisting and Caring for Others	Providing personal assistance, medical attention, emotional support, or other personal care to others such as coworkers, customers, or patients.
Repairing and Maintaining Mechanical Equipment	Servicing, repairing, adjusting, and testing machines, devices, moving parts, and equipment that operate primarily on the basis of mechanical (not electronic) principles.
Processing Information	Compiling, coding, categorizing, calculating, tabulating, auditing, or verifying information or data.
Guiding, Directing, and Motivating Subordinates	Providing guidance and direction to subordinates, including setting performance standards and monitoring performance.
Developing and Building Teams	Encouraging and building mutual trust, respect, and cooperation among team members.
Controlling Machines and Processes	Using either control mechanisms or direct physical activity to operate machines or processes (not including computers or vehicles).
Provide Consultation and Advice to Others	Providing guidance and expert advice to management or other groups on technical, systems-, or process-related topics.
Developing Objectives and Strategies	Establishing long-range objectives and specifying the strategies and actions to achieve them.
Communicating with Persons Outside Organization	Communicating with people outside the organization, representing the organization to customers, the public, government, and other external sources. This information can be exchanged in person, in writing, or by telephone or e-mail.
Analyzing Data or Information	Identifying the underlying principles, reasons, or facts of information by breaking down information or data into separate parts.
Operating Vehicles, Mechanized Devices, or Equipme	Running, maneuvering, navigating, or driving vehicles or mechanized equipment, such as forklifts, passenger vehicles, aircraft, or water craft.
Performing Administrative Activities	Performing day-to-day administrative tasks such as maintaining information files and processing paperwork.
Interacting With Computers	Using computers and computer systems (including hardware and software) to program, write software, set up functions, enter data, or process information.
Documenting/Recording Information	Entering, transcribing, recording, storing, or maintaining information in written or electronic/magnetic form.
Repairing and Maintaining Electronic Equipment	Servicing, repairing, calibrating, regulating, fine-tuning, or testing machines, devices, and equipment that operate primarily on the basis of electrical or electronic (not mechanical) principles.
Drafting, Laying Out, and Specifying Technical Dev	Providing documentation, detailed instructions, drawings, or specifications to tell others about how devices, parts, equipment, or structures are to be fabricated, constructed, assembled, modified, maintained, or used.

Work_Context	Work_Context Definitions
Structured versus Unstructured Work	To what extent is this job structured for the worker, rather than allowing the worker to determine tasks, priorities, and goals?
Indoors, Environmentally Controlled	How often does this job require working indoors in environmentally controlled conditions?
Face-to-Face Discussions	How often do you have to have face-to-face discussions with individuals or teams in this job?
Work With Work Group or Team	How important is it to work with others in a group or team in this job?
Contact With Others	How much does this job require the worker to be in contact with others (face-to-face, by telephone, or otherwise) in order to perform it?
Telephone	How often do you have telephone conversations in this job?
Spend Time Standing	How much does this job require standing?
Spend Time Walking and Running	How much does this job require walking and running?
Freedom to Make Decisions	How much decision making freedom, without supervision, does the job offer?
Spend Time Using Your Hands to Handle, Control, or	How much does this job require using your hands to handle, control, or feel objects, tools or controls?

Responsible for Others' Health and Safety	How much responsibility is there for the health and safety of others in this job?
Deal With External Customers	How important is it to work with external customers or the public in this job?
Importance of Being Exact or Accurate	How important is being very exact or highly accurate in performing this job?
Frequency of Decision Making	How frequently is the worker required to make decisions that affect other people, the financial resources, and/or the image and reputation of the organization?
Physical Proximity	To what extent does this job require the worker to perform job tasks in close physical proximity to other people?
Responsibility for Outcomes and Results	How responsible is the worker for work outcomes and results of other workers?
Coordinate or Lead Others	How important is it to coordinate or lead others in accomplishing work activities in this job?
Spend Time Making Repetitive Motions	How much does this job require making repetitive motions?
Spend Time Bending or Twisting the Body	How much does this job require bending or twisting your body?
Spend Time Kneeling, Crouching, Stooping, or Crawl	How much does this job require kneeling, crouching, stooping or crawling?
Spend Time Keeping or Regaining Balance	How much does this job require keeping or regaining your balance?
Impact of Decisions on Co-workers or Company Resul	How do the decisions an employee makes impact the results of co-workers, clients or the company?
Level of Competition	To what extent does this job require the worker to compete or to be aware of competitive pressures?
Degree of Automation	How automated is the job?
Time Pressure	How often does this job require the worker to meet strict deadlines?
Importance of Repeating Same Tasks	How important is repeating the same physical activities (e.g., key entry) or mental activities (e.g., checking entries in a ledger) over and over, without stopping, to performing this job?
Electronic Mail	How often do you use electronic mail in this job?
Exposed to Hazardous Conditions	How often does this job require exposure to hazardous conditions?
Public Speaking	How often do you have to perform public speaking in this job?
Exposed to High Places	How often does this job require exposure to high places?
Deal With Unpleasant or Angry People	How frequently does the worker have to deal with unpleasant, angry, or discourteous individuals as part of the job requirements?
Spend Time Sitting	How much does this job require sitting?
Frequency of Conflict Situations	How often are there conflict situations the employee has to face in this job?
Pace Determined by Speed of Equipment	How important is it to this job that the pace is determined by the speed of equipment or machinery? (This does not refer to keeping busy at all times on this job)
Consequence of Error	How serious would the result usually be if the worker made a mistake that was not readily correctable?
Exposed to Contaminants	How often does this job require working exposed to contaminants (such as pollutants, gases, dust or odors)?
Wear Common Protective or Safety Equipment such as	How much does this job require wearing common protective or safety equipment such as safety shoes, glasses, gloves, hard hats or live jackets?
Sounds, Noise Levels Are Distracting or Uncomforta	How often does this job require working exposed to sounds and noise levels that are distracting or uncomfortable?
Spend Time Climbing Ladders, Scaffolds, or Poles	How much does this job require climbing ladders, scaffolds, or poles?
Letters and Memos	How often does the job require written letters and memos?
Exposed to Minor Burns, Cuts, Bites, or Stings	How often does this job require exposure to minor burns, cuts, bites, or stings?
Cramped Work Space, Awkward Positions	How often does this job require working in cramped work spaces that requires getting into awkward positions?
Exposed to Disease or Infections	How often does this job require exposure to disease/infections?
Exposed to Hazardous Equipment	How often does this job require exposure to hazardous equipment?
Indoors, Not Environmentally Controlled	How often does this job require working indoors in non-controlled environmental conditions (e.g., warehouse without heat)?
In an Open Vehicle or Equipment	How often does this job require working in an open vehicle or equipment (e.g., tractor)?
In an Enclosed Vehicle or Equipment	How often does this job require working in a closed vehicle or equipment (e.g., car)?

Very Hot or Cold Temperatures	How often does this job require working in very hot (above 90 F degrees) or very cold (below 32 F degrees) temperatures?
Outdoors, Under Cover	How often does this job require working outdoors, under cover (e.g., structure with roof but no walls)?
Outdoors, Exposed to Weather	How often does this job require working outdoors, exposed to all weather conditions?
Deal With Physically Aggressive People	How frequently does this job require the worker to deal with physical aggression of violent individuals?
Extremely Bright or Inadequate Lighting	How often does this job require working in extremely bright or inadequate lighting conditions?
Exposed to Radiation	How often does this job require exposure to radiation?
Wear Specialized Protective or Safety Equipment su	How much does this job require wearing specialized protective or safety equipment such as breathing apparatus, safety harness, full protection suits, or radiation protection?
Exposed to Whole Body Vibration	How often does this job require exposure to whole body vibration (e.g., operate a jackhammer)?

Job Zone Component	Job Zone Component Definitions
Title	Job Zone One: Little or No Preparation Needed
Overall Experience	No previous work-related skill, knowledge, or experience is needed for these occupations. For example, a person can become a general office clerk even if he/she has never worked in an office before.
Job Training	Employees in these occupations need anywhere from a few days to a few months of training. Usually, an experienced worker could show you how to do the job.
Job Zone Examples	These occupations involve following instructions and helping others. Examples include bus drivers, forest and conservation workers, general office clerks, home health aides, and waiters/waitresses.
SVP Range	(Below 4.0)
Education	These occupations may require a high school diploma or GED certificate. Some may require a formal training course to obtain a license.

Work_Styles	Work_Styles Definitions
Integrity	Job requires being honest and ethical.
Dependability	Job requires being reliable, responsible, and dependable, and fulfilling obligations.
Independence	Job requires developing one's own ways of doing things, guiding oneself with little or no supervision, and depending on oneself to get things done.
Stress Tolerance	Job requires accepting criticism and dealing calmly and effectively with high stress situations.
Cooperation	Job requires being pleasant with others on the job and displaying a good-natured, cooperative attitude.
Self Control	Job requires maintaining composure, keeping emotions in check, controlling anger, and avoiding aggressive behavior, even in very difficult situations.
Social Orientation	Job requires preferring to work with others rather than alone, and being personally connected with others on the job.
Adaptability/Flexibility	Job requires being open to change (positive or negative) and to considerable variety in the workplace.
Attention to Detail	Job requires being careful about detail and thorough in completing work tasks.
Concern for Others	Job requires being sensitive to others' needs and feelings and being understanding and helpful on the job.
Analytical Thinking	Job requires analyzing information and using logic to address work-related issues and problems.
Achievement/Effort	Job requires establishing and maintaining personally challenging achievement goals and exerting effort toward mastering tasks.
Persistence	Job requires persistence in the face of obstacles.
Innovation	Job requires creativity and alternative thinking to develop new ideas for and answers to work-related problems.
Initiative	Job requires a willingness to take on responsibilities and challenges.
Leadership	Job requires a willingness to lead, take charge, and offer opinions and direction.

39-4011.00 - Embalmers

Prepare bodies for interment in conformity with legal requirements.

Tasks

1) Reshape or reconstruct disfigured or maimed bodies when necessary, using derma-surgery techniques and materials such as clay, cotton, plaster of paris, and wax.

2) Wash and dry bodies, using germicidal soap and towels or hot air dryers.

3) Make incisions in arms or thighs and drain blood from circulatory system and replace it with embalming fluid, using pump.

4) Dress bodies and place them in caskets.

5) Maintain records such as itemized lists of clothing or valuables delivered with body and names of persons embalmed.

6) Incise stomach and abdominal walls and probe internal organs, using trocar, to withdraw blood and waste matter from organs.

7) Apply cosmetics to impart lifelike appearance to the deceased.

8) Pack body orifices with cotton saturated with embalming fluid to prevent escape of gases or waste matter.

9) Insert convex celluloid or cotton between eyeballs and eyelids to prevent slipping and sinking of eyelids.

10) Assist with placing caskets in hearses, and organize cemetery processions.

11) Join lips, using needles and thread or wire.

12) Attach trocar to pump-tube, start pump, and repeat probing to force embalming fluid into organs.

13) Arrange for transporting the deceased to another state for interment.

14) Arrange funeral home equipment and perform general maintenance.

15) Direct casket and floral display placement and arrange guest seating.

16) Serve as pallbearers, attend visiting rooms, and provide other assistance to the bereaved.

17) Perform the duties of funeral directors, including coordinating funeral activities.

18) Conduct interviews to arrange for the preparation of obituary notices, to assist with the selection of caskets or urns, and to determine the location and time of burials or cremations.

19) Supervise funeral attendants and other funeral home staff.

20) Assist coroners at death scenes or at autopsies, file police reports, and testify at inquests or in court, if employed by a coroner.

21) Press diaphragm to evacuate air from lungs.

22) Conform to laws of health and sanitation, and ensure that legal requirements concerning embalming are met.

23) Perform special procedures necessary for remains that are to be transported to other states or overseas, or where death was caused by infectious disease.

Knowledge	Knowledge Definitions
Chemistry	Knowledge of the chemical composition, structure, and properties of substances and of the chemical processes and transformations that they undergo. This includes uses of chemicals and their interactions, danger signs, production techniques, and disposal methods.
Customer and Personal Service	Knowledge of principles and processes for providing customer and personal services. This includes customer needs assessment, meeting quality standards for services, and evaluation of customer satisfaction.
Biology	Knowledge of plant and animal organisms, their tissues, cells, functions, interdependencies, and interactions with each other and the environment.
English Language	Knowledge of the structure and content of the English language including the meaning and spelling of words, rules of composition, and grammar.
Law and Government	Knowledge of laws, legal codes, court procedures, precedents, government regulations, executive orders, agency rules, and the democratic political process.
Clerical	Knowledge of administrative and clerical procedures and systems such as word processing, managing files and records, stenography and transcription, designing forms, and other office procedures and terminology.
Education and Training	Knowledge of principles and methods for curriculum and training design, teaching and instruction for individuals and groups, and the measurement of training effects.
Psychology	Knowledge of human behavior and performance; individual differences in ability, personality, and interests; learning and motivation; psychological research methods; and the assessment and treatment of behavioral and affective disorders.
Administration and Management	Knowledge of business and management principles involved in strategic planning, resource allocation, human resources modeling, leadership technique, production methods, and coordination of people and resources.
Philosophy and Theology	Knowledge of different philosophical systems and religions. This includes their basic principles, values, ethics, ways of thinking, customs, practices, and their impact on human culture.
Transportation	Knowledge of principles and methods for moving people or goods by air, rail, sea, or road, including the relative costs and benefits.
Sales and Marketing	Knowledge of principles and methods for showing, promoting, and selling products or services. This includes marketing strategy and tactics, product demonstration, sales techniques, and sales control systems.
Personnel and Human Resources	Knowledge of principles and procedures for personnel recruitment, selection, training, compensation and benefits, labor relations and negotiation, and personnel information systems.
Sociology and Anthropology	Knowledge of group behavior and dynamics, societal trends and influences, human migrations, ethnicity, cultures and their history and origins.
Public Safety and Security	Knowledge of relevant equipment, policies, procedures, and strategies to promote effective local, state, or national security operations for the protection of people, data, property, and institutions.
Economics and Accounting	Knowledge of economic and accounting principles and practices, the financial markets, banking and the analysis and reporting of financial data.
Therapy and Counseling	Knowledge of principles, methods, and procedures for diagnosis, treatment, and rehabilitation of physical and mental dysfunctions, and for career counseling and guidance.
Production and Processing	Knowledge of raw materials, production processes, quality control, costs, and other techniques for maximizing the effective manufacture and distribution of goods.
Mathematics	Knowledge of arithmetic, algebra, geometry, calculus, statistics, and their applications.
Medicine and Dentistry	Knowledge of the information and techniques needed to diagnose and treat human injuries, diseases, and deformities. This includes symptoms, treatment alternatives, drug properties and interactions, and preventive health-care measures.
Mechanical	Knowledge of machines and tools, including their designs, uses, repair, and maintenance.
Computers and Electronics	Knowledge of circuit boards, processors, chips, electronic equipment, and computer hardware and software, including applications and programming.
Communications and Media	Knowledge of media production, communication, and dissemination techniques and methods. This includes alternative ways to inform and entertain via written, oral, and visual media.
Physics	Knowledge and prediction of physical principles, laws, their interrelationships, and applications to understanding fluid, material, and atmospheric dynamics, and mechanical, electrical, atomic and sub- atomic structures and processes.
History and Archeology	Knowledge of historical events and their causes, indicators, and effects on civilizations and cultures.
Design	Knowledge of design techniques, tools, and principles involved in production of precision technical plans, blueprints, drawings, and models.
Engineering and Technology	Knowledge of the practical application of engineering science and technology. This includes applying principles, techniques, procedures, and equipment to the design and production of various goods and services.
Geography	Knowledge of principles and methods for describing the features of land, sea, and air masses, including their physical characteristics, locations, interrelationships, and distribution of plant, animal, and human life.
Telecommunications	Knowledge of transmission, broadcasting, switching, control, and operation of telecommunications systems.

Building and Construction	Knowledge of materials, methods, and the tools involved in the construction or repair of houses, buildings, or other structures such as highways and roads.
Foreign Language	Knowledge of the structure and content of a foreign (non-English) language including the meaning and spelling of words, rules of composition and grammar, and pronunciation.
Fine Arts	Knowledge of the theory and techniques required to compose, produce, and perform works of music, dance, visual arts, drama, and sculpture.
Food Production	Knowledge of techniques and equipment for planting, growing, and harvesting food products (both plant and animal) for consumption, including storage/handling techniques.

Skills	**Skills Definitions**
Active Listening	Giving full attention to what other people are saying, taking time to understand the points being made, asking questions as appropriate, and not interrupting at inappropriate times.
Service Orientation	Actively looking for ways to help people.
Speaking	Talking to others to convey information effectively.
Coordination	Adjusting actions in relation to others' actions.
Science	Using scientific rules and methods to solve problems.
Reading Comprehension	Understanding written sentences and paragraphs in work related documents.
Social Perceptiveness	Being aware of others' reactions and understanding why they react as they do.
Instructing	Teaching others how to do something.
Time Management	Managing one's own time and the time of others.
Critical Thinking	Using logic and reasoning to identify the strengths and weaknesses of alternative solutions, conclusions or approaches to problems.
Judgment and Decision Making	Considering the relative costs and benefits of potential actions to choose the most appropriate one.
Equipment Selection	Determining the kind of tools and equipment needed to do a job.
Writing	Communicating effectively in writing as appropriate for the needs of the audience.
Active Learning	Understanding the implications of new information for both current and future problem-solving and decision-making.
Complex Problem Solving	Identifying complex problems and reviewing related information to develop and evaluate options and implement solutions.
Monitoring	Monitoring/Assessing performance of yourself, other individuals, or organizations to make improvements or take corrective action.
Management of Material Resources	Obtaining and seeing to the appropriate use of equipment, facilities, and materials needed to do certain work.
Learning Strategies	Selecting and using training/instructional methods and procedures appropriate for the situation when learning or teaching new things.
Mathematics	Using mathematics to solve problems.
Equipment Maintenance	Performing routine maintenance on equipment and determining when and what kind of maintenance is needed.
Operation Monitoring	Watching gauges, dials, or other indicators to make sure a machine is working properly.
Management of Personnel Resources	Motivating, developing, and directing people as they work, identifying the best people for the job.
Operation and Control	Controlling operations of equipment or systems.
Negotiation	Bringing others together and trying to reconcile differences.
Troubleshooting	Determining causes of operating errors and deciding what to do about it.
Operations Analysis	Analyzing needs and product requirements to create a design.
Management of Financial Resources	Determining how money will be spent to get the work done, and accounting for these expenditures.
Quality Control Analysis	Conducting tests and inspections of products, services, or processes to evaluate quality or performance.
Persuasion	Persuading others to change their minds or behavior.
Repairing	Repairing machines or systems using the needed tools.
Technology Design	Generating or adapting equipment and technology to serve user needs.
Installation	Installing equipment, machines, wiring, or programs to meet specifications.
Systems Evaluation	Identifying measures or indicators of system performance and the actions needed to improve or correct performance, relative to the goals of the system.
Systems Analysis	Determining how a system should work and how changes in conditions, operations, and the environment will affect outcomes.

Programming	Writing computer programs for various purposes.

Ability	**Ability Definitions**
Problem Sensitivity	The ability to tell when something is wrong or is likely to go wrong. It does not involve solving the problem, only recognizing there is a problem.
Near Vision	The ability to see details at close range (within a few feet of the observer).
Oral Comprehension	The ability to listen to and understand information and ideas presented through spoken words and sentences.
Arm-Hand Steadiness	The ability to keep your hand and arm steady while moving your arm or while holding your arm and hand in one position.
Deductive Reasoning	The ability to apply general rules to specific problems to produce answers that make sense.
Oral Expression	The ability to communicate information and ideas in speaking so others will understand.
Information Ordering	The ability to arrange things or actions in a certain order or pattern according to a specific rule or set of rules (e.g., patterns of numbers, letters, words, pictures, mathematical operations).
Finger Dexterity	The ability to make precisely coordinated movements of the fingers of one or both hands to grasp, manipulate, or assemble very small objects.
Speech Recognition	The ability to identify and understand the speech of another person.
Manual Dexterity	The ability to quickly move your hand, your hand together with your arm, or your two hands to grasp, manipulate, or assemble objects.
Inductive Reasoning	The ability to combine pieces of information to form general rules or conclusions (includes finding a relationship among seemingly unrelated events).
Visualization	The ability to imagine how something will look after it is moved around or when its parts are moved or rearranged.
Visual Color Discrimination	The ability to match or detect differences between colors, including shades of color and brightness.
Written Expression	The ability to communicate information and ideas in writing so others will understand.
Static Strength	The ability to exert maximum muscle force to lift, push, pull, or carry objects.
Speech Clarity	The ability to speak clearly so others can understand you.
Written Comprehension	The ability to read and understand information and ideas presented in writing.
Trunk Strength	The ability to use your abdominal and lower back muscles to support part of the body repeatedly or continuously over time without 'giving out' or fatiguing.
Control Precision	The ability to quickly and repeatedly adjust the controls of a machine or a vehicle to exact positions.
Multilimb Coordination	The ability to coordinate two or more limbs (for example, two arms, two legs, or one leg and one arm) while sitting, standing, or lying down. It does not involve performing the activities while the whole body is in motion.
Category Flexibility	The ability to generate or use different sets of rules for combining or grouping things in different ways.
Flexibility of Closure	The ability to identify or detect a known pattern (a figure, object, word, or sound) that is hidden in other distracting material.
Fluency of Ideas	The ability to come up with a number of ideas about a topic (the number of ideas is important, not their quality, correctness, or creativity).
Depth Perception	The ability to judge which of several objects is closer or farther away from you, or to judge the distance between you and an object.
Selective Attention	The ability to concentrate on a task over a period of time without being distracted.
Originality	The ability to come up with unusual or clever ideas about a given topic or situation, or to develop creative ways to solve a problem.
Far Vision	The ability to see details at a distance.
Stamina	The ability to exert yourself physically over long periods of time without getting winded or out of breath.
Dynamic Strength	The ability to exert muscle force repeatedly or continuously over time. This involves muscular endurance and resistance to muscle fatigue.
Extent Flexibility	The ability to bend, stretch, twist, or reach with your body, arms, and/or legs.
Gross Body Coordination	The ability to coordinate the movement of your arms, legs, and torso together when the whole body is in motion.

Time Sharing	The ability to shift back and forth between two or more activities or sources of information (such as speech, sounds, touch, or other sources).
Perceptual Speed	The ability to quickly and accurately compare similarities and differences among sets of letters, numbers, objects, pictures, or patterns. The things to be compared may be presented at the same time or one after the other. This ability also includes comparing a presented object with a remembered object.
Memorization	The ability to remember information such as words, numbers, pictures, and procedures.
Wrist-Finger Speed	The ability to make fast, simple, repeated movements of the fingers, hands, and wrists.
Mathematical Reasoning	The ability to choose the right mathematical methods or formulas to solve a problem.
Number Facility	The ability to add, subtract, multiply, or divide quickly and correctly.
Speed of Limb Movement	The ability to quickly move the arms and legs.
Speed of Closure	The ability to quickly make sense of, combine, and organize information into meaningful patterns.
Auditory Attention	The ability to focus on a single source of sound in the presence of other distracting sounds.
Reaction Time	The ability to quickly respond (with the hand, finger, or foot) to a signal (sound, light, picture) when it appears.
Response Orientation	The ability to choose quickly between two or more movements in response to two or more different signals (lights, sounds, pictures). It includes the speed with which the correct response is started with the hand, foot, or other body part.
Hearing Sensitivity	The ability to detect or tell the differences between sounds that vary in pitch and loudness.
Peripheral Vision	The ability to see objects or movement of objects to one's side when the eyes are looking ahead.
Spatial Orientation	The ability to know your location in relation to the environment or to know where other objects are in relation to you.
Rate Control	The ability to time your movements or the movement of a piece of equipment in anticipation of changes in the speed and/or direction of a moving object or scene.
Gross Body Equilibrium	The ability to keep or regain your body balance or stay upright when in an unstable position.
Glare Sensitivity	The ability to see objects in the presence of glare or bright lighting.
Sound Localization	The ability to tell the direction from which a sound originated.
Night Vision	The ability to see under low light conditions.
Dynamic Flexibility	The ability to quickly and repeatedly bend, stretch, twist, or reach out with your body, arms, and/or legs.
Explosive Strength	The ability to use short bursts of muscle force to propel oneself (as in jumping or sprinting), or to throw an object.

Work_Activity	Work_Activity Definitions
Getting Information	Observing, receiving, and otherwise obtaining information from all relevant sources.
Documenting/Recording Information	Entering, transcribing, recording, storing, or maintaining information in written or electronic/magnetic form.
Assisting and Caring for Others	Providing personal assistance, medical attention, emotional support, or other personal care to others such as coworkers, customers, or patients.
Updating and Using Relevant Knowledge	Keeping up-to-date technically and applying new knowledge to your job.
Performing for or Working Directly with the Public	Performing for people or dealing directly with the public. This includes serving customers in restaurants and stores, and receiving clients or guests.
Communicating with Supervisors, Peers, or Subordin	Providing information to supervisors, co-workers, and subordinates by telephone, in written form, e-mail, or in person.
Making Decisions and Solving Problems	Analyzing information and evaluating results to choose the best solution and solve problems.
Monitor Processes, Materials, or Surroundings	Monitoring and reviewing information from materials, events, or the environment, to detect or assess problems.
Organizing, Planning, and Prioritizing Work	Developing specific goals and plans to prioritize, organize, and accomplish your work.
Communicating with Persons Outside Organization	Communicating with people outside the organization, representing the organization to customers, the public, government, and other external sources. This information can be exchanged in person, in writing, or by telephone or e-mail.
Evaluating Information to Determine Compliance wit	Using relevant information and individual judgment to determine whether events or processes comply with laws, regulations, or standards.

Identifying Objects, Actions, and Events	Identifying information by categorizing, estimating, recognizing differences or similarities, and detecting changes in circumstances or events.
Performing General Physical Activities	Performing physical activities that require considerable use of your arms and legs and moving your whole body, such as climbing, lifting, balancing, walking, stooping, and handling of materials.
Establishing and Maintaining Interpersonal Relatio	Developing constructive and cooperative working relationships with others, and maintaining them over time.
Handling and Moving Objects	Using hands and arms in handling, installing, positioning, and moving materials, and manipulating things.
Inspecting Equipment, Structures, or Material	Inspecting equipment, structures, or materials to identify the cause of errors or other problems or defects.
Processing Information	Compiling, coding, categorizing, calculating, tabulating, auditing, or verifying information or data.
Scheduling Work and Activities	Scheduling events, programs, and activities, as well as the work of others.
Thinking Creatively	Developing, designing, or creating new applications, ideas, relationships, systems, or products, including artistic contributions.
Coordinating the Work and Activities of Others	Getting members of a group to work together to accomplish tasks.
Performing Administrative Activities	Performing day-to-day administrative tasks such as maintaining information files and processing paperwork.
Judging the Qualities of Things, Services, or Peop	Assessing the value, importance, or quality of things or people.
Controlling Machines and Processes	Using either control mechanisms or direct physical activity to operate machines or processes (not including computers or vehicles).
Interpreting the Meaning of Information for Others	Translating or explaining what information means and how it can be used.
Resolving Conflicts and Negotiating with Others	Handling complaints, settling disputes, and resolving grievances and conflicts, or otherwise negotiating with others.
Operating Vehicles, Mechanized Devices, or Equipme	Running, maneuvering, navigating, or driving vehicles or mechanized equipment, such as forklifts, passenger vehicles, aircraft, or water craft.
Provide Consultation and Advice to Others	Providing guidance and expert advice to management or other groups on technical, systems-, or process-related topics.
Analyzing Data or Information	Identifying the underlying principles, reasons, or facts of information by breaking down information or data into separate parts.
Training and Teaching Others	Identifying the educational needs of others, developing formal educational or training programs or classes, and teaching or instructing others.
Guiding, Directing, and Motivating Subordinates	Providing guidance and direction to subordinates, including setting performance standards and monitoring performance.
Estimating the Quantifiable Characteristics of Pro	Estimating sizes, distances, and quantities; or determining time, costs, resources, or materials needed to perform a work activity.
Developing and Building Teams	Encouraging and building mutual trust, respect, and cooperation among team members.
Selling or Influencing Others	Convincing others to buy merchandise/goods or to otherwise change their minds or actions.
Interacting With Computers	Using computers and computer systems (including hardware and software) to program, write software, set up functions, enter data, or process information.
Developing Objectives and Strategies	Establishing long-range objectives and specifying the strategies and actions to achieve them.
Repairing and Maintaining Mechanical Equipment	Servicing, repairing, adjusting, and testing machines, devices, moving parts, and equipment that operate primarily on the basis of mechanical (not electronic) principles.
Coaching and Developing Others	Identifying the developmental needs of others and coaching, mentoring, or otherwise helping others to improve their knowledge or skills.
Monitoring and Controlling Resources	Monitoring and controlling resources and overseeing the spending of money.
Staffing Organizational Units	Recruiting, interviewing, selecting, hiring, and promoting employees in an organization.
Repairing and Maintaining Electronic Equipment	Servicing, repairing, calibrating, regulating, fine-tuning, or testing machines, devices, and equipment that operate primarily on the basis of electrical or electronic (not mechanical) principles.
Drafting, Laying Out, and Specifying Technical Dev	Providing documentation, detailed instructions, drawings, or specifications to tell others about how devices, parts, equipment, or structures are to be fabricated, constructed, assembled, modified, maintained, or used.

Work_Context	Work_Context Definitions
Telephone	How often do you have telephone conversations in this job?
Face-to-Face Discussions	How often do you have to have face-to-face discussions with individuals or teams in this job?
Impact of Decisions on Co-workers or Company Resul	How do the decisions an employee makes impact the results of co-workers, clients or the company?
Contact With Others	How much does this job require the worker to be in contact with others (face-to-face, by telephone, or otherwise) in order to perform it?
Freedom to Make Decisions	How much decision making freedom, without supervision, does the job offer?
Structured versus Unstructured Work	To what extent is this job structured for the worker, rather than allowing the worker to determine tasks, priorities, and goals?
Frequency of Decision Making	How frequently is the worker required to make decisions that affect other people, the financial resources, and/or the image and reputation of the organization?
Importance of Being Exact or Accurate	How important is being very exact or highly accurate in performing this job?
Responsible for Others' Health and Safety	How much responsibility is there for the health and safety of others in this job?
Deal With External Customers	How important is it to work with external customers or the public in this job?
Exposed to Disease or Infections	How often does this job require exposure to disease/infections?
Wear Common Protective or Safety Equipment such as	How much does this job require wearing common protective or safety equipment such as safety shoes, glasses, gloves, hard hats or live jackets?
Indoors, Environmentally Controlled	How often does this job require working indoors in environmentally controlled conditions?
Exposed to Hazardous Conditions	How often does this job require exposure to hazardous conditions?
Time Pressure	How often does this job require the worker to meet strict deadlines?
Exposed to Contaminants	How often does this job require working exposed to contaminants (such as pollutants, gases, dust or odors)?
Work With Work Group or Team	How important is it to work with others in a group or team in this job?
Coordinate or Lead Others	How important is it to coordinate or lead others in accomplishing work activities in this job?
In an Enclosed Vehicle or Equipment	How often does this job require working in a closed vehicle or equipment (e.g., car)?
Spend Time Standing	How much does this job require standing?
Physical Proximity	To what extent does this job require the worker to perform job tasks in close physical proximity to other people?
Letters and Memos	How often does the job require written letters and memos?
Responsibility for Outcomes and Results	How responsible is the worker for work outcomes and results of other workers?
Spend Time Using Your Hands to Handle, Control, or	How much does this job require using your hands to handle, control, or feel objects, tools or controls?
Outdoors, Exposed to Weather	How often does this job require working outdoors, exposed to all weather conditions?
Electronic Mail	How often do you use electronic mail in this job?
Consequence of Error	How serious would the result usually be if the worker made a mistake that was not readily correctable?
Importance of Repeating Same Tasks	How important is repeating the same physical activities (e.g., key entry) or mental activities (e.g., checking entries in a ledger) over and over, without stopping, to performing this job?
Wear Specialized Protective or Safety Equipment su	How much does this job require wearing specialized protective or safety equipment such as breathing apparatus, safety harness, full protection suits, or radiation protection?
Level of Competition	To what extent does this job require the worker to compete or to be aware of competitive pressures?
Public Speaking	How often do you have to perform public speaking in this job?
Very Hot or Cold Temperatures	How often does this job require working in very hot (above 90 F degrees) or very cold (below 32 F degrees) temperatures?
Deal With Unpleasant or Angry People	How frequently does the worker have to deal with unpleasant, angry, or discourteous individuals as part of the job requirements?
Frequency of Conflict Situations	How often are there conflict situations the employee has to face in this job?
Spend Time Walking and Running	How much does this job require walking and running?
Spend Time Bending or Twisting the Body	How much does this job require bending or twisting your body?
Spend Time Making Repetitive Motions	How much does this job require making repetitive motions?
Spend Time Sitting	How much does this job require sitting?
Outdoors, Under Cover	How often does this job require working outdoors, under cover (e.g., structure with roof but no walls)?
Extremely Bright or Inadequate Lighting	How often does this job require working in extremely bright or inadequate lighting conditions?
Degree of Automation	How automated is the job?
Exposed to Hazardous Equipment	How often does this job require exposure to hazardous equipment?
Spend Time Kneeling, Crouching, Stooping, or Crawl	How much does this job require kneeling, crouching, stooping, or crawling?
Sounds, Noise Levels Are Distracting or Uncomforta	How often does this job require working exposed to sounds and noise levels that are distracting or uncomfortable?
Indoors, Not Environmentally Controlled	How often does this job require working indoors in non-controlled environmental conditions (e.g., warehouse without heat)?
Exposed to Minor Burns, Cuts, Bites, or Stings	How often does this job require exposure to minor burns, cuts, bites, or stings?
Deal With Physically Aggressive People	How frequently does this job require the worker to deal with physical aggression of violent individuals?
Pace Determined by Speed of Equipment	How important is it to this job that the pace is determined by the speed of equipment or machinery? (This does not refer to keeping busy at all times on this job.)
Cramped Work Space, Awkward Positions	How often does this job require working in cramped work spaces that requires getting into awkward positions?
Spend Time Keeping or Regaining Balance	How much does this job require keeping or regaining your balance?
In an Open Vehicle or Equipment	How much does this job require working in an open vehicle or equipment (e.g., tractor)?
Exposed to High Places	How often does this job require exposure to high places?
Exposed to Radiation	How often does this job require exposure to radiation?
Spend Time Climbing Ladders, Scaffolds, or Poles	How much does this job require climbing ladders, scaffolds, or poles?
Exposed to Whole Body Vibration	How often does this job require exposure to whole body vibration (e.g., operate a jackhammer)?

Job Zone Component	Job Zone Component Definitions
Title	Job Zone Three: Medium Preparation Needed
Overall Experience	Previous work-related skill, knowledge, or experience is required for these occupations. For example, an electrician must have completed three or four years of apprenticeship or several years of vocational training, and often must have passed a licensing exam, in order to perform the job.
Job Training	Employees in these occupations usually need one or two years of training involving both on-the-job experience and informal training with experienced workers.
Job Zone Examples	These occupations usually involve using communication and organizational skills to coordinate, supervise, manage, or train others to accomplish goals. Examples include dental assistants, electricians, fish and game wardens, legal secretaries, personnel recruiters, and recreation workers.
SVP Range	(6.0 to < 7.0)
Education	Most occupations in this zone require training in vocational schools, related on-the-job experience, or an associate's degree. Some may require a bachelor's degree.

Work_Styles	Work_Styles Definitions
Attention to Detail	Job requires being careful about detail and thorough in completing work tasks.
Dependability	Job requires being reliable, responsible, and dependable, and fulfilling obligations.
Integrity	Job requires being honest and ethical.
Concern for Others	Job requires being sensitive to others' needs and feelings and being understanding and helpful on the job.
Self Control	Job requires maintaining composure, keeping emotions in check, controlling anger, and avoiding aggressive behavior, even in very difficult situations.
Innovation	Job requires creativity and alternative thinking to develop new ideas for and answers to work-related problems.
Analytical Thinking	Job requires analyzing information and using logic to address work-related issues and problems.

Initiative	Job requires a willingness to take on responsibilities and challenges.
Independence	Job requires developing one's own ways of doing things, guiding oneself with little or no supervision, and depending on oneself to get things done.
Adaptability/Flexibility	Job requires being open to change (positive or negative) and to considerable variety in the workplace.
Persistence	Job requires persistence in the face of obstacles.
Stress Tolerance	Job requires accepting criticism and dealing calmly and effectively with high stress situations.
Cooperation	Job requires being pleasant with others on the job and displaying a good-natured, cooperative attitude.
Achievement/Effort	Job requires establishing and maintaining personally challenging achievement goals and exerting effort toward mastering tasks.
Leadership	Job requires a willingness to lead, take charge, and offer opinions and direction.
Social Orientation	Job requires preferring to work with others rather than alone, and being personally connected with others on the job.

39-4021.00 - Funeral Attendants

Perform variety of tasks during funeral, such as placing casket in parlor or chapel prior to service; arranging floral offerings or lights around casket; directing or escorting mourners; closing casket; and issuing and storing funeral equipment.

Tasks

1) Perform a variety of tasks during funerals to assist funeral directors and to ensure that services run smoothly and as planned.

2) Direct or escort mourners to parlors or chapels in which wakes or funerals are being held.

3) Arrange floral offerings or lights around caskets.

4) Carry flowers to hearses or limousines for transportation to places of interment.

5) Clean funeral parlors and chapels.

6) Place caskets in parlors or chapels prior to wakes or funerals.

7) Clean and drive funeral vehicles such as cars or hearses in funeral processions.

8) Offer assistance to mourners as they enter or exit limousines.

9) Close caskets at appropriate point in services.

10) Perform general maintenance duties for funeral homes.

11) Transfer the deceased to funeral homes.

12) Provide advice to mourners on how to make charitable donations in honor of the deceased.

13) Issue and store funeral equipment.

14) Obtain burial permits and register deaths.

15) Act as pallbearers.

16) Assist with cremations, and with the processing and packaging of cremated remains.

Knowledge	Knowledge Definitions
Customer and Personal Service	Knowledge of principles and processes for providing customer and personal services. This includes customer needs assessment, meeting quality standards for services, and evaluation of customer satisfaction.
English Language	Knowledge of the structure and content of the English language including the meaning and spelling of words, rules of composition, and grammar.
Psychology	Knowledge of human behavior and performance; individual differences in ability, personality, and interests; learning and motivation; psychological research methods; and the assessment and treatment of behavioral and affective disorders.
Clerical	Knowledge of administrative and clerical procedures and systems such as word processing, managing files and records, stenography and transcription, designing forms, and other office procedures and terminology.
Transportation	Knowledge of principles and methods for moving people or goods by air, rail, sea, or road, including the relative costs and benefits.

Public Safety and Security	Knowledge of relevant equipment, policies, procedures, and strategies to promote effective local, state, or national security operations for the protection of people, data, property, and institutions.
Administration and Management	Knowledge of business and management principles involved in strategic planning, resource allocation, human resources modeling, leadership technique, production methods, and coordination of people and resources.
Law and Government	Knowledge of laws, legal codes, court procedures, precedents, government regulations, executive orders, agency rules, and the democratic political process.
Mathematics	Knowledge of arithmetic, algebra, geometry, calculus, statistics, and their applications.
Computers and Electronics	Knowledge of circuit boards, processors, chips, electronic equipment, and computer hardware and software, including applications and programming.
Philosophy and Theology	Knowledge of different philosophical systems and religions. This includes their basic principles, values, ethics, ways of thinking, customs, practices, and their impact on human culture.
Therapy and Counseling	Knowledge of principles, methods, and procedures for diagnosis, treatment, and rehabilitation of physical and mental dysfunctions, and for career counseling and guidance.
Economics and Accounting	Knowledge of economic and accounting principles and practices, the financial markets, banking and the analysis and reporting of financial data.
Communications and Media	Knowledge of media production, communication, and dissemination techniques and methods. This includes alternative ways to inform and entertain via written, oral, and visual media.
Personnel and Human Resources	Knowledge of principles and procedures for personnel recruitment, selection, training, compensation and benefits, labor relations and negotiation, and personnel information systems.
Sales and Marketing	Knowledge of principles and methods for showing, promoting, and selling products or services. This includes marketing strategy and tactics, product demonstration, sales techniques, and sales control systems.
Telecommunications	Knowledge of transmission, broadcasting, switching, control, and operation of telecommunications systems.
Education and Training	Knowledge of principles and methods for curriculum and training design, teaching and instruction for individuals and groups, and the measurement of training effects.
Sociology and Anthropology	Knowledge of group behavior and dynamics, societal trends and influences, human migrations, ethnicity, cultures and their history and origins.
Production and Processing	Knowledge of raw materials, production processes, quality control, costs, and other techniques for maximizing the effective manufacture and distribution of goods.
Chemistry	Knowledge of the chemical composition, structure, and properties of substances and of the chemical processes and transformations that they undergo. This includes uses of chemicals and their interactions, danger signs, production techniques, and disposal methods.
Biology	Knowledge of plant and animal organisms, their tissues, cells, functions, interdependencies, and interactions with each other and the environment.
Mechanical	Knowledge of machines and tools, including their designs, uses, repair, and maintenance.
Geography	Knowledge of principles and methods for describing the features of land, sea, and air masses, including their physical characteristics, locations, interrelationships, and distribution of plant, animal, and human life.
Foreign Language	Knowledge of the structure and content of a foreign (non-English) language including the meaning and spelling of words, rules of composition and grammar, and pronunciation.
Medicine and Dentistry	Knowledge of the information and techniques needed to diagnose and treat human injuries, diseases, and deformities. This includes symptoms, treatment alternatives, drug properties and interactions, and preventive health-care measures.
Engineering and Technology	Knowledge of the practical application of engineering science and technology. This includes applying principles, techniques, procedures, and equipment to the design and production of various goods and services.
Design	Knowledge of design techniques, tools, and principles involved in production of precision technical plans, blueprints, drawings, and models.

History and Archeology	Knowledge of historical events and their causes, indicators, and effects on civilizations and cultures.
Fine Arts	Knowledge of the theory and techniques required to compose, produce, and perform works of music, dance, visual arts, drama, and sculpture.
Building and Construction	Knowledge of materials, methods, and the tools involved in the construction or repair of houses, buildings, or other structures such as highways and roads.
Physics	Knowledge and prediction of physical principles, laws, their interrelationships, and applications to understanding fluid, material, and atmospheric dynamics, and mechanical, electrical, atomic and sub- atomic structures and processes.
Food Production	Knowledge of techniques and equipment for planting, growing, and harvesting food products (both plant and animal) for consumption, including storage/handling techniques.

Skills	Skills Definitions
Active Listening	Giving full attention to what other people are saying, taking time to understand the points being made, asking questions as appropriate, and not interrupting at inappropriate times.
Service Orientation	Actively looking for ways to help people.
Speaking	Talking to others to convey information effectively.
Reading Comprehension	Understanding written sentences and paragraphs in work related documents.
Social Perceptiveness	Being aware of others' reactions and understanding why they react as they do.
Coordination	Adjusting actions in relation to others' actions.
Writing	Communicating effectively in writing as appropriate for the needs of the audience.
Time Management	Managing one's own time and the time of others.
Critical Thinking	Using logic and reasoning to identify the strengths and weaknesses of alternative solutions, conclusions or approaches to problems.
Learning Strategies	Selecting and using training/instructional methods and procedures appropriate for the situation when learning or teaching new things.
Active Learning	Understanding the implications of new information for both current and future problem-solving and decision-making.
Instructing	Teaching others how to do something.
Judgment and Decision Making	Considering the relative costs and benefits of potential actions to choose the most appropriate one.
Monitoring	Monitoring/Assessing performance of yourself, other individuals, or organizations to make improvements or take corrective action.
Mathematics	Using mathematics to solve problems.
Persuasion	Persuading others to change their minds or behavior.
Complex Problem Solving	Identifying complex problems and reviewing related information to develop and evaluate options and implement solutions.
Management of Financial Resources	Determining how money will be spent to get the work done, and accounting for these expenditures.
Negotiation	Bringing others together and trying to reconcile differences.
Equipment Maintenance	Performing routine maintenance on equipment and determining when and what kind of maintenance is needed.
Troubleshooting	Determining causes of operating errors and deciding what to do about it.
Management of Material Resources	Obtaining and seeing to the appropriate use of equipment, facilities, and materials needed to do certain work.
Equipment Selection	Determining the kind of tools and equipment needed to do a job.
Management of Personnel Resources	Motivating, developing, and directing people as they work, identifying the best people for the job.
Operation and Control	Controlling operations of equipment or systems.
Quality Control Analysis	Conducting tests and inspections of products, services, or processes to evaluate quality or performance.
Science	Using scientific rules and methods to solve problems.
Operation Monitoring	Watching gauges, dials, or other indicators to make sure a machine is working properly.
Installation	Installing equipment, machines, wiring, or programs to meet specifications.
Systems Analysis	Determining how a system should work and how changes in conditions, operations, and the environment will affect outcomes.
Operations Analysis	Analyzing needs and product requirements to create a design.
Systems Evaluation	Identifying measures or indicators of system performance and the actions needed to improve or correct performance, relative to the goals of the system.

Repairing	Repairing machines or systems using the needed tools.
Technology Design	Generating or adapting equipment and technology to serve user needs.
Programming	Writing computer programs for various purposes.

Ability	Ability Definitions
Oral Comprehension	The ability to listen to and understand information and ideas presented through spoken words and sentences.
Oral Expression	The ability to communicate information and ideas in speaking so others will understand.
Speech Clarity	The ability to speak clearly so others can understand you.
Speech Recognition	The ability to identify and understand the speech of another person.
Near Vision	The ability to see details at close range (within a few feet of the observer).
Problem Sensitivity	The ability to tell when something is wrong or is likely to go wrong. It does not involve solving the problem, only recognizing there is a problem.
Static Strength	The ability to exert maximum muscle force to lift, push, pull, or carry objects.
Information Ordering	The ability to arrange things or actions in a certain order or pattern according to a specific rule or set of rules (e.g., patterns of numbers, letters, words, pictures, mathematical operations).
Inductive Reasoning	The ability to combine pieces of information to form general rules or conclusions (includes finding a relationship among seemingly unrelated events).
Trunk Strength	The ability to use your abdominal and lower back muscles to support part of the body repeatedly or continuously over time without 'giving out' or fatiguing.
Written Comprehension	The ability to read and understand information and ideas presented in writing.
Written Expression	The ability to communicate information and ideas in writing so others will understand.
Deductive Reasoning	The ability to apply general rules to specific problems to produce answers that make sense.
Multilimb Coordination	The ability to coordinate two or more limbs (for example, two arms, two legs, or one leg and one arm) while sitting, standing, or lying down. It does not involve performing the activities while the whole body is in motion.
Control Precision	The ability to quickly and repeatedly adjust the controls of a machine or a vehicle to exact positions.
Far Vision	The ability to see details at a distance.
Category Flexibility	The ability to generate or use different sets of rules for combining or grouping things in different ways.
Arm-Hand Steadiness	The ability to keep your hand and arm steady while moving your arm or while holding your arm and hand in one position.
Selective Attention	The ability to concentrate on a task over a period of time without being distracted.
Time Sharing	The ability to shift back and forth between two or more activities or sources of information (such as speech, sounds, touch, or other sources).
Depth Perception	The ability to judge which of several objects is closer or farther away from you, or to judge the distance between you and an
Spatial Orientation	The ability to know your location in relation to the environment or to know where other objects are in relation to you.
Visualization	The ability to imagine how something will look after it is moved around or when its parts are moved or rearranged.
Manual Dexterity	The ability to quickly move your hand, your hand together with your arm, or your two hands to grasp, manipulate, or assemble objects.
Stamina	The ability to exert yourself physically over long periods of time without getting winded or out of breath.
Reaction Time	The ability to quickly respond (with the hand, finger, or foot) to a signal (sound, light, picture) when it appears.
Fluency of Ideas	The ability to come up with a number of ideas about a topic (the number of ideas is important, not their quality, correctness, or creativity).
Gross Body Coordination	The ability to coordinate the movement of your arms, legs, and torso together when the whole body is in motion.
Originality	The ability to come up with unusual or clever ideas about a given topic or situation, or to develop creative ways to solve a problem.
Memorization	The ability to remember information such as words, numbers, pictures, and procedures.

Dynamic Strength	The ability to exert muscle force repeatedly or continuously over time. This involves muscular endurance and resistance to muscle fatigue.
Rate Control	The ability to time your movements or the movement of a piece of equipment in anticipation of changes in the speed and/or direction of a moving object or scene.
Visual Color Discrimination	The ability to match or detect differences between colors, including shades of color and brightness.
Extent Flexibility	The ability to bend, stretch, twist, or reach with your body, arms, and/or legs.
Number Facility	The ability to add, subtract, multiply, or divide quickly and correctly.
Glare Sensitivity	The ability to see objects in the presence of glare or bright lighting.
Auditory Attention	The ability to focus on a single source of sound in the presence of other distracting sounds.
Perceptual Speed	The ability to quickly and accurately compare similarities and differences among sets of letters, numbers, objects, pictures, or patterns. The things to be compared may be presented at the same time or one after the other. This ability also includes comparing a presented object with a remembered object.
Peripheral Vision	The ability to see objects or movement of objects to one's side when the eyes are looking ahead.
Finger Dexterity	The ability to make precisely coordinated movements of the fingers of one or both hands to grasp, manipulate, or assemble very small objects.
Speed of Limb Movement	The ability to quickly move the arms and legs.
Response Orientation	The ability to choose quickly between two or more movements in response to two or more different signals (lights, sounds, pictures). It includes the speed with which the correct response is started with the hand, foot, or other body part.
Flexibility of Closure	The ability to identify or detect a known pattern (a figure, object, word, or sound) that is hidden in other distracting material.
Mathematical Reasoning	The ability to choose the right mathematical methods or formulas to solve a problem.
Speed of Closure	The ability to quickly make sense of, combine, and organize information into meaningful patterns.
Night Vision	The ability to see under low light conditions.
Hearing Sensitivity	The ability to detect or tell the differences between sounds that vary in pitch and loudness.
Sound Localization	The ability to tell the direction from which a sound originated.
Gross Body Equilibrium	The ability to keep or regain your body balance or stay upright when in an unstable position.
Explosive Strength	The ability to use short bursts of muscle force to propel oneself (as in jumping or sprinting), or to throw an object.
Wrist-Finger Speed	The ability to make fast, simple, repeated movements of the fingers, hands, and wrists.
Dynamic Flexibility	The ability to quickly and repeatedly bend, stretch, twist, or reach out with your body, arms, and/or legs.

Work_Activity	Work_Activity Definitions
Performing for or Working Directly with the Public	Performing for people or dealing directly with the public. This includes serving customers in restaurants and stores, and receiving clients or guests.
Assisting and Caring for Others	Providing personal assistance, medical attention, emotional support, or other personal care to others such as coworkers, customers, or patients.
Getting Information	Observing, receiving, and otherwise obtaining information from all relevant sources.
Establishing and Maintaining Interpersonal Relatio	Developing constructive and cooperative working relationships with others, and maintaining them over time.
Communicating with Persons Outside Organization	Communicating with people outside the organization, representing the organization to customers, the public, government, and other external sources. This information can be exchanged in person, in writing, or by telephone or e-mail.
Communicating with Supervisors, Peers, or Subordin	Providing information to supervisors, co-workers, and subordinates by telephone, in written form, e-mail, or in person.
Handling and Moving Objects	Using hands and arms in handling, installing, positioning, and moving materials, and manipulating things.
Making Decisions and Solving Problems	Analyzing information and evaluating results to choose the best solution and solve problems.
Identifying Objects, Actions, and Events	Identifying information by categorizing, estimating, recognizing differences or similarities, and detecting changes in circumstances or events.

Operating Vehicles, Mechanized Devices, or Equipme	Running, maneuvering, navigating, or driving vehicles or mechanized equipment, such as forklifts, passenger vehicles, aircraft, or water craft.
Organizing, Planning, and Prioritizing Work	Developing specific goals and plans to prioritize, organize, and accomplish your work.
Judging the Qualities of Things, Services, or Peop	Assessing the value, importance, or quality of things or people.
Performing General Physical Activities	Performing physical activities that require considerable use of your arms and legs and moving your whole body, such as climbing, lifting, balancing, walking, stooping, and handling of materials.
Updating and Using Relevant Knowledge	Keeping up-to-date technically and applying new knowledge to your job.
Monitor Processes, Materials, or Surroundings	Monitoring and reviewing information from materials, events, or the environment, to detect or assess problems.
Documenting/Recording Information	Entering, transcribing, recording, storing, or maintaining information in written or electronic/magnetic form.
Thinking Creatively	Developing, designing, or creating new applications, ideas, relationships, systems, or products, including artistic contributions.
Evaluating Information to Determine Compliance wit	Using relevant information and individual judgment to determine whether events or processes comply with laws, regulations, or standards.
Coordinating the Work and Activities of Others	Getting members of a group to work together to accomplish tasks.
Processing Information	Compiling, coding, categorizing, calculating, tabulating, auditing, or verifying information or data.
Inspecting Equipment, Structures, or Material	Inspecting equipment, structures, or materials to identify the cause of errors or other problems or defects.
Developing and Building Teams	Encouraging and building mutual trust, respect, and cooperation among team members.
Scheduling Work and Activities	Scheduling events, programs, and activities, as well as the work of others.
Performing Administrative Activities	Performing day-to-day administrative tasks such as maintaining information files and processing paperwork.
Resolving Conflicts and Negotiating with Others	Handling complaints, settling disputes, and resolving grievances and conflicts, or otherwise negotiating with others.
Interpreting the Meaning of Information for Others	Translating or explaining what information means and how it can be used.
Training and Teaching Others	Identifying the educational needs of others, developing formal educational or training programs or classes, and teaching or instructing others.
Analyzing Data or Information	Identifying the underlying principles, reasons, or facts of information by breaking down information or data into separate parts.
Interacting With Computers	Using computers and computer systems (including hardware and software) to program, write software, set up functions, enter data, or process information.
Selling or Influencing Others	Convincing others to buy merchandise/goods or to otherwise change their minds or actions.
Provide Consultation and Advice to Others	Providing guidance and expert advice to management or other groups on technical, systems-, or process-related topics.
Estimating the Quantifiable Characteristics of Pro	Estimating sizes, distances, and quantities; or determining time, costs, resources, or materials needed to perform a work activity.
Coaching and Developing Others	Identifying the developmental needs of others and coaching, mentoring, or otherwise helping others to improve their knowledge or skills.
Developing Objectives and Strategies	Establishing long-range objectives and specifying the strategies and actions to achieve them.
Guiding, Directing, and Motivating Subordinates	Providing guidance and direction to subordinates, including setting performance standards and monitoring performance.
Monitoring and Controlling Resources	Monitoring and controlling resources and overseeing the spending of money.
Controlling Machines and Processes	Using either control mechanisms or direct physical activity to operate machines or processes (not including computers or vehicles).
Repairing and Maintaining Mechanical Equipment	Servicing, repairing, adjusting, and testing machines, devices, moving parts, and equipment that operate primarily on the basis of mechanical (not electronic) principles.
Staffing Organizational Units	Recruiting, interviewing, selecting, hiring, and promoting employees in an organization.
Repairing and Maintaining Electronic Equipment	Servicing, repairing, calibrating, regulating, fine-tuning, or testing machines, devices, and equipment that operate primarily on the basis of electrical or electronic (not mechanical) principles.

789

Drafting, Laying Out, and Specifying Technical Dev	Providing documentation, detailed instructions, drawings, or specifications to tell others about how devices, parts, equipment, or structures are to be fabricated, constructed, assembled, modified, maintained, or used.

Work_Context	Work_Context Definitions
Contact With Others	How much does this job require the worker to be in contact with others (face-to-face, by telephone, or otherwise) in order to perform it?
Telephone	How often do you have telephone conversations in this job?
Face-to-Face Discussions	How often do you have to have face-to-face discussions with individuals or teams in this job?
Work With Work Group or Team	How important is it to work with others in a group or team in this job?
Physical Proximity	To what extent does this job require the worker to perform job tasks in close physical proximity to other people?
Indoors, Environmentally Controlled	How often does this job require working indoors in environmentally controlled conditions?
Deal With External Customers	How important is it to work with external customers or the public in this job?
In an Enclosed Vehicle or Equipment	How often does this job require working in a closed vehicle or equipment (e.g., car)?
Freedom to Make Decisions	How much decision making freedom, without supervision, does the job offer?
Structured versus Unstructured Work	To what extent is this job structured for the worker, rather than allowing the worker to determine tasks, priorities, and goals?
Importance of Being Exact or Accurate	How important is being very exact or highly accurate in performing this job?
Impact of Decisions on Co-workers or Company Resul	How do the decisions an employee makes impact the results of co-workers, clients or the company?
Spend Time Standing	How much does this job require standing?
Outdoors, Exposed to Weather	How often does this job require working outdoors, exposed to all weather conditions?
Frequency of Decision Making	How frequently is the worker required to make decisions that affect other people, the financial resources, and/or the image and reputation of the organization?
Time Pressure	How often does this job require the worker to meet strict deadlines?
Coordinate or Lead Others	How important is it to coordinate or lead others in accomplishing work activities in this job?
Responsible for Others' Health and Safety	How much responsibility is there for the health and safety of others in this job?
Responsibility for Outcomes and Results	How responsible is the worker for work outcomes and results of other workers?
Letters and Memos	How often does the job require written letters and memos?
Exposed to Disease or Infections	How often does this job require exposure to disease/infections?
Importance of Repeating Same Tasks	How important is repeating the same physical activities (e.g., key entry) or mental activities (e.g., checking entries in a ledger) over and over, without stopping, to performing this job?
Very Hot or Cold Temperatures	How often does this job require working in very hot (above 90 F degrees) or very cold (below 32 F degrees) temperatures?
Exposed to Contaminants	How often does this job require working exposed to contaminants (such as pollutants, gases, dust or odors)?
Consequence of Error	How serious would the result usually be if the worker made a mistake that was not readily correctable?
Spend Time Sitting	How much does this job require sitting?
Deal With Unpleasant or Angry People	How frequently does the worker have to deal with unpleasant, angry, or discourteous individuals as part of the job requirements?
Spend Time Walking and Running	How much does this job require walking and running?
Frequency of Conflict Situations	How often are there conflict situations the employee has to face in this job?
Outdoors, Under Cover	How often does this job require working outdoors, under cover (e.g., structure with roof but no walls)?
Level of Competition	To what extent does this job require the worker to compete or to be aware of competitive pressures?
Spend Time Using Your Hands to Handle, Control, or	How much does this job require using your hands to handle, control, or feel objects, tools or controls?
Wear Common Protective or Safety Equipment such as	How much does this job require wearing common protective or safety equipment such as safety shoes, glasses, gloves, hard hats or life jackets?
Spend Time Bending or Twisting the Body	How much does this job require bending or twisting your body?

Spend Time Making Repetitive Motions	How much does this job require making repetitive motions?
Exposed to Hazardous Conditions	How often does this job require exposure to hazardous conditions?
Public Speaking	How often do you have to perform public speaking in this job?
Indoors, Not Environmentally Controlled	How often does this job require working indoors in non-controlled environmental conditions (e.g., warehouse without heat)?
Degree of Automation	How automated is the job?
Exposed to Minor Burns, Cuts, Bites, or Stings	How often does this job require exposure to minor burns, cuts, bites, or stings?
Electronic Mail	How often do you use electronic mail in this job?
Cramped Work Space, Awkward Positions	How often does this job require working in cramped work spaces that requires getting into awkward positions?
Extremely Bright or Inadequate Lighting	How often does this job require working in extremely bright or inadequate lighting conditions?
Wear Specialized Protective or Safety Equipment su	How much does this job require wearing specialized protective or safety equipment such as breathing apparatus, safety harness, full protection suits, or radiation protection?
Sounds, Noise Levels Are Distracting or Uncomforta	How often does this job require working exposed to sounds and noise levels that are distracting or uncomfortable?
Exposed to Hazardous Equipment	How often does this job require exposure to hazardous equipment?
Deal With Physically Aggressive People	How frequently does this job require the worker to deal with physical aggression of violent individuals?
Spend Time Kneeling, Crouching, Stooping, or Crawl	How much does this job require kneeling, crouching, stooping, or crawling?
Spend Time Keeping or Regaining Balance	How much does this job require keeping or regaining your balance?
In an Open Vehicle or Equipment	How often does this job require working in an open vehicle or equipment (e.g., tractor)?
Pace Determined by Speed of Equipment	How important is it to this job that the pace is determined by the speed of equipment or machinery? (This does not refer to keeping busy at all times on this job.)
Exposed to High Places	How often does this job require exposure to high places?
Spend Time Climbing Ladders, Scaffolds, or Poles	How much does this job require climbing ladders, scaffolds, or poles?
Exposed to Radiation	How often does this job require exposure to radiation?
Exposed to Whole Body Vibration	How often does this job require exposure to whole body vibration (e.g., operate a jackhammer)?

Job Zone Component	Job Zone Component Definitions
Title	Job Zone Two: Some Preparation Needed
Overall Experience	Some previous work-related skill, knowledge, or experience may be helpful in these occupations, but usually is not needed. For example, a drywall installer might benefit from experience installing drywall, but an inexperienced person could still learn to be an installer with little difficulty.
Job Training	Employees in these occupations need anywhere from a few months to one year of working with experienced employees.
Job Zone Examples	These occupations often involve using your knowledge and skills to help others. Examples include drywall installers, fire inspectors, flight attendants, pharmacy technicians, salespersons (retail), and tellers.
SVP Range	(4.0 to < 6.0)
Education	These occupations usually require a high school diploma and may require some vocational training or job-related course work. In some cases, an associate's or bachelor's degree could be needed.

Work_Styles	Work_Styles Definitions
Attention to Detail	Job requires being careful about detail and thorough in completing work tasks.
Dependability	Job requires being reliable, responsible, and dependable, and fulfilling obligations.
Integrity	Job requires being honest and ethical.
Concern for Others	Job requires being sensitive to others' needs and feelings and being understanding and helpful on the job.
Self Control	Job requires maintaining composure, keeping emotions in check, controlling anger, and avoiding aggressive behavior, even in very difficult situations.
Cooperation	Job requires being pleasant with others on the job and displaying a good-natured, cooperative attitude.

Adaptability/Flexibility	Job requires being open to change (positive or negative) and to considerable variety in the workplace.
Stress Tolerance	Job requires accepting criticism and dealing calmly and effectively with high stress situations.
Initiative	Job requires a willingness to take on responsibilities and challenges.
Social Orientation	Job requires preferring to work with others rather than alone, and being personally connected with others on the job.
Independence	Job requires developing one's own ways of doing things, guiding oneself with little or no supervision, and depending on oneself to get things done.
Persistence	Job requires persistence in the face of obstacles.
Achievement/Effort	Job requires establishing and maintaining personally challenging achievement goals and exerting effort toward mastering tasks.
Leadership	Job requires a willingness to lead, take charge, and offer opinions and direction.
Innovation	Job requires creativity and alternative thinking to develop new ideas for and answers to work-related problems.
Analytical Thinking	Job requires analyzing information and using logic to address work-related issues and problems.

39-5011.00 - Barbers

Provide barbering services, such as cutting, trimming, shampooing, and styling hair, trimming beards, or giving shaves.

Tasks

1) Question patrons regarding desired services and haircut styles.

2) Cut and trim hair according to clients' instructions and/or current hairstyles, using clippers, combs, hand-held blow driers, and scissors.

3) Curl, color, or straighten hair, using special chemical solutions and equipment.

4) Clean work stations and sweep floors.

5) Clean and sterilize scissors, combs, clippers, and other instruments.

6) Record services provided on cashiers' tickets or receive payment from customers.

7) Provide skin care and nail treatments.

8) Shape and trim beards and moustaches, using scissors.

9) Identify hair problems, using microscopes and testing devices, or by sending clients' hair samples out to independent laboratories for analysis.

10) Drape and pin protective cloths around customers' shoulders.

11) Provide face, neck, and scalp massages.

12) Perform clerical and administrative duties such as keeping records, paying bills, and hiring and supervising personnel.

13) Order supplies.

14) Keep card files on clientele, recording notes of work done, products used and fees charged after each visit.

15) Stay informed of the latest styles and hair care techniques.

16) Suggest treatments to alleviate hair problems.

17) Shampoo hair.

18) Apply lather; and shave beards, or neck and temple hair contours, using razors.

19) Measure, fit, and groom hairpieces.

39-5012.00 - Hairdressers, Hairstylists, and Cosmetologists

Provide beauty services, such as shampooing, cutting, coloring, and styling hair, and massaging and treating scalp. May also apply makeup, dress wigs, perform hair removal, and provide nail and skin care services.

Tasks

1) Apply water, setting, straightening or waving solutions to hair and use curlers, rollers, hot combs and curling irons to press and curl hair.

2) Keep work stations clean and sanitize tools such as scissors and combs.

3) Shampoo, rinse, condition and dry hair and scalp or hairpieces with water, liquid soap, or other solutions.

4) Cut, trim and shape hair or hairpieces, based on customers' instructions, hair type and facial features, using clippers, scissors, trimmers and razors.

5) Develop new styles and techniques.

6) Demonstrate and sell hair care products and cosmetics.

7) Shave, trim and shape beards and moustaches.

8) Schedule client appointments.

9) Comb, brush, and spray hair or wigs to set style.

10) Massage and treat scalp for hygienic and remedial purposes, using hands, fingers, or vibrating equipment.

11) Shape eyebrows and remove facial hair, using depilatory cream, tweezers, electrolysis or wax.

12) Administer therapeutic medication and advise patron to seek medical treatment for chronic or contagious scalp conditions.

13) Operate cash registers to receive payments from patrons.

14) Attach wigs or hairpieces to model heads and dress wigs and hairpieces according to instructions, samples, sketches or photographs.

15) Train or supervise other hairstylists, hairdressers and assistants.

16) Recommend and explain the use of cosmetics, lotions, and creams to soften and lubricate skin and enhance and restore natural appearance.

17) Clean, shape, and polish fingernails and toenails, using files and nail polish.

18) Apply artificial fingernails.

19) Give facials to patrons, using special compounds such as lotions and creams.

20) Analyze patrons' hair and other physical features to determine and recommend beauty treatment or suggest hair styles.

21) Bleach, dye, or tint hair, using applicator or brush.

Knowledge	Knowledge Definitions
Customer and Personal Service	Knowledge of principles and processes for providing customer and personal services. This includes customer needs assessment, meeting quality standards for services, and evaluation of customer satisfaction.
English Language	Knowledge of the structure and content of the English language including the meaning and spelling of words, rules of composition, and grammar.
Chemistry	Knowledge of the chemical composition, structure, and properties of substances and of the chemical processes and transformations that they undergo. This includes uses of chemicals and their interactions, danger signs, production techniques, and disposal methods.
Administration and Management	Knowledge of business and management principles involved in strategic planning, resource allocation, human resources modeling, leadership technique, production methods, and coordination of people and resources.
Education and Training	Knowledge of principles and methods for curriculum and training design, teaching and instruction for individuals and groups, and the measurement of training effects.
Sales and Marketing	Knowledge of principles and methods for showing, promoting, and selling products or services. This includes marketing strategy and tactics, product demonstration, sales techniques, and sales control systems.
Mathematics	Knowledge of arithmetic, algebra, geometry, calculus, statistics, and their applications.
Psychology	Knowledge of human behavior and performance; individual differences in ability, personality, and interests; learning and motivation; psychological research methods; and the assessment and treatment of behavioral and affective disorders.
Communications and Media	Knowledge of media production, communication, and dissemination techniques and methods. This includes alternative ways to inform and entertain via written, oral, and visual media.
Law and Government	Knowledge of laws, legal codes, court procedures, precedents, government regulations, executive orders, agency rules, and the democratic political process.

Public Safety and Security	Knowledge of relevant equipment, policies, procedures, and strategies to promote effective local, state, or national security operations for the protection of people, data, property, and institutions.
Clerical	Knowledge of administrative and clerical procedures and systems such as word processing, managing files and records, stenography and transcription, designing forms, and other office procedures and terminology.
Personnel and Human Resources	Knowledge of principles and procedures for personnel recruitment, selection, training, compensation and benefits, labor relations and negotiation, and personnel information systems.
Economics and Accounting	Knowledge of economic and accounting principles and practices, the financial markets, banking and the analysis and reporting of financial data.
Biology	Knowledge of plant and animal organisms, their tissues, cells, functions, interdependencies, and interactions with each other and the environment.
Telecommunications	Knowledge of transmission, broadcasting, switching, control, and operation of telecommunications systems.
Production and Processing	Knowledge of raw materials, production processes, quality control, costs, and other techniques for maximizing the effective manufacture and distribution of goods.
Physics	Knowledge and prediction of physical principles, laws, their interrelationships, and applications to understanding fluid, material, and atmospheric dynamics, and mechanical, electrical, atomic and sub-atomic structures and processes.
Therapy and Counseling	Knowledge of principles, methods, and procedures for diagnosis, treatment, and rehabilitation of physical and mental dysfunctions, and for career counseling and guidance.
Design	Knowledge of design techniques, tools, and principles involved in production of precision technical plans, blueprints, drawings, and models.
Philosophy and Theology	Knowledge of different philosophical systems and religions. This includes their basic principles, values, ethics, ways of thinking, customs, practices, and their impact on human culture.
Computers and Electronics	Knowledge of circuit boards, processors, chips, electronic equipment, and computer hardware and software, including applications and programming.
Engineering and Technology	Knowledge of the practical application of engineering science and technology. This includes applying principles, techniques, procedures, and equipment to the design and production of various goods and services.
Medicine and Dentistry	Knowledge of the information and techniques needed to diagnose and treat human injuries, diseases, and deformities. This includes symptoms, treatment alternatives, drug properties and interactions, and preventive health-care measures.
Mechanical	Knowledge of machines and tools, including their designs, uses, repair, and maintenance.
History and Archeology	Knowledge of historical events and their causes, indicators, and effects on civilizations and cultures.
Sociology and Anthropology	Knowledge of group behavior and dynamics, societal trends and influences, human migrations, ethnicity, cultures and their history and origins.
Transportation	Knowledge of principles and methods for moving people or goods by air, rail, sea, or road, including the relative costs and benefits.
Foreign Language	Knowledge of the structure and content of a foreign (non-English) language including the meaning and spelling of words, rules of composition and grammar, and pronunciation.
Fine Arts	Knowledge of the theory and techniques required to compose, produce, and perform works of music, dance, visual arts, drama, and sculpture.
Building and Construction	Knowledge of materials, methods, and the tools involved in construction or repair of houses, buildings, or other structures such as highways and roads.
Food Production	Knowledge of techniques and equipment for planting, growing, and harvesting food products (both plant and animal) for consumption, including storage/handling techniques.
Geography	Knowledge of principles and methods for describing the features of land, sea, and air masses, including their physical characteristics, locations, interrelationships, and distribution of plant, animal, and human life.

Skills	Skills Definitions
Active Listening	Giving full attention to what other people are saying, taking time to understand the points being made, asking questions as appropriate, and not interrupting at inappropriate times.
Speaking	Talking to others to convey information effectively.
Time Management	Managing one's own time and the time of others.
Social Perceptiveness	Being aware of others' reactions and understanding why they react as they do.
Coordination	Adjusting actions in relation to others' actions.
Reading Comprehension	Understanding written sentences and paragraphs in work related documents.
Learning Strategies	Selecting and using training/instructional methods and procedures appropriate for the situation when learning or teaching new things.
Active Learning	Understanding the implications of new information for both current and future problem-solving and decision-making.
Equipment Selection	Determining the kind of tools and equipment needed to do a job.
Critical Thinking	Using logic and reasoning to identify the strengths and weaknesses of alternative solutions, conclusions or approaches to problems.
Service Orientation	Actively looking for ways to help people.
Monitoring	Monitoring/Assessing performance of yourself, other individuals, or organizations to make improvements or take corrective action.
Operations Analysis	Analyzing needs and product requirements to create a design.
Judgment and Decision Making	Considering the relative costs and benefits of potential actions to choose the most appropriate one.
Writing	Communicating effectively in writing as appropriate for the needs of the audience.
Management of Material Resources	Obtaining and seeing to the appropriate use of equipment, facilities, and materials needed to do certain work.
Equipment Maintenance	Performing routine maintenance on equipment and determining when and what kind of maintenance is needed.
Instructing	Teaching others how to do something.
Complex Problem Solving	Identifying complex problems and reviewing related information to develop and evaluate options and implement solutions.
Persuasion	Persuading others to change their minds or behavior.
Mathematics	Using mathematics to solve problems.
Science	Using scientific rules and methods to solve problems.
Negotiation	Bringing others together and trying to reconcile differences.
Management of Personnel Resources	Motivating, developing, and directing people as they work, identifying the best people for the job.
Management of Financial Resources	Determining how money will be spent to get the work done, and accounting for these expenditures.
Troubleshooting	Determining causes of operating errors and deciding what to do about it.
Technology Design	Generating or adapting equipment and technology to serve user needs.
Quality Control Analysis	Conducting tests and inspections of products, services, or processes to evaluate quality or performance.
Installation	Installing equipment, machines, wiring, or programs to meet specifications.
Repairing	Repairing machines or systems using the needed tools.
Operation and Control	Controlling operations of equipment or systems.
Systems Evaluation	Identifying measures or indicators of system performance and the actions needed to improve or correct performance, relative to the goals of the system.
Programming	Writing computer programs for various purposes.
Systems Analysis	Determining how a system should work and how changes in conditions, operations, and the environment will affect outcomes.
Operation Monitoring	Watching gauges, dials, or other indicators to make sure a machine is working properly.

Ability	Ability Definitions
Manual Dexterity	The ability to quickly move your hand, your hand together with your arm, or your two hands to grasp, manipulate, or assemble objects.
Arm-Hand Steadiness	The ability to keep your hand and arm steady while moving your arm or while holding your arm and hand in one position.
Finger Dexterity	The ability to make precisely coordinated movements of the fingers of one or both hands to grasp, manipulate, or assemble very small objects.
Oral Comprehension	The ability to listen to and understand information and ideas presented through spoken words and sentences.

Originality	The ability to come up with unusual or clever ideas about a given topic or situation, or to develop creative ways to solve a problem.
Near Vision	The ability to see details at close range (within a few feet of the observer).
Speech Recognition	The ability to identify and understand the speech of another person.
Oral Expression	The ability to communicate information and ideas in speaking so others will understand.
Visualization	The ability to imagine how something will look after it is moved around or when its parts are moved or rearranged.
Speech Clarity	The ability to speak clearly so others can understand you.
Fluency of Ideas	The ability to come up with a number of ideas about a topic (the number of ideas is important, not their quality, correctness, or creativity).
Trunk Strength	The ability to use your abdominal and lower back muscles to support part of the body repeatedly or continuously over time without 'giving out' or fatiguing.
Selective Attention	The ability to concentrate on a task over a period of time without being distracted.
Multilimb Coordination	The ability to coordinate two or more limbs (for example, two arms, two legs, or one leg and one arm) while sitting, standing, or lying down. It does not involve performing the activities while the whole body is in motion.
Problem Sensitivity	The ability to tell when something is wrong or is likely to go wrong. It does not involve solving the problem, only recognizing there is a problem.
Visual Color Discrimination	The ability to match or detect differences between colors, including shades of color and brightness.
Inductive Reasoning	The ability to combine pieces of information to form general rules or conclusions (includes finding a relationship among seemingly unrelated events).
Deductive Reasoning	The ability to apply general rules to specific problems to produce answers that make sense.
Written Comprehension	The ability to read and understand information and ideas presented in writing.
Time Sharing	The ability to shift back and forth between two or more activities or sources of information (such as speech, sounds, touch, or other sources).
Flexibility of Closure	The ability to identify or detect a known pattern (a figure, object, word, or sound) that is hidden in other distracting material.
Information Ordering	The ability to arrange things or actions in a certain order or pattern according to a specific rule or set of rules (e.g., patterns of numbers, letters, words, pictures, mathematical operations).
Extent Flexibility	The ability to bend, stretch, twist, or reach with your body, arms, and/or legs.
Category Flexibility	The ability to generate or use different sets of rules for combining or grouping things in different ways.
Control Precision	The ability to quickly and repeatedly adjust the controls of a machine or a vehicle to exact positions.
Written Expression	The ability to communicate information and ideas in writing so others will understand.
Mathematical Reasoning	The ability to choose the right mathematical methods or formulas to solve a problem.
Perceptual Speed	The ability to quickly and accurately compare similarities and differences among sets of letters, numbers, objects, pictures, or patterns. The things to be compared may be presented at the same time or one after the other. This ability also includes comparing a presented object with a remembered object.
Auditory Attention	The ability to focus on a single source of sound in the presence of other distracting sounds.
Far Vision	The ability to see details at a distance.
Stamina	The ability to exert yourself physically over long periods of time without getting winded or out of breath.
Speed of Closure	The ability to quickly make sense of, combine, and organize information into meaningful patterns.
Depth Perception	The ability to judge which of several objects is closer or farther away from you, or to judge the distance between you and an object.
Dynamic Strength	The ability to exert muscle force repeatedly or continuously over time. This involves muscular endurance and resistance to muscle fatigue.
Number Facility	The ability to add, subtract, multiply, or divide quickly and correctly.
Wrist-Finger Speed	The ability to make fast, simple, repeated movements of the fingers, hands, and wrists.

Memorization	The ability to remember information such as words, numbers, pictures, and procedures.
Static Strength	The ability to exert maximum muscle force to lift, push, pull, or carry objects.
Hearing Sensitivity	The ability to detect or tell the differences between sounds that vary in pitch and loudness.
Gross Body Coordination	The ability to coordinate the movement of your arms, legs, and torso together when the whole body is in motion.
Gross Body Equilibrium	The ability to keep or regain your body balance or stay upright when in an unstable position.
Glare Sensitivity	The ability to see objects in the presence of glare or bright lighting.
Speed of Limb Movement	The ability to quickly move the arms and legs.
Rate Control	The ability to time your movements or the movement of a piece of equipment in anticipation of changes in the speed and/or direction of a moving object or scene.
Explosive Strength	The ability to use short bursts of muscle force to propel oneself (as in jumping or sprinting), or to throw an object.
Sound Localization	The ability to tell the direction from which a sound originated.
Reaction Time	The ability to quickly respond (with the hand, finger, or foot) to a signal (sound, light, picture) when it appears.
Night Vision	The ability to see under low light conditions.
Response Orientation	The ability to choose quickly between two or more movements in response to two or more different signals (lights, sounds, pictures). It includes the speed with which the correct response is started with the hand, foot, or other body part.
Peripheral Vision	The ability to see objects or movement of objects to one's side when the eyes are looking ahead.
Dynamic Flexibility	The ability to quickly and repeatedly bend, stretch, twist, or reach out with your body, arms, and/or legs.
Spatial Orientation	The ability to know your location in relation to the environment or to know where other objects are in relation to you.

Work_Activity	Work_Activity Definitions
Performing for or Working Directly with the Public	Performing for people or dealing directly with the public. This includes serving customers in restaurants and stores, and receiving clients or guests.
Thinking Creatively	Developing, designing, or creating new applications, ideas, relationships, systems, or products, including artistic contributions.
Updating and Using Relevant Knowledge	Keeping up-to-date technically and applying new knowledge to your job.
Assisting and Caring for Others	Providing personal assistance, medical attention, emotional support, or other personal care to others such as coworkers, customers, or patients.
Getting Information	Observing, receiving, and otherwise obtaining information from all relevant sources.
Establishing and Maintaining Interpersonal Relatio	Developing constructive and cooperative working relationships with others, and maintaining them over time.
Performing General Physical Activities	Performing physical activities that require considerable use of your arms and legs and moving your whole body, such as climbing, lifting, balancing, walking, stooping, and handling of materials.
Provide Consultation and Advice to Others	Providing guidance and expert advice to management or other groups on technical, systems-, or process-related topics.
Making Decisions and Solving Problems	Analyzing information and evaluating results to choose the best solution and solve problems.
Handling and Moving Objects	Using hands and arms in handling, installing, positioning, and moving materials, and manipulating things.
Resolving Conflicts and Negotiating with Others	Handling complaints, settling disputes, and resolving grievances and conflicts, or otherwise negotiating with others.
Judging the Qualities of Things, Services, or Peop	Assessing the value, importance, or quality of things or people.
Communicating with Persons Outside Organization	Communicating with people outside the organization, representing the organization to customers, the public, government, and other external sources. This information can be exchanged in person, in writing, or by telephone or e-mail.
Selling or Influencing Others	Convincing others to buy merchandise/goods or to otherwise change their minds or actions.
Estimating the Quantifiable Characteristics of Pro	Estimating sizes, distances, and quantities; or determining time, costs, resources, or materials needed to perform a work activity.
Communicating with Supervisors, Peers, or Subordin	Providing information to supervisors, co-workers, and subordinates by telephone, in written form, e-mail, or in person.

Inspecting Equipment, Structures, or Material	Inspecting equipment, structures, or materials to identify the cause of errors or other problems or defects.
Monitor Processes, Materials, or Surroundings	Monitoring and reviewing information from materials, events, or the environment, to detect or assess problems.
Organizing, Planning, and Prioritizing Work	Developing specific goals and plans to prioritize, organize, and accomplish your work.
Documenting/Recording Information	Entering, transcribing, recording, storing, or maintaining information in written or electronic/magnetic form.
Developing Objectives and Strategies	Establishing long-range objectives and specifying the strategies and actions to achieve them.
Evaluating Information to Determine Compliance wit	Using relevant information and individual judgment to determine whether events or processes comply with laws, regulations, or standards.
Identifying Objects, Actions, and Events	Identifying information by categorizing, estimating, recognizing differences or similarities, and detecting changes in circumstances or events.
Scheduling Work and Activities	Scheduling events, programs, and activities, as well as the work of others.
Interpreting the Meaning of Information for Others	Translating or explaining what information means and how it can be used.
Analyzing Data or Information	Identifying the underlying principles, reasons, or facts of information by breaking down information or data into separate parts.
Developing and Building Teams	Encouraging and building mutual trust, respect, and cooperation among team members.
Coaching and Developing Others	Identifying the developmental needs of others and coaching, mentoring, or otherwise helping others to improve their knowledge or skills.
Training and Teaching Others	Identifying the educational needs of others, developing formal educational or training programs or classes, and teaching or instructing others.
Guiding, Directing, and Motivating Subordinates	Providing guidance and direction to subordinates, including setting performance standards and monitoring performance.
Performing Administrative Activities	Performing day-to-day administrative tasks such as maintaining information files and processing paperwork.
Processing Information	Compiling, coding, categorizing, calculating, tabulating, auditing, or verifying information or data.
Coordinating the Work and Activities of Others	Getting members of a group to work together to accomplish tasks.
Controlling Machines and Processes	Using either control mechanisms or direct physical activity to operate machines or processes (not including computers or vehicles).
Monitoring and Controlling Resources	Monitoring and controlling resources and overseeing the spending of money.
Repairing and Maintaining Mechanical Equipment	Servicing, repairing, adjusting, and testing machines, devices, moving parts, and equipment that operate primarily on the basis of mechanical (not electronic) principles.
Interacting With Computers	Using computers and computer systems (including hardware and software) to program, write software, set up functions, enter data, or process information.
Staffing Organizational Units	Recruiting, interviewing, selecting, hiring, and promoting employees in an organization.
Repairing and Maintaining Electronic Equipment	Servicing, repairing, calibrating, regulating, fine-tuning, or testing machines, devices, and equipment that operate primarily on the basis of electrical or electronic (not mechanical) principles.
Operating Vehicles, Mechanized Devices, or Equipme	Running, maneuvering, navigating, or driving vehicles or mechanized equipment, such as forklifts, passenger vehicles, aircraft, or water craft.
Drafting, Laying Out, and Specifying Technical Dev	Providing documentation, detailed instructions, drawings, or specifications to tell others about how devices, parts, equipment, or structures are to be fabricated, constructed, assembled, modified, maintained, or used.

Work_Context	**Work_Context Definitions**
Freedom to Make Decisions	How much decision making freedom, without supervision, does the job offer?
Structured versus Unstructured Work	To what extent is this job structured for the worker, rather than allowing the worker to determine tasks, priorities, and goals?
Face-to-Face Discussions	How often do you have to have face-to-face discussions with individuals or teams in this job?
Spend Time Standing	How much does this job require standing?
Telephone	How often do you have telephone conversations in this job?
Contact With Others	How much does this job require the worker to be in contact with others (face-to-face, by telephone, or otherwise) in order to perform it?

Spend Time Making Repetitive Motions	How much does this job require making repetitive motions?
Spend Time Using Your Hands to Handle, Control, or	How much does this job require using your hands to handle, control, or feel objects, tools or controls?
Deal With External Customers	How important is it to work with external customers or the public in this job?
Exposed to Contaminants	How often does this job require working exposed to contaminants (such as pollutants, gases, dust or odors)?
Indoors, Environmentally Controlled	How often does this job require working indoors in environmentally controlled conditions?
Frequency of Decision Making	How frequently is the worker required to make decisions that affect other people, the financial resources, and/or the image and reputation of the organization?
Work With Work Group or Team	How important is it to work with others in a group or team in this job?
Importance of Being Exact or Accurate	How important is being very exact or highly accurate in performing this job?
Exposed to Minor Burns, Cuts, Bites, or Stings	How often does this job require exposure to minor burns, cuts, bites, or stings?
Physical Proximity	To what extent does this job require the worker to perform job tasks in close physical proximity to other people?
Spend Time Bending or Twisting the Body	How much does this job require bending or twisting your body?
Impact of Decisions on Co-workers or Company Resul	How do the decisions an employee makes impact the results of co-workers, clients or the company?
Importance of Repeating Same Tasks	How important is repeating the same physical activities (e.g., key entry) or mental activities (e.g., checking entries in a ledger) over and over, without stopping, to performing this job?
Level of Competition	To what extent does this job require the worker to compete or to be aware of competitive pressures?
Wear Common Protective or Safety Equipment such as	How much does this job require wearing common protective or safety equipment such as safety shoes, glasses, gloves, hard hats or live jackets?
Exposed to Hazardous Conditions	How often does this job require exposure to hazardous conditions?
Time Pressure	How often does this job require the worker to meet strict deadlines?
Deal With Unpleasant or Angry People	How frequently does the worker have to deal with unpleasant, angry, or discourteous individuals as part of the job requirements?
Sounds, Noise Levels Are Distracting or Uncomforta	How often does this job require working exposed to sounds and noise levels that are distracting or uncomfortable?
Exposed to Disease or Infections	How often does this job require exposure to disease/infections?
Coordinate or Lead Others	How important is it to coordinate or lead others in accomplishing work activities in this job?
Frequency of Conflict Situations	How often are there conflict situations the employee has to face in this job?
Letters and Memos	How often does the job require written letters and memos?
Spend Time Walking and Running	How much does this job require walking and running?
Public Speaking	How often do you have to perform public speaking in this job?
Consequence of Error	How serious would the result usually be if the worker made a mistake that was not readily correctable?
Responsible for Others' Health and Safety	How much responsibility is there for the health and safety of others in this job?
Responsibility for Outcomes and Results	How responsible is the worker for work outcomes and results of other workers?
Spend Time Kneeling, Crouching, Stooping, or Crawl	How much does this job require kneeling, crouching, stooping, or crawling?
Extremely Bright or Inadequate Lighting	How often does this job require working in extremely bright or inadequate lighting conditions?
Electronic Mail	How often do you use electronic mail in this job?
Cramped Work Space, Awkward Positions	How often does this job require working in cramped work spaces that requires getting into awkward positions?
Deal With Physically Aggressive People	How frequently does this job require the worker to deal with physical aggression of violent individuals?
Degree of Automation	How automated is the job?
Spend Time Keeping or Regaining Balance	How much does this job require keeping or regaining your balance?
Spend Time Sitting	How much does this job require sitting?
Very Hot or Cold Temperatures	How often does this job require working in very hot (above 90 F degrees) or very cold (below 32 F degrees) temperatures?

Pace Determined by Speed of Equipment	How important is it to this job that the pace is determined by the speed of equipment or machinery? (This does not refer to keeping busy at all times on this job.)
Wear Specialized Protective or Safety Equipment su	How much does this job require wearing specialized protective or safety equipment such as breathing apparatus, safety harness, full protection suits, or radiation protection?
Indoors, Not Environmentally Controlled	How often does this job require working indoors in non-controlled environmental conditions (e.g., warehouse without heat)?
Exposed to Hazardous Equipment	How often does this job require exposure to hazardous equipment?
In an Enclosed Vehicle or Equipment	How often does this job require working in a closed vehicle or equipment (e.g., car)?
Outdoors, Under Cover	How often does this job require working outdoors, under cover (e.g., structure with roof but no walls)?
Outdoors, Exposed to Weather	How often does this job require working outdoors, exposed to all weather conditions?
Spend Time Climbing Ladders, Scaffolds, or Poles	How much does this job require climbing ladders, scaffolds, or poles?
Exposed to High Places	How often does this job require exposure to high places?
Exposed to Radiation	How often does this job require exposure to radiation?
Exposed to Whole Body Vibration	How often does this job require exposure to whole body vibration (e.g., operate a jackhammer)?
In an Open Vehicle or Equipment	How often does this job require working in an open vehicle or equipment (e.g., tractor)?

Job Zone Component	Job Zone Component Definitions
Title	Job Zone Three: Medium Preparation Needed
Overall Experience	Previous work-related skill, knowledge, or experience is required for these occupations. For example, an electrician must have completed three or four years of apprenticeship or several years of vocational training, and often must have passed a licensing exam, in order to perform the job.
Job Training	Employees in these occupations usually need one or two years of training involving both on-the-job experience and informal training with experienced workers.
Job Zone Examples	These occupations usually involve using communication and organizational skills to coordinate, supervise, manage, or train others to accomplish goals. Examples include dental assistants, electricians, fish and game wardens, legal secretaries, personnel recruiters, and recreation workers.
SVP Range	(6.0 to < 7.0)
Education	Most occupations in this zone require training in vocational schools, related on-the-job experience, or an associate's degree. Some may require a bachelor's degree.

Work_Styles	Work_Styles Definitions
Cooperation	Job requires being pleasant with others on the job and displaying a good-natured, cooperative attitude.
Self Control	Job requires maintaining composure, keeping emotions in check, controlling anger, and avoiding aggressive behavior, even in very difficult situations.
Attention to Detail	Job requires being careful about detail and thorough in completing work tasks.
Integrity	Job requires being honest and ethical.
Dependability	Job requires being reliable, responsible, and dependable, and fulfilling obligations.
Innovation	Job requires creativity and alternative thinking to develop new ideas for and answers to work-related problems.
Concern for Others	Job requires being sensitive to others' needs and feelings and being understanding and helpful on the job.
Social Orientation	Job requires preferring to work with others rather than alone, and being personally connected with others on the job.
Independence	Job requires developing one's own ways of doing things, guiding oneself with little or no supervision, and depending on oneself to get things done.
Initiative	Job requires a willingness to take on responsibilities and challenges.
Achievement/Effort	Job requires establishing and maintaining personally challenging achievement goals and exerting effort toward mastering tasks.
Persistence	Job requires persistence in the face of obstacles.
Stress Tolerance	Job requires accepting criticism and dealing calmly and effectively with high stress situations.

Adaptability/Flexibility	Job requires being open to change (positive or negative) and to considerable variety in the workplace.
Leadership	Job requires a willingness to lead, take charge, and offer opinions and direction.
Analytical Thinking	Job requires analyzing information and using logic to address work-related issues and problems.

39-5091.00 - Makeup Artists, Theatrical and Performance

Apply makeup to performers to reflect period, setting, and situation of their role.

Tasks

1) Apply makeup to enhance, and/or alter the appearance of people appearing in productions such as movies.

2) Cleanse and tone the skin in order to prepare it for makeup application.

3) Confer with stage or motion picture officials and performers in order to determine desired effects.

4) Design rubber or plastic prostheses that can be used to change performers' appearances.

5) Duplicate work precisely in order to replicate characters' appearances on a daily basis.

6) Evaluate environmental characteristics such as venue size and lighting plans in order to determine makeup requirements.

7) Establish budgets, and work within budgetary limits.

8) Assess performers' skin-type in order to ensure that make-up will not cause break-outs or skin irritations.

9) Advise hairdressers on the hairstyles required for character parts.

10) Attach prostheses to performers and apply makeup in order to create special features or effects such as scars, aging, or illness.

11) Create character drawings or models, based upon independent research, in order to augment period production files.

12) Select desired makeup shades from stock, or mix oil, grease, and coloring in order to achieve specific color effects.

13) Write makeup sheets and take photos in order to document specific looks and the products that were used to achieve the looks.

14) Wash and reset wigs.

15) Study production information, such as character descriptions, period settings, and situations in order to determine makeup requirements.

16) Examine sketches, photographs, and plaster models in order to obtain desired character image depiction.

17) Provide performers with makeup removal assistance after performances have been completed.

18) Requisition or acquire needed materials for special effects, including wigs, beards, and special cosmetics.

19) Analyze a script, noting events that affect each character's appearance, so that plans can be made for each scene.

20) Demonstrate products to clients, and provide instruction in makeup application.

39-5092.00 - Manicurists and Pedicurists

Clean and shape customers' fingernails and toenails. May polish or decorate nails.

Tasks

1) Soften nail cuticles with water and oil, push back cuticles, using cuticle knife, and trim cuticles, using scissors or nippers.

2) Polish nails, using powdered polish and buffer.

3) Apply undercoat and clear or colored polish onto nails with brush.

4) Attach paper forms to tips of customers' fingers to support and shape artificial nails.

5) Brush powder and solvent onto nails and paper forms to maintain nail appearance and to extend nails, then remove forms and shape and smooth nail edges using rotary abrasive

795

wheel.

6) Clean customers' nails in soapy water, using swabs, files, and orange sticks.

7) Remove previously applied nail polish, using liquid remover and swabs.

8) Roughen surfaces of fingernails, using abrasive wheel.

9) Whiten underside of nails with white paste or pencil.

10) Advise clients on nail care and use of products and colors.

11) Assess the condition of clients' hands, remove dead skin from the hands and massage them.

12) Decorate clients' nails by piercing them or attaching ornaments or designs.

13) Maintain supply inventories and records of client services.

14) Promote and sell nail care products.

15) Treat nails to repair or improve strength and resilience by wrapping, or provide treatment to nail biters.

16) Clean and sanitize tools and work environment.

17) Shape and smooth ends of nails, using scissors, files, and emery boards.

39-5093.00 - Shampooers

Shampoo and rinse customers' hair.

Tasks

1) Maintain treatment records.

2) Massage, shampoo, and condition patron's hair and scalp to clean them and remove excess oil.

3) Advise patrons with chronic or potentially contagious scalp conditions to seek medical treatment.

39-5094.00 - Skin Care Specialists

Provide skin care treatments to face and body to enhance an individual's appearance.

Tasks

1) Remove body and facial hair by applying wax.

2) Keep records of client needs and preferences, and the services provided.

3) Apply chemical peels in order to reduce fine lines and age spots.

4) Tint eyelashes and eyebrows.

5) Cleanse clients' skin with water, creams and/or lotions.

6) Demonstrate how to clean and care for skin properly, and recommend skin-care regimens.

7) Determine which products or colors will improve clients' skin quality and appearance.

8) Examine clients' skin, using magnifying lamps or visors when necessary, in order to evaluate skin condition and appearance.

9) Advise clients about colors and types of makeup, and instruct them in makeup application techniques.

10) Select and apply cosmetic products such as creams, lotions, and tonics.

11) Sterilize equipment, and clean work areas.

12) Collaborate with plastic surgeons and dermatologists in order to provide patients with preoperative and postoperative skin care.

13) Provide facial and body massages.

14) Sell makeup to clients.

15) Treat the facial skin to maintain and improve its appearance, using specialized techniques and products such as peels and masks.

16) Refer clients to medical personnel for treatment of serious skin problems.

17) Perform simple extractions to remove blackheads.

39-6011.00 - Baggage Porters and Bellhops

Handle baggage for travelers at transportation terminals or for guests at hotels or similar establishments.

Tasks

1) Transfer luggage, trunks, and packages to and from rooms, loading areas, vehicles, or transportation terminals, by hand or using baggage carts.

2) Receive and mark baggage by completing and attaching claim checks.

3) Act as part of the security team at transportation terminals, hotels, or similar establishments.

4) Greet incoming guests and escort them to their rooms.

5) Transport guests about premises and local areas, or arrange for transportation.

6) Pick up and return items for laundry and valet service.

7) Explain the operation of room features such as locks, ventilation systems, and televisions.

8) Deliver messages and room service orders, and run errands for guests.

9) Maintain clean lobbies or entrance areas for travelers or guests.

10) Inspect guests' rooms to ensure that they are adequately stocked, orderly, and comfortable.

11) Complete baggage insurance forms.

12) Page guests in hotel lobbies, dining rooms, or other areas.

13) Arrange for shipments of baggage, express mail, and parcels by providing weighing and billing services.

14) Compute and complete charge slips for services rendered and maintain records.

15) Set up conference rooms, display tables, racks, or shelves, and arrange merchandise displays for sales personnel.

16) Supply guests or travelers with directions, travel information, and other information such as available services and points of interest.

Knowledge	Knowledge Definitions
Transportation	Knowledge of principles and methods for moving people or goods by air, rail, sea, or road, including the relative costs and benefits.
Telecommunications	Knowledge of transmission, broadcasting, switching, control, and operation of telecommunications systems.
Public Safety and Security	Knowledge of relevant equipment, policies, procedures, and strategies to promote effective local, state, or national security operations for the protection of people, data, property, and institutions.
English Language	Knowledge of the structure and content of the English language including the meaning and spelling of words, rules of composition, and grammar.
Customer and Personal Service	Knowledge of principles and processes for providing customer and personal services. This includes customer needs assessment, meeting quality standards for services, and evaluation of customer satisfaction.
Mathematics	Knowledge of arithmetic, algebra, geometry, calculus, statistics, and their applications.
Clerical	Knowledge of administrative and clerical procedures and systems such as word processing, managing files and records, stenography and transcription, designing forms, and other office procedures and terminology.
Computers and Electronics	Knowledge of circuit boards, processors, chips, electronic equipment, and computer hardware and software, including applications and programming.
Law and Government	Knowledge of laws, legal codes, court procedures, precedents, government regulations, executive orders, agency rules, and the democratic political process.
Foreign Language	Knowledge of the structure and content of a foreign (non-English) language including the meaning and spelling of words, rules of composition and grammar, and pronunciation.
Administration and Management	Knowledge of business and management principles involved in strategic planning, resource allocation, human resources modeling, leadership technique, production methods, and coordination of people and resources.

		Skills	Skills Definitions

Psychology — Knowledge of human behavior and performance; individual differences in ability, personality, and interests; learning and motivation; psychological research methods; and the assessment and treatment of behavioral and affective disorders.

Geography — Knowledge of principles and methods for describing the features of land, sea, and air masses, including their physical characteristics, locations, interrelationships, and distribution of plant, animal, and human life.

Education and Training — Knowledge of principles and methods for curriculum and training design, teaching and instruction for individuals and groups, and the measurement of training effects.

Sociology and Anthropology — Knowledge of group behavior and dynamics, societal trends and influences, human migrations, ethnicity, cultures and their history and origins.

Communications and Media — Knowledge of media production, communication, and dissemination techniques and methods. This includes alternative ways to inform and entertain via written, oral, and visual media.

Sales and Marketing — Knowledge of principles and methods for showing, promoting, and selling products or services. This includes marketing strategy and tactics, product demonstration, sales techniques, and sales control systems.

Personnel and Human Resources — Knowledge of principles and procedures for personnel recruitment, selection, training, compensation and benefits, labor relations and negotiation, and personnel information systems.

Philosophy and Theology — Knowledge of different philosophical systems and religions. This includes their basic principles, values, ethics, ways of thinking, customs, practices, and their impact on human culture.

Economics and Accounting — Knowledge of economic and accounting principles and practices, the financial markets, banking and the analysis and reporting of financial data.

Production and Processing — Knowledge of raw materials, production processes, quality control, costs, and other techniques for maximizing the effective manufacture and distribution of goods.

History and Archeology — Knowledge of historical events and their causes, indicators, and effects on civilizations and cultures.

Mechanical — Knowledge of machines and tools, including their designs, uses, repair, and maintenance.

Engineering and Technology — Knowledge of the practical application of engineering science and technology. This includes applying principles, techniques, procedures, and equipment to the design and production of various goods and services.

Building and Construction — Knowledge of materials, methods, and the tools involved in the construction or repair of houses, buildings, or other structures such as highways and roads.

Physics — Knowledge and prediction of physical principles, laws, their interrelationships, and applications to understanding fluid, material, and atmospheric dynamics, and mechanical, electrical, atomic and sub-atomic structures and processes.

Fine Arts — Knowledge of the theory and techniques required to compose, produce, and perform works of music, dance, visual arts, drama, and sculpture.

Medicine and Dentistry — Knowledge of the information and techniques needed to diagnose and treat human injuries, diseases, and deformities. This includes symptoms, treatment alternatives, drug properties and interactions, and preventive health-care measures.

Therapy and Counseling — Knowledge of principles, methods, and procedures for diagnosis, treatment, and rehabilitation of physical and mental dysfunctions, and for career counseling and guidance.

Biology — Knowledge of plant and animal organisms, their tissues, cells, functions, interdependencies, and interactions with each other and the environment.

Food Production — Knowledge of techniques and equipment for planting, growing, and harvesting food products (both plant and animal) for consumption, including storage/handling techniques.

Chemistry — Knowledge of the chemical composition, structure, and properties of substances and of the chemical processes and transformations that they undergo. This includes uses of chemicals and their interactions, danger signs, production techniques, and disposal methods.

Design — Knowledge of design techniques, tools, and principles involved in production of precision technical plans, blueprints, drawings, and models.

Skills / Skills Definitions

Speaking — Talking to others to convey information effectively.

Active Listening — Giving full attention to what other people are saying, taking time to understand the points being made, asking questions as appropriate, and not interrupting at inappropriate times.

Service Orientation — Actively looking for ways to help people.

Social Perceptiveness — Being aware of others' reactions and understanding why they react as they do.

Coordination — Adjusting actions in relation to others' actions.

Critical Thinking — Using logic and reasoning to identify the strengths and weaknesses of alternative solutions, conclusions or approaches to problems.

Reading Comprehension — Understanding written sentences and paragraphs in work related documents.

Active Learning — Understanding the implications of new information for both current and future problem-solving and decision-making.

Instructing — Teaching others how to do something.

Learning Strategies — Selecting and using training/instructional methods and procedures appropriate for the situation when learning or teaching new things.

Monitoring — Monitoring/Assessing performance of yourself, other individuals, or organizations to make improvements or take corrective action.

Time Management — Managing one's own time and the time of others.

Judgment and Decision Making — Considering the relative costs and benefits of potential actions to choose the most appropriate one.

Complex Problem Solving — Identifying complex problems and reviewing related information to develop and evaluate options and implement solutions.

Writing — Communicating effectively in writing as appropriate for the needs of the audience.

Management of Personnel Resources — Motivating, developing, and directing people as they work, identifying the best people for the job.

Mathematics — Using mathematics to solve problems.

Quality Control Analysis — Conducting tests and inspections of products, services, or processes to evaluate quality or performance.

Management of Material Resources — Obtaining and seeing to the appropriate use of equipment, facilities, and materials needed to do certain work.

Persuasion — Persuading others to change their minds or behavior.

Equipment Selection — Determining the kind of tools and equipment needed to do a job.

Negotiation — Bringing others together and trying to reconcile differences.

Operation and Control — Controlling operations of equipment or systems.

Systems Evaluation — Identifying measures or indicators of system performance and the actions needed to improve or correct performance, relative to the goals of the system.

Management of Financial Resources — Determining how money will be spent to get the work done, and accounting for these expenditures.

Troubleshooting — Determining causes of operating errors and deciding what to do about it.

Operations Analysis — Analyzing needs and product requirements to create a design.

Operation Monitoring — Watching gauges, dials, or other indicators to make sure a machine is working properly.

Equipment Maintenance — Performing routine maintenance on equipment and determining when and what kind of maintenance is needed.

Science — Using scientific rules and methods to solve problems.

Technology Design — Generating or adapting equipment and technology to serve user needs.

Installation — Installing equipment, machines, wiring, or programs to meet specifications.

Systems Analysis — Determining how a system should work and how changes in conditions, operations, and the environment will affect outcomes.

Repairing — Repairing machines or systems using the needed tools.

Programming — Writing computer programs for various purposes.

Ability / Ability Definitions

Oral Expression — The ability to communicate information and ideas in speaking so others will understand.

Oral Comprehension — The ability to listen to and understand information and ideas presented through spoken words and sentences.

Speech Recognition — The ability to identify and understand the speech of another person.

Speech Clarity — The ability to speak clearly so others can understand you.

Static Strength — The ability to exert maximum muscle force to lift, push, pull, or carry objects.

797

Gross Body Coordination	The ability to coordinate the movement of your arms, legs, and torso together when the whole body is in motion.
Problem Sensitivity	The ability to tell when something is wrong or is likely to go wrong. It does not involve solving the problem, only recognizing there is a problem.
Trunk Strength	The ability to use your abdominal and lower back muscles to support part of the body repeatedly or continuously over time without 'giving out' or fatiguing.
Stamina	The ability to exert yourself physically over long periods of time without getting winded or out of breath.
Extent Flexibility	The ability to bend, stretch, twist, or reach with your body, arms, and/or legs.
Deductive Reasoning	The ability to apply general rules to specific problems to produce answers that make sense.
Multilimb Coordination	The ability to coordinate two or more limbs (for example, two arms, two legs, or one leg and one arm) while sitting, standing, or lying down. It does not involve performing the activities while the whole body is in motion.
Selective Attention	The ability to concentrate on a task over a period of time without being distracted.
Near Vision	The ability to see details at close range (within a few feet of the observer).
Information Ordering	The ability to arrange things or actions in a certain order or pattern according to a specific rule or set of rules (e.g., patterns of numbers, letters, words, pictures, mathematical operations).
Manual Dexterity	The ability to quickly move your hand, your hand together with your arm, or your two hands to grasp, manipulate, or assemble objects.
Memorization	The ability to remember information such as words, numbers, pictures, and procedures.
Inductive Reasoning	The ability to combine pieces of information to form general rules or conclusions (includes finding a relationship among seemingly unrelated events).
Written Comprehension	The ability to read and understand information and ideas presented in writing.
Speed of Limb Movement	The ability to quickly move the arms and legs.
Written Expression	The ability to communicate information and ideas in writing so others will understand.
Arm-Hand Steadiness	The ability to keep your hand and arm steady while moving your arm or while holding your arm and hand in one position.
Auditory Attention	The ability to focus on a single source of sound in the presence of other distracting sounds.
Dynamic Strength	The ability to exert muscle force repeatedly or continuously over time. This involves muscular endurance and resistance to muscle fatigue.
Far Vision	The ability to see details at a distance.
Category Flexibility	The ability to generate or use different sets of rules for combining or grouping things in different ways.
Time Sharing	The ability to shift back and forth between two or more activities or sources of information (such as speech, sounds, touch, or other sources).
Spatial Orientation	The ability to know your location in relation to the environment or to know where other objects are in relation to you.
Perceptual Speed	The ability to quickly and accurately compare similarities and differences among sets of letters, numbers, objects, pictures, or patterns. The things to be compared may be presented at the same time or one after the other. This ability also includes comparing a presented object with a remembered object.
Fluency of Ideas	The ability to come up with a number of ideas about a topic (the number of ideas is important, not their quality, correctness, or creativity).
Originality	The ability to come up with unusual or clever ideas about a given topic or situation, or to develop creative ways to solve a problem.
Glare Sensitivity	The ability to see objects in the presence of glare or bright lighting.
Mathematical Reasoning	The ability to choose the right mathematical methods or formulas to solve a problem.
Visual Color Discrimination	The ability to match or detect differences between colors, including shades of color and brightness.
Speed of Closure	The ability to quickly make sense of, combine, and organize information into meaningful patterns.
Finger Dexterity	The ability to make precisely coordinated movements of the fingers of one or both hands to grasp, manipulate, or assemble very small objects.
Flexibility of Closure	The ability to identify or detect a known pattern (a figure, object, word, or sound) that is hidden in other distracting material.

Depth Perception	The ability to judge which of several objects is closer or farther away from you, or to judge the distance between you and an object.
Number Facility	The ability to add, subtract, multiply, or divide quickly and correctly.
Control Precision	The ability to quickly and repeatedly adjust the controls of a machine or a vehicle to exact positions.
Visualization	The ability to imagine how something will look after it is moved around or when its parts are moved or rearranged.
Dynamic Flexibility	The ability to quickly and repeatedly bend, stretch, twist, or reach out with your body, arms, and/or legs.
Gross Body Equilibrium	The ability to keep or regain your body balance or stay upright when in an unstable position.
Hearing Sensitivity	The ability to detect or tell the differences between sounds that vary in pitch and loudness.
Wrist-Finger Speed	The ability to make fast, simple, repeated movements of the fingers, hands, and wrists.
Night Vision	The ability to see under low light conditions.
Peripheral Vision	The ability to see objects or movement of objects to one's side when the eyes are looking ahead.
Response Orientation	The ability to choose quickly between two or more movements in response to two or more different signals (lights, sounds, pictures). It includes the speed with which the correct response is started with the hand, foot, or other body part.
Reaction Time	The ability to quickly respond (with the hand, finger, or foot) to a signal (sound, light, picture) when it appears.
Explosive Strength	The ability to use short bursts of muscle force to propel oneself (as in jumping or sprinting), or to throw an object.
Sound Localization	The ability to tell the direction from which a sound originated.
Rate Control	The ability to time your movements or the movement of a piece of equipment in anticipation of changes in the speed and/or direction of a moving object or scene.

Work_Activity	Work_Activity Definitions
Identifying Objects, Actions, and Events	Identifying information by categorizing, estimating, recognizing differences or similarities, and detecting changes in circumstances or events.
Performing for or Working Directly with the Public	Performing for people or dealing directly with the public. This includes serving customers in restaurants and stores, and receiving clients or guests.
Judging the Qualities of Things, Services, or Peop	Assessing the value, importance, or quality of things or people.
Performing General Physical Activities	Performing physical activities that require considerable use of your arms and legs and moving your whole body, such as climbing, lifting, balancing, walking, stooping, and handling of materials.
Handling and Moving Objects	Using hands and arms in handling, installing, positioning, and moving materials, and manipulating things.
Communicating with Supervisors, Peers, or Subordin	Providing information to supervisors, co-workers, and subordinates by telephone, in written form, e-mail, or in person.
Monitor Processes, Materials, or Surroundings	Monitoring and reviewing information from materials, events, or the environment, to detect or assess problems.
Making Decisions and Solving Problems	Analyzing information and evaluating results to choose the best solution and solve problems.
Getting Information	Observing, receiving, and otherwise obtaining information from all relevant sources.
Analyzing Data or Information	Identifying the underlying principles, reasons, or facts of information by breaking down information or data into separate parts.
Updating and Using Relevant Knowledge	Keeping up-to-date technically and applying new knowledge to your job.
Establishing and Maintaining Interpersonal Relatio	Developing constructive and cooperative working relationships with others, and maintaining them over time.
Processing Information	Compiling, coding, categorizing, calculating, tabulating, auditing, or verifying information or data.
Interpreting the Meaning of Information for Others	Translating or explaining what information means and how it can be used.
Resolving Conflicts and Negotiating with Others	Handling complaints, settling disputes, and resolving grievances and conflicts, or otherwise negotiating with others.
Communicating with Persons Outside Organization	Communicating with people outside the organization, representing the organization to customers, the public, government, and other external sources. This information can be exchanged in person, in writing, or by telephone or e-mail.

Training and Teaching Others	Identifying the educational needs of others, developing formal educational or training programs or classes, and teaching or instructing others.
Thinking Creatively	Developing, designing, or creating new applications, ideas, relationships, systems, or products, including artistic contributions.
Estimating the Quantifiable Characteristics of Pro	Estimating sizes, distances, and quantities; or determining time, costs, resources, or materials needed to perform a work activity.
Assisting and Caring for Others	Providing personal assistance, medical attention, emotional support, or other personal care to others such as coworkers, customers, or patients.
Developing and Building Teams	Encouraging and building mutual trust, respect, and cooperation among team members.
Coordinating the Work and Activities of Others	Getting members of a group to work together to accomplish tasks.
Provide Consultation and Advice to Others	Providing guidance and expert advice to management or other groups on technical, systems-, or process-related topics.
Evaluating Information to Determine Compliance wit	Using relevant information and individual judgment to determine whether events or processes comply with laws, regulations, or standards.
Coaching and Developing Others	Identifying the developmental needs of others and coaching, mentoring, or otherwise helping others to improve their knowledge or skills.
Monitoring and Controlling Resources	Monitoring and controlling resources and overseeing the spending of money.
Controlling Machines and Processes	Using either control mechanisms or direct physical activity to operate machines or processes (not including computers or vehicles).
Guiding, Directing, and Motivating Subordinates	Providing guidance and direction to subordinates, including setting performance standards and monitoring performance.
Interacting With Computers	Using computers and computer systems (including hardware and software) to program, write software, set up functions, enter data, or process information.
Documenting/Recording Information	Entering, transcribing, recording, storing, or maintaining information in written or electronic/magnetic form.
Inspecting Equipment, Structures, or Material	Inspecting equipment, structures, or materials to identify the cause of errors or other problems or defects.
Scheduling Work and Activities	Scheduling events, programs, and activities, as well as the work of others.
Operating Vehicles, Mechanized Devices, or Equipme	Running, maneuvering, navigating, or driving vehicles or mechanized equipment, such as forklifts, passenger vehicles, aircraft, or water craft.
Selling or Influencing Others	Convincing others to buy merchandise/goods or to otherwise change their minds or actions.
Organizing, Planning, and Prioritizing Work	Developing specific goals and plans to prioritize, organize, and accomplish your work.
Performing Administrative Activities	Performing day-to-day administrative tasks such as maintaining information files and processing paperwork.
Repairing and Maintaining Mechanical Equipment	Servicing, repairing, adjusting, and testing machines, devices, moving parts, and equipment that operate primarily on the basis of mechanical (not electronic) principles.
Developing Objectives and Strategies	Establishing long-range objectives and specifying the strategies and actions to achieve them.
Drafting, Laying Out, and Specifying Technical Dev	Providing documentation, detailed instructions, drawings, or specifications to tell others about how devices, parts, equipment, or structures are to be fabricated, constructed, assembled, modified, maintained, or used.
Staffing Organizational Units	Recruiting, interviewing, selecting, hiring, and promoting employees in an organization.
Repairing and Maintaining Electronic Equipment	Servicing, repairing, calibrating, regulating, fine-tuning, or testing machines, devices, and equipment that operate primarily on the basis of electrical or electronic (not mechanical) principles.

Work_Context	Work_Context Definitions
Contact With Others	How much does this job require the worker to be in contact with others (face-to-face, by telephone, or otherwise) in order to perform it?
Face-to-Face Discussions	How often do you have to have face-to-face discussions with individuals or teams in this job?
Outdoors, Exposed to Weather	How often does this job require working outdoors, exposed to all weather conditions?
Work With Work Group or Team	How important is it to work with others in a group or team in this job?

Frequency of Decision Making	How frequently is the worker required to make decisions that affect other people, the financial resources, and/or the image and reputation of the organization?
Spend Time Walking and Running	How much does this job require walking and running?
Importance of Being Exact or Accurate	How important is being very exact or highly accurate in performing this job?
Deal With External Customers	How important is it to work with external customers or the public in this job?
Very Hot or Cold Temperatures	How often does this job require working in very hot (above 90 F degrees) or very cold (below 32 F degrees) temperatures?
Outdoors, Under Cover	How often does this job require working outdoors, under cover (e.g., structure with roof but no walls)?
Telephone	How often do you have telephone conversations in this job?
Spend Time Standing	How much does this job require standing?
Spend Time Making Repetitive Motions	How much does this job require making repetitive motions?
Extremely Bright or Inadequate Lighting	How often does this job require working in extremely bright or inadequate lighting conditions?
Time Pressure	How often does this job require the worker to meet strict deadlines?
Freedom to Make Decisions	How much decision making freedom, without supervision, does the job offer?
Physical Proximity	To what extent does this job require the worker to perform job tasks in close physical proximity to other people?
Sounds, Noise Levels Are Distracting or Uncomforta	How often does this job require working exposed to sounds and noise levels that are distracting or uncomfortable?
Exposed to Contaminants	How often does this job require working exposed to contaminants (such as pollutants, gases, dust or odors)?
Deal With Unpleasant or Angry People	How frequently does the worker have to deal with unpleasant, angry, or discourteous individuals as part of the job requirements?
Cramped Work Space, Awkward Positions	How often does this job require working in cramped work spaces that requires getting into awkward positions?
Coordinate or Lead Others	How important is it to coordinate or lead others in accomplishing work activities in this job?
Structured versus Unstructured Work	To what extent is this job structured for the worker, rather than allowing the worker to determine tasks, priorities, and goals?
Responsibility for Outcomes and Results	How responsible is the worker for work outcomes and results of other workers?
Degree of Automation	How automated is the job?
Impact of Decisions on Co-workers or Company Resul	How do the decisions an employee makes impact the results of co-workers, clients or the company?
Importance of Repeating Same Tasks	How important is repeating the same physical activities (e.g., key entry) or mental activities (e.g., checking entries in a ledger) over and over, without stopping, to performing this job?
Spend Time Bending or Twisting the Body	How much does this job require bending or twisting your body?
Indoors, Environmentally Controlled	How often does this job require working indoors in environmentally controlled conditions?
Consequence of Error	How serious would the result usually be if the worker made a mistake that was not readily correctable?
Spend Time Using Your Hands to Handle, Control, or	How much does this job require using your hands to handle, control, or feel objects, tools or controls?
Frequency of Conflict Situations	How often are there conflict situations the employee has to face in this job?
Level of Competition	To what extent does this job require the worker to compete or to be aware of competitive pressures?
Responsible for Others' Health and Safety	How much responsibility is there for the health and safety of others in this job?
In an Enclosed Vehicle or Equipment	How often does this job require working in a closed vehicle or equipment (e.g., car)?
Letters and Memos	How often does the job require written letters and memos?
Exposed to Minor Burns, Cuts, Bites, or Stings	How often does this job require exposure to minor burns, cuts, bites, or stings?
Spend Time Kneeling, Crouching, Stooping, or Crawl	How much does this job require kneeling, crouching, stooping or crawling?
Spend Time Keeping or Regaining Balance	How much does this job require keeping or regaining your balance?
Spend Time Sitting	How much does this job require sitting?
Indoors, Not Environmentally Controlled	How often does this job require working indoors in non-controlled environmental conditions (e.g., warehouse without heat)?

Wear Common Protective or Safety Equipment such as	How much does this job require wearing common protective or safety equipment such as safety shoes, glasses, gloves, hard hats or life jackets?
Wear Specialized Protective or Safety Equipment su	How much does this job require wearing specialized protective or safety equipment such as breathing apparatus, safety harness, full protection suits, or radiation protection?
In an Open Vehicle or Equipment	How often does this job require working in an open vehicle or equipment (e.g., tractor)?
Public Speaking	How often do you have to perform public speaking in this job?
Deal With Physically Aggressive People	How frequently does this job require the worker to deal with physical aggression of violent individuals?
Pace Determined by Speed of Equipment	How important is it to this job that the pace is determined by the speed of equipment or machinery? (This does not refer to keeping busy at all times on this job.)
Electronic Mail	How often do you use electronic mail in this job?
Exposed to Disease or Infections	How often does this job require exposure to disease/infections?
Exposed to Hazardous Equipment	How often does this job require exposure to hazardous equipment?
Exposed to High Places	How often does this job require exposure to high places?
Exposed to Hazardous Conditions	How often does this job require exposure to hazardous conditions?
Spend Time Climbing Ladders, Scaffolds, or Poles	How much does this job require climbing ladders, scaffolds, or poles?
Exposed to Whole Body Vibration	How often does this job require exposure to whole body vibration (e.g., operate a jackhammer)?
Exposed to Radiation	How often does this job require exposure to radiation?

Job Zone Component	Job Zone Component Definitions
Title	Job Zone One: Little or No Preparation Needed
Overall Experience	No previous work-related skill, knowledge, or experience is needed for these occupations. For example, a person can become a general office clerk even if he/she has never worked in an office before.
Job Training	Employees in these occupations need anywhere from a few days to a few months of training. Usually, an experienced worker could show you how to do the job.
Job Zone Examples	These occupations involve following instructions and helping others. Examples include bus drivers, forest and conservation workers, general office clerks, home health aides, and waiters/waitresses.
SVP Range	(Below 4.0)
Education	These occupations may require a high school diploma or GED certificate. Some may require a formal training course to obtain a license.

Work_Styles	Work_Styles Definitions
Integrity	Job requires being honest and ethical.
Dependability	Job requires being reliable, responsible, and dependable, and fulfilling obligations.
Attention to Detail	Job requires being careful about detail and thorough in completing work tasks.
Self Control	Job requires maintaining composure, keeping emotions in check, controlling anger, and avoiding aggressive behavior, even in very difficult situations.
Concern for Others	Job requires being sensitive to others' needs and feelings and being understanding and helpful on the job.
Cooperation	Job requires being pleasant with others on the job and displaying a good-natured, cooperative attitude.
Stress Tolerance	Job requires accepting criticism and dealing calmly and effectively with high stress situations.
Independence	Job requires developing one's own ways of doing things, guiding oneself with little or no supervision, and depending on oneself to get things done.
Adaptability/Flexibility	Job requires being open to change (positive or negative) and to considerable variety in the workplace.
Initiative	Job requires a willingness to take on responsibilities and challenges.
Social Orientation	Job requires preferring to work with others rather than alone, and being personally connected with others on the job.
Persistence	Job requires persistence in the face of obstacles.
Innovation	Job requires creativity and alternative thinking to develop new ideas for and answers to work-related problems.

Leadership	Job requires a willingness to lead, take charge, and offer opinions and direction.
Achievement/Effort	Job requires establishing and maintaining personally challenging achievement goals and exerting effort toward mastering tasks.
Analytical Thinking	Job requires analyzing information and using logic to address work-related issues and problems.

39-6012.00 - Concierges

Assist patrons at hotel, apartment or office building with personal services. May take messages, arrange or give advice on transportation, business services or entertainment, or monitor guest requests for housekeeping and maintenance.

Tasks

1) Pick up and deliver items, or run errands for guests.

2) Perform office duties on a temporary basis when needed.

3) Receive, store, and deliver luggage and mail.

4) Make travel arrangements for sightseeing and other tours.

5) Carry out unusual requests such as searching for hard-to-find items and arranging for exotic services such as hot-air balloon rides.

6) Arrange for the replacement of items lost by travelers.

7) Arrange for interpreters or translators when patrons require such services.

8) Plan special events, parties, and meetings, which may include booking musicians or celebrities to appear.

9) Provide information about local features such as shopping, dining, nightlife, and recreational destinations.

Knowledge	Knowledge Definitions
Customer and Personal Service	Knowledge of principles and processes for providing customer and personal services. This includes customer needs assessment, meeting quality standards for services, and evaluation of customer satisfaction.
English Language	Knowledge of the structure and content of the English language including the meaning and spelling of words, rules of composition, and grammar.
Telecommunications	Knowledge of transmission, broadcasting, switching, control, and operation of telecommunications systems.
Public Safety and Security	Knowledge of relevant equipment, policies, procedures, and strategies to promote effective local, state, or national security operations for the protection of people, data, property, and institutions.
Clerical	Knowledge of administrative and clerical procedures and systems such as word processing, managing files and records, stenography and transcription, designing forms, and other office procedures and terminology.
Psychology	Knowledge of human behavior and performance; individual differences in ability, personality, and interests; learning and motivation; psychological research methods; and the assessment and treatment of behavioral and affective disorders.
Communications and Media	Knowledge of media production, communication, and dissemination techniques and methods. This includes alternative ways to inform and entertain via written, oral, and visual media.
Administration and Management	Knowledge of business and management principles involved in strategic planning, resource allocation, human resources modeling, leadership technique, production methods, and coordination of people and resources.
Transportation	Knowledge of principles and methods for moving people or goods by air, rail, sea, or road, including the relative costs and benefits.
Philosophy and Theology	Knowledge of different philosophical systems and religions. This includes their basic principles, values, ethics, ways of thinking, customs, practices, and their impact on human culture.
Education and Training	Knowledge of principles and methods for curriculum and training design, teaching and instruction for individuals and groups, and the measurement of training effects.

Sales and Marketing	Knowledge of principles and methods for showing, promoting, and selling products or services. This includes marketing strategy and tactics, product demonstration, sales techniques, and sales control systems.
Sociology and Anthropology	Knowledge of group behavior and dynamics, societal trends and influences, human migrations, ethnicity, cultures and their history and origins.
Computers and Electronics	Knowledge of circuit boards, processors, chips, electronic equipment, and computer hardware and software, including applications and programming.
History and Archeology	Knowledge of historical events and their causes, indicators, and effects on civilizations and cultures.
Mathematics	Knowledge of arithmetic, algebra, geometry, calculus, statistics, and their applications.
Geography	Knowledge of principles and methods for describing the features of land, sea, and air masses, including their physical characteristics, locations, interrelationships, and distribution of plant, animal, and human life.
Foreign Language	Knowledge of the structure and content of a foreign (non-English) language including the meaning and spelling of words, rules of composition and grammar, and pronunciation.
Economics and Accounting	Knowledge of economic and accounting principles and practices, the financial markets, banking and the analysis and reporting of financial data.
Mechanical	Knowledge of machines and tools, including their designs, uses, repair, and maintenance.
Personnel and Human Resources	Knowledge of principles and procedures for personnel recruitment, selection, training, compensation and benefits, labor relations and negotiation, and personnel information systems.
Law and Government	Knowledge of laws, legal codes, court procedures, precedents, government regulations, executive orders, agency rules, and the democratic political process.
Food Production	Knowledge of techniques and equipment for planting, growing, and harvesting food products (both plant and animal) for consumption, including storage/handling techniques.
Fine Arts	Knowledge of the theory and techniques required to compose, produce, and perform works of music, dance, visual arts, drama, and sculpture.
Production and Processing	Knowledge of raw materials, production processes, quality control, costs, and other techniques for maximizing the effective manufacture and distribution of goods.
Therapy and Counseling	Knowledge of principles, methods, and procedures for diagnosis, treatment, and rehabilitation of physical and mental dysfunctions, and for career counseling and guidance.
Engineering and Technology	Knowledge of the practical application of engineering science and technology. This includes applying principles, techniques, procedures, and equipment to the design and production of various goods and services.
Design	Knowledge of design techniques, tools, and principles involved in production of precision technical plans, blueprints, drawings, and models.
Medicine and Dentistry	Knowledge of the information and techniques needed to diagnose and treat human injuries, diseases, and deformities. This includes symptoms, treatment alternatives, drug properties and interactions, and preventive health-care measures.
Chemistry	Knowledge of the chemical composition, structure, and properties of substances and of the chemical processes and transformations that they undergo. This includes uses of chemicals and their interactions, danger signs, production techniques, and disposal methods.
Building and Construction	Knowledge of materials, methods, and the tools involved in the construction or repair of houses, buildings, or other structures such as highways and roads.
Physics	Knowledge and prediction of physical principles, laws, their interrelationships, and applications to understanding fluid, material, atomic and atmospheric dynamics, and mechanical, electrical, atomic and sub- atomic structures and processes.
Biology	Knowledge of plant and animal organisms, their tissues, cells, functions, interdependencies, and interactions with each other and the environment.

Skills	Skills Definitions
Active Listening	Giving full attention to what other people are saying, taking time to understand the points being made, asking questions as appropriate, and not interrupting at inappropriate times.
Service Orientation	Actively looking for ways to help people.

Speaking	Talking to others to convey information effectively.
Social Perceptiveness	Being aware of others' reactions and understanding why they react as they do.
Reading Comprehension	Understanding written sentences and paragraphs in work related documents.
Critical Thinking	Using logic and reasoning to identify the strengths and weaknesses of alternative solutions, conclusions or approaches to problems.
Time Management	Managing one's own time and the time of others.
Writing	Communicating effectively in writing as appropriate for the needs of the audience.
Coordination	Adjusting actions in relation to others' actions.
Learning Strategies	Selecting and using training/instructional methods and procedures appropriate for the situation when learning or teaching new things.
Instructing	Teaching others how to do something.
Judgment and Decision Making	Considering the relative costs and benefits of potential actions to choose the most appropriate one.
Active Learning	Understanding the implications of new information for both current and future problem-solving and decision-making.
Monitoring	Monitoring/Assessing performance of yourself, other individuals, or organizations to make improvements or take corrective action.
Management of Personnel Resources	Motivating, developing, and directing people as they work, identifying the best people for the job.
Complex Problem Solving	Identifying complex problems and reviewing related information to develop and evaluate options and implement solutions.
Persuasion	Persuading others to change their minds or behavior.
Mathematics	Using mathematics to solve problems.
Negotiation	Bringing others together and trying to reconcile differences.
Equipment Selection	Determining the kind of tools and equipment needed to do a job.
Operations Analysis	Analyzing needs and product requirements to create a design.
Systems Evaluation	Identifying measures or indicators of system performance and the actions needed to improve or correct performance, relative to the goals of the system.
Management of Material Resources	Obtaining and seeing to the appropriate use of equipment, facilities, and materials needed to do certain work.
Operation and Control	Controlling operations of equipment or systems.
Systems Analysis	Determining how a system should work and how changes in conditions, operations, and the environment will affect outcomes.
Management of Financial Resources	Determining how money will be spent to get the work done, and accounting for these expenditures.
Quality Control Analysis	Conducting tests and inspections of products, services, or processes to evaluate quality or performance.
Troubleshooting	Determining causes of operating errors and deciding what to do about it.
Technology Design	Generating or adapting equipment and technology to serve user needs.
Equipment Maintenance	Performing routine maintenance on equipment and determining when and what kind of maintenance is needed.
Programming	Writing computer programs for various purposes.
Repairing	Repairing machines or systems using the needed tools.
Installation	Installing equipment, machines, wiring, or programs to meet specifications.
Operation Monitoring	Watching gauges, dials, or other indicators to make sure a machine is working properly.
Science	Using scientific rules and methods to solve problems.

Ability	Ability Definitions
Oral Comprehension	The ability to listen to and understand information and ideas presented through spoken words and sentences.
Oral Expression	The ability to communicate information and ideas in speaking so others will understand.
Speech Clarity	The ability to speak clearly so others can understand you.
Speech Recognition	The ability to identify and understand the speech of another person.
Problem Sensitivity	The ability to tell when something is wrong or is likely to go wrong. It does not involve solving the problem, only recognizing there is a problem.
Written Comprehension	The ability to read and understand information and ideas presented in writing.
Deductive Reasoning	The ability to apply general rules to specific problems to produce answers that make sense.

Inductive Reasoning	The ability to combine pieces of information to form general rules or conclusions (includes finding a relationship among seemingly unrelated events).
Fluency of Ideas	The ability to come up with a number of ideas about a topic (the number of ideas is important, not their quality, correctness, or creativity).
Originality	The ability to come up with unusual or clever ideas about a given topic or situation, or to develop creative ways to solve a problem.
Information Ordering	The ability to arrange things or actions in a certain order or pattern according to a specific rule or set of rules (e.g., patterns of numbers, letters, words, pictures, mathematical operations).
Near Vision	The ability to see details at close range (within a few feet of the observer).
Written Expression	The ability to communicate information and ideas in writing so others will understand.
Selective Attention	The ability to concentrate on a task over a period of time without being distracted.
Category Flexibility	The ability to generate or use different sets of rules for combining or grouping things in different ways.
Time Sharing	The ability to shift back and forth between two or more activities or sources of information (such as speech, sounds, touch, or other sources).
Flexibility of Closure	The ability to identify or detect a known pattern (a figure, object, word, or sound) that is hidden in other distracting material.
Auditory Attention	The ability to focus on a single source of sound in the presence of other distracting sounds.
Speed of Closure	The ability to quickly make sense of, combine, and organize information into meaningful patterns.
Memorization	The ability to remember information such as words, numbers, pictures, and procedures.
Trunk Strength	The ability to use your abdominal and lower back muscles to support part of the body repeatedly or continuously over time without 'giving out' or fatiguing.
Far Vision	The ability to see details at a distance.
Visual Color Discrimination	The ability to match or detect differences between colors, including shades of color and brightness.
Stamina	The ability to exert yourself physically over long periods of time without getting winded or out of breath.
Perceptual Speed	The ability to quickly and accurately compare similarities and differences among sets of letters, numbers, objects, pictures, or patterns. The things to be compared may be presented at the same time or one after the other. This ability also includes comparing a presented object with a remembered object.
Hearing Sensitivity	The ability to detect or tell the differences between sounds that vary in pitch and loudness.
Visualization	The ability to imagine how something will look after it is moved around or when its parts are moved or rearranged.
Finger Dexterity	The ability to make precisely coordinated movements of the fingers of one or both hands to grasp, manipulate, or assemble very small objects.
Mathematical Reasoning	The ability to choose the right mathematical methods or formulas to solve a problem.
Static Strength	The ability to exert maximum muscle force to lift, push, pull, or carry objects.
Number Facility	The ability to add, subtract, multiply, or divide quickly and correctly.
Arm-Hand Steadiness	The ability to keep your hand and arm steady while moving your arm or while holding your arm and hand in one position.
Gross Body Coordination	The ability to coordinate the movement of your arms, legs, and torso together when the whole body is in motion.
Depth Perception	The ability to judge which of several objects is closer or farther away from you, or to judge the distance between you and an object.
Extent Flexibility	The ability to bend, stretch, twist, or reach with your body, arms, and/or legs.
Dynamic Strength	The ability to exert muscle force repeatedly or continuously over time. This involves muscular endurance and resistance to muscle fatigue.
Control Precision	The ability to quickly and repeatedly adjust the controls of a machine or a vehicle to exact positions.
Gross Body Equilibrium	The ability to keep or regain your body balance or stay upright when in an unstable position.
Multilimb Coordination	The ability to coordinate two or more limbs (for example, two arms, two legs, or one leg and one arm) while sitting, standing, or lying down. It does not involve performing the activities while the whole body is in motion.

Manual Dexterity	The ability to quickly move your hand, your hand together with your arm, or your two hands to grasp, manipulate, or assemble objects.
Speed of Limb Movement	The ability to quickly move the arms and legs.
Spatial Orientation	The ability to know your location in relation to the environment or to know where other objects are in relation to you.
Response Orientation	The ability to choose quickly between two or more movements in response to two or more different signals (lights, sounds, pictures). It includes the speed with which the correct response is started with the hand, foot, or other body part.
Wrist-Finger Speed	The ability to make fast, simple, repeated movements of the fingers, hands, and wrists.
Glare Sensitivity	The ability to see objects in the presence of glare or bright lighting.
Sound Localization	The ability to tell the direction from which a sound originated.
Dynamic Flexibility	The ability to quickly and repeatedly bend, stretch, twist, or reach out with your body, arms, and/or legs.
Rate Control	The ability to time your movements or the movement of a piece of equipment in anticipation of changes in the speed and/or direction of a moving object or scene.
Peripheral Vision	The ability to see objects or movement of objects to one's side when the eyes are looking ahead.
Night Vision	The ability to see under low light conditions.
Reaction Time	The ability to quickly respond (with the hand, finger, or foot) to a signal (sound, light, picture) when it appears.
Explosive Strength	The ability to use short bursts of muscle force to propel oneself (as in jumping or sprinting), or to throw an object.

Work_Activity	Work_Activity Definitions
Getting Information	Observing, receiving, and otherwise obtaining information from all relevant sources.
Performing for or Working Directly with the Public	Performing for people or dealing directly with the public. This includes serving customers in restaurants and stores, and receiving clients or guests.
Communicating with Supervisors, Peers, or Subordin	Providing information to supervisors, co-workers, and subordinates by telephone, in written form, e-mail, or in person.
Communicating with Persons Outside Organization	Communicating with people outside the organization, representing the organization to customers, the public, government, and other external sources. This information can be exchanged in person, in writing, or by telephone or e-mail.
Making Decisions and Solving Problems	Analyzing information and evaluating results to choose the best solution and solve problems.
Identifying Objects, Actions, and Events	Identifying information by categorizing, estimating, recognizing differences or similarities, and detecting changes in circumstances or events.
Establishing and Maintaining Interpersonal Relatio	Developing constructive and cooperative working relationships with others, and maintaining them over time.
Judging the Qualities of Things, Services, or Peop	Assessing the value, importance, or quality of things or people.
Updating and Using Relevant Knowledge	Keeping up-to-date technically and applying new knowledge to your job.
Interacting With Computers	Using computers and computer systems (including hardware and software) to program, write software, set up functions, enter data, or process information.
Thinking Creatively	Developing, designing, or creating new applications, ideas, relationships, systems, or products, including artistic contributions.
Resolving Conflicts and Negotiating with Others	Handling complaints, settling disputes, and resolving grievances and conflicts, or otherwise negotiating with others.
Assisting and Caring for Others	Providing personal assistance, medical attention, emotional support, or other personal care to others such as coworkers, customers, or patients.
Organizing, Planning, and Prioritizing Work	Developing specific goals and plans to prioritize, organize, and accomplish your work.
Documenting/Recording Information	Entering, transcribing, recording, storing, or maintaining information in written or electronic/magnetic form.
Developing and Building Teams	Encouraging and building mutual trust, respect, and cooperation among team members.
Monitor Processes, Materials, or Surroundings	Monitoring and reviewing information from materials, events, or the environment, to detect or assess problems.
Coordinating the Work and Activities of Others	Getting members of a group to work together to accomplish tasks.
Selling or Influencing Others	Convincing others to buy merchandise/goods or to otherwise change their minds or actions.

Interpreting the Meaning of Information for Others	Translating or explaining what information means and how it can be used.
Training and Teaching Others	Identifying the educational needs of others, developing formal educational or training programs or classes, and teaching or instructing others.
Performing Administrative Activities	Performing day-to-day administrative tasks such as maintaining information files and processing paperwork.
Processing Information	Compiling, coding, categorizing, calculating, tabulating, auditing, or verifying information or data.
Scheduling Work and Activities	Scheduling events, programs, and activities, as well as the work of others.
Coaching and Developing Others	Identifying the developmental needs of others and coaching, mentoring, or otherwise helping others to improve their knowledge or skills.
Estimating the Quantifiable Characteristics of Pro	Estimating sizes, distances, and quantities; or determining time, costs, resources, or materials needed to perform a work activity.
Evaluating Information to Determine Compliance wit	Using relevant information and individual judgment to determine whether events or processes comply with laws, regulations, or standards.
Guiding, Directing, and Motivating Subordinates	Providing guidance and direction to subordinates, including setting performance standards and monitoring performance.
Provide Consultation and Advice to Others	Providing guidance and expert advice to management or other groups on technical, systems-, or process-related topics.
Performing General Physical Activities	Performing physical activities that require considerable use of your arms and legs and moving your whole body, such as climbing, lifting, balancing, walking, stooping, and handling of materials.
Developing Objectives and Strategies	Establishing long-range objectives and specifying the strategies and actions to achieve them.
Analyzing Data or Information	Identifying the underlying principles, reasons, or facts of information by breaking down information or data into separate parts.
Monitoring and Controlling Resources	Monitoring and controlling resources and overseeing the spending of money.
Handling and Moving Objects	Using hands and arms in handling, installing, positioning, and moving materials, and manipulating things.
Inspecting Equipment, Structures, or Material	Inspecting equipment, structures, or materials to identify the cause of errors or other problems or defects.
Staffing Organizational Units	Recruiting, interviewing, selecting, hiring, and promoting employees in an organization.
Controlling Machines and Processes	Using either control mechanisms or direct physical activity to operate machines or processes (not including computers or vehicles).
Repairing and Maintaining Electronic Equipment	Servicing, repairing, calibrating, regulating, fine-tuning, or testing machines, devices, and equipment that operate primarily on the basis of electrical or electronic (not mechanical) principles.
Operating Vehicles, Mechanized Devices, or Equipme	Running, maneuvering, navigating, or driving vehicles or mechanized equipment, such as forklifts, passenger vehicles, aircraft, or water craft.
Repairing and Maintaining Mechanical Equipment	Servicing, repairing, adjusting, and testing machines, devices, moving parts, and equipment that operate primarily on the basis of mechanical (not electronic) principles.
Drafting, Laying Out, and Specifying Technical Dev	Providing documentation, detailed instructions, drawings, or specifications to tell others about how devices, parts, equipment, or structures are to be fabricated, constructed, assembled, modified, maintained, or used.

Work_Context | Work_Context Definitions

Contact With Others	How much does this job require the worker to be in contact with others (face-to-face, by telephone, or otherwise) in order to perform it?
Telephone	How often do you have telephone conversations in this job?
Deal With External Customers	How important is it to work with external customers or the public in this job?
Face-to-Face Discussions	How often do you have to have face-to-face discussions with individuals or teams in this job?
Work With Work Group or Team	How important is it to work with others in a group or team in this job?
Frequency of Decision Making	How frequently is the worker required to make decisions that affect other people, the financial resources, and/or the image and reputation of the organization?
Freedom to Make Decisions	How much decision making freedom, without supervision, does the job offer?
Physical Proximity	To what extent does this job require the worker to perform job tasks in close physical proximity to other people?

Impact of Decisions on Co-workers or Company Resul	How do the decisions an employee makes impact the results of co-workers, clients or the company?
Importance of Being Exact or Accurate	How important is being very exact or highly accurate in performing this job?
Deal With Unpleasant or Angry People	How frequently does the worker have to deal with unpleasant, angry, or discourteous individuals as part of the job requirements?
Structured versus Unstructured Work	To what extent is this job structured for the worker, rather than allowing the worker to determine tasks, priorities, and goals?
Letters and Memos	How often does the job require written letters and memos?
Indoors, Environmentally Controlled	How often does this job require working indoors in environmentally controlled conditions?
Time Pressure	How often does this job require the worker to meet strict deadlines?
Spend Time Standing	How much does this job require standing?
Frequency of Conflict Situations	How often are there conflict situations the employee has to face in this job?
Electronic Mail	How often do you use electronic mail in this job?
Coordinate or Lead Others	How important is it to coordinate or lead others in accomplishing work activities in this job?
Importance of Repeating Same Tasks	How important is repeating the same physical activities (e.g., key entry) or mental activities (e.g., checking entries in a ledger) over and over, without stopping, to performing this job?
Spend Time Making Repetitive Motions	How much does this job require making repetitive motions?
Responsibility for Outcomes and Results	How responsible is the worker for work outcomes and results of other workers?
Sounds, Noise Levels Are Distracting or Uncomforta	How often does this job require working exposed to sounds and noise levels that are distracting or uncomfortable?
Spend Time Using Your Hands to Handle, Control, or	How much does this job require using your hands to handle, control, or feel objects, tools or controls?
Level of Competition	To what extent does this job require the worker to compete or to be aware of competitive pressures?
Spend Time Walking and Running	How much does this job require walking and running?
Responsible for Others' Health and Safety	How much responsibility is there for the health and safety of others in this job?
Public Speaking	How often do you have to perform public speaking in this job?
Spend Time Sitting	How much does this job require sitting?
Degree of Automation	How automated is the job?
Spend Time Bending or Twisting the Body	How much does this job require bending or twisting your body?
Cramped Work Space, Awkward Positions	How often does this job require working in cramped work spaces that requires getting into awkward positions?
Consequence of Error	How serious would the result usually be if the worker made a mistake that was not readily correctable?
Exposed to Contaminants	How often does this job require working exposed to contaminants (such as pollutants, gases, dust or odors)?
Deal With Physically Aggressive People	How frequently does this job require the worker to deal with physical aggression of violent individuals?
Spend Time Kneeling, Crouching, Stooping, or Crawl	How much does this job require kneeling, crouching, stooping or crawling?
Very Hot or Cold Temperatures	How often does this job require working in very hot (above 90 F degrees) or very cold (below 32 F degrees) temperatures?
Spend Time Keeping or Regaining Balance	How much does this job require keeping or regaining your balance?
Exposed to Minor Burns, Cuts, Bites, or Stings	How often does this job require exposure to minor burns, cuts, bites, or stings?
Extremely Bright or Inadequate Lighting	How often does this job require working in extremely bright or inadequate lighting conditions?
Outdoors, Exposed to Weather	How often does this job require working outdoors, exposed to all weather conditions?
In an Enclosed Vehicle or Equipment	How often does this job require working in a closed vehicle or equipment (e.g., car)?
Pace Determined by Speed of Equipment	How important is it to this job that the pace is determined by the speed of equipment or machinery? (This does not refer to keeping busy at all times on this job.)
Indoors, Not Environmentally Controlled	How often does this job require working indoors in non-controlled environmental conditions (e.g., warehouse without heat)?
Outdoors, Under Cover	How often does this job require working outdoors, under cover (e.g., structure with roof but no walls)?
Exposed to Disease or Infections	How often does this job require exposure to disease/infections?
Exposed to Radiation	How often does this job require exposure to radiation?

Wear Common Protective or Safety Equipment such as	How much does this job require wearing common protective or safety equipment such as safety shoes, glasses, gloves, hard hats or live jackets?
Exposed to Hazardous Conditions	How often does this job require exposure to hazardous conditions?
Exposed to Hazardous Equipment	How often does this job require exposure to hazardous equipment?
Exposed to High Places	How often does this job require exposure to high places?
Exposed to Whole Body Vibration	How often does this job require exposure to whole body vibration (e.g., operate a jackhammer)?
Wear Specialized Protective or Safety Equipment su	How much does this job require wearing specialized protective or safety equipment such as breathing apparatus, safety harness, full protection suits, or radiation protection?
In an Open Vehicle or Equipment	How often does this job require working in an open vehicle or equipment (e.g., tractor)?
Spend Time Climbing Ladders, Scaffolds, or Poles	How much does this job require climbing ladders, scaffolds, or poles?

Job Zone Component	Job Zone Component Definitions
Title	Job Zone Two: Some Preparation Needed
Overall Experience	Some previous work-related skill, knowledge, or experience may be helpful in these occupations, but usually is not needed. For example, a drywall installer might benefit from experience installing drywall, but an inexperienced person could still learn to be an installer with little difficulty.
Job Training	Employees in these occupations need anywhere from a few months to one year of working with experienced employees. These occupations often involve using your knowledge and skills to help others. Examples include drywall installers, fire inspectors, flight attendants, pharmacy technicians, salespersons (retail), and tellers.
Job Zone Examples	
SVP Range	(4.0 to < 6.0)
Education	These occupations usually require a high school diploma and may require some vocational training or job-related course work. In some cases, an associate's or bachelor's degree could be needed.

Work_Styles	Work_Styles Definitions
Dependability	Job requires being reliable, responsible, and dependable, and fulfilling obligations.
Self Control	Job requires maintaining composure, keeping emotions in check, controlling anger, and avoiding aggressive behavior, even in very difficult situations.
Cooperation	Job requires being pleasant with others on the job and displaying a good-natured, cooperative attitude.
Concern for Others	Job requires being sensitive to others' needs and feelings and being understanding and helpful on the job.
Stress Tolerance	Job requires accepting criticism and dealing calmly and effectively with high stress situations.
Attention to Detail	Job requires being careful about detail and thorough in completing work tasks.
Integrity	Job requires being honest and ethical.
Independence	Job requires developing one's own ways of doing things, guiding oneself with little or no supervision, and depending on oneself to get things done.
Adaptability/Flexibility	Job requires being open to change (positive or negative) and to considerable variety in the workplace.
Initiative	Job requires a willingness to take on responsibilities and challenges.
Leadership	Job requires a willingness to lead, take charge, and offer opinions and direction.
Persistence	Job requires persistence in the face of obstacles.
Social Orientation	Job requires preferring to work with others rather than alone, and being personally connected with others on the job.
Innovation	Job requires creativity and alternative thinking to develop new ideas for and answers to work-related problems.
Analytical Thinking	Job requires analyzing information and using logic to address work-related issues and problems.
Achievement/Effort	Job requires establishing and maintaining personally challenging achievement goals and exerting effort toward mastering tasks.

39-6021.00 - Tour Guides and Escorts

Escort individuals or groups on sightseeing tours or through places of interest, such as industrial establishments, public buildings, and art galleries

Tasks

1) Provide directions and other pertinent information to visitors.

2) Conduct educational activities for school children.

3) Monitor visitors' activities in order to ensure compliance with establishment or tour regulations and safety practices.

4) Distribute brochures, show audiovisual presentations, and explain establishment processes and operations at tour sites.

5) Escort individuals or groups on cruises, sightseeing tours, or through places of interest such as industrial establishments, public buildings, and art galleries.

6) Greet and register visitors, and issue any required identification badges and/or safety devices.

7) Select travel routes and sites to be visited based on knowledge of specific areas.

8) Provide for physical safety of groups, performing such activities as providing first aid and directing emergency evacuations.

9) Collect fees and tickets from group members.

10) Perform clerical duties such as filing, typing, operating switchboards, and routing mail and messages.

11) Provide information about wildlife varieties and habitats, as well as any relevant regulations, such as those pertaining to hunting and fishing.

12) Solicit tour patronage and sell souvenirs.

13) Speak foreign languages in order to communicate with foreign visitors.

14) Assemble and check the required supplies and equipment prior to departure.

15) Research environmental conditions and clients' skill and ability levels in order to plan expeditions, instruction, and commentary that are appropriate.

16) Teach skills, such as proper climbing methods, and demonstrate and advise on the use of equipment.

17) Drive motor vehicles in order to transport visitors to establishments and tour site locations.

Knowledge	Knowledge Definitions
Customer and Personal Service	Knowledge of principles and processes for providing customer and personal services. This includes customer needs assessment, meeting quality standards for services, and evaluation of customer satisfaction.
History and Archeology	Knowledge of historical events and their causes, indicators, and effects on civilizations and cultures.
English Language	Knowledge of the structure and content of the English language including the meaning and spelling of words, rules of composition, and grammar.
Public Safety and Security	Knowledge of relevant equipment, policies, procedures, and strategies to promote effective local, state, or national security operations for the protection of people, data, property, and institutions.
Education and Training	Knowledge of principles and methods for curriculum and training design, teaching and instruction for individuals and groups, and the measurement of training effects.
Communications and Media	Knowledge of media production, communication, and dissemination techniques and methods. This includes alternative ways to inform and entertain via written, oral, and visual media.
Fine Arts	Knowledge of the theory and techniques required to compose, produce, and perform works of music, dance, visual arts, drama, and sculpture.
Philosophy and Theology	Knowledge of different philosophical systems and religions. This includes their basic principles, values, ethics, ways of thinking, customs, practices, and their impact on human culture.
Sociology and Anthropology	Knowledge of group behavior and dynamics, societal trends and influences, human migrations, ethnicity, cultures and their history and origins.

Sales and Marketing	Knowledge of principles and methods for showing, promoting, and selling products or services. This includes marketing strategy and tactics, product demonstration, sales techniques, and sales control systems.
Biology	Knowledge of plant and animal organisms, their tissues, cells, functions, interdependencies, and interactions with each other and the environment.
Psychology	Knowledge of human behavior and performance; individual differences in ability, personality, and interests; learning and motivation; psychological research methods; and the assessment and treatment of behavioral and affective disorders.
Geography	Knowledge of principles and methods for describing the features of land, sea, and air masses, including their physical characteristics, locations, interrelationships, and distribution of plant, animal, and human life.
Administration and Management	Knowledge of business and management principles involved in strategic planning, resource allocation, human resources modeling, leadership technique, production methods, and coordination of people and resources.
Computers and Electronics	Knowledge of circuit boards, processors, chips, electronic equipment, and computer hardware and software, including applications and programming.
Clerical	Knowledge of administrative and clerical procedures and systems such as word processing, managing files and records, stenography and transcription, designing forms, and other office procedures and terminology.
Personnel and Human Resources	Knowledge of principles and procedures for personnel recruitment, selection, training, compensation and benefits, labor relations and negotiation, and personnel information systems.
Foreign Language	Knowledge of the structure and content of a foreign (non-English) language including the meaning and spelling of words, rules of composition and grammar, and pronunciation.
Transportation	Knowledge of principles and methods for moving people or goods by air, rail, sea, or road, including the relative costs and benefits.
Telecommunications	Knowledge of transmission, broadcasting, switching, control, and operation of telecommunications systems.
Mathematics	Knowledge of arithmetic, algebra, geometry, calculus, statistics, and their applications.
Physics	Knowledge of physical principles, laws, their interrelationships, and applications to understanding fluid, material, and atmospheric dynamics, and mechanical, electrical, atomic and sub-atomic structures and processes.
Economics and Accounting	Knowledge of economic and accounting principles and practices, the financial markets, banking and the analysis and reporting of financial data.
Law and Government	Knowledge of laws, legal codes, court procedures, precedents, government regulations, executive orders, agency rules, and the democratic political process.
Design	Knowledge of design techniques, tools, and principles involved in production of precision technical plans, blueprints, drawings, and models.
Chemistry	Knowledge of the chemical composition, structure, and properties of substances and of the chemical processes and transformations that they undergo. This includes uses of chemicals and their interactions, danger signs, production techniques, and disposal methods.
Mechanical	Knowledge of machines and tools, including their designs, uses, repair, and maintenance.
Therapy and Counseling	Knowledge of principles, methods, and procedures for diagnosis, treatment, and rehabilitation of physical and mental dysfunctions, and for career counseling and guidance.
Production and Processing	Knowledge of raw materials, production processes, quality control, costs, and other techniques for maximizing the effective manufacture and distribution of goods.
Building and Construction	Knowledge of materials, methods, and the tools involved in the construction or repair of houses, buildings, or other structures such as highways and roads.
Engineering and Technology	Knowledge of the practical application of engineering science and technology. This includes applying principles, techniques, procedures, and equipment to the design and production of various goods and services.
Food Production	Knowledge of techniques and equipment for planting, growing, and harvesting food products (both plant and animal) for consumption, including storage/handling techniques.

Medicine and Dentistry	Knowledge of the information and techniques needed to diagnose and treat human injuries, diseases, and deformities. This includes symptoms, treatment alternatives, drug properties and interactions, and preventive health-care measures.

Skills	Skills Definitions
Speaking	Talking to others to convey information effectively.
Active Listening	Giving full attention to what other people are saying, taking time to understand the points being made, asking questions as appropriate, and not interrupting at inappropriate times.
Reading Comprehension	Understanding written sentences and paragraphs in work related documents.
Social Perceptiveness	Being aware of others' reactions and understanding why they react as they do.
Active Learning	Understanding the implications of new information for both current and future problem-solving and decision-making.
Instructing	Teaching others how to do something.
Learning Strategies	Selecting and using training/instructional methods and procedures appropriate for the situation when learning or teaching new things.
Monitoring	Monitoring/Assessing performance of yourself, other individuals, or organizations to make improvements or take corrective action.
Time Management	Managing one's own time and the time of others.
Critical Thinking	Using logic and reasoning to identify the strengths and weaknesses of alternative solutions, conclusions or approaches to problems.
Service Orientation	Actively looking for ways to help people.
Writing	Communicating effectively in writing as appropriate for the needs of the audience.
Coordination	Adjusting actions in relation to others' actions.
Persuasion	Persuading others to change their minds or behavior.
Judgment and Decision Making	Considering the relative costs and benefits of potential actions to choose the most appropriate one.
Complex Problem Solving	Identifying complex problems and reviewing related information to develop and evaluate options and implement solutions.
Negotiation	Bringing others together and trying to reconcile differences.
Management of Personnel Resources	Motivating, developing, and directing people as they work, identifying the best people for the job.
Science	Using scientific rules and methods to solve problems.
Mathematics	Using mathematics to solve problems.
Equipment Selection	Determining the kind of tools and equipment needed to do a job.
Systems Evaluation	Identifying measures or indicators of system performance and the actions needed to improve or correct performance, relative to the goals of the system.
Operations Analysis	Analyzing needs and product requirements to create a design.
Quality Control Analysis	Conducting tests and inspections of products, services, or processes to evaluate quality or performance.
Repairing	Repairing machines or systems using the needed tools.
Troubleshooting	Determining causes of operating errors and deciding what to do about it.
Systems Analysis	Determining how a system should work and how changes in conditions, operations, and the environment will affect outcomes.
Equipment Maintenance	Performing routine maintenance on equipment and determining when and what kind of maintenance is needed.
Operation and Control	Controlling operations of equipment or systems.
Management of Material Resources	Obtaining and seeing to the appropriate use of equipment, facilities, and materials needed to do certain work.
Management of Financial Resources	Determining how money will be spent to get the work done, and accounting for these expenditures.
Installation	Installing equipment, machines, wiring, or programs to meet specifications.
Operation Monitoring	Watching gauges, dials, or other indicators to make sure a machine is working properly.
Programming	Writing computer programs for various purposes.
Technology Design	Generating or adapting equipment and technology to serve user needs.

Ability	Ability Definitions
Oral Expression	The ability to communicate information and ideas in speaking so others will understand.
Speech Clarity	The ability to speak clearly so others can understand you.

Oral Comprehension	The ability to listen to and understand information and ideas presented through spoken words and sentences.
Speech Recognition	The ability to identify and understand the speech of another person.
Problem Sensitivity	The ability to tell when something is wrong or is likely to go wrong. It does not involve solving the problem, only recognizing there is a problem.
Deductive Reasoning	The ability to apply general rules to specific problems to produce answers that make sense.
Information Ordering	The ability to arrange things or actions in a certain order or pattern according to a specific rule or set of rules (e.g., patterns of numbers, letters, words, pictures, mathematical operations).
Inductive Reasoning	The ability to combine pieces of information to form general rules or conclusions (includes finding a relationship among seemingly unrelated events).
Near Vision	The ability to see details at close range (within a few feet of the observer).
Written Comprehension	The ability to read and understand information and ideas presented in writing.
Far Vision	The ability to see details at a distance.
Originality	The ability to come up with unusual or clever ideas about a given topic or situation, or to develop creative ways to solve a problem.
Selective Attention	The ability to concentrate on a task over a period of time without being distracted.
Memorization	The ability to remember information such as words, numbers, pictures, and procedures.
Trunk Strength	The ability to use your abdominal and lower back muscles to support part of the body repeatedly or continuously over time without 'giving out' or fatiguing.
Category Flexibility	The ability to generate or use different sets of rules for combining or grouping things in different ways.
Written Expression	The ability to communicate information and ideas in writing so others will understand.
Fluency of Ideas	The ability to come up with a number of ideas about a topic (the number of ideas is important, not their quality, correctness, or creativity).
Stamina	The ability to exert yourself physically over long periods of time without getting winded or out of breath.
Manual Dexterity	The ability to quickly move your hand, your hand together with your arm, or your two hands to grasp, manipulate, or assemble objects.
Time Sharing	The ability to shift back and forth between two or more activities or sources of information (such as speech, sounds, touch, or other sources).
Multilimb Coordination	The ability to coordinate two or more limbs (for example, two arms, two legs, or one leg and one arm) while sitting, standing, or lying down. It does not involve performing the activities while the whole body is in motion.
Gross Body Coordination	The ability to coordinate the movement of your arms, legs, and torso together when the whole body is in motion.
Arm-Hand Steadiness	The ability to keep your hand and arm steady while moving your arm or while holding your arm and hand in one position.
Static Strength	The ability to exert maximum muscle force to lift, push, pull, or carry objects.
Extent Flexibility	The ability to bend, stretch, twist, or reach with your body, arms, and/or legs.
Dynamic Strength	The ability to exert muscle force repeatedly or continuously over time. This involves muscular endurance and resistance to muscle fatigue.
Finger Dexterity	The ability to make precisely coordinated movements of the fingers of one or both hands to grasp, manipulate, or assemble very small objects.
Flexibility of Closure	The ability to identify or detect a known pattern (a figure, object, word, or sound) that is hidden in other distracting material.
Speed of Closure	The ability to quickly make sense of, combine, and organize information into meaningful patterns.
Perceptual Speed	The ability to quickly and accurately compare similarities and differences among sets of letters, numbers, objects, pictures, or patterns. The things to be compared may be presented at the same time or one after the other. This ability also includes comparing a presented object with a remembered object.
Spatial Orientation	The ability to know your location in relation to the environment or to know where other objects are in relation to you.
Mathematical Reasoning	The ability to choose the right mathematical methods or formulas to solve a problem.

Number Facility	The ability to add, subtract, multiply, or divide quickly and correctly.
Gross Body Equilibrium	The ability to keep or regain your body balance or stay upright when in an unstable position.
Visualization	The ability to imagine how something will look after it is moved around or when its parts are moved or rearranged.
Visual Color Discrimination	The ability to match or detect differences between colors, including shades of color and brightness.
Reaction Time	The ability to quickly respond (with the hand, finger, or foot) to a signal (sound, light, picture) when it appears.
Sound Localization	The ability to tell the direction from which a sound originated.
Auditory Attention	The ability to focus on a single source of sound in the presence of other distracting sounds.
Depth Perception	The ability to judge which of several objects is closer or farther away from you, or to judge the distance between you and an object.
Hearing Sensitivity	The ability to detect or tell the differences between sounds that vary in pitch and loudness.
Glare Sensitivity	The ability to see objects in the presence of glare or bright lighting.
Speed of Limb Movement	The ability to quickly move the arms and legs.
Peripheral Vision	The ability to see objects or movement of objects to one's side when the eyes are looking ahead.
Control Precision	The ability to quickly and repeatedly adjust the controls of a machine or a vehicle to exact positions.
Night Vision	The ability to see under low light conditions.
Response Orientation	The ability to choose quickly between two or more movements in response to two or more different signals (lights, sounds, pictures). It includes the speed with which the correct response is started with the hand, foot, or other body part.
Explosive Strength	The ability to use short bursts of muscle force to propel oneself (as in jumping or sprinting), or to throw an object.
Rate Control	The ability to time your movements or the movement of a piece of equipment in anticipation of changes in the speed and/or direction of a moving object or scene.
Wrist-Finger Speed	The ability to make fast, simple, repeated movements of the fingers, hands, and wrists.
Dynamic Flexibility	The ability to quickly and repeatedly bend, stretch, twist, or reach out with your body, arms, and/or legs.

Work_Activity	Work_Activity Definitions
Performing for or Working Directly with the Public	Performing for people or dealing directly with the public. This includes serving customers in restaurants and stores, and receiving clients or guests.
Getting Information	Observing, receiving, and otherwise obtaining information from all relevant sources.
Establishing and Maintaining Interpersonal Relatio	Developing constructive and cooperative working relationships with others, and maintaining them over time.
Interpreting the Meaning of Information for Others	Translating or explaining what information means and how it can be used.
Thinking Creatively	Developing, designing, or creating new applications, ideas, relationships, systems, or products, including artistic contributions.
Communicating with Supervisors, Peers, or Subordin	Providing information to supervisors, co-workers, and subordinates by telephone, in written form, e-mail, or in person.
Identifying Objects, Actions, and Events	Identifying information by categorizing, estimating, recognizing differences or similarities, and detecting changes in circumstances or events.
Training and Teaching Others	Identifying the educational needs of others, developing formal educational or training programs or classes, and teaching or instructing others.
Updating and Using Relevant Knowledge	Keeping up-to-date technically and applying new knowledge to your job.
Communicating with Persons Outside Organization	Communicating with people outside the organization, representing the organization to customers, the public, government, and other external sources. This information can be exchanged in person, in writing, or by telephone or e-mail.
Performing General Physical Activities	Performing physical activities that require considerable use of your arms and legs and moving your whole body, such as climbing, lifting, balancing, walking, stooping, and handling of materials.
Organizing, Planning, and Prioritizing Work	Developing specific goals and plans to prioritize, organize, and accomplish your work.

Assisting and Caring for Others	Providing personal assistance, medical attention, emotional support, or other personal care to others such as coworkers, customers, or patients.
Making Decisions and Solving Problems	Analyzing information and evaluating results to choose the best solution and solve problems.
Judging the Qualities of Things, Services, or Peop	Assessing the value, importance, or quality of things or people.
Handling and Moving Objects	Using hands and arms in handling, installing, positioning, and moving materials, and manipulating things.
Monitor Processes, Materials, or Surroundings	Monitoring and reviewing information from materials, events, or the environment, to detect or assess problems.
Developing and Building Teams	Encouraging and building mutual trust, respect, and cooperation among team members.
Resolving Conflicts and Negotiating with Others	Handling complaints, settling disputes, and resolving grievances and conflicts, or otherwise negotiating with others.
Coordinating the Work and Activities of Others	Getting members of a group to work together to accomplish tasks.
Inspecting Equipment, Structures, or Material	Inspecting equipment, structures, or materials to identify the cause of errors or other problems or defects.
Processing Information	Compiling, coding, categorizing, calculating, tabulating, auditing, or verifying information or data.
Selling or Influencing Others	Convincing others to buy merchandise/goods or to otherwise change their minds or actions.
Documenting/Recording Information	Entering, transcribing, recording, storing, or maintaining information in written or electronic/magnetic form.
Analyzing Data or Information	Identifying the underlying principles, reasons, or facts of information by breaking down information or data into separate parts.
Coaching and Developing Others	Identifying the developmental needs of others and coaching, mentoring, or otherwise helping others to improve their knowledge or skills.
Evaluating Information to Determine Compliance wit	Using relevant information and individual judgment to determine whether events or processes comply with laws, regulations, or standards.
Developing Objectives and Strategies	Establishing long-range objectives and specifying the strategies and actions to achieve them.
Guiding, Directing, and Motivating Subordinates	Providing guidance and direction to subordinates, including setting performance standards and monitoring performance.
Scheduling Work and Activities	Scheduling events, programs, and activities, as well as the work of others.
Provide Consultation and Advice to Others	Providing guidance and expert advice to management or other groups on technical, systems-, or process-related topics.
Estimating the Quantifiable Characteristics of Pro	Estimating sizes, distances, and quantities; or determining time, costs, resources, or materials needed to perform a work activity.
Interacting With Computers	Using computers and computer systems (including hardware and software) to program, write software, set up functions, enter data, or process information.
Controlling Machines and Processes	Using either control mechanisms or direct physical activity to operate machines or processes (not including computers or vehicles).
Monitoring and Controlling Resources	Monitoring and controlling resources and overseeing the spending of money.
Performing Administrative Activities	Performing day-to-day administrative tasks such as maintaining information files and processing paperwork.
Operating Vehicles, Mechanized Devices, or Equipme	Running, maneuvering, navigating, or driving vehicles or mechanized equipment, such as forklifts, passenger vehicles, aircraft, or water craft.
Drafting, Laying Out, and Specifying Technical Dev	Providing documentation, detailed instructions, drawings, or specifications to tell others about how devices, parts, equipment, or structures are to be fabricated, constructed, assembled, modified, maintained, or used.
Repairing and Maintaining Electronic Equipment	Servicing, repairing, calibrating, regulating, fine-tuning, or testing machines, devices, and equipment that operate primarily on the basis of electrical or electronic (not mechanical) principles.
Staffing Organizational Units	Recruiting, interviewing, selecting, hiring, and promoting employees in an organization.
Repairing and Maintaining Mechanical Equipment	Servicing, repairing, adjusting, and testing machines, devices, moving parts, and equipment that operate primarily on the basis of mechanical (not electronic) principles.

Work_Context	Work_Context Definitions
Contact With Others	How much does this job require the worker to be in contact with others (face-to-face, by telephone, or otherwise) in order to perform it?

Face-to-Face Discussions	How often do you have to have face-to-face discussions with individuals or teams in this job?
Deal With External Customers	How important is it to work with external customers or the public in this job?
Public Speaking	How often do you have to perform public speaking in this job?
Physical Proximity	To what extent does this job require the worker to perform job tasks in close physical proximity to other people?
Work With Work Group or Team	How important is it to work with others in a group or team in this job?
Structured versus Unstructured Work	To what extent is this job structured for the worker, rather than allowing the worker to determine tasks, priorities, and goals?
Freedom to Make Decisions	How much decision making freedom, without supervision, does the job offer?
Spend Time Standing	How much does this job require standing?
Indoors, Not Environmentally Controlled	How often does this job require working indoors in non-controlled environmental conditions (e.g., warehouse without heat)?
Frequency of Decision Making	How frequently is the worker required to make decisions that affect other people, the financial resources, and/or the image and reputation of the organization?
Importance of Being Exact or Accurate	How important is being very exact or highly accurate in performing this job?
Impact of Decisions on Co-workers or Company Resul	How do the decisions an employee makes impact the results of co-workers, clients or the company?
Indoors, Environmentally Controlled	How often does this job require working indoors in environmentally controlled conditions?
Time Pressure	How often does this job require the worker to meet strict deadlines?
Telephone	How often do you have telephone conversations in this job?
Coordinate or Lead Others	How important is it to coordinate or lead others in accomplishing work activities in this job?
Outdoors, Exposed to Weather	How often does this job require working outdoors, exposed to all weather conditions?
Spend Time Sitting	How much does this job require sitting?
Spend Time Walking and Running	How much does this job require walking and running?
Electronic Mail	How often do you use electronic mail in this job?
Outdoors, Under Cover	How often does this job require working outdoors, under cover (e.g., structure with roof but no walls)?
Very Hot or Cold Temperatures	How often does this job require working in very hot (above 90 F degrees) or very cold (below 32 F degrees) temperatures?
Sounds, Noise Levels Are Distracting or Uncomforta	How often does this job require working exposed to sounds and noise levels that are distracting or uncomfortable?
Extremely Bright or Inadequate Lighting	How often does this job require working in extremely bright or inadequate lighting conditions?
Letters and Memos	How often does the job require written letters and memos?
Deal With Unpleasant or Angry People	How frequently does the worker have to deal with unpleasant, angry, or discourteous individuals as part of the job requirements?
Frequency of Conflict Situations	How often are there conflict situations the employee has to face in this job?
Spend Time Using Your Hands to Handle, Control, or	How much does this job require using your hands to handle, control, or feel objects, tools or controls?
Responsibility for Outcomes and Results	How responsible is the worker for work outcomes and results of other workers?
Exposed to Contaminants	How often does this job require working exposed to contaminants (such as pollutants, gases, dust or odors)?
Consequence of Error	How serious would the result usually be if the worker made a mistake that was not readily correctable?
Exposed to Minor Burns, Cuts, Bites, or Stings	How often does this job require exposure to minor burns, cuts, bites, or stings?
Responsible for Others' Health and Safety	How much responsibility is there for the health and safety of others in this job?
Importance of Repeating Same Tasks	How important is repeating the same physical activities (e.g., key entry) or mental activities (e.g., checking entries in a ledger) over and over, without stopping, to performing this job?
Spend Time Bending or Twisting the Body	How much does this job require bending or twisting your body?
In an Enclosed Vehicle or Equipment	How often does this job require working in a closed vehicle or equipment (e.g., car)?
Spend Time Making Repetitive Motions	How much does this job require making repetitive motions?
Level of Competition	To what extent does this job require the worker to compete or to be aware of competitive pressures?
Cramped Work Space, Awkward Positions	How often does this job require working in cramped work spaces that requires getting into awkward positions?

Spend Time Kneeling, Crouching, Stooping, or Crawl	How much does this job require kneeling, crouching, stooping, or crawling?
Exposed to High Places	How often does this job require exposure to high places?
Exposed to Hazardous Equipment	How often does this job require exposure to hazardous equipment?
Wear Common Protective or Safety Equipment such as	How much does this job require wearing common protective or safety equipment such as safety shoes, glasses, gloves, hard hats or life jackets?
Degree of Automation	How automated is the job?
Exposed to Whole Body Vibration	How often does this job require exposure to whole body vibration (e.g., operate a jackhammer)?
Exposed to Disease or Infections	How often does this job require exposure to disease/infections?
Wear Specialized Protective or Safety Equipment su	How much does this job require wearing specialized protective or safety equipment such as breathing apparatus, safety harness, full protection suits, or radiation protection?
Spend Time Climbing Ladders, Scaffolds, or Poles	How much does this job require climbing ladders, scaffolds, or poles?
Deal With Physically Aggressive People	How frequently does this job require the worker to deal with physical aggression of violent individuals?
Spend Time Keeping or Regaining Balance	How much does this job require keeping or regaining your balance?
Exposed to Hazardous Conditions	How often does this job require exposure to hazardous conditions?
Pace Determined by Speed of Equipment	How important is it to this job that the pace is determined by the speed of equipment or machinery? (This does not refer to keeping busy at all times on this job.)
In an Open Vehicle or Equipment	How often does this job require working in an open vehicle or equipment (e.g., tractor)?
Exposed to Radiation	How often does this job require exposure to radiation?

Job Zone Component	Job Zone Component Definitions
Title	Job Zone Three: Medium Preparation Needed
Overall Experience	Previous work-related skill, knowledge, or experience is required for these occupations. For example, an electrician must have completed three or four years of apprenticeship or several years of vocational training, and often must have passed a licensing exam, in order to perform the job.
Job Training	Employees in these occupations usually need one or two years of training involving both on-the-job experience and informal training with experienced workers.
Job Zone Examples	These occupations usually involve using communication and organizational skills to coordinate, supervise, manage, or train others to accomplish goals. Examples include dental assistants, electricians, fish and game wardens, legal secretaries, personnel recruiters, and recreation workers.
SVP Range	(6.0 to < 7.0)
Education	Most occupations in this zone require training in vocational schools, related on-the-job experience, or an associate's degree. Some may require a bachelor's degree.

Work_Styles	Work_Styles Definitions
Cooperation	Job requires being pleasant with others on the job and displaying a good-natured, cooperative attitude.
Dependability	Job requires being reliable, responsible, and dependable, and fulfilling obligations.
Self Control	Job requires maintaining composure, keeping emotions in check, controlling anger, and avoiding aggressive behavior, even in very difficult situations.
Concern for Others	Job requires being sensitive to others' needs and feelings and being understanding and helpful on the job.
Integrity	Job requires being honest and ethical.
Adaptability/Flexibility	Job requires being open to change (positive or negative) and to considerable variety in the workplace.
Stress Tolerance	Job requires accepting criticism and dealing calmly and effectively with high stress situations.
Social Orientation	Job requires preferring to work with others rather than alone, and being personally connected with others on the job.
Independence	Job requires developing one's own ways of doing things, guiding oneself with little or no supervision, and depending on oneself to get things done.
Attention to Detail	Job requires being careful about detail and thorough in completing work tasks.

Initiative	Job requires a willingness to take on responsibilities and challenges.
Leadership	Job requires a willingness to lead, take charge, and offer opinions and direction.
Persistence	Job requires persistence in the face of obstacles.
Achievement/Effort	Job requires establishing and maintaining personally challenging achievement goals and exerting effort toward mastering tasks.
Innovation	Job requires creativity and alternative thinking to develop new ideas for and answers to work-related problems.
Analytical Thinking	Job requires analyzing information and using logic to address work-related issues and problems.

39-6022.00 - Travel Guides

Plan, organize, and conduct long distance cruises, tours, and expeditions for individuals and groups.

Tasks

1) Sell travel packages.

2) Plan tour itineraries, applying knowledge of travel routes and destination sites.

3) Instruct novices in climbing techniques, mountaineering, and wilderness survival, and demonstrate use of hunting, fishing, and climbing equipment.

4) Sell or rent equipment, clothing, and supplies related to expeditions.

5) Set up camps, and prepare meals for tour group members.

6) Attend to special needs of tour participants.

7) Pay bills and record checks issued.

8) Provide tourists with assistance in obtaining permits and documents such as visas, passports, and health certificates, and in converting currency.

9) Lead individuals or groups to tour site locations and describe points of interest.

10) Resolve any problems with itineraries, service, or accommodations.

11) Verify amounts and quality of equipment prior to expeditions or tours.

12) Administer first aid to injured group participants.

13) Pilot airplanes or drive land and water vehicles to transport tourists to activity/tour sites.

14) Evaluate services received on the tour, and report findings to tour organizers.

15) Explain hunting and fishing laws to groups in order to ensure compliance.

16) Give advice on sightseeing and shopping.

39-6031.00 - Flight Attendants

Provide personal services to ensure the safety and comfort of airline passengers during flight. Greet passengers, verify tickets, explain use of safety equipment, and serve food or beverages.

Tasks

1) Answer passengers' questions about flights, aircraft, weather, travel routes and services, arrival times, and/or schedules.

2) Assist passengers in placing carry-on luggage in overhead, garment, or under-seat storage.

3) Attend preflight briefings concerning weather, altitudes, routes, emergency procedures, crew coordination, lengths of flights, food and beverage services offered, and numbers of passengers.

4) Assist passengers while entering or disembarking the aircraft.

5) Determine special assistance needs of passengers such as small children, the elderly, or disabled persons.

6) Prepare reports showing places of departure and destination, passenger ticket numbers, meal and beverage inventories, the conditions of cabin equipment, and any problems encountered by passengers.

7) Inspect passenger tickets to verify information and to obtain destination information.

8) Operate audio and video systems.

9) Verify that first aid kits and other emergency equipment. including fire extinguishers and oxygen bottles. are in working order.

10) Reassure passengers when situations such as turbulence are encountered.

11) Prepare passengers and aircraft for landing, following procedures.

12) Sell alcoholic beverages to passengers.

13) Check to ensure that food, beverages, blankets, reading material, emergency equipment, and other supplies are aboard and are in adequate supply.

14) Collect money for meals and beverages.

15) Walk aisles of planes to verify that passengers have complied with federal regulations prior to take-offs and landings.

16) Administer first aid to passengers in distress.

17) Heat and serve prepared foods.

18) Greet passengers boarding aircraft and direct them to assigned seats.

19) Inspect and clean cabins, checking for any problems and making sure that cabins are in order.

20) Announce flight delays and descent preparations.

21) Direct and assist passengers in the event of an emergency, such as directing passengers to evacuate a plane following an emergency landing.

22) Conduct periodic trips through the cabin to ensure passenger comfort, and to distribute reading material. headphones, pillows, playing cards, and blankets.

23) Take inventory of headsets, alcoholic beverages, and money collected.

39-9011.00 - Child Care Workers

Attend to children at schools, businesses, private households, and child care institutions. Perform a variety of tasks, such as dressing, feeding, bathing, and overseeing play.

Tasks

1) Support children's emotional and social development, encouraging understanding of others and positive self-concepts.

2) Organize and participate in recreational activities, such as games.

3) Discipline children and recommend or initiate other measures to control behavior, such as caring for own clothing and picking up toys and books.

4) Instruct children in health and personal habits such as eating, resting, and toilet habits.

5) Read to children, and teach them simple painting, drawing, handicrafts, and songs.

6) Assist in preparing food for children and serve meals and refreshments to children and regulate rest periods.

7) Organize and store toys and materials to ensure order in activity areas.

8) Keep records on individual children, including daily observations and information about activities, meals served, and medications administered.

9) Identify signs of emotional or developmental problems in children and bring them to parents' or guardians' attention.

10) Sanitize toys and play equipment.

11) Care for children in institutional setting, such as group homes, nursery schools, private businesses, or schools for the handicapped.

12) Perform housekeeping duties such as laundry, cleaning, dishwashing, and changing of linens.

13) Dress children and change diapers.

14) Help children with homework and school work.

15) Sterilize bottles and prepare formulas.

16) Accompany children to and from school, on outings, and to medical appointments.

17) Place or hoist children into baths or pools.

18) Provide counseling or therapy to mentally disturbed, delinquent, or handicapped children.

19) Operate in-house daycare centers within businesses.

Knowledge	Knowledge Definitions
Customer and Personal Service	Knowledge of principles and processes for providing customer and personal services. This includes customer needs assessment. meeting quality standards for services, and evaluation of customer satisfaction.
Psychology	Knowledge of human behavior and performance; individual differences in ability, personality, and interests; learning and motivation; psychological research methods; and the assessment and treatment of behavioral and affective disorders.
English Language	Knowledge of the structure and content of the English language including the meaning and spelling of words, rules of composition, and grammar.
Public Safety and Security	Knowledge of relevant equipment, policies, procedures, and strategies to promote effective local, state, or national security operations for the protection of people, data, property, and institutions.
Education and Training	Knowledge of principles and methods for curriculum and training design, teaching and instruction for individuals and groups, and the measurement of training effects.
Medicine and Dentistry	Knowledge of the information and techniques needed to diagnose and treat human injuries, diseases, and deformities. This includes symptoms, treatment alternatives, drug properties and interactions, and preventive health-care measures.
Sociology and Anthropology	Knowledge of group behavior and dynamics, societal trends and influences, human migrations, ethnicity, cultures and their history and origins.
Therapy and Counseling	Knowledge of principles, methods, and procedures for diagnosis, treatment, and rehabilitation of physical and mental dysfunctions, and for career counseling and guidance.
Mathematics	Knowledge of arithmetic, algebra, geometry, calculus, statistics, and their applications.
Personnel and Human Resources	Knowledge of principles and procedures for personnel recruitment, selection, training, compensation and benefits, labor relations and negotiation, and personnel information systems.
Geography	Knowledge of principles and methods for describing the features of land, sea, and air masses, including their physical characteristics, locations, interrelationships, and distribution of plant, animal, and human life.
Philosophy and Theology	Knowledge of different philosophical systems and religions. This includes their basic principles, values, ethics, ways of thinking, customs, practices, and their impact on human culture.
Law and Government	Knowledge of laws, legal codes, court procedures, precedents, government regulations, executive orders, agency rules, and the democratic political process.
Administration and Management	Knowledge of business and management principles involved in strategic planning, resource allocation, human resources modeling, leadership technique, production methods, and coordination of people and resources.
Transportation	Knowledge of principles and methods for moving people or goods by air, rail, sea, or road, including the relative costs and benefits.
Communications and Media	Knowledge of media production, communication, and dissemination techniques and methods. This includes alternative ways to inform and entertain via written, oral, and visual media.
Clerical	Knowledge of administrative and clerical procedures and systems such as word processing, managing files and records, stenography and transcription, designing forms, and other office procedures and terminology.
Computers and Electronics	Knowledge of circuit boards, processors, chips, electronic equipment, and computer hardware and software, including applications and programming.
Chemistry	Knowledge of the chemical composition, structure, and properties of substances and of the chemical processes and transformations that they undergo. This includes uses of chemicals and their interactions, danger signs, production techniques, and disposal methods.
History and Archeology	Knowledge of historical events and their causes, indicators, and effects on civilizations and cultures.
Economics and Accounting	Knowledge of economic and accounting principles and practices, the financial markets, banking and the analysis and reporting of financial data.
Foreign Language	Knowledge of the structure and content of a foreign (non-English) language including the meaning and spelling of words, rules of composition and grammar, and pronunciation.

Fine Arts	Knowledge of the theory and techniques required to compose, produce, and perform works of music, dance, visual arts, drama, and sculpture.
Sales and Marketing	Knowledge of principles and methods for showing, promoting, and selling products or services. This includes marketing strategy and tactics, product demonstration, sales techniques, and sales control systems.
Telecommunications	Knowledge of transmission, broadcasting, switching, control, and operation of telecommunications systems.
Design	Knowledge of design techniques, tools, and principles involved in production of precision technical plans, blueprints, drawings, and models.
Production and Processing	Knowledge of raw materials, production processes, quality control, costs, and other techniques for maximizing the effective manufacture and distribution of goods.
Mechanical	Knowledge of machines and tools, including their designs, uses, repair, and maintenance.
Biology	Knowledge of plant and animal organisms, their tissues, cells, functions, interdependencies, and interactions with each other and the environment.
Food Production	Knowledge of techniques and equipment for planting, growing, and harvesting food products (both plant and animal) for consumption, including storage/handling techniques.
Physics	Knowledge and prediction of physical principles, laws, their interrelationships, and applications to understanding fluid, material, and atmospheric dynamics, and mechanical, electrical, atomic and sub-atomic structures and processes.
Building and Construction	Knowledge of materials, methods, and the tools involved in the construction or repair of houses, buildings, or other structures such as highways and roads.
Engineering and Technology	Knowledge of the practical application of engineering science and technology. This includes applying principles, techniques, procedures, and equipment to the design and production of various goods and services.

Skills	**Skills Definitions**
Active Listening	Giving full attention to what other people are saying, taking time to understand the points being made, asking questions as appropriate, and not interrupting at inappropriate times.
Learning Strategies	Selecting and using training/instructional methods and procedures appropriate for the situation when learning or teaching new things.
Social Perceptiveness	Being aware of others' reactions and understanding why they react as they do.
Instructing	Teaching others how to do something.
Speaking	Talking to others to convey information effectively.
Monitoring	Monitoring/Assessing performance of yourself, other individuals, or organizations to make improvements or take corrective action.
Critical Thinking	Using logic and reasoning to identify the strengths and weaknesses of alternative solutions, conclusions or approaches to problems.
Active Learning	Understanding the implications of new information for both current and future problem-solving and decision-making.
Negotiation	Bringing others together and trying to reconcile differences.
Time Management	Managing one's own time and the time of others.
Service Orientation	Actively looking for ways to help people.
Judgment and Decision Making	Considering the relative costs and benefits of potential actions to choose the most appropriate one.
Reading Comprehension	Understanding written sentences and paragraphs in work related documents.
Persuasion	Persuading others to change their minds or behavior.
Writing	Communicating effectively in writing as appropriate for the needs of the audience.
Coordination	Adjusting actions in relation to others' actions.
Complex Problem Solving	Identifying complex problems and reviewing related information to develop and evaluate options and implement solutions.
Management of Personnel Resources	Motivating, developing, and directing people as they work, identifying the best people for the job.
Management of Material Resources	Obtaining and seeing to the appropriate use of equipment, facilities, and materials needed to do certain work.
Quality Control Analysis	Conducting tests and inspections of products, services, or processes to evaluate quality or performance.
Mathematics	Using mathematics to solve problems.
Management of Financial Resources	Determining how money will be spent to get the work done, and accounting for these expenditures.

Equipment Selection	Determining the kind of tools and equipment needed to do a job.
Systems Evaluation	Identifying measures or indicators of system performance and the actions needed to improve or correct performance, relative to the goals of the system.
Equipment Maintenance	Performing routine maintenance on equipment and determining when and what kind of maintenance is needed.
Repairing	Repairing machines or systems using the needed tools.
Operation and Control	Controlling operations of equipment or systems.
Technology Design	Generating or adapting equipment and technology to serve user needs.
Troubleshooting	Determining causes of operating errors and deciding what to do about it.
Systems Analysis	Determining how a system should work and how changes in conditions, operations, and the environment will affect outcomes.
Operations Analysis	Analyzing needs and product requirements to create a design.
Science	Using scientific rules and methods to solve problems.
Operation Monitoring	Watching gauges, dials, or other indicators to make sure a machine is working properly.
Installation	Installing equipment, machines, wiring, or programs to meet specifications.
Programming	Writing computer programs for various purposes.

Ability	**Ability Definitions**
Problem Sensitivity	The ability to tell when something is wrong or is likely to go wrong. It does not involve solving the problem, only recognizing there is a problem.
Speech Clarity	The ability to speak clearly so others can understand you.
Oral Expression	The ability to communicate information and ideas in speaking so others will understand.
Oral Comprehension	The ability to listen to and understand information and ideas presented through spoken words and sentences.
Speech Recognition	The ability to identify and understand the speech of another person.
Fluency of Ideas	The ability to come up with a number of ideas about a topic (the number of ideas is important, not their quality, correctness, or creativity).
Inductive Reasoning	The ability to combine pieces of information to form general rules or conclusions (includes finding a relationship among seemingly unrelated events).
Originality	The ability to come up with unusual or clever ideas about a given topic or situation, or to develop creative ways to solve a problem.
Time Sharing	The ability to shift back and forth between two or more activities or sources of information (such as speech, sounds, touch, or other sources).
Deductive Reasoning	The ability to apply general rules to specific problems to produce answers that make sense.
Written Comprehension	The ability to read and understand information and ideas presented in writing.
Selective Attention	The ability to concentrate on a task over a period of time without being distracted.
Written Expression	The ability to communicate information and ideas in writing so others will understand.
Information Ordering	The ability to arrange things or actions in a certain order or pattern according to a specific rule or set of rules (e.g., patterns of numbers, letters, words, pictures, mathematical operations).
Flexibility of Closure	The ability to identify or detect a known pattern (a figure, object, word, or sound) that is hidden in other distracting material.
Category Flexibility	The ability to generate or use different sets of rules for combining or grouping things in different ways.
Near Vision	The ability to see details at close range (within a few feet of the observer).
Extent Flexibility	The ability to bend, stretch, twist, or reach with your body, arms, and/or legs.
Far Vision	The ability to see details at a distance.
Speed of Closure	The ability to quickly make sense of, combine, and organize information into meaningful patterns.
Trunk Strength	The ability to use your abdominal and lower back muscles to support part of the body repeatedly or continuously over time without 'giving out' or fatiguing.
Stamina	The ability to exert yourself physically over long periods of time without getting winded or out of breath.
Visualization	The ability to imagine how something will look after it is moved around or when its parts are moved or rearranged.

Ability	Definition
Hearing Sensitivity	The ability to detect or tell the differences between sounds that vary in pitch and loudness.
Visual Color Discrimination	The ability to match or detect differences between colors, including shades of color and brightness.
Memorization	The ability to remember information such as words, numbers, pictures, and procedures.
Finger Dexterity	The ability to make precisely coordinated movements of the fingers of one or both hands to grasp, manipulate, or assemble very small objects.
Static Strength	The ability to exert maximum muscle force to lift, push, pull, or carry objects.
Arm-Hand Steadiness	The ability to keep your hand and arm steady while moving your arm or while holding your arm and hand in one position.
Auditory Attention	The ability to focus on a single source of sound in the presence of other distracting sounds.
Perceptual Speed	The ability to quickly and accurately compare similarities and differences among sets of letters, numbers, objects, pictures, or patterns. The things to be compared may be presented at the same time or one after the other. This ability also includes comparing a presented object with a remembered object.
Manual Dexterity	The ability to quickly move your hand, your hand together with your arm, or your two hands to grasp, manipulate, or assemble objects.
Multilimb Coordination	The ability to coordinate two or more limbs (for example, two arms, two legs, or one leg and one arm) while sitting, standing, or lying down. It does not involve performing the activities while the whole body is in motion.
Gross Body Coordination	The ability to coordinate the movement of your arms, legs, and torso together when the whole body is in motion.
Speed of Limb Movement	The ability to quickly move the arms and legs.
Dynamic Strength	The ability to exert muscle force repeatedly or continuously over time. This involves muscular endurance and resistance to muscle fatigue.
Gross Body Equilibrium	The ability to keep or regain your body balance or stay upright when in an unstable position.
Number Facility	The ability to add, subtract, multiply, or divide quickly and correctly.
Control Precision	The ability to quickly and repeatedly adjust the controls of a machine or a vehicle to exact positions.
Sound Localization	The ability to tell the direction from which a sound originated.
Response Orientation	The ability to choose quickly between two or more movements in response to two or more different signals (lights, sounds, pictures). It includes the speed with which the correct response is started with the hand, foot, or other body part.
Reaction Time	The ability to quickly respond (with the hand, finger, or foot) to a signal (sound, light, picture) when it appears.
Depth Perception	The ability to judge which of several objects is closer or farther away from you, or to judge the distance between you and an object.
Peripheral Vision	The ability to see objects or movement of objects to one's side when the eyes are looking ahead.
Wrist-Finger Speed	The ability to make fast, simple, repeated movements of the fingers, hands, and wrists.
Mathematical Reasoning	The ability to choose the right mathematical methods or formulas to solve a problem.
Spatial Orientation	The ability to know your location in relation to the environment or to know where other objects are in relation to you.
Explosive Strength	The ability to use short bursts of muscle force to propel oneself (as in jumping or sprinting), or to throw an object.
Night Vision	The ability to see under low light conditions.
Rate Control	The ability to time your movements or the movement of a piece of equipment in anticipation of changes in the speed and/or direction of a moving object or scene.
Dynamic Flexibility	The ability to quickly and repeatedly bend, stretch, twist, or reach out with your body, arms, and/or legs.
Glare Sensitivity	The ability to see objects in the presence of glare or bright lighting.

Work_Activity	Work_Activity Definitions
Assisting and Caring for Others	Providing personal assistance, medical attention, emotional support, or other personal care to others such as coworkers, customers, or patients.
Thinking Creatively	Developing, designing, or creating new applications, ideas, relationships, systems, or products, including artistic contributions.
Communicating with Supervisors, Peers, or Subordin	Providing information to supervisors, co-workers, and subordinates by telephone, in written form, e-mail, or in person.
Establishing and Maintaining Interpersonal Relatio	Developing constructive and cooperative working relationships with others, and maintaining them over time.
Organizing, Planning, and Prioritizing Work	Developing specific goals and plans to prioritize, organize, and accomplish your work.
Getting Information	Observing, receiving, and otherwise obtaining information from all relevant sources.
Resolving Conflicts and Negotiating with Others	Handling complaints, settling disputes, and resolving grievances and conflicts, or otherwise negotiating with others.
Making Decisions and Solving Problems	Analyzing information and evaluating results to choose the best solution and solve problems.
Training and Teaching Others	Identifying the educational needs of others, developing formal educational or training programs or classes, and teaching or instructing others.
Performing General Physical Activities	Performing physical activities that require considerable use of your arms and legs and moving your whole body, such as climbing, lifting, balancing, walking, stooping, and handling of materials.
Documenting/Recording Information	Entering, transcribing, recording, storing, or maintaining information in written or electronic/magnetic form.
Evaluating Information to Determine Compliance wit	Using relevant information and individual judgment to determine whether events or processes comply with laws, regulations, or standards.
Updating and Using Relevant Knowledge	Keeping up-to-date technically and applying new knowledge to your job.
Coordinating the Work and Activities of Others	Getting members of a group to work together to accomplish tasks.
Scheduling Work and Activities	Scheduling events, programs, and activities, as well as the work of others.
Monitor Processes, Materials, or Surroundings	Monitoring and reviewing information from materials, events, or the environment, to detect or assess problems.
Coaching and Developing Others	Identifying the developmental needs of others and coaching, mentoring, or otherwise helping others to improve their knowledge or skills.
Developing and Building Teams	Encouraging and building mutual trust, respect, and cooperation among team members.
Identifying Objects, Actions, and Events	Identifying information by categorizing, estimating, recognizing differences or similarities, and detecting changes in circumstances or events.
Performing for or Working Directly with the Public	Performing for people or dealing directly with the public. This includes serving customers in restaurants and stores, and receiving clients or guests.
Communicating with Persons Outside Organization	Communicating with people outside the organization, representing the organization to customers, the public, government, and other external sources. This information can be exchanged in person, in writing, or by telephone or e-mail.
Developing Objectives and Strategies	Establishing long-range objectives and specifying the strategies and actions to achieve them.
Guiding, Directing, and Motivating Subordinates	Providing guidance and direction to subordinates, including setting performance standards and monitoring performance.
Inspecting Equipment, Structures, or Material	Inspecting equipment, structures, or materials to identify the cause of errors or other problems or defects.
Interpreting the Meaning of Information for Others	Translating or explaining what information means and how it can be used.
Performing Administrative Activities	Performing day-to-day administrative tasks such as maintaining information files and processing paperwork.
Judging the Qualities of Things, Services, or Peop	Assessing the value, importance, or quality of things or people.
Handling and Moving Objects	Using hands and arms in handling, installing, positioning, and moving materials, and manipulating things.
Processing Information	Compiling, coding, categorizing, calculating, tabulating, auditing, or verifying information or data.
Analyzing Data or Information	Identifying the underlying principles, reasons, or facts of information by breaking down information or data into separate parts.
Monitoring and Controlling Resources	Monitoring and controlling resources and overseeing the spending of money.
Estimating the Quantifiable Characteristics of Pro	Estimating sizes, distances, and quantities; or determining time, costs, resources, or materials needed to perform a work activity.
Selling or Influencing Others	Convincing others to buy merchandise/goods or to otherwise change their minds or actions.
Provide Consultation and Advice to Others	Providing guidance and expert advice to management or other groups on technical, systems-, or process-related topics.

Staffing Organizational Units	Recruiting, interviewing, selecting, hiring, and promoting employees in an organization.
Interacting With Computers	Using computers and computer systems (including hardware and software) to program, write software, set up functions, enter data, or process information.
Operating Vehicles, Mechanized Devices, or Equipme	Running, maneuvering, navigating, or driving vehicles or mechanized equipment, such as forklifts, passenger vehicles, aircraft, or water craft.
Controlling Machines and Processes	Using either control mechanisms or direct physical activity to operate machines or processes (not including computers or vehicles).
Repairing and Maintaining Mechanical Equipment	Servicing, repairing, adjusting, and testing machines, devices, moving parts, and equipment that operate primarily on the basis of mechanical (not electronic) principles.
Drafting, Laying Out, and Specifying Technical Dev	Providing documentation, detailed instructions, drawings, or specifications to tell others about how devices, parts, equipment, or structures are to be fabricated, constructed, assembled, modified, maintained, or used.
Repairing and Maintaining Electronic Equipment	Servicing, repairing, calibrating, regulating, fine-tuning, or testing machines, devices, and equipment that operate primarily on the basis of electrical or electronic (not mechanical) principles.

Work_Context	Work_Context Definitions
Face-to-Face Discussions	How often do you have to have face-to-face discussions with individuals or teams in this job?
Contact With Others	How much does this job require the worker to be in contact with others (face-to-face, by telephone, or otherwise) in order to perform it?
Work With Work Group or Team	How important is it to work with others in a group or team in this job?
Freedom to Make Decisions	How much decision making freedom, without supervision, does the job offer?
Structured versus Unstructured Work	To what extent is this job structured for the worker, rather than allowing the worker to determine tasks, priorities, and goals?
Physical Proximity	To what extent does this job require the worker to perform job tasks in close physical proximity to other people?
Responsible for Others' Health and Safety	How much responsibility is there for the health and safety of others in this job?
Telephone	How often do you have telephone conversations in this job?
Coordinate or Lead Others	How important is it to coordinate or lead others in accomplishing work activities in this job?
Indoors, Environmentally Controlled	How often does this job require working indoors in environmentally controlled conditions?
Spend Time Standing	How much does this job require standing?
Impact of Decisions on Co-workers or Company Resul	How do the decisions an employee makes impact the results of co-workers, clients or the company?
Sounds, Noise Levels Are Distracting or Uncomforta	How often does this job require working exposed to sounds and noise levels that are distracting or uncomfortable?
Importance of Being Exact or Accurate	How important is being very exact or highly accurate in performing this job?
Exposed to Disease or Infections	How often does this job require exposure to disease/infections?
Deal With Unpleasant or Angry People	How frequently does the worker have to deal with unpleasant, angry, or discourteous individuals as part of the job requirements?
Frequency of Conflict Situations	How often are there conflict situations the employee has to face in this job?
Letters and Memos	How often does the job require written letters and memos?
Spend Time Kneeling, Crouching, Stooping, or Crawl	How much does this job require kneeling, crouching, stooping, or crawling?
Frequency of Decision Making	How frequently is the worker required to make decisions that affect other people, the financial resources, and/or the image and reputation of the organization?
Spend Time Walking and Running	How much does this job require walking and running?
Exposed to Minor Burns, Cuts, Bites, or Stings	How often does this job require exposure to minor burns, cuts, bites, or stings?
Deal With External Customers	How important is it to work with external customers or the public in this job?
Spend Time Bending or Twisting the Body	How much does this job require bending or twisting your body?
Responsibility for Outcomes and Results	How responsible is the worker for work outcomes and results of other workers?

Time Pressure	How often does this job require the worker to meet strict deadlines?
Spend Time Using Your Hands to Handle, Control, or	How much does this job require using your hands to handle, control, or feel objects, tools or controls?
Spend Time Sitting	How much does this job require sitting?
Wear Common Protective or Safety Equipment such as	How much does this job require wearing common protective or safety equipment such as safety shoes, glasses, gloves, hard hats or live jackets?
Spend Time Making Repetitive Motions	How much does this job require making repetitive motions?
Outdoors, Exposed to Weather	How often does this job require working outdoors, exposed to all weather conditions?
Consequence of Error	How serious would the result usually be if the worker made a mistake that was not readily correctable?
Importance of Repeating Same Tasks	How important is repeating the same physical activities (e.g., key entry) or mental activities (e.g., checking entries in a ledger) over and over, without stopping, to performing this job?
Level of Competition	To what extent does this job require the worker to compete or to be aware of competitive pressures?
Deal With Physically Aggressive People	How frequently does this job require the worker to deal with physical aggression of violent individuals?
Public Speaking	How often do you have to perform public speaking in this job?
Exposed to Contaminants	How often does this job require working exposed to contaminants (such as pollutants, gases, dust or odors)?
Electronic Mail	How often do you use electronic mail in this job?
Degree of Automation	How automated is the job?
Cramped Work Space, Awkward Positions	How often does this job require working in cramped work spaces that requires getting into awkward positions?
Very Hot or Cold Temperatures	How often does this job require working in very hot (above 90 F degrees) or very cold (below 32 F degrees) temperatures?
Spend Time Keeping or Regaining Balance	How much does this job require keeping or regaining your balance?
Outdoors, Under Cover	How often does this job require working outdoors, under cover (e.g., structure with roof but no walls)?
Indoors, Not Environmentally Controlled	How often does this job require working indoors in non-controlled environmental conditions (e.g., warehouse without heat)?
Extremely Bright or Inadequate Lighting	How often does this job require working in extremely bright or inadequate lighting conditions?
In an Enclosed Vehicle or Equipment	How often does this job require working in a closed vehicle or equipment (e.g., car)?
Exposed to Hazardous Conditions	How often does this job require exposure to hazardous conditions?
Exposed to Radiation	How often does this job require exposure to radiation?
Exposed to Hazardous Equipment	How often does this job require exposure to hazardous equipment?
Pace Determined by Speed of Equipment	How important is it to this job that the pace is determined by the speed of equipment or machinery? (This does not refer to keeping busy at all times on this job.)
Exposed to High Places	How often does this job require exposure to high places?
Exposed to Whole Body Vibration	How often does this job require exposure to whole body vibration (e.g., operate a jackhammer)?
In an Open Vehicle or Equipment	How often does this job require working in an open vehicle or equipment (e.g., tractor)?
Wear Specialized Protective or Safety Equipment su	How much does this job require wearing specialized protective or safety equipment such as breathing apparatus, safety harness, full protection suits, or radiation protection?
Spend Time Climbing Ladders, Scaffolds, or Poles	How much does this job require climbing ladders, scaffolds, or poles?

Job Zone Component	Job Zone Component Definitions
Title	Job Zone Three: Medium Preparation Needed
Overall Experience	Previous work-related skill, knowledge, or experience is required for these occupations. For example, an electrician must have completed three or four years of apprenticeship or several years of vocational training, and often must have passed a licensing exam, in order to perform the job.
Job Training	Employees in these occupations usually need one or two years of training involving both on-the-job experience and informal training with experienced workers.

Job Zone Examples	These occupations usually involve using communication and organizational skills to coordinate, supervise, manage, or train others to accomplish goals. Examples include dental assistants, electricians, fish and game wardens, legal secretaries, personnel recruiters, and recreation workers.
SVP Range	(6.0 to 7.0)
Education	Most occupations in this zone require training in vocational schools, related on-the-job experience, or an associate's degree. Some may require a bachelor's degree.

Work_Styles	Work_Styles Definitions
Dependability	Job requires being reliable, responsible, and dependable, and fulfilling obligations.
Self Control	Job requires maintaining composure, keeping emotions in check, controlling anger, and avoiding aggressive behavior, even in very difficult situations.
Concern for Others	Job requires being sensitive to others' needs and feelings and being understanding and helpful on the job.
Integrity	Job requires being honest and ethical.
Cooperation	Job requires being pleasant with others on the job and displaying a good-natured, cooperative attitude.
Stress Tolerance	Job requires accepting criticism and dealing calmly and effectively with high stress situations.
Social Orientation	Job requires preferring to work with others rather than alone, and being personally connected with others on the job.
Adaptability/Flexibility	Job requires being open to change (positive or negative) and to considerable variety in the workplace.
Leadership	Job requires a willingness to lead, take charge, and offer opinions and direction.
Attention to Detail	Job requires being careful about detail and thorough in completing work tasks.
Initiative	Job requires a willingness to take on responsibilities and challenges.
Independence	Job requires developing one's own ways of doing things, guiding oneself with little or no supervision, and depending on oneself to get things done.
Persistence	Job requires persistence in the face of obstacles.
Innovation	Job requires creativity and alternative thinking to develop new ideas for and answers to work-related problems.
Achievement/Effort	Job requires establishing and maintaining personally challenging achievement goals and exerting effort toward mastering tasks.
Analytical Thinking	Job requires analyzing information and using logic to address work-related issues and problems.

39-9021.00 - Personal and Home Care Aides

Assist elderly or disabled adults with daily living activities at the person's home or in a daytime non-residential facility. Duties performed at a place of residence may include keeping house (making beds, doing laundry, washing dishes) and preparing meals. May provide meals and supervised activities at non-residential care facilities. May advise families, the elderly, and disabled on such things as nutrition, cleanliness, and household utilities.

Tasks

1) Prepare and maintain records of client progress and services performed, reporting changes in client condition to manager or supervisor.

2) Plan, shop for, and prepare meals, including special diets, and assist families in planning, shopping for, and preparing nutritious meals.

3) Participate in case reviews, consulting with the team caring for the client, to evaluate the client's needs and plan for continuing services.

4) Care for individuals and families during periods of incapacitation, family disruption or convalescence, providing companionship, personal care and help in adjusting to new lifestyles.

5) Administer bedside and personal care, such as ambulation and personal hygiene assistance

6) Perform health-care related tasks, such as monitoring vital signs and medication, under the direction of registered nurses and physiotherapists.

7) Transport clients to locations outside the home, such as to physicians' offices or on outings, using a motor vehicle.

8) Instruct and advise clients on issues such as household cleanliness, utilities, hygiene,

nutrition and infant care.

9) Provide clients with communication assistance, typing their correspondence and obtaining information for them.

10) Train family members to provide bedside care.

Knowledge	Knowledge Definitions
Customer and Personal Service	Knowledge of principles and processes for providing customer and personal services. This includes customer needs assessment, meeting quality standards for services, and evaluation of customer satisfaction.
English Language	Knowledge of the structure and content of the English language including the meaning and spelling of words, rules of composition, and grammar.
Medicine and Dentistry	Knowledge of the information and techniques needed to diagnose and treat human injuries, diseases, and deformities. This includes symptoms, treatment alternatives, drug properties and interactions, and preventive health-care measures.
Psychology	Knowledge of human behavior and performance; individual differences in ability, personality, and interests; learning and motivation; psychological research methods; and the assessment and treatment of behavioral and affective disorders.
Therapy and Counseling	Knowledge of principles, methods, and procedures for diagnosis, treatment, and rehabilitation of physical and mental dysfunctions, and for career counseling and guidance.
Education and Training	Knowledge of principles and methods for curriculum and training design, teaching and instruction for individuals and groups, and the measurement of training effects.
Communications and Media	Knowledge of media production, communication, and dissemination techniques and methods. This includes alternative ways to inform and entertain via written, oral, and visual media.
Sociology and Anthropology	Knowledge of group behavior and dynamics, societal trends and influences, human migrations, ethnicity, cultures and their history and origins.
Transportation	Knowledge of principles and methods for moving people or goods by air, rail, sea, or road, including the relative costs and benefits.
Mathematics	Knowledge of arithmetic, algebra, geometry, calculus, statistics, and their applications.
Public Safety and Security	Knowledge of relevant equipment, policies, procedures, and strategies to promote effective local, state, or national security operations for the protection of people, data, property, and institutions.
Telecommunications	Knowledge of transmission, broadcasting, switching, control, and operation of telecommunications systems.
Chemistry	Knowledge of the chemical composition, structure, and properties of substances and of the chemical processes and transformations that they undergo. This includes uses of chemicals and their interactions, danger signs, production techniques, and disposal methods.
Biology	Knowledge of plant and animal organisms, their tissues, cells, functions, interdependencies, and interactions with each other and the environment.
Philosophy and Theology	Knowledge of different philosophical systems and religions. This includes their basic principles, values, ethics, ways of thinking, customs, practices, and their impact on human culture.
History and Archeology	Knowledge of historical events and their causes, indicators, and effects on civilizations and cultures.
Law and Government	Knowledge of laws, legal codes, court procedures, precedents, government regulations, executive orders, agency rules, and the democratic political process.
Foreign Language	Knowledge of the structure and content of a foreign (non-English) language including the meaning and spelling of words, rules of composition and grammar, and pronunciation.
Geography	Knowledge of principles and methods for describing the features of land, sea, and air masses, including their physical characteristics, locations, interrelationships, and distribution of plant, animal, and human life.
Clerical	Knowledge of administrative and clerical procedures and systems such as word processing, managing files and records, stenography and transcription, designing forms, and other office procedures and terminology.
Administration and Management	Knowledge of business and management principles involved in strategic planning, resource allocation, human resources modeling, leadership technique, production methods, and coordination of people and resources.

Food Production	Knowledge of techniques and equipment for planting, growing, and harvesting food products (both plant and animal) for consumption, including storage/handling techniques.
Economics and Accounting	Knowledge of economic and accounting principles and practices, the financial markets, banking and the analysis and reporting of financial data.
Personnel and Human Resources	Knowledge of principles and procedures for personnel recruitment, selection, training, compensation and benefits, labor relations and negotiation, and personnel information systems.
Sales and Marketing	Knowledge of principles and methods for showing, promoting, and selling products or services. This includes marketing strategy and tactics, product demonstration, sales techniques, and sales control systems.
Mechanical	Knowledge of machines and tools, including their designs, uses, repair, and maintenance.
Computers and Electronics	Knowledge of circuit boards, processors, chips, electronic equipment, and computer hardware and software, including applications and programming.
Fine Arts	Knowledge of the theory and techniques required to compose, produce, and perform works of music, dance, visual arts, drama, and sculpture.
Production and Processing	Knowledge of raw materials, production processes, quality control, costs, and other techniques for maximizing the effective manufacture and distribution of goods.
Physics	Knowledge and prediction of physical principles, laws, their interrelationships, and applications to understanding fluid, material, and atmospheric dynamics, and mechanical, electrical, atomic and sub- atomic structures and processes.
Engineering and Technology	Knowledge of the practical application of engineering science and technology. This includes applying principles, techniques, procedures, and equipment to the design and production of various goods and services.
Design	Knowledge of design techniques, tools, and principles involved in production of precision technical plans, blueprints, drawings, and models.
Building and Construction	Knowledge of materials, methods, and the tools involved in the construction or repair of houses, buildings, or other structures such as highways and roads.

Skills	**Skills Definitions**
Social Perceptiveness	Being aware of others' reactions and understanding why they react as they do.
Active Listening	Giving full attention to what other people are saying, taking time to understand the points being made, asking questions as appropriate, and not interrupting at inappropriate times.
Coordination	Adjusting actions in relation to others' actions.
Service Orientation	Actively looking for ways to help people.
Time Management	Managing one's own time and the time of others.
Monitoring	Monitoring/Assessing performance of yourself, other individuals, or organizations to make improvements or take corrective action.
Speaking	Talking to others to convey information effectively.
Critical Thinking	Using logic and reasoning to identify the strengths and weaknesses of alternative solutions, conclusions or approaches to problems.
Reading Comprehension	Understanding written sentences and paragraphs in work related documents.
Learning Strategies	Selecting and using training/instructional methods and procedures appropriate for the situation when learning or teaching new things.
Active Learning	Understanding the implications of new information for both current and future problem-solving and decision-making.
Writing	Communicating effectively in writing as appropriate for the needs of the audience.
Persuasion	Persuading others to change their minds or behavior.
Instructing	Teaching others how to do something.
Equipment Selection	Determining the kind of tools and equipment needed to do a job.
Management of Personnel Resources	Motivating, developing, and directing people as they work, identifying the best people for the job.
Complex Problem Solving	Identifying complex problems and reviewing related information to develop and evaluate options and implement solutions.
Judgment and Decision Making	Considering the relative costs and benefits of potential actions to choose the most appropriate one.

Management of Material Resources	Obtaining and seeing to the appropriate use of equipment, facilities, and materials needed to do certain work.
Negotiation	Bringing others together and trying to reconcile differences.
Technology Design	Generating or adapting equipment and technology to serve user needs.
Troubleshooting	Determining causes of operating errors and deciding what to do about it.
Equipment Maintenance	Performing routine maintenance on equipment and determining when and what kind of maintenance is needed.
Operation Monitoring	Watching gauges, dials, or other indicators to make sure a machine is working properly.
Operation and Control	Controlling operations of equipment or systems.
Management of Financial Resources	Determining how money will be spent to get the work done, and accounting for these expenditures.
Mathematics	Using mathematics to solve problems.
Operations Analysis	Analyzing needs and product requirements to create a design.
Quality Control Analysis	Conducting tests and inspections of products, services, or processes to evaluate quality or performance.
Science	Using scientific rules and methods to solve problems.
Repairing	Repairing machines or systems using the needed tools.
Systems Evaluation	Identifying measures or indicators of system performance and the actions needed to improve or correct performance, relative to the goals of the system.
Installation	Installing equipment, machines, wiring, or programs to meet specifications.
Systems Analysis	Determining how a system should work and how changes in conditions, operations, and the environment will affect outcomes.
Programming	Writing computer programs for various purposes.

Ability	**Ability Definitions**
Speech Clarity	The ability to speak clearly so others can understand you.
Problem Sensitivity	The ability to tell when something is wrong or is likely to go wrong. It does not involve solving the problem, only recognizing there is a problem.
Oral Comprehension	The ability to listen to and understand information and ideas presented through spoken words and sentences.
Oral Expression	The ability to communicate information and ideas in speaking so others will understand.
Speech Recognition	The ability to identify and understand the speech of another person.
Written Comprehension	The ability to read and understand information and ideas presented in writing.
Written Expression	The ability to communicate information and ideas in writing so others will understand.
Deductive Reasoning	The ability to apply general rules to specific problems to produce answers that make sense.
Information Ordering	The ability to arrange things or actions in a certain order or pattern according to a specific rule or set of rules (e.g., patterns of numbers, letters, words, pictures, mathematical operations).
Near Vision	The ability to see details at close range (within a few feet of the observer).
Inductive Reasoning	The ability to combine pieces of information to form general rules or conclusions (includes finding a relationship among seemingly unrelated events).
Multilimb Coordination	The ability to coordinate two or more limbs (for example, two arms, two legs, or one leg and one arm) while sitting, standing, or lying down. It does not involve performing the activities while the whole body is in motion.
Trunk Strength	The ability to use your abdominal and lower back muscles to support part of the body repeatedly or continuously over time without 'giving out' or fatiguing.
Flexibility of Closure	The ability to identify or detect a known pattern (a figure, object, word, or sound) that is hidden in other distracting material.
Static Strength	The ability to exert maximum muscle force to lift, push, pull, or carry objects.
Category Flexibility	The ability to generate or use different sets of rules for combining or grouping things in different ways.
Finger Dexterity	The ability to make precisely coordinated movements of the fingers of one or both hands to grasp, manipulate, or assemble very small objects.
Far Vision	The ability to see details at a distance.
Selective Attention	The ability to concentrate on a task over a period of time without being distracted.
Stamina	The ability to exert yourself physically over long periods of time without getting winded or out of breath.

Depth Perception	The ability to judge which of several objects is closer or farther away from you, or to judge the distance between you and an object.
Control Precision	The ability to quickly and repeatedly adjust the controls of a machine or a vehicle to exact positions.
Arm-Hand Steadiness	The ability to keep your hand and arm steady while moving your arm or while holding your arm and hand in one position.
Time Sharing	The ability to shift back and forth between two or more activities or sources of information (such as speech, sounds, touch, or other sources).
Speed of Closure	The ability to quickly make sense of, combine, and organize information into meaningful patterns.
Extent Flexibility	The ability to bend, stretch, twist, or reach with your body, arms, and/or legs.
Visual Color Discrimination	The ability to match or detect differences between colors, including shades of color and brightness.
Perceptual Speed	The ability to quickly and accurately compare similarities and differences among sets of letters, numbers, objects, pictures, or patterns. The things to be compared may be presented at the same time or one after the other. This ability also includes comparing a presented object with a remembered object.
Fluency of Ideas	The ability to come up with a number of ideas about a topic (the number of ideas is important, not their quality, correctness, or creativity).
Gross Body Coordination	The ability to coordinate the movement of your arms, legs, and torso together when the whole body is in motion.
Dynamic Strength	The ability to exert muscle force repeatedly or continuously over time. This involves muscular endurance and resistance to muscle fatigue.
Hearing Sensitivity	The ability to detect or tell the differences between sounds that vary in pitch and loudness.
Memorization	The ability to remember information such as words, numbers, pictures, and procedures.
Originality	The ability to come up with unusual or clever ideas about a given topic or situation, or to develop creative ways to solve a problem.
Visualization	The ability to imagine how something will look after it is moved around or when its parts are moved or rearranged.
Auditory Attention	The ability to focus on a single source of sound in the presence of other distracting sounds.
Gross Body Equilibrium	The ability to keep or regain your body balance or stay upright when in an unstable position.
Number Facility	The ability to add, subtract, multiply, or divide quickly and correctly.
Reaction Time	The ability to quickly respond (with the hand, finger, or foot) to a signal (sound, light, picture) when it appears.
Manual Dexterity	The ability to quickly move your hand, your hand together with your arm, or your two hands to grasp, manipulate, or assemble objects.
Response Orientation	The ability to choose quickly between two or more movements in response to two or more different signals (lights, sounds, pictures). It includes the speed with which the correct response is started with the hand, foot, or other body part.
Speed of Limb Movement	The ability to quickly move the arms and legs.
Spatial Orientation	The ability to know your location in relation to the environment or to know where other objects are in relation to you.
Mathematical Reasoning	The ability to choose the right mathematical methods or formulas to solve a problem.
Glare Sensitivity	The ability to see objects in the presence of glare or bright lighting.
Night Vision	The ability to see under low light conditions.
Peripheral Vision	The ability to see objects or movement of objects to one's side when the eyes are looking ahead.
Sound Localization	The ability to tell the direction from which a sound originated.
Wrist-Finger Speed	The ability to make fast, simple, repeated movements of the fingers, hands, and wrists.
Explosive Strength	The ability to use short bursts of muscle force to propel oneself (as in jumping or sprinting), or to throw an object.
Dynamic Flexibility	The ability to quickly and repeatedly bend, stretch, twist, or reach out with your body, arms, and/or legs.
Rate Control	The ability to time your movements or the movement of a piece of equipment in anticipation of changes in the speed and/or direction of a moving object or scene.

Work_Activity	Work_Activity Definitions
Assisting and Caring for Others	Providing personal assistance, medical attention, emotional support, or other personal care to others such as coworkers, customers, or patients.
Establishing and Maintaining Interpersonal Relatio	Developing constructive and cooperative working relationships with others, and maintaining them over time.
Making Decisions and Solving Problems	Analyzing information and evaluating results to choose the best solution and solve problems.
Getting Information	Observing, receiving, and otherwise obtaining information from all relevant sources.
Identifying Objects, Actions, and Events	Identifying information by categorizing, estimating, recognizing differences or similarities, and detecting changes in circumstances or events.
Communicating with Supervisors, Peers, or Subordin	Providing information to supervisors, co-workers, and subordinates by telephone, in written form, e-mail, or in person.
Monitor Processes, Materials, or Surroundings	Monitoring and reviewing information from materials, events, or the environment, to detect or assess problems.
Documenting/Recording Information	Entering, transcribing, recording, storing, or maintaining information in written or electronic/magnetic form.
Performing General Physical Activities	Performing physical activities that require considerable use of your arms and legs and moving your whole body, such as climbing, lifting, balancing, walking, stooping, and handling of materials.
Organizing, Planning, and Prioritizing Work	Developing specific goals and plans to prioritize, organize, and accomplish your work.
Performing for or Working Directly with the Public	Performing for people or dealing directly with the public. This includes serving customers in restaurants and stores, and receiving clients or guests.
Developing and Building Teams	Encouraging and building mutual trust, respect, and cooperation among team members.
Resolving Conflicts and Negotiating with Others	Handling complaints, settling disputes, and resolving grievances and conflicts, or otherwise negotiating with others.
Updating and Using Relevant Knowledge	Keeping up-to-date technically and applying new knowledge to your job.
Scheduling Work and Activities	Scheduling events, programs, and activities, as well as the work of others.
Communicating with Persons Outside Organization	Communicating with people outside the organization, representing the organization to customers, the public, government, and other external sources. This information can be exchanged in person, in writing, or by telephone or e-mail.
Processing Information	Compiling, coding, categorizing, calculating, tabulating, auditing, or verifying information or data.
Evaluating Information to Determine Compliance wit	Using relevant information and individual judgment to determine whether events or processes comply with laws, regulations, or standards.
Handling and Moving Objects	Using hands and arms in handling, installing, positioning, and moving materials, and manipulating things.
Inspecting Equipment, Structures, or Material	Inspecting equipment, structures, or materials to identify the cause of errors or other problems or defects.
Coaching and Developing Others	Identifying the developmental needs of others and coaching, mentoring, or otherwise helping others to improve their knowledge or skills.
Thinking Creatively	Developing, designing, or creating new applications, ideas, relationships, systems, or products, including artistic contributions.
Judging the Qualities of Things, Services, or Peop	Assessing the value, importance, or quality of things or people.
Training and Teaching Others	Identifying the educational needs of others, developing formal educational or training programs or classes, and teaching or instructing others.
Estimating the Quantifiable Characteristics of Pro	Estimating sizes, distances, and quantities; or determining time, costs, resources, or materials needed to perform a work activity.
Interpreting the Meaning of Information for Others	Translating or explaining what information means and how it can be used.
Operating Vehicles, Mechanized Devices, or Equipme	Running, maneuvering, navigating, or driving vehicles or mechanized equipment, such as forklifts, passenger vehicles, aircraft, or water craft.
Coordinating the Work and Activities of Others	Getting members of a group to work together to accomplish tasks.
Developing Objectives and Strategies	Establishing long-range objectives and specifying the strategies and actions to achieve them.

Analyzing Data or Information	Identifying the underlying principles, reasons, or facts of information by breaking down information or data into separate parts.
Performing Administrative Activities	Performing day-to-day administrative tasks such as maintaining information files and processing paperwork.
Controlling Machines and Processes	Using either control mechanisms or direct physical activity to operate machines or processes (not including computers or vehicles).
Provide Consultation and Advice to Others	Providing guidance and expert advice to management or other groups on technical, systems-, or process-related topics.
Monitoring and Controlling Resources	Monitoring and controlling resources and overseeing the spending of money.
Drafting, Laying Out, and Specifying Technical Dev	Providing documentation, detailed instructions, drawings, or specifications to tell others about how devices, parts, equipment, or structures are to be fabricated, constructed, assembled, modified, maintained, or used.
Guiding, Directing, and Motivating Subordinates	Providing guidance and direction to subordinates, including setting performance standards and monitoring performance.
Staffing Organizational Units	Recruiting, interviewing, selecting, hiring, and promoting employees in an organization.
Interacting With Computers	Using computers and computer systems (including hardware and software) to program, write software, set up functions, enter data, or process information.
Selling or Influencing Others	Convincing others to buy merchandise/goods or to otherwise change their minds or actions.
Repairing and Maintaining Electronic Equipment	Servicing, repairing, calibrating, regulating, fine-tuning, or testing machines, devices, and equipment that operate primarily on the basis of electrical or electronic (not mechanical) principles.
Repairing and Maintaining Mechanical Equipment	Servicing, repairing, adjusting, and testing machines, devices, moving parts, and equipment that operate primarily on the basis of mechanical (not electronic) principles.

Work_Context	Work_Context Definitions
Physical Proximity	To what extent does this job require the worker to perform job tasks in close physical proximity to other people?
Face-to-Face Discussions	How often do you have to have face-to-face discussions with individuals or teams in this job?
Contact With Others	How much does this job require the worker to be in contact with others (face-to-face, by telephone, or otherwise) in order to perform it?
Structured versus Unstructured Work	To what extent is this job structured for the worker, rather than allowing the worker to determine tasks, priorities, and goals?
Telephone	How often do you have telephone conversations in this job?
Frequency of Decision Making	How frequently is the worker required to make decisions that affect other people, the financial resources, and/or the image and reputation of the organization?
Freedom to Make Decisions	How much decision making freedom, without supervision, does the job offer?
In an Enclosed Vehicle or Equipment	How often does this job require working in a closed vehicle or equipment (e.g., car)?
Work With Work Group or Team	How important is it to work with others in a group or team in this job?
Wear Common Protective or Safety Equipment such as	How much does this job require wearing common protective or safety equipment such as safety shoes, glasses, gloves, hard hats or life jackets?
Consequence of Error	How serious would the result usually be if the worker made a mistake that was not readily correctable?
Letters and Memos	How often does the job require written letters and memos?
Spend Time Standing	How much does this job require standing?
Impact of Decisions on Co-workers or Company Resul	How do the decisions an employee makes impact the results of co-workers, clients or the company?
Importance of Being Exact or Accurate	How important is being very exact or highly accurate in performing this job?
Exposed to Disease or Infections	How often does this job require exposure to disease/infections?
Frequency of Conflict Situations	How often are there conflict situations the employee has to face in this job?
Deal With Unpleasant or Angry People	How frequently does the worker have to deal with unpleasant, angry, or discourteous individuals as part of the job requirements?
Time Pressure	How often does this job require the worker to meet strict deadlines?
Coordinate or Lead Others	How important is it to coordinate or lead others in accomplishing work activities in this job?

Exposed to Minor Burns, Cuts, Bites, or Stings	How often does this job require exposure to minor burns, cuts, bites, or stings?
Deal With Physically Aggressive People	How frequently does this job require the worker to deal with physical aggression of violent individuals?
Indoors, Environmentally Controlled	How often does this job require working indoors in environmentally controlled conditions?
Deal With External Customers	How important is it to work with external customers or the public in this job?
Level of Competition	To what extent does this job require the worker to compete or to be aware of competitive pressures?
Spend Time Sitting	How much does this job require sitting?
Spend Time Walking and Running	How much does this job require walking and running?
Spend Time Bending or Twisting the Body	How much does this job require bending or twisting your body?
Spend Time Making Repetitive Motions	How much does this job require making repetitive motions?
Importance of Repeating Same Tasks	How important is repeating the same physical activities (e.g., key entry) or mental activities (e.g., checking entries in a ledger) over and over, without stopping, to performing this job?
Responsible for Others' Health and Safety	How much responsibility is there for the health and safety of others in this job?
Cramped Work Space, Awkward Positions	How often does this job require working in cramped work spaces that requires getting into awkward positions?
Spend Time Kneeling, Crouching, Stooping, or Crawl	How much does this job require kneeling, crouching, stooping or crawling?
Responsibility for Outcomes and Results	How responsible is the worker for work outcomes and results of other workers?
Very Hot or Cold Temperatures	How often does this job require working in very hot (above 90 F degrees) or very cold (below 32 F degrees) temperatures?
Exposed to Contaminants	How often does this job require working exposed to contaminants (such as pollutants, gases, dust or odors)?
Spend Time Using Your Hands to Handle, Control, or	How much does this job require using your hands to handle, control, or feel objects, tools or controls?
Degree of Automation	How automated is the job?
Extremely Bright or Inadequate Lighting	How often does this job require working in extremely bright or inadequate lighting conditions?
Sounds, Noise Levels Are Distracting or Uncomforta	How often does this job require working exposed to sounds and noise levels that are distracting or uncomfortable?
Indoors, Not Environmentally Controlled	How often does this job require working indoors in non-controlled environmental conditions (e.g., warehouse without heat)?
Outdoors, Exposed to Weather	How often does this job require working outdoors, exposed to all weather conditions?
Spend Time Keeping or Regaining Balance	How much does this job require keeping or regaining your balance?
Public Speaking	How often do you have to perform public speaking in this job?
In an Open Vehicle or Equipment	How often does this job require working in an open vehicle or equipment (e.g., tractor)?
Wear Specialized Protective or Safety Equipment su	How much does this job require wearing specialized protective or safety equipment such as breathing apparatus, safety harness, full protection suits, or radiation protection?
Outdoors, Under Cover	How often does this job require working outdoors, under cover (e.g., structure with roof but no walls)?
Pace Determined by Speed of Equipment	How important is it to this job that the pace is determined by the speed of equipment or machinery? (This does not refer to keeping busy at all times on this job.)
Exposed to High Places	How often does this job require exposure to high places?
Electronic Mail	How often do you use electronic mail in this job?
Spend Time Climbing Ladders, Scaffolds, or Poles	How much does this job require climbing ladders, scaffolds, or poles?
Exposed to Hazardous Conditions	How often does this job require exposure to hazardous conditions?
Exposed to Whole Body Vibration	How often does this job require exposure to whole body vibration (e.g., operate a jackhammer)?
Exposed to Hazardous Equipment	How often does this job require exposure to hazardous equipment?
Exposed to Radiation	How often does this job require exposure to radiation?

Job Zone Component	Job Zone Component Definitions
Title	Job Zone Two: Some Preparation Needed

Overall Experience	Some previous work-related skill, knowledge, or experience may be helpful in these occupations, but usually is not needed. For example, a drywall installer might benefit from experience installing drywall, but an inexperienced person could still learn to be an installer with little difficulty.
Job Training	Employees in these occupations need anywhere from a few months to one year of working with experienced employees. These occupations often involve using your knowledge and skills to help others. Examples include drywall installers, fire inspectors, flight attendants, pharmacy technicians, salespersons (retail), and tellers.
Job Zone Examples	
SVP Range	(4.0 to < 6.0)
Education	These occupations usually require a high school diploma and may require some vocational training or job-related course work. In some cases, an associate's or bachelor's degree could be needed.

Work_Styles	Work_Styles Definitions
Concern for Others	Job requires being sensitive to others' needs and feelings and being understanding and helpful on the job.
Self Control	Job requires maintaining composure, keeping emotions in check, controlling anger, and avoiding aggressive behavior, even in very difficult situations.
Integrity	Job requires being honest and ethical.
Dependability	Job requires being reliable, responsible, and dependable, and fulfilling obligations.
Cooperation	Job requires being pleasant with others on the job and displaying a good-natured, cooperative attitude.
Stress Tolerance	Job requires accepting criticism and dealing calmly and effectively with high stress situations.
Attention to Detail	Job requires being careful about detail and thorough in completing work tasks.
Adaptability/Flexibility	Job requires being open to change (positive or negative) and to considerable variety in the workplace.
Independence	Job requires developing one's own ways of doing things, guiding oneself with little or no supervision, and depending on oneself to get things done.
Social Orientation	Job requires preferring to work with others rather than alone, and being personally connected with others on the job.
Initiative	Job requires a willingness to take on responsibilities and challenges.
Persistence	Job requires persistence in the face of obstacles.
Analytical Thinking	Job requires analyzing information and using logic to address work-related issues and problems.
Leadership	Job requires a willingness to lead, take charge, and offer opinions and direction.
Achievement/Effort	Job requires establishing and maintaining personally challenging achievement goals and exerting effort toward mastering tasks.
Innovation	Job requires creativity and alternative thinking to develop new ideas for and answers to work-related problems.

39-9031.00 - Fitness Trainers and Aerobics Instructors

Instruct or coach groups or individuals in exercise activities and the fundamentals of sports. Demonstrate techniques and methods of participation. Observe participants and inform them of corrective measures necessary to improve their skills. Those required to hold teaching degrees should be reported in the appropriate teaching category.

Tasks

1) Instruct participants in maintaining exertion levels in order to maximize benefits from exercise routines.

2) Observe participants and inform them of corrective measures necessary for skill improvement.

3) Monitor participants' progress and adapt programs as needed.

4) Teach proper breathing techniques used during physical exertion.

5) Advise clients about proper clothing and shoes.

6) Offer alternatives during classes to accommodate different levels of fitness.

7) Evaluate individuals' abilities, needs, and physical conditions, and develop suitable

training programs to meet any special requirements.

8) Conduct therapeutic, recreational, or athletic activities.

9) Provide students with information and resources regarding nutrition, weight control, and lifestyle issues.

10) Administer emergency first aid, wrap injuries, treat minor chronic disabilities, or refer injured persons to physicians.

11) Plan routines, choose appropriate music, and choose different movements for each set of muscles, depending on participants' capabilities and limitations.

12) Teach and demonstrate use of gymnastic and training equipment such as trampolines and weights.

13) Plan physical education programs to promote development of participants' physical attributes and social skills.

14) Maintain fitness equipment.

15) Promote health clubs through membership sales and record member information.

16) Maintain equipment inventories; and select, store, and issue equipment as needed.

17) Teach individual and team sports to participants through instruction and demonstration, utilizing knowledge of sports techniques and of participants' physical capabilities.

18) Organize and conduct competitions and tournaments.

19) Massage body parts to relieve soreness, strains, and bruises.

20) Advise participants in use of heat or ultraviolet treatments and hot baths.

21) Organize, lead, and referee indoor and outdoor games such as volleyball, baseball, and basketball.

22) Wrap ankles, fingers, wrists, or other body parts with synthetic skin, gauze, or adhesive tape, in order to support muscles and ligaments.

Knowledge	Knowledge Definitions
Customer and Personal Service	Knowledge of principles and processes for providing customer and personal services. This includes customer needs assessment, meeting quality standards for services, and evaluation of customer satisfaction.
Education and Training	Knowledge of principles and methods for curriculum and training design, teaching and instruction for individuals and groups, and the measurement of training effects.
Psychology	Knowledge of human behavior and performance; individual differences in ability, personality, and interests; learning and motivation; psychological research methods; and the assessment and treatment of behavioral and affective disorders.
English Language	Knowledge of the structure and content of the English language including the meaning and spelling of words, rules of composition, and grammar.
Sales and Marketing	Knowledge of principles and methods for showing, promoting, and selling products or services. This includes marketing strategy and tactics, product demonstration, sales techniques, and sales control systems.
Sociology and Anthropology	Knowledge of group behavior and dynamics, societal trends and influences, human migrations, ethnicity, cultures and their history and origins.
Administration and Management	Knowledge of business and management principles involved in strategic planning, resource allocation, human resources modeling, leadership technique, production methods, and coordination of people and resources.
Personnel and Human Resources	Knowledge of principles and procedures for personnel recruitment, selection, training, compensation and benefits, labor relations and negotiation, and personnel information systems.
Clerical	Knowledge of administrative and clerical procedures and systems such as word processing, managing files and records, stenography and transcription, designing forms, and other office procedures and terminology.
Mathematics	Knowledge of arithmetic, algebra, geometry, calculus, statistics, and their applications.
Fine Arts	Knowledge of the theory and techniques required to compose, produce, and perform works of music, dance, visual arts, drama, and sculpture.
Medicine and Dentistry	Knowledge of the information and techniques needed to diagnose and treat human injuries, diseases, and deformities. This includes symptoms, treatment alternatives, drug properties and interactions, and preventive health-care measures.

Communications and Media	Knowledge of media production, communication, and dissemination techniques and methods. This includes alternative ways to inform and entertain via written, oral, and visual media.
Public Safety and Security	Knowledge of relevant equipment, policies, procedures, and strategies to promote effective local, state, or national security operations for the protection of people, data, property, and institutions.
Therapy and Counseling	Knowledge of principles, methods, and procedures for diagnosis, treatment, and rehabilitation of physical and mental dysfunctions, and for career counseling and guidance.
Biology	Knowledge of plant and animal organisms, their tissues, cells, functions, interdependencies, and interactions with each other and the environment.
Chemistry	Knowledge of the chemical composition, structure, and properties of substances and of the chemical processes and transformations that they undergo. This includes uses of chemicals and their interactions, danger signs, production techniques, and disposal methods.
Computers and Electronics	Knowledge of circuit boards, processors, chips, electronic equipment, and computer hardware and software, including applications and programming.
Law and Government	Knowledge of laws, legal codes, court procedures, precedents, government regulations, executive orders, agency rules, and the democratic political process.
Economics and Accounting	Knowledge of economic and accounting principles and practices, the financial markets, banking and the analysis and reporting of financial data.
Mechanical	Knowledge of machines and tools, including their designs, uses, repair, and maintenance.
Transportation	Knowledge of principles and methods for moving people or goods by air, rail, sea, or road, including the relative costs and benefits.
Telecommunications	Knowledge of transmission, broadcasting, switching, control, and operation of telecommunications systems.
Physics	Knowledge and prediction of physical principles, laws, their interrelationships, and applications to understanding fluid, material, and atmospheric dynamics, and mechanical, electrical, atomic and sub- atomic structures and processes.
Engineering and Technology	Knowledge of the practical application of engineering science and technology. This includes applying principles, techniques, procedures, and equipment to the design and production of various goods and services.
Foreign Language	Knowledge of the structure and content of a foreign (non-English) language including the meaning and spelling of words, rules of composition and grammar, and pronunciation.
Design	Knowledge of design techniques, tools, and principles involved in production of precision technical plans, blueprints, drawings, and models.
Production and Processing	Knowledge of raw materials, production processes, quality control, costs, and other techniques for maximizing the effective manufacture and distribution of goods.
Food Production	Knowledge of techniques and equipment for planting, growing, and harvesting food products (both plant and animal) for consumption, including storage/handling techniques.
Geography	Knowledge of principles and methods for describing the features of land, sea, and air masses, including their physical characteristics, locations, interrelationships, and distribution of plant, animal, and human life.
Philosophy and Theology	Knowledge of different philosophical systems and religions. This includes their basic principles, values, ethics, ways of thinking, customs, practices, and their impact on human culture.
History and Archeology	Knowledge of historical events and their causes, indicators, and effects on civilizations and cultures.
Building and Construction	Knowledge of materials, methods, and the tools involved in the construction or repair of houses, buildings, or other structures such as highways and roads.

Skills	**Skills Definitions**
Instructing	Teaching others how to do something.
Speaking	Talking to others to convey information effectively.
Coordination	Adjusting actions in relation to others' actions.
Monitoring	Monitoring/Assessing performance of yourself, other individuals, or organizations to make improvements or take corrective action.

Learning Strategies	Selecting and using training/instructional methods and procedures appropriate for the situation when learning or teaching new things.
Time Management	Managing one's own time and the time of others.
Service Orientation	Actively looking for ways to help people.
Active Learning	Understanding the implications of new information for both current and future problem-solving and decision-making.
Equipment Selection	Determining the kind of tools and equipment needed to do a job.
Social Perceptiveness	Being aware of others' reactions and understanding why they react as they do.
Active Listening	Giving full attention to what other people are saying, taking time to understand the points being made, asking questions as appropriate, and not interrupting at inappropriate times.
Complex Problem Solving	Identifying complex problems and reviewing related information to develop and evaluate options and implement solutions.
Critical Thinking	Using logic and reasoning to identify the strengths and weaknesses of alternative solutions, conclusions or approaches to problems.
Judgment and Decision Making	Considering the relative costs and benefits of potential actions to choose the most appropriate one.
Troubleshooting	Determining causes of operating errors and deciding what to do about it.
Technology Design	Generating or adapting equipment and technology to serve user needs.
Equipment Maintenance	Performing routine maintenance on equipment and determining when and what kind of maintenance is needed.
Science	Using scientific rules and methods to solve problems.
Reading Comprehension	Understanding written sentences and paragraphs in work related documents.
Negotiation	Bringing others together and trying to reconcile differences.
Persuasion	Persuading others to change their minds or behavior.
Operations Analysis	Analyzing needs and product requirements to create a design.
Management of Material Resources	Obtaining and seeing to the appropriate use of equipment, facilities, and materials needed to do certain work.
Installation	Installing equipment, machines, wiring, or programs to meet specifications.
Writing	Communicating effectively in writing as appropriate for the needs of the audience.
Management of Financial Resources	Determining how money will be spent to get the work done, and accounting for these expenditures.
Mathematics	Using mathematics to solve problems.
Systems Evaluation	Identifying measures or indicators of system performance and the actions needed to improve or correct performance, relative to the goals of the system.
Repairing	Repairing machines or systems using the needed tools.
Operation Monitoring	Watching gauges, dials, or other indicators to make sure a machine is working properly.
Operation and Control	Controlling operations of equipment or systems.
Management of Personnel Resources	Motivating, developing, and directing people as they work, identifying the best people for the job.
Systems Analysis	Determining how a system should work and how changes in conditions, operations, and the environment will affect outcomes.
Quality Control Analysis	Conducting tests and inspections of products, services, or processes to evaluate quality or performance.
Programming	Writing computer programs for various purposes.

Ability	**Ability Definitions**
Oral Expression	The ability to communicate information and ideas in speaking so others will understand.
Stamina	The ability to exert yourself physically over long periods of time without getting winded or out of breath.
Gross Body Coordination	The ability to coordinate the movement of your arms, legs, and torso together when the whole body is in motion.
Static Strength	The ability to exert maximum muscle force to lift, push, pull, or carry objects.
Oral Comprehension	The ability to listen to and understand information and ideas presented through spoken words and sentences.
Trunk Strength	The ability to use your abdominal and lower back muscles to support part of the body repeatedly or continuously over time without 'giving out' or fatiguing.
Dynamic Strength	The ability to exert muscle force repeatedly or continuously over time. This involves muscular endurance and resistance to muscle fatigue.
Speech Clarity	The ability to speak clearly so others can understand you.

Problem Sensitivity	The ability to tell when something is wrong or is likely to go wrong. It does not involve solving the problem, only recognizing there is a problem.
Deductive Reasoning	The ability to apply general rules to specific problems to produce answers that make sense.
Speech Recognition	The ability to identify and understand the speech of another person.
Information Ordering	The ability to arrange things or actions in a certain order or pattern according to a specific rule or set of rules (e.g., patterns of numbers, letters, words, pictures, mathematical operations).
Extent Flexibility	The ability to bend, stretch, twist, or reach with your body, arms, and/or legs.
Multilimb Coordination	The ability to coordinate two or more limbs (for example, two arms, two legs, or one leg and one arm) while sitting, standing, or lying down. It does not involve performing the activities while the whole body is in motion.
Originality	The ability to come up with unusual or clever ideas about a given topic or situation, or to develop creative ways to solve a problem.
Near Vision	The ability to see details at close range (within a few feet of the observer).
Speed of Limb Movement	The ability to quickly move the arms and legs.
Fluency of Ideas	The ability to come up with a number of ideas about a topic (the number of ideas is important, not their quality, correctness, or creativity).
Inductive Reasoning	The ability to combine pieces of information to form general rules or conclusions (includes finding a relationship among seemingly unrelated events).
Gross Body Equilibrium	The ability to keep or regain your body balance or stay upright when in an unstable position.
Dynamic Flexibility	The ability to quickly and repeatedly bend, stretch, twist, or reach out with your body, arms, and/or legs.
Written Expression	The ability to communicate information and ideas in writing so others will understand.
Far Vision	The ability to see details at a distance.
Category Flexibility	The ability to generate or use different sets of rules for combining or grouping things in different ways.
Written Comprehension	The ability to read and understand information and ideas presented in writing.
Selective Attention	The ability to concentrate on a task over a period of time without being distracted.
Arm-Hand Steadiness	The ability to keep your hand and arm steady while moving your arm or while holding your arm and hand in one position.
Manual Dexterity	The ability to quickly move your hand, your hand together with your arm, or your two hands to grasp, manipulate, or assemble objects.
Memorization	The ability to remember information such as words, numbers, pictures, and procedures.
Time Sharing	The ability to shift back and forth between two or more activities or sources of information (such as speech, sounds, touch, or other sources).
Finger Dexterity	The ability to make precisely coordinated movements of the fingers of one or both hands to grasp, manipulate, or assemble very small objects.
Visualization	The ability to imagine how something will look after it is moved around or when its parts are moved or rearranged.
Visual Color Discrimination	The ability to match or detect differences between colors, including shades of color and brightness.
Depth Perception	The ability to judge which of several objects is closer or farther away from you, or to judge the distance between you and an object.
Perceptual Speed	The ability to quickly and accurately compare similarities and differences among sets of letters, numbers, objects, pictures, or patterns. The things to be compared may be presented at the same time or one after the other. This ability also includes comparing a presented object with a remembered object.
Flexibility of Closure	The ability to identify or detect a known pattern (a figure, object, word, or sound) that is hidden in other distracting material.
Explosive Strength	The ability to use short bursts of muscle force to propel oneself (as in jumping or sprinting), or to throw an object.
Speed of Closure	The ability to quickly make sense of, combine, and organize information into meaningful patterns.
Auditory Attention	The ability to focus on a single source of sound in the presence of other distracting sounds.
Control Precision	The ability to quickly and repeatedly adjust the controls of a machine or a vehicle to exact positions.

Response Orientation	The ability to choose quickly between two or more movements in response to two or more different signals (lights, sounds, pictures). It includes the speed with which the correct response is started with the hand, foot, or other body part.
Mathematical Reasoning	The ability to choose the right mathematical methods or formulas to solve a problem.
Peripheral Vision	The ability to see objects or movement of objects to one's side when the eyes are looking ahead.
Reaction Time	The ability to quickly respond (with the hand, finger, or foot) to a signal (sound, light, picture) when it appears.
Number Facility	The ability to add, subtract, multiply, or divide quickly and correctly.
Wrist-Finger Speed	The ability to make fast, simple, repeated movements of the fingers, hands, and wrists.
Rate Control	The ability to time your movements or the movement of a piece of equipment in anticipation of changes in the speed and/or direction of a moving object or scene.
Spatial Orientation	The ability to know your location in relation to the environment or to know where other objects are in relation to you.
Hearing Sensitivity	The ability to detect or tell the differences between sounds that vary in pitch and loudness.
Night Vision	The ability to see under low light conditions.
Sound Localization	The ability to tell the direction from which a sound originated.
Glare Sensitivity	The ability to see objects in the presence of glare or bright lighting.

Work_Activity	Work_Activity Definitions
Performing for or Working Directly with the Public	Performing for people or dealing directly with the public. This includes serving customers in restaurants and stores, and receiving clients or guests.
Performing General Physical Activities	Performing physical activities that require considerable use of your arms and legs and moving your whole body, such as climbing, lifting, balancing, walking, stooping, and handling of materials.
Establishing and Maintaining Interpersonal Relatio	Developing constructive and cooperative working relationships with others, and maintaining them over time.
Coaching and Developing Others	Identifying the developmental needs of others and coaching, mentoring, or otherwise helping others to improve their knowledge or skills.
Assisting and Caring for Others	Providing personal assistance, medical attention, emotional support, or other personal care to others such as coworkers, customers, or patients.
Monitor Processes, Materials, or Surroundings	Monitoring and reviewing information from materials, events, or the environment, to detect or assess problems.
Communicating with Supervisors, Peers, or Subordin	Providing information to supervisors, co-workers, and subordinates by telephone, in written form, e-mail, or in person.
Updating and Using Relevant Knowledge	Keeping up-to-date technically and applying new knowledge to your job.
Getting Information	Observing, receiving, and otherwise obtaining information from all relevant sources.
Handling and Moving Objects	Using hands and arms in handling, installing, positioning, and moving materials, and manipulating things.
Making Decisions and Solving Problems	Analyzing information and evaluating results to choose the best solution and solve problems.
Inspecting Equipment, Structures, or Material	Inspecting equipment, structures, or materials to identify the cause of errors or other problems or defects.
Identifying Objects, Actions, and Events	Identifying information by categorizing, estimating, recognizing differences or similarities, and detecting changes in circumstances or events.
Training and Teaching Others	Identifying the educational needs of others, developing formal educational or training programs or classes, and teaching or instructing others.
Thinking Creatively	Developing, designing, or creating new applications, ideas, relationships, systems, or products, including artistic contributions.
Communicating with Persons Outside Organization	Communicating with people outside the organization, representing the organization to customers, the public, government, and other external sources. This information can be exchanged in person, in writing, or by telephone or e-mail.
Interpreting the Meaning of Information for Others	Translating or explaining what information means and how it can be used.
Documenting/Recording Information	Entering, transcribing, recording, storing, or maintaining information in written or electronic/magnetic form.

819

Judging the Qualities of Things, Services, or Peop	Assessing the value, importance, or quality of things or people.
Developing and Building Teams	Encouraging and building mutual trust, respect, and cooperation among team members.
Coordinating the Work and Activities of Others	Getting members of a group to work together to accomplish tasks.
Provide Consultation and Advice to Others	Providing guidance and expert advice to management or other groups on technical, systems-, or process-related topics.
Guiding, Directing, and Motivating Subordinates	Providing guidance and direction to subordinates, including setting performance standards and monitoring performance.
Processing Information	Compiling, coding, categorizing, calculating, tabulating, auditing, or verifying information or data.
Organizing, Planning, and Prioritizing Work	Developing specific goals and plans to prioritize, organize, and accomplish your work.
Interacting With Computers	Using computers and computer systems (including hardware and software) to program, write software, set up functions, enter data, or process information.
Resolving Conflicts and Negotiating with Others	Handling complaints, settling disputes, and resolving grievances and conflicts, or otherwise negotiating with others.
Evaluating Information to Determine Compliance wit	Using relevant information and individual judgment to determine whether events or processes comply with laws, regulations, or standards.
Controlling Machines and Processes	Using either control mechanisms or direct physical activity to operate machines or processes (not including computers or vehicles).
Performing Administrative Activities	Performing day-to-day administrative tasks such as maintaining information files and processing paperwork.
Developing Objectives and Strategies	Establishing long-range objectives and specifying the strategies and actions to achieve them.
Scheduling Work and Activities	Scheduling events, programs, and activities, as well as the work of others.
Analyzing Data or Information	Identifying the underlying principles, reasons, or facts of information by breaking down information or data into separate parts.
Estimating the Quantifiable Characteristics of Pro	Estimating sizes, distances, and quantities; or determining time, costs, resources, or materials needed to perform a work activity.
Selling or Influencing Others	Convincing others to buy merchandise/goods or to otherwise change their minds or actions.
Monitoring and Controlling Resources	Monitoring and controlling resources and overseeing the spending of money.
Operating Vehicles, Mechanized Devices, or Equipme	Running, maneuvering, navigating, or driving vehicles or mechanized equipment, such as forklifts, passenger vehicles, aircraft, or water craft.
Staffing Organizational Units	Recruiting, interviewing, selecting, hiring, and promoting employees in an organization.
Repairing and Maintaining Mechanical Equipment	Servicing, repairing, adjusting, and testing machines, devices, moving parts, and equipment that operate primarily on the basis of mechanical (not electronic) principles.
Drafting, Laying Out, and Specifying Technical Dev	Providing documentation, detailed instructions, drawings, or specifications to tell others about how devices, parts, equipment, or structures are to be fabricated, constructed, assembled, modified, maintained, or used.
Repairing and Maintaining Electronic Equipment	Servicing, repairing, calibrating, regulating, fine-tuning, or testing machines, devices, and equipment that operate primarily on the basis of electrical or electronic (not mechanical) principles.

Work_Context

Work_Context	Work_Context Definitions
Contact With Others	How much does this job require the worker to be in contact with others (face-to-face, by telephone, or otherwise) in order to perform it?
Face-to-Face Discussions	How often do you have to have face-to-face discussions with individuals or teams in this job?
Freedom to Make Decisions	How much decision making freedom, without supervision, does the job offer?
Deal With External Customers	How important is it to work with external customers or the public in this job?
Spend Time Standing	How much does this job require standing?
Public Speaking	How often do you have to perform public speaking in this job?
Structured versus Unstructured Work	To what extent is this job structured for the worker, rather than allowing the worker to determine tasks, priorities, and goals?
Indoors, Environmentally Controlled	How often does this job require working indoors in environmentally controlled conditions?
Physical Proximity	To what extent does this job require the worker to perform job tasks in close physical proximity to other people?

Spend Time Walking and Running	How much does this job require walking and running?
Impact of Decisions on Co-workers or Company Resul	How do the decisions an employee makes impact the results of co-workers, clients or the company?
Telephone	How often do you have telephone conversations in this job?
Frequency of Decision Making	How frequently is the worker required to make decisions that affect other people, the financial resources, and/or the image and reputation of the organization?
Work With Work Group or Team	How important is it to work with others in a group or team in this job?
Spend Time Making Repetitive Motions	How much does this job require making repetitive motions?
Responsible for Others' Health and Safety	How much responsibility is there for the health and safety of others in this job?
Frequency of Conflict Situations	How often are there conflict situations the employee has to face in this job?
Letters and Memos	How often does the job require written letters and memos?
Coordinate or Lead Others	How important is it to coordinate or lead others in accomplishing work activities in this job?
Deal With Unpleasant or Angry People	How often does the worker have to deal with unpleasant, angry, or discourteous individuals as part of the job requirements?
Spend Time Bending or Twisting the Body	How much does this job require bending or twisting your body?
Responsibility for Outcomes and Results	How responsible is the worker for work outcomes and results of other workers?
Importance of Being Exact or Accurate	How important is being very exact or highly accurate in performing this job?
Electronic Mail	How often do you use electronic mail in this job?
Indoors, Not Environmentally Controlled	How often does this job require working indoors in non-controlled environmental conditions (e.g., warehouse without heat)?
Spend Time Keeping or Regaining Balance	How much does this job require keeping or regaining your balance?
Level of Competition	To what extent does this job require the worker to compete or to be aware of competitive pressures?
Importance of Repeating Same Tasks	How important is repeating the same physical activities (e.g., key entry) or mental activities (e.g., checking entries in a ledger) over and over, without stopping, to performing this job?
Sounds, Noise Levels Are Distracting or Uncomforta	How often does this job require working exposed to sounds and noise levels that are distracting or uncomfortable?
Spend Time Using Your Hands to Handle, Control, or	How much does this job require using your hands to handle, control, or feel objects, tools or controls?
Time Pressure	How often does this job require the worker to meet strict deadlines?
Exposed to Contaminants	How often does this job require working exposed to contaminants (such as pollutants, gases, dust or odors)?
Spend Time Sitting	How much does this job require sitting?
Consequence of Error	How serious would the result usually be if the worker made a mistake that was not readily correctable?
Degree of Automation	How automated is the job?
Exposed to Minor Burns, Cuts, Bites, or Stings	How often does this job require exposure to minor burns, cuts, bites, or stings?
Deal With Physically Aggressive People	How frequently does this job require the worker to deal with physical aggression of violent individuals?
Outdoors, Exposed to Weather	How often does this job require working outdoors, exposed to all weather conditions?
Spend Time Kneeling, Crouching, Stooping, or Crawl	How much does this job require kneeling, crouching, stooping or crawling?
Exposed to Disease or Infections	How often does this job require exposure to disease/infections?
Outdoors, Under Cover	How often does this job require working outdoors, under cover (e.g., structure with roof but no walls)?
Pace Determined by Speed of Equipment	How important is it to this job that the pace is determined by the speed of equipment or machinery? (This does not refer to keeping busy at all times on this job.)
In an Enclosed Vehicle or Equipment	How often does this job require working in a closed vehicle or equipment (e.g., car)?
Extremely Bright or Inadequate Lighting	How often does this job require working in extremely bright or inadequate lighting conditions?
Spend Time Climbing Ladders, Scaffolds, or Poles	How much does this job require climbing ladders, scaffolds, or poles?
Very Hot or Cold Temperatures	How often does this job require working in very hot (above 90 F degrees) or very cold (below 32 F degrees) temperatures?

Cramped Work Space, Awkward Positions	How often does this job require working in cramped work spaces that requires getting into awkward positions?
Exposed to Hazardous Conditions	How often does this job require exposure to hazardous conditions?
Exposed to Hazardous Equipment	How often does this job require exposure to hazardous equipment?
Wear Common Protective or Safety Equipment such as	How much does this job require wearing common protective or safety equipment such as safety shoes, glasses, gloves, hard hats or life jackets?
Exposed to Whole Body Vibration	How often does this job require exposure to whole body vibration (e.g., operate a jackhammer)?
Exposed to Radiation	How often does this job require exposure to radiation?
Exposed to High Places	How often does this job require exposure to high places?
Wear Specialized Protective or Safety Equipment su	How much does this job require wearing specialized protective or safety equipment such as breathing apparatus, safety harness, full protection suits, or radiation protection?
In an Open Vehicle or Equipment	How often does this job require working in an open vehicle or equipment (e.g., tractor)?

Job Zone Component	Job Zone Component Definitions
Title	Job Zone Three: Medium Preparation Needed
Overall Experience	Previous work-related skill, knowledge, or experience is required for these occupations. For example, an electrician must have completed three or four years of apprenticeship or several years of vocational training, and often must have passed a licensing exam, in order to perform the job.
Job Training	Employees in these occupations usually need one or two years of training involving both on-the-job experience and informal training with experienced workers.
Job Zone Examples	These occupations usually involve using communication and organizational skills to coordinate, supervise, manage, or train others to accomplish goals. Examples include dental assistants, electricians, fish and game wardens, legal secretaries, personnel recruiters, and recreation workers.
SVP Range	(6.0 to < 7.0)
Education	Most occupations in this zone require training in vocational schools, related on-the-job experience, or an associate's degree. Some may require a bachelor's degree.

Work_Styles	Work_Styles Definitions
Dependability	Job requires being reliable, responsible, and dependable, and fulfilling obligations.
Integrity	Job requires being honest and ethical.
Leadership	Job requires a willingness to lead, take charge, and offer opinions and direction.
Concern for Others	Job requires being sensitive to others' needs and feelings and being understanding and helpful on the job.
Social Orientation	Job requires preferring to work with others rather than alone, and being personally connected with others on the job.
Self Control	Job requires maintaining composure, keeping emotions in check, controlling anger, and avoiding aggressive behavior, even in very difficult situations.
Cooperation	Job requires being pleasant with others on the job and displaying a good-natured, cooperative attitude.
Adaptability/Flexibility	Job requires being open to change (positive or negative) and to considerable variety in the workplace.
Independence	Job requires developing one's own ways of doing things, guiding oneself with little or no supervision, and depending on oneself to get things done.
Attention to Detail	Job requires being careful about detail and thorough in completing work tasks.
Innovation	Job requires creativity and alternative thinking to develop new ideas for and answers to work-related problems.
Stress Tolerance	Job requires accepting criticism and dealing calmly and effectively with high stress situations.
Achievement/Effort	Job requires establishing and maintaining personally challenging achievement goals and exerting effort toward mastering tasks.
Initiative	Job requires a willingness to take on responsibilities and challenges.
Persistence	Job requires persistence in the face of obstacles.
Analytical Thinking	Job requires analyzing information and using logic to address work-related issues and problems.

39-9032.00 - Recreation Workers

Conduct recreation activities with groups in public, private, or volunteer agencies or recreation facilities. Organize and promote activities, such as arts and crafts, sports, games, music, dramatics, social recreation, camping, and hobbies, taking into account the needs and interests of individual members.

Tasks

1) Greet new arrivals to activities, introducing them to other participants, explaining facility rules, and encouraging their participation.

2) Enforce rules and regulations of recreational facilities in order to maintain discipline and ensure safety.

3) Confer with management in order to discuss and resolve participant complaints.

4) Complete and maintain time and attendance forms and inventory lists.

5) Ascertain and interpret group interests, evaluate equipment and facilities, and adapt activities to meet participant needs.

6) Administer first aid according to prescribed procedures, and notify emergency medical personnel when necessary.

7) Explain principles, techniques, and safety procedures to participants in recreational activities, and demonstrate use of materials and equipment.

8) Manage the daily operations of recreational facilities.

9) Provide for entertainment and set up related decorations and equipment.

10) Meet with staff to discuss rules, regulations, and work-related problems.

11) Meet and collaborate with agency personnel, community organizations, and other professional personnel to plan balanced recreational programs for participants.

12) Schedule maintenance and use of facilities.

13) Evaluate recreation areas, facilities, and services in order to determine if they are producing desired results.

14) Direct special activities or events such as aquatics, gymnastics, or performing arts.

15) Encourage participants to develop their own activities and leadership skills through group discussions.

16) Supervise and coordinate the work activities of personnel, such as training staff members and assigning work duties.

17) Serve as liaison between park or recreation administrators and activity instructors.

18) Evaluate staff performance, recording evaluations on appropriate forms.

19) Oversee the purchase, planning, design, construction, and upkeep of recreation facilities and areas.

Knowledge	Knowledge Definitions
Customer and Personal Service	Knowledge of principles and processes for providing customer and personal services. This includes customer needs assessment, meeting quality standards for services, and evaluation of customer satisfaction.
Psychology	Knowledge of human behavior and performance; individual differences in ability, personality, and interests; learning and motivation; psychological research methods; and the assessment and treatment of behavioral and affective disorders.
Education and Training	Knowledge of principles and methods for curriculum and training design, teaching and instruction for individuals and groups, and the measurement of training effects.
English Language	Knowledge of the structure and content of the English language including the meaning and spelling of words, rules of composition, and grammar.
Administration and Management	Knowledge of business and management principles involved in strategic planning, resource allocation, human resources modeling, leadership technique, production methods, and coordination of people and resources.
Public Safety and Security	Knowledge of relevant equipment, policies, procedures, and strategies to promote effective local, state, or national security operations for the protection of people, data, property, and institutions.
Clerical	Knowledge of administrative and clerical procedures and systems such as word processing, managing files and records, stenography and transcription, designing forms, and other office procedures and terminology.

Personnel and Human Resources	Knowledge of principles and procedures for personnel recruitment. selection. training. compensation and benefits. labor relations and negotiation. and personnel information systems.
Sociology and Anthropology	Knowledge of group behavior and dynamics, societal trends and influences. human migrations. ethnicity, cultures and their history and origins.
Sales and Marketing	Knowledge of principles and methods for showing, promoting, and selling products or services. This includes marketing strategy and tactics. product demonstration, sales techniques, and sales control systems.
Communications and Media	Knowledge of media production, communication, and dissemination techniques and methods. This includes alternative ways to inform and entertain via written, oral, and visual media.
Therapy and Counseling	Knowledge of principles, methods, and procedures for diagnosis, treatment, and rehabilitation of physical and mental dysfunctions, and for career counseling and guidance.
Computers and Electronics	Knowledge of circuit boards, processors, chips, electronic equipment. and computer hardware and software, including applications and programming.
Mathematics	Knowledge of arithmetic, algebra, geometry, calculus, statistics, and their applications.
Law and Government	Knowledge of laws. legal codes, court procedures, precedents, government regulations. executive orders, agency rules, and the democratic political process.
Medicine and Dentistry	Knowledge of the information and techniques needed to diagnose and treat human injuries, diseases, and deformities. This includes symptoms, treatment alternatives, drug properties and interactions, and preventive health-care measures.
Economics and Accounting	Knowledge of economic and accounting principles and practices, the financial markets, banking and the analysis and reporting of financial data.
Philosophy and Theology	Knowledge of different philosophical systems and religions. This includes their basic principles, values, ethics, ways of thinking, customs, practices, and their impact on human culture.
Production and Processing	Knowledge of raw materials, production processes, quality control, costs, and other techniques for maximizing the effective manufacture and distribution of goods.
Telecommunications	Knowledge of transmission, broadcasting, switching, control, and operation of telecommunications systems.
Transportation	Knowledge of principles and methods for moving people or goods by air, rail, sea, or road, including the relative costs and benefits.
History and Archeology	Knowledge of historical events and their causes, indicators, and effects on civilizations and cultures.
Foreign Language	Knowledge of the structure and content of a foreign (non-English) language including the meaning and spelling of words, rules of composition and grammar, and pronunciation.
Geography	Knowledge of principles and methods for describing the features of land, sea, and air masses, including their physical characteristics, locations, interrelationships, and distribution of plant, animal, and human life.
Fine Arts	Knowledge of the theory and techniques required to compose, produce, and perform works of music, dance, visual arts, drama, and sculpture.
Mechanical	Knowledge of machines and tools, including their designs, uses, repair, and maintenance.
Biology	Knowledge of plant and animal organisms, their tissues, cells, functions, interdependencies, and interactions with each other and the environment.
Food Production	Knowledge of techniques and equipment for planting, growing, and harvesting food products (both plant and animal) for consumption, including storage/handling techniques.
Design	Knowledge of design techniques, tools, and principles involved in production of precision technical plans, blueprints, drawings, and models.
Physics	Knowledge and prediction of physical principles, laws, their interrelationships, and applications to understanding fluid, material, and atmospheric dynamics, and mechanical, electrical, atomic and sub- atomic structures and processes.
Chemistry	Knowledge of the chemical composition, structure, and properties of substances and of the chemical processes and transformations that they undergo. This includes uses of chemicals and their interactions. danger signs, production techniques, and disposal methods.

Engineering and Technology	Knowledge of the practical application of engineering science and technology. This includes applying principles. techniques. procedures, and equipment to the design and production of various goods and services.
Building and Construction	Knowledge of materials, methods, and the tools involved in the construction or repair of houses, buildings, or other structures such as highways and roads.

Skills	Skills Definitions
Service Orientation	Actively looking for ways to help people.
Active Listening	Giving full attention to what other people are saying. taking time to understand the points being made. asking questions as appropriate, and not interrupting at inappropriate times.
Speaking	Talking to others to convey information effectively.
Instructing	Teaching others how to do something.
Judgment and Decision Making	Considering the relative costs and benefits of potential actions to choose the most appropriate one.
Time Management	Managing one's own time and the time of others.
Management of Personnel Resources	Motivating, developing, and directing people as they work, identifying the best people for the job.
Social Perceptiveness	Being aware of others' reactions and understanding why they react as they do.
Reading Comprehension	Understanding written sentences and paragraphs in work related documents.
Critical Thinking	Using logic and reasoning to identify the strengths and weaknesses of alternative solutions, conclusions or approaches to problems.
Writing	Communicating effectively in writing as appropriate for the needs of the audience.
Monitoring	Monitoring/Assessing performance of yourself. other individuals, or organizations to make improvements or take corrective action.
Active Learning	Understanding the implications of new information for both current and future problem-solving and decision-making.
Coordination	Adjusting actions in relation to others' actions.
Equipment Selection	Determining the kind of tools and equipment needed to do a job.
Learning Strategies	Selecting and using training/instructional methods and procedures appropriate for the situation when learning or teaching new things.
Negotiation	Bringing others together and trying to reconcile differences.
Complex Problem Solving	Identifying complex problems and reviewing related information to develop and evaluate options and implement solutions.
Management of Financial Resources	Determining how money will be spent to get the work done, and accounting for these expenditures.
Management of Material Resources	Obtaining and seeing to the appropriate use of equipment, facilities, and materials needed to do certain work.
Persuasion	Persuading others to change their minds or behavior.
Mathematics	Using mathematics to solve problems.
Systems Evaluation	Identifying measures or indicators of system performance and the actions needed to improve or correct performance, relative to the goals of the system.
Technology Design	Generating or adapting equipment and technology to serve user needs.
Operations Analysis	Analyzing needs and product requirements to create a design.
Systems Analysis	Determining how a system should work and how changes in conditions, operations, and the environment will affect outcomes.
Troubleshooting	Determining causes of operating errors and deciding what to do about it.
Operation and Control	Controlling operations of equipment or systems.
Science	Using scientific rules and methods to solve problems.
Quality Control Analysis	Conducting tests and inspections of products, services, or processes to evaluate quality or performance.
Equipment Maintenance	Performing routine maintenance on equipment and determining when and what kind of maintenance is needed.
Repairing	Repairing machines or systems using the needed tools.
Programming	Writing computer programs for various purposes.
Installation	Installing equipment, machines, wiring. or programs to meet specifications.
Operation Monitoring	Watching gauges, dials, or other indicators to make sure a machine is working properly.

Ability	Ability Definitions
Oral Expression	The ability to communicate information and ideas in speaking so others will understand.
Oral Comprehension	The ability to listen to and understand information and ideas presented through spoken words and sentences.
Speech Clarity	The ability to speak clearly so others can understand you.
Problem Sensitivity	The ability to tell when something is wrong or is likely to go wrong. It does not involve solving the problem, only recognizing there is a problem.
Information Ordering	The ability to arrange things or actions in a certain order or pattern according to a specific rule or set of rules (e.g., patterns of numbers, letters, words, pictures, mathematical operations).
Speech Recognition	The ability to identify and understand the speech of another person.
Fluency of Ideas	The ability to come up with a number of ideas about a topic (the number of ideas is important, not their quality, correctness, or creativity).
Originality	The ability to come up with unusual or clever ideas about a given topic or situation, or to develop creative ways to solve a problem.
Deductive Reasoning	The ability to apply general rules to specific problems to produce answers that make sense.
Inductive Reasoning	The ability to combine pieces of information to form general rules or conclusions (includes finding a relationship among seemingly unrelated events).
Near Vision	The ability to see details at close range (within a few feet of the observer).
Time Sharing	The ability to shift back and forth between two or more activities or sources of information (such as speech, sounds, touch, or other sources).
Selective Attention	The ability to concentrate on a task over a period of time without being distracted.
Written Comprehension	The ability to read and understand information and ideas presented in writing.
Written Expression	The ability to communicate information and ideas in writing so others will understand.
Category Flexibility	The ability to generate or use different sets of rules for combining or grouping things in different ways.
Memorization	The ability to remember information such as words, numbers, pictures, and procedures.
Far Vision	The ability to see details at a distance.
Visualization	The ability to imagine how something will look after it is moved around or when its parts are moved or rearranged.
Arm-Hand Steadiness	The ability to keep your hand and arm steady while moving your arm or while holding your arm and hand in one position.
Multilimb Coordination	The ability to coordinate two or more limbs (for example, two arms, two legs, or one leg and one arm) while sitting, standing, or lying down. It does not involve performing the activities while the whole body is in motion.
Trunk Strength	The ability to use your abdominal and lower back muscles to support part of the body repeatedly or continuously over time without 'giving out' or fatiguing.
Gross Body Coordination	The ability to coordinate the movement of your arms, legs, and torso together when the whole body is in motion.
Mathematical Reasoning	The ability to choose the right mathematical methods or formulas to solve a problem.
Depth Perception	The ability to judge which of several objects is closer or farther away from you, or to judge the distance between you and an object.
Manual Dexterity	The ability to quickly move your hand, your hand together with your arm, or your two hands to grasp, manipulate, or assemble objects.
Static Strength	The ability to exert maximum muscle force to lift, push, pull, or carry objects.
Flexibility of Closure	The ability to identify or detect a known pattern (a figure, object, word, or sound) that is hidden in other distracting material.
Speed of Closure	The ability to quickly make sense of, combine, and organize information into meaningful patterns.
Auditory Attention	The ability to focus on a single source of sound in the presence of other distracting sounds.
Stamina	The ability to exert yourself physically over long periods of time without getting winded or out of breath.
Extent Flexibility	The ability to bend, stretch, twist, or reach with your body, arms, and/or legs.
Spatial Orientation	The ability to know your location in relation to the environment or to know where other objects are in relation to you.
Dynamic Strength	The ability to exert muscle force repeatedly or continuously over time. This involves muscular endurance and resistance to muscle fatigue.
Perceptual Speed	The ability to quickly and accurately compare similarities and differences among sets of letters, numbers, objects, pictures, or patterns. The things to be compared may be presented at the same time or one after the other. This ability also includes comparing a presented object with a remembered object.
Finger Dexterity	The ability to make precisely coordinated movements of the fingers of one or both hands to grasp, manipulate, or assemble very small objects.
Peripheral Vision	The ability to see objects or movement of objects to one's side when the eyes are looking ahead.
Visual Color Discrimination	The ability to match or detect differences between colors, including shades of color and brightness.
Control Precision	The ability to quickly and repeatedly adjust the controls of a machine or a vehicle to exact positions.
Explosive Strength	The ability to use short bursts of muscle force to propel oneself (as in jumping or sprinting), or to throw an object.
Glare Sensitivity	The ability to see objects in the presence of glare or bright lighting.
Response Orientation	The ability to choose quickly between two or more movements in response to two or more different signals (lights, sounds, pictures). It includes the speed with which the correct response is started with the hand, foot, or other body part.
Speed of Limb Movement	The ability to quickly move the arms and legs.
Number Facility	The ability to add, subtract, multiply, or divide quickly and correctly.
Reaction Time	The ability to quickly respond (with the hand, finger, or foot) to a signal (sound, light, picture) when it appears.
Gross Body Equilibrium	The ability to keep or regain your body balance or stay upright when in an unstable position.
Sound Localization	The ability to tell the direction from which a sound originated.
Night Vision	The ability to see under low light conditions.
Wrist-Finger Speed	The ability to make fast, simple, repeated movements of the fingers, hands, and wrists.
Hearing Sensitivity	The ability to detect or tell the differences between sounds that vary in pitch and loudness.
Dynamic Flexibility	The ability to quickly and repeatedly bend, stretch, twist, or reach out with your body, arms, and/or legs.
Rate Control	The ability to time your movements or the movement of a piece of equipment in anticipation of changes in the speed and/or direction of a moving object or scene.

Work_Activity	Work_Activity Definitions
Scheduling Work and Activities	Scheduling events, programs, and activities, as well as the work of others.
Establishing and Maintaining Interpersonal Relatio	Developing constructive and cooperative working relationships with others, and maintaining them over time.
Thinking Creatively	Developing, designing, or creating new applications, ideas, relationships, systems, or products, including artistic contributions.
Coordinating the Work and Activities of Others	Getting members of a group to work together to accomplish tasks.
Organizing, Planning, and Prioritizing Work	Developing specific goals and plans to prioritize, organize, and accomplish your work.
Communicating with Supervisors, Peers, or Subordin	Providing information to supervisors, co-workers, and subordinates by telephone, in written form, e-mail, or in person.
Communicating with Persons Outside Organization	Communicating with people outside the organization, representing the organization to customers, the public, government, and other external sources. This information can be exchanged in person, in writing, or by telephone or e-mail.
Resolving Conflicts and Negotiating with Others	Handling complaints, settling disputes, and resolving grievances and conflicts, or otherwise negotiating with others.
Making Decisions and Solving Problems	Analyzing information and evaluating results to choose the best solution and solve problems.
Assisting and Caring for Others	Providing personal assistance, medical attention, emotional support, or other personal care to others such as coworkers, customers, or patients.
Getting Information	Observing, receiving, and otherwise obtaining information from all relevant sources.
Performing General Physical Activities	Performing physical activities that require considerable use of your arms and legs and moving your whole body, such as climbing, lifting, balancing, walking, stooping, and handling of materials.

		Work_Context	Work_Context Definitions

Coaching and Developing Others — Identifying the developmental needs of others and coaching, mentoring, or otherwise helping others to improve their knowledge or skills.

Documenting/Recording Information — Entering, transcribing, recording, storing, or maintaining information in written or electronic/magnetic form.

Updating and Using Relevant Knowledge — Keeping up-to-date technically and applying new knowledge to your job.

Identifying Objects, Actions, and Events — Identifying information by categorizing, estimating, recognizing differences or similarities, and detecting changes in circumstances or events.

Training and Teaching Others — Identifying the educational needs of others, developing formal educational or training programs or classes, and teaching or instructing others.

Developing and Building Teams — Encouraging and building mutual trust, respect, and cooperation among team members.

Handling and Moving Objects — Using hands and arms in handling, installing, positioning, and moving materials, and manipulating things.

Performing for or Working Directly with the Public — Performing for people or dealing directly with the public. This includes serving customers in restaurants and stores, and receiving clients or guests.

Developing Objectives and Strategies — Establishing long-range objectives and specifying the strategies and actions to achieve them.

Interpreting the Meaning of Information for Others — Translating or explaining what information means and how it can be used.

Guiding, Directing, and Motivating Subordinates — Providing guidance and direction to subordinates, including setting performance standards and monitoring performance.

Evaluating Information to Determine Compliance with — Using relevant information and individual judgment to determine whether events or processes comply with laws, regulations, or standards.

Inspecting Equipment, Structures, or Material — Inspecting equipment, structures, or materials to identify the cause of errors or other problems or defects.

Judging the Qualities of Things, Services, or Peop — Assessing the value, importance, or quality of things or people.

Monitor Processes, Materials, or Surroundings — Monitoring and reviewing information from materials, events, or the environment, to detect or assess problems.

Interacting With Computers — Using computers and computer systems (including hardware and software) to program, write software, set up functions, enter data, or process information.

Analyzing Data or Information — Identifying the underlying principles, reasons, or facts of information by breaking down information or data into separate parts.

Processing Information — Compiling, coding, categorizing, calculating, tabulating, auditing, or verifying information or data.

Performing Administrative Activities — Performing day-to-day administrative tasks such as maintaining information files and processing paperwork.

Monitoring and Controlling Resources — Monitoring and controlling resources and overseeing the spending of money.

Selling or Influencing Others — Convincing others to buy merchandise/goods or to otherwise change their minds or actions.

Estimating the Quantifiable Characteristics of Pro — Estimating sizes, distances, and quantities; or determining time, costs, resources, or materials needed to perform a work activity.

Staffing Organizational Units — Recruiting, interviewing, selecting, hiring, and promoting employees in an organization.

Provide Consultation and Advice to Others — Providing guidance and expert advice to management or other groups on technical, systems-, or process-related topics.

Controlling Machines and Processes — Using either control mechanisms or direct physical activity to operate machines or processes (not including computers or vehicles).

Operating Vehicles, Mechanized Devices, or Equipme — Running, maneuvering, navigating, or driving vehicles or mechanized equipment, such as forklifts, passenger vehicles, aircraft, or water craft.

Drafting, Laying Out, and Specifying Technical Dev — Providing documentation, detailed instructions, drawings, or specifications to tell others about how devices, parts, equipment, or structures are to be fabricated, constructed, assembled, modified, maintained, or used.

Repairing and Maintaining Mechanical Equipment — Servicing, repairing, adjusting, and testing machines, devices, moving parts, and equipment that operate primarily on the basis of mechanical (not electronic) principles.

Repairing and Maintaining Electronic Equipment — Servicing, repairing, calibrating, regulating, fine-tuning, or testing machines, devices, and equipment that operate primarily on the basis of electrical or electronic (not mechanical) principles.

Face-to-Face Discussions — How often do you have to have face-to-face discussions with individuals or teams in this job?

Contact With Others — How much does this job require the worker to be in contact with others (face-to-face, by telephone, or otherwise) in order to perform it?

Structured versus Unstructured Work — To what extent is this job structured for the worker, rather than allowing the worker to determine tasks, priorities, and goals?

Work With Work Group or Team — How important is it to work with others in a group or team in this job?

Freedom to Make Decisions — How much decision making freedom, without supervision, does the job offer?

Coordinate or Lead Others — How important is it to coordinate or lead others in accomplishing work activities in this job?

Frequency of Decision Making — How frequently is the worker required to make decisions that affect other people, the financial resources, and/or the image and reputation of the organization?

Telephone — How often do you have telephone conversations in this job?

Impact of Decisions on Co-workers or Company Resul — How do the decisions an employee makes impact the results of co-workers, clients or the company?

Deal With External Customers — How important is it to work with external customers or the public in this job?

Physical Proximity — To what extent does this job require the worker to perform job tasks in close physical proximity to other people?

Indoors, Environmentally Controlled — How often does this job require working indoors in environmentally controlled conditions?

Sounds, Noise Levels Are Distracting or Uncomforta — How often does this job require working exposed to sounds and noise levels that are distracting or uncomfortable?

Importance of Being Exact or Accurate — How important is being very exact or highly accurate in performing this job?

Frequency of Conflict Situations — How often are there conflict situations the employee has to face in this job?

Deal With Unpleasant or Angry People — How frequently does the worker have to deal with unpleasant, angry, or discourteous individuals as part of the job requirements?

Spend Time Using Your Hands to Handle, Control, or — How much does this job require using your hands to handle, control, or feel objects, tools or controls?

Spend Time Standing — How much does this job require standing?

Letters and Memos — How often does the job require written letters and memos?

Responsibility for Outcomes and Results — How responsible is the worker for work outcomes and results of other workers?

Responsible for Others' Health and Safety — How much responsibility is there for the health and safety of others in this job?

Public Speaking — How often do you have to perform public speaking in this job?

Spend Time Sitting — How much does this job require sitting?

Spend Time Making Repetitive Motions — How much does this job require making repetitive motions?

Spend Time Walking and Running — How much does this job require walking and running?

Importance of Repeating Same Tasks — How important is repeating the same physical activities (e.g., key entry) or mental activities (e.g., checking entries in a ledger) over and over, without stopping, to performing this job?

Electronic Mail — How often do you use electronic mail in this job?

In an Enclosed Vehicle or Equipment — How often does this job require working in a closed vehicle or equipment (e.g., car)?

Level of Competition — To what extent does this job require the worker to compete or to be aware of competitive pressures?

Spend Time Bending or Twisting the Body — How much does this job require bending or twisting your body?

Exposed to Contaminants — How often does this job require working exposed to contaminants (such as pollutants, gases, dust or odors)?

Time Pressure — How often does this job require the worker to meet strict deadlines?

Indoors, Not Environmentally Controlled — How often does this job require working indoors in non-controlled environmental conditions (e.g., warehouse without heat)?

Very Hot or Cold Temperatures — How often does this job require working in very hot (above 90 F degrees) or very cold (below 32 F degrees) temperatures?

Consequence of Error — How serious would the result usually be if the worker made a mistake that was not readily correctable?

Exposed to Minor Burns, Cuts, Bites, or Stings — How often does this job require exposure to minor burns, cuts, bites, or stings?

Outdoors, Exposed to Weather — How often does this job require working outdoors, exposed to all weather conditions?

Deal With Physically Aggressive People	How frequently does this job require the worker to deal with physical aggression of violent individuals?
Outdoors, Under Cover	How often does this job require working outdoors, under cover (e.g., structure with roof but no walls)?
Degree of Automation	How automated is the job?
Extremely Bright or Inadequate Lighting	How often does this job require working in extremely bright or inadequate lighting conditions?
Spend Time Kneeling, Crouching, Stooping, or Crawl	How much does this job require kneeling, crouching, stooping or crawling?
Spend Time Keeping or Regaining Balance	How much does this job require keeping or regaining your balance?
Exposed to Disease or Infections	How often does this job require exposure to disease/infections?
Cramped Work Space, Awkward Positions	How often does this job require working in cramped work spaces that requires getting into awkward positions?
Exposed to Hazardous Conditions	How often does this job require exposure to hazardous conditions?
Wear Common Protective or Safety Equipment such as	How much does this job require wearing common protective or safety equipment such as safety shoes, glasses, gloves, hard hats or live jackets?
Exposed to High Places	How often does this job require exposure to high places?
In an Open Vehicle or Equipment	How often does this job require working in an open vehicle or equipment (e.g., tractor)?
Exposed to Hazardous Equipment	How often does this job require exposure to hazardous equipment?
Spend Time Climbing Ladders, Scaffolds, or Poles	How much does this job require climbing ladders, scaffolds, or poles?
Pace Determined by Speed of Equipment	How important is it to this job that the pace is determined by the speed of equipment or machinery? (This does not refer to keeping busy at all times on this job.)
Wear Specialized Protective or Safety Equipment su	How much does this job require wearing specialized protective or safety equipment such as breathing apparatus, safety harness, full protection suits, or radiation protection?
Exposed to Radiation	How often does this job require exposure to radiation?
Exposed to Whole Body Vibration	How often does this job require exposure to whole body vibration (e.g., operate a jackhammer)?

Job Zone Component	Job Zone Component Definitions
Title	Job Zone Four: Considerable Preparation Needed
Overall Experience	A minimum of two to four years of work-related skill, knowledge, or experience is needed for these occupations. For example, an accountant must complete four years of college and work for several years in accounting to be considered qualified.
Job Training	Employees in these occupations usually need several years of work-related experience, on-the-job training, and/or vocational training.
Job Zone Examples	Many of these occupations involve coordinating, supervising, managing, or training others. Examples include accountants, chefs and head cooks, computer programmers, historians, pharmacists, and police detectives.
SVP Range	(7.0 to < 8.0)
Education	Most of these occupations require a four - year bachelor's degree, but some do not.

Work_Styles	Work_Styles Definitions
Cooperation	Job requires being pleasant with others on the job and displaying a good-natured, cooperative attitude.
Integrity	Job requires being honest and ethical.
Self Control	Job requires maintaining composure, keeping emotions in check, controlling anger, and avoiding aggressive behavior, even in very difficult situations.
Dependability	Job requires being reliable, responsible, and dependable, and fulfilling obligations.
Adaptability/Flexibility	Job requires being open to change (positive or negative) and to considerable variety in the workplace.
Leadership	Job requires a willingness to lead, take charge, and offer opinions and direction.
Concern for Others	Job requires being sensitive to others' needs and feelings and being understanding and helpful on the job.
Social Orientation	Job requires preferring to work with others rather than alone, and being personally connected with others on the job.

Stress Tolerance	Job requires accepting criticism and dealing calmly and effectively with high stress situations.
Initiative	Job requires a willingness to take on responsibilities and challenges.
Attention to Detail	Job requires being careful about detail and thorough in completing work tasks.
Independence	Job requires developing one's own ways of doing things, guiding oneself with little or no supervision, and depending on oneself to get things done.
Persistence	Job requires persistence in the face of obstacles.
Achievement/Effort	Job requires establishing and maintaining personally challenging achievement goals and exerting effort toward mastering tasks.
Innovation	Job requires creativity and alternative thinking to develop new ideas for and answers to work-related problems.
Analytical Thinking	Job requires analyzing information and using logic to address work-related issues and problems.

41-1011.00 - First-Line Supervisors/Managers of Retail Sales Workers

Directly supervise sales workers in a retail establishment or department. Duties may include management functions, such as purchasing, budgeting, accounting, and personnel work, in addition to supervisory duties.

Tasks

1) Enforce safety, health, and security rules.

2) Monitor sales activities to ensure that customers receive satisfactory service and quality goods.

3) Perform work activities of subordinates, such as cleaning and organizing shelves and displays and selling merchandise.

4) Examine products purchased for resale or received for storage to assess the condition of each product or item.

5) Direct and supervise employees engaged in sales, inventory-taking, reconciling cash receipts, or in performing services for customers.

6) Instruct staff on how to handle difficult and complicated sales.

7) Inventory stock and reorder when inventory drops to a specified level.

8) Establish and implement policies, goals, objectives, and procedures for their department.

9) Keep records of purchases, sales, and requisitions.

10) Hire, train, and evaluate personnel in sales or marketing establishments, promoting or firing workers when appropriate.

11) Confer with company officials to develop methods and procedures to increase sales, expand markets, and promote business.

12) Plan and prepare work schedules and keep records of employees' work schedules and time cards.

13) Examine merchandise to ensure that it is correctly priced and displayed and that it functions as advertised.

14) Estimate consumer demand and determine the types and amounts of goods to be sold.

15) Establish credit policies and operating procedures.

16) Review inventory and sales records to prepare reports for management and budget departments.

17) Plan budgets and authorize payments and merchandise returns.

18) Formulate pricing policies for merchandise, according to profitability requirements.

19) Plan and coordinate advertising campaigns and sales promotions, and prepare merchandise displays and advertising copy.

20) Provide customer service by greeting and assisting customers, and responding to customer inquiries and complaints.

Knowledge	Knowledge Definitions
Customer and Personal Service	Knowledge of principles and processes for providing customer and personal services. This includes customer needs assessment, meeting quality standards for services, and evaluation of customer satisfaction.

Administration and Management	Knowledge of business and management principles involved in strategic planning, resource allocation, human resources modeling, leadership technique, production methods, and coordination of people and resources.
English Language	Knowledge of the structure and content of the English language including the meaning and spelling of words, rules of composition, and grammar.
Mathematics	Knowledge of arithmetic, algebra, geometry, calculus, statistics, and their applications.
Personnel and Human Resources	Knowledge of principles and procedures for personnel recruitment, selection, training, compensation and benefits, labor relations and negotiation, and personnel information systems.
Food Production	Knowledge of techniques and equipment for planting, growing, and harvesting food products (both plant and animal) for consumption, including storage/handling techniques.
Sales and Marketing	Knowledge of principles and methods for showing, promoting, and selling products or services. This includes marketing strategy and tactics, product demonstration, sales techniques, and sales control systems.
Public Safety and Security	Knowledge of relevant equipment, policies, procedures, and strategies to promote effective local, state, or national security operations for the protection of people, data, property, and institutions.
Economics and Accounting	Knowledge of economic and accounting principles and practices, the financial markets, banking and the analysis and reporting of financial data.
Education and Training	Knowledge of principles and methods for curriculum and training design, teaching and instruction for individuals and groups, and the measurement of training effects.
Clerical	Knowledge of administrative and clerical procedures and systems such as word processing, managing files and records, stenography and transcription, designing forms, and other office procedures and terminology.
Mechanical	Knowledge of machines and tools, including their designs, uses, repair, and maintenance.
Computers and Electronics	Knowledge of circuit boards, processors, chips, electronic equipment, and computer hardware and software, including applications and programming.
Production and Processing	Knowledge of raw materials, production processes, quality control, costs, and other techniques for maximizing the effective manufacture and distribution of goods.
Communications and Media	Knowledge of media production, communication, and dissemination techniques and methods. This includes alternative ways to inform and entertain via written, oral, and visual media.
Telecommunications	Knowledge of transmission, broadcasting, switching, control, and operation of telecommunications systems.
Law and Government	Knowledge of laws, legal codes, court procedures, precedents, government regulations, executive orders, agency rules, and the democratic political process.
Psychology	Knowledge of human behavior and performance; individual differences in ability, personality, and interests; learning and motivation; psychological research methods; and the assessment and treatment of behavioral and affective disorders.
Engineering and Technology	Knowledge of the practical application of engineering science and technology. This includes applying principles, techniques, procedures, and equipment to the design and production of various goods and services.
Building and Construction	Knowledge of materials, methods, and the tools involved in the construction or repair of houses, buildings, or other structures such as highways and roads.
Therapy and Counseling	Knowledge of principles, methods, and procedures for diagnosis, treatment, and rehabilitation of physical and mental dysfunctions, and for career counseling and guidance.
Transportation	Knowledge of principles and methods for moving people or goods by air, rail, sea, or road, including the relative costs and benefits.
Physics	Knowledge and prediction of physical principles, laws, their interrelationships, and applications to understanding fluid, material, and atmospheric dynamics, and mechanical, electrical, atomic and sub-atomic structures and processes.
Foreign Language	Knowledge of the structure and content of a foreign (non-English) language including the meaning and spelling of words, rules of composition and grammar, and pronunciation.
Chemistry	Knowledge of the chemical composition, structure, and properties of substances and of the chemical processes and transformations that they undergo. This includes uses of chemicals and their interactions, danger signs, production techniques, and disposal methods.
Geography	Knowledge of principles and methods for describing the features of land, sea, and air masses, including their physical characteristics, locations, interrelationships, and distribution of plant, animal, and human life.
Sociology and Anthropology	Knowledge of group behavior and dynamics, societal trends and influences, human migrations, ethnicity, cultures and their history and origins.
Medicine and Dentistry	Knowledge of the information and techniques needed to diagnose and treat human injuries, diseases, and deformities. This includes symptoms, treatment alternatives, drug properties and interactions, and preventive health-care measures.
Design	Knowledge of design techniques, tools, and principles involved in production of precision technical plans, blueprints, drawings, and models.
Philosophy and Theology	Knowledge of different philosophical systems and religions. This includes their basic principles, values, ethics, ways of thinking, customs, practices, and their impact on human culture.
Biology	Knowledge of plant and animal organisms, their tissues, cells, functions, interdependencies, and interactions with each other and the environment.
Fine Arts	Knowledge of the theory and techniques required to compose, produce, and perform works of music, dance, visual arts, drama, and sculpture.
History and Archeology	Knowledge of historical events and their causes, indicators, and effects on civilizations and cultures.

Skills	**Skills Definitions**
Management of Personnel Resources	Motivating, developing, and directing people as they work, identifying the best people for the job.
Active Listening	Giving full attention to what other people are saying, taking time to understand the points being made, asking questions as appropriate, and not interrupting at inappropriate times.
Service Orientation	Actively looking for ways to help people.
Time Management	Managing one's own time and the time of others.
Instructing	Teaching others how to do something.
Monitoring	Monitoring/Assessing performance of yourself, other individuals, or organizations to make improvements or take corrective action.
Reading Comprehension	Understanding written sentences and paragraphs in work related documents.
Judgment and Decision Making	Considering the relative costs and benefits of potential actions to choose the most appropriate one.
Critical Thinking	Using logic and reasoning to identify the strengths and weaknesses of alternative solutions, conclusions or approaches to problems.
Active Learning	Understanding the implications of new information for both current and future problem-solving and decision-making.
Speaking	Talking to others to convey information effectively.
Mathematics	Using mathematics to solve problems.
Social Perceptiveness	Being aware of others' reactions and understanding why they react as they do.
Persuasion	Persuading others to change their minds or behavior.
Troubleshooting	Determining causes of operating errors and deciding what to do about it.
Equipment Maintenance	Performing routine maintenance on equipment and determining when and what kind of maintenance is needed.
Learning Strategies	Selecting and using training/instructional methods and procedures appropriate for the situation when learning or teaching new things.
Writing	Communicating effectively in writing as appropriate for the needs of the audience.
Complex Problem Solving	Identifying complex problems and reviewing related information to develop and evaluate options and implement solutions.
Negotiation	Bringing others together and trying to reconcile differences.
Coordination	Adjusting actions in relation to others' actions.
Quality Control Analysis	Conducting tests and inspections of products, services, or processes to evaluate quality or performance.
Operation and Control	Controlling operations of equipment or systems.
Equipment Selection	Determining the kind of tools and equipment needed to do a job.

826

Management of Financial Resources	Determining how money will be spent to get the work done, and accounting for these expenditures.
Operation Monitoring	Watching gauges, dials, or other indicators to make sure a machine is working properly.
Operations Analysis	Analyzing needs and product requirements to create a design.
Repairing	Repairing machines or systems using the needed tools.
Systems Analysis	Determining how a system should work and how changes in conditions, operations, and the environment will affect outcomes.
Management of Material Resources	Obtaining and seeing to the appropriate use of equipment, facilities, and materials needed to do certain work.
Systems Evaluation	Identifying measures or indicators of system performance and the actions needed to improve or correct performance, relative to the goals of the system.
Science	Using scientific rules and methods to solve problems.
Installation	Installing equipment, machines, wiring, or programs to meet specifications.
Programming	Writing computer programs for various purposes.
Technology Design	Generating or adapting equipment and technology to serve user needs.

Ability	Ability Definitions
Oral Expression	The ability to communicate information and ideas in speaking so others will understand.
Oral Comprehension	The ability to listen to and understand information and ideas presented through spoken words and sentences.
Speech Clarity	The ability to speak clearly so others can understand you.
Deductive Reasoning	The ability to apply general rules to specific problems to produce answers that make sense.
Problem Sensitivity	The ability to tell when something is wrong or is likely to go wrong. It does not involve solving the problem, only recognizing there is a problem.
Speech Recognition	The ability to identify and understand the speech of another person.
Inductive Reasoning	The ability to combine pieces of information to form general rules or conclusions (includes finding a relationship among seemingly unrelated events).
Originality	The ability to come up with unusual or clever ideas about a given topic or situation, or to develop creative ways to solve a problem.
Information Ordering	The ability to arrange things or actions in a certain order or pattern according to a specific rule or set of rules (e.g., patterns of numbers, letters, words, pictures, mathematical operations).
Written Expression	The ability to communicate information and ideas in writing so others will understand.
Time Sharing	The ability to shift back and forth between two or more activities or sources of information (such as speech, sounds, touch, or other sources).
Written Comprehension	The ability to read and understand information and ideas presented in writing.
Near Vision	The ability to see details at close range (within a few feet of the observer).
Mathematical Reasoning	The ability to choose the right mathematical methods or formulas to solve a problem.
Category Flexibility	The ability to generate or use different sets of rules for combining or grouping things in different ways.
Fluency of Ideas	The ability to come up with a number of ideas about a topic (the number of ideas is important, not their quality, correctness, or creativity).
Number Facility	The ability to add, subtract, multiply, or divide quickly and correctly.
Trunk Strength	The ability to use your abdominal and lower back muscles to support part of the body repeatedly or continuously over time without 'giving out' or fatiguing.
Memorization	The ability to remember information such as words, numbers, pictures, and procedures.
Selective Attention	The ability to concentrate on a task over a period of time without being distracted.
Stamina	The ability to exert yourself physically over long periods of time without getting winded or out of breath.
Finger Dexterity	The ability to make precisely coordinated movements of the fingers of one or both hands to grasp, manipulate, or assemble very small objects.
Static Strength	The ability to exert maximum muscle force to lift, push, pull, or carry objects.
Extent Flexibility	The ability to bend, stretch, twist, or reach with your body, arms, and/or legs.

Far Vision	The ability to see details at a distance.
Perceptual Speed	The ability to quickly and accurately compare similarities and differences among sets of letters, numbers, objects, pictures, or patterns. The things to be compared may be presented at the same time or one after the other. This ability also includes comparing a presented object with a remembered object.
Flexibility of Closure	The ability to identify or detect a known pattern (a figure, object, word, or sound) that is hidden in other distracting material.
Visualization	The ability to imagine how something will look after it is moved around or when its parts are moved or rearranged.
Manual Dexterity	The ability to quickly move your hand, your hand together with your arm, or your two hands to grasp, manipulate, or assemble objects.
Speed of Limb Movement	The ability to quickly move the arms and legs.
Visual Color Discrimination	The ability to match or detect differences between colors, including shades of color and brightness.
Auditory Attention	The ability to focus on a single source of sound in the presence of other distracting sounds.
Multilimb Coordination	The ability to coordinate two or more limbs (for example, two arms, two legs, or one leg and one arm) while sitting, standing, or lying down. It does not involve performing the activities while the whole body is in motion.
Speed of Closure	The ability to quickly make sense of, combine, and organize information into meaningful patterns.
Gross Body Coordination	The ability to coordinate the movement of your arms, legs, and torso together when the whole body is in motion.
Arm-Hand Steadiness	The ability to keep your hand and arm steady while moving your arm or while holding your arm and hand in one position.
Hearing Sensitivity	The ability to detect or tell the differences between sounds that vary in pitch and loudness.
Gross Body Equilibrium	The ability to keep or regain your body balance or stay upright when in an unstable position.
Dynamic Strength	The ability to exert muscle force repeatedly or continuously over time. This involves muscular endurance and resistance to muscle fatigue.
Reaction Time	The ability to quickly respond (with the hand, finger, or foot) to a signal (sound, light, picture) when it appears.
Control Precision	The ability to quickly and repeatedly adjust the controls of a machine or a vehicle to exact positions.
Depth Perception	The ability to judge which of several objects is closer or farther away from you, or to judge the distance between you and an object.
Wrist-Finger Speed	The ability to make fast, simple, repeated movements of the fingers, hands, and wrists.
Dynamic Flexibility	The ability to quickly and repeatedly bend, stretch, twist, or reach out with your body, arms, and/or legs.
Night Vision	The ability to see under low light conditions.
Explosive Strength	The ability to use short bursts of muscle force to propel oneself (as in jumping or sprinting), or to throw an object.
Response Orientation	The ability to choose quickly between two or more movements in response to two or more different signals (lights, sounds, pictures). It includes the speed with which the correct response is started with the hand, foot, or other body part.
Spatial Orientation	The ability to know your location in relation to the environment or to know where other objects are in relation to you.
Peripheral Vision	The ability to see objects or movement of objects to one's side when the eyes are looking ahead.
Sound Localization	The ability to tell the direction from which a sound originated.
Glare Sensitivity	The ability to see objects in the presence of glare or bright lighting.
Rate Control	The ability to time your movements or the movement of a piece of equipment in anticipation of changes in the speed and/or direction of a moving object or scene.

Work_Activity	Work_Activity Definitions
Performing for or Working Directly with the Public	Performing for people or dealing directly with the public. This includes serving customers in restaurants and stores, and receiving clients or guests.
Organizing, Planning, and Prioritizing Work	Developing specific goals and plans to prioritize, organize, and accomplish your work.
Establishing and Maintaining Interpersonal Relatio	Developing constructive and cooperative working relationships with others, and maintaining them over time.

Communicating with Persons Outside Organization	Communicating with people outside the organization, representing the organization to customers. the public. government. and other external sources. This information can be exchanged in person, in writing, or by telephone or e-mail.
Communicating with Supervisors, Peers, or Subordin	Providing information to supervisors, co-workers, and subordinates by telephone, in written form, e-mail, or in person.
Coaching and Developing Others	Identifying the developmental needs of others and coaching, mentoring, or otherwise helping others to improve their knowledge or skills.
Coordinating the Work and Activities of Others	Getting members of a group to work together to accomplish tasks.
Guiding, Directing, and Motivating Subordinates	Providing guidance and direction to subordinates, including setting performance standards and monitoring performance.
Thinking Creatively	Developing, designing, or creating new applications, ideas, relationships, systems, or products, including artistic contributions.
Making Decisions and Solving Problems	Analyzing information and evaluating results to choose the best solution and solve problems.
Performing General Physical Activities	Performing physical activities that require considerable use of your arms and legs and moving your whole body, such as climbing, lifting, balancing, walking, stooping, and handling of materials.
Resolving Conflicts and Negotiating with Others	Handling complaints, settling disputes, and resolving grievances and conflicts, or otherwise negotiating with others.
Training and Teaching Others	Identifying the educational needs of others, developing formal educational or training programs or classes, and teaching or instructing others.
Documenting/Recording Information	Entering, transcribing, recording, storing, or maintaining information in written or electronic/magnetic form.
Developing and Building Teams	Encouraging and building mutual trust, respect, and cooperation among team members.
Scheduling Work and Activities	Scheduling events, programs, and activities, as well as the work of others.
Getting Information	Observing, receiving, and otherwise obtaining information from all relevant sources.
Selling or Influencing Others	Convincing others to buy merchandise/goods or to otherwise change their minds or actions.
Handling and Moving Objects	Using hands and arms in handling, installing, positioning, and moving materials, and manipulating things.
Updating and Using Relevant Knowledge	Keeping up-to-date technically and applying new knowledge to your job.
Interacting With Computers	Using computers and computer systems (including hardware and software) to program, write software, set up functions, enter data, or process information.
Evaluating Information to Determine Compliance wit	Using relevant information and individual judgment to determine whether events or processes comply with laws, regulations, or standards.
Inspecting Equipment, Structures, or Material	Inspecting equipment, structures, or materials to identify the cause of errors or other problems or defects.
Monitor Processes, Materials, or Surroundings	Monitoring and reviewing information from materials, events, or the environment, to detect or assess problems.
Assisting and Caring for Others	Providing personal assistance, medical attention, emotional support, or other personal care to others such as coworkers, customers, or patients.
Staffing Organizational Units	Recruiting, interviewing, selecting, hiring, and promoting employees in an organization.
Performing Administrative Activities	Performing day-to-day administrative tasks such as maintaining information files and processing paperwork.
Processing Information	Compiling, coding, categorizing, calculating, tabulating, auditing, or verifying information or data.
Judging the Qualities of Things, Services, or Peop	Assessing the value, importance, or quality of things or people.
Provide Consultation and Advice to Others	Providing guidance and expert advice to management or other groups on technical, systems-, or process-related topics.
Identifying Objects, Actions, and Events	Identifying information by categorizing, estimating, recognizing differences or similarities, and detecting changes in circumstances or events.
Monitoring and Controlling Resources	Monitoring and controlling resources and overseeing the spending of money.
Developing Objectives and Strategies	Establishing long-range objectives and specifying the strategies and actions to achieve them.
Analyzing Data or Information	Identifying the underlying principles, reasons, or facts of information by breaking down information or data into separate parts.

Controlling Machines and Processes	Using either control mechanisms or direct physical activity to operate machines or processes (not including computers or vehicles).
Estimating the Quantifiable Characteristics of Pro	Estimating sizes, distances, and quantities; or determining time, costs, resources. or materials needed to perform a work activity.
Repairing and Maintaining Mechanical Equipment	Servicing. repairing, adjusting, and testing machines, devices, moving parts, and equipment that operate primarily on the basis of mechanical (not electronic) principles.
Repairing and Maintaining Electronic Equipment	Servicing, repairing, calibrating, regulating, fine-tuning, or testing machines, devices, and equipment that operate primarily on the basis of electrical or electronic (not mechanical) principles.
Operating Vehicles, Mechanized Devices, or Equipme	Running, maneuvering, navigating, or driving vehicles or mechanized equipment, such as forklifts, passenger vehicles, aircraft, or water craft.
Interpreting the Meaning of Information for Others	Translating or explaining what information means and how it can be used.
Drafting, Laying Out, and Specifying Technical Dev	Providing documentation, detailed instructions, drawings, or specifications to tell others about how devices, parts, equipment, or structures are to be fabricated, constructed, assembled, modified, maintained, or used.

Work_Context	Work_Context Definitions
Frequency of Decision Making	How frequently is the worker required to make decisions that affect other people. the financial resources, and/or the image and reputation of the organization?
Deal With External Customers	How important is it to work with external customers or the public in this job?
Indoors, Environmentally Controlled	How often does this job require working indoors in environmentally controlled conditions?
Contact With Others	How much does this job require the worker to be in contact with others (face-to-face, by telephone, or otherwise) in order to perform it?
Telephone	How often do you have telephone conversations in this job?
Spend Time Standing	How much does this job require standing?
Coordinate or Lead Others	How important is it to coordinate or lead others in accomplishing work activities in this job?
Responsibility for Outcomes and Results	How responsible is the worker for work outcomes and results of other workers?
Work With Work Group or Team	How important is it to work with others in a group or team in this job?
Face-to-Face Discussions	How often do you have to have face-to-face discussions with individuals or teams in this job?
Freedom to Make Decisions	How much decision making freedom, without supervision, does the job offer?
Physical Proximity	To what extent does this job require the worker to perform job tasks in close physical proximity to other people?
Impact of Decisions on Co-workers or Company Resul	How do the decisions an employee makes impact the results of co-workers, clients or the company?
Time Pressure	How often does this job require the worker to meet strict deadlines?
Spend Time Walking and Running	How much does this job require walking and running?
Structured versus Unstructured Work	To what extent is this job structured for the worker, rather than allowing the worker to determine tasks, priorities, and goals?
Responsible for Others' Health and Safety	How much responsibility is there for the health and safety of others in this job?
Deal With Unpleasant or Angry People	How frequently does the worker have to deal with unpleasant, angry, or discourteous individuals as part of the job requirements?
Letters and Memos	How often does the job require written letters and memos?
Level of Competition	To what extent does this job require the worker to compete or to be aware of competitive pressures?
Importance of Being Exact or Accurate	How important is being very exact or highly accurate in performing this job?
Spend Time Using Your Hands to Handle, Control, or	How much does this job require using your hands to handle, control, or feel objects, tools or controls?
Exposed to Hazardous Equipment	How often does this job require exposure to hazardous equipment?
Frequency of Conflict Situations	How often are there conflict situations the employee has to face in this job?
Wear Common Protective or Safety Equipment such as	How much does this job require wearing common protective or safety equipment such as safety shoes, glasses, gloves, hard hats or live jackets?

Exposed to Minor Burns, Cuts, Bites, or Stings	How often does this job require exposure to minor burns, cuts, bites, or stings?
Importance of Repeating Same Tasks	How important is repeating the same physical activities (e.g., key entry) or mental activities (e.g., checking entries in a ledger) over and over, without stopping, to performing this job?
Consequence of Error	How serious would the result usually be if the worker made a mistake that was not readily correctable?
Sounds, Noise Levels Are Distracting or Uncomforta	How often does this job require working exposed to sounds and noise levels that are distracting or uncomfortable?
Deal With Physically Aggressive People	How frequently does this job require the worker to deal with physical aggression of violent individuals?
Cramped Work Space, Awkward Positions	How often does this job require working in cramped work spaces that requires getting into awkward positions?
Spend Time Making Repetitive Motions	How much does this job require making repetitive motions?
Degree of Automation	How automated is the job?
Pace Determined by Speed of Equipment	How important is it to this job that the pace is determined by the speed of equipment or machinery? (This does not refer to keeping busy at all times on this job.)
In an Enclosed Vehicle or Equipment	How often does this job require working in a closed vehicle or equipment (e.g., car)?
Spend Time Sitting	How much does this job require sitting?
Electronic Mail	How often do you use electronic mail in this job?
Spend Time Bending or Twisting the Body	How much does this job require bending or twisting your body?
Public Speaking	How often do you have to perform public speaking in this job?
Very Hot or Cold Temperatures	How often does this job require working in very hot (above 90 F degrees) or very cold (below 32 F degrees) temperatures?
Indoors, Not Environmentally Controlled	How often does this job require working indoors in non-controlled environmental conditions (e.g., warehouse without heat)?
Outdoors, Exposed to Weather	How often does this job require working outdoors, exposed to all weather conditions?
Extremely Bright or Inadequate Lighting	How often does this job require working in extremely bright or inadequate lighting conditions?
Spend Time Kneeling, Crouching, Stooping, or Crawl	How much does this job require kneeling, crouching, stooping or crawling?
Outdoors, Under Cover	How often does this job require working outdoors, under cover (e.g., structure with roof but no walls)?
Exposed to Contaminants	How often does this job require working exposed to contaminants (such as pollutants, gases, dust or odors)?
Spend Time Keeping or Regaining Balance	How much does this job require keeping or regaining your balance?
Exposed to Hazardous Conditions	How often does this job require exposure to hazardous conditions?
Exposed to Disease or Infections	How often does this job require exposure to disease/infections?
Exposed to High Places	How often does this job require exposure to high places?
Spend Time Climbing Ladders, Scaffolds, or Poles	How much does this job require climbing ladders, scaffolds, or poles?
In an Open Vehicle or Equipment	How often does this job require working in an open vehicle or equipment (e.g., tractor)?
Exposed to Radiation	How often does this job require exposure to radiation?
Exposed to Whole Body Vibration	How often does this job require exposure to whole body vibration (e.g., operate a jackhammer)?
Wear Specialized Protective or Safety Equipment su	How much does this job require wearing specialized protective or safety equipment such as breathing apparatus, safety harness, full protection suits, or radiation protection?

Job Zone Component	Job Zone Component Definitions
Title	Job Zone Two: Some Preparation Needed
Overall Experience	Some previous work-related skill, knowledge, or experience may be helpful in these occupations, but usually is not needed. For example, a drywall installer might benefit from experience installing drywall, but an inexperienced person could still learn to be an installer with little difficulty.
Job Training	Employees in these occupations need anywhere from a few months to one year of working with experienced employees.
Job Zone Examples	These occupations often involve using your knowledge and skills to help others. Examples include drywall installers, fire inspectors, flight attendants, pharmacy technicians, salespersons (retail), and tellers.
SVP Range	(4.0 to 6.0)

These occupations usually require a high school diploma and may require some vocational training or job-related course work. In some cases, an associate's or bachelor's degree could be needed.

Work_Styles	Work_Styles Definitions
Stress Tolerance	Job requires accepting criticism and dealing calmly and effectively with high stress situations.
Dependability	Job requires being reliable, responsible, and dependable, and fulfilling obligations.
Integrity	Job requires being honest and ethical.
Self Control	Job requires maintaining composure, keeping emotions in check, controlling anger, and avoiding aggressive behavior, even in very difficult situations.
Adaptability/Flexibility	Job requires being open to change (positive or negative) and to considerable variety in the workplace.
Leadership	Job requires a willingness to lead, take charge, and offer opinions and direction.
Attention to Detail	Job requires being careful about detail and thorough in completing work tasks.
Cooperation	Job requires being pleasant with others on the job and displaying a good-natured, cooperative attitude.
Achievement/Effort	Job requires establishing and maintaining personally challenging achievement goals and exerting effort toward mastering tasks.
Independence	Job requires developing one's own ways of doing things, guiding oneself with little or no supervision, and depending on oneself to get things done.
Concern for Others	Job requires being sensitive to others' needs and feelings and being understanding and helpful on the job.
Persistence	Job requires persistence in the face of obstacles.
Initiative	Job requires a willingness to take on responsibilities and challenges.
Social Orientation	Job requires preferring to work with others rather than alone, and being personally connected with others on the job.
Analytical Thinking	Job requires analyzing information and using logic to address work-related issues and problems.
Innovation	Job requires creativity and alternative thinking to develop new ideas for and answers to work-related problems.

41-1012.00 - First-Line Supervisors/Managers of Non-Retail Sales Workers

Directly supervise and coordinate activities of sales workers other than retail sales workers. May perform duties, such as budgeting, accounting, and personnel work, in addition to supervisory duties.

Tasks

1) Visit retailers and sales representatives to promote products and gather information.

2) Monitor sales staff performance to ensure that goals are met.

3) Examine merchandise to ensure correct pricing and display, and that it functions as advertised.

4) Confer with company officials to develop methods and procedures to increase sales, expand markets, and promote business.

5) Attend company meetings to exchange product information and coordinate work activities with other departments.

6) Provide staff with assistance in performing difficult or complicated duties.

7) Analyze details of sales territories to assess their growth potential, and to set quotas.

8) Direct and supervise employees engaged in sales, inventory-taking, reconciling cash receipts, or performing specific services such as pumping gasoline for customers.

9) Listen to and resolve customer complaints regarding services, products, or personnel.

10) Keep records pertaining to purchases, sales, and requisitions.

11) Inventory stock, and reorder when inventories drop to specified levels.

12) Examine products purchased for resale or received for storage to determine product condition.

13) Hire, train, and evaluate personnel.

14) Prepare rental or lease agreements. specifying charges and payment procedures for use of machinery, tools, or other items.

15) Prepare sales and inventory reports for management and budget departments.

16) Formulate pricing policies on merchandise according to profitability requirements.

17) Plan and prepare work schedules, and assign employees to specific duties.

41-2011.00 - Cashiers

Receive and disburse money in establishments other than financial institutions. Usually involves use of electronic scanners, cash registers, or related equipment. Often involved in processing credit or debit card transactions and validating checks.

Tasks

1) Maintain clean and orderly checkout areas.

2) Establish or identify prices of goods, services or admission, and tabulate bills using calculators, cash registers, or optical price scanners.

3) Receive payment by cash, check, credit cards, vouchers, or automatic debits.

4) Answer customers' questions, and provide information on procedures or policies.

5) Greet customers entering establishments.

6) Resolve customer complaints.

7) Count money in cash drawers at the beginning of shifts to ensure that amounts are correct and that there is adequate change.

8) Cash checks for customers.

9) Issue trading stamps, and redeem food stamps and coupons.

10) Sell tickets and other items to customers.

11) Request information or assistance using paging systems.

12) Calculate total payments received during a time period, and reconcile this with total sales.

13) Process merchandise returns and exchanges.

14) Sort, count, and wrap currency and coins.

15) Stock shelves, and mark prices on shelves and items.

16) Bag, box, wrap, or gift-wrap merchandise, and prepare packages for shipment.

17) Monitor checkout stations to ensure that they have adequate cash available and that they are staffed appropriately.

18) Weigh items sold by weight in order to determine prices.

19) Compute and record totals of transactions.

20) Offer customers carry-out service at the completion of transactions.

21) Compile and maintain non-monetary reports and records.

22) Keep periodic balance sheets of amounts and numbers of transactions.

23) Pay company bills by cash, vouchers, or checks.

24) Post charges against guests' or patients' accounts.

Knowledge	Knowledge Definitions
Customer and Personal Service	Knowledge of principles and processes for providing customer and personal services. This includes customer needs assessment, meeting quality standards for services, and evaluation of customer satisfaction.
Mathematics	Knowledge of arithmetic, algebra, geometry, calculus, statistics, and their applications.
English Language	Knowledge of the structure and content of the English language including the meaning and spelling of words, rules of composition, and grammar.
Public Safety and Security	Knowledge of relevant equipment, policies, procedures, and strategies to promote effective local, state, or national security operations for the protection of people, data, property, and institutions.
Education and Training	Knowledge of principles and methods for curriculum and training design, teaching and instruction for individuals and groups, and the measurement of training effects.
Administration and Management	Knowledge of business and management principles involved in strategic planning, resource allocation, human resources modeling, leadership technique, production methods, and coordination of people and resources.
Computers and Electronics	Knowledge of circuit boards, processors, chips, electronic equipment, and computer hardware and software, including applications and programming.
Sales and Marketing	Knowledge of principles and methods for showing, promoting, and selling products or services. This includes marketing strategy and tactics, product demonstration, sales techniques, and sales control systems.
Communications and Media	Knowledge of media production, communication, and dissemination techniques and methods. This includes alternative ways to inform and entertain via written, oral, and visual media.
Personnel and Human Resources	Knowledge of principles and procedures for personnel recruitment, selection, training, compensation and benefits, labor relations and negotiation, and personnel information systems.
Foreign Language	Knowledge of the structure and content of a foreign (non-English) language including the meaning and spelling of words, rules of composition and grammar, and pronunciation.
Telecommunications	Knowledge of transmission, broadcasting, switching, control, and operation of telecommunications systems.
Clerical	Knowledge of administrative and clerical procedures and systems such as word processing, managing files and records, stenography and transcription, designing forms, and other office procedures and terminology.
Transportation	Knowledge of principles and methods for moving people or goods by air, rail, sea, or road, including the relative costs and benefits.
Law and Government	Knowledge of laws, legal codes, court procedures, precedents, government regulations, executive orders, agency rules, and the democratic political process.
Economics and Accounting	Knowledge of economic and accounting principles and practices, the financial markets, banking and the analysis and reporting of financial data.
Psychology	Knowledge of human behavior and performance; individual differences in ability, personality, and interests; learning and motivation; psychological research methods; and the assessment and treatment of behavioral and affective disorders.
Production and Processing	Knowledge of raw materials, production processes, quality control, costs, and other techniques for maximizing the effective manufacture and distribution of goods.
Mechanical	Knowledge of machines and tools, including their designs, uses, repair, and maintenance.
Medicine and Dentistry	Knowledge of the information and techniques needed to diagnose and treat human injuries, diseases, and deformities. This includes symptoms, treatment alternatives, drug properties and interactions, and preventive health-care measures.
Food Production	Knowledge of techniques and equipment for planting, growing, and harvesting food products (both plant and animal) for consumption, including storage/handling techniques.
Sociology and Anthropology	Knowledge of group behavior and dynamics, societal trends and influences, human migrations, ethnicity, cultures and their history and origins.
Therapy and Counseling	Knowledge of principles, methods, and procedures for diagnosis, treatment, and rehabilitation of physical and mental dysfunctions, and for career counseling and guidance.
Engineering and Technology	Knowledge of the practical application of engineering science and technology. This includes applying principles, techniques, procedures, and equipment to the design and production of various goods and services.
Chemistry	Knowledge of the chemical composition, structure, and properties of substances and of the chemical processes and transformations that they undergo. This includes uses of chemicals and their interactions, danger signs, production techniques, and disposal methods.
Philosophy and Theology	Knowledge of different philosophical systems and religions. This includes their basic principles, values, ethics, ways of thinking, customs, practices, and their impact on human culture.
Physics	Knowledge and prediction of physical principles, laws, their interrelationships, and applications to understanding fluid, material, and atmospheric dynamics, and mechanical, electrical, atomic and sub-atomic structures and processes.
History and Archeology	Knowledge of historical events and their causes, indicators, and effects on civilizations and cultures.

Design	Knowledge of design techniques, tools, and principles involved in production of precision technical plans, blueprints, drawings, and models.
Fine Arts	Knowledge of the theory and techniques required to compose, produce, and perform works of music, dance, visual arts, drama, and sculpture.
Building and Construction	Knowledge of materials, methods, and the tools involved in the construction or repair of houses, buildings, or other structures such as highways and roads.
Geography	Knowledge of principles and methods for describing the features of land, sea, and air masses, including their physical characteristics, locations, interrelationships, and distribution of plant, animal, and human life.
Biology	Knowledge of plant and animal organisms, their tissues, cells, functions, interdependencies, and interactions with each other and the environment.

Skills

Skills	Skills Definitions
Active Listening	Giving full attention to what other people are saying, taking time to understand the points being made, asking questions as appropriate, and not interrupting at inappropriate times.
Mathematics	Using mathematics to solve problems.
Speaking	Talking to others to convey information effectively.
Instructing	Teaching others how to do something.
Social Perceptiveness	Being aware of others' reactions and understanding why they react as they do.
Service Orientation	Actively looking for ways to help people.
Learning Strategies	Selecting and using training/instructional methods and procedures appropriate for the situation when learning or teaching new things.
Critical Thinking	Using logic and reasoning to identify the strengths and weaknesses of alternative solutions, conclusions or approaches to problems.
Writing	Communicating effectively in writing as appropriate for the needs of the audience.
Reading Comprehension	Understanding written sentences and paragraphs in work related documents.
Active Learning	Understanding the implications of new information for both current and future problem-solving and decision-making.
Judgment and Decision Making	Considering the relative costs and benefits of potential actions to choose the most appropriate one.
Monitoring	Monitoring/Assessing performance of yourself, other individuals, or organizations to make improvements or take corrective action.
Negotiation	Bringing others together and trying to reconcile differences.
Persuasion	Persuading others to change their minds or behavior.
Operation and Control	Controlling operations of equipment or systems.
Management of Personnel Resources	Motivating, developing, and directing people as they work, identifying the best people for the job.
Coordination	Adjusting actions in relation to others' actions.
Systems Analysis	Determining how a system should work and how changes in conditions, operations, and the environment will affect outcomes.
Troubleshooting	Determining causes of operating errors and deciding what to do about it.
Operation Monitoring	Watching gauges, dials, or other indicators to make sure a machine is working properly.
Complex Problem Solving	Identifying complex problems and reviewing related information to develop and evaluate options and implement solutions.
Equipment Maintenance	Performing routine maintenance on equipment and determining when and what kind of maintenance is needed.
Management of Financial Resources	Determining how money will be spent to get the work done, and accounting for these expenditures.
Systems Evaluation	Identifying measures or indicators of system performance and the actions needed to improve or correct performance, relative to the goals of the system.
Equipment Selection	Determining the kind of tools and equipment needed to do a job.
Time Management	Managing one's own time and the time of others.
Quality Control Analysis	Conducting tests and inspections of products, services, or processes to evaluate quality or performance.
Operations Analysis	Analyzing needs and product requirements to create a design.
Installation	Installing equipment, machines, wiring, or programs to meet specifications.
Repairing	Repairing machines or systems using the needed tools.
Programming	Writing computer programs for various purposes.

Technology Design	Generating or adapting equipment and technology to serve user needs.
Management of Material Resources	Obtaining and seeing to the appropriate use of equipment, facilities, and materials needed to do certain work.
Science	Using scientific rules and methods to solve problems.

Ability

Ability	Ability Definitions
Oral Expression	The ability to communicate information and ideas in speaking so others will understand.
Speech Clarity	The ability to speak clearly so others can understand you.
Speech Recognition	The ability to identify and understand the speech of another person.
Number Facility	The ability to add, subtract, multiply, or divide quickly and correctly.
Oral Comprehension	The ability to listen to and understand information and ideas presented through spoken words and sentences.
Near Vision	The ability to see details at close range (within a few feet of the observer).
Problem Sensitivity	The ability to tell when something is wrong or is likely to go wrong. It does not involve solving the problem, only recognizing there is a problem.
Information Ordering	The ability to arrange things or actions in a certain order or pattern according to a specific rule or set of rules (e.g., patterns of numbers, letters, words, pictures, mathematical operations).
Selective Attention	The ability to concentrate on a task over a period of time without being distracted.
Mathematical Reasoning	The ability to choose the right mathematical methods or formulas to solve a problem.
Deductive Reasoning	The ability to apply general rules to specific problems to produce answers that make sense.
Arm-Hand Steadiness	The ability to keep your hand and arm steady while moving your arm or while holding your arm and hand in one position.
Finger Dexterity	The ability to make precisely coordinated movements of the fingers of one or both hands to grasp, manipulate, or assemble very small objects.
Extent Flexibility	The ability to bend, stretch, twist, or reach with your body, arms, and/or legs.
Manual Dexterity	The ability to quickly move your hand, your hand together with your arm, or your two hands to grasp, manipulate, or assemble objects.
Inductive Reasoning	The ability to combine pieces of information to form general rules or conclusions (includes finding a relationship among seemingly unrelated events).
Perceptual Speed	The ability to quickly and accurately compare similarities and differences among sets of letters, numbers, objects, pictures, or patterns. The things to be compared may be presented at the same time or one after the other. This ability also includes comparing a presented object with a remembered object.
Written Comprehension	The ability to read and understand information and ideas presented in writing.
Time Sharing	The ability to shift back and forth between two or more activities or sources of information (such as speech, sounds, touch, or other sources).
Static Strength	The ability to exert maximum muscle force to lift, push, pull, or carry objects.
Category Flexibility	The ability to generate or use different sets of rules for combining or grouping things in different ways.
Memorization	The ability to remember information such as words, numbers, pictures, and procedures.
Written Expression	The ability to communicate information and ideas in writing so others will understand.
Speed of Closure	The ability to quickly make sense of, combine, and organize information into meaningful patterns.
Trunk Strength	The ability to use your abdominal and lower back muscles to support part of the body repeatedly or continuously over time without 'giving out' or fatiguing.
Wrist-Finger Speed	The ability to make fast, simple, repeated movements of the fingers, hands, and wrists.
Flexibility of Closure	The ability to identify or detect a known pattern (a figure, object, word, or sound) that is hidden in other distracting material.
Multilimb Coordination	The ability to coordinate two or more limbs (for example, two arms, two legs, or one leg and one arm) while sitting, standing, or lying down. It does not involve performing the activities while the whole body is in motion.
Control Precision	The ability to quickly and repeatedly adjust the controls of a machine or a vehicle to exact positions.

Auditory Attention	The ability to focus on a single source of sound in the presence of other distracting sounds.
Far Vision	The ability to see details at a distance.
Stamina	The ability to exert yourself physically over long periods of time without getting winded or out of breath.
Reaction Time	The ability to quickly respond (with the hand, finger, or foot) to a signal (sound, light, picture) when it appears.
Fluency of Ideas	The ability to come up with a number of ideas about a topic (the number of ideas is important, not their quality, correctness, or creativity).
Hearing Sensitivity	The ability to detect or tell the differences between sounds that vary in pitch and loudness.
Visualization	The ability to imagine how something will look after it is moved around or when its parts are moved or rearranged.
Rate Control	The ability to time your movements or the movement of a piece of equipment in anticipation of changes in the speed and/or direction of a moving object or scene.
Gross Body Equilibrium	The ability to keep or regain your body balance or stay upright when in an unstable position.
Gross Body Coordination	The ability to coordinate the movement of your arms, legs, and torso together when the whole body is in motion.
Visual Color Discrimination	The ability to match or detect differences between colors, including shades of color and brightness.
Originality	The ability to come up with unusual or clever ideas about a given topic or situation, or to develop creative ways to solve a problem.
Depth Perception	The ability to judge which of several objects is closer or farther away from you, or to judge the distance between you and an object.
Speed of Limb Movement	The ability to quickly move the arms and legs.
Dynamic Strength	The ability to exert muscle force repeatedly or continuously over time. This involves muscular endurance and resistance to muscle fatigue.
Response Orientation	The ability to choose quickly between two or more movements in response to two or more different signals (lights, sounds, pictures). It includes the speed with which the correct response is started with the hand, foot, or other body part.
Dynamic Flexibility	The ability to quickly and repeatedly bend, stretch, twist, or reach out with your body, arms, and/or legs.
Spatial Orientation	The ability to know your location in relation to the environment or to know where other objects are in relation to you.
Explosive Strength	The ability to use short bursts of muscle force to propel oneself (as in jumping or sprinting), or to throw an object.
Glare Sensitivity	The ability to see objects in the presence of glare or bright lighting.
Night Vision	The ability to see under low light conditions.
Peripheral Vision	The ability to see objects or movement of objects to one's side when the eyes are looking ahead.
Sound Localization	The ability to tell the direction from which a sound originated.

Work_Activity	**Work_Activity Definitions**
Performing for or Working Directly with the Public	Performing for people or dealing directly with the public. This includes serving customers in restaurants and stores, and receiving clients or guests.
Establishing and Maintaining Interpersonal Relatio	Developing constructive and cooperative working relationships with others, and maintaining them over time.
Getting Information	Observing, receiving, and otherwise obtaining information from all relevant sources.
Identifying Objects, Actions, and Events	Identifying information by categorizing, estimating, recognizing differences or similarities, and detecting changes in circumstances or events.
Processing Information	Compiling, coding, categorizing, calculating, tabulating, auditing, or verifying information or data.
Communicating with Supervisors, Peers, or Subordin	Providing information to supervisors, co-workers, and subordinates by telephone, in written form, e-mail, or in person.
Updating and Using Relevant Knowledge	Keeping up-to-date technically and applying new knowledge to your job.
Interacting With Computers	Using computers and computer systems (including hardware and software) to program, write software, set up functions, enter data, or process information.
Assisting and Caring for Others	Providing personal assistance, medical attention, emotional support, or other personal care to others such as coworkers, customers, or patients.
Resolving Conflicts and Negotiating with Others	Handling complaints, settling disputes, and resolving grievances and conflicts, or otherwise negotiating with others.

Handling and Moving Objects	Using hands and arms in handling, installing, positioning, and moving materials, and manipulating things.
Communicating with Persons Outside Organization	Communicating with people outside the organization, representing the organization to customers, the public, government, and other external sources. This information can be exchanged in person, in writing, or by telephone or e-mail.
Training and Teaching Others	Identifying the educational needs of others, developing formal educational or training programs or classes, and teaching or instructing others.
Coordinating the Work and Activities of Others	Getting members of a group to work together to accomplish tasks.
Controlling Machines and Processes	Using either control mechanisms or direct physical activity to operate machines or processes (not including computers or vehicles).
Performing General Physical Activities	Performing physical activities that require considerable use of your arms and legs and moving your whole body, such as climbing, lifting, balancing, walking, stooping, and handling of materials.
Making Decisions and Solving Problems	Analyzing information and evaluating results to choose the best solution and solve problems.
Judging the Qualities of Things, Services, or Peop	Assessing the value, importance, or quality of things or people.
Selling or Influencing Others	Convincing others to buy merchandise/goods or to otherwise change their minds or actions.
Monitor Processes, Materials, or Surroundings	Monitoring and reviewing information from materials, events, or the environment, to detect or assess problems.
Organizing, Planning, and Prioritizing Work	Developing specific goals and plans to prioritize, organize, and accomplish your work.
Inspecting Equipment, Structures, or Material	Inspecting equipment, structures, or materials to identify the cause of errors or other problems or defects.
Coaching and Developing Others	Identifying the developmental needs of others and coaching, mentoring, or otherwise helping others to improve their knowledge or skills.
Documenting/Recording Information	Entering, transcribing, recording, storing, or maintaining information in written or electronic/magnetic form.
Guiding, Directing, and Motivating Subordinates	Providing guidance and direction to subordinates, including setting performance standards and monitoring performance.
Estimating the Quantifiable Characteristics of Pro	Estimating sizes, distances, and quantities; or determining time, costs, resources, or materials needed to perform a work activity.
Evaluating Information to Determine Compliance wit	Using relevant information and individual judgment to determine whether events or processes comply with laws, regulations, or standards.
Analyzing Data or Information	Identifying the underlying principles, reasons, or facts of information by breaking down information or data into separate parts.
Performing Administrative Activities	Performing day-to-day administrative tasks such as maintaining information files and processing paperwork.
Provide Consultation and Advice to Others	Providing guidance and expert advice to management or other groups on technical, systems-, or process-related topics.
Scheduling Work and Activities	Scheduling events, programs, and activities, as well as the work of others.
Interpreting the Meaning of Information for Others	Translating or explaining what information means and how it can be used.
Repairing and Maintaining Electronic Equipment	Servicing, repairing, calibrating, regulating, fine-tuning, or testing machines, devices, and equipment that operate primarily on the basis of electrical or electronic (not mechanical) principles.
Developing and Building Teams	Encouraging and building mutual trust, respect, and cooperation among team members.
Thinking Creatively	Developing, designing, or creating new applications, ideas, relationships, systems, or products, including artistic contributions.
Repairing and Maintaining Mechanical Equipment	Servicing, repairing, adjusting, and testing machines, devices, moving parts, and equipment that operate primarily on the basis of mechanical (not electronic) principles.
Monitoring and Controlling Resources	Monitoring and controlling resources and overseeing the spending of money.
Staffing Organizational Units	Recruiting, interviewing, selecting, hiring, and promoting employees in an organization.
Drafting, Laying Out, and Specifying Technical Dev	Providing documentation, detailed instructions, drawings, or specifications to tell others about how devices, parts, equipment, or structures are to be fabricated, constructed, assembled, modified, maintained, or used.
Developing Objectives and Strategies	Establishing long-range objectives and specifying the strategies and actions to achieve them.

Work_Context	Work_Context Definitions
Spend Time Standing	How much does this job require standing?
Deal With External Customers	How important is it to work with external customers or the public in this job?
Contact With Others	How much does this job require the worker to be in contact with others (face-to-face, by telephone, or otherwise) in order to perform it?
Spend Time Making Repetitive Motions	How much does this job require making repetitive motions?
Importance of Being Exact or Accurate	How important is being very exact or highly accurate in performing this job?
Face-to-Face Discussions	How often do you have to have face-to-face discussions with individuals or teams in this job?
Deal With Unpleasant or Angry People	How frequently does the worker have to deal with unpleasant, angry, or discourteous individuals as part of the job requirements?
Impact of Decisions on Co-workers or Company Resul	How do the decisions an employee makes impact the results of co-workers, clients or the company?
Spend Time Using Your Hands to Handle, Control, or	How much does this job require using your hands to handle, control, or feel objects, tools or controls?
Work With Work Group or Team	How important is it to work with others in a group or team in this job?
Physical Proximity	To what extent does this job require the worker to perform job tasks in close physical proximity to other people?
Frequency of Decision Making	How frequently is the worker required to make decisions that affect other people, the financial resources, and/or the image and reputation of the organization?
Importance of Repeating Same Tasks	How important is repeating the same physical activities (e.g., key entry) or mental activities (e.g., checking entries in a ledger) over and over, without stopping, to performing this job?
Indoors, Environmentally Controlled	How often does this job require working indoors in environmentally controlled conditions?
Freedom to Make Decisions	How much decision making freedom, without supervision, does the job offer?
Spend Time Bending or Twisting the Body	How much does this job require bending or twisting your body?
Coordinate or Lead Others	How important is it to coordinate or lead others in accomplishing work activities in this job?
Telephone	How often do you have telephone conversations in this job?
Structured versus Unstructured Work	To what extent is this job structured for the worker, rather than allowing the worker to determine tasks, priorities, and goals?
Spend Time Walking and Running	How much does this job require walking and running?
Exposed to Contaminants	How often does this job require working exposed to contaminants (such as pollutants, gases, dust or odors)?
Sounds, Noise Levels Are Distracting or Uncomforta	How often does this job require working exposed to sounds and noise levels that are distracting or uncomfortable?
Degree of Automation	How automated is the job?
Time Pressure	How often does this job require the worker to meet strict deadlines?
Pace Determined by Speed of Equipment	How important is it to this job that the pace is determined by the speed of equipment or machinery? (This does not refer to keeping busy at all times on this job.)
Responsible for Others' Health and Safety	How much responsibility is there for the health and safety of others in this job?
Very Hot or Cold Temperatures	How often does this job require working in very hot (above 90 F degrees) or very cold (below 32 F degrees) temperatures?
Exposed to Minor Burns, Cuts, Bites, or Stings	How often does this job require exposure to minor burns, cuts, bites, or stings?
Frequency of Conflict Situations	How often are there conflict situations the employee has to face in this job?
Deal With Physically Aggressive People	How frequently does this job require the worker to deal with physical aggression of violent individuals?
Consequence of Error	How serious would the result usually be if the worker made a mistake that was not readily correctable?
Level of Competition	To what extent does this job require the worker to compete or to be aware of competitive pressures?
Spend Time Keeping or Regaining Balance	How much does this job require keeping or regaining your balance?
Responsibility for Outcomes and Results	How responsible is the worker for work outcomes and results of other workers?

Operating Vehicles, Mechanized Devices, or Equipme Running, maneuvering, navigating, or driving vehicles or mechanized equipment, such as forklifts, passenger vehicles, aircraft, or water craft.

Cramped Work Space. Awkward Positions	How often does this job require working in cramped work spaces that requires getting into awkward positions?
Spend Time Kneeling. Crouching. Stooping. or Crawl	How much does this job require kneeling, crouching, stooping or crawling?
Letters and Memos	How often does the job require written letters and memos?
Public Speaking	How often do you have to perform public speaking in this job?
Outdoors. Exposed to Weather	How often does this job require working outdoors, exposed to all weather conditions?
Exposed to Disease or Infections	How often does this job require exposure to disease/infections?
Extremely Bright or Inadequate Lighting	How often does this job require working in extremely bright or inadequate lighting conditions?
Spend Time Sitting	How much does this job require sitting?
Spend Time Climbing Ladders, Scaffolds, or Poles	How much does this job require climbing ladders, scaffolds, or poles?
Electronic Mail	How often do you use electronic mail in this job?
Indoors, Not Environmentally Controlled	How often does this job require working indoors in non-controlled environmental conditions (e.g., warehouse without heat)?
Wear Common Protective or Safety Equipment such as	How much does this job require wearing common protective or safety equipment such as safety shoes, glasses, gloves, hard hats or live jackets?
In an Open Vehicle or Equipment	How often does this job require working in an open vehicle or equipment (e.g., tractor)?
Exposed to Hazardous Equipment	How often does this job require exposure to hazardous equipment?
Exposed to Hazardous Conditions	How often does this job require exposure to hazardous conditions?
Exposed to High Places	How often does this job require exposure to high places?
Outdoors, Under Cover	How often does this job require working outdoors, under cover (e.g., structure with roof but no walls)?
Wear Specialized Protective or Safety Equipment su	How much does this job require wearing specialized protective or safety equipment such as breathing apparatus, safety harness, full protection suits, or radiation protection?
Exposed to Radiation	How often does this job require exposure to radiation?
Exposed to Whole Body Vibration	How often does this job require exposure to whole body vibration (e.g., operate a jackhammer)?
In an Enclosed Vehicle or Equipment	How often does this job require working in a closed vehicle or equipment (e.g., car)?

Job Zone Component	Job Zone Component Definitions
Title	Job Zone One: Little or No Preparation Needed
Overall Experience	No previous work-related skill, knowledge, or experience is needed for these occupations. For example, a person can become a general office clerk even if he/she has never worked in an office before.
Job Training	Employees in these occupations need anywhere from a few days to a few months of training. Usually, an experienced worker could show you how to do the job.
Job Zone Examples	These occupations involve following instructions and helping others. Examples include bus drivers, forest and conservation workers, general office clerks, home health aides, and waiters/waitresses.
SVP Range	(Below 4.0)
Education	These occupations may require a high school diploma or GED certificate. Some may require a formal training course to obtain a license.

Work_Styles	Work_Styles Definitions
Integrity	Job requires being honest and ethical.
Cooperation	Job requires being pleasant with others on the job and displaying a good-natured, cooperative attitude.
Self Control	Job requires maintaining composure, keeping emotions in check, controlling anger, and avoiding aggressive behavior, even in very difficult situations.
Dependability	Job requires being reliable, responsible, and dependable, and fulfilling obligations.
Attention to Detail	Job requires being careful about detail and thorough in completing work tasks.
Stress Tolerance	Job requires accepting criticism and dealing calmly and effectively with high stress situations.
Concern for Others	Job requires being sensitive to others' needs and feelings and being understanding and helpful on the job.

Adaptability/Flexibility	Job requires being open to change (positive or negative) and to considerable variety in the workplace.
Social Orientation	Job requires preferring to work with others rather than alone, and being personally connected with others on the job.
Independence	Job requires developing one's own ways of doing things, guiding oneself with little or no supervision, and depending on oneself to get things done.
Initiative	Job requires a willingness to take on responsibilities and challenges.
Leadership	Job requires a willingness to lead, take charge, and offer opinions and direction.
Achievement/Effort	Job requires establishing and maintaining personally challenging achievement goals and exerting effort toward mastering tasks.
Innovation	Job requires creativity and alternative thinking to develop new ideas for and answers to work-related problems.
Analytical Thinking	Job requires analyzing information and using logic to address work-related issues and problems.
Persistence	Job requires persistence in the face of obstacles.

41-2021.00 - Counter and Rental Clerks

Receive orders for repairs, rentals, and services. May describe available options, compute cost, and accept payment.

Tasks

1) Answer telephones to provide information and receive orders.

2) Prepare merchandise for display, or for purchase or rental.

3) Recommend and provide advice on a wide variety of products and services.

4) Greet customers and discuss the type, quality and quantity of merchandise sought for rental.

5) Advise customers on use and care of merchandise.

6) Inspect and adjust rental items to meet needs of customer.

7) Receive orders for services, such as rentals, repairs, dry cleaning, and storage.

8) Keep records of transactions, and of the number of customers entering an establishment.

9) Explain rental fees, policies and procedures.

10) Provide information about rental items, such as availability, operation or description.

11) Receive, examine, and tag articles to be altered, cleaned, stored, or repaired.

12) Reserve items for requested times and keep records of items rented.

13) Prepare rental forms, obtaining customer signature and other information, such as required licenses.

14) Rent items, arrange for provision of services to customers and accept returns.

15) Allocate equipment to participants in sporting events or recreational activities.

Knowledge	Knowledge Definitions
English Language	Knowledge of the structure and content of the English language including the meaning and spelling of words, rules of composition, and grammar.
Customer and Personal Service	Knowledge of principles and processes for providing customer and personal services. This includes customer needs assessment, meeting quality standards for services, and evaluation of customer satisfaction.
Administration and Management	Knowledge of business and management principles involved in strategic planning, resource allocation, human resources modeling, leadership technique, production methods, and coordination of people and resources.
Mathematics	Knowledge of arithmetic, algebra, geometry, calculus, statistics, and their applications.
Sales and Marketing	Knowledge of principles and methods for showing, promoting, and selling products or services. This includes marketing strategy and tactics, product demonstration, sales techniques, and sales control systems.
Economics and Accounting	Knowledge of economic and accounting principles and practices, the financial markets, banking and the analysis and reporting of financial data.
Transportation	Knowledge of principles and methods for moving people or goods by air, rail, sea, or road, including the relative costs and benefits.
Clerical	Knowledge of administrative and clerical procedures and systems such as word processing, managing files and records, stenography and transcription, designing forms, and other office procedures and terminology.
Food Production	Knowledge of techniques and equipment for planting, growing, and harvesting food products (both plant and animal) for consumption, including storage/handling techniques.
Production and Processing	Knowledge of raw materials, production processes, quality control, costs, and other techniques for maximizing the effective manufacture and distribution of goods.
Personnel and Human Resources	Knowledge of principles and procedures for personnel recruitment, selection, training, compensation and benefits, labor relations and negotiation, and personnel information systems.
Computers and Electronics	Knowledge of circuit boards, processors, chips, electronic equipment, and computer hardware and software, including applications and programming.
Public Safety and Security	Knowledge of relevant equipment, policies, procedures, and strategies to promote effective local, state, or national security operations for the protection of people, data, property, and institutions.
Law and Government	Knowledge of laws, legal codes, court procedures, precedents, government regulations, executive orders, agency rules, and the democratic political process.
Chemistry	Knowledge of the chemical composition, structure, and properties of substances and of the chemical processes and transformations that they undergo. This includes uses of chemicals and their interactions, danger signs, production techniques, and disposal methods.
Education and Training	Knowledge of principles and methods for curriculum and training design, teaching and instruction for individuals and groups, and the measurement of training effects.
Medicine and Dentistry	Knowledge of the information and techniques needed to diagnose and treat human injuries, diseases, and deformities. This includes symptoms, treatment alternatives, drug properties and interactions, and preventive health-care measures.
Foreign Language	Knowledge of the structure and content of a foreign (non-English) language including the meaning and spelling of words, rules of composition and grammar, and pronunciation.
Communications and Media	Knowledge of media production, communication, and dissemination techniques and methods. This includes alternative ways to inform and entertain via written, oral, and visual media.
Design	Knowledge of design techniques, tools, and principles involved in production of precision technical plans, blueprints, drawings, and models.
Telecommunications	Knowledge of transmission, broadcasting, switching, control, and operation of telecommunications systems.
Psychology	Knowledge of human behavior and performance; individual differences in ability, personality, and interests; learning and motivation; psychological research methods; and the assessment and treatment of behavioral and affective disorders.
Engineering and Technology	Knowledge of the practical application of engineering science and technology. This includes applying principles, techniques, procedures, and equipment to the design and production of various goods and services.
Physics	Knowledge and prediction of physical principles, laws, their interrelationships, and applications to understanding fluid, material, and atmospheric dynamics, and mechanical, electrical, atomic and sub-atomic structures and processes.
Biology	Knowledge of plant and animal organisms, their tissues, cells, functions, interdependencies, and interactions with each other and the environment.
Mechanical	Knowledge of machines and tools, including their designs, uses, repair, and maintenance.
Building and Construction	Knowledge of materials, methods, and the tools involved in the construction or repair of houses, buildings, or other structures such as highways and roads.
Therapy and Counseling	Knowledge of principles, methods, and procedures for diagnosis, treatment, and rehabilitation of physical and mental dysfunctions, and for career counseling and guidance.
Geography	Knowledge of principles and methods for describing the features of land, sea, and air masses, including their physical characteristics, locations, interrelationships, and distribution of plant, animal, and human life.

History and Archeology	Knowledge of historical events and their causes. indicators, and effects on civilizations and cultures.
Philosophy and Theology	Knowledge of different philosophical systems and religions. This includes their basic principles, values, ethics, ways of thinking, customs, practices, and their impact on human culture.
Sociology and Anthropology	Knowledge of group behavior and dynamics, societal trends and influences, human migrations, ethnicity, cultures and their history and origins.
Fine Arts	Knowledge of the theory and techniques required to compose, produce, and perform works of music, dance, visual arts, drama, and sculpture.

Skills	Skills Definitions
Active Listening	Giving full attention to what other people are saying, taking time to understand the points being made, asking questions as appropriate, and not interrupting at inappropriate times.
Reading Comprehension	Understanding written sentences and paragraphs in work related documents.
Speaking	Talking to others to convey information effectively.
Mathematics	Using mathematics to solve problems.
Service Orientation	Actively looking for ways to help people.
Social Perceptiveness	Being aware of others' reactions and understanding why they react as they do.
Monitoring	Monitoring/Assessing performance of yourself, other individuals, or organizations to make improvements or take corrective action.
Time Management	Managing one's own time and the time of others.
Instructing	Teaching others how to do something.
Critical Thinking	Using logic and reasoning to identify the strengths and weaknesses of alternative solutions, conclusions or approaches to problems.
Negotiation	Bringing others together and trying to reconcile differences.
Active Learning	Understanding the implications of new information for both current and future problem-solving and decision-making.
Writing	Communicating effectively in writing as appropriate for the needs of the audience.
Operation and Control	Controlling operations of equipment or systems.
Judgment and Decision Making	Considering the relative costs and benefits of potential actions to choose the most appropriate one.
Equipment Maintenance	Performing routine maintenance on equipment and determining when and what kind of maintenance is needed.
Repairing	Repairing machines or systems using the needed tools.
Learning Strategies	Selecting and using training/instructional methods and procedures appropriate for the situation when learning or teaching new things.
Troubleshooting	Determining causes of operating errors and deciding what to do about it.
Systems Evaluation	Identifying measures or indicators of system performance and the actions needed to improve or correct performance, relative to the goals of the system.
Persuasion	Persuading others to change their minds or behavior.
Coordination	Adjusting actions in relation to others' actions.
Equipment Selection	Determining the kind of tools and equipment needed to do a job.
Management of Material Resources	Obtaining and seeing to the appropriate use of equipment, facilities, and materials needed to do certain work.
Systems Analysis	Determining how a system should work and how changes in conditions, operations, and the environment will affect outcomes.
Management of Personnel Resources	Motivating, developing, and directing people as they work, identifying the best people for the job.
Complex Problem Solving	Identifying complex problems and reviewing related information to develop and evaluate options and implement solutions.
Operations Analysis	Analyzing needs and product requirements to create a design.
Quality Control Analysis	Conducting tests and inspections of products, services, or processes to evaluate quality or performance.
Management of Financial Resources	Determining how money will be spent to get the work done, and accounting for these expenditures.
Science	Using scientific rules and methods to solve problems.
Installation	Installing equipment, machines, wiring, or programs to meet specifications.
Operation Monitoring	Watching gauges, dials, or other indicators to make sure a machine is working properly.
Programming	Writing computer programs for various purposes.

Technology Design	Generating or adapting equipment and technology to serve user needs.

Ability	Ability Definitions
Oral Comprehension	The ability to listen to and understand information and ideas presented through spoken words and sentences.
Oral Expression	The ability to communicate information and ideas in speaking so others will understand.
Speech Clarity	The ability to speak clearly so others can understand you.
Speech Recognition	The ability to identify and understand the speech of another person.
Near Vision	The ability to see details at close range (within a few feet of the observer).
Trunk Strength	The ability to use your abdominal and lower back muscles to support part of the body repeatedly or continuously over time without 'giving out' or fatiguing.
Information Ordering	The ability to arrange things or actions in a certain order or pattern according to a specific rule or set of rules (e.g., patterns of numbers, letters, words, pictures, mathematical operations).
Problem Sensitivity	The ability to tell when something is wrong or is likely to go wrong. It does not involve solving the problem, only recognizing there is a problem.
Selective Attention	The ability to concentrate on a task over a period of time without being distracted.
Deductive Reasoning	The ability to apply general rules to specific problems to produce answers that make sense.
Number Facility	The ability to add, subtract, multiply, or divide quickly and correctly.
Inductive Reasoning	The ability to combine pieces of information to form general rules or conclusions (includes finding a relationship among seemingly unrelated events).
Category Flexibility	The ability to generate or use different sets of rules for combining or grouping things in different ways.
Written Expression	The ability to communicate information and ideas in writing so others will understand.
Mathematical Reasoning	The ability to choose the right mathematical methods or formulas to solve a problem.
Written Comprehension	The ability to read and understand information and ideas presented in writing.
Manual Dexterity	The ability to quickly move your hand, your hand together with your arm, or your two hands to grasp, manipulate, or assemble objects.
Far Vision	The ability to see details at a distance.
Time Sharing	The ability to shift back and forth between two or more activities or sources of information (such as speech, sounds, touch, or other sources).
Arm-Hand Steadiness	The ability to keep your hand and arm steady while moving your arm or while holding your arm and hand in one position.
Stamina	The ability to exert yourself physically over long periods of time without getting winded or out of breath.
Extent Flexibility	The ability to bend, stretch, twist, or reach with your body, arms, and/or legs.
Gross Body Coordination	The ability to coordinate the movement of your arms, legs, and torso together when the whole body is in motion.
Originality	The ability to come up with unusual or clever ideas about a given topic or situation, or to develop creative ways to solve a problem.
Auditory Attention	The ability to focus on a single source of sound in the presence of other distracting sounds.
Finger Dexterity	The ability to make precisely coordinated movements of the fingers of one or both hands to grasp, manipulate, or assemble very small objects.
Fluency of Ideas	The ability to come up with a number of ideas about a topic (the number of ideas is important, not their quality, correctness, or creativity).
Memorization	The ability to remember information such as words, numbers, pictures, and procedures.
Visual Color Discrimination	The ability to match or detect differences between colors, including shades of color and brightness.
Flexibility of Closure	The ability to identify or detect a known pattern (a figure, object, word, or sound) that is hidden in other distracting material.
Perceptual Speed	The ability to quickly and accurately compare similarities and differences among sets of letters, numbers, objects, pictures, or patterns. The things to be compared may be presented at the same time or one after the other. This ability also includes comparing a presented object with a remembered object.

Visualization	The ability to imagine how something will look after it is moved around or when its parts are moved or rearranged.
Speed of Limb Movement	The ability to quickly move the arms and legs.
Speed of Closure	The ability to quickly make sense of, combine, and organize information into meaningful patterns.
Hearing Sensitivity	The ability to detect or tell the differences between sounds that vary in pitch and loudness.
Static Strength	The ability to exert maximum muscle force to lift, push, pull, or carry objects.
Control Precision	The ability to quickly and repeatedly adjust the controls of a machine or a vehicle to exact positions.
Depth Perception	The ability to judge which of several objects is closer or farther away from you, or to judge the distance between you and an object.
Reaction Time	The ability to quickly respond (with the hand, finger, or foot) to a signal (sound, light, picture) when it appears.
Sound Localization	The ability to tell the direction from which a sound originated.
Multilimb Coordination	The ability to coordinate two or more limbs (for example, two arms, two legs, or one leg and one arm) while sitting, standing, or lying down. It does not involve performing the activities while the whole body is in motion.
Wrist-Finger Speed	The ability to make fast, simple, repeated movements of the fingers, hands, and wrists.
Night Vision	The ability to see under low light conditions.
Glare Sensitivity	The ability to see objects in the presence of glare or bright lighting.
Dynamic Flexibility	The ability to quickly and repeatedly bend, stretch, twist, or reach out with your body, arms, and/or legs.
Gross Body Equilibrium	The ability to keep or regain your body balance or stay upright when in an unstable position.
Peripheral Vision	The ability to see objects or movement of objects to one's side when the eyes are looking ahead.
Response Orientation	The ability to choose quickly between two or more movements in response to two or more different signals (lights, sounds, pictures). It includes the speed with which the correct response is started with the hand, foot, or other body part.
Rate Control	The ability to time your movements or the movement of a piece of equipment in anticipation of changes in the speed and/or direction of a moving object or scene.
Dynamic Strength	The ability to exert muscle force repeatedly or continuously over time. This involves muscular endurance and resistance to muscle fatigue.
Explosive Strength	The ability to use short bursts of muscle force to propel oneself (as in jumping or sprinting), or to throw an object.
Spatial Orientation	The ability to know your location in relation to the environment or to know where other objects are in relation to you.

Work_Activity	Work_Activity Definitions
Performing for or Working Directly with the Public	Performing for people or dealing directly with the public. This includes serving customers in restaurants and stores, and receiving clients or guests.
Getting Information	Observing, receiving, and otherwise obtaining information from all relevant sources.
Identifying Objects, Actions, and Events	Identifying information by categorizing, estimating, recognizing differences or similarities, and detecting changes in circumstances or events.
Developing and Building Teams	Encouraging and building mutual trust, respect, and cooperation among team members.
Establishing and Maintaining Interpersonal Relatio	Developing constructive and cooperative working relationships with others, and maintaining them over time.
Making Decisions and Solving Problems	Analyzing information and evaluating results to choose the best solution and solve problems.
Updating and Using Relevant Knowledge	Keeping up-to-date technically and applying new knowledge to your job.
Evaluating Information to Determine Compliance wit	Using relevant information and individual judgment to determine whether events or processes comply with laws, regulations, or standards.
Judging the Qualities of Things, Services, or Peop	Assessing the value, importance, or quality of things or people.
Assisting and Caring for Others	Providing personal assistance, medical attention, emotional support, or other personal care to others such as coworkers, customers, or patients.
Monitor Processes, Materials, or Surroundings	Monitoring and reviewing information from materials, events, or the environment, to detect or assess problems.

Resolving Conflicts and Negotiating with Others	Handling complaints, settling disputes, and resolving grievances and conflicts, or otherwise negotiating with others.
Estimating the Quantifiable Characteristics of Pro	Estimating sizes, distances, and quantities; or determining time, costs, resources, or materials needed to perform a work activity.
Organizing, Planning, and Prioritizing Work	Developing specific goals and plans to prioritize, organize, and accomplish your work.
Performing Administrative Activities	Performing day-to-day administrative tasks such as maintaining information files and processing paperwork.
Communicating with Persons Outside Organization	Communicating with people outside the organization, representing the organization to customers, the public, government, and other external sources. This information can be exchanged in person, in writing, or by telephone or e-mail.
Performing General Physical Activities	Performing physical activities that require considerable use of your arms and legs and moving your whole body, such as climbing, lifting, balancing, walking, stooping, and handling of materials.
Coaching and Developing Others	Identifying the developmental needs of others and coaching, mentoring, or otherwise helping others to improve their knowledge or skills.
Selling or Influencing Others	Convincing others to buy merchandise/goods or to otherwise change their minds or actions.
Interacting With Computers	Using computers and computer systems (including hardware and software) to program, write software, set up functions, enter data, or process information.
Provide Consultation and Advice to Others	Providing guidance and expert advice to management or other groups on technical, systems-, or process-related topics.
Communicating with Supervisors, Peers, or Subordin	Providing information to supervisors, co-workers, and subordinates by telephone, in written form, e-mail, or in person.
Handling and Moving Objects	Using hands and arms in handling, installing, positioning, and moving materials, and manipulating things.
Inspecting Equipment, Structures, or Material	Inspecting equipment, structures, or materials to identify the cause of errors or other problems or defects.
Interpreting the Meaning of Information for Others	Translating or explaining what information means and how it can be used.
Documenting/Recording Information	Entering, transcribing, recording, storing, or maintaining information in written or electronic/magnetic form.
Coordinating the Work and Activities of Others	Getting members of a group to work together to accomplish tasks.
Processing Information	Compiling, coding, categorizing, calculating, tabulating, auditing, or verifying information or data.
Training and Teaching Others	Identifying the educational needs of others, developing formal educational or training programs or classes, and teaching or instructing others.
Thinking Creatively	Developing, designing, or creating new applications, ideas, relationships, systems, or products, including artistic contributions.
Guiding, Directing, and Motivating Subordinates	Providing guidance and direction to subordinates, including setting performance standards and monitoring performance.
Scheduling Work and Activities	Scheduling events, programs, and activities, as well as the work of others.
Analyzing Data or Information	Identifying the underlying principles, reasons, or facts of information by breaking down information or data into separate parts.
Controlling Machines and Processes	Using either control mechanisms or direct physical activity to operate machines or processes (not including computers or vehicles).
Monitoring and Controlling Resources	Monitoring and controlling resources and overseeing the spending of money.
Repairing and Maintaining Mechanical Equipment	Servicing, repairing, adjusting, and testing machines, devices, moving parts, and equipment that operate primarily on the basis of mechanical (not electronic) principles.
Staffing Organizational Units	Recruiting, interviewing, selecting, hiring, and promoting employees in an organization.
Operating Vehicles, Mechanized Devices, or Equipme	Running, maneuvering, navigating, or driving vehicles or mechanized equipment, such as forklifts, passenger vehicles, aircraft, or water craft.
Developing Objectives and Strategies	Establishing long-range objectives and specifying the strategies and actions to achieve them.
Repairing and Maintaining Electronic Equipment	Servicing, repairing, calibrating, regulating, fine-tuning, or testing machines, devices, and equipment that operate primarily on the basis of electrical or electronic (not mechanical) principles.
Drafting, Laying Out, and Specifying Technical Dev	Providing documentation, detailed instructions, drawings, or specifications to tell others about how devices, parts, equipment, or structures are to be fabricated, constructed, assembled, modified, maintained, or used.

Work_Context	Work_Context Definitions
Contact With Others	How much does this job require the worker to be in contact with others (face-to-face, by telephone, or otherwise) in order to perform it?
Deal With External Customers	How important is it to work with external customers or the public in this job?
Spend Time Standing	How much does this job require standing?
Face-to-Face Discussions	How often do you have to have face-to-face discussions with individuals or teams in this job?
Indoors, Environmentally Controlled	How often does this job require working indoors in environmentally controlled conditions?
Physical Proximity	To what extent does this job require the worker to perform job tasks in close physical proximity to other people?
Freedom to Make Decisions	How much decision making freedom, without supervision, does the job offer?
Work With Work Group or Team	How important is it to work with others in a group or team in this job?
Coordinate or Lead Others	How important is it to coordinate or lead others in accomplishing work activities in this job?
Frequency of Decision Making	How frequently is the worker required to make decisions that affect other people, the financial resources, and/or the image and reputation of the organization?
Structured versus Unstructured Work	To what extent is this job structured for the worker, rather than allowing the worker to determine tasks, priorities, and goals?
Importance of Being Exact or Accurate	How important is being very exact or highly accurate in performing this job?
Level of Competition	To what extent does this job require the worker to compete or to be aware of competitive pressures?
Spend Time Using Your Hands to Handle, Control, or	How much does this job require using your hands to handle, control, or feel objects, tools or controls?
Spend Time Walking and Running	How much does this job require walking and running?
Impact of Decisions on Co-workers or Company Resul	How do the decisions an employee makes impact the results of co-workers, clients or the company?
Importance of Repeating Same Tasks	How important is repeating the same physical activities (e.g., key entry) or mental activities (e.g., checking entries in a ledger) over and over, without stopping, to performing this job?
Deal With Unpleasant or Angry People	How frequently does the worker have to deal with unpleasant, angry, or discourteous individuals as part of the job requirements?
Sounds, Noise Levels Are Distracting or Uncomforta	How often does this job require working exposed to sounds and noise levels that are distracting or uncomfortable?
Frequency of Conflict Situations	How often are there conflict situations the employee has to face in this job?
Public Speaking	How often do you have to perform public speaking in this job?
Telephone	How often do you have telephone conversations in this job?
Exposed to Minor Burns, Cuts, Bites, or Stings	How often does this job require exposure to minor burns, cuts, bites, or stings?
Exposed to Hazardous Equipment	How often does this job require exposure to hazardous equipment?
Exposed to Contaminants	How often does this job require working exposed to contaminants (such as pollutants, gases, dust or odors)?
Responsibility for Outcomes and Results	How responsible is the worker for work outcomes and results of other workers?
Degree of Automation	How automated is the job?
Spend Time Kneeling, Crouching, Stooping, or Crawl	How much does this job require kneeling, crouching, stooping or crawling?
Responsible for Others' Health and Safety	How much responsibility is there for the health and safety of others in this job?
Pace Determined by Speed of Equipment	How important is it to this job that the pace is determined by the speed of equipment or machinery? (This does not refer to keeping busy at all times on this job.)
Letters and Memos	How often does the job require written letters and memos?
Time Pressure	How often does this job require the worker to meet strict deadlines?
Spend Time Making Repetitive Motions	How much does this job require making repetitive motions?
Consequence of Error	How serious would the result usually be if the worker made a mistake that was not readily correctable?
Spend Time Sitting	How much does this job require sitting?
Spend Time Bending or Twisting the Body	How much does this job require bending or twisting your body?
Deal With Physically Aggressive People	How frequently does this job require the worker to deal with physical aggression of violent individuals?
Indoors, Not Environmentally Controlled	How often does this job require working indoors in non-controlled environmental conditions (e.g., warehouse without heat)?
Extremely Bright or Inadequate Lighting	How often does this job require working in extremely bright or inadequate lighting conditions?
Very Hot or Cold Temperatures	How often does this job require working in very hot (above 90 F degrees) or very cold (below 32 F degrees) temperatures?
In an Enclosed Vehicle or Equipment	How often does this job require working in a closed vehicle or equipment (e.g., car)?
Exposed to Hazardous Conditions	How often does this job require exposure to hazardous conditions?
Electronic Mail	How often do you use electronic mail in this job?
Spend Time Keeping or Regaining Balance	How much does this job require keeping or regaining your balance?
Cramped Work Space, Awkward Positions	How often does this job require working in cramped work spaces that requires getting into awkward positions?
In an Open Vehicle or Equipment	How often does this job require working in an open vehicle or equipment (e.g., tractor)?
Wear Common Protective or Safety Equipment such as	How much does this job require wearing common protective or safety equipment such as safety shoes, glasses, gloves, hard hats or live jackets?
Exposed to High Places	How often does this job require exposure to high places?
Outdoors, Exposed to Weather	How often does this job require working outdoors, exposed to all weather conditions?
Exposed to Disease or Infections	How often does this job require exposure to disease/infections?
Exposed to Radiation	How often does this job require exposure to radiation?
Spend Time Climbing Ladders, Scaffolds, or Poles	How much does this job require climbing ladders, scaffolds, or poles?
Outdoors, Under Cover	How often does this job require working outdoors, under cover (e.g., structure with roof but no walls)?
Wear Specialized Protective or Safety Equipment su	How much does this job require wearing specialized protective or safety equipment such as breathing apparatus, safety harness, full protection suits, or radiation protection?
Exposed to Whole Body Vibration	How often does this job require exposure to whole body vibration (e.g., operate a jackhammer)?

Job Zone Component	Job Zone Component Definitions
Title	Job Zone One:　Little or No Preparation Needed
Overall Experience	No previous work-related skill, knowledge, or experience is needed for these occupations. For example, a person can become a general office clerk even if he/she has never worked in an office before.
Job Training	Employees in these occupations need anywhere from a few days to a few months of training. Usually, an experienced worker could show you how to do the job.
Job Zone Examples	These occupations involve following instructions and helping others. Examples include bus drivers, forest and conservation workers, general office clerks, home health aides, and waiters/waitresses.
SVP Range	(Below 4.0)
Education	These occupations may require a high school diploma or GED certificate. Some may require a formal training course to obtain a license.

Work_Styles	Work_Styles Definitions
Integrity	Job requires being honest and ethical.
Self Control	Job requires maintaining composure, keeping emotions in check, controlling anger, and avoiding aggressive behavior, even in very difficult situations.
Dependability	Job requires being reliable, responsible, and dependable, and fulfilling obligations.
Attention to Detail	Job requires being careful about detail and thorough in completing work tasks.
Adaptability/Flexibility	Job requires being open to change (positive or negative) and to considerable variety in the workplace.
Cooperation	Job requires being pleasant with others on the job and displaying a good-natured, cooperative attitude.
Stress Tolerance	Job requires accepting criticism and dealing calmly and effectively with high stress situations.
Leadership	Job requires a willingness to lead, take charge, and offer opinions and direction.

Concern for Others	Job requires being sensitive to others' needs and feelings and being understanding and helpful on the job.
Achievement/Effort	Job requires establishing and maintaining personally challenging achievement goals and exerting effort toward mastering tasks.
Independence	Job requires developing one's own ways of doing things, guiding oneself with little or no supervision, and depending on oneself to get things done.
Social Orientation	Job requires preferring to work with others rather than alone, and being personally connected with others on the job.
Initiative	Job requires a willingness to take on responsibilities and challenges.
Persistence	Job requires persistence in the face of obstacles.
Innovation	Job requires creativity and alternative thinking to develop new ideas for and answers to work-related problems.
Analytical Thinking	Job requires analyzing information and using logic to address work-related issues and problems.

41-2022.00 - Parts Salespersons

Sell spare and replacement parts and equipment in repair shop or parts store.

Tasks

1) Advise customers on substitution or modification of parts when identical replacements are not available.

2) Read catalogs, microfiche viewers, or computer displays in order to determine replacement part stock numbers and prices.

3) Examine returned parts for defects, and exchange defective parts or refund money.

4) Determine replacement parts required, according to inspections of old parts, customer requests, or customers' descriptions of malfunctions.

5) Fill customer orders from stock.

6) Receive payment or obtain credit authorization.

7) Take inventory of stock.

8) Prepare sales slips or sales contracts.

9) Discuss use and features of various parts, based on knowledge of machines or equipment.

10) Mark and store parts in stockrooms according to prearranged systems.

11) Demonstrate equipment to customers and explain functioning of equipment.

12) Place new merchandise on display.

13) Measure parts, using precision measuring instruments, in order to determine whether similar parts may be machined to required sizes.

14) Repair parts or equipment.

Knowledge	Knowledge Definitions
Customer and Personal Service	Knowledge of principles and processes for providing customer and personal services. This includes customer needs assessment, meeting quality standards for services, and evaluation of customer satisfaction.
Sales and Marketing	Knowledge of principles and methods for showing, promoting, and selling products or services. This includes marketing strategy and tactics, product demonstration, sales techniques, and sales control systems.
Computers and Electronics	Knowledge of circuit boards, processors, chips, electronic equipment, and computer hardware and software, including applications and programming.
Mechanical	Knowledge of machines and tools, including their designs, uses, repair, and maintenance.
Mathematics	Knowledge of arithmetic, algebra, geometry, calculus, statistics, and their applications.
English Language	Knowledge of the structure and content of the English language including the meaning and spelling of words, rules of composition, and grammar.
Administration and Management	Knowledge of business and management principles involved in strategic planning, resource allocation, human resources modeling, leadership technique, production methods, and coordination of people and resources.

Education and Training	Knowledge of principles and methods for curriculum and training design, teaching and instruction for individuals and groups, and the measurement of training effects.
Production and Processing	Knowledge of raw materials, production processes, quality control, costs, and other techniques for maximizing the effective manufacture and distribution of goods.
Clerical	Knowledge of administrative and clerical procedures and systems such as word processing, managing files and records, stenography and transcription, designing forms, and other office procedures and terminology.
Personnel and Human Resources	Knowledge of principles and procedures for personnel recruitment, selection, training, compensation and benefits, labor relations and negotiation, and personnel information systems.
Economics and Accounting	Knowledge of economic and accounting principles and practices, the financial markets, banking and the analysis and reporting of financial data.
Law and Government	Knowledge of laws, legal codes, court procedures, precedents, government regulations, executive orders, agency rules, and the democratic political process.
Public Safety and Security	Knowledge of relevant equipment, policies, procedures, and strategies to promote effective local, state, or national security operations for the protection of people, data, property, and institutions.
Transportation	Knowledge of principles and methods for moving people or goods by air, rail, sea, or road, including the relative costs and benefits.
Engineering and Technology	Knowledge of the practical application of engineering science and technology. This includes applying principles, techniques, procedures, and equipment to the design and production of various goods and services.
Telecommunications	Knowledge of transmission, broadcasting, switching, control, and operation of telecommunications systems.
Design	Knowledge of design techniques, tools, and principles involved in production of precision technical plans, blueprints, drawings, and models.
Psychology	Knowledge of human behavior and performance; individual differences in ability, personality, and interests; learning and motivation; psychological research methods; and the assessment and treatment of behavioral and affective disorders.
Communications and Media	Knowledge of media production, communication, and dissemination techniques and methods. This includes alternative ways to inform and entertain via written, oral, and visual media.
Foreign Language	Knowledge of the structure and content of a foreign (non-English) language including the meaning and spelling of words, rules of composition and grammar, and pronunciation.
Chemistry	Knowledge of the chemical composition, structure, and properties of substances and of the chemical processes and transformations that they undergo. This includes uses of chemicals and their interactions, danger signs, production techniques, and disposal methods.
Physics	Knowledge and prediction of physical principles, laws, their interrelationships, and applications to understanding fluid, material, and atmospheric dynamics, and mechanical, electrical, atomic and sub-atomic structures and processes.
Building and Construction	Knowledge of materials, methods, and the tools involved in the construction or repair of houses, buildings, or other structures such as highways and roads.
Geography	Knowledge of principles and methods for describing the features of land, sea, and air masses, including their physical characteristics, locations, interrelationships, and distribution of plant, animal, and human life.
Biology	Knowledge of plant and animal organisms, their tissues, cells, functions, interdependencies, and interactions with each other and the environment.
Sociology and Anthropology	Knowledge of group behavior and dynamics, societal trends and influences, human migrations, ethnicity, cultures and their history and origins.
History and Archeology	Knowledge of historical events and their causes, indicators, and effects on civilizations and cultures.
Philosophy and Theology	Knowledge of different philosophical systems and religions. This includes their basic principles, values, ethics, ways of thinking, customs, practices, and their impact on human culture.

Medicine and Dentistry	Knowledge of the information and techniques needed to diagnose and treat human injuries, diseases, and deformities. This includes symptoms, treatment alternatives, drug properties and interactions, and preventive health-care measures.
Food Production	Knowledge of techniques and equipment for planting, growing, and harvesting food products (both plant and animal) for consumption, including storage/handling techniques.
Fine Arts	Knowledge of the theory and techniques required to compose, produce, and perform works of music, dance, visual arts, drama, and sculpture.
Therapy and Counseling	Knowledge of principles, methods, and procedures for diagnosis, treatment, and rehabilitation of physical and mental dysfunctions, and for career counseling and guidance.

Skills	Skills Definitions
Active Listening	Giving full attention to what other people are saying, taking time to understand the points being made, asking questions as appropriate, and not interrupting at inappropriate times.
Speaking	Talking to others to convey information effectively.
Reading Comprehension	Understanding written sentences and paragraphs in work related documents.
Time Management	Managing one's own time and the time of others.
Instructing	Teaching others how to do something.
Critical Thinking	Using logic and reasoning to identify the strengths and weaknesses of alternative solutions, conclusions or approaches to problems.
Social Perceptiveness	Being aware of others' reactions and understanding why they react as they do.
Service Orientation	Actively looking for ways to help people.
Active Learning	Understanding the implications of new information for both current and future problem-solving and decision-making.
Monitoring	Monitoring/Assessing performance of yourself, other individuals, or organizations to make improvements or take corrective action.
Judgment and Decision Making	Considering the relative costs and benefits of potential actions to choose the most appropriate one.
Learning Strategies	Selecting and using training/instructional methods and procedures appropriate for the situation when learning or teaching new things.
Coordination	Adjusting actions in relation to others' actions.
Mathematics	Using mathematics to solve problems.
Writing	Communicating effectively in writing as appropriate for the needs of the audience.
Equipment Selection	Determining the kind of tools and equipment needed to do a job.
Persuasion	Persuading others to change their minds or behavior.
Negotiation	Bringing others together and trying to reconcile differences.
Complex Problem Solving	Identifying complex problems and reviewing related information to develop and evaluate options and implement solutions.
Management of Personnel Resources	Motivating, developing, and directing people as they work, identifying the best people for the job.
Operations Analysis	Analyzing needs and product requirements to create a design.
Management of Financial Resources	Determining how money will be spent to get the work done, and accounting for these expenditures.
Troubleshooting	Determining causes of operating errors and deciding what to do about it.
Management of Material Resources	Obtaining and seeing to the appropriate use of equipment, facilities, and materials needed to do certain work.
Systems Evaluation	Identifying measures or indicators of system performance and the actions needed to improve or correct performance, relative to the goals of the system.
Systems Analysis	Determining how a system should work and how changes in conditions, operations, and the environment will affect outcomes.
Installation	Installing equipment, machines, wiring, or programs to meet specifications.
Quality Control Analysis	Conducting tests and inspections of products, services, or processes to evaluate quality or performance.
Operation and Control	Controlling operations of equipment or systems.
Technology Design	Generating or adapting equipment and technology to serve user needs.
Repairing	Repairing machines or systems using the needed tools.
Equipment Maintenance	Performing routine maintenance on equipment and determining when and what kind of maintenance is needed.
Science	Using scientific rules and methods to solve problems.
Programming	Writing computer programs for various purposes.

Operation Monitoring	Watching gauges, dials, or other indicators to make sure a machine is working properly.

Ability	Ability Definitions
Oral Comprehension	The ability to listen to and understand information and ideas presented through spoken words and sentences.
Oral Expression	The ability to communicate information and ideas in speaking so others will understand.
Speech Clarity	The ability to speak clearly so others can understand you.
Written Comprehension	The ability to read and understand information and ideas presented in writing.
Speech Recognition	The ability to identify and understand the speech of another person.
Near Vision	The ability to see details at close range (within a few feet of the observer).
Information Ordering	The ability to arrange things or actions in a certain order or pattern according to a specific rule or set of rules (e.g., patterns of numbers, letters, words, pictures, mathematical operations).
Selective Attention	The ability to concentrate on a task over a period of time without being distracted.
Written Expression	The ability to communicate information and ideas in writing so others will understand.
Inductive Reasoning	The ability to combine pieces of information to form general rules or conclusions (includes finding a relationship among seemingly unrelated events).
Problem Sensitivity	The ability to tell when something is wrong or is likely to go wrong. It does not involve solving the problem, only recognizing there is a problem.
Flexibility of Closure	The ability to identify or detect a known pattern (a figure, object, word, or sound) that is hidden in other distracting material.
Perceptual Speed	The ability to quickly and accurately compare similarities and differences among sets of letters, numbers, objects, pictures, or patterns. The things to be compared may be presented at the same time or one after the other. This ability also includes comparing a presented object with a remembered object.
Deductive Reasoning	The ability to apply general rules to specific problems to produce answers that make sense.
Category Flexibility	The ability to generate or use different sets of rules for combining or grouping things in different ways.
Fluency of Ideas	The ability to come up with a number of ideas about a topic (the number of ideas is important, not their quality, correctness, or creativity).
Time Sharing	The ability to shift back and forth between two or more activities or sources of information (such as speech, sounds, touch, or other sources).
Static Strength	The ability to exert maximum muscle force to lift, push, pull, or carry objects.
Arm-Hand Steadiness	The ability to keep your hand and arm steady while moving your arm or while holding your arm and hand in one position.
Originality	The ability to come up with unusual or clever ideas about a given topic or situation, or to develop creative ways to solve a problem.
Finger Dexterity	The ability to make precisely coordinated movements of the fingers of one or both hands to grasp, manipulate, or assemble very small objects.
Speed of Closure	The ability to quickly make sense of, combine, and organize information into meaningful patterns.
Number Facility	The ability to add, subtract, multiply, or divide quickly and correctly.
Far Vision	The ability to see details at a distance.
Trunk Strength	The ability to use your abdominal and lower back muscles to support part of the body repeatedly or continuously over time without 'giving out' or fatiguing.
Visual Color Discrimination	The ability to match or detect differences between colors, including shades of color and brightness.
Auditory Attention	The ability to focus on a single source of sound in the presence of other distracting sounds.
Visualization	The ability to imagine how something will look after it is moved around or when its parts are moved or rearranged.
Manual Dexterity	The ability to quickly move your hand, your hand together with your arm, or your two hands to grasp, manipulate, or assemble objects.
Mathematical Reasoning	The ability to choose the right mathematical methods or formulas to solve a problem.

Multilimb Coordination	The ability to coordinate two or more limbs (for example, two arms, two legs, or one leg and one arm) while sitting, standing, or lying down. It does not involve performing the activities while the whole body is in motion.
Memorization	The ability to remember information such as words, numbers, pictures, and procedures.
Hearing Sensitivity	The ability to detect or tell the differences between sounds that vary in pitch and loudness.
Extent Flexibility	The ability to bend, stretch, twist, or reach with your body, arms, and/or legs.
Gross Body Equilibrium	The ability to keep or regain your body balance or stay upright when in an unstable position.
Stamina	The ability to exert yourself physically over long periods of time without getting winded or out of breath.
Gross Body Coordination	The ability to coordinate the movement of your arms, legs, and torso together when the whole body is in motion.
Control Precision	The ability to quickly and repeatedly adjust the controls of a machine or a vehicle to exact positions.
Speed of Limb Movement	The ability to quickly move the arms and legs.
Dynamic Strength	The ability to exert muscle force repeatedly or continuously over time. This involves muscular endurance and resistance to muscle fatigue.
Wrist-Finger Speed	The ability to make fast, simple, repeated movements of the fingers, hands, and wrists.
Spatial Orientation	The ability to know your location in relation to the environment or to know where other objects are in relation to you.
Explosive Strength	The ability to use short bursts of muscle force to propel oneself (as in jumping or sprinting), or to throw an object.
Sound Localization	The ability to tell the direction from which a sound originated.
Depth Perception	The ability to judge which of several objects is closer or farther away from you, or to judge the distance between you and an object.
Response Orientation	The ability to choose quickly between two or more movements in response to two or more different signals (lights, sounds, pictures). It includes the speed with which the correct response is started with the hand, foot, or other body part.
Night Vision	The ability to see under low light conditions.
Dynamic Flexibility	The ability to quickly and repeatedly bend, stretch, twist, or reach out with your body, arms, and/or legs.
Glare Sensitivity	The ability to see objects in the presence of glare or bright lighting.
Reaction Time	The ability to quickly respond (with the hand, finger, or foot) to a signal (sound, light, picture) when it appears.
Rate Control	The ability to time your movements or the movement of a piece of equipment in anticipation of changes in the speed and/or direction of a moving object or scene.
Peripheral Vision	The ability to see objects or movement of objects to one's side when the eyes are looking ahead.

Work_Activity	Work_Activity Definitions
Getting Information	Observing, receiving, and otherwise obtaining information from all relevant sources.
Performing for or Working Directly with the Public	Performing for people or dealing directly with the public. This includes serving customers in restaurants and stores, and receiving clients or guests.
Selling or Influencing Others	Convincing others to buy merchandise/goods or to otherwise change their minds or actions.
Identifying Objects, Actions, and Events	Identifying information by categorizing, estimating, recognizing differences or similarities, and detecting changes in circumstances or events.
Communicating with Persons Outside Organization	Communicating with people outside the organization, representing the organization to customers, the public, government, and other external sources. This information can be exchanged in person, in writing, or by telephone or e-mail.
Establishing and Maintaining Interpersonal Relatio	Developing constructive and cooperative working relationships with others, and maintaining them over time.
Communicating with Supervisors, Peers, or Subordin	Providing information to supervisors, co-workers, and subordinates by telephone, in written form, e-mail, or in person.
Interacting With Computers	Using computers and computer systems (including hardware and software) to program, write software, set up functions, enter data, or process information.
Updating and Using Relevant Knowledge	Keeping up-to-date technically and applying new knowledge to your job.
Making Decisions and Solving Problems	Analyzing information and evaluating results to choose the best solution and solve problems.

Processing Information	Compiling, coding, categorizing, calculating, tabulating, auditing, or verifying information or data.
Monitor Processes, Materials, or Surroundings	Monitoring and reviewing information from materials, events, or the environment, to detect or assess problems.
Resolving Conflicts and Negotiating with Others	Handling complaints, settling disputes, and resolving grievances and conflicts, or otherwise negotiating with others.
Interpreting the Meaning of Information for Others	Translating or explaining what information means and how it can be used.
Judging the Qualities of Things, Services, or Peop	Assessing the value, importance, or quality of things or people.
Analyzing Data or Information	Identifying the underlying principles, reasons, or facts of information by breaking down information or data into separate parts.
Organizing, Planning, and Prioritizing Work	Developing specific goals and plans to prioritize, organize, and accomplish your work.
Handling and Moving Objects	Using hands and arms in handling, installing, positioning, and moving materials, and manipulating things.
Performing General Physical Activities	Performing physical activities that require considerable use of your arms and legs and moving your whole body, such as climbing, lifting, balancing, walking, stooping, and handling of materials.
Performing Administrative Activities	Performing day-to-day administrative tasks such as maintaining information files and processing paperwork.
Documenting/Recording Information	Entering, transcribing, recording, storing, or maintaining information in written or electronic/magnetic form.
Assisting and Caring for Others	Providing personal assistance, medical attention, emotional support, or other personal care to others such as coworkers, customers, or patients.
Scheduling Work and Activities	Scheduling events, programs, and activities, as well as the work of others.
Inspecting Equipment, Structures, or Material	Inspecting equipment, structures, or materials to identify the cause of errors or other problems or defects.
Thinking Creatively	Developing, designing, or creating new applications, ideas, relationships, systems, or products, including artistic contributions.
Coaching and Developing Others	Identifying the developmental needs of others and coaching, mentoring, or otherwise helping others to improve their knowledge or skills.
Coordinating the Work and Activities of Others	Getting members of a group to work together to accomplish tasks.
Developing Objectives and Strategies	Establishing long-range objectives and specifying the strategies and actions to achieve them.
Estimating the Quantifiable Characteristics of Pro	Estimating sizes, distances, and quantities; or determining time, costs, resources, or materials needed to perform a work activity.
Monitoring and Controlling Resources	Monitoring and controlling resources and overseeing the spending of money.
Evaluating Information to Determine Compliance wit	Using relevant information and individual judgment to determine whether events or processes comply with laws, regulations, or standards.
Developing and Building Teams	Encouraging and building mutual trust, respect, and cooperation among team members.
Training and Teaching Others	Identifying the educational needs of others, developing formal educational or training programs or classes, and teaching or instructing others.
Operating Vehicles, Mechanized Devices, or Equipme	Running, maneuvering, navigating, or driving vehicles or mechanized equipment, such as forklifts, passenger vehicles, aircraft, or water craft.
Guiding, Directing, and Motivating Subordinates	Providing guidance and direction to subordinates, including setting performance standards and monitoring performance.
Provide Consultation and Advice to Others	Providing guidance and expert advice to management or other groups on technical, systems-, or process-related topics.
Controlling Machines and Processes	Using either control mechanisms or direct physical activity to operate machines or processes (not including computers or vehicles).
Staffing Organizational Units	Recruiting, interviewing, selecting, hiring, and promoting employees in an organization.
Drafting, Laying Out, and Specifying Technical Dev	Providing documentation, detailed instructions, drawings, or specifications to tell others about how devices, parts, equipment, or structures are to be fabricated, constructed, assembled, modified, maintained, or used.
Repairing and Maintaining Electronic Equipment	Servicing, repairing, calibrating, regulating, fine-tuning, or testing machines, devices, and equipment that operate primarily on the basis of electrical or electronic (not mechanical) principles.

Repairing and Maintaining Mechanical Equipment	Servicing, repairing, adjusting, and testing machines, devices, moving parts, and equipment that operate primarily on the basis of mechanical (not electronic) principles.

Work_Context	**Work_Context Definitions**
Telephone	How often do you have telephone conversations in this job?
Contact With Others	How much does this job require the worker to be in contact with others (face-to-face, by telephone, or otherwise) in order to perform it?
Deal With External Customers	How important is it to work with external customers or the public in this job?
Indoors, Environmentally Controlled	How often does this job require working indoors in environmentally controlled conditions?
Frequency of Decision Making	How frequently is the worker required to make decisions that affect other people, the financial resources, and/or the image and reputation of the organization?
Importance of Being Exact or Accurate	How important is being very exact or highly accurate in performing this job?
Freedom to Make Decisions	How much decision making freedom, without supervision, does the job offer?
Face-to-Face Discussions	How often do you have to have face-to-face discussions with individuals or teams in this job?
Structured versus Unstructured Work	To what extent is this job structured for the worker, rather than allowing the worker to determine tasks, priorities, and goals?
Work With Work Group or Team	How important is it to work with others in a group or team in this job?
Importance of Repeating Same Tasks	How important is repeating the same physical activities (e.g., key entry) or mental activities (e.g., checking entries in a ledger) over and over, without stopping, to performing this job?
Time Pressure	How often does this job require the worker to meet strict deadlines?
Impact of Decisions on Co-workers or Company Resul	How do the decisions an employee makes impact the results of co-workers, clients or the company?
Physical Proximity	To what extent does this job require the worker to perform job tasks in close physical proximity to other people?
Exposed to Contaminants	How often does this job require working exposed to contaminants (such as pollutants, gases, dust or odors)?
Sounds, Noise Levels Are Distracting or Uncomforta	How often does this job require working exposed to sounds and noise levels that are distracting or uncomfortable?
Deal With Unpleasant or Angry People	How frequently does the worker have to deal with unpleasant, angry, or discourteous individuals as part of the job requirements?
Electronic Mail	How often do you use electronic mail in this job?
Coordinate or Lead Others	How important is it to coordinate or lead others in accomplishing work activities in this job?
Spend Time Standing	How much does this job require standing?
Spend Time Making Repetitive Motions	How much does this job require making repetitive motions?
Indoors, Not Environmentally Controlled	How often does this job require working indoors in non-controlled environmental conditions (e.g., warehouse without heat)?
Frequency of Conflict Situations	How often are there conflict situations the employee has to face in this job?
Responsibility for Outcomes and Results	How responsible is the worker for work outcomes and results of other workers?
Level of Competition	To what extent does this job require the worker to compete or to be aware of competitive pressures?
Spend Time Walking and Running	How much does this job require walking and running?
Spend Time Sitting	How much does this job require sitting?
Degree of Automation	How automated is the job?
Responsible for Others' Health and Safety	How much responsibility is there for the health and safety of others in this job?
Spend Time Using Your Hands to Handle, Control, or	How much does this job require using your hands to handle, control, or feel objects, tools or controls?
Letters and Memos	How often does the job require written letters and memos?
Exposed to Hazardous Conditions	How often does this job require exposure to hazardous conditions?
Wear Common Protective or Safety Equipment such as	How much does this job require wearing common protective or safety equipment such as safety shoes, glasses, gloves, hard hats or life jackets?
Very Hot or Cold Temperatures	How often does this job require working in very hot (above 90 F degrees) or very cold (below 32 F degrees) temperatures?
Outdoors, Exposed to Weather	How often does this job require working outdoors, exposed to all weather conditions?
Exposed to Hazardous Equipment	How often does this job require exposure to hazardous equipment?
Spend Time Bending or Twisting the Body	How much does this job require bending or twisting your body?
Extremely Bright or Inadequate Lighting	How often does this job require working in extremely bright or inadequate lighting conditions?
Spend Time Kneeling, Crouching, Stooping, or Crawl	How much does this job require kneeling, crouching, stooping or crawling?
In an Enclosed Vehicle or Equipment	How often does this job require working in a closed vehicle or equipment (e.g., car)?
Consequence of Error	How serious would the result usually be if the worker made a mistake that was not readily correctable?
Exposed to Minor Burns, Cuts, Bites, or Stings	How often does this job require exposure to minor burns, cuts, bites, or stings?
Cramped Work Space, Awkward Positions	How often does this job require working in cramped work spaces that requires getting into awkward positions?
Outdoors, Under Cover	How often does this job require working outdoors, under cover (e.g., structure with roof but no walls)?
Public Speaking	How often do you have to perform public speaking in this job?
Exposed to High Places	How often does this job require exposure to high places?
Spend Time Keeping or Regaining Balance	How much does this job require keeping or regaining your balance?
Spend Time Climbing Ladders, Scaffolds, or Poles	How much does this job require climbing ladders, scaffolds, or poles?
Pace Determined by Speed of Equipment	How important is it to this job that the pace is determined by the speed of equipment or machinery? (This does not refer to keeping busy at all times on this job.)
Deal With Physically Aggressive People	How frequently does this job require the worker to deal with physical aggression of violent individuals?
In an Open Vehicle or Equipment	How often does this job require working in an open vehicle or equipment (e.g., tractor)?
Exposed to Disease or Infections	How often does this job require exposure to disease/infections?
Wear Specialized Protective or Safety Equipment su	How much does this job require wearing specialized protective or safety equipment such as breathing apparatus, safety harness, full protection suits, or radiation protection?
Exposed to Whole Body Vibration	How often does this job require exposure to whole body vibration (e.g., operate a jackhammer)?
Exposed to Radiation	How often does this job require exposure to radiation?

Job Zone Component	**Job Zone Component Definitions**
Title	Job Zone Two: Some Preparation Needed
Overall Experience	Some previous work-related skill, knowledge, or experience may be helpful in these occupations, but usually is not needed. For example, a drywall installer might benefit from experience installing drywall, but an inexperienced person could still learn to be an installer with little difficulty.
Job Training	Employees in these occupations need anywhere from a few months to one year of working with experienced employees.
Job Zone Examples	These occupations often involve using your knowledge and skills to help others. Examples include drywall installers, fire inspectors, flight attendants, pharmacy technicians, salespersons (retail), and tellers.
SVP Range	(4.0 to < 6.0)
Education	These occupations usually require a high school diploma and may require some vocational training or job-related course work. In some cases, an associate's or bachelor's degree could be needed.

Work_Styles	**Work_Styles Definitions**
Cooperation	Job requires being pleasant with others on the job and displaying a good-natured, cooperative attitude.
Self Control	Job requires maintaining composure, keeping emotions in check, controlling anger, and avoiding aggressive behavior, even in very difficult situations.
Attention to Detail	Job requires being careful about detail and thorough in completing work tasks.
Stress Tolerance	Job requires accepting criticism and dealing calmly and effectively with high stress situations.
Independence	Job requires developing one's own ways of doing things, guiding oneself with little or no supervision, and depending on oneself to get things done.

Dependability	Job requires being reliable, responsible, and dependable, and fulfilling obligations.
Integrity	Job requires being honest and ethical.
Concern for Others	Job requires being sensitive to others' needs and feelings and being understanding and helpful on the job.
Adaptability/Flexibility	Job requires being open to change (positive or negative) and to considerable variety in the workplace.
Initiative	Job requires a willingness to take on responsibilities and challenges.
Achievement/Effort	Job requires establishing and maintaining personally challenging achievement goals and exerting effort toward mastering tasks.
Persistence	Job requires persistence in the face of obstacles.
Social Orientation	Job requires preferring to work with others rather than alone, and being personally connected with others on the job.
Analytical Thinking	Job requires analyzing information and using logic to address work-related issues and problems.
Leadership	Job requires a willingness to lead, take charge, and offer opinions and direction.
Innovation	Job requires creativity and alternative thinking to develop new ideas for and answers to work-related problems.

41-2031.00 - Retail Salespersons

Sell merchandise, such as furniture, motor vehicles, appliances, or apparel in a retail establishment.

Tasks

1) Greet customers and ascertain what each customer wants or needs.

2) Recommend, select, and help locate or obtain merchandise based on customer needs and desires.

3) Clean shelves, counters, and tables.

4) Maintain knowledge of current sales and promotions, policies regarding payment and exchanges, and security practices.

5) Ticket, arrange and display merchandise to promote sales.

6) Compute sales prices, total purchases and receive and process cash or credit payment.

7) Watch for and recognize security risks and thefts, and know how to prevent or handle these situations.

8) Describe merchandise and explain use, operation, and care of merchandise to customers.

9) Bag or package purchases, and wrap gifts.

10) Exchange merchandise for customers and accept returns.

11) Open and close cash registers, performing tasks such as counting money, separating charge slips, coupons, and vouchers, balancing cash drawers, and making deposits.

12) Demonstrate use or operation of merchandise.

13) Maintain records related to sales.

14) Prepare sales slips or sales contracts.

15) Place special orders or call other stores to find desired items.

16) Inventory stock and requisition new stock.

17) Prepare merchandise for purchase or rental.

18) Help customers try on or fit merchandise.

19) Sell or arrange for delivery, insurance, financing, or service contracts for merchandise.

20) Estimate cost of repair or alteration of merchandise.

21) Estimate quantity and cost of merchandise required, such as paint or floor covering.

22) Estimate and quote trade-in allowances.

23) Rent merchandise to customers.

Knowledge	Knowledge Definitions
Customer and Personal Service	Knowledge of principles and processes for providing customer and personal services. This includes customer needs assessment, meeting quality standards for services, and evaluation of customer satisfaction.
Sales and Marketing	Knowledge of principles and methods for showing, promoting, and selling products or services. This includes marketing strategy and tactics, product demonstration, sales techniques, and sales control systems.
Administration and Management	Knowledge of business and management principles involved in strategic planning, resource allocation, human resources modeling, leadership technique, production methods, and coordination of people and resources.
Education and Training	Knowledge of principles and methods for curriculum and training design, teaching and instruction for individuals and groups, and the measurement of training effects.
Mathematics	Knowledge of arithmetic, algebra, geometry, calculus, statistics, and their applications.
English Language	Knowledge of the structure and content of the English language including the meaning and spelling of words, rules of composition, and grammar.
Public Safety and Security	Knowledge of relevant equipment, policies, procedures, and strategies to promote effective local, state, or national security operations for the protection of people, data, property, and institutions.
Personnel and Human Resources	Knowledge of principles and procedures for personnel recruitment, selection, training, compensation and benefits, labor relations and negotiation, and personnel information systems.
Clerical	Knowledge of administrative and clerical procedures and systems such as word processing, managing files and records, stenography and transcription, designing forms, and other office procedures and terminology.
Economics and Accounting	Knowledge of economic and accounting principles and practices, the financial markets, banking and the analysis and reporting of financial data.
Psychology	Knowledge of human behavior and performance; individual differences in ability, personality, and interests; learning and motivation; psychological research methods; and the assessment and treatment of behavioral and affective disorders.
Telecommunications	Knowledge of transmission, broadcasting, switching, control, and operation of telecommunications systems.
Law and Government	Knowledge of laws, legal codes, court procedures, precedents, government regulations, executive orders, agency rules, and the democratic political process.
Computers and Electronics	Knowledge of circuit boards, processors, chips, electronic equipment, and computer hardware and software, including applications and programming.
Transportation	Knowledge of principles and methods for moving people or goods by air, rail, sea, or road, including the relative costs and benefits.
Production and Processing	Knowledge of raw materials, production processes, quality control, costs, and other techniques for maximizing the effective manufacture and distribution of goods.
Communications and Media	Knowledge of media production, communication, and dissemination techniques and methods. This includes alternative ways to inform and entertain via written, oral, and visual media.
Sociology and Anthropology	Knowledge of group behavior and dynamics, societal trends and influences, human migrations, ethnicity, cultures and their history and origins.
Mechanical	Knowledge of machines and tools, including their designs, uses, repair, and maintenance.
Foreign Language	Knowledge of the structure and content of a foreign (non-English) language including the meaning and spelling of words, rules of composition and grammar, and pronunciation.
Geography	Knowledge of principles and methods for describing the features of land, sea, and air masses, including their physical characteristics, locations, interrelationships, and distribution of plant, animal, and human life.
Therapy and Counseling	Knowledge of principles, methods, and procedures for diagnosis, treatment, and rehabilitation of physical and mental dysfunctions, and for career counseling and guidance.
Medicine and Dentistry	Knowledge of the information and techniques needed to diagnose and treat human injuries, diseases, and deformities. This includes symptoms, treatment alternatives, drug properties and interactions, and preventive health-care measures.
Engineering and Technology	Knowledge of the practical application of engineering science and technology. This includes applying principles, techniques, procedures, and equipment to the design and production of various goods and services.

Design	Knowledge of design techniques, tools, and principles involved in production of precision technical plans, blueprints, drawings, and models.
Chemistry	Knowledge of the chemical composition, structure, and properties of substances and of the chemical processes and transformations that they undergo. This includes uses of chemicals and their interactions, danger signs, production techniques, and disposal methods.
Food Production	Knowledge of techniques and equipment for planting, growing, and harvesting food products (both plant and animal) for consumption, including storage/handling techniques.
Fine Arts	Knowledge of the theory and techniques required to compose, produce, and perform works of music, dance, visual arts, drama, and sculpture.
Biology	Knowledge of plant and animal organisms, their tissues, cells, functions, interdependencies, and interactions with each other and the environment.
Physics	Knowledge and prediction of physical principles, laws, their interrelationships, and applications to understanding fluid, material, and atmospheric dynamics, and mechanical, electrical, atomic and sub-atomic structures and processes.
Philosophy and Theology	Knowledge of different philosophical systems and religions. This includes their basic principles, values, ethics, ways of thinking, customs, practices, and their impact on human culture.
History and Archeology	Knowledge of historical events and their causes, indicators, and effects on civilizations and cultures.
Building and Construction	Knowledge of materials, methods, and the tools involved in the construction or repair of houses, buildings, or other structures such as highways and roads.

Skills	Skills Definitions
Active Listening	Giving full attention to what other people are saying, taking time to understand the points being made, asking questions as appropriate, and not interrupting at inappropriate times.
Mathematics	Using mathematics to solve problems.
Speaking	Talking to others to convey information effectively.
Social Perceptiveness	Being aware of others' reactions and understanding why they react as they do.
Critical Thinking	Using logic and reasoning to identify the strengths and weaknesses of alternative solutions, conclusions or approaches to problems.
Writing	Communicating effectively in writing as appropriate for the needs of the audience.
Judgment and Decision Making	Considering the relative costs and benefits of potential actions to choose the most appropriate one.
Instructing	Teaching others how to do something.
Reading Comprehension	Understanding written sentences and paragraphs in work related documents.
Time Management	Managing one's own time and the time of others.
Negotiation	Bringing others together and trying to reconcile differences.
Learning Strategies	Selecting and using training/instructional methods and procedures appropriate for the situation when learning or teaching new things.
Active Learning	Understanding the implications of new information for both current and future problem-solving and decision-making.
Service Orientation	Actively looking for ways to help people.
Operation and Control	Controlling operations of equipment or systems.
Management of Personnel Resources	Motivating, developing, and directing people as they work, identifying the best people for the job.
Coordination	Adjusting actions in relation to others' actions.
Systems Analysis	Determining how a system should work and how changes in conditions, operations, and the environment will affect outcomes.
Systems Evaluation	Identifying measures or indicators of system performance and the actions needed to improve or correct performance, relative to the goals of the system.
Monitoring	Monitoring/Assessing performance of yourself, other individuals, or organizations to make improvements or take corrective action.
Persuasion	Persuading others to change their minds or behavior.
Operations Analysis	Analyzing needs and product requirements to create a design.
Complex Problem Solving	Identifying complex problems and reviewing related information to develop and evaluate options and implement solutions.
Equipment Maintenance	Performing routine maintenance on equipment and determining when and what kind of maintenance is needed.

Troubleshooting	Determining causes of operating errors and deciding what to do about it.
Equipment Selection	Determining the kind of tools and equipment needed to do a job.
Management of Financial Resources	Determining how money will be spent to get the work done, and accounting for these expenditures.
Operation Monitoring	Watching gauges, dials, or other indicators to make sure a machine is working properly.
Repairing	Repairing machines or systems using the needed tools.
Quality Control Analysis	Conducting tests and inspections of products, services, or processes to evaluate quality or performance.
Management of Material Resources	Obtaining and seeing to the appropriate use of equipment, facilities, and materials needed to do certain work.
Programming	Writing computer programs for various purposes.
Technology Design	Generating or adapting equipment and technology to serve user needs.
Installation	Installing equipment, machines, wiring, or programs to meet specifications.
Science	Using scientific rules and methods to solve problems.

Ability	Ability Definitions
Oral Expression	The ability to communicate information and ideas in speaking so others will understand.
Oral Comprehension	The ability to listen to and understand information and ideas presented through spoken words and sentences.
Speech Clarity	The ability to speak clearly so others can understand you.
Trunk Strength	The ability to use your abdominal and lower back muscles to support part of the body repeatedly or continuously over time without 'giving out' or fatiguing.
Speech Recognition	The ability to identify and understand the speech of another person.
Problem Sensitivity	The ability to tell when something is wrong or is likely to go wrong. It does not involve solving the problem, only recognizing there is a problem.
Information Ordering	The ability to arrange things or actions in a certain order or pattern according to a specific rule or set of rules (e.g., patterns of numbers, letters, words, pictures, mathematical operations).
Deductive Reasoning	The ability to apply general rules to specific problems to produce answers that make sense.
Inductive Reasoning	The ability to combine pieces of information to form general rules or conclusions (includes finding a relationship among seemingly unrelated events).
Number Facility	The ability to add, subtract, multiply, or divide quickly and correctly.
Manual Dexterity	The ability to quickly move your hand, your hand together with your arm, or your two hands to grasp, manipulate, or assemble objects.
Category Flexibility	The ability to generate or use different sets of rules for combining or grouping things in different ways.
Finger Dexterity	The ability to make precisely coordinated movements of the fingers of one or both hands to grasp, manipulate, or assemble very small objects.
Time Sharing	The ability to shift back and forth between two or more activities or sources of information (such as speech, sounds, touch, or other sources).
Near Vision	The ability to see details at close range (within a few feet of the observer).
Mathematical Reasoning	The ability to choose the right mathematical methods or formulas to solve a problem.
Written Comprehension	The ability to read and understand information and ideas presented in writing.
Selective Attention	The ability to concentrate on a task over a period of time without being distracted.
Multilimb Coordination	The ability to coordinate two or more limbs (for example, two arms, two legs, or one leg and one arm) while sitting, standing, or lying down. It does not involve performing the activities while the whole body is in motion.
Written Expression	The ability to communicate information and ideas in writing so others will understand.
Memorization	The ability to remember information such as words, numbers, pictures, and procedures.
Perceptual Speed	The ability to quickly and accurately compare similarities and differences among sets of letters, numbers, objects, pictures, or patterns. The things to be compared may be presented at the same time or one after the other. This ability also includes comparing a presented object with a remembered object.

Visual Color Discrimination	The ability to match or detect differences between colors, including shades of color and brightness.
Far Vision	The ability to see details at a distance.
Stamina	The ability to exert yourself physically over long periods of time without getting winded or out of breath.
Arm-Hand Steadiness	The ability to keep your hand and arm steady while moving your arm or while holding your arm and hand in one position.
Fluency of Ideas	The ability to come up with a number of ideas about a topic (the number of ideas is important, not their quality, correctness, or creativity).
Static Strength	The ability to exert maximum muscle force to lift, push, pull, or carry objects.
Originality	The ability to come up with unusual or clever ideas about a given topic or situation, or to develop creative ways to solve a problem.
Extent Flexibility	The ability to bend, stretch, twist, or reach with your body, arms, and/or legs.
Visualization	The ability to imagine how something will look after it is moved around or when its parts are moved or rearranged.
Gross Body Coordination	The ability to coordinate the movement of your arms, legs, and torso together when the whole body is in motion.
Flexibility of Closure	The ability to identify or detect a known pattern (a figure, object, word, or sound) that is hidden in other distracting material.
Speed of Closure	The ability to quickly make sense of, combine, and organize information into meaningful patterns.
Gross Body Equilibrium	The ability to keep or regain your body balance or stay upright when in an unstable position.
Speed of Limb Movement	The ability to quickly move the arms and legs.
Control Precision	The ability to quickly and repeatedly adjust the controls of a machine or a vehicle to exact positions.
Wrist-Finger Speed	The ability to make fast, simple, repeated movements of the fingers, hands, and wrists.
Dynamic Strength	The ability to exert muscle force repeatedly or continuously over time. This involves muscular endurance and resistance to muscle fatigue.
Spatial Orientation	The ability to know your location in relation to the environment or to know where other objects are in relation to you.
Hearing Sensitivity	The ability to detect or tell the differences between sounds that vary in pitch and loudness.
Peripheral Vision	The ability to see objects or movement of objects to one's side when the eyes are looking ahead.
Auditory Attention	The ability to focus on a single source of sound in the presence of other distracting sounds.
Response Orientation	The ability to choose quickly between two or more movements in response to two or more different signals (lights, sounds, pictures). It includes the speed with which the correct response is started with the hand, foot, or other body part.
Depth Perception	The ability to judge which of several objects is closer or farther away from you, or to judge the distance between you and an object.
Glare Sensitivity	The ability to see objects in the presence of glare or bright lighting.
Rate Control	The ability to time your movements or the movement of a piece of equipment in anticipation of changes in the speed and/or direction of a moving object or scene.
Reaction Time	The ability to quickly respond (with the hand, finger, or foot) to a signal (sound, light, picture) when it appears.
Dynamic Flexibility	The ability to quickly and repeatedly bend, stretch, twist, or reach out with your body, arms, and/or legs.
Night Vision	The ability to see under low light conditions.
Explosive Strength	The ability to use short bursts of muscle force to propel oneself (as in jumping or sprinting), or to throw an object.
Sound Localization	The ability to tell the direction from which a sound originated.

Work_Activity	Work_Activity Definitions
Performing for or Working Directly with the Public	Performing for people or dealing directly with the public. This includes serving customers in restaurants and stores, and receiving clients or guests.
Selling or Influencing Others	Convincing others to buy merchandise/goods or to otherwise change their minds or actions.
Getting Information	Observing, receiving, and otherwise obtaining information from all relevant sources.
Establishing and Maintaining Interpersonal Relatio	Developing constructive and cooperative working relationships with others, and maintaining them over time.

Communicating with Supervisors, Peers, or Subordin	Providing information to supervisors, co-workers, and subordinates by telephone, in written form, e-mail, or in person.
Updating and Using Relevant Knowledge	Keeping up-to-date technically and applying new knowledge to your job.
Resolving Conflicts and Negotiating with Others	Handling complaints, settling disputes, and resolving grievances and conflicts, or otherwise negotiating with others.
Training and Teaching Others	Identifying the educational needs of others, developing formal educational or training programs or classes, and teaching or instructing others.
Communicating with Persons Outside Organization	Communicating with people outside the organization, representing the organization to customers, the public, government, and other external sources. This information can be exchanged in person, in writing, or by telephone or e-mail.
Assisting and Caring for Others	Providing personal assistance, medical attention, emotional support, or other personal care to others such as coworkers, customers, or patients.
Handling and Moving Objects	Using hands and arms in handling, installing, positioning, and moving materials, and manipulating things.
Making Decisions and Solving Problems	Analyzing information and evaluating results to choose the best solution and solve problems.
Identifying Objects, Actions, and Events	Identifying information by categorizing, estimating, recognizing differences or similarities, and detecting changes in circumstances or events.
Documenting/Recording Information	Entering, transcribing, recording, storing, or maintaining information in written or electronic/magnetic form.
Performing General Physical Activities	Performing physical activities that require considerable use of your arms and legs and moving your whole body, such as climbing, lifting, balancing, walking, stooping, and handling of materials.
Interacting With Computers	Using computers and computer systems (including hardware and software) to program, write software, set up functions, enter data, or process information.
Thinking Creatively	Developing, designing, or creating new applications, ideas, relationships, systems, or products, including artistic contributions.
Performing Administrative Activities	Performing day-to-day administrative tasks such as maintaining information files and processing paperwork.
Processing Information	Compiling, coding, categorizing, calculating, tabulating, auditing, or verifying information or data.
Organizing, Planning, and Prioritizing Work	Developing specific goals and plans to prioritize, organize, and accomplish your work.
Judging the Qualities of Things, Services, or Peop	Assessing the value, importance, or quality of things or people.
Monitor Processes, Materials, or Surroundings	Monitoring and reviewing information from materials, events, or the environment, to detect or assess problems.
Interpreting the Meaning of Information for Others	Translating or explaining what information means and how it can be used.
Scheduling Work and Activities	Scheduling events, programs, and activities, as well as the work of others.
Developing and Building Teams	Encouraging and building mutual trust, respect, and cooperation among team members.
Estimating the Quantifiable Characteristics of Pro	Estimating sizes, distances, and quantities; or determining time, costs, resources, or materials needed to perform a work activity.
Analyzing Data or Information	Identifying the underlying principles, reasons, or facts of information by breaking down information or data into separate parts.
Controlling Machines and Processes	Using either control mechanisms or direct physical activity to operate machines or processes (not including computers or vehicles).
Inspecting Equipment, Structures, or Material	Inspecting equipment, structures, or materials to identify the cause of errors or other problems or defects.
Coordinating the Work and Activities of Others	Getting members of a group to work together to accomplish tasks.
Coaching and Developing Others	Identifying the developmental needs of others and coaching, mentoring, or otherwise helping others to improve their knowledge or skills.
Evaluating Information to Determine Compliance wit	Using relevant information and individual judgment to determine whether events or processes comply with laws, regulations, or standards.
Provide Consultation and Advice to Others	Providing guidance and expert advice to management or other groups on technical, systems-, or process-related topics.
Developing Objectives and Strategies	Establishing long-range objectives and specifying the strategies and actions to achieve them.

Operating Vehicles, Mechanized Devices, or Equipme	Running, maneuvering, navigating, or driving vehicles or mechanized equipment, such as forklifts, passenger vehicles, aircraft, or water craft.
Monitoring and Controlling Resources	Monitoring and controlling resources and overseeing the spending of money.
Guiding, Directing, and Motivating Subordinates	Providing guidance and direction to subordinates, including setting performance standards and monitoring performance.
Repairing and Maintaining Mechanical Equipment	Servicing, repairing, adjusting, and testing machines, devices, moving parts, and equipment that operate primarily on the basis of mechanical (not electronic) principles.
Repairing and Maintaining Electronic Equipment	Servicing, repairing, calibrating, regulating, fine-tuning, or testing machines, devices, and equipment that operate primarily on the basis of electrical or electronic (not mechanical) principles.
Staffing Organizational Units	Recruiting, interviewing, selecting, hiring, and promoting employees in an organization.
Drafting, Laying Out, and Specifying Technical Dev	Providing documentation, detailed instructions, drawings, or specifications to tell others about how devices, parts, equipment, or structures are to be fabricated, constructed, assembled, modified, maintained, or used.

Work_Context — Work_Context Definitions

Work_Context	Work_Context Definitions
Spend Time Standing	How much does this job require standing?
Deal With External Customers	How important is it to work with external customers or the public in this job?
Telephone	How often do you have telephone conversations in this job?
Contact With Others	How much does this job require the worker to be in contact with others (face-to-face, by telephone, or otherwise) in order to perform it?
Face-to-Face Discussions	How often do you have to have face-to-face discussions with individuals or teams in this job?
Indoors, Environmentally Controlled	How often does this job require working indoors in environmentally controlled conditions?
Frequency of Decision Making	How frequently is the worker required to make decisions that affect other people, the financial resources, and/or the image and reputation of the organization?
Work With Work Group or Team	How important is it to work with others in a group or team in this job?
Physical Proximity	To what extent does this job require the worker to perform job tasks in close physical proximity to other people?
Structured versus Unstructured Work	To what extent is this job structured for the worker, rather than allowing the worker to determine tasks, priorities, and goals?
Time Pressure	How often does this job require the worker to meet strict deadlines?
Freedom to Make Decisions	How much decision making freedom, without supervision, does the job offer?
Impact of Decisions on Co-workers or Company Resul	How do the decisions an employee makes impact the results of co-workers, clients or the company?
Coordinate or Lead Others	How important is it to coordinate or lead others in accomplishing work activities in this job?
Deal With Unpleasant or Angry People	How frequently does the worker have to deal with unpleasant, angry, or discourteous individuals as part of the job requirements?
Importance of Being Exact or Accurate	How important is being very exact or highly accurate in performing this job?
Level of Competition	To what extent does this job require the worker to compete or to be aware of competitive pressures?
Spend Time Walking and Running	How much does this job require walking and running?
Spend Time Making Repetitive Motions	How much does this job require making repetitive motions?
Responsible for Others' Health and Safety	How much responsibility is there for the health and safety of others in this job?
Spend Time Using Your Hands to Handle, Control, or	How much does this job require using your hands to handle, control, or feel objects, tools or controls?
Frequency of Conflict Situations	How often are there conflict situations the employee has to face in this job?
Responsibility for Outcomes and Results	How responsible is the worker for work outcomes and results of other workers?
Importance of Repeating Same Tasks	How important is repeating the same physical activities (e.g., key entry) or mental activities (e.g., checking entries in a ledger) over and over, without stopping, to performing this job?
Letters and Memos	How often does the job require written letters and memos?
Sounds, Noise Levels Are Distracting or Uncomforta	How often does this job require working exposed to sounds and noise levels that are distracting or uncomfortable?

Degree of Automation	How automated is the job?
Spend Time Kneeling, Crouching, Stooping, or Crawl	How much does this job require kneeling, crouching, stooping or crawling?
Exposed to Contaminants	How often does this job require working exposed to contaminants (such as pollutants, gases, dust or odors)?
Exposed to Minor Burns, Cuts, Bites, or Stings	How often does this job require exposure to minor burns, cuts, bites, or stings?
Very Hot or Cold Temperatures	How often does this job require working in very hot (above 90 F degrees) or very cold (below 32 F degrees) temperatures?
Spend Time Bending or Twisting the Body	How much does this job require bending or twisting your body?
Spend Time Sitting	How much does this job require sitting?
Consequence of Error	How serious would the result usually be if the worker made a mistake that was not readily correctable?
Spend Time Keeping or Regaining Balance	How much does this job require keeping or regaining your balance?
Electronic Mail	How often do you use electronic mail in this job?
Cramped Work Space, Awkward Positions	How often does this job require working in cramped work spaces that requires getting into awkward positions?
Extremely Bright or Inadequate Lighting	How often does this job require working in extremely bright or inadequate lighting conditions?
Outdoors, Exposed to Weather	How often does this job require working outdoors, exposed to all weather conditions?
Deal With Physically Aggressive People	How frequently does this job require the worker to deal with physical aggression of violent individuals?
Wear Common Protective or Safety Equipment such as	How much does this job require wearing common protective or safety equipment such as safety shoes, glasses, gloves, hard hats or live jackets?
Public Speaking	How often do you have to perform public speaking in this job?
Exposed to Hazardous Equipment	How often does this job require exposure to hazardous equipment?
Pace Determined by Speed of Equipment	How important is it to this job that the pace is determined by the speed of equipment or machinery? (This does not refer to keeping busy at all times on this job.)
Spend Time Climbing Ladders, Scaffolds, or Poles	How much does this job require climbing ladders, scaffolds, or poles?
Exposed to Hazardous Conditions	How often does this job require exposure to hazardous conditions?
Exposed to High Places	How often does this job require exposure to high places?
Indoors, Not Environmentally Controlled	How often does this job require working indoors in non-controlled environmental conditions (e.g., warehouse without heat)?
In an Enclosed Vehicle or Equipment	How often does this job require working in a closed vehicle or equipment (e.g., car)?
In an Open Vehicle or Equipment	How often does this job require working in an open vehicle or equipment (e.g., tractor)?
Outdoors, Under Cover	How often does this job require working outdoors, under cover (e.g., structure with roof but no walls)?
Exposed to Disease or Infections	How often does this job require exposure to disease/infections?
Exposed to Whole Body Vibration	How often does this job require exposure to whole body vibration (e.g., operate a jackhammer)?
Wear Specialized Protective or Safety Equipment su	How much does this job require wearing specialized protective or safety equipment such as breathing apparatus, safety harness, full protection suits, or radiation protection?
Exposed to Radiation	How often does this job require exposure to radiation?

Job Zone Component — Job Zone Component Definitions

Job Zone Component	Job Zone Component Definitions
Title	Job Zone Two: Some Preparation Needed
Overall Experience	Some previous work-related skill, knowledge, or experience may be helpful in these occupations, but usually is not needed. For example, a drywall installer might benefit from experience installing drywall, but an inexperienced person could still learn to be an installer with little difficulty.
Job Training	Employees in these occupations need anywhere from a few months to one year of working with experienced employees.
Job Zone Examples	These occupations often involve using your knowledge and skills to help others. Examples include drywall installers, fire inspectors, flight attendants, pharmacy technicians, salespersons (retail), and tellers.
SVP Range	(4.0 to < 6.0)

845

Education	These occupations usually require a high school diploma and may require some vocational training or job-related course work. In some cases, an associate's or bachelor's degree could be needed.

Work_Styles	Work_Styles Definitions
Dependability	Job requires being reliable, responsible, and dependable, and fulfilling obligations.
Cooperation	Job requires being pleasant with others on the job and displaying a good-natured, cooperative attitude.
Self Control	Job requires maintaining composure, keeping emotions in check, controlling anger, and avoiding aggressive behavior, even in very difficult situations.
Integrity	Job requires being honest and ethical.
Adaptability/Flexibility	Job requires being open to change (positive or negative) and to considerable variety in the workplace.
Concern for Others	Job requires being sensitive to others' needs and feelings and being understanding and helpful on the job.
Stress Tolerance	Job requires accepting criticism and dealing calmly and effectively with high stress situations.
Attention to Detail	Job requires being careful about detail and thorough in completing work tasks.
Initiative	Job requires a willingness to take on responsibilities and challenges.
Persistence	Job requires persistence in the face of obstacles.
Achievement/Effort	Job requires establishing and maintaining personally challenging achievement goals and exerting effort toward mastering tasks.
Leadership	Job requires a willingness to lead, take charge, and offer opinions and direction.
Independence	Job requires developing one's own ways of doing things, guiding oneself with little or no supervision, and depending on oneself to get things done.
Social Orientation	Job requires preferring to work with others rather than alone, and being personally connected with others on the job.
Innovation	Job requires creativity and alternative thinking to develop new ideas for and answers to work-related problems.
Analytical Thinking	Job requires analyzing information and using logic to address work-related issues and problems.

41-3011.00 - Advertising Sales Agents

Sell or solicit advertising, including graphic art, advertising space in publications, custom made signs, or TV and radio advertising time. May obtain leases for outdoor advertising sites or persuade retailer to use sales promotion display items.

Tasks

1) Process all correspondence and paperwork related to accounts.

2) Prepare and deliver sales presentations to new and existing customers in order to sell new advertising programs, and to protect and increase existing advertising.

3) Attend sales meetings, industry trade shows, and training seminars in order to gather information, promote products, expand network of contacts, and increase knowledge.

4) Maintain assigned account bases while developing new accounts.

5) Consult with company officials, sales departments, and advertising agencies in order to develop promotional plans.

6) Draw up contracts for advertising work, and collect payments due.

7) Obtain and study information about clients' products, needs, problems, advertising history, and business practices in order to offer effective sales presentations and appropriate product assistance.

8) Deliver advertising or illustration proofs to customers for approval.

9) Determine advertising medium to be used, and prepare sample advertisements within the selected medium for presentation to customers.

10) Prepare promotional plans, sales literature, media kits, and sales contracts, using computer.

11) Inform customers of available options for advertisement artwork, and provide samples.

12) Explain to customers how specific types of advertising will help promote their products or services in the most effective way possible.

13) Identify new advertising markets, and propose products to serve them.

14) Write copy as part of layout.

15) Recommend appropriate sizes and formats for advertising, depending on medium being used.

16) Write sales outlines for use by staff.

17) Gather all relevant material for bid processes, and coordinate bidding and contract approval.

18) Arrange for commercial taping sessions, and accompany clients to sessions.

19) Locate and contact potential clients in order to offer advertising services.

Knowledge	Knowledge Definitions
English Language	Knowledge of the structure and content of the English language including the meaning and spelling of words, rules of composition, and grammar.
Sales and Marketing	Knowledge of principles and methods for showing, promoting, and selling products or services. This includes marketing strategy and tactics, product demonstration, sales techniques, and sales control systems.
Customer and Personal Service	Knowledge of principles and processes for providing customer and personal services. This includes customer needs assessment, meeting quality standards for services, and evaluation of customer satisfaction.
Communications and Media	Knowledge of media production, communication, and dissemination techniques and methods. This includes alternative ways to inform and entertain via written, oral, and visual media.
Mathematics	Knowledge of arithmetic, algebra, geometry, calculus, statistics, and their applications.
Administration and Management	Knowledge of business and management principles involved in strategic planning, resource allocation, human resources modeling, leadership technique, production methods, and coordination of people and resources.
Clerical	Knowledge of administrative and clerical procedures and systems such as word processing, managing files and records, stenography and transcription, designing forms, and other office procedures and terminology.
Personnel and Human Resources	Knowledge of principles and procedures for personnel recruitment, selection, training, compensation and benefits, labor relations and negotiation, and personnel information systems.
Economics and Accounting	Knowledge of economic and accounting principles and practices, the financial markets, banking and the analysis and reporting of financial data.
Transportation	Knowledge of principles and methods for moving people or goods by air, rail, sea, or road, including the relative costs and benefits.
Education and Training	Knowledge of principles and methods for curriculum and training design, teaching and instruction for individuals and groups, and the measurement of training effects.
Telecommunications	Knowledge of transmission, broadcasting, switching, control, and operation of telecommunications systems.
Design	Knowledge of design techniques, tools, and principles involved in production of precision technical plans, blueprints, drawings, and models.
Psychology	Knowledge of human behavior and performance; individual differences in ability, personality, and interests; learning and motivation; psychological research methods; and the assessment and treatment of behavioral and affective disorders.
Production and Processing	Knowledge of raw materials, production processes, quality control, costs, and other techniques for maximizing the effective manufacture and distribution of goods.
Geography	Knowledge of principles and methods for describing the features of land, sea, and air masses, including their physical characteristics, locations, interrelationships, and distribution of plant, animal, and human life.
Sociology and Anthropology	Knowledge of group behavior and dynamics, societal trends and influences, human migrations, ethnicity, cultures and their history and origins.
Computers and Electronics	Knowledge of circuit boards, processors, chips, electronic equipment, and computer hardware and software, including applications and programming.
Public Safety and Security	Knowledge of relevant equipment, policies, procedures, and strategies to promote effective local, state, or national security operations for the protection of people, data, property, and institutions.

Law and Government	Knowledge of laws, legal codes, court procedures, precedents, government regulations, executive orders, agency rules, and the democratic political process.	Persuasion	Persuading others to change their minds or behavior.
Philosophy and Theology	Knowledge of different philosophical systems and religions. This includes their basic principles, values, ethics, ways of thinking, customs, practices, and their impact on human culture.	Learning Strategies	Selecting and using training/instructional methods and procedures appropriate for the situation when learning or teaching new things.
Fine Arts	Knowledge of the theory and techniques required to compose, produce, and perform works of music, dance, visual arts, drama, and sculpture.	Management of Financial Resources	Determining how money will be spent to get the work done, and accounting for these expenditures.
Therapy and Counseling	Knowledge of principles, methods, and procedures for diagnosis, treatment, and rehabilitation of physical and mental dysfunctions, and for career counseling and guidance.	Troubleshooting	Determining causes of operating errors and deciding what to do about it.
History and Archeology	Knowledge of historical events and their causes, indicators, and effects on civilizations and cultures.	Operations Analysis	Analyzing needs and product requirements to create a design.
Foreign Language	Knowledge of the structure and content of a foreign (non-English) language including the meaning and spelling of words, rules of composition and grammar, and pronunciation.	Management of Material Resources	Obtaining and seeing to the appropriate use of equipment, facilities, and materials needed to do certain work.
Engineering and Technology	Knowledge of the practical application of engineering science and technology. This includes applying principles, techniques, procedures, and equipment to the design and production of various goods and services.	Management of Personnel Resources	Motivating, developing, and directing people as they work, identifying the best people for the job.
Building and Construction	Knowledge of materials, methods, and the tools involved in the construction or repair of houses, buildings, or other structures such as highways and roads.	Equipment Selection	Determining the kind of tools and equipment needed to do a job.
Chemistry	Knowledge of the chemical composition, structure, and properties of substances and of the chemical processes and transformations that they undergo. This includes uses of chemicals and their interactions, danger signs, production techniques, and disposal methods.	Systems Analysis	Determining how a system should work and how changes in conditions, operations, and the environment will affect outcomes.
Mechanical	Knowledge of machines and tools, including their designs, uses, repair, and maintenance.	Operation and Control	Controlling operations of equipment or systems.
Biology	Knowledge of plant and animal organisms, their tissues, cells, functions, interdependencies, and interactions with each other and the environment.	Systems Evaluation	Identifying measures or indicators of system performance and the actions needed to improve or correct performance, relative to the goals of the system.
Physics	Knowledge and prediction of physical principles, laws, their interrelationships, and applications to understanding fluid, material, and atmospheric dynamics, and mechanical, electrical, atomic and sub- atomic structures and processes.	Operation Monitoring	Watching gauges, dials, or other indicators to make sure a machine is working properly.
Medicine and Dentistry	Knowledge of the information and techniques needed to diagnose and treat human injuries, diseases, and deformities. This includes symptoms, treatment alternatives, drug properties and interactions, and preventive health-care measures.	Installation	Installing equipment, machines, wiring, or programs to meet specifications.
		Quality Control Analysis	Conducting tests and inspections of products, services, or processes to evaluate quality or performance.
Food Production	Knowledge of techniques and equipment for planting, growing, and harvesting food products (both plant and animal) for consumption, including storage/handling techniques.	Equipment Maintenance	Performing routine maintenance on equipment and determining when and what kind of maintenance is needed.
		Programming	Writing computer programs for various purposes.
		Repairing	Repairing machines or systems using the needed tools.
		Science	Using scientific rules and methods to solve problems.
		Technology Design	Generating or adapting equipment and technology to serve user needs.

Skills	Skills Definitions	Ability	Ability Definitions
Active Listening	Giving full attention to what other people are saying, taking time to understand the points being made, asking questions as appropriate, and not interrupting at inappropriate times.	Oral Expression	The ability to communicate information and ideas in speaking so others will understand.
Time Management	Managing one's own time and the time of others.	Oral Comprehension	The ability to listen to and understand information and ideas presented through spoken words and sentences.
Speaking	Talking to others to convey information effectively.	Written Expression	The ability to communicate information and ideas in writing so others will understand.
Mathematics	Using mathematics to solve problems.	Speech Clarity	The ability to speak clearly so others can understand you.
Negotiation	Bringing others together and trying to reconcile differences.	Written Comprehension	The ability to read and understand information and ideas presented in writing.
Active Learning	Understanding the implications of new information for both current and future problem-solving and decision-making.	Originality	The ability to come up with unusual or clever ideas about a given topic or situation, or to develop creative ways to solve a problem.
Reading Comprehension	Understanding written sentences and paragraphs in work related documents.	Fluency of Ideas	The ability to come up with a number of ideas about a topic (the number of ideas is important, not their quality, correctness, or creativity).
Service Orientation	Actively looking for ways to help people.	Speech Recognition	The ability to identify and understand the speech of another person.
Writing	Communicating effectively in writing as appropriate for the needs of the audience.	Inductive Reasoning	The ability to combine pieces of information to form general rules or conclusions (includes finding a relationship among seemingly unrelated events).
Social Perceptiveness	Being aware of others' reactions and understanding why they react as they do.	Near Vision	The ability to see details at close range (within a few feet of the observer).
Coordination	Adjusting actions in relation to others' actions.	Problem Sensitivity	The ability to tell when something is wrong or is likely to go wrong. It does not involve solving the problem, only recognizing there is a problem.
Critical Thinking	Using logic and reasoning to identify the strengths and weaknesses of alternative solutions, conclusions or approaches to problems.	Deductive Reasoning	The ability to apply general rules to specific problems to produce answers that make sense.
Complex Problem Solving	Identifying complex problems and reviewing related information to develop and evaluate options and implement solutions.	Information Ordering	The ability to arrange things or actions in a certain order or pattern according to a specific rule or set of rules (e.g., patterns of numbers, letters, words, pictures, mathematical operations).
Monitoring	Monitoring/Assessing performance of yourself, other individuals, or organizations to make improvements or take corrective action.	Category Flexibility	The ability to generate or use different sets of rules for combining or grouping things in different ways.
		Flexibility of Closure	The ability to identify or detect a known pattern (a figure, object, word, or sound) that is hidden in other distracting material.
Judgment and Decision Making	Considering the relative costs and benefits of potential actions to choose the most appropriate one.	Selective Attention	The ability to concentrate on a task over a period of time without being distracted.
Instructing	Teaching others how to do something.	Mathematical Reasoning	The ability to choose the right mathematical methods or formulas to solve a problem.

Time Sharing	The ability to shift back and forth between two or more activities or sources of information (such as speech, sounds, touch, or other sources).
Visualization	The ability to imagine how something will look after it is moved around or when its parts are moved or rearranged.
Number Facility	The ability to add, subtract, multiply, or divide quickly and correctly.
Speed of Closure	The ability to quickly make sense of, combine, and organize information into meaningful patterns.
Memorization	The ability to remember information such as words, numbers, pictures, and procedures.
Far Vision	The ability to see details at a distance.
Visual Color Discrimination	The ability to match or detect differences between colors, including shades of color and brightness.
Depth Perception	The ability to judge which of several objects is closer or farther away from you, or to judge the distance between you and an object.
Auditory Attention	The ability to focus on a single source of sound in the presence of other distracting sounds.
Multilimb Coordination	The ability to coordinate two or more limbs (for example, two arms, two legs, or one leg and one arm) while sitting, standing, or lying down. It does not involve performing the activities while the whole body is in motion.
Perceptual Speed	The ability to quickly and accurately compare similarities and differences among sets of letters, numbers, objects, pictures, or patterns. The things to be compared may be presented at the same time or one after the other. This ability also includes comparing a presented object with a remembered object.
Control Precision	The ability to quickly and repeatedly adjust the controls of a machine or a vehicle to exact positions.
Trunk Strength	The ability to use your abdominal and lower back muscles to support part of the body repeatedly or continuously over time without 'giving out' or fatiguing.
Manual Dexterity	The ability to quickly move your hand, your hand together with your arm, or your two hands to grasp, manipulate, or assemble objects.
Finger Dexterity	The ability to make precisely coordinated movements of the fingers of one or both hands to grasp, manipulate, or assemble very small objects.
Gross Body Coordination	The ability to coordinate the movement of your arms, legs, and torso together when the whole body is in motion.
Arm-Hand Steadiness	The ability to keep your hand and arm steady while moving your arm or while holding your arm and hand in one position.
Stamina	The ability to exert yourself physically over long periods of time without getting winded or out of breath.
Reaction Time	The ability to quickly respond (with the hand, finger, or foot) to a signal (sound, light, picture) when it appears.
Speed of Limb Movement	The ability to quickly move the arms and legs.
Glare Sensitivity	The ability to see objects in the presence of glare or bright lighting.
Peripheral Vision	The ability to see objects or movement of objects to one's side when the eyes are looking ahead.
Night Vision	The ability to see under low light conditions.
Spatial Orientation	The ability to know your location in relation to the environment or to know where other objects are in relation to you.
Sound Localization	The ability to tell the direction from which a sound originated.
Response Orientation	The ability to choose quickly between two or more movements in response to two or more different signals (lights, sounds, pictures). It includes the speed with which the correct response is started with the hand, foot, or other body part.
Rate Control	The ability to time your movements or the movement of a piece of equipment in anticipation of changes in the speed and/or direction of a moving object or scene.
Wrist-Finger Speed	The ability to make fast, simple, repeated movements of the fingers, hands, and wrists.
Hearing Sensitivity	The ability to detect or tell the differences between sounds that vary in pitch and loudness.
Gross Body Equilibrium	The ability to keep or regain your body balance or stay upright when in an unstable position.
Dynamic Strength	The ability to exert muscle force repeatedly or continuously over time. This involves muscular endurance and resistance to muscle fatigue.
Dynamic Flexibility	The ability to quickly and repeatedly bend, stretch, twist, or reach out with your body, arms, and/or legs.
Explosive Strength	The ability to use short bursts of muscle force to propel oneself (as in jumping or sprinting), or to throw an object.
Extent Flexibility	The ability to bend, stretch, twist, or reach with your body, arms, and/or legs.

Static Strength	The ability to exert maximum muscle force to lift, push, pull, or carry objects.

Work_Activity	Work_Activity Definitions
Selling or Influencing Others	Convincing others to buy merchandise/goods or to otherwise change their minds or actions.
Getting Information	Observing, receiving, and otherwise obtaining information from all relevant sources.
Communicating with Persons Outside Organization	Communicating with people outside the organization, representing the organization to customers, the public, government, and other external sources. This information can be exchanged in person, in writing, or by telephone or e-mail.
Establishing and Maintaining Interpersonal Relatio	Developing constructive and cooperative working relationships with others, and maintaining them over time.
Organizing, Planning, and Prioritizing Work	Developing specific goals and plans to prioritize, organize, and accomplish your work.
Performing for or Working Directly with the Public	Performing for people or dealing directly with the public. This includes serving customers in restaurants and stores, and receiving clients or guests.
Communicating with Supervisors, Peers, or Subordin	Providing information to supervisors, co-workers, and subordinates by telephone, in written form, e-mail, or in person.
Making Decisions and Solving Problems	Analyzing information and evaluating results to choose the best solution and solve problems.
Resolving Conflicts and Negotiating with Others	Handling complaints, settling disputes, and resolving grievances and conflicts, or otherwise negotiating with others.
Thinking Creatively	Developing, designing, or creating new applications, ideas, relationships, systems, or products, including artistic contributions.
Updating and Using Relevant Knowledge	Keeping up-to-date technically and applying new knowledge to your job.
Identifying Objects, Actions, and Events	Identifying information by categorizing, estimating, recognizing differences or similarities, and detecting changes in circumstances or events.
Interacting With Computers	Using computers and computer systems (including hardware and software) to program, write software, set up functions, enter data, or process information.
Performing Administrative Activities	Performing day-to-day administrative tasks such as maintaining information files and processing paperwork.
Developing Objectives and Strategies	Establishing long-range objectives and specifying the strategies and actions to achieve them.
Provide Consultation and Advice to Others	Providing guidance and expert advice to management or other groups on technical, systems-, or process-related topics.
Analyzing Data or Information	Identifying the underlying principles, reasons, or facts of information by breaking down information or data into separate parts.
Processing Information	Compiling, coding, categorizing, calculating, tabulating, auditing, or verifying information or data.
Coordinating the Work and Activities of Others	Getting members of a group to work together to accomplish tasks.
Developing and Building Teams	Encouraging and building mutual trust, respect, and cooperation among team members.
Scheduling Work and Activities	Scheduling events, programs, and activities, as well as the work of others.
Judging the Qualities of Things, Services, or Peop	Assessing the value, importance, or quality of things or people.
Interpreting the Meaning of Information for Others	Translating or explaining what information means and how it can be used.
Monitor Processes, Materials, or Surroundings	Monitoring and reviewing information from materials, events, or the environment, to detect or assess problems.
Documenting/Recording Information	Entering, transcribing, recording, storing, or maintaining information in written or electronic/magnetic form.
Operating Vehicles, Mechanized Devices, or Equipme	Running, maneuvering, navigating, or driving vehicles or mechanized equipment, such as forklifts, passenger vehicles, aircraft, or water craft.
Estimating the Quantifiable Characteristics of Pro	Estimating sizes, distances, and quantities; or determining time, costs, resources, or materials needed to perform a work activity.
Assisting and Caring for Others	Providing personal assistance, medical attention, emotional support, or other personal care to others such as coworkers, customers, or patients.
Guiding, Directing, and Motivating Subordinates	Providing guidance and direction to subordinates, including setting performance standards and monitoring performance.

Evaluating Information to Determine Compliance wit	Using relevant information and individual judgment to determine whether events or processes comply with laws, regulations, or standards.
Coaching and Developing Others	Identifying the developmental needs of others and coaching, mentoring, or otherwise helping others to improve their knowledge or skills.
Monitoring and Controlling Resources	Monitoring and controlling resources and overseeing the spending of money.
Controlling Machines and Processes	Using either control mechanisms or direct physical activity to operate machines or processes (not including computers or vehicles).
Handling and Moving Objects	Using hands and arms in handling, installing, positioning, and moving materials, and manipulating things.
Performing General Physical Activities	Performing physical activities that require considerable use of your arms and legs and moving your whole body, such as climbing, lifting, balancing, walking, stooping, and handling of materials.
Staffing Organizational Units	Recruiting, interviewing, selecting, hiring, and promoting employees in an organization.
Inspecting Equipment, Structures, or Material	Inspecting equipment, structures, or materials to identify the cause of errors or other problems or defects.
Drafting, Laying Out, and Specifying Technical Dev	Providing documentation, detailed instructions, drawings, or specifications to tell others about how devices, parts, equipment, or structures are to be fabricated, constructed, assembled, modified, maintained, or used.
Training and Teaching Others	Identifying the educational needs of others, developing formal educational or training programs or classes, and teaching or instructing others.
Repairing and Maintaining Electronic Equipment	Servicing, repairing, calibrating, regulating, fine-tuning, or testing machines, devices, and equipment that operate primarily on the basis of electrical or electronic (not mechanical) principles.
Repairing and Maintaining Mechanical Equipment	Servicing, repairing, adjusting, and testing machines, devices, moving parts, and equipment that operate primarily on the basis of mechanical (not electronic) principles.

Work_Context	Work_Context Definitions
Telephone	How often do you have telephone conversations in this job?
Deal With External Customers	How important is it to work with external customers or the public in this job?
Contact With Others	How much does this job require the worker to be in contact with others (face-to-face, by telephone, or otherwise) in order to perform it?
Face-to-Face Discussions	How often do you have to have face-to-face discussions with individuals or teams in this job?
Time Pressure	How often does this job require the worker to meet strict deadlines?
In an Enclosed Vehicle or Equipment	How often does this job require working in a closed vehicle or equipment (e.g., car)?
Level of Competition	To what extent does this job require the worker to compete or to be aware of competitive pressures?
Letters and Memos	How often does the job require written letters and memos?
Importance of Being Exact or Accurate	How important is being very exact or highly accurate in performing this job?
Outdoors, Exposed to Weather	How often does this job require working outdoors, exposed to all weather conditions?
Indoors, Environmentally Controlled	How often does this job require working indoors in environmentally controlled conditions?
Frequency of Decision Making	How frequently is the worker required to make decisions that affect other people, the financial resources, and/or the image and reputation of the organization?
Structured versus Unstructured Work	To what extent is this job structured for the worker, rather than allowing the worker to determine tasks, priorities, and goals?
Freedom to Make Decisions	How much decision making freedom, without supervision, does the job offer?
Impact of Decisions on Co-workers or Company Resul	How do the decisions an employee makes impact the results of co-workers, clients or the company?
Coordinate or Lead Others	How important is it to coordinate or lead others in accomplishing work activities in this job?
Work With Work Group or Team	How important is it to work with others in a group or team in this job?
Frequency of Conflict Situations	How often are there conflict situations the employee has to face in this job?
Physical Proximity	To what extent does this job require the worker to perform job tasks in close physical proximity to other people?

Deal With Unpleasant or Angry People	How frequently does the worker have to deal with unpleasant, angry, or discourteous individuals as part of the job requirements?
Spend Time Standing	How much does this job require standing?
Spend Time Sitting	How much does this job require sitting?
Very Hot or Cold Temperatures	How often does this job require working in very hot (above 90 F degrees) or very cold (below 32 F degrees) temperatures?
Sounds, Noise Levels Are Distracting or Uncomforta	How often does this job require working exposed to sounds and noise levels that are distracting or uncomfortable?
Electronic Mail	How often do you use electronic mail in this job?
Spend Time Walking and Running	How much does this job require walking and running?
Importance of Repeating Same Tasks	How important is repeating the same physical activities (e.g., key entry) or mental activities (e.g., checking entries in a ledger) over and over, without stopping, to performing this job?
Consequence of Error	How serious would the result usually be if the worker made a mistake that was not readily correctable?
Public Speaking	How often do you have to perform public speaking in this job?
Exposed to Contaminants	How often does this job require working exposed to contaminants (such as pollutants, gases, dust or odors)?
Responsibility for Outcomes and Results	How responsible is the worker for work outcomes and results of other workers?
Pace Determined by Speed of Equipment	How important is it to this job that the pace is determined by the speed of equipment or machinery? (This does not refer to keeping busy at all times on this job.)
Spend Time Making Repetitive Motions	How much does this job require making repetitive motions?
Degree of Automation	How automated is the job?
Spend Time Bending or Twisting the Body	How much does this job require bending or twisting your body?
Extremely Bright or Inadequate Lighting	How often does this job require working in extremely bright or inadequate lighting conditions?
Indoors, Not Environmentally Controlled	How often does this job require working indoors in non-controlled environmental conditions (e.g., warehouse without heat)?
Responsible for Others' Health and Safety	How much responsibility is there for the health and safety of others in this job?
Outdoors, Under Cover	How often does this job require working outdoors, under cover (e.g., structure with roof but no walls)?
In an Open Vehicle or Equipment	How often does this job require working in an open vehicle or equipment (e.g., tractor)?
Spend Time Using Your Hands to Handle, Control, or	How much does this job require using your hands to handle, control, or feel objects, tools or controls?
Spend Time Keeping or Regaining Balance	How much does this job require keeping or regaining your balance?
Spend Time Kneeling, Crouching, Stooping, or Crawl	How much does this job require kneeling, crouching, stooping or crawling?
Deal With Physically Aggressive People	How frequently does this job require the worker to deal with physical aggression of violent individuals?
Exposed to Minor Burns, Cuts, Bites, or Stings	How often does this job require exposure to minor burns, cuts, bites, or stings?
Exposed to Hazardous Equipment	How often does this job require exposure to hazardous equipment?
Cramped Work Space, Awkward Positions	How often does this job require working in cramped work spaces that requires getting into awkward positions?
Exposed to High Places	How often does this job require exposure to high places?
Exposed to Radiation	How often does this job require exposure to radiation?
Exposed to Whole Body Vibration	How often does this job require exposure to whole body vibration (e.g., operate a jackhammer)?
Wear Common Protective or Safety Equipment such as	How much does this job require wearing common protective or safety equipment such as safety shoes, glasses, gloves, hard hats or live jackets?
Spend Time Climbing Ladders, Scaffolds, or Poles	How much does this job require climbing ladders, scaffolds, or poles?
Wear Specialized Protective or Safety Equipment su	How much does this job require wearing specialized protective or safety equipment such as breathing apparatus, safety harness, full protection suits, or radiation protection?
Exposed to Hazardous Conditions	How often does this job require exposure to hazardous conditions?
Exposed to Disease or Infections	How often does this job require exposure to disease/infections?

Job Zone Component	Job Zone Component Definitions
Title	Job Zone Three: Medium Preparation Needed
Overall Experience	Previous work-related skill, knowledge, or experience is required for these occupations. For example, an electrician must have completed three or four years of apprenticeship or several years of vocational training, and often must have passed a licensing exam, in order to perform the job.
Job Training	Employees in these occupations usually need one or two years of training involving both on-the-job experience and informal training with experienced workers.
Job Zone Examples	These occupations usually involve using communication and organizational skills to coordinate, supervise, manage, or train others to accomplish goals. Examples include dental assistants, electricians, fish and game wardens, legal secretaries, personnel recruiters, and recreation workers.
SVP Range	(6.0 to < 7.0)
Education	Most occupations in this zone require training in vocational schools, related on-the-job experience, or an associate's degree. Some may require a bachelor's degree.

Work_Styles	Work_Styles Definitions
Dependability	Job requires being reliable, responsible, and dependable, and fulfilling obligations.
Persistence	Job requires persistence in the face of obstacles.
Initiative	Job requires a willingness to take on responsibilities and challenges.
Achievement/Effort	Job requires establishing and maintaining personally challenging achievement goals and exerting effort toward mastering tasks.
Attention to Detail	Job requires being careful about detail and thorough in completing work tasks.
Adaptability/Flexibility	Job requires being open to change (positive or negative) and to considerable variety in the workplace.
Stress Tolerance	Job requires accepting criticism and dealing calmly and effectively with high stress situations.
Integrity	Job requires being honest and ethical.
Cooperation	Job requires being pleasant with others on the job and displaying a good-natured, cooperative attitude.
Social Orientation	Job requires preferring to work with others rather than alone, and being personally connected with others on the job.
Independence	Job requires developing one's own ways of doing things, guiding oneself with little or no supervision, and depending on oneself to get things done.
Self Control	Job requires maintaining composure, keeping emotions in check, controlling anger, and avoiding aggressive behavior, even in very difficult situations.
Innovation	Job requires creativity and alternative thinking to develop new ideas for and answers to work-related problems.
Concern for Others	Job requires being sensitive to others' needs and feelings and being understanding and helpful on the job.
Leadership	Job requires a willingness to lead, take charge, and offer opinions and direction.
Analytical Thinking	Job requires analyzing information and using logic to address work-related issues and problems.

41-3021.00 - Insurance Sales Agents

Sell life, property, casualty, health, automotive, or other types of insurance. May refer clients to independent brokers, work as independent broker, or be employed by an insurance company.

Tasks

1) Interview prospective clients to obtain data about their financial resources and needs, the physical condition of the person or property to be insured, and to discuss any existing coverage.

2) Call on policyholders to deliver and explain policy, to analyze insurance program and suggest additions or changes, or to change beneficiaries.

3) Explain features, advantages and disadvantages of various policies to promote sale of insurance plans.

4) Customize insurance programs to suit individual customers, often covering a variety of risks.

5) Perform administrative tasks, such as maintaining records and handling policy renewals.

6) Contact underwriter and submit forms to obtain binder coverage.

7) Confer with clients to obtain and provide information when claims are made on a policy.

8) Ensure that policy requirements are fulfilled, including any necessary medical examinations and the completion of appropriate forms.

9) Seek out new clients and develop clientele by networking to find new customers and generate lists of prospective clients.

10) Sell various types of insurance policies to businesses and individuals on behalf of insurance companies, including automobile, fire, life, property, medical and dental insurance or specialized policies such as marine, farm/crop, and medical malpractice.

11) Develop marketing strategies to compete with other individuals or companies who sell insurance.

12) Monitor insurance claims to ensure they are settled equitably for both the client and the insurer.

13) Select company that offers type of coverage requested by client to underwrite policy.

14) Inspect property, examining its general condition, type of construction, age, and other characteristics, to decide if it is a good insurance risk.

15) Explain necessary bookkeeping requirements for customer to implement and provide group insurance program.

16) Plan and oversee incorporation of insurance program into bookkeeping system of company.

17) Install bookkeeping systems and resolve system problems.

18) Attend meetings, seminars and programs to learn about new products and services, learn new skills, and receive technical assistance in developing new accounts.

Knowledge	Knowledge Definitions
Customer and Personal Service	Knowledge of principles and processes for providing customer and personal services. This includes customer needs assessment, meeting quality standards for services, and evaluation of customer satisfaction.
Sales and Marketing	Knowledge of principles and methods for showing, promoting, and selling products or services. This includes marketing strategy and tactics, product demonstration, sales techniques, and sales control systems.
English Language	Knowledge of the structure and content of the English language including the meaning and spelling of words, rules of composition, and grammar.
Computers and Electronics	Knowledge of circuit boards, processors, chips, electronic equipment, and computer hardware and software, including applications and programming.
Administration and Management	Knowledge of business and management principles involved in strategic planning, resource allocation, human resources modeling, leadership technique, production methods, and coordination of people and resources.
Clerical	Knowledge of administrative and clerical procedures and systems such as word processing, managing files and records, stenography and transcription, designing forms, and other office procedures and terminology.
Economics and Accounting	Knowledge of economic and accounting principles and practices, the financial markets, banking and the analysis and reporting of financial data.
Mathematics	Knowledge of arithmetic, algebra, geometry, calculus, statistics, and their applications.
Personnel and Human Resources	Knowledge of principles and procedures for personnel recruitment, selection, training, compensation and benefits, labor relations and negotiation, and personnel information systems.
Education and Training	Knowledge of principles and methods for curriculum and training design, teaching and instruction for individuals and groups, and the measurement of training effects.
Law and Government	Knowledge of laws, legal codes, court procedures, precedents, government regulations, executive orders, agency rules, and the democratic political process.
Communications and Media	Knowledge of media production, communication, and dissemination techniques and methods. This includes alternative ways to inform and entertain via written, oral, and visual media.

Psychology	Knowledge of human behavior and performance; individual differences in ability, personality, and interests; learning and motivation; psychological research methods; and the assessment and treatment of behavioral and affective disorders.
Production and Processing	Knowledge of raw materials, production processes, quality control, costs, and other techniques for maximizing the effective manufacture and distribution of goods.
Telecommunications	Knowledge of transmission, broadcasting, switching, control, and operation of telecommunications systems.
Transportation	Knowledge of principles and methods for moving people or goods by air, rail, sea, or road, including the relative costs and benefits.
Public Safety and Security	Knowledge of relevant equipment, policies, procedures, and strategies to promote effective local, state, or national security operations for the protection of people, data, property, and institutions.
Geography	Knowledge of principles and methods for describing the features of land, sea, and air masses, including their physical characteristics, locations, interrelationships, and distribution of plant, animal, and human life.
Therapy and Counseling	Knowledge of principles, methods, and procedures for diagnosis, treatment, and rehabilitation of physical and mental dysfunctions, and for career counseling and guidance.
Sociology and Anthropology	Knowledge of group behavior and dynamics, societal trends and influences, human migrations, ethnicity, cultures and their history and origins.
Philosophy and Theology	Knowledge of different philosophical systems and religions. This includes their basic principles, values, ethics, ways of thinking, customs, practices, and their impact on human culture.
Building and Construction	Knowledge of materials, methods, and the tools involved in the construction or repair of houses, buildings, or other structures such as highways and roads.
Foreign Language	Knowledge of the structure and content of a foreign (non-English) language including the meaning and spelling of words, rules of composition and grammar, and pronunciation.
Engineering and Technology	Knowledge of the practical application of engineering science and technology. This includes applying principles, techniques, procedures, and equipment to the design and production of various goods and services.
History and Archeology	Knowledge of historical events and their causes, indicators, and effects on civilizations and cultures.
Design	Knowledge of design techniques, tools, and principles involved in production of precision technical plans, blueprints, drawings, and models.
Fine Arts	Knowledge of the theory and techniques required to compose, produce, and perform works of music, dance, visual arts, drama, and sculpture.
Mechanical	Knowledge of machines and tools, including their designs, uses, repair, and maintenance.
Medicine and Dentistry	Knowledge of the information and techniques needed to diagnose and treat human injuries, diseases, and deformities. This includes symptoms, treatment alternatives, drug properties and interactions, and preventive health-care measures.
Physics	Knowledge and prediction of physical principles, laws, their interrelationships, and applications to understanding fluid, material, and atmospheric dynamics, and mechanical, electrical, atomic and sub- atomic structures and processes.
Food Production	Knowledge of techniques and equipment for planting, growing, and harvesting food products (both plant and animal) for consumption, including storage/handling techniques.
Biology	Knowledge of plant and animal organisms, their tissues, cells, functions, interdependencies, and interactions with each other and the environment.
Chemistry	Knowledge of the chemical composition, structure, and properties of substances and of the chemical processes and transformations that they undergo. This includes uses of chemicals and their interactions, danger signs, production techniques, and disposal methods.

Skills	Skills Definitions
Active Listening	Giving full attention to what other people are saying, taking time to understand the points being made, asking questions as appropriate, and not interrupting at inappropriate times.
Speaking	Talking to others to convey information effectively.
Time Management	Managing one's own time and the time of others.

Reading Comprehension	Understanding written sentences and paragraphs in work related documents.
Persuasion	Persuading others to change their minds or behavior.
Service Orientation	Actively looking for ways to help people.
Social Perceptiveness	Being aware of others' reactions and understanding why they react as they do.
Active Learning	Understanding the implications of new information for both current and future problem-solving and decision-making.
Judgment and Decision Making	Considering the relative costs and benefits of potential actions to choose the most appropriate one.
Critical Thinking	Using logic and reasoning to identify the strengths and weaknesses of alternative solutions, conclusions or approaches to problems.
Writing	Communicating effectively in writing as appropriate for the needs of the audience.
Mathematics	Using mathematics to solve problems.
Negotiation	Bringing others together and trying to reconcile differences.
Complex Problem Solving	Identifying complex problems and reviewing related information to develop and evaluate options and implement solutions.
Coordination	Adjusting actions in relation to others' actions.
Learning Strategies	Selecting and using training/instructional methods and procedures appropriate for the situation when learning or teaching new things.
Monitoring	Monitoring/Assessing performance of yourself, other individuals, or organizations to make improvements or take corrective action.
Instructing	Teaching others how to do something.
Management of Personnel Resources	Motivating, developing, and directing people as they work, identifying the best people for the job.
Management of Financial Resources	Determining how money will be spent to get the work done, and accounting for these expenditures.
Operations Analysis	Analyzing needs and product requirements to create a design.
Troubleshooting	Determining causes of operating errors and deciding what to do about it.
Management of Material Resources	Obtaining and seeing to the appropriate use of equipment, facilities, and materials needed to do certain work.
Equipment Selection	Determining the kind of tools and equipment needed to do a job.
Systems Evaluation	Identifying measures or indicators of system performance and the actions needed to improve or correct performance, relative to the goals of the system.
Quality Control Analysis	Conducting tests and inspections of products, services, or processes to evaluate quality or performance.
Technology Design	Generating or adapting equipment and technology to serve user needs.
Operation and Control	Controlling operations of equipment or systems.
Operation Monitoring	Watching gauges, dials, or other indicators to make sure a machine is working properly.
Installation	Installing equipment, machines, wiring, or programs to meet specifications.
Equipment Maintenance	Performing routine maintenance on equipment and determining when and what kind of maintenance is needed.
Programming	Writing computer programs for various purposes.
Systems Analysis	Determining how a system should work and how changes in conditions, operations, and the environment will affect outcomes.
Repairing	Repairing machines or systems using the needed tools.
Science	Using scientific rules and methods to solve problems.

Ability	Ability Definitions
Oral Expression	The ability to communicate information and ideas in speaking so others will understand.
Oral Comprehension	The ability to listen to and understand information and ideas presented through spoken words and sentences.
Written Comprehension	The ability to read and understand information and ideas presented in writing.
Written Expression	The ability to communicate information and ideas in writing so others will understand.
Speech Recognition	The ability to identify and understand the speech of another person.
Deductive Reasoning	The ability to apply general rules to specific problems to produce answers that make sense.
Speech Clarity	The ability to speak clearly so others can understand you.
Near Vision	The ability to see details at close range (within a few feet of the observer).

Problem Sensitivity	The ability to tell when something is wrong or is likely to go wrong. It does not involve solving the problem, only recognizing there is a problem.
Category Flexibility	The ability to generate or use different sets of rules for combining or grouping things in different ways.
Inductive Reasoning	The ability to combine pieces of information to form general rules or conclusions (includes finding a relationship among seemingly unrelated events).
Fluency of Ideas	The ability to come up with a number of ideas about a topic (the number of ideas is important, not their quality, correctness, or creativity).
Selective Attention	The ability to concentrate on a task over a period of time without being distracted.
Mathematical Reasoning	The ability to choose the right mathematical methods or formulas to solve a problem.
Information Ordering	The ability to arrange things or actions in a certain order or pattern according to a specific rule or set of rules (e.g., patterns of numbers, letters, words, pictures, mathematical operations).
Originality	The ability to come up with unusual or clever ideas about a given topic or situation, or to develop creative ways to solve a problem.
Speed of Closure	The ability to quickly make sense of, combine, and organize information into meaningful patterns.
Number Facility	The ability to add, subtract, multiply, or divide quickly and correctly.
Far Vision	The ability to see details at a distance.
Flexibility of Closure	The ability to identify or detect a known pattern (a figure, object, word, or sound) that is hidden in other distracting material.
Finger Dexterity	The ability to make precisely coordinated movements of the fingers of one or both hands to grasp, manipulate, or assemble very small objects.
Memorization	The ability to remember information such as words, numbers, pictures, and procedures.
Perceptual Speed	The ability to quickly and accurately compare similarities and differences among sets of letters, numbers, objects, pictures, or patterns. The things to be compared may be presented at the same time or one after the other. This ability also includes comparing a presented object with a remembered object.
Time Sharing	The ability to shift back and forth between two or more activities or sources of information (such as speech, sounds, touch, or other sources).
Depth Perception	The ability to judge which of several objects is closer or farther away from you, or to judge the distance between you and an object.
Multilimb Coordination	The ability to coordinate two or more limbs (for example, two arms, two legs, or one leg and one arm) while sitting, standing, or lying down. It does not involve performing the activities while the whole body is in motion.
Visualization	The ability to imagine how something will look after it is moved around or when its parts are moved or rearranged.
Visual Color Discrimination	The ability to match or detect differences between colors, including shades of color and brightness.
Control Precision	The ability to quickly and repeatedly adjust the controls of a machine or a vehicle to exact positions.
Auditory Attention	The ability to focus on a single source of sound in the presence of other distracting sounds.
Hearing Sensitivity	The ability to detect or tell the differences between sounds that vary in pitch and loudness.
Trunk Strength	The ability to use your abdominal and lower back muscles to support part of the body repeatedly or continuously over time without 'giving out' or fatiguing.
Manual Dexterity	The ability to quickly move your hand, your hand together with your arm, or your two hands to grasp, manipulate, or assemble objects.
Reaction Time	The ability to quickly respond (with the hand, finger, or foot) to a signal (sound, light, picture) when it appears.
Extent Flexibility	The ability to bend, stretch, twist, or reach with your body, arms, and/or legs.
Gross Body Coordination	The ability to coordinate the movement of your arms, legs, and torso together when the whole body is in motion.
Rate Control	The ability to time your movements or the movement of a piece of equipment in anticipation of changes in the speed and/or direction of a moving object or scene.
Response Orientation	The ability to choose quickly between two or more movements in response to two or more different signals (lights, sounds, pictures). It includes the speed with which the correct response is started with the hand, foot, or other body part.

Glare Sensitivity	The ability to see objects in the presence of glare or bright lighting.
Night Vision	The ability to see under low light conditions.
Explosive Strength	The ability to use short bursts of muscle force to propel oneself (as in jumping or sprinting), or to throw an object.
Dynamic Strength	The ability to exert muscle force repeatedly or continuously over time. This involves muscular endurance and resistance to muscle fatigue.
Stamina	The ability to exert yourself physically over long periods of time without getting winded or out of breath.
Dynamic Flexibility	The ability to quickly and repeatedly bend, stretch, twist, or reach out with your body, arms, and/or legs.
Speed of Limb Movement	The ability to quickly move the arms and legs.
Gross Body Equilibrium	The ability to keep or regain your body balance or stay upright when in an unstable position.
Static Strength	The ability to exert maximum muscle force to lift, push, pull, or carry objects.
Sound Localization	The ability to tell the direction from which a sound originated.
Arm-Hand Steadiness	The ability to keep your hand and arm steady while moving your arm or while holding your arm and hand in one position.
Spatial Orientation	The ability to know your location in relation to the environment or to know where other objects are in relation to you.
Peripheral Vision	The ability to see objects or movement of objects to one's side when the eyes are looking ahead.
Wrist-Finger Speed	The ability to make fast, simple, repeated movements of the fingers, hands, and wrists.

Work_Activity	Work_Activity Definitions
Getting Information	Observing, receiving, and otherwise obtaining information from all relevant sources.
Establishing and Maintaining Interpersonal Relatio	Developing constructive and cooperative working relationships with others, and maintaining them over time.
Making Decisions and Solving Problems	Analyzing information and evaluating results to choose the best solution and solve problems.
Processing Information	Compiling, coding, categorizing, calculating, tabulating, auditing, or verifying information or data.
Interacting With Computers	Using computers and computer systems (including hardware and software) to program, write software, set up functions, enter data, or process information.
Evaluating Information to Determine Compliance wit	Using relevant information and individual judgment to determine whether events or processes comply with laws, regulations, or standards.
Communicating with Supervisors, Peers, or Subordin	Providing information to supervisors, co-workers, and subordinates by telephone, in written form, e-mail, or in person.
Identifying Objects, Actions, and Events	Identifying information by categorizing, estimating, recognizing differences or similarities, and detecting changes in circumstances or events.
Selling or Influencing Others	Convincing others to buy merchandise/goods or to otherwise change their minds or actions.
Resolving Conflicts and Negotiating with Others	Handling complaints, settling disputes, and resolving grievances and conflicts, or otherwise negotiating with others.
Communicating with Persons Outside Organization	Communicating with people outside the organization, representing the organization to customers, the public, government, and other external sources. This information can be exchanged in person, in writing, or by telephone or e-mail.
Performing for or Working Directly with the Public	Performing for people or dealing directly with the public. This includes serving customers in restaurants and stores, and receiving clients or guests.
Thinking Creatively	Developing, designing, or creating new applications, ideas, relationships, systems, or products, including artistic contributions.
Developing Objectives and Strategies	Establishing long-range objectives and specifying the strategies and actions to achieve them.
Documenting/Recording Information	Entering, transcribing, recording, storing, or maintaining information in written or electronic/magnetic form.
Performing Administrative Activities	Performing day-to-day administrative tasks such as maintaining information files and processing paperwork.
Analyzing Data or Information	Identifying the underlying principles, reasons, or facts of information by breaking down information or data into separate parts.
Judging the Qualities of Things, Services, or Peop	Assessing the value, importance, or quality of things or people.
Updating and Using Relevant Knowledge	Keeping up-to-date technically and applying new knowledge to your job.

Interpreting the Meaning of Information for Others	Translating or explaining what information means and how it can be used.
Organizing, Planning, and Prioritizing Work	Developing specific goals and plans to prioritize, organize, and accomplish your work.
Coaching and Developing Others	Identifying the developmental needs of others and coaching, mentoring, or otherwise helping others to improve their knowledge or skills.
Developing and Building Teams	Encouraging and building mutual trust, respect, and cooperation among team members.
Training and Teaching Others	Identifying the educational needs of others, developing formal educational or training programs or classes, and teaching or instructing others.
Assisting and Caring for Others	Providing personal assistance, medical attention, emotional support, or other personal care to others such as coworkers, customers, or patients.
Scheduling Work and Activities	Scheduling events, programs, and activities, as well as the work of others.
Monitor Processes, Materials, or Surroundings	Monitoring and reviewing information from materials, events, or the environment, to detect or assess problems.
Coordinating the Work and Activities of Others	Getting members of a group to work together to accomplish tasks.
Estimating the Quantifiable Characteristics of Pro	Estimating sizes, distances, and quantities; or determining time, costs, resources, or materials needed to perform a work activity.
Provide Consultation and Advice to Others	Providing guidance and expert advice to management or other groups on technical, systems-, or process-related topics.
Monitoring and Controlling Resources	Monitoring and controlling resources and overseeing the spending of money.
Guiding, Directing, and Motivating Subordinates	Providing guidance and direction to subordinates, including setting performance standards and monitoring performance.
Performing General Physical Activities	Performing physical activities that require considerable use of your arms and legs and moving your whole body, such as climbing, lifting, balancing, walking, stooping, and handling of materials.
Inspecting Equipment, Structures, or Material	Inspecting equipment, structures, or materials to identify the cause of errors or other problems or defects.
Operating Vehicles, Mechanized Devices, or Equipme	Running, maneuvering, navigating, or driving vehicles or mechanized equipment, such as forklifts, passenger vehicles, aircraft, or water craft.
Controlling Machines and Processes	Using either control mechanisms or direct physical activity to operate machines or processes (not including computers or vehicles).
Handling and Moving Objects	Using hands and arms in handling, installing, positioning, and moving materials, and manipulating things.
Staffing Organizational Units	Recruiting, interviewing, selecting, hiring, and promoting employees in an organization.
Repairing and Maintaining Electronic Equipment	Servicing, repairing, calibrating, regulating, fine-tuning, or testing machines, devices, and equipment that operate primarily on the basis of electrical or electronic (not mechanical) principles.
Repairing and Maintaining Mechanical Equipment	Servicing, repairing, adjusting, and testing machines, devices, moving parts, and equipment that operate primarily on the basis of mechanical (not electronic) principles.
Drafting, Laying Out, and Specifying Technical Dev	Providing documentation, detailed instructions, drawings, or specifications to tell others about how devices, parts, equipment, or structures are to be fabricated, constructed, assembled, modified, maintained, or used.

Work Context

	Work_Context Definitions
Telephone	How often do you have telephone conversations in this job?
Letters and Memos	How often does the job require written letters and memos?
Level of Competition	To what extent does this job require the worker to compete or to be aware of competitive pressures?
Structured versus Unstructured Work	To what extent is this job structured for the worker, rather than allowing the worker to determine tasks, priorities, and goals?
Contact With Others	How much does this job require the worker to be in contact with others (face-to-face, by telephone, or otherwise) in order to perform it?
Face-to-Face Discussions	How often do you have to have face-to-face discussions with individuals or teams in this job?
Freedom to Make Decisions	How much decision making freedom, without supervision, does the job offer?
Frequency of Decision Making	How frequently is the worker required to make decisions that affect other people, the financial resources, and/or the image and reputation of the organization?
Spend Time Sitting	How much does this job require sitting?

Importance of Being Exact or Accurate	How important is being very exact or highly accurate in performing this job?
Deal With External Customers	How important is it to work with external customers or the public in this job?
Impact of Decisions on Co-workers or Company Resul	How do the decisions an employee makes impact the results of co-workers, clients or the company?
Indoors, Environmentally Controlled	How often does this job require working indoors in environmentally controlled conditions?
Importance of Repeating Same Tasks	How important is repeating the same physical activities (e.g., key entry) or mental activities (e.g., checking entries in a ledger) over and over, without stopping, to performing this job?
Work With Work Group or Team	How important is it to work with others in a group or team in this job?
Time Pressure	How often does this job require the worker to meet strict deadlines?
Electronic Mail	How often do you use electronic mail in this job?
Physical Proximity	To what extent does this job require the worker to perform job tasks in close physical proximity to other people?
Deal With Unpleasant or Angry People	How frequently does the worker have to deal with unpleasant, angry, or discourteous individuals as part of the job requirements?
In an Enclosed Vehicle or Equipment	How often does this job require working in a closed vehicle or equipment (e.g., car)?
Frequency of Conflict Situations	How often are there conflict situations the employee has to face in this job?
Degree of Automation	How automated is the job?
Coordinate or Lead Others	How important is it to coordinate or lead others in accomplishing work activities in this job?
Sounds, Noise Levels Are Distracting or Uncomforta	How often does this job require working exposed to sounds and noise levels that are distracting or uncomfortable?
Spend Time Making Repetitive Motions	How much does this job require making repetitive motions?
Consequence of Error	How serious would the result usually be if the worker made a mistake that was not readily correctable?
Public Speaking	How often do you have to perform public speaking in this job?
Responsibility for Outcomes and Results	How responsible is the worker for work outcomes and results of other workers?
Indoors, Not Environmentally Controlled	How often does this job require working indoors in non-controlled environmental conditions (e.g., warehouse without heat)?
Extremely Bright or Inadequate Lighting	How often does this job require working in extremely bright or inadequate lighting conditions?
Outdoors, Exposed to Weather	How often does this job require working outdoors, exposed to all weather conditions?
Spend Time Standing	How much does this job require standing?
Exposed to Contaminants	How often does this job require working exposed to contaminants (such as pollutants, gases, dust or odors)?
Responsible for Others' Health and Safety	How much responsibility is there for the health and safety of others in this job?
Spend Time Walking and Running	How much does this job require walking and running?
Very Hot or Cold Temperatures	How often does this job require working in very hot (above 90 F degrees) or very cold (below 32 F degrees) temperatures?
Spend Time Using Your Hands to Handle, Control, or	How much does this job require using your hands to handle, control, or feel objects, tools or controls?
Spend Time Bending or Twisting the Body	How much does this job require bending or twisting your body?
Outdoors, Under Cover	How often does this job require working outdoors, under cover (e.g., structure with roof but no walls)?
Spend Time Kneeling, Crouching, Stooping, or Crawl	How much does this job require kneeling, crouching, stooping or crawling?
Cramped Work Space, Awkward Positions	How often does this job require working in cramped work spaces that requires getting into awkward positions?
Pace Determined by Speed of Equipment	How important is it to this job that the pace is determined by the speed of equipment or machinery? (This does not refer to keeping busy at all times on this job.)
Deal With Physically Aggressive People	How frequently does this job require the worker to deal with physical aggression of violent individuals?
Exposed to Hazardous Conditions	How often does this job require exposure to hazardous conditions?
Wear Common Protective or Safety Equipment such as	How much does this job require wearing common protective or safety equipment such as safety shoes, glasses, gloves, hard hats or live jackets?
Exposed to Minor Burns, Cuts, Bites, or Stings	How often does this job require exposure to minor burns, cuts, bites, or stings?

In an Open Vehicle or Equipment	How often does this job require working in an open vehicle or equipment (e.g., tractor)?
Exposed to Disease or Infections	How often does this job require exposure to disease/infections?
Exposed to Whole Body Vibration	How often does this job require exposure to whole body vibration (e.g., operate a jackhammer)?
Spend Time Climbing Ladders, Scaffolds, or Poles	How much does this job require climbing ladders, scaffolds, or poles?
Spend Time Keeping or Regaining Balance	How much does this job require keeping or regaining your balance?
Exposed to Radiation	How often does this job require exposure to radiation?
Exposed to Hazardous Equipment	How often does this job require exposure to hazardous equipment?
Wear Specialized Protective or Safety Equipment su	How much does this job require wearing specialized protective or safety equipment such as breathing apparatus, safety harness, full protection suits, or radiation protection?
Exposed to High Places	How often does this job require exposure to high places?

Job Zone Component	Job Zone Component Definitions
Title	Job Zone Three: Medium Preparation Needed
Overall Experience	Previous work-related skill, knowledge, or experience is required for these occupations. For example, an electrician must have completed three or four years of apprenticeship or several years of vocational training, and often must have passed a licensing exam, in order to perform the job.
Job Training	Employees in these occupations usually need one or two years of training involving both on-the-job experience and informal training with experienced workers.
Job Zone Examples	These occupations usually involve using communication and organizational skills to coordinate, supervise, manage, or train others to accomplish goals. Examples include dental assistants, electricians, fish and game wardens, legal secretaries, personnel recruiters, and recreation workers.
SVP Range	(6.0 to < 7.0)
Education	Most occupations in this zone require training in vocational schools, related on-the-job experience, or an associate's degree. Some may require a bachelor's degree.

Work_Styles	Work_Styles Definitions
Integrity	Job requires being honest and ethical.
Dependability	Job requires being reliable, responsible, and dependable, and fulfilling obligations.
Attention to Detail	Job requires being careful about detail and thorough in completing work tasks.
Self Control	Job requires maintaining composure, keeping emotions in check, controlling anger, and avoiding aggressive behavior, even in very difficult situations.
Initiative	Job requires a willingness to take on responsibilities and challenges.
Persistence	Job requires persistence in the face of obstacles.
Stress Tolerance	Job requires accepting criticism and dealing calmly and effectively with high stress situations.
Cooperation	Job requires being pleasant with others on the job and displaying a good-natured, cooperative attitude.
Concern for Others	Job requires being sensitive to others' needs and feelings and being understanding and helpful on the job.
Independence	Job requires developing one's own ways of doing things, guiding oneself with little or no supervision, and depending on oneself to get things done.
Achievement/Effort	Job requires establishing and maintaining personally challenging achievement goals and exerting effort toward mastering tasks.
Adaptability/Flexibility	Job requires being open to change (positive or negative) and to considerable variety in the workplace.
Social Orientation	Job requires preferring to work with others rather than alone, and being personally connected with others on the job.
Leadership	Job requires a willingness to lead, take charge, and offer opinions and direction.
Analytical Thinking	Job requires analyzing information and using logic to address work-related issues and problems.
Innovation	Job requires creativity and alternative thinking to develop new ideas for and answers to work-related problems.

41-3031.01 - Sales Agents, Securities and Commodities

Buy and sell securities in investment and trading firms and develop and implement financial plans for individuals, businesses, and organizations.

Tasks

1) Review financial periodicals, stock and bond reports, business publications and other material in order to identify potential investments for clients and to keep abreast of trends affecting market conditions.

2) Record transactions accurately, and keep clients informed about transactions.

3) Contact prospective customers to determine customer needs, present information, and explain available services.

4) Explain stock market terms and trading practices to clients.

5) Offer advice on the purchase or sale of particular securities.

6) Identify potential clients, using advertising campaigns, mailing lists, and personal contacts.

7) Relay buy or sell orders to securities exchanges or to firm trading departments.

8) Analyze market conditions in order to determine optimum times to execute securities transactions.

9) Read corporate reports and calculate ratios to determine best prospects for profit on stock purchases and to monitor client accounts.

10) Review all securities transactions to ensure accuracy of information and that trades conform to regulations of governing agencies.

11) Prepare documents needed to implement plans selected by clients.

12) Interview clients to determine clients' assets, liabilities, cash flow, insurance coverage, tax status, and financial objectives.

13) Prepare financial reports to monitor client or corporate finances.

14) Develop financial plans based on analysis of clients' financial status, and discuss financial options with clients.

15) Calculate costs for billings and commissions purposes.

16) Supply the latest price quotes on any security, as well as information on the activities and financial positions of the corporations issuing these securities.

17) Complete sales order tickets and submit for processing of client requested transactions.

41-3031.02 - Sales Agents, Financial Services

Sell financial services, such as loan, tax, and securities counseling to customers of financial institutions and business establishments.

Tasks

1) Evaluate costs and revenue of agreements in order to determine continued profitability.

2) Make presentations on financial services to groups in order to attract new clients.

3) Review business trends in order to advise customers regarding expected fluctuations.

4) Contact prospective customers in order to present information and explain available services.

5) Determine customers' financial services needs, and prepare proposals to sell services that address these needs.

6) Develop prospects from current commercial customers, referral leads, and sales and trade meetings.

7) Prepare forms or agreements to complete sales.

41-3041.00 - Travel Agents

Plan and sell transportation and accommodations for travel agency customers. Determine destination, modes of transportation, travel dates, costs, and accommodations required.

Tasks

1) Book transportation and hotel reservations, using computer terminal or telephone.

2) Print or request transportation carrier tickets, using computer printer system or system link to travel carrier.

3) Plan, describe, arrange, and sell itinerary tour packages and promotional travel incentives offered by various travel carriers.

4) Converse with customer to determine destination, mode of transportation, travel dates, financial considerations, and accommodations required.

5) Compute cost of travel and accommodations, using calculator, computer, carrier tariff books, and hotel rate books, or quote package tour's costs.

6) Provide customer with brochures and publications containing travel information, such as local customs, points of interest, or foreign country regulations.

Knowledge	Knowledge Definitions
Customer and Personal Service	Knowledge of principles and processes for providing customer and personal services. This includes customer needs assessment, meeting quality standards for services, and evaluation of customer satisfaction.
Geography	Knowledge of principles and methods for describing the features of land, sea, and air masses, including their physical characteristics, locations, interrelationships, and distribution of plant, animal, and human life.
Sales and Marketing	Knowledge of principles and methods for showing, promoting, and selling products or services. This includes marketing strategy and tactics, product demonstration, sales techniques, and sales control systems.
Transportation	Knowledge of principles and methods for moving people or goods by air, rail, sea, or road, including the relative costs and benefits.
English Language	Knowledge of the structure and content of the English language including the meaning and spelling of words, rules of composition, and grammar.
Clerical	Knowledge of administrative and clerical procedures and systems such as word processing, managing files and records, stenography and transcription, designing forms, and other office procedures and terminology.
Computers and Electronics	Knowledge of circuit boards, processors, chips, electronic equipment, and computer hardware and software, including applications and programming.
Economics and Accounting	Knowledge of economic and accounting principles and practices, the financial markets, banking and the analysis and reporting of financial data.
Administration and Management	Knowledge of business and management principles involved in strategic planning, resource allocation, human resources modeling, leadership technique, production methods, and coordination of people and resources.
Mathematics	Knowledge of arithmetic, algebra, geometry, calculus, statistics, and their applications.
Education and Training	Knowledge of principles and methods for curriculum and training design, teaching and instruction for individuals and groups, and the measurement of training effects.
Foreign Language	Knowledge of the structure and content of a foreign (non-English) language including the meaning and spelling of words, rules of composition and grammar, and pronunciation.
Law and Government	Knowledge of laws, legal codes, court procedures, precedents, government regulations, executive orders, agency rules, and the democratic political process.
History and Archeology	Knowledge of historical events and their causes, indicators, and effects on civilizations and cultures.
Telecommunications	Knowledge of transmission, broadcasting, switching, control, and operation of telecommunications systems.
Communications and Media	Knowledge of media production, communication, and dissemination techniques and methods. This includes alternative ways to inform and entertain via written, oral, and visual media.
Psychology	Knowledge of human behavior and performance; individual differences in ability, personality, and interests; learning and motivation; psychological research methods; and the assessment and treatment of behavioral and affective disorders.
Public Safety and Security	Knowledge of relevant equipment, policies, procedures, and strategies to promote effective local, state, or national security operations for the protection of people, data, property, and institutions.
Personnel and Human Resources	Knowledge of principles and procedures for personnel recruitment, selection, training, compensation and benefits, labor relations and negotiation, and personnel information systems.
Sociology and Anthropology	Knowledge of group behavior and dynamics, societal trends and influences, human migrations, ethnicity, cultures and their history and origins.
Production and Processing	Knowledge of raw materials, production processes, quality control, costs, and other techniques for maximizing the effective manufacture and distribution of goods.
Mechanical	Knowledge of machines and tools, including their designs, uses, repair, and maintenance.
Design	Knowledge of design techniques, tools, and principles involved in production of precision technical plans, blueprints, drawings, and models.
Philosophy and Theology	Knowledge of different philosophical systems and religions. This includes their basic principles, values, ethics, ways of thinking, customs, practices, and their impact on human culture.
Engineering and Technology	Knowledge of the practical application of engineering science and technology. This includes applying principles, techniques, procedures, and equipment to the design and production of various goods and services.
Therapy and Counseling	Knowledge of principles, methods, and procedures for diagnosis, treatment, and rehabilitation of physical and mental dysfunctions, and for career counseling and guidance.
Fine Arts	Knowledge of the theory and techniques required to compose, produce, and perform works of music, dance, visual arts, drama, and sculpture.
Medicine and Dentistry	Knowledge of the information and techniques needed to diagnose and treat human injuries, diseases, and deformities. This includes symptoms, treatment alternatives, drug properties and interactions, and preventive health-care measures.
Building and Construction	Knowledge of materials, methods, and the tools involved in the construction or repair of houses, buildings, or other structures such as highways and roads.
Food Production	Knowledge of techniques and equipment for planting, growing, and harvesting food products (both plant and animal) for consumption, including storage/handling techniques.
Biology	Knowledge of plant and animal organisms, their tissues, cells, functions, interdependencies, and interactions with each other and the environment.
Chemistry	Knowledge of the chemical composition, structure, and properties of substances and of the chemical processes and transformations that they undergo. This includes uses of chemicals and their interactions, danger signs, production techniques, and disposal methods.
Physics	Knowledge and prediction of physical principles, laws, their interrelationships, and applications to understanding fluid, material, and atmospheric dynamics, and mechanical, electrical, atomic and sub-atomic structures and processes.

Skills	Skills Definitions
Active Listening	Giving full attention to what other people are saying, taking time to understand the points being made, asking questions as appropriate, and not interrupting at inappropriate times.
Service Orientation	Actively looking for ways to help people.
Reading Comprehension	Understanding written sentences and paragraphs in work related documents.
Speaking	Talking to others to convey information effectively.
Time Management	Managing one's own time and the time of others.
Social Perceptiveness	Being aware of others' reactions and understanding why they react as they do.
Coordination	Adjusting actions in relation to others' actions.
Active Learning	Understanding the implications of new information for both current and future problem-solving and decision-making.
Mathematics	Using mathematics to solve problems.
Writing	Communicating effectively in writing as appropriate for the needs of the audience.
Persuasion	Persuading others to change their minds or behavior.
Learning Strategies	Selecting and using training/instructional methods and procedures appropriate for the situation when learning or teaching new things.
Critical Thinking	Using logic and reasoning to identify the strengths and weaknesses of alternative solutions, conclusions or approaches to problems.

Judgment and Decision Making	Considering the relative costs and benefits of potential actions to choose the most appropriate one.
Monitoring	Monitoring/Assessing performance of yourself, other individuals, or organizations to make improvements or take corrective action.
Management of Personnel Resources	Motivating, developing, and directing people as they work, identifying the best people for the job.
Instructing	Teaching others how to do something.
Complex Problem Solving	Identifying complex problems and reviewing related information to develop and evaluate options and implement solutions.
Negotiation	Bringing others together and trying to reconcile differences.
Technology Design	Generating or adapting equipment and technology to serve user needs.
Operation and Control	Controlling operations of equipment or systems.
Quality Control Analysis	Conducting tests and inspections of products, services, or processes to evaluate quality or performance.
Operations Analysis	Analyzing needs and product requirements to create a design.
Equipment Selection	Determining the kind of tools and equipment needed to do a job.
Management of Financial Resources	Determining how money will be spent to get the work done, and accounting for these expenditures.
Systems Evaluation	Identifying measures or indicators of system performance and the actions needed to improve or correct performance, relative to the goals of the system.
Equipment Maintenance	Performing routine maintenance on equipment and determining when and what kind of maintenance is needed.
Troubleshooting	Determining causes of operating errors and deciding what to do about it.
Operation Monitoring	Watching gauges, dials, or other indicators to make sure a machine is working properly.
Management of Material Resources	Obtaining and seeing to the appropriate use of equipment, facilities, and materials needed to do certain work.
Systems Analysis	Determining how a system should work and how changes in conditions, operations, and the environment will affect outcomes.
Repairing	Repairing machines or systems using the needed tools.
Installation	Installing equipment, machines, wiring, or programs to meet specifications.
Programming	Writing computer programs for various purposes.
Science	Using scientific rules and methods to solve problems.

Ability	Ability Definitions
Oral Expression	The ability to communicate information and ideas in speaking so others will understand.
Oral Comprehension	The ability to listen to and understand information and ideas presented through spoken words and sentences.
Speech Clarity	The ability to speak clearly so others can understand you.
Speech Recognition	The ability to identify and understand the speech of another person.
Written Comprehension	The ability to read and understand information and ideas presented in writing.
Near Vision	The ability to see details at close range (within a few feet of the observer).
Problem Sensitivity	The ability to tell when something is wrong or is likely to go wrong. It does not involve solving the problem, only recognizing there is a problem.
Information Ordering	The ability to arrange things or actions in a certain order or pattern according to a specific rule or set of rules (e.g., patterns of numbers, letters, words, pictures, mathematical operations).
Selective Attention	The ability to concentrate on a task over a period of time without being distracted.
Number Facility	The ability to add, subtract, multiply, or divide quickly and correctly.
Deductive Reasoning	The ability to apply general rules to specific problems to produce answers that make sense.
Category Flexibility	The ability to generate or use different sets of rules for combining or grouping things in different ways.
Fluency of Ideas	The ability to come up with a number of ideas about a topic (the number of ideas is important, not their quality, correctness, or creativity).
Originality	The ability to come up with unusual or clever ideas about a given topic or situation, or to develop creative ways to solve a problem.
Inductive Reasoning	The ability to combine pieces of information to form general rules or conclusions (includes finding a relationship among seemingly unrelated events).

Time Sharing	The ability to shift back and forth between two or more activities or sources of information (such as speech, sounds, touch, or other sources).
Written Expression	The ability to communicate information and ideas in writing so others will understand.
Memorization	The ability to remember information such as words, numbers, pictures, and procedures.
Mathematical Reasoning	The ability to choose the right mathematical methods or formulas to solve a problem.
Finger Dexterity	The ability to make precisely coordinated movements of the fingers of one or both hands to grasp, manipulate, or assemble very small objects.
Auditory Attention	The ability to focus on a single source of sound in the presence of other distracting sounds.
Flexibility of Closure	The ability to identify or detect a known pattern (a figure, object, word, or sound) that is hidden in other distracting material.
Visualization	The ability to imagine how something will look after it is moved around or when its parts are moved or rearranged.
Perceptual Speed	The ability to quickly and accurately compare similarities and differences among sets of letters, numbers, objects, pictures, or patterns. The things to be compared may be presented at the same time or one after the other. This ability also includes comparing a presented object with a remembered object.
Wrist-Finger Speed	The ability to make fast, simple, repeated movements of the fingers, hands, and wrists.
Speed of Closure	The ability to make sense of, combine, and organize information into meaningful patterns.
Far Vision	The ability to see details at a distance.
Hearing Sensitivity	The ability to detect or tell the differences between sounds that vary in pitch and loudness.
Trunk Strength	The ability to use your abdominal and lower back muscles to support part of the body repeatedly or continuously over time without 'giving out' or fatiguing.
Visual Color Discrimination	The ability to match or detect differences between colors, including shades of color and brightness.
Depth Perception	The ability to judge which of several objects is closer or farther away from you, or to judge the distance between you and an object.
Manual Dexterity	The ability to quickly move your hand, your hand together with your arm, or your two hands to grasp, manipulate, or assemble objects.
Multilimb Coordination	The ability to coordinate two or more limbs (for example, two arms, two legs, or one leg and one arm) while sitting, standing, or lying down. It does not involve performing the activities while the whole body is in motion.
Arm-Hand Steadiness	The ability to keep your hand and arm steady while moving your arm or while holding your arm and hand in one position.
Static Strength	The ability to exert maximum muscle force to lift, push, pull, or carry objects.
Glare Sensitivity	The ability to see objects in the presence of glare or bright lighting.
Extent Flexibility	The ability to bend, stretch, twist, or reach with your body, arms, and/or legs.
Spatial Orientation	The ability to know your location in relation to the environment or to know where other objects are in relation to you.
Sound Localization	The ability to tell the direction from which a sound originated.
Explosive Strength	The ability to use short bursts of muscle force to propel oneself (as in jumping or sprinting), or to throw an object.
Control Precision	The ability to quickly and repeatedly adjust the controls of a machine or a vehicle to exact positions.
Gross Body Coordination	The ability to coordinate the movement of your arms, legs, and torso together when the whole body is in motion.
Dynamic Flexibility	The ability to quickly and repeatedly bend, stretch, twist, or reach out with your body, arms, and/or legs.
Dynamic Strength	The ability to exert muscle force repeatedly or continuously over time. This involves muscular endurance and resistance to muscle fatigue.
Speed of Limb Movement	The ability to quickly move the arms and legs.
Stamina	The ability to exert yourself physically over long periods of time without getting winded or out of breath.
Response Orientation	The ability to choose quickly between two or more movements in response to two or more different signals (lights, sounds, pictures). It includes the speed with which the correct response is started with the hand, foot, or other body part.
Peripheral Vision	The ability to see objects or movement of objects to one's side when the eyes are looking ahead.

Gross Body Equilibrium	The ability to keep or regain your body balance or stay upright when in an unstable position.
Rate Control	The ability to time your movements or the movement of a piece of equipment in anticipation of changes in the speed and/or direction of a moving object or scene.
Night Vision	The ability to see under low light conditions.
Reaction Time	The ability to quickly respond (with the hand, finger, or foot) to a signal (sound, light, picture) when it appears.

Work_Activity	Work_Activity Definitions
Performing for or Working Directly with the Public	Performing for people or dealing directly with the public. This includes serving customers in restaurants and stores, and receiving clients or guests.
Selling or Influencing Others	Convincing others to buy merchandise/goods or to otherwise change their minds or actions.
Interacting With Computers	Using computers and computer systems (including hardware and software) to program, write software, set up functions, enter data, or process information.
Getting Information	Observing, receiving, and otherwise obtaining information from all relevant sources.
Communicating with Persons Outside Organization	Communicating with people outside the organization, representing the organization to customers, the public, government, and other external sources. This information can be exchanged in person, in writing, or by telephone or e-mail.
Updating and Using Relevant Knowledge	Keeping up-to-date technically and applying new knowledge to your job.
Establishing and Maintaining Interpersonal Relatio	Developing constructive and cooperative working relationships with others, and maintaining them over time.
Organizing, Planning, and Prioritizing Work	Developing specific goals and plans to prioritize, organize, and accomplish your work.
Communicating with Supervisors, Peers, or Subordin	Providing information to supervisors, co-workers, and subordinates by telephone, in written form, e-mail, or in person.
Making Decisions and Solving Problems	Analyzing information and evaluating results to choose the best solution and solve problems.
Documenting/Recording Information	Entering, transcribing, recording, storing, or maintaining information in written or electronic/magnetic form.
Interpreting the Meaning of Information for Others	Translating or explaining what information means and how it can be used.
Resolving Conflicts and Negotiating with Others	Handling complaints, settling disputes, and resolving grievances and conflicts, or otherwise negotiating with others.
Performing Administrative Activities	Performing day-to-day administrative tasks such as maintaining information files and processing paperwork.
Judging the Qualities of Things, Services, or Peop	Assessing the value, importance, or quality of things or people.
Processing Information	Compiling, coding, categorizing, calculating, tabulating, auditing, or verifying information or data.
Thinking Creatively	Developing, designing, or creating new applications, ideas, relationships, systems, or products, including artistic contributions.
Analyzing Data or Information	Identifying the underlying principles, reasons, or facts of information by breaking down information or data into separate parts.
Assisting and Caring for Others	Providing personal assistance, medical attention, emotional support, or other personal care to others such as coworkers, customers, or patients.
Coordinating the Work and Activities of Others	Getting members of a group to work together to accomplish tasks.
Scheduling Work and Activities	Scheduling events, programs, and activities, as well as the work of others.
Monitoring and Controlling Resources	Monitoring and controlling resources and overseeing the spending of money.
Training and Teaching Others	Identifying the educational needs of others, developing formal educational or training programs or classes, and teaching or instructing others.
Developing Objectives and Strategies	Establishing long-range objectives and specifying the strategies and actions to achieve them.
Identifying Objects, Actions, and Events	Identifying information by categorizing, estimating, recognizing differences or similarities, and detecting changes in circumstances or events.
Estimating the Quantifiable Characteristics of Pro	Estimating sizes, distances, and quantities; or determining time, costs, resources, or materials needed to perform a work activity.
Provide Consultation and Advice to Others	Providing guidance and expert advice to management or other groups on technical, systems-, or process-related topics.

Developing and Building Teams	Encouraging and building mutual trust, respect, and cooperation among team members.
Coaching and Developing Others	Identifying the developmental needs of others and coaching, mentoring, or otherwise helping others to improve their knowledge or skills.
Evaluating Information to Determine Compliance wit	Using relevant information and individual judgment to determine whether events or processes comply with laws, regulations, or standards.
Monitor Processes, Materials, or Surroundings	Monitoring and reviewing information from materials, events, or the environment, to detect or assess problems.
Guiding, Directing, and Motivating Subordinates	Providing guidance and direction to subordinates, including setting performance standards and monitoring performance.
Staffing Organizational Units	Recruiting, interviewing, selecting, hiring, and promoting employees in an organization.
Handling and Moving Objects	Using hands and arms in handling, installing, positioning, and moving materials, and manipulating things.
Controlling Machines and Processes	Using either control mechanisms or direct physical activity to operate machines or processes (not including computers or vehicles).
Performing General Physical Activities	Performing physical activities that require considerable use of your arms and legs and moving your whole body, such as climbing, lifting, balancing, walking, stooping, and handling of materials.
Inspecting Equipment, Structures, or Material	Inspecting equipment, structures, or materials to identify the cause of errors or other problems or defects.
Drafting, Laying Out, and Specifying Technical Dev	Providing documentation, detailed instructions, drawings, or specifications to tell others about how devices, parts, equipment, or structures are to be fabricated, constructed, assembled, modified, maintained, or used.
Repairing and Maintaining Electronic Equipment	Servicing, repairing, calibrating, regulating, fine-tuning, or testing machines, devices, and equipment that operate primarily on the basis of electrical or electronic (not mechanical) principles.
Repairing and Maintaining Mechanical Equipment	Servicing, repairing, adjusting, and testing machines, devices, moving parts, and equipment that operate primarily on the basis of mechanical (not electronic) principles.
Operating Vehicles, Mechanized Devices, or Equipme	Running, maneuvering, navigating, or driving vehicles or mechanized equipment, such as forklifts, passenger vehicles, aircraft, or water craft.

Work_Context	Work_Context Definitions
Contact With Others	How much does this job require the worker to be in contact with others (face-to-face, by telephone, or otherwise) in order to perform it?
Telephone	How often do you have telephone conversations in this job?
Electronic Mail	How often do you use electronic mail in this job?
Spend Time Sitting	How much does this job require sitting?
Face-to-Face Discussions	How often do you have to have face-to-face discussions with individuals or teams in this job?
Deal With External Customers	How important is it to work with external customers or the public in this job?
Importance of Being Exact or Accurate	How important is being very exact or highly accurate in performing this job?
Freedom to Make Decisions	How much decision making freedom, without supervision, does the job offer?
Letters and Memos	How often does the job require written letters and memos?
Level of Competition	To what extent does this job require the worker to compete or to be aware of competitive pressures?
Impact of Decisions on Co-workers or Company Resul	How do the decisions an employee makes impact the results of co-workers, clients or the company?
Structured versus Unstructured Work	To what extent is this job structured for the worker, rather than allowing the worker to determine tasks, priorities, and goals?
Indoors, Environmentally Controlled	How often does this job require working indoors in environmentally controlled conditions?
Degree of Automation	How automated is the job?
Time Pressure	How often does this job require the worker to meet strict deadlines?
Consequence of Error	How serious would the result usually be if the worker made a mistake that was not readily correctable?
Work With Work Group or Team	How important is it to work with others in a group or team in this job?
Frequency of Decision Making	How frequently is the worker required to make decisions that affect other people, the financial resources, and/or the image and reputation of the organization?

Importance of Repeating Same Tasks	How important is repeating the same physical activities (e.g., key entry) or mental activities (e.g., checking entries in a ledger) over and over, without stopping, to performing this job?
Deal With Unpleasant or Angry People	How frequently does the worker have to deal with unpleasant, angry, or discourteous individuals as part of the job requirements?
Physical Proximity	To what extent does this job require the worker to perform job tasks in close physical proximity to other people?
Frequency of Conflict Situations	How often are there conflict situations the employee has to face in this job?
Sounds, Noise Levels Are Distracting or Uncomfortable	How often does this job require working exposed to sounds and noise levels that are distracting or uncomfortable?
Spend Time Making Repetitive Motions	How much does this job require making repetitive motions?
Responsibility for Outcomes and Results	How responsible is the worker for work outcomes and results of other workers?
Spend Time Using Your Hands to Handle, Control, or	How much does this job require using your hands to handle, control, or feel objects, tools or controls?
Responsible for Others' Health and Safety	How much responsibility is there for the health and safety of others in this job?
Public Speaking	How often do you have to perform public speaking in this job?
Coordinate or Lead Others	How important is it to coordinate or lead others in accomplishing work activities in this job?
Spend Time Bending or Twisting the Body	How much does this job require bending or twisting your body?
Spend Time Standing	How much does this job require standing?
In an Enclosed Vehicle or Equipment	How often does this job require working in a closed vehicle or equipment (e.g., car)?
Pace Determined by Speed of Equipment	How important is it to this job that the pace is determined by the speed of equipment or machinery? (This does not refer to keeping busy at all times on this job.)
Spend Time Walking and Running	How much does this job require walking and running?
Exposed to Contaminants	How often does this job require working exposed to contaminants (such as pollutants, gases, dust or odors)?
Indoors, Not Environmentally Controlled	How often does this job require working indoors in non-controlled environmental conditions (e.g., warehouse without heat)?
Outdoors, Exposed to Weather	How often does this job require working outdoors, exposed to all weather conditions?
Cramped Work Space, Awkward Positions	How often does this job require working in cramped work spaces that requires getting into awkward positions?
Deal With Physically Aggressive People	How frequently does this job require the worker to deal with physical aggression of violent individuals?
Outdoors, Under Cover	How often does this job require working outdoors, under cover (e.g., structure with roof but no walls)?
In an Open Vehicle or Equipment	How often does this job require working in an open vehicle or equipment (e.g., tractor)?
Extremely Bright or Inadequate Lighting	How often does this job require working in extremely bright or inadequate lighting conditions?
Spend Time Kneeling, Crouching, Stooping, or Crawl	How much does this job require kneeling, crouching, stooping, or crawling?
Spend Time Keeping or Regaining Balance	How much does this job require keeping or regaining your balance?
Very Hot or Cold Temperatures	How often does this job require working in very hot (above 90 F degrees) or very cold (below 32 F degrees) temperatures?
Exposed to Hazardous Equipment	How often does this job require exposure to hazardous equipment?
Wear Common Protective or Safety Equipment such as	How much does this job require wearing common protective or safety equipment such as safety shoes, glasses, gloves, hard hats or life jackets?
Spend Time Climbing Ladders, Scaffolds, or Poles	How much does this job require climbing ladders, scaffolds, or poles?
Exposed to Minor Burns, Cuts, Bites, or Stings	How often does this job require exposure to minor burns, cuts, bites, or stings?
Wear Specialized Protective or Safety Equipment su	How often does this job require wearing specialized protective or safety equipment such as breathing apparatus, safety harness, full protection suits, or radiation protection?
Exposed to High Places	How often does this job require exposure to high places?
Exposed to Radiation	How often does this job require exposure to radiation?
Exposed to Whole Body Vibration	How often does this job require exposure to whole body vibration (e.g., operate a jackhammer)?
Exposed to Disease or Infections	How often does this job require exposure to disease/infections?

Exposed to Hazardous Conditions	How often does this job require exposure to hazardous conditions?

Job Zone Component	Job Zone Component Definitions
Title	Job Zone Three: Medium Preparation Needed
Overall Experience	Previous work-related skill, knowledge, or experience is required for these occupations. For example, an electrician must have completed three or four years of apprenticeship or several years of vocational training, and often must have passed a licensing exam, in order to perform the job.
Job Training	Employees in these occupations usually need one or two years of training involving both on-the-job experience and informal training with experienced workers.
Job Zone Examples	These occupations usually involve using communication and organizational skills to coordinate, supervise, manage, or train others to accomplish goals. Examples include dental assistants, electricians, fish and game wardens, legal secretaries, personnel recruiters, and recreation workers.
SVP Range	(6.0 to < 7.0)
Education	Most occupations in this zone require training in vocational schools, related on-the-job experience, or an associate's degree. Some may require a bachelor's degree.

Work_Styles	Work_Styles Definitions
Attention to Detail	Job requires being careful about detail and thorough in completing work tasks.
Dependability	Job requires being reliable, responsible, and dependable, and fulfilling obligations.
Integrity	Job requires being honest and ethical.
Cooperation	Job requires being pleasant with others on the job and displaying a good-natured, cooperative attitude.
Self Control	Job requires maintaining composure, keeping emotions in check, controlling anger, and avoiding aggressive behavior, even in very difficult situations.
Independence	Job requires developing one's own ways of doing things, guiding oneself with little or no supervision, and depending on oneself to get things done.
Initiative	Job requires a willingness to take on responsibilities and challenges.
Stress Tolerance	Job requires accepting criticism and dealing calmly and effectively with high stress situations.
Concern for Others	Job requires being sensitive to others' needs and feelings and being understanding and helpful on the job.
Adaptability/Flexibility	Job requires being open to change (positive or negative) and to considerable variety in the workplace.
Leadership	Job requires a willingness to lead, take charge, and offer opinions and direction.
Persistence	Job requires persistence in the face of obstacles.
Achievement/Effort	Job requires establishing and maintaining personally challenging achievement goals and exerting effort toward mastering tasks.
Social Orientation	Job requires preferring to work with others rather than alone, and being personally connected with others on the job.
Analytical Thinking	Job requires analyzing information and using logic to address work-related issues and problems.
Innovation	Job requires creativity and alternative thinking to develop new ideas for and answers to work-related problems.

41-4011.00 - Sales Representatives, Wholesale and Manufacturing, Technical and Scientific Products

Sell goods for wholesalers or manufacturers where technical or scientific knowledge is required in such areas as biology, engineering, chemistry, and electronics, normally obtained from at least 2 years of post-secondary education.

Tasks

1) Sell service contracts for products.

2) Arrange for installation and test-operation of machinery.

3) Verify customers' credit ratings, and appraise equipment in order to determine contract

858

terms and trade-in values.

4) Recommend ways for customers to alter product usage in order to improve production.

5) Verify that materials lists are accurate and that delivery schedules meet project deadlines.

6) Complete expense reports, sales reports, and other paperwork.

7) Select the correct products or assist customers in making product selections, based on customers' needs, product specifications, and applicable regulations.

8) Answer customers' questions about products, prices, availability, product uses, and credit terms.

9) Write specifications to order custom-made surgical appliances, using customers' measurements and physicians' prescriptions.

10) Obtain building blueprints and specifications for use by engineering departments in bid preparations.

11) Inspect, test, and observe chemical changes in water system equipment, using test kits, reference manuals, and knowledge of chemical treatments.

12) Provide feedback to company's product design team so that products can be tailored to clients' needs.

13) Select surgical appliances from stock, and fit and sell appliances to customers.

14) Emphasize product features based on analyses of customers' needs, and on technical knowledge of product capabilities and limitations.

15) Stock and distribute resources such as samples and promotional and educational materials.

16) Study information about new products so that equipment and supplies can be accurately depicted and proper recommendations made.

17) Inform customers of estimated delivery schedules, service contracts, warranties, or other information pertaining to purchased products.

18) Review existing machinery/equipment placement, and create diagrams to illustrate efficient space utilization, using standard measuring devices and templates.

19) Compute customer's installation or production costs, and estimate savings from new services, products, or equipment.

20) Initiate sales campaigns and follow marketing plan guidelines in order to meet sales and production expectations.

21) Visit establishments to evaluate needs and to promote product or service sales.

22) Attend medical procedures in order to provide medical personnel with product assistance.

23) Advise customers regarding office layouts, legal and insurance regulations, cost analyses, and collection methods.

24) Contact new and existing customers to discuss their needs, and to explain how these needs could be met by specific products and services.

25) Identify prospective customers by using business directories, following leads from existing clients, participating in organizations and clubs, and attending trade shows and conferences.

26) Train establishment personnel in equipment use.

27) Attend sales and trade meetings, and read related publications in order to obtain information about market conditions, business trends, and industry developments.

28) Maintain customer records, using automated systems.

29) Prepare sales contracts for orders obtained, and submit orders for processing.

30) Demonstrate and explain the operation and use of products.

31) Negotiate prices and terms of sales and service agreements.

32) Consult with engineers regarding technical problems.

33) Prepare sales presentations and proposals that explain product specifications and applications.

34) Quote prices, credit terms and other bid specifications.

35) Visit establishments such as pharmacies in order to check product sales.

36) Collaborate with colleagues to exchange information such as selling strategies and marketing information.

37) Design and fabricate custom-made medical appliances.

38) Complete product and development training as required.

41-4012.00 - Sales Representatives, Wholesale and Manufacturing, Except Technical and Scientific Products

Sell goods for wholesalers or manufacturers to businesses or groups of individuals. Work requires substantial knowledge of items sold.

Tasks

1) Provide customers with product samples and catalogs.

2) Answer customers' questions about products, prices, availability, product uses, and credit terms.

3) Arrange and direct delivery and installation of products and equipment.

4) Contact regular and prospective customers to demonstrate products, explain product features, and solicit orders.

5) Obtain credit information about prospective customers.

6) Train customers' employees to operate and maintain new equipment.

7) Perform administrative duties, such as preparing sales budgets and reports, keeping sales records, and filing expense account reports.

8) Estimate or quote prices, credit or contract terms, warranties, and delivery dates.

9) Prepare drawings, estimates, and bids that meet specific customer needs.

10) Check stock levels and reorder merchandise as necessary.

11) Recommend products to customers, based on customers' needs and interests.

12) Negotiate details of contracts and payments, and prepare sales contracts and order forms.

13) Plan, assemble, and stock product displays in retail stores, or make recommendations to retailers regarding product displays, promotional programs, and advertising.

14) Forward orders to manufacturers.

15) Identify prospective customers by using business directories, following leads from existing clients, participating in organizations and clubs, and attending trade shows and conferences.

16) Consult with clients after sales or contract signings in order to resolve problems and to provide ongoing support.

17) Buy products from manufacturers or brokerage firms, and distribute them to wholesale and retail clients.

18) Monitor market conditions, product innovations, and competitors' products, prices, and sales.

41-9011.00 - Demonstrators and Product Promoters

Demonstrate merchandise and answer questions for the purpose of creating public interest in buying the product. May sell demonstrated merchandise.

Tasks

1) Keep areas neat while working, and return items to correct locations following demonstrations.

2) Practice demonstrations to ensure that they will run smoothly.

3) Prepare and alter presentation contents to target specific audiences.

4) Provide product information, using lectures, films, charts, and/or slide shows.

5) Visit trade shows, stores, community organizations, and other venues to demonstrate products or services, and to answer questions from potential customers.

6) Provide product samples, coupons, informational brochures, and other incentives to persuade people to buy products.

7) Record and report demonstration-related information such as the number of questions asked by the audience and the number of coupons distributed.

8) Suggest specific product purchases to meet customers' needs.

9) Collect fees or accept donations.

10) Research and investigate products to be presented to prepare for demonstrations.

11) Contact businesses and civic establishments to arrange to exhibit and sell merchandise.

12) Stock shelves with products.

13) Work as part of a team of demonstrators to accommodate large crowds.

14) Demonstrate and explain products, methods, or services in order to persuade customers to purchase products or utilize services.

15) Learn about competitors' products and consumers' interests and concerns in order to answer questions and provide more complete information.

16) Write articles and pamphlets about products.

17) Train demonstrators to present a company's products or services.

18) Sell products being promoted, and keep records of sales.

19) Recommend product or service improvements to employers.

20) Instruct customers in alteration of products.

21) Give tours of plants where specific products are made.

22) Develop lists of prospective clients from sources such as newspaper items, company records, local merchants, and customers.

23) Identify interested and qualified customers in order to provide them with additional information.

24) Wear costumes or sign boards and walk in public to promote merchandise, services, or events.

25) Set up and arrange displays and demonstration areas to attract the attention of prospective customers.

41-9021.00 - Real Estate Brokers

Operate real estate office, or work for commercial real estate firm, overseeing real estate transactions. Other duties usually include selling real estate or renting properties and arranging loans.

Tasks

1) Sell, for a fee, real estate owned by others.

2) Maintain awareness of current income tax regulations, local zoning, building and tax laws, and growth possibilities of the area where a property is located.

3) Compare a property with similar properties that have recently sold, in order to determine its competitive market price.

4) Generate lists of properties for sale, their locations and descriptions, and available financing options, using computers.

5) Check work completed by loan officers, attorneys, and other professionals to ensure that it is performed properly.

6) Obtain agreements from property owners to place properties for sale with real estate firms.

7) Act as an intermediary in negotiations between buyers and sellers over property prices and settlement details, and during the closing of sales.

8) Monitor fulfillment of purchase contract terms to ensure that they are handled in a timely manner.

9) Arrange for financing of property purchases.

10) Appraise property values, assessing income potential when relevant.

11) Review property details to ensure that environmental regulations are met.

12) Arrange for title searches of properties being sold.

13) Give buyers virtual tours of properties in which they are interested, using computers.

14) Rent properties or manage rental properties.

15) Manage and operate real estate offices, handling associated business details.

16) Supervise agents who handle real estate transactions.

17) Develop, sell, or lease property used for industry or manufacturing.

18) Maintain working knowledge of various factors that determine a farm's capacity to produce, including agricultural variables and proximity to market centers and transportation facilities.

Knowledge	Knowledge Definitions
Sales and Marketing	Knowledge of principles and methods for showing, promoting, and selling products or services. This includes marketing strategy and tactics, product demonstration, sales techniques, and sales control systems.
Customer and Personal Service	Knowledge of principles and processes for providing customer and personal services. This includes customer needs assessment, meeting quality standards for services, and evaluation of customer satisfaction.
English Language	Knowledge of the structure and content of the English language including the meaning and spelling of words, rules of composition, and grammar.
Administration and Management	Knowledge of business and management principles involved in strategic planning, resource allocation, human resources modeling, leadership technique, production methods, and coordination of people and resources.
Clerical	Knowledge of administrative and clerical procedures and systems such as word processing, managing files and records, stenography and transcription, designing forms, and other office procedures and terminology.
Mathematics	Knowledge of arithmetic, algebra, geometry, calculus, statistics, and their applications.
Law and Government	Knowledge of laws, legal codes, court procedures, precedents, government regulations, executive orders, agency rules, and the democratic political process.
Computers and Electronics	Knowledge of circuit boards, processors, chips, electronic equipment, and computer hardware and software, including applications and programming.
Economics and Accounting	Knowledge of economic and accounting principles and practices, the financial markets, banking and the analysis and reporting of financial data.
Building and Construction	Knowledge of materials, methods, and the tools involved in the construction or repair of houses, buildings, or other structures such as highways and roads.
Personnel and Human Resources	Knowledge of principles and procedures for personnel recruitment, selection, training, compensation and benefits, labor relations and negotiation, and personnel information systems.
Public Safety and Security	Knowledge of relevant equipment, policies, procedures, and strategies to promote effective local, state, or national security operations for the protection of people, data, property, and institutions.
Education and Training	Knowledge of principles and methods for curriculum and training design, teaching and instruction for individuals and groups, and the measurement of training effects.
Psychology	Knowledge of human behavior and performance; individual differences in ability, personality, and interests; learning and motivation; psychological research methods; and the assessment and treatment of behavioral and affective disorders.
Communications and Media	Knowledge of media production, communication, and dissemination techniques and methods. This includes alternative ways to inform and entertain via written, oral, and visual media.
Geography	Knowledge of principles and methods for describing the features of land, sea, and air masses, including their physical characteristics, locations, interrelationships, and distribution of plant, animal, and human life.
Telecommunications	Knowledge of transmission, broadcasting, switching, control, and operation of telecommunications systems.
Mechanical	Knowledge of machines and tools, including their designs, uses, repair, and maintenance.
Production and Processing	Knowledge of raw materials, production processes, quality control, costs, and other techniques for maximizing the effective manufacture and distribution of goods.
Foreign Language	Knowledge of the structure and content of a foreign (non-English) language including the meaning and spelling of words, rules of composition and grammar, and pronunciation.
Transportation	Knowledge of principles and methods for moving people or goods by air, rail, sea, or road, including the relative costs and benefits.
Sociology and Anthropology	Knowledge of group behavior and dynamics, societal trends and influences, human migrations, ethnicity, cultures and their history and origins.
Design	Knowledge of design techniques, tools, and principles involved in production of precision technical plans, blueprints, drawings, and models.
Therapy and Counseling	Knowledge of principles, methods, and procedures for diagnosis, treatment, and rehabilitation of physical and mental dysfunctions, and for career counseling and guidance.
Philosophy and Theology	Knowledge of different philosophical systems and religions. This includes their basic principles, values, ethics, ways of thinking, customs, practices, and their impact on human culture.
Engineering and Technology	Knowledge of the practical application of engineering science and technology. This includes applying principles, techniques, procedures, and equipment to the design and production of various goods and services.

Physics	Knowledge and prediction of physical principles, laws, their interrelationships, and applications to understanding fluid, material, and atmospheric dynamics, and mechanical, electrical, atomic and sub-atomic structures and processes.
Biology	Knowledge of plant and animal organisms, their tissues, cells, functions, interdependencies, and interactions with each other and the environment.
History and Archeology	Knowledge of historical events and their causes, indicators, and effects on civilizations and cultures.
Chemistry	Knowledge of the chemical composition, structure, and properties of substances and of the chemical processes and transformations that they undergo. This includes uses of chemicals and their interactions, danger signs, production techniques, and disposal methods.
Fine Arts	Knowledge of the theory and techniques required to compose, produce, and perform works of music, dance, visual arts, drama, and sculpture.
Medicine and Dentistry	Knowledge of the information and techniques needed to diagnose and treat human injuries, diseases, and deformities. This includes symptoms, treatment alternatives, drug properties and interactions, and preventive health-care measures.
Food Production	Knowledge of techniques and equipment for planting, growing, and harvesting food products (both plant and animal) for consumption, including storage/handling techniques.

Skills	**Skills Definitions**
Negotiation	Bringing others together and trying to reconcile differences.
Time Management	Managing one's own time and the time of others.
Active Listening	Giving full attention to what other people are saying, taking time to understand the points being made, asking questions as appropriate, and not interrupting at inappropriate times.
Reading Comprehension	Understanding written sentences and paragraphs in work related documents.
Management of Financial Resources	Determining how money will be spent to get the work done, and accounting for these expenditures.
Judgment and Decision Making	Considering the relative costs and benefits of potential actions to choose the most appropriate one.
Critical Thinking	Using logic and reasoning to identify the strengths and weaknesses of alternative solutions, conclusions or approaches to problems.
Active Learning	Understanding the implications of new information for both current and future problem-solving and decision-making.
Speaking	Talking to others to convey information effectively.
Service Orientation	Actively looking for ways to help people.
Coordination	Adjusting actions in relation to others' actions.
Mathematics	Using mathematics to solve problems.
Writing	Communicating effectively in writing as appropriate for the needs of the audience.
Persuasion	Persuading others to change their minds or behavior.
Social Perceptiveness	Being aware of others' reactions and understanding why they react as they do.
Complex Problem Solving	Identifying complex problems and reviewing related information to develop and evaluate options and implement solutions.
Monitoring	Monitoring/Assessing performance of yourself, other individuals, or organizations to make improvements or take corrective action.
Management of Personnel Resources	Motivating, developing, and directing people as they work, identifying the best people for the job.
Learning Strategies	Selecting and using training/instructional methods and procedures appropriate for the situation when learning or teaching new things.
Instructing	Teaching others how to do something.
Management of Material Resources	Obtaining and seeing to the appropriate use of equipment, facilities, and materials needed to do certain work.
Equipment Selection	Determining the kind of tools and equipment needed to do a job.
Operations Analysis	Analyzing needs and product requirements to create a design.
Technology Design	Generating or adapting equipment and technology to serve user needs.
Quality Control Analysis	Conducting tests and inspections of products, services, or processes to evaluate quality or performance.
Systems Evaluation	Identifying measures or indicators of system performance and the actions needed to improve or correct performance, relative to the goals of the system.

Systems Analysis	Determining how a system should work and how changes in conditions, operations, and the environment will affect outcomes.
Troubleshooting	Determining causes of operating errors and deciding what to do about it.
Science	Using scientific rules and methods to solve problems.
Installation	Installing equipment, machines, wiring, or programs to meet specifications.
Operation and Control	Controlling operations of equipment or systems.
Programming	Writing computer programs for various purposes.
Equipment Maintenance	Performing routine maintenance on equipment and determining when and what kind of maintenance is needed.
Operation Monitoring	Watching gauges, dials, or other indicators to make sure a machine is working properly.
Repairing	Repairing machines or systems using the needed tools.

Ability	**Ability Definitions**
Oral Expression	The ability to communicate information and ideas in speaking so others will understand.
Oral Comprehension	The ability to listen to and understand information and ideas presented through spoken words and sentences.
Written Comprehension	The ability to read and understand information and ideas presented in writing.
Near Vision	The ability to see details at close range (within a few feet of the observer).
Speech Recognition	The ability to identify and understand the speech of another person.
Deductive Reasoning	The ability to apply general rules to specific problems to produce answers that make sense.
Speech Clarity	The ability to speak clearly so others can understand you.
Problem Sensitivity	The ability to tell when something is wrong or is likely to go wrong. It does not involve solving the problem, only recognizing there is a problem.
Written Expression	The ability to communicate information and ideas in writing so others will understand.
Inductive Reasoning	The ability to combine pieces of information to form general rules or conclusions (includes finding a relationship among seemingly unrelated events).
Information Ordering	The ability to arrange things or actions in a certain order or pattern according to a specific rule or set of rules (e.g., patterns of numbers, letters, words, pictures, mathematical operations).
Mathematical Reasoning	The ability to choose the right mathematical methods or formulas to solve a problem.
Category Flexibility	The ability to generate or use different sets of rules for combining or grouping things in different ways.
Fluency of Ideas	The ability to come up with a number of ideas about a topic (the number of ideas is important, not their quality, correctness, or creativity).
Selective Attention	The ability to concentrate on a task over a period of time without being distracted.
Originality	The ability to come up with unusual or clever ideas about a given topic or situation, or to develop creative ways to solve a problem.
Flexibility of Closure	The ability to identify or detect a known pattern (a figure, object, word, or sound) that is hidden in other distracting material.
Far Vision	The ability to see details at a distance.
Time Sharing	The ability to shift back and forth between two or more activities or sources of information (such as speech, sounds, touch, or other sources).
Perceptual Speed	The ability to quickly and accurately compare similarities and differences among sets of letters, numbers, objects, pictures, or patterns. The things to be compared may be presented at the same time or one after the other. This ability also includes comparing a presented object with a remembered object.
Control Precision	The ability to quickly and repeatedly adjust the controls of a machine or a vehicle to exact positions.
Memorization	The ability to remember information such as words, numbers, pictures, and procedures.
Number Facility	The ability to add, subtract, multiply, or divide quickly and correctly.
Depth Perception	The ability to judge which of several objects is closer or farther away from you, or to judge the distance between you and an object.
Trunk Strength	The ability to use your abdominal and lower back muscles to support part of the body repeatedly or continuously over time without 'giving out' or fatiguing.

861

Multilimb Coordination	The ability to coordinate two or more limbs (for example, two arms, two legs, or one leg and one arm) while sitting, standing, or lying down. It does not involve performing the activities while the whole body is in motion.
Visualization	The ability to imagine how something will look after it is moved around or when its parts are moved or rearranged.
Speed of Closure	The ability to quickly make sense of, combine, and organize information into meaningful patterns.
Visual Color Discrimination	The ability to match or detect differences between colors, including shades of color and brightness.
Auditory Attention	The ability to focus on a single source of sound in the presence of other distracting sounds.
Spatial Orientation	The ability to know your location in relation to the environment or to know where other objects are in relation to you.
Finger Dexterity	The ability to make precisely coordinated movements of the fingers of one or both hands to grasp, manipulate, or assemble very small objects.
Glare Sensitivity	The ability to see objects in the presence of glare or bright lighting.
Night Vision	The ability to see under low light conditions.
Reaction Time	The ability to quickly respond (with the hand, finger, or foot) to a signal (sound, light, picture) when it appears.
Manual Dexterity	The ability to quickly move your hand, your hand together with your arm, or your two hands to grasp, manipulate, or assemble objects.
Speed of Limb Movement	The ability to quickly move the arms and legs.
Response Orientation	The ability to choose quickly between two or more movements in response to two or more different signals (lights, sounds, pictures). It includes the speed with which the correct response is started with the hand, foot, or other body part.
Rate Control	The ability to time your movements or the movement of a piece of equipment in anticipation of changes in the speed and/or direction of a moving object or scene.
Arm-Hand Steadiness	The ability to keep your hand and arm steady while moving your arm or while holding your arm and hand in one position.
Hearing Sensitivity	The ability to detect or tell the differences between sounds that vary in pitch and loudness.
Peripheral Vision	The ability to see objects or movement of objects to one's side when the eyes are looking ahead.
Sound Localization	The ability to tell the direction from which a sound originated.
Wrist-Finger Speed	The ability to make fast, simple, repeated movements of the fingers, hands, and wrists.
Stamina	The ability to exert yourself physically over long periods of time without getting winded or out of breath.
Static Strength	The ability to exert maximum muscle force to lift, push, pull, or carry objects.
Dynamic Strength	The ability to exert muscle force repeatedly or continuously over time. This involves muscular endurance and resistance to muscle fatigue.
Gross Body Equilibrium	The ability to keep or regain your body balance or stay upright when in an unstable position.
Gross Body Coordination	The ability to coordinate the movement of your arms, legs, and torso together when the whole body is in motion.
Dynamic Flexibility	The ability to quickly and repeatedly bend, stretch, twist, or reach out with your body, arms, and/or legs.
Extent Flexibility	The ability to bend, stretch, twist, or reach with your body, arms, and/or legs.
Explosive Strength	The ability to use short bursts of muscle force to propel oneself (as in jumping or sprinting), or to throw an object.

Work_Activity	Work_Activity Definitions
Getting Information	Observing, receiving, and otherwise obtaining information from all relevant sources.
Communicating with Persons Outside Organization	Communicating with people outside the organization, representing the organization to customers, the public, government, and other external sources. This information can be exchanged in person, in writing, or by telephone or e-mail.
Making Decisions and Solving Problems	Analyzing information and evaluating results to choose the best solution and solve problems.
Performing for or Working Directly with the Public	Performing for people or dealing directly with the public. This includes serving customers in restaurants and stores, and receiving clients or guests.
Resolving Conflicts and Negotiating with Others	Handling complaints, settling disputes, and resolving grievances and conflicts, or otherwise negotiating with others.
Organizing, Planning, and Prioritizing Work	Developing specific goals and plans to prioritize, organize, and accomplish your work.

Performing Administrative Activities	Performing day-to-day administrative tasks such as maintaining information files and processing paperwork.
Establishing and Maintaining Interpersonal Relatio	Developing constructive and cooperative working relationships with others, and maintaining them over time.
Interacting With Computers	Using computers and computer systems (including hardware and software) to program, write software, set up functions, enter data, or process information.
Communicating with Supervisors, Peers, or Subordin	Providing information to supervisors, co-workers, and subordinates by telephone, in written form, e-mail, or in person.
Documenting/Recording Information	Entering, transcribing, recording, storing, or maintaining information in written or electronic/magnetic form.
Scheduling Work and Activities	Scheduling events, programs, and activities, as well as the work of others.
Thinking Creatively	Developing, designing, or creating new applications, ideas, relationships, systems, or products, including artistic contributions.
Judging the Qualities of Things, Services, or Peop	Assessing the value, importance, or quality of things or people.
Interpreting the Meaning of Information for Others	Translating or explaining what information means and how it can be used.
Identifying Objects, Actions, and Events	Identifying information by categorizing, estimating, recognizing differences or similarities, and detecting changes in circumstances or events.
Selling or Influencing Others	Convincing others to buy merchandise/goods or to otherwise change their minds or actions.
Processing Information	Compiling, coding, categorizing, calculating, tabulating, auditing, or verifying information or data.
Analyzing Data or Information	Identifying the underlying principles, reasons, or facts of information by breaking down information or data into separate parts.
Updating and Using Relevant Knowledge	Keeping up-to-date technically and applying new knowledge to your job.
Evaluating Information to Determine Compliance wit	Using relevant information and individual judgment to determine whether events or processes comply with laws, regulations, or standards.
Developing Objectives and Strategies	Establishing long-range objectives and specifying the strategies and actions to achieve them.
Monitoring and Controlling Resources	Monitoring and controlling resources and overseeing the spending of money.
Monitor Processes, Materials, or Surroundings	Monitoring and reviewing information from materials, events, or the environment, to detect or assess problems.
Coordinating the Work and Activities of Others	Getting members of a group to work together to accomplish tasks.
Inspecting Equipment, Structures, or Material	Inspecting equipment, structures, or materials to identify the cause of errors or other problems or defects.
Developing and Building Teams	Encouraging and building mutual trust, respect, and cooperation among team members.
Estimating the Quantifiable Characteristics of Pro	Estimating sizes, distances, and quantities; or determining time, costs, resources, or materials needed to perform a work activity.
Operating Vehicles, Mechanized Devices, or Equipme	Running, maneuvering, navigating, or driving vehicles or mechanized equipment, such as forklifts, passenger vehicles, aircraft, or water craft.
Provide Consultation and Advice to Others	Providing guidance and expert advice to management or other groups on technical, systems-, or process-related topics.
Training and Teaching Others	Identifying the educational needs of others, developing formal educational or training programs or classes, and teaching or instructing others.
Guiding, Directing, and Motivating Subordinates	Providing guidance and direction to subordinates, including setting performance standards and monitoring performance.
Assisting and Caring for Others	Providing personal assistance, medical attention, emotional support, or other personal care to others such as coworkers, customers, or patients.
Coaching and Developing Others	Identifying the developmental needs of others and coaching, mentoring, or otherwise helping others to improve their knowledge or skills.
Performing General Physical Activities	Performing physical activities that require considerable use of your arms and legs and moving your whole body, such as climbing, lifting, balancing, walking, stooping, and handling of materials.
Staffing Organizational Units	Recruiting, interviewing, selecting, hiring, and promoting employees in an organization.
Handling and Moving Objects	Using hands and arms in handling, installing, positioning, and moving materials, and manipulating things.

Controlling Machines and Processes	Using either control mechanisms or direct physical activity to operate machines or processes (not including computers or vehicles).
Drafting, Laying Out, and Specifying Technical Dev	Providing documentation, detailed instructions, drawings, or specifications to tell others about how devices, parts, equipment, or structures are to be fabricated, constructed, assembled, modified, maintained, or used.
Repairing and Maintaining Electronic Equipment	Servicing, repairing, calibrating, regulating, fine-tuning, or testing machines, devices, and equipment that operate primarily on the basis of electrical or electronic (not mechanical) principles.
Repairing and Maintaining Mechanical Equipment	Servicing, repairing, adjusting, and testing machines, devices, moving parts, and equipment that operate primarily on the basis of mechanical (not electronic) principles.

Work_Context	Work_Context Definitions
Telephone	How often do you have telephone conversations in this job?
Face-to-Face Discussions	How often do you have to have face-to-face discussions with individuals or teams in this job?
In an Enclosed Vehicle or Equipment	How often does this job require working in a closed vehicle or equipment (e.g., car)?
Deal With External Customers	How important is it to work with external customers or the public in this job?
Contact With Others	How much does this job require the worker to be in contact with others (face-to-face, by telephone, or otherwise) in order to perform it?
Structured versus Unstructured Work	To what extent is this job structured for the worker, rather than allowing the worker to determine tasks, priorities, and goals?
Freedom to Make Decisions	How much decision making freedom, without supervision, does the job offer?
Frequency of Decision Making	How frequently is the worker required to make decisions that affect other people, the financial resources, and/or the image and reputation of the organization?
Electronic Mail	How often do you use electronic mail in this job?
Impact of Decisions on Co-workers or Company Resul	How do the decisions an employee makes impact the results of co-workers, clients or the company?
Indoors, Environmentally Controlled	How often does this job require working indoors in environmentally controlled conditions?
Letters and Memos	How often does the job require written letters and memos?
Level of Competition	To what extent does this job require the worker to compete or to be aware of competitive pressures?
Coordinate or Lead Others	How important is it to coordinate or lead others in accomplishing work activities in this job?
Importance of Being Exact or Accurate	How important is being very exact or highly accurate in performing this job?
Work With Work Group or Team	How important is it to work with others in a group or team in this job?
Outdoors, Exposed to Weather	How often does this job require working outdoors, exposed to all weather conditions?
Physical Proximity	To what extent does this job require the worker to perform job tasks in close physical proximity to other people?
Time Pressure	How often does this job require the worker to meet strict deadlines?
Spend Time Sitting	How much does this job require sitting?
Frequency of Conflict Situations	How often are there conflict situations the employee has to face in this job?
Importance of Repeating Same Tasks	How important is repeating the same physical activities (e.g., key entry) or mental activities (e.g., checking entries in a ledger) over and over, without stopping, to performing this job?
Deal With Unpleasant or Angry People	How frequently does the worker have to deal with unpleasant, angry, or discourteous individuals as part of the job requirements?
Consequence of Error	How serious would the result usually be if the worker made a mistake that was not readily correctable?
Responsibility for Outcomes and Results	How responsible is the worker for work outcomes and results of other workers?
Indoors, Not Environmentally Controlled	How often does this job require working indoors in non-controlled environmental conditions (e.g., warehouse without heat)?
Spend Time Standing	How much does this job require standing?
Responsible for Others' Health and Safety	How much responsibility is there for the health and safety of others in this job?
Spend Time Making Repetitive Motions	How much does this job require making repetitive motions?
Public Speaking	How often do you have to perform public speaking in this job?

Spend Time Walking and Running	How much does this job require walking and running?
Degree of Automation	How automated is the job?
Very Hot or Cold Temperatures	How often does this job require working in very hot (above 90 F degrees) or very cold (below 32 F degrees) temperatures?
Exposed to Contaminants	How often does this job require working exposed to contaminants (such as pollutants, gases, dust or odors)?
Sounds, Noise Levels Are Distracting or Uncomforta	How often does this job require working exposed to sounds and noise levels that are distracting or uncomfortable?
Extremely Bright or Inadequate Lighting	How often does this job require working in extremely bright or inadequate lighting conditions?
Spend Time Bending or Twisting the Body	How much does this job require bending or twisting your body?
Spend Time Using Your Hands to Handle, Control, or	How much does this job require using your hands to handle, control, or feel objects, tools or controls?
Spend Time Kneeling, Crouching, Stooping, or Crawl	How much does this job require kneeling, crouching, stooping or crawling?
Exposed to High Places	How often does this job require exposure to high places?
Cramped Work Space, Awkward Positions	How often does this job require working in cramped work spaces that requires getting into awkward positions?
Deal With Physically Aggressive People	How frequently does this job require the worker to deal with physical aggression of violent individuals?
Exposed to Minor Burns, Cuts, Bites, or Stings	How often does this job require exposure to minor burns, cuts, bites, or stings?
Exposed to Hazardous Equipment	How often does this job require exposure to hazardous equipment?
Exposed to Hazardous Conditions	How often does this job require exposure to hazardous conditions?
Spend Time Climbing Ladders, Scaffolds, or Poles	How much does this job require climbing ladders, scaffolds, or poles?
Exposed to Disease or Infections	How often does this job require exposure to disease/infections?
Outdoors, Under Cover	How often does this job require working outdoors, under cover (e.g., structure with roof but no walls)?
Wear Common Protective or Safety Equipment such as	How much does this job require wearing common protective or safety equipment such as safety shoes, glasses, gloves, hard hats or live jackets?
In an Open Vehicle or Equipment	How much does this job require working in an open vehicle or equipment (e.g., tractor)?
Spend Time Keeping or Regaining Balance	How much does this job require keeping or regaining your balance?
Pace Determined by Speed of Equipment	How important is it to this job that the pace is determined by the speed of equipment or machinery? (This does not refer to keeping busy at all times on this job.)
Exposed to Radiation	How often does this job require exposure to radiation?
Exposed to Whole Body Vibration	How often does this job require exposure to whole body vibration (e.g., operate a jackhammer)?
Wear Specialized Protective or Safety Equipment su	How much does this job require wearing specialized protective or safety equipment such as breathing apparatus, safety harness, full protection suits, or radiation protection?

Job Zone Component	Job Zone Component Definitions
Title	Job Zone Three: Medium Preparation Needed
Overall Experience	Previous work-related skill, knowledge, or experience is required for these occupations. For example, an electrician must have completed three or four years of apprenticeship or several years of vocational training, and often must have passed a licensing exam, in order to perform the job.
Job Training	Employees in these occupations usually need one or two years of training involving both on-the-job experience and informal training with experienced workers.
Job Zone Examples	These occupations usually involve using communication and organizational skills to coordinate, supervise, manage, or train others to accomplish goals. Examples include dental assistants, electricians, fish and game wardens, legal secretaries, personnel recruiters, and recreation workers.
SVP Range	(6.0 to < 7.0)
Education	Most occupations in this zone require training in vocational schools, related on-the-job experience, or an associate's degree. Some may require a bachelor's degree.

Work_Styles	Work_Styles Definitions
Integrity	Job requires being honest and ethical.
Dependability	Job requires being reliable, responsible, and dependable, and fulfilling obligations.
Attention to Detail	Job requires being careful about detail and thorough in completing work tasks.
Stress Tolerance	Job requires accepting criticism and dealing calmly and effectively with high stress situations.
Initiative	Job requires a willingness to take on responsibilities and challenges.
Leadership	Job requires a willingness to lead, take charge, and offer opinions and direction.
Independence	Job requires developing one's own ways of doing things, guiding oneself with little or no supervision, and depending on oneself to get things done.
Cooperation	Job requires being pleasant with others on the job and displaying a good-natured, cooperative attitude.
Self Control	Job requires maintaining composure, keeping emotions in check, controlling anger, and avoiding aggressive behavior, even in very difficult situations.
Persistence	Job requires persistence in the face of obstacles.
Achievement/Effort	Job requires establishing and maintaining personally challenging achievement goals and exerting effort toward mastering tasks.
Adaptability/Flexibility	Job requires being open to change (positive or negative) and to considerable variety in the workplace.
Innovation	Job requires creativity and alternative thinking to develop new ideas for and answers to work-related problems.
Concern for Others	Job requires being sensitive to others' needs and feelings and being understanding and helpful on the job.
Social Orientation	Job requires preferring to work with others rather than alone, and being personally connected with others on the job.
Analytical Thinking	Job requires analyzing information and using logic to address work-related issues and problems.

41-9022.00 - Real Estate Sales Agents

Rent, buy, or sell property for clients. Perform duties, such as study property listings, interview prospective clients, accompany clients to property site, discuss conditions of sale, and draw up real estate contracts. Includes agents who represent buyer.

Tasks

1) Review property listings, trade journals, and relevant literature, and attend conventions, seminars, and staff and association meetings in order to remain knowledgeable about real estate markets.

2) Visit properties to assess them before showing them to clients.

3) Interview clients to determine what kinds of properties they are seeking.

4) Act as an intermediary in negotiations between buyers and sellers, generally representing one or the other.

5) Generate lists of properties that are compatible with buyers' needs and financial resources.

6) Coordinate appointments to show homes to prospective buyers.

7) Accompany buyers during visits to and inspections of property, advising them on the suitability and value of the homes they are visiting.

8) Compare a property with similar properties that have recently sold in order to determine its competitive market price.

9) Present purchase offers to sellers for consideration.

10) Advise sellers on how to make homes more appealing to potential buyers.

11) Promote sales of properties through advertisements, open houses, and participation in multiple listing services.

12) Contact property owners and advertise services in order to solicit property sales listings.

13) Advise clients on market conditions, prices, mortgages, legal requirements and related matters.

14) Prepare documents such as representation contracts, purchase agreements, closing statements, deeds and leases.

15) Display commercial, industrial, agricultural, and residential properties to clients and explain their features.

16) Arrange for title searches to determine whether clients have clear property titles.

17) Inspect condition of premises, and arrange for necessary maintenance or notify owners of maintenance needs.

18) Develop networks of attorneys, mortgage lenders, and contractors to whom clients may be referred.

19) Answer clients' questions regarding construction work, financing, maintenance, repairs, and appraisals.

20) Contact utility companies for service hookups to clients' property.

21) Evaluate mortgage options to help clients obtain financing at the best prevailing rates and terms.

22) Coordinate property closings, overseeing signing of documents and disbursement of funds.

23) Investigate clients' financial and credit status in order to determine eligibility for financing.

24) Review plans for new construction with clients, enumerating and recommending available options and features.

25) Arrange meetings between buyers and sellers when details of transactions need to be negotiated.

26) Secure construction or purchase financing with own firm or mortgage company.

27) Solicit and compile listings of available rental properties.

28) Rent or lease properties on behalf of clients.

29) Locate and appraise undeveloped areas for building sites, based on evaluations of area market conditions.

30) Appraise properties to determine loan values.

31) Conduct seminars and training sessions for sales agents in order to improve sales techniques.

Knowledge	Knowledge Definitions
Customer and Personal Service	Knowledge of principles and processes for providing customer and personal services. This includes customer needs assessment, meeting quality standards for services, and evaluation of customer satisfaction.
Sales and Marketing	Knowledge of principles and methods for showing, promoting, and selling products or services. This includes marketing strategy and tactics, product demonstration, sales techniques, and sales control systems.
Clerical	Knowledge of administrative and clerical procedures and systems such as word processing, managing files and records, stenography and transcription, designing forms, and other office procedures and terminology.
Administration and Management	Knowledge of business and management principles involved in strategic planning, resource allocation, human resources modeling, leadership technique, production methods, and coordination of people and resources.
English Language	Knowledge of the structure and content of the English language including the meaning and spelling of words, rules of composition, and grammar.
Economics and Accounting	Knowledge of economic and accounting principles and practices, the financial markets, banking and the analysis and reporting of financial data.
Law and Government	Knowledge of laws, legal codes, court procedures, precedents, government regulations, executive orders, agency rules, and the democratic political process.
Building and Construction	Knowledge of materials, methods, and the tools involved in the construction or repair of houses, buildings, or other structures such as highways and roads.
Computers and Electronics	Knowledge of circuit boards, processors, chips, electronic equipment, and computer hardware and software, including applications and programming.
Mathematics	Knowledge of arithmetic, algebra, geometry, calculus, statistics, and their applications.
Education and Training	Knowledge of principles and methods for curriculum and training design, teaching and instruction for individuals and groups, and the measurement of training effects.
Personnel and Human Resources	Knowledge of principles and procedures for personnel recruitment, selection, training, compensation and benefits, labor relations and negotiation, and personnel information systems.

Public Safety and Security	Knowledge of relevant equipment, policies, procedures, and strategies to promote effective local, state, or national security operations for the protection of people, data, property, and institutions.
Communications and Media	Knowledge of media production, communication, and dissemination techniques and methods. This includes alternative ways to inform and entertain via written, oral, and visual media.
Transportation	Knowledge of principles and methods for moving people or goods by air, rail, sea, or road, including the relative costs and benefits.
Telecommunications	Knowledge of transmission, broadcasting, switching, control, and operation of telecommunications systems.
Production and Processing	Knowledge of raw materials, production processes, quality control, costs, and other techniques for maximizing the effective manufacture and distribution of goods.
Foreign Language	Knowledge of the structure and content of a foreign (non-English) language including the meaning and spelling of words, rules of composition and grammar, and pronunciation.
Sociology and Anthropology	Knowledge of group behavior and dynamics, societal trends and influences, human migrations, ethnicity, cultures and their history and origins.
Psychology	Knowledge of human behavior and performance; individual differences in ability, personality, and interests; learning and motivation; psychological research methods; and the assessment and treatment of behavioral and affective disorders.
Geography	Knowledge of principles and methods for describing the features of land, sea, and air masses, including their physical characteristics, locations, interrelationships, and distribution of plant, animal, and human life.
Design	Knowledge of design techniques, tools, and principles involved in production of precision technical plans, blueprints, drawings, and models.
Therapy and Counseling	Knowledge of principles, methods, and procedures for diagnosis, treatment, and rehabilitation of physical and mental dysfunctions, and for career counseling and guidance.
Philosophy and Theology	Knowledge of different philosophical systems and religions. This includes their basic principles, values, ethics, ways of thinking, customs, practices, and their impact on human culture.
Mechanical	Knowledge of machines and tools, including their designs, uses, repair, and maintenance.
Engineering and Technology	Knowledge of the practical application of engineering science and technology. This includes applying principles, techniques, procedures, and equipment to the design and production of various goods and services.
History and Archeology	Knowledge of historical events and their causes, indicators, and effects on civilizations and cultures.
Chemistry	Knowledge of the chemical composition, structure, and properties of substances and of the chemical processes and transformations that they undergo. This includes uses of chemicals and their interactions, danger signs, production techniques, and disposal methods.
Physics	Knowledge and prediction of physical principles, laws, their interrelationships, and applications to understanding fluid, material, and atmospheric dynamics, and mechanical, electrical, atomic and sub-atomic structures and processes.
Biology	Knowledge of plant and animal organisms, their tissues, cells, functions, interdependencies, and interactions with each other and the environment.
Fine Arts	Knowledge of the theory and techniques required to compose, produce, and perform works of music, dance, visual arts, drama, and sculpture.
Medicine and Dentistry	Knowledge of the information and techniques needed to diagnose and treat human injuries, diseases, and deformities. This includes symptoms, treatment alternatives, drug properties and interactions, and preventive health-care measures.
Food Production	Knowledge of techniques and equipment for planting, growing, and harvesting food products (both plant and animal) for consumption, including storage/handling techniques.

Skills	Skills Definitions
Active Listening	Giving full attention to what other people are saying, taking time to understand the points being made, asking questions as appropriate, and not interrupting at inappropriate times.
Time Management	Managing one's own time and the time of others.
Negotiation	Bringing others together and trying to reconcile differences.

Speaking	Talking to others to convey information effectively.
Reading Comprehension	Understanding written sentences and paragraphs in work related documents.
Coordination	Adjusting actions in relation to others' actions.
Mathematics	Using mathematics to solve problems.
Service Orientation	Actively looking for ways to help people.
Social Perceptiveness	Being aware of others' reactions and understanding why they react as they do.
Writing	Communicating effectively in writing as appropriate for the needs of the audience.
Monitoring	Monitoring/Assessing performance of yourself, other individuals, or organizations to make improvements or take corrective action.
Judgment and Decision Making	Considering the relative costs and benefits of potential actions to choose the most appropriate one.
Active Learning	Understanding the implications of new information for both current and future problem-solving and decision-making.
Critical Thinking	Using logic and reasoning to identify the strengths and weaknesses of alternative solutions, conclusions or approaches to problems.
Learning Strategies	Selecting and using training/instructional methods and procedures appropriate for the situation when learning or teaching new things.
Management of Financial Resources	Determining how money will be spent to get the work done, and accounting for these expenditures.
Complex Problem Solving	Identifying complex problems and reviewing related information to develop and evaluate options and implement solutions.
Persuasion	Persuading others to change their minds or behavior.
Instructing	Teaching others how to do something.
Management of Personnel Resources	Motivating, developing, and directing people as they work, identifying the best people for the job.
Technology Design	Generating or adapting equipment and technology to serve user needs.
Troubleshooting	Determining causes of operating errors and deciding what to do about it.
Management of Material Resources	Obtaining and seeing to the appropriate use of equipment, facilities, and materials needed to do certain work.
Operations Analysis	Analyzing needs and product requirements to create a design.
Quality Control Analysis	Conducting tests and inspections of products, services, or processes to evaluate quality or performance.
Equipment Selection	Determining the kind of tools and equipment needed to do a job.
Repairing	Repairing machines or systems using the needed tools.
Science	Using scientific rules and methods to solve problems.
Installation	Installing equipment, machines, wiring, or programs to meet specifications.
Operation and Control	Controlling operations of equipment or systems.
Equipment Maintenance	Performing routine maintenance on equipment and determining when and what kind of maintenance is needed.
Operation Monitoring	Watching gauges, dials, or other indicators to make sure a machine is working properly.
Systems Analysis	Determining how a system should work and how changes in conditions, operations, and the environment will affect outcomes.
Systems Evaluation	Identifying measures or indicators of system performance and the actions needed to improve or correct performance, relative to the goals of the system.
Programming	Writing computer programs for various purposes.

Ability	Ability Definitions
Oral Expression	The ability to communicate information and ideas in speaking so others will understand.
Oral Comprehension	The ability to listen to and understand information and ideas presented through spoken words and sentences.
Near Vision	The ability to see details at close range (within a few feet of the observer).
Written Comprehension	The ability to read and understand information and ideas presented in writing.
Speech Recognition	The ability to identify and understand the speech of another person.
Inductive Reasoning	The ability to combine pieces of information to form general rules or conclusions (includes finding a relationship among seemingly unrelated events).
Speech Clarity	The ability to speak clearly so others can understand you.
Written Expression	The ability to communicate information and ideas in writing so others will understand.

Deductive Reasoning	The ability to apply general rules to specific problems to produce answers that make sense.
Information Ordering	The ability to arrange things or actions in a certain order or pattern according to a specific rule or set of rules (e.g., patterns of numbers, letters, words, pictures, mathematical operations).
Problem Sensitivity	The ability to tell when something is wrong or is likely to go wrong. It does not involve solving the problem, only recognizing there is a problem.
Flexibility of Closure	The ability to identify or detect a known pattern (a figure, object, word, or sound) that is hidden in other distracting material.
Far Vision	The ability to see details at a distance.
Originality	The ability to come up with unusual or clever ideas about a given topic or situation, or to develop creative ways to solve a problem.
Category Flexibility	The ability to generate or use different sets of rules for combining or grouping things in different ways.
Fluency of Ideas	The ability to come up with a number of ideas about a topic (the number of ideas is important, not their quality, correctness, or creativity).
Perceptual Speed	The ability to quickly and accurately compare similarities and differences among sets of letters, numbers, objects, pictures, or patterns. The things to be compared may be presented at the same time or one after the other. This ability also includes comparing a presented object with a remembered object.
Selective Attention	The ability to concentrate on a task over a period of time without being distracted.
Mathematical Reasoning	The ability to choose the right mathematical methods or formulas to solve a problem.
Speed of Closure	The ability to quickly make sense of, combine, and organize information into meaningful patterns.
Time Sharing	The ability to shift back and forth between two or more activities or sources of information (such as speech, sounds, touch, or other sources).
Memorization	The ability to remember information such as words, numbers, pictures, and procedures.
Finger Dexterity	The ability to make precisely coordinated movements of the fingers of one or both hands to grasp, manipulate, or assemble very small objects.
Visualization	The ability to imagine how something will look after it is moved around or when its parts are moved or rearranged.
Number Facility	The ability to add, subtract, multiply, or divide quickly and correctly.
Visual Color Discrimination	The ability to match or detect differences between colors, including shades of color and brightness.
Depth Perception	The ability to judge which of several objects is closer or farther away from you, or to judge the distance between you and an object.
Auditory Attention	The ability to focus on a single source of sound in the presence of other distracting sounds.
Trunk Strength	The ability to use your abdominal and lower back muscles to support part of the body repeatedly or continuously over time without 'giving out' or fatiguing.
Hearing Sensitivity	The ability to detect or tell the differences between sounds that vary in pitch and loudness.
Control Precision	The ability to quickly and repeatedly adjust the controls of a machine or a vehicle to exact positions.
Spatial Orientation	The ability to know your location in relation to the environment or to know where other objects are in relation to you.
Multilimb Coordination	The ability to coordinate two or more limbs (for example, two arms, two legs, or one leg and one arm) while sitting, standing, or lying down. It does not involve performing the activities while the whole body is in motion.
Stamina	The ability to exert yourself physically over long periods of time without getting winded or out of breath.
Wrist-Finger Speed	The ability to make fast, simple, repeated movements of the fingers, hands, and wrists.
Arm-Hand Steadiness	The ability to keep your hand and arm steady while moving your arm or while holding your arm and hand in one position.
Night Vision	The ability to see under low light conditions.
Static Strength	The ability to exert maximum muscle force to lift, push, pull, or carry objects.
Peripheral Vision	The ability to see objects or movement of objects to one's side when the eyes are looking ahead.
Glare Sensitivity	The ability to see objects in the presence of glare or bright lighting.

Manual Dexterity	The ability to quickly move your hand, your hand together with your arm, or your two hands to grasp, manipulate, or assemble objects.
Rate Control	The ability to time your movements or the movement of a piece of equipment in anticipation of changes in the speed and/or direction of a moving object or scene.
Reaction Time	The ability to quickly respond (with the hand, finger, or foot) to a signal (sound, light, picture) when it appears.
Gross Body Coordination	The ability to coordinate the movement of your arms, legs, and torso together when the whole body is in motion.
Extent Flexibility	The ability to bend, stretch, twist, or reach with your body, arms, and/or legs.
Speed of Limb Movement	The ability to quickly move the arms and legs.
Response Orientation	The ability to choose quickly between two or more movements in response to two or more different signals (lights, sounds, pictures). It includes the speed with which the correct response is started with the hand, foot, or other body part.
Sound Localization	The ability to tell the direction from which a sound originated.
Gross Body Equilibrium	The ability to keep or regain your body balance or stay upright when in an unstable position.
Dynamic Flexibility	The ability to quickly and repeatedly bend, stretch, twist, or reach out with your body, arms, and/or legs.
Dynamic Strength	The ability to exert muscle force repeatedly or continuously over time. This involves muscular endurance and resistance to muscle fatigue.
Explosive Strength	The ability to use short bursts of muscle force to propel oneself (as in jumping or sprinting), or to throw an object.

Work_Activity	Work_Activity Definitions
Getting Information	Observing, receiving, and otherwise obtaining information from all relevant sources.
Performing for or Working Directly with the Public	Performing for people or dealing directly with the public. This includes serving customers in restaurants and stores, and receiving clients or guests.
Communicating with Persons Outside Organization	Communicating with people outside the organization, representing the organization to customers, the public, government, and other external sources. This information can be exchanged in person, in writing, or by telephone or e-mail.
Making Decisions and Solving Problems	Analyzing information and evaluating results to choose the best solution and solve problems.
Identifying Objects, Actions, and Events	Identifying information by categorizing, estimating, recognizing differences or similarities, and detecting changes in circumstances or events.
Interacting With Computers	Using computers and computer systems (including hardware and software) to program, write software, set up functions, enter data, or process information.
Organizing, Planning, and Prioritizing Work	Developing specific goals and plans to prioritize, organize, and accomplish your work.
Updating and Using Relevant Knowledge	Keeping up-to-date technically and applying new knowledge to your job.
Establishing and Maintaining Interpersonal Relatio	Developing constructive and cooperative working relationships with others, and maintaining them over time.
Resolving Conflicts and Negotiating with Others	Handling complaints, settling disputes, and resolving grievances and conflicts, or otherwise negotiating with others.
Selling or Influencing Others	Convincing others to buy merchandise/goods or to otherwise change their minds or actions.
Communicating with Supervisors, Peers, or Subordin	Providing information to supervisors, co-workers, and subordinates by telephone, in written form, e-mail, or in person.
Documenting/Recording Information	Entering, transcribing, recording, storing, or maintaining information in written or electronic/magnetic form.
Scheduling Work and Activities	Scheduling events, programs, and activities, as well as the work of others.
Judging the Qualities of Things, Services, or Peop	Assessing the value, importance, or quality of things or people.
Performing Administrative Activities	Performing day-to-day administrative tasks such as maintaining information files and processing paperwork.
Assisting and Caring for Others	Providing personal assistance, medical attention, emotional support, or other personal care to others such as coworkers, customers, or patients.
Developing Objectives and Strategies	Establishing long-range objectives and specifying the strategies and actions to achieve them.
Evaluating Information to Determine Compliance wit	Using relevant information and individual judgment to determine whether events or processes comply with laws, regulations, or standards.

Thinking Creatively	Developing, designing, or creating new applications, ideas, relationships, systems, or products, including artistic contributions.
Interpreting the Meaning of Information for Others	Translating or explaining what information means and how it can be used.
Inspecting Equipment, Structures, or Material	Inspecting equipment, structures, or materials to identify the cause of errors or other problems or defects.
Processing Information	Compiling, coding, categorizing, calculating, tabulating, auditing, or verifying information or data.
Monitor Processes, Materials, or Surroundings	Monitoring and reviewing information from materials, events, or the environment, to detect or assess problems.
Developing and Building Teams	Encouraging and building mutual trust, respect, and cooperation among team members.
Monitoring and Controlling Resources	Monitoring and controlling resources and overseeing the spending of money.
Performing General Physical Activities	Performing physical activities that require considerable use of your arms and legs and moving your whole body, such as climbing, lifting, balancing, walking, stooping, and handling of materials.
Operating Vehicles, Mechanized Devices, or Equipme	Running, maneuvering, navigating, or driving vehicles or mechanized equipment, such as forklifts, passenger vehicles, aircraft, or water craft.
Handling and Moving Objects	Using hands and arms in handling, installing, positioning, and moving materials, and manipulating things.
Analyzing Data or Information	Identifying the underlying principles, reasons, or facts of information by breaking down information or data into separate parts.
Controlling Machines and Processes	Using either control mechanisms or direct physical activity to operate machines or processes (not including computers or vehicles).
Estimating the Quantifiable Characteristics of Pro	Estimating sizes, distances, and quantities; or determining time, costs, resources, or materials needed to perform a work activity.
Coordinating the Work and Activities of Others	Getting members of a group to work together to accomplish tasks.
Provide Consultation and Advice to Others	Providing guidance and expert advice to management or other groups on technical, systems-, or process-related topics.
Coaching and Developing Others	Identifying the developmental needs of others and coaching, mentoring, or otherwise helping others to improve their knowledge or skills.
Training and Teaching Others	Identifying the educational needs of others, developing formal educational or training programs or classes, and teaching or instructing others.
Guiding, Directing, and Motivating Subordinates	Providing guidance and direction to subordinates, including setting performance standards and monitoring performance.
Staffing Organizational Units	Recruiting, interviewing, selecting, hiring, and promoting employees in an organization.
Repairing and Maintaining Mechanical Equipment	Servicing, repairing, adjusting, and testing machines, devices, moving parts, and equipment that operate primarily on the basis of mechanical (not electronic) principles.
Drafting, Laying Out, and Specifying Technical Dev	Providing documentation, detailed instructions, drawings, or specifications to tell others about how devices, parts, equipment, or structures are to be fabricated, constructed, assembled, modified, maintained, or used.
Repairing and Maintaining Electronic Equipment	Servicing, repairing, calibrating, regulating, fine-tuning, or testing machines, devices, and equipment that operate primarily on the basis of electrical or electronic (not mechanical) principles.

Work_Context	Work_Context Definitions
Telephone	How often do you have telephone conversations in this job?
Contact With Others	How much does this job require the worker to be in contact with others (face-to-face, by telephone, or otherwise) in order to perform it?
Face-to-Face Discussions	How often do you have to have face-to-face discussions with individuals or teams in this job?
Structured versus Unstructured Work	To what extent is this job structured for the worker, rather than allowing the worker to determine tasks, priorities, and goals?
Electronic Mail	How often do you use electronic mail in this job?
Freedom to Make Decisions	How much decision making freedom, without supervision, does the job offer?
Importance of Being Exact or Accurate	How important is being very exact or highly accurate in performing this job?
Level of Competition	To what extent does this job require the worker to compete or to be aware of competitive pressures?
Letters and Memos	How often does the job require written letters and memos?

In an Enclosed Vehicle or Equipment	How often does this job require working in a closed vehicle or equipment (e.g., car)?
Impact of Decisions on Co-workers or Company Resul	How do the decisions an employee makes impact the results of co-workers, clients or the company?
Frequency of Decision Making	How frequently is the worker required to make decisions that affect other people, the financial resources, and/or the image and reputation of the organization?
Indoors, Environmentally Controlled	How often does this job require working indoors in environmentally controlled conditions?
Work With Work Group or Team	How important is it to work with others in a group or team in this job?
Outdoors, Exposed to Weather	How often does this job require working outdoors, exposed to all weather conditions?
Spend Time Sitting	How much does this job require sitting?
Physical Proximity	To what extent does this job require the worker to perform job tasks in close physical proximity to other people?
Time Pressure	How often does this job require the worker to meet strict deadlines?
Deal With External Customers	How important is it to work with external customers or the public in this job?
Consequence of Error	How serious would the result usually be if the worker made a mistake that was not readily correctable?
Frequency of Conflict Situations	How often are there conflict situations the employee has to face in this job?
Importance of Repeating Same Tasks	How important is repeating the same physical activities (e.g., key entry) or mental activities (e.g., checking entries in a ledger) over and over, without stopping, to performing this job?
Coordinate or Lead Others	How important is it to coordinate or lead others in accomplishing work activities in this job?
Spend Time Standing	How much does this job require standing?
Very Hot or Cold Temperatures	How often does this job require working in very hot (above 90 F degrees) or very cold (below 32 F degrees) temperatures?
Deal With Unpleasant or Angry People	How frequently does the worker have to deal with unpleasant, angry, or discourteous individuals as part of the job requirements?
Sounds, Noise Levels Are Distracting or Uncomforta	How often does this job require working exposed to sounds and noise levels that are distracting or uncomfortable?
Exposed to Contaminants	How often does this job require working exposed to contaminants (such as pollutants, gases, dust or odors)?
Public Speaking	How often do you have to perform public speaking in this job?
Responsibility for Outcomes and Results	How responsible is the worker for work outcomes and results of other workers?
Spend Time Walking and Running	How much does this job require walking and running?
Outdoors, Under Cover	How often does this job require working outdoors, under cover (e.g., structure with roof but no walls)?
Spend Time Using Your Hands to Handle, Control, or	How much does this job require using your hands to handle, control, or feel objects, tools or controls?
Indoors, Not Environmentally Controlled	How often does this job require working indoors in non-controlled environmental conditions (e.g., warehouse without heat)?
Cramped Work Space, Awkward Positions	How often does this job require working in cramped work spaces that requires getting into awkward positions?
Extremely Bright or Inadequate Lighting	How often does this job require working in extremely bright or inadequate lighting conditions?
Degree of Automation	How automated is the job?
Spend Time Kneeling, Crouching, Stooping, or Crawl	How much does this job require kneeling, crouching, stooping or crawling?
Spend Time Making Repetitive Motions	How much does this job require making repetitive motions?
Spend Time Bending or Twisting the Body	How much does this job require bending or twisting your body?
Exposed to Disease or Infections	How often does this job require exposure to disease/infections?
Spend Time Keeping or Regaining Balance	How much does this job require keeping or regaining your balance?
Exposed to Minor Burns, Cuts, Bites, or Stings	How often does this job require exposure to minor burns, cuts, bites, or stings?
Responsible for Others' Health and Safety	How much responsibility is there for the health and safety of others in this job?
Exposed to Hazardous Conditions	How often does this job require exposure to hazardous conditions?
Exposed to High Places	How often does this job require exposure to high places?
Deal With Physically Aggressive People	How frequently does this job require the worker to deal with physical aggression of violent individuals?

Spend Time Climbing Ladders, Scaffolds, or Poles	How much does this job require climbing ladders, scaffolds, or poles?
Pace Determined by Speed of Equipment	How important is it to this job that the pace is determined by the speed of equipment or machinery? (This does not refer to keeping busy at all times on this job.)
Exposed to Whole Body Vibration	How often does this job require exposure to whole body vibration (e.g., operate a jackhammer)?
Exposed to Hazardous Equipment	How often does this job require exposure to hazardous equipment?
In an Open Vehicle or Equipment	How often does this job require working in an open vehicle or equipment (e.g., tractor)?
Wear Specialized Protective or Safety Equipment su	How much does this job require wearing specialized protective or safety equipment such as breathing apparatus, safety harness, full protection suits, or radiation protection?
Exposed to Radiation	How often does this job require exposure to radiation?
Wear Common Protective or Safety Equipment such as	How much does this job require wearing common protective or safety equipment such as safety shoes, glasses, gloves, hard hats or live jackets?

Job Zone Component	Job Zone Component Definitions
Title	Job Zone Two: Some Preparation Needed
Overall Experience	Some previous work-related skill, knowledge, or experience may be helpful in these occupations, but usually is not needed. For example, a drywall installer might benefit from experience installing drywall, but an inexperienced person could still learn to be an installer with little difficulty.
Job Training	Employees in these occupations need anywhere from a few months to one year of working with experienced employees. These occupations often involve using your knowledge and skills to help others.
Job Zone Examples	Examples include drywall installers, fire inspectors, flight attendants, pharmacy technicians, salespersons (retail), and tellers.
SVP Range	(4.0 to < 6.0)
Education	These occupations usually require a high school diploma and may require some vocational training or job-related course work. In some cases, an associate's or bachelor's degree could be needed.

Work_Styles	Work_Styles Definitions
Integrity	Job requires being honest and ethical.
Attention to Detail	Job requires being careful about detail and thorough in completing work tasks.
Dependability	Job requires being reliable, responsible, and dependable, and fulfilling obligations.
Initiative	Job requires a willingness to take on responsibilities and challenges.
Persistence	Job requires persistence in the face of obstacles.
Cooperation	Job requires being pleasant with others on the job and displaying a good-natured, cooperative attitude.
Self Control	Job requires maintaining composure, keeping emotions in check, controlling anger, and avoiding aggressive behavior, even in very difficult situations.
Independence	Job requires developing one's own ways of doing things, guiding oneself with little or no supervision, and depending on oneself to get things done.
Achievement/Effort	Job requires establishing and maintaining personally challenging achievement goals and exerting effort toward mastering tasks.
Concern for Others	Job requires being sensitive to others' needs and feelings and being understanding and helpful on the job.
Leadership	Job requires a willingness to lead, take charge, and offer opinions and direction.
Adaptability/Flexibility	Job requires being open to change (positive or negative) and to considerable variety in the workplace.
Stress Tolerance	Job requires accepting criticism and dealing calmly and effectively with high stress situations.
Social Orientation	Job requires preferring to work with others rather than alone, and being personally connected with others on the job.
Innovation	Job requires creativity and alternative thinking to develop new ideas for and answers to work-related problems.
Analytical Thinking	Job requires analyzing information and using logic to address work-related issues and problems.

41-9031.00 - Sales Engineers

Sell business goods or services, the selling of which requires a technical background equivalent to a baccalaureate degree in engineering.

Tasks

1) Provide information needed for the development of custom-made machinery.

2) Recommend improved materials or machinery to customers, documenting how such changes will lower costs or increase production.

3) Keep informed on industry news and trends, products, services, competitors, relevant information about legacy, existing, and emerging technologies, and the latest product-line developments.

4) Collaborate with sales teams to understand customer requirements, to promote the sale of company products, and to provide sales support.

5) Visit prospective buyers at commercial, industrial, or other establishments to show samples or catalogs, and to inform them about product pricing, availability, and advantages.

6) Prepare and deliver technical presentations that explain products or services to customers and prospective customers.

7) Write technical documentation for products.

8) Document account activities, generate reports, and keep records of business transactions with customers and suppliers.

9) Research and identify potential customers for products or services.

10) Train team members in the customer applications of technologies.

11) Report to supervisors about prospective firms' credit ratings.

12) Provide technical and non-technical support and services to clients or other staff members regarding the use, operation, and maintenance of equipment.

13) Maintain sales forecasting reports.

14) Secure and renew orders and arrange delivery.

15) Attend trade shows and seminars to promote products or to learn about industry developments.

16) Identify resale opportunities, and support them to achieve sales plans.

17) Attend company training seminars to become familiar with product lines.

18) Sell products requiring extensive technical expertise and support for installation and use, such as material handling equipment, numerical-control machinery, and computer systems.

19) Develop, present, or respond to proposals for specific customer requirements, including request for proposal responses and industry-specific solutions.

20) Confer with customers and engineers to assess equipment needs, and to determine system requirements.

21) Arrange for demonstrations or trial installations of equipment.

22) Create sales or service contracts for products or services.

23) Develop sales plans to introduce products in new markets.

24) Diagnose problems with installed equipment.

41-9041.00 - Telemarketers

Solicit orders for goods or services over the telephone.

Tasks

1) Obtain customer information such as name, address, and payment method, and enter orders into computers.

2) Deliver prepared sales talks, reading from scripts that describe products or services, in order to persuade potential customers to purchase a product or service or to make a donation.

3) Record names, addresses, purchases, and reactions of prospects contacted.

4) Adjust sales scripts to better target the needs and interests of specific individuals.

5) Contact businesses or private individuals by telephone in order to solicit sales for goods or services, or to request donations for charitable causes.

6) Maintain records of contacts, accounts, and orders.

7) Conduct client or market surveys in order to obtain information about potential customers.

8) Telephone or write letters to respond to correspondence from customers or to follow up initial sales contacts.

9) Answer telephone calls from potential customers who have been solicited through advertisements.

10) Schedule appointments for sales representatives to meet with prospective customers or for customers to attend sales presentations.

11) Obtain names and telephone numbers of potential customers from sources such as telephone directories, magazine reply cards, and lists purchased from other organizations.

Knowledge	Knowledge Definitions
Sales and Marketing	Knowledge of principles and methods for showing, promoting, and selling products or services. This includes marketing strategy and tactics, product demonstration, sales techniques, and sales control systems.
English Language	Knowledge of the structure and content of the English language including the meaning and spelling of words, rules of composition, and grammar.
Customer and Personal Service	Knowledge of principles and processes for providing customer and personal services. This includes customer needs assessment, meeting quality standards for services, and evaluation of customer satisfaction.
Telecommunications	Knowledge of transmission, broadcasting, switching, control, and operation of telecommunications systems.
Communications and Media	Knowledge of media production, communication, and dissemination techniques and methods. This includes alternative ways to inform and entertain via written, oral, and visual media.
Computers and Electronics	Knowledge of circuit boards, processors, chips, electronic equipment, and computer hardware and software, including applications and programming.
Education and Training	Knowledge of principles and methods for curriculum and training design, teaching and instruction for individuals and groups, and the measurement of training effects.
Clerical	Knowledge of administrative and clerical procedures and systems such as word processing, managing files and records, stenography and transcription, designing forms, and other office procedures and terminology.
Mathematics	Knowledge of arithmetic, algebra, geometry, calculus, statistics, and their applications.
Transportation	Knowledge of principles and methods for moving people or goods by air, rail, sea, or road, including the relative costs and benefits.
Production and Processing	Knowledge of raw materials, production processes, quality control, costs, and other techniques for maximizing the effective manufacture and distribution of goods.
Psychology	Knowledge of human behavior and performance; individual differences in ability, personality, and interests; learning and motivation; psychological research methods; and the assessment and treatment of behavioral and affective disorders.
Economics and Accounting	Knowledge of economic and accounting principles and practices, the financial markets, banking and the analysis and reporting of financial data.
Administration and Management	Knowledge of business and management principles involved in strategic planning, resource allocation, human resources modeling, leadership technique, production methods, and coordination of people and resources.
Public Safety and Security	Knowledge of relevant equipment, policies, procedures, and strategies to promote effective local, state, or national security operations for the protection of people, data, property, and institutions.
Geography	Knowledge of principles and methods for describing the features of land, sea, and air masses, including their physical characteristics, locations, interrelationships, and distribution of plant, animal, and human life.
Law and Government	Knowledge of laws, legal codes, court procedures, precedents, government regulations, executive orders, agency rules, and the democratic political process.
Personnel and Human Resources	Knowledge of principles and procedures for personnel recruitment, selection, training, compensation and benefits, labor relations and negotiation, and personnel information systems.
Sociology and Anthropology	Knowledge of group behavior and dynamics, societal trends and influences, human migrations, ethnicity, cultures and their history and origins.
Foreign Language	Knowledge of the structure and content of a foreign (non-English) language including the meaning and spelling of words, rules of composition and grammar, and pronunciation.
Engineering and Technology	Knowledge of the practical application of engineering science and technology. This includes applying principles, techniques, procedures, and equipment to the design and production of various goods and services.
Design	Knowledge of design techniques, tools, and principles involved in production of precision technical plans, blueprints, drawings, and models.
Fine Arts	Knowledge of the theory and techniques required to compose, produce, and perform works of music, dance, visual arts, drama, and sculpture.
Philosophy and Theology	Knowledge of different philosophical systems and religions. This includes their basic principles, values, ethics, ways of thinking, customs, practices, and their impact on human culture.
Therapy and Counseling	Knowledge of principles, methods, and procedures for diagnosis, treatment, and rehabilitation of physical and mental dysfunctions, and for career counseling and guidance.
Mechanical	Knowledge of machines and tools, including their designs, uses, repair, and maintenance.
History and Archeology	Knowledge of historical events and their causes, indicators, and effects on civilizations and cultures.
Food Production	Knowledge of techniques and equipment for planting, growing, and harvesting food products (both plant and animal) for consumption, including storage/handling techniques.
Medicine and Dentistry	Knowledge of the information and techniques needed to diagnose and treat human injuries, diseases, and deformities. This includes symptoms, treatment alternatives, drug properties and interactions, and preventive health-care measures.
Biology	Knowledge of plant and animal organisms, their tissues, cells, functions, interdependencies, and interactions with each other and the environment.
Building and Construction	Knowledge of materials, methods, and the tools involved in the construction or repair of houses, buildings, or other structures such as highways and roads.
Physics	Knowledge and prediction of physical principles, laws, their interrelationships, and applications to understanding fluid, material, and atmospheric dynamics, and mechanical, electrical, atomic and sub-atomic structures and processes.
Chemistry	Knowledge of the chemical composition, structure, and properties of substances and of the chemical processes and transformations that they undergo. This includes uses of chemicals and their interactions, danger signs, production techniques, and disposal methods.

Skills	Skills Definitions
Active Listening	Giving full attention to what other people are saying, taking time to understand the points being made, asking questions as appropriate, and not interrupting at inappropriate times.
Speaking	Talking to others to convey information effectively.
Persuasion	Persuading others to change their minds or behavior.
Reading Comprehension	Understanding written sentences and paragraphs in work related documents.
Time Management	Managing one's own time and the time of others.
Monitoring	Monitoring/Assessing performance of yourself, other individuals, or organizations to make improvements or take corrective action.
Negotiation	Bringing others together and trying to reconcile differences.
Social Perceptiveness	Being aware of others' reactions and understanding why they react as they do.
Critical Thinking	Using logic and reasoning to identify the strengths and weaknesses of alternative solutions, conclusions or approaches to problems.
Learning Strategies	Selecting and using training/instructional methods and procedures appropriate for the situation when learning or teaching new things.
Service Orientation	Actively looking for ways to help people.
Active Learning	Understanding the implications of new information for both current and future problem-solving and decision-making.
Instructing	Teaching others how to do something.
Judgment and Decision Making	Considering the relative costs and benefits of potential actions to choose the most appropriate one.
Management of Personnel Resources	Motivating, developing, and directing people as they work, identifying the best people for the job.
Coordination	Adjusting actions in relation to others' actions.

Troubleshooting	Determining causes of operating errors and deciding what to do about it.
Writing	Communicating effectively in writing as appropriate for the needs of the audience.
Complex Problem Solving	Identifying complex problems and reviewing related information to develop and evaluate options and implement solutions.
Mathematics	Using mathematics to solve problems.
Quality Control Analysis	Conducting tests and inspections of products, services, or processes to evaluate quality or performance.
Systems Evaluation	Identifying measures or indicators of system performance and the actions needed to improve or correct performance, relative to the goals of the system.
Management of Financial Resources	Determining how money will be spent to get the work done, and accounting for these expenditures.
Operations Analysis	Analyzing needs and product requirements to create a design.
Operation and Control	Controlling operations of equipment or systems.
Equipment Selection	Determining the kind of tools and equipment needed to do a job.
Technology Design	Generating or adapting equipment and technology to serve user needs.
Operation Monitoring	Watching gauges, dials, or other indicators to make sure a machine is working properly.
Repairing	Repairing machines or systems using the needed tools.
Systems Analysis	Determining how a system should work and how changes in conditions, operations, and the environment will affect outcomes.
Equipment Maintenance	Performing routine maintenance on equipment and determining when and what kind of maintenance is needed.
Management of Material Resources	Obtaining and seeing to the appropriate use of equipment, facilities, and materials needed to do certain work.
Installation	Installing equipment, machines, wiring, or programs to meet specifications.
Programming	Writing computer programs for various purposes.
Science	Using scientific rules and methods to solve problems.

Ability	Ability Definitions
Oral Expression	The ability to communicate information and ideas in speaking so others will understand.
Oral Comprehension	The ability to listen to and understand information and ideas presented through spoken words and sentences.
Speech Clarity	The ability to speak clearly so others can understand you.
Speech Recognition	The ability to identify and understand the speech of another person.
Written Comprehension	The ability to read and understand information and ideas presented in writing.
Selective Attention	The ability to concentrate on a task over a period of time without being distracted.
Written Expression	The ability to communicate information and ideas in writing so others will understand.
Near Vision	The ability to see details at close range (within a few feet of the observer).
Problem Sensitivity	The ability to tell when something is wrong or is likely to go wrong. It does not involve solving the problem, only recognizing there is a problem.
Deductive Reasoning	The ability to apply general rules to specific problems to produce answers that make sense.
Inductive Reasoning	The ability to combine pieces of information to form general rules or conclusions (includes finding a relationship among seemingly unrelated events).
Information Ordering	The ability to arrange things or actions in a certain order or pattern according to a specific rule or set of rules (e.g., patterns of numbers, letters, words, pictures, mathematical operations).
Time Sharing	The ability to shift back and forth between two or more activities or sources of information (such as speech, sounds, touch, or other sources).
Originality	The ability to come up with unusual or clever ideas about a given topic or situation, or to develop creative ways to solve a problem.
Fluency of Ideas	The ability to come up with a number of ideas about a topic (the number of ideas is important, not their quality, correctness, or creativity).
Category Flexibility	The ability to generate or use different sets of rules for combining or grouping things in different ways.
Finger Dexterity	The ability to make precisely coordinated movements of the fingers of one or both hands to grasp, manipulate, or assemble very small objects.

Number Facility	The ability to add, subtract, multiply, or divide quickly and correctly.
Memorization	The ability to remember information such as words, numbers, pictures, and procedures.
Auditory Attention	The ability to focus on a single source of sound in the presence of other distracting sounds.
Mathematical Reasoning	The ability to choose the right mathematical methods or formulas to solve a problem.
Manual Dexterity	The ability to quickly move your hand, your hand together with your arm, or your two hands to grasp, manipulate, or assemble objects.
Trunk Strength	The ability to use your abdominal and lower back muscles to support part of the body repeatedly or continuously over time without 'giving out' or fatiguing.
Flexibility of Closure	The ability to identify or detect a known pattern (a figure, object, word, or sound) that is hidden in other distracting material.
Arm-Hand Steadiness	The ability to keep your hand and arm steady while moving your arm or while holding your arm and hand in one position.
Visual Color Discrimination	The ability to match or detect differences between colors, including shades of color and brightness.
Speed of Closure	The ability to quickly make sense of, combine, and organize information into meaningful patterns.
Control Precision	The ability to quickly and repeatedly adjust the controls of a machine or a vehicle to exact positions.
Perceptual Speed	The ability to quickly and accurately compare similarities and differences among sets of letters, numbers, objects, pictures, or patterns. The things to be compared may be presented at the same time or one after the other. This ability also includes comparing a presented object with a remembered object.
Far Vision	The ability to see details at a distance.
Hearing Sensitivity	The ability to detect or tell the differences between sounds that vary in pitch and loudness.
Visualization	The ability to imagine how something will look after it is moved around or when its parts are moved or rearranged.
Wrist-Finger Speed	The ability to make fast, simple, repeated movements of the fingers, hands, and wrists.
Stamina	The ability to exert yourself physically over long periods of time without getting winded or out of breath.
Multilimb Coordination	The ability to coordinate two or more limbs (for example, two arms, two legs, or one leg and one arm) while sitting, standing, or lying down. It does not involve performing the activities while the whole body is in motion.
Response Orientation	The ability to choose quickly between two or more movements in response to two or more different signals (lights, sounds, pictures). It includes the speed with which the correct response is started with the hand, foot, or other body part.
Rate Control	The ability to time your movements or the movement of a piece of equipment in anticipation of changes in the speed and/or direction of a moving object or scene.
Reaction Time	The ability to quickly respond (with the hand, finger, or foot) to a signal (sound, light, picture) when it appears.
Gross Body Equilibrium	The ability to keep or regain your body balance or stay upright when in an unstable position.
Dynamic Strength	The ability to exert muscle force repeatedly or continuously over time. This involves muscular endurance and resistance to muscle fatigue.
Spatial Orientation	The ability to know your location in relation to the environment or to know where other objects are in relation to you.
Explosive Strength	The ability to use short bursts of muscle force to propel oneself (as in jumping or sprinting), or to throw an object.
Dynamic Flexibility	The ability to quickly and repeatedly bend, stretch, twist, or reach out with your body, arms, and/or legs.
Gross Body Coordination	The ability to coordinate the movement of your arms, legs, and torso together when the whole body is in motion.
Night Vision	The ability to see under low light conditions.
Speed of Limb Movement	The ability to quickly move the arms and legs.
Peripheral Vision	The ability to see objects or movement of objects to one's side when the eyes are looking ahead.
Depth Perception	The ability to judge which of several objects is closer or farther away from you, or to judge the distance between you and an object.
Glare Sensitivity	The ability to see objects in the presence of glare or bright lighting.
Sound Localization	The ability to tell the direction from which a sound originated.
Static Strength	The ability to exert maximum muscle force to lift, push, pull, or carry objects.

Work_Activity	Work_Activity Definitions

Extent Flexibility — The ability to bend, stretch, twist, or reach with your body, arms, and/or legs.

Selling or Influencing Others — Convincing others to buy merchandise/goods or to otherwise change their minds or actions.

Interacting With Computers — Using computers and computer systems (including hardware and software) to program, write software, set up functions, enter data, or process information.

Communicating with Persons Outside Organization — Communicating with people outside the organization, representing the organization to customers, the public, government, and other external sources. This information can be exchanged in person, in writing, or by telephone or e-mail.

Getting Information — Observing, receiving, and otherwise obtaining information from all relevant sources.

Establishing and Maintaining Interpersonal Relatio — Developing constructive and cooperative working relationships with others, and maintaining them over time.

Documenting/Recording Information — Entering, transcribing, recording, storing, or maintaining information in written or electronic/magnetic form.

Communicating with Supervisors, Peers, or Subordin — Providing information to supervisors, co-workers, and subordinates by telephone, in written form, e-mail, or in person.

Processing Information — Compiling, coding, categorizing, calculating, tabulating, auditing, or verifying information or data.

Identifying Objects, Actions, and Events — Identifying information by categorizing, estimating, recognizing differences or similarities, and detecting changes in circumstances or events.

Resolving Conflicts and Negotiating with Others — Handling complaints, settling disputes, and resolving grievances and conflicts, or otherwise negotiating with others.

Making Decisions and Solving Problems — Analyzing information and evaluating results to choose the best solution and solve problems.

Updating and Using Relevant Knowledge — Keeping up-to-date technically and applying new knowledge to your job.

Interpreting the Meaning of Information for Others — Translating or explaining what information means and how it can be used.

Thinking Creatively — Developing, designing, or creating new applications, ideas, relationships, systems, or products, including artistic contributions.

Evaluating Information to Determine Compliance wit — Using relevant information and individual judgment to determine whether events or processes comply with laws, regulations, or standards.

Performing Administrative Activities — Performing day-to-day administrative tasks such as maintaining information files and processing paperwork.

Organizing, Planning, and Prioritizing Work — Developing specific goals and plans to prioritize, organize, and accomplish your work.

Performing for or Working Directly with the Public — Performing for people or dealing directly with the public. This includes serving customers in restaurants and stores, and receiving clients or guests.

Judging the Qualities of Things, Services, or Peop — Assessing the value, importance, or quality of things or people.

Monitor Processes, Materials, or Surroundings — Monitoring and reviewing information from materials, events, or the environment, to detect or assess problems.

Analyzing Data or Information — Identifying the underlying principles, reasons, or facts of information by breaking down information or data into separate parts.

Developing Objectives and Strategies — Establishing long-range objectives and specifying the strategies and actions to achieve them.

Assisting and Caring for Others — Providing personal assistance, medical attention, emotional support, or other personal care to others such as coworkers, customers, or patients.

Coaching and Developing Others — Identifying the developmental needs of others and coaching, mentoring, or otherwise helping others to improve their knowledge or skills.

Training and Teaching Others — Identifying the educational needs of others, developing formal educational or training programs or classes, and teaching or instructing others.

Estimating the Quantifiable Characteristics of Pro — Estimating sizes, distances, and quantities; or determining time, costs, resources, or materials needed to perform a work activity.

Developing and Building Teams — Encouraging and building mutual trust, respect, and cooperation among team members.

Coordinating the Work and Activities of Others — Getting members of a group to work together to accomplish tasks.

Provide Consultation and Advice to Others — Providing guidance and expert advice to management or other groups on technical, systems-, or process-related topics.

Inspecting Equipment, Structures, or Material — Inspecting equipment, structures, or materials to identify the cause of errors or other problems or defects.

Handling and Moving Objects — Using hands and arms in handling, installing, positioning, and moving materials, and manipulating things.

Scheduling Work and Activities — Scheduling events, programs, and activities, as well as the work of others.

Controlling Machines and Processes — Using either control mechanisms or direct physical activity to operate machines or processes (not including computers or vehicles).

Guiding, Directing, and Motivating Subordinates — Providing guidance and direction to subordinates, including setting performance standards and monitoring performance.

Staffing Organizational Units — Recruiting, interviewing, selecting, hiring, and promoting employees in an organization.

Repairing and Maintaining Electronic Equipment — Servicing, repairing, calibrating, regulating, fine-tuning, or testing machines, devices, and equipment that operate primarily on the basis of electrical or electronic (not mechanical) principles.

Monitoring and Controlling Resources — Monitoring and controlling resources and overseeing the spending of money.

Drafting, Laying Out, and Specifying Technical Dev — Providing documentation, detailed instructions, drawings, or specifications to tell others about how devices, parts, equipment, or structures are to be fabricated, constructed, assembled, modified, maintained, or used.

Repairing and Maintaining Mechanical Equipment — Servicing, repairing, adjusting, and testing machines, devices, moving parts, and equipment that operate primarily on the basis of mechanical (not electronic) principles.

Performing General Physical Activities — Performing physical activities that require considerable use of your arms and legs and moving your whole body, such as climbing, lifting, balancing, walking, stooping, and handling of materials.

Operating Vehicles, Mechanized Devices, or Equipme — Running, maneuvering, navigating, or driving vehicles or mechanized equipment, such as forklifts, passenger vehicles, aircraft, or water craft.

Work_Context	Work_Context Definitions

Telephone — How often do you have telephone conversations in this job?

Contact With Others — How much does this job require the worker to be in contact with others (face-to-face, by telephone, or otherwise) in order to perform it?

Spend Time Sitting — How much does this job require sitting?

Deal With Unpleasant or Angry People — How frequently does the worker have to deal with unpleasant, angry, or discourteous individuals as part of the job requirements?

Face-to-Face Discussions — How often do you have to have face-to-face discussions with individuals or teams in this job?

Indoors, Environmentally Controlled — How often does this job require working indoors in environmentally controlled conditions?

Physical Proximity — To what extent does this job require the worker to perform job tasks in close physical proximity to other people?

Importance of Being Exact or Accurate — How important is being very exact or highly accurate in performing this job?

Deal With External Customers — How important is it to work with external customers or the public in this job?

Work With Work Group or Team — How important is it to work with others in a group or team in this job?

Level of Competition — To what extent does this job require the worker to compete or to be aware of competitive pressures?

Importance of Repeating Same Tasks — How important is repeating the same physical activities (e.g., key entry) or mental activities (e.g., checking entries in a ledger) over and over, without stopping, to performing this job?

Spend Time Using Your Hands to Handle, Control, or — How much does this job require using your hands to handle, control, or feel objects, tools or controls?

Freedom to Make Decisions — How much decision making freedom, without supervision, does the job offer?

Sounds, Noise Levels Are Distracting or Uncomforta — How often does this job require working exposed to sounds and noise levels that are distracting or uncomfortable?

Structured versus Unstructured Work — To what extent is this job structured for the worker, rather than allowing the worker to determine tasks, priorities, and goals?

Frequency of Decision Making — How frequently is the worker required to make decisions that affect other people, the financial resources, and/or the image and reputation of the organization?

Spend Time Making Repetitive Motions — How much does this job require making repetitive motions?

Impact of Decisions on Co-workers or Company Resul — How do the decisions an employee makes impact the results of co-workers, clients or the company?

871

Time Pressure	How often does this job require the worker to meet strict deadlines?
Degree of Automation	How automated is the job?
Letters and Memos	How often does the job require written letters and memos?
Consequence of Error	How serious would the result usually be if the worker made a mistake that was not readily correctable?
Frequency of Conflict Situations	How often are there conflict situations the employee has to face in this job?
Coordinate or Lead Others	How important is it to coordinate or lead others in accomplishing work activities in this job?
Responsible for Others' Health and Safety	How much responsibility is there for the health and safety of others in this job?
Pace Determined by Speed of Equipment	How important is it to this job that the pace is determined by the speed of equipment or machinery? (This does not refer to keeping busy at all times on this job.)
Electronic Mail	How often do you use electronic mail in this job?
Public Speaking	How often do you have to perform public speaking in this job?
Responsibility for Outcomes and Results	How responsible is the worker for work outcomes and results of other workers?
Spend Time Standing	How much does this job require standing?
Exposed to Contaminants	How often does this job require working exposed to contaminants (such as pollutants, gases, dust or odors)?
Deal With Physically Aggressive People	How frequently does this job require the worker to deal with physical aggression of violent individuals?
Spend Time Walking and Running	How much does this job require walking and running?
Cramped Work Space, Awkward Positions	How often does this job require working in cramped work spaces that requires getting into awkward positions?
Exposed to Disease or Infections	How often does this job require exposure to disease/infections?
Spend Time Bending or Twisting the Body	How much does this job require bending or twisting your body?
Extremely Bright or Inadequate Lighting	How often does this job require working in extremely bright or inadequate lighting conditions?
Exposed to Hazardous Conditions	How often does this job require exposure to hazardous conditions?
Spend Time Keeping or Regaining Balance	How much does this job require keeping or regaining your balance?
Very Hot or Cold Temperatures	How often does this job require working in very hot (above 90 F degrees) or very cold (below 32 F degrees) temperatures?
Indoors, Not Environmentally Controlled	How often does this job require working indoors in non-controlled environmental conditions (e.g., warehouse without heat)?
Exposed to Minor Burns, Cuts, Bites, or Stings	How often does this job require exposure to minor burns, cuts, bites, or stings?
Exposed to High Places	How often does this job require exposure to high places?
In an Enclosed Vehicle or Equipment	How often does this job require working in a closed vehicle or equipment (e.g., car)?
Spend Time Climbing Ladders, Scaffolds, or Poles	How much does this job require climbing ladders, scaffolds, or poles?
Outdoors, Exposed to Weather	How often does this job require working outdoors, exposed to all weather conditions?
In an Open Vehicle or Equipment	How often does this job require working in an open vehicle or equipment (e.g., tractor)?
Exposed to Hazardous Equipment	How often does this job require exposure to hazardous equipment?
Wear Common Protective or Safety Equipment such as	How much does this job require wearing common protective or safety equipment such as safety shoes, glasses, gloves, hard hats or live jackets?
Outdoors, Under Cover	How often does this job require working outdoors, under cover (e.g., structure with roof but no walls)?
Exposed to Whole Body Vibration	How often does this job require exposure to whole body vibration (e.g., operate a jackhammer)?
Exposed to Radiation	How often does this job require exposure to radiation?
Spend Time Kneeling, Crouching, Stooping, or Crawl	How much does this job require kneeling, crouching, stooping, or crawling?
Wear Specialized Protective or Safety Equipment su	How much does this job require wearing specialized protective or safety equipment such as breathing apparatus, safety harness, full protection suits, or radiation protection?

Job Zone Component	Job Zone Component Definitions
Title	Job Zone Two: Some Preparation Needed

Overall Experience	Some previous work-related skill, knowledge, or experience may be helpful in these occupations, but usually is not needed. For example, a drywall installer might benefit from experience installing drywall, but an inexperienced person could still learn to be an installer with little difficulty.
Job Training	Employees in these occupations need anywhere from a few months to one year of working with experienced employees.
Job Zone Examples	These occupations often involve using your knowledge and skills to help others. Examples include drywall installers, fire inspectors, flight attendants, pharmacy technicians, salespersons (retail), and tellers.
SVP Range	(4.0 to < 6.0)
Education	These occupations usually require a high school diploma and may require some vocational training or job-related course work. In some cases, an associate's or bachelor's degree could be needed.

Work_Styles	Work_Styles Definitions
Stress Tolerance	Job requires accepting criticism and dealing calmly and effectively with high stress situations.
Integrity	Job requires being honest and ethical.
Persistence	Job requires persistence in the face of obstacles.
Dependability	Job requires being reliable, responsible, and dependable, and fulfilling obligations.
Achievement/Effort	Job requires establishing and maintaining personally challenging achievement goals and exerting effort toward mastering tasks.
Self Control	Job requires maintaining composure, keeping emotions in check, controlling anger, and avoiding aggressive behavior, even in very difficult situations.
Adaptability/Flexibility	Job requires being open to change (positive or negative) and to considerable variety in the workplace.
Attention to Detail	Job requires being careful about detail and thorough in completing work tasks.
Initiative	Job requires a willingness to take on responsibilities and challenges.
Cooperation	Job requires being pleasant with others on the job and displaying a good-natured, cooperative attitude.
Independence	Job requires developing one's own ways of doing things, guiding oneself with little or no supervision, and depending on oneself to get things done.
Concern for Others	Job requires being sensitive to others' needs and feelings and being understanding and helpful on the job.
Analytical Thinking	Job requires analyzing information and using logic to address work-related issues and problems.
Leadership	Job requires a willingness to lead, take charge, and offer opinions and direction.
Social Orientation	Job requires preferring to work with others rather than alone, and being personally connected with others on the job.
Innovation	Job requires creativity and alternative thinking to develop new ideas for and answers to work-related problems.

43-1011.00 - First-Line Supervisors/Managers of Office and Administrative Support Workers

Supervise and coordinate the activities of clerical and administrative support workers.

Tasks

1) Develop and/or update procedures, policies, and standards.

2) Evaluate employees' job performance and conformance to regulations, and recommend appropriate personnel action.

3) Interpret and communicate work procedures and company policies to staff.

4) Implement corporate and departmental policies, procedures, and service standards in conjunction with management.

5) Discuss job performance problems with employees in order to identify causes and issues, and to work on resolving problems.

6) Develop work schedules according to budgets and workloads.

7) Coordinate activities with other supervisory personnel, and with other work units or departments.

8) Consult with managers and other personnel to resolve problems in areas such as equipment performance, output quality, and work schedules.

9) Analyze financial activities of establishments or departments, and provide input into budget planning and preparation processes.

10) Make recommendations to management concerning such issues as staffing decisions and procedural changes.

11) Research, compile, and prepare reports, manuals, correspondence, and other information required by management or governmental agencies.

12) Discuss work problems or grievances with union representatives.

13) Recruit, interview, and select employees.

14) Maintain records pertaining to inventory, personnel, orders, supplies, and machine maintenance.

15) Plan layouts of stockrooms, warehouses, or other storage areas, considering turnover, size, weight, and related factors pertaining to items stored.

16) Plan for and coordinate office services such as equipment and supply acquisition and organization, disposal of assets, relocation, parking, maintenance, and security services.

17) Coordinate or perform activities associated with shipping, receiving, distribution, and transportation.

18) Keep informed of provisions of labor-management agreements and their effects on departmental operations.

19) Provide employees with guidance in handling difficult or complex problems, and in resolving escalated complaints or disputes.

20) Review records and reports pertaining to activities such as production, payroll, and shipping in order to verify details, monitor work activities, and evaluate performance.

21) Arrange for necessary maintenance and repair work.

22) Participate in the work of subordinates in order to facilitate productivity or to overcome difficult aspects of work.

23) Supervise the work of office, administrative, or customer service employees to ensure adherence to quality standards, deadlines, and proper procedures, correcting errors or problems.

24) Prepare and issue work schedules, deadlines, and duty assignments of office or administrative staff.

25) Train and instruct employees in job duties and company policies, or arrange for training to be provided.

26) Design, implement, and evaluate staff training and development programs, customer service initiatives, and performance measurement criteria.

27) Compute figures such as balances, totals, and commissions.

28) Resolve customer complaints, and answer customers' questions regarding policies and procedures.

43-2011.00 - Switchboard Operators, Including Answering Service

Operate telephone business systems equipment or switchboards to relay incoming, outgoing, and interoffice calls. May supply information to callers and record messages.

Tasks

1) Operate communication systems, such as telephone, switchboard, intercom, two-way radio, or public address.

2) Route emergency calls appropriately.

3) Relay and route written and verbal messages.

4) Page individuals to inform them of telephone calls, using paging and interoffice communication equipment.

5) Perform clerical duties, such as typing, proofreading, accepting orders, scheduling appointments, and sorting mail.

6) Place telephone calls or arrange conference calls as instructed.

7) Contact security staff members when necessary, using radio-telephones.

8) Stamp messages with time and date, and file them appropriately.

9) Answer simple questions about clients' businesses, using reference files.

10) Monitor alarm systems in order to ensure that secure conditions are maintained.

11) Record messages, suggesting rewording for clarity and conciseness.

12) Keep records of calls placed and charges incurred.

13) Complete forms for sales orders.

Knowledge	Knowledge Definitions
Customer and Personal Service	Knowledge of principles and processes for providing customer and personal services. This includes customer needs assessment, meeting quality standards for services, and evaluation of customer satisfaction.
Clerical	Knowledge of administrative and clerical procedures and systems such as word processing, managing files and records, stenography and transcription, designing forms, and other office procedures and terminology.
English Language	Knowledge of the structure and content of the English language including the meaning and spelling of words, rules of composition, and grammar.
Telecommunications	Knowledge of transmission, broadcasting, switching, control, and operation of telecommunications systems.
Computers and Electronics	Knowledge of circuit boards, processors, chips, electronic equipment, and computer hardware and software, including applications and programming.
Public Safety and Security	Knowledge of relevant equipment, policies, procedures, and strategies to promote effective local, state, or national security operations for the protection of people, data, property, and institutions.
Psychology	Knowledge of human behavior and performance; individual differences in ability, personality, and interests; learning and motivation; psychological research methods; and the assessment and treatment of behavioral and affective disorders.
Communications and Media	Knowledge of media production, communication, and dissemination techniques and methods. This includes alternative ways to inform and entertain via written, oral, and visual media.
Administration and Management	Knowledge of business and management principles involved in strategic planning, resource allocation, human resources modeling, leadership technique, production methods, and coordination of people and resources.
Mathematics	Knowledge of arithmetic, algebra, geometry, calculus, statistics, and their applications.
Foreign Language	Knowledge of the structure and content of a foreign (non-English) language including the meaning and spelling of words, rules of composition and grammar, and pronunciation.
Personnel and Human Resources	Knowledge of principles and procedures for personnel recruitment, selection, training, compensation and benefits, labor relations and negotiation, and personnel information systems.
Education and Training	Knowledge of principles and methods for curriculum and training design, teaching and instruction for individuals and groups, and the measurement of training effects.
Sales and Marketing	Knowledge of principles and methods for showing, promoting, and selling products or services. This includes marketing strategy and tactics, product demonstration, sales techniques, and sales control systems.
Economics and Accounting	Knowledge of economic and accounting principles and practices, the financial markets, banking and the analysis and reporting of financial data.
Law and Government	Knowledge of laws, legal codes, court procedures, precedents, government regulations, executive orders, agency rules, and the democratic political process.
Sociology and Anthropology	Knowledge of group behavior and dynamics, societal trends and influences, human migrations, ethnicity, cultures and their history and origins.
Production and Processing	Knowledge of raw materials, production processes, quality control, costs, and other techniques for maximizing the effective manufacture and distribution of goods.
Philosophy and Theology	Knowledge of different philosophical systems and religions. This includes their basic principles, values, ethics, ways of thinking, customs, practices, and their impact on human culture.
Geography	Knowledge of principles and methods for describing the features of land, sea, and air masses, including their physical characteristics, locations, interrelationships, and distribution of plant, animal, and human life.

Medicine and Dentistry	Knowledge of the information and techniques needed to diagnose and treat human injuries, diseases, and deformities. This includes symptoms, treatment alternatives, drug properties and interactions, and preventive health-care measures.
Therapy and Counseling	Knowledge of principles, methods, and procedures for diagnosis, treatment, and rehabilitation of physical and mental dysfunctions, and for career counseling and guidance.
Engineering and Technology	Knowledge of the practical application of engineering science and technology. This includes applying principles, techniques, procedures, and equipment to the design and production of various goods and services.
Transportation	Knowledge of principles and methods for moving people or goods by air, rail, sea, or road, including the relative costs and benefits.
Mechanical	Knowledge of machines and tools, including their designs, uses, repair, and maintenance.
Chemistry	Knowledge of the chemical composition, structure, and properties of substances and of the chemical processes and transformations that they undergo. This includes uses of chemicals and their interactions, danger signs, production techniques, and disposal methods.
Fine Arts	Knowledge of the theory and techniques required to compose, produce, and perform works of music, dance, visual arts, drama, and sculpture.
History and Archeology	Knowledge of historical events and their causes, indicators, and effects on civilizations and cultures.
Design	Knowledge of design techniques, tools, and principles involved in production of precision technical plans, blueprints, drawings, and models.
Biology	Knowledge of plant and animal organisms, their tissues, cells, functions, interdependencies, and interactions with each other and the environment.
Building and Construction	Knowledge of materials, methods, and the tools involved in the construction or repair of houses, buildings, or other structures such as highways and roads.
Physics	Knowledge and prediction of physical principles, laws, their interrelationships, and applications to understanding fluid, material, and atmospheric dynamics, and mechanical, electrical, atomic and sub- atomic structures and processes.
Food Production	Knowledge of techniques and equipment for planting, growing, and harvesting food products (both plant and animal) for consumption, including storage/handling techniques.

Skills	**Skills Definitions**
Active Listening	Giving full attention to what other people are saying, taking time to understand the points being made, asking questions as appropriate, and not interrupting at inappropriate times.
Speaking	Talking to others to convey information effectively.
Service Orientation	Actively looking for ways to help people.
Social Perceptiveness	Being aware of others' reactions and understanding why they react as they do.
Reading Comprehension	Understanding written sentences and paragraphs in work related documents.
Critical Thinking	Using logic and reasoning to identify the strengths and weaknesses of alternative solutions, conclusions or approaches to problems.
Writing	Communicating effectively in writing as appropriate for the needs of the audience.
Learning Strategies	Selecting and using training/instructional methods and procedures appropriate for the situation when learning or teaching new things.
Instructing	Teaching others how to do something.
Active Learning	Understanding the implications of new information for both current and future problem-solving and decision-making.
Time Management	Managing one's own time and the time of others.
Coordination	Adjusting actions in relation to others' actions.
Monitoring	Monitoring/Assessing performance of yourself, other individuals, or organizations to make improvements or take corrective action.
Judgment and Decision Making	Considering the relative costs and benefits of potential actions to choose the most appropriate one.
Operation and Control	Controlling operations of equipment or systems.
Persuasion	Persuading others to change their minds or behavior.
Mathematics	Using mathematics to solve problems.
Negotiation	Bringing others together and trying to reconcile differences.

Complex Problem Solving	Identifying complex problems and reviewing related information to develop and evaluate options and implement solutions.
Equipment Selection	Determining the kind of tools and equipment needed to do a job.
Troubleshooting	Determining causes of operating errors and deciding what to do about it.
Management of Personnel Resources	Motivating, developing, and directing people as they work, identifying the best people for the job.
Operation Monitoring	Watching gauges, dials, or other indicators to make sure a machine is working properly.
Quality Control Analysis	Conducting tests and inspections of products, services, or processes to evaluate quality or performance.
Systems Evaluation	Identifying measures or indicators of system performance and the actions needed to improve or correct performance, relative to the goals of the system.
Systems Analysis	Determining how a system should work and how changes in conditions, operations, and the environment will affect outcomes.
Equipment Maintenance	Performing routine maintenance on equipment and determining when and what kind of maintenance is needed.
Operations Analysis	Analyzing needs and product requirements to create a design.
Repairing	Repairing machines or systems using the needed tools.
Technology Design	Generating or adapting equipment and technology to serve user needs.
Management of Financial Resources	Determining how money will be spent to get the work done, and accounting for these expenditures.
Management of Material Resources	Obtaining and seeing to the appropriate use of equipment, facilities, and materials needed to do certain work.
Installation	Installing equipment, machines, wiring, or programs to meet specifications.
Programming	Writing computer programs for various purposes.
Science	Using scientific rules and methods to solve problems.

Ability	**Ability Definitions**
Speech Recognition	The ability to identify and understand the speech of another person.
Speech Clarity	The ability to speak clearly so others can understand you.
Oral Comprehension	The ability to listen to and understand information and ideas presented through spoken words and sentences.
Oral Expression	The ability to communicate information and ideas in speaking so others will understand.
Problem Sensitivity	The ability to tell when something is wrong or is likely to go wrong. It does not involve solving the problem, only recognizing there is a problem.
Written Comprehension	The ability to read and understand information and ideas presented in writing.
Selective Attention	The ability to concentrate on a task over a period of time without being distracted.
Written Expression	The ability to communicate information and ideas in writing so others will understand.
Near Vision	The ability to see details at close range (within a few feet of the observer).
Deductive Reasoning	The ability to apply general rules to specific problems to produce answers that make sense.
Information Ordering	The ability to arrange things or actions in a certain order or pattern according to a specific rule or set of rules (e.g., patterns of numbers, letters, words, pictures, mathematical operations).
Category Flexibility	The ability to generate or use different sets of rules for combining or grouping things in different ways.
Inductive Reasoning	The ability to combine pieces of information to form general rules or conclusions (includes finding a relationship among seemingly unrelated events).
Perceptual Speed	The ability to quickly and accurately compare similarities and differences among sets of letters, numbers, objects, pictures, or patterns. The things to be compared may be presented at the same time or one after the other. This ability also includes comparing a presented object with a remembered object.
Finger Dexterity	The ability to make precisely coordinated movements of the fingers of one or both hands to grasp, manipulate, or assemble very small objects.
Time Sharing	The ability to shift back and forth between two or more activities or sources of information (such as speech, sounds, touch, or other sources).
Flexibility of Closure	The ability to identify or detect a known pattern (a figure, object, word, or sound) that is hidden in other distracting material.

Auditory Attention	The ability to focus on a single source of sound in the presence of other distracting sounds.
Far Vision	The ability to see details at a distance.
Hearing Sensitivity	The ability to detect or tell the differences between sounds that vary in pitch and loudness.
Fluency of Ideas	The ability to come up with a number of ideas about a topic (the number of ideas is important, not their quality, correctness, or creativity).
Speed of Closure	The ability to quickly make sense of, combine, and organize information into meaningful patterns.
Originality	The ability to come up with unusual or clever ideas about a given topic or situation, or to develop creative ways to solve a problem.
Manual Dexterity	The ability to quickly move your hand, your hand together with your arm, or your two hands to grasp, manipulate, or assemble objects.
Arm-Hand Steadiness	The ability to keep your hand and arm steady while moving your arm or while holding your arm and hand in one position.
Mathematical Reasoning	The ability to choose the right mathematical methods or formulas to solve a problem.
Control Precision	The ability to quickly and repeatedly adjust the controls of a machine or a vehicle to exact positions.
Number Facility	The ability to add, subtract, multiply, or divide quickly and correctly.
Visualization	The ability to imagine how something will look after it is moved around or when its parts are moved or rearranged.
Visual Color Discrimination	The ability to match or detect differences between colors, including shades of color and brightness.
Memorization	The ability to remember information such as words, numbers, pictures, and procedures.
Trunk Strength	The ability to use your abdominal and lower back muscles to support part of the body repeatedly or continuously over time without 'giving out' or fatiguing.
Wrist-Finger Speed	The ability to make fast, simple, repeated movements of the fingers, hands, and wrists.
Response Orientation	The ability to choose quickly between two or more movements in response to two or more different signals (lights, sounds, pictures). It includes the speed with which the correct response is started with the hand, foot, or other body part.
Reaction Time	The ability to quickly respond (with the hand, finger, or foot) to a signal (sound, light, picture) when it appears.
Sound Localization	The ability to tell the direction from which a sound originated.
Multilimb Coordination	The ability to coordinate two or more limbs (for example, two arms, two legs, or one leg and one arm) while sitting, standing, or lying down. It does not involve performing the activities while the whole body is in motion.
Speed of Limb Movement	The ability to quickly move the arms and legs.
Extent Flexibility	The ability to bend, stretch, twist, or reach with your body, arms, and/or legs.
Explosive Strength	The ability to use short bursts of muscle force to propel oneself (as in jumping or sprinting), or to throw an object.
Peripheral Vision	The ability to see objects or movement of objects to one's side when the eyes are looking ahead.
Dynamic Flexibility	The ability to quickly and repeatedly bend, stretch, twist, or reach out with your body, arms, and/or legs.
Glare Sensitivity	The ability to see objects in the presence of glare or bright lighting.
Gross Body Coordination	The ability to coordinate the movement of your arms, legs, and torso together when the whole body is in motion.
Gross Body Equilibrium	The ability to keep or regain your body balance or stay upright when in an unstable position.
Dynamic Strength	The ability to exert muscle force repeatedly or continuously over time. This involves muscular endurance and resistance to muscle fatigue.
Night Vision	The ability to see under low light conditions.
Depth Perception	The ability to judge which of several objects is closer or farther away from you, or to judge the distance between you and an object.
Stamina	The ability to exert yourself physically over long periods of time without getting winded or out of breath.
Spatial Orientation	The ability to know your location in relation to the environment or to know where other objects are in relation to you.
Static Strength	The ability to exert maximum muscle force to lift, push, pull, or carry objects.
Rate Control	The ability to time your movements or the movement of a piece of equipment in anticipation of changes in the speed and/or direction of a moving object or scene.

Work_Activity	Work_Activity Definitions
Getting Information	Observing, receiving, and otherwise obtaining information from all relevant sources.
Communicating with Persons Outside Organization	Communicating with people outside the organization, representing the organization to customers, the public, government, and other external sources. This information can be exchanged in person, in writing, or by telephone or e-mail.
Establishing and Maintaining Interpersonal Relatio	Developing constructive and cooperative working relationships with others, and maintaining them over time.
Communicating with Supervisors, Peers, or Subordin	Providing information to supervisors, co-workers, and subordinates by telephone, in written form, e-mail, or in person.
Performing for or Working Directly with the Public	Performing for people or dealing directly with the public. This includes serving customers in restaurants and stores, and receiving clients or guests.
Identifying Objects, Actions, and Events	Identifying information by categorizing, estimating, recognizing differences or similarities, and detecting changes in circumstances or events.
Interacting With Computers	Using computers and computer systems (including hardware and software) to program, write software, set up functions, enter data, or process information.
Processing Information	Compiling, coding, categorizing, calculating, tabulating, auditing, or verifying information or data.
Updating and Using Relevant Knowledge	Keeping up-to-date technically and applying new knowledge to your job.
Making Decisions and Solving Problems	Analyzing information and evaluating results to choose the best solution and solve problems.
Monitor Processes, Materials, or Surroundings	Monitoring and reviewing information from materials, events, or the environment, to detect or assess problems.
Assisting and Caring for Others	Providing personal assistance, medical attention, emotional support, or other personal care to others such as coworkers, customers, or patients.
Documenting/Recording Information	Entering, transcribing, recording, storing, or maintaining information in written or electronic/magnetic form.
Organizing, Planning, and Prioritizing Work	Developing specific goals and plans to prioritize, organize, and accomplish your work.
Judging the Qualities of Things, Services, or Peop	Assessing the value, importance, or quality of things or people.
Performing Administrative Activities	Performing day-to-day administrative tasks such as maintaining information files and processing paperwork.
Interpreting the Meaning of Information for Others	Translating or explaining what information means and how it can be used.
Resolving Conflicts and Negotiating with Others	Handling complaints, settling disputes, and resolving grievances and conflicts, or otherwise negotiating with others.
Evaluating Information to Determine Compliance wit	Using relevant information and individual judgment to determine whether events or processes comply with laws, regulations, or standards.
Analyzing Data or Information	Identifying the underlying principles, reasons, or facts of information by breaking down information or data into separate parts.
Thinking Creatively	Developing, designing, or creating new applications, ideas, relationships, systems, or products, including artistic contributions.
Training and Teaching Others	Identifying the educational needs of others, developing formal educational or training programs or classes, and teaching or instructing others.
Developing and Building Teams	Encouraging and building mutual trust, respect, and cooperation among team members.
Inspecting Equipment, Structures, or Material	Inspecting equipment, structures, or materials to identify the cause of errors or other problems or defects.
Scheduling Work and Activities	Scheduling events, programs, and activities, as well as the work of others.
Coaching and Developing Others	Identifying the developmental needs of others and coaching, mentoring, or otherwise helping others to improve their knowledge or skills.
Estimating the Quantifiable Characteristics of Pro	Estimating sizes, distances, and quantities; or determining time, costs, resources, or materials needed to perform a work activity.
Coordinating the Work and Activities of Others	Getting members of a group to work together to accomplish tasks.
Selling or Influencing Others	Convincing others to buy merchandise/goods or to otherwise change their minds or actions.
Developing Objectives and Strategies	Establishing long-range objectives and specifying the strategies and actions to achieve them.

Performing General Physical Activities	Performing physical activities that require considerable use of your arms and legs and moving your whole body, such as climbing, lifting, balancing, walking, stooping, and handling of materials.
Provide Consultation and Advice to Others	Providing guidance and expert advice to management or other groups on technical, systems-, or process-related topics.
Guiding, Directing, and Motivating Subordinates	Providing guidance and direction to subordinates, including setting performance standards and monitoring performance.
Controlling Machines and Processes	Using either control mechanisms or direct physical activity to operate machines or processes (not including computers or vehicles).
Handling and Moving Objects	Using hands and arms in handling, installing, positioning, and moving materials, and manipulating things.
Monitoring and Controlling Resources	Monitoring and controlling resources and overseeing the spending of money.
Operating Vehicles, Mechanized Devices, or Equipme	Running, maneuvering, navigating, or driving vehicles or mechanized equipment, such as forklifts, passenger vehicles, aircraft, or water craft.
Repairing and Maintaining Electronic Equipment	Servicing, repairing, calibrating, regulating, fine-tuning, or testing machines, devices, and equipment that operate primarily on the basis of electrical or electronic (not mechanical) principles.
Staffing Organizational Units	Recruiting, interviewing, selecting, hiring, and promoting employees in an organization.
Repairing and Maintaining Mechanical Equipment	Servicing, repairing, adjusting, and testing machines, devices, moving parts, and equipment that operate primarily on the basis of mechanical (not electronic) principles.
Drafting, Laying Out, and Specifying Technical Dev	Providing documentation, detailed instructions, drawings, or specifications to tell others about how devices, parts, equipment, or structures are to be fabricated, constructed, assembled, modified, maintained, or used.

Work_Context	Work_Context Definitions
Telephone	How often do you have telephone conversations in this job?
Contact With Others	How much does this job require the worker to be in contact with others (face-to-face, by telephone, or otherwise) in order to perform it?
Spend Time Sitting	How much does this job require sitting?
Indoors, Environmentally Controlled	How often does this job require working indoors in environmentally controlled conditions?
Face-to-Face Discussions	How often do you have to have face-to-face discussions with individuals or teams in this job?
Importance of Being Exact or Accurate	How important is being very exact or highly accurate in performing this job?
Spend Time Using Your Hands to Handle, Control, or	How much does this job require using your hands to handle, control, or feel objects, tools or controls?
Deal With Unpleasant or Angry People	How frequently does the worker have to deal with unpleasant, angry, or discourteous individuals as part of the job requirements?
Work With Work Group or Team	How important is it to work with others in a group or team in this job?
Importance of Repeating Same Tasks	How important is repeating the same physical activities (e.g., key entry) or mental activities (e.g., checking entries in a ledger) over and over, without stopping, to performing this job?
Deal With External Customers	How important is it to work with external customers or the public in this job?
Freedom to Make Decisions	How much decision making freedom, without supervision, does the job offer?
Spend Time Making Repetitive Motions	How much does this job require making repetitive motions?
Letters and Memos	How often does the job require written letters and memos?
Impact of Decisions on Co-workers or Company Resul	How do the decisions an employee makes impact the results of co-workers, clients or the company?
Structured versus Unstructured Work	To what extent is this job structured for the worker, rather than allowing the worker to determine tasks, priorities, and goals?
Frequency of Decision Making	How frequently is the worker required to make decisions that affect other people, the financial resources, and/or the image and reputation of the organization?
Frequency of Conflict Situations	How often are there conflict situations the employee has to face in this job?
Electronic Mail	How often do you use electronic mail in this job?
Physical Proximity	To what extent does this job require the worker to perform job tasks in close physical proximity to other people?
Coordinate or Lead Others	How important is it to coordinate or lead others in accomplishing work activities in this job?

Sounds, Noise Levels Are Distracting or Uncomforta	How often does this job require working exposed to sounds and noise levels that are distracting or uncomfortable?
Time Pressure	How often does this job require the worker to meet strict deadlines?
Responsibility for Outcomes and Results	How responsible is the worker for work outcomes and results of other workers?
Consequence of Error	How serious would the result usually be if the worker made a mistake that was not readily correctable?
Degree of Automation	How automated is the job?
Pace Determined by Speed of Equipment	How important is it to this job that the pace is determined by the speed of equipment or machinery? (This does not refer to keeping busy at all times on this job.)
Responsible for Others' Health and Safety	How much responsibility is there for the health and safety of others in this job?
Exposed to Disease or Infections	How often does this job require exposure to disease/infections?
Spend Time Bending or Twisting the Body	How much does this job require bending or twisting your body?
Exposed to Contaminants	How often does this job require working exposed to contaminants (such as pollutants, gases, dust or odors)?
Level of Competition	To what extent does this job require the worker to compete or to be aware of competitive pressures?
Extremely Bright or Inadequate Lighting	How often does this job require working in extremely bright or inadequate lighting conditions?
Spend Time Standing	How much does this job require standing?
Spend Time Walking and Running	How much does this job require walking and running?
Public Speaking	How often do you have to perform public speaking in this job?
Spend Time Kneeling, Crouching, Stooping, or Crawl	How much does this job require kneeling, crouching, stooping or crawling?
Cramped Work Space, Awkward Positions	How often does this job require working in cramped work spaces that requires getting into awkward positions?
Exposed to Minor Burns, Cuts, Bites, or Stings	How often does this job require exposure to minor burns, cuts, bites, or stings?
Deal With Physically Aggressive People	How frequently does this job require the worker to deal with physical aggression of violent individuals?
In an Enclosed Vehicle or Equipment	How often does this job require working in a closed vehicle or equipment (e.g., car)?
Exposed to Radiation	How often does this job require exposure to radiation?
Indoors, Not Environmentally Controlled	How often does this job require working indoors in non-controlled environmental conditions (e.g., warehouse without heat)?
Very Hot or Cold Temperatures	How often does this job require working in very hot (above 90 F degrees) or very cold (below 32 F degrees) temperatures?
Exposed to Hazardous Conditions	How often does this job require exposure to hazardous conditions?
Spend Time Keeping or Regaining Balance	How much does this job require keeping or regaining your balance?
Wear Common Protective or Safety Equipment such as	How much does this job require wearing common protective or safety equipment such as safety shoes, glasses, gloves, hard hats or live jackets?
Outdoors, Under Cover	How often does this job require working outdoors, under cover (e.g., structure with roof but no walls)?
Wear Specialized Protective or Safety Equipment su	How much does this job require wearing specialized protective or safety equipment such as breathing apparatus, safety harness, full protection suits, or radiation protection?
Spend Time Climbing Ladders, Scaffolds, or Poles	How much does this job require climbing ladders, scaffolds, or poles?
Exposed to Whole Body Vibration	How often does this job require exposure to whole body vibration (e.g., operate a jackhammer)?
Exposed to High Places	How often does this job require exposure to high places?
Outdoors, Exposed to Weather	How often does this job require working outdoors, exposed to all weather conditions?
In an Open Vehicle or Equipment	How often does this job require working in an open vehicle or equipment (e.g., tractor)?
Exposed to Hazardous Equipment	How often does this job require exposure to hazardous equipment?

Job Zone Component	Job Zone Component Definitions
Title	Job Zone Two: Some Preparation Needed

876

Overall Experience	Some previous work-related skill, knowledge, or experience may be helpful in these occupations, but usually is not needed. For example, a drywall installer might benefit from experience installing drywall, but an inexperienced person could still learn to be an installer with little difficulty.
Job Training	Employees in these occupations need anywhere from a few months to one year of working with experienced employees.
Job Zone Examples	These occupations often involve using your knowledge and skills to help others. Examples include drywall installers, fire inspectors, flight attendants, pharmacy technicians, salespersons (retail), and tellers.
SVP Range	(4.0 to < 6.0)
Education	These occupations usually require a high school diploma and may require some vocational training or job-related course work. In some cases, an associate's or bachelor's degree could be needed.

Work_Styles	Work_Styles Definitions
Cooperation	Job requires being pleasant with others on the job and displaying a good-natured, cooperative attitude.
Concern for Others	Job requires being sensitive to others' needs and feelings and being understanding and helpful on the job.
Integrity	Job requires being honest and ethical.
Self Control	Job requires maintaining composure, keeping emotions in check, controlling anger, and avoiding aggressive behavior, even in very difficult situations.
Dependability	Job requires being reliable, responsible, and dependable, and fulfilling obligations.
Attention to Detail	Job requires being careful about detail and thorough in completing work tasks.
Stress Tolerance	Job requires accepting criticism and dealing calmly and effectively with high stress situations.
Adaptability/Flexibility	Job requires being open to change (positive or negative) and to considerable variety in the workplace.
Social Orientation	Job requires preferring to work with others rather than alone, and being personally connected with others on the job.
Independence	Job requires developing one's own ways of doing things, guiding oneself with little or no supervision, and depending on oneself to get things done.
Initiative	Job requires a willingness to take on responsibilities and challenges.
Achievement/Effort	Job requires establishing and maintaining personally challenging achievement goals and exerting effort toward mastering tasks.
Persistence	Job requires persistence in the face of obstacles.
Innovation	Job requires creativity and alternative thinking to develop new ideas for and answers to work-related problems.
Analytical Thinking	Job requires analyzing information and using logic to address work-related issues and problems.
Leadership	Job requires a willingness to lead, take charge, and offer opinions and direction.

43-2021.00 - Telephone Operators

Provide information by accessing alphabetical and geographical directories. Assist customers with special billing requests, such as charges to a third party and credits or refunds for incorrectly dialed numbers or bad connections. May handle emergency calls and assist children or people with physical disabilities to make telephone calls.

Tasks

1) Offer special assistance to persons such as those who are unable to dial or who are in emergency situations.

2) Perform clerical duties such as typing, proofreading, and sorting mail.

3) Insert tickets in calculagraphs (time-stamping devices) to record times of toll calls.

4) Update directory information.

5) Record messages to be used on telephone systems.

6) Provide assistance for customers with special billing requests.

7) Promote company products, services, and savings plans when appropriate.

8) Listen to customer requests, referring to alphabetical or geographical directories to answer questions and provide telephone information.

9) Interrupt busy lines if an emergency warrants.

10) Monitor automated systems for placing collect calls and intervene for a callers needing assistance.

11) Observe signal lights on switchboards, and dial or press buttons to make connections.

12) Operate telephone switchboards and systems to advance and complete connections, including those for local, long distance, pay telephone, mobile, person-to-person, and emergency calls.

13) Provide relay service for hearing-impaired users.

14) Set up conference calls in different locations and time zones.

15) Suggest and check alternate spellings, locations, and/or listing formats to customers lacking details or complete information.

16) Calculate and quote charges for services such as long-distance connections.

17) Consult charts to determine charges for pay-telephone calls, requesting coin deposits for calls as necessary.

18) Operate paging systems or other systems of bells or buzzers to notify recipients of incoming calls.

43-3011.00 - Bill and Account Collectors

Locate and notify customers of delinquent accounts by mail, telephone, or personal visit to solicit payment. Duties include receiving payment and posting amount to customer's account; preparing statements to credit department if customer fails to respond; initiating repossession proceedings or service disconnection; keeping records of collection and status of accounts.

Tasks

1) Locate and notify customers of delinquent accounts by mail, telephone, or personal visits in order to solicit payment.

2) Record information about financial status of customers and status of collection efforts.

3) Perform various administrative functions for assigned accounts, such as recording address changes and purging the records of deceased customers.

4) Locate and monitor overdue accounts, using computers and a variety of automated systems.

5) Sort and file correspondence, and perform miscellaneous clerical duties such as answering correspondence and writing reports.

6) Receive payments and post amounts paid to customer accounts.

7) Arrange for debt repayment or establish repayment schedules, based on customers' financial situations.

8) Advise customers of necessary actions and strategies for debt repayment.

9) Persuade customers to pay amounts due on credit accounts, damage claims, or nonpayable checks, or to return merchandise.

10) Negotiate credit extensions when necessary.

11) Notify credit departments, order merchandise repossession or service disconnection, and turn over account records to attorneys when customers fail to respond to collection attempts.

12) Trace delinquent customers to new addresses by inquiring at post offices, telephone companies, credit bureaus, or through the questioning of neighbors.

13) Drive vehicles to visit customers, return merchandise to creditors, or deliver bills.

Knowledge	Knowledge Definitions
Customer and Personal Service	Knowledge of principles and processes for providing customer and personal services. This includes customer needs assessment, meeting quality standards for services, and evaluation of customer satisfaction.
Clerical	Knowledge of administrative and clerical procedures and systems such as word processing, managing files and records, stenography and transcription, designing forms, and other office procedures and terminology.
English Language	Knowledge of the structure and content of the English language including the meaning and spelling of words, rules of composition, and grammar.
Economics and Accounting	Knowledge of economic and accounting principles and practices, the financial markets, banking and the analysis and reporting of financial data.

Mathematics	Knowledge of arithmetic, algebra, geometry, calculus, statistics, and their applications.
Administration and Management	Knowledge of business and management principles involved in strategic planning, resource allocation, human resources modeling, leadership technique, production methods, and coordination of people and resources.
Computers and Electronics	Knowledge of circuit boards, processors, chips, electronic equipment, and computer hardware and software, including applications and programming.
Law and Government	Knowledge of laws, legal codes, court procedures, precedents, government regulations, executive orders, agency rules, and the democratic political process.
Personnel and Human Resources	Knowledge of principles and procedures for personnel recruitment, selection, training, compensation and benefits, labor relations and negotiation, and personnel information systems.
Education and Training	Knowledge of principles and methods for curriculum and training design, teaching and instruction for individuals and groups, and the measurement of training effects.
Communications and Media	Knowledge of media production, communication, and dissemination techniques and methods. This includes alternative ways to inform and entertain via written, oral, and visual media.
Telecommunications	Knowledge of transmission, broadcasting, switching, control, and operation of telecommunications systems.
Psychology	Knowledge of human behavior and performance; individual differences in ability, personality, and interests; learning and motivation; psychological research methods; and the assessment and treatment of behavioral and affective disorders.
Sales and Marketing	Knowledge of principles and methods for showing, promoting, and selling products or services. This includes marketing strategy and tactics, product demonstration, sales techniques, and sales control systems.
Therapy and Counseling	Knowledge of principles, methods, and procedures for diagnosis, treatment, and rehabilitation of physical and mental dysfunctions, and for career counseling and guidance.
Production and Processing	Knowledge of raw materials, production processes, quality control, costs, and other techniques for maximizing the effective manufacture and distribution of goods.
Public Safety and Security	Knowledge of relevant equipment, policies, procedures, and strategies to promote effective local, state, or national security operations for the protection of people, data, property, and institutions.
Transportation	Knowledge of principles and methods for moving people or goods by air, rail, sea, or road, including the relative costs and benefits.
Medicine and Dentistry	Knowledge of the information and techniques needed to diagnose and treat human injuries, diseases, and deformities. This includes symptoms, treatment alternatives, drug properties and interactions, and preventive health-care measures.
Philosophy and Theology	Knowledge of different philosophical systems and religions. This includes their basic principles, values, ethics, ways of thinking, customs, practices, and their impact on human culture.
Foreign Language	Knowledge of the structure and content of a foreign (non-English) language including the meaning and spelling of words, rules of composition and grammar, and pronunciation.
Sociology and Anthropology	Knowledge of group behavior and dynamics, societal trends and influences, human migrations, ethnicity, cultures and their history and origins.
Geography	Knowledge of principles and methods for describing the features of land, sea, and air masses, including their physical characteristics, locations, interrelationships, and distribution of plant, animal, and human life.
Fine Arts	Knowledge of the theory and techniques required to compose, produce, and perform works of music, dance, visual arts, drama, and sculpture.
History and Archeology	Knowledge of historical events and their causes, indicators, and effects on civilizations and cultures.
Mechanical	Knowledge of machines and tools, including their designs, uses, repair, and maintenance.
Biology	Knowledge of plant and animal organisms, their tissues, cells, functions, interdependencies, and interactions with each other and the environment.

Chemistry	Knowledge of the chemical composition, structure, and properties of substances and of the chemical processes and transformations that they undergo. This includes uses of chemicals and their interactions, danger signs, production techniques, and disposal methods.
Physics	Knowledge and prediction of physical principles, laws, their interrelationships, and applications to understanding fluid, material, and atmospheric dynamics, and mechanical, electrical, atomic and sub-atomic structures and processes.
Engineering and Technology	Knowledge of the practical application of engineering science and technology. This includes applying principles, techniques, procedures, and equipment to the design and production of various goods and services.
Building and Construction	Knowledge of materials, methods, and the tools involved in the construction or repair of houses, buildings, or other structures such as highways and roads.
Food Production	Knowledge of techniques and equipment for planting, growing, and harvesting food products (both plant and animal) for consumption, including storage/handling techniques.
Design	Knowledge of design techniques, tools, and principles involved in production of precision technical plans, blueprints, drawings, and models.

Skills	Skills Definitions
Active Listening	Giving full attention to what other people are saying, taking time to understand the points being made, asking questions as appropriate, and not interrupting at inappropriate times.
Speaking	Talking to others to convey information effectively.
Reading Comprehension	Understanding written sentences and paragraphs in work related documents.
Time Management	Managing one's own time and the time of others.
Mathematics	Using mathematics to solve problems.
Social Perceptiveness	Being aware of others' reactions and understanding why they react as they do.
Writing	Communicating effectively in writing as appropriate for the needs of the audience.
Active Learning	Understanding the implications of new information for both current and future problem-solving and decision-making.
Judgment and Decision Making	Considering the relative costs and benefits of potential actions to choose the most appropriate one.
Critical Thinking	Using logic and reasoning to identify the strengths and weaknesses of alternative solutions, conclusions or approaches to problems.
Monitoring	Monitoring/Assessing performance of yourself, other individuals, or organizations to make improvements or take corrective action.
Service Orientation	Actively looking for ways to help people.
Learning Strategies	Selecting and using training/instructional methods and procedures appropriate for the situation when learning or teaching new things.
Persuasion	Persuading others to change their minds or behavior.
Instructing	Teaching others how to do something.
Coordination	Adjusting actions in relation to others' actions.
Management of Personnel Resources	Motivating, developing, and directing people as they work, identifying the best people for the job.
Negotiation	Bringing others together and trying to reconcile differences.
Troubleshooting	Determining causes of operating errors and deciding what to do about it.
Complex Problem Solving	Identifying complex problems and reviewing related information to develop and evaluate options and implement solutions.
Equipment Selection	Determining the kind of tools and equipment needed to do a job.
Management of Financial Resources	Determining how money will be spent to get the work done, and accounting for these expenditures.
Operations Analysis	Analyzing needs and product requirements to create a design.
Systems Evaluation	Identifying measures or indicators of system performance and the actions needed to improve or correct performance, relative to the goals of the system.
Management of Material Resources	Obtaining and seeing to the appropriate use of equipment, facilities, and materials needed to do certain work.
Operation and Control	Controlling operations of equipment or systems.
Technology Design	Generating or adapting equipment and technology to serve user needs.
Installation	Installing equipment, machines, wiring, or programs to meet specifications.

Systems Analysis	Determining how a system should work and how changes in conditions, operations, and the environment will affect outcomes.
Quality Control Analysis	Conducting tests and inspections of products, services, or processes to evaluate quality or performance.
Programming	Writing computer programs for various purposes.
Repairing	Repairing machines or systems using the needed tools.
Equipment Maintenance	Performing routine maintenance on equipment and determining when and what kind of maintenance is needed.
Science	Using scientific rules and methods to solve problems.
Operation Monitoring	Watching gauges, dials, or other indicators to make sure a machine is working properly.

Ability	**Ability Definitions**
Oral Expression	The ability to communicate information and ideas in speaking so others will understand.
Speech Clarity	The ability to speak clearly so others can understand you.
Oral Comprehension	The ability to listen to and understand information and ideas presented through spoken words and sentences.
Near Vision	The ability to see details at close range (within a few feet of the observer).
Problem Sensitivity	The ability to tell when something is wrong or is likely to go wrong. It does not involve solving the problem, only recognizing there is a problem.
Written Comprehension	The ability to read and understand information and ideas presented in writing.
Speech Recognition	The ability to identify and understand the speech of another person.
Written Expression	The ability to communicate information and ideas in writing so others will understand.
Information Ordering	The ability to arrange things or actions in a certain order or pattern according to a specific rule or set of rules (e.g., patterns of numbers, letters, words, pictures, mathematical operations).
Deductive Reasoning	The ability to apply general rules to specific problems to produce answers that make sense.
Inductive Reasoning	The ability to combine pieces of information to form general rules or conclusions (includes finding a relationship among seemingly unrelated events).
Category Flexibility	The ability to generate or use different sets of rules for combining or grouping things in different ways.
Selective Attention	The ability to concentrate on a task over a period of time without being distracted.
Time Sharing	The ability to shift back and forth between two or more activities or sources of information (such as speech, sounds, touch, or other sources).
Mathematical Reasoning	The ability to choose the right mathematical methods or formulas to solve a problem.
Memorization	The ability to remember information such as words, numbers, pictures, and procedures.
Fluency of Ideas	The ability to come up with a number of ideas about a topic (the number of ideas is important, not their quality, correctness, or creativity).
Originality	The ability to come up with unusual or clever ideas about a given topic or situation, or to develop creative ways to solve a problem.
Flexibility of Closure	The ability to identify or detect a known pattern (a figure, object, word, or sound) that is hidden in other distracting material.
Far Vision	The ability to see details at a distance.
Perceptual Speed	The ability to quickly and accurately compare similarities and differences among sets of letters, numbers, objects, pictures, or patterns. The things to be compared may be presented at the same time or one after the other. This ability also includes comparing a presented object with a remembered object.
Number Facility	The ability to add, subtract, multiply, or divide quickly and correctly.
Speed of Closure	The ability to quickly make sense of, combine, and organize information into meaningful patterns.
Auditory Attention	The ability to focus on a single source of sound in the presence of other distracting sounds.
Finger Dexterity	The ability to make precisely coordinated movements of the fingers of one or both hands to grasp, manipulate, or assemble very small objects.
Manual Dexterity	The ability to quickly move your hand, your hand together with your arm, or your two hands to grasp, manipulate, or assemble objects.

Gross Body Coordination	The ability to coordinate the movement of your arms, legs, and torso together when the whole body is in motion.
Control Precision	The ability to quickly and repeatedly adjust the controls of a machine or a vehicle to exact positions.
Depth Perception	The ability to judge which of several objects is closer or farther away from you, or to judge the distance between you and an object.
Arm-Hand Steadiness	The ability to keep your hand and arm steady while moving your arm or while holding your arm and hand in one position.
Multilimb Coordination	The ability to coordinate two or more limbs (for example, two arms, two legs, or one leg and one arm) while sitting, standing, or lying down. It does not involve performing the activities while the whole body is in motion.
Reaction Time	The ability to quickly respond (with the hand, finger, or foot) to a signal (sound, light, picture) when it appears.
Visualization	The ability to imagine how something will look after it is moved around or when its parts are moved or rearranged.
Trunk Strength	The ability to use your abdominal and lower back muscles to support part of the body repeatedly or continuously over time without 'giving out' or fatiguing.
Response Orientation	The ability to choose quickly between two or more movements in response to two or more different signals (lights, sounds, pictures). It includes the speed with which the correct response is started with the hand, foot, or other body part.
Explosive Strength	The ability to use short bursts of muscle force to propel oneself (as in jumping or sprinting), or to throw an object.
Stamina	The ability to exert yourself physically over long periods of time without getting winded or out of breath.
Rate Control	The ability to time your movements or the movement of a piece of equipment in anticipation of changes in the speed and/or direction of a moving object or scene.
Static Strength	The ability to exert maximum muscle force to lift, push, pull, or carry objects.
Wrist-Finger Speed	The ability to make fast, simple, repeated movements of the fingers, hands, and wrists.
Peripheral Vision	The ability to see objects or movement of objects to one's side when the eyes are looking ahead.
Gross Body Equilibrium	The ability to keep or regain your body balance or stay upright when in an unstable position.
Visual Color Discrimination	The ability to match or detect differences between colors, including shades of color and brightness.
Glare Sensitivity	The ability to see objects in the presence of glare or bright lighting.
Hearing Sensitivity	The ability to detect or tell the differences between sounds that vary in pitch and loudness.
Dynamic Flexibility	The ability to quickly and repeatedly bend, stretch, twist, or reach out with your body, arms, and/or legs.
Extent Flexibility	The ability to bend, stretch, twist, or reach with your body, arms, and/or legs.
Night Vision	The ability to see under low light conditions.
Dynamic Strength	The ability to exert muscle force repeatedly or continuously over time. This involves muscular endurance and resistance to muscle fatigue.
Spatial Orientation	The ability to know your location in relation to the environment or to know where other objects are in relation to you.
Sound Localization	The ability to tell the direction from which a sound originated.
Speed of Limb Movement	The ability to quickly move the arms and legs.

Work_Activity	**Work_Activity Definitions**
Interacting With Computers	Using computers and computer systems (including hardware and software) to program, write software, set up functions, enter data, or process information.
Getting Information	Observing, receiving, and otherwise obtaining information from all relevant sources.
Processing Information	Compiling, coding, categorizing, calculating, tabulating, auditing, or verifying information or data.
Making Decisions and Solving Problems	Analyzing information and evaluating results to choose the best solution and solve problems.
Evaluating Information to Determine Compliance wit	Using relevant information and individual judgment to determine whether events or processes comply with laws, regulations, or standards.
Organizing, Planning, and Prioritizing Work	Developing specific goals and plans to prioritize, organize, and accomplish your work.
Communicating with Persons Outside Organization	Communicating with people outside the organization, representing the organization to customers, the public, government, and other external sources. This information can be exchanged in person, in writing, or by telephone or e-mail.

Documenting/Recording Information	Entering, transcribing, recording, storing, or maintaining information in written or electronic/magnetic form.
Updating and Using Relevant Knowledge	Keeping up-to-date technically and applying new knowledge to your job.
Communicating with Supervisors, Peers, or Subordin	Providing information to supervisors, co-workers, and subordinates by telephone, in written form, e-mail, or in person.
Resolving Conflicts and Negotiating with Others	Handling complaints, settling disputes, and resolving grievances and conflicts, or otherwise negotiating with others.
Performing Administrative Activities	Performing day-to-day administrative tasks such as maintaining information files and processing paperwork.
Establishing and Maintaining Interpersonal Relatio	Developing constructive and cooperative working relationships with others, and maintaining them over time.
Analyzing Data or Information	Identifying the underlying principles, reasons, or facts of information by breaking down information or data into separate parts.
Identifying Objects, Actions, and Events	Identifying information by categorizing, estimating, recognizing differences or similarities, and detecting changes in circumstances or events.
Monitor Processes, Materials, or Surroundings	Monitoring and reviewing information from materials, events, or the environment, to detect or assess problems.
Performing for or Working Directly with the Public	Performing for people or dealing directly with the public. This includes serving customers in restaurants and stores, and receiving clients or guests.
Interpreting the Meaning of Information for Others	Translating or explaining what information means and how it can be used.
Judging the Qualities of Things, Services, or Peop	Assessing the value, importance, or quality of things or people.
Estimating the Quantifiable Characteristics of Pro	Estimating sizes, distances, and quantities; or determining time, costs, resources, or materials needed to perform a work activity.
Coordinating the Work and Activities of Others	Getting members of a group to work together to accomplish tasks.
Developing Objectives and Strategies	Establishing long-range objectives and specifying the strategies and actions to achieve them.
Coaching and Developing Others	Identifying the developmental needs of others and coaching, mentoring, or otherwise helping others to improve their knowledge or skills.
Training and Teaching Others	Identifying the educational needs of others, developing formal educational or training programs or classes, and teaching or instructing others.
Inspecting Equipment, Structures, or Material	Inspecting equipment, structures, or materials to identify the cause of errors or other problems or defects.
Developing and Building Teams	Encouraging and building mutual trust, respect, and cooperation among team members.
Provide Consultation and Advice to Others	Providing guidance and expert advice to management or other groups on technical, systems-, or process-related topics.
Assisting and Caring for Others	Providing personal assistance, medical attention, emotional support, or other personal care to others such as coworkers, customers, or patients.
Selling or Influencing Others	Convincing others to buy merchandise/goods or to otherwise change their minds or actions.
Scheduling Work and Activities	Scheduling events, programs, and activities, as well as the work of others.
Monitoring and Controlling Resources	Monitoring and controlling resources and overseeing the spending of money.
Thinking Creatively	Developing, designing, or creating new applications, ideas, relationships, systems, or products, including artistic contributions.
Guiding, Directing, and Motivating Subordinates	Providing guidance and direction to subordinates, including setting performance standards and monitoring performance.
Handling and Moving Objects	Using hands and arms in handling, installing, positioning, and moving materials, and manipulating things.
Performing General Physical Activities	Performing physical activities that require considerable use of your arms and legs and moving your whole body, such as climbing, lifting, balancing, walking, stooping, and handling of materials.
Controlling Machines and Processes	Using either control mechanisms or direct physical activity to operate machines or processes (not including computers or vehicles).
Staffing Organizational Units	Recruiting, interviewing, selecting, hiring, and promoting employees in an organization.
Operating Vehicles, Mechanized Devices, or Equipme	Running, maneuvering, navigating, or driving vehicles or mechanized equipment, such as forklifts, passenger vehicles, aircraft, or water craft.

Repairing and Maintaining Electronic Equipment	Servicing, repairing, calibrating, regulating, fine-tuning, or testing machines, devices, and equipment that operate primarily on the basis of electrical or electronic (not mechanical) principles.
Repairing and Maintaining Mechanical Equipment	Servicing, repairing, adjusting, and testing machines, devices, moving parts, and equipment that operate primarily on the basis of mechanical (not electronic) principles.
Drafting, Laying Out, and Specifying Technical Dev	Providing documentation, detailed instructions, drawings, or specifications to tell others about how devices, parts, equipment, or structures are to be fabricated, constructed, assembled, modified, maintained, or used.

Work_Context	Work_Context Definitions
Telephone	How often do you have telephone conversations in this job?
Contact With Others	How much does this job require the worker to be in contact with others (face-to-face, by telephone, or otherwise) in order to perform it?
Importance of Being Exact or Accurate	How important is being very exact or highly accurate in performing this job?
Importance of Repeating Same Tasks	How important is repeating the same physical activities (e.g., key entry) or mental activities (e.g., checking entries in a ledger) over and over, without stopping, to performing this job?
Indoors, Environmentally Controlled	How often does this job require working indoors in environmentally controlled conditions?
Frequency of Decision Making	How frequently is the worker required to make decisions that affect other people, the financial resources, and/or the image and reputation of the organization?
Deal With Unpleasant or Angry People	How frequently does the worker have to deal with unpleasant, angry, or discourteous individuals as part of the job requirements?
Spend Time Sitting	How much does this job require sitting?
Deal With External Customers	How important is it to work with external customers or the public in this job?
Time Pressure	How often does this job require the worker to meet strict deadlines?
Work With Work Group or Team	How important is it to work with others in a group or team in this job?
Letters and Memos	How often does the job require written letters and memos?
Spend Time Making Repetitive Motions	How much does this job require making repetitive motions?
Face-to-Face Discussions	How often do you have to have face-to-face discussions with individuals or teams in this job?
Impact of Decisions on Co-workers or Company Resul	How do the decisions an employee makes impact the results of co-workers, clients or the company?
Frequency of Conflict Situations	How often are there conflict situations the employee has to face in this job?
Freedom to Make Decisions	How much decision making freedom, without supervision, does the job offer?
Structured versus Unstructured Work	To what extent is this job structured for the worker, rather than allowing the worker to determine tasks, priorities, and goals?
Spend Time Using Your Hands to Handle, Control, or	How much does this job require using your hands to handle, control, or feel objects, tools or controls?
Electronic Mail	How often do you use electronic mail in this job?
Coordinate or Lead Others	How important is it to coordinate or lead others in accomplishing work activities in this job?
Physical Proximity	To what extent does this job require the worker to perform job tasks in close physical proximity to other people?
Responsibility for Outcomes and Results	How responsible is the worker for work outcomes and results of other workers?
Degree of Automation	How automated is the job?
Sounds, Noise Levels Are Distracting or Uncomforta	How often does this job require working exposed to sounds and noise levels that are distracting or uncomfortable?
Level of Competition	To what extent does this job require the worker to compete or to be aware of competitive pressures?
Responsible for Others' Health and Safety	How much responsibility is there for the health and safety of others in this job?
Consequence of Error	How serious would the result usually be if the worker made a mistake that was not readily correctable?
Exposed to Contaminants	How often does this job require working exposed to contaminants (such as pollutants, gases, dust or odors)?
Spend Time Walking and Running	How much does this job require walking and running?
Spend Time Standing	How much does this job require standing?
Spend Time Bending or Twisting the Body	How much does this job require bending or twisting your body?

Deal With Physically Aggressive People	How frequently does this job require the worker to deal with physical aggression of violent individuals?
Public Speaking	How often do you have to perform public speaking in this job?
Cramped Work Space, Awkward Positions	How often does this job require working in cramped work spaces that requires getting into awkward positions?
Pace Determined by Speed of Equipment	How important is it to this job that the pace is determined by the speed of equipment or machinery? (This does not refer to keeping busy at all times on this job.)
Extremely Bright or Inadequate Lighting	How often does this job require working in extremely bright or inadequate lighting conditions?
In an Enclosed Vehicle or Equipment	How often does this job require working in a closed vehicle or equipment (e.g., car)?
Exposed to Disease or Infections	How often does this job require exposure to disease/infections?
Spend Time Kneeling, Crouching, Stooping, or Crawl	How much does this job require kneeling, crouching, stooping, or crawling?
Outdoors, Exposed to Weather	How often does this job require working outdoors, exposed to all weather conditions?
Very Hot or Cold Temperatures	How often does this job require working in very hot (above 90 F degrees) or very cold (below 32 F degrees) temperatures?
Spend Time Keeping or Regaining Balance	How much does this job require keeping or regaining your balance?
Indoors, Not Environmentally Controlled	How often does this job require working indoors in non-controlled environmental conditions (e.g.. warehouse without heat)?
Exposed to Hazardous Conditions	How often does this job require exposure to hazardous conditions?
Wear Common Protective or Safety Equipment such as	How much does this job require wearing common protective or safety equipment such as safety shoes, glasses, gloves, hard hats or live jackets?
Exposed to Minor Burns, Cuts, Bites, or Stings	How often does this job require exposure to minor burns, cuts, bites, or stings?
Exposed to Radiation	How often does this job require exposure to radiation?
Outdoors, Under Cover	How often does this job require working outdoors, under cover (e.g., structure with roof but no walls)?
In an Open Vehicle or Equipment	How often does this job require working in an open vehicle or equipment (e.g., tractor)?
Wear Specialized Protective or Safety Equipment su	How much does this job require wearing specialized protective or safety equipment such as breathing apparatus, safety harness, full protection suits, or radiation protection?
Exposed to Hazardous Equipment	How often does this job require exposure to hazardous equipment?
Exposed to High Places	How often does this job require exposure to high places?
Spend Time Climbing Ladders, Scaffolds, or Poles	How much does this job require climbing ladders, scaffolds, or poles?
Exposed to Whole Body Vibration	How often does this job require exposure to whole body vibration (e.g., operate a jackhammer)?

Job Zone Component	Job Zone Component Definitions
Title	Job Zone Three: Medium Preparation Needed
Overall Experience	Previous work-related skill, knowledge, or experience is required for these occupations. For example, an electrician must have completed three or four years of apprenticeship or several years of vocational training, and often must have passed a licensing exam, in order to perform the job.
Job Training	Employees in these occupations usually need one or two years of training involving both on-the-job experience and informal training with experienced workers.
Job Zone Examples	These occupations usually involve using communication and organizational skills to coordinate, supervise, manage, or train others to accomplish goals. Examples include dental assistants, electricians,fish and game wardens, legal secretaries, personnel recruiters, and recreation workers.
SVP Range	(6.0 to < 7.0)
Education	Most occupations in this zone require training in vocational schools, related on-the-job experience, or an associate's degree. Some may require a bachelor's degree.

Work_Styles	Work_Styles Definitions
Attention to Detail	Job requires being careful about detail and thorough in completing work tasks.
Integrity	Job requires being honest and ethical.
Dependability	Job requires being reliable. responsible, and dependable, and fulfilling obligations.
Self Control	Job requires maintaining composure, keeping emotions in check, controlling anger. and avoiding aggressive behavior, even in very difficult situations.
Independence	Job requires developing one's own ways of doing things, guiding oneself with little or no supervision, and depending on oneself to get things done.
Cooperation	Job requires being pleasant with others on the job and displaying a good-natured, cooperative attitude.
Stress Tolerance	Job requires accepting criticism and dealing calmly and effectively with high stress situations.
Adaptability/Flexibility	Job requires being open to change (positive or negative) and to considerable variety in the workplace.
Persistence	Job requires persistence in the face of obstacles.
Initiative	Job requires a willingness to take on responsibilities and challenges.
Concern for Others	Job requires being sensitive to others' needs and feelings and being understanding and helpful on the job.
Achievement/Effort	Job requires establishing and maintaining personally challenging achievement goals and exerting effort toward mastering tasks.
Analytical Thinking	Job requires analyzing information and using logic to address work-related issues and problems.
Social Orientation	Job requires preferring to work with others rather than alone, and being personally connected with others on the job.
Innovation	Job requires creativity and alternative thinking to develop new ideas for and answers to work-related problems.
Leadership	Job requires a willingness to lead, take charge, and offer opinions and direction.

43-3021.01 - Statement Clerks

Prepare and distribute bank statements to customers, answer inquiries, and reconcile discrepancies in records and accounts.

Tasks

1) Take orders for imprinted checks.

2) Monitor equipment in order to ensure proper operation.

3) Post stop-payment notices in order to prevent payment of protested checks.

4) Fix minor problems, such as equipment jams, and notify repair personnel of major equipment problems.

5) Verify signatures and required information on checks.

6) Match statements with batches of canceled checks by account numbers.

7) Maintain files of canceled checks and customers' signatures.

8) Load machines with statements, cancelled checks, and envelopes in order to prepare statements for distribution to customers, or stuff envelopes by hand.

9) Encode and cancel checks, using bank machines.

10) Compare previously prepared bank statements with canceled checks, and reconcile discrepancies.

11) Route statements for mailing or over-the-counter delivery to customers.

12) Weigh envelopes containing statements in order to determine correct postage and affix postage using stamps or metering equipment.

43-3021.02 - Billing, Cost, and Rate Clerks

Compile data, compute fees and charges, and prepare invoices for billing purposes. Duties include computing costs and calculating rates for goods, services, and shipment of goods; posting data; and keeping other relevant records. May involve use of computer or typewriter, calculator, and adding and bookkeeping machines.

Tasks

1) Operate typing, adding, calculating, and billing machines.

2) Contact customers in order to obtain or relay account information.

3) Perform bookkeeping work, including posting data and keeping other records concerning costs of goods and services and the shipment of goods.

4) Prepare itemized statements, bills, or invoices; and record amounts due for items purchased or services rendered.

5) Resolve discrepancies in accounting records.

6) Type billing documents, shipping labels, credit memorandums, and credit forms, using typewriters or computers.

7) Keep records of invoices and support documents.

8) Review documents such as purchase orders, sales tickets, charge slips, or hospital records in order to compute fees and charges due.

9) Answer mail and telephone inquiries regarding rates, routing, and procedures.

10) Compute credit terms, discounts, shipment charges, and rates for goods and services in order to complete billing documents.

11) Update manuals when rates, rules, or regulations are amended.

12) Consult sources such as rate books, manuals, and insurance company representatives in order to determine specific charges and information such as rules, regulations, and government tax and tariff information.

13) Compile reports of cost factors, such as labor, production, storage, and equipment.

14) Estimate market value of products or services.

15) Track accumulated hours and dollar amounts charged to each client job in order to calculate client fees for professional services such as legal and accounting services.

16) Review compiled data on operating costs and revenues in order to set rates.

Knowledge	Knowledge Definitions
Clerical	Knowledge of administrative and clerical procedures and systems such as word processing, managing files and records, stenography and transcription, designing forms, and other office procedures and terminology.
English Language	Knowledge of the structure and content of the English language including the meaning and spelling of words, rules of composition, and grammar.
Mathematics	Knowledge of arithmetic, algebra, geometry, calculus, statistics, and their applications.
Customer and Personal Service	Knowledge of principles and processes for providing customer and personal services. This includes customer needs assessment, meeting quality standards for services, and evaluation of customer satisfaction.
Computers and Electronics	Knowledge of circuit boards, processors, chips, electronic equipment, and computer hardware and software, including applications and programming.
Administration and Management	Knowledge of business and management principles involved in strategic planning, resource allocation, human resources modeling, leadership technique, production methods, and coordination of people and resources.
Economics and Accounting	Knowledge of economic and accounting principles and practices, the financial markets, banking and the analysis and reporting of financial data.
Education and Training	Knowledge of principles and methods for curriculum and training design, teaching and instruction for individuals and groups, and the measurement of training effects.
Law and Government	Knowledge of laws, legal codes, court procedures, precedents, government regulations, executive orders, agency rules, and the democratic political process.
Medicine and Dentistry	Knowledge of the information and techniques needed to diagnose and treat human injuries, diseases, and deformities. This includes symptoms, treatment alternatives, drug properties and interactions, and preventive health-care measures.
Transportation	Knowledge of principles and methods for moving people or goods by air, rail, sea, or road, including the relative costs and benefits.
Communications and Media	Knowledge of media production, communication, and dissemination techniques and methods. This includes alternative ways to inform and entertain via written, oral, and visual media.
Personnel and Human Resources	Knowledge of principles and procedures for personnel recruitment, selection, training, compensation and benefits, labor relations and negotiation, and personnel information systems.

Sales and Marketing	Knowledge of principles and methods for showing, promoting, and selling products or services. This includes marketing strategy and tactics, product demonstration, sales techniques, and sales control systems.
Telecommunications	Knowledge of transmission, broadcasting, switching, control, and operation of telecommunications systems.
Public Safety and Security	Knowledge of relevant equipment, policies, procedures, and strategies to promote effective local, state, or national security operations for the protection of people, data, property, and institutions.
Psychology	Knowledge of human behavior and performance; individual differences in ability, personality, and interests; learning and motivation; psychological research methods; and the assessment and treatment of behavioral and affective disorders.
Philosophy and Theology	Knowledge of different philosophical systems and religions. This includes their basic principles, values, ethics, ways of thinking, customs, practices, and their impact on human culture.
Sociology and Anthropology	Knowledge of group behavior and dynamics, societal trends and influences, human migrations, ethnicity, cultures and their history and origins.
Therapy and Counseling	Knowledge of principles, methods, and procedures for diagnosis, treatment, and rehabilitation of physical and mental dysfunctions, and for career counseling and guidance.
Mechanical	Knowledge of machines and tools, including their designs, uses, repair, and maintenance.
Production and Processing	Knowledge of raw materials, production processes, quality control, costs, and other techniques for maximizing the effective manufacture and distribution of goods.
Foreign Language	Knowledge of the structure and content of a foreign (non-English) language including the meaning and spelling of words, rules of composition and grammar, and pronunciation.
Engineering and Technology	Knowledge of the practical application of engineering science and technology. This includes applying principles, techniques, procedures, and equipment to the design and production of various goods and services.
Design	Knowledge of design techniques, tools, and principles involved in production of precision technical plans, blueprints, drawings, and models.
Geography	Knowledge of principles and methods for describing the features of land, sea, and air masses, including their physical characteristics, locations, interrelationships, and distribution of plant, animal, and human life.
History and Archeology	Knowledge of historical events and their causes, indicators, and effects on civilizations and cultures.
Physics	Knowledge and prediction of physical principles, laws, their interrelationships, and applications to understanding fluid, material, and atmospheric dynamics, and mechanical, electrical, atomic and sub-atomic structures and processes.
Chemistry	Knowledge of the chemical composition, structure, and properties of substances and of the chemical processes and transformations that they undergo. This includes uses of chemicals and their interactions, danger signs, production techniques, and disposal methods.
Food Production	Knowledge of techniques and equipment for planting, growing, and harvesting food products (both plant and animal) for consumption, including storage/handling techniques.
Building and Construction	Knowledge of materials, methods, and the tools involved in the construction or repair of houses, buildings, or other structures such as highways and roads.
Biology	Knowledge of plant and animal organisms, their tissues, cells, functions, interdependencies, and interactions with each other and the environment.
Fine Arts	Knowledge of the theory and techniques required to compose, produce, and perform works of music, dance, visual arts, drama, and sculpture.

Skills	Skills Definitions
Active Listening	Giving full attention to what other people are saying, taking time to understand the points being made, asking questions as appropriate, and not interrupting at inappropriate times.
Speaking	Talking to others to convey information effectively.
Mathematics	Using mathematics to solve problems.
Reading Comprehension	Understanding written sentences and paragraphs in work related documents.
Writing	Communicating effectively in writing as appropriate for the needs of the audience.

Time Management	Managing one's own time and the time of others.	Inductive Reasoning	The ability to combine pieces of information to form general rules or conclusions (includes finding a relationship among seemingly unrelated events).
Social Perceptiveness	Being aware of others' reactions and understanding why they react as they do.	Category Flexibility	The ability to generate or use different sets of rules for combining or grouping things in different ways.
Instructing	Teaching others how to do something.	Mathematical Reasoning	The ability to choose the right mathematical methods or formulas to solve a problem.
Critical Thinking	Using logic and reasoning to identify the strengths and weaknesses of alternative solutions, conclusions or approaches to problems.	Number Facility	The ability to add, subtract, multiply, or divide quickly and correctly.
Active Learning	Understanding the implications of new information for both current and future problem-solving and decision-making.	Selective Attention	The ability to concentrate on a task over a period of time without being distracted.
Monitoring	Monitoring/Assessing performance of yourself, other individuals, or organizations to make improvements or take corrective action.	Written Expression	The ability to communicate information and ideas in writing so others will understand.
Service Orientation	Actively looking for ways to help people.		
Learning Strategies	Selecting and using training/instructional methods and procedures appropriate for the situation when learning or teaching new things.	Perceptual Speed	The ability to quickly and accurately compare similarities and differences among sets of letters, numbers, objects, pictures, or patterns. The things to be compared may be presented at the same time or one after the other. This ability also includes comparing a presented object with a remembered object.
Complex Problem Solving	Identifying complex problems and reviewing related information to develop and evaluate options and implement solutions.	Flexibility of Closure	The ability to identify or detect a known pattern (a figure, object, word, or sound) that is hidden in other distracting material.
Coordination	Adjusting actions in relation to others' actions.		
Management of Personnel Resources	Motivating, developing, and directing people as they work, identifying the best people for the job.	Speed of Closure	The ability to quickly make sense of, combine, and organize information into meaningful patterns.
Negotiation	Bringing others together and trying to reconcile differences.	Finger Dexterity	The ability to make precisely coordinated movements of the fingers of one or both hands to grasp, manipulate, or assemble very small objects.
Judgment and Decision Making	Considering the relative costs and benefits of potential actions to choose the most appropriate one.	Memorization	The ability to remember information such as words, numbers, pictures, and procedures.
Persuasion	Persuading others to change their minds or behavior.		
Equipment Selection	Determining the kind of tools and equipment needed to do a job.	Originality	The ability to come up with unusual or clever ideas about a given topic or situation, or to develop creative ways to solve a problem.
Operation and Control	Controlling operations of equipment or systems.	Far Vision	The ability to see details at a distance.
Technology Design	Generating or adapting equipment and technology to serve user needs.	Fluency of Ideas	The ability to come up with a number of ideas about a topic (the number of ideas is important, not their quality, correctness, or creativity).
Troubleshooting	Determining causes of operating errors and deciding what to do about it.		
Management of Financial Resources	Determining how money will be spent to get the work done, and accounting for these expenditures.	Time Sharing	The ability to shift back and forth between two or more activities or sources of information (such as speech, sounds, touch, or other sources).
Operations Analysis	Analyzing needs and product requirements to create a design.	Hearing Sensitivity	The ability to detect or tell the differences between sounds that vary in pitch and loudness.
Systems Evaluation	Identifying measures or indicators of system performance and the actions needed to improve or correct performance, relative to the goals of the system.	Visualization	The ability to imagine how something will look after it is moved around or when its parts are moved or rearranged.
Equipment Maintenance	Performing routine maintenance on equipment and determining when and what kind of maintenance is needed.	Manual Dexterity	The ability to quickly move your hand, your hand together with your arm, or your two hands to grasp, manipulate, or assemble objects.
Repairing	Repairing machines or systems using the needed tools.		
Systems Analysis	Determining how a system should work and how changes in conditions, operations, and the environment will affect outcomes.	Control Precision	The ability to quickly and repeatedly adjust the controls of a machine or a vehicle to exact positions.
Quality Control Analysis	Conducting tests and inspections of products, services, or processes to evaluate quality or performance.	Visual Color Discrimination	The ability to match or detect differences between colors, including shades of color and brightness.
Installation	Installing equipment, machines, wiring, or programs to meet specifications.	Arm-Hand Steadiness	The ability to keep your hand and arm steady while moving your arm or while holding your arm and hand in one position.
Management of Material Resources	Obtaining and seeing to the appropriate use of equipment, facilities, and materials needed to do certain work.	Wrist-Finger Speed	The ability to make fast, simple, repeated movements of the fingers, hands, and wrists.
Operation Monitoring	Watching gauges, dials, or other indicators to make sure a machine is working properly.	Auditory Attention	The ability to focus on a single source of sound in the presence of other distracting sounds.
Programming	Writing computer programs for various purposes.		
Science	Using scientific rules and methods to solve problems.	Trunk Strength	The ability to use your abdominal and lower back muscles to support part of the body repeatedly or continuously over time without 'giving out' or fatiguing.
Ability	**Ability Definitions**	Reaction Time	The ability to quickly respond (with the hand, finger, or foot) to a signal (sound, light, picture) when it appears.
Oral Expression	The ability to communicate information and ideas in speaking so others will understand.	Gross Body Coordination	The ability to coordinate the movement of your arms, legs, and torso together when the whole body is in motion.
Oral Comprehension	The ability to listen to and understand information and ideas presented through spoken words and sentences.	Dynamic Flexibility	The ability to quickly and repeatedly bend, stretch, twist, or reach out with your body, arms, and/or legs.
Speech Clarity	The ability to speak clearly so others can understand you.	Dynamic Strength	The ability to exert muscle force repeatedly or continuously over time. This involves muscular endurance and resistance to muscle fatigue.
Speech Recognition	The ability to identify and understand the speech of another person.		
Problem Sensitivity	The ability to tell when something is wrong or is likely to go wrong. It does not involve solving the problem, only recognizing there is a problem.	Stamina	The ability to exert yourself physically over long periods of time without getting winded or out of breath.
Deductive Reasoning	The ability to apply general rules to specific problems to produce answers that make sense.	Explosive Strength	The ability to use short bursts of muscle force to propel oneself (as in jumping or sprinting), or to throw an object.
Written Comprehension	The ability to read and understand information and ideas presented in writing.	Static Strength	The ability to exert maximum muscle force to lift, push, pull, or carry objects.
Near Vision	The ability to see details at close range (within a few feet of the observer).	Speed of Limb Movement	The ability to quickly move the arms and legs.
		Gross Body Equilibrium	The ability to keep or regain your body balance or stay upright when in an unstable position.
Information Ordering	The ability to arrange things or actions in a certain order or pattern according to a specific rule or set of rules (e.g., patterns of numbers, letters, words, pictures, mathematical operations).	Spatial Orientation	The ability to know your location in relation to the environment or to know where other objects are in relation to you.

Extent Flexibility	The ability to bend, stretch, twist, or reach with your body, arms, and/or legs.
Response Orientation	The ability to choose quickly between two or more movements in response to two or more different signals (lights, sounds, pictures). It includes the speed with which the correct response is started with the hand, foot, or other body part.
Sound Localization	The ability to tell the direction from which a sound originated.
Depth Perception	The ability to judge which of several objects is closer or farther away from you, or to judge the distance between you and an object.
Peripheral Vision	The ability to see objects or movement of objects to one's side when the eyes are looking ahead.
Night Vision	The ability to see under low light conditions.
Multilimb Coordination	The ability to coordinate two or more limbs (for example, two arms, two legs, or one leg and one arm) while sitting, standing, or lying down. It does not involve performing the activities while the whole body is in motion.
Rate Control	The ability to time your movements or the movement of a piece of equipment in anticipation of changes in the speed and/or direction of a moving object or scene.
Glare Sensitivity	The ability to see objects in the presence of glare or bright lighting.

Work_Activity	Work_Activity Definitions
Interacting With Computers	Using computers and computer systems (including hardware and software) to program, write software, set up functions, enter data, or process information.
Communicating with Supervisors, Peers, or Subordin	Providing information to supervisors, co-workers, and subordinates by telephone, in written form, e-mail, or in person.
Getting Information	Observing, receiving, and otherwise obtaining information from all relevant sources.
Establishing and Maintaining Interpersonal Relatio	Developing constructive and cooperative working relationships with others, and maintaining them over time.
Updating and Using Relevant Knowledge	Keeping up-to-date technically and applying new knowledge to your job.
Processing Information	Compiling, coding, categorizing, calculating, tabulating, auditing, or verifying information or data.
Analyzing Data or Information	Identifying the underlying principles, reasons, or facts of information by breaking down information or data into separate parts.
Organizing, Planning, and Prioritizing Work	Developing specific goals and plans to prioritize, organize, and accomplish your work.
Documenting/Recording Information	Entering, transcribing, recording, storing, or maintaining information in written or electronic/magnetic form.
Performing Administrative Activities	Performing day-to-day administrative tasks such as maintaining information files and processing paperwork.
Evaluating Information to Determine Compliance wit	Using relevant information and individual judgment to determine whether events or processes comply with laws, regulations, or standards.
Making Decisions and Solving Problems	Analyzing information and evaluating results to choose the best solution and solve problems.
Communicating with Persons Outside Organization	Communicating with people outside the organization, representing the organization to customers, the public, government, and other external sources. This information can be exchanged in person, in writing, or by telephone or e-mail.
Identifying Objects, Actions, and Events	Identifying information by categorizing, estimating, recognizing differences or similarities, and detecting changes in circumstances or events.
Interpreting the Meaning of Information for Others	Translating or explaining what information means and how it can be used.
Assisting and Caring for Others	Providing personal assistance, medical attention, emotional support, or other personal care to others such as coworkers, customers, or patients.
Resolving Conflicts and Negotiating with Others	Handling complaints, settling disputes, and resolving grievances and conflicts, or otherwise negotiating with others.
Monitor Processes, Materials, or Surroundings	Monitoring and reviewing information from materials, events, or the environment, to detect or assess problems.
Judging the Qualities of Things, Services, or Peop	Assessing the value, importance, or quality of things or people.
Estimating the Quantifiable Characteristics of Pro	Estimating sizes, distances, and quantities; or determining time, costs, resources, or materials needed to perform a work activity.

Thinking Creatively	Developing, designing, or creating new applications, ideas, relationships, systems, or products, including artistic contributions.
Developing Objectives and Strategies	Establishing long-range objectives and specifying the strategies and actions to achieve them.
Developing and Building Teams	Encouraging and building mutual trust, respect, and cooperation among team members.
Training and Teaching Others	Identifying the educational needs of others, developing formal educational or training programs or classes, and teaching or instructing others.
Coordinating the Work and Activities of Others	Getting members of a group to work together to accomplish tasks.
Performing for or Working Directly with the Public	Performing for people or dealing directly with the public. This includes serving customers in restaurants and stores, and receiving clients or guests.
Provide Consultation and Advice to Others	Providing guidance and expert advice to management or other groups on technical, systems-, or process-related topics.
Scheduling Work and Activities	Scheduling events, programs, and activities, as well as the work of others.
Coaching and Developing Others	Identifying the developmental needs of others and coaching, mentoring, or otherwise helping others to improve their knowledge or skills.
Staffing Organizational Units	Recruiting, interviewing, selecting, hiring, and promoting employees in an organization.
Handling and Moving Objects	Using hands and arms in handling, installing, positioning, and moving materials, and manipulating things.
Monitoring and Controlling Resources	Monitoring and controlling resources and overseeing the spending of money.
Performing General Physical Activities	Performing physical activities that require considerable use of your arms and legs and moving your whole body, such as climbing, lifting, balancing, walking, stooping, and handling of materials.
Guiding, Directing, and Motivating Subordinates	Providing guidance and direction to subordinates, including setting performance standards and monitoring performance.
Selling or Influencing Others	Convincing others to buy merchandise/goods or to otherwise change their minds or actions.
Inspecting Equipment, Structures, or Material	Inspecting equipment, structures, or materials to identify the cause of errors or other problems or defects.
Controlling Machines and Processes	Using either control mechanisms or direct physical activity to operate machines or processes (not including computers or vehicles).
Repairing and Maintaining Electronic Equipment	Servicing, repairing, calibrating, regulating, fine-tuning, or testing machines, devices, and equipment that operate primarily on the basis of electrical or electronic (not mechanical) principles.
Repairing and Maintaining Mechanical Equipment	Servicing, repairing, adjusting, and testing machines, devices, moving parts, and equipment that operate primarily on the basis of mechanical (not electronic) principles.
Operating Vehicles, Mechanized Devices, or Equipme	Running, maneuvering, navigating, or driving vehicles or mechanized equipment, such as forklifts, passenger vehicles, aircraft, or water craft.
Drafting, Laying Out, and Specifying Technical Dev	Providing documentation, detailed instructions, drawings, or specifications to tell others about how devices, parts, equipment, or structures are to be fabricated, constructed, assembled, modified, maintained, or used.

Work_Context	Work_Context Definitions
Telephone	How often do you have telephone conversations in this job?
Face-to-Face Discussions	How often do you have to have face-to-face discussions with individuals or teams in this job?
Contact With Others	How much does this job require the worker to be in contact with others (face-to-face, by telephone, or otherwise) in order to perform it?
Frequency of Decision Making	How frequently is the worker required to make decisions that affect other people, the financial resources, and/or the image and reputation of the organization?
Freedom to Make Decisions	How much decision making freedom, without supervision, does the job offer?
Importance of Being Exact or Accurate	How important is being very exact or highly accurate in performing this job?
Spend Time Sitting	How much does this job require sitting?
Indoors, Environmentally Controlled	How often does this job require working indoors in environmentally controlled conditions?
Structured versus Unstructured Work	To what extent is this job structured for the worker, rather than allowing the worker to determine tasks, priorities, and goals?
Electronic Mail	How often do you use electronic mail in this job?

Work With Work Group or Team	How important is it to work with others in a group or team in this job?
Letters and Memos	How often does the job require written letters and memos?
Deal With External Customers	How important is it to work with external customers or the public in this job?
Importance of Repeating Same Tasks	How important is repeating the same physical activities (e.g., key entry) or mental activities (e.g., checking entries in a ledger) over and over, without stopping, to performing this job?
Impact of Decisions on Co-workers or Company Resul	How do the decisions an employee makes impact the results of co-workers, clients or the company?
Time Pressure	How often does this job require the worker to meet strict deadlines?
Responsibility for Outcomes and Results	How responsible is the worker for work outcomes and results of other workers?
Coordinate or Lead Others	How important is it to coordinate or lead others in accomplishing work activities in this job?
Deal With Unpleasant or Angry People	How frequently does the worker have to deal with unpleasant, angry, or discourteous individuals as part of the job requirements?
Physical Proximity	To what extent does this job require the worker to perform job tasks in close physical proximity to other people?
Frequency of Conflict Situations	How often are there conflict situations the employee has to face in this job?
Spend Time Using Your Hands to Handle, Control, or	How much does this job require using your hands to handle, control, or feel objects, tools or controls?
Level of Competition	To what extent does this job require the worker to compete or to be aware of competitive pressures?
Spend Time Making Repetitive Motions	How much does this job require making repetitive motions?
Consequence of Error	How serious would the result usually be if the worker made a mistake that was not readily correctable?
Degree of Automation	How automated is the job?
Responsible for Others' Health and Safety	How much responsibility is there for the health and safety of others in this job?
Exposed to Contaminants	How often does this job require working exposed to contaminants (such as pollutants, gases, dust or odors)?
Spend Time Standing	How much does this job require standing?
Spend Time Walking and Running	How much does this job require walking and running?
Sounds, Noise Levels Are Distracting or Uncomforta	How often does this job require working exposed to sounds and noise levels that are distracting or uncomfortable?
Spend Time Bending or Twisting the Body	How much does this job require bending or twisting your body?
In an Enclosed Vehicle or Equipment	How often does this job require working in a closed vehicle or equipment (e.g., car)?
Exposed to Radiation	How often does this job require exposure to radiation?
Wear Common Protective or Safety Equipment such as	How much does this job require wearing common protective or safety equipment such as safety shoes, glasses, gloves, hard hats or live jackets?
Spend Time Kneeling, Crouching, Stooping, or Crawl	How much does this job require kneeling, crouching, stooping or crawling?
Outdoors, Exposed to Weather	How often does this job require working outdoors, exposed to all weather conditions?
Exposed to Hazardous Conditions	How often does this job require exposure to hazardous conditions?
Outdoors, Under Cover	How often does this job require working outdoors, under cover (e.g., structure with roof but no walls)?
Public Speaking	How often do you have to perform public speaking in this job?
Pace Determined by Speed of Equipment	How important is it to this job that the pace is determined by the speed of equipment or machinery? (This does not refer to keeping busy at all times on this job.)
Exposed to Disease or Infections	How often does this job require exposure to disease/infections?
Exposed to Minor Burns, Cuts, Bites, or Stings	How often does this job require exposure to minor burns, cuts, bites, or stings?
Very Hot or Cold Temperatures	How often does this job require working in very hot (above 90 F degrees) or very cold (below 32 F degrees) temperatures?
Deal With Physically Aggressive People	How frequently does this job require the worker to deal with physical aggression of violent individuals?
Indoors, Not Environmentally Controlled	How often does this job require working indoors in non-controlled environmental conditions (e.g., warehouse without heat)?
Exposed to High Places	How often does this job require exposure to high places?
Cramped Work Space, Awkward Positions	How often does this job require working in cramped work spaces that requires getting into awkward positions?

Extremely Bright or Inadequate Lighting	How often does this job require working in extremely bright or inadequate lighting conditions?
Wear Specialized Protective or Safety Equipment su	How much does this job require wearing specialized protective or safety equipment such as breathing apparatus, safety harness, full protection suits, or radiation protection?
Spend Time Climbing Ladders, Scaffolds, or Poles	How much does this job require climbing ladders, scaffolds, or poles?
Spend Time Keeping or Regaining Balance	How much does this job require keeping or regaining your balance?
In an Open Vehicle or Equipment	How often does this job require working in an open vehicle or equipment (e.g., tractor)?
Exposed to Hazardous Equipment	How often does this job require exposure to hazardous equipment?
Exposed to Whole Body Vibration	How often does this job require exposure to whole body vibration (e.g., operate a jackhammer)?

Job Zone Component	Job Zone Component Definitions
Title	Job Zone Three: Medium Preparation Needed
Overall Experience	Previous work-related skill, knowledge, or experience is required for these occupations. For example, an electrician must have completed three or four years of apprenticeship or several years of vocational training, and often must have passed a licensing exam, in order to perform the job.
Job Training	Employees in these occupations usually need one or two years of training involving both on-the-job experience and informal training with experienced workers.
Job Zone Examples	These occupations usually involve using communication and organizational skills to coordinate, supervise, manage, or train others to accomplish goals. Examples include dental assistants, electricians, fish and game wardens, legal secretaries, personnel recruiters, and recreation workers.
SVP Range	(6.0 to < 7.0)
Education	Most occupations in this zone require training in vocational schools, related on-the-job experience, or an associate's degree. Some may require a bachelor's degree.

Work_Styles	Work_Styles Definitions
Attention to Detail	Job requires being careful about detail and thorough in completing work tasks.
Dependability	Job requires being reliable, responsible, and dependable, and fulfilling obligations.
Integrity	Job requires being honest and ethical.
Cooperation	Job requires being pleasant with others on the job and displaying a good-natured, cooperative attitude.
Initiative	Job requires a willingness to take on responsibilities and challenges.
Self Control	Job requires maintaining composure, keeping emotions in check, controlling anger, and avoiding aggressive behavior, even in very difficult situations.
Stress Tolerance	Job requires accepting criticism and dealing calmly and effectively with high stress situations.
Independence	Job requires developing one's own ways of doing things, guiding oneself with little or no supervision, and depending on oneself to get things done.
Adaptability/Flexibility	Job requires being open to change (positive or negative) and to considerable variety in the workplace.
Concern for Others	Job requires being sensitive to others' needs and feelings and being understanding and helpful on the job.
Persistence	Job requires persistence in the face of obstacles.
Achievement/Effort	Job requires establishing and maintaining personally challenging achievement goals and exerting effort toward mastering tasks.
Social Orientation	Job requires preferring to work with others rather than alone, and being personally connected with others on the job.
Analytical Thinking	Job requires analyzing information and using logic to address work-related issues and problems.
Leadership	Job requires a willingness to lead, take charge, and offer opinions and direction.
Innovation	Job requires creativity and alternative thinking to develop new ideas for and answers to work-related problems.

43-3031.00 - Bookkeeping, Accounting, and Auditing Clerks

Compute, classify, and record numerical data to keep financial records complete. Perform any combination of routine calculating, posting, and verifying duties to obtain primary financial data for use in maintaining accounting records. May also check the accuracy of figures, calculations, and postings pertaining to business transactions recorded by other workers.

Tasks

1) Perform general office duties such as filing, answering telephones, and handling routine correspondence.

2) Operate computers programmed with accounting software to record, store, and analyze information.

3) Check figures, postings, and documents for correct entry, mathematical accuracy, and proper codes.

4) Access computerized financial information to answer general questions as well as those related to specific accounts.

5) Comply with federal, state, and company policies, procedures, and regulations.

6) Debit, credit, and total accounts on computer spreadsheets and databases, using specialized accounting software.

7) Classify, record, and summarize numerical and financial data in order to compile and keep financial records, using journals and ledgers or computers.

8) Reconcile or note and report discrepancies found in records.

9) Compile statistical, financial, accounting or auditing reports and tables pertaining to such matters as cash receipts, expenditures, accounts payable and receivable, and profits and losses.

10) Perform financial calculations such as amounts due, interest charges, balances, discounts, equity, and principal.

11) Calculate, prepare, and issue bills, invoices, account statements, and other financial statements according to established procedures.

12) Code documents according to company procedures.

13) Reconcile records of bank transactions.

14) Receive, record, and bank cash, checks, and vouchers.

15) Transfer details from separate journals to general ledgers and/or data processing sheets.

16) Calculate and prepare checks for utilities, taxes, and other payments.

17) Compare computer printouts to manually maintained journals in order to determine if they match.

18) Prepare bank deposits by compiling data from cashiers, verifying and balancing receipts, and sending cash, checks, or other forms of payment to banks.

19) Match order forms with invoices, and record the necessary information.

20) Monitor status of loans and accounts to ensure that payments are up to date.

21) Compile budget data and documents, based on estimated revenues and expenses and previous budgets.

22) Calculate costs of materials, overhead and other expenses, based on estimates, quotations and price lists.

23) Prepare trial balances of books.

24) Complete and submit tax forms and returns, workers' compensation forms, pension contribution forms, and other government documents.

25) Maintain inventory records.

26) Prepare purchase orders and expense reports.

27) Perform personal bookkeeping services.

28) Compute deductions for income and social security taxes.

Knowledge	Knowledge Definitions
Clerical	Knowledge of administrative and clerical procedures and systems such as word processing, managing files and records, stenography and transcription, designing forms, and other office procedures and terminology.
Mathematics	Knowledge of arithmetic, algebra, geometry, calculus, statistics, and their applications.
English Language	Knowledge of the structure and content of the English language including the meaning and spelling of words, rules of composition, and grammar.
Economics and Accounting	Knowledge of economic and accounting principles and practices, the financial markets, banking and the analysis and reporting of financial data.
Customer and Personal Service	Knowledge of principles and processes for providing customer and personal services. This includes customer needs assessment, meeting quality standards for services, and evaluation of customer satisfaction.
Computers and Electronics	Knowledge of circuit boards, processors, chips, electronic equipment, and computer hardware and software, including applications and programming.
Administration and Management	Knowledge of business and management principles involved in strategic planning, resource allocation, human resources modeling, leadership technique, production methods, and coordination of people and resources.
Sales and Marketing	Knowledge of principles and methods for showing, promoting, and selling products or services. This includes marketing strategy and tactics, product demonstration, sales techniques, and sales control systems.
Telecommunications	Knowledge of transmission, broadcasting, switching, control, and operation of telecommunications systems.
Education and Training	Knowledge of principles and methods for curriculum and training design, teaching and instruction for individuals and groups, and the measurement of training effects.
Personnel and Human Resources	Knowledge of principles and procedures for personnel recruitment, selection, training, compensation and benefits, labor relations and negotiation, and personnel information systems.
Communications and Media	Knowledge of media production, communication, and dissemination techniques and methods. This includes alternative ways to inform and entertain via written, oral, and visual media.
Production and Processing	Knowledge of raw materials, production processes, quality control, costs, and other techniques for maximizing the effective manufacture and distribution of goods.
Public Safety and Security	Knowledge of relevant equipment, policies, procedures, and strategies to promote effective local, state, or national security operations for the protection of people, data, property, and institutions.
Law and Government	Knowledge of laws, legal codes, court procedures, precedents, government regulations, executive orders, agency rules, and the democratic political process.
Mechanical	Knowledge of machines and tools, including their designs, uses, repair, and maintenance.
Transportation	Knowledge of principles and methods for moving people or goods by air, rail, sea, or road, including the relative costs and benefits.
Foreign Language	Knowledge of the structure and content of a foreign (non-English) language including the meaning and spelling of words, rules of composition and grammar, and pronunciation.
Psychology	Knowledge of human behavior and performance; individual differences in ability, personality, and interests; learning and motivation; psychological research methods; and the assessment and treatment of behavioral and affective disorders.
Therapy and Counseling	Knowledge of principles, methods, and procedures for diagnosis, treatment, and rehabilitation of physical and mental dysfunctions, and for career counseling and guidance.
Geography	Knowledge of principles and methods for describing the features of land, sea, and air masses, including their physical characteristics, locations, interrelationships, and distribution of plant, animal, and human life.
Sociology and Anthropology	Knowledge of group behavior and dynamics, societal trends and influences, human migrations, ethnicity, cultures and their history and origins.
Engineering and Technology	Knowledge of the practical application of engineering science and technology. This includes applying principles, techniques, procedures, and equipment to the design and production of various goods and services.
Food Production	Knowledge of techniques and equipment for planting, growing, and harvesting food products (both plant and animal) for consumption, including storage/handling techniques.
Philosophy and Theology	Knowledge of different philosophical systems and religions. This includes their basic principles, values, ethics, ways of thinking, customs, practices, and their impact on human culture.

Medicine and Dentistry	Knowledge of the information and techniques needed to diagnose and treat human injuries, diseases, and deformities. This includes symptoms, treatment alternatives, drug properties and interactions, and preventive health-care measures.
History and Archeology	Knowledge of historical events and their causes, indicators, and effects on civilizations and cultures.
Chemistry	Knowledge of the chemical composition, structure, and properties of substances and of the chemical processes and transformations that they undergo. This includes uses of chemicals and their interactions, danger signs, production techniques, and disposal methods.
Building and Construction	Knowledge of materials, methods, and the tools involved in the construction or repair of houses, buildings, or other structures such as highways and roads.
Fine Arts	Knowledge of the theory and techniques required to compose, produce, and perform works of music, dance, visual arts, drama, and sculpture.
Design	Knowledge of design techniques, tools, and principles involved in production of precision technical plans, blueprints, drawings, and models.
Physics	Knowledge and prediction of physical principles, laws, their interrelationships, and applications to understanding fluid, material, and atmospheric dynamics, and mechanical, electrical, atomic and sub- atomic structures and processes.
Biology	Knowledge of plant and animal organisms, their tissues, cells, functions, interdependencies, and interactions with each other and the environment.

Skills	Skills Definitions
Mathematics	Using mathematics to solve problems.
Reading Comprehension	Understanding written sentences and paragraphs in work related documents.
Time Management	Managing one's own time and the time of others.
Active Listening	Giving full attention to what other people are saying, taking time to understand the points being made, asking questions as appropriate, and not interrupting at inappropriate times.
Critical Thinking	Using logic and reasoning to identify the strengths and weaknesses of alternative solutions, conclusions or approaches to problems.
Active Learning	Understanding the implications of new information for both current and future problem-solving and decision-making.
Learning Strategies	Selecting and using training/instructional methods and procedures appropriate for the situation when learning or teaching new things.
Social Perceptiveness	Being aware of others' reactions and understanding why they react as they do.
Writing	Communicating effectively in writing as appropriate for the needs of the audience.
Speaking	Talking to others to convey information effectively.
Management of Financial Resources	Determining how money will be spent to get the work done, and accounting for these expenditures.
Instructing	Teaching others how to do something.
Complex Problem Solving	Identifying complex problems and reviewing related information to develop and evaluate options and implement solutions.
Monitoring	Monitoring/Assessing performance of yourself, other individuals, or organizations to make improvements or take corrective action.
Coordination	Adjusting actions in relation to others' actions.
Service Orientation	Actively looking for ways to help people.
Persuasion	Persuading others to change their minds or behavior.
Troubleshooting	Determining causes of operating errors and deciding what to do about it.
Negotiation	Bringing others together and trying to reconcile differences.
Judgment and Decision Making	Considering the relative costs and benefits of potential actions to choose the most appropriate one.
Equipment Selection	Determining the kind of tools and equipment needed to do a job.
Management of Personnel Resources	Motivating, developing, and directing people as they work, identifying the best people for the job.
Quality Control Analysis	Conducting tests and inspections of products, services, or processes to evaluate quality or performance.
Systems Analysis	Determining how a system should work and how changes in conditions, operations, and the environment will affect outcomes.
Management of Material Resources	Obtaining and seeing to the appropriate use of equipment, facilities, and materials needed to do certain work.

Technology Design	Generating or adapting equipment and technology to serve user needs.
Systems Evaluation	Identifying measures or indicators of system performance and the actions needed to improve or correct performance, relative to the goals of the system.
Programming	Writing computer programs for various purposes.
Operations Analysis	Analyzing needs and product requirements to create a design.
Science	Using scientific rules and methods to solve problems.
Operation and Control	Controlling operations of equipment or systems.
Equipment Maintenance	Performing routine maintenance on equipment and determining when and what kind of maintenance is needed.
Operation Monitoring	Watching gauges, dials, or other indicators to make sure a machine is working properly.
Repairing	Repairing machines or systems using the needed tools.
Installation	Installing equipment, machines, wiring, or programs to meet specifications.

Ability	Ability Definitions
Near Vision	The ability to see details at close range (within a few feet of the observer).
Mathematical Reasoning	The ability to choose the right mathematical methods or formulas to solve a problem.
Problem Sensitivity	The ability to tell when something is wrong or is likely to go wrong. It does not involve solving the problem, only recognizing there is a problem.
Oral Comprehension	The ability to listen to and understand information and ideas presented through spoken words and sentences.
Information Ordering	The ability to arrange things or actions in a certain order or pattern according to a specific rule or set of rules (e.g., patterns of numbers, letters, words, pictures, mathematical operations).
Written Comprehension	The ability to read and understand information and ideas presented in writing.
Deductive Reasoning	The ability to apply general rules to specific problems to produce answers that make sense.
Written Expression	The ability to communicate information and ideas in writing so others will understand.
Speech Clarity	The ability to speak clearly so others can understand you.
Oral Expression	The ability to communicate information and ideas in speaking so others will understand.
Speech Recognition	The ability to identify and understand the speech of another person.
Number Facility	The ability to add, subtract, multiply, or divide quickly and correctly.
Selective Attention	The ability to concentrate on a task over a period of time without being distracted.
Perceptual Speed	The ability to quickly and accurately compare similarities and differences among sets of letters, numbers, objects, pictures, or patterns. The things to be compared may be presented at the same time or one after the other. This ability also includes comparing a presented object with a remembered object.
Inductive Reasoning	The ability to combine pieces of information to form general rules or conclusions (includes finding a relationship among seemingly unrelated events).
Category Flexibility	The ability to generate or use different sets of rules for combining or grouping things in different ways.
Time Sharing	The ability to shift back and forth between two or more activities or sources of information (such as speech, sounds, touch, or other sources).
Flexibility of Closure	The ability to identify or detect a known pattern (a figure, object, word, or sound) that is hidden in other distracting material.
Memorization	The ability to remember information such as words, numbers, pictures, and procedures.
Finger Dexterity	The ability to make precisely coordinated movements of the fingers of one or both hands to grasp, manipulate, or assemble very small objects.
Wrist-Finger Speed	The ability to make fast, simple, repeated movements of the fingers, hands, and wrists.
Speed of Closure	The ability to quickly make sense of, combine, and organize information into meaningful patterns.
Auditory Attention	The ability to focus on a single source of sound in the presence of other distracting sounds.
Trunk Strength	The ability to use your abdominal and lower back muscles to support part of the body repeatedly or continuously over time without 'giving out' or fatiguing.
Stamina	The ability to exert yourself physically over long periods of time without getting winded or out of breath.

Arm-Hand Steadiness	The ability to keep your hand and arm steady while moving your arm or while holding your arm and hand in one position.
Visualization	The ability to imagine how something will look after it is moved around or when its parts are moved or rearranged.
Manual Dexterity	The ability to quickly move your hand, your hand together with your arm, or your two hands to grasp, manipulate, or assemble objects.
Control Precision	The ability to quickly and repeatedly adjust the controls of a machine or a vehicle to exact positions.
Originality	The ability to come up with unusual or clever ideas about a given topic or situation, or to develop creative ways to solve a problem.
Gross Body Coordination	The ability to coordinate the movement of your arms, legs, and torso together when the whole body is in motion.
Fluency of Ideas	The ability to come up with a number of ideas about a topic (the number of ideas is important, not their quality, correctness, or creativity).
Far Vision	The ability to see details at a distance.
Hearing Sensitivity	The ability to detect or tell the differences between sounds that vary in pitch and loudness.
Multilimb Coordination	The ability to coordinate two or more limbs (for example, two arms, two legs, or one leg and one arm) while sitting, standing, or lying down. It does not involve performing the activities while the whole body is in motion.
Extent Flexibility	The ability to bend, stretch, twist, or reach with your body, arms, and/or legs.
Gross Body Equilibrium	The ability to keep or regain your body balance or stay upright when in an unstable position.
Visual Color Discrimination	The ability to match or detect differences between colors, including shades of color and brightness.
Speed of Limb Movement	The ability to quickly move the arms and legs.
Static Strength	The ability to exert maximum muscle force to lift, push, pull, or carry objects.
Night Vision	The ability to see under low light conditions.
Spatial Orientation	The ability to know your location in relation to the environment or to know where other objects are in relation to you.
Response Orientation	The ability to choose quickly between two or more movements in response to two or more different signals (lights, sounds, pictures). It includes the speed with which the correct response is started with the hand, foot, or other body part.
Rate Control	The ability to time your movements or the movement of a piece of equipment in anticipation of changes in the speed and/or direction of a moving object or scene.
Explosive Strength	The ability to use short bursts of muscle force to propel oneself (as in jumping or sprinting), or to throw an object.
Reaction Time	The ability to quickly respond (with the hand, finger, or foot) to a signal (sound, light, picture) when it appears.
Peripheral Vision	The ability to see objects or movement of objects to one's side when the eyes are looking ahead.
Depth Perception	The ability to judge which of several objects is closer or farther away from you, or to judge the distance between you and an object.
Sound Localization	The ability to tell the direction from which a sound originated.
Glare Sensitivity	The ability to see objects in the presence of glare or bright lighting.
Dynamic Strength	The ability to exert muscle force repeatedly or continuously over time. This involves muscular endurance and resistance to muscle fatigue.
Dynamic Flexibility	The ability to quickly and repeatedly bend, stretch, twist, or reach out with your body, arms, and/or legs.

Work_Activity	Work_Activity Definitions
Interacting With Computers	Using computers and computer systems (including hardware and software) to program, write software, set up functions, enter data, or process information.
Getting Information	Observing, receiving, and otherwise obtaining information from all relevant sources.
Processing Information	Compiling, coding, categorizing, calculating, tabulating, auditing, or verifying information or data.
Establishing and Maintaining Interpersonal Relatio	Developing constructive and cooperative working relationships with others, and maintaining them over time.
Organizing, Planning, and Prioritizing Work	Developing specific goals and plans to prioritize, organize, and accomplish your work.
Communicating with Supervisors, Peers, or Subordin	Providing information to supervisors, co-workers, and subordinates by telephone, in written form, e-mail, or in person.

Documenting/Recording Information	Entering, transcribing, recording, storing, or maintaining information in written or electronic/magnetic form.
Making Decisions and Solving Problems	Analyzing information and evaluating results to choose the best solution and solve problems.
Performing Administrative Activities	Performing day-to-day administrative tasks such as maintaining information files and processing paperwork.
Analyzing Data or Information	Identifying the underlying principles, reasons, or facts of information by breaking down information or data into separate parts.
Identifying Objects, Actions, and Events	Identifying information by categorizing, estimating, recognizing differences or similarities, and detecting changes in circumstances or events.
Updating and Using Relevant Knowledge	Keeping up-to-date technically and applying new knowledge to your job.
Monitor Processes, Materials, or Surroundings	Monitoring and reviewing information from materials, events, or the environment, to detect or assess problems.
Evaluating Information to Determine Compliance wit	Using relevant information and individual judgment to determine whether events or processes comply with laws, regulations, or standards.
Communicating with Persons Outside Organization	Communicating with people outside the organization, representing the organization to customers, the public, government, and other external sources. This information can be exchanged in person, in writing, or by telephone or e-mail.
Coaching and Developing Others	Identifying the developmental needs of others and coaching, mentoring, or otherwise helping others to improve their knowledge or skills.
Resolving Conflicts and Negotiating with Others	Handling complaints, settling disputes, and resolving grievances and conflicts, or otherwise negotiating with others.
Estimating the Quantifiable Characteristics of Pro	Estimating sizes, distances, and quantities; or determining time, costs, resources, or materials needed to perform a work activity.
Provide Consultation and Advice to Others	Providing guidance and expert advice to management or other groups on technical, systems-, or process-related topics.
Assisting and Caring for Others	Providing personal assistance, medical attention, emotional support, or other personal care to others such as coworkers, customers, or patients.
Coordinating the Work and Activities of Others	Getting members of a group to work together to accomplish tasks.
Interpreting the Meaning of Information for Others	Translating or explaining what information means and how it can be used.
Judging the Qualities of Things, Services, or Peop	Assessing the value, importance, or quality of things or people.
Developing Objectives and Strategies	Establishing long-range objectives and specifying the strategies and actions to achieve them.
Training and Teaching Others	Identifying the educational needs of others, developing formal educational or training programs or classes, and teaching or instructing others.
Developing and Building Teams	Encouraging and building mutual trust, respect, and cooperation among team members.
Scheduling Work and Activities	Scheduling events, programs, and activities, as well as the work of others.
Performing for or Working Directly with the Public	Performing for people or dealing directly with the public. This includes serving customers in restaurants and stores, and receiving clients or guests.
Staffing Organizational Units	Recruiting, interviewing, selecting, hiring, and promoting employees in an organization.
Monitoring and Controlling Resources	Monitoring and controlling resources and overseeing the spending of money.
Thinking Creatively	Developing, designing, or creating new applications, ideas, relationships, systems, or products, including artistic contributions.
Guiding, Directing, and Motivating Subordinates	Providing guidance and direction to subordinates, including setting performance standards and monitoring performance.
Inspecting Equipment, Structures, or Material	Inspecting equipment, structures, or materials to identify the cause of errors or other problems or defects.
Handling and Moving Objects	Using hands and arms in handling, installing, positioning, and moving materials, and manipulating things.
Repairing and Maintaining Mechanical Equipment	Servicing, repairing, adjusting, and testing machines, devices, moving parts, and equipment that operate primarily on the basis of mechanical (not electronic) principles.
Selling or Influencing Others	Convincing others to buy merchandise/goods or to otherwise change their minds or actions.
Repairing and Maintaining Electronic Equipment	Servicing, repairing, calibrating, regulating, fine-tuning, or testing machines, devices, and equipment that operate primarily on the basis of electrical or electronic (not mechanical) principles.

Performing General Physical Activities	Performing physical activities that require considerable use of your arms and legs and moving your whole body, such as climbing, lifting, balancing, walking, stooping, and handling of materials.
Controlling Machines and Processes	Using either control mechanisms or direct physical activity to operate machines or processes (not including computers or vehicles).
Operating Vehicles, Mechanized Devices, or Equipme	Running, maneuvering, navigating, or driving vehicles or mechanized equipment, such as forklifts, passenger vehicles, aircraft, or water craft.
Drafting, Laying Out, and Specifying Technical Dev	Providing documentation, detailed instructions, drawings, or specifications to tell others about how devices, parts, equipment, or structures are to be fabricated, constructed, assembled, modified, maintained, or used.

Work_Context	Work_Context Definitions
Telephone	How often do you have telephone conversations in this job?
Electronic Mail	How often do you use electronic mail in this job?
Importance of Being Exact or Accurate	How important is being very exact or highly accurate in performing this job?
Importance of Repeating Same Tasks	How important is repeating the same physical activities (e.g., key entry) or mental activities (e.g., checking entries in a ledger) over and over, without stopping, to performing this job?
Face-to-Face Discussions	How often do you have to have face-to-face discussions with individuals or teams in this job?
Contact With Others	How much does this job require the worker to be in contact with others (face-to-face, by telephone, or otherwise) in order to perform it?
Spend Time Sitting	How much does this job require sitting?
Structured versus Unstructured Work	To what extent is this job structured for the worker, rather than allowing the worker to determine tasks, priorities, and goals?
Time Pressure	How often does this job require the worker to meet strict deadlines?
Freedom to Make Decisions	How much decision making freedom, without supervision, does the job offer?
Work With Work Group or Team	How important is it to work with others in a group or team in this job?
Frequency of Decision Making	How frequently is the worker required to make decisions that affect other people, the financial resources, and/or the image and reputation of the organization?
Impact of Decisions on Co-workers or Company Resul	How do the decisions an employee makes impact the results of co-workers, clients or the company?
Letters and Memos	How often does the job require written letters and memos?
Indoors, Environmentally Controlled	How often does this job require working indoors in environmentally controlled conditions?
Deal With External Customers	How important is it to work with external customers or the public in this job?
Degree of Automation	How automated is the job?
Spend Time Making Repetitive Motions	How much does this job require making repetitive motions?
Deal With Unpleasant or Angry People	How frequently does the worker have to deal with unpleasant, angry, or discourteous individuals as part of the job requirements?
Coordinate or Lead Others	How important is it to coordinate or lead others in accomplishing work activities in this job?
Level of Competition	To what extent does this job require the worker to compete or to be aware of competitive pressures?
Physical Proximity	To what extent does this job require the worker to perform job tasks in close physical proximity to other people?
Frequency of Conflict Situations	How often are there conflict situations the employee has to face in this job?
Responsibility for Outcomes and Results	How responsible is the worker for work outcomes and results of other workers?
Sounds, Noise Levels Are Distracting or Uncomforta	How often does this job require working exposed to sounds and noise levels that are distracting or uncomfortable?
Spend Time Using Your Hands to Handle, Control, or	How much does this job require using your hands to handle, control, or feel objects, tools or controls?
Consequence of Error	How serious would the result usually be if the worker made a mistake that was not readily correctable?
Spend Time Walking and Running	How much does this job require walking and running?
Exposed to Contaminants	How often does this job require working exposed to contaminants (such as pollutants, gases, dust or odors)?
Spend Time Standing	How much does this job require standing?

Pace Determined by Speed of Equipment	How important is it to this job that the pace is determined by the speed of equipment or machinery? (This does not refer to keeping busy at all times on this job.)
Responsible for Others' Health and Safety	How much responsibility is there for the health and safety of others in this job?
Spend Time Bending or Twisting the Body	How much does this job require bending or twisting your body?
Spend Time Kneeling, Crouching, Stooping, or Crawl	How much does this job require kneeling, crouching, stooping or crawling?
Public Speaking	How often do you have to perform public speaking in this job?
Very Hot or Cold Temperatures	How often does this job require working in very hot (above 90 F degrees) or very cold (below 32 F degrees) temperatures?
Exposed to Disease or Infections	How often does this job require exposure to disease/infections?
Wear Common Protective or Safety Equipment such as	How much does this job require wearing common protective or safety equipment such as safety shoes, glasses, gloves, hard hats or life jackets?
In an Enclosed Vehicle or Equipment	How often does this job require working in a closed vehicle or equipment (e.g., car)?
Extremely Bright or Inadequate Lighting	How often does this job require working in extremely bright or inadequate lighting conditions?
Cramped Work Space, Awkward Positions	How often does this job require working in cramped work spaces that requires getting into awkward positions?
Indoors, Not Environmentally Controlled	How often does this job require working indoors in non-controlled environmental conditions (e.g., warehouse without heat)?
Deal With Physically Aggressive People	How frequently does this job require the worker to deal with physical aggression of violent individuals?
Exposed to Minor Burns, Cuts, Bites, or Stings	How often does this job require exposure to minor burns, cuts, bites, or stings?
Exposed to Hazardous Equipment	How often does this job require exposure to hazardous equipment?
Outdoors, Exposed to Weather	How often does this job require working outdoors, exposed to all weather conditions?
Outdoors, Under Cover	How often does this job require working outdoors, under cover (e.g., structure with roof but no walls)?
Exposed to Radiation	How often does this job require exposure to radiation?
Spend Time Keeping or Regaining Balance	How much does this job require keeping or regaining your balance?
Spend Time Climbing Ladders, Scaffolds, or Poles	How much does this job require climbing ladders, scaffolds, or poles?
Exposed to Whole Body Vibration	How often does this job require exposure to whole body vibration (e.g., operate a jackhammer)?
In an Open Vehicle or Equipment	How often does this job require working in an open vehicle or equipment (e.g., tractor)?
Exposed to High Places	How often does this job require exposure to high places?
Exposed to Hazardous Conditions	How often does this job require exposure to hazardous conditions?
Wear Specialized Protective or Safety Equipment su	How much does this job require wearing specialized protective or safety equipment such as breathing apparatus, safety harness, full protection suits, or radiation protection?

Job Zone Component	Job Zone Component Definitions
Title	Job Zone Three: Medium Preparation Needed
Overall Experience	Previous work-related skill, knowledge, or experience is required for these occupations. For example, an electrician must have completed three or four years of apprenticeship or several years of vocational training, and often must have passed a licensing exam, in order to perform the job.
Job Training	Employees in these occupations usually need one or two years of training involving both on-the-job experience and informal training with experienced workers.
Job Zone Examples	These occupations usually involve using communication and organizational skills to coordinate, supervise, manage, or train others to accomplish goals. Examples include dental assistants, electricians, fish and game wardens, legal secretaries, personnel recruiters, and recreation workers.
SVP Range	(6.0 to < 7.0)
Education	Most occupations in this zone require training in vocational schools, related on-the-job experience, or an associate's degree. Some may require a bachelor's degree.

889

Work_Styles	Work_Styles Definitions
Attention to Detail	Job requires being careful about detail and thorough in completing work tasks.
Integrity	Job requires being honest and ethical.
Dependability	Job requires being reliable, responsible, and dependable, and fulfilling obligations.
Cooperation	Job requires being pleasant with others on the job and displaying a good-natured, cooperative attitude.
Independence	Job requires developing one's own ways of doing things, guiding oneself with little or no supervision, and depending on oneself to get things done.
Self Control	Job requires maintaining composure, keeping emotions in check, controlling anger, and avoiding aggressive behavior, even in very difficult situations.
Initiative	Job requires a willingness to take on responsibilities and challenges.
Persistence	Job requires persistence in the face of obstacles.
Stress Tolerance	Job requires accepting criticism and dealing calmly and effectively with high stress situations.
Concern for Others	Job requires being sensitive to others' needs and feelings and being understanding and helpful on the job.
Adaptability/Flexibility	Job requires being open to change (positive or negative) and to considerable variety in the workplace.
Achievement/Effort	Job requires establishing and maintaining personally challenging achievement goals and exerting effort toward mastering tasks.
Social Orientation	Job requires preferring to work with others rather than alone, and being personally connected with others on the job.
Leadership	Job requires a willingness to lead, take charge, and offer opinions and direction.
Innovation	Job requires creativity and alternative thinking to develop new ideas for and answers to work-related problems.
Analytical Thinking	Job requires analyzing information and using logic to address work-related issues and problems.

43-3041.00 - Gaming Cage Workers

In a gaming establishment, conduct financial transactions for patrons. May reconcile daily summaries of transactions to balance books. Accept patron's credit application and verify credit references to provide check-cashing authorization or to establish house credit accounts. May sell gambling chips, tokens, or tickets to patrons, or to other workers for resale to patrons. May convert gaming chips, tokens, or tickets to currency upon patron's request. May use a cash register or computer to record transaction.

Tasks

1) Convert gaming checks, coupons, tokens, and coins to currency for gaming patrons.

2) Cash checks and process credit card advances for patrons.

3) Maintain confidentiality of customers' transactions.

4) Count funds and reconcile daily summaries of transactions to balance books.

5) Determine cash requirements for windows, and order all necessary currency, coins, and chips.

6) Provide customers with information about casino operations.

7) Perform removal and rotation of cash, coin, and chip inventories as necessary.

8) Provide assistance in the training and orientation of new cashiers.

9) Maintain cage security.

10) Supply currency, coins, chips, and gaming checks to other departments as needed.

11) Sell gambling chips, tokens, or tickets to patrons or to other workers for resale to patrons.

12) Verify accuracy of reports such as authorization forms, transaction reconciliations, and exchange summary reports.

13) Prepare bank deposits, balancing assigned funds as necessary.

14) Record casino exchange transactions, using cash registers.

15) Prepare reports, including assignment of company funds and recording of department revenues.

16) Establish new computer accounts.

Knowledge	Knowledge Definitions
Mathematics	Knowledge of arithmetic, algebra, geometry, calculus, statistics, and their applications.
Customer and Personal Service	Knowledge of principles and processes for providing customer and personal services. This includes customer needs assessment, meeting quality standards for services, and evaluation of customer satisfaction.
English Language	Knowledge of the structure and content of the English language including the meaning and spelling of words, rules of composition, and grammar.
Economics and Accounting	Knowledge of economic and accounting principles and practices, the financial markets, banking and the analysis and reporting of financial data.
Administration and Management	Knowledge of business and management principles involved in strategic planning, resource allocation, human resources modeling, leadership technique, production methods, and coordination of people and resources.
Public Safety and Security	Knowledge of relevant equipment, policies, procedures, and strategies to promote effective local, state, or national security operations for the protection of people, data, property, and institutions.
Clerical	Knowledge of administrative and clerical procedures and systems such as word processing, managing files and records, stenography and transcription, designing forms, and other office procedures and terminology.
Computers and Electronics	Knowledge of circuit boards, processors, chips, electronic equipment, and computer hardware and software, including applications and programming.
Law and Government	Knowledge of laws, legal codes, court procedures, precedents, government regulations, executive orders, agency rules, and the democratic political process.
Education and Training	Knowledge of principles and methods for curriculum and training design, teaching and instruction for individuals and groups, and the measurement of training effects.
Personnel and Human Resources	Knowledge of principles and procedures for personnel recruitment, selection, training, compensation and benefits, labor relations and negotiation, and personnel information systems.
Psychology	Knowledge of human behavior and performance; individual differences in ability, personality, and interests; learning and motivation; psychological research methods; and the assessment and treatment of behavioral and affective disorders.
Sales and Marketing	Knowledge of principles and methods for showing, promoting, and selling products or services. This includes marketing strategy and tactics, product demonstration, sales techniques, and sales control systems.
Communications and Media	Knowledge of media production, communication, and dissemination techniques and methods. This includes alternative ways to inform and entertain via written, oral, and visual media.
Telecommunications	Knowledge of transmission, broadcasting, switching, control, and operation of telecommunications systems.
Production and Processing	Knowledge of raw materials, production processes, quality control, costs, and other techniques for maximizing the effective manufacture and distribution of goods.
Transportation	Knowledge of principles and methods for moving people or goods by air, rail, sea, or road, including the relative costs and benefits.
Foreign Language	Knowledge of the structure and content of a foreign (non-English) language including the meaning and spelling of words, rules of composition and grammar, and pronunciation.
Mechanical	Knowledge of machines and tools, including their designs, uses, repair, and maintenance.
Sociology and Anthropology	Knowledge of group behavior and dynamics, societal trends and influences, human migrations, ethnicity, cultures and their history and origins.
Philosophy and Theology	Knowledge of different philosophical systems and religions. This includes their basic principles, values, ethics, ways of thinking, customs, practices, and their impact on human culture.
Medicine and Dentistry	Knowledge of the information and techniques needed to diagnose and treat human injuries, diseases, and deformities. This includes symptoms, treatment alternatives, drug properties and interactions, and preventive health-care measures.

Engineering and Technology	Knowledge of the practical application of engineering science and technology. This includes applying principles, techniques, procedures, and equipment to the design and production of various goods and services.
Food Production	Knowledge of techniques and equipment for planting, growing, and harvesting food products (both plant and animal) for consumption, including storage/handling techniques.
Geography	Knowledge of principles and methods for describing the features of land, sea, and air masses, including their physical characteristics, locations, interrelationships, and distribution of plant, animal, and human life.
Therapy and Counseling	Knowledge of principles, methods, and procedures for diagnosis, treatment, and rehabilitation of physical and mental dysfunctions, and for career counseling and guidance.
Chemistry	Knowledge of the chemical composition, structure, and properties of substances and of the chemical processes and transformations that they undergo. This includes uses of chemicals and their interactions, danger signs, production techniques, and disposal methods.
Physics	Knowledge and prediction of physical principles, laws, their interrelationships, and applications to understanding fluid, material, and atmospheric dynamics, and mechanical, electrical, atomic and sub-atomic structures and processes.
History and Archeology	Knowledge of historical events and their causes, indicators, and effects on civilizations and cultures.
Design	Knowledge of design techniques, tools, and principles involved in production of precision technical plans, blueprints, drawings, and models.
Fine Arts	Knowledge of the theory and techniques required to compose, produce, and perform works of music, dance, visual arts, drama, and sculpture.
Building and Construction	Knowledge of materials, methods, and the tools involved in the construction or repair of houses, buildings, or other structures such as highways and roads.
Biology	Knowledge of plant and animal organisms, their tissues, cells, functions, interdependencies, and interactions with each other and the environment.

Skills — Skills Definitions

Mathematics	Using mathematics to solve problems.
Active Listening	Giving full attention to what other people are saying, taking time to understand the points being made, asking questions as appropriate, and not interrupting at inappropriate times.
Speaking	Talking to others to convey information effectively.
Reading Comprehension	Understanding written sentences and paragraphs in work related documents.
Service Orientation	Actively looking for ways to help people.
Instructing	Teaching others how to do something.
Critical Thinking	Using logic and reasoning to identify the strengths and weaknesses of alternative solutions, conclusions or approaches to problems.
Learning Strategies	Selecting and using training/instructional methods and procedures appropriate for the situation when learning or teaching new things.
Time Management	Managing one's own time and the time of others.
Social Perceptiveness	Being aware of others' reactions and understanding why they react as they do.
Writing	Communicating effectively in writing as appropriate for the needs of the audience.
Judgment and Decision Making	Considering the relative costs and benefits of potential actions to choose the most appropriate one.
Active Learning	Understanding the implications of new information for both current and future problem-solving and decision-making.
Monitoring	Monitoring/Assessing performance of yourself, other individuals, or organizations to make improvements or take corrective action.
Coordination	Adjusting actions in relation to others' actions.
Management of Personnel Resources	Motivating, developing, and directing people as they work, identifying the best people for the job.
Troubleshooting	Determining causes of operating errors and deciding what to do about it.
Operation and Control	Controlling operations of equipment or systems.
Complex Problem Solving	Identifying complex problems and reviewing related information to develop and evaluate options and implement solutions.
Management of Material Resources	Obtaining and seeing to the appropriate use of equipment, facilities, and materials needed to do certain work.

Persuasion	Persuading others to change their minds or behavior.
Management of Financial Resources	Determining how money will be spent to get the work done, and accounting for these expenditures.
Operation Monitoring	Watching gauges, dials, or other indicators to make sure a machine is working properly.
Equipment Maintenance	Performing routine maintenance on equipment and determining when and what kind of maintenance is needed.
Negotiation	Bringing others together and trying to reconcile differences.
Equipment Selection	Determining the kind of tools and equipment needed to do a job.
Systems Evaluation	Identifying measures or indicators of system performance and the actions needed to improve or correct performance, relative to the goals of the system.
Repairing	Repairing machines or systems using the needed tools.
Quality Control Analysis	Conducting tests and inspections of products, services, or processes to evaluate quality or performance.
Systems Analysis	Determining how a system should work and how changes in conditions, operations, and the environment will affect outcomes.
Installation	Installing equipment, machines, wiring, or programs to meet specifications.
Operations Analysis	Analyzing needs and product requirements to create a design.
Programming	Writing computer programs for various purposes.
Technology Design	Generating or adapting equipment and technology to serve user needs.
Science	Using scientific rules and methods to solve problems.

Ability — Ability Definitions

Number Facility	The ability to add, subtract, multiply, or divide quickly and correctly.
Problem Sensitivity	The ability to tell when something is wrong or is likely to go wrong. It does not involve solving the problem, only recognizing there is a problem.
Oral Expression	The ability to communicate information and ideas in speaking so others will understand.
Near Vision	The ability to see details at close range (within a few feet of the observer).
Mathematical Reasoning	The ability to choose the right mathematical methods or formulas to solve a problem.
Oral Comprehension	The ability to listen to and understand information and ideas presented through spoken words and sentences.
Speech Clarity	The ability to speak clearly so others can understand you.
Speech Recognition	The ability to identify and understand the speech of another person.
Information Ordering	The ability to arrange things or actions in a certain order or pattern according to a specific rule or set of rules (e.g., patterns of numbers, letters, words, pictures, mathematical operations).
Selective Attention	The ability to concentrate on a task over a period of time without being distracted.
Deductive Reasoning	The ability to apply general rules to specific problems to produce answers that make sense.
Written Comprehension	The ability to read and understand information and ideas presented in writing.
Trunk Strength	The ability to use your abdominal and lower back muscles to support part of the body repeatedly or continuously over time without 'giving out' or fatiguing.
Perceptual Speed	The ability to quickly and accurately compare similarities and differences among sets of letters, numbers, objects, pictures, or patterns. The things to be compared may be presented at the same time or one after the other. This ability also includes comparing a presented object with a remembered object.
Inductive Reasoning	The ability to combine pieces of information to form general rules or conclusions (includes finding a relationship among seemingly unrelated events).
Written Expression	The ability to communicate information and ideas in writing so others will understand.
Category Flexibility	The ability to generate or use different sets of rules for combining or grouping things in different ways.
Extent Flexibility	The ability to bend, stretch, twist, or reach with your body, arms, and/or legs.
Memorization	The ability to remember information such as words, numbers, pictures, and procedures.
Time Sharing	The ability to shift back and forth between two or more activities or sources of information (such as speech, sounds, touch, or other sources).

Finger Dexterity	The ability to make precisely coordinated movements of the fingers of one or both hands to grasp, manipulate, or assemble very small objects.
Auditory Attention	The ability to focus on a single source of sound in the presence of other distracting sounds.
Manual Dexterity	The ability to quickly move your hand, your hand together with your arm, or your two hands to grasp, manipulate, or assemble objects.
Fluency of Ideas	The ability to come up with a number of ideas about a topic (the number of ideas is important, not their quality, correctness, or creativity).
Arm-Hand Steadiness	The ability to keep your hand and arm steady while moving your arm or while holding your arm and hand in one position.
Control Precision	The ability to quickly and repeatedly adjust the controls of a machine or a vehicle to exact positions.
Visual Color Discrimination	The ability to match or detect differences between colors, including shades of color and brightness.
Stamina	The ability to exert yourself physically over long periods of time without getting winded or out of breath.
Originality	The ability to come up with unusual or clever ideas about a given topic or situation, or to develop creative ways to solve a problem.
Gross Body Coordination	The ability to coordinate the movement of your arms, legs, and torso together when the whole body is in motion.
Static Strength	The ability to exert maximum muscle force to lift, push, pull, or carry objects.
Speed of Closure	The ability to quickly make sense of, combine, and organize information into meaningful patterns.
Flexibility of Closure	The ability to identify or detect a known pattern (a figure, object, word, or sound) that is hidden in other distracting material.
Multilimb Coordination	The ability to coordinate two or more limbs (for example, two arms, two legs, or one leg and one arm) while sitting, standing, or lying down. It does not involve performing the activities while the whole body is in motion.
Far Vision	The ability to see details at a distance.
Speed of Limb Movement	The ability to quickly move the arms and legs.
Visualization	The ability to imagine how something will look after it is moved around or when its parts are moved or rearranged.
Depth Perception	The ability to judge which of several objects is closer or farther away from you, or to judge the distance between you and an object.
Dynamic Strength	The ability to exert muscle force repeatedly or continuously over time. This involves muscular endurance and resistance to muscle fatigue.
Wrist-Finger Speed	The ability to make fast, simple, repeated movements of the fingers, hands, and wrists.
Hearing Sensitivity	The ability to detect or tell the differences between sounds that vary in pitch and loudness.
Reaction Time	The ability to quickly respond (with the hand, finger, or foot) to a signal (sound, light, picture) when it appears.
Response Orientation	The ability to choose quickly between two or more movements in response to two or more different signals (lights, sounds, pictures). It includes the speed with which the correct response is started with the hand, foot, or other body part.
Gross Body Equilibrium	The ability to keep or regain your body balance or stay upright when in an unstable position.
Rate Control	The ability to time your movements or the movement of a piece of equipment in anticipation of changes in the speed and/or direction of a moving object or scene.
Explosive Strength	The ability to use short bursts of muscle force to propel oneself (as in jumping or sprinting), or to throw an object.
Night Vision	The ability to see under low light conditions.
Peripheral Vision	The ability to see objects or movement of objects to one's side when the eyes are looking ahead.
Glare Sensitivity	The ability to see objects in the presence of glare or bright lighting.
Sound Localization	The ability to tell the direction from which a sound originated.
Spatial Orientation	The ability to know your location in relation to the environment or to know where other objects are in relation to you.
Dynamic Flexibility	The ability to quickly and repeatedly bend, stretch, twist, or reach out with your body, arms, and/or legs.

Work Activity	Work_Activity Definitions
Performing for or Working Directly with the Public	Performing for people or dealing directly with the public. This includes serving customers in restaurants and stores, and receiving clients or guests.

Getting Information	Observing, receiving, and otherwise obtaining information from all relevant sources.
Identifying Objects, Actions, and Events	Identifying information by categorizing, estimating, recognizing differences or similarities, and detecting changes in circumstances or events.
Communicating with Supervisors, Peers, or Subordin	Providing information to supervisors, co-workers, and subordinates by telephone, in written form, e-mail, or in person.
Documenting/Recording Information	Entering, transcribing, recording, storing, or maintaining information in written or electronic/magnetic form.
Evaluating Information to Determine Compliance wit	Using relevant information and individual judgment to determine whether events or processes comply with laws, regulations, or standards.
Interacting With Computers	Using computers and computer systems (including hardware and software) to program, write software, set up functions, enter data, or process information.
Processing Information	Compiling, coding, categorizing, calculating, tabulating, auditing, or verifying information or data.
Judging the Qualities of Things, Services, or Peop	Assessing the value, importance, or quality of things or people.
Monitor Processes, Materials, or Surroundings	Monitoring and reviewing information from materials, events, or the environment, to detect or assess problems.
Handling and Moving Objects	Using hands and arms in handling, installing, positioning, and moving materials, and manipulating things.
Performing General Physical Activities	Performing physical activities that require considerable use of your arms and legs and moving your whole body, such as climbing, lifting, balancing, walking, stooping, and handling of materials.
Developing and Building Teams	Encouraging and building mutual trust, respect, and cooperation among team members.
Establishing and Maintaining Interpersonal Relatio	Developing constructive and cooperative working relationships with others, and maintaining them over time.
Making Decisions and Solving Problems	Analyzing information and evaluating results to choose the best solution and solve problems.
Communicating with Persons Outside Organization	Communicating with people outside the organization, representing the organization to customers, the public, government, and other external sources. This information can be exchanged in person, in writing, or by telephone or e-mail.
Updating and Using Relevant Knowledge	Keeping up-to-date technically and applying new knowledge to your job.
Resolving Conflicts and Negotiating with Others	Handling complaints, settling disputes, and resolving grievances and conflicts, or otherwise negotiating with others.
Inspecting Equipment, Structures, or Material	Inspecting equipment, structures, or materials to identify the cause of errors or other problems or defects.
Training and Teaching Others	Identifying the educational needs of others, developing formal educational or training programs or classes, and teaching or instructing others.
Coordinating the Work and Activities of Others	Getting members of a group to work together to accomplish tasks.
Performing Administrative Activities	Performing day-to-day administrative tasks such as maintaining information files and processing paperwork.
Assisting and Caring for Others	Providing personal assistance, medical attention, emotional support, or other personal care to others such as coworkers, customers, or patients.
Controlling Machines and Processes	Using either control mechanisms or direct physical activity to operate machines or processes (not including computers or vehicles).
Organizing, Planning, and Prioritizing Work	Developing specific goals and plans to prioritize, organize, and accomplish your work.
Coaching and Developing Others	Identifying the developmental needs of others and coaching, mentoring, or otherwise helping others to improve their knowledge or skills.
Analyzing Data or Information	Identifying the underlying principles, reasons, or facts of information by breaking down information or data into separate parts.
Scheduling Work and Activities	Scheduling events, programs, and activities, as well as the work of others.
Interpreting the Meaning of Information for Others	Translating or explaining what information means and how it can be used.
Estimating the Quantifiable Characteristics of Pro	Estimating sizes, distances, and quantities; or determining time, costs, resources, or materials needed to perform a work activity.
Guiding, Directing, and Motivating Subordinates	Providing guidance and direction to subordinates, including setting performance standards and monitoring performance.
Monitoring and Controlling Resources	Monitoring and controlling resources and overseeing the spending of money.

Thinking Creatively	Developing, designing, or creating new applications, ideas, relationships, systems, or products, including artistic contributions.
Developing Objectives and Strategies	Establishing long-range objectives and specifying the strategies and actions to achieve them.
Selling or Influencing Others	Convincing others to buy merchandise/goods or to otherwise change their minds or actions.
Provide Consultation and Advice to Others	Providing guidance and expert advice to management or other groups on technical, systems-, or process-related topics.
Staffing Organizational Units	Recruiting, interviewing, selecting, hiring, and promoting employees in an organization.
Repairing and Maintaining Electronic Equipment	Servicing, repairing, calibrating, regulating, fine-tuning, or testing machines, devices, and equipment that operate primarily on the basis of electrical or electronic (not mechanical) principles.
Operating Vehicles, Mechanized Devices, or Equipme	Running, maneuvering, navigating, or driving vehicles or mechanized equipment, such as forklifts, passenger vehicles, aircraft, or water craft.
Repairing and Maintaining Mechanical Equipment	Servicing, repairing, adjusting, and testing machines, devices, moving parts, and equipment that operate primarily on the basis of mechanical (not electronic) principles.
Drafting, Laying Out, and Specifying Technical Dev	Providing documentation, detailed instructions, drawings, or specifications to tell others about how devices, parts, equipment, or structures are to be fabricated, constructed, assembled, modified, maintained, or used.

Work_Context	Work_Context Definitions
Importance of Being Exact or Accurate	How important is being very exact or highly accurate in performing this job?
Contact With Others	How much does this job require the worker to be in contact with others (face-to-face, by telephone, or otherwise) in order to perform it?
Importance of Repeating Same Tasks	How important is repeating the same physical activities (e.g., key entry) or mental activities (e.g., checking entries in a ledger) over and over, without stopping, to performing this job?
Indoors, Environmentally Controlled	How often does this job require working indoors in environmentally controlled conditions?
Spend Time Standing	How much does this job require standing?
Work With Work Group or Team	How important is it to work with others in a group or team in this job?
Deal With External Customers	How important is it to work with external customers or the public in this job?
Face-to-Face Discussions	How often do you have to have face-to-face discussions with individuals or teams in this job?
Impact of Decisions on Co-workers or Company Resul	How do the decisions an employee makes impact the results of co-workers, clients or the company?
Frequency of Decision Making	How frequently is the worker required to make decisions that affect other people, the financial resources, and/or the image and reputation of the organization?
Spend Time Making Repetitive Motions	How much does this job require making repetitive motions?
Telephone	How often do you have telephone conversations in this job?
Sounds, Noise Levels Are Distracting or Uncomforta	How often does this job require working exposed to sounds and noise levels that are distracting or uncomfortable?
Physical Proximity	To what extent does this job require the worker to perform job tasks in close physical proximity to other people?
Spend Time Using Your Hands to Handle, Control, or	How much does this job require using your hands to handle, control, or feel objects, tools or controls?
Time Pressure	How often does this job require the worker to meet strict deadlines?
Deal With Unpleasant or Angry People	How frequently does the worker have to deal with unpleasant, angry, or discourteous individuals as part of the job requirements?
Coordinate or Lead Others	How important is it to coordinate or lead others in accomplishing work activities in this job?
Spend Time Bending or Twisting the Body	How much does this job require bending or twisting your body?
Consequence of Error	How serious would the result usually be if the worker made a mistake that was not readily correctable?
Frequency of Conflict Situations	How often are there conflict situations the employee has to face in this job?
Structured versus Unstructured Work	To what extent is this job structured for the worker, rather than allowing the worker to determine tasks, priorities, and goals?
Freedom to Make Decisions	How much decision making freedom, without supervision, does the job offer?

Responsible for Others' Health and Safety	How much responsibility is there for the health and safety of others in this job?
Letters and Memos	How often does the job require written letters and memos?
Exposed to Contaminants	How often does this job require working exposed to contaminants (such as pollutants, gases, dust or odors)?
Level of Competition	To what extent does this job require the worker to compete or to be aware of competitive pressures?
Cramped Work Space, Awkward Positions	How often does this job require working in cramped work spaces that requires getting into awkward positions?
Responsibility for Outcomes and Results	How responsible is the worker for work outcomes and results of other workers?
Spend Time Walking and Running	How much does this job require walking and running?
Degree of Automation	How automated is the job?
Spend Time Kneeling, Crouching, Stooping, or Crawl	How much does this job require kneeling, crouching, stooping or crawling?
Deal With Physically Aggressive People	How frequently does this job require the worker to deal with physical aggression of violent individuals?
Pace Determined by Speed of Equipment	How important is it to this job that the pace is determined by the speed of equipment or machinery? (This does not refer to keeping busy at all times on this job.)
Spend Time Keeping or Regaining Balance	How much does this job require keeping or regaining your balance?
Exposed to Minor Burns, Cuts, Bites, or Stings	How often does this job require exposure to minor burns, cuts, bites, or stings?
Public Speaking	How often do you have to perform public speaking in this job?
Exposed to Disease or Infections	How often does this job require exposure to disease/infections?
Spend Time Sitting	How much does this job require sitting?
Extremely Bright or Inadequate Lighting	How often does this job require working in extremely bright or inadequate lighting conditions?
Electronic Mail	How often do you use electronic mail in this job?
Very Hot or Cold Temperatures	How often does this job require working in very hot (above 90 F degrees) or very cold (below 32 F degrees) temperatures?
Wear Common Protective or Safety Equipment such as	How much does this job require wearing common protective or safety equipment such as safety shoes, glasses, gloves, hard hats or live jackets?
Indoors, Not Environmentally Controlled	How often does this job require working indoors in non-controlled environmental conditions (e.g., warehouse without heat)?
Spend Time Climbing Ladders, Scaffolds, or Poles	How much does this job require climbing ladders, scaffolds, or poles?
Exposed to Hazardous Equipment	How often does this job require exposure to hazardous equipment?
Exposed to Hazardous Conditions	How often does this job require exposure to hazardous conditions?
Outdoors, Under Cover	How often does this job require working outdoors, under cover (e.g., structure with roof but no walls)?
Wear Specialized Protective or Safety Equipment su	How much does this job require wearing specialized protective or safety equipment such as breathing apparatus, safety harness, full protection suits, or radiation protection?
Exposed to Radiation	How often does this job require exposure to radiation?
Exposed to Whole Body Vibration	How often does this job require exposure to whole body vibration (e.g., operate a jackhammer)?
Outdoors, Exposed to Weather	How often does this job require working outdoors, exposed to all weather conditions?
In an Open Vehicle or Equipment	How often does this job require working in an open vehicle or equipment (e.g., tractor)?
Exposed to High Places	How often does this job require exposure to high places?
In an Enclosed Vehicle or Equipment	How often does this job require working in a closed vehicle or equipment (e.g., car)?

Job Zone Component	Job Zone Component Definitions
Title	Job Zone Two: Some Preparation Needed
Overall Experience	Some previous work-related skill, knowledge, or experience may be helpful in these occupations, but usually is not needed. For example, a drywall installer might benefit from experience installing drywall, but an inexperienced person could still learn to be an installer with little difficulty.
Job Training	Employees in these occupations need anywhere from a few months to one year of working with experienced employees.

Job Zone Examples	These occupations often involve using your knowledge and skills to help others. Examples include drywall installers, fire inspectors, flight attendants, pharmacy technicians, salespersons (retail), and tellers.
SVP Range	(4.0 to < 6.0)
Education	These occupations usually require a high school diploma and may require some vocational training or job-related course work. In some cases, an associate's or bachelor's degree could be needed.

Work_Styles	Work_Styles Definitions
Integrity	Job requires being honest and ethical.
Dependability	Job requires being reliable, responsible, and dependable, and fulfilling obligations.
Attention to Detail	Job requires being careful about detail and thorough in completing work tasks.
Self Control	Job requires maintaining composure, keeping emotions in check, controlling anger, and avoiding aggressive behavior, even in very difficult situations.
Cooperation	Job requires being pleasant with others on the job and displaying a good-natured, cooperative attitude.
Stress Tolerance	Job requires accepting criticism and dealing calmly and effectively with high stress situations.
Independence	Job requires developing one's own ways of doing things, guiding oneself with little or no supervision, and depending on oneself to get things done.
Adaptability/Flexibility	Job requires being open to change (positive or negative) and to considerable variety in the workplace.
Concern for Others	Job requires being sensitive to others' needs and feelings and being understanding and helpful on the job.
Achievement/Effort	Job requires establishing and maintaining personally challenging achievement goals and exerting effort toward mastering tasks.
Social Orientation	Job requires preferring to work with others rather than alone, and being personally connected with others on the job.
Initiative	Job requires a willingness to take on responsibilities and challenges.
Persistence	Job requires persistence in the face of obstacles.
Analytical Thinking	Job requires analyzing information and using logic to address work-related issues and problems.
Leadership	Job requires a willingness to lead, take charge, and offer opinions and direction.
Innovation	Job requires creativity and alternative thinking to develop new ideas for and answers to work-related problems.

43-3051.00 - Payroll and Timekeeping Clerks

Compile and post employee time and payroll data. May compute employees' time worked, production, and commission. May compute and post wages and deductions. May prepare paychecks.

Tasks

1) Compile employee time, production, and payroll data from time sheets and other records.

2) Verify attendance, hours worked, and pay adjustments, and post information onto designated records.

3) Process and issue employee paychecks and statements of earnings and deductions.

4) Record employee information, such as exemptions, transfers, and resignations, in order to maintain and update payroll records.

5) Issue and record adjustments to pay related to previous errors or retroactive increases.

6) Provide information to employees and managers on payroll matters, tax issues, benefit plans, and collective agreement provisions.

7) Compute wages and deductions, and enter data into computers.

8) Keep informed about changes in tax and deduction laws that apply to the payroll process.

9) Distribute and collect timecards each pay period.

10) Complete time sheets showing employees' arrival and departure times.

11) Compile statistical reports, statements, and summaries related to pay and benefits accounts, and submit them to appropriate departments.

12) Prepare and balance period-end reports, and reconcile issued payrolls to bank statements.

13) Complete, verify, and process forms and documentation for administration of benefits such as pension plans, and unemployment and medical insurance.

14) Coordinate special programs, such as United Way campaigns, that involve payroll deductions.

15) Post relevant work hours to client files in order to bill clients properly.

Knowledge	Knowledge Definitions
Clerical	Knowledge of administrative and clerical procedures and systems such as word processing, managing files and records, stenography and transcription, designing forms, and other office procedures and terminology.
Customer and Personal Service	Knowledge of principles and processes for providing customer and personal services. This includes customer needs assessment, meeting quality standards for services, and evaluation of customer satisfaction.
Administration and Management	Knowledge of business and management principles involved in strategic planning, resource allocation, human resources modeling, leadership technique, production methods, and coordination of people and resources.
Personnel and Human Resources	Knowledge of principles and procedures for personnel recruitment, selection, training, compensation and benefits, labor relations and negotiation, and personnel information systems.
Mathematics	Knowledge of arithmetic, algebra, geometry, calculus, statistics, and their applications.
English Language	Knowledge of the structure and content of the English language including the meaning and spelling of words, rules of composition, and grammar.
Economics and Accounting	Knowledge of economic and accounting principles and practices, the financial markets, banking and the analysis and reporting of financial data.
Computers and Electronics	Knowledge of circuit boards, processors, chips, electronic equipment, and computer hardware and software, including applications and programming.
Communications and Media	Knowledge of media production, communication, and dissemination techniques and methods. This includes alternative ways to inform and entertain via written, oral, and visual media.
Education and Training	Knowledge of principles and methods for curriculum and training design, teaching and instruction for individuals and groups, and the measurement of training effects.
Sales and Marketing	Knowledge of principles and methods for showing, promoting, and selling products or services. This includes marketing strategy and tactics, product demonstration, sales techniques, and sales control systems.
Telecommunications	Knowledge of transmission, broadcasting, switching, control, and operation of telecommunications systems.
Law and Government	Knowledge of laws, legal codes, court procedures, precedents, government regulations, executive orders, agency rules, and the democratic political process.
Production and Processing	Knowledge of raw materials, production processes, quality control, costs, and other techniques for maximizing the effective manufacture and distribution of goods.
Psychology	Knowledge of human behavior and performance; individual differences in ability, personality, and interests; learning and motivation; psychological research methods; and the assessment and treatment of behavioral and affective disorders.
Public Safety and Security	Knowledge of relevant equipment, policies, procedures, and strategies to promote effective local, state, or national security operations for the protection of people, data, property, and institutions.
Mechanical	Knowledge of machines and tools, including their designs, uses, repair, and maintenance.
Sociology and Anthropology	Knowledge of group behavior and dynamics, societal trends and influences, human migrations, ethnicity, cultures and their history and origins.
Transportation	Knowledge of principles and methods for moving people or goods by air, rail, sea, or road, including the relative costs and benefits.
Philosophy and Theology	Knowledge of different philosophical systems and religions. This includes their basic principles, values, ethics, ways of thinking, customs, practices, and their impact on human culture.

Foreign Language	Knowledge of the structure and content of a foreign (non-English) language including the meaning and spelling of words, rules of composition and grammar, and pronunciation.
Design	Knowledge of design techniques, tools, and principles involved in production of precision technical plans, blueprints, drawings, and models.
Engineering and Technology	Knowledge of the practical application of engineering science and technology. This includes applying principles, techniques, procedures, and equipment to the design and production of various goods and services.
Geography	Knowledge of principles and methods for describing the features of land, sea, and air masses, including their physical characteristics, locations, interrelationships, and distribution of plant, animal, and human life.
Therapy and Counseling	Knowledge of principles, methods, and procedures for diagnosis, treatment, and rehabilitation of physical and mental dysfunctions, and for career counseling and guidance.
Chemistry	Knowledge of the chemical composition, structure, and properties of substances and of the chemical processes and transformations that they undergo. This includes uses of chemicals and their interactions, danger signs, production techniques, and disposal methods.
Medicine and Dentistry	Knowledge of the information and techniques needed to diagnose and treat human injuries, diseases, and deformities. This includes symptoms, treatment alternatives, drug properties and interactions, and preventive health-care measures.
Fine Arts	Knowledge of the theory and techniques required to compose, produce, and perform works of music, dance, visual arts, drama, and sculpture.
Biology	Knowledge of plant and animal organisms, their tissues, cells, functions, interdependencies, and interactions with each other and the environment.
History and Archeology	Knowledge of historical events and their causes, indicators, and effects on civilizations and cultures.
Food Production	Knowledge of techniques and equipment for planting, growing, and harvesting food products (both plant and animal) for consumption, including storage/handling techniques.
Physics	Knowledge and prediction of physical principles, laws, their interrelationships, and applications to understanding fluid, material, and atmospheric dynamics, and mechanical, electrical, atomic and sub-atomic structures and processes.
Building and Construction	Knowledge of materials, methods, and the tools involved in the construction or repair of houses, buildings, or other structures such as highways and roads.

Skills	Skills Definitions
Time Management	Managing one's own time and the time of others.
Mathematics	Using mathematics to solve problems.
Reading Comprehension	Understanding written sentences and paragraphs in work related documents.
Active Listening	Giving full attention to what other people are saying, taking time to understand the points being made, asking questions as appropriate, and not interrupting at inappropriate times.
Speaking	Talking to others to convey information effectively.
Active Learning	Understanding the implications of new information for both current and future problem-solving and decision-making.
Judgment and Decision Making	Considering the relative costs and benefits of potential actions to choose the most appropriate one.
Learning Strategies	Selecting and using training/instructional methods and procedures appropriate for the situation when learning or teaching new things.
Critical Thinking	Using logic and reasoning to identify the strengths and weaknesses of alternative solutions, conclusions or approaches to problems.
Writing	Communicating effectively in writing as appropriate for the needs of the audience.
Monitoring	Monitoring/Assessing performance of yourself, other individuals, or organizations to make improvements or take corrective action.
Coordination	Adjusting actions in relation to others' actions.
Instructing	Teaching others how to do something.
Social Perceptiveness	Being aware of others' reactions and understanding why they react as they do.
Service Orientation	Actively looking for ways to help people.
Complex Problem Solving	Identifying complex problems and reviewing related information to develop and evaluate options and implement solutions.

Equipment Selection	Determining the kind of tools and equipment needed to do a job.
Negotiation	Bringing others together and trying to reconcile differences.
Operations Analysis	Analyzing needs and product requirements to create a design.
Management of Financial Resources	Determining how money will be spent to get the work done, and accounting for these expenditures.
Persuasion	Persuading others to change their minds or behavior.
Troubleshooting	Determining causes of operating errors and deciding what to do about it.
Operation and Control	Controlling operations of equipment or systems.
Management of Material Resources	Obtaining and seeing to the appropriate use of equipment, facilities, and materials needed to do certain work.
Technology Design	Generating or adapting equipment and technology to serve user needs.
Systems Evaluation	Identifying measures or indicators of system performance and the actions needed to improve or correct performance, relative to the goals of the system.
Systems Analysis	Determining how a system should work and how changes in conditions, operations, and the environment will affect outcomes.
Management of Personnel Resources	Motivating, developing, and directing people as they work, identifying the best people for the job.
Quality Control Analysis	Conducting tests and inspections of products, services, or processes to evaluate quality or performance.
Installation	Installing equipment, machines, wiring, or programs to meet specifications.
Programming	Writing computer programs for various purposes.
Operation Monitoring	Watching gauges, dials, or other indicators to make sure a machine is working properly.
Equipment Maintenance	Performing routine maintenance on equipment and determining when and what kind of maintenance is needed.
Repairing	Repairing machines or systems using the needed tools.
Science	Using scientific rules and methods to solve problems.

Ability	Ability Definitions
Information Ordering	The ability to arrange things or actions in a certain order or pattern according to a specific rule or set of rules (e.g., patterns of numbers, letters, words, pictures, mathematical operations).
Mathematical Reasoning	The ability to choose the right mathematical methods or formulas to solve a problem.
Problem Sensitivity	The ability to tell when something is wrong or is likely to go wrong. It does not involve solving the problem, only recognizing there is a problem.
Oral Comprehension	The ability to listen to and understand information and ideas presented through spoken words and sentences.
Oral Expression	The ability to communicate information and ideas in speaking so others will understand.
Near Vision	The ability to see details at close range (within a few feet of the observer).
Deductive Reasoning	The ability to apply general rules to specific problems to produce answers that make sense.
Written Comprehension	The ability to read and understand information and ideas presented in writing.
Speech Clarity	The ability to speak clearly so others can understand you.
Speech Recognition	The ability to identify and understand the speech of another person.
Written Expression	The ability to communicate information and ideas in writing so others will understand.
Inductive Reasoning	The ability to combine pieces of information to form general rules or conclusions (includes finding a relationship among seemingly unrelated events).
Selective Attention	The ability to concentrate on a task over a period of time without being distracted.
Category Flexibility	The ability to generate or use different sets of rules for combining or grouping things in different ways.
Number Facility	The ability to add, subtract, multiply, or divide quickly and correctly.
Perceptual Speed	The ability to quickly and accurately compare similarities and differences among sets of letters, numbers, objects, pictures, or patterns. The things to be compared may be presented at the same time or one after the other. This ability also includes comparing a presented object with a remembered object.
Flexibility of Closure	The ability to identify or detect a known pattern (a figure, object, word, or sound) that is hidden in other distracting material.
Memorization	The ability to remember information such as words, numbers, pictures, and procedures.

Time Sharing	The ability to shift back and forth between two or more activities or sources of information (such as speech. sounds, touch, or other sources).		

Time Sharing	The ability to shift back and forth between two or more activities or sources of information (such as speech. sounds, touch, or other sources).
Speed of Closure	The ability to quickly make sense of, combine, and organize information into meaningful patterns.
Auditory Attention	The ability to focus on a single source of sound in the presence of other distracting sounds.
Wrist-Finger Speed	The ability to make fast, simple, repeated movements of the fingers, hands, and wrists.
Trunk Strength	The ability to use your abdominal and lower back muscles to support part of the body repeatedly or continuously over time without 'giving out' or fatiguing.
Manual Dexterity	The ability to quickly move your hand, your hand together with your arm, or your two hands to grasp, manipulate, or assemble objects.
Fluency of Ideas	The ability to come up with a number of ideas about a topic (the number of ideas is important, not their quality, correctness, or creativity).
Finger Dexterity	The ability to make precisely coordinated movements of the fingers of one or both hands to grasp, manipulate, or assemble very small objects.
Arm-Hand Steadiness	The ability to keep your hand and arm steady while moving your arm or while holding your arm and hand in one position.
Control Precision	The ability to quickly and repeatedly adjust the controls of a machine or a vehicle to exact positions.
Stamina	The ability to exert yourself physically over long periods of time without getting winded or out of breath.
Visualization	The ability to imagine how something will look after it is moved around or when its parts are moved or rearranged.
Far Vision	The ability to see details at a distance.
Hearing Sensitivity	The ability to detect or tell the differences between sounds that vary in pitch and loudness.
Extent Flexibility	The ability to bend, stretch, twist, or reach with your body, arms, and/or legs.
Visual Color Discrimination	The ability to match or detect differences between colors, including shades of color and brightness.
Originality	The ability to come up with unusual or clever ideas about a given topic or situation, or to develop creative ways to solve a problem.
Explosive Strength	The ability to use short bursts of muscle force to propel oneself (as in jumping or sprinting), or to throw an object.
Glare Sensitivity	The ability to see objects in the presence of glare or bright lighting.
Multilimb Coordination	The ability to coordinate two or more limbs (for example, two arms, two legs, or one leg and one arm) while sitting, standing, or lying down. It does not involve performing the activities while the whole body is in motion.
Response Orientation	The ability to choose quickly between two or more movements in response to two or more different signals (lights, sounds, pictures). It includes the speed with which the correct response is started with the hand, foot, or other body part.
Rate Control	The ability to time your movements or the movement of a piece of equipment in anticipation of changes in the speed and/or direction of a moving object or scene.
Reaction Time	The ability to quickly respond (with the hand, finger, or foot) to a signal (sound, light, picture) when it appears.
Speed of Limb Movement	The ability to quickly move the arms and legs.
Static Strength	The ability to exert maximum muscle force to lift, push, pull, or carry objects.
Dynamic Flexibility	The ability to quickly and repeatedly bend, stretch, twist, or reach out with your body, arms, and/or legs.
Gross Body Coordination	The ability to coordinate the movement of your arms, legs, and torso together when the whole body is in motion.
Night Vision	The ability to see under low light conditions.
Sound Localization	The ability to tell the direction from which a sound originated.
Spatial Orientation	The ability to know your location in relation to the environment or to know where other objects are in relation to you.
Gross Body Equilibrium	The ability to keep or regain your body balance or stay upright when in an unstable position.
Depth Perception	The ability to judge which of several objects is closer or farther away from you, or to judge the distance between you and an object.
Peripheral Vision	The ability to see objects or movement of objects to one's side when the eyes are looking ahead.
Dynamic Strength	The ability to exert muscle force repeatedly or continuously over time. This involves muscular endurance and resistance to muscle fatigue.

Work_Activity	Work_Activity Definitions
Processing Information	Compiling. coding. categorizing. calculating. tabulating, auditing, or verifying information or data.
Documenting/Recording Information	Entering. transcribing, recording, storing, or maintaining information in written or electronic/magnetic form.
Performing Administrative Activities	Performing day-to-day administrative tasks such as maintaining information files and processing paperwork.
Getting Information	Observing, receiving, and otherwise obtaining information from all relevant sources.
Interacting With Computers	Using computers and computer systems (including hardware and software) to program, write software, set up functions, enter data, or process information.
Establishing and Maintaining Interpersonal Relatio	Developing constructive and cooperative working relationships with others, and maintaining them over time.
Communicating with Supervisors, Peers, or Subordin	Providing information to supervisors, co-workers, and subordinates by telephone. in written form, e-mail, or in person.
Organizing, Planning, and Prioritizing Work	Developing specific goals and plans to prioritize, organize, and accomplish your work.
Updating and Using Relevant Knowledge	Keeping up-to-date technically and applying new knowledge to your job.
Evaluating Information to Determine Compliance wit	Using relevant information and individual judgment to determine whether events or processes comply with laws, regulations. or standards.
Making Decisions and Solving Problems	Analyzing information and evaluating results to choose the best solution and solve problems.
Communicating with Persons Outside Organization	Communicating with people outside the organization, representing the organization to customers, the public, government. and other external sources. This information can be exchanged in person, in writing, or by telephone or e-mail.
Analyzing Data or Information	Identifying the underlying principles, reasons, or facts of information by breaking down information or data into separate parts.
Interpreting the Meaning of Information for Others	Translating or explaining what information means and how it can be used.
Identifying Objects, Actions, and Events	Identifying information by categorizing, estimating, recognizing differences or similarities, and detecting changes in circumstances or events.
Scheduling Work and Activities	Scheduling events, programs, and activities, as well as the work of others.
Resolving Conflicts and Negotiating with Others	Handling complaints, settling disputes, and resolving grievances and conflicts, or otherwise negotiating with others.
Monitor Processes, Materials, or Surroundings	Monitoring and reviewing information from materials, events, or the environment, to detect or assess problems.
Thinking Creatively	Developing, designing, or creating new applications, ideas, relationships, systems, or products, including artistic contributions.
Judging the Qualities of Things, Services, or Peop	Assessing the value, importance, or quality of things or people.
Training and Teaching Others	Identifying the educational needs of others, developing formal educational or training programs or classes, and teaching or instructing others.
Developing Objectives and Strategies	Establishing long-range objectives and specifying the strategies and actions to achieve them.
Assisting and Caring for Others	Providing personal assistance, medical attention, emotional support, or other personal care to others such as coworkers, customers, or patients.
Developing and Building Teams	Encouraging and building mutual trust, respect, and cooperation among team members.
Monitoring and Controlling Resources	Monitoring and controlling resources and overseeing the spending of money.
Coordinating the Work and Activities of Others	Getting members of a group to work together to accomplish tasks.
Coaching and Developing Others	Identifying the developmental needs of others and coaching, mentoring, or otherwise helping others to improve their knowledge or skills.
Estimating the Quantifiable Characteristics of Pro	Estimating sizes, distances, and quantities; or determining time, costs, resources, or materials needed to perform a work activity.
Provide Consultation and Advice to Others	Providing guidance and expert advice to management or other groups on technical, systems-, or process-related topics.
Inspecting Equipment, Structures, or Material	Inspecting equipment, structures, or materials to identify the cause of errors or other problems or defects.
Staffing Organizational Units	Recruiting, interviewing, selecting, hiring, and promoting employees in an organization.

Guiding, Directing, and Motivating Subordinates	Providing guidance and direction to subordinates, including setting performance standards and monitoring performance.
Controlling Machines and Processes	Using either control mechanisms or direct physical activity to operate machines or processes (not including computers or vehicles).
Handling and Moving Objects	Using hands and arms in handling, installing, positioning, and moving materials, and manipulating things.
Performing for or Working Directly with the Public	Performing for people or dealing directly with the public. This includes serving customers in restaurants and stores, and receiving clients or guests.
Selling or Influencing Others	Convincing others to buy merchandise/goods or to otherwise change their minds or actions.
Performing General Physical Activities	Performing physical activities that require considerable use of your arms and legs and moving your whole body, such as climbing, lifting, balancing, walking, stooping, and handling of materials.
Drafting, Laying Out, and Specifying Technical Dev	Providing documentation, detailed instructions, drawings, or specifications to tell others about how devices, parts, equipment, or structures are to be fabricated, constructed, assembled, modified, maintained, or used.
Operating Vehicles, Mechanized Devices, or Equipme	Running, maneuvering, navigating, or driving vehicles or mechanized equipment, such as forklifts, passenger vehicles, aircraft, or water craft.
Repairing and Maintaining Electronic Equipment	Servicing, repairing, calibrating, regulating, fine-tuning, or testing machines, devices, and equipment that operate primarily on the basis of electrical or electronic (not mechanical) principles.
Repairing and Maintaining Mechanical Equipment	Servicing, repairing, adjusting, and testing machines, devices, moving parts, and equipment that operate primarily on the basis of mechanical (not electronic) principles.

Work_Context   Work_Context Definitions

Telephone	How often do you have telephone conversations in this job?
Importance of Being Exact or Accurate	How important is being very exact or highly accurate in performing this job?
Face-to-Face Discussions	How often do you have to have face-to-face discussions with individuals or teams in this job?
Importance of Repeating Same Tasks	How important is repeating the same physical activities (e.g., key entry) or mental activities (e.g., checking entries in a ledger) over and over, without stopping, to performing this job?
Spend Time Sitting	How much does this job require sitting?
Indoors, Environmentally Controlled	How often does this job require working indoors in environmentally controlled conditions?
Structured versus Unstructured Work	To what extent is this job structured for the worker, rather than allowing the worker to determine tasks, priorities, and goals?
Contact With Others	How much does this job require the worker to be in contact with others (face-to-face, by telephone, or otherwise) in order to perform it?
Work With Work Group or Team	How important is it to work with others in a group or team in this job?
Electronic Mail	How often do you use electronic mail in this job?
Freedom to Make Decisions	How much decision making freedom, without supervision, does the job offer?
Letters and Memos	How often does the job require written letters and memos?
Time Pressure	How often does this job require the worker to meet strict deadlines?
Deal With External Customers	How important is it to work with external customers or the public in this job?
Spend Time Making Repetitive Motions	How much does this job require making repetitive motions?
Sounds, Noise Levels Are Distracting or Uncomforta	How often does this job require working exposed to sounds and noise levels that are distracting or uncomfortable?
Frequency of Decision Making	How frequently is the worker required to make decisions that affect other people, the financial resources, and/or the image and reputation of the organization?
Coordinate or Lead Others	How important is it to coordinate or lead others in accomplishing work activities in this job?
Deal With Unpleasant or Angry People	How frequently does the worker have to deal with unpleasant, angry, or discourteous individuals as part of the job requirements?
Frequency of Conflict Situations	How often are there conflict situations the employee has to face in this job?
Impact of Decisions on Co-workers or Company Resul	How do the decisions an employee makes impact the results of co-workers, clients or the company?

Spend Time Using Your Hands to Handle, Control, or	How much does this job require using your hands to handle, control, or feel objects, tools or controls?
Responsibility for Outcomes and Results	How responsible is the worker for work outcomes and results of other workers?
Physical Proximity	To what extent does this job require the worker to perform job tasks in close physical proximity to other people?
Degree of Automation	How automated is the job?
Level of Competition	To what extent does this job require the worker to compete or to be aware of competitive pressures?
Consequence of Error	How serious would the result usually be if the worker made a mistake that was not readily correctable?
Spend Time Standing	How much does this job require standing?
Responsible for Others' Health and Safety	How much responsibility is there for the health and safety of others in this job?
Exposed to Contaminants	How often does this job require working exposed to contaminants (such as pollutants, gases, dust or odors)?
Spend Time Bending or Twisting the Body	How much does this job require bending or twisting your body?
Spend Time Walking and Running	How much does this job require walking and running?
Spend Time Kneeling, Crouching, Stooping, or Crawl	How much does this job require kneeling, crouching, stooping or crawling?
Wear Common Protective or Safety Equipment such as	How much does this job require wearing common protective or safety equipment such as safety shoes, glasses, gloves, hard hats or live jackets?
Cramped Work Space, Awkward Positions	How often does this job require working in cramped work spaces that requires getting into awkward positions?
Public Speaking	How often do you have to perform public speaking in this job?
Indoors, Not Environmentally Controlled	How often does this job require working indoors in non-controlled environmental conditions (e.g., warehouse without heat)?
Extremely Bright or Inadequate Lighting	How often does this job require working in extremely bright or inadequate lighting conditions?
Pace Determined by Speed of Equipment	How important is it to this job that the pace is determined by the speed of equipment or machinery? (This does not refer to keeping busy at all times on this job.)
Deal With Physically Aggressive People	How frequently does this job require the worker to deal with physical aggression of violent individuals?
Outdoors, Exposed to Weather	How often does this job require working outdoors, exposed to all weather conditions?
Very Hot or Cold Temperatures	How often does this job require working in very hot (above 90 F degrees) or very cold (below 32 F degrees) temperatures?
Exposed to Minor Burns, Cuts, Bites, or Stings	How often does this job require exposure to minor burns, cuts, bites, or stings?
In an Enclosed Vehicle or Equipment	How often does this job require working in a closed vehicle or equipment (e.g., car)?
Exposed to Disease or Infections	How often does this job require exposure to disease/infections?
Exposed to Whole Body Vibration	How often does this job require exposure to whole body vibration (e.g., operate a jackhammer)?
Outdoors, Under Cover	How often does this job require working outdoors, under cover (e.g., structure with roof but no walls)?
Spend Time Keeping or Regaining Balance	How much does this job require keeping or regaining your balance?
Exposed to Hazardous Conditions	How often does this job require exposure to hazardous conditions?
Exposed to Hazardous Equipment	How often does this job require exposure to hazardous equipment?
In an Open Vehicle or Equipment	How often does this job require working in an open vehicle or equipment (e.g., tractor)?
Wear Specialized Protective or Safety Equipment su	How much does this job require wearing specialized protective or safety equipment such as breathing apparatus, safety harness, full protection suits, or radiation protection?
Spend Time Climbing Ladders, Scaffolds, or Poles	How much does this job require climbing ladders, scaffolds, or poles?
Exposed to High Places	How often does this job require exposure to high places?
Exposed to Radiation	How often does this job require exposure to radiation?

Job Zone Component   Job Zone Component Definitions

Title	Job Zone Three: Medium Preparation Needed

Overall Experience	Previous work-related skill, knowledge, or experience is required for these occupations. For example, an electrician must have completed three or four years of apprenticeship or several years of vocational training, and often must have passed a licensing exam, in order to perform the job.
Job Training	Employees in these occupations usually need one or two years of training involving both on-the-job experience and informal training with experienced workers.
Job Zone Examples	These occupations usually involve using communication and organizational skills to coordinate, supervise, manage, or train others to accomplish goals. Examples include dental assistants, electricians, fish and game wardens, legal secretaries, personnel recruiters, and recreation workers.
SVP Range	(6.0 to < 7.0)
Education	Most occupations in this zone require training in vocational schools, related on-the-job experience, or an associate's degree. Some may require a bachelor's degree.

Work_Styles	Work_Styles Definitions
Attention to Detail	Job requires being careful about detail and thorough in completing work tasks.
Integrity	Job requires being honest and ethical.
Dependability	Job requires being reliable, responsible, and dependable, and fulfilling obligations.
Cooperation	Job requires being pleasant with others on the job and displaying a good-natured, cooperative attitude.
Independence	Job requires developing one's own ways of doing things, guiding oneself with little or no supervision, and depending on oneself to get things done.
Self Control	Job requires maintaining composure, keeping emotions in check, controlling anger, and avoiding aggressive behavior, even in very difficult situations.
Initiative	Job requires a willingness to take on responsibilities and challenges.
Concern for Others	Job requires being sensitive to others' needs and feelings and being understanding and helpful on the job.
Adaptability/Flexibility	Job requires being open to change (positive or negative) and to considerable variety in the workplace.
Stress Tolerance	Job requires accepting criticism and dealing calmly and effectively with high stress situations.
Persistence	Job requires persistence in the face of obstacles.
Achievement/Effort	Job requires establishing and maintaining personally challenging achievement goals and exerting effort toward mastering tasks.
Analytical Thinking	Job requires analyzing information and using logic to address work-related issues and problems.
Leadership	Job requires a willingness to lead, take charge, and offer opinions and direction.
Social Orientation	Job requires preferring to work with others rather than alone, and being personally connected with others on the job.
Innovation	Job requires creativity and alternative thinking to develop new ideas for and answers to work-related problems.

43-3061.00 - Procurement Clerks

Compile information and records to draw up purchase orders for procurement of materials and services.

Tasks

1) Track the status of requisitions, contracts, and orders.

2) Perform buying duties when necessary.

3) Contact suppliers in order to schedule or expedite deliveries and to resolve shortages, missed or late deliveries, and other problems.

4) Prepare purchase orders and send copies to suppliers and to departments originating requests.

5) Review requisition orders in order to verify accuracy, terminology, and specifications.

6) Determine if inventory quantities are sufficient for needs, ordering more materials when necessary.

7) Prepare, maintain, and review purchasing files, reports and price lists.

8) Compare suppliers' bills with bids and purchase orders in order to verify accuracy.

9) Locate suppliers, using sources such as catalogs and the internet, and interview them to gather information about products to be ordered.

10) Calculate costs of orders, and charge or forward invoices to appropriate accounts.

11) Compare prices, specifications, and delivery dates in order to determine the best bid among potential suppliers.

12) Check shipments when they arrive to ensure that orders have been filled correctly and that goods meet specifications.

13) Approve bills for payment.

14) Maintain knowledge of all organizational and governmental rules affecting purchases, and provide information about these rules to organization staff members and to vendors.

15) Monitor in-house inventory movement and complete inventory transfer forms for bookkeeping purposes.

16) Prepare invitation-of-bid forms, and mail forms to supplier firms or distribute forms for public posting.

17) Monitor contractor performance, recommending contract modifications when necessary.

Knowledge	Knowledge Definitions
Clerical	Knowledge of administrative and clerical procedures and systems such as word processing, managing files and records, stenography and transcription, designing forms, and other office procedures and terminology.
Customer and Personal Service	Knowledge of principles and processes for providing customer and personal services. This includes customer needs assessment, meeting quality standards for services, and evaluation of customer satisfaction.
English Language	Knowledge of the structure and content of the English language including the meaning and spelling of words, rules of composition, and grammar.
Mathematics	Knowledge of arithmetic, algebra, geometry, calculus, statistics, and their applications.
Administration and Management	Knowledge of business and management principles involved in strategic planning, resource allocation, human resources modeling, leadership technique, production methods, and coordination of people and resources.
Computers and Electronics	Knowledge of circuit boards, processors, chips, electronic equipment, and computer hardware and software, including applications and programming.
Production and Processing	Knowledge of raw materials, production processes, quality control, costs, and other techniques for maximizing the effective manufacture and distribution of goods.
Economics and Accounting	Knowledge of economic and accounting principles and practices, the financial markets, banking and the analysis and reporting of financial data.
Communications and Media	Knowledge of media production, communication, and dissemination techniques and methods. This includes alternative ways to inform and entertain via written, oral, and visual media.
Law and Government	Knowledge of laws, legal codes, court procedures, precedents, government regulations, executive orders, agency rules, and the democratic political process.
Personnel and Human Resources	Knowledge of principles and procedures for personnel recruitment, selection, training, compensation and benefits, labor relations and negotiation, and personnel information systems.
Education and Training	Knowledge of principles and methods for curriculum and training design, teaching and instruction for individuals and groups, and the measurement of training effects.
Telecommunications	Knowledge of transmission, broadcasting, switching, control, and operation of telecommunications systems.
Transportation	Knowledge of principles and methods for moving people or goods by air, rail, sea, or road, including the relative costs and benefits.
Mechanical	Knowledge of machines and tools, including their designs, uses, repair, and maintenance.
Public Safety and Security	Knowledge of relevant equipment, policies, procedures, and strategies to promote effective local, state, or national security operations for the protection of people, data, property, and institutions.
Sales and Marketing	Knowledge of principles and methods for showing, promoting, and selling products or services. This includes marketing strategy and tactics, product demonstration, sales techniques, and sales control systems.

Design	Knowledge of design techniques, tools, and principles involved in production of precision technical plans, blueprints, drawings, and models.
Psychology	Knowledge of human behavior and performance; individual differences in ability, personality, and interests; learning and motivation; psychological research methods; and the assessment and treatment of behavioral and affective disorders.
Geography	Knowledge of principles and methods for describing the features of land, sea, and air masses, including their physical characteristics, locations, interrelationships, and distribution of plant, animal, and human life.
Building and Construction	Knowledge of materials, methods, and the tools involved in the construction or repair of houses, buildings, or other structures such as highways and roads.
Foreign Language	Knowledge of the structure and content of a foreign (non-English) language including the meaning and spelling of words, rules of composition and grammar, and pronunciation.
History and Archeology	Knowledge of historical events and their causes, indicators, and effects on civilizations and cultures.
Therapy and Counseling	Knowledge of principles, methods, and procedures for diagnosis, treatment, and rehabilitation of physical and mental dysfunctions, and for career counseling and guidance.
Chemistry	Knowledge of the chemical composition, structure, and properties of substances and of the chemical processes and transformations that they undergo. This includes uses of chemicals and their interactions, danger signs, production techniques, and disposal methods.
Engineering and Technology	Knowledge of the practical application of engineering science and technology. This includes applying principles, techniques, procedures, and equipment to the design and production of various goods and services.
Medicine and Dentistry	Knowledge of the information and techniques needed to diagnose and treat human injuries, diseases, and deformities. This includes symptoms, treatment alternatives, drug properties and interactions, and preventive health-care measures.
Philosophy and Theology	Knowledge of different philosophical systems and religions. This includes their basic principles, values, ethics, ways of thinking, customs, practices, and their impact on human culture.
Biology	Knowledge of plant and animal organisms, their tissues, cells, functions, interdependencies, and interactions with each other and the environment.
Food Production	Knowledge of techniques and equipment for planting, growing, and harvesting food products (both plant and animal) for consumption, including storage/handling techniques.
Sociology and Anthropology	Knowledge of group behavior and dynamics, societal trends and influences, human migrations, ethnicity, cultures and their history and origins.
Physics	Knowledge and prediction of physical principles, laws, their interrelationships, and applications to understanding fluid, material, and atmospheric dynamics, and mechanical, electrical, atomic and sub- atomic structures and processes.
Fine Arts	Knowledge of the theory and techniques required to compose, produce, and perform works of music, dance, visual arts, drama, and sculpture.

Skills	Skills Definitions
Time Management	Managing one's own time and the time of others.
Reading Comprehension	Understanding written sentences and paragraphs in work related documents.
Speaking	Talking to others to convey information effectively.
Active Listening	Giving full attention to what other people are saying, taking time to understand the points being made, asking questions as appropriate, and not interrupting at inappropriate times.
Critical Thinking	Using logic and reasoning to identify the strengths and weaknesses of alternative solutions, conclusions or approaches to problems.
Writing	Communicating effectively in writing as appropriate for the needs of the audience.
Monitoring	Monitoring/Assessing performance of yourself, other individuals, or organizations to make improvements or take corrective action.
Management of Material Resources	Obtaining and seeing to the appropriate use of equipment, facilities, and materials needed to do certain work.
Mathematics	Using mathematics to solve problems.
Service Orientation	Actively looking for ways to help people.

Judgment and Decision Making	Considering the relative costs and benefits of potential actions to choose the most appropriate one.
Negotiation	Bringing others together and trying to reconcile differences.
Persuasion	Persuading others to change their minds or behavior.
Instructing	Teaching others how to do something.
Coordination	Adjusting actions in relation to others' actions.
Active Learning	Understanding the implications of new information for both current and future problem-solving and decision-making.
Management of Financial Resources	Determining how money will be spent to get the work done, and accounting for these expenditures.
Learning Strategies	Selecting and using training/instructional methods and procedures appropriate for the situation when learning or teaching new things.
Social Perceptiveness	Being aware of others' reactions and understanding why they react as they do.
Complex Problem Solving	Identifying complex problems and reviewing related information to develop and evaluate options and implement solutions.
Operations Analysis	Analyzing needs and product requirements to create a design.
Management of Personnel Resources	Motivating, developing, and directing people as they work, identifying the best people for the job.
Systems Evaluation	Identifying measures or indicators of system performance and the actions needed to improve or correct performance, relative to the goals of the system.
Quality Control Analysis	Conducting tests and inspections of products, services, or processes to evaluate quality or performance.
Systems Analysis	Determining how a system should work and how changes in conditions, operations, and the environment will affect outcomes.
Equipment Selection	Determining the kind of tools and equipment needed to do a job.
Operation Monitoring	Watching gauges, dials, or other indicators to make sure a machine is working properly.
Troubleshooting	Determining causes of operating errors and deciding what to do about it.
Science	Using scientific rules and methods to solve problems.
Technology Design	Generating or adapting equipment and technology to serve user needs.
Operation and Control	Controlling operations of equipment or systems.
Equipment Maintenance	Performing routine maintenance on equipment and determining when and what kind of maintenance is needed.
Installation	Installing equipment, machines, wiring, or programs to meet specifications.
Programming	Writing computer programs for various purposes.
Repairing	Repairing machines or systems using the needed tools.

Ability	Ability Definitions
Oral Expression	The ability to communicate information and ideas in speaking so others will understand.
Oral Comprehension	The ability to listen to and understand information and ideas presented through spoken words and sentences.
Written Comprehension	The ability to read and understand information and ideas presented in writing.
Information Ordering	The ability to arrange things or actions in a certain order or pattern according to a specific rule or set of rules (e.g., patterns of numbers, letters, words, pictures, mathematical operations).
Speech Clarity	The ability to speak clearly so others can understand you.
Deductive Reasoning	The ability to apply general rules to specific problems to produce answers that make sense.
Problem Sensitivity	The ability to tell when something is wrong or is likely to go wrong. It does not involve solving the problem, only recognizing there is a problem.
Written Expression	The ability to communicate information and ideas in writing so others will understand.
Near Vision	The ability to see details at close range (within a few feet of the observer).
Speech Recognition	The ability to identify and understand the speech of another person.
Inductive Reasoning	The ability to combine pieces of information to form general rules or conclusions (includes finding a relationship among seemingly unrelated events).
Mathematical Reasoning	The ability to choose the right mathematical methods or formulas to solve a problem.
Category Flexibility	The ability to generate or use different sets of rules for combining or grouping things in different ways.

Perceptual Speed	The ability to quickly and accurately compare similarities and differences among sets of letters, numbers, objects, pictures, or patterns. The things to be compared may be presented at the same time or one after the other. This ability also includes comparing a presented object with a remembered object.
Selective Attention	The ability to concentrate on a task over a period of time without being distracted.
Time Sharing	The ability to shift back and forth between two or more activities or sources of information (such as speech, sounds, touch, or other sources).
Number Facility	The ability to add, subtract, multiply, or divide quickly and correctly.
Fluency of Ideas	The ability to come up with a number of ideas about a topic (the number of ideas is important, not their quality, correctness, or creativity).
Memorization	The ability to remember information such as words, numbers, pictures, and procedures.
Originality	The ability to come up with unusual or clever ideas about a given topic or situation, or to develop creative ways to solve a problem.
Flexibility of Closure	The ability to identify or detect a known pattern (a figure, object, word, or sound) that is hidden in other distracting material.
Speed of Closure	The ability to quickly make sense of, combine, and organize information into meaningful patterns.
Manual Dexterity	The ability to quickly move your hand, your hand together with your arm, or your two hands to grasp, manipulate, or assemble objects.
Auditory Attention	The ability to focus on a single source of sound in the presence of other distracting sounds.
Control Precision	The ability to quickly and repeatedly adjust the controls of a machine or a vehicle to exact positions.
Finger Dexterity	The ability to make precisely coordinated movements of the fingers of one or both hands to grasp, manipulate, or assemble very small objects.
Arm-Hand Steadiness	The ability to keep your hand and arm steady while moving your arm or while holding your arm and hand in one position.
Far Vision	The ability to see details at a distance.
Visual Color Discrimination	The ability to match or detect differences between colors, including shades of color and brightness.
Visualization	The ability to imagine how something will look after it is moved around or when its parts are moved or rearranged.
Hearing Sensitivity	The ability to detect or tell the differences between sounds that vary in pitch and loudness.
Dynamic Flexibility	The ability to quickly and repeatedly bend, stretch, twist, or reach out with your body, arms, and/or legs.
Wrist-Finger Speed	The ability to make fast, simple, repeated movements of the fingers, hands, and wrists.
Gross Body Coordination	The ability to coordinate the movement of your arms, legs, and torso together when the whole body is in motion.
Static Strength	The ability to exert maximum muscle force to lift, push, pull, or carry objects.
Explosive Strength	The ability to use short bursts of muscle force to propel oneself (as in jumping or sprinting), or to throw an object.
Rate Control	The ability to time your movements or the movement of a piece of equipment in anticipation of changes in the speed and/or direction of a moving object or scene.
Trunk Strength	The ability to use your abdominal and lower back muscles to support part of the body repeatedly or continuously over time without 'giving out' or fatiguing.
Peripheral Vision	The ability to see objects or movement of objects to one's side when the eyes are looking ahead.
Extent Flexibility	The ability to bend, stretch, twist, or reach with your body, arms, and/or legs.
Dynamic Strength	The ability to exert muscle force repeatedly or continuously over time. This involves muscular endurance and resistance to muscle fatigue.
Response Orientation	The ability to choose quickly between two or more movements in response to two or more different signals (lights, sounds, pictures). It includes the speed with which the correct response is started with the hand, foot, or other body part.
Multilimb Coordination	The ability to coordinate two or more limbs (for example, two arms, two legs, or one leg and one arm) while sitting, standing, or lying down. It does not involve performing the activities while the whole body is in motion.
Spatial Orientation	The ability to know your location in relation to the environment or to know where other objects are in relation to you.
Speed of Limb Movement	The ability to quickly move the arms and legs.

Night Vision	The ability to see under low light conditions.
Depth Perception	The ability to judge which of several objects is closer or farther away from you, or to judge the distance between you and an object.
Glare Sensitivity	The ability to see objects in the presence of glare or bright lighting.
Gross Body Equilibrium	The ability to keep or regain your body balance or stay upright when in an unstable position.
Stamina	The ability to exert yourself physically over long periods of time without getting winded or out of breath.
Reaction Time	The ability to quickly respond (with the hand, finger, or foot) to a signal (sound, light, picture) when it appears.
Sound Localization	The ability to tell the direction from which a sound originated.

Work_Activity	Work_Activity Definitions
Getting Information	Observing, receiving, and otherwise obtaining information from all relevant sources.
Interacting With Computers	Using computers and computer systems (including hardware and software) to program, write software, set up functions, enter data, or process information.
Establishing and Maintaining Interpersonal Relatio	Developing constructive and cooperative working relationships with others, and maintaining them over time.
Communicating with Supervisors, Peers, or Subordin	Providing information to supervisors, co-workers, and subordinates by telephone, in written form, e-mail, or in person.
Processing Information	Compiling, coding, categorizing, calculating, tabulating, auditing, or verifying information or data.
Communicating with Persons Outside Organization	Communicating with people outside the organization, representing the organization to customers, the public, government, and other external sources. This information can be exchanged in person, in writing, or by telephone or e-mail.
Organizing, Planning, and Prioritizing Work	Developing specific goals and plans to prioritize, organize, and accomplish your work.
Identifying Objects, Actions, and Events	Identifying information by categorizing, estimating, recognizing differences or similarities, and detecting changes in circumstances or events.
Making Decisions and Solving Problems	Analyzing information and evaluating results to choose the best solution and solve problems.
Performing Administrative Activities	Performing day-to-day administrative tasks such as maintaining information files and processing paperwork.
Updating and Using Relevant Knowledge	Keeping up-to-date technically and applying new knowledge to your job.
Analyzing Data or Information	Identifying the underlying principles, reasons, or facts of information by breaking down information or data into separate parts.
Documenting/Recording Information	Entering, transcribing, recording, storing, or maintaining information in written or electronic/magnetic form.
Judging the Qualities of Things, Services, or Peop	Assessing the value, importance, or quality of things or people.
Monitor Processes, Materials, or Surroundings	Monitoring and reviewing information from materials, events, or the environment, to detect or assess problems.
Estimating the Quantifiable Characteristics of Pro	Estimating sizes, distances, and quantities; or determining time, costs, resources, or materials needed to perform a work activity.
Monitoring and Controlling Resources	Monitoring and controlling resources and overseeing the spending of money.
Evaluating Information to Determine Compliance wit	Using relevant information and individual judgment to determine whether events or processes comply with laws, regulations, or standards.
Resolving Conflicts and Negotiating with Others	Handling complaints, settling disputes, and resolving grievances and conflicts, or otherwise negotiating with others.
Performing for or Working Directly with the Public	Performing for people or dealing directly with the public. This includes serving customers in restaurants and stores, and receiving clients or guests.
Coordinating the Work and Activities of Others	Getting members of a group to work together to accomplish tasks.
Scheduling Work and Activities	Scheduling events, programs, and activities, as well as the work of others.
Thinking Creatively	Developing, designing, or creating new applications, ideas, relationships, systems, or products, including artistic contributions.
Selling or Influencing Others	Convincing others to buy merchandise/goods or to otherwise change their minds or actions.

Coaching and Developing Others	Identifying the developmental needs of others and coaching, mentoring, or otherwise helping others to improve their knowledge or skills.
Developing and Building Teams	Encouraging and building mutual trust, respect, and cooperation among team members.
Training and Teaching Others	Identifying the educational needs of others, developing formal educational or training programs or classes, and teaching or instructing others.
Provide Consultation and Advice to Others	Providing guidance and expert advice to management or other groups on technical, systems-, or process-related topics.
Guiding, Directing, and Motivating Subordinates	Providing guidance and direction to subordinates, including setting performance standards and monitoring performance.
Inspecting Equipment, Structures, or Material	Inspecting equipment, structures, or materials to identify the cause of errors or other problems or defects.
Developing Objectives and Strategies	Establishing long-range objectives and specifying the strategies and actions to achieve them.
Interpreting the Meaning of Information for Others	Translating or explaining what information means and how it can be used.
Handling and Moving Objects	Using hands and arms in handling, installing, positioning, and moving materials, and manipulating things.
Assisting and Caring for Others	Providing personal assistance, medical attention, emotional support, or other personal care to others such as coworkers, customers, or patients.
Performing General Physical Activities	Performing physical activities that require considerable use of your arms and legs and moving your whole body, such as climbing, lifting, balancing, walking, stooping, and handling of materials.
Controlling Machines and Processes	Using either control mechanisms or direct physical activity to operate machines or processes (not including computers or vehicles).
Drafting, Laying Out, and Specifying Technical Dev	Providing documentation, detailed instructions, drawings, or specifications to tell others about how devices, parts, equipment, or structures are to be fabricated, constructed, assembled, modified, maintained, or used.
Staffing Organizational Units	Recruiting, interviewing, selecting, hiring, and promoting employees in an organization.
Operating Vehicles, Mechanized Devices, or Equipme	Running, maneuvering, navigating, or driving vehicles or mechanized equipment, such as forklifts, passenger vehicles, aircraft, or water craft.
Repairing and Maintaining Mechanical Equipment	Servicing, repairing, adjusting, and testing machines, devices, moving parts, and equipment that operate primarily on the basis of mechanical (not electronic) principles.
Repairing and Maintaining Electronic Equipment	Servicing, repairing, calibrating, regulating, fine-tuning, or testing machines, devices, and equipment that operate primarily on the basis of electrical or electronic (not mechanical) principles.

Work_Context	Work_Context Definitions
Telephone	How often do you have telephone conversations in this job?
Face-to-Face Discussions	How often do you have to have face-to-face discussions with individuals or teams in this job?
Indoors, Environmentally Controlled	How often does this job require working indoors in environmentally controlled conditions?
Contact With Others	How much does this job require the worker to be in contact with others (face-to-face, by telephone, or otherwise) in order to perform it?
Electronic Mail	How often do you use electronic mail in this job?
Work With Work Group or Team	How important is it to work with others in a group or team in this job?
Frequency of Decision Making	How frequently is the worker required to make decisions that affect other people, the financial resources, and/or the image and reputation of the organization?
Structured versus Unstructured Work	To what extent is this job structured for the worker, rather than allowing the worker to determine tasks, priorities, and goals?
Deal With External Customers	How important is it to work with external customers or the public in this job?
Freedom to Make Decisions	How much decision making freedom, without supervision, does the job offer?
Importance of Being Exact or Accurate	How important is being very exact or highly accurate in performing this job?
Impact of Decisions on Co-workers or Company Resul	How do the decisions an employee makes impact the results of co-workers, clients or the company?
Importance of Repeating Same Tasks	How important is repeating the same physical activities (e.g., key entry) or mental activities (e.g., checking entries in a ledger) over and over, without stopping, to performing this job?
Spend Time Sitting	How much does this job require sitting?

Time Pressure	How often does this job require the worker to meet strict deadlines?
Letters and Memos	How often does the job require written letters and memos?
Responsible for Others' Health and Safety	How much responsibility is there for the health and safety of others in this job?
Spend Time Making Repetitive Motions	How much does this job require making repetitive motions?
Level of Competition	To what extent does this job require the worker to compete or to be aware of competitive pressures?
Sounds, Noise Levels Are Distracting or Uncomforta	How often does this job require working exposed to sounds and noise levels that are distracting or uncomfortable?
Deal With Unpleasant or Angry People	How frequently does the worker have to deal with unpleasant, angry, or discourteous individuals as part of the job requirements?
Responsibility for Outcomes and Results	How responsible is the worker for work outcomes and results of other workers?
Frequency of Conflict Situations	How often are there conflict situations the employee has to face in this job?
Coordinate or Lead Others	How important is it to coordinate or lead others in accomplishing work activities in this job?
Exposed to Contaminants	How often does this job require working exposed to contaminants (such as pollutants, gases, dust or odors)?
Consequence of Error	How serious would the result usually be if the worker made a mistake that was not readily correctable?
Spend Time Using Your Hands to Handle, Control, or	How much does this job require using your hands to handle, control, or feel objects, tools or controls?
Physical Proximity	To what extent does this job require the worker to perform job tasks in close physical proximity to other people?
Degree of Automation	How automated is the job?
Spend Time Walking and Running	How much does this job require walking and running?
Spend Time Standing	How much does this job require standing?
Pace Determined by Speed of Equipment	How important is it to this job that the pace is determined by the speed of equipment or machinery? (This does not refer to keeping busy at all times on this job.)
Exposed to Minor Burns, Cuts, Bites, or Stings	How often does this job require exposure to minor burns, cuts, bites, or stings?
In an Enclosed Vehicle or Equipment	How often does this job require working in a closed vehicle or equipment (e.g., car)?
Exposed to Hazardous Equipment	How often does this job require exposure to hazardous equipment?
Exposed to Hazardous Conditions	How often does this job require exposure to hazardous conditions?
Indoors, Not Environmentally Controlled	How often does this job require working indoors in non-controlled environmental conditions (e.g., warehouse without heat)?
Very Hot or Cold Temperatures	How often does this job require working in very hot (above 90 F degrees) or very cold (below 32 F degrees) temperatures?
Spend Time Bending or Twisting the Body	How much does this job require bending or twisting your body?
Wear Common Protective or Safety Equipment such as	How much does this job require wearing common protective or safety equipment such as safety shoes, glasses, gloves, hard hats or live jackets?
Outdoors, Exposed to Weather	How often does this job require working outdoors, exposed to all weather conditions?
Outdoors, Under Cover	How often does this job require working outdoors, under cover (e.g., structure with roof but no walls)?
Public Speaking	How often do you have to perform public speaking in this job?
Spend Time Kneeling, Crouching, Stooping, or Crawl	How much does this job require kneeling, crouching, stooping, or crawling?
Deal With Physically Aggressive People	How frequently does this job require the worker to deal with physical aggression of violent individuals?
Extremely Bright or Inadequate Lighting	How often does this job require working in extremely bright or inadequate lighting conditions?
Cramped Work Space, Awkward Positions	How often does this job require working in cramped work spaces that requires getting into awkward positions?
In an Open Vehicle or Equipment	How often does this job require working in an open vehicle or equipment (e.g., tractor)?
Exposed to Disease or Infections	How often does this job require exposure to disease/infections?
Spend Time Keeping or Regaining Balance	How much does this job require keeping or regaining your balance?
Exposed to High Places	How often does this job require exposure to high places?
Spend Time Climbing Ladders, Scaffolds, or Poles	How much does this job require climbing ladders, scaffolds, or poles?

Exposed to Radiation	How often does this job require exposure to radiation?
Wear Specialized Protective or Safety Equipment su	How much does this job require wearing specialized protective or safety equipment such as breathing apparatus, safety harness, full protection suits, or radiation protection?
Exposed to Whole Body Vibration	How often does this job require exposure to whole body vibration (e.g., operate a jackhammer)?

Job Zone Component	Job Zone Component Definitions
Title	Job Zone Three: Medium Preparation Needed
Overall Experience	Previous work-related skill, knowledge, or experience is required for these occupations. For example, an electrician must have completed three or four years of apprenticeship or several years of vocational training, and often must have passed a licensing exam, in order to perform the job.
Job Training	Employees in these occupations usually need one or two years of training involving both on-the-job experience and informal training with experienced workers.
Job Zone Examples	These occupations usually involve using communication and organizational skills to coordinate, supervise, manage, or train others to accomplish goals. Examples include dental assistants, electricians, fish and game wardens, legal secretaries, personnel recruiters, and recreation workers.
SVP Range	(6.0 to < 7.0)
Education	Most occupations in this zone require training in vocational schools, related on-the-job experience, or an associate's degree. Some may require a bachelor's degree.

Work_Styles	Work_Styles Definitions
Dependability	Job requires being reliable, responsible, and dependable, and fulfilling obligations.
Attention to Detail	Job requires being careful about detail and thorough in completing work tasks.
Integrity	Job requires being honest and ethical.
Independence	Job requires developing one's own ways of doing things, guiding oneself with little or no supervision, and depending on oneself to get things done.
Adaptability/Flexibility	Job requires being open to change (positive or negative) and to considerable variety in the workplace.
Cooperation	Job requires being pleasant with others on the job and displaying a good-natured, cooperative attitude.
Self Control	Job requires maintaining composure, keeping emotions in check, controlling anger, and avoiding aggressive behavior, even in very difficult situations.
Stress Tolerance	Job requires accepting criticism and dealing calmly and effectively with high stress situations.
Initiative	Job requires a willingness to take on responsibilities and challenges.
Concern for Others	Job requires being sensitive to others' needs and feelings and being understanding and helpful on the job.
Achievement/Effort	Job requires establishing and maintaining personally challenging achievement goals and exerting effort toward mastering tasks.
Analytical Thinking	Job requires analyzing information and using logic to address work-related issues and problems.
Persistence	Job requires persistence in the face of obstacles.
Leadership	Job requires a willingness to lead, take charge, and offer opinions and direction.
Innovation	Job requires creativity and alternative thinking to develop new ideas for and answers to work-related problems.
Social Orientation	Job requires preferring to work with others rather than alone, and being personally connected with others on the job.

43-3071.00 - Tellers

Receive and pay out money. Keep records of money and negotiable instruments involved in a financial institution's various transactions.

Tasks

1) Examine checks for endorsements and to verify other information such as dates, bank names, identification of the persons receiving payments and the legality of the documents.

2) Cash checks and pay out money after verifying that signatures are correct, that written and numerical amounts agree, and that accounts have sufficient funds.

3) Explain, promote, or sell products or services such as travelers' checks, savings bonds, money orders, and cashier's checks, using computerized information about customers to tailor recommendations.

4) Prepare and verify cashier's checks.

5) Process transactions such as term deposits, retirement savings plan contributions, automated teller transactions, night deposits, and mail deposits.

6) Identify transaction mistakes when debits and credits do not balance.

7) Receive mortgage, loan, or public utility bill payments, verifying payment dates and amounts due.

8) Resolve problems or discrepancies concerning customers' accounts.

9) Count currency, coins, and checks received, by hand or using currency-counting machine, in order to prepare them for deposit or shipment to branch banks or the Federal Reserve Bank.

10) Enter customers' transactions into computers in order to record transactions and issue computer-generated receipts.

11) Arrange monies received in cash boxes and coin dispensers according to denomination.

12) Perform clerical tasks such as typing, filing, and microfilm photography.

13) Receive and count daily inventories of cash, drafts, and travelers' checks.

14) Carry out special services for customers, such as ordering bank cards and checks.

15) Monitor bank vaults to ensure cash balances are correct.

16) Inform customers about foreign currency regulations, and compute transaction fees for currency exchanges.

17) Obtain and process information required for the provision of services, such as opening accounts, savings plans, and purchasing bonds.

18) Order a supply of cash to meet daily needs.

19) Compute financial fees, interest, and service charges.

20) Count, verify, and post armored car deposits.

21) Sort and file deposit slips and checks.

22) Compose, type, and mail customer statements and other correspondence related to issues such as discrepancies and outstanding unpaid items.

23) Issue checks to bond owners in settlement of transactions.

24) Quote unit exchange rates, following daily international rate sheets or computer displays.

25) Process and maintain records of customer loans.

26) Prepare work schedules for staff.

27) Receive checks and cash for deposit, verify amounts, and check accuracy of deposit slips.

Knowledge	Knowledge Definitions
Customer and Personal Service	Knowledge of principles and processes for providing customer and personal services. This includes customer needs assessment, meeting quality standards for services, and evaluation of customer satisfaction.
English Language	Knowledge of the structure and content of the English language including the meaning and spelling of words, rules of composition, and grammar.
Mathematics	Knowledge of arithmetic, algebra, geometry, calculus, statistics, and their applications.
Clerical	Knowledge of administrative and clerical procedures and systems such as word processing, managing files and records, stenography and transcription, designing forms, and other office procedures and terminology.
Sales and Marketing	Knowledge of principles and methods for showing, promoting, and selling products or services. This includes marketing strategy and tactics, product demonstration, sales techniques, and sales control systems.
Public Safety and Security	Knowledge of relevant equipment, policies, procedures, and strategies to promote effective local, state, or national security operations for the protection of people, data, property, and institutions.
Economics and Accounting	Knowledge of economic and accounting principles and practices, the financial markets, banking and the analysis and reporting of financial data.

Administration and Management	Knowledge of business and management principles involved in strategic planning, resource allocation, human resources modeling, leadership technique, production methods, and coordination of people and resources.
Law and Government	Knowledge of laws, legal codes, court procedures, precedents, government regulations, executive orders, agency rules, and the democratic political process.
Computers and Electronics	Knowledge of circuit boards, processors, chips, electronic equipment, and computer hardware and software, including applications and programming.
Production and Processing	Knowledge of raw materials, production processes, quality control, costs, and other techniques for maximizing the effective manufacture and distribution of goods.
Education and Training	Knowledge of principles and methods for curriculum and training design, teaching and instruction for individuals and groups, and the measurement of training effects.
Communications and Media	Knowledge of media production, communication, and dissemination techniques and methods. This includes alternative ways to inform and entertain via written, oral, and visual media.
Telecommunications	Knowledge of transmission, broadcasting, switching, control, and operation of telecommunications systems.
Personnel and Human Resources	Knowledge of principles and procedures for personnel recruitment, selection, training, compensation and benefits, labor relations and negotiation, and personnel information systems.
Psychology	Knowledge of human behavior and performance; individual differences in ability, personality, and interests; learning and motivation; psychological research methods; and the assessment and treatment of behavioral and affective disorders.
Foreign Language	Knowledge of the structure and content of a foreign (non-English) language including the meaning and spelling of words, rules of composition and grammar, and pronunciation.
Sociology and Anthropology	Knowledge of group behavior and dynamics, societal trends and influences, human migrations, ethnicity, cultures and their history and origins.
Geography	Knowledge of principles and methods for describing the features of land, sea, and air masses, including their physical characteristics, locations, interrelationships, and distribution of plant, animal, and human life.
Transportation	Knowledge of principles and methods for moving people or goods by air, rail, sea, or road, including the relative costs and benefits.
Physics	Knowledge and prediction of physical principles, laws, their interrelationships, and applications to understanding fluid, material, and atmospheric dynamics, and mechanical, electrical, atomic and sub- atomic structures and processes.
History and Archeology	Knowledge of historical events and their causes, indicators, and effects on civilizations and cultures.
Philosophy and Theology	Knowledge of different philosophical systems and religions. This includes their basic principles, values, ethics, ways of thinking, customs, practices, and their impact on human culture.
Therapy and Counseling	Knowledge of principles, methods, and procedures for diagnosis, treatment, and rehabilitation of physical and mental dysfunctions, and for career counseling and guidance.
Medicine and Dentistry	Knowledge of the information and techniques needed to diagnose and treat human injuries, diseases, and deformities. This includes symptoms, treatment alternatives, drug properties and interactions, and preventive health-care measures.
Mechanical	Knowledge of machines and tools, including their designs, uses, repair, and maintenance.
Chemistry	Knowledge of the chemical composition, structure, and properties of substances and of the chemical processes and transformations that they undergo. This includes uses of chemicals and their interactions, danger signs, production techniques, and disposal methods.
Fine Arts	Knowledge of the theory and techniques required to compose, produce, and perform works of music, dance, visual arts, drama, and sculpture.
Design	Knowledge of design techniques, tools, and principles involved in production of precision technical plans, blueprints, drawings, and models.
Food Production	Knowledge of techniques and equipment for planting, growing, and harvesting food products (both plant and animal) for consumption, including storage/handling techniques.
Biology	Knowledge of plant and animal organisms, their tissues, cells, functions, interdependencies, and interactions with each other and the environment.
Building and Construction	Knowledge of materials, methods, and the tools involved in the construction or repair of houses, buildings, or other structures such as highways and roads.
Engineering and Technology	Knowledge of the practical application of engineering science and technology. This includes applying principles, techniques, procedures, and equipment to the design and production of various goods and services.

Skills	Skills Definitions
Mathematics	Using mathematics to solve problems.
Active Listening	Giving full attention to what other people are saying, taking time to understand the points being made, asking questions as appropriate, and not interrupting at inappropriate times.
Service Orientation	Actively looking for ways to help people.
Social Perceptiveness	Being aware of others' reactions and understanding why they react as they do.
Reading Comprehension	Understanding written sentences and paragraphs in work related documents.
Speaking	Talking to others to convey information effectively.
Active Learning	Understanding the implications of new information for both current and future problem-solving and decision-making.
Time Management	Managing one's own time and the time of others.
Monitoring	Monitoring/Assessing performance of yourself, other individuals, or organizations to make improvements or take corrective action.
Critical Thinking	Using logic and reasoning to identify the strengths and weaknesses of alternative solutions, conclusions or approaches to problems.
Writing	Communicating effectively in writing as appropriate for the needs of the audience.
Learning Strategies	Selecting and using training/instructional methods and procedures appropriate for the situation when learning or teaching new things.
Instructing	Teaching others how to do something.
Coordination	Adjusting actions in relation to others' actions.
Complex Problem Solving	Identifying complex problems and reviewing related information to develop and evaluate options and implement solutions.
Judgment and Decision Making	Considering the relative costs and benefits of potential actions to choose the most appropriate one.
Persuasion	Persuading others to change their minds or behavior.
Operation and Control	Controlling operations of equipment or systems.
Quality Control Analysis	Conducting tests and inspections of products, services, or processes to evaluate quality or performance.
Negotiation	Bringing others together and trying to reconcile differences.
Operations Analysis	Analyzing needs and product requirements to create a design.
Systems Evaluation	Identifying measures or indicators of system performance and the actions needed to improve or correct performance, relative to the goals of the system.
Equipment Selection	Determining the kind of tools and equipment needed to do a job.
Management of Personnel Resources	Motivating, developing, and directing people as they work, identifying the best people for the job.
Equipment Maintenance	Performing routine maintenance on equipment and determining when and what kind of maintenance is needed.
Troubleshooting	Determining causes of operating errors and deciding what to do about it.
Management of Financial Resources	Determining how money will be spent to get the work done, and accounting for these expenditures.
Systems Analysis	Determining how a system should work and how changes in conditions, operations, and the environment will affect outcomes.
Operation Monitoring	Watching gauges, dials, or other indicators to make sure a machine is working properly.
Management of Material Resources	Obtaining and seeing to the appropriate use of equipment, facilities, and materials needed to do certain work.
Technology Design	Generating or adapting equipment and technology to serve user needs.
Installation	Installing equipment, machines, wiring, or programs to meet specifications.
Repairing	Repairing machines or systems using the needed tools.
Programming	Writing computer programs for various purposes.
Science	Using scientific rules and methods to solve problems.

Ability	Ability Definitions
Oral Expression	The ability to communicate information and ideas in speaking so others will understand.
Oral Comprehension	The ability to listen to and understand information and ideas presented through spoken words and sentences.
Problem Sensitivity	The ability to tell when something is wrong or is likely to go wrong. It does not involve solving the problem, only recognizing there is a problem.
Information Ordering	The ability to arrange things or actions in a certain order or pattern according to a specific rule or set of rules (e.g., patterns of numbers, letters, words, pictures, mathematical operations).
Number Facility	The ability to add, subtract, multiply, or divide quickly and correctly.
Speech Clarity	The ability to speak clearly so others can understand you.
Near Vision	The ability to see details at close range (within a few feet of the observer).
Speech Recognition	The ability to identify and understand the speech of another person.
Mathematical Reasoning	The ability to choose the right mathematical methods or formulas to solve a problem.
Written Comprehension	The ability to read and understand information and ideas presented in writing.
Perceptual Speed	The ability to quickly and accurately compare similarities and differences among sets of letters, numbers, objects, pictures, or patterns. The things to be compared may be presented at the same time or one after the other. This ability also includes comparing a presented object with a remembered object.
Deductive Reasoning	The ability to apply general rules to specific problems to produce answers that make sense.
Selective Attention	The ability to concentrate on a task over a period of time without being distracted.
Inductive Reasoning	The ability to combine pieces of information to form general rules or conclusions (includes finding a relationship among seemingly unrelated events).
Written Expression	The ability to communicate information and ideas in writing so others will understand.
Category Flexibility	The ability to generate or use different sets of rules for combining or grouping things in different ways.
Manual Dexterity	The ability to quickly move your hand, your hand together with your arm, or your two hands to grasp, manipulate, or assemble objects.
Time Sharing	The ability to shift back and forth between two or more activities or sources of information (such as speech, sounds, touch, or other sources).
Memorization	The ability to remember information such as words, numbers, pictures, and procedures.
Flexibility of Closure	The ability to identify or detect a known pattern (a figure, object, word, or sound) that is hidden in other distracting material.
Speed of Closure	The ability to quickly make sense of, combine, and organize information into meaningful patterns.
Finger Dexterity	The ability to make precisely coordinated movements of the fingers of one or both hands to grasp, manipulate, or assemble very small objects.
Wrist-Finger Speed	The ability to make fast, simple, repeated movements of the fingers, hands, and wrists.
Trunk Strength	The ability to use your abdominal and lower back muscles to support part of the body repeatedly or continuously over time without 'giving out' or fatiguing.
Arm-Hand Steadiness	The ability to keep your hand and arm steady while moving your arm or while holding your arm and hand in one position.
Multilimb Coordination	The ability to coordinate two or more limbs (for example, two arms, two legs, or one leg and one arm) while sitting, standing, or lying down. It does not involve performing the activities while the whole body is in motion.
Visual Color Discrimination	The ability to match or detect differences between colors, including shades of color and brightness.
Fluency of Ideas	The ability to come up with a number of ideas about a topic (the number of ideas is important, not their quality, correctness, or creativity).
Control Precision	The ability to quickly and repeatedly adjust the controls of a machine or a vehicle to exact positions.
Far Vision	The ability to see details at a distance.
Originality	The ability to come up with unusual or clever ideas about a given topic or situation, or to develop creative ways to solve a problem.

Ability	Ability Definitions
Static Strength	The ability to exert maximum muscle force to lift, push, pull, or carry objects.
Extent Flexibility	The ability to bend, stretch, twist, or reach with your body, arms, and/or legs.
Auditory Attention	The ability to focus on a single source of sound in the presence of other distracting sounds.
Visualization	The ability to imagine how something will look after it is moved around or when its parts are moved or rearranged.
Hearing Sensitivity	The ability to detect or tell the differences between sounds that vary in pitch and loudness.
Dynamic Strength	The ability to exert muscle force repeatedly or continuously over time. This involves muscular endurance and resistance to muscle fatigue.
Gross Body Coordination	The ability to coordinate the movement of your arms, legs, and torso together when the whole body is in motion.
Rate Control	The ability to time your movements or the movement of a piece of equipment in anticipation of changes in the speed and/or direction of a moving object or scene.
Response Orientation	The ability to choose quickly between two or more movements in response to two or more different signals (lights, sounds, pictures). It includes the speed with which the correct response is started with the hand, foot, or other body part.
Gross Body Equilibrium	The ability to keep or regain your body balance or stay upright when in an unstable position.
Stamina	The ability to exert yourself physically over long periods of time without getting winded or out of breath.
Depth Perception	The ability to judge which of several objects is closer or farther away from you, or to judge the distance between you and an object.
Reaction Time	The ability to quickly respond (with the hand, finger, or foot) to a signal (sound, light, picture) when it appears.
Explosive Strength	The ability to use short bursts of muscle force to propel oneself (as in jumping or sprinting), or to throw an object.
Spatial Orientation	The ability to know your location in relation to the environment or to know where other objects are in relation to you.
Sound Localization	The ability to tell the direction from which a sound originated.
Peripheral Vision	The ability to see objects or movement of objects to one's side when the eyes are looking ahead.
Night Vision	The ability to see under low light conditions.
Speed of Limb Movement	The ability to quickly move the arms and legs.
Dynamic Flexibility	The ability to quickly and repeatedly bend, stretch, twist, or reach out with your body, arms, and/or legs.
Glare Sensitivity	The ability to see objects in the presence of glare or bright lighting.

Work_Activity	Work_Activity Definitions
Communicating with Supervisors, Peers, or Subordin	Providing information to supervisors, co-workers, and subordinates by telephone, in written form, e-mail, or in person.
Establishing and Maintaining Interpersonal Relatio	Developing constructive and cooperative working relationships with others, and maintaining them over time.
Performing for or Working Directly with the Public	Performing for people or dealing directly with the public. This includes serving customers in restaurants and stores, and receiving clients or guests.
Interacting With Computers	Using computers and computer systems (including hardware and software) to program, write software, set up functions, enter data, or process information.
Documenting/Recording Information	Entering, transcribing, recording, storing, or maintaining information in written or electronic/magnetic form.
Evaluating Information to Determine Compliance wit	Using relevant information and individual judgment to determine whether events or processes comply with laws, regulations, or standards.
Getting Information	Observing, receiving, and otherwise obtaining information from all relevant sources.
Making Decisions and Solving Problems	Analyzing information and evaluating results to choose the best solution and solve problems.
Processing Information	Compiling, coding, categorizing, calculating, tabulating, auditing, or verifying information or data.
Communicating with Persons Outside Organization	Communicating with people outside the organization, representing the organization to customers, the public, government, and other external sources. This information can be exchanged in person, in writing, or by telephone or e-mail.
Updating and Using Relevant Knowledge	Keeping up-to-date technically and applying new knowledge to your job.
Interpreting the Meaning of Information for Others	Translating or explaining what information means and how it can be used.

Identifying Objects, Actions, and Events	Identifying information by categorizing, estimating, recognizing differences or similarities, and detecting changes in circumstances or events.
Organizing, Planning, and Prioritizing Work	Developing specific goals and plans to prioritize, organize, and accomplish your work.
Analyzing Data or Information	Identifying the underlying principles, reasons, or facts of information by breaking down information or data into separate parts.
Resolving Conflicts and Negotiating with Others	Handling complaints, settling disputes, and resolving grievances and conflicts, or otherwise negotiating with others.
Judging the Qualities of Things, Services, or Peop	Assessing the value, importance, or quality of things or people.
Monitor Processes, Materials, or Surroundings	Monitoring and reviewing information from materials, events, or the environment, to detect or assess problems.
Selling or Influencing Others	Convincing others to buy merchandise/goods or to otherwise change their minds or actions.
Developing and Building Teams	Encouraging and building mutual trust, respect, and cooperation among team members.
Assisting and Caring for Others	Providing personal assistance, medical attention, emotional support, or other personal care to others such as coworkers, customers, or patients.
Performing Administrative Activities	Performing day-to-day administrative tasks such as maintaining information files and processing paperwork.
Controlling Machines and Processes	Using either control mechanisms or direct physical activity to operate machines or processes (not including computers or vehicles).
Performing General Physical Activities	Performing physical activities that require considerable use of your arms and legs and moving your whole body, such as climbing, lifting, balancing, walking, stooping, and handling of materials.
Handling and Moving Objects	Using hands and arms in handling, installing, positioning, and moving materials, and manipulating things.
Inspecting Equipment, Structures, or Material	Inspecting equipment, structures, or materials to identify the cause of errors or other problems or defects.
Coaching and Developing Others	Identifying the developmental needs of others and coaching, mentoring, or otherwise helping others to improve their knowledge or skills.
Developing Objectives and Strategies	Establishing long-range objectives and specifying the strategies and actions to achieve them.
Training and Teaching Others	Identifying the educational needs of others, developing formal educational or training programs or classes, and teaching or instructing others.
Estimating the Quantifiable Characteristics of Pro	Estimating sizes, distances, and quantities; or determining time, costs, resources, or materials needed to perform a work activity.
Thinking Creatively	Developing, designing, or creating new applications, ideas, relationships, systems, or products, including artistic contributions.
Coordinating the Work and Activities of Others	Getting members of a group to work together to accomplish tasks.
Provide Consultation and Advice to Others	Providing guidance and expert advice to management or other groups on technical, systems-, or process-related topics.
Scheduling Work and Activities	Scheduling events, programs, and activities, as well as the work of others.
Guiding, Directing, and Motivating Subordinates	Providing guidance and direction to subordinates, including setting performance standards and monitoring performance.
Monitoring and Controlling Resources	Monitoring and controlling resources and overseeing the spending of money.
Repairing and Maintaining Electronic Equipment	Servicing, repairing, calibrating, regulating, fine-tuning, or testing machines, devices, and equipment that operate primarily on the basis of electrical or electronic (not mechanical) principles.
Drafting, Laying Out, and Specifying Technical Dev	Providing documentation, detailed instructions, drawings, or specifications to tell others about how devices, parts, equipment, or structures are to be fabricated, constructed, assembled, modified, maintained, or used.
Operating Vehicles, Mechanized Devices, or Equipme	Running, maneuvering, navigating, or driving vehicles or mechanized equipment, such as forklifts, passenger vehicles, aircraft, or water craft.
Staffing Organizational Units	Recruiting, interviewing, selecting, hiring, and promoting employees in an organization.
Repairing and Maintaining Mechanical Equipment	Servicing, repairing, adjusting, and testing machines, devices, moving parts, and equipment that operate primarily on the basis of mechanical (not electronic) principles.

Work_Context	Work_Context Definitions
Contact With Others	How much does this job require the worker to be in contact with others (face-to-face, by telephone, or otherwise) in order to perform it?
Telephone	How often do you have telephone conversations in this job?
Face-to-Face Discussions	How often do you have to have face-to-face discussions with individuals or teams in this job?
Importance of Being Exact or Accurate	How important is being very exact or highly accurate in performing this job?
Work With Work Group or Team	How important is it to work with others in a group or team in this job?
Importance of Repeating Same Tasks	How important is repeating the same physical activities (e.g., key entry) or mental activities (e.g., checking entries in a ledger) over and over, without stopping, to performing this job?
Spend Time Making Repetitive Motions	How much does this job require making repetitive motions?
Time Pressure	How often does this job require the worker to meet strict deadlines?
Physical Proximity	To what extent does this job require the worker to perform job tasks in close physical proximity to other people?
Frequency of Decision Making	How frequently is the worker required to make decisions that affect other people, the financial resources, and/or the image and reputation of the organization?
Impact of Decisions on Co-workers or Company Resul	How do the decisions an employee makes impact the results of co-workers, clients or the company?
Indoors, Environmentally Controlled	How often does this job require working indoors in environmentally controlled conditions?
Deal With External Customers	How important is it to work with external customers or the public in this job?
Electronic Mail	How often do you use electronic mail in this job?
Structured versus Unstructured Work	To what extent is this job structured for the worker, rather than allowing the worker to determine tasks, priorities, and goals?
Freedom to Make Decisions	How much decision making freedom, without supervision, does the job offer?
Deal With Unpleasant or Angry People	How frequently does the worker have to deal with unpleasant, angry, or discourteous individuals as part of the job requirements?
Spend Time Standing	How much does this job require standing?
Spend Time Using Your Hands to Handle, Control, or	How much does this job require using your hands to handle, control, or feel objects, tools or controls?
Spend Time Sitting	How much does this job require sitting?
Coordinate or Lead Others	How important is it to coordinate or lead others in accomplishing work activities in this job?
Letters and Memos	How often does the job require written letters and memos?
Level of Competition	To what extent does this job require the worker to compete or to be aware of competitive pressures?
Consequence of Error	How serious would the result usually be if the worker made a mistake that was not readily correctable?
Frequency of Conflict Situations	How often are there conflict situations the employee has to face in this job?
Responsibility for Outcomes and Results	How responsible is the worker for work outcomes and results of other workers?
Responsible for Others' Health and Safety	How much responsibility is there for the health and safety of others in this job?
Exposed to Minor Burns, Cuts, Bites, or Stings	How often does this job require exposure to minor burns, cuts, bites, or stings?
Degree of Automation	How automated is the job?
Public Speaking	How often do you have to perform public speaking in this job?
Spend Time Bending or Twisting the Body	How much does this job require bending or twisting your body?
Spend Time Walking and Running	How much does this job require walking and running?
Exposed to Contaminants	How often does this job require working exposed to contaminants (such as pollutants, gases, dust or odors)?
Spend Time Keeping or Regaining Balance	How much does this job require keeping or regaining your balance?
Sounds, Noise Levels Are Distracting or Uncomforta	How often does this job require working exposed to sounds and noise levels that are distracting or uncomfortable?
Cramped Work Space, Awkward Positions	How often does this job require working in cramped work spaces that requires getting into awkward positions?
Spend Time Kneeling, Crouching, Stooping, or Crawl	How much does this job require kneeling, crouching, stooping or crawling?
Extremely Bright or Inadequate Lighting	How often does this job require working in extremely bright or inadequate lighting conditions?

Deal With Physically Aggressive People	How frequently does this job require the worker to deal with physical aggression of violent individuals?
Exposed to Disease or Infections	How often does this job require exposure to disease/infections?
Very Hot or Cold Temperatures	How often does this job require working in very hot (above 90 F degrees) or very cold (below 32 F degrees) temperatures?
Outdoors, Exposed to Weather	How often does this job require working outdoors, exposed to all weather conditions?
Pace Determined by Speed of Equipment	How important is it to this job that the pace is determined by the speed of equipment or machinery? (This does not refer to keeping busy at all times on this job.)
Outdoors, Under Cover	How often does this job require working outdoors, under cover (e.g., structure with roof but no walls)?
In an Enclosed Vehicle or Equipment	How often does this job require working in a closed vehicle or equipment (e.g., car)?
Exposed to Whole Body Vibration	How often does this job require exposure to whole body vibration (e.g., operate a jackhammer)?
Wear Specialized Protective or Safety Equipment su	How much does this job require wearing specialized protective or safety equipment such as breathing apparatus, safety harness, full protection suits, or radiation protection?
Exposed to Radiation	How often does this job require exposure to radiation?
Spend Time Climbing Ladders, Scaffolds, or Poles	How much does this job require climbing ladders, scaffolds, or poles?
Exposed to High Places	How often does this job require exposure to high places?
In an Open Vehicle or Equipment	How often does this job require working in an open vehicle or equipment (e.g., tractor)?
Wear Common Protective or Safety Equipment such as	How much does this job require wearing common protective or safety equipment such as safety shoes, glasses, gloves, hard hats or life jackets?
Exposed to Hazardous Equipment	How often does this job require exposure to hazardous equipment?
Indoors, Not Environmentally Controlled	How often does this job require working indoors in non-controlled environmental conditions (e.g., warehouse without heat)?
Exposed to Hazardous Conditions	How often does this job require exposure to hazardous conditions?

Job Zone Component	Job Zone Component Definitions
Title	Job Zone Two: Some Preparation Needed
Overall Experience	Some previous work-related skill, knowledge, or experience may be helpful in these occupations, but usually is not needed. For example, a drywall installer might benefit from experience installing drywall, but an inexperienced person could still learn to be an installer with little difficulty.
Job Training	Employees in these occupations need anywhere from a few months to one year of working with experienced employees.
Job Zone Examples	These occupations often involve using your knowledge and skills to help others. Examples include drywall installers, fire inspectors, flight attendants, pharmacy technicians, salespersons (retail), and tellers.
SVP Range	(4.0 to < 6.0)
Education	These occupations usually require a high school diploma and may require some vocational training or job-related course work. In some cases, an associate's or bachelor's degree could be needed.

Work_Styles	Work_Styles Definitions
Integrity	Job requires being honest and ethical.
Attention to Detail	Job requires being careful about detail and thorough in completing work tasks.
Concern for Others	Job requires being sensitive to others' needs and feelings and being understanding and helpful on the job.
Cooperation	Job requires being pleasant with others on the job and displaying a good-natured, cooperative attitude.
Dependability	Job requires being reliable, responsible, and dependable, and fulfilling obligations.
Self Control	Job requires maintaining composure, keeping emotions in check, controlling anger, and avoiding aggressive behavior, even in very difficult situations.
Stress Tolerance	Job requires accepting criticism and dealing calmly and effectively with high stress situations.
Social Orientation	Job requires preferring to work with others rather than alone, and being personally connected with others on the job.

Adaptability/Flexibility	Job requires being open to change (positive or negative) and to considerable variety in the workplace.
Leadership	Job requires a willingness to lead, take charge, and offer opinions and direction.
Initiative	Job requires a willingness to take on responsibilities and challenges.
Achievement/Effort	Job requires establishing and maintaining personally challenging achievement goals and exerting effort toward mastering tasks.
Independence	Job requires developing one's own ways of doing things, guiding oneself with little or no supervision, and depending on oneself to get things done.
Persistence	Job requires persistence in the face of obstacles.
Analytical Thinking	Job requires analyzing information and using logic to address work-related issues and problems.
Innovation	Job requires creativity and alternative thinking to develop new ideas for and answers to work-related problems.

43-4011.00 - Brokerage Clerks

Perform clerical duties involving the purchase or sale of securities. Duties include writing orders for stock purchases and sales, computing transfer taxes, verifying stock transactions, accepting and delivering securities, tracking stock price fluctuations, computing equity, distributing dividends, and keeping records of daily transactions and holdings.

Tasks

1) Record and document security transactions, such as purchases, sales, conversions, redemptions, and payments, using computers, accounting ledgers, and certificate records.

2) Prepare reports summarizing daily transactions and earnings for individual customer accounts.

3) Compute total holdings, dividends, interest, transfer taxes, brokerage fees, and commissions, and allocate appropriate payments to customers.

4) Prepare forms, such as receipts, withdrawal orders, transmittal papers, and transfer confirmations, based on transaction requests from stockholders.

5) Schedule and coordinate transfer and delivery of security certificates between companies, departments, and customers.

6) Verify ownership and transaction information and dividend distribution instructions to ensure conformance with governmental regulations, using stock records and reports.

7) Monitor daily stock prices, and compute fluctuations in order to determine the need for additional collateral to secure loans.

8) File, type, and operate standard office machines.

43-4021.00 - Correspondence Clerks

Compose letters in reply to requests for merchandise, damage claims, credit and other information, delinquent accounts, incorrect billings, or unsatisfactory services. Duties may include gathering data to formulate reply and typing correspondence.

Tasks

1) Compose correspondence requesting medical information and records.

2) Present clear and concise explanations of governing rules and regulations.

3) Compose letters in reply to correspondence concerning such items as requests for merchandise, damage claims, credit information requests, delinquent accounts, incorrect billing, or unsatisfactory service.

4) Review correspondence for format and typographical accuracy, assemble the information into a prescribed form with the correct number of copies, and submit it to an authorized official for signature.

5) Route correspondence to other departments for reply.

6) Type acknowledgment letters to persons sending correspondence.

7) Compile data pertinent to manufacture of special products for customers.

8) Respond to internal and external requests for the release of information contained in medical records, copying medical records, and selective extracts in accordance with laws and regulations.

9) Confer with company personnel regarding feasibility of complying with writers' requests.

10) Ensure that money collected is properly recorded and secured.

11) Maintain files and control records to show correspondence activities.

12) Prepare records for shipment by certified mail.

13) Compile data from records to prepare periodic reports.

14) Prepare documents and correspondence such as damage claims, credit and billing inquiries, invoices, and service complaints.

15) Obtain written authorization to access required medical information.

16) Gather records pertinent to specific problems, review them for completeness and accuracy, and attach records to correspondence as necessary.

17) Compute costs of records furnished to requesters, and write letters to obtain payment.

18) Complete form letters in response to requests or problems identified by correspondence.

19) Read incoming correspondence to ascertain nature of writers' concerns and to determine disposition of correspondence.

20) Process orders for goods requested in correspondence.

43-4031.01 - Court Clerks

Perform clerical duties in court of law; prepare docket of cases to be called; secure information for judges; and contact witnesses, attorneys, and litigants to obtain information for court.

Tasks

1) Explain procedures or forms to parties in cases or to the general public.

2) Record case dispositions, court orders, and arrangements made for payment of court fees.

3) Prepare documents recording the outcomes of court proceedings.

4) Prepare and issue orders of the court, including probation orders, release documentation, sentencing information, and summonses.

5) Prepare dockets or calendars of cases to be called, using typewriters or computers.

6) Instruct parties about timing of court appearances.

7) Search files, and contact witnesses, attorneys, and litigants, in order to obtain information for the court.

8) Collect court fees or fines, and record amounts collected.

9) Prepare courtrooms with paper, pens, water, easels, and electronic equipment, and ensure that recording equipment is working.

10) Examine legal documents submitted to courts for adherence to laws or court procedures.

11) Meet with judges, lawyers, parole officers, police, and social agency officials in order to coordinate the functions of the court.

12) Swear in jury members, interpreters, witnesses and defendants.

13) Direct support staff in handling of paperwork processed by clerks' offices.

14) Prepare and mark all applicable court exhibits and evidence.

15) Read charges and related information to the court and, if necessary, record defendants' pleas.

16) Record court proceedings, using recording equipment, or record minutes of court proceedings using stenotype machines or shorthand.

17) Follow procedures to secure courtrooms and exhibits such as money, drugs, and weapons.

18) Conduct roll calls, and poll jurors.

19) Open courts, calling them to order and announcing judges.

20) Amend indictments when necessary, and endorse indictments with pertinent information.

Knowledge	Knowledge Definitions
Clerical	Knowledge of administrative and clerical procedures and systems such as word processing, managing files and records, stenography and transcription, designing forms, and other office procedures and terminology.
Law and Government	Knowledge of laws, legal codes, court procedures, precedents, government regulations, executive orders, agency rules, and the democratic political process.
Computers and Electronics	Knowledge of circuit boards, processors, chips, electronic equipment, and computer hardware and software, including applications and programming.
Customer and Personal Service	Knowledge of principles and processes for providing customer and personal services. This includes customer needs assessment, meeting quality standards for services, and evaluation of customer satisfaction.
English Language	Knowledge of the structure and content of the English language including the meaning and spelling of words, rules of composition, and grammar.
Mathematics	Knowledge of arithmetic, algebra, geometry, calculus, statistics, and their applications.
Administration and Management	Knowledge of business and management principles involved in strategic planning, resource allocation, human resources modeling, leadership technique, production methods, and coordination of people and resources.
Public Safety and Security	Knowledge of relevant equipment, policies, procedures, and strategies to promote effective local, state, or national security operations for the protection of people, data, property, and institutions.
Education and Training	Knowledge of principles and methods for curriculum and training design, teaching and instruction for individuals and groups, and the measurement of training effects.
Telecommunications	Knowledge of transmission, broadcasting, switching, control, and operation of telecommunications systems.
Psychology	Knowledge of human behavior and performance; individual differences in ability, personality, and interests; learning and motivation; psychological research methods; and the assessment and treatment of behavioral and affective disorders.
Economics and Accounting	Knowledge of economic and accounting principles and practices, the financial markets, banking and the analysis and reporting of financial data.
Geography	Knowledge of principles and methods for describing the features of land, sea, and air masses, including their physical characteristics, locations, interrelationships, and distribution of plant, animal, and human life.
Communications and Media	Knowledge of media production, communication, and dissemination techniques and methods. This includes alternative ways to inform and entertain via written, oral, and visual media.
Production and Processing	Knowledge of raw materials, production processes, quality control, costs, and other techniques for maximizing the effective manufacture and distribution of goods.
Personnel and Human Resources	Knowledge of principles and procedures for personnel recruitment, selection, training, compensation and benefits, labor relations and negotiation, and personnel information systems.
Mechanical	Knowledge of machines and tools, including their designs, uses, repair, and maintenance.
Transportation	Knowledge of principles and methods for moving people or goods by air, rail, sea, or road, including the relative costs and benefits.
Foreign Language	Knowledge of the structure and content of a foreign (non-English) language including the meaning and spelling of words, rules of composition and grammar, and pronunciation.
Sociology and Anthropology	Knowledge of group behavior and dynamics, societal trends and influences, human migrations, ethnicity, cultures and their history and origins.
Sales and Marketing	Knowledge of principles and methods for showing, promoting, and selling products or services. This includes marketing strategy and tactics, product demonstration, sales techniques, and sales control systems.
Philosophy and Theology	Knowledge of different philosophical systems and religions. This includes their basic principles, values, ethics, ways of thinking, customs, practices, and their impact on human culture.
Design	Knowledge of design techniques, tools, and principles involved in production of precision technical plans, blueprints, drawings, and models.
Therapy and Counseling	Knowledge of principles, methods, and procedures for diagnosis, treatment, and rehabilitation of physical and mental dysfunctions, and for career counseling and guidance.
History and Archeology	Knowledge of historical events and their causes, indicators, and effects on civilizations and cultures.
Medicine and Dentistry	Knowledge of the information and techniques needed to diagnose and treat human injuries, diseases, and deformities. This includes symptoms, treatment alternatives, drug properties and interactions, and preventive health-care measures.

Engineering and Technology	Knowledge of the practical application of engineering science and technology. This includes applying principles, techniques, procedures, and equipment to the design and production of various goods and services.
Biology	Knowledge of plant and animal organisms, their tissues, cells, functions, interdependencies, and interactions with each other and the environment.
Fine Arts	Knowledge of the theory and techniques required to compose, produce, and perform works of music, dance, visual arts, drama, and sculpture.
Chemistry	Knowledge of the chemical composition, structure, and properties of substances and of the chemical processes and transformations that they undergo. This includes uses of chemicals and their interactions, danger signs, production techniques, and disposal methods.
Building and Construction	Knowledge of materials, methods, and the tools involved in the construction or repair of houses, buildings, or other structures such as highways and roads.
Physics	Knowledge and prediction of physical principles, laws, their interrelationships, and applications to understanding fluid, material, and atmospheric dynamics, and mechanical, electrical, atomic and sub- atomic structures and processes.
Food Production	Knowledge of techniques and equipment for planting, growing, and harvesting food products (both plant and animal) for consumption, including storage/handling techniques.

Skills	Skills Definitions
Reading Comprehension	Understanding written sentences and paragraphs in work related documents.
Active Listening	Giving full attention to what other people are saying, taking time to understand the points being made, asking questions as appropriate, and not interrupting at inappropriate times.
Writing	Communicating effectively in writing as appropriate for the needs of the audience.
Coordination	Adjusting actions in relation to others' actions.
Speaking	Talking to others to convey information effectively.
Instructing	Teaching others how to do something.
Time Management	Managing one's own time and the time of others.
Service Orientation	Actively looking for ways to help people.
Critical Thinking	Using logic and reasoning to identify the strengths and weaknesses of alternative solutions, conclusions or approaches to problems.
Learning Strategies	Selecting and using training/instructional methods and procedures appropriate for the situation when learning or teaching new things.
Social Perceptiveness	Being aware of others' reactions and understanding why they react as they do.
Active Learning	Understanding the implications of new information for both current and future problem-solving and decision-making.
Mathematics	Using mathematics to solve problems.
Monitoring	Monitoring/Assessing performance of yourself, other individuals, or organizations to make improvements or take corrective action.
Management of Personnel Resources	Motivating, developing, and directing people as they work, identifying the best people for the job.
Complex Problem Solving	Identifying complex problems and reviewing related information to develop and evaluate options and implement solutions.
Negotiation	Bringing others together and trying to reconcile differences.
Equipment Selection	Determining the kind of tools and equipment needed to do a job.
Judgment and Decision Making	Considering the relative costs and benefits of potential actions to choose the most appropriate one.
Operations Analysis	Analyzing needs and product requirements to create a design.
Technology Design	Generating or adapting equipment and technology to serve user needs.
Systems Analysis	Determining how a system should work and how changes in conditions, operations, and the environment will affect outcomes.
Management of Financial Resources	Determining how money will be spent to get the work done, and accounting for these expenditures.
Persuasion	Persuading others to change their minds or behavior.
Programming	Writing computer programs for various purposes.
Operation and Control	Controlling operations of equipment or systems.
Systems Evaluation	Identifying measures or indicators of system performance and the actions needed to improve or correct performance, relative to the goals of the system.

Equipment Maintenance	Performing routine maintenance on equipment and determining when and what kind of maintenance is needed.
Installation	Installing equipment, machines, wiring, or programs to meet specifications.
Management of Material Resources	Obtaining and seeing to the appropriate use of equipment, facilities, and materials needed to do certain work.
Troubleshooting	Determining causes of operating errors and deciding what to do about it.
Quality Control Analysis	Conducting tests and inspections of products, services, or processes to evaluate quality or performance.
Operation Monitoring	Watching gauges, dials, or other indicators to make sure a machine is working properly.
Repairing	Repairing machines or systems using the needed tools.
Science	Using scientific rules and methods to solve problems.

Ability	Ability Definitions
Oral Comprehension	The ability to listen to and understand information and ideas presented through spoken words and sentences.
Written Expression	The ability to communicate information and ideas in writing so others will understand.
Written Comprehension	The ability to read and understand information and ideas presented in writing.
Oral Expression	The ability to communicate information and ideas in speaking so others will understand.
Information Ordering	The ability to arrange things or actions in a certain order or pattern according to a specific rule or set of rules (e.g., patterns of numbers, letters, words, pictures, mathematical operations).
Near Vision	The ability to see details at close range (within a few feet of the observer).
Speech Recognition	The ability to identify and understand the speech of another person.
Speech Clarity	The ability to speak clearly so others can understand you.
Problem Sensitivity	The ability to tell when something is wrong or is likely to go wrong. It does not involve solving the problem, only recognizing there is a problem.
Deductive Reasoning	The ability to apply general rules to specific problems to produce answers that make sense.
Inductive Reasoning	The ability to combine pieces of information to form general rules or conclusions (includes finding a relationship among seemingly unrelated events).
Category Flexibility	The ability to generate or use different sets of rules for combining or grouping things in different ways.
Selective Attention	The ability to concentrate on a task over a period of time without being distracted.
Time Sharing	The ability to shift back and forth between two or more activities or sources of information (such as speech, sounds, touch, or other sources).
Auditory Attention	The ability to focus on a single source of sound in the presence of other distracting sounds.
Finger Dexterity	The ability to make precisely coordinated movements of the fingers of one or both hands to grasp, manipulate, or assemble very small objects.
Manual Dexterity	The ability to quickly move your hand, your hand together with your arm, or your two hands to grasp, manipulate, or assemble objects.
Memorization	The ability to remember information such as words, numbers, pictures, and procedures.
Control Precision	The ability to quickly and repeatedly adjust the controls of a machine or a vehicle to exact positions.
Extent Flexibility	The ability to bend, stretch, twist, or reach with your body, arms, and/or legs.
Number Facility	The ability to add, subtract, multiply, or divide quickly and correctly.
Fluency of Ideas	The ability to come up with a number of ideas about a topic (the number of ideas is important, not their quality, correctness, or creativity).
Far Vision	The ability to see details at a distance.
Perceptual Speed	The ability to quickly and accurately compare similarities and differences among sets of letters, numbers, objects, pictures, or patterns. The things to be compared may be presented at the same time or one after the other. This ability also includes comparing a presented object with a remembered object.
Glare Sensitivity	The ability to see objects in the presence of glare or bright lighting.
Visual Color Discrimination	The ability to match or detect differences between colors, including shades of color and brightness.

908

Flexibility of Closure	The ability to identify or detect a known pattern (a figure, object, word, or sound) that is hidden in other distracting material.
Originality	The ability to come up with unusual or clever ideas about a given topic or situation, or to develop creative ways to solve a problem.
Mathematical Reasoning	The ability to choose the right mathematical methods or formulas to solve a problem.
Wrist-Finger Speed	The ability to make fast, simple, repeated movements of the fingers, hands, and wrists.
Arm-Hand Steadiness	The ability to keep your hand and arm steady while moving your arm or while holding your arm and hand in one position.
Visualization	The ability to imagine how something will look after it is moved around or when its parts are moved or rearranged.
Speed of Closure	The ability to quickly make sense of, combine, and organize information into meaningful patterns.
Depth Perception	The ability to judge which of several objects is closer or farther away from you, or to judge the distance between you and an object.
Hearing Sensitivity	The ability to detect or tell the differences between sounds that vary in pitch and loudness.
Static Strength	The ability to exert maximum muscle force to lift, push, pull, or carry objects.
Trunk Strength	The ability to use your abdominal and lower back muscles to support part of the body repeatedly or continuously over time without 'giving out' or fatiguing.
Multilimb Coordination	The ability to coordinate two or more limbs (for example, two arms, two legs, or one leg and one arm) while sitting, standing, or lying down. It does not involve performing the activities while the whole body is in motion.
Explosive Strength	The ability to use short bursts of muscle force to propel oneself (as in jumping or sprinting), or to throw an object.
Gross Body Equilibrium	The ability to keep or regain your body balance or stay upright when in an unstable position.
Sound Localization	The ability to tell the direction from which a sound originated.
Night Vision	The ability to see under low light conditions.
Peripheral Vision	The ability to see objects or movement of objects to one's side when the eyes are looking ahead.
Spatial Orientation	The ability to know your location in relation to the environment or to know where other objects are in relation to you.
Rate Control	The ability to time your movements or the movement of a piece of equipment in anticipation of changes in the speed and/or direction of a moving object or scene.
Reaction Time	The ability to quickly respond (with the hand, finger, or foot) to a signal (sound, light, picture) when it appears.
Dynamic Flexibility	The ability to quickly and repeatedly bend, stretch, twist, or reach out with your body, arms, and/or legs.
Dynamic Strength	The ability to exert muscle force repeatedly or continuously over time. This involves muscular endurance and resistance to muscle fatigue.
Speed of Limb Movement	The ability to quickly move the arms and legs.
Response Orientation	The ability to choose quickly between two or more movements in response to two or more different signals (lights, sounds, pictures). It includes the speed with which the correct response is started with the hand, foot, or other body part.
Stamina	The ability to exert yourself physically over long periods of time without getting winded or out of breath.
Gross Body Coordination	The ability to coordinate the movement of your arms, legs, and torso together when the whole body is in motion.

Work_Activity	Work_Activity Definitions
Interacting With Computers	Using computers and computer systems (including hardware and software) to program, write software, set up functions, enter data, or process information.
Documenting/Recording Information	Entering, transcribing, recording, storing, or maintaining information in written or electronic/magnetic form.
Getting Information	Observing, receiving, and otherwise obtaining information from all relevant sources.
Processing Information	Compiling, coding, categorizing, calculating, tabulating, auditing, or verifying information or data.
Communicating with Persons Outside Organization	Communicating with people outside the organization, representing the organization to customers, the public, government, and other external sources. This information can be exchanged in person, in writing, or by telephone or e-mail.
Organizing, Planning, and Prioritizing Work	Developing specific goals and plans to prioritize, organize, and accomplish your work.

Establishing and Maintaining Interpersonal Relatio	Developing constructive and cooperative working relationships with others, and maintaining them over time.
Communicating with Supervisors, Peers, or Subordin	Providing information to supervisors, co-workers, and subordinates by telephone, in written form, e-mail, or in person.
Updating and Using Relevant Knowledge	Keeping up-to-date technically and applying new knowledge to your job.
Performing Administrative Activities	Performing day-to-day administrative tasks such as maintaining information files and processing paperwork.
Performing for or Working Directly with the Public	Performing for people or dealing directly with the public. This includes serving customers in restaurants and stores, and receiving clients or guests.
Evaluating Information to Determine Compliance wit	Using relevant information and individual judgment to determine whether events or processes comply with laws, regulations, or standards.
Identifying Objects, Actions, and Events	Identifying information by categorizing, estimating, recognizing differences or similarities, and detecting changes in circumstances or events.
Making Decisions and Solving Problems	Analyzing information and evaluating results to choose the best solution and solve problems.
Monitor Processes, Materials, or Surroundings	Monitoring and reviewing information from materials, events, or the environment, to detect or assess problems.
Developing and Building Teams	Encouraging and building mutual trust, respect, and cooperation among team members.
Assisting and Caring for Others	Providing personal assistance, medical attention, emotional support, or other personal care to others such as coworkers, customers, or patients.
Scheduling Work and Activities	Scheduling events, programs, and activities, as well as the work of others.
Training and Teaching Others	Identifying the educational needs of others, developing formal educational or training programs or classes, and teaching or instructing others.
Inspecting Equipment, Structures, or Material	Inspecting equipment, structures, or materials to identify the cause of errors or other problems or defects.
Analyzing Data or Information	Identifying the underlying principles, reasons, or facts of information by breaking down information or data into separate parts.
Guiding, Directing, and Motivating Subordinates	Providing guidance and direction to subordinates, including setting performance standards and monitoring performance.
Resolving Conflicts and Negotiating with Others	Handling complaints, settling disputes, and resolving grievances and conflicts, or otherwise negotiating with others.
Interpreting the Meaning of Information for Others	Translating or explaining what information means and how it can be used.
Developing Objectives and Strategies	Establishing long-range objectives and specifying the strategies and actions to achieve them.
Handling and Moving Objects	Using hands and arms in handling, installing, positioning, and moving materials, and manipulating things.
Coordinating the Work and Activities of Others	Getting members of a group to work together to accomplish tasks.
Performing General Physical Activities	Performing physical activities that require considerable use of your arms and legs and moving your whole body, such as climbing, lifting, balancing, walking, stooping, and handling of materials.
Thinking Creatively	Developing, designing, or creating new applications, ideas, relationships, systems, or products, including artistic contributions.
Coaching and Developing Others	Identifying the developmental needs of others and coaching, mentoring, or otherwise helping others to improve their knowledge or skills.
Judging the Qualities of Things, Services, or Peop	Assessing the value, importance, or quality of things or people.
Estimating the Quantifiable Characteristics of Pro	Estimating sizes, distances, and quantities; or determining time, costs, resources, or materials needed to perform a work activity.
Monitoring and Controlling Resources	Monitoring and controlling resources and overseeing the spending of money.
Controlling Machines and Processes	Using either control mechanisms or direct physical activity to operate machines or processes (not including computers or vehicles).
Provide Consultation and Advice to Others	Providing guidance and expert advice to management or other groups on technical, systems-, or process-related topics.
Staffing Organizational Units	Recruiting, interviewing, selecting, hiring, and promoting employees in an organization.
Selling or Influencing Others	Convincing others to buy merchandise/goods or to otherwise change their minds or actions.

Repairing and Maintaining Electronic Equipment — Servicing, repairing, calibrating, regulating, fine-tuning, or testing machines, devices, and equipment that operate primarily on the basis of electrical or electronic (not mechanical) principles.

Operating Vehicles, Mechanized Devices, or Equipme — Running, maneuvering, navigating, or driving vehicles or mechanized equipment, such as forklifts, passenger vehicles, aircraft, or water craft.

Drafting, Laying Out, and Specifying Technical Dev — Providing documentation, detailed instructions, drawings, or specifications to tell others about how devices, parts, equipment, or structures are to be fabricated, constructed, assembled, modified, maintained, or used.

Repairing and Maintaining Mechanical Equipment — Servicing, repairing, adjusting, and testing machines, devices, moving parts, and equipment that operate primarily on the basis of mechanical (not electronic) principles.

Work_Context	Work_Context Definitions
Telephone	How often do you have telephone conversations in this job?
Face-to-Face Discussions	How often do you have to have face-to-face discussions with individuals or teams in this job?
Contact With Others	How much does this job require the worker to be in contact with others (face-to-face, by telephone, or otherwise) in order to perform it?
Importance of Being Exact or Accurate	How important is being very exact or highly accurate in performing this job?
Indoors, Environmentally Controlled	How often does this job require working indoors in environmentally controlled conditions?
Spend Time Sitting	How much does this job require sitting?
Deal With External Customers	How important is it to work with external customers or the public in this job?
Importance of Repeating Same Tasks	How important is repeating the same physical activities (e.g., key entry) or mental activities (e.g., checking entries in a ledger) over and over, without stopping, to performing this job?
Structured versus Unstructured Work	To what extent is this job structured for the worker, rather than allowing the worker to determine tasks, priorities, and goals?
Spend Time Making Repetitive Motions	How much does this job require making repetitive motions?
Deal With Unpleasant or Angry People	How frequently does the worker have to deal with unpleasant, angry, or discourteous individuals as part of the job requirements?
Work With Work Group or Team	How important is it to work with others in a group or team in this job?
Frequency of Decision Making	How frequently is the worker required to make decisions that affect other people, the financial resources, and/or the image and reputation of the organization?
Time Pressure	How often does this job require the worker to meet strict deadlines?
Impact of Decisions on Co-workers or Company Resul	How do the decisions an employee makes impact the results of co-workers, clients or the company?
Spend Time Using Your Hands to Handle, Control, or	How much does this job require using your hands to handle, control, or feel objects, tools or controls?
Frequency of Conflict Situations	How often are there conflict situations the employee has to face in this job?
Freedom to Make Decisions	How much decision making freedom, without supervision, does the job offer?
Physical Proximity	To what extent does this job require the worker to perform job tasks in close physical proximity to other people?
Letters and Memos	How often does the job require written letters and memos?
Degree of Automation	How automated is the job?
Electronic Mail	How often do you use electronic mail in this job?
Coordinate or Lead Others	How important is it to coordinate or lead others in accomplishing work activities in this job?
Sounds, Noise Levels Are Distracting or Uncomforta	How often does this job require working exposed to sounds and noise levels that are distracting or uncomfortable?
Consequence of Error	How serious would the result usually be if the worker made a mistake that was not readily correctable?
Exposed to Contaminants	How often does this job require working exposed to contaminants (such as pollutants, gases, dust or odors)?
Spend Time Bending or Twisting the Body	How much does this job require bending or twisting your body?
Cramped Work Space, Awkward Positions	How often does this job require working in cramped work spaces that requires getting into awkward positions?
Extremely Bright or Inadequate Lighting	How often does this job require working in extremely bright or inadequate lighting conditions?
Level of Competition	To what extent does this job require the worker to compete or to be aware of competitive pressures?
Responsibility for Outcomes and Results	How responsible is the worker for work outcomes and results of other workers?
Spend Time Standing	How much does this job require standing?
Spend Time Walking and Running	How much does this job require walking and running?
Exposed to Disease or Infections	How often does this job require exposure to disease/infections?
Public Speaking	How often do you have to perform public speaking in this job?
Deal With Physically Aggressive People	How frequently does this job require the worker to deal with physical aggression of violent individuals?
Responsible for Others' Health and Safety	How much responsibility is there for the health and safety of others in this job?
Spend Time Kneeling, Crouching, Stooping, or Crawl	How much does this job require kneeling, crouching, stooping, or crawling?
Very Hot or Cold Temperatures	How often does this job require working in very hot (above 90 F degrees) or very cold (below 32 F degrees) temperatures?
Exposed to Radiation	How often does this job require exposure to radiation?
Pace Determined by Speed of Equipment	How important is it to this job that the pace is determined by the speed of equipment or machinery? (This does not refer to keeping busy at all times on this job.)
Spend Time Keeping or Regaining Balance	How much does this job require keeping or regaining your balance?
Spend Time Climbing Ladders, Scaffolds, or Poles	How much does this job require climbing ladders, scaffolds, or poles?
In an Enclosed Vehicle or Equipment	How often does this job require working in a closed vehicle or equipment (e.g., car)?
Outdoors, Exposed to Weather	How often does this job require working outdoors, exposed to all weather conditions?
Exposed to Minor Burns, Cuts, Bites, or Stings	How often does this job require exposure to minor burns, cuts, bites, or stings?
Outdoors, Under Cover	How often does this job require working outdoors, under cover (e.g., structure with roof but no walls)?
Indoors, Not Environmentally Controlled	How often does this job require working indoors in non-controlled environmental conditions (e.g., warehouse without heat)?
Wear Common Protective or Safety Equipment such as	How much does this job require wearing common protective or safety equipment such as safety shoes, glasses, gloves, hard hats or life jackets?
Exposed to Hazardous Equipment	How often does this job require exposure to hazardous equipment?
Exposed to Hazardous Conditions	How often does this job require exposure to hazardous conditions?
Exposed to High Places	How often does this job require exposure to high places?
Exposed to Whole Body Vibration	How often does this job require exposure to whole body vibration (e.g., operate a jackhammer)?
In an Open Vehicle or Equipment	How often does this job require working in an open vehicle or equipment (e.g., tractor)?
Wear Specialized Protective or Safety Equipment su	How much does this job require wearing specialized protective or safety equipment such as breathing apparatus, safety harness, full protection suits, or radiation protection?

Job Zone Component	Job Zone Component Definitions
Title	Job Zone Two: Some Preparation Needed
Overall Experience	Some previous work-related skill, knowledge, or experience may be helpful in these occupations, but usually is not needed. For example, a drywall installer might benefit from experience installing drywall, but an inexperienced person could still learn to be an installer with little difficulty.
Job Training	Employees in these occupations need anywhere from a few months to one year of working with experienced employees.
Job Zone Examples	These occupations often involve using your knowledge and skills to help others. Examples include drywall installers, fire inspectors, flight attendants, pharmacy technicians, salespersons (retail), and tellers.
SVP Range	(4.0 to < 6.0)
Education	These occupations usually require a high school diploma and may require some vocational training or job-related course work. In some cases, an associate's or bachelor's degree could be needed.

Work_Styles	Work_Styles Definitions
Integrity	Job requires being honest and ethical.

Attention to Detail	Job requires being careful about detail and thorough in completing work tasks.
Dependability	Job requires being reliable, responsible, and dependable, and fulfilling obligations.
Self Control	Job requires maintaining composure, keeping emotions in check, controlling anger, and avoiding aggressive behavior, even in very difficult situations.
Cooperation	Job requires being pleasant with others on the job and displaying a good-natured, cooperative attitude.
Stress Tolerance	Job requires accepting criticism and dealing calmly and effectively with high stress situations.
Independence	Job requires developing one's own ways of doing things, guiding oneself with little or no supervision, and depending on oneself to get things done.
Concern for Others	Job requires being sensitive to others' needs and feelings and being understanding and helpful on the job.
Initiative	Job requires a willingness to take on responsibilities and challenges.
Social Orientation	Job requires preferring to work with others rather than alone, and being personally connected with others on the job.
Adaptability/Flexibility	Job requires being open to change (positive or negative) and to considerable variety in the workplace.
Achievement/Effort	Job requires establishing and maintaining personally challenging achievement goals and exerting effort toward mastering tasks.
Analytical Thinking	Job requires analyzing information and using logic to address work-related issues and problems.
Leadership	Job requires a willingness to lead, take charge, and offer opinions and direction.
Innovation	Job requires creativity and alternative thinking to develop new ideas for and answers to work-related problems.
Persistence	Job requires persistence in the face of obstacles.

43-4031.02 - Municipal Clerks

Draft agendas and bylaws for town or city council; record minutes of council meetings; answer official correspondence; keep fiscal records and accounts; and prepare reports on civic needs.

Tasks

1) Research information in the municipal archives upon request of public officials and private citizens.

2) Respond to requests for information from the public, other municipalities, state officials, and state and federal legislative offices.

3) Perform general office duties such as taking and transcribing dictation, typing and proofreading correspondence, distributing and filing official forms, and scheduling appointments.

4) Issue public notification of all official activities and meetings.

5) Collaborate with other staff to assist in the development and implementation of goals, objectives, policies, and priorities.

6) Plan and direct the maintenance, filing, safekeeping, and computerization of all municipal documents.

7) Prepare meeting agendas and packets of related information.

8) Perform budgeting duties, including assisting in budget preparation, expenditure review, and budget administration.

9) Prepare ordinances, resolutions, and proclamations so that they can be executed, recorded, archived, and distributed.

10) Coordinate and maintain office-tracking systems for correspondence and follow-up actions.

11) Maintain fiscal records and accounts.

12) Represent municipalities at community events, and serve as liaisons on community committees.

13) Serve as a notary of the public.

14) Maintain and update documents such as municipal codes and city charters.

15) Participate in the administration of municipal elections, including preparation and distribution of ballots, appointment and training of election officers, and tabulation and certification of results.

16) Perform contract administration duties, assisting with bid openings and the awarding of contracts.

17) Issue various permits and licenses, including marriage, fishing, hunting, and dog licenses, and collect appropriate fees.

18) Process claims against the municipality, maintaining files and log of claims, and coordinate claim response and handling with municipal claims administrators.

19) Provide assistance to persons with disabilities in reaching less accessible areas of municipal facilities.

20) Develop and conduct orientation programs for candidates for political office.

21) Prepare reports on civic needs.

22) Provide assistance with events such as police department auctions of abandoned automobiles.

Knowledge	Knowledge Definitions
Clerical	Knowledge of administrative and clerical procedures and systems such as word processing, managing files and records, stenography and transcription, designing forms, and other office procedures and terminology.
English Language	Knowledge of the structure and content of the English language including the meaning and spelling of words, rules of composition, and grammar.
Administration and Management	Knowledge of business and management principles involved in strategic planning, resource allocation, human resources modeling, leadership technique, production methods, and coordination of people and resources.
Law and Government	Knowledge of laws, legal codes, court procedures, precedents, government regulations, executive orders, agency rules, and the democratic political process.
Personnel and Human Resources	Knowledge of principles and procedures for personnel recruitment, selection, training, compensation and benefits, labor relations and negotiation, and personnel information systems.
Customer and Personal Service	Knowledge of principles and processes for providing customer and personal services. This includes customer needs assessment, meeting quality standards for services, and evaluation of customer satisfaction.
Mathematics	Knowledge of arithmetic, algebra, geometry, calculus, statistics, and their applications.
Economics and Accounting	Knowledge of economic and accounting principles and practices, the financial markets, banking and the analysis and reporting of financial data.
Communications and Media	Knowledge of media production, communication, and dissemination techniques and methods. This includes alternative ways to inform and entertain via written, oral, and visual media.
Computers and Electronics	Knowledge of circuit boards, processors, chips, electronic equipment, and computer hardware and software, including applications and programming.
Education and Training	Knowledge of principles and methods for curriculum and training design, teaching and instruction for individuals and groups, and the measurement of training effects.
Foreign Language	Knowledge of the structure and content of a foreign (non-English) language including the meaning and spelling of words, rules of composition and grammar, and pronunciation.
Psychology	Knowledge of human behavior and performance; individual differences in ability, personality, and interests; learning and motivation; psychological research methods; and the assessment and treatment of behavioral and affective disorders.
History and Archeology	Knowledge of historical events and their causes, indicators, and effects on civilizations and cultures.
Public Safety and Security	Knowledge of relevant equipment, policies, procedures, and strategies to promote effective local, state, or national security operations for the protection of people, data, property, and institutions.
Telecommunications	Knowledge of transmission, broadcasting, switching, control, and operation of telecommunications systems.
Sociology and Anthropology	Knowledge of group behavior and dynamics, societal trends and influences, human migrations, ethnicity, cultures and their history and origins.
Production and Processing	Knowledge of raw materials, production processes, quality control, costs, and other techniques for maximizing the effective manufacture and distribution of goods.

Geography	Knowledge of principles and methods for describing the features of land, sea, and air masses, including their physical characteristics, locations, interrelationships, and distribution of plant, animal, and human life.
Transportation	Knowledge of principles and methods for moving people or goods by air, rail, sea, or road, including the relative costs and benefits.
Sales and Marketing	Knowledge of principles and methods for showing, promoting, and selling products or services. This includes marketing strategy and tactics, product demonstration, sales techniques, and sales control systems.
Mechanical	Knowledge of machines and tools, including their designs, uses, repair, and maintenance.
Philosophy and Theology	Knowledge of different philosophical systems and religions. This includes their basic principles, values, ethics, ways of thinking, customs, practices, and their impact on human culture.
Building and Construction	Knowledge of materials, methods, and the tools involved in the construction or repair of houses, buildings, or other structures such as highways and roads.
Medicine and Dentistry	Knowledge of the information and techniques needed to diagnose and treat human injuries, diseases, and deformities. This includes symptoms, treatment alternatives, drug properties and interactions, and preventive health-care measures.
Engineering and Technology	Knowledge of the practical application of engineering science and technology. This includes applying principles, techniques, procedures, and equipment to the design and production of various goods and services.
Biology	Knowledge of plant and animal organisms, their tissues, cells, functions, interdependencies, and interactions with each other and the environment.
Physics	Knowledge and prediction of physical principles, laws, their interrelationships, and applications to understanding fluid, material, and atmospheric dynamics, and mechanical, electrical, atomic and sub-atomic structures and processes.
Chemistry	Knowledge of the chemical composition, structure, and properties of substances and of the chemical processes and transformations that they undergo. This includes uses of chemicals and their interactions, danger signs, production techniques, and disposal methods.
Therapy and Counseling	Knowledge of principles, methods, and procedures for diagnosis, treatment, and rehabilitation of physical and mental dysfunctions, and for career counseling and guidance.
Design	Knowledge of design techniques, tools, and principles involved in production of precision technical plans, blueprints, drawings, and models.
Fine Arts	Knowledge of the theory and techniques required to compose, produce, and perform works of music, dance, visual arts, drama, and sculpture.
Food Production	Knowledge of techniques and equipment for planting, growing, and harvesting food products (both plant and animal) for consumption, including storage/handling techniques.

Skills	Skills Definitions
Active Listening	Giving full attention to what other people are saying, taking time to understand the points being made, asking questions as appropriate, and not interrupting at inappropriate times.
Time Management	Managing one's own time and the time of others.
Writing	Communicating effectively in writing as appropriate for the needs of the audience.
Reading Comprehension	Understanding written sentences and paragraphs in work related documents.
Speaking	Talking to others to convey information effectively.
Social Perceptiveness	Being aware of others' reactions and understanding why they react as they do.
Service Orientation	Actively looking for ways to help people.
Critical Thinking	Using logic and reasoning to identify the strengths and weaknesses of alternative solutions, conclusions or approaches to problems.
Active Learning	Understanding the implications of new information for both current and future problem-solving and decision-making.
Coordination	Adjusting actions in relation to others' actions.
Mathematics	Using mathematics to solve problems.
Judgment and Decision Making	Considering the relative costs and benefits of potential actions to choose the most appropriate one.

Monitoring	Monitoring/Assessing performance of yourself, other individuals, or organizations to make improvements or take corrective action.
Management of Personnel Resources	Motivating, developing, and directing people as they work, identifying the best people for the job.
Management of Financial Resources	Determining how money will be spent to get the work done, and accounting for these expenditures.
Instructing	Teaching others how to do something.
Learning Strategies	Selecting and using training/instructional methods and procedures appropriate for the situation when learning or teaching new things.
Persuasion	Persuading others to change their minds or behavior.
Complex Problem Solving	Identifying complex problems and reviewing related information to develop and evaluate options and implement solutions.
Negotiation	Bringing others together and trying to reconcile differences.
Equipment Selection	Determining the kind of tools and equipment needed to do a job.
Operations Analysis	Analyzing needs and product requirements to create a design.
Management of Material Resources	Obtaining and seeing to the appropriate use of equipment, facilities, and materials needed to do certain work.
Troubleshooting	Determining causes of operating errors and deciding what to do about it.
Technology Design	Generating or adapting equipment and technology to serve user needs.
Operation and Control	Controlling operations of equipment or systems.
Systems Evaluation	Identifying measures or indicators of system performance and the actions needed to improve or correct performance, relative to the goals of the system.
Systems Analysis	Determining how a system should work and how changes in conditions, operations, and the environment will affect outcomes.
Quality Control Analysis	Conducting tests and inspections of products, services, or processes to evaluate quality or performance.
Equipment Maintenance	Performing routine maintenance on equipment and determining when and what kind of maintenance is needed.
Operation Monitoring	Watching gauges, dials, or other indicators to make sure a machine is working properly.
Installation	Installing equipment, machines, wiring, or programs to meet specifications.
Repairing	Repairing machines or systems using the needed tools.
Science	Using scientific rules and methods to solve problems.
Programming	Writing computer programs for various purposes.

Ability	Ability Definitions
Oral Comprehension	The ability to listen to and understand information and ideas presented through spoken words and sentences.
Oral Expression	The ability to communicate information and ideas in speaking so others will understand.
Written Comprehension	The ability to read and understand information and ideas presented in writing.
Written Expression	The ability to communicate information and ideas in writing so others will understand.
Near Vision	The ability to see details at close range (within a few feet of the observer).
Speech Recognition	The ability to identify and understand the speech of another person.
Information Ordering	The ability to arrange things or actions in a certain order or pattern according to a specific rule or set of rules (e.g., patterns of numbers, letters, words, pictures, mathematical operations).
Speech Clarity	The ability to speak clearly so others can understand you.
Deductive Reasoning	The ability to apply general rules to specific problems to produce answers that make sense.
Problem Sensitivity	The ability to tell when something is wrong or is likely to go wrong. It does not involve solving the problem, only recognizing there is a problem.
Inductive Reasoning	The ability to combine pieces of information to form general rules or conclusions (includes finding a relationship among seemingly unrelated events).
Category Flexibility	The ability to generate or use different sets of rules for combining or grouping things in different ways.
Mathematical Reasoning	The ability to choose the right mathematical methods or formulas to solve a problem.
Selective Attention	The ability to concentrate on a task over a period of time without being distracted.

Fluency of Ideas	The ability to come up with a number of ideas about a topic (the number of ideas is important, not their quality, correctness, or creativity).
Memorization	The ability to remember information such as words, numbers, pictures, and procedures.
Originality	The ability to come up with unusual or clever ideas about a given topic or situation, or to develop creative ways to solve a problem.
Number Facility	The ability to add, subtract, multiply, or divide quickly and correctly.
Flexibility of Closure	The ability to identify or detect a known pattern (a figure, object, word, or sound) that is hidden in other distracting material.
Time Sharing	The ability to shift back and forth between two or more activities or sources of information (such as speech, sounds, touch, or other sources).
Perceptual Speed	The ability to quickly and accurately compare similarities and differences among sets of letters, numbers, objects, pictures, or patterns. The things to be compared may be presented at the same time or one after the other. This ability also includes comparing a presented object with a remembered object.
Finger Dexterity	The ability to make precisely coordinated movements of the fingers of one or both hands to grasp, manipulate, or assemble very small objects.
Speed of Closure	The ability to quickly make sense of, combine, and organize information into meaningful patterns.
Visual Color Discrimination	The ability to match or detect differences between colors, including shades of color and brightness.
Auditory Attention	The ability to focus on a single source of sound in the presence of other distracting sounds.
Far Vision	The ability to see details at a distance.
Visualization	The ability to imagine how something will look after it is moved around or when its parts are moved or rearranged.
Hearing Sensitivity	The ability to detect or tell the differences between sounds that vary in pitch and loudness.
Wrist-Finger Speed	The ability to make fast, simple, repeated movements of the fingers, hands, and wrists.
Multilimb Coordination	The ability to coordinate two or more limbs (for example, two arms, two legs, or one leg and one arm) while sitting, standing, or lying down. It does not involve performing the activities while the whole body is in motion.
Trunk Strength	The ability to use your abdominal and lower back muscles to support part of the body repeatedly or continuously over time without 'giving out' or fatiguing.
Static Strength	The ability to exert maximum muscle force to lift, push, pull, or carry objects.
Manual Dexterity	The ability to quickly move your hand, your hand together with your arm, or your two hands to grasp, manipulate, or assemble objects.
Rate Control	The ability to time your movements or the movement of a piece of equipment in anticipation of changes in the speed and/or direction of a moving object or scene.
Arm-Hand Steadiness	The ability to keep your hand and arm steady while moving your arm or while holding your arm and hand in one position.
Extent Flexibility	The ability to bend, stretch, twist, or reach with your body, arms, and/or legs.
Speed of Limb Movement	The ability to quickly move the arms and legs.
Dynamic Flexibility	The ability to quickly and repeatedly bend, stretch, twist, or reach out with your body, arms, and/or legs.
Explosive Strength	The ability to use short bursts of muscle force to propel oneself (as in jumping or sprinting), or to throw an object.
Reaction Time	The ability to quickly respond (with the hand, finger, or foot) to a signal (sound, light, picture) when it appears.
Control Precision	The ability to quickly and repeatedly adjust the controls of a machine or a vehicle to exact positions.
Gross Body Coordination	The ability to coordinate the movement of your arms, legs, and torso together when the whole body is in motion.
Depth Perception	The ability to judge which of several objects is closer or farther away from you, or to judge the distance between you and an object.
Stamina	The ability to exert yourself physically over long periods of time without getting winded or out of breath.
Sound Localization	The ability to tell the direction from which a sound originated.
Dynamic Strength	The ability to exert muscle force repeatedly or continuously over time. This involves muscular endurance and resistance to muscle fatigue.
Peripheral Vision	The ability to see objects or movement of objects to one's side when the eyes are looking ahead.

Night Vision	The ability to see under low light conditions.
Glare Sensitivity	The ability to see objects in the presence of glare or bright lighting.
Response Orientation	The ability to choose quickly between two or more movements in response to two or more different signals (lights, sounds, pictures). It includes the speed with which the correct response is started with the hand, foot, or other body part.
Spatial Orientation	The ability to know your location in relation to the environment or to know where other objects are in relation to you.
Gross Body Equilibrium	The ability to keep or regain your body balance or stay upright when in an unstable position.

Work_Activity	Work Activity Definitions
Performing for or Working Directly with the Public	Performing for people or dealing directly with the public. This includes serving customers in restaurants and stores, and receiving clients or guests.
Documenting/Recording Information	Entering, transcribing, recording, storing, or maintaining information in written or electronic/magnetic form.
Communicating with Supervisors, Peers, or Subordin	Providing information to supervisors, co-workers, and subordinates by telephone, in written form, e-mail, or in person.
Interacting With Computers	Using computers and computer systems (including hardware and software) to program, write software, set up functions, enter data, or process information.
Communicating with Persons Outside Organization	Communicating with people outside the organization, representing the organization to customers, the public, government, and other external sources. This information can be exchanged in person, in writing, or by telephone or e-mail.
Getting Information	Observing, receiving, and otherwise obtaining information from all relevant sources.
Establishing and Maintaining Interpersonal Relatio	Developing constructive and cooperative working relationships with others, and maintaining them over time.
Processing Information	Compiling, coding, categorizing, calculating, tabulating, auditing, or verifying information or data.
Evaluating Information to Determine Compliance wit	Using relevant information and individual judgment to determine whether events or processes comply with laws, regulations, or standards.
Performing Administrative Activities	Performing day-to-day administrative tasks such as maintaining information files and processing paperwork.
Organizing, Planning, and Prioritizing Work	Developing specific goals and plans to prioritize, organize, and accomplish your work.
Updating and Using Relevant Knowledge	Keeping up-to-date technically and applying new knowledge to your job.
Making Decisions and Solving Problems	Analyzing information and evaluating results to choose the best solution and solve problems.
Resolving Conflicts and Negotiating with Others	Handling complaints, settling disputes, and resolving grievances and conflicts, or otherwise negotiating with others.
Coordinating the Work and Activities of Others	Getting members of a group to work together to accomplish tasks.
Interpreting the Meaning of Information for Others	Translating or explaining what information means and how it can be used.
Identifying Objects, Actions, and Events	Identifying information by categorizing, estimating, recognizing differences or similarities, and detecting changes in circumstances or events.
Monitoring and Controlling Resources	Monitoring and controlling resources and overseeing the spending of money.
Provide Consultation and Advice to Others	Providing guidance and expert advice to management or other groups on technical, systems-, or process-related topics.
Monitor Processes, Materials, or Surroundings	Monitoring and reviewing information from materials, events, or the environment, to detect or assess problems.
Judging the Qualities of Things, Services, or Peop	Assessing the value, importance, or quality of things or people.
Scheduling Work and Activities	Scheduling events, programs, and activities, as well as the work of others.
Developing Objectives and Strategies	Establishing long-range objectives and specifying the strategies and actions to achieve them.
Analyzing Data or Information	Identifying the underlying principles, reasons, or facts of information by breaking down information or data into separate parts.
Thinking Creatively	Developing, designing, or creating new applications, ideas, relationships, systems, or products, including artistic contributions.
Assisting and Caring for Others	Providing personal assistance, medical attention, emotional support, or other personal care to others such as coworkers, customers, or patients.

Training and Teaching Others	Identifying the educational needs of others, developing formal educational or training programs or classes, and teaching or instructing others.
Coaching and Developing Others	Identifying the developmental needs of others and coaching, mentoring, or otherwise helping others to improve their knowledge or skills.
Handling and Moving Objects	Using hands and arms in handling, installing, positioning, and moving materials, and manipulating things.
Developing and Building Teams	Encouraging and building mutual trust, respect, and cooperation among team members.
Guiding, Directing, and Motivating Subordinates	Providing guidance and direction to subordinates, including setting performance standards and monitoring performance.
Estimating the Quantifiable Characteristics of Pro	Estimating sizes, distances, and quantities; or determining time, costs, resources, or materials needed to perform a work activity.
Controlling Machines and Processes	Using either control mechanisms or direct physical activity to operate machines or processes (not including computers or vehicles).
Staffing Organizational Units	Recruiting, interviewing, selecting, hiring, and promoting employees in an organization.
Selling or Influencing Others	Convincing others to buy merchandise/goods or to otherwise change their minds or actions.
Performing General Physical Activities	Performing physical activities that require considerable use of your arms and legs and moving your whole body, such as climbing, lifting, balancing, walking, stooping, and handling of materials.
Inspecting Equipment, Structures, or Material	Inspecting equipment, structures, or materials to identify the cause of errors or other problems or defects.
Operating Vehicles, Mechanized Devices, or Equipme	Running, maneuvering, navigating, or driving vehicles or mechanized equipment, such as forklifts, passenger vehicles, aircraft, or water craft.
Drafting, Laying Out, and Specifying Technical Dev	Providing documentation, detailed instructions, drawings, or specifications to tell others about how devices, parts, equipment, or structures are to be fabricated, constructed, assembled, modified, maintained, or used.
Repairing and Maintaining Electronic Equipment	Servicing, repairing, calibrating, regulating, fine-tuning, or testing machines, devices, and equipment that operate primarily on the basis of electrical or electronic (not mechanical) principles.
Repairing and Maintaining Mechanical Equipment	Servicing, repairing, adjusting, and testing machines, devices, moving parts, and equipment that operate primarily on the basis of mechanical (not electronic) principles.

Work_Context	Work_Context Definitions
Telephone	How often do you have telephone conversations in this job?
Structured versus Unstructured Work	To what extent is this job structured for the worker, rather than allowing the worker to determine tasks, priorities, and goals?
Freedom to Make Decisions	How much decision making freedom, without supervision, does the job offer?
Importance of Repeating Same Tasks	How important is repeating the same physical activities (e.g., key entry) or mental activities (e.g., checking entries in a ledger) over and over, without stopping, to performing this job?
Importance of Being Exact or Accurate	How important is being very exact or highly accurate in performing this job?
Contact With Others	How much does this job require the worker to be in contact with others (face-to-face, by telephone, or otherwise) in order to perform it?
Indoors, Environmentally Controlled	How often does this job require working indoors in environmentally controlled conditions?
Letters and Memos	How often does the job require written letters and memos?
Spend Time Sitting	How much does this job require sitting?
Electronic Mail	How often do you use electronic mail in this job?
Face-to-Face Discussions	How often do you have to have face-to-face discussions with individuals or teams in this job?
Time Pressure	How often does this job require the worker to meet strict deadlines?
Impact of Decisions on Co-workers or Company Resul	How do the decisions an employee makes impact the results of co-workers, clients or the company?
Deal With External Customers	How important is it to work with external customers or the public in this job?
Work With Work Group or Team	How important is it to work with others in a group or team in this job?
Frequency of Decision Making	How frequently is the worker required to make decisions that affect other people, the financial resources, and/or the image and reputation of the organization?

Coordinate or Lead Others	How important is it to coordinate or lead others in accomplishing work activities in this job?
Responsible for Others' Health and Safety	How much responsibility is there for the health and safety of others in this job?
Deal With Unpleasant or Angry People	How frequently does the worker have to deal with unpleasant, angry, or discourteous individuals as part of the job requirements?
Responsibility for Outcomes and Results	How responsible is the worker for work outcomes and results of other workers?
Physical Proximity	To what extent does this job require the worker to perform job tasks in close physical proximity to other people?
Frequency of Conflict Situations	How often are there conflict situations the employee has to face in this job?
Degree of Automation	How automated is the job?
Spend Time Using Your Hands to Handle, Control, or	How much does this job require using your hands to handle, control, or feel objects, tools or controls?
Sounds, Noise Levels Are Distracting or Uncomforta	How often does this job require working exposed to sounds and noise levels that are distracting or uncomfortable?
Public Speaking	How often do you have to perform public speaking in this job?
In an Enclosed Vehicle or Equipment	How often does this job require working in a closed vehicle or equipment (e.g., car)?
Spend Time Standing	How much does this job require standing?
Consequence of Error	How serious would the result usually be if the worker made a mistake that was not readily correctable?
Spend Time Making Repetitive Motions	How much does this job require making repetitive motions?
Spend Time Walking and Running	How much does this job require walking and running?
Spend Time Bending or Twisting the Body	How much does this job require bending or twisting your body?
Level of Competition	To what extent does this job require the worker to compete or to be aware of competitive pressures?
Deal With Physically Aggressive People	How frequently does this job require the worker to deal with physical aggression of violent individuals?
Spend Time Kneeling, Crouching, Stooping, or Crawl	How much does this job require kneeling, crouching, stooping or crawling?
Outdoors, Exposed to Weather	How often does this job require working outdoors, exposed to all weather conditions?
Exposed to Minor Burns, Cuts, Bites, or Stings	How often does this job require exposure to minor burns, cuts, bites, or stings?
Cramped Work Space, Awkward Positions	How often does this job require working in cramped work spaces that requires getting into awkward positions?
Exposed to Contaminants	How often does this job require working exposed to contaminants (such as pollutants, gases, dust or odors)?
Outdoors, Under Cover	How often does this job require working outdoors, under cover (e.g., structure with roof but no walls)?
Indoors, Not Environmentally Controlled	How often does this job require working indoors in non-controlled environmental conditions (e.g., warehouse without heat)?
Spend Time Keeping or Regaining Balance	How much does this job require keeping or regaining your balance?
Spend Time Climbing Ladders, Scaffolds, or Poles	How much does this job require climbing ladders, scaffolds, or poles?
Extremely Bright or Inadequate Lighting	How often does this job require working in extremely bright or inadequate lighting conditions?
Exposed to High Places	How often does this job require exposure to high places?
Wear Specialized Protective or Safety Equipment su	How much does this job require wearing specialized protective or safety equipment such as breathing apparatus, safety harness, full protection suits, or radiation protection?
Very Hot or Cold Temperatures	How often does this job require working in very hot (above 90 F degrees) or very cold (below 32 F degrees) temperatures?
Wear Common Protective or Safety Equipment such as	How much does this job require wearing common protective or safety equipment such as safety shoes, glasses, gloves, hard hats or live jackets?
Exposed to Disease or Infections	How often does this job require exposure to disease/infections?
Exposed to Hazardous Equipment	How often does this job require exposure to hazardous equipment?
Pace Determined by Speed of Equipment	How important is it to this job that the pace is determined by the speed of equipment or machinery? (This does not refer to keeping busy at all times on this job.)
Exposed to Radiation	How often does this job require exposure to radiation?
In an Open Vehicle or Equipment	How often does this job require working in an open vehicle or equipment (e.g., tractor)?

| Exposed to Whole Body Vibration | How often does this job require exposure to whole body vibration (e.g., operate a jackhammer)? |
| Exposed to Hazardous Conditions | How often does this job require exposure to hazardous conditions? |

Job Zone Component	Job Zone Component Definitions
Title	Job Zone Three: Medium Preparation Needed
Overall Experience	Previous work-related skill, knowledge, or experience is required for these occupations. For example, an electrician must have completed three or four years of apprenticeship or several years of vocational training, and often must have passed a licensing exam, in order to perform the job.
Job Training	Employees in these occupations usually need one or two years of training involving both on-the-job experience and informal training with experienced workers.
Job Zone Examples	These occupations usually involve using communication and organizational skills to coordinate, supervise, manage, or train others to accomplish goals. Examples include dental assistants, electricians, fish and game wardens, legal secretaries, personnel recruiters, and recreation workers.
SVP Range	(6.0 to < 7.0)
Education	Most occupations in this zone require training in vocational schools, related on-the-job experience, or an associate's degree. Some may require a bachelor's degree.

Work_Styles	Work_Styles Definitions
Integrity	Job requires being honest and ethical.
Attention to Detail	Job requires being careful about detail and thorough in completing work tasks.
Dependability	Job requires being reliable, responsible, and dependable, and fulfilling obligations.
Cooperation	Job requires being pleasant with others on the job and displaying a good-natured, cooperative attitude.
Stress Tolerance	Job requires accepting criticism and dealing calmly and effectively with high stress situations.
Initiative	Job requires a willingness to take on responsibilities and challenges.
Leadership	Job requires a willingness to lead, take charge, and offer opinions and direction.
Concern for Other	Job requires being sensitive to others' needs and feelings and being understanding and helpful on the job.
Self Control	Job requires maintaining composure, keeping emotions in check, controlling anger, and avoiding aggressive behavior, even in very difficult situations.
Adaptability/Flexibility	Job requires being open to change (positive or negative) and to considerable variety in the workplace.
Achievement/Effort	Job requires establishing and maintaining personally challenging achievement goals and exerting effort toward mastering tasks.
Persistence	Job requires persistence in the face of obstacles.
Independence	Job requires developing one's own ways of doing things, guiding oneself with little or no supervision, and depending on oneself to get things done.
Social Orientation	Job requires preferring to work with others rather than alone, and being personally connected with others on the job.
Analytical Thinking	Job requires analyzing information and using logic to address work-related issues and problems.
Innovation	Job requires creativity and alternative thinking to develop new ideas for and answers to work-related problems.

43-4031.03 - License Clerks

Issue licenses or permits to qualified applicants. Obtain necessary information; record data; advise applicants on requirements; collect fees; and issue licenses. May conduct oral, written, visual, or performance testing.

Tasks

1) Maintain records of applications made and licensing fees collected.

2) Perform routine data entry and other office support activities including creating, sorting, photocopying, distributing, and filing documents.

3) Evaluate information on applications to verify completeness and accuracy and to determine whether applicants are qualified to obtain desired licenses.

4) Conduct and score oral, visual, written, or performance tests to determine applicant qualifications, and notify applicants of their scores.

5) Collect prescribed fees for licenses.

6) Assemble photographs with printed license information in order to produce completed documents.

7) Answer questions and provide advice to the public regarding licensing policies, procedures, and regulations.

8) Operate specialized photographic equipment in order to obtain photographs for drivers' licenses and photo identification cards.

9) Question applicants to obtain required information, such as name, address, and age, and record data on prescribed forms.

10) Stock counters with adequate supplies of forms, film, licenses, and other required materials.

11) Code information on license applications for entry into computers.

12) Train other workers, and coordinate their work as necessary.

13) Prepare lists of overdue accounts, license suspensions and issuances.

14) Perform driver education program enrollments for participating schools.

15) Send by mail drivers' licenses to out-of-county or out-of-state applicants.

16) Enforce canine licensing regulations, contacting non-compliant owners in person or by mail to inform them of the required regulations and potential enforcement actions.

17) Respond to correspondence from insurance companies regarding the licensure of agents, brokers and adjusters.

18) Provide assistance in the preparation of insurance examinations covering a variety of types of insurance.

19) Inform customers by mail or telephone of additional steps they need to take to obtain licenses.

20) Prepare bank deposits, and take them to banks.

21) Perform record checks on past and current licensees, as required by investigations.

22) Update operational records and licensing information, using computer terminals.

43-4041.01 - Credit Authorizers

Authorize credit charges against customers' accounts.

Tasks

1) Receive charge slips or credit applications by mail, or receive information from salespeople or merchants by telephone.

2) Evaluate customers' computerized credit records and payment histories to decide whether to approve new credit, based on predetermined standards.

3) File sales slips in customers' ledgers for billing purposes.

4) Prepare credit cards or charge account plates.

5) Mail charge statements to customers.

43-4041.02 - Credit Checkers

Investigate history and credit standing of individuals or business establishments applying for credit. Telephone or write to credit departments of business and service establishments to obtain information about applicant's credit standing.

Tasks

1) Examine city directories and public records in order to verify residence property ownership, bankruptcies, liens, arrest record, or unpaid taxes of applicants.

2) Obtain information about potential creditors from banks, credit bureaus, and other credit services, and provide reciprocal information if requested.

3) Compile and analyze credit information gathered by investigation.

4) Interview credit applicants by telephone or in person in order to obtain personal and financial data needed to complete credit report.

5) Relay credit report information to subscribers by mail or by telephone.

6) Prepare reports of findings and recommendations, using typewriters or computers.

43-4051.00 - Customer Service Representatives

Interact with customers to provide information in response to inquiries about products and services and to handle and resolve complaints.

Tasks

1) Refer unresolved customer grievances to designated departments for further investigation.

2) Keep records of customer interactions and transactions, recording details of inquiries, complaints, and comments, as well as actions taken.

3) Confer with customers by telephone or in person in order to provide information about products and services, to take orders or cancel accounts, or to obtain details of complaints.

4) Resolve customers' service or billing complaints by performing activities such as exchanging merchandise, refunding money, and adjusting bills.

5) Contact customers in order to respond to inquiries or to notify them of claim investigation results and any planned adjustments.

6) Determine charges for services requested, collect deposits or payments, and/or arrange for billing.

7) Complete contract forms, prepare change of address records, and issue service discontinuance orders, using computers.

8) Solicit sale of new or additional services or products.

9) Compare disputed merchandise with original requisitions and information from invoices, and prepare invoices for returned goods.

10) Recommend improvements in products, packaging, shipping, service, or billing methods and procedures in order to prevent future problems.

11) Obtain and examine all relevant information in order to assess validity of complaints and to determine possible causes, such as extreme weather conditions that could increase utility bills.

12) Review insurance policy terms in order to determine whether a particular loss is covered by insurance.

13) Order tests that could determine the causes of product malfunctions.

14) Review claims adjustments with dealers, examining parts claimed to be defective and approving or disapproving dealers' claims.

Knowledge	Knowledge Definitions
Customer and Personal Service	Knowledge of principles and processes for providing customer and personal services. This includes customer needs assessment, meeting quality standards for services, and evaluation of customer satisfaction.
English Language	Knowledge of the structure and content of the English language including the meaning and spelling of words, rules of composition, and grammar.
Clerical	Knowledge of administrative and clerical procedures and systems such as word processing, managing files and records, stenography and transcription, designing forms, and other office procedures and terminology.
Mathematics	Knowledge of arithmetic, algebra, geometry, calculus, statistics, and their applications.
Computers and Electronics	Knowledge of circuit boards, processors, chips, electronic equipment, and computer hardware and software, including applications and programming.
Administration and Management	Knowledge of business and management principles involved in strategic planning, resource allocation, human resources modeling, leadership technique, production methods, and coordination of people and resources.
Sales and Marketing	Knowledge of principles and methods for showing, promoting, and selling products or services. This includes marketing strategy and tactics, product demonstration, sales techniques, and sales control systems.
Communications and Media	Knowledge of media production, communication, and dissemination techniques and methods. This includes alternative ways to inform and entertain via written, oral, and visual media.
Telecommunications	Knowledge of transmission, broadcasting, switching, control, and operation of telecommunications systems.
Personnel and Human Resources	Knowledge of principles and procedures for personnel recruitment, selection, training, compensation and benefits, labor relations and negotiation, and personnel information systems.
Education and Training	Knowledge of principles and methods for curriculum and training design, teaching and instruction for individuals and groups, and the measurement of training effects.
Psychology	Knowledge of human behavior and performance; individual differences in ability, personality, and interests; learning and motivation; psychological research methods; and the assessment and treatment of behavioral and affective disorders.
Production and Processing	Knowledge of raw materials, production processes, quality control, costs, and other techniques for maximizing the effective manufacture and distribution of goods.
Economics and Accounting	Knowledge of economic and accounting principles and practices, the financial markets, banking and the analysis and reporting of financial data.
Foreign Language	Knowledge of the structure and content of a foreign (non-English) language including the meaning and spelling of words, rules of composition and grammar, and pronunciation.
Public Safety and Security	Knowledge of relevant equipment, policies, procedures, and strategies to promote effective local, state, or national security operations for the protection of people, data, property, and institutions.
Law and Government	Knowledge of laws, legal codes, court procedures, precedents, government regulations, executive orders, agency rules, and the democratic political process.
Sociology and Anthropology	Knowledge of group behavior and dynamics, societal trends and influences, human migrations, ethnicity, cultures and their history and origins.
Geography	Knowledge of principles and methods for describing the features of land, sea, and air masses, including their physical characteristics, locations, interrelationships, and distribution of plant, animal, and human life.
Transportation	Knowledge of principles and methods for moving people or goods by air, rail, sea, or road, including the relative costs and benefits.
Medicine and Dentistry	Knowledge of the information and techniques needed to diagnose and treat human injuries, diseases, and deformities. This includes symptoms, treatment alternatives, drug properties and interactions, and preventive health-care measures.
Therapy and Counseling	Knowledge of principles, methods, and procedures for diagnosis, treatment, and rehabilitation of physical and mental dysfunctions, and for career counseling and guidance.
Engineering and Technology	Knowledge of the practical application of engineering science and technology. This includes applying principles, techniques, procedures, and equipment to the design and production of various goods and services.
Design	Knowledge of design techniques, tools, and principles involved in production of precision technical plans, blueprints, drawings, and models.
Building and Construction	Knowledge of materials, methods, and the tools involved in the construction or repair of houses, buildings, or other structures such as highways and roads.
Philosophy and Theology	Knowledge of different philosophical systems and religions. This includes their basic principles, values, ethics, ways of thinking, customs, practices, and their impact on human culture.
Mechanical	Knowledge of machines and tools, including their designs, uses, repair, and maintenance.
Biology	Knowledge of plant and animal organisms, their tissues, cells, functions, interdependencies, and interactions with each other and the environment.
Physics	Knowledge and prediction of physical principles, laws, their interrelationships, and applications to understanding fluid, material, and atmospheric dynamics, and mechanical, electrical, atomic and sub- atomic structures and processes.
Fine Arts	Knowledge of the theory and techniques required to compose, produce, and perform works of music, dance, visual arts, drama, and sculpture.

Chemistry	Knowledge of the chemical composition, structure, and properties of substances and of the chemical processes and transformations that they undergo. This includes uses of chemicals and their interactions, danger signs, production techniques, and disposal methods.
Food Production	Knowledge of techniques and equipment for planting, growing, and harvesting food products (both plant and animal) for consumption, including storage/handling techniques.
History and Archeology	Knowledge of historical events and their causes, indicators, and effects on civilizations and cultures.

Skills	Skills Definitions
Active Listening	Giving full attention to what other people are saying, taking time to understand the points being made, asking questions as appropriate, and not interrupting at inappropriate times.
Reading Comprehension	Understanding written sentences and paragraphs in work related documents.
Speaking	Talking to others to convey information effectively.
Monitoring	Monitoring/Assessing performance of yourself, other individuals, or organizations to make improvements or take corrective action.
Time Management	Managing one's own time and the time of others.
Service Orientation	Actively looking for ways to help people.
Active Learning	Understanding the implications of new information for both current and future problem-solving and decision-making.
Learning Strategies	Selecting and using training/instructional methods and procedures appropriate for the situation when learning or teaching new things.
Writing	Communicating effectively in writing as appropriate for the needs of the audience.
Critical Thinking	Using logic and reasoning to identify the strengths and weaknesses of alternative solutions, conclusions or approaches to problems.
Social Perceptiveness	Being aware of others' reactions and understanding why they react as they do.
Coordination	Adjusting actions in relation to others' actions.
Instructing	Teaching others how to do something.
Persuasion	Persuading others to change their minds or behavior.
Judgment and Decision Making	Considering the relative costs and benefits of potential actions to choose the most appropriate one.
Troubleshooting	Determining causes of operating errors and deciding what to do about it.
Mathematics	Using mathematics to solve problems.
Negotiation	Bringing others together and trying to reconcile differences.
Complex Problem Solving	Identifying complex problems and reviewing related information to develop and evaluate options and implement solutions.
Systems Analysis	Determining how a system should work and how changes in conditions, operations, and the environment will affect outcomes.
Systems Evaluation	Identifying measures or indicators of system performance and the actions needed to improve or correct performance, relative to the goals of the system.
Operations Analysis	Analyzing needs and product requirements to create a design.
Operation and Control	Controlling operations of equipment or systems.
Quality Control Analysis	Conducting tests and inspections of products, services, or processes to evaluate quality or performance.
Technology Design	Generating or adapting equipment and technology to serve user needs.
Management of Material Resources	Obtaining and seeing to the appropriate use of equipment, facilities, and materials needed to do certain work.
Equipment Selection	Determining the kind of tools and equipment needed to do a job.
Management of Financial Resources	Determining how money will be spent to get the work done, and accounting for these expenditures.
Equipment Maintenance	Performing routine maintenance on equipment and determining when and what kind of maintenance is needed.
Operation Monitoring	Watching gauges, dials, or other indicators to make sure a machine is working properly.
Repairing	Repairing machines or systems using the needed tools.
Management of Personnel Resources	Motivating, developing, and directing people as they work, identifying the best people for the job.
Installation	Installing equipment, machines, wiring, or programs to meet specifications.
Programming	Writing computer programs for various purposes.
Science	Using scientific rules and methods to solve problems.

Ability	Ability Definitions
Oral Comprehension	The ability to listen to and understand information and ideas presented through spoken words and sentences.
Oral Expression	The ability to communicate information and ideas in speaking so others will understand.
Deductive Reasoning	The ability to apply general rules to specific problems to produce answers that make sense.
Problem Sensitivity	The ability to tell when something is wrong or is likely to go wrong. It does not involve solving the problem, only recognizing there is a problem.
Speech Recognition	The ability to identify and understand the speech of another person.
Speech Clarity	The ability to speak clearly so others can understand you.
Written Comprehension	The ability to read and understand information and ideas presented in writing.
Inductive Reasoning	The ability to combine pieces of information to form general rules or conclusions (includes finding a relationship among seemingly unrelated events).
Near Vision	The ability to see details at close range (within a few feet of the observer).
Information Ordering	The ability to arrange things or actions in a certain order or pattern according to a specific rule or set of rules (e.g., patterns of numbers, letters, words, pictures, mathematical operations).
Written Expression	The ability to communicate information and ideas in writing so others will understand.
Mathematical Reasoning	The ability to choose the right mathematical methods or formulas to solve a problem.
Category Flexibility	The ability to generate or use different sets of rules for combining or grouping things in different ways.
Selective Attention	The ability to concentrate on a task over a period of time without being distracted.
Fluency of Ideas	The ability to come up with a number of ideas about a topic (the number of ideas is important, not their quality, correctness, or creativity).
Flexibility of Closure	The ability to identify or detect a known pattern (a figure, object, word, or sound) that is hidden in other distracting material.
Finger Dexterity	The ability to make precisely coordinated movements of the fingers of one or both hands to grasp, manipulate, or assemble very small objects.
Perceptual Speed	The ability to quickly and accurately compare similarities and differences among sets of letters, numbers, objects, pictures, or patterns. The things to be compared may be presented at the same time or one after the other. This ability also includes comparing a presented object with a remembered object.
Time Sharing	The ability to shift back and forth between two or more activities or sources of information (such as speech, sounds, touch, or other sources).
Speed of Closure	The ability to quickly make sense of, combine, and organize information into meaningful patterns.
Number Facility	The ability to add, subtract, multiply, or divide quickly and correctly.
Originality	The ability to come up with unusual or clever ideas about a given topic or situation, or to develop creative ways to solve a problem.
Memorization	The ability to remember information such as words, numbers, pictures, and procedures.
Auditory Attention	The ability to focus on a single source of sound in the presence of other distracting sounds.
Far Vision	The ability to see details at a distance.
Visualization	The ability to imagine how something will look after it is moved around or when its parts are moved or rearranged.
Visual Color Discrimination	The ability to match or detect differences between colors, including shades of color and brightness.
Arm-Hand Steadiness	The ability to keep your hand and arm steady while moving your arm or while holding your arm and hand in one position.
Manual Dexterity	The ability to quickly move your hand, your hand together with your arm, or your two hands to grasp, manipulate, or assemble objects.
Control Precision	The ability to quickly and repeatedly adjust the controls of a machine or a vehicle to exact positions.
Hearing Sensitivity	The ability to detect or tell the differences between sounds that vary in pitch and loudness.
Depth Perception	The ability to judge which of several objects is closer or farther away from you, or to judge the distance between you and an object.

Wrist-Finger Speed	The ability to make fast, simple, repeated movements of the fingers, hands, and wrists.
Trunk Strength	The ability to use your abdominal and lower back muscles to support part of the body repeatedly or continuously over time without 'giving out' or fatiguing.
Multilimb Coordination	The ability to coordinate two or more limbs (for example, two arms, two legs, or one leg and one arm) while sitting, standing, or lying down. It does not involve performing the activities while the whole body is in motion.
Speed of Limb Movement	The ability to quickly move the arms and legs.
Reaction Time	The ability to quickly respond (with the hand, finger, or foot) to a signal (sound, light, picture) when it appears.
Sound Localization	The ability to tell the direction from which a sound originated.
Response Orientation	The ability to choose quickly between two or more movements in response to two or more different signals (lights, sounds, pictures). It includes the speed with which the correct response is started with the hand, foot, or other body part.
Static Strength	The ability to exert maximum muscle force to lift, push, pull, or carry objects.
Glare Sensitivity	The ability to see objects in the presence of glare or bright lighting.
Extent Flexibility	The ability to bend, stretch, twist, or reach with your body, arms, and/or legs.
Dynamic Flexibility	The ability to quickly and repeatedly bend, stretch, twist, or reach out with your body, arms, and/or legs.
Spatial Orientation	The ability to know your location in relation to the environment or to know where other objects are in relation to you.
Rate Control	The ability to time your movements or the movement of a piece of equipment in anticipation of changes in the speed and/or direction of a moving object or scene.
Dynamic Strength	The ability to exert muscle force repeatedly or continuously over time. This involves muscular endurance and resistance to muscle fatigue.
Gross Body Coordination	The ability to coordinate the movement of your arms, legs, and torso together when the whole body is in motion.
Gross Body Equilibrium	The ability to keep or regain your body balance or stay upright when in an unstable position.
Night Vision	The ability to see under low light conditions.
Peripheral Vision	The ability to see objects or movement of objects to one's side when the eyes are looking ahead.
Stamina	The ability to exert yourself physically over long periods of time without getting winded or out of breath.
Explosive Strength	The ability to use short bursts of muscle force to propel oneself (as in jumping or sprinting), or to throw an object.

Work_Activity	Work_Activity Definitions
Interacting With Computers	Using computers and computer systems (including hardware and software) to program, write software, set up functions, enter data, or process information.
Getting Information	Observing, receiving, and otherwise obtaining information from all relevant sources.
Making Decisions and Solving Problems	Analyzing information and evaluating results to choose the best solution and solve problems.
Documenting/Recording Information	Entering, transcribing, recording, storing, or maintaining information in written or electronic/magnetic form.
Communicating with Supervisors, Peers, or Subordin	Providing information to supervisors, co-workers, and subordinates by telephone, in written form, e-mail, or in person.
Monitor Processes, Materials, or Surroundings	Monitoring and reviewing information from materials, events, or the environment, to detect or assess problems.
Identifying Objects, Actions, and Events	Identifying information by categorizing, estimating, recognizing differences or similarities, and detecting changes in circumstances or events.
Processing Information	Compiling, coding, categorizing, calculating, tabulating, auditing, or verifying information or data.
Establishing and Maintaining Interpersonal Relatio	Developing constructive and cooperative working relationships with others, and maintaining them over time.
Evaluating Information to Determine Compliance wit	Using relevant information and individual judgment to determine whether events or processes comply with laws, regulations, or standards.
Resolving Conflicts and Negotiating with Others	Handling complaints, settling disputes, and resolving grievances and conflicts, or otherwise negotiating with others.
Updating and Using Relevant Knowledge	Keeping up-to-date technically and applying new knowledge to your job.

Organizing, Planning, and Prioritizing Work	Developing specific goals and plans to prioritize, organize, and accomplish your work.
Judging the Qualities of Things, Services, or Peop	Assessing the value, importance, or quality of things or people.
Communicating with Persons Outside Organization	Communicating with people outside the organization, representing the organization to customers, the public, government, and other external sources. This information can be exchanged in person, in writing, or by telephone or e-mail.
Performing Administrative Activities	Performing day-to-day administrative tasks such as maintaining information files and processing paperwork.
Analyzing Data or Information	Identifying the underlying principles, reasons, or facts of information by breaking down information or data into separate parts.
Interpreting the Meaning of Information for Others	Translating or explaining what information means and how it can be used.
Coordinating the Work and Activities of Others	Getting members of a group to work together to accomplish tasks.
Training and Teaching Others	Identifying the educational needs of others, developing formal educational or training programs or classes, and teaching or instructing others.
Thinking Creatively	Developing, designing, or creating new applications, ideas, relationships, systems, or products, including artistic contributions.
Developing and Building Teams	Encouraging and building mutual trust, respect, and cooperation among team members.
Assisting and Caring for Others	Providing personal assistance, medical attention, emotional support, or other personal care to others such as coworkers, customers, or patients.
Inspecting Equipment, Structures, or Material	Inspecting equipment, structures, or materials to identify the cause of errors or other problems or defects.
Estimating the Quantifiable Characteristics of Pro	Estimating sizes, distances, and quantities; or determining time, costs, resources, or materials needed to perform a work activity.
Performing for or Working Directly with the Public	Performing for people or dealing directly with the public. This includes serving customers in restaurants and stores, and receiving clients or guests.
Scheduling Work and Activities	Scheduling events, programs, and activities, as well as the work of others.
Coaching and Developing Others	Identifying the developmental needs of others and coaching, mentoring, or otherwise helping others to improve their knowledge or skills.
Developing Objectives and Strategies	Establishing long-range objectives and specifying the strategies and actions to achieve them.
Guiding, Directing, and Motivating Subordinates	Providing guidance and direction to subordinates, including setting performance standards and monitoring performance.
Selling or Influencing Others	Convincing others to buy merchandise/goods or to otherwise change their minds or actions.
Provide Consultation and Advice to Others	Providing guidance and expert advice to management or other groups on technical, systems-, or process-related topics.
Drafting, Laying Out, and Specifying Technical Dev	Providing documentation, detailed instructions, drawings, or specifications to tell others about how devices, parts, equipment, or structures are to be fabricated, constructed, assembled, modified, maintained, or used.
Performing General Physical Activities	Performing physical activities that require considerable use of your arms and legs and moving your whole body, such as climbing, lifting, balancing, walking, stooping, and handling of materials.
Handling and Moving Objects	Using hands and arms in handling, installing, positioning, and moving materials, and manipulating things.
Staffing Organizational Units	Recruiting, interviewing, selecting, hiring, and promoting employees in an organization.
Monitoring and Controlling Resources	Monitoring and controlling resources and overseeing the spending of money.
Operating Vehicles, Mechanized Devices, or Equipme	Running, maneuvering, navigating, or driving vehicles or mechanized equipment, such as forklifts, passenger vehicles, aircraft, or water craft.
Repairing and Maintaining Electronic Equipment	Servicing, repairing, calibrating, regulating, fine-tuning, or testing machines, devices, and equipment that operate primarily on the basis of electrical or electronic (not mechanical) principles.
Controlling Machines and Processes	Using either control mechanisms or direct physical activity to operate machines or processes (not including computers or vehicles).
Repairing and Maintaining Mechanical Equipment	Servicing, repairing, adjusting, and testing machines, devices, moving parts, and equipment that operate primarily on the basis of mechanical (not electronic) principles.

Work_Context	Work_Context Definitions
Contact With Others	How much does this job require the worker to be in contact with others (face-to-face, by telephone, or otherwise) in order to perform it?
Telephone	How often do you have telephone conversations in this job?
Indoors, Environmentally Controlled	How often does this job require working indoors in environmentally controlled conditions?
Face-to-Face Discussions	How often do you have to have face-to-face discussions with individuals or teams in this job?
Spend Time Sitting	How much does this job require sitting?
Time Pressure	How often does this job require the worker to meet strict deadlines?
Work With Work Group or Team	How important is it to work with others in a group or team in this job?
Electronic Mail	How often do you use electronic mail in this job?
Freedom to Make Decisions	How much decision making freedom, without supervision, does the job offer?
Deal With External Customers	How important is it to work with external customers or the public in this job?
Frequency of Decision Making	How frequently is the worker required to make decisions that affect other people, the financial resources, and/or the image and reputation of the organization?
Spend Time Using Your Hands to Handle, Control, or	How much does this job require using your hands to handle, control, or feel objects, tools or controls?
Importance of Being Exact or Accurate	How important is being very exact or highly accurate in performing this job?
Importance of Repeating Same Tasks	How important is repeating the same physical activities (e.g., key entry) or mental activities (e.g., checking entries in a ledger) over and over, without stopping, to performing this job?
Deal With Unpleasant or Angry People	How frequently does the worker have to deal with unpleasant, angry, or discourteous individuals as part of the job requirements?
Structured versus Unstructured Work	To what extent is this job structured for the worker, rather than allowing the worker to determine tasks, priorities, and goals?
Spend Time Making Repetitive Motions	How much does this job require making repetitive motions?
Physical Proximity	To what extent does this job require the worker to perform job tasks in close physical proximity to other people?
Impact of Decisions on Co-workers or Company Resul	How do the decisions an employee makes impact the results of co-workers, clients or the company?
Letters and Memos	How often does the job require written letters and memos?
Frequency of Conflict Situations	How often are there conflict situations the employee has to face in this job?
Coordinate or Lead Others	How important is it to coordinate or lead others in accomplishing work activities in this job?
Sounds, Noise Levels Are Distracting or Uncomforta	How often does this job require working exposed to sounds and noise levels that are distracting or uncomfortable?
Level of Competition	To what extent does this job require the worker to compete or to be aware of competitive pressures?
Degree of Automation	How automated is the job?
Responsible for Others' Health and Safety	How much responsibility is there for the health and safety of others in this job?
Consequence of Error	How serious would the result usually be if the worker made a mistake that was not readily correctable?
Responsibility for Outcomes and Results	How responsible is the worker for work outcomes and results of other workers?
Spend Time Bending or Twisting the Body	How much does this job require bending or twisting your body?
Spend Time Standing	How much does this job require standing?
Exposed to Contaminants	How often does this job require working exposed to contaminants (such as pollutants, gases, dust or odors)?
Spend Time Walking and Running	How much does this job require walking and running?
Pace Determined by Speed of Equipment	How important is it to this job that the pace is determined by the speed of equipment or machinery? (This does not refer to keeping busy at all times on this job.)
Cramped Work Space, Awkward Positions	How often does this job require working in cramped work spaces that requires getting into awkward positions?
Spend Time Kneeling, Crouching, Stooping, or Crawl	How much does this job require kneeling, crouching, stooping or crawling?
Public Speaking	How often do you have to perform public speaking in this job?
Exposed to Minor Burns, Cuts, Bites, or Stings	How often does this job require exposure to minor burns, cuts, bites, or stings?

Extremely Bright or Inadequate Lighting	How often does this job require working in extremely bright or inadequate lighting conditions?
In an Enclosed Vehicle or Equipment	How often does this job require working in a closed vehicle or equipment (e.g., car)?
Indoors, Not Environmentally Controlled	How often does this job require working indoors in non-controlled environmental conditions (e.g., warehouse without heat)?
Very Hot or Cold Temperatures	How often does this job require working in very hot (above 90 F degrees) or very cold (below 32 F degrees) temperatures?
Outdoors, Exposed to Weather	How often does this job require working outdoors, exposed to all weather conditions?
Spend Time Climbing Ladders, Scaffolds, or Poles	How much does this job require climbing ladders, scaffolds, or poles?
Outdoors, Under Cover	How often does this job require working outdoors, under cover (e.g., structure with roof but no walls)?
Exposed to High Places	How often does this job require exposure to high places?
Spend Time Keeping or Regaining Balance	How much does this job require keeping or regaining your balance?
Deal With Physically Aggressive People	How frequently does this job require the worker to deal with physical aggression of violent individuals?
Wear Common Protective or Safety Equipment such as	How much does this job require wearing common protective or safety equipment such as safety shoes, glasses, gloves, hard hats or live jackets?
Exposed to Hazardous Equipment	How often does this job require exposure to hazardous equipment?
In an Open Vehicle or Equipment	How often does this job require working in an open vehicle or equipment (e.g., tractor)?
Exposed to Whole Body Vibration	How often does this job require exposure to whole body vibration (e.g., operate a jackhammer)?
Exposed to Hazardous Conditions	How often does this job require exposure to hazardous conditions?
Exposed to Disease or Infections	How often does this job require exposure to disease/infections?
Exposed to Radiation	How often does this job require exposure to radiation?
Wear Specialized Protective or Safety Equipment su	How much does this job require wearing specialized protective or safety equipment such as breathing apparatus, safety harness, full protection suits, or radiation protection?

Job Zone Component	Job Zone Component Definitions
Title	Job Zone Two: Some Preparation Needed
Overall Experience	Some previous work-related skill, knowledge, or experience may be helpful in these occupations, but usually is not needed. For example, a drywall installer might benefit from experience installing drywall, but an inexperienced person could still learn to be an installer with little difficulty.
Job Training	Employees in these occupations need anywhere from a few months to one year of working with experienced employees.
Job Zone Examples	These occupations often involve using your knowledge and skills to help others. Examples include drywall installers, fire inspectors, flight attendants, pharmacy technicians, salespersons (retail), and tellers.
SVP Range	(4.0 to < 6.0)
Education	These occupations usually require a high school diploma and may require some vocational training or job-related course work. In some cases, an associate's or bachelor's degree could be needed.

Work_Styles	Work_Styles Definitions
Cooperation	Job requires being pleasant with others on the job and displaying a good-natured, cooperative attitude.
Dependability	Job requires being reliable, responsible, and dependable, and fulfilling obligations.
Self Control	Job requires maintaining composure, keeping emotions in check, controlling anger, and avoiding aggressive behavior, even in very difficult situations.
Attention to Detail	Job requires being careful about detail and thorough in completing work tasks.
Stress Tolerance	Job requires accepting criticism and dealing calmly and effectively with high stress situations.
Initiative	Job requires a willingness to take on responsibilities and challenges.
Adaptability/Flexibility	Job requires being open to change (positive or negative) and to considerable variety in the workplace.

Concern for Others	Job requires being sensitive to others' needs and feelings and being understanding and helpful on the job.
Independence	Job requires developing one's own ways of doing things, guiding oneself with little or no supervision, and depending on oneself to get things done.
Persistence	Job requires persistence in the face of obstacles.
Social Orientation	Job requires preferring to work with others rather than alone, and being personally connected with others on the job.
Integrity	Job requires being honest and ethical.
Analytical Thinking	Job requires analyzing information and using logic to address work-related issues and problems.
Achievement/Effort	Job requires establishing and maintaining personally challenging achievement goals and exerting effort toward mastering tasks.
Leadership	Job requires a willingness to lead, take charge, and offer opinions and direction.
Innovation	Job requires creativity and alternative thinking to develop new ideas for and answers to work-related problems.

43-4061.00 - Eligibility Interviewers, Government Programs

Determine eligibility of persons applying to receive assistance from government programs and agency resources, such as welfare, unemployment benefits, social security, and public housing.

Tasks

1) Interpret and explain information such as eligibility requirements, application details, payment methods, and applicants' legal rights.

2) Check with employers or other references to verify answers and obtain further information.

3) Answer applicants' questions about benefits and claim procedures.

4) Compile, record, and evaluate personal and financial data in order to verify completeness and accuracy, and to determine eligibility status.

5) Provide applicants with assistance in completing application forms such as those for job referrals or unemployment compensation claims.

6) Prepare applications and forms for applicants for such purposes as school enrollment, employment, and medical services.

7) Receive and record security deposits and advance rents from tenants receiving housing assistance.

8) Investigate claimants for the possibility of fraud or abuse.

9) Interview benefits recipients at specified intervals to certify their eligibility for continuing benefits.

10) Refer applicants to job openings or to interviews with other staff, in accordance with administrative guidelines or office procedures.

11) Initiate procedures to grant, modify, deny, or terminate assistance, or refer applicants to other agencies for assistance.

12) Provide social workers with pertinent information gathered during applicant interviews.

13) Interview and investigate applicants for public assistance to gather information pertinent to their applications.

14) Conduct annual, interim, and special housing reviews and home visits to ensure conformance to regulations.

15) Keep records of assigned cases, and prepare required reports.

16) Compute and authorize amounts of assistance for programs such as grants, monetary payments, and food stamps.

17) Schedule benefits claimants for adjudication interviews to address questions of eligibility.

43-4071.00 - File Clerks

File correspondence, cards, invoices, receipts, and other records in alphabetical or numerical order or according to the filing system used. Locate and remove material from file when requested.

Tasks

1) Answer questions about records and files.

2) Add new material to file records, and create new records as necessary.

3) Perform general office duties such as typing, operating office machines, and sorting mail.

4) Eliminate outdated or unnecessary materials, destroying them or transferring them to inactive storage according to file maintenance guidelines and/or legal requirements.

5) Find and retrieve information from files in response to requests from authorized users.

6) Sort or classify information according to guidelines such as content, purpose, user criteria, or chronological, alphabetical, or numerical order.

7) Keep records of materials filed or removed, using logbooks or computers.

8) Perform periodic inspections of materials or files in order to ensure correct placement, legibility, and proper condition.

9) Assign and record or stamp identification numbers or codes in order to index materials for filing.

10) Gather materials to be filed from departments and employees.

11) Track materials removed from files in order to ensure that borrowed files are returned.

12) Modify and improve filing systems, or implement new filing systems.

13) Scan or read incoming materials in order to determine how and where they should be classified or filed.

14) Enter document identification codes into systems in order to determine locations of documents to be retrieved.

15) Design forms related to filing systems.

16) Retrieve documents stored in microfilm or microfiche and place them in viewers for reading.

17) Operate mechanized files that rotate to bring needed records to a particular location.

Knowledge	Knowledge Definitions
Clerical	Knowledge of administrative and clerical procedures and systems such as word processing, managing files and records, stenography and transcription, designing forms, and other office procedures and terminology.
English Language	Knowledge of the structure and content of the English language including the meaning and spelling of words, rules of composition, and grammar.
Customer and Personal Service	Knowledge of principles and processes for providing customer and personal services. This includes customer needs assessment, meeting quality standards for services, and evaluation of customer satisfaction.
Computers and Electronics	Knowledge of circuit boards, processors, chips, electronic equipment, and computer hardware and software, including applications and programming.
Mathematics	Knowledge of arithmetic, algebra, geometry, calculus, statistics, and their applications.
Administration and Management	Knowledge of business and management principles involved in strategic planning, resource allocation, human resources modeling, leadership technique, production methods, and coordination of people and resources.
Personnel and Human Resources	Knowledge of principles and procedures for personnel recruitment, selection, training, compensation and benefits, labor relations and negotiation, and personnel information systems.
Education and Training	Knowledge of principles and methods for curriculum and training design, teaching and instruction for individuals and groups, and the measurement of training effects.
Communications and Media	Knowledge of media production, communication, and dissemination techniques and methods. This includes alternative ways to inform and entertain via written, oral, and visual media.
Economics and Accounting	Knowledge of economic and accounting principles and practices, the financial markets, banking and the analysis and reporting of financial data.
Telecommunications	Knowledge of transmission, broadcasting, switching, control, and operation of telecommunications systems.
Law and Government	Knowledge of laws, legal codes, court procedures, precedents, government regulations, executive orders, agency rules, and the democratic political process.

Sales and Marketing	Knowledge of principles and methods for showing, promoting, and selling products or services. This includes marketing strategy and tactics, product demonstration, sales techniques, and sales control systems.
Production and Processing	Knowledge of raw materials, production processes, quality control, costs, and other techniques for maximizing the effective manufacture and distribution of goods.
Therapy and Counseling	Knowledge of principles, methods, and procedures for diagnosis, treatment, and rehabilitation of physical and mental dysfunctions, and for career counseling and guidance.
Medicine and Dentistry	Knowledge of the information and techniques needed to diagnose and treat human injuries, diseases, and deformities. This includes symptoms, treatment alternatives, drug properties and interactions, and preventive health-care measures.
Transportation	Knowledge of principles and methods for moving people or goods by air, rail, sea, or road, including the relative costs and benefits.
Public Safety and Security	Knowledge of relevant equipment, policies, procedures, and strategies to promote effective local, state, or national security operations for the protection of people, data, property, and institutions.
Psychology	Knowledge of human behavior and performance; individual differences in ability, personality, and interests; learning and motivation; psychological research methods; and the assessment and treatment of behavioral and affective disorders.
Geography	Knowledge of principles and methods for describing the features of land, sea, and air masses, including their physical characteristics, locations, interrelationships, and distribution of plant, animal, and human life.
Mechanical	Knowledge of machines and tools, including their designs, uses, repair, and maintenance.
Engineering and Technology	Knowledge of the practical application of engineering science and technology. This includes applying principles, techniques, procedures, and equipment to the design and production of various goods and services.
Sociology and Anthropology	Knowledge of group behavior and dynamics, societal trends and influences, human migrations, ethnicity, cultures and their history and origins.
Design	Knowledge of design techniques, tools, and principles involved in production of precision technical plans, blueprints, drawings, and models.
Physics	Knowledge and prediction of physical principles, laws, their interrelationships, and applications to understanding fluid, material, and atmospheric dynamics, and mechanical, electrical, atomic and sub-atomic structures and processes.
Foreign Language	Knowledge of the structure and content of a foreign (non-English) language including the meaning and spelling of words, rules of composition and grammar, and pronunciation.
Chemistry	Knowledge of the chemical composition, structure, and properties of substances and of the chemical processes and transformations that they undergo. This includes uses of chemicals and their interactions, danger signs, production techniques, and disposal methods.
Building and Construction	Knowledge of materials, methods, and the tools involved in the construction or repair of houses, buildings, or other structures such as highways and roads.
Biology	Knowledge of plant and animal organisms, their tissues, cells, functions, interdependencies, and interactions with each other and the environment.
Philosophy and Theology	Knowledge of different philosophical systems and religions. This includes their basic principles, values, ethics, ways of thinking, customs, practices, and their impact on human culture.
History and Archeology	Knowledge of historical events and their causes, indicators, and effects on civilizations and cultures.
Food Production	Knowledge of techniques and equipment for planting, growing, and harvesting food products (both plant and animal) for consumption, including storage/handling techniques.
Fine Arts	Knowledge of the theory and techniques required to compose, produce, and perform works of music, dance, visual arts, drama, and sculpture.

Skills	Skills Definitions
Active Listening	Giving full attention to what other people are saying, taking time to understand the points being made, asking questions as appropriate, and not interrupting at inappropriate times.
Speaking	Talking to others to convey information effectively.

Reading Comprehension	Understanding written sentences and paragraphs in work related documents.
Time Management	Managing one's own time and the time of others.
Active Learning	Understanding the implications of new information for both current and future problem-solving and decision-making.
Service Orientation	Actively looking for ways to help people.
Instructing	Teaching others how to do something.
Learning Strategies	Selecting and using training/instructional methods and procedures appropriate for the situation when learning or teaching new things.
Social Perceptiveness	Being aware of others' reactions and understanding why they react as they do.
Coordination	Adjusting actions in relation to others' actions.
Critical Thinking	Using logic and reasoning to identify the strengths and weaknesses of alternative solutions, conclusions or approaches to problems.
Writing	Communicating effectively in writing as appropriate for the needs of the audience.
Complex Problem Solving	Identifying complex problems and reviewing related information to develop and evaluate options and implement solutions.
Mathematics	Using mathematics to solve problems.
Monitoring	Monitoring/Assessing performance of yourself, other individuals, or organizations to make improvements or take corrective action.
Judgment and Decision Making	Considering the relative costs and benefits of potential actions to choose the most appropriate one.
Operation and Control	Controlling operations of equipment or systems.
Persuasion	Persuading others to change their minds or behavior.
Negotiation	Bringing others together and trying to reconcile differences.
Troubleshooting	Determining causes of operating errors and deciding what to do about it.
Quality Control Analysis	Conducting tests and inspections of products, services, or processes to evaluate quality or performance.
Systems Evaluation	Identifying measures or indicators of system performance and the actions needed to improve or correct performance, relative to the goals of the system.
Operations Analysis	Analyzing needs and product requirements to create a design.
Equipment Selection	Determining the kind of tools and equipment needed to do a job.
Management of Material Resources	Obtaining and seeing to the appropriate use of equipment, facilities, and materials needed to do certain work.
Equipment Maintenance	Performing routine maintenance on equipment and determining when and what kind of maintenance is needed.
Operation Monitoring	Watching gauges, dials, or other indicators to make sure a machine is working properly.
Technology Design	Generating or adapting equipment and technology to serve user needs.
Management of Personnel Resources	Motivating, developing, and directing people as they work, identifying the best people for the job.
Systems Analysis	Determining how a system should work and how changes in conditions, operations, and the environment will affect outcomes.
Management of Financial Resources	Determining how money will be spent to get the work done, and accounting for these expenditures.
Installation	Installing equipment, machines, wiring, or programs to meet specifications.
Repairing	Repairing machines or systems using the needed tools.
Programming	Writing computer programs for various purposes.
Science	Using scientific rules and methods to solve problems.

Ability	Ability Definitions
Information Ordering	The ability to arrange things or actions in a certain order or pattern according to a specific rule or set of rules (e.g., patterns of numbers, letters, words, pictures, mathematical operations).
Written Comprehension	The ability to read and understand information and ideas presented in writing.
Category Flexibility	The ability to generate or use different sets of rules for combining or grouping things in different ways.
Near Vision	The ability to see details at close range (within a few feet of the observer).
Oral Comprehension	The ability to listen to and understand information and ideas presented through spoken words and sentences.
Written Expression	The ability to communicate information and ideas in writing so others will understand.

Perceptual Speed	The ability to quickly and accurately compare similarities and differences among sets of letters, numbers. objects, pictures, or patterns. The things to be compared may be presented at the same time or one after the other. This ability also includes comparing a presented object with a remembered object.
Oral Expression	The ability to communicate information and ideas in speaking so others will understand.
Flexibility of Closure	The ability to identify or detect a known pattern (a figure, object, word, or sound) that is hidden in other distracting material.
Speech Clarity	The ability to speak clearly so others can understand you.
Speech Recognition	The ability to identify and understand the speech of another person.
Problem Sensitivity	The ability to tell when something is wrong or is likely to go wrong. It does not involve solving the problem, only recognizing there is a problem.
Selective Attention	The ability to concentrate on a task over a period of time without being distracted.
Inductive Reasoning	The ability to combine pieces of information to form general rules or conclusions (includes finding a relationship among seemingly unrelated events).
Deductive Reasoning	The ability to apply general rules to specific problems to produce answers that make sense.
Finger Dexterity	The ability to make precisely coordinated movements of the fingers of one or both hands to grasp, manipulate. or assemble very small objects.
Fluency of Ideas	The ability to come up with a number of ideas about a topic (the number of ideas is important, not their quality, correctness, or creativity).
Manual Dexterity	The ability to quickly move your hand, your hand together with your arm, or your two hands to grasp, manipulate, or assemble objects.
Memorization	The ability to remember information such as words, numbers, pictures, and procedures.
Originality	The ability to come up with unusual or clever ideas about a given topic or situation, or to develop creative ways to solve a problem.
Arm-Hand Steadiness	The ability to keep your hand and arm steady while moving your arm or while holding your arm and hand in one position.
Far Vision	The ability to see details at a distance.
Wrist-Finger Speed	The ability to make fast, simple, repeated movements of the fingers, hands, and wrists.
Number Facility	The ability to add, subtract, multiply, or divide quickly and correctly.
Time Sharing	The ability to shift back and forth between two or more activities or sources of information (such as speech, sounds, touch, or other sources).
Multilimb Coordination	The ability to coordinate two or more limbs (for example, two arms, two legs, or one leg and one arm) while sitting, standing, or lying down. It does not involve performing the activities while the whole body is in motion.
Trunk Strength	The ability to use your abdominal and lower back muscles to support part of the body repeatedly or continuously over time without 'giving out' or fatiguing.
Speed of Closure	The ability to quickly make sense of, combine, and organize information into meaningful patterns.
Visualization	The ability to imagine how something will look after it is moved around or when its parts are moved or rearranged.
Static Strength	The ability to exert maximum muscle force to lift, push, pull, or carry objects.
Stamina	The ability to exert yourself physically over long periods of time without getting winded or out of breath.
Visual Color Discrimination	The ability to match or detect differences between colors, including shades of color and brightness.
Extent Flexibility	The ability to bend, stretch, twist, or reach with your body, arms, and/or legs.
Gross Body Coordination	The ability to coordinate the movement of your arms, legs, and torso together when the whole body is in motion.
Mathematical Reasoning	The ability to choose the right mathematical methods or formulas to solve a problem.
Control Precision	The ability to quickly and repeatedly adjust the controls of a machine or a vehicle to exact positions.
Gross Body Equilibrium	The ability to keep or regain your body balance or stay upright when in an unstable position.
Depth Perception	The ability to judge which of several objects is closer or farther away from you, or to judge the distance between you and an object.
Speed of Limb Movement	The ability to quickly move the arms and legs.

Dynamic Strength	The ability to exert muscle force repeatedly or continuously over time. This involves muscular endurance and resistance to muscle fatigue.
Hearing Sensitivity	The ability to detect or tell the differences between sounds that vary in pitch and loudness.
Auditory Attention	The ability to focus on a single source of sound in the presence of other distracting sounds.
Dynamic Flexibility	The ability to quickly and repeatedly bend, stretch, twist, or reach out with your body, arms, and/or legs.
Glare Sensitivity	The ability to see objects in the presence of glare or bright lighting.
Spatial Orientation	The ability to know your location in relation to the environment or to know where other objects are in relation to you.
Rate Control	The ability to time your movements or the movement of a piece of equipment in anticipation of changes in the speed and/or direction of a moving object or scene.
Peripheral Vision	The ability to see objects or movement of objects to one's side when the eyes are looking ahead.
Sound Localization	The ability to tell the direction from which a sound originated.
Explosive Strength	The ability to use short bursts of muscle force to propel oneself (as in jumping or sprinting), or to throw an object.
Night Vision	The ability to see under low light conditions.
Reaction Time	The ability to quickly respond (with the hand, finger, or foot) to a signal (sound, light, picture) when it appears.
Response Orientation	The ability to choose quickly between two or more movements in response to two or more different signals (lights, sounds, pictures). It includes the speed with which the correct response is started with the hand, foot, or other body part.

Work_Activity	Work_Activity Definitions
Documenting/Recording Information	Entering, transcribing, recording, storing, or maintaining information in written or electronic/magnetic form.
Performing Administrative Activities	Performing day-to-day administrative tasks such as maintaining information files and processing paperwork.
Organizing, Planning, and Prioritizing Work	Developing specific goals and plans to prioritize, organize, and accomplish your work.
Establishing and Maintaining Interpersonal Relatio	Developing constructive and cooperative working relationships with others, and maintaining them over time.
Interacting With Computers	Using computers and computer systems (including hardware and software) to program, write software, set up functions, enter data, or process information.
Processing Information	Compiling, coding, categorizing, calculating, tabulating, auditing, or verifying information or data.
Communicating with Supervisors, Peers, or Subordin	Providing information to supervisors, co-workers, and subordinates by telephone, in written form, e-mail, or in person.
Getting Information	Observing, receiving, and otherwise obtaining information from all relevant sources.
Evaluating Information to Determine Compliance wit	Using relevant information and individual judgment to determine whether events or processes comply with laws, regulations, or standards.
Updating and Using Relevant Knowledge	Keeping up-to-date technically and applying new knowledge to your job.
Monitoring and Controlling Resources	Monitoring and controlling resources and overseeing the spending of money.
Performing General Physical Activities	Performing physical activities that require considerable use of your arms and legs and moving your whole body, such as climbing, lifting, balancing, walking, stooping, and handling of materials.
Communicating with Persons Outside Organization	Communicating with people outside the organization, representing the organization to customers, the public, government, and other external sources. This information can be exchanged in person, in writing, or by telephone or e-mail.
Training and Teaching Others	Identifying the educational needs of others, developing formal educational or training programs or classes, and teaching or instructing others.
Analyzing Data or Information	Identifying the underlying principles, reasons, or facts of information by breaking down information or data into separate parts.
Interpreting the Meaning of Information for Others	Translating or explaining what information means and how it can be used.
Handling and Moving Objects	Using hands and arms in handling, installing, positioning, and moving materials, and manipulating things.
Performing for or Working Directly with the Public	Performing for people or dealing directly with the public. This includes serving customers in restaurants and stores, and receiving clients or guests.

Scheduling Work and Activities	Scheduling events, programs, and activities, as well as the work of others.
Resolving Conflicts and Negotiating with Others	Handling complaints, settling disputes, and resolving grievances and conflicts, or otherwise negotiating with others.
Assisting and Caring for Others	Providing personal assistance, medical attention, emotional support, or other personal care to others such as coworkers, customers, or patients.
Identifying Objects, Actions, and Events	Identifying information by categorizing, estimating, recognizing differences or similarities, and detecting changes in circumstances or events.
Thinking Creatively	Developing, designing, or creating new applications, ideas, relationships, systems, or products, including artistic contributions.
Developing Objectives and Strategies	Establishing long-range objectives and specifying the strategies and actions to achieve them.
Coaching and Developing Others	Identifying the developmental needs of others and coaching, mentoring, or otherwise helping others to improve their knowledge or skills.
Making Decisions and Solving Problems	Analyzing information and evaluating results to choose the best solution and solve problems.
Monitor Processes, Materials, or Surroundings	Monitoring and reviewing information from materials, events, or the environment, to detect or assess problems.
Guiding, Directing, and Motivating Subordinates	Providing guidance and direction to subordinates, including setting performance standards and monitoring performance.
Inspecting Equipment, Structures, or Material	Inspecting equipment, structures, or materials to identify the cause of errors or other problems or defects.
Coordinating the Work and Activities of Others	Getting members of a group to work together to accomplish tasks.
Judging the Qualities of Things, Services, or Peop	Assessing the value, importance, or quality of things or people.
Developing and Building Teams	Encouraging and building mutual trust, respect, and cooperation among team members.
Estimating the Quantifiable Characteristics of Pro	Estimating sizes, distances, and quantities; or determining time, costs, resources, or materials needed to perform a work activity.
Controlling Machines and Processes	Using either control mechanisms or direct physical activity to operate machines or processes (not including computers or vehicles).
Selling or Influencing Others	Convincing others to buy merchandise/goods or to otherwise change their minds or actions.
Provide Consultation and Advice to Others	Providing guidance and expert advice to management or other groups on technical, systems-, or process-related topics.
Operating Vehicles, Mechanized Devices, or Equipme	Running, maneuvering, navigating, or driving vehicles or mechanized equipment, such as forklifts, passenger vehicles, aircraft, or water craft.
Repairing and Maintaining Electronic Equipment	Servicing, repairing, calibrating, regulating, fine-tuning, or testing machines, devices, and equipment that operate primarily on the basis of electrical or electronic (not mechanical) principles.
Staffing Organizational Units	Recruiting, interviewing, selecting, hiring, and promoting employees in an organization.
Repairing and Maintaining Mechanical Equipment	Servicing, repairing, adjusting, and testing machines, devices, moving parts, and equipment that operate primarily on the basis of mechanical (not electronic) principles.
Drafting, Laying Out, and Specifying Technical Dev	Providing documentation, detailed instructions, drawings, or specifications to tell others about how devices, parts, equipment, or structures are to be fabricated, constructed, assembled, modified, maintained, or used.

Work_Context	Work_Context Definitions
Face-to-Face Discussions	How often do you have to have face-to-face discussions with individuals or teams in this job?
Telephone	How often do you have telephone conversations in this job?
Contact With Others	How much does this job require the worker to be in contact with others (face-to-face, by telephone, or otherwise) in order to perform it?
Indoors, Environmentally Controlled	How often does this job require working indoors in environmentally controlled conditions?
Structured versus Unstructured Work	To what extent is this job structured for the worker, rather than allowing the worker to determine tasks, priorities, and goals?
Time Pressure	How often does this job require the worker to meet strict deadlines?
Work With Work Group or Team	How important is it to work with others in a group or team in this job?
Importance of Being Exact or Accurate	How important is being very exact or highly accurate in performing this job?

Importance of Repeating Same Tasks	How important is repeating the same physical activities (e.g., key entry) or mental activities (e.g., checking entries in a ledger) over and over, without stopping, to performing this job?
Deal With External Customers	How important is it to work with external customers or the public in this job?
Freedom to Make Decisions	How much decision making freedom, without supervision, does the job offer?
Spend Time Sitting	How much does this job require sitting?
Spend Time Making Repetitive Motions	How much does this job require making repetitive motions?
Responsibility for Outcomes and Results	How responsible is the worker for work outcomes and results of other workers?
Spend Time Using Your Hands to Handle, Control, or	How much does this job require using your hands to handle, control, or feel objects, tools or controls?
Frequency of Decision Making	How frequently is the worker required to make decisions that affect other people, the financial resources, and/or the image and reputation of the organization?
Impact of Decisions on Co-workers or Company Resul	How do the decisions an employee makes impact the results of co-workers, clients or the company?
Physical Proximity	To what extent does this job require the worker to perform job tasks in close physical proximity to other people?
Coordinate or Lead Others	How important is it to coordinate or lead others in accomplishing work activities in this job?
Electronic Mail	How often do you use electronic mail in this job?
Letters and Memos	How often does the job require written letters and memos?
Frequency of Conflict Situations	How often are there conflict situations the employee has to face in this job?
Spend Time Walking and Running	How much does this job require walking and running?
Consequence of Error	How serious would the result usually be if the worker made a mistake that was not readily correctable?
Spend Time Bending or Twisting the Body	How much does this job require bending or twisting your body?
Responsible for Others' Health and Safety	How much responsibility is there for the health and safety of others in this job?
Sounds, Noise Levels Are Distracting or Uncomforta	How often does this job require working exposed to sounds and noise levels that are distracting or uncomfortable?
Spend Time Standing	How much does this job require standing?
Deal With Unpleasant or Angry People	How frequently does the worker have to deal with unpleasant, angry, or discourteous individuals as part of the job requirements?
Degree of Automation	How automated is the job?
Exposed to Disease or Infections	How often does this job require exposure to disease/infections?
Level of Competition	To what extent does this job require the worker to compete or to be aware of competitive pressures?
Spend Time Kneeling, Crouching, Stooping, or Crawl	How much does this job require kneeling, crouching, stooping, or crawling?
Pace Determined by Speed of Equipment	How important is it to this job that the pace is determined by the speed of equipment or machinery? (This does not refer to keeping busy at all times on this job.)
Exposed to Contaminants	How often does this job require working exposed to contaminants (such as pollutants, gases, dust or odors)?
Cramped Work Space, Awkward Positions	How often does this job require working in cramped work spaces that requires getting into awkward positions?
Spend Time Keeping or Regaining Balance	How much does this job require keeping or regaining your balance?
Exposed to Radiation	How often does this job require exposure to radiation?
Extremely Bright or Inadequate Lighting	How often does this job require working in extremely bright or inadequate lighting conditions?
Public Speaking	How often do you have to perform public speaking in this job?
Wear Common Protective or Safety Equipment such as	How much does this job require wearing common protective or safety equipment such as safety shoes, glasses, gloves, hard hats or live jackets?
In an Enclosed Vehicle or Equipment	How often does this job require working in a closed vehicle or equipment (e.g., car)?
Exposed to Minor Burns, Cuts, Bites, or Stings	How often does this job require exposure to minor burns, cuts, bites, or stings?
Very Hot or Cold Temperatures	How often does this job require working in very hot (above 90 F degrees) or very cold (below 32 F degrees) temperatures?
Deal With Physically Aggressive People	How frequently does this job require the worker to deal with physical aggression of violent individuals?
Spend Time Climbing Ladders, Scaffolds, or Poles	How much does this job require climbing ladders, scaffolds, or poles?

Indoors, Not Environmentally Controlled	How often does this job require working indoors in non-controlled environmental conditions (e.g., warehouse without heat)?
Outdoors, Under Cover	How often does this job require working outdoors, under cover (e.g., structure with roof but no walls)?
Outdoors, Exposed to Weather	How often does this job require working outdoors, exposed to all weather conditions?
Exposed to Hazardous Equipment	How often does this job require exposure to hazardous equipment?
Exposed to Hazardous Conditions	How often does this job require exposure to hazardous conditions?
Wear Specialized Protective or Safety Equipment su	How much does this job require wearing specialized protective or safety equipment such as breathing apparatus, safety harness, full protection suits, or radiation protection?
In an Open Vehicle or Equipment	How often does this job require working in an open vehicle or equipment (e.g., tractor)?
Exposed to High Places	How often does this job require exposure to high places?
Exposed to Whole Body Vibration	How often does this job require exposure to whole body vibration (e.g., operate a jackhammer)?

Job Zone Component	Job Zone Component Definitions
Title	Job Zone Three: Medium Preparation Needed
Overall Experience	Previous work-related skill, knowledge, or experience is required for these occupations. For example, an electrician must have completed three or four years of apprenticeship or several years of vocational training, and often must have passed a licensing exam, in order to perform the job.
Job Training	Employees in these occupations usually need one or two years of training involving both on-the-job experience and informal training with experienced workers.
Job Zone Examples	These occupations usually involve using communication and organizational skills to coordinate, supervise, manage, or train others to accomplish goals. Examples include dental assistants, electricians, fish and game wardens, legal secretaries, personnel recruiters, and recreation workers.
SVP Range	(6.0 to < 7.0)
Education	Most occupations in this zone require training in vocational schools, related on-the-job experience, or an associate's degree. Some may require a bachelor's degree.

Work_Styles	Work_Styles Definitions
Attention to Detail	Job requires being careful about detail and thorough in completing work tasks.
Independence	Job requires developing one's own ways of doing things, guiding oneself with little or no supervision, and depending on oneself to get things done.
Dependability	Job requires being reliable, responsible, and dependable, and fulfilling obligations.
Cooperation	Job requires being pleasant with others on the job and displaying a good-natured, cooperative attitude.
Integrity	Job requires being honest and ethical.
Initiative	Job requires a willingness to take on responsibilities and challenges.
Innovation	Job requires creativity and alternative thinking to develop new ideas for and answers to work-related problems.
Concern for Others	Job requires being sensitive to others' needs and feelings and being understanding and helpful on the job.
Adaptability/Flexibility	Job requires being open to change (positive or negative) and to considerable variety in the workplace.
Self Control	Job requires maintaining composure, keeping emotions in check, controlling anger, and avoiding aggressive behavior, even in very difficult situations.
Persistence	Job requires persistence in the face of obstacles.
Achievement/Effort	Job requires establishing and maintaining personally challenging achievement goals and exerting effort toward mastering tasks.
Analytical Thinking	Job requires analyzing information and using logic to address work-related issues and problems.
Stress Tolerance	Job requires accepting criticism and dealing calmly and effectively with high stress situations.
Social Orientation	Job requires preferring to work with others rather than alone, and being personally connected with others on the job.
Leadership	Job requires a willingness to lead, take charge, and offer opinions and direction.

43-4081.00 - Hotel, Motel, and Resort Desk Clerks

Accommodate hotel, motel, and resort patrons by registering and assigning rooms to guests, issuing room keys, transmitting and receiving messages, keeping records of occupied rooms and guests' accounts, making and confirming reservations, and presenting statements to and collecting payments from departing guests.

Tasks

1) Contact housekeeping or maintenance staff when guests report problems.

2) Keep records of room availability and guests' accounts, manually or using computers.

3) Greet, register, and assign rooms to guests of hotels or motels.

4) Post charges, such those for rooms, food, liquor, or telephone calls, to ledgers manually, or by using computers.

5) Compute bills, collect payments, and make change for guests.

6) Verify customers' credit, and establish how the customer will pay for the accommodation.

7) Make and confirm reservations.

8) Review accounts and charges with guests during the check out process.

9) Transmit and receive messages, using telephones or telephone switchboards.

10) Issue room keys and escort instructions to bellhops.

11) Perform simple bookkeeping activities, such as balancing cash accounts.

12) Arrange tours, taxis, and restaurants for customers.

13) Advise housekeeping staff when rooms have been vacated and are ready for cleaning.

14) Deposit guests' valuables in hotel safes or safe-deposit boxes.

15) Date-stamp, sort, and rack incoming mail and messages.

16) Answer inquiries pertaining to hotel services, registration of guests, and shopping, dining, entertainment, and travel directions.

Knowledge	Knowledge Definitions
Customer and Personal Service	Knowledge of principles and processes for providing customer and personal services. This includes customer needs assessment, meeting quality standards for services, and evaluation of customer satisfaction.
Administration and Management	Knowledge of business and management principles involved in strategic planning, resource allocation, human resources modeling, leadership technique, production methods, and coordination of people and resources.
Clerical	Knowledge of administrative and clerical procedures and systems such as word processing, managing files and records, stenography and transcription, designing forms, and other office procedures and terminology.
English Language	Knowledge of the structure and content of the English language including the meaning and spelling of words, rules of composition, and grammar.
Mathematics	Knowledge of arithmetic, algebra, geometry, calculus, statistics, and their applications.
Sales and Marketing	Knowledge of principles and methods for showing, promoting, and selling products or services. This includes marketing strategy and tactics, product demonstration, sales techniques, and sales control systems.
Computers and Electronics	Knowledge of circuit boards, processors, chips, electronic equipment, and computer hardware and software, including applications and programming.
Public Safety and Security	Knowledge of relevant equipment, policies, procedures, and strategies to promote effective local, state, or national security operations for the protection of people, data, property, and institutions.
Telecommunications	Knowledge of transmission, broadcasting, switching, control, and operation of telecommunications systems.
Economics and Accounting	Knowledge of economic and accounting principles and practices, the financial markets, banking and the analysis and reporting of financial data.
Communications and Media	Knowledge of media production, communication, and dissemination techniques and methods. This includes alternative ways to inform and entertain via written, oral, and visual media.

Personnel and Human Resources	Knowledge of principles and procedures for personnel recruitment, selection, training, compensation and benefits, labor relations and negotiation, and personnel information systems.
Education and Training	Knowledge of principles and methods for curriculum and training design, teaching and instruction for individuals and groups, and the measurement of training effects.
Transportation	Knowledge of principles and methods for moving people or goods by air, rail, sea, or road, including the relative costs and benefits.
Geography	Knowledge of principles and methods for describing the features of land, sea, and air masses, including their physical characteristics, locations, interrelationships, and distribution of plant, animal, and human life.
Psychology	Knowledge of human behavior and performance; individual differences in ability, personality, and interests; learning and motivation; psychological research methods; and the assessment and treatment of behavioral and affective disorders.
Foreign Language	Knowledge of the structure and content of a foreign (non-English) language including the meaning and spelling of words, rules of composition and grammar, and pronunciation.
Engineering and Technology	Knowledge of the practical application of engineering science and technology. This includes applying principles, techniques, procedures, and equipment to the design and production of various goods and services.
Sociology and Anthropology	Knowledge of group behavior and dynamics, societal trends and influences, human migrations, ethnicity, cultures and their history and origins.
Law and Government	Knowledge of laws, legal codes, court procedures, precedents, government regulations, executive orders, agency rules, and the democratic political process.
Production and Processing	Knowledge of raw materials, production processes, quality control, costs, and other techniques for maximizing the effective manufacture and distribution of goods.
History and Archeology	Knowledge of historical events and their causes, indicators, and effects on civilizations and cultures.
Therapy and Counseling	Knowledge of principles, methods, and procedures for diagnosis, treatment, and rehabilitation of physical and mental dysfunctions, and for career counseling and guidance.
Philosophy and Theology	Knowledge of different philosophical systems and religions. This includes their basic principles, values, ethics, ways of thinking, customs, practices, and their impact on human culture.
Mechanical	Knowledge of machines and tools, including their designs, uses, repair, and maintenance.
Chemistry	Knowledge of the chemical composition, structure, and properties of substances and of the chemical processes and transformations that they undergo. This includes uses of chemicals and their interactions, danger signs, production techniques, and disposal methods.
Medicine and Dentistry	Knowledge of the information and techniques needed to diagnose and treat human injuries, diseases, and deformities. This includes symptoms, treatment alternatives, drug properties and interactions, and preventive health-care measures.
Fine Arts	Knowledge of the theory and techniques required to compose, produce, and perform works of music, dance, visual arts, drama, and sculpture.
Food Production	Knowledge of techniques and equipment for planting, growing, and harvesting food products (both plant and animal) for consumption, including storage/handling techniques.
Design	Knowledge of design techniques, tools, and principles involved in production of precision technical plans, blueprints, drawings, and models.
Building and Construction	Knowledge of materials, methods, and the tools involved in the construction or repair of houses, buildings, or other structures such as highways and roads.
Physics	Knowledge and prediction of physical principles, laws, their interrelationships, and applications to understanding fluid, material, and atmospheric dynamics, and mechanical, electrical, atomic and sub-atomic structures and processes.
Biology	Knowledge of plant and animal organisms, their tissues, cells, functions, interdependencies, and interactions with each other and the environment.

Skills	**Skills Definitions**
Active Listening	Giving full attention to what other people are saying, taking time to understand the points being made, asking questions as appropriate, and not interrupting at inappropriate times.
Speaking	Talking to others to convey information effectively.
Service Orientation	Actively looking for ways to help people.
Social Perceptiveness	Being aware of others' reactions and understanding why they react as they do.
Critical Thinking	Using logic and reasoning to identify the strengths and weaknesses of alternative solutions, conclusions or approaches to problems.
Reading Comprehension	Understanding written sentences and paragraphs in work related documents.
Mathematics	Using mathematics to solve problems.
Instructing	Teaching others how to do something.
Monitoring	Monitoring/Assessing performance of yourself, other individuals, or organizations to make improvements or take corrective action.
Coordination	Adjusting actions in relation to others' actions.
Learning Strategies	Selecting and using training/instructional methods and procedures appropriate for the situation when learning or teaching new things.
Writing	Communicating effectively in writing as appropriate for the needs of the audience.
Active Learning	Understanding the implications of new information for both current and future problem-solving and decision-making.
Judgment and Decision Making	Considering the relative costs and benefits of potential actions to choose the most appropriate one.
Negotiation	Bringing others together and trying to reconcile differences.
Time Management	Managing one's own time and the time of others.
Persuasion	Persuading others to change their minds or behavior.
Management of Personnel Resources	Motivating, developing, and directing people as they work, identifying the best people for the job.
Complex Problem Solving	Identifying complex problems and reviewing related information to develop and evaluate options and implement solutions.
Operations Analysis	Analyzing needs and product requirements to create a design.
Equipment Selection	Determining the kind of tools and equipment needed to do a job.
Operation and Control	Controlling operations of equipment or systems.
Systems Evaluation	Identifying measures or indicators of system performance and the actions needed to improve or correct performance, relative to the goals of the system.
Quality Control Analysis	Conducting tests and inspections of products, services, or processes to evaluate quality or performance.
Troubleshooting	Determining causes of operating errors and deciding what to do about it.
Systems Analysis	Determining how a system should work and how changes in conditions, operations, and the environment will affect outcomes.
Technology Design	Generating or adapting equipment and technology to serve user needs.
Management of Financial Resources	Determining how money will be spent to get the work done, and accounting for these expenditures.
Installation	Installing equipment, machines, wiring, or programs to meet specifications.
Repairing	Repairing machines or systems using the needed tools.
Management of Material Resources	Obtaining and seeing to the appropriate use of equipment, facilities, and materials needed to do certain work.
Programming	Writing computer programs for various purposes.
Operation Monitoring	Watching gauges, dials, or other indicators to make sure a machine is working properly.
Science	Using scientific rules and methods to solve problems.
Equipment Maintenance	Performing routine maintenance on equipment and determining when and what kind of maintenance is needed.

Ability	**Ability Definitions**
Oral Comprehension	The ability to listen to and understand information and ideas presented through spoken words and sentences.
Oral Expression	The ability to communicate information and ideas in speaking so others will understand.
Speech Clarity	The ability to speak clearly so others can understand you.
Written Comprehension	The ability to read and understand information and ideas presented in writing.
Near Vision	The ability to see details at close range (within a few feet of the observer).

Speech Recognition	The ability to identify and understand the speech of another person.
Problem Sensitivity	The ability to tell when something is wrong or is likely to go wrong. It does not involve solving the problem, only recognizing there is a problem.
Inductive Reasoning	The ability to combine pieces of information to form general rules or conclusions (includes finding a relationship among seemingly unrelated events).
Written Expression	The ability to communicate information and ideas in writing so others will understand.
Information Ordering	The ability to arrange things or actions in a certain order or pattern according to a specific rule or set of rules (e.g., patterns of numbers, letters, words, pictures, mathematical operations).
Number Facility	The ability to add, subtract, multiply, or divide quickly and correctly.
Time Sharing	The ability to shift back and forth between two or more activities or sources of information (such as speech, sounds, touch, or other sources).
Originality	The ability to come up with unusual or clever ideas about a given topic or situation, or to develop creative ways to solve a problem.
Mathematical Reasoning	The ability to choose the right mathematical methods or formulas to solve a problem.
Deductive Reasoning	The ability to apply general rules to specific problems to produce answers that make sense.
Fluency of Ideas	The ability to come up with a number of ideas about a topic (the number of ideas is important, not their quality, correctness, or creativity).
Category Flexibility	The ability to generate or use different sets of rules for combining or grouping things in different ways.
Selective Attention	The ability to concentrate on a task over a period of time without being distracted.
Finger Dexterity	The ability to make precisely coordinated movements of the fingers of one or both hands to grasp, manipulate, or assemble very small objects.
Flexibility of Closure	The ability to identify or detect a known pattern (a figure, object, word, or sound) that is hidden in other distracting material.
Far Vision	The ability to see details at a distance.
Memorization	The ability to remember information such as words, numbers, pictures, and procedures.
Perceptual Speed	The ability to quickly and accurately compare similarities and differences among sets of letters, numbers, objects, pictures, or patterns. The things to be compared may be presented at the same time or one after the other. This ability also includes comparing a presented object with a remembered object.
Speed of Closure	The ability to quickly make sense of, combine, and organize information into meaningful patterns.
Trunk Strength	The ability to use your abdominal and lower back muscles to support part of the body repeatedly or continuously over time without 'giving out' or fatiguing.
Visualization	The ability to imagine how something will look after it is moved around or when its parts are moved or rearranged.
Hearing Sensitivity	The ability to detect or tell the differences between sounds that vary in pitch and loudness.
Arm-Hand Steadiness	The ability to keep your hand and arm steady while moving your arm or while holding your arm and hand in one position.
Visual Color Discrimination	The ability to match or detect differences between colors, including shades of color and brightness.
Manual Dexterity	The ability to quickly move your hand, your hand together with your arm, or your two hands to grasp, manipulate, or assemble objects.
Auditory Attention	The ability to focus on a single source of sound in the presence of other distracting sounds.
Control Precision	The ability to quickly and repeatedly adjust the controls of a machine or a vehicle to exact positions.
Spatial Orientation	The ability to know your location in relation to the environment or to know where other objects are in relation to you.
Static Strength	The ability to exert maximum muscle force to lift, push, pull, or carry objects.
Wrist-Finger Speed	The ability to make fast, simple, repeated movements of the fingers, hands, and wrists.
Response Orientation	The ability to choose quickly between two or more movements in response to two or more different signals (lights, sounds, pictures). It includes the speed with which the correct response is started with the hand, foot, or other body part.
Extent Flexibility	The ability to bend, stretch, twist, or reach with your body, arms, and/or legs.
Glare Sensitivity	The ability to see objects in the presence of glare or bright lighting.
Depth Perception	The ability to judge which of several objects is closer or farther away from you, or to judge the distance between you and an object.
Sound Localization	The ability to tell the direction from which a sound originated.
Speed of Limb Movement	The ability to quickly move the arms and legs.
Rate Control	The ability to time your movements or the movement of a piece of equipment in anticipation of changes in the speed and/or direction of a moving object or scene.
Gross Body Equilibrium	The ability to keep or regain your body balance or stay upright when in an unstable position.
Reaction Time	The ability to quickly respond (with the hand, finger, or foot) to a signal (sound, light, picture) when it appears.
Explosive Strength	The ability to use short bursts of muscle force to propel oneself (as in jumping or sprinting), or to throw an object.
Dynamic Strength	The ability to exert muscle force repeatedly or continuously over time. This involves muscular endurance and resistance to muscle fatigue.
Dynamic Flexibility	The ability to quickly and repeatedly bend, stretch, twist, or reach out with your body, arms, and/or legs.
Multilimb Coordination	The ability to coordinate two or more limbs (for example, two arms, two legs, or one leg and one arm) while sitting, standing, or lying down. It does not involve performing the activities while the whole body is in motion.
Gross Body Coordination	The ability to coordinate the movement of your arms, legs, and torso together when the whole body is in motion.
Night Vision	The ability to see under low light conditions.
Peripheral Vision	The ability to see objects or movement of objects to one's side when the eyes are looking ahead.
Stamina	The ability to exert yourself physically over long periods of time without getting winded or out of breath.

Work_Activity	Work_Activity Definitions
Performing for or Working Directly with the Public	Performing for people or dealing directly with the public. This includes serving customers in restaurants and stores, and receiving clients or guests.
Interacting With Computers	Using computers and computer systems (including hardware and software) to program, write software, set up functions, enter data, or process information.
Communicating with Supervisors, Peers, or Subordin	Providing information to supervisors, co-workers, and subordinates by telephone, in written form, e-mail, or in person.
Getting Information	Observing, receiving, and otherwise obtaining information from all relevant sources.
Resolving Conflicts and Negotiating with Others	Handling complaints, settling disputes, and resolving grievances and conflicts, or otherwise negotiating with others.
Making Decisions and Solving Problems	Analyzing information and evaluating results to choose the best solution and solve problems.
Documenting/Recording Information	Entering, transcribing, recording, storing, or maintaining information in written or electronic/magnetic form.
Communicating with Persons Outside Organization	Communicating with people outside the organization, representing the organization to customers, the public, government, and other external sources. This information can be exchanged in person, in writing, or by telephone or e-mail.
Assisting and Caring for Others	Providing personal assistance, medical attention, emotional support, or other personal care to others such as coworkers, customers, or patients.
Establishing and Maintaining Interpersonal Relatio	Developing constructive and cooperative working relationships with others, and maintaining them over time.
Performing Administrative Activities	Performing day-to-day administrative tasks such as maintaining information files and processing paperwork.
Processing Information	Compiling, coding, categorizing, calculating, tabulating, auditing, or verifying information or data.
Judging the Qualities of Things, Services, or Peop	Assessing the value, importance, or quality of things or people.
Organizing, Planning, and Prioritizing Work	Developing specific goals and plans to prioritize, organize, and accomplish your work.
Identifying Objects, Actions, and Events	Identifying information by categorizing, estimating, recognizing differences or similarities, and detecting changes in circumstances or events.
Interpreting the Meaning of Information for Others	Translating or explaining what information means and how it can be used.
Analyzing Data or Information	Identifying the underlying principles, reasons, or facts of information by breaking down information or data into separate parts.

Updating and Using Relevant Knowledge	Keeping up-to-date technically and applying new knowledge to your job.
Evaluating Information to Determine Compliance wit	Using relevant information and individual judgment to determine whether events or processes comply with laws, regulations, or standards.
Selling or Influencing Others	Convincing others to buy merchandise/goods or to otherwise change their minds or actions.
Developing and Building Teams	Encouraging and building mutual trust, respect, and cooperation among team members.
Training and Teaching Others	Identifying the educational needs of others, developing formal educational or training programs or classes, and teaching or instructing others.
Monitor Processes, Materials, or Surroundings	Monitoring and reviewing information from materials, events, or the environment, to detect or assess problems.
Scheduling Work and Activities	Scheduling events, programs, and activities, as well as the work of others.
Coordinating the Work and Activities of Others	Getting members of a group to work together to accomplish tasks.
Thinking Creatively	Developing, designing, or creating new applications, ideas, relationships, systems, or products, including artistic contributions.
Provide Consultation and Advice to Others	Providing guidance and expert advice to management or other groups on technical, systems-, or process-related topics.
Coaching and Developing Others	Identifying the developmental needs of others and coaching, mentoring, or otherwise helping others to improve their knowledge or skills.
Developing Objectives and Strategies	Establishing long-range objectives and specifying the strategies and actions to achieve them.
Guiding, Directing, and Motivating Subordinates	Providing guidance and direction to subordinates, including setting performance standards and monitoring performance.
Inspecting Equipment, Structures, or Material	Inspecting equipment, structures, or materials to identify the cause of errors or other problems or defects.
Estimating the Quantifiable Characteristics of Pro	Estimating sizes, distances, and quantities; or determining time, costs, resources, or materials needed to perform a work activity.
Monitoring and Controlling Resources	Monitoring and controlling resources and overseeing the spending of money.
Handling and Moving Objects	Using hands and arms in handling, installing, positioning, and moving materials, and manipulating things.
Performing General Physical Activities	Performing physical activities that require considerable use of your arms and legs and moving your whole body, such as climbing, lifting, balancing, walking, stooping, and handling of materials.
Staffing Organizational Units	Recruiting, interviewing, selecting, hiring, and promoting employees in an organization.
Operating Vehicles, Mechanized Devices, or Equipme	Running, maneuvering, navigating, or driving vehicles or mechanized equipment, such as forklifts, passenger vehicles, aircraft, or water craft.
Repairing and Maintaining Electronic Equipment	Servicing, repairing, calibrating, regulating, fine-tuning, or testing machines, devices, and equipment that operate primarily on the basis of electrical or electronic (not mechanical) principles.
Controlling Machines and Processes	Using either control mechanisms or direct physical activity to operate machines or processes (not including computers or vehicles).
Repairing and Maintaining Mechanical Equipment	Servicing, repairing, adjusting, and testing machines, devices, moving parts, and equipment that operate primarily on the basis of mechanical (not electronic) principles.
Drafting, Laying Out, and Specifying Technical Dev	Providing documentation, detailed instructions, drawings, or specifications to tell others about how devices, parts, equipment, or structures are to be fabricated, constructed, assembled, modified, maintained, or used.

Work_Context	**Work_Context Definitions**
Telephone	How often do you have telephone conversations in this job?
Contact With Others	How much does this job require the worker to be in contact with others (face-to-face, by telephone, or otherwise) in order to perform it?
Deal With External Customers	How important is it to work with external customers or the public in this job?
Face-to-Face Discussions	How often do you have to have face-to-face discussions with individuals or teams in this job?
Deal With Unpleasant or Angry People	How frequently does the worker have to deal with unpleasant, angry, or discourteous individuals as part of the job requirements?

Work With Work Group or Team	How important is it to work with others in a group or team in this job?
Importance of Repeating Same Tasks	How important is repeating the same physical activities (e.g., key entry) or mental activities (e.g., checking entries in a ledger) over and over, without stopping, to performing this job?
Spend Time Standing	How much does this job require standing?
Indoors, Environmentally Controlled	How often does this job require working indoors in environmentally controlled conditions?
Freedom to Make Decisions	How much decision making freedom, without supervision, does the job offer?
Frequency of Conflict Situations	How often are there conflict situations the employee has to face in this job?
Importance of Being Exact or Accurate	How important is being very exact or highly accurate in performing this job?
Coordinate or Lead Others	How important is it to coordinate or lead others in accomplishing work activities in this job?
Frequency of Decision Making	How frequently is the worker required to make decisions that affect other people, the financial resources, and/or the image and reputation of the organization?
Impact of Decisions on Co-workers or Company Resul	How do the decisions an employee makes impact the results of co-workers, clients or the company?
Physical Proximity	To what extent does this job require the worker to perform job tasks in close physical proximity to other people?
Structured versus Unstructured Work	To what extent is this job structured for the worker, rather than allowing the worker to determine tasks, priorities, and goals?
Spend Time Making Repetitive Motions	How much does this job require making repetitive motions?
Letters and Memos	How often does the job require written letters and memos?
Spend Time Using Your Hands to Handle, Control, or	How much does this job require using your hands to handle, control, or feel objects, tools or controls?
Responsibility for Outcomes and Results	How responsible is the worker for work outcomes and results of other workers?
Time Pressure	How often does this job require the worker to meet strict deadlines?
Spend Time Walking and Running	How much does this job require walking and running?
Degree of Automation	How automated is the job?
Sounds, Noise Levels Are Distracting or Uncomforta	How often does this job require working exposed to sounds and noise levels that are distracting or uncomfortable?
Responsible for Others' Health and Safety	How much responsibility is there for the health and safety of others in this job?
Spend Time Sitting	How much does this job require sitting?
Level of Competition	To what extent does this job require the worker to compete or to be aware of competitive pressures?
Electronic Mail	How often do you use electronic mail in this job?
Public Speaking	How often do you have to perform public speaking in this job?
Spend Time Bending or Twisting the Body	How much does this job require bending or twisting your body?
Consequence of Error	How serious would the result usually be if the worker made a mistake that was not readily correctable?
Deal With Physically Aggressive People	How frequently does this job require the worker to deal with physical aggression of violent individuals?
Very Hot or Cold Temperatures	How often does this job require working in very hot (above 90 F degrees) or very cold (below 32 F degrees) temperatures?
Spend Time Kneeling, Crouching, Stooping, or Crawl	How much does this job require kneeling, crouching, stooping or crawling?
Pace Determined by Speed of Equipment	How important is it to this job that the pace is determined by the speed of equipment or machinery? (This does not refer to keeping busy at all times on this job.)
Exposed to Contaminants	How often does this job require working exposed to contaminants (such as pollutants, gases, dust or odors)?
Extremely Bright or Inadequate Lighting	How often does this job require working in extremely bright or inadequate lighting conditions?
In an Enclosed Vehicle or Equipment	How often does this job require working in a closed vehicle or equipment (e.g., car)?
Exposed to Minor Burns, Cuts, Bites, or Stings	How often does this job require exposure to minor burns, cuts, bites, or stings?
Spend Time Keeping or Regaining Balance	How much does this job require keeping or regaining your balance?
Outdoors, Exposed to Weather	How often does this job require working outdoors, exposed to all weather conditions?
Cramped Work Space, Awkward Positions	How often does this job require working in cramped work spaces that requires getting into awkward positions?
Outdoors, Under Cover	How often does this job require working outdoors, under cover (e.g., structure with roof but no walls)?

927

Wear Common Protective or Safety Equipment such as	How much does this job require wearing common protective or safety equipment such as safety shoes, glasses, gloves, hard hats or live jackets?
Exposed to Disease or Infections	How often does this job require exposure to disease/infections?
Exposed to Hazardous Conditions	How often does this job require exposure to hazardous conditions?
Indoors, Not Environmentally Controlled	How often does this job require working indoors in non-controlled environmental conditions (e.g., warehouse without heat)?
Exposed to High Places	How often does this job require exposure to high places?
Spend Time Climbing Ladders, Scaffolds, or Poles	How much does this job require climbing ladders, scaffolds, or poles?
Exposed to Hazardous Equipment	How often does this job require exposure to hazardous equipment?
Exposed to Whole Body Vibration	How often does this job require exposure to whole body vibration (e.g., operate a jackhammer)?
In an Open Vehicle or Equipment	How often does this job require working in an open vehicle or equipment (e.g., tractor)?
Exposed to Radiation	How often does this job require exposure to radiation?
Wear Specialized Protective or Safety Equipment su	How much does this job require wearing specialized protective or safety equipment such as breathing apparatus, safety harness, full protection suits, or radiation protection?

Job Zone Component	Job Zone Component Definitions
Title	Job Zone Two: Some Preparation Needed
Overall Experience	Some previous work-related skill, knowledge, or experience may be helpful in these occupations, but usually is not needed. For example, a drywall installer might benefit from experience installing drywall, but an inexperienced person could still learn to be an installer with little difficulty.
Job Training	Employees in these occupations need anywhere from a few months to one year of working with experienced employees.
Job Zone Examples	These occupations often involve using your knowledge and skills to help others. Examples include drywall installers, fire inspectors, flight attendants, pharmacy technicians, salespersons (retail), and tellers.
SVP Range	(4.0 to < 6.0)
Education	These occupations usually require a high school diploma and may require some vocational training or job-related course work. In some cases, an associate's or bachelor's degree could be needed.

Work_Styles	Work_Styles Definitions
Dependability	Job requires being reliable, responsible, and dependable, and fulfilling obligations.
Self Control	Job requires maintaining composure, keeping emotions in check, controlling anger, and avoiding aggressive behavior, even in very difficult situations.
Cooperation	Job requires being pleasant with others on the job and displaying a good-natured, cooperative attitude.
Concern for Others	Job requires being sensitive to others' needs and feelings and being understanding and helpful on the job.
Integrity	Job requires being honest and ethical.
Attention to Detail	Job requires being careful about detail and thorough in completing work tasks.
Stress Tolerance	Job requires accepting criticism and dealing calmly and effectively with high stress situations.
Independence	Job requires developing one's own ways of doing things, guiding oneself with little or no supervision, and depending on oneself to get things done.
Adaptability/Flexibility	Job requires being open to change (positive or negative) and to considerable variety in the workplace.
Social Orientation	Job requires preferring to work with others rather than alone, and being personally connected with others on the job.
Leadership	Job requires a willingness to lead, take charge, and offer opinions and direction.
Initiative	Job requires a willingness to take on responsibilities and challenges.
Persistence	Job requires persistence in the face of obstacles.
Analytical Thinking	Job requires analyzing information and using logic to address work-related issues and problems.
Innovation	Job requires creativity and alternative thinking to develop new ideas for and answers to work-related problems.

Achievement/Effort	Job requires establishing and maintaining personally challenging achievement goals and exerting effort toward mastering tasks.

43-4111.00 - Interviewers, Except Eligibility and Loan

Interview persons by telephone, mail, in person, or by other means for the purpose of completing forms, applications, or questionnaires. Ask specific questions, record answers, and assist persons with completing form. May sort, classify, and file forms.

Tasks

1) Identify and resolve inconsistencies in interviewees' responses by means of appropriate questioning and/or explanation.

2) Assist individuals in filling out applications or questionnaires.

3) Compile, record and code results and data from interview or survey, using computer or specified form.

4) Review data obtained from interview for completeness and accuracy.

5) Contact individuals to be interviewed at home, place of business, or field location, by telephone, mail, or in person.

6) Locate and list addresses and households.

7) Explain survey objectives and procedures to interviewees, and interpret survey questions to help interviewees' comprehension.

8) Perform patient services, such as answering the telephone and assisting patients with financial and medical questions.

9) Identify and report problems in obtaining valid data.

10) Meet with supervisor daily to submit completed assignments and discuss progress.

11) Prepare reports to provide answers in response to specific problems.

12) Perform other office duties as needed, such as telemarketing and customer service inquiries, billing patients and receiving payments.

13) Ensure payment for services by verifying benefits with the person's insurance provider or working out financing options.

14) Collect and analyze data, such as studying old records, tallying the number of outpatients entering each day or week, or participating in federal, state, or local population surveys as a Census Enumerator.

Knowledge	Knowledge Definitions
Customer and Personal Service	Knowledge of principles and processes for providing customer and personal services. This includes customer needs assessment, meeting quality standards for services, and evaluation of customer satisfaction.
Education and Training	Knowledge of principles and methods for curriculum and training design, teaching and instruction for individuals and groups, and the measurement of training effects.
English Language	Knowledge of the structure and content of the English language including the meaning and spelling of words, rules of composition, and grammar.
Administration and Management	Knowledge of business and management principles involved in strategic planning, resource allocation, human resources modeling, leadership technique, production methods, and coordination of people and resources.
Psychology	Knowledge of human behavior and performance; individual differences in ability, personality, and interests; learning and motivation; psychological research methods; and the assessment and treatment of behavioral and affective disorders.
Clerical	Knowledge of administrative and clerical procedures and systems such as word processing, managing files and records, stenography and transcription, designing forms, and other office procedures and terminology.
Therapy and Counseling	Knowledge of principles, methods, and procedures for diagnosis, treatment, and rehabilitation of physical and mental dysfunctions, and for career counseling and guidance.
Sales and Marketing	Knowledge of principles and methods for showing, promoting, and selling products or services. This includes marketing strategy and tactics, product demonstration, sales techniques, and sales control systems.

Medicine and Dentistry	Knowledge of the information and techniques needed to diagnose and treat human injuries, diseases, and deformities. This includes symptoms, treatment alternatives, drug properties and interactions, and preventive health-care measures.
Mathematics	Knowledge of arithmetic, algebra, geometry, calculus, statistics, and their applications.
Public Safety and Security	Knowledge of relevant equipment, policies, procedures, and strategies to promote effective local, state, or national security operations for the protection of people, data, property, and institutions.
Computers and Electronics	Knowledge of circuit boards, processors, chips, electronic equipment, and computer hardware and software, including applications and programming.
Personnel and Human Resources	Knowledge of principles and procedures for personnel recruitment, selection, training, compensation and benefits, labor relations and negotiation, and personnel information systems.
Sociology and Anthropology	Knowledge of group behavior and dynamics, societal trends and influences, human migrations, ethnicity, cultures and their history and origins.
Production and Processing	Knowledge of raw materials, production processes, quality control, costs, and other techniques for maximizing the effective manufacture and ion of goods.
Law and Government	Knowledge of laws, legal codes, court procedures, precedents, government regulations, executive orders, agency rules, and the democratic political process.
Economics and Accounting	Knowledge of economic and accounting principles and practices, the financial markets, banking and the analysis and reporting of financial data.
Philosophy and Theology	Knowledge of different philosophical systems and religions. This includes their basic principles, values, ethics, ways of thinking, customs, practices, and their impact on human culture.
Communications and Media	Knowledge of media production, communication, and dissemination techniques and methods. This includes alternative ways to inform and entertain via written, oral, and visual media.
Telecommunications	Knowledge of transmission, broadcasting, switching, control, and operation of telecommunications systems.
Transportation	Knowledge of principles and methods for moving people or goods by air, rail, sea, or road, including the relative costs and benefits.
Foreign Language	Knowledge of the structure and content of a foreign (non-English) language including the meaning and spelling of words, rules of composition and grammar, and pronunciation.
Chemistry	Knowledge of the chemical composition, structure, and properties of substances and of the chemical processes and transformations that they undergo. This includes uses of chemicals and their interactions, danger signs, production techniques, and disposal methods.
Mechanical	Knowledge of machines and tools, including their designs, uses, repair, and maintenance.
Biology	Knowledge of plant and animal organisms, their tissues, cells, functions, interdependencies, and interactions with each other and the environment.
Engineering and Technology	Knowledge of the practical application of engineering science and technology. This includes applying principles, techniques, procedures, and equipment to the design and production of various goods and services.
History and Archeology	Knowledge of historical events and their causes, indicators, and effects on civilizations and cultures.
Design	Knowledge of design techniques, tools, and principles involved in production of precision technical plans, blueprints, drawings, and models.
Fine Arts	Knowledge of the theory and techniques required to compose, produce, and perform works of music, dance, visual arts, drama, and sculpture.
Physics	Knowledge and prediction of physical principles, laws, their interrelationships, and applications to understanding fluid, material, and atmospheric dynamics, and mechanical, electrical, atomic and sub- atomic structures and processes.
Geography	Knowledge of principles and methods for describing the features of land, sea, and air masses, including their physical characteristics, locations, interrelationships, and distribution of plant, animal, and human life.
Food Production	Knowledge of techniques and equipment for planting, growing, and harvesting food products (both plant and animal) for consumption, including storage/handling techniques.

Building and Construction	Knowledge of materials, methods, and the tools involved in the construction or repair of houses, buildings, or other structures such as highways and roads.

Skills	Skills Definitions
Active Listening	Giving full attention to what other people are saying, taking time to understand the points being made, asking questions as appropriate, and not interrupting at inappropriate times.
Reading Comprehension	Understanding written sentences and paragraphs in work related documents.
Speaking	Talking to others to convey information effectively.
Service Orientation	Actively looking for ways to help people.
Writing	Communicating effectively in writing as appropriate for the needs of the audience.
Social Perceptiveness	Being aware of others' reactions and understanding why they react as they do.
Learning Strategies	Selecting and using training/instructional methods and procedures appropriate for the situation when learning or teaching new things.
Critical Thinking	Using logic and reasoning to identify the strengths and weaknesses of alternative solutions, conclusions or approaches to problems.
Time Management	Managing one's own time and the time of others.
Monitoring	Monitoring/Assessing performance of yourself, other individuals, or organizations to make improvements or take corrective action.
Judgment and Decision Making	Considering the relative costs and benefits of potential actions to choose the most appropriate one.
Active Learning	Understanding the implications of new information for both current and future problem-solving and decision-making.
Persuasion	Persuading others to change their minds or behavior.
Coordination	Adjusting actions in relation to others' actions.
Negotiation	Bringing others together and trying to reconcile differences.
Mathematics	Using mathematics to solve problems.
Complex Problem Solving	Identifying complex problems and reviewing related information to develop and evaluate options and implement solutions.
Instructing	Teaching others how to do something.
Systems Evaluation	Identifying measures or indicators of system performance and the actions needed to improve or correct performance, relative to the goals of the system.
Management of Personnel Resources	Motivating, developing, and directing people as they work, identifying the best people for the job.
Quality Control Analysis	Conducting tests and inspections of products, services, or processes to evaluate quality or performance.
Operation and Control	Controlling operations of equipment or systems.
Systems Analysis	Determining how a system should work and how changes in conditions, operations, and the environment will affect outcomes.
Management of Material Resources	Obtaining and seeing to the appropriate use of equipment, facilities, and materials needed to do certain work.
Operations Analysis	Analyzing needs and product requirements to create a design.
Management of Financial Resources	Determining how money will be spent to get the work done, and accounting for these expenditures.
Troubleshooting	Determining causes of operating errors and deciding what to do about it.
Equipment Maintenance	Performing routine maintenance on equipment and determining when and what kind of maintenance is needed.
Operation Monitoring	Watching gauges, dials, or other indicators to make sure a machine is working properly.
Equipment Selection	Determining the kind of tools and equipment needed to do a job.
Technology Design	Generating or adapting equipment and technology to serve user needs.
Science	Using scientific rules and methods to solve problems.
Repairing	Repairing machines or systems using the needed tools.
Installation	Installing equipment, machines, wiring, or programs to meet specifications.
Programming	Writing computer programs for various purposes.

Ability	Ability Definitions
Speech Clarity	The ability to speak clearly so others can understand you.
Oral Comprehension	The ability to listen to and understand information and ideas presented through spoken words and sentences.
Oral Expression	The ability to communicate information and ideas in speaking so others will understand.

Speech Recognition	The ability to identify and understand the speech of another person.
Problem Sensitivity	The ability to tell when something is wrong or is likely to go wrong. It does not involve solving the problem, only recognizing there is a problem.
Inductive Reasoning	The ability to combine pieces of information to form general rules or conclusions (includes finding a relationship among seemingly unrelated events).
Information Ordering	The ability to arrange things or actions in a certain order or pattern according to a specific rule or set of rules (e.g., patterns of numbers, letters, words, pictures, mathematical operations).
Near Vision	The ability to see details at close range (within a few feet of the observer).
Selective Attention	The ability to concentrate on a task over a period of time without being distracted.
Written Expression	The ability to communicate information and ideas in writing so others will understand.
Written Comprehension	The ability to read and understand information and ideas presented in writing.
Deductive Reasoning	The ability to apply general rules to specific problems to produce answers that make sense.
Category Flexibility	The ability to generate or use different sets of rules for combining or grouping things in different ways.
Speed of Closure	The ability to quickly make sense of, combine, and organize information into meaningful patterns.
Flexibility of Closure	The ability to identify or detect a known pattern (a figure, object, word, or sound) that is hidden in other distracting material.
Time Sharing	The ability to shift back and forth between two or more activities or sources of information (such as speech, sounds, touch, or other sources).
Perceptual Speed	The ability to quickly and accurately compare similarities and differences among sets of letters, numbers, objects, pictures, or patterns. The things to be compared may be presented at the same time or one after the other. This ability also includes comparing a presented object with a remembered object.
Fluency of Ideas	The ability to come up with a number of ideas about a topic (the number of ideas is important, not their quality, correctness, or creativity).
Auditory Attention	The ability to focus on a single source of sound in the presence of other distracting sounds.
Mathematical Reasoning	The ability to choose the right mathematical methods or formulas to solve a problem.
Originality	The ability to come up with unusual or clever ideas about a given topic or situation, or to develop creative ways to solve a problem.
Memorization	The ability to remember information such as words, numbers, pictures, and procedures.
Wrist-Finger Speed	The ability to make fast, simple, repeated movements of the fingers, hands, and wrists.
Trunk Strength	The ability to use your abdominal and lower back muscles to support part of the body repeatedly or continuously over time without 'giving out' or fatiguing.
Number Facility	The ability to add, subtract, multiply, or divide quickly and correctly.
Finger Dexterity	The ability to make precisely coordinated movements of the fingers of one or both hands to grasp, manipulate, or assemble very small objects.
Multilimb Coordination	The ability to coordinate two or more limbs (for example, two arms, two legs, or one leg and one arm) while sitting, standing, or lying down. It does not involve performing the activities while the whole body is in motion.
Stamina	The ability to exert yourself physically over long periods of time without getting winded or out of breath.
Arm-Hand Steadiness	The ability to keep your hand and arm steady while moving your arm or while holding your arm and hand in one position.
Extent Flexibility	The ability to bend, stretch, twist, or reach with your body, arms, and/or legs.
Hearing Sensitivity	The ability to detect or tell the differences between sounds that vary in pitch and loudness.
Gross Body Coordination	The ability to coordinate the movement of your arms, legs, and torso together when the whole body is in motion.
Manual Dexterity	The ability to quickly move your hand, your hand together with your arm, or your two hands to grasp, manipulate, or assemble objects.
Visual Color Discrimination	The ability to match or detect differences between colors, including shades of color and brightness.

Static Strength	The ability to exert maximum muscle force to lift, push, pull, or carry objects.
Speed of Limb Movement	The ability to quickly move the arms and legs.
Control Precision	The ability to quickly and repeatedly adjust the controls of a machine or a vehicle to exact positions.
Visualization	The ability to imagine how something will look after it is moved around or when its parts are moved or rearranged.
Response Orientation	The ability to choose quickly between two or more movements in response to two or more different signals (lights, sounds, pictures). It includes the speed with which the correct response is started with the hand, foot, or other body part.
Reaction Time	The ability to quickly respond (with the hand, finger, or foot) to a signal (sound, light, picture) when it appears.
Dynamic Strength	The ability to exert muscle force repeatedly or continuously over time. This involves muscular endurance and resistance to muscle fatigue.
Far Vision	The ability to see details at a distance.
Peripheral Vision	The ability to see objects or movement of objects to one's side when the eyes are looking ahead.
Dynamic Flexibility	The ability to quickly and repeatedly bend, stretch, twist, or reach out with your body, arms, and/or legs.
Explosive Strength	The ability to use short bursts of muscle force to propel oneself (as in jumping or sprinting), or to throw an object.
Spatial Orientation	The ability to know your location in relation to the environment or to know where other objects are in relation to you.
Sound Localization	The ability to tell the direction from which a sound originated.
Glare Sensitivity	The ability to see objects in the presence of glare or bright lighting.
Depth Perception	The ability to judge which of several objects is closer or farther away from you, or to judge the distance between you and an object.
Night Vision	The ability to see under low light conditions.
Gross Body Equilibrium	The ability to keep or regain your body balance or stay upright when in an unstable position.
Rate Control	The ability to time your movements or the movement of a piece of equipment in anticipation of changes in the speed and/or direction of a moving object or scene.

Work_Activity	Work_Activity Definitions
Getting Information	Observing, receiving, and otherwise obtaining information from all relevant sources.
Communicating with Supervisors, Peers, or Subordin	Providing information to supervisors, co-workers, and subordinates by telephone, in written form, e-mail, or in person.
Interacting With Computers	Using computers and computer systems (including hardware and software) to program, write software, set up functions, enter data, or process information.
Performing for or Working Directly with the Public	Performing for people or dealing directly with the public. This includes serving customers in restaurants and stores, and receiving clients or guests.
Documenting/Recording Information	Entering, transcribing, recording, storing, or maintaining information in written or electronic/magnetic form.
Communicating with Persons Outside Organization	Communicating with people outside the organization, representing the organization to customers, the public, government, and other external sources. This information can be exchanged in person, in writing, or by telephone or e-mail.
Making Decisions and Solving Problems	Analyzing information and evaluating results to choose the best solution and solve problems.
Assisting and Caring for Others	Providing personal assistance, medical attention, emotional support, or other personal care to others such as coworkers, customers, or patients.
Establishing and Maintaining Interpersonal Relatio	Developing constructive and cooperative working relationships with others, and maintaining them over time.
Evaluating Information to Determine Compliance wit	Using relevant information and individual judgment to determine whether events or processes comply with laws, regulations, or standards.
Updating and Using Relevant Knowledge	Keeping up-to-date technically and applying new knowledge to your job.
Identifying Objects, Actions, and Events	Identifying information by categorizing, estimating, recognizing differences or similarities, and detecting changes in circumstances or events.
Organizing, Planning, and Prioritizing Work	Developing specific goals and plans to prioritize, organize, and accomplish your work.
Processing Information	Compiling, coding, categorizing, calculating, tabulating, auditing, or verifying information or data.

930

Performing Administrative Activities	Performing day-to-day administrative tasks such as maintaining information files and processing paperwork.
Analyzing Data or Information	Identifying the underlying principles, reasons, or facts of information by breaking down information or data into separate parts.
Interpreting the Meaning of Information for Others	Translating or explaining what information means and how it can be used.
Developing and Building Teams	Encouraging and building mutual trust, respect, and cooperation among team members.
Judging the Qualities of Things, Services, or Peop	Assessing the value, importance, or quality of things or people.
Coordinating the Work and Activities of Others	Getting members of a group to work together to accomplish tasks.
Training and Teaching Others	Identifying the educational needs of others, developing formal educational or training programs or classes, and teaching or instructing others.
Coaching and Developing Others	Identifying the developmental needs of others and coaching, mentoring, or otherwise helping others to improve their knowledge or skills.
Monitor Processes, Materials, or Surroundings	Monitoring and reviewing information from materials, events, or the environment, to detect or assess problems.
Scheduling Work and Activities	Scheduling events, programs, and activities, as well as the work of others.
Resolving Conflicts and Negotiating with Others	Handling complaints, settling disputes, and resolving grievances and conflicts, or otherwise negotiating with others.
Provide Consultation and Advice to Others	Providing guidance and expert advice to management or other groups on technical, systems-, or process-related topics.
Developing Objectives and Strategies	Establishing long-range objectives and specifying the strategies and actions to achieve them.
Thinking Creatively	Developing, designing, or creating new applications, ideas, relationships, systems, or products, including artistic contributions.
Performing General Physical Activities	Performing physical activities that require considerable use of your arms and legs and moving your whole body, such as climbing, lifting, balancing, walking, stooping, and handling of materials.
Inspecting Equipment, Structures, or Material	Inspecting equipment, structures, or materials to identify the cause of errors or other problems or defects.
Selling or Influencing Others	Convincing others to buy merchandise/goods or to otherwise change their minds or actions.
Handling and Moving Objects	Using hands and arms in handling, installing, positioning, and moving materials, and manipulating things.
Guiding, Directing, and Motivating Subordinates	Providing guidance and direction to subordinates, including setting performance standards and monitoring performance.
Estimating the Quantifiable Characteristics of Pro	Estimating sizes, distances, and quantities; or determining time, costs, resources, or materials needed to perform a work activity.
Staffing Organizational Units	Recruiting, interviewing, selecting, hiring, and promoting employees in an organization.
Controlling Machines and Processes	Using either control mechanisms or direct physical activity to operate machines or processes (not including computers or vehicles).
Monitoring and Controlling Resources	Monitoring and controlling resources and overseeing the spending of money.
Operating Vehicles, Mechanized Devices, or Equipme	Running, maneuvering, navigating, or driving vehicles or mechanized equipment, such as forklifts, passenger vehicles, aircraft, or water craft.
Repairing and Maintaining Mechanical Equipment	Servicing, repairing, adjusting, and testing machines, devices, moving parts, and equipment that operate primarily on the basis of mechanical (not electronic) principles.
Repairing and Maintaining Electronic Equipment	Servicing, repairing, calibrating, regulating, fine-tuning, or testing machines, devices, and equipment that operate primarily on the basis of electrical or electronic (not mechanical) principles.
Drafting, Laying Out, and Specifying Technical Dev	Providing documentation, detailed instructions, drawings, or specifications to tell others about how devices, parts, equipment, or structures are to be fabricated, constructed, assembled, modified, maintained, or used.

Work_Context	Work_Context Definitions
Telephone	How often do you have telephone conversations in this job?
Contact With Others	How much does this job require the worker to be in contact with others (face-to-face, by telephone, or otherwise) in order to perform it?
Spend Time Sitting	How much does this job require sitting?

Deal With Unpleasant or Angry People	How frequently does the worker have to deal with unpleasant, angry, or discourteous individuals as part of the job requirements?
Importance of Being Exact or Accurate	How important is being very exact or highly accurate in performing this job?
Face-to-Face Discussions	How often do you have to have face-to-face discussions with individuals or teams in this job?
Importance of Repeating Same Tasks	How important is repeating the same physical activities (e.g., key entry) or mental activities (e.g., checking entries in a ledger) over and over, without stopping, to performing this job?
Indoors, Environmentally Controlled	How often does this job require working indoors in environmentally controlled conditions?
Work With Work Group or Team	How important is it to work with others in a group or team in this job?
Time Pressure	How often does this job require the worker to meet strict deadlines?
Physical Proximity	To what extent does this job require the worker to perform job tasks in close physical proximity to other people?
Structured versus Unstructured Work	To what extent is this job structured for the worker, rather than allowing the worker to determine tasks, priorities, and goals?
Spend Time Making Repetitive Motions	How much does this job require making repetitive motions?
Frequency of Decision Making	How frequently is the worker required to make decisions that affect other people, the financial resources, and/or the image and reputation of the organization?
Spend Time Using Your Hands to Handle, Control, or	How much does this job require using your hands to handle, control, or feel objects, tools or controls?
Freedom to Make Decisions	How much decision making freedom, without supervision, does the job offer?
Impact of Decisions on Co-workers or Company Resul	How do the decisions an employee makes impact the results of co-workers, clients or the company?
Frequency of Conflict Situations	How often are there conflict situations the employee has to face in this job?
Level of Competition	To what extent does this job require the worker to compete or to be aware of competitive pressures?
Degree of Automation	How automated is the job?
Deal With External Customers	How important is it to work with external customers or the public in this job?
Responsibility for Outcomes and Results	How responsible is the worker for work outcomes and results of other workers?
Coordinate or Lead Others	How important is it to coordinate or lead others in accomplishing work activities in this job?
Letters and Memos	How often does this job require written letters and memos?
Electronic Mail	How often do you use electronic mail in this job?
Pace Determined by Speed of Equipment	How important is it to this job that the pace is determined by the speed of equipment or machinery? (This does not refer to keeping busy at all times on this job.)
Public Speaking	How often do you have to perform public speaking in this job?
Sounds, Noise Levels Are Distracting or Uncomforta	How often does this job require working exposed to sounds and noise levels that are distracting or uncomfortable?
Consequence of Error	How serious would the result usually be if the worker made a mistake that was not readily correctable?
Exposed to Disease or Infections	How often does this job require exposure to disease/infections?
Deal With Physically Aggressive People	How frequently does this job require the worker to deal with physical aggression of violent individuals?
Exposed to Hazardous Conditions	How often does this job require exposure to hazardous conditions?
Exposed to Contaminants	How often does this job require working exposed to contaminants (such as pollutants, gases, dust or odors)?
Spend Time Walking and Running	How much does this job require walking and running?
Spend Time Standing	How much does this job require standing?
Cramped Work Space, Awkward Positions	How often does this job require working in cramped work spaces that requires getting into awkward positions?
Responsible for Others' Health and Safety	How much responsibility is there for the health and safety of others in this job?
Very Hot or Cold Temperatures	How often does this job require working in very hot (above 90 F degrees) or very cold (below 32 F degrees) temperatures?
Spend Time Bending or Twisting the Body	How much does this job require bending or twisting your body?
Extremely Bright or Inadequate Lighting	How often does this job require working in extremely bright or inadequate lighting conditions?
Spend Time Kneeling, Crouching, Stooping, or Crawl	How much does this job require kneeling, crouching, stooping or crawling?

Exposed to Minor Burns, Cuts, Bites, or Stings	How often does this job require exposure to minor burns, cuts, bites, or stings?
Spend Time Keeping or Regaining Balance	How much does this job require keeping or regaining your balance?
Indoors, Not Environmentally Controlled	How often does this job require working indoors in non-controlled environmental conditions (e.g., warehouse without heat)?
Wear Common Protective or Safety Equipment such as	How much does this job require wearing common protective or safety equipment such as safety shoes, glasses, gloves, hard hats or live jackets?
Exposed to Radiation	How often does this job require exposure to radiation?
Outdoors, Under Cover	How often does this job require working outdoors, under cover (e.g., structure with roof but no walls)?
Wear Specialized Protective or Safety Equipment su	How much does this job require wearing specialized protective or safety equipment such as breathing apparatus, safety harness, full protection suits, or radiation protection?
Outdoors, Exposed to Weather	How often does this job require working outdoors, exposed to all weather conditions?
Exposed to Whole Body Vibration	How often does this job require exposure to whole body vibration (e.g., operate a jackhammer)?
Spend Time Climbing Ladders, Scaffolds, or Poles	How much does this job require climbing ladders, scaffolds, or poles?
In an Open Vehicle or Equipment	How often does this job require working in an open vehicle or equipment (e.g., tractor)?
In an Enclosed Vehicle or Equipment	How often does this job require working in a closed vehicle or equipment (e.g., car)?
Exposed to Hazardous Equipment	How often does this job require exposure to hazardous equipment?
Exposed to High Places	How often does this job require exposure to high places?

Job Zone Component	Job Zone Component Definitions
Title	Job Zone Three: Medium Preparation Needed
Overall Experience	Previous work-related skill, knowledge, or experience is required for these occupations. For example, an electrician must have completed three or four years of apprenticeship or several years of vocational training, and often must have passed a licensing exam, in order to perform the job.
Job Training	Employees in these occupations usually need one or two years of training involving both on-the-job experience and informal training with experienced workers.
Job Zone Examples	These occupations usually involve using communication and organizational skills to coordinate, supervise, manage, or train others to accomplish goals. Examples include dental assistants, electricians, fish and game wardens, legal secretaries, personnel recruiters, and recreation workers.
SVP Range	(6.0 to < 7.0)
Education	Most occupations in this zone require training in vocational schools, related on-the-job experience, or an associate's degree. Some may require a bachelor's degree.

Work_Styles	Work_Styles Definitions
Attention to Detail	Job requires being careful about detail and thorough in completing work tasks.
Cooperation	Job requires being pleasant with others on the job and displaying a good-natured, cooperative attitude.
Integrity	Job requires being honest and ethical.
Self Control	Job requires maintaining composure, keeping emotions in check, controlling anger, and avoiding aggressive behavior, even in very difficult situations.
Stress Tolerance	Job requires accepting criticism and dealing calmly and effectively with high stress situations.
Dependability	Job requires being reliable, responsible, and dependable, and fulfilling obligations.
Social Orientation	Job requires preferring to work with others rather than alone, and being personally connected with others on the job.
Concern for Others	Job requires being sensitive to others' needs and feelings and being understanding and helpful on the job.
Analytical Thinking	Job requires analyzing information and using logic to address work-related issues and problems.
Independence	Job requires developing one's own ways of doing things, guiding oneself with little or no supervision, and depending on oneself to get things done.
Initiative	Job requires a willingness to take on responsibilities and challenges.

Innovation	Job requires creativity and alternative thinking to develop new ideas for and answers to work-related problems.
Leadership	Job requires a willingness to lead, take charge, and offer opinions and direction.
Adaptability/Flexibility	Job requires being open to change (positive or negative) and to considerable variety in the workplace.
Achievement/Effort	Job requires establishing and maintaining personally challenging achievement goals and exerting effort toward mastering tasks.
Persistence	Job requires persistence in the face of obstacles.

43-4121.00 - Library Assistants, Clerical

Compile records, sort and shelve books, and issue and receive library materials such as pictures, cards, slides and microfilm. Locate library materials for loan and replace material in shelving area, stacks, or files according to identification number and title. Register patrons to permit them to borrow books, periodicals, and other library materials.

Tasks

1) Sort books, publications, and other items according to established procedure and return them to shelves, files, or other designated storage areas.

2) Perform clerical activities such as filing, typing, word processing, photocopying and mailing out material, and mail sorting.

3) Answer routine inquiries, and refer patrons in need of professional assistance to librarians.

4) Provide assistance to librarians in the maintenance of collections of books, periodicals, magazines, newspapers, and audiovisual and other materials.

5) Instruct patrons on how to use reference sources, card catalogs, and automated information systems.

6) Process new materials including books, audiovisual materials, and computer software.

7) Take action to deal with disruptive or problem patrons.

8) Enter and update patrons' records on computers.

9) Lend and collect books, periodicals, videotapes, and other materials at circulation desks.

10) Inspect returned books for condition and due-date status, and compute any applicable fines.

11) Maintain records of items received, stored, issued, and returned, and file catalog cards according to system used.

12) Send out notices and accept fine payments for lost or overdue books.

13) Deliver and retrieve items to and from departments by hand or using push carts.

14) Register new patrons and issue borrower identification cards that permit patrons to borrow books and other materials.

15) Repair books, using mending tape, paste, and brushes.

16) Classify and catalog items according to content and purpose.

17) Select substitute titles when requested materials are unavailable following criteria such as age, education, and interests.

18) Prepare, store, and retrieve classification and catalog information, lecture notes, or other information related to stored documents, using computers.

19) Assist in the preparation of book displays.

20) Review records, such as microfilm and issue cards, in order to identify titles of overdue materials and delinquent borrowers.

21) Schedule and supervise clerical workers, volunteers, and student assistants.

22) Operate and maintain audiovisual equipment.

23) Facilitate the acquisition of books, pamphlets, periodicals, and audiovisual materials by checking prices, figuring costs, and preparing appropriate order forms.

24) Place books in mailing containers, affix address labels, and secure containers with straps for mailing to blind library patrons.

25) Operate small branch libraries, under the direction of off-site librarian supervisors.

Knowledge	Knowledge Definitions
Clerical	Knowledge of administrative and clerical procedures and systems such as word processing, managing files and records, stenography and transcription, designing forms, and other office procedures and terminology.
Customer and Personal Service	Knowledge of principles and processes for providing customer and personal services. This includes customer needs assessment, meeting quality standards for services, and evaluation of customer satisfaction.
English Language	Knowledge of the structure and content of the English language including the meaning and spelling of words, rules of composition, and grammar.
Computers and Electronics	Knowledge of circuit boards, processors, chips, electronic equipment, and computer hardware and software, including applications and programming.
Education and Training	Knowledge of principles and methods for curriculum and training design, teaching and instruction for individuals and groups, and the measurement of training effects.
Communications and Media	Knowledge of media production, communication, and dissemination techniques and methods. This includes alternative ways to inform and entertain via written, oral, and visual media.
Mathematics	Knowledge of arithmetic, algebra, geometry, calculus, statistics, and their applications.
Administration and Management	Knowledge of business and management principles involved in strategic planning, resource allocation, human resources modeling, leadership technique, production methods, and coordination of people and resources.
Public Safety and Security	Knowledge of relevant equipment, policies, procedures, and strategies to promote effective local, state, or national security operations for the protection of people, data, property, and institutions.
Production and Processing	Knowledge of raw materials, production processes, quality control, costs, and other techniques for maximizing the effective manufacture and distribution of goods.
Psychology	Knowledge of human behavior and performance; individual differences in ability, personality, and interests; learning and motivation; psychological research methods; and the assessment and treatment of behavioral and affective disorders.
Law and Government	Knowledge of laws, legal codes, court procedures, precedents, government regulations, executive orders, agency rules, and the democratic political process.
Telecommunications	Knowledge of transmission, broadcasting, switching, control, and operation of telecommunications systems.
Personnel and Human Resources	Knowledge of principles and procedures for personnel recruitment, selection, training, compensation and benefits, labor relations and negotiation, and personnel information systems.
Geography	Knowledge of principles and methods for describing the features of land, sea, and air masses, including their physical characteristics, locations, interrelationships, and distribution of plant, animal, and human life.
History and Archeology	Knowledge of historical events and their causes, indicators, and effects on civilizations and cultures.
Economics and Accounting	Knowledge of economic and accounting principles and practices, the financial markets, banking and the analysis and reporting of financial data.
Sociology and Anthropology	Knowledge of group behavior and dynamics, societal trends and influences, human migrations, ethnicity, cultures and their history and origins.
Mechanical	Knowledge of machines and tools, including their designs, uses, repair, and maintenance.
Transportation	Knowledge of principles and methods for moving people or goods by air, rail, sea, or road, including the relative costs and benefits.
Philosophy and Theology	Knowledge of different philosophical systems and religions. This includes their basic principles, values, ethics, ways of thinking, customs, practices, and their impact on human culture.
Foreign Language	Knowledge of the structure and content of a foreign (non-English) language including the meaning and spelling of words, rules of composition and grammar, and pronunciation.
Sales and Marketing	Knowledge of principles and methods for showing, promoting, and selling products or services. This includes marketing strategy and tactics, product demonstration, sales techniques, and sales control systems.

Fine Arts	Knowledge of the theory and techniques required to compose, produce, and perform works of music, dance, visual arts, drama, and sculpture.
Therapy and Counseling	Knowledge of principles, methods, and procedures for diagnosis, treatment, and rehabilitation of physical and mental dysfunctions, and for career counseling and guidance.
Engineering and Technology	Knowledge of the practical application of engineering science and technology. This includes applying principles, techniques, procedures, and equipment to the design and production of various goods and services.
Design	Knowledge of design techniques, tools, and principles involved in production of precision technical plans, blueprints, drawings, and models.
Physics	Knowledge and prediction of physical principles, laws, their interrelationships, and applications to understanding fluid, material, and atmospheric dynamics, and mechanical, electrical, atomic and sub- atomic structures and processes.
Chemistry	Knowledge of the chemical composition, structure, and properties of substances and of the chemical processes and transformations that they undergo. This includes uses of chemicals and their interactions, danger signs, production techniques, and disposal methods.
Medicine and Dentistry	Knowledge of the information and techniques needed to diagnose and treat human injuries, diseases, and deformities. This includes symptoms, treatment alternatives, drug properties and interactions, and preventive health-care measures.
Biology	Knowledge of plant and animal organisms, their tissues, cells, functions, interdependencies, and interactions with each other and the environment.
Building and Construction	Knowledge of materials, methods, and the tools involved in the construction or repair of houses, buildings, or other structures such as highways and roads.
Food Production	Knowledge of techniques and equipment for planting, growing, and harvesting food products (both plant and animal) for consumption, including storage/handling techniques.

Skills	Skills Definitions
Reading Comprehension	Understanding written sentences and paragraphs in work related documents.
Active Listening	Giving full attention to what other people are saying, taking time to understand the points being made, asking questions as appropriate, and not interrupting at inappropriate times.
Service Orientation	Actively looking for ways to help people.
Time Management	Managing one's own time and the time of others.
Active Learning	Understanding the implications of new information for both current and future problem-solving and decision-making.
Speaking	Talking to others to convey information effectively.
Instructing	Teaching others how to do something.
Writing	Communicating effectively in writing as appropriate for the needs of the audience.
Social Perceptiveness	Being aware of others' reactions and understanding why they react as they do.
Learning Strategies	Selecting and using training/instructional methods and procedures appropriate for the situation when learning or teaching new things.
Critical Thinking	Using logic and reasoning to identify the strengths and weaknesses of alternative solutions, conclusions or approaches to problems.
Coordination	Adjusting actions in relation to others' actions.
Monitoring	Monitoring/Assessing performance of yourself, other individuals, or organizations to make improvements or take corrective action.
Judgment and Decision Making	Considering the relative costs and benefits of potential actions to choose the most appropriate one.
Complex Problem Solving	Identifying complex problems and reviewing related information to develop and evaluate options and implement solutions.
Equipment Selection	Determining the kind of tools and equipment needed to do a job.
Mathematics	Using mathematics to solve problems.
Operation and Control	Controlling operations of equipment or systems.
Negotiation	Bringing others together and trying to reconcile differences.
Persuasion	Persuading others to change their minds or behavior.
Equipment Maintenance	Performing routine maintenance on equipment and determining when and what kind of maintenance is needed.
Technology Design	Generating or adapting equipment and technology to serve user needs.

Troubleshooting	Determining causes of operating errors and deciding what to do about it.
Systems Evaluation	Identifying measures or indicators of system performance and the actions needed to improve or correct performance, relative to the goals of the system.
Operations Analysis	Analyzing needs and product requirements to create a design.
Management of Material Resources	Obtaining and seeing to the appropriate use of equipment, facilities, and materials needed to do certain work.
Management of Personnel Resources	Motivating, developing, and directing people as they work, identifying the best people for the job.
Quality Control Analysis	Conducting tests and inspections of products, services, or processes to evaluate quality or performance.
Operation Monitoring	Watching gauges, dials, or other indicators to make sure a machine is working properly.
Systems Analysis	Determining how a system should work and how changes in conditions, operations, and the environment will affect outcomes.
Installation	Installing equipment, machines, wiring, or programs to meet specifications.
Management of Financial Resources	Determining how money will be spent to get the work done, and accounting for these expenditures.
Repairing	Repairing machines or systems using the needed tools.
Science	Using scientific rules and methods to solve problems.
Programming	Writing computer programs for various purposes.

Ability	Ability Definitions
Oral Expression	The ability to communicate information and ideas in speaking so others will understand.
Written Comprehension	The ability to read and understand information and ideas presented in writing.
Near Vision	The ability to see details at close range (within a few feet of the observer).
Information Ordering	The ability to arrange things or actions in a certain order or pattern according to a specific rule or set of rules (e.g., patterns of numbers, letters, words, pictures, mathematical operations).
Oral Comprehension	The ability to listen to and understand information and ideas presented through spoken words and sentences.
Category Flexibility	The ability to generate or use different sets of rules for combining or grouping things in different ways.
Speech Clarity	The ability to speak clearly so others can understand you.
Flexibility of Closure	The ability to identify or detect a known pattern (a figure, object, word, or sound) that is hidden in other distracting material.
Speech Recognition	The ability to identify and understand the speech of another person.
Inductive Reasoning	The ability to combine pieces of information to form general rules or conclusions (includes finding a relationship among seemingly unrelated events).
Written Expression	The ability to communicate information and ideas in writing so others will understand.
Selective Attention	The ability to concentrate on a task over a period of time without being distracted.
Perceptual Speed	The ability to quickly and accurately compare similarities and differences among sets of letters, numbers, objects, pictures, or patterns. The things to be compared may be presented at the same time or one after the other. This ability also includes comparing a presented object with a remembered object.
Deductive Reasoning	The ability to apply general rules to specific problems to produce answers that make sense.
Problem Sensitivity	The ability to tell when something is wrong or is likely to go wrong. It does not involve solving the problem, only recognizing there is a problem.
Fluency of Ideas	The ability to come up with a number of ideas about a topic (the number of ideas is important, not their quality, correctness, or creativity).
Finger Dexterity	The ability to make precisely coordinated movements of the fingers of one or both hands to grasp, manipulate, or assemble very small objects.
Far Vision	The ability to see details at a distance.
Static Strength	The ability to exert maximum muscle force to lift, push, pull, or carry objects.
Arm-Hand Steadiness	The ability to keep your hand and arm steady while moving your arm or while holding your arm and hand in one position.
Memorization	The ability to remember information such as words, numbers, pictures, and procedures.

Time Sharing	The ability to shift back and forth between two or more activities or sources of information (such as speech, sounds, touch, or other sources).
Trunk Strength	The ability to use your abdominal and lower back muscles to support part of the body repeatedly or continuously over time without 'giving out' or fatiguing.
Originality	The ability to come up with unusual or clever ideas about a given topic or situation, or to develop creative ways to solve a problem.
Multilimb Coordination	The ability to coordinate two or more limbs (for example, two arms, two legs, or one leg and one arm) while sitting, standing, or lying down. It does not involve performing the activities while the whole body is in motion.
Manual Dexterity	The ability to quickly move your hand, your hand together with your arm, or your two hands to grasp, manipulate, or assemble objects.
Visual Color Discrimination	The ability to match or detect differences between colors, including shades of color and brightness.
Visualization	The ability to imagine how something will look after it is moved around or when its parts are moved or rearranged.
Number Facility	The ability to add, subtract, multiply, or divide quickly and correctly.
Speed of Closure	The ability to quickly make sense of, combine, and organize information into meaningful patterns.
Hearing Sensitivity	The ability to detect or tell the differences between sounds that vary in pitch and loudness.
Mathematical Reasoning	The ability to choose the right mathematical methods or formulas to solve a problem.
Extent Flexibility	The ability to bend, stretch, twist, or reach with your body, arms, and/or legs.
Stamina	The ability to exert yourself physically over long periods of time without getting winded or out of breath.
Depth Perception	The ability to judge which of several objects is closer or farther away from you, or to judge the distance between you and an object.
Gross Body Equilibrium	The ability to keep or regain your body balance or stay upright when in an unstable position.
Auditory Attention	The ability to focus on a single source of sound in the presence of other distracting sounds.
Gross Body Coordination	The ability to coordinate the movement of your arms, legs, and torso together when the whole body is in motion.
Dynamic Strength	The ability to exert muscle force repeatedly or continuously over time. This involves muscular endurance and resistance to muscle fatigue.
Spatial Orientation	The ability to know your location in relation to the environment or to know where other objects are in relation to you.
Wrist-Finger Speed	The ability to make fast, simple, repeated movements of the fingers, hands, and wrists.
Control Precision	The ability to quickly and repeatedly adjust the controls of a machine or a vehicle to exact positions.
Dynamic Flexibility	The ability to quickly and repeatedly bend, stretch, twist, or reach out with your body, arms, and/or legs.
Response Orientation	The ability to choose quickly between two or more movements in response to two or more different signals (lights, sounds, pictures). It includes the speed with which the correct response is started with the hand, foot, or other body part.
Night Vision	The ability to see under low light conditions.
Sound Localization	The ability to tell the direction from which a sound originated.
Speed of Limb Movement	The ability to quickly move the arms and legs.
Peripheral Vision	The ability to see objects or movement of objects to one's side when the eyes are looking ahead.
Rate Control	The ability to time your movements or the movement of a piece of equipment in anticipation of changes in the speed and/or direction of a moving object or scene.
Explosive Strength	The ability to use short bursts of muscle force to propel oneself (as in jumping or sprinting), or to throw an object.
Reaction Time	The ability to quickly respond (with the hand, finger, or foot) to a signal (sound, light, picture) when it appears.
Glare Sensitivity	The ability to see objects in the presence of glare or bright lighting.

Work_Activity	Work_Activity Definitions
Interacting With Computers	Using computers and computer systems (including hardware and software) to program, write software, set up functions, enter data, or process information.

Establishing and Maintaining Interpersonal Relatio
Developing constructive and cooperative working relationships with others, and maintaining them over time.

Communicating with Supervisors, Peers, or Subordin
Providing information to supervisors, co-workers, and subordinates by telephone, in written form, e-mail, or in person.

Getting Information
Observing, receiving, and otherwise obtaining information from all relevant sources.

Identifying Objects, Actions, and Events
Identifying information by categorizing, estimating, recognizing differences or similarities, and detecting changes in circumstances or events.

Performing for or Working Directly with the Public
Performing for people or dealing directly with the public. This includes serving customers in restaurants and stores, and receiving clients or guests.

Organizing, Planning, and Prioritizing Work
Developing specific goals and plans to prioritize, organize, and accomplish your work.

Documenting/Recording Information
Entering, transcribing, recording, storing, or maintaining information in written or electronic/magnetic form.

Processing Information
Compiling, coding, categorizing, calculating, tabulating, auditing, or verifying information or data.

Monitor Processes, Materials, or Surroundings
Monitoring and reviewing information from materials, events, or the environment, to detect or assess problems.

Updating and Using Relevant Knowledge
Keeping up-to-date technically and applying new knowledge to your job.

Handling and Moving Objects
Using hands and arms in handling, installing, positioning, and moving materials, and manipulating things.

Making Decisions and Solving Problems
Analyzing information and evaluating results to choose the best solution and solve problems.

Assisting and Caring for Others
Providing personal assistance, medical attention, emotional support, or other personal care to others such as coworkers, customers, or patients.

Interpreting the Meaning of Information for Others
Translating or explaining what information means and how it can be used.

Performing Administrative Activities
Performing day-to-day administrative tasks such as maintaining information files and processing paperwork.

Performing General Physical Activities
Performing physical activities that require considerable use of your arms and legs and moving your whole body, such as climbing, lifting, balancing, walking, stooping, and handling of materials.

Judging the Qualities of Things, Services, or Peop
Assessing the value, importance, or quality of things or people.

Resolving Conflicts and Negotiating with Others
Handling complaints, settling disputes, and resolving grievances and conflicts, or otherwise negotiating with others.

Thinking Creatively
Developing, designing, or creating new applications, ideas, relationships, systems, or products, including artistic contributions.

Coaching and Developing Others
Identifying the developmental needs of others and coaching, mentoring, or otherwise helping others to improve their knowledge or skills.

Coordinating the Work and Activities of Others
Getting members of a group to work together to accomplish tasks.

Inspecting Equipment, Structures, or Material
Inspecting equipment, structures, or materials to identify the cause of errors or other problems or defects.

Communicating with Persons Outside Organization
Communicating with people outside the organization, representing the organization to customers, the public, government, and other external sources. This information can be exchanged in person, in writing, or by telephone or e-mail.

Training and Teaching Others
Identifying the educational needs of others, developing formal educational or training programs or classes, and teaching or instructing others.

Analyzing Data or Information
Identifying the underlying principles, reasons, or facts of information by breaking down information or data into separate parts.

Scheduling Work and Activities
Scheduling events, programs, and activities, as well as the work of others.

Guiding, Directing, and Motivating Subordinates
Providing guidance and direction to subordinates, including setting performance standards and monitoring performance.

Evaluating Information to Determine Compliance wit
Using relevant information and individual judgment to determine whether events or processes comply with laws, regulations, or standards.

Developing and Building Teams
Encouraging and building mutual trust, respect, and cooperation among team members.

Developing Objectives and Strategies
Establishing long-range objectives and specifying the strategies and actions to achieve them.

Controlling Machines and Processes
Using either control mechanisms or direct physical activity to operate machines or processes (not including computers or vehicles).

Estimating the Quantifiable Characteristics of Pro
Estimating sizes, distances, and quantities; or determining time, costs, resources, or materials needed to perform a work activity.

Monitoring and Controlling Resources
Monitoring and controlling resources and overseeing the spending of money.

Staffing Organizational Units
Recruiting, interviewing, selecting, hiring, and promoting employees in an organization.

Provide Consultation and Advice to Others
Providing guidance and expert advice to management or other groups on technical, systems-, or process-related topics.

Repairing and Maintaining Electronic Equipment
Servicing, repairing, calibrating, regulating, fine-tuning, or testing machines, devices, and equipment that operate primarily on the basis of electrical or electronic (not mechanical) principles.

Repairing and Maintaining Mechanical Equipment
Servicing, repairing, adjusting, and testing machines, devices, moving parts, and equipment that operate primarily on the basis of mechanical (not electronic) principles.

Selling or Influencing Others
Convincing others to buy merchandise/goods or to otherwise change their minds or actions.

Drafting, Laying Out, and Specifying Technical Dev
Providing documentation, detailed instructions, drawings, or specifications to tell others about how devices, parts, equipment, or structures are to be fabricated, constructed, assembled, modified, maintained, or used.

Operating Vehicles, Mechanized Devices, or Equipme
Running, maneuvering, navigating, or driving vehicles or mechanized equipment, such as forklifts, passenger vehicles, aircraft, or water craft.

Work_Context	Work_Context Definitions
Face-to-Face Discussions	How often do you have to have face-to-face discussions with individuals or teams in this job?
Contact With Others	How much does this job require the worker to be in contact with others (face-to-face, by telephone, or otherwise) in order to perform it?
Telephone	How often do you have telephone conversations in this job?
Structured versus Unstructured Work	To what extent is this job structured for the worker, rather than allowing the worker to determine tasks, priorities, and goals?
Importance of Being Exact or Accurate	How important is being very exact or highly accurate in performing this job?
Indoors, Environmentally Controlled	How often does this job require working indoors in environmentally controlled conditions?
Importance of Repeating Same Tasks	How important is repeating the same physical activities (e.g., key entry) or mental activities (e.g., checking entries in a ledger) over and over, without stopping, to performing this job?
Electronic Mail	How often do you use electronic mail in this job?
Freedom to Make Decisions	How much decision making freedom, without supervision, does the job offer?
Work With Work Group or Team	How important is it to work with others in a group or team in this job?
Physical Proximity	To what extent does this job require the worker to perform job tasks in close physical proximity to other people?
Spend Time Making Repetitive Motions	How much does this job require making repetitive motions?
Deal With External Customers	How important is it to work with external customers or the public in this job?
Spend Time Using Your Hands to Handle, Control, or	How much does this job require using your hands to handle, control, or feel objects, tools or controls?
Spend Time Sitting	How much does this job require sitting?
Degree of Automation	How automated is the job?
Letters and Memos	How often does the job require written letters and memos?
Spend Time Standing	How much does this job require standing?
Impact of Decisions on Co-workers or Company Resul	How do the decisions an employee makes impact the results of co-workers, clients or the company?
Time Pressure	How often does this job require the worker to meet strict deadlines?
Frequency of Decision Making	How frequently is the worker required to make decisions that affect other people, the financial resources, and/or the image and reputation of the organization?
Coordinate or Lead Others	How important is it to coordinate or lead others in accomplishing work activities in this job?
Deal With Unpleasant or Angry People	How frequently does the worker have to deal with unpleasant, angry, or discourteous individuals as part of the job requirements?
Responsibility for Outcomes and Results	How responsible is the worker for work outcomes and results of other workers?
Frequency of Conflict Situations	How often are there conflict situations the employee has to face in this job?

935

Responsible for Others' Health and Safety	How much responsibility is there for the health and safety of others in this job?	
Exposed to Contaminants	How often does this job require working exposed to contaminants (such as pollutants, gases, dust or odors)?	
Sounds, Noise Levels Are Distracting or Uncomfortable	How often does this job require working exposed to sounds and noise levels that are distracting or uncomfortable?	
Spend Time Bending or Twisting the Body	How much does this job require bending or twisting your body?	
Spend Time Walking and Running	How much does this job require walking and running?	
Level of Competition	To what extent does this job require the worker to compete or to be aware of competitive pressures?	
Public Speaking	How often do you have to perform public speaking in this job?	
Consequence of Error	How serious would the result usually be if the worker made a mistake that was not readily correctable?	
Spend Time Kneeling, Crouching, Stooping, or Crawl	How much does this job require kneeling, crouching, stooping or crawling?	
Exposed to Minor Burns, Cuts, Bites, or Stings	How often does this job require exposure to minor burns, cuts, bites, or stings?	
Pace Determined by Speed of Equipment	How important is it to this job that the pace is determined by the speed of equipment or machinery? (This does not refer to keeping busy at all times on this job.)	
Spend Time Keeping or Regaining Balance	How much does this job require keeping or regaining your balance?	
Very Hot or Cold Temperatures	How often does this job require working in very hot (above 90 F degrees) or very cold (below 32 F degrees) temperatures?	
Outdoors, Exposed to Weather	How often does this job require working outdoors, exposed to all weather conditions?	
Cramped Work Space, Awkward Positions	How often does this job require working in cramped work spaces that requires getting into awkward positions?	
Deal With Physically Aggressive People	How frequently does this job require the worker to deal with physical aggression of violent individuals?	
Extremely Bright or Inadequate Lighting	How often does this job require working in extremely bright or inadequate lighting conditions?	
Exposed to Hazardous Equipment	How often does this job require exposure to hazardous equipment?	
Spend Time Climbing Ladders, Scaffolds, or Poles	How much does this job require climbing ladders, scaffolds, or poles?	
Wear Common Protective or Safety Equipment such as	How much does this job require wearing common protective or safety equipment such as safety shoes, glasses, gloves, hard hats or live jackets?	
In an Enclosed Vehicle or Equipment	How often does this job require working in a closed vehicle or equipment (e.g., car)?	
Indoors, Not Environmentally Controlled	How often does this job require working indoors in non-controlled environmental conditions (e.g., warehouse without heat)?	
In an Open Vehicle or Equipment	How often does this job require working in an open vehicle or equipment (e.g., tractor)?	
Exposed to Disease or Infections	How often does this job require exposure to disease/infections?	
Exposed to High Places	How often does this job require exposure to high places?	
Outdoors, Under Cover	How often does this job require working outdoors, under cover (e.g., structure with roof but no walls)?	
Exposed to Radiation	How often does this job require exposure to radiation?	
Exposed to Whole Body Vibration	How often does this job require exposure to whole body vibration (e.g., operate a jackhammer)?	
Wear Specialized Protective or Safety Equipment su	How much does this job require wearing specialized protective or safety equipment such as breathing apparatus, safety harness, full protection suits, or radiation protection?	
Exposed to Hazardous Conditions	How often does this job require exposure to hazardous conditions?	

Job Zone Component	Job Zone Component Definitions
Title	Job Zone Three: Medium Preparation Needed
Overall Experience	Previous work-related skill, knowledge, or experience is required for these occupations. For example, an electrician must have completed three or four years of apprenticeship or several years of vocational training, and often must have passed a licensing exam, in order to perform the job.
Job Training	Employees in these occupations usually need one or two years of training involving both on-the-job experience and informal training with experienced workers.

These occupations usually involve using communication and organizational skills to coordinate, supervise, manage, or train others to accomplish goals. Examples include dental assistants, electricians, fish and game wardens, legal secretaries, personnel recruiters, and recreation workers.

Job Zone Examples	
SVP Range	(6.0 to < 7.0)
Education	Most occupations in this zone require training in vocational schools, related on-the-job experience, or an associate's degree. Some may require a bachelor's degree.

Work_Styles	Work_Styles Definitions
Attention to Detail	Job requires being careful about detail and thorough in completing work tasks.
Integrity	Job requires being honest and ethical.
Cooperation	Job requires being pleasant with others on the job and displaying a good-natured, cooperative attitude.
Dependability	Job requires being reliable, responsible, and dependable, and fulfilling obligations.
Concern for Others	Job requires being sensitive to others' needs and feelings and being understanding and helpful on the job.
Independence	Job requires developing one's own ways of doing things, guiding oneself with little or no supervision, and depending on oneself to get things done.
Self Control	Job requires maintaining composure, keeping emotions in check, controlling anger, and avoiding aggressive behavior, even in very difficult situations.
Adaptability/Flexibility	Job requires being open to change (positive or negative) and to considerable variety in the workplace.
Social Orientation	Job requires preferring to work with others rather than alone, and being personally connected with others on the job.
Stress Tolerance	Job requires accepting criticism and dealing calmly and effectively with high stress situations.
Initiative	Job requires a willingness to take on responsibilities and challenges.
Persistence	Job requires persistence in the face of obstacles.
Achievement/Effort	Job requires establishing and maintaining personally challenging achievement goals and exerting effort toward mastering tasks.
Innovation	Job requires creativity and alternative thinking to develop new ideas for and answers to work-related problems.
Leadership	Job requires a willingness to lead, take charge, and offer opinions and direction.
Analytical Thinking	Job requires analyzing information and using logic to address work-related issues and problems.

43-4131.00 - Loan Interviewers and Clerks

Interview loan applicants to elicit information; investigate applicants' backgrounds and verify references; prepare loan request papers; and forward findings, reports, and documents to appraisal department. Review loan papers to ensure completeness, and complete transactions between loan establishment, borrowers, and sellers upon approval of loan.

Tasks

1) Accept payment on accounts.

2) Verify and examine information and accuracy of loan application and closing documents.

3) File and maintain loan records.

4) Answer questions and advise customers regarding loans and transactions.

5) Schedule and conduct closings of mortgage transactions.

6) Present loan and repayment schedules to customers.

7) Establish credit limits and grant extensions of credit on overdue accounts.

8) Interview loan applicants in order to obtain personal and financial data, and to assist in completing applications.

9) Order property insurance or mortgage insurance policies in order to ensure protection against loss on mortgaged property.

10) Calculate, review, and correct errors on interest, principal, payment, and closing costs, using computers or calculators.

11) Assemble and compile documents for loan closings, such as title abstracts, insurance

forms, loan forms, and tax receipts.

12) Record applications for loan and credit, loan information, and disbursements of funds, using computers.

13) Submit loan applications with recommendation for underwriting approval.

14) Contact customers by mail, telephone, or in person concerning acceptance or rejection of applications.

15) Contact credit bureaus, employers, and other sources in order to check applicants' credit and personal references.

16) Check value of customer collateral to be held as loan security.

17) Prepare and type loan applications, closing documents, legal documents, letters, forms, government notices, and checks, using computers.

43-4141.00 - New Accounts Clerks

Interview persons desiring to open bank accounts. Explain banking services available to prospective customers and assist them in preparing application form.

Tasks

1) Answer customers' questions, and explain available services such as deposit accounts, bonds, and securities.

2) Refer customers to appropriate bank personnel in order to meet their financial needs.

3) Compile information about new accounts, enter account information into computers, and file related forms or other documents.

4) Investigate and correct errors upon customers' request, according to customer and bank records.

5) Collect and record customer deposits and fees, and issue receipts using computers.

6) Obtain credit records from reporting agencies.

7) Execute wire transfers of funds.

8) Perform teller duties as required.

9) Issue initial and replacement safe-deposit keys to customers, and admit customers to vaults.

10) Duplicate records for distribution to branch offices.

11) Perform foreign currency transactions and sell traveler's checks.

12) Schedule repairs for locks on safe-deposit boxes.

13) Inform customers of procedures for applying for services such as ATM cards, direct deposit of checks, and certificates of deposit.

Knowledge	Knowledge Definitions
Customer and Personal Service	Knowledge of principles and processes for providing customer and personal services. This includes customer needs assessment, meeting quality standards for services, and evaluation of customer satisfaction.
Mathematics	Knowledge of arithmetic, algebra, geometry, calculus, statistics, and their applications.
Economics and Accounting	Knowledge of economic and accounting principles and practices, the financial markets, banking and the analysis and reporting of financial data.
English Language	Knowledge of the structure and content of the English language including the meaning and spelling of words, rules of composition, and grammar.
Sales and Marketing	Knowledge of principles and methods for showing, promoting, and selling products or services. This includes marketing strategy and tactics, product demonstration, sales techniques, and sales control systems.
Clerical	Knowledge of administrative and clerical procedures and systems such as word processing, managing files and records, stenography and transcription, designing forms, and other office procedures and terminology.
Administration and Management	Knowledge of business and management principles involved in strategic planning, resource allocation, human resources modeling, leadership technique, production methods, and coordination of people and resources.
Computers and Electronics	Knowledge of circuit boards, processors, chips, electronic equipment, and computer hardware and software, including applications and programming.
Law and Government	Knowledge of laws, legal codes, court procedures, precedents, government regulations, executive orders, agency rules, and the democratic political process.
Personnel and Human Resources	Knowledge of principles and procedures for personnel recruitment, selection, training, compensation and benefits, labor relations and negotiation, and personnel information systems.
Education and Training	Knowledge of principles and methods for curriculum and training design, teaching and instruction for individuals and groups, and the measurement of training effects.
Public Safety and Security	Knowledge of relevant equipment, policies, procedures, and strategies to promote effective local, state, or national security operations for the protection of people, data, property, and institutions.
Communications and Media	Knowledge of media production, communication, and dissemination techniques and methods. This includes alternative ways to inform and entertain via written, oral, and visual media.
Psychology	Knowledge of human behavior and performance; individual differences in ability, personality, and interests; learning and motivation; psychological research methods; and the assessment and treatment of behavioral and affective disorders.
Foreign Language	Knowledge of the structure and content of a foreign (non-English) language including the meaning and spelling of words, rules of composition and grammar, and pronunciation.
Telecommunications	Knowledge of transmission, broadcasting, switching, control, and operation of telecommunications systems.
Production and Processing	Knowledge of raw materials, production processes, quality control, costs, and other techniques for maximizing the effective manufacture and distribution of goods.
Sociology and Anthropology	Knowledge of group behavior and dynamics, societal trends and influences, human migrations, ethnicity, cultures and their history and origins.
Transportation	Knowledge of principles and methods for moving people or goods by air, rail, sea, or road, including the relative costs and benefits.
Philosophy and Theology	Knowledge of different philosophical systems and religions. This includes their basic principles, values, ethics, ways of thinking, customs, practices, and their impact on human culture.
Engineering and Technology	Knowledge of the practical application of engineering science and technology. This includes applying principles, techniques, procedures, and equipment to the design and production of various goods and services.
Geography	Knowledge of principles and methods for describing the features of land, sea, and air masses, including their physical characteristics, locations, interrelationships, and distribution of plant, animal, and human life.
History and Archeology	Knowledge of historical events and their causes, indicators, and effects on civilizations and cultures.
Medicine and Dentistry	Knowledge of the information and techniques needed to diagnose and treat human injuries, diseases, and deformities. This includes symptoms, treatment alternatives, drug properties and interactions, and preventive health-care measures.
Therapy and Counseling	Knowledge of principles, methods, and procedures for diagnosis, treatment, and rehabilitation of physical and mental dysfunctions, and for career counseling and guidance.
Fine Arts	Knowledge of the theory and techniques required to compose, produce, and perform works of music, dance, visual arts, drama, and sculpture.
Mechanical	Knowledge of machines and tools, including their designs, uses, repair, and maintenance.
Food Production	Knowledge of techniques and equipment for planting, growing, and harvesting food products (both plant and animal) for consumption, including storage/handling techniques.
Biology	Knowledge of plant and animal organisms, their tissues, cells, functions, interdependencies, and interactions with each other and the environment.
Design	Knowledge of design techniques, tools, and principles involved in production of precision technical plans, blueprints, drawings, and models.
Chemistry	Knowledge of the chemical composition, structure, and properties of substances and of the chemical processes and transformations that they undergo. This includes uses of chemicals and their interactions, danger signs, production techniques, and disposal methods.

Building and Construction	Knowledge of materials, methods, and the tools involved in the construction or repair of houses, buildings, or other structures such as highways and roads.
Physics	Knowledge and prediction of physical principles, laws, their interrelationships, and applications to understanding fluid, material, and atmospheric dynamics, and mechanical, electrical, atomic and sub-atomic structures and processes.

Skills	Skills Definitions
Active Listening	Giving full attention to what other people are saying, taking time to understand the points being made, asking questions as appropriate, and not interrupting at inappropriate times.
Speaking	Talking to others to convey information effectively.
Reading Comprehension	Understanding written sentences and paragraphs in work related documents.
Mathematics	Using mathematics to solve problems.
Critical Thinking	Using logic and reasoning to identify the strengths and weaknesses of alternative solutions, conclusions or approaches to problems.
Service Orientation	Actively looking for ways to help people.
Social Perceptiveness	Being aware of others' reactions and understanding why they react as they do.
Writing	Communicating effectively in writing as appropriate for the needs of the audience.
Learning Strategies	Selecting and using training/instructional methods and procedures appropriate for the situation when learning or teaching new things.
Judgment and Decision Making	Considering the relative costs and benefits of potential actions to choose the most appropriate one.
Time Management	Managing one's own time and the time of others.
Active Learning	Understanding the implications of new information for both current and future problem-solving and decision-making.
Instructing	Teaching others how to do something.
Monitoring	Monitoring/Assessing performance of yourself, other individuals, or organizations to make improvements or take corrective action.
Complex Problem Solving	Identifying complex problems and reviewing related information to develop and evaluate options and implement solutions.
Coordination	Adjusting actions in relation to others' actions.
Negotiation	Bringing others together and trying to reconcile differences.
Persuasion	Persuading others to change their minds or behavior.
Operation and Control	Controlling operations of equipment or systems.
Troubleshooting	Determining causes of operating errors and deciding what to do about it.
Equipment Selection	Determining the kind of tools and equipment needed to do a job.
Systems Evaluation	Identifying measures or indicators of system performance and the actions needed to improve or correct performance, relative to the goals of the system.
Management of Personnel Resources	Motivating, developing, and directing people as they work, identifying the best people for the job.
Operations Analysis	Analyzing needs and product requirements to create a design.
Technology Design	Generating or adapting equipment and technology to serve user needs.
Operation Monitoring	Watching gauges, dials, or other indicators to make sure a machine is working properly.
Systems Analysis	Determining how a system should work and how changes in conditions, operations, and the environment will affect outcomes.
Equipment Maintenance	Performing routine maintenance on equipment and determining when and what kind of maintenance is needed.
Management of Financial Resources	Determining how money will be spent to get the work done, and accounting for these expenditures.
Management of Material Resources	Obtaining and seeing to the appropriate use of equipment, facilities, and materials needed to do certain work.
Quality Control Analysis	Conducting tests and inspections of products, services, or processes to evaluate quality or performance.
Repairing	Repairing machines or systems using the needed tools.
Science	Using scientific rules and methods to solve problems.
Installation	Installing equipment, machines, wiring, or programs to meet specifications.
Programming	Writing computer programs for various purposes.

Ability	Ability Definitions
Oral Comprehension	The ability to listen to and understand information and ideas presented through spoken words and sentences.
Oral Expression	The ability to communicate information and ideas in speaking so others will understand.
Speech Clarity	The ability to speak clearly so others can understand you.
Speech Recognition	The ability to identify and understand the speech of another person.
Near Vision	The ability to see details at close range (within a few feet of the observer).
Problem Sensitivity	The ability to tell when something is wrong or is likely to go wrong. It does not involve solving the problem, only recognizing there is a problem.
Information Ordering	The ability to arrange things or actions in a certain order or pattern according to a specific rule or set of rules (e.g., patterns of numbers, letters, words, pictures, mathematical operations).
Written Comprehension	The ability to read and understand information and ideas presented in writing.
Selective Attention	The ability to concentrate on a task over a period of time without being distracted.
Written Expression	The ability to communicate information and ideas in writing so others will understand.
Deductive Reasoning	The ability to apply general rules to specific problems to produce answers that make sense.
Category Flexibility	The ability to generate or use different sets of rules for combining or grouping things in different ways.
Number Facility	The ability to add, subtract, multiply, or divide quickly and correctly.
Inductive Reasoning	The ability to combine pieces of information to form general rules or conclusions (includes finding a relationship among seemingly unrelated events).
Perceptual Speed	The ability to quickly and accurately compare similarities and differences among sets of letters, numbers, objects, pictures, or patterns. The things to be compared may be presented at the same time or one after the other. This ability also includes comparing a presented object with a remembered object.
Speed of Closure	The ability to quickly make sense of, combine, and organize information into meaningful patterns.
Mathematical Reasoning	The ability to choose the right mathematical methods or formulas to solve a problem.
Time Sharing	The ability to shift back and forth between two or more activities or sources of information (such as speech, sounds, touch, or other sources).
Flexibility of Closure	The ability to identify or detect a known pattern (a figure, object, word, or sound) that is hidden in other distracting material.
Auditory Attention	The ability to focus on a single source of sound in the presence of other distracting sounds.
Fluency of Ideas	The ability to come up with a number of ideas about a topic (the number of ideas is important, not their quality, correctness, or creativity).
Finger Dexterity	The ability to make precisely coordinated movements of the fingers of one or both hands to grasp, manipulate, or assemble very small objects.
Visualization	The ability to imagine how something will look after it is moved around or when its parts are moved or rearranged.
Memorization	The ability to remember information such as words, numbers, pictures, and procedures.
Originality	The ability to come up with unusual or clever ideas about a given topic or situation, or to develop creative ways to solve a problem.
Far Vision	The ability to see details at a distance.
Hearing Sensitivity	The ability to detect or tell the differences between sounds that vary in pitch and loudness.
Visual Color Discrimination	The ability to match or detect differences between colors, including shades of color and brightness.
Manual Dexterity	The ability to quickly move your hand, your hand together with your arm, or your two hands to grasp, manipulate, or assemble objects.
Arm-Hand Steadiness	The ability to keep your hand and arm steady while moving your arm or while holding your arm and hand in one position.
Control Precision	The ability to quickly and repeatedly adjust the controls of a machine or a vehicle to exact positions.
Wrist-Finger Speed	The ability to make fast, simple, repeated movements of the fingers, hands, and wrists.

Trunk Strength	The ability to use your abdominal and lower back muscles to support part of the body repeatedly or continuously over time without 'giving out' or fatiguing.
Response Orientation	The ability to choose quickly between two or more movements in response to two or more different signals (lights, sounds, pictures). It includes the speed with which the correct response is started with the hand, foot, or other body part.
Rate Control	The ability to time your movements or the movement of a piece of equipment in anticipation of changes in the speed and/or direction of a moving object or scene.
Gross Body Coordination	The ability to coordinate the movement of your arms, legs, and torso together when the whole body is in motion.
Extent Flexibility	The ability to bend, stretch, twist, or reach with your body, arms, and/or legs.
Dynamic Strength	The ability to exert muscle force repeatedly or continuously over time. This involves muscular endurance and resistance to muscle fatigue.
Explosive Strength	The ability to use short bursts of muscle force to propel oneself (as in jumping or sprinting), or to throw an object.
Static Strength	The ability to exert maximum muscle force to lift, push, pull, or carry objects.
Reaction Time	The ability to quickly respond (with the hand, finger, or foot) to a signal (sound, light, picture) when it appears.
Multilimb Coordination	The ability to coordinate two or more limbs (for example, two arms, two legs, or one leg and one arm) while sitting, standing, or lying down. It does not involve performing the activities while the whole body is in motion.
Spatial Orientation	The ability to know your location in relation to the environment or to know where other objects are in relation to you.
Gross Body Equilibrium	The ability to keep or regain your body balance or stay upright when in an unstable position.
Speed of Limb Movement	The ability to quickly move the arms and legs.
Depth Perception	The ability to judge which of several objects is closer or farther away from you, or to judge the distance between you and an object.
Sound Localization	The ability to tell the direction from which a sound originated.
Glare Sensitivity	The ability to see objects in the presence of glare or bright lighting.
Peripheral Vision	The ability to see objects or movement of objects to one's side when the eyes are looking ahead.
Night Vision	The ability to see under low light conditions.
Stamina	The ability to exert yourself physically over long periods of time without getting winded or out of breath.
Dynamic Flexibility	The ability to quickly and repeatedly bend, stretch, twist, or reach out with your body, arms, and/or legs.

Work_Activity	Work_Activity Definitions
Performing for or Working Directly with the Public	Performing for people or dealing directly with the public. This includes serving customers in restaurants and stores, and receiving clients or guests.
Communicating with Supervisors, Peers, or Subordin	Providing information to supervisors, co-workers, and subordinates by telephone, in written form, e-mail, or in person.
Communicating with Persons Outside Organization	Communicating with people outside the organization, representing the organization to customers, the public, government, and other external sources. This information can be exchanged in person, in writing, or by telephone or e-mail.
Getting Information	Observing, receiving, and otherwise obtaining information from all relevant sources.
Identifying Objects, Actions, and Events	Identifying information by categorizing, estimating, recognizing differences or similarities, and detecting changes in circumstances or events.
Interacting With Computers	Using computers and computer systems (including hardware and software) to program, write software, set up functions, enter data, or process information.
Processing Information	Compiling, coding, categorizing, calculating, tabulating, auditing, or verifying information or data.
Establishing and Maintaining Interpersonal Relatio	Developing constructive and cooperative working relationships with others, and maintaining them over time.
Performing Administrative Activities	Performing day-to-day administrative tasks such as maintaining information files and processing paperwork.
Selling or Influencing Others	Convincing others to buy merchandise/goods or to otherwise change their minds or actions.
Making Decisions and Solving Problems	Analyzing information and evaluating results to choose the best solution and solve problems.

Organizing, Planning, and Prioritizing Work	Developing specific goals and plans to prioritize, organize, and accomplish your work.
Judging the Qualities of Things, Services, or Peop	Assessing the value, importance, or quality of things or people.
Monitor Processes, Materials, or Surroundings	Monitoring and reviewing information from materials, events, or the environment, to detect or assess problems.
Resolving Conflicts and Negotiating with Others	Handling complaints, settling disputes, and resolving grievances and conflicts, or otherwise negotiating with others.
Evaluating Information to Determine Compliance wit	Using relevant information and individual judgment to determine whether events or processes comply with laws, regulations, or standards.
Interpreting the Meaning of Information for Others	Translating or explaining what information means and how it can be used.
Developing and Building Teams	Encouraging and building mutual trust, respect, and cooperation among team members.
Training and Teaching Others	Identifying the educational needs of others, developing formal educational or training programs or classes, and teaching or instructing others.
Updating and Using Relevant Knowledge	Keeping up-to-date technically and applying new knowledge to your job.
Coordinating the Work and Activities of Others	Getting members of a group to work together to accomplish tasks.
Coaching and Developing Others	Identifying the developmental needs of others and coaching, mentoring, or otherwise helping others to improve their knowledge or skills.
Documenting/Recording Information	Entering, transcribing, recording, storing, or maintaining information in written or electronic/magnetic form.
Provide Consultation and Advice to Others	Providing guidance and expert advice to management or other groups on technical, systems-, or process-related topics.
Thinking Creatively	Developing, designing, or creating new applications, ideas, relationships, systems, or products, including artistic contributions.
Analyzing Data or Information	Identifying the underlying principles, reasons, or facts of information by breaking down information or data into separate parts.
Estimating the Quantifiable Characteristics of Pro	Estimating sizes, distances, and quantities; or determining time, costs, resources, or materials needed to perform a work activity.
Assisting and Caring for Others	Providing personal assistance, medical attention, emotional support, or other personal care to others such as coworkers, customers, or patients.
Scheduling Work and Activities	Scheduling events, programs, and activities, as well as the work of others.
Developing Objectives and Strategies	Establishing long-range objectives and specifying the strategies and actions to achieve them.
Controlling Machines and Processes	Using either control mechanisms or direct physical activity to operate machines or processes (not including computers or vehicles).
Guiding, Directing, and Motivating Subordinates	Providing guidance and direction to subordinates, including setting performance standards and monitoring performance.
Monitoring and Controlling Resources	Monitoring and controlling resources and overseeing the spending of money.
Performing General Physical Activities	Performing physical activities that require considerable use of your arms and legs and moving your whole body, such as climbing, lifting, balancing, walking, stooping, and handling of materials.
Handling and Moving Objects	Using hands and arms in handling, installing, positioning, and moving materials, and manipulating things.
Staffing Organizational Units	Recruiting, interviewing, selecting, hiring, and promoting employees in an organization.
Inspecting Equipment, Structures, or Material	Inspecting equipment, structures, or materials to identify the cause of errors or other problems or defects.
Repairing and Maintaining Mechanical Equipment	Servicing, repairing, adjusting, and testing machines, devices, moving parts, and equipment that operate primarily on the basis of mechanical (not electronic) principles.
Drafting, Laying Out, and Specifying Technical Dev	Providing documentation, detailed instructions, drawings, or specifications to tell others about how devices, parts, equipment, or structures are to be fabricated, constructed, assembled, modified, maintained, or used.
Operating Vehicles, Mechanized Devices, or Equipme	Running, maneuvering, navigating, or driving vehicles or mechanized equipment, such as forklifts, passenger vehicles, aircraft, or water craft.
Repairing and Maintaining Electronic Equipment	Servicing, repairing, calibrating, regulating, fine-tuning, or testing machines, devices, and equipment that operate primarily on the basis of electrical or electronic (not mechanical) principles.

Work_Context	Work_Context Definitions
Telephone	How often do you have telephone conversations in this job?
Face-to-Face Discussions	How often do you have to have face-to-face discussions with individuals or teams in this job?
Importance of Being Exact or Accurate	How important is being very exact or highly accurate in performing this job?
Contact With Others	How much does this job require the worker to be in contact with others (face-to-face, by telephone, or otherwise) in order to perform it?
Deal With External Customers	How important is it to work with external customers or the public in this job?
Freedom to Make Decisions	How much decision making freedom, without supervision, does the job offer?
Frequency of Decision Making	How frequently is the worker required to make decisions that affect other people, the financial resources, and/or the image and reputation of the organization?
Work With Work Group or Team	How important is it to work with others in a group or team in this job?
Impact of Decisions on Co-workers or Company Resul	How do the decisions an employee makes impact the results of co-workers, clients or the company?
Letters and Memos	How often does the job require written letters and memos?
Structured versus Unstructured Work	To what extent is this job structured for the worker, rather than allowing the worker to determine tasks, priorities, and goals?
Indoors, Environmentally Controlled	How often does this job require working indoors in environmentally controlled conditions?
Spend Time Sitting	How much does this job require sitting?
Electronic Mail	How often do you use electronic mail in this job?
Importance of Repeating Same Tasks	How important is repeating the same physical activities (e.g., key entry) or mental activities (e.g., checking entries in a ledger) over and over, without stopping, to performing this job?
Deal With Unpleasant or Angry People	How frequently does the worker have to deal with unpleasant, angry, or discourteous individuals as part of the job requirements?
Time Pressure	How often does this job require the worker to meet strict deadlines?
Coordinate or Lead Others	How important is it to coordinate or lead others in accomplishing work activities in this job?
Frequency of Conflict Situations	How often are there conflict situations the employee has to face in this job?
Degree of Automation	How automated is the job?
Sounds, Noise Levels Are Distracting or Uncomforta	How often does this job require working exposed to sounds and noise levels that are distracting or uncomfortable?
Physical Proximity	To what extent does this job require the worker to perform job tasks in close physical proximity to other people?
Responsibility for Outcomes and Results	How responsible is the worker for work outcomes and results of other workers?
Level of Competition	To what extent does this job require the worker to compete or to be aware of competitive pressures?
Consequence of Error	How serious would the result usually be if the worker made a mistake that was not readily correctable?
Spend Time Making Repetitive Motions	How much does this job require making repetitive motions?
Spend Time Using Your Hands to Handle, Control, or	How much does this job require using your hands to handle, control, or feel objects, tools or controls?
Spend Time Standing	How much does this job require standing?
Responsible for Others' Health and Safety	How much responsibility is there for the health and safety of others in this job?
Deal With Physically Aggressive People	How frequently does this job require the worker to deal with physical aggression of violent individuals?
Public Speaking	How often do you have to perform public speaking in this job?
Spend Time Walking and Running	How much does this job require walking and running?
Cramped Work Space, Awkward Positions	How often does this job require working in cramped work spaces that requires getting into awkward positions?
Spend Time Bending or Twisting the Body	How much does this job require bending or twisting your body?
Extremely Bright or Inadequate Lighting	How often does this job require working in extremely bright or inadequate lighting conditions?
Exposed to Contaminants	How often does this job require working exposed to contaminants (such as pollutants, gases, dust or odors)?
Very Hot or Cold Temperatures	How often does this job require working in very hot (above 90 F degrees) or very cold (below 32 F degrees) temperatures?
Spend Time Keeping or Regaining Balance	How much does this job require keeping or regaining your balance?

In an Enclosed Vehicle or Equipment	How often does this job require working in a closed vehicle or equipment (e.g., car)?
Exposed to Disease or Infections	How often does this job require exposure to disease/infections?
Spend Time Kneeling, Crouching, Stooping, or Crawl	How much does this job require kneeling, crouching, stooping, or crawling?
Pace Determined by Speed of Equipment	How important is it to this job that the pace is determined by the speed of equipment or machinery? (This does not refer to keeping busy at all times on this job.)
Outdoors, Exposed to Weather	How often does this job require working outdoors, exposed to all weather conditions?
Spend Time Climbing Ladders, Scaffolds, or Poles	How much does this job require climbing ladders, scaffolds, or poles?
Wear Common Protective or Safety Equipment such as	How much does this job require wearing common protective or safety equipment such as safety shoes, glasses, gloves, hard hats or life jackets?
In an Open Vehicle or Equipment	How often does this job require working in an open vehicle or equipment (e.g., tractor)?
Outdoors, Under Cover	How often does this job require working outdoors, under cover (e.g., structure with roof but no walls)?
Exposed to Radiation	How often does this job require exposure to radiation?
Exposed to Hazardous Equipment	How often does this job require exposure to hazardous equipment?
Exposed to High Places	How often does this job require exposure to high places?
Wear Specialized Protective or Safety Equipment su	How much does this job require wearing specialized protective or safety equipment such as breathing apparatus, safety harness, full protection suits, or radiation protection?
Exposed to Hazardous Conditions	How often does this job require exposure to hazardous conditions?
Indoors, Not Environmentally Controlled	How often does this job require working indoors in non-controlled environmental conditions (e.g., warehouse without heat)?
Exposed to Minor Burns, Cuts, Bites, or Stings	How often does this job require exposure to minor burns, cuts, bites, or stings?
Exposed to Whole Body Vibration	How often does this job require exposure to whole body vibration (e.g., operate a jackhammer)?

Job Zone Component	Job Zone Component Definitions
Title	Job Zone Two: Some Preparation Needed
Overall Experience	Some previous work-related skill, knowledge, or experience may be helpful in these occupations, but usually is not needed. For example, a drywall installer might benefit from experience installing drywall, but an inexperienced person could still learn to be an installer with little difficulty.
Job Training	Employees in these occupations need anywhere from a few months to one year of working with experienced employees.
Job Zone Examples	These occupations often involve using your knowledge and skills to help others. Examples include drywall installers, fire inspectors, flight attendants, pharmacy technicians, salespersons (retail), and tellers.
SVP Range	(4.0 to < 6.0)
Education	These occupations usually require a high school diploma and may require some vocational training or job-related course work. In some cases, an associate's or bachelor's degree could be needed.

Work_Styles	Work_Styles Definitions
Integrity	Job requires being honest and ethical.
Attention to Detail	Job requires being careful about detail and thorough in completing work tasks.
Dependability	Job requires being reliable, responsible, and dependable, and fulfilling obligations.
Stress Tolerance	Job requires accepting criticism and dealing calmly and effectively with high stress situations.
Cooperation	Job requires being pleasant with others on the job and displaying a good-natured, cooperative attitude.
Self Control	Job requires maintaining composure, keeping emotions in check, controlling anger, and avoiding aggressive behavior, even in very difficult situations.
Concern for Others	Job requires being sensitive to others' needs and feelings and being understanding and helpful on the job.
Initiative	Job requires a willingness to take on responsibilities and challenges.

940

Independence	Job requires developing one's own ways of doing things, guiding oneself with little or no supervision, and depending on oneself to get things done.
Social Orientation	Job requires preferring to work with others rather than alone, and being personally connected with others on the job.
Adaptability/Flexibility	Job requires being open to change (positive or negative) and to considerable variety in the workplace.
Achievement/Effort	Job requires establishing and maintaining personally challenging achievement goals and exerting effort toward mastering tasks.
Analytical Thinking	Job requires analyzing information and using logic to address work-related issues and problems.
Leadership	Job requires a willingness to lead, take charge, and offer opinions and direction.
Persistence	Job requires persistence in the face of obstacles.
Innovation	Job requires creativity and alternative thinking to develop new ideas for and answers to work-related problems.

43-4151.00 - Order Clerks

Receive and process incoming orders for materials, merchandise, classified ads, or services such as repairs, installations, or rental of facilities. Duties include informing customers of receipt, prices, shipping dates, and delays; preparing contracts; and handling complaints.

Tasks

1) Obtain customers' names, addresses, and billing information, product numbers, and specifications of items to be purchased, and enter this information on order forms.

2) Inform customers by mail or telephone of order information, such as unit prices, shipping dates, and any anticipated delays.

3) Receive and respond to customer complaints.

4) File copies of orders received, or post orders on records.

5) Prepare invoices, shipping documents, and contracts.

6) Review orders for completeness according to reporting procedures and forward incomplete orders for further processing.

7) Direct specified departments or units to prepare and ship orders to designated locations.

8) Compute total charges for merchandise or services and shipping charges.

9) Confer with production, sales, shipping, warehouse, or common carrier personnel in order to expedite or trace shipments.

10) Check inventory records to determine availability of requested merchandise.

11) Recommend merchandise or services that will meet customers' needs.

12) Attempt to sell additional merchandise or services to prospective or current customers by telephone or through visits.

13) Notify departments when supplies of specific items are low, or when orders would deplete available supplies.

14) Calculate and compile order-related statistics, and prepare reports for management.

15) Collect payment for merchandise, record transactions, and send items such as checks or money orders for further processing.

16) Inspect outgoing work for compliance with customers' specifications.

17) Recommend type of packing or labeling needed on order.

18) Adjust inventory records to reflect product movement.

Knowledge / Knowledge Definitions

Knowledge	Knowledge Definitions
Customer and Personal Service	Knowledge of principles and processes for providing customer and personal services. This includes customer needs assessment, meeting quality standards for services, and evaluation of customer satisfaction.
Sales and Marketing	Knowledge of principles and methods for showing, promoting, and selling products or services. This includes marketing strategy and tactics, product demonstration, sales techniques, and sales control systems.
Clerical	Knowledge of administrative and clerical procedures and systems such as word processing, managing files and records, stenography and transcription, designing forms, and other office procedures and terminology.
Mathematics	Knowledge of arithmetic, algebra, geometry, calculus, statistics, and their applications.
Administration and Management	Knowledge of business and management principles involved in strategic planning, resource allocation, human resources modeling, leadership technique, production methods, and coordination of people and resources.
Production and Processing	Knowledge of raw materials, production processes, quality control, costs, and other techniques for maximizing the effective manufacture and distribution of goods.
Building and Construction	Knowledge of materials, methods, and the tools involved in the construction or repair of houses, buildings, or other structures such as highways and roads.
English Language	Knowledge of the structure and content of the English language including the meaning and spelling of words, rules of composition, and grammar.
Computers and Electronics	Knowledge of circuit boards, processors, chips, electronic equipment, and computer hardware and software, including applications and programming.
Economics and Accounting	Knowledge of economic and accounting principles and practices, the financial markets, banking and the analysis and reporting of financial data.
Public Safety and Security	Knowledge of relevant equipment, policies, procedures, and strategies to promote effective local, state, or national security operations for the protection of people, data, property, and institutions.
Telecommunications	Knowledge of transmission, broadcasting, switching, control, and operation of telecommunications systems.
Design	Knowledge of design techniques, tools, and principles involved in production of precision technical plans, blueprints, drawings, and models.
Communications and Media	Knowledge of media production, communication, and dissemination techniques and methods. This includes alternative ways to inform and entertain via written, oral, and visual media.
Mechanical	Knowledge of machines and tools, including their designs, uses, repair, and maintenance.
Chemistry	Knowledge of the chemical composition, structure, and properties of substances and of the chemical processes and transformations that they undergo. This includes uses of chemicals and their interactions, danger signs, production techniques, and disposal methods.
Transportation	Knowledge of principles and methods for moving people or goods by air, rail, sea, or road, including the relative costs and benefits.
Personnel and Human Resources	Knowledge of principles and procedures for personnel recruitment, selection, training, compensation and benefits, labor relations and negotiation, and personnel information systems.
Physics	Knowledge and prediction of physical principles, laws, their interrelationships, and applications to understanding fluid, material, and atmospheric dynamics, and mechanical, electrical, atomic and sub-atomic structures and processes.
Education and Training	Knowledge of principles and methods for curriculum and training design, teaching and instruction for individuals and groups, and the measurement of training effects.
Geography	Knowledge of principles and methods for describing the features of land, sea, and air masses, including their physical characteristics, locations, interrelationships, and distribution of plant, animal, and human life.
Psychology	Knowledge of human behavior and performance; individual differences in ability, personality, and interests; learning and motivation; psychological research methods; and the assessment and treatment of behavioral and affective disorders.
Foreign Language	Knowledge of the structure and content of a foreign (non-English) language including the meaning and spelling of words, rules of composition and grammar, and pronunciation.
Food Production	Knowledge of techniques and equipment for planting, growing, and harvesting food products (both plant and animal) for consumption, including storage/handling techniques.
Philosophy and Theology	Knowledge of different philosophical systems and religions. This includes their basic principles, values, ethics, ways of thinking, customs, practices, and their impact on human culture.
Biology	Knowledge of plant and animal organisms, their tissues, cells, functions, interdependencies, and interactions with each other and the environment.

Engineering and Technology	Knowledge of the practical application of engineering science and technology. This includes applying principles, techniques, procedures, and equipment to the design and production of various goods and services.
Sociology and Anthropology	Knowledge of group behavior and dynamics, societal trends and influences, human migrations, ethnicity, cultures and their history and origins.
Law and Government	Knowledge of laws, legal codes, court procedures, precedents, government regulations, executive orders, agency rules, and the democratic political process.
Medicine and Dentistry	Knowledge of the information and techniques needed to diagnose and treat human injuries, diseases, and deformities. This includes symptoms, treatment alternatives, drug properties and interactions, and preventive health-care measures.
History and Archeology	Knowledge of historical events and their causes, indicators, and effects on civilizations and cultures.
Fine Arts	Knowledge of the theory and techniques required to compose, produce, and perform works of music, dance, visual arts, drama, and sculpture.
Therapy and Counseling	Knowledge of principles, methods, and procedures for diagnosis, treatment, and rehabilitation of physical and mental dysfunctions, and for career counseling and guidance.

Skills	Skills Definitions
Reading Comprehension	Understanding written sentences and paragraphs in work related documents.
Active Listening	Giving full attention to what other people are saying, taking time to understand the points being made, asking questions as appropriate, and not interrupting at inappropriate times.
Speaking	Talking to others to convey information effectively.
Time Management	Managing one's own time and the time of others.
Writing	Communicating effectively in writing as appropriate for the needs of the audience.
Service Orientation	Actively looking for ways to help people.
Mathematics	Using mathematics to solve problems.
Active Learning	Understanding the implications of new information for both current and future problem-solving and decision-making.
Coordination	Adjusting actions in relation to others' actions.
Critical Thinking	Using logic and reasoning to identify the strengths and weaknesses of alternative solutions, conclusions or approaches to problems.
Monitoring	Monitoring/Assessing performance of yourself, other individuals, or organizations to make improvements or take corrective action.
Social Perceptiveness	Being aware of others' reactions and understanding why they react as they do.
Persuasion	Persuading others to change their minds or behavior.
Negotiation	Bringing others together and trying to reconcile differences.
Learning Strategies	Selecting and using training/instructional methods and procedures appropriate for the situation when learning or teaching new things.
Troubleshooting	Determining causes of operating errors and deciding what to do about it.
Equipment Selection	Determining the kind of tools and equipment needed to do a job.
Management of Personnel Resources	Motivating, developing, and directing people as they work, identifying the best people for the job.
Judgment and Decision Making	Considering the relative costs and benefits of potential actions to choose the most appropriate one.
Instructing	Teaching others how to do something.
Complex Problem Solving	Identifying complex problems and reviewing related information to develop and evaluate options and implement solutions.
Management of Financial Resources	Determining how money will be spent to get the work done, and accounting for these expenditures.
Quality Control Analysis	Conducting tests and inspections of products, services, or processes to evaluate quality or performance.
Equipment Maintenance	Performing routine maintenance on equipment and determining when and what kind of maintenance is needed.
Systems Evaluation	Identifying measures or indicators of system performance and the actions needed to improve or correct performance, relative to the goals of the system.
Repairing	Repairing machines or systems using the needed tools.
Technology Design	Generating or adapting equipment and technology to serve user needs.

Systems Analysis	Determining how a system should work and how changes in conditions, operations, and the environment will affect outcomes.
Installation	Installing equipment, machines, wiring, or programs to meet specifications.
Operation and Control	Controlling operations of equipment or systems.
Programming	Writing computer programs for various purposes.
Management of Material Resources	Obtaining and seeing to the appropriate use of equipment, facilities, and materials needed to do certain work.
Operations Analysis	Analyzing needs and product requirements to create a design.
Operation Monitoring	Watching gauges, dials, or other indicators to make sure a machine is working properly.
Science	Using scientific rules and methods to solve problems.

Ability	Ability Definitions
Oral Expression	The ability to communicate information and ideas in speaking so others will understand.
Oral Comprehension	The ability to listen to and understand information and ideas presented through spoken words and sentences.
Near Vision	The ability to see details at close range (within a few feet of the observer).
Speech Clarity	The ability to speak clearly so others can understand you.
Speech Recognition	The ability to identify and understand the speech of another person.
Problem Sensitivity	The ability to tell when something is wrong or is likely to go wrong. It does not involve solving the problem, only recognizing there is a problem.
Written Comprehension	The ability to read and understand information and ideas presented in writing.
Written Expression	The ability to communicate information and ideas in writing so others will understand.
Selective Attention	The ability to concentrate on a task over a period of time without being distracted.
Inductive Reasoning	The ability to combine pieces of information to form general rules or conclusions (includes finding a relationship among seemingly unrelated events).
Information Ordering	The ability to arrange things or actions in a certain order or pattern according to a specific rule or set of rules (e.g., patterns of numbers, letters, words, pictures, mathematical operations).
Deductive Reasoning	The ability to apply general rules to specific problems to produce answers that make sense.
Finger Dexterity	The ability to make precisely coordinated movements of the fingers of one or both hands to grasp, manipulate, or assemble very small objects.
Perceptual Speed	The ability to quickly and accurately compare similarities and differences among sets of letters, numbers, objects, pictures, or patterns. The things to be compared may be presented at the same time or one after the other. This ability also includes comparing a presented object with a remembered object.
Category Flexibility	The ability to generate or use different sets of rules for combining or grouping things in different ways.
Flexibility of Closure	The ability to identify or detect a known pattern (a figure, object, word, or sound) that is hidden in other distracting material.
Speed of Closure	The ability to quickly make sense of, combine, and organize information into meaningful patterns.
Number Facility	The ability to add, subtract, multiply, or divide quickly and correctly.
Auditory Attention	The ability to focus on a single source of sound in the presence of other distracting sounds.
Mathematical Reasoning	The ability to choose the right mathematical methods or formulas to solve a problem.
Fluency of Ideas	The ability to come up with a number of ideas about a topic (the number of ideas is important, not their quality, correctness, or creativity).
Time Sharing	The ability to shift back and forth between two or more activities or sources of information (such as speech, sounds, touch, or other sources).
Visualization	The ability to imagine how something will look after it is moved around or when its parts are moved or rearranged.
Originality	The ability to come up with unusual or clever ideas about a given topic or situation, or to develop creative ways to solve a problem.
Far Vision	The ability to see details at a distance.
Memorization	The ability to remember information such as words, numbers, pictures, and procedures.

Trunk Strength	The ability to use your abdominal and lower back muscles to support part of the body repeatedly or continuously over time without 'giving out' or fatiguing.
Visual Color Discrimination	The ability to match or detect differences between colors, including shades of color and brightness.
Arm-Hand Steadiness	The ability to keep your hand and arm steady while moving your arm or while holding your arm and hand in one position.
Hearing Sensitivity	The ability to detect or tell the differences between sounds that vary in pitch and loudness.
Depth Perception	The ability to judge which of several objects is closer or farther away from you, or to judge the distance between you and an object.
Manual Dexterity	The ability to quickly move your hand, your hand together with your arm, or your two hands to grasp, manipulate, or assemble objects.
Control Precision	The ability to quickly and repeatedly adjust the controls of a machine or a vehicle to exact positions.
Wrist-Finger Speed	The ability to make fast, simple, repeated movements of the fingers, hands, and wrists.
Static Strength	The ability to exert maximum muscle force to lift, push, pull, or carry objects.
Multilimb Coordination	The ability to coordinate two or more limbs (for example, two arms, two legs, or one leg and one arm) while sitting, standing, or lying down. It does not involve performing the activities while the whole body is in motion.
Extent Flexibility	The ability to bend, stretch, twist, or reach with your body, arms, and/or legs.
Response Orientation	The ability to choose quickly between two or more movements in response to two or more different signals (lights, sounds, pictures). It includes the speed with which the correct response is started with the hand, foot, or other body part.
Reaction Time	The ability to quickly respond (with the hand, finger, or foot) to a signal (sound, light, picture) when it appears.
Speed of Limb Movement	The ability to quickly move the arms and legs.
Gross Body Equilibrium	The ability to keep or regain your body balance or stay upright when in an unstable position.
Spatial Orientation	The ability to know your location in relation to the environment or to know where other objects are in relation to you.
Rate Control	The ability to time your movements or the movement of a piece of equipment in anticipation of changes in the speed and/or direction of a moving object or scene.
Explosive Strength	The ability to use short bursts of muscle force to propel oneself (as in jumping or sprinting), or to throw an object.
Dynamic Strength	The ability to exert muscle force repeatedly or continuously over time. This involves muscular endurance and resistance to muscle fatigue.
Dynamic Flexibility	The ability to quickly and repeatedly bend, stretch, twist, or reach out with your body, arms, and/or legs.
Night Vision	The ability to see under low light conditions.
Peripheral Vision	The ability to see objects or movement of objects to one's side when the eyes are looking ahead.
Sound Localization	The ability to tell the direction from which a sound originated.
Glare Sensitivity	The ability to see objects in the presence of glare or bright lighting.
Stamina	The ability to exert yourself physically over long periods of time without getting winded or out of breath.
Gross Body Coordination	The ability to coordinate the movement of your arms, legs, and torso together when the whole body is in motion.

Work_Activity	Work_Activity Definitions
Interacting With Computers	Using computers and computer systems (including hardware and software) to program, write software, set up functions, enter data, or process information.
Getting Information	Observing, receiving, and otherwise obtaining information from all relevant sources.
Establishing and Maintaining Interpersonal Relatio	Developing constructive and cooperative working relationships with others, and maintaining them over time.
Identifying Objects, Actions, and Events	Identifying information by categorizing, estimating, recognizing differences or similarities, and detecting changes in circumstances or events.
Performing Administrative Activities	Performing day-to-day administrative tasks such as maintaining information files and processing paperwork.
Processing Information	Compiling, coding, categorizing, calculating, tabulating, auditing, or verifying information or data.
Updating and Using Relevant Knowledge	Keeping up-to-date technically and applying new knowledge to your job.

Communicating with Persons Outside Organization	Communicating with people outside the organization, representing the organization to customers, the public, government, and other external sources. This information can be exchanged in person, in writing, or by telephone or e-mail.
Documenting/Recording Information	Entering, transcribing, recording, storing, or maintaining information in written or electronic/magnetic form.
Making Decisions and Solving Problems	Analyzing information and evaluating results to choose the best solution and solve problems.
Analyzing Data or Information	Identifying the underlying principles, reasons, or facts of information by breaking down information or data into separate parts.
Communicating with Supervisors, Peers, or Subordin	Providing information to supervisors, co-workers, and subordinates by telephone, in written form, e-mail, or in person.
Resolving Conflicts and Negotiating with Others	Handling complaints, settling disputes, and resolving grievances and conflicts, or otherwise negotiating with others.
Organizing, Planning, and Prioritizing Work	Developing specific goals and plans to prioritize, organize, and accomplish your work.
Selling or Influencing Others	Convincing others to buy merchandise/goods or to otherwise change their minds or actions.
Interpreting the Meaning of Information for Others	Translating or explaining what information means and how it can be used.
Estimating the Quantifiable Characteristics of Pro	Estimating sizes, distances, and quantities; or determining time, costs, resources, or materials needed to perform a work activity.
Monitor Processes, Materials, or Surroundings	Monitoring and reviewing information from materials, events, or the environment, to detect or assess problems.
Performing for or Working Directly with the Public	Performing for people or dealing directly with the public. This includes serving customers in restaurants and stores, and receiving clients or guests.
Training and Teaching Others	Identifying the educational needs of others, developing formal educational or training programs or classes, and teaching or instructing others.
Coordinating the Work and Activities of Others	Getting members of a group to work together to accomplish tasks.
Judging the Qualities of Things, Services, or Peop	Assessing the value, importance, or quality of things or people.
Evaluating Information to Determine Compliance wit	Using relevant information and individual judgment to determine whether events or processes comply with laws, regulations, or standards.
Monitoring and Controlling Resources	Monitoring and controlling resources and overseeing the spending of money.
Guiding, Directing, and Motivating Subordinates	Providing guidance and direction to subordinates, including setting performance standards and monitoring performance.
Controlling Machines and Processes	Using either control mechanisms or direct physical activity to operate machines or processes (not including computers or vehicles).
Performing General Physical Activities	Performing physical activities that require considerable use of your arms and legs and moving your whole body, such as climbing, lifting, balancing, walking, stooping, and handling of materials.
Scheduling Work and Activities	Scheduling events, programs, and activities, as well as the work of others.
Assisting and Caring for Others	Providing personal assistance, medical attention, emotional support, or other personal care to others such as coworkers, customers, or patients.
Developing and Building Teams	Encouraging and building mutual trust, respect, and cooperation among team members.
Inspecting Equipment, Structures, or Material	Inspecting equipment, structures, or materials to identify the cause of errors or other problems or defects.
Handling and Moving Objects	Using hands and arms in handling, installing, positioning, and moving materials, and manipulating things.
Coaching and Developing Others	Identifying the developmental needs of others and coaching, mentoring, or otherwise helping others to improve their knowledge or skills.
Provide Consultation and Advice to Others	Providing guidance and expert advice to management or other groups on technical, systems-, or process-related topics.
Operating Vehicles, Mechanized Devices, or Equipme	Running, maneuvering, navigating, or driving vehicles or mechanized equipment, such as forklifts, passenger vehicles, aircraft, or water craft.
Drafting, Laying Out, and Specifying Technical Dev	Providing documentation, detailed instructions, drawings, or specifications to tell others about how devices, parts, equipment, or structures are to be fabricated, constructed, assembled, modified, maintained, or used.
Developing Objectives and Strategies	Establishing long-range objectives and specifying the strategies and actions to achieve them.

Thinking Creatively	Developing, designing, or creating new applications, ideas, relationships, systems, or products, including artistic contributions.
Repairing and Maintaining Electronic Equipment	Servicing, repairing, calibrating, regulating, fine-tuning, or testing machines, devices, and equipment that operate primarily on the basis of electrical or electronic (not mechanical) principles.
Staffing Organizational Units	Recruiting, interviewing, selecting, hiring, and promoting employees in an organization.
Repairing and Maintaining Mechanical Equipment	Servicing, repairing, adjusting, and testing machines, devices, moving parts, and equipment that operate primarily on the basis of mechanical (not electronic) principles.

Work_Context	Work_Context Definitions
Indoors, Environmentally Controlled	How often does this job require working indoors in environmentally controlled conditions?
Importance of Repeating Same Tasks	How important is repeating the same physical activities (e.g., key entry) or mental activities (e.g., checking entries in a ledger) over and over, without stopping, to performing this job?
Importance of Being Exact or Accurate	How important is being very exact or highly accurate in performing this job?
Contact With Others	How much does this job require the worker to be in contact with others (face-to-face, by telephone, or otherwise) in order to perform it?
Deal With External Customers	How important is it to work with external customers or the public in this job?
Deal With Unpleasant or Angry People	How frequently does the worker have to deal with unpleasant, angry, or discourteous individuals as part of the job requirements?
Telephone	How often do you have telephone conversations in this job?
Freedom to Make Decisions	How much decision making freedom, without supervision, does the job offer?
Structured versus Unstructured Work	To what extent is this job structured for the worker, rather than allowing the worker to determine tasks, priorities, and goals?
Face-to-Face Discussions	How often do you have to have face-to-face discussions with individuals or teams in this job?
Frequency of Conflict Situations	How often are there conflict situations the employee has to face in this job?
Electronic Mail	How often do you use electronic mail in this job?
Physical Proximity	To what extent does this job require the worker to perform job tasks in close physical proximity to other people?
Spend Time Sitting	How much does this job require sitting?
Exposed to Contaminants	How often does this job require working exposed to contaminants (such as pollutants, gases, dust or odors)?
Very Hot or Cold Temperatures	How often does this job require working in very hot (above 90 F degrees) or very cold (below 32 F degrees) temperatures?
Work With Work Group or Team	How important is it to work with others in a group or team in this job?
Time Pressure	How often does this job require the worker to meet strict deadlines?
Frequency of Decision Making	How frequently is the worker required to make decisions that affect other people, the financial resources, and/or the image and reputation of the organization?
Coordinate or Lead Others	How important is it to coordinate or lead others in accomplishing work activities in this job?
Sounds, Noise Levels Are Distracting or Uncomforta	How often does this job require working exposed to sounds and noise levels that are distracting or uncomfortable?
Spend Time Making Repetitive Motions	How much does this job require making repetitive motions?
Responsible for Others' Health and Safety	How much responsibility is there for the health and safety of others in this job?
Impact of Decisions on Co-workers or Company Resul	How do the decisions an employee makes impact the results of co-workers, clients or the company?
Letters and Memos	How often does the job require written letters and memos?
Level of Competition	To what extent does this job require the worker to compete or to be aware of competitive pressures?
Consequence of Error	How serious would the result usually be if the worker made a mistake that was not readily correctable?
Outdoors, Exposed to Weather	How often does this job require working outdoors, exposed to all weather conditions?
Spend Time Using Your Hands to Handle, Control, or	How much does this job require using your hands to handle, control, or feel objects, tools or controls?
Indoors, Not Environmentally Controlled	How often does this job require working indoors in non-controlled environmental conditions (e.g., warehouse without heat)?

Outdoors, Under Cover	How often does this job require working outdoors, under cover (e.g., structure with roof but no walls)?
Spend Time Standing	How much does this job require standing?
Responsibility for Outcomes and Results	How responsible is the worker for work outcomes and results of other workers?
Degree of Automation	How automated is the job?
Pace Determined by Speed of Equipment	How important is it to this job that the pace is determined by the speed of equipment or machinery? (This does not refer to keeping busy at all times on this job.)
Exposed to Hazardous Equipment	How often does this job require exposure to hazardous equipment?
Spend Time Walking and Running	How much does this job require walking and running?
Cramped Work Space, Awkward Positions	How often does this job require working in cramped work spaces that requires getting into awkward positions?
Extremely Bright or Inadequate Lighting	How often does this job require working in extremely bright or inadequate lighting conditions?
Deal With Physically Aggressive People	How frequently does this job require the worker to deal with physical aggression of violent individuals?
Exposed to Minor Burns, Cuts, Bites, or Stings	How often does this job require exposure to minor burns, cuts, bites, or stings?
Wear Specialized Protective or Safety Equipment su	How much does this job require wearing specialized protective or safety equipment such as breathing apparatus, safety harness, full protection suits, or radiation protection?
Public Speaking	How often do you have to perform public speaking in this job?
Spend Time Kneeling, Crouching, Stooping, or Crawl	How much does this job require kneeling, crouching, stooping, or crawling?
Exposed to Hazardous Conditions	How often does this job require exposure to hazardous conditions?
Spend Time Bending or Twisting the Body	How much does this job require bending or twisting your body?
Wear Common Protective or Safety Equipment such as	How much does this job require wearing common protective or safety equipment such as safety shoes, glasses, gloves, hard hats or live jackets?
Exposed to High Places	How often does this job require exposure to high places?
Spend Time Climbing Ladders, Scaffolds, or Poles	How much does this job require climbing ladders, scaffolds, or poles?
Exposed to Disease or Infections	How often does this job require exposure to disease/infections?
In an Enclosed Vehicle or Equipment	How often does this job require working in a closed vehicle or equipment (e.g., car)?
Spend Time Keeping or Regaining Balance	How much does this job require keeping or regaining your balance?
In an Open Vehicle or Equipment	How often does this job require working in an open vehicle or equipment (e.g., tractor)?
Exposed to Whole Body Vibration	How often does this job require exposure to whole body vibration (e.g., operate a jackhammer)?
Exposed to Radiation	How often does this job require exposure to radiation?

Job Zone Component	Job Zone Component Definitions
Title	Job Zone Two: Some Preparation Needed
Overall Experience	Some previous work-related skill, knowledge, or experience may be helpful in these occupations, but usually is not needed. For example, a drywall installer might benefit from experience installing drywall, but an inexperienced person could still learn to be an installer with little difficulty.
Job Training	Employees in these occupations need anywhere from a few months to one year of working with experienced employees.
Job Zone Examples	These occupations often involve using your knowledge and skills to help others. Examples include drywall installers, fire inspectors, flight attendants, pharmacy technicians, salespersons (retail), and tellers.
SVP Range	(4.0 to < 6.0)
Education	These occupations usually require a high school diploma and may require some vocational training or job-related course work. In some cases, an associate's or bachelor's degree could be needed.

Work_Styles	Work_Styles Definitions
Dependability	Job requires being reliable, responsible, and dependable, and fulfilling obligations.
Integrity	Job requires being honest and ethical.

Attention to Detail	Job requires being careful about detail and thorough in completing work tasks.
Persistence	Job requires persistence in the face of obstacles.
Cooperation	Job requires being pleasant with others on the job and displaying a good-natured, cooperative attitude.
Self Control	Job requires maintaining composure, keeping emotions in check, controlling anger, and avoiding aggressive behavior, even in very difficult situations.
Initiative	Job requires a willingness to take on responsibilities and challenges.
Independence	Job requires developing one's own ways of doing things, guiding oneself with little or no supervision, and depending on oneself to get things done.
Stress Tolerance	Job requires accepting criticism and dealing calmly and effectively with high stress situations.
Achievement/Effort	Job requires establishing and maintaining personally challenging achievement goals and exerting effort toward mastering tasks.
Adaptability/Flexibility	Job requires being open to change (positive or negative) and to considerable variety in the workplace.
Social Orientation	Job requires preferring to work with others rather than alone, and being personally connected with others on the job.
Leadership	Job requires a willingness to lead, take charge, and offer opinions and direction.
Innovation	Job requires creativity and alternative thinking to develop new ideas for and answers to work-related problems.
Analytical Thinking	Job requires analyzing information and using logic to address work-related issues and problems.
Concern for Others	Job requires being sensitive to others' needs and feelings and being understanding and helpful on the job.

43-4161.00 - Human Resources Assistants, Except Payroll and Timekeeping

Compile and keep personnel records. Record data for each employee, such as address, weekly earnings, absences, amount of sales or production, supervisory reports on ability, and date of and reason for termination. Compile and type reports from employment records. File employment records. Search employee files and furnish information to authorized persons.

Tasks

1) Examine employee files to answer inquiries and provide information for personnel actions.

2) Answer questions regarding examinations, eligibility, salaries, benefits, and other pertinent information.

3) Record data for each employee, including such information as addresses, weekly earnings, absences, amount of sales or production, supervisory reports on performance, and dates of and reasons for terminations.

4) Process, verify, and maintain documentation relating to personnel activities such as staffing, recruitment, training, grievances, performance evaluations, and classifications.

5) Gather personnel records from other departments and/or employees.

6) Search employee files in order to obtain information for authorized persons and organizations, such as credit bureaus and finance companies.

7) Process and review employment applications in order to evaluate qualifications or eligibility of applicants.

8) Arrange for advertising or posting of job vacancies, and notify eligible workers of position availability.

9) Compile and prepare reports and documents pertaining to personnel activities.

10) Provide assistance in administering employee benefit programs and worker's compensation plans.

11) Inform job applicants of their acceptance or rejection of employment.

12) Request information from law enforcement officials, previous employers, and other references in order to determine applicants' employment acceptability.

13) Select applicants meeting specified job requirements and refer them to hiring personnel.

14) Interview job applicants to obtain and verify information used to screen and evaluate them.

15) Arrange for in-house and external training activities.

16) Prepare badges, passes, and identification cards, and perform other security-related duties.

17) Administer and score applicant and employee aptitude, personality, and interest assessment instruments.

Knowledge	Knowledge Definitions
Clerical	Knowledge of administrative and clerical procedures and systems such as word processing, managing files and records, stenography and transcription, designing forms, and other office procedures and terminology.
Personnel and Human Resources	Knowledge of principles and procedures for personnel recruitment, selection, training, compensation and benefits, labor relations and negotiation, and personnel information systems.
English Language	Knowledge of the structure and content of the English language including the meaning and spelling of words, rules of composition, and grammar.
Customer and Personal Service	Knowledge of principles and processes for providing customer and personal services. This includes customer needs assessment, meeting quality standards for services, and evaluation of customer satisfaction.
Administration and Management	Knowledge of business and management principles involved in strategic planning, resource allocation, human resources modeling, leadership technique, production methods, and coordination of people and resources.
Computers and Electronics	Knowledge of circuit boards, processors, chips, electronic equipment, and computer hardware and software, including applications and programming.
Mathematics	Knowledge of arithmetic, algebra, geometry, calculus, statistics, and their applications.
Education and Training	Knowledge of principles and methods for curriculum and training design, teaching and instruction for individuals and groups, and the measurement of training effects.
Law and Government	Knowledge of laws, legal codes, court procedures, precedents, government regulations, executive orders, agency rules, and the democratic political process.
Psychology	Knowledge of human behavior and performance; individual differences in ability, personality, and interests; learning and motivation; psychological research methods; and the assessment and treatment of behavioral and affective disorders.
Communications and Media	Knowledge of media production, communication, and dissemination techniques and methods. This includes alternative ways to inform and entertain via written, oral, and visual media.
Economics and Accounting	Knowledge of economic and accounting principles and practices, the financial markets, banking and the analysis and reporting of financial data.
Telecommunications	Knowledge of transmission, broadcasting, switching, control, and operation of telecommunications systems.
Public Safety and Security	Knowledge of relevant equipment, policies, procedures, and strategies to promote effective local, state, or national security operations for the protection of people, data, property, and institutions.
Sociology and Anthropology	Knowledge of group behavior and dynamics, societal trends and influences, human migrations, ethnicity, cultures and their history and origins.
Production and Processing	Knowledge of raw materials, production processes, quality control, costs, and other techniques for maximizing the effective manufacture and distribution of goods.
Therapy and Counseling	Knowledge of principles, methods, and procedures for diagnosis, treatment, and rehabilitation of physical and mental dysfunctions, and for career counseling and guidance.
Transportation	Knowledge of principles and methods for moving people or goods by air, rail, sea, or road, including the relative costs and benefits.
Philosophy and Theology	Knowledge of different philosophical systems and religions. This includes their basic principles, values, ethics, ways of thinking, customs, practices, and their impact on human culture.
Geography	Knowledge of principles and methods for describing the features of land, sea, and air masses, including their physical characteristics, locations, interrelationships, and distribution of plant, animal, and human life.
Medicine and Dentistry	Knowledge of the information and techniques needed to diagnose and treat human injuries, diseases, and deformities. This includes symptoms, treatment alternatives, drug properties and interactions, and preventive health-care measures.

Foreign Language	Knowledge of the structure and content of a foreign (non-English) language including the meaning and spelling of words, rules of composition and grammar, and pronunciation.
Sales and Marketing	Knowledge of principles and methods for showing, promoting, and selling products or services. This includes marketing strategy and tactics, product demonstration, sales techniques, and sales control systems.
History and Archeology	Knowledge of historical events and their causes, indicators, and effects on civilizations and cultures.
Fine Arts	Knowledge of the theory and techniques required to compose, produce, and perform works of music, dance, visual arts, drama, and sculpture.
Biology	Knowledge of plant and animal organisms, their tissues, cells, functions, interdependencies, and interactions with each other and the environment.
Engineering and Technology	Knowledge of the practical application of engineering science and technology. This includes applying principles, techniques, procedures, and equipment to the design and production of various goods and services.
Mechanical	Knowledge of machines and tools, including their designs, uses, repair, and maintenance.
Physics	Knowledge and prediction of physical principles, laws, their interrelationships, and applications to understanding fluid, material, and atmospheric dynamics, and mechanical, electrical, atomic and sub-atomic structures and processes.
Chemistry	Knowledge of the chemical composition, structure, and properties of substances and of the chemical processes and transformations that they undergo. This includes uses of chemicals and their interactions, danger signs, production techniques, and disposal methods.
Design	Knowledge of design techniques, tools, and principles involved in production of precision technical plans, blueprints, drawings, and models.
Food Production	Knowledge of techniques and equipment for planting, growing, and harvesting food products (both plant and animal) for consumption, including storage/handling techniques.
Building and Construction	Knowledge of materials, methods, and the tools involved in the construction or repair of houses, buildings, or other structures such as highways and roads.

Skills	Skills Definitions
Active Listening	Giving full attention to what other people are saying, taking time to understand the points being made, asking questions as appropriate, and not interrupting at inappropriate times.
Reading Comprehension	Understanding written sentences and paragraphs in work related documents.
Speaking	Talking to others to convey information effectively.
Time Management	Managing one's own time and the time of others.
Critical Thinking	Using logic and reasoning to identify the strengths and weaknesses of alternative solutions, conclusions or approaches to problems.
Writing	Communicating effectively in writing as appropriate for the needs of the audience.
Mathematics	Using mathematics to solve problems.
Learning Strategies	Selecting and using training/instructional methods and procedures appropriate for the situation when learning or teaching new things.
Instructing	Teaching others how to do something.
Social Perceptiveness	Being aware of others' reactions and understanding why they react as they do.
Service Orientation	Actively looking for ways to help people.
Active Learning	Understanding the implications of new information for both current and future problem-solving and decision-making.
Monitoring	Monitoring/Assessing performance of yourself, other individuals, or organizations to make improvements or take corrective action.
Coordination	Adjusting actions in relation to others' actions.
Judgment and Decision Making	Considering the relative costs and benefits of potential actions to choose the most appropriate one.
Management of Personnel Resources	Motivating, developing, and directing people as they work, identifying the best people for the job.
Complex Problem Solving	Identifying complex problems and reviewing related information to develop and evaluate options and implement solutions.
Negotiation	Bringing others together and trying to reconcile differences.
Management of Financial Resources	Determining how money will be spent to get the work done, and accounting for these expenditures.

Persuasion	Persuading others to change their minds or behavior.
Operations Analysis	Analyzing needs and product requirements to create a design.
Equipment Selection	Determining the kind of tools and equipment needed to do a job.
Operation and Control	Controlling operations of equipment or systems.
Systems Evaluation	Identifying measures or indicators of system performance and the actions needed to improve or correct performance, relative to the goals of the system.
Quality Control Analysis	Conducting tests and inspections of products, services, or processes to evaluate quality or performance.
Systems Analysis	Determining how a system should work and how changes in conditions, operations, and the environment will affect outcomes.
Troubleshooting	Determining causes of operating errors and deciding what to do about it.
Management of Material Resources	Obtaining and seeing to the appropriate use of equipment, facilities, and materials needed to do certain work.
Operation Monitoring	Watching gauges, dials, or other indicators to make sure a machine is working properly.
Technology Design	Generating or adapting equipment and technology to serve user needs.
Programming	Writing computer programs for various purposes.
Equipment Maintenance	Performing routine maintenance on equipment and determining when and what kind of maintenance is needed.
Science	Using scientific rules and methods to solve problems.
Installation	Installing equipment, machines, wiring, or programs to meet specifications.
Repairing	Repairing machines or systems using the needed tools.

Ability	Ability Definitions
Written Comprehension	The ability to read and understand information and ideas presented in writing.
Oral Comprehension	The ability to listen to and understand information and ideas presented through spoken words and sentences.
Oral Expression	The ability to communicate information and ideas in speaking so others will understand.
Written Expression	The ability to communicate information and ideas in writing so others will understand.
Speech Clarity	The ability to speak clearly so others can understand you.
Near Vision	The ability to see details at close range (within a few feet of the observer).
Problem Sensitivity	The ability to tell when something is wrong or is likely to go wrong. It does not involve solving the problem, only recognizing there is a problem.
Speech Recognition	The ability to identify and understand the speech of another person.
Information Ordering	The ability to arrange things or actions in a certain order or pattern according to a specific rule or set of rules (e.g., patterns of numbers, letters, words, pictures, mathematical operations).
Selective Attention	The ability to concentrate on a task over a period of time without being distracted.
Inductive Reasoning	The ability to combine pieces of information to form general rules or conclusions (includes finding a relationship among seemingly unrelated events).
Deductive Reasoning	The ability to apply general rules to specific problems to produce answers that make sense.
Flexibility of Closure	The ability to identify or detect a known pattern (a figure, object, word, or sound) that is hidden in other distracting material.
Category Flexibility	The ability to generate or use different sets of rules for combining or grouping things in different ways.
Perceptual Speed	The ability to quickly and accurately compare similarities and differences among sets of letters, numbers, objects, pictures, or patterns. The things to be compared may be presented at the same time or one after the other. This ability also includes comparing a presented object with a remembered object.
Finger Dexterity	The ability to make precisely coordinated movements of the fingers of one or both hands to grasp, manipulate, or assemble very small objects.
Time Sharing	The ability to shift back and forth between two or more activities or sources of information (such as speech, sounds, touch, or other sources).
Fluency of Ideas	The ability to come up with a number of ideas about a topic (the number of ideas is important, not their quality, correctness, or creativity).
Far Vision	The ability to see details at a distance.

946

		Work_Activity	Work_Activity Definitions
Speed of Closure	The ability to quickly make sense of, combine, and organize information into meaningful patterns.	Establishing and Maintaining Interpersonal Relatio	Developing constructive and cooperative working relationships with others, and maintaining them over time.
Originality	The ability to come up with unusual or clever ideas about a given topic or situation, or to develop creative ways to solve a problem.	Communicating with Supervisors, Peers, or Subordin	Providing information to supervisors, co-workers, and subordinates by telephone, in written form, e-mail, or in person.
Number Facility	The ability to add, subtract, multiply, or divide quickly and correctly.	Interacting With Computers	Using computers and computer systems (including hardware and software) to program, write software, set up functions, enter data, or process information.
Auditory Attention	The ability to focus on a single source of sound in the presence of other distracting sounds.	Performing Administrative Activities	Performing day-to-day administrative tasks such as maintaining information files and processing paperwork.
Memorization	The ability to remember information such as words, numbers, pictures, and procedures.	Organizing, Planning, and Prioritizing Work	Developing specific goals and plans to prioritize, organize, and accomplish your work.
Visualization	The ability to imagine how something will look after it is moved around or when its parts are moved or rearranged.	Getting Information	Observing, receiving, and otherwise obtaining information from all relevant sources.
Mathematical Reasoning	The ability to choose the right mathematical methods or formulas to solve a problem.	Evaluating Information to Determine Compliance wit	Using relevant information and individual judgment to determine whether events or processes comply with laws, regulations, or standards.
Visual Color Discrimination	The ability to match or detect differences between colors, including shades of color and brightness.	Communicating with Persons Outside Organization	Communicating with people outside the organization, representing the organization to customers, the public, government, and other external sources. This information can be exchanged in person, in writing, or by telephone or e-mail.
Hearing Sensitivity	The ability to detect or tell the differences between sounds that vary in pitch and loudness.		
Trunk Strength	The ability to use your abdominal and lower back muscles to support part of the body repeatedly or continuously over time without 'giving out' or fatiguing.	Processing Information	Compiling, coding, categorizing, calculating, tabulating, auditing, or verifying information or data.
Arm-Hand Steadiness	The ability to keep your hand and arm steady while moving your arm or while holding your arm and hand in one position.	Making Decisions and Solving Problems	Analyzing information and evaluating results to choose the best solution and solve problems.
Static Strength	The ability to exert maximum muscle force to lift, push, pull, or carry objects.	Documenting/Recording Information	Entering, transcribing, recording, storing, or maintaining information in written or electronic/magnetic form.
Wrist-Finger Speed	The ability to make fast, simple, repeated movements of the fingers, hands, and wrists.	Updating and Using Relevant Knowledge	Keeping up-to-date technically and applying new knowledge to your job.
Extent Flexibility	The ability to bend, stretch, twist, or reach with your body, arms, and/or legs.	Judging the Qualities of Things, Services, or Peop	Assessing the value, importance, or quality of things or people.
Manual Dexterity	The ability to quickly move your hand, your hand together with your arm, or your two hands to grasp, manipulate, or assemble objects.	Identifying Objects, Actions, and Events	Identifying information by categorizing, estimating, recognizing differences or similarities, and detecting changes in circumstances or events.
Response Orientation	The ability to choose quickly between two or more movements in response to two or more different signals (lights, sounds, pictures). It includes the speed with which the correct response is started with the hand, foot, or other body part.	Resolving Conflicts and Negotiating with Others	Handling complaints, settling disputes, and resolving grievances and conflicts, or otherwise negotiating with others.
Multilimb Coordination	The ability to coordinate two or more limbs (for example, two arms, two legs, or one leg and one arm) while sitting, standing, or lying down. It does not involve performing the activities while the whole body is in motion.	Analyzing Data or Information	Identifying the underlying principles, reasons, or facts of information by breaking down information or data into separate parts.
Control Precision	The ability to quickly and repeatedly adjust the controls of a machine or a vehicle to exact positions.	Scheduling Work and Activities	Scheduling events, programs, and activities, as well as the work of others.
Spatial Orientation	The ability to know your location in relation to the environment or to know where other objects are in relation to you.	Monitor Processes, Materials, or Surroundings	Monitoring and reviewing information from materials, events, or the environment, to detect or assess problems.
Rate Control	The ability to time your movements or the movement of a piece of equipment in anticipation of changes in the speed and/or direction of a moving object or scene.		
Gross Body Equilibrium	The ability to keep or regain your body balance or stay upright when in an unstable position.	Thinking Creatively	Developing, designing, or creating new applications, ideas, relationships, systems, or products, including artistic contributions.
Reaction Time	The ability to quickly respond (with the hand, finger, or foot) to a signal (sound, light, picture) when it appears.	Coordinating the Work and Activities of Others	Getting members of a group to work together to accomplish tasks.
Speed of Limb Movement	The ability to quickly move the arms and legs.	Interpreting the Meaning of Information for Others	Translating or explaining what information means and how it can be used.
Stamina	The ability to exert yourself physically over long periods of time without getting winded or out of breath.	Staffing Organizational Units	Recruiting, interviewing, selecting, hiring, and promoting employees in an organization.
Dynamic Strength	The ability to exert muscle force repeatedly or continuously over time. This involves muscular endurance and resistance to muscle fatigue.	Assisting and Caring for Others	Providing personal assistance, medical attention, emotional support, or other personal care to others such as coworkers, customers, or patients.
Gross Body Coordination	The ability to coordinate the movement of your arms, legs, and torso together when the whole body is in motion.	Performing for or Working Directly with the Public	Performing for people or dealing directly with the public. This includes serving customers in restaurants and stores, and receiving clients or guests.
Explosive Strength	The ability to use short bursts of muscle force to propel oneself (as in jumping or sprinting), or to throw an object.	Developing Objectives and Strategies	Establishing long-range objectives and specifying the strategies and actions to achieve them.
Night Vision	The ability to see under low light conditions.	Provide Consultation and Advice to Others	Providing guidance and expert advice to management or other groups on technical, systems-, or process-related topics.
Peripheral Vision	The ability to see objects or movement of objects to one's side when the eyes are looking ahead.	Developing and Building Teams	Encouraging and building mutual trust, respect, and cooperation among team members.
Depth Perception	The ability to judge which of several objects is closer or farther away from you, or to judge the distance between you and an object.	Monitoring and Controlling Resources	Monitoring and controlling resources and overseeing the spending of money.
Glare Sensitivity	The ability to see objects in the presence of glare or bright lighting.	Training and Teaching Others	Identifying the educational needs of others, developing formal educational or training programs or classes, and teaching or instructing others.
Sound Localization	The ability to tell the direction from which a sound originated.		
Dynamic Flexibility	The ability to quickly and repeatedly bend, stretch, twist, or reach out with your body, arms, and/or legs.	Estimating the Quantifiable Characteristics of Pro	Estimating sizes, distances, and quantities; or determining time, costs, resources, or materials needed to perform a work activity.

947

Coaching and Developing Others	Identifying the developmental needs of others and coaching, mentoring, or otherwise helping others to improve their knowledge or skills.	Degree of Automation	How automated is the job?
Inspecting Equipment, Structures, or Material	Inspecting equipment, structures, or materials to identify the cause of errors or other problems or defects.	Frequency of Conflict Situations	How often are there conflict situations the employee has to face in this job?
Guiding, Directing, and Motivating Subordinates	Providing guidance and direction to subordinates, including setting performance standards and monitoring performance.	Physical Proximity	To what extent does this job require the worker to perform job tasks in close physical proximity to other people?
Handling and Moving Objects	Using hands and arms in handling, installing, positioning, and moving materials, and manipulating things.	Responsible for Others' Health and Safety	How much responsibility is there for the health and safety of others in this job?
Selling or Influencing Others	Convincing others to buy merchandise/goods or to otherwise change their minds or actions.	Consequence of Error	How serious would the result usually be if the worker made a mistake that was not readily correctable?
Performing General Physical Activities	Performing physical activities that require considerable use of your arms and legs and moving your whole body, such as climbing, lifting, balancing, walking, stooping, and handling of materials.	Public Speaking	How often do you have to perform public speaking in this job?
		Spend Time Using Your Hands to Handle, Control, or	How much does this job require using your hands to handle, control, or feel objects, tools or controls?
Controlling Machines and Processes	Using either control mechanisms or direct physical activity to operate machines or processes (not including computers or vehicles).	Spend Time Standing	How much does this job require standing?
Operating Vehicles, Mechanized Devices, or Equipme	Running, maneuvering, navigating, or driving vehicles or mechanized equipment, such as forklifts, passenger vehicles, aircraft, or water craft.	Exposed to Contaminants	How often does this job require working exposed to contaminants (such as pollutants, gases, dust or odors)?
		Spend Time Walking and Running	How much does this job require walking and running?
Drafting, Laying Out, and Specifying Technical Dev	Providing documentation, detailed instructions, drawings, or specifications to tell others about how devices, parts, equipment, or structures are to be fabricated, constructed, assembled, modified, maintained, or used.	Level of Competition	To what extent does this job require the worker to compete or to be aware of competitive pressures?
		Spend Time Bending or Twisting the Body	How much does this job require bending or twisting your body?
Repairing and Maintaining Electronic Equipment	Servicing, repairing, calibrating, regulating, fine-tuning, or testing machines, devices, and equipment that operate primarily on the basis of electrical or electronic (not mechanical) principles.	Extremely Bright or Inadequate Lighting	How often does this job require working in extremely bright or inadequate lighting conditions?
		Spend Time Kneeling, Crouching, Stooping, or Crawl	How much does this job require kneeling, crouching, stooping, or crawling?
Repairing and Maintaining Mechanical Equipment	Servicing, repairing, adjusting, and testing machines, devices, moving parts, and equipment that operate primarily on the basis of mechanical (not electronic) principles.	Cramped Work Space, Awkward Positions	How often does this job require working in cramped work spaces that requires getting into awkward positions?
		In an Enclosed Vehicle or Equipment	How often does this job require working in a closed vehicle or equipment (e.g., car)?
		Exposed to Minor Burns, Cuts, Bites, or Stings	How often does this job require exposure to minor burns, cuts, bites, or stings?

Work_Context	Work_Context Definitions		
Telephone	How often do you have telephone conversations in this job?	Very Hot or Cold Temperatures	How often does this job require working in very hot (above 90 F degrees) or very cold (below 32 F degrees) temperatures?
Face-to-Face Discussions	How often do you have to have face-to-face discussions with individuals or teams in this job?	Wear Common Protective or Safety Equipment such as	How much does this job require wearing common protective or safety equipment such as safety shoes, glasses, gloves, hard hats or live jackets?
Contact With Others	How much does this job require the worker to be in contact with others (face-to-face, by telephone, or otherwise) in order to perform it?	Exposed to Radiation	How often does this job require exposure to radiation?
Electronic Mail	How often do you use electronic mail in this job?	Indoors, Not Environmentally Controlled	How often does this job require working indoors in non-controlled environmental conditions (e.g., warehouse without heat)?
Spend Time Sitting	How much does this job require sitting?		
Importance of Being Exact or Accurate	How important is being very exact or highly accurate in performing this job?	Pace Determined by Speed of Equipment	How important is it to this job that the pace is determined by the speed of equipment or machinery? (This does not refer to keeping busy at all times on this job.)
Structured versus Unstructured Work	To what extent is this job structured for the worker, rather than allowing the worker to determine tasks, priorities, and goals?	Deal With Physically Aggressive People	How frequently does this job require the worker to deal with physical aggression of violent individuals?
Work With Work Group or Team	How important is it to work with others in a group or team in this job?	Outdoors, Under Cover	How often does this job require working outdoors, under cover (e.g., structure with roof but no walls)?
Importance of Repeating Same Tasks	How important is repeating the same physical activities (e.g., key entry) or mental activities (e.g., checking entries in a ledger) over and over, without stopping, to performing this job?	Exposed to Hazardous Equipment	How often does this job require exposure to hazardous equipment?
		Outdoors, Exposed to Weather	How often does this job require working outdoors, exposed to all weather conditions?
Indoors, Environmentally Controlled	How often does this job require working indoors in environmentally controlled conditions?	Exposed to Disease or Infections	How often does this job require exposure to disease/infections?
Letters and Memos	How often does the job require written letters and memos?	In an Open Vehicle or Equipment	How often does this job require working in an open vehicle or equipment (e.g., tractor)?
Time Pressure	How often does this job require the worker to meet strict deadlines?	Spend Time Keeping or Regaining Balance	How much does this job require keeping or regaining your balance?
Frequency of Decision Making	How frequently is the worker required to make decisions that affect other people, the financial resources, and/or the image and reputation of the organization?	Exposed to Hazardous Conditions	How often does this job require exposure to hazardous conditions?
Freedom to Make Decisions	How much decision making freedom, without supervision, does the job offer?	Spend Time Climbing Ladders, Scaffolds, or Poles	How much does this job require climbing ladders, scaffolds, or poles?
Impact of Decisions on Co-workers or Company Resul	How do the decisions an employee makes impact the results of co-workers, clients or the company?	Exposed to Whole Body Vibration	How often does this job require exposure to whole body vibration (e.g., operate a jackhammer)?
Deal With External Customers	How important is it to work with external customers or the public in this job?	Wear Specialized Protective or Safety Equipment su	How much does this job require wearing specialized protective or safety equipment such as breathing apparatus, safety harness, full protection suits, or radiation protection?
Coordinate or Lead Others	How important is it to coordinate or lead others in accomplishing work activities in this job?	Exposed to High Places	How often does this job require exposure to high places?
Sounds, Noise Levels Are Distracting or Uncomforta	How often does this job require working exposed to sounds and noise levels that are distracting or uncomfortable?		
Deal With Unpleasant or Angry People	How frequently does the worker have to deal with unpleasant, angry, or discourteous individuals as part of the job requirements?		
Responsibility for Outcomes and Results	How responsible is the worker for work outcomes and results of other workers?	Job Zone Component	Job Zone Component Definitions
Spend Time Making Repetitive Motions	How much does this job require making repetitive motions?	Title	Job Zone Three: Medium Preparation Needed

948

Overall Experience	Previous work-related skill, knowledge, or experience is required for these occupations. For example, an electrician must have completed three or four years of apprenticeship or several years of vocational training, and often must have passed a licensing exam, in order to perform the job.
Job Training	Employees in these occupations usually need one or two years of training involving both on-the-job experience and informal training with experienced workers.
Job Zone Examples	These occupations usually involve using communication and organizational skills to coordinate, supervise, manage, or train others to accomplish goals. Examples include dental assistants, electricians, fish and game wardens, legal secretaries, personnel recruiters, and recreation workers.
SVP Range	(6.0 to < 7.0)
Education	Most occupations in this zone require training in vocational schools, related on-the-job experience, or an associate's degree. Some may require a bachelor's degree.

Work_Styles	Work_Styles Definitions
Cooperation	Job requires being pleasant with others on the job and displaying a good-natured, cooperative attitude.
Integrity	Job requires being honest and ethical.
Attention to Detail	Job requires being careful about detail and thorough in completing work tasks.
Dependability	Job requires being reliable, responsible, and dependable, and fulfilling obligations.
Self Control	Job requires maintaining composure, keeping emotions in check, controlling anger, and avoiding aggressive behavior, even in very difficult situations.
Concern for Others	Job requires being sensitive to others' needs and feelings and being understanding and helpful on the job.
Adaptability/Flexibility	Job requires being open to change (positive or negative) and to considerable variety in the workplace.
Stress Tolerance	Job requires accepting criticism and dealing calmly and effectively with high stress situations.
Initiative	Job requires a willingness to take on responsibilities and challenges.
Independence	Job requires developing one's own ways of doing things, guiding oneself with little or no supervision, and depending on oneself to get things done.
Social Orientation	Job requires preferring to work with others rather than alone, and being personally connected with others on the job.
Leadership	Job requires a willingness to lead, take charge, and offer opinions and direction.
Achievement/Effort	Job requires establishing and maintaining personally challenging achievement goals and exerting effort toward mastering tasks.
Analytical Thinking	Job requires analyzing information and using logic to address work-related issues and problems.
Persistence	Job requires persistence in the face of obstacles.
Innovation	Job requires creativity and alternative thinking to develop new ideas for and answers to work-related problems.

43-4171.00 - Receptionists and Information Clerks

Answer inquiries and obtain information for general public, customers, visitors, and other interested parties. Provide information regarding activities conducted at establishment; location of departments, offices, and employees within organization.

Tasks

1) Greet persons entering establishment, determine nature and purpose of visit, and direct or escort them to specific destinations.

2) File and maintain records.

3) Collect, sort, distribute and prepare mail, messages and courier deliveries.

4) Provide information about establishment, such as location of departments or offices, employees within the organization, or services provided.

5) Transmit information or documents to customers, using computer, mail, or facsimile machine.

6) Perform administrative support tasks such as proofreading, transcribing handwritten information, and operating calculators or computers to work with pay records, invoices,

balance sheets and other documents.

7) Hear and resolve complaints from customers and public.

8) Receive payment and record receipts for services.

9) Perform duties such as taking care of plants and straightening magazines to maintain lobby or reception area.

10) Keep a current record of staff members' whereabouts and availability.

11) Analyze data to determine answers to questions from customers or members of the public.

12) Schedule appointments, and maintain and update appointment calendars.

13) Process and prepare memos, correspondence, travel vouchers, or other documents.

14) Take orders for merchandise or materials and send them to the proper departments to be filled.

15) Schedule space and equipment for special programs and prepare lists of participants.

16) Enroll individuals to participate in programs and notify them of their acceptance.

17) Calculate and quote rates for tours, stocks, insurance policies, and other products and services.

18) Conduct tours or deliver talks describing features of public facility, such as historic site or national park.

Knowledge	Knowledge Definitions
Customer and Personal Service	Knowledge of principles and processes for providing customer and personal services. This includes customer needs assessment, meeting quality standards for services, and evaluation of customer satisfaction.
Clerical	Knowledge of administrative and clerical procedures and systems such as word processing, managing files and records, stenography and transcription, designing forms, and other office procedures and terminology.
English Language	Knowledge of the structure and content of the English language including the meaning and spelling of words, rules of composition, and grammar.
Computers and Electronics	Knowledge of circuit boards, processors, chips, electronic equipment, and computer hardware and software, including applications and programming.
Mathematics	Knowledge of arithmetic, algebra, geometry, calculus, statistics, and their applications.
Administration and Management	Knowledge of business and management principles involved in strategic planning, resource allocation, human resources modeling, leadership technique, production methods, and coordination of people and resources.
Transportation	Knowledge of principles and methods for moving people or goods by air, rail, sea, or road, including the relative costs and benefits.
Psychology	Knowledge of human behavior and performance; individual differences in ability, personality, and interests; learning and motivation; psychological research methods; and the assessment and treatment of behavioral and affective disorders.
Telecommunications	Knowledge of transmission, broadcasting, switching, control, and operation of telecommunications systems.
Sales and Marketing	Knowledge of principles and methods for showing, promoting, and selling products or services. This includes marketing strategy and tactics, product demonstration, sales techniques, and sales control systems.
Economics and Accounting	Knowledge of economic and accounting principles and practices, the financial markets, banking and the analysis and reporting of financial data.
Education and Training	Knowledge of principles and methods for curriculum and training design, teaching and instruction for individuals and groups, and the measurement of training effects.
Public Safety and Security	Knowledge of relevant equipment, policies, procedures, and strategies to promote effective local, state, or national security operations for the protection of people, data, property, and institutions.
Geography	Knowledge of principles and methods for describing the features of land, sea, and air masses, including their physical characteristics, locations, interrelationships, and distribution of plant, animal, and human life.
Personnel and Human Resources	Knowledge of principles and procedures for personnel recruitment, selection, training, compensation and benefits, labor relations and negotiation, and personnel information systems.

Sociology and Anthropology	Knowledge of group behavior and dynamics, societal trends and influences, human migrations, ethnicity, cultures and their history and origins.
Communications and Media	Knowledge of media production, communication, and dissemination techniques and methods. This includes alternative ways to inform and entertain via written, oral, and visual media.
Foreign Language	Knowledge of the structure and content of a foreign (non-English) language including the meaning and spelling of words, rules of composition and grammar, and pronunciation.
Law and Government	Knowledge of laws, legal codes, court procedures, precedents, government regulations, executive orders, agency rules, and the democratic political process.
Production and Processing	Knowledge of raw materials, production processes, quality control, costs, and other techniques for maximizing the effective manufacture and distribution of goods.
Philosophy and Theology	Knowledge of different philosophical systems and religions. This includes their basic principles, values, ethics, ways of thinking, customs, practices, and their impact on human culture.
Therapy and Counseling	Knowledge of principles, methods, and procedures for diagnosis, treatment, and rehabilitation of physical and mental dysfunctions, and for career counseling and guidance.
Medicine and Dentistry	Knowledge of the information and techniques needed to diagnose and treat human injuries, diseases, and deformities. This includes symptoms, treatment alternatives, drug properties and interactions, and preventive health-care measures.
Mechanical	Knowledge of machines and tools, including their designs, uses, repair, and maintenance.
Engineering and Technology	Knowledge of the practical application of engineering science and technology. This includes applying principles, techniques, procedures, and equipment to the design and production of various goods and services.
Design	Knowledge of design techniques, tools, and principles involved in production of precision technical plans, blueprints, drawings, and models.
Chemistry	Knowledge of the chemical composition, structure, and properties of substances and of the chemical processes and transformations that they undergo. This includes uses of chemicals and their interactions, danger signs, production techniques, and disposal methods.
Biology	Knowledge of plant and animal organisms, their tissues, cells, functions, interdependencies, and interactions with each other and the environment.
Building and Construction	Knowledge of materials, methods, and the tools involved in the construction or repair of houses, buildings, or other structures such as highways and roads.
Physics	Knowledge and prediction of physical principles, laws, their interrelationships, and applications to understanding fluid, material, and atmospheric dynamics, and mechanical, electrical, atomic and sub- atomic structures and processes.
History and Archeology	Knowledge of historical events and their causes, indicators, and effects on civilizations and cultures.
Fine Arts	Knowledge of the theory and techniques required to compose, produce, and perform works of music, dance, visual arts, drama, and sculpture.
Food Production	Knowledge of techniques and equipment for planting, growing, and harvesting food products (both plant and animal) for consumption, including storage/handling techniques.

Skills	Skills Definitions
Active Listening	Giving full attention to what other people are saying, taking time to understand the points being made, asking questions as appropriate, and not interrupting at inappropriate times.
Speaking	Talking to others to convey information effectively.
Reading Comprehension	Understanding written sentences and paragraphs in work related documents.
Writing	Communicating effectively in writing as appropriate for the needs of the audience.
Service Orientation	Actively looking for ways to help people.
Learning Strategies	Selecting and using training/instructional methods and procedures appropriate for the situation when learning or teaching new things.
Social Perceptiveness	Being aware of others' reactions and understanding why they react as they do.

Critical Thinking	Using logic and reasoning to identify the strengths and weaknesses of alternative solutions, conclusions or approaches to problems.
Time Management	Managing one's own time and the time of others.
Active Learning	Understanding the implications of new information for both current and future problem-solving and decision-making.
Judgment and Decision Making	Considering the relative costs and benefits of potential actions to choose the most appropriate one.
Coordination	Adjusting actions in relation to others' actions.
Mathematics	Using mathematics to solve problems.
Negotiation	Bringing others together and trying to reconcile differences.
Instructing	Teaching others how to do something.
Persuasion	Persuading others to change their minds or behavior.
Monitoring	Monitoring/Assessing performance of yourself, other individuals, or organizations to make improvements or take corrective action.
Complex Problem Solving	Identifying complex problems and reviewing related information to develop and evaluate options and implement solutions.
Management of Personnel Resources	Motivating, developing, and directing people as they work, identifying the best people for the job.
Equipment Selection	Determining the kind of tools and equipment needed to do a job.
Management of Financial Resources	Determining how money will be spent to get the work done, and accounting for these expenditures.
Operations Analysis	Analyzing needs and product requirements to create a design.
Systems Analysis	Determining how a system should work and how changes in conditions, operations, and the environment will affect outcomes.
Technology Design	Generating or adapting equipment and technology to serve user needs.
Equipment Maintenance	Performing routine maintenance on equipment and determining when and what kind of maintenance is needed.
Quality Control Analysis	Conducting tests and inspections of products, services, or processes to evaluate quality or performance.
Operation and Control	Controlling operations of equipment or systems.
Programming	Writing computer programs for various purposes.
Installation	Installing equipment, machines, wiring, or programs to meet specifications.
Management of Material Resources	Obtaining and seeing to the appropriate use of equipment, facilities, and materials needed to do certain work.
Troubleshooting	Determining causes of operating errors and deciding what to do about it.
Science	Using scientific rules and methods to solve problems.
Systems Evaluation	Identifying measures or indicators of system performance and the actions needed to improve or correct performance, relative to the goals of the system.
Repairing	Repairing machines or systems using the needed tools.
Operation Monitoring	Watching gauges, dials, or other indicators to make sure a machine is working properly.

Ability	Ability Definitions
Oral Comprehension	The ability to listen to and understand information and ideas presented through spoken words and sentences.
Oral Expression	The ability to communicate information and ideas in speaking so others will understand.
Speech Recognition	The ability to identify and understand the speech of another person.
Speech Clarity	The ability to speak clearly so others can understand you.
Written Comprehension	The ability to read and understand information and ideas presented in writing.
Near Vision	The ability to see details at close range (within a few feet of the observer).
Information Ordering	The ability to arrange things or actions in a certain order or pattern according to a specific rule or set of rules (e.g., patterns of numbers, letters, words, pictures, mathematical operations).
Selective Attention	The ability to concentrate on a task over a period of time without being distracted.
Written Expression	The ability to communicate information and ideas in writing so others will understand.
Mathematical Reasoning	The ability to choose the right mathematical methods or formulas to solve a problem.
Problem Sensitivity	The ability to tell when something is wrong or is likely to go wrong. It does not involve solving the problem, only recognizing there is a problem.
Category Flexibility	The ability to generate or use different sets of rules for combining or grouping things in different ways.

950

Inductive Reasoning	The ability to combine pieces of information to form general rules or conclusions (includes finding a relationship among seemingly unrelated events).
Deductive Reasoning	The ability to apply general rules to specific problems to produce answers that make sense.
Number Facility	The ability to add, subtract, multiply, or divide quickly and correctly.
Finger Dexterity	The ability to make precisely coordinated movements of the fingers of one or both hands to grasp, manipulate, or assemble very small objects.
Time Sharing	The ability to shift back and forth between two or more activities or sources of information (such as speech, sounds, touch, or other sources).
Originality	The ability to come up with unusual or clever ideas about a given topic or situation, or to develop creative ways to solve a problem.
Memorization	The ability to remember information such as words, numbers, pictures, and procedures.
Fluency of Ideas	The ability to come up with a number of ideas about a topic (the number of ideas is important, not their quality, correctness, or creativity).
Flexibility of Closure	The ability to identify or detect a known pattern (a figure, object, word, or sound) that is hidden in other distracting material.
Far Vision	The ability to see details at a distance.
Perceptual Speed	The ability to quickly and accurately compare similarities and differences among sets of letters, numbers, objects, pictures, or patterns. The things to be compared may be presented at the same time or one after the other. This ability also includes comparing a presented object with a remembered object.
Manual Dexterity	The ability to quickly move your hand, your hand together with your arm, or your two hands to grasp, manipulate, or assemble objects.
Speed of Closure	The ability to quickly make sense of, combine, and organize information into meaningful patterns.
Arm-Hand Steadiness	The ability to keep your hand and arm steady while moving your arm or while holding your arm and hand in one position.
Visualization	The ability to imagine how something will look after it is moved around or when its parts are moved or rearranged.
Control Precision	The ability to quickly and repeatedly adjust the controls of a machine or a vehicle to exact positions.
Multilimb Coordination	The ability to coordinate two or more limbs (for example, two arms, two legs, or one leg and one arm) while sitting, standing, or lying down. It does not involve performing the activities while the whole body is in motion.
Static Strength	The ability to exert maximum muscle force to lift, push, pull, or carry objects.
Response Orientation	The ability to choose quickly between two or more movements in response to two or more different signals (lights, sounds, pictures). It includes the speed with which the correct response is started with the hand, foot, or other body part.
Hearing Sensitivity	The ability to detect or tell the differences between sounds that vary in pitch and loudness.
Wrist-Finger Speed	The ability to make fast, simple, repeated movements of the fingers, hands, and wrists.
Auditory Attention	The ability to focus on a single source of sound in the presence of other distracting sounds.
Reaction Time	The ability to quickly respond (with the hand, finger, or foot) to a signal (sound, light, picture) when it appears.
Trunk Strength	The ability to use your abdominal and lower back muscles to support part of the body repeatedly or continuously over time without 'giving out' or fatiguing.
Extent Flexibility	The ability to bend, stretch, twist, or reach with your body, arms, and/or legs.
Visual Color Discrimination	The ability to match or detect differences between colors, including shades of color and brightness.
Spatial Orientation	The ability to know your location in relation to the environment or to know where other objects are in relation to you.
Gross Body Coordination	The ability to coordinate the movement of your arms, legs, and torso together when the whole body is in motion.
Explosive Strength	The ability to use short bursts of muscle force to propel oneself (as in jumping or sprinting), or to throw an object.
Speed of Limb Movement	The ability to quickly move the arms and legs.
Gross Body Equilibrium	The ability to keep or regain your body balance or stay upright when in an unstable position.
Dynamic Strength	The ability to exert muscle force repeatedly or continuously over time. This involves muscular endurance and resistance to muscle fatigue.

Stamina	The ability to exert yourself physically over long periods of time without getting winded or out of breath.
Sound Localization	The ability to tell the direction from which a sound originated.
Dynamic Flexibility	The ability to quickly and repeatedly bend, stretch, twist, or reach out with your body, arms, and/or legs.
Peripheral Vision	The ability to see objects or movement of objects to one's side when the eyes are looking ahead.
Depth Perception	The ability to judge which of several objects is closer or farther away from you, or to judge the distance between you and an object.
Glare Sensitivity	The ability to see objects in the presence of glare or bright lighting.
Night Vision	The ability to see under low light conditions.
Rate Control	The ability to time your movements or the movement of a piece of equipment in anticipation of changes in the speed and/or direction of a moving object or scene.

Work_Activity	Work_Activity Definitions
Interacting With Computers	Using computers and computer systems (including hardware and software) to program, write software, set up functions, enter data, or process information.
Getting Information	Observing, receiving, and otherwise obtaining information from all relevant sources.
Performing Administrative Activities	Performing day-to-day administrative tasks such as maintaining information files and processing paperwork.
Communicating with Supervisors, Peers, or Subordin	Providing information to supervisors, co-workers, and subordinates by telephone, in written form, e-mail, or in person.
Communicating with Persons Outside Organization	Communicating with people outside the organization, representing the organization to customers, the public, government, and other external sources. This information can be exchanged in person, in writing, or by telephone or e-mail.
Organizing, Planning, and Prioritizing Work	Developing specific goals and plans to prioritize, organize, and accomplish your work.
Establishing and Maintaining Interpersonal Relatio	Developing constructive and cooperative working relationships with others, and maintaining them over time.
Documenting/Recording Information	Entering, transcribing, recording, storing, or maintaining information in written or electronic/magnetic form.
Performing for or Working Directly with the Public	Performing for people or dealing directly with the public. This includes serving customers in restaurants and stores, and receiving clients or guests.
Assisting and Caring for Others	Providing personal assistance, medical attention, emotional support, or other personal care to others such as coworkers, customers, or patients.
Processing Information	Compiling, coding, categorizing, calculating, tabulating, auditing, or verifying information or data.
Updating and Using Relevant Knowledge	Keeping up-to-date technically and applying new knowledge to your job.
Making Decisions and Solving Problems	Analyzing information and evaluating results to choose the best solution and solve problems.
Resolving Conflicts and Negotiating with Others	Handling complaints, settling disputes, and resolving grievances and conflicts, or otherwise negotiating with others.
Thinking Creatively	Developing, designing, or creating new applications, ideas, relationships, systems, or products, including artistic contributions.
Scheduling Work and Activities	Scheduling events, programs, and activities, as well as the work of others.
Handling and Moving Objects	Using hands and arms in handling, installing, positioning, and moving materials, and manipulating things.
Interpreting the Meaning of Information for Others	Translating or explaining what information means and how it can be used.
Monitor Processes, Materials, or Surroundings	Monitoring and reviewing information from materials, events, or the environment, to detect or assess problems.
Monitoring and Controlling Resources	Monitoring and controlling resources and overseeing the spending of money.
Identifying Objects, Actions, and Events	Identifying information by categorizing, estimating, recognizing differences or similarities, and detecting changes in circumstances or events.
Analyzing Data or Information	Identifying the underlying principles, reasons, or facts of information by breaking down information or data into separate parts.
Training and Teaching Others	Identifying the educational needs of others, developing formal educational or training programs or classes, and teaching or instructing others.

Evaluating Information to Determine Compliance wit	Using relevant information and individual judgment to determine whether events or processes comply with laws, regulations, or standards.
Selling or Influencing Others	Convincing others to buy merchandise/goods or to otherwise change their minds or actions.
Coaching and Developing Others	Identifying the developmental needs of others and coaching, mentoring, or otherwise helping others to improve their knowledge or skills.
Judging the Qualities of Things, Services, or Peop	Assessing the value, importance, or quality of things or people.
Performing General Physical Activities	Performing physical activities that require considerable use of your arms and legs and moving your whole body, such as climbing, lifting, balancing, walking, stooping, and handling of materials.
Coordinating the Work and Activities of Others	Getting members of a group to work together to accomplish tasks.
Guiding, Directing, and Motivating Subordinates	Providing guidance and direction to subordinates, including setting performance standards and monitoring performance.
Developing and Building Teams	Encouraging and building mutual trust, respect, and cooperation among team members.
Provide Consultation and Advice to Others	Providing guidance and expert advice to management or other groups on technical, systems-, or process-related topics.
Controlling Machines and Processes	Using either control mechanisms or direct physical activity to operate machines or processes (not including computers or vehicles).
Staffing Organizational Units	Recruiting, interviewing, selecting, hiring, and promoting employees in an organization.
Developing Objectives and Strategies	Establishing long-range objectives and specifying the strategies and actions to achieve them.
Inspecting Equipment, Structures, or Material	Inspecting equipment, structures, or materials to identify the cause of errors or other problems or defects.
Estimating the Quantifiable Characteristics of Pro	Estimating sizes, distances, and quantities; or determining time, costs, resources, or materials needed to perform a work activity.
Repairing and Maintaining Electronic Equipment	Servicing, repairing, calibrating, regulating, fine-tuning, or testing machines, devices, and equipment that operate primarily on the basis of electrical or electronic (not mechanical) principles.
Drafting, Laying Out, and Specifying Technical Dev	Providing documentation, detailed instructions, drawings, or specifications to tell others about how devices, parts, equipment, or structures are to be fabricated, constructed, assembled, modified, maintained, or used.
Operating Vehicles, Mechanized Devices, or Equipme	Running, maneuvering, navigating, or driving vehicles or mechanized equipment, such as forklifts, passenger vehicles, aircraft, or water craft.
Repairing and Maintaining Mechanical Equipment	Servicing, repairing, adjusting, and testing machines, devices, moving parts, and equipment that operate primarily on the basis of mechanical (not electronic) principles.

Work_Context	**Work_Context Definitions**
Telephone	How often do you have telephone conversations in this job?
Contact With Others	How much does this job require the worker to be in contact with others (face-to-face, by telephone, or otherwise) in order to perform it?
Face-to-Face Discussions	How often do you have to have face-to-face discussions with individuals or teams in this job?
Structured versus Unstructured Work	To what extent is this job structured for the worker, rather than allowing the worker to determine tasks, priorities, and goals?
Importance of Being Exact or Accurate	How important is being very exact or highly accurate in performing this job?
Spend Time Sitting	How much does this job require sitting?
Work With Work Group or Team	How important is it to work with others in a group or team in this job?
Importance of Repeating Same Tasks	How important is repeating the same physical activities (e.g., key entry) or mental activities (e.g., checking entries in a ledger) over and over, without stopping, to performing this job?
Letters and Memos	How often does the job require written letters and memos?
Indoors, Environmentally Controlled	How often does this job require working indoors in environmentally controlled conditions?
Freedom to Make Decisions	How much decision making freedom, without supervision, does the job offer?
Deal With External Customers	How important is it to work with external customers or the public in this job?
Frequency of Decision Making	How frequently is the worker required to make decisions that affect other people, the financial resources, and/or the image and reputation of the organization?

Time Pressure	How often does this job require the worker to meet strict deadlines?
Physical Proximity	To what extent does this job require the worker to perform job tasks in close physical proximity to other people?
Impact of Decisions on Co-workers or Company Resul	How do the decisions an employee makes impact the results of co-workers, clients or the company?
Electronic Mail	How often do you use electronic mail in this job?
Spend Time Making Repetitive Motions	How much does this job require making repetitive motions?
Deal With Unpleasant or Angry People	How frequently does the worker have to deal with unpleasant, angry, or discourteous individuals as part of the job requirements?
Coordinate or Lead Others	How important is it to coordinate or lead others in accomplishing work activities in this job?
Spend Time Using Your Hands to Handle, Control, or	How much does this job require using your hands to handle, control, or feel objects, tools or controls?
Frequency of Conflict Situations	How often are there conflict situations the employee has to face in this job?
Sounds, Noise Levels Are Distracting or Uncomforta	How often does this job require working exposed to sounds and noise levels that are distracting or uncomfortable?
Exposed to Contaminants	How often does this job require working exposed to contaminants (such as pollutants, gases, dust or odors)?
Responsibility for Outcomes and Results	How responsible is the worker for work outcomes and results of other workers?
Consequence of Error	How serious would the result usually be if the worker made a mistake that was not readily correctable?
Spend Time Standing	How much does this job require standing?
Degree of Automation	How automated is the job?
Indoors, Not Environmentally Controlled	How often does this job require working indoors in non-controlled environmental conditions (e.g., warehouse without heat)?
Level of Competition	To what extent does this job require the worker to compete or to be aware of competitive pressures?
Spend Time Walking and Running	How much does this job require walking and running?
Extremely Bright or Inadequate Lighting	How often does this job require working in extremely bright or inadequate lighting conditions?
Responsible for Others' Health and Safety	How much responsibility is there for the health and safety of others in this job?
Spend Time Bending or Twisting the Body	How much does this job require bending or twisting your body?
Exposed to Disease or Infections	How often does this job require exposure to disease/infections?
Pace Determined by Speed of Equipment	How important is it to this job that the pace is determined by the speed of equipment or machinery? (This does not refer to keeping busy at all times on this job.)
Spend Time Kneeling, Crouching, Stooping, or Crawl	How much does this job require kneeling, crouching, stooping or crawling?
Exposed to Minor Burns, Cuts, Bites, or Stings	How often does this job require exposure to minor burns, cuts, bites, or stings?
Deal With Physically Aggressive People	How frequently does this job require the worker to deal with physical aggression of violent individuals?
Public Speaking	How often do you have to perform public speaking in this job?
In an Enclosed Vehicle or Equipment	How often does this job require working in a closed vehicle or equipment (e.g., car)?
Very Hot or Cold Temperatures	How often does this job require working in very hot (above 90 F degrees) or very cold (below 32 F degrees) temperatures?
Cramped Work Space, Awkward Positions	How often does this job require working in cramped work spaces that requires getting into awkward positions?
Wear Common Protective or Safety Equipment such as	How much does this job require wearing common protective or safety equipment such as safety shoes, glasses, gloves, hard hats or live jackets?
Spend Time Keeping or Regaining Balance	How much does this job require keeping or regaining your balance?
Exposed to Radiation	How often does this job require exposure to radiation?
Exposed to High Places	How often does this job require exposure to high places?
Outdoors, Under Cover	How often does this job require working outdoors, under cover (e.g., structure with roof but no walls)?
Exposed to Hazardous Equipment	How often does this job require exposure to hazardous equipment?
Outdoors, Exposed to Weather	How often does this job require working outdoors, exposed to all weather conditions?
Exposed to Hazardous Conditions	How often does this job require exposure to hazardous conditions?

Spend Time Climbing Ladders, Scaffolds, or Poles	How much does this job require climbing ladders, scaffolds, or poles?
Wear Specialized Protective or Safety Equipment su	How much does this job require wearing specialized protective or safety equipment such as breathing apparatus, safety harness, full protection suits, or radiation protection?
Exposed to Whole Body Vibration	How often does this job require exposure to whole body vibration (e.g., operate a jackhammer)?
In an Open Vehicle or Equipment	How often does this job require working in an open vehicle or equipment (e.g., tractor)?

Job Zone Component	Job Zone Component Definitions
Title	Job Zone Two: Some Preparation Needed
Overall Experience	Some previous work-related skill, knowledge, or experience may be helpful in these occupations, but usually is not needed. For example, a drywall installer might benefit from experience installing drywall, but an inexperienced person could still learn to be an installer with little difficulty.
Job Training	Employees in these occupations need anywhere from a few months to one year of working with experienced employees.
Job Zone Examples	These occupations often involve using your knowledge and skills to help others. Examples include drywall installers, fire inspectors, flight attendants, pharmacy technicians, salespersons (retail), and tellers.
SVP Range	(4.0 to < 6.0)
Education	These occupations usually require a high school diploma and may require some vocational training or job-related course work. In some cases, an associate's or bachelor's degree could be needed.

Work_Styles	Work_Styles Definitions
Cooperation	Job requires being pleasant with others on the job and displaying a good-natured, cooperative attitude.
Dependability	Job requires being reliable, responsible, and dependable, and fulfilling obligations.
Integrity	Job requires being honest and ethical.
Stress Tolerance	Job requires accepting criticism and dealing calmly and effectively with high stress situations.
Self Control	Job requires maintaining composure, keeping emotions in check, controlling anger, and avoiding aggressive behavior, even in very difficult situations.
Attention to Detail	Job requires being careful about detail and thorough in completing work tasks.
Concern for Others	Job requires being sensitive to others' needs and feelings and being understanding and helpful on the job.
Independence	Job requires developing one's own ways of doing things, guiding oneself with little or no supervision, and depending on oneself to get things done.
Social Orientation	Job requires preferring to work with others rather than alone, and being personally connected with others on the job.
Initiative	Job requires a willingness to take on responsibilities and challenges.
Adaptability/Flexibility	Job requires being open to change (positive or negative) and to considerable variety in the workplace.
Persistence	Job requires persistence in the face of obstacles.
Achievement/Effort	Job requires establishing and maintaining personally challenging achievement goals and exerting effort toward mastering tasks.
Leadership	Job requires a willingness to lead, take charge, and offer opinions and direction.
Innovation	Job requires creativity and alternative thinking to develop new ideas for and answers to work-related problems.
Analytical Thinking	Job requires analyzing information and using logic to address work-related issues and problems.

43-4181.00 - Reservation and Transportation Ticket Agents and Travel Clerks

Make and confirm reservations and sell tickets to passengers for large hotel or motel chains. May check baggage and direct passengers to designated concourse, pier, or track; make reservations, deliver tickets, arrange for visas, contact individuals and groups to inform them of package tours, or provide tourists with travel information, such as points of interest, restaurants, rates, and emergency service.

Tasks

1) Examine passenger documentation to determine destinations and to assign boarding passes.

2) Provide clients with assistance in preparing required travel documents and forms.

3) Inform clients of essential travel information such as travel times, transportation connections, and medical and visa requirements.

4) Maintain computerized inventories of available passenger space, and provide information on space reserved or available.

5) Make and confirm reservations for transportation and accommodations, using telephones, faxes, mail, and computers.

6) Contact customers or travel agents to advise them of travel conveyance changes or to confirm reservations.

7) Plan routes, itineraries, and accommodation details, and compute fares and fees, using schedules, rate books, and computers.

8) Answer inquiries regarding such information as schedules, accommodations, procedures, and policies.

9) Provide boarding or disembarking assistance to passengers needing special assistance.

10) Check baggage and cargo, and direct passengers to designated locations for loading.

11) Confer with customers to determine their service requirements and travel preferences.

12) Assemble and issue required documentation such as tickets, travel insurance policies, and itineraries.

13) Provide customers with travel suggestions and information such as guides, directories, brochures, and maps.

14) Contact motel, hotel, resort, and travel operators to obtain current advertising literature.

15) Announce arrival and departure information, using public-address systems.

16) Sell travel insurance.

17) Prepare customer invoices, and accept payment.

18) Sell a range of goods such as stamps, souvenirs, postcards, and maps.

19) Open and close information facilities, and keep them clean during operation.

20) Gather and compile visitor statistics such as the numbers and types of visitor inquiries.

21) Trace lost, delayed, or misdirected baggage for customers.

22) Promote particular destinations, tour packages, and other travel services.

43-5011.00 - Cargo and Freight Agents

Expedite and route movement of incoming and outgoing cargo and freight shipments in airline, train, and trucking terminals, and shipping docks. Take orders from customers and arrange pickup of freight and cargo for delivery to loading platform. Prepare and examine bills of lading to determine shipping charges and tariffs.

Tasks

1) Coordinate and supervise activities of workers engaged in packing and shipping merchandise.

2) Attach address labels, identification codes, and shipping instructions to containers.

3) Inspect and count items received and check them against invoices or other documents, recording shortages and rejecting damaged goods.

4) Keep records of all goods shipped, received, and stored.

5) Estimate freight or postal rates, and record shipment costs and weights.

6) Enter shipping information into a computer by hand or by using a hand-held scanner that reads bar codes on goods.

7) Direct or participate in cargo loading in order to ensure completeness of load and even distribution of weight.

8) Direct delivery trucks to shipping doors or designated marshalling areas, and help load and unload goods safely.

9) Determine method of shipment, and prepare bills of lading, invoices, and other shipping documents.

10) Contact vendors and/or claims adjustment departments in order to resolve problems with

953

shipments, or contact service depots to arrange for repairs.

11) Check import/export documentation to determine cargo contents, and classify goods into different fee or tariff groups, using a tariff coding system.

12) Advise clients on transportation and payment methods.

13) Arrange insurance coverage for goods.

14) Remove ramps after airplane loading is complete, and signal pilots that personnel and equipment are clear of plane.

15) Route received goods to first available flight or to appropriate storage areas or departments, using forklifts, handtrucks, or other equipment.

16) Pack goods for shipping, using tools such as staplers, strapping machines, and hammers.

17) Shovel loose materials into machine hoppers or into vehicles and containers.

18) Send samples of merchandise to quality control units for inspection.

19) Notify consignees, passengers, or customers of the arrival of freight or baggage, and arrange for delivery.

20) Assemble containers and crates used to transport items such as machines or vehicles.

21) Position ramps for loading of airplanes.

22) Negotiate and arrange transport of goods with shipping or freight companies.

23) Open cargo containers and unwrap contents, using steel cutters, crowbars, or other hand tools.

24) Obtain flight numbers, airplane numbers, and names of crew members from dispatchers, and record data on airplane flight papers.

25) Maintain a supply of packing materials.

26) Install straps, braces, and padding to loads in order to prevent shifting or damage during shipment.

27) Inspect trucks and vans to ensure cleanliness when shipping such items as grain, flour, and milk.

28) Force conditioned air into interiors of planes prior to departure, using mobile aircraft-air-conditioning-units.

29) Prepare manifests showing baggage, mail, and freight weights, and number of passengers on airplanes, and transmit data to destinations.

43-5031.00 - Police, Fire, and Ambulance Dispatchers

Receive complaints from public concerning crimes and police emergencies. Broadcast orders to police patrol units in vicinity of complaint to investigate. Operate radio, telephone, or computer equipment to receive reports of fires and medical emergencies and relay information or orders to proper officials.

Tasks

1) Record details of calls, dispatches, and messages.

2) Determine response requirements and relative priorities of situations, and dispatch units in accordance with established procedures.

3) Question callers to determine their locations, and the nature of their problems in order to determine type of response needed.

4) Learn material and pass required tests for certification.

5) Relay information and messages to and from emergency sites, to law enforcement agencies, and to all other individuals or groups requiring notification.

6) Enter, update, and retrieve information from teletype networks and computerized data systems regarding such things as wanted persons, stolen property, vehicle registration, and stolen vehicles.

7) Receive incoming telephone or alarm system calls regarding emergency and non-emergency police and fire service, emergency ambulance service, information and after hours calls for departments within a city.

8) Maintain access to, and security of, highly sensitive materials.

9) Scan status charts and computer screens, and contact emergency response field units in order to determine emergency units available for dispatch.

10) Maintain files of information relating to emergency calls such as personnel rosters, and emergency call-out and pager files.

11) Read and effectively interpret small-scale maps and information from a computer screen in order to determine locations and provide directions.

12) Observe alarm registers and scan maps in order to determine whether a specific emergency is in the dispatch service area.

13) Monitor various radio frequencies such as those used by public works departments, school security, and civil defense in order to keep apprised of developing situations.

14) Test and adjust communication and alarm systems, and report malfunctions to maintenance units.

15) Provide emergency medical instructions to callers.

16) Operate and maintain mobile dispatch vehicles and equipment.

17) Monitor alarm systems to detect emergencies such as fires and illegal entry into establishments.

Knowledge	Knowledge Definitions
Telecommunications	Knowledge of transmission, broadcasting, switching, control, and operation of telecommunications systems.
Public Safety and Security	Knowledge of relevant equipment, policies, procedures, and strategies to promote effective local, state, or national security operations for the protection of people, data, property, and institutions.
Customer and Personal Service	Knowledge of principles and processes for providing customer and personal services. This includes customer needs assessment, meeting quality standards for services, and evaluation of customer satisfaction.
Law and Government	Knowledge of laws, legal codes, court procedures, precedents, government regulations, executive orders, agency rules, and the democratic political process.
English Language	Knowledge of the structure and content of the English language including the meaning and spelling of words, rules of composition, and grammar.
Clerical	Knowledge of administrative and clerical procedures and systems such as word processing, managing files and records, stenography and transcription, designing forms, and other office procedures and terminology.
Computers and Electronics	Knowledge of circuit boards, processors, chips, electronic equipment, and computer hardware and software, including applications and programming.
Administration and Management	Knowledge of business and management principles involved in strategic planning, resource allocation, human resources modeling, leadership technique, production methods, and coordination of people and resources.
Communications and Media	Knowledge of media production, communication, and dissemination techniques and methods. This includes alternative ways to inform and entertain via written, oral, and visual media.
Education and Training	Knowledge of principles and methods for curriculum and training design, teaching and instruction for individuals and groups, and the measurement of training effects.
Psychology	Knowledge of human behavior and performance; individual differences in ability, personality, and interests; learning and motivation; psychological research methods; and the assessment and treatment of behavioral and affective disorders.
Geography	Knowledge of principles and methods for describing the features of land, sea, and air masses, including their physical characteristics, locations, interrelationships, and distribution of plant, animal, and human life.
Personnel and Human Resources	Knowledge of principles and procedures for personnel recruitment, selection, training, compensation and benefits, labor relations and negotiation, and personnel information systems.
Transportation	Knowledge of principles and methods for moving people or goods by air, rail, sea, or road, including the relative costs and benefits.
Therapy and Counseling	Knowledge of principles, methods, and procedures for diagnosis, treatment, and rehabilitation of physical and mental dysfunctions, and for career counseling and guidance.
Sociology and Anthropology	Knowledge of group behavior and dynamics, societal trends and influences, human migrations, ethnicity, cultures and their history and origins.
Foreign Language	Knowledge of the structure and content of a foreign (non-English) language including the meaning and spelling of words, rules of composition and grammar, and pronunciation.
Mathematics	Knowledge of arithmetic, algebra, geometry, calculus, statistics, and their applications.

Philosophy and Theology	Knowledge of different philosophical systems and religions. This includes their basic principles, values, ethics, ways of thinking, customs, practices, and their impact on human culture.
Medicine and Dentistry	Knowledge of the information and techniques needed to diagnose and treat human injuries, diseases, and deformities. This includes symptoms, treatment alternatives, drug properties and interactions, and preventive health-care measures.
Chemistry	Knowledge of the chemical composition, structure, and properties of substances and of the chemical processes and transformations that they undergo. This includes uses of chemicals and their interactions, danger signs, production techniques, and disposal methods.
Economics and Accounting	Knowledge of economic and accounting principles and practices, the financial markets, banking and the analysis and reporting of financial data.
Production and Processing	Knowledge of raw materials, production processes, quality control, costs, and other techniques for maximizing the effective manufacture and distribution of goods.
Design	Knowledge of design techniques, tools, and principles involved in production of precision technical plans, blueprints, drawings, and models.
Mechanical	Knowledge of machines and tools, including their designs, uses, repair, and maintenance.
Engineering and Technology	Knowledge of the practical application of engineering science and technology. This includes applying principles, techniques, procedures, and equipment to the design and production of various goods and services.
Sales and Marketing	Knowledge of principles and methods for showing, promoting, and selling products or services. This includes marketing strategy and tactics, product demonstration, sales techniques, and sales control systems.
Building and Construction	Knowledge of materials, methods, and the tools involved in the construction or repair of houses, buildings, or other structures such as highways and roads.
History and Archeology	Knowledge of historical events and their causes, indicators, and effects on civilizations and cultures.
Physics	Knowledge and prediction of physical principles, laws, their interrelationships, and applications to understanding fluid, material, and atmospheric dynamics, and mechanical, electrical, atomic and sub- atomic structures and processes.
Food Production	Knowledge of techniques and equipment for planting, growing, and harvesting food products (both plant and animal) for consumption, including storage/handling techniques.
Biology	Knowledge of plant and animal organisms, their tissues, cells, functions, interdependencies, and interactions with each other and the environment.
Fine Arts	Knowledge of the theory and techniques required to compose, produce, and perform works of music, dance, visual arts, drama, and sculpture.

Skills	Skills Definitions
Active Listening	Giving full attention to what other people are saying, taking time to understand the points being made, asking questions as appropriate, and not interrupting at inappropriate times.
Speaking	Talking to others to convey information effectively.
Critical Thinking	Using logic and reasoning to identify the strengths and weaknesses of alternative solutions, conclusions or approaches to problems.
Reading Comprehension	Understanding written sentences and paragraphs in work related documents.
Judgment and Decision Making	Considering the relative costs and benefits of potential actions to choose the most appropriate one.
Active Learning	Understanding the implications of new information for both current and future problem-solving and decision-making.
Coordination	Adjusting actions in relation to others' actions.
Writing	Communicating effectively in writing as appropriate for the needs of the audience.
Service Orientation	Actively looking for ways to help people.
Social Perceptiveness	Being aware of others' reactions and understanding why they react as they do.
Learning Strategies	Selecting and using training/instructional methods and procedures appropriate for the situation when learning or teaching new things.
Instructing	Teaching others how to do something.

Monitoring	Monitoring/Assessing performance of yourself, other individuals, or organizations to make improvements or take corrective action.
Complex Problem Solving	Identifying complex problems and reviewing related information to develop and evaluate options and implement solutions.
Operation and Control	Controlling operations of equipment or systems.
Negotiation	Bringing others together and trying to reconcile differences.
Persuasion	Persuading others to change their minds or behavior.
Time Management	Managing one's own time and the time of others.
Equipment Selection	Determining the kind of tools and equipment needed to do a job.
Troubleshooting	Determining causes of operating errors and deciding what to do about it.
Equipment Maintenance	Performing routine maintenance on equipment and determining when and what kind of maintenance is needed.
Operation Monitoring	Watching gauges, dials, or other indicators to make sure a machine is working properly.
Quality Control Analysis	Conducting tests and inspections of products, services, or processes to evaluate quality or performance.
Management of Personnel Resources	Motivating, developing, and directing people as they work, identifying the best people for the job.
Systems Evaluation	Identifying measures or indicators of system performance and the actions needed to improve or correct performance, relative to the goals of the system.
Mathematics	Using mathematics to solve problems.
Systems Analysis	Determining how a system should work and how changes in conditions, operations, and the environment will affect outcomes.
Installation	Installing equipment, machines, wiring, or programs to meet specifications.
Technology Design	Generating or adapting equipment and technology to serve user needs.
Operations Analysis	Analyzing needs and product requirements to create a design.
Repairing	Repairing machines or systems using the needed tools.
Management of Material Resources	Obtaining and seeing to the appropriate use of equipment, facilities, and materials needed to do certain work.
Programming	Writing computer programs for various purposes.
Science	Using scientific rules and methods to solve problems.
Management of Financial Resources	Determining how money will be spent to get the work done, and accounting for these expenditures.

Ability	Ability Definitions
Oral Comprehension	The ability to listen to and understand information and ideas presented through spoken words and sentences.
Problem Sensitivity	The ability to tell when something is wrong or is likely to go wrong. It does not involve solving the problem, only recognizing there is a problem.
Oral Expression	The ability to communicate information and ideas in speaking so others will understand.
Inductive Reasoning	The ability to combine pieces of information to form general rules or conclusions (includes finding a relationship among seemingly unrelated events).
Speech Recognition	The ability to identify and understand the speech of another person.
Speech Clarity	The ability to speak clearly so others can understand you.
Written Expression	The ability to communicate information and ideas in writing so others will understand.
Near Vision	The ability to see details at close range (within a few feet of the observer).
Written Comprehension	The ability to read and understand information and ideas presented in writing.
Deductive Reasoning	The ability to apply general rules to specific problems to produce answers that make sense.
Information Ordering	The ability to arrange things or actions in a certain order or pattern according to a specific rule or set of rules (e.g., patterns of numbers, letters, words, pictures, mathematical operations).
Selective Attention	The ability to concentrate on a task over a period of time without being distracted.
Perceptual Speed	The ability to quickly and accurately compare similarities and differences among sets of letters, numbers, objects, pictures, or patterns. The things to be compared may be presented at the same time or one after the other. This ability also includes comparing a presented object with a remembered object.
Flexibility of Closure	The ability to identify or detect a known pattern (a figure, object, word, or sound) that is hidden in other distracting material.

Speed of Closure	The ability to quickly make sense of, combine, and organize information into meaningful patterns.
Time Sharing	The ability to shift back and forth between two or more activities or sources of information (such as speech, sounds, touch, or other sources).
Finger Dexterity	The ability to make precisely coordinated movements of the fingers of one or both hands to grasp, manipulate, or assemble very small objects.
Category Flexibility	The ability to generate or use different sets of rules for combining or grouping things in different ways.
Auditory Attention	The ability to focus on a single source of sound in the presence of other distracting sounds.
Memorization	The ability to remember information such as words, numbers, pictures, and procedures.
Fluency of Ideas	The ability to come up with a number of ideas about a topic (the number of ideas is important, not their quality, correctness, or creativity).
Hearing Sensitivity	The ability to detect or tell the differences between sounds that vary in pitch and loudness.
Far Vision	The ability to see details at a distance.
Visualization	The ability to imagine how something will look after it is moved around or when its parts are moved or rearranged.
Originality	The ability to come up with unusual or clever ideas about a given topic or situation, or to develop creative ways to solve a problem.
Visual Color Discrimination	The ability to match or detect differences between colors, including shades of color and brightness.
Response Orientation	The ability to choose quickly between two or more movements in response to two or more different signals (lights, sounds, pictures). It includes the speed with which the correct response is started with the hand, foot, or other body part.
Manual Dexterity	The ability to quickly move your hand, your hand together with your arm, or your two hands to grasp, manipulate, or assemble objects.
Arm-Hand Steadiness	The ability to keep your hand and arm steady while moving your arm or while holding your arm and hand in one position.
Reaction Time	The ability to quickly respond (with the hand, finger, or foot) to a signal (sound, light, picture) when it appears.
Control Precision	The ability to quickly and repeatedly adjust the controls of a machine or a vehicle to exact positions.
Number Facility	The ability to add, subtract, multiply, or divide quickly and correctly.
Mathematical Reasoning	The ability to choose the right mathematical methods or formulas to solve a problem.
Spatial Orientation	The ability to know your location in relation to the environment or to know where other objects are in relation to you.
Wrist-Finger Speed	The ability to make fast, simple, repeated movements of the fingers, hands, and wrists.
Gross Body Coordination	The ability to coordinate the movement of your arms, legs, and torso together when the whole body is in motion.
Stamina	The ability to exert yourself physically over long periods of time without getting winded or out of breath.
Gross Body Equilibrium	The ability to keep or regain your body balance or stay upright when in an unstable position.
Static Strength	The ability to exert maximum muscle force to lift, push, pull, or carry objects.
Explosive Strength	The ability to use short bursts of muscle force to propel oneself (as in jumping or sprinting), or to throw an object.
Glare Sensitivity	The ability to see objects in the presence of glare or bright lighting.
Trunk Strength	The ability to use your abdominal and lower back muscles to support part of the body repeatedly or continuously over time without 'giving out' or fatiguing.
Extent Flexibility	The ability to bend, stretch, twist, or reach with your body, arms, and/or legs.
Multilimb Coordination	The ability to coordinate two or more limbs (for example, two arms, two legs, or one leg and one arm) while sitting, standing, or lying down. It does not involve performing the activities while the whole body is in motion.
Sound Localization	The ability to tell the direction from which a sound originated.
Depth Perception	The ability to judge which of several objects is closer or farther away from you, or to judge the distance between you and an object.
Speed of Limb Movement	The ability to quickly move the arms and legs.
Peripheral Vision	The ability to see objects or movement of objects to one's side when the eyes are looking ahead.
Night Vision	The ability to see under low light conditions.

Dynamic Flexibility	The ability to quickly and repeatedly bend, stretch, twist, or reach out with your body, arms, and/or legs.
Dynamic Strength	The ability to exert muscle force repeatedly or continuously over time. This involves muscular endurance and resistance to muscle fatigue.
Rate Control	The ability to time your movements or the movement of a piece of equipment in anticipation of changes in the speed and/or direction of a moving object or scene.

Work_Activity	Work_Activity Definitions
Getting Information	Observing, receiving, and otherwise obtaining information from all relevant sources.
Performing for or Working Directly with the Public	Performing for people or dealing directly with the public. This includes serving customers in restaurants and stores, and receiving clients or guests.
Interacting With Computers	Using computers and computer systems (including hardware and software) to program, write software, set up functions, enter data, or process information.
Documenting/Recording Information	Entering, transcribing, recording, storing, or maintaining information in written or electronic/magnetic form.
Identifying Objects, Actions, and Events	Identifying information by categorizing, estimating, recognizing differences or similarities, and detecting changes in circumstances or events.
Communicating with Supervisors, Peers, or Subordin	Providing information to supervisors, co-workers, and subordinates by telephone, in written form, e-mail, or in person.
Assisting and Caring for Others	Providing personal assistance, medical attention, emotional support, or other personal care to others such as coworkers, customers, or patients.
Processing Information	Compiling, coding, categorizing, calculating, tabulating, auditing, or verifying information or data.
Updating and Using Relevant Knowledge	Keeping up-to-date technically and applying new knowledge to your job.
Communicating with Persons Outside Organization	Communicating with people outside the organization, representing the organization to customers, the public, government, and other external sources. This information can be exchanged in person, in writing, or by telephone or e-mail.
Resolving Conflicts and Negotiating with Others	Handling complaints, settling disputes, and resolving grievances and conflicts, or otherwise negotiating with others.
Monitor Processes, Materials, or Surroundings	Monitoring and reviewing information from materials, events, or the environment, to detect or assess problems.
Establishing and Maintaining Interpersonal Relatio	Developing constructive and cooperative working relationships with others, and maintaining them over time.
Making Decisions and Solving Problems	Analyzing information and evaluating results to choose the best solution and solve problems.
Interpreting the Meaning of Information for Others	Translating or explaining what information means and how it can be used.
Evaluating Information to Determine Compliance wit	Using relevant information and individual judgment to determine whether events or processes comply with laws, regulations, or standards.
Organizing, Planning, and Prioritizing Work	Developing specific goals and plans to prioritize, organize, and accomplish your work.
Developing and Building Teams	Encouraging and building mutual trust, respect, and cooperation among team members.
Analyzing Data or Information	Identifying the underlying principles, reasons, or facts of information by breaking down information or data into separate parts.
Training and Teaching Others	Identifying the educational needs of others, developing formal educational or training programs or classes, and teaching or instructing others.
Coordinating the Work and Activities of Others	Getting members of a group to work together to accomplish tasks.
Performing Administrative Activities	Performing day-to-day administrative tasks such as maintaining information files and processing paperwork.
Provide Consultation and Advice to Others	Providing guidance and expert advice to management or other groups on technical, systems-, or process-related topics.
Coaching and Developing Others	Identifying the developmental needs of others and coaching, mentoring, or otherwise helping others to improve their knowledge or skills.
Judging the Qualities of Things, Services, or Peop	Assessing the value, importance, or quality of things or people.
Thinking Creatively	Developing, designing, or creating new applications, ideas, relationships, systems, or products, including artistic contributions.

Guiding, Directing, and Motivating Subordinates	Providing guidance and direction to subordinates, including setting performance standards and monitoring performance.
Developing Objectives and Strategies	Establishing long-range objectives and specifying the strategies and actions to achieve them.
Monitoring and Controlling Resources	Monitoring and controlling resources and overseeing the spending of money.
Selling or Influencing Others	Convincing others to buy merchandise/goods or to otherwise change their minds or actions.
Estimating the Quantifiable Characteristics of Pro	Estimating sizes, distances, and quantities; or determining time, costs, resources, or materials needed to perform a work activity.
Scheduling Work and Activities	Scheduling events, programs, and activities, as well as the work of others.
Controlling Machines and Processes	Using either control mechanisms or direct physical activity to operate machines or processes (not including computers or vehicles).
Inspecting Equipment, Structures, or Material	Inspecting equipment, structures, or materials to identify the cause of errors or other problems or defects.
Staffing Organizational Units	Recruiting, interviewing, selecting, hiring, and promoting employees in an organization.
Handling and Moving Objects	Using hands and arms in handling, installing, positioning, and moving materials, and manipulating things.
Repairing and Maintaining Electronic Equipment	Servicing, repairing, calibrating, regulating, fine-tuning, or testing machines, devices, and equipment that operate primarily on the basis of electrical or electronic (not mechanical) principles.
Performing General Physical Activities	Performing physical activities that require considerable use of your arms and legs and moving your whole body, such as climbing, lifting, balancing, walking, stooping, and handling of materials.
Drafting, Laying Out, and Specifying Technical Dev	Providing documentation, detailed instructions, drawings, or specifications to tell others about how devices, parts, equipment, or structures are to be fabricated, constructed, assembled, modified, maintained, or used.
Repairing and Maintaining Mechanical Equipment	Servicing, repairing, adjusting, and testing machines, devices, moving parts, and equipment that operate primarily on the basis of mechanical (not electronic) principles.
Operating Vehicles, Mechanized Devices, or Equipme	Running, maneuvering, navigating, or driving vehicles or mechanized equipment, such as forklifts, passenger vehicles, aircraft, or water craft.

Work_Context	Work_Context Definitions
Telephone	How often do you have telephone conversations in this job?
Indoors, Environmentally Controlled	How often does this job require working indoors in environmentally controlled conditions?
Spend Time Sitting	How much does this job require sitting?
Frequency of Decision Making	How frequently is the worker required to make decisions that affect other people, the financial resources, and/or the image and reputation of the organization?
Deal With Unpleasant or Angry People	How frequently does the worker have to deal with unpleasant, angry, or discourteous individuals as part of the job requirements?
Contact With Others	How much does this job require the worker to be in contact with others (face-to-face, by telephone, or otherwise) in order to perform it?
Deal With External Customers	How important is it to work with external customers or the public in this job?
Work With Work Group or Team	How important is it to work with others in a group or team in this job?
Importance of Being Exact or Accurate	How important is being very exact or highly accurate in performing this job?
Frequency of Conflict Situations	How often are there conflict situations the employee has to face in this job?
Importance of Repeating Same Tasks	How important is repeating the same physical activities (e.g., key entry) or mental activities (e.g., checking entries in a ledger) over and over, without stopping, to performing this job?
Impact of Decisions on Co-workers or Company Resul	How do the decisions an employee makes impact the results of co-workers, clients or the company?
Face-to-Face Discussions	How often do you have to have face-to-face discussions with individuals or teams in this job?
Spend Time Using Your Hands to Handle, Control, or	How much does this job require using your hands to handle, control, or feel objects, tools or controls?
Time Pressure	How often does this job require the worker to meet strict deadlines?

Coordinate or Lead Others	How important is it to coordinate or lead others in accomplishing work activities in this job?
Spend Time Making Repetitive Motions	How much does this job require making repetitive motions?
Freedom to Make Decisions	How much decision making freedom, without supervision, does the job offer?
Sounds, Noise Levels Are Distracting or Uncomforta	How often does this job require working exposed to sounds and noise levels that are distracting or uncomfortable?
Consequence of Error	How serious would the result usually be if the worker made a mistake that was not readily correctable?
Physical Proximity	To what extent does this job require the worker to perform job tasks in close physical proximity to other people?
Structured versus Unstructured Work	To what extent is this job structured for the worker, rather than allowing the worker to determine tasks, priorities, and goals?
Electronic Mail	How often do you use electronic mail in this job?
Responsible for Others' Health and Safety	How much responsibility is there for the health and safety of others in this job?
Deal With Physically Aggressive People	How frequently does this job require the worker to deal with physical aggression of violent individuals?
Responsibility for Outcomes and Results	How responsible is the worker for work outcomes and results of other workers?
Letters and Memos	How often does the job require written letters and memos?
Degree of Automation	How automated is the job?
Exposed to Contaminants	How often does this job require working exposed to contaminants (such as pollutants, gases, dust or odors)?
Spend Time Bending or Twisting the Body	How much does this job require bending or twisting your body?
Extremely Bright or Inadequate Lighting	How often does this job require working in extremely bright or inadequate lighting conditions?
Level of Competition	To what extent does this job require the worker to compete or to be aware of competitive pressures?
Cramped Work Space, Awkward Positions	How often does this job require working in cramped work spaces that requires getting into awkward positions?
Spend Time Standing	How much does this job require standing?
Exposed to Disease or Infections	How often does this job require exposure to disease/infections?
Pace Determined by Speed of Equipment	How important is it to this job that the pace is determined by the speed of equipment or machinery? (This does not refer to keeping busy at all times on this job.)
Public Speaking	How often do you have to perform public speaking in this job?
Spend Time Walking and Running	How much does this job require walking and running?
Spend Time Kneeling, Crouching, Stooping, or Crawl	How much does this job require kneeling, crouching, stooping or crawling?
Exposed to Hazardous Equipment	How often does this job require exposure to hazardous equipment?
Very Hot or Cold Temperatures	How often does this job require working in very hot (above 90 F degrees) or very cold (below 32 F degrees) temperatures?
Exposed to Minor Burns, Cuts, Bites, or Stings	How often does this job require exposure to minor burns, cuts, bites, or stings?
In an Enclosed Vehicle or Equipment	How often does this job require working in a closed vehicle or equipment (e.g., car)?
Spend Time Keeping or Regaining Balance	How much does this job require keeping or regaining your balance?
Indoors, Not Environmentally Controlled	How often does this job require working indoors in non-controlled environmental conditions (e.g., warehouse without heat)?
Outdoors, Exposed to Weather	How often does this job require working outdoors, exposed to all weather conditions?
Outdoors, Under Cover	How often does this job require working outdoors, under cover (e.g., structure with roof but no walls)?
Spend Time Climbing Ladders, Scaffolds, or Poles	How much does this job require climbing ladders, scaffolds, or poles?
Exposed to Radiation	How often does this job require exposure to radiation?
Wear Specialized Protective or Safety Equipment su	How much does this job require wearing specialized protective or safety equipment such as breathing apparatus, safety harness, full protection suits, or radiation protection?
Exposed to High Places	How often does this job require exposure to high places?
Exposed to Hazardous Conditions	How often does this job require exposure to hazardous conditions?
In an Open Vehicle or Equipment	How often does this job require working in an open vehicle or equipment (e.g., tractor)?
Wear Common Protective or Safety Equipment such as	How much does this job require wearing common protective or safety equipment such as safety shoes, glasses, gloves, hard hats or live jackets?

Exposed to Whole Body Vibration	How often does this job require exposure to whole body vibration (e.g., operate a jackhammer)?

Job Zone Component	Job Zone Component Definitions
Title	Job Zone Two: Some Preparation Needed
Overall Experience	Some previous work-related skill, knowledge, or experience may be helpful in these occupations, but usually is not needed. For example, a drywall installer might benefit from experience installing drywall, but an inexperienced person could still learn to be an installer with little difficulty.
Job Training	Employees in these occupations need anywhere from a few months to one year of working with experienced employees.
Job Zone Examples	These occupations often involve using your knowledge and skills to help others. Examples include drywall installers, fire inspectors, flight attendants, pharmacy technicians, salespersons (retail), and tellers.
SVP Range	(4.0 to < 6.0)
Education	These occupations usually require a high school diploma and may require some vocational training or job-related course work. In some cases, an associate's or bachelor's degree could be needed.

Work_Styles	Work_Styles Definitions
Stress Tolerance	Job requires accepting criticism and dealing calmly and effectively with high stress situations.
Self Control	Job requires maintaining composure, keeping emotions in check, controlling anger, and avoiding aggressive behavior, even in very difficult situations.
Dependability	Job requires being reliable, responsible, and dependable, and fulfilling obligations.
Integrity	Job requires being honest and ethical.
Attention to Detail	Job requires being careful about detail and thorough in completing work tasks.
Cooperation	Job requires being pleasant with others on the job and displaying a good-natured, cooperative attitude.
Adaptability/Flexibility	Job requires being open to change (positive or negative) and to considerable variety in the workplace.
Persistence	Job requires persistence in the face of obstacles.
Concern for Others	Job requires being sensitive to others' needs and feelings and being understanding and helpful on the job.
Initiative	Job requires a willingness to take on responsibilities and challenges.
Achievement/Effort	Job requires establishing and maintaining personally challenging achievement goals and exerting effort toward mastering tasks.
Social Orientation	Job requires preferring to work with others rather than alone, and being personally connected with others on the job.
Leadership	Job requires a willingness to lead, take charge, and offer opinions and direction.
Independence	Job requires developing one's own ways of doing things, guiding oneself with little or no supervision, and depending on oneself to get things done.
Analytical Thinking	Job requires analyzing information and using logic to address work-related issues and problems.
Innovation	Job requires creativity and alternative thinking to develop new ideas for and answers to work-related problems.

43-5032.00 - Dispatchers, Except Police, Fire, and Ambulance

Schedule and dispatch workers, work crews, equipment, or service vehicles for conveyance of materials, freight, or passengers, or for normal installation, service, or emergency repairs rendered outside the place of business. Duties may include using radio, telephone, or computer to transmit assignments and compiling statistics and reports on work progress.

Tasks

1) Confer with customers or supervising personnel in order to address questions, problems, and requests for service or equipment.

2) Advise personnel about traffic problems such as construction areas, accidents, congestion, weather conditions, and other hazards.

3) Record and maintain files and records of customer requests, work or services performed, charges, expenses, inventory, and other dispatch information.

4) Schedule and dispatch workers, work crews, equipment, or service vehicles to appropriate locations according to customer requests, specifications, or needs, using radios or telephones.

5) Prepare daily work and run schedules.

6) Receive or prepare work orders.

7) Monitor personnel and/or equipment locations and utilization in order to coordinate service and schedules.

8) Oversee all communications within specifically assigned territories.

9) Determine types or amounts of equipment, vehicles, materials, or personnel required according to work orders or specifications.

10) Arrange for necessary repairs in order to restore service and schedules.

11) Order supplies and equipment, and issue them to personnel.

12) Ensure timely and efficient movement of trains according to train orders and schedules.

Knowledge	Knowledge Definitions
Transportation	Knowledge of principles and methods for moving people or goods by air, rail, sea, or road, including the relative costs and benefits.
Clerical	Knowledge of administrative and clerical procedures and systems such as word processing, managing files and records, stenography and transcription, designing forms, and other office procedures and terminology.
English Language	Knowledge of the structure and content of the English language including the meaning and spelling of words, rules of composition, and grammar.
Public Safety and Security	Knowledge of relevant equipment, policies, procedures, and strategies to promote effective local, state, or national security operations for the protection of people, data, property, and institutions.
Administration and Management	Knowledge of business and management principles involved in strategic planning, resource allocation, human resources modeling, leadership technique, production methods, and coordination of people and resources.
Customer and Personal Service	Knowledge of principles and processes for providing customer and personal services. This includes customer needs assessment, meeting quality standards for services, and evaluation of customer satisfaction.
Telecommunications	Knowledge of transmission, broadcasting, switching, control, and operation of telecommunications systems.
Mathematics	Knowledge of arithmetic, algebra, geometry, calculus, statistics, and their applications.
Computers and Electronics	Knowledge of circuit boards, processors, chips, electronic equipment, and computer hardware and software, including applications and programming.
Communications and Media	Knowledge of media production, communication, and dissemination techniques and methods. This includes alternative ways to inform and entertain via written, oral, and visual media.
Education and Training	Knowledge of principles and methods for curriculum and training design, teaching and instruction for individuals and groups, and the measurement of training effects.
Geography	Knowledge of principles and methods for describing the features of land, sea, and air masses, including their physical characteristics, locations, interrelationships, and distribution of plant, animal, and human life.
Personnel and Human Resources	Knowledge of principles and procedures for personnel recruitment, selection, training, compensation and benefits, labor relations and negotiation, and personnel information systems.
Psychology	Knowledge of human behavior and performance; individual differences in ability, personality, and interests; learning and motivation; psychological research methods; and the assessment and treatment of behavioral and affective disorders.
Law and Government	Knowledge of laws, legal codes, court procedures, precedents, government regulations, executive orders, agency rules, and the democratic political process.
Production and Processing	Knowledge of raw materials, production processes, quality control, costs, and other techniques for maximizing the effective manufacture and distribution of goods.
Mechanical	Knowledge of machines and tools, including their designs, uses, repair, and maintenance.

Economics and Accounting	Knowledge of economic and accounting principles and practices, the financial markets, banking and the analysis and reporting of financial data.
Sales and Marketing	Knowledge of principles and methods for showing, promoting, and selling products or services. This includes marketing strategy and tactics, product demonstration, sales techniques, and sales control systems.
Physics	Knowledge and prediction of physical principles, laws, their interrelationships, and applications to understanding fluid, material, and atmospheric dynamics, and mechanical, electrical, atomic and sub- atomic structures and processes.
Chemistry	Knowledge of the chemical composition, structure, and properties of substances and of the chemical processes and transformations that they undergo. This includes uses of chemicals and their interactions, danger signs, production techniques, and disposal methods.
Engineering and Technology	Knowledge of the practical application of engineering science and technology. This includes applying principles, techniques, procedures, and equipment to the design and production of various goods and services.
Design	Knowledge of design techniques, tools, and principles involved in production of precision technical plans, blueprints, drawings, and models.
Medicine and Dentistry	Knowledge of the information and techniques needed to diagnose and treat human injuries, diseases, and deformities. This includes symptoms, treatment alternatives, drug properties and interactions, and preventive health-care measures.
Therapy and Counseling	Knowledge of principles, methods, and procedures for diagnosis, treatment, and rehabilitation of physical and mental dysfunctions, and for career counseling and guidance.
History and Archeology	Knowledge of historical events and their causes, indicators, and effects on civilizations and cultures.
Building and Construction	Knowledge of materials, methods, and the tools involved in the construction or repair of houses, buildings, or other structures such as highways and roads.
Food Production	Knowledge of techniques and equipment for planting, growing, and harvesting food products (both plant and animal) for consumption, including storage/handling techniques.
Foreign Language	Knowledge of the structure and content of a foreign (non-English) language including the meaning and spelling of words, rules of composition and grammar, and pronunciation.
Sociology and Anthropology	Knowledge of group behavior and dynamics, societal trends and influences, human migrations, ethnicity, cultures and their history and origins.
Biology	Knowledge of plant and animal organisms, their tissues, cells, functions, interdependencies, and interactions with each other and the environment.
Philosophy and Theology	Knowledge of different philosophical systems and religions. This includes their basic principles, values, ethics, ways of thinking, customs, practices, and their impact on human culture.
Fine Arts	Knowledge of the theory and techniques required to compose, produce, and perform works of music, dance, visual arts, drama, and sculpture.

Skills	Skills Definitions
Active Listening	Giving full attention to what other people are saying, taking time to understand the points being made, asking questions as appropriate, and not interrupting at inappropriate times.
Judgment and Decision Making	Considering the relative costs and benefits of potential actions to choose the most appropriate one.
Reading Comprehension	Understanding written sentences and paragraphs in work related documents.
Speaking	Talking to others to convey information effectively.
Time Management	Managing one's own time and the time of others.
Critical Thinking	Using logic and reasoning to identify the strengths and weaknesses of alternative solutions, conclusions or approaches to problems.
Monitoring	Monitoring/Assessing performance of yourself, other individuals, or organizations to make improvements or take corrective action.
Learning Strategies	Selecting and using training/instructional methods and procedures appropriate for the situation when learning or teaching new things.
Active Learning	Understanding the implications of new information for both current and future problem-solving and decision-making.
Instructing	Teaching others how to do something.

Troubleshooting	Determining causes of operating errors and deciding what to do about it.
Service Orientation	Actively looking for ways to help people.
Coordination	Adjusting actions in relation to others' actions.
Operations Analysis	Analyzing needs and product requirements to create a design.
Social Perceptiveness	Being aware of others' reactions and understanding why they react as they do.
Management of Personnel Resources	Motivating, developing, and directing people as they work, identifying the best people for the job.
Systems Evaluation	Identifying measures or indicators of system performance and the actions needed to improve or correct performance, relative to the goals of the system.
Writing	Communicating effectively in writing as appropriate for the needs of the audience.
Systems Analysis	Determining how a system should work and how changes in conditions, operations, and the environment will affect outcomes.
Complex Problem Solving	Identifying complex problems and reviewing related information to develop and evaluate options and implement solutions.
Equipment Selection	Determining the kind of tools and equipment needed to do a job.
Quality Control Analysis	Conducting tests and inspections of products, services, or processes to evaluate quality or performance.
Operation and Control	Controlling operations of equipment or systems.
Operation Monitoring	Watching gauges, dials, or other indicators to make sure a machine is working properly.
Negotiation	Bringing others together and trying to reconcile differences.
Persuasion	Persuading others to change their minds or behavior.
Technology Design	Generating or adapting equipment and technology to serve user needs.
Management of Material Resources	Obtaining and seeing to the appropriate use of equipment, facilities, and materials needed to do certain work.
Mathematics	Using mathematics to solve problems.
Programming	Writing computer programs for various purposes.
Equipment Maintenance	Performing routine maintenance on equipment and determining when and what kind of maintenance is needed.
Management of Financial Resources	Determining how money will be spent to get the work done, and accounting for these expenditures.
Installation	Installing equipment, machines, wiring, or programs to meet specifications.
Repairing	Repairing machines or systems using the needed tools.
Science	Using scientific rules and methods to solve problems.

Ability	Ability Definitions
Oral Expression	The ability to communicate information and ideas in speaking so others will understand.
Speech Clarity	The ability to speak clearly so others can understand you.
Oral Comprehension	The ability to listen to and understand information and ideas presented through spoken words and sentences.
Problem Sensitivity	The ability to tell when something is wrong or is likely to go wrong. It does not involve solving the problem, only recognizing there is a problem.
Information Ordering	The ability to arrange things or actions in a certain order or pattern according to a specific rule or set of rules (e.g., patterns of numbers, letters, words, pictures, mathematical operations).
Speech Recognition	The ability to identify and understand the speech of another person.
Deductive Reasoning	The ability to apply general rules to specific problems to produce answers that make sense.
Inductive Reasoning	The ability to combine pieces of information to form general rules or conclusions (includes finding a relationship among seemingly unrelated events).
Near Vision	The ability to see details at close range (within a few feet of the observer).
Written Comprehension	The ability to read and understand information and ideas presented in writing.
Selective Attention	The ability to concentrate on a task over a period of time without being distracted.
Category Flexibility	The ability to generate or use different sets of rules for combining or grouping things in different ways.
Written Expression	The ability to communicate information and ideas in writing so others will understand.
Time Sharing	The ability to shift back and forth between two or more activities or sources of information (such as speech, sounds, touch, or other sources).

Auditory Attention	The ability to focus on a single source of sound in the presence of other distracting sounds.
Memorization	The ability to remember information such as words, numbers, pictures, and procedures.
Visualization	The ability to imagine how something will look after it is moved around or when its parts are moved or rearranged.
Flexibility of Closure	The ability to identify or detect a known pattern (a figure, object, word, or sound) that is hidden in other distracting material.
Originality	The ability to come up with unusual or clever ideas about a given topic or situation, or to develop creative ways to solve a problem.
Fluency of Ideas	The ability to come up with a number of ideas about a topic (the number of ideas is important, not their quality, correctness, or creativity).
Speed of Closure	The ability to quickly make sense of, combine, and organize information into meaningful patterns.
Finger Dexterity	The ability to make precisely coordinated movements of the fingers of one or both hands to grasp, manipulate, or assemble very small objects.
Mathematical Reasoning	The ability to choose the right mathematical methods or formulas to solve a problem.
Perceptual Speed	The ability to quickly and accurately compare similarities and differences among sets of letters, numbers, objects, pictures, or patterns. The things to be compared may be presented at the same time or one after the other. This ability also includes comparing a presented object with a remembered object.
Manual Dexterity	The ability to quickly move your hand, your hand together with your arm, or your two hands to grasp, manipulate, or assemble objects.
Arm-Hand Steadiness	The ability to keep your hand and arm steady while moving your arm or while holding your arm and hand in one position.
Control Precision	The ability to quickly and repeatedly adjust the controls of a machine or a vehicle to exact positions.
Trunk Strength	The ability to use your abdominal and lower back muscles to support part of the body repeatedly or continuously over time without 'giving out' or fatiguing.
Hearing Sensitivity	The ability to detect or tell the differences between sounds that vary in pitch and loudness.
Number Facility	The ability to add, subtract, multiply, or divide quickly and correctly.
Reaction Time	The ability to quickly respond (with the hand, finger, or foot) to a signal (sound, light, picture) when it appears.
Rate Control	The ability to time your movements or the movement of a piece of equipment in anticipation of changes in the speed and/or direction of a moving object or scene.
Spatial Orientation	The ability to know your location in relation to the environment or to know where other objects are in relation to you.
Stamina	The ability to exert yourself physically over long periods of time without getting winded or out of breath.
Gross Body Coordination	The ability to coordinate the movement of your arms, legs, and torso together when the whole body is in motion.
Far Vision	The ability to see details at a distance.
Visual Color Discrimination	The ability to match or detect differences between colors, including shades of color and brightness.
Depth Perception	The ability to judge which of several objects is closer or farther away from you, or to judge the distance between you and an object.
Response Orientation	The ability to choose quickly between two or more movements in response to two or more different signals (lights, sounds, pictures). It includes the speed with which the correct response is started with the hand, foot, or other body part.
Extent Flexibility	The ability to bend, stretch, twist, or reach with your body, arms, and/or legs.
Speed of Limb Movement	The ability to quickly move the arms and legs.
Sound Localization	The ability to tell the direction from which a sound originated.
Multilimb Coordination	The ability to coordinate two or more limbs (for example, two arms, two legs, or one leg and one arm) while sitting, standing, or lying down. It does not involve performing the activities while the whole body is in motion.
Glare Sensitivity	The ability to see objects in the presence of glare or bright lighting.
Gross Body Equilibrium	The ability to keep or regain your body balance or stay upright when in an unstable position.
Dynamic Flexibility	The ability to quickly and repeatedly bend, stretch, twist, or reach out with your body, arms, and/or legs.

Dynamic Strength	The ability to exert muscle force repeatedly or continuously over time. This involves muscular endurance and resistance to muscle fatigue.
Explosive Strength	The ability to use short bursts of muscle force to propel oneself (as in jumping or sprinting), or to throw an object.
Static Strength	The ability to exert maximum muscle force to lift, push, pull, or carry objects.
Wrist-Finger Speed	The ability to make fast, simple, repeated movements of the fingers, hands, and wrists.
Night Vision	The ability to see under low light conditions.
Peripheral Vision	The ability to see objects or movement of objects to one's side when the eyes are looking ahead.

Work_Activity	Work_Activity Definitions
Getting Information	Observing, receiving, and otherwise obtaining information from all relevant sources.
Making Decisions and Solving Problems	Analyzing information and evaluating results to choose the best solution and solve problems.
Documenting/Recording Information	Entering, transcribing, recording, storing, or maintaining information in written or electronic/magnetic form.
Processing Information	Compiling, coding, categorizing, calculating, tabulating, auditing, or verifying information or data.
Interacting With Computers	Using computers and computer systems (including hardware and software) to program, write software, set up functions, enter data, or process information.
Identifying Objects, Actions, and Events	Identifying information by categorizing, estimating, recognizing differences or similarities, and detecting changes in circumstances or events.
Communicating with Supervisors, Peers, or Subordin	Providing information to supervisors, co-workers, and subordinates by telephone, in written form, e-mail, or in person.
Organizing, Planning, and Prioritizing Work	Developing specific goals and plans to prioritize, organize, and accomplish your work.
Scheduling Work and Activities	Scheduling events, programs, and activities, as well as the work of others.
Estimating the Quantifiable Characteristics of Pro	Estimating sizes, distances, and quantities; or determining time, costs, resources, or materials needed to perform a work activity.
Monitor Processes, Materials, or Surroundings	Monitoring and reviewing information from materials, events, or the environment, to detect or assess problems.
Updating and Using Relevant Knowledge	Keeping up-to-date technically and applying new knowledge to your job.
Evaluating Information to Determine Compliance wit	Using relevant information and individual judgment to determine whether events or processes comply with laws, regulations, or standards.
Judging the Qualities of Things, Services, or Peop	Assessing the value, importance, or quality of things or people.
Analyzing Data or Information	Identifying the underlying principles, reasons, or facts of information by breaking down information or data into separate parts.
Thinking Creatively	Developing, designing, or creating new applications, ideas, relationships, systems, or products, including artistic contributions.
Establishing and Maintaining Interpersonal Relatio	Developing constructive and cooperative working relationships with others, and maintaining them over time.
Interpreting the Meaning of Information for Others	Translating or explaining what information means and how it can be used.
Coordinating the Work and Activities of Others	Getting members of a group to work together to accomplish tasks.
Performing Administrative Activities	Performing day-to-day administrative tasks such as maintaining information files and processing paperwork.
Communicating with Persons Outside Organization	Communicating with people outside the organization, representing the organization to customers, the public, government, and other external sources. This information can be exchanged in person, in writing, or by telephone or e-mail.
Training and Teaching Others	Identifying the educational needs of others, developing formal educational or training programs or classes, and teaching or instructing others.
Monitoring and Controlling Resources	Monitoring and controlling resources and overseeing the spending of money.
Resolving Conflicts and Negotiating with Others	Handling complaints, settling disputes, and resolving grievances and conflicts, or otherwise negotiating with others.
Developing Objectives and Strategies	Establishing long-range objectives and specifying the strategies and actions to achieve them.

Guiding, Directing, and Motivating Subordinates	Providing guidance and direction to subordinates, including setting performance standards and monitoring performance.
Inspecting Equipment, Structures, or Material	Inspecting equipment, structures, or materials to identify the cause of errors or other problems or defects.
Assisting and Caring for Others	Providing personal assistance, medical attention, emotional support, or other personal care to others such as coworkers, customers, or patients.
Provide Consultation and Advice to Others	Providing guidance and expert advice to management or other groups on technical, systems-, or process-related topics.
Operating Vehicles, Mechanized Devices, or Equipme	Running, maneuvering, navigating, or driving vehicles or mechanized equipment, such as forklifts, passenger vehicles, aircraft, or water craft.
Coaching and Developing Others	Identifying the developmental needs of others and coaching, mentoring, or otherwise helping others to improve their knowledge or skills.
Developing and Building Teams	Encouraging and building mutual trust, respect, and cooperation among team members.
Performing for or Working Directly with the Public	Performing for people or dealing directly with the public. This includes serving customers in restaurants and stores, and receiving clients or guests.
Selling or Influencing Others	Convincing others to buy merchandise/goods or to otherwise change their minds or actions.
Controlling Machines and Processes	Using either control mec or direct physical activity to operate machines or process not including computers or vehicles).
Handling and Moving Objects	Using hands and arms in handling, installing, positioning, and moving materials, and manipulating things.
Performing General Physical Activities	Performing physical activities that require considerable use of your arms and legs and moving your whole body, such as climbing, lifting, balancing, walking, stooping, and handling of materials.
Staffing Organizational Units	Recruiting, interviewing, selecting, hiring, and promoting employees in an organization.
Drafting, Laying Out, and Specifying Technical Dev	Providing documentation, detailed instructions, drawings, or specifications to tell others about how devices, parts, equipment, or structures are to be fabricated, constructed, assembled, modified, maintained, or used.
Repairing and Maintaining Electronic Equipment	Servicing, repairing, calibrating, regulating, fine-tuning, or testing machines, devices, and equipment that operate primarily on the basis of electrical or electronic (not mechanical) principles.
Repairing and Maintaining Mechanical Equipment	Servicing, repairing, adjusting, and testing machines, devices, moving parts, and equipment that operate primarily on the basis of mechanical (not electronic) principles.

Work_Context	Work_Context Definitions
Telephone	How often do you have telephone conversations in this job?
Contact With Others	How much does this job require the worker to be in contact with others (face-to-face, by telephone, or otherwise) in order to perform it?
Freedom to Make Decisions	How much decision making freedom, without supervision, does the job offer?
Structured versus Unstructured Work	To what extent is this job structured for the worker, rather than allowing the worker to determine tasks, priorities, and goals?
Importance of Repeating Same Tasks	How important is repeating the same physical activities (e.g., key entry) or mental activities (e.g., checking entries in a ledger) over and over, without stopping, to performing this job?
Importance of Being Exact or Accurate	How important is being very exact or highly accurate in performing this job?
Work With Work Group or Team	How important is it to work with others in a group or team in this job?
Spend Time Sitting	How much does this job require sitting?
Spend Time Making Repetitive Motions	How much does this job require making repetitive motions?
Deal With External Customers	How important is it to work with external customers or the public in this job?
Face-to-Face Discussions	How often do you have to have face-to-face discussions with individuals or teams in this job?
Frequency of Decision Making	How frequently is the worker required to make decisions that affect other people, the financial resources, and/or the image and reputation of the organization?
Indoors, Environmentally Controlled	How often does this job require working indoors in environmentally controlled conditions?
Deal With Unpleasant or Angry People	How frequently does the worker have to deal with unpleasant, angry, or discourteous individuals as part of the job requirements?

Impact of Decisions on Co-workers or Company Resul	How do the decisions an employee makes impact the results of co-workers, clients or the company?
Physical Proximity	To what extent does this job require the worker to perform job tasks in close physical proximity to other people?
Time Pressure	How often does this job require the worker to meet strict deadlines?
Sounds, Noise Levels Are Distracting or Uncomforta	How often does this job require working exposed to sounds and noise levels that are distracting or uncomfortable?
Frequency of Conflict Situations	How often are there conflict situations the employee has to face in this job?
Spend Time Using Your Hands to Handle, Control, or	How much does this job require using your hands to handle, control, or feel objects, tools or controls?
Degree of Automation	How automated is the job?
Coordinate or Lead Others	How important is it to coordinate or lead others in accomplishing work activities in this job?
Electronic Mail	How often do you use electronic mail in this job?
Responsibility for Outcomes and Results	How responsible is the worker for work outcomes and results of other workers?
Level of Competition	To what extent does this job require the worker to compete or to be aware of competitive pressures?
Responsible for Others' Health and Safety	How much responsibility is there for the health and safety of others in this job?
Consequence of Error	How serious would the result usually be if the worker made a mistake that was not readily correctable?
Pace Determined by Speed of Equipment	How important is it to this job that the pace is determined by the speed of equipment or machinery? (This does not refer to keeping busy at all times on this job.)
Letters and Memos	How often does the job require written letters and memos?
Exposed to Contaminants	How often does this job require working exposed to contaminants (such as pollutants, gases, dust or odors)?
Spend Time Standing	How much does this job require standing?
Exposed to Hazardous Equipment	How often does this job require exposure to hazardous equipment?
Deal With Physically Aggressive People	How frequently does this job require the worker to deal with physical aggression of violent individuals?
Public Speaking	How often do you have to perform public speaking in this job?
In an Enclosed Vehicle or Equipment	How often does this job require working in a closed vehicle or equipment (e.g., car)?
Spend Time Bending or Twisting the Body	How much does this job require bending or twisting your body?
Spend Time Walking and Running	How much does this job require walking and running?
Outdoors, Exposed to Weather	How often does this job require working outdoors, exposed to all weather conditions?
Indoors, Not Environmentally Controlled	How often does this job require working indoors in non-controlled environmental conditions (e.g., warehouse without heat)?
Very Hot or Cold Temperatures	How often does this job require working in very hot (above 90 F degrees) or very cold (below 32 F degrees) temperatures?
Wear Common Protective or Safety Equipment such as	How much does this job require wearing common protective or safety equipment such as safety shoes, glasses, gloves, hard hats or live jackets?
Extremely Bright or Inadequate Lighting	How often does this job require working in extremely bright or inadequate lighting conditions?
Outdoors, Under Cover	How often does this job require working outdoors, under cover (e.g., structure with roof but no walls)?
In an Open Vehicle or Equipment	How often does this job require working in an open vehicle or equipment (e.g., tractor)?
Cramped Work Space, Awkward Positions	How often does this job require working in cramped work spaces that requires getting into awkward positions?
Spend Time Kneeling, Crouching, Stooping, or Crawl	How much does this job require kneeling, crouching, stooping or crawling?
Exposed to Minor Burns, Cuts, Bites, or Stings	How often does this job require exposure to minor burns, cuts, bites, or stings?
Exposed to Whole Body Vibration	How often does this job require exposure to whole body vibration (e.g., operate a jackhammer)?
Exposed to Hazardous Conditions	How often does this job require exposure to hazardous conditions?
Exposed to High Places	How often does this job require exposure to high places?
Exposed to Disease or Infections	How often does this job require exposure to disease/infections?
Spend Time Keeping or Regaining Balance	How much does this job require keeping or regaining your balance?

Spend Time Climbing Ladders, Scaffolds, or Poles	How much does this job require climbing ladders, scaffolds, or poles?
Exposed to Radiation	How often does this job require exposure to radiation?
Wear Specialized Protective or Safety Equipment su	How much does this job require wearing specialized protective or safety equipment such as breathing apparatus, safety harness, full protection suits, or radiation protection?

Job Zone Component	Job Zone Component Definitions
Title	Job Zone Two: Some Preparation Needed
Overall Experience	Some previous work-related skill, knowledge, or experience may be helpful in these occupations, but usually is not needed. For example, a drywall installer might benefit from experience installing drywall, but an inexperienced person could still learn to be an installer with little difficulty.
Job Training	Employees in these occupations need anywhere from a few months to one year of working with experienced employees.
Job Zone Examples	These occupations often involve using your knowledge and skills to help others. Examples include drywall installers, fire inspectors, flight attendants, pharmacy technicians, salespersons (retail), and tellers.
SVP Range	(4.0 to < 6.0)
Education	These occupations usually require a high school diploma and may require some vocational training or job-related course work. In some cases, an associate's or bachelor's degree could be needed.

Work_Styles	Work_Styles Definitions
Dependability	Job requires being reliable, responsible, and dependable, and fulfilling obligations.
Attention to Detail	Job requires being careful about detail and thorough in completing work tasks.
Initiative	Job requires a willingness to take on responsibilities and challenges.
Cooperation	Job requires being pleasant with others on the job and displaying a good-natured, cooperative attitude.
Stress Tolerance	Job requires accepting criticism and dealing calmly and effectively with high stress situations.
Integrity	Job requires being honest and ethical.
Analytical Thinking	Job requires analyzing information and using logic to address work-related issues and problems.
Independence	Job requires developing one's own ways of doing things, guiding oneself with little or no supervision, and depending on oneself to get things done.
Self Control	Job requires maintaining composure, keeping emotions in check, controlling anger, and avoiding aggressive behavior, even in very difficult situations.
Leadership	Job requires a willingness to lead, take charge, and offer opinions and direction.
Innovation	Job requires creativity and alternative thinking to develop new ideas for and answers to work-related problems.
Adaptability/Flexibility	Job requires being open to change (positive or negative) and to considerable variety in the workplace.
Achievement/Effort	Job requires establishing and maintaining personally challenging achievement goals and exerting effort toward mastering tasks.
Persistence	Job requires persistence in the face of obstacles.
Concern for Others	Job requires being sensitive to others' needs and feelings and being understanding and helpful on the job.
Social Orientation	Job requires preferring to work with others rather than alone, and being personally connected with others on the job.

43-5041.00 - Meter Readers, Utilities

Read meter and record consumption of electricity, gas, water, or steam.

Tasks

1) Verify readings in cases where consumption appears to be abnormal, and record possible reasons for fluctuations.

2) Report lost or broken keys.

3) Answer customers' questions about services and charges, or direct them to customer service centers.

4) Report to service departments any problems such as meter irregularities, damaged equipment, or impediments to meter access, including dogs.

5) Read electric, gas, water, or steam consumption meters and enter data in route books or hand-held computers.

6) Leave messages to arrange different times to read meters in cases in which meters are not accessible.

7) Collect past-due bills.

8) Inspect meters for unauthorized connections, defects, and damage such as broken seals.

9) Walk or drive vehicles along established routes to take readings of meter dials.

10) Upload into office computers all information collected on hand-held computers during meter rounds, or return route books or hand-hand computers to business offices so that data can be compiled.

11) Connect and disconnect utility services at specific locations.

43-5051.00 - Postal Service Clerks

Perform any combination of tasks in a post office, such as receive letters and parcels; sell postage and revenue stamps, postal cards, and stamped envelopes; fill out and sell money orders; place mail in pigeon holes of mail rack or in bags according to State, address, or other scheme; and examine mail for correct postage.

Tasks

1) Put undelivered parcels away, retrieve them when customers come to claim them, and complete any related documentation.

2) Respond to complaints regarding mail theft, delivery problems, and lost or damaged mail, filling out forms and making appropriate referrals for investigation.

3) Post announcements or government information on public bulletin boards.

4) Cash money orders.

5) Sort incoming and outgoing mail, according to type and destination, by hand or by operating electronic mail-sorting and scanning devices.

6) Provide assistance to the public in complying with federal regulations of Postal Service and other federal agencies.

7) Transport mail from one work station to another.

8) Answer questions regarding mail regulations and procedures, postage rates, and post office boxes.

9) Sell and collect payment for products such as stamps, prepaid mail envelopes, and money orders.

10) Set postage meters, and calibrate them to ensure correct operation.

11) Complete forms regarding changes of address, or theft or loss of mail, or for special services such as registered or priority mail.

12) Provide customers with assistance in filing claims for mail theft, or lost or damaged mail.

13) Receive letters and parcels, and place mail into bags.

14) Register, certify, and insure letters and parcels.

15) Check mail in order to ensure correct postage and that packages and letters are in proper condition for mailing.

16) Obtain signatures from recipients of registered or special delivery mail.

17) Rent post office boxes to customers.

18) Weigh letters and parcels; compute mailing costs based on type, weight, and destination; and affix correct postage.

19) Feed mail into postage canceling devices or hand stamp mail to cancel postage.

43-5052.00 - Postal Service Mail Carriers

Sort mail for delivery. Deliver mail on established route by vehicle or on foot.

Tasks

1) Sort mail for delivery, arranging it in delivery sequence.

2) Maintain accurate records of deliveries.

3) Sell stamps and money orders.

4) Report any unusual circumstances concerning mail delivery, including the condition of street letter boxes.

5) Answer customers' questions about postal services and regulations.

6) Complete forms that notify publishers of address changes.

7) Travel to post offices to pick up the mail for routes and/or pick up mail from postal relay boxes.

8) Sign for cash-on-delivery and registered mail before leaving the post office.

9) Obtain signed receipts for registered, certified, and insured mail; collect associated charges; and complete any necessary paperwork.

10) Leave notices telling patrons where to collect mail that could not be delivered.

11) Bundle mail in preparation for delivery or transportation to relay boxes.

12) Hold mail for customers who are away from delivery locations.

13) Return to the post office with mail collected from homes, businesses, and public mailboxes.

14) Record address changes and redirect mail for those addresses.

15) Provide customers with change of address cards and other forms.

16) Register, certify, and insure parcels and letters.

17) Return incorrectly addressed mail to senders.

18) Deliver mail to residences and business establishments along specified routes by walking and/or driving, using a combination of satchels, carts, cars, and small trucks.

19) Turn in money and receipts collected along mail routes.

20) Meet schedules for the collection and return of mail.

43-5053.00 - Postal Service Mail Sorters, Processors, and Processing Machine Operators

Prepare incoming and outgoing mail for distribution. Examine, sort, and route mail by State, type of mail, or other scheme. Load, operate, and occasionally adjust and repair mail processing, sorting, and canceling machinery. Keep records of shipments, pouches, and sacks; and other duties related to mail handling within the postal service. Must complete a competitive exam.

Tasks

1) Direct items according to established routing schemes, using computer controlled keyboards or voice recognition equipment.

2) Weigh articles to determine required postage.

3) Sort odd-sized mail by hand, sort mail that other workers have been unable to sort, and segregate items requiring special handling.

4) Remove envelopes or tape from postmarking machines.

5) Operate various types of equipment, such as computer scanning equipment, addressographs, mimeographs, optical character readers, and bar-code sorters.

6) Operate machines that seal envelopes and print postage and postmarks.

7) Rewrap soiled or broken parcels.

8) Dump sacks of mail onto conveyors for culling and sorting.

9) Search directories to find correct addresses for redirected mail.

10) Distribute incoming mail into the correct boxes or pigeonholes.

11) Load and unload mail trucks, sometimes lifting containers of mail onto equipment that transports items to sorting stations.

12) Clear jams in sorting equipment.

13) Check items to ensure that addresses are legible and correct, that sufficient postage has been paid or the appropriate documentation is attached, and that items are in a suitable condition for processing.

14) Cancel letter or parcel post stamps by hand.

15) Bundle, label, and route sorted mail to designated areas depending on destinations and according to established procedures and deadlines.

16) Move containers of mail, using equipment such as forklifts and automated trains.

17) Serve the public at counters or windows, such as by selling stamps and weighing parcels.

18) Supervise other mail sorters.

19) Accept and check containers of mail from large volume mailers, couriers, and contractors.

20) Open and label mail containers.

43-5071.00 - Shipping, Receiving, and Traffic Clerks

Verify and keep records on incoming and outgoing shipments. Prepare items for shipment. Duties include assembling, addressing, stamping, and shipping merchandise or material; receiving, unpacking, verifying and recording incoming merchandise or material; and arranging for the transportation of products.

Tasks

1) Confer and correspond with establishment representatives to rectify problems, such as damages, shortages, and nonconformance to specifications.

2) Contact carrier representative to make arrangements and to issue instructions for shipping and delivery of materials.

3) Requisition and store shipping materials and supplies to maintain inventory of stock.

4) Record shipment data, such as weight, charges, space availability, and damages and discrepancies, for reporting, accounting, and record-keeping purposes.

5) Prepare documents, such as work orders, bills of lading, and shipping orders to route materials.

6) Determine shipping method for materials, using knowledge of shipping procedures, routes, and rates.

7) Deliver or route materials to departments, using work devices, such as handtruck, conveyor, or sorting bins.

8) Compute amounts, such as space available, and shipping, storage, and demurrage charges, using calculator or price list.

9) Pack, seal, label, and affix postage to prepare materials for shipping, using work devices such as hand tools, power tools, and postage meter.

Knowledge	Knowledge Definitions
Transportation	Knowledge of principles and methods for moving people or goods by air, rail, sea, or road, including the relative costs and benefits.
English Language	Knowledge of the structure and content of the English language including the meaning and spelling of words, rules of composition, and grammar.
Clerical	Knowledge of administrative and clerical procedures and systems such as word processing, managing files and records, stenography and transcription, designing forms, and other office procedures and terminology.
Customer and Personal Service	Knowledge of principles and processes for providing customer and personal services. This includes customer needs assessment, meeting quality standards for services, and evaluation of customer satisfaction.
Production and Processing	Knowledge of raw materials, production processes, quality control, costs, and other techniques for maximizing the effective manufacture and distribution of goods.
Mathematics	Knowledge of arithmetic, algebra, geometry, calculus, statistics, and their applications.
Administration and Management	Knowledge of business and management principles involved in strategic planning, resource allocation, human resources modeling, leadership technique, production methods, and coordination of people and resources.
Computers and Electronics	Knowledge of circuit boards, processors, chips, electronic equipment, and computer hardware and software, including applications and programming.
Education and Training	Knowledge of principles and methods for curriculum and training design, teaching and instruction for individuals and groups, and the measurement of training effects.

Public Safety and Security	Knowledge of relevant equipment. policies. procedures. and strategies to promote effective local, state, or national security operations for the protection of people, data, property, and institutions.
Personnel and Human Resources	Knowledge of principles and procedures for personnel recruitment. selection, training, compensation and benefits, labor relations and negotiation, and personnel information systems.
Economics and Accounting	Knowledge of economic and accounting principles and practices. the financial markets, banking and the analysis and reporting of financial data.
Telecommunications	Knowledge of transmission, broadcasting, switching, control, and operation of telecommunications systems.
Sales and Marketing	Knowledge of principles and methods for showing, promoting, and selling products or services. This includes marketing strategy and tactics, product demonstration, sales techniques, and sales control systems.
Foreign Language	Knowledge of the structure and content of a foreign (non-English) language including the meaning and spelling of words, rules of composition and grammar, and pronunciation.
Law and Government	Knowledge of laws, legal codes, court procedures, precedents, government regulations, executive orders, agency rules, and the democratic political process.
Communications and Media	Knowledge of media production, communication, and dissemination techniques and methods. This includes alternative ways to inform and entertain via written, oral, and visual media.
Chemistry	Knowledge of the chemical composition, structure, and properties of substances and of the chemical processes and transformations that they undergo. This includes uses of chemicals and their interactions, danger signs, production techniques. and disposal methods.
Geography	Knowledge of principles and methods for describing the features of land, sea, and air masses, including their physical characteristics. locations, interrelationships, and distribution of plant, animal, and human life.
Psychology	Knowledge of human behavior and performance; individual differences in ability, personality, and interests; learning and motivation; psychological research methods; and the assessment and treatment of behavioral and affective disorders.
Mechanical	Knowledge of machines and tools, including their designs, uses, repair, and maintenance.
Philosophy and Theology	Knowledge of different philosophical systems and religions. This includes their basic principles, values, ethics, ways of thinking, customs, practices, and their impact on human culture.
Sociology and Anthropology	Knowledge of group behavior and dynamics, societal trends and influences, human migrations, ethnicity, cultures and their history and origins.
Engineering and Technology	Knowledge of the practical application of engineering science and technology. This includes applying principles, techniques, procedures, and equipment to the design and production of various goods and services.
Medicine and Dentistry	Knowledge of the information and techniques needed to diagnose and treat human injuries, diseases, and deformities. This includes symptoms, treatment alternatives, drug properties and interactions, and preventive health-care measures.
Physics	Knowledge and prediction of physical principles, laws, their interrelationships, and applications to understanding fluid, material, and atmospheric dynamics, and mechanical, electrical, atomic and sub- atomic structures and processes.
Food Production	Knowledge of techniques and equipment for planting, growing, and harvesting food products (both plant and animal) for consumption, including storage/handling techniques.
Design	Knowledge of design techniques, tools, and principles involved in production of precision technical plans, blueprints, drawings, and models.
Building and Construction	Knowledge of materials, methods, and the tools involved in the construction or repair of houses, buildings, or other structures such as highways and roads.
Therapy and Counseling	Knowledge of principles, methods, and procedures for diagnosis. treatment, and rehabilitation of physical and mental dysfunctions, and for career counseling and guidance.
History and Archeology	Knowledge of historical events and their causes. indicators, and effects on civilizations and cultures.
Biology	Knowledge of plant and animal organisms, their tissues, cells, functions, interdependencies, and interactions with each other and the environment.

Fine Arts	Knowledge of the theory and techniques required to compose. produce. and perform works of music, dance, visual arts. drama. and sculpture.

Skills	Skills Definitions
Active Listening	Giving full attention to what other people are saying, taking time to understand the points being made, asking questions as appropriate, and not interrupting at inappropriate times.
Reading Comprehension	Understanding written sentences and paragraphs in work related documents.
Speaking	Talking to others to convey information effectively.
Time Management	Managing one's own time and the time of others.
Writing	Communicating effectively in writing as appropriate for the needs of the audience.
Mathematics	Using mathematics to solve problems.
Learning Strategies	Selecting and using training/instructional methods and procedures appropriate for the situation when learning or teaching new things.
Monitoring	Monitoring/Assessing performance of yourself, other individuals, or organizations to make improvements or take corrective action.
Social Perceptiveness	Being aware of others' reactions and understanding why they react as they do.
Critical Thinking	Using logic and reasoning to identify the strengths and weaknesses of alternative solutions, conclusions or approaches to problems.
Coordination	Adjusting actions in relation to others' actions.
Judgment and Decision Making	Considering the relative costs and benefits of potential actions to choose the most appropriate one.
Service Orientation	Actively looking for ways to help people.
Instructing	Teaching others how to do something.
Active Learning	Understanding the implications of new information for both current and future problem-solving and decision-making.
Negotiation	Bringing others together and trying to reconcile differences.
Management of Personnel Resources	Motivating, developing, and directing people as they work, identifying the best people for the job.
Systems Evaluation	Identifying measures or indicators of system performance and the actions needed to improve or correct performance, relative to the goals of the system.
Management of Financial Resources	Determining how money will be spent to get the work done, and accounting for these expenditures.
Persuasion	Persuading others to change their minds or behavior.
Complex Problem Solving	Identifying complex problems and reviewing related information to develop and evaluate options and implement solutions.
Management of Material Resources	Obtaining and seeing to the appropriate use of equipment, facilities, and materials needed to do certain work.
Quality Control Analysis	Conducting tests and inspections of products, services, or processes to evaluate quality or performance.
Systems Analysis	Determining how a system should work and how changes in conditions, operations, and the environment will affect outcomes.
Equipment Maintenance	Performing routine maintenance on equipment and determining when and what kind of maintenance is needed.
Operation and Control	Controlling operations of equipment or systems.
Equipment Selection	Determining the kind of tools and equipment needed to do a job.
Troubleshooting	Determining causes of operating errors and deciding what to do about it.
Science	Using scientific rules and methods to solve problems.
Operations Analysis	Analyzing needs and product requirements to create a design.
Repairing	Repairing machines or systems using the needed tools.
Operation Monitoring	Watching gauges, dials, or other indicators to make sure a machine is working properly.
Installation	Installing equipment, machines, wiring, or programs to meet specifications.
Technology Design	Generating or adapting equipment and technology to serve user needs.
Programming	Writing computer programs for various purposes.

Ability	Ability Definitions
Oral Expression	The ability to communicate information and ideas in speaking so others will understand.
Problem Sensitivity	The ability to tell when something is wrong or is likely to go wrong. It does not involve solving the problem, only recognizing there is a problem.

Written Comprehension	The ability to read and understand information and ideas presented in writing.
Oral Comprehension	The ability to listen to and understand information and ideas presented through spoken words and sentences.
Information Ordering	The ability to arrange things or actions in a certain order or pattern according to a specific rule or set of rules (e.g., patterns of numbers, letters, words, pictures, mathematical operations).
Speech Clarity	The ability to speak clearly so others can understand you.
Speech Recognition	The ability to identify and understand the speech of another person.
Near Vision	The ability to see details at close range (within a few feet of the observer).
Deductive Reasoning	The ability to apply general rules to specific problems to produce answers that make sense.
Category Flexibility	The ability to generate or use different sets of rules for combining or grouping things in different ways.
Inductive Reasoning	The ability to combine pieces of information to form general rules or conclusions (includes finding a relationship among seemingly unrelated events).
Written Expression	The ability to communicate information and ideas in writing so others will understand.
Perceptual Speed	The ability to quickly and accurately compare similarities and differences among sets of letters, numbers, objects, pictures, or patterns. The things to be compared may be presented at the same time or one after the other. This ability also includes comparing a presented object with a remembered object.
Manual Dexterity	The ability to quickly move your hand, your hand together with your arm, or your two hands to grasp, manipulate, or assemble objects.
Selective Attention	The ability to concentrate on a task over a period of time without being distracted.
Static Strength	The ability to exert maximum muscle force to lift, push, pull, or carry objects.
Multilimb Coordination	The ability to coordinate two or more limbs (for example, two arms, two legs, or one leg and one arm) while sitting, standing, or lying down. It does not involve performing the activities while the whole body is in motion.
Finger Dexterity	The ability to make precisely coordinated movements of the fingers of one or both hands to grasp, manipulate, or assemble very small objects.
Visual Color Discrimination	The ability to match or detect differences between colors, including shades of color and brightness.
Arm-Hand Steadiness	The ability to keep your hand and arm steady while moving your arm or while holding your arm and hand in one position.
Far Vision	The ability to see details at a distance.
Time Sharing	The ability to shift back and forth between two or more activities or sources of information (such as speech, sounds, touch, or other sources).
Extent Flexibility	The ability to bend, stretch, twist, or reach with your body, arms, and/or legs.
Visualization	The ability to imagine how something will look after it is moved around or when its parts are moved or rearranged.
Originality	The ability to come up with unusual or clever ideas about a given topic or situation, or to develop creative ways to solve a problem.
Flexibility of Closure	The ability to identify or detect a known pattern (a figure, object, word, or sound) that is hidden in other distracting material.
Speed of Closure	The ability to quickly make sense of, combine, and organize information into meaningful patterns.
Number Facility	The ability to add, subtract, multiply, or divide quickly and correctly.
Fluency of Ideas	The ability to come up with a number of ideas about a topic (the number of ideas is important, not their quality, correctness, or creativity).
Trunk Strength	The ability to use your abdominal and lower back muscles to support part of the body repeatedly or continuously over time without 'giving out' or fatiguing.
Depth Perception	The ability to judge which of several objects is closer or farther away from you, or to judge the distance between you and an object.
Auditory Attention	The ability to focus on a single source of sound in the presence of other distracting sounds.
Gross Body Coordination	The ability to coordinate the movement of your arms, legs, and torso together when the whole body is in motion.
Mathematical Reasoning	The ability to choose the right mathematical methods or formulas to solve a problem.

Stamina	The ability to exert yourself physically over long periods of time without getting winded or out of breath.
Speed of Limb Movement	The ability to quickly move the arms and legs.
Hearing Sensitivity	The ability to detect or tell the differences between sounds that vary in pitch and loudness.
Control Precision	The ability to quickly and repeatedly adjust the controls of a machine or a vehicle to exact positions.
Dynamic Strength	The ability to exert muscle force repeatedly or continuously over time. This involves muscular endurance and resistance to muscle fatigue.
Spatial Orientation	The ability to know your location in relation to the environment or to know where other objects are in relation to you.
Sound Localization	The ability to tell the direction from which a sound originated.
Memorization	The ability to remember information such as words, numbers, pictures, and procedures.
Peripheral Vision	The ability to see objects or movement of objects to one's side when the eyes are looking ahead.
Gross Body Equilibrium	The ability to keep or regain your body balance or stay upright when in an unstable position.
Glare Sensitivity	The ability to see objects in the presence of glare or bright lighting.
Night Vision	The ability to see under low light conditions.
Response Orientation	The ability to choose quickly between two or more movements in response to two or more different signals (lights, sounds, pictures). It includes the speed with which the correct response is started with the hand, foot, or other body part.
Rate Control	The ability to time your movements or the movement of a piece of equipment in anticipation of changes in the speed and/or direction of a moving object or scene.
Reaction Time	The ability to quickly respond (with the hand, finger, or foot) to a signal (sound, light, picture) when it appears.
Wrist-Finger Speed	The ability to make fast, simple, repeated movements of the fingers, hands, and wrists.
Dynamic Flexibility	The ability to quickly and repeatedly bend, stretch, twist, or reach out with your body, arms, and/or legs.
Explosive Strength	The ability to use short bursts of muscle force to propel oneself (as in jumping or sprinting), or to throw an object.

Work_Activity	Work_Activity Definitions
Getting Information	Observing, receiving, and otherwise obtaining information from all relevant sources.
Communicating with Supervisors, Peers, or Subordin	Providing information to supervisors, co-workers, and subordinates by telephone, in written form, e-mail, or in person.
Performing Administrative Activities	Performing day-to-day administrative tasks such as maintaining information files and processing paperwork.
Identifying Objects, Actions, and Events	Identifying information by categorizing, estimating, recognizing differences or similarities, and detecting changes in circumstances or events.
Interacting With Computers	Using computers and computer systems (including hardware and software) to program, write software, set up functions, enter data, or process information.
Establishing and Maintaining Interpersonal Relatio	Developing constructive and cooperative working relationships with others, and maintaining them over time.
Communicating with Persons Outside Organization	Communicating with people outside the organization, representing the organization to customers, the public, government, and other external sources. This information can be exchanged in person, in writing, or by telephone or e-mail.
Making Decisions and Solving Problems	Analyzing information and evaluating results to choose the best solution and solve problems.
Analyzing Data or Information	Identifying the underlying principles, reasons, or facts of information by breaking down information or data into separate parts.
Assisting and Caring for Others	Providing personal assistance, medical attention, emotional support, or other personal care to others such as coworkers, customers, or patients.
Organizing, Planning, and Prioritizing Work	Developing specific goals and plans to prioritize, organize, and accomplish your work.
Selling or Influencing Others	Convincing others to buy merchandise/goods or to otherwise change their minds or actions.
Processing Information	Compiling, coding, categorizing, calculating, tabulating, auditing, or verifying information or data.
Monitor Processes, Materials, or Surroundings	Monitoring and reviewing information from materials, events, or the environment, to detect or assess problems.

Documenting/Recording Information	Entering. transcribing, recording, storing, or maintaining information in written or electronic/magnetic form.
Training and Teaching Others	Identifying the educational needs of others, developing formal educational or training programs or classes, and teaching or instructing others.
Resolving Conflicts and Negotiating with Others	Handling complaints, settling disputes, and resolving grievances and conflicts, or otherwise negotiating with others.
Handling and Moving Objects	Using hands and arms in handling, installing, positioning, and moving materials, and manipulating things.
Updating and Using Relevant Knowledge	Keeping up-to-date technically and applying new knowledge to your job.
Performing General Physical Activities	Performing physical activities that require considerable use of your arms and legs and moving your whole body, such as climbing, lifting, balancing, walking, stooping, and handling of materials.
Coordinating the Work and Activities of Others	Getting members of a group to work together to accomplish tasks.
Operating Vehicles, Mechanized Devices, or Equipme	Running. maneuvering, navigating, or driving vehicles or mechanized equipment, such as forklifts, passenger vehicles, aircraft, or water craft.
Inspecting Equipment, Structures, or Material	Inspecting equipment, structures, or materials to identify the cause of errors or other problems or defects.
Developing and Building Teams	Encouraging and building mutual trust, respect, and cooperation among team members.
Evaluating Information to Determine Compliance wit	Using relevant information and individual judgment to determine whether events or processes comply with laws, regulations, or standards.
Scheduling Work and Activities	Scheduling events, programs, and activities, as well as the work of others.
Judging the Qualities of Things, Services. or Peop	Assessing the value, importance, or quality of things or people.
Performing for or Working Directly with the Public	Performing for people or dealing directly with the public. This includes serving customers in restaurants and stores, and receiving clients or guests.
Monitoring and Controlling Resources	Monitoring and controlling resources and overseeing the spending of money.
Controlling Machines and Processes	Using either control mechanisms or direct physical activity to operate machines or processes (not including computers or vehicles).
Coaching and Developing Others	Identifying the developmental needs of others and coaching, mentoring, or otherwise helping others to improve their knowledge or skills.
Guiding, Directing, and Motivating Subordinates	Providing guidance and direction to subordinates, including setting performance standards and monitoring performance.
Interpreting the Meaning of Information for Others	Translating or explaining what information means and how it can be used.
Estimating the Quantifiable Characteristics of Pro	Estimating sizes, distances, and quantities; or determining time, costs, resources, or materials needed to perform a work activity.
Thinking Creatively	Developing, designing, or creating new applications, ideas, relationships, systems, or products, including artistic contributions.
Developing Objectives and Strategies	Establishing long-range objectives and specifying the strategies and actions to achieve them.
Provide Consultation and Advice to Others	Providing guidance and expert advice to management or other groups on technical, systems-, or process-related topics.
Repairing and Maintaining Mechanical Equipment	Servicing, repairing, adjusting, and testing machines, devices, moving parts, and equipment that operate primarily on the basis of mechanical (not electronic) principles.
Staffing Organizational Units	Recruiting, interviewing, selecting, hiring, and promoting employees in an organization.
Repairing and Maintaining Electronic Equipment	Servicing, repairing, calibrating, regulating, fine-tuning, or testing machines, devices, and equipment that operate primarily on the basis of electrical or electronic (not mechanical) principles.
Drafting, Laying Out, and Specifying Technical Dev	Providing documentation, detailed instructions, drawings, or specifications to tell others about how devices, parts, equipment, or structures are to be fabricated, constructed, assembled, modified, maintained, or used.

Work_Context	Work_Context Definitions
Telephone	How often do you have telephone conversations in this job?
Contact With Others	How much does this job require the worker to be in contact with others (face-to-face, by telephone, or otherwise) in order to perform it?
Face-to-Face Discussions	How often do you have to have face-to-face discussions with individuals or teams in this job?

Importance of Being Exact or Accurate	How important is being very exact or highly accurate in performing this job?
Time Pressure	How often does this job require the worker to meet strict deadlines?
Work With Work Group or Team	How important is it to work with others in a group or team in this job?
Frequency of Decision Making	How frequently is the worker required to make decisions that affect other people, the financial resources, and/or the image and reputation of the organization?
Impact of Decisions on Co-workers or Company Resul	How do the decisions an employee makes impact the results of co-workers, clients or the company?
Structured versus Unstructured Work	To what extent is this job structured for the worker, rather than allowing the worker to determine tasks, priorities, and goals?
Electronic Mail	How often do you use electronic mail in this job?
Freedom to Make Decisions	How much decision making freedom, without supervision, does the job offer?
Coordinate or Lead Others	How important is it to coordinate or lead others in accomplishing work activities in this job?
Physical Proximity	To what extent does this job require the worker to perform job tasks in close physical proximity to other people?
Indoors, Environmentally Controlled	How often does this job require working indoors in environmentally controlled conditions?
Letters and Memos	How often does the job require written letters and memos?
Importance of Repeating Same Tasks	How important is repeating the same physical activities (e.g., key entry) or mental activities (e.g., checking entries in a ledger) over and over, without stopping, to performing this job?
Spend Time Using Your Hands to Handle, Control, or	How much does this job require using your hands to handle, control, or feel objects, tools or controls?
Sounds, Noise Levels Are Distracting or Uncomforta	How often does this job require working exposed to sounds and noise levels that are distracting or uncomfortable?
Responsibility for Outcomes and Results	How responsible is the worker for work outcomes and results of other workers?
Spend Time Walking and Running	How much does this job require walking and running?
Exposed to Contaminants	How often does this job require working exposed to contaminants (such as pollutants, gases, dust or odors)?
Responsible for Others' Health and Safety	How much responsibility is there for the health and safety of others in this job?
Spend Time Sitting	How much does this job require sitting?
Spend Time Standing	How much does this job require standing?
Spend Time Bending or Twisting the Body	How much does this job require bending or twisting your body?
Indoors, Not Environmentally Controlled	How often does this job require working indoors in non-controlled environmental conditions (e.g., warehouse without heat)?
Consequence of Error	How serious would the result usually be if the worker made a mistake that was not readily correctable?
Deal With Unpleasant or Angry People	How frequently does the worker have to deal with unpleasant, angry, or discourteous individuals as part of the job requirements?
Spend Time Making Repetitive Motions	How much does this job require making repetitive motions?
Deal With External Customers	How important is it to work with external customers or the public in this job?
Wear Common Protective or Safety Equipment such as	How much does this job require wearing common protective or safety equipment such as safety shoes, glasses, gloves, hard hats or live jackets?
Frequency of Conflict Situations	How often are there conflict situations the employee has to face in this job?
Degree of Automation	How automated is the job?
Pace Determined by Speed of Equipment	How important is it to this job that the pace is determined by the speed of equipment or machinery? (This does not refer to keeping busy at all times on this job.)
Level of Competition	To what extent does this job require the worker to compete or to be aware of competitive pressures?
In an Enclosed Vehicle or Equipment	How often does this job require working in a closed vehicle or equipment (e.g., car)?
Very Hot or Cold Temperatures	How often does this job require working in very hot (above 90 F degrees) or very cold (below 32 F degrees) temperatures?
Spend Time Kneeling, Crouching, Stooping, or Crawl	How much does this job require kneeling, crouching, stooping or crawling?
Outdoors, Exposed to Weather	How often does this job require working outdoors, exposed to all weather conditions?
Exposed to High Places	How often does this job require exposure to high places?

Exposed to Minor Burns, Cuts, Bites, or Stings	How often does this job require exposure to minor burns, cuts, bites, or stings?
In an Open Vehicle or Equipment	How often does this job require working in an open vehicle or equipment (e.g., tractor)?
Exposed to Hazardous Equipment	How often does this job require exposure to hazardous equipment?
Exposed to Hazardous Conditions	How often does this job require exposure to hazardous conditions?
Extremely Bright or Inadequate Lighting	How often does this job require working in extremely bright or inadequate lighting conditions?
Spend Time Keeping or Regaining Balance	How much does this job require keeping or regaining your balance?
Cramped Work Space, Awkward Positions	How often does this job require working in cramped work spaces that requires getting into awkward positions?
Outdoors, Under Cover	How often does this job require working outdoors, under cover (e.g., structure with roof but no walls)?
Exposed to Disease or Infections	How often does this job require exposure to disease/infections?
Spend Time Climbing Ladders, Scaffolds, or Poles	How much does this job require climbing ladders, scaffolds, or poles?
Exposed to Whole Body Vibration	How often does this job require exposure to whole body vibration (e.g., operate a jackhammer)?
Public Speaking	How often do you have to perform public speaking in this job?
Wear Specialized Protective or Safety Equipment su	How much does this job require wearing specialized protective or safety equipment such as breathing apparatus, safety harness, full protection suits, or radiation protection?
Deal With Physically Aggressive People	How frequently does this job require the worker to deal with physical aggression of violent individuals?
Exposed to Radiation	How often does this job require exposure to radiation?

Job Zone Component	Job Zone Component Definitions
Title	Job Zone Two: Some Preparation Needed
Overall Experience	Some previous work-related skill, knowledge, or experience may be helpful in these occupations, but usually is not needed. For example, a drywall installer might benefit from experience installing drywall, but an inexperienced person could still learn to be an installer with little difficulty.
Job Training	Employees in these occupations need anywhere from a few months to one year of working with experienced employees.
Job Zone Examples	These occupations often involve using your knowledge and skills to help others. Examples include drywall installers, fire inspectors, flight attendants, pharmacy technicians, salespersons (retail), and tellers.
SVP Range	(4.0 to < 6.0)
Education	These occupations usually require a high school diploma and may require some vocational training or job-related course work. In some cases, an associate's or bachelor's degree could be needed.

Work_Styles	Work_Styles Definitions
Attention to Detail	Job requires being careful about detail and thorough in completing work tasks.
Integrity	Job requires being honest and ethical.
Cooperation	Job requires being pleasant with others on the job and displaying a good-natured, cooperative attitude.
Dependability	Job requires being reliable, responsible, and dependable, and fulfilling obligations.
Stress Tolerance	Job requires accepting criticism and dealing calmly and effectively with high stress situations.
Concern for Others	Job requires being sensitive to others' needs and feelings and being understanding and helpful on the job.
Initiative	Job requires a willingness to take on responsibilities and challenges.
Self Control	Job requires maintaining composure, keeping emotions in check, controlling anger, and avoiding aggressive behavior, even in very difficult situations.
Adaptability/Flexibility	Job requires being open to change (positive or negative) and to considerable variety in the workplace.
Independence	Job requires developing one's own ways of doing things, guiding oneself with little or no supervision, and depending on oneself to get things done.
Leadership	Job requires a willingness to lead, take charge, and offer opinions and direction.

Achievement Effort	Job requires establishing and maintaining personally challenging achievement goals and exerting effort toward mastering tasks.
Analytical Thinking	Job requires analyzing information and using logic to address work-related issues and problems.
Persistence	Job requires persistence in the face of obstacles.
Social Orientation	Job requires preferring to work with others rather than alone, and being personally connected with others on the job.
Innovation	Job requires creativity and alternative thinking to develop new ideas for and answers to work-related problems.

43-5081.01 - Stock Clerks, Sales Floor

Receive, store, and issue sales floor merchandise. Stock shelves, racks, cases, bins, and tables with merchandise and arrange merchandise displays to attract customers. May periodically take physical count of stock or check and mark merchandise.

Tasks

1) Stock shelves, racks, cases, bins, and tables with new or transferred merchandise.

2) Receive, open, unpack and issue sales floor merchandise.

3) Clean display cases, shelves, and aisles.

4) Take inventory or examine merchandise to identify items to be reordered or replenished.

5) Itemize and total customer merchandise selection at checkout counter, using cash register, and accept cash or charge card for purchases.

6) Pack customer purchases in bags or cartons.

7) Compare merchandise invoices to items actually received to ensure that shipments are correct.

8) Design and set up advertising signs and displays of merchandise on shelves, counters, or tables to attract customers and promote sales.

9) Transport packages to customers' vehicles.

10) Requisition merchandise from supplier based on available space, merchandise on hand, customer demand, or advertised specials.

11) Stamp, attach, or change price tags on merchandise, referring to price list.

Knowledge	Knowledge Definitions
Customer and Personal Service	Knowledge of principles and processes for providing customer and personal services. This includes customer needs assessment, meeting quality standards for services, and evaluation of customer satisfaction.
Mathematics	Knowledge of arithmetic, algebra, geometry, calculus, statistics, and their applications.
English Language	Knowledge of the structure and content of the English language including the meaning and spelling of words, rules of composition, and grammar.
Administration and Management	Knowledge of business and management principles involved in strategic planning, resource allocation, human resources modeling, leadership technique, production methods, and coordination of people and resources.
Public Safety and Security	Knowledge of relevant equipment, policies, procedures, and strategies to promote effective local, state, or national security operations for the protection of people, data, property, and institutions.
Sales and Marketing	Knowledge of principles and methods for showing, promoting, and selling products or services. This includes marketing strategy and tactics, product demonstration, sales techniques, and sales control systems.
Computers and Electronics	Knowledge of circuit boards, processors, chips, electronic equipment, and computer hardware and software, including applications and programming.
Education and Training	Knowledge of principles and methods for curriculum and training design, teaching and instruction for individuals and groups, and the measurement of training effects.
Clerical	Knowledge of administrative and clerical procedures and systems such as word processing, managing files and records, stenography and transcription, designing forms, and other office procedures and terminology.

Economics and Accounting	Knowledge of economic and accounting principles and practices, the financial markets, banking and the analysis and reporting of financial data.	Fine Arts	Knowledge of the theory and techniques required to compose, produce, and perform works of music, dance, visual arts, drama, and sculpture.
Personnel and Human Resources	Knowledge of principles and procedures for personnel recruitment, selection, training, compensation and benefits, labor relations and negotiation, and personnel information systems.	**Skills**	**Skills Definitions**
Psychology	Knowledge of human behavior and performance; individual differences in ability, personality, and interests; learning and motivation; psychological research methods; and the assessment and treatment of behavioral and affective disorders.	Active Listening	Giving full attention to what other people are saying, taking time to understand the points being made, asking questions as appropriate, and not interrupting at inappropriate times.
Law and Government	Knowledge of laws, legal codes, court procedures, precedents, government regulations, executive orders, agency rules, and the democratic political process.	Speaking	Talking to others to convey information effectively.
		Reading Comprehension	Understanding written sentences and paragraphs in work related documents.
Production and Processing	Knowledge of raw materials, production processes, quality control, costs, and other techniques for maximizing the effective manufacture and distribution of goods.	Coordination	Adjusting actions in relation to others' actions.
		Social Perceptiveness	Being aware of others' reactions and understanding why they react as they do.
Transportation	Knowledge of principles and methods for moving people or goods by air, rail, sea, or road, including the relative costs and benefits.	Service Orientation	Actively looking for ways to help people.
		Time Management	Managing one's own time and the time of others.
		Mathematics	Using mathematics to solve problems.
Communications and Media	Knowledge of media production, communication, and dissemination techniques and methods. This includes alternative ways to inform and entertain via written, oral, and visual media.	Active Learning	Understanding the implications of new information for both current and future problem-solving and decision-making.
Telecommunications	Knowledge of transmission, broadcasting, switching, control, and operation of telecommunications systems.	Learning Strategies	Selecting and using training/instructional methods and procedures appropriate for the situation when learning or teaching new things.
Mechanical	Knowledge of machines and tools, including their designs, uses, repair, and maintenance.	Judgment and Decision Making	Considering the relative costs and benefits of potential actions to choose the most appropriate one.
Geography	Knowledge of principles and methods for describing the features of land, sea, and air masses, including their physical characteristics, locations, interrelationships, and distribution of plant, animal, and human life.	Instructing	Teaching others how to do something.
		Critical Thinking	Using logic and reasoning to identify the strengths and weaknesses of alternative solutions, conclusions or approaches to problems.
Chemistry	Knowledge of the chemical composition, structure, and properties of substances and of the chemical processes and transformations that they undergo. This includes uses of chemicals and their interactions, danger signs, production techniques, and disposal methods.	Management of Personnel Resources	Motivating, developing, and directing people as they work, identifying the best people for the job.
		Writing	Communicating effectively in writing as appropriate for the needs of the audience.
Food Production	Knowledge of techniques and equipment for planting, growing, and harvesting food products (both plant and animal) for consumption, including storage/handling techniques.	Monitoring	Monitoring/Assessing performance of yourself, other individuals, or organizations to make improvements or take corrective action.
		Negotiation	Bringing others together and trying to reconcile differences.
Medicine and Dentistry	Knowledge of the information and techniques needed to diagnose and treat human injuries, diseases, and deformities. This includes symptoms, treatment alternatives, drug properties and interactions, and preventive health-care measures.	Complex Problem Solving	Identifying complex problems and reviewing related information to develop and evaluate options and implement solutions.
Therapy and Counseling	Knowledge of principles, methods, and procedures for diagnosis, treatment, and rehabilitation of physical and mental dysfunctions, and for career counseling and guidance.	Persuasion	Persuading others to change their minds or behavior.
		Operation and Control	Controlling operations of equipment or systems.
		Repairing	Repairing machines or systems using the needed tools.
Sociology and Anthropology	Knowledge of group behavior and dynamics, societal trends and influences, human migrations, ethnicity, cultures and their history and origins.	Troubleshooting	Determining causes of operating errors and deciding what to do about it.
Physics	Knowledge and prediction of physical principles, laws, their interrelationships, and applications to understanding fluid, material, and atmospheric dynamics, and mechanical, electrical, atomic and sub- atomic structures and processes.	Equipment Maintenance	Performing routine maintenance on equipment and determining when and what kind of maintenance is needed.
		Operations Analysis	Analyzing needs and product requirements to create a design.
		Systems Evaluation	Identifying measures or indicators of system performance and the actions needed to improve or correct performance, relative to the goals of the system.
Foreign Language	Knowledge of the structure and content of a foreign (non-English) language including the meaning and spelling of words, rules of composition and grammar, and pronunciation.	Management of Financial Resources	Determining how money will be spent to get the work done, and accounting for these expenditures.
Building and Construction	Knowledge of materials, methods, and the tools involved in the construction or repair of houses, buildings, or other structures such as highways and roads.	Equipment Selection	Determining the kind of tools and equipment needed to do a job.
Engineering and Technology	Knowledge of the practical application of engineering science and technology. This includes applying principles, techniques, procedures, and equipment to the design and production of various goods and services.	Management of Material Resources	Obtaining and seeing to the appropriate use of equipment, facilities, and materials needed to do certain work.
		Science	Using scientific rules and methods to solve problems.
Philosophy and Theology	Knowledge of different philosophical systems and religions. This includes their basic principles, values, ethics, ways of thinking, customs, practices, and their impact on human culture.	Systems Analysis	Determining how a system should work and how changes in conditions, operations, and the environment will affect outcomes.
		Technology Design	Generating or adapting equipment and technology to serve user needs.
Design	Knowledge of design techniques, tools, and principles involved in production of precision technical plans, blueprints, drawings, and models.	Quality Control Analysis	Conducting tests and inspections of products, services, or processes to evaluate quality or performance.
Biology	Knowledge of plant and animal organisms, their tissues, cells, functions, interdependencies, and interactions with each other and the environment.	Operation Monitoring	Watching gauges, dials, or other indicators to make sure a machine is working properly.
		Installation	Installing equipment, machines, wiring, or programs to meet specifications.
History and Archeology	Knowledge of historical events and their causes, indicators, and effects on civilizations and cultures.	Programming	Writing computer programs for various purposes.
		Ability	**Ability Definitions**
		Oral Expression	The ability to communicate information and ideas in speaking so others will understand.
		Speech Clarity	The ability to speak clearly so others can understand you.
		Oral Comprehension	The ability to listen to and understand information and ideas presented through spoken words and sentences.

Trunk Strength	The ability to use your abdominal and lower back muscles to support part of the body repeatedly or continuously over time without 'giving out' or fatiguing.
Category Flexibility	The ability to generate or use different sets of rules for combining or grouping things in different ways.
Speech Recognition	The ability to identify and understand the speech of another person.
Information Ordering	The ability to arrange things or actions in a certain order or pattern according to a specific rule or set of rules (e.g., patterns of numbers, letters, words, pictures, mathematical operations).
Near Vision	The ability to see details at close range (within a few feet of the observer).
Problem Sensitivity	The ability to tell when something is wrong or is likely to go wrong. It does not involve solving the problem, only recognizing there is a problem.
Deductive Reasoning	The ability to apply general rules to specific problems to produce answers that make sense.
Static Strength	The ability to exert maximum muscle force to lift, push, pull, or carry objects.
Inductive Reasoning	The ability to combine pieces of information to form general rules or conclusions (includes finding a relationship among seemingly unrelated events).
Extent Flexibility	The ability to bend, stretch, twist, or reach with your body, arms, and/or legs.
Multilimb Coordination	The ability to coordinate two or more limbs (for example, two arms, two legs, or one leg and one arm) while sitting, standing, or lying down. It does not involve performing the activities while the whole body is in motion.
Time Sharing	The ability to shift back and forth between two or more activities or sources of information (such as speech, sounds, touch, or other sources).
Written Comprehension	The ability to read and understand information and ideas presented in writing.
Stamina	The ability to exert yourself physically over long periods of time without getting winded or out of breath.
Mathematical Reasoning	The ability to choose the right mathematical methods or formulas to solve a problem.
Number Facility	The ability to add, subtract, multiply, or divide quickly and correctly.
Manual Dexterity	The ability to quickly move your hand, your hand together with your arm, or your two hands to grasp, manipulate, or assemble objects.
Originality	The ability to come up with unusual or clever ideas about a given topic or situation, or to develop creative ways to solve a problem.
Gross Body Coordination	The ability to coordinate the movement of your arms, legs, and torso together when the whole body is in motion.
Visualization	The ability to imagine how something will look after it is moved around or when its parts are moved or rearranged.
Arm-Hand Steadiness	The ability to keep your hand and arm steady while moving your arm or while holding your arm and hand in one position.
Selective Attention	The ability to concentrate on a task over a period of time without being distracted.
Perceptual Speed	The ability to quickly and accurately compare similarities and differences among sets of letters, numbers, objects, pictures, or patterns. The things to be compared may be presented at the same time or one after the other. This ability also includes comparing a presented object with a remembered object.
Far Vision	The ability to see details at a distance.
Fluency of Ideas	The ability to come up with a number of ideas about a topic (the number of ideas is important, not their quality, correctness, or creativity).
Memorization	The ability to remember information such as words, numbers, pictures, and procedures.
Written Expression	The ability to communicate information and ideas in writing so others will understand.
Auditory Attention	The ability to focus on a single source of sound in the presence of other distracting sounds.
Speed of Limb Movement	The ability to quickly move the arms and legs.
Dynamic Strength	The ability to exert muscle force repeatedly or continuously over time. This involves muscular endurance and resistance to muscle fatigue.
Spatial Orientation	The ability to know your location in relation to the environment or to know where other objects are in relation to you.
Depth Perception	The ability to judge which of several objects is closer or farther away from you, or to judge the distance between you and an object.

Gross Body Equilibrium	The ability to keep or regain your body balance or stay upright when in an unstable position.
Finger Dexterity	The ability to make precisely coordinated movements of the fingers of one or both hands to grasp, manipulate, or assemble very small objects.
Glare Sensitivity	The ability to see objects in the presence of glare or bright lighting.
Visual Color Discrimination	The ability to match or detect differences between colors, including shades of color and brightness.
Flexibility of Closure	The ability to identify or detect a known pattern (a figure, object, word, or sound) that is hidden in other distracting material.
Speed of Closure	The ability to quickly make sense of, combine, and organize information into meaningful patterns.
Wrist-Finger Speed	The ability to make fast, simple, repeated movements of the fingers, hands, and wrists.
Control Precision	The ability to quickly and repeatedly adjust the controls of a machine or a vehicle to exact positions.
Dynamic Flexibility	The ability to quickly and repeatedly bend, stretch, twist, or reach out with your body, arms, and/or legs.
Peripheral Vision	The ability to see objects or movement of objects to one's side when the eyes are looking ahead.
Reaction Time	The ability to quickly respond (with the hand, finger, or foot) to a signal (sound, light, picture) when it appears.
Response Orientation	The ability to choose quickly between two or more movements in response to two or more different signals (lights, sounds, pictures). It includes the speed with which the correct response is started with the hand, foot, or other body part.
Hearing Sensitivity	The ability to detect or tell the differences between sounds that vary in pitch and loudness.
Night Vision	The ability to see under low light conditions.
Rate Control	The ability to time your movements or the movement of a piece of equipment in anticipation of changes in the speed and/or direction of a moving object or scene.
Sound Localization	The ability to tell the direction from which a sound originated.
Explosive Strength	The ability to use short bursts of muscle force to propel oneself (as in jumping or sprinting), or to throw an object.

Work_Activity	Work_Activity Definitions
Communicating with Supervisors, Peers, or Subordin	Providing information to supervisors, co-workers, and subordinates by telephone, in written form, e-mail, or in person.
Performing for or Working Directly with the Public	Performing for people or dealing directly with the public. This includes serving customers in restaurants and stores, and receiving clients or guests.
Handling and Moving Objects	Using hands and arms in handling, installing, positioning, and moving materials, and manipulating things.
Performing General Physical Activities	Performing physical activities that require considerable use of your arms and legs and moving your whole body, such as climbing, lifting, balancing, walking, stooping, and handling of materials.
Controlling Machines and Processes	Using either control mechanisms or direct physical activity to operate machines or processes (not including computers or vehicles).
Training and Teaching Others	Identifying the educational needs of others, developing formal educational or training programs or classes, and teaching or instructing others.
Establishing and Maintaining Interpersonal Relatio	Developing constructive and cooperative working relationships with others, and maintaining them over time.
Identifying Objects, Actions, and Events	Identifying information by categorizing, estimating, recognizing differences or similarities, and detecting changes in circumstances or events.
Judging the Qualities of Things, Services, or Peop	Assessing the value, importance, or quality of things or people.
Getting Information	Observing, receiving, and otherwise obtaining information from all relevant sources.
Updating and Using Relevant Knowledge	Keeping up-to-date technically and applying new knowledge to your job.
Resolving Conflicts and Negotiating with Others	Handling complaints, settling disputes, and resolving grievances and conflicts, or otherwise negotiating with others.
Developing and Building Teams	Encouraging and building mutual trust, respect, and cooperation among team members.
Coordinating the Work and Activities of Others	Getting members of a group to work together to accomplish tasks.
Processing Information	Compiling, coding, categorizing, calculating, tabulating, auditing, or verifying information or data.

Selling or Influencing Others	Convincing others to buy merchandise/goods or to otherwise change their minds or actions.
Organizing, Planning, and Prioritizing Work	Developing specific goals and plans to prioritize, organize, and accomplish your work.
Assisting and Caring for Others	Providing personal assistance, medical attention, emotional support, or other personal care to others such as coworkers, customers, or patients.
Making Decisions and Solving Problems	Analyzing information and evaluating results to choose the best solution and solve problems.
Inspecting Equipment, Structures, or Material	Inspecting equipment, structures, or materials to identify the cause of errors or other problems or defects.
Documenting/Recording Information	Entering, transcribing, recording, storing, or maintaining information in written or electronic/magnetic form.
Operating Vehicles, Mechanized Devices, or Equipme	Running, maneuvering, navigating, or driving vehicles or mechanized equipment, such as forklifts, passenger vehicles, aircraft, or water craft.
Evaluating Information to Determine Compliance wit	Using relevant information and individual judgment to determine whether events or processes comply with laws, regulations, or standards.
Estimating the Quantifiable Characteristics of Pro	Estimating sizes, distances, and quantities; or determining time, costs, resources, or materials needed to perform a work activity.
Coaching and Developing Others	Identifying the developmental needs of others and coaching, mentoring, or otherwise helping others to improve their knowledge or skills.
Monitoring and Controlling Resources	Monitoring and controlling resources and overseeing the spending of money.
Analyzing Data or Information	Identifying the underlying principles, reasons, or facts of information by breaking down information or data into separate parts.
Interpreting the Meaning of Information for Others	Translating or explaining what information means and how it can be used.
Provide Consultation and Advice to Others	Providing guidance and expert advice to management or other groups on technical, systems-, or process-related topics.
Guiding, Directing, and Motivating Subordinates	Providing guidance and direction to subordinates, including setting performance standards and monitoring performance.
Thinking Creatively	Developing, designing, or creating new applications, ideas, relationships, systems, or products, including artistic contributions.
Interacting With Computers	Using computers and computer systems (including hardware and software) to program, write software, set up functions, enter data, or process information.
Monitor Processes, Materials, or Surroundings	Monitoring and reviewing information from materials, events, or the environment, to detect or assess problems.
Communicating with Persons Outside Organization	Communicating with people outside the organization, representing the organization to customers, the public, government, and other external sources. This information can be exchanged in person, in writing, or by telephone or e-mail.
Scheduling Work and Activities	Scheduling events, programs, and activities, as well as the work of others.
Performing Administrative Activities	Performing day-to-day administrative tasks such as maintaining information files and processing paperwork.
Developing Objectives and Strategies	Establishing long-range objectives and specifying the strategies and actions to achieve them.
Staffing Organizational Units	Recruiting, interviewing, selecting, hiring, and promoting employees in an organization.
Drafting, Laying Out, and Specifying Technical Dev	Providing documentation, detailed instructions, drawings, or specifications to tell others about how devices, parts, equipment, or structures are to be fabricated, constructed, assembled, modified, maintained, or used.
Repairing and Maintaining Electronic Equipment	Servicing, repairing, calibrating, regulating, fine-tuning, or testing machines, devices, and equipment that operate primarily on the basis of electrical or electronic (not mechanical) principles.
Repairing and Maintaining Mechanical Equipment	Servicing, repairing, adjusting, and testing machines, devices, moving parts, and equipment that operate primarily on the basis of mechanical (not electronic) principles.

Work_Context	**Work_Context Definitions**
Deal With External Customers	How important is it to work with external customers or the public in this job?
Contact With Others	How much does this job require the worker to be in contact with others (face-to-face, by telephone, or otherwise) in order to perform it?
Indoors, Environmentally Controlled	How often does this job require working indoors in environmentally controlled conditions?

Spend Time Standing	How much does this job require standing?
Face-to-Face Discussions	How often do you have to have face-to-face discussions with individuals or teams in this job?
Work With Work Group or Team	How important is it to work with others in a group or team in this job?
Importance of Being Exact or Accurate	How important is being very exact or highly accurate in performing this job?
Spend Time Using Your Hands to Handle, Control, or	How much does this job require using your hands to handle, control, or feel objects, tools or controls?
Time Pressure	How often does this job require the worker to meet strict deadlines?
Spend Time Walking and Running	How much does this job require walking and running?
Freedom to Make Decisions	How much decision making freedom, without supervision, does the job offer?
Telephone	How often do you have telephone conversations in this job?
Structured versus Unstructured Work	To what extent is this job structured for the worker, rather than allowing the worker to determine tasks, priorities, and goals?
Coordinate or Lead Others	How important is it to coordinate or lead others in accomplishing work activities in this job?
Spend Time Kneeling, Crouching, Stooping, or Crawl	How much does this job require kneeling, crouching, stooping, or crawling?
Responsible for Others' Health and Safety	How much responsibility is there for the health and safety of others in this job?
Spend Time Bending or Twisting the Body	How much does this job require bending or twisting your body?
Spend Time Making Repetitive Motions	How much does this job require making repetitive motions?
Physical Proximity	To what extent does this job require the worker to perform job tasks in close physical proximity to other people?
Importance of Repeating Same Tasks	How important is repeating the same physical activities (e.g., key entry) or mental activities (e.g., checking entries in a ledger) over and over, without stopping, to performing this job?
Sounds, Noise Levels Are Distracting or Uncomforta	How often does this job require working exposed to sounds and noise levels that are distracting or uncomfortable?
Frequency of Conflict Situations	How often are there conflict situations the employee has to face in this job?
Impact of Decisions on Co-workers or Company Resul	How do the decisions an employee makes impact the results of co-workers, clients or the company?
Deal With Unpleasant or Angry People	How frequently does the worker have to deal with unpleasant, angry, or discourteous individuals as part of the job requirements?
Frequency of Decision Making	How frequently is the worker required to make decisions that affect other people, the financial resources, and/or the image and reputation of the organization?
Exposed to Contaminants	How often does this job require working exposed to contaminants (such as pollutants, gases, dust or odors)?
Wear Common Protective or Safety Equipment such as	How much does this job require wearing common protective or safety equipment such as safety shoes, glasses, gloves, hard hats or live jackets?
Responsibility for Outcomes and Results	How responsible is the worker for work outcomes and results of other workers?
Extremely Bright or Inadequate Lighting	How often does this job require working in extremely bright or inadequate lighting conditions?
Level of Competition	To what extent does this job require the worker to compete or to be aware of competitive pressures?
Pace Determined by Speed of Equipment	How important is it to this job that the pace is determined by the speed of equipment or machinery? (This does not refer to keeping busy at all times on this job.)
Very Hot or Cold Temperatures	How often does this job require working in very hot (above 90 F degrees) or very cold (below 32 F degrees) temperatures?
Indoors, Not Environmentally Controlled	How often does this job require working indoors in non-controlled environmental conditions (e.g., warehouse without heat)?
Letters and Memos	How often does the job require written letters and memos?
Spend Time Sitting	How much does this job require sitting?
Electronic Mail	How often do you use electronic mail in this job?
Consequence of Error	How serious would the result usually be if the worker made a mistake that was not readily correctable?
Outdoors, Exposed to Weather	How often does this job require working outdoors, exposed to all weather conditions?
Degree of Automation	How automated is the job?
Exposed to Minor Burns, Cuts, Bites, or Stings	How often does this job require exposure to minor burns, cuts, bites, or stings?

In an Open Vehicle or Equipment	How often does this job require working in an open vehicle or equipment (e.g., tractor)?
Public Speaking	How often do you have to perform public speaking in this job?
Spend Time Climbing Ladders, Scaffolds, or Poles	How much does this job require climbing ladders, scaffolds, or poles?
Exposed to Hazardous Conditions	How often does this job require exposure to hazardous conditions?
Outdoors, Under Cover	How often does this job require working outdoors, under cover (e.g., structure with roof but no walls)?
Spend Time Keeping or Regaining Balance	How much does this job require keeping or regaining your balance?
Cramped Work Space, Awkward Positions	How often does this job require working in cramped work spaces that requires getting into awkward positions?
Deal With Physically Aggressive People	How frequently does this job require the worker to deal with physical aggression of violent individuals?
Exposed to High Places	How often does this job require exposure to high places?
Exposed to Disease or Infections	How often does this job require exposure to disease/infections?
Exposed to Hazardous Equipment	How often does this job require exposure to hazardous equipment?
In an Enclosed Vehicle or Equipment	How often does this job require working in a closed vehicle or equipment (e.g., car)?
Exposed to Whole Body Vibration	How often does this job require exposure to whole body vibration (e.g., operate a jackhammer)?
Wear Specialized Protective or Safety Equipment su	How much does this job require wearing specialized protective or safety equipment such as breathing apparatus, safety harness, full protection suits, or radiation protection?
Exposed to Radiation	How often does this job require exposure to radiation?

Job Zone Component	Job Zone Component Definitions
Title	Job Zone One: Little or No Preparation Needed
Overall Experience	No previous work-related skill, knowledge, or experience is needed for these occupations. For example, a person can become a general office clerk even if he/she has never worked in an office before.
Job Training	Employees in these occupations need anywhere from a few days to a few months of training. Usually, an experienced worker could show you how to do the job.
Job Zone Examples	These occupations involve following instructions and helping others. Examples include bus drivers, forest and conservation workers, general office clerks, home health aides, and waiters/waitresses.
SVP Range	(Below 4.0)
Education	These occupations may require a high school diploma or GED certificate. Some may require a formal training course to obtain a license.

Work_Styles	Work_Styles Definitions
Self Control	Job requires maintaining composure, keeping emotions in check, controlling anger, and avoiding aggressive behavior, even in very difficult situations.
Dependability	Job requires being reliable, responsible, and dependable, and fulfilling obligations.
Integrity	Job requires being honest and ethical.
Cooperation	Job requires being pleasant with others on the job and displaying a good-natured, cooperative attitude.
Attention to Detail	Job requires being careful about detail and thorough in completing work tasks.
Stress Tolerance	Job requires accepting criticism and dealing calmly and effectively with high stress situations.
Concern for Others	Job requires being sensitive to others' needs and feelings and being understanding and helpful on the job.
Social Orientation	Job requires preferring to work with others rather than alone, and being personally connected with others on the job.
Independence	Job requires developing one's own ways of doing things, guiding oneself with little or no supervision, and depending on oneself to get things done.
Leadership	Job requires a willingness to lead, take charge, and offer opinions and direction.
Initiative	Job requires a willingness to take on responsibilities and challenges.
Adaptability/Flexibility	Job requires being open to change (positive or negative) and to considerable variety in the workplace.

Achievement/Effort	Job requires establishing and maintaining personally challenging achievement goals and exerting effort toward mastering tasks.
Innovation	Job requires creativity and alternative thinking to develop new ideas for and answers to work-related problems.
Persistence	Job requires persistence in the face of obstacles.
Analytical Thinking	Job requires analyzing information and using logic to address work-related issues and problems.

43-5081.02 - Marking Clerks

Print and attach price tickets to articles of merchandise using one or several methods, such as marking price on tickets by hand or using ticket-printing machine.

Tasks

1) Pin, paste, sew, tie, or staple tickets, tags, or labels to article.

2) Put price information on tickets, marking by hand or using ticket-printing machine.

3) Keep records of production, returned goods, and related transactions.

4) Record price, buyer, and grade of product on tickets attached to products auctioned.

5) Mark selling price by hand on boxes containing merchandise.

6) Indicate item size, style, color, and inspection results on tags, tickets, and labels, using rubber stamp or writing instrument.

7) Compare printed price tickets with entries on purchase orders to verify accuracy and notify supervisor of discrepancies.

8) Change the price of books in a warehouse.

43-5081.03 - Stock Clerks- Stockroom, Warehouse, or Storage Yard

Receive, store, and issue materials, equipment, and other items from stockroom, warehouse, or storage yard. Keep records and compile stock reports.

Tasks

1) Pack and unpack items to be stocked on shelves in stockrooms, warehouses, or storage yards.

2) Dispose of damaged or defective items, or return them to vendors.

3) Clean and maintain supplies, tools, equipment, and storage areas in order to ensure compliance with safety regulations.

4) Receive and count stock items, and record data manually or using computer.

5) Examine and inspect stock items for wear or defects, reporting any damage to supervisors.

6) Mark stock items using identification tags, stamps, electric marking tools, or other labeling equipment.

7) Verify inventory computations by comparing them to physical counts of stock, and investigate discrepancies or adjust errors.

8) Provide assistance or direction to other stockroom, warehouse, or storage yard workers.

9) Keep records on the use and/or damage of stock or stock handling equipment.

10) Determine proper storage methods, identification, and stock location based on turnover, environmental factors, and physical capabilities of facilities.

11) Recommend disposal of excess, defective, or obsolete stock.

12) Issue or distribute materials, products, parts, and supplies to customers or coworkers, based on information from incoming requisitions.

13) Purchase new or additional stock, or prepare documents that provide for such purchases.

14) Sell materials, equipment, and other items from stock in retail settings.

15) Advise retail customers or internal users on the appropriateness of parts, supplies, or materials requested.

16) Prepare and maintain records and reports of inventories, price lists, shortages, shipments, expenditures, and goods used or issued.

17) Prepare products, supplies, equipment, or other items for use by adjusting, repairing or

assembling them as necessary.

18) Confer with engineering and purchasing personnel and vendors regarding stock procurement and availability.

19) Determine sequence and release of back orders according to stock availability.

20) Compile, review, and maintain data from contracts, purchase orders, requisitions, and other documents in order to assess supply needs.

21) Drive trucks in order to pick up incoming stock or to deliver parts to designated locations.

Knowledge	Knowledge Definitions
Administration and Management	Knowledge of business and management principles involved in strategic planning, resource allocation, human resources modeling, leadership technique, production methods, and coordination of people and resources.
Customer and Personal Service	Knowledge of principles and processes for providing customer and personal services. This includes customer needs assessment, meeting quality standards for services, and evaluation of customer satisfaction.
English Language	Knowledge of the structure and content of the English language including the meaning and spelling of words, rules of composition, and grammar.
Production and Processing	Knowledge of raw materials, production processes, quality control, costs, and other techniques for maximizing the effective manufacture and distribution of goods.
Mathematics	Knowledge of arithmetic, algebra, geometry, calculus, statistics, and their applications.
Public Safety and Security	Knowledge of relevant equipment, policies, procedures, and strategies to promote effective local, state, or national security operations for the protection of people, data, property, and institutions.
Clerical	Knowledge of administrative and clerical procedures and systems such as word processing, managing files and records, stenography and transcription, designing forms, and other office procedures and terminology.
Sales and Marketing	Knowledge of principles and methods for showing, promoting, and selling products or services. This includes marketing strategy and tactics, product demonstration, sales techniques, and sales control systems.
Personnel and Human Resources	Knowledge of principles and procedures for personnel recruitment, selection, training, compensation and benefits, labor relations and negotiation, and personnel information systems.
Computers and Electronics	Knowledge of circuit boards, processors, chips, electronic equipment, and computer hardware and software, including applications and programming.
Education and Training	Knowledge of principles and methods for curriculum and training design, teaching and instruction for individuals and groups, and the measurement of training effects.
Economics and Accounting	Knowledge of economic and accounting principles and practices, the financial markets, banking and the analysis and reporting of financial data.
Transportation	Knowledge of principles and methods for moving people or goods by air, rail, sea, or road, including the relative costs and benefits.
Mechanical	Knowledge of machines and tools, including their designs, uses, repair, and maintenance.
Law and Government	Knowledge of laws, legal codes, court procedures, precedents, government regulations, executive orders, agency rules, and the democratic political process.
Food Production	Knowledge of techniques and equipment for planting, growing, and harvesting food products (both plant and animal) for consumption, including storage/handling techniques.
Psychology	Knowledge of human behavior and performance; individual differences in ability, personality, and interests; learning and motivation; psychological research methods; and the assessment and treatment of behavioral and affective disorders.
Chemistry	Knowledge of the chemical composition, structure, and properties of substances and of the chemical processes and transformations that they undergo. This includes uses of chemicals and their interactions, danger signs, production techniques, and disposal methods.
Engineering and Technology	Knowledge of the practical application of engineering science and technology. This includes applying principles, techniques, procedures, and equipment to the design and production of various goods and services.
Design	Knowledge of design techniques, tools, and principles involved in production of precision technical plans, blueprints, drawings, and models.
Sociology and Anthropology	Knowledge of group behavior and dynamics, societal trends and influences, human migrations, ethnicity, cultures and their history and origins.
Telecommunications	Knowledge of transmission, broadcasting, switching, control, and operation of telecommunications systems.
Building and Construction	Knowledge of materials, methods, and the tools involved in the construction or repair of houses, buildings, or other structures such as highways and roads.
Communications and Media	Knowledge of media production, communication, and dissemination techniques and methods. This includes alternative ways to inform and entertain via written, oral, and visual media.
Therapy and Counseling	Knowledge of principles, methods, and procedures for diagnosis, treatment, and rehabilitation of physical and mental dysfunctions, and for career counseling and guidance.
Foreign Language	Knowledge of the structure and content of a foreign (non-English) language including the meaning and spelling of words, rules of composition and grammar, and pronunciation.
Geography	Knowledge of principles and methods for describing the features of land, sea, and air masses, including their physical characteristics, locations, interrelationships, and distribution of plant, animal, and human life.
Medicine and Dentistry	Knowledge of the information and techniques needed to diagnose and treat human injuries, diseases, and deformities. This includes symptoms, treatment alternatives, drug properties and interactions, and preventive health-care measures.
Physics	Knowledge and prediction of physical principles, laws, their interrelationships, and applications to understanding fluid, material, and atmospheric dynamics, and mechanical, electrical, atomic and sub- atomic structures and processes.
History and Archeology	Knowledge of historical events and their causes, indicators, and effects on civilizations and cultures.
Biology	Knowledge of plant and animal organisms, their tissues, cells, functions, interdependencies, and interactions with each other and the environment.
Fine Arts	Knowledge of the theory and techniques required to compose, produce, and perform works of music, dance, visual arts, drama, and sculpture.
Philosophy and Theology	Knowledge of different philosophical systems and religions. This includes their basic principles, values, ethics, ways of thinking, customs, practices, and their impact on human culture.

Skills	Skills Definitions
Speaking	Talking to others to convey information effectively.
Active Listening	Giving full attention to what other people are saying, taking time to understand the points being made, asking questions as appropriate, and not interrupting at inappropriate times.
Active Learning	Understanding the implications of new information for both current and future problem-solving and decision-making.
Mathematics	Using mathematics to solve problems.
Critical Thinking	Using logic and reasoning to identify the strengths and weaknesses of alternative solutions, conclusions or approaches to problems.
Coordination	Adjusting actions in relation to others' actions.
Learning Strategies	Selecting and using training/instructional methods and procedures appropriate for the situation when learning or teaching new things.
Social Perceptiveness	Being aware of others' reactions and understanding why they react as they do.
Reading Comprehension	Understanding written sentences and paragraphs in work related documents.
Service Orientation	Actively looking for ways to help people.
Instructing	Teaching others how to do something.
Time Management	Managing one's own time and the time of others.
Monitoring	Monitoring/Assessing performance of yourself, other individuals, or organizations to make improvements or take corrective action.
Judgment and Decision Making	Considering the relative costs and benefits of potential actions to choose the most appropriate one.
Negotiation	Bringing others together and trying to reconcile differences.
Quality Control Analysis	Conducting tests and inspections of products, services, or processes to evaluate quality or performance.

Writing	Communicating effectively in writing as appropriate for the needs of the audience.
Management of Personnel Resources	Motivating, developing, and directing people as they work, identifying the best people for the job.
Equipment Selection	Determining the kind of tools and equipment needed to do a job.
Persuasion	Persuading others to change their minds or behavior.
Management of Financial Resources	Determining how money will be spent to get the work done, and accounting for these expenditures.
Operation and Control	Controlling operations of equipment or systems.
Complex Problem Solving	Identifying complex problems and reviewing related information to develop and evaluate options and implement solutions.
Equipment Maintenance	Performing routine maintenance on equipment and determining when and what kind of maintenance is needed.
Troubleshooting	Determining causes of operating errors and deciding what to do about it.
Operation Monitoring	Watching gauges, dials, or other indicators to make sure a machine is working properly.
Systems Analysis	Determining how a system should work and how changes in conditions, operations, and the environment will affect outcomes.
Operations Analysis	Analyzing needs and product requirements to create a design.
Management of Material Resources	Obtaining and seeing to the appropriate use of equipment, facilities, and materials needed to do certain work.
Technology Design	Generating or adapting equipment and technology to serve user needs.
Systems Evaluation	Identifying measures or indicators of system performance and the actions needed to improve or correct performance, relative to the goals of the system.
Science	Using scientific rules and methods to solve problems.
Installation	Installing equipment, machines, wiring, or programs to meet specifications.
Repairing	Repairing machines or systems using the needed tools.
Programming	Writing computer programs for various purposes.

Ability	Ability Definitions
Problem Sensitivity	The ability to tell when something is wrong or is likely to go wrong. It does not involve solving the problem, only recognizing there is a problem.
Deductive Reasoning	The ability to apply general rules to specific problems to produce answers that make sense.
Oral Comprehension	The ability to listen to and understand information and ideas presented through spoken words and sentences.
Information Ordering	The ability to arrange things or actions in a certain order or pattern according to a specific rule or set of rules (e.g., patterns of numbers, letters, words, pictures, mathematical operations).
Manual Dexterity	The ability to quickly move your hand, your hand together with your arm, or your two hands to grasp, manipulate, or assemble objects.
Near Vision	The ability to see details at close range (within a few feet of the observer).
Multilimb Coordination	The ability to coordinate two or more limbs (for example, two arms, two legs, or one leg and one arm) while sitting, standing, or lying down. It does not involve performing the activities while the whole body is in motion.
Speech Clarity	The ability to speak clearly so others can understand you.
Oral Expression	The ability to communicate information and ideas in speaking so others will understand.
Extent Flexibility	The ability to bend, stretch, twist, or reach with your body, arms, and/or legs.
Inductive Reasoning	The ability to combine pieces of information to form general rules or conclusions (includes finding a relationship among seemingly unrelated events).
Static Strength	The ability to exert maximum muscle force to lift, push, pull, or carry objects.
Trunk Strength	The ability to use your abdominal and lower back muscles to support part of the body repeatedly or continuously over time without 'giving out' or fatiguing.
Speech Recognition	The ability to identify and understand the speech of another person.
Written Expression	The ability to communicate information and ideas in writing so others will understand.
Stamina	The ability to exert yourself physically over long periods of time without getting winded or out of breath.
Written Comprehension	The ability to read and understand information and ideas presented in writing.

Gross Body Coordination	The ability to coordinate the movement of your arms, legs, and torso together when the whole body is in motion.
Category Flexibility	The ability to generate or use different sets of rules for combining or grouping things in different ways.
Arm-Hand Steadiness	The ability to keep your hand and arm steady while moving your arm or while holding your arm and hand in one position.
Depth Perception	The ability to judge which of several objects is closer or farther away from you, or to judge the distance between you and an object.
Mathematical Reasoning	The ability to choose the right mathematical methods or formulas to solve a problem.
Selective Attention	The ability to concentrate on a task over a period of time without being distracted.
Far Vision	The ability to see details at a distance.
Finger Dexterity	The ability to make precisely coordinated movements of the fingers of one or both hands to grasp, manipulate, or assemble very small objects.
Control Precision	The ability to quickly and repeatedly adjust the controls of a machine or a vehicle to exact positions.
Speed of Limb Movement	The ability to quickly move the arms and legs.
Perceptual Speed	The ability to quickly and accurately compare similarities and differences among sets of letters, numbers, objects, pictures, or patterns. The things to be compared may be presented at the same time or one after the other. This ability also includes comparing a presented object with a remembered object.
Number Facility	The ability to add, subtract, multiply, or divide quickly and correctly.
Dynamic Strength	The ability to exert muscle force repeatedly or continuously over time. This involves muscular endurance and resistance to muscle fatigue.
Time Sharing	The ability to shift back and forth between two or more activities or sources of information (such as speech, sounds, touch, or other sources).
Flexibility of Closure	The ability to identify or detect a known pattern (a figure, object, word, or sound) that is hidden in other distracting material.
Visualization	The ability to imagine how something will look after it is moved around or when its parts are moved or rearranged.
Spatial Orientation	The ability to know your location in relation to the environment or to know where other objects are in relation to you.
Speed of Closure	The ability to quickly make sense of, combine, and organize information into meaningful patterns.
Wrist-Finger Speed	The ability to make fast, simple, repeated movements of the fingers, hands, and wrists.
Auditory Attention	The ability to focus on a single source of sound in the presence of other distracting sounds.
Visual Color Discrimination	The ability to match or detect differences between colors, including shades of color and brightness.
Originality	The ability to come up with unusual or clever ideas about a given topic or situation, or to develop creative ways to solve a problem.
Fluency of Ideas	The ability to come up with a number of ideas about a topic (the number of ideas is important, not their quality, correctness, or creativity).
Gross Body Equilibrium	The ability to keep or regain your body balance or stay upright when in an unstable position.
Memorization	The ability to remember information such as words, numbers, pictures, and procedures.
Response Orientation	The ability to choose quickly between two or more movements in response to two or more different signals (lights, sounds, pictures). It includes the speed with which the correct response is started with the hand, foot, or other body part.
Reaction Time	The ability to quickly respond (with the hand, finger, or foot) to a signal (sound, light, picture) when it appears.
Rate Control	The ability to time your movements or the movement of a piece of equipment in anticipation of changes in the speed and/or direction of a moving object or scene.
Hearing Sensitivity	The ability to detect or tell the differences between sounds that vary in pitch and loudness.
Peripheral Vision	The ability to see objects or movement of objects to one's side when the eyes are looking ahead.
Dynamic Flexibility	The ability to quickly and repeatedly bend, stretch, twist, or reach out with your body, arms, and/or legs.
Night Vision	The ability to see under low light conditions.
Explosive Strength	The ability to use short bursts of muscle force to propel oneself (as in jumping or sprinting), or to throw an object.
Glare Sensitivity	The ability to see objects in the presence of glare or bright lighting.

973

Sound Localization	The ability to tell the direction from which a sound originated.

Work_Activity	Work_Activity Definitions
Handling and Moving Objects	Using hands and arms in handling, installing, positioning, and moving materials, and manipulating things.
Performing General Physical Activities	Performing physical activities that require considerable use of your arms and legs and moving your whole body, such as climbing, lifting, balancing, walking, stooping, and handling of materials.
Getting Information	Observing, receiving, and otherwise obtaining information from all relevant sources.
Establishing and Maintaining Interpersonal Relatio	Developing constructive and cooperative working relationships with others, and maintaining them over time.
Communicating with Supervisors, Peers, or Subordin	Providing information to supervisors, co-workers, and subordinates by telephone, in written form, e-mail, or in person.
Performing for or Working Directly with the Public	Performing for people or dealing directly with the public. This includes serving customers in restaurants and stores, and receiving clients or guests.
Controlling Machines and Processes	Using either control mechanisms or direct physical activity to operate machines or processes (not including computers or vehicles).
Organizing, Planning, and Prioritizing Work	Developing specific goals and plans to prioritize, organize, and accomplish your work.
Identifying Objects, Actions, and Events	Identifying information by categorizing, estimating, recognizing differences or similarities, and detecting changes in circumstances or events.
Processing Information	Compiling, coding, categorizing, calculating, tabulating, auditing, or verifying information or data.
Making Decisions and Solving Problems	Analyzing information and evaluating results to choose the best solution and solve problems.
Estimating the Quantifiable Characteristics of Pro	Estimating sizes, distances, and quantities; or determining time, costs, resources, or materials needed to perform a work activity.
Assisting and Caring for Others	Providing personal assistance, medical attention, emotional support, or other personal care to others such as coworkers, customers, or patients.
Monitor Processes, Materials, or Surroundings	Monitoring and reviewing information from materials, events, or the environment, to detect or assess problems.
Documenting/Recording Information	Entering, transcribing, recording, storing, or maintaining information in written or electronic/magnetic form.
Selling or Influencing Others	Convincing others to buy merchandise/goods or to otherwise change their minds or actions.
Resolving Conflicts and Negotiating with Others	Handling complaints, settling disputes, and resolving grievances and conflicts, or otherwise negotiating with others.
Operating Vehicles, Mechanized Devices, or Equipme	Running, maneuvering, navigating, or driving vehicles or mechanized equipment, such as forklifts, passenger vehicles, aircraft, or water craft.
Developing and Building Teams	Encouraging and building mutual trust, respect, and cooperation among team members.
Interacting With Computers	Using computers and computer systems (including hardware and software) to program, write software, set up functions, enter data, or process information.
Scheduling Work and Activities	Scheduling events, programs, and activities, as well as the work of others.
Inspecting Equipment, Structures, or Material	Inspecting equipment, structures, or materials to identify the cause of errors or other problems or defects.
Judging the Qualities of Things, Services, or Peop	Assessing the value, importance, or quality of things or people.
Guiding, Directing, and Motivating Subordinates	Providing guidance and direction to subordinates, including setting performance standards and monitoring performance.
Thinking Creatively	Developing, designing, or creating new applications, ideas, relationships, systems, or products, including artistic contributions.
Evaluating Information to Determine Compliance wit	Using relevant information and individual judgment to determine whether events or processes comply with laws, regulations, or standards.
Updating and Using Relevant Knowledge	Keeping up-to-date technically and applying new knowledge to your job.
Training and Teaching Others	Identifying the educational needs of others, developing formal educational or training programs or classes, and teaching or instructing others.
Interpreting the Meaning of Information for Others	Translating or explaining what information means and how it can be used.

Performing Administrative Activities	Performing day-to-day administrative tasks such as maintaining information files and processing paperwork.
Communicating with Persons Outside Organization	Communicating with people outside the organization, representing the organization to customers, the public, government, and other external sources. This information can be exchanged in person, in writing, or by telephone or e-mail.
Analyzing Data or Information	Identifying the underlying principles, reasons, or facts of information by breaking down information or data into separate parts.
Coordinating the Work and Activities of Others	Getting members of a group to work together to accomplish tasks.
Developing Objectives and Strategies	Establishing long-range objectives and specifying the strategies and actions to achieve them.
Coaching and Developing Others	Identifying the developmental needs of others and coaching, mentoring, or otherwise helping others to improve their knowledge or skills.
Repairing and Maintaining Mechanical Equipment	Servicing, repairing, adjusting, and testing machines, devices, moving parts, and equipment that operate primarily on the basis of mechanical (not electronic) principles.
Monitoring and Controlling Resources	Monitoring and controlling resources and overseeing the spending of money.
Provide Consultation and Advice to Others	Providing guidance and expert advice to management or other groups on technical, systems-, or process-related topics.
Staffing Organizational Units	Recruiting, interviewing, selecting, hiring, and promoting employees in an organization.
Repairing and Maintaining Electronic Equipment	Servicing, repairing, calibrating, regulating, fine-tuning, or testing machines, devices, and equipment that operate primarily on the basis of electrical or electronic (not mechanical) principles.
Drafting, Laying Out, and Specifying Technical Dev	Providing documentation, detailed instructions, drawings, or specifications to tell others about how devices, parts, equipment, or structures are to be fabricated, constructed, assembled, modified, maintained, or used.

Work_Context	Work_Context Definitions
Work With Work Group or Team	How important is it to work with others in a group or team in this job?
Contact With Others	How much does this job require the worker to be in contact with others (face-to-face, by telephone, or otherwise) in order to perform it?
Face-to-Face Discussions	How often do you have to have face-to-face discussions with individuals or teams in this job?
Spend Time Standing	How much does this job require standing?
Frequency of Decision Making	How frequently is the worker required to make decisions that affect other people, the financial resources, and/or the image and reputation of the organization?
Importance of Being Exact or Accurate	How important is being very exact or highly accurate in performing this job?
Freedom to Make Decisions	How much decision making freedom, without supervision, does the job offer?
Spend Time Using Your Hands to Handle, Control, or	How much does this job require using your hands to handle, control, or feel objects, tools or controls?
Impact of Decisions on Co-workers or Company Resul	How do the decisions an employee makes impact the results of co-workers, clients or the company?
Telephone	How often do you have telephone conversations in this job?
Time Pressure	How often does this job require the worker to meet strict deadlines?
Deal With External Customers	How important is it to work with external customers or the public in this job?
Structured versus Unstructured Work	To what extent is this job structured for the worker, rather than allowing the worker to determine tasks, priorities, and goals?
Spend Time Walking and Running	How much does this job require walking and running?
Physical Proximity	To what extent does this job require the worker to perform job tasks in close physical proximity to other people?
Spend Time Making Repetitive Motions	How much does this job require making repetitive motions?
Spend Time Bending or Twisting the Body	How much does this job require bending or twisting your body?
Deal With Unpleasant or Angry People	How frequently does the worker have to deal with unpleasant, angry, or discourteous individuals as part of the job requirements?
Indoors, Environmentally Controlled	How often does this job require working indoors in environmentally controlled conditions?

974

Exposed to Contaminants	How often does this job require working exposed to contaminants (such as pollutants, gases, dust or odors)?
Responsible for Others' Health and Safety	How much responsibility is there for the health and safety of others in this job?
Frequency of Conflict Situations	How often are there conflict situations the employee has to face in this job?
Importance of Repeating Same Tasks	How important is repeating the same physical activities (e.g., key entry) or mental activities (e.g., checking entries in a ledger) over and over, without stopping, to performing this job?
Sounds, Noise Levels Are Distracting or Uncomforta	How often does this job require working exposed to sounds and noise levels that are distracting or uncomfortable?
Letters and Memos	How often does the job require written letters and memos?
Very Hot or Cold Temperatures	How often does this job require working in very hot (above 90 F degrees) or very cold (below 32 F degrees) temperatures?
Spend Time Kneeling, Crouching, Stooping, or Crawl	How much does this job require kneeling, crouching, stooping or crawling?
Indoors, Not Environmentally Controlled	How often does this job require working indoors in non-controlled environmental conditions (e.g., warehouse without heat)?
Level of Competition	To what extent does this job require the worker to compete or to be aware of competitive pressures?
Coordinate or Lead Others	How important is it to coordinate or lead others in accomplishing work activities in this job?
In an Open Vehicle or Equipment	How often does this job require working in an open vehicle or equipment (e.g., tractor)?
Responsibility for Outcomes and Results	How responsible is the worker for work outcomes and results of other workers?
Spend Time Keeping or Regaining Balance	How much does this job require keeping or regaining your balance?
Extremely Bright or Inadequate Lighting	How often does this job require working in extremely bright or inadequate lighting conditions?
Pace Determined by Speed of Equipment	How important is it to this job that the pace is determined by the speed of equipment or machinery? (This does not refer to keeping busy at all times on this job.)
Outdoors, Exposed to Weather	How often does this job require working outdoors, exposed to all weather conditions?
Consequence of Error	How serious would the result usually be if the worker made a mistake that was not readily correctable?
In an Enclosed Vehicle or Equipment	How often does this job require working in a closed vehicle or equipment (e.g., car)?
Exposed to Minor Burns, Cuts, Bites, or Stings	How often does this job require exposure to minor burns, cuts, bites, or stings?
Exposed to Hazardous Equipment	How often does this job require exposure to hazardous equipment?
Exposed to High Places	How often does this job require exposure to high places?
Wear Common Protective or Safety Equipment such as	How much does this job require wearing common protective or safety equipment such as safety shoes, glasses, gloves, hard hats or live jackets?
Cramped Work Space, Awkward Positions	How often does this job require working in cramped work spaces that requires getting into awkward positions?
Spend Time Sitting	How much does this job require sitting?
Exposed to Disease or Infections	How often does this job require exposure to disease/infections?
Exposed to Whole Body Vibration	How often does this job require exposure to whole body vibration (e.g., operate a jackhammer)?
Electronic Mail	How often do you use electronic mail in this job?
Outdoors, Under Cover	How often does this job require working outdoors, under cover (e.g., structure with roof but no walls)?
Degree of Automation	How automated is the job?
Exposed to Hazardous Conditions	How often does this job require exposure to hazardous conditions?
Spend Time Climbing Ladders, Scaffolds, or Poles	How much does this job require climbing ladders, scaffolds, or poles?
Public Speaking	How often do you have to perform public speaking in this job?
Deal With Physically Aggressive People	How frequently does this job require the worker to deal with physical aggression of violent individuals?
Exposed to Radiation	How often does this job require exposure to radiation?
Wear Specialized Protective or Safety Equipment su	How much does this job require wearing specialized protective or safety equipment such as breathing apparatus, safety harness, full protection suits, or radiation protection?

Job Zone Component	Job Zone Component Definitions
Title	Job Zone One: Little or No Preparation Needed

Overall Experience	No previous work-related skill, knowledge, or experience is needed for these occupations. For example, a person can become a general office clerk even if he/she has never worked in an office before.
Job Training	Employees in these occupations need anywhere from a few days to a few months of training. Usually, an experienced worker could show you how to do the job.
Job Zone Examples	These occupations involve following instructions and helping others. Examples include bus drivers, forest and conservation workers, general office clerks, home health aides, and waiters/waitresses.
SVP Range	(Below 4.0)
Education	These occupations may require a high school diploma or GED certificate. Some may require a formal training course to obtain a license.

Work_Styles	Work_Styles Definitions
Dependability	Job requires being reliable, responsible, and dependable, and fulfilling obligations.
Attention to Detail	Job requires being careful about detail and thorough in completing work tasks.
Cooperation	Job requires being pleasant with others on the job and displaying a good-natured, cooperative attitude.
Concern for Others	Job requires being sensitive to others' needs and feelings and being understanding and helpful on the job.
Self Control	Job requires maintaining composure, keeping emotions in check, controlling anger, and avoiding aggressive behavior, even in very difficult situations.
Integrity	Job requires being honest and ethical.
Independence	Job requires developing one's own ways of doing things, guiding oneself with little or no supervision, and depending on oneself to get things done.
Persistence	Job requires persistence in the face of obstacles.
Initiative	Job requires a willingness to take on responsibilities and challenges.
Social Orientation	Job requires preferring to work with others rather than alone, and being personally connected with others on the job.
Achievement/Effort	Job requires establishing and maintaining personally challenging achievement goals and exerting effort toward mastering tasks.
Stress Tolerance	Job requires accepting criticism and dealing calmly and effectively with high stress situations.
Adaptability/Flexibility	Job requires being open to change (positive or negative) and to considerable variety in the workplace.
Innovation	Job requires creativity and alternative thinking to develop new ideas for and answers to work-related problems.
Analytical Thinking	Job requires analyzing information and using logic to address work-related issues and problems.
Leadership	Job requires a willingness to lead, take charge, and offer opinions and direction.

43-5081.04 - Order Fillers, Wholesale and Retail Sales

Fill customers' mail and telephone orders from stored merchandise in accordance with specifications on sales slips or order forms. Duties include computing prices of items, completing order receipts, keeping records of out-going orders, and requisitioning additional materials, supplies, and equipment.

Tasks

1) Read orders to ascertain catalog numbers, sizes, colors, and quantities of merchandise.

2) Requisition additional materials, supplies, and equipment.

3) Compute prices of items or groups of items.

4) Keep records of out-going orders.

5) Complete order receipts.

6) Place merchandise on conveyors leading to wrapping areas.

Knowledge	Knowledge Definitions
Sales and Marketing	Knowledge of principles and methods for showing, promoting, and selling products or services. This includes marketing strategy and tactics, product demonstration, sales techniques, and sales control systems.
Production and Processing	Knowledge of raw materials, production processes, quality control, costs, and other techniques for maximizing the effective manufacture and distribution of goods.
Public Safety and Security	Knowledge of relevant equipment, policies, procedures, and strategies to promote effective local, state, or national security operations for the protection of people, data, property, and institutions.
English Language	Knowledge of the structure and content of the English language including the meaning and spelling of words, rules of composition, and grammar.
Mathematics	Knowledge of arithmetic, algebra, geometry, calculus, statistics, and their applications.
Administration and Management	Knowledge of business and management principles involved in strategic planning, resource allocation, human resources modeling, leadership technique, production methods, and coordination of people and resources.
Customer and Personal Service	Knowledge of principles and processes for providing customer and personal services. This includes customer needs assessment, meeting quality standards for services, and evaluation of customer satisfaction.
Education and Training	Knowledge of principles and methods for curriculum and training design, teaching and instruction for individuals and groups, and the measurement of training effects.
Clerical	Knowledge of administrative and clerical procedures and systems such as word processing, managing files and records, stenography and transcription, designing forms, and other office procedures and terminology.
Design	Knowledge of design techniques, tools, and principles involved in production of precision technical plans, blueprints, drawings, and models.
Telecommunications	Knowledge of transmission, broadcasting, switching, control, and operation of telecommunications systems.
Food Production	Knowledge of techniques and equipment for planting, growing, and harvesting food products (both plant and animal) for consumption, including storage/handling techniques.
Transportation	Knowledge of principles and methods for moving people or goods by air, rail, sea, or road, including the relative costs and benefits.
Mechanical	Knowledge of machines and tools, including their designs, uses, repair, and maintenance.
Communications and Media	Knowledge of media production, communication, and dissemination techniques and methods. This includes alternative ways to inform and entertain via written, oral, and visual media.
Computers and Electronics	Knowledge of circuit boards, processors, chips, electronic equipment, and computer hardware and software, including applications and programming.
Law and Government	Knowledge of laws, legal codes, court procedures, precedents, government regulations, executive orders, agency rules, and the democratic political process.
Psychology	Knowledge of human behavior and performance; individual differences in ability, personality, and interests; learning and motivation; psychological research methods; and the assessment and treatment of behavioral and affective disorders.
Chemistry	Knowledge of the chemical composition, structure, and properties of substances and of the chemical processes and transformations that they undergo. This includes uses of chemicals and their interactions, danger signs, production techniques, and disposal methods.
Physics	Knowledge and prediction of physical principles, laws, their interrelationships, and applications to understanding fluid, material, and atmospheric dynamics, and mechanical, electrical, atomic and sub-atomic structures and processes.
Engineering and Technology	Knowledge of the practical application of engineering science and technology. This includes applying principles, techniques, procedures, and equipment to the design and production of various goods and services.
Personnel and Human Resources	Knowledge of principles and procedures for personnel recruitment, selection, training, compensation and benefits, labor relations and negotiation, and personnel information systems.

Economics and Accounting	Knowledge of economic and accounting principles and practices, the financial markets, banking and the analysis and reporting of financial data.
Geography	Knowledge of principles and methods for describing the features of land, sea, and air masses, including their physical characteristics, locations, interrelationships, and distribution of plant, animal, and human life.
Therapy and Counseling	Knowledge of principles, methods, and procedures for diagnosis, treatment, and rehabilitation of physical and mental dysfunctions, and for career counseling and guidance.
Sociology and Anthropology	Knowledge of group behavior and dynamics, societal trends and influences, human migrations, ethnicity, cultures and their history and origins.
Building and Construction	Knowledge of materials, methods, and the tools involved in the construction or repair of houses, buildings, or other structures such as highways and roads.
Philosophy and Theology	Knowledge of different philosophical systems and religions. This includes their basic principles, values, ethics, ways of thinking, customs, practices, and their impact on human culture.
Medicine and Dentistry	Knowledge of the information and techniques needed to diagnose and treat human injuries, diseases, and deformities. This includes symptoms, treatment alternatives, drug properties and interactions, and preventive health-care measures.
Foreign Language	Knowledge of the structure and content of a foreign (non-English) language including the meaning and spelling of words, rules of composition and grammar, and pronunciation.
Biology	Knowledge of plant and animal organisms, their tissues, cells, functions, interdependencies, and interactions with each other and the environment.
Fine Arts	Knowledge of the theory and techniques required to compose, produce, and perform works of music, dance, visual arts, drama, and sculpture.
History and Archeology	Knowledge of historical events and their causes, indicators, and effects on civilizations and cultures.

Skills	Skills Definitions
Reading Comprehension	Understanding written sentences and paragraphs in work related documents.
Active Listening	Giving full attention to what other people are saying, taking time to understand the points being made, asking questions as appropriate, and not interrupting at inappropriate times.
Mathematics	Using mathematics to solve problems.
Quality Control Analysis	Conducting tests and inspections of products, services, or processes to evaluate quality or performance.
Speaking	Talking to others to convey information effectively.
Social Perceptiveness	Being aware of others' reactions and understanding why they react as they do.
Learning Strategies	Selecting and using training/instructional methods and procedures appropriate for the situation when learning or teaching new things.
Time Management	Managing one's own time and the time of others.
Critical Thinking	Using logic and reasoning to identify the strengths and weaknesses of alternative solutions, conclusions or approaches to problems.
Operation and Control	Controlling operations of equipment or systems.
Troubleshooting	Determining causes of operating errors and deciding what to do about it.
Instructing	Teaching others how to do something.
Equipment Selection	Determining the kind of tools and equipment needed to do a job.
Monitoring	Monitoring/Assessing performance of yourself, other individuals, or organizations to make improvements or take corrective action.
Coordination	Adjusting actions in relation to others' actions.
Writing	Communicating effectively in writing as appropriate for the needs of the audience.
Judgment and Decision Making	Considering the relative costs and benefits of potential actions to choose the most appropriate one.
Complex Problem Solving	Identifying complex problems and reviewing related information to develop and evaluate options and implement solutions.
Management of Personnel Resources	Motivating, developing, and directing people as they work, identifying the best people for the job.
Active Learning	Understanding the implications of new information for both current and future problem-solving and decision-making.

Equipment Maintenance	Performing routine maintenance on equipment and determining when and what kind of maintenance is needed.
Repairing	Repairing machines or systems using the needed tools.
Negotiation	Bringing others together and trying to reconcile differences.
Management of Material Resources	Obtaining and seeing to the appropriate use of equipment, facilities, and materials needed to do certain work.
Systems Analysis	Determining how a system should work and how changes in conditions, operations, and the environment will affect outcomes.
Operation Monitoring	Watching gauges, dials, or other indicators to make sure a machine is working properly.
Operations Analysis	Analyzing needs and product requirements to create a design.
Management of Financial Resources	Determining how money will be spent to get the work done, and accounting for these expenditures.
Systems Evaluation	Identifying measures or indicators of system performance and the actions needed to improve or correct performance, relative to the goals of the system.
Persuasion	Persuading others to change their minds or behavior.
Technology Design	Generating or adapting equipment and technology to serve user needs.
Installation	Installing equipment, machines, wiring, or programs to meet specifications.
Service Orientation	Actively looking for ways to help people.
Programming	Writing computer programs for various purposes.
Science	Using scientific rules and methods to solve problems.

Ability	Ability Definitions
Written Comprehension	The ability to read and understand information and ideas presented in writing.
Near Vision	The ability to see details at close range (within a few feet of the observer).
Information Ordering	The ability to arrange things or actions in a certain order or pattern according to a specific rule or set of rules (e.g., patterns of numbers, letters, words, pictures, mathematical operations).
Oral Comprehension	The ability to listen to and understand information and ideas presented through spoken words and sentences.
Problem Sensitivity	The ability to tell when something is wrong or is likely to go wrong. It does not involve solving the problem, only recognizing there is a problem.
Speech Clarity	The ability to speak clearly so others can understand you.
Manual Dexterity	The ability to quickly move your hand, your hand together with your arm, or your two hands to grasp, manipulate, or assemble objects.
Speech Recognition	The ability to identify and understand the speech of another person.
Oral Expression	The ability to communicate information and ideas in speaking so others will understand.
Selective Attention	The ability to concentrate on a task over a period of time without being distracted.
Deductive Reasoning	The ability to apply general rules to specific problems to produce answers that make sense.
Category Flexibility	The ability to generate or use different sets of rules for combining or grouping things in different ways.
Mathematical Reasoning	The ability to choose the right mathematical methods or formulas to solve a problem.
Written Expression	The ability to communicate information and ideas in writing so others will understand.
Perceptual Speed	The ability to quickly and accurately compare similarities and differences among sets of letters, numbers, objects, pictures, or patterns. The things to be compared may be presented at the same time or one after the other. This ability also includes comparing a presented object with a remembered object.
Inductive Reasoning	The ability to combine pieces of information to form general rules or conclusions (includes finding a relationship among seemingly unrelated events).
Extent Flexibility	The ability to bend, stretch, twist, or reach with your body, arms, and/or legs.
Trunk Strength	The ability to use your abdominal and lower back muscles to support part of the body repeatedly or continuously over time without 'giving out' or fatiguing.
Number Facility	The ability to add, subtract, multiply, or divide quickly and correctly.
Static Strength	The ability to exert maximum muscle force to lift, push, pull, or carry objects.
Auditory Attention	The ability to focus on a single source of sound in the presence of other distracting sounds.

Flexibility of Closure	The ability to identify or detect a known pattern (a figure, object, word, or sound) that is hidden in other distracting material.
Arm-Hand Steadiness	The ability to keep your hand and arm steady while moving your arm or while holding your arm and hand in one position.
Multilimb Coordination	The ability to coordinate two or more limbs (for example, two arms, two legs, or one leg and one arm) while sitting, standing, or lying down. It does not involve performing the activities while the whole body is in motion.
Stamina	The ability to exert yourself physically over long periods of time without getting winded or out of breath.
Gross Body Coordination	The ability to coordinate the movement of your arms, legs, and torso together when the whole body is in motion.
Visual Color Discrimination	The ability to match or detect differences between colors, including shades of color and brightness.
Time Sharing	The ability to shift back and forth between two or more activities or sources of information (such as speech, sounds, touch, or other sources).
Far Vision	The ability to see details at a distance.
Finger Dexterity	The ability to make precisely coordinated movements of the fingers of one or both hands to grasp, manipulate, or assemble very small objects.
Control Precision	The ability to quickly and repeatedly adjust the controls of a machine or a vehicle to exact positions.
Reaction Time	The ability to quickly respond (with the hand, finger, or foot) to a signal (sound, light, picture) when it appears.
Speed of Limb Movement	The ability to quickly move the arms and legs.
Fluency of Ideas	The ability to come up with a number of ideas about a topic (the number of ideas is important, not their quality, correctness, or creativity).
Memorization	The ability to remember information such as words, numbers, pictures, and procedures.
Visualization	The ability to imagine how something will look after it is moved around or when its parts are moved or rearranged.
Originality	The ability to come up with unusual or clever ideas about a given topic or situation, or to develop creative ways to solve a problem.
Explosive Strength	The ability to use short bursts of muscle force to propel oneself (as in jumping or sprinting), or to throw an object.
Response Orientation	The ability to choose quickly between two or more movements in response to two or more different signals (lights, sounds, pictures). It includes the speed with which the correct response is started with the hand, foot, or other body part.
Speed of Closure	The ability to quickly make sense of, combine, and organize information into meaningful patterns.
Peripheral Vision	The ability to see objects or movement of objects to one's side when the eyes are looking ahead.
Spatial Orientation	The ability to know your location in relation to the environment or to know where other objects are in relation to you.
Hearing Sensitivity	The ability to detect or tell the differences between sounds that vary in pitch and loudness.
Depth Perception	The ability to judge which of several objects is closer or farther away from you, or to judge the distance between you and an object.
Sound Localization	The ability to tell the direction from which a sound originated.
Glare Sensitivity	The ability to see objects in the presence of glare or bright lighting.
Rate Control	The ability to time your movements or the movement of a piece of equipment in anticipation of changes in the speed and/or direction of a moving object or scene.
Night Vision	The ability to see under low light conditions.
Dynamic Flexibility	The ability to quickly and repeatedly bend, stretch, twist, or reach out with your body, arms, and/or legs.
Dynamic Strength	The ability to exert muscle force repeatedly or continuously over time. This involves muscular endurance and resistance to muscle fatigue.
Wrist-Finger Speed	The ability to make fast, simple, repeated movements of the fingers, hands, and wrists.
Gross Body Equilibrium	The ability to keep or regain your body balance or stay upright when in an unstable position.

Work_Activity	Work_Activity Definitions
Identifying Objects, Actions, and Events	Identifying information by categorizing, estimating, recognizing differences or similarities, and detecting changes in circumstances or events.

Communicating with Persons Outside Organization	Communicating with people outside the organization, representing the organization to customers, the public, government, and other external sources. This information can be exchanged in person, in writing, or by telephone or e-mail.
Interacting With Computers	Using computers and computer systems (including hardware and software) to program, write software, set up functions, enter data, or process information.
Processing Information	Compiling, coding, categorizing, calculating, tabulating, auditing, or verifying information or data.
Selling or Influencing Others	Convincing others to buy merchandise/goods or to otherwise change their minds or actions.
Updating and Using Relevant Knowledge	Keeping up-to-date technically and applying new knowledge to your job.
Making Decisions and Solving Problems	Analyzing information and evaluating results to choose the best solution and solve problems.
Evaluating Information to Determine Compliance wit	Using relevant information and individual judgment to determine whether events or processes comply with laws, regulations, or standards.
Establishing and Maintaining Interpersonal Relatio	Developing constructive and cooperative working relationships with others, and maintaining them over time.
Getting Information	Observing, receiving, and otherwise obtaining information from all relevant sources.
Communicating with Supervisors, Peers, or Subordin	Providing information to supervisors, co-workers, and subordinates by telephone, in written form, e-mail, or in person.
Estimating the Quantifiable Characteristics of Pro	Estimating sizes, distances, and quantities; or determining time, costs, resources, or materials needed to perform a work activity.
Handling and Moving Objects	Using hands and arms in handling, installing, positioning, and moving materials, and manipulating things.
Assisting and Caring for Others	Providing personal assistance, medical attention, emotional support, or other personal care to others such as coworkers, customers, or patients.
Operating Vehicles, Mechanized Devices, or Equipme	Running, maneuvering, navigating, or driving vehicles or mechanized equipment, such as forklifts, passenger vehicles, aircraft, or water craft.
Analyzing Data or Information	Identifying the underlying principles, reasons, or facts of information by breaking down information or data into separate parts.
Judging the Qualities of Things, Services, or Peop	Assessing the value, importance, or quality of things or people.
Performing General Physical Activities	Performing physical activities that require considerable use of your arms and legs and moving your whole body, such as climbing, lifting, balancing, walking, stooping, and handling of materials.
Performing for or Working Directly with the Public	Performing for people or dealing directly with the public. This includes serving customers in restaurants and stores, and receiving clients or guests.
Coordinating the Work and Activities of Others	Getting members of a group to work together to accomplish tasks.
Performing Administrative Activities	Performing day-to-day administrative tasks such as maintaining information files and processing paperwork.
Resolving Conflicts and Negotiating with Others	Handling complaints, settling disputes, and resolving grievances and conflicts, or otherwise negotiating with others.
Documenting/Recording Information	Entering, transcribing, recording, storing, or maintaining information in written or electronic/magnetic form.
Developing Objectives and Strategies	Establishing long-range objectives and specifying the strategies and actions to achieve them.
Controlling Machines and Processes	Using either control mechanisms or direct physical activity to operate machines or processes (not including computers or vehicles).
Organizing, Planning, and Prioritizing Work	Developing specific goals and plans to prioritize, organize, and accomplish your work.
Interpreting the Meaning of Information for Others	Translating or explaining what information means and how it can be used.
Repairing and Maintaining Mechanical Equipment	Servicing, repairing, adjusting, and testing machines, devices, moving parts, and equipment that operate primarily on the basis of mechanical (not electronic) principles.
Monitor Processes, Materials, or Surroundings	Monitoring and reviewing information from materials, events, or the environment, to detect or assess problems.
Thinking Creatively	Developing, designing, or creating new applications, ideas, relationships, systems, or products, including artistic contributions.
Developing and Building Teams	Encouraging and building mutual trust, respect, and cooperation among team members.

Inspecting Equipment, Structures, or Material	Inspecting equipment, structures, or materials to identify the cause of errors or other problems or defects.
Guiding, Directing, and Motivating Subordinates	Providing guidance and direction to subordinates, including setting performance standards and monitoring performance.
Training and Teaching Others	Identifying the educational needs of others, developing formal educational or training programs or classes, and teaching or instructing others.
Coaching and Developing Others	Identifying the developmental needs of others and coaching, mentoring, or otherwise helping others to improve their knowledge or skills.
Scheduling Work and Activities	Scheduling events, programs, and activities, as well as the work of others.
Provide Consultation and Advice to Others	Providing guidance and expert advice to management or other groups on technical, systems-, or process-related topics.
Staffing Organizational Units	Recruiting, interviewing, selecting, hiring, and promoting employees in an organization.
Repairing and Maintaining Electronic Equipment	Servicing, repairing, calibrating, regulating, fine-tuning, or testing machines, devices, and equipment that operate primarily on the basis of electrical or electronic (not mechanical) principles.
Monitoring and Controlling Resources	Monitoring and controlling resources and overseeing the spending of money.
Drafting, Laying Out, and Specifying Technical Dev	Providing documentation, detailed instructions, drawings, or specifications to tell others about how devices, parts, equipment, or structures are to be fabricated, constructed, assembled, modified, maintained, or used.

Work_Context	**Work_Context Definitions**
Face-to-Face Discussions	How often do you have to have face-to-face discussions with individuals or teams in this job?
Time Pressure	How often does this job require the worker to meet strict deadlines?
Importance of Being Exact or Accurate	How important is being very exact or highly accurate in performing this job?
Spend Time Making Repetitive Motions	How much does this job require making repetitive motions?
Telephone	How often do you have telephone conversations in this job?
Indoors, Environmentally Controlled	How often does this job require working indoors in environmentally controlled conditions?
Spend Time Using Your Hands to Handle, Control, or	How much does this job require using your hands to handle, control, or feel objects, tools or controls?
Structured versus Unstructured Work	To what extent is this job structured for the worker, rather than allowing the worker to determine tasks, priorities, and goals?
Sounds, Noise Levels Are Distracting or Uncomforta	How often does this job require working exposed to sounds and noise levels that are distracting or uncomfortable?
Frequency of Decision Making	How frequently is the worker required to make decisions that affect other people, the financial resources, and/or the image and reputation of the organization?
Work With Work Group or Team	How important is it to work with others in a group or team in this job?
Freedom to Make Decisions	How much decision making freedom, without supervision, does the job offer?
Contact With Others	How much does this job require the worker to be in contact with others (face-to-face, by telephone, or otherwise) in order to perform it?
Letters and Memos	How often does the job require written letters and memos?
Impact of Decisions on Co-workers or Company Resul	How do the decisions an employee makes impact the results of co-workers, clients or the company?
Exposed to Contaminants	How often does this job require working exposed to contaminants (such as pollutants, gases, dust or odors)?
Spend Time Standing	How much does this job require standing?
Importance of Repeating Same Tasks	How important is repeating the same physical activities (e.g., key entry) or mental activities (e.g., checking entries in a ledger) over and over, without stopping, to performing this job?
Physical Proximity	To what extent does this job require the worker to perform job tasks in close physical proximity to other people?
Electronic Mail	How often do you use electronic mail in this job?
Coordinate or Lead Others	How important is it to coordinate or lead others in accomplishing work activities in this job?
Deal With External Customers	How important is it to work with external customers or the public in this job?
Responsibility for Outcomes and Results	How responsible is the worker for work outcomes and results of other workers?
Responsible for Others' Health and Safety	How much responsibility is there for the health and safety of others in this job?

Spend Time Sitting	How much does this job require sitting?
Deal With Unpleasant or Angry People	How frequently does the worker have to deal with unpleasant, angry, or discourteous individuals as part of the job requirements?
Frequency of Conflict Situations	How often are there conflict situations the employee has to face in this job?
Spend Time Walking and Running	How much does this job require walking and running?
Spend Time Bending or Twisting the Body	How much does this job require bending or twisting your body?
Exposed to Hazardous Equipment	How often does this job require exposure to hazardous equipment?
Cramped Work Space, Awkward Positions	How often does this job require working in cramped work spaces that requires getting into awkward positions?
Wear Common Protective or Safety Equipment such as	How much does this job require wearing common protective or safety equipment such as safety shoes, glasses, gloves, hard hats or live jackets?
Degree of Automation	How automated is the job?
Level of Competition	To what extent does this job require the worker to compete or to be aware of competitive pressures?
Indoors, Not Environmentally Controlled	How often does this job require working indoors in non-controlled environmental conditions (e.g., warehouse without heat)?
Spend Time Kneeling, Crouching, Stooping, or Crawl	How much does this job require kneeling, crouching, stooping or crawling?
Outdoors, Exposed to Weather	How often does this job require working outdoors, exposed to all weather conditions?
Very Hot or Cold Temperatures	How often does this job require working in very hot (above 90 F degrees) or very cold (below 32 F degrees) temperatures?
Extremely Bright or Inadequate Lighting	How often does this job require working in extremely bright or inadequate lighting conditions?
Exposed to High Places	How often does this job require exposure to high places?
Outdoors, Under Cover	How often does this job require working outdoors, under cover (e.g., structure with roof but no walls)?
Public Speaking	How often do you have to perform public speaking in this job?
In an Enclosed Vehicle or Equipment	How often does this job require working in a closed vehicle or equipment (e.g., car)?
Consequence of Error	How serious would the result usually be if the worker made a mistake that was not readily correctable?
Exposed to Minor Burns, Cuts, Bites, or Stings	How often does this job require exposure to minor burns, cuts, bites, or stings?
Spend Time Climbing Ladders, Scaffolds, or Poles	How much does this job require climbing ladders, scaffolds, or poles?
Spend Time Keeping or Regaining Balance	How much does this job require keeping or regaining your balance?
In an Open Vehicle or Equipment	How often does this job require working in an open vehicle or equipment (e.g., tractor)?
Pace Determined by Speed of Equipment	How important is it to this job that the pace is determined by the speed of equipment or machinery? (This does not refer to keeping busy at all times on this job.)
Exposed to Hazardous Conditions	How often does this job require exposure to hazardous conditions?
Deal With Physically Aggressive People	How frequently does this job require the worker to deal with physical aggression of violent individuals?
Exposed to Disease or Infections	How often does this job require exposure to disease/infections?
Wear Specialized Protective or Safety Equipment su	How much does this job require wearing specialized protective or safety equipment such as breathing apparatus, safety harness, full protection suits, or radiation protection?
Exposed to Whole Body Vibration	How often does this job require exposure to whole body vibration (e.g., operate a jackhammer)?
Exposed to Radiation	How often does this job require exposure to radiation?

Job Zone Component	Job Zone Component Definitions
Title	Job Zone Two: Some Preparation Needed
Overall Experience	Some previous work-related skill, knowledge, or experience may be helpful in these occupations, but usually is not needed. For example, a drywall installer might benefit from experience installing drywall, but an inexperienced person could still learn to be an installer with little difficulty.
Job Training	Employees in these occupations need anywhere from a few months to one year of working with experienced employees.

Job Zone Examples	These occupations often involve using your knowledge and skills to help others. Examples include drywall installers, tire inspectors, flight attendants, pharmacy technicians, salespersons (retail), and tellers.
SVP Range	(4.0 to < 6.0)
Education	These occupations usually require a high school diploma and may require some vocational training or job-related course work. In some cases, an associate's or bachelor's degree could be needed.

Work_Styles	Work_Styles Definitions
Self Control	Job requires maintaining composure, keeping emotions in check, controlling anger, and avoiding aggressive behavior, even in very difficult situations.
Stress Tolerance	Job requires accepting criticism and dealing calmly and effectively with high stress situations.
Cooperation	Job requires being pleasant with others on the job and displaying a good-natured, cooperative attitude.
Integrity	Job requires being honest and ethical.
Independence	Job requires developing one's own ways of doing things, guiding oneself with little or no supervision, and depending on oneself to get things done.
Attention to Detail	Job requires being careful about detail and thorough in completing work tasks.
Dependability	Job requires being reliable, responsible, and dependable, and fulfilling obligations.
Social Orientation	Job requires preferring to work with others rather than alone, and being personally connected with others on the job.
Persistence	Job requires persistence in the face of obstacles.
Adaptability/Flexibility	Job requires being open to change (positive or negative) and to considerable variety in the workplace.
Concern for Others	Job requires being sensitive to others' needs and feelings and being understanding and helpful on the job.
Achievement/Effort	Job requires establishing and maintaining personally challenging achievement goals and exerting effort toward mastering tasks.
Initiative	Job requires a willingness to take on responsibilities and challenges.
Innovation	Job requires creativity and alternative thinking to develop new ideas for and answers to work-related problems.
Leadership	Job requires a willingness to lead, take charge, and offer opinions and direction.
Analytical Thinking	Job requires analyzing information and using logic to address work-related issues and problems.

43-6011.00 - Executive Secretaries and Administrative Assistants

Provide high-level administrative support by conducting research, preparing statistical reports, handling information requests, and performing clerical functions such as preparing correspondence, receiving visitors, arranging conference calls, and scheduling meetings. May also train and supervise lower-level clerical staff.

Tasks

1) Open, sort, and distribute incoming correspondence, including faxes and email.

2) Perform general office duties such as ordering supplies, maintaining records management systems, and performing basic bookkeeping work.

3) File and retrieve corporate documents, records, and reports.

4) Prepare responses to correspondence containing routine inquiries.

5) Prepare agendas and make arrangements for committee, board, and other meetings.

6) Greet visitors and determine whether they should be given access to specific individuals.

7) Read and analyze incoming memos, submissions, and reports in order to determine their significance and plan their distribution.

8) Manage and maintain executives' schedules.

9) Conduct research, compile data, and prepare papers for consideration and presentation by executives, committees and boards of directors.

10) Coordinate and direct office services, such as records and budget preparation, personnel, and housekeeping, in order to aid executives.

11) Supervise and train other clerical staff.

12) Compile, transcribe, and distribute minutes of meetings.

13) Make travel arrangements for executives.

14) Review operating practices and procedures in order to determine whether improvements can be made in areas such as workflow, reporting procedures, or expenditures.

15) Interpret administrative and operating policies and procedures for employees.

16) Set up and oversee administrative policies and procedures for offices and/or organizations.

17) Attend meetings in order to record minutes.

18) Meet with individuals, special interest groups and others on behalf of executives, committees and boards of directors.

Knowledge	Knowledge Definitions
Clerical	Knowledge of administrative and clerical procedures and systems such as word processing, managing files and records, stenography and transcription, designing forms, and other office procedures and terminology.
English Language	Knowledge of the structure and content of the English language including the meaning and spelling of words, rules of composition, and grammar.
Customer and Personal Service	Knowledge of principles and processes for providing customer and personal services. This includes customer needs assessment, meeting quality standards for services, and evaluation of customer satisfaction.
Computers and Electronics	Knowledge of circuit boards, processors, chips, electronic equipment, and computer hardware and software, including applications and programming.
Administration and Management	Knowledge of business and management principles involved in strategic planning, resource allocation, human resources modeling, leadership technique, production methods, and coordination of people and resources.
Mathematics	Knowledge of arithmetic, algebra, geometry, calculus, statistics, and their applications.
Communications and Media	Knowledge of media production, communication, and dissemination techniques and methods. This includes alternative ways to inform and entertain via written, oral, and visual media.
Law and Government	Knowledge of laws, legal codes, court procedures, precedents, government regulations, executive orders, agency rules, and the democratic political process.
Personnel and Human Resources	Knowledge of principles and procedures for personnel recruitment, selection, training, compensation and benefits, labor relations and negotiation, and personnel information systems.
Economics and Accounting	Knowledge of economic and accounting principles and practices, the financial markets, banking and the analysis and reporting of financial data.
Telecommunications	Knowledge of transmission, broadcasting, switching, control, and operation of telecommunications systems.
Public Safety and Security	Knowledge of relevant equipment, policies, procedures, and strategies to promote effective local, state, or national security operations for the protection of people, data, property, and institutions.
Education and Training	Knowledge of principles and methods for curriculum and training design, teaching and instruction for individuals and groups, and the measurement of training effects.
Psychology	Knowledge of human behavior and performance; individual differences in ability, personality, and interests; learning and motivation; psychological research methods; and the assessment and treatment of behavioral and affective disorders.
Geography	Knowledge of principles and methods for describing the features of land, sea, and air masses, including their physical characteristics, locations, interrelationships, and distribution of plant, animal, and human life.
Transportation	Knowledge of principles and methods for moving people or goods by air, rail, sea, or road, including the relative costs and benefits.
Sales and Marketing	Knowledge of principles and methods for showing, promoting, and selling products or services. This includes marketing strategy and tactics, product demonstration, sales techniques, and sales control systems.
Philosophy and Theology	Knowledge of different philosophical systems and religions. This includes their basic principles, values, ethics, ways of thinking, customs, practices, and their impact on human culture.
Production and Processing	Knowledge of raw materials, production processes, quality control, costs, and other techniques for maximizing the effective manufacture and distribution of goods.
Sociology and Anthropology	Knowledge of group behavior and dynamics, societal trends and influences, human migrations, ethnicity, cultures and their history and origins.
Foreign Language	Knowledge of the structure and content of a foreign (non-English) language including the meaning and spelling of words, rules of composition and grammar, and pronunciation.
Therapy and Counseling	Knowledge of principles, methods, and procedures for diagnosis, treatment, and rehabilitation of physical and mental dysfunctions, and for career counseling and guidance.
Design	Knowledge of design techniques, tools, and principles involved in production of precision technical plans, blueprints, drawings, and models.
History and Archeology	Knowledge of historical events and their causes, indicators, and effects on civilizations and cultures.
Mechanical	Knowledge of machines and tools, including their designs, uses, repair, and maintenance.
Medicine and Dentistry	Knowledge of the information and techniques needed to diagnose and treat human injuries, diseases, and deformities. This includes symptoms, treatment alternatives, drug properties and interactions, and preventive health-care measures.
Fine Arts	Knowledge of the theory and techniques required to compose, produce, and perform works of music, dance, visual arts, drama, and sculpture.
Engineering and Technology	Knowledge of the practical application of engineering science and technology. This includes applying principles, techniques, procedures, and equipment to the design and production of various goods and services.
Biology	Knowledge of plant and animal organisms, their tissues, cells, functions, interdependencies, and interactions with each other and the environment.
Chemistry	Knowledge of the chemical composition, structure, and properties of substances and of the chemical processes and transformations that they undergo. This includes uses of chemicals and their interactions, danger signs, production techniques, and disposal methods.
Food Production	Knowledge of techniques and equipment for planting, growing, and harvesting food products (both plant and animal) for consumption, including storage/handling techniques.
Building and Construction	Knowledge of materials, methods, and the tools involved in the construction or repair of houses, buildings, or other structures such as highways and roads.
Physics	Knowledge and prediction of physical principles, laws, their interrelationships, and applications to understanding fluid, material, and atmospheric dynamics, and mechanical, electrical, atomic and sub-atomic structures and processes.

Skills	Skills Definitions
Active Listening	Giving full attention to what other people are saying, taking time to understand the points being made, asking questions as appropriate, and not interrupting at inappropriate times.
Reading Comprehension	Understanding written sentences and paragraphs in work related documents.
Time Management	Managing one's own time and the time of others.
Speaking	Talking to others to convey information effectively.
Writing	Communicating effectively in writing as appropriate for the needs of the audience.
Critical Thinking	Using logic and reasoning to identify the strengths and weaknesses of alternative solutions, conclusions or approaches to problems.
Active Learning	Understanding the implications of new information for both current and future problem-solving and decision-making.
Coordination	Adjusting actions in relation to others' actions.
Monitoring	Monitoring/Assessing performance of yourself, other individuals, or organizations to make improvements or take corrective action.
Service Orientation	Actively looking for ways to help people.
Social Perceptiveness	Being aware of others' reactions and understanding why they react as they do.
Judgment and Decision Making	Considering the relative costs and benefits of potential actions to choose the most appropriate one.

Instructing	Teaching others how to do something.
Mathematics	Using mathematics to solve problems.
Learning Strategies	Selecting and using training/instructional methods and procedures appropriate for the situation when learning or teaching new things.
Management of Financial Resources	Determining how money will be spent to get the work done, and accounting for these expenditures.
Persuasion	Persuading others to change their minds or behavior.
Management of Personnel Resources	Motivating, developing, and directing people as they work, identifying the best people for the job.
Equipment Selection	Determining the kind of tools and equipment needed to do a job.
Operations Analysis	Analyzing needs and product requirements to create a design.
Complex Problem Solving	Identifying complex problems and reviewing related information to develop and evaluate options and implement solutions.
Negotiation	Bringing others together and trying to reconcile differences.
Management of Material Resources	Obtaining and seeing to the appropriate use of equipment, facilities, and materials needed to do certain work.
Operation and Control	Controlling operations of equipment or systems.
Quality Control Analysis	Conducting tests and inspections of products, services, or processes to evaluate quality or performance.
Troubleshooting	Determining causes of operating errors and deciding what to do about it.
Systems Evaluation	Identifying measures or indicators of system performance and the actions needed to improve or correct performance, relative to the goals of the system.
Technology Design	Generating or adapting equipment and technology to serve user needs.
Equipment Maintenance	Performing routine maintenance on equipment and determining when and what kind of maintenance is needed.
Systems Analysis	Determining how a system should work and how changes in conditions, operations, and the environment will affect outcomes.
Installation	Installing equipment, machines, wiring, or programs to meet specifications.
Operation Monitoring	Watching gauges, dials, or other indicators to make sure a machine is working properly.
Repairing	Repairing machines or systems using the needed tools.
Programming	Writing computer programs for various purposes.
Science	Using scientific rules and methods to solve problems.

Ability	Ability Definitions
Written Expression	The ability to communicate information and ideas in writing so others will understand.
Oral Comprehension	The ability to listen to and understand information and ideas presented through spoken words and sentences.
Written Comprehension	The ability to read and understand information and ideas presented in writing.
Oral Expression	The ability to communicate information and ideas in speaking so others will understand.
Speech Clarity	The ability to speak clearly so others can understand you.
Near Vision	The ability to see details at close range (within a few feet of the observer).
Speech Recognition	The ability to identify and understand the speech of another person.
Problem Sensitivity	The ability to tell when something is wrong or is likely to go wrong. It does not involve solving the problem, only recognizing there is a problem.
Information Ordering	The ability to arrange things or actions in a certain order or pattern according to a specific rule or set of rules (e.g., patterns of numbers, letters, words, pictures, mathematical operations).
Deductive Reasoning	The ability to apply general rules to specific problems to produce answers that make sense.
Category Flexibility	The ability to generate or use different sets of rules for combining or grouping things in different ways.
Inductive Reasoning	The ability to combine pieces of information to form general rules or conclusions (includes finding a relationship among seemingly unrelated events).
Selective Attention	The ability to concentrate on a task over a period of time without being distracted.
Time Sharing	The ability to shift back and forth between two or more activities or sources of information (such as speech, sounds, touch, or other sources).
Memorization	The ability to remember information such as words, numbers, pictures, and procedures.

Speed of Closure	The ability to quickly make sense of, combine, and organize information into meaningful patterns.
Wrist-Finger Speed	The ability to make fast, simple, repeated movements of the fingers, hands, and wrists.
Flexibility of Closure	The ability to identify or detect a known pattern (a figure, object, word, or sound) that is hidden in other distracting material.
Mathematical Reasoning	The ability to choose the right mathematical methods or formulas to solve a problem.
Fluency of Ideas	The ability to come up with a number of ideas about a topic (the number of ideas is important, not their quality, correctness, or creativity).
Auditory Attention	The ability to focus on a single source of sound in the presence of other distracting sounds.
Visualization	The ability to imagine how something will look after it is moved around or when its parts are moved or rearranged.
Originality	The ability to come up with unusual or clever ideas about a given topic or situation, or to develop creative ways to solve a problem.
Number Facility	The ability to add, subtract, multiply, or divide quickly and correctly.
Far Vision	The ability to see details at a distance.
Finger Dexterity	The ability to make precisely coordinated movements of the fingers of one or both hands to grasp, manipulate, or assemble very small objects.
Perceptual Speed	The ability to quickly and accurately compare similarities and differences among sets of letters, numbers, objects, pictures, or patterns. The things to be compared may be presented at the same time or one after the other. This ability also includes comparing a presented object with a remembered object.
Trunk Strength	The ability to use your abdominal and lower back muscles to support part of the body repeatedly or continuously over time without 'giving out' or fatiguing.
Visual Color Discrimination	The ability to match or detect differences between colors, including shades of color and brightness.
Response Orientation	The ability to choose quickly between two or more movements in response to two or more different signals (lights, sounds, pictures). It includes the speed with which the correct response is started with the hand, foot, or other body part.
Hearing Sensitivity	The ability to detect or tell the differences between sounds that vary in pitch and loudness.
Manual Dexterity	The ability to quickly move your hand, your hand together with your arm, or your two hands to grasp, manipulate, or assemble objects.
Extent Flexibility	The ability to bend, stretch, twist, or reach with your body, arms, and/or legs.
Depth Perception	The ability to judge which of several objects is closer or farther away from you, or to judge the distance between you and an object.
Multilimb Coordination	The ability to coordinate two or more limbs (for example, two arms, two legs, or one leg and one arm) while sitting, standing, or lying down. It does not involve performing the activities while the whole body is in motion.
Static Strength	The ability to exert maximum muscle force to lift, push, pull, or carry objects.
Peripheral Vision	The ability to see objects or movement of objects to one's side when the eyes are looking ahead.
Speed of Limb Movement	The ability to quickly move the arms and legs.
Gross Body Equilibrium	The ability to keep or regain your body balance or stay upright when in an unstable position.
Arm-Hand Steadiness	The ability to keep your hand and arm steady while moving your arm or while holding your arm and hand in one position.
Control Precision	The ability to quickly and repeatedly adjust the controls of a machine or a vehicle to exact positions.
Rate Control	The ability to time your movements or the movement of a piece of equipment in anticipation of changes in the speed and/or direction of a moving object or scene.
Spatial Orientation	The ability to know your location in relation to the environment or to know where other objects are in relation to you.
Reaction Time	The ability to quickly respond (with the hand, finger, or foot) to a signal (sound, light, picture) when it appears.
Dynamic Strength	The ability to exert muscle force repeatedly or continuously over time. This involves muscular endurance and resistance to muscle fatigue.
Stamina	The ability to exert yourself physically over long periods of time without being winded or out of breath.
Dynamic Flexibility	The ability to quickly and repeatedly bend, stretch, twist, or reach out with your body, arms, and/or legs.

981

Gross Body Coordination	The ability to coordinate the movement of your arms, legs, and torso together when the whole body is in motion.
Glare Sensitivity	The ability to see objects in the presence of glare or bright lighting.
Night Vision	The ability to see under low light conditions.
Sound Localization	The ability to tell the direction from which a sound originated.
Explosive Strength	The ability to use short bursts of muscle force to propel oneself (as in jumping or sprinting), or to throw an object.

Work_Activity	Work_Activity Definitions
Performing Administrative Activities	Performing day-to-day administrative tasks such as maintaining information files and processing paperwork.
Interacting With Computers	Using computers and computer systems (including hardware and software) to program, write software, set up functions, enter data, or process information.
Getting Information	Observing, receiving, and otherwise obtaining information from all relevant sources.
Communicating with Supervisors, Peers, or Subordin	Providing information to supervisors, co-workers, and subordinates by telephone, in written form, e-mail, or in person.
Establishing and Maintaining Interpersonal Relatio	Developing constructive and cooperative working relationships with others, and maintaining them over time.
Organizing, Planning, and Prioritizing Work	Developing specific goals and plans to prioritize, organize, and accomplish your work.
Communicating with Persons Outside Organization	Communicating with people outside the organization, representing the organization to customers, the public, government, and other external sources. This information can be exchanged in person, in writing, or by telephone or e-mail.
Documenting/Recording Information	Entering, transcribing, recording, storing, or maintaining information in written or electronic/magnetic form.
Identifying Objects, Actions, and Events	Identifying information by categorizing, estimating, recognizing differences or similarities, and detecting changes in circumstances or events.
Updating and Using Relevant Knowledge	Keeping up-to-date technically and applying new knowledge to your job.
Scheduling Work and Activities	Scheduling events, programs, and activities, as well as the work of others.
Processing Information	Compiling, coding, categorizing, calculating, tabulating, auditing, or verifying information or data.
Making Decisions and Solving Problems	Analyzing information and evaluating results to choose the best solution and solve problems.
Monitor Processes, Materials, or Surroundings	Monitoring and reviewing information from materials, events, or the environment, to detect or assess problems.
Performing for or Working Directly with the Public	Performing for people or dealing directly with the public. This includes serving customers in restaurants and stores, and receiving clients or guests.
Thinking Creatively	Developing, designing, or creating new applications, ideas, relationships, systems, or products, including artistic contributions.
Resolving Conflicts and Negotiating with Others	Handling complaints, settling disputes, and resolving grievances and conflicts, or otherwise negotiating with others.
Evaluating Information to Determine Compliance wit	Using relevant information and individual judgment to determine whether events or processes comply with laws, regulations, or standards.
Interpreting the Meaning of Information for Others	Translating or explaining what information means and how it can be used.
Developing and Building Teams	Encouraging and building mutual trust, respect, and cooperation among team members.
Coordinating the Work and Activities of Others	Getting members of a group to work together to accomplish tasks.
Analyzing Data or Information	Identifying the underlying principles, reasons, or facts of information by breaking down information or data into separate parts.
Judging the Qualities of Things, Services, or Peop	Assessing the value, importance, or quality of things or people.
Assisting and Caring for Others	Providing personal assistance, medical attention, emotional support, or other personal care to others such as coworkers, customers, or patients.
Monitoring and Controlling Resources	Monitoring and controlling resources and overseeing the spending of money.
Estimating the Quantifiable Characteristics of Pro	Estimating sizes, distances, and quantities; or determining time, costs, resources, or materials needed to perform a work activity.
Developing Objectives and Strategies	Establishing long-range objectives and specifying the strategies and actions to achieve them.

Coaching and Developing Others	Identifying the developmental needs of others and coaching, mentoring, or otherwise helping others to improve their knowledge or skills.
Guiding, Directing, and Motivating Subordinates	Providing guidance and direction to subordinates, including setting performance standards and monitoring performance.
Provide Consultation and Advice to Others	Providing guidance and expert advice to management or other groups on technical, systems-, or process-related topics.
Training and Teaching Others	Identifying the educational needs of others, developing formal educational or training programs or classes, and teaching or instructing others.
Handling and Moving Objects	Using hands and arms in handling, installing, positioning, and moving materials, and manipulating things.
Selling or Influencing Others	Convincing others to buy merchandise/goods or to otherwise change their minds or actions.
Inspecting Equipment, Structures, or Material	Inspecting equipment, structures, or materials to identify the cause of errors or other problems or defects.
Controlling Machines and Processes	Using either control mechanisms or direct physical activity to operate machines or processes (not including computers or vehicles).
Performing General Physical Activities	Performing physical activities that require considerable use of your arms and legs and moving your whole body, such as climbing, lifting, balancing, walking, stooping, and handling of materials.
Staffing Organizational Units	Recruiting, interviewing, selecting, hiring, and promoting employees in an organization.
Repairing and Maintaining Electronic Equipment	Servicing, repairing, calibrating, regulating, fine-tuning, or testing machines, devices, and equipment that operate primarily on the basis of electrical or electronic (not mechanical) principles.
Operating Vehicles, Mechanized Devices, or Equipme	Running, maneuvering, navigating, or driving vehicles or mechanized equipment, such as forklifts, passenger vehicles, aircraft, or water craft.
Repairing and Maintaining Mechanical Equipment	Servicing, repairing, adjusting, and testing machines, devices, moving parts, and equipment that operate primarily on the basis of mechanical (not electronic) principles.
Drafting, Laying Out, and Specifying Technical Dev	Providing documentation, detailed instructions, drawings, or specifications to tell others about how devices, parts, equipment, or structures are to be fabricated, constructed, assembled, modified, maintained, or used.

Work_Context	Work_Context Definitions
Telephone	How often do you have telephone conversations in this job?
Contact With Others	How much does this job require the worker to be in contact with others (face-to-face, by telephone, or otherwise) in order to perform it?
Face-to-Face Discussions	How often do you have to have face-to-face discussions with individuals or teams in this job?
Electronic Mail	How often do you use electronic mail in this job?
Letters and Memos	How often does the job require written letters and memos?
Importance of Being Exact or Accurate	How important is being very exact or highly accurate in performing this job?
Work With Work Group or Team	How important is it to work with others in a group or team in this job?
Structured versus Unstructured Work	To what extent is this job structured for the worker, rather than allowing the worker to determine tasks, priorities, and goals?
Importance of Repeating Same Tasks	How important is repeating the same physical activities (e.g., key entry) or mental activities (e.g., checking entries in a ledger) over and over, without stopping, to performing this job?
Spend Time Sitting	How much does this job require sitting?
Freedom to Make Decisions	How much decision making freedom, without supervision, does the job offer?
Deal With External Customers	How important is it to work with external customers or the public in this job?
Coordinate or Lead Others	How important is it to coordinate or lead others in accomplishing work activities in this job?
Indoors, Environmentally Controlled	How often does this job require working indoors in environmentally controlled conditions?
Time Pressure	How often does this job require the worker to meet strict deadlines?
Spend Time Making Repetitive Motions	How much does this job require making repetitive motions?
Frequency of Decision Making	How frequently is the worker required to make decisions that affect other people, the financial resources, and/or the image and reputation of the organization?
Impact of Decisions on Co-workers or Company Resul	How do the decisions an employee makes impact the results of co-workers, clients or the company?

Responsibility for Outcomes and Results	How responsible is the worker for work outcomes and results of other workers?
Physical Proximity	To what extent does this job require the worker to perform job tasks in close physical proximity to other people?
Sounds, Noise Levels Are Distracting or Uncomforta	How often does this job require working exposed to sounds and noise levels that are distracting or uncomfortable?
Frequency of Conflict Situations	How often are there conflict situations the employee has to face in this job?
Degree of Automation	How automated is the job?
Deal With Unpleasant or Angry People	How frequently does the worker have to deal with unpleasant, angry, or discourteous individuals as part of the job requirements?
Level of Competition	To what extent does this job require the worker to compete or to be aware of competitive pressures?
Spend Time Using Your Hands to Handle, Control, or	How much does this job require using your hands to handle, control, or feel objects, tools or controls?
Responsible for Others' Health and Safety	How much responsibility is there for the health and safety of others in this job?
Spend Time Standing	How much does this job require standing?
Consequence of Error	How serious would the result usually be if the worker made a mistake that was not readily correctable?
Spend Time Walking and Running	How much does this job require walking and running?
Public Speaking	How often do you have to perform public speaking in this job?
Spend Time Bending or Twisting the Body	How much does this job require bending or twisting your body?
Exposed to Disease or Infections	How often does this job require exposure to disease/infections?
Pace Determined by Speed of Equipment	How important is it to this job that the pace is determined by the speed of equipment or machinery? (This does not refer to keeping busy at all times on this job.)
Cramped Work Space, Awkward Positions	How often does this job require working in cramped work spaces that requires getting into awkward positions?
Spend Time Kneeling, Crouching, Stooping, or Crawl	How much does this job require kneeling, crouching, stooping or crawling?
Exposed to Contaminants	How often does this job require working exposed to contaminants (such as pollutants, gases, dust or odors)?
In an Enclosed Vehicle or Equipment	How often does this job require working in a closed vehicle or equipment (e.g., car)?
Exposed to Minor Burns, Cuts, Bites, or Stings	How often does this job require exposure to minor burns, cuts, bites, or stings?
Very Hot or Cold Temperatures	How often does this job require working in very hot (above 90 F degrees) or very cold (below 32 F degrees) temperatures?
Extremely Bright or Inadequate Lighting	How often does this job require working in extremely bright or inadequate lighting conditions?
Outdoors, Exposed to Weather	How often does this job require working outdoors, exposed to all weather conditions?
Spend Time Keeping or Regaining Balance	How much does this job require keeping or regaining your balance?
Deal With Physically Aggressive People	How frequently does this job require the worker to deal with physical aggression of violent individuals?
Indoors, Not Environmentally Controlled	How often does this job require working indoors in non-controlled environmental conditions (e.g., warehouse without heat)?
Exposed to Radiation	How often does this job require exposure to radiation?
Outdoors, Under Cover	How often does this job require working outdoors, under cover (e.g., structure with roof but no walls)?
Wear Common Protective or Safety Equipment such as	How much does this job require wearing common protective or safety equipment such as safety shoes, glasses, gloves, hard hats or live jackets?
Exposed to Hazardous Conditions	How often does this job require exposure to hazardous conditions?
Spend Time Climbing Ladders, Scaffolds, or Poles	How much does this job require climbing ladders, scaffolds, or poles?
Exposed to Hazardous Equipment	How often does this job require exposure to hazardous equipment?
In an Open Vehicle or Equipment	How often does this job require working in an open vehicle or equipment (e.g., tractor)?
Exposed to Whole Body Vibration	How often does this job require exposure to whole body vibration (e.g., operate a jackhammer)?
Wear Specialized Protective or Safety Equipment su	How much does this job require wearing specialized protective or safety equipment such as breathing apparatus, safety harness, full protection suits, or radiation protection?
Exposed to High Places	How often does this job require exposure to high places?

Job Zone Component	Job Zone Component Definitions
Title	Job Zone Three: Medium Preparation Needed
Overall Experience	Previous work-related skill, knowledge, or experience is required for these occupations. For example, an electrician must have completed three or four years of apprenticeship or several years of vocational training, and often must have passed a licensing exam, in order to perform the job.
Job Training	Employees in these occupations usually need one or two years of training involving both on-the-job experience and informal training with experienced workers.
Job Zone Examples	These occupations usually involve using communication and organizational skills to coordinate, supervise, manage, or train others to accomplish goals. Examples include dental assistants, electricians.fish and game wardens, legal secretaries, personnel recruiters, and recreation workers.
SVP Range	(6.0 to < 7.0)
Education	Most occupations in this zone require training in vocational schools, related on-the-job experience, or an associate's degree. Some may require a bachelor's degree.

Work_Styles	Work_Styles Definitions
Cooperation	Job requires being pleasant with others on the job and displaying a good-natured, cooperative attitude.
Attention to Detail	Job requires being careful about detail and thorough in completing work tasks.
Dependability	Job requires being reliable, responsible, and dependable, and fulfilling obligations.
Integrity	Job requires being honest and ethical.
Concern for Others	Job requires being sensitive to others' needs and feelings and being understanding and helpful on the job.
Self Control	Job requires maintaining composure, keeping emotions in check, controlling anger, and avoiding aggressive behavior, even in very difficult situations.
Adaptability/Flexibility	Job requires being open to change (positive or negative) and to considerable variety in the workplace.
Stress Tolerance	Job requires accepting criticism and dealing calmly and effectively with high stress situations.
Independence	Job requires developing one's own ways of doing things, guiding oneself with little or no supervision, and depending on oneself to get things done.
Initiative	Job requires a willingness to take on responsibilities and challenges.
Innovation	Job requires creativity and alternative thinking to develop new ideas for and answers to work-related problems.
Social Orientation	Job requires preferring to work with others rather than alone, and being personally connected with others on the job.
Achievement/Effort	Job requires establishing and maintaining personally challenging achievement goals and exerting effort toward mastering tasks.
Persistence	Job requires persistence in the face of obstacles.
Analytical Thinking	Job requires analyzing information and using logic to address work-related issues and problems.
Leadership	Job requires a willingness to lead, take charge, and offer opinions and direction.

43-6012.00 - Legal Secretaries

Perform secretarial duties utilizing legal terminology, procedures, and documents. Prepare legal papers and correspondence, such as summonses, complaints, motions, and subpoenas. May also assist with legal research.

Tasks

1) Mail, fax, or arrange for delivery of legal correspondence to clients, witnesses, and court officials.

2) Prepare and process legal documents and papers, such as summonses, subpoenas, complaints, appeals, motions, and pretrial agreements.

3) Make photocopies of correspondence, document, and other printed matter.

4) Schedule and make appointments.

5) Assist attorneys in collecting information such as employment, medical, and other records.

6) Draft and type office memos.

7) Organize and maintain law libraries and document and case files.

8) Attend legal meetings, such as client interviews, hearings, or depositions, and take notes.

9) Complete various forms, such as accident reports, trial and courtroom requests, and applications for clients.

10) Submit articles and information from searches to attorneys for review and approval for use.

11) Review legal publications and perform data base searches to identify laws and court decisions relevant to pending cases.

Knowledge	Knowledge Definitions
Clerical	Knowledge of administrative and clerical procedures and systems such as word processing, managing files and records, stenography and transcription, designing forms, and other office procedures and terminology.
Law and Government	Knowledge of laws, legal codes, court procedures, precedents, government regulations, executive orders, agency rules, and the democratic political process.
English Language	Knowledge of the structure and content of the English language including the meaning and spelling of words, rules of composition, and grammar.
Customer and Personal Service	Knowledge of principles and processes for providing customer and personal services. This includes customer needs assessment, meeting quality standards for services, and evaluation of customer satisfaction.
Economics and Accounting	Knowledge of economic and accounting principles and practices, the financial markets, banking and the analysis and reporting of financial data.
Computers and Electronics	Knowledge of circuit boards, processors, chips, electronic equipment, and computer hardware and software, including applications and programming.
Administration and Management	Knowledge of business and management principles involved in strategic planning, resource allocation, human resources modeling, leadership technique, production methods, and coordination of people and resources.
Mathematics	Knowledge of arithmetic, algebra, geometry, calculus, statistics, and their applications.
Communications and Media	Knowledge of media production, communication, and dissemination techniques and methods. This includes alternative ways to inform and entertain via written, oral, and visual media.
Geography	Knowledge of principles and methods for describing the features of land, sea, and air masses, including their physical characteristics, locations, interrelationships, and distribution of plant, animal, and human life.
Personnel and Human Resources	Knowledge of principles and procedures for personnel recruitment, selection, training, compensation and benefits, labor relations and negotiation, and personnel information systems.
Psychology	Knowledge of human behavior and performance; individual differences in ability, personality, and interests; learning and motivation; psychological research methods; and the assessment and treatment of behavioral and affective disorders.
Sales and Marketing	Knowledge of principles and methods for showing, promoting, and selling products or services. This includes marketing strategy and tactics, product demonstration, sales techniques, and sales control systems.
Sociology and Anthropology	Knowledge of group behavior and dynamics, societal trends and influences, human migrations, ethnicity, cultures and their history and origins.
Education and Training	Knowledge of principles and methods for curriculum and training design, teaching and instruction for individuals and groups, and the measurement of training effects.
Telecommunications	Knowledge of transmission, broadcasting, switching, control, and operation of telecommunications systems.
History and Archeology	Knowledge of historical events and their causes, indicators, and effects on civilizations and cultures.
Public Safety and Security	Knowledge of relevant equipment, policies, procedures, and strategies to promote effective local, state, or national security operations for the protection of people, data, property, and institutions.
Foreign Language	Knowledge of the structure and content of a foreign (non-English) language including the meaning and spelling of words, rules of composition and grammar, and pronunciation.
Philosophy and Theology	Knowledge of different philosophical systems and religions. This includes their basic principles, values, ethics, ways of thinking, customs, practices, and their impact on human culture.
Mechanical	Knowledge of machines and tools, including their designs, uses, repair, and maintenance.
Transportation	Knowledge of principles and methods for moving people or goods by air, rail, sea, or road, including the relative costs and benefits.
Production and Processing	Knowledge of raw materials, production processes, quality control, costs, and other techniques for maximizing the effective manufacture and distribution of goods.
Therapy and Counseling	Knowledge of principles, methods, and procedures for diagnosis, treatment, and rehabilitation of physical and mental dysfunctions, and for career counseling and guidance.
Engineering and Technology	Knowledge of the practical application of engineering science and technology. This includes applying principles, techniques, procedures, and equipment to the design and production of various goods and services.
Medicine and Dentistry	Knowledge of the information and techniques needed to diagnose and treat human injuries, diseases, and deformities. This includes symptoms, treatment alternatives, drug properties and interactions, and preventive health-care measures.
Design	Knowledge of design techniques, tools, and principles involved in production of precision technical plans, blueprints, drawings, and models.
Physics	Knowledge and prediction of physical principles, laws, their interrelationships, and applications to understanding fluid, material, and atmospheric dynamics, and mechanical, electrical, atomic and sub-atomic structures and processes.
Biology	Knowledge of plant and animal organisms, their tissues, cells, functions, interdependencies, and interactions with each other and the environment.
Food Production	Knowledge of techniques and equipment for planting, growing, and harvesting food products (both plant and animal) for consumption, including storage/handling techniques.
Fine Arts	Knowledge of the theory and techniques required to compose, produce, and perform works of music, dance, visual arts, drama, and sculpture.
Building and Construction	Knowledge of materials, methods, and the tools involved in the construction or repair of houses, buildings, or other structures such as highways and roads.
Chemistry	Knowledge of the chemical composition, structure, and properties of substances and of the chemical processes and transformations that they undergo. This includes uses of chemicals and their interactions, danger signs, production techniques, and disposal methods.

Skills	Skills Definitions
Reading Comprehension	Understanding written sentences and paragraphs in work related documents.
Active Listening	Giving full attention to what other people are saying, taking time to understand the points being made, asking questions as appropriate, and not interrupting at inappropriate times.
Time Management	Managing one's own time and the time of others.
Writing	Communicating effectively in writing as appropriate for the needs of the audience.
Active Learning	Understanding the implications of new information for both current and future problem-solving and decision-making.
Speaking	Talking to others to convey information effectively.
Learning Strategies	Selecting and using training/instructional methods and procedures appropriate for the situation when learning or teaching new things.
Judgment and Decision Making	Considering the relative costs and benefits of potential actions to choose the most appropriate one.
Coordination	Adjusting actions in relation to others' actions.
Critical Thinking	Using logic and reasoning to identify the strengths and weaknesses of alternative solutions, conclusions or approaches to problems.
Social Perceptiveness	Being aware of others' reactions and understanding why they react as they do.
Complex Problem Solving	Identifying complex problems and reviewing related information to develop and evaluate options and implement solutions.
Service Orientation	Actively looking for ways to help people.

Monitoring	Monitoring/Assessing performance of yourself, other individuals, or organizations to make improvements or take corrective action.
Mathematics	Using mathematics to solve problems.
Instructing	Teaching others how to do something.
Persuasion	Persuading others to change their minds or behavior.
Operation and Control	Controlling operations of equipment or systems.
Quality Control Analysis	Conducting tests and inspections of products, services, or processes to evaluate quality or performance.
Negotiation	Bringing others together and trying to reconcile differences.
Equipment Selection	Determining the kind of tools and equipment needed to do a job.
Management of Personnel Resources	Motivating, developing, and directing people as they work, identifying the best people for the job.
Technology Design	Generating or adapting equipment and technology to serve user needs.
Management of Financial Resources	Determining how money will be spent to get the work done, and accounting for these expenditures.
Troubleshooting	Determining causes of operating errors and deciding what to do about it.
Equipment Maintenance	Performing routine maintenance on equipment and determining when and what kind of maintenance is needed.
Management of Material Resources	Obtaining and seeing to the appropriate use of equipment, facilities, and materials needed to do certain work.
Operations Analysis	Analyzing needs and product requirements to create a design.
Systems Evaluation	Identifying measures or indicators of system performance and the actions needed to improve or correct performance, relative to the goals of the system.
Installation	Installing equipment, machines, wiring, or programs to meet specifications.
Operation Monitoring	Watching gauges, dials, or other indicators to make sure a machine is working properly.
Systems Analysis	Determining how a system should work and how changes in conditions, operations, and the environment will affect outcomes.
Repairing	Repairing machines or systems using the needed tools.
Programming	Writing computer programs for various purposes.
Science	Using scientific rules and methods to solve problems.

Ability	Ability Definitions
Oral Comprehension	The ability to listen to and understand information and ideas presented through spoken words and sentences.
Speech Recognition	The ability to identify and understand the speech of another person.
Oral Expression	The ability to communicate information and ideas in speaking so others will understand.
Information Ordering	The ability to arrange things or actions in a certain order or pattern according to a specific rule or set of rules (e.g., patterns of numbers, letters, words, pictures, mathematical operations).
Written Comprehension	The ability to read and understand information and ideas presented in writing.
Speech Clarity	The ability to speak clearly so others can understand you.
Near Vision	The ability to see details at close range (within a few feet of the observer).
Written Expression	The ability to communicate information and ideas in writing so others will understand.
Problem Sensitivity	The ability to tell when something is wrong or is likely to go wrong. It does not involve solving the problem, only recognizing there is a problem.
Selective Attention	The ability to concentrate on a task over a period of time without being distracted.
Deductive Reasoning	The ability to apply general rules to specific problems to produce answers that make sense.
Category Flexibility	The ability to generate or use different sets of rules for combining or grouping things in different ways.
Inductive Reasoning	The ability to combine pieces of information to form general rules or conclusions (includes finding a relationship among seemingly unrelated events).
Time Sharing	The ability to shift back and forth between two or more activities or sources of information (such as speech, sounds, touch, or other sources).
Speed of Closure	The ability to quickly make sense of, combine, and organize information into meaningful patterns.
Flexibility of Closure	The ability to identify or detect a known pattern (a figure, object, word, or sound) that is hidden in other distracting material.

Originality	The ability to come up with unusual or clever ideas about a given topic or situation, or to develop creative ways to solve a problem.
Manual Dexterity	The ability to quickly move your hand, your hand together with your arm, or your two hands to grasp, manipulate, or assemble objects.
Fluency of Ideas	The ability to come up with a number of ideas about a topic (the number of ideas is important, not their quality, correctness, or creativity).
Finger Dexterity	The ability to make precisely coordinated movements of the fingers of one or both hands to grasp, manipulate, or assemble very small objects.
Wrist-Finger Speed	The ability to make fast, simple, repeated movements of the fingers, hands, and wrists.
Memorization	The ability to remember information such as words, numbers, pictures, and procedures.
Number Facility	The ability to add, subtract, multiply, or divide quickly and correctly.
Far Vision	The ability to see details at a distance.
Arm-Hand Steadiness	The ability to keep your hand and arm steady while moving your arm or while holding your arm and hand in one position.
Auditory Attention	The ability to focus on a single source of sound in the presence of other distracting sounds.
Perceptual Speed	The ability to quickly and accurately compare similarities and differences among sets of letters, numbers, objects, pictures, or patterns. The things to be compared may be presented at the same time or one after the other. This ability also includes comparing a presented object with a remembered object.
Control Precision	The ability to quickly and repeatedly adjust the controls of a machine or a vehicle to exact positions.
Visualization	The ability to imagine how something will look after it is moved around or when its parts are moved or rearranged.
Mathematical Reasoning	The ability to choose the right mathematical methods or formulas to solve a problem.
Trunk Strength	The ability to use your abdominal and lower back muscles to support part of the body repeatedly or continuously over time without 'giving out' or fatiguing.
Sound Localization	The ability to tell the direction from which a sound originated.
Night Vision	The ability to see under low light conditions.
Extent Flexibility	The ability to bend, stretch, twist, or reach with your body, arms, and/or legs.
Static Strength	The ability to exert maximum muscle force to lift, push, pull, or carry objects.
Hearing Sensitivity	The ability to detect or tell the differences between sounds that vary in pitch and loudness.
Multilimb Coordination	The ability to coordinate two or more limbs (for example, two arms, two legs, or one leg and one arm) while sitting, standing, or lying down. It does not involve performing the activities while the whole body is in motion.
Reaction Time	The ability to quickly respond (with the hand, finger, or foot) to a signal (sound, light, picture) when it appears.
Explosive Strength	The ability to use short bursts of muscle force to propel oneself (as in jumping or sprinting), or to throw an object.
Dynamic Strength	The ability to exert muscle force repeatedly or continuously over time. This involves muscular endurance and resistance to muscle fatigue.
Stamina	The ability to exert yourself physically over long periods of time without getting winded or out of breath.
Spatial Orientation	The ability to know your location in relation to the environment or to know where other objects are in relation to you.
Response Orientation	The ability to choose quickly between two or more movements in response to two or more different signals (lights, sounds, pictures). It includes the speed with which the correct response is started with the hand, foot, or other body part.
Rate Control	The ability to time your movements or the movement of a piece of equipment in anticipation of changes in the speed and/or direction of a moving object or scene.
Glare Sensitivity	The ability to see objects in the presence of glare or bright lighting.
Gross Body Coordination	The ability to coordinate the movement of your arms, legs, and torso together when the whole body is in motion.
Speed of Limb Movement	The ability to quickly move the arms and legs.
Gross Body Equilibrium	The ability to keep or regain your body balance or stay upright when in an unstable position.
Visual Color Discrimination	The ability to match or detect differences between colors, including shades of color and brightness.
Peripheral Vision	The ability to see objects or movement of objects to one's side when the eyes are looking ahead.

Depth Perception	The ability to judge which of several objects is closer or farther away from you, or to judge the distance between you and an object.
Dynamic Flexibility	The ability to quickly and repeatedly bend, stretch, twist, or reach out with your body, arms, and/or legs.

Work_Activity	Work_Activity Definitions
Interacting With Computers	Using computers and computer systems (including hardware and software) to program, write software, set up functions, enter data, or process information.
Performing Administrative Activities	Performing day-to-day administrative tasks such as maintaining information files and processing paperwork.
Getting Information	Observing, receiving, and otherwise obtaining information from all relevant sources.
Communicating with Persons Outside Organization	Communicating with people outside the organization, representing the organization to customers, the public, government, and other external sources. This information can be exchanged in person, in writing, or by telephone or e-mail.
Communicating with Supervisors, Peers, or Subordin	Providing information to supervisors, co-workers, and subordinates by telephone, in written form, e-mail, or in person.
Organizing, Planning, and Prioritizing Work	Developing specific goals and plans to prioritize, organize, and accomplish your work.
Documenting/Recording Information	Entering, transcribing, recording, storing, or maintaining information in written or electronic/magnetic form.
Performing for or Working Directly with the Public	Performing for people or dealing directly with the public. This includes serving customers in restaurants and stores, and receiving clients or guests.
Monitoring and Controlling Resources	Monitoring and controlling resources and overseeing the spending of money.
Processing Information	Compiling, coding, categorizing, calculating, tabulating, auditing, or verifying information or data.
Updating and Using Relevant Knowledge	Keeping up-to-date technically and applying new knowledge to your job.
Establishing and Maintaining Interpersonal Relatio	Developing constructive and cooperative working relationships with others, and maintaining them over time.
Scheduling Work and Activities	Scheduling events, programs, and activities, as well as the work of others.
Making Decisions and Solving Problems	Analyzing information and evaluating results to choose the best solution and solve problems.
Resolving Conflicts and Negotiating with Others	Handling complaints, settling disputes, and resolving grievances and conflicts, or otherwise negotiating with others.
Interpreting the Meaning of Information for Others	Translating or explaining what information means and how it can be used.
Monitor Processes, Materials, or Surroundings	Monitoring and reviewing information from materials, events, or the environment, to detect or assess problems.
Coordinating the Work and Activities of Others	Getting members of a group to work together to accomplish tasks.
Identifying Objects, Actions, and Events	Identifying information by categorizing, estimating, recognizing differences or similarities, and detecting changes in circumstances or events.
Evaluating Information to Determine Compliance wit	Using relevant information and individual judgment to determine whether events or processes comply with laws, regulations, or standards.
Assisting and Caring for Others	Providing personal assistance, medical attention, emotional support, or other personal care to others such as coworkers, customers, or patients.
Analyzing Data or Information	Identifying the underlying principles, reasons, or facts of information by breaking down information or data into separate parts.
Developing Objectives and Strategies	Establishing long-range objectives and specifying the strategies and actions to achieve them.
Developing and Building Teams	Encouraging and building mutual trust, respect, and cooperation among team members.
Thinking Creatively	Developing, designing, or creating new applications, ideas, relationships, systems, or products, including artistic contributions.
Judging the Qualities of Things, Services, or Peop	Assessing the value, importance, or quality of things or people.
Coaching and Developing Others	Identifying the developmental needs of others and coaching, mentoring, or otherwise helping others to improve their knowledge or skills.
Training and Teaching Others	Identifying the educational needs of others, developing formal educational or training programs or classes, and teaching or instructing others.

Controlling Machines and Processes	Using either control mechanisms or direct physical activity to operate machines or processes (not including computers or vehicles).
Handling and Moving Objects	Using hands and arms in handling, installing, positioning, and moving materials, and manipulating things.
Performing General Physical Activities	Performing physical activities that require considerable use of your arms and legs and moving your whole body, such as climbing, lifting, balancing, walking, stooping, and handling of materials.
Inspecting Equipment, Structures, or Material	Inspecting equipment, structures, or materials to identify the cause of errors or other problems or defects.
Provide Consultation and Advice to Others	Providing guidance and expert advice to management or other groups on technical, systems-, or process-related topics.
Selling or Influencing Others	Convincing others to buy merchandise/goods or to otherwise change their minds or actions.
Guiding, Directing, and Motivating Subordinates	Providing guidance and direction to subordinates, including setting performance standards and monitoring performance.
Estimating the Quantifiable Characteristics of Pro	Estimating sizes, distances, and quantities; or determining time, costs, resources, or materials needed to perform a work activity.
Repairing and Maintaining Electronic Equipment	Servicing, repairing, calibrating, regulating, fine-tuning, or testing machines, devices, and equipment that operate primarily on the basis of electrical or electronic (not mechanical) principles.
Staffing Organizational Units	Recruiting, interviewing, selecting, hiring, and promoting employees in an organization.
Operating Vehicles, Mechanized Devices, or Equipme	Running, maneuvering, navigating, or driving vehicles or mechanized equipment, such as forklifts, passenger vehicles, aircraft, or water craft.
Drafting, Laying Out, and Specifying Technical Dev	Providing documentation, detailed instructions, drawings, or specifications to tell others about how devices, parts, equipment, or structures are to be fabricated, constructed, assembled, modified, maintained, or used.
Repairing and Maintaining Mechanical Equipment	Servicing, repairing, adjusting, and testing machines, devices, moving parts, and equipment that operate primarily on the basis of mechanical (not electronic) principles.

Work_Context	Work_Context Definitions
Letters and Memos	How often does the job require written letters and memos?
Telephone	How often do you have telephone conversations in this job?
Importance of Being Exact or Accurate	How important is being very exact or highly accurate in performing this job?
Contact With Others	How much does this job require the worker to be in contact with others (face-to-face, by telephone, or otherwise) in order to perform it?
Face-to-Face Discussions	How often do you have to have face-to-face discussions with individuals or teams in this job?
Importance of Repeating Same Tasks	How important is repeating the same physical activities (e.g., key entry) or mental activities (e.g., checking entries in a ledger) over and over, without stopping, to performing this job?
Time Pressure	How often does this job require the worker to meet strict deadlines?
Structured versus Unstructured Work	To what extent is this job structured for the worker, rather than allowing the worker to determine tasks, priorities, and goals?
Spend Time Sitting	How much does this job require sitting?
Indoors, Environmentally Controlled	How often does this job require working indoors in environmentally controlled conditions?
Frequency of Decision Making	How frequently is the worker required to make decisions that affect other people, the financial resources, and/or the image and reputation of the organization?
Spend Time Making Repetitive Motions	How much does this job require making repetitive motions?
Impact of Decisions on Co-workers or Company Resul	How do the decisions an employee makes impact the results of co-workers, clients or the company?
Electronic Mail	How often do you use electronic mail in this job?
Freedom to Make Decisions	How much decision making freedom, without supervision, does the job offer?
Deal With Unpleasant or Angry People	How frequently does the worker have to deal with unpleasant, angry, or discourteous individuals as part of the job requirements?
Deal With External Customers	How important is it to work with external customers or the public in this job?
Consequence of Error	How serious would the result usually be if the worker made a mistake that was not readily correctable?
Level of Competition	To what extent does this job require the worker to compete or to be aware of competitive pressures?

Spend Time Using Your Hands to Handle, Control, or	How much does this job require using your hands to handle, control, or feel objects, tools or controls?
Physical Proximity	To what extent does this job require the worker to perform job tasks in close physical proximity to other people?
Work With Work Group or Team	How important is it to work with others in a group or team in this job?
Coordinate or Lead Others	How important is it to coordinate or lead others in accomplishing work activities in this job?
Spend Time Standing	How much does this job require standing?
Frequency of Conflict Situations	How often are there conflict situations the employee has to face in this job?
Spend Time Walking and Running	How much does this job require walking and running?
Degree of Automation	How automated is the job?
Public Speaking	How often do you have to perform public speaking in this job?
Sounds, Noise Levels Are Distracting or Uncomforta	How often does this job require working exposed to sounds and noise levels that are distracting or uncomfortable?
Pace Determined by Speed of Equipment	How important is it to this job that the pace is determined by the speed of equipment or machinery? (This does not refer to keeping busy at all times on this job.)
In an Enclosed Vehicle or Equipment	How often does this job require working in a closed vehicle or equipment (e.g., car)?
Responsibility for Outcomes and Results	How responsible is the worker for work outcomes and results of other workers?
Responsible for Others' Health and Safety	How much responsibility is there for the health and safety of others in this job?
Spend Time Bending or Twisting the Body	How much does this job require bending or twisting your body?
Extremely Bright or Inadequate Lighting	How often does this job require working in extremely bright or inadequate lighting conditions?
Deal With Physically Aggressive People	How frequently does this job require the worker to deal with physical aggression of violent individuals?
Spend Time Kneeling, Crouching, Stooping, or Crawl	How much does this job require kneeling, crouching, stooping, or crawling?
Exposed to Contaminants	How often does this job require working exposed to contaminants (such as pollutants, gases, dust or odors)?
Cramped Work Space, Awkward Positions	How often does this job require working in cramped work spaces that requires getting into awkward positions?
Outdoors, Exposed to Weather	How often does this job require working outdoors, exposed to all weather conditions?
Exposed to Minor Burns, Cuts, Bites, or Stings	How often does this job require exposure to minor burns, cuts, bites, or stings?
Exposed to Whole Body Vibration	How often does this job require exposure to whole body vibration (e.g., operate a jackhammer)?
Exposed to Hazardous Conditions	How often does this job require exposure to hazardous conditions?
Wear Specialized Protective or Safety Equipment su	How much does this job require wearing specialized protective or safety equipment such as breathing apparatus, safety harness, full protection suits, or radiation protection?
Exposed to Disease or Infections	How often does this job require exposure to disease/infections?
Exposed to Radiation	How often does this job require exposure to radiation?
Exposed to High Places	How often does this job require exposure to high places?
Spend Time Keeping or Regaining Balance	How much does this job require keeping or regaining your balance?
Outdoors, Under Cover	How often does this job require working outdoors, under cover (e.g., structure with roof but no walls)?
Very Hot or Cold Temperatures	How often does this job require working in very hot (above 90 F degrees) or very cold (below 32 F degrees) temperatures?
Indoors, Not Environmentally Controlled	How often does this job require working indoors in non-controlled environmental conditions (e.g., warehouse without heat)?
Spend Time Climbing Ladders, Scaffolds, or Poles	How much does this job require climbing ladders, scaffolds, or poles?
In an Open Vehicle or Equipment	How often does this job require working in an open vehicle or equipment (e.g., tractor)?
Exposed to Hazardous Equipment	How often does this job require exposure to hazardous equipment?
Wear Common Protective or Safety Equipment such as	How much does this job require wearing common protective or safety equipment such as safety shoes, glasses, gloves, hard hats or life jackets?

Job Zone Component	Job Zone Component Definitions
Title	Job Zone Three: Medium Preparation Needed
Overall Experience	Previous work-related skill, knowledge, or experience is required for these occupations. For example, an electrician must have completed three or four years of apprenticeship or several years of vocational training, and often must have passed a licensing exam, in order to perform the job.
Job Training	Employees in these occupations usually need one or two years of training involving both on-the-job experience and informal training with experienced workers.
Job Zone Examples	These occupations usually involve using communication and organizational skills to coordinate, supervise, manage, or train others to accomplish goals. Examples include dental assistants, electricians, fish and game wardens, legal secretaries, personnel recruiters, and recreation workers.
SVP Range	(6.0 to < 7.0)
Education	Most occupations in this zone require training in vocational schools, related on-the-job experience, or an associate's degree. Some may require a bachelor's degree.

Work_Styles	Work_Styles Definitions
Attention to Detail	Job requires being careful about detail and thorough in completing work tasks.
Integrity	Job requires being honest and ethical.
Dependability	Job requires being reliable, responsible, and dependable, and fulfilling obligations.
Cooperation	Job requires being pleasant with others on the job and displaying a good-natured, cooperative attitude.
Independence	Job requires developing one's own ways of doing things, guiding oneself with little or no supervision, and depending on oneself to get things done.
Stress Tolerance	Job requires accepting criticism and dealing calmly and effectively with high stress situations.
Initiative	Job requires a willingness to take on responsibilities and challenges.
Self Control	Job requires maintaining composure, keeping emotions in check, controlling anger, and avoiding aggressive behavior, even in very difficult situations.
Achievement/Effort	Job requires establishing and maintaining personally challenging achievement goals and exerting effort toward mastering tasks.
Persistence	Job requires persistence in the face of obstacles.
Adaptability/Flexibility	Job requires being open to change (positive or negative) and to considerable variety in the workplace.
Concern for Others	Job requires being sensitive to others' needs and feelings and being understanding and helpful on the job.
Leadership	Job requires a willingness to lead, take charge, and offer opinions and direction.
Innovation	Job requires creativity and alternative thinking to develop new ideas for and answers to work-related problems.
Analytical Thinking	Job requires analyzing information and using logic to address work-related issues and problems.
Social Orientation	Job requires preferring to work with others rather than alone, and being personally connected with others on the job.

43-6013.00 - Medical Secretaries

Perform secretarial duties utilizing specific knowledge of medical terminology and hospital, clinic, or laboratory procedures. Duties include scheduling appointments, billing patients, and compiling and recording medical charts, reports, and correspondence.

Tasks

1) Greet visitors, ascertain purpose of visit, and direct them to appropriate staff.

2) Compile and record medical charts, reports, and correspondence, using typewriter or personal computer.

3) Transmit correspondence and medical records by mail, e-mail, or fax.

4) Perform various clerical and administrative functions, such as ordering and maintaining an inventory of supplies.

5) Maintain medical records, technical library and correspondence files.

6) Operate office equipment such as voice mail messaging systems, and use word processing, spreadsheet, and other software applications to prepare reports, invoices, financial statements, letters, case histories and medical records.

7) Schedule and confirm patient diagnostic appointments, surgeries and medical consultations.

8) Interview patients in order to complete documents, case histories, and forms such as intake and insurance forms.

9) Complete insurance and other claim forms.

10) Transcribe recorded messages and practitioners' diagnoses and recommendations into patients' medical records.

11) Perform bookkeeping duties, such as credits and collections, preparing and sending financial statements and bills, and keeping financial records.

12) Prepare correspondence and assist physicians or medical scientists with preparation of reports, speeches, articles and conference proceedings.

13) Arrange hospital admissions for patients.

14) Answer telephones, and direct calls to appropriate staff.

Knowledge	Knowledge Definitions
Customer and Personal Service	Knowledge of principles and processes for providing customer and personal services. This includes customer needs assessment, meeting quality standards for services, and evaluation of customer satisfaction.
Clerical	Knowledge of administrative and clerical procedures and systems such as word processing, managing files and records, stenography and transcription, designing forms, and other office procedures and terminology.
English Language	Knowledge of the structure and content of the English language including the meaning and spelling of words, rules of composition, and grammar.
Computers and Electronics	Knowledge of circuit boards, processors, chips, electronic equipment, and computer hardware and software, including applications and programming.
Telecommunications	Knowledge of transmission, broadcasting, switching, control, and operation of telecommunications systems.
Communications and Media	Knowledge of media production, communication, and dissemination techniques and methods. This includes alternative ways to inform and entertain via written, oral, and visual media.
Education and Training	Knowledge of principles and methods for curriculum and training design, teaching and instruction for individuals and groups, and the measurement of training effects.
Mathematics	Knowledge of arithmetic, algebra, geometry, calculus, statistics, and their applications.
Administration and Management	Knowledge of business and management principles involved in strategic planning, resource allocation, human resources modeling, leadership technique, production methods, and coordination of people and resources.
Transportation	Knowledge of principles and methods for moving people or goods by air, rail, sea, or road, including the relative costs and benefits.
Public Safety and Security	Knowledge of relevant equipment, policies, procedures, and strategies to promote effective local, state, or national security operations for the protection of people, data, property, and institutions.
Medicine and Dentistry	Knowledge of the information and techniques needed to diagnose and treat human injuries, diseases, and deformities. This includes symptoms, treatment alternatives, drug properties and interactions, and preventive health-care measures.
Philosophy and Theology	Knowledge of different philosophical systems and religions. This includes their basic principles, values, ethics, ways of thinking, customs, practices, and their impact on human culture.
Food Production	Knowledge of techniques and equipment for planting, growing, and harvesting food products (both plant and animal) for consumption, including storage/handling techniques.
Economics and Accounting	Knowledge of economic and accounting principles and practices, the financial markets, banking and the analysis and reporting of financial data.
Law and Government	Knowledge of laws, legal codes, court procedures, precedents, government regulations, executive orders, agency rules, and the democratic political process.
Sociology and Anthropology	Knowledge of group behavior and dynamics, societal trends and influences, human migrations, ethnicity, cultures and their history and origins.
Production and Processing	Knowledge of raw materials, production processes, quality control, costs, and other techniques for maximizing the effective manufacture and distribution of goods.
Personnel and Human Resources	Knowledge of principles and procedures for personnel recruitment, selection, training, compensation and benefits, labor relations and negotiation, and personnel information systems.
Psychology	Knowledge of human behavior and performance; individual differences in ability, personality, and interests; learning and motivation; psychological research methods; and the assessment and treatment of behavioral and affective disorders.
Mechanical	Knowledge of machines and tools, including their designs, uses, repair, and maintenance.
Geography	Knowledge of principles and methods for describing the features of land, sea, and air masses, including their physical characteristics, locations, interrelationships, and distribution of plant, animal, and human life.
Therapy and Counseling	Knowledge of principles, methods, and procedures for diagnosis, treatment, and rehabilitation of physical and mental dysfunctions, and for career counseling and guidance.
Foreign Language	Knowledge of the structure and content of a foreign (non-English) language including the meaning and spelling of words, rules of composition and grammar, and pronunciation.
Biology	Knowledge of plant and animal organisms, their tissues, cells, functions, interdependencies, and interactions with each other and the environment.
Sales and Marketing	Knowledge of principles and methods for showing, promoting, and selling products or services. This includes marketing strategy and tactics, product demonstration, sales techniques, and sales control systems.
Engineering and Technology	Knowledge of the practical application of engineering science and technology. This includes applying principles, techniques, procedures, and equipment to the design and production of various goods and services.
Chemistry	Knowledge of the chemical composition, structure, and properties of substances and of the chemical processes and transformations that they undergo. This includes uses of chemicals and their interactions, danger signs, production techniques, and disposal methods.
History and Archeology	Knowledge of historical events and their causes, indicators, and effects on civilizations and cultures.
Design	Knowledge of design techniques, tools, and principles involved in production of precision technical plans, blueprints, drawings, and models.
Fine Arts	Knowledge of the theory and techniques required to compose, produce, and perform works of music, dance, visual arts, drama, and sculpture.
Physics	Knowledge and prediction of physical principles, laws, their interrelationships, and applications to understanding fluid, material, and atmospheric dynamics, and mechanical, electrical, atomic and sub-atomic structures and processes.
Building and Construction	Knowledge of materials, methods, and the tools involved in the construction or repair of houses, buildings, or other structures such as highways and roads.

Skills	Skills Definitions
Active Listening	Giving full attention to what other people are saying, taking time to understand the points being made, asking questions as appropriate, and not interrupting at inappropriate times.
Reading Comprehension	Understanding written sentences and paragraphs in work related documents.
Speaking	Talking to others to convey information effectively.
Coordination	Adjusting actions in relation to others' actions.
Active Learning	Understanding the implications of new information for both current and future problem-solving and decision-making.
Time Management	Managing one's own time and the time of others.
Instructing	Teaching others how to do something.
Writing	Communicating effectively in writing as appropriate for the needs of the audience.
Service Orientation	Actively looking for ways to help people.
Learning Strategies	Selecting and using training/instructional methods and procedures appropriate for the situation when learning or teaching new things.

Social Perceptiveness	Being aware of others' reactions and understanding why they react as they do.
Management of Material Resources	Obtaining and seeing to the appropriate use of equipment, facilities, and materials needed to do certain work.
Operation and Control	Controlling operations of equipment or systems.
Monitoring	Monitoring/Assessing performance of yourself, other individuals, or organizations to make improvements or take corrective action.
Judgment and Decision Making	Considering the relative costs and benefits of potential actions to choose the most appropriate one.
Equipment Selection	Determining the kind of tools and equipment needed to do a job.
Critical Thinking	Using logic and reasoning to identify the strengths and weaknesses of alternative solutions, conclusions or approaches to problems.
Negotiation	Bringing others together and trying to reconcile differences.
Management of Personnel Resources	Motivating, developing, and directing people as they work, identifying the best people for the job.
Mathematics	Using mathematics to solve problems.
Systems Evaluation	Identifying measures or indicators of system performance and the actions needed to improve or correct performance, relative to the goals of the system.
Persuasion	Persuading others to change their minds or behavior.
Quality Control Analysis	Conducting tests and inspections of products, services, or processes to evaluate quality or performance.
Equipment Maintenance	Performing routine maintenance on equipment and determining when and what kind of maintenance is needed.
Complex Problem Solving	Identifying complex problems and reviewing related information to develop and evaluate options and implement solutions.
Technology Design	Generating or adapting equipment and technology to serve user needs.
Troubleshooting	Determining causes of operating errors and deciding what to do about it.
Operations Analysis	Analyzing needs and product requirements to create a design.
Repairing	Repairing machines or systems using the needed tools.
Installation	Installing equipment, machines, wiring, or programs to meet specifications.
Management of Financial Resources	Determining how money will be spent to get the work done, and accounting for these expenditures.
Operation Monitoring	Watching gauges, dials, or other indicators to make sure a machine is working properly.
Science	Using scientific rules and methods to solve problems.
Systems Analysis	Determining how a system should work and how changes in conditions, operations, and the environment will affect outcomes.
Programming	Writing computer programs for various purposes.

Ability	Ability Definitions
Oral Comprehension	The ability to listen to and understand information and ideas presented through spoken words and sentences.
Oral Expression	The ability to communicate information and ideas in speaking so others will understand.
Speech Clarity	The ability to speak clearly so others can understand you.
Near Vision	The ability to see details at close range (within a few feet of the observer).
Information Ordering	The ability to arrange things or actions in a certain order or pattern according to a specific rule or set of rules (e.g., patterns of numbers, letters, words, pictures, mathematical operations).
Speech Recognition	The ability to identify and understand the speech of another person.
Written Comprehension	The ability to read and understand information and ideas presented in writing.
Time Sharing	The ability to shift back and forth between two or more activities or sources of information (such as speech, sounds, touch, or other sources).
Problem Sensitivity	The ability to tell when something is wrong or is likely to go wrong. It does not involve solving the problem, only recognizing there is a problem.
Written Expression	The ability to communicate information and ideas in writing so others will understand.
Selective Attention	The ability to concentrate on a task over a period of time without being distracted.
Inductive Reasoning	The ability to combine pieces of information to form general rules or conclusions (includes finding a relationship among seemingly unrelated events).

Deductive Reasoning	The ability to apply general rules to specific problems to produce answers that make sense.
Category Flexibility	The ability to generate or use different sets of rules for combining or grouping things in different ways.
Finger Dexterity	The ability to make precisely coordinated movements of the fingers of one or both hands to grasp, manipulate, or assemble very small objects.
Perceptual Speed	The ability to quickly and accurately compare similarities and differences among sets of letters, numbers, objects, pictures, or patterns. The things to be compared may be presented at the same time or one after the other. This ability also includes comparing a presented object with a remembered object.
Originality	The ability to come up with unusual or clever ideas about a given topic or situation, or to develop creative ways to solve a problem.
Mathematical Reasoning	The ability to choose the right mathematical methods or formulas to solve a problem.
Auditory Attention	The ability to focus on a single source of sound in the presence of other distracting sounds.
Fluency of Ideas	The ability to come up with a number of ideas about a topic (the number of ideas is important, not their quality, correctness, or creativity).
Arm-Hand Steadiness	The ability to keep your hand and arm steady while moving your arm or while holding your arm and hand in one position.
Number Facility	The ability to add, subtract, multiply, or divide quickly and correctly.
Memorization	The ability to remember information such as words, numbers, pictures, and procedures.
Trunk Strength	The ability to use your abdominal and lower back muscles to support part of the body repeatedly or continuously over time without 'giving out' or fatiguing.
Manual Dexterity	The ability to quickly move your hand, your hand together with your arm, or your two hands to grasp, manipulate, or assemble objects.
Flexibility of Closure	The ability to identify or detect a known pattern (a figure, object, word, or sound) that is hidden in other distracting material.
Static Strength	The ability to exert maximum muscle force to lift, push, pull, or carry objects.
Gross Body Coordination	The ability to coordinate the movement of your arms, legs, and torso together when the whole body is in motion.
Speed of Closure	The ability to quickly make sense of, combine, and organize information into meaningful patterns.
Stamina	The ability to exert yourself physically over long periods of time without getting winded or out of breath.
Far Vision	The ability to see details at a distance.
Multilimb Coordination	The ability to coordinate two or more limbs (for example, two arms, two legs, or one leg and one arm) while sitting, standing, or lying down. It does not involve performing the activities while the whole body is in motion.
Control Precision	The ability to quickly and repeatedly adjust the controls of a machine or a vehicle to exact positions.
Hearing Sensitivity	The ability to detect or tell the differences between sounds that vary in pitch and loudness.
Speed of Limb Movement	The ability to quickly move the arms and legs.
Visual Color Discrimination	The ability to match or detect differences between colors, including shades of color and brightness.
Wrist-Finger Speed	The ability to make fast, simple, repeated movements of the fingers, hands, and wrists.
Visualization	The ability to imagine how something will look after it is moved around or when its parts are moved or rearranged.
Depth Perception	The ability to judge which of several objects is closer or farther away from you, or to judge the distance between you and an object.
Reaction Time	The ability to quickly respond (with the hand, finger, or foot) to a signal (sound, light, picture) when it appears.
Response Orientation	The ability to choose quickly between two or more movements in response to two or more different signals (lights, sounds, pictures). It includes the speed with which the correct response is started with the hand, foot, or other body part.
Sound Localization	The ability to tell the direction from which a sound originated.
Extent Flexibility	The ability to bend, stretch, twist, or reach with your body, arms, and/or legs.
Peripheral Vision	The ability to see objects or movement of objects to one's side when the eyes are looking ahead.
Dynamic Flexibility	The ability to quickly and repeatedly bend, stretch, twist, or reach out with your body, arms, and/or legs.

Dynamic Strength	The ability to exert muscle force repeatedly or continuously over time. This involves muscular endurance and resistance to muscle fatigue.	Handling and Moving Objects	Using hands and arms in handling, installing, positioning, and moving materials, and manipulating things.
Spatial Orientation	The ability to know your location in relation to the environment or to know where other objects are in relation to you.	Coaching and Developing Others	Identifying the developmental needs of others and coaching, mentoring, or otherwise helping others to improve their knowledge or skills.
Night Vision	The ability to see under low light conditions.	Analyzing Data or Information	Identifying the underlying principles, reasons, or facts of information by breaking down information or data into separate parts.
Glare Sensitivity	The ability to see objects in the presence of glare or bright lighting.		
Rate Control	The ability to time your movements or the movement of a piece of equipment in anticipation of changes in the speed and/or direction of a moving object or scene.	Developing Objectives and Strategies	Establishing long-range objectives and specifying the strategies and actions to achieve them.
Explosive Strength	The ability to use short bursts of muscle force to propel oneself (as in jumping or sprinting), or to throw an object.	Judging the Qualities of Things, Services, or Peop	Assessing the value, importance, or quality of things or people.
Gross Body Equilibrium	The ability to keep or regain your body balance or stay upright when in an unstable position.	Selling or Influencing Others	Convincing others to buy merchandise/goods or to otherwise change their minds or actions.
		Performing General Physical Activities	Performing physical activities that require considerable use of your arms and legs and moving your whole body, such as climbing, lifting, balancing, walking, stooping, and handling of materials.

Work_Activity	**Work_Activity Definitions**		
Getting Information	Observing, receiving, and otherwise obtaining information from all relevant sources.	Monitoring and Controlling Resources	Monitoring and controlling resources and overseeing the spending of money.
Communicating with Supervisors, Peers, or Subordin	Providing information to supervisors, co-workers, and subordinates by telephone, in written form, e-mail, or in person.	Inspecting Equipment, Structures, or Material	Inspecting equipment, structures, or materials to identify the cause of errors or other problems or defects.
Communicating with Persons Outside Organization	Communicating with people outside the organization, representing the organization to customers, the public, government, and other external sources. This information can be exchanged in person, in writing, or by telephone or e-mail.	Controlling Machines and Processes	Using either control mechanisms or direct physical activity to operate machines or processes (not including computers or vehicles).
Interacting With Computers	Using computers and computer systems (including hardware and software) to program, write software, set up functions, enter data, or process information.	Training and Teaching Others	Identifying the educational needs of others, developing formal educational or training programs or classes, and teaching or instructing others.
Establishing and Maintaining Interpersonal Relatio	Developing constructive and cooperative working relationships with others, and maintaining them over time.	Guiding, Directing, and Motivating Subordinates	Providing guidance and direction to subordinates, including setting performance standards and monitoring performance.
Assisting and Caring for Others	Providing personal assistance, medical attention, emotional support, or other personal care to others such as coworkers, customers, or patients.	Staffing Organizational Units	Recruiting, interviewing, selecting, hiring, and promoting employees in an organization.
Documenting/Recording Information	Entering, transcribing, recording, storing, or maintaining information in written or electronic/magnetic form.	Repairing and Maintaining Mechanical Equipment	Servicing, repairing, adjusting, and testing machines, devices, moving parts, and equipment that operate primarily on the basis of mechanical (not electronic) principles.
Organizing, Planning, and Prioritizing Work	Developing specific goals and plans to prioritize, organize, and accomplish your work.	Repairing and Maintaining Electronic Equipment	Servicing, repairing, calibrating, regulating, fine-tuning, or testing machines, devices, and equipment that operate primarily on the basis of electrical or electronic (not mechanical) principles.
Performing Administrative Activities	Performing day-to-day administrative tasks such as maintaining information files and processing paperwork.		
Processing Information	Compiling, coding, categorizing, calculating, tabulating, auditing, or verifying information or data.	Drafting, Laying Out, and Specifying Technical Dev	Providing documentation, detailed instructions, drawings, or specifications to tell others about how devices, parts, equipment, or structures are to be fabricated, constructed, assembled, modified, maintained, or used.
Performing for or Working Directly with the Public	Performing for people or dealing directly with the public. This includes serving customers in restaurants and stores, and receiving clients or guests.	Operating Vehicles, Mechanized Devices, or Equipme	Running, maneuvering, navigating, or driving vehicles or mechanized equipment, such as forklifts, passenger vehicles, aircraft, or water craft.
Making Decisions and Solving Problems	Analyzing information and evaluating results to choose the best solution and solve problems.		
Updating and Using Relevant Knowledge	Keeping up-to-date technically and applying new knowledge to your job.	**Work_Context**	**Work_Context Definitions**
Monitor Processes, Materials, or Surroundings	Monitoring and reviewing information from materials, events, or the environment, to detect or assess problems.	Telephone	How often do you have telephone conversations in this job?
Scheduling Work and Activities	Scheduling events, programs, and activities, as well as the work of others.	Contact With Others	How much does this job require the worker to be in contact with others (face-to-face, by telephone, or otherwise) in order to perform it?
Interpreting the Meaning of Information for Others	Translating or explaining what information means and how it can be used.	Face-to-Face Discussions	How often do you have to have face-to-face discussions with individuals or teams in this job?
Coordinating the Work and Activities of Others	Getting members of a group to work together to accomplish tasks.	Work With Work Group or Team	How important is it to work with others in a group or team in this job?
Resolving Conflicts and Negotiating with Others	Handling complaints, settling disputes, and resolving grievances and conflicts, or otherwise negotiating with others.	Structured versus Unstructured Work	To what extent is this job structured for the worker, rather than allowing the worker to determine tasks, priorities, and goals?
Evaluating Information to Determine Compliance wit	Using relevant information and individual judgment to determine whether events or processes comply with laws, regulations, or standards.	Spend Time Using Your Hands to Handle, Control, or	How much does this job require using your hands to handle, control, or feel objects, tools or controls?
Identifying Objects, Actions, and Events	Identifying information by categorizing, estimating, recognizing differences or similarities, and detecting changes in circumstances or events.	Importance of Being Exact or Accurate	How important is being very exact or highly accurate in performing this job?
Developing and Building Teams	Encouraging and building mutual trust, respect, and cooperation among team members.	Frequency of Decision Making	How frequently is the worker required to make decisions that affect other people, the financial resources, and/or the image and reputation of the organization?
Estimating the Quantifiable Characteristics of Pro	Estimating sizes, distances, and quantities; or determining time, costs, resources, or materials needed to perform a work activity.	Time Pressure	How often does this job require the worker to meet strict deadlines?
Thinking Creatively	Developing, designing, or creating new applications, ideas, relationships, systems, or products, including artistic contributions.	Deal With Unpleasant or Angry People	How frequently does the worker have to deal with unpleasant, angry, or discourteous individuals as part of the job requirements?
Provide Consultation and Advice to Others	Providing guidance and expert advice to management or other groups on technical, systems-, or process-related topics.	Deal With External Customers	How important is it to work with external customers or the public in this job?
		Exposed to Disease or Infections	How often does this job require exposure to disease/infections?
		Frequency of Conflict Situations	How often are there conflict situations the employee has to face in this job?

Impact of Decisions on Co-workers or Company Resul	How do the decisions an employee makes impact the results of co-workers, clients or the company?
Coordinate or Lead Others	How important is it to coordinate or lead others in accomplishing work activities in this job?
Physical Proximity	To what extent does this job require the worker to perform job tasks in close physical proximity to other people?
Sounds, Noise Levels Are Distracting or Uncomforta	How often does this job require working exposed to sounds and noise levels that are distracting or uncomfortable?
Freedom to Make Decisions	How much decision making freedom, without supervision, does the job offer?
Spend Time Sitting	How much does this job require sitting?
Consequence of Error	How serious would the result usually be if the worker made a mistake that was not readily correctable?
Letters and Memos	How often does the job require written letters and memos?
Importance of Repeating Same Tasks	How important is repeating the same physical activities (e.g., key entry) or mental activities (e.g., checking entries in a ledger) over and over, without stopping, to performing this job?
Spend Time Making Repetitive Motions	How much does this job require making repetitive motions?
Indoors, Environmentally Controlled	How often does this job require working indoors in environmentally controlled conditions?
Responsibility for Outcomes and Results	How responsible is the worker for work outcomes and results of other workers?
Spend Time Walking and Running	How much does this job require walking and running?
Electronic Mail	How often do you use electronic mail in this job?
Level of Competition	To what extent does this job require the worker to compete or to be aware of competitive pressures?
Degree of Automation	How automated is the job?
Responsible for Others' Health and Safety	How much responsibility is there for the health and safety of others in this job?
Spend Time Standing	How much does this job require standing?
Cramped Work Space, Awkward Positions	How often does this job require working in cramped work spaces that requires getting into awkward positions?
Exposed to Radiation	How often does this job require exposure to radiation?
Spend Time Bending or Twisting the Body	How much does this job require bending or twisting your body?
Wear Common Protective or Safety Equipment such as	How much does this job require wearing common protective or safety equipment such as safety shoes, glasses, gloves, hard hats or live jackets?
Spend Time Kneeling, Crouching, Stooping, or Crawl	How much does this job require kneeling, crouching, stooping or crawling?
Pace Determined by Speed of Equipment	How important is it to this job that the pace is determined by the speed of equipment or machinery? (This does not refer to keeping busy at all times on this job.)
Deal With Physically Aggressive People	How frequently does this job require the worker to deal with physical aggression of violent individuals?
Extremely Bright or Inadequate Lighting	How often does this job require working in extremely bright or inadequate lighting conditions?
Public Speaking	How often do you have to perform public speaking in this job?
Indoors, Not Environmentally Controlled	How often does this job require working indoors in non-controlled environmental conditions (e.g., warehouse without heat)?
Exposed to Minor Burns, Cuts, Bites, or Stings	How often does this job require exposure to minor burns, cuts, bites, or stings?
Exposed to Contaminants	How often does this job require working exposed to contaminants (such as pollutants, gases, dust or odors)?
Spend Time Climbing Ladders, Scaffolds, or Poles	How much does this job require climbing ladders, scaffolds, or poles?
Very Hot or Cold Temperatures	How often does this job require working in very hot (above 90 F degrees) or very cold (below 32 F degrees) temperatures?
Exposed to Hazardous Equipment	How often does this job require exposure to hazardous equipment?
Exposed to Hazardous Conditions	How often does this job require exposure to hazardous conditions?
Exposed to Whole Body Vibration	How often does this job require exposure to whole body vibration (e.g., operate a jackhammer)?
Spend Time Keeping or Regaining Balance	How much does this job require keeping or regaining your balance?
Outdoors, Under Cover	How often does this job require working outdoors, under cover (e.g., structure with roof but no walls)?
In an Open Vehicle or Equipment	How often does this job require working in an open vehicle or equipment (e.g., tractor)?
In an Enclosed Vehicle or Equipment	How often does this job require working in a closed vehicle or equipment (e.g., car)?

Wear Specialized Protective or Safety Equipment su	How much does this job require wearing specialized protective or safety equipment such as breathing apparatus, safety harness, full protection suits, or radiation protection?
Outdoors, Exposed to Weather	How often does this job require working outdoors, exposed to all weather conditions?
Exposed to High Places	How often does this job require exposure to high places?

Job Zone Component	Job Zone Component Definitions
Title	Job Zone Two: Some Preparation Needed
Overall Experience	Some previous work-related skill, knowledge, or experience may be helpful in these occupations, but usually is not needed. For example, a drywall installer might benefit from experience installing drywall, but an inexperienced person could still learn to be an installer with little difficulty.
Job Training	Employees in these occupations need anywhere from a few months to one year of working with experienced employees. These occupations often involve using your knowledge and skills to help others. Examples include drywall installers, fire inspectors, flight attendants, pharmacy technicians, salespersons (retail), and tellers.
Job Zone Examples	
SVP Range	(4.0 to 6.0)
Education	These occupations usually require a high school diploma and may require some vocational training or job-related course work. In some cases, an associate's or bachelor's degree could be needed.

Work_Styles	Work_Styles Definitions
Cooperation	Job requires being pleasant with others on the job and displaying a good-natured, cooperative attitude.
Dependability	Job requires being reliable, responsible, and dependable, and fulfilling obligations.
Attention to Detail	Job requires being careful about detail and thorough in completing work tasks.
Self Control	Job requires maintaining composure, keeping emotions in check, controlling anger, and avoiding aggressive behavior, even in very difficult situations.
Adaptability/Flexibility	Job requires being open to change (positive or negative) and to considerable variety in the workplace.
Stress Tolerance	Job requires accepting criticism and dealing calmly and effectively with high stress situations.
Integrity	Job requires being honest and ethical.
Concern for Others	Job requires being sensitive to others' needs and feelings and being understanding and helpful on the job.
Independence	Job requires developing one's own ways of doing things, guiding oneself with little or no supervision, and depending on oneself to get things done.
Initiative	Job requires a willingness to take on responsibilities and challenges.
Social Orientation	Job requires preferring to work with others rather than alone, and being personally connected with others on the job.
Achievement/Effort	Job requires establishing and maintaining personally challenging achievement goals and exerting effort toward mastering tasks.
Persistence	Job requires persistence in the face of obstacles.
Innovation	Job requires creativity and alternative thinking to develop new ideas for and answers to work-related problems.
Leadership	Job requires a willingness to lead, take charge, and offer opinions and direction.
Analytical Thinking	Job requires analyzing information and using logic to address work-related issues and problems.

43-6014.00 - Secretaries, Except Legal, Medical, and Executive

Perform routine clerical and administrative functions such as drafting correspondence, scheduling appointments, organizing and maintaining paper and electronic files, or providing information to callers.

Tasks

1) Make copies of correspondence and other printed material.

2) Answer telephones and give information to callers, take messages, or transfer calls to

appropriate individuals.

3) Greet visitors and callers, handle their inquiries, and direct them to the appropriate persons according to their needs.

4) Learn to operate new office technologies as they are developed and implemented.

5) Set up and maintain paper and electronic filing systems for records, correspondence, and other material.

6) Compose, type, and distribute meeting notes, routine correspondence, and reports.

7) Complete forms in accordance with company procedures.

8) Schedule and confirm appointments for clients, customers, or supervisors.

9) Conduct searches to find needed information, using such sources as the Internet.

10) Order and dispense supplies.

11) Open, read, route, and distribute incoming mail and other material, and prepare answers to routine letters.

12) Locate and attach appropriate files to incoming correspondence requiring replies.

13) Maintain scheduling and event calendars.

14) Manage projects, and contribute to committee and team work.

15) Mail newsletters, promotional material, and other information.

16) Review work done by others to check for correct spelling and grammar, ensure that company format policies are followed, and recommend revisions.

17) Operate electronic mail systems and coordinate the flow of information both internally and with other organizations.

18) Provide services to customers, such as order placement and account information.

19) Arrange conferences, meetings, and travel reservations for office personnel.

20) Supervise other clerical staff, and provide training and orientation to new staff.

21) Coordinate conferences and meetings.

22) Collect and disburse funds from cash accounts, and keep records of collections and disbursements.

23) Prepare and mail checks.

24) Establish work procedures and schedules, and keep track of the daily work of clerical staff.

25) Take dictation in shorthand or by machine, and transcribe information.

Knowledge	Knowledge Definitions
Clerical	Knowledge of administrative and clerical procedures and systems such as word processing, managing files and records, stenography and transcription, designing forms, and other office procedures and terminology.
Customer and Personal Service	Knowledge of principles and processes for providing customer and personal services. This includes customer needs assessment, meeting quality standards for services, and evaluation of customer satisfaction.
English Language	Knowledge of the structure and content of the English language including the meaning and spelling of words, rules of composition, and grammar.
Computers and Electronics	Knowledge of circuit boards, processors, chips, electronic equipment, and computer hardware and software, including applications and programming.
Administration and Management	Knowledge of business and management principles involved in strategic planning, resource allocation, human resources modeling, leadership technique, production methods, and coordination of people and resources.
Mathematics	Knowledge of arithmetic, algebra, geometry, calculus, statistics, and their applications.
Economics and Accounting	Knowledge of economic and accounting principles and practices, the financial markets, banking and the analysis and reporting of financial data.
Personnel and Human Resources	Knowledge of principles and procedures for personnel recruitment, selection, training, compensation and benefits, labor relations and negotiation, and personnel information systems.
Communications and Media	Knowledge of media production, communication, and dissemination techniques and methods. This includes alternative ways to inform and entertain via written, oral, and visual media.
Telecommunications	Knowledge of transmission, broadcasting, switching, control, and operation of telecommunications systems.

Public Safety and Security	Knowledge of relevant equipment, policies, procedures, and strategies to promote effective local, state, or national security operations for the protection of people, data, property, and institutions.
Education and Training	Knowledge of principles and methods for curriculum and training design, teaching and instruction for individuals and groups, and the measurement of training effects.
Production and Processing	Knowledge of raw materials, production processes, quality control, costs, and other techniques for maximizing the effective manufacture and distribution of goods.
Psychology	Knowledge of human behavior and performance; individual differences in ability, personality, and interests; learning and motivation; psychological research methods; and the assessment and treatment of behavioral and affective disorders.
Law and Government	Knowledge of laws, legal codes, court procedures, precedents, government regulations, executive orders, agency rules, and the democratic political process.
Sales and Marketing	Knowledge of principles and methods for showing, promoting, and selling products or services. This includes marketing strategy and tactics, product demonstration, sales techniques, and sales control systems.
Transportation	Knowledge of principles and methods for moving people or goods by air, rail, sea, or road, including the relative costs and benefits.
Geography	Knowledge of principles and methods for describing the features of land, sea, and air masses, including their physical characteristics, locations, interrelationships, and distribution of plant, animal, and human life.
Therapy and Counseling	Knowledge of principles, methods, and procedures for diagnosis, treatment, and rehabilitation of physical and mental dysfunctions, and for career counseling and guidance.
Medicine and Dentistry	Knowledge of the information and techniques needed to diagnose and treat human injuries, diseases, and deformities. This includes symptoms, treatment alternatives, drug properties and interactions, and preventive health-care measures.
Sociology and Anthropology	Knowledge of group behavior and dynamics, societal trends and influences, human migrations, ethnicity, cultures and their history and origins.
Design	Knowledge of design techniques, tools, and principles involved in production of precision technical plans, blueprints, drawings, and models.
Engineering and Technology	Knowledge of the practical application of engineering science and technology. This includes applying principles, techniques, procedures, and equipment to the design and production of various goods and services.
Foreign Language	Knowledge of the structure and content of a foreign (non-English) language including the meaning and spelling of words, rules of composition and grammar, and pronunciation.
Mechanical	Knowledge of machines and tools, including their designs, uses, repair, and maintenance.
Philosophy and Theology	Knowledge of different philosophical systems and religions. This includes their basic principles, values, ethics, ways of thinking, customs, practices, and their impact on human culture.
History and Archeology	Knowledge of historical events and their causes, indicators, and effects on civilizations and cultures.
Fine Arts	Knowledge of the theory and techniques required to compose, produce, and perform works of music, dance, visual arts, drama, and sculpture.
Building and Construction	Knowledge of materials, methods, and the tools involved in the construction or repair of houses, buildings, or other structures such as highways and roads.
Food Production	Knowledge of techniques and equipment for planting, growing, and harvesting food products (both plant and animal) for consumption, including storage/handling techniques.
Chemistry	Knowledge of the chemical composition, structure, and properties of substances and of the chemical processes and transformations that they undergo. This includes uses of chemicals and their interactions, danger signs, production techniques, and disposal methods.
Biology	Knowledge of plant and animal organisms, their tissues, cells, functions, interdependencies, and interactions with each other and the environment.
Physics	Knowledge and prediction of physical principles, laws, their interrelationships, and applications to understanding fluid, material, and atmospheric dynamics, and mechanical, electrical, atomic and sub-atomic structures and processes.

Skills	Skills Definitions
Active Listening	Giving full attention to what other people are saying, taking time to understand the points being made, asking questions as appropriate, and not interrupting at inappropriate times.
Reading Comprehension	Understanding written sentences and paragraphs in work related documents.
Time Management	Managing one's own time and the time of others.
Speaking	Talking to others to convey information effectively.
Writing	Communicating effectively in writing as appropriate for the needs of the audience.
Social Perceptiveness	Being aware of others' reactions and understanding why they react as they do.
Critical Thinking	Using logic and reasoning to identify the strengths and weaknesses of alternative solutions, conclusions or approaches to problems.
Active Learning	Understanding the implications of new information for both current and future problem-solving and decision-making.
Monitoring	Monitoring/Assessing performance of yourself, other individuals, or organizations to make improvements or take corrective action.
Learning Strategies	Selecting and using training/instructional methods and procedures appropriate for _____ ation when learning or teaching new things.
Coordination	Adjusting actions in relation to others' actions.
Mathematics	Using mathematics to solve problems.
Instructing	Teaching others how to do something.
Service Orientation	Actively looking for ways to help people.
Judgment and Decision Making	Considering the relative costs and benefits of potential actions to choose the most appropriate one.
Persuasion	Persuading others to change their minds or behavior.
Management of Personnel Resources	Motivating, developing, and directing people as they work, identifying the best people for the job.
Complex Problem Solving	Identifying complex problems and reviewing related information to develop and evaluate options and implement solutions.
Negotiation	Bringing others together and trying to reconcile differences.
Management of Financial Resources	Determining how money will be spent to get the work done, and accounting for these expenditures.
Operation and Control	Controlling operations of equipment or systems.
Equipment Selection	Determining the kind of tools and equipment needed to do a job.
Management of Material Resources	Obtaining and seeing to the appropriate use of equipment, facilities, and materials needed to do certain work.
Quality Control Analysis	Conducting tests and inspections of products, services, or processes to evaluate quality or performance.
Troubleshooting	Determining causes of operating errors and deciding what to do about it.
Operations Analysis	Analyzing needs and product requirements to create a design.
Equipment Maintenance	Performing routine maintenance on equipment and determining when and what kind of maintenance is needed.
Systems Evaluation	Identifying measures or indicators of system performance and the actions needed to improve or correct performance, relative to the goals of the system.
Technology Design	Generating or adapting equipment and technology to serve user needs.
Installation	Installing equipment, machines, wiring, or programs to meet specifications.
Systems Analysis	Determining how a system should work and how changes in conditions, operations, and the environment will affect outcomes.
Repairing	Repairing machines or systems using the needed tools.
Operation Monitoring	Watching gauges, dials, or other indicators to make sure a machine is working properly.
Programming	Writing computer programs for various purposes.
Science	Using scientific rules and methods to solve problems.

Ability	Ability Definitions
Oral Comprehension	The ability to listen to and understand information and ideas presented through spoken words and sentences.
Oral Expression	The ability to communicate information and ideas in speaking so others will understand.
Written Comprehension	The ability to read and understand information and ideas presented in writing.
Speech Recognition	The ability to identify and understand the speech of another person.
Speech Clarity	The ability to speak clearly so others can understand you.

Information Ordering	The ability to arrange things or actions in a certain order or pattern according to a specific rule or set of rules (e.g., patterns of numbers, letters, words, pictures, mathematical operations).
Near Vision	The ability to see details at close range (within a few feet of the observer).
Written Expression	The ability to communicate information and ideas in writing so others will understand.
Problem Sensitivity	The ability to tell when something is wrong or is likely to go wrong. It does not involve solving the problem, only recognizing there is a problem.
Deductive Reasoning	The ability to apply general rules to specific problems to produce answers that make sense.
Category Flexibility	The ability to generate or use different sets of rules for combining or grouping things in different ways.
Selective Attention	The ability to concentrate on a task over a period of time without being distracted.
Inductive Reasoning	The ability to combine pieces of information to form general rules or conclusions (includes finding a relationship among seemingly unrelated events).
Time Sharing	The ability to shift back and forth between two or more activities or sources of information (such as speech, sounds, touch, or other sources).
Memorization	The ability to remember information such as words, numbers, pictures, and procedures.
Originality	The ability to come up with unusual or clever ideas about a given topic or situation, or to develop creative ways to solve a problem.
Speed of Closure	The ability to quickly make sense of, combine, and organize information into meaningful patterns.
Perceptual Speed	The ability to quickly and accurately compare similarities and differences among sets of letters, numbers, objects, pictures, or patterns. The things to be compared may be presented at the same time or one after the other. This ability also includes comparing a presented object with a remembered object.
Fluency of Ideas	The ability to come up with a number of ideas about a topic (the number of ideas is important, not their quality, correctness, or creativity).
Flexibility of Closure	The ability to identify or detect a known pattern (a figure, object, word, or sound) that is hidden in other distracting material.
Visualization	The ability to imagine how something will look after it is moved around or when its parts are moved or rearranged.
Wrist-Finger Speed	The ability to make fast, simple, repeated movements of the fingers, hands, and wrists.
Mathematical Reasoning	The ability to choose the right mathematical methods or formulas to solve a problem.
Auditory Attention	The ability to focus on a single source of sound in the presence of other distracting sounds.
Arm-Hand Steadiness	The ability to keep your hand and arm steady while moving your arm or while holding your arm and hand in one position.
Manual Dexterity	The ability to quickly move your hand, your hand together with your arm, or your two hands to grasp, manipulate, or assemble objects.
Visual Color Discrimination	The ability to match or detect differences between colors, including shades of color and brightness.
Far Vision	The ability to see details at a distance.
Control Precision	The ability to quickly and repeatedly adjust the controls of a machine or a vehicle to exact positions.
Number Facility	The ability to add, subtract, multiply, or divide quickly and correctly.
Trunk Strength	The ability to use your abdominal and lower back muscles to support part of the body repeatedly or continuously over time without 'giving out' or fatiguing.
Finger Dexterity	The ability to make precisely coordinated movements of the fingers of one or both hands to grasp, manipulate, or assemble very small objects.
Multilimb Coordination	The ability to coordinate two or more limbs (for example, two arms, two legs, or one leg and one arm) while sitting, standing, or lying down. It does not involve performing the activities while the whole body is in motion.
Response Orientation	The ability to choose quickly between two or more movements in response to two or more different signals (lights, sounds, pictures). It includes the speed with which the correct response is started with the hand, foot, or other body part.
Hearing Sensitivity	The ability to detect or tell the differences between sounds that vary in pitch and loudness.
Extent Flexibility	The ability to bend, stretch, twist, or reach with your body, arms, and/or legs.

Dynamic Flexibility	The ability to quickly and repeatedly bend, stretch, twist, or reach out with your body, arms, and/or legs.
Spatial Orientation	The ability to know your location in relation to the environment or to know where other objects are in relation to you.
Rate Control	The ability to time your movements or the movement of a piece of equipment in anticipation of changes in the speed and/or direction of a moving object or scene.
Reaction Time	The ability to quickly respond (with the hand, finger, or foot) to a signal (sound, light, picture) when it appears.
Stamina	The ability to exert yourself physically over long periods of time without getting winded or out of breath.
Dynamic Strength	The ability to exert muscle force repeatedly or continuously over time. This involves muscular endurance and resistance to muscle fatigue.
Explosive Strength	The ability to use short bursts of muscle force to propel oneself (as in jumping or sprinting), or to throw an object.
Gross Body Equilibrium	The ability to keep or regain your body balance or stay upright when in an unstable position.
Sound Localization	The ability to tell the direction from which a sound originated.
Night Vision	The ability to see under low light conditions.
Peripheral Vision	The ability to see objects or movement of objects to one's side when the eyes are looking ahead.
Depth Perception	The ability to judge which of several objects is closer or farther away from you, or to judge the distance between you and an object.
Glare Sensitivity	The ability to see objects in the presence of glare or bright lighting.
Speed of Limb Movement	The ability to quickly move the arms and legs.
Static Strength	The ability to exert maximum muscle force to lift, push, pull, or carry objects.
Gross Body Coordination	The ability to coordinate the movement of your arms, legs, and torso together when the whole body is in motion.

Work_Activity	Work_Activity Definitions
Interacting With Computers	Using computers and computer systems (including hardware and software) to program, write software, set up functions, enter data, or process information.
Communicating with Supervisors, Peers, or Subordin	Providing information to supervisors, co-workers, and subordinates by telephone, in written form, e-mail, or in person.
Performing Administrative Activities	Performing day-to-day administrative tasks such as maintaining information files and processing paperwork.
Getting Information	Observing, receiving, and otherwise obtaining information from all relevant sources.
Documenting/Recording Information	Entering, transcribing, recording, storing, or maintaining information in written or electronic/magnetic form.
Establishing and Maintaining Interpersonal Relatio	Developing constructive and cooperative working relationships with others, and maintaining them over time.
Processing Information	Compiling, coding, categorizing, calculating, tabulating, auditing, or verifying information or data.
Organizing, Planning, and Prioritizing Work	Developing specific goals and plans to prioritize, organize, and accomplish your work.
Communicating with Persons Outside Organization	Communicating with people outside the organization, representing the organization to customers, the public, government, and other external sources. This information can be exchanged in person, in writing, or by telephone or e-mail.
Scheduling Work and Activities	Scheduling events, programs, and activities, as well as the work of others.
Performing for or Working Directly with the Public	Performing for people or dealing directly with the public. This includes serving customers in restaurants and stores, and receiving clients or guests.
Updating and Using Relevant Knowledge	Keeping up-to-date technically and applying new knowledge to your job.
Identifying Objects, Actions, and Events	Identifying information by categorizing, estimating, recognizing differences or similarities, and detecting changes in circumstances or events.
Making Decisions and Solving Problems	Analyzing information and evaluating results to choose the best solution and solve problems.
Monitor Processes, Materials, or Surroundings	Monitoring and reviewing information from materials, events, or the environment, to detect or assess problems.
Resolving Conflicts and Negotiating with Others	Handling complaints, settling disputes, and resolving grievances and conflicts, or otherwise negotiating with others.
Thinking Creatively	Developing, designing, or creating new applications, ideas, relationships, systems, or products, including artistic contributions.

Evaluating Information to Determine Compliance wit	Using relevant information and individual judgment to determine whether events or processes comply with laws, regulations, or standards.
Coordinating the Work and Activities of Others	Getting members of a group to work together to accomplish tasks.
Analyzing Data or Information	Identifying the underlying principles, reasons, or facts of information by breaking down information or data into separate parts.
Monitoring and Controlling Resources	Monitoring and controlling resources and overseeing the spending of money.
Judging the Qualities of Things, Services, or Peop	Assessing the value, importance, or quality of things or people.
Assisting and Caring for Others	Providing personal assistance, medical attention, emotional support, or other personal care to others such as coworkers, customers, or patients.
Training and Teaching Others	Identifying the educational needs of others, developing formal educational or training programs or classes, and teaching or instructing others.
Developing Objectives and Strategies	Establishing long-range objectives and specifying the strategies and actions to achieve them.
Handling and Moving Objects	Using hands and arms in handling, installing, positioning, and moving materials, and manipulating things.
Interpreting the Meaning of Information for Others	Translating or explaining what information means and how it can be used.
Estimating the Quantifiable Characteristics of Pro	Estimating sizes, distances, and quantities; or determining time, costs, resources, or materials needed to perform a work activity.
Coaching and Developing Others	Identifying the developmental needs of others and coaching, mentoring, or otherwise helping others to improve their knowledge or skills.
Controlling Machines and Processes	Using either control mechanisms or direct physical activity to operate machines or processes (not including computers or vehicles).
Guiding, Directing, and Motivating Subordinates	Providing guidance and direction to subordinates, including setting performance standards and monitoring performance.
Inspecting Equipment, Structures, or Material	Inspecting equipment, structures, or materials to identify the cause of errors or other problems or defects.
Provide Consultation and Advice to Others	Providing guidance and expert advice to management or other groups on technical, systems-, or process-related topics.
Developing and Building Teams	Encouraging and building mutual trust, respect, and cooperation among team members.
Selling or Influencing Others	Convincing others to buy merchandise/goods or to otherwise change their minds or actions.
Staffing Organizational Units	Recruiting, interviewing, selecting, hiring, and promoting employees in an organization.
Performing General Physical Activities	Performing physical activities that require considerable use of your arms and legs and moving your whole body, such as climbing, lifting, balancing, walking, stooping, and handling of materials.
Repairing and Maintaining Electronic Equipment	Servicing, repairing, calibrating, regulating, fine-tuning, or testing machines, devices, and equipment that operate primarily on the basis of electrical or electronic (not mechanical) principles.
Operating Vehicles, Mechanized Devices, or Equipme	Running, maneuvering, navigating, or driving vehicles or mechanized equipment, such as forklifts, passenger vehicles, aircraft, or water craft.
Repairing and Maintaining Mechanical Equipment	Servicing, repairing, adjusting, and testing machines, devices, moving parts, and equipment that operate primarily on the basis of mechanical (not electronic) principles.
Drafting, Laying Out, and Specifying Technical Dev	Providing documentation, detailed instructions, drawings, or specifications to tell others about how devices, parts, equipment, or structures are to be fabricated, constructed, assembled, modified, maintained, or used.

Work_Context	Work_Context Definitions
Telephone	How often do you have telephone conversations in this job?
Face-to-Face Discussions	How often do you have to have face-to-face discussions with individuals or teams in this job?
Contact With Others	How much does this job require the worker to be in contact with others (face-to-face, by telephone, or otherwise) in order to perform it?
Structured versus Unstructured Work	To what extent is this job structured for the worker, rather than allowing the worker to determine tasks, priorities, and goals?
Spend Time Sitting	How much does this job require sitting?
Indoors, Environmentally Controlled	How often does this job require working indoors in environmentally controlled conditions?

Importance of Being Exact or Accurate	How important is being very exact or highly accurate in performing this job?
Importance of Repeating Same Tasks	How important is repeating the same physical activities (e.g., key entry) or mental activities (e.g., checking entries in a ledger) over and over, without stopping, to performing this job?
Letters and Memos	How often does the job require written letters and memos?
Electronic Mail	How often do you use electronic mail in this job?
Freedom to Make Decisions	How much decision making freedom, without supervision, does the job offer?
Work With Work Group or Team	How important is it to work with others in a group or team in this job?
Deal With External Customers	How important is it to work with external customers or the public in this job?
Time Pressure	How often does this job require the worker to meet strict deadlines?
Spend Time Making Repetitive Motions	How much does this job require making repetitive motions?
Frequency of Decision Making	How frequently is the worker required to make decisions that affect other people, the financial resources, and/or the image and reputation of the organization?
Impact of Decisions on Co-workers or Company Resul	How do the decisions an employee makes impact the results of co-workers, clients or the company?
Coordinate or Lead Others	How important is it to coordinate or lead others in accomplishing work activities in this job?
Deal With Unpleasant or Angry People	How frequently does the worker have to deal with unpleasant, angry, or discourteous individuals as part of the job requirements?
Physical Proximity	To what extent does this job require the worker to perform job tasks in close physical proximity to other people?
Spend Time Using Your Hands to Handle, Control, or	How much does this job require using your hands to handle, control, or feel objects, tools or controls?
Frequency of Conflict Situations	How often are there conflict situations the employee has to face in this job?
Degree of Automation	How automated is the job?
Sounds, Noise Levels Are Distracting or Uncomforta	How often does this job require working exposed to sounds and noise levels that are distracting or uncomfortable?
Level of Competition	To what extent does this job require the worker to compete or to be aware of competitive pressures?
Spend Time Walking and Running	How much does this job require walking and running?
Spend Time Standing	How much does this job require standing?
Exposed to Contaminants	How often does this job require working exposed to contaminants (such as pollutants, gases, dust or odors)?
Responsibility for Outcomes and Results	How responsible is the worker for work outcomes and results of other workers?
Consequence of Error	How serious would the result usually be if the worker made a mistake that was not readily correctable?
Responsible for Others' Health and Safety	How much responsibility is there for the health and safety of others in this job?
Spend Time Bending or Twisting the Body	How much does this job require bending or twisting your body?
Public Speaking	How often do you have to perform public speaking in this job?
Spend Time Kneeling, Crouching, Stooping, or Crawl	How much does this job require kneeling, crouching, stooping or crawling?
Exposed to Minor Burns, Cuts, Bites, or Stings	How often does this job require exposure to minor burns, cuts, bites, or stings?
In an Enclosed Vehicle or Equipment	How often does this job require working in a closed vehicle or equipment (e.g., car)?
Pace Determined by Speed of Equipment	How important is it to this job that the pace is determined by the speed of equipment or machinery? (This does not refer to keeping busy at all times on this job.)
Extremely Bright or Inadequate Lighting	How often does this job require working in extremely bright or inadequate lighting conditions?
Deal With Physically Aggressive People	How frequently does this job require the worker to deal with physical aggression of violent individuals?
Very Hot or Cold Temperatures	How often does this job require working in very hot (above 90 F degrees) or very cold (below 32 F degrees) temperatures?
Indoors, Not Environmentally Controlled	How often does this job require working indoors in non-controlled environmental conditions (e.g., warehouse without heat)?
Cramped Work Space, Awkward Positions	How often does this job require working in cramped work spaces that requires getting into awkward positions?
Exposed to Disease or Infections	How often does this job require exposure to disease/infections?
Outdoors, Exposed to Weather	How often does this job require working outdoors, exposed to all weather conditions?
Outdoors, Under Cover	How often does this job require working outdoors, under cover (e.g., structure with roof but no walls)?
Spend Time Keeping or Regaining Balance	How much does this job require keeping or regaining your balance?
Exposed to Hazardous Conditions	How often does this job require exposure to hazardous conditions?
Wear Common Protective or Safety Equipment such as	How much does this job require wearing common protective or safety equipment such as safety shoes, glasses, gloves, hard hats or life jackets?
Exposed to High Places	How often does this job require exposure to high places?
Spend Time Climbing Ladders, Scaffolds, or Poles	How much does this job require climbing ladders, scaffolds, or poles?
Exposed to Hazardous Equipment	How often does this job require exposure to hazardous equipment?
Wear Specialized Protective or Safety Equipment su	How much does this job require wearing specialized protective or safety equipment such as breathing apparatus, safety harness, full protection suits, or radiation protection?
Exposed to Radiation	How often does this job require exposure to radiation?
Exposed to Whole Body Vibration	How often does this job require exposure to whole body vibration (e.g., operate a jackhammer)?
In an Open Vehicle or Equipment	How often does this job require working in an open vehicle or equipment (e.g., tractor)?

Job Zone Component	Job Zone Component Definitions
Title	Job Zone Two: Some Preparation Needed
Overall Experience	Some previous work-related skill, knowledge, or experience may be helpful in these occupations, but usually is not needed. For example, a drywall installer might benefit from experience installing drywall, but an inexperienced person could still learn to be an installer with little difficulty.
Job Training	Employees in these occupations need anywhere from a few months to one year of working with experienced employees.
Job Zone Examples	These occupations often involve using your knowledge and skills to help others. Examples include drywall installers, fire inspectors, flight attendants, pharmacy technicians, salespersons (retail), and tellers.
SVP Range	(4.0 to < 6.0)
Education	These occupations usually require a high school diploma and may require some vocational training or job-related course work. In some cases, an associate's or bachelor's degree could be needed.

Work_Styles	Work_Styles Definitions
Dependability	Job requires being reliable, responsible, and dependable, and fulfilling obligations.
Attention to Detail	Job requires being careful about detail and thorough in completing work tasks.
Integrity	Job requires being honest and ethical.
Cooperation	Job requires being pleasant with others on the job and displaying a good-natured, cooperative attitude.
Self Control	Job requires maintaining composure, keeping emotions in check, controlling anger, and avoiding aggressive behavior, even in very difficult situations.
Independence	Job requires developing one's own ways of doing things, guiding oneself with little or no supervision, and depending on oneself to get things done.
Concern for Others	Job requires being sensitive to others' needs and feelings and being understanding and helpful on the job.
Stress Tolerance	Job requires accepting criticism and dealing calmly and effectively with high stress situations.
Adaptability/Flexibility	Job requires being open to change (positive or negative) and to considerable variety in the workplace.
Initiative	Job requires a willingness to take on responsibilities and challenges.
Achievement/Effort	Job requires establishing and maintaining personally challenging achievement goals and exerting effort toward mastering tasks.
Analytical Thinking	Job requires analyzing information and using logic to address work-related issues and problems.
Persistence	Job requires persistence in the face of obstacles.
Leadership	Job requires a willingness to lead, take charge, and offer opinions and direction.

Social Orientation	Job requires preferring to work with others rather than alone, and being personally connected with others on the job.
Innovation	Job requires creativity and alternative thinking to develop new ideas for and answers to work-related problems.

43-9011.00 - Computer Operators

Monitor and control electronic computer and peripheral electronic data processing equipment to process business, scientific, engineering, and other data according to operating instructions. May enter commands at a computer terminal and set controls on computer and peripheral devices. Monitor and respond to operating and error messages.

Tasks

1) Enter commands, using computer terminal, and activate controls on computer and peripheral equipment to integrate and operate equipment.

2) Respond to program error messages by finding and correcting problems or terminating the program.

3) Operate spreadsheet programs and other types of software to load and manipulate data and to produce reports.

4) Monitor the system for equipment failure or errors in performance.

5) Retrieve, separate and sort program output as needed, and send data to specified users.

6) Answer telephone calls to assist computer users encountering problems.

7) Read job set-up instructions to determine equipment to be used, order of use, material such as disks and paper to be loaded, and control settings.

8) Oversee the operation of computer hardware systems, including coordinating and scheduling the use of computer terminals and networks to ensure efficient use.

9) Record information such as computer operating time, problems that occurred, and actions taken.

10) Load peripheral equipment with selected materials for operating runs, or oversee loading of peripheral equipment by peripheral equipment operators.

11) Clear equipment at end of operating run and review schedule to determine next assignment.

12) Help programmers and systems analysts test and debug new programs.

13) Type command on keyboard to transfer encoded data from memory unit to magnetic tape and assist in labeling, classifying, cataloging and maintaining tapes.

14) Supervise and train peripheral equipment operators and computer operator trainees.

Knowledge	Knowledge Definitions
Computers and Electronics	Knowledge of circuit boards, processors, chips, electronic equipment, and computer hardware and software, including applications and programming.
Customer and Personal Service	Knowledge of principles and processes for providing customer and personal services. This includes customer needs assessment, meeting quality standards for services, and evaluation of customer satisfaction.
Sales and Marketing	Knowledge of principles and methods for showing, promoting, and selling products or services. This includes marketing strategy and tactics, product demonstration, sales techniques, and sales control systems.
Clerical	Knowledge of administrative and clerical procedures and systems such as word processing, managing files and records, stenography and transcription, designing forms, and other office procedures and terminology.
Administration and Management	Knowledge of business and management principles involved in strategic planning, resource allocation, human resources modeling, leadership technique, production methods, and coordination of people and resources.
English Language	Knowledge of the structure and content of the English language including the meaning and spelling of words, rules of composition, and grammar.
Telecommunications	Knowledge of transmission, broadcasting, switching, control, and operation of telecommunications systems.
Education and Training	Knowledge of principles and methods for curriculum and training design, teaching and instruction for individuals and groups, and the measurement of training effects.
Mathematics	Knowledge of arithmetic, algebra, geometry, calculus, statistics, and their applications.
Communications and Media	Knowledge of media production, communication, and dissemination techniques and methods. This includes alternative ways to inform and entertain via written, oral, and visual media.
Economics and Accounting	Knowledge of economic and accounting principles and practices, the financial markets, banking and the analysis and reporting of financial data.
Production and Processing	Knowledge of raw materials, production processes, quality control, costs, and other techniques for maximizing the effective manufacture and distribution of goods.
Engineering and Technology	Knowledge of the practical application of engineering science and technology. This includes applying principles, techniques, procedures, and equipment to the design and production of various goods and services.
Personnel and Human Resources	Knowledge of principles and procedures for personnel recruitment, selection, training, compensation and benefits, labor relations and negotiation, and personnel information systems.
Transportation	Knowledge of principles and methods for moving people or goods by air, rail, sea, or road, including the relative costs and benefits.
Law and Government	Knowledge of laws, legal codes, court procedures, precedents, government regulations, executive orders, agency rules, and the democratic political process.
Psychology	Knowledge of human behavior and performance; individual differences in ability, personality, and interests; learning and motivation; psychological research methods; and the assessment and treatment of behavioral and affective disorders.
Geography	Knowledge of principles and methods for describing the features of land, sea, and air masses, including their physical characteristics, locations, interrelationships, and distribution of plant, animal, and human life.
Sociology and Anthropology	Knowledge of group behavior and dynamics, societal trends and influences, human migrations, ethnicity, cultures and their history and origins.
Fine Arts	Knowledge of the theory and techniques required to compose, produce, and perform works of music, dance, visual arts, drama, and sculpture.
Foreign Language	Knowledge of the structure and content of a foreign (non-English) language including the meaning and spelling of words, rules of composition and grammar, and pronunciation.
Design	Knowledge of design techniques, tools, and principles involved in production of precision technical plans, blueprints, drawings, and models.
Food Production	Knowledge of techniques and equipment for planting, growing, and harvesting food products (both plant and animal) for consumption, including storage/handling techniques.
Mechanical	Knowledge of machines and tools, including their designs, uses, repair, and maintenance.
Public Safety and Security	Knowledge of relevant equipment, policies, procedures, and strategies to promote effective local, state, or national security operations for the protection of people, data, property, and institutions.
Therapy and Counseling	Knowledge of principles, methods, and procedures for diagnosis, treatment, and rehabilitation of physical and mental dysfunctions, and for career counseling and guidance.
Biology	Knowledge of plant and animal organisms, their tissues, cells, functions, interdependencies, and interactions with each other and the environment.
History and Archeology	Knowledge of historical events and their causes, indicators, and effects on civilizations and cultures.
Medicine and Dentistry	Knowledge of the information and techniques needed to diagnose and treat human injuries, diseases, and deformities. This includes symptoms, treatment alternatives, drug properties and interactions, and preventive health-care measures.
Philosophy and Theology	Knowledge of different philosophical systems and religions. This includes their basic principles, values, ethics, ways of thinking, customs, practices, and their impact on human culture.
Building and Construction	Knowledge of materials, methods, and the tools involved in the construction or repair of houses, buildings, or other structures such as highways and roads.
Chemistry	Knowledge of the chemical composition, structure, and properties of substances and of the chemical processes that they undergo. This includes uses of chemicals and their interactions, danger signs, production techniques, and disposal methods.

Physics	Knowledge and prediction of physical principles, laws, their interrelationships, and applications to understanding fluid, material, and atmospheric dynamics, and mechanical, electrical, atomic and sub- atomic structures and processes.

Skills	Skills Definitions
Active Listening	Giving full attention to what other people are saying, taking time to understand the points being made, asking questions as appropriate, and not interrupting at inappropriate times.
Reading Comprehension	Understanding written sentences and paragraphs in work related documents.
Critical Thinking	Using logic and reasoning to identify the strengths and weaknesses of alternative solutions, conclusions or approaches to problems.
Active Learning	Understanding the implications of new information for both current and future problem-solving and decision-making.
Time Management	Managing one's own time and the time of others.
Troubleshooting	Determining causes of operating errors and deciding what to do about it.
Instructing	Teaching others how to do something.
Speaking	Talking to others to convey information effectively.
Service Orientation	Actively looking for ways to help people.
Judgment and Decision Making	Considering the relative costs and benefits of potential actions to choose the most appropriate one.
Coordination	Adjusting actions in relation to others' actions.
Operation and Control	Controlling operations of equipment or systems.
Writing	Communicating effectively in writing as appropriate for the needs of the audience.
Social Perceptiveness	Being aware of others' reactions and understanding why they react as they do.
Monitoring	Monitoring/Assessing performance of yourself, other individuals, or organizations to make improvements or take corrective action.
Mathematics	Using mathematics to solve problems.
Systems Evaluation	Identifying measures or indicators of system performance and the actions needed to improve or correct performance, relative to the goals of the system.
Complex Problem Solving	Identifying complex problems and reviewing related information to develop and evaluate options and implement solutions.
Learning Strategies	Selecting and using training/instructional methods and procedures appropriate for the situation when learning or teaching new things.
Negotiation	Bringing others together and trying to reconcile differences.
Equipment Maintenance	Performing routine maintenance on equipment and determining when and what kind of maintenance is needed.
Systems Analysis	Determining how a system should work and how changes in conditions, operations, and the environment will affect outcomes.
Quality Control Analysis	Conducting tests and inspections of products, services, or processes to evaluate quality or performance.
Persuasion	Persuading others to change their minds or behavior.
Management of Financial Resources	Determining how money will be spent to get the work done, and accounting for these expenditures.
Equipment Selection	Determining the kind of tools and equipment needed to do a job.
Management of Material Resources	Obtaining and seeing to the appropriate use of equipment, facilities, and materials needed to do certain work.
Operations Analysis	Analyzing needs and product requirements to create a design.
Management of Personnel Resources	Motivating, developing, and directing people as they work, identifying the best people for the job.
Operation Monitoring	Watching gauges, dials, or other indicators to make sure a machine is working properly.
Installation	Installing equipment, machines, wiring, or programs to meet specifications.
Programming	Writing computer programs for various purposes.
Technology Design	Generating or adapting equipment and technology to serve user needs.
Repairing	Repairing machines or systems using the needed tools.
Science	Using scientific rules and methods to solve problems.

Ability	Ability Definitions
Written Comprehension	The ability to read and understand information and ideas presented in writing.
Problem Sensitivity	The ability to tell when something is wrong or is likely to go wrong. It does not involve solving the problem, only recognizing there is a problem.
Information Ordering	The ability to arrange things or actions in a certain order or pattern according to a specific rule or set of rules (e.g., patterns of numbers, letters, words, pictures, mathematical operations).
Oral Comprehension	The ability to listen to and understand information and ideas presented through spoken words and sentences.
Deductive Reasoning	The ability to apply general rules to specific problems to produce answers that make sense.
Oral Expression	The ability to communicate information and ideas in speaking so others will understand.
Near Vision	The ability to see details at close range (within a few feet of the observer).
Written Expression	The ability to communicate information and ideas in writing so others will understand.
Inductive Reasoning	The ability to combine pieces of information to form general rules or conclusions (includes finding a relationship among seemingly unrelated events).
Speech Recognition	The ability to identify and understand the speech of another person.
Speech Clarity	The ability to speak clearly so others can understand you.
Category Flexibility	The ability to generate or use different sets of rules for combining or grouping things in different ways.
Flexibility of Closure	The ability to identify or detect a known pattern (a figure, object, word, or sound) that is hidden in other distracting material.
Selective Attention	The ability to concentrate on a task over a period of time without being distracted.
Originality	The ability to come up with unusual or clever ideas about a given topic or situation, or to develop creative ways to solve a problem.
Fluency of Ideas	The ability to come up with a number of ideas about a topic (the number of ideas is important, not their quality, correctness, or creativity).
Visualization	The ability to imagine how something will look after it is moved around or when its parts are moved or rearranged.
Perceptual Speed	The ability to quickly and accurately compare similarities and differences among sets of letters, numbers, objects, pictures, or patterns. The things to be compared may be presented at the same time or one after the other. This ability also includes comparing a presented object with a remembered object.
Manual Dexterity	The ability to quickly move your hand, your hand together with your arm, or your two hands to grasp, manipulate, or assemble objects.
Arm-Hand Steadiness	The ability to keep your hand and arm steady while moving your arm or while holding your arm and hand in one position.
Control Precision	The ability to quickly and repeatedly adjust the controls of a machine or a vehicle to exact positions.
Time Sharing	The ability to shift back and forth between two or more activities or sources of information (such as speech, sounds, touch, or other sources).
Mathematical Reasoning	The ability to choose the right mathematical methods or formulas to solve a problem.
Finger Dexterity	The ability to make precisely coordinated movements of the fingers of one or both hands to grasp, manipulate, or assemble very small objects.
Speed of Closure	The ability to quickly make sense of, combine, and organize information into meaningful patterns.
Memorization	The ability to remember information such as words, numbers, pictures, and procedures.
Wrist-Finger Speed	The ability to make fast, simple, repeated movements of the fingers, hands, and wrists.
Multilimb Coordination	The ability to coordinate two or more limbs (for example, two arms, two legs, or one leg and one arm) while sitting, standing, or lying down. It does not involve performing the activities while the whole body is in motion.
Auditory Attention	The ability to focus on a single source of sound in the presence of other distracting sounds.
Number Facility	The ability to add, subtract, multiply, or divide quickly and correctly.
Far Vision	The ability to see details at a distance.
Visual Color Discrimination	The ability to match or detect differences between colors, including shades of color and brightness.
Depth Perception	The ability to judge which of several objects is closer or farther away from you, or to judge the distance between you and an object.

Trunk Strength	The ability to use your abdominal and lower back muscles to support part of the body repeatedly or continuously over time without 'giving out' or fatiguing.
Hearing Sensitivity	The ability to detect or tell the differences between sounds that vary in pitch and loudness.
Reaction Time	The ability to quickly respond (with the hand, finger, or foot) to a signal (sound, light, picture) when it appears.
Glare Sensitivity	The ability to see objects in the presence of glare or bright lighting.
Spatial Orientation	The ability to know your location in relation to the environment or to know where other objects are in relation to you.
Speed of Limb Movement	The ability to quickly move the arms and legs.
Gross Body Coordination	The ability to coordinate the movement of your arms, legs, and torso together when the whole body is in motion.
Dynamic Flexibility	The ability to quickly and repeatedly bend, stretch, twist, or reach out with your body, arms, and/or legs.
Extent Flexibility	The ability to bend, stretch, twist, or reach with your body, arms, and/or legs.
Stamina	The ability to exert yourself physically over long periods of time without getting winded or out of breath.
Explosive Strength	The ability to use short bursts of muscle force to propel oneself (as in jumping or sprinting), or to throw an object.
Static Strength	The ability to exert maximum muscle force to lift, push, pull, or carry objects.
Gross Body Equilibrium	The ability to keep or regain your body balance or stay upright when in an unstable position.
Peripheral Vision	The ability to see objects or movement of objects to one's side when the eyes are looking ahead.
Dynamic Strength	The ability to exert muscle force repeatedly or continuously over time. This involves muscular endurance and resistance to muscle fatigue.
Response Orientation	The ability to choose quickly between two or more movements in response to two or more different signals (lights, sounds, pictures). It includes the speed with which the correct response is started with the hand, foot, or other body part.
Sound Localization	The ability to tell the direction from which a sound originated.
Night Vision	The ability to see under low light conditions.
Rate Control	The ability to time your movements or the movement of a piece of equipment in anticipation of changes in the speed and/or direction of a moving object or scene.

Work_Activity	Work_Activity Definitions
Making Decisions and Solving Problems	Analyzing information and evaluating results to choose the best solution and solve problems.
Getting Information	Observing, receiving, and otherwise obtaining information from all relevant sources.
Processing Information	Compiling, coding, categorizing, calculating, tabulating, auditing, or verifying information or data.
Communicating with Supervisors, Peers, or Subordin	Providing information to supervisors, co-workers, and subordinates by telephone, in written form, e-mail, or in person.
Updating and Using Relevant Knowledge	Keeping up-to-date technically and applying new knowledge to your job.
Documenting/Recording Information	Entering, transcribing, recording, storing, or maintaining information in written or electronic/magnetic form.
Interacting With Computers	Using computers and computer systems (including hardware and software) to program, write software, set up functions, enter data, or process information.
Organizing, Planning, and Prioritizing Work	Developing specific goals and plans to prioritize, organize, and accomplish your work.
Performing Administrative Activities	Performing day-to-day administrative tasks such as maintaining information files and processing paperwork.
Analyzing Data or Information	Identifying the underlying principles, reasons, or facts of information by breaking down information or data into separate parts.
Scheduling Work and Activities	Scheduling events, programs, and activities, as well as the work of others.
Establishing and Maintaining Interpersonal Relatio	Developing constructive and cooperative working relationships with others, and maintaining them over time.
Evaluating Information to Determine Compliance wit	Using relevant information and individual judgment to determine whether events or processes comply with laws, regulations, or standards.
Communicating with Persons Outside Organization	Communicating with people outside the organization, representing the organization to customers, the public, government, and other external sources. This information can be exchanged in person, in writing, or by telephone or e-mail.

Thinking Creatively	Developing, designing, or creating new applications, ideas, relationships, systems, or products, including artistic contributions.
Coordinating the Work and Activities of Others	Getting members of a group to work together to accomplish tasks.
Identifying Objects, Actions, and Events	Identifying information by categorizing, estimating, recognizing differences or similarities, and detecting changes in circumstances or events.
Interpreting the Meaning of Information for Others	Translating or explaining what information means and how it can be used.
Provide Consultation and Advice to Others	Providing guidance and expert advice to management or other groups on technical, systems-, or process-related topics.
Training and Teaching Others	Identifying the educational needs of others, developing formal educational or training programs or classes, and teaching or instructing others.
Developing and Building Teams	Encouraging and building mutual trust, respect, and cooperation among team members.
Monitor Processes, Materials, or Surroundings	Monitoring and reviewing information from materials, events, or the environment, to detect or assess problems.
Coaching and Developing Others	Identifying the developmental needs of others and coaching, mentoring, or otherwise helping others to improve their knowledge or skills.
Developing Objectives and Strategies	Establishing long-range objectives and specifying the strategies and actions to achieve them.
Assisting and Caring for Others	Providing personal assistance, medical attention, emotional support, or other personal care to others such as coworkers, customers, or patients.
Judging the Qualities of Things, Services, or Peop	Assessing the value, importance, or quality of things or people.
Resolving Conflicts and Negotiating with Others	Handling complaints, settling disputes, and resolving grievances and conflicts, or otherwise negotiating with others.
Guiding, Directing, and Motivating Subordinates	Providing guidance and direction to subordinates, including setting performance standards and monitoring performance.
Performing for or Working Directly with the Public	Performing for people or dealing directly with the public. This includes serving customers in restaurants and stores, and receiving clients or guests.
Selling or Influencing Others	Convincing others to buy merchandise/goods or to otherwise change their minds or actions.
Estimating the Quantifiable Characteristics of Pro	Estimating sizes, distances, and quantities; or determining time, costs, resources, or materials needed to perform a work activity.
Staffing Organizational Units	Recruiting, interviewing, selecting, hiring, and promoting employees in an organization.
Monitoring and Controlling Resources	Monitoring and controlling resources and overseeing the spending of money.
Handling and Moving Objects	Using hands and arms in handling, installing, positioning, and moving materials, and manipulating things.
Inspecting Equipment, Structures, or Material	Inspecting equipment, structures, or materials to identify the cause of errors or other problems or defects.
Performing General Physical Activities	Performing physical activities that require considerable use of your arms and legs and moving your whole body, such as climbing, lifting, balancing, walking, stooping, and handling of materials.
Drafting, Laying Out, and Specifying Technical Dev	Providing documentation, detailed instructions, drawings, or specifications to tell others about how devices, parts, equipment, or structures are to be fabricated, constructed, assembled, modified, maintained, or used.
Controlling Machines and Processes	Using either control mechanisms or direct physical activity to operate machines or processes (not including computers or vehicles).
Repairing and Maintaining Mechanical Equipment	Servicing, repairing, adjusting, and testing machines, devices, moving parts, and equipment that operate primarily on the basis of mechanical (not electronic) principles.
Repairing and Maintaining Electronic Equipment	Servicing, repairing, calibrating, regulating, fine-tuning, or testing machines, devices, and equipment that operate primarily on the basis of electrical or electronic (not mechanical) principles.
Operating Vehicles, Mechanized Devices, or Equipme	Running, maneuvering, navigating, or driving vehicles or mechanized equipment, such as forklifts, passenger vehicles, aircraft, or water craft.

Work_Context	Work_Context Definitions
Telephone	How often do you have telephone conversations in this job?
Contact With Others	How much does this job require the worker to be in contact with others (face-to-face, by telephone, or otherwise) in order to perform it?

Importance of Being Exact or Accurate	How important is being very exact or highly accurate in performing this job?
Indoors, Environmentally Controlled	How often does this job require working indoors in environmentally controlled conditions?
Time Pressure	How often does this job require the worker to meet strict deadlines?
Spend Time Sitting	How much does this job require sitting?
Work With Work Group or Team	How important is it to work with others in a group or team in this job?
Importance of Repeating Same Tasks	How important is repeating the same physical activities (e.g., key entry) or mental activities (e.g., checking entries in a ledger) over and over, without stopping, to performing this job?
Face-to-Face Discussions	How often do you have to have face-to-face discussions with individuals or teams in this job?
Structured versus Unstructured Work	To what extent is this job structured for the worker, rather than allowing the worker to determine tasks, priorities, and goals?
Impact of Decisions on Co-workers or Company Resul	How do the decisions an employee makes impact the results of co-workers, clients or the company?
Frequency of Decision Making	How frequently is the worker required to make decisions that affect other people, the financial resources, and/or the image and reputation of the organization?
Spend Time Using Your Hands to Handle, Control, or	How much does this job require using your hands to handle, control, or feel objects, tools or controls?
Deal With External Customers	How important is it to work with external customers or the public in this job?
Spend Time Making Repetitive Motions	How much does this job require making repetitive motions?
Freedom to Make Decisions	How much decision making freedom, without supervision, does the job offer?
Electronic Mail	How often do you use electronic mail in this job?
Coordinate or Lead Others	How important is it to coordinate or lead others in accomplishing work activities in this job?
Consequence of Error	How serious would the result usually be if the worker made a mistake that was not readily correctable?
Letters and Memos	How often does the job require written letters and memos?
Degree of Automation	How automated is the job?
Deal With Unpleasant or Angry People	How frequently does the worker have to deal with unpleasant, angry, or discourteous individuals as part of the job requirements?
Frequency of Conflict Situations	How often are there conflict situations the employee has to face in this job?
Responsibility for Outcomes and Results	How responsible is the worker for work outcomes and results of other workers?
Sounds, Noise Levels Are Distracting or Uncomforta	How often does this job require working exposed to sounds and noise levels that are distracting or uncomfortable?
Responsible for Others' Health and Safety	How much responsibility is there for the health and safety of others in this job?
In an Enclosed Vehicle or Equipment	How often does this job require working in a closed vehicle or equipment (e.g., car)?
Physical Proximity	To what extent does this job require the worker to perform job tasks in close physical proximity to other people?
Spend Time Standing	How much does this job require standing?
Deal With Physically Aggressive People	How frequently does this job require the worker to deal with physical aggression of violent individuals?
Public Speaking	How often do you have to perform public speaking in this job?
Exposed to Disease or Infections	How often does this job require exposure to disease/infections?
Spend Time Walking and Running	How much does this job require walking and running?
Spend Time Bending or Twisting the Body	How much does this job require bending or twisting your body?
Spend Time Kneeling, Crouching, Stooping, or Crawl	How much does this job require kneeling, crouching, stooping or crawling?
Exposed to Minor Burns, Cuts, Bites, or Stings	How often does this job require exposure to minor burns, cuts, bites, or stings?
Level of Competition	To what extent does this job require the worker to compete or to be aware of competitive pressures?
Pace Determined by Speed of Equipment	How important is it to this job that the pace is determined by the speed of equipment or machinery? (This does not refer to keeping busy at all times on this job.)
Wear Common Protective or Safety Equipment such as	How much does this job require wearing common protective or safety equipment such as safety shoes, glasses, gloves, hard hats or life jackets?
Outdoors, Exposed to Weather	How often does this job require working outdoors, exposed to all weather conditions?

Exposed to Contaminants	How often does this job require working exposed to contaminants (such as pollutants, gases, dust or odors)?
Indoors, Not Environmentally Controlled	How often does this job require working indoors in non-controlled environmental conditions (e.g., warehouse without heat)?
Very Hot or Cold Temperatures	How often does this job require working in very hot (above 90 F degrees) or very cold (below 32 F degrees) temperatures?
Exposed to High Places	How often does this job require exposure to high places?
Exposed to Hazardous Equipment	How often does this job require exposure to hazardous equipment?
Cramped Work Space, Awkward Positions	How often does this job require working in cramped work spaces that requires getting into awkward positions?
Extremely Bright or Inadequate Lighting	How often does this job require working in extremely bright or inadequate lighting conditions?
Exposed to Hazardous Conditions	How often does this job require exposure to hazardous conditions?
Spend Time Climbing Ladders, Scaffolds, or Poles	How much does this job require climbing ladders, scaffolds, or poles?
Outdoors, Under Cover	How often does this job require working outdoors, under cover (e.g., structure with roof but no walls)?
In an Open Vehicle or Equipment	How often does this job require working in an open vehicle or equipment (e.g., tractor)?
Spend Time Keeping or Regaining Balance	How much does this job require keeping or regaining your balance?
Wear Specialized Protective or Safety Equipment su	How much does this job require wearing specialized protective or safety equipment such as breathing apparatus, safety harness, full protection suits, or radiation protection?
Exposed to Whole Body Vibration	How often does this job require exposure to whole body vibration (e.g., operate a jackhammer)?
Exposed to Radiation	How often does this job require exposure to radiation?

Job Zone Component	**Job Zone Component Definitions**
Title	Job Zone Three: Medium Preparation Needed
Overall Experience	Previous work-related skill, knowledge, or experience is required for these occupations. For example, an electrician must have completed three or four years of apprenticeship or several years of vocational training, and often must have passed a licensing exam, in order to perform the job.
Job Training	Employees in these occupations usually need one or two years of training involving both on-the-job experience and informal training with experienced workers.
Job Zone Examples	These occupations usually involve using communication and organizational skills to coordinate, supervise, manage, or train others to accomplish goals. Examples include dental assistants, electricians, fish and game wardens, legal secretaries, personnel recruiters, and recreation workers.
SVP Range	(6.0 to < 7.0)
Education	Most occupations in this zone require training in vocational schools, related on-the-job experience, or an associate's degree. Some may require a bachelor's degree.

Work_Styles	**Work_Styles Definitions**
Attention to Detail	Job requires being careful about detail and thorough in completing work tasks.
Dependability	Job requires being reliable, responsible, and dependable, and fulfilling obligations.
Initiative	Job requires a willingness to take on responsibilities and challenges.
Innovation	Job requires creativity and alternative thinking to develop new ideas and for answers to work-related problems.
Independence	Job requires developing one's own ways of doing things, guiding oneself with little or no supervision, and depending on oneself to get things done.
Achievement/Effort	Job requires establishing and maintaining personally challenging achievement goals and exerting effort toward mastering tasks.
Adaptability/Flexibility	Job requires being open to change (positive or negative) and to considerable variety in the workplace.
Analytical Thinking	Job requires analyzing information and using logic to address work-related issues and problems.
Self Control	Job requires maintaining composure, keeping emotions in check, controlling anger, and avoiding aggressive behavior, even in very difficult situations.

Leadership	Job requires a willingness to lead, take charge, and offer opinions and direction.
Persistence	Job requires persistence in the face of obstacles.
Stress Tolerance	Job requires accepting criticism and dealing calmly and effectively with high stress situations.
Cooperation	Job requires being pleasant with others on the job and displaying a good-natured, cooperative attitude.
Integrity	Job requires being honest and ethical.
Concern for Others	Job requires being sensitive to others' needs and feelings and being understanding and helpful on the job.
Social Orientation	Job requires preferring to work with others rather than alone, and being personally connected with others on the job.

43-9021.00 - Data Entry Keyers

Operate data entry device, such as keyboard or photo composing perforator. Duties may include verifying data and preparing materials for printing.

Tasks

1) Select materials needed to complete work assignments.

2) Resolve garbled or indecipherable messages, using cryptographic procedures and equipment.

3) Load machines with required input or output media such as paper, cards, disks, tape or Braille media.

4) Read source documents such as canceled checks, sales reports, or bills, and enter data in specific data fields or onto tapes or disks for subsequent entry, using keyboards or scanners.

5) Maintain logs of activities and completed work.

6) Compile, sort and verify the accuracy of data before it is entered.

7) Store completed documents in appropriate locations.

8) Locate and correct data entry errors, or report them to supervisors.

43-9022.00 - Word Processors and Typists

Use word processor/computer or typewriter to type letters, reports, forms, or other material from rough draft, corrected copy, or voice recording. May perform other clerical duties as assigned.

Tasks

1) Perform other clerical duties such as answering telephone, sorting and distributing mail, running errands or sending faxes.

2) Type correspondence, reports, text and other written material from rough drafts, corrected copies, voice recordings, dictation or previous versions, using a computer, word processor, or typewriter.

3) Address envelopes or prepare envelope labels, using typewriter or computer.

4) Adjust settings for format, page layout, line spacing, and other style requirements.

5) File and store completed documents on computer hard drive or disk, and/or maintain a computer filing system to store, retrieve, update and delete documents.

6) Collate pages of reports and other documents prepared.

7) Check completed work for spelling, grammar, punctuation, and format.

8) Operate and resupply printers and computers, changing print wheels or fluid cartridges, adding paper, and loading blank tapes, cards, or disks into equipment.

9) Electronically sort and compile text and numerical data, retrieving, updating, and merging documents as required.

10) Reformat documents, moving paragraphs and/or columns.

11) Gather, register, and arrange the material to be typed, following instructions.

12) Search for specific sets of stored, typed characters in order to make changes.

13) Compute and verify totals on report forms, requisitions, or bills, using adding machine or calculator.

14) Keep records of work performed.

15) Transmit work electronically to other locations.

16) Work with technical material, preparing statistical reports, planning and typing statistical tables, and combining and rearranging material from different sources.

17) Use data entry devices, such as optical scanners, to input data into computers for revision or editing.

18) Transcribe stenotyped notes of court proceedings.

Knowledge	Knowledge Definitions
Clerical	Knowledge of administrative and clerical procedures and systems such as word processing, managing files and records, stenography and transcription, designing forms, and other office procedures and terminology.
English Language	Knowledge of the structure and content of the English language including the meaning and spelling of words, rules of composition, and grammar.
Customer and Personal Service	Knowledge of principles and processes for providing customer and personal services. This includes customer needs assessment, meeting quality standards for services, and evaluation of customer satisfaction.
Computers and Electronics	Knowledge of circuit boards, processors, chips, electronic equipment, and computer hardware and software, including applications and programming.
Administration and Management	Knowledge of business and management principles involved in strategic planning, resource allocation, human resources modeling, leadership technique, production methods, and coordination of people and resources.
Mathematics	Knowledge of arithmetic, algebra, geometry, calculus, statistics, and their applications.
Sales and Marketing	Knowledge of principles and methods for showing, promoting, and selling products or services. This includes marketing strategy and tactics, product demonstration, sales techniques, and sales control systems.
Economics and Accounting	Knowledge of economic and accounting principles and practices, the financial markets, banking and the analysis and reporting of financial data.
Personnel and Human Resources	Knowledge of principles and procedures for personnel recruitment, selection, training, compensation and benefits, labor relations and negotiation, and personnel information systems.
Psychology	Knowledge of human behavior and performance; individual differences in ability, personality, and interests; learning and motivation; psychological research methods; and the assessment and treatment of behavioral and affective disorders.
Law and Government	Knowledge of laws, legal codes, court procedures, precedents, government regulations, executive orders, agency rules, and the democratic political process.
Production and Processing	Knowledge of raw materials, production processes, quality control, costs, and other techniques for maximizing the effective manufacture and distribution of goods.
Communications and Media	Knowledge of media production, communication, and dissemination techniques and methods. This includes alternative ways to inform and entertain via written, oral, and visual media.
Telecommunications	Knowledge of transmission, broadcasting, switching, control, and operation of telecommunications systems.
Transportation	Knowledge of principles and methods for moving people or goods by air, rail, sea, or road, including the relative costs and benefits.
Education and Training	Knowledge of principles and methods for curriculum and training design, teaching and instruction for individuals and groups, and the measurement of training effects.
Public Safety and Security	Knowledge of relevant equipment, policies, procedures, and strategies to promote effective local, state, or national security operations for the protection of people, data, property, and institutions.
Therapy and Counseling	Knowledge of principles, methods, and procedures for diagnosis, treatment, and rehabilitation of physical and mental dysfunctions, and for career counseling and guidance.
Foreign Language	Knowledge of the structure and content of a foreign (non-English) language including the meaning and spelling of words, rules of composition and grammar, and pronunciation.
Philosophy and Theology	Knowledge of different philosophical systems and religions. This includes their basic principles, values, ethics, ways of thinking, customs, practices, and their impact on human culture.

Geography	Knowledge of principles and methods for describing the features of land, sea, and air masses, including their physical characteristics, locations, interrelationships, and distribution of plant, animal, and human life.
History and Archeology	Knowledge of historical events and their causes, indicators, and effects on civilizations and cultures.
Sociology and Anthropology	Knowledge of group behavior and dynamics, societal trends and influences, human migrations, ethnicity, cultures and their history and origins.
Mechanical	Knowledge of machines and tools, including their designs, uses, repair, and maintenance.
Engineering and Technology	Knowledge of the practical application of engineering science and technology. This includes applying principles, techniques, procedures, and equipment to the design and production of various goods and services.
Building and Construction	Knowledge of materials, methods, and the tools involved in the construction or repair of houses, buildings, or other structures such as highways and roads.
Food Production	Knowledge of techniques and equipment for planting, growing, and harvesting food products (both plant and animal) for consumption, including storage/handling techniques.
Medicine and Dentistry	Knowledge of the information and techniques needed to diagnose and treat human injuries, diseases, and deformities. This includes symptoms, treatment alternatives, drug properties and interactions, and preventive health-care measures.
Chemistry	Knowledge of the chemical composition, structure, and properties of substances and of the chemical processes and transformations that they undergo. This includes uses of chemicals and their interactions, danger signs, production techniques, and disposal methods.
Physics	Knowledge and prediction of physical principles, laws, their interrelationships, and applications to understanding fluid, material, and atmospheric dynamics, and mechanical, electrical, atomic and sub-atomic structures and processes.
Design	Knowledge of design techniques, tools, and principles involved in production of precision technical plans, blueprints, drawings, and models.
Biology	Knowledge of plant and animal organisms, their tissues, cells, functions, interdependencies, and interactions with each other and the environment.
Fine Arts	Knowledge of the theory and techniques required to compose, produce, and perform works of music, dance, visual arts, drama, and sculpture.

Skills | Skills Definitions

Skills	Skills Definitions
Writing	Communicating effectively in writing as appropriate for the needs of the audience.
Active Listening	Giving full attention to what other people are saying, taking time to understand the points being made, asking questions as appropriate, and not interrupting at inappropriate times.
Time Management	Managing one's own time and the time of others.
Reading Comprehension	Understanding written sentences and paragraphs in work related documents.
Speaking	Talking to others to convey information effectively.
Mathematics	Using mathematics to solve problems.
Critical Thinking	Using logic and reasoning to identify the strengths and weaknesses of alternative solutions, conclusions or approaches to problems.
Learning Strategies	Selecting and using training/instructional methods and procedures appropriate for the situation when learning or teaching new things.
Coordination	Adjusting actions in relation to others' actions.
Judgment and Decision Making	Considering the relative costs and benefits of potential actions to choose the most appropriate one.
Instructing	Teaching others how to do something.
Social Perceptiveness	Being aware of others' reactions and understanding why they react as they do.
Active Learning	Understanding the implications of new information for both current and future problem-solving and decision-making.
Service Orientation	Actively looking for ways to help people.
Troubleshooting	Determining causes of operating errors and deciding what to do about it.
Equipment Selection	Determining the kind of tools and equipment needed to do a job.
Complex Problem Solving	Identifying complex problems and reviewing related information to develop and evaluate options and implement solutions.

Negotiation	Bringing others together and trying to reconcile differences.
Operation Monitoring	Watching gauges, dials, or other indicators to make sure a machine is working properly.
Equipment Maintenance	Performing routine maintenance on equipment and determining when and what kind of maintenance is needed.
Monitoring	Monitoring/Assessing performance of yourself, other individuals, or organizations to make improvements or take corrective action.
Installation	Installing equipment, machines, wiring, or programs to meet specifications.
Persuasion	Persuading others to change their minds or behavior.
Systems Evaluation	Identifying measures or indicators of system performance and the actions needed to improve or correct performance, relative to the goals of the system.
Management of Financial Resources	Determining how money will be spent to get the work done, and accounting for these expenditures.
Systems Analysis	Determining how a system should work and how changes in conditions, operations, and the environment will affect outcomes.
Repairing	Repairing machines or systems using the needed tools.
Operation and Control	Controlling operations of equipment or systems.
Management of Personnel Resources	Motivating, developing, and directing people as they work, identifying the best people for the job.
Operations Analysis	Analyzing needs and product requirements to create a design.
Technology Design	Generating or adapting equipment and technology to serve user needs.
Programming	Writing computer programs for various purposes.
Quality Control Analysis	Conducting tests and inspections of products, services, or processes to evaluate quality or performance.
Management of Material Resources	Obtaining and seeing to the appropriate use of equipment, facilities, and materials needed to do certain work.
Science	Using scientific rules and methods to solve problems.

Ability | Ability Definitions

Ability	Ability Definitions
Near Vision	The ability to see details at close range (within a few feet of the observer).
Written Comprehension	The ability to read and understand information and ideas presented in writing.
Oral Comprehension	The ability to listen to and understand information and ideas presented through spoken words and sentences.
Speech Recognition	The ability to identify and understand the speech of another person.
Information Ordering	The ability to arrange things or actions in a certain order or pattern according to a specific rule or set of rules (e.g., patterns of numbers, letters, words, pictures, mathematical operations).
Oral Expression	The ability to communicate information and ideas in speaking so others will understand.
Perceptual Speed	The ability to quickly and accurately compare similarities and differences among sets of letters, numbers, objects, pictures, or patterns. The things to be compared may be presented at the same time or one after the other. This ability also includes comparing a presented object with a remembered object.
Speech Clarity	The ability to speak clearly so others can understand you.
Finger Dexterity	The ability to make precisely coordinated movements of the fingers of one or both hands to grasp, manipulate, or assemble very small objects.
Written Expression	The ability to communicate information and ideas in writing so others will understand.
Category Flexibility	The ability to generate or use different sets of rules for combining or grouping things in different ways.
Wrist-Finger Speed	The ability to make fast, simple, repeated movements of the fingers, hands, and wrists.
Deductive Reasoning	The ability to apply general rules to specific problems to produce answers that make sense.
Problem Sensitivity	The ability to tell when something is wrong or is likely to go wrong. It does not involve solving the problem, only recognizing there is a problem.
Selective Attention	The ability to concentrate on a task over a period of time without being distracted.
Mathematical Reasoning	The ability to choose the right mathematical methods or formulas to solve a problem.
Time Sharing	The ability to shift back and forth between two or more activities or sources of information (such as speech, sounds, touch, or other sources).
Inductive Reasoning	The ability to combine pieces of information to form general rules or conclusions (includes finding a relationship among seemingly unrelated events).

		Work_Activity	Work_Activity Definitions
Number Facility	The ability to add, subtract, multiply, or divide quickly and correctly.	Getting Information	Observing, receiving, and otherwise obtaining information from all relevant sources.
Auditory Attention	The ability to focus on a single source of sound in the presence of other distracting sounds.	Interacting With Computers	Using computers and computer systems (including hardware and software) to program, write software, set up functions, enter data, or process information.
Visualization	The ability to imagine how something will look after it is moved around or when its parts are moved or rearranged.	Communicating with Supervisors, Peers, or Subordin	Providing information to supervisors, co-workers, and subordinates by telephone, in written form, e-mail, or in person.
Flexibility of Closure	The ability to identify or detect a known pattern (a figure, object, word, or sound) that is hidden in other distracting material.	Performing Administrative Activities	Performing day-to-day administrative tasks such as maintaining information files and processing paperwork.
Fluency of Ideas	The ability to come up with a number of ideas about a topic (the number of ideas is important, not their quality, correctness, or creativity).	Establishing and Maintaining Interpersonal Relatio	Developing constructive and cooperative working relationships with others, and maintaining them over time.
Manual Dexterity	The ability to quickly move your hand, your hand together with your arm, or your two hands to grasp, manipulate, or assemble objects.	Organizing, Planning, and Prioritizing Work	Developing specific goals and plans to prioritize, organize, and accomplish your work.
Originality	The ability to come up with unusual or clever ideas about a given topic or situation, or to develop creative ways to solve a problem.	Processing Information	Compiling, coding, categorizing, calculating, tabulating, auditing, or verifying information or data.
Visual Color Discrimination	The ability to match or detect differences between colors, including shades of color and brightness.	Thinking Creatively	Developing, designing, or creating new applications, ideas, relationships, systems, or products, including artistic contributions.
Far Vision	The ability to see details at a distance.		
Speed of Closure	The ability to quickly make sense of, combine, and organize information into meaningful patterns.	Communicating with Persons Outside Organization	Communicating with people outside the organization, representing the organization to customers, the public, government, and other external sources. This information can be exchanged in person, in writing, or by telephone or e-mail.
Memorization	The ability to remember information such as words, numbers, pictures, and procedures.	Documenting/Recording Information	Entering, transcribing, recording, storing, or maintaining information in written or electronic/magnetic form.
Control Precision	The ability to quickly and repeatedly adjust the controls of a machine or a vehicle to exact positions.	Updating and Using Relevant Knowledge	Keeping up-to-date technically and applying new knowledge to your job.
Hearing Sensitivity	The ability to detect or tell the differences between sounds that vary in pitch and loudness.	Identifying Objects, Actions, and Events	Identifying information by categorizing, estimating, recognizing differences or similarities, and detecting changes in circumstances or events.
Arm-Hand Steadiness	The ability to keep your hand and arm steady while moving your arm or while holding your arm and hand in one position.	Scheduling Work and Activities	Scheduling events, programs, and activities, as well as the work of others.
Trunk Strength	The ability to use your abdominal and lower back muscles to support part of the body repeatedly or continuously over time without 'giving out' or fatiguing.	Assisting and Caring for Others	Providing personal assistance, medical attention, emotional support, or other personal care to others such as coworkers, customers, or patients.
Response Orientation	The ability to choose quickly between two or more movements in response to two or more different signals (lights, sounds, pictures). It includes the speed with which the correct response is started with the hand, foot, or other body part.	Making Decisions and Solving Problems	Analyzing information and evaluating results to choose the best solution and solve problems.
Multilimb Coordination	The ability to coordinate two or more limbs (for example, two arms, two legs, or one leg and one arm) while sitting, standing, or lying down. It does not involve performing the activities while the whole body is in motion.	Performing for or Working Directly with the Public	Performing for people or dealing directly with the public. This includes serving customers in restaurants and stores, and receiving clients or guests.
Reaction Time	The ability to quickly respond (with the hand, finger, or foot) to a signal (sound, light, picture) when it appears.	Interpreting the Meaning of Information for Others	Translating or explaining what information means and how it can be used.
Extent Flexibility	The ability to bend, stretch, twist, or reach with your body, arms, and/or legs.	Developing and Building Teams	Encouraging and building mutual trust, respect, and cooperation among team members.
Speed of Limb Movement	The ability to quickly move the arms and legs.	Judging the Qualities of Things, Services, or Peop	Assessing the value, importance, or quality of things or people.
Dynamic Strength	The ability to exert muscle force repeatedly or continuously over time. This involves muscular endurance and resistance to muscle fatigue.	Monitor Processes, Materials, or Surroundings	Monitoring and reviewing information from materials, events, or the environment, to detect or assess problems.
Stamina	The ability to exert yourself physically over long periods of time without getting winded or out of breath.	Coordinating the Work and Activities of Others	Getting members of a group to work together to accomplish tasks.
Gross Body Coordination	The ability to coordinate the movement of your arms, legs, and torso together when the whole body is in motion.	Developing Objectives and Strategies	Establishing long-range objectives and specifying the strategies and actions to achieve them.
Spatial Orientation	The ability to know your location in relation to the environment or to know where other objects are in relation to you.	Analyzing Data or Information	Identifying the underlying principles, reasons, or facts of information by breaking down information or data into separate parts.
Rate Control	The ability to time your movements or the movement of a piece of equipment in anticipation of changes in the speed and/or direction of a moving object or scene.	Evaluating Information to Determine Compliance wit	Using relevant information and individual judgment to determine whether events or processes comply with laws, regulations, or standards.
Static Strength	The ability to exert maximum muscle force to lift, push, pull, or carry objects.	Resolving Conflicts and Negotiating with Others	Handling complaints, settling disputes, and resolving grievances and conflicts, or otherwise negotiating with others.
Glare Sensitivity	The ability to see objects in the presence of glare or bright lighting.	Coaching and Developing Others	Identifying the developmental needs of others and coaching, mentoring, or otherwise helping others to improve their knowledge or skills.
Sound Localization	The ability to tell the direction from which a sound originated.		
Explosive Strength	The ability to use short bursts of muscle force to propel oneself (as in jumping or sprinting), or to throw an object.	Training and Teaching Others	Identifying the educational needs of others, developing formal educational or training programs or classes, and teaching or instructing others.
Gross Body Equilibrium	The ability to keep or regain your body balance or stay upright when in an unstable position.	Inspecting Equipment, Structures, or Material	Inspecting equipment, structures, or materials to identify the cause of errors or other problems or defects.
Night Vision	The ability to see under low light conditions.	Monitoring and Controlling Resources	Monitoring and controlling resources and overseeing the spending of money.
Peripheral Vision	The ability to see objects or movement of objects to one's side when the eyes are looking ahead.	Handling and Moving Objects	Using hands and arms in handling, installing, positioning, and moving materials, and manipulating things.
Depth Perception	The ability to judge which of several objects is closer or farther away from you, or to judge the distance between you and an object.		
Dynamic Flexibility	The ability to quickly and repeatedly bend, stretch, twist, or reach out with your body, arms, and/or legs.		

Estimating the Quantifiable Characteristics of Pro	Estimating sizes, distances, and quantities; or determining time, costs, resources, or materials needed to perform a work activity.
Provide Consultation and Advice to Others	Providing guidance and expert advice to management or other groups on technical, systems-, or process-related topics.
Performing General Physical Activities	Performing physical activities that require considerable use of your arms and legs and moving your whole body, such as climbing, lifting, balancing, walking, stooping, and handling of materials.
Guiding, Directing, and Motivating Subordinates	Providing guidance and direction to subordinates, including setting performance standards and monitoring performance.
Controlling Machines and Processes	Using either control mechanisms or direct physical activity to operate machines or processes (not including computers or vehicles).
Repairing and Maintaining Electronic Equipment	Servicing, repairing, calibrating, regulating, fine-tuning, or testing machines, devices, and equipment that operate primarily on the basis of electrical or electronic (not mechanical) principles.
Staffing Organizational Units	Recruiting, interviewing, selecting, hiring, and promoting employees in an organization.
Operating Vehicles, Mechanized Devices, or Equipme	Running, maneuvering, navigating, or driving vehicles or mechanized equipment, such as forklifts, passenger vehicles, aircraft, or water craft.
Selling or Influencing Others	Convincing others to buy merchandise/goods or to otherwise change their minds or actions.
Repairing and Maintaining Mechanical Equipment	Servicing, repairing, adjusting, and testing machines, devices, moving parts, and equipment that operate primarily on the basis of mechanical (not electronic) principles.
Drafting, Laying Out, and Specifying Technical Dev	Providing documentation, detailed instructions, drawings, or specifications to tell others about how devices, parts, equipment, or structures are to be fabricated, constructed, assembled, modified, maintained, or used.

Work_Context	**Work_Context Definitions**
Face-to-Face Discussions	How often do you have to have face-to-face discussions with individuals or teams in this job?
Spend Time Sitting	How much does this job require sitting?
Importance of Being Exact or Accurate	How important is being very exact or highly accurate in performing this job?
Telephone	How often do you have telephone conversations in this job?
Structured versus Unstructured Work	To what extent is this job structured for the worker, rather than allowing the worker to determine tasks, priorities, and goals?
Indoors, Environmentally Controlled	How often does this job require working indoors in environmentally controlled conditions?
Letters and Memos	How often does the job require written letters and memos?
Work With Work Group or Team	How important is it to work with others in a group or team in this job?
Contact With Others	How much does this job require the worker to be in contact with others (face-to-face, by telephone, or otherwise) in order to perform it?
Electronic Mail	How often do you use electronic mail in this job?
Freedom to Make Decisions	How much decision making freedom, without supervision, does the job offer?
Time Pressure	How often does this job require the worker to meet strict deadlines?
Importance of Repeating Same Tasks	How important is repeating the same physical activities (e.g., key entry) or mental activities (e.g., checking entries in a ledger) over and over, without stopping, to performing this job?
Deal With External Customers	How important is it to work with external customers or the public in this job?
Coordinate or Lead Others	How important is it to coordinate or lead others in accomplishing work activities in this job?
Impact of Decisions on Co-workers or Company Resul	How do the decisions an employee makes impact the results of co-workers, clients or the company?
Frequency of Decision Making	How frequently is the worker required to make decisions that affect other people, the financial resources, and/or the image and reputation of the organization?
Physical Proximity	To what extent does this job require the worker to perform job tasks in close physical proximity to other people?
Level of Competition	To what extent does this job require the worker to compete or to be aware of competitive pressures?
Frequency of Conflict Situations	How often are there conflict situations the employee has to face in this job?
Degree of Automation	How automated is the job?

Spend Time Using Your Hands to Handle, Control, or	How much does this job require using your hands to handle, control, or feel objects, tools or controls?
Sounds, Noise Levels Are Distracting or Uncomforta	How often does this job require working exposed to sounds and noise levels that are distracting or uncomfortable?
Spend Time Making Repetitive Motions	How much does this job require making repetitive motions?
Responsibility for Outcomes and Results	How responsible is the worker for work outcomes and results of other workers?
Deal With Unpleasant or Angry People	How frequently does the worker have to deal with unpleasant, angry, or discourteous individuals as part of the job requirements?
Consequence of Error	How serious would the result usually be if the worker made a mistake that was not readily correctable?
Spend Time Standing	How much does this job require standing?
Pace Determined by Speed of Equipment	How important is it to this job that the pace is determined by the speed of equipment or machinery? (This does not refer to keeping busy at all times on this job.)
Spend Time Walking and Running	How much does this job require walking and running?
Public Speaking	How often do you have to perform public speaking in this job?
Responsible for Others' Health and Safety	How much responsibility is there for the health and safety of others in this job?
Spend Time Bending or Twisting the Body	How much does this job require bending or twisting your body?
Exposed to Contaminants	How often does this job require working exposed to contaminants (such as pollutants, gases, dust or odors)?
Cramped Work Space, Awkward Positions	How often does this job require working in cramped work spaces that requires getting into awkward positions?
Very Hot or Cold Temperatures	How often does this job require working in very hot (above 90 F degrees) or very cold (below 32 F degrees) temperatures?
Outdoors, Exposed to Weather	How often does this job require working outdoors, exposed to all weather conditions?
Indoors, Not Environmentally Controlled	How often does this job require working indoors in non-controlled environmental conditions (e.g., warehouse without heat)?
Deal With Physically Aggressive People	How frequently does this job require the worker to deal with physical aggression of violent individuals?
Extremely Bright or Inadequate Lighting	How often does this job require working in extremely bright or inadequate lighting conditions?
In an Enclosed Vehicle or Equipment	How often does this job require working in a closed vehicle or equipment (e.g., car)?
Exposed to Disease or Infections	How often does this job require exposure to disease/infections?
In an Open Vehicle or Equipment	How often does this job require working in an open vehicle or equipment (e.g., tractor)?
Spend Time Keeping or Regaining Balance	How much does this job require keeping or regaining your balance?
Spend Time Kneeling, Crouching, Stooping, or Crawl	How much does this job require kneeling, crouching, stooping or crawling?
Exposed to Minor Burns, Cuts, Bites, or Stings	How often does this job require exposure to minor burns, cuts, bites, or stings?
Exposed to Radiation	How often does this job require exposure to radiation?
Spend Time Climbing Ladders, Scaffolds, or Poles	How much does this job require climbing ladders, scaffolds, or poles?
Wear Specialized Protective or Safety Equipment su	How much does this job require wearing specialized protective or safety equipment such as breathing apparatus, safety harness, full protection suits, or radiation protection?
Exposed to Whole Body Vibration	How often does this job require exposure to whole body vibration (e.g., operate a jackhammer)?
Exposed to Hazardous Conditions	How often does this job require exposure to hazardous conditions?
Wear Common Protective or Safety Equipment such as	How much does this job require wearing common protective or safety equipment such as safety shoes, glasses, gloves, hard hats or live jackets?
Exposed to Hazardous Equipment	How often does this job require exposure to hazardous equipment?
Outdoors, Under Cover	How often does this job require working outdoors, under cover (e.g., structure with roof but no walls)?
Exposed to High Places	How often does this job require exposure to high places?

Job Zone Component	**Job Zone Component Definitions**
Title	Job Zone Two: Some Preparation Needed

Overall Experience	Some previous work-related skill, knowledge, or experience may be helpful in these occupations, but usually is not needed. For example, a drywall installer might benefit from experience installing drywall, but an inexperienced person could still learn to be an installer with little difficulty.
Job Training	Employees in these occupations need anywhere from a few months to one year of working with experienced employees.
Job Zone Examples	These occupations often involve using your knowledge and skills to help others. Examples include drywall installers, fire inspectors, flight attendants, pharmacy technicians, salespersons (retail), and tellers.
SVP Range	(4.0 to 6.0)
Education	These occupations usually require a high school diploma and may require some vocational training or job-related course work. In some cases, an associate's or bachelor's degree could be needed.

Work_Styles	Work_Styles Definitions
Attention to Detail	Job requires being careful about detail and thorough in completing work tasks.
Integrity	Job requires being honest and ethical.
Dependability	Job requires being reliable, responsible, and dependable, and fulfilling obligations.
Cooperation	Job requires being pleasant with others on the job and displaying a good-natured, cooperative attitude.
Concern for Others	Job requires being sensitive to others' needs and feelings and being understanding and helpful on the job.
Self Control	Job requires maintaining composure, keeping emotions in check, controlling anger, and avoiding aggressive behavior, even in very difficult situations.
Social Orientation	Job requires preferring to work with others rather than alone, and being personally connected with others on the job.
Initiative	Job requires a willingness to take on responsibilities and challenges.
Independence	Job requires developing one's own ways of doing things, guiding oneself with little or no supervision, and depending on oneself to get things done.
Achievement/Effort	Job requires establishing and maintaining personally challenging achievement goals and exerting effort toward mastering tasks.
Adaptability/Flexibility	Job requires being open to change (positive or negative) and to considerable variety in the workplace.
Persistence	Job requires persistence in the face of obstacles.
Stress Tolerance	Job requires accepting criticism and dealing calmly and effectively with high stress situations.
Innovation	Job requires creativity and alternative thinking to develop new ideas for and answers to work-related problems.
Analytical Thinking	Job requires analyzing information and using logic to address work-related issues and problems.
Leadership	Job requires a willingness to lead, take charge, and offer opinions and direction.

43-9031.00 - Desktop Publishers

Format typescript and graphic elements using computer software to produce publication-ready material.

Tasks

1) Check preliminary and final proofs for errors and make necessary corrections.

2) Study layout or other design instructions to determine work to be done and sequence of operations.

3) Import text and art elements such as electronic clip-art or electronic files from photographs that have been scanned or produced with a digital camera, using computer software.

4) Prepare sample layouts for approval, using computer software.

5) Operate desktop publishing software and equipment to design, lay out, and produce camera-ready copy.

6) Position text and art elements from a variety of databases in a visually appealing way in order to design print or web pages, using knowledge of type styles and size and layout patterns.

7) Load floppy disks or tapes containing information into system.

8) Convert various types of files for printing or for the Internet, using computer software.

9) Store copies of publications on paper, magnetic tape, film or diskette.

10) Edit graphics and photos using pixel or bitmap editing, airbrushing, masking, or image retouching.

11) Enter digitized data into electronic prepress system computer memory, using scanner, camera, keyboard, or mouse.

12) Select number of colors and determine color separations.

13) Enter data, such as coordinates of images and color specifications, into system to retouch and make color corrections.

14) View monitors for visual representation of work in progress and for instructions and feedback throughout process, making modifications as necessary.

15) Collaborate with graphic artists, editors and writers to produce master copies according to design specifications.

16) Transmit, deliver or mail publication master to printer for production into film and plates.

17) Create special effects such as vignettes, mosaics, and image combining, and add elements such as sound and animation to electronic publications.

Knowledge	Knowledge Definitions
Computers and Electronics	Knowledge of circuit boards, processors, chips, electronic equipment, and computer hardware and software, including applications and programming.
English Language	Knowledge of the structure and content of the English language including the meaning and spelling of words, rules of composition, and grammar.
Production and Processing	Knowledge of raw materials, production processes, quality control, costs, and other techniques for maximizing the effective manufacture and distribution of goods.
Customer and Personal Service	Knowledge of principles and processes for providing customer and personal services. This includes customer needs assessment, meeting quality standards for services, and evaluation of customer satisfaction.
Clerical	Knowledge of administrative and clerical procedures and systems such as word processing, managing files and records, stenography and transcription, designing forms, and other office procedures and terminology.
Administration and Management	Knowledge of business and management principles involved in strategic planning, resource allocation, human resources modeling, leadership technique, production methods, and coordination of people and resources.
Communications and Media	Knowledge of media production, communication, and dissemination techniques and methods. This includes alternative ways to inform and entertain via written, oral, and visual media.
Mathematics	Knowledge of arithmetic, algebra, geometry, calculus, statistics, and their applications.
Mechanical	Knowledge of machines and tools, including their designs, uses, repair, and maintenance.
Design	Knowledge of design techniques, tools, and principles involved in production of precision technical plans, blueprints, drawings, and models.
Telecommunications	Knowledge of transmission, broadcasting, switching, control, and operation of telecommunications systems.
Education and Training	Knowledge of principles and methods for curriculum and training design, teaching and instruction for individuals and groups, and the measurement of training effects.
Personnel and Human Resources	Knowledge of principles and procedures for personnel recruitment, selection, training, compensation and benefits, labor relations and negotiation, and personnel information systems.
Public Safety and Security	Knowledge of relevant equipment, policies, procedures, and strategies to promote effective local, state, or national security operations for the protection of people, data, property, and institutions.
Engineering and Technology	Knowledge of the practical application of engineering science and technology. This includes applying principles, techniques, procedures, and equipment to the design and production of various goods and services.
Law and Government	Knowledge of laws, legal codes, court procedures, precedents, government regulations, executive orders, agency rules, and the democratic political process.

Economics and Accounting	Knowledge of economic and accounting principles and practices, the financial markets, banking and the analysis and reporting of financial data.
Chemistry	Knowledge of the chemical composition, structure, and properties of substances and of the chemical processes and transformations that they undergo. This includes uses of chemicals and their interactions, danger signs, production techniques, and disposal methods.
Transportation	Knowledge of principles and methods for moving people or goods by air, rail, sea, or road, including the relative costs and benefits.
Sales and Marketing	Knowledge of principles and methods for showing, promoting, and selling products or services. This includes marketing strategy and tactics, product demonstration, sales techniques, and sales control systems.
Philosophy and Theology	Knowledge of different philosophical systems and religions. This includes their basic principles, values, ethics, ways of thinking, customs, practices, and their impact on human culture.
Physics	Knowledge and prediction of physical principles, laws, their interrelationships, and applications to understanding fluid, material, and atmospheric dynamics, and mechanical, electrical, atomic and sub-atomic structures and processes.
Fine Arts	Knowledge of the theory and techniques required to compose, produce, and perform works of music, dance, visual arts, drama, and sculpture.
Psychology	Knowledge of human behavior and performance; individual differences in ability, personality, and interests; learning and motivation; psychological research methods; and the assessment and treatment of behavioral and affective disorders.
Foreign Language	Knowledge of the structure and content of a foreign (non-English) language including the meaning and spelling of words, rules of composition and grammar, and pronunciation.
Geography	Knowledge of principles and methods for describing the features of land, sea, and air masses, including their physical characteristics, locations, interrelationships, and distribution of plant, animal, and human life.
Medicine and Dentistry	Knowledge of the information and techniques needed to diagnose and treat human injuries, diseases, and deformities. This includes symptoms, treatment alternatives, drug properties and interactions, and preventive health-care measures.
History and Archeology	Knowledge of historical events and their causes, indicators, and effects on civilizations and cultures.
Sociology and Anthropology	Knowledge of group behavior and dynamics, societal trends and influences, human migrations, ethnicity, cultures and their history and origins.
Biology	Knowledge of plant and animal organisms, their tissues, cells, functions, interdependencies, and interactions with each other and the environment.
Building and Construction	Knowledge of materials, methods, and the tools involved in the construction or repair of houses, buildings, or other structures such as highways and roads.
Food Production	Knowledge of techniques and equipment for planting, growing, and harvesting food products (both plant and animal) for consumption, including storage/handling techniques.
Therapy and Counseling	Knowledge of principles, methods, and procedures for diagnosis, treatment, and rehabilitation of physical and mental dysfunctions, and for career counseling and guidance.

Skills	Skills Definitions
Active Listening	Giving full attention to what other people are saying, taking time to understand the points being made, asking questions as appropriate, and not interrupting at inappropriate times.
Reading Comprehension	Understanding written sentences and paragraphs in work related documents.
Time Management	Managing one's own time and the time of others.
Writing	Communicating effectively in writing as appropriate for the needs of the audience.
Critical Thinking	Using logic and reasoning to identify the strengths and weaknesses of alternative solutions, conclusions or approaches to problems.
Service Orientation	Actively looking for ways to help people.
Speaking	Talking to others to convey information effectively.
Active Learning	Understanding the implications of new information for both current and future problem-solving and decision-making.
Coordination	Adjusting actions in relation to others' actions.

Equipment Selection	Determining the kind of tools and equipment needed to do a job.
Troubleshooting	Determining causes of operating errors and deciding what to do about it.
Monitoring	Monitoring/Assessing performance of yourself, other individuals, or organizations to make improvements or take corrective action.
Quality Control Analysis	Conducting tests and inspections of products, services, or processes to evaluate quality or performance.
Judgment and Decision Making	Considering the relative costs and benefits of potential actions to choose the most appropriate one.
Complex Problem Solving	Identifying complex problems and reviewing related information to develop and evaluate options and implement solutions.
Learning Strategies	Selecting and using training/instructional methods and procedures appropriate for the situation when learning or teaching new things.
Operations Analysis	Analyzing needs and product requirements to create a design.
Social Perceptiveness	Being aware of others' reactions and understanding why they react as they do.
Operation and Control	Controlling operations of equipment or systems.
Instructing	Teaching others how to do something.
Mathematics	Using mathematics to solve problems.
Technology Design	Generating or adapting equipment and technology to serve user needs.
Equipment Maintenance	Performing routine maintenance on equipment and determining when and what kind of maintenance is needed.
Persuasion	Persuading others to change their minds or behavior.
Negotiation	Bringing others together and trying to reconcile differences.
Systems Evaluation	Identifying measures or indicators of system performance and the actions needed to improve or correct performance, relative to the goals of the system.
Systems Analysis	Determining how a system should work and how changes in conditions, operations, and the environment will affect outcomes.
Management of Material Resources	Obtaining and seeing to the appropriate use of equipment, facilities, and materials needed to do certain work.
Programming	Writing computer programs for various purposes.
Operation Monitoring	Watching gauges, dials, or other indicators to make sure a machine is working properly.
Management of Financial Resources	Determining how money will be spent to get the work done, and accounting for these expenditures.
Management of Personnel Resources	Motivating, developing, and directing people as they work, identifying the best people for the job.
Repairing	Repairing machines or systems using the needed tools.
Installation	Installing equipment, machines, wiring, or programs to meet specifications.
Science	Using scientific rules and methods to solve problems.

Ability	Ability Definitions
Written Comprehension	The ability to read and understand information and ideas presented in writing.
Near Vision	The ability to see details at close range (within a few feet of the observer).
Visualization	The ability to imagine how something will look after it is moved around or when its parts are moved or rearranged.
Written Expression	The ability to communicate information and ideas in writing so others will understand.
Oral Comprehension	The ability to listen to and understand information and ideas presented through spoken words and sentences.
Fluency of Ideas	The ability to come up with a number of ideas about a topic (the number of ideas is important, not their quality, correctness, or creativity).
Problem Sensitivity	The ability to tell when something is wrong or is likely to go wrong. It does not involve solving the problem, only recognizing there is a problem.
Originality	The ability to come up with unusual or clever ideas about a given topic or situation, or to develop creative ways to solve a problem.
Speech Clarity	The ability to speak clearly so others can understand you.
Oral Expression	The ability to communicate information and ideas in speaking so others will understand.
Category Flexibility	The ability to generate or use different sets of rules for combining or grouping things in different ways.
Selective Attention	The ability to concentrate on a task over a period of time without being distracted.

Flexibility of Closure	The ability to identify or detect a known pattern (a figure, object, word, or sound) that is hidden in other distracting material.
Speech Recognition	The ability to identify and understand the speech of another person.
Visual Color Discrimination	The ability to match or detect differences between colors, including shades of color and brightness.
Information Ordering	The ability to arrange things or actions in a certain order or pattern according to a specific rule or set of rules (e.g., patterns of numbers, letters, words, pictures, mathematical operations).
Inductive Reasoning	The ability to combine pieces of information to form general rules or conclusions (includes finding a relationship among seemingly unrelated events).
Deductive Reasoning	The ability to apply general rules to specific problems to produce answers that make sense.
Finger Dexterity	The ability to make precisely coordinated movements of the fingers of one or both hands to grasp, manipulate, or assemble very small objects.
Far Vision	The ability to see details at a distance.
Perceptual Speed	The ability to quickly and accurately compare similarities and differences among sets of letters, numbers, objects, pictures, or patterns. The things to be compared may be presented at the same time or one after the other. This ability also includes comparing a presented object with a remembered object.
Arm-Hand Steadiness	The ability to keep your hand and arm steady while moving your arm or while holding your arm and hand in one position.
Time Sharing	The ability to shift back and forth between two or more activities or sources of information (such as speech, sounds, touch, or other sources).
Control Precision	The ability to quickly and repeatedly adjust the controls of a machine or a vehicle to exact positions.
Memorization	The ability to remember information such as words, numbers, pictures, and procedures.
Number Facility	The ability to add, subtract, multiply, or divide quickly and correctly.
Depth Perception	The ability to judge which of several objects is closer or farther away from you, or to judge the distance between you and an object.
Manual Dexterity	The ability to quickly move your hand, your hand together with your arm, or your two hands to grasp, manipulate, or assemble objects.
Mathematical Reasoning	The ability to choose the right mathematical methods or formulas to solve a problem.
Hearing Sensitivity	The ability to detect or tell the differences between sounds that vary in pitch and loudness.
Speed of Closure	The ability to quickly make sense of, combine, and organize information into meaningful patterns.
Auditory Attention	The ability to focus on a single source of sound in the presence of other distracting sounds.
Wrist-Finger Speed	The ability to make fast, simple, repeated movements of the fingers, hands, and wrists.
Trunk Strength	The ability to use your abdominal and lower back muscles to support part of the body repeatedly or continuously over time without 'giving out' or fatiguing.
Multilimb Coordination	The ability to coordinate two or more limbs (for example, two arms, two legs, or one leg and one arm) while sitting, standing, or lying down. It does not involve performing the activities while the whole body is in motion.
Peripheral Vision	The ability to see objects or movement of objects to one's side when the eyes are looking ahead.
Sound Localization	The ability to tell the direction from which a sound originated.
Glare Sensitivity	The ability to see objects in the presence of glare or bright lighting.
Speed of Limb Movement	The ability to quickly move the arms and legs.
Spatial Orientation	The ability to know your location in relation to the environment or to know where other objects are in relation to you.
Response Orientation	The ability to choose quickly between two or more movements in response to two or more different signals (lights, sounds, pictures). It includes the speed with which the correct response is started with the hand, foot, or other body part.
Extent Flexibility	The ability to bend, stretch, twist, or reach with your body, arms, and/or legs.
Stamina	The ability to exert yourself physically over long periods of time without getting winded or out of breath.
Static Strength	The ability to exert maximum muscle force to lift, push, pull, or carry objects.
Reaction Time	The ability to quickly respond (with the hand, finger, or foot) to a signal (sound, light, picture) when it appears.

Gross Body Equilibrium	The ability to keep or regain your body balance or stay upright when in an unstable position.
Dynamic Flexibility	The ability to quickly and repeatedly bend, stretch, twist, or reach out with your body, arms, and/or legs.
Rate Control	The ability to time your movements or the movement of a piece of equipment in anticipation of changes in the speed and/or direction of a moving object or scene.
Explosive Strength	The ability to use short bursts of muscle force to propel oneself (as in jumping or sprinting), or to throw an object.
Night Vision	The ability to see under low light conditions.
Gross Body Coordination	The ability to coordinate the movement of your arms, legs, and torso together when the whole body is in motion.
Dynamic Strength	The ability to exert muscle force repeatedly or continuously over time. This involves muscular endurance and resistance to muscle fatigue.

Work_Activity	Work_Activity Definitions
Interacting With Computers	Using computers and computer systems (including hardware and software) to program, write software, set up functions, enter data, or process information.
Getting Information	Observing, receiving, and otherwise obtaining information from all relevant sources.
Thinking Creatively	Developing, designing, or creating new applications, ideas, relationships, systems, or products, including artistic contributions.
Updating and Using Relevant Knowledge	Keeping up-to-date technically and applying new knowledge to your job.
Organizing, Planning, and Prioritizing Work	Developing specific goals and plans to prioritize, organize, and accomplish your work.
Establishing and Maintaining Interpersonal Relatio	Developing constructive and cooperative working relationships with others, and maintaining them over time.
Communicating with Supervisors, Peers, or Subordin	Providing information to supervisors, co-workers, and subordinates by telephone, in written form, e-mail, or in person.
Making Decisions and Solving Problems	Analyzing information and evaluating results to choose the best solution and solve problems.
Processing Information	Compiling, coding, categorizing, calculating, tabulating, auditing, or verifying information or data.
Identifying Objects, Actions, and Events	Identifying information by categorizing, estimating, recognizing differences or similarities, and detecting changes in circumstances or events.
Communicating with Persons Outside Organization	Communicating with people outside the organization, representing the organization to customers, the public, government, and other external sources. This information can be exchanged in person, in writing, or by telephone or e-mail.
Documenting/Recording Information	Entering, transcribing, recording, storing, or maintaining information in written or electronic/magnetic form.
Monitor Processes, Materials, or Surroundings	Monitoring and reviewing information from materials, events, or the environment, to detect or assess problems.
Estimating the Quantifiable Characteristics of Pro	Estimating sizes, distances, and quantities; or determining time, costs, resources, or materials needed to perform a work activity.
Performing Administrative Activities	Performing day-to-day administrative tasks such as maintaining information files and processing paperwork.
Scheduling Work and Activities	Scheduling events, programs, and activities, as well as the work of others.
Interpreting the Meaning of Information for Others	Translating or explaining what information means and how it can be used.
Judging the Qualities of Things, Services, or Peop	Assessing the value, importance, or quality of things or people.
Performing for or Working Directly with the Public	Performing for people or dealing directly with the public. This includes serving customers in restaurants and stores, and receiving clients or guests.
Inspecting Equipment, Structures, or Material	Inspecting equipment, structures, or materials to identify the cause of errors or other problems or defects.
Coordinating the Work and Activities of Others	Getting members of a group to work together to accomplish tasks.
Evaluating Information to Determine Compliance wit	Using relevant information and individual judgment to determine whether events or processes comply with laws, regulations, or standards.
Provide Consultation and Advice to Others	Providing guidance and expert advice to management or other groups on technical, systems-, or process-related topics.
Analyzing Data or Information	Identifying the underlying principles, reasons, or facts of information by breaking down information or data into separate parts.

Resolving Conflicts and Negotiating with Others	Handling complaints, settling disputes, and resolving grievances and conflicts, or otherwise negotiating with others.
Drafting, Laying Out, and Specifying Technical Dev	Providing documentation, detailed instructions, drawings, or specifications to tell others about how devices, parts, equipment, or structures are to be fabricated, constructed, assembled, modified, maintained, or used.
Coaching and Developing Others	Identifying the developmental needs of others and coaching, mentoring, or otherwise helping others to improve their knowledge or skills.
Developing and Building Teams	Encouraging and building mutual trust, respect, and cooperation among team members.
Training and Teaching Others	Identifying the educational needs of others, developing formal educational or training programs or classes, and teaching or instructing others.
Guiding, Directing, and Motivating Subordinates	Providing guidance and direction to subordinates, including setting performance standards and monitoring performance.
Monitoring and Controlling Resources	Monitoring and controlling resources and overseeing the spending of money.
Controlling Machines and Processes	Using either control mechanisms or direct physical activity to operate machines or processes (not including computers or vehicles).
Developing Objectives and Strategies	Establishing long-range objectives and specifying the strategies and actions to achieve them.
Selling or Influencing Others	Convincing others to buy merchandise/goods or to otherwise change their minds or actions.
Staffing Organizational Units	Recruiting, interviewing, selecting, hiring, and promoting employees in an organization.
Operating Vehicles, Mechanized Devices, or Equipme	Running, maneuvering, navigating, or driving vehicles or mechanized equipment, such as forklifts, passenger vehicles, aircraft, or water craft.
Repairing and Maintaining Electronic Equipment	Servicing, repairing, calibrating, regulating, fine-tuning, or testing machines, devices, and equipment that operate primarily on the basis of electrical or electronic (not mechanical) principles.
Assisting and Caring for Others	Providing personal assistance, medical attention, emotional support, or other personal care to others such as coworkers, customers, or patients.
Handling and Moving Objects	Using hands and arms in handling, installing, positioning, and moving materials, and manipulating things.
Performing General Physical Activities	Performing physical activities that require considerable use of your arms and legs and moving your whole body, such as climbing, lifting, balancing, walking, stooping, and handling of materials.
Repairing and Maintaining Mechanical Equipment	Servicing, repairing, adjusting, and testing machines, devices, moving parts, and equipment that operate primarily on the basis of mechanical (not electronic) principles.

Work_Context

Work_Context	Work_Context Definitions
Telephone	How often do you have telephone conversations in this job?
Electronic Mail	How often do you use electronic mail in this job?
Face-to-Face Discussions	How often do you have to have face-to-face discussions with individuals or teams in this job?
Importance of Being Exact or Accurate	How important is being very exact or highly accurate in performing this job?
Time Pressure	How often does this job require the worker to meet strict deadlines?
Indoors, Environmentally Controlled	How often does this job require working indoors in environmentally controlled conditions?
Structured versus Unstructured Work	To what extent is this job structured for the worker, rather than allowing the worker to determine tasks, priorities, and goals?
Spend Time Sitting	How much does this job require sitting?
Work With Work Group or Team	How important is it to work with others in a group or team in this job?
Contact With Others	How much does this job require the worker to be in contact with others (face-to-face, by telephone, or otherwise) in order to perform it?
Importance of Repeating Same Tasks	How important is repeating the same physical activities (e.g., key entry) or mental activities (e.g., checking entries in a ledger) over and over, without stopping, to performing this job?
Freedom to Make Decisions	How much decision making freedom, without supervision, does the job offer?
Deal With External Customers	How important is it to work with external customers or the public in this job?
Spend Time Making Repetitive Motions	How much does this job require making repetitive motions?

Frequency of Decision Making	How frequently is the worker required to make decisions that affect other people, the financial resources, and/or the image and reputation of the organization?
Letters and Memos	How often does the job require written letters and memos?
Coordinate or Lead Others	How important is it to coordinate or lead others in accomplishing work activities in this job?
Impact of Decisions on Co-workers or Company Resul	How do the decisions an employee makes impact the results of co-workers, clients or the company?
Spend Time Using Your Hands to Handle, Control, or	How much does this job require using your hands to handle, control, or feel objects, tools or controls?
Responsibility for Outcomes and Results	How responsible is the worker for work outcomes and results of other workers?
Degree of Automation	How automated is the job?
Physical Proximity	To what extent does this job require the worker to perform job tasks in close physical proximity to other people?
Consequence of Error	How serious would the result usually be if the worker made a mistake that was not readily correctable?
Frequency of Conflict Situations	How often are there conflict situations the employee has to face in this job?
Deal With Unpleasant or Angry People	How frequently does the worker have to deal with unpleasant, angry, or discourteous individuals as part of the job requirements?
Sounds, Noise Levels Are Distracting or Uncomforta	How often does this job require working exposed to sounds and noise levels that are distracting or uncomfortable?
Exposed to Contaminants	How often does this job require working exposed to contaminants (such as pollutants, gases, dust or odors)?
Level of Competition	To what extent does this job require the worker to compete or to be aware of competitive pressures?
Spend Time Standing	How much does this job require standing?
Responsible for Others' Health and Safety	How much responsibility is there for the health and safety of others in this job?
Pace Determined by Speed of Equipment	How important is it to this job that the pace is determined by the speed of equipment or machinery? (This does not refer to keeping busy at all times on this job.)
Spend Time Walking and Running	How much does this job require walking and running?
Cramped Work Space, Awkward Positions	How often does this job require working in cramped work spaces that requires getting into awkward positions?
In an Enclosed Vehicle or Equipment	How often does this job require working in a closed vehicle or equipment (e.g., car)?
Spend Time Bending or Twisting the Body	How much does this job require bending or twisting your body?
Public Speaking	How often do you have to perform public speaking in this job?
Extremely Bright or Inadequate Lighting	How often does this job require working in extremely bright or inadequate lighting conditions?
Spend Time Kneeling, Crouching, Stooping, or Crawl	How much does this job require kneeling, crouching, stooping or crawling?
Exposed to Hazardous Conditions	How often does this job require exposure to hazardous conditions?
Indoors, Not Environmentally Controlled	How often does this job require working indoors in non-controlled environmental conditions (e.g., warehouse without heat)?
Exposed to Minor Burns, Cuts, Bites, or Stings	How often does this job require exposure to minor burns, cuts, bites, or stings?
Outdoors, Under Cover	How often does this job require working outdoors, under cover (e.g., structure with roof but no walls)?
Exposed to Radiation	How often does this job require exposure to radiation?
Outdoors, Exposed to Weather	How often does this job require working outdoors, exposed to all weather conditions?
Very Hot or Cold Temperatures	How often does this job require working in very hot (above 90 F degrees) or very cold (below 32 F degrees) temperatures?
Spend Time Keeping or Regaining Balance	How much does this job require keeping or regaining your balance?
Wear Common Protective or Safety Equipment such as	How much does this job require wearing common protective or safety equipment such as safety shoes, glasses, gloves, hard hats or live jackets?
Exposed to Disease or Infections	How often does this job require exposure to disease/infections?
Exposed to Hazardous Equipment	How often does this job require exposure to hazardous equipment?
In an Open Vehicle or Equipment	How often does this job require working in an open vehicle or equipment (e.g., tractor)?
Deal With Physically Aggressive People	How frequently does this job require the worker to deal with physical aggression of violent individuals?

Wear Specialized Protective or Safety Equipment su	How much does this job require wearing specialized protective or safety equipment such as breathing apparatus, safety harness, full protection suits, or radiation protection?
Exposed to High Places	How often does this job require exposure to high places?
Spend Time Climbing Ladders. Scaffolds, or Poles	How much does this job require climbing ladders, scaffolds, or poles?
Exposed to Whole Body Vibration	How often does this job require exposure to whole body vibration (e.g., operate a jackhammer)?

Job Zone Component	Job Zone Component Definitions
Title	Job Zone Three: Medium Preparation Needed
Overall Experience	Previous work-related skill, knowledge, or experience is required for these occupations. For example, an electrician must have completed three or four years of apprenticeship or several years of vocational training, and often must have passed a licensing exam, in order to perform the job.
Job Training	Employees in these occupations usually need one or two years of training involving both on-the-job experience and informal training with experienced workers.
Job Zone Examples	These occupations usually involve using communication and organizational skills to coordinate, supervise, manage, or train others to accomplish goals. Examples include dental assistants, electricians, fish and game wardens, legal secretaries, personnel recruiters, and recreation workers.
SVP Range	(6.0 to < 7.0)
Education	Most occupations in this zone require training in vocational schools, related on-the-job experience, or an associate's degree. Some may require a bachelor's degree.

Work_Styles	Work_Styles Definitions
Attention to Detail	Job requires being careful about detail and thorough in completing work tasks.
Dependability	Job requires being reliable, responsible, and dependable, and fulfilling obligations.
Cooperation	Job requires being pleasant with others on the job and displaying a good-natured, cooperative attitude.
Independence	Job requires developing one's own ways of doing things, guiding oneself with little or no supervision, and depending on oneself to get things done.
Innovation	Job requires creativity and alternative thinking to develop new ideas for and answers to work-related problems.
Self Control	Job requires maintaining composure, keeping emotions in check, controlling anger, and avoiding aggressive behavior, even in very difficult situations.
Integrity	Job requires being honest and ethical.
Stress Tolerance	Job requires accepting criticism and dealing calmly and effectively with high stress situations.
Adaptability/Flexibility	Job requires being open to change (positive or negative) and to considerable variety in the workplace.
Initiative	Job requires a willingness to take on responsibilities and challenges.
Achievement/Effort	Job requires establishing and maintaining personally challenging achievement goals and exerting effort toward mastering tasks.
Social Orientation	Job requires preferring to work with others rather than alone, and being personally connected with others on the job.
Persistence	Job requires persistence in the face of obstacles.
Analytical Thinking	Job requires analyzing information and using logic to address work-related issues and problems.
Concern for Others	Job requires being sensitive to others' needs and feelings and being understanding and helpful on the job.
Leadership	Job requires a willingness to lead, take charge, and offer opinions and direction.

43-9041.01 - Insurance Claims Clerks

Obtain information from insured or designated persons for purpose of settling claim with insurance carrier.

Tasks

1) Provide customer service, such as giving limited instructions on how to proceed with claims or providing referrals to auto repair facilities or local contractors.

2) Prepare and review insurance-claim forms and related documents for completeness.

3) Review insurance policy to determine coverage.

4) Post or attach information to claim file.

5) Calculate amount of claim.

6) Contact insured or other involved persons to obtain missing information.

7) Pay small claims.

8) Apply insurance rating systems.

9) Transmit claims for payment or further investigation.

43-9041.02 - Insurance Policy Processing Clerks

Process applications for, changes to, reinstatement of, and cancellation of insurance policies. Duties include reviewing insurance applications to ensure that all questions have been answered, compiling data on insurance policy changes, changing policy records to conform to insured party's specifications, compiling data on lapsed insurance policies to determine automatic reinstatement according to company policies, canceling insurance policies as requested by agents, and verifying the accuracy of insurance company records.

Tasks

1) Examine letters from policyholders or agents, original insurance applications, and other company documents to determine if changes are needed and effects of changes.

2) Process and record new insurance policies and claims.

3) Modify, update, and process existing policies and claims to reflect any change in beneficiary, amount of coverage, or type of insurance.

4) Organize and work with detailed office or warehouse records, maintaining files for each policyholder, including policies that are to be reinstated or cancelled.

5) Review and verify data, such as age, name, address, and principal sum and value of property on insurance applications and policies.

6) Notify insurance agent and accounting department of policy cancellation.

7) Transcribe data to worksheets and enter data into computer for use in preparing documents and adjusting accounts.

8) Collect initial premiums and issue receipts.

9) Calculate premiums, refunds, commissions, adjustments, and new reserve requirements, using insurance rate standards.

10) Interview clients and take their calls in order to provide customer service and obtain information on claims.

11) Compare information from application to criteria for policy reinstatement and approve reinstatement when criteria are met.

12) Compose business correspondence for supervisors, managers and professionals.

13) Obtain computer printout of policy cancellations or retrieve cancellation cards from file.

14) Process, prepare, and submit business or government forms, such as submitting applications for coverage to insurance carriers.

15) Check computations of interest accrued, premiums due, and settlement surrender on loan values.

Knowledge	Knowledge Definitions
Customer and Personal Service	Knowledge of principles and processes for providing customer and personal services. This includes customer needs assessment, meeting quality standards for services, and evaluation of customer satisfaction.
Clerical	Knowledge of administrative and clerical procedures and systems such as word processing, managing files and records, stenography and transcription, designing forms, and other office procedures and terminology.
English Language	Knowledge of the structure and content of the English language including the meaning and spelling of words, rules of composition, and grammar.

Computers and Electronics	Knowledge of circuit boards, processors, chips, electronic equipment, and computer hardware and software, including applications and programming.	Therapy and Counseling	Knowledge of principles, methods, and procedures for diagnosis, treatment, and rehabilitation of physical and mental dysfunctions, and for career counseling and guidance.
Mathematics	Knowledge of arithmetic, algebra, geometry, calculus, statistics, and their applications.	Chemistry	Knowledge of the chemical composition, structure, and properties of substances and of the chemical processes and transformations that they undergo. This includes uses of chemicals and their interactions, danger signs, production techniques, and disposal methods.
Administration and Management	Knowledge of business and management principles involved in strategic planning, resource allocation, human resources modeling, leadership technique, production methods, and coordination of people and resources.		
Sales and Marketing	Knowledge of principles and methods for showing, promoting, and selling products or services. This includes marketing strategy and tactics, product demonstration, sales techniques, and sales control systems.	History and Archeology	Knowledge of historical events and their causes, indicators, and effects on civilizations and cultures.
		Physics	Knowledge and prediction of physical principles, laws, their interrelationships, and applications to understanding fluid, material, and atmospheric dynamics, and mechanical, electrical, atomic and sub-atomic structures and processes.
Production and Processing	Knowledge of raw materials, production processes, quality control, costs, and other techniques for maximizing the effective manufacture and distribution of goods.	Fine Arts	Knowledge of the theory and techniques required to compose, produce, and perform works of music, dance, visual arts, drama, and sculpture.
Economics and Accounting	Knowledge of economic and accounting principles and practices, the financial markets, banking and the analysis and reporting of financial data.	Biology	Knowledge of plant and animal organisms, their tissues, cells, functions, interdependencies, and interactions with each other and the environment.
Communications and Media	Knowledge of media production, communication, and dissemination techniques and methods. This includes alternative ways to inform and entertain via written, oral, and visual media.	Food Production	Knowledge of techniques and equipment for planting, growing, and harvesting food products (both plant and animal) for consumption, including storage/handling techniques.
Telecommunications	Knowledge of transmission, broadcasting, switching, control, and operation of telecommunications systems.	**Skills**	**Skills Definitions**
Education and Training	Knowledge of principles and methods for curriculum and training design, teaching and instruction for individuals and groups, and the measurement of training effects.	Active Listening	Giving full attention to what other people are saying, taking time to understand the points being made, asking questions as appropriate, and not interrupting at inappropriate times.
Law and Government	Knowledge of laws, legal codes, court procedures, precedents, government regulations, executive orders, agency rules, and the democratic political process.	Speaking	Talking to others to convey information effectively.
		Reading Comprehension	Understanding written sentences and paragraphs in work related documents.
Personnel and Human Resources	Knowledge of principles and procedures for personnel recruitment, selection, training, compensation and benefits, labor relations and negotiation, and personnel information systems.	Critical Thinking	Using logic and reasoning to identify the strengths and weaknesses of alternative solutions, conclusions or approaches to problems.
Public Safety and Security	Knowledge of relevant equipment, policies, procedures, and strategies to promote effective local, state, or national security operations for the protection of people, data, property, and institutions.	Active Learning	Understanding the implications of new information for both current and future problem-solving and decision-making.
		Mathematics	Using mathematics to solve problems.
Transportation	Knowledge of principles and methods for moving people or goods by air, rail, sea, or road, including the relative costs and benefits.	Complex Problem Solving	Identifying complex problems and reviewing related information to develop and evaluate options and implement solutions.
		Time Management	Managing one's own time and the time of others.
Geography	Knowledge of principles and methods for describing the features of land, sea, and air masses, including their physical characteristics, locations, interrelationships, and distribution of plant, animal, and human life.	Coordination	Adjusting actions in relation to others' actions.
		Service Orientation	Actively looking for ways to help people.
		Writing	Communicating effectively in writing as appropriate for the needs of the audience.
Psychology	Knowledge of human behavior and performance; individual differences in ability, personality, and interests; learning and motivation; psychological research methods; and the assessment and treatment of behavioral and affective disorders.	Social Perceptiveness	Being aware of others' reactions and understanding why they react as they do.
		Instructing	Teaching others how to do something.
Engineering and Technology	Knowledge of the practical application of engineering science and technology. This includes applying principles, techniques, procedures, and equipment to the design and production of various goods and services.	Learning Strategies	Selecting and using training/instructional methods and procedures appropriate for the situation when learning or teaching new things.
		Judgment and Decision Making	Considering the relative costs and benefits of potential actions to choose the most appropriate one.
Medicine and Dentistry	Knowledge of the information and techniques needed to diagnose and treat human injuries, diseases, and deformities. This includes symptoms, treatment alternatives, drug properties and interactions, and preventive health-care measures.	Monitoring	Monitoring/Assessing performance of yourself, other individuals, or organizations to make improvements or take corrective action.
		Persuasion	Persuading others to change their minds or behavior.
Foreign Language	Knowledge of the structure and content of a foreign (non-English) language including the meaning and spelling of words, rules of composition and grammar, and pronunciation.	Negotiation	Bringing others together and trying to reconcile differences.
		Quality Control Analysis	Conducting tests and inspections of products, services, or processes to evaluate quality or performance.
Building and Construction	Knowledge of materials, methods, and the tools involved in the construction or repair of houses, buildings, or other structures such as highways and roads.	Management of Personnel Resources	Motivating, developing, and directing people as they work, identifying the best people for the job.
		Troubleshooting	Determining causes of operating errors and deciding what to do about it.
Philosophy and Theology	Knowledge of different philosophical systems and religions. This includes their basic principles, values, ethics, ways of thinking, customs, practices, and their impact on human culture.	Operations Analysis	Analyzing needs and product requirements to create a design.
		Technology Design	Generating or adapting equipment and technology to serve user needs.
Mechanical	Knowledge of machines and tools, including their designs, uses, repair, and maintenance.	Equipment Selection	Determining the kind of tools and equipment needed to do a job.
		Operation and Control	Controlling operations of equipment or systems.
Sociology and Anthropology	Knowledge of group behavior and dynamics, societal trends and influences, human migrations, ethnicity, cultures and their history and origins.	Systems Evaluation	Identifying measures or indicators of system performance and the actions needed to improve or correct performance, relative to the goals of the system.
Design	Knowledge of design techniques, tools, and principles involved in production of precision technical plans, blueprints, drawings, and models.	Equipment Maintenance	Performing routine maintenance on equipment and determining when and what kind of maintenance is needed.
		Management of Material Resources	Obtaining and seeing to the appropriate use of equipment, facilities, and materials needed to do certain work.

Operation Monitoring	Watching gauges, dials, or other indicators to make sure a machine is working properly.
Science	Using scientific rules and methods to solve problems.
Systems Analysis	Determining how a system should work and how changes in conditions, operations, and the environment will affect outcomes.
Management of Financial Resources	Determining how money will be spent to get the work done, and accounting for these expenditures.
Repairing	Repairing machines or systems using the needed tools.
Installation	Installing equipment, machines, wiring, or programs to meet specifications.
Programming	Writing computer programs for various purposes.

Ability	Ability Definitions
Written Comprehension	The ability to read and understand information and ideas presented in writing.
Information Ordering	The ability to arrange things or actions in a certain order or pattern according to a specific rule or set of rules (e.g., patterns of numbers, letters, words, pictures, mathematical operations).
Speech Clarity	The ability to speak clearly so others can understand you.
Problem Sensitivity	The ability to tell when something is wrong or is likely to go wrong. It does not involve solving the problem, only recognizing there is a problem.
Near Vision	The ability to see details at close range (within a few feet of the observer).
Written Expression	The ability to communicate information and ideas in writing so others will understand.
Oral Expression	The ability to communicate information and ideas in speaking so others will understand.
Speech Recognition	The ability to identify and understand the speech of another person.
Oral Comprehension	The ability to listen to and understand information and ideas presented through spoken words and sentences.
Deductive Reasoning	The ability to apply general rules to specific problems to produce answers that make sense.
Selective Attention	The ability to concentrate on a task over a period of time without being distracted.
Inductive Reasoning	The ability to combine pieces of information to form general rules or conclusions (includes finding a relationship among seemingly unrelated events).
Category Flexibility	The ability to generate or use different sets of rules for combining or grouping things in different ways.
Finger Dexterity	The ability to make precisely coordinated movements of the fingers of one or both hands to grasp, manipulate, or assemble very small objects.
Mathematical Reasoning	The ability to choose the right mathematical methods or formulas to solve a problem.
Number Facility	The ability to add, subtract, multiply, or divide quickly and correctly.
Perceptual Speed	The ability to quickly and accurately compare similarities and differences among sets of letters, numbers, objects, pictures, or patterns. The things to be compared may be presented at the same time or one after the other. This ability also includes comparing a presented object with a remembered object.
Flexibility of Closure	The ability to identify or detect a known pattern (a figure, object, word, or sound) that is hidden in other distracting material.
Speed of Closure	The ability to quickly make sense of, combine, and organize information into meaningful patterns.
Time Sharing	The ability to shift back and forth between two or more activities or sources of information (such as speech, sounds, touch, or other sources).
Originality	The ability to come up with unusual or clever ideas about a given topic or situation, or to develop creative ways to solve a problem.
Memorization	The ability to remember information such as words, numbers, pictures, and procedures.
Fluency of Ideas	The ability to come up with a number of ideas about a topic (the number of ideas is important, not their quality, correctness, or creativity).
Auditory Attention	The ability to focus on a single source of sound in the presence of other distracting sounds.
Far Vision	The ability to see details at a distance.
Visualization	The ability to imagine how something will look after it is moved around or when its parts are moved or rearranged.
Wrist-Finger Speed	The ability to make fast, simple, repeated movements of the fingers, hands, and wrists.

Trunk Strength	The ability to use your abdominal and lower back muscles to support part of the body repeatedly or continuously over time without 'giving out' or fatiguing.
Manual Dexterity	The ability to quickly move your hand, your hand together with your arm, or your two hands to grasp, manipulate, or assemble objects.
Hearing Sensitivity	The ability to detect or tell the differences between sounds that vary in pitch and loudness.
Visual Color Discrimination	The ability to match or detect differences between colors, including shades of color and brightness.
Reaction Time	The ability to quickly respond (with the hand, finger, or foot) to a signal (sound, light, picture) when it appears.
Multilimb Coordination	The ability to coordinate two or more limbs (for example, two arms, two legs, or one leg and one arm) while sitting, standing, or lying down. It does not involve performing the activities while the whole body is in motion.
Speed of Limb Movement	The ability to quickly move the arms and legs.
Spatial Orientation	The ability to know your location in relation to the environment or to know where other objects are in relation to you.
Arm-Hand Steadiness	The ability to keep your hand and arm steady while moving your arm or while holding your arm and hand in one position.
Control Precision	The ability to quickly and repeatedly adjust the controls of a machine or a vehicle to exact positions.
Dynamic Strength	The ability to exert muscle force repeatedly or continuously over time. This involves muscular endurance and resistance to muscle fatigue.
Rate Control	The ability to time your movements or the movement of a piece of equipment in anticipation of changes in the speed and/or direction of a moving object or scene.
Extent Flexibility	The ability to bend, stretch, twist, or reach with your body, arms, and/or legs.
Static Strength	The ability to exert maximum muscle force to lift, push, pull, or carry objects.
Explosive Strength	The ability to use short bursts of muscle force to propel oneself (as in jumping or sprinting), or to throw an object.
Dynamic Flexibility	The ability to quickly and repeatedly bend, stretch, twist, or reach out with your body, arms, and/or legs.
Gross Body Coordination	The ability to coordinate the movement of your arms, legs, and torso together when the whole body is in motion.
Depth Perception	The ability to judge which of several objects is closer or farther away from you, or to judge the distance between you and an object.
Sound Localization	The ability to tell the direction from which a sound originated.
Glare Sensitivity	The ability to see objects in the presence of glare or bright lighting.
Gross Body Equilibrium	The ability to keep or regain your body balance or stay upright when in an unstable position.
Night Vision	The ability to see under low light conditions.
Peripheral Vision	The ability to see objects or movement of objects to one's side when the eyes are looking ahead.
Response Orientation	The ability to choose quickly between two or more movements in response to two or more different signals (lights, sounds, pictures). It includes the speed with which the correct response is started with the hand, foot, or other body part.
Stamina	The ability to exert yourself physically over long periods of time without getting winded or out of breath.

Work_Activity	Work_Activity Definitions
Getting Information	Observing, receiving, and otherwise obtaining information from all relevant sources.
Interacting With Computers	Using computers and computer systems (including hardware and software) to program, write software, set up functions, enter data, or process information.
Communicating with Supervisors, Peers, or Subordin	Providing information to supervisors, co-workers, and subordinates by telephone, in written form, e-mail, or in person.
Updating and Using Relevant Knowledge	Keeping up-to-date technically and applying new knowledge to your job.
Organizing, Planning, and Prioritizing Work	Developing specific goals and plans to prioritize, organize, and accomplish your work.
Making Decisions and Solving Problems	Analyzing information and evaluating results to choose the best solution and solve problems.
Evaluating Information to Determine Compliance wit	Using relevant information and individual judgment to determine whether events or processes comply with laws, regulations, or standards.

Communicating with Persons Outside Organization	Communicating with people outside the organization, representing the organization to customers, the public, government, and other external sources. This information can be exchanged in person, in writing, or by telephone or e-mail.
Performing for or Working Directly with the Public	Performing for people or dealing directly with the public. This includes serving customers in restaurants and stores, and receiving clients or guests.
Processing Information	Compiling, coding, categorizing, calculating, tabulating, auditing, or verifying information or data.
Identifying Objects, Actions, and Events	Identifying information by categorizing, estimating, recognizing differences or similarities, and detecting changes in circumstances or events.
Analyzing Data or Information	Identifying the underlying principles, reasons, or facts of information by breaking down information or data into separate parts.
Establishing and Maintaining Interpersonal Relatio	Developing constructive and cooperative working relationships with others, and maintaining them over time.
Performing Administrative Activities	Performing day-to-day administrative tasks such as maintaining information files and processing paperwork.
Documenting/Recording Information	Entering, transcribing, recording, storing, or maintaining information in written or electronic/magnetic form.
Monitor Processes, Materials, or Surroundings	Monitoring and reviewing information from materials, events, or the environment, to detect or assess problems.
Resolving Conflicts and Negotiating with Others	Handling complaints, settling disputes, and resolving grievances and conflicts, or otherwise negotiating with others.
Selling or Influencing Others	Convincing others to buy merchandise/goods or to otherwise change their minds or actions.
Judging the Qualities of Things, Services, or Peop	Assessing the value, importance, or quality of things or people.
Developing Objectives and Strategies	Establishing long-range objectives and specifying the strategies and actions to achieve them.
Interpreting the Meaning of Information for Others	Translating or explaining what information means and how it can be used.
Thinking Creatively	Developing, designing, or creating new applications, ideas, relationships, systems, or products, including artistic contributions.
Assisting and Caring for Others	Providing personal assistance, medical attention, emotional support, or other personal care to others such as coworkers, customers, or patients.
Scheduling Work and Activities	Scheduling events, programs, and activities, as well as the work of others.
Performing General Physical Activities	Performing physical activities that require considerable use of your arms and legs and moving your whole body, such as climbing, lifting, balancing, walking, stooping, and handling of materials.
Provide Consultation and Advice to Others	Providing guidance and expert advice to management or other groups on technical, systems-, or process-related topics.
Handling and Moving Objects	Using hands and arms in handling, installing, positioning, and moving materials, and manipulating things.
Estimating the Quantifiable Characteristics of Pro	Estimating sizes, distances, and quantities; or determining time, costs, resources, or materials needed to perform a work activity.
Coordinating the Work and Activities of Others	Getting members of a group to work together to accomplish tasks.
Training and Teaching Others	Identifying the educational needs of others, developing formal educational or training programs or classes, and teaching or instructing others.
Guiding, Directing, and Motivating Subordinates	Providing guidance and direction to subordinates, including setting performance standards and monitoring performance.
Coaching and Developing Others	Identifying the developmental needs of others and coaching, mentoring, or otherwise helping others to improve their knowledge or skills.
Developing and Building Teams	Encouraging and building mutual trust, respect, and cooperation among team members.
Inspecting Equipment, Structures, or Material	Inspecting equipment, structures, or materials to identify the cause of errors or other problems or defects.
Controlling Machines and Processes	Using either control mechanisms or direct physical activity to operate machines or processes (not including computers or vehicles).
Operating Vehicles, Mechanized Devices, or Equipme	Running, maneuvering, navigating, or driving vehicles or mechanized equipment, such as forklifts, passenger vehicles, aircraft, or water craft.
Staffing Organizational Units	Recruiting, interviewing, selecting, hiring, and promoting employees in an organization.
Monitoring and Controlling Resources	Monitoring and controlling resources and overseeing the spending of money.

Repairing and Maintaining Electronic Equipment	Servicing, repairing, calibrating, regulating, fine-tuning, or testing machines, devices, and equipment that operate primarily on the basis of electrical or electronic (not mechanical) principles.
Drafting, Laying Out, and Specifying Technical Dev	Providing documentation, detailed instructions, drawings, or specifications to tell others about how devices, parts, equipment, or structures are to be fabricated, constructed, assembled, modified, maintained, or used.
Repairing and Maintaining Mechanical Equipment	Servicing, repairing, adjusting, and testing machines, devices, moving parts, and equipment that operate primarily on the basis of mechanical (not electronic) principles.

Work_Context	Work_Context Definitions
Importance of Being Exact or Accurate	How important is being very exact or highly accurate in performing this job?
Structured versus Unstructured Work	To what extent is this job structured for the worker, rather than allowing the worker to determine tasks, priorities, and goals?
Freedom to Make Decisions	How much decision making freedom, without supervision, does the job offer?
Telephone	How often do you have telephone conversations in this job?
Importance of Repeating Same Tasks	How important is repeating the same physical activities (e.g., key entry) or mental activities (e.g., checking entries in a ledger) over and over, without stopping, to performing this job?
Spend Time Sitting	How much does this job require sitting?
Face-to-Face Discussions	How often do you have to have face-to-face discussions with individuals or teams in this job?
Contact With Others	How much does this job require the worker to be in contact with others (face-to-face, by telephone, or otherwise) in order to perform it?
Time Pressure	How often does this job require the worker to meet strict deadlines?
Deal With External Customers	How important is it to work with external customers or the public in this job?
Frequency of Decision Making	How frequently is the worker required to make decisions that affect other people, the financial resources, and/or the image and reputation of the organization?
Electronic Mail	How often do you use electronic mail in this job?
Impact of Decisions on Co-workers or Company Resul	How do the decisions an employee makes impact the results of co-workers, clients or the company?
Letters and Memos	How often does the job require written letters and memos?
Work With Work Group or Team	How important is it to work with others in a group or team in this job?
Coordinate or Lead Others	How important is it to coordinate or lead others in accomplishing work activities in this job?
Degree of Automation	How automated is the job?
Deal With Unpleasant or Angry People	How frequently does the worker have to deal with unpleasant, angry, or discourteous individuals as part of the job requirements?
Spend Time Making Repetitive Motions	How much does this job require making repetitive motions?
Physical Proximity	To what extent does this job require the worker to perform job tasks in close physical proximity to other people?
Responsibility for Outcomes and Results	How responsible is the worker for work outcomes and results of other workers?
Indoors, Environmentally Controlled	How often does this job require working indoors in environmentally controlled conditions?
Frequency of Conflict Situations	How often are there conflict situations the employee has to face in this job?
Consequence of Error	How serious would the result usually be if the worker made a mistake that was not readily correctable?
Level of Competition	To what extent does this job require the worker to compete or to be aware of competitive pressures?
Spend Time Using Your Hands to Handle, Control, or	How much does this job require using your hands to handle, control, or feel objects, tools or controls?
Spend Time Standing	How much does this job require standing?
Sounds, Noise Levels Are Distracting or Uncomforta	How often does this job require working exposed to sounds and noise levels that are distracting or uncomfortable?
Responsible for Others' Health and Safety	How much responsibility is there for the health and safety of others in this job?
Spend Time Walking and Running	How much does this job require walking and running?
Deal With Physically Aggressive People	How frequently does this job require the worker to deal with physical aggression of violent individuals?

Pace Determined by Speed of Equipment	How important is it to this job that the pace is determined by the speed of equipment or machinery? (This does not refer to keeping busy at all times on this job.)
In an Enclosed Vehicle or Equipment	How often does this job require working in a closed vehicle or equipment (e.g., car)?
Extremely Bright or Inadequate Lighting	How often does this job require working in extremely bright or inadequate lighting conditions?
Exposed to Contaminants	How often does this job require working exposed to contaminants (such as pollutants, gases, dust or odors)?
Public Speaking	How often do you have to perform public speaking in this job?
Spend Time Bending or Twisting the Body	How much does this job require bending or twisting your body?
Very Hot or Cold Temperatures	How often does this job require working in very hot (above 90 F degrees) or very cold (below 32 F degrees) temperatures?
Cramped Work Space, Awkward Positions	How often does this job require working in cramped work spaces that requires getting into awkward positions?
Exposed to Minor Burns, Cuts, Bites, or Stings	How often does this job require exposure to minor burns, cuts, bites, or stings?
Exposed to Disease or Infections	How often does this job require exposure to disease/infections?
Spend Time Climbing Ladders, Scaffolds, or Poles	How much does this job require climbing ladders, scaffolds, or poles?
Spend Time Kneeling, Crouching, Stooping, or Crawl	How much does this job require kneeling, crouching, stooping, or crawling?
Exposed to High Places	How often does this job require exposure to high places?
Exposed to Hazardous Conditions	How often does this job require exposure to hazardous conditions?
Wear Specialized Protective or Safety Equipment su	How much does this job require wearing specialized protective or safety equipment such as breathing apparatus, safety harness, full protection suits, or radiation protection?
Spend Time Keeping or Regaining Balance	How much does this job require keeping or regaining your balance?
Exposed to Hazardous Equipment	How often does this job require exposure to hazardous equipment?
Wear Common Protective or Safety Equipment such as	How much does this job require wearing common protective or safety equipment such as safety shoes, glasses, gloves, hard hats or live jackets?
Outdoors, Under Cover	How often does this job require working outdoors, under cover (e.g., structure with roof but no walls)?
Outdoors, Exposed to Weather	How often does this job require working outdoors, exposed to all weather conditions?
Indoors, Not Environmentally Controlled	How often does this job require working indoors in non-controlled environmental conditions (e.g., warehouse without heat)?
Exposed to Whole Body Vibration	How often does this job require exposure to whole body vibration (e.g., operate a jackhammer)?
Exposed to Radiation	How often does this job require exposure to radiation?
In an Open Vehicle or Equipment	How often does this job require working in an open vehicle or equipment (e.g., tractor)?

Job Zone Component	Job Zone Component Definitions
Title	Job Zone Two: Some Preparation Needed
Overall Experience	Some previous work-related skill, knowledge, or experience may be helpful in these occupations, but usually is not needed. For example, a drywall installer might benefit from experience installing drywall, but an inexperienced person could still learn to be an installer with little difficulty.
Job Training	Employees in these occupations need anywhere from a few months to one year of working with experienced employees.
Job Zone Examples	These occupations often involve using your knowledge and skills to help others. Examples include drywall installers, fire inspectors, flight attendants, pharmacy technicians, salespersons (retail), and tellers.
SVP Range	(4.0 to < 6.0)
Education	These occupations usually require a high school diploma and may require some vocational training or job-related course work. In some cases, an associate's or bachelor's degree could be needed.

Work_Styles	Work_Styles Definitions
Attention to Detail	Job requires being careful about detail and thorough in completing work tasks.
Integrity	Job requires being honest and ethical.

Cooperation	Job requires being pleasant with others on the job and displaying a good-natured, cooperative attitude.
Dependability	Job requires being reliable, responsible, and dependable, and fulfilling obligations.
Achievement/Effort	Job requires establishing and maintaining personally challenging achievement goals and exerting effort toward mastering tasks.
Initiative	Job requires a willingness to take on responsibilities and challenges.
Concern for Others	Job requires being sensitive to others' needs and feelings and being understanding and helpful on the job.
Stress Tolerance	Job requires accepting criticism and dealing calmly and effectively with high stress situations.
Self Control	Job requires maintaining composure, keeping emotions in check, controlling anger, and avoiding aggressive behavior, even in very difficult situations.
Adaptability/Flexibility	Job requires being open to change (positive or negative) and to considerable variety in the workplace.
Independence	Job requires developing one's own ways of doing things, guiding oneself with little or no supervision, and depending on oneself to get things done.
Social Orientation	Job requires preferring to work with others rather than alone, and being personally connected with others on the job.
Persistence	Job requires persistence in the face of obstacles.
Analytical Thinking	Job requires analyzing information and using logic to address work-related issues and problems.
Leadership	Job requires a willingness to lead, take charge, and offer opinions and direction.
Innovation	Job requires creativity and alternative thinking to develop new ideas for and answers to work-related problems.

43-9051.00 - Mail Clerks and Mail Machine Operators, Except Postal Service

Prepare incoming and outgoing mail for distribution. Use hand or mail handling machines to time stamp, open, read, sort, and route incoming mail; and address, seal, stamp, fold, stuff, and affix postage to outgoing mail or packages. Duties may also include keeping necessary records and completed forms.

Tasks

1) Answer inquiries regarding shipping or mailing policies.

2) Adjust guides, rollers, loose card inserters, weighing machines, and tying arms, using rules and hand tools.

3) Operate computer-controlled keyboards or voice recognition equipment in order to direct items according to established routing schemes.

4) Wrap packages or bundles by hand, or by using tying machines.

5) Remove containers of sorted mail/parcels, and transfer them to designated areas according to established procedures.

6) Use equipment such as forklifts and automated trains to move containers of mail.

7) Fold letters or circulars and insert them in envelopes.

8) Place incoming or outgoing letters or packages into sacks or bins based on destination or type, and place identifying tags on sacks or bins.

9) Sell mail products, and accept payment for products and mailing charges.

10) Seal or open envelopes, by hand or by using machines.

11) Release packages or letters to customers upon presentation of written notices or other identification.

12) Operate embossing machines or typewriters to make corrections, additions, and changes to address plates.

13) Mail merchandise samples or promotional literature in response to requests.

14) Add ink, fill paste reservoirs, and change machine ribbons when necessary.

15) Clear jams in sortation equipment.

16) Lift and unload containers of mail or parcels onto equipment for transportation to sortation stations.

17) Weigh packages or letters to determine postage needed, using weighing scales and rate charts.

18) Verify that items are addressed correctly, marked with the proper postage, and in suitable condition for processing.

19) Stamp dates and times of receipt of incoming mail.

20) Remove from machines printed materials such as labeled articles, postmarked envelopes or tape, and folded sheets.

21) Contact delivery or courier services to arrange delivery of letters and parcels.

22) Accept and check containers of mail or parcels from large volume mailers, couriers, and contractors.

23) Start machines that automatically feed plates, stencils, or tapes through mechanisms, and observe machine operations in order to detect any malfunctions.

24) Sort and route incoming mail, and collect outgoing mail, using carts as necessary.

25) Insert material for printing or addressing into loading racks on machines, select type or die sizes, and position plates, stencils, or tapes in machine magazines.

26) Affix postage to packages or letters by hand, or stamp materials, using postage meters.

27) Determine manner in which mail is to be sent, and prepare it for delivery to mailing facilities.

28) Read production orders to determine types and sizes of items scheduled for printing and mailing.

43-9061.00 - Office Clerks, General

Perform duties too varied and diverse to be classified in any specific office clerical occupation, requiring limited knowledge of office management systems and procedures. Clerical duties may be assigned in accordance with the office procedures of individual establishments and may include a combination of answering telephones, bookkeeping, typing or word processing, stenography, office machine operation, and filing.

Tasks

1) Answer telephones, direct calls and take messages.

2) Operate office machines, such as photocopiers and scanners, facsimile machines, voice mail systems and personal computers.

3) Compile, copy, sort, and file records of office activities, business transactions, and other activities.

4) Maintain and update filing, inventory, mailing, and database systems, either manually or using a computer.

5) Compute, record, and proofread data and other information, such as records or reports.

6) Open, sort and route incoming mail, answer correspondence, and prepare outgoing mail.

7) Deliver messages and run errands.

8) Inventory and order materials, supplies, and services.

9) Complete and mail bills, contracts, policies, invoices, or checks.

10) Collect, count, and disburse money, do basic bookkeeping and complete banking transactions.

11) Review files, records, and other documents to obtain information to respond to requests.

12) Complete work schedules, manage calendars and arrange appointments.

13) Type, format, proofread and edit correspondence and other documents, from notes or dictating machines, using computers or typewriters.

14) Train other staff members to perform work activities, such as using computer applications.

15) Troubleshoot problems involving office equipment, such as computer hardware and software.

16) Process and prepare documents, such as business or government forms and expense reports.

17) Prepare meeting agendas, attend meetings, and record and transcribe minutes.

18) Count, weigh, measure, and/or organize materials.

19) Monitor and direct the work of lower-level clerks.

20) Make travel arrangements for office personnel.

Knowledge	Knowledge Definitions
Customer and Personal Service	Knowledge of principles and processes for providing customer and personal services. This includes customer needs assessment, meeting quality standards for services, and evaluation of customer satisfaction.
Clerical	Knowledge of administrative and clerical procedures and systems such as word processing, managing files and records, stenography and transcription, designing forms, and other office procedures and terminology.
English Language	Knowledge of the structure and content of the English language including the meaning and spelling of words, rules of composition, and grammar.
Mathematics	Knowledge of arithmetic, algebra, geometry, calculus, statistics, and their applications.
Economics and Accounting	Knowledge of economic and accounting principles and practices, the financial markets, banking and the analysis and reporting of financial data.
Computers and Electronics	Knowledge of circuit boards, processors, chips, electronic equipment, and computer hardware and software, including applications and programming.
Administration and Management	Knowledge of business and management principles involved in strategic planning, resource allocation, human resources modeling, leadership technique, production methods, and coordination of people and resources.
Personnel and Human Resources	Knowledge of principles and procedures for personnel recruitment, selection, training, compensation and benefits, labor relations and negotiation, and personnel information systems.
Communications and Media	Knowledge of media production, communication, and dissemination techniques and methods. This includes alternative ways to inform and entertain via written, oral, and visual media.
Education and Training	Knowledge of principles and methods for curriculum and training design, teaching and instruction for individuals and groups, and the measurement of training effects.
Telecommunications	Knowledge of transmission, broadcasting, switching, control, and operation of telecommunications systems.
Law and Government	Knowledge of laws, legal codes, court procedures, precedents, government regulations, executive orders, agency rules, and the democratic political process.
Psychology	Knowledge of human behavior and performance; individual differences in ability, personality, and interests; learning and motivation; psychological research methods; and the assessment and treatment of behavioral and affective disorders.
Sales and Marketing	Knowledge of principles and methods for showing, promoting, and selling products or services. This includes marketing strategy and tactics, product demonstration, sales techniques, and sales control systems.
Public Safety and Security	Knowledge of relevant equipment, policies, procedures, and strategies to promote effective local, state, or national security operations for the protection of people, data, property, and institutions.
Transportation	Knowledge of principles and methods for moving people or goods by air, rail, sea, or road, including the relative costs and benefits.
Mechanical	Knowledge of machines and tools, including their designs, uses, repair, and maintenance.
Production and Processing	Knowledge of raw materials, production processes, quality control, costs, and other techniques for maximizing the effective manufacture and distribution of goods.
Chemistry	Knowledge of the chemical composition, structure, and properties of substances and of the chemical processes and transformations that they undergo. This includes uses of chemicals and their interactions, danger signs, production techniques, and disposal methods.
Foreign Language	Knowledge of the structure and content of a foreign (non-English) language including the meaning and spelling of words, rules of composition and grammar, and pronunciation.
Design	Knowledge of design techniques, tools, and principles involved in production of precision technical plans, blueprints, drawings, and models.
Geography	Knowledge of principles and methods for describing the features of land, sea, and air masses, including their physical characteristics, locations, interrelationships, and distribution of plant, animal, and human life.

Therapy and Counseling	Knowledge of principles, methods, and procedures for diagnosis, treatment, and rehabilitation of physical and mental dysfunctions, and for career counseling and guidance.
Philosophy and Theology	Knowledge of different philosophical systems and religions. This includes their basic principles, values, ethics, ways of thinking, customs, practices, and their impact on human culture.
Medicine and Dentistry	Knowledge of the information and techniques needed to diagnose and treat human injuries, diseases, and deformities. This includes symptoms, treatment alternatives, drug properties and interactions, and preventive health-care measures.
Sociology and Anthropology	Knowledge of group behavior and dynamics, societal trends and influences, human migrations, ethnicity, cultures and their history and origins.
Fine Arts	Knowledge of the theory and techniques required to compose, produce, and perform works of music, dance, visual arts, drama, and sculpture.
Physics	Knowledge and prediction of physical principles, laws, their interrelationships, and applications to understanding fluid, material, and atmospheric dynamics, and mechanical, electrical, atomic and sub- atomic structures and processes.
Building and Construction	Knowledge of materials, methods, and the tools involved in the construction or repair of houses, buildings, or other structures such as highways and roads.
History and Archeology	Knowledge of historical events and their causes, indicators, and effects on civilizations and cultures.
Engineering and Technology	Knowledge of the practical application of engineering science and technology. This includes applying principles, techniques, procedures, and equipment to the design and production of various goods and services.
Food Production	Knowledge of techniques and equipment for planting, growing, and harvesting food products (both plant and animal) for consumption, including storage/handling techniques.
Biology	Knowledge of plant and animal organisms, their tissues, cells, functions, interdependencies, and interactions with each other and the environment.

Skills	Skills Definitions
Active Listening	Giving full attention to what other people are saying, taking time to understand the points being made, asking questions as appropriate, and not interrupting at inappropriate times.
Reading Comprehension	Understanding written sentences and paragraphs in work related documents.
Speaking	Talking to others to convey information effectively.
Writing	Communicating effectively in writing as appropriate for the needs of the audience.
Social Perceptiveness	Being aware of others' reactions and understanding why they react as they do.
Mathematics	Using mathematics to solve problems.
Learning Strategies	Selecting and using training/instructional methods and procedures appropriate for the situation when learning or teaching new things.
Service Orientation	Actively looking for ways to help people.
Critical Thinking	Using logic and reasoning to identify the strengths and weaknesses of alternative solutions, conclusions or approaches to problems.
Time Management	Managing one's own time and the time of others.
Coordination	Adjusting actions in relation to others' actions.
Active Learning	Understanding the implications of new information for both current and future problem-solving and decision-making.
Instructing	Teaching others how to do something.
Judgment and Decision Making	Considering the relative costs and benefits of potential actions to choose the most appropriate one.
Monitoring	Monitoring/Assessing performance of yourself, other individuals, or organizations to make improvements or take corrective action.
Persuasion	Persuading others to change their minds or behavior.
Negotiation	Bringing others together and trying to reconcile differences.
Equipment Selection	Determining the kind of tools and equipment needed to do a job.
Operation and Control	Controlling operations of equipment or systems.
Complex Problem Solving	Identifying complex problems and reviewing related information to develop and evaluate options and implement solutions.
Management of Personnel Resources	Motivating, developing, and directing people as they work, identifying the best people for the job.

Troubleshooting	Determining causes of operating errors and deciding what to do about it.
Management of Financial Resources	Determining how money will be spent to get the work done, and accounting for these expenditures.
Operations Analysis	Analyzing needs and product requirements to create a design.
Quality Control Analysis	Conducting tests and inspections of products, services, or processes to evaluate quality or performance.
Management of Material Resources	Obtaining and seeing to the appropriate use of equipment, facilities, and materials needed to do certain work.
Technology Design	Generating or adapting equipment and technology to serve user needs.
Systems Evaluation	Identifying measures or indicators of system performance and the actions needed to improve or correct performance, relative to the goals of the system.
Equipment Maintenance	Performing routine maintenance on equipment and determining when and what kind of maintenance is needed.
Operation Monitoring	Watching gauges, dials, or other indicators to make sure a machine is working properly.
Systems Analysis	Determining how a system should work and how changes in conditions, operations, and the environment will affect outcomes.
Installation	Installing equipment, machines, wiring, or programs to meet specifications.
Repairing	Repairing machines or systems using the needed tools.
Science	Using scientific rules and methods to solve problems.
Programming	Writing computer programs for various purposes.

Ability	Ability Definitions
Oral Comprehension	The ability to listen to and understand information and ideas presented through spoken words and sentences.
Oral Expression	The ability to communicate information and ideas in speaking so others will understand.
Speech Recognition	The ability to identify and understand the speech of another person.
Speech Clarity	The ability to speak clearly so others can understand you.
Near Vision	The ability to see details at close range (within a few feet of the observer).
Written Comprehension	The ability to read and understand information and ideas presented in writing.
Number Facility	The ability to add, subtract, multiply, or divide quickly and correctly.
Information Ordering	The ability to arrange things or actions in a certain order or pattern according to a specific rule or set of rules (e.g., patterns of numbers, letters, words, pictures, mathematical operations).
Selective Attention	The ability to concentrate on a task over a period of time without being distracted.
Mathematical Reasoning	The ability to choose the right mathematical methods or formulas to solve a problem.
Written Expression	The ability to communicate information and ideas in writing so others will understand.
Perceptual Speed	The ability to quickly and accurately compare similarities and differences among sets of letters, numbers, objects, pictures, or patterns. The things to be compared may be presented at the same time or one after the other. This ability also includes comparing a presented object with a remembered object.
Category Flexibility	The ability to generate or use different sets of rules for combining or grouping things in different ways.
Problem Sensitivity	The ability to tell when something is wrong or is likely to go wrong. It does not involve solving the problem, only recognizing there is a problem.
Inductive Reasoning	The ability to combine pieces of information to form general rules or conclusions (includes finding a relationship among seemingly unrelated events).
Deductive Reasoning	The ability to apply general rules to specific problems to produce answers that make sense.
Finger Dexterity	The ability to make precisely coordinated movements of the fingers of one or both hands to grasp, manipulate, or assemble very small objects.
Time Sharing	The ability to shift back and forth between two or more activities or sources of information (such as speech, sounds, touch, or other sources).
Far Vision	The ability to see details at a distance.
Manual Dexterity	The ability to quickly move your hand, your hand together with your arm, or your two hands to grasp, manipulate, or assemble objects.
Wrist-Finger Speed	The ability to make fast, simple, repeated movements of the fingers, hands, and wrists.

Arm-Hand Steadiness	The ability to keep your hand and arm steady while moving your arm or while holding your arm and hand in one position.
Flexibility of Closure	The ability to identify or detect a known pattern (a figure, object, word, or sound) that is hidden in other distracting material.
Speed of Closure	The ability to quickly make sense of, combine, and organize information into meaningful patterns.
Visualization	The ability to imagine how something will look after it is moved around or when its parts are moved or rearranged.
Originality	The ability to come up with unusual or clever ideas about a given topic or situation, or to develop creative ways to solve a problem.
Fluency of Ideas	The ability to come up with a number of ideas about a topic (the number of ideas is important, not their quality, correctness, or creativity).
Auditory Attention	The ability to focus on a single source of sound in the presence of other distracting sounds.
Control Precision	The ability to quickly and repeatedly adjust the controls of a machine or a vehicle to exact positions.
Visual Color Discrimination	The ability to match or detect differences between colors, including shades of color and brightness.
Hearing Sensitivity	The ability to detect or tell the differences between sounds that vary in pitch and loudness.
Memorization	The ability to remember information such as words, numbers, pictures, and procedures.
Trunk Strength	The ability to use your abdominal and lower back muscles to support part of the body repeatedly or continuously over time without 'giving out' or fatiguing.
Extent Flexibility	The ability to bend, stretch, twist, or reach with your body, arms, and/or legs.
Gross Body Coordination	The ability to coordinate the movement of your arms, legs, and torso together when the whole body is in motion.
Gross Body Equilibrium	The ability to keep or regain your body balance or stay upright when in an unstable position.
Depth Perception	The ability to judge which of several objects is closer or farther away from you, or to judge the distance between you and an object.
Multilimb Coordination	The ability to coordinate two or more limbs (for example, two arms, two legs, or one leg and one arm) while sitting, standing, or lying down. It does not involve performing the activities while the whole body is in motion.
Static Strength	The ability to exert maximum muscle force to lift, push, pull, or carry objects.
Stamina	The ability to exert yourself physically over long periods of time without getting winded or out of breath.
Peripheral Vision	The ability to see objects or movement of objects to one's side when the eyes are looking ahead.
Sound Localization	The ability to tell the direction from which a sound originated.
Dynamic Strength	The ability to exert muscle force repeatedly or continuously over time. This involves muscular endurance and resistance to muscle fatigue.
Explosive Strength	The ability to use short bursts of muscle force to propel oneself (as in jumping or sprinting), or to throw an object.
Night Vision	The ability to see under low light conditions.
Dynamic Flexibility	The ability to quickly and repeatedly bend, stretch, twist, or reach out with your body, arms, and/or legs.
Rate Control	The ability to time your movements or the movement of a piece of equipment in anticipation of changes in the speed and/or direction of a moving object or scene.
Speed of Limb Movement	The ability to quickly move the arms and legs.
Response Orientation	The ability to choose quickly between two or more movements in response to two or more different signals (lights, sounds, pictures). It includes the speed with which the correct response is started with the hand, foot, or other body part.
Spatial Orientation	The ability to know your location in relation to the environment or to know where other objects are in relation to you.
Reaction Time	The ability to quickly respond (with the hand, finger, or foot) to a signal (sound, light, picture) when it appears.
Glare Sensitivity	The ability to see objects in the presence of glare or bright lighting.

Work_Activity	Work_Activity Definitions
Interacting With Computers	Using computers and computer systems (including hardware and software) to program, write software, set up functions, enter data, or process information.
Getting Information	Observing, receiving, and otherwise obtaining information from all relevant sources.
Communicating with Supervisors, Peers, or Subordin	Providing information to supervisors, co-workers, and subordinates by telephone, in written form, e-mail, or in person.
Performing Administrative Activities	Performing day-to-day administrative tasks such as maintaining information files and processing paperwork.
Processing Information	Compiling, coding, categorizing, calculating, tabulating, auditing, or verifying information or data.
Establishing and Maintaining Interpersonal Relatio	Developing constructive and cooperative working relationships with others, and maintaining them over time.
Documenting/Recording Information	Entering, transcribing, recording, storing, or maintaining information in written or electronic/magnetic form.
Performing for or Working Directly with the Public	Performing for people or dealing directly with the public. This includes serving customers in restaurants and stores, and receiving clients or guests.
Organizing, Planning, and Prioritizing Work	Developing specific goals and plans to prioritize, organize, and accomplish your work.
Making Decisions and Solving Problems	Analyzing information and evaluating results to choose the best solution and solve problems.
Identifying Objects, Actions, and Events	Identifying information by categorizing, estimating, recognizing differences or similarities, and detecting changes in circumstances or events.
Communicating with Persons Outside Organization	Communicating with people outside the organization, representing the organization to customers, the public, government, and other external sources. This information can be exchanged in person, in writing, or by telephone or e-mail.
Updating and Using Relevant Knowledge	Keeping up-to-date technically and applying new knowledge to your job.
Monitor Processes, Materials, or Surroundings	Monitoring and reviewing information from materials, events, or the environment, to detect or assess problems.
Analyzing Data or Information	Identifying the underlying principles, reasons, or facts of information by breaking down information or data into separate parts.
Evaluating Information to Determine Compliance wit	Using relevant information and individual judgment to determine whether events or processes comply with laws, regulations, or standards.
Coordinating the Work and Activities of Others	Getting members of a group to work together to accomplish tasks.
Resolving Conflicts and Negotiating with Others	Handling complaints, settling disputes, and resolving grievances and conflicts, or otherwise negotiating with others.
Scheduling Work and Activities	Scheduling events, programs, and activities, as well as the work of others.
Assisting and Caring for Others	Providing personal assistance, medical attention, emotional support, or other personal care to others such as coworkers, customers, or patients.
Thinking Creatively	Developing, designing, or creating new applications, ideas, relationships, systems, or products, including artistic contributions.
Interpreting the Meaning of Information for Others	Translating or explaining what information means and how it can be used.
Training and Teaching Others	Identifying the educational needs of others, developing formal educational or training programs or classes, and teaching or instructing others.
Coaching and Developing Others	Identifying the developmental needs of others and coaching, mentoring, or otherwise helping others to improve their knowledge or skills.
Judging the Qualities of Things, Services, or Peop	Assessing the value, importance, or quality of things or people.
Estimating the Quantifiable Characteristics of Pro	Estimating sizes, distances, and quantities; or determining time, costs, resources, or materials needed to perform a work activity.
Developing and Building Teams	Encouraging and building mutual trust, respect, and cooperation among team members.
Inspecting Equipment, Structures, or Material	Inspecting equipment, structures, or materials to identify the cause of errors or other problems or defects.
Developing Objectives and Strategies	Establishing long-range objectives and specifying the strategies and actions to achieve them.
Provide Consultation and Advice to Others	Providing guidance and expert advice to management or other groups on technical, systems-, or process-related topics.
Guiding, Directing, and Motivating Subordinates	Providing guidance and direction to subordinates, including setting performance standards and monitoring performance.
Monitoring and Controlling Resources	Monitoring and controlling resources and overseeing the spending of money.
Handling and Moving Objects	Using hands and arms in handling, installing, positioning, and moving materials, and manipulating things.

Controlling Machines and Processes	Using either control mechanisms or direct physical activity to operate machines or processes (not including computers or vehicles).	Degree of Automation	How automated is the job?
Selling or Influencing Others	Convincing others to buy merchandise/goods or to otherwise change their minds or actions.	Spend Time Standing	How much does this job require standing?
Performing General Physical Activities	Performing physical activities that require considerable use of your arms and legs and moving your whole body, such as climbing, lifting, balancing, walking, stooping, and handling of materials.	Consequence of Error	How serious would the result usually be if the worker made a mistake that was not readily correctable?
		Level of Competition	To what extent does this job require the worker to compete or to be aware of competitive pressures?
Staffing Organizational Units	Recruiting, interviewing, selecting, hiring, and promoting employees in an organization.	Responsible for Others' Health and Safety	How much responsibility is there for the health and safety of others in this job?
Repairing and Maintaining Electronic Equipment	Servicing, repairing, calibrating, regulating, fine-tuning, or testing machines, devices, and equipment that operate primarily on the basis of electrical or electronic (not mechanical) principles.	Cramped Work Space, Awkward Positions	How often does this job require working in cramped work spaces that requires getting into awkward positions?
		Spend Time Walking and Running	How much does this job require walking and running?
Repairing and Maintaining Mechanical Equipment	Servicing, repairing, adjusting, and testing machines, devices, moving parts, and equipment that operate primarily on the basis of mechanical (not electronic) principles.	Pace Determined by Speed of Equipment	How important is it to this job that the pace is determined by the speed of equipment or machinery? (This does not refer to keeping busy at all times on this job.)
Operating Vehicles, Mechanized Devices, or Equipme	Running, maneuvering, navigating, or driving vehicles or mechanized equipment, such as forklifts, passenger vehicles, aircraft, or water craft.	In an Enclosed Vehicle or Equipment	How often does this job require working in a closed vehicle or equipment (e.g., car)?
		Spend Time Bending or Twisting the Body	How much does this job require bending or twisting your body?
Drafting, Laying Out, and Specifying Technical Dev	Providing documentation, detailed instructions, drawings, or specifications to tell others about how devices, parts, equipment, or structures are to be fabricated, constructed, assembled, modified, maintained, or used.	Exposed to Disease or Infections	How often does this job require exposure to disease/infections?
		Wear Common Protective or Safety Equipment such as	How much does this job require wearing common protective or safety equipment such as safety shoes, glasses, gloves, hard hats or live jackets?

Work_Context	**Work_Context Definitions**	Deal With Physically Aggressive People	How frequently does this job require the worker to deal with physical aggression of violent individuals?
Telephone	How often do you have telephone conversations in this job?	Spend Time Kneeling, Crouching, Stooping, or Crawl	How much does this job require kneeling, crouching, stooping, or crawling?
Contact With Others	How much does this job require the worker to be in contact with others (face-to-face, by telephone, or otherwise) in order to perform it?	Exposed to Contaminants	How often does this job require working exposed to contaminants (such as pollutants, gases, dust or odors)?
Face-to-Face Discussions	How often do you have to have face-to-face discussions with individuals or teams in this job?	Indoors, Not Environmentally Controlled	How often does this job require working indoors in non-controlled environmental conditions (e.g., warehouse without heat)?
Importance of Being Exact or Accurate	How important is being very exact or highly accurate in performing this job?	Public Speaking	How often do you have to perform public speaking in this job?
Spend Time Sitting	How much does this job require sitting?	Exposed to Minor Burns, Cuts, Bites, or Stings	How often does this job require exposure to minor burns, cuts, bites, or stings?
Structured versus Unstructured Work	To what extent is this job structured for the worker, rather than allowing the worker to determine tasks, priorities, and goals?	Spend Time Keeping or Regaining Balance	How much does this job require keeping or regaining your balance?
Importance of Repeating Same Tasks	How important is repeating the same physical activities (e.g., key entry) or mental activities (e.g., checking entries in a ledger) over and over, without stopping, to performing this job?	Exposed to Hazardous Equipment	How often does this job require exposure to hazardous equipment?
Indoors, Environmentally Controlled	How often does this job require working indoors in environmentally controlled conditions?	Extremely Bright or Inadequate Lighting	How often does this job require working in extremely bright or inadequate lighting conditions?
Electronic Mail	How often do you use electronic mail in this job?	Outdoors, Exposed to Weather	How often does this job require working outdoors, exposed to all weather conditions?
Work With Work Group or Team	How important is it to work with others in a group or team in this job?	Exposed to Hazardous Conditions	How often does this job require exposure to hazardous conditions?
Deal With External Customers	How important is it to work with external customers or the public in this job?	Exposed to High Places	How often does this job require exposure to high places?
Freedom to Make Decisions	How much decision making freedom, without supervision, does the job offer?	Outdoors, Under Cover	How often does this job require working outdoors, under cover (e.g., structure with roof but no walls)?
Impact of Decisions on Co-workers or Company Resul	How do the decisions an employee makes impact the results of co-workers, clients or the company?	Wear Specialized Protective or Safety Equipment su	How much does this job require wearing specialized protective or safety equipment such as breathing apparatus, safety harness, full protection suits, or radiation protection?
Time Pressure	How often does this job require the worker to meet strict deadlines?	Spend Time Climbing Ladders, Scaffolds, or Poles	How much does this job require climbing ladders, scaffolds, or poles?
Frequency of Decision Making	How frequently is the worker required to make decisions that affect other people, the financial resources, and/or the image and reputation of the organization?	Very Hot or Cold Temperatures	How often does this job require working in very hot (above 90 F degrees) or very cold (below 32 F degrees) temperatures?
Deal With Unpleasant or Angry People	How frequently does the worker have to deal with unpleasant, angry, or discourteous individuals as part of the job requirements?	In an Open Vehicle or Equipment	How often does this job require working in an open vehicle or equipment (e.g., tractor)?
Letters and Memos	How often does the job require written letters and memos?	Exposed to Whole Body Vibration	How often does this job require exposure to whole body vibration (e.g., operate a jackhammer)?
Physical Proximity	To what extent does this job require the worker to perform job tasks in close physical proximity to other people?	Exposed to Radiation	How often does this job require exposure to radiation?
Spend Time Using Your Hands to Handle, Control, or	How much does this job require using your hands to handle, control, or feel objects, tools or controls?		
Coordinate or Lead Others	How important is it to coordinate or lead others in accomplishing work activities in this job?	**Job Zone Component**	**Job Zone Component Definitions**
Frequency of Conflict Situations	How often are there conflict situations the employee has to face in this job?	Title	Job Zone Two: Some Preparation Needed
Spend Time Making Repetitive Motions	How much does this job require making repetitive motions?	Overall Experience	Some previous work-related skill, knowledge, or experience may be helpful in these occupations, but usually is not needed. For example, a drywall installer might benefit from experience installing drywall, but an inexperienced person could still learn to be an installer with little difficulty.
Responsibility for Outcomes and Results	How responsible is the worker for work outcomes and results of other workers?	Job Training	Employees in these occupations need anywhere from a few months to one year of working with experienced employees.
Sounds, Noise Levels Are Distracting : Uncomforta	How often does this job require working exposed to sounds and noise levels that are distracting or uncomfortable?		

Job Zone Examples	These occupations often involve using your knowledge and skills to help others. Examples include drywall installers, fire inspectors, flight attendants, pharmacy technicians, salespersons (retail), and tellers.
SVP Range	(4.0 to < 6.0)
Education	These occupations usually require a high school diploma and may require some vocational training or job-related course work. In some cases, an associate's or bachelor's degree could be needed.

Work_Styles	Work_Styles Definitions
Cooperation	Job requires being pleasant with others on the job and displaying a good-natured, cooperative attitude.
Dependability	Job requires being reliable, responsible, and dependable, and fulfilling obligations.
Integrity	Job requires being honest and ethical.
Attention to Detail	Job requires being careful about detail and thorough in completing work tasks.
Concern for Others	Job requires being sensitive to others' needs and feelings and being understanding and helpful on the job.
Self Control	Job requires maintaining composure, keeping emotions in check, controlling anger, and avoiding aggressive behavior, even in very difficult situations.
Independence	Job requires developing one's own ways of doing things, guiding oneself with little or no supervision, and depending on oneself to get things done.
Stress Tolerance	Job requires accepting criticism and dealing calmly and effectively with high stress situations.
Initiative	Job requires a willingness to take on responsibilities and challenges.
Social Orientation	Job requires preferring to work with others rather than alone, and being personally connected with others on the job.
Adaptability/Flexibility	Job requires being open to change (positive or negative) and to considerable variety in the workplace.
Persistence	Job requires persistence in the face of obstacles.
Leadership	Job requires a willingness to lead, take charge, and offer opinions and direction.
Achievement/Effort	Job requires establishing and maintaining personally challenging achievement goals and exerting effort toward mastering tasks.
Analytical Thinking	Job requires analyzing information and using logic to address work-related issues and problems.
Innovation	Job requires creativity and alternative thinking to develop new ideas for and answers to work-related problems.

43-9071.00 - Office Machine Operators, Except Computer

Operate one or more of a variety of office machines, such as photocopying, photographic, and duplicating machines, or other office machines.

Tasks

1) Monitor machine operation, and make adjustments as necessary to ensure proper operation.

2) Compute prices for services and receive payment, or provide supervisors with billing information.

3) Deliver completed work.

4) Maintain stock of supplies, and requisition any needed items.

5) Load machines with materials such as blank paper or film.

6) Move heat units and clamping frames over screen beds to form Braille impressions on pages; then raise frames to release individual copies.

7) File and store completed documents.

8) Place original copies in feed trays, feed originals into feed rolls, or position originals on tables beneath camera lenses.

9) Read job orders to determine the type of work to be done, the quantities to be produced, and the materials needed.

10) Set up and adjust machines, regulating factors such as speed, ink flow, focus, and number of copies.

11) Prepare and process papers for use in scanning, microfilming, and microfiche.

12) Clean and file master copies or plates.

13) Clean machines, perform minor repairs, and report major repair needs.

14) Cut copies apart and write identifying information, such as page numbers or titles, on copies.

15) Operate auxiliary machines such as collators, pad and tablet making machines, staplers, and paper punching, folding, cutting, and perforating machines.

16) Sort, assemble, and proof completed work.

17) Operate office machines such as high speed business photocopiers, reader/scanners, addressing machines, stencil-cutting machines, microfilm reader/printers, folding and inserting, bursting, and binder machines.

43-9111.00 - Statistical Assistants

Compile and compute data according to statistical formulas for use in statistical studies. May perform actuarial computations and compile charts and graphs for use by actuaries. Includes actuarial clerks.

Tasks

1) Compile reports, charts, and graphs that describe and interpret findings of analyses.

2) File data and related information, and maintain and update databases.

3) Check source data in order to verify its completeness and accuracy.

4) Check survey responses for errors such as the use of pens instead of pencils, and set aside response forms that cannot be used.

5) Compute and analyze data, using statistical formulas and computers or calculators.

6) Feed response sheets through optical scanners that read responses and store data in a format that computers can read.

7) Organize paperwork such as survey forms and reports for distribution and for analysis.

8) Select statistical tests for analyzing data.

9) Interview people and keep track of their responses.

10) Send out surveys.

11) Discuss data presentation requirements with clients.

12) Enter data into computers for use in analyses and reports.

13) Participate in the publication of data and information.

14) Code data as necessary prior to computer entry, using lists of codes.

45-1011.05 - First-Line Supervisors and Manager/Supervisors - Logging Workers

Directly supervise and coordinate activities of logging workers. Manager/Supervisors are generally found in smaller establishments where they perform both supervisory and management functions, such as accounting, marketing, and personnel work, and may also engage in the same logging work as the workers they supervise.

Tasks

1) Supervise and coordinate the activities of workers engaged in logging operations and silvicultural operations.

2) Change logging operations or methods to eliminate unsafe conditions.

3) Prepare production and personnel time records for management.

4) Coordinate the selection and movement of logs from storage areas, according to transportation schedules or production requirements.

5) Train workers in tree felling and bucking, operation of tractors and loading machines, yarding and loading techniques, and safety regulations.

6) Monitor workers to ensure that safety regulations are followed, warning or disciplining those who violate safety regulations.

7) Monitor logging operations to identify and solve problems, improve work methods, and ensure compliance with safety, company, and government regulations.

8) Assign to workers duties such as trees to be cut, cutting sequences and specifications, and loading of trucks, railcars, or rafts.

9) Plan and schedule logging operations such as felling and bucking trees; and grading, sorting, yarding or loading logs.

10) Coordinate dismantling, moving, and setting up equipment at new work sites.

11) Determine logging operation methods, crew sizes, and equipment requirements, conferring with mill, company, and forestry officials as necessary.

12) Schedule work crews, equipment, and transportation for several different work locations.

45-2021.00 - Animal Breeders

Breed animals, including cattle, goats, horses, sheep, swine, poultry, dogs, cats, or pet birds. Select and breed animals according to their genealogy, characteristics, and offspring. May require a knowledge of artificial insemination techniques and equipment use. May involve keeping records on heats, birth intervals, or pedigree.

Tasks

1) Measure specified amounts of semen into calibrated syringes, and insert syringes into inseminating guns.

2) Feed and water animals, and clean and disinfect pens, cages, yards, and hutches.

3) Exhibit animals at shows.

4) Clip or shear hair on animals.

5) Build hutches, pens, and fenced yards.

6) Examine semen microscopically in order to assess and record density and motility of gametes, and dilute semen with prescribed diluents according to formulas.

7) Treat minor injuries and ailments, and contact veterinarians in order to obtain treatment for animals with serious illnesses or injuries.

8) Milk cows and goats.

9) Package and label semen to be used for artificial insemination, recording information such as the date, source, quality, and concentration.

10) Record animal characteristics such as weights, growth patterns, and diets.

11) Perform procedures such as animal dehorning or castration.

12) Arrange for sale of animals and eggs to hospitals, research centers, pet shops, and food processing plants.

13) Place vaccines in drinking water, inject vaccines, or dust air with vaccine powder, in order to protect animals from diseases.

14) Brand, tattoo, or tag animals in order to allow animal identification.

15) Incubate eggs to induce hatching.

16) Inject prepared animal semen into female animals for breeding purposes, by inserting nozzle of syringe into vagina and depressing syringe plunger.

17) Inject semen into hens' oviducts or through holes in egg shells.

18) Maintain logs of semen specimens used and animals bred.

19) Observe animals in heat in order to detect approach of estrus, and exercise animals to induce or hasten estrus, if necessary.

20) Confine roosters (pinioning) in order to collect semen in vial.

21) Attach rubber collecting sheaths to genitals of tethered bull, and stimulate animal's organ in order to induce ejaculation.

22) Adjust controls in order to maintain specific building temperatures required for animals' health and safety.

23) Examine animals in order to detect symptoms of illness or injury.

24) Select animals to be bred, and semen specimens to be used, according to knowledge of animals, genealogies, traits, and desired offspring characteristics.

25) Kill animals, remove their pelts, and arrange for sale of pelts.

45-4021.00 - Fallers

Use axes or chainsaws to fell trees using knowledge of tree characteristics and cutting techniques to control direction of fall and minimize tree damage.

Tasks

1) Place supporting limbs or poles under felled trees in order to avoid splitting undersides, and to prevent logs from rolling.

2) Assemble floating logs into rafts for towing to mills.

3) Trim off the tops and limbs of trees, using chainsaws, delimbers, or axes.

4) Stop saw engines, pull cutting bars from cuts, and run to safety as tree falls.

5) Appraise trees for certain characteristics, such as twist, rot, and heavy limb growth, and gauge amount and direction of lean, in order to determine how to control the direction of a tree's fall with the least damage.

6) Select trees to be cut down, assessing factors such as site, terrain, and weather conditions before beginning work.

7) Mark logs for identification.

8) Maintain and repair chainsaws and other equipment, cleaning, oiling, and greasing equipment, and sharpening equipment properly.

9) Split logs, using axes, wedges, and mauls, and stack wood in ricks or cord lots.

10) Work as a member of a team, rotating between chain saw operation and skidder operation.

11) Control the direction of a tree's fall by scoring cutting lines with axes, sawing undercuts along scored lines with chainsaws, knocking slabs from cuts with single-bit axes, and driving wedges.

12) Secure steel cables or chains to logs for dragging by tractors or for pulling by cable yarding systems.

13) Assess logs after cutting to ensure that the quality and length are correct.

14) Load logs or wood onto trucks, trailers, or railroad cars, by hand or using loaders or winches.

15) Measure felled trees and cut them into specified log lengths, using chain saws and axes.

16) Clear brush from work areas and escape routes, and cut saplings and other trees from direction of falls, using axes, chainsaws, or bulldozers.

17) Tag unsafe trees with high-visibility ribbons.

18) Saw back-cuts, leaving sufficient sound wood to control direction of fall.

19) Determine position, direction, and depth of cuts to be made, and placement of wedges or jacks.

45-4022.00 - Logging Equipment Operators

Drive logging tractor or wheeled vehicle equipped with one or more accessories, such as bulldozer blade, frontal shear, grapple, logging arch, cable winches, hoisting rack, or crane boom, to fell tree; to skid, load, unload, or stack logs; or to pull stumps or clear brush.

Tasks

1) Drive and maneuver tractors and tree harvesters to shear the tops off of trees, cut and limb the trees, and then cut the logs into desired lengths.

2) Fill out required job or shift report forms.

3) Grade logs according to characteristics such as knot size and straightness, and according to established industry or company standards.

4) Inspect equipment for safety prior to use, and perform necessary basic maintenance tasks.

5) Control hydraulic tractors equipped with tree clamps and booms to lift, swing, and bunch sheared trees.

6) Drive crawler or wheeled tractors to drag or transport logs from felling sites to log landing areas for processing and loading.

7) Drive tractors for the purpose of building or repairing logging and skid roads.

8) Drive straight or articulated tractors equipped with accessories such as bulldozer blades, grapples, logging arches, cable winches, and crane booms, to skid, load, unload, or stack logs, pull stumps, or clear brush.

45-4023.00 - Log Graders and Scalers

Grade logs or estimate the marketable content or value of logs or pulpwood in sorting yards, millpond, log deck, or similar locations. Inspect logs for defects or measure logs to determine volume.

Tasks

1) Drive to sawmills, wharfs, or skids to inspect logs or pulpwood.

2) Saw felled trees into lengths.

3) Paint identification marks of specified colors on logs to identify grades or species, using spray cans, or call out grades to log markers.

4) Tend conveyor chains that move logs to and from scaling stations.

5) Weigh log trucks before and after unloading, and record load weights and supplier identities.

6) Record data about individual trees or load volumes into tally books or hand-held collection terminals.

7) Measure felled logs or loads of pulpwood to calculate volume, weight, dimensions, and marketable value, using measuring devices and conversion tables.

8) Jab logs with metal ends of scale sticks, and inspect logs to ascertain characteristics or defects such as water damage, splits, knots, broken ends, rotten areas, twists, and curves.

9) Identify logs of substandard or special grade so that they can be returned to shippers, regraded, recut, or transferred for other processing.

10) Evaluate log characteristics and determine grades, using established criteria.

11) Measure log lengths and mark boles for bucking into logs, according to specifications.

47-2011.00 - Boilermakers

Construct, assemble, maintain, and repair stationary steam boilers and boiler house auxiliaries. Align structures or plate sections to assemble boiler frame tanks or vats, following blueprints. Work involves use of hand and power tools, plumb bobs, levels, wedges, dogs, or turnbuckles. Assist in testing assembled vessels. Direct cleaning of boilers and boiler furnaces. Inspect and repair boiler fittings, such as safety valves, regulators, automatic-control mechanisms, water columns, and auxiliary machines.

Tasks

1) Inspect assembled vessels and individual components, such as tubes, fittings, valves, controls, and auxiliary mechanisms, to locate any defects.

2) Locate and mark reference points for columns or plates on boiler foundations, following blueprints and using straightedges, squares, transits, and measuring instruments.

3) Clean pressure vessel equipment, using scrapers, wire brushes, and cleaning solvents.

4) Assemble large vessels in an on-site fabrication shop prior to installation, in order to ensure proper fit.

5) Straighten or reshape bent pressure vessel plates and structure parts, using hammers, jacks, and torches.

6) Position, align, and secure structural parts and related assemblies to boiler frames, tanks, or vats of pressure vessels, following blueprints.

7) Lay out plate, sheet steel, or other heavy metal, and locate and mark bending and cutting lines, using protractors, compasses, and drawing instruments or templates.

8) Shape seams, joints, and irregular edges of pressure vessel sections and structural parts in order to attain specified fit of parts, using cutting torches, hammers, files, and metalworking machines.

9) Install manholes, handholes, taps, tubes, valves, gauges, and feedwater connections in drums of water tube boilers, using hand tools.

10) Examine boilers, pressure vessels, tanks, and vats to locate defects such as leaks, weak spots, and defective sections so that they can be repaired.

11) Bolt or arc-weld pressure vessel structures and parts together, using wrenches and welding equipment.

12) Bell, bead with power hammers, or weld pressure vessel tube ends, in order to ensure leakproof joints.

13) Attach rigging, and signal crane or hoist operators to lift heavy frame and plate sections and other parts into place.

14) Repair or replace defective pressure vessel parts, such as safety valves and regulators, using torches, jacks, caulking hammers, power saws, threading dies, welding equipment, and metalworking machinery.

15) Shape and fabricate parts, such as stacks, uptakes, and chutes, in order to adapt pressure

vessels, heat exchangers, and piping to premises, using heavy-metalworking machines such as brakes, rolls, and drill presses.

16) Install refractory bricks and other heat-resistant materials in fireboxes of pressure vessels.

47-2021.00 - Brickmasons and Blockmasons

Lay and bind building materials, such as brick, structural tile, concrete block, cinder block, glass block, and terra-cotta block, with mortar and other substances to construct or repair walls, partitions, arches, sewers, and other structures.

Tasks

1) Apply and smooth mortar or other mixture over work surface.

2) Calculate angles and courses and determine vertical and horizontal alignment of courses.

3) Interpret blueprints and drawings to determine specifications and to calculate the materials required.

4) Clean working surface to remove scale, dust, soot, or chips of brick and mortar, using broom, wire brush, or scraper.

5) Fasten or fuse brick or other building material to structure with wire clamps, anchor holes, torch, or cement.

6) Examine brickwork or structure to determine need for repair.

7) Remove burned or damaged brick or mortar, using sledgehammer, crowbar, chipping gun, or chisel.

8) Mix specified amounts of sand, clay, dirt, or mortar powder with water to form refractory mixtures.

9) Lay and align bricks, blocks, or tiles to build or repair structures or high temperature equipment, such as cupola, kilns, ovens, or furnaces.

10) Spray or spread refractory material over brickwork to protect against deterioration.

11) Remove excess mortar with trowels and hand tools, and finish mortar joints with jointing tools, for a sealed, uniform appearance.

12) Break or cut bricks, tiles, or blocks to size, using trowel edge, hammer, or power saw.

13) Construct corners by fastening in plumb position a corner pole or building a corner pyramid of bricks, then filling in between the corners using a line from corner to corner to guide each course, or layer, of brick.

Knowledge	Knowledge Definitions
Building and Construction	Knowledge of materials, methods, and the tools involved in the construction or repair of houses, buildings, or other structures such as highways and roads.
Mathematics	Knowledge of arithmetic, algebra, geometry, calculus, statistics, and their applications.
Design	Knowledge of design techniques, tools, and principles involved in production of precision technical plans, blueprints, drawings, and models.
Production and Processing	Knowledge of raw materials, production processes, quality control, costs, and other techniques for maximizing the effective manufacture and distribution of goods.
English Language	Knowledge of the structure and content of the English language including the meaning and spelling of words, rules of composition, and grammar.
Administration and Management	Knowledge of business and management principles involved in strategic planning, resource allocation, human resources modeling, leadership technique, production methods, and coordination of people and resources.
Public Safety and Security	Knowledge of relevant equipment, policies, procedures, and strategies to promote effective local, state, or national security operations for the protection of people, data, property, and institutions.
Mechanical	Knowledge of machines and tools, including their designs, uses, repair, and maintenance.
Customer and Personal Service	Knowledge of principles and processes for providing customer and personal services. This includes customer needs assessment, meeting quality standards for services, and evaluation of customer satisfaction.
Education and Training	Knowledge of principles and methods for curriculum and training design, teaching and instruction for individuals and groups, and the measurement of training effects.

Engineering and Technology	Knowledge of the practical application of engineering science and technology. This includes applying principles, techniques, procedures, and equipment to the design and production of various goods and services.
Personnel and Human Resources	Knowledge of principles and procedures for personnel recruitment, selection, training, compensation and benefits, labor relations and negotiation, and personnel information systems.
Transportation	Knowledge of principles and methods for moving people or goods by air, rail, sea, or road, including the relative costs and benefits.
Psychology	Knowledge of human behavior and performance; individual differences in ability, personality, and interests; learning and motivation; psychological research methods; and the assessment and treatment of behavioral and affective disorders.
Law and Government	Knowledge of laws, legal codes, court procedures, precedents, government regulations, executive orders, agency rules, and the democratic political process.
Sales and Marketing	Knowledge of principles and methods for showing, promoting, and selling products or services. This includes marketing strategy and tactics, product demonstration, sales techniques, and sales control systems.
Physics	Knowledge and prediction of physical principles, laws, their interrelationships, and applications to understanding fluid, material, and atmospheric dynamics, and mechanical, electrical, atomic and sub-atomic structures and processes.
Sociology and Anthropology	Knowledge of group behavior and dynamics, societal trends and influences, human migrations, ethnicity, cultures and their history and origins.
Chemistry	Knowledge of the chemical composition, structure, and properties of substances and of the chemical processes and transformations that they undergo. This includes uses of chemicals and their interactions, danger signs, production techniques, and disposal methods.
Economics and Accounting	Knowledge of economic and accounting principles and practices, the financial markets, banking and the analysis and reporting of financial data.
Clerical	Knowledge of administrative and clerical procedures and systems such as word processing, managing files and records, stenography and transcription, designing forms, and other office procedures and terminology.
Geography	Knowledge of principles and methods for describing the features of land, sea, and air masses, including their physical characteristics, locations, interrelationships, and distribution of plant, animal, and human life.
Therapy and Counseling	Knowledge of principles, methods, and procedures for diagnosis, treatment, and rehabilitation of physical and mental dysfunctions, and for career counseling and guidance.
Philosophy and Theology	Knowledge of different philosophical systems and religions. This includes their basic principles, values, ethics, ways of thinking, customs, practices, and their impact on human culture.
Foreign Language	Knowledge of the structure and content of a foreign (non-English) language including the meaning and spelling of words, rules of composition and grammar, and pronunciation.
Telecommunications	Knowledge of transmission, broadcasting, switching, control, and operation of telecommunications systems.
Computers and Electronics	Knowledge of circuit boards, processors, chips, electronic equipment, and computer hardware and software, including applications and programming.
Medicine and Dentistry	Knowledge of the information and techniques needed to diagnose and treat human injuries, diseases, and deformities. This includes symptoms, treatment alternatives, drug properties and interactions, and preventive health-care measures.
History and Archeology	Knowledge of historical events and their causes, indicators, and effects on civilizations and cultures.
Communications and Media	Knowledge of media production, communication, and dissemination techniques and methods. This includes alternative ways to inform and entertain via written, oral, and visual media.
Fine Arts	Knowledge of the theory and techniques required to compose, produce, and perform works of music, dance, visual arts, drama, and sculpture.
Biology	Knowledge of plant and animal organisms, their tissues, cells, functions, interdependencies, and interactions with each other and the environment.

Food Production	Knowledge of techniques and equipment for planting, growing, and harvesting food products (both plant and animal) for consumption, including storage/handling techniques.

Skills	Skills Definitions
Active Listening	Giving full attention to what other people are saying, taking time to understand the points being made, asking questions as appropriate, and not interrupting at inappropriate times.
Coordination	Adjusting actions in relation to others' actions.
Mathematics	Using mathematics to solve problems.
Time Management	Managing one's own time and the time of others.
Equipment Selection	Determining the kind of tools and equipment needed to do a job.
Speaking	Talking to others to convey information effectively.
Equipment Maintenance	Performing routine maintenance on equipment and determining when and what kind of maintenance is needed.
Reading Comprehension	Understanding written sentences and paragraphs in work related documents.
Critical Thinking	Using logic and reasoning to identify the strengths and weaknesses of alternative solutions, conclusions or approaches to problems.
Judgment and Decision Making	Considering the relative costs and benefits of potential actions to choose the most appropriate one.
Monitoring	Monitoring/Assessing performance of yourself, other individuals, or organizations to make improvements or take corrective action.
Active Learning	Understanding the implications of new information for both current and future problem-solving and decision-making.
Instructing	Teaching others how to do something.
Installation	Installing equipment, machines, wiring, or programs to meet specifications.
Learning Strategies	Selecting and using training/instructional methods and procedures appropriate for the situation when learning or teaching new things.
Management of Material Resources	Obtaining and seeing to the appropriate use of equipment, facilities, and materials needed to do certain work.
Social Perceptiveness	Being aware of others' reactions and understanding why they react as they do.
Complex Problem Solving	Identifying complex problems and reviewing related information to develop and evaluate options and implement solutions.
Troubleshooting	Determining causes of operating errors and deciding what to do about it.
Management of Financial Resources	Determining how money will be spent to get the work done, and accounting for these expenditures.
Service Orientation	Actively looking for ways to help people.
Management of Personnel Resources	Motivating, developing, and directing people as they work, identifying the best people for the job.
Technology Design	Generating or adapting equipment and technology to serve user needs.
Writing	Communicating effectively in writing as appropriate for the needs of the audience.
Operations Analysis	Analyzing needs and product requirements to create a design.
Quality Control Analysis	Conducting tests and inspections of products, services, or processes to evaluate quality or performance.
Repairing	Repairing machines or systems using the needed tools.
Negotiation	Bringing others together and trying to reconcile differences.
Operation and Control	Controlling operations of equipment or systems.
Persuasion	Persuading others to change their minds or behavior.
Operation Monitoring	Watching gauges, dials, or other indicators to make sure a machine is working properly.
Science	Using scientific rules and methods to solve problems.
Systems Evaluation	Identifying measures or indicators of system performance and the actions needed to improve or correct performance, relative to the goals of the system.
Systems Analysis	Determining how a system should work and how changes in conditions, operations, and the environment will affect outcomes.
Programming	Writing computer programs for various purposes.

Ability	Ability Definitions
Trunk Strength	The ability to use your abdominal and lower back muscles to support part of the body repeatedly or continuously over time without 'giving out' or fatiguing.

Manual Dexterity	The ability to quickly move your hand, your hand together with your arm, or your two hands to grasp, manipulate, or assemble objects.
Near Vision	The ability to see details at close range (within a few feet of the observer).
Visualization	The ability to imagine how something will look after it is moved around or when its parts are moved or rearranged.
Problem Sensitivity	The ability to tell when something is wrong or is likely to go wrong. It does not involve solving the problem, only recognizing there is a problem.
Information Ordering	The ability to arrange things or actions in a certain order or pattern according to a specific rule or set of rules (e.g., patterns of numbers, letters, words, pictures, mathematical operations).
Oral Comprehension	The ability to listen to and understand information and ideas presented through spoken words and sentences.
Extent Flexibility	The ability to bend, stretch, twist, or reach with your body, arms, and/or legs.
Arm-Hand Steadiness	The ability to keep your hand and arm steady while moving your arm or while holding your arm and hand in one position.
Stamina	The ability to exert yourself physically over long periods of time without getting winded or out of breath.
Static Strength	The ability to exert maximum muscle force to lift, push, pull, or carry objects.
Multilimb Coordination	The ability to coordinate two or more limbs (for example, two arms, two legs, or one leg and one arm) while sitting, standing, or lying down. It does not involve performing the activities while the whole body is in motion.
Gross Body Coordination	The ability to coordinate the movement of your arms, legs, and torso together when the whole body is in motion.
Oral Expression	The ability to communicate information and ideas in speaking so others will understand.
Finger Dexterity	The ability to make precisely coordinated movements of the fingers of one or both hands to grasp, manipulate, or assemble very small objects.
Gross Body Equilibrium	The ability to keep or regain your body balance or stay upright when in an unstable position.
Dynamic Strength	The ability to exert muscle force repeatedly or continuously over time. This involves muscular endurance and resistance to muscle fatigue.
Selective Attention	The ability to concentrate on a task over a period of time without being distracted.
Reaction Time	The ability to quickly respond (with the hand, finger, or foot) to a signal (sound, light, picture) when it appears.
Speech Recognition	The ability to identify and understand the speech of another person.
Deductive Reasoning	The ability to apply general rules to specific problems to produce answers that make sense.
Speech Clarity	The ability to speak clearly so others can understand you.
Mathematical Reasoning	The ability to choose the right mathematical methods or formulas to solve a problem.
Inductive Reasoning	The ability to combine pieces of information to form general rules or conclusions (includes finding a relationship among seemingly unrelated events).
Category Flexibility	The ability to generate or use different sets of rules for combining or grouping things in different ways.
Control Precision	The ability to quickly and repeatedly adjust the controls of a machine or a vehicle to exact positions.
Speed of Limb Movement	The ability to quickly move the arms and legs.
Written Comprehension	The ability to read and understand information and ideas presented in writing.
Depth Perception	The ability to judge which of several objects is closer or farther away from you, or to judge the distance between you and an object.
Flexibility of Closure	The ability to identify or detect a known pattern (a figure, object, word, or sound) that is hidden in other distracting material.
Number Facility	The ability to add, subtract, multiply, or divide quickly and correctly.
Fluency of Ideas	The ability to come up with a number of ideas about a topic (the number of ideas is important, not their quality, correctness, or creativity).
Far Vision	The ability to see details at a distance.
Time Sharing	The ability to shift back and forth between two or more activities or sources of information (such as speech, sounds, touch, or other sources).
Explosive Strength	The ability to use short bursts of muscle force to propel oneself (as in jumping or sprinting), or to throw an object.

Glare Sensitivity	The ability to see objects in the presence of glare or bright lighting.
Perceptual Speed	The ability to quickly and accurately compare similarities and differences among sets of letters, numbers, objects, pictures, or patterns. The things to be compared may be presented at the same time or one after the other. This ability also includes comparing a presented object with a remembered object.
Speed of Closure	The ability to quickly make sense of, combine, and organize information into meaningful patterns.
Auditory Attention	The ability to focus on a single source of sound in the presence of other distracting sounds.
Written Expression	The ability to communicate information and ideas in writing so others will understand.
Visual Color Discrimination	The ability to match or detect differences between colors, including shades of color and brightness.
Spatial Orientation	The ability to know your location in relation to the environment or to know where other objects are in relation to you.
Wrist-Finger Speed	The ability to make fast, simple, repeated movements of the fingers, hands, and wrists.
Dynamic Flexibility	The ability to quickly and repeatedly bend, stretch, twist, or reach out with your body, arms, and/or legs.
Originality	The ability to come up with unusual or clever ideas about a given topic or situation, or to develop creative ways to solve a problem.
Memorization	The ability to remember information such as words, numbers, pictures, and procedures.
Response Orientation	The ability to choose quickly between two or more movements in response to two or more different signals (lights, sounds, pictures). It includes the speed with which the correct response is started with the hand, foot, or other body part.
Night Vision	The ability to see under low light conditions.
Peripheral Vision	The ability to see objects or movement of objects to one's side when the eyes are looking ahead.
Rate Control	The ability to time your movements or the movement of a piece of equipment in anticipation of changes in the speed and/or direction of a moving object or scene.
Sound Localization	The ability to tell the direction from which a sound originated.
Hearing Sensitivity	The ability to detect or tell the differences between sounds that vary in pitch and loudness.

Work_Activity	Work_Activity Definitions
Getting Information	Observing, receiving, and otherwise obtaining information from all relevant sources.
Performing General Physical Activities	Performing physical activities that require considerable use of your arms and legs and moving your whole body, such as climbing, lifting, balancing, walking, stooping, and handling of materials.
Handling and Moving Objects	Using hands and arms in handling, installing, positioning, and moving materials, and manipulating things.
Inspecting Equipment, Structures, or Material	Inspecting equipment, structures, or materials to identify the cause of errors or other problems or defects.
Making Decisions and Solving Problems	Analyzing information and evaluating results to choose the best solution and solve problems.
Coordinating the Work and Activities of Others	Getting members of a group to work together to accomplish tasks.
Drafting, Laying Out, and Specifying Technical Dev	Providing documentation, detailed instructions, drawings, or specifications to tell others about how devices, parts, equipment, or structures are to be fabricated, constructed, assembled, modified, maintained, or used.
Communicating with Supervisors, Peers, or Subordin	Providing information to supervisors, co-workers, and subordinates by telephone, in written form, e-mail, or in person.
Organizing, Planning, and Prioritizing Work	Developing specific goals and plans to prioritize, organize, and accomplish your work.
Identifying Objects, Actions, and Events	Identifying information by categorizing, estimating, recognizing differences or similarities, and detecting changes in circumstances or events.
Establishing and Maintaining Interpersonal Relatio	Developing constructive and cooperative working relationships with others, and maintaining them over time.
Coaching and Developing Others	Identifying the developmental needs of others and coaching, mentoring, or otherwise helping others to improve their knowledge or skills.
Scheduling Work and Activities	Scheduling events, programs, and activities, as well as the work of others.
Judging the Qualities of Things, Services, or Peop	Assessing the value, importance, or quality of things or people.

Operating Vehicles, Mechanized Devices, or Equipme	Running, maneuvering, navigating, or driving vehicles or mechanized equipment, such as forklifts, passenger vehicles, aircraft, or water craft.
Thinking Creatively	Developing, designing, or creating new applications, ideas, relationships, systems, or products, including artistic contributions.
Communicating with Persons Outside Organization	Communicating with people outside the organization, representing the organization to customers, the public, government, and other external sources. This information can be exchanged in person, in writing, or by telephone or e-mail.
Developing and Building Teams	Encouraging and building mutual trust, respect, and cooperation among team members.
Interpreting the Meaning of Information for Others	Translating or explaining what information means and how it can be used.
Evaluating Information to Determine Compliance wit	Using relevant information and individual judgment to determine whether events or processes comply with laws, regulations, or standards.
Training and Teaching Others	Identifying the educational needs of others, developing formal educational or training programs or classes, and teaching or instructing others.
Estimating the Quantifiable Characteristics of Pro	Estimating sizes, distances, and quantities; or determining time, costs, resources, or materials needed to perform a work activity.
Assisting and Caring for Others	Providing personal assistance, medical attention, emotional support, or other personal care to others such as coworkers, customers, or patients.
Resolving Conflicts and Negotiating with Others	Handling complaints, settling disputes, and resolving grievances and conflicts, or otherwise negotiating with others.
Guiding, Directing, and Motivating Subordinates	Providing guidance and direction to subordinates, including setting performance standards and monitoring performance.
Updating and Using Relevant Knowledge	Keeping up-to-date technically and applying new knowledge to your job.
Monitor Processes, Materials, or Surroundings	Monitoring and reviewing information from materials, events, or the environment, to detect or assess problems.
Processing Information	Compiling, coding, categorizing, calculating, tabulating, auditing, or verifying information or data.
Controlling Machines and Processes	Using either control mechanisms or direct physical activity to operate machines or processes (not including computers or vehicles).
Provide Consultation and Advice to Others	Providing guidance and expert advice to management or other groups on technical, systems-, or process-related topics.
Monitoring and Controlling Resources	Monitoring and controlling resources and overseeing the spending of money.
Repairing and Maintaining Mechanical Equipment	Servicing, repairing, adjusting, and testing machines, devices, moving parts, and equipment that operate primarily on the basis of mechanical (not electronic) principles.
Performing Administrative Activities	Performing day-to-day administrative tasks such as maintaining information files and processing paperwork.
Developing Objectives and Strategies	Establishing long-range objectives and specifying the strategies and actions to achieve them.
Documenting/Recording Information	Entering, transcribing, recording, storing, or maintaining information in written or electronic/magnetic form.
Analyzing Data or Information	Identifying the underlying principles, reasons, or facts of information by breaking down information or data into separate parts.
Selling or Influencing Others	Convincing others to buy merchandise/goods or to otherwise change their minds or actions.
Performing for or Working Directly with the Public	Performing for people or dealing directly with the public. This includes serving customers in restaurants and stores, and receiving clients or guests.
Staffing Organizational Units	Recruiting, interviewing, selecting, hiring, and promoting employees in an organization.
Repairing and Maintaining Electronic Equipment	Servicing, repairing, calibrating, regulating, fine-tuning, or testing machines, devices, and equipment that operate primarily on the basis of electrical or electronic (not mechanical) principles.
Interacting With Computers	Using computers and computer systems (including hardware and software) to program, write software, set up functions, enter data, or process information.

Work_Context	Work_Context Definitions
Wear Common Protective or Safety Equipment such as	How much does this job require wearing common protective or safety equipment such as safety shoes, glasses, gloves, hard hats or live jackets?
Outdoors, Exposed to Weather	How often does this job require working outdoors, exposed to all weather conditions?

Spend Time Standing	How much does this job require standing?
Spend Time Using Your Hands to Handle, Control, or	How much does this job require using your hands to handle, control, or feel objects, tools or controls?
Face-to-Face Discussions	How often do you have to have face-to-face discussions with individuals or teams in this job?
Exposed to Hazardous Equipment	How often does this job require exposure to hazardous equipment?
Spend Time Bending or Twisting the Body	How much does this job require bending or twisting your body?
Very Hot or Cold Temperatures	How often does this job require working in very hot (above 90 F degrees) or very cold (below 32 F degrees) temperatures?
Freedom to Make Decisions	How much decision making freedom, without supervision, does the job offer?
Exposed to High Places	How often does this job require exposure to high places?
Contact With Others	How much does this job require the worker to be in contact with others (face-to-face, by telephone, or otherwise) in order to perform it?
Telephone	How often do you have telephone conversations in this job?
Time Pressure	How often does this job require the worker to meet strict deadlines?
Exposed to Contaminants	How often does this job require working exposed to contaminants (such as pollutants, gases, dust or odors)?
Spend Time Making Repetitive Motions	How much does this job require making repetitive motions?
Importance of Being Exact or Accurate	How important is being very exact or highly accurate in performing this job?
Spend Time Walking and Running	How much does this job require walking and running?
Exposed to Minor Burns, Cuts, Bites, or Stings	How often does this job require exposure to minor burns, cuts, bites, or stings?
Sounds, Noise Levels Are Distracting or Uncomforta	How often does this job require working exposed to sounds and noise levels that are distracting or uncomfortable?
Work With Work Group or Team	How important is it to work with others in a group or team in this job?
Impact of Decisions on Co-workers or Company Resul	How do the decisions an employee makes impact the results of co-workers, clients or the company?
Responsible for Others' Health and Safety	How much responsibility is there for the health and safety of others in this job?
Structured versus Unstructured Work	To what extent is this job structured for the worker, rather than allowing the worker to determine tasks, priorities, and goals?
Level of Competition	To what extent does this job require the worker to compete or to be aware of competitive pressures?
Spend Time Kneeling, Crouching, Stooping, or Crawl	How much does this job require kneeling, crouching, stooping or crawling?
Coordinate or Lead Others	How important is it to coordinate or lead others in accomplishing work activities in this job?
Extremely Bright or Inadequate Lighting	How often does this job require working in extremely bright or inadequate lighting conditions?
Responsibility for Outcomes and Results	How responsible is the worker for work outcomes and results of other workers?
Spend Time Climbing Ladders, Scaffolds, or Poles	How much does this job require climbing ladders, scaffolds, or poles?
Spend Time Keeping or Regaining Balance	How much does this job require keeping or regaining your balance?
Frequency of Decision Making	How frequently is the worker required to make decisions that affect other people, the financial resources, and/or the image and reputation of the organization?
Physical Proximity	To what extent does this job require the worker to perform job tasks in close physical proximity to other people?
Frequency of Conflict Situations	How often are there conflict situations the employee has to face in this job?
Cramped Work Space, Awkward Positions	How often does this job require working in cramped work spaces that requires getting into awkward positions?
Importance of Repeating Same Tasks	How important is repeating the same physical activities (e.g., key entry) or mental activities (e.g., checking entries in a ledger) over and over, without stopping, to performing this job?
Deal With Unpleasant or Angry People	How frequently does the worker have to deal with unpleasant, angry, or discourteous individuals as part of the job requirements?
Consequence of Error	How serious would the result usually be if the worker made a mistake that was not readily correctable?
In an Enclosed Vehicle or Equipment	How often does this job require working in a closed vehicle or equipment (e.g., car)?

Outdoors, Under Cover	How often does this job require working outdoors, under cover (e.g., structure with roof but no walls)?
Deal With External Customers	How important is it to work with external customers or the public in this job?
Pace Determined by Speed of Equipment	How important is it to this job that the pace is determined by the speed of equipment or machinery? (This does not refer to keeping busy at all times on this job.)
Exposed to Hazardous Conditions	How often does this job require exposure to hazardous conditions?
Exposed to Whole Body Vibration	How often does this job require exposure to whole body vibration (e.g., operate a jackhammer)?
Wear Specialized Protective or Safety Equipment su	How much does this job require wearing specialized protective or safety equipment such as breathing apparatus, safety harness, full protection suits, or radiation protection?
Letters and Memos	How often does the job require written letters and memos?
Indoors, Not Environmentally Controlled	How often does this job require working indoors in non-controlled environmental conditions (e.g., warehouse without heat)?
Degree of Automation	How automated is the job?
Deal With Physically Aggressive People	How frequently does this job require the worker to deal with physical aggression of violent individuals?
In an Open Vehicle or Equipment	How often does this job require working in an open vehicle or equipment (e.g., tractor)?
Electronic Mail	How often do you use electronic mail in this job?
Public Speaking	How often do you have to perform public speaking in this job?
Indoors, Environmentally Controlled	How often does this job require working indoors in environmentally controlled conditions?
Spend Time Sitting	How much does this job require sitting?
Exposed to Disease or Infections	How often does this job require exposure to disease/infections?
Exposed to Radiation	How often does this job require exposure to radiation?

Job Zone Component	Job Zone Component Definitions
Title	Job Zone Two: Some Preparation Needed
Overall Experience	Some previous work-related skill, knowledge, or experience may be helpful in these occupations, but usually is not needed. For example, a drywall installer might benefit from experience installing drywall, but an inexperienced person could still learn to be an installer with little difficulty.
Job Training	Employees in these occupations need anywhere from a few months to one year of working with experienced employees.
Job Zone Examples	These occupations often involve using your knowledge and skills to help others. Examples include drywall installers, fire inspectors, flight attendants, pharmacy technicians, salespersons (retail), and tellers.
SVP Range	(4.0 to < 6.0)
Education	These occupations usually require a high school diploma and may require some vocational training or job-related course work. In some cases, an associate's or bachelor's degree could be needed.

Work_Styles	Work_Styles Definitions
Attention to Detail	Job requires being careful about detail and thorough in completing work tasks.
Dependability	Job requires being reliable, responsible, and dependable, and fulfilling obligations.
Initiative	Job requires a willingness to take on responsibilities and challenges.
Integrity	Job requires being honest and ethical.
Persistence	Job requires persistence in the face of obstacles.
Independence	Job requires developing one's own ways of doing things, guiding oneself with little or no supervision, and depending on oneself to get things done.
Achievement/Effort	Job requires establishing and maintaining personally challenging achievement goals and exerting effort toward mastering tasks.
Analytical Thinking	Job requires analyzing information and using logic to address work-related issues and problems.
Leadership	Job requires a willingness to lead, take charge, and offer opinions and direction.
Cooperation	Job requires being pleasant with others on the job and displaying a good-natured, cooperative attitude.
Self Control	Job requires maintaining composure, keeping emotions in check, controlling anger, and avoiding aggressive behavior, even in very difficult situations.

Stress Tolerance	Job requires accepting criticism and dealing calmly and effectively with high stress situations.
Adaptability/Flexibility	Job requires being open to change (positive or negative) and to considerable variety in the workplace.
Innovation	Job requires creativity and alternative thinking to develop new ideas for and answers to work-related problems.
Social Orientation	Job requires preferring to work with others rather than alone, and being personally connected with others on the job.
Concern for Others	Job requires being sensitive to others' needs and feelings and being understanding and helpful on the job.

47-2022.00 - Stonemasons

Build stone structures, such as piers, walls, and abutments. Lay walks, curbstones, or special types of masonry for vats, tanks, and floors.

Tasks

1) Replace broken or missing masonry units in walls or floors.

2) Drill holes in marble or ornamental stone and anchor brackets in holes.

3) Clean excess mortar or grout from surface of marble, stone, or monument, using sponge, brush, water, or acid.

4) Lay out wall patterns or foundations, using straight edge, rule, or staked lines.

5) Mix mortar or grout and pour or spread mortar or grout on marble slabs, stone, or foundation.

6) Remove wedges, fill joints between stones, finish joints between stones, using a trowel, and smooth the mortar to an attractive finish, using a tuck pointer.

7) Set stone or marble in place, according to layout or pattern.

8) Shape, trim, face and cut marble or stone preparatory to setting, using power saws, cutting equipment, and hand tools.

9) Line interiors of molds with treated paper and fill molds with composition-stone mixture.

10) Position mold along guidelines of wall, press mold in place, and remove mold and paper from wall.

11) Remove sections of monument from truck bed, and guide stone onto foundation, using skids, hoist, or truck crane.

12) Repair cracked or chipped areas of stone or marble, using blowtorch and mastic, and remove rough or defective spots from concrete, using power grinder or chisel and hammer.

13) Lay brick to build shells of chimneys and smokestacks or to line or reline industrial furnaces, kilns, boilers and similar installations.

14) Smooth, polish, and bevel surfaces, using hand tools and power tools.

15) Dig trench for foundation of monument, using pick and shovel.

16) Set vertical and horizontal alignment of structures, using plumb bob, gauge line, and level.

47-2031.01 - Construction Carpenters

Construct, erect, install, and repair structures and fixtures of wood, plywood, and wallboard, using carpenter's hand tools and power tools.

Tasks

1) Shape or cut materials to specified measurements, using hand tools, machines, or power saw.

2) Follow established safety rules and regulations and maintain a safe and clean environment.

3) Build or repair cabinets, doors, frameworks, floors, and other wooden fixtures used in buildings, using woodworking machines, carpenter's hand tools, and power tools.

4) Study specifications in blueprints, sketches or building plans to prepare project layout and determine dimensions and materials required.

5) Verify trueness of structure, using plumb bob and level.

6) Install structures and fixtures, such as windows, frames, floorings, and trim, or hardware, using carpenter's hand and power tools.

7) Remove damaged or defective parts or sections of structures and repair or replace, using hand tools.

8) Erect scaffolding and ladders for assembling structures above ground level.

9) Select and order lumber and other required materials.

10) Maintain records, document actions and present written progress reports.

11) Apply shock-absorbing, sound-deadening, and decorative paneling to ceilings and walls.

12) Perform minor plumbing, welding and/or concrete mixing work.

13) Inspect ceiling or floor tile, wall coverings, siding, glass, or woodwork to detect broken or damaged structures.

14) Finish surfaces of woodwork or wallboard in houses and buildings, using paint, hand tools, and paneling.

15) Fill cracks and other defects in plaster or plasterboard and sand patch, using patching plaster, trowel, and sanding tool.

16) Cover subfloors with building paper to keep out moisture and lay hardwood, parquet, and wood-strip-block floors by nailing floors to subfloor or cementing them to mastic or asphalt base.

17) Construct forms and chutes for pouring concrete.

18) Arrange for subcontractors to deal with special areas such as heating and electrical wiring work.

19) Prepare cost estimates for clients or employers.

20) Work with and/or remove hazardous material.

21) Assemble and fasten materials to make framework or props, using hand tools and wood screws, nails, dowel pins, or glue.

Knowledge	Knowledge Definitions
Building and Construction	Knowledge of materials, methods, and the tools involved in the construction or repair of houses, buildings, or other structures such as highways and roads.
Mathematics	Knowledge of arithmetic, algebra, geometry, calculus, statistics, and their applications.
Design	Knowledge of design techniques, tools, and principles involved in production of precision technical plans, blueprints, drawings, and models.
Production and Processing	Knowledge of raw materials, production processes, quality control, costs, and other techniques for maximizing the effective manufacture and distribution of goods.
Engineering and Technology	Knowledge of the practical application of engineering science and technology. This includes applying principles, techniques, procedures, and equipment to the design and production of various goods and services.
Mechanical	Knowledge of machines and tools, including their designs, uses, repair, and maintenance.
Public Safety and Security	Knowledge of relevant equipment, policies, procedures, and strategies to promote effective local, state, or national security operations for the protection of people, data, property, and institutions.
Law and Government	Knowledge of laws, legal codes, court procedures, precedents, government regulations, executive orders, agency rules, and the democratic political process.
Customer and Personal Service	Knowledge of principles and processes for providing customer and personal services. This includes customer needs assessment, meeting quality standards for services, and evaluation of customer satisfaction.
English Language	Knowledge of the structure and content of the English language including the meaning and spelling of words, rules of composition, and grammar.
Transportation	Knowledge of principles and methods for moving people or goods by air, rail, sea, or road, including the relative costs and benefits.
Education and Training	Knowledge of principles and methods for curriculum and training design, teaching and instruction for individuals and groups, and the measurement of training effects.
Psychology	Knowledge of human behavior and performance; individual differences in ability, personality, and interests; learning and motivation; psychological research methods; and the assessment and treatment of behavioral and affective disorders.
Administration and Management	Knowledge of business and management principles involved in strategic planning, resource allocation, human resources modeling, leadership technique, production methods, and coordination of people and resources.
Physics	Knowledge and prediction of physical principles, laws, their interrelationships, and applications to understanding fluid, material, and atmospheric dynamics, and mechanical, electrical, atomic and sub- atomic structures and processes.
Personnel and Human Resources	Knowledge of principles and procedures for personnel recruitment, selection, training, compensation and benefits, labor relations and negotiation, and personnel information systems.
Computers and Electronics	Knowledge of circuit boards, processors, chips, electronic equipment, and computer hardware and software, including applications and programming.
Telecommunications	Knowledge of transmission, broadcasting, switching, control, and operation of telecommunications systems.
Clerical	Knowledge of administrative and clerical procedures and systems such as word processing, managing files and records, stenography and transcription, designing forms, and other office procedures and terminology.
Communications and Media	Knowledge of media production, communication, and dissemination techniques and methods. This includes alternative ways to inform and entertain via written, oral, and visual media.
Economics and Accounting	Knowledge of economic and accounting principles and practices, the financial markets, banking and the analysis and reporting of financial data.
Sales and Marketing	Knowledge of principles and methods for showing, promoting, and selling products or services. This includes marketing strategy and tactics, product demonstration, sales techniques, and sales control systems.
Chemistry	Knowledge of the chemical composition, structure, and properties of substances and of the chemical processes and transformations that they undergo. This includes uses of chemicals and their interactions, danger signs, production techniques, and disposal methods.
Geography	Knowledge of principles and methods for describing the features of land, sea, and air masses, including their physical characteristics, locations, interrelationships, and distribution of plant, animal, and human life.
Medicine and Dentistry	Knowledge of the information and techniques needed to diagnose and treat human injuries, diseases, and deformities. This includes symptoms, treatment alternatives, drug properties and interactions, and preventive health-care measures.
History and Archeology	Knowledge of historical events and their causes, indicators, and effects on civilizations and cultures.
Foreign Language	Knowledge of the structure and content of a foreign (non-English) language including the meaning and spelling of words, rules of composition and grammar, and pronunciation.
Therapy and Counseling	Knowledge of principles, methods, and procedures for diagnosis, treatment, and rehabilitation of physical and mental dysfunctions, and for career counseling and guidance.
Fine Arts	Knowledge of the theory and techniques required to compose, produce, and perform works of music, dance, visual arts, drama, and sculpture.
Biology	Knowledge of plant and animal organisms, their tissues, cells, functions, interdependencies, and interactions with each other and the environment.
Philosophy and Theology	Knowledge of different philosophical systems and religions. This includes their basic principles, values, ethics, ways of thinking, customs, practices, and their impact on human culture.
Sociology and Anthropology	Knowledge of group behavior and dynamics, societal trends and influences, human migrations, ethnicity, cultures and their history and origins.
Food Production	Knowledge of techniques and equipment for planting, growing, and harvesting food products (both plant and animal) for consumption, including storage/handling techniques.

Skills	Skills Definitions
Mathematics	Using mathematics to solve problems.
Time Management	Managing one's own time and the time of others.
Critical Thinking	Using logic and reasoning to identify the strengths and weaknesses of alternative solutions, conclusions or approaches to problems.
Active Listening	Giving full attention to what other people are saying, taking time to understand the points being made, asking questions as appropriate, and not interrupting at inappropriate times.
Judgment and Decision Making	Considering the relative costs and benefits of potential actions to choose the most appropriate one.

Quality Control Analysis	Conducting tests and inspections of products, services, or processes to evaluate quality or performance.
Management of Material Resources	Obtaining and seeing to the appropriate use of equipment, facilities, and materials needed to do certain work.
Active Learning	Understanding the implications of new information for both current and future problem-solving and decision-making.
Installation	Installing equipment, machines, wiring, or programs to meet specifications.
Management of Financial Resources	Determining how money will be spent to get the work done, and accounting for these expenditures.
Equipment Maintenance	Performing routine maintenance on equipment and determining when and what kind of maintenance is needed.
Management of Personnel Resources	Motivating, developing, and directing people as they work, identifying the best people for the job.
Speaking	Talking to others to convey information effectively.
Service Orientation	Actively looking for ways to help people.
Complex Problem Solving	Identifying complex problems and reviewing related information to develop and evaluate options and implement solutions.
Monitoring	Monitoring/Assessing performance of yourself, other individuals, or organizations to make improvements or take corrective action.
Equipment Selection	Determining the kind of equipment needed to do a job.
Instructing	Teaching others how to do something.
Coordination	Adjusting actions in relation to others' actions.
Repairing	Repairing machines or systems using the needed tools.
Learning Strategies	Selecting and using training/instructional methods and procedures appropriate for the situation when learning or teaching new things.
Troubleshooting	Determining causes of operating errors and deciding what to do about it.
Reading Comprehension	Understanding written sentences and paragraphs in work related documents.
Technology Design	Generating or adapting equipment and technology to serve user needs.
Operation and Control	Controlling operations of equipment or systems.
Social Perceptiveness	Being aware of others' reactions and understanding why they react as they do.
Persuasion	Persuading others to change their minds or behavior.
Operations Analysis	Analyzing needs and product requirements to create a design.
Operation Monitoring	Watching gauges, dials, or other indicators to make sure a machine is working properly.
Negotiation	Bringing others together and trying to reconcile differences.
Science	Using scientific rules and methods to solve problems.
Systems Evaluation	Identifying measures or indicators of system performance and the actions needed to improve or correct performance, relative to the goals of the system.
Writing	Communicating effectively in writing as appropriate for the needs of the audience.
Systems Analysis	Determining how a system should work and how changes in conditions, operations, and the environment will affect outcomes.
Programming	Writing computer programs for various purposes.

Ability	**Ability Definitions**
Arm-Hand Steadiness	The ability to keep your hand and arm steady while moving your arm or while holding your arm and hand in one position.
Multilimb Coordination	The ability to coordinate two or more limbs (for example, two arms, two legs, or one leg and one arm) while sitting, standing, or lying down. It does not involve performing the activities while the whole body is in motion.
Trunk Strength	The ability to use your abdominal and lower back muscles to support part of the body repeatedly or continuously over time without 'giving out' or fatiguing.
Near Vision	The ability to see details at close range (within a few feet of the observer).
Problem Sensitivity	The ability to tell when something is wrong or is likely to go wrong. It does not involve solving the problem, only recognizing there is a problem.
Information Ordering	The ability to arrange things or actions in a certain order or pattern according to a specific rule or set of rules (e.g., patterns of numbers, letters, words, pictures, mathematical operations).
Manual Dexterity	The ability to quickly move your hand, your hand together with your arm, or your two hands to grasp, manipulate, or assemble objects.

Visualization	The ability to imagine how something will look after it is moved around or when its parts are moved or rearranged.
Deductive Reasoning	The ability to apply general rules to specific problems to produce answers that make sense.
Oral Comprehension	The ability to listen to and understand information and ideas presented through spoken words and sentences.
Static Strength	The ability to exert maximum muscle force to lift, push, pull, or carry objects.
Speech Recognition	The ability to identify and understand the speech of another person.
Finger Dexterity	The ability to make precisely coordinated movements of the fingers of one or both hands to grasp, manipulate, or assemble very small objects.
Dynamic Strength	The ability to exert muscle force repeatedly or continuously over time. This involves muscular endurance and resistance to muscle fatigue.
Originality	The ability to come up with unusual or clever ideas about a given topic or situation, or to develop creative ways to solve a problem.
Control Precision	The ability to quickly and repeatedly adjust the controls of a machine or a vehicle to exact positions.
Oral Expression	The ability to communicate information and ideas in speaking so others will understand.
Speech Clarity	The ability to speak clearly so others can understand you.
Far Vision	The ability to see details at a distance.
Depth Perception	The ability to judge which of several objects is closer or farther away from you, or to judge the distance between you and an object.
Stamina	The ability to exert yourself physically over long periods of time without getting winded or out of breath.
Selective Attention	The ability to concentrate on a task over a period of time without being distracted.
Written Comprehension	The ability to read and understand information and ideas presented in writing.
Extent Flexibility	The ability to bend, stretch, twist, or reach with your body, arms, and/or legs.
Inductive Reasoning	The ability to combine pieces of information to form general rules or conclusions (includes finding a relationship among seemingly unrelated events).
Category Flexibility	The ability to generate or use different sets of rules for combining or grouping things in different ways.
Gross Body Coordination	The ability to coordinate the movement of your arms, legs, and torso together when the whole body is in motion.
Gross Body Equilibrium	The ability to keep or regain your body balance or stay upright when in an unstable position.
Flexibility of Closure	The ability to identify or detect a known pattern (a figure, object, word, or sound) that is hidden in other distracting material.
Perceptual Speed	The ability to quickly and accurately compare similarities and differences among sets of letters, numbers, objects, pictures, or patterns. The things to be compared may be presented at the same time or one after the other. This ability also includes comparing a presented object with a remembered object.
Reaction Time	The ability to quickly respond (with the hand, finger, or foot) to a signal (sound, light, picture) when it appears.
Speed of Limb Movement	The ability to quickly move the arms and legs.
Fluency of Ideas	The ability to come up with a number of ideas about a topic (the number of ideas is important, not their quality, correctness, or creativity).
Auditory Attention	The ability to focus on a single source of sound in the presence of other distracting sounds.
Visual Color Discrimination	The ability to match or detect differences between colors, including shades of color and brightness.
Written Expression	The ability to communicate information and ideas in writing so others will understand.
Wrist-Finger Speed	The ability to make fast, simple, repeated movements of the fingers, hands, and wrists.
Memorization	The ability to remember information such as words, numbers, pictures, and procedures.
Spatial Orientation	The ability to know your location in relation to the environment or to know where other objects are in relation to you.
Explosive Strength	The ability to use short bursts of muscle force to propel oneself (as in jumping or sprinting), or to throw an object.
Response Orientation	The ability to choose quickly between two or more movements in response to two or more different signals (lights, sounds, pictures). It includes the speed with which the correct response is started with the hand, foot, or other body part.

Mathematical Reasoning	The ability to choose the right mathematical methods or formulas to solve a problem.
Glare Sensitivity	The ability to see objects in the presence of glare or bright lighting.
Hearing Sensitivity	The ability to detect or tell the differences between sounds that vary in pitch and loudness.
Speed of Closure	The ability to quickly make sense of, combine, and organize information into meaningful patterns.
Rate Control	The ability to time your movements or the movement of a piece of equipment in anticipation of changes in the speed and/or direction of a moving object or scene.
Time Sharing	The ability to shift back and forth between two or more activities or sources of information (such as speech, sounds, touch, or other sources).
Number Facility	The ability to add, subtract, multiply, or divide quickly and correctly.
Peripheral Vision	The ability to see objects or movement of objects to one's side when the eyes are looking ahead.
Sound Localization	The ability to tell the direction from which a sound originated.
Night Vision	The ability to see under low light conditions.
Dynamic Flexibility	The ability to quickly and repeatedly bend, stretch, twist, or reach out with your body, arms, and/or legs.

Work_Activity	Work_Activity Definitions
Controlling Machines and Processes	Using either control mechanisms or direct physical activity to operate machines or processes (not including computers or vehicles).
Judging the Qualities of Things, Services, or Peop	Assessing the value, importance, or quality of things or people.
Monitor Processes, Materials, or Surroundings	Monitoring and reviewing information from materials, events, or the environment, to detect or assess problems.
Communicating with Supervisors, Peers, or Subordin	Providing information to supervisors, co-workers, and subordinates by telephone, in written form, e-mail, or in person.
Coordinating the Work and Activities of Others	Getting members of a group to work together to accomplish tasks.
Performing General Physical Activities	Performing physical activities that require considerable use of your arms and legs and moving your whole body, such as climbing, lifting, balancing, walking, stooping, and handling of materials.
Scheduling Work and Activities	Scheduling events, programs, and activities, as well as the work of others.
Getting Information	Observing, receiving, and otherwise obtaining information from all relevant sources.
Communicating with Persons Outside Organization	Communicating with people outside the organization, representing the organization to customers, the public, government, and other external sources. This information can be exchanged in person, in writing, or by telephone or e-mail.
Making Decisions and Solving Problems	Analyzing information and evaluating results to choose the best solution and solve problems.
Organizing, Planning, and Prioritizing Work	Developing specific goals and plans to prioritize, organize, and accomplish your work.
Training and Teaching Others	Identifying the educational needs of others, developing formal educational or training programs or classes, and teaching or instructing others.
Inspecting Equipment, Structures, or Material	Inspecting equipment, structures, or materials to identify the cause of errors or other problems or defects.
Thinking Creatively	Developing, designing, or creating new applications, ideas, relationships, systems, or products, including artistic contributions.
Handling and Moving Objects	Using hands and arms in handling, installing, positioning, and moving materials, and manipulating things.
Identifying Objects, Actions, and Events	Identifying information by categorizing, estimating, recognizing differences or similarities, and detecting changes in circumstances or events.
Operating Vehicles, Mechanized Devices, or Equipme	Running, maneuvering, navigating, or driving vehicles or mechanized equipment, such as forklifts, passenger vehicles, aircraft, or water craft.
Updating and Using Relevant Knowledge	Keeping up-to-date technically and applying new knowledge to your job.
Guiding, Directing, and Motivating Subordinates	Providing guidance and direction to subordinates, including setting performance standards and monitoring performance.
Evaluating Information to Determine Compliance wit	Using relevant information and individual judgment to determine whether events or processes comply with laws, regulations, or standards.

Estimating the Quantifiable Characteristics of Pro	Estimating sizes, distances, and quantities; or determining time, costs, resources, or materials needed to perform a work activity.
Repairing and Maintaining Mechanical Equipment	Servicing, repairing, adjusting, and testing machines, devices, moving parts, and equipment that operate primarily on the basis of mechanical (not electronic) principles.
Establishing and Maintaining Interpersonal Relatio	Developing constructive and cooperative working relationships with others, and maintaining them over time.
Developing Objectives and Strategies	Establishing long-range objectives and specifying the strategies and actions to achieve them.
Developing and Building Teams	Encouraging and building mutual trust, respect, and cooperation among team members.
Analyzing Data or Information	Identifying the underlying principles, reasons, or facts of information by breaking down information or data into separate parts.
Interpreting the Meaning of Information for Others	Translating or explaining what information means and how it can be used.
Drafting, Laying Out, and Specifying Technical Dev	Providing documentation, detailed instructions, drawings, or specifications to tell others about how devices, parts, equipment, or structures are to be fabricated, constructed, assembled, modified, maintained, or used.
Documenting/Recording Information	Entering, transcribing, recording, storing, or maintaining information in written or electronic/magnetic form.
Processing Information	Compiling, coding, categorizing, calculating, tabulating, auditing, or verifying information or data.
Coaching and Developing Others	Identifying the developmental needs of others and coaching, mentoring, or otherwise helping others to improve their knowledge or skills.
Resolving Conflicts and Negotiating with Others	Handling complaints, settling disputes, and resolving grievances and conflicts, or otherwise negotiating with others.
Performing for or Working Directly with the Public	Performing for people or dealing directly with the public. This includes serving customers in restaurants and stores, and receiving clients or guests.
Provide Consultation and Advice to Others	Providing guidance and expert advice to management or other groups on technical, systems-, or process-related topics.
Assisting and Caring for Others	Providing personal assistance, medical attention, emotional support, or other personal care to others such as coworkers, customers, or patients.
Repairing and Maintaining Electronic Equipment	Servicing, repairing, calibrating, regulating, fine-tuning, or testing machines, devices, and equipment that operate primarily on the basis of electrical or electronic (not mechanical) principles.
Performing Administrative Activities	Performing day-to-day administrative tasks such as maintaining information files and processing paperwork.
Interacting With Computers	Using computers and computer systems (including hardware and software) to program, write software, set up functions, enter data, or process information.
Selling or Influencing Others	Convincing others to buy merchandise/goods or to otherwise change their minds or actions.
Staffing Organizational Units	Recruiting, interviewing, selecting, hiring, and promoting employees in an organization.
Monitoring and Controlling Resources	Monitoring and controlling resources and overseeing the spending of money.

Work_Context	Work_Context Definitions
Spend Time Standing	How much does this job require standing?
Spend Time Using Your Hands to Handle, Control, or	How much does this job require using your hands to handle, control, or feel objects, tools or controls?
Wear Common Protective or Safety Equipment such as	How much does this job require wearing common protective or safety equipment such as safety shoes, glasses, gloves, hard hats or live jackets?
Face-to-Face Discussions	How often do you have to have face-to-face discussions with individuals or teams in this job?
Exposed to Hazardous Equipment	How often does this job require exposure to hazardous equipment?
Sounds, Noise Levels Are Distracting or Uncomforta	How often does this job require working exposed to sounds and noise levels that are distracting or uncomfortable?
Importance of Being Exact or Accurate	How important is being very exact or highly accurate in performing this job?
Freedom to Make Decisions	How much decision making freedom, without supervision, does the job offer?
Outdoors, Exposed to Weather	How often does this job require working outdoors, exposed to all weather conditions?
Telephone	How often do you have telephone conversations in this job?

1026

Work With Work Group or Team	How important is it to work with others in a group or team in this job?
Structured versus Unstructured Work	To what extent is this job structured for the worker, rather than allowing the worker to determine tasks, priorities, and goals?
Frequency of Decision Making	How frequently is the worker required to make decisions that affect other people, the financial resources, and/or the image and reputation of the organization?
Physical Proximity	To what extent does this job require the worker to perform job tasks in close physical proximity to other people?
Contact With Others	How much does this job require the worker to be in contact with others (face-to-face, by telephone, or otherwise) in order to perform it?
Impact of Decisions on Co-workers or Company Resul	How do the decisions an employee makes impact the results of co-workers, clients or the company?
Level of Competition	To what extent does this job require the worker to compete or to be aware of competitive pressures?
Coordinate or Lead Others	How important is it to coordinate or lead others in accomplishing work activities in this job?
Spend Time Walking and Running	How much does this job require walking and running?
Exposed to Contaminants	How often does this job require working exposed to contaminants (such as pollutants, gases, dust or odors)?
Exposed to Minor Burns, Cuts, Bites, or Stings	How often does this job require exposure to minor burns, cuts, bites, or stings?
Time Pressure	How often does this job require the worker to meet strict deadlines?
Responsibility for Outcomes and Results	How responsible is the worker for work outcomes and results of other workers?
Very Hot or Cold Temperatures	How often does this job require working in very hot (above 90 F degrees) or very cold (below 32 F degrees) temperatures?
Exposed to High Places	How often does this job require exposure to high places?
Responsible for Others' Health and Safety	How much responsibility is there for the health and safety of others in this job?
Spend Time Bending or Twisting the Body	How much does this job require bending or twisting your body?
Spend Time Making Repetitive Motions	How much does this job require making repetitive motions?
Spend Time Kneeling, Crouching, Stooping, or Crawl	How much does this job require kneeling, crouching, stooping, or crawling?
Deal With External Customers	How important is it to work with external customers or the public in this job?
Outdoors, Under Cover	How often does this job require working outdoors, under cover (e.g., structure with roof but no walls)?
Indoors, Not Environmentally Controlled	How often does this job require working indoors in non-controlled environmental conditions (e.g., warehouse without heat)?
Cramped Work Space, Awkward Positions	How often does this job require working in cramped work spaces that requires getting into awkward positions?
Extremely Bright or Inadequate Lighting	How often does this job require working in extremely bright or inadequate lighting conditions?
In an Enclosed Vehicle or Equipment	How often does this job require working in a closed vehicle or equipment (e.g., car)?
Spend Time Climbing Ladders, Scaffolds, or Poles	How much does this job require climbing ladders, scaffolds, or poles?
In an Open Vehicle or Equipment	How often does this job require working in an open vehicle or equipment (e.g., tractor)?
Letters and Memos	How often does the job require written letters and memos?
Importance of Repeating Same Tasks	How important is repeating the same physical activities (e.g., key entry) or mental activities (e.g., checking entries in a ledger) over and over, without stopping, to performing this job?
Frequency of Conflict Situations	How often are there conflict situations the employee has to face in this job?
Spend Time Keeping or Regaining Balance	How much does this job require keeping or regaining your balance?
Deal With Unpleasant or Angry People	How frequently does the worker have to deal with unpleasant, angry, or discourteous individuals as part of the job requirements?
Indoors, Environmentally Controlled	How often does this job require working indoors in environmentally controlled conditions?
Wear Specialized Protective or Safety Equipment su	How much does this job require wearing specialized protective or safety equipment such as breathing apparatus, safety harness, full protection suits, or radiation protection?
Consequence of Error	How serious would the result usually be if the worker made a mistake that was not readily correctable?

Pace Determined by Speed of Equipment	How important is it to this job that the pace is determined by the speed of equipment or machinery? (This does not refer to keeping busy at all times on this job.)
Degree of Automation	How automated is the job?
Public Speaking	How often do you have to perform public speaking in this job?
Electronic Mail	How often do you use electronic mail in this job?
Exposed to Disease or Infections	How often does this job require exposure to disease/infections?
Exposed to Whole Body Vibration	How often does this job require exposure to whole body vibration (e.g., operate a jackhammer)?
Deal With Physically Aggressive People	How frequently does this job require the worker to deal with physical aggression of violent individuals?
Spend Time Sitting	How much does this job require sitting?
Exposed to Hazardous Conditions	How often does this job require exposure to hazardous conditions?
Exposed to Radiation	How often does this job require exposure to radiation?

Job Zone Component	Job Zone Component Definitions
Title	Job Zone Three: Medium Preparation Needed
Overall Experience	Previous work-related skill, knowledge, or experience is required for these occupations. For example, an electrician must have completed three or four years of apprenticeship or several years of vocational training, and often must have passed a licensing exam, in order to perform the job.
Job Training	Employees in these occupations usually need one or two years of training involving both on-the-job experience and informal training with experienced workers.
Job Zone Examples	These occupations usually involve using communication and organizational skills to coordinate, supervise, manage, or train others to accomplish goals. Examples include dental assistants, electricians, fish and game wardens, legal secretaries, personnel recruiters, and recreation workers.
SVP Range	(6.0 to < 7.0)
Education	Most occupations in this zone require training in vocational schools, related on-the-job experience, or an associate's degree. Some may require a bachelor's degree.

Work_Styles	Work_Styles Definitions
Attention to Detail	Job requires being careful about detail and thorough in completing work tasks.
Dependability	Job requires being reliable, responsible, and dependable, and fulfilling obligations.
Persistence	Job requires persistence in the face of obstacles.
Cooperation	Job requires being pleasant with others on the job and displaying a good-natured, cooperative attitude.
Integrity	Job requires being honest and ethical.
Adaptability/Flexibility	Job requires being open to change (positive or negative) and to considerable variety in the workplace.
Analytical Thinking	Job requires analyzing information and using logic to address work-related issues and problems.
Innovation	Job requires creativity and alternative thinking to develop new ideas for and answers to work-related problems.
Initiative	Job requires a willingness to take on responsibilities and challenges.
Self Control	Job requires maintaining composure, keeping emotions in check, controlling anger, and avoiding aggressive behavior, even in very difficult situations.
Independence	Job requires developing one's own ways of doing things, guiding oneself with little or no supervision, and depending on oneself to get things done.
Stress Tolerance	Job requires accepting criticism and dealing calmly and effectively with high stress situations.
Achievement/Effort	Job requires establishing and maintaining personally challenging achievement goals and exerting effort toward mastering tasks.
Concern for Others	Job requires being sensitive to others' needs and feelings and being understanding and helpful on the job.
Leadership	Job requires a willingness to lead, take charge, and offer opinions and direction.
Social Orientation	Job requires preferring to work with others rather than alone, and being personally connected with others on the job.

47-2031.02 - Rough Carpenters

Build rough wooden structures, such as concrete forms, scaffolds, tunnel, bridge, or sewer supports, billboard signs, and temporary frame shelters, according to sketches, blueprints, or oral instructions.

Tasks

1) Mark cutting lines on materials, using pencil and scriber.

2) Bore boltholes in timber, masonry or concrete walls, using power drill.

3) Erect forms, framework, scaffolds, hoists, roof supports, or chutes, using hand tools, plumb rule, and level.

4) Study blueprints and diagrams to determine dimensions of structure or form to be constructed.

5) Install rough door and window frames, subflooring, fixtures, or temporary supports in structures undergoing construction or repair.

6) Fabricate parts, using woodworking and metalworking machines.

7) Examine structural timbers and supports to detect decay, and replace timbers as required, using hand tools, nuts, and bolts.

8) Dig or direct digging of post holes and set poles to support structures.

9) Build chutes for pouring concrete.

10) Build sleds from logs and timbers for use in hauling camp buildings and machinery through wooded areas.

11) Measure materials or distances, using square, measuring tape, or rule to lay out work.

12) Cut or saw boards, timbers, or plywood to required size, using handsaw, power saw, or woodworking machine.

13) Assemble and fasten material together to construct wood or metal framework of structure, using bolts, nails, or screws.

Knowledge	Knowledge Definitions
Building and Construction	Knowledge of materials, methods, and the tools involved in the construction or repair of houses, buildings, or other structures such as highways and roads.
Design	Knowledge of design techniques, tools, and principles involved in production of precision technical plans, blueprints, drawings, and models.
Mathematics	Knowledge of arithmetic, algebra, geometry, calculus, statistics, and their applications.
Mechanical	Knowledge of machines and tools, including their designs, uses, repair, and maintenance.
Engineering and Technology	Knowledge of the practical application of engineering science and technology. This includes applying principles, techniques, procedures, and equipment to the design and production of various goods and services.
Production and Processing	Knowledge of raw materials, production processes, quality control, costs, and other techniques for maximizing the effective manufacture and distribution of goods.
English Language	Knowledge of the structure and content of the English language including the meaning and spelling of words, rules of composition, and grammar.
Public Safety and Security	Knowledge of relevant equipment, policies, procedures, and strategies to promote effective local, state, or national security operations for the protection of people, data, property, and institutions.
Administration and Management	Knowledge of business and management principles involved in strategic planning, resource allocation, human resources modeling, leadership technique, production methods, and coordination of people and resources.
Education and Training	Knowledge of principles and methods for curriculum and training design, teaching and instruction for individuals and groups, and the measurement of training effects.
Law and Government	Knowledge of laws, legal codes, court procedures, precedents, government regulations, executive orders, agency rules, and the democratic political process.
Psychology	Knowledge of human behavior and performance; individual differences in ability, personality, and interests; learning and motivation; psychological research methods; and the assessment and treatment of behavioral and affective disorders.
Physics	Knowledge and prediction of physical principles, laws, their interrelationships, and applications to understanding fluid, material, and atmospheric dynamics, and mechanical, electrical, atomic and sub-atomic structures and processes.
Customer and Personal Service	Knowledge of principles and processes for providing customer and personal services. This includes customer needs assessment, meeting quality standards for services, and evaluation of customer satisfaction.
Chemistry	Knowledge of the chemical composition, structure, and properties of substances and of the chemical processes and transformations that they undergo. This includes uses of chemicals and their interactions, danger signs, production techniques, and disposal methods.
Transportation	Knowledge of principles and methods for moving people or goods by air, rail, sea, or road, including the relative costs and benefits.
Personnel and Human Resources	Knowledge of principles and procedures for personnel recruitment, selection, training, compensation and benefits, labor relations and negotiation, and personnel information systems.
Economics and Accounting	Knowledge of economic and accounting principles and practices, the financial markets, banking and the analysis and reporting of financial data.
Telecommunications	Knowledge of transmission, broadcasting, switching, control, and operation of telecommunications systems.
Clerical	Knowledge of administrative and clerical procedures and systems such as word processing, managing files and records, stenography and transcription, designing forms, and other office procedures and terminology.
Sales and Marketing	Knowledge of principles and methods for showing, promoting, and selling products or services. This includes marketing strategy and tactics, product demonstration, sales techniques, and sales control systems.
Medicine and Dentistry	Knowledge of the information and techniques needed to diagnose and treat human injuries, diseases, and deformities. This includes symptoms, treatment alternatives, drug properties and interactions, and preventive health-care measures.
Biology	Knowledge of plant and animal organisms, their tissues, cells, functions, interdependencies, and interactions with each other and the environment.
Sociology and Anthropology	Knowledge of group behavior and dynamics, societal trends and influences, human migrations, ethnicity, cultures and their history and origins.
Computers and Electronics	Knowledge of circuit boards, processors, chips, electronic equipment, and computer hardware and software, including applications and programming.
History and Archeology	Knowledge of historical events and their causes, indicators, and effects on civilizations and cultures.
Philosophy and Theology	Knowledge of different philosophical systems and religions. This includes their basic principles, values, ethics, ways of thinking, customs, practices, and their impact on human culture.
Fine Arts	Knowledge of the theory and techniques required to compose, produce, and perform works of music, dance, visual arts, drama, and sculpture.
Therapy and Counseling	Knowledge of principles, methods, and procedures for diagnosis, treatment, and rehabilitation of physical and mental dysfunctions, and for career counseling and guidance.
Communications and Media	Knowledge of media production, communication, and dissemination techniques and methods. This includes alternative ways to inform and entertain via written, oral, and visual media.
Geography	Knowledge of principles and methods for describing the features of land, sea, and air masses, including their physical characteristics, locations, interrelationships, and distribution of plant, animal, and human life.
Foreign Language	Knowledge of the structure and content of a foreign (non-English) language including the meaning and spelling of words, rules of composition and grammar, and pronunciation.
Food Production	Knowledge of techniques and equipment for planting, growing, and harvesting food products (both plant and animal) for consumption, including storage/handling techniques.

Skills	Skills Definitions
Active Listening	Giving full attention to what other people are saying, taking time to understand the points being made, asking questions as appropriate, and not interrupting at inappropriate times.

Mathematics	Using mathematics to solve problems.
Equipment Selection	Determining the kind of tools and equipment needed to do a job.
Reading Comprehension	Understanding written sentences and paragraphs in work related documents.
Coordination	Adjusting actions in relation to others' actions.
Installation	Installing equipment, machines, wiring, or programs to meet specifications.
Management of Personnel Resources	Motivating, developing, and directing people as they work, identifying the best people for the job.
Repairing	Repairing machines or systems using the needed tools.
Critical Thinking	Using logic and reasoning to identify the strengths and weaknesses of alternative solutions, conclusions or approaches to problems.
Speaking	Talking to others to convey information effectively.
Instructing	Teaching others how to do something.
Time Management	Managing one's own time and the time of others.
Complex Problem Solving	Identifying complex problems and reviewing related information to develop and evaluate options and implement solutions.
Equipment Maintenance	Performing routine maintenance on equipment and determining when and what kind of maintenance is needed.
Management of Material Resources	Obtaining and seeing to the appropriate use of equipment, facilities, and materials needed to do certain work.
Troubleshooting	Determining causes of operating errors and deciding what to do about it.
Active Learning	Understanding the implications of new information for both current and future problem-solving and decision-making.
Quality Control Analysis	Conducting tests and inspections of products, services, or processes to evaluate quality or performance.
Writing	Communicating effectively in writing as appropriate for the needs of the audience.
Judgment and Decision Making	Considering the relative costs and benefits of potential actions to choose the most appropriate one.
Social Perceptiveness	Being aware of others' reactions and understanding why they react as they do.
Learning Strategies	Selecting and using training/instructional methods and procedures appropriate for the situation when learning or teaching new things.
Technology Design	Generating or adapting equipment and technology to serve user needs.
Monitoring	Monitoring/Assessing performance of yourself, other individuals, or organizations to make improvements or take corrective action.
Operation and Control	Controlling operations of equipment or systems.
Operations Analysis	Analyzing needs and product requirements to create a design.
Persuasion	Persuading others to change their minds or behavior.
Negotiation	Bringing others together and trying to reconcile differences.
Systems Analysis	Determining how a system should work and how changes in conditions, operations, and the environment will affect outcomes.
Service Orientation	Actively looking for ways to help people.
Management of Financial Resources	Determining how money will be spent to get the work done, and accounting for these expenditures.
Operation Monitoring	Watching gauges, dials, or other indicators to make sure a machine is working properly.
Science	Using scientific rules and methods to solve problems.
Systems Evaluation	Identifying measures or indicators of system performance and the actions needed to improve or correct performance, relative to the goals of the system.
Programming	Writing computer programs for various purposes.

Ability	Ability Definitions
Problem Sensitivity	The ability to tell when something is wrong or is likely to go wrong. It does not involve solving the problem, only recognizing there is a problem.
Manual Dexterity	The ability to quickly move your hand, your hand together with your arm, or your two hands to grasp, manipulate, or assemble objects.
Deductive Reasoning	The ability to apply general rules to specific problems to produce answers that make sense.
Trunk Strength	The ability to use your abdominal and lower back muscles to support part of the body repeatedly or continuously over time without 'giving out' or fatiguing.
Arm-Hand Steadiness	The ability to keep your hand and arm steady while moving your arm or while holding your arm and hand in one position.

Near Vision	The ability to see details at close range (within a few feet of the observer).
Oral Comprehension	The ability to listen to and understand information and ideas presented through spoken words and sentences.
Information Ordering	The ability to arrange things or actions in a certain order or pattern according to a specific rule or set of rules (e.g., patterns of numbers, letters, words, pictures, mathematical operations).
Inductive Reasoning	The ability to combine pieces of information to form general rules or conclusions (includes finding a relationship among seemingly unrelated events).
Static Strength	The ability to exert maximum muscle force to lift, push, pull, or carry objects.
Depth Perception	The ability to judge which of several objects is closer or farther away from you, or to judge the distance between you and an object.
Far Vision	The ability to see details at a distance.
Visualization	The ability to imagine how something will look after it is moved around or when its parts are moved or rearranged.
Speech Clarity	The ability to speak clearly so others can understand you.
Selective Attention	The ability to concentrate on a task over a period of time without being distracted.
Extent Flexibility	The ability to bend, stretch, twist, or reach with your body, arms, and/or legs.
Speech Recognition	The ability to identify and understand the speech of another person.
Category Flexibility	The ability to generate or use different sets of rules for combining or grouping things in different ways.
Oral Expression	The ability to communicate information and ideas in speaking so others will understand.
Written Comprehension	The ability to read and understand information and ideas presented in writing.
Multilimb Coordination	The ability to coordinate two or more limbs (for example, two arms, two legs, or one leg and one arm) while sitting, standing, or lying down. It does not involve performing the activities while the whole body is in motion.
Control Precision	The ability to quickly and repeatedly adjust the controls of a machine or a vehicle to exact positions.
Finger Dexterity	The ability to make precisely coordinated movements of the fingers of one or both hands to grasp, manipulate, or assemble very small objects.
Hearing Sensitivity	The ability to detect or tell the differences between sounds that vary in pitch and loudness.
Stamina	The ability to exert yourself physically over long periods of time without getting winded or out of breath.
Perceptual Speed	The ability to quickly and accurately compare similarities and differences among sets of letters, numbers, objects, pictures, or patterns. The things to be compared may be presented at the same time or one after the other. This ability also includes comparing a presented object with a remembered object.
Fluency of Ideas	The ability to come up with a number of ideas about a topic (the number of ideas is important, not their quality, correctness, or creativity).
Gross Body Equilibrium	The ability to keep or regain your body balance or stay upright when in an unstable position.
Dynamic Strength	The ability to exert muscle force repeatedly or continuously over time. This involves muscular endurance and resistance to muscle fatigue.
Gross Body Coordination	The ability to coordinate the movement of your arms, legs, and torso together when the whole body is in motion.
Originality	The ability to come up with unusual or clever ideas about a given topic or situation, or to develop creative ways to solve a problem.
Reaction Time	The ability to quickly respond (with the hand, finger, or foot) to a signal (sound, light, picture) when it appears.
Time Sharing	The ability to shift back and forth between two or more activities or sources of information (such as speech, sounds, touch, or other sources).
Flexibility of Closure	The ability to identify or detect a known pattern (a figure, object, word, or sound) that is hidden in other distracting material.
Speed of Closure	The ability to quickly make sense of, combine, and organize information into meaningful patterns.
Auditory Attention	The ability to focus on a single source of sound in the presence of other distracting sounds.
Visual Color Discrimination	The ability to match or detect differences between colors, including shades of color and brightness.
Wrist-Finger Speed	The ability to make fast, simple, repeated movements of the fingers, hands, and wrists.

Number Facility	The ability to add, subtract, multiply, or divide quickly and correctly.
Written Expression	The ability to communicate information and ideas in writing so others will understand.
Glare Sensitivity	The ability to see objects in the presence of glare or bright lighting.
Response Orientation	The ability to choose quickly between two or more movements in response to two or more different signals (lights, sounds, pictures). It includes the speed with which the correct response is started with the hand, foot, or other body part.
Memorization	The ability to remember information such as words, numbers, pictures, and procedures.
Speed of Limb Movement	The ability to quickly move the arms and legs.
Mathematical Reasoning	The ability to choose the right mathematical methods or formulas to solve a problem.
Rate Control	The ability to time your movements or the movement of a piece of equipment in anticipation of changes in the speed and/or direction of a moving object or scene.
Sound Localization	The ability to tell the direction from which a sound originated.
Peripheral Vision	The ability to see objects or movement of objects to one's side when the eyes are looking ahead.
Spatial Orientation	The ability to know your location in relation to the environment or to know where other objects are in relation to you.
Explosive Strength	The ability to use short bursts of muscle force to propel oneself (as in jumping or sprinting), or to throw an object.
Night Vision	The ability to see under low light conditions.
Dynamic Flexibility	The ability to quickly and repeatedly bend, stretch, twist, or reach out with your body, arms, and/or legs.

Work_Activity	**Work_Activity Definitions**
Getting Information	Observing, receiving, and otherwise obtaining information from all relevant sources.
Inspecting Equipment, Structures, or Material	Inspecting equipment, structures, or materials to identify the cause of errors or other problems or defects.
Handling and Moving Objects	Using hands and arms in handling, installing, positioning, and moving materials, and manipulating things.
Controlling Machines and Processes	Using either control mechanisms or direct physical activity to operate machines or processes (not including computers or vehicles).
Communicating with Supervisors, Peers, or Subordin	Providing information to supervisors, co-workers, and subordinates by telephone, in written form, e-mail, or in person.
Performing General Physical Activities	Performing physical activities that require considerable use of your arms and legs and moving your whole body, such as climbing, lifting, balancing, walking, stooping, and handling of materials.
Making Decisions and Solving Problems	Analyzing information and evaluating results to choose the best solution and solve problems.
Coordinating the Work and Activities of Others	Getting members of a group to work together to accomplish tasks.
Monitor Processes, Materials, or Surroundings	Monitoring and reviewing information from materials, events, or the environment, to detect or assess problems.
Identifying Objects, Actions, and Events	Identifying information by categorizing, estimating, recognizing differences or similarities, and detecting changes in circumstances or events.
Evaluating Information to Determine Compliance wit	Using relevant information and individual judgment to determine whether events or processes comply with laws, regulations, or standards.
Developing and Building Teams	Encouraging and building mutual trust, respect, and cooperation among team members.
Operating Vehicles, Mechanized Devices, or Equipme	Running, maneuvering, navigating, or driving vehicles or mechanized equipment, such as forklifts, passenger vehicles, aircraft, or water craft.
Organizing, Planning, and Prioritizing Work	Developing specific goals and plans to prioritize, organize, and accomplish your work.
Interpreting the Meaning of Information for Others	Translating or explaining what information means and how it can be used.
Establishing and Maintaining Interpersonal Relatio	Developing constructive and cooperative working relationships with others, and maintaining them over time.
Processing Information	Compiling, coding, categorizing, calculating, tabulating, auditing, or verifying information or data.
Communicating with Persons Outside Organization	Communicating with people outside the organization, representing the organization to customers, the public, government, and other external sources. This information can be exchanged in person, in writing, or by telephone or e-mail.

Judging the Qualities of Things, Services, or Peop	Assessing the value, importance, or quality of things or people.
Coaching and Developing Others	Identifying the developmental needs of others and coaching, mentoring, or otherwise helping others to improve their knowledge or skills.
Estimating the Quantifiable Characteristics of Pro	Estimating sizes, distances, and quantities; or determining time, costs, resources, or materials needed to perform a work activity.
Scheduling Work and Activities	Scheduling events, programs, and activities, as well as the work of others.
Drafting, Laying Out, and Specifying Technical Dev	Providing documentation, detailed instructions, drawings, or specifications to tell others about how devices, parts, equipment, or structures are to be fabricated, constructed, assembled, modified, maintained, or used.
Guiding, Directing, and Motivating Subordinates	Providing guidance and direction to subordinates, including setting performance standards and monitoring performance.
Resolving Conflicts and Negotiating with Others	Handling complaints, settling disputes, and resolving grievances and conflicts, or otherwise negotiating with others.
Training and Teaching Others	Identifying the educational needs of others, developing formal educational or training programs or classes, and teaching or instructing others.
Updating and Using Relevant Knowledge	Keeping up-to-date technically and applying new knowledge to your job.
Analyzing Data or Information	Identifying the underlying principles, reasons, or facts of information by breaking down information or data into separate parts.
Thinking Creatively	Developing, designing, or creating new applications, ideas, relationships, systems, or products, including artistic contributions.
Developing Objectives and Strategies	Establishing long-range objectives and specifying the strategies and actions to achieve them.
Monitoring and Controlling Resources	Monitoring and controlling resources and overseeing the spending of money.
Assisting and Caring for Others	Providing personal assistance, medical attention, emotional support, or other personal care to others such as coworkers, customers, or patients.
Performing for or Working Directly with the Public	Performing for people or dealing directly with the public. This includes serving customers in restaurants and stores, and receiving clients or guests.
Repairing and Maintaining Mechanical Equipment	Servicing, repairing, adjusting, and testing machines, devices, moving parts, and equipment that operate primarily on the basis of mechanical (not electronic) principles.
Performing Administrative Activities	Performing day-to-day administrative tasks such as maintaining information files and processing paperwork.
Documenting/Recording Information	Entering, transcribing, recording, storing, or maintaining information in written or electronic/magnetic form.
Selling or Influencing Others	Convincing others to buy merchandise/goods or to otherwise change their minds or actions.
Staffing Organizational Units	Recruiting, interviewing, selecting, hiring, and promoting employees in an organization.
Provide Consultation and Advice to Others	Providing guidance and expert advice to management or other groups on technical, systems-, or process-related topics.
Repairing and Maintaining Electronic Equipment	Servicing, repairing, calibrating, regulating, fine-tuning, or testing machines, devices, and equipment that operate primarily on the basis of electrical or electronic (not mechanical) principles.
Interacting With Computers	Using computers and computer systems (including hardware and software) to program, write software, set up functions, enter data, or process information.

Work_Context	**Work_Context Definitions**
Contact With Others	How much does this job require the worker to be in contact with others (face-to-face, by telephone, or otherwise) in order to perform it?
Face-to-Face Discussions	How often do you have to have face-to-face discussions with individuals or teams in this job?
Spend Time Standing	How much does this job require standing?
Wear Common Protective or Safety Equipment such as	How much does this job require wearing common protective or safety equipment such as safety shoes, glasses, gloves, hard hats or live jackets?
Spend Time Using Your Hands to Handle, Control, or	How much does this job require using your hands to handle, control, or feel objects, tools or controls?
Very Hot or Cold Temperatures	How often does this job require working in very hot (above 90 F degrees) or very cold (below 32 F degrees) temperatures?
Freedom to Make Decisions	How much decision making freedom, without supervision, does the job offer?

Outdoors, Exposed to Weather	How often does this job require working outdoors, exposed to all weather conditions?
Telephone	How often do you have telephone conversations in this job?
Sounds, Noise Levels Are Distracting or Uncomforta	How often does this job require working exposed to sounds and noise levels that are distracting or uncomfortable?
Structured versus Unstructured Work	To what extent is this job structured for the worker, rather than allowing the worker to determine tasks, priorities, and goals?
Responsible for Others' Health and Safety	How much responsibility is there for the health and safety of others in this job?
Responsibility for Outcomes and Results	How responsible is the worker for work outcomes and results of other workers?
Exposed to Contaminants	How often does this job require working exposed to contaminants (such as pollutants, gases, dust or odors)?
Work With Work Group or Team	How important is it to work with others in a group or team in this job?
Importance of Being Exact or Accurate	How important is being very exact or highly accurate in performing this job?
Physical Proximity	To what extent does this job require the worker to perform job tasks in close physical proximity to other people?
Extremely Bright or Inadequate Lighting	How often does this job require working in extremely bright or inadequate lighting conditions?
Exposed to High Places	How often does this job require exposure to high places?
Frequency of Decision Making	How frequently is the worker required to make decisions that affect other people, the financial resources, and/or the image and reputation of the organization?
Impact of Decisions on Co-workers or Company Resul	How do the decisions an employee makes impact the results of co-workers, clients or the company?
Level of Competition	To what extent does this job require the worker to compete or to be aware of competitive pressures?
Indoors, Not Environmentally Controlled	How often does this job require working indoors in non-controlled environmental conditions (e.g., warehouse without heat)?
Exposed to Hazardous Equipment	How often does this job require exposure to hazardous equipment?
Coordinate or Lead Others	How important is it to coordinate or lead others in accomplishing work activities in this job?
Cramped Work Space, Awkward Positions	How often does this job require working in cramped work spaces that requires getting into awkward positions?
Spend Time Walking and Running	How much does this job require walking and running?
Spend Time Bending or Twisting the Body	How much does this job require bending or twisting your body?
Time Pressure	How often does this job require the worker to meet strict deadlines?
Deal With External Customers	How important is it to work with external customers or the public in this job?
Exposed to Minor Burns, Cuts, Bites, or Stings	How often does this job require exposure to minor burns, cuts, bites, or stings?
Spend Time Making Repetitive Motions	How much does this job require making repetitive motions?
Spend Time Climbing Ladders, Scaffolds, or Poles	How much does this job require climbing ladders, scaffolds, or poles?
Spend Time Kneeling, Crouching, Stooping, or Crawl	How much does this job require kneeling, crouching, stooping or crawling?
Outdoors, Under Cover	How often does this job require working outdoors, under cover (e.g., structure with roof but no walls)?
Frequency of Conflict Situations	How often are there conflict situations the employee has to face in this job?
Importance of Repeating Same Tasks	How important is repeating the same physical activities (e.g., key entry) or mental activities (e.g., checking entries in a ledger) over and over, without stopping, to performing this job?
Deal With Unpleasant or Angry People	How frequently does the worker have to deal with unpleasant, angry, or discourteous individuals as part of the job requirements?
In an Enclosed Vehicle or Equipment	How often does this job require working in a closed vehicle or equipment (e.g., car)?
Indoors, Environmentally Controlled	How often does this job require working indoors in environmentally controlled conditions?
Letters and Memos	How often does the job require written letters and memos?
In an Open Vehicle or Equipment	How often does this job require working in an open vehicle or equipment (e.g., tractor)?
Exposed to Hazardous Conditions	How often does this job require exposure to hazardous conditions?

Wear Specialized Protective or Safety Equipment su	How much does this job require wearing specialized protective or safety equipment such as breathing apparatus, safety harness, full protection suits, or radiation protection?
Consequence of Error	How serious would the result usually be if the worker made a mistake that was not readily correctable?
Exposed to Whole Body Vibration	How often does this job require exposure to whole body vibration (e.g., operate a jackhammer)?
Electronic Mail	How often do you use electronic mail in this job?
Spend Time Keeping or Regaining Balance	How much does this job require keeping or regaining your balance?
Spend Time Sitting	How much does this job require sitting?
Pace Determined by Speed of Equipment	How important is it to this job that the pace is determined by the speed of equipment or machinery? (This does not refer to keeping busy at all times on this job.)
Degree of Automation	How automated is the job?
Public Speaking	How often do you have to perform public speaking in this job?
Deal With Physically Aggressive People	How frequently does this job require the worker to deal with physical aggression of violent individuals?
Exposed to Radiation	How often does this job require exposure to radiation?
Exposed to Disease or Infections	How often does this job require exposure to disease/infections?

Job Zone Component

Job Zone Component	Job Zone Component Definitions
Title	Job Zone Two: Some Preparation Needed
Overall Experience	Some previous work-related skill, knowledge, or experience may be helpful in these occupations, but usually is not needed. For example, a drywall installer might benefit from experience installing drywall, but an inexperienced person could still learn to be an installer with little difficulty.
Job Training	Employees in these occupations need anywhere from a few months to one year of working with experienced employees.
Job Zone Examples	These occupations often involve using your knowledge and skills to help others. Examples include drywall installers, fire inspectors, flight attendants, pharmacy technicians, salespersons (retail), and tellers.
SVP Range	(4.0 to < 6.0)
Education	These occupations usually require a high school diploma and may require some vocational training or job-related course work. In some cases, an associate's or bachelor's degree could be needed.

Work_Styles	Work_Styles Definitions
Dependability	Job requires being reliable, responsible, and dependable, and fulfilling obligations.
Attention to Detail	Job requires being careful about detail and thorough in completing work tasks.
Integrity	Job requires being honest and ethical.
Initiative	Job requires a willingness to take on responsibilities and challenges.
Stress Tolerance	Job requires accepting criticism and dealing calmly and effectively with high stress situations.
Self Control	Job requires maintaining composure, keeping emotions in check, controlling anger, and avoiding aggressive behavior, even in very difficult situations.
Persistence	Job requires persistence in the face of obstacles.
Independence	Job requires developing one's own ways of doing things, guiding oneself with little or no supervision, and depending on oneself to get things done.
Adaptability/Flexibility	Job requires being open to change (positive or negative) and to considerable variety in the workplace.
Analytical Thinking	Job requires analyzing information and using logic to address work-related issues and problems.
Cooperation	Job requires being pleasant with others on the job and displaying a good-natured, cooperative attitude.
Leadership	Job requires a willingness to lead, take charge, and offer opinions and direction.
Achievement/Effort	Job requires establishing and maintaining personally challenging achievement goals and exerting effort toward mastering tasks.
Innovation	Job requires creativity and alternative thinking to develop new ideas for and answers to work-related problems.
Concern for Others	Job requires being sensitive to others' needs and feelings and being understanding and helpful on the job.
Social Orientation	Job requires preferring to work with others rather than alone, and being personally connected with others on the job.

47-2041.00 - Carpet Installers

Lay and install carpet from rolls or blocks on floors. Install padding and trim flooring materials.

Tasks

1) Nail tack strips around area to be carpeted or use old strips to attach edges of new carpet.

2) Plan the layout of the carpet, allowing for expected traffic patterns and placing seams for best appearance and longest wear.

3) Stretch carpet to align with walls and ensure a smooth surface, and press carpet in place over tack strips or use staples, tape, tacks or glue to hold carpet in place.

4) Measure, cut and install tackless strips along the baseboard or wall.

5) Roll out, measure, mark, and cut carpeting to size with a carpet knife, following floor sketches and allowing extra carpet for final fitting.

6) Move furniture from area to be carpeted and remove old carpet and padding.

7) Join edges of carpet and seam edges where necessary, by sewing or by using tape with glue and heated carpet iron.

8) Take measurements and study floor sketches to calculate the area to be carpeted and the amount of material needed.

9) Draw building diagrams and record dimensions.

10) Cut and bind material.

11) Inspect the surface to be covered to determine its condition, and correct any imperfections that might show through carpet or cause carpet to wear unevenly.

12) Install carpet on some floors using adhesive, following prescribed method.

13) Cut carpet padding to size and install padding, following prescribed method.

14) Cut and trim carpet to fit along wall edges, openings, and projections, finishing the edges with a wall trimmer.

Knowledge	Knowledge Definitions
Customer and Personal Service	Knowledge of principles and processes for providing customer and personal services. This includes customer needs assessment, meeting quality standards for services, and evaluation of customer satisfaction.
Mathematics	Knowledge of arithmetic, algebra, geometry, calculus, statistics, and their applications.
Public Safety and Security	Knowledge of relevant equipment, policies, procedures, and strategies to promote effective local, state, or national security operations for the protection of people, data, property, and institutions.
Mechanical	Knowledge of machines and tools, including their designs, uses, repair, and maintenance.
English Language	Knowledge of the structure and content of the English language including the meaning and spelling of words, rules of composition, and grammar.
Production and Processing	Knowledge of raw materials, production processes, quality control, costs, and other techniques for maximizing the effective manufacture and distribution of goods.
Design	Knowledge of design techniques, tools, and principles involved in production of precision technical plans, blueprints, drawings, and models.
Building and Construction	Knowledge of materials, methods, and the tools involved in the construction or repair of houses, buildings, or other structures such as highways and roads.
Sales and Marketing	Knowledge of principles and methods for showing, promoting, and selling products or services. This includes marketing strategy and tactics, product demonstration, sales techniques, and sales control systems.
Engineering and Technology	Knowledge of the practical application of engineering science and technology. This includes applying principles, techniques, procedures, and equipment to the design and production of various goods and services.
Education and Training	Knowledge of principles and methods for curriculum and training design, teaching and instruction for individuals and groups, and the measurement of training effects.
Transportation	Knowledge of principles and methods for moving people or goods by air, rail, sea, or road, including the relative costs and benefits.
Administration and Management	Knowledge of business and management principles involved in strategic planning, resource allocation, human resources modeling, leadership technique, production methods, and coordination of people and resources.
Personnel and Human Resources	Knowledge of principles and procedures for personnel recruitment, selection, training, compensation and benefits, labor relations and negotiation, and personnel information systems.
Economics and Accounting	Knowledge of economic and accounting principles and practices, the financial markets, banking and the analysis and reporting of financial data.
Clerical	Knowledge of administrative and clerical procedures and systems such as word processing, managing files and records, stenography and transcription, designing forms, and other office procedures and terminology.
Law and Government	Knowledge of laws, legal codes, court procedures, precedents, government regulations, executive orders, agency rules, and the democratic political process.
Geography	Knowledge of principles and methods for describing the features of land, sea, and air masses, including their physical characteristics, locations, interrelationships, and distribution of plant, animal, and human life.
Therapy and Counseling	Knowledge of principles, methods, and procedures for diagnosis, treatment, and rehabilitation of physical and mental dysfunctions, and for career counseling and guidance.
Foreign Language	Knowledge of the structure and content of a foreign (non-English) language including the meaning and spelling of words, rules of composition and grammar, and pronunciation.
Chemistry	Knowledge of the chemical composition, structure, and properties of substances and of the chemical processes and transformations that they undergo. This includes uses of chemicals and their interactions, danger signs, production techniques, and disposal methods.
Psychology	Knowledge of human behavior and performance; individual differences in ability, personality, and interests; learning and motivation; psychological research methods; and the assessment and treatment of behavioral and affective disorders.
Telecommunications	Knowledge of transmission, broadcasting, switching, control, and operation of telecommunications systems.
Computers and Electronics	Knowledge of circuit boards, processors, chips, electronic equipment, and computer hardware and software, including applications and programming.
Communications and Media	Knowledge of media production, communication, and dissemination techniques and methods. This includes alternative ways to inform and entertain via written, oral, and visual media.
Physics	Knowledge and prediction of physical principles, laws, their interrelationships, and applications to understanding fluid, material, and atmospheric dynamics, and mechanical, electrical, atomic and sub- atomic structures and processes.
Philosophy and Theology	Knowledge of different philosophical systems and religions. This includes their basic principles, values, ethics, ways of thinking, customs, practices, and their impact on human culture.
Medicine and Dentistry	Knowledge of the information and techniques needed to diagnose and treat human injuries, diseases, and deformities. This includes symptoms, treatment alternatives, drug properties and interactions, and preventive health-care measures.
History and Archeology	Knowledge of historical events and their causes, indicators, and effects on civilizations and cultures.
Sociology and Anthropology	Knowledge of group behavior and dynamics, societal trends and influences, human migrations, ethnicity, cultures and their history and origins.
Biology	Knowledge of plant and animal organisms, their tissues, cells, functions, interdependencies, and interactions with each other and the environment.
Fine Arts	Knowledge of the theory and techniques required to compose, produce, and perform works of music, dance, visual arts, drama, and sculpture.
Food Production	Knowledge of techniques and equipment for planting, growing, and harvesting food products (both plant and animal) for consumption, including storage/handling techniques.

Skills	Skills Definitions
Mathematics	Using mathematics to solve problems.
Installation	Installing equipment, machines, wiring, or programs to meet specifications.
Time Management	Managing one's own time and the time of others.
Instructing	Teaching others how to do something.
Equipment Selection	Determining the kind of tools and equipment needed to do a job.
Coordination	Adjusting actions in relation to others' actions.
Judgment and Decision Making	Considering the relative costs and benefits of potential actions to choose the most appropriate one.
Complex Problem Solving	Identifying complex problems and reviewing related information to develop and evaluate options and implement solutions.
Management of Personnel Resources	Motivating, developing, and directing people as they work, identifying the best people for the job.
Speaking	Talking to others to convey information effectively.
Repairing	Repairing machines or systems using the needed tools.
Active Learning	Understanding the implications of new information for both current and future problem-solving and decision-making.
Active Listening	Giving full attention to what other people are saying, taking time to understand the points being made, asking questions as appropriate, and not interrupting at inappropriate times.
Learning Strategies	Selecting and using training/instructional methods and procedures appropriate for the situation when learning or teaching new things.
Critical Thinking	Using logic and reasoning to identify the strengths and weaknesses of alternative solutions, conclusions or approaches to problems.
Troubleshooting	Determining causes of operating errors and deciding what to do about it.
Reading Comprehension	Understanding written sentences and paragraphs in work related documents.
Social Perceptiveness	Being aware of others' reactions and understanding why they react as they do.
Service Orientation	Actively looking for ways to help people.
Equipment Maintenance	Performing routine maintenance on equipment and determining when and what kind of maintenance is needed.
Quality Control Analysis	Conducting tests and inspections of products, services, or processes to evaluate quality or performance.
Management of Material Resources	Obtaining and seeing to the appropriate use of equipment, facilities, and materials needed to do certain work.
Systems Evaluation	Identifying measures or indicators of system performance and the actions needed to improve or correct performance, relative to the goals of the system.
Persuasion	Persuading others to change their minds or behavior.
Negotiation	Bringing others together and trying to reconcile differences.
Writing	Communicating effectively in writing as appropriate for the needs of the audience.
Monitoring	Monitoring/Assessing performance of yourself, other individuals, or organizations to make improvements or take corrective action.
Operation and Control	Controlling operations of equipment or systems.
Management of Financial Resources	Determining how money will be spent to get the work done, and accounting for these expenditures.
Operations Analysis	Analyzing needs and product requirements to create a design.
Technology Design	Generating or adapting equipment and technology to serve user needs.
Operation Monitoring	Watching gauges, dials, or other indicators to make sure a machine is working properly.
Science	Using scientific rules and methods to solve problems.
Systems Analysis	Determining how a system should work and how changes in conditions, operations, and the environment will affect outcomes.
Programming	Writing computer programs for various purposes.

Ability	Ability Definitions
Extent Flexibility	The ability to bend, stretch, twist, or reach with your body, arms, and/or legs.
Near Vision	The ability to see details at close range (within a few feet of the observer).
Static Strength	The ability to exert maximum muscle force to lift, push, pull, or carry objects.
Arm-Hand Steadiness	The ability to keep your hand and arm steady while moving your arm or while holding your arm and hand in one position.
Multilimb Coordination	The ability to coordinate two or more limbs (for example, two arms, two legs, or one leg and one arm) while sitting, standing, or lying down. It does not involve performing the activities while the whole body is in motion.
Inductive Reasoning	The ability to combine pieces of information to form general rules or conclusions (includes finding a relationship among seemingly unrelated events).
Trunk Strength	The ability to use your abdominal and lower back muscles to support part of the body repeatedly or continuously over time without 'giving out' or fatiguing.
Problem Sensitivity	The ability to tell when something is wrong or is likely to go wrong. It does not involve solving the problem, only recognizing there is a problem.
Stamina	The ability to exert yourself physically over long periods of time without getting winded or out of breath.
Oral Expression	The ability to communicate information and ideas in speaking so others will understand.
Oral Comprehension	The ability to listen to and understand information and ideas presented through spoken words and sentences.
Information Ordering	The ability to arrange things or actions in a certain order or pattern according to a specific rule or set of rules (e.g., patterns of numbers, letters, words, pictures, mathematical operations).
Dynamic Strength	The ability to exert muscle force repeatedly or continuously over time. This involves muscular endurance and resistance to muscle fatigue.
Far Vision	The ability to see details at a distance.
Manual Dexterity	The ability to quickly move your hand, your hand together with your arm, or your two hands to grasp, manipulate, or assemble objects.
Visualization	The ability to imagine how something will look after it is moved around or when its parts are moved or rearranged.
Finger Dexterity	The ability to make precisely coordinated movements of the fingers of one or both hands to grasp, manipulate, or assemble very small objects.
Deductive Reasoning	The ability to apply general rules to specific problems to produce answers that make sense.
Speech Recognition	The ability to identify and understand the speech of another person.
Gross Body Coordination	The ability to coordinate the movement of your arms, legs, and torso together when the whole body is in motion.
Control Precision	The ability to quickly and repeatedly adjust the controls of a machine or a vehicle to exact positions.
Gross Body Equilibrium	The ability to keep or regain your body balance or stay upright when in an unstable position.
Speech Clarity	The ability to speak clearly so others can understand you.
Written Comprehension	The ability to read and understand information and ideas presented in writing.
Depth Perception	The ability to judge which of several objects is closer or farther away from you, or to judge the distance between you and an object.
Selective Attention	The ability to concentrate on a task over a period of time without being distracted.
Flexibility of Closure	The ability to identify or detect a known pattern (a figure, object, word, or sound) that is hidden in other distracting material.
Mathematical Reasoning	The ability to choose the right mathematical methods or formulas to solve a problem.
Category Flexibility	The ability to generate or use different sets of rules for combining or grouping things in different ways.
Time Sharing	The ability to shift back and forth between two or more activities or sources of information (such as speech, sounds, touch, or other sources).
Visual Color Discrimination	The ability to match or detect differences between colors, including shades of color and brightness.
Reaction Time	The ability to quickly respond (with the hand, finger, or foot) to a signal (sound, light, picture) when it appears.
Speed of Limb Movement	The ability to quickly move the arms and legs.
Number Facility	The ability to add, subtract, multiply, or divide quickly and correctly.
Written Expression	The ability to communicate information and ideas in writing so others will understand.
Fluency of Ideas	The ability to come up with a number of ideas about a topic (the number of ideas is important, not their quality, correctness, or creativity).

Perceptual Speed	The ability to quickly and accurately compare similarities and differences among sets of letters, numbers, objects, pictures, or patterns. The things to be compared may be presented at the same time or one after the other. This ability also includes comparing a presented object with a remembered object.
Wrist-Finger Speed	The ability to make fast, simple, repeated movements of the fingers, hands, and wrists.
Originality	The ability to come up with unusual or clever ideas about a given topic or situation, or to develop creative ways to solve a problem.
Memorization	The ability to remember information such as words, numbers, pictures, and procedures.
Spatial Orientation	The ability to know your location in relation to the environment or to know where other objects are in relation to you.
Explosive Strength	The ability to use short bursts of muscle force to propel oneself (as in jumping or sprinting), or to throw an object.
Glare Sensitivity	The ability to see objects in the presence of glare or bright lighting.
Response Orientation	The ability to choose quickly between two or more movements in response to two or more different signals (lights, sounds, pictures). It includes the speed with which the correct response is started with the hand, foot, or other body part.
Speed of Closure	The ability to quickly make sense of, combine, and organize information into meaningful patterns.
Auditory Attention	The ability to focus on a single source of sound in the presence of other distracting sounds.
Hearing Sensitivity	The ability to detect or tell the differences between sounds that vary in pitch and loudness.
Peripheral Vision	The ability to see objects or movement of objects to one's side when the eyes are looking ahead.
Rate Control	The ability to time your movements or the movement of a piece of equipment in anticipation of changes in the speed and/or direction of a moving object or scene.
Night Vision	The ability to see under low light conditions.
Dynamic Flexibility	The ability to quickly and repeatedly bend, stretch, twist, or reach out with your body, arms, and/or legs.
Sound Localization	The ability to tell the direction from which a sound originated.

Work_Activity	Work_Activity Definitions
Performing General Physical Activities	Performing physical activities that require considerable use of your arms and legs and moving your whole body, such as climbing, lifting, balancing, walking, stooping, and handling of materials.
Training and Teaching Others	Identifying the educational needs of others, developing formal educational or training programs or classes, and teaching or instructing others.
Communicating with Supervisors, Peers, or Subordin	Providing information to supervisors, co-workers, and subordinates by telephone, in written form, e-mail, or in person.
Handling and Moving Objects	Using hands and arms in handling, installing, positioning, and moving materials, and manipulating things.
Judging the Qualities of Things, Services, or Peop	Assessing the value, importance, or quality of things or people.
Getting Information	Observing, receiving, and otherwise obtaining information from all relevant sources.
Performing for or Working Directly with the Public	Performing for people or dealing directly with the public. This includes serving customers in restaurants and stores, and receiving clients or guests.
Coaching and Developing Others	Identifying the developmental needs of others and coaching, mentoring, or otherwise helping others to improve their knowledge or skills.
Inspecting Equipment, Structures, or Material	Inspecting equipment, structures, or materials to identify the cause of errors or other problems or defects.
Operating Vehicles, Mechanized Devices, or Equipme	Running, maneuvering, navigating, or driving vehicles or mechanized equipment, such as forklifts, passenger vehicles, aircraft, or water craft.
Communicating with Persons Outside Organization	Communicating with people outside the organization, representing the organization to customers, the public, government, and other external sources. This information can be exchanged in person, in writing, or by telephone or e-mail.
Controlling Machines and Processes	Using either control mechanisms or direct physical activity to operate machines or processes (not including computers or vehicles).
Making Decisions and Solving Problems	Analyzing information and evaluating results to choose the best solution and solve problems.
Organizing, Planning, and Prioritizing Work	Developing specific goals and plans to prioritize, organize, and accomplish your work.

Estimating the Quantifiable Characteristics of Pro	Estimating sizes, distances, and quantities; or determining time, costs, resources, or materials needed to perform a work activity.
Guiding, Directing, and Motivating Subordinates	Providing guidance and direction to subordinates, including setting performance standards and monitoring performance.
Documenting/Recording Information	Entering, transcribing, recording, storing, or maintaining information in written or electronic/magnetic form.
Evaluating Information to Determine Compliance wit	Using relevant information and individual judgment to determine whether events or processes comply with laws, regulations, or standards.
Resolving Conflicts and Negotiating with Others	Handling complaints, settling disputes, and resolving grievances and conflicts, or otherwise negotiating with others.
Developing and Building Teams	Encouraging and building mutual trust, respect, and cooperation among team members.
Monitor Processes, Materials, or Surroundings	Monitoring and reviewing information from materials, events, or the environment, to detect or assess problems.
Establishing and Maintaining Interpersonal Relatio	Developing constructive and cooperative working relationships with others, and maintaining them over time.
Provide Consultation and Advice to Others	Providing guidance and expert advice to management or other groups on technical, systems-, or process-related topics.
Interpreting the Meaning of Information for Others	Translating or explaining what information means and how it can be used.
Identifying Objects, Actions, and Events	Identifying information by categorizing, estimating, recognizing differences or similarities, and detecting changes in circumstances or events.
Monitoring and Controlling Resources	Monitoring and controlling resources and overseeing the spending of money.
Scheduling Work and Activities	Scheduling events, programs, and activities, as well as the work of others.
Performing Administrative Activities	Performing day-to-day administrative tasks such as maintaining information files and processing paperwork.
Selling or Influencing Others	Convincing others to buy merchandise/goods or to otherwise change their minds or actions.
Repairing and Maintaining Mechanical Equipment	Servicing, repairing, adjusting, and testing machines, devices, moving parts, and equipment that operate primarily on the basis of mechanical (not electronic) principles.
Thinking Creatively	Developing, designing, or creating new applications, ideas, relationships, systems, or products, including artistic contributions.
Processing Information	Compiling, coding, categorizing, calculating, tabulating, auditing, or verifying information or data.
Updating and Using Relevant Knowledge	Keeping up-to-date technically and applying new knowledge to your job.
Coordinating the Work and Activities of Others	Getting members of a group to work together to accomplish tasks.
Analyzing Data or Information	Identifying the underlying principles, reasons, or facts of information by breaking down information or data into separate parts.
Repairing and Maintaining Electronic Equipment	Servicing, repairing, calibrating, regulating, fine-tuning, or testing machines, devices, and equipment that operate primarily on the basis of electrical or electronic (not mechanical) principles.
Drafting, Laying Out, and Specifying Technical Dev	Providing documentation, detailed instructions, drawings, or specifications to tell others about how devices, parts, equipment, or structures are to be fabricated, constructed, assembled, modified, maintained, or used.
Developing Objectives and Strategies	Establishing long-range objectives and specifying the strategies and actions to achieve them.
Staffing Organizational Units	Recruiting, interviewing, selecting, hiring, and promoting employees in an organization.
Assisting and Caring for Others	Providing personal assistance, medical attention, emotional support, or other personal care to others such as coworkers, customers, or patients.
Interacting With Computers	Using computers and computer systems (including hardware and software) to program, write software, set up functions, enter data, or process information.

Work_Context	Work_Context Definitions
Spend Time Using Your Hands to Handle, Control, or	How much does this job require using your hands to handle, control, or feel objects, tools or controls?
Spend Time Kneeling, Crouching, Stooping, or Crawl	How much does this job require kneeling, crouching, stooping or crawling?

Freedom to Make Decisions	How much decision making freedom, without supervision, does the job offer?
Contact With Others	How important is it to this job require the worker to be in contact with others (face-to-face, by telephone, or otherwise) in order to perform it?
Structured versus Unstructured Work	To what extent is this job structured for the worker, rather than allowing the worker to determine tasks, priorities, and goals?
Time Pressure	How often does this job require the worker to meet strict deadlines?
Importance of Being Exact or Accurate	How important is being very exact or highly accurate in performing this job?
Spend Time Bending or Twisting the Body	How much does this job require bending or twisting your body?
Deal With External Customers	How important is it to work with external customers or the public in this job?
Telephone	How often do you have telephone conversations in this job?
Exposed to Minor Burns, Cuts, Bites, or Stings	How often does this job require exposure to minor burns, cuts, bites, or stings?
Spend Time Standing	How much does this job require standing?
In an Enclosed Vehicle or Equipment	How often does this job require working in a closed vehicle or equipment (e.g., car)?
Work With Work Group or Team	How important is it to work with others in a group or team in this job?
Spend Time Walking and Running	How much does this job require walking and running?
Impact of Decisions on Co-workers or Company Resul	How do the decisions an employee makes impact the results of co-workers, clients or the company?
Spend Time Making Repetitive Motions	How much does this job require making repetitive motions?
Very Hot or Cold Temperatures	How often does this job require working in very hot (above 90 F degrees) or very cold (below 32 F degrees) temperatures?
Spend Time Keeping or Regaining Balance	How much does this job require keeping or regaining your balance?
Coordinate or Lead Others	How important is it to coordinate or lead others in accomplishing work activities in this job?
Face-to-Face Discussions	How often do you have to have face-to-face discussions with individuals or teams in this job?
Outdoors, Under Cover	How often does this job require working outdoors, under cover (e.g., structure with roof but no walls)?
Level of Competition	To what extent does this job require the worker to compete or to be aware of competitive pressures?
Extremely Bright or Inadequate Lighting	How often does this job require working in extremely bright or inadequate lighting conditions?
Exposed to Whole Body Vibration	How often does this job require exposure to whole body vibration (e.g., operate a jackhammer)?
Exposed to Hazardous Equipment	How often does this job require exposure to hazardous equipment?
Responsibility for Outcomes and Results	How responsible is the worker for work outcomes and results of other workers?
Responsible for Others' Health and Safety	How much responsibility is there for the health and safety of others in this job?
Frequency of Decision Making	How frequently is the worker required to make decisions that affect other people, the financial resources, and/or the image and reputation of the organization?
Exposed to Contaminants	How often does this job require working exposed to contaminants (such as pollutants, gases, dust or odors)?
Indoors, Environmentally Controlled	How often does this job require working indoors in environmentally controlled conditions?
Indoors, Not Environmentally Controlled	How often does this job require working indoors in non-controlled environmental conditions (e.g., warehouse without heat)?
Consequence of Error	How serious would the result usually be if the worker made a mistake that was not readily correctable?
Importance of Repeating Same Tasks	How important is repeating the same physical activities (e.g., key entry) or mental activities (e.g., checking entries in a ledger) over and over, without stopping, to performing this job?
Physical Proximity	To what extent does this job require the worker to perform job tasks in close physical proximity to other people?
Cramped Work Space, Awkward Positions	How often does this job require working in cramped work spaces that requires getting into awkward positions?
Deal With Unpleasant or Angry People	How frequently does the worker have to deal with unpleasant, angry, or discourteous individuals as part of the job requirements?
Wear Common Protective or Safety Equipment such as	How much does this job require wearing common protective or safety equipment such as safety shoes, glasses, gloves, hard hats or live jackets?
Frequency of Conflict	How often are there conflict situations the employee has to face

Sounds, Noise Levels Are Distracting or Uncomforta	How often does this job require working exposed to sounds and noise levels that are distracting or uncomfortable?
Pace Determined by Speed of Equipment	How important is it to this job that the pace is determined by the speed of equipment or machinery? (This does not refer to keeping busy at all times on this job.)
Letters and Memos	How often does the job require written letters and memos?
Spend Time Sitting	How much does this job require sitting?
Outdoors, Exposed to Weather	How often does this job require working outdoors, exposed to all weather conditions?
Wear Specialized Protective or Safety Equipment su	How much does this job require wearing specialized protective or safety equipment such as breathing apparatus, safety harness, full protection suits, or radiation protection?
Exposed to Hazardous Conditions	How often does this job require exposure to hazardous conditions?
Public Speaking	How often do you have to perform public speaking in this job?
Deal With Physically Aggressive People	How frequently does this job require the worker to deal with physical aggression of violent individuals?
Spend Time Climbing Ladders, Scaffolds, or Poles	How much does this job require climbing ladders, scaffolds, or poles?
Exposed to Disease or Infections	How often does this job require exposure to disease/infections?
Exposed to High Places	How often does this job require exposure to high places?
In an Open Vehicle or Equipment	How often does this job require working in an open vehicle or equipment (e.g., tractor)?
Degree of Automation	How automated is the job?
Electronic Mail	How often do you use electronic mail in this job?
Exposed to Radiation	How often does this job require exposure to radiation?

Job Zone Component	Job Zone Component Definitions
Title	Job Zone One: Little or No Preparation Needed
Overall Experience	No previous work-related skill, knowledge, or experience is needed for these occupations. For example, a person can become a general office clerk even if he/she has never worked in an office before.
Job Training	Employees in these occupations need anywhere from a few days to a few months of training. Usually, an experienced worker could show you how to do the job.
Job Zone Examples	These occupations involve following instructions and helping others. Examples include bus drivers, forest and conservation workers, general office clerks, home health aides, and waiters/waitresses.
SVP Range	(Below 4.0)
Education	These occupations may require a high school diploma or GED certificate. Some may require a formal training course to obtain a license.

Work_Styles	Work_Styles Definitions
Attention to Detail	Job requires being careful about detail and thorough in completing work tasks.
Dependability	Job requires being reliable, responsible, and dependable, and fulfilling obligations.
Integrity	Job requires being honest and ethical.
Self Control	Job requires maintaining composure, keeping emotions in check, controlling anger, and avoiding aggressive behavior, even in very difficult situations.
Cooperation	Job requires being pleasant with others on the job and displaying a good-natured, cooperative attitude.
Innovation	Job requires creativity and alternative thinking to develop new ideas for and answers to work-related problems.
Stress Tolerance	Job requires accepting criticism and dealing calmly and effectively with high stress situations.
Concern for Others	Job requires being sensitive to others' needs and feelings and being understanding and helpful on the job.
Adaptability/Flexibility	Job requires being open to change (positive or negative) and to considerable variety in the workplace.
Initiative	Job requires a willingness to take on responsibilities and challenges.
Analytical Thinking	Job requires analyzing information and using logic to address work-related issues and problems.
Social Orientation	Job requires preferring to work with others rather than alone, and being personally connected with others on the job.
Leadership	Job requires a willingness to lead, take charge, and offer opinions and direction.
Persistence	Job requires persistence in the face of obstacles.

	Job requires developing one's own ways of doing things,
Independence	guiding oneself with little or no supervision, and depending on oneself to get things done.
Achievement/Effort	Job requires establishing and maintaining personally challenging achievement goals and exerting effort toward mastering tasks.

47-2042.00 - Floor Layers, Except Carpet, Wood, and Hard Tiles

Apply blocks, strips, or sheets of shock-absorbing, sound-deadening, or decorative coverings to floors.

Tasks

1) Remove excess cement to clean finished surface.

2) Cut covering and foundation materials, according to blueprints and sketches.

3) Disconnect and remove appliances, light fixtures, and worn floor and wall covering from floors, walls, and cabinets.

4) Cut flooring material to fit around obstructions.

5) Roll and press sheet wall and floor covering into cement base to smooth and finish surface, using hand roller.

6) Inspect surface to be covered to ensure that it is firm and dry.

7) Apply adhesive cement to floor or wall material to join and adhere foundation material.

8) Determine traffic areas and decide location of seams.

9) Sweep, scrape, sand, or chip dirt and irregularities to clean base surfaces, correcting imperfections that may show through the covering.

10) Trim excess covering materials, tack edges, and join sections of covering material to form tight joint.

11) Heat and soften floor covering materials to patch cracks or fit floor coverings around irregular surfaces, using blowtorch.

12) Form a smooth foundation by stapling plywood or Masonite over the floor or by brushing waterproof compound onto surface and filling cracks with plaster, putty, or grout to seal pores.

13) Measure and mark guidelines on surfaces or foundations, using chalk lines and dividers.

47-2044.00 - Tile and Marble Setters

Apply hard tile, marble, and wood tile to walls, floors, ceilings, and roof decks.

Tasks

1) Mix, apply, and spread plaster, concrete, mortar, cement, mastic, glue or other adhesives to form a bed for the tiles, using brush, trowel and screed.

2) Determine and implement the best layout to achieve a desired pattern.

3) Apply mortar to tile back, position the tile and press or tap with trowel handle to affix tile to base.

4) Remove and replace cracked or damaged tile.

5) Align and straighten tile using levels, squares and straightedges.

6) Finish and dress the joints and wipe excess grout from between tiles, using damp sponge.

7) Measure and mark surfaces to be tiled, following blueprints.

8) Study blueprints and examine surface to be covered to determine amount of material needed.

9) Remove any old tile, grout and adhesive using chisels and scrapers and clean the surface carefully.

10) Lay and set mosaic tiles to create decorative wall, mural and floor designs.

11) Prepare surfaces for tiling by attaching lath or waterproof paper, or by applying a cement mortar coat onto a metal screen.

12) Apply a sealer to make grout stain- and water-resistant.

13) Assist customers in selection of tile and grout.

14) Install and anchor fixtures in designated positions, using hand tools.

15) Cut, surface, polish and install marble and granite and/or install pre-cast terrazzo, granite or marble units.

16) Measure and cut metal lath to size for walls and ceilings, using tin snips.

17) Prepare cost and labor estimates based on calculations of time and materials needed for project.

18) Level concrete and allow to dry.

19) Build underbeds and install anchor bolts, wires and brackets.

20) Cut tile backing to required size, using shears.

21) Mix and apply mortar or cement to edges and ends of drain tiles to seal halves and joints.

22) Select and order tile and other items to be installed, such as bathroom accessories, walls, panels, and cabinets, according to specifications.

23) Brush glue onto manila paper on which design has been drawn and position tiles finished side down onto paper.

24) Spread mastic or other adhesive base on roof deck to form base for promenade tile, using serrated spreader.

Knowledge	Knowledge Definitions
Building and Construction	Knowledge of materials, methods, and the tools involved in the construction or repair of houses, buildings, or other structures such as highways and roads.
Administration and Management	Knowledge of business and management principles involved in strategic planning, resource allocation, human resources modeling, leadership technique, production methods, and coordination of people and resources.
Customer and Personal Service	Knowledge of principles and processes for providing customer and personal services. This includes customer needs assessment, meeting quality standards for services, and evaluation of customer satisfaction.
Mathematics	Knowledge of arithmetic, algebra, geometry, calculus, statistics, and their applications.
Production and Processing	Knowledge of raw materials, production processes, quality control, costs, and other techniques for maximizing the effective manufacture and distribution of goods.
Economics and Accounting	Knowledge of economic and accounting principles and practices, the financial markets, banking and the analysis and reporting of financial data.
Design	Knowledge of design techniques, tools, and principles involved in production of precision technical plans, blueprints, drawings, and models.
Clerical	Knowledge of administrative and clerical procedures and systems such as word processing, managing files and records, stenography and transcription, designing forms, and other office procedures and terminology.
Education and Training	Knowledge of principles and methods for curriculum and training design, teaching and instruction for individuals and groups, and the measurement of training effects.
Mechanical	Knowledge of machines and tools, including their designs, uses, repair, and maintenance.
Public Safety and Security	Knowledge of relevant equipment, policies, procedures, and strategies to promote effective local, state, or national security operations for the protection of people, data, property, and institutions.
Transportation	Knowledge of principles and methods for moving people or goods by air, rail, sea, or road, including the relative costs and benefits.
English Language	Knowledge of the structure and content of the English language including the meaning and spelling of words, rules of composition, and grammar.
Sales and Marketing	Knowledge of principles and methods for showing, promoting, and selling products or services. This includes marketing strategy and tactics, product demonstration, sales techniques, and sales control systems.
Personnel and Human Resources	Knowledge of principles and procedures for personnel recruitment, selection, training, compensation and benefits, labor relations and negotiation, and personnel information systems.
Physics	Knowledge and prediction of physical principles, laws, their interrelationships, and applications to understanding fluid, material, and atmospheric dynamics, and mechanical, electrical, atomic and sub-atomic structures and processes.

Chemistry	Knowledge of the chemical composition, structure, and properties of substances and of the chemical processes and transformations that they undergo. This includes uses of chemicals and their interactions, danger signs, production techniques, and disposal methods.
Telecommunications	Knowledge of transmission, broadcasting, switching, control, and operation of telecommunications systems.
Engineering and Technology	Knowledge of the practical application of engineering science and technology. This includes applying principles, techniques, procedures, and equipment to the design and production of various goods and services.
Communications and Media	Knowledge of media production, communication, and dissemination techniques and methods. This includes alternative ways to inform and entertain via written, oral, and visual media.
Law and Government	Knowledge of laws, legal codes, court procedures, precedents, government regulations, executive orders, agency rules, and the democratic political process.
Computers and Electronics	Knowledge of circuit boards, processors, chips, electronic equipment, and computer hardware and software, including applications and programming.
Foreign Language	Knowledge of the structure and content of a foreign (non-English) language including the meaning and spelling of words, rules of composition and grammar, and pronunciation.
Biology	Knowledge of plant and animal organisms, their tissues, cells, functions, interdependencies, and interactions with each other and the environment.
Psychology	Knowledge of human behavior and performance; individual differences in ability, personality, and interests; learning and motivation; psychological research methods; and the assessment and treatment of behavioral and affective disorders.
Sociology and Anthropology	Knowledge of group behavior and dynamics, societal trends and influences, human migrations, ethnicity, cultures and their history and origins.
Geography	Knowledge of principles and methods for describing the features of land, sea, and air masses, including their physical characteristics, locations, interrelationships, and distribution of plant, animal, and human life.
Philosophy and Theology	Knowledge of different philosophical systems and religions. This includes their basic principles, values, ethics, ways of thinking, customs, practices, and their impact on human culture.
History and Archeology	Knowledge of historical events and their causes, indicators, and effects on civilizations and cultures.
Medicine and Dentistry	Knowledge of the information and techniques needed to diagnose and treat human injuries, diseases, and deformities. This includes symptoms, treatment alternatives, drug properties and interactions, and preventive health-care measures.
Therapy and Counseling	Knowledge of principles, methods, and procedures for diagnosis, treatment, and rehabilitation of physical and mental dysfunctions, and for career counseling and guidance.
Fine Arts	Knowledge of the theory and techniques required to compose, produce, and perform works of music, dance, visual arts, drama, and sculpture.
Food Production	Knowledge of techniques and equipment for planting, growing, and harvesting food products (both plant and animal) for consumption, including storage/handling techniques.

Skills	Skills Definitions
Mathematics	Using mathematics to solve problems.
Coordination	Adjusting actions in relation to others' actions.
Active Listening	Giving full attention to what other people are saying, taking time to understand the points being made, asking questions as appropriate, and not interrupting at inappropriate times.
Judgment and Decision Making	Considering the relative costs and benefits of potential actions to choose the most appropriate one.
Time Management	Managing one's own time and the time of others.
Equipment Selection	Determining the kind of tools and equipment needed to do a job.
Critical Thinking	Using logic and reasoning to identify the strengths and weaknesses of alternative solutions, conclusions or approaches to problems.
Social Perceptiveness	Being aware of others' reactions and understanding why they react as they do.
Complex Problem Solving	Identifying complex problems and reviewing related information to develop and evaluate options and implement solutions.

Skills	Skills Definitions
Reading Comprehension	Understanding written sentences and paragraphs in work related documents.
Monitoring	Monitoring/Assessing performance of yourself, other individuals, or organizations to make improvements or take corrective action.
Installation	Installing equipment, machines, wiring, or programs to meet specifications.
Active Learning	Understanding the implications of new information for both current and future problem-solving and decision-making.
Instructing	Teaching others how to do something.
Speaking	Talking to others to convey information effectively.
Management of Material Resources	Obtaining and seeing to the appropriate use of equipment, facilities, and materials needed to do certain work.
Service Orientation	Actively looking for ways to help people.
Learning Strategies	Selecting and using training/instructional methods and procedures appropriate for the situation when learning or teaching new things.
Management of Financial Resources	Determining how money will be spent to get the work done, and accounting for these expenditures.
Writing	Communicating effectively in writing as appropriate for the needs of the audience.
Management of Personnel Resources	Motivating, developing, and directing people as they work, identifying the best people for the job.
Negotiation	Bringing others together and trying to reconcile differences.
Equipment Maintenance	Performing routine maintenance on equipment and determining when and what kind of maintenance is needed.
Persuasion	Persuading others to change their minds or behavior.
Operations Analysis	Analyzing needs and product requirements to create a design.
Quality Control Analysis	Conducting tests and inspections of products, services, or processes to evaluate quality or performance.
Technology Design	Generating or adapting equipment and technology to serve user needs.
Troubleshooting	Determining causes of operating errors and deciding what to do about it.
Operation and Control	Controlling operations of equipment or systems.
Repairing	Repairing machines or systems using the needed tools.
Systems Analysis	Determining how a system should work and how changes in conditions, operations, and the environment will affect outcomes.
Operation Monitoring	Watching gauges, dials, or other indicators to make sure a machine is working properly.
Systems Evaluation	Identifying measures or indicators of system performance and the actions needed to improve or correct performance, relative to the goals of the system.
Science	Using scientific rules and methods to solve problems.
Programming	Writing computer programs for various purposes.

Ability	Ability Definitions
Visualization	The ability to imagine how something will look after it is moved around or when its parts are moved or rearranged.
Arm-Hand Steadiness	The ability to keep your hand and arm steady while moving your arm or while holding your arm and hand in one position.
Multilimb Coordination	The ability to coordinate two or more limbs (for example, two arms, two legs, or one leg and one arm) while sitting, standing, or lying down. It does not involve performing the activities while the whole body is in motion.
Near Vision	The ability to see details at close range (within a few feet of the observer).
Problem Sensitivity	The ability to tell when something is wrong or is likely to go wrong. It does not involve solving the problem, only recognizing there is a problem.
Oral Expression	The ability to communicate information and ideas in speaking so others will understand.
Oral Comprehension	The ability to listen to and understand information and ideas presented through spoken words and sentences.
Trunk Strength	The ability to use your abdominal and lower back muscles to support part of the body repeatedly or continuously over time without 'giving out' or fatiguing.
Speech Recognition	The ability to identify and understand the speech of another person.
Manual Dexterity	The ability to quickly move your hand, your hand together with your arm, or your two hands to grasp, manipulate, or assemble objects.
Information Ordering	The ability to arrange things or actions in a certain order or pattern according to a specific rule or set of rules (e.g., patterns of numbers, letters, words, pictures, mathematical operations).
Speech Clarity	The ability to speak clearly so others can understand you.

Extent Flexibility	The ability to bend, stretch, twist, or reach with your body, arms, and/or legs.
Deductive Reasoning	The ability to apply general rules to specific problems to produce answers that make sense.
Mathematical Reasoning	The ability to choose the right mathematical methods or formulas to solve a problem.
Originality	The ability to come up with unusual or clever ideas about a given topic or situation, or to develop creative ways to solve a problem.
Dynamic Strength	The ability to exert muscle force repeatedly or continuously over time. This involves muscular endurance and resistance to muscle fatigue.
Static Strength	The ability to exert maximum muscle force to lift, push, pull, or carry objects.
Inductive Reasoning	The ability to combine pieces of information to form general rules or conclusions (includes finding a relationship among seemingly unrelated events).
Depth Perception	The ability to judge which of several objects is closer or farther away from you, or to judge the distance between you and an object.
Gross Body Coordination	The ability to coordinate the movement of your arms, legs, and torso together when the whole body is in motion.
Fluency of Ideas	The ability to come up with a number of ideas about a topic (the number of ideas is important, not their quality, correctness, or creativity).
Stamina	The ability to exert yourself physically over long periods of time without getting winded or out of breath.
Number Facility	The ability to add, subtract, multiply, or divide quickly and correctly.
Selective Attention	The ability to concentrate on a task over a period of time without being distracted.
Written Expression	The ability to communicate information and ideas in writing so others will understand.
Category Flexibility	The ability to generate or use different sets of rules for combining or grouping things in different ways.
Written Comprehension	The ability to read and understand information and ideas presented in writing.
Dynamic Flexibility	The ability to quickly and repeatedly bend, stretch, twist, or reach out with your body, arms, and/or legs.
Time Sharing	The ability to shift back and forth between two or more activities or sources of information (such as speech, sounds, touch, or other sources).
Visual Color Discrimination	The ability to match or detect differences between colors, including shades of color and brightness.
Control Precision	The ability to quickly and repeatedly adjust the controls of a machine or a vehicle to exact positions.
Memorization	The ability to remember information such as words, numbers, pictures, and procedures.
Finger Dexterity	The ability to make precisely coordinated movements of the fingers of one or both hands to grasp, manipulate, or assemble very small objects.
Wrist-Finger Speed	The ability to make fast, simple, repeated movements of the fingers, hands, and wrists.
Gross Body Equilibrium	The ability to keep or regain your body balance or stay upright when in an unstable position.
Spatial Orientation	The ability to know your location in relation to the environment or to know where other objects are in relation to you.
Rate Control	The ability to time your movements or the movement of a piece of equipment in anticipation of changes in the speed and/or direction of a moving object or scene.
Perceptual Speed	The ability to quickly and accurately compare similarities and differences among sets of letters, numbers, objects, pictures, or patterns. The things to be compared may be presented at the same time or one after the other. This ability also includes comparing a presented object with a remembered object.
Speed of Limb Movement	The ability to quickly move the arms and legs.
Speed of Closure	The ability to quickly make sense of, combine, and organize information into meaningful patterns.
Reaction Time	The ability to quickly respond (with the hand, finger, or foot) to a signal (sound, light, picture) when it appears.
Flexibility of Closure	The ability to identify or detect a known pattern (a figure, object, word, or sound) that is hidden in other distracting material.
Far Vision	The ability to see details at a distance.
Explosive Strength	The ability to use short bursts of muscle force to propel oneself (as in jumping or sprinting), or to throw an object.
Peripheral Vision	The ability to see objects or movement of objects to one's side when the eyes are looking ahead.

Hearing Sensitivity	The ability to detect or tell the differences between sounds that vary in pitch and loudness.
Auditory Attention	The ability to focus on a single source of sound in the presence of other distracting sounds.
Response Orientation	The ability to choose quickly between two or more movements in response to two or more different signals (lights, sounds, pictures). It includes the speed with which the correct response is started with the hand, foot, or other body part.
Glare Sensitivity	The ability to see objects in the presence of glare or bright lighting.
Sound Localization	The ability to tell the direction from which a sound originated.
Night Vision	The ability to see under low light conditions.

Work_Activity	Work_Activity Definitions
Handling and Moving Objects	Using hands and arms in handling, installing, positioning, and moving materials, and manipulating things.
Performing General Physical Activities	Performing physical activities that require considerable use of your arms and legs and moving your whole body, such as climbing, lifting, balancing, walking, stooping, and handling of materials.
Getting Information	Observing, receiving, and otherwise obtaining information from all relevant sources.
Making Decisions and Solving Problems	Analyzing information and evaluating results to choose the best solution and solve problems.
Estimating the Quantifiable Characteristics of Pro	Estimating sizes, distances, and quantities; or determining time, costs, resources, or materials needed to perform a work activity.
Training and Teaching Others	Identifying the educational needs of others, developing formal educational or training programs or classes, and teaching or instructing others.
Identifying Objects, Actions, and Events	Identifying information by categorizing, estimating, recognizing differences or similarities, and detecting changes in circumstances or events.
Establishing and Maintaining Interpersonal Relatio	Developing constructive and cooperative working relationships with others, and maintaining them over time.
Operating Vehicles, Mechanized Devices, or Equipme	Running, maneuvering, navigating, or driving vehicles or mechanized equipment, such as forklifts, passenger vehicles, aircraft, or water craft.
Communicating with Supervisors, Peers, or Subordin	Providing information to supervisors, co-workers, and subordinates by telephone, in written form, e-mail, or in person.
Thinking Creatively	Developing, designing, or creating new applications, ideas, relationships, systems, or products, including artistic contributions.
Monitor Processes, Materials, or Surroundings	Monitoring and reviewing information from materials, events, or the environment, to detect or assess problems.
Controlling Machines and Processes	Using either control mechanisms or direct physical activity to operate machines or processes (not including computers or vehicles).
Organizing, Planning, and Prioritizing Work	Developing specific goals and plans to prioritize, organize, and accomplish your work.
Coordinating the Work and Activities of Others	Getting members of a group to work together to accomplish tasks.
Communicating with Persons Outside Organization	Communicating with people outside the organization, representing the organization to customers, the public, government, and other external sources. This information can be exchanged in person, in writing, or by telephone or e-mail.
Inspecting Equipment, Structures, or Material	Inspecting equipment, structures, or materials to identify the cause of errors or other problems or defects.
Guiding, Directing, and Motivating Subordinates	Providing guidance and direction to subordinates, including setting performance standards and monitoring performance.
Scheduling Work and Activities	Scheduling events, programs, and activities, as well as the work of others.
Performing for or Working Directly with the Public	Performing for people or dealing directly with the public. This includes serving customers in restaurants and stores, and receiving clients or guests.
Coaching and Developing Others	Identifying the developmental needs of others and coaching, mentoring, or otherwise helping others to improve their knowledge or skills.
Judging the Qualities of Things, Services, or Peop	Assessing the value, importance, or quality of things or people.
Interpreting the Meaning of Information for Others	Translating or explaining what information means and how it can be used.

Evaluating Information to Determine Compliance wit	Using relevant information and individual judgment to determine whether events or processes comply with laws, regulations, or standards.
Resolving Conflicts and Negotiating with Others	Handling complaints, settling disputes, and resolving · grievances and conflicts, or otherwise negotiating with others.
Processing Information	Compiling, coding, categorizing, calculating, tabulating, auditing, or verifying information or data.
Drafting, Laying Out, and Specifying Technical Dev	Providing documentation, detailed instructions, drawings, or specifications to tell others about how devices, parts, equipment, or structures are to be fabricated, constructed, assembled, modified, maintained, or used.
Developing and Building Teams	Encouraging and building mutual trust, respect, and cooperation among team members.
Updating and Using Relevant Knowledge	Keeping up-to-date technically and applying new knowledge to your job.
Developing Objectives and Strategies	Establishing long-range objectives and specifying the strategies and actions to achieve them.
Documenting/Recording Information	Entering, transcribing, recording, storing, or maintaining information in written or electronic/magnetic form.
Analyzing Data or Information	Identifying the underlying principles, reasons, or facts of information by breaking down information or data into separate parts.
Provide Consultation and Advice to Others	Providing guidance and expert advice to management or other groups on technical, systems-, or process-related topics.
Monitoring and Controlling Resources	Monitoring and controlling resources and overseeing the spending of money.
Assisting and Caring for Others	Providing personal assistance, medical attention, emotional support, or other personal care to others such as coworkers, customers, or patients.
Repairing and Maintaining Mechanical Equipment	Servicing, repairing, adjusting, and testing machines, devices, moving parts, and equipment that operate primarily on the basis of mechanical (not electronic) principles.
Selling or Influencing Others	Convincing others to buy merchandise/goods or to otherwise change their minds or actions.
Performing Administrative Activities	Performing day-to-day administrative tasks such as maintaining information files and processing paperwork.
Interacting With Computers	Using computers and computer systems (including hardware and software) to program, write software, set up functions, enter data, or process information.
Staffing Organizational Units	Recruiting, interviewing, selecting, hiring, and promoting employees in an organization.
Repairing and Maintaining Electronic Equipment	Servicing, repairing, calibrating, regulating, fine-tuning, or testing machines, devices, and equipment that operate primarily on the basis of electrical or electronic (not mechanical) principles.

Work_Context	Work_Context Definitions
Telephone	How often do you have telephone conversations in this job?
Face-to-Face Discussions	How often do you have to have face-to-face discussions with individuals or teams in this job?
Spend Time Using Your Hands to Handle, Control, or	How much does this job require using your hands to handle, control, or feel objects, tools or controls?
Impact of Decisions on Co-workers or Company Resul	How do the decisions an employee makes impact the results of co-workers, clients or the company?
Importance of Being Exact or Accurate	How important is being very exact or highly accurate in performing this job?
Contact With Others	How much does this job require the worker to be in contact with others (face-to-face, by telephone, or otherwise) in order to perform it?
Wear Common Protective or Safety Equipment such as	How much does this job require wearing common protective or safety equipment such as safety shoes, glasses, gloves, hard hats or live jackets?
Time Pressure	How often does this job require the worker to meet strict deadlines?
Responsibility for Outcomes and Results	How responsible is the worker for work outcomes and results of other workers?
Structured versus Unstructured Work	To what extent is this job structured for the worker, rather than allowing the worker to determine tasks, priorities, and goals?
Frequency of Decision Making	How frequently is the worker required to make decisions that affect other people, the financial resources, and/or the image and reputation of the organization?
Freedom to Make Decisions	How much decision making freedom, without supervision, does the job offer?
Sounds, Noise Levels Are Distracting or Uncomforta	How often does this job require working exposed to sounds and noise levels that are distracting or uncomfortable?

Spend Time Bending or Twisting the Body	How much does this job require bending or twisting your body?
Spend Time Standing	How much does this job require standing?
Responsible for Others' Health and Safety	How much responsibility is there for the health and safety of others in this job?
Exposed to Contaminants	How often does this job require working exposed to contaminants (such as pollutants, gases, dust or odors)?
Cramped Work Space, Awkward Positions	How often does this job require working in cramped work spaces that requires getting into awkward positions?
Physical Proximity	To what extent does this job require the worker to perform job tasks in close physical proximity to other people?
Spend Time Kneeling, Crouching, Stooping, or Crawl	How much does this job require kneeling, crouching, stooping or crawling?
Indoors, Not Environmentally Controlled	How often does this job require working indoors in non-controlled environmental conditions (e.g., warehouse without heat)?
Work With Work Group or Team	How important is it to work with others in a group or team in this job?
Coordinate or Lead Others	How important is it to coordinate or lead others in accomplishing work activities in this job?
Exposed to Hazardous Equipment	How often does this job require exposure to hazardous equipment?
Spend Time Making Repetitive Motions	How much does this job require making repetitive motions?
Letters and Memos	How often does the job require written letters and memos?
Level of Competition	To what extent does this job require the worker to compete or to be aware of competitive pressures?
Outdoors, Exposed to Weather	How often does this job require working outdoors, exposed to all weather conditions?
In an Enclosed Vehicle or Equipment	How often does this job require working in a closed vehicle or equipment (e.g., car)?
Indoors, Environmentally Controlled	How often does this job require working indoors in environmentally controlled conditions?
Deal With External Customers	How important is it to work with external customers or the public in this job?
Frequency of Conflict Situations	How often are there conflict situations the employee has to face in this job?
Outdoors, Under Cover	How often does this job require working outdoors, under cover (e.g., structure with roof but no walls)?
Consequence of Error	How serious would the result usually be if the worker made a mistake that was not readily correctable?
Extremely Bright or Inadequate Lighting	How often does this job require working in extremely bright or inadequate lighting conditions?
Exposed to Whole Body Vibration	How often does this job require exposure to whole body vibration (e.g., operate a jackhammer)?
Wear Specialized Protective or Safety Equipment su	How much does this job require wearing specialized protective or safety equipment such as breathing apparatus, safety harness, full protection suits, or radiation protection?
Spend Time Climbing Ladders, Scaffolds, or Poles	How much does this job require climbing ladders, scaffolds, or poles?
Very Hot or Cold Temperatures	How often does this job require working in very hot (above 90 F degrees) or very cold (below 32 F degrees) temperatures?
Exposed to Hazardous Conditions	How often does this job require exposure to hazardous conditions?
Spend Time Walking and Running	How much does this job require walking and running?
Deal With Unpleasant or Angry People	How frequently does the worker have to deal with unpleasant, angry, or discourteous individuals as part of the job requirements?
Exposed to Minor Burns, Cuts, Bites, or Stings	How often does this job require exposure to minor burns, cuts, bites, or stings?
Importance of Repeating Same Tasks	How important is repeating the same physical activities (e.g., key entry) or mental activities (e.g., checking entries in a ledger) over and over, without stopping, to performing this job?
Electronic Mail	How often do you use electronic mail in this job?
Spend Time Keeping or Regaining Balance	How much does this job require keeping or regaining your balance?
Exposed to High Places	How often does this job require exposure to high places?
Spend Time Sitting	How much does this job require sitting?
Degree of Automation	How automated is the job?
Pace Determined by Speed of Equipment	How important is it to this job that the pace is determined by the speed of equipment or machinery? (This does not refer to keeping busy at all times on this job.)
Deal With Physically Aggressive People	How frequently does this job require the worker to deal with physical aggression of violent individuals?

In an Open Vehicle or Equipment	How often does this job require working in an open vehicle or equipment (e.g., tractor)?
Public Speaking	How often do you have to perform public speaking in this job?
Exposed to Disease or Infections	How often does this job require exposure to disease/infections?
Exposed to Radiation	How often does this job require exposure to radiation?

Job Zone Component	Job Zone Component Definitions
Title	Job Zone Two: Some Preparation Needed
Overall Experience	Some previous work-related skill, knowledge, or experience may be helpful in these occupations, but usually is not needed. For example, a drywall installer might benefit from experience installing drywall, but an inexperienced person could still learn to be an installer with little difficulty.
Job Training	Employees in these occupations need anywhere from a few months to one year of working with experienced employees. These occupations often involve using your knowledge and skills to help others.
Job Zone Examples	Examples include drywall installers, fire inspectors, flight attendants, pharmacy technicians, salespersons (retail), and tellers.
SVP Range	(4.0 to < 6.0)
Education	These occupations usually require a high school diploma and may require some vocational training or job-related course work. In some cases, an associate's or bachelor's degree could be needed.

Work_Styles	Work_Styles Definitions
Attention to Detail	Job requires being careful about detail and thorough in completing work tasks.
Integrity	Job requires being honest and ethical.
Dependability	Job requires being reliable, responsible, and dependable, and fulfilling obligations.
Cooperation	Job requires being pleasant with others on the job and displaying a good-natured, cooperative attitude.
Self Control	Job requires maintaining composure, keeping emotions in check, controlling anger, and avoiding aggressive behavior, even in very difficult situations.
Stress Tolerance	Job requires accepting criticism and dealing calmly and effectively with high stress situations.
Independence	Job requires developing one's own ways of doing things, guiding oneself with little or no supervision, and depending on oneself to get things done.
Analytical Thinking	Job requires analyzing information and using logic to address work-related issues and problems.
Initiative	Job requires a willingness to take on responsibilities and challenges.
Persistence	Job requires persistence in the face of obstacles.
Achievement/Effort	Job requires establishing and maintaining personally challenging achievement goals and exerting effort toward mastering tasks.
Leadership	Job requires a willingness to lead, take charge, and offer opinions and direction.
Adaptability/Flexibility	Job requires being open to change (positive or negative) and to considerable variety in the workplace.
Innovation	Job requires creativity and alternative thinking to develop new ideas for and answers to work-related problems.
Concern for Others	Job requires being sensitive to others' needs and feelings and being understanding and helpful on the job.
Social Orientation	Job requires preferring to work with others rather than alone, and being personally connected with others on the job.

47-2053.00 - Terrazzo Workers and Finishers

Apply a mixture of cement, sand, pigment, or marble chips to floors, stairways, and cabinet fixtures to fashion durable and decorative surfaces.

Tasks

1) Spread roofing paper on surface of foundation, and spread concrete onto roofing paper with trowel to form terrazzo base.

2) Spread, level, and smooth concrete and terrazzo mixtures to form bases and finished surfaces, using rakes, shovels, hand or power trowels, hand or power screeds, and floats.

3) Sprinkle colored marble or stone chips, powdered steel, or coloring powder over surface to produce prescribed finish.

4) Wash polished terrazzo surface, using cleaner and water, and apply sealer and curing agent according to manufacturer's specifications, using brush or sprayer.

5) Precast terrazzo blocks in wooden forms.

6) Grind surfaces with a power grinder and polish surfaces with polishing or surfacing machines.

7) Mix cement, sand, and water to produce concrete, grout, or slurry, using hoe, trowel, tamper, scraper, or concrete-mixing machine.

8) Cut metal division strips and press them into the terrazzo base wherever there is to be a joint or change of color, to form desired designs or patterns, and to help prevent cracks.

9) Wet concrete surface, and rub with stone to smooth surface and obtain specified finish.

10) Wet surface to prepare for bonding, fill holes and cracks with grout or slurry, and smooth, using trowel.

11) Measure designated amounts of ingredients for terrazzo or grout according to standard formulas and specifications, using graduated containers and scale, and load ingredients into portable mixer.

12) Modify mixing, grouting, grinding, and cleaning procedures according to type of installation or material used.

13) Mold expansion joints and edges, using edging tools, jointers, and straightedges.

14) Grind curved surfaces and areas inaccessible to surfacing machine, such as stairways and cabinet tops, with portable hand grinder.

15) Fill slight depressions left by grinding with a matching grout material, and then hand trowel for a smooth, uniform surface.

16) Position and secure moisture membrane and wire mesh prior to pouring base materials for terrazzo installation.

17) Move terrazzo installation materials, tools, machines, and work devices to work areas, manually or using wheelbarrow.

18) Remove frames once the foundation is dry.

19) Cut out damaged areas, drill holes for reinforcing rods, and position reinforcing rods to repair concrete, using power saw and drill.

20) Clean installation site, mixing and storage areas, tools, machines, and equipment, and store materials and equipment.

21) Clean chipped area, using wire brush, and feel and observe surface to determine if it is rough or uneven.

22) Chip, scrape, and grind high spots, ridges, and rough projections to finish concrete, using pneumatic chisel, hand chisel, or other hand tools.

23) Build wooden molds, clamping molds around areas to be repaired, and setting up frames to the proper depth and alignment.

24) Blend marble chip mixtures and place into panels, then push a roller over the surface to embed the chips.

25) Produce rough concrete surface, using broom.

47-2071.00 - Paving, Surfacing, and Tamping Equipment Operators

Operate equipment used for applying concrete, asphalt, or other materials to road beds, parking lots, or airport runways and taxiways, or equipment used for tamping gravel, dirt, or other materials. Includes concrete and asphalt paving machine operators, form tampers, tamping machine operators, and stone spreader operators.

Tasks

1) Shovel blacktop.

2) Drive machines onto truck trailers, and drive trucks to transport machines and material to and from job sites.

3) Coordinate truck dumping.

4) Operate tamping machines or manually roll surfaces to compact earth fills, foundation forms, and finished road materials, according to grade specifications.

5) Operate machines to spread, smooth, level, or steel-reinforce stone, concrete, or asphalt on

road beds.

6) Operate oil distributors, loaders, chip spreaders, dump trucks, and snow plows.

7) Set up and tear down equipment.

8) Start machine, engage clutch, and push and move levers to guide machine along forms or guidelines and to control the operation of machine attachments.

9) Fill tanks, hoppers, or machines with paving materials.

10) Observe distribution of paving material in order to adjust machine settings or material flow, and indicate low spots for workers to add material.

11) Control paving machines to push dump trucks and to maintain a constant flow of asphalt or other material into hoppers or screeds.

12) Light burners or start heating units of machines, and regulate screed temperatures and asphalt flow rates.

13) Set up forms and lay out guidelines for curbs, according to written specifications, using string, spray paint, and concrete/water mixes.

14) Cut or break up pavement and drive guardrail posts, using machines equipped with interchangeable hammers.

15) Operate machines that clean or cut expansion joints in concrete or asphalt and that rout out cracks in pavement.

16) Install dies, cutters, and extensions to screeds onto machines, using hand tools.

17) Place strips of material such as cork, asphalt, or steel into joints, or place rolls of expansion-joint material on machines that automatically insert material.

18) Drive and operate curbing machines to extrude concrete or asphalt curbing.

Knowledge	Knowledge Definitions
Building and Construction	Knowledge of materials, methods, and the tools involved in the construction or repair of houses, buildings, or other structures such as highways and roads.
Mechanical	Knowledge of machines and tools, including their designs, uses, repair, and maintenance.
Public Safety and Security	Knowledge of relevant equipment, policies, procedures, and strategies to promote effective local, state, or national security operations for the protection of people, data, property, and institutions.
Transportation	Knowledge of principles and methods for moving people or goods by air, rail, sea, or road, including the relative costs and benefits.
English Language	Knowledge of the structure and content of the English language including the meaning and spelling of words, rules of composition, and grammar.
Administration and Management	Knowledge of business and management principles involved in strategic planning, resource allocation, human resources modeling, leadership technique, production methods, and coordination of people and resources.
Mathematics	Knowledge of arithmetic, algebra, geometry, calculus, statistics, and their applications.
Customer and Personal Service	Knowledge of principles and processes for providing customer and personal services. This includes customer needs assessment, meeting quality standards for services, and evaluation of customer satisfaction.
Engineering and Technology	Knowledge of the practical application of engineering science and technology. This includes applying principles, techniques, procedures, and equipment to the design and production of various goods and services.
Production and Processing	Knowledge of raw materials, production processes, quality control, costs, and other techniques for maximizing the effective manufacture and distribution of goods.
Personnel and Human Resources	Knowledge of principles and procedures for personnel recruitment, selection, training, compensation and benefits, labor relations and negotiation, and personnel information systems.
Law and Government	Knowledge of laws, legal codes, court procedures, precedents, government regulations, executive orders, agency rules, and the democratic political process.
Education and Training	Knowledge of principles and methods for curriculum and training design, teaching and instruction for individuals and groups, and the measurement of training effects.
Psychology	Knowledge of human behavior and performance; individual differences in ability, personality, and interests; learning and motivation; psychological research methods; and the assessment and treatment of behavioral and affective disorders.
Design	Knowledge of design techniques, tools, and principles involved in production of precision technical plans, blueprints, drawings, and models.
Chemistry	Knowledge of the chemical composition, structure, and properties of substances and of the chemical processes and transformations that they undergo. This includes uses of chemicals and their interactions, danger signs, production techniques, and disposal methods.
Communications and Media	Knowledge of media production, communication, and dissemination techniques and methods. This includes alternative ways to inform and entertain via written, oral, and visual media.
Physics	Knowledge and prediction of physical principles, laws, their interrelationships, and applications to understanding fluid, material, and atmospheric dynamics, and mechanical, electrical, atomic and sub-atomic structures and processes.
Computers and Electronics	Knowledge of circuit boards, processors, chips, electronic equipment, and computer hardware and software, including applications and programming.
Geography	Knowledge of principles and methods for describing the features of land, sea, and air masses, including their physical characteristics, locations, interrelationships, and distribution of plant, animal, and human life.
Sociology and Anthropology	Knowledge of group behavior and dynamics, societal trends and influences, human migrations, ethnicity, cultures and their history and origins.
Clerical	Knowledge of administrative and clerical procedures and systems such as word processing, managing files and records, stenography and transcription, designing forms, and other office procedures and terminology.
Telecommunications	Knowledge of transmission, broadcasting, switching, control, and operation of telecommunications systems.
Biology	Knowledge of plant and animal organisms, their tissues, cells, functions, interdependencies, and interactions with each other and the environment.
Foreign Language	Knowledge of the structure and content of a foreign (non-English) language including the meaning and spelling of words, rules of composition and grammar, and pronunciation.
Medicine and Dentistry	Knowledge of the information and techniques needed to diagnose and treat human injuries, diseases, and deformities. This includes symptoms, treatment alternatives, drug properties and interactions, and preventive health-care measures.
Economics and Accounting	Knowledge of economic and accounting principles and practices, the financial markets, banking and the analysis and reporting of financial data.
Sales and Marketing	Knowledge of principles and methods for showing, promoting, and selling products or services. This includes marketing strategy and tactics, product demonstration, sales techniques, and sales control systems.
History and Archeology	Knowledge of historical events and their causes, indicators, and effects on civilizations and cultures.
Therapy and Counseling	Knowledge of principles, methods, and procedures for diagnosis, treatment, and rehabilitation of physical and mental dysfunctions, and for career counseling and guidance.
Philosophy and Theology	Knowledge of different philosophical systems and religions. This includes their basic principles, values, ethics, ways of thinking, customs, practices, and their impact on human culture.
Fine Arts	Knowledge of the theory and techniques required to compose, produce, and perform works of music, dance, visual arts, drama, and sculpture.
Food Production	Knowledge of techniques and equipment for planting, growing, and harvesting food products (both plant and animal) for consumption, including storage/handling techniques.

Skills	Skills Definitions
Equipment Maintenance	Performing routine maintenance on equipment and determining when and what kind of maintenance is needed.
Instructing	Teaching others how to do something.
Critical Thinking	Using logic and reasoning to identify the strengths and weaknesses of alternative solutions, conclusions or approaches to problems.
Operation and Control	Controlling operations of equipment or systems.
Equipment Selection	Determining the kind of tools and equipment needed to do a job.

Active Listening	Giving full attention to what other people are saying, taking time to understand the points being made, asking questions as appropriate, and not interrupting at inappropriate times.
Troubleshooting	Determining causes of operating errors and deciding what to do about it.
Speaking	Talking to others to convey information effectively.
Operation Monitoring	Watching gauges, dials, or other indicators to make sure a machine is working properly.
Coordination	Adjusting actions in relation to others' actions.
Judgment and Decision Making	Considering the relative costs and benefits of potential actions to choose the most appropriate one.
Repairing	Repairing machines or systems using the needed tools.
Learning Strategies	Selecting and using training/instructional methods and procedures appropriate for the situation when learning or teaching new things.
Monitoring	Monitoring/Assessing performance of yourself, other individuals, or organizations to make improvements or take corrective action.
Active Learning	Understanding the implications of new information for both current and future problem-solving and decision-making.
Reading Comprehension	Understanding written sentences and paragraphs in work related documents.
Complex Problem Solving	Identifying complex problems and reviewing related information to develop and evaluate options and implement solutions.
Persuasion	Persuading others to change their minds or behavior.
Social Perceptiveness	Being aware of others' reactions and understanding why they react as they do.
Installation	Installing equipment, machines, wiring, or programs to meet specifications.
Mathematics	Using mathematics to solve problems.
Negotiation	Bringing others together and trying to reconcile differences.
Service Orientation	Actively looking for ways to help people.
Systems Analysis	Determining how a system should work and how changes in conditions, operations, and the environment will affect outcomes.
Systems Evaluation	Identifying measures or indicators of system performance and the actions needed to improve or correct performance, relative to the goals of the system.
Operations Analysis	Analyzing needs and product requirements to create a design.
Management of Personnel Resources	Motivating, developing, and directing people as they work, identifying the best people for the job.
Time Management	Managing one's own time and the time of others.
Management of Material Resources	Obtaining and seeing to the appropriate use of equipment, facilities, and materials needed to do certain work.
Technology Design	Generating or adapting equipment and technology to serve user needs.
Quality Control Analysis	Conducting tests and inspections of products, services, or processes to evaluate quality or performance.
Writing	Communicating effectively in writing as appropriate for the needs of the audience.
Science	Using scientific rules and methods to solve problems.
Management of Financial Resources	Determining how money will be spent to get the work done, and accounting for these expenditures.
Programming	Writing computer programs for various purposes.

Ability	**Ability Definitions**
Problem Sensitivity	The ability to tell when something is wrong or is likely to go wrong. It does not involve solving the problem, only recognizing there is a problem.
Multilimb Coordination	The ability to coordinate two or more limbs (for example, two arms, two legs, or one leg and one arm) while sitting, standing, or lying down. It does not involve performing the activities while the whole body is in motion.
Control Precision	The ability to quickly and repeatedly adjust the controls of a machine or a vehicle to exact positions.
Depth Perception	The ability to judge which of several objects is closer or farther away from you, or to judge the distance between you and an object.
Arm-Hand Steadiness	The ability to keep your hand and arm steady while moving your arm or while holding your arm and hand in one position.
Manual Dexterity	The ability to quickly move your hand, your hand together with your arm, or your two hands to grasp, manipulate, or assemble objects.
Oral Comprehension	The ability to listen to and understand information and ideas presented through spoken words and sentences.

Deductive Reasoning	The ability to apply general rules to specific problems to produce answers that make sense.
Oral Expression	The ability to communicate information and ideas in speaking so others will understand.
Information Ordering	The ability to arrange things or actions in a certain order or pattern according to a specific rule or set of rules (e.g., patterns of numbers, letters, words, pictures, mathematical operations).
Speech Clarity	The ability to speak clearly so others can understand you.
Speech Recognition	The ability to identify and understand the speech of another person.
Inductive Reasoning	The ability to combine pieces of information to form general rules or conclusions (includes finding a relationship among seemingly unrelated events).
Near Vision	The ability to see details at close range (within a few feet of the observer).
Rate Control	The ability to time your movements or the movement of a piece of equipment in anticipation of changes in the speed and/or direction of a moving object or scene.
Hearing Sensitivity	The ability to detect or tell the differences between sounds that vary in pitch and loudness.
Reaction Time	The ability to quickly respond (with the hand, finger, or foot) to a signal (sound, light, picture) when it appears.
Far Vision	The ability to see details at a distance.
Selective Attention	The ability to concentrate on a task over a period of time without being distracted.
Perceptual Speed	The ability to quickly and accurately compare similarities and differences among sets of letters, numbers, objects, pictures, or patterns. The things to be compared may be presented at the same time or one after the other. This ability also includes comparing a presented object with a remembered object.
Finger Dexterity	The ability to make precisely coordinated movements of the fingers of one or both hands to grasp, manipulate, or assemble very small objects.
Trunk Strength	The ability to use your abdominal and lower back muscles to support part of the body repeatedly or continuously over time without 'giving out' or fatiguing.
Flexibility of Closure	The ability to identify or detect a known pattern (a figure, object, word, or sound) that is hidden in other distracting material.
Static Strength	The ability to exert maximum muscle force to lift, push, pull, or carry objects.
Extent Flexibility	The ability to bend, stretch, twist, or reach with your body, arms, and/or legs.
Visualization	The ability to imagine how something will look after it is moved around or when its parts are moved or rearranged.
Visual Color Discrimination	The ability to match or detect differences between colors, including shades of color and brightness.
Category Flexibility	The ability to generate or use different sets of rules for combining or grouping things in different ways.
Glare Sensitivity	The ability to see objects in the presence of glare or bright lighting.
Response Orientation	The ability to choose quickly between two or more movements in response to two or more different signals (lights, sounds, pictures). It includes the speed with which the correct response is started with the hand, foot, or other body part.
Written Comprehension	The ability to read and understand information and ideas presented in writing.
Spatial Orientation	The ability to know your location in relation to the environment or to know where other objects are in relation to you.
Time Sharing	The ability to shift back and forth between two or more activities or sources of information (such as speech, sounds, touch, or other sources).
Gross Body Coordination	The ability to coordinate the movement of your arms, legs, and torso together when the whole body is in motion.
Auditory Attention	The ability to focus on a single source of sound in the presence of other distracting sounds.
Fluency of Ideas	The ability to come up with a number of ideas about a topic (the number of ideas is important, not their quality, correctness, or creativity).
Written Expression	The ability to communicate information and ideas in writing so others will understand.
Speed of Limb Movement	The ability to quickly move the arms and legs.
Peripheral Vision	The ability to see objects or movement of objects to one's side when the eyes are looking ahead.
Speed of Closure	The ability to quickly make sense of, combine, and organize information into meaningful patterns.
Stamina	The ability to exert yourself physically over long periods of time without getting winded or out of breath.

Originality	The ability to come up with unusual or clever ideas about a given topic or situation, or to develop creative ways to solve a problem.
Wrist-Finger Speed	The ability to make fast, simple, repeated movements of the fingers, hands, and wrists.
Memorization	The ability to remember information such as words, numbers, pictures, and procedures.
Number Facility	The ability to add, subtract, multiply, or divide quickly and correctly.
Sound Localization	The ability to tell the direction from which a sound originated.
Dynamic Strength	The ability to exert muscle force repeatedly or continuously over time. This involves muscular endurance and resistance to muscle fatigue.
Gross Body Equilibrium	The ability to keep or regain your body balance or stay upright when in an unstable position.
Mathematical Reasoning	The ability to choose the right mathematical methods or formulas to solve a problem.
Night Vision	The ability to see under low light conditions.
Explosive Strength	The ability to use short bursts of muscle force to propel oneself (as in jumping or sprinting), or to throw an object.
Dynamic Flexibility	The ability to quickly and repeatedly bend, stretch, twist, or reach out with your body, arms, and/or legs.

Work_Activity	Work_Activity Definitions
Operating Vehicles, Mechanized Devices, or Equipme	Running, maneuvering, navigating, or driving vehicles or mechanized equipment, such as forklifts, passenger vehicles, aircraft, or water craft.
Getting Information	Observing, receiving, and otherwise obtaining information from all relevant sources.
Handling and Moving Objects	Using hands and arms in handling, installing, positioning, and moving materials, and manipulating things.
Controlling Machines and Processes	Using either control mechanisms or direct physical activity to operate machines or processes (not including computers or vehicles).
Identifying Objects, Actions, and Events	Identifying information by categorizing, estimating, recognizing differences or similarities, and detecting changes in circumstances or events.
Inspecting Equipment, Structures, or Material	Inspecting equipment, structures, or materials to identify the cause of errors or other problems or defects.
Performing General Physical Activities	Performing physical activities that require considerable use of your arms and legs and moving your whole body, such as climbing, lifting, balancing, walking, stooping, and handling of materials.
Monitor Processes, Materials, or Surroundings	Monitoring and reviewing information from materials, events, or the environment, to detect or assess problems.
Communicating with Persons Outside Organization	Communicating with people outside the organization, representing the organization to customers, the public, government, and other external sources. This information can be exchanged in person, in writing, or by telephone or e-mail.
Repairing and Maintaining Mechanical Equipment	Servicing, repairing, adjusting, and testing machines, devices, moving parts, and equipment that operate primarily on the basis of mechanical (not electronic) principles.
Communicating with Supervisors, Peers, or Subordin	Providing information to supervisors, co-workers, and subordinates by telephone, in written form, e-mail, or in person.
Organizing, Planning, and Prioritizing Work	Developing specific goals and plans to prioritize, organize, and accomplish your work.
Making Decisions and Solving Problems	Analyzing information and evaluating results to choose the best solution and solve problems.
Developing Objectives and Strategies	Establishing long-range objectives and specifying the strategies and actions to achieve them.
Coordinating the Work and Activities of Others	Getting members of a group to work together to accomplish tasks.
Updating and Using Relevant Knowledge	Keeping up-to-date technically and applying new knowledge to your job.
Establishing and Maintaining Interpersonal Relatio	Developing constructive and cooperative working relationships with others, and maintaining them over time.
Performing for or Working Directly with the Public	Performing for people or dealing directly with the public. This includes serving customers in restaurants and stores, and receiving clients or guests.
Scheduling Work and Activities	Scheduling events, programs, and activities, as well as the work of others.
Thinking Creatively	Developing, designing, or creating new applications, ideas, relationships, systems, or products, including artistic contributions.

Guiding, Directing, and Motivating Subordinates	Providing guidance and direction to subordinates, including setting performance standards and monitoring performance.
Developing and Building Teams	Encouraging and building mutual trust, respect, and cooperation among team members.
Training and Teaching Others	Identifying the educational needs of others, developing formal educational or training programs or classes, and teaching or instructing others.
Coaching and Developing Others	Identifying the developmental needs of others and coaching, mentoring, or otherwise helping others to improve their knowledge or skills.
Estimating the Quantifiable Characteristics of Pro	Estimating sizes, distances, and quantities; or determining time, costs, resources, or materials needed to perform a work activity.
Judging the Qualities of Things, Services, or Peop	Assessing the value, importance, or quality of things or people.
Assisting and Caring for Others	Providing personal assistance, medical attention, emotional support, or other personal care to others such as coworkers, customers, or patients.
Interpreting the Meaning of Information for Others	Translating or explaining what information means and how it can be used.
Provide Consultation and Advice to Others	Providing guidance and expert advice to management or other groups on technical, systems-, or process-related topics.
Processing Information	Compiling, coding, categorizing, calculating, tabulating, auditing, or verifying information or data.
Resolving Conflicts and Negotiating with Others	Handling complaints, settling disputes, and resolving grievances and conflicts, or otherwise negotiating with others.
Evaluating Information to Determine Compliance wit	Using relevant information and individual judgment to determine whether events or processes comply with laws, regulations, or standards.
Drafting, Laying Out, and Specifying Technical Dev	Providing documentation, detailed instructions, drawings, or specifications to tell others about how devices, parts, equipment, or structures are to be fabricated, constructed, assembled, modified, maintained, or used.
Documenting/Recording Information	Entering, transcribing, recording, storing, or maintaining information in written or electronic/magnetic form.
Repairing and Maintaining Electronic Equipment	Servicing, repairing, calibrating, regulating, fine-tuning, or testing machines, devices, and equipment that operate primarily on the basis of electrical or electronic (not mechanical) principles.
Analyzing Data or Information	Identifying the underlying principles, reasons, or facts of information by breaking down information or data into separate parts.
Monitoring and Controlling Resources	Monitoring and controlling resources and overseeing the spending of money.
Selling or Influencing Others	Convincing others to buy merchandise/goods or to otherwise change their minds or actions.
Performing Administrative Activities	Performing day-to-day administrative tasks such as maintaining information files and processing paperwork.
Staffing Organizational Units	Recruiting, interviewing, selecting, hiring, and promoting employees in an organization.
Interacting With Computers	Using computers and computer systems (including hardware and software) to program, write software, set up functions, enter data, or process information.

Work_Context	Work_Context Definitions
Outdoors, Exposed to Weather	How often does this job require working outdoors, exposed to all weather conditions?
Wear Common Protective or Safety Equipment such as	How much does this job require wearing common protective or safety equipment such as safety shoes, glasses, gloves, hard hats or live jackets?
Spend Time Using Your Hands to Handle, Control, or	How much does this job require using your hands to handle, control, or feel objects, tools or controls?
Exposed to Contaminants	How often does this job require working exposed to contaminants (such as pollutants, gases, dust or odors)?
Face-to-Face Discussions	How often do you have to have face-to-face discussions with individuals or teams in this job?
Exposed to Hazardous Equipment	How often does this job require exposure to hazardous equipment?
Very Hot or Cold Temperatures	How often does this job require working in very hot (above 90 F degrees) or very cold (below 32 F degrees) temperatures?
In an Open Vehicle or Equipment	How often does this job require working in an open vehicle or equipment (e.g., tractor)?
Sounds, Noise Levels Are Distracting or Uncomforta	How often does this job require working exposed to sounds and noise levels that are distracting or uncomfortable?

Pace Determined by Speed of Equipment	How important is it to this job that the pace is determined by the speed of equipment or machinery? (This does not refer to keeping busy at all times on this job.)
Exposed to Minor Burns, Cuts, Bites, or Stings	How often does this job require exposure to minor burns, cuts, bites, or stings?
Freedom to Make Decisions	How much decision making freedom, without supervision, does the job offer?
Work With Work Group or Team	How important is it to work with others in a group or team in this job?
Contact With Others	How much does this job require the worker to be in contact with others (face-to-face, by telephone, or otherwise) in order to perform it?
Responsible for Others' Health and Safety	How much responsibility is there for the health and safety of others in this job?
Time Pressure	How often does this job require the worker to meet strict deadlines?
Frequency of Decision Making	How frequently is the worker required to make decisions that affect other people, the financial resources, and/or the image and reputation of the organization?
Impact of Decisions on Co-workers or Company Resul	How do the decisions an employee makes impact the results of co-workers, clients or the company?
Spend Time Making Repetitive Motions	How much does this job require making repetitive motions?
Physical Proximity	To what extent does this job require the worker to perform job tasks in close physical proximity to other people?
Extremely Bright or Inadequate Lighting	How often does this job require working in extremely bright or inadequate lighting conditions?
Deal With External Customers	How important is it to work with external customers or the public in this job?
Spend Time Bending or Twisting the Body	How much does this job require bending or twisting your body?
Exposed to Whole Body Vibration	How often does this job require exposure to whole body vibration (e.g., operate a jackhammer)?
Importance of Being Exact or Accurate	How important is being very exact or highly accurate in performing this job?
Structured versus Unstructured Work	To what extent is this job structured for the worker, rather than allowing the worker to determine tasks, priorities, and goals?
Spend Time Standing	How much does this job require standing?
Responsibility for Outcomes and Results	How responsible is the worker for work outcomes and results of other workers?
In an Enclosed Vehicle or Equipment	How often does this job require working in a closed vehicle or equipment (e.g., car)?
Frequency of Conflict Situations	How often are there conflict situations the employee has to face in this job?
Spend Time Walking and Running	How much does this job require walking and running?
Coordinate or Lead Others	How important is it to coordinate or lead others in accomplishing work activities in this job?
Telephone	How often do you have telephone conversations in this job?
Indoors, Not Environmentally Controlled	How often does this job require working indoors in non-controlled environmental conditions (e.g., warehouse without heat)?
Cramped Work Space, Awkward Positions	How often does this job require working in cramped work spaces that requires getting into awkward positions?
Importance of Repeating Same Tasks	How important is repeating the same physical activities (e.g., key entry) or mental activities (e.g., checking entries in a ledger) over and over, without stopping, to performing this job?
Deal With Unpleasant or Angry People	How frequently does the worker have to deal with unpleasant, angry, or discourteous individuals as part of the job requirements?
Consequence of Error	How serious would the result usually be if the worker made a mistake that was not readily correctable?
Spend Time Sitting	How much does this job require sitting?
Exposed to Hazardous Conditions	How often does this job require exposure to hazardous conditions?
Level of Competition	To what extent does this job require the worker to compete or to be aware of competitive pressures?
Degree of Automation	How automated is the job?
Outdoors, Under Cover	How often does this job require working outdoors, under cover (e.g., structure with roof but no walls)?
Spend Time Kneeling, Crouching, Stooping, or Crawl	How much does this job require kneeling, crouching, stooping or crawling?
Exposed to High Places	How often does this job require exposure to high places?
Letters and Memos	How often does the job require written letters and memos?
Spend Time Keeping or Regaining Balance	How much does this job require keeping or regaining your balance?

Wear Specialized Protective or Safety Equipment su	How much does this job require wearing specialized protective or safety equipment such as breathing apparatus, safety harness, full protection suits, or radiation protection?
Electronic Mail	How often do you use electronic mail in this job?
Public Speaking	How often do you have to perform public speaking in this job?
Spend Time Climbing Ladders, Scaffolds, or Poles	How much does this job require climbing ladders, scaffolds, or poles?
Deal With Physically Aggressive People	How frequently does this job require the worker to deal with physical aggression of violent individuals?
Exposed to Radiation	How often does this job require exposure to radiation?
Exposed to Disease or Infections	How often does this job require exposure to disease/infections?
Indoors, Environmentally Controlled	How often does this job require working indoors in environmentally controlled conditions?

Job Zone Component	Job Zone Component Definitions
Title	Job Zone Two: Some Preparation Needed
Overall Experience	Some previous work-related skill, knowledge, or experience may be helpful in these occupations, but usually is not needed. For example, a drywall installer might benefit from experience installing drywall, but an inexperienced person could still learn to be an installer with little difficulty.
Job Training	Employees in these occupations need anywhere from a few months to one year of working with experienced employees. These occupations often involve using your knowledge and skills to help others.
Job Zone Examples	Examples include drywall installers, fire inspectors, flight attendants, pharmacy technicians, salespersons (retail), and tellers.
SVP Range	(4.0 to < 6.0)
Education	These occupations usually require a high school diploma and may require some vocational training or job-related course work. In some cases, an associate's or bachelor's degree could be needed.

Work_Styles	Work_Styles Definitions
Cooperation	Job requires being pleasant with others on the job and displaying a good-natured, cooperative attitude.
Dependability	Job requires being reliable, responsible, and dependable, and fulfilling obligations.
Attention to Detail	Job requires being careful about detail and thorough in completing work tasks.
Stress Tolerance	Job requires accepting criticism and dealing calmly and effectively with high stress situations.
Integrity	Job requires being honest and ethical.
Initiative	Job requires a willingness to take on responsibilities and challenges.
Self Control	Job requires maintaining composure, keeping emotions in check, controlling anger, and avoiding aggressive behavior, even in very difficult situations.
Persistence	Job requires persistence in the face of obstacles.
Social Orientation	Job requires preferring to work with others rather than alone, and being personally connected with others on the job.
Concern for Others	Job requires being sensitive to others' needs and feelings and being understanding and helpful on the job.
Achievement/Effort	Job requires establishing and maintaining personally challenging achievement goals and exerting effort toward mastering tasks.
Independence	Job requires developing one's own ways of doing things, guiding oneself with little or no supervision, and depending on oneself to get things done.
Adaptability/Flexibility	Job requires being open to change (positive or negative) and to considerable variety in the workplace.
Leadership	Job requires a willingness to lead, take charge, and offer opinions and direction.
Analytical Thinking	Job requires analyzing information and using logic to address work-related issues and problems.
Innovation	Job requires creativity and alternative thinking to develop new ideas for and answers to work-related problems.

47-2111.00 - Electricians

Install, maintain, and repair electrical wiring, equipment, and fixtures. Ensure that work is in accordance with relevant codes. May install or service street lights, intercom systems, or electrical control systems.

Tasks

1) Work from ladders, scaffolds, and roofs to install, maintain or repair electrical wiring, equipment, and fixtures.

2) Assemble, install, test, and maintain electrical or electronic wiring, equipment, appliances, apparatus, and fixtures, using hand tools and power tools.

3) Place conduit (pipes or tubing) inside designated partitions, walls, or other concealed areas, and pull insulated wires or cables through the conduit to complete circuits between boxes.

4) Connect wires to circuit breakers, transformers, or other components.

5) Install ground leads and connect power cables to equipment, such as motors.

6) Use a variety of tools and equipment such as power construction equipment, measuring devices, power tools, and testing equipment including oscilloscopes, ammeters, and test lamps.

7) Fasten small metal or plastic boxes to walls to house electrical switches or outlets.

8) Diagnose malfunctioning systems, apparatus, and components, using test equipment and hand tools, to locate the cause of a breakdown and correct the problem.

9) Test electrical systems and continuity of circuits in electrical wiring, equipment, and fixtures, using testing devices such as ohmmeters, voltmeters, and oscilloscopes, to ensure compatibility and safety of system.

10) Plan layout and installation of electrical wiring, equipment and fixtures, based on job specifications and local codes.

11) Construct and fabricate parts, using hand tools and specifications.

12) Inspect electrical systems, equipment, and components to identify hazards, defects, and the need for adjustment or repair, and to ensure compliance with codes.

13) Perform physically demanding tasks, such as digging trenches to lay conduit and moving and lifting heavy objects.

14) Advise management on whether continued operation of equipment could be hazardous.

15) Direct and train workers to install, maintain, or repair electrical wiring, equipment, and fixtures.

16) Prepare sketches or follow blueprints to determine the location of wiring and equipment and to ensure conformance to building and safety codes.

17) Maintain current electrician's license or identification card to meet governmental regulations.

18) Perform business management duties such as maintaining records and files, preparing reports and ordering supplies and equipment.

19) Provide assistance during emergencies by operating floodlights and generators, placing flares, and driving needed vehicles.

20) Provide preliminary sketches and cost estimates for materials and services.

Knowledge	Knowledge Definitions
Building and Construction	Knowledge of materials, methods, and the tools involved in the construction or repair of houses, buildings, or other structures such as highways and roads.
Mechanical	Knowledge of machines and tools, including their designs, uses, repair, and maintenance.
Mathematics	Knowledge of arithmetic, algebra, geometry, calculus, statistics, and their applications.
English Language	Knowledge of the structure and content of the English language including the meaning and spelling of words, rules of composition, and grammar.
Public Safety and Security	Knowledge of relevant equipment, policies, procedures, and strategies to promote effective local, state, or national security operations for the protection of people, data, property, and institutions.
Customer and Personal Service	Knowledge of principles and processes for providing customer and personal services. This includes customer needs assessment, meeting quality standards for services, and evaluation of customer satisfaction.
Administration and Management	Knowledge of business and management principles involved in strategic planning, resource allocation, human resources modeling, leadership technique, production methods, and coordination of people and resources.
Design	Knowledge of design techniques, tools, and principles involved in production of precision technical plans, blueprints, drawings, and models.
Production and Processing	Knowledge of raw materials, production processes, quality control, costs, and other techniques for maximizing the effective manufacture and distribution of goods.
Education and Training	Knowledge of principles and methods for curriculum and training design, teaching and instruction for individuals and groups, and the measurement of training effects.
Law and Government	Knowledge of laws, legal codes, court procedures, precedents, government regulations, executive orders, agency rules, and the democratic political process.
Psychology	Knowledge of human behavior and performance; individual differences in ability, personality, and interests; learning and motivation; psychological research methods; and the assessment and treatment of behavioral and affective disorders.
Physics	Knowledge and prediction of physical principles, laws, their interrelationships, and applications to understanding fluid, material, and atmospheric dynamics, and mechanical, electrical, atomic and sub-atomic structures and processes.
Transportation	Knowledge of principles and methods for moving people or goods by air, rail, sea, or road, including the relative costs and benefits.
Economics and Accounting	Knowledge of economic and accounting principles and practices, the financial markets, banking and the analysis and reporting of financial data.
Clerical	Knowledge of administrative and clerical procedures and systems such as word processing, managing files and records, stenography and transcription, designing forms, and other office procedures and terminology.
Telecommunications	Knowledge of transmission, broadcasting, switching, control, and operation of telecommunications systems.
Engineering and Technology	Knowledge of the practical application of engineering science and technology. This includes applying principles, techniques, procedures, and equipment to the design and production of various goods and services.
Sales and Marketing	Knowledge of principles and methods for showing, promoting, and selling products or services. This includes marketing strategy and tactics, product demonstration, sales techniques, and sales control systems.
Personnel and Human Resources	Knowledge of principles and procedures for personnel recruitment, selection, training, compensation and benefits, labor relations and negotiation, and personnel information systems.
Communications and Media	Knowledge of media production, communication, and dissemination techniques and methods. This includes alternative ways to inform and entertain via written, oral, and visual media.
Chemistry	Knowledge of the chemical composition, structure, and properties of substances and of the chemical processes and transformations that they undergo. This includes uses of chemicals and their interactions, danger signs, production techniques, and disposal methods.
Computers and Electronics	Knowledge of circuit boards, processors, chips, electronic equipment, and computer hardware and software, including applications and programming.
Philosophy and Theology	Knowledge of different philosophical systems and religions. This includes their basic principles, values, ethics, ways of thinking, customs, practices, and their impact on human culture.
Geography	Knowledge of principles and methods for describing the features of land, sea, and air masses, including their physical characteristics, locations, interrelationships, and distribution of plant, animal, and human life.
Sociology and Anthropology	Knowledge of group behavior and dynamics, societal trends and influences, human migrations, ethnicity, cultures and their history and origins.
Therapy and Counseling	Knowledge of principles, methods, and procedures for diagnosis, treatment, and rehabilitation of physical and mental dysfunctions, and for career counseling and guidance.
Medicine and Dentistry	Knowledge of the information and techniques needed to diagnose and treat human injuries, diseases, and deformities. This includes symptoms, treatment alternatives, drug properties and interactions, and preventive health-care measures.

Biology	Knowledge of plant and animal organisms, their tissues, cells, functions, interdependencies, and interactions with each other and the environment.	Programming	Writing computer programs for various purposes.
		Negotiation	Bringing others together and trying to reconcile differences.
History and Archeology	Knowledge of historical events and their causes, indicators, and effects on civilizations and cultures.	Persuasion	Persuading others to change their minds or behavior.

Ability	Ability Definitions
Arm-Hand Steadiness	The ability to keep your hand and arm steady while moving your arm or while holding your arm and hand in one position.

Foreign Language — Knowledge of the structure and content of a foreign (non-English) language including the meaning and spelling of words, rules of composition and grammar, and pronunciation.

Food Production — Knowledge of techniques and equipment for planting, growing, and harvesting food products (both plant and animal) for consumption, including storage/handling techniques.

Fine Arts — Knowledge of the theory and techniques required to compose, produce, and perform works of music, dance, visual arts, drama, and sculpture.

Skills	Skills Definitions		Ability	Ability Definitions

Skills	Skills Definitions
Installation	Installing equipment, machines, wiring, or programs to meet specifications.
Reading Comprehension	Understanding written sentences and paragraphs in work related documents.
Active Listening	Giving full attention to what other people are saying, taking time to understand the points being made, asking questions as appropriate, and not interrupting at inappropriate times.
Troubleshooting	Determining causes of operating errors and deciding what to do about it.
Equipment Selection	Determining the kind of tools and equipment needed to do a job.
Repairing	Repairing machines or systems using the needed tools.
Judgment and Decision Making	Considering the relative costs and benefits of potential actions to choose the most appropriate one.
Time Management	Managing one's own time and the time of others.
Mathematics	Using mathematics to solve problems.
Active Learning	Understanding the implications of new information for both current and future problem-solving and decision-making.
Speaking	Talking to others to convey information effectively.
Coordination	Adjusting actions in relation to others' actions.
Critical Thinking	Using logic and reasoning to identify the strengths and weaknesses of alternative solutions, conclusions or approaches to problems.
Equipment Maintenance	Performing routine maintenance on equipment and determining when and what kind of maintenance is needed.
Learning Strategies	Selecting and using training/instructional methods and procedures appropriate for the situation when learning or teaching new things.
Complex Problem Solving	Identifying complex problems and reviewing related information to develop and evaluate options and implement solutions.
Operation and Control	Controlling operations of equipment or systems.
Instructing	Teaching others how to do something.
Monitoring	Monitoring/Assessing performance of yourself, other individuals, or organizations to make improvements or take corrective action.
Technology Design	Generating or adapting equipment and technology to serve user needs.
Writing	Communicating effectively in writing as appropriate for the needs of the audience.
Operation Monitoring	Watching gauges, dials, or other indicators to make sure a machine is working properly.
Service Orientation	Actively looking for ways to help people.
Management of Material Resources	Obtaining and seeing to the appropriate use of equipment, facilities, and materials needed to do certain work.
Systems Analysis	Determining how a system should work and how changes in conditions, operations, and the environment will affect outcomes.
Operations Analysis	Analyzing needs and product requirements to create a design.
Quality Control Analysis	Conducting tests and inspections of products, services, or processes to evaluate quality or performance.
Systems Evaluation	Identifying measures or indicators of system performance and the actions needed to improve or correct performance, relative to the goals of the system.
Management of Personnel Resources	Motivating, developing, and directing people as they work, identifying the best people for the job.
Science	Using scientific rules and methods to solve problems.
Management of Financial Resources	Determining how money will be spent to get the work done, and accounting for these expenditures.
Social Perceptiveness	Being aware of others' reactions and understanding why they react as they do.

Ability	Ability Definitions
Arm-Hand Steadiness	The ability to keep your hand and arm steady while moving your arm or while holding your arm and hand in one position.
Problem Sensitivity	The ability to tell when something is wrong or is likely to go wrong. It does not involve solving the problem, only recognizing there is a problem.
Near Vision	The ability to see details at close range (within a few feet of the observer).
Finger Dexterity	The ability to make precisely coordinated movements of the fingers of one or both hands to grasp, manipulate, or assemble very small objects.
Extent Flexibility	The ability to bend, stretch, twist, or reach with your body, arms, and/or legs.
Deductive Reasoning	The ability to apply general rules to specific problems to produce answers that make sense.
Trunk Strength	The ability to use your abdominal and lower back muscles to support part of the body repeatedly or continuously over time without 'giving out' or fatiguing.
Manual Dexterity	The ability to quickly move your hand, your hand together with your arm, or your two hands to grasp, manipulate, or assemble objects.
Information Ordering	The ability to arrange things or actions in a certain order or pattern according to a specific rule or set of rules (e.g., patterns of numbers, letters, words, pictures, mathematical operations).
Oral Expression	The ability to communicate information and ideas in speaking so others will understand.
Gross Body Equilibrium	The ability to keep or regain your body balance or stay upright when in an unstable position.
Static Strength	The ability to exert maximum muscle force to lift, push, pull, or carry objects.
Oral Comprehension	The ability to listen to and understand information and ideas presented through spoken words and sentences.
Inductive Reasoning	The ability to combine pieces of information to form general rules or conclusions (includes finding a relationship among seemingly unrelated events).
Stamina	The ability to exert yourself physically over long periods of time without getting winded or out of breath.
Speech Clarity	The ability to speak clearly so others can understand you.
Visual Color Discrimination	The ability to match or detect differences between colors, including shades of color and brightness.
Speech Recognition	The ability to identify and understand the speech of another person.
Visualization	The ability to imagine how something will look after it is moved around or when its parts are moved or rearranged.
Selective Attention	The ability to concentrate on a task over a period of time without being distracted.
Flexibility of Closure	The ability to identify or detect a known pattern (a figure, object, word, or sound) that is hidden in other distracting material.
Dynamic Strength	The ability to exert muscle force repeatedly or continuously over time. This involves muscular endurance and resistance to muscle fatigue.
Written Comprehension	The ability to read and understand information and ideas presented in writing.
Multilimb Coordination	The ability to coordinate two or more limbs (for example, two arms, two legs, or one leg and one arm) while sitting, standing, or lying down. It does not involve performing the activities while the whole body is in motion.
Gross Body Coordination	The ability to coordinate the movement of your arms, legs, and torso together when the whole body is in motion.
Category Flexibility	The ability to generate or use different sets of rules for combining or grouping things in different ways.
Perceptual Speed	The ability to quickly and accurately compare similarities and differences among sets of letters, numbers, objects, pictures, or patterns. The things to be compared may be presented at the same time or one after the other. This ability also includes comparing a presented object with a remembered object.
Control Precision	The ability to quickly and repeatedly adjust the controls of a machine or a vehicle to exact positions.
Fluency of Ideas	The ability to come up with a number of ideas about a topic (the number of ideas is important, not their quality, correctness, or creativity).
Far Vision	The ability to see details at a distance.

Depth Perception	The ability to judge which of several objects is closer or farther away from you, or to judge the distance between you and an object.
Written Expression	The ability to communicate information and ideas in writing so others will understand.
Memorization	The ability to remember information such as words, numbers, pictures, and procedures.
Number Facility	The ability to add, subtract, multiply, or divide quickly and correctly.
Time Sharing	The ability to shift back and forth between two or more activities or sources of information (such as speech, sounds, touch, or other sources).
Speed of Closure	The ability to quickly make sense of, combine, and organize information into meaningful patterns.
Originality	The ability to come up with unusual or clever ideas about a given topic or situation, or to develop creative ways to solve a problem.
Reaction Time	The ability to quickly respond (with the hand, finger, or foot) to a signal (sound, light, picture) when it appears.
Hearing Sensitivity	The ability to detect or tell the differences between sounds that vary in pitch and loudness.
Spatial Orientation	The ability to know your location in relation to the environment or to know where other objects are in relation to you.
Auditory Attention	The ability to focus on a single source of sound in the presence of other distracting sounds.
Speed of Limb Movement	The ability to quickly move the arms and legs.
Wrist-Finger Speed	The ability to make fast, simple, repeated movements of the fingers, hands, and wrists.
Mathematical Reasoning	The ability to choose the right mathematical methods or formulas to solve a problem.
Glare Sensitivity	The ability to see objects in the presence of glare or bright lighting.
Response Orientation	The ability to choose quickly between two or more movements in response to two or more different signals (lights, sounds, pictures). It includes the speed with which the correct response is started with the hand, foot, or other body part.
Rate Control	The ability to time your movements or the movement of a piece of equipment in anticipation of changes in the speed and/or direction of a moving object or scene.
Night Vision	The ability to see under low light conditions.
Sound Localization	The ability to tell the direction from which a sound originated.
Peripheral Vision	The ability to see objects or movement of objects to one's side when the eyes are looking ahead.
Explosive Strength	The ability to use short bursts of muscle force to propel oneself (as in jumping or sprinting), or to throw an object.
Dynamic Flexibility	The ability to quickly and repeatedly bend, stretch, twist, or reach out with your body, arms, and/or legs.

Work_Activity	Work_Activity Definitions
Making Decisions and Solving Problems	Analyzing information and evaluating results to choose the best solution and solve problems.
Communicating with Supervisors, Peers, or Subordin	Providing information to supervisors, co-workers, and subordinates by telephone, in written form, e-mail, or in person.
Performing General Physical Activities	Performing physical activities that require considerable use of your arms and legs and moving your whole body, such as climbing, lifting, balancing, walking, stooping, and handling of materials.
Organizing, Planning, and Prioritizing Work	Developing specific goals and plans to prioritize, organize, and accomplish your work.
Updating and Using Relevant Knowledge	Keeping up-to-date technically and applying new knowledge to your job.
Getting Information	Observing, receiving, and otherwise obtaining information from all relevant sources.
Evaluating Information to Determine Compliance wit	Using relevant information and individual judgment to determine whether events or processes comply with laws, regulations, or standards.
Handling and Moving Objects	Using hands and arms in handling, installing, positioning, and moving materials, and manipulating things.
Scheduling Work and Activities	Scheduling events, programs, and activities, as well as the work of others.
Inspecting Equipment, Structures, or Material	Inspecting equipment, structures, or materials to identify the cause of errors or other problems or defects.
Repairing and Maintaining Electronic Equipment	Servicing, repairing, calibrating, regulating, fine-tuning, or testing machines, devices, and equipment that operate primarily on the basis of electrical or electronic (not mechanical) principles.

Establishing and Maintaining Interpersonal Relatio	Developing constructive and cooperative working relationships with others, and maintaining them over time.
Identifying Objects, Actions, and Events	Identifying information by categorizing, estimating, recognizing differences or similarities, and detecting changes in circumstances or events.
Judging the Qualities of Things, Services, or Peop	Assessing the value, importance, or quality of things or people.
Monitor Processes, Materials, or Surroundings	Monitoring and reviewing information from materials, events, or the environment, to detect or assess problems.
Training and Teaching Others	Identifying the educational needs of others, developing formal educational or training programs or classes, and teaching or instructing others.
Controlling Machines and Processes	Using either control mechanisms or direct physical activity to operate machines or processes (not including computers or vehicles).
Communicating with Persons Outside Organization	Communicating with people outside the organization, representing the organization to customers, the public, government, and other external sources. This information can be exchanged in person, in writing, or by telephone or e-mail.
Estimating the Quantifiable Characteristics of Pro	Estimating sizes, distances, and quantities; or determining time, costs, resources, or materials needed to perform a work activity.
Operating Vehicles, Mechanized Devices, or Equipme	Running, maneuvering, navigating, or driving vehicles or mechanized equipment, such as forklifts, passenger vehicles, aircraft, or water craft.
Processing Information	Compiling, coding, categorizing, calculating, tabulating, auditing, or verifying information or data.
Coordinating the Work and Activities of Others	Getting members of a group to work together to accomplish tasks.
Interpreting the Meaning of Information for Others	Translating or explaining what information means and how it can be used.
Repairing and Maintaining Mechanical Equipment	Servicing, repairing, adjusting, and testing machines, devices, moving parts, and equipment that operate primarily on the basis of mechanical (not electronic) principles.
Thinking Creatively	Developing, designing, or creating new applications, ideas, relationships, systems, or products, including artistic contributions.
Guiding, Directing, and Motivating Subordinates	Providing guidance and direction to subordinates, including setting performance standards and monitoring performance.
Resolving Conflicts and Negotiating with Others	Handling complaints, settling disputes, and resolving grievances and conflicts, or otherwise negotiating with others.
Analyzing Data or Information	Identifying the underlying principles, reasons, or facts of information by breaking down information or data into separate parts.
Developing and Building Teams	Encouraging and building mutual trust, respect, and cooperation among team members.
Documenting/Recording Information	Entering, transcribing, recording, storing, or maintaining information in written or electronic/magnetic form.
Developing Objectives and Strategies	Establishing long-range objectives and specifying the strategies and actions to achieve them.
Coaching and Developing Others	Identifying the developmental needs of others and coaching, mentoring, or otherwise helping others to improve their knowledge or skills.
Performing for or Working Directly with the Public	Performing for people or dealing directly with the public. This includes serving customers in restaurants and stores, and receiving clients or guests.
Drafting, Laying Out, and Specifying Technical Dev	Providing documentation, detailed instructions, drawings, or specifications to tell others about how devices, parts, equipment, or structures are to be fabricated, constructed, assembled, modified, maintained, or used.
Provide Consultation and Advice to Others	Providing guidance and expert advice to management or other groups on technical, systems-, or process-related topics.
Selling or Influencing Others	Convincing others to buy merchandise/goods or to otherwise change their minds or actions.
Monitoring and Controlling Resources	Monitoring and controlling resources and overseeing the spending of money.
Performing Administrative Activities	Performing day-to-day administrative tasks such as maintaining information files and processing paperwork.
Assisting and Caring for Others	Providing personal assistance, medical attention, emotional support, or other personal care to others such as coworkers, customers, or patients.
Interacting With Computers	Using computers and computer systems (including hardware and software) to program, write software, set up functions, enter data, or process information.
Staffing Organizational Units	Recruiting, interviewing, selecting, hiring, and promoting employees in an organization.

Work_Context	Work_Context Definitions
Freedom to Make Decisions	How much decision making freedom, without supervision, does the job offer?
Spend Time Standing	How much does this job require standing?
Structured versus Unstructured Work	To what extent is this job structured for the worker, rather than allowing the worker to determine tasks, priorities, and goals?
Contact With Others	How much does this job require the worker to be in contact with others (face-to-face, by telephone, or otherwise) in order to perform it?
Telephone	How often do you have telephone conversations in this job?
Importance of Being Exact or Accurate	How important is being very exact or highly accurate in performing this job?
Face-to-Face Discussions	How often do you have to have face-to-face discussions with individuals or teams in this job?
Indoors, Not Environmentally Controlled	How often does this job require working indoors in non-controlled environmental conditions (e.g., warehouse without heat)?
Frequency of Decision Making	How frequently is the worker required to make decisions that affect other people, the financial resources, and/or the image and reputation of the organization?
Impact of Decisions on Co-workers or Company Resul	How do the decisions an employee makes impact the results of co-workers, clients or the company?
Work With Work Group or Team	How important is it to work with others in a group or team in this job?
Time Pressure	How often does this job require the worker to meet strict deadlines?
Spend Time Walking and Running	How much does this job require walking and running?
Coordinate or Lead Others	How important is it to coordinate or lead others in accomplishing work activities in this job?
Spend Time Using Your Hands to Handle, Control, or	How much does this job require using your hands to handle, control, or feel objects, tools or controls?
Responsible for Others' Health and Safety	How much responsibility is there for the health and safety of others in this job?
Outdoors, Exposed to Weather	How often does this job require working outdoors, exposed to all weather conditions?
Sounds, Noise Levels Are Distracting or Uncomforta	How often does this job require working exposed to sounds and noise levels that are distracting or uncomfortable?
Wear Common Protective or Safety Equipment such as	How much does this job require wearing common protective or safety equipment such as safety shoes, glasses, gloves, hard hats or live jackets?
Responsibility for Outcomes and Results	How responsible is the worker for work outcomes and results of other workers?
Exposed to Minor Burns, Cuts, Bites, or Stings	How often does this job require exposure to minor burns, cuts, bites, or stings?
Deal With External Customers	How important is it to work with external customers or the public in this job?
Exposed to High Places	How often does this job require exposure to high places?
Cramped Work Space, Awkward Positions	How often does this job require working in cramped work spaces that requires getting into awkward positions?
Very Hot or Cold Temperatures	How often does this job require working in very hot (above 90 F degrees) or very cold (below 32 F degrees) temperatures?
Spend Time Climbing Ladders, Scaffolds, or Poles	How much does this job require climbing ladders, scaffolds, or poles?
Extremely Bright or Inadequate Lighting	How often does this job require working in extremely bright or inadequate lighting conditions?
Spend Time Kneeling, Crouching, Stooping, or Crawl	How much does this job require kneeling, crouching, stooping or crawling?
Indoors, Environmentally Controlled	How often does this job require working indoors in environmentally controlled conditions?
Level of Competition	To what extent does this job require the worker to compete or to be aware of competitive pressures?
Spend Time Bending or Twisting the Body	How much does this job require bending or twisting your body?
Physical Proximity	To what extent does this job require the worker to perform job tasks in close physical proximity to other people?
Outdoors, Under Cover	How often does this job require working outdoors, under cover (e.g., structure with roof but no walls)?
Importance of Repeating Same Tasks	How important is repeating the same physical activities (e.g., key entry) or mental activities (e.g., checking entries in a ledger) over and over, without stopping, to performing this job?

In an Enclosed Vehicle or Equipment	How often does this job require working in a closed vehicle or equipment (e.g., car)?
Frequency of Conflict Situations	How often are there conflict situations the employee has to face in this job?
Consequence of Error	How serious would the result usually be if the worker made a mistake that was not readily correctable?
Exposed to Contaminants	How often does this job require working exposed to contaminants (such as pollutants, gases, dust or odors)?
Exposed to Hazardous Conditions	How often does this job require exposure to hazardous conditions?
Exposed to Hazardous Equipment	How often does this job require exposure to hazardous equipment?
Deal With Unpleasant or Angry People	How frequently does the worker have to deal with unpleasant, angry, or discourteous individuals as part of the job requirements?
Spend Time Making Repetitive Motions	How much does this job require making repetitive motions?
Letters and Memos	How often does the job require written letters and memos?
Spend Time Keeping or Regaining Balance	How much does this job require keeping or regaining your balance?
Exposed to Whole Body Vibration	How often does this job require exposure to whole body vibration (e.g., operate a jackhammer)?
Electronic Mail	How often do you use electronic mail in this job?
In an Open Vehicle or Equipment	How often does this job require working in an open vehicle or equipment (e.g., tractor)?
Pace Determined by Speed of Equipment	How important is it to this job that the pace is determined by the speed of equipment or machinery? (This does not refer to keeping busy at all times on this job.)
Wear Specialized Protective or Safety Equipment su	How much does this job require wearing specialized protective or safety equipment such as breathing apparatus, safety harness, full protection suits, or radiation protection?
Spend Time Sitting	How much does this job require sitting?
Degree of Automation	How automated is the job?
Exposed to Disease or Infections	How often does this job require exposure to disease/infections?
Public Speaking	How often do you have to perform public speaking in this job?
Deal With Physically Aggressive People	How frequently does this job require the worker to deal with physical aggression of violent individuals?
Exposed to Radiation	How often does this job require exposure to radiation?

Job Zone Component	Job Zone Component Definitions
Title	Job Zone Three: Medium Preparation Needed
Overall Experience	Previous work-related skill, knowledge, or experience is required for these occupations. For example, an electrician must have completed three or four years of apprenticeship or several years of vocational training, and often must have passed a licensing exam, in order to perform the job.
Job Training	Employees in these occupations usually need one or two years of training involving both on-the-job experience and informal training with experienced workers.
Job Zone Examples	These occupations usually involve using communication and organizational skills to coordinate, supervise, manage, or train others to accomplish goals. Examples include dental assistants, electricians, fish and game wardens, legal secretaries, personnel recruiters, and recreation workers.
SVP Range	(6.0 to < 7.0)
Education	Most occupations in this zone require training in vocational schools, related on-the-job experience, or an associate's degree. Some may require a bachelor's degree.

Work_Styles	Work_Styles Definitions
Attention to Detail	Job requires being careful about detail and thorough in completing work tasks.
Dependability	Job requires being reliable, responsible, and dependable, and fulfilling obligations.
Initiative	Job requires a willingness to take on responsibilities and challenges.
Integrity	Job requires being honest and ethical.
Cooperation	Job requires being pleasant with others on the job and displaying a good-natured, cooperative attitude.
Independence	Job requires developing one's own ways of doing things, guiding oneself with little or no supervision, and depending on oneself to get things done.
Adaptability/Flexibility	Job requires being open to change (positive or negative) and to considerable variety in the workplace.

Leadership	Job requires a willingness to lead, take charge, and offer opinions and direction.
Innovation	Job requires creativity and alternative thinking to develop new ideas for and answers to work-related problems.
Persistence	Job requires persistence in the face of obstacles.
Self Control	Job requires maintaining composure, keeping emotions in check, controlling anger, and avoiding aggressive behavior, even in very difficult situations.
Achievement/Effort	Job requires establishing and maintaining personally challenging achievement goals and exerting effort toward mastering tasks.
Analytical Thinking	Job requires analyzing information and using logic to address work-related issues and problems.
Stress Tolerance	Job requires accepting criticism and dealing calmly and effectively with high stress situations.
Concern for Others	Job requires being sensitive to others' needs and feelings and being understanding and helpful on the job.
Social Orientation	Job requires preferring to work with others rather than alone, and being personally connected with others on the job.

47-2152.01 - Pipe Fitters

Lay out, assemble, install, and maintain pipe systems, pipe supports, and related hydraulic and pneumatic equipment for steam, hot water, heating, cooling, lubricating, sprinkling, and industrial production and processing systems.

Tasks

1) Lay out full scale drawings of pipe systems, supports, and related equipment, following blueprints.

2) Plan pipe system layout, installation, or repair according to specifications.

3) Measure and mark pipes for cutting and threading.

4) Assemble and secure pipes, tubes, fittings, and related equipment, according to specifications, by welding, brazing, cementing, soldering, and threading joints.

5) Cut, thread, and hammer pipe to specifications, using tools such as saws, cutting torches, and pipe threaders and benders.

6) Modify, clean, and maintain pipe systems, units, fittings, and related machines and equipment, following specifications and using hand and power tools.

7) Turn valves to shut off steam, water, or other gases or liquids from pipe sections, using valve keys or wrenches.

8) Cut and bore holes in structures, such as bulkheads, decks, walls, and mains, prior to pipe installation, using hand and power tools.

9) Select pipe sizes and types and related materials, such as supports, hangers, and hydraulic cylinders, according to specifications.

10) Remove and replace worn components.

11) Attach pipes to walls, structures and fixtures, such as radiators or tanks, using brackets, clamps, tools or welding equipment.

12) Install automatic controls used to regulate pipe systems.

13) Operate motorized pumps to remove water from flooded manholes, basements, or facility floors.

14) Inspect work sites for obstructions and to ensure that holes will not cause structural weakness.

15) Prepare cost estimates for clients.

16) Dip nonferrous piping materials in a mixture of molten tin and lead to obtain a coating that prevents erosion or galvanic and electrolytic action.

Knowledge	Knowledge Definitions
Mechanical	Knowledge of machines and tools, including their designs, uses, repair, and maintenance.
Design	Knowledge of design techniques, tools, and principles involved in production of precision technical plans, blueprints, drawings, and models.
Building and Construction	Knowledge of materials, methods, and the tools involved in the construction or repair of houses, buildings, or other structures such as highways and roads.
English Language	Knowledge of the structure and content of the English language including the meaning and spelling of words, rules of composition, and grammar.
Engineering and Technology	Knowledge of the practical application of engineering science and technology. This includes applying principles, techniques, procedures, and equipment to the design and production of various goods and services.
Public Safety and Security	Knowledge of relevant equipment, policies, procedures, and strategies to promote effective local, state, or national security operations for the protection of people, data, property, and institutions.
Mathematics	Knowledge of arithmetic, algebra, geometry, calculus, statistics, and their applications.
Economics and Accounting	Knowledge of economic and accounting principles and practices, the financial markets, banking and the analysis and reporting of financial data.
Education and Training	Knowledge of principles and methods for curriculum and training design, teaching and instruction for individuals and groups, and the measurement of training effects.
Computers and Electronics	Knowledge of circuit boards, processors, chips, electronic equipment, and computer hardware and software, including applications and programming.
Customer and Personal Service	Knowledge of principles and processes for providing customer and personal services. This includes customer needs assessment, meeting quality standards for services, and evaluation of customer satisfaction.
Law and Government	Knowledge of laws, legal codes, court procedures, precedents, government regulations, executive orders, agency rules, and the democratic political process.
Transportation	Knowledge of principles and methods for moving people or goods by air, rail, sea, or road, including the relative costs and benefits.
Personnel and Human Resources	Knowledge of principles and procedures for personnel recruitment, selection, training, compensation and benefits, labor relations and negotiation, and personnel information systems.
Administration and Management	Knowledge of business and management principles involved in strategic planning, resource allocation, human resources modeling, leadership technique, production methods, and coordination of people and resources.
Clerical	Knowledge of administrative and clerical procedures and systems such as word processing, managing files and records, stenography and transcription, designing forms, and other office procedures and terminology.
Sales and Marketing	Knowledge of principles and methods for showing, promoting, and selling products or services. This includes marketing strategy and tactics, product demonstration, sales techniques, and sales control systems.
Geography	Knowledge of principles and methods for describing the features of land, sea, and air masses, including their physical characteristics, locations, interrelationships, and distribution of plant, animal, and human life.
Production and Processing	Knowledge of raw materials, production processes, quality control, costs, and other techniques for maximizing the effective manufacture and distribution of goods.
Communications and Media	Knowledge of media production, communication, and dissemination techniques and methods. This includes alternative ways to inform and entertain via written, oral, and visual media.
Foreign Language	Knowledge of the structure and content of a foreign (non-English) language including the meaning and spelling of words, rules of composition and grammar, and pronunciation.
Physics	Knowledge and prediction of physical principles, laws, their interrelationships, and applications to understanding fluid, material, and atmospheric dynamics, and mechanical, electrical, atomic and sub- atomic structures and processes.
Therapy and Counseling	Knowledge of principles, methods, and procedures for diagnosis, treatment, and rehabilitation of physical and mental dysfunctions, and for career counseling and guidance.
Biology	Knowledge of plant and animal organisms, their tissues, cells, functions, interdependencies, and interactions with each other and the environment.
Chemistry	Knowledge of the chemical composition, structure, and properties of substances and of the chemical processes and transformations that they undergo. This includes uses of chemicals and their interactions, danger signs, production techniques, and disposal methods.

History and Archeology	Knowledge of historical events and their causes, indicators, and effects on civilizations and cultures.
Food Production	Knowledge of techniques and equipment for planting, growing, and harvesting food products (both plant and animal) for consumption, including storage/handling techniques.
Telecommunications	Knowledge of transmission, broadcasting, switching, control, and operation of telecommunications systems.
Psychology	Knowledge of human behavior and performance; individual differences in ability, personality, and interests; learning and motivation; psychological research methods; and the assessment and treatment of behavioral and affective disorders.
Sociology and Anthropology	Knowledge of group behavior and dynamics, societal trends and influences, human migrations, ethnicity, cultures and their history and origins.
Philosophy and Theology	Knowledge of different philosophical systems and religions. This includes their basic principles, values, ethics, ways of thinking, customs, practices, and their impact on human culture.
Medicine and Dentistry	Knowledge of the information and techniques needed to diagnose and treat human injuries, diseases, and deformities. This includes symptoms, treatment alternatives, drug properties and interactions, and preventive health-care measures.
Fine Arts	Knowledge of the theory and techniques required to compose, produce, and perform works of music, dance, visual arts, drama, and sculpture.

Skills	Skills Definitions
Installation	Installing equipment, machines, wiring, or programs to meet specifications.
Instructing	Teaching others how to do something.
Critical Thinking	Using logic and reasoning to identify the strengths and weaknesses of alternative solutions, conclusions or approaches to problems.
Active Learning	Understanding the implications of new information for both current and future problem-solving and decision-making.
Equipment Selection	Determining the kind of tools and equipment needed to do a job.
Judgment and Decision Making	Considering the relative costs and benefits of potential actions to choose the most appropriate one.
Active Listening	Giving full attention to what other people are saying, taking time to understand the points being made, asking questions as appropriate, and not interrupting at inappropriate times.
Repairing	Repairing machines or systems using the needed tools.
Time Management	Managing one's own time and the time of others.
Reading Comprehension	Understanding written sentences and paragraphs in work related documents.
Coordination	Adjusting actions in relation to others' actions.
Troubleshooting	Determining causes of operating errors and deciding what to do about it.
Service Orientation	Actively looking for ways to help people.
Management of Personnel Resources	Motivating, developing, and directing people as they work, identifying the best people for the job.
Mathematics	Using mathematics to solve problems.
Persuasion	Persuading others to change their minds or behavior.
Equipment Maintenance	Performing routine maintenance on equipment and determining when and what kind of maintenance is needed.
Systems Analysis	Determining how a system should work and how changes in conditions, operations, and the environment will affect outcomes.
Operation Monitoring	Watching gauges, dials, or other indicators to make sure a machine is working properly.
Negotiation	Bringing others together and trying to reconcile differences.
Quality Control Analysis	Conducting tests and inspections of products, services, or processes to evaluate quality or performance.
Monitoring	Monitoring/Assessing performance of yourself, other individuals, or organizations to make improvements or take corrective action.
Operation and Control	Controlling operations of equipment or systems.
Speaking	Talking to others to convey information effectively.
Learning Strategies	Selecting and using training/instructional methods and procedures appropriate for the situation when learning or teaching new things.
Complex Problem Solving	Identifying complex problems and reviewing related information to develop and evaluate options and implement solutions.

Systems Evaluation	Identifying measures or indicators of system performance and the actions needed to improve or correct performance, relative to the goals of the system.
Social Perceptiveness	Being aware of others' reactions and understanding why they react as they do.
Management of Material Resources	Obtaining and seeing to the appropriate use of equipment, facilities, and materials needed to do certain work.
Writing	Communicating effectively in writing as appropriate for the needs of the audience.
Technology Design	Generating or adapting equipment and technology to serve user needs.
Operations Analysis	Analyzing needs and product requirements to create a design.
Science	Using scientific rules and methods to solve problems.
Management of Financial Resources	Determining how money will be spent to get the work done, and accounting for these expenditures.
Programming	Writing computer programs for various purposes.

Ability	Ability Definitions
Information Ordering	The ability to arrange things or actions in a certain order or pattern according to a specific rule or set of rules (e.g., patterns of numbers, letters, words, pictures, mathematical operations).
Near Vision	The ability to see details at close range (within a few feet of the observer).
Problem Sensitivity	The ability to tell when something is wrong or is likely to go wrong. It does not involve solving the problem, only recognizing there is a problem.
Deductive Reasoning	The ability to apply general rules to specific problems to produce answers that make sense.
Arm-Hand Steadiness	The ability to keep your hand and arm steady while moving your arm or while holding your arm and hand in one position.
Visualization	The ability to imagine how something will look after it is moved around or when its parts are moved or rearranged.
Oral Comprehension	The ability to listen to and understand information and ideas presented through spoken words and sentences.
Oral Expression	The ability to communicate information and ideas in speaking so others will understand.
Speech Clarity	The ability to speak clearly so others can understand you.
Speech Recognition	The ability to identify and understand the speech of another person.
Manual Dexterity	The ability to quickly move your hand, your hand together with your arm, or your two hands to grasp, manipulate, or assemble objects.
Inductive Reasoning	The ability to combine pieces of information to form general rules or conclusions (includes finding a relationship among seemingly unrelated events).
Multilimb Coordination	The ability to coordinate two or more limbs (for example, two arms, two legs, or one leg and one arm) while sitting, standing, or lying down. It does not involve performing the activities while the whole body is in motion.
Written Comprehension	The ability to read and understand information and ideas presented in writing.
Finger Dexterity	The ability to make precisely coordinated movements of the fingers of one or both hands to grasp, manipulate, or assemble very small objects.
Control Precision	The ability to quickly and repeatedly adjust the controls of a machine or a vehicle to exact positions.
Trunk Strength	The ability to use your abdominal and lower back muscles to support part of the body repeatedly or continuously over time without 'giving out' or fatiguing.
Gross Body Coordination	The ability to coordinate the movement of your arms, legs, and torso together when the whole body is in motion.
Static Strength	The ability to exert maximum muscle force to lift, push, pull, or carry objects.
Fluency of Ideas	The ability to come up with a number of ideas about a topic (the number of ideas is important, not their quality, correctness, or creativity).
Category Flexibility	The ability to generate or use different sets of rules for combining or grouping things in different ways.
Mathematical Reasoning	The ability to choose the right mathematical methods or formulas to solve a problem.
Extent Flexibility	The ability to bend, stretch, twist, or reach with your body, arms, and/or legs.
Stamina	The ability to exert yourself physically over long periods of time without getting winded or out of breath.
Written Expression	The ability to communicate information and ideas in writing so others will understand.

Dynamic Strength	The ability to exert muscle force repeatedly or continuously over time. This involves muscular endurance and resistance to muscle fatigue.
Flexibility of Closure	The ability to identify or detect a known pattern (a figure, object, word, or sound) that is hidden in other distracting material.
Gross Body Equilibrium	The ability to keep or regain your body balance or stay upright when in an unstable position.
Depth Perception	The ability to judge which of several objects is closer or farther away from you, or to judge the distance between you and an object.
Perceptual Speed	The ability to quickly and accurately compare similarities and differences among sets of letters, numbers, objects, pictures, or patterns. The things to be compared may be presented at the same time or one after the other. This ability also includes comparing a presented object with a remembered object.
Selective Attention	The ability to concentrate on a task over a period of time without being distracted.
Originality	The ability to come up with unusual or clever ideas about a given topic or situation, or to develop creative ways to solve a problem.
Reaction Time	The ability to quickly respond (with the hand, finger, or foot) to a signal (sound, light, picture) when it appears.
Far Vision	The ability to see details at a distance.
Speed of Closure	The ability to quickly make sense of, combine, and organize information into meaningful patterns.
Number Facility	The ability to add, subtract, multiply, or divide quickly and correctly.
Memorization	The ability to remember information such as words, numbers, pictures, and procedures.
Auditory Attention	The ability to focus on a single source of sound in the presence of other distracting sounds.
Wrist-Finger Speed	The ability to make fast, simple, repeated movements of the fingers, hands, and wrists.
Speed of Limb Movement	The ability to quickly move the arms and legs.
Explosive Strength	The ability to use short bursts of muscle force to propel oneself (as in jumping or sprinting), or to throw an object.
Time Sharing	The ability to shift back and forth between two or more activities or sources of information (such as speech, sounds, touch, or other sources).
Glare Sensitivity	The ability to see objects in the presence of glare or bright lighting.
Visual Color Discrimination	The ability to match or detect differences between colors, including shades of color and brightness.
Spatial Orientation	The ability to know your location in relation to the environment or to know where other objects are in relation to you.
Sound Localization	The ability to tell the direction from which a sound originated.
Hearing Sensitivity	The ability to detect or tell the differences between sounds that vary in pitch and loudness.
Night Vision	The ability to see under low light conditions.
Response Orientation	The ability to choose quickly between two or more movements in response to two or more different signals (lights, sounds, pictures). It includes the speed with which the correct response is started with the hand, foot, or other body part.
Dynamic Flexibility	The ability to quickly and repeatedly bend, stretch, twist, or reach out with your body, arms, and/or legs.
Rate Control	The ability to time your movements or the movement of a piece of equipment in anticipation of changes in the speed and/or direction of a moving object or scene.
Peripheral Vision	The ability to see objects or movement of objects to one's side when the eyes are looking ahead.

Work_Activity	Work_Activity Definitions
Getting Information	Observing, receiving, and otherwise obtaining information from all relevant sources.
Inspecting Equipment, Structures, or Material	Inspecting equipment, structures, or materials to identify the cause of errors or other problems or defects.
Making Decisions and Solving Problems	Analyzing information and evaluating results to choose the best solution and solve problems.
Communicating with Supervisors, Peers, or Subordin	Providing information to supervisors, co-workers, and subordinates by telephone, in written form, e-mail, or in person.
Analyzing Data or Information	Identifying the underlying principles, reasons, or facts of information by breaking down information or data into separate parts.

Repairing and Maintaining Mechanical Equipment	Servicing, repairing, adjusting, and testing machines, devices, moving parts, and equipment that operate primarily on the basis of mechanical (not electronic) principles.
Processing Information	Compiling, coding, categorizing, calculating, tabulating, auditing, or verifying information or data.
Organizing, Planning, and Prioritizing Work	Developing specific goals and plans to prioritize, organize, and accomplish your work.
Performing General Physical Activities	Performing physical activities that require considerable use of your arms and legs and moving your whole body, such as climbing, lifting, balancing, walking, stooping, and handling of materials.
Scheduling Work and Activities	Scheduling events, programs, and activities, as well as the work of others.
Handling and Moving Objects	Using hands and arms in handling, installing, positioning, and moving materials, and manipulating things.
Updating and Using Relevant Knowledge	Keeping up-to-date technically and applying new knowledge to your job.
Judging the Qualities of Things, Services, or Peop	Assessing the value, importance, or quality of things or people.
Interacting With Computers	Using computers and computer systems (including hardware and software) to program, write software, set up functions, enter data, or process information.
Interpreting the Meaning of Information for Others	Translating or explaining what information means and how it can be used.
Developing Objectives and Strategies	Establishing long-range objectives and specifying the strategies and actions to achieve them.
Drafting, Laying Out, and Specifying Technical Dev	Providing documentation, detailed instructions, drawings, or specifications to tell others about how devices, parts, equipment, or structures are to be fabricated, constructed, assembled, modified, maintained, or used.
Developing and Building Teams	Encouraging and building mutual trust, respect, and cooperation among team members.
Training and Teaching Others	Identifying the educational needs of others, developing formal educational or training programs or classes, and teaching or instructing others.
Guiding, Directing, and Motivating Subordinates	Providing guidance and direction to subordinates, including setting performance standards and monitoring performance.
Coaching and Developing Others	Identifying the developmental needs of others and coaching, mentoring, or otherwise helping others to improve their knowledge or skills.
Selling or Influencing Others	Convincing others to buy merchandise/goods or to otherwise change their minds or actions.
Performing for or Working Directly with the Public	Performing for people or dealing directly with the public. This includes serving customers in restaurants and stores, and receiving clients or guests.
Repairing and Maintaining Electronic Equipment	Servicing, repairing, calibrating, regulating, fine-tuning, or testing machines, devices, and equipment that operate primarily on the basis of electrical or electronic (not mechanical) principles.
Estimating the Quantifiable Characteristics of Pro	Estimating sizes, distances, and quantities; or determining time, costs, resources, or materials needed to perform a work activity.
Coordinating the Work and Activities of Others	Getting members of a group to work together to accomplish tasks.
Communicating with Persons Outside Organization	Communicating with people outside the organization, representing the organization to customers, the public, government, and other external sources. This information can be exchanged in person, in writing, or by telephone or e-mail.
Documenting/Recording Information	Entering, transcribing, recording, storing, or maintaining information in written or electronic/magnetic form.
Provide Consultation and Advice to Others	Providing guidance and expert advice to management or other groups on technical, systems-, or process-related topics.
Resolving Conflicts and Negotiating with Others	Handling complaints, settling disputes, and resolving grievances and conflicts, or otherwise negotiating with others.
Identifying Objects, Actions, and Events	Identifying information by categorizing, estimating, recognizing differences or similarities, and detecting changes in circumstances or events.
Monitor Processes, Materials, or Surroundings	Monitoring and reviewing information from materials, events, or the environment, to detect or assess problems.
Performing Administrative Activities	Performing day-to-day administrative tasks such as maintaining information files and processing paperwork.
Staffing Organizational Units	Recruiting, interviewing, selecting, hiring, and promoting employees in an organization.
Evaluating Information to Determine Compliance wit	Using relevant information and individual judgment to determine whether events or processes comply with laws, regulations, or standards.

Controlling Machines and Processes	Using either control mechanisms or direct physical activity to operate machines or processes (not including computers or vehicles).
Operating Vehicles, Mechanized Devices, or Equipme	Running. maneuvering, navigating, or driving vehicles or mechanized equipment, such as forklifts, passenger vehicles, aircraft, or water craft.
Establishing and Maintaining Interpersonal Relatio	Developing constructive and cooperative working relationships with others, and maintaining them over time.
Thinking Creatively	Developing, designing, or creating new applications, ideas, relationships, systems, or products, including artistic contributions.
Assisting and Caring for Others	Providing personal assistance, medical attention, emotional support, or other personal care to others such as coworkers, customers, or patients.
Monitoring and Controlling Resources	Monitoring and controlling resources and overseeing the spending of money.

Work_Context	**Work_Context Definitions**
Face-to-Face Discussions	How often do you have to have face-to-face discussions with individuals or teams in this job?
Freedom to Make Decisions	How much decision making freedom, without supervision, does the job offer?
Contact With Others	How much does this job require the worker to be in contact with others (face-to-face, by telephone, or otherwise) in order to perform it?
Responsible for Others' Health and Safety	How much responsibility is there for the health and safety of others in this job?
Impact of Decisions on Co-workers or Company Resul	How do the decisions an employee makes impact the results of co-workers, clients or the company?
Frequency of Decision Making	How frequently is the worker required to make decisions that affect other people, the financial resources, and/or the image and reputation of the organization?
Work With Work Group or Team	How important is it to work with others in a group or team in this job?
Structured versus Unstructured Work	To what extent is this job structured for the worker, rather than allowing the worker to determine tasks, priorities, and goals?
Telephone	How often do you have telephone conversations in this job?
Wear Common Protective or Safety Equipment such as	How much does this job require wearing common protective or safety equipment such as safety shoes, glasses, gloves, hard hats or live jackets?
Responsibility for Outcomes and Results	How responsible is the worker for work outcomes and results of other workers?
Level of Competition	To what extent does this job require the worker to compete or to be aware of competitive pressures?
Outdoors, Exposed to Weather	How often does this job require working outdoors, exposed to all weather conditions?
Exposed to Hazardous Equipment	How often does this job require exposure to hazardous equipment?
Indoors, Not Environmentally Controlled	How often does this job require working indoors in non-controlled environmental conditions (e.g., warehouse without heat)?
Importance of Being Exact or Accurate	How important is being very exact or highly accurate in performing this job?
Time Pressure	How often does this job require the worker to meet strict deadlines?
Spend Time Using Your Hands to Handle, Control, or	How much does this job require using your hands to handle, control, or feel objects, tools or controls?
Exposed to Minor Burns, Cuts, Bites, or Stings	How often does this job require exposure to minor burns, cuts, bites, or stings?
In an Enclosed Vehicle or Equipment	How often does this job require working in a closed vehicle or equipment (e.g., car)?
Spend Time Making Repetitive Motions	How much does this job require making repetitive motions?
Physical Proximity	To what extent does this job require the worker to perform job tasks in close physical proximity to other people?
Frequency of Conflict Situations	How often are there conflict situations the employee has to face in this job?
Spend Time Standing	How much does this job require standing?
Very Hot or Cold Temperatures	How often does this job require working in very hot (above 90 F degrees) or very cold (below 32 F degrees) temperatures?
Indoors, Environmentally Controlled	How often does this job require working indoors in environmentally controlled conditions?
Extremely Bright or Inadequate Lighting	How often does this job require working in extremely bright or inadequate lighting conditions?

Exposed to Contaminants	How often does this job require working exposed to contaminants (such as pollutants, gases. dust or odors)?
Sounds, Noise Levels Are Distracting or Uncomforta	How often does this job require working exposed to sounds and noise levels that are distracting or uncomfortable?
Cramped Work Space, Awkward Positions	How often does this job require working in cramped work spaces that requires getting into awkward positions?
Importance of Repeating Same Tasks	How important is repeating the same physical activities (e.g., key entry) or mental activities (e.g., checking entries in a ledger) over and over, without stopping, to performing this job?
Spend Time Sitting	How much does this job require sitting?
Spend Time Walking and Running	How much does this job require walking and running?
Exposed to High Places	How often does this job require exposure to high places?
Letters and Memos	How often does the job require written letters and memos?
Spend Time Climbing Ladders, Scaffolds, or Poles	How much does this job require climbing ladders, scaffolds, or poles?
Exposed to Hazardous Conditions	How often does this job require exposure to hazardous conditions?
Outdoors, Under Cover	How often does this job require working outdoors, under cover (e.g., structure with roof but no walls)?
Spend Time Bending or Twisting the Body	How much does this job require bending or twisting your body?
Electronic Mail	How often do you use electronic mail in this job?
Consequence of Error	How serious would the result usually be if the worker made a mistake that was not readily correctable?
Deal With Unpleasant or Angry People	How frequently does the worker have to deal with unpleasant, angry, or discourteous individuals as part of the job requirements?
Spend Time Kneeling, Crouching, Stooping, or Crawl	How much does this job require kneeling, crouching, stooping or crawling?
Coordinate or Lead Others	How important is it to coordinate or lead others in accomplishing work activities in this job?
Spend Time Keeping or Regaining Balance	How much does this job require keeping or regaining your balance?
Exposed to Whole Body Vibration	How often does this job require exposure to whole body vibration (e.g., operate a jackhammer)?
Wear Specialized Protective or Safety Equipment su	How much does this job require wearing specialized protective or safety equipment such as breathing apparatus, safety harness, full protection suits, or radiation protection?
In an Open Vehicle or Equipment	How often does this job require working in an open vehicle or equipment (e.g., tractor)?
Deal With External Customers	How important is it to work with external customers or the public in this job?
Deal With Physically Aggressive People	How frequently does the worker require the worker to deal with physical aggression of violent individuals?
Public Speaking	How often do you have to perform public speaking in this job?
Pace Determined by Speed of Equipment	How important is it to this job that the pace is determined by the speed of equipment or machinery? (This does not refer to keeping busy at all times on this job.)
Degree of Automation	How automated is the job?
Exposed to Disease or Infections	How often does this job require exposure to disease/infections?
Exposed to Radiation	How often does this job require exposure to radiation?

Job Zone Component	**Job Zone Component Definitions**
Title	Job Zone Three: Medium Preparation Needed
	Previous work-related skill, knowledge, or experience is required for these occupations. For example, an electrician must
Overall Experience	have completed three or four years of apprenticeship or several years of vocational training, and often must have passed a licensing exam, in order to perform the job.
Job Training	Employees in these occupations usually need one or two years of training involving both on-the-job experience and informal training with experienced workers.
Job Zone Examples	These occupations usually involve using communication and organizational skills to coordinate, supervise, manage, or train others to accomplish goals. Examples include dental assistants, electricians, fish and game wardens, legal secretaries, personnel recruiters, and recreation workers.
SVP Range	(6.0 to < 7.0)
Education	Most occupations in this zone require training in vocational schools, related on-the-job experience, or an associate's degree. Some may require a bachelor's degree.

Work_Styles	Work_Styles Definitions
Integrity	Job requires being honest and ethical.
Dependability	Job requires being reliable, responsible, and dependable, and fulfilling obligations.
Attention to Detail	Job requires being careful about detail and thorough in completing work tasks.
Self Control	Job requires maintaining composure, keeping emotions in check, controlling anger, and avoiding aggressive behavior, even in very difficult situations.
Cooperation	Job requires being pleasant with others on the job and displaying a good-natured, cooperative attitude.
Stress Tolerance	Job requires accepting criticism and dealing calmly and effectively with high stress situations.
Independence	Job requires developing one's own ways of doing things, guiding oneself with little or no supervision, and depending on oneself to get things done.
Analytical Thinking	Job requires analyzing information and using logic to address work-related issues and problems.
Leadership	Job requires a willingness to lead, take charge, and offer opinions and direction.
Persistence	Job requires persistence in the face of obstacles.
Initiative	Job requires a willingness to take on responsibilities and challenges.
Achievement/Effort	Job requires establishing and maintaining personally challenging achievement goals and exerting effort toward mastering tasks.
Innovation	Job requires creativity and alternative thinking to develop new ideas for and answers to work-related problems.
Adaptability/Flexibility	Job requires being open to change (positive or negative) and to considerable variety in the workplace.
Social Orientation	Job requires preferring to work with others rather than alone, and being personally connected with others on the job.
Concern for Others	Job requires being sensitive to others' needs and feelings and being understanding and helpful on the job.

47-2152.02 - Plumbers

Assemble, install, and repair pipes, fittings, and fixtures of heating, water, and drainage systems, according to specifications and plumbing codes.

Tasks

1) Cut openings in structures to accommodate pipes and pipe fittings, using hand and power tools.

2) Repair and maintain plumbing, replacing defective washers, replacing or mending broken pipes, and opening clogged drains.

3) Install underground storm, sanitary and water piping systems and extend piping to connect fixtures and plumbing to these systems.

4) Fill pipes or plumbing fixtures with water or air and observe pressure gauges to detect and locate leaks.

5) Install pipe assemblies, fittings, valves, appliances such as dishwashers and water heaters, and fixtures such as sinks and toilets, using hand and power tools.

6) Measure, cut, thread, and bend pipe to required angle, using hand and power tools or machines such as pipe cutters, pipe-threading machines, and pipe-bending machines.

7) Study building plans and inspect structures to assess material and equipment needs, to establish the sequence of pipe installations, and to plan installation around obstructions such as electrical wiring.

8) Hang steel supports from ceiling joists to hold pipes in place.

9) Locate and mark the position of pipe installations, connections, passage holes, and fixtures in structures, using measuring instruments such as rulers and levels.

10) Clear away debris in a renovation.

11) Keep records of assignments and produce detailed work reports.

12) Direct workers engaged in pipe cutting and preassembly and installation of plumbing systems and components.

13) Perform complex calculations and planning for special or very large jobs.

14) Review blueprints and building codes and specifications to determine work details and procedures.

15) Prepare written work cost estimates and negotiate contracts.

16) Install oxygen and medical gas in hospitals.

17) Use specialized techniques, equipment, or materials, such as performing computer-assisted welding of small pipes, or working with the special piping used in microchip fabrication.

Knowledge	Knowledge Definitions
Customer and Personal Service	Knowledge of principles and processes for providing customer and personal services. This includes customer needs assessment, meeting quality standards for services, and evaluation of customer satisfaction.
Mechanical	Knowledge of machines and tools, including their designs, uses, repair, and maintenance.
English Language	Knowledge of the structure and content of the English language including the meaning and spelling of words, rules of composition, and grammar.
Building and Construction	Knowledge of materials, methods, and the tools involved in the construction or repair of houses, buildings, or other structures such as highways and roads.
Mathematics	Knowledge of arithmetic, algebra, geometry, calculus, statistics, and their applications.
Public Safety and Security	Knowledge of relevant equipment, policies, procedures, and strategies to promote effective local, state, or national security operations for the protection of people, data, property, and institutions.
Chemistry	Knowledge of the chemical composition, structure, and properties of substances and of the chemical processes and transformations that they undergo. This includes uses of chemicals and their interactions, danger signs, production techniques, and disposal methods.
Design	Knowledge of design techniques, tools, and principles involved in production of precision technical plans, blueprints, drawings, and models.
Sales and Marketing	Knowledge of principles and methods for showing, promoting, and selling products or services. This includes marketing strategy and tactics, product demonstration, sales techniques, and sales control systems.
Education and Training	Knowledge of principles and methods for curriculum and training design, teaching and instruction for individuals and groups, and the measurement of training effects.
Transportation	Knowledge of principles and methods for moving people or goods by air, rail, sea, or road, including the relative costs and benefits.
Communications and Media	Knowledge of media production, communication, and dissemination techniques and methods. This includes alternative ways to inform and entertain via written, oral, and visual media.
Physics	Knowledge and prediction of physical principles, laws, their interrelationships, and applications to understanding fluid, material, and atmospheric dynamics, and mechanical, electrical, atomic and sub-atomic structures and processes.
Administration and Management	Knowledge of business and management principles involved in strategic planning, resource allocation, human resources modeling, leadership technique, production methods, and coordination of people and resources.
Telecommunications	Knowledge of transmission, broadcasting, switching, control, and operation of telecommunications systems.
Law and Government	Knowledge of laws, legal codes, court procedures, precedents, government regulations, executive orders, agency rules, and the democratic political process.
Production and Processing	Knowledge of raw materials, production processes, quality control, costs, and other techniques for maximizing the effective manufacture and distribution of goods.
Clerical	Knowledge of administrative and clerical procedures and systems such as word processing, managing files and records, stenography and transcription, designing forms, and other office procedures and terminology.
Economics and Accounting	Knowledge of economic and accounting principles and practices, the financial markets, banking and the analysis and reporting of financial data.
Geography	Knowledge of principles and methods for describing the features of land, sea, and air masses, including their physical characteristics, locations, interrelationships, and distribution of plant, animal, and human life.

Personnel and Human Resources	Knowledge of principles and procedures for personnel recruitment, selection, training, compensation and benefits, labor relations and negotiation, and personnel information systems.
Foreign Language	Knowledge of the structure and content of a foreign (non-English) language including the meaning and spelling of words, rules of composition and grammar, and pronunciation.
Food Production	Knowledge of techniques and equipment for planting, growing, and harvesting food products (both plant and animal) for consumption, including storage/handling techniques.
Engineering and Technology	Knowledge of the practical application of engineering science and technology. This includes applying principles, techniques, procedures, and equipment to the design and production of various goods and services.
Psychology	Knowledge of human behavior and performance; individual differences in ability, personality, and interests; learning and motivation; psychological research methods; and the assessment and treatment of behavioral and affective disorders.
Biology	Knowledge of plant and animal organisms, their tissues, cells, functions, interdependencies, and interactions with each other and the environment.
Medicine and Dentistry	Knowledge of the information and techniques needed to diagnose and treat human injuries, diseases, and deformities. This includes symptoms, treatment alternatives, drug properties and interactions, and preventive health-care measures.
Computers and Electronics	Knowledge of circuit boards, processors, chips, electronic equipment, and computer hardware and software, including applications and programming.
Therapy and Counseling	Knowledge of principles, methods, and procedures for diagnosis, treatment, and rehabilitation of physical and mental dysfunctions, and for career counseling and guidance.
History and Archeology	Knowledge of historical events and their causes, indicators, and effects on civilizations and cultures.
Philosophy and Theology	Knowledge of different philosophical systems and religions. This includes their basic principles, values, ethics, ways of thinking, customs, practices, and their impact on human culture.
Sociology and Anthropology	Knowledge of group behavior and dynamics, societal trends and influences, human migrations, ethnicity, cultures and their history and origins.
Fine Arts	Knowledge of the theory and techniques required to compose, produce, and perform works of music, dance, visual arts, drama, and sculpture.

Skills — Skills Definitions

Active Listening	Giving full attention to what other people are saying, taking time to understand the points being made, asking questions as appropriate, and not interrupting at inappropriate times.
Mathematics	Using mathematics to solve problems.
Troubleshooting	Determining causes of operating errors and deciding what to do about it.
Repairing	Repairing machines or systems using the needed tools.
Complex Problem Solving	Identifying complex problems and reviewing related information to develop and evaluate options and implement solutions.
Installation	Installing equipment, machines, wiring, or programs to meet specifications.
Time Management	Managing one's own time and the time of others.
Equipment Selection	Determining the kind of tools and equipment needed to do a job.
Reading Comprehension	Understanding written sentences and paragraphs in work related documents.
Management of Material Resources	Obtaining and seeing to the appropriate use of equipment, facilities, and materials needed to do certain work.
Quality Control Analysis	Conducting tests and inspections of products, services, or processes to evaluate quality or performance.
Critical Thinking	Using logic and reasoning to identify the strengths and weaknesses of alternative solutions, conclusions or approaches to problems.
Speaking	Talking to others to convey information effectively.
Coordination	Adjusting actions in relation to others' actions.
Service Orientation	Actively looking for ways to help people.
Judgment and Decision Making	Considering the relative costs and benefits of potential actions to choose the most appropriate one.
Instructing	Teaching others how to do something.
Equipment Maintenance	Performing routine maintenance on equipment and determining when and what kind of maintenance is needed.

Persuasion	Persuading others to change their minds or behavior.
Management of Financial Resources	Determining how money will be spent to get the work done, and accounting for these expenditures.
Monitoring	Monitoring/Assessing performance of yourself, other individuals, or organizations to make improvements or take corrective action.
Learning Strategies	Selecting and using training/instructional methods and procedures appropriate for the situation when learning or teaching new things.
Systems Analysis	Determining how a system should work and how changes in conditions, operations, and the environment will affect outcomes.
Science	Using scientific rules and methods to solve problems.
Management of Personnel Resources	Motivating, developing, and directing people as they work, identifying the best people for the job.
Social Perceptiveness	Being aware of others' reactions and understanding why they react as they do.
Systems Evaluation	Identifying measures or indicators of system performance and the actions needed to improve or correct performance, relative to the goals of the system.
Active Learning	Understanding the implications of new information for both current and future problem-solving and decision-making.
Operations Analysis	Analyzing needs and product requirements to create a design.
Operation and Control	Controlling operations of equipment or systems.
Writing	Communicating effectively in writing as appropriate for the needs of the audience.
Operation Monitoring	Watching gauges, dials, or other indicators to make sure a machine is working properly.
Technology Design	Generating or adapting equipment and technology to serve user needs.
Negotiation	Bringing others together and trying to reconcile differences.
Programming	Writing computer programs for various purposes.

Ability — Ability Definitions

Arm-Hand Steadiness	The ability to keep your hand and arm steady while moving your arm or while holding your arm and hand in one position.
Static Strength	The ability to exert maximum muscle force to lift, push, pull, or carry objects.
Problem Sensitivity	The ability to tell when something is wrong or is likely to go wrong. It does not involve solving the problem, only recognizing there is a problem.
Manual Dexterity	The ability to quickly move your hand, your hand together with your arm, or your two hands to grasp, manipulate, or assemble objects.
Visualization	The ability to imagine how something will look after it is moved around or when its parts are moved or rearranged.
Finger Dexterity	The ability to make precisely coordinated movements of the fingers of one or both hands to grasp, manipulate, or assemble very small objects.
Extent Flexibility	The ability to bend, stretch, twist, or reach with your body, arms, and/or legs.
Information Ordering	The ability to arrange things or actions in a certain order or pattern according to a specific rule or set of rules (e.g., patterns of numbers, letters, words, pictures, mathematical operations).
Near Vision	The ability to see details at close range (within a few feet of the observer).
Oral Expression	The ability to communicate information and ideas in speaking so others will understand.
Oral Comprehension	The ability to listen to and understand information and ideas presented through spoken words and sentences.
Deductive Reasoning	The ability to apply general rules to specific problems to produce answers that make sense.
Trunk Strength	The ability to use your abdominal and lower back muscles to support part of the body repeatedly or continuously over time without 'giving out' or fatiguing.
Speech Clarity	The ability to speak clearly so others can understand you.
Speech Recognition	The ability to identify and understand the speech of another person.
Written Comprehension	The ability to read and understand information and ideas presented in writing.
Multilimb Coordination	The ability to coordinate two or more limbs (for example, two arms, two legs, or one leg and one arm) while sitting, standing, or lying down. It does not involve performing the activities while the whole body is in motion.
Inductive Reasoning	The ability to combine pieces of information to form general rules or conclusions (includes finding a relationship among seemingly unrelated events).

		Work_Activity	Work_Activity Definitions
Gross Body Equilibrium	The ability to keep or regain your body balance or stay upright when in an unstable position.	Performing General Physical Activities	Performing physical activities that require considerable use of your arms and legs and moving your whole body, such as climbing, lifting, balancing, walking, stooping, and handling of materials.
Dynamic Strength	The ability to exert muscle force repeatedly or continuously over time. This involves muscular endurance and resistance to muscle fatigue.	Getting Information	Observing, receiving, and otherwise obtaining information from all relevant sources.
Control Precision	The ability to quickly and repeatedly adjust the controls of a machine or a vehicle to exact positions.	Handling and Moving Objects	Using hands and arms in handling, installing, positioning, and moving materials, and manipulating things.
Written Expression	The ability to communicate information and ideas in writing so others will understand.	Identifying Objects, Actions, and Events	Identifying information by categorizing, estimating, recognizing differences or similarities, and detecting changes in circumstances or events.
Flexibility of Closure	The ability to identify or detect a known pattern (a figure, object, word, or sound) that is hidden in other distracting material.	Repairing and Maintaining Mechanical Equipment	Servicing, repairing, adjusting, and testing machines, devices, moving parts, and equipment that operate primarily on the basis of mechanical (not electronic) principles.
Category Flexibility	The ability to generate or use different sets of rules for combining or grouping things in different ways.	Performing for or Working Directly with the Public	Performing for people or dealing directly with the public. This includes serving customers in restaurants and stores, and receiving clients or guests.
Speed of Closure	The ability to quickly make sense of, combine, and organize information into meaningful patterns.	Making Decisions and Solving Problems	Analyzing information and evaluating results to choose the best solution and solve problems.
Selective Attention	The ability to concentrate on a task over a period of time without being distracted.	Controlling Machines and Processes	Using either control mechanisms or direct physical activity to operate machines or processes (not including computers or vehicles).
Depth Perception	The ability to judge which of several objects is closer or farther away from you, or to judge the distance between you and an object.	Inspecting Equipment, Structures, or Material	Inspecting equipment, structures, or materials to identify the cause of errors or other problems or defects.
Mathematical Reasoning	The ability to choose the right mathematical methods or formulas to solve a problem.	Monitor Processes, Materials, or Surroundings	Monitoring and reviewing information from materials, events, or the environment, to detect or assess problems.
Spatial Orientation	The ability to know your location in relation to the environment or to know where other objects are in relation to you.	Organizing, Planning, and Prioritizing Work	Developing specific goals and plans to prioritize, organize, and accomplish your work.
Stamina	The ability to exert yourself physically over long periods of time without getting winded or out of breath.	Communicating with Supervisors, Peers, or Subordin	Providing information to supervisors, co-workers, and subordinates by telephone, in written form, e-mail, or in person.
Originality	The ability to come up with unusual or clever ideas about a given topic or situation, or to develop creative ways to solve a problem.	Operating Vehicles, Mechanized Devices, or Equipme	Running, maneuvering, navigating, or driving vehicles or mechanized equipment, such as forklifts, passenger vehicles, aircraft, or water craft.
Fluency of Ideas	The ability to come up with a number of ideas about a topic (the number of ideas is important, not their quality, correctness, or creativity).	Scheduling Work and Activities	Scheduling events, programs, and activities, as well as the work of others.
Memorization	The ability to remember information such as words, numbers, pictures, and procedures.	Updating and Using Relevant Knowledge	Keeping up-to-date technically and applying new knowledge to your job.
Reaction Time	The ability to quickly respond (with the hand, finger, or foot) to a signal (sound, light, picture) when it appears.	Drafting, Laying Out, and Specifying Technical Dev	Providing documentation, detailed instructions, drawings, or specifications to tell others about how devices, parts, equipment, or structures are to be fabricated, constructed, assembled, modified, maintained, or used.
Gross Body Coordination	The ability to coordinate the movement of your arms, legs, and torso together when the whole body is in motion.	Evaluating Information to Determine Compliance wit	Using relevant information and individual judgment to determine whether events or processes comply with laws, regulations, or standards.
Far Vision	The ability to see details at a distance.	Establishing and Maintaining Interpersonal Relatio	Developing constructive and cooperative working relationships with others, and maintaining them over time.
Time Sharing	The ability to shift back and forth between two or more activities or sources of information (such as speech, sounds, touch, or other sources).	Training and Teaching Others	Identifying the educational needs of others, developing formal educational or training programs or classes, and teaching or instructing others.
Hearing Sensitivity	The ability to detect or tell the differences between sounds that vary in pitch and loudness.	Estimating the Quantifiable Characteristics of Pro	Estimating sizes, distances, and quantities; or determining time, costs, resources, or materials needed to perform a work activity.
Visual Color Discrimination	The ability to match or detect differences between colors, including shades of color and brightness.	Thinking Creatively	Developing, designing, or creating new applications, ideas, relationships, systems, or products, including artistic contributions.
Perceptual Speed	The ability to quickly and accurately compare similarities and differences among sets of letters, numbers, objects, pictures, or patterns. The things to be compared may be presented at the same time or one after the other. This ability also includes comparing a presented object with a remembered object.	Selling or Influencing Others	Convincing others to buy merchandise/goods or to otherwise change their minds or actions.
Rate Control	The ability to time your movements or the movement of a piece of equipment in anticipation of changes in the speed and/or direction of a moving object or scene.	Coordinating the Work and Activities of Others	Getting members of a group to work together to accomplish tasks.
Wrist-Finger Speed	The ability to make fast, simple, repeated movements of the fingers, hands, and wrists.	Resolving Conflicts and Negotiating with Others	Handling complaints, settling disputes, and resolving grievances and conflicts, or otherwise negotiating with others.
Number Facility	The ability to add, subtract, multiply, or divide quickly and correctly.	Judging the Qualities of Things, Services, or Peop	Assessing the value, importance, or quality of things or people.
Speed of Limb Movement	The ability to quickly move the arms and legs.	Assisting and Caring for Others	Providing personal assistance, medical attention, emotional support, or other personal care to others such as coworkers, customers, or patients.
Auditory Attention	The ability to focus on a single source of sound in the presence of other distracting sounds.	Performing Administrative Activities	Performing day-to-day administrative tasks such as maintaining information files and processing paperwork.
Glare Sensitivity	The ability to see objects in the presence of glare or bright lighting.	Monitoring and Controlling Resources	Monitoring and controlling resources and overseeing the spending of money.
Response Orientation	The ability to choose quickly between two or more movements in response to two or more different signals (lights, sounds, pictures). It includes the speed with which the correct response is started with the hand, foot, or other body part.		
Peripheral Vision	The ability to see objects or movement of objects to one's side when the eyes are looking ahead.		
Sound Localization	The ability to tell the direction from which a sound originated.		
Night Vision	The ability to see under low light conditions.		
Explosive Strength	The ability to use short bursts of muscle force to propel oneself (as in jumping or sprinting), or to throw an object.		
Dynamic Flexibility	The ability to quickly and repeatedly bend, stretch, twist, or reach out with your body, arms, and/or legs.		

Communicating with Persons Outside Organization	Communicating with people outside the organization, representing the organization to customers, the public, government, and other external sources. This information can be exchanged in person, in writing, or by telephone or e-mail.
Documenting/Recording Information	Entering, transcribing, recording, storing, or maintaining information in written or electronic/magnetic form.
Coaching and Developing Others	Identifying the developmental needs of others and coaching, mentoring, or otherwise helping others to improve their knowledge or skills.
Repairing and Maintaining Electronic Equipment	Servicing, repairing, calibrating, regulating, fine-tuning, or testing machines, devices, and equipment that operate primarily on the basis of electrical or electronic (not mechanical) principles.
Processing Information	Compiling, coding, categorizing, calculating, tabulating, auditing, or verifying information or data.
Analyzing Data or Information	Identifying the underlying principles, reasons, or facts of information by breaking down information or data into separate parts.
Interacting With Computers	Using computers and computer systems (including hardware and software) to program, write software, set up functions, enter data, or process information.
Staffing Organizational Units	Recruiting, interviewing, selecting, hiring, and promoting employees in an organization.
Provide Consultation and Advice to Others	Providing guidance and expert advice to management or other groups on technical, systems-, or process-related topics.
Developing Objectives and Strategies	Establishing long-range objectives and specifying the strategies and actions to achieve them.
Guiding, Directing, and Motivating Subordinates	Providing guidance and direction to subordinates, including setting performance standards and monitoring performance.
Developing and Building Teams	Encouraging and building mutual trust, respect, and cooperation among team members.
Interpreting the Meaning of Information for Others	Translating or explaining what information means and how it can be used.

Work_Context	Work_Context Definitions
Face-to-Face Discussions	How often do you have to have face-to-face discussions with individuals or teams in this job?
Contact With Others	How much does this job require the worker to be in contact with others (face-to-face, by telephone, or otherwise) in order to perform it?
Outdoors, Exposed to Weather	How often does this job require working outdoors, exposed to all weather conditions?
Spend Time Using Your Hands to Handle, Control, or	How much does this job require using your hands to handle, control, or feel objects, tools or controls?
Exposed to Minor Burns, Cuts, Bites, or Stings	How often does this job require exposure to minor burns, cuts, bites, or stings?
Importance of Being Exact or Accurate	How important is being very exact or highly accurate in performing this job?
Telephone	How often do you have telephone conversations in this job?
Indoors, Not Environmentally Controlled	How often does this job require working indoors in non-controlled environmental conditions (e.g., warehouse without heat)?
Exposed to Hazardous Equipment	How often does this job require exposure to hazardous equipment?
Cramped Work Space, Awkward Positions	How often does this job require working in cramped work spaces that requires getting into awkward positions?
Frequency of Decision Making	How frequently is the worker required to make decisions that affect other people, the financial resources, and/or the image and reputation of the organization?
Freedom to Make Decisions	How much decision making freedom, without supervision, does the job offer?
Responsibility for Outcomes and Results	How responsible is the worker for work outcomes and results of other workers?
Impact of Decisions on Co-workers or Company Resul	How do the decisions an employee makes impact the results of co-workers, clients or the company?
In an Enclosed Vehicle or Equipment	How often does this job require working in a closed vehicle or equipment (e.g., car)?
Exposed to Contaminants	How often does this job require working exposed to contaminants (such as pollutants, gases, dust or odors)?
Coordinate or Lead Others	How important is it to coordinate or lead others in accomplishing work activities in this job?
Responsible for Others' Health and Safety	How much responsibility is there for the health and safety of others in this job?
Structured versus Unstructured Work	To what extent is this job structured for the worker, rather than allowing the worker to determine tasks, priorities, and goals?

Very Hot or Cold Temperatures	How often does this job require working in very hot (above 90 F degrees) or very cold (below 32 F degrees) temperatures?
Spend Time Kneeling, Crouching, Stooping, or Crawl	How much does this job require kneeling, crouching, stooping or crawling?
Wear Common Protective or Safety Equipment such as	How much does this job require wearing common protective or safety equipment such as safety shoes, glasses, gloves, hard hats or live jackets?
Work With Work Group or Team	How important is it to work with others in a group or team in this job?
Spend Time Standing	How much does this job require standing?
Deal With External Customers	How important is it to work with external customers or the public in this job?
Spend Time Bending or Twisting the Body	How much does this job require bending or twisting your body?
Physical Proximity	To what extent does this job require the worker to perform job tasks in close physical proximity to other people?
Outdoors, Under Cover	How often does this job require working outdoors, under cover (e.g., structure with roof but no walls)?
Sounds, Noise Levels Are Distracting or Uncomforta	How often does this job require working exposed to sounds and noise levels that are distracting or uncomfortable?
Indoors, Environmentally Controlled	How often does this job require working indoors in environmentally controlled conditions?
Exposed to High Places	How often does this job require exposure to high places?
Spend Time Walking and Running	How much does this job require walking and running?
Exposed to Disease or Infections	How often does this job require exposure to disease/infections?
Time Pressure	How often does this job require the worker to meet strict deadlines?
Level of Competition	To what extent does this job require the worker to compete or to be aware of competitive pressures?
Spend Time Making Repetitive Motions	How much does this job require making repetitive motions?
Extremely Bright or Inadequate Lighting	How often does this job require working in extremely bright or inadequate lighting conditions?
Consequence of Error	How serious would the result usually be if the worker made a mistake that was not readily correctable?
Frequency of Conflict Situations	How often are there conflict situations the employee has to face in this job?
Letters and Memos	How often does the job require written letters and memos?
Exposed to Hazardous Conditions	How often does this job require exposure to hazardous conditions?
Importance of Repeating Same Tasks	How important is repeating the same physical activities (e.g., key entry) or mental activities (e.g., checking entries in a ledger) over and over, without stopping, to performing this job?
Deal With Unpleasant or Angry People	How frequently does the worker have to deal with unpleasant, angry, or discourteous individuals as part of the job requirements?
Exposed to Whole Body Vibration	How often does this job require exposure to whole body vibration (e.g., operate a jackhammer)?
Pace Determined by Speed of Equipment	How important is it to this job that the pace is determined by the speed of equipment or machinery? (This does not refer to keeping busy at all times on this job.)
Spend Time Climbing Ladders, Scaffolds, or Poles	How much does this job require climbing ladders, scaffolds, or poles?
Spend Time Sitting	How much does this job require sitting?
Spend Time Keeping or Regaining Balance	How much does this job require keeping or regaining your balance?
In an Open Vehicle or Equipment	How often does this job require working in an open vehicle or equipment (e.g., tractor)?
Public Speaking	How often do you have to perform public speaking in this job?
Wear Specialized Protective or Safety Equipment su	How much does this job require wearing specialized protective or safety equipment such as breathing apparatus, safety harness, full protection suits, or radiation protection?
Degree of Automation	How automated is the job?
Deal With Physically Aggressive People	How frequently does this job require the worker to deal with physical aggression of violent individuals?
Exposed to Radiation	How often does this job require exposure to radiation?
Electronic Mail	How often do you use electronic mail in this job?

Job Zone Component Title	Job Zone Component Definitions
Title	Job Zone Three: Medium Preparation Needed

Overall Experience	Previous work-related skill, knowledge, or experience is required for these occupations. For example, an electrician must have completed three or four years of apprenticeship or several years of vocational training, and often must have passed a licensing exam, in order to perform the job.
Job Training	Employees in these occupations usually need one or two years of training involving both on-the-job experience and informal training with experienced workers.
Job Zone Examples	These occupations usually involve using communication and organizational skills to coordinate, supervise, manage, or train others to accomplish goals. Examples include dental assistants, electricians, fish and game wardens, legal secretaries, personnel recruiters, and recreation workers.
SVP Range	(6.0 to < 7.0)
Education	Most occupations in this zone require training in vocational schools, related on-the-job experience, or an associate's degree. Some may require a bachelor's degree.

Work_Styles	Work_Styles Definitions
Dependability	Job requires being reliable, responsible, and dependable, and fulfilling obligations.
Attention to Detail	Job requires being careful a_____ ail and thorough in completing work tasks.
Self Control	Job requires maintaining composure, keeping emotions in check, controlling anger, and avoiding aggressive behavior, even in very difficult situations.
Cooperation	Job requires being pleasant with others on the job and displaying a good-natured, cooperative attitude.
Integrity	Job requires being honest and ethical.
Persistence	Job requires persistence in the face of obstacles.
Stress Tolerance	Job requires accepting criticism and dealing calmly and effectively with high stress situations.
Independence	Job requires developing one's own ways of doing things, guiding oneself with little or no supervision, and depending on oneself to get things done.
Adaptability/Flexibility	Job requires being open to change (positive or negative) and to considerable variety in the workplace.
Initiative	Job requires a willingness to take on responsibilities and challenges.
Innovation	Job requires creativity and alternative thinking to develop new ideas for and answers to work-related problems.
Analytical Thinking	Job requires analyzing information and using logic to address work-related issues and problems.
Achievement/Effort	Job requires establishing and maintaining personally challenging achievement goals and exerting effort toward mastering tasks.
Leadership	Job requires a willingness to lead, take charge, and offer opinions and direction.
Concern for Others	Job requires being sensitive to others' needs and feelings and being understanding and helpful on the job.
Social Orientation	Job requires preferring to work with others rather than alone, and being personally connected with others on the job.

47-2152.03 - Pipelaying Fitters

Align pipeline section in preparation of welding. Signal tractor driver for placement of pipeline sections in proper alignment. Insert steel spacer.

Tasks

1) Correct misalignments of pipe, using a sledge hammer.

2) Guide pipe into trench and signal hoist operator to move pipe until alignment is achieved, so that pipes can be welded together.

3) Inspect joints to ensure uniform spacing and proper alignment of pipe surfaces.

47-2161.00 - Plasterers and Stucco Masons

Apply interior or exterior plaster, cement, stucco, or similar materials. May also set ornamental plaster.

Tasks

1) Apply weatherproof, decorative coverings to exterior surfaces of buildings, such as troweling or spraying on coats of stucco.

2) Apply coats of plaster or stucco to walls, ceilings, or partitions of buildings, using trowels, brushes, or spray guns.

3) Mix mortar and plaster to desired consistency or direct workers who perform mixing.

4) Mold and install ornamental plaster pieces, panels, and trim.

5) Rough the undercoat surface with a scratcher so the finish coat will adhere.

6) Spray acoustic materials or texture finish over walls and ceilings.

7) Apply insulation to building exteriors by installing prefabricated insulation systems over existing walls or by covering the outer wall with insulation board, reinforcing mesh, and a base coat.

8) Create decorative textures in finish coat, using brushes or trowels, sand, pebbles, or stones.

9) Clean and prepare surfaces for applications of plaster, cement, stucco, or similar materials, such as by drywall taping.

10) Install guidewires on exterior surfaces of buildings to indicate thickness of plaster or stucco, and nail wire mesh, lath, or similar materials to the outside surface to hold stucco in place.

47-2171.00 - Reinforcing Iron and Rebar Workers

Position and secure steel bars or mesh in concrete forms in order to reinforce concrete. Use a variety of fasteners, rod-bending machines, blowtorches, and hand tools.

Tasks

1) Position and secure steel bars, rods, cables, or mesh in concrete forms, using fasteners, rod-bending machines, blowtorches, and hand tools.

2) Determine quantities, sizes, shapes, and locations of reinforcing rods from blueprints, sketches, or oral instructions.

3) Bend steel rods with hand tools and rodbending machines, and weld them with arc-welding equipment.

4) Cut rods to required lengths, using metal shears, hacksaws, bar cutters, or acetylene torches.

5) Cut and fit wire mesh or fabric, using hooked rods, and position fabric or mesh in concrete to reinforce concrete.

6) Place blocks under rebar to hold the bars off the deck when reinforcing floors.

47-2221.00 - Structural Iron and Steel Workers

Raise, place, and unite iron or steel girders, columns, and other structural members to form completed structures or structural frameworks. May erect metal storage tanks and assemble prefabricated metal buildings.

Tasks

1) Unload and position prefabricated steel units for hoisting as needed.

2) Insert sealing strips, wiring, insulating material, ladders, flanges, gauges, and valves, depending on types of structures being assembled.

3) Hoist steel beams, girders, and columns into place, using cranes, or signal hoisting equipment operators to lift and position structural-steel members.

4) Catch hot rivets in buckets, and insert rivets in holes, using tongs.

5) Bolt aligned structural-steel members in position for permanent riveting, bolting, or welding into place.

6) Assemble hoisting equipment and rigging, such as cables, pulleys, and hooks, to move heavy equipment and materials.

7) Connect columns, beams, and girders with bolts, following blueprints and instructions from supervisors.

8) Fabricate metal parts such as steel frames, columns, beams, and girders, according to blueprints or instructions from supervisors.

9) Place blocks under reinforcing bars used to reinforce floors.

10) Ride on girders or other structural-steel members to position them, or use rope to guide them into position.

11) Cut, bend, and weld steel pieces, using metal shears, torches, and welding equipment.

12) Pull, push, or pry structural-steel members into approximate positions for bolting into place.

13) Fasten structural-steel members to hoist cables, using chains, cables, or rope.

14) Erect metal and precast concrete components for structures such as buildings, bridges, dams, towers, storage tanks, fences, and highway guard rails.

15) Drive drift pins through rivet holes in order to align rivet holes in structural-steel members with corresponding holes in previously placed members.

16) Dismantle structures and equipment.

17) Verify vertical and horizontal alignment of structural-steel members, using plumb bobs, laser equipment, transits, and/or levels.

18) Read specifications and blueprints to determine the locations, quantities, and sizes of materials required.

19) Force structural-steel members into final positions, using turnbuckles, crowbars, jacks, and hand tools.

47-3012.00 - Helpers--Carpenters

Help carpenters by performing duties of lesser skill. Duties include using, supplying or holding materials or tools, and cleaning work area and equipment.

Tasks

1) Select tools, equipment, and materials from storage and transport items to work site.

2) Position and hold timbers, lumber, and paneling in place for fastening or cutting.

3) Hold plumb bobs, sighting rods, and other equipment, to aid in establishing reference points and lines.

4) Secure stakes to grids for constructions of footings, nail scabs to footing forms, and vibrate and float concrete.

5) Cut timbers, lumber and/or paneling to specified dimensions, and drill holes in timbers or lumber.

6) Glue and clamp edges or joints of assembled parts.

7) Clean work areas, machines, and equipment, to maintain a clean and safe jobsite.

8) Align, straighten, plumb and square forms for installation.

9) Perform tie spacing layout, then measure, mark, drill and/or cut.

10) Smooth and sand surfaces to remove ridges, tool marks, glue, or caulking.

11) Cut and install insulating or sound-absorbing material.

12) Fasten timbers and/or lumber with glue, screws, pegs, or nails, and install hardware.

13) Cut tile or linoleum to fit, and spread adhesives on flooring to install tile or linoleum.

14) Construct forms, then assist in raising them to the required elevation.

15) Install handrails under the direction of a carpenter.

16) Cover surfaces with laminated plastic covering material.

47-3013.00 - Helpers--Electricians

Help electricians by performing duties of lesser skill. Duties include using, supplying or holding materials or tools, and cleaning work area and equipment.

Tasks

1) Measure, cut, and bend wire and conduit, using measuring instruments and hand tools.

2) Maintain tools, vehicles, and equipment and keep parts and supplies in order.

3) Transport tools, materials, equipment, and supplies to work site by hand, handtruck, or heavy, motorized truck.

4) Examine electrical units for loose connections and broken insulation and tighten connections, using hand tools.

5) Perform semi-skilled and unskilled laboring duties related to the installation, maintenance and repair of a wide variety of electrical systems and equipment.

6) Thread conduit ends, connect couplings, and fabricate and secure conduit support brackets, using hand tools.

7) Clean work area and wash parts.

8) Disassemble defective electrical equipment, replace defective or worn parts, and reassemble equipment, using hand tools.

9) Trace out short circuits in wiring, using test meter.

10) Dig trenches or holes for installation of conduit or supports.

11) Construct controllers and panels, using power drills, drill presses, taps, saws and punches.

12) String transmission lines or cables through ducts or conduits, under the ground, through equipment, or to towers.

13) Strip insulation from wire ends, using wire stripping pliers, and attach wires to terminals for subsequent soldering.

14) Erect electrical system components and barricades, and rig scaffolds, hoists, and shoring.

15) Raise, lower, or position equipment, tools, and materials, using hoist, hand line, or block and tackle.

16) Install copper-clad ground rods, using a manual post driver.

17) Break up concrete, using airhammer, to facilitate installation, construction, or repair of equipment.

18) Paint a variety of objects related to electrical functions.

19) Requisition materials, using warehouse requisition or release forms.

20) Solder electrical connections, using soldering iron.

21) Bolt component parts together to form tower assemblies, using hand tools.

22) Operate cutting torches and welding equipment, while working with conduit and metal components to construct devices associated with electrical functions.

23) Trim trees and clear undergrowth along right-of-way.

Knowledge	Knowledge Definitions
Building and Construction	Knowledge of materials, methods, and the tools involved in the construction or repair of houses, buildings, or other structures such as highways and roads.
Mechanical	Knowledge of machines and tools, including their designs, uses, repair, and maintenance.
Mathematics	Knowledge of arithmetic, algebra, geometry, calculus, statistics, and their applications.
Customer and Personal Service	Knowledge of principles and processes for providing customer and personal services. This includes customer needs assessment, meeting quality standards for services, and evaluation of customer satisfaction.
Design	Knowledge of design techniques, tools, and principles involved in production of precision technical plans, blueprints, drawings, and models.
English Language	Knowledge of the structure and content of the English language including the meaning and spelling of words, rules of composition, and grammar.
Public Safety and Security	Knowledge of relevant equipment, policies, procedures, and strategies to promote effective local, state, or national security operations for the protection of people, data, property, and institutions.
Education and Training	Knowledge of principles and methods for curriculum and training design, teaching and instruction for individuals and groups, and the measurement of training effects.
Administration and Management	Knowledge of business and management principles involved in strategic planning, resource allocation, human resources modeling, leadership technique, production methods, and coordination of people and resources.
Production and Processing	Knowledge of raw materials, production processes, quality control, costs, and other techniques for maximizing the effective manufacture and distribution of goods.
Engineering and Technology	Knowledge of the practical application of engineering science and technology. This includes applying principles, techniques, procedures, and equipment to the design and production of various goods and services.
Computers and Electronics	Knowledge of circuit boards, processors, chips, electronic equipment, and computer hardware and software, including applications and programming.

Law and Government	Knowledge of laws, legal codes, court procedures, precedents, government regulations, executive orders, agency rules, and the democratic political process.
Physics	Knowledge and prediction of physical principles, laws, their interrelationships, and applications to understanding fluid, material, and atmospheric dynamics, and mechanical, electrical, atomic and sub-atomic structures and processes.
Transportation	Knowledge of principles and methods for moving people or goods by air, rail, sea, or road, including the relative costs and benefits.
Telecommunications	Knowledge of transmission, broadcasting, switching, control, and operation of telecommunications systems.
Personnel and Human Resources	Knowledge of principles and procedures for personnel recruitment, selection, training, compensation and benefits, labor relations and negotiation, and personnel information systems.
Communications and Media	Knowledge of media production, communication, and dissemination techniques and methods. This includes alternative ways to inform and entertain via written, oral, and visual media.
Economics and Accounting	Knowledge of economic and accounting principles and practices, the financial markets, banking and the analysis and reporting of financial data.
Psychology	Knowledge of human behavior and performance; individual differences in ability, personality, and interests; learning and motivation; psychological research methods; and the assessment and treatment of behavioral and affective disorders.
Chemistry	Knowledge of the chemical composition, structure, and properties of substances and of the chemical processes and transformations that they undergo. This includes uses of chemicals and their interactions, danger signs, production techniques, and disposal methods.
Sales and Marketing	Knowledge of principles and methods for showing, promoting, and selling products or services. This includes marketing strategy and tactics, product demonstration, sales techniques, and sales control systems.
Geography	Knowledge of principles and methods for describing the features of land, sea, and air masses, including their physical characteristics, locations, interrelationships, and distribution of plant, animal, and human life.
Clerical	Knowledge of administrative and clerical procedures and systems such as word processing, managing files and records, stenography and transcription, designing forms, and other office procedures and terminology.
Medicine and Dentistry	Knowledge of the information and techniques needed to diagnose and treat human injuries, diseases, and deformities. This includes symptoms, treatment alternatives, drug properties and interactions, and preventive health-care measures.
Biology	Knowledge of plant and animal organisms, their tissues, cells, functions, interdependencies, and interactions with each other and the environment.
Foreign Language	Knowledge of the structure and content of a foreign (non-English) language including the meaning and spelling of words, rules of composition and grammar, and pronunciation.
Sociology and Anthropology	Knowledge of group behavior and dynamics, societal trends and influences, human migrations, ethnicity, cultures and their history and origins.
Philosophy and Theology	Knowledge of different philosophical systems and religions. This includes their basic principles, values, ethics, ways of thinking, customs, practices, and their impact on human culture.
Therapy and Counseling	Knowledge of principles, methods, and procedures for diagnosis, treatment, and rehabilitation of physical and mental dysfunctions, and for career counseling and guidance.
Fine Arts	Knowledge of the theory and techniques required to compose, produce, and perform works of music, dance, visual arts, drama, and sculpture.
History and Archeology	Knowledge of historical events and their causes, indicators, and effects on civilizations and cultures.
Food Production	Knowledge of techniques and equipment for planting, growing, and harvesting food products (both plant and animal) for consumption, including storage/handling techniques.

Skills	**Skills Definitions**
Troubleshooting	Determining causes of operating errors and deciding what to do about it.
Mathematics	Using mathematics to solve problems.

Installation	Installing equipment, machines, wiring, or programs to meet specifications.
Active Listening	Giving full attention to what other people are saying, taking time to understand the points being made, asking questions as appropriate, and not interrupting at inappropriate times.
Speaking	Talking to others to convey information effectively.
Reading Comprehension	Understanding written sentences and paragraphs in work related documents.
Time Management	Managing one's own time and the time of others.
Equipment Selection	Determining the kind of tools and equipment needed to do a job.
Critical Thinking	Using logic and reasoning to identify the strengths and weaknesses of alternative solutions, conclusions or approaches to problems.
Complex Problem Solving	Identifying complex problems and reviewing related information to develop and evaluate options and implement solutions.
Learning Strategies	Selecting and using training/instructional methods and procedures appropriate for the situation when learning or teaching new things.
Active Learning	Understanding the implications of new information for both current and future problem-solving and decision-making.
Monitoring	Monitoring/Assessing performance of yourself, other individuals, or organizations to make improvements or take corrective action.
Instructing	Teaching others how to do something.
Repairing	Repairing machines or systems using the needed tools.
Judgment and Decision Making	Considering the relative costs and benefits of potential actions to choose the most appropriate one.
Coordination	Adjusting actions in relation to others' actions.
Writing	Communicating effectively in writing as appropriate for the needs of the audience.
Operation and Control	Controlling operations of equipment or systems.
Management of Personnel Resources	Motivating, developing, and directing people as they work, identifying the best people for the job.
Operation Monitoring	Watching gauges, dials, or other indicators to make sure a machine is working properly.
Service Orientation	Actively looking for ways to help people.
Equipment Maintenance	Performing routine maintenance on equipment and determining when and what kind of maintenance is needed.
Science	Using scientific rules and methods to solve problems.
Operations Analysis	Analyzing needs and product requirements to create a design.
Management of Material Resources	Obtaining and seeing to the appropriate use of equipment, facilities, and materials needed to do certain work.
Social Perceptiveness	Being aware of others' reactions and understanding why they react as they do.
Technology Design	Generating or adapting equipment and technology to serve user needs.
Quality Control Analysis	Conducting tests and inspections of products, services, or processes to evaluate quality or performance.
Systems Analysis	Determining how a system should work and how changes in conditions, operations, and the environment will affect outcomes.
Management of Financial Resources	Determining how money will be spent to get the work done, and accounting for these expenditures.
Negotiation	Bringing others together and trying to reconcile differences.
Persuasion	Persuading others to change their minds or behavior.
Systems Evaluation	Identifying measures or indicators of system performance and the actions needed to improve or correct performance, relative to the goals of the system.
Programming	Writing computer programs for various purposes.

Ability	**Ability Definitions**
Manual Dexterity	The ability to quickly move your hand, your hand together with your arm, or your two hands to grasp, manipulate, or assemble objects.
Near Vision	The ability to see details at close range (within a few feet of the observer).
Extent Flexibility	The ability to bend, stretch, twist, or reach with your body, arms, and/or legs.
Problem Sensitivity	The ability to tell when something is wrong or is likely to go wrong. It does not involve solving the problem, only recognizing there is a problem.
Information Ordering	The ability to arrange things or actions in a certain order or pattern according to a specific rule or set of rules (e.g., patterns of numbers, letters, words, pictures, mathematical operations).

Finger Dexterity	The ability to make precisely coordinated movements of the fingers of one or both hands to grasp, manipulate, or assemble very small objects.
Arm-Hand Steadiness	The ability to keep your hand and arm steady while moving your arm or while holding your arm and hand in one position.
Trunk Strength	The ability to use your abdominal and lower back muscles to support part of the body repeatedly or continuously over time without 'giving out' or fatiguing.
Control Precision	The ability to quickly and repeatedly adjust the controls of a machine or a vehicle to exact positions.
Multilimb Coordination	The ability to coordinate two or more limbs (for example, two arms, two legs, or one leg and one arm) while sitting, standing, or lying down. It does not involve performing the activities while the whole body is in motion.
Oral Comprehension	The ability to listen to and understand information and ideas presented through spoken words and sentences.
Static Strength	The ability to exert maximum muscle force to lift, push, pull, or carry objects.
Visual Color Discrimination	The ability to match or detect differences between colors, including shades of color and brightness.
Visualization	The ability to imagine how something will look after it is moved around or when its parts are moved or rearranged.
Gross Body Equilibrium	The ability to keep or regain your body balance or stay upright when in an unstable position.
Deductive Reasoning	The ability to apply general rules to specific problems to produce answers that make sense.
Gross Body Coordination	The ability to coordinate the movement of your arms, legs, and torso together when the whole body is in motion.
Oral Expression	The ability to communicate information and ideas in speaking so others will understand.
Speech Recognition	The ability to identify and understand the speech of another person.
Dynamic Strength	The ability to exert muscle force repeatedly or continuously over time. This involves muscular endurance and resistance to muscle fatigue.
Selective Attention	The ability to concentrate on a task over a period of time without being distracted.
Speech Clarity	The ability to speak clearly so others can understand you.
Stamina	The ability to exert yourself physically over long periods of time without getting winded or out of breath.
Category Flexibility	The ability to generate or use different sets of rules for combining or grouping things in different ways.
Inductive Reasoning	The ability to combine pieces of information to form general rules or conclusions (includes finding a relationship among seemingly unrelated events).
Depth Perception	The ability to judge which of several objects is closer or farther away from you, or to judge the distance between you and an object.
Flexibility of Closure	The ability to identify or detect a known pattern (a figure, object, word, or sound) that is hidden in other distracting material.
Reaction Time	The ability to quickly respond (with the hand, finger, or foot) to a signal (sound, light, picture) when it appears.
Written Comprehension	The ability to read and understand information and ideas presented in writing.
Far Vision	The ability to see details at a distance.
Written Expression	The ability to communicate information and ideas in writing so others will understand.
Fluency of Ideas	The ability to come up with a number of ideas about a topic (the number of ideas is important, not their quality, correctness, or creativity).
Auditory Attention	The ability to focus on a single source of sound in the presence of other distracting sounds.
Perceptual Speed	The ability to quickly and accurately compare similarities and differences among sets of letters, numbers, objects, pictures, or patterns. The things to be compared may be presented at the same time or one after the other. This ability also includes comparing a presented object with a remembered object.
Originality	The ability to come up with unusual or clever ideas about a given topic or situation, or to develop creative ways to solve a problem.
Time Sharing	The ability to shift back and forth between two or more activities or sources of information (such as speech, sounds, touch, or other sources).
Glare Sensitivity	The ability to see objects in the presence of glare or bright lighting.
Memorization	The ability to remember information such as words, numbers, pictures, and procedures.

Wrist-Finger Speed	The ability to make fast, simple, repeated movements of the fingers, hands, and wrists.
Number Facility	The ability to add, subtract, multiply, or divide quickly and correctly.
Speed of Limb Movement	The ability to quickly move the arms and legs.
Response Orientation	The ability to choose quickly between two or more movements in response to two or more different signals (lights, sounds, pictures). It includes the speed with which the correct response is started with the hand, foot, or other body part.
Mathematical Reasoning	The ability to choose the right mathematical methods or formulas to solve a problem.
Spatial Orientation	The ability to know your location in relation to the environment or to know where other objects are in relation to you.
Speed of Closure	The ability to quickly make sense of, combine, and organize information into meaningful patterns.
Dynamic Flexibility	The ability to quickly and repeatedly bend, stretch, twist, or reach out with your body, arms, and/or legs.
Rate Control	The ability to time your movements or the movement of a piece of equipment in anticipation of changes in the speed and/or direction of a moving object or scene.
Explosive Strength	The ability to use short bursts of muscle force to propel oneself (as in jumping or sprinting), or to throw an object.
Hearing Sensitivity	The ability to detect or tell the differences between sounds that vary in pitch and loudness.
Peripheral Vision	The ability to see objects or movement of objects to one's side when the eyes are looking ahead.
Night Vision	The ability to see under low light conditions.
Sound Localization	The ability to tell the direction from which a sound originated.

Work_Activity	Work_Activity Definitions
Getting Information	Observing, receiving, and otherwise obtaining information from all relevant sources.
Handling and Moving Objects	Using hands and arms in handling, installing, positioning, and moving materials, and manipulating things.
Communicating with Supervisors, Peers, or Subordin	Providing information to supervisors, co-workers, and subordinates by telephone, in written form, e-mail, or in person.
Performing General Physical Activities	Performing physical activities that require considerable use of your arms and legs and moving your whole body, such as climbing, lifting, balancing, walking, stooping, and handling of materials.
Organizing, Planning, and Prioritizing Work	Developing specific goals and plans to prioritize, organize, and accomplish your work.
Evaluating Information to Determine Compliance wit	Using relevant information and individual judgment to determine whether events or processes comply with laws, regulations, or standards.
Updating and Using Relevant Knowledge	Keeping up-to-date technically and applying new knowledge to your job.
Making Decisions and Solving Problems	Analyzing information and evaluating results to choose the best solution and solve problems.
Inspecting Equipment, Structures, or Material	Inspecting equipment, structures, or materials to identify the cause of errors or other problems or defects.
Establishing and Maintaining Interpersonal Relatio	Developing constructive and cooperative working relationships with others, and maintaining them over time.
Training and Teaching Others	Identifying the educational needs of others, developing formal educational or training programs or classes, and teaching or instructing others.
Identifying Objects, Actions, and Events	Identifying information by categorizing, estimating, recognizing differences or similarities, and detecting changes in circumstances or events.
Monitor Processes, Materials, or Surroundings	Monitoring and reviewing information from materials, events, or the environment, to detect or assess problems.
Thinking Creatively	Developing, designing, or creating new applications, ideas, relationships, systems, or products, including artistic contributions.
Estimating the Quantifiable Characteristics of Pro	Estimating sizes, distances, and quantities; or determining time, costs, resources, or materials needed to perform a work activity.
Developing and Building Teams	Encouraging and building mutual trust, respect, and cooperation among team members.
Coordinating the Work and Activities of Others	Getting members of a group to work together to accomplish tasks.
Judging the Qualities of Things, Services, or Peop	Assessing the value, importance, or quality of things or people.

Communicating with Persons Outside Organization	Communicating with people outside the organization, representing the organization to customers, the public, government, and other external sources. This information can be exchanged in person, in writing, or by telephone or e-mail.
Processing Information	Compiling, coding, categorizing, calculating, tabulating, auditing, or verifying information or data.
Scheduling Work and Activities	Scheduling events, programs, and activities, as well as the work of others.
Controlling Machines and Processes	Using either control mechanisms or direct physical activity to operate machines or processes (not including computers or vehicles).
Developing Objectives and Strategies	Establishing long-range objectives and specifying the strategies and actions to achieve them.
Interpreting the Meaning of Information for Others	Translating or explaining what information means and how it can be used.
Operating Vehicles, Mechanized Devices, or Equipme	Running, maneuvering, navigating, or driving vehicles or mechanized equipment, such as forklifts, passenger vehicles, aircraft, or water craft.
Guiding, Directing, and Motivating Subordinates	Providing guidance and direction to subordinates, including setting performance standards and monitoring performance.
Repairing and Maintaining Mechanical Equipment	Servicing, repairing, adjusting, and testing machines, devices, moving parts, and equipment that operate primarily on the basis of mechanical (not electronic) principles.
Assisting and Caring for Others	Providing personal assistance, medical attention, emotional support, or other personal care to others such as coworkers, customers, or patients.
Documenting/Recording Information	Entering, transcribing, recording, storing, or maintaining information in written or electronic/magnetic form.
Analyzing Data or Information	Identifying the underlying principles, reasons, or facts of information by breaking down information or data into separate parts.
Repairing and Maintaining Electronic Equipment	Servicing, repairing, calibrating, regulating, fine-tuning, or testing machines, devices, and equipment that operate primarily on the basis of electrical or electronic (not mechanical) principles.
Coaching and Developing Others	Identifying the developmental needs of others and coaching, mentoring, or otherwise helping others to improve their knowledge or skills.
Performing for or Working Directly with the Public	Performing for people or dealing directly with the public. This includes serving customers in restaurants and stores, and receiving clients or guests.
Drafting, Laying Out, and Specifying Technical Dev	Providing documentation, detailed instructions, drawings, or specifications to tell others about how devices, parts, equipment, or structures are to be fabricated, constructed, assembled, modified, maintained, or used.
Resolving Conflicts and Negotiating with Others	Handling complaints, settling disputes, and resolving grievances and conflicts, or otherwise negotiating with others.
Provide Consultation and Advice to Others	Providing guidance and expert advice to management or other groups on technical, systems-, or process-related topics.
Selling or Influencing Others	Convincing others to buy merchandise/goods or to otherwise change their minds or actions.
Performing Administrative Activities	Performing day-to-day administrative tasks such as maintaining information files and processing paperwork.
Monitoring and Controlling Resources	Monitoring and controlling resources and overseeing the spending of money.
Interacting With Computers	Using computers and computer systems (including hardware and software) to program, write software, set up functions, enter data, or process information.
Staffing Organizational Units	Recruiting, interviewing, selecting, hiring, and promoting employees in an organization.

Work_Context	Work_Context Definitions
Face-to-Face Discussions	How often do you have to have face-to-face discussions with individuals or teams in this job?
Wear Common Protective or Safety Equipment such as	How much does this job require wearing common protective or safety equipment such as safety shoes, glasses, gloves, hard hats or life jackets?
Spend Time Using Your Hands to Handle, Control, or	How much does this job require using your hands to handle, control, or feel objects, tools or controls?
Spend Time Standing	How much does this job require standing?
Contact With Others	How much does this job require the worker to be in contact with others (face-to-face, by telephone, or otherwise) in order to perform it?
Work With Work Group or Team	How important is it to work with others in a group or team in this job?

Outdoors, Exposed to Weather	How often does this job require working outdoors, exposed to all weather conditions?
Importance of Being Exact or Accurate	How important is being very exact or highly accurate in performing this job?
Exposed to Contaminants	How often does this job require working exposed to contaminants (such as pollutants, gases, dust or odors)?
Responsible for Others' Health and Safety	How much responsibility is there for the health and safety of others in this job?
Frequency of Decision Making	How frequently is the worker required to make decisions that affect other people, the financial resources, and/or the image and reputation of the organization?
Very Hot or Cold Temperatures	How often does this job require working in very hot (above 90 F degrees) or very cold (below 32 F degrees) temperatures?
Exposed to High Places	How often does this job require exposure to high places?
Time Pressure	How often does this job require the worker to meet strict deadlines?
Exposed to Hazardous Equipment	How often does this job require exposure to hazardous equipment?
Spend Time Kneeling, Crouching, Stooping, or Crawl	How much does this job require kneeling, crouching, stooping or crawling?
Indoors, Not Environmentally Controlled	How often does this job require working indoors in non-controlled environmental conditions (e.g., warehouse without heat)?
Sounds, Noise Levels Are Distracting or Uncomforta	How often does this job require working exposed to sounds and noise levels that are distracting or uncomfortable?
Spend Time Climbing Ladders, Scaffolds, or Poles	How much does this job require climbing ladders, scaffolds, or poles?
Spend Time Bending or Twisting the Body	How much does this job require bending or twisting your body?
Cramped Work Space, Awkward Positions	How often does this job require working in cramped work spaces that requires getting into awkward positions?
Freedom to Make Decisions	How much decision making freedom, without supervision, does the job offer?
Impact of Decisions on Co-workers or Company Resul	How do the decisions an employee makes impact the results of co-workers, clients or the company?
Extremely Bright or Inadequate Lighting	How often does this job require working in extremely bright or inadequate lighting conditions?
Physical Proximity	To what extent does this job require the worker to perform job tasks in close physical proximity to other people?
Spend Time Walking and Running	How much does this job require walking and running?
Structured versus Unstructured Work	To what extent is this job structured for the worker, rather than allowing the worker to determine tasks, priorities, and goals?
Exposed to Hazardous Conditions	How often does this job require exposure to hazardous conditions?
Spend Time Making Repetitive Motions	How much does this job require making repetitive motions?
Outdoors, Under Cover	How often does this job require working outdoors, under cover (e.g., structure with roof but no walls)?
Exposed to Minor Burns, Cuts, Bites, or Stings	How often does this job require exposure to minor burns, cuts, bites, or stings?
Telephone	How often do you have telephone conversations in this job?
Deal With External Customers	How important is it to work with external customers or the public in this job?
Consequence of Error	How serious would the result usually be if the worker made a mistake that was not readily correctable?
Indoors, Environmentally Controlled	How often does this job require working indoors in environmentally controlled conditions?
Responsibility for Outcomes and Results	How responsible is the worker for work outcomes and results of other workers?
Spend Time Keeping or Regaining Balance	How much does this job require keeping or regaining your balance?
Coordinate or Lead Others	How important is it to coordinate or lead others in accomplishing work activities in this job?
Level of Competition	To what extent does this job require the worker to compete or to be aware of competitive pressures?
Deal With Unpleasant or Angry People	How frequently does the worker have to deal with unpleasant, angry, or discourteous individuals as part of the job requirements?
Frequency of Conflict Situations	How often are there conflict situations the employee has to face in this job?
In an Enclosed Vehicle or Equipment	How often does this job require working in a closed vehicle or equipment (e.g., car)?
Letters and Memos	How often does the job require written letters and memos?

In an Open Vehicle or Equipment	How often does this job require working in an open vehicle or equipment (e.g., tractor)?
Exposed to Whole Body Vibration	How often does this job require exposure to whole body vibration (e.g., operate a jackhammer)?
Wear Specialized Protective or Safety Equipment su	How much does this job require wearing specialized protective or safety equipment such as breathing apparatus, safety harness, full protection suits, or radiation protection?
Importance of Repeating Same Tasks	How important is repeating the same physical activities (e.g., key entry) or mental activities (e.g., checking entries in a ledger) over and over, without stopping, to performing this job?
Pace Determined by Speed of Equipment	How important is it to this job that the pace is determined by the speed of equipment or machinery? (This does not refer to keeping busy at all times on this job.)
Public Speaking	How often do you have to perform public speaking in this job?
Deal With Physically Aggressive People	How frequently does this job require the worker to deal with physical aggression of violent individuals?
Exposed to Disease or Infections	How often does this job require exposure to disease/infections?
Spend Time Sitting	How much does this job require sitting?
Degree of Automation	How automated is the job?
Electronic Mail	How often do you use electronic mail in this job?
Exposed to Radiation	How often does this job require exposure to radiation?

Job Zone Component	Job Zone Component Definitions
Title	Job Zone Two: Some Preparation Needed
Overall Experience	Some previous work-related skill, knowledge, or experience may be helpful in these occupations, but usually is not needed. For example, a drywall installer might benefit from experience installing drywall, but an inexperienced person could still learn to be an installer with little difficulty.
Job Training	Employees in these occupations need anywhere from a few months to one year of working with experienced employees.
Job Zone Examples	These occupations often involve using your knowledge and skills to help others. Examples include drywall installers, fire inspectors, flight attendants, pharmacy technicians, salespersons (retail), and tellers.
SVP Range	(4.0 to < 6.0)
Education	These occupations usually require a high school diploma and may require some vocational training or job-related course work. In some cases, an associate's or bachelor's degree could be needed.

Work_Styles	Work_Styles Definitions
Attention to Detail	Job requires being careful about detail and thorough in completing work tasks.
Cooperation	Job requires being pleasant with others on the job and displaying a good-natured, cooperative attitude.
Dependability	Job requires being reliable, responsible, and dependable, and fulfilling obligations.
Integrity	Job requires being honest and ethical.
Initiative	Job requires a willingness to take on responsibilities and challenges.
Self Control	Job requires maintaining composure, keeping emotions in check, controlling anger, and avoiding aggressive behavior, even in very difficult situations.
Concern for Others	Job requires being sensitive to others' needs and feelings and being understanding and helpful on the job.
Adaptability/Flexibility	Job requires being open to change (positive or negative) and to considerable variety in the workplace.
Analytical Thinking	Job requires analyzing information and using logic to address work-related issues and problems.
Stress Tolerance	Job requires accepting criticism and dealing calmly and effectively with high stress situations.
Achievement/Effort	Job requires establishing and maintaining personally challenging achievement goals and exerting effort toward mastering tasks.
Independence	Job requires developing one's own ways of doing things, guiding oneself with little or no supervision, and depending on oneself to get things done.
Leadership	Job requires a willingness to lead, take charge, and offer opinions and direction.
Innovation	Job requires creativity and alternative thinking to develop new ideas for and answers to work-related problems.
Persistence	Job requires persistence in the face of obstacles.

Social Orientation	Job requires preferring to work with others rather than alone, and being personally connected with others on the job.

47-3015.00 - Helpers--Pipelayers, Plumbers, Pipefitters, and Steamfitters

Help plumbers, pipefitters, steamfitters, or pipelayers by performing duties of lesser skill. Duties include using, supplying or holding materials or tools, and cleaning work area and equipment.

Tasks

1) Disassemble and remove damaged or worn pipe.

2) Measure, cut, thread and assemble new pipe, placing the assembled pipe in hangers or other supports.

3) Cut or drill holes in walls or floors to accommodate the passage of pipes.

4) Mount brackets and hangers on walls and ceilings to hold pipes, and set sleeves or inserts to provide support for pipes.

5) Assist plumbers by performing rough-ins, repairing and replacing fixtures, and locating and repairing leaking or broken pipes.

6) Clean shop, work area, and machines, using solvent and rags.

7) Cut pipe and lift up to fitters.

8) Excavate and grade ditches, and lay and join pipe for water and sewer service.

9) Assist pipefitters in the layout, assembly, and installation of piping for air, ammonia, gas, and water systems.

10) Requisition tools and equipment, select type and size of pipe, and collect and transport materials and equipment to work site.

11) Fill pipes with sand or resin to prevent distortion, and hold pipes during bending and installation.

12) Clean and renew steam traps.

13) Immerse pipe in chemical solution to remove dirt, oil, and scale.

14) Install gas burners to convert furnaces from wood, coal, or oil.

Knowledge	Knowledge Definitions
Building and Construction	Knowledge of materials, methods, and the tools involved in the construction or repair of houses, buildings, or other structures such as highways and roads.
Public Safety and Security	Knowledge of relevant equipment, policies, procedures, and strategies to promote effective local, state, or national security operations for the protection of people, data, property, and institutions.
Mechanical	Knowledge of machines and tools, including their designs, uses, repair, and maintenance.
English Language	Knowledge of the structure and content of the English language including the meaning and spelling of words, rules of composition, and grammar.
Mathematics	Knowledge of arithmetic, algebra, geometry, calculus, statistics, and their applications.
Customer and Personal Service	Knowledge of principles and processes for providing customer and personal services. This includes customer needs assessment, meeting quality standards for services, and evaluation of customer satisfaction.
Administration and Management	Knowledge of business and management principles involved in strategic planning, resource allocation, human resources modeling, leadership technique, production methods, and coordination of people and resources.
Production and Processing	Knowledge of raw materials, production processes, quality control, costs, and other techniques for maximizing the effective manufacture and distribution of goods.
Education and Training	Knowledge of principles and methods for curriculum and training design, teaching and instruction for individuals and groups, and the measurement of training effects.
Design	Knowledge of design techniques, tools, and principles involved in production of precision technical plans, blueprints, drawings, and models.
Transportation	Knowledge of principles and methods for moving people or goods by air, rail, sea, or road, including the relative costs and benefits.

Engineering and Technology	Knowledge of the practical application of engineering science and technology. This includes applying principles, techniques, procedures, and equipment to the design and production of various goods and services.
Law and Government	Knowledge of laws, legal codes, court procedures, precedents, government regulations, executive orders, agency rules, and the democratic political process.
Personnel and Human Resources	Knowledge of principles and procedures for personnel recruitment, selection, training, compensation and benefits, labor relations and negotiation, and personnel information systems.
Physics	Knowledge and prediction of physical principles, laws, their interrelationships, and applications to understanding fluid, material, and atmospheric dynamics, and mechanical, electrical, atomic and sub- atomic structures and processes.
Chemistry	Knowledge of the chemical composition, structure, and properties of substances and of the chemical processes and transformations that they undergo. This includes uses of chemicals and their interactions, danger signs, production techniques, and disposal methods.
Sales and Marketing	Knowledge of principles and methods for showing, promoting, and selling products or services. This includes marketing strategy and tactics, product demonstration, sales techniques, and sales control systems.
Clerical	Knowledge of administrative and clerical procedures and systems such as word processing, managing files and records, stenography and transcription, designing forms, and other office procedures and terminology.
Computers and Electronics	Knowledge of circuit boards, processors, chips, electronic equipment, and computer hardware and software, including applications and programming.
Telecommunications	Knowledge of transmission, broadcasting, switching, control, and operation of telecommunications systems.
Psychology	Knowledge of human behavior and performance; individual differences in ability, personality, and interests; learning and motivation; psychological research methods; and the assessment and treatment of behavioral and affective disorders.
Foreign Language	Knowledge of the structure and content of a foreign (non-English) language including the meaning and spelling of words, rules of composition and grammar, and pronunciation.
Economics and Accounting	Knowledge of economic and accounting principles and practices, the financial markets, banking and the analysis and reporting of financial data.
Communications and Media	Knowledge of media production, communication, and dissemination techniques and methods. This includes alternative ways to inform and entertain via written, oral, and visual media.
Sociology and Anthropology	Knowledge of group behavior and dynamics, societal trends and influences, human migrations, ethnicity, cultures and their history and origins.
Medicine and Dentistry	Knowledge of the information and techniques needed to diagnose and treat human injuries, diseases, and deformities. This includes symptoms, treatment alternatives, drug properties and interactions, and preventive health-care measures.
Biology	Knowledge of plant and animal organisms, their tissues, cells, functions, interdependencies, and interactions with each other and the environment.
Geography	Knowledge of principles and methods for describing the features of land, sea, and air masses, including their physical characteristics, locations, interrelationships, and distribution of plant, animal, and human life.
Therapy and Counseling	Knowledge of principles, methods, and procedures for diagnosis, treatment, and rehabilitation of physical and mental dysfunctions, and for career counseling and guidance.
Food Production	Knowledge of techniques and equipment for planting, growing, and harvesting food products (both plant and animal) for consumption, including storage/handling techniques.
Philosophy and Theology	Knowledge of different philosophical systems and religions. This includes their basic principles, values, ethics, ways of thinking, customs, practices, and their impact on human culture.
Fine Arts	Knowledge of the theory and techniques required to compose, produce, and perform works of music, dance, visual arts, drama, and sculpture.
History and Archeology	Knowledge of historical events and their causes, indicators, and effects on civilizations and cultures.

Skills	Skills Definitions
Active Listening	Giving full attention to what other people are saying, taking time to understand the points being made, asking questions as appropriate, and not interrupting at inappropriate times.
Mathematics	Using mathematics to solve problems.
Equipment Selection	Determining the kind of tools and equipment needed to do a job.
Installation	Installing equipment, machines, wiring, or programs to meet specifications.
Coordination	Adjusting actions in relation to others' actions.
Active Learning	Understanding the implications of new information for both current and future problem-solving and decision making.
Critical Thinking	Using logic and reasoning to identify the strengths and weaknesses of alternative solutions, conclusions or approaches to problems.
Instructing	Teaching others how to do something.
Learning Strategies	Selecting and using training/instructional methods and procedures appropriate for the situation when learning or teaching new things.
Speaking	Talking to others to convey information effectively.
Reading Comprehension	Understanding written sentences and paragraphs in work related documents.
Time Management	Managing one's own time and the time of others.
Troubleshooting	Determining causes of operating errors and deciding what to do about it.
Equipment Maintenance	Performing routine maintenance on equipment and determining when and what kind of maintenance is needed.
Monitoring	Monitoring/Assessing performance of yourself, other individuals, or organizations to make improvements or take corrective action.
Complex Problem Solving	Identifying complex problems and reviewing related information to develop and evaluate options and implement solutions.
Quality Control Analysis	Conducting tests and inspections of products, services, or processes to evaluate quality or performance.
Repairing	Repairing machines or systems using the needed tools.
Writing	Communicating effectively in writing as appropriate for the needs of the audience.
Judgment and Decision Making	Considering the relative costs and benefits of potential actions to choose the most appropriate one.
Social Perceptiveness	Being aware of others' reactions and understanding why they react as they do.
Operation Monitoring	Watching gauges, dials, or other indicators to make sure a machine is working properly.
Operation and Control	Controlling operations of equipment or systems.
Negotiation	Bringing others together and trying to reconcile differences.
Management of Material Resources	Obtaining and seeing to the appropriate use of equipment, facilities, and materials needed to do certain work.
Persuasion	Persuading others to change their minds or behavior.
Technology Design	Generating or adapting equipment and technology to serve user needs.
Management of Personnel Resources	Motivating, developing, and directing people as they work, identifying the best people for the job.
Service Orientation	Actively looking for ways to help people.
Operations Analysis	Analyzing needs and product requirements to create a design.
Science	Using scientific rules and methods to solve problems.
Systems Analysis	Determining how a system should work and how changes in conditions, operations, and the environment will affect outcomes.
Systems Evaluation	Identifying measures or indicators of system performance and the actions needed to improve or correct performance, relative to the goals of the system.
Management of Financial Resources	Determining how money will be spent to get the work done, and accounting for these expenditures.
Programming	Writing computer programs for various purposes.

Ability	Ability Definitions
Manual Dexterity	The ability to quickly move your hand, your hand together with your arm, or your two hands to grasp, manipulate, or assemble objects.
Near Vision	The ability to see details at close range (within a few feet of the observer).
Extent Flexibility	The ability to bend, stretch, twist, or reach with your body, arms, and/or legs.

Information Ordering	The ability to arrange things or actions in a certain order or pattern according to a specific rule or set of rules (e.g., patterns of numbers, letters, words, pictures, mathematical operations).
Oral Comprehension	The ability to listen to and understand information and ideas presented through spoken words and sentences.
Trunk Strength	The ability to use your abdominal and lower back muscles to support part of the body repeatedly or continuously over time without 'giving out' or fatiguing.
Arm-Hand Steadiness	The ability to keep your hand and arm steady while moving your arm or while holding your arm and hand in one position.
Problem Sensitivity	The ability to tell when something is wrong or is likely to go wrong. It does not involve solving the problem, only recognizing there is a problem.
Multilimb Coordination	The ability to coordinate two or more limbs (for example, two arms, two legs, or one leg and one arm) while sitting, standing, or lying down. It does not involve performing the activities while the whole body is in motion.
Static Strength	The ability to exert maximum muscle force to lift, push, pull, or carry objects.
Visualization	The ability to imagine how something will look after it is moved around or when its parts are moved or rearranged.
Control Precision	The ability to quickly and repeatedly adjust the controls of a machine or a vehicle to exact positions.
Speech Recognition	The ability to identify and understand the speech of another person.
Speech Clarity	The ability to speak clearly so others can understand you.
Oral Expression	The ability to communicate information and ideas in speaking so others will understand.
Category Flexibility	The ability to generate or use different sets of rules for combining or grouping things in different ways.
Deductive Reasoning	The ability to apply general rules to specific problems to produce answers that make sense.
Selective Attention	The ability to concentrate on a task over a period of time without being distracted.
Inductive Reasoning	The ability to combine pieces of information to form general rules or conclusions (includes finding a relationship among seemingly unrelated events).
Gross Body Equilibrium	The ability to keep or regain your body balance or stay upright when in an unstable position.
Depth Perception	The ability to judge which of several objects is closer or farther away from you, or to judge the distance between you and an object.
Finger Dexterity	The ability to make precisely coordinated movements of the fingers of one or both hands to grasp, manipulate, or assemble very small objects.
Gross Body Coordination	The ability to coordinate the movement of your arms, legs, and torso together when the whole body is in motion.
Dynamic Strength	The ability to exert muscle force repeatedly or continuously over time. This involves muscular endurance and resistance to muscle fatigue.
Stamina	The ability to exert yourself physically over long periods of time without getting winded or out of breath.
Speed of Limb Movement	The ability to quickly move the arms and legs.
Auditory Attention	The ability to focus on a single source of sound in the presence of other distracting sounds.
Reaction Time	The ability to quickly respond (with the hand, finger, or foot) to a signal (sound, light, picture) when it appears.
Flexibility of Closure	The ability to identify or detect a known pattern (a figure, object, word, or sound) that is hidden in other distracting material.
Far Vision	The ability to see details at a distance.
Spatial Orientation	The ability to know your location in relation to the environment or to know where other objects are in relation to you.
Originality	The ability to come up with unusual or clever ideas about a given topic or situation, or to develop creative ways to solve a problem.
Wrist-Finger Speed	The ability to make fast, simple, repeated movements of the fingers, hands, and wrists.
Written Comprehension	The ability to read and understand information and ideas presented in writing.
Time Sharing	The ability to shift back and forth between two or more activities or sources of information (such as speech, sounds, touch, or other sources).
Mathematical Reasoning	The ability to choose the right mathematical methods or formulas to solve a problem.
Glare Sensitivity	The ability to see objects in the presence of glare or bright lighting.

Perceptual Speed	The ability to quickly and accurately compare similarities and differences among sets of letters, numbers, objects, pictures, or patterns. The things to be compared may be presented at the same time or one after the other. This ability also includes comparing a presented object with a remembered object.
Fluency of Ideas	The ability to come up with a number of ideas about a topic (the number of ideas is important, not their quality, correctness, or creativity).
Visual Color Discrimination	The ability to match or detect differences between colors, including shades of color and brightness.
Response Orientation	The ability to choose quickly between two or more movements in response to two or more different signals (lights, sounds, pictures). It includes the speed with which the correct response is started with the hand, foot, or other body part.
Speed of Closure	The ability to quickly make sense of, combine, and organize information into meaningful patterns.
Written Expression	The ability to communicate information and ideas in writing so others will understand.
Number Facility	The ability to add, subtract, multiply, or divide quickly and correctly.
Memorization	The ability to remember information such as words, numbers, pictures, and procedures.
Hearing Sensitivity	The ability to detect or tell the differences between sounds that vary in pitch and loudness.
Rate Control	The ability to time your movements or the movement of a piece of equipment in anticipation of changes in the speed and/or direction of a moving object or scene.
Explosive Strength	The ability to use short bursts of muscle force to propel oneself (as in jumping or sprinting), or to throw an object.
Peripheral Vision	The ability to see objects or movement of objects to one's side when the eyes are looking ahead.
Night Vision	The ability to see under low light conditions.
Dynamic Flexibility	The ability to quickly and repeatedly bend, stretch, twist, or reach out with your body, arms, and/or legs.
Sound Localization	The ability to tell the direction from which a sound originated.

Work_Activity	Work_Activity Definitions
Performing General Physical Activities	Performing physical activities that require considerable use of your arms and legs and moving your whole body, such as climbing, lifting, balancing, walking, stooping, and handling of materials.
Handling and Moving Objects	Using hands and arms in handling, installing, positioning, and moving materials, and manipulating things.
Inspecting Equipment, Structures, or Material	Inspecting equipment, structures, or materials to identify the cause of errors or other problems or defects.
Getting Information	Observing, receiving, and otherwise obtaining information from all relevant sources.
Operating Vehicles, Mechanized Devices, or Equipme	Running, maneuvering, navigating, or driving vehicles or mechanized equipment, such as forklifts, passenger vehicles, aircraft, or water craft.
Evaluating Information to Determine Compliance wit	Using relevant information and individual judgment to determine whether events or processes comply with laws, regulations, or standards.
Identifying Objects, Actions, and Events	Identifying information by categorizing, estimating, recognizing differences or similarities, and detecting changes in circumstances or events.
Communicating with Supervisors, Peers, or Subordin	Providing information to supervisors, co-workers, and subordinates by telephone, in written form, e-mail, or in person.
Updating and Using Relevant Knowledge	Keeping up-to-date technically and applying new knowledge to your job.
Controlling Machines and Processes	Using either control mechanisms or direct physical activity to operate machines or processes (not including computers or vehicles).
Establishing and Maintaining Interpersonal Relatio	Developing constructive and cooperative working relationships with others, and maintaining them over time.
Repairing and Maintaining Mechanical Equipment	Servicing, repairing, adjusting, and testing machines, devices, moving parts, and equipment that operate primarily on the basis of mechanical (not electronic) principles.
Organizing, Planning, and Prioritizing Work	Developing specific goals and plans to prioritize, organize, and accomplish your work.
Judging the Qualities of Things, Services, or Peop	Assessing the value, importance, or quality of things or people.
Processing Information	Compiling, coding, categorizing, calculating, tabulating, auditing, or verifying information or data.

Making Decisions and Solving Problems	Analyzing information and evaluating results to choose the best solution and solve problems.
Monitor Processes, Materials, or Surroundings	Monitoring and reviewing information from materials, events, or the environment, to detect or assess problems.
Estimating the Quantifiable Characteristics of Pro	Estimating sizes, distances, and quantities; or determining time, costs, resources, or materials needed to perform a work activity.
Assisting and Caring for Others	Providing personal assistance, medical attention, emotional support, or other personal care to others such as coworkers, customers, or patients.
Developing Objectives and Strategies	Establishing long-range objectives and specifying the strategies and actions to achieve them.
Coaching and Developing Others	Identifying the developmental needs of others and coaching, mentoring, or otherwise helping others to improve their knowledge or skills.
Resolving Conflicts and Negotiating with Others	Handling complaints, settling disputes, and resolving grievances and conflicts, or otherwise negotiating with others.
Interpreting the Meaning of Information for Others	Translating or explaining what information means and how it can be used.
Coordinating the Work and Activities of Others	Getting members of a group to work together to accomplish tasks.
Analyzing Data or Information	Identifying the underlying principles, reasons, or facts of information by breaking down information or data into separate parts.
Thinking Creatively	Developing, designing, or creating new applications, ideas, relationships, systems, or products, including artistic contributions.
Communicating with Persons Outside Organization	Communicating with people outside the organization, representing the organization to customers, the public, government, and other external sources. This information can be exchanged in person, in writing, or by telephone or e-mail.
Guiding, Directing, and Motivating Subordinates	Providing guidance and direction to subordinates, including setting performance standards and monitoring performance.
Training and Teaching Others	Identifying the educational needs of others, developing formal educational or training programs or classes, and teaching or instructing others.
Drafting, Laying Out, and Specifying Technical Dev	Providing documentation, detailed instructions, drawings, or specifications to tell others about how devices, parts, equipment, or structures are to be fabricated, constructed, assembled, modified, maintained, or used.
Provide Consultation and Advice to Others	Providing guidance and expert advice to management or other groups on technical, systems-, or process-related topics.
Developing and Building Teams	Encouraging and building mutual trust, respect, and cooperation among team members.
Monitoring and Controlling Resources	Monitoring and controlling resources and overseeing the spending of money.
Scheduling Work and Activities	Scheduling events, programs, and activities, as well as the work of others.
Performing Administrative Activities	Performing day-to-day administrative tasks such as maintaining information files and processing paperwork.
Repairing and Maintaining Electronic Equipment	Servicing, repairing, calibrating, regulating, fine-tuning, or testing machines, devices, and equipment that operate primarily on the basis of electrical or electronic (not mechanical) principles.
Performing for or Working Directly with the Public	Performing for people or dealing directly with the public. This includes serving customers in restaurants and stores, and receiving clients or guests.
Documenting/Recording Information	Entering, transcribing, recording, storing, or maintaining information in written or electronic/magnetic form.
Selling or Influencing Others	Convincing others to buy merchandise/goods or to otherwise change their minds or actions.
Staffing Organizational Units	Recruiting, interviewing, selecting, hiring, and promoting employees in an organization.
Interacting With Computers	Using computers and computer systems (including hardware and software) to program, write software, set up functions, enter data, or process information.

Work_Context

Work_Context	Work_Context Definitions
Face-to-Face Discussions	How often do you have to have face-to-face discussions with individuals or teams in this job?
Wear Common Protective or Safety Equipment such as	How much does this job require wearing common protective or safety equipment such as safety shoes, glasses, gloves, hard hats or life jackets?
Outdoors, Exposed to Weather	How often does this job require working outdoors, exposed to all weather conditions?

Spend Time Using Your Hands to Handle, Control, or	How much does this job require using your hands to handle, control, or feel objects, tools or controls?
Contact With Others	How much does this job require the worker to be in contact with others (face-to-face, by telephone, or otherwise) in order to perform it?
Exposed to Hazardous Equipment	How often does this job require exposure to hazardous equipment?
Sounds, Noise Levels Are Distracting or Uncomforta	How often does this job require working exposed to sounds and noise levels that are distracting or uncomfortable?
Importance of Being Exact or Accurate	How important is being very exact or highly accurate in performing this job?
Spend Time Standing	How much does this job require standing?
Work With Work Group or Team	How important is it to work with others in a group or team in this job?
Time Pressure	How often does this job require the worker to meet strict deadlines?
Exposed to Contaminants	How often does this job require working exposed to contaminants (such as pollutants, gases, dust or odors)?
Exposed to Minor Burns, Cuts, Bites, or Stings	How often does this job require exposure to minor burns, cuts, bites, or stings?
Very Hot or Cold Temperatures	How often does this job require working in very hot (above 90 F degrees) or very cold (below 32 F degrees) temperatures?
Cramped Work Space, Awkward Positions	How often does this job require working in cramped work spaces that requires getting into awkward positions?
Physical Proximity	To what extent does this job require the worker to perform job tasks in close physical proximity to other people?
Outdoors, Under Cover	How often does this job require working outdoors, under cover (e.g., structure with roof but no walls)?
Responsible for Others' Health and Safety	How much responsibility is there for the health and safety of others in this job?
Spend Time Kneeling, Crouching, Stooping, or Crawl	How much does this job require kneeling, crouching, stooping, or crawling?
Freedom to Make Decisions	How much decision making freedom, without supervision, does the job offer?
Impact of Decisions on Co-workers or Company Resul	How do the decisions an employee makes impact the results of co-workers, clients or the company?
Indoors, Not Environmentally Controlled	How often does this job require working indoors in non-controlled environmental conditions (e.g., warehouse without heat)?
Exposed to Whole Body Vibration	How often does this job require exposure to whole body vibration (e.g., operate a jackhammer)?
Exposed to High Places	How often does this job require exposure to high places?
Frequency of Decision Making	How frequently is the worker required to make decisions that affect other people, the financial resources, and/or the image and reputation of the organization?
Spend Time Bending or Twisting the Body	How much does this job require bending or twisting your body?
Responsibility for Outcomes and Results	How responsible is the worker for work outcomes and results of other workers?
Extremely Bright or Inadequate Lighting	How often does this job require working in extremely bright or inadequate lighting conditions?
Spend Time Making Repetitive Motions	How much does this job require making repetitive motions?
Spend Time Walking and Running	How much does this job require walking and running?
Coordinate or Lead Others	How important is it to coordinate or lead others in accomplishing work activities in this job?
Telephone	How often do you have telephone conversations in this job?
In an Enclosed Vehicle or Equipment	How often does this job require working in a closed vehicle or equipment (e.g., car)?
Consequence of Error	How serious would the result usually be if the worker made a mistake that was not readily correctable?
Structured versus Unstructured Work	To what extent is this job structured for the worker, rather than allowing the worker to determine tasks, priorities, and goals?
Spend Time Climbing Ladders, Scaffolds, or Poles	How much does this job require climbing ladders, scaffolds, or poles?
Deal With External Customers	How important is it to work with external customers or the public in this job?
In an Open Vehicle or Equipment	How often does this job require working in an open vehicle or equipment (e.g., tractor)?
Level of Competition	To what extent does this job require the worker to compete or to be aware of competitive pressures?
Indoors, Environmentally Controlled	How often does this job require working indoors in environmentally controlled conditions?

1065

Importance of Repeating Same Tasks	How important is repeating the same physical activities (e.g., key entry) or mental activities (e.g., checking entries in a ledger) over and over, without stopping, to performing this job?
Frequency of Conflict Situations	How often are there conflict situations the employee has to face in this job?
Wear Specialized Protective or Safety Equipment su	How much does this job require wearing specialized protective or safety equipment such as breathing apparatus, safety harness, full protection suits, or radiation protection?
Pace Determined by Speed of Equipment	How important is it to this job that the pace is determined by the speed of equipment or machinery? (This does not refer to keeping busy at all times on this job.)
Exposed to Hazardous Conditions	How often does this job require exposure to hazardous conditions?
Spend Time Keeping or Regaining Balance	How much does this job require keeping or regaining your balance?
Deal With Unpleasant or Angry People	How frequently does the worker have to deal with unpleasant, angry, or discourteous individuals as part of the job requirements?
Spend Time Sitting	How much does this job require sitting?
Degree of Automation	How automated is the job?
Exposed to Disease or Infections	How often does this job require exposure to disease/infections?
Letters and Memos	How often does the job require written letters and memos?
Public Speaking	How often do you have to perform public speaking in this job?
Deal With Physically Aggressive People	How frequently does this job require the worker to deal with physical aggression of violent individuals?
Electronic Mail	How often do you use electronic mail in this job?
Exposed to Radiation	How often does this job require exposure to radiation?

Job Zone Component	Job Zone Component Definitions
Title	Job Zone Two: Some Preparation Needed
Overall Experience	Some previous work-related skill, knowledge, or experience may be helpful in these occupations, but usually is not needed. For example, a drywall installer might benefit from experience installing drywall, but an inexperienced person could still learn to be an installer with little difficulty.
Job Training	Employees in these occupations need anywhere from a few months to one year of working with experienced employees.
Job Zone Examples	These occupations often involve using your knowledge and skills to help others. Examples include drywall installers, fire inspectors, flight attendants, pharmacy technicians, salespersons (retail), and tellers.
SVP Range	(4.0 to < 6.0)
Education	These occupations usually require a high school diploma and may require some vocational training or job-related course work. In some cases, an associate's or bachelor's degree could be needed.

Work_Styles	Work_Styles Definitions
Cooperation	Job requires being pleasant with others on the job and displaying a good-natured, cooperative attitude.
Dependability	Job requires being reliable, responsible, and dependable, and fulfilling obligations.
Attention to Detail	Job requires being careful about detail and thorough in completing work tasks.
Initiative	Job requires a willingness to take on responsibilities and challenges.
Adaptability/Flexibility	Job requires being open to change (positive or negative) and to considerable variety in the workplace.
Integrity	Job requires being honest and ethical.
Persistence	Job requires persistence in the face of obstacles.
Leadership	Job requires a willingness to lead, take charge, and offer opinions and direction.
Stress Tolerance	Job requires accepting criticism and dealing calmly and effectively with high stress situations.
Independence	Job requires developing one's own ways of doing things, guiding oneself with little or no supervision, and depending on oneself to get things done.
Self Control	Job requires maintaining composure, keeping emotions in check, controlling anger, and avoiding aggressive behavior, even in very difficult situations.
Achievement/Effort	Job requires establishing and maintaining personally challenging achievement goals and exerting effort toward mastering tasks.

Innovation	Job requires creativity and alternative thinking to develop new ideas for and answers to work-related problems.
Concern for Others	Job requires being sensitive to others' needs and feelings and being understanding and helpful on the job.
Analytical Thinking	Job requires analyzing information and using logic to address work-related issues and problems.
Social Orientation	Job requires preferring to work with others rather than alone, and being personally connected with others on the job.

47-4011.00 - Construction and Building Inspectors

Inspect structures using engineering skills to determine structural soundness and compliance with specifications, building codes, and other regulations. Inspections may be general in nature or may be limited to a specific area, such as electrical systems or plumbing.

Tasks

1) Inspect bridges, dams, highways, buildings, wiring, plumbing, electrical circuits, sewers, heating systems, and foundations during and after construction for structural quality, general safety and conformance to specifications and codes.

2) Review and interpret plans, blueprints, site layouts, specifications, and construction methods to ensure compliance to legal requirements and safety regulations.

3) Use survey instruments, metering devices, tape measures, and test equipment, such as concrete strength measurers, to perform inspections.

4) Inspect and monitor construction sites to ensure adherence to safety standards, building codes, and specifications.

5) Measure dimensions and verify level, alignment, and elevation of structures and fixtures to ensure compliance to building plans and codes.

6) Issue violation notices and stop-work orders, conferring with owners, violators, and authorities to explain regulations and recommend rectifications.

7) Train, direct and supervise other construction inspectors.

8) Approve and sign plans that meet required specifications.

9) Monitor installation of plumbing, wiring, equipment, and appliances to ensure that installation is performed properly and is in compliance with applicable regulations.

10) Compute estimates of work completed or of needed renovations or upgrades, and approve payment for contractors.

11) Evaluate premises for cleanliness, including proper garbage disposal and lack of vermin infestation.

12) Issue permits for construction, relocation, demolition and occupancy.

13) Examine lifting and conveying devices, such as elevators, escalators, moving sidewalks, lifts and hoists, inclined railways, ski lifts, and amusement rides to ensure safety and proper functioning.

Knowledge	Knowledge Definitions
Building and Construction	Knowledge of materials, methods, and the tools involved in the construction or repair of houses, buildings, or other structures such as highways and roads.
Engineering and Technology	Knowledge of the practical application of engineering science and technology. This includes applying principles, techniques, procedures, and equipment to the design and production of various goods and services.
Customer and Personal Service	Knowledge of principles and processes for providing customer and personal services. This includes customer needs assessment, meeting quality standards for services, and evaluation of customer satisfaction.
Public Safety and Security	Knowledge of relevant equipment, policies, procedures, and strategies to promote effective local, state, or national security operations for the protection of people, data, property, and institutions.
Design	Knowledge of design techniques, tools, and principles involved in production of precision technical plans, blueprints, drawings, and models.
English Language	Knowledge of the structure and content of the English language including the meaning and spelling of words, rules of composition, and grammar.
Mathematics	Knowledge of arithmetic, algebra, geometry, calculus, statistics, and their applications.

Administration and Management	Knowledge of business and management principles involved in strategic planning, resource allocation, human resources modeling, leadership technique, production methods, and coordination of people and resources.	Therapy and Counseling	Knowledge of principles, methods, and procedures for diagnosis, treatment, and rehabilitation of physical and mental dysfunctions, and for career counseling and guidance.
Computers and Electronics	Knowledge of circuit boards, processors, chips, electronic equipment, and computer hardware and software, including applications and programming.	Foreign Language	Knowledge of the structure and content of a foreign (non-English) language including the meaning and spelling of words, rules of composition and grammar, and pronunciation.
Clerical	Knowledge of administrative and clerical procedures and systems such as word processing, managing files and records, stenography and transcription, designing forms, and other office procedures and terminology.	Medicine and Dentistry	Knowledge of the information and techniques needed to diagnose and treat human injuries, diseases, and deformities. This includes symptoms, treatment alternatives, drug properties and interactions, and preventive health-care measures.

Skills   **Skills Definitions**

Education and Training	Knowledge of principles and methods for curriculum and training design, teaching and instruction for individuals and groups, and the measurement of training effects.	Reading Comprehension	Understanding written sentences and paragraphs in work related documents.
Mechanical	Knowledge of machines and tools, including their designs, uses, repair, and maintenance.	Active Listening	Giving full attention to what other people are saying, taking time to understand the points being made, asking questions as appropriate, and not interrupting at inappropriate times.
Geography	Knowledge of principles and methods for describing the features of land, sea, and air masses, including their physical characteristics, locations, interrelationships, and distribution of plant, animal, and human life.	Mathematics	Using mathematics to solve problems.
		Critical Thinking	Using logic and reasoning to identify the strengths and weaknesses of alternative solutions, conclusions or approaches to problems.
Personnel and Human Resources	Knowledge of principles and procedures for personnel recruitment, selection, training, compensation and benefits, labor relations and negotiation, and personnel information systems.	Active Learning	Understanding the implications of new information for both current and future problem-solving and decision-making.
Telecommunications	Knowledge of transmission, broadcasting, switching, control, and operation of telecommunications systems.	Time Management	Managing one's own time and the time of others.
		Coordination	Adjusting actions in relation to others' actions.
Communications and Media	Knowledge of media production, communication, and dissemination techniques and methods. This includes alternative ways to inform and entertain via written, oral, and visual media.	Writing	Communicating effectively in writing as appropriate for the needs of the audience.
		Social Perceptiveness	Being aware of others' reactions and understanding why they react as they do.
Transportation	Knowledge of principles and methods for moving people or goods by air, rail, sea, or road, including the relative costs and benefits.	Complex Problem Solving	Identifying complex problems and reviewing related information to develop and evaluate options and implement solutions.
Physics	Knowledge and prediction of physical principles, laws, their interrelationships, and applications to understanding fluid, material, and atmospheric dynamics, and mechanical, electrical, atomic and sub- atomic structures and processes.	Quality Control Analysis	Conducting tests and inspections of products, services, or processes to evaluate quality or performance.
		Speaking	Talking to others to convey information effectively.
Production and Processing	Knowledge of raw materials, production processes, quality control, costs, and other techniques for maximizing the effective manufacture and distribution of goods.	Judgment and Decision Making	Considering the relative costs and benefits of potential actions to choose the most appropriate one.
		Instructing	Teaching others how to do something.
Sales and Marketing	Knowledge of principles and methods for showing, promoting, and selling products or services. This includes marketing strategy and tactics, product demonstration, sales techniques, and sales control systems.	Learning Strategies	Selecting and using training/instructional methods and procedures appropriate for the situation when learning or teaching new things.
		Persuasion	Persuading others to change their minds or behavior.
Law and Government	Knowledge of laws, legal codes, court procedures, precedents, government regulations, executive orders, agency rules, and the democratic political process.	Monitoring	Monitoring/Assessing performance of yourself, other individuals, or organizations to make improvements or take corrective action.
Economics and Accounting	Knowledge of economic and accounting principles and practices, the financial markets, banking and the analysis and reporting of financial data.	Troubleshooting	Determining causes of operating errors and deciding what to do about it.
		Science	Using scientific rules and methods to solve problems.
		Service Orientation	Actively looking for ways to help people.
Psychology	Knowledge of human behavior and performance; individual differences in ability, personality, and interests; learning and motivation; psychological research methods; and the assessment and treatment of behavioral and affective disorders.	Negotiation	Bringing others together and trying to reconcile differences.
		Equipment Selection	Determining the kind of tools and equipment needed to do a job.
Chemistry	Knowledge of the chemical composition, structure, and properties of substances and of the chemical processes and transformations that they undergo. This includes uses of chemicals and their interactions, danger signs, production techniques, and disposal methods.	Equipment Maintenance	Performing routine maintenance on equipment and determining when and what kind of maintenance is needed.
		Operation Monitoring	Watching gauges, dials, or other indicators to make sure a machine is working properly.
Biology	Knowledge of plant and animal organisms, their tissues, cells, functions, interdependencies, and interactions with each other and the environment.	Installation	Installing equipment, machines, wiring, or programs to meet specifications.
		Technology Design	Generating or adapting equipment and technology to serve user needs.
Sociology and Anthropology	Knowledge of group behavior and dynamics, societal trends and influences, human migrations, ethnicity, cultures and their history and origins.	Operations Analysis	Analyzing needs and product requirements to create a design.
		Operation and Control	Controlling operations of equipment or systems.
Food Production	Knowledge of techniques and equipment for planting, growing, and harvesting food products (both plant and animal) for consumption, including storage/handling techniques.	Management of Material Resources	Obtaining and seeing to the appropriate use of equipment, facilities, and materials needed to do certain work.
Fine Arts	Knowledge of the theory and techniques required to compose, produce, and perform works of music, dance, visual arts, drama, and sculpture.	Systems Analysis	Determining how a system should work and how changes in conditions, operations, and the environment will affect outcomes.
History and Archeology	Knowledge of historical events and their causes, indicators, and effects on civilizations and cultures.	Systems Evaluation	Identifying measures or indicators of system performance and the actions needed to improve or correct performance, relative to the goals of the system.
Philosophy and Theology	Knowledge of different philosophical systems and religions. This includes their basic principles, values, ethics, ways of thinking, customs, practices, and their impact on human culture.	Management of Personnel Resources	Motivating, developing, and directing people as they work, identifying the best people for the job.
		Management of Financial Resources	Determining how money will be spent to get the work done, and accounting for these expenditures.
		Repairing	Repairing machines or systems using the needed tools.
		Programming	Writing computer programs for various purposes.

Ability	Ability Definitions
Problem Sensitivity	The ability to tell when something is wrong or is likely to go wrong. It does not involve solving the problem, only recognizing there is a problem.
Oral Expression	The ability to communicate information and ideas in speaking so others will understand.
Inductive Reasoning	The ability to combine pieces of information to form general rules or conclusions (includes finding a relationship among seemingly unrelated events).
Near Vision	The ability to see details at close range (within a few feet of the observer).
Oral Comprehension	The ability to listen to and understand information and ideas presented through spoken words and sentences.
Speech Clarity	The ability to speak clearly so others can understand you.
Deductive Reasoning	The ability to apply general rules to specific problems to produce answers that make sense.
Written Comprehension	The ability to read and understand information and ideas presented in writing.
Speech Recognition	The ability to identify and understand the speech of another person.
Flexibility of Closure	The ability to identify or detect a known pattern (a figure, object, word, or sound) that is hidden in other distracting material.
Information Ordering	The ability to arrange things or actions in a certain order or pattern according to a specific rule or set of rules (e.g., patterns of numbers, letters, words, pictures, mathematical operations).
Written Expression	The ability to communicate information and ideas in writing so others will understand.
Visualization	The ability to imagine how something will look after it is moved around or when its parts are moved or rearranged.
Far Vision	The ability to see details at a distance.
Selective Attention	The ability to concentrate on a task over a period of time without being distracted.
Arm-Hand Steadiness	The ability to keep your hand and arm steady while moving your arm or while holding your arm and hand in one position.
Visual Color Discrimination	The ability to match or detect differences between colors, including shades of color and brightness.
Depth Perception	The ability to judge which of several objects is closer or farther away from you, or to judge the distance between you and an object.
Speed of Closure	The ability to quickly make sense of, combine, and organize information into meaningful patterns.
Perceptual Speed	The ability to quickly and accurately compare similarities and differences among sets of letters, numbers, objects, pictures, or patterns. The things to be compared may be presented at the same time or one after the other. This ability also includes comparing a presented object with a remembered object.
Time Sharing	The ability to shift back and forth between two or more activities or sources of information (such as speech, sounds, touch, or other sources).
Mathematical Reasoning	The ability to choose the right mathematical methods or formulas to solve a problem.
Number Facility	The ability to add, subtract, multiply, or divide quickly and correctly.
Control Precision	The ability to quickly and repeatedly adjust the controls of a machine or a vehicle to exact positions.
Auditory Attention	The ability to focus on a single source of sound in the presence of other distracting sounds.
Category Flexibility	The ability to generate or use different sets of rules for combining or grouping things in different ways.
Finger Dexterity	The ability to make precisely coordinated movements of the fingers of one or both hands to grasp, manipulate, or assemble very small objects.
Originality	The ability to come up with unusual or clever ideas about a given topic or situation, or to develop creative ways to solve a problem.
Multilimb Coordination	The ability to coordinate two or more limbs (for example, two arms, two legs, or one leg and one arm) while sitting, standing, or lying down. It does not involve performing the activities while the whole body is in motion.
Gross Body Coordination	The ability to coordinate the movement of your arms, legs, and torso together when the whole body is in motion.
Spatial Orientation	The ability to know your location in relation to the environment or to know where other objects are in relation to you.
Memorization	The ability to remember information such as words, numbers, pictures, and procedures.

Ability	Ability Definitions
Extent Flexibility	The ability to bend, stretch, twist, or reach with your body, arms, and/or legs.
Trunk Strength	The ability to use your abdominal and lower back muscles to support part of the body repeatedly or continuously over time without 'giving out' or fatiguing.
Manual Dexterity	The ability to quickly move your hand, your hand together with your arm, or your two hands to grasp, manipulate, or assemble objects.
Gross Body Equilibrium	The ability to keep or regain your body balance or stay upright when in an unstable position.
Fluency of Ideas	The ability to come up with a number of ideas about a topic (the number of ideas is important, not their quality, correctness, or creativity).
Glare Sensitivity	The ability to see objects in the presence of glare or bright lighting.
Reaction Time	The ability to quickly respond (with the hand, finger, or foot) to a signal (sound, light, picture) when it appears.
Stamina	The ability to exert yourself physically over long periods of time without getting winded or out of breath.
Static Strength	The ability to exert maximum muscle force to lift, push, pull, or carry objects.
Peripheral Vision	The ability to see objects or movement of objects to one's side when the eyes are looking ahead.
Sound Localization	The ability to tell the direction from which a sound originated.
Rate Control	The ability to time your movements or the movement of a piece of equipment in anticipation of changes in the speed and/or direction of a moving object or scene.
Hearing Sensitivity	The ability to detect or tell the differences between sounds that vary in pitch and loudness.
Speed of Limb Movement	The ability to quickly move the arms and legs.
Response Orientation	The ability to choose quickly between two or more movements in response to two or more different signals (lights, sounds, pictures). It includes the speed with which the correct response is started with the hand, foot, or other body part.
Wrist-Finger Speed	The ability to make fast, simple, repeated movements of the fingers, hands, and wrists.
Night Vision	The ability to see under low light conditions.
Dynamic Strength	The ability to exert muscle force repeatedly or continuously over time. This involves muscular endurance and resistance to muscle fatigue.
Dynamic Flexibility	The ability to quickly and repeatedly bend, stretch, twist, or reach out with your body, arms, and/or legs.
Explosive Strength	The ability to use short bursts of muscle force to propel oneself (as in jumping or sprinting), or to throw an object.

Work_Activity	Work_Activity Definitions
Inspecting Equipment, Structures, or Material	Inspecting equipment, structures, or materials to identify the cause of errors or other problems or defects.
Evaluating Information to Determine Compliance wit	Using relevant information and individual judgment to determine whether events or processes comply with laws, regulations, or standards.
Getting Information	Observing, receiving, and otherwise obtaining information from all relevant sources.
Monitor Processes, Materials, or Surroundings	Monitoring and reviewing information from materials, events, or the environment, to detect or assess problems.
Identifying Objects, Actions, and Events	Identifying information by categorizing, estimating, recognizing differences or similarities, and detecting changes in circumstances or events.
Documenting/Recording Information	Entering, transcribing, recording, storing, or maintaining information in written or electronic/magnetic form.
Communicating with Supervisors, Peers, or Subordin	Providing information to supervisors, co-workers, and subordinates by telephone, in written form, e-mail, or in person.
Communicating with Persons Outside Organization	Communicating with people outside the organization, representing the organization to customers, the public, government, and other external sources. This information can be exchanged in person, in writing, or by telephone or e-mail.
Making Decisions and Solving Problems	Analyzing information and evaluating results to choose the best solution and solve problems.
Processing Information	Compiling, coding, categorizing, calculating, tabulating, auditing, or verifying information or data.
Resolving Conflicts and Negotiating with Others	Handling complaints, settling disputes, and resolving grievances and conflicts, or otherwise negotiating with others.
Performing Administrative Activities	Performing day-to-day administrative tasks such as maintaining information files and processing paperwork.

Establishing and Maintaining Interpersonal Relatio	Developing constructive and cooperative working relationships with others, and maintaining them over time.
Analyzing Data or Information	Identifying the underlying principles, reasons, or facts of information by breaking down information or data into separate parts.
Performing for or Working Directly with the Public	Performing for people or dealing directly with the public. This includes serving customers in restaurants and stores, and receiving clients or guests.
Estimating the Quantifiable Characteristics of Pro	Estimating sizes, distances, and quantities; or determining time, costs, resources, or materials needed to perform a work activity.
Interacting With Computers	Using computers and computer systems (including hardware and software) to program, write software, set up functions, enter data, or process information.
Organizing, Planning, and Prioritizing Work	Developing specific goals and plans to prioritize, organize, and accomplish your work.
Interpreting the Meaning of Information for Others	Translating or explaining what information means and how it can be used.
Updating and Using Relevant Knowledge	Keeping up-to-date technically and applying new knowledge to your job.
Scheduling Work and Activities	Scheduling events, programs, and activities, as well as the work of others.
Judging the Qualities of Things, Services, or Peop	Assessing the value, importance, or quality of things or people.
Monitoring and Controlling Resources	Monitoring and controlling resources and overseeing the spending of money.
Drafting, Laying Out, and Specifying Technical Dev	Providing documentation, detailed instructions, drawings, or specifications to tell others about how devices, parts, equipment, or structures are to be fabricated, constructed, assembled, modified, maintained, or used.
Thinking Creatively	Developing, designing, or creating new applications, ideas, relationships, systems, or products, including artistic contributions.
Performing General Physical Activities	Performing physical activities that require considerable use of your arms and legs and moving your whole body, such as climbing, lifting, balancing, walking, stooping, and handling of materials.
Provide Consultation and Advice to Others	Providing guidance and expert advice to management or other groups on technical, systems-, or process-related topics.
Controlling Machines and Processes	Using either control mechanisms or direct physical activity to operate machines or processes (not including computers or vehicles).
Operating Vehicles, Mechanized Devices, or Equipme	Running, maneuvering, navigating, or driving vehicles or mechanized equipment, such as forklifts, passenger vehicles, aircraft, or water craft.
Developing and Building Teams	Encouraging and building mutual trust, respect, and cooperation among team members.
Developing Objectives and Strategies	Establishing long-range objectives and specifying the strategies and actions to achieve them.
Coordinating the Work and Activities of Others	Getting members of a group to work together to accomplish tasks.
Handling and Moving Objects	Using hands and arms in handling, installing, positioning, and moving materials, and manipulating things.
Coaching and Developing Others	Identifying the developmental needs of others and coaching, mentoring, or otherwise helping others to improve their knowledge or skills.
Training and Teaching Others	Identifying the educational needs of others, developing formal educational or training programs or classes, and teaching or instructing others.
Assisting and Caring for Others	Providing personal assistance, medical attention, emotional support, or other personal care to others such as coworkers, customers, or patients.
Repairing and Maintaining Electronic Equipment	Servicing, repairing, calibrating, regulating, fine-tuning, or testing machines, devices, and equipment that operate primarily on the basis of electrical or electronic (not mechanical) principles.
Repairing and Maintaining Mechanical Equipment	Servicing, repairing, adjusting, and testing machines, devices, moving parts, and equipment that operate primarily on the basis of mechanical (not electronic) principles.
Guiding, Directing, and Motivating Subordinates	Providing guidance and direction to subordinates, including setting performance standards and monitoring performance.
Selling or Influencing Others	Convincing others to buy merchandise/goods or to otherwise change their minds or actions.
Staffing Organizational Units	Recruiting, interviewing, selecting, hiring, and promoting employees in an organization.

Work_Context	Work_Context Definitions
Face-to-Face Discussions	How often do you have to have face-to-face discussions with individuals or teams in this job?
Telephone	How often do you have telephone conversations in this job?
Contact With Others	How much does this job require the worker to be in contact with others (face-to-face, by telephone, or otherwise) in order to perform it?
Frequency of Decision Making	How frequently is the worker required to make decisions that affect other people, the financial resources, and/or the image and reputation of the organization?
Freedom to Make Decisions	How much decision making freedom, without supervision, does the job offer?
Outdoors, Exposed to Weather	How often does this job require working outdoors, exposed to all weather conditions?
In an Enclosed Vehicle or Equipment	How often does this job require working in a closed vehicle or equipment (e.g., car)?
Letters and Memos	How often does the job require written letters and memos?
Structured versus Unstructured Work	To what extent is this job structured for the worker, rather than allowing the worker to determine tasks, priorities, and goals?
Time Pressure	How often does this job require the worker to meet strict deadlines?
Importance of Being Exact or Accurate	How important is being very exact or highly accurate in performing this job?
Work With Work Group or Team	How important is it to work with others in a group or team in this job?
Sounds, Noise Levels Are Distracting or Uncomforta	How often does this job require working exposed to sounds and noise levels that are distracting or uncomfortable?
Impact of Decisions on Co-workers or Company Resul	How do the decisions an employee makes impact the results of co-workers, clients or the company?
Frequency of Conflict Situations	How often are there conflict situations the employee has to face in this job?
Exposed to Hazardous Equipment	How often does this job require exposure to hazardous equipment?
Wear Common Protective or Safety Equipment such as	How much does this job require wearing common protective or safety equipment such as safety shoes, glasses, gloves, hard hats or live jackets?
Deal With Unpleasant or Angry People	How frequently does the worker have to deal with unpleasant, angry, or discourteous individuals as part of the job requirements?
Exposed to Contaminants	How often does this job require working exposed to contaminants (such as pollutants, gases, dust or odors)?
Physical Proximity	To what extent does this job require the worker to perform job tasks in close physical proximity to other people?
Indoors, Environmentally Controlled	How often does this job require working indoors in environmentally controlled conditions?
Responsibility for Outcomes and Results	How responsible is the worker for work outcomes and results of other workers?
Spend Time Standing	How much does this job require standing?
Coordinate or Lead Others	How important is it to coordinate or lead others in accomplishing work activities in this job?
Very Hot or Cold Temperatures	How often does this job require working in very hot (above 90 F degrees) or very cold (below 32 F degrees) temperatures?
Extremely Bright or Inadequate Lighting	How often does this job require working in extremely bright or inadequate lighting conditions?
Importance of Repeating Same Tasks	How important is repeating the same physical activities (e.g., key entry) or mental activities (e.g., checking entries in a ledger) over and over, without stopping, to performing this job?
Cramped Work Space, Awkward Positions	How often does this job require working in cramped work spaces that requires getting into awkward positions?
Exposed to Minor Burns, Cuts, Bites, or Stings	How often does this job require exposure to minor burns, cuts, bites, or stings?
Deal With External Customers	How important is it to work with external customers or the public in this job?
Spend Time Walking and Running	How much does this job require walking and running?
Responsible for Others' Health and Safety	How much responsibility is there for the health and safety of others in this job?
Spend Time Sitting	How much does this job require sitting?
Electronic Mail	How often do you use electronic mail in this job?
Consequence of Error	How serious would the result usually be if the worker made a mistake that was not readily correctable?
Indoors, Not Environmentally Controlled	How often does this job require working indoors in non-controlled environmental conditions (e.g., warehouse without heat)?
Exposed to Radiation	How often does this job require exposure to radiation?
Exposed to High Places	How often does this job require exposure to high places?

Spend Time Using Your Hands to Handle. Control. or Spend Time Making Repetitive Motions	How much does this job require using your hands to handle, control, or feel objects. tools or controls? How much does this job require making repetitive motions?
Pace Determined by Speed of Equipment	How important is it to this job that the pace is determined by the speed of equipment or machinery? (This does not refer to keeping busy at all times on this job.)
Level of Competition	To what extent does this job require the worker to compete or to be aware of competitive pressures?
Degree of Automation	How automated is the job?
Spend Time Bending or Twisting the Body	How much does this job require bending or twisting your body?
Spend Time Kneeling. Crouching. Stooping, or Crawl	How much does this job require kneeling. crouching. stooping or crawling?
Exposed to Whole Body Vibration	How often does this job require exposure to whole body vibration (e.g., operate a jackhammer)?
Wear Specialized Protective or Safety Equipment su	How much does this job require wearing specialized protective or safety equipment such as breathing apparatus. safety harness, full protection suits, or radiation protection?
Exposed to Hazardous Conditions	How often does this job require exposure to hazardous conditions?
Spend Time Climbing Ladders. Scaffolds, or Poles	How much does this job require climbing ladders, scaffolds, or poles?
Spend Time Keeping or Regaining Balance	How much does this job require keeping or regaining your balance?
Outdoors, Under Cover	How often does this job require working outdoors, under cover (e.g., structure with roof but no walls)?
Public Speaking	How often do you have to perform public speaking in this job?
Exposed to Disease or Infections	How often does this job require exposure to disease/infections?
Deal With Physically Aggressive People	How frequently does this job require the worker to deal with physical aggression of violent individuals?
In an Open Vehicle or Equipment	How often does this job require working in an open vehicle or equipment (e.g., tractor)?

Job Zone Component	Job Zone Component Definitions
Title	Job Zone Three: Medium Preparation Needed
Overall Experience	Previous work-related skill, knowledge, or experience is required for these occupations. For example, an electrician must have completed three or four years of apprenticeship or several years of vocational training, and often must have passed a licensing exam, in order to perform the job.
Job Training	Employees in these occupations usually need one or two years of training involving both on-the-job experience and informal training with experienced workers.
Job Zone Examples	These occupations usually involve using communication and organizational skills to coordinate, supervise, manage, or train others to accomplish goals. Examples include dental assistants, electricians, fish and game wardens, legal secretaries, personnel recruiters, and recreation workers.
SVP Range	(6.0 to < 7.0)
Education	Most occupations in this zone require training in vocational schools, related on-the-job experience, or an associate's degree. Some may require a bachelor's degree.

Work_Styles	Work_Styles Definitions
Dependability	Job requires being reliable, responsible, and dependable, and fulfilling obligations.
Integrity	Job requires being honest and ethical.
Attention to Detail	Job requires being careful about detail and thorough in completing work tasks.
Cooperation	Job requires being pleasant with others on the job and displaying a good-natured, cooperative attitude.
Stress Tolerance	Job requires accepting criticism and dealing calmly and effectively with high stress situations.
Self Control	Job requires maintaining composure, keeping emotions in check, controlling anger, and avoiding aggressive behavior, even in very difficult situations.
Adaptability/Flexibility	Job requires being open to change (positive or negative) and to considerable variety in the workplace.

Independence	Job requires developing one's own ways of doing things, guiding oneself with little or no supervision, and depending on oneself to get things done.
Leadership	Job requires a willingness to lead, take charge, and offer opinions and direction.
Initiative	Job requires a willingness to take on responsibilities and challenges.
Concern for Others	Job requires being sensitive to others' needs and feelings and being understanding and helpful on the job.
Social Orientation	Job requires preferring to work with others rather than alone, and being personally connected with others on the job.
Innovation	Job requires creativity and alternative thinking to develop new ideas for and answers to work-related problems.
Persistence	Job requires persistence in the face of obstacles.
Analytical Thinking	Job requires analyzing information and using logic to address work-related issues and problems.
Achievement/Effort	Job requires establishing and maintaining personally challenging achievement goals and exerting effort toward mastering tasks.

47-4021.00 - Elevator Installers and Repairers

Assemble, install, repair, or maintain electric or hydraulic freight or passenger elevators, escalators, or dumbwaiters.

Tasks

1) Connect car frames to counterweights, using steel cables.

2) Attach guide shoes and rollers to minimize the lateral motion of cars as they travel through shafts.

3) Assemble elevator cars, installing each car's platform, walls, and doors.

4) Check that safety regulations and building codes are met, and complete service reports verifying conformance to standards.

5) Inspect wiring connections, control panel hookups, door installations, and alignments and clearances of cars and hoistways to ensure that equipment will operate properly.

6) Assemble electrically powered stairs, steel frameworks, and tracks, and install associated motors and electrical wiring.

7) Maintain log books that detail all repairs and checks performed.

8) Connect electrical wiring to control panels and electric motors.

9) Bolt or weld steel rails to the walls of shafts to guide elevators, working from scaffolding or platforms.

10) Disassemble defective units, and repair or replace parts such as locks, gears, cables, and electric wiring.

11) Install electrical wires and controls by attaching conduit along shaft walls from floor to floor, then pulling plastic-covered wires through the conduit.

12) Participate in additional training to keep skills up-to-date.

13) Locate malfunctions in brakes, motors, switches, and signal and control systems, using test equipment.

14) Operate elevators to determine power demands, and test power consumption to detect overload factors.

15) Read and interpret blueprints to determine the layout of system components, frameworks, and foundations, and to select installation equipment.

16) Test newly installed equipment to ensure that it meets specifications, such as stopping at floors for set amounts of time.

17) Install outer doors and door frames at elevator entrances on each floor of a structure.

18) Adjust safety controls, counterweights, door mechanisms, and components such as valves, ratchets, seals, and brake linings.

19) Cut prefabricated sections of framework, rails, and other components to specified dimensions.

47-4041.00 - Hazardous Materials Removal Workers

Identify, remove, pack, transport, or dispose of hazardous materials, including asbestos, lead-based paint. waste oil. fuel, transmission fluid. radioactive materials, contaminated soil, etc. Specialized training and certification in hazardous materials handling or a confined entry permit are generally required. May operate earth-moving equipment or trucks.

Tasks

1) Identify asbestos, lead, or other hazardous materials that need to be removed, using monitoring devices.

2) Unload baskets of irradiated elements onto packaging machines that automatically insert fuel elements into canisters and secure lids.

3) Clean contaminated equipment or areas for re-use, using detergents and solvents. sandblasters, filter pumps, and steam cleaners.

4) Follow prescribed safety procedures, and comply with federal laws regulating waste disposal methods.

5) Operate cranes to move and load baskets, casks, and canisters.

6) Drive trucks or other heavy equipment to convey contaminated waste to designated sea or ground locations.

7) Load and unload materials into containers and onto trucks, using hoists or forklifts.

8) Pull tram cars along underwater tracks, and position cars to receive irradiated fuel elements; then pull loaded cars to mechanisms that automatically unload elements onto underwater tables.

9) Operate machines and equipment to remove, package, store, or transport loads of waste materials.

10) Record numbers of containers stored at disposal sites, and specify amounts and types of equipment and waste disposed.

11) Apply chemical compounds to lead-based paint, allow compounds to dry, then scrape the hazardous material into containers for removal and/or storage.

12) Manipulate handgrips of mechanical arms to place irradiated fuel elements into baskets.

13) Organize and track the locations of hazardous items in landfills.

14) Package, store, and move irradiated fuel elements in the underwater storage basin of a nuclear reactor plant, using machines and equipment.

15) Remove asbestos and/or lead from surfaces, using hand and power tools such as scrapers, vacuums, and high-pressure sprayers.

16) Mix and pour concrete into forms to encase waste material for disposal.

47-4051.00 - Highway Maintenance Workers

Maintain highways, municipal and rural roads, airport runways, and rights-of-way. Duties include patching broken or eroded pavement, repairing guard rails, highway markers, and snow fences. May also mow or clear brush from along road or plow snow from roadway.

Tasks

1) Flag motorists to warn them of obstacles or repair work ahead.

2) Drive trucks to transport crews and equipment to work sites.

3) Clean and clear debris from culverts, catch basins, drop inlets, ditches, and other drain structures.

4) Drive trucks or tractors with adjustable attachments to sweep debris from paved surfaces, mow grass and weeds, and remove snow and ice.

5) Haul and spread sand, gravel, and clay to fill washouts and repair road shoulders.

6) Remove litter and debris from roadways, including debris from rock and mud slides.

7) Dump, spread, and tamp asphalt, using pneumatic tampers, to repair joints and patch broken pavement.

8) Erect, install, or repair guardrails, road shoulders, berms, highway markers, warning signals, and highway lighting, using hand tools and power tools.

9) Perform roadside landscaping work, such as clearing weeds and brush, and planting and trimming trees.

10) Inspect, clean, and repair drainage systems, bridges, tunnels, and other structures.

11) Apply poisons along roadsides and in animal burrows to eliminate unwanted roadside vegetation and rodents.

12) Apply oil to road surfaces, using sprayers.

13) Inspect markers to verify accurate installation.

14) Measure and mark locations for installation of markers, using tape, string, or chalk.

15) Paint traffic control lines and place pavement traffic messages, by hand or using machines.

16) Place and remove snow fences used to prevent the accumulation of drifting snow on highways.

17) Blend compounds to form adhesive mixtures used for marker installation.

Knowledge	Knowledge Definitions
Public Safety and Security	Knowledge of relevant equipment. policies. procedures, and strategies to promote effective local, state, or national security operations for the protection of people, data, property, and institutions.
Transportation	Knowledge of principles and methods for moving people or goods by air, rail, sea, or road, including the relative costs and benefits.
Mechanical	Knowledge of machines and tools, including their designs, uses, repair, and maintenance.
Building and Construction	Knowledge of materials, methods, and the tools involved in the construction or repair of houses, buildings, or other structures such as highways and roads.
Customer and Personal Service	Knowledge of principles and processes for providing customer and personal services. This includes customer needs assessment, meeting quality standards for services, and evaluation of customer satisfaction.
Education and Training	Knowledge of principles and methods for curriculum and training design, teaching and instruction for individuals and groups, and the measurement of training effects.
Administration and Management	Knowledge of business and management principles involved in strategic planning, resource allocation, human resources modeling, leadership technique, production methods, and coordination of people and resources.
English Language	Knowledge of the structure and content of the English language including the meaning and spelling of words, rules of composition, and grammar.
Clerical	Knowledge of administrative and clerical procedures and systems such as word processing, managing files and records, stenography and transcription, designing forms, and other office procedures and terminology.
Law and Government	Knowledge of laws, legal codes, court procedures, precedents, government regulations, executive orders, agency rules, and the democratic political process.
Engineering and Technology	Knowledge of the practical application of engineering science and technology. This includes applying principles, techniques, procedures, and equipment to the design and production of various goods and services.
Mathematics	Knowledge of arithmetic, algebra, geometry, calculus, statistics, and their applications.
Geography	Knowledge of principles and methods for describing the features of land, sea, and air masses, including their physical characteristics, locations, interrelationships, and distribution of plant, animal, and human life.
Production and Processing	Knowledge of raw materials, production processes, quality control, costs, and other techniques for maximizing the effective manufacture and distribution of goods.
Design	Knowledge of design techniques, tools, and principles involved in production of precision technical plans, blueprints, drawings, and models.
Computers and Electronics	Knowledge of circuit boards, processors, chips, electronic equipment, and computer hardware and software, including applications and programming.
Telecommunications	Knowledge of transmission, broadcasting, switching, control, and operation of telecommunications systems.
Personnel and Human Resources	Knowledge of principles and procedures for personnel recruitment, selection, training, compensation and benefits, labor relations and negotiation, and personnel information systems.
Communications and Media	Knowledge of media production, communication, and dissemination techniques and methods. This includes alternative ways to inform and entertain via written, oral, and visual media.
Physics	Knowledge and prediction of physical principles, laws, their interrelationships, and applications to understanding fluid, material, and atmospheric dynamics, and mechanical, electrical, atomic and sub-atomic structures and processes.

Psychology	Knowledge of human behavior and performance: individual differences in ability. personality. and interests: learning and motivation; psychological research methods; and the assessment and treatment of behavioral and affective disorders.
Chemistry	Knowledge of the chemical composition. structure, and properties of substances and of the chemical processes and transformations that they undergo. This includes uses of chemicals and their interactions. danger signs, production techniques, and disposal methods.
Economics and Accounting	Knowledge of economic and accounting principles and practices, the financial markets, banking and the analysis and reporting of financial data.
Therapy and Counseling	Knowledge of principles, methods, and procedures for diagnosis, treatment, and rehabilitation of physical and mental dysfunctions, and for career counseling and guidance.
Medicine and Dentistry	Knowledge of the information and techniques needed to diagnose and treat human injuries, diseases, and deformities. This includes symptoms, treatment alternatives, drug properties and interactions, and preventive health-care measures.
Biology	Knowledge of plant and animal organisms, their tissues, cells, functions, interdependencies. and interactions with each other and the environment.
Sociology and Anthropology	Knowledge of group behavior and dynamics, societal trends and influences, human migrations, ethnicity, cultures and their history and origins.
History and Archeology	Knowledge of historical events and their causes, indicators, and effects on civilizations and cultures.
Foreign Language	Knowledge of the structure and content of a foreign (non-English) language including the meaning and spelling of words, rules of composition and grammar, and pronunciation.
Philosophy and Theology	Knowledge of different philosophical systems and religions. This includes their basic principles, values, ethics, ways of thinking, customs, practices, and their impact on human culture.
Sales and Marketing	Knowledge of principles and methods for showing, promoting, and selling products or services. This includes marketing strategy and tactics, product demonstration, sales techniques, and sales control systems.
Food Production	Knowledge of techniques and equipment for planting, growing, and harvesting food products (both plant and animal) for consumption, including storage/handling techniques.
Fine Arts	Knowledge of the theory and techniques required to compose, produce, and perform works of music, dance, visual arts, drama, and sculpture.

Skills	Skills Definitions
Equipment Maintenance	Performing routine maintenance on equipment and determining when and what kind of maintenance is needed.
Equipment Selection	Determining the kind of tools and equipment needed to do a job.
Coordination	Adjusting actions in relation to others' actions.
Speaking	Talking to others to convey information effectively.
Judgment and Decision Making	Considering the relative costs and benefits of potential actions to choose the most appropriate one.
Critical Thinking	Using logic and reasoning to identify the strengths and weaknesses of alternative solutions, conclusions or approaches to problems.
Active Listening	Giving full attention to what other people are saying, taking time to understand the points being made, asking questions as appropriate, and not interrupting at inappropriate times.
Reading Comprehension	Understanding written sentences and paragraphs in work related documents.
Repairing	Repairing machines or systems using the needed tools.
Active Learning	Understanding the implications of new information for both current and future problem-solving and decision-making.
Time Management	Managing one's own time and the time of others.
Instructing	Teaching others how to do something.
Learning Strategies	Selecting and using training/instructional methods and procedures appropriate for the situation when learning or teaching new things.
Writing	Communicating effectively in writing as appropriate for the needs of the audience.
Operation and Control	Controlling operations of equipment or systems.
Troubleshooting	Determining causes of operating errors and deciding what to do about it.
Management of Material Resources	Obtaining and seeing to the appropriate use of equipment, facilities, and materials needed to do certain work.

Social Perceptiveness	Being aware of others' reactions and understanding why they react as they do.
Mathematics	Using mathematics to solve problems.
Operation Monitoring	Watching gauges. dials, or other indicators to make sure a machine is working properly.
Monitoring	Monitoring/Assessing performance of yourself, other individuals. or organizations to make improvements or take corrective action.
Installation	Installing equipment, machines, wiring, or programs to meet specifications.
Management of Personnel Resources	Motivating, developing, and directing people as they work, identifying the best people for the job.
Service Orientation	Actively looking for ways to help people.
Complex Problem Solving	Identifying complex problems and reviewing related information to develop and evaluate options and implement solutions.
Quality Control Analysis	Conducting tests and inspections of products, services, or processes to evaluate quality or performance.
Systems Analysis	Determining how a system should work and how changes in conditions. operations, and the environment will affect outcomes.
Persuasion	Persuading others to change their minds or behavior.
Technology Design	Generating or adapting equipment and technology to serve user needs.
Negotiation	Bringing others together and trying to reconcile differences.
Systems Evaluation	Identifying measures or indicators of system performance and the actions needed to improve or correct performance, relative to the goals of the system.
Operations Analysis	Analyzing needs and product requirements to create a design.
Science	Using scientific rules and methods to solve problems.
Management of Financial Resources	Determining how money will be spent to get the work done, and accounting for these expenditures.
Programming	Writing computer programs for various purposes.

Ability	Ability Definitions
Control Precision	The ability to quickly and repeatedly adjust the controls of a machine or a vehicle to exact positions.
Multilimb Coordination	The ability to coordinate two or more limbs (for example, two arms, two legs, or one leg and one arm) while sitting, standing, or lying down. It does not involve performing the activities while the whole body is in motion.
Static Strength	The ability to exert maximum muscle force to lift, push, pull, or carry objects.
Depth Perception	The ability to judge which of several objects is closer or farther away from you, or to judge the distance between you and an object.
Manual Dexterity	The ability to quickly move your hand, your hand together with your arm, or your two hands to grasp, manipulate, or assemble objects.
Near Vision	The ability to see details at close range (within a few feet of the observer).
Far Vision	The ability to see details at a distance.
Arm-Hand Steadiness	The ability to keep your hand and arm steady while moving your arm or while holding your arm and hand in one position.
Problem Sensitivity	The ability to tell when something is wrong or is likely to go wrong. It does not involve solving the problem, only recognizing there is a problem.
Trunk Strength	The ability to use your abdominal and lower back muscles to support part of the body repeatedly or continuously over time without 'giving out' or fatiguing.
Stamina	The ability to exert yourself physically over long periods of time without getting winded or out of breath.
Speech Recognition	The ability to identify and understand the speech of another person.
Deductive Reasoning	The ability to apply general rules to specific problems to produce answers that make sense.
Inductive Reasoning	The ability to combine pieces of information to form general rules or conclusions (includes finding a relationship among seemingly unrelated events).
Extent Flexibility	The ability to bend, stretch, twist, or reach with your body, arms, and/or legs.
Peripheral Vision	The ability to see objects or movement of objects to one's side when the eyes are looking ahead.
Information Ordering	The ability to arrange things or actions in a certain order or pattern according to a specific rule or set of rules (e.g., patterns of numbers, letters, words, pictures, mathematical operations).

Reaction Time	The ability to quickly respond (with the hand, finger, or foot) to a signal (sound, light, picture) when it appears.
Speech Clarity	The ability to speak clearly so others can understand you.
Oral Expression	The ability to communicate information and ideas in speaking so others will understand.
Oral Comprehension	The ability to listen to and understand information and ideas presented through spoken words and sentences.
Rate Control	The ability to time your movements or the movement of a piece of equipment in anticipation of changes in the speed and/or direction of a moving object or scene.
Response Orientation	The ability to choose quickly between two or more movements in response to two or more different signals (lights, sounds, pictures). It includes the speed with which the correct response is started with the hand, foot, or other body part.
Time Sharing	The ability to shift back and forth between two or more activities or sources of information (such as speech, sounds, touch, or other sources).
Written Comprehension	The ability to read and understand information and ideas presented in writing.
Category Flexibility	The ability to generate or use different sets of rules for combining or grouping things in different ways.
Visualization	The ability to imagine how something will look after it is moved around or when its parts are moved or rearranged.
Selective Attention	The ability to concentrate on a task over a period of time without being distracted.
Visual Color Discrimination	The ability to match or detect differences between colors, including shades of color and brightness.
Hearing Sensitivity	The ability to detect or tell the differences between sounds that vary in pitch and loudness.
Gross Body Coordination	The ability to coordinate the movement of your arms, legs, and torso together when the whole body is in motion.
Glare Sensitivity	The ability to see objects in the presence of glare or bright lighting.
Dynamic Strength	The ability to exert muscle force repeatedly or continuously over time. This involves muscular endurance and resistance to muscle fatigue.
Auditory Attention	The ability to focus on a single source of sound in the presence of other distracting sounds.
Sound Localization	The ability to tell the direction from which a sound originated.
Speed of Limb Movement	The ability to quickly move the arms and legs.
Finger Dexterity	The ability to make precisely coordinated movements of the fingers of one or both hands to grasp, manipulate, or assemble very small objects.
Spatial Orientation	The ability to know your location in relation to the environment or to know where other objects are in relation to you.
Gross Body Equilibrium	The ability to keep or regain your body balance or stay upright when in an unstable position.
Night Vision	The ability to see under low light conditions.
Originality	The ability to come up with unusual or clever ideas about a given topic or situation, or to develop creative ways to solve a problem.
Fluency of Ideas	The ability to come up with a number of ideas about a topic (the number of ideas is important, not their quality, correctness, or creativity).
Perceptual Speed	The ability to quickly and accurately compare similarities and differences among sets of letters, numbers, objects, pictures, or patterns. The things to be compared may be presented at the same time or one after the other. This ability also includes comparing a presented object with a remembered object.
Wrist-Finger Speed	The ability to make fast, simple, repeated movements of the fingers, hands, and wrists.
Memorization	The ability to remember information such as words, numbers, pictures, and procedures.
Flexibility of Closure	The ability to identify or detect a known pattern (a figure, object, word, or sound) that is hidden in other distracting material.
Speed of Closure	The ability to quickly make sense of, combine, and organize information into meaningful patterns.
Number Facility	The ability to add, subtract, multiply, or divide quickly and correctly.
Written Expression	The ability to communicate information and ideas in writing so others will understand.
Mathematical Reasoning	The ability to choose the right mathematical methods or formulas to solve a problem.
Dynamic Flexibility	The ability to quickly and repeatedly bend, stretch, twist, or reach out with your body, arms, and/or legs.
Explosive Strength	The ability to use short bursts of muscle force to propel oneself (as in jumping or sprinting), or to throw an object.

Work_Activity	Work_Activity Definitions
Operating Vehicles, Mechanized Devices, or Equipme	Running, maneuvering, navigating, or driving vehicles or mechanized equipment, such as forklifts, passenger vehicles, aircraft, or water craft.
Inspecting Equipment, Structures, or Material	Inspecting equipment, structures, or materials to identify the cause of errors or other problems or defects.
Handling and Moving Objects	Using hands and arms in handling, installing, positioning, and moving materials, and manipulating things.
Repairing and Maintaining Mechanical Equipment	Servicing, repairing, adjusting, and testing machines, devices, moving parts, and equipment that operate primarily on the basis of mechanical (not electronic) principles.
Getting Information	Observing, receiving, and otherwise obtaining information from all relevant sources.
Performing General Physical Activities	Performing physical activities that require considerable use of your arms and legs and moving your whole body, such as climbing, lifting, balancing, walking, stooping, and handling of materials.
Controlling Machines and Processes	Using either control mechanisms or direct physical activity to operate machines or processes (not including computers or vehicles).
Coordinating the Work and Activities of Others	Getting members of a group to work together to accomplish tasks.
Making Decisions and Solving Problems	Analyzing information and evaluating results to choose the best solution and solve problems.
Communicating with Supervisors, Peers, or Subordin	Providing information to supervisors, co-workers, and subordinates by telephone, in written form, e-mail, or in person.
Identifying Objects, Actions, and Events	Identifying information by categorizing, estimating, recognizing differences or similarities, and detecting changes in circumstances or events.
Scheduling Work and Activities	Scheduling events, programs, and activities, as well as the work of others.
Establishing and Maintaining Interpersonal Relatio	Developing constructive and cooperative working relationships with others, and maintaining them over time.
Judging the Qualities of Things, Services, or Peop	Assessing the value, importance, or quality of things or people.
Communicating with Persons Outside Organization	Communicating with people outside the organization, representing the organization to customers, the public, government, and other external sources. This information can be exchanged in person, in writing, or by telephone or e-mail.
Training and Teaching Others	Identifying the educational needs of others, developing formal educational or training programs or classes, and teaching or instructing others.
Estimating the Quantifiable Characteristics of Pro	Estimating sizes, distances, and quantities; or determining time, costs, resources, or materials needed to perform a work activity.
Organizing, Planning, and Prioritizing Work	Developing specific goals and plans to prioritize, organize, and accomplish your work.
Performing for or Working Directly with the Public	Performing for people or dealing directly with the public. This includes serving customers in restaurants and stores, and receiving clients or guests.
Monitor Processes, Materials, or Surroundings	Monitoring and reviewing information from materials, events, or the environment, to detect or assess problems.
Thinking Creatively	Developing, designing, or creating new applications, ideas, relationships, systems, or products, including artistic contributions.
Updating and Using Relevant Knowledge	Keeping up-to-date technically and applying new knowledge to your job.
Developing and Building Teams	Encouraging and building mutual trust, respect, and cooperation among team members.
Evaluating Information to Determine Compliance wit	Using relevant information and individual judgment to determine whether events or processes comply with laws, regulations, or standards.
Coaching and Developing Others	Identifying the developmental needs of others and coaching, mentoring, or otherwise helping others to improve their knowledge or skills.
Developing Objectives and Strategies	Establishing long-range objectives and specifying the strategies and actions to achieve them.
Guiding, Directing, and Motivating Subordinates	Providing guidance and direction to subordinates, including setting performance standards and monitoring performance.
Assisting and Caring for Others	Providing personal assistance, medical attention, emotional support, or other personal care to others such as coworkers, customers, or patients.

Resolving Conflicts and Negotiating with Others	Handling complaints, settling disputes, and resolving grievances and conflicts, or otherwise negotiating with others.
Documenting/Recording Information	Entering, transcribing, recording, storing, or maintaining information in written or electronic/magnetic form.
Processing Information	Compiling, coding, categorizing, calculating, tabulating, auditing, or verifying information or data.
Drafting, Laying Out, and Specifying Technical Dev	Providing documentation, detailed instructions, drawings, or specifications to tell others about how devices, parts, equipment, or structures are to be fabricated, constructed, assembled, modified, maintained, or used.
Provide Consultation and Advice to Others	Providing guidance and expert advice to management or other groups on technical, systems-, or process-related topics.
Analyzing Data or Information	Identifying the underlying principles, reasons, or facts of information by breaking down information or data into separate parts.
Interpreting the Meaning of Information for Others	Translating or explaining what information means and how it can be used.
Monitoring and Controlling Resources	Monitoring and controlling resources and overseeing the spending of money.
Repairing and Maintaining Electronic Equipment	Servicing, repairing, calibrating, regulating, fine-tuning, or testing machines, devices, and equipment that operate primarily on the basis of electrical or electronic (not mechanical) principles.
Selling or Influencing Others	Convincing others to buy merchandise/goods or to otherwise change their minds or actions.
Performing Administrative Activities	Performing day-to-day administrative tasks such as maintaining information files and processing paperwork.
Interacting With Computers	Using computers and computer systems (including hardware and software) to program, write software, set up functions, enter data, or process information.
Staffing Organizational Units	Recruiting, interviewing, selecting, hiring, and promoting employees in an organization.

Work_Context	Work_Context Definitions
Wear Common Protective or Safety Equipment such as	How much does this job require wearing common protective or safety equipment such as safety shoes, glasses, gloves, hard hats or live jackets?
Outdoors, Exposed to Weather	How often does this job require working outdoors, exposed to all weather conditions?
Spend Time Using Your Hands to Handle, Control, or	How much does this job require using your hands to handle, control, or feel objects, tools or controls?
Very Hot or Cold Temperatures	How often does this job require working in very hot (above 90 F degrees) or very cold (below 32 F degrees) temperatures?
In an Enclosed Vehicle or Equipment	How often does this job require working in a closed vehicle or equipment (e.g., car)?
Face-to-Face Discussions	How often do you have to have face-to-face discussions with individuals or teams in this job?
Responsible for Others' Health and Safety	How much responsibility is there for the health and safety of others in this job?
Contact With Others	How much does this job require the worker to be in contact with others (face-to-face, by telephone, or otherwise) in order to perform it?
In an Open Vehicle or Equipment	How often does this job require working in an open vehicle or equipment (e.g., tractor)?
Work With Work Group or Team	How important is it to work with others in a group or team in this job?
Exposed to Contaminants	How often does this job require working exposed to contaminants (such as pollutants, gases, dust or odors)?
Freedom to Make Decisions	How much decision making freedom, without supervision, does the job offer?
Sounds, Noise Levels Are Distracting or Uncomforta	How often does this job require working exposed to sounds and noise levels that are distracting or uncomfortable?
Physical Proximity	To what extent does this job require the worker to perform job tasks in close physical proximity to other people?
Telephone	How often do you use telephone conversations in this job?
Exposed to Hazardous Equipment	How often does this job require exposure to hazardous equipment?
Spend Time Standing	How much does this job require standing?
Spend Time Bending or Twisting the Body	How much does this job require bending or twisting your body?
Importance of Being Exact or Accurate	How important is being very exact or highly accurate in performing this job?
Frequency of Decision Making	How frequently is the worker required to make decisions that affect other people, the financial resources, and/or the image and reputation of the organization?

Extremely Bright or Inadequate Lighting	How often does this job require working in extremely bright or inadequate lighting conditions?
Responsibility for Outcomes and Results	How responsible is the worker for work outcomes and results of other workers?
Indoors, Not Environmentally Controlled	How often does this job require working indoors in non-controlled environmental conditions (e.g., warehouse without heat)?
Exposed to Minor Burns, Cuts, Bites, or Stings	How often does this job require exposure to minor burns, cuts, bites, or stings?
Coordinate or Lead Others	How important is it to coordinate or lead others in accomplishing work activities in this job?
Impact of Decisions on Co-workers or Company Resul	How do the decisions an employee makes impact the results of co-workers, clients or the company?
Structured versus Unstructured Work	To what extent is this job structured for the worker, rather than allowing the worker to determine tasks, priorities, and goals?
Spend Time Walking and Running	How much does this job require walking and running?
Consequence of Error	How serious would the result usually be if the worker made a mistake that was not readily correctable?
Deal With External Customers	How important is it to work with external customers or the public in this job?
Spend Time Making Repetitive Motions	How much does this job require making repetitive motions?
Time Pressure	How often does this job require the worker to meet strict deadlines?
Pace Determined by Speed of Equipment	How important is it to this job that the pace is determined by the speed of equipment or machinery? (This does not refer to keeping busy at all times on this job.)
Spend Time Sitting	How much does this job require sitting?
Exposed to Whole Body Vibration	How often does this job require exposure to whole body vibration (e.g., operate a jackhammer)?
Frequency of Conflict Situations	How often are there conflict situations the employee has to face in this job?
Deal With Unpleasant or Angry People	How frequently does the worker have to deal with unpleasant, angry, or discourteous individuals as part of the job requirements?
Spend Time Kneeling, Crouching, Stooping, or Crawl	How much does this job require kneeling, crouching, stooping or crawling?
Letters and Memos	How often does the job require written letters and memos?
Importance of Repeating Same Tasks	How important is repeating the same physical activities (e.g., key entry) or mental activities (e.g., checking entries in a ledger) over and over, without stopping, to performing this job?
Exposed to Hazardous Conditions	How often does this job require exposure to hazardous conditions?
Cramped Work Space, Awkward Positions	How often does this job require working in cramped work spaces that requires getting into awkward positions?
Outdoors, Under Cover	How often does this job require working outdoors, under cover (e.g., structure with roof but no walls)?
Level of Competition	To what extent does this job require the worker to compete or to be aware of competitive pressures?
Electronic Mail	How often do you use electronic mail in this job?
Degree of Automation	How automated is the job?
Exposed to High Places	How often does this job require exposure to high places?
Spend Time Keeping or Regaining Balance	How much does this job require keeping or regaining your balance?
Deal With Physically Aggressive People	How frequently does this job require the worker to deal with physical aggression of violent individuals?
Wear Specialized Protective or Safety Equipment su	How much does this job require wearing specialized protective or safety equipment such as breathing apparatus, safety harness, full protection suits, or radiation protection?
Public Speaking	How often do you have to perform public speaking in this job?
Indoors, Environmentally Controlled	How often does this job require working indoors in environmentally controlled conditions?
Exposed to Disease or Infections	How often does this job require exposure to disease/infections?
Spend Time Climbing Ladders, Scaffolds, or Poles	How much does this job require climbing ladders, scaffolds, or poles?
Exposed to Radiation	How often does this job require exposure to radiation?

Job Zone Component	Job Zone Component Definitions
Title	Job Zone Two: Some Preparation Needed

Overall Experience	Some previous work-related skill, knowledge, or experience may be helpful in these occupations, but usually is not needed. For example, a drywall installer might benefit from experience installing drywall, but an inexperienced person could still learn to be an installer with little difficulty.
Job Training	Employees in these occupations need anywhere from a few months to one year of working with experienced employees. These occupations often involve using your knowledge and skills to help others. Examples include drywall installers, fire inspectors, flight attendants, pharmacy technicians, salespersons (retail), and tellers.
Job Zone Examples	
SVP Range	(4.0 to < 6.0)
Education	These occupations usually require a high school diploma and may require some vocational training or job-related course work. In some cases, an associate's or bachelor's degree could be needed.

Work_Styles	Work_Styles Definitions
Dependability	Job requires being reliable, responsible, and dependable, and fulfilling obligations.
Self Control	Job requires maintaining composure, keeping emotions in check, controlling anger, and avoiding aggressive behavior, even in very difficult situations.
Attention to Detail	Job requires being careful about detail and thorough in completing work tasks.
Cooperation	Job requires being pleasant with others on the job and displaying a good-natured, cooperative attitude.
Adaptability/Flexibility	Job requires being open to change (positive or negative) and to considerable variety in the workplace.
Integrity	Job requires being honest and ethical.
Concern for Others	Job requires being sensitive to others' needs and feelings and being understanding and helpful on the job.
Stress Tolerance	Job requires accepting criticism and dealing calmly and effectively with high stress situations.
Initiative	Job requires a willingness to take on responsibilities and challenges.
Social Orientation	Job requires preferring to work with others rather than alone, and being personally connected with others on the job.
Independence	Job requires developing one's own ways of doing things, guiding oneself with little or no supervision, and depending on oneself to get things done.
Achievement/Effort	Job requires establishing and maintaining personally challenging achievement goals and exerting effort toward mastering tasks.
Leadership	Job requires a willingness to lead, take charge, and offer opinions and direction.
Persistence	Job requires persistence in the face of obstacles.
Analytical Thinking	Job requires analyzing information and using logic to address work-related issues and problems.
Innovation	Job requires creativity and alternative thinking to develop new ideas for and answers to work-related problems.

47-4061.00 - Rail-Track Laying and Maintenance Equipment Operators

Lay, repair, and maintain track for standard or narrow-gauge railroad equipment used in regular railroad service or in plant yards, quarries, sand and gravel pits, and mines. Includes ballast cleaning machine operators and road bed tamping machine operators.

Tasks

1) Operate single- or multiple-head spike driving machines to drive spikes into ties and secure rails.

2) Drive graders, tamping machines, brooms, and ballast cleaning/spreading machines to redistribute gravel and ballast between rails.

3) Clean and make minor repairs to machines and equipment.

4) Operate track-wrench machines to tighten or loosen bolts at joints that hold ends of rails together.

5) Operate single- or multiple-head spike pullers to pull old spikes from ties.

6) Patrol assigned track sections so that damaged or broken track can be located and reported.

7) Paint railroad signs, such as speed limits and gate-crossing warnings.

8) Clean tracks, and clear ice and snow from tracks and switch boxes.

9) Turn wheels of machines, using lever controls, to adjust guidelines for track alignments and grades, following specifications.

10) Dress and reshape worn or damaged railroad switch points and frogs, using portable power grinders.

11) Spray ties, fishplates, and joints with oil to protect them from weathering.

12) Drive vehicles that automatically move and lay tracks or rails over sections of track to be constructed, repaired, or maintained.

13) Push controls to close grasping devices on track or rail sections so that they can be raised or moved.

14) Operate tie-adzing machines to cut ties and permit insertion of fishplates that hold rails.

15) Lubricate machines, change oil, and fill hydraulic reservoirs to specified levels.

16) Grind ends of new or worn rails to attain smooth joints, using portable grinders.

17) Raise rails, using hydraulic jacks, to allow for tie removal and replacement.

18) Engage mechanisms that lay tracks or rails to specified gauges.

19) Adjust controls of machines that spread, shape, raise, level, and align track, according to specifications.

20) Drill holes through rails, tie plates, and fishplates for insertion of bolts and spikes, using power drills.

21) Clean, grade, and level ballast on railroad tracks.

22) Cut rails to specified lengths, using rail saws.

23) String and attach wire-guidelines machine to rails so that tracks or rails can be aligned or leveled.

24) Observe leveling indicator arms to verify levelness and alignment of tracks.

47-4071.00 - Septic Tank Servicers and Sewer Pipe Cleaners

Clean and repair septic tanks, sewer lines, or drains. May patch walls and partitions of tank, replace damaged drain tile, or repair breaks in underground piping.

Tasks

1) Communicate with supervisors and other workers, using equipment such as wireless phones, pagers, or radio telephones.

2) Withdraw cables from pipes and examine them for evidence of mud, roots, grease, and other deposits indicating broken or clogged sewer lines.

3) Requisition or order tools and equipment.

4) Update sewer maps and manhole charts.

5) Rotate cleaning rods manually, using turning pins.

6) Clean and disinfect domestic basements and other areas flooded by sewer stoppages.

7) Dig out sewer lines manually, using shovels.

8) Prepare and keep records of actions taken, including maintenance and repair work.

9) Tap mainline sewers to install sewer saddles.

10) Ensure that repaired sewer line joints are tightly sealed before backfilling begins.

11) Start machines to feed revolving cables or rods into openings, stopping machines and changing knives to conform to pipe sizes.

12) Cover repaired pipes with dirt, and pack backfilled excavations, using air and gasoline tampers.

13) Cut damaged sections of pipe with cutters, remove broken sections from ditches, and replace pipe sections, using pipe sleeves.

14) Install rotary knives on flexible cables mounted on machine reels, according to the diameters of pipes to be cleaned.

15) Locate problems, using specially designed equipment, and mark where digging must occur to reach damaged tanks or pipes.

16) Measure excavation sites, using plumbers' snakes, tapelines, or lengths of cutting heads within sewers, and mark areas for digging.

17) Inspect manholes to locate sewer line stoppages.

1075

18) Operate sewer cleaning equipment, including power rodders, high velocity water jets, sewer flushers, bucket machines, wayne balls, and vac-alls.

19) Break asphalt and other pavement so that pipes can be accessed, using airhammers, picks, and shovels.

20) Drive trucks to transport crews, materials, and equipment.

21) Service, adjust, and make minor repairs to equipment, machines, and attachments.

47-4091.00 - Segmental Pavers

Lay out, cut, and paste segmental paving units. Includes installers of bedding and restraining materials for the paving units.

Tasks

1) Supply and place base materials, edge restraints, bedding sand and jointing sand.

2) Set pavers, aligning and spacing them correctly.

3) Sweep sand into the joints and compact pavement until the joints are full.

4) Resurface an outside area with cobblestones, terracotta tiles, concrete or other materials.

5) Discuss the design with the client.

6) Prepare base for installation by removing unstable or unsuitable materials, compacting and grading the soil, draining or stabilizing weak or saturated soils and taking measures to prevent water penetration and migration of bedding sand.

7) Compact bedding sand and pavers to finish the paved area, using a plate compactor.

8) Cut paving stones to size and for edges, using a splitter and a masonry saw.

9) Cement the edges of the paved area.

10) Sweep sand from the surface prior to opening to traffic.

11) Design paver installation layout pattern and create markings for directional references of joints and stringlines.

47-5011.00 - Derrick Operators, Oil and Gas

Rig derrick equipment and operate pumps to circulate mud through drill hole.

Tasks

1) Prepare mud reports, and instruct crews about the handling of any chemical additives.

2) Listen to mud pumps and check regularly for vibration and other problems, in order to ensure that rig pumps and drilling mud systems are working properly.

3) Start pumps that circulate mud through drill pipes and boreholes to cool drill bits and flush out drill-cuttings.

4) Repair pumps, mud tanks, and related equipment.

5) Supervise crew members, and provide assistance in training them.

6) Weigh clay, and mix with water and chemicals in order to make drilling mud, using portable mixers.

7) String cables through pulleys and blocks.

8) Inspect derricks, or order their inspection, prior to being raised or lowered.

9) Control the viscosity and weight of the drilling fluid.

10) Clamp holding fixtures on ends of hoisting cables.

11) Position and align derrick elements, using harnesses and platform climbing devices.

12) Guide lengths of pipe into and out of elevators.

13) Steady pipes during connection to or disconnection from drill or casing strings.

14) Inspect derricks for flaws, and clean and oil derricks in order to maintain proper working conditions.

47-5012.00 - Rotary Drill Operators, Oil and Gas

Set up or operate a variety of drills to remove petroleum products from the earth and to find

and remove core samples for testing during oil and gas exploration.

Tasks

1) Train crews, and introduce procedures to make drill work more safe and effective.

2) Repair or replace defective parts of machinery, such as rotary drill rigs, water trucks, air compressors, and pumps, using hand tools.

3) Remove core samples during drilling in order to determine the nature of the strata being drilled.

4) Cap wells with packers, or turn valves, in order to regulate outflow of oil from wells.

5) Line drilled holes with pipes, and install all necessary hardware, in order to prepare new wells.

6) Direct rig crews in drilling and other activities, such as setting up rigs and completing or servicing wells.

7) Dig holes, set forms, and mix and pour concrete, for foundations of steel or wooden derricks.

8) Clean and oil pulleys, blocks, and cables.

9) Bolt together pump and engine parts, and connect tanks and flow lines.

10) Connect sections of drill pipe, using hand tools and powered wrenches and tongs.

11) Maintain and adjust machinery in order to ensure proper performance.

12) Maintain records of footage drilled, location and nature of strata penetrated, materials and tools used, services rendered, and time required.

13) Weigh clay, and mix with water and chemicals to make drilling mud.

14) Start and examine operation of slush pumps in order to ensure circulation and consistency of drilling fluid or mud in well.

15) Plug observation wells, and restore sites.

16) Push levers and brake pedals in order to control gasoline, diesel, electric, or steam draw works that lower and raise drill pipes and casings in and out of wells.

17) Locate and recover lost or broken bits, casings, and drill pipes from wells, using special tools.

18) Lower and explode charges in boreholes in order to start flow of oil from wells.

19) Monitor progress of drilling operations, and select and change drill bits according to the nature of strata, using hand tools.

20) Observe pressure gauge and move throttles and levers in order to control the speed of rotary tables, and to regulate pressure of tools at bottoms of boreholes.

21) Count sections of drill rod in order to determine depths of boreholes.

47-5061.00 - Roof Bolters, Mining

Operate machinery to install roof support bolts in underground mine.

Tasks

1) Position bolting machines, and insert drill bits into chucks.

2) Test bolts for specified tension, using torque wrenches.

3) Remove drill bits from chucks after drilling holes, then insert bolts into chucks.

4) Force bolts into holes, using hydraulic mechanisms of self-propelled bolting machines.

5) Position safety jacks to support underground mine roofs until bolts can be installed.

6) Rotate chucks to turn bolts and open expansion heads against rock formations.

7) Install truss bolts traversing entire ceiling spans.

8) Tighten ends of anchored truss bolts, using turnbuckles.

Knowledge	Knowledge Definitions
Mechanical	Knowledge of machines and tools, including their designs, uses, repair, and maintenance.
Education and Training	Knowledge of principles and methods for curriculum and training design, teaching and instruction for individuals and groups, and the measurement of training effects.
Law and Government	Knowledge of laws, legal codes, court procedures, precedents, government regulations, executive orders, agency rules, and the democratic political process.

Production and Processing	Knowledge of raw materials, production processes, quality control, costs, and other techniques for maximizing the effective manufacture and distribution of goods.	Clerical	Knowledge of administrative and clerical procedures and systems such as word processing, managing files and records, stenography and transcription, designing forms, and other office procedures and terminology.
Transportation	Knowledge of principles and methods for moving people or goods by air, rail, sea, or road, including the relative costs and benefits.	Biology	Knowledge of plant and animal organisms, their tissues, cells, functions, interdependencies, and interactions with each other and the environment.
Public Safety and Security	Knowledge of relevant equipment, policies, procedures, and strategies to promote effective local, state, or national security operations for the protection of people, data, property, and institutions.	Philosophy and Theology	Knowledge of different philosophical systems and religions. This includes their basic principles, values, ethics, ways of thinking, customs, practices, and their impact on human culture.
Administration and Management	Knowledge of business and management principles involved in strategic planning, resource allocation, human resources modeling, leadership technique, production methods, and coordination of people and resources.	Sociology and Anthropology	Knowledge of group behavior and dynamics, societal trends and influences, human migrations, ethnicity, cultures and their history and origins.
Engineering and Technology	Knowledge of the practical application of engineering science and technology. This includes applying principles, techniques, procedures, and equipment to the design and production of various goods and services.	Fine Arts	Knowledge of the theory and techniques required to compose, produce, and perform works of music, dance, visual arts, drama, and sculpture.
Medicine and Dentistry	Knowledge of the information and techniques needed to diagnose and treat human injuries, diseases, and deformities. This includes symptoms, treatment alternatives, drug properties and interactions, and preventive health-care measures.	Food Production	Knowledge of techniques and equipment for planting, growing, and harvesting food products (both plant and animal) for consumption, including storage/handling techniques.
Mathematics	Knowledge of arithmetic, algebra, geometry, calculus, statistics, and their applications.	Foreign Language	Knowledge of the structure and content of a foreign (non-English) language including the meaning and spelling of words, rules of composition and grammar, and pronunciation.
Physics	Knowledge and prediction of physical principles, laws, their interrelationships, and applications to understanding fluid, material, and atmospheric dynamics, and mechanical, electrical, atomic and sub-atomic structures and processes.	History and Archeology	Knowledge of historical events and their causes, indicators, and effects on civilizations and cultures.
English Language	Knowledge of the structure and content of the English language including the meaning and spelling of words, rules of composition, and grammar.	**Skills**	**Skills Definitions**
		Operation and Control	Controlling operations of equipment or systems.
Customer and Personal Service	Knowledge of principles and processes for providing customer and personal services. This includes customer needs assessment, meeting quality standards for services, and evaluation of customer satisfaction.	Equipment Selection	Determining the kind of tools and equipment needed to do a job.
Sales and Marketing	Knowledge of principles and methods for showing, promoting, and selling products or services. This includes marketing strategy and tactics, product demonstration, sales techniques, and sales control systems.	Equipment Maintenance	Performing routine maintenance on equipment and determining when and what kind of maintenance is needed.
		Active Listening	Giving full attention to what other people are saying, taking time to understand the points being made, asking questions as appropriate, and not interrupting at inappropriate times.
Personnel and Human Resources	Knowledge of principles and procedures for personnel recruitment, selection, training, compensation and benefits, labor relations and negotiation, and personnel information systems.	Speaking	Talking to others to convey information effectively.
		Installation	Installing equipment, machines, wiring, or programs to meet specifications.
		Instructing	Teaching others how to do something.
Chemistry	Knowledge of the chemical composition, structure, and properties of substances and of the chemical processes and transformations that they undergo. This includes uses of chemicals and their interactions, danger signs, production techniques, and disposal methods.	Critical Thinking	Using logic and reasoning to identify the strengths and weaknesses of alternative solutions, conclusions or approaches to problems.
		Judgment and Decision Making	Considering the relative costs and benefits of potential actions to choose the most appropriate one.
Design	Knowledge of design techniques, tools, and principles involved in production of precision technical plans, blueprints, drawings, and models.	Operation Monitoring	Watching gauges, dials, or other indicators to make sure a machine is working properly.
Economics and Accounting	Knowledge of economic and accounting principles and practices, the financial markets, banking and the analysis and reporting of financial data.	Troubleshooting	Determining causes of operating errors and deciding what to do about it.
Telecommunications	Knowledge of transmission, broadcasting, switching, control, and operation of telecommunications systems.	Active Learning	Understanding the implications of new information for both current and future problem-solving and decision-making.
		Repairing	Repairing machines or systems using the needed tools.
Therapy and Counseling	Knowledge of principles, methods, and procedures for diagnosis, treatment, and rehabilitation of physical and mental dysfunctions, and for career counseling and guidance.	Learning Strategies	Selecting and using training/instructional methods and procedures appropriate for the situation when learning or teaching new things.
		Time Management	Managing one's own time and the time of others.
Computers and Electronics	Knowledge of circuit boards, processors, chips, electronic equipment, and computer hardware and software, including applications and programming.	Coordination	Adjusting actions in relation to others' actions.
		Management of Material Resources	Obtaining and seeing to the appropriate use of equipment, facilities, and materials needed to do certain work.
Geography	Knowledge of principles and methods for describing the features of land, sea, and air masses, including their physical characteristics, locations, interrelationships, and distribution of plant, animal, and human life.	Systems Analysis	Determining how a system should work and how changes in conditions, operations, and the environment will affect outcomes.
		Service Orientation	Actively looking for ways to help people.
Psychology	Knowledge of human behavior and performance; individual differences in ability, personality, and interests; learning and motivation; psychological research methods; and the assessment and treatment of behavioral and affective disorders.	Complex Problem Solving	Identifying complex problems and reviewing related information to develop and evaluate options and implement solutions.
		Systems Evaluation	Identifying measures or indicators of system performance and the actions needed to improve or correct performance, relative to the goals of the system.
Building and Construction	Knowledge of materials, methods, and the tools involved in the construction or repair of houses, buildings, or other structures such as highways and roads.	Social Perceptiveness	Being aware of others' reactions and understanding why they react as they do.
		Reading Comprehension	Understanding written sentences and paragraphs in work related documents.
Communications and Media	Knowledge of media production, communication, and dissemination techniques and methods. This includes alternative ways to inform and entertain via written, oral, and visual media.	Technology Design	Generating or adapting equipment and technology to serve user needs.
		Monitoring	Monitoring/Assessing performance of yourself, other individuals, or organizations to make improvements or take corrective action.

Management of Personnel Resources	Motivating, developing, and directing people as they work, identifying the best people for the job.
Mathematics	Using mathematics to solve problems.
Quality Control Analysis	Conducting tests and inspections of products, services, or processes to evaluate quality or performance.
Management of Financial Resources	Determining how money will be spent to get the work done, and accounting for these expenditures.
Operations Analysis	Analyzing needs and product requirements to create a design.
Persuasion	Persuading others to change their minds or behavior.
Negotiation	Bringing others together and trying to reconcile differences.
Science	Using scientific rules and methods to solve problems.
Writing	Communicating effectively in writing as appropriate for the needs of the audience.
Programming	Writing computer programs for various purposes.

Ability	Ability Definitions
Control Precision	The ability to quickly and repeatedly adjust the controls of a machine or a vehicle to exact positions.
Reaction Time	The ability to quickly respond (with the hand, finger, or foot) to a signal (sound, light, picture) when it appears.
Problem Sensitivity	The ability to tell when something is wrong or is likely to go wrong. It does not involve solving the problem, only recognizing there is a problem.
Multilimb Coordination	The ability to coordinate two or more limbs (for example, two arms, two legs, or one leg and one arm) while sitting, standing, or lying down. It does not involve performing the activities while the whole body is in motion.
Static Strength	The ability to exert maximum muscle force to lift, push, pull, or carry objects.
Arm-Hand Steadiness	The ability to keep your hand and arm steady while moving your arm or while holding your arm and hand in one position.
Manual Dexterity	The ability to quickly move your hand, your hand together with your arm, or your two hands to grasp, manipulate, or assemble objects.
Depth Perception	The ability to judge which of several objects is closer or farther away from you, or to judge the distance between you and an object.
Extent Flexibility	The ability to bend, stretch, twist, or reach with your body, arms, and/or legs.
Near Vision	The ability to see details at close range (within a few feet of the observer).
Selective Attention	The ability to concentrate on a task over a period of time without being distracted.
Information Ordering	The ability to arrange things or actions in a certain order or pattern according to a specific rule or set of rules (e.g., patterns of numbers, letters, words, pictures, mathematical operations).
Response Orientation	The ability to choose quickly between two or more movements in response to two or more different signals (lights, sounds, pictures). It includes the speed with which the correct response is started with the hand, foot, or other body part.
Auditory Attention	The ability to focus on a single source of sound in the presence of other distracting sounds.
Rate Control	The ability to time your movements or the movement of a piece of equipment in anticipation of changes in the speed and/or direction of a moving object or scene.
Trunk Strength	The ability to use your abdominal and lower back muscles to support part of the body repeatedly or continuously over time without 'giving out' or fatiguing.
Stamina	The ability to exert yourself physically over long periods of time without getting winded or out of breath.
Speech Recognition	The ability to identify and understand the speech of another person.
Deductive Reasoning	The ability to apply general rules to specific problems to produce answers that make sense.
Oral Comprehension	The ability to listen to and understand information and ideas presented through spoken words and sentences.
Glare Sensitivity	The ability to see objects in the presence of glare or bright lighting.
Dynamic Strength	The ability to exert muscle force repeatedly or continuously over time. This involves muscular endurance and resistance to muscle fatigue.
Wrist-Finger Speed	The ability to make fast, simple, repeated movements of the fingers, hands, and wrists.
Speed of Limb Movement	The ability to quickly move the arms and legs.
Hearing Sensitivity	The ability to detect or tell the differences between sounds that vary in pitch and loudness.

Inductive Reasoning	The ability to combine pieces of information to form general rules or conclusions (includes finding a relationship among seemingly unrelated events).
Visualization	The ability to imagine how something will look after it is moved around or when its parts are moved or rearranged.
Spatial Orientation	The ability to know your location in relation to the environment or to know where other objects are in relation to you.
Speech Clarity	The ability to speak clearly so others can understand you.
Perceptual Speed	The ability to quickly and accurately compare similarities and differences among sets of letters, numbers, objects, pictures, or patterns. The things to be compared may be presented at the same time or one after the other. This ability also includes comparing a presented object with a remembered object.
Time Sharing	The ability to shift back and forth between two or more activities or sources of information (such as speech, sounds, touch, or other sources).
Oral Expression	The ability to communicate information and ideas in speaking so others will understand.
Far Vision	The ability to see details at a distance.
Finger Dexterity	The ability to make precisely coordinated movements of the fingers of one or both hands to grasp, manipulate, or assemble very small objects.
Night Vision	The ability to see under low light conditions.
Sound Localization	The ability to tell the direction from which a sound originated.
Gross Body Equilibrium	The ability to keep or regain your body balance or stay upright when in an unstable position.
Category Flexibility	The ability to generate or use different sets of rules for combining or grouping things in different ways.
Flexibility of Closure	The ability to identify or detect a known pattern (a figure, object, word, or sound) that is hidden in other distracting material.
Gross Body Coordination	The ability to coordinate the movement of your arms, legs, and torso together when the whole body is in motion.
Peripheral Vision	The ability to see objects or movement of objects to one's side when the eyes are looking ahead.
Visual Color Discrimination	The ability to match or detect differences between colors, including shades of color and brightness.
Written Comprehension	The ability to read and understand information and ideas presented in writing.
Originality	The ability to come up with unusual or clever ideas about a given topic or situation, or to develop creative ways to solve a problem.
Speed of Closure	The ability to quickly make sense of, combine, and organize information into meaningful patterns.
Fluency of Ideas	The ability to come up with a number of ideas about a topic (the number of ideas is important, not their quality, correctness, or creativity).
Number Facility	The ability to add, subtract, multiply, or divide quickly and correctly.
Memorization	The ability to remember information such as words, numbers, pictures, and procedures.
Mathematical Reasoning	The ability to choose the right mathematical methods or formulas to solve a problem.
Written Expression	The ability to communicate information and ideas in writing so others will understand.
Explosive Strength	The ability to use short bursts of muscle force to propel oneself (as in jumping or sprinting), or to throw an object.
Dynamic Flexibility	The ability to quickly and repeatedly bend, stretch, twist, or reach out with your body, arms, and/or legs.

Work_Activity	Work_Activity Definitions
Controlling Machines and Processes	Using either control mechanisms or direct physical activity to operate machines or processes (not including computers or vehicles).
Operating Vehicles, Mechanized Devices, or Equipme	Running, maneuvering, navigating, or driving vehicles or mechanized equipment, such as forklifts, passenger vehicles, aircraft, or water craft.
Evaluating Information to Determine Compliance wit	Using relevant information and individual judgment to determine whether events or processes comply with laws, regulations, or standards.
Inspecting Equipment, Structures, or Material	Inspecting equipment, structures, or materials to identify the cause of errors or other problems or defects.
Handling and Moving Objects	Using hands and arms in handling, installing, positioning, and moving materials, and manipulating things.

Performing General Physical Activities	Performing physical activities that require considerable use of your arms and legs and moving your whole body, such as climbing, lifting, balancing, walking, stooping, and handling of materials.
Identifying Objects, Actions, and Events	Identifying information by categorizing, estimating, recognizing differences or similarities, and detecting changes in circumstances or events.
Getting Information	Observing, receiving, and otherwise obtaining information from all relevant sources.
Monitor Processes, Materials, or Surroundings	Monitoring and reviewing information from materials, events, or the environment, to detect or assess problems.
Communicating with Supervisors, Peers, or Subordin	Providing information to supervisors, co-workers, and subordinates by telephone, in written form, e-mail, or in person.
Making Decisions and Solving Problems	Analyzing information and evaluating results to choose the best solution and solve problems.
Repairing and Maintaining Mechanical Equipment	Servicing, repairing, adjusting, and testing machines, devices, moving parts, and equipment that operate primarily on the basis of mechanical (not electronic) principles.
Training and Teaching Others	Identifying the educational needs of others, developing formal educational or training programs or classes, and teaching or instructing others.
Coordinating the Work and Activities of Others	Getting members of a group to work together to accomplish tasks.
Establishing and Maintaining Interpersonal Relatio	Developing constructive and cooperative working relationships with others, and maintaining them over time.
Organizing, Planning, and Prioritizing Work	Developing specific goals and plans to prioritize, organize, and accomplish your work.
Updating and Using Relevant Knowledge	Keeping up-to-date technically and applying new knowledge to your job.
Developing and Building Teams	Encouraging and building mutual trust, respect, and cooperation among team members.
Assisting and Caring for Others	Providing personal assistance, medical attention, emotional support, or other personal care to others such as coworkers, customers, or patients.
Coaching and Developing Others	Identifying the developmental needs of others and coaching, mentoring, or otherwise helping others to improve their knowledge or skills.
Judging the Qualities of Things, Services, or Peop	Assessing the value, importance, or quality of things or people.
Estimating the Quantifiable Characteristics of Pro	Estimating sizes, distances, and quantities; or determining time, costs, resources, or materials needed to perform a work activity.
Interpreting the Meaning of Information for Others	Translating or explaining what information means and how it can be used.
Thinking Creatively	Developing, designing, or creating new applications, ideas, relationships, systems, or products, including artistic contributions.
Monitoring and Controlling Resources	Monitoring and controlling resources and overseeing the spending of money.
Repairing and Maintaining Electronic Equipment	Servicing, repairing, calibrating, regulating, fine-tuning, or testing machines, devices, and equipment that operate primarily on the basis of electrical or electronic (not mechanical) principles.
Resolving Conflicts and Negotiating with Others	Handling complaints, settling disputes, and resolving grievances and conflicts, or otherwise negotiating with others.
Drafting, Laying Out, and Specifying Technical Dev	Providing documentation, detailed instructions, drawings, or specifications to tell others about how devices, parts, equipment, or structures are to be fabricated, constructed, assembled, modified, maintained, or used.
Guiding, Directing, and Motivating Subordinates	Providing guidance and direction to subordinates, including setting performance standards and monitoring performance.
Provide Consultation and Advice to Others	Providing guidance and expert advice to management or other groups on technical, systems-, or process-related topics.
Developing Objectives and Strategies	Establishing long-range objectives and specifying the strategies and actions to achieve them.
Scheduling Work and Activities	Scheduling events, programs, and activities, as well as the work of others.
Processing Information	Compiling, coding, categorizing, calculating, tabulating, auditing, or verifying information or data.
Analyzing Data or Information	Identifying the underlying principles, reasons, or facts of information by breaking down information or data into separate parts.
Documenting/Recording Information	Entering, transcribing, recording, storing, or maintaining information in written or electronic/magnetic form.

Staffing Organizational Units	Recruiting, interviewing, selecting, hiring, and promoting employees in an organization.
Selling or Influencing Others	Convincing others to buy merchandise/goods or to otherwise change their minds or actions.
Performing Administrative Activities	Performing day-to-day administrative tasks such as maintaining information files and processing paperwork.
Performing for or Working Directly with the Public	Performing for people or dealing directly with the public. This includes serving customers in restaurants and stores, and receiving clients or guests.
Communicating with Persons Outside Organization	Communicating with people outside the organization, representing the organization to customers, the public, government, and other external sources. This information can be exchanged in person, in writing, or by telephone or e-mail.
Interacting With Computers	Using computers and computer systems (including hardware and software) to program, write software, set up functions, enter data, or process information.

Work_Context	Work_Context Definitions
Wear Common Protective or Safety Equipment such as	How much does this job require wearing common protective or safety equipment such as safety shoes, glasses, gloves, hard hats or life jackets?
Spend Time Using Your Hands to Handle, Control, or	How much does this job require using your hands to handle, control, or feel objects, tools or controls?
Sounds, Noise Levels Are Distracting or Uncomforta	How often does this job require working exposed to sounds and noise levels that are distracting or uncomfortable?
Exposed to Contaminants	How often does this job require working exposed to contaminants (such as pollutants, gases, dust or odors)?
Exposed to Hazardous Equipment	How often does this job require exposure to hazardous equipment?
Spend Time Making Repetitive Motions	How much does this job require making repetitive motions?
Frequency of Decision Making	How frequently is the worker required to make decisions that affect other people, the financial resources, and/or the image and reputation of the organization?
Spend Time Bending or Twisting the Body	How much does this job require bending or twisting your body?
Responsible for Others' Health and Safety	How much responsibility is there for the health and safety of others in this job?
Impact of Decisions on Co-workers or Company Resul	How do the decisions an employee makes impact the results of co-workers, clients or the company?
Cramped Work Space, Awkward Positions	How often does this job require working in cramped work spaces that requires getting into awkward positions?
Pace Determined by Speed of Equipment	How important is it to this job that the pace is determined by the speed of equipment or machinery? (This does not refer to keeping busy at all times on this job.)
Exposed to Hazardous Conditions	How often does this job require exposure to hazardous conditions?
Work With Work Group or Team	How important is it to work with others in a group or team in this job?
Exposed to Minor Burns, Cuts, Bites, or Stings	How often does this job require exposure to minor burns, cuts, bites, or stings?
Freedom to Make Decisions	How much decision making freedom, without supervision, does the job offer?
Importance of Being Exact or Accurate	How important is being very exact or highly accurate in performing this job?
Face-to-Face Discussions	How often do you have to have face-to-face discussions with individuals or teams in this job?
Time Pressure	How often does this job require the worker to meet strict deadlines?
Contact With Others	How much does this job require the worker to be in contact with others (face-to-face, by telephone, or otherwise) in order to perform it?
Extremely Bright or Inadequate Lighting	How often does this job require working in extremely bright or inadequate lighting conditions?
Spend Time Standing	How much does this job require standing?
In an Open Vehicle or Equipment	How often does this job require working in an open vehicle or equipment (e.g., tractor)?
Coordinate or Lead Others	How important is it to coordinate or lead others in accomplishing work activities in this job?
Physical Proximity	To what extent does this job require the worker to perform job tasks in close physical proximity to other people?
Structured versus Unstructured Work	To what extent is this job structured for the worker, rather than allowing the worker to determine tasks, priorities, and goals?
Consequence of Error	How serious would the result usually be if the worker made a mistake that was not readily correctable?

Responsibility for Outcomes and Results	How responsible is the worker for work outcomes and results of other workers?
Exposed to Whole Body Vibration	How often does this job require exposure to whole body vibration (e.g., operate a jackhammer)?
Spend Time Kneeling, Crouching, Stooping, or Crawl	How much does this job require kneeling, crouching, stooping or crawling?
Indoors, Not Environmentally Controlled	How often does this job require working indoors in non-controlled environmental conditions (e.g., warehouse without heat)?
Importance of Repeating Same Tasks	How important is repeating the same physical activities (e.g., key entry) or mental activities (e.g., checking entries in a ledger) over and over, without stopping, to performing this job?
Very Hot or Cold Temperatures	How often does this job require working in very hot (above 90 F degrees) or very cold (below 32 F degrees) temperatures?
Level of Competition	To what extent does this job require the worker to compete or to be aware of competitive pressures?
Spend Time Walking and Running	How much does this job require walking and running?
Deal With Unpleasant or Angry People	How frequently does the worker have to deal with unpleasant, angry, or discourteous individuals as part of the job requirements?
Wear Specialized Protective or Safety Equipment su	How much does this job require wearing specialized protective or safety equipment such as breathing apparatus, safety harness, full protection suits, or radiation protection?
Frequency of Conflict Situations	How often are there conflict situations the employee has to face in this job?
In an Enclosed Vehicle or Equipment	How often does this job require working in a closed vehicle or equipment (e.g., car)?
Spend Time Keeping or Regaining Balance	How much does this job require keeping or regaining your balance?
Degree of Automation	How automated is the job?
Public Speaking	How often do you have to perform public speaking in this job?
Letters and Memos	How often does the job require written letters and memos?
Telephone	How often do you have telephone conversations in this job?
Exposed to Disease or Infections	How often does this job require exposure to disease/infections?
Outdoors, Exposed to Weather	How often does this job require working outdoors, exposed to all weather conditions?
Outdoors, Under Cover	How often does this job require working outdoors, under cover (e.g., structure with roof but no walls)?
Exposed to High Places	How often does this job require exposure to high places?
Deal With External Customers	How important is it to work with external customers or the public in this job?
Deal With Physically Aggressive People	How frequently does this job require the worker to deal with physical aggression of violent individuals?
Spend Time Sitting	How much does this job require sitting?
Indoors, Environmentally Controlled	How often does this job require working indoors in environmentally controlled conditions?
Electronic Mail	How often do you use electronic mail in this job?
Spend Time Climbing Ladders, Scaffolds, or Poles	How much does this job require climbing ladders, scaffolds, or poles?
Exposed to Radiation	How often does this job require exposure to radiation?

Job Zone Component	Job Zone Component Definitions
Title	Job Zone Two: Some Preparation Needed
Overall Experience	Some previous work-related skill, knowledge, or experience may be helpful in these occupations, but usually is not needed. For example, a drywall installer might benefit from experience installing drywall, but an inexperienced person could still learn to be an installer with little difficulty.
Job Training	Employees in these occupations need anywhere from a few months to one year of working with experienced employees.
Job Zone Examples	These occupations often involve using your knowledge and skills to help others. Examples include drywall installers, fire inspectors, flight attendants, pharmacy technicians, salespersons (retail), and tellers.
SVP Range	(4.0 to < 6.0)
Education	These occupations usually require a high school diploma and may require some vocational training or job-related course work. In some cases, an associate's or bachelor's degree could be needed.

Work_Styles	Work_Styles Definitions
Dependability	Job requires being reliable, responsible, and dependable, and fulfilling obligations.
Attention to Detail	Job requires being careful about detail and thorough in completing work tasks.
Independence	Job requires developing one's own ways of doing things, guiding oneself with little or no supervision, and depending on oneself to get things done.
Initiative	Job requires a willingness to take on responsibilities and challenges.
Concern for Others	Job requires being sensitive to others' needs and feelings and being understanding and helpful on the job.
Self Control	Job requires maintaining composure, keeping emotions in check, controlling anger, and avoiding aggressive behavior, even in very difficult situations.
Cooperation	Job requires being pleasant with others on the job and displaying a good-natured, cooperative attitude.
Achievement/Effort	Job requires establishing and maintaining personally challenging achievement goals and exerting effort toward mastering tasks.
Integrity	Job requires being honest and ethical.
Persistence	Job requires persistence in the face of obstacles.
Social Orientation	Job requires preferring to work with others rather than alone, and being personally connected with others on the job.
Stress Tolerance	Job requires accepting criticism and dealing calmly and effectively with high stress situations.
Adaptability/Flexibility	Job requires being open to change (positive or negative) and to considerable variety in the workplace.
Leadership	Job requires a willingness to lead, take charge, and offer opinions and direction.
Analytical Thinking	Job requires analyzing information and using logic to address work-related issues and problems.
Innovation	Job requires creativity and alternative thinking to develop new ideas for and answers to work-related problems.

47-5081.00 - Helpers--Extraction Workers

Help extraction craft workers, such as earth drillers, blasters and explosives workers, derrick operators, and mining machine operators, by performing duties of lesser skill. Duties include supplying equipment or cleaning work area.

Tasks

1) Load materials into well holes or into equipment, using hand tools.

2) Dig trenches.

3) Collect and examine geological matter, using hand tools and testing devices.

4) Unload materials, devices and machine parts, using hand tools.

5) Clean and prepare sites for excavation or boring.

6) Signal workers to start geological material extraction or boring.

7) Organize materials in order to prepare for use.

8) Clean up work areas and remove debris after extraction activities are complete.

9) Dismantle extracting and boring equipment used for excavation, using hand tools.

10) Drive moving equipment in order to transport materials and parts to excavation sites.

11) Repair and maintain automotive and drilling equipment, using hand tools.

12) Provide assistance to extraction craft workers such as earth drillers and derrick operators.

13) Set up and adjust equipment used to excavate geological materials.

49-1011.00 - First-Line Supervisors/Managers of Mechanics, Installers, and Repairers

Supervise and coordinate the activities of mechanics, installers, and repairers.

Tasks

1) Monitor employees' work levels and review work performance.

2) Patrol and monitor work areas and examine tools and equipment in order to detect unsafe conditions or violations of procedures or safety rules.

3) Examine objects, systems, or facilities); and analyze information to determine needed installations, services, or repairs.

4) Conduct or arrange for worker training in safety, repair, and maintenance techniques); operational procedures); and equipment use.

5) Requisition materials and supplies, such as tools, equipment, and replacement parts.

6) Determine schedules, sequences, and assignments for work activities, based on work priority, quantity of equipment and skill of personnel.

7) Recommend or initiate personnel actions, such as hires, promotions, transfers, discharges, and disciplinary measures.

8) Develop, implement, and evaluate maintenance policies and procedures.

9) Meet with vendors and suppliers in order to discuss products used in repair work.

10) Confer with personnel, such as management, engineering, quality control, customer, and union workers' representatives, in order to coordinate work activities, resolve employee grievances, and identify and review resource needs.

11) Monitor tool inventories and the condition and maintenance of shops in order to ensure adequate working conditions.

12) Compute estimates and actual costs of factors such as materials, labor, and outside contractors.

13) Participate in budget preparation and administration, coordinating purchasing and documentation, and monitoring departmental expenditures.

14) Investigate accidents and injuries, and prepare reports of findings.

15) Compile operational and personnel records, such as time and production records, inventory data, repair and maintenance statistics, and test results.

16) Perform skilled repair and maintenance operations, using equipment such as hand and power tools, hydraulic presses and shears, and welding equipment.

17) Inspect, test, and measure completed work, using devices such as hand tools and gauges to verify conformance to standards and repair requirements.

18) Interpret specifications, blueprints, and job orders in order to construct templates and lay out reference points for workers.

19) Develop and implement electronic maintenance programs and computer information management systems.

20) Design equipment configurations to meet personnel needs.

Knowledge	Knowledge Definitions
Mechanical	Knowledge of machines and tools, including their designs, uses, repair, and maintenance.
Administration and Management	Knowledge of business and management principles involved in strategic planning, resource allocation, human resources modeling, leadership technique, production methods, and coordination of people and resources.
Customer and Personal Service	Knowledge of principles and processes for providing customer and personal services. This includes customer needs assessment, meeting quality standards for services, and evaluation of customer satisfaction.
English Language	Knowledge of the structure and content of the English language including the meaning and spelling of words, rules of composition, and grammar.
Engineering and Technology	Knowledge of the practical application of engineering science and technology. This includes applying principles, techniques, procedures, and equipment to the design and production of various goods and services.
Building and Construction	Knowledge of materials, methods, and the tools involved in the construction or repair of houses, buildings, or other structures such as highways and roads.
Public Safety and Security	Knowledge of relevant equipment, policies, procedures, and strategies to promote effective local, state, or national security operations for the protection of people, data, property, and institutions.
Personnel and Human Resources	Knowledge of principles and procedures for personnel recruitment, selection, training, compensation and benefits, labor relations and negotiation, and personnel information systems.
Production and Processing	Knowledge of raw materials, production processes, quality control, costs, and other techniques for maximizing the effective manufacture and distribution of goods.
Design	Knowledge of design techniques, tools, and principles involved in production of precision technical plans, blueprints, drawings, and models.
Clerical	Knowledge of administrative and clerical procedures and systems such as word processing, managing files and records, stenography and transcription, designing forms, and other office procedures and terminology.
Computers and Electronics	Knowledge of circuit boards, processors, chips, electronic equipment, and computer hardware and software, including applications and programming.
Mathematics	Knowledge of arithmetic, algebra, geometry, calculus, statistics, and their applications.
Education and Training	Knowledge of principles and methods for curriculum and training design, teaching and instruction for individuals and groups, and the measurement of training effects.
Law and Government	Knowledge of laws, legal codes, court procedures, precedents, government regulations, executive orders, agency rules, and the democratic political process.
Psychology	Knowledge of human behavior and performance; individual differences in ability, personality, and interests; learning and motivation; psychological research methods; and the assessment and treatment of behavioral and affective disorders.
Chemistry	Knowledge of the chemical composition, structure, and properties of substances and of the chemical processes and transformations that they undergo. This includes uses of chemicals and their interactions, danger signs, production techniques, and disposal methods.
Physics	Knowledge and prediction of physical principles, laws, their interrelationships, and applications to understanding fluid, material, and atmospheric dynamics, and mechanical, electrical, atomic and sub-atomic structures and processes.
Transportation	Knowledge of principles and methods for moving people or goods by air, rail, sea, or road, including the relative costs and benefits.
Economics and Accounting	Knowledge of economic and accounting principles and practices, the financial markets, banking and the analysis and reporting of financial data.
Telecommunications	Knowledge of transmission, broadcasting, switching, control, and operation of telecommunications systems.
Communications and Media	Knowledge of media production, communication, and dissemination techniques and methods. This includes alternative ways to inform and entertain via written, oral, and visual media.
Sales and Marketing	Knowledge of principles and methods for showing, promoting, and selling products or services. This includes marketing strategy and tactics, product demonstration, sales techniques, and sales control systems.
Therapy and Counseling	Knowledge of principles, methods, and procedures for diagnosis, treatment, and rehabilitation of physical and mental dysfunctions, and for career counseling and guidance.
Biology	Knowledge of plant and animal organisms, their tissues, cells, functions, interdependencies, and interactions with each other and the environment.
Sociology and Anthropology	Knowledge of group behavior and dynamics, societal trends and influences, human migrations, ethnicity, cultures and their history and origins.
Geography	Knowledge of principles and methods for describing the features of land, sea, and air masses, including their physical characteristics, locations, interrelationships, and distribution of plant, animal, and human life.
Medicine and Dentistry	Knowledge of the information and techniques needed to diagnose and treat human injuries, diseases, and deformities. This includes symptoms, treatment alternatives, drug properties and interactions, and preventive health-care measures.
Philosophy and Theology	Knowledge of different philosophical systems and religions. This includes their basic principles, values, ethics, ways of thinking, customs, practices, and their impact on human culture.
Foreign Language	Knowledge of the structure and content of a foreign (non-English) language including the meaning and spelling of words, rules of composition and grammar, and pronunciation.
History and Archeology	Knowledge of historical events and their causes, indicators, and effects on civilizations and cultures.

Food Production	Knowledge of techniques and equipment for planting, growing, and harvesting food products (both plant and animal) for consumption, including storage/handling techniques.
Fine Arts	Knowledge of the theory and techniques required to compose, produce, and perform works of music, dance, visual arts, drama, and sculpture.

Skills	**Skills Definitions**
Management of Personnel Resources	Motivating, developing, and directing people as they work, identifying the best people for the job.
Reading Comprehension	Understanding written sentences and paragraphs in work related documents.
Equipment Selection	Determining the kind of tools and equipment needed to do a job.
Active Listening	Giving full attention to what other people are saying, taking time to understand the points being made, asking questions as appropriate, and not interrupting at inappropriate times.
Instructing	Teaching others how to do something.
Installation	Installing equipment, machines, wiring, or programs to meet specifications.
Time Management	Managing one's own time and the time of others.
Troubleshooting	Determining causes of operating errors and deciding what to do about it.
Critical Thinking	Using logic and reasoning to identify the strengths and weaknesses of alternative solutions, conclusions or approaches to problems.
Equipment Maintenance	Performing routine maintenance on equipment and determining when and what kind of maintenance is needed.
Monitoring	Monitoring/Assessing performance of yourself, other individuals, or organizations to make improvements or take corrective action.
Complex Problem Solving	Identifying complex problems and reviewing related information to develop and evaluate options and implement solutions.
Coordination	Adjusting actions in relation to others' actions.
Judgment and Decision Making	Considering the relative costs and benefits of potential actions to choose the most appropriate one.
Management of Material Resources	Obtaining and seeing to the appropriate use of equipment, facilities, and materials needed to do certain work.
Repairing	Repairing machines or systems using the needed tools.
Speaking	Talking to others to convey information effectively.
Learning Strategies	Selecting and using training/instructional methods and procedures appropriate for the situation when learning or teaching new things.
Negotiation	Bringing others together and trying to reconcile differences.
Active Learning	Understanding the implications of new information for both current and future problem-solving and decision-making.
Quality Control Analysis	Conducting tests and inspections of products, services, or processes to evaluate quality or performance.
Social Perceptiveness	Being aware of others' reactions and understanding why they react as they do.
Mathematics	Using mathematics to solve problems
Writing	Communicating effectively in writing as appropriate for the needs of the audience.
Service Orientation	Actively looking for ways to help people.
Management of Financial Resources	Determining how money will be spent to get the work done, and accounting for these expenditures.
Persuasion	Persuading others to change their minds or behavior.
Operations Analysis	Analyzing needs and product requirements to create a design.
Systems Evaluation	Identifying measures or indicators of system performance and the actions needed to improve or correct performance, relative to the goals of the system.
Operation Monitoring	Watching gauges, dials, or other indicators to make sure a machine is working properly.
Technology Design	Generating or adapting equipment and technology to serve user needs.
Operation and Control	Controlling operations of equipment or systems.
Systems Analysis	Determining how a system should work and how changes in conditions, operations, and the environment will affect outcomes.
Science	Using scientific rules and methods to solve problems.
Programming	Writing computer programs for various purposes.

Ability	**Ability Definitions**
Oral Expression	The ability to communicate information and ideas in speaking so others will understand.
Problem Sensitivity	The ability to tell when something is wrong or is likely to go wrong. It does not involve solving the problem, only recognizing there is a problem.
Oral Comprehension	The ability to listen to and understand information and ideas presented through spoken words and sentences.
Written Comprehension	The ability to read and understand information and ideas presented in writing.
Deductive Reasoning	The ability to apply general rules to specific problems to produce answers that make sense.
Speech Recognition	The ability to identify and understand the speech of another person.
Speech Clarity	The ability to speak clearly so others can understand you.
Inductive Reasoning	The ability to combine pieces of information to form general rules or conclusions (includes finding a relationship among seemingly unrelated events).
Near Vision	The ability to see details at close range (within a few feet of the observer).
Written Expression	The ability to communicate information and ideas in writing so others will understand.
Fluency of Ideas	The ability to come up with a number of ideas about a topic (the number of ideas is important, not their quality, correctness, or creativity).
Information Ordering	The ability to arrange things or actions in a certain order or pattern according to a specific rule or set of rules (e.g., patterns of numbers, letters, words, pictures, mathematical operations).
Selective Attention	The ability to concentrate on a task over a period of time without being distracted.
Far Vision	The ability to see details at a distance.
Flexibility of Closure	The ability to identify or detect a known pattern (a figure, object, word, or sound) that is hidden in other distracting material.
Category Flexibility	The ability to generate or use different sets of rules for combining or grouping things in different ways.
Visualization	The ability to imagine how something will look after it is moved around or when its parts are moved or rearranged.
Time Sharing	The ability to shift back and forth between two or more activities or sources of information (such as speech, sounds, touch, or other sources).
Hearing Sensitivity	The ability to detect or tell the differences between sounds that vary in pitch and loudness.
Perceptual Speed	The ability to quickly and accurately compare similarities and differences among sets of letters, numbers, objects, pictures, or patterns. The things to be compared may be presented at the same time or one after the other. This ability also includes comparing a presented object with a remembered object.
Visual Color Discrimination	The ability to match or detect differences between colors, including shades of color and brightness.
Originality	The ability to come up with unusual or clever ideas about a given topic or situation, or to develop creative ways to solve a problem.
Mathematical Reasoning	The ability to choose the right mathematical methods or formulas to solve a problem.
Speed of Closure	The ability to quickly make sense of, combine, and organize information into meaningful patterns.
Finger Dexterity	The ability to make precisely coordinated movements of the fingers of one or both hands to grasp, manipulate, or assemble very small objects.
Arm-Hand Steadiness	The ability to keep your hand and arm steady while moving your arm or while holding your arm and hand in one position.
Number Facility	The ability to add, subtract, multiply, or divide quickly and correctly.
Auditory Attention	The ability to focus on a single source of sound in the presence of other distracting sounds.
Multilimb Coordination	The ability to coordinate two or more limbs (for example, two arms, two legs, or one leg and one arm) while sitting, standing, or lying down. It does not involve performing the activities while the whole body is in motion.
Control Precision	The ability to quickly and repeatedly adjust the controls of a machine or a vehicle to exact positions.
Depth Perception	The ability to judge which of several objects is closer or farther away from you, or to judge the distance between you and an object.
Extent Flexibility	The ability to bend, stretch, twist, or reach with your body, arms, and/or legs.
Memorization	The ability to remember information such as words, numbers, pictures, and procedures.

Manual Dexterity	The ability to quickly move your hand, your hand together with your arm, or your two hands to grasp, manipulate, or assemble objects.
Trunk Strength	The ability to use your abdominal and lower back muscles to support part of the body repeatedly or continuously over time without 'giving out' or fatiguing.
Reaction Time	The ability to quickly respond (with the hand, finger, or foot) to a signal (sound, light, picture) when it appears.
Gross Body Coordination	The ability to coordinate the movement of your arms, legs, and torso together when the whole body is in motion.
Static Strength	The ability to exert maximum muscle force to lift, push, pull, or carry objects.
Stamina	The ability to exert yourself physically over long periods of time without getting winded or out of breath.
Response Orientation	The ability to choose quickly between two or more movements in response to two or more different signals (lights, sounds, pictures). It includes the speed with which the correct response is started with the hand, foot, or other body part.
Gross Body Equilibrium	The ability to keep or regain your body balance or stay upright when in an unstable position.
Wrist-Finger Speed	The ability to make fast, simple, repeated movements of the fingers, hands, and wrists.
Dynamic Strength	The ability to exert muscle force repeatedly or continuously over time. This involves muscular endurance and resistance to muscle fatigue.
Glare Sensitivity	The ability to see objects in the presence of glare or bright lighting.
Rate Control	The ability to time your movements or the movement of a piece of equipment in anticipation of changes in the speed and/or direction of a moving object or scene.
Speed of Limb Movement	The ability to quickly move the arms and legs.
Spatial Orientation	The ability to know your location in relation to the environment or to know where other objects are in relation to you.
Peripheral Vision	The ability to see objects or movement of objects to one's side when the eyes are looking ahead.
Sound Localization	The ability to tell the direction from which a sound originated.
Explosive Strength	The ability to use short bursts of muscle force to propel oneself (as in jumping or sprinting), or to throw an object.
Night Vision	The ability to see under low light conditions.
Dynamic Flexibility	The ability to quickly and repeatedly bend, stretch, twist, or reach out with your body, arms, and/or legs.

Work_Activity	**Work_Activity Definitions**
Communicating with Supervisors, Peers, or Subordin	Providing information to supervisors, co-workers, and subordinates by telephone, in written form, e-mail, or in person.
Getting Information	Observing, receiving, and otherwise obtaining information from all relevant sources.
Monitor Processes, Materials, or Surroundings	Monitoring and reviewing information from materials, events, or the environment, to detect or assess problems.
Making Decisions and Solving Problems	Analyzing information and evaluating results to choose the best solution and solve problems.
Inspecting Equipment, Structures, or Material	Inspecting equipment, structures, or materials to identify the cause of errors or other problems or defects.
Developing and Building Teams	Encouraging and building mutual trust, respect, and cooperation among team members.
Updating and Using Relevant Knowledge	Keeping up-to-date technically and applying new knowledge to your job.
Guiding, Directing, and Motivating Subordinates	Providing guidance and direction to subordinates, including setting performance standards and monitoring performance.
Organizing, Planning, and Prioritizing Work	Developing specific goals and plans to prioritize, organize, and accomplish your work.
Identifying Objects, Actions, and Events	Identifying information by categorizing, estimating, recognizing differences or similarities, and detecting changes in circumstances or events.
Establishing and Maintaining Interpersonal Relatio	Developing constructive and cooperative working relationships with others, and maintaining them over time.
Scheduling Work and Activities	Scheduling events, programs, and activities, as well as the work of others.
Coordinating the Work and Activities of Others	Getting members of a group to work together to accomplish tasks.
Judging the Qualities of Things, Services, or Peop	Assessing the value, importance, or quality of things or people.

Analyzing Data or Information	Identifying the underlying principles, reasons, or facts of information by breaking down information or data into separate parts.
Evaluating Information to Determine Compliance wit	Using relevant information and individual judgment to determine whether events or processes comply with laws, regulations, or standards.
Interacting With Computers	Using computers and computer systems (including hardware and software) to program, write software, set up functions, enter data, or process information.
Provide Consultation and Advice to Others	Providing guidance and expert advice to management or other groups on technical, systems-, or process-related topics.
Developing Objectives and Strategies	Establishing long-range objectives and specifying the strategies and actions to achieve them.
Performing Administrative Activities	Performing day-to-day administrative tasks such as maintaining information files and processing paperwork.
Coaching and Developing Others	Identifying the developmental needs of others and coaching, mentoring, or otherwise helping others to improve their knowledge or skills.
Processing Information	Compiling, coding, categorizing, calculating, tabulating, auditing, or verifying information or data.
Resolving Conflicts and Negotiating with Others	Handling complaints, settling disputes, and resolving grievances and conflicts, or otherwise negotiating with others.
Thinking Creatively	Developing, designing, or creating new applications, ideas, relationships, systems, or products, including artistic contributions.
Interpreting the Meaning of Information for Others	Translating or explaining what information means and how it can be used.
Documenting/Recording Information	Entering, transcribing, recording, storing, or maintaining information in written or electronic/magnetic form.
Communicating with Persons Outside Organization	Communicating with people outside the organization, representing the organization to customers, the public, government, and other external sources. This information can be exchanged in person, in writing, or by telephone or e-mail.
Estimating the Quantifiable Characteristics of Pro	Estimating sizes, distances, and quantities; or determining time, costs, resources, or materials needed to perform a work activity
Training and Teaching Others	Identifying the educational needs of others, developing formal educational or training programs or classes, and teaching or instructing others.
Monitoring and Controlling Resources	Monitoring and controlling resources and overseeing the spending of money.
Repairing and Maintaining Mechanical Equipment	Servicing, repairing, adjusting, and testing machines, devices, moving parts, and equipment that operate primarily on the basis of mechanical (not electronic) principles.
Staffing Organizational Units	Recruiting, interviewing, selecting, hiring, and promoting employees in an organization.
Drafting, Laying Out, and Specifying Technical Dev	Providing documentation, detailed instructions, drawings, or specifications to tell others about how devices, parts, equipment, or structures are to be fabricated, constructed, assembled, modified, maintained, or used.
Repairing and Maintaining Electronic Equipment	Servicing, repairing, calibrating, regulating, fine-tuning, or testing machines, devices, and equipment that operate primarily on the basis of electrical or electronic (not mechanical) principles.
Controlling Machines and Processes	Using either control mechanisms or direct physical activity to operate machines or processes (not including computers or vehicles).
Assisting and Caring for Others	Providing personal assistance, medical attention, emotional support, or other personal care to others such as coworkers, customers, or patients.
Performing General Physical Activities	Performing physical activities that require considerable use of your arms and legs and moving your whole body, such as climbing, lifting, balancing, walking, stooping, and handling of materials.
Operating Vehicles, Mechanized Devices, or Equipme	Running, maneuvering, navigating, or driving vehicles or mechanized equipment, such as forklifts, passenger vehicles, aircraft, or water craft.
Handling and Moving Objects	Using hands and arms in handling, installing, positioning, and moving materials, and manipulating things.
Selling or Influencing Others	Convincing others to buy merchandise/goods or to otherwise change their minds or actions.
Performing for or Working Directly with the Public	Performing for people or dealing directly with the public. This includes serving customers in restaurants and stores, and receiving clients or guests.

Work_Context	Work_Context Definitions
Face-to-Face Discussions	How often do you have to have face-to-face discussions with individuals or teams in this job?
Telephone	How often do you have telephone conversations in this job?
Responsibility for Outcomes and Results	How responsible is the worker for work outcomes and results of other workers?
Responsible for Others' Health and Safety	How much responsibility is there for the health and safety of others in this job?
Electronic Mail	How often do you use electronic mail in this job?
Work With Work Group or Team	How important is it to work with others in a group or team in this job?
Contact With Others	How much does this job require the worker to be in contact with others (face-to-face, by telephone, or otherwise) in order to perform it?
Freedom to Make Decisions	How much decision making freedom, without supervision, does the job offer?
Structured versus Unstructured Work	To what extent is this job structured for the worker, rather than allowing the worker to determine tasks, priorities, and goals?
Impact of Decisions on Co-workers or Company Resul	How do the decisions an employee makes impact the results of co-workers, clients or the company?
Indoors, Environmentally Controlled	How often does this job require working indoors in environmentally controlled conditions?
Coordinate or Lead Others	How important is it to coordinate or lead others in accomplishing work activities in this job?
Frequency of Decision Making	How frequently is the worker required to make decisions that affect other people, the financial resources, and/or the image and reputation of the organization?
Outdoors, Exposed to Weather	How often does this job require working outdoors, exposed to all weather conditions?
Exposed to Contaminants	How often does this job require working exposed to contaminants (such as pollutants, gases, dust or odors)?
Letters and Memos	How often does the job require written letters and memos?
Time Pressure	How often does this job require the worker to meet strict deadlines?
Wear Common Protective or Safety Equipment such as	How much does this job require wearing common protective or safety equipment such as safety shoes, glasses, gloves, hard hats or live jackets?
Indoors, Not Environmentally Controlled	How often does this job require working indoors in non-controlled environmental conditions (e.g., warehouse without heat)?
In an Enclosed Vehicle or Equipment	How often does this job require working in a closed vehicle or equipment (e.g., car)?
Importance of Being Exact or Accurate	How important is being very exact or highly accurate in performing this job?
Spend Time Standing	How much does this job require standing?
Level of Competition	To what extent does this job require the worker to compete or to be aware of competitive pressures?
Deal With External Customers	How important is it to work with external customers or the public in this job?
Sounds, Noise Levels Are Distracting or Uncomforta	How often does this job require working exposed to sounds and noise levels that are distracting or uncomfortable?
Very Hot or Cold Temperatures	How often does this job require working in very hot (above 90 F degrees) or very cold (below 32 F degrees) temperatures?
Physical Proximity	To what extent does this job require the worker to perform job tasks in close physical proximity to other people?
Importance of Repeating Same Tasks	How important is repeating the same physical activities (e.g., key entry) or mental activities (e.g., checking entries in a ledger) over and over, without stopping, to performing this job?
Public Speaking	How often do you have to perform public speaking in this job?
Consequence of Error	How serious would the result usually be if the worker made a mistake that was not readily correctable?
Frequency of Conflict Situations	How often are there conflict situations the employee has to face in this job?
Spend Time Walking and Running	How much does this job require walking and running?
Spend Time Using Your Hands to Handle, Control, or	How much does this job require using your hands to handle, control, or feel objects, tools or controls?
Spend Time Sitting	How much does this job require sitting?
Exposed to Hazardous Equipment	How often does this job require exposure to hazardous equipment?
Spend Time Bending or Twisting the Body	How much does this job require bending or twisting your body?
Extremely Bright or Inadequate Lighting	How often does this job require working in extremely bright or inadequate lighting conditions?

Cramped Work Space, Awkward Positions	How often does this job require working in cramped work spaces that requires getting into awkward positions?
Deal With Unpleasant or Angry People	How frequently does the worker have to deal with unpleasant, angry, or discourteous individuals as part of the job requirements?
Outdoors, Under Cover	How often does this job require working outdoors, under cover (e.g., structure with roof but no walls)?
Exposed to Minor Burns, Cuts, Bites, or Stings	How often does this job require exposure to minor burns, cuts, bites, or stings?
Pace Determined by Speed of Equipment	How important is it to this job that the pace is determined by the speed of equipment or machinery? (This does not refer to keeping busy at all times on this job.)
Spend Time Making Repetitive Motions	How much does this job require making repetitive motions?
Exposed to Hazardous Conditions	How often does this job require exposure to hazardous conditions?
Exposed to High Places	How often does this job require exposure to high places?
In an Open Vehicle or Equipment	How often does this job require working in an open vehicle or equipment (e.g., tractor)?
Spend Time Kneeling, Crouching, Stooping, or Crawl	How much does this job require kneeling, crouching, stooping or crawling?
Degree of Automation	How automated is the job?
Spend Time Climbing Ladders, Scaffolds, or Poles	How much does this job require climbing ladders, scaffolds, or poles?
Exposed to Disease or Infections	How often does this job require exposure to disease/infections?
Spend Time Keeping or Regaining Balance	How much does this job require keeping or regaining your balance?
Exposed to Whole Body Vibration	How often does this job require exposure to whole body vibration (e.g., operate a jackhammer)?
Wear Specialized Protective or Safety Equipment su	How much does this job require wearing specialized protective or safety equipment such as breathing apparatus, safety harness, full protection suits, or radiation protection?
Deal With Physically Aggressive People	How frequently does this job require the worker to deal with physical aggression of violent individuals?
Exposed to Radiation	How often does this job require exposure to radiation?

Job Zone Component	Job Zone Component Definitions
Title	Job Zone Four: Considerable Preparation Needed
Overall Experience	A minimum of two to four years of work-related skill, knowledge, or experience is needed for these occupations. For example, an accountant must complete four years of college and work for several years in accounting to be considered qualified.
Job Training	Employees in these occupations usually need several years of work-related experience, on-the-job training, and/or vocational training.
Job Zone Examples	Many of these occupations involve coordinating, supervising, managing, or training others. Examples include accountants, chefs and head cooks, computer programmers, historians, pharmacists, and police detectives.
SVP Range	(7.0 to < 8.0)
Education	Most of these occupations require a four - year bachelor's degree, but some do not.

Work_Styles	Work_Styles Definitions
Dependability	Job requires being reliable, responsible, and dependable, and fulfilling obligations.
Attention to Detail	Job requires being careful about detail and thorough in completing work tasks.
Initiative	Job requires a willingness to take on responsibilities and challenges.
Integrity	Job requires being honest and ethical.
Leadership	Job requires a willingness to lead, take charge, and offer opinions and direction.
Self Control	Job requires maintaining composure, keeping emotions in check, controlling anger, and avoiding aggressive behavior, even in very difficult situations.
Cooperation	Job requires being pleasant with others on the job and displaying a good-natured, cooperative attitude.
Stress Tolerance	Job requires accepting criticism and dealing calmly and effectively with high stress situations.
Persistence	Job requires persistence in the face of obstacles.

Adaptability/Flexibility	Job requires being open to change (positive or negative) and to considerable variety in the workplace.
Achievement/Effort	Job requires establishing and maintaining personally challenging achievement goals and exerting effort toward mastering tasks.
Concern for Others	Job requires being sensitive to others' needs and feelings and being understanding and helpful on the job.
Independence	Job requires developing one's own ways of doing things, guiding oneself with little or no supervision, and depending on oneself to get things done.
Analytical Thinking	Job requires analyzing information and using logic to address work-related issues and problems.
Social Orientation	Job requires preferring to work with others rather than alone, and being personally connected with others on the job.
Innovation	Job requires creativity and alternative thinking to develop new ideas for and answers to work-related problems.

49-2011.00 - Computer, Automated Teller, and Office Machine Repairers

Repair, maintain, or install computers, word processing systems, automated teller machines, and electronic office machines, such as duplicating and fax machines.

Tasks

1) Fill machines with toners, inks, or other duplicating fluids.

2) Reassemble machines after making repairs or replacing parts.

3) Reinstall software programs or adjust settings on existing software in order to fix machine malfunctions.

4) Enter information into computers to copy programs from one electronic component to another, or to draw, modify, or store schematics.

5) Calibrate testing instruments.

6) Update existing equipment, performing tasks such as installing updated circuit boards or additional memory.

7) Test new systems in order to ensure that they are in working order.

8) Test components and circuits of faulty equipment in order to locate defects, using oscilloscopes, signal generators, ammeters, voltmeters, or special diagnostic software programs.

9) Train new repairers.

10) Install and configure new equipment, including operating software and peripheral equipment.

11) Travel to customers' stores or offices to service machines, or to provide emergency repair service.

12) Analyze equipment performance records in order to assess equipment functioning.

13) Maintain parts inventories, and order any additional parts needed for repairs.

14) Repair, adjust, or replace electrical and mechanical components and parts, using hand tools, power tools, and soldering or welding equipment.

15) Align, adjust, and calibrate equipment according to specifications.

16) Read specifications such as blueprints, charts, and schematics in order to determine machine settings and adjustments.

17) Assemble machines according to specifications, using hand tools, power tools, and measuring devices.

18) Clean, oil, and adjust mechanical parts to maintain machines' operating efficiency and to prevent breakdowns.

19) Complete repair bills, shop records, time cards, and expense reports.

20) Converse with customers in order to determine details of equipment problems.

21) Disassemble machine to examine parts such as wires, gears, and bearings for wear and defects, using hand tools, power tools, and measuring devices.

22) Lay cable and hook up electrical connections between machines, power sources, and phone lines.

23) Maintain records of equipment maintenance work and repairs.

24) Advise customers concerning equipment operation, maintenance and programming.

49-2022.00 - Telecommunications Equipment Installers and Repairers, Except Line Installers

Set-up, rearrange, or remove switching and dialing equipment used in central offices. Service or repair telephones and other communication equipment on customers' property. May install equipment in new locations or install wiring and telephone jacks in buildings under construction.

Tasks

1) Climb poles and ladders, use truck-mounted booms, and enter areas such as manholes and cable vaults, in order to install, maintain, or inspect equipment.

2) Adjust or modify equipment to enhance equipment performance or to respond to customer requests.

3) Remove and replace plug-in circuit equipment.

4) Note differences in wire and cable colors so that work can be performed correctly.

5) Install telephone station equipment, such as intercommunication systems, transmitters, receivers, relays, and ringers, and related apparatus, such as coin collectors, telephone booths, and switching-key equipment.

6) Diagnose and correct problems from remote locations, using special switchboards to find the sources of problems.

7) Designate cables available for use.

8) Clean switches and replace contact points, using vacuum hoses, solvents, and hand tools.

9) Measure distances from landmarks to identify exact installation sites for equipment.

10) Test repaired, newly installed, or updated equipment to ensure that it functions properly and conforms to specifications, using test equipment and observation.

11) Request support from technical service centers when on-site procedures fail to solve installation or maintenance problems.

12) Remove loose wires and other debris after work is completed.

13) Provide input into the design and manufacturing of new equipment.

14) Demonstrate equipment to customers and explain how it is to be used, and respond to any inquiries or complaints.

15) Clean and maintain tools, test equipment, and motor vehicles.

16) Determine viability of sites through observation, and discuss site locations and construction requirements with customers.

17) Dig holes or trenches as necessary for equipment installation and access.

18) Drive crew trucks to and from work areas.

19) Examine telephone transmission facilities to determine requirements for new or additional telephone services.

20) Install updated software, and programs that maintain existing software and/or provide requested features such as time-correlated call routing.

21) Perform database verifications, using computers.

22) Collaborate with other workers in order to locate and correct malfunctions.

23) Run wires between components and to outside cable systems, connecting them to wires from telephone poles or underground cable accesses.

24) Perform routine maintenance on equipment, including adjusting and lubricating components, and painting worn or exposed areas.

25) Place intercept circuits on terminals to handle vacant lines in central office installations.

26) Maintain computer and manual records pertaining to facilities and equipment.

27) Inspect equipment on a regular basis in order to ensure proper functioning.

28) Enter codes needed to correct electronic switching system programming.

29) Program computerized switches and switchboards to provide requested features.

30) Test circuits and components of malfunctioning telecommunications equipment to isolate sources of malfunctions, using test meters, circuit diagrams, polarity probes, and other hand tools.

31) Assemble and install communication equipment such as data and telephone communication lines, wiring, switching equipment, wiring frames, power apparatus, computer systems, and networks.

32) Route and connect cables and lines to switches, switchboard equipment, and distributing frames, using wire-wrap guns or soldering irons to connect wires to terminals.

33) Review manufacturer's instructions, manuals, technical specifications, building permits, and ordinances in order to determine communication equipment requirements and procedures.

34) Repair or replace faulty equipment such as defective and damaged telephones, wires, switching system components, and associated equipment.

35) Remove and remake connections in order to change circuit layouts, following work orders or diagrams.

36) Refer to manufacturers' manuals to obtain maintenance instructions pertaining to specific malfunctions.

37) Address special issues or situations, such as illegal or unauthorized use of equipment, or cases of electrical or acoustic shock.

38) Test connections to ensure that power supplies are adequate and that communications links function.

39) Communicate with bases, using telephones or two-way radios to receive instructions or technical advice, or to report equipment status.

49-2091.00 - Avionics Technicians

Install, inspect, test, adjust, or repair avionics equipment, such as radar, radio, navigation, and missile control systems in aircraft or space vehicles.

Tasks

1) Fabricate parts and test aids as required.

2) Lay out installation of aircraft assemblies and systems, following documentation such as blueprints, manuals, and wiring diagrams.

3) Adjust, repair, or replace malfunctioning components or assemblies, using hand tools and/or soldering irons.

4) Set up and operate ground support and test equipment to perform functional flight tests of electrical and electronic systems.

5) Keep records of maintenance and repair work.

6) Coordinate work with that of engineers, technicians, and other aircraft maintenance personnel.

7) Test and troubleshoot instruments, components, and assemblies, using circuit testers, oscilloscopes, and voltmeters.

8) Interpret flight test data in order to diagnose malfunctions and systemic performance problems.

9) Install electrical and electronic components, assemblies, and systems in aircraft, using hand tools, power tools, and/or soldering irons.

10) Connect components to assemblies such as radio systems, instruments, magnetos, inverters, and in-flight refueling systems, using hand tools and soldering irons.

11) Assemble components such as switches, electrical controls, and junction boxes, using hand tools and soldering irons.

12) Assemble prototypes or models of circuits, instruments, and systems so that they can be used for testing.

49-2093.00 - Electrical and Electronics Installers and Repairers, Transportation Equipment

Install, adjust, or maintain mobile electronics communication equipment, including sound, sonar, security, navigation, and surveillance systems on trains, watercraft, or other mobile equipment.

Tasks

1) Inspect and test electrical systems and equipment to locate and diagnose malfunctions, using visual inspections, testing devices, and computer software.

2) Measure, cut, and install frameworks and conduit to support and connect wiring, control panels, and junction boxes, using hand tools.

3) Repair or rebuild equipment such as starters, generators, distributors, or door controls, using electrician's tools.

4) Refer to schematics and manufacturers' specifications that show connections and provide

instructions on how to locate problems.

5) Reassemble and test equipment after repairs.

6) Locate and remove or repair circuit defects such as blown fuses or malfunctioning transistors.

7) Install new fuses, electrical cables, or power sources as required.

8) Install fixtures, outlets, terminal boards, switches, and wall boxes, using hand tools.

9) Adjust, repair, or replace defective wiring and relays in ignition, lighting, air-conditioning, and safety control systems, using electrician's tools.

10) Estimate costs of repairs based on parts and labor requirements.

11) Maintain equipment service records.

12) Confer with customers to determine the nature of malfunctions.

13) Splice wires with knives or cutting pliers, and solder connections to fixtures, outlets, and equipment.

14) Install electrical equipment such as air-conditioning, heating, or ignition systems and components such as generator brushes and commutators, using hand tools.

49-2094.00 - Electrical and Electronics Repairers, Commercial and Industrial Equipment

Repair, test, adjust, or install electronic equipment, such as industrial controls, transmitters, and antennas.

Tasks

1) Operate equipment to demonstrate proper use and to analyze malfunctions.

2) Perform scheduled preventive maintenance tasks, such as checking, cleaning, and repairing equipment, to detect and prevent problems.

3) Examine work orders and converse with equipment operators to detect equipment problems and to ascertain whether mechanical or human errors contributed to the problems.

4) Test faulty equipment to diagnose malfunctions, using test equipment and software, and applying knowledge of the functional operation of electronic units and systems.

5) Repair and adjust equipment, machines, and defective components, replacing worn parts such as gaskets and seals in watertight electrical equipment.

6) Inspect components of industrial equipment for accurate assembly and installation and for defects such as loose connections and frayed wires.

7) Coordinate efforts with other workers involved in installing and maintaining equipment or components.

8) Consult with customers, supervisors, and engineers to plan layout of equipment and to resolve problems in system operation and maintenance.

9) Calibrate testing instruments and installed or repaired equipment to prescribed specifications.

10) Set up and test industrial equipment to ensure that it functions properly.

11) Maintain equipment logs that record performance problems, repairs, calibrations, and tests.

12) Advise management regarding customer satisfaction, product performance, and suggestions for product improvements.

13) Send defective units to the manufacturer or to a specialized repair shop for repair.

14) Maintain inventory of spare parts.

15) Install repaired equipment in various settings, such as industrial or military establishments.

16) Determine feasibility of using standardized equipment, and develop specifications for equipment required to perform additional functions.

17) Develop or modify industrial electronic devices, circuits, and equipment according to available specifications.

18) Enter information into computer to copy program or to draw, modify, or store schematics, applying knowledge of software package used.

19) Sign overhaul documents for equipment replaced or repaired.

Knowledge	Knowledge Definitions
Mechanical	Knowledge of machines and tools, including their designs, uses, repair, and maintenance.

Computers and Electronics	Knowledge of circuit boards. processors. chips. electronic equipment, and computer hardware and software. including applications and programming.
Engineering and Technology	Knowledge of the practical application of engineering science and technology. This includes applying principles. techniques. procedures, and equipment to the design and production of various goods and services.
Telecommunications	Knowledge of transmission, broadcasting, switching, control. and operation of telecommunications systems.
Customer and Personal Service	Knowledge of principles and processes for providing customer and personal services. This includes customer needs assessment, meeting quality standards for services, and evaluation of customer satisfaction.
Mathematics	Knowledge of arithmetic, algebra, geometry, calculus, statistics, and their applications.
Production and Processing	Knowledge of raw materials. production processes, quality control, costs, and other techniques for maximizing the effective manufacture and distribution of goods.
English Language	Knowledge of the structure and content of the English language including the meaning and spelling of words, rules of composition, and grammar.
Design	Knowledge of design techniques, tools, and principles involved in production of precision technical plans, blueprints, drawings, and models.
Communications and Media	Knowledge of media production, communication, and dissemination techniques and methods. This includes alternative ways to inform and entertain via written, oral, and visual media.
Transportation	Knowledge of principles and methods for moving people or goods by air, rail, sea, or road, including the relative costs and benefits.
Administration and Management	Knowledge of business and management principles involved in strategic planning, resource allocation, human resources modeling, leadership technique, production methods, and coordination of people and resources.
Public Safety and Security	Knowledge of relevant equipment, policies, procedures, and strategies to promote effective local, state, or national security operations for the protection of people, data, property, and institutions.
Building and Construction	Knowledge of materials, methods, and the tools involved in the construction or repair of houses, buildings, or other structures such as highways and roads.
Education and Training	Knowledge of principles and methods for curriculum and training design, teaching and instruction for individuals and groups, and the measurement of training effects.
Clerical	Knowledge of administrative and clerical procedures and systems such as word processing, managing files and records, stenography and transcription, designing forms, and other office procedures and terminology.
Physics	Knowledge and prediction of physical principles, laws, their interrelationships, and applications to understanding fluid, material, and atmospheric dynamics, and mechanical, electrical, atomic and sub- atomic structures and processes.
Sales and Marketing	Knowledge of principles and methods for showing, promoting, and selling products or services. This includes marketing strategy and tactics, product demonstration, sales techniques, and sales control systems.
Chemistry	Knowledge of the chemical composition, structure, and properties of substances and of the chemical processes and transformations that they undergo. This includes uses of chemicals and their interactions, danger signs, production techniques, and disposal methods.
Law and Government	Knowledge of laws, legal codes, court procedures, precedents, government regulations, executive orders, agency rules, and the democratic political process.
Personnel and Human Resources	Knowledge of principles and procedures for personnel recruitment, selection, training, compensation and benefits, labor relations and negotiation, and personnel information systems.
Economics and Accounting	Knowledge of economic and accounting principles and practices, the financial markets, banking and the analysis and reporting of financial data.
Psychology	Knowledge of human behavior and performance; individual differences in ability, personality, and interests; learning and motivation; psychological research methods; and the assessment and treatment of behavioral and affective disorders.

Geography	Knowledge of principles and methods for describing the features of land. sea. and air masses, including their physical characteristics, locations. interrelationships, and distribution of plant, animal, and human life.
Biology	Knowledge of plant and animal organisms, their tissues, cells, functions, interdependencies, and interactions with each other and the environment.
Food Production	Knowledge of techniques and equipment for planting, growing, and harvesting food products (both plant and animal) for consumption, including storage/handling techniques.
Therapy and Counseling	Knowledge of principles, methods, and procedures for diagnosis, treatment, and rehabilitation of physical and mental dysfunctions, and for career counseling and guidance.
Philosophy and Theology	Knowledge of different philosophical systems and religions. This includes their basic principles, values, ethics, ways of thinking, customs, practices, and their impact on human culture.
Medicine and Dentistry	Knowledge of the information and techniques needed to diagnose and treat human injuries, diseases, and deformities. This includes symptoms, treatment alternatives, drug properties and interactions, and preventive health-care measures.
History and Archeology	Knowledge of historical events and their causes, indicators, and effects on civilizations and cultures.
Sociology and Anthropology	Knowledge of group behavior and dynamics, societal trends and influences, human migrations, ethnicity, cultures and their history and origins.
Foreign Language	Knowledge of the structure and content of a foreign (non-English) language including the meaning and spelling of words, rules of composition and grammar, and pronunciation.
Fine Arts	Knowledge of the theory and techniques required to compose, produce, and perform works of music, dance, visual arts, drama, and sculpture.

Skills	**Skills Definitions**
Troubleshooting	Determining causes of operating errors and deciding what to do about it.
Repairing	Repairing machines or systems using the needed tools.
Reading Comprehension	Understanding written sentences and paragraphs in work related documents.
Installation	Installing equipment, machines, wiring, or programs to meet specifications.
Active Listening	Giving full attention to what other people are saying, taking time to understand the points being made, asking questions as appropriate, and not interrupting at inappropriate times.
Operation Monitoring	Watching gauges, dials, or other indicators to make sure a machine is working properly.
Coordination	Adjusting actions in relation to others' actions.
Equipment Maintenance	Performing routine maintenance on equipment and determining when and what kind of maintenance is needed.
Critical Thinking	Using logic and reasoning to identify the strengths and weaknesses of alternative solutions, conclusions or approaches to problems.
Active Learning	Understanding the implications of new information for both current and future problem-solving and decision-making.
Equipment Selection	Determining the kind of tools and equipment needed to do a job.
Operation and Control	Controlling operations of equipment or systems.
Learning Strategies	Selecting and using training/instructional methods and procedures appropriate for the situation when learning or teaching new things.
Writing	Communicating effectively in writing as appropriate for the needs of the audience.
Judgment and Decision Making	Considering the relative costs and benefits of potential actions to choose the most appropriate one.
Complex Problem Solving	Identifying complex problems and reviewing related information to develop and evaluate options and implement solutions.
Instructing	Teaching others how to do something.
Time Management	Managing one's own time and the time of others.
Speaking	Talking to others to convey information effectively.
Monitoring	Monitoring/Assessing performance of yourself, other individuals, or organizations to make improvements or take corrective action.
Systems Analysis	Determining how a system should work and how changes in conditions, operations, and the environment will affect outcomes.
· Mathematics	Using mathematics to solve problems.
Technology Design	Generating or adapting equipment and technology to serve user needs.

Social Perceptiveness	Being aware of others' reactions and understanding why they react as they do.
Systems Evaluation	Identifying measures or indicators of system performance and the actions needed to improve or correct performance, relative to the goals of the system.
Service Orientation	Actively looking for ways to help people.
Quality Control Analysis	Conducting tests and inspections of products, services, or processes to evaluate quality or performance.
Persuasion	Persuading others to change their minds or behavior.
Negotiation	Bringing others together and trying to reconcile differences.
Science	Using scientific rules and methods to solve problems.
Operations Analysis	Analyzing needs and product requirements to create a design.
Management of Personnel Resources	Motivating, developing, and directing people as they work, identifying the best people for the job.
Management of Material Resources	Obtaining and seeing to the appropriate use of equipment, facilities, and materials needed to do certain work.
Programming	Writing computer programs for various purposes.
Management of Financial Resources	Determining how money will be spent to get the work done, and accounting for these expenditures.

Ability	Ability Definitions
Problem Sensitivity	The ability to tell when something is wrong or is likely to go wrong. It does not involve solving the problem, only recognizing there is a problem.
Near Vision	The ability to see details at close range (within a few feet of the observer).
Deductive Reasoning	The ability to apply general rules to specific problems to produce answers that make sense.
Oral Comprehension	The ability to listen to and understand information and ideas presented through spoken words and sentences.
Oral Expression	The ability to communicate information and ideas in speaking so others will understand.
Speech Clarity	The ability to speak clearly so others can understand you.
Information Ordering	The ability to arrange things or actions in a certain order or pattern according to a specific rule or set of rules (e.g., patterns of numbers, letters, words, pictures, mathematical operations).
Written Comprehension	The ability to read and understand information and ideas presented in writing.
Control Precision	The ability to quickly and repeatedly adjust the controls of a machine or a vehicle to exact positions.
Arm-Hand Steadiness	The ability to keep your hand and arm steady while moving your arm or while holding your arm and hand in one position.
Selective Attention	The ability to concentrate on a task over a period of time without being distracted.
Extent Flexibility	The ability to bend, stretch, twist, or reach with your body, arms, and/or legs.
Finger Dexterity	The ability to make precisely coordinated movements of the fingers of one or both hands to grasp, manipulate, or assemble very small objects.
Inductive Reasoning	The ability to combine pieces of information to form general rules or conclusions (includes finding a relationship among seemingly unrelated events).
Visual Color Discrimination	The ability to match or detect differences between colors, including shades of color and brightness.
Speech Recognition	The ability to identify and understand the speech of another person.
Multilimb Coordination	The ability to coordinate two or more limbs (for example, two arms, two legs, or one leg and one arm) while sitting, standing, or lying down. It does not involve performing the activities while the whole body is in motion.
Memorization	The ability to remember information such as words, numbers, pictures, and procedures.
Written Expression	The ability to communicate information and ideas in writing so others will understand.
Manual Dexterity	The ability to quickly move your hand, your hand together with your arm, or your two hands to grasp, manipulate, or assemble objects.
Trunk Strength	The ability to use your abdominal and lower back muscles to support part of the body repeatedly or continuously over time without 'giving out' or fatiguing.
Visualization	The ability to imagine how something will look after it is moved around or when its parts are moved or rearranged.
Flexibility of Closure	The ability to identify or detect a known pattern (a figure, object, word, or sound) that is hidden in other distracting material.

Perceptual Speed	The ability to quickly and accurately compare similarities and differences among sets of letters, numbers, objects, pictures, or patterns. The things to be compared may be presented at the same time or one after the other. This ability also includes comparing a presented object with a remembered object.
Category Flexibility	The ability to generate or use different sets of rules for combining or grouping things in different ways.
Hearing Sensitivity	The ability to detect or tell the differences between sounds that vary in pitch and loudness.
Auditory Attention	The ability to focus on a single source of sound in the presence of other distracting sounds.
Far Vision	The ability to see details at a distance.
Gross Body Coordination	The ability to coordinate the movement of your arms, legs, and torso together when the whole body is in motion.
Time Sharing	The ability to shift back and forth between two or more activities or sources of information (such as speech, sounds, touch, or other sources).
Fluency of Ideas	The ability to come up with a number of ideas about a topic (the number of ideas is important, not their quality, correctness, or creativity).
Depth Perception	The ability to judge which of several objects is closer or farther away from you, or to judge the distance between you and an object.
Static Strength	The ability to exert maximum muscle force to lift, push, pull, or carry objects.
Stamina	The ability to exert yourself physically over long periods of time without getting winded or out of breath.
Speed of Closure	The ability to quickly make sense of, combine, and organize information into meaningful patterns.
Originality	The ability to come up with unusual or clever ideas about a given topic or situation, or to develop creative ways to solve a problem.
Mathematical Reasoning	The ability to choose the right mathematical methods or formulas to solve a problem.
Number Facility	The ability to add, subtract, multiply, or divide quickly and correctly.
Reaction Time	The ability to quickly respond (with the hand, finger, or foot) to a signal (sound, light, picture) when it appears.
Peripheral Vision	The ability to see objects or movement of objects to one's side when the eyes are looking ahead.
Spatial Orientation	The ability to know your location in relation to the environment or to know where other objects are in relation to you.
Response Orientation	The ability to choose quickly between two or more movements in response to two or more different signals (lights, sounds, pictures). It includes the speed with which the correct response is started with the hand, foot, or other body part.
Dynamic Strength	The ability to exert muscle force repeatedly or continuously over time. This involves muscular endurance and resistance to muscle fatigue.
Speed of Limb Movement	The ability to quickly move the arms and legs.
Sound Localization	The ability to tell the direction from which a sound originated.
Rate Control	The ability to time your movements or the movement of a piece of equipment in anticipation of changes in the speed and/or direction of a moving object or scene.
Glare Sensitivity	The ability to see objects in the presence of glare or bright lighting.
Gross Body Equilibrium	The ability to keep or regain your body balance or stay upright when in an unstable position.
Night Vision	The ability to see under low light conditions.
Wrist-Finger Speed	The ability to make fast, simple, repeated movements of the fingers, hands, and wrists.
Dynamic Flexibility	The ability to quickly and repeatedly bend, stretch, twist, or reach out with your body, arms, and/or legs.
Explosive Strength	The ability to use short bursts of muscle force to propel oneself (as in jumping or sprinting), or to throw an object.

Work_Activity	Work_Activity Definitions
Making Decisions and Solving Problems	Analyzing information and evaluating results to choose the best solution and solve problems.
Repairing and Maintaining Electronic Equipment	Servicing, repairing, calibrating, regulating, fine-tuning, or testing machines, devices, and equipment that operate primarily on the basis of electrical or electronic (not mechanical) principles.
Communicating with Supervisors, Peers, or Subordin	Providing information to supervisors, co-workers, and subordinates by telephone, in written form, e-mail, or in person.
Getting Information	Observing, receiving, and otherwise obtaining information from all relevant sources.

Interacting With Computers	Using computers and computer systems (including hardware and software) to program, write software, set up functions, enter data, or process information.
Establishing and Maintaining Interpersonal Relatio	Developing constructive and cooperative working relationships with others, and maintaining them over time.
Updating and Using Relevant Knowledge	Keeping up-to-date technically and applying new knowledge to your job.
Interpreting the Meaning of Information for Others	Translating or explaining what information means and how it can be used.
Communicating with Persons Outside Organization	Communicating with people outside the organization, representing the organization to customers, the public, government, and other external sources. This information can be exchanged in person, in writing, or by telephone or e-mail.
Inspecting Equipment, Structures, or Material	Inspecting equipment, structures, or materials to identify the cause of errors or other problems or defects.
Identifying Objects, Actions, and Events	Identifying information by categorizing, estimating, recognizing differences or similarities, and detecting changes in circumstances or events.
Evaluating Information to Determine Compliance wit	Using relevant information and individual judgment to determine whether events or processes comply with laws, regulations, or standards.
Handling and Moving Objects	Using hands and arms in handling, installing, positioning, and moving materials, and m...ng things.
Monitor Processes, Materials, or Surroundings	Monitoring and reviewing i...ation from materials, events, or the environment, to detect or assess problems.
Training and Teaching Others	Identifying the educational needs of others, developing formal educational or training programs or classes, and teaching or instructing others.
Organizing, Planning, and Prioritizing Work	Developing specific goals and plans to prioritize, organize, and accomplish your work.
Performing General Physical Activities	Performing physical activities that require considerable use of your arms and legs and moving your whole body, such as climbing, lifting, balancing, walking, stooping, and handling of materials.
Documenting/Recording Information	Entering, transcribing, recording, storing, or maintaining information in written or electronic/magnetic form.
Operating Vehicles, Mechanized Devices, or Equipme	Running, maneuvering, navigating, or driving vehicles or mechanized equipment, such as forklifts, passenger vehicles, aircraft, or water craft.
Repairing and Maintaining Mechanical Equipment	Servicing, repairing, adjusting, and testing machines, devices, moving parts, and equipment that operate primarily on the basis of mechanical (not electronic) principles.
Scheduling Work and Activities	Scheduling events, programs, and activities, as well as the work of others.
Provide Consultation and Advice to Others	Providing guidance and expert advice to management or other groups on technical, systems-, or process-related topics.
Analyzing Data or Information	Identifying the underlying principles, reasons, or facts of information by breaking down information or data into separate parts.
Judging the Qualities of Things, Services, or Peop	Assessing the value, importance, or quality of things or people.
Assisting and Caring for Others	Providing personal assistance, medical attention, emotional support, or other personal care to others such as coworkers, customers, or patients.
Processing Information	Compiling, coding, categorizing, calculating, tabulating, auditing, or verifying information or data.
Performing Administrative Activities	Performing day-to-day administrative tasks such as maintaining information files and processing paperwork.
Thinking Creatively	Developing, designing, or creating new applications, ideas, relationships, systems, or products, including artistic contributions.
Coordinating the Work and Activities of Others	Getting members of a group to work together to accomplish tasks.
Controlling Machines and Processes	Using either control mechanisms or direct physical activity to operate machines or processes (not including computers or vehicles).
Performing for or Working Directly with the Public	Performing for people or dealing directly with the public. This includes serving customers in restaurants and stores, and receiving clients or guests.
Estimating the Quantifiable Characteristics of Pro	Estimating sizes, distances, and quantities; or determining time, costs, resources, or materials needed to perform a work activity.
Coaching and Developing Others	Identifying the developmental needs of others and coaching, mentoring, or otherwise helping others to improve their knowledge or skills.

Drafting, Laying Out, and Specifying Technical Dev	Providing documentation, detailed instructions, drawings, or specifications to tell others about how devices, parts, equipment, or structures are to be fabricated, constructed, assembled, modified, maintained, or used.
Developing and Building Teams	Encouraging and building mutual trust, respect, and cooperation among team members.
Developing Objectives and Strategies	Establishing long-range objectives and specifying the strategies and actions to achieve them.
Guiding, Directing, and Motivating Subordinates	Providing guidance and direction to subordinates, including setting performance standards and monitoring performance.
Resolving Conflicts and Negotiating with Others	Handling complaints, settling disputes, and resolving grievances and conflicts, or otherwise negotiating with others.
Monitoring and Controlling Resources	Monitoring and controlling resources and overseeing the spending of money.
Staffing Organizational Units	Recruiting, interviewing, selecting, hiring, and promoting employees in an organization.
Selling or Influencing Others	Convincing others to buy merchandise/goods or to otherwise change their minds or actions.

Work_Context	Work_Context Definitions
Face-to-Face Discussions	How often do you have to have face-to-face discussions with individuals or teams in this job?
Importance of Being Exact or Accurate	How important is being very exact or highly accurate in performing this job?
Contact With Others	How much does this job require the worker to be in contact with others (face-to-face, by telephone, or otherwise) in order to perform it?
Telephone	How often do you have telephone conversations in this job?
Indoors, Environmentally Controlled	How often does this job require working indoors in environmentally controlled conditions?
Spend Time Using Your Hands to Handle, Control, or	How much does this job require using your hands to handle, control, or feel objects, tools or controls?
Structured versus Unstructured Work	To what extent is this job structured for the worker, rather than allowing the worker to determine tasks, priorities, and goals?
Freedom to Make Decisions	How much decision making freedom, without supervision, does the job offer?
Time Pressure	How often does this job require the worker to meet strict deadlines?
Wear Common Protective or Safety Equipment such as	How much does this job require wearing common protective or safety equipment such as safety shoes, glasses, gloves, hard hats or live jackets?
Cramped Work Space, Awkward Positions	How often does this job require working in cramped work spaces that requires getting into awkward positions?
Physical Proximity	To what extent does this job require the worker to perform job tasks in close physical proximity to other people?
Sounds, Noise Levels Are Distracting or Uncomforta	How often does this job require working exposed to sounds and noise levels that are distracting or uncomfortable?
Work With Work Group or Team	How important is it to work with others in a group or team in this job?
Indoors, Not Environmentally Controlled	How often does this job require working indoors in non-controlled environmental conditions (e.g., warehouse without heat)?
Frequency of Decision Making	How frequently is the worker required to make decisions that affect other people, the financial resources, and/or the image and reputation of the organization?
Impact of Decisions on Co-workers or Company Resul	How do the decisions an employee makes impact the results of co-workers, clients or the company?
Exposed to Hazardous Conditions	How often does this job require exposure to hazardous conditions?
Spend Time Standing	How much does this job require standing?
Consequence of Error	How serious would the result usually be if the worker made a mistake that was not readily correctable?
Responsible for Others' Health and Safety	How much responsibility is there for the health and safety of others in this job?
Coordinate or Lead Others	How important is it to coordinate or lead others in accomplishing work activities in this job?
Electronic Mail	How often do you use electronic mail in this job?
Exposed to Contaminants	How often does this job require working exposed to contaminants (such as pollutants, gases, dust or odors)?
Deal With External Customers	How important is it to work with external customers or the public in this job?
Level of Competition	To what extent does this job require the worker to compete or to be aware of competitive pressures?
Letters and Memos	How often does the job require written letters and memos?
Spend Time Bending or Twisting the Body	How much does this job require bending or twisting your body?

		Work_Styles	Work_Styles Definitions
Very Hot or Cold Temperatures	How often does this job require working in very hot (above 90 F degrees) or very cold (below 32 F degrees) temperatures?	Attention to Detail	Job requires being careful about detail and thorough in completing work tasks.
Spend Time Walking and Running	How much does this job require walking and running?	Dependability	Job requires being reliable, responsible, and dependable, and fulfilling obligations.
Spend Time Kneeling, Crouching, Stooping, or Crawl	How much does this job require kneeling, crouching, stooping or crawling?	Initiative	Job requires a willingness to take on responsibilities and challenges.
In an Enclosed Vehicle or Equipment	How often does this job require working in a closed vehicle or equipment (e.g., car)?	Persistence	Job requires persistence in the face of obstacles.
Frequency of Conflict Situations	How often are there conflict situations the employee has to face in this job?	Stress Tolerance	Job requires accepting criticism and dealing calmly and effectively with high stress situations.
Importance of Repeating Same Tasks	How important is repeating the same physical activities (e.g., key entry) or mental activities (e.g., checking entries in a ledger) over and over, without stopping, to performing this job?	Self Control	Job requires maintaining composure, keeping emotions in check, controlling anger, and avoiding aggressive behavior, even in very difficult situations.
Deal With Unpleasant or Angry People	How frequently does the worker have to deal with unpleasant, angry, or discourteous individuals as part of the job requirements?	Integrity	Job requires being honest and ethical.
		Cooperation	Job requires being pleasant with others on the job and displaying a good-natured, cooperative attitude.
Exposed to Hazardous Equipment	How often does this job require exposure to hazardous equipment?	Independence	Job requires developing one's own ways of doing things, guiding oneself with little or no supervision, and depending on oneself to get things done.
Exposed to Minor Burns, Cuts, Bites, or Stings	How often does this job require exposure to minor burns, cuts, bites, or stings?	Analytical Thinking	Job requires analyzing information and using logic to address work-related issues and problems.
Spend Time Sitting	How much does this job require sitting?	Innovation	Job requires creativity and alternative thinking to develop new ideas for and answers to work-related problems.
Outdoors, Exposed to Weather	How often does this job require working outdoors, exposed to all weather conditions?	Achievement/Effort	Job requires establishing and maintaining personally challenging achievement goals and exerting effort toward mastering tasks.
Spend Time Making Repetitive Motions	How much does this job require making repetitive motions?	Leadership	Job requires a willingness to lead, take charge, and offer opinions and direction.
Responsibility for Outcomes and Results	How responsible is the worker for work outcomes and results of other workers?	Adaptability/Flexibility	Job requires being open to change (positive or negative) and to considerable variety in the workplace.
Extremely Bright or Inadequate Lighting	How often does this job require working in extremely bright or inadequate lighting conditions?	Concern for Others	Job requires being sensitive to others' needs and feelings and being understanding and helpful on the job.
Exposed to High Places	How often does this job require exposure to high places?	Social Orientation	Job requires preferring to work with others rather than alone, and being personally connected with others on the job.
Wear Specialized Protective or Safety Equipment su	How much does this job require wearing specialized protective or safety equipment such as breathing apparatus, safety harness, full protection suits, or radiation protection?		
Pace Determined by Speed of Equipment	How important is it to this job that the pace is determined by the speed of equipment or machinery? (This does not refer to keeping busy at all times on this job.)		

49-2095.00 - Electrical and Electronics Repairers, Powerhouse, Substation, and Relay

Outdoors, Under Cover	How often does this job require working outdoors, under cover (e.g., structure with roof but no walls)?
Degree of Automation	How automated is the job?
Spend Time Climbing Ladders, Scaffolds, or Poles	How much does this job require climbing ladders, scaffolds, or poles?
Spend Time Keeping or Regaining Balance	How much does this job require keeping or regaining your balance?
Exposed to Whole Body Vibration	How often does this job require exposure to whole body vibration (e.g., operate a jackhammer)?
Exposed to Radiation	How often does this job require exposure to radiation?
In an Open Vehicle or Equipment	How often does this job require working in an open vehicle or equipment (e.g., tractor)?
Public Speaking	How often do you have to perform public speaking in this job?
Exposed to Disease or Infections	How often does this job require exposure to disease/infections?
Deal With Physically Aggressive People	How frequently does this job require the worker to deal with physical aggression of violent individuals?

Inspect, test, repair, or maintain electrical equipment in generating stations, substations, and in-service relays.

Tasks

1) Repair, replace, and clean equipment and components such as circuit breakers, brushes, and commutators.

2) Set forms and pour concrete footings for installation of heavy equipment.

3) Inspect and test equipment and circuits to identify malfunctions or defects, using wiring diagrams and testing devices such as ohmmeters, voltmeters, or ammeters.

4) Test insulators and bushings of equipment by inducing voltage across insulation, testing current, and calculating insulation loss.

5) Disconnect voltage regulators, bolts, and screws, and connect replacement regulators to high-voltage lines.

6) Maintain inventories of spare parts for all equipment, requisitioning parts as necessary.

7) Notify facility personnel of equipment shutdowns.

8) Prepare and maintain records detailing tests, repairs, and maintenance.

9) Schedule and supervise splicing or termination of cables in color-code order.

10) Consult manuals, schematics, wiring diagrams, and engineering personnel in order to troubleshoot and solve equipment problems and to determine optimum equipment functioning.

11) Analyze test data in order to diagnose malfunctions, to determine performance characteristics of systems, and to evaluate effects of system modifications.

12) Schedule and supervise the construction and testing of special devices and the implementation of unique monitoring or control systems.

13) Construct, test, maintain, and repair substation relay and control systems.

14) Test oil in circuit breakers and transformers for dielectric strength, refilling oil periodically.

15) Run signal quality and connectivity tests for individual cables, and record results.

Job Zone Component	Job Zone Component Definitions
Title	Job Zone Three: Medium Preparation Needed
Overall Experience	Previous work-related skill, knowledge, or experience is required for these occupations. For example, an electrician must have completed three or four years of apprenticeship or several years of vocational training, and often must have passed a licensing exam, in order to perform the job.
Job Training	Employees in these occupations usually need one or two years of training involving both on-the-job experience and informal training with experienced workers.
Job Zone Examples	These occupations usually involve using communication and organizational skills to coordinate, supervise, manage, or train others to accomplish goals. Examples include dental assistants, electricians, fish and game wardens, legal secretaries, personnel recruiters, and recreation workers.
SVP Range	(6.0 to < 7.0)
Education	Most occupations in this zone require training in vocational schools, related on-the-job experience, or an associate's degree. Some may require a bachelor's degree.

49-2098.00 - Security and Fire Alarm Systems Installers

Install, program, maintain, and repair security and fire alarm wiring and equipment. Ensure that work is in accordance with relevant codes.

Tasks

1) Mount raceways and conduits, and fasten wires to wood framing, using staplers.

2) Test and repair circuits and sensors, following wiring and system specifications.

3) Examine systems to locate problems such as loose connections or broken insulation.

4) Drill holes for wiring in wall studs, joists, ceilings, and floors.

5) Prepare documents such as invoices and warranties.

6) Test backup batteries, keypad programming, sirens, and all security features in order to ensure proper functioning, and to diagnose malfunctions.

7) Mount and fasten control panels, door and window contacts, sensors, and video cameras, and attach electrical and telephone wiring in order to connect components.

8) Provide customers with cost estimates for equipment installation.

9) Order replacement parts.

10) Keep informed of new products and developments.

11) Install, maintain, or repair security systems, alarm devices, and related equipment, following blueprints of electrical layouts and building plans.

12) Inspect installation sites and study work orders, building plans, and installation manuals in order to determine materials requirements and installation procedures.

13) Demonstrate systems for customers, and explain details such as the causes and consequences of false alarms.

14) Feed cables through access holes, roof spaces, and cavity walls to reach fixture outlets; then position and terminate cables, wires and strapping.

15) Consult with clients to assess risks and to determine security requirements.

49-3011.00 - Aircraft Mechanics and Service Technicians

Diagnose, adjust, repair, or overhaul aircraft engines and assemblies, such as hydraulic and pneumatic systems.

Tasks

1) Inspect completed work to certify that maintenance meets standards and that aircraft are ready for operation.

2) Determine repair limits for engine hot section parts.

3) Clean, strip, prime, and sand structural surfaces and materials to prepare them for bonding.

4) Reassemble engines following repair or inspection, and re-install engines in aircraft.

5) Maintain, repair, and rebuild aircraft structures, functional components, and parts such as wings and fuselage, rigging, hydraulic units, oxygen systems, fuel systems, electrical systems, gaskets, and seals.

6) Measure parts for wear, using precision instruments.

7) Measure the tension of control cables.

8) Obtain fuel and oil samples, and check them for contamination.

9) Read and interpret pilots' descriptions of problems in order to diagnose causes.

10) Replace or repair worn, defective, or damaged components, using hand tools, gauges, and testing equipment.

11) Service and maintain aircraft and related apparatus by performing activities such as flushing crankcases, cleaning screens, and lubricating moving parts.

12) Test operation of engines and other systems, using test equipment such as ignition analyzers, compression checkers, distributor timers, and ammeters.

13) Read and interpret maintenance manuals, service bulletins, and other specifications to determine the feasibility and method of repairing or replacing malfunctioning or damaged components.

14) Install and align repaired or replacement parts for subsequent riveting or welding, using clamps and wrenches.

15) Communicate with other workers to coordinate fitting and alignment of heavy parts, or to facilitate processing of repair parts.

16) Remove, inspect, repair, and install in-flight refueling stores and external fuel tanks.

17) Inspect airframes for wear or other defects.

18) Listen to operating engines to detect and diagnose malfunctions such as sticking or burned valves.

19) Assemble and install electrical, plumbing, mechanical, hydraulic, and structural components and accessories, using hand tools and power tools.

20) Check for corrosion, distortion, and invisible cracks in the fuselage, wings, and tail, using x-ray and magnetic inspection equipment.

21) Maintain repair logs, documenting all preventive and corrective aircraft maintenance.

22) Examine engines through specially designed openings while working from ladders or scaffolds, or use hoists or lifts to remove the entire engine from an aircraft.

23) Cure bonded structures, using portable or stationary curing equipment.

24) Accompany aircraft on flights in order to make in-flight adjustments and corrections.

25) Trim and shape replacement body sections to specified sizes and fits, and secure sections in place, using adhesives, hand tools, and power tools.

26) Clean, refuel, and change oil in line service aircraft.

27) Inventory and requisition or order supplies, parts, materials, and equipment.

28) Remove or install aircraft engines, using hoists or forklift trucks.

29) Prepare and paint aircraft surfaces.

30) Examine and inspect aircraft components, including landing gear, hydraulic systems, and de-icers to locate cracks, breaks, leaks, or other problem.

31) Locate and mark dimensions and reference lines on defective or replacement parts, using templates, scribes, compasses, and steel rules.

32) Clean engines, sediment bulk and screens, and carburetors, adjusting carburetor float levels.

33) Modify aircraft structures, space vehicles, systems, or components, following drawings, schematics, charts, engineering orders, and technical publications.

34) Disassemble engines, and inspect parts such as turbine blades and cylinders for corrosion, wear, warping, cracks, and leaks, using precision measuring instruments, x-rays, and magnetic inspection equipment.

35) Fabricate defective sections or parts, using metal fabricating machines, saws, brakes, shears, and grinders.

36) Spread plastic film over areas to be repaired in order to prevent damage to surrounding areas.

37) Conduct routine and special inspections as required by regulations.

49-3021.00 - Automotive Body and Related Repairers

Repair and refinish automotive vehicle bodies and straighten vehicle frames.

Tasks

1) Mix polyester resins and hardeners to be used in restoring damaged areas.

2) Fill small dents that cannot be worked out with plastic or solder.

3) Remove upholstery, accessories, electrical window-and-seat-operating equipment, and trim in order to gain access to vehicle bodies and fenders.

4) Position dolly blocks against surfaces of dented areas and beat opposite surfaces to remove dents, using hammers.

5) Sand body areas to be painted and cover bumpers, windows, and trim with masking tape or paper to protect them from the paint.

6) Cut and tape plastic separating film to outside repair areas in order to avoid damaging surrounding surfaces during repair procedure, and remove tape and wash surfaces after repairs are complete.

7) Remove small pits and dimples in body metal using pick hammers and punches.

8) Adjust or align headlights, wheels, and brake systems.

9) Fit and weld replacement parts into place, using wrenches and welding equipment, and grind down welds to smooth them, using power grinders and other tools.

10) Remove damaged sections of vehicles using metal-cutting guns, air grinders and

wrenches, and install replacement parts using wrenches or welding equipment.

11) Chain or clamp frames and sections to alignment machines that use hydraulic pressure to align damaged components.

12) Prime and paint repaired surfaces, using paint sprayguns and motorized sanders.

13) Clean work areas, using air hoses, in order to remove damaged material and discarded fiberglass strips used in repair procedures.

14) Apply heat to plastic panels, using hot-air welding guns or immersion in hot water, and press the softened panels back into shape by hand.

15) Review damage reports, prepare or review repair cost estimates, and plan work to be performed.

16) Follow supervisors' instructions as to which parts to restore or replace and how much time the job should take.

17) Inspect repaired vehicles for dimensional accuracy and test drive them to ensure proper alignment and handling.

18) Remove damaged panels, and identify the family and properties of the plastic used on a vehicle.

19) Soak fiberglass matting in resin mixtures, and apply layers of matting over repair areas to specified thicknesses.

20) Replace damaged glass on vehicles.

21) Fit and secure windows, vinyl roofs, and metal trim to vehicle bodies, using caulking guns, adhesive brushes, and mallets.

22) Cut openings in vehicle bodies for the installation of customized windows, using templates and power shears or chisels.

23) Read specifications or confer with customers in order to determine the desired custom modifications for altering the appearance of vehicles.

24) Measure and mark vinyl material and cut material to size for roof installation, using rules, straightedges, and hand shears.

Knowledge	Knowledge Definitions
Mechanical	Knowledge of machines and tools, including their designs, uses, repair, and maintenance.
Administration and Management	Knowledge of business and management principles involved in strategic planning, resource allocation, human resources modeling, leadership technique, production methods, and coordination of people and resources.
Customer and Personal Service	Knowledge of principles and processes for providing customer and personal services. This includes customer needs assessment, meeting quality standards for services, and evaluation of customer satisfaction.
English Language	Knowledge of the structure and content of the English language including the meaning and spelling of words, rules of composition, and grammar.
Education and Training	Knowledge of principles and methods for curriculum and training design, teaching and instruction for individuals and groups, and the measurement of training effects.
Chemistry	Knowledge of the chemical composition, structure, and properties of substances and of the chemical processes and transformations that they undergo. This includes uses of chemicals and their interactions, danger signs, production techniques, and disposal methods.
Production and Processing	Knowledge of raw materials, production processes, quality control, costs, and other techniques for maximizing the effective manufacture and distribution of goods.
Sales and Marketing	Knowledge of principles and methods for showing, promoting, and selling products or services. This includes marketing strategy and tactics, product demonstration, sales techniques, and sales control systems.
Building and Construction	Knowledge of materials, methods, and the tools involved in the construction or repair of houses, buildings, or other structures such as highways and roads.
Mathematics	Knowledge of arithmetic, algebra, geometry, calculus, statistics, and their applications.
Transportation	Knowledge of principles and methods for moving people or goods by air, rail, sea, or road, including the relative costs and benefits.
Public Safety and Security	Knowledge of relevant equipment, policies, procedures, and strategies to promote effective local, state, or national security operations for the protection of people, data, property, and institutions.
Clerical	Knowledge of administrative and clerical procedures and systems such as word processing, managing files and records, stenography and transcription, designing forms, and other office procedures and terminology.
Computers and Electronics	Knowledge of circuit boards, processors, chips, electronic equipment, and computer hardware and software, including applications and programming.
Geography	Knowledge of principles and methods for describing the features of land, sea, and air masses, including their physical characteristics, locations, interrelationships, and distribution of plant, animal, and human life.
Law and Government	Knowledge of laws, legal codes, court procedures, precedents, government regulations, executive orders, agency rules, and the democratic political process.
Fine Arts	Knowledge of the theory and techniques required to compose, produce, and perform works of music, dance, visual arts, drama, and sculpture.
Physics	Knowledge and prediction of physical principles, laws, their interrelationships, and applications to understanding fluid, material, and atmospheric dynamics, and mechanical, electrical, atomic and sub- atomic structures and processes.
Design	Knowledge of design techniques, tools, and principles involved in production of precision technical plans, blueprints, drawings, and models.
Engineering and Technology	Knowledge of the practical application of engineering science and technology. This includes applying principles, techniques, procedures, and equipment to the design and production of various goods and services.
Psychology	Knowledge of human behavior and performance; individual differences in ability, personality, and interests; learning and motivation; psychological research methods; and the assessment and treatment of behavioral and affective disorders.
Communications and Media	Knowledge of media production, communication, and dissemination techniques and methods. This includes alternative ways to inform and entertain via written, oral, and visual media.
Economics and Accounting	Knowledge of economic and accounting principles and practices, the financial markets, banking and the analysis and reporting of financial data.
Telecommunications	Knowledge of transmission, broadcasting, switching, control, and operation of telecommunications systems.
Therapy and Counseling	Knowledge of principles, methods, and procedures for diagnosis, treatment, and rehabilitation of physical and mental dysfunctions, and for career counseling and guidance.
Personnel and Human Resources	Knowledge of principles and procedures for personnel recruitment, selection, training, compensation and benefits, labor relations and negotiation, and personnel information systems.
Foreign Language	Knowledge of the structure and content of a foreign (non-English) language including the meaning and spelling of words, rules of composition and grammar, and pronunciation.
Biology	Knowledge of plant and animal organisms, their tissues, cells, functions, interdependencies, and interactions with each other and the environment.
Philosophy and Theology	Knowledge of different philosophical systems and religions. This includes their basic principles, values, ethics, ways of thinking, customs, practices, and their impact on human culture.
Medicine and Dentistry	Knowledge of the information and techniques needed to diagnose and treat human injuries, diseases, and deformities. This includes symptoms, treatment alternatives, drug properties and interactions, and preventive health-care measures.
Sociology and Anthropology	Knowledge of group behavior and dynamics, societal trends and influences, human migrations, ethnicity, cultures and their history and origins.
History and Archeology	Knowledge of historical events and their causes, indicators, and effects on civilizations and cultures.
Food Production	Knowledge of techniques and equipment for planting, growing, and harvesting food products (both plant and animal) for consumption, including storage/handling techniques.

Skills	Skills Definitions
Equipment Selection	Determining the kind of tools and equipment needed to do a job.
Repairing	Repairing machines or systems using the needed tools.
Troubleshooting	Determining causes of operating errors and deciding what to do about it.

Installation	Installing equipment, machines, wiring, or programs to meet specifications.
Learning Strategies	Selecting and using training/instructional methods and procedures appropriate for the situation when learning or teaching new things.
Complex Problem Solving	Identifying complex problems and reviewing related information to develop and evaluate options and implement solutions.
Reading Comprehension	Understanding written sentences and paragraphs in work related documents.
Equipment Maintenance	Performing routine maintenance on equipment and determining when and what kind of maintenance is needed.
Time Management	Managing one's own time and the time of others.
Speaking	Talking to others to convey information effectively.
Critical Thinking	Using logic and reasoning to identify the strengths and weaknesses of alternative solutions, conclusions or approaches to problems.
Social Perceptiveness	Being aware of others' reactions and understanding why they react as they do.
Judgment and Decision Making	Considering the relative costs and benefits of potential actions to choose the most appropriate one.
Monitoring	Monitoring/Assessing performance of yourself, other individuals, or organizations to make improvements or take corrective action.
Mathematics	Using mathematics to solve problems.
Active Learning	Understanding the implications of new information for both current and future problem-solving and decision-making.
Active Listening	Giving full attention to what other people are saying, taking time to understand the points being made, asking questions as appropriate, and not interrupting at inappropriate times.
Systems Evaluation	Identifying measures or indicators of system performance and the actions needed to improve or correct performance, relative to the goals of the system.
Persuasion	Persuading others to change their minds or behavior.
Instructing	Teaching others how to do something.
Quality Control Analysis	Conducting tests and inspections of products, services, or processes to evaluate quality or performance.
Operation and Control	Controlling operations of equipment or systems.
Management of Material Resources	Obtaining and seeing to the appropriate use of equipment, facilities, and materials needed to do certain work.
Negotiation	Bringing others together and trying to reconcile differences.
Coordination	Adjusting actions in relation to others' actions.
Operation Monitoring	Watching gauges, dials, or other indicators to make sure a machine is working properly.
Management of Financial Resources	Determining how money will be spent to get the work done, and accounting for these expenditures.
Operations Analysis	Analyzing needs and product requirements to create a design.
Writing	Communicating effectively in writing as appropriate for the needs of the audience.
Systems Analysis	Determining how a system should work and how changes in conditions, operations, and the environment will affect outcomes.
Management of Personnel Resources	Motivating, developing, and directing people as they work, identifying the best people for the job.
Science	Using scientific rules and methods to solve problems.
Technology Design	Generating or adapting equipment and technology to serve user needs.
Service Orientation	Actively looking for ways to help people.
Programming	Writing computer programs for various purposes.

Ability	**Ability Definitions**
Arm-Hand Steadiness	The ability to keep your hand and arm steady while moving your arm or while holding your arm and hand in one position.
Extent Flexibility	The ability to bend, stretch, twist, or reach with your body, arms, and/or legs.
Near Vision	The ability to see details at close range (within a few feet of the observer).
Control Precision	The ability to quickly and repeatedly adjust the controls of a machine or a vehicle to exact positions.
Problem Sensitivity	The ability to tell when something is wrong or is likely to go wrong. It does not involve solving the problem, only recognizing there is a problem.
Manual Dexterity	The ability to quickly move your hand, your hand together with your arm, or your two hands to grasp, manipulate, or assemble objects.
Selective Attention	The ability to concentrate on a task over a period of time without being distracted.

Oral Expression	The ability to communicate information and ideas in speaking so others will understand.
Oral Comprehension	The ability to listen to and understand information and ideas presented through spoken words and sentences.
Visual Color Discrimination	The ability to match or detect differences between colors, including shades of color and brightness.
Visualization	The ability to imagine how something will look after it is moved around or when its parts are moved or rearranged.
Trunk Strength	The ability to use your abdominal and lower back muscles to support part of the body repeatedly or continuously over time without 'giving out' or fatiguing.
Depth Perception	The ability to judge which of several objects is closer or farther away from you, or to judge the distance between you and an object.
Deductive Reasoning	The ability to apply general rules to specific problems to produce answers that make sense.
Finger Dexterity	The ability to make precisely coordinated movements of the fingers of one or both hands to grasp, manipulate, or assemble very small objects.
Multilimb Coordination	The ability to coordinate two or more limbs (for example, two arms, two legs, or one leg and one arm) while sitting, standing, or lying down. It does not involve performing the activities while the whole body is in motion.
Speech Clarity	The ability to speak clearly so others can understand you.
Inductive Reasoning	The ability to combine pieces of information to form general rules or conclusions (includes finding a relationship among seemingly unrelated events).
Static Strength	The ability to exert maximum muscle force to lift, push, pull, or carry objects.
Hearing Sensitivity	The ability to detect or tell the differences between sounds that vary in pitch and loudness.
Speech Recognition	The ability to identify and understand the speech of another person.
Perceptual Speed	The ability to quickly and accurately compare similarities and differences among sets of letters, numbers, objects, pictures, or patterns. The things to be compared may be presented at the same time or one after the other. This ability also includes comparing a presented object with a remembered object.
Information Ordering	The ability to arrange things or actions in a certain order or pattern according to a specific rule or set of rules (e.g., patterns of numbers, letters, words, pictures, mathematical operations).
Far Vision	The ability to see details at a distance.
Reaction Time	The ability to quickly respond (with the hand, finger, or foot) to a signal (sound, light, picture) when it appears.
Flexibility of Closure	The ability to identify or detect a known pattern (a figure, object, word, or sound) that is hidden in other distracting material.
Dynamic Strength	The ability to exert muscle force repeatedly or continuously over time. This involves muscular endurance and resistance to muscle fatigue.
Response Orientation	The ability to choose quickly between two or more movements in response to two or more different signals (lights, sounds, pictures). It includes the speed with which the correct response is started with the hand, foot, or other body part.
Auditory Attention	The ability to focus on a single source of sound in the presence of other distracting sounds.
Written Comprehension	The ability to read and understand information and ideas presented in writing.
Category Flexibility	The ability to generate or use different sets of rules for combining or grouping things in different ways.
Wrist-Finger Speed	The ability to make fast, simple, repeated movements of the fingers, hands, and wrists.
Time Sharing	The ability to shift back and forth between two or more activities or sources of information (such as speech, sounds, touch, or other sources).
Written Expression	The ability to communicate information and ideas in writing so others will understand.
Rate Control	The ability to time your movements or the movement of a piece of equipment in anticipation of changes in the speed and/or direction of a moving object or scene.
Mathematical Reasoning	The ability to choose the right mathematical methods or formulas to solve a problem.
Stamina	The ability to exert yourself physically over long periods of time without getting winded or out of breath.
Gross Body Coordination	The ability to coordinate the movement of your arms, legs, and torso together when the whole body is in motion.
Speed of Limb Movement	The ability to quickly move the arms and legs.

Gross Body Equilibrium	The ability to keep or regain your body balance or stay upright when in an unstable position.
Speed of Closure	The ability to quickly make sense of, combine, and organize information into meaningful patterns.
Sound Localization	The ability to tell the direction from which a sound originated.
Spatial Orientation	The ability to know your location in relation to the environment or to know where other objects are in relation to you.
Fluency of Ideas	The ability to come up with a number of ideas about a topic (the number of ideas is important, not their quality, correctness, or creativity).
Peripheral Vision	The ability to see objects or movement of objects to one's side when the eyes are looking ahead.
Memorization	The ability to remember information such as words, numbers, pictures, and procedures.
Originality	The ability to come up with unusual or clever ideas about a given topic or situation, or to develop creative ways to solve a problem.
Glare Sensitivity	The ability to see objects in the presence of glare or bright lighting.
Number Facility	The ability to add, subtract, multiply, or divide quickly and correctly.
Night Vision	The ability to see under low light conditions.
Explosive Strength	The ability to use short bursts of muscle force to propel oneself (as in jumping or sprinting), or to throw an object.
Dynamic Flexibility	The ability to quickly and repeatedly bend, stretch, twist, or reach out with your body, arms, and/or legs.

Work_Activity	Work_Activity Definitions
Inspecting Equipment, Structures, or Material	Inspecting equipment, structures, or materials to identify the cause of errors or other problems or defects.
Operating Vehicles, Mechanized Devices, or Equipme	Running, maneuvering, navigating, or driving vehicles or mechanized equipment, such as forklifts, passenger vehicles, aircraft, or water craft.
Getting Information	Observing, receiving, and otherwise obtaining information from all relevant sources.
Establishing and Maintaining Interpersonal Relatio	Developing constructive and cooperative working relationships with others, and maintaining them over time.
Handling and Moving Objects	Using hands and arms in handling, installing, positioning, and moving materials, and manipulating things.
Making Decisions and Solving Problems	Analyzing information and evaluating results to choose the best solution and solve problems.
Updating and Using Relevant Knowledge	Keeping up-to-date technically and applying new knowledge to your job.
Identifying Objects, Actions, and Events	Identifying information by categorizing, estimating, recognizing differences or similarities, and detecting changes in circumstances or events.
Judging the Qualities of Things, Services, or Peop	Assessing the value, importance, or quality of things or people.
Performing General Physical Activities	Performing physical activities that require considerable use of your arms and legs and moving your whole body, such as climbing, lifting, balancing, walking, stooping, and handling of materials.
Controlling Machines and Processes	Using either control mechanisms or direct physical activity to operate machines or processes (not including computers or vehicles).
Monitor Processes, Materials, or Surroundings	Monitoring and reviewing information from materials, events, or the environment, to detect or assess problems.
Organizing, Planning, and Prioritizing Work	Developing specific goals and plans to prioritize, organize, and accomplish your work.
Evaluating Information to Determine Compliance wit	Using relevant information and individual judgment to determine whether events or processes comply with laws, regulations, or standards.
Communicating with Persons Outside Organization	Communicating with people outside the organization, representing the organization to customers, the public, government, and other external sources. This information can be exchanged in person, in writing, or by telephone or e-mail.
Communicating with Supervisors, Peers, or Subordin	Providing information to supervisors, co-workers, and subordinates by telephone, in written form, e-mail, or in person.
Processing Information	Compiling, coding, categorizing, calculating, tabulating, auditing, or verifying information or data.
Estimating the Quantifiable Characteristics of Pro	Estimating sizes, distances, and quantities; or determining time, costs, resources, or materials needed to perform a work activity.

Repairing and Maintaining Mechanical Equipment	Servicing, repairing, adjusting, and testing machines, devices, moving parts, and equipment that operate primarily on the basis of mechanical (not electronic) principles.
Performing for or Working Directly with the Public	Performing for people or dealing directly with the public. This includes serving customers in restaurants and stores, and receiving clients or guests.
Assisting and Caring for Others	Providing personal assistance, medical attention, emotional support, or other personal care to others such as coworkers, customers, or patients.
Monitoring and Controlling Resources	Monitoring and controlling resources and overseeing the spending of money.
Thinking Creatively	Developing, designing, or creating new applications, ideas, relationships, systems, or products, including artistic contributions.
Developing Objectives and Strategies	Establishing long-range objectives and specifying the strategies and actions to achieve them.
Documenting/Recording Information	Entering, transcribing, recording, storing, or maintaining information in written or electronic/magnetic form.
Selling or Influencing Others	Convincing others to buy merchandise/goods or to otherwise change their minds or actions.
Analyzing Data or Information	Identifying the underlying principles, reasons, or facts of information by breaking down information or data into separate parts.
Resolving Conflicts and Negotiating with Others	Handling complaints, settling disputes, and resolving grievances and conflicts, or otherwise negotiating with others.
Performing Administrative Activities	Performing day-to-day administrative tasks such as maintaining information files and processing paperwork.
Scheduling Work and Activities	Scheduling events, programs, and activities, as well as the work of others.
Interpreting the Meaning of Information for Others	Translating or explaining what information means and how it can be used.
Training and Teaching Others	Identifying the educational needs of others, developing formal educational or training programs or classes, and teaching or instructing others.
Developing and Building Teams	Encouraging and building mutual trust, respect, and cooperation among team members.
Coaching and Developing Others	Identifying the developmental needs of others and coaching, mentoring, or otherwise helping others to improve their knowledge or skills.
Provide Consultation and Advice to Others	Providing guidance and expert advice to management or other groups on technical, systems-, or process-related topics.
Repairing and Maintaining Electronic Equipment	Servicing, repairing, calibrating, regulating, fine-tuning, or testing machines, devices, and equipment that operate primarily on the basis of electrical or electronic (not mechanical) principles.
Interacting With Computers	Using computers and computer systems (including hardware and software) to program, write software, set up functions, enter data, or process information.
Drafting, Laying Out, and Specifying Technical Dev	Providing documentation, detailed instructions, drawings, or specifications to tell others about how devices, parts, equipment, or structures are to be fabricated, constructed, assembled, modified, maintained, or used.
Coordinating the Work and Activities of Others	Getting members of a group to work together to accomplish tasks.
Guiding, Directing, and Motivating Subordinates	Providing guidance and direction to subordinates, including setting performance standards and monitoring performance.
Staffing Organizational Units	Recruiting, interviewing, selecting, hiring, and promoting employees in an organization.

Work_Context	Work_Context Definitions
Wear Common Protective or Safety Equipment such as	How much does this job require wearing common protective or safety equipment such as safety shoes, glasses, gloves, hard hats or life jackets?
Spend Time Using Your Hands to Handle, Control, or	How much does this job require using your hands to handle, control, or feel objects, tools or controls?
Spend Time Standing	How much does this job require standing?
Exposed to Contaminants	How often does this job require working exposed to contaminants (such as pollutants, gases, dust or odors)?
Freedom to Make Decisions	How much decision making freedom, without supervision, does the job offer?
Importance of Being Exact or Accurate	How important is being very exact or highly accurate in performing this job?
Spend Time Making Repetitive Motions	How much does this job require making repetitive motions?
Time Pressure	How often does this job require the worker to meet strict deadlines?

Sounds, Noise Levels Are Distracting or Uncomforta	How often does this job require working exposed to sounds and noise levels that are distracting or uncomfortable?
Face-to-Face Discussions	How often do you have to have face-to-face discussions with individuals or teams in this job?
Exposed to Hazardous Equipment	How often does this job require exposure to hazardous equipment?
Structured versus Unstructured Work	To what extent is this job structured for the worker, rather than allowing the worker to determine tasks, priorities, and goals?
Exposed to Minor Burns, Cuts, Bites, or Stings	How often does this job require exposure to minor burns, cuts, bites, or stings?
Spend Time Bending or Twisting the Body	How much does this job require bending or twisting your body?
Importance of Repeating Same Tasks	How important is repeating the same physical activities (e.g., key entry) or mental activities (e.g., checking entries in a ledger) over and over, without stopping, to performing this job?
Spend Time Kneeling, Crouching, Stooping, or Crawl	How much does this job require kneeling, crouching, stooping or crawling?
Frequency of Decision Making	How frequently is the worker required to make decisions that affect other people, the financial resources, and/or the image and reputation of the organization?
Exposed to Hazardous Conditions	How often does this job require exposure to hazardous conditions?
Impact of Decisions on Co-workers or Company Resul	How do the decisions an employee makes impact the results of co-workers, clients or the company?
Level of Competition	To what extent does this job require the worker to compete or to be aware of competitive pressures?
Work With Work Group or Team	How important is it to work with others in a group or team in this job?
Contact With Others	How much does this job require the worker to be in contact with others (face-to-face, by telephone, or otherwise) in order to perform it?
Responsible for Others' Health and Safety	How much responsibility is there for the health and safety of others in this job?
Responsibility for Outcomes and Results	How responsible is the worker for work outcomes and results of other workers?
Telephone	How often do you have telephone conversations in this job?
Cramped Work Space, Awkward Positions	How often does this job require working in cramped work spaces that requires getting into awkward positions?
Wear Specialized Protective or Safety Equipment su	How much does this job require wearing specialized protective or safety equipment such as breathing apparatus, safety harness, full protection suits, or radiation protection?
Spend Time Walking and Running	How much does this job require walking and running?
Coordinate or Lead Others	How important is it to coordinate or lead others in accomplishing work activities in this job?
Very Hot or Cold Temperatures	How often does this job require working in very hot (above 90 F degrees) or very cold (below 32 F degrees) temperatures?
Deal With External Customers	How important is it to work with external customers or the public in this job?
Consequence of Error	How serious would the result usually be if the worker made a mistake that was not readily correctable?
Extremely Bright or Inadequate Lighting	How often does this job require working in extremely bright or inadequate lighting conditions?
Frequency of Conflict Situations	How often are there conflict situations the employee has to face in this job?
Electronic Mail	How often do you use electronic mail in this job?
Indoors, Not Environmentally Controlled	How often does this job require working indoors in non-controlled environmental conditions (e.g., warehouse without heat)?
Spend Time Keeping or Regaining Balance	How much does this job require keeping or regaining your balance?
Indoors, Environmentally Controlled	How often does this job require working indoors in environmentally controlled conditions?
Pace Determined by Speed of Equipment	How important is it to this job that the pace is determined by the speed of equipment or machinery? (This does not refer to keeping busy at all times on this job.)
Physical Proximity	To what extent does this job require the worker to perform job tasks in close physical proximity to other people?
In an Enclosed Vehicle or Equipment	How often does this job require working in a closed vehicle or equipment (e.g., car)?
Letters and Memos	How often does the job require written letters and memos?
Deal With Unpleasant or Angry People	How frequently does the worker have to deal with unpleasant, angry, or discourteous individuals as part of the job requirements?
Spend Time Sitting	How much does this job require sitting?
Degree of Automation	How automated is the job?

In an Open Vehicle or Equipment	How often does this job require working in an open vehicle or equipment (e.g., tractor)?
Outdoors, Exposed to Weather	How often does this job require working outdoors, exposed to all weather conditions?
Exposed to Whole Body Vibration	How often does this job require exposure to whole body vibration (e.g., operate a jackhammer)?
Outdoors, Under Cover	How often does this job require working outdoors, under cover (e.g., structure with roof but no walls)?
Spend Time Climbing Ladders, Scaffolds, or Poles	How much does this job require climbing ladders, scaffolds, or poles?
Deal With Physically Aggressive People	How frequently does this job require the worker to deal with physical aggression of violent individuals?
Public Speaking	How often do you have to perform public speaking in this job?
Exposed to Radiation	How often does this job require exposure to radiation?
Exposed to High Places	How often does this job require exposure to high places?
Exposed to Disease or Infections	How often does this job require exposure to disease/infections?

Job Zone Component	Job Zone Component Definitions
Title	Job Zone Two: Some Preparation Needed
Overall Experience	Some previous work-related skill, knowledge, or experience may be helpful in these occupations, but usually is not needed. For example, a drywall installer might benefit from experience installing drywall, but an inexperienced person could still learn to be an installer with little difficulty.
Job Training	Employees in these occupations need anywhere from a few months to one year of working with experienced employees. These occupations often involve using your knowledge and skills to help others. Examples include drywall installers, fire inspectors, flight attendants, pharmacy technicians, salespersons (retail), and tellers.
Job Zone Examples	
SVP Range	(4.0 to < 6.0)
Education	These occupations usually require a high school diploma and may require some vocational training or job-related course work. In some cases, an associate's or bachelor's degree could be needed.

Work_Styles	Work_Styles Definitions
Attention to Detail	Job requires being careful about detail and thorough in completing work tasks.
Dependability	Job requires being reliable, responsible, and dependable, and fulfilling obligations.
Cooperation	Job requires being pleasant with others on the job and displaying a good-natured, cooperative attitude.
Self Control	Job requires maintaining composure, keeping emotions in check, controlling anger, and avoiding aggressive behavior, even in very difficult situations.
Achievement/Effort	Job requires establishing and maintaining personally challenging achievement goals and exerting effort toward mastering tasks.
Leadership	Job requires a willingness to lead, take charge, and offer opinions and direction.
Integrity	Job requires being honest and ethical.
Persistence	Job requires persistence in the face of obstacles.
Analytical Thinking	Job requires analyzing information and using logic to address work-related issues and problems.
Initiative	Job requires a willingness to take on responsibilities and challenges.
Independence	Job requires developing one's own ways of doing things, guiding oneself with little or no supervision, and depending on oneself to get things done.
Innovation	Job requires creativity and alternative thinking to develop new ideas for and answers to work-related problems.
Concern for Others	Job requires being sensitive to others' needs and feelings and being understanding and helpful on the job.
Stress Tolerance	Job requires accepting criticism and dealing calmly and effectively with high stress situations.
Social Orientation	Job requires preferring to work with others rather than alone, and being personally connected with others on the job.
Adaptability/Flexibility	Job requires being open to change (positive or negative) and to considerable variety in the workplace.

49-3022.00 - Automotive Glass Installers and Repairers

Replace or repair broken windshields and window glass in motor vehicles.

Tasks

1) Install replacement glass in vehicles after old glass has been removed and all necessary preparations have been made.

2) Install rubber-channeling strips around edges of glass or frames in order to weatherproof windows or to prevent rattling.

3) Install new foam dams on pinchwelds if required.

4) Remove broken or damaged glass windshields or window-glass from motor vehicles, using hand tools to remove screws from frames holding glass.

5) Remove all dirt, foreign matter, and loose glass from damaged areas; then apply primer along windshield or window edges and allow it to dry.

6) Hold cut or uneven edges of glass against automated abrasive belts in order to shape or smooth edges.

7) Check for moisture or contamination in damaged areas, dry out any moisture prior to making repairs, and keep damaged areas dry until repairs are complete.

8) Apply a bead of urethane around the perimeter of each pinchweld, and dress the remaining urethane on the pinchwelds so that it is of uniform level and thickness all the way around.

9) Cool or warm glass in the event of temperature extremes.

10) Obtain windshields or windows for specific automobile makes and models from stock, and examine them for defects prior to installation.

11) Prime all scratches on pinchwelds with primer, and allow primed scratches to dry.

12) Cut flat safety glass according to specified patterns, or perform precision pattern-making and glass-cutting to custom-fit replacement windows.

13) Remove all moldings, clips, windshield wipers, screws, bolts, and inside A-pillar moldings; then lower headliners prior to beginning installation or repair work.

14) Replace all moldings, clips, windshield wipers, and any other parts that were removed prior to glass replacement or repair.

15) Replace or adjust motorized or manual window-raising mechanisms.

16) Allow all glass parts installed with urethane ample time to cure, taking temperature and humidity into account.

17) Install, repair, and replace safety glass and related materials, such as backglass heating-elements, on vehicles and equipment.

49-3023.01 - Automotive Master Mechanics

Repair automobiles, trucks, buses, and other vehicles. Master mechanics repair virtually any part on the vehicle or specialize in the transmission system.

Tasks

1) Perform routine and scheduled maintenance services such as oil changes, lubrications, and tune-ups.

2) Repair, reline, replace, and adjust brakes.

3) Install and repair accessories such as radios, heaters, mirrors, and windshield wipers.

4) Test drive vehicles, and test components and systems, using equipment such as infrared engine analyzers, compression gauges, and computerized diagnostic devices.

5) Replace and adjust headlights.

6) Repair and service air conditioning, heating, engine-cooling, and electrical systems.

7) Repair or replace shock absorbers.

8) Test and adjust repaired systems to meet manufacturers' performance specifications.

9) Tear down, repair, and rebuild faulty assemblies such as power systems, steering systems, and linkages.

10) Follow checklists to ensure all important parts are examined, including belts, hoses, steering systems, spark plugs, brake and fuel systems, wheel bearings, and other potentially troublesome areas.

11) Review work orders and discuss work with supervisors.

12) Disassemble units and inspect parts for wear, using micrometers, calipers, and gauges.

13) Plan work procedures, using charts, technical manuals, and experience.

14) Overhaul or replace carburetors, blowers, generators, distributors, starters, and pumps.

15) Rewire ignition systems, lights, and instrument panels.

16) Confer with customers to obtain descriptions of vehicle problems, and to discuss work to be performed and future repair requirements.

17) Repair or replace parts such as pistons, rods, gears, valves, and bearings.

18) Repair radiator leaks.

19) Repair manual and automatic transmissions.

20) Align vehicles' front ends.

21) Rebuild parts such as crankshafts and cylinder blocks.

22) Repair damaged automobile bodies.

Knowledge	Knowledge Definitions
Mechanical	Knowledge of machines and tools, including their designs, uses, repair, and maintenance.
Computers and Electronics	Knowledge of circuit boards, processors, chips, electronic equipment, and computer hardware and software, including applications and programming.
Customer and Personal Service	Knowledge of principles and processes for providing customer and personal services. This includes customer needs assessment, meeting quality standards for services, and evaluation of customer satisfaction.
Education and Training	Knowledge of principles and methods for curriculum and training design, teaching and instruction for individuals and groups, and the measurement of training effects.
Mathematics	Knowledge of arithmetic, algebra, geometry, calculus, statistics, and their applications.
Public Safety and Security	Knowledge of relevant equipment, policies, procedures, and strategies to promote effective local, state, or national security operations for the protection of people, data, property, and institutions.
Engineering and Technology	Knowledge of the practical application of engineering science and technology. This includes applying principles, techniques, procedures, and equipment to the design and production of various goods and services.
Physics	Knowledge and prediction of physical principles, laws, their interrelationships, and applications to understanding fluid, material, and atmospheric dynamics, and mechanical, electrical, atomic and sub-atomic structures and processes.
Chemistry	Knowledge of the chemical composition, structure, and properties of substances and of the chemical processes and transformations that they undergo. This includes uses of chemicals and their interactions, danger signs, production techniques, and disposal methods.
English Language	Knowledge of the structure and content of the English language including the meaning and spelling of words, rules of composition, and grammar.
Transportation	Knowledge of principles and methods for moving people or goods by air, rail, sea, or road, including the relative costs and benefits.
Telecommunications	Knowledge of transmission, broadcasting, switching, control, and operation of telecommunications systems.
Administration and Management	Knowledge of business and management principles involved in strategic planning, resource allocation, human resources modeling, leadership technique, production methods, and coordination of people and resources.
Sales and Marketing	Knowledge of principles and methods for showing, promoting, and selling products or services. This includes marketing strategy and tactics, product demonstration, sales techniques, and sales control systems.
Communications and Media	Knowledge of media production, communication, and dissemination techniques and methods. This includes alternative ways to inform and entertain via written, oral, and visual media.
Psychology	Knowledge of human behavior and performance; individual differences in ability, personality, and interests; learning and motivation; psychological research methods; and the assessment and treatment of behavioral and affective disorders.
Design	Knowledge of design techniques, tools, and principles involved in production of precision technical plans, blueprints, drawings, and models.

Building and Construction	Knowledge of materials, methods, and the tools involved in the construction or repair of houses, buildings, or other structures such as highways and roads.
Economics and Accounting	Knowledge of economic and accounting principles and practices, the financial markets, banking and the analysis and reporting of financial data.
Law and Government	Knowledge of laws, legal codes, court procedures, precedents, government regulations, executive orders, agency rules, and the democratic political process.
Production and Processing	Knowledge of raw materials, production processes, quality control, costs, and other techniques for maximizing the effective manufacture and distribution of goods.
Personnel and Human Resources	Knowledge of principles and procedures for personnel recruitment, selection, training, compensation and benefits, labor relations and negotiation, and personnel information systems.
Clerical	Knowledge of administrative and clerical procedures and systems such as word processing, managing files and records, stenography and transcription, designing forms, and other office procedures and terminology.
Medicine and Dentistry	Knowledge of the information and techniques needed to diagnose and treat human injuries, diseases, and deformities. This includes symptoms, treatment alternatives, drug properties and interactions, and preventive health-care measures.
Foreign Language	Knowledge of the structure and content of a foreign (non-English) language including the meaning and spelling of words, rules of composition and grammar, and pronunciation.
Therapy and Counseling	Knowledge of principles, methods, and procedures for diagnosis, treatment, and rehabilitation of physical and mental dysfunctions, and for career counseling and guidance.
Geography	Knowledge of principles and methods for describing the features of land, sea, and air masses, including their physical characteristics, locations, interrelationships, and distribution of plant, animal, and human life.
History and Archeology	Knowledge of historical events and their causes, indicators, and effects on civilizations and cultures.
Food Production	Knowledge of techniques and equipment for planting, growing, and harvesting food products (both plant and animal) for consumption, including storage/handling techniques.
Philosophy and Theology	Knowledge of different philosophical systems and religions. This includes their basic principles, values, ethics, ways of thinking, customs, practices, and their impact on human culture.
Sociology and Anthropology	Knowledge of group behavior and dynamics, societal trends and influences, human migrations, ethnicity, cultures and their history and origins.
Fine Arts	Knowledge of the theory and techniques required to compose, produce, and perform works of music, dance, visual arts, drama, and sculpture.
Biology	Knowledge of plant and animal organisms, their tissues, cells, functions, interdependencies, and interactions with each other and the environment.

Skills	Skills Definitions
Troubleshooting	Determining causes of operating errors and deciding what to do about it.
Repairing	Repairing machines or systems using the needed tools.
Equipment Selection	Determining the kind of tools and equipment needed to do a job.
Active Learning	Understanding the implications of new information for both current and future problem-solving and decision-making.
Reading Comprehension	Understanding written sentences and paragraphs in work related documents.
Critical Thinking	Using logic and reasoning to identify the strengths and weaknesses of alternative solutions, conclusions or approaches to problems.
Installation	Installing equipment, machines, wiring, or programs to meet specifications.
Complex Problem Solving	Identifying complex problems and reviewing related information to develop and evaluate options and implement solutions.
Active Listening	Giving full attention to what other people are saying, taking time to understand the points being made, asking questions as appropriate, and not interrupting at inappropriate times.
Speaking	Talking to others to convey information effectively.

Learning Strategies	Selecting and using training/instructional methods and procedures appropriate for the situation when learning or teaching new things.
Equipment Maintenance	Performing routine maintenance on equipment and determining when and what kind of maintenance is needed.
Time Management	Managing one's own time and the time of others.
Coordination	Adjusting actions in relation to others' actions.
Writing	Communicating effectively in writing as appropriate for the needs of the audience.
Instructing	Teaching others how to do something.
Mathematics	Using mathematics to solve problems.
Judgment and Decision Making	Considering the relative costs and benefits of potential actions to choose the most appropriate one.
Operation Monitoring	Watching gauges, dials, or other indicators to make sure a machine is working properly.
Operation and Control	Controlling operations of equipment or systems.
Monitoring	Monitoring/Assessing performance of yourself, other individuals, or organizations to make improvements or take corrective action.
Quality Control Analysis	Conducting tests and inspections of products, services, or processes to evaluate quality or performance.
Technology Design	Generating or adapting equipment and technology to serve user needs.
Science	Using scientific rules and methods to solve problems.
Systems Analysis	Determining how a system should work and how changes in conditions, operations, and the environment will affect outcomes.
Systems Evaluation	Identifying measures or indicators of system performance and the actions needed to improve or correct performance, relative to the goals of the system.
Social Perceptiveness	Being aware of others' reactions and understanding why they react as they do.
Operations Analysis	Analyzing needs and product requirements to create a design.
Service Orientation	Actively looking for ways to help people.
Management of Material Resources	Obtaining and seeing to the appropriate use of equipment, facilities, and materials needed to do certain work.
Persuasion	Persuading others to change their minds or behavior.
Negotiation	Bringing others together and trying to reconcile differences.
Management of Financial Resources	Determining how money will be spent to get the work done, and accounting for these expenditures.
Programming	Writing computer programs for various purposes.
Management of Personnel Resources	Motivating, developing, and directing people as they work, identifying the best people for the job.

Ability	Ability Definitions
Problem Sensitivity	The ability to tell when something is wrong or is likely to go wrong. It does not involve solving the problem, only recognizing there is a problem.
Information Ordering	The ability to arrange things or actions in a certain order or pattern according to a specific rule or set of rules (e.g., patterns of numbers, letters, words, pictures, mathematical operations).
Inductive Reasoning	The ability to combine pieces of information to form general rules or conclusions (includes finding a relationship among seemingly unrelated events).
Deductive Reasoning	The ability to apply general rules to specific problems to produce answers that make sense.
Arm-Hand Steadiness	The ability to keep your hand and arm steady while moving your arm or while holding your arm and hand in one position.
Near Vision	The ability to see details at close range (within a few feet of the observer).
Flexibility of Closure	The ability to identify or detect a known pattern (a figure, object, word, or sound) that is hidden in other distracting material.
Manual Dexterity	The ability to quickly move your hand, your hand together with your arm, or your two hands to grasp, manipulate, or assemble objects.
Hearing Sensitivity	The ability to detect or tell the differences between sounds that vary in pitch and loudness.
Finger Dexterity	The ability to make precisely coordinated movements of the fingers of one or both hands to grasp, manipulate, or assemble very small objects.
Oral Comprehension	The ability to listen to and understand information and ideas presented through spoken words and sentences.
Control Precision	The ability to quickly and repeatedly adjust the controls of a machine or a vehicle to exact positions.
Oral Expression	The ability to communicate information and ideas in speaking so others will understand.

Perceptual Speed	The ability to quickly and accurately compare similarities and differences among sets of letters, numbers, objects, pictures, or patterns. The things to be compared may be presented at the same time or one after the other. This ability also includes comparing a presented object with a remembered object.	Wrist-Finger Speed	The ability to make fast, simple, repeated movements of the fingers, hands, and wrists.
Speech Clarity	The ability to speak clearly so others can understand you.	Dynamic Strength	The ability to exert muscle force repeatedly or continuously over time. This involves muscular endurance and resistance to muscle fatigue.
Selective Attention	The ability to concentrate on a task over a period of time without being distracted.	Explosive Strength	The ability to use short bursts of muscle force to propel oneself (as in jumping or sprinting), or to throw an object.
Written Comprehension	The ability to read and understand information and ideas presented in writing.	Dynamic Flexibility	The ability to quickly and repeatedly bend, stretch, twist, or reach out with your body, arms, and/or legs.
Visualization	The ability to imagine how something will look after it is moved around or when its parts are moved or rearranged.		

Work_Activity	Work_Activity Definitions
Speech Recognition — The ability to identify and understand the speech of another person.	Repairing and Maintaining Mechanical Equipment — Servicing, repairing, adjusting, and testing machines, devices, moving parts, and equipment that operate primarily on the basis of mechanical (not electronic) principles.

Auditory Attention	The ability to focus on a single source of sound in the presence of other distracting sounds.
Depth Perception	The ability to judge which of several objects is closer or farther away from you, or to judge the distance between you and an object.
Category Flexibility	The ability to generate or use different sets of rules for combining or grouping things in different ways.
Far Vision	The ability to see details at a distance.
Visual Color Discrimination	The ability to match or detect differences between colors, including shades of color and brightness.
Extent Flexibility	The ability to bend, stretch, twist, or reach with your body, arms, and/or legs.
Multilimb Coordination	The ability to coordinate two or more limbs (for example, two arms, two legs, or one leg and one arm) while sitting, standing, or lying down. It does not involve performing the activities while the whole body is in motion.
Speed of Closure	The ability to quickly make sense of, combine, and organize information into meaningful patterns.
Static Strength	The ability to exert maximum muscle force to lift, push, pull, or carry objects.
Memorization	The ability to remember information such as words, numbers, pictures, and procedures.
Reaction Time	The ability to quickly respond (with the hand, finger, or foot) to a signal (sound, light, picture) when it appears.
Originality	The ability to come up with unusual or clever ideas about a given topic or situation, or to develop creative ways to solve a problem.
Fluency of Ideas	The ability to come up with a number of ideas about a topic (the number of ideas is important, not their quality, correctness, or creativity).
Sound Localization	The ability to tell the direction from which a sound originated.
Response Orientation	The ability to choose quickly between two or more movements in response to two or more different signals (lights, sounds, pictures). It includes the speed with which the correct response is started with the hand, foot, or other body part.
Trunk Strength	The ability to use your abdominal and lower back muscles to support part of the body repeatedly or continuously over time without 'giving out' or fatiguing.
Spatial Orientation	The ability to know your location in relation to the environment or to know where other objects are in relation to you.
Written Expression	The ability to communicate information and ideas in writing so others will understand.
Mathematical Reasoning	The ability to choose the right mathematical methods or formulas to solve a problem.
Time Sharing	The ability to shift back and forth between two or more activities or sources of information (such as speech, sounds, touch, or other sources).
Gross Body Coordination	The ability to coordinate the movement of your arms, legs, and torso together when the whole body is in motion.
Night Vision	The ability to see under low light conditions.
Rate Control	The ability to time your movements or the movement of a piece of equipment in anticipation of changes in the speed and/or direction of a moving object or scene.
Number Facility	The ability to add, subtract, multiply, or divide quickly and correctly.
Peripheral Vision	The ability to see objects or movement of objects to one's side when the eyes are looking ahead.
Glare Sensitivity	The ability to see objects in the presence of glare or bright lighting.
Stamina	The ability to exert yourself physically over long periods of time without getting winded or out of breath.
Gross Body Equilibrium	The ability to keep or regain your body balance or stay upright when in an unstable position.
Speed of Limb Movement	The ability to quickly move the arms and legs.

Making Decisions and Solving Problems	Analyzing information and evaluating results to choose the best solution and solve problems.
Getting Information	Observing, receiving, and otherwise obtaining information from all relevant sources.
Updating and Using Relevant Knowledge	Keeping up-to-date technically and applying new knowledge to your job.
Identifying Objects, Actions, and Events	Identifying information by categorizing, estimating, recognizing differences or similarities, and detecting changes in circumstances or events.
Inspecting Equipment, Structures, or Material	Inspecting equipment, structures, or materials to identify the cause of errors or other problems or defects.
Analyzing Data or Information	Identifying the underlying principles, reasons, or facts of information by breaking down information or data into separate parts.
Operating Vehicles, Mechanized Devices, or Equipme	Running, maneuvering, navigating, or driving vehicles or mechanized equipment, such as forklifts, passenger vehicles, aircraft, or water craft.
Processing Information	Compiling, coding, categorizing, calculating, tabulating, auditing, or verifying information or data.
Communicating with Supervisors, Peers, or Subordin	Providing information to supervisors, co-workers, and subordinates by telephone, in written form, e-mail, or in person.
Interpreting the Meaning of Information for Others	Translating or explaining what information means and how it can be used.
Evaluating Information to Determine Compliance wit	Using relevant information and individual judgment to determine whether events or processes comply with laws, regulations, or standards.
Interacting With Computers	Using computers and computer systems (including hardware and software) to program, write software, set up functions, enter data, or process information.
Monitor Processes, Materials, or Surroundings	Monitoring and reviewing information from materials, events, or the environment, to detect or assess problems.
Handling and Moving Objects	Using hands and arms in handling, installing, positioning, and moving materials, and manipulating things.
Communicating with Persons Outside Organization	Communicating with people outside the organization, representing the organization to customers, the public, government, and other external sources. This information can be exchanged in person, in writing, or by telephone or e-mail.
Controlling Machines and Processes	Using either control mechanisms or direct physical activity to operate machines or processes (not including computers or vehicles).
Repairing and Maintaining Electronic Equipment	Servicing, repairing, calibrating, regulating, fine-tuning, or testing machines, devices, and equipment that operate primarily on the basis of electrical or electronic (not mechanical) principles.
Thinking Creatively	Developing, designing, or creating new applications, ideas, relationships, systems, or products, including artistic contributions.
Estimating the Quantifiable Characteristics of Pro	Estimating sizes, distances, and quantities; or determining time, costs, resources, or materials needed to perform a work activity.
Judging the Qualities of Things, Services, or Peop	Assessing the value, importance, or quality of things or people.
Organizing, Planning, and Prioritizing Work	Developing specific goals and plans to prioritize, organize, and accomplish your work.
Performing General Physical Activities	Performing physical activities that require considerable use of your arms and legs and moving your whole body, such as climbing, lifting, balancing, walking, stooping, and handling of materials.
Selling or Influencing Others	Convincing others to buy merchandise/goods or to otherwise change their minds or actions.

Documenting/Recording Information	Entering, transcribing, recording, storing, or maintaining information in written or electronic/magnetic form.
Establishing and Maintaining Interpersonal Relatio	Developing constructive and cooperative working relationships with others, and maintaining them over time.
Developing Objectives and Strategies	Establishing long-range objectives and specifying the strategies and actions to achieve them.
Training and Teaching Others	Identifying the educational needs of others, developing formal educational or training programs or classes, and teaching or instructing others.
Scheduling Work and Activities	Scheduling events, programs, and activities, as well as the work of others.
Provide Consultation and Advice to Others	Providing guidance and expert advice to management or other groups on technical, systems- or process-related topics.
Resolving Conflicts and Negotiating with Others	Handling complaints, settling disputes, and resolving grievances and conflicts, or otherwise negotiating with others.
Drafting, Laying Out, and Specifying Technical Dev	Providing documentation, detailed instructions, drawings, or specifications to tell others about how devices, parts, equipment, or structures are to be fabricated, constructed, assembled, modified, maintained, or used.
Performing for or Working Directly with the Public	Performing for people or dealing directly with the public. This includes serving customers in restaurants and stores, and receiving clients or guests.
Monitoring and Controlling Resources	Monitoring and controlling resources and overseeing the spending of money.
Assisting and Caring for Others	Providing personal assistance, medical attention, emotional support, or other personal care to others such as coworkers, customers, or patients.
Guiding, Directing, and Motivating Subordinates	Providing guidance and direction to subordinates, including setting performance standards and monitoring performance.
Coaching and Developing Others	Identifying the developmental needs of others and coaching, mentoring, or otherwise helping others to improve their knowledge or skills.
Coordinating the Work and Activities of Others	Getting members of a group to work together to accomplish tasks.
Performing Administrative Activities	Performing day-to-day administrative tasks such as maintaining information files and processing paperwork.
Developing and Building Teams	Encouraging and building mutual trust, respect, and cooperation among team members.
Staffing Organizational Units	Recruiting, interviewing, selecting, hiring, and promoting employees in an organization.

Work_Context	Work_Context Definitions
Exposed to Contaminants	How often does this job require working exposed to contaminants (such as pollutants, gases, dust or odors)?
In an Enclosed Vehicle or Equipment	How often does this job require working in a closed vehicle or equipment (e.g., car)?
Spend Time Using Your Hands to Handle, Control, or	How much does this job require using your hands to handle, control, or feel objects, tools or controls?
Time Pressure	How often does this job require the worker to meet strict deadlines?
Freedom to Make Decisions	How much decision making freedom, without supervision, does the job offer?
Importance of Being Exact or Accurate	How important is being very exact or highly accurate in performing this job?
Spend Time Standing	How much does this job require standing?
Contact With Others	How much does this job require the worker to be in contact with others (face-to-face, by telephone, or otherwise) in order to perform it?
Face-to-Face Discussions	How often do you have to have face-to-face discussions with individuals or teams in this job?
Exposed to Minor Burns, Cuts, Bites, or Stings	How often does this job require exposure to minor burns, cuts, bites, or stings?
Exposed to Hazardous Equipment	How often does this job require exposure to hazardous equipment?
Sounds, Noise Levels Are Distracting or Uncomforta	How often does this job require working exposed to sounds and noise levels that are distracting or uncomfortable?
Cramped Work Space, Awkward Positions	How often does this job require working in cramped work spaces that requires getting into awkward positions?
Wear Common Protective or Safety Equipment such as	How often does this job require wearing common protective or safety equipment such as safety shoes, glasses, gloves, hard hats or live jackets?
Structured versus Unstructured Work	To what extent is this job structured for the worker, rather than allowing the worker to determine tasks, priorities, and goals?
Spend Time Bending or Twisting the Body	How much does this job require bending or twisting your body?

Impact of Decisions on Co-workers or Company Resul	How do the decisions an employee makes impact the results of co-workers, clients or the company?
Frequency of Decision Making	How frequently is the worker required to make decisions that affect other people, the financial resources, and/or the image and reputation of the organization?
Indoors, Not Environmentally Controlled	How often does this job require working indoors in non-controlled environmental conditions (e.g., warehouse without heat)?
Spend Time Making Repetitive Motions	How much does this job require making repetitive motions?
Exposed to Hazardous Conditions	How often does this job require exposure to hazardous conditions?
Telephone	How often do you have telephone conversations in this job?
Deal With External Customers	How important is it to work with external customers or the public in this job?
Deal With Unpleasant or Angry People	How frequently does the worker have to deal with unpleasant, angry, or discourteous individuals as part of the job requirements?
Work With Work Group or Team	How important is it to work with others in a group or team in this job?
Extremely Bright or Inadequate Lighting	How often does this job require working in extremely bright or inadequate lighting conditions?
Very Hot or Cold Temperatures	How often does this job require working in very hot (above 90 F degrees) or very cold (below 32 F degrees) temperatures?
Frequency of Conflict Situations	How often are there conflict situations the employee has to face in this job?
Physical Proximity	To what extent does this job require the worker to perform job tasks in close physical proximity to other people?
Spend Time Kneeling, Crouching, Stooping, or Crawl	How much does this job require kneeling, crouching, stooping or crawling?
Level of Competition	To what extent does this job require the worker to compete or to be aware of competitive pressures?
Indoors, Environmentally Controlled	How often does this job require working indoors in environmentally controlled conditions?
Spend Time Walking and Running	How much does this job require walking and running?
Letters and Memos	How often does the job require written letters and memos?
Responsible for Others' Health and Safety	How much responsibility is there for the health and safety of others in this job?
Coordinate or Lead Others	How important is it to coordinate or lead others in accomplishing work activities in this job?
Outdoors, Exposed to Weather	How often does this job require working outdoors, exposed to all weather conditions?
Importance of Repeating Same Tasks	How important is repeating the same physical activities (e.g., key entry) or mental activities (e.g., checking entries in a ledger) over and over, without stopping, to performing this job?
Responsibility for Outcomes and Results	How responsible is the worker for work outcomes and results of other workers?
Consequence of Error	How serious would the result usually be if the worker made a mistake that was not readily correctable?
Outdoors, Under Cover	How often does this job require working outdoors, under cover (e.g., structure with roof but no walls)?
In an Open Vehicle or Equipment	How often does this job require working in an open vehicle or equipment (e.g., tractor)?
Electronic Mail	How often do you use electronic mail in this job?
Exposed to Whole Body Vibration	How often does this job require exposure to whole body vibration (e.g., operate a jackhammer)?
Spend Time Keeping or Regaining Balance	How much does this job require keeping or regaining your balance?
Deal With Physically Aggressive People	How frequently does this job require the worker to deal with physical aggression of violent individuals?
Pace Determined by Speed of Equipment	How important is it to this job that the pace is determined by the speed of equipment or machinery? (This does not refer to keeping busy at all times on this job.)
Spend Time Sitting	How much does this job require sitting?
Wear Specialized Protective or Safety Equipment su	How much does this job require wearing specialized protective or safety equipment such as breathing apparatus, safety harness, full protection suits, or radiation protection?
Exposed to Disease or Infections	How often does this job require exposure to disease/infections?
Degree of Automation	How automated is the job?
Exposed to High Places	How often does this job require exposure to high places?
Spend Time Climbing Ladders, Scaffolds, or Poles	How much does this job require climbing ladders, scaffolds, or poles?
Public Speaking	How often do you have to perform public speaking in this job?

1099

| Exposed to Radiation | How often does this job require exposure to radiation? |

raise and lower automobile windows, seats, and tops.

5) Align and repair wheels, axles, frames, torsion bars, and steering mechanisms of automobiles, using special alignment equipment and wheel-balancing machines.

6) Rebuild, repair, and test automotive fuel injection units.

7) Repair and rebuild clutch systems.

8) Remove and replace defective mufflers and tailpipes.

9) Repair and replace automobile leaf springs.

10) Repair and replace defective balljoint suspensions, brakeshoes, and wheelbearings.

11) Repair, overhaul, and adjust automobile brake systems.

12) Test electronic computer components in automobiles to ensure that they are working properly.

13) Tune automobile engines to ensure proper and efficient functioning.

14) Repair, replace, and adjust defective carburetor parts and gasoline filters.

15) Install and repair air conditioners, and service components such as compressors, condensers, and controls.

Job Zone Component	Job Zone Component Definitions
Title	Job Zone Three: Medium Preparation Needed
Overall Experience	Previous work-related skill, knowledge, or experience is required for these occupations. For example, an electrician must have completed three or four years of apprenticeship or several years of vocational training, and often must have passed a licensing exam, in order to perform the job.
Job Training	Employees in these occupations usually need one or two years of training involving both on-the-job experience and informal training with experienced workers.
Job Zone Examples	These occupations usually involve using communication and organizational skills to coordinate, supervise, manage, or train others to accomplish goals. Examples include dental assistants, electricians, fish and game wardens, legal secretaries, personnel recruiters, and recreation workers.
SVP Range	(6.0 to < 7.0)
Education	Most occupations in this zone require training in vocational schools, related on-the-job experience, or an associate's degree. Some may require a bachelor's degree.

49-3031.00 - Bus and Truck Mechanics and Diesel Engine Specialists

Diagnose, adjust, repair, or overhaul trucks, buses, and all types of diesel engines. Includes mechanics working primarily with automobile diesel engines.

Tasks

1) Inspect, test, and listen to defective equipment to diagnose malfunctions, using test instruments such as handheld computers, motor analyzers, chassis charts, and pressure gauges.

2) Raise trucks, buses, and heavy parts or equipment using hydraulic jacks or hoists.

3) Examine and adjust protective guards, loose bolts, and specified safety devices.

4) Perform routine maintenance such as changing oil, checking batteries, and lubricating equipment and machinery.

5) Adjust and reline brakes, align wheels, tighten bolts and screws, and reassemble equipment.

6) Test drive trucks and buses to diagnose malfunctions or to ensure that they are working properly.

7) Inspect and verify dimensions and clearances of parts to ensure conformance to factory specifications.

8) Inspect brake systems, steering mechanisms, wheel bearings, and other important parts to ensure that they are in proper operating condition.

9) Repair and adjust seats, doors, and windows, and install and repair accessories.

10) Specialize in repairing and maintaining parts of the engine, such as fuel injection systems.

11) Rewire ignition systems, lights, and instrument panels.

12) Recondition and replace parts, pistons, bearings, gears, and valves.

13) Disassemble and overhaul internal combustion engines, pumps, generators, transmissions, clutches, and differential units.

14) Inspect, repair, and maintain automotive and mechanical equipment and machinery such as pumps and compressors.

15) Rebuild gas and/or diesel engines.

16) Align front ends and suspension systems.

17) Operate valve-grinding machines to grind and reset valves.

18) Use handtools such as screwdrivers, pliers, wrenches, pressure gauges, and precision instruments, as well as power tools such as pneumatic wrenches, lathes, welding equipment, and jacks and hoists.

Work_Styles	Work_Styles Definitions
Attention to Detail	Job requires being careful about detail and thorough in completing work tasks.
Persistence	Job requires persistence in the face of obstacles.
Cooperation	Job requires being pleasant with others on the job and displaying a good-natured, cooperative attitude.
Integrity	Job requires being honest and ethical.
Analytical Thinking	Job requires analyzing information and using logic to address work-related issues and problems.
Self Control	Job requires maintaining composure, keeping emotions in check, controlling anger, and avoiding aggressive behavior, even in very difficult situations.
Innovation	Job requires creativity and alternative thinking to develop new ideas for and answers to work-related problems.
Achievement/Effort	Job requires establishing and maintaining personally challenging achievement goals and exerting effort toward mastering tasks.
Initiative	Job requires a willingness to take on responsibilities and challenges.
Dependability	Job requires being reliable, responsible, and dependable, and fulfilling obligations.
Independence	Job requires developing one's own ways of doing things, guiding oneself with little or no supervision, and depending on oneself to get things done.
Adaptability/Flexibility	Job requires being open to change (positive or negative) and to considerable variety in the workplace.
Stress Tolerance	Job requires accepting criticism and dealing calmly and effectively with high stress situations.
Concern for Others	Job requires being sensitive to others' needs and feelings and being understanding and helpful on the job.
Social Orientation	Job requires preferring to work with others rather than alone, and being personally connected with others on the job.
Leadership	Job requires a willingness to lead, take charge, and offer opinions and direction.

49-3023.02 - Automotive Specialty Technicians

Repair only one system or component on a vehicle, such as brakes, suspension, or radiator.

Tasks

1) Examine vehicles, compile estimates of repair costs, and secure customers' approval to perform repairs.

2) Convert vehicle fuel systems from gasoline to butane gas operations, and repair and service operating butane fuel units.

3) Use electronic test equipment to locate and correct malfunctions in fuel, ignition, and emissions control systems.

4) Repair, install, and adjust hydraulic and electromagnetic automatic lift mechanisms used to

Knowledge	Knowledge Definitions
Mechanical	Knowledge of machines and tools, including their designs, uses, repair, and maintenance.
Transportation	Knowledge of principles and methods for moving people or goods by air, rail, sea, or road, including the relative costs and benefits.

Public Safety and Security	Knowledge of relevant equipment, policies, procedures, and strategies to promote effective local, state, or national security operations for the protection of people, data, property, and institutions.
Engineering and Technology	Knowledge of the practical application of engineering science and technology. This includes applying principles, techniques, procedures, and equipment to the design and production of various goods and services.
English Language	Knowledge of the structure and content of the English language including the meaning and spelling of words, rules of composition, and grammar.
Law and Government	Knowledge of laws, legal codes, court procedures, precedents, government regulations, executive orders, agency rules, and the democratic political process.
Customer and Personal Service	Knowledge of principles and processes for providing customer and personal services. This includes customer needs assessment, meeting quality standards for services, and evaluation of customer satisfaction.
Education and Training	Knowledge of principles and methods for curriculum and training design, teaching and instruction for individuals and groups, and the measurement of training effects.
Mathematics	Knowledge of arithmetic, algebra, geometry, calculus, statistics, and their applications.
Physics	Knowledge and prediction of physical principles, laws, their interrelationships, and applications to understanding fluid, material, and atmospheric dynamics, and mechanical, electrical, atomic and sub-atomic structures and processes.
Production and Processing	Knowledge of raw materials, production processes, quality control, costs, and other techniques for maximizing the effective manufacture and distribution of goods.
Chemistry	Knowledge of the chemical composition, structure, and properties of substances and of the chemical processes and transformations that they undergo. This includes uses of chemicals and their interactions, danger signs, production techniques, and disposal methods.
Computers and Electronics	Knowledge of circuit boards, processors, chips, electronic equipment, and computer hardware and software, including applications and programming.
Clerical	Knowledge of administrative and clerical procedures and systems such as word processing, managing files and records, stenography and transcription, designing forms, and other office procedures and terminology.
Design	Knowledge of design techniques, tools, and principles involved in production of precision technical plans, blueprints, drawings, and models.
Administration and Management	Knowledge of business and management principles involved in strategic planning, resource allocation, human resources modeling, leadership technique, production methods, and coordination of people and resources.
Psychology	Knowledge of human behavior and performance; individual differences in ability, personality, and interests; learning and motivation; psychological research methods; and the assessment and treatment of behavioral and affective disorders.
Medicine and Dentistry	Knowledge of the information and techniques needed to diagnose and treat human injuries, diseases, and deformities. This includes symptoms, treatment alternatives, drug properties and interactions, and preventive health-care measures.
Geography	Knowledge of principles and methods for describing the features of land, sea, and air masses, including their physical characteristics, locations, interrelationships, and distribution of plant, animal, and human life.
Telecommunications	Knowledge of transmission, broadcasting, switching, control, and operation of telecommunications systems.
Communications and Media	Knowledge of media production, communication, and dissemination techniques and methods. This includes alternative ways to inform and entertain via written, oral, and visual media.
Personnel and Human Resources	Knowledge of principles and procedures for personnel recruitment, selection, training, compensation and benefits, labor relations and negotiation, and personnel information systems.
Building and Construction	Knowledge of materials, methods, and the tools involved in the construction or repair of houses, buildings, or other structures such as highways and roads.
Economics and Accounting	Knowledge of economic and accounting principles and practices, the financial markets, banking and the analysis and reporting of financial data.

Philosophy and Theology	Knowledge of different philosophical systems and religions. This includes their basic principles, values, ethics, ways of thinking, customs, practices, and their impact on human culture.
Foreign Language	Knowledge of the structure and content of a foreign (non-English) language including the meaning and spelling of words, rules of composition and grammar, and pronunciation.
Sociology and Anthropology	Knowledge of group behavior and dynamics, societal trends and influences, human migrations, ethnicity, cultures and their history and origins.
Therapy and Counseling	Knowledge of principles, methods, and procedures for diagnosis, treatment, and rehabilitation of physical and mental dysfunctions, and for career counseling and guidance.
History and Archeology	Knowledge of historical events and their causes, indicators, and effects on civilizations and cultures.
Sales and Marketing	Knowledge of principles and methods for showing, promoting, and selling products or services. This includes marketing strategy and tactics, product demonstration, sales techniques, and sales control systems.
Food Production	Knowledge of techniques and equipment for planting, growing, and harvesting food products (both plant and animal) for consumption, including storage/handling techniques.
Biology	Knowledge of plant and animal organisms, their tissues, cells, functions, interdependencies, and interactions with each other and the environment.
Fine Arts	Knowledge of the theory and techniques required to compose, produce, and perform works of music, dance, visual arts, drama, and sculpture.

Skills	Skills Definitions
Equipment Maintenance	Performing routine maintenance on equipment and determining when and what kind of maintenance is needed.
Troubleshooting	Determining causes of operating errors and deciding what to do about it.
Repairing	Repairing machines or systems using the needed tools.
Reading Comprehension	Understanding written sentences and paragraphs in work related documents.
Installation	Installing equipment, machines, wiring, or programs to meet specifications.
Equipment Selection	Determining the kind of tools and equipment needed to do a job.
Coordination	Adjusting actions in relation to others' actions.
Judgment and Decision Making	Considering the relative costs and benefits of potential actions to choose the most appropriate one.
Active Listening	Giving full attention to what other people are saying, taking time to understand the points being made, asking questions as appropriate, and not interrupting at inappropriate times.
Time Management	Managing one's own time and the time of others.
Learning Strategies	Selecting and using training/instructional methods and procedures appropriate for the situation when learning or teaching new things.
Social Perceptiveness	Being aware of others' reactions and understanding why they react as they do.
Active Learning	Understanding the implications of new information for both current and future problem-solving and decision-making.
Instructing	Teaching others how to do something.
Speaking	Talking to others to convey information effectively.
Writing	Communicating effectively in writing as appropriate for the needs of the audience.
Critical Thinking	Using logic and reasoning to identify the strengths and weaknesses of alternative solutions, conclusions or approaches to problems.
Complex Problem Solving	Identifying complex problems and reviewing related information to develop and evaluate options and implement solutions.
Monitoring	Monitoring/Assessing performance of yourself, other individuals, or organizations to make improvements or take corrective action.
Mathematics	Using mathematics to solve problems.
Science	Using scientific rules and methods to solve problems.
Systems Analysis	Determining how a system should work and how changes in conditions, operations, and the environment will affect outcomes.
Technology Design	Generating or adapting equipment and technology to serve user needs.
Service Orientation	Actively looking for ways to help people.
Negotiation	Bringing others together and trying to reconcile differences.

Systems Evaluation	Identifying measures or indicators of system performance and the actions needed to improve or correct performance, relative to the goals of the system.
Operation and Control	Controlling operations of equipment or systems.
Quality Control Analysis	Conducting tests and inspections of products, services, or processes to evaluate quality or performance.
Persuasion	Persuading others to change their minds or behavior.
Operation Monitoring	Watching gauges, dials, or other indicators to make sure a machine is working properly.
Management of Material Resources	Obtaining and seeing to the appropriate use of equipment, facilities, and materials needed to do certain work.
Management of Personnel Resources	Motivating, developing, and directing people as they work, identifying the best people for the job.
Operations Analysis	Analyzing needs and product requirements to create a design.
Management of Financial Resources	Determining how money will be spent to get the work done, and accounting for these expenditures.
Programming	Writing computer programs for various purposes.

Ability	Ability Definitions
Problem Sensitivity	The ability to tell when something is wrong or is likely to go wrong. It does not involve solving the problem, only recognizing there is a problem.
Manual Dexterity	The ability to quickly move your hand, your hand together with your arm, or your two hands to grasp, manipulate, or assemble objects.
Multilimb Coordination	The ability to coordinate two or more limbs (for example, two arms, two legs, or one leg and one arm) while sitting, standing, or lying down. It does not involve performing the activities while the whole body is in motion.
Near Vision	The ability to see details at close range (within a few feet of the observer).
Control Precision	The ability to quickly and repeatedly adjust the controls of a machine or a vehicle to exact positions.
Oral Comprehension	The ability to listen to and understand information and ideas presented through spoken words and sentences.
Arm-Hand Steadiness	The ability to keep your hand and arm steady while moving your arm or while holding your arm and hand in one position.
Oral Expression	The ability to communicate information and ideas in speaking so others will understand.
Inductive Reasoning	The ability to combine pieces of information to form general rules or conclusions (includes finding a relationship among seemingly unrelated events).
Hearing Sensitivity	The ability to detect or tell the differences between sounds that vary in pitch and loudness.
Finger Dexterity	The ability to make precisely coordinated movements of the fingers of one or both hands to grasp, manipulate, or assemble very small objects.
Selective Attention	The ability to concentrate on a task over a period of time without being distracted.
Information Ordering	The ability to arrange things or actions in a certain order or pattern according to a specific rule or set of rules (e.g., patterns of numbers, letters, words, pictures, mathematical operations).
Trunk Strength	The ability to use your abdominal and lower back muscles to support part of the body repeatedly or continuously over time without 'giving out' or fatiguing.
Deductive Reasoning	The ability to apply general rules to specific problems to produce answers that make sense.
Visualization	The ability to imagine how something will look after it is moved around or when its parts are moved or rearranged.
Extent Flexibility	The ability to bend, stretch, twist, or reach with your body, arms, and/or legs.
Auditory Attention	The ability to focus on a single source of sound in the presence of other distracting sounds.
Speech Clarity	The ability to speak clearly so others can understand you.
Static Strength	The ability to exert maximum muscle force to lift, push, pull, or carry objects.
Depth Perception	The ability to judge which of several objects is closer or farther away from you, or to judge the distance between you and an object.
Speech Recognition	The ability to identify and understand the speech of another person.
Flexibility of Closure	The ability to identify or detect a known pattern (a figure, object, word, or sound) that is hidden in other distracting material.
Gross Body Equilibrium	The ability to keep or regain your body balance or stay upright when in an unstable position.

Visual Color Discrimination	The ability to match or detect differences between colors, including shades of color and brightness.
Gross Body Coordination	The ability to coordinate the movement of your arms, legs, and torso together when the whole body is in motion.
Speed of Closure	The ability to quickly make sense of, combine, and organize information into meaningful patterns.
Glare Sensitivity	The ability to see objects in the presence of glare or bright lighting.
Written Expression	The ability to communicate information and ideas in writing so others will understand.
Written Comprehension	The ability to read and understand information and ideas presented in writing.
Time Sharing	The ability to shift back and forth between two or more activities or sources of information (such as speech, sounds, touch, or other sources).
Reaction Time	The ability to quickly respond (with the hand, finger, or foot) to a signal (sound, light, picture) when it appears.
Category Flexibility	The ability to generate or use different sets of rules for combining or grouping things in different ways.
Dynamic Strength	The ability to exert muscle force repeatedly or continuously over time. This involves muscular endurance and resistance to muscle fatigue.
Stamina	The ability to exert yourself physically over long periods of time without getting winded or out of breath.
Memorization	The ability to remember information such as words, numbers, pictures, and procedures.
Perceptual Speed	The ability to quickly and accurately compare similarities and differences among sets of letters, numbers, objects, pictures, or patterns. The things to be compared may be presented at the same time or one after the other. This ability also includes comparing a presented object with a remembered object.
Sound Localization	The ability to tell the direction from which a sound originated.
Far Vision	The ability to see details at a distance.
Spatial Orientation	The ability to know your location in relation to the environment or to know where other objects are in relation to you.
Response Orientation	The ability to choose quickly between two or more movements in response to two or more different signals (lights, sounds, pictures). It includes the speed with which the correct response is started with the hand, foot, or other body part.
Peripheral Vision	The ability to see objects or movement of objects to one's side when the eyes are looking ahead.
Speed of Limb Movement	The ability to quickly move the arms and legs.
Rate Control	The ability to time your movements or the movement of a piece of equipment in anticipation of changes in the speed and/or direction of a moving object or scene.
Wrist-Finger Speed	The ability to make fast, simple, repeated movements of the fingers, hands, and wrists.
Fluency of Ideas	The ability to come up with a number of ideas about a topic (the number of ideas is important, not their quality, correctness, or creativity).
Mathematical Reasoning	The ability to choose the right mathematical methods or formulas to solve a problem.
Originality	The ability to come up with unusual or clever ideas about a given topic or situation, or to develop creative ways to solve a problem.
Night Vision	The ability to see under low light conditions.
Explosive Strength	The ability to use short bursts of muscle force to propel oneself (as in jumping or sprinting), or to throw an object.
Dynamic Flexibility	The ability to quickly and repeatedly bend, stretch, twist, or reach out with your body, arms, and/or legs.
Number Facility	The ability to add, subtract, multiply, or divide quickly and correctly.

Work_Activity	Work_Activity Definitions
Repairing and Maintaining Mechanical Equipment	Servicing, repairing, adjusting, and testing machines, devices, moving parts, and equipment that operate primarily on the basis of mechanical (not electronic) principles.
Inspecting Equipment, Structures, or Material	Inspecting equipment, structures, or materials to identify the cause of errors or other problems or defects.
Operating Vehicles, Mechanized Devices, or Equipme	Running, maneuvering, navigating, or driving vehicles or mechanized equipment, such as forklifts, passenger vehicles, aircraft, or water craft.
Handling and Moving Objects	Using hands and arms in handling, installing, positioning, and moving materials, and manipulating things.
Getting Information	Observing, receiving, and otherwise obtaining information from all relevant sources.

Performing General Physical Activities	Performing physical activities that require considerable use of your arms and legs and moving your whole body, such as climbing, lifting, balancing, walking, stooping, and handling of materials.
Communicating with Supervisors, Peers, or Subordin	Providing information to supervisors, co-workers, and subordinates by telephone, in written form, e-mail, or in person.
Identifying Objects, Actions, and Events	Identifying information by categorizing, estimating, recognizing differences or similarities, and detecting changes in circumstances or events.
Updating and Using Relevant Knowledge	Keeping up-to-date technically and applying new knowledge to your job.
Establishing and Maintaining Interpersonal Relatio	Developing constructive and cooperative working relationships with others, and maintaining them over time.
Making Decisions and Solving Problems	Analyzing information and evaluating results to choose the best solution and solve problems.
Monitor Processes, Materials, or Surroundings	Monitoring and reviewing information from materials, events, or the environment, to detect or assess problems.
Interpreting the Meaning of Information for Others	Translating or explaining what information means and how it can be used.
Controlling Machines and Processes	Using either control mechanisms or direct physical activity to operate machines or processes (not including computers or vehicles).
Evaluating Information to Determine Compliance wit	Using relevant information and individual judgment to determine whether events or processes comply with laws, regulations, or standards.
Coaching and Developing Others	Identifying the developmental needs of others and coaching, mentoring, or otherwise helping others to improve their knowledge or skills.
Documenting/Recording Information	Entering, transcribing, recording, storing, or maintaining information in written or electronic/magnetic form.
Judging the Qualities of Things, Services, or Peop	Assessing the value, importance, or quality of things or people.
Repairing and Maintaining Electronic Equipment	Servicing, repairing, calibrating, regulating, fine-tuning, or testing machines, devices, and equipment that operate primarily on the basis of electrical or electronic (not mechanical) principles.
Organizing, Planning, and Prioritizing Work	Developing specific goals and plans to prioritize, organize, and accomplish your work.
Estimating the Quantifiable Characteristics of Pro	Estimating sizes, distances, and quantities; or determining time, costs, resources, or materials needed to perform a work activity.
Assisting and Caring for Others	Providing personal assistance, medical attention, emotional support, or other personal care to others such as coworkers, customers, or patients.
Processing Information	Compiling, coding, categorizing, calculating, tabulating, auditing, or verifying information or data.
Analyzing Data or Information	Identifying the underlying principles, reasons, or facts of information by breaking down information or data into separate parts.
Developing and Building Teams	Encouraging and building mutual trust, respect, and cooperation among team members.
Training and Teaching Others	Identifying the educational needs of others, developing formal educational or training programs or classes, and teaching or instructing others.
Resolving Conflicts and Negotiating with Others	Handling complaints, settling disputes, and resolving grievances and conflicts, or otherwise negotiating with others.
Interacting With Computers	Using computers and computer systems (including hardware and software) to program, write software, set up functions, enter data, or process information.
Provide Consultation and Advice to Others	Providing guidance and expert advice to management or other groups on technical, systems-, or process-related topics.
Thinking Creatively	Developing, designing, or creating new applications, ideas, relationships, systems, or products, including artistic contributions.
Monitoring and Controlling Resources	Monitoring and controlling resources and overseeing the spending of money.
Guiding, Directing, and Motivating Subordinates	Providing guidance and direction to subordinates, including setting performance standards and monitoring performance.
Communicating with Persons Outside Organization	Communicating with people outside the organization, representing the organization to customers, the public, government, and other external sources. This information can be exchanged in person, in writing, or by telephone or e-mail.
Scheduling Work and Activities	Scheduling events, programs, and activities, as well as the work of others.
Coordinating the Work and Activities of Others	Getting members of a group to work together to accomplish tasks.
Performing Administrative Activities	Performing day-to-day administrative tasks such as maintaining information files and processing paperwork.
Developing Objectives and Strategies	Establishing long-range objectives and specifying the strategies and actions to achieve them.
Performing for or Working Directly with the Public	Performing for people or dealing directly with the public. This includes serving customers in restaurants and stores, and receiving clients or guests.
Selling or Influencing Others	Convincing others to buy merchandise/goods or to otherwise change their minds or actions.
Drafting, Laying Out, and Specifying Technical Dev	Providing documentation, detailed instructions, drawings, or specifications to tell others about how devices, parts, equipment, or structures are to be fabricated, constructed, assembled, modified, maintained, or used.
Staffing Organizational Units	Recruiting, interviewing, selecting, hiring, and promoting employees in an organization.

Work_Context	Work_Context Definitions
Exposed to Contaminants	How often does this job require working exposed to contaminants (such as pollutants, gases, dust or odors)?
Spend Time Using Your Hands to Handle, Control, or	How much does this job require using your hands to handle, control, or feel objects, tools or controls?
Wear Common Protective or Safety Equipment such as	How much does this job require wearing common protective or safety equipment such as safety shoes, glasses, gloves, hard hats or life jackets?
Sounds, Noise Levels Are Distracting or Uncomforta	How often does this job require working exposed to sounds and noise levels that are distracting or uncomfortable?
Indoors, Not Environmentally Controlled	How often does this job require working indoors in non-controlled environmental conditions (e.g., warehouse without heat)?
Exposed to Hazardous Equipment	How often does this job require exposure to hazardous equipment?
Extremely Bright or Inadequate Lighting	How often does this job require working in extremely bright or inadequate lighting conditions?
Spend Time Standing	How much does this job require standing?
Exposed to Minor Burns, Cuts, Bites, or Stings	How often does this job require exposure to minor burns, cuts, bites, or stings?
Freedom to Make Decisions	How much decision making freedom, without supervision, does the job offer?
Outdoors, Exposed to Weather	How often does this job require working outdoors, exposed to all weather conditions?
Importance of Being Exact or Accurate	How important is being very exact or highly accurate in performing this job?
Contact With Others	How much does this job require the worker to be in contact with others (face-to-face, by telephone, or otherwise) in order to perform it?
Face-to-Face Discussions	How often do you have to have face-to-face discussions with individuals or teams in this job?
In an Open Vehicle or Equipment	How often does this job require working in an open vehicle or equipment (e.g., tractor)?
Cramped Work Space, Awkward Positions	How often does this job require working in cramped work spaces that requires getting into awkward positions?
Structured versus Unstructured Work	To what extent is this job structured for the worker, rather than allowing the worker to determine tasks, priorities, and goals?
Spend Time Making Repetitive Motions	How much does this job require making repetitive motions?
Exposed to Hazardous Conditions	How often does this job require exposure to hazardous conditions?
Spend Time Bending or Twisting the Body	How much does this job require bending or twisting your body?
Impact of Decisions on Co-workers or Company Resul	How do the decisions an employee makes impact the results of co-workers, clients or the company?
Frequency of Decision Making	How frequently is the worker required to make decisions that affect other people, the financial resources, and/or the image and reputation of the organization?
Very Hot or Cold Temperatures	How often does this job require working in very hot (above 90 F degrees) or very cold (below 32 F degrees) temperatures?
Outdoors, Under Cover	How often does this job require working outdoors, under cover (e.g., structure with roof but no walls)?
In an Enclosed Vehicle or Equipment	How often does this job require working in a closed vehicle or equipment (e.g., car)?
Telephone	How often do you have telephone conversations in this job?
Time Pressure	How often does this job require the worker to meet strict deadlines?

Responsible for Others' Health and Safety	How much responsibility is there for the health and safety of others in this job?
Importance of Repeating Same Tasks	How important is repeating the same physical activities (e.g., key entry) or mental activities (e.g., checking entries in a ledger) over and over, without stopping, to performing this job?
Consequence of Error	How serious would the result usually be if the worker made a mistake that was not readily correctable?
Physical Proximity	To what extent does this job require the worker to perform job tasks in close physical proximity to other people?
Spend Time Kneeling, Crouching, Stooping, or Crawl	How much does this job require kneeling, crouching, stooping or crawling?
Work With Work Group or Team	How important is it to work with others in a group or team in this job?
Responsibility for Outcomes and Results	How responsible is the worker for work outcomes and results of other workers?
Spend Time Keeping or Regaining Balance	How much does this job require keeping or regaining your balance?
Exposed to High Places	How often does this job require exposure to high places?
Coordinate or Lead Others	How important is it to coordinate or lead others in accomplishing work activities in this job?
Exposed to Disease or Infections	How often does this job require exposure to disease/infections?
Spend Time Walking and Running	How much does this job require walking and running?
Exposed to Whole Body Vibration	How often does this job require exposure to whole body vibration (e.g., operate a jackhammer)?
Deal With Unpleasant or Angry People	How frequently does the worker have to deal with unpleasant, angry, or discourteous individuals as part of the job requirements?
Frequency of Conflict Situations	How often are there conflict situations the employee has to face in this job?
Letters and Memos	How often does the job require written letters and memos?
Electronic Mail	How often do you use electronic mail in this job?
Level of Competition	To what extent does this job require the worker to compete or to be aware of competitive pressures?
Spend Time Sitting	How much does this job require sitting?
Pace Determined by Speed of Equipment	How important is it to this job that the pace is determined by the speed of equipment or machinery? (This does not refer to keeping busy at all times on this job.)
Deal With External Customers	How important is it to work with external customers or the public in this job?
Spend Time Climbing Ladders, Scaffolds, or Poles	How much does this job require climbing ladders, scaffolds, or poles?
Indoors, Environmentally Controlled	How often does this job require working indoors in environmentally controlled conditions?
Exposed to Radiation	How often does this job require exposure to radiation?
Wear Specialized Protective or Safety Equipment su	How much does this job require wearing specialized protective or safety equipment such as breathing apparatus, safety harness, full protection suits, or radiation protection?
Degree of Automation	How automated is the job?
Deal With Physically Aggressive People	How frequently does this job require the worker to deal with physical aggression of violent individuals?
Public Speaking	How often do you have to perform public speaking in this job?

Job Zone Component	Job Zone Component Definitions
Title	Job Zone Three: Medium Preparation Needed
Overall Experience	Previous work-related skill, knowledge, or experience is required for these occupations. For example, an electrician must have completed three or four years of apprenticeship or several years of vocational training, and often must have passed a licensing exam, in order to perform the job.
Job Training	Employees in these occupations usually need one or two years of training involving both on-the-job experience and informal training with experienced workers.
Job Zone Examples	These occupations usually involve using communication and organizational skills to coordinate, supervise, manage, or train others to accomplish goals. Examples include dental assistants, electricians, fish and game wardens, legal secretaries, personnel recruiters, and recreation workers.
SVP Range	(6.0 to < 7.0)
Education	Most occupations in this zone require training in vocational schools, related on-the-job experience, or an associate's degree. Some may require a bachelor's degree.

Work_Styles	Work_Styles Definitions
Dependability	Job requires being reliable, responsible, and dependable, and fulfilling obligations.
Attention to Detail	Job requires being careful about detail and thorough in completing work tasks.
Independence	Job requires developing one's own ways of doing things, guiding oneself with little or no supervision, and depending on oneself to get things done.
Cooperation	Job requires being pleasant with others on the job and displaying a good-natured, cooperative attitude.
Integrity	Job requires being honest and ethical.
Self Control	Job requires maintaining composure, keeping emotions in check, controlling anger, and avoiding aggressive behavior, even in very difficult situations.
Analytical Thinking	Job requires analyzing information and using logic to address work-related issues and problems.
Innovation	Job requires creativity and alternative thinking to develop new ideas for and answers to work-related problems.
Persistence	Job requires persistence in the face of obstacles.
Concern for Others	Job requires being sensitive to others' needs and feelings and being understanding and helpful on the job.
Achievement/Effort	Job requires establishing and maintaining personally challenging achievement goals and exerting effort toward mastering tasks.
Stress Tolerance	Job requires accepting criticism and dealing calmly and effectively with high stress situations.
Initiative	Job requires a willingness to take on responsibilities and challenges.
Adaptability/Flexibility	Job requires being open to change (positive or negative) and to considerable variety in the workplace.
Leadership	Job requires a willingness to lead, take charge, and offer opinions and direction.
Social Orientation	Job requires preferring to work with others rather than alone, and being personally connected with others on the job.

49-3042.00 - Mobile Heavy Equipment Mechanics, Except Engines

Diagnose, adjust, repair, or overhaul mobile mechanical, hydraulic, and pneumatic equipment, such as cranes, bulldozers, graders, and conveyors, used in construction, logging, and surface mining.

Tasks

1) Fit bearings to adjust, repair, or overhaul mobile mechanical, hydraulic, and pneumatic equipment.

2) Read and understand operating manuals, blueprints, and technical drawings.

3) Dismantle and reassemble heavy equipment using hoists and hand tools.

4) Test mechanical products and equipment after repair or assembly to ensure proper performance and compliance with manufacturers' specifications.

5) Clean, lubricate, and perform other routine maintenance work on equipment and vehicles.

6) Repair and replace damaged or worn parts.

7) Clean parts by spraying them with grease solvent or immersing them in tanks of solvent.

8) Operate and inspect machines or heavy equipment in order to diagnose defects.

9) Weld or solder broken parts and structural members, using electric or gas welders and soldering tools.

10) Diagnose faults or malfunctions to determine required repairs, using engine diagnostic equipment such as computerized test equipment and calibration devices.

11) Assemble gear systems, and align frames and gears.

12) Examine parts for damage or excessive wear, using micrometers and gauges.

13) Fabricate needed parts or items from sheet metal.

14) Adjust and maintain industrial machinery, using control and regulating devices.

15) Adjust, maintain, and repair or replace subassemblies, such as transmissions and crawler heads, using hand tools, jacks, and cranes.

16) Schedule maintenance for industrial machines and equipment, and keep equipment service records.

17) Direct workers who are assembling or disassembling equipment or cleaning parts.

Knowledge	Knowledge Definitions
Mechanical	Knowledge of machines and tools, including their designs, uses, repair, and maintenance.
Customer and Personal Service	Knowledge of principles and processes for providing customer and personal services. This includes customer needs assessment, meeting quality standards for services, and evaluation of customer satisfaction.
Mathematics	Knowledge of arithmetic, algebra, geometry, calculus, statistics, and their applications.
Administration and Management	Knowledge of business and management principles involved in strategic planning, resource allocation, human resources modeling, leadership technique, production methods, and coordination of people and resources.
Production and Processing	Knowledge of raw materials, production processes, quality control, costs, and other techniques for maximizing the effective manufacture and distribution of goods.
English Language	Knowledge of the structure and content of the English language including the meaning and spelling of words, rules of composition, and grammar.
Engineering and Technology	Knowledge of the practical application of engineering science and technology. This includes applying principles, techniques, procedures, and equipment to the design and production of various goods and services.
Clerical	Knowledge of administrative and clerical procedures and systems such as word processing, managing files and records, stenography and transcription, designing forms, and other office procedures and terminology.
Computers and Electronics	Knowledge of circuit boards, processors, chips, electronic equipment, and computer hardware and software, including applications and programming.
Physics	Knowledge and prediction of physical principles, laws, their interrelationships, and applications to understanding fluid, material, and atmospheric dynamics, and mechanical, electrical, atomic and sub-atomic structures and processes.
Transportation	Knowledge of principles and methods for moving people or goods by air, rail, sea, or road, including the relative costs and benefits.
Design	Knowledge of design techniques, tools, and principles involved in production of precision technical plans, blueprints, drawings, and models.
Public Safety and Security	Knowledge of relevant equipment, policies, procedures, and strategies to promote effective local, state, or national security operations for the protection of people, data, property, and institutions.
Building and Construction	Knowledge of materials, methods, and the tools involved in the construction or repair of houses, buildings, or other structures such as highways and roads.
Personnel and Human Resources	Knowledge of principles and procedures for personnel recruitment, selection, training, compensation and benefits, labor relations and negotiation, and personnel information systems.
Education and Training	Knowledge of principles and methods for curriculum and training design, teaching and instruction for individuals and groups, and the measurement of training effects.
Chemistry	Knowledge of the chemical composition, structure, and properties of substances and of the chemical processes and transformations that they undergo. This includes uses of chemicals and their interactions, danger signs, production techniques, and disposal methods.
Economics and Accounting	Knowledge of economic and accounting principles and practices, the financial markets, banking and the analysis and reporting of financial data.
Law and Government	Knowledge of laws, legal codes, court procedures, precedents, government regulations, executive orders, agency rules, and the democratic political process.
Sales and Marketing	Knowledge of principles and methods for showing, promoting, and selling products or services. This includes marketing strategy and tactics, product demonstration, sales techniques, and sales control systems.
Geography	Knowledge of principles and methods for describing the features of land, sea, and air masses, including their physical characteristics, locations, interrelationships, and distribution of plant, animal, and human life.
Foreign Language	Knowledge of the structure and content of a foreign (non-English) language including the meaning and spelling of words, rules of composition and grammar, and pronunciation.
Psychology	Knowledge of human behavior and performance; individual differences in ability, personality, and interests; learning and motivation; psychological research methods; and the assessment and treatment of behavioral and affective disorders.
Telecommunications	Knowledge of transmission, broadcasting, switching, control, and operation of telecommunications systems.
Communications and Media	Knowledge of media production, communication, and dissemination techniques and methods. This includes alternative ways to inform and entertain via written, oral, and visual media.
Sociology and Anthropology	Knowledge of group behavior and dynamics, societal trends and influences, human migrations, ethnicity, cultures and their history and origins.
Food Production	Knowledge of techniques and equipment for planting, growing, and harvesting food products (both plant and animal) for consumption, including storage/handling techniques.
Medicine and Dentistry	Knowledge of the information and techniques needed to diagnose and treat human injuries, diseases, and deformities. This includes symptoms, treatment alternatives, drug properties and interactions, and preventive health-care measures.
Therapy and Counseling	Knowledge of principles, methods, and procedures for diagnosis, treatment, and rehabilitation of physical and mental dysfunctions, and for career counseling and guidance.
Philosophy and Theology	Knowledge of different philosophical systems and religions. This includes their basic principles, values, ethics, ways of thinking, customs, practices, and their impact on human culture.
Biology	Knowledge of plant and animal organisms, their tissues, cells, functions, interdependencies, and interactions with each other and the environment.
Fine Arts	Knowledge of the theory and techniques required to compose, produce, and perform works of music, dance, visual arts, drama, and sculpture.
History and Archeology	Knowledge of historical events and their causes, indicators, and effects on civilizations and cultures.

Skills	Skills Definitions
Troubleshooting	Determining causes of operating errors and deciding what to do about it.
Repairing	Repairing machines or systems using the needed tools.
Equipment Maintenance	Performing routine maintenance on equipment and determining when and what kind of maintenance is needed.
Equipment Selection	Determining the kind of tools and equipment needed to do a job.
Installation	Installing equipment, machines, wiring, or programs to meet specifications.
Operation Monitoring	Watching gauges, dials, or other indicators to make sure a machine is working properly.
Operation and Control	Controlling operations of equipment or systems.
Complex Problem Solving	Identifying complex problems and reviewing related information to develop and evaluate options and implement solutions.
Judgment and Decision Making	Considering the relative costs and benefits of potential actions to choose the most appropriate one.
Critical Thinking	Using logic and reasoning to identify the strengths and weaknesses of alternative solutions, conclusions or approaches to problems.
Time Management	Managing one's own time and the time of others.
Reading Comprehension	Understanding written sentences and paragraphs in work related documents.
Service Orientation Instructing	Actively looking for ways to help people. Teaching others how to do something.
Active Learning	Understanding the implications of new information for both current and future problem-solving and decision-making.
Coordination	Adjusting actions in relation to others' actions.
Persuasion	Persuading others to change their minds or behavior.
Learning Strategies	Selecting and using training/instructional methods and procedures appropriate for the situation when learning or teaching new things.
Mathematics	Using mathematics to solve problems.
Speaking	Talking to others to convey information effectively.
Technology Design	Generating or adapting equipment and technology to serve user needs.
Monitoring	Monitoring/Assessing performance of yourself, other individuals, or organizations to make improvements or take corrective action.

Active Listening	Giving full attention to what other people are saying, taking time to understand the points being made, asking questions as appropriate, and not interrupting at inappropriate times.
Writing	Communicating effectively in writing as appropriate for the needs of the audience.
Systems Evaluation	Identifying measures or indicators of system performance and the actions needed to improve or correct performance, relative to the goals of the system.
Quality Control Analysis	Conducting tests and inspections of products, services, or processes to evaluate quality or performance.
Systems Analysis	Determining how a system should work and how changes in conditions, operations, and the environment will affect outcomes.
Negotiation	Bringing others together and trying to reconcile differences.
Social Perceptiveness	Being aware of others' reactions and understanding why they react as they do.
Science	Using scientific rules and methods to solve problems.
Operations Analysis	Analyzing needs and product requirements to create a design.
Management of Material Resources	Obtaining and seeing to the appropriate use of equipment, facilities, and materials needed to do certain work.
Management of Financial Resources	Determining how money will be spent to get the work done, and accounting for these expenditures.
Management of Personnel Resources	Motivating, developing, and directing people as they work, identifying the best people for the job.
Programming	Writing computer programs for various purposes.

Ability	Ability Definitions
Information Ordering	The ability to arrange things or actions in a certain order or pattern according to a specific rule or set of rules (e.g., patterns of numbers, letters, words, pictures, mathematical operations).
Near Vision	The ability to see details at close range (within a few feet of the observer).
Manual Dexterity	The ability to quickly move your hand, your hand together with your arm, or your two hands to grasp, manipulate, or assemble objects.
Problem Sensitivity	The ability to tell when something is wrong or is likely to go wrong. It does not involve solving the problem, only recognizing there is a problem.
Multilimb Coordination	The ability to coordinate two or more limbs (for example, two arms, two legs, or one leg and one arm) while sitting, standing, or lying down. It does not involve performing the activities while the whole body is in motion.
Control Precision	The ability to quickly and repeatedly adjust the controls of a machine or a vehicle to exact positions.
Selective Attention	The ability to concentrate on a task over a period of time without being distracted.
Visualization	The ability to imagine how something will look after it is moved around or when its parts are moved or rearranged.
Arm-Hand Steadiness	The ability to keep your hand and arm steady while moving your arm or while holding your arm and hand in one position.
Deductive Reasoning	The ability to apply general rules to specific problems to produce answers that make sense.
Depth Perception	The ability to judge which of several objects is closer or farther away from you, or to judge the distance between you and an object.
Written Comprehension	The ability to read and understand information and ideas presented in writing.
Finger Dexterity	The ability to make precisely coordinated movements of the fingers of one or both hands to grasp, manipulate, or assemble very small objects.
Inductive Reasoning	The ability to combine pieces of information to form general rules or conclusions (includes finding a relationship among seemingly unrelated events).
Auditory Attention	The ability to focus on a single source of sound in the presence of other distracting sounds.
Extent Flexibility	The ability to bend, stretch, twist, or reach with your body, arms, and/or legs.
Oral Comprehension	The ability to listen to and understand information and ideas presented through spoken words and sentences.
Oral Expression	The ability to communicate information and ideas in speaking so others will understand.
Speech Clarity	The ability to speak clearly so others can understand you.
Trunk Strength	The ability to use your abdominal and lower back muscles to support part of the body repeatedly or continuously over time without 'giving out' or fatiguing.
Static Strength	The ability to exert maximum muscle force to lift, push, pull, or carry objects.

Reaction Time	The ability to quickly respond (with the hand, finger, or foot) to a signal (sound, light, picture) when it appears.
Flexibility of Closure	The ability to identify or detect a known pattern (a figure, object, word, or sound) that is hidden in other distracting material.
Speech Recognition	The ability to identify and understand the speech of another person.
Category Flexibility	The ability to generate or use different sets of rules for combining or grouping things in different ways.
Hearing Sensitivity	The ability to detect or tell the differences between sounds that vary in pitch and loudness.
Far Vision	The ability to see details at a distance.
Written Expression	The ability to communicate information and ideas in writing so others will understand.
Perceptual Speed	The ability to quickly and accurately compare similarities and differences among sets of letters, numbers, objects, pictures, or patterns. The things to be compared may be presented at the same time or one after the other. This ability also includes comparing a presented object with a remembered object.
Time Sharing	The ability to shift back and forth between two or more activities or sources of information (such as speech, sounds, touch, or other sources).
Gross Body Coordination	The ability to coordinate the movement of your arms, legs, and torso together when the whole body is in motion.
Rate Control	The ability to time your movements or the movement of a piece of equipment in anticipation of changes in the speed and/or direction of a moving object or scene.
Spatial Orientation	The ability to know your location in relation to the environment or to know where other objects are in relation to you.
Memorization	The ability to remember information such as words, numbers, pictures, and procedures.
Glare Sensitivity	The ability to see objects in the presence of glare or bright lighting.
Visual Color Discrimination	The ability to match or detect differences between colors, including shades of color and brightness.
Speed of Closure	The ability to quickly make sense of, combine, and organize information into meaningful patterns.
Dynamic Strength	The ability to exert muscle force repeatedly or continuously over time. This involves muscular endurance and resistance to muscle fatigue.
Response Orientation	The ability to choose quickly between two or more movements in response to two or more different signals (lights, sounds, pictures). It includes the speed with which the correct response is started with the hand, foot, or other body part.
Stamina	The ability to exert yourself physically over long periods of time without getting winded or out of breath.
Speed of Limb Movement	The ability to quickly move the arms and legs.
Wrist-Finger Speed	The ability to make fast, simple, repeated movements of the fingers, hands, and wrists.
Originality	The ability to come up with unusual or clever ideas about a given topic or situation, or to develop creative ways to solve a problem.
Mathematical Reasoning	The ability to choose the right mathematical methods or formulas to solve a problem.
Peripheral Vision	The ability to see objects or movement of objects to one's side when the eyes are looking ahead.
Gross Body Equilibrium	The ability to keep or regain your body balance or stay upright when in an unstable position.
Fluency of Ideas	The ability to come up with a number of ideas about a topic (the number of ideas is important, not their quality, correctness, or creativity).
Number Facility	The ability to add, subtract, multiply, or divide quickly and correctly.
Night Vision	The ability to see under low light conditions.
Explosive Strength	The ability to use short bursts of muscle force to propel oneself (as in jumping or sprinting), or to throw an object.
Sound Localization	The ability to tell the direction from which a sound originated.
Dynamic Flexibility	The ability to quickly and repeatedly bend, stretch, twist, or reach out with your body, arms, and/or legs.

Work_Activity	Work_Activity Definitions
Repairing and Maintaining Mechanical Equipment	Servicing, repairing, adjusting, and testing machines, devices, moving parts, and equipment that operate primarily on the basis of mechanical (not electronic) principles.
Operating Vehicles, Mechanized Devices, or Equipme	Running, maneuvering, navigating, or driving vehicles or mechanized equipment, such as forklifts, passenger vehicles, aircraft, or water craft.

Making Decisions and Solving Problems	Analyzing information and evaluating results to choose the best solution and solve problems.
Updating and Using Relevant Knowledge	Keeping up-to-date technically and applying new knowledge to your job.
Inspecting Equipment, Structures, or Material	Inspecting equipment, structures, or materials to identify the cause of errors or other problems or defects.
Getting Information	Observing, receiving, and otherwise obtaining information from all relevant sources.
Identifying Objects, Actions, and Events	Identifying information by categorizing, estimating, recognizing differences or similarities, and detecting changes in circumstances or events.
Communicating with Supervisors, Peers, or Subordin	Providing information to supervisors, co-workers, and subordinates by telephone, in written form, e-mail, or in person.
Controlling Machines and Processes	Using either control mechanisms or direct physical activity to operate machines or processes (not including computers or vehicles).
Analyzing Data or Information	Identifying the underlying principles, reasons, or facts of information by breaking down information or data into separate parts.
Handling and Moving Objects	Using hands and arms in handling, installing, positioning, and moving materials, and manipulating things.
Performing General Physical Activities	Performing physical activities that require considerable use of your arms and legs and moving your whole body, such as climbing, lifting, balancing, walking, stooping, and handling of materials.
Monitor Processes, Materials, or Surroundings	Monitoring and reviewing information from materials, events, or the environment, to detect or assess problems.
Documenting/Recording Information	Entering, transcribing, recording, storing, or maintaining information in written or electronic/magnetic form.
Communicating with Persons Outside Organization	Communicating with people outside the organization, representing the organization to customers, the public, government, and other external sources. This information can be exchanged in person, in writing, or by telephone or e-mail.
Estimating the Quantifiable Characteristics of Pro	Estimating sizes, distances, and quantities; or determining time, costs, resources, or materials needed to perform a work activity.
Repairing and Maintaining Electronic Equipment	Servicing, repairing, calibrating, regulating, fine-tuning, or testing machines, devices, and equipment that operate primarily on the basis of electrical or electronic (not mechanical) principles.
Scheduling Work and Activities	Scheduling events, programs, and activities, as well as the work of others.
Judging the Qualities of Things, Services, or Peop	Assessing the value, importance, or quality of things or people.
Processing Information	Compiling, coding, categorizing, calculating, tabulating, auditing, or verifying information or data.
Organizing, Planning, and Prioritizing Work	Developing specific goals and plans to prioritize, organize, and accomplish your work.
Provide Consultation and Advice to Others	Providing guidance and expert advice to management or other groups on technical, systems-, or process-related topics.
Establishing and Maintaining Interpersonal Relatio	Developing constructive and cooperative working relationships with others, and maintaining them over time.
Coordinating the Work and Activities of Others	Getting members of a group to work together to accomplish tasks.
Thinking Creatively	Developing, designing, or creating new applications, ideas, relationships, systems, or products, including artistic contributions.
Interpreting the Meaning of Information for Others	Translating or explaining what information means and how it can be used.
Resolving Conflicts and Negotiating with Others	Handling complaints, settling disputes, and resolving grievances and conflicts, or otherwise negotiating with others.
Guiding, Directing, and Motivating Subordinates	Providing guidance and direction to subordinates, including setting performance standards and monitoring performance.
Evaluating Information to Determine Compliance wit	Using relevant information and individual judgment to determine whether events or processes comply with laws, regulations, or standards.
Performing for or Working Directly with the Public	Performing for people or dealing directly with the public. This includes serving customers in restaurants and stores, and receiving clients or guests.
Developing Objectives and Strategies	Establishing long-range objectives and specifying the strategies and actions to achieve them.
Developing and Building Teams	Encouraging and building mutual trust, respect, and cooperation among team members.
Monitoring and Controlling Resources	Monitoring and controlling resources and overseeing the spending of money.

Interacting With Computers	Using computers and computer systems (including hardware and software) to program, write software, set up functions, enter data, or process information.
Assisting and Caring for Others	Providing personal assistance, medical attention, emotional support, or other personal care to others such as coworkers, customers, or patients.
Selling or Influencing Others	Convincing others to buy merchandise/goods or to otherwise change their minds or actions.
Performing Administrative Activities	Performing day-to-day administrative tasks such as maintaining information files and processing paperwork.
Training and Teaching Others	Identifying the educational needs of others, developing formal educational or training programs or classes, and teaching or instructing others.
Coaching and Developing Others	Identifying the developmental needs of others and coaching, mentoring, or otherwise helping others to improve their knowledge or skills.
Drafting, Laying Out, and Specifying Technical Dev	Providing documentation, detailed instructions, drawings, or specifications to tell others about how devices, parts, equipment, or structures are to be fabricated, constructed, assembled, modified, maintained, or used.
Staffing Organizational Units	Recruiting, interviewing, selecting, hiring, and promoting employees in an organization.

Work_Context	Work_Context Definitions
Sounds, Noise Levels Are Distracting or Uncomforta	How often does this job require working exposed to sounds and noise levels that are distracting or uncomfortable?
Exposed to Contaminants	How often does this job require working exposed to contaminants (such as pollutants, gases, dust or odors)?
Exposed to Hazardous Equipment	How often does this job require exposure to hazardous equipment?
Wear Common Protective or Safety Equipment such as	How often does this job require wearing common protective or safety equipment such as safety shoes, glasses, gloves, hard hats or live jackets?
Spend Time Using Your Hands to Handle, Control, or	How much does this job require using your hands to handle, control, or feel objects, tools or controls?
Face-to-Face Discussions	How often do you have to have face-to-face discussions with individuals or teams in this job?
Indoors, Not Environmentally Controlled	How often does this job require working indoors in non-controlled environmental conditions (e.g., warehouse without heat)?
Time Pressure	How often does this job require the worker to meet strict deadlines?
Frequency of Decision Making	How frequently is the worker required to make decisions that affect other people, the financial resources, and/or the image and reputation of the organization?
Exposed to Minor Burns, Cuts, Bites, or Stings	How often does this job require exposure to minor burns, cuts, bites, or stings?
In an Open Vehicle or Equipment	How often does this job require working in an open vehicle or equipment (e.g., tractor)?
Structured versus Unstructured Work	To what extent is this job structured for the worker, rather than allowing the worker to determine tasks, priorities, and goals?
Contact With Others	How much does this job require the worker to be in contact with others (face-to-face, by telephone, or otherwise) in order to perform it?
Spend Time Standing	How much does this job require standing?
Freedom to Make Decisions	How much decision making freedom, without supervision, does the job offer?
In an Enclosed Vehicle or Equipment	How often does this job require working in a closed vehicle or equipment (e.g., car)?
Cramped Work Space, Awkward Positions	How often does this job require working in cramped work spaces that requires getting into awkward positions?
Impact of Decisions on Co-workers or Company Resul	How do the decisions an employee makes impact the results of co-workers, clients or the company?
Outdoors, Exposed to Weather	How often does this job require working outdoors, exposed to all weather conditions?
Telephone	How often do you have telephone conversations in this job?
Exposed to Hazardous Conditions	How often does this job require exposure to hazardous conditions?
Work With Work Group or Team	How important is it to work with others in a group or team in this job?
Importance of Being Exact or Accurate	How important is being very exact or highly accurate in performing this job?
Very Hot or Cold Temperatures	How often does this job require working in very hot (above 90 F degrees) or very cold (below 32 F degrees) temperatures?

1107

Extremely Bright or Inadequate Lighting	How often does this job require working in extremely bright or inadequate lighting conditions?
Consequence of Error	How serious would the result usually be if the worker made a mistake that was not readily correctable?
Spend Time Kneeling, Crouching, Stooping, or Crawl	How much does this job require kneeling, crouching, stooping or crawling?
Responsible for Others' Health and Safety	How much responsibility is there for the health and safety of others in this job?
Coordinate or Lead Others	How important is it to coordinate or lead others in accomplishing work activities in this job?
Exposed to Whole Body Vibration	How often does this job require exposure to whole body vibration (e.g., operate a jackhammer)?
Responsibility for Outcomes and Results	How responsible is the worker for work outcomes and results of other workers?
Deal With Unpleasant or Angry People	How frequently does the worker have to deal with unpleasant, angry, or discourteous individuals as part of the job requirements?
Spend Time Making Repetitive Motions	How much does this job require making repetitive motions?
Spend Time Bending or Twisting the Body	How much does this job require bending or twisting your body?
Physical Proximity	To what extent does this job require the worker to perform job tasks in close physical proximity to other people?
Spend Time Walking and Running	How much does this job require walking and running?
Deal With External Customers	How important is it to work with external customers or the public in this job?
Frequency of Conflict Situations	How often are there conflict situations the employee has to face in this job?
Letters and Memos	How often does the job require written letters and memos?
Level of Competition	To what extent does this job require the worker to compete or to be aware of competitive pressures?
Importance of Repeating Same Tasks	How important is repeating the same physical activities (e.g., key entry) or mental activities (e.g., checking entries in a ledger) over and over, without stopping, to performing this job?
Exposed to High Places	How often does this job require exposure to high places?
Spend Time Keeping or Regaining Balance	How much does this job require keeping or regaining your balance?
Indoors, Environmentally Controlled	How often does this job require working indoors in environmentally controlled conditions?
Pace Determined by Speed of Equipment	How important is it to this job that the pace is determined by the speed of equipment or machinery? (This does not refer to keeping busy at all times on this job.)
Outdoors, Under Cover	How often does this job require working outdoors, under cover (e.g., structure with roof but no walls)?
Spend Time Climbing Ladders, Scaffolds, or Poles	How much does this job require climbing ladders, scaffolds, or poles?
Wear Specialized Protective or Safety Equipment su	How much does this job require wearing specialized protective or safety equipment such as breathing apparatus, safety harness, full protection suits, or radiation protection?
Spend Time Sitting	How much does this job require sitting?
Deal With Physically Aggressive People	How frequently does this job require the worker to deal with physical aggression of violent individuals?
Exposed to Disease or Infections	How often does this job require exposure to disease/infections?
Electronic Mail	How often do you use electronic mail in this job?
Degree of Automation	How automated is the job?
Public Speaking	How often do you have to perform public speaking in this job?
Exposed to Radiation	How often does this job require exposure to radiation?

Job Zone Component	Job Zone Component Definitions
Title	Job Zone Four: Considerable Preparation Needed
Overall Experience	A minimum of two to four years of work-related skill, knowledge, or experience is needed for these occupations. For example, an accountant must complete four years of college and work for several years in accounting to be considered qualified.
Job Training	Employees in these occupations usually need several years of work-related experience, on-the-job training, and/or vocational training.
Job Zone Examples	Many of these occupations involve coordinating, supervising, managing, or training others. Examples include accountants, chefs and head cooks, computer programmers, historians, pharmacists, and police detectives.

SVP Range	(7.0 to < 8.0)
Education	Most of these occupations require a four - year bachelor's degree, but some do not.

Work_Styles	Work_Styles Definitions
Dependability	Job requires being reliable, responsible, and dependable, and fulfilling obligations.
Integrity	Job requires being honest and ethical.
Attention to Detail	Job requires being careful about detail and thorough in completing work tasks.
Independence	Job requires developing one's own ways of doing things, guiding oneself with little or no supervision, and depending on oneself to get things done.
Initiative	Job requires a willingness to take on responsibilities and challenges.
Analytical Thinking	Job requires analyzing information and using logic to address work-related issues and problems.
Cooperation	Job requires being pleasant with others on the job and displaying a good-natured, cooperative attitude.
Adaptability/Flexibility	Job requires being open to change (positive or negative) and to considerable variety in the workplace.
Persistence	Job requires persistence in the face of obstacles.
Innovation	Job requires creativity and alternative thinking to develop new ideas for and answers to work-related problems.
Self Control	Job requires maintaining composure, keeping emotions in check, controlling anger, and avoiding aggressive behavior, even in very difficult situations.
Achievement/Effort	Job requires establishing and maintaining personally challenging achievement goals and exerting effort toward mastering tasks.
Social Orientation	Job requires preferring to work with others rather than alone, and being personally connected with others on the job.
Stress Tolerance	Job requires accepting criticism and dealing calmly and effectively with high stress situations.
Leadership	Job requires a willingness to lead, take charge, and offer opinions and direction.
Concern for Others	Job requires being sensitive to others' needs and feelings and being understanding and helpful on the job.

49-3043.00 - Rail Car Repairers

Diagnose, adjust, repair, or overhaul railroad rolling stock, mine cars, or mass transit rail cars.

Tasks

1) Perform scheduled maintenance, and clean units and components.

2) Measure diameters of axle wheel seats, using micrometers, and mark dimensions on axles so that wheels can be bored to specified dimensions.

3) Inspect the interior and exterior of rail cars coming into rail yards in order to identify defects and to determine the extent of wear and damage.

4) Test units for operability before and after repairs.

5) Repair or replace defective or worn parts such as bearings, pistons, and gears, using hand tools, torque wrenches, power tools, and welding equipment.

6) Test electrical systems of cars by operating systems and using testing equipment such as ammeters.

7) Replace defective wiring and insulation, and tighten electrical connections, using hand tools.

8) Repair, fabricate, and install steel or wood fittings, using blueprints, shop sketches, and instruction manuals.

9) Align car sides for installation of car ends and crossties, using width gauges, turnbuckles, and wrenches.

10) Repair and maintain electrical and electronic controls for propulsion and braking systems.

11) Record conditions of cars, and repair and maintenance work performed or to be performed.

12) Install and repair interior flooring, fixtures, walls, plumbing, steps, and platforms.

13) Remove locomotives, car mechanical units, or other components, using pneumatic hoists

and jacks. pinch bars, hand tools, and cutting torches.

14) Repair car upholstery.

15) Adjust repaired or replaced units as needed to ensure proper operation.

16) Disassemble units such as water pumps. control valves, and compressors so that repairs can be made.

17) Examine car roofs for wear and damage, and repair defective sections, using roofing material. cement, nails, and waterproof paint.

18) Repair window sash frames, attach weather stripping and channels to frames, and replace window glass, using hand tools.

19) Inspect components such as bearings, seals, gaskets, wheels, and coupler assemblies to determine if repairs are needed.

49-3051.00 - Motorboat Mechanics

Repairs and adjusts electrical and mechanical equipment of gasoline or diesel powered inboard or inboard-outboard boat engines.

Tasks

1) Mount motors to boats and operate boats at various speeds on waterways to conduct operational tests.

2) Repair or rework parts, using machine tools such as lathes, mills, drills, and grinders.

3) Idle motors and observe thermometers to determine the effectiveness of cooling systems.

4) Disassemble and inspect motors to locate defective parts, using mechanic's hand tools and gauges.

5) Repair engine mechanical equipment such as power-tilts, bilge pumps, or power take-offs.

6) Document inspection and test results, and work performed or to be performed.

7) Adjust carburetor mixtures, electrical point settings, and timing while motors are running in water-filled test tanks.

8) Replace parts such as gears, magneto points, piston rings, and spark plugs, and reassemble engines.

9) Start motors, and monitor performance for signs of malfunctioning such as smoke, excessive vibration, and misfiring.

10) Adjust generators and replace faulty wiring, using hand tools and soldering irons.

11) Set starter locks, and align and repair steering or throttle controls, using gauges, screwdrivers, and wrenches.

49-3052.00 - Motorcycle Mechanics

Diagnose, adjust, repair, or overhaul motorcycles, scooters, mopeds, dirt bikes, or similar motorized vehicles.

Tasks

1) Disassemble subassembly units and examine condition, movement or alignment of parts visually or using gauges.

2) Listen to engines, examine vehicle frames, and confer with customers in order to determine nature and extent of malfunction or damage.

3) Reassemble and test subassembly units.

4) Replace defective parts, using hand tools, arbor presses, flexible power presses, or power tools.

5) Repair and adjust motorcycle subassemblies such as forks, transmissions, brakes, and drive chains, according to specifications.

6) Repair or replace other parts, such as headlights, horns, handlebar controls, gasoline and oil tanks, starters, and mufflers.

7) Remove cylinder heads, grind valves, and scrape off carbon, and replace defective valves, pistons, cylinders and rings, using hand tools and power tools.

8) Dismantle engines and repair or replace defective parts, such as magnetos, carburetors, and generators.

9) Connect test panels to engines and measure generator output, ignition timing, and other engine performance indicators.

49-3093.00 - Tire Repairers and Changers

Repair and replace tires.

Tasks

1) Buff defective areas of inner tubes, using scrapers.

2) Drive automobile or service trucks to industrial sites in order to provide services, and respond to emergency calls.

3) Remount wheels onto vehicles.

4) Reassemble tires onto wheels.

5) Raise vehicles using hydraulic jacks.

6) Prepare rims and wheel drums for reassembly by scraping, grinding, or sandblasting.

7) Place wheels on balancing machines to determine counterweights required to balance wheels.

8) Place casing-camelback assemblies in tire molds for the vulcanization process, and exert pressure on the camelbacks to ensure good adhesion.

9) Patch tubes with adhesive rubber patches, or seal rubber patches to tubes using hot vulcanizing plates.

10) Locate punctures in tubeless tires by visual inspection or by immersing inflated tires in water baths and observing air bubbles.

11) Replace valve stems and remove puncturing objects.

12) Inflate inner tubes and immerse them in water to locate leaks.

13) Glue boots (tire patches) over ruptures in tire casings, using rubber cement.

14) Apply rubber cement to buffed tire casings prior to vulcanization process.

15) Rotate tires to different positions on vehicles, using hand tools.

16) Seal punctures in tubeless tires by inserting adhesive material and expanding rubber plugs into punctures, using hand tools.

17) Order replacements for tires and tubes.

18) Identify and inflate tires correctly for the size and ply.

19) Clean sides of whitewall tires.

20) Unbolt wheels from vehicles and remove them, using lug wrenches and other hand and power tools.

21) Separate tubed tires from wheels, using rubber mallets and metal bars, or mechanical tire changers.

22) Inspect tire casings for defects, such as holes and tears.

23) Roll new rubber treads, known as camelbacks, over tire casings, and mold the semi-raw rubber treads onto the buffed casings.

24) Hammer required counterweights onto rims of wheels.

49-9011.00 - Mechanical Door Repairers

Install, service, or repair opening and closing mechanisms of automatic doors and hydraulic door closers. Includes garage door mechanics.

Tasks

1) Bore and cut holes in flooring as required for installation, using hand tools and power tools.

2) Complete required paperwork, such as work orders, according to services performed or required.

3) Operate lifts, winches, or chain falls in order to move heavy curtain doors.

4) Wind large springs with upward motion of arm.

5) Order replacement springs, sections, and slats.

6) Study blueprints and schematic diagrams in order to determine appropriate methods of installing and repairing automated door openers.

7) Adjust doors to open or close with the correct amount of effort, and make simple adjustments to electric openers.

8) Apply hardware to door sections, such as drilling holes to install locks.

9) Assemble and fasten tracks to structures or bucks, using impact wrenches or welding equipment.

10) Repair or replace worn or broken door parts, using hand tools.

11) Clean door closer parts, using caustic soda, rotary brushes, and grinding wheels.

12) Install dock seals, bumpers, and shelters.

13) Cut door stops and angle irons to fit openings.

14) Inspect job sites, assessing headroom, side room, and other conditions in order to determine appropriateness of door for a given location.

15) Install door frames, rails, steel rolling curtains, electronic-eye mechanisms, and electric door openers and closers, using power tools, hand tools, and electronic test equipment.

16) Lubricate door closer oil chambers and pack spindles with leather washers.

17) Set in and secure floor treadles for door activating mechanisms; then connect power packs and electrical panelboards to treadles.

18) Collect payment upon job completion.

19) Fasten angle iron back-hangers to ceilings and tracks, using fasteners or welding equipment.

20) Run low voltage wiring on ceiling surfaces, using insulated staples.

21) Set doors into place or stack hardware sections into openings after rail or track installation.

22) Remove or disassemble defective automatic mechanical door closers, using hand tools.

23) Fabricate replacements for worn or broken parts, using welders, lathes, drill presses, and shaping and milling machines.

24) Carry springs to tops of doors, using ladders or scaffolding, and attach springs to tracks in order to install spring systems.

49-9012.00 - Control and Valve Installers and Repairers, Except Mechanical Door

Install, repair, and maintain mechanical regulating and controlling devices, such as electric meters, gas regulators, thermostats, safety and flow valves, and other mechanical governors.

Tasks

1) Mount and install meters and other electric equipment such as time clocks, transformers, and circuit breakers, using electricians' hand tools.

2) Dip valves and regulators in molten lead to prevent leakage, and paint valves, fittings, and other devices, using spray guns.

3) Clean plant growth, scale, paint, soil, and/or rust from meter housings, using wire brushes, scrapers, buffers, sandblasters, and/or cleaning compounds.

4) Clamp regulator units into vises on stages above water tanks, and attach compressed air hoses to intake ports.

5) Attach pressurized meters to fixtures which submerge them in water, and observe meters for leaks.

6) Attach air hoses to meter inlets; then plug outlets and observe gauges for pressure losses in order to test internal seams for leaks.

7) Advise customers on proper installation of valves or regulators and related equipment.

8) Disconnect and/or remove defective or unauthorized meters, using hand tools.

9) Cut seats to receive new orifices, tap inspection ports, and perform other repairs in order to salvage usable materials, using hand tools and machine tools.

10) Make adjustments to meter components, such as setscrews or timing mechanisms, so that they conform to specifications.

11) Install, inspect, and test electric meters, relays, and power sources to detect causes of malfunctions and inaccuracies, using hand tools and testing equipment.

12) Measure tolerances of assembled and salvageable parts for conformance to standards or specifications, using gauges, micrometers, and calipers.

13) Lubricate wearing surfaces of mechanical parts, using oils or other lubricants.

14) Calibrate thermostats for specified temperature or pressure settings.

15) Clean internal compartments and moving parts, using rags and cleaning compounds.

16) Connect regulators to test stands, and turn screw adjustments until gauges indicate that inlet and outlet pressures meet specifications.

17) Dismantle meters, and replace or adjust defective parts such as cases, shafts, gears, disks, and recording mechanisms, using soldering irons and hand tools.

18) Examine valves or mechanical control device parts for defects, dents, or loose attachments, and mark malfunctioning areas of defective units.

19) Recondition displacement type gas meters and governors, fabricating, machining, and/or modifying parts needed for repairs.

20) Repair leaks in valve seats or bellows of automotive heater thermostats, using soft solder, flux, and acetylene torches.

21) Turn meters on or off to establish or close service.

22) Disassemble and repair mechanical control devices or valves, such as regulators, thermostats, or hydrants, using power tools, hand tools, and cutting torches.

23) Turn valves to allow measured amounts of air or gas to pass through meters at specified flow rates.

24) Reassemble repaired equipment, and solder top, front, and back case panels in place, using soldering guns, power tools, and hand tools.

25) Vary air pressure flowing into regulators and turn handles to assess functioning of valves and pistons.

26) Record maintenance information, including test results, material usage, and repairs made.

27) Replace defective parts, such as bellows, range springs, and toggle switches, and reassemble units according to blueprints, using cam presses and hand tools.

28) Record meter readings and installation data on meter cards, work orders, or field service orders, or enter data into hand-held computers.

29) Trace and tag meters or house lines.

30) Operate power-driven foot pedals to raise and/or lower regulators into and out of water tanks.

31) Collect money due on delinquent accounts.

32) Investigate instances of illegal tapping into service lines.

33) Test valves and regulators for leaks and accurate temperature and pressure settings, using precision testing equipment.

34) Recommend and write up specifications for changes in hardware, such as house wiring.

35) Shut off service and notify repair crews when major repairs are required, such as the replacement of underground pipes or wiring.

36) Connect hoses from provers to meter inlets and outlets, and raise prover bells until prover gauges register zero.

37) Repair electric meters and components, such as transformers and relays, and replace metering devices, dial glasses, and faulty or incorrect wiring, using hand tools.

38) Splice and connect cables from meters or current transformers to pull boxes or switchboards, using hand tools.

39) Report hazardous field situations and damaged or missing meters.

49-9021.01 - Heating and Air Conditioning Mechanics

Install, service, and repair heating and air conditioning systems in residences and commercial establishments.

Tasks

1) Test pipe or tubing joints and connections for leaks, using pressure gauge or soap-and-water solution.

2) Test electrical circuits and components for continuity, using electrical test equipment.

3) Install, connect, and adjust thermostats, humidistats and timers, using hand tools.

4) Discuss heating-cooling system malfunctions with users to isolate problems or to verify that malfunctions have been corrected.

5) Recommend, develop, and perform preventive and general maintenance procedures such as cleaning, power-washing and vacuuming equipment, oiling parts, and changing filters.

6) Lay out and connect electrical wiring between controls and equipment according to wiring diagram, using electrician's hand tools.

7) Install auxiliary components to heating-cooling equipment, such as expansion and discharge valves, air ducts, pipes, blowers, dampers, flues and stokers, following blueprints.

8) Adjust system controls to setting recommended by manufacturer to balance system, using

hand tools.

9) Record and report all faults, deficiencies, and other unusual occurrences, as well as the time and materials expended on work orders.

10) Cut and drill holes in floors, walls, and roof to install equipment, using power saws and drills.

11) Join pipes or tubing to equipment and to fuel, water, or refrigerant source, to form complete circuit.

12) Inspect and test system to verify system compliance with plans and specifications and to detect and locate malfunctions.

13) Obtain and maintain required certification(s).

14) Study blueprints, design specifications, and manufacturers¹ recommendations to ascertain the configuration of heating or cooling equipment components and to ensure the proper installation of components.

15) Reassemble and test equipment following repairs.

16) Assemble, position and mount heating or cooling equipment, following blueprints.

17) Measure, cut, thread, and bend pipe or tubing, using pipefitter's tools.

18) Assist with other work in coordination with repair and maintenance teams.

19) Wrap pipes in insulation, securing it in place with cement or wire bands.

20) Generate work orders that address deficiencies in need of correction.

21) Fabricate, assemble and install duct work and chassis parts, using portable metal-working tools and welding equipment.

22) Comply with all applicable standards, policies, and procedures, including safety procedures and the maintenance of a clean work area.

Knowledge	Knowledge Definitions
Mechanical	Knowledge of machines and tools, including their designs, uses, repair, and maintenance.
Customer and Personal Service	Knowledge of principles and processes for providing customer and personal services. This includes customer needs assessment, meeting quality standards for services, and evaluation of customer satisfaction.
Engineering and Technology	Knowledge of the practical application of engineering science and technology. This includes applying principles, techniques, procedures, and equipment to the design and production of various goods and services.
Design	Knowledge of design techniques, tools, and principles involved in production of precision technical plans, blueprints, drawings, and models.
English Language	Knowledge of the structure and content of the English language including the meaning and spelling of words, rules of composition, and grammar.
Building and Construction	Knowledge of materials, methods, and the tools involved in the construction or repair of houses, buildings, or other structures such as highways and roads.
Mathematics	Knowledge of arithmetic, algebra, geometry, calculus, statistics, and their applications.
Sales and Marketing	Knowledge of principles and methods for showing, promoting, and selling products or services. This includes marketing strategy and tactics, product demonstration, sales techniques, and sales control systems.
Computers and Electronics	Knowledge of circuit boards, processors, chips, electronic equipment, and computer hardware and software, including applications and programming.
Physics	Knowledge and prediction of physical principles, laws, their interrelationships, and applications to understanding fluid, material, and atmospheric dynamics, and mechanical, electrical, atomic and sub- atomic structures and processes.
Education and Training	Knowledge of principles and methods for curriculum and training design, teaching and instruction for individuals and groups, and the measurement of training effects.
Public Safety and Security	Knowledge of relevant equipment, policies, procedures, and strategies to promote effective local, state, or national security operations for the protection of people, data, property, and institutions.
Administration and Management	Knowledge of business and management principles involved in strategic planning, resource allocation, human resources modeling, leadership technique, production methods, and coordination of people and resources.
Law and Government	Knowledge of laws, legal codes, court procedures, precedents, government regulations, executive orders, agency rules, and the democratic political process.
Chemistry	Knowledge of the chemical composition, structure, and properties of substances and of the chemical processes and transformations that they undergo. This includes uses of chemicals and their interactions, danger signs, production techniques, and disposal methods.
Production and Processing	Knowledge of raw materials, production processes, quality control, costs, and other techniques for maximizing the effective manufacture and distribution of goods.
Economics and Accounting	Knowledge of economic and accounting principles and practices, the financial markets, banking and the analysis and reporting of financial data.
Clerical	Knowledge of administrative and clerical procedures and systems such as word processing, managing files and records, stenography and transcription, designing forms, and other office procedures and terminology.
Transportation	Knowledge of principles and methods for moving people or goods by air, rail, sea, or road, including the relative costs and benefits.
Personnel and Human Resources	Knowledge of principles and procedures for personnel recruitment, selection, training, compensation and benefits, labor relations and negotiation, and personnel information systems.
Psychology	Knowledge of human behavior and performance; individual differences in ability, personality, and interests; learning and motivation; psychological research methods; and the assessment and treatment of behavioral and affective disorders.
Communications and Media	Knowledge of media production, communication, and dissemination techniques and methods. This includes alternative ways to inform and entertain via written, oral, and visual media.
Telecommunications	Knowledge of transmission, broadcasting, switching, control, and operation of telecommunications systems.
Biology	Knowledge of plant and animal organisms, their tissues, cells, functions, interdependencies, and interactions with each other and the environment.
Therapy and Counseling	Knowledge of principles, methods, and procedures for diagnosis, treatment, and rehabilitation of physical and mental dysfunctions, and for career counseling and guidance.
Geography	Knowledge of principles and methods for describing the features of land, sea, and air masses, including their physical characteristics, locations, interrelationships, and distribution of plant, animal, and human life.
Medicine and Dentistry	Knowledge of the information and techniques needed to diagnose and treat human injuries, diseases, and deformities. This includes symptoms, treatment alternatives, drug properties and interactions, and preventive health-care measures.
Food Production	Knowledge of techniques and equipment for planting, growing, and harvesting food products (both plant and animal) for consumption, including storage/handling techniques.
Sociology and Anthropology	Knowledge of group behavior and dynamics, societal trends and influences, human migrations, ethnicity, cultures and their history and origins.
Foreign Language	Knowledge of the structure and content of a foreign (non-English) language including the meaning and spelling of words, rules of composition and grammar, and pronunciation.
Philosophy and Theology	Knowledge of different philosophical systems and religions. This includes their basic principles, values, ethics, ways of thinking, customs, practices, and their impact on human culture.
History and Archeology	Knowledge of historical events and their causes, indicators, and effects on civilizations and cultures.
Fine Arts	Knowledge of the theory and techniques required to compose, produce, and perform works of music, dance, visual arts, drama, and sculpture.

Skills	Skills Definitions
Troubleshooting	Determining causes of operating errors and deciding what to do about it.
Repairing	Repairing machines or systems using the needed tools.
Active Listening	Giving full attention to what other people are saying, taking time to understand the points being made, asking questions as appropriate, and not interrupting at inappropriate times.
Equipment Maintenance	Performing routine maintenance on equipment and determining when and what kind of maintenance is needed.
Installation	Installing equipment, machines, wiring, or programs to meet specifications.

Social Perceptiveness	Being aware of others' reactions and understanding why they react as they do.
Critical Thinking	Using logic and reasoning to identify the strengths and weaknesses of alternative solutions, conclusions or approaches to problems.
Active Learning	Understanding the implications of new information for both current and future problem-solving and decision-making.
Coordination	Adjusting actions in relation to others' actions.
Reading Comprehension	Understanding written sentences and paragraphs in work related documents.
Time Management	Managing one's own time and the time of others.
Learning Strategies	Selecting and using training/instructional methods and procedures appropriate for the situation when learning or teaching new things.
Speaking	Talking to others to convey information effectively.
Operation Monitoring	Watching gauges, dials, or other indicators to make sure a machine is working properly.
Complex Problem Solving	Identifying complex problems and reviewing related information to develop and evaluate options and implement solutions.
Equipment Selection	Determining the kind of tools and equipment needed to do a job.
Science	Using scientific rules and methods to solve problems.
Systems Evaluation	Identifying measures or indicators of system performance and the actions needed to improve or correct performance, relative to the goals of the system.
Persuasion	Persuading others to change their minds or behavior.
Systems Analysis	Determining how a system should work and how changes in conditions, operations, and the environment will affect outcomes.
Mathematics	Using mathematics to solve problems.
Monitoring	Monitoring/Assessing performance of yourself, other individuals, or organizations to make improvements or take corrective action.
Instructing	Teaching others how to do something.
Negotiation	Bringing others together and trying to reconcile differences.
Service Orientation	Actively looking for ways to help people.
Judgment and Decision Making	Considering the relative costs and benefits of potential actions to choose the most appropriate one.
Writing	Communicating effectively in writing as appropriate for the needs of the audience.
Quality Control Analysis	Conducting tests and inspections of products, services, or processes to evaluate quality or performance.
Operations Analysis	Analyzing needs and product requirements to create a design.
Management of Material Resources	Obtaining and seeing to the appropriate use of equipment, facilities, and materials needed to do certain work.
Technology Design	Generating or adapting equipment and technology to serve user needs.
Operation and Control	Controlling operations of equipment or systems.
Management of Personnel Resources	Motivating, developing, and directing people as they work, identifying the best people for the job.
Management of Financial Resources	Determining how money will be spent to get the work done, and accounting for these expenditures.
Programming	Writing computer programs for various purposes.

Ability	Ability Definitions
Extent Flexibility	The ability to bend, stretch, twist, or reach with your body, arms, and/or legs.
Problem Sensitivity	The ability to tell when something is wrong or is likely to go wrong. It does not involve solving the problem, only recognizing there is a problem.
Finger Dexterity	The ability to make precisely coordinated movements of the fingers of one or both hands to grasp, manipulate, or assemble very small objects.
Manual Dexterity	The ability to quickly move your hand, your hand together with your arm, or your two hands to grasp, manipulate, or assemble objects.
Arm-Hand Steadiness	The ability to keep your hand and arm steady while moving your arm or while holding your arm and hand in one position.
Trunk Strength	The ability to use your abdominal and lower back muscles to support part of the body repeatedly or continuously over time without 'giving out' or fatiguing.
Inductive Reasoning	The ability to combine pieces of information to form general rules or conclusions (includes finding a relationship among seemingly unrelated events).
Deductive Reasoning	The ability to apply general rules to specific problems to produce answers that make sense.

Control Precision	The ability to quickly and repeatedly adjust the controls of a machine or a vehicle to exact positions.
Information Ordering	The ability to arrange things or actions in a certain order or pattern according to a specific rule or set of rules (e.g., patterns of numbers, letters, words, pictures, mathematical operations).
Oral Comprehension	The ability to listen to and understand information and ideas presented through spoken words and sentences.
Oral Expression	The ability to communicate information and ideas in speaking so others will understand.
Near Vision	The ability to see details at close range (within a few feet of the observer).
Multilimb Coordination	The ability to coordinate two or more limbs (for example, two arms, two legs, or one leg and one arm) while sitting, standing, or lying down. It does not involve performing the activities while the whole body is in motion.
Static Strength	The ability to exert maximum muscle force to lift, push, pull, or carry objects.
Selective Attention	The ability to concentrate on a task over a period of time without being distracted.
Speech Clarity	The ability to speak clearly so others can understand you.
Gross Body Coordination	The ability to coordinate the movement of your arms, legs, and torso together when the whole body is in motion.
Gross Body Equilibrium	The ability to keep or regain your body balance or stay upright when in an unstable position.
Visualization	The ability to imagine how something will look after it is moved around or when its parts are moved or rearranged.
Stamina	The ability to exert yourself physically over long periods of time without getting winded or out of breath.
Hearing Sensitivity	The ability to detect or tell the differences between sounds that vary in pitch and loudness.
Written Comprehension	The ability to read and understand information and ideas presented in writing.
Visual Color Discrimination	The ability to match or detect differences between colors, including shades of color and brightness.
Reaction Time	The ability to quickly respond (with the hand, finger, or foot) to a signal (sound, light, picture) when it appears.
Speech Recognition	The ability to identify and understand the speech of another person.
Speed of Limb Movement	The ability to quickly move the arms and legs.
Perceptual Speed	The ability to quickly and accurately compare similarities and differences among sets of letters, numbers, objects, pictures, or patterns. The things to be compared may be presented at the same time or one after the other. This ability also includes comparing a presented object with a remembered object.
Category Flexibility	The ability to generate or use different sets of rules for combining or grouping things in different ways.
Auditory Attention	The ability to focus on a single source of sound in the presence of other distracting sounds.
Speed of Closure	The ability to quickly make sense of, combine, and organize information into meaningful patterns.
Flexibility of Closure	The ability to identify or detect a known pattern (a figure, object, word, or sound) that is hidden in other distracting material.
Far Vision	The ability to see details at a distance.
Written Expression	The ability to communicate information and ideas in writing so others will understand.
Dynamic Strength	The ability to exert muscle force repeatedly or continuously over time. This involves muscular endurance and resistance to muscle fatigue.
Depth Perception	The ability to judge which of several objects is closer or farther away from you, or to judge the distance between you and an object.
Fluency of Ideas	The ability to come up with a number of ideas about a topic (the number of ideas is important, not their quality, correctness, or creativity).
Wrist-Finger Speed	The ability to make fast, simple, repeated movements of the fingers, hands, and wrists.
Originality	The ability to come up with unusual or clever ideas about a given topic or situation, or to develop creative ways to solve a problem.
Memorization	The ability to remember information such as words, numbers, pictures, and procedures.
Glare Sensitivity	The ability to see objects in the presence of glare or bright lighting.
Time Sharing	The ability to shift back and forth between two or more activities or sources of information (such as speech, sounds, touch, or other sources).
Sound Localization	The ability to tell the direction from which a sound originated.

Spatial Orientation	The ability to know your location in relation to the environment or to know where other objects are in relation to you.
Response Orientation	The ability to choose quickly between two or more movements in response to two or more different signals (lights, sounds, pictures). It includes the speed with which the correct response is started with the hand, foot, or other body part.
Rate Control	The ability to time your movements or the movement of a piece of equipment in anticipation of changes in the speed and/or direction of a moving object or scene.
Night Vision	The ability to see under low light conditions.
Peripheral Vision	The ability to see objects or movement of objects to one's side when the eyes are looking ahead.
Mathematical Reasoning	The ability to choose the right mathematical methods or formulas to solve a problem.
Number Facility	The ability to add, subtract, multiply, or divide quickly and correctly.
Explosive Strength	The ability to use short bursts of muscle force to propel oneself (as in jumping or sprinting), or to throw an object.
Dynamic Flexibility	The ability to quickly and repeatedly bend, stretch, twist, or reach out with your body, arms, and/or legs.

Work_Activity	Work_Activity Definitions
Performing General Physical Activities	Performing physical activities that require considerable use of your arms and legs and moving your whole body, such as climbing, lifting, balancing, walking, stooping, and handling of materials.
Repairing and Maintaining Mechanical Equipment	Servicing, repairing, adjusting, and testing machines, devices, moving parts, and equipment that operate primarily on the basis of mechanical (not electronic) principles.
Handling and Moving Objects	Using hands and arms in handling, installing, positioning, and moving materials, and manipulating things.
Getting Information	Observing, receiving, and otherwise obtaining information from all relevant sources.
Operating Vehicles, Mechanized Devices, or Equipme	Running, maneuvering, navigating, or driving vehicles or mechanized equipment, such as forklifts, passenger vehicles, aircraft, or water craft.
Performing for or Working Directly with the Public	Performing for people or dealing directly with the public. This includes serving customers in restaurants and stores, and receiving clients or guests.
Making Decisions and Solving Problems	Analyzing information and evaluating results to choose the best solution and solve problems.
Communicating with Persons Outside Organization	Communicating with people outside the organization, representing the organization to customers, the public, government, and other external sources. This information can be exchanged in person, in writing, or by telephone or e-mail.
Inspecting Equipment, Structures, or Material	Inspecting equipment, structures, or materials to identify the cause of errors or other problems or defects.
Communicating with Supervisors, Peers, or Subordin	Providing information to supervisors, co-workers, and subordinates by telephone, in written form, e-mail, or in person.
Thinking Creatively	Developing, designing, or creating new applications, ideas, relationships, systems, or products, including artistic contributions.
Organizing, Planning, and Prioritizing Work	Developing specific goals and plans to prioritize, organize, and accomplish your work.
Updating and Using Relevant Knowledge	Keeping up-to-date technically and applying new knowledge to your job.
Establishing and Maintaining Interpersonal Relatio	Developing constructive and cooperative working relationships with others, and maintaining them over time.
Coordinating the Work and Activities of Others	Getting members of a group to work together to accomplish tasks.
Repairing and Maintaining Electronic Equipment	Servicing, repairing, calibrating, regulating, fine-tuning, or testing machines, devices, and equipment that operate primarily on the basis of electrical or electronic (not mechanical) principles.
Selling or Influencing Others	Convincing others to buy merchandise/goods or to otherwise change their minds or actions.
Identifying Objects, Actions, and Events	Identifying information by categorizing, estimating, recognizing differences or similarities, and detecting changes in circumstances or events.
Controlling Machines and Processes	Using either control mechanisms or direct physical activity to operate machines or processes (not including computers or vehicles).

Drafting, Laying Out, and Specifying Technical Dev	Providing documentation, detailed instructions, drawings, or specifications to tell others about how devices, parts, equipment, or structures are to be fabricated, constructed, assembled, modified, maintained, or used.
Training and Teaching Others	Identifying the educational needs of others, developing formal educational or training programs or classes, and teaching or instructing others.
Estimating the Quantifiable Characteristics of Pro	Estimating sizes, distances, and quantities; or determining time, costs, resources, or materials needed to perform a work activity.
Judging the Qualities of Things, Services, or Peop	Assessing the value, importance, or quality of things or people.
Developing and Building Teams	Encouraging and building mutual trust, respect, and cooperation among team members.
Coaching and Developing Others	Identifying the developmental needs of others and coaching, mentoring, or otherwise helping others to improve their knowledge or skills.
Evaluating Information to Determine Compliance wit	Using relevant information and individual judgment to determine whether events or processes comply with laws, regulations, or standards.
Documenting/Recording Information	Entering, transcribing, recording, storing, or maintaining information in written or electronic/magnetic form.
Developing Objectives and Strategies	Establishing long-range objectives and specifying the strategies and actions to achieve them.
Resolving Conflicts and Negotiating with Others	Handling complaints, settling disputes, and resolving grievances and conflicts, or otherwise negotiating with others.
Provide Consultation and Advice to Others	Providing guidance and expert advice to management or other groups on technical, systems-, or process-related topics.
Guiding, Directing, and Motivating Subordinates	Providing guidance and direction to subordinates, including setting performance standards and monitoring performance.
Interpreting the Meaning of Information for Others	Translating or explaining what information means and how it can be used.
Analyzing Data or Information	Identifying the underlying principles, reasons, or facts of information by breaking down information or data into separate parts.
Monitor Processes, Materials, or Surroundings	Monitoring and reviewing information from materials, events, or the environment, to detect or assess problems.
Processing Information	Compiling, coding, categorizing, calculating, tabulating, auditing, or verifying information or data.
Assisting and Caring for Others	Providing personal assistance, medical attention, emotional support, or other personal care to others such as coworkers, customers, or patients.
Scheduling Work and Activities	Scheduling events, programs, and activities, as well as the work of others.
Performing Administrative Activities	Performing day-to-day administrative tasks such as maintaining information files and processing paperwork.
Interacting With Computers	Using computers and computer systems (including hardware and software) to program, write software, set up functions, enter data, or process information.
Monitoring and Controlling Resources	Monitoring and controlling resources and overseeing the spending of money.
Staffing Organizational Units	Recruiting, interviewing, selecting, hiring, and promoting employees in an organization.

Work_Context	Work_Context Definitions
Face-to-Face Discussions	How often do you have to have face-to-face discussions with individuals or teams in this job?
Telephone	How often do you have telephone conversations in this job?
Freedom to Make Decisions	How much decision making freedom, without supervision, does the job offer?
Contact With Others	How much does this job require the worker to be in contact with others (face-to-face, by telephone, or otherwise) in order to perform it?
Exposed to Contaminants	How often does this job require working exposed to contaminants (such as pollutants, gases, dust or odors)?
Exposed to Hazardous Conditions	How often does this job require exposure to hazardous conditions?
Structured versus Unstructured Work	To what extent is this job structured for the worker, rather than allowing the worker to determine tasks, priorities, and goals?
In an Enclosed Vehicle or Equipment	How often does this job require working in a closed vehicle or equipment (e.g., car)?
Outdoors, Exposed to Weather	How often does this job require working outdoors, exposed to all weather conditions?
Spend Time Using Your Hands to Handle, Control, or	How much does this job require using your hands to handle, control, or feel objects, tools or controls?

Exposed to Minor Burns, Cuts, Bites, or Stings	How often does this job require exposure to minor burns, cuts, bites, or stings?
Impact of Decisions on Co-workers or Company Resul	How do the decisions an employee makes impact the results of co-workers, clients or the company?
Spend Time Standing	How much does this job require standing?
Very Hot or Cold Temperatures	How often does this job require working in very hot (above 90 F degrees) or very cold (below 32 F degrees) temperatures?
Sounds, Noise Levels Are Distracting or Uncomforta	How often does this job require working exposed to sounds and noise levels that are distracting or uncomfortable?
Cramped Work Space, Awkward Positions	How often does this job require working in cramped work spaces that requires getting into awkward positions?
Exposed to High Places	How often does this job require exposure to high places?
Frequency of Decision Making	How frequently is the worker required to make decisions that affect other people, the financial resources, and/or the image and reputation of the organization?
Spend Time Bending or Twisting the Body	How much does this job require bending or twisting your body?
Exposed to Hazardous Equipment	How much does this job require exposure to hazardous equipment?
Wear Common Protective or Safety Equipment such as	How much does this job require wearing common protective or safety equipment such as safety shoes, glasses, gloves, hard hats or life jackets?
Time Pressure	How often does this job require the worker to meet strict deadlines?
Indoors, Not Environmentally Controlled	How often does this job require working indoors in non-controlled environmental conditions (e.g., warehouse without heat)?
Level of Competition	To what extent does this job require the worker to compete or to be aware of competitive pressures?
Consequence of Error	How serious would the result usually be if the worker made a mistake that was not readily correctable?
Responsibility for Outcomes and Results	How responsible is the worker for work outcomes and results of other workers?
Deal With External Customers	How important is it to work with external customers or the public in this job?
Spend Time Kneeling, Crouching, Stooping, or Crawl	How much does this job require kneeling, crouching, stooping, or crawling?
Importance of Being Exact or Accurate	How important is being very exact or highly accurate in performing this job?
Indoors, Environmentally Controlled	How often does this job require working indoors in environmentally controlled conditions?
Spend Time Climbing Ladders, Scaffolds, or Poles	How much does this job require climbing ladders, scaffolds, or poles?
Physical Proximity	To what extent does this job require the worker to perform job tasks in close physical proximity to other people?
Spend Time Making Repetitive Motions	How much does this job require making repetitive motions?
Spend Time Walking and Running	How much does this job require walking and running?
Extremely Bright or Inadequate Lighting	How often does this job require working in extremely bright or inadequate lighting conditions?
Work With Work Group or Team	How important is it to work with others in a group or team in this job?
Outdoors, Under Cover	How often does this job require working outdoors, under cover (e.g., structure with roof but no walls)?
Letters and Memos	How often does the job require written letters and memos?
Spend Time Keeping or Regaining Balance	How much does this job require keeping or regaining your balance?
Coordinate or Lead Others	How important is it to coordinate or lead others in accomplishing work activities in this job?
Frequency of Conflict Situations	How often are there conflict situations the employee has to face in this job?
Responsible for Others' Health and Safety	How much responsibility is there for the health and safety of others in this job?
Deal With Unpleasant or Angry People	How frequently does the worker have to deal with unpleasant, angry, or discourteous individuals as part of the job requirements?
Wear Specialized Protective or Safety Equipment su	How much does this job require wearing specialized protective or safety equipment such as breathing apparatus, safety harness, full protection suits, or radiation protection?
Exposed to Whole Body Vibration	How often does this job require exposure to whole body vibration (e.g., operate a jackhammer)?
Importance of Repeating Same Tasks	How important is repeating the same physical activities (e.g., key entry) or mental activities (e.g., checking entries in a ledger) over and over, without stopping, to performing this job?

Pace Determined by Speed of Equipment	How important is it to this job that the pace is determined by the speed of equipment or machinery? (This does not refer to keeping busy at all times on this job.)
Degree of Automation	How automated is the job?
In an Open Vehicle or Equipment	How often does this job require working in an open vehicle or equipment (e.g., tractor)?
Exposed to Disease or Infections	How often does this job require exposure to disease/infections?
Spend Time Sitting	How much does this job require sitting?
Electronic Mail	How often do you use electronic mail in this job?
Public Speaking	How often do you have to perform public speaking in this job?
Exposed to Radiation	How often does this job require exposure to radiation?
Deal With Physically Aggressive People	How frequently does this job require the worker to deal with physical aggression of violent individuals?

Job Zone Component	**Job Zone Component Definitions**
Title	Job Zone Three: Medium Preparation Needed
Overall Experience	Previous work-related skill, knowledge, or experience is required for these occupations. For example, an electrician must have completed three or four years of apprenticeship or several years of vocational training, and often must have passed a licensing exam, in order to perform the job.
Job Training	Employees in these occupations usually need one or two years of training involving both on-the-job experience and informal training with experienced workers.
Job Zone Examples	These occupations usually involve using communication and organizational skills to coordinate, supervise, manage, or train others to accomplish goals. Examples include dental assistants, electricians, fish and game wardens, legal secretaries, personnel recruiters, and recreation workers.
SVP Range	(6.0 to < 7.0)
Education	Most occupations in this zone require training in vocational schools, related on-the-job experience, or an associate's degree. Some may require a bachelor's degree.

Work_Styles	**Work_Styles Definitions**
Dependability	Job requires being reliable, responsible, and dependable, and fulfilling obligations.
Integrity	Job requires being honest and ethical.
Cooperation	Job requires being pleasant with others on the job and displaying a good-natured, cooperative attitude.
Stress Tolerance	Job requires accepting criticism and dealing calmly and effectively with high stress situations.
Attention to Detail	Job requires being careful about detail and thorough in completing work tasks.
Initiative	Job requires a willingness to take on responsibilities and challenges.
Self Control	Job requires maintaining composure, keeping emotions in check, controlling anger, and avoiding aggressive behavior, even in very difficult situations.
Independence	Job requires developing one's own ways of doing things, guiding oneself with little or no supervision, and depending on oneself to get things done.
Persistence	Job requires persistence in the face of obstacles.
Leadership	Job requires a willingness to lead, take charge, and offer opinions and direction.
Analytical Thinking	Job requires analyzing information and using logic to address work-related issues and problems.
Achievement/Effort	Job requires establishing and maintaining personally challenging achievement goals and exerting effort toward mastering tasks.
Adaptability/Flexibility	Job requires being open to change (positive or negative) and to considerable variety in the workplace.
Concern for Others	Job requires being sensitive to others' needs and feelings and being understanding and helpful on the job.
Innovation	Job requires creativity and alternative thinking to develop new ideas for and answers to work-related problems.
Social Orientation	Job requires preferring to work with others rather than alone, and being personally connected with others on the job.

49-9021.02 - Refrigeration Mechanics

Install and repair industrial and commercial refrigerating systems.

Tasks

1) Test lines, components, and connections for leaks.

2) Braze or solder parts to repair defective joints and leaks.

3) Install expansion and control valves, using acetylene torches and wrenches.

4) Perform mechanical overhauls and refrigerant reclaiming.

5) Adjust valves according to specifications and charge system with proper type of refrigerant by pumping the specified gas or fluid into the system.

6) Estimate, order, pick up, deliver, and install materials and supplies needed to maintain equipment in good working condition.

7) Cut, bend, thread, and connect pipe to functional components and water, power, or refrigeration system.

8) Dismantle malfunctioning systems and test components, using electrical, mechanical, and pneumatic testing equipment.

9) Schedule work with customers and initiate work orders, house requisitions and orders from stock.

10) Drill holes and install mounting brackets and hangers into floor and walls of building.

11) Install wiring to connect components to an electric power source.

12) Fabricate and assemble structural and functional components of refrigeration system, using hand tools, power tools, and welding equipment.

13) Mount compressor, condenser, and other components in specified locations on frames, using hand tools and acetylene welding equipment.

14) Keep records of repairs and replacements made and causes of malfunctions.

15) Supervise and instruct assistants.

16) Lift and align components into position, using hoist or block and tackle.

17) Lay out reference points for installation of structural and functional components, using measuring instruments.

18) Read blueprints to determine location, size, capacity, and type of components needed to build refrigeration system.

19) Insulate shells and cabinets of systems.

20) Adjust or replace worn or defective mechanisms and parts, and reassemble repaired systems.

Knowledge	Knowledge Definitions
Mechanical	Knowledge of machines and tools, including their designs, uses, repair, and maintenance.
Customer and Personal Service	Knowledge of principles and processes for providing customer and personal services. This includes customer needs assessment, meeting quality standards for services, and evaluation of customer satisfaction.
Engineering and Technology	Knowledge of the practical application of engineering science and technology. This includes applying principles, techniques, procedures, and equipment to the design and production of various goods and services.
Mathematics	Knowledge of arithmetic, algebra, geometry, calculus, statistics, and their applications.
Public Safety and Security	Knowledge of relevant equipment, policies, procedures, and strategies to promote effective local, state, or national security operations for the protection of people, data, property, and institutions.
Building and Construction	Knowledge of materials, methods, and the tools involved in the construction or repair of houses, buildings, or other structures such as highways and roads.
Design	Knowledge of design techniques, tools, and principles involved in production of precision technical plans, blueprints, drawings, and models.
English Language	Knowledge of the structure and content of the English language including the meaning and spelling of words, rules of composition, and grammar.
Sales and Marketing	Knowledge of principles and methods for showing, promoting, and selling products or services. This includes marketing strategy and tactics, product demonstration, sales techniques, and sales control systems.
Physics	Knowledge and prediction of physical principles, laws, their interrelationships, and applications to understanding fluid, material, and atmospheric dynamics, and mechanical, electrical, atomic and sub- atomic structures and processes.
Administration and Management	Knowledge of business and management principles involved in strategic planning, resource allocation, human resources modeling, leadership technique, production methods, and coordination of people and resources.
Education and Training	Knowledge of principles and methods for curriculum and training design, teaching and instruction for individuals and groups, and the measurement of training effects.
Economics and Accounting	Knowledge of economic and accounting principles and practices, the financial markets, banking and the analysis and reporting of financial data.
Chemistry	Knowledge of the chemical composition, structure, and properties of substances and of the chemical processes and transformations that they undergo. This includes uses of chemicals and their interactions, danger signs, production techniques, and disposal methods.
Personnel and Human Resources	Knowledge of principles and procedures for personnel recruitment, selection, training, compensation and benefits, labor relations and negotiation, and personnel information systems.
Law and Government	Knowledge of laws, legal codes, court procedures, precedents, government regulations, executive orders, agency rules, and the democratic political process.
Production and Processing	Knowledge of raw materials, production processes, quality control, costs, and other techniques for maximizing the effective manufacture and distribution of goods.
Psychology	Knowledge of human behavior and performance; individual differences in ability, personality, and interests; learning and motivation; psychological research methods; and the assessment and treatment of behavioral and affective disorders.
Telecommunications	Knowledge of transmission, broadcasting, switching, control, and operation of telecommunications systems.
Transportation	Knowledge of principles and methods for moving people or goods by air, rail, sea, or road, including the relative costs and benefits.
Clerical	Knowledge of administrative and clerical procedures and systems such as word processing, managing files and records, stenography and transcription, designing forms, and other office procedures and terminology.
Geography	Knowledge of principles and methods for describing the features of land, sea, and air masses, including their physical characteristics, locations, interrelationships, and distribution of plant, animal, and human life.
Computers and Electronics	Knowledge of circuit boards, processors, chips, electronic equipment, and computer hardware and software, including applications and programming.
Communications and Media	Knowledge of media production, communication, and dissemination techniques and methods. This includes alternative ways to inform and entertain via written, oral, and visual media.
Therapy and Counseling	Knowledge of principles, methods, and procedures for diagnosis, treatment, and rehabilitation of physical and mental dysfunctions, and for career counseling and guidance.
Sociology and Anthropology	Knowledge of group behavior and dynamics, societal trends and influences, human migrations, ethnicity, cultures and their history and origins.
Philosophy and Theology	Knowledge of different philosophical systems and religions. This includes their basic principles, values, ethics, ways of thinking, customs, practices, and their impact on human culture.
Medicine and Dentistry	Knowledge of the information and techniques needed to diagnose and treat human injuries, diseases, and deformities. This includes symptoms, treatment alternatives, drug properties and interactions, and preventive health-care measures.
History and Archeology	Knowledge of historical events and their causes, indicators, and effects on civilizations and cultures.
Biology	Knowledge of plant and animal organisms, their tissues, cells, functions, interdependencies, and interactions with each other and the environment.

		Ability	Ability Definitions
Fine Arts	Knowledge of the theory and techniques required to compose, produce, and perform works of music, dance, visual arts, drama, and sculpture.	Problem Sensitivity	The ability to tell when something is wrong or is likely to go wrong. It does not involve solving the problem, only recognizing there is a problem.
Foreign Language	Knowledge of the structure and content of a foreign (non-English) language including the meaning and spelling of words, rules of composition and grammar, and pronunciation.	Manual Dexterity	The ability to quickly move your hand, your hand together with your arm, or your two hands to grasp, manipulate, or assemble objects.
Food Production	Knowledge of techniques and equipment for planting, growing, and harvesting food products (both plant and animal) for consumption, including storage/handling techniques.	Near Vision	The ability to see details at close range (within a few feet of the observer).

Skills	Skills Definitions	Ability	Ability Definitions
Troubleshooting	Determining causes of operating errors and deciding what to do about it.	Oral Comprehension	The ability to listen to and understand information and ideas presented through spoken words and sentences.
Installation	Installing equipment, machines, wiring, or programs to meet specifications.	Arm-Hand Steadiness	The ability to keep your hand and arm steady while moving your arm or while holding your arm and hand in one position.
Reading Comprehension	Understanding written sentences and paragraphs in work related documents.	Deductive Reasoning	The ability to apply general rules to specific problems to produce answers that make sense.
Operation Monitoring	Watching gauges, dials, or other indicators to make sure a machine is working properly.	Oral Expression	The ability to communicate information and ideas in speaking so others will understand.
Repairing	Repairing machines or systems using the needed tools.	Control Precision	The ability to quickly and repeatedly adjust the controls of a machine or a vehicle to exact positions.
Active Listening	Giving full attention to what other people are saying, taking time to understand the points being made, asking questions as appropriate, and not interrupting at inappropriate times.	Information Ordering	The ability to arrange things or actions in a certain order or pattern according to a specific rule or set of rules (e.g., patterns of numbers, letters, words, pictures, mathematical operations).
Equipment Selection	Determining the kind of tools and equipment needed to do a job.	Visualization	The ability to imagine how something will look after it is moved around or when its parts are moved or rearranged.
Active Learning	Understanding the implications of new information for both current and future problem-solving and decision-making.	Multilimb Coordination	The ability to coordinate two or more limbs (for example, two arms, two legs, or one leg and one arm) while sitting, standing, or lying down. It does not involve performing the activities while the whole body is in motion.
Equipment Maintenance	Performing routine maintenance on equipment and determining when and what kind of maintenance is needed.	Finger Dexterity	The ability to make precisely coordinated movements of the fingers of one or both hands to grasp, manipulate, or assemble very small objects.
Operation and Control	Controlling operations of equipment or systems.		
Learning Strategies	Selecting and using training/instructional methods and procedures appropriate for the situation when learning or teaching new things.	Inductive Reasoning	The ability to combine pieces of information to form general rules or conclusions (includes finding a relationship among seemingly unrelated events).
Mathematics	Using mathematics to solve problems.	Speech Clarity	The ability to speak clearly so others can understand you.
Coordination	Adjusting actions in relation to others' actions.	Extent Flexibility	The ability to bend, stretch, twist, or reach with your body, arms, and/or legs.
Writing	Communicating effectively in writing as appropriate for the needs of the audience.	Static Strength	The ability to exert maximum muscle force to lift, push, pull, or carry objects.
Time Management	Managing one's own time and the time of others.		
Speaking	Talking to others to convey information effectively.	Flexibility of Closure	The ability to identify or detect a known pattern (a figure, object, word, or sound) that is hidden in other distracting material.
Critical Thinking	Using logic and reasoning to identify the strengths and weaknesses of alternative solutions, conclusions or approaches to problems.	Speech Recognition	The ability to identify and understand the speech of another person.
Instructing	Teaching others how to do something.	Written Comprehension	The ability to read and understand information and ideas presented in writing.
Complex Problem Solving	Identifying complex problems and reviewing related information to develop and evaluate options and implement solutions.	Trunk Strength	The ability to use your abdominal and lower back muscles to support part of the body repeatedly or continuously over time without 'giving out' or fatiguing.
Systems Evaluation	Identifying measures or indicators of system performance and the actions needed to improve or correct performance, relative to the goals of the system.	Selective Attention	The ability to concentrate on a task over a period of time without being distracted.
Monitoring	Monitoring/Assessing performance of yourself, other individuals, or organizations to make improvements or take corrective action.	Category Flexibility	The ability to generate or use different sets of rules for combining or grouping things in different ways.
Systems Analysis	Determining how a system should work and how changes in conditions, operations, and the environment will affect outcomes.	Written Expression	The ability to communicate information and ideas in writing so others will understand.
Judgment and Decision Making	Considering the relative costs and benefits of potential actions to choose the most appropriate one.	Gross Body Coordination	The ability to coordinate the movement of your arms, legs, and torso together when the whole body is in motion.
Service Orientation	Actively looking for ways to help people.	Depth Perception	The ability to judge which of several objects is closer or farther away from you, or to judge the distance between you and an object.
Science	Using scientific rules and methods to solve problems.		
Management of Material Resources	Obtaining and seeing to the appropriate use of equipment, facilities, and materials needed to do certain work.	Perceptual Speed	The ability to quickly and accurately compare similarities and differences among sets of letters, numbers, objects, pictures, or patterns. The things to be compared may be presented at the same time or one after the other. This ability also includes comparing a presented object with a remembered object.
Social Perceptiveness	Being aware of others' reactions and understanding why they react as they do.		
Technology Design	Generating or adapting equipment and technology to serve user needs.	Visual Color Discrimination	The ability to match or detect differences between colors, including shades of color and brightness.
Negotiation	Bringing others together and trying to reconcile differences.	Hearing Sensitivity	The ability to detect or tell the differences between sounds that vary in pitch and loudness.
Operations Analysis	Analyzing needs and product requirements to create a design.		
Management of Personnel Resources	Motivating, developing, and directing people as they work, identifying the best people for the job.	Fluency of Ideas	The ability to come up with a number of ideas about a topic (the number of ideas is important, not their quality, correctness, or creativity).
Persuasion	Persuading others to change their minds or behavior.		
Quality Control Analysis	Conducting tests and inspections of products, services, or processes to evaluate quality or performance.	Originality	The ability to come up with unusual or clever ideas about a given topic or situation, or to develop creative ways to solve a problem.
Management of Financial Resources	Determining how money will be spent to get the work done, and accounting for these expenditures.	Reaction Time	The ability to quickly respond (with the hand, finger, or foot) to a signal (sound, light, picture) when it appears.
Programming	Writing computer programs for various purposes.		

Auditory Attention	The ability to focus on a single source of sound in the presence of other distracting sounds.
Memorization	The ability to remember information such as words, numbers, pictures, and procedures.
Stamina	The ability to exert yourself physically over long periods of time without getting winded or out of breath.
Gross Body Equilibrium	The ability to keep or regain your body balance or stay upright when in an unstable position.
Glare Sensitivity	The ability to see objects in the presence of glare or bright lighting.
Far Vision	The ability to see details at a distance.
Number Facility	The ability to add, subtract, multiply, or divide quickly and correctly.
Speed of Closure	The ability to quickly make sense of, combine, and organize information into meaningful patterns.
Time Sharing	The ability to shift back and forth between two or more activities or sources of information (such as speech, sounds, touch, or other sources).
Dynamic Strength	The ability to exert muscle force repeatedly or continuously over time. This involves muscular endurance and resistance to muscle fatigue.
Mathematical Reasoning	The ability to choose the right mathematical methods or formulas to solve a problem.
Speed of Limb Movement	The ability to quickly move the arms and legs.
Response Orientation	The ability to choose quickly between two or more movements in response to two or more different signals (lights, sounds, pictures). It includes the speed with which the correct response is started with the hand, foot, or other body part.
Spatial Orientation	The ability to know your location in relation to the environment or to know where other objects are in relation to you.
Wrist-Finger Speed	The ability to make fast, simple, repeated movements of the fingers, hands, and wrists.
Night Vision	The ability to see under low light conditions.
Rate Control	The ability to time your movements or the movement of a piece of equipment in anticipation of changes in the speed and/or direction of a moving object or scene.
Peripheral Vision	The ability to see objects or movement of objects to one's side when the eyes are looking ahead.
Explosive Strength	The ability to use short bursts of muscle force to propel oneself (as in jumping or sprinting), or to throw an object.
Sound Localization	The ability to tell the direction from which a sound originated.
Dynamic Flexibility	The ability to quickly and repeatedly bend, stretch, twist, or reach out with your body, arms, and/or legs.

Work_Activity	Work_Activity Definitions
Repairing and Maintaining Mechanical Equipment	Servicing, repairing, adjusting, and testing machines, devices, moving parts, and equipment that operate primarily on the basis of mechanical (not electronic) principles.
Handling and Moving Objects	Using hands and arms in handling, installing, positioning, and moving materials, and manipulating things.
Monitor Processes, Materials, or Surroundings	Monitoring and reviewing information from materials, events, or the environment, to detect or assess problems.
Getting Information	Observing, receiving, and otherwise obtaining information from all relevant sources.
Identifying Objects, Actions, and Events	Identifying information by categorizing, estimating, recognizing differences or similarities, and detecting changes in circumstances or events.
Repairing and Maintaining Electronic Equipment	Servicing, repairing, calibrating, regulating, fine-tuning, or testing machines, devices, and equipment that operate primarily on the basis of electrical or electronic (not mechanical) principles.
Performing General Physical Activities	Performing physical activities that require considerable use of your arms and legs and moving your whole body, such as climbing, lifting, balancing, walking, stooping, and handling of materials.
Operating Vehicles, Mechanized Devices, or Equipme	Running, maneuvering, navigating, or driving vehicles or mechanized equipment, such as forklifts, passenger vehicles, aircraft, or water craft.
Inspecting Equipment, Structures, or Material	Inspecting equipment, structures, or materials to identify the cause of errors or other problems or defects.
Making Decisions and Solving Problems	Analyzing information and evaluating results to choose the best solution and solve problems.
Communicating with Persons Outside Organization	Communicating with people outside the organization, representing the organization to customers, the public, government, and other external sources. This information can be exchanged in person, in writing, or by telephone or e-mail.

Organizing, Planning, and Prioritizing Work	Developing specific goals and plans to prioritize, organize, and accomplish your work.
Controlling Machines and Processes	Using either control mechanisms or direct physical activity to operate machines or processes (not including computers or vehicles).
Updating and Using Relevant Knowledge	Keeping up-to-date technically and applying new knowledge to your job.
Communicating with Supervisors, Peers, or Subordin	Providing information to supervisors, co-workers, and subordinates by telephone, in written form, e-mail, or in person.
Establishing and Maintaining Interpersonal Relatio	Developing constructive and cooperative working relationships with others, and maintaining them over time.
Coordinating the Work and Activities of Others	Getting members of a group to work together to accomplish tasks.
Performing for or Working Directly with the Public	Performing for people or dealing directly with the public. This includes serving customers in restaurants and stores, and receiving clients or guests.
Coaching and Developing Others	Identifying the developmental needs of others and coaching, mentoring, or otherwise helping others to improve their knowledge or skills.
Training and Teaching Others	Identifying the educational needs of others, developing formal educational or training programs or classes, and teaching or instructing others.
Estimating the Quantifiable Characteristics of Pro	Estimating sizes, distances, and quantities; or determining time, costs, resources, or materials needed to perform a work activity.
Drafting, Laying Out, and Specifying Technical Dev	Providing documentation, detailed instructions, drawings, or specifications to tell others about how devices, parts, equipment, or structures are to be fabricated, constructed, assembled, modified, maintained, or used.
Evaluating Information to Determine Compliance wit	Using relevant information and individual judgment to determine whether events or processes comply with laws, regulations, or standards.
Processing Information	Compiling, coding, categorizing, calculating, tabulating, auditing, or verifying information or data.
Scheduling Work and Activities	Scheduling events, programs, and activities, as well as the work of others.
Analyzing Data or Information	Identifying the underlying principles, reasons, or facts of information by breaking down information or data into separate parts.
Interacting With Computers	Using computers and computer systems (including hardware and software) to program, write software, set up functions, enter data, or process information.
Interpreting the Meaning of Information for Others	Translating or explaining what information means and how it can be used.
Developing and Building Teams	Encouraging and building mutual trust, respect, and cooperation among team members.
Documenting/Recording Information	Entering, transcribing, recording, storing, or maintaining information in written or electronic/magnetic form.
Judging the Qualities of Things, Services, or Peop	Assessing the value, importance, or quality of things or people.
Thinking Creatively	Developing, designing, or creating new applications, ideas, relationships, systems, or products, including artistic contributions.
Provide Consultation and Advice to Others	Providing guidance and expert advice to management or other groups on technical, systems-, or process-related topics.
Guiding, Directing, and Motivating Subordinates	Providing guidance and direction to subordinates, including setting performance standards and monitoring performance.
Resolving Conflicts and Negotiating with Others	Handling complaints, settling disputes, and resolving grievances and conflicts, or otherwise negotiating with others.
Selling or Influencing Others	Convincing others to buy merchandise/goods or to otherwise change their minds or actions.
Assisting and Caring for Others	Providing personal assistance, medical attention, emotional support, or other personal care to others such as coworkers, customers, or patients.
Monitoring and Controlling Resources	Monitoring and controlling resources and overseeing the spending of money.
Performing Administrative Activities	Performing day-to-day administrative tasks such as maintaining information files and processing paperwork.
Staffing Organizational Units	Recruiting, interviewing, selecting, hiring, and promoting employees in an organization.
Developing Objectives and Strategies	Establishing long-range objectives and specifying the strategies and actions to achieve them.

Work_Context	Work_Context Definitions
Impact of Decisions on Co-workers or Company Resul	How do the decisions an employee makes impact the results of co-workers, clients or the company?
Frequency of Decision Making	How frequently is the worker required to make decisions that affect other people, the financial resources, and/or the image and reputation of the organization?
Importance of Being Exact or Accurate	How important is being very exact or highly accurate in performing this job?
Freedom to Make Decisions	How much decision making freedom, without supervision, does the job offer?
Face-to-Face Discussions	How often do you have to have face-to-face discussions with individuals or teams in this job?
Wear Common Protective or Safety Equipment such as	How much does this job require wearing common protective or safety equipment such as safety shoes, glasses, gloves, hard hats or life jackets?
Structured versus Unstructured Work	To what extent is this job structured for the worker, rather than allowing the worker to determine tasks, priorities, and goals?
In an Enclosed Vehicle or Equipment	How often does this job require working in a closed vehicle or equipment (e.g., car)?
Spend Time Using Your Hands to Handle, Control, or	How much does this job require using your hands to handle, control, or feel objects, tools or controls?
Contact With Others	How much does this job require the worker to be in contact with others (face-to-face, by telephone, or otherwise) in order to perform it?
Spend Time Standing	How much does this job require standing?
Telephone	How often do you have telephone conversations in this job?
Outdoors, Exposed to Weather	How often does this job require working outdoors, exposed to all weather conditions?
Exposed to Minor Burns, Cuts, Bites, or Stings	How often does this job require exposure to minor burns, cuts, bites, or stings?
Very Hot or Cold Temperatures	How often does this job require working in very hot (above 90 F degrees) or very cold (below 32 F degrees) temperatures?
Cramped Work Space, Awkward Positions	How often does this job require working in cramped work spaces that requires getting into awkward positions?
Time Pressure	How often does this job require the worker to meet strict deadlines?
Indoors, Environmentally Controlled	How often does this job require working indoors in environmentally controlled conditions?
Exposed to Hazardous Equipment	How often does this job require exposure to hazardous equipment?
Extremely Bright or Inadequate Lighting	How often does this job require working in extremely bright or inadequate lighting conditions?
Work With Work Group or Team	How important is it to work with others in a group or team in this job?
Exposed to Contaminants	How often does this job require working exposed to contaminants (such as pollutants, gases, dust or odors)?
Deal With External Customers	How important is it to work with external customers or the public in this job?
Physical Proximity	To what extent does this job require the worker to perform job tasks in close physical proximity to other people?
Consequence of Error	How serious would the result usually be if the worker made a mistake that was not readily correctable?
Spend Time Walking and Running	How much does this job require walking and running?
Exposed to High Places	How often does this job require exposure to high places?
Responsible for Others' Health and Safety	How much responsibility is there for the health and safety of others in this job?
Importance of Repeating Same Tasks	How important is repeating the same physical activities (e.g., key entry) or mental activities (e.g., checking entries in a ledger) over and over, without stopping, to performing this job?
Indoors, Not Environmentally Controlled	How often does this job require working indoors in non-controlled environmental conditions (e.g., warehouse without heat)?
Letters and Memos	How often does the job require written letters and memos?
Responsibility for Outcomes and Results	How responsible is the worker for work outcomes and results of other workers?
Exposed to Hazardous Conditions	How often does this job require exposure to hazardous conditions?
Coordinate or Lead Others	How important is it to coordinate or lead others in accomplishing work activities in this job?
Level of Competition	To what extent does this job require the worker to compete or to be aware of competitive pressures?
Spend Time Kneeling, Crouching, Stooping, or Crawl	How much does this job require kneeling, crouching, stooping or crawling?
Spend Time Bending or	How much does this job require bending or twisting your body?

Sounds, Noise Levels Are Distracting or Uncomforta	How often does this job require working exposed to sounds and noise levels that are distracting or uncomfortable?
Frequency of Conflict Situations	How often are there conflict situations the employee has to face in this job?
Spend Time Climbing Ladders, Scaffolds, or Poles	How much does this job require climbing ladders, scaffolds, or poles?
Deal With Unpleasant or Angry People	How frequently does the worker have to deal with unpleasant, angry, or discourteous individuals as part of the job requirements?
Outdoors, Under Cover	How often does this job require working outdoors, under cover (e.g., structure with roof but no walls)?
Spend Time Making Repetitive Motions	How much does this job require making repetitive motions?
Pace Determined by Speed of Equipment	How important is it to this job that the pace is determined by the speed of equipment or machinery? (This does not refer to keeping busy at all times on this job.)
Wear Specialized Protective or Safety Equipment su	How much does this job require wearing specialized protective or safety equipment such as breathing apparatus, safety harness, full protection suits, or radiation protection?
Public Speaking	How often do you have to perform public speaking in this job?
Spend Time Keeping or Regaining Balance	How much does this job require keeping or regaining your balance?
Exposed to Whole Body Vibration	How often does this job require exposure to whole body vibration (e.g., operate a jackhammer)?
Spend Time Sitting	How much does this job require sitting?
In an Open Vehicle or Equipment	How often does this job require working in an open vehicle or equipment (e.g., tractor)?
Exposed to Disease or Infections	How often does this job require exposure to disease/infections?
Degree of Automation	How automated is the job?
Deal With Physically Aggressive People	How frequently does this job require the worker to deal with physical aggression of violent individuals?
Electronic Mail	How often do you use electronic mail in this job?
Exposed to Radiation	How often does this job require exposure to radiation?

Job Zone Component	Job Zone Component Definitions
Title	Job Zone Three: Medium Preparation Needed
Overall Experience	Previous work-related skill, knowledge, or experience is required for these occupations. For example, an electrician must have completed three or four years of apprenticeship or several years of vocational training, and often must have passed a licensing exam, in order to perform the job.
Job Training	Employees in these occupations usually need one or two years of training involving both on-the-job experience and informal training with experienced workers.
Job Zone Examples	These occupations usually involve using communication and organizational skills to coordinate, supervise, manage, or train others to accomplish goals. Examples include dental assistants, electricians, fish and game wardens, legal secretaries, personnel recruiters, and recreation workers.
SVP Range	(6.0 to < 7.0)
Education	Most occupations in this zone require training in vocational schools, related on-the-job experience, or an associate's degree. Some may require a bachelor's degree.

Work_Styles	Work_Styles Definitions
Dependability	Job requires being reliable, responsible, and dependable, and fulfilling obligations.
Attention to Detail	Job requires being careful about detail and thorough in completing work tasks.
Independence	Job requires developing one's own ways of doing things, guiding oneself with little or no supervision, and depending on oneself to get things done.
Cooperation	Job requires being pleasant with others on the job and displaying a good-natured, cooperative attitude.
Initiative	Job requires a willingness to take on responsibilities and challenges.
Self Control	Job requires maintaining composure, keeping emotions in check, controlling anger, and avoiding aggressive behavior, even in very difficult situations.
Persistence	Job requires persistence in the face of obstacles.
Leadership	Job requires a willingness to lead, take charge, and offer opinions and direction.

Adaptability/Flexibility	Job requires being open to change (positive or negative) and to considerable variety in the workplace.
Innovation	Job requires creativity and alternative thinking to develop new ideas for and answers to work-related problems.
Integrity	Job requires being honest and ethical.
Stress Tolerance	Job requires accepting criticism and dealing calmly and effectively with high stress situations.
Concern for Others	Job requires being sensitive to others' needs and feelings and being understanding and helpful on the job.
Analytical Thinking	Job requires analyzing information and using logic to address work-related issues and problems.
Achievement/Effort	Job requires establishing and maintaining personally challenging achievement goals and exerting effort toward mastering tasks.
Social Orientation	Job requires preferring to work with others rather than alone, and being personally connected with others on the job.

49-9031.00 - Home Appliance Repairers

Repair, adjust, or install all types of electric or gas household appliances, such as refrigerators, washers, dryers, and ovens.

Tasks

1) Take measurements to determine if appliances will fit in installation locations; perform minor carpentry work when necessary to ensure proper installation.

2) Disassemble appliances so that problems can be diagnosed and repairs can be made.

3) Clean and reinstall parts.

4) Observe and examine appliances during operation to detect specific malfunctions such as loose parts or leaking fluid.

5) Reassemble units after repairs are made, making adjustments and cleaning and lubricating parts as needed.

6) Talk to customers or refer to work orders in order to establish the nature of appliance malfunctions.

7) Replace worn and defective parts such as switches, bearings, transmissions, belts, gears, circuit boards, or defective wiring.

8) Hang steel supports from beams or joists to hold hoses, vents, and gas pipes in place.

9) Light and adjust pilot lights on gas stoves, and examine valves and burners for gas leakage and specified flame.

10) Install appliances such as refrigerators, washing machines, and stoves.

11) Assemble new or reconditioned appliances.

12) Disassemble and reinstall existing kitchen cabinets, or assemble and install prefabricated kitchen cabinets and trim in conjunction with appliance installation.

13) Record maintenance and repair work performed on appliances.

14) Provide repair cost estimates, and recommend whether appliance repair or replacement is a better choice.

15) Level washing machines and connect hoses to water pipes, using hand tools.

16) Trace electrical circuits, following diagrams, and conduct tests with circuit testers and other equipment to locate shorts and grounds.

17) Measure, cut, and thread pipe, and connect it to feeder lines and equipment or appliances, using rules and hand tools.

18) Conserve, recover, and recycle refrigerants used in cooling systems.

19) Respond to emergency calls for problems such as gas leaks.

20) Level refrigerators, adjust doors, and connect water lines to water pipes for ice makers and water dispensers, using hand tools.

21) Instruct customers regarding operation and care of appliances, and provide information such as emergency service numbers.

22) Install gas pipes and water lines to connect appliances to existing gas lines or plumbing.

23) Observe and test operation of appliances following installation, and make any initial installation adjustments that are necessary.

24) Set appliance thermostats, and check to ensure that they are functioning properly.

25) Test and examine gas pipelines and equipment to locate leaks and faulty connections, and to determine the pressure and flow of gas.

26) Maintain stocks of parts used in on-site installation, maintenance, and repair of appliances.

27) Bill customers for repair work, and collect payment.

28) Contact supervisors or offices to receive repair assignments.

29) Clean, lubricate, and touch up minor defects on newly installed or repaired appliances.

30) Service and repair domestic electrical and/or gas appliances such as clothes washers, refrigerators, stoves, and dryers.

49-9042.00 - Maintenance and Repair Workers, General

Perform work involving the skills of two or more maintenance or craft occupations to keep machines, mechanical equipment, or the structure of an establishment in repair. Duties may involve pipe fitting; boiler making; insulating; welding; machining; carpentry; repairing electrical or mechanical equipment; installing, aligning, and balancing new equipment; and repairing buildings, floors, or stairs.

Tasks

1) Perform routine preventive maintenance to ensure that machines continue to run smoothly, building systems operate efficiently, and the physical condition of buildings does not deteriorate.

2) Repair or replace defective equipment parts using hand tools and power tools, and reassemble equipment.

3) Diagnose mechanical problems and determine how to correct them, checking blueprints, repair manuals, and parts catalogs as necessary.

4) Order parts, supplies, and equipment from catalogs and suppliers, or obtain them from storerooms.

5) Assemble, install and/or repair wiring, electrical and electronic components, pipe systems and plumbing, machinery, and equipment.

6) Dismantle devices to gain access to and remove defective parts, using hoists, cranes, hand tools, and power tools.

7) Adjust functional parts of devices and control instruments, using hand tools, levels, plumb bobs, and straightedges.

8) Inspect drives, motors, and belts, check fluid levels, replace filters, and perform other maintenance actions, following checklists.

9) Inspect, operate, and test machinery and equipment in order to diagnose machine malfunctions.

10) Clean and lubricate shafts, bearings, gears, and other parts of machinery.

11) Plan and lay out repair work using diagrams, drawings, blueprints, maintenance manuals, and schematic diagrams.

12) Paint and repair roofs, windows, doors, floors, woodwork, plaster, drywall, and other parts of building structures.

13) Record maintenance and repair work performed and the costs of the work.

14) Operate cutting torches or welding equipment to cut or join metal parts.

15) Align and balance new equipment after installation.

16) Maintain and repair specialized equipment and machinery found in cafeterias, laundries, hospitals, stores, offices, and factories.

17) Inspect used parts to determine changes in dimensional requirements, using rules, calipers, micrometers, and other measuring instruments.

18) Fabricate and repair counters, benches, partitions, and other wooden structures such as sheds and outbuildings.

19) Estimate repair costs.

20) Set up and operate machine tools to repair or fabricate machine parts, jigs and fixtures, and tools.

21) Lay brick to repair and maintain buildings, walls, arches and other structures.

22) Grind and reseat valves, using valve-grinding machines.

Knowledge	Knowledge Definitions
Mechanical	Knowledge of machines and tools, including their designs, uses, repair, and maintenance.

Building and Construction	Knowledge of materials, methods, and the tools involved in the construction or repair of houses, buildings, or other structures such as highways and roads.	Economics and Accounting	Knowledge of economic and accounting principles and practices, the financial markets, banking and the analysis and reporting of financial data.
Public Safety and Security	Knowledge of relevant equipment, policies, procedures, and strategies to promote effective local, state, or national security operations for the protection of people, data, property, and institutions.	Communications and Media	Knowledge of media production, communication, and dissemination techniques and methods. This includes alternative ways to inform and entertain via written, oral, and visual media.
Design	Knowledge of design techniques, tools, and principles involved in production of precision technical plans, blueprints, drawings, and models.	Biology	Knowledge of plant and animal organisms, their tissues, cells, functions, interdependencies, and interactions with each other and the environment.
English Language	Knowledge of the structure and content of the English language including the meaning and spelling of words, rules of composition, and grammar.	Sales and Marketing	Knowledge of principles and methods for showing, promoting, and selling products or services. This includes marketing strategy and tactics, product demonstration, sales techniques, and sales control systems.
Engineering and Technology	Knowledge of the practical application of engineering science and technology. This includes applying principles, techniques, procedures, and equipment to the design and production of various goods and services.	Food Production	Knowledge of techniques and equipment for planting, growing, and harvesting food products (both plant and animal) for consumption, including storage/handling techniques.
Mathematics	Knowledge of arithmetic, algebra, geometry, calculus, statistics, and their applications.	Foreign Language	Knowledge of the structure and content of a foreign (non-English) language including the meaning and spelling of words, rules of composition and grammar, and pronunciation.
Education and Training	Knowledge of principles and methods for curriculum and training design, teaching and instruction for individuals and groups, and the measurement of training effects.	Therapy and Counseling	Knowledge of principles, methods, and procedures for diagnosis, treatment, and rehabilitation of physical and mental dysfunctions, and for career counseling and guidance.
Physics	Knowledge and prediction of physical principles, laws, their interrelationships, and applications to understanding fluid, material, and atmospheric dynamics, and mechanical, electrical, atomic and sub-atomic structures and processes.	History and Archeology	Knowledge of historical events and their causes, indicators, and effects on civilizations and cultures.
Customer and Personal Service	Knowledge of principles and processes for providing customer and personal services. This includes customer needs assessment, meeting quality standards for services, and evaluation of customer satisfaction.	Fine Arts	Knowledge of the theory and techniques required to compose, produce, and perform works of music, dance, visual arts, drama, and sculpture.
Production and Processing	Knowledge of raw materials, production processes, quality control, costs, and other techniques for maximizing the effective manufacture and distribution of goods.	Philosophy and Theology	Knowledge of different philosophical systems and religions. This includes their basic principles, values, ethics, ways of thinking, customs, practices, and their impact on human culture.
Chemistry	Knowledge of the chemical composition, structure, and properties of substances and of the chemical processes and transformations that they undergo. This includes uses of chemicals and their interactions, danger signs, production techniques, and disposal methods.	**Skills**	**Skills Definitions**
Administration and Management	Knowledge of business and management principles involved in strategic planning, resource allocation, human resources modeling, leadership technique, production methods, and coordination of people and resources.	Equipment Maintenance	Performing routine maintenance on equipment and determining when and what kind of maintenance is needed.
Computers and Electronics	Knowledge of circuit boards, processors, chips, electronic equipment, and computer hardware and software, including applications and programming.	Repairing	Repairing machines or systems using the needed tools.
		Troubleshooting	Determining causes of operating errors and deciding what to do about it.
Transportation	Knowledge of principles and methods for moving people or goods by air, rail, sea, or road, including the relative costs and benefits.	Installation	Installing equipment, machines, wiring, or programs to meet specifications.
Law and Government	Knowledge of laws, legal codes, court procedures, precedents, government regulations, executive orders, agency rules, and the democratic political process.	Active Listening	Giving full attention to what other people are saying, taking time to understand the points being made, asking questions as appropriate, and not interrupting at inappropriate times.
Clerical	Knowledge of administrative and clerical procedures and systems such as word processing, managing files and records, stenography and transcription, designing forms, and other office procedures and terminology.	Equipment Selection	Determining the kind of tools and equipment needed to do a job.
		Reading Comprehension	Understanding written sentences and paragraphs in work related documents.
Personnel and Human Resources	Knowledge of principles and procedures for personnel recruitment, selection, training, compensation and benefits, labor relations and negotiation, and personnel information systems.	Critical Thinking	Using logic and reasoning to identify the strengths and weaknesses of alternative solutions, conclusions or approaches to problems.
		Operation Monitoring	Watching gauges, dials, or other indicators to make sure a machine is working properly.
Psychology	Knowledge of human behavior and performance; individual differences in ability, personality, and interests; learning and motivation; psychological research methods; and the assessment and treatment of behavioral and affective disorders.	Coordination	Adjusting actions in relation to others' actions.
		Active Learning	Understanding the implications of new information for both current and future problem-solving and decision-making.
Sociology and Anthropology	Knowledge of group behavior and dynamics, societal trends and influences, human migrations, ethnicity, cultures and their history and origins.	Operation and Control	Controlling operations of equipment or systems.
		Judgment and Decision Making	Considering the relative costs and benefits of potential actions to choose the most appropriate one.
Telecommunications	Knowledge of transmission, broadcasting, switching, control, and operation of telecommunications systems.	Learning Strategies	Selecting and using training/instructional methods and procedures appropriate for the situation when learning or teaching new things.
Geography	Knowledge of principles and methods for describing the features of land, sea, and air masses, including their physical characteristics, locations, interrelationships, and distribution of plant, animal, and human life.	Speaking	Talking to others to convey information effectively.
		Monitoring	Monitoring/Assessing performance of yourself, other individuals, or organizations to make improvements or take corrective action.
		Complex Problem Solving	Identifying complex problems and reviewing related information to develop and evaluate options and implement solutions.
Medicine and Dentistry	Knowledge of the information and techniques needed to diagnose and treat human injuries, diseases, and deformities. This includes symptoms, treatment alternatives, drug properties and interactions, and preventive health-care measures.	Instructing	Teaching others how to do something.
		Quality Control Analysis	Conducting tests and inspections of products, services, or processes to evaluate quality or performance.
		Service Orientation	Actively looking for ways to help people.
		Social Perceptiveness	Being aware of others' reactions and understanding why they react as they do.
		Time Management	Managing one's own time and the time of others.

Systems Evaluation	Identifying measures or indicators of system performance and the actions needed to improve or correct performance, relative to the goals of the system.
Writing	Communicating effectively in writing as appropriate for the needs of the audience.
Mathematics	Using mathematics to solve problems.
Systems Analysis	Determining how a system should work and how changes in conditions, operations, and the environment will affect outcomes.
Technology Design	Generating or adapting equipment and technology to serve user needs.
Operations Analysis	Analyzing needs and product requirements to create a design.
Management of Material Resources	Obtaining and seeing to the appropriate use of equipment, facilities, and materials needed to do certain work.
Persuasion	Persuading others to change their minds or behavior.
Negotiation	Bringing others together and trying to reconcile differences.
Management of Personnel Resources	Motivating, developing, and directing people as they work, identifying the best people for the job.
Science	Using scientific rules and methods to solve problems.
Management of Financial Resources	Determining how money will be spent to get the work done, and accounting for these expenditures.
Programming	Writing computer programs for various purposes.

Ability	Ability Definitions
Problem Sensitivity	The ability to tell when something is wrong or is likely to go wrong. It does not involve solving the problem, only recognizing there is a problem.
Manual Dexterity	The ability to quickly move your hand, your hand together with your arm, or your two hands to grasp, manipulate, or assemble objects.
Information Ordering	The ability to arrange things or actions in a certain order or pattern according to a specific rule or set of rules (e.g., patterns of numbers, letters, words, pictures, mathematical operations).
Near Vision	The ability to see details at close range (within a few feet of the observer).
Multilimb Coordination	The ability to coordinate two or more limbs (for example, two arms, two legs, or one leg and one arm) while sitting, standing, or lying down. It does not involve performing the activities while the whole body is in motion.
Arm-Hand Steadiness	The ability to keep your hand and arm steady while moving your arm or while holding your arm and hand in one position.
Inductive Reasoning	The ability to combine pieces of information to form general rules or conclusions (includes finding a relationship among seemingly unrelated events).
Visualization	The ability to imagine how something will look after it is moved around or when its parts are moved or rearranged.
Static Strength	The ability to exert maximum muscle force to lift, push, pull, or carry objects.
Deductive Reasoning	The ability to apply general rules to specific problems to produce answers that make sense.
Finger Dexterity	The ability to make precisely coordinated movements of the fingers of one or both hands to grasp, manipulate, or assemble very small objects.
Selective Attention	The ability to concentrate on a task over a period of time without being distracted.
Speech Clarity	The ability to speak clearly so others can understand you.
Control Precision	The ability to quickly and repeatedly adjust the controls of a machine or a vehicle to exact positions.
Oral Expression	The ability to communicate information and ideas in speaking so others will understand.
Oral Comprehension	The ability to listen to and understand information and ideas presented through spoken words and sentences.
Speech Recognition	The ability to identify and understand the speech of another person.
Flexibility of Closure	The ability to identify or detect a known pattern (a figure, object, word, or sound) that is hidden in other distracting material.
Extent Flexibility	The ability to bend, stretch, twist, or reach with your body, arms, and/or legs.
Trunk Strength	The ability to use your abdominal and lower back muscles to support part of the body repeatedly or continuously over time without 'giving out' or fatiguing.
Speed of Closure	The ability to quickly make sense of, combine, and organize information into meaningful patterns.
Written Comprehension	The ability to read and understand information and ideas presented in writing.

Visual Color Discrimination	The ability to match or detect differences between colors, including shades of color and brightness.
Auditory Attention	The ability to focus on a single source of sound in the presence of other distracting sounds.
Speed of Limb Movement	The ability to quickly move the arms and legs.
Gross Body Coordination	The ability to coordinate the movement of your arms, legs, and torso together when the whole body is in motion.
Depth Perception	The ability to judge which of several objects is closer or farther away from you, or to judge the distance between you and an object.
Reaction Time	The ability to quickly respond (with the hand, finger, or foot) to a signal (sound, light, picture) when it appears.
Stamina	The ability to exert yourself physically over long periods of time without getting winded or out of breath.
Hearing Sensitivity	The ability to detect or tell the differences between sounds that vary in pitch and loudness.
Written Expression	The ability to communicate information and ideas in writing so others will understand.
Far Vision	The ability to see details at a distance.
Perceptual Speed	The ability to quickly and accurately compare similarities and differences among sets of letters, numbers, objects, pictures, or patterns. The things to be compared may be presented at the same time or one after the other. This ability also includes comparing a presented object with a remembered object.
Dynamic Strength	The ability to exert muscle force repeatedly or continuously over time. This involves muscular endurance and resistance to muscle fatigue.
Gross Body Equilibrium	The ability to keep or regain your body balance or stay upright when in an unstable position.
Memorization	The ability to remember information such as words, numbers, pictures, and procedures.
Spatial Orientation	The ability to know your location in relation to the environment or to know where other objects are in relation to you.
Originality	The ability to come up with unusual or clever ideas about a given topic or situation, or to develop creative ways to solve a problem.
Glare Sensitivity	The ability to see objects in the presence of glare or bright lighting.
Category Flexibility	The ability to generate or use different sets of rules for combining or grouping things in different ways.
Time Sharing	The ability to shift back and forth between two or more activities or sources of information (such as speech, sounds, touch, or other sources).
Rate Control	The ability to time your movements or the movement of a piece of equipment in anticipation of changes in the speed and/or direction of a moving object or scene.
Mathematical Reasoning	The ability to choose the right mathematical methods or formulas to solve a problem.
Response Orientation	The ability to choose quickly between two or more movements in response to two or more different signals (lights, sounds, pictures). It includes the speed with which the correct response is started with the hand, foot, or other body part.
Wrist-Finger Speed	The ability to make fast, simple, repeated movements of the fingers, hands, and wrists.
Fluency of Ideas	The ability to come up with a number of ideas about a topic (the number of ideas is important, not their quality, correctness, or creativity).
Number Facility	The ability to add, subtract, multiply, or divide quickly and correctly.
Night Vision	The ability to see under low light conditions.
Explosive Strength	The ability to use short bursts of muscle force to propel oneself (as in jumping or sprinting), or to throw an object.
Peripheral Vision	The ability to see objects or movement of objects to one's side when the eyes are looking ahead.
Dynamic Flexibility	The ability to quickly and repeatedly bend, stretch, twist, or reach out with your body, arms, and/or legs.
Sound Localization	The ability to tell the direction from which a sound originated.

Work_Activity	Work_Activity Definitions
Inspecting Equipment, Structures, or Material	Inspecting equipment, structures, or materials to identify the cause of errors or other problems or defects.
Performing General Physical Activities	Performing physical activities that require considerable use of your arms and legs and moving your whole body, such as climbing, lifting, balancing, walking, stooping, and handling of materials.

Repairing and Maintaining Mechanical Equipment	Servicing, repairing, adjusting, and testing machines, devices, moving parts, and equipment that operate primarily on the basis of mechanical (not electronic) principles.
Handling and Moving Objects	Using hands and arms in handling, installing, positioning, and moving materials, and manipulating things.
Getting Information	Observing, receiving, and otherwise obtaining information from all relevant sources.
Communicating with Supervisors, Peers, or Subordin	Providing information to supervisors, co-workers, and subordinates by telephone, in written form, e-mail, or in person.
Making Decisions and Solving Problems	Analyzing information and evaluating results to choose the best solution and solve problems.
Identifying Objects, Actions, and Events	Identifying information by categorizing, estimating, recognizing differences or similarities, and detecting changes in circumstances or events.
Controlling Machines and Processes	Using either control mechanisms or direct physical activity to operate machines or processes (not including computers or vehicles).
Operating Vehicles, Mechanized Devices, or Equipme	Running, maneuvering, navigating, or driving vehicles or mechanized equipment, such as forklifts, passenger vehicles, aircraft, or water craft.
Monitor Processes, Materials, or Surroundings	Monitoring and reviewing information from materials, events, or the environment, to detect or assess problems.
Establishing and Maintaining Interpersonal Relatio	Developing constructive and cooperative working relationships with others, and maintaining them over time.
Updating and Using Relevant Knowledge	Keeping up-to-date technically and applying new knowledge to your job.
Organizing, Planning, and Prioritizing Work	Developing specific goals and plans to prioritize, organize, and accomplish your work.
Thinking Creatively	Developing, designing, or creating new applications, ideas, relationships, systems, or products, including artistic contributions.
Coordinating the Work and Activities of Others	Getting members of a group to work together to accomplish tasks.
Training and Teaching Others	Identifying the educational needs of others, developing formal educational or training programs or classes, and teaching or instructing others.
Assisting and Caring for Others	Providing personal assistance, medical attention, emotional support, or other personal care to others such as coworkers, customers, or patients.
Repairing and Maintaining Electronic Equipment	Servicing, repairing, calibrating, regulating, fine-tuning, or testing machines, devices, and equipment that operate primarily on the basis of electrical or electronic (not mechanical) principles.
Judging the Qualities of Things, Services, or Peop	Assessing the value, importance, or quality of things or people.
Documenting/Recording Information	Entering, transcribing, recording, storing, or maintaining information in written or electronic/magnetic form.
Scheduling Work and Activities	Scheduling events, programs, and activities, as well as the work of others.
Evaluating Information to Determine Compliance wit	Using relevant information and individual judgment to determine whether events or processes comply with laws, regulations, or standards.
Processing Information	Compiling, coding, categorizing, calculating, tabulating, auditing, or verifying information or data.
Analyzing Data or Information	Identifying the underlying principles, reasons, or facts of information by breaking down information or data into separate parts.
Resolving Conflicts and Negotiating with Others	Handling complaints, settling disputes, and resolving grievances and conflicts, or otherwise negotiating with others.
Performing for or Working Directly with the Public	Performing for people or dealing directly with the public. This includes serving customers in restaurants and stores, and receiving clients or guests.
Performing Administrative Activities	Performing day-to-day administrative tasks such as maintaining information files and processing paperwork.
Developing and Building Teams	Encouraging and building mutual trust, respect, and cooperation among team members.
Coaching and Developing Others	Identifying the developmental needs of others and coaching, mentoring, or otherwise helping others to improve their knowledge or skills.
Estimating the Quantifiable Characteristics of Pro	Estimating sizes, distances, and quantities; or determining time, costs, resources, or materials needed to perform a work activity.
Developing Objectives and Strategies	Establishing long-range objectives and specifying the strategies and actions to achieve them.
Drafting, Laying Out, and Specifying Technical Dev	Providing documentation, detailed instructions, drawings, or specifications to tell others about how devices, parts, equipment, or structures are to be fabricated, constructed, assembled, modified, maintained, or used.
Monitoring and Controlling Resources	Monitoring and controlling resources and overseeing the spending of money.
Interpreting the Meaning of Information for Others	Translating or explaining what information means and how it can be used.
Communicating with Persons Outside Organization	Communicating with people outside the organization, representing the organization to customers, the public, government, and other external sources. This information can be exchanged in person, in writing, or by telephone or e-mail.
Interacting With Computers	Using computers and computer systems (including hardware and software) to program, write software, set up functions, enter data, or process information.
Guiding, Directing, and Motivating Subordinates	Providing guidance and direction to subordinates, including setting performance standards and monitoring performance.
Selling or Influencing Others	Convincing others to buy merchandise/goods or to otherwise change their minds or actions.
Provide Consultation and Advice to Others	Providing guidance and expert advice to management or other groups on technical, systems-, or process-related topics.
Staffing Organizational Units	Recruiting, interviewing, selecting, hiring, and promoting employees in an organization.

Work_Context	Work_Context Definitions
Face-to-Face Discussions	How often do you have to have face-to-face discussions with individuals or teams in this job?
Spend Time Using Your Hands to Handle, Control, or	How much does this job require using your hands to handle, control, or feel objects, tools or controls?
Freedom to Make Decisions	How much decision making freedom, without supervision, does the job offer?
Telephone	How often do you have telephone conversations in this job?
Contact With Others	How much does this job require the worker to be in contact with others (face-to-face, by telephone, or otherwise) in order to perform it?
Spend Time Standing	How much does this job require standing?
Indoors, Environmentally Controlled	How often does this job require working indoors in environmentally controlled conditions?
Wear Common Protective or Safety Equipment such as	How much does this job require wearing common protective or safety equipment such as safety shoes, glasses, gloves, hard hats or live jackets?
Structured versus Unstructured Work	To what extent is this job structured for the worker, rather than allowing the worker to determine tasks, priorities, and goals?
Exposed to Minor Burns, Cuts, Bites, or Stings	How often does this job require exposure to minor burns, cuts, bites, or stings?
Importance of Being Exact or Accurate	How important is being very exact or highly accurate in performing this job?
Indoors, Not Environmentally Controlled	How often does this job require working indoors in non-controlled environmental conditions (e.g., warehouse without heat)?
Sounds, Noise Levels Are Distracting or Uncomforta	How often does this job require working exposed to sounds and noise levels that are distracting or uncomfortable?
Spend Time Walking and Running	How much does this job require walking and running?
Outdoors, Exposed to Weather	How often does this job require working outdoors, exposed to all weather conditions?
Exposed to Contaminants	How often does this job require working exposed to contaminants (such as pollutants, gases, dust or odors)?
Very Hot or Cold Temperatures	How often does this job require working in very hot (above 90 F degrees) or very cold (below 32 F degrees) temperatures?
Exposed to Hazardous Equipment	How often does this job require exposure to hazardous equipment?
Responsible for Others' Health and Safety	How much responsibility is there for the health and safety of others in this job?
Time Pressure	How often does this job require the worker to meet strict deadlines?
Frequency of Decision Making	How frequently is the worker required to make decisions that affect other people, the financial resources, and/or the image and reputation of the organization?
Work With Work Group or Team	How important is it to work with others in a group or team in this job?
Impact of Decisions on Co-workers or Company Resul	How do the decisions an employee makes impact the results of co-workers, clients or the company?
Cramped Work Space, Awkward Positions	How often does this job require working in cramped work spaces that requires getting into awkward positions?

Consequence of Error	How serious would the result usually be if the worker made a mistake that was not readily correctable?
Extremely Bright or Inadequate Lighting	How often does this job require working in extremely bright or inadequate lighting conditions?
Exposed to Hazardous Conditions	How often does this job require exposure to hazardous conditions?
Coordinate or Lead Others	How important is it to coordinate or lead others in accomplishing work activities in this job?
Physical Proximity	To what extent does this job require the worker to perform job tasks in close physical proximity to other people?
Letters and Memos	How often does the job require written letters and memos?
Exposed to High Places	How often does this job require exposure to high places?
Deal With External Customers	How important is it to work with external customers or the public in this job?
Responsibility for Outcomes and Results	How responsible is the worker for work outcomes and results of other workers?
Spend Time Bending or Twisting the Body	How much does this job require bending or twisting your body?
In an Enclosed Vehicle or Equipment	How often does this job require working in a closed vehicle or equipment (e.g., car)?
Importance of Repeating Same Tasks	How important is repeating the same physical activities (e.g., key entry) or mental activities (e.g., checking entries in a ledger) over and over, without stopping, to performing this job?
Frequency of Conflict Situations	How often are there conflict situations the employee has to face in this job?
Deal With Unpleasant or Angry People	How frequently does the worker have to deal with unpleasant, angry, or discourteous individuals as part of the job requirements?
Spend Time Making Repetitive Motions	How much does this job require making repetitive motions?
Spend Time Kneeling, Crouching, Stooping, or Crawl	How much does this job require kneeling, crouching, stooping or crawling?
Outdoors, Under Cover	How often does this job require working outdoors, under cover (e.g., structure with roof but no walls)?
In an Open Vehicle or Equipment	How often does this job require working in an open vehicle or equipment (e.g., tractor)?
Exposed to Disease or Infections	How often does this job require exposure to disease/infections?
Electronic Mail	How often do you use electronic mail in this job?
Spend Time Climbing Ladders, Scaffolds, or Poles	How much does this job require climbing ladders, scaffolds, or poles?
Level of Competition	To what extent does this job require the worker to compete or to be aware of competitive pressures?
Exposed to Whole Body Vibration	How often does this job require exposure to whole body vibration (e.g., operate a jackhammer)?
Wear Specialized Protective or Safety Equipment su	How much does this job require wearing specialized protective or safety equipment such as breathing apparatus, safety harness, full protection suits, or radiation protection?
Pace Determined by Speed of Equipment	How important is it to this job that the pace is determined by the speed of equipment or machinery? (This does not refer to keeping busy at all times on this job.)
Spend Time Sitting	How much does this job require sitting?
Spend Time Keeping or Regaining Balance	How much does this job require keeping or regaining your balance?
Degree of Automation	How automated is the job?
Public Speaking	How often do you have to perform public speaking in this job?
Deal With Physically Aggressive People	How frequently does this job require the worker to deal with physical aggression of violent individuals?
Exposed to Radiation	How often does this job require exposure to radiation?

Job Zone Component	Job Zone Component Definitions
Title	Job Zone Three: Medium Preparation Needed
Overall Experience	Previous work-related skill, knowledge, or experience is required for these occupations. For example, an electrician must have completed three or four years of apprenticeship or several years of vocational training, and often must have passed a licensing exam, in order to perform the job.
Job Training	Employees in these occupations usually need one or two years of training involving both on-the-job experience and informal training with experienced workers.

Job Zone Examples	These occupations usually involve using communication and organizational skills to coordinate, supervise, manage, or train others to accomplish goals. Examples include dental assistants, electricians, fish and game wardens, legal secretaries, personnel recruiters, and recreation workers.
SVP Range	(6.0 to < 7.0)
Education	Most occupations in this zone require training in vocational schools, related on-the-job experience, or an associate's degree. Some may require a bachelor's degree.

Work_Styles	Work_Styles Definitions
Dependability	Job requires being reliable, responsible, and dependable, and fulfilling obligations.
Attention to Detail	Job requires being careful about detail and thorough in completing work tasks.
Cooperation	Job requires being pleasant with others on the job and displaying a good-natured, cooperative attitude.
Self Control	Job requires maintaining composure, keeping emotions in check, controlling anger, and avoiding aggressive behavior, even in very difficult situations.
Integrity	Job requires being honest and ethical.
Initiative	Job requires a willingness to take on responsibilities and challenges.
Analytical Thinking	Job requires analyzing information and using logic to address work-related issues and problems.
Concern for Others	Job requires being sensitive to others' needs and feelings and being understanding and helpful on the job.
Stress Tolerance	Job requires accepting criticism and dealing calmly and effectively with high stress situations.
Adaptability/Flexibility	Job requires being open to change (positive or negative) and to considerable variety in the workplace.
Achievement/Effort	Job requires establishing and maintaining personally challenging achievement goals and exerting effort toward mastering tasks.
Independence	Job requires developing one's own ways of doing things, guiding oneself with little or no supervision, and depending on oneself to get things done.
Persistence	Job requires persistence in the face of obstacles.
Leadership	Job requires a willingness to lead, take charge, and offer opinions and direction.
Innovation	Job requires creativity and alternative thinking to develop new ideas for and answers to work-related problems.
Social Orientation	Job requires preferring to work with others rather than alone, and being personally connected with others on the job.

49-9044.00 - Millwrights

Install, dismantle, or move machinery and heavy equipment according to layout plans, blueprints, or other drawings.

Tasks

1) Lay out mounting holes, using measuring instruments, and drill holes with power drill.

2) Move machinery and equipment, using hoists, dollies, rollers, and trucks.

3) Insert shims, adjust tension on nuts and bolts, or position parts, using hand tools and measuring instruments, to set specified clearances between moving and stationary parts.

4) Align machines and equipment, using hoists, jacks, hand tools, squares, rules, micrometers, and plumb bobs.

5) Replace defective parts of machine or adjust clearances and alignment of moving parts.

6) Repair and lubricate machines and equipment.

7) Assemble machines, and bolt, weld, rivet, or otherwise fasten them to foundation or other structures, using hand tools and power tools.

8) Dismantle machines, using hammers, wrenches, crowbars, and other hand tools.

9) Attach moving parts and subassemblies to basic assembly unit, using hand tools and power tools.

10) Level bedplate and establish centerline, using straightedge, levels, and transit.

11) Signal crane operator to lower basic assembly units to bedplate, and align unit to centerline.

12) Shrink-fit bushings, sleeves, rings, liners, gears, and wheels to specified items, using portable gas heating equipment.

13) Position steel beams to support bedplates of machines and equipment, using blueprints and schematic drawings, to determine work procedures.

14) Bolt parts, such as side and deck plates, jaw plates, and journals, to basic assembly unit.

15) Connect power unit to machines or steam piping to equipment, and test unit to evaluate its mechanical operation.

16) Construct foundation for machines, using hand tools and building materials such as wood, cement, and steel.

17) Dismantle machinery and equipment for shipment to installation site, usually performing installation and maintenance work as part of team.

18) Operate engine lathe to grind, file, and turn machine parts to dimensional specifications.

19) Install robot and modify its program, using teach pendant.

Knowledge	Knowledge Definitions
Mechanical	Knowledge of machines and tools, including their designs, uses, repair, and maintenance.
Building and Construction	Knowledge of materials, methods, and the tools involved in the construction or repair of houses, buildings, or other structures such as highways and roads.
Design	Knowledge of design techniques, tools, and principles involved in production of precision technical plans, blueprints, drawings, and models.
English Language	Knowledge of the structure and content of the English language including the meaning and spelling of words, rules of composition, and grammar.
Mathematics	Knowledge of arithmetic, algebra, geometry, calculus, statistics, and their applications.
Engineering and Technology	Knowledge of the practical application of engineering science and technology. This includes applying principles, techniques, procedures, and equipment to the design and production of various goods and services.
Physics	Knowledge and prediction of physical principles, laws, their interrelationships, and applications to understanding fluid, material, and atmospheric dynamics, and mechanical, electrical, atomic and sub-atomic structures and processes.
Public Safety and Security	Knowledge of relevant equipment, policies, procedures, and strategies to promote effective local, state, or national security operations for the protection of people, data, property, and institutions.
Education and Training	Knowledge of principles and methods for curriculum and training design, teaching and instruction for individuals and groups, and the measurement of training effects.
Production and Processing	Knowledge of raw materials, production processes, quality control, costs, and other techniques for maximizing the effective manufacture and distribution of goods.
Administration and Management	Knowledge of business and management principles involved in strategic planning, resource allocation, human resources modeling, leadership technique, production methods, and coordination of people and resources.
Chemistry	Knowledge of the chemical composition, structure, and properties of substances and of the chemical processes and transformations that they undergo. This includes uses of chemicals and their interactions, danger signs, production techniques, and disposal methods.
Clerical	Knowledge of administrative and clerical procedures and systems such as word processing, managing files and records, stenography and transcription, designing forms, and other office procedures and terminology.
Customer and Personal Service	Knowledge of principles and processes for providing customer and personal services. This includes customer needs assessment, meeting quality standards for services, and evaluation of customer satisfaction.
Transportation	Knowledge of principles and methods for moving people or goods by air, rail, sea, or road, including the relative costs and benefits.
Computers and Electronics	Knowledge of circuit boards, processors, chips, electronic equipment, and computer hardware and software, including applications and programming.
Personnel and Human Resources	Knowledge of principles and procedures for personnel recruitment, selection, training, compensation and benefits, labor relations and negotiation, and personnel information systems.
Law and Government	Knowledge of laws, legal codes, court procedures, precedents, government regulations, executive orders, agency rules, and the democratic political process.
Sales and Marketing	Knowledge of principles and methods for showing, promoting, and selling products or services. This includes marketing strategy and tactics, product demonstration, sales techniques, and sales control systems.
Psychology	Knowledge of human behavior and performance; individual differences in ability, personality, and interests; learning and motivation; psychological research methods; and the assessment and treatment of behavioral and affective disorders.
Telecommunications	Knowledge of transmission, broadcasting, switching, control, and operation of telecommunications systems.
Communications and Media	Knowledge of media production, communication, and dissemination techniques and methods. This includes alternative ways to inform and entertain via written, oral, and visual media.
Economics and Accounting	Knowledge of economic and accounting principles and practices, the financial markets, banking and the analysis and reporting of financial data.
Medicine and Dentistry	Knowledge of the information and techniques needed to diagnose and treat human injuries, diseases, and deformities. This includes symptoms, treatment alternatives, drug properties and interactions, and preventive health-care measures.
Geography	Knowledge of principles and methods for describing the features of land, sea, and air masses, including their physical characteristics, locations, interrelationships, and distribution of plant, animal, and human life.
Philosophy and Theology	Knowledge of different philosophical systems and religions. This includes their basic principles, values, ethics, ways of thinking, customs, practices, and their impact on human culture.
Biology	Knowledge of plant and animal organisms, their tissues, cells, functions, interdependencies, and interactions with each other and the environment.
Foreign Language	Knowledge of the structure and content of a foreign (non-English) language including the meaning and spelling of words, rules of composition and grammar, and pronunciation.
Sociology and Anthropology	Knowledge of group behavior and dynamics, societal trends and influences, human migrations, ethnicity, cultures and their history and origins.
Therapy and Counseling	Knowledge of principles, methods, and procedures for diagnosis, treatment, and rehabilitation of physical and mental dysfunctions, and for career counseling and guidance.
Fine Arts	Knowledge of the theory and techniques required to compose, produce, and perform works of music, dance, visual arts, drama, and sculpture.
History and Archeology	Knowledge of historical events and their causes, indicators, and effects on civilizations and cultures.
Food Production	Knowledge of techniques and equipment for planting, growing, and harvesting food products (both plant and animal) for consumption, including storage/handling techniques.

Skills	Skills Definitions
Equipment Selection	Determining the kind of tools and equipment needed to do a job.
Repairing	Repairing machines or systems using the needed tools.
Installation	Installing equipment, machines, wiring, or programs to meet specifications.
Troubleshooting	Determining causes of operating errors and deciding what to do about it.
Mathematics	Using mathematics to solve problems.
Active Listening	Giving full attention to what other people are saying, taking time to understand the points being made, asking questions as appropriate, and not interrupting at inappropriate times.
Instructing	Teaching others how to do something.
Complex Problem Solving	Identifying complex problems and reviewing related information to develop and evaluate options and implement solutions.
Equipment Maintenance	Performing routine maintenance on equipment and determining when and what kind of maintenance is needed.
Coordination	Adjusting actions in relation to others' actions.
Reading Comprehension	Understanding written sentences and paragraphs in work related documents.
Active Learning	Understanding the implications of new information for both current and future problem-solving and decision-making.
Time Management	Managing one's own time and the time of others.

Critical Thinking	Using logic and reasoning to identify the strengths and weaknesses of alternative solutions, conclusions or approaches to problems.
Judgment and Decision Making	Considering the relative costs and benefits of potential actions to choose the most appropriate one.
Learning Strategies	Selecting and using training/instructional methods and procedures appropriate for the situation when learning or teaching new things.
Operation and Control	Controlling operations of equipment or systems.
Operation Monitoring	Watching gauges, dials, or other indicators to make sure a machine is working properly.
Management of Material Resources	Obtaining and seeing to the appropriate use of equipment, facilities, and materials needed to do certain work.
Monitoring	Monitoring/Assessing performance of yourself, other individuals, or organizations to make improvements or take corrective action.
Systems Analysis	Determining how a system should work and how changes in conditions, operations, and the environment will affect outcomes.
Technology Design	Generating or adapting equipment and technology to serve user needs.
Writing	Communicating effectively in writing as appropriate for the needs of the audience.
Service Orientation	Actively looking for ways to help people.
Speaking	Talking to others to convey information effectively.
Quality Control Analysis	Conducting tests and inspections of products, services, or processes to evaluate quality or performance.
Systems Evaluation	Identifying measures or indicators of system performance and the actions needed to improve or correct performance, relative to the goals of the system.
Management of Personnel Resources	Motivating, developing, and directing people as they work, identifying the best people for the job.
Negotiation	Bringing others together and trying to reconcile differences.
Science	Using scientific rules and methods to solve problems.
Persuasion	Persuading others to change their minds or behavior.
Social Perceptiveness	Being aware of others' reactions and understanding why they react as they do.
Operations Analysis	Analyzing needs and product requirements to create a design.
Management of Financial Resources	Determining how money will be spent to get the work done, and accounting for these expenditures.
Programming	Writing computer programs for various purposes.

Ability	Ability Definitions
Information Ordering	The ability to arrange things or actions in a certain order or pattern according to a specific rule or set of rules (e.g., patterns of numbers, letters, words, pictures, mathematical operations).
Manual Dexterity	The ability to quickly move your hand, your hand together with your arm, or your two hands to grasp, manipulate, or assemble objects.
Near Vision	The ability to see details at close range (within a few feet of the observer).
Visualization	The ability to imagine how something will look after it is moved around or when its parts are moved or rearranged.
Problem Sensitivity	The ability to tell when something is wrong or is likely to go wrong. It does not involve solving the problem, only recognizing there is a problem.
Multilimb Coordination	The ability to coordinate two or more limbs (for example, two arms, two legs, or one leg and one arm) while sitting, standing, or lying down. It does not involve performing the activities while the whole body is in motion.
Deductive Reasoning	The ability to apply general rules to specific problems to produce answers that make sense.
Speech Clarity	The ability to speak clearly so others can understand you.
Arm-Hand Steadiness	The ability to keep your hand and arm steady while moving your arm or while holding your arm and hand in one position.
Selective Attention	The ability to concentrate on a task over a period of time without being distracted.
Control Precision	The ability to quickly and repeatedly adjust the controls of a machine or a vehicle to exact positions.
Depth Perception	The ability to judge which of several objects is closer or farther away from you, or to judge the distance between you and an object.
Static Strength	The ability to exert maximum muscle force to lift, push, pull, or carry objects.
Speech Recognition	The ability to identify and understand the speech of another person.

Auditory Attention	The ability to focus on a single source of sound in the presence of other distracting sounds.
Oral Comprehension	The ability to listen to and understand information and ideas presented through spoken words and sentences.
Oral Expression	The ability to communicate information and ideas in speaking so others will understand.
Finger Dexterity	The ability to make precisely coordinated movements of the fingers of one or both hands to grasp, manipulate, or assemble very small objects.
Extent Flexibility	The ability to bend, stretch, twist, or reach with your body, arms, and/or legs.
Trunk Strength	The ability to use your abdominal and lower back muscles to support part of the body repeatedly or continuously over time without 'giving out' or fatiguing.
Reaction Time	The ability to quickly respond (with the hand, finger, or foot) to a signal (sound, light, picture) when it appears.
Perceptual Speed	The ability to quickly and accurately compare similarities and differences among sets of letters, numbers, objects, pictures, or patterns. The things to be compared may be presented at the same time or one after the other. This ability also includes comparing a presented object with a remembered object.
Gross Body Equilibrium	The ability to keep or regain your body balance or stay upright when in an unstable position.
Inductive Reasoning	The ability to combine pieces of information to form general rules or conclusions (includes finding a relationship among seemingly unrelated events).
Spatial Orientation	The ability to know your location in relation to the environment or to know where other objects are in relation to you.
Dynamic Strength	The ability to exert muscle force repeatedly or continuously over time. This involves muscular endurance and resistance to muscle fatigue.
Rate Control	The ability to time your movements or the movement of a piece of equipment in anticipation of changes in the speed and/or direction of a moving object or scene.
Stamina	The ability to exert yourself physically over long periods of time without getting winded or out of breath.
Far Vision	The ability to see details at a distance.
Flexibility of Closure	The ability to identify or detect a known pattern (a figure, object, word, or sound) that is hidden in other distracting material.
Hearing Sensitivity	The ability to detect or tell the differences between sounds that vary in pitch and loudness.
Gross Body Coordination	The ability to coordinate the movement of your arms, legs, and torso together when the whole body is in motion.
Written Comprehension	The ability to read and understand information and ideas presented in writing.
Written Expression	The ability to communicate information and ideas in writing so others will understand.
Visual Color Discrimination	The ability to match or detect differences between colors, including shades of color and brightness.
Category Flexibility	The ability to generate or use different sets of rules for combining or grouping things in different ways.
Glare Sensitivity	The ability to see objects in the presence of glare or bright lighting.
Time Sharing	The ability to shift back and forth between two or more activities or sources of information (such as speech, sounds, touch, or other sources).
Wrist-Finger Speed	The ability to make fast, simple, repeated movements of the fingers, hands, and wrists.
Originality	The ability to come up with unusual or clever ideas about a given topic or situation, or to develop creative ways to solve a problem.
Memorization	The ability to remember information such as words, numbers, pictures, and procedures.
Speed of Limb Movement	The ability to quickly move the arms and legs.
Response Orientation	The ability to choose quickly between two or more movements in response to two or more different signals (lights, sounds, pictures). It includes the speed with which the correct response is started with the hand, foot, or other body part.
Mathematical Reasoning	The ability to choose the right mathematical methods or formulas to solve a problem.
Fluency of Ideas	The ability to come up with a number of ideas about a topic (the number of ideas is important, not their quality, correctness, or creativity).
Peripheral Vision	The ability to see objects or movement of objects to one's side when the eyes are looking ahead.
Speed of Closure	The ability to quickly make sense of, combine, and organize information into meaningful patterns.

Number Facility	The ability to add, subtract, multiply, or divide quickly and correctly.
Sound Localization	The ability to tell the direction from which a sound originated.
Explosive Strength	The ability to use short bursts of muscle force to propel oneself (as in jumping or sprinting), or to throw an object.
Dynamic Flexibility	The ability to quickly and repeatedly bend, stretch, twist, or reach out with your body, arms, and/or legs.
Night Vision	The ability to see under low light conditions.

Work_Activity	Work_Activity Definitions
Repairing and Maintaining Mechanical Equipment	Servicing, repairing, adjusting, and testing machines, devices, moving parts, and equipment that operate primarily on the basis of mechanical (not electronic) principles.
Operating Vehicles, Mechanized Devices, or Equipme	Running, maneuvering, navigating, or driving vehicles or mechanized equipment, such as forklifts, passenger vehicles, aircraft, or water craft.
Getting Information	Observing, receiving, and otherwise obtaining information from all relevant sources.
Inspecting Equipment, Structures, or Material	Inspecting equipment, structures, or materials to identify the cause of errors or other problems or defects.
Making Decisions and Solving Problems	Analyzing information and evaluating results to choose the best solution and solve problems.
Updating and Using Relevant Knowledge	Keeping up-to-date technically and applying new knowledge to your job.
Handling and Moving Objects	Using hands and arms in handling, installing, positioning, and moving materials, and manipulating things.
Performing General Physical Activities	Performing physical activities that require considerable use of your arms and legs and moving your whole body, such as climbing, lifting, balancing, walking, stooping, and handling of materials.
Identifying Objects, Actions, and Events	Identifying information by categorizing, estimating, recognizing differences or similarities, and detecting changes in circumstances or events.
Monitor Processes, Materials, or Surroundings	Monitoring and reviewing information from materials, events, or the environment, to detect or assess problems.
Communicating with Supervisors, Peers, or Subordin	Providing information to supervisors, co-workers, and subordinates by telephone, in written form, e-mail, or in person.
Coordinating the Work and Activities of Others	Getting members of a group to work together to accomplish tasks.
Establishing and Maintaining Interpersonal Relatio	Developing constructive and cooperative working relationships with others, and maintaining them over time.
Estimating the Quantifiable Characteristics of Pro	Estimating sizes, distances, and quantities; or determining time, costs, resources, or materials needed to perform a work activity.
Interpreting the Meaning of Information for Others	Translating or explaining what information means and how it can be used.
Judging the Qualities of Things, Services, or Peop	Assessing the value, importance, or quality of things or people.
Evaluating Information to Determine Compliance wit	Using relevant information and individual judgment to determine whether events or processes comply with laws, regulations, or standards.
Analyzing Data or Information	Identifying the underlying principles, reasons, or facts of information by breaking down information or data into separate parts.
Controlling Machines and Processes	Using either control mechanisms or direct physical activity to operate machines or processes (not including computers or vehicles).
Processing Information	Compiling, coding, categorizing, calculating, tabulating, auditing, or verifying information or data.
Thinking Creatively	Developing, designing, or creating new applications, ideas, relationships, systems, or products, including artistic contributions.
Coaching and Developing Others	Identifying the developmental needs of others and coaching, mentoring, or otherwise helping others to improve their knowledge or skills.
Drafting, Laying Out, and Specifying Technical Dev	Providing documentation, detailed instructions, drawings, or specifications to tell others about how devices, parts, equipment, or structures are to be fabricated, constructed, assembled, modified, maintained, or used.
Organizing, Planning, and Prioritizing Work	Developing specific goals and plans to prioritize, organize, and accomplish your work.
Provide Consultation and Advice to Others	Providing guidance and expert advice to management or other groups on technical, systems-, or process-related topics.

Developing and Building Teams	Encouraging and building mutual trust, respect, and cooperation among team members.
Scheduling Work and Activities	Scheduling events, programs, and activities, as well as the work of others.
Guiding, Directing, and Motivating Subordinates	Providing guidance and direction to subordinates, including setting performance standards and monitoring performance.
Developing Objectives and Strategies	Establishing long-range objectives and specifying the strategies and actions to achieve them.
Training and Teaching Others	Identifying the educational needs of others, developing formal educational or training programs or classes, and teaching or instructing others.
Documenting/Recording Information	Entering, transcribing, recording, storing, or maintaining information in written or electronic/magnetic form.
Assisting and Caring for Others	Providing personal assistance, medical attention, emotional support, or other personal care to others such as coworkers, customers, or patients.
Interacting With Computers	Using computers and computer systems (including hardware and software) to program, write software, set up functions, enter data, or process information.
Repairing and Maintaining Electronic Equipment	Servicing, repairing, calibrating, regulating, fine-tuning, or testing machines, devices, and equipment that operate primarily on the basis of electrical or electronic (not mechanical) principles.
Performing Administrative Activities	Performing day-to-day administrative tasks such as maintaining information files and processing paperwork.
Monitoring and Controlling Resources	Monitoring and controlling resources and overseeing the spending of money.
Communicating with Persons Outside Organization	Communicating with people outside the organization, representing the organization to customers, the public, government, and other external sources. This information can be exchanged in person, in writing, or by telephone or e-mail.
Resolving Conflicts and Negotiating with Others	Handling complaints, settling disputes, and resolving grievances and conflicts, or otherwise negotiating with others.
Staffing Organizational Units	Recruiting, interviewing, selecting, hiring, and promoting employees in an organization.
Selling or Influencing Others	Convincing others to buy merchandise/goods or to otherwise change their minds or actions.
Performing for or Working Directly with the Public	Performing for people or dealing directly with the public. This includes serving customers in restaurants and stores, and receiving clients or guests.

Work_Context	Work_Context Definitions
Wear Common Protective or Safety Equipment such as	How much does this job require wearing common protective or safety equipment such as safety shoes, glasses, gloves, hard hats or live jackets?
Face-to-Face Discussions	How often do you have to have face-to-face discussions with individuals or teams in this job?
Sounds, Noise Levels Are Distracting or Uncomforta	How often does this job require working exposed to sounds and noise levels that are distracting or uncomfortable?
Very Hot or Cold Temperatures	How often does this job require working in very hot (above 90 F degrees) or very cold (below 32 F degrees) temperatures?
Indoors, Not Environmentally Controlled	How often does this job require working indoors in non-controlled environmental conditions (e.g., warehouse without heat)?
Exposed to Hazardous Equipment	How often does this job require exposure to hazardous equipment?
Freedom to Make Decisions	How much decision making freedom, without supervision, does the job offer?
Structured versus Unstructured Work	To what extent is this job structured for the worker, rather than allowing the worker to determine tasks, priorities, and goals?
Frequency of Decision Making	How frequently is the worker required to make decisions that affect other people, the financial resources, and/or the image and reputation of the organization?
Exposed to Contaminants	How often does this job require working exposed to contaminants (such as pollutants, gases, dust or odors)?
Spend Time Using Your Hands to Handle, Control, or	How much does this job require using your hands to handle, control, or feel objects, tools or controls?
Physical Proximity	To what extent does this job require the worker to perform job tasks in close physical proximity to other people?
Extremely Bright or Inadequate Lighting	How often does this job require working in extremely bright or inadequate lighting conditions?
Cramped Work Space, Awkward Positions	How often does this job require working in cramped work spaces that requires getting into awkward positions?
Telephone	How often do you have telephone conversations in this job?
Time Pressure	How often does this job require the worker to meet strict deadlines?

Spend Time Standing	How much does this job require standing?
Exposed to Hazardous Conditions	How often does this job require exposure to hazardous conditions?
Impact of Decisions on Co-workers or Company Resul	How do the decisions an employee makes impact the results of co-workers, clients or the company?
Responsible for Others' Health and Safety	How much responsibility is there for the health and safety of others in this job?
Importance of Being Exact or Accurate	How important is being very exact or highly accurate in performing this job?
Exposed to High Places	How often does this job require exposure to high places?
Spend Time Bending or Twisting the Body	How much does this job require bending or twisting your body?
Work With Work Group or Team	How important is it to work with others in a group or team in this job?
Contact With Others	How much does this job require the worker to be in contact with others (face-to-face, by telephone, or otherwise) in order to perform it?
Exposed to Minor Burns, Cuts, Bites, or Stings	How often does this job require exposure to minor burns, cuts, bites, or stings?
Coordinate or Lead Others	How important is it to coordinate or lead others in accomplishing work activities in this job?
Consequence of Error	How serious would the result usually be if the worker made a mistake that was not readily correctable?
Outdoors, Exposed to Weather	How often does this job require working outdoors, exposed to all weather conditions?
Responsibility for Outcomes and Results	How responsible is the worker for work outcomes and results of other workers?
Spend Time Making Repetitive Motions	How much does this job require making repetitive motions?
Wear Specialized Protective or Safety Equipment su	How much does this job require wearing specialized protective or safety equipment such as breathing apparatus, safety harness, full protection suits, or radiation protection?
Level of Competition	To what extent does this job require the worker to compete or to be aware of competitive pressures?
Outdoors, Under Cover	How often does this job require working outdoors, under cover (e.g., structure with roof but no walls)?
Deal With Unpleasant or Angry People	How frequently does the worker have to deal with unpleasant, angry, or discourteous individuals as part of the job requirements?
Spend Time Walking and Running	How much does this job require walking and running?
In an Open Vehicle or Equipment	How often does this job require working in an open vehicle or equipment (e.g., tractor)?
Spend Time Keeping or Regaining Balance	How much does this job require keeping or regaining your balance?
Spend Time Kneeling, Crouching, Stooping, or Crawl	How much does this job require kneeling, crouching, stooping or crawling?
Letters and Memos	How often does the job require written letters and memos?
Pace Determined by Speed of Equipment	How important is it to this job that the pace is determined by the speed of equipment or machinery? (This does not refer to keeping busy at all times on this job.)
Importance of Repeating Same Tasks	How important is repeating the same physical activities (e.g., key entry) or mental activities (e.g., checking entries in a ledger) over and over, without stopping, to performing this job?
Exposed to Whole Body Vibration	How often does this job require exposure to whole body vibration (e.g., operate a jackhammer)?
Frequency of Conflict Situations	How often are there conflict situations the employee has to face in this job?
Spend Time Climbing Ladders, Scaffolds, or Poles	How much does this job require climbing ladders, scaffolds, or poles?
Deal With External Customers	How important is it to work with external customers or the public in this job?
Degree of Automation	How automated is the job?
Indoors, Environmentally Controlled	How often does this job require working indoors in environmentally controlled conditions?
Exposed to Disease or Infections	How often does this job require exposure to disease/infections?
Electronic Mail	How often do you use electronic mail in this job?
Public Speaking	How often do you have to perform public speaking in this job?
In an Enclosed Vehicle or Equipment	How often does this job require working in a closed vehicle or equipment (e.g., car)?
Spend Time Sitting	How much does this job require sitting?
Exposed to Radiation	How often does this job require exposure to radiation?
Deal With Physically Aggressive People	How frequently does this job require the worker to deal with physical aggression of violent individuals?

Job Zone Component	Job Zone Component Definitions
Title	Job Zone Three: Medium Preparation Needed
Overall Experience	Previous work-related skill, knowledge, or experience is required for these occupations. For example, an electrician must have completed three or four years of apprenticeship or several years of vocational training, and often must have passed a licensing exam, in order to perform the job.
Job Training	Employees in these occupations usually need one or two years of training involving both on-the-job experience and informal training with experienced workers.
Job Zone Examples	These occupations usually involve using communication and organizational skills to coordinate, supervise, manage, or train others to accomplish goals. Examples include dental assistants, electricians, fish and game wardens, legal secretaries, personnel recruiters, and recreation workers.
SVP Range	(6.0 to < 7.0)
Education	Most occupations in this zone require training in vocational schools, related on-the-job experience, or an associate's degree. Some may require a bachelor's degree.

Work_Styles	Work_Styles Definitions
Attention to Detail	Job requires being careful about detail and thorough in completing work tasks.
Independence	Job requires developing one's own ways of doing things, guiding oneself with little or no supervision, and depending on oneself to get things done.
Dependability	Job requires being reliable, responsible, and dependable, and fulfilling obligations.
Concern for Others	Job requires being sensitive to others' needs and feelings and being understanding and helpful on the job.
Analytical Thinking	Job requires analyzing information and using logic to address work-related issues and problems.
Innovation	Job requires creativity and alternative thinking to develop new ideas for and answers to work-related problems.
Initiative	Job requires a willingness to take on responsibilities and challenges.
Cooperation	Job requires being pleasant with others on the job and displaying a good-natured, cooperative attitude.
Self Control	Job requires maintaining composure, keeping emotions in check, controlling anger, and avoiding aggressive behavior, even in very difficult situations.
Persistence	Job requires persistence in the face of obstacles.
Adaptability/Flexibility	Job requires being open to change (positive or negative) and to considerable variety in the workplace.
Achievement/Effort	Job requires establishing and maintaining personally challenging achievement goals and exerting effort toward mastering tasks.
Stress Tolerance	Job requires accepting criticism and dealing calmly and effectively with high stress situations.
Integrity	Job requires being honest and ethical.
Leadership	Job requires a willingness to lead, take charge, and offer opinions and direction.
Social Orientation	Job requires preferring to work with others rather than alone, and being personally connected with others on the job.

49-9045.00 - Refractory Materials Repairers, Except Brickmasons

Build or repair furnaces, kilns, cupolas, boilers, converters, ladles, soaking pits, ovens, etc., using refractory materials.

Tasks

1) Reline or repair ladles and pouring spouts with refractory clay, using trowels.

2) Spread mortar on stopper heads and rods, using trowels, and slide brick sleeves over rods to form refractory jackets.

3) Tighten locknuts holding refractory stopper assemblies together, spread mortar on jackets to seal sleeve joints, and dry mortar in ovens.

4) Climb scaffolding, carrying hoses, and spray surfaces of cupolas with refractory mixtures.

using spray equipment.

5) Install preformed metal scaffolding in interiors of cupolas, using hand tools.

6) Chip slag from linings of ladles or remove linings when beyond repair, using hammers and chisels.

7) Disassemble molds, and cut, chip, and smooth clay structures such as floaters, drawbars, and L-blocks.

8) Drill holes in furnace walls, bolt overlapping layers of plastic to walls, and hammer surfaces to compress layers into solid sheets.

9) Measure furnace walls to determine dimensions, then cut required number of sheets from plastic block, using saws.

10) Install clay structures in melting tanks and drawing kilns to control the flow and temperature of molten glass, using hoists and hand tools.

11) Fasten stopper heads to rods with metal pins to assemble refractory stoppers used to plug pouring nozzles of steel ladles.

12) Dump and tamp clay in molds, using tamping tools.

13) Dry and bake new linings by placing inverted linings over burners, building fires in ladles, or by using blowtorches.

14) Bolt sections of wooden molds together, using wrenches, and line molds with paper to prevent clay from sticking to molds.

15) Mix specified amounts of sand, clay, mortar powder, and water to form refractory clay or mortar, using shovels or mixing machines.

16) Transfer clay structures to curing ovens, melting tanks, and drawing kilns, using forklifts.

49-9051.00 - Electrical Power-Line Installers and Repairers

Install or repair cables or wires used in electrical power or distribution systems. May erect poles and light or heavy duty transmission towers.

Tasks

1) Install watt-hour meters and connect service drops between power lines and consumers' facilities.

2) Travel in trucks, helicopters, and airplanes to inspect lines for freedom from obstruction and adequacy of insulation.

3) Trim trees that could be hazardous to the functioning of cables or wires.

4) Place insulating or fireproofing materials over conductors and joints.

5) Clean, tin, and splice corresponding conductors by twisting ends together or by joining ends with metal clamps and soldering connections.

6) Attach crossarms, insulators, and auxiliary equipment to poles prior to installing them.

7) Identify defective sectionalizing devices, circuit breakers, fuses, voltage regulators, transformers, switches, relays, or wiring, using wiring diagrams and electrical-testing instruments.

8) Climb poles or use truck-mounted buckets to access equipment.

9) Dig holes using augers, and set poles, using cranes and power equipment.

10) Splice or solder cables together or to overhead transmission lines, customer service lines, or street light lines, using hand tools, epoxies, or specialized equipment.

11) Open switches or attach grounding devices in order to remove electrical hazards from disturbed or fallen lines or to facilitate repairs.

12) Cut and peel lead sheathing and insulation from defective or newly installed cables and conduits prior to splicing.

13) Replace damaged poles with new poles, and straighten the poles.

14) Test conductors, according to electrical diagrams and specifications, to identify corresponding conductors and to prevent incorrect connections.

15) Cut trenches for laying underground cables, using trenchers and cable plows.

16) Inspect and test power lines and auxiliary equipment to locate and identify problems, using reading and testing instruments.

17) Lay underground cable directly in trenches, or string it through conduit running through the trenches.

18) Adhere to safety practices and procedures, such as checking equipment regularly and erecting barriers around work areas.

19) Pull up cable by hand from large reels mounted on trucks.

20) Install, maintain, and repair electrical distribution and transmission systems, including conduits, cables, wires, and related equipment such as transformers, circuit breakers, and switches.

21) String wire conductors and cables between poles, towers, trenches, pylons, and buildings, setting lines in place and using winches to adjust tension.

22) Coordinate work assignment preparation and completion with other workers.

49-9052.00 - Telecommunications Line Installers and Repairers

String and repair telephone and television cable, including fiber optics and other equipment for transmitting messages or television programming.

Tasks

1) Splice cables, using hand tools, epoxy, or mechanical equipment.

2) Lay underground cable directly in trenches, or string it through conduits running through trenches.

3) Travel to customers' premises to install, maintain, and repair audio and visual electronic reception equipment and accessories.

4) Use a variety of construction equipment to complete installations, including digger derricks, trenchers, and cable plows.

5) Measure signal strength at utility poles, using electronic test equipment.

6) Clean and maintain tools and test equipment.

7) Set up service for customers, installing, connecting, testing, and adjusting equipment.

8) String cables between structures and lines from poles, towers, or trenches and pull lines to proper tension.

9) Inspect and test lines and cables, recording and analyzing test results, to assess transmission characteristics and locate faults and malfunctions.

10) Fill and tamp holes, using cement, earth, and tamping devices.

11) Place insulation over conductors, and seal splices with moisture-proof covering.

12) Participate in the construction and removal of telecommunication towers and associated support structures.

13) Dig trenches for underground wires and cables.

14) Pull up cable by hand from large reels mounted on trucks; then pull lines through ducts by hand or with winches.

15) Install equipment such as amplifiers and repeaters in order to maintain the strength of communications transmissions.

16) Compute impedance of wires from poles to houses in order to determine additional resistance needed for reducing signals to desired levels.

17) Dig holes for power poles, using power augers or shovels, set poles in place with cranes, and hoist poles upright, using winches.

18) Access specific areas to string lines and install terminal boxes, auxiliary equipment, and appliances, using bucket trucks, or by climbing poles and ladders or entering tunnels, trenches, or crawl spaces.

49-9061.00 - Camera and Photographic Equipment Repairers

Repair and adjust cameras and photographic equipment, including commercial video and motion picture camera equipment.

Tasks

1) Record test data and document fabrication techniques on reports.

2) Disassemble equipment to gain access to defect, using hand tools.

3) Assemble aircraft cameras, still and motion picture cameras, photographic equipment, and frames, using diagrams, blueprints, bench machines, hand tools, and power tools.

4) Fabricate or modify defective electronic, electrical, and mechanical components, using bench lathe, milling machine, shaper, grinder, and precision hand tools according to specifications.

5) Install film in aircraft camera and electrical assemblies and wiring in camera housing, following blueprints, using hand tools and soldering equipment.

6) Requisition parts and materials.

7) Measure parts to verify specified dimensions/settings, such as camera shutter speed and light meter reading accuracy, using measuring instruments.

8) Adjust cameras, photographic mechanisms, and equipment, such as range and view finders, shutters, light meters, and lens systems, using hand tools.

9) Test equipment performance, focus of lens system, alignment of diaphragm, lens mounts, and film transport, using precision gauges.

10) Calibrate and verify accuracy of light meters, shutter diaphragm operation, and lens carriers, using timing instruments.

11) Clean and lubricate cameras and polish camera lenses, using cleaning materials and work aids.

12) Lay out reference points and dimensions on parts and metal stock to be machined, using precision measuring instruments.

13) Recommend design changes or upgrades of micro-filming, film-developing, and photographic equipment.

14) Examine cameras, equipment, processed film, and laboratory reports to diagnose malfunction, using work aids and specifications.

49-9062.00 - Medical Equipment Repairers

Test, adjust, or repair biomedical or electromedical equipment.

Tasks

1) Disassemble malfunctioning equipment and remove, repair and replace defective parts such as motors, clutches or transformers.

2) Inspect and test malfunctioning medical and related equipment following manufacturers' specifications, using test and analysis instruments.

3) Perform preventive maintenance or service such as cleaning, lubricating and adjusting equipment.

4) Explain and demonstrate correct operation and preventive maintenance of medical equipment to personnel.

5) Study technical manuals and attend training sessions provided by equipment manufacturers to maintain current knowledge.

6) Keep records of maintenance, repair, and required updates of equipment.

7) Plan and carry out work assignments, using blueprints, schematic drawings, technical manuals, wiring diagrams, and liquid and air flow sheets, while following prescribed regulations, directives, and other instructions as required.

8) Examine medical equipment and facility's structural environment and check for proper use of equipment, to protect patients and staff from electrical or mechanical hazards and to ensure compliance with safety regulations.

9) Evaluate technical specifications to identify equipment and systems best suited for intended use and possible purchase based on specifications, user needs and technical requirements.

10) Solder loose connections, using soldering iron.

11) Research catalogs and repair part lists to locate sources for repair parts, requisitioning parts and recording their receipt.

12) Contribute expertise to develop medical maintenance standard operating procedures.

13) Test, evaluate, and classify excess or in-use medial equipment and determine serviceability, condition, and disposition in accordance with regulations.

14) Compute power and space requirements for installing medical, dental or related equipment and install units to manufacturers' specifications.

15) Repair shop equipment, metal furniture, and hospital equipment, including welding broken parts and replacing missing parts, or bring item into local shop for major repairs.

16) Fabricate, dress down, or substitute parts or major new items to modify equipment to meet unique operational or research needs, working from job orders, sketches, modification orders, samples or discussions with operating officials.

17) Supervise and advise subordinate personnel.

18) Make computations relating to load requirements of wiring and equipment, using algebraic expressions and standard formulas.

Knowledge	Knowledge Definitions
Computers and Electronics	Knowledge of circuit boards, processors, chips, electronic equipment, and computer hardware and software, including applications and programming.
Customer and Personal Service	Knowledge of principles and processes for providing customer and personal services. This includes customer needs assessment, meeting quality standards for services, and evaluation of customer satisfaction.
Mechanical	Knowledge of machines and tools, including their designs, uses, repair, and maintenance.
Engineering and Technology	Knowledge of the practical application of engineering science and technology. This includes applying principles, techniques, procedures, and equipment to the design and production of various goods and services.
English Language	Knowledge of the structure and content of the English language including the meaning and spelling of words, rules of composition, and grammar.
Clerical	Knowledge of administrative and clerical procedures and systems such as word processing, managing files and records, stenography and transcription, designing forms, and other office procedures and terminology.
Public Safety and Security	Knowledge of relevant equipment, policies, procedures, and strategies to promote effective local, state, or national security operations for the protection of people, data, property, and institutions.
Physics	Knowledge and prediction of physical principles, laws, their interrelationships, and applications to understanding fluid, material, and atmospheric dynamics, and mechanical, electrical, atomic and sub-atomic structures and processes.
Education and Training	Knowledge of principles and methods for curriculum and training design, teaching and instruction for individuals and groups, and the measurement of training effects.
Law and Government	Knowledge of laws, legal codes, court procedures, precedents, government regulations, executive orders, agency rules, and the democratic political process.
Telecommunications	Knowledge of transmission, broadcasting, switching, control, and operation of telecommunications systems.
Mathematics	Knowledge of arithmetic, algebra, geometry, calculus, statistics, and their applications.
Medicine and Dentistry	Knowledge of the information and techniques needed to diagnose and treat human injuries, diseases, and deformities. This includes symptoms, treatment alternatives, drug properties and interactions, and preventive health-care measures.
Administration and Management	Knowledge of business and management principles involved in strategic planning, resource allocation, human resources modeling, leadership technique, production methods, and coordination of people and resources.
Chemistry	Knowledge of the chemical composition, structure, and properties of substances and of the chemical processes and transformations that they undergo. This includes uses of chemicals and their interactions, danger signs, production techniques, and disposal methods.
Communications and Media	Knowledge of media production, communication, and dissemination techniques and methods. This includes alternative ways to inform and entertain via written, oral, and visual media.
Biology	Knowledge of plant and animal organisms, their tissues, cells, functions, interdependencies, and interactions with each other and the environment.
Transportation	Knowledge of principles and methods for moving people or goods by air, rail, sea, or road, including the relative costs and benefits.
Psychology	Knowledge of human behavior and performance; individual differences in ability, personality, and interests; learning and motivation; psychological research methods; and the assessment and treatment of behavioral and affective disorders.
Design	Knowledge of design techniques, tools, and principles involved in production of precision technical plans, blueprints, drawings, and models.
Production and Processing	Knowledge of raw materials, production processes, quality control, costs, and other techniques for maximizing the effective manufacture and distribution of goods.
Personnel and Human Resources	Knowledge of principles and procedures for personnel recruitment, selection, training, compensation and benefits, labor relations and negotiation, and personnel information systems.

Building and Construction	Knowledge of materials, methods, and the tools involved in the construction or repair of houses, buildings, or other structures such as highways and roads.
Economics and Accounting	Knowledge of economic and accounting principles and practices, the financial markets, banking and the analysis and reporting of financial data.
Sales and Marketing	Knowledge of principles and methods for showing, promoting, and selling products or services. This includes marketing strategy and tactics, product demonstration, sales techniques, and sales control systems.
Therapy and Counseling	Knowledge of principles, methods, and procedures for diagnosis, treatment, and rehabilitation of physical and mental dysfunctions, and for career counseling and guidance.
Sociology and Anthropology	Knowledge of group behavior and dynamics, societal trends and influences, human migrations, ethnicity, cultures and their history and origins.
Foreign Language	Knowledge of the structure and content of a foreign (non-English) language including the meaning and spelling of words, rules of composition and grammar, and pronunciation.
Philosophy and Theology	Knowledge of different philosophical systems and religions. This includes their basic principles, values, ethics, ways of thinking, customs, practices, and their impact on human culture.
Geography	Knowledge of principles and methods for describing the features of land, sea, and air masses, including their physical characteristics, locations, interrelationships, and distribution of plant, animal, and human life.
History and Archeology	Knowledge of historical events and their causes, indicators, and effects on civilizations and cultures.
Food Production	Knowledge of techniques and equipment for planting, growing, and harvesting food products (both plant and animal) for consumption, including storage/handling techniques.
Fine Arts	Knowledge of the theory and techniques required to compose, produce, and perform works of music, dance, visual arts, drama, and sculpture.

Skills	**Skills Definitions**
Troubleshooting	Determining causes of operating errors and deciding what to do about it.
Equipment Maintenance	Performing routine maintenance on equipment and determining when and what kind of maintenance is needed.
Repairing	Repairing machines or systems using the needed tools.
Reading Comprehension	Understanding written sentences and paragraphs in work related documents.
Critical Thinking	Using logic and reasoning to identify the strengths and weaknesses of alternative solutions, conclusions or approaches to problems.
Installation	Installing equipment, machines, wiring, or programs to meet specifications.
Equipment Selection	Determining the kind of tools and equipment needed to do a job.
Active Learning	Understanding the implications of new information for both current and future problem-solving and decision-making.
Complex Problem Solving	Identifying complex problems and reviewing related information to develop and evaluate options and implement solutions.
Active Listening	Giving full attention to what other people are saying, taking time to understand the points being made, asking questions as appropriate, and not interrupting at inappropriate times.
Coordination	Adjusting actions in relation to others' actions.
Speaking	Talking to others to convey information effectively.
Quality Control Analysis	Conducting tests and inspections of products, services, or processes to evaluate quality or performance.
Judgment and Decision Making	Considering the relative costs and benefits of potential actions to choose the most appropriate one.
Instructing	Teaching others how to do something.
Operation and Control	Controlling operations of equipment or systems.
Learning Strategies	Selecting and using training/instructional methods and procedures appropriate for the situation when learning or teaching new things.
Service Orientation	Actively looking for ways to help people.
Time Management	Managing one's own time and the time of others.
Operation Monitoring	Watching gauges, dials, or other indicators to make sure a machine is working properly.
Monitoring	Monitoring/Assessing performance of yourself, other individuals, or organizations to make improvements or take corrective action.

Social Perceptiveness	Being aware of others' reactions and understanding why they react as they do.
Systems Evaluation	Identifying measures or indicators of system performance and the actions needed to improve or correct performance, relative to the goals of the system.
Systems Analysis	Determining how a system should work and how changes in conditions, operations, and the environment will affect outcomes.
Mathematics	Using mathematics to solve problems.
Management of Material Resources	Obtaining and seeing to the appropriate use of equipment, facilities, and materials needed to do certain work.
Science	Using scientific rules and methods to solve problems.
Writing	Communicating effectively in writing as appropriate for the needs of the audience.
Operations Analysis	Analyzing needs and product requirements to create a design.
Technology Design	Generating or adapting equipment and technology to serve user needs.
Persuasion	Persuading others to change their minds or behavior.
Negotiation	Bringing others together and trying to reconcile differences.
Management of Personnel Resources	Motivating, developing, and directing people as they work, identifying the best people for the job.
Programming	Writing computer programs for various purposes.
Management of Financial Resources	Determining how money will be spent to get the work done, and accounting for these expenditures.

Ability	**Ability Definitions**
Problem Sensitivity	The ability to tell when something is wrong or is likely to go wrong. It does not involve solving the problem, only recognizing there is a problem.
Near Vision	The ability to see details at close range (within a few feet of the observer).
Information Ordering	The ability to arrange things or actions in a certain order or pattern according to a specific rule or set of rules (e.g., patterns of numbers, letters, words, pictures, mathematical operations).
Deductive Reasoning	The ability to apply general rules to specific problems to produce answers that make sense.
Written Comprehension	The ability to read and understand information and ideas presented in writing.
Oral Comprehension	The ability to listen to and understand information and ideas presented through spoken words and sentences.
Oral Expression	The ability to communicate information and ideas in speaking so others will understand.
Finger Dexterity	The ability to make precisely coordinated movements of the fingers of one or both hands to grasp, manipulate, or assemble very small objects.
Inductive Reasoning	The ability to combine pieces of information to form general rules or conclusions (includes finding a relationship among seemingly unrelated events).
Arm-Hand Steadiness	The ability to keep your hand and arm steady while moving your arm or while holding your arm and hand in one position.
Flexibility of Closure	The ability to identify or detect a known pattern (a figure, object, word, or sound) that is hidden in other distracting material.
Visualization	The ability to imagine how something will look after it is moved around or when its parts are moved or rearranged.
Speech Clarity	The ability to speak clearly so others can understand you.
Written Expression	The ability to communicate information and ideas in writing so others will understand.
Perceptual Speed	The ability to quickly and accurately compare similarities and differences among sets of letters, numbers, objects, pictures, or patterns. The things to be compared may be presented at the same time or one after the other. This ability also includes comparing a presented object with a remembered object.
Visual Color Discrimination	The ability to match or detect differences between colors, including shades of color and brightness.
Manual Dexterity	The ability to quickly move your hand, your hand together with your arm, or your two hands to grasp, manipulate, or assemble objects.
Category Flexibility	The ability to generate or use different sets of rules for combining or grouping things in different ways.
Memorization	The ability to remember information such as words, numbers, pictures, and procedures.
Hearing Sensitivity	The ability to detect or tell the differences between sounds that vary in pitch and loudness.
Control Precision	The ability to quickly and repeatedly adjust the controls of a machine or a vehicle to exact positions.

Selective Attention	The ability to concentrate on a task over a period of time without being distracted.
Speech Recognition	The ability to identify and understand the speech of another person.
Far Vision	The ability to see details at a distance.
Fluency of Ideas	The ability to come up with a number of ideas about a topic (the number of ideas is important, not their quality, correctness, or creativity).
Depth Perception	The ability to judge which of several objects is closer or farther away from you, or to judge the distance between you and an object.
Time Sharing	The ability to shift back and forth between two or more activities or sources of information (such as speech, sounds, touch, or other sources).
Speed of Closure	The ability to quickly make sense of, combine, and organize information into meaningful patterns.
Multilimb Coordination	The ability to coordinate two or more limbs (for example, two arms, two legs, or one leg and one arm) while sitting, standing, or lying down. It does not involve performing the activities while the whole body is in motion.
Originality	The ability to come up with unusual or clever ideas about a given topic or situation, or to develop creative ways to solve a problem.
Mathematical Reasoning	The ability to choose the right mathematical methods or formulas to solve a problem.
Static Strength	The ability to exert maximum muscle force to lift, push, pull, or carry objects.
Extent Flexibility	The ability to bend, stretch, twist, or reach with your body, arms, and/or legs.
Auditory Attention	The ability to focus on a single source of sound in the presence of other distracting sounds.
Stamina	The ability to exert yourself physically over long periods of time without getting winded or out of breath.
Number Facility	The ability to add, subtract, multiply, or divide quickly and correctly.
Speed of Limb Movement	The ability to quickly move the arms and legs.
Dynamic Strength	The ability to exert muscle force repeatedly or continuously over time. This involves muscular endurance and resistance to muscle fatigue.
Trunk Strength	The ability to use your abdominal and lower back muscles to support part of the body repeatedly or continuously over time without 'giving out' or fatiguing.
Reaction Time	The ability to quickly respond (with the hand, finger, or foot) to a signal (sound, light, picture) when it appears.
Gross Body Coordination	The ability to coordinate the movement of your arms, legs, and torso together when the whole body is in motion.
Response Orientation	The ability to choose quickly between two or more movements in response to two or more different signals (lights, sounds, pictures). It includes the speed with which the correct response is started with the hand, foot, or other body part.
Spatial Orientation	The ability to know your location in relation to the environment or to know where other objects are in relation to you.
Sound Localization	The ability to tell the direction from which a sound originated.
Rate Control	The ability to time your movements or the movement of a piece of equipment in anticipation of changes in the speed and/or direction of a moving object or scene.
Wrist-Finger Speed	The ability to make fast, simple, repeated movements of the fingers, hands, and wrists.
Night Vision	The ability to see under low light conditions.
Glare Sensitivity	The ability to see objects in the presence of glare or bright lighting.
Peripheral Vision	The ability to see objects or movement of objects to one's side when the eyes are looking ahead.
Gross Body Equilibrium	The ability to keep or regain your body balance or stay upright when in an unstable position.
Dynamic Flexibility	The ability to quickly and repeatedly bend, stretch, twist, or reach out with your body, arms, and/or legs.
Explosive Strength	The ability to use short bursts of muscle force to propel oneself (as in jumping or sprinting), or to throw an object.

Work_Activity	Work_Activity Definitions
Repairing and Maintaining Electronic Equipment	Servicing, repairing, calibrating, regulating, fine-tuning, or testing machines, devices, and equipment that operate primarily on the basis of electrical or electronic (not mechanical) principles.
Inspecting Equipment, Structures, or Material	Inspecting equipment, structures, or materials to identify the cause of errors or other problems or defects.

Getting Information	Observing, receiving, and otherwise obtaining information from all relevant sources.
Identifying Objects, Actions, and Events	Identifying information by categorizing, estimating, recognizing differences or similarities, and detecting changes in circumstances or events.
Updating and Using Relevant Knowledge	Keeping up-to-date technically and applying new knowledge to your job.
Making Decisions and Solving Problems	Analyzing information and evaluating results to choose the best solution and solve problems.
Repairing and Maintaining Mechanical Equipment	Servicing, repairing, adjusting, and testing machines, devices, moving parts, and equipment that operate primarily on the basis of mechanical (not electronic) principles.
Documenting/Recording Information	Entering, transcribing, recording, storing, or maintaining information in written or electronic/magnetic form.
Communicating with Supervisors, Peers, or Subordin	Providing information to supervisors, co-workers, and subordinates by telephone, in written form, e-mail, or in person.
Interacting With Computers	Using computers and computer systems (including hardware and software) to program, write software, set up functions, enter data, or process information.
Establishing and Maintaining Interpersonal Relatio	Developing constructive and cooperative working relationships with others, and maintaining them over time.
Evaluating Information to Determine Compliance wit	Using relevant information and individual judgment to determine whether events or processes comply with laws, regulations, or standards.
Organizing, Planning, and Prioritizing Work	Developing specific goals and plans to prioritize, organize, and accomplish your work.
Monitor Processes, Materials, or Surroundings	Monitoring and reviewing information from materials, events, or the environment, to detect or assess problems.
Communicating with Persons Outside Organization	Communicating with people outside the organization, representing the organization to customers, the public, government, and other external sources. This information can be exchanged in person, in writing, or by telephone or e-mail.
Handling and Moving Objects	Using hands and arms in handling, installing, positioning, and moving materials, and manipulating things.
Performing General Physical Activities	Performing physical activities that require considerable use of your arms and legs and moving your whole body, such as climbing, lifting, balancing, walking, stooping, and handling of materials.
Training and Teaching Others	Identifying the educational needs of others, developing formal educational or training programs or classes, and teaching or instructing others.
Controlling Machines and Processes	Using either control mechanisms or direct physical activity to operate machines or processes (not including computers or vehicles).
Processing Information	Compiling, coding, categorizing, calculating, tabulating, auditing, or verifying information or data.
Judging the Qualities of Things, Services, or Peop	Assessing the value, importance, or quality of things or people.
Scheduling Work and Activities	Scheduling events, programs, and activities, as well as the work of others.
Performing Administrative Activities	Performing day-to-day administrative tasks such as maintaining information files and processing paperwork.
Analyzing Data or Information	Identifying the underlying principles, reasons, or facts of information by breaking down information or data into separate parts.
Provide Consultation and Advice to Others	Providing guidance and expert advice to management or other groups on technical, systems-, or process-related topics.
Performing for or Working Directly with the Public	Performing for people or dealing directly with the public. This includes serving customers in restaurants and stores, and receiving clients or guests.
Operating Vehicles, Mechanized Devices, or Equipme	Running, maneuvering, navigating, or driving vehicles or mechanized equipment, such as forklifts, passenger vehicles, aircraft, or water craft.
Interpreting the Meaning of Information for Others	Translating or explaining what information means and how it can be used.
Resolving Conflicts and Negotiating with Others	Handling complaints, settling disputes, and resolving grievances and conflicts, or otherwise negotiating with others.
Developing and Building Teams	Encouraging and building mutual trust, respect, and cooperation among team members.
Estimating the Quantifiable Characteristics of Pro	Estimating sizes, distances, and quantities; or determining time, costs, resources, or materials needed to perform a work activity.
Thinking Creatively	Developing, designing, or creating new applications, ideas, relationships, systems, or products, including artistic contributions.

Assisting and Caring for Others	Providing personal assistance, medical attention, emotional support, or other personal care to others such as coworkers, customers, or patients.
Developing Objectives and Strategies	Establishing long-range objectives and specifying the strategies and actions to achieve them.
Drafting, Laying Out, and Specifying Technical Dev	Providing documentation, detailed instructions, drawings, or specifications to tell others about how devices, parts, equipment, or structures are to be fabricated, constructed, assembled, modified, maintained, or used.
Coaching and Developing Others	Identifying the developmental needs of others and coaching, mentoring, or otherwise helping others to improve their knowledge or skills.
Monitoring and Controlling Resources	Monitoring and controlling resources and overseeing the spending of money.
Selling or Influencing Others	Convincing others to buy merchandise/goods or to otherwise change their minds or actions.
Coordinating the Work and Activities of Others	Getting members of a group to work together to accomplish tasks.
Guiding, Directing, and Motivating Subordinates	Providing guidance and direction to subordinates, including setting performance standards and monitoring performance.
Staffing Organizational Units	Recruiting, interviewing, selecting, hiring, and promoting employees in an organization.

Work_Context	**Work_Context Definitions**
Face-to-Face Discussions	How often do you have to have face-to-face discussions with individuals or teams in this job?
Indoors, Environmentally Controlled	How often does this job require working indoors in environmentally controlled conditions?
Telephone	How often do you have telephone conversations in this job?
Importance of Being Exact or Accurate	How important is being very exact or highly accurate in performing this job?
Contact With Others	How much does this job require the worker to be in contact with others (face-to-face, by telephone, or otherwise) in order to perform it?
Frequency of Decision Making	How frequently is the worker required to make decisions that affect other people, the financial resources, and/or the image and reputation of the organization?
Time Pressure	How often does this job require the worker to meet strict deadlines?
Freedom to Make Decisions	How much decision making freedom, without supervision, does the job offer?
Impact of Decisions on Co-workers or Company Resul	How do the decisions an employee makes impact the results of co-workers, clients or the company?
Structured versus Unstructured Work	To what extent is this job structured for the worker, rather than allowing the worker to determine tasks, priorities, and goals?
Work With Work Group or Team	How important is it to work with others in a group or team in this job?
Spend Time Using Your Hands to Handle, Control, or	How much does this job require using your hands to handle, control, or feel objects, tools or controls?
Physical Proximity	To what extent does this job require the worker to perform job tasks in close physical proximity to other people?
Spend Time Standing	How much does this job require standing?
Deal With External Customers	How important is it to work with external customers or the public in this job?
Responsible for Others' Health and Safety	How much responsibility is there for the health and safety of others in this job?
Electronic Mail	How often do you use electronic mail in this job?
Exposed to Disease or Infections	How often does this job require exposure to disease/infections?
Wear Common Protective or Safety Equipment such as	How much does this job require wearing common protective or safety equipment such as safety shoes, glasses, gloves, hard hats or life jackets?
Consequence of Error	How serious would the result usually be if the worker made a mistake that was not readily correctable?
Exposed to Contaminants	How often does this job require working exposed to contaminants (such as pollutants, gases, dust or odors)?
Coordinate or Lead Others	How important is it to coordinate or lead others in accomplishing work activities in this job?
Responsibility for Outcomes and Results	How responsible is the worker for work outcomes and results of other workers?
Cramped Work Space, Awkward Positions	How often does this job require working in cramped work spaces that requires getting into awkward positions?
Letters and Memos	How often does the job require written letters and memos?

Importance of Repeating Same Tasks	How important is repeating the same physical activities (e.g., key entry) or mental activities (e.g., checking entries in a ledger) over and over, without stopping, to performing this job?
In an Enclosed Vehicle or Equipment	How often does this job require working in a closed vehicle or equipment (e.g., car)?
Sounds, Noise Levels Are Distracting or Uncomforta	How often does this job require working exposed to sounds and noise levels that are distracting or uncomfortable?
Level of Competition	To what extent does this job require the worker to compete or to be aware of competitive pressures?
Frequency of Conflict Situations	How often are there conflict situations the employee has to face in this job?
Exposed to Hazardous Conditions	How often does this job require exposure to hazardous conditions?
Spend Time Walking and Running	How much does this job require walking and running?
Extremely Bright or Inadequate Lighting	How often does this job require working in extremely bright or inadequate lighting conditions?
Deal With Unpleasant or Angry People	How frequently does the worker have to deal with unpleasant, angry, or discourteous individuals as part of the job requirements?
Exposed to Hazardous Equipment	How often does this job require exposure to hazardous equipment?
Spend Time Sitting	How much does this job require sitting?
Wear Specialized Protective or Safety Equipment su	How much does this job require wearing specialized protective or safety equipment such as breathing apparatus, safety harness, full protection suits, or radiation protection?
Exposed to Radiation	How often does this job require exposure to radiation?
Spend Time Making Repetitive Motions	How much does this job require making repetitive motions?
Exposed to Minor Burns, Cuts, Bites, or Stings	How often does this job require exposure to minor burns, cuts, bites, or stings?
Spend Time Bending or Twisting the Body	How much does this job require bending or twisting your body?
Indoors, Not Environmentally Controlled	How often does this job require working indoors in non-controlled environmental conditions (e.g., warehouse without heat)?
Spend Time Kneeling, Crouching, Stooping, or Crawl	How much does this job require kneeling, crouching, stooping or crawling?
Public Speaking	How often do you have to perform public speaking in this job?
Outdoors, Exposed to Weather	How often does this job require working outdoors, exposed to all weather conditions?
Degree of Automation	How automated is the job?
Very Hot or Cold Temperatures	How often does this job require working in very hot (above 90 F degrees) or very cold (below 32 F degrees) temperatures?
Spend Time Climbing Ladders, Scaffolds, or Poles	How much does this job require climbing ladders, scaffolds, or poles?
Exposed to Whole Body Vibration	How often does this job require exposure to whole body vibration (e.g., operate a jackhammer)?
Spend Time Keeping or Regaining Balance	How much does this job require keeping or regaining your balance?
Outdoors, Under Cover	How often does this job require working outdoors, under cover (e.g., structure with roof but no walls)?
Exposed to High Places	How often does this job require exposure to high places?
In an Open Vehicle or Equipment	How often does this job require working in an open vehicle or equipment (e.g., tractor)?
Pace Determined by Speed of Equipment	How important is it to this job that the pace is determined by the speed of equipment or machinery? (This does not refer to keeping busy at all times on this job.)
Deal With Physically Aggressive People	How frequently does this job require the worker to deal with physical aggression of violent individuals?

Job Zone Component	**Job Zone Component Definitions**
Title	Job Zone Three: Medium Preparation Needed
Overall Experience	Previous work-related skill, knowledge, or experience is required for these occupations. For example, an electrician must have completed three or four years of apprenticeship or several years of vocational training, and often must have passed a licensing exam, in order to perform the job.
Job Training	Employees in these occupations usually need one or two years of training involving both on-the-job experience and informal training with experienced workers.

Job Zone Examples	These occupations usually involve using communication and organizational skills to coordinate, supervise, manage, or train others to accomplish goals. Examples include dental assistants, electricians, fish and game wardens, legal secretaries, personnel recruiters, and recreation workers.
SVP Range	(6.0 to < 7.0)
Education	Most occupations in this zone require training in vocational schools, related on-the-job experience, or an associate's degree. Some may require a bachelor's degree.

Work_Styles	Work_Styles Definitions
Attention to Detail	Job requires being careful about detail and thorough in completing work tasks.
Integrity	Job requires being honest and ethical.
Dependability	Job requires being reliable, responsible, and dependable, and fulfilling obligations.
Analytical Thinking	Job requires analyzing information and using logic to address work-related issues and problems.
Cooperation	Job requires being pleasant with others on the job and displaying a good-natured, cooperative attitude.
Independence	Job requires developing one's own ways of doing things, guiding oneself with little or no supervision, and depending on oneself to get things done.
Stress Tolerance	Job requires accepting criticism and dealing calmly and effectively with high stress situations.
Self Control	Job requires maintaining composure, keeping emotions in check, controlling anger, and avoiding aggressive behavior, even in very difficult situations.
Concern for Others	Job requires being sensitive to others' needs and feelings and being understanding and helpful on the job.
Initiative	Job requires a willingness to take on responsibilities and challenges.
Persistence	Job requires persistence in the face of obstacles.
Adaptability/Flexibility	Job requires being open to change (positive or negative) and to considerable variety in the workplace.
Innovation	Job requires creativity and alternative thinking to develop new ideas for and answers to work-related problems.
Achievement/Effort	Job requires establishing and maintaining personally challenging achievement goals and exerting effort toward mastering tasks.
Leadership	Job requires a willingness to lead, take charge, and offer opinions and direction.
Social Orientation	Job requires preferring to work with others rather than alone, and being personally connected with others on the job.

49-9064.00 - Watch Repairers

Repair, clean, and adjust mechanisms of timing instruments, such as watches and clocks.

Tasks

1) Reassemble timepieces, replacing glass faces and batteries, before returning them to customers.

2) Perform regular adjustment and maintenance on timepieces, watch cases, and watch bands.

3) Oil moving parts of timepieces.

4) Gather information from customers about a timepiece's problems and its service history.

5) Disassemble timepieces and inspect them for defective, worn, misaligned, or rusty parts, using loupes.

6) Repair or replace broken, damaged, or worn parts on timepieces, using lathes, drill presses, and hand tools.

7) Record quantities and types of timepieces repaired, serial and model numbers of items, work performed, and charges for repairs.

8) Clean, rinse, and dry timepiece parts, using solutions and ultrasonic or mechanical watch-cleaning machines.

9) Test and replace batteries and other electronic components.

10) Test timepiece accuracy and performance, using meters and other electronic instruments.

11) Fabricate parts for watches and clocks, using small lathes and other machines.

12) Demagnetize mechanisms, using demagnetizing machines.

13) Estimate repair costs and timepiece values.

49-9092.00 - Commercial Divers

Work below surface of water, using scuba gear to inspect, repair, remove, or install equipment and structures. May use a variety of power and hand tools, such as drills, sledgehammers, torches, and welding equipment. May conduct tests or experiments, rig explosives, or photograph structures or marine life.

Tasks

1) Set up dive sites for recreational instruction.

2) Remove rubbish and pollution from the sea.

3) Cultivate and harvest marine species, and perform routine work on fish farms.

4) Communicate with workers on the surface while underwater, using signal lines or telephones.

5) Carry out non-destructive testing such as tests for cracks on the legs of oil rigs at sea.

6) Cut and weld steel, using underwater welding equipment, jigs, and supports.

7) Descend into water with the aid of diver helpers, using scuba gear or diving suits.

8) Inspect and test docks, ships, bouyage systems, plant intakes and outflows, and underwater pipelines, cables, and sewers, using closed circuit television, still photography, and testing equipment.

9) Install pilings or footings for piers and bridges.

10) Remove obstructions from strainers and marine railway or launching ways, using pneumatic and power hand tools.

11) Supervise and train other divers, including hobby divers.

12) Salvage wrecked ships and/or their cargo, using pneumatic power velocity and hydraulic tools, and explosive charges when necessary.

13) Install, inspect, clean, and repair piping and valves.

14) Obtain information about diving tasks and environmental conditions.

15) Set or guide placement of pilings and sandbags to provide support for structures such as docks, bridges, cofferdams, and platforms.

16) Perform activities related to underwater search and rescue, salvage, recovery, and cleanup operations.

17) Perform offshore oil and gas exploration and extraction duties such as conducting underwater surveys and repairing and maintaining drilling rigs and platforms.

18) Recover objects by placing rigging around sunken objects, hooking rigging to crane lines, and operating winches, derricks, or cranes to raise objects.

19) Repair ships, bridge foundations, and other structures below the water line, using caulk, bolts, and hand tools.

20) Take appropriate safety precautions, such as monitoring dive lengths and depths, and registering with authorities before diving expeditions begin.

21) Drill holes in rock, and rig explosives for underwater demolitions.

22) Operate underwater video, sonar, recording, and related equipment to investigate underwater structures or marine life.

23) Check and maintain diving equipment such as helmets, masks, air tanks, harnesses and gauges.

49-9096.00 - Riggers

Set up or repair rigging for construction projects, manufacturing plants, logging yards, ships and shipyards, or for the entertainment industry.

Tasks

1) Signal or verbally direct workers engaged in hoisting and moving loads, in order to ensure safety of workers and materials.

2) Control movement of heavy equipment through narrow openings or confined spaces, using chainfalls, gin poles, gallows frames, and other equipment.

3) Attach pulleys and blocks to fixed overhead structures such as beams, ceilings, and gin

pole booms, using bolts and clamps.

4) Align, level, and anchor machinery.

5) Test rigging to ensure safety and reliability.

6) Attach loads to rigging to provide support or prepare them for moving, using hand and power tools.

7) Clean and dress machine surfaces and component parts.

8) Fabricate, set up, and repair rigging, supporting structures, hoists, and pulling gear, using hand and power tools.

9) Select gear such as cables, pulleys, and winches, according to load weights and sizes, facilities, and work schedules.

10) Tilt, dip, and turn suspended loads to maneuver over, under, and/or around obstacles, using multi-point suspension techniques.

11) Install ground rigging for yarding lines, attaching chokers to logs and then to the lines.

12) Manipulate rigging lines, hoists, and pulling gear to move or support materials such as heavy equipment, ships, or theatrical sets.

49-9097.00 - Signal and Track Switch Repairers

Install, inspect, test, maintain, or repair electric gate crossings, signals, signal equipment, track switches, section lines, or intercommunications systems within a railroad system.

Tasks

1) Tighten loose bolts, using wrenches, and test circuits and connections by opening and closing gates.

2) Record and report information about mileage or track inspected, repairs performed, and equipment requiring replacement.

3) Test air lines and air cylinders on pneumatically operated gates.

4) Install, inspect, maintain, and repair various railroad service equipment on the road or in the shop, including railroad signal systems.

5) Replace defective wiring, broken lenses, or burned-out light bulbs.

6) Maintain high tension lines, de-energizing lines for power companies when repairs are requested.

7) Drive motor vehicles to job sites.

8) Inspect and test operation, mechanical parts, and circuitry of gate crossings, signals, and signal equipment such as interlocks and hotbox detectors.

9) Inspect electrical units of railroad grade crossing gates and repair loose bolts and defective electrical connections and parts.

10) Clean lenses of lamps with cloths and solvents.

11) Lubricate moving parts on gate-crossing mechanisms and swinging signals.

12) Inspect switch-controlling mechanisms on trolley wires and in track beds, using hand tools and test equipment.

49-9098.00 - Helpers--Installation, Maintenance, and Repair Workers

Help installation, maintenance, and repair workers in maintenance, parts replacement, and repair of vehicles, industrial machinery, and electrical and electronic equipment. Perform duties, such as furnishing tools, materials, and supplies to other workers; cleaning work area, machines, and tools; and holding materials or tools for other workers.

Tasks

1) Install or replace machinery, equipment, and new or replacement parts and instruments, using hand tools or power tools.

2) Clean or lubricate vehicles, machinery, equipment, instruments, tools, work areas, and other objects, using hand tools, power tools, and cleaning equipment.

3) Disassemble broken or defective equipment in order to facilitate repair; reassemble equipment when repairs are complete.

4) Examine and test machinery, equipment, components, and parts for defects, and to ensure proper functioning.

5) Position vehicles, machinery, equipment, physical structures, and other objects for assembly or installation, using hand tools, power tools, and moving equipment.

6) Adjust, connect, or disconnect wiring, piping, tubing, and other parts, using hand tools or power tools.

7) Tend and observe equipment and machinery in order to verify efficient and safe operation.

8) Hold or supply tools, parts, equipment, and supplies for other workers.

9) Provide assistance to more skilled workers involved in the adjustment, maintenance, part replacement, and repair of tools, equipment, and machines.

10) Assemble and maintain physical structures, using hand tools or power tools.

11) Apply protective materials to equipment, components, and parts in order to prevent defects and corrosion.

12) Prepare work stations so mechanics and repairers can conduct work.

Knowledge	Knowledge Definitions
Mechanical	Knowledge of machines and tools, including their designs, uses, repair, and maintenance.
Public Safety and Security	Knowledge of relevant equipment, policies, procedures, and strategies to promote effective local, state, or national security operations for the protection of people, data, property, and institutions.
Mathematics	Knowledge of arithmetic, algebra, geometry, calculus, statistics, and their applications.
Engineering and Technology	Knowledge of the practical application of engineering science and technology. This includes applying principles, techniques, procedures, and equipment to the design and production of various goods and services.
Design	Knowledge of design techniques, tools, and principles involved in production of precision technical plans, blueprints, drawings, and models.
English Language	Knowledge of the structure and content of the English language including the meaning and spelling of words, rules of composition, and grammar.
Building and Construction	Knowledge of materials, methods, and the tools involved in the construction or repair of houses, buildings, or other structures such as highways and roads.
Chemistry	Knowledge of the chemical composition, structure, and properties of substances and of the chemical processes and transformations that they undergo. This includes uses of chemicals and their interactions, danger signs, production techniques, and disposal methods.
Production and Processing	Knowledge of raw materials, production processes, quality control, costs, and other techniques for maximizing the effective manufacture and distribution of goods.
Administration and Management	Knowledge of business and management principles involved in strategic planning, resource allocation, human resources modeling, leadership technique, production methods, and coordination of people and resources.
Physics	Knowledge and prediction of physical principles, laws, their interrelationships, and applications to understanding fluid, material, and atmospheric dynamics, and mechanical, electrical, atomic and sub- atomic structures and processes.
Customer and Personal Service	Knowledge of principles and processes for providing customer and personal services. This includes customer needs assessment, meeting quality standards for services, and evaluation of customer satisfaction.
Education and Training	Knowledge of principles and methods for curriculum and training design, teaching and instruction for individuals and groups, and the measurement of training effects.
Law and Government	Knowledge of laws, legal codes, court procedures, precedents, government regulations, executive orders, agency rules, and the democratic political process.
Computers and Electronics	Knowledge of circuit boards, processors, chips, electronic equipment, and computer hardware and software, including applications and programming.
Telecommunications	Knowledge of transmission, broadcasting, switching, control, and operation of telecommunications systems.
Transportation	Knowledge of principles and methods for moving people or goods by air, rail, sea, or road, including the relative costs and benefits.
Clerical	Knowledge of administrative and clerical procedures and systems such as word processing, managing files and records, stenography and transcription, designing forms, and other office procedures and terminology.

Psychology	Knowledge of human behavior and performance; individual differences in ability, personality, and interests; learning and motivation; psychological research methods; and the assessment and treatment of behavioral and affective disorders.
Personnel and Human Resources	Knowledge of principles and procedures for personnel recruitment, selection, training, compensation and benefits, labor relations and negotiation, and personnel information systems.
Sociology and Anthropology	Knowledge of group behavior and dynamics, societal trends and influences, human migrations, ethnicity, cultures and their history and origins.
Communications and Media	Knowledge of media production, communication, and dissemination techniques and methods. This includes alternative ways to inform and entertain via written, oral, and visual media.
Foreign Language	Knowledge of the structure and content of a foreign (non-English) language including the meaning and spelling of words, rules of composition and grammar, and pronunciation.
Geography	Knowledge of principles and methods for describing the features of land, sea, and air masses, including their physical characteristics, locations, interrelationships, and distribution of plant, animal, and human life.
Medicine and Dentistry	Knowledge of the information and techniques needed to diagnose and treat human injuries, diseases, and deformities. This includes symptoms, treatment alternatives, drug properties and interactions, and preventive health-care measures.
Economics and Accounting	Knowledge of economic and accounting principles and practices, the financial markets, banking and the analysis and reporting of financial data.
Philosophy and Theology	Knowledge of different philosophical systems and religions. This includes their basic principles, values, ethics, ways of thinking, customs, practices, and their impact on human culture.
Therapy and Counseling	Knowledge of principles, methods, and procedures for diagnosis, treatment, and rehabilitation of physical and mental dysfunctions, and for career counseling and guidance.
Sales and Marketing	Knowledge of principles and methods for showing, promoting, and selling products or services. This includes marketing strategy and tactics, product demonstration, sales techniques, and sales control systems.
History and Archeology	Knowledge of historical events and their causes, indicators, and effects on civilizations and cultures.
Biology	Knowledge of plant and animal organisms, their tissues, cells, functions, interdependencies, and interactions with each other and the environment.
Food Production	Knowledge of techniques and equipment for planting, growing, and harvesting food products (both plant and animal) for consumption, including storage/handling techniques.
Fine Arts	Knowledge of the theory and techniques required to compose, produce, and perform works of music, dance, visual arts, drama, and sculpture.

Skills	Skills Definitions
Equipment Maintenance	Performing routine maintenance on equipment and determining when and what kind of maintenance is needed.
Active Listening	Giving full attention to what other people are saying, taking time to understand the points being made, asking questions as appropriate, and not interrupting at inappropriate times.
Repairing	Repairing machines or systems using the needed tools.
Installation	Installing equipment, machines, wiring, or programs to meet specifications.
Troubleshooting	Determining causes of operating errors and deciding what to do about it.
Critical Thinking	Using logic and reasoning to identify the strengths and weaknesses of alternative solutions, conclusions or approaches to problems.
Operation Monitoring	Watching gauges, dials, or other indicators to make sure a machine is working properly.
Operation and Control	Controlling operations of equipment or systems.
Equipment Selection	Determining the kind of tools and equipment needed to do a job.
Active Learning	Understanding the implications of new information for both current and future problem-solving and decision-making.
Speaking	Talking to others to convey information effectively.
Reading Comprehension	Understanding written sentences and paragraphs in work related documents.
Coordination	Adjusting actions in relation to others' actions.

Service Orientation	Actively looking for ways to help people.
Mathematics	Using mathematics to solve problems.
Judgment and Decision Making	Considering the relative costs and benefits of potential actions to choose the most appropriate one.
Complex Problem Solving	Identifying complex problems and reviewing related information to develop and evaluate options and implement solutions.
Instructing	Teaching others how to do something.
Social Perceptiveness	Being aware of others' reactions and understanding why they react as they do.
Learning Strategies	Selecting and using training/instructional methods and procedures appropriate for the situation when learning or teaching new things.
Time Management	Managing one's own time and the time of others.
Monitoring	Monitoring/Assessing performance of yourself, other individuals, or organizations to make improvements or take corrective action.
Operations Analysis	Analyzing needs and product requirements to create a design.
Writing	Communicating effectively in writing as appropriate for the needs of the audience.
Systems Analysis	Determining how a system should work and how changes in conditions, operations, and the environment will affect outcomes.
Quality Control Analysis	Conducting tests and inspections of products, services, or processes to evaluate quality or performance.
Systems Evaluation	Identifying measures or indicators of system performance and the actions needed to improve or correct performance, relative to the goals of the system.
Management of Financial Resources	Determining how money will be spent to get the work done, and accounting for these expenditures.
Persuasion	Persuading others to change their minds or behavior.
Management of Material Resources	Obtaining and seeing to the appropriate use of equipment, facilities, and materials needed to do certain work.
Management of Personnel Resources	Motivating, developing, and directing people as they work, identifying the best people for the job.
Technology Design	Generating or adapting equipment and technology to serve user needs.
Negotiation	Bringing others together and trying to reconcile differences.
Science	Using scientific rules and methods to solve problems.
Programming	Writing computer programs for various purposes.

Ability	Ability Definitions
Arm-Hand Steadiness	The ability to keep your hand and arm steady while moving your arm or while holding your arm and hand in one position.
Problem Sensitivity	The ability to tell when something is wrong or is likely to go wrong. It does not involve solving the problem, only recognizing there is a problem.
Near Vision	The ability to see details at close range (within a few feet of the observer).
Oral Comprehension	The ability to listen to and understand information and ideas presented through spoken words and sentences.
Extent Flexibility	The ability to bend, stretch, twist, or reach with your body, arms, and/or legs.
Inductive Reasoning	The ability to combine pieces of information to form general rules or conclusions (includes finding a relationship among seemingly unrelated events).
Information Ordering	The ability to arrange things or actions in a certain order or pattern according to a specific rule or set of rules (e.g., patterns of numbers, letters, words, pictures, mathematical operations).
Far Vision	The ability to see details at a distance.
Static Strength	The ability to exert maximum muscle force to lift, push, pull, or carry objects.
Finger Dexterity	The ability to make precisely coordinated movements of the fingers of one or both hands to grasp, manipulate, or assemble very small objects.
Trunk Strength	The ability to use your abdominal and lower back muscles to support part of the body repeatedly or continuously over time without 'giving out' or fatiguing.
Control Precision	The ability to quickly and repeatedly adjust the controls of a machine or a vehicle to exact positions.
Oral Expression	The ability to communicate information and ideas in speaking so others will understand.
Deductive Reasoning	The ability to apply general rules to specific problems to produce answers that make sense.
Speech Recognition	The ability to identify and understand the speech of another person.

Multilimb Coordination	The ability to coordinate two or more limbs (for example, two arms, two legs, or one leg and one arm) while sitting, standing, or lying down. It does not involve performing the activities while the whole body is in motion.
Flexibility of Closure	The ability to identify or detect a known pattern (a figure, object, word, or sound) that is hidden in other distracting material.
Manual Dexterity	The ability to quickly move your hand, your hand together with your arm, or your two hands to grasp, manipulate, or assemble objects.
Gross Body Equilibrium	The ability to keep or regain your body balance or stay upright when in an unstable position.
Selective Attention	The ability to concentrate on a task over a period of time without being distracted.
Category Flexibility	The ability to generate or use different sets of rules for combining or grouping things in different ways.
Hearing Sensitivity	The ability to detect or tell the differences between sounds that vary in pitch and loudness.
Speech Clarity	The ability to speak clearly so others can understand you.
Visualization	The ability to imagine how something will look after it is moved around or when its parts are moved or rearranged.
Dynamic Strength	The ability to exert muscle force repeatedly or continuously over time. This involves muscular endurance and resistance to muscle fatigue.
Perceptual Speed	The ability to quickly and accurately compare similarities and differences among sets of letters, numbers, objects, pictures, or patterns. The things to be compared may be presented at the same time or one after the other. This ability also includes comparing a presented object with a remembered object.
Visual Color Discrimination	The ability to match or detect differences between colors, including shades of color and brightness.
Stamina	The ability to exert yourself physically over long periods of time without getting winded or out of breath.
Depth Perception	The ability to judge which of several objects is closer or farther away from you, or to judge the distance between you and an object.
Written Comprehension	The ability to read and understand information and ideas presented in writing.
Gross Body Coordination	The ability to coordinate the movement of your arms, legs, and torso together when the whole body is in motion.
Time Sharing	The ability to shift back and forth between two or more activities or sources of information (such as speech, sounds, touch, or other sources).
Auditory Attention	The ability to focus on a single source of sound in the presence of other distracting sounds.
Reaction Time	The ability to quickly respond (with the hand, finger, or foot) to a signal (sound, light, picture) when it appears.
Originality	The ability to come up with unusual or clever ideas about a given topic or situation, or to develop creative ways to solve a problem.
Fluency of Ideas	The ability to come up with a number of ideas about a topic (the number of ideas is important, not their quality, correctness, or creativity).
Glare Sensitivity	The ability to see objects in the presence of glare or bright lighting.
Wrist-Finger Speed	The ability to make fast, simple, repeated movements of the fingers, hands, and wrists.
Rate Control	The ability to time your movements or the movement of a piece of equipment in anticipation of changes in the speed and/or direction of a moving object or scene.
Written Expression	The ability to communicate information and ideas in writing so others will understand.
Memorization	The ability to remember information such as words, numbers, pictures, and procedures.
Speed of Closure	The ability to quickly make sense of, combine, and organize information into meaningful patterns.
Speed of Limb Movement	The ability to quickly move the arms and legs.
Response Orientation	The ability to choose quickly between two or more movements in response to two or more different signals (lights, sounds, pictures). It includes the speed with which the correct response is started with the hand, foot, or other body part.
Sound Localization	The ability to tell the direction from which a sound originated.
Peripheral Vision	The ability to see objects or movement of objects to one's side when the eyes are looking ahead.
Number Facility	The ability to add, subtract, multiply, or divide quickly and correctly.
Spatial Orientation	The ability to know your location in relation to the environment or to know where other objects are in relation to you.

Night Vision	The ability to see under low light conditions.
Mathematical Reasoning	The ability to choose the right mathematical methods or formulas to solve a problem.
Explosive Strength	The ability to use short bursts of muscle force to propel oneself (as in jumping or sprinting), or to throw an object.
Dynamic Flexibility	The ability to quickly and repeatedly bend, stretch, twist, or reach out with your body, arms, and/or legs.

Work_Activity	Work_Activity Definitions
Communicating with Supervisors, Peers, or Subordin	Providing information to supervisors, co-workers, and subordinates by telephone, in written form, e-mail, or in person.
Inspecting Equipment, Structures, or Material	Inspecting equipment, structures, or materials to identify the cause of errors or other problems or defects.
Performing General Physical Activities	Performing physical activities that require considerable use of your arms and legs and moving your whole body, such as climbing, lifting, balancing, walking, stooping, and handling of materials.
Monitor Processes, Materials, or Surroundings	Monitoring and reviewing information from materials, events, or the environment, to detect or assess problems.
Evaluating Information to Determine Compliance wit	Using relevant information and individual judgment to determine whether events or processes comply with laws, regulations, or standards.
Handling and Moving Objects	Using hands and arms in handling, installing, positioning, and moving materials, and manipulating things.
Identifying Objects, Actions, and Events	Identifying information by categorizing, estimating, recognizing differences or similarities, and detecting changes in circumstances or events.
Getting Information	Observing, receiving, and otherwise obtaining information from all relevant sources.
Controlling Machines and Processes	Using either control mechanisms or direct physical activity to operate machines or processes (not including computers or vehicles).
Organizing, Planning, and Prioritizing Work	Developing specific goals and plans to prioritize, organize, and accomplish your work.
Updating and Using Relevant Knowledge	Keeping up-to-date technically and applying new knowledge to your job.
Communicating with Persons Outside Organization	Communicating with people outside the organization, representing the organization to customers, the public, government, and other external sources. This information can be exchanged in person, in writing, or by telephone or e-mail.
Thinking Creatively	Developing, designing, or creating new applications, ideas, relationships, systems, or products, including artistic contributions.
Establishing and Maintaining Interpersonal Relatio	Developing constructive and cooperative working relationships with others, and maintaining them over time.
Repairing and Maintaining Mechanical Equipment	Servicing, repairing, adjusting, and testing machines, devices, moving parts, and equipment that operate primarily on the basis of mechanical (not electronic) principles.
Judging the Qualities of Things, Services, or Peop	Assessing the value, importance, or quality of things or people.
Operating Vehicles, Mechanized Devices, or Equipme	Running, maneuvering, navigating, or driving vehicles or mechanized equipment, such as forklifts, passenger vehicles, aircraft, or water craft.
Coordinating the Work and Activities of Others	Getting members of a group to work together to accomplish tasks.
Making Decisions and Solving Problems	Analyzing information and evaluating results to choose the best solution and solve problems.
Estimating the Quantifiable Characteristics of Pro	Estimating sizes, distances, and quantities; or determining time, costs, resources, or materials needed to perform a work activity.
Scheduling Work and Activities	Scheduling events, programs, and activities, as well as the work of others.
Drafting, Laying Out, and Specifying Technical Dev	Providing documentation, detailed instructions, drawings, or specifications to tell others about how devices, parts, equipment, or structures are to be fabricated, constructed, assembled, modified, maintained, or used.
Training and Teaching Others	Identifying the educational needs of others, developing formal educational or training programs or classes, and teaching or instructing others.
Processing Information	Compiling, coding, categorizing, calculating, tabulating, auditing, or verifying information or data.
Assisting and Caring for Others	Providing personal assistance, medical attention, emotional support, or other personal care to others such as coworkers, customers, or patients.

Interpreting the Meaning of Information for Others	Translating or explaining what information means and how it can be used.
Developing and Building Teams	Encouraging and building mutual trust, respect, and cooperation among team members.
Documenting/Recording Information	Entering, transcribing, recording, storing, or maintaining information in written or electronic/magnetic form.
Coaching and Developing Others	Identifying the developmental needs of others and coaching, mentoring, or otherwise helping others to improve their knowledge or skills.
Resolving Conflicts and Negotiating with Others	Handling complaints, settling disputes, and resolving grievances and conflicts, or otherwise negotiating with others.
Repairing and Maintaining Electronic Equipment	Servicing, repairing, calibrating, regulating, fine-tuning, or testing machines, devices, and equipment that operate primarily on the basis of electrical or electronic (not mechanical) principles.
Performing Administrative Activities	Performing day-to-day administrative tasks such as maintaining information files and processing paperwork.
Performing for or Working Directly with the Public	Performing for people or dealing directly with the public. This includes serving customers in restaurants and stores, and receiving clients or guests.
Guiding, Directing, and Motivating Subordinates	Providing guidance and direction to subordinates, including setting performance standards and monitoring performance.
Analyzing Data or Information	Identifying the underlying principles, reasons, or facts of information by breaking down information or data into separate parts.
Developing Objectives and Strategies	Establishing long-range objectives and specifying the strategies and actions to achieve them.
Monitoring and Controlling Resources	Monitoring and controlling resources and overseeing the spending of money.
Interacting With Computers	Using computers and computer systems (including hardware and software) to program, write software, set up functions, enter data, or process information.
Provide Consultation and Advice to Others	Providing guidance and expert advice to management or other groups on technical, systems-, or process-related topics.
Staffing Organizational Units	Recruiting, interviewing, selecting, hiring, and promoting employees in an organization.
Selling or Influencing Others	Convincing others to buy merchandise/goods or to otherwise change their minds or actions.

Work_Context

Work_Context	Work_Context Definitions
Spend Time Using Your Hands to Handle, Control, or	How much does this job require using your hands to handle, control, or feel objects, tools or controls?
Face-to-Face Discussions	How often do you have to have face-to-face discussions with individuals or teams in this job?
Contact With Others	How much does this job require the worker to be in contact with others (face-to-face, by telephone, or otherwise) in order to perform it?
Exposed to Hazardous Equipment	How often does this job require exposure to hazardous equipment?
Wear Common Protective or Safety Equipment such as	How much does this job require wearing common protective or safety equipment such as safety shoes, glasses, gloves, hard hats or life jackets?
Frequency of Decision Making	How frequently is the worker required to make decisions that affect other people, the financial resources, and/or the image and reputation of the organization?
Freedom to Make Decisions	How much decision making freedom, without supervision, does the job offer?
Physical Proximity	To what extent does this job require the worker to perform job tasks in close physical proximity to other people?
Work With Work Group or Team	How important is it to work with others in a group or team in this job?
Exposed to Hazardous Conditions	How often does this job require exposure to hazardous conditions?
Consequence of Error	How serious would the result usually be if the worker made a mistake that was not readily correctable?
Telephone	How often do you have telephone conversations in this job?
Time Pressure	How often does this job require the worker to meet strict deadlines?
Importance of Being Exact or Accurate	How important is being very exact or highly accurate in performing this job?
Spend Time Standing	How much does this job require standing?
Sounds, Noise Levels Are Distracting or Uncomforta	How often does this job require working exposed to sounds and noise levels that are distracting or uncomfortable?
Spend Time Bending or Twisting the Body	How much does this job require bending or twisting your body?

Spend Time Making Repetitive Motions	How much does this job require making repetitive motions?
Indoors, Environmentally Controlled	How often does this job require working indoors in environmentally controlled conditions?
Exposed to Contaminants	How often does this job require working exposed to contaminants (such as pollutants, gases, dust or odors)?
Extremely Bright or Inadequate Lighting	How often does this job require working in extremely bright or inadequate lighting conditions?
Exposed to Minor Burns, Cuts, Bites, or Stings	How often does this job require exposure to minor burns, cuts, bites, or stings?
Outdoors, Exposed to Weather	How often does this job require working outdoors, exposed to all weather conditions?
Responsible for Others' Health and Safety	How much responsibility is there for the health and safety of others in this job?
Cramped Work Space, Awkward Positions	How often does this job require working in cramped work spaces that requires getting into awkward positions?
Very Hot or Cold Temperatures	How often does this job require working in very hot (above 90 F degrees) or very cold (below 32 F degrees) temperatures?
Structured versus Unstructured Work	To what extent is this job structured for the worker, rather than allowing the worker to determine tasks, priorities, and goals?
Responsibility for Outcomes and Results	How responsible is the worker for work outcomes and results of other workers?
Exposed to High Places	How often does this job require exposure to high places?
Letters and Memos	How often does the job require written letters and memos?
Spend Time Kneeling, Crouching, Stooping, or Crawl	How much does this job require kneeling, crouching, stooping or crawling?
Coordinate or Lead Others	How important is it to coordinate or lead others in accomplishing work activities in this job?
Impact of Decisions on Co-workers or Company Resul	How do the decisions an employee makes impact the results of co-workers, clients or the company?
Spend Time Walking and Running	How much does this job require walking and running?
Deal With Unpleasant or Angry People	How frequently does the worker have to deal with unpleasant, angry, or discourteous individuals as part of the job requirements?
Level of Competition	To what extent does this job require the worker to compete or to be aware of competitive pressures?
In an Enclosed Vehicle or Equipment	How often does this job require working in a closed vehicle or equipment (e.g., car)?
Importance of Repeating Same Tasks	How important is repeating the same physical activities (e.g., key entry) or mental activities (e.g., checking entries in a ledger) over and over, without stopping, to performing this job?
Indoors, Not Environmentally Controlled	How often does this job require working indoors in non-controlled environmental conditions (e.g., warehouse without heat)?
Spend Time Climbing Ladders, Scaffolds, or Poles	How much does this job require climbing ladders, scaffolds, or poles?
Deal With External Customers	How important is it to work with external customers or the public in this job?
Wear Specialized Protective or Safety Equipment su	How much does this job require wearing specialized protective or safety equipment such as breathing apparatus, safety harness, full protection suits, or radiation protection?
Pace Determined by Speed of Equipment	How important is it to this job that the pace is determined by the speed of equipment or machinery? (This does not refer to keeping busy at all times on this job.)
Degree of Automation	How automated is the job?
Outdoors, Under Cover	How often does this job require working outdoors, under cover (e.g., structure with roof but no walls)?
Spend Time Keeping or Regaining Balance	How much does this job require keeping or regaining your balance?
Spend Time Sitting	How much does this job require sitting?
Exposed to Disease or Infections	How often does this job require exposure to disease/infections?
Exposed to Whole Body Vibration	How often does this job require exposure to whole body vibration (e.g., operate a jackhammer)?
Electronic Mail	How often do you use electronic mail in this job?
Frequency of Conflict Situations	How often are there conflict situations the employee has to face in this job?
Exposed to Radiation	How often does this job require exposure to radiation?
In an Open Vehicle or Equipment	How often does this job require working in an open vehicle or equipment (e.g., tractor)?
Public Speaking	How often do you have to perform public speaking in this job?
Deal With Physically Aggressive People	How frequently does this job require the worker to deal with physical aggression of violent individuals?

Job Zone Component	Job Zone Component Definitions
Title	Job Zone Two: Some Preparation Needed
Overall Experience	Some previous work-related skill. knowledge, or experience may be helpful in these occupations, but usually is not needed. For example. a drywall installer might benefit from experience installing drywall, but an inexperienced person could still learn to be an installer with little difficulty.
Job Training	Employees in these occupations need anywhere from a few months to one year of working with experienced employees.
Job Zone Examples	These occupations often involve using your knowledge and skills to help others. Examples include drywall installers, fire inspectors, flight attendants, pharmacy technicians, salespersons (retail), and tellers.
SVP Range	(4.0 to < 6.0)
Education	These occupations usually require a high school diploma and may require some vocational training or job-related course work. In some cases, an associate's or bachelor's degree could be needed.

Work_Styles	Work_Styles Definitions
Attention to Detail	Job requires being careful about detail and thorough in completing work tasks.
Dependability	Job requires being reliable, responsible, and dependable, and fulfilling obligations.
Cooperation	Job requires being pleasant with others on the job and displaying a good-natured, cooperative attitude.
Integrity	Job requires being honest and ethical.
Self Control	Job requires maintaining composure, keeping emotions in check, controlling anger, and avoiding aggressive behavior, even in very difficult situations.
Stress Tolerance	Job requires accepting criticism and dealing calmly and effectively with high stress situations.
Concern for Others	Job requires being sensitive to others' needs and feelings and being understanding and helpful on the job.
Adaptability/Flexibility	Job requires being open to change (positive or negative) and to considerable variety in the workplace.
Independence	Job requires developing one's own ways of doing things, guiding oneself with little or no supervision, and depending on oneself to get things done.
Persistence	Job requires persistence in the face of obstacles.
Analytical Thinking	Job requires analyzing information and using logic to address work-related issues and problems.
Initiative	Job requires a willingness to take on responsibilities and challenges.
Social Orientation	Job requires preferring to work with others rather than alone, and being personally connected with others on the job.
Leadership	Job requires a willingness to lead, take charge, and offer opinions and direction.
Innovation	Job requires creativity and alternative thinking to develop new ideas for and answers to work-related problems.
Achievement/Effort	Job requires establishing and maintaining personally challenging achievement goals and exerting effort toward mastering tasks.

51-1011.00 - First-Line Supervisors/Managers of Production and Operating Workers

Supervise and coordinate the activities of production and operating workers, such as inspectors, precision workers, machine setters and operators, assemblers, fabricators, and plant and system operators.

Tasks

1) Recommend or implement measures to motivate employees and to improve production methods. equipment performance, product quality, or efficiency.

2) Determine standards, budgets, production goals, and rates, based on company policies, equipment and labor availability, and workloads.

3) Enforce safety and sanitation regulations.

4) Plan and develop new products and production processes.

5) Read and analyze charts, work orders, production schedules, and other records and reports, in order to determine production requirements and to evaluate current production estimates

and outputs.

6) Recommend personnel actions such as hirings and promotions.

7) Inspect materials, products, or equipment to detect defects or malfunctions.

8) Interpret specifications, blueprints, job orders, and company policies and procedures for workers.

9) Maintain operations data such as time, production, and cost records, and prepare management reports of production results.

10) Confer with other supervisors to coordinate operations and activities within or between departments.

11) Calculate labor and equipment requirements and production specifications. using standard formulas.

12) Confer with management or subordinates to resolve worker problems, complaints, or grievances.

13) Demonstrate equipment operations and work and safety procedures to new employees, or assign employees to experienced workers for training.

14) Direct and coordinate the activities of employees engaged in the production or processing of goods, such as inspectors, machine setters, and fabricators.

15) Plan and establish work schedules, assignments, and production sequences to meet production goals.

16) Set up and adjust machines and equipment.

17) Observe work, and monitor gauges, dials, and other indicators to ensure that operators conform to production or processing standards.

51-2011.00 - Aircraft Structure, Surfaces, Rigging, and Systems Assemblers

Assemble, fit, fasten, and install parts of airplanes, space vehicles, or missiles, such as tails, wings, fuselage, bulkheads, stabilizers, landing gear, rigging and control equipment, or heating and ventilating systems

Tasks

1) Select and install accessories in swaging machines, using hand tools.

2) Prepare and load live ammunition, missiles, and bombs onto aircraft, according to established procedures.

3) Participate in operational checkouts of entire armament systems on the ground or during test flights.

4) Mark identifying information on tubing or cable assemblies, using etching devices, labels, rubber stamps, or other methods.

5) Install and connect control cables to electronically controlled units, using hand tools, ring locks, cotter keys, threaded connectors, turnbuckles, and related devices

6) Install mechanical linkages and actuators, and verify tension of cables, using tensiometers.

7) Clean, oil, and/or coat system components as necessary before assembling and attaching them.

8) Weld tubing and fittings, and solder cable ends, using tack-welders, induction brazing chambers, or other equipment.

9) Verify dimensions of cable assemblies and positions of fittings, using measuring instruments.

10) Swage fittings onto cables, using swaging machines.

11) Set up and operate machines and systems to crimp, cut, bend, form, swage, flare, bead, burr, and straighten tubing, according to specifications.

12) Fabricate parts needed for assembly and installation, using shop equipment.

13) Align and fit structural assemblies manually, or signal crane operators to position assemblies for joining.

14) Inspect and test installed units, parts, systems, and assemblies for fit, alignment, performance, defects, and compliance with standards, using measuring instruments and test equipment.

15) Align, fit, assemble, connect, and install system components, using jigs, fixtures, measuring instruments, hand tools, and power tools.

16) Assemble and fit prefabricated parts to form subassemblies.

17) Assemble, install, and connect parts, fittings, and assemblies on aircraft, using layout

tools, hand tools, power tools, and fasteners such as bolts, screws, rivets, and clamps.

18) Attach brackets, hinges, or clips to secure or support components and subassemblies, using bolts, screws, rivets, chemical bonding, or welding.

19) Cut, trim, file, bend, and smooth parts, and verify sizes and fitting tolerances in order to ensure proper fit and clearance of parts.

20) Form loops or splices in cables, using clamps and fittings, or reweave cable strands.

21) Adjust, repair, rework, or replace parts and assemblies to eliminate malfunctions and to ensure proper operation.

22) Join structural assemblies such as wings, tails, and fuselage.

23) Fit and fasten sheet metal coverings to surface areas and other sections of aircraft prior to welding or riveting.

24) Measure and cut cables and tubing, using master templates, measuring instruments, and cable cutters or saws.

25) Position and align subassemblies in jigs or fixtures, using measuring instruments and following blueprint lines and index points.

26) Read and interpret blueprints, illustrations, and specifications to determine layouts, sequences of operations, or identities and relationships of parts.

27) Lay out and mark reference points and locations for installation of parts and components, using jigs, templates, and measuring and marking instruments.

51-2031.00 - Engine and Other Machine Assemblers

Construct, assemble, or rebuild machines, such as engines, turbines, and similar equipment used in such industries as construction, extraction, textiles, and paper manufacturing.

Tasks

1) Maintain and lubricate parts and components.

2) Set and verify parts clearances.

3) Set up and operate metalworking machines, such as milling and grinding machines, to shape or fabricate parts.

4) Rework, repair, and replace damaged parts or assemblies.

5) Remove rough spots, and smooth surfaces to fit, trim, or clean parts, using hand tools and power tools.

6) Read and interpret assembly blueprints and specifications manuals, and plan assembly or building operations.

7) Lay out and drill, ream, tap, and cut parts for assembly.

8) Inspect, operate, and test completed products to verify functioning, machine capabilities, and conformance to customer specifications.

9) Fasten and install piping, fixtures, or wiring and electrical components to form assemblies or subassemblies, using hand tools, rivet guns, and welding equipment.

10) Position and align components for assembly, manually or using hoists.

11) Assemble systems of gears by aligning and meshing gears in gearboxes.

51-2041.00 - Structural Metal Fabricators and Fitters

Fabricate, lay out, position, align, and fit parts of structural metal products.

Tasks

1) Set up face blocks, jigs, and fixtures.

2) Hammer, chip, and grind workpieces in order to cut, bend, and straighten metal.

3) Set up and operate fabricating machines such as brakes, rolls, shears, flame cutters, grinders, and drill presses to bend, cut, form, punch, drill, or otherwise form and assemble metal components.

4) Remove high spots and cut bevels, using hand files, portable grinders, and cutting torches.

5) Install boilers, containers, and other structures.

6) Lay out and examine metal stock or workpieces to be processed in order to ensure that specifications are met.

7) Align and fit parts according to specifications, using jacks, turnbuckles, wedges, drift pins, pry bars, and hammers.

8) Locate and mark workpiece bending and cutting lines, allowing for stock thickness, machine and welding shrinkage, and other component specifications.

9) Smooth workpiece edges, and fix taps, tubes, and valves.

10) Straighten warped or bent parts, using sledges, hand torches, straightening presses, or bulldozers.

11) Position or tighten braces, jacks, clamps, ropes, and/or bolt straps, or bolt parts in position for welding or riveting.

12) Position, align, fit, and weld parts to form complete units or subunits, following blueprints and layout specifications, and using jigs, welding torches, and hand tools.

13) Lift or move materials and finished products, using large cranes.

14) Tack-weld fitted parts together.

15) Verify conformance of workpieces to specifications, using squares, rulers, and measuring tapes.

16) Design and construct templates and fixtures, using hand tools.

17) Direct welders to build up low spots or short pieces with weld.

18) Erect ladders and scaffolding to fit together large assemblies.

19) Preheat workpieces to make them malleable, using hand torches or furnaces.

20) Heat-treat parts, using acetylene torches.

21) Study engineering drawings and blueprints to determine materials requirements and task sequences.

22) Move parts into position, manually or by using hoists or cranes.

51-2091.00 - Fiberglass Laminators and Fabricators

Laminate layers of fiberglass on molds to form boat decks and hulls, bodies for golf carts, automobiles, or other products.

Tasks

1) Check all dies, templates, and cutout patterns to be used in the manufacturing process to ensure that they conform to dimensional data, photographs, blueprints, samples, and/or customer specifications.

2) Mix catalysts into resins, and saturate cloth and mats with mixtures, using brushes.

3) Trim excess materials from molds, using hand shears or trimming knives.

4) Cure materials by letting them set at room temperature, placing them under heat lamps, or baking them in ovens.

5) Repair or modify damaged or defective glass-fiber parts, checking thicknesses, densities, and contours to ensure a close fit after repair.

6) Mask off mold areas which are not to be laminated, using cellophane, wax paper, masking tape, or special sprays containing mold-release substances.

7) Spray chopped fiberglass, resins, and catalysts onto prepared molds or dies using pneumatic spray guns with chopper attachments.

8) Trim cured materials by sawing them with diamond-impregnated cutoff wheels.

9) Check completed products for conformance to specifications and for defects by measuring with rulers or micrometers, by checking them visually, or by tapping them to detect bubbles or dead spots.

10) Apply lacquers and waxes to mold surfaces to facilitate assembly and removal of laminated parts.

11) Inspect, clean, and assemble molds before beginning work.

12) Release air bubbles and smooth seams, using rollers.

13) Select precut fiberglass mats, cloth, and woodbracing materials as required by projects being assembled.

14) Pat or press layers of saturated mat or cloth into place on molds, using brushes or hands, and smooth out wrinkles and air bubbles with hands or squeegees.

15) Apply layers of plastic resin to mold surfaces prior to placement of fiberglass mats, repeating layers until products have the desired thicknesses and plastics have jelled.

51-2092.00 - Team Assemblers

Work as part of a team having responsibility for assembling an entire product or component of a product. Team assemblers can perform all tasks conducted by the team in the assembly process and rotate through all or most of them rather than being assigned to a specific task on a permanent basis. May participate in making management decisions affecting the work. Team leaders who work as part of the team should be included.

Tasks

1) Determine work assignments and procedures.

2) Provide assistance in the production of wiring assemblies.

3) Shovel and sweep work areas.

4) Rotate through all the tasks required in a particular production process.

51-3021.00 - Butchers and Meat Cutters

Cut, trim, or prepare consumer-sized portions of meat for use or sale in retail establishments.

Tasks

1) Wrap, weigh, label and price cuts of meat.

2) Estimate requirements and order or requisition meat supplies to maintain inventories.

3) Prepare special cuts of meat ordered by customers.

4) Prepare and place meat cuts and products in display counter, so they will appear attractive and catch the shopper's eye.

5) Negotiate with representatives from supply companies to determine order details.

6) Shape, lace, and tie roasts, using boning knife, skewer, and twine.

7) Total sales, and collect money from customers.

8) Supervise other butchers or meat cutters.

9) Cure, smoke, tenderize and preserve meat.

10) Record quantity of meat received and issued to cooks and/or keep records of meat sales.

11) Cut, trim, bone, tie, and grind meats, such as beef, pork, poultry, and fish, to prepare meat in cooking form.

51-3022.00 - Meat, Poultry, and Fish Cutters and Trimmers

Use hand tools to perform routine cutting and trimming of meat, poultry, and fish.

Tasks

1) Separate meats and byproducts into specified containers and seal containers.

2) Clean, trim, slice, and section carcasses for future processing.

3) Obtain and distribute specified meat or carcass.

4) Inspect meat products for defects, bruises or blemishes and remove them along with any excess fat.

5) Process primal parts into cuts that are ready for retail use.

6) Produce hamburger meat and meat trimmings.

7) Remove parts, such as skin, feathers, scales or bones, from carcass.

8) Slaughter live animals, using stunning devices and knives.

9) Cut and trim meat to prepare for packing.

10) Weigh meats and tag containers for weight and contents.

11) Prepare ready-to-heat foods by filleting meat or fish or cutting it into bite-sized pieces, preparing and adding vegetables or applying sauces or breading.

12) Prepare sausages, luncheon meats, hot dogs, and other fabricated meat products, using meat trimmings and hamburger meat.

13) Clean and salt hides.

51-3023.00 - Slaughterers and Meat Packers

Work in slaughtering, meat packing, or wholesale establishments performing precision functions involving the preparation of meat. Work may include specialized slaughtering tasks, cutting standard or premium cuts of meat for marketing, making sausage, or wrapping meats.

Tasks

1) Saw, split, or scribe carcasses into smaller portions to facilitate handling.

2) Remove bones, and cut meat into standard cuts in preparation for marketing.

3) Skin sections of animals or whole animals.

4) Stun animals prior to slaughtering.

5) Grind meat into hamburger, and into trimmings used to prepare sausages, luncheon meats, and other meat products.

6) Tend assembly lines, performing a few of the many cuts needed to process a carcass.

7) Sever jugular veins to drain blood and facilitate slaughtering.

8) Shave or singe and defeather carcasses, and wash them in preparation for further processing or packaging.

9) Slaughter animals in accordance with religious law, and determine that carcasses meet specified religious standards.

10) Slit open, eviscerate, and trim carcasses of slaughtered animals.

11) Wrap dressed carcasses and/or meat cuts.

12) Trim, clean, and/or cure animal hides.

13) Shackle hind legs of animals to raise them for slaughtering or skinning.

14) Trim head meat, and sever or remove parts of animals' heads or skulls.

51-3091.00 - Food and Tobacco Roasting, Baking, and Drying Machine Operators and Tenders

Operate or tend food or tobacco roasting, baking, or drying equipment, including hearth ovens, kiln driers, roasters, char kilns, and vacuum drying equipment.

Tasks

1) Observe temperature, humidity, pressure gauges, and product samples, and adjust controls, such as thermostats and valves, in order to maintain prescribed operating conditions for specific stages.

2) Operate or tend equipment that roasts, bakes, dries, or cures food items such as cocoa and coffee beans, grains, nuts, and bakery products.

3) Test products for moisture content, using moisture meters.

4) Weigh or measure products, using scale hoppers or scale conveyors.

5) Smooth out products in bins, pans, trays, or conveyors, using rakes or shovels.

6) Observe flow of materials and listen for machine malfunctions, such as jamming or spillage, and notify supervisors if corrective actions fail.

7) Record production data, such as weight and amount of product processed, type of product, and time and temperature of processing.

8) Clear or dislodge blockages in bins, screens, or other equipment, using poles, brushes, or mallets.

9) Take product samples during and/or after processing for laboratory analyses.

10) Lift racks of fish from washing tanks and place racks in smoke chambers.

11) Remove salt-cured fish from barrels, hang fish on racks, and place racks in washing tank, turning valves to regulate fresh water flow.

12) Set temperature and time controls; light ovens, burners, driers, or roasters; and start equipment, such as conveyors, cylinders, blowers, driers, or pumps.

13) Read work orders in order to determine quantities and types of products to be baked, dried, or roasted.

14) Install equipment, such as spray units, cutting blades, or screens, using hand tools.

15) Clean equipment with steam, hot water, and hoses.

16) Signal coworkers in order to synchronize flow of materials.

17) Observe, feel, taste, or otherwise examine products during and after processing, in order to ensure conformance to standards.

18) Push racks or carts in order to transfer products to storage, cooling stations, or the next stage of processing.

19) Dump sugar dust from collectors into melting tanks and add water, in order to reclaim sugar lost during processing.

20) Open valves, gates, or chutes, or use shovels in order to load or remove products from ovens or other equipment.

21) Fill or remove product from trays, carts, hoppers, or equipment, using scoops, peels, or shovels, or by hand.

51-3092.00 - Food Batchmakers

Set up and operate equipment that mixes or blends ingredients used in the manufacturing of food products. Includes candy makers and cheese makers.

Tasks

1) Mix or blend ingredients, according to recipes, using a paddle or an agitator, or by controlling vats that heat and mix ingredients.

2) Turn valve controls to start equipment and to adjust operation in order to maintain product quality.

3) Select and measure or weigh ingredients, using English or metric measures and balance scales.

4) Follow recipes to produce food products of specified flavor, texture, clarity, bouquet, and/or color.

5) Press switches and turn knobs to start, adjust, and regulate equipment such as beaters, extruders, discharge pipes, and salt pumps.

6) Observe and listen to equipment in order to detect possible malfunctions, such as leaks or plugging, and report malfunctions or undesirable tastes to supervisors.

7) Determine mixing sequences, based on knowledge of temperature effects and of the solubility of specific ingredients.

8) Record production and test data for each food product batch, such as the ingredients used, temperature, test results, and time cycle.

9) Give directions to other workers who are assisting in the batchmaking process.

10) Clean and sterilize vats and factory processing areas.

11) Fill processing or cooking containers, such as kettles, rotating cookers, pressure cookers, or vats, with ingredients, by opening valves, by starting pumps or injectors, or by hand.

12) Observe gauges and thermometers to determine if the mixing chamber temperature is within specified limits, and turn valves to control the temperature.

13) Inspect vats after cleaning in order to ensure that fermentable residue has been removed.

14) Examine, feel, and taste product samples during production in order to evaluate quality, color, texture, flavor, and bouquet, and document the results.

15) Modify cooking and forming operations based on the results of sampling processes, adjusting time cycles and ingredients in order to achieve desired qualities, such as firmness or texture.

16) Test food product samples for moisture content, acidity level, specific gravity, and/or butter-fat content, and continue processing until desired levels are reached.

17) Manipulate products, by hand or using machines, in order to separate, spread, knead, spin, cast, cut, pull, or roll products.

18) Operate refining machines in order to reduce the particle size of cooked batches.

19) Place products on carts or conveyors in order to transfer them to the next stage of processing.

20) Inspect and pack the final product.

21) Formulate and/or modify recipes for specific kinds of food products.

22) Grade food products according to government regulations or according to type, color, bouquet, and moisture content.

23) Cool food product batches on slabs or in water-cooled kettles.

24) Homogenize or pasteurize material to prevent separation or to obtain prescribed butterfat content, using a homogenizing device.

Knowledge	Knowledge Definitions
Production and Processing	Knowledge of raw materials, production processes, quality control, costs, and other techniques for maximizing the effective manufacture and distribution of goods.
Mathematics	Knowledge of arithmetic, algebra, geometry, calculus, statistics, and their applications.
Public Safety and Security	Knowledge of relevant equipment, policies, procedures, and strategies to promote effective local, state, or national security operations for the protection of people, data, property, and institutions.
English Language	Knowledge of the structure and content of the English language including the meaning and spelling of words, rules of composition, and grammar.
Education and Training	Knowledge of principles and methods for curriculum and training design, teaching and instruction for individuals and groups, and the measurement of training effects.
Food Production	Knowledge of techniques and equipment for planting, growing, and harvesting food products (both plant and animal) for consumption, including storage/handling techniques.
Mechanical	Knowledge of machines and tools, including their designs, uses, repair, and maintenance.
Administration and Management	Knowledge of business and management principles involved in strategic planning, resource allocation, human resources modeling, leadership technique, production methods, and coordination of people and resources.
Chemistry	Knowledge of the chemical composition, structure, and properties of substances and of the chemical processes and transformations that they undergo. This includes uses of chemicals and their interactions, danger signs, production techniques, and disposal methods.
Computers and Electronics	Knowledge of circuit boards, processors, chips, electronic equipment, and computer hardware and software, including applications and programming.
Personnel and Human Resources	Knowledge of principles and procedures for personnel recruitment, selection, training, compensation and benefits, labor relations and negotiation, and personnel information systems.
Customer and Personal Service	Knowledge of principles and processes for providing customer and personal services. This includes customer needs assessment, meeting quality standards for services, and evaluation of customer satisfaction.
Foreign Language	Knowledge of the structure and content of a foreign (non-English) language including the meaning and spelling of words, rules of composition and grammar, and pronunciation.
Engineering and Technology	Knowledge of the practical application of engineering science and technology. This includes applying principles, techniques, procedures, and equipment to the design and production of various goods and services.
Physics	Knowledge and prediction of physical principles, laws, their interrelationships, and applications to understanding fluid, material, and atmospheric dynamics, and mechanical, electrical, atomic and sub-atomic structures and processes.
Law and Government	Knowledge of laws, legal codes, court procedures, precedents, government regulations, executive orders, agency rules, and the democratic political process.
Psychology	Knowledge of human behavior and performance; individual differences in ability, personality, and interests; learning and motivation; psychological research methods; and the assessment and treatment of behavioral and affective disorders.
Communications and Media	Knowledge of media production, communication, and dissemination techniques and methods. This includes alternative ways to inform and entertain via written, oral, and visual media.
Clerical	Knowledge of administrative and clerical procedures and systems such as word processing, managing files and records, stenography and transcription, designing forms, and other office procedures and terminology.
Philosophy and Theology	Knowledge of different philosophical systems and religions. This includes their basic principles, values, ethics, ways of thinking, customs, practices, and their impact on human culture.
Transportation	Knowledge of principles and methods for moving people or goods by air, rail, sea, or road, including the relative costs and benefits.

Sales and Marketing	Knowledge of principles and methods for showing, promoting, and selling products or services. This includes marketing strategy and tactics, product demonstration, sales techniques, and sales control systems.
Design	Knowledge of design techniques, tools, and principles involved in production of precision technical plans, blueprints, drawings, and models.
Fine Arts	Knowledge of the theory and techniques required to compose, produce, and perform works of music, dance, visual arts, drama, and sculpture.
Biology	Knowledge of plant and animal organisms, their tissues, cells, functions, interdependencies, and interactions with each other and the environment.
Telecommunications	Knowledge of transmission, broadcasting, switching, control, and operation of telecommunications systems.
Economics and Accounting	Knowledge of economic and accounting principles and practices, the financial markets, banking and the analysis and reporting of financial data.
Medicine and Dentistry	Knowledge of the information and techniques needed to diagnose and treat human injuries, diseases, and deformities. This includes symptoms, treatment alternatives, drug properties and interactions, and preventive health-care measures.
Geography	Knowledge of principles and methods for describing the features of land, sea, and air masses, including their physical characteristics, locations, interrelationships, and distribution of plant, animal, and human life.
Building and Construction	Knowledge of materials, methods, and the tools involved in construction or repair of houses, buildings, or other structures such as highways and roads.
History and Archeology	Knowledge of historical events and their causes, indicators, and effects on civilizations and cultures.
Sociology and Anthropology	Knowledge of group behavior and dynamics, societal trends and influences, human migrations, ethnicity, cultures and their history and origins.
Therapy and Counseling	Knowledge of principles, methods, and procedures for diagnosis, treatment, and rehabilitation of physical and mental dysfunctions, and for career counseling and guidance.

Skills — Skills Definitions

Active Listening	Giving full attention to what other people are saying, taking time to understand the points being made, asking questions as appropriate, and not interrupting at inappropriate times.
Operation Monitoring	Watching gauges, dials, or other indicators to make sure a machine is working properly.
Mathematics	Using mathematics to solve problems.
Reading Comprehension	Understanding written sentences and paragraphs in work related documents.
Operation and Control	Controlling operations of equipment or systems.
Time Management	Managing one's own time and the time of others.
Active Learning	Understanding the implications of new information for both current and future problem-solving and decision-making.
Troubleshooting	Determining causes of operating errors and deciding what to do about it.
Critical Thinking	Using logic and reasoning to identify the strengths and weaknesses of alternative solutions, conclusions or approaches to problems.
Coordination	Adjusting actions in relation to others' actions.
Speaking	Talking to others to convey information effectively.
Learning Strategies	Selecting and using training/instructional methods and procedures appropriate for the situation when learning or teaching new things.
Quality Control Analysis	Conducting tests and inspections of products, services, or processes to evaluate quality or performance.
Instructing	Teaching others how to do something.
Equipment Maintenance	Performing routine maintenance on equipment and determining when and what kind of maintenance is needed.
Monitoring	Monitoring/Assessing performance of yourself, other individuals, or organizations to make improvements or take corrective action.
Writing	Communicating effectively in writing as appropriate for the needs of the audience.
Judgment and Decision Making	Considering the relative costs and benefits of potential actions to choose the most appropriate one.
Equipment Selection	Determining the kind of tools and equipment needed to do a job.
Repairing	Repairing machines or systems using the needed tools.

Complex Problem Solving	Identifying complex problems and reviewing related information to develop and evaluate options and implement solutions.
Social Perceptiveness	Being aware of others' reactions and understanding why they react as they do.
Management of Material Resources	Obtaining and seeing to the appropriate use of equipment, facilities, and materials needed to do certain work.
Service Orientation	Actively looking for ways to help people.
Systems Analysis	Determining how a system should work and how changes in conditions, operations, and the environment will affect outcomes.
Management of Personnel Resources	Motivating, developing, and directing people as they work, identifying the best people for the job.
Negotiation	Bringing others together and trying to reconcile differences.
Operations Analysis	Analyzing needs and product requirements to create a design.
Programming	Writing computer programs for various purposes.
Technology Design	Generating or adapting equipment and technology to serve user needs.
Systems Evaluation	Identifying measures or indicators of system performance and the actions needed to improve or correct performance, relative to the goals of the system.
Persuasion	Persuading others to change their minds or behavior.
Installation	Installing equipment, machines, wiring, or programs to meet specifications.
Management of Financial Resources	Determining how money will be spent to get the work done, and accounting for these expenditures.
Science	Using scientific rules and methods to solve problems.

Ability — Ability Definitions

Information Ordering	The ability to arrange things or actions in a certain order or pattern according to a specific rule or set of rules (e.g., patterns of numbers, letters, words, pictures, mathematical operations).
Near Vision	The ability to see details at close range (within a few feet of the observer).
Control Precision	The ability to quickly and repeatedly adjust the controls of a machine or a vehicle to exact positions.
Manual Dexterity	The ability to quickly move your hand, your hand together with your arm, or your two hands to grasp, manipulate, or assemble objects.
Trunk Strength	The ability to use your abdominal and lower back muscles to support part of the body repeatedly or continuously over time without 'giving out' or fatiguing.
Problem Sensitivity	The ability to tell when something is wrong or is likely to go wrong. It does not involve solving the problem, only recognizing there is a problem.
Oral Expression	The ability to communicate information and ideas in speaking so others will understand.
Category Flexibility	The ability to generate or use different sets of rules for combining or grouping things in different ways.
Arm-Hand Steadiness	The ability to keep your hand and arm steady while moving your arm or while holding your arm and hand in one position.
Speech Recognition	The ability to identify and understand the speech of another person.
Deductive Reasoning	The ability to apply general rules to specific problems to produce answers that make sense.
Written Comprehension	The ability to read and understand information and ideas presented in writing.
Oral Comprehension	The ability to listen to and understand information and ideas presented through spoken words and sentences.
Auditory Attention	The ability to focus on a single source of sound in the presence of other distracting sounds.
Selective Attention	The ability to concentrate on a task over a period of time without being distracted.
Perceptual Speed	The ability to quickly and accurately compare similarities and differences among sets of letters, numbers, objects, pictures, or patterns. The things to be compared may be presented at the same time or one after the other. This ability also includes comparing a presented object with a remembered object.
Extent Flexibility	The ability to bend, stretch, twist, or reach with your body, arms, and/or legs.
Hearing Sensitivity	The ability to detect or tell the differences between sounds that vary in pitch and loudness.
Inductive Reasoning	The ability to combine pieces of information to form general rules or conclusions (includes finding a relationship among seemingly unrelated events).
Speech Clarity	The ability to speak clearly so others can understand you.

Flexibility of Closure	The ability to identify or detect a known pattern (a figure, object, word, or sound) that is hidden in other distracting material.
Rate Control	The ability to time your movements or the movement of a piece of equipment in anticipation of changes in the speed and/or direction of a moving object or scene.
Reaction Time	The ability to quickly respond (with the hand, finger, or foot) to a signal (sound, light, picture) when it appears.
Written Expression	The ability to communicate information and ideas in writing so others will understand.
Finger Dexterity	The ability to make precisely coordinated movements of the fingers of one or both hands to grasp, manipulate, or assemble very small objects.
Multilimb Coordination	The ability to coordinate two or more limbs (for example, two arms, two legs, or one leg and one arm) while sitting, standing, or lying down. It does not involve performing the activities while the whole body is in motion.
Time Sharing	The ability to shift back and forth between two or more activities or sources of information (such as speech, sounds, touch, or other sources).
Visual Color Discrimination	The ability to match or detect differences between colors, including shades of color and brightness.
Number Facility	The ability to add, subtract, multiply, or divide quickly and correctly.
Static Strength	The ability to exert maximum muscle force to lift, push, pull, or carry objects.
Stamina	The ability to exert yourself physically over long periods of time without getting winded or out of breath.
Response Orientation	The ability to choose quickly between two or more movements in response to two or more different signals (lights, sounds, pictures). It includes the speed with which the correct response is started with the hand, foot, or other body part.
Wrist-Finger Speed	The ability to make fast, simple, repeated movements of the fingers, hands, and wrists.
Visualization	The ability to imagine how something will look after it is moved around or when its parts are moved or rearranged.
Speed of Limb Movement	The ability to quickly move the arms and legs.
Dynamic Strength	The ability to exert muscle force repeatedly or continuously over time. This involves muscular endurance and resistance to muscle fatigue.
Mathematical Reasoning	The ability to choose the right mathematical methods or formulas to solve a problem.
Speed of Closure	The ability to quickly make sense of, combine, and organize information into meaningful patterns.
Gross Body Coordination	The ability to coordinate the movement of your arms, legs, and torso together when the whole body is in motion.
Depth Perception	The ability to judge which of several objects is closer or farther away from you, or to judge the distance between you and an object.
Far Vision	The ability to see details at a distance.
Memorization	The ability to remember information such as words, numbers, pictures, and procedures.
Sound Localization	The ability to tell the direction from which a sound originated.
Fluency of Ideas	The ability to come up with a number of ideas about a topic (the number of ideas is important, not their quality, correctness, or creativity).
Originality	The ability to come up with unusual or clever ideas about a given topic or situation, or to develop creative ways to solve a problem.
Gross Body Equilibrium	The ability to keep or regain your body balance or stay upright when in an unstable position.
Dynamic Flexibility	The ability to quickly and repeatedly bend, stretch, twist, or reach out with your body, arms, and/or legs.
Peripheral Vision	The ability to see objects or movement of objects to one's side when the eyes are looking ahead.
Spatial Orientation	The ability to know your location in relation to the environment or to know where other objects are in relation to you.
Night Vision	The ability to see under low light conditions.
Glare Sensitivity	The ability to see objects in the presence of glare or bright lighting.
Explosive Strength	The ability to use short bursts of muscle force to propel oneself (as in jumping or sprinting), or to throw an object.

Work_Activity	**Work_Activity Definitions**
Getting Information	Observing, receiving, and otherwise obtaining information from all relevant sources.
Monitor Processes, Materials, or Surroundings	Monitoring and reviewing information from materials, events, or the environment, to detect or assess problems.
Handling and Moving Objects	Using hands and arms in handling, installing, positioning, and moving materials, and manipulating things.
Communicating with Supervisors, Peers, or Subordin	Providing information to supervisors, co-workers, and subordinates by telephone, in written form, e-mail, or in person.
Identifying Objects, Actions, and Events	Identifying information by categorizing, estimating, recognizing differences or similarities, and detecting changes in circumstances or events.
Controlling Machines and Processes	Using either control mechanisms or direct physical activity to operate machines or processes (not including computers or vehicles).
Performing General Physical Activities	Performing physical activities that require considerable use of your arms and legs and moving your whole body, such as climbing, lifting, balancing, walking, stooping, and handling of materials.
Processing Information	Compiling, coding, categorizing, calculating, tabulating, auditing, or verifying information or data.
Evaluating Information to Determine Compliance wit	Using relevant information and individual judgment to determine whether events or processes comply with laws, regulations, or standards.
Estimating the Quantifiable Characteristics of Pro	Estimating sizes, distances, and quantities; or determining time, costs, resources, or materials needed to perform a work activity.
Training and Teaching Others	Identifying the educational needs of others, developing formal educational or training programs or classes, and teaching or instructing others.
Documenting/Recording Information	Entering, transcribing, recording, storing, or maintaining information in written or electronic/magnetic form.
Establishing and Maintaining Interpersonal Relatio	Developing constructive and cooperative working relationships with others, and maintaining them over time.
Inspecting Equipment, Structures, or Material	Inspecting equipment, structures, or materials to identify the cause of errors or other problems or defects.
Making Decisions and Solving Problems	Analyzing information and evaluating results to choose the best solution and solve problems.
Updating and Using Relevant Knowledge	Keeping up-to-date technically and applying new knowledge to your job.
Operating Vehicles, Mechanized Devices, or Equipme	Running, maneuvering, navigating, or driving vehicles or mechanized equipment, such as forklifts, passenger vehicles, aircraft, or water craft.
Judging the Qualities of Things, Services, or Peop	Assessing the value, importance, or quality of things or people.
Analyzing Data or Information	Identifying the underlying principles, reasons, or facts of information by breaking down information or data into separate parts.
Coaching and Developing Others	Identifying the developmental needs of others and coaching, mentoring, or otherwise helping others to improve their knowledge or skills.
Organizing, Planning, and Prioritizing Work	Developing specific goals and plans to prioritize, organize, and accomplish your work.
Interpreting the Meaning of Information for Others	Translating or explaining what information means and how it can be used.
Assisting and Caring for Others	Providing personal assistance, medical attention, emotional support, or other personal care to others such as coworkers, customers, or patients.
Coordinating the Work and Activities of Others	Getting members of a group to work together to accomplish tasks.
Developing and Building Teams	Encouraging and building mutual trust, respect, and cooperation among team members.
Resolving Conflicts and Negotiating with Others	Handling complaints, settling disputes, and resolving grievances and conflicts, or otherwise negotiating with others.
Interacting With Computers	Using computers and computer systems (including hardware and software) to program, write software, set up functions, enter data, or process information.
Guiding, Directing, and Motivating Subordinates	Providing guidance and direction to subordinates, including setting performance standards and monitoring performance.
Provide Consultation and Advice to Others	Providing guidance and expert advice to management or other groups on technical, systems-, or process-related topics.
Scheduling Work and Activities	Scheduling events, programs, and activities, as well as the work of others.
Performing Administrative Activities	Performing day-to-day administrative tasks such as maintaining information files and processing paperwork.
Thinking Creatively	Developing, designing, or creating new applications, ideas, relationships, systems, or products, including artistic contributions.

Developing Objectives and Strategies	Establishing long-range objectives and specifying the strategies and actions to achieve them.
Performing for or Working Directly with the Public	Performing for people or dealing directly with the public. This includes serving customers in restaurants and stores, and receiving clients or guests.
Communicating with Persons Outside Organization	Communicating with people outside the organization, representing the organization to customers, the public, government, and other external sources. This information can be exchanged in person, in writing, or by telephone or e-mail.
Selling or Influencing Others	Convincing others to buy merchandise/goods or to otherwise change their minds or actions.
Monitoring and Controlling Resources	Monitoring and controlling resources and overseeing the spending of money.
Repairing and Maintaining Mechanical Equipment	Servicing, repairing, adjusting, and testing machines, devices, moving parts, and equipment that operate primarily on the basis of mechanical (not electronic) principles.
Repairing and Maintaining Electronic Equipment	Servicing, repairing, calibrating, regulating, fine-tuning, or testing machines, devices, and equipment that operate primarily on the basis of electrical or electronic (not mechanical) principles.
Drafting, Laying Out, and Specifying Technical Dev	Providing documentation, detailed instructions, drawings, or specifications to tell others about how devices, parts, equipment, or structures are to be fabricated, constructed, assembled, modified, maintained, or used.
Staffing Organizational Units	Recruiting, interviewing, selecting, hiring, and promoting employees in an organization.

Work_Context	**Work_Context Definitions**
Spend Time Standing	How much does this job require standing?
Wear Common Protective or Safety Equipment such as	How much does this job require wearing common protective or safety equipment such as safety shoes, glasses, gloves, hard hats or live jackets?
Sounds, Noise Levels Are Distracting or Uncomforta	How often does this job require working exposed to sounds and noise levels that are distracting or uncomfortable?
Face-to-Face Discussions	How often do you have to have face-to-face discussions with individuals or teams in this job?
Spend Time Using Your Hands to Handle, Control, or	How much does this job require using your hands to handle, control, or feel objects, tools or controls?
Contact With Others	How much does this job require the worker to be in contact with others (face-to-face, by telephone, or otherwise) in order to perform it?
Pace Determined by Speed of Equipment	How important is it to this job that the pace is determined by the speed of equipment or machinery? (This does not refer to keeping busy at all times on this job.)
Time Pressure	How often does this job require the worker to meet strict deadlines?
Spend Time Making Repetitive Motions	How much does this job require making repetitive motions?
Spend Time Bending or Twisting the Body	How much does this job require bending or twisting your body?
Importance of Repeating Same Tasks	How important is repeating the same physical activities (e.g., key entry) or mental activities (e.g., checking entries in a ledger) over and over, without stopping, to performing this job?
Work With Work Group or Team	How important is it to work with others in a group or team in this job?
Importance of Being Exact or Accurate	How important is being very exact or highly accurate in performing this job?
Exposed to Contaminants	How often does this job require working exposed to contaminants (such as pollutants, gases, dust or odors)?
Indoors, Not Environmentally Controlled	How often does this job require working indoors in non-controlled environmental conditions (e.g., warehouse without heat)?
Responsible for Others' Health and Safety	How much responsibility is there for the health and safety of others in this job?
Freedom to Make Decisions	How much decision making freedom, without supervision, does the job offer?
Coordinate or Lead Others	How important is it to coordinate or lead others in accomplishing work activities in this job?
Structured versus Unstructured Work	To what extent is this job structured for the worker, rather than allowing the worker to determine tasks, priorities, and goals?
Spend Time Walking and Running	How much does this job require walking and running?
Consequence of Error	How serious would the result usually be if the worker made a mistake that was not readily correctable?

Impact of Decisions on Co-workers or Company Resul	How do the decisions an employee makes impact the results of co-workers, clients or the company?
Frequency of Decision Making	How frequently is the worker required to make decisions that affect other people, the financial resources, and/or the image and reputation of the organization?
Responsibility for Outcomes and Results	How responsible is the worker for work outcomes and results of other workers?
Indoors, Environmentally Controlled	How often does this job require working indoors in environmentally controlled conditions?
Degree of Automation	How automated is the job?
Exposed to Minor Burns, Cuts, Bites, or Stings	How often does this job require exposure to minor burns, cuts, bites, or stings?
Very Hot or Cold Temperatures	How often does this job require working in very hot (above 90 F degrees) or very cold (below 32 F degrees) temperatures?
Physical Proximity	To what extent does this job require the worker to perform job tasks in close physical proximity to other people?
Deal With Unpleasant or Angry People	How frequently does the worker have to deal with unpleasant, angry, or discourteous individuals as part of the job requirements?
Level of Competition	To what extent does this job require the worker to compete or to be aware of competitive pressures?
Telephone	How often do you have telephone conversations in this job?
Frequency of Conflict Situations	How often are there conflict situations the employee has to face in this job?
Spend Time Kneeling, Crouching, Stooping, or Crawl	How much does this job require kneeling, crouching, stooping or crawling?
Cramped Work Space, Awkward Positions	How often does this job require working in cramped work spaces that requires getting into awkward positions?
Exposed to Hazardous Equipment	How often does this job require exposure to hazardous equipment?
Exposed to High Places	How often does this job require exposure to high places?
Deal With External Customers	How important is it to work with external customers or the public in this job?
Exposed to Hazardous Conditions	How often does this job require exposure to hazardous conditions?
Wear Specialized Protective or Safety Equipment su	How much does this job require wearing specialized protective or safety equipment such as breathing apparatus, safety harness, full protection suits, or radiation protection?
Extremely Bright or Inadequate Lighting	How often does this job require working in extremely bright or inadequate lighting conditions?
Letters and Memos	How often does the job require written letters and memos?
Spend Time Keeping or Regaining Balance	How much does this job require keeping or regaining your balance?
Spend Time Climbing Ladders, Scaffolds, or Poles	How much does this job require climbing ladders, scaffolds, or poles?
In an Enclosed Vehicle or Equipment	How often does this job require working in a closed vehicle or equipment (e.g., car)?
Spend Time Sitting	How much does this job require sitting?
Deal With Physically Aggressive People	How frequently does this job require the worker to deal with physical aggression of violent individuals?
Exposed to Disease or Infections	How often does this job require exposure to disease/infections?
Outdoors, Exposed to Weather	How often does this job require working outdoors, exposed to all weather conditions?
In an Open Vehicle or Equipment	How often does this job require working in an open vehicle or equipment (e.g., tractor)?
Electronic Mail	How often do you use electronic mail in this job?
Exposed to Whole Body Vibration	How often does this job require exposure to whole body vibration (e.g., operate a jackhammer)?
Outdoors, Under Cover	How often does this job require working outdoors, under cover (e.g., structure with roof but no walls)?
Public Speaking	How often do you have to perform public speaking in this job?
Exposed to Radiation	How often does this job require exposure to radiation?

Job Zone Component	**Job Zone Component Definitions**
Title	Job Zone Two: Some Preparation Needed
Overall Experience	Some previous work-related skill, knowledge, or experience may be helpful in these occupations, but usually is not needed. For example, a drywall installer might benefit from experience installing drywall, but an inexperienced person could still learn to be an installer with little difficulty.
Job Training	Employees in these occupations need anywhere from a few months to one year of working with experienced employees.

Job Zone Examples	These occupations often involve using your knowledge and skills to help others. Examples include drywall installers, fire inspectors, flight attendants, pharmacy technicians, salespersons (retail), and tellers.	
SVP Range	(4.0 to < 6.0)	
Education	These occupations usually require a high school diploma and may require some vocational training or job-related course work. In some cases, an associate's or bachelor's degree could be needed.	

Work_Styles	Work_Styles Definitions
Attention to Detail	Job requires being careful about detail and thorough in completing work tasks.
Dependability	Job requires being reliable, responsible, and dependable, and fulfilling obligations.
Integrity	Job requires being honest and ethical.
Cooperation	Job requires being pleasant with others on the job and displaying a good-natured, cooperative attitude.
Initiative	Job requires a willingness to take on responsibilities and challenges.
Self Control	Job requires maintaining composure, keeping emotions in check, controlling anger, and avoiding aggressive behavior, even in very difficult situations.
Independence	Job requires developing one's own ways of doing things, guiding oneself with little or no supervision, and depending on oneself to get things done.
Concern for Others	Job requires being sensitive to others' needs and feelings and being understanding and helpful on the job.
Persistence	Job requires persistence in the face of obstacles.
Adaptability/Flexibility	Job requires being open to change (positive or negative) and to considerable variety in the workplace.
Achievement/Effort	Job requires establishing and maintaining personally challenging achievement goals and exerting effort toward mastering tasks.
Stress Tolerance	Job requires accepting criticism and dealing calmly and effectively with high stress situations.
Innovation	Job requires creativity and alternative thinking to develop new ideas for and answers to work-related problems.
Analytical Thinking	Job requires analyzing information and using logic to address work-related issues and problems.
Social Orientation	Job requires preferring to work with others rather than alone, and being personally connected with others on the job.
Leadership	Job requires a willingness to lead, take charge, and offer opinions and direction.

51-3093.00 - Food Cooking Machine Operators and Tenders

Operate or tend cooking equipment, such as steam cooking vats, deep fry cookers, pressure cookers, kettles, and boilers, to prepare food products.

Tasks

1) Set temperature, pressure, and time controls; and start conveyers, machines, or pumps.

2) Tend or operate and control equipment such as kettles, cookers, vats and tanks, and boilers, in order to cook ingredients or prepare products for further processing.

3) Listen for malfunction alarms, and shut down equipment and notify supervisors when necessary.

4) Record production and test data, such as processing steps, temperature and steam readings, cooking time, batches processed, and test results.

5) Measure or weigh ingredients, using scales or measuring containers.

6) Notify or signal other workers to operate equipment or when processing is complete.

7) Read work orders, recipes, or formulas in order to determine cooking times and temperatures, and ingredient specifications.

8) Observe gauges, dials, and product characteristics, and adjust controls in order to maintain appropriate temperature, pressure, and flow of ingredients.

9) Remove cooked material or products from equipment.

10) Admit required amounts of water, steam, cooking oils, or compressed air into equipment, such as by opening water valves to cool mixtures to the desired consistency.

11) Turn valves or start pumps to add ingredients or drain products from equipment and to transfer products for storage, cooling, or further processing.

12) Collect and examine product samples during production in order to test them for quality, color, content, consistency, viscosity, acidity, and/or specific gravity.

13) Pour, dump, or load prescribed quantities of ingredients or products into cooking equipment, manually or using a hoist.

14) Activate agitators and paddles in order to mix or stir ingredients, stopping machines when ingredients are thoroughly mixed.

15) Place products on conveyers or carts, and monitor product flow.

16) Operate auxiliary machines and equipment, such as grinders, canners, and molding presses, in order to prepare or further process products.

Knowledge	Knowledge Definitions
Production and Processing	Knowledge of raw materials, production processes, quality control, costs, and other techniques for maximizing the effective manufacture and distribution of goods.
Food Production	Knowledge of techniques and equipment for planting, growing, and harvesting food products (both plant and animal) for consumption, including storage/handling techniques.
Customer and Personal Service	Knowledge of principles and processes for providing customer and personal services. This includes customer needs assessment, meeting quality standards for services, and evaluation of customer satisfaction.
Administration and Management	Knowledge of business and management principles involved in strategic planning, resource allocation, human resources modeling, leadership technique, production methods, and coordination of people and resources.
Computers and Electronics	Knowledge of circuit boards, processors, chips, electronic equipment, and computer hardware and software, including applications and programming.
Education and Training	Knowledge of principles and methods for curriculum and training design, teaching and instruction for individuals and groups, and the measurement of training effects.
Mechanical	Knowledge of machines and tools, including their designs, uses, repair, and maintenance.
Mathematics	Knowledge of arithmetic, algebra, geometry, calculus, statistics, and their applications.
Chemistry	Knowledge of the chemical composition, structure, and properties of substances and of the chemical processes and transformations that they undergo. This includes uses of chemicals and their interactions, danger signs, production techniques, and disposal methods.
English Language	Knowledge of the structure and content of the English language including the meaning and spelling of words, rules of composition, and grammar.
Personnel and Human Resources	Knowledge of principles and procedures for personnel recruitment, selection, training, compensation and benefits, labor relations and negotiation, and personnel information systems.
Psychology	Knowledge of human behavior and performance; individual differences in ability, personality, and interests; learning and motivation; psychological research methods; and the assessment and treatment of behavioral and affective disorders.
Clerical	Knowledge of administrative and clerical procedures and systems such as word processing, managing files and records, stenography and transcription, designing forms, and other office procedures and terminology.
Economics and Accounting	Knowledge of economic and accounting principles and practices, the financial markets, banking and the analysis and reporting of financial data.
Public Safety and Security	Knowledge of relevant equipment, policies, procedures, and strategies to promote effective local, state, or national security operations for the protection of people, data, property, and institutions.
Transportation	Knowledge of principles and methods for moving people or goods by air, rail, sea, or road, including the relative costs and benefits.
Sales and Marketing	Knowledge of principles and methods for showing, promoting, and selling products or services. This includes marketing strategy and tactics, product demonstration, sales techniques, and sales control systems.
Engineering and Technology	Knowledge of the practical application of engineering science and technology. This includes applying principles, techniques, procedures, and equipment to the design and production of various goods and services.

Design	Knowledge of design techniques, tools, and principles involved in production of precision technical plans, blueprints, drawings, and models.
Law and Government	Knowledge of laws, legal codes, court procedures, precedents, government regulations, executive orders, agency rules, and the democratic political process.
Communications and Media	Knowledge of media production, communication, and dissemination techniques and methods. This includes alternative ways to inform and entertain via written, oral, and visual media.
Physics	Knowledge and prediction of physical principles, laws, their interrelationships, and applications to understanding fluid, material, and atmospheric dynamics, and mechanical, electrical, atomic and sub- atomic structures and processes.
Biology	Knowledge of plant and animal organisms, their tissues, cells, functions, interdependencies, and interactions with each other and the environment.
Telecommunications	Knowledge of transmission, broadcasting, switching, control, and operation of telecommunications systems.
Medicine and Dentistry	Knowledge of the information and techniques needed to diagnose and treat human injuries, diseases, and deformities. This includes symptoms, treatment alternatives, drug properties and interactions, and preventive health-care measures.
Building and Construction	Knowledge of materials, methods, and the tools involved in the construction or repair of houses, buildings, or other structures such as highways and roads.
Therapy and Counseling	Knowledge of principles, methods, and procedures for diagnosis, treatment, and rehabilitation of physical and mental dysfunctions, and for career counseling and guidance.
Philosophy and Theology	Knowledge of different philosophical systems and religions. This includes their basic principles, values, ethics, ways of thinking, customs, practices, and their impact on human culture.
Sociology and Anthropology	Knowledge of group behavior and dynamics, societal trends and influences, human migrations, ethnicity, cultures and their history and origins.
Foreign Language	Knowledge of the structure and content of a foreign (non-English) language including the meaning and spelling of words, rules of composition and grammar, and pronunciation.
Geography	Knowledge of principles and methods for describing the features of land, sea, and air masses, including their physical characteristics, locations, interrelationships, and distribution of plant, animal, and human life.
Fine Arts	Knowledge of the theory and techniques required to compose, produce, and perform works of music, dance, visual arts, drama, and sculpture.
History and Archeology	Knowledge of historical events and their causes, indicators, and effects on civilizations and cultures.

Skills	**Skills Definitions**
Operation Monitoring	Watching gauges, dials, or other indicators to make sure a machine is working properly.
Instructing	Teaching others how to do something.
Quality Control Analysis	Conducting tests and inspections of products, services, or processes to evaluate quality or performance.
Speaking	Talking to others to convey information effectively.
Active Listening	Giving full attention to what other people are saying, taking time to understand the points being made, asking questions as appropriate, and not interrupting at inappropriate times.
Operation and Control	Controlling operations of equipment or systems.
Learning Strategies	Selecting and using training/instructional methods and procedures appropriate for the situation when learning or teaching new things.
Coordination	Adjusting actions in relation to others' actions.
Active Learning	Understanding the implications of new information for both current and future problem-solving and decision-making.
Reading Comprehension	Understanding written sentences and paragraphs in work related documents.
Time Management	Managing one's own time and the time of others.
Writing	Communicating effectively in writing as appropriate for the needs of the audience.
Monitoring	Monitoring/Assessing performance of yourself, other individuals, or organizations to make improvements or take corrective action.
Mathematics	Using mathematics to solve problems.
Troubleshooting	Determining causes of operating errors and deciding what to do about it.

Service Orientation	Actively looking for ways to help people.
Critical Thinking	Using logic and reasoning to identify the strengths and weaknesses of alternative solutions, conclusions or approaches to problems.
Social Perceptiveness	Being aware of others' reactions and understanding why they react as they do.
Equipment Selection	Determining the kind of tools and equipment needed to do a job.
Negotiation	Bringing others together and trying to reconcile differences.
Systems Analysis	Determining how a system should work and how changes in conditions, operations, and the environment will affect outcomes.
Systems Evaluation	Identifying measures or indicators of system performance and the actions needed to improve or correct performance, relative to the goals of the system.
Management of Personnel Resources	Motivating, developing, and directing people as they work, identifying the best people for the job.
Complex Problem Solving	Identifying complex problems and reviewing related information to develop and evaluate options and implement solutions.
Judgment and Decision Making	Considering the relative costs and benefits of potential actions to choose the most appropriate one.
Equipment Maintenance	Performing routine maintenance on equipment and determining when and what kind of maintenance is needed.
Operations Analysis	Analyzing needs and product requirements to create a design.
Technology Design	Generating or adapting equipment and technology to serve user needs.
Installation	Installing equipment, machines, wiring, or programs to meet specifications.
Persuasion	Persuading others to change their minds or behavior.
Repairing	Repairing machines or systems using the needed tools.
Management of Material Resources	Obtaining and seeing to the appropriate use of equipment, facilities, and materials needed to do certain work.
Science	Using scientific rules and methods to solve problems.
Programming	Writing computer programs for various purposes.
Management of Financial Resources	Determining how money will be spent to get the work done, and accounting for these expenditures.

Ability	**Ability Definitions**
Information Ordering	The ability to arrange things or actions in a certain order or pattern according to a specific rule or set of rules (e.g., patterns of numbers, letters, words, pictures, mathematical operations).
Near Vision	The ability to see details at close range (within a few feet of the observer).
Problem Sensitivity	The ability to tell when something is wrong or is likely to go wrong. It does not involve solving the problem, only recognizing there is a problem.
Written Comprehension	The ability to read and understand information and ideas presented in writing.
Oral Comprehension	The ability to listen to and understand information and ideas presented through spoken words and sentences.
Selective Attention	The ability to concentrate on a task over a period of time without being distracted.
Control Precision	The ability to quickly and repeatedly adjust the controls of a machine or a vehicle to exact positions.
Oral Expression	The ability to communicate information and ideas in speaking so others will understand.
Deductive Reasoning	The ability to apply general rules to specific problems to produce answers that make sense.
Manual Dexterity	The ability to quickly move your hand, your hand together with your arm, or your two hands to grasp, manipulate, or assemble objects.
Reaction Time	The ability to quickly respond (with the hand, finger, or foot) to a signal (sound, light, picture) when it appears.
Rate Control	The ability to time your movements or the movement of a piece of equipment in anticipation of changes in the speed and/or direction of a moving object or scene.
Category Flexibility	The ability to generate or use different sets of rules for combining or grouping things in different ways.
Speech Recognition	The ability to identify and understand the speech of another person.
Auditory Attention	The ability to focus on a single source of sound in the presence of other distracting sounds.
Written Expression	The ability to communicate information and ideas in writing so others will understand.
Arm-Hand Steadiness	The ability to keep your hand and arm steady while moving your arm or while holding your arm and hand in one position.

Speech Clarity	The ability to speak clearly so others can understand you.
Hearing Sensitivity	The ability to detect or tell the differences between sounds that vary in pitch and loudness.
Perceptual Speed	The ability to quickly and accurately compare similarities and differences among sets of letters, numbers, objects, pictures, or patterns. The things to be compared may be presented at the same time or one after the other. This ability also includes comparing a presented object with a remembered object.
Inductive Reasoning	The ability to combine pieces of information to form general rules or conclusions (includes finding a relationship among seemingly unrelated events).
Multilimb Coordination	The ability to coordinate two or more limbs (for example, two arms, two legs, or one leg and one arm) while sitting, standing, or lying down. It does not involve performing the activities while the whole body is in motion.
Trunk Strength	The ability to use your abdominal and lower back muscles to support part of the body repeatedly or continuously over time without 'giving out' or fatiguing.
Static Strength	The ability to exert maximum muscle force to lift, push, pull, or carry objects.
Flexibility of Closure	The ability to identify or detect a known pattern (a figure, object, word, or sound) that is hidden in other distracting material.
Finger Dexterity	The ability to make precisely coordinated movements of the fingers of one or both hands to grasp, manipulate, or assemble very small objects.
Number Facility	The ability to add, subtract, multiply, or divide quickly and correctly.
Extent Flexibility	The ability to bend, stretch, twist, or reach with your body, arms, and/or legs.
Visual Color Discrimination	The ability to match or detect differences between colors, including shades of color and brightness.
Mathematical Reasoning	The ability to choose the right mathematical methods or formulas to solve a problem.
Visualization	The ability to imagine how something will look after it is moved around or when its parts are moved or rearranged.
Memorization	The ability to remember information such as words, numbers, pictures, and procedures.
Gross Body Coordination	The ability to coordinate the movement of your arms, legs, and torso together when the whole body is in motion.
Stamina	The ability to exert yourself physically over long periods of time without getting winded or out of breath.
Fluency of Ideas	The ability to come up with a number of ideas about a topic (the number of ideas is important, not their quality, correctness, or creativity).
Response Orientation	The ability to choose quickly between two or more movements in response to two or more different signals (lights, sounds, pictures). It includes the speed with which the correct response is started with the hand, foot, or other body part.
Time Sharing	The ability to shift back and forth between two or more activities or sources of information (such as speech, sounds, touch, or other sources).
Speed of Limb Movement	The ability to quickly move the arms and legs.
Wrist-Finger Speed	The ability to make fast, simple, repeated movements of the fingers, hands, and wrists.
Speed of Closure	The ability to quickly make sense of, combine, and organize information into meaningful patterns.
Far Vision	The ability to see details at a distance.
Depth Perception	The ability to judge which of several objects is closer or farther away from you, or to judge the distance between you and an object.
Dynamic Strength	The ability to exert muscle force repeatedly or continuously over time. This involves muscular endurance and resistance to muscle fatigue.
Originality	The ability to come up with unusual or clever ideas about a given topic or situation, or to develop creative ways to solve a problem.
Gross Body Equilibrium	The ability to keep or regain your body balance or stay upright when in an unstable position.
Sound Localization	The ability to tell the direction from which a sound originated.
Dynamic Flexibility	The ability to quickly and repeatedly bend, stretch, twist, or reach out with your body, arms, and/or legs.
Explosive Strength	The ability to use short bursts of muscle force to propel oneself (as in jumping or sprinting), or to throw an object.
Glare Sensitivity	The ability to see objects in the presence of glare or bright lighting.
Peripheral Vision	The ability to see objects or movement of objects to one's side when the eyes are looking ahead.

Night Vision	The ability to see under low light conditions.
Spatial Orientation	The ability to know your location in relation to the environment or to know where other objects are in relation to you.

Work_Activity	**Work_Activity Definitions**
Monitor Processes, Materials, or Surroundings	Monitoring and reviewing information from materials, events, or the environment, to detect or assess problems.
Controlling Machines and Processes	Using either control mechanisms or direct physical activity to operate machines or processes (not including computers or vehicles).
Getting Information	Observing, receiving, and otherwise obtaining information from all relevant sources.
Identifying Objects, Actions, and Events	Identifying information by categorizing, estimating, recognizing differences or similarities, and detecting changes in circumstances or events.
Communicating with Supervisors, Peers, or Subordin	Providing information to supervisors, co-workers, and subordinates by telephone, in written form, e-mail, or in person.
Inspecting Equipment, Structures, or Material	Inspecting equipment, structures, or materials to identify the cause of errors or other problems or defects.
Evaluating Information to Determine Compliance wit	Using relevant information and individual judgment to determine whether events or processes comply with laws, regulations, or standards.
Documenting/Recording Information	Entering, transcribing, recording, storing, or maintaining information in written or electronic/magnetic form.
Training and Teaching Others	Identifying the educational needs of others, developing formal educational or training programs or classes, and teaching or instructing others.
Making Decisions and Solving Problems	Analyzing information and evaluating results to choose the best solution and solve problems.
Processing Information	Compiling, coding, categorizing, calculating, tabulating, auditing, or verifying information or data.
Handling and Moving Objects	Using hands and arms in handling, installing, positioning, and moving materials, and manipulating things.
Performing General Physical Activities	Performing physical activities that require considerable use of your arms and legs and moving your whole body, such as climbing, lifting, balancing, walking, stooping, and handling of materials.
Estimating the Quantifiable Characteristics of Pro	Estimating sizes, distances, and quantities; or determining time, costs, resources, or materials needed to perform a work activity.
Interpreting the Meaning of Information for Others	Translating or explaining what information means and how it can be used.
Updating and Using Relevant Knowledge	Keeping up-to-date technically and applying new knowledge to your job.
Coaching and Developing Others	Identifying the developmental needs of others and coaching, mentoring, or otherwise helping others to improve their knowledge or skills.
Developing and Building Teams	Encouraging and building mutual trust, respect, and cooperation among team members.
Establishing and Maintaining Interpersonal Relatio	Developing constructive and cooperative working relationships with others, and maintaining them over time.
Repairing and Maintaining Mechanical Equipment	Servicing, repairing, adjusting, and testing machines, devices, moving parts, and equipment that operate primarily on the basis of mechanical (not electronic) principles.
Scheduling Work and Activities	Scheduling events, programs, and activities, as well as the work of others.
Interacting With Computers	Using computers and computer systems (including hardware and software) to program, write software, set up functions, enter data, or process information.
Judging the Qualities of Things, Services, or Peop	Assessing the value, importance, or quality of things or people.
Guiding, Directing, and Motivating Subordinates	Providing guidance and direction to subordinates, including setting performance standards and monitoring performance.
Analyzing Data or Information	Identifying the underlying principles, reasons, or facts of information by breaking down information or data into separate parts.
Assisting and Caring for Others	Providing personal assistance, medical attention, emotional support, or other personal care to others such as coworkers, customers, or patients.
Resolving Conflicts and Negotiating with Others	Handling complaints, settling disputes, and resolving grievances and conflicts, or otherwise negotiating with others.
Monitoring and Controlling Resources	Monitoring and controlling resources and overseeing the spending of money.

Repairing and Maintaining Electronic Equipment	Servicing. repairing. calibrating. regulating. fine-tuning, or testing machines. devices and equipment that operate primarily on the basis of electrical or electronic (not mechanical) principles.
Organizing, Planning, and Prioritizing Work	Developing specific goals and plans to prioritize, organize, and accomplish your work.
Coordinating the Work and Activities of Others	Getting members of a group to work together to accomplish tasks.
Provide Consultation and Advice to Others	Providing guidance and expert advice to management or other groups on technical, systems-, or process-related topics.
Performing Administrative Activities	Performing day-to-day administrative tasks such as maintaining information files and processing paperwork.
Operating Vehicles, Mechanized Devices, or Equipme	Running, maneuvering, navigating, or driving vehicles or mechanized equipment. such as forklifts, passenger vehicles, aircraft, or water craft.
Thinking Creatively	Developing, designing, or creating new applications, ideas, relationships, systems, or products, including artistic contributions.
Selling or Influencing Others	Convincing others to buy merchandise/goods or to otherwise change their minds or actions.
Developing Objectives and Strategies	Establishing long-range objectives and specifying the strategies and actions to achieve them.
Communicating with Persons Outside Organization	Communicating with people outside the organization, representing the organization to customers, the public, government, and other external sources. This information can be exchanged in person, in writing, or by telephone or e-mail.
Performing for or Working Directly with the Public	Performing for people or dealing directly with the public. This includes serving customers in restaurants and stores, and receiving clients or guests.
Staffing Organizational Units	Recruiting, interviewing, selecting, hiring, and promoting employees in an organization.
Drafting, Laying Out, and Specifying Technical Dev	Providing documentation. detailed instructions, drawings, or specifications to tell others about how devices, parts, equipment, or structures are to be fabricated, constructed, assembled, modified, maintained, or used.

Work_Context	Work_Context Definitions
Wear Common Protective or Safety Equipment such as	How much does this job require wearing common protective or safety equipment such as safety shoes, glasses, gloves, hard hats or live jackets?
Spend Time Standing	How much does this job require standing?
Contact With Others	How much does this job require the worker to be in contact with others (face-to-face, by telephone, or otherwise) in order to perform it?
Spend Time Using Your Hands to Handle, Control, or	How much does this job require using your hands to handle, control, or feel objects, tools or controls?
Importance of Being Exact or Accurate	How important is being very exact or highly accurate in performing this job?
Work With Work Group or Team	How important is it to work with others in a group or team in this job?
Face-to-Face Discussions	How often do you have to have face-to-face discussions with individuals or teams in this job?
Physical Proximity	To what extent does this job require the worker to perform job tasks in close physical proximity to other people?
Sounds, Noise Levels Are Distracting or Uncomforta	How often does this job require working exposed to sounds and noise levels that are distracting or uncomfortable?
Pace Determined by Speed of Equipment	How important is it to this job that the pace is determined by the speed of equipment or machinery? (This does not refer to keeping busy at all times on this job.)
Time Pressure	How often does this job require the worker to meet strict deadlines?
Spend Time Walking and Running	How much does this job require walking and running?
Frequency of Decision Making	How frequently is the worker required to make decisions that affect other people, the financial resources, and/or the image and reputation of the organization?
Importance of Repeating Same Tasks	How important is repeating the same physical activities (e.g., key entry) or mental activities (e.g., checking entries in a ledger) over and over, without stopping, to performing this job?
Very Hot or Cold Temperatures	How often does this job require working in very hot (above 90 F degrees) or very cold (below 32 F degrees) temperatures?
Exposed to Minor Burns, Cuts, Bites, or Stings	How often does this job require exposure to minor burns, cuts, bites, or stings?
Spend Time Making Repetitive Motions	How much does this job require making repetitive motions?

Impact of Decisions on Co-workers or Company Resul	How do the decisions an employee makes impact the results of co-workers, clients or the company?
Structured versus Unstructured Work	To what extent is this job structured for the worker, rather than allowing the worker to determine tasks, priorities, and goals?
Freedom to Make Decisions	How much decision making freedom. without supervision. does the job offer?
Responsible for Others' Health and Safety	How much responsibility is there for the health and safety of others in this job?
Indoors, Environmentally Controlled	How often does this job require working indoors in environmentally controlled conditions?
Consequence of Error	How serious would the result usually be if the worker made a mistake that was not readily correctable?
Responsibility for Outcomes and Results	How responsible is the worker for work outcomes and results of other workers?
Spend Time Bending or Twisting the Body	How much does this job require bending or twisting your body?
Level of Competition	To what extent does this job require the worker to compete or to be aware of competitive pressures?
Degree of Automation	How automated is the job?
Coordinate or Lead Others	How important is it to coordinate or lead others in accomplishing work activities in this job?
Exposed to Contaminants	How often does this job require working exposed to contaminants (such as pollutants, gases, dust or odors)?
Indoors, Not Environmentally Controlled	How often does this job require working indoors in non-controlled environmental conditions (e.g.. warehouse without heat)?
Exposed to Hazardous Equipment	How often does this job require exposure to hazardous equipment?
Telephone	How often do you have telephone conversations in this job?
Frequency of Conflict Situations	How often are there conflict situations the employee has to face in this job?
Deal With Unpleasant or Angry People	How frequently does the worker have to deal with unpleasant, angry, or discourteous individuals as part of the job requirements?
Cramped Work Space, Awkward Positions	How often does this job require working in cramped work spaces that requires getting into awkward positions?
Wear Specialized Protective or Safety Equipment su	How much does this job require wearing specialized protective or safety equipment such as breathing apparatus, safety harness, full protection suits, or radiation protection?
Exposed to Hazardous Conditions	How often does this job require exposure to hazardous conditions?
Deal With External Customers	How important is it to work with external customers or the public in this job?
Exposed to High Places	How often does this job require exposure to high places?
Spend Time Kneeling, Crouching, Stooping, or Crawl	How much does this job require kneeling, crouching, stooping or crawling?
Letters and Memos	How often does the job require written letters and memos?
Electronic Mail	How often do you use electronic mail in this job?
Spend Time Climbing Ladders, Scaffolds, or Poles	How much does this job require climbing ladders, scaffolds, or poles?
Extremely Bright or Inadequate Lighting	How often does this job require working in extremely bright or inadequate lighting conditions?
Spend Time Keeping or Regaining Balance	How much does this job require keeping or regaining your balance?
Spend Time Sitting	How much does this job require sitting?
Public Speaking	How often do you have to perform public speaking in this job?
In an Open Vehicle or Equipment	How often does this job require working in an open vehicle or equipment (e.g., tractor)?
Deal With Physically Aggressive People	How frequently does this job require the worker to deal with physical aggression of violent individuals?
Exposed to Disease or Infections	How often does this job require exposure to disease/infections?
Exposed to Whole Body Vibration	How often does this job require exposure to whole body vibration (e.g., operate a jackhammer)?
Outdoors, Exposed to Weather	How often does this job require working outdoors, exposed to all weather conditions?
Outdoors, Under Cover	How often does this job require working outdoors, under cover (e.g., structure with roof but no walls)?
In an Enclosed Vehicle or Equipment	How often does this job require working in a closed vehicle or equipment (e.g., car)?
Exposed to Radiation	How often does this job require exposure to radiation?

Job Zone Component	Job Zone Component Definitions
Title	Job Zone Two: Some Preparation Needed
Overall Experience	Some previous work-related skill, knowledge, or experience may be helpful in these occupations, but usually is not needed. For example, a drywall installer might benefit from experience installing drywall, but an inexperienced person could still learn to be an installer with little difficulty.
Job Training	Employees in these occupations need anywhere from a few months to one year of working with experienced employees.
Job Zone Examples	These occupations often involve using your knowledge and skills to help others. Examples include drywall installers, fire inspectors, flight attendants, pharmacy technicians, salespersons (retail), and tellers.
SVP Range	(4.0 to < 6.0)
Education	These occupations usually require a high school diploma and may require some vocational training or job-related course work. In some cases, an associate's or bachelor's degree could be needed.

Work_Styles	Work_Styles Definitions
Dependability	Job requires being reliable, responsible, and dependable, and fulfilling obligations.
Cooperation	Job requires being pleasant with others on the job and displaying a good-natured, cooperative attitude.
Attention to Detail	Job requires being careful about detail and thorough in completing work tasks.
Self Control	Job requires maintaining composure, keeping emotions in check, controlling anger, and avoiding aggressive behavior, even in very difficult situations.
Stress Tolerance	Job requires accepting criticism and dealing calmly and effectively with high stress situations.
Integrity	Job requires being honest and ethical.
Leadership	Job requires a willingness to lead, take charge, and offer opinions and direction.
Independence	Job requires developing one's own ways of doing things, guiding oneself with little or no supervision, and depending on oneself to get things done.
Concern for Others	Job requires being sensitive to others' needs and feelings and being understanding and helpful on the job.
Initiative	Job requires a willingness to take on responsibilities and challenges.
Social Orientation	Job requires preferring to work with others rather than alone, and being personally connected with others on the job.
Achievement/Effort	Job requires establishing and maintaining personally challenging achievement goals and exerting effort toward mastering tasks.
Adaptability/Flexibility	Job requires being open to change (positive or negative) and to considerable variety in the workplace.
Persistence	Job requires persistence in the face of obstacles.
Innovation	Job requires creativity and alternative thinking to develop new ideas for and answers to work-related problems.
Analytical Thinking	Job requires analyzing information and using logic to address work-related issues and problems.

51-4021.00 - Extruding and Drawing Machine Setters, Operators, and Tenders, Metal and Plastic

Set up, operate, or tend machines to extrude or draw thermoplastic or metal materials into tubes, rods, hoses, wire, bars, or structural shapes.

Tasks

1) Troubleshoot, maintain, and make minor repairs to equipment.

2) Adjust controls to draw or press metal into specified shapes and diameters.

3) Start machines and set controls to regulate vacuum, air pressure, sizing rings, and temperature, and to synchronize speed of extrusion.

4) Reel extruded products into rolls of specified lengths and weights.

5) Change dies on extruding machines according to production line changes.

6) Install dies, machine screws, and sizing rings on machines that extrude thermoplastic or metal materials.

7) Load machine hoppers with mixed materials, using augers, or stuff rolls of plastic dough into machine cylinders.

8) Replace worn dies when products vary from specifications.

9) Determine setup procedures and select machine dies and parts, according to specifications.

10) Maintain an inventory of materials.

11) Clean work areas.

12) Operate shearing mechanisms to cut rods to specified lengths.

13) Test physical properties of products with testing devices such as acid-bath testers, burst testers, and impact testers.

14) Weigh and mix pelletized, granular, or powdered thermoplastic materials and coloring pigments.

15) Select nozzles, spacers, and wire guides, according to diameters and lengths of rods.

51-4022.00 - Forging Machine Setters, Operators, and Tenders, Metal and Plastic

Set up, operate, or tend forging machines to taper, shape, or form metal or plastic parts.

Tasks

1) Start machines to produce sample workpieces, and observe operations to detect machine malfunctions and to verify that machine setups conform to specifications.

2) Set up, operate, or tend presses and forging machines to perform hot or cold forging by flattening, straightening, bending, cutting, piercing, or other operations to taper, shape, or form metal.

3) Position and move metal wires or workpieces through a series of dies that compress and shape stock to form die impressions.

4) Measure and inspect machined parts to ensure conformance to product specifications.

5) Install, adjust, and remove dies, synchronizing cams, forging hammers, and stop guides, using overhead cranes or other hoisting devices, and hand tools.

6) Confer with other workers about machine setups and operational specifications.

7) Place metal pieces in furnaces, then remove them, using hand tongs or overhead cranes, when metal color indicates proper forging temperatures.

8) Repair, maintain, and replace parts on dies.

9) Trim and compress finished forgings to specified tolerances.

10) Sharpen cutting tools and drill bits, using bench grinders.

11) Select, align, and bolt positioning fixtures, stops and specified dies to rams and anvils, forging rolls, or presses and hammers.

12) Turn handles or knobs to set pressures and depths of ram strokes and to synchronize machine operations.

13) Operate gas or oil furnaces to heat metal to proper temperature prior to forging.

14) Read work orders or blueprints to determine specified tolerances and sequences of operations for machine setup.

51-4023.00 - Rolling Machine Setters, Operators, and Tenders, Metal and Plastic

Set up, operate, or tend machines to roll steel or plastic forming bends, beads, knurls, rolls, or plate or to flatten, temper, or reduce gauge of material.

Tasks

1) Thread or feed sheets or rods through rolling mechanisms, or start and control mechanisms that automatically feed steel into rollers.

2) Set distance points between rolls, guides, meters, and stops, according to specifications.

3) Read rolling orders, blueprints, and mill schedules to determine setup specifications, work sequences, product dimensions, and installation procedures.

4) Direct and train other workers to change rolls, operate mill equipment, remove coils and cobbles, and band and load material.

5) Manipulate controls and observe dial indicators in order to monitor, adjust, and regulate speeds of machine mechanisms.

6) Signal and assist other workers to remove and position equipment, fill hoppers, and feed materials into machines.

7) Select rolls, dies, roll stands, and chucks from data charts in order to form specified contours and to fabricate products.

8) Disassemble sizing mills removed from rolling lines, and sort and store parts.

9) Position, align, and secure arbors, spindles, coils, mandrels, dies, and slitting knives.

10) Record mill production on schedule sheets.

11) Remove scratches and polish roll surfaces, using polishing stones and electric buffers.

12) Calculate draft space and roll speed for each mill stand in order to plan rolling sequences and specified dimensions and tempers.

13) Examine, inspect, and measure raw materials and finished products to verify conformance to specifications.

14) Fill oil cups, adjust valves, and observe gauges to control flow of metal coolants and lubricants onto workpieces.

15) Install equipment such as guides, guards, gears, cooling equipment, and rolls, using hand tools.

16) Start operation of rolling and milling machines to flatten, temper, form, and reduce sheet metal sections and to produce steel strips.

17) Activate shears and grinders to trim workpieces.

18) Adjust and correct machine set-ups to reduce thicknesses, reshape products, and eliminate product defects.

51-4031.00 - Cutting, Punching, and Press Machine Setters, Operators, and Tenders, Metal and Plastic

Set up, operate, or tend machines to saw, cut, shear, slit, punch, crimp, notch, bend, or straighten metal or plastic material.

Tasks

1) Remove housings, feed tubes, tool holders, and other accessories in order to replace worn or broken parts such as springs and bushings.

2) Scribe reference lines on workpieces as guides for cutting operations, according to blueprints, templates, sample parts, or specifications.

3) Select, clean, and install spacers, rubber sleeves, and cutters on arbors.

4) Hand-form, cut, or finish workpieces, using tools such as table saws, hand sledges, and anvils.

5) Start machines, monitor their operations, and record operational data.

6) Set blade tensions, heights, and angles to perform prescribed cuts, using wrenches.

7) Test and adjust machine speeds and actions, according to product specifications, and using gauges and hand tools.

8) Turn controls to set cutting speeds, feed rates, and table angles for specified operations.

9) Turn valves to start flow of coolant against cutting areas and to start airflow that blows cuttings away from kerfs.

10) Clean and lubricate machines.

11) Grind out burrs and sharp edges, using portable grinders, speed lathes, and polishing jacks.

12) Set up, operate, or tend machines to saw, cut, shear, slit, punch, crimp, notch, bend, or straighten metal or plastic material.

13) Sharpen dulled blades, using bench grinders, abrasive wheels, or lathes.

14) Examine completed workpieces for defects such as chipped edges and marred surfaces, and sort defective pieces according to types of flaws.

15) Replace defective blades or wheels, using hand tools.

16) Preheat workpieces, using heating furnaces or hand torches.

17) Mark identifying data on workpieces.

18) Lubricate workpieces with oil.

19) Hone cutters with oilstones to remove nicks.

20) Position guides, stops, holding blocks, or other fixtures to secure and direct workpieces, using hand tools and measuring devices.

21) Read work orders and production schedules to determine specifications, such as materials

to be used, locations of cutting lines, and dimensions and tolerances.

22) Adjust ram strokes of presses to specified lengths, using hand tools.

23) Position, align, and secure workpieces against fixtures or stops on machine beds or on dies.

24) Plan sequences of operations, applying knowledge of physical properties of workpiece materials.

25) Place workpieces on cutting tables, manually or using hoists, cranes, or sledges.

26) Measure completed workpieces to verify conformance to specifications, using micrometers, gauges, calipers, templates, or rulers.

27) Load workpieces, plastic material, or chemical solutions into machines.

28) Install, align, and lock specified punches, dies, cutting blades or other fixtures in rams or beds of machines, using gauges, templates, feelers, shims, and hand tools.

29) Thread ends of metal coils from reels through slitters, and secure ends on recoilers.

51-4041.00 - Machinists

Set up and operate a variety of machine tools to produce precision parts and instruments. Includes precision instrument makers who fabricate, modify, or repair mechanical instruments. May also fabricate and modify parts to make or repair machine tools or maintain industrial machines, applying knowledge of mechanics, shop mathematics, metal properties, layout, and machining procedures.

Tasks

1) Calculate dimensions and tolerances using knowledge of mathematics and instruments such as micrometers and vernier calipers.

2) Maintain industrial machines, applying knowledge of mechanics, shop mathematics, metal properties, layout, and machining procedures.

3) Align and secure holding fixtures, cutting tools, attachments, accessories, and materials onto machines.

4) Select the appropriate tools, machines, and materials to be used in preparation of machinery work.

5) Measure, examine, and test completed units in order to detect defects and ensure conformance to specifications, using precision instruments such as micrometers.

6) Position and fasten workpieces.

7) Machine parts to specifications using machine tools such as lathes, milling machines, shapers, or grinders.

8) Clean and lubricate machines, tools, and equipment in order to remove grease, rust, stains, and foreign matter.

9) Set up, adjust, and operate all of the basic machine tools and many specialized or advanced variation tools in order to perform precision machining operations.

10) Study sample parts, blueprints, drawings, and engineering information in order to determine methods and sequences of operations needed to fabricate products, and determine product dimensions and tolerances.

11) Check workpieces to ensure that they are properly lubricated and cooled.

12) Observe and listen to operating machines or equipment in order to diagnose machine malfunctions and to determine need for adjustments or repairs.

13) Operate equipment to verify operational efficiency.

14) Lay out, measure, and mark metal stock in order to display placement of cuts.

15) Install repaired parts into equipment, or install new equipment.

16) Confer with engineering, supervisory, and manufacturing personnel in order to exchange technical information.

17) Dismantle machines or equipment, using hand tools and power tools, in order to examine parts for defects and replace defective parts where needed.

18) Evaluate experimental procedures, and recommend changes or modifications for improved efficiency and adaptability to setup and production.

19) Support metalworking projects from planning and fabrication through assembly, inspection, and testing, using knowledge of machine functions, metal properties and mathematics.

20) Set controls to regulate machining, or enter commands to retrieve, input, or edit computerized machine control media.

21) Fit and assemble parts to make or repair machine tools.

22) Establish work procedures for fabricating new structural products. using a variety of metalworking machines.

23) Design fixtures. tooling, and experimental parts to meet special engineering needs.

24) Program computers and electronic instruments such as numerically controlled machine tools.

25) Confer with numerical control programmers in order to check and ensure that new programs or machinery will function properly, and that output will meet specifications.

26) Set up and operate metalworking, brazing, heat-treating, welding, and cutting equipment.

27) Prepare working sketches for the illustration of product appearance.

28) Install experimental parts and assemblies such as hydraulic systems. electrical wiring, lubricants, and batteries into machines and mechanisms.

29) Advise clients about the materials being used for finished products.

30) Test experimental models under simulated operating conditions for such purposes as development, standardization, and feasibility of design.

Knowledge	Knowledge Definitions
Mechanical	Knowledge of machines and tools, including their designs, uses. repair, and maintenance.
Mathematics	Knowledge of arithmetic. algebra, geometry, calculus, statistics, and their applications.
Engineering and Technology	Knowledge of the practical application of engineering science and technology. This includes applying principles, techniques, procedures, and equipment to the design and production of various goods and services.
Computers and Electronics	Knowledge of circuit boards, processors, chips, electronic equipment, and computer hardware and software, including applications and programming.
Production and Processing	Knowledge of raw materials, production processes, quality control, costs, and other techniques for maximizing the effective manufacture and distribution of goods.
Design	Knowledge of design techniques, tools, and principles involved in production of precision technical plans, blueprints, drawings, and models.
Education and Training	Knowledge of principles and methods for curriculum and training design, teaching and instruction for individuals and groups, and the measurement of training effects.
English Language	Knowledge of the structure and content of the English language including the meaning and spelling of words, rules of composition, and grammar.
Customer and Personal Service	Knowledge of principles and processes for providing customer and personal services. This includes customer needs assessment, meeting quality standards for services, and evaluation of customer satisfaction.
Administration and Management	Knowledge of business and management principles involved in strategic planning, resource allocation, human resources modeling, leadership technique, production methods, and coordination of people and resources.
Chemistry	Knowledge of the chemical composition, structure, and properties of substances and of the chemical processes and transformations that they undergo. This includes uses of chemicals and their interactions, danger signs, production techniques, and disposal methods.
Public Safety and Security	Knowledge of relevant equipment, policies, procedures, and strategies to promote effective local, state, or national security operations for the protection of people, data, property, and institutions.
Psychology	Knowledge of human behavior and performance; individual differences in ability, personality, and interests; learning and motivation; psychological research methods; and the assessment and treatment of behavioral and affective disorders.
Physics	Knowledge and prediction of physical principles, laws, their interrelationships, and applications to understanding fluid, material, and atmospheric dynamics, and mechanical, electrical, atomic and sub- atomic structures and processes.
Clerical	Knowledge of administrative and clerical procedures and systems such as word processing, managing files and records, stenography and transcription, designing forms, and other office procedures and terminology.
Foreign Language	Knowledge of the structure and content of a foreign (non-English) language including the meaning and spelling of words, rules of composition and grammar, and pronunciation.
Transportation	Knowledge of principles and methods for moving people or goods by air, rail, sea, or road, including the relative costs and benefits.
Law and Government	Knowledge of laws, legal codes, court procedures, precedents, government regulations, executive orders, agency rules, and the democratic political process.
Telecommunications	Knowledge of transmission, broadcasting, switching, control, and operation of telecommunications systems.
Medicine and Dentistry	Knowledge of the information and techniques needed to diagnose and treat human injuries, diseases, and deformities. This includes symptoms, treatment alternatives, drug properties and interactions, and preventive health-care measures.
Therapy and Counseling	Knowledge of principles, methods, and procedures for diagnosis, treatment, and rehabilitation of physical and mental dysfunctions, and for career counseling and guidance.
Personnel and Human Resources	Knowledge of principles and procedures for personnel recruitment, selection, training, compensation and benefits, labor relations and negotiation, and personnel information systems.
Building and Construction	Knowledge of materials, methods, and the tools involved in the construction or repair of houses, buildings, or other structures such as highways and roads.
Communications and Media	Knowledge of media production, communication, and dissemination techniques and methods. This includes alternative ways to inform and entertain via written, oral, and visual media.
Sales and Marketing	Knowledge of principles and methods for showing, promoting, and selling products or services. This includes marketing strategy and tactics, product demonstration, sales techniques, and sales control systems.
Economics and Accounting	Knowledge of economic and accounting principles and practices, the financial markets, banking and the analysis and reporting of financial data.
Philosophy and Theology	Knowledge of different philosophical systems and religions. This includes their basic principles, values, ethics, ways of thinking, customs, practices, and their impact on human culture.
Biology	Knowledge of plant and animal organisms, their tissues, cells, functions, interdependencies, and interactions with each other and the environment.
Geography	Knowledge of principles and methods for describing the features of land, sea, and air masses, including their physical characteristics, locations, interrelationships, and distribution of plant, animal, and human life.
History and Archeology	Knowledge of historical events and their causes, indicators, and effects on civilizations and cultures.
Sociology and Anthropology	Knowledge of group behavior and dynamics, societal trends and influences, human migrations, ethnicity, cultures and their history and origins.
Fine Arts	Knowledge of the theory and techniques required to compose, produce, and perform works of music, dance, visual arts, drama, and sculpture.
Food Production	Knowledge of techniques and equipment for planting, growing, and harvesting food products (both plant and animal) for consumption, including storage/handling techniques.

Skills	Skills Definitions
Operation and Control	Controlling operations of equipment or systems.
Operation Monitoring	Watching gauges, dials, or other indicators to make sure a machine is working properly.
Mathematics	Using mathematics to solve problems.
Equipment Selection	Determining the kind of tools and equipment needed to do a job.
Troubleshooting	Determining causes of operating errors and deciding what to do about it.
Reading Comprehension	Understanding written sentences and paragraphs in work related documents.
Quality Control Analysis	Conducting tests and inspections of products, services, or processes to evaluate quality or performance.
Equipment Maintenance	Performing routine maintenance on equipment and determining when and what kind of maintenance is needed.
Repairing	Repairing machines or systems using the needed tools.
Active Listening	Giving full attention to what other people are saying, taking time to understand the points being made, asking questions as appropriate, and not interrupting at inappropriate times.
Active Learning	Understanding the implications of new information for both current and future problem-solving and decision-making.
Judgment and Decision Making	Considering the relative costs and benefits of potential actions to choose the most appropriate one.

Critical Thinking	Using logic and reasoning to identify the strengths and weaknesses of alternative solutions, conclusions or approaches to problems.
Complex Problem Solving	Identifying complex problems and reviewing related information to develop and evaluate options and implement solutions.
Time Management	Managing one's own time and the time of others.
Installation	Installing equipment, machines, wiring, or programs to meet specifications.
Technology Design	Generating or adapting equipment and technology to serve user needs.
Coordination	Adjusting actions in relation to others' actions.
Learning Strategies	Selecting and using training/instructional methods and procedures appropriate for the situation when learning or teaching new things.
Speaking	Talking to others to convey information effectively.
Monitoring	Monitoring/Assessing performance of yourself, other individuals, or organizations to make improvements or take corrective action.
Systems Analysis	Determining how a system should work and how changes in conditions, operations, and the environment will affect outcomes.
Instructing	Teaching others how to do something.
Operations Analysis	Analyzing needs and product requirements to create a design.
Systems Evaluation	Identifying measures or indicators of system performance and the actions needed to improve or correct performance, relative to the goals of the system.
Writing	Communicating effectively in writing as appropriate for the needs of the audience.
Social Perceptiveness	Being aware of others' reactions and understanding why they react as they do.
Programming	Writing computer programs for various purposes.
Service Orientation	Actively looking for ways to help people.
Negotiation	Bringing others together and trying to reconcile differences.
Persuasion	Persuading others to change their minds or behavior.
Management of Material Resources	Obtaining and seeing to the appropriate use of equipment, facilities, and materials needed to do certain work.
Science	Using scientific rules and methods to solve problems.
Management of Personnel Resources	Motivating, developing, and directing people as they work, identifying the best people for the job.
Management of Financial Resources	Determining how money will be spent to get the work done, and accounting for these expenditures.

Ability	Ability Definitions
Problem Sensitivity	The ability to tell when something is wrong or is likely to go wrong. It does not involve solving the problem, only recognizing there is a problem.
Arm-Hand Steadiness	The ability to keep your hand and arm steady while moving your arm or while holding your arm and hand in one position.
Near Vision	The ability to see details at close range (within a few feet of the observer).
Information Ordering	The ability to arrange things or actions in a certain order or pattern according to a specific rule or set of rules (e.g., patterns of numbers, letters, words, pictures, mathematical operations).
Control Precision	The ability to quickly and repeatedly adjust the controls of a machine or a vehicle to exact positions.
Mathematical Reasoning	The ability to choose the right mathematical methods or formulas to solve a problem.
Deductive Reasoning	The ability to apply general rules to specific problems to produce answers that make sense.
Inductive Reasoning	The ability to combine pieces of information to form general rules or conclusions (includes finding a relationship among seemingly unrelated events).
Visualization	The ability to imagine how something will look after it is moved around or when its parts are moved or rearranged.
Oral Comprehension	The ability to listen to and understand information and ideas presented through spoken words and sentences.
Speech Clarity	The ability to speak clearly so others can understand you.
Selective Attention	The ability to concentrate on a task over a period of time without being distracted.
Manual Dexterity	The ability to quickly move your hand, your hand together with your arm, or your two hands to grasp, manipulate, or assemble objects.
Oral Expression	The ability to communicate information and ideas in speaking so others will understand.
Speech Recognition	The ability to identify and understand the speech of another person.

Multilimb Coordination	The ability to coordinate two or more limbs (for example, two arms, two legs, or one leg and one arm) while sitting, standing, or lying down. It does not involve performing the activities while the whole body is in motion.
Auditory Attention	The ability to focus on a single source of sound in the presence of other distracting sounds.
Written Comprehension	The ability to read and understand information and ideas presented in writing.
Rate Control	The ability to time your movements or the movement of a piece of equipment in anticipation of changes in the speed and/or direction of a moving object or scene.
Hearing Sensitivity	The ability to detect or tell the differences between sounds that vary in pitch and loudness.
Finger Dexterity	The ability to make precisely coordinated movements of the fingers of one or both hands to grasp, manipulate, or assemble very small objects.
Depth Perception	The ability to judge which of several objects is closer or farther away from you, or to judge the distance between you and an object.
Static Strength	The ability to exert maximum muscle force to lift, push, pull, or carry objects.
Extent Flexibility	The ability to bend, stretch, twist, or reach with your body, arms, and/or legs.
Trunk Strength	The ability to use your abdominal and lower back muscles to support part of the body repeatedly or continuously over time without 'giving out' or fatiguing.
Flexibility of Closure	The ability to identify or detect a known pattern (a figure, object, word, or sound) that is hidden in other distracting material.
Written Expression	The ability to communicate information and ideas in writing so others will understand.
Reaction Time	The ability to quickly respond (with the hand, finger, or foot) to a signal (sound, light, picture) when it appears.
Number Facility	The ability to add, subtract, multiply, or divide quickly and correctly.
Speed of Closure	The ability to quickly make sense of, combine, and organize information into meaningful patterns.
Category Flexibility	The ability to generate or use different sets of rules for combining or grouping things in different ways.
Wrist-Finger Speed	The ability to make fast, simple, repeated movements of the fingers, hands, and wrists.
Perceptual Speed	The ability to quickly and accurately compare similarities and differences among sets of letters, numbers, objects, pictures, or patterns. The things to be compared may be presented at the same time or one after the other. This ability also includes comparing a presented object with a remembered object.
Originality	The ability to come up with unusual or clever ideas about a given topic or situation, or to develop creative ways to solve a problem.
Fluency of Ideas	The ability to come up with a number of ideas about a topic (the number of ideas is important, not their quality, correctness, or creativity).
Memorization	The ability to remember information such as words, numbers, pictures, and procedures.
Time Sharing	The ability to shift back and forth between two or more activities or sources of information (such as speech, sounds, touch, or other sources).
Far Vision	The ability to see details at a distance.
Response Orientation	The ability to choose quickly between two or more movements in response to two or more different signals (lights, sounds, pictures). It includes the speed with which the correct response is started with the hand, foot, or other body part.
Speed of Limb Movement	The ability to quickly move the arms and legs.
Spatial Orientation	The ability to know your location in relation to the environment or to know where other objects are in relation to you.
Sound Localization	The ability to tell the direction from which a sound originated.
Gross Body Coordination	The ability to coordinate the movement of your arms, legs, and torso together when the whole body is in motion.
Dynamic Strength	The ability to exert muscle force repeatedly or continuously over time. This involves muscular endurance and resistance to muscle fatigue.
Stamina	The ability to exert yourself physically over long periods of time without getting winded or out of breath.
Peripheral Vision	The ability to see objects or movement of objects to one's side when the eyes are looking ahead.
Visual Color Discrimination	The ability to match or detect differences between colors, including shades of color and brightness.

Gross Body Equilibrium	The ability to keep or regain your body balance or stay upright when in an unstable position.
Dynamic Flexibility	The ability to quickly and repeatedly bend, stretch, twist, or reach out with your body, arms, and/or legs.
Explosive Strength	The ability to use short bursts of muscle force to propel oneself (as in jumping or sprinting), or to throw an object.
Night Vision	The ability to see under low light conditions.
Glare Sensitivity	The ability to see objects in the presence of glare or bright lighting.

Work_Activity	Work_Activity Definitions
Controlling Machines and Processes	Using either control mechanisms or direct physical activity to operate machines or processes (not including computers or vehicles).
Communicating with Supervisors, Peers, or Subordin	Providing information to supervisors, co-workers, and subordinates by telephone, in written form, e-mail, or in person.
Getting Information	Observing, receiving, and otherwise obtaining information from all relevant sources.
Handling and Moving Objects	Using hands and arms in handling, installing, positioning, and moving materials, and manipulating things.
Monitor Processes, Materials, or Surroundings	Monitoring and reviewing information from materials, events, or the environment, to detect or assess problems.
Inspecting Equipment, Structures, or Material	Inspecting equipment, structures, or materials to identify the cause of errors or other problems or defects.
Making Decisions and Solving Problems	Analyzing information and evaluating results to choose the best solution and solve problems.
Judging the Qualities of Things, Services, or Peop	Assessing the value, importance, or quality of things or people.
Identifying Objects, Actions, and Events	Identifying information by categorizing, estimating, recognizing differences or similarities, and detecting changes in circumstances or events.
Updating and Using Relevant Knowledge	Keeping up-to-date technically and applying new knowledge to your job.
Performing General Physical Activities	Performing physical activities that require considerable use of your arms and legs and moving your whole body, such as climbing, lifting, balancing, walking, stooping, and handling of materials.
Documenting/Recording Information	Entering, transcribing, recording, storing, or maintaining information in written or electronic/magnetic form.
Evaluating Information to Determine Compliance wit	Using relevant information and individual judgment to determine whether events or processes comply with laws, regulations, or standards.
Organizing, Planning, and Prioritizing Work	Developing specific goals and plans to prioritize, organize, and accomplish your work.
Processing Information	Compiling, coding, categorizing, calculating, tabulating, auditing, or verifying information or data.
Repairing and Maintaining Mechanical Equipment	Servicing, repairing, adjusting, and testing machines, devices, moving parts, and equipment that operate primarily on the basis of mechanical (not electronic) principles.
Operating Vehicles, Mechanized Devices, or Equipme	Running, maneuvering, navigating, or driving vehicles or mechanized equipment, such as forklifts, passenger vehicles, aircraft, or water craft.
Establishing and Maintaining Interpersonal Relatio	Developing constructive and cooperative working relationships with others, and maintaining them over time.
Training and Teaching Others	Identifying the educational needs of others, developing formal educational or training programs or classes, and teaching or instructing others.
Interpreting the Meaning of Information for Others	Translating or explaining what information means and how it can be used.
Developing and Building Teams	Encouraging and building mutual trust, respect, and cooperation among team members.
Coordinating the Work and Activities of Others	Getting members of a group to work together to accomplish tasks.
Thinking Creatively	Developing, designing, or creating new applications, ideas, relationships, systems, or products, including artistic contributions.
Guiding, Directing, and Motivating Subordinates	Providing guidance and direction to subordinates, including setting performance standards and monitoring performance.
Estimating the Quantifiable Characteristics of Pro	Estimating sizes, distances, and quantities; or determining time, costs, resources, or materials needed to perform a work activity.
Developing Objectives and Strategies	Establishing long-range objectives and specifying the strategies and actions to achieve them.

Communicating with Persons Outside Organization	Communicating with people outside the organization, representing the organization to customers, the public, government, and other external sources. This information can be exchanged in person, in writing, or by telephone or e-mail.
Analyzing Data or Information	Identifying the underlying principles, reasons, or facts of information by breaking down information or data into separate parts.
Interacting With Computers	Using computers and computer systems (including hardware and software) to program, write software, set up functions, enter data, or process information.
Drafting, Laying Out, and Specifying Technical Dev	Providing documentation, detailed instructions, drawings, or specifications to tell others about how devices, parts, equipment, or structures are to be fabricated, constructed, assembled, modified, maintained, or used.
Scheduling Work and Activities	Scheduling events, programs, and activities, as well as the work of others.
Resolving Conflicts and Negotiating with Others	Handling complaints, settling disputes, and resolving grievances and conflicts, or otherwise negotiating with others.
Repairing and Maintaining Electronic Equipment	Servicing, repairing, calibrating, regulating, fine-tuning, or testing machines, devices, and equipment that operate primarily on the basis of electrical or electronic (not mechanical) principles.
Coaching and Developing Others	Identifying the developmental needs of others and coaching, mentoring, or otherwise helping others to improve their knowledge or skills.
Assisting and Caring for Others	Providing personal assistance, medical attention, emotional support, or other personal care to others such as coworkers, customers, or patients.
Performing for or Working Directly with the Public	Performing for people or dealing directly with the public. This includes serving customers in restaurants and stores, and receiving clients or guests.
Provide Consultation and Advice to Others	Providing guidance and expert advice to management or other groups on technical, systems-, or process-related topics.
Selling or Influencing Others	Convincing others to buy merchandise/goods or to otherwise change their minds or actions.
Performing Administrative Activities	Performing day-to-day administrative tasks such as maintaining information files and processing paperwork.
Staffing Organizational Units	Recruiting, interviewing, selecting, hiring, and promoting employees in an organization.
Monitoring and Controlling Resources	Monitoring and controlling resources and overseeing the spending of money.

Work_Context	Work_Context Definitions
Wear Common Protective or Safety Equipment such as	How much does this job require wearing common protective or safety equipment such as safety shoes, glasses, gloves, hard hats or live jackets?
Spend Time Using Your Hands to Handle, Control, or	How much does this job require using your hands to handle, control, or feel objects, tools or controls?
Sounds, Noise Levels Are Distracting or Uncomforta	How often does this job require working exposed to sounds and noise levels that are distracting or uncomfortable?
Importance of Being Exact or Accurate	How important is being very exact or highly accurate in performing this job?
Face-to-Face Discussions	How often do you have to have face-to-face discussions with individuals or teams in this job?
Spend Time Standing	How much does this job require standing?
Exposed to Hazardous Equipment	How often does this job require exposure to hazardous equipment?
Indoors, Not Environmentally Controlled	How often does this job require working indoors in non-controlled environmental conditions (e.g., warehouse without heat)?
Contact With Others	How often does this job require the worker to be in contact with others (face-to-face, by telephone, or otherwise) in order to perform it?
Time Pressure	How often does this job require the worker to meet strict deadlines?
Freedom to Make Decisions	How much decision making freedom, without supervision, does the job offer?
Frequency of Decision Making	How frequently is the worker required to make decisions that affect other people, the financial resources, and/or the image and reputation of the organization?
Responsibility for Outcomes and Results	How responsible is the worker for work outcomes and results of other workers?
Pace Determined by Speed of Equipment	How important is it to this job that the pace is determined by the speed of equipment or machinery? (This does not refer to keeping busy at all times on this job.)

Structured versus Unstructured Work — To what extent is this job structured for the worker, rather than allowing the worker to determine tasks, priorities, and goals?

Spend Time Making Repetitive Motions — How much does this job require making repetitive motions?

Physical Proximity — To what extent does this job require the worker to perform job tasks in close physical proximity to other people?

Work With Work Group or Team — How important is it to work with others in a group or team in this job?

Indoors, Environmentally Controlled — How often does this job require working indoors in environmentally controlled conditions?

Exposed to Contaminants — How often does this job require working exposed to contaminants (such as pollutants, gases, dust or odors)?

Impact of Decisions on Co-workers or Company Resul — How do the decisions an employee makes impact the results of co-workers, clients or the company?

Responsible for Others' Health and Safety — How much responsibility is there for the health and safety of others in this job?

Consequence of Error — How serious would the result usually be if the worker made a mistake that was not readily correctable?

Exposed to Minor Burns, Cuts, Bites, or Stings — How often does this job require exposure to minor burns, cuts, bites, or stings?

Telephone — How often do you have telephone conversations in this job?

Level of Competition — To what extent does this job require the worker to compete or to be aware of competitive pressures?

Coordinate or Lead Others — How important is it to coordinate or lead others in accomplishing work activities in this job?

Spend Time Bending or Twisting the Body — How much does this job require bending or twisting your body?

Very Hot or Cold Temperatures — How often does this job require working in very hot (above 90 F degrees) or very cold (below 32 F degrees) temperatures?

Importance of Repeating Same Tasks — How important is repeating the same physical activities (e.g., key entry) or mental activities (e.g., checking entries in a ledger) over and over, without stopping, to performing this job?

Electronic Mail — How often do you use electronic mail in this job?

Deal With External Customers — How important is it to work with external customers or the public in this job?

Deal With Unpleasant or Angry People — How frequently does the worker have to deal with unpleasant, angry, or discourteous individuals as part of the job requirements?

Spend Time Walking and Running — How much does this job require walking and running?

Exposed to Hazardous Conditions — How often does this job require exposure to hazardous conditions?

Letters and Memos — How often does the job require written letters and memos?

Frequency of Conflict Situations — How often are there conflict situations the employee has to face in this job?

Degree of Automation — How automated is the job?

Cramped Work Space, Awkward Positions — How often does this job require working in cramped work spaces that requires getting into awkward positions?

Outdoors, Exposed to Weather — How often does this job require working outdoors, exposed to all weather conditions?

Extremely Bright or Inadequate Lighting — How often does this job require working in extremely bright or inadequate lighting conditions?

Outdoors, Under Cover — How often does this job require working outdoors, under cover (e.g., structure with roof but no walls)?

Spend Time Sitting — How much does this job require sitting?

Spend Time Kneeling, Crouching, Stooping, or Crawl — How much does this job require kneeling, crouching, stooping or crawling?

Public Speaking — How often do you have to perform public speaking in this job?

Wear Specialized Protective or Safety Equipment su — How much does this job require wearing specialized protective or safety equipment such as breathing apparatus, safety harness, full protection suits, or radiation protection?

In an Open Vehicle or Equipment — How often does this job require working in an open vehicle or equipment (e.g., tractor)?

Exposed to High Places — How often does this job require exposure to high places?

Exposed to Disease or Infections — How often does this job require exposure to disease/infections?

Exposed to Whole Body Vibration — How often does this job require exposure to whole body vibration (e.g., operate a jackhammer)?

Spend Time Climbing Ladders, Scaffolds, or Poles — How much does this job require climbing ladders, scaffolds, or poles?

Spend Time Keeping or Regaining Balance — How much does this job require keeping or regaining your balance?

In an Enclosed Vehicle or Equipment — How often does this job require working in a closed vehicle or equipment (e.g., car)?

Deal With Physically Aggressive People — How frequently does this job require the worker to deal with physical aggression of violent individuals?

Exposed to Radiation — How often does this job require exposure to radiation?

Job Zone Component	Job Zone Component Definitions
Title	Job Zone Three: Medium Preparation Needed
Overall Experience	Previous work-related skill, knowledge, or experience is required for these occupations. For example, an electrician must have completed three or four years of apprenticeship or several years of vocational training, and often must have passed a licensing exam, in order to perform the job.
Job Training	Employees in these occupations usually need one or two years of training involving both on-the-job experience and informal training with experienced workers.
Job Zone Examples	These occupations usually involve using communication and organizational skills to coordinate, supervise, manage, or train others to accomplish goals. Examples include dental assistants, electricians, fish and game wardens, legal secretaries, personnel recruiters, and recreation workers.
SVP Range	(6.0 to < 7.0)
Education	Most occupations in this zone require training in vocational schools, related on-the-job experience, or an associate's degree. Some may require a bachelor's degree.

Work_Styles	Work_Styles Definitions
Attention to Detail	Job requires being careful about detail and thorough in completing work tasks.
Analytical Thinking	Job requires analyzing information and using logic to address work-related issues and problems.
Dependability	Job requires being reliable, responsible, and dependable, and fulfilling obligations.
Initiative	Job requires a willingness to take on responsibilities and challenges.
Innovation	Job requires creativity and alternative thinking to develop new ideas for and answers to work-related problems.
Independence	Job requires developing one's own ways of doing things, guiding oneself with little or no supervision, and depending on oneself to get things done.
Persistence	Job requires persistence in the face of obstacles.
Adaptability/Flexibility	Job requires being open to change (positive or negative) and to considerable variety in the workplace.
Cooperation	Job requires being pleasant with others on the job and displaying a good-natured, cooperative attitude.
Integrity	Job requires being honest and ethical.
Achievement/Effort	Job requires establishing and maintaining personally challenging achievement goals and exerting effort toward mastering tasks.
Leadership	Job requires a willingness to lead, take charge, and offer opinions and direction.
Self Control	Job requires maintaining composure, keeping emotions in check, controlling anger, and avoiding aggressive behavior, even in very difficult situations.
Stress Tolerance	Job requires accepting criticism and dealing calmly and effectively with high stress situations.
Concern for Others	Job requires being sensitive to others' needs and feelings and being understanding and helpful on the job.
Social Orientation	Job requires preferring to work with others rather than alone, and being personally connected with others on the job.

51-4051.00 - Metal-Refining Furnace Operators and Tenders

Operate or tend furnaces, such as gas, oil, coal, electric-arc or electric induction, open-hearth, or oxygen furnaces, to melt and refine metal before casting or to produce specified types of steel.

Tasks

1) Remove impurities from the surface of molten metal, using strainers.

2) Scrape accumulations of metal oxides from floors, molds, and crucibles, and sift and store them for reclamation.

3) Drain, transfer, or remove molten metal from furnaces, and place it into molds, using hoists, pumps, or ladles.

4) Draw smelted metal samples from furnaces or kettles for analysis, and calculate types and amounts of materials needed to ensure that materials meet specifications.

5) Kindle fires, and shovel fuel and other materials into furnaces or onto conveyors by hand, with hoists, or by directing crane operators.

6) Observe air and temperature gauges or metal color and fluidity, and turn fuel valves or adjust controls to maintain required temperatures.

7) Operate controls to move or discharge metal workpieces from furnaces.

8) Sprinkle chemicals over molten metal to bring impurities to the surface.

9) Direct work crews in the cleaning and repair of furnace walls and flooring.

10) Inspect furnaces and equipment to locate defects and wear.

11) Record production data, and maintain production logs.

12) Prepare material to load into furnaces, including cleaning, crushing, or applying chemicals, by using crushing-machines, shovels, rakes, or sprayers.

13) Regulate supplies of fuel and air, or control flow of electric current and water coolant to heat furnaces and adjust temperatures.

14) Observe operations inside furnaces, using television screens, to ensure that problems do not occur.

51-4052.00 - Pourers and Casters, Metal

Operate hand-controlled mechanisms to pour and regulate the flow of molten metal into molds to produce castings or ingots.

Tasks

1) Examine molds to ensure they are clean, smooth, and properly coated.

2) Repair and maintain metal forms and equipment, using hand tools, sledges, and bars.

3) Transport metal ingots to storage areas, using forklifts.

4) Remove solidified steel or slag from pouring nozzles, using long bars or oxygen burners.

5) Add metal to molds to compensate for shrinkage.

6) Turn valves to circulate water through cores, or spray water on filled molds to cool and solidify metal.

7) Stencil identifying information on ingots and pigs, using special hand tools.

8) Pull levers to lift ladle stoppers and to allow molten steel to flow into ingot molds to specified heights.

9) Load specified amounts of metal and flux into furnaces or clay crucibles.

10) Pour and regulate the flow of molten metal into molds and forms to produce ingots or other castings, using ladles or hand-controlled mechanisms.

11) Read temperature gauges and observe color changes; then adjust furnace flames, torches, or electrical heating units as necessary to melt metal to specifications.

12) Remove metal ingots or cores from molds, using hand tools, cranes, and chain hoists.

13) Collect samples, or signal workers to sample metal for analysis.

14) Position equipment such as ladles, grinding wheels, pouring nozzles, or crucibles, or signal other workers to position equipment.

15) Skim slag or remove excess metal from ingots or equipment, using hand tools, strainers, rakes, or burners; collect scrap for recycling.

51-4071.00 - Foundry Mold and Coremakers

Make or form wax or sand cores or molds used in the production of metal castings in foundries.

Tasks

1) Sprinkle or spray parting agents onto patterns and mold sections to facilitate removal of patterns from molds.

2) Tend machines that bond cope and drag together to form completed shell molds.

3) Rotate sweep boards around spindles in order to make symmetrical molds for convex impressions.

4) Pour molten metal into molds, manually or using crane ladles.

5) Operate ovens or furnaces to bake cores or to melt, skim, and flux metal.

6) Move and position workpieces such as mold sections, patterns, and bottom boards, using cranes, or signal others to move workpieces.

7) Clean and smooth molds, cores, and core boxes, and repair surface imperfections.

8) Sift and pack sand into mold sections, core boxes, and pattern contours, using hand or pneumatic ramming tools.

9) Position patterns inside mold sections and clamp sections together.

10) Position cores into lower sections of molds, and reassemble molds for pouring.

11) Form and assemble slab cores around patterns and position wire in mold sections to reinforce molds, using hand tools and glue.

12) Cut spouts, runner holes, and sprue holes into molds.

51-4072.00 - Molding, Coremaking, and Casting Machine Setters, Operators, and Tenders, Metal and Plastic

Set up, operate, or tend metal or plastic molding, casting, or coremaking machines to mold or cast metal or thermoplastic parts or products.

Tasks

1) Select and install blades, tools, or other attachments for each operation.

2) Obtain and move specified patterns to work stations, manually or using hoists, and secure patterns to machines, using wrenches.

3) Preheat tools, dies, plastic materials, or patterns, using blowtorches or other equipment.

4) Remove finished or cured products from dies or molds, using hand tools, air hoses and other equipment; stamp identifying information on products when necessary.

5) Read specifications, blueprints, and work orders to determine setups, temperatures, and time settings required to mold, form, or cast plastic materials, as well as to plan production sequences.

6) Pull level and toggle latches to fill molds, to regulate tension on sheeting, and to release mold covers.

7) Install dies onto machines or presses, then coat dies with parting agents, according to work order specifications.

8) Position and secure workpieces on machines, and start feeding mechanisms.

9) Unload finished products from conveyor belts, pack them in containers, and place containers in warehouses.

10) Observe meters and gauges to verify and record temperatures, pressures, and press-cycle times.

11) Observe continuous operation of automatic machines to ensure that products meet specifications and to detect jams or malfunctions, making adjustments as necessary.

12) Mix and measure compounds, or weigh premixed compounds; then dump them into machine tubs, cavities, or molds.

13) Measure and visually inspect products for surface and dimension defects in order to ensure conformance to specifications, using precision measuring instruments.

14) Trim excess material from parts, using knives, and grind scrap plastic into powder for reuse.

15) Turn valves and dials of machines to regulate pressure, temperature, and speed and feed rates, and to set cycle times.

16) Set up, operate, or tend metal or plastic molding, casting, or coremaking machines to mold or cast metal or thermoplastic parts or products.

17) Operate hoists to position dies or patterns on foundry floors.

18) Cut spouts and pouring holes in molds, and size hardened cores, using saws.

19) Adjust equipment and workpiece holding fixtures, such as mold frames, tubs, and cutting tables, to ensure proper functioning.

20) Skim or pour dross, slag, or impurities from molten metal, using ladles, rakes, hoes, spatulas, or spoons.

21) Repair or replace damaged molds, pipes, belts, chains, or other equipment, using hand

tools, hand-powered presses, or jib cranes.

22) Pour or load metal or sand into melting pots, furnaces, molds, or hoppers, using shovels, ladles, or machines.

23) Place reels of controller paper on holders, thread paper around reels, and attach to winding rolls.

24) Maintain inventories of materials.

25) Pack material around an exact model of the finished product in a molding box to create a metal casting mold.

26) Set up matrices in assembly sticks by hand, according to specifications.

27) Inventory and record quantities of materials and finished products; requisition additional supplies as necessary.

28) Shape molds to specified contours, using sand, and trowels and related tools.

29) Smooth and clean inner surfaces of molds, using brushes, scrapers, air hoses, or grinding wheels, and fill imperfections with refractory material.

30) Spray, smoke, or coat molds with compounds to lubricate or insulate molds, using acetylene torches or sprayers.

31) Remove parts such as dies from machines after production runs are finished.

32) Select coolants and lubricants, and start their flow.

33) Perform maintenance work such as cleaning and oiling machines.

34) Assemble shell halves, patterns, and foundry flasks, and reinforce core boxes, using glue, clamps, wire, bolts, rams, or machines.

35) Clamp metal and plywood strips around dies or patterns to form molds.

36) Connect water hoses to cooling systems of dies, using hand tools.

37) Cool products after processing to prevent distortion.

38) Fill core boxes and mold patterns with sand or powders, using ramming tools or pneumatic hammers, and remove excess.

39) Position, measure, and mark out metal stock or castings.

51-4081.00 - Multiple Machine Tool Setters, Operators, and Tenders, Metal and Plastic

Set up, operate, or tend more than one type of cutting or forming machine tool or robot.

Tasks

1) Position, adjust, and secure stock material or workpieces against stops, on arbors, or in chucks, fixtures, or automatic feeding mechanisms, manually or using hoists.

2) Align layout marks with dies or blades.

3) Compute data such as gear dimensions and machine settings, applying knowledge of shop mathematics.

4) Inspect workpieces for defects, and measure workpieces to determine accuracy of machine operation, using rules, templates, or other measuring instruments.

5) Extract or lift jammed pieces from machines, using fingers, wire hooks, or lift bars.

6) Set up and operate machines such as lathes, cutters, shears, borers, millers, grinders, presses, drills, and auxiliary machines in order to make metallic and plastic workpieces.

7) Move controls or mount gears, cams, or templates in machines to set feed rates and cutting speeds, depths, and angles.

8) Read blueprints or job orders to determine product specifications and tooling instructions, and to plan operational sequences.

9) Make minor electrical and mechanical repairs and adjustments to machines, and notify supervisors when major service is required.

10) Measure and mark reference points and cutting lines on workpieces, using traced templates, compasses, and rules.

11) Select, install, and adjust alignment of drills, cutters, dies, guides, and holding devices, using templates, measuring instruments, and hand tools.

12) Set machine stops or guides to specified lengths as indicated by scales, rules, or templates.

13) Remove burrs, sharp edges, rust, or scale from workpieces, using files, hand grinders, wire brushes, or power tools.

14) Record operational data such as pressure readings, lengths of strokes, feed rates, and speeds.

15) Perform minor machine maintenance, such as oiling or cleaning machines, dies, or workpieces, or adding coolant to machine reservoirs.

16) Instruct other workers in machine setup and operation.

17) Change worn machine accessories such as cutting tools and brushes, using hand tools.

18) Start machines, and turn handwheels or valves to engage feeding, cooling, and lubricating mechanisms.

19) Observe machine operation to detect workpiece defects or machine malfunctions; adjust machines as necessary.

51-4111.00 - Tool and Die Makers

Analyze specifications, lay out metal stock, set up and operate machine tools, and fit and assemble parts to make and repair dies, cutting tools, jigs, fixtures, gauges, and machinists' hand tools.

Tasks

1) Develop and design new tools and dies, using computer-aided design software.

2) Set pyrometer controls of heat-treating furnaces, and feed or place parts, tools, or assemblies into furnaces to harden.

3) Verify dimensions, alignments, and clearances of finished parts for conformance to specifications, using measuring instruments such as calipers, gauge blocks, micrometers, and dial indicators.

4) Cut, shape, and trim blanks or blocks to specified lengths or shapes, using power saws, power shears, rules, and hand tools.

5) Conduct test runs with completed tools or dies to ensure that parts meet specifications; make adjustments as necessary.

6) Measure, mark, and scribe metal or plastic stock to lay out machining, using instruments such as protractors, micrometers, scribes, and rulers.

7) Visualize and compute dimensions, sizes, shapes, and tolerances of assemblies, based on specifications.

8) Design jigs, fixtures, and templates for use as work aids in the fabrication of parts or products.

9) File, grind, shim, and adjust different parts to properly fit them together.

10) Fit and assemble parts to make, repair, or modify dies, jigs, gauges, and tools, using machine tools and hand tools.

11) Cast plastic tools or parts, or tungsten-carbide cutting tips, using pre-made molds.

12) Lift, position, and secure machined parts on surface plates or worktables, using hoists, vises, v-blocks, or angle plates.

13) Select metals to be used from a range of metals and alloys, based on properties such as hardness and heat tolerance.

14) Set up and operate conventional or computer numerically controlled machine tools such as lathes, milling machines, and grinders to cut, bore, grind, or otherwise shape parts to prescribed dimensions and finishes.

15) Set up and operate drill presses to drill and tap holes in parts for assembly.

16) Smooth and polish flat and contoured surfaces of parts or tools, using scrapers, abrasive stones, files, emery cloths, or power grinders.

17) Study blueprints, sketches, models, or specifications to plan sequences of operations for fabricating tools, dies, or assemblies.

51-4122.00 - Welding, Soldering, and Brazing Machine Setters, Operators, and Tenders

Set up, operate, or tend welding, soldering, or brazing machines or robots that weld, braze, solder, or heat treat metal products, components, or assemblies.

Tasks

1) Dress electrodes, using tip dressers, files, emery cloths, or dressing wheels.

2) Set up, operate, and tend welding machines that join or bond components to fabricate metal products or assemblies.

3) Tend auxiliary equipment used in welding processes.

4) Conduct trial runs before welding, soldering or brazing; make necessary adjustments to equipment.

5) Transfer components, metal products, and assemblies, using moving equipment.

6) Assemble, align, and clamp workpieces into holding fixtures to bond, heat-treat, or solder fabricated metal components.

7) Add chemicals and materials to workpieces or machines to facilitate bonding or to cool workpieces.

8) Anneal finished workpieces to relieve internal stress.

9) Turn and press knobs and buttons, or enter operating instructions into computers to adjust and start welding machines.

10) Start, monitor, and adjust robotic welding production lines.

11) Inspect, measure, or test completed metal workpieces to ensure conformance to specifications, using measuring and testing devices.

12) Prepare metal surfaces and workpieces, using hand-operated equipment such as grinders, cutters, or drills.

13) Fill hoppers and position spouts to direct flow of flux, or manually brush flux onto seams of workpieces.

14) Observe meters, gauges, and machine operations to ensure that soldering or brazing processes meet specifications.

15) Mark weld points and positions of components on workpieces, using rules, squares, templates, and scribes.

16) Load or feed workpieces into welding machines in order to join or bond components.

17) Select torch tips, alloys, flux, coil, tubing, and wire, according to metal types and thicknesses, data charts, and records.

18) Set dials and timing controls to regulate electrical current, gas flow pressure, heating/cooling cycles, and shut-off.

19) Read blueprints, work orders, and production schedules to determine product or job instructions and specifications.

20) Remove workpieces and parts from machinery after work is complete, using hand tools.

21) Give directions to other workers regarding machine setup and use.

22) Select, position, align, and bolt jigs, holding fixtures, guides, and stops onto machines, using measuring instruments and hand tools.

23) Correct problems by adjusting controls, or by stopping machines and opening holding devices.

24) Immerse completed workpieces into water or acid baths to cool and clean components.

25) Lay out, fit, or connect parts to be bonded, calculating production measurements as necessary.

26) Clean, lubricate, maintain, and adjust equipment to maintain efficient operation, using air hoses, cleaning fluids, and hand tools.

27) Devise and build fixtures and jigs used to hold parts in place during welding, brazing, or soldering.

28) Record operational information on specified production reports.

51-4191.00 - Heat Treating Equipment Setters, Operators, and Tenders, Metal and Plastic

Set up, operate, or tend heating equipment, such as heat-treating furnaces, flame-hardening machines, induction machines, soaking pits, or vacuum equipment to temper, harden, anneal, or heat-treat metal or plastic objects.

Tasks

1) Place completed workpieces on conveyors, using cold rods, tongs, or chain hoists, or signal crane operators to transport them to subsequent stations.

2) Start conveyors and open furnace doors to load stock, or signal crane operators to uncover soaking pits and lower ingots into them.

3) Set up and operate or tend machines, such as furnaces, baths, flame-hardening machines, and electronic induction machines, that harden, anneal, and heat-treat metal.

4) Mount workpieces in fixtures, on arbors, or between centers of machines.

5) Remove parts from furnaces after specified times, and air dry or cool parts in water, oil brine, or other baths.

6) Move controls to light gas burners and to adjust gas and water flow and flame temperature.

7) Set and adjust speeds of reels and conveyors for prescribed time cycles in order to pass parts through continuous furnaces.

8) Cover parts with charcoal before inserting them in furnaces, in order to prevent discoloration caused by rapid heating.

9) Impregnate fabrics with plastic resins, and cut fabrics into strips.

10) Insert vacuum tubes into bags, and seal bags around tubes, using tape.

11) Set up and operate die-quenching machines to prevent parts from warping.

12) Position stock in furnaces, using tongs, chain hoists, or pry bars.

13) Test parts for hardness, using hardness testing equipment, or by examining and feeling samples.

14) Reduce heat when processing is complete in order to allow parts to cool in furnaces or machinery.

15) Repair, replace, and maintain furnace equipment as needed, using hand tools.

16) Place parts on carts, connect vacuum lines to vacuum tubes, and smooth bags around parts to ensure vacuum.

17) Mount fixtures and industrial coils on machines, using hand tools.

18) Instruct new workers in machine operation.

19) Load parts into containers and place containers on conveyors to be inserted into furnaces, or insert parts into furnaces.

20) Signal forklift operators to deposit or extract containers of parts into and from furnaces and quenching rinse tanks.

21) Examine parts to ensure metal shades and colors conform to specifications, utilizing knowledge of metal heat-treating.

22) Clean oxides and scales from parts or fittings, using steam sprays or chemical and water baths.

23) Stamp heat-treatment identification marks on parts, using hammers and punches.

24) Read production schedules and work orders to determine processing sequences, furnace temperatures, and heat cycle requirements for objects to be heat-treated.

25) Position plastic sheets and molds in plastic bags, heat material under lamps, and force confrontation of sheets to molds by vacuum pressure.

26) Determine flame temperatures, current frequencies, heating cycles, and induction heating coils needed, based on degree of hardness required and properties of stock to be treated.

27) Record times that parts are removed from furnaces to document that objects have attained specified temperatures for specified times.

28) Remove parts from autoclaves, and cut away plastic bags.

29) Determine types and temperatures of baths and quenching media needed to attain specified part hardness, toughness, and ductility, using heat-treating charts and knowledge of methods, equipment, and metals.

30) Position parts in plastic bags, and seal bags with irons.

31) Adjust controls to maintain temperatures and heating times, using thermal instruments and charts, dials and gauges of furnaces, and color of stock in furnaces to make setting determinations.

32) Heat billets, bars, plates, rods, and other stock to specified temperatures preparatory to forging, rolling, or processing, using oil, gas, or electrical furnaces.

51-4192.00 - Lay-Out Workers, Metal and Plastic

Lay out reference points and dimensions on metal or plastic stock or workpieces, such as sheets, plates, tubes, structural shapes, castings, or machine parts, for further processing. Includes shipfitters.

Tasks

1) Brace parts in position within hulls or ships for riveting or welding.

2) Mark curves, lines, holes, dimensions, and welding symbols onto workpieces, using scribes, soapstones, punches, and hand drills.

3) Compute layout dimensions, and determine and mark reference points on metal stock or workpieces for further processing, such as welding and assembly.

4) Add dimensional details to blueprints or drawings made by other workers.

5) Inspect machined parts to verify conformance to specifications.

6) Lift and position workpieces in relation to surface plates, manually or with hoists, and using parallel blocks and angle plates.

7) Design and prepare templates of wood, paper, or metal.

8) Locate center lines and verify template positions, using measuring instruments such as gauge blocks, height gauges, and dial indicators.

9) Install doors, hatches, brackets, and clips.

10) Lay out and fabricate metal structural parts such as plates, bulkheads, and frames.

11) Fit and align fabricated parts to be welded or assembled.

12) Plan locations and sequences of cutting, drilling, bending, rolling, punching, and welding operations, using compasses, protractors, dividers, and rules.

13) Plan and develop layouts from blueprints and templates, applying knowledge of trigonometry, design, effects of heat, and properties of metals.

51-4193.00 - Plating and Coating Machine Setters, Operators, and Tenders, Metal and Plastic

Set up, operate, or tend plating or coating machines to coat metal or plastic products with chromium, zinc, copper, cadmium, nickel, or other metal to protect or decorate surfaces. Includes electrolytic processes.

Tasks

1) Set up, operate, or tend plating or coating machines to coat metal or plastic products with chromium, zinc, copper, cadmium, nickel, or other metal to protect or decorate surfaces.

2) Cut metal or other materials, using shears or band saws.

3) Clean workpieces, using wire brushes.

4) Preheat workpieces in ovens.

5) Charge furnaces.

6) Examine completed objects to determine thicknesses of metal deposits, or measure thicknesses by using instruments such as micrometers.

7) Spray coating in specified patterns according to instructions.

8) Test machinery to ensure that it is operating properly.

9) Maintain production records.

10) Place plated or coated materials on racks and transfer them to ovens to dry for specified periods of time.

11) Suspend objects such as parts or molds from cathode rods (negative terminals), and immerse objects in plating solutions.

12) Monitor and measure thicknesses of electroplating on component parts in order to verify conformance to specifications, using micrometers.

13) Measure, mark, and mask areas to be excluded from plating.

14) Measure and set stops, rolls, brushes, and guides on automatic feeders and conveying equipment or coating machines, using micrometers, rules, and hand tools.

15) Inspect coated or plated areas for defects such as air bubbles or uneven coverage.

16) Mix and test solutions, and turn valves to fill tanks with solutions.

17) Immerse workpieces in coating solutions or liquid metal or plastic for specified times.

18) Immerse objects to be coated or plated into cleaning solutions, or spray objects with conductive solutions to prepare them for plating.

19) Attach nozzles, position guns, connect hoses, and thread wire in order to set up metal-spraying machines.

20) Measure or weigh materials, using rulers, calculators, and scales.

21) Clean and maintain equipment, using water hoses and scrapers.

22) Suspend sticks or pieces of plating metal from anodes (positive terminals) and immerse metal in plating solutions.

23) Rinse coated objects in cleansing liquids; then dry them with cloths, centrifugal driers, or by tumbling in sawdust-filled barrels.

24) Determine sizes and compositions of objects to be plated, and amounts of electrical current and time required.

25) Adjust controls to set temperatures of coating substances and speeds of machines and equipment.

26) Adjust dials to regulate flow of current and voltage supplied to terminals in order to control plating processes.

27) Position and feed materials into processing machines, by hand or by using automated equipment.

28) Position objects to be plated in frames, or suspend them from positive or negative terminals of power supplies.

29) Read production schedules to determine setups of equipment and machines.

30) Operate sandblasting equipment to roughen and clean surfaces of workpieces.

31) Remove excess materials or impurities from objects, using air hoses or grinding machines.

32) Operate hoists to place workpieces onto machine feed carriages or spindles.

33) Perform equipment maintenance such as cleaning tanks and lubricating moving parts of conveyors.

34) Plate small objects such as nuts or bolts, using motor-driven barrels.

35) Position containers to receive parts, and load or unload materials in containers, using dollies or handtrucks.

36) Replace worn parts and adjust equipment components, using hand tools.

37) Install gears and holding devices on conveyor equipment.

38) Remove objects from solutions at periodic intervals and observe objects to verify conformance to specifications.

51-4194.00 - Tool Grinders, Filers, and Sharpeners

Perform precision smoothing, sharpening, polishing, or grinding of metal objects.

Tasks

1) Inspect dies to detect defects, assess wear, and verify specifications, using micrometers, steel gauge pins, and loupes.

2) Straighten workpieces and remove dents, using straightening presses and hammers.

3) Fit parts together in preassembly to ensure that dimensions are accurate.

4) File or finish surfaces of workpieces, using prescribed hand tools.

5) Compute numbers, widths, and angles of cutting tools, micrometers, scales, and gauges, and adjust tools to produce specified cuts.

6) Select and mount grinding wheels on machines, according to specifications, using hand tools and applying knowledge of abrasives and grinding procedures.

7) Monitor machine operations to determine whether adjustments are necessary; stop machines when problems occur.

8) Inspect, feel, and measure workpieces to ensure that surfaces and dimensions meet specifications.

9) Place workpieces in electroplating solutions or apply pigments to surfaces of workpieces to highlight ridges and grooves.

10) Turn valves to direct flow of coolant against cutting wheels and workpieces during grinding.

11) Set up and operate grinding or polishing machines to grind metal workpieces such as dies, parts, and tools.

12) Duplicate workpiece contours, using tracer attachments.

13) Perform basic maintenance, such as cleaning and lubricating machine parts.

14) Remove finished workpieces from machines and place them in boxes or on racks; set aside pieces that are defective.

15) Remove and replace worn or broken machine parts, using hand tools.

16) Study blueprints or layouts of metal workpieces to determine grinding procedures, and to plan machine setups and operational sequences.

17) Dress grinding wheels, according to specifications.

51-5011.00 - Bindery Workers

Set up or operate binding machines that produce books and other printed materials.

Tasks

1) Clean work areas, and maintain equipment and work stations, using hand tools.

2) Record production sheet information such as the amount of time spent on specific tasks.

3) Stitch or glue endpapers. bindings. and signatures to attach them.

4) Maintain records of daily production. using specified forms.

5) Train workers to set up. operate. and use automatic bindery machines.

6) Lubricate and clean machine parts. and make minor repairs in order to keep machines in working condition.

7) Stop machines. cut threads that connect books. and stack separated books.

8) Mount and secure rolls or reels of wire, cloth, paper, or other material onto machine spindles.

9) Move controls to adjust and activate bindery machines.

10) Observe and monitor machine operations to detect malfunctions and to determine whether adjustments are needed.

11) Open machines and remove and replace damaged covers and books. using hand tools.

12) Read work orders to determine setup specifications and instructions.

13) Remove broken wire pieces from machines, and load machines with new spools of wire.

14) Fill machine paper feeds.

15) Punch holes in paper sheets. and fasten sheets. signatures. or other material. using hand or machine punches or staplers.

16) Feed books and related articles such as periodicals and pamphlets into binding machines. following specifications.

17) Examine stitched, collated, bound. and unbound product samples for defects such as imperfect bindings, ink spots. torn or loose pages, and loose and uncut threads.

18) Set machine controls to adjust lengths and thicknesses of folds, stitches, or cuts, to synchronize speed of feeding devices and stitching, and to adjust tension on creasing blades and folding rollers.

19) Set up, or set up and operate. machines that perform binding operations such as pressing, folding, and trimming on books and related articles.

20) Start machines and make trial runs to verify accuracy of machine setups.

21) Thread spirals in perforated holes of items to be bound, using spindles or rollers.

22) Install and adjust bindery machine devices, such as knives, guides, rollers, rounding forms, creasing rams, and clamps. in order to accommodate sheets, signatures, or books of specified sizes, using hand tools.

23) Secure reels of stitching wire on spindles, and thread wire through feeding, cutting, stitch forming, and driving mechanisms to load stitcher heads for stapling.

24) Remove printed material or finished products from machines or conveyors, wrap products in plastic, and stack them on pallets or skids or pack them in boxes.

25) Fill glue reservoirs, turn switches to activate heating elements, and adjust flow of glue and speed of conveyors.

26) Crease or compress signatures before affixing covers; then place paper jackets on finished books.

51-5012.00 - Bookbinders

Perform highly skilled hand finishing operations, such as grooving and lettering to bind books.

Tasks

1) Attach endpapers to tops and bottoms of book bodies, using sewing machines, or glue endpapers and signatures together along spines, using brushes or glue machines.

2) Apply color to edges of signatures, using brushes, pads, or atomizers.

3) Pack and weigh books, and stack them on pallets to prepare them for shipment.

4) Repair, restore, and rebind old or damaged books, including rare books.

5) Design original or special bindings for limited editions.

6) Trim edges of books to size, using cutting or book trimming machines or hand cutters.

7) Cut binder boards to specified dimensions, using board shears, hand cutters, or cutting machines.

8) Place bound books in presses that exert pressure on covers until glue dries.

9) Imprint and emboss lettering, designs, or numbers on covers, using gold, silver, or colored foil, and stamping machines.

10) Glue outside endpapers to covers.

11) Establish production procedures based on job orders.

12) Fold and sew printed sheets to form signatures. and assemble signatures in numerical order to form book bodies.

13) Perform highly skilled hand finishing operations. such as grooving and lettering. to bind books.

14) Cut cover material to specified dimensions, and fit and glue material to binder boards manually or by machine.

15) Compress sewed or glued signatures to reduce books to required thicknesses. using hand presses or smashing machines.

16) Meet with clients. printers. and/or designers to discuss job requirements and binding plans.

17) Apply glue to backs of books, using brushes or glue machines. and attach cloth backing and headbands.

18) Insert book bodies in devices that form back edges of books into convex shapes and produce grooves that facilitate attachment of covers.

51-5021.00 - Job Printers

Set type according to copy; operate press to print job order; and read proof for errors and clarity of impression, and correct imperfections. Job printers are often found in small establishments where work combines several job skills.

Tasks

1) Tap typefaces with hammers to improve the quality of impressions.

2) Lay forms on proof presses; then ink type, fasten paper to press rollers, and pull rollers over forms to make proof copies.

3) Slide type from sticks into galleys.

4) Remove assembled type from galleys and place type on composing stones.

5) Insert spacers between words and leads between lines.

6) Clean ink rollers after runs are completed.

7) Design and set up product compositions and page layouts.

8) Examine proofs or printed sheets in order to detect errors and to evaluate the adequacy of impression clarity.

9) Fill ink fountains and move levers to adjust the flow of ink.

10) Operate cylinder or automatic platen presses to print job orders.

11) Set feed guides according to sizes and thicknesses of paper.

12) Reset type to correct typographical errors.

13) Select type from type cases, and insert type in printers' sticks to reproduce material in copy.

14) Position forms (type in locked chases) on beds of presses; then tighten clamps, using wrenches.

51-5022.00 - Prepress Technicians and Workers

Set up and prepare material for printing presses.

Tasks

1) Examine unexposed photographic plates to detect flaws or foreign particles prior to printing.

2) Activate scanners to produce positive or negative films for the black-and-white, cyan, yellow, and magenta separations from each original copy.

3) Analyze originals to evaluate color density, gradation highlights, middle tones, and shadows, using densitometers and knowledge of light and color.

4) Cut plates to fit printing presses, using plate curving machines.

5) Inspect developed film for specified results and quality, using magnifying glasses and scopes; forward acceptable negatives or positives to other workers or to customers.

6) Examine photographic images for obvious imperfections prior to plate making.

7) Enter, store, and retrieve information on computer-aided equipment.

8) Mount negatives and plates in cameras, set exposure controls, and expose plates to light through negatives in order to transfer images onto plates.

9) Lower vacuum frames onto plate-film assemblies, activate vacuums to establish contact between film and plates, and set timers to activate ultraviolet lights that expose plates.

10) Mount finished plates on wood or metal blocks, using hammers and nails or thermoplastic adhesives and heat presses.

11) Operate and maintain laser plate-making equipment that converts electronic data to plates without the use of film.

12) Perform minor deletions, additions, or corrections to completed plates, on or off printing presses, using tusche, printing ink, erasers, and needles.

13) Improve plate quality by raising, lowering, or repairing imperfections, outlining images, cutting borders, blocking out backgrounds, and raising halftone dots, using engraving tools.

14) Monitor contact between cover glass and masks inside vacuum frames, in order to prevent flaws resulting from overexposure or light reflection.

15) Perform tests to determine lengths of exposures, by exposing plates, scanning line copy, and comparing exposures to tone range scales.

16) Place masking paper on areas of plates not covered by positives or negatives, in order to prevent exposure.

17) Scale copy for reductions and enlargements, using proportion wheels.

18) Perform close alignment or registration of double and single flats to sensitized plates prior to exposure, in order to produce composite images.

19) Unload exposed film from scanners, and place film in automatic processors to develop images.

20) Examine finished plates to detect flaws, verify conformity with master plates, and measure dot sizes and centers, using light-boxes and microscopes.

21) Reposition lamps and adjust aperture controls in order to provide high quality images.

22) Remove plate-film assemblies from vacuum frames, and place exposed plates in automatic processors to develop images and dry plates.

23) Select proper types of plates according to press run lengths.

24) Punch holes in light-sensitive plates and insert pins in holes to prepare plates for contact with positive or negative film.

25) Position color transparencies, negatives, or reflection copies on scanning drums, and mount drums and heads on scanners.

26) Rub plate surfaces with finishing materials to reveal any unevenness.

27) Set scanners to specific color densities, sizes, screen rulings, and exposure adjustments, using scanner keyboards or computers.

28) Position and angle screens for proper exposure.

29) Shave and smooth plates to specified thicknesses, using cutting tools.

30) Maintain, adjust, and clean equipment, and perform minor repairs.

31) Mix solutions such as developing solutions and colored coating solutions.

32) Tap uneven plates with hammers and blocks to flatten them until they are even.

33) Operate and maintain a variety of cameras and equipment, such as process, line, halftone, and color separation cameras, enlargers, electronic scanners, and contact equipment.

34) Operate presses to print proofs of plates, monitoring printing quality to ensure that it is adequate.

35) Prepare microfiche duplicates of microfilm, using contact printers and developing machines.

36) Enter, position, and alter text size, using computers, to make up and arrange pages so that printed materials can be produced.

37) Correct minor film mask defects with litho tape or opaquing fluid.

38) Arrange and mount typeset material and illustrations into paste-ups for printing reproduction, based on artists' or editors' layouts.

39) Transfer images from master plates to unexposed plates, and immerse plates in developing solutions to develop images.

51-5023.00 - Printing Machine Operators

Set up or operate various types of printing machines, such as offset, letterset, intaglio, or gravure presses or screen printers to produce print on paper or other materials.

Tasks

1) Inspect and examine printed products for print clarity, color accuracy, conformance to specifications, and external defects.

2) Monitor stocks of materials such as paper, ink, and metal in order to maintain supplies during equipment operation.

3) Coordinate printing activities with activities of workers who set up, clean, and feed machines.

4) Monitor feeding, printing, and racking processes of presses in order to maintain specified operating levels and to detect malfunctions; make any necessary adjustments.

5) Input instructions in order to program automated machinery, using a computer keyboard.

6) Set and adjust speed, temperature, ink flow, and positions and pressure tolerances of equipment.

7) Examine job orders to determine details such as quantities to be printed, production times, stock specifications, colors, and color sequences.

8) Correct misprinted materials, using materials such as ink eradicators or solvents.

9) Push buttons, turn handles or move controls and levers to start and control printing machines.

10) Remove printed materials from presses, using handtrucks, electric lifts, or hoists, and transport them to drying, storage or finishing areas.

11) Reposition printing plates, adjust pressure rolls, or otherwise adjust machines to improve print quality, using knobs, handwheels, or hand tools.

12) Select and install printing plates, rollers, feed guides, gauges, screens, stencils, type, dies, and cylinders in machines according to specifications, using hand tools.

13) Blend and test paint, inks, stains, and solvents according to types of material being printed and work order specifications.

14) Load, position, and adjust unprinted materials on holding fixtures or in equipment loading and feeding mechanisms.

15) Accept orders from customers, calculate and quote prices, and receive payment.

16) Place printed items in ovens to dry or set ink.

17) Operate equipment at slow speed to ensure proper ink coverage, alignment, and registration.

18) Pour ink into pans, and smooth paint onto stencils, using flat-bladed knives.

19) Direct and monitor activities of workers feeding, inspecting, and tending printing machines and materials.

20) Monitor and control operation of auxiliary equipment used to assemble and finish products.

21) Place spools of thread or wire on holders, and thread through machines.

22) Position knives at specified distances from edges of plastic material in order to trim excess material from edges.

23) Pack and label cartons, boxes, or bins of finished products.

24) Measure screens, and use measurements to center and align screens in proper positions and sequences on machines, using gauges and hand tools.

25) Repair, maintain, or adjust equipment.

26) Apply glue or tape to holes in screens in order to repair leaks.

27) Thin printing compounds, using specified thinners.

28) Clean and lubricate printing machines and components, using oil, solvents, brushes, rags, and hoses.

29) Squeeze or spread ink on plates, pads, or rollers, using putty knives, brushes, or sponges.

30) Attach cloth to take-up rollers, placing it in feeding position and threading it through equipment as necessary.

31) Requisition supplies, materials, and equipment, and receive stock when it arrives.

32) Prepare and treat lithographic plates with various chemicals to clean and preserve plates and fix images.

33) Maintain records of goods produced, supplies used, production costs, and machine

maintenance and repair activities.

34) Provide assistance in the design and layout of forms and materials to be printed.

51-6052.00 - Tailors, Dressmakers, and Custom Sewers

Design, make, alter, repair, or fit garments.

Tasks

1) Put in padding and shaping materials.

2) Examine tags on garments to determine alterations that are needed.

3) Estimate how much a garment will cost to make, based on factors such as time and material requirements.

4) Develop, copy, or adapt designs for garments, and design patterns to fit measurements, applying knowledge of garment design, construction, styling, and fabric.

5) Take up or let down hems to shorten or lengthen garment parts such as sleeves.

6) Sew garments, using needles and thread or sewing machines.

7) Trim excess material, using scissors.

8) Assemble garment parts and join parts with basting stitches, using needles and thread or sewing machines.

9) Sew buttonholes and attach buttons in order to finish garments.

10) Repair or replace defective garment parts such as pockets, zippers, snaps, buttons, and linings.

11) Confer with customers to determine types of material and garment styles desired.

12) Fit and study garments on customers to determine required alterations.

13) Fit, alter, repair, and make made-to-measure clothing, according to customers' and clothing manufacturers' specifications and fit, and applying principles of garment design, construction, and styling.

14) Remove stitches from garments to be altered, using rippers or razor blades.

15) Measure parts such as sleeves or pant legs, and mark or pin-fold alteration lines.

16) Record required alterations and instructions on tags, and attach them to garments.

17) Make garment style changes, such as tapering pant legs, narrowing lapels, and adding or removing padding.

18) Maintain garment drape and proportions as alterations are performed.

19) Press garments, using hand irons or pressing machines.

20) Position patterns of garment parts on fabric, and cut fabric along outlines, using scissors.

21) Measure customers, using tape measures, and record measurements.

51-6091.00 - Extruding and Forming Machine Setters, Operators, and Tenders, Synthetic and Glass Fibers

Set up, operate, or tend machines that extrude and form continuous filaments from synthetic materials, such as liquid polymer, rayon, and fiberglass.

Tasks

1) Turn petcocks to adjust the flow of binding fluid to sleeves.

2) Notify other workers of defects, and direct them to adjust extruding and forming machines.

3) Start metering pumps and observe operation of machines and equipment to ensure continuous flow of filaments extruded through spinnerettes and to detect processing defects.

4) Observe machine operations, control boards, and gauges to detect malfunctions such as clogged bushings and defective binder applicators.

5) Open cabinet doors to cut multifilament threadlines away from guides, using scissors.

6) Pass sliver strands through openings in floors to workers on floors below who wind slivers onto tubes.

7) Move controls to activate and adjust extruding and forming machines.

8) Observe flow of finish across finish rollers, and turn valves to adjust flow to specifications.

9) Set up, operate, or tend machines that extrude and form filaments from synthetic materials

such as rayon, fiberglass, or liquid polymers.

10) Turn rheostats to obtain specified temperatures in electric furnaces where glass is melted.

11) Clean and maintain extruding and forming machines, using hand tools.

12) Lower pans inside cabinets to catch molten filaments until flow of polymer through packs has stopped.

13) Record details of machine malfunctions.

14) Load materials into extruding and forming machines, using hand tools, and adjust feed mechanisms to set feed rates.

15) Remove polymer deposits from spinnerettes and equipment, using silicone spray, brass chisels, and bronze-wool pads.

16) Wipe finish rollers with cloths and wash finish trays with water when necessary.

17) Press metering-pump buttons and turn valves to stop flow of polymers.

18) Press buttons to stop machines when processes are complete or when malfunctions are detected.

19) Pull extruded fiberglass filaments over sleeves where binding solution is applied, then into grooves of graphite shoes that bind filaments into single strands of sliver.

20) Record operational data on tags, and attach tags to machines.

51-8011.00 - Nuclear Power Reactor Operators

Control nuclear reactors.

Tasks

1) Record operating data such as the results of surveillance tests.

2) Note malfunctions of equipment, instruments, or controls, and report these conditions to supervisors.

3) Conduct inspections and operations outside of control rooms as necessary.

4) Direct reactor operators in emergency situations, in accordance with emergency operating procedures.

5) Monitor all systems for normal running conditions, performing activities such as checking gauges to assess output or assess the effects of generator loading on other equipment.

6) Participate in nuclear fuel element handling activities such as preparation, transfer, loading, and unloading.

7) Implement operational procedures such as those controlling start-up and shut-down activities.

8) Adjust controls to position rod and to regulate flux level, reactor period, coolant temperature, and rate of power flow, following standard procedures.

9) Dispatch orders and instructions to personnel through radiotelephone or intercommunication systems to coordinate auxiliary equipment operation.

10) Authorize maintenance activities on units and changes in equipment and system operational status.

11) Monitor and operate boilers, turbines, wells, and auxiliary power plant equipment.

51-8012.00 - Power Distributors and Dispatchers

Coordinate, regulate, or distribute electricity or steam.

Tasks

1) Distribute and regulate the flow of power between entities such as generating stations, substations, distribution lines, and users, keeping track of the status of circuits and connections.

2) Track conditions that could affect power needs, such as changes in the weather, and adjust equipment to meet any anticipated changes.

3) Control, monitor, or operate equipment that regulates or distributes electricity or steam, using data obtained from instruments or computers.

4) Repair, maintain, and clean equipment and machinery, using hand tools.

5) Tend auxiliary equipment used in the power distribution process.

6) Monitor and record switchboard and control board readings to ensure that electrical or steam distribution equipment is operating properly.

7) Manipulate controls to adjust and activate power distribution equipment and machines.

8) Inspect equipment to ensure that specifications are met, and to detect any defects.

9) Coordinate with engineers, planners, field personnel, and other utility workers to provide information such as clearances, switching orders, and distribution process changes.

10) Calculate and determine load estimates or equipment requirements, in order to determine required control settings.

11) Accept and implement energy schedules, including real-time transmission reservations and schedules.

12) Prepare switching orders that will isolate work areas without causing power outages, referring to drawings of power systems.

13) Record and compile operational data, such as chart and meter readings, power demands, and usage and operating times, using transmission system maps.

14) Direct personnel engaged in controlling and operating distribution equipment and machinery, for example, instructing control room operators to start boilers and generators.

51-8013.00 - Power Plant Operators

Control, operate, or maintain machinery to generate electric power. Includes auxiliary equipment operators.

Tasks

1) Communicate with systems operators to regulate and coordinate transmission loads and frequencies, and line voltages.

2) Examine and test electrical power distribution machinery and equipment, using testing devices.

3) Receive outage calls and call in necessary personnel during power outages and emergencies.

4) Operate or control power generating equipment, including boilers, turbines, generators, and reactors, using control boards or semi-automatic equipment.

5) Start or stop generators, auxiliary pumping equipment, turbines, and other power plant equipment, and connect or disconnect equipment from circuits.

6) Collect oil, water, and electrolyte samples for laboratory analysis.

7) Control and maintain auxiliary equipment, such as pumps, fans, compressors, condensers, feedwater heaters, filters, and chlorinators, to supply water, fuel, lubricants, air, and auxiliary power.

8) Control generator output to match the phase, frequency, and voltage of electricity supplied to panels.

9) Inspect records and log book entries, and communicate with other plant personnel, in order to assess equipment operating status.

10) Take readings from charts, meters and gauges at established intervals, and take corrective steps as necessary.

11) Make adjustments or minor repairs, such as tightening leaking gland and pipe joints; report any needs for major repairs.

12) Replenish electrolytes in batteries and oil in voltage transformers, and reset tripped electric relays.

13) Place standby emergency electrical generators on line in emergencies and monitor the temperature, output, and lubrication of the system.

14) Open and close valves and switches in sequence upon signals from other workers, in order to start or shut down auxiliary units.

15) Monitor and inspect power plant equipment and indicators to detect evidence of operating problems.

16) Clean, lubricate, and maintain equipment such as generators, turbines, pumps, and compressors in order to prevent equipment failure or deterioration.

17) Regulate equipment operations and conditions such as water levels, based on data from recording and indicating instruments or from computers.

18) Adjust controls to generate specified electrical power, or to regulate the flow of power between generating stations and substations.

51-8021.00 - Stationary Engineers and Boiler Operators

Operate or maintain stationary engines, boilers, or other mechanical equipment to provide utilities for buildings or industrial processes. Operate equipment, such as steam engines, generators, motors, turbines, and steam boilers.

Tasks

1) Supervise the work of assistant stationary engineers, turbine operators, boiler tenders, and/or air-conditioning and refrigeration operators and mechanics.

2) Contact equipment manufacturers or appropriate specialists when necessary to resolve equipment problems.

3) Maintain daily logs of operation, maintenance, and safety activities, including test results, instrument readings, and details of equipment malfunctions and maintenance work.

4) Monitor boiler water, chemical, and fuel levels, and make adjustments to maintain required levels.

5) Monitor and inspect equipment, computer terminals, switches, valves, gauges, alarms, safety devices, and meters to detect leaks or malfunctions, and to ensure that equipment is operating efficiently and safely.

6) Ignite fuel in burners, using torches or flames.

7) Fire coal furnaces by hand or with stokers and gas- or oil-fed boilers, using automatic gas feeds or oil pumps.

8) Operate mechanical hoppers, and provide assistance in their adjustment and repair.

9) Receive instructions from steam engineers regarding steam plant and air compressor operations.

10) Perform or arrange for repairs, such as complete overhauls, replacement of defective valves, gaskets, or bearings, and/or fabrication of new parts.

11) Operate or tend stationary engines, boilers, and auxiliary equipment such as pumps, compressors and air-conditioning equipment, in order to supply and maintain steam or heat for buildings, marine vessels, or pneumatic tools.

12) Weigh, measure, and record fuel used.

13) Switch from automatic controls to manual controls, and isolate equipment mechanically and electrically, in order to allow for safe inspection and repair work.

14) Test electrical systems to determine voltages, using voltage meters.

15) Provide assistance to plumbers in repairing or replacing water, sewer, or waste lines, and in daily maintenance activities.

16) Check the air quality of ventilation systems and make adjustments to ensure compliance with mandated safety codes.

17) Activate valves to maintain required amounts of water in boilers, to adjust supplies of combustion air, and to control the flow of fuel into burners.

18) Adjust controls and/or valves on equipment to provide power, and to regulate and set operations of system and/or industrial processes.

19) Analyze problems and take appropriate action to ensure continuous and reliable operation of equipment and systems.

20) Clean and lubricate boilers and auxiliary equipment and make minor adjustments as needed, using hand tools.

21) Test boiler water quality or arrange for testing; and take any necessary corrective action, such as adding chemicals to prevent corrosion and harmful deposits.

22) Develop operation, safety, and maintenance procedures, or assist in their development.

23) Install burners and auxiliary equipment, using hand tools.

24) Investigate and report on accidents.

51-8031.00 - Water and Liquid Waste Treatment Plant and System Operators

Operate or control an entire process or system of machines, often through the use of control boards, to transfer or treat water or liquid waste.

Tasks

1) Record operational data, personnel attendance, and meter and gauge readings on specified forms.

2) Operate and adjust controls on equipment to purify and clarify water, process or dispose of sewage, and generate power.

3) Collect and test water and sewage samples, using test equipment and color analysis standards.

4) Maintain, repair, and lubricate equipment, using hand tools and power tools.

5) Clean and maintain tanks and filter beds, using hand tools and power tools.

6) Direct and coordinate plant workers engaged in routine operations and maintenance activities.

7) Inspect equipment and monitor operating conditions, meters, and gauges to determine load requirements and detect malfunctions.

Knowledge	Knowledge Definitions
Biology	Knowledge of plant and animal organisms, their tissues, cells, functions, interdependencies, and interactions with each other and the environment.
Chemistry	Knowledge of the chemical composition, structure, and properties of substances and of the chemical processes and transformations that they undergo. This includes uses of chemicals and their interactions, danger signs, production techniques, and disposal methods.
Public Safety and Security	Knowledge of relevant equipment, policies, procedures, and strategies to promote effective local, state, or national security operations for the protection of people, data, property, and institutions.
Mathematics	Knowledge of arithmetic, algebra, geometry, calculus, statistics, and their applications.
English Language	Knowledge of the structure and content of the English language including the meaning and spelling of words, rules of composition, and grammar.
Mechanical	Knowledge of machines and tools, including their designs, uses, repair, and maintenance.
Physics	Knowledge and prediction of physical principles, laws, their interrelationships, and applications to understanding fluid, material, and atmospheric dynamics, and mechanical, electrical, atomic and sub- atomic structures and processes.
Law and Government	Knowledge of laws, legal codes, court procedures, precedents, government regulations, executive orders, agency rules, and the democratic political process.
Computers and Electronics	Knowledge of circuit boards, processors, chips, electronic equipment, and computer hardware and software, including applications and programming.
Customer and Personal Service	Knowledge of principles and processes for providing customer and personal services. This includes customer needs assessment, meeting quality standards for services, and evaluation of customer satisfaction.
Administration and Management	Knowledge of business and management principles involved in strategic planning, resource allocation, human resources modeling, leadership technique, production methods, and coordination of people and resources.
Engineering and Technology	Knowledge of the practical application of engineering science and technology. This includes applying principles, techniques, procedures, and equipment to the design and production of various goods and services.
Education and Training	Knowledge of principles and methods for curriculum and training design, teaching and instruction for individuals and groups, and the measurement of training effects.
Production and Processing	Knowledge of raw materials, production processes, quality control, costs, and other techniques for maximizing the effective manufacture and distribution of goods.
Clerical	Knowledge of administrative and clerical procedures and systems such as word processing, managing files and records, stenography and transcription, designing forms, and other office procedures and terminology.
Building and Construction	Knowledge of materials, methods, and the tools involved in the construction or repair of houses, buildings, or other structures such as highways and roads.
Geography	Knowledge of principles and methods for describing the features of land, sea, and air masses, including their physical characteristics, locations, interrelationships, and distribution of plant, animal, and human life.
Telecommunications	Knowledge of transmission, broadcasting, switching, control, and operation of telecommunications systems.
Personnel and Human Resources	Knowledge of principles and procedures for personnel recruitment, selection, training, compensation and benefits, labor relations and negotiation, and personnel information systems.
Communications and Media	Knowledge of media production, communication, and dissemination techniques and methods. This includes alternative ways to inform and entertain via written, oral, and visual media.
Design	Knowledge of design techniques, tools, and principles involved in production of precision technical plans, blueprints, drawings, and models.
Medicine and Dentistry	Knowledge of the information and techniques needed to diagnose and treat human injuries, diseases, and deformities. This includes symptoms, treatment alternatives, drug properties and interactions, and preventive health-care measures.
Transportation	Knowledge of principles and methods for moving people or goods by air, rail, sea, or road, including the relative costs and benefits.
Psychology	Knowledge of human behavior and performance; individual differences in ability, personality, and interests; learning and motivation; psychological research methods; and the assessment and treatment of behavioral and affective disorders.
Economics and Accounting	Knowledge of economic and accounting principles and practices, the financial markets, banking and the analysis and reporting of financial data.
Sociology and Anthropology	Knowledge of group behavior and dynamics, societal trends and influences, human migrations, ethnicity, cultures and their history and origins.
History and Archeology	Knowledge of historical events and their causes, indicators, and effects on civilizations and cultures.
Therapy and Counseling	Knowledge of principles, methods, and procedures for diagnosis, treatment, and rehabilitation of physical and mental dysfunctions, and for career counseling and guidance.
Philosophy and Theology	Knowledge of different philosophical systems and religions. This includes their basic principles, values, ethics, ways of thinking, customs, practices, and their impact on human culture.
Foreign Language	Knowledge of the structure and content of a foreign (non-English) language including the meaning and spelling of words, rules of composition and grammar, and pronunciation.
Food Production	Knowledge of techniques and equipment for planting, growing, and harvesting food products (both plant and animal) for consumption, including storage/handling techniques.
Sales and Marketing	Knowledge of principles and methods for showing, promoting, and selling products or services. This includes marketing strategy and tactics, product demonstration, sales techniques, and sales control systems.
Fine Arts	Knowledge of the theory and techniques required to compose, produce, and perform works of music, dance, visual arts, drama, and sculpture.

Skills	Skills Definitions
Reading Comprehension	Understanding written sentences and paragraphs in work related documents.
Operation and Control	Controlling operations of equipment or systems.
Troubleshooting	Determining causes of operating errors and deciding what to do about it.
Active Listening	Giving full attention to what other people are saying, taking time to understand the points being made, asking questions as appropriate, and not interrupting at inappropriate times.
Monitoring	Monitoring/Assessing performance of yourself, other individuals, or organizations to make improvements or take corrective action.
Operation Monitoring	Watching gauges, dials, or other indicators to make sure a machine is working properly.
Equipment Maintenance	Performing routine maintenance on equipment and determining when and what kind of maintenance is needed.
Learning Strategies	Selecting and using training/instructional methods and procedures appropriate for the situation when learning or teaching new things.
Critical Thinking	Using logic and reasoning to identify the strengths and weaknesses of alternative solutions, conclusions or approaches to problems.
Writing	Communicating effectively in writing as appropriate for the needs of the audience.
Mathematics	Using mathematics to solve problems.

Active Learning	Understanding the implications of new information for both current and future problem-solving and decision-making.
Judgment and Decision Making	Considering the relative costs and benefits of potential actions to choose the most appropriate one.
Installation	Installing equipment, machines, wiring, or programs to meet specifications.
Speaking	Talking to others to convey information effectively.
Coordination	Adjusting actions in relation to others' actions.
Management of Material Resources	Obtaining and seeing to the appropriate use of equipment, facilities, and materials needed to do certain work.
Quality Control Analysis	Conducting tests and inspections of products, services, or processes to evaluate quality or performance.
Instructing	Teaching others how to do something.
Complex Problem Solving	Identifying complex problems and reviewing related information to develop and evaluate options and implement solutions.
Management of Personnel Resources	Motivating, developing, and directing people as they work, identifying the best people for the job.
Repairing	Repairing machines or systems using the needed tools.
Systems Evaluation	Identifying measures or indicators of system performance and the actions needed to improve or correct performance, relative to the goals of the system.
Systems Analysis	Determining how a system should work and how changes in conditions, operations, and the environment will affect outcomes.
Operations Analysis	Analyzing needs and product requirements to create a design.
Equipment Selection	Determining the kind of tools and equipment needed to do a job.
Technology Design	Generating or adapting equipment and technology to serve user needs.
Social Perceptiveness	Being aware of others' reactions and understanding why they react as they do.
Time Management	Managing one's own time and the time of others.
Science	Using scientific rules and methods to solve problems.
Service Orientation	Actively looking for ways to help people.
Programming	Writing computer programs for various purposes.
Negotiation	Bringing others together and trying to reconcile differences.
Management of Financial Resources	Determining how money will be spent to get the work done, and accounting for these expenditures.
Persuasion	Persuading others to change their minds or behavior.

Ability	**Ability Definitions**
Near Vision	The ability to see details at close range (within a few feet of the observer).
Problem Sensitivity	The ability to tell when something is wrong or is likely to go wrong. It does not involve solving the problem, only recognizing there is a problem.
Deductive Reasoning	The ability to apply general rules to specific problems to produce answers that make sense.
Control Precision	The ability to quickly and repeatedly adjust the controls of a machine or a vehicle to exact positions.
Information Ordering	The ability to arrange things or actions in a certain order or pattern according to a specific rule or set of rules (e.g., patterns of numbers, letters, words, pictures, mathematical operations).
Oral Comprehension	The ability to listen to and understand information and ideas presented through spoken words and sentences.
Multilimb Coordination	The ability to coordinate two or more limbs (for example, two arms, two legs, or one leg and one arm) while sitting, standing, or lying down. It does not involve performing the activities while the whole body is in motion.
Arm-Hand Steadiness	The ability to keep your hand and arm steady while moving your arm or while holding your arm and hand in one position.
Oral Expression	The ability to communicate information and ideas in speaking so others will understand.
Inductive Reasoning	The ability to combine pieces of information to form general rules or conclusions (includes finding a relationship among seemingly unrelated events).
Speech Clarity	The ability to speak clearly so others can understand you.
Selective Attention	The ability to concentrate on a task over a period of time without being distracted.
Manual Dexterity	The ability to quickly move your hand, your hand together with your arm, or your two hands to grasp, manipulate, or assemble objects.
Trunk Strength	The ability to use your abdominal and lower back muscles to support part of the body repeatedly or continuously over time without 'giving out' or fatiguing.
Far Vision	The ability to see details at a distance.

Depth Perception	The ability to judge which of several objects is closer or farther away from you, or to judge the distance between you and an object.
Visual Color Discrimination	The ability to match or detect differences between colors, including shades of color and brightness.
Flexibility of Closure	The ability to identify or detect a known pattern (a figure, object, word, or sound) that is hidden in other distracting material.
Perceptual Speed	The ability to quickly and accurately compare similarities and differences among sets of letters, numbers, objects, pictures, or patterns. The things to be compared may be presented at the same time or one after the other. This ability also includes comparing a presented object with a remembered object.
Category Flexibility	The ability to generate or use different sets of rules for combining or grouping things in different ways.
Speech Recognition	The ability to identify and understand the speech of another person.
Written Comprehension	The ability to read and understand information and ideas presented in writing.
Written Expression	The ability to communicate information and ideas in writing so others will understand.
Spatial Orientation	The ability to know your location in relation to the environment or to know where other objects are in relation to you.
Rate Control	The ability to time your movements or the movement of a piece of equipment in anticipation of changes in the speed and/or direction of a moving object or scene.
Time Sharing	The ability to shift back and forth between two or more activities or sources of information (such as speech, sounds, touch, or other sources).
Reaction Time	The ability to quickly respond (with the hand, finger, or foot) to a signal (sound, light, picture) when it appears.
Visualization	The ability to imagine how something will look after it is moved around or when its parts are moved or rearranged.
Extent Flexibility	The ability to bend, stretch, twist, or reach with your body, arms, and/or legs.
Finger Dexterity	The ability to make precisely coordinated movements of the fingers of one or both hands to grasp, manipulate, or assemble very small objects.
Static Strength	The ability to exert maximum muscle force to lift, push, pull, or carry objects.
Hearing Sensitivity	The ability to detect or tell the differences between sounds that vary in pitch and loudness.
Auditory Attention	The ability to focus on a single source of sound in the presence of other distracting sounds.
Glare Sensitivity	The ability to see objects in the presence of glare or bright lighting.
Response Orientation	The ability to choose quickly between two or more movements in response to two or more different signals (lights, sounds, pictures). It includes the speed with which the correct response is started with the hand, foot, or other body part.
Memorization	The ability to remember information such as words, numbers, pictures, and procedures.
Gross Body Coordination	The ability to coordinate the movement of your arms, legs, and torso together when the whole body is in motion.
Originality	The ability to come up with unusual or clever ideas about a given topic or situation, or to develop creative ways to solve a problem.
Speed of Closure	The ability to quickly make sense of, combine, and organize information into meaningful patterns.
Sound Localization	The ability to tell the direction from which a sound originated.
Stamina	The ability to exert yourself physically over long periods of time without getting winded or out of breath.
Gross Body Equilibrium	The ability to keep or regain your body balance or stay upright when in an unstable position.
Dynamic Strength	The ability to exert muscle force repeatedly or continuously over time. This involves muscular endurance and resistance to muscle fatigue.
Number Facility	The ability to add, subtract, multiply, or divide quickly and correctly.
Peripheral Vision	The ability to see objects or movement of objects to one's side when the eyes are looking ahead.
Wrist-Finger Speed	The ability to make fast, simple, repeated movements of the fingers, hands, and wrists.
Fluency of Ideas	The ability to come up with a number of ideas about a topic (the number of ideas is important, not their quality, correctness, or creativity).
Speed of Limb Movement	The ability to quickly move the arms and legs.

Mathematical Reasoning	The ability to choose the right mathematical methods or formulas to solve a problem.
Night Vision	The ability to see under low light conditions.
Dynamic Flexibility	The ability to quickly and repeatedly bend, stretch, twist, or reach out with your body, arms, and/or legs.
Explosive Strength	The ability to use short bursts of muscle force to propel oneself (as in jumping or sprinting), or to throw an object.

Work_Activity	Work_Activity Definitions
Monitor Processes, Materials, or Surroundings	Monitoring and reviewing information from materials, events, or the environment, to detect or assess problems.
Performing General Physical Activities	Performing physical activities that require considerable use of your arms and legs and moving your whole body, such as climbing, lifting, balancing, walking, stooping, and handling of materials.
Inspecting Equipment, Structures, or Material	Inspecting equipment, structures, or materials to identify the cause of errors or other problems or defects.
Evaluating Information to Determine Compliance wit	Using relevant information and individual judgment to determine whether events or processes comply with laws, regulations, or standards.
Handling and Moving Objects	Using hands and arms in handling, installing, positioning, and moving materials, and manipulating things.
Making Decisions and Solving Problems	Analyzing information and evaluating results to choose the best solution and solve problems.
Updating and Using Relevant Knowledge	Keeping up-to-date technically and applying new knowledge to your job.
Identifying Objects, Actions, and Events	Identifying information by categorizing, estimating, recognizing differences or similarities, and detecting changes in circumstances or events.
Documenting/Recording Information	Entering, transcribing, recording, storing, or maintaining information in written or electronic/magnetic form.
Getting Information	Observing, receiving, and otherwise obtaining information from all relevant sources.
Communicating with Supervisors, Peers, or Subordin	Providing information to supervisors, co-workers, and subordinates by telephone, in written form, e-mail, or in person.
Operating Vehicles, Mechanized Devices, or Equipme	Running, maneuvering, navigating, or driving vehicles or mechanized equipment, such as forklifts, passenger vehicles, aircraft, or water craft.
Controlling Machines and Processes	Using either control mechanisms or direct physical activity to operate machines or processes (not including computers or vehicles).
Organizing, Planning, and Prioritizing Work	Developing specific goals and plans to prioritize, organize, and accomplish your work.
Analyzing Data or Information	Identifying the underlying principles, reasons, or facts of information by breaking down information or data into separate parts.
Processing Information	Compiling, coding, categorizing, calculating, tabulating, auditing, or verifying information or data.
Monitoring and Controlling Resources	Monitoring and controlling resources and overseeing the spending of money.
Thinking Creatively	Developing, designing, or creating new applications, ideas, relationships, systems, or products, including artistic contributions.
Performing for or Working Directly with the Public	Performing for people or dealing directly with the public. This includes serving customers in restaurants and stores, and receiving clients or guests.
Establishing and Maintaining Interpersonal Relatio	Developing constructive and cooperative working relationships with others, and maintaining them over time.
Developing Objectives and Strategies	Establishing long-range objectives and specifying the strategies and actions to achieve them.
Communicating with Persons Outside Organization	Communicating with people outside the organization, representing the organization to customers, the public, government, and other external sources. This information can be exchanged in person, in writing, or by telephone or e-mail.
Repairing and Maintaining Mechanical Equipment	Servicing, repairing, adjusting, and testing machines, devices, moving parts, and equipment that operate primarily on the basis of mechanical (not electronic) principles.
Repairing and Maintaining Electronic Equipment	Servicing, repairing, calibrating, regulating, fine-tuning, or testing machines, devices, and equipment that operate primarily on the basis of electrical or electronic (not mechanical) principles.
Estimating the Quantifiable Characteristics of Pro	Estimating sizes, distances, and quantities; or determining time, costs, resources, or materials needed to perform a work activity.

Resolving Conflicts and Negotiating with Others	Handling complaints, settling disputes, and resolving grievances and conflicts, or otherwise negotiating with others.
Scheduling Work and Activities	Scheduling events, programs, and activities, as well as the work of others.
Training and Teaching Others	Identifying the educational needs of others, developing formal educational or training programs or classes, and teaching or instructing others.
Interpreting the Meaning of Information for Others	Translating or explaining what information means and how it can be used.
Interacting With Computers	Using computers and computer systems (including hardware and software) to program, write software, set up functions, enter data, or process information.
Judging the Qualities of Things, Services, or Peop	Assessing the value, importance, or quality of things or people.
Guiding, Directing, and Motivating Subordinates	Providing guidance and direction to subordinates, including setting performance standards and monitoring performance.
Assisting and Caring for Others	Providing personal assistance, medical attention, emotional support, or other personal care to others such as coworkers, customers, or patients.
Coaching and Developing Others	Identifying the developmental needs of others and coaching, mentoring, or otherwise helping others to improve their knowledge or skills.
Coordinating the Work and Activities of Others	Getting members of a group to work together to accomplish tasks.
Provide Consultation and Advice to Others	Providing guidance and expert advice to management or other groups on technical, systems-, or process-related topics.
Performing Administrative Activities	Performing day-to-day administrative tasks such as maintaining information files and processing paperwork.
Developing and Building Teams	Encouraging and building mutual trust, respect, and cooperation among team members.
Selling or Influencing Others	Convincing others to buy merchandise/goods or to otherwise change their minds or actions.
Drafting, Laying Out, and Specifying Technical Dev	Providing documentation, detailed instructions, drawings, or specifications to tell others about how devices, parts, equipment, or structures are to be fabricated, constructed, assembled, modified, maintained, or used.
Staffing Organizational Units	Recruiting, interviewing, selecting, hiring, and promoting employees in an organization.

Work_Context	Work_Context Definitions
Outdoors, Exposed to Weather	How often does this job require working outdoors, exposed to all weather conditions?
Freedom to Make Decisions	How much decision making freedom, without supervision, does the job offer?
In an Enclosed Vehicle or Equipment	How often does this job require working in a closed vehicle or equipment (e.g., car)?
Wear Common Protective or Safety Equipment such as	How much does this job require wearing common protective or safety equipment such as safety shoes, glasses, gloves, hard hats or live jackets?
Structured versus Unstructured Work	To what extent is this job structured for the worker, rather than allowing the worker to determine tasks, priorities, and goals?
Impact of Decisions on Co-workers or Company Resul	How do the decisions an employee makes impact the results of co-workers, clients or the company?
Frequency of Decision Making	How frequently is the worker required to make decisions that affect other people, the financial resources, and/or the image and reputation of the organization?
Face-to-Face Discussions	How often do you have to have face-to-face discussions with individuals or teams in this job?
Indoors, Environmentally Controlled	How often does this job require working indoors in environmentally controlled conditions?
Exposed to Contaminants	How often does this job require working exposed to contaminants (such as pollutants, gases, dust or odors)?
Importance of Being Exact or Accurate	How important is being very exact or highly accurate in performing this job?
Sounds, Noise Levels Are Distracting or Uncomforta	How often does this job require working exposed to sounds and noise levels that are distracting or uncomfortable?
Telephone	How often do you have telephone conversations in this job?
Indoors, Not Environmentally Controlled	How often does this job require working indoors in non-controlled environmental conditions (e.g., warehouse without heat)?
Consequence of Error	How serious would the result usually be if the worker made a mistake that was not readily correctable?
Responsibility for Outcomes and Results	How responsible is the worker for work outcomes and results of other workers?
Very Hot or Cold Temperatures	How often does this job require working in very hot (above 90 F degrees) or very cold (below 32 F degrees) temperatures?

Exposed to Minor Burns, Cuts, Bites, or Stings	How often does this job require exposure to minor burns, cuts, bites, or stings?
Responsible for Others' Health and Safety	How much responsibility is there for the health and safety of others in this job?
Spend Time Standing	How much does this job require standing?
Exposed to Hazardous Equipment	How often does this job require exposure to hazardous equipment?
Exposed to Hazardous Conditions	How often does this job require exposure to hazardous conditions?
Spend Time Using Your Hands to Handle, Control, or	How much does this job require using your hands to handle, control, or feel objects, tools or controls?
Work With Work Group or Team	How important is it to work with others in a group or team in this job?
Importance of Repeating Same Tasks	How important is repeating the same physical activities (e.g., key entry) or mental activities (e.g., checking entries in a ledger) over and over, without stopping, to performing this job?
Exposed to Disease or Infections	How often does this job require exposure to disease/infections?
Time Pressure	How often does this job require the worker to meet strict deadlines?
Exposed to High Places	How often does this job require exposure to high places?
Contact With Others	How much does this job require the worker to be in contact with others (face-to-face, by telephone, or otherwise) in order to perform it?
Spend Time Walking and Running	How much does this job require walking and running?
Coordinate or Lead Others	How important is it to coordinate or lead others in accomplishing work activities in this job?
Degree of Automation	How automated is the job?
Outdoors, Under Cover	How often does this job require working outdoors, under cover (e.g., structure with roof but no walls)?
Letters and Memos	How often does the job require written letters and memos?
Cramped Work Space, Awkward Positions	How often does this job require working in cramped work spaces that requires getting into awkward positions?
Deal With External Customers	How important is it to work with external customers or the public in this job?
Extremely Bright or Inadequate Lighting	How often does this job require working in extremely bright or inadequate lighting conditions?
Pace Determined by Speed of Equipment	How important is it to this job that the pace is determined by the speed of equipment or machinery? (This does not refer to keeping busy at all times on this job.)
Spend Time Sitting	How much does this job require sitting?
Electronic Mail	How often do you use electronic mail in this job?
Deal With Unpleasant or Angry People	How frequently does the worker have to deal with unpleasant, angry, or discourteous individuals as part of the job requirements?
Physical Proximity	To what extent does this job require the worker to perform job tasks in close physical proximity to other people?
Spend Time Making Repetitive Motions	How much does this job require making repetitive motions?
Spend Time Climbing Ladders, Scaffolds, or Poles	How much does this job require climbing ladders, scaffolds, or poles?
Frequency of Conflict Situations	How often are there conflict situations the employee has to face in this job?
Level of Competition	To what extent does this job require the worker to compete or to be aware of competitive pressures?
Spend Time Bending or Twisting the Body	How much does this job require bending or twisting your body?
In an Open Vehicle or Equipment	How often does this job require working in an open vehicle or equipment (e.g., tractor)?
Wear Specialized Protective or Safety Equipment su	How much does this job require wearing specialized protective or safety equipment such as breathing apparatus, safety harness, full protection suits, or radiation protection?
Spend Time Keeping or Regaining Balance	How much does this job require keeping or regaining your balance?
Exposed to Whole Body Vibration	How often does this job require exposure to whole body vibration (e.g., operate a jackhammer)?
Spend Time Kneeling, Crouching, Stooping, or Crawl	How much does this job require kneeling, crouching, stooping or crawling?
Public Speaking	How often do you have to perform public speaking in this job?
Deal With Physically Aggressive People	How frequently does this job require the worker to deal with physical aggression of violent individuals?
Exposed to Radiation	How often does this job require exposure to radiation?

51-8031.00

Job Zone Component	Job Zone Component Definitions
Title	Job Zone Three: Medium Preparation Needed
Overall Experience	Previous work-related skill, knowledge, or experience is required for these occupations. For example, an electrician must have completed three or four years of apprenticeship or several years of vocational training, and often must have passed a licensing exam, in order to perform the job.
Job Training	Employees in these occupations usually need one or two years of training involving both on-the-job experience and informal training with experienced workers.
Job Zone Examples	These occupations usually involve using communication and organizational skills to coordinate, supervise, manage, or train others to accomplish goals. Examples include dental assistants, electricians, fish and game wardens, legal secretaries, personnel recruiters, and recreation workers.
SVP Range	(6.0 to < 7.0)
Education	Most occupations in this zone require training in vocational schools, related on-the-job experience, or an associate's degree. Some may require a bachelor's degree.

Work_Styles	Work_Styles Definitions
Dependability	Job requires being reliable, responsible, and dependable, and fulfilling obligations.
Attention to Detail	Job requires being careful about detail and thorough in completing work tasks.
Cooperation	Job requires being pleasant with others on the job and displaying a good-natured, cooperative attitude.
Self Control	Job requires maintaining composure, keeping emotions in check, controlling anger, and avoiding aggressive behavior, even in very difficult situations.
Analytical Thinking	Job requires analyzing information and using logic to address work-related issues and problems.
Integrity	Job requires being honest and ethical.
Initiative	Job requires a willingness to take on responsibilities and challenges.
Leadership	Job requires a willingness to lead, take charge, and offer opinions and direction.
Adaptability/Flexibility	Job requires being open to change (positive or negative) and to considerable variety in the workplace.
Independence	Job requires developing one's own ways of doing things, guiding oneself with little or no supervision, and depending on oneself to get things done.
Persistence	Job requires persistence in the face of obstacles.
Stress Tolerance	Job requires accepting criticism and dealing calmly and effectively with high stress situations.
Achievement/Effort	Job requires establishing and maintaining personally challenging achievement goals and exerting effort toward mastering tasks.
Concern for Others	Job requires being sensitive to others' needs and feelings and being understanding and helpful on the job.
Innovation	Job requires creativity and alternative thinking to develop new ideas for and answers to work-related problems.
Social Orientation	Job requires preferring to work with others rather than alone, and being personally connected with others on the job.

51-8091.00 - Chemical Plant and System Operators

Control or operate an entire chemical process or system of machines.

Tasks

1) Notify maintenance, stationary-engineering, and other auxiliary personnel to correct equipment malfunctions and to adjust power, steam, water, or air supplies.

2) Control or operate chemical processes or systems of machines, using panelboards, control boards, or semi-automatic equipment.

3) Direct workers engaged in operating machinery that regulates the flow of materials and products.

4) Regulate or shut down equipment during emergency situations, as directed by supervisory personnel.

5) Patrol work areas to ensure that solutions in tanks and troughs are not in danger of overflowing.

6) Move control settings to make necessary adjustments on equipment units affecting speeds of chemical reactions, quality, and yields.

7) Monitor recording instruments, flowmeters, panel lights, and other indicators, and listen for warning signals, in order to verify conformity of process conditions.

8) Record operating data such as process conditions, test results, and instrument readings.

9) Start pumps to wash and rinse reactor vessels, to exhaust gases and vapors, to regulate the flow of oil, steam, air, and perfume to towers, and to add products to converter or blending vessels.

10) Turn valves to regulate flow of products or byproducts through agitator tanks, storage drums, or neutralizer tanks.

11) Interpret chemical reactions visible through sight glasses or on television monitors, and review laboratory test reports for process adjustments.

12) Calculate material requirements or yields according to formulas.

13) Supervise the cleaning of towers, strainers, and spray tips.

14) Gauge tank levels, using calibrated rods.

15) Draw samples of products, and conduct quality control tests in order to monitor processing, and to ensure that standards are met.

16) Confer with technical and supervisory personnel to report or resolve conditions affecting safety, efficiency, and product quality.

17) Inspect operating units such as towers, soap-spray storage tanks, scrubbers, collectors, and driers to ensure that all are functioning, and to maintain maximum efficiency.

18) Repair and replace damaged equipment.

51-8092.00 - Gas Plant Operators

Distribute or process gas for utility companies and others by controlling compressors to maintain specified pressures on main pipelines.

Tasks

1) Control equipment to regulate flow and pressure of gas to feedlines of boilers, furnaces, and related steam-generating or heating equipment.

2) Clean, maintain, and repair equipment, using hand tools, or request that repair and maintenance work be performed.

3) Operate construction equipment to install and maintain gas distribution systems.

4) Signal or direct workers who tend auxiliary equipment.

5) Record, review, and compile operations records, test results, and gauge readings such as temperatures, pressures, concentrations, and flows.

6) Read logsheets to determine product demand and disposition, or to detect malfunctions.

7) Monitor transportation and storage of flammable and other potentially dangerous products to ensure that safety guidelines are followed.

8) Contact maintenance crews when necessary.

9) Change charts in recording meters.

10) Test gas, chemicals, and air during processing to assess factors such as purity and moisture content, and to detect quality problems or gas or chemical leaks.

11) Adjust temperature, pressure, vacuum, level, flow rate, and/or transfer of gas to maintain processes at required levels or to correct problems.

12) Calculate gas ratios to detect deviations from specifications, using testing apparatus.

13) Control fractioning columns, compressors, purifying towers, heat exchangers, and related equipment in order to extract nitrogen and oxygen from air.

14) Determine causes of abnormal pressure variances, and make corrective recommendations, such as installation of pipes to relieve overloading.

15) Distribute or process gas for utility companies or industrial plants, using panel boards, control boards, and semi-automatic equipment.

16) Monitor equipment functioning, observe temperature, level, and flow gauges, and perform regular unit checks, in order to ensure that all equipment is operating as it should.

17) Collaborate with other operators to solve unit problems.

18) Control operation of compressors, scrubbers, evaporators, and refrigeration equipment in order to liquefy, compress, or regasify natural gas.

51-8093.00 - Petroleum Pump System Operators, Refinery Operators, and Gaugers

Control the operation of petroleum refining or processing units. May specialize in controlling manifold and pumping systems, gauging or testing oil in storage tanks, or regulating the flow of oil into pipelines.

Tasks

1) Coordinate shutdowns and major projects.

2) Inspect pipelines, tightening connections and lubricating valves as necessary.

3) Lower thermometers into tanks to obtain temperature readings.

4) Maintain and repair equipment, or report malfunctioning equipment to supervisors so that repairs can be scheduled.

5) Operate auxiliary equipment and control multiple processing units during distilling or treating operations, moving controls that regulate valves, pumps, compressors, and auxiliary equipment.

6) Patrol units to monitor the amount of oil in storage tanks, and to verify that activities and operations are safe, efficient, and in compliance with regulations.

7) Prepare calculations for receipts and deliveries of oil and oil products.

8) Operate control panels to coordinate and regulate process variables such as temperature and pressure, and to direct product flow rate, according to process schedules.

9) Calculate test result values, using standard formulas.

10) Clean interiors of processing units by circulating chemicals and solvents within units.

11) Start pumps and open valves or use automated equipment to regulate the flow of oil in pipelines and into and out of tanks.

12) Read and analyze specifications, schedules, logs, test results, and laboratory recommendations to determine how to set equipment controls to produce the required qualities and quantities of products.

13) Control or operate manifold and pumping systems to circulate liquids through a petroleum refinery.

14) Clamp seals around valves to secure tanks.

15) Monitor process indicators, instruments, gauges, and meters in order to detect and report any possible problems.

16) Plan movement of products through lines to processing, storage, and shipping units, utilizing knowledge of system interconnections and capacities.

17) Collect product samples by turning bleeder valves, or by lowering containers into tanks to obtain oil samples.

18) Read automatic gauges at specified intervals to determine the flow rate of oil into or from tanks, and the amount of oil in tanks.

19) Record and compile operating data, instrument readings, documentation, and results of laboratory analyses.

20) Signal other workers by telephone or radio to operate pumps, open and close valves, and check temperatures.

21) Synchronize activities with other pumphouses to ensure a continuous flow of products and a minimum of contamination between products.

22) Verify that incoming and outgoing products are moving through the correct meters, and that meters are working properly.

23) Perform tests to check the qualities and grades of products, such as assessing levels of bottom sediment, water, and foreign materials in oil samples, using centrifugal testers.

51-9011.00 - Chemical Equipment Operators and Tenders

Operate or tend equipment to control chemical changes or reactions in the processing of industrial or consumer products. Equipment used includes devulcanizers, steam-jacketed kettles, and reactor vessels.

Tasks

1) Draw samples of products at specified stages so that analyses can be performed.

2) Drain equipment, and pump water or other solutions through in order to flush and clean tanks and equipment.

3) Control and operate equipment in which chemical changes or reactions take place during the processing of industrial or consumer products.

4) Test product samples for specific gravity, chemical characteristics, pH levels, and concentrations or viscosities, or send them to laboratories for testing.

5) Record operational data such as temperatures, pressures, ingredients used, processing times, or test results.

6) Monitor gauges, recording instruments, flowmeters, or products to ensure that specified conditions are maintained.

7) Adjust controls to regulate temperature, pressure, feed, and flow of liquids and gases, and times of prescribed reactions, according to knowledge of equipment and processes.

8) Notify maintenance engineers of equipment malfunctions.

9) Inspect equipment or units to detect leaks and malfunctions, shutting equipment down if necessary.

10) Observe and compare colors and consistencies of products to instrument readings, and to laboratory and standard test results.

11) Open valves or start pumps, agitators, reactors, blowers, or automatic feed of materials.

12) Measure, weigh, and mix chemical ingredients, according to specifications.

13) Observe safety precautions to prevent fires and explosions.

14) Add treating or neutralizing agents to products, and pump products through filters or centrifuges in order to remove impurities or to precipitate products.

15) Direct activities of workers assisting in control or verification of processes, or in unloading of materials.

16) Estimate materials required for production and manufacturing of products.

17) Implement appropriate industrial emergency response procedures.

18) Inventory supplies received and consumed.

19) Make minor repairs, and lubricate and maintain equipment, using hand tools.

20) Read plant specifications to determine products, ingredients, and prescribed modifications of plant procedures.

21) Flush or clean equipment, using steam hoses or mechanical reamers.

22) Dump or scoop prescribed solid, granular, or powdered materials into equipment.

51-9012.00 - Separating, Filtering, Clarifying, Precipitating, and Still Machine Setters, Operators, and Tenders

Set up, operate, or tend continuous flow or vat-type equipment; filter presses; shaker screens; centrifuges; condenser tubes; precipitating, fermenting, or evaporating tanks; scrubbing towers; or batch stills. These machines extract, sort, or separate liquids, gases, or solids from other materials to recover a refined product. Includes dairy processing equipment operators.

Tasks

1) Test samples to determine viscosity, acidity, specific gravity, or degree of concentration, using test equipment such as viscometers, pH meters, and hydrometers.

2) Remove full bags or containers from discharge outlets, and replace them with empty ones.

3) Pack bottles into cartons or crates, using machines.

4) Maintain logs of instrument readings, test results, and shift production, and send production information to computer databases.

5) Install and maintain or repair hoses, pumps, filters, or screens in order to maintain processing equipment, using hand tools.

6) Turn valves to pump sterilizing solutions and rinsewater through pipes and equipment, and to spray vats with atomizers.

7) Inspect machines and equipment for hazards, operating efficiency, malfunctions, wear, and leaks.

8) Measure or weigh materials to be refined, mixed, transferred, stored, or otherwise processed.

9) Set or adjust machine controls to regulate conditions such as material flow, temperature, and pressure.

10) Remove clogs, defects, and impurities from machines, tanks, conveyors, screens, or other processing equipment.

11) Start agitators, shakers, conveyors, pumps, or centrifuge machines, then turn valves or move controls to admit, drain, separate, filter, clarify, mix, or transfer materials.

12) Assemble fittings, valves, bowls, plates, disks, impeller shafts, and other parts to equipment in order to prepare equipment for operation.

13) Collect samples of materials or products for laboratory analysis.

14) Dump, pour, or load specified amounts of refined or unrefined materials into equipment or containers for further processing or storage.

15) Monitor material flow and instruments such as temperature and pressure gauges, indicators, and meters, in order to ensure optimal processing conditions.

16) Examine samples visually or by hand to verify qualities such as clarity, cleanliness, consistency, dryness, and texture.

17) Connect pipes between vats and processing equipment.

18) Clean and sterilize tanks, screens, inflow pipes, production areas, and equipment, using hoses, brushes, scrapers, or chemical solutions.

51-9023.00 - Mixing and Blending Machine Setters, Operators, and Tenders

Set up, operate, or tend machines to mix or blend materials, such as chemicals, tobacco, liquids, color pigments, or explosive ingredients.

Tasks

1) Add or mix chemicals and ingredients for processing, using hand tools or other devices.

2) Dislodge and clear jammed materials or other items from machinery and equipment, using hand tools.

3) Dump or pour specified amounts of materials into machinery and equipment.

4) Examine materials, ingredients, or products visually or with hands, in order to ensure conformance to established standards.

5) Read work orders to determine production specifications and information.

6) Open valves to drain slurry from mixers into storage tanks.

7) Operate or tend machines to mix or blend any of a wide variety of materials such as spices, dough batter, tobacco, fruit juices, chemicals, livestock feed, food products, color pigments, or explosive ingredients.

8) Observe production and monitor equipment to ensure safe and efficient operation.

9) Weigh or measure materials, ingredients, and products to ensure conformance to requirements.

10) Start machines to mix or blend ingredients; then allow them to mix for specified times.

11) Stop mixing or blending machines when specified product qualities are obtained, and open valves and start pumps to transfer mixtures.

12) Tend accessory equipment such as pumps and conveyors to move materials or ingredients through production processes.

13) Collect samples of materials or products for laboratory testing.

14) Test samples of materials or products to ensure compliance with specifications, using test equipment.

15) Transfer materials, supplies, and products between work areas, using moving equipment and hand tools.

16) Unload mixtures into containers or onto conveyors for further processing.

17) Compound and process ingredients or dyes according to formulas.

18) Clean and maintain equipment, using hand tools.

51-9041.00 - Extruding, Forming, Pressing, and Compacting Machine Setters, Operators, and Tenders

Set up, operate, or tend machines, such as glass forming machines, plodder machines, and tuber machines, to shape and form products, such as glassware, food, rubber, soap, brick, tile, clay, wax, tobacco, or cosmetics.

Tasks

1) Measure, mix, cut, shape, soften, and join materials and ingredients such as powder, cornmeal, or rubber in order to prepare them for machine processing.

2) Examine, measure, and weigh materials or products to verify conformance to standards, using measuring devices such as templates, micrometers, or scales.

3) Complete work tickets, and place them with products.

4) Clean dies, arbors, compression chambers, and molds, using swabs, sponges, or air hoses.

5) Turn controls to adjust machine functions, such as regulating air pressure, creating vacuums, and adjusting coolant flow.

6) Select and install machine components such as dies, molds, and cutters, according to specifications, using hand tools and measuring devices.

7) Notify supervisors when extruded filaments fail to meet standards.

8) Clear jams, and remove defective or substandard materials or products.

9) Feed products into machines by hand or conveyor.

10) Couple air and gas lines to machines to maintain plasticity of material and to regulate solidification of final products.

11) Activate machines to shape or form products such as candy bars, light bulbs, balloons, or insulation panels.

12) Remove molds, mold components, and feeder tubes from machinery after production is complete.

13) Pour, scoop, or dump specified ingredients, metal assemblies, or mixtures into sections of machine prior to starting machines.

14) Measure arbors and dies to verify sizes specified on work tickets.

15) Review work orders, specifications, or instructions to determine materials, ingredients, procedures, components, settings, and adjustments for extruding, forming, pressing, or compacting machines.

16) Install, align, and adjust neck rings, press plungers, and feeder tubes.

17) Monitor machine operations and observe lights and gauges in order to detect malfunctions.

18) Disassemble equipment to repair it or to replace parts such as nozzles, punches, and filters.

19) Remove materials or products from molds or from extruding, forming, pressing, or compacting machines, and stack or store them for additional processing.

20) Ignite burners to preheat products, or use torches to apply heat.

21) Thread extruded strips through water tanks and hold-down bars, or attach strands to wires and draw them through tubes.

22) Synchronize speeds of sections of machines when producing products involving several steps or processes.

23) Swab molds with solutions to prevent products from sticking.

24) Send product samples to laboratories for analysis.

25) Record and maintain production data such as meter readings, and quantities, types, and dimensions of materials produced.

26) Move materials, supplies, components, and finished products between storage and work areas, using work aids such as racks, hoists, and handtrucks.

27) Press control buttons to activate machinery and equipment.

51-9051.00 - Furnace, Kiln, Oven, Drier, and Kettle Operators and Tenders

Operate or tend heating equipment other than basic metal, plastic, or food processing equipment. Includes activities, such as annealing glass, drying lumber, curing rubber, removing moisture from materials, or boiling soap.

Tasks

1) Confer with supervisors or other equipment operators in order to report equipment malfunctions or to resolve production problems.

2) Record gauge readings, test results, and shift production in log books.

3) Read and interpret work orders and instructions in order to determine work assignments, process specifications, and production schedules.

4) Transport materials and products to and from work areas, manually or using carts,

handtrucks, or hoists.

5) Press and adjust controls in order to activate, set, and regulate equipment according to specifications.

6) Examine or test samples of processed substances, or collect samples for laboratory testing, in order to ensure conformance to specifications.

7) Remove products from equipment, manually or using hoists, and prepare them for storage, shipment, or additional processing.

8) Clean, lubricate, and adjust equipment, using scrapers, solvents, air hoses, oil, and hand tools.

9) Weigh or measure specified amounts of ingredients or materials for processing, using devices such as scales and calipers.

10) Stop equipment and clear blockages or jams, using fingers, wire, or hand tools.

11) Replace worn or defective equipment parts, using hand tools.

12) Load equipment receptacles or conveyors with material to be processed, by hand or using hoists.

13) Calculate amounts of materials to be loaded into furnaces, adjusting amounts as necessary for specific conditions.

14) Sprinkle chemicals on the surface of molten metal in order to bring impurities to surface and remove impurities, using strainers.

15) Feed fuel, such as coal and coke, into fireboxes or onto conveyors, and remove ashes from furnaces, using shovels and buckets.

16) Melt or refine metal before casting, calculating required temperatures; and observe metal color and adjust controls as necessary in order to maintain required temperatures.

17) Direct crane operators and crew members to load vessels with materials to be processed.

Knowledge	Knowledge Definitions
Production and Processing	Knowledge of raw materials, production processes, quality control, costs, and other techniques for maximizing the effective manufacture and distribution of goods.
Mechanical	Knowledge of machines and tools, including their designs, uses, repair, and maintenance.
Public Safety and Security	Knowledge of relevant equipment, policies, procedures, and strategies to promote effective local, state, or national security operations for the protection of people, data, property, and institutions.
Education and Training	Knowledge of principles and methods for curriculum and training design, teaching and instruction for individuals and groups, and the measurement of training effects.
Mathematics	Knowledge of arithmetic, algebra, geometry, calculus, statistics, and their applications.
English Language	Knowledge of the structure and content of the English language including the meaning and spelling of words, rules of composition, and grammar.
Engineering and Technology	Knowledge of the practical application of engineering science and technology. This includes applying principles, techniques, procedures, and equipment to the design and production of various goods and services.
Administration and Management	Knowledge of business and management principles involved in strategic planning, resource allocation, human resources modeling, leadership technique, production methods, and coordination of people and resources.
Chemistry	Knowledge of the chemical composition, structure, and properties of substances and of the chemical processes and transformations that they undergo. This includes uses of chemicals and their interactions, danger signs, production techniques, and disposal methods.
Physics	Knowledge and prediction of physical principles, laws, their interrelationships, and applications to understanding fluid, material, and atmospheric dynamics, and mechanical, electrical, atomic and sub-atomic structures and processes.
Computers and Electronics	Knowledge of circuit boards, processors, chips, electronic equipment, and computer hardware and software, including applications and programming.
Law and Government	Knowledge of laws, legal codes, court procedures, precedents, government regulations, executive orders, agency rules, and the democratic political process.
Transportation	Knowledge of principles and methods for moving people or goods by air, rail, sea, or road, including the relative costs and benefits.
Clerical	Knowledge of administrative and clerical procedures and systems such as word processing, managing files and records, stenography and transcription, designing forms, and other office procedures and terminology.

Sales and Marketing	Knowledge of principles and methods for showing, promoting, and selling products or services. This includes marketing strategy and tactics. product demonstration, sales techniques, and sales control systems.
Personnel and Human Resources	Knowledge of principles and procedures for personnel recruitment, selection, training, compensation and benefits, labor relations and negotiation, and personnel information systems.
Customer and Personal Service	Knowledge of principles and processes for providing customer and personal services. This includes customer needs assessment, meeting quality standards for services, and evaluation of customer satisfaction.
Telecommunications	Knowledge of transmission, broadcasting, switching, control, and operation of telecommunications systems.
Design	Knowledge of design techniques, tools, and principles involved in production of precision technical plans, blueprints, drawings, and models.
Building and Construction	Knowledge of materials, methods, and the tools involved in the construction or repair of houses, buildings, or other structures such as highways and roads.
Economics and Accounting	Knowledge of economic and accounting principles and practices. the financial markets, banking and the analysis and reporting of financial data.
Medicine and Dentistry	Knowledge of the information and techniques needed to diagnose and treat human injuries, diseases, and deformities. This includes symptoms, treatment alternatives, drug properties and interactions, and preventive health-care measures.
Communications and Media	Knowledge of media production, communication, and dissemination techniques and methods. This includes alternative ways to inform and entertain via written, oral, and visual media.
Psychology	Knowledge of human behavior and performance; individual differences in ability, personality, and interests; learning and motivation; psychological research methods; and the assessment and treatment of behavioral and affective disorders.
Philosophy and Theology	Knowledge of different philosophical systems and religions. This includes their basic principles, values, ethics, ways of thinking, customs, practices, and their impact on human culture.
Foreign Language	Knowledge of the structure and content of a foreign (non-English) language including the meaning and spelling of words, rules of composition and grammar, and pronunciation.
Food Production	Knowledge of techniques and equipment for planting, growing, and harvesting food products (both plant and animal) for consumption, including storage/handling techniques.
Biology	Knowledge of plant and animal organisms, their tissues, cells, functions, interdependencies, and interactions with each other and the environment.
Therapy and Counseling	Knowledge of principles, methods, and procedures for diagnosis, treatment, and rehabilitation of physical and mental dysfunctions, and for career counseling and guidance.
Sociology and Anthropology	Knowledge of group behavior and dynamics, societal trends and influences, human migrations, ethnicity, cultures and their history and origins.
Geography	Knowledge of principles and methods for describing the features of land, sea, and air masses, including their physical characteristics, locations, interrelationships, and distribution of plant, animal, and human life.
Fine Arts	Knowledge of the theory and techniques required to compose, produce, and perform works of music, dance, visual arts, drama, and sculpture.
History and Archeology	Knowledge of historical events and their causes, indicators, and effects on civilizations and cultures.

Skills	Skills Definitions
Operation Monitoring	Watching gauges, dials, or other indicators to make sure a machine is working properly.
Instructing	Teaching others how to do something.
Operation and Control	Controlling operations of equipment or systems.
Active Listening	Giving full attention to what other people are saying, taking time to understand the points being made, asking questions as appropriate, and not interrupting at inappropriate times.
Troubleshooting	Determining causes of operating errors and deciding what to do about it.
Reading Comprehension	Understanding written sentences and paragraphs in work related documents.

Monitoring	Monitoring/Assessing performance of yourself, other individuals, or organizations to make improvements or take corrective action.
Coordination	Adjusting actions in relation to others' actions.
Learning Strategies	Selecting and using training/instructional methods and procedures appropriate for the situation when learning or teaching new things.
Speaking	Talking to others to convey information effectively.
Active Learning	Understanding the implications of new information for both current and future problem-solving and decision-making.
Time Management	Managing one's own time and the time of others.
Equipment Selection	Determining the kind of tools and equipment needed to do a job.
Repairing	Repairing machines or systems using the needed tools.
Equipment Maintenance	Performing routine maintenance on equipment and determining when and what kind of maintenance is needed.
Mathematics	Using mathematics to solve problems.
Quality Control Analysis	Conducting tests and inspections of products, services, or processes to evaluate quality or performance.
Service Orientation	Actively looking for ways to help people.
Complex Problem Solving	Identifying complex problems and reviewing related information to develop and evaluate options and implement solutions.
Judgment and Decision Making	Considering the relative costs and benefits of potential actions to choose the most appropriate one.
Writing	Communicating effectively in writing as appropriate for the needs of the audience.
Systems Analysis	Determining how a system should work and how changes in conditions, operations, and the environment will affect outcomes.
Social Perceptiveness	Being aware of others' reactions and understanding why they react as they do.
Critical Thinking	Using logic and reasoning to identify the strengths and weaknesses of alternative solutions, conclusions or approaches to problems.
Systems Evaluation	Identifying measures or indicators of system performance and the actions needed to improve or correct performance, relative to the goals of the system.
Management of Personnel Resources	Motivating, developing, and directing people as they work, identifying the best people for the job.
Persuasion	Persuading others to change their minds or behavior.
Management of Material Resources	Obtaining and seeing to the appropriate use of equipment, facilities, and materials needed to do certain work.
Science	Using scientific rules and methods to solve problems.
Negotiation	Bringing others together and trying to reconcile differences.
Operations Analysis	Analyzing needs and product requirements to create a design.
Technology Design	Generating or adapting equipment and technology to serve user needs.
Installation	Installing equipment, machines, wiring, or programs to meet specifications.
Programming	Writing computer programs for various purposes.
Management of Financial Resources	Determining how money will be spent to get the work done, and accounting for these expenditures.

Ability	Ability Definitions
Control Precision	The ability to quickly and repeatedly adjust the controls of a machine or a vehicle to exact positions.
Problem Sensitivity	The ability to tell when something is wrong or is likely to go wrong. It does not involve solving the problem, only recognizing there is a problem.
Near Vision	The ability to see details at close range (within a few feet of the observer).
Selective Attention	The ability to concentrate on a task over a period of time without being distracted.
Oral Comprehension	The ability to listen to and understand information and ideas presented through spoken words and sentences.
Oral Expression	The ability to communicate information and ideas in speaking so others will understand.
Perceptual Speed	The ability to quickly and accurately compare similarities and differences among sets of letters, numbers, objects, pictures, or patterns. The things to be compared may be presented at the same time or one after the other. This ability also includes comparing a presented object with a remembered object.
Information Ordering	The ability to arrange things or actions in a certain order or pattern according to a specific rule or set of rules (e.g., patterns of numbers, letters, words, pictures, mathematical operations).

Speech Recognition	The ability to identify and understand the speech of another person.
Written Comprehension	The ability to read and understand information and ideas presented in writing.
Multilimb Coordination	The ability to coordinate two or more limbs (for example, two arms, two legs, or one leg and one arm) while sitting, standing, or lying down. It does not involve performing the activities while the whole body is in motion.
Reaction Time	The ability to quickly respond (with the hand, finger, or foot) to a signal (sound, light, picture) when it appears.
Arm-Hand Steadiness	The ability to keep your hand and arm steady while moving your arm or while holding your arm and hand in one position.
Manual Dexterity	The ability to quickly move your hand, your hand together with your arm, or your two hands to grasp, manipulate, or assemble objects.
Written Expression	The ability to communicate information and ideas in writing so others will understand.
Speech Clarity	The ability to speak clearly so others can understand you.
Inductive Reasoning	The ability to combine pieces of information to form general rules or conclusions (includes finding a relationship among seemingly unrelated events).
Trunk Strength	The ability to use your abdominal and lower back muscles to support part of the body repeatedly or continuously over time without 'giving out' or fatiguing.
Static Strength	The ability to exert maximum muscle force to lift, push, pull, or carry objects.
Gross Body Equilibrium	The ability to keep or regain your body balance or stay upright when in an unstable position.
Category Flexibility	The ability to generate or use different sets of rules for combining or grouping things in different ways.
Extent Flexibility	The ability to bend, stretch, twist, or reach with your body, arms, and/or legs.
Deductive Reasoning	The ability to apply general rules to specific problems to produce answers that make sense.
Auditory Attention	The ability to focus on a single source of sound in the presence of other distracting sounds.
Finger Dexterity	The ability to make precisely coordinated movements of the fingers of one or both hands to grasp, manipulate, or assemble very small objects.
Flexibility of Closure	The ability to identify or detect a known pattern (a figure, object, word, or sound) that is hidden in other distracting material.
Rate Control	The ability to time your movements or the movement of a piece of equipment in anticipation of changes in the speed and/or direction of a moving object or scene.
Depth Perception	The ability to judge which of several objects is closer or farther away from you, or to judge the distance between you and an object.
Mathematical Reasoning	The ability to choose the right mathematical methods or formulas to solve a problem.
Gross Body Coordination	The ability to coordinate the movement of your arms, legs, and torso together when the whole body is in motion.
Stamina	The ability to exert yourself physically over long periods of time without getting winded or out of breath.
Dynamic Strength	The ability to exert muscle force repeatedly or continuously over time. This involves muscular endurance and resistance to muscle fatigue.
Time Sharing	The ability to shift back and forth between two or more activities or sources of information (such as speech, sounds, touch, or other sources).
Response Orientation	The ability to choose quickly between two or more movements in response to two or more different signals (lights, sounds, pictures). It includes the speed with which the correct response is started with the hand, foot, or other body part.
Number Facility	The ability to add, subtract, multiply, or divide quickly and correctly.
Far Vision	The ability to see details at a distance.
Visual Color Discrimination	The ability to match or detect differences between colors, including shades of color and brightness.
Wrist-Finger Speed	The ability to make fast, simple, repeated movements of the fingers, hands, and wrists.
Speed of Limb Movement	The ability to quickly move the arms and legs.
Fluency of Ideas	The ability to come up with a number of ideas about a topic (the number of ideas is important, not their quality, correctness, or creativity).
Visualization	The ability to imagine how something will look after it is moved around or when its parts are moved or rearranged.
Hearing Sensitivity	The ability to detect or tell the differences between sounds that vary in pitch and loudness.
Originality	The ability to come up with unusual or clever ideas about a given topic or situation, or to develop creative ways to solve a problem.
Memorization	The ability to remember information such as words, numbers, pictures, and procedures.
Speed of Closure	The ability to quickly make sense of, combine, and organize information into meaningful patterns.
Spatial Orientation	The ability to know your location in relation to the environment or to know where other objects are in relation to you.
Dynamic Flexibility	The ability to quickly and repeatedly bend, stretch, twist, or reach out with your body, arms, and/or legs.
Peripheral Vision	The ability to see objects or movement of objects to one's side when the eyes are looking ahead.
Night Vision	The ability to see under low light conditions.
Glare Sensitivity	The ability to see objects in the presence of glare or bright lighting.
Sound Localization	The ability to tell the direction from which a sound originated.
Explosive Strength	The ability to use short bursts of muscle force to propel oneself (as in jumping or sprinting), or to throw an object.

Work_Activity	Work_Activity Definitions
Controlling Machines and Processes	Using either control mechanisms or direct physical activity to operate machines or processes (not including computers or vehicles).
Performing General Physical Activities	Performing physical activities that require considerable use of your arms and legs and moving your whole body, such as climbing, lifting, balancing, walking, stooping, and handling of materials.
Communicating with Supervisors, Peers, or Subordin	Providing information to supervisors, co-workers, and subordinates by telephone, in written form, e-mail, or in person.
Documenting/Recording Information	Entering, transcribing, recording, storing, or maintaining information in written or electronic/magnetic form.
Handling and Moving Objects	Using hands and arms in handling, installing, positioning, and moving materials, and manipulating things.
Monitor Processes, Materials, or Surroundings	Monitoring and reviewing information from materials, events, or the environment, to detect or assess problems.
Inspecting Equipment, Structures, or Material	Inspecting equipment, structures, or materials to identify the cause of errors or other problems or defects.
Getting Information	Observing, receiving, and otherwise obtaining information from all relevant sources.
Operating Vehicles, Mechanized Devices, or Equipme	Running, maneuvering, navigating, or driving vehicles or mechanized equipment, such as forklifts, passenger vehicles, aircraft, or water craft.
Coaching and Developing Others	Identifying the developmental needs of others and coaching, mentoring, or otherwise helping others to improve their knowledge or skills.
Interacting With Computers	Using computers and computer systems (including hardware and software) to program, write software, set up functions, enter data, or process information.
Coordinating the Work and Activities of Others	Getting members of a group to work together to accomplish tasks.
Establishing and Maintaining Interpersonal Relatio	Developing constructive and cooperative working relationships with others, and maintaining them over time.
Processing Information	Compiling, coding, categorizing, calculating, tabulating, auditing, or verifying information or data.
Training and Teaching Others	Identifying the educational needs of others, developing formal educational or training programs or classes, and teaching or instructing others.
Developing and Building Teams	Encouraging and building mutual trust, respect, and cooperation among team members.
Making Decisions and Solving Problems	Analyzing information and evaluating results to choose the best solution and solve problems.
Identifying Objects, Actions, and Events	Identifying information by categorizing, estimating, recognizing differences or similarities, and detecting changes in circumstances or events.
Evaluating Information to Determine Compliance wit	Using relevant information and individual judgment to determine whether events or processes comply with laws, regulations, or standards.
Organizing, Planning, and Prioritizing Work	Developing specific goals and plans to prioritize, organize, and accomplish your work.
Updating and Using Relevant Knowledge	Keeping up-to-date technically and applying new knowledge to your job.
Judging the Qualities of Things, Services, or Peop	Assessing the value, importance, or quality of things or people.
Provide Consultation and Advice to Others	Providing guidance and expert advice to management or other groups on technical, systems-, or process-related topics.

Assisting and Caring for Others	Providing personal assistance, medical attention, emotional support, or other personal care to others such as coworkers, customers, or patients.
Interpreting the Meaning of Information for Others	Translating or explaining what information means and how it can be used.
Monitoring and Controlling Resources	Monitoring and controlling resources and overseeing the spending of money.
Analyzing Data or Information	Identifying the underlying principles, reasons, or facts of information by breaking down information or data into separate parts.
Performing Administrative Activities	Performing day-to-day administrative tasks such as maintaining information files and processing paperwork.
Thinking Creatively	Developing, designing, or creating new applications, ideas, relationships, systems, or products, including artistic contributions.
Resolving Conflicts and Negotiating with Others	Handling complaints, settling disputes, and resolving grievances and conflicts, or otherwise negotiating with others.
Repairing and Maintaining Electronic Equipment	Servicing, repairing, calibrating, regulating, fine-tuning, or testing machines, devices, and equipment that operate primarily on the basis of electrical or electronic (not mechanical) principles.
Estimating the Quantifiable Characteristics of Pro	Estimating sizes, distances, and quantities; or determining time, costs, resources, or materials needed to perform a work activity.
Selling or Influencing Others	Convincing others to buy merchandise/goods or to otherwise change their minds or actions.
Guiding, Directing, and Motivating Subordinates	Providing guidance and direction to subordinates, including setting performance standards and monitoring performance.
Repairing and Maintaining Mechanical Equipment	Servicing, repairing, adjusting, and testing machines, devices, moving parts, and equipment that operate primarily on the basis of mechanical (not electronic) principles.
Developing Objectives and Strategies	Establishing long-range objectives and specifying the strategies and actions to achieve them.
Scheduling Work and Activities	Scheduling events, programs, and activities, as well as the work of others.
Staffing Organizational Units	Recruiting, interviewing, selecting, hiring, and promoting employees in an organization.
Drafting, Laying Out, and Specifying Technical Dev	Providing documentation, detailed instructions, drawings, or specifications to tell others about how devices, parts, equipment, or structures are to be fabricated, constructed, assembled, modified, or used.
Communicating with Persons Outside Organization	Communicating with people outside the organization, representing the organization to customers, the public, government, and other external sources. This information can be exchanged in person, in writing, or by telephone or e-mail.
Performing for or Working Directly with the Public	Performing for people or dealing directly with the public. This includes serving customers in restaurants and stores, and receiving clients or guests.

Work_Context	**Work_Context Definitions**
Wear Common Protective or Safety Equipment such as	How much does this job require wearing common protective or safety equipment such as safety shoes, glasses, gloves, hard hats or live jackets?
Sounds, Noise Levels Are Distracting or Uncomforta	How often does this job require working exposed to sounds and noise levels that are distracting or uncomfortable?
Exposed to Hazardous Equipment	How often does this job require exposure to hazardous equipment?
Exposed to Contaminants	How often does this job require working exposed to contaminants (such as pollutants, gases, dust or odors)?
Exposed to Hazardous Conditions	How often does this job require exposure to hazardous conditions?
In an Open Vehicle or Equipment	How often does this job require working in an open vehicle or equipment (e.g., tractor)?
Exposed to High Places	How often does this job require exposure to high places?
Importance of Being Exact or Accurate	How important is being very exact or highly accurate in performing this job?
Contact With Others	How much does this job require the worker to be in contact with others (face-to-face, by telephone, or otherwise) in order to perform it?
Responsible for Others' Health and Safety	How much responsibility is there for the health and safety of others in this job?
Exposed to Minor Burns, Cuts, Bites, or Stings	How often does this job require exposure to minor burns, cuts, bites, or stings?
Face-to-Face Discussions	How often do you have to have face-to-face discussions with individuals or teams in this job?
Indoors, Environmentally Controlled	How often does this job require working indoors in environmentally controlled conditions?

Spend Time Using Your Hands to Handle, Control, or	How much does this job require using your hands to handle, control, or feel objects, tools or controls?
Responsibility for Outcomes and Results	How responsible is the worker for work outcomes and results of other workers?
Coordinate or Lead Others	How important is it to coordinate or lead others in accomplishing work activities in this job?
Structured versus Unstructured Work	To what extent is this job structured for the worker, rather than allowing the worker to determine tasks, priorities, and goals?
Telephone	How often do you have telephone conversations in this job?
Deal With Unpleasant or Angry People	How frequently does the worker have to deal with unpleasant, angry, or discourteous individuals as part of the job requirements?
Spend Time Standing	How much does this job require standing?
Very Hot or Cold Temperatures	How often does this job require working in very hot (above 90 F degrees) or very cold (below 32 F degrees) temperatures?
Spend Time Walking and Running	How much does this job require walking and running?
Spend Time Bending or Twisting the Body	How much does this job require bending or twisting your body?
Pace Determined by Speed of Equipment	How important is it to this job that the pace is determined by the speed of equipment or machinery? (This does not refer to keeping busy at all times on this job.)
Consequence of Error	How serious would the result usually be if the worker made a mistake that was not readily correctable?
Frequency of Conflict Situations	How often are there conflict situations the employee has to face in this job?
Freedom to Make Decisions	How much decision making freedom, without supervision, does the job offer?
Importance of Repeating Same Tasks	How important is repeating the same physical activities (e.g., key entry) or mental activities (e.g., checking entries in a ledger) over and over, without stopping, to performing this job?
Cramped Work Space, Awkward Positions	How often does this job require working in cramped work spaces that requires getting into awkward positions?
Time Pressure	How often does this job require the worker to meet strict deadlines?
Work With Work Group or Team	How important is it to work with others in a group or team in this job?
Physical Proximity	To what extent does this job require the worker to perform job tasks in close physical proximity to other people?
Spend Time Making Repetitive Motions	How much does this job require making repetitive motions?
Wear Specialized Protective or Safety Equipment su	How much does this job require wearing specialized protective or safety equipment such as breathing apparatus, safety harness, full protection suits, or radiation protection?
Impact of Decisions on Co-workers or Company Resul	How do the decisions an employee makes impact the results of co-workers, clients or the company?
Indoors, Not Environmentally Controlled	How often does this job require working indoors in non-controlled environmental conditions (e.g., warehouse without heat)?
Level of Competition	To what extent does this job require the worker to compete or to be aware of competitive pressures?
Spend Time Keeping or Regaining Balance	How much does this job require keeping or regaining your balance?
Frequency of Decision Making	How frequently is the worker required to make decisions that affect other people, the financial resources, and/or the image and reputation of the organization?
Degree of Automation	How automated is the job?
Letters and Memos	How often does the job require written letters and memos?
Extremely Bright or Inadequate Lighting	How often does this job require working in extremely bright or inadequate lighting conditions?
Outdoors, Exposed to Weather	How often does this job require working outdoors, exposed to all weather conditions?
Outdoors, Under Cover	How often does this job require working outdoors, under cover (e.g., structure with roof but no walls)?
Spend Time Climbing Ladders, Scaffolds, or Poles	How much does this job require climbing ladders, scaffolds, or poles?
Spend Time Sitting	How much does this job require sitting?
In an Enclosed Vehicle or Equipment	How often does this job require working in a closed vehicle or equipment (e.g., car)?
Deal With Physically Aggressive People	How frequently does this job require the worker to deal with physical aggression of violent individuals?
Spend Time Kneeling, Crouching, Stooping, or Crawl	How much does this job require kneeling, crouching, stooping, or crawling?
Electronic Mail	How often do you use electronic mail in this job?

Deal With External Customers	How important is it to work with external customers or the public in this job?
Exposed to Radiation	How often does this job require exposure to radiation?
Exposed to Whole Body Vibration	How often does this job require exposure to whole body vibration (e.g., operate a jackhammer)?
Public Speaking	How often do you have to perform public speaking in this job?
Exposed to Disease or Infections	How often does this job require exposure to disease/infections?

Job Zone Component	Job Zone Component Definitions
Title	Job Zone Two: Some Preparation Needed
Overall Experience	Some previous work-related skill, knowledge, or experience may be helpful in these occupations, but usually is not needed. For example, a drywall installer might benefit from experience installing drywall, but an inexperienced person could still learn to be an installer with little difficulty.
Job Training	Employees in these occupations need anywhere from a few months to one year of working with experienced employees.
Job Zone Examples	These occupations often involve using your knowledge and skills to help others. Examples include drywall installers, fire inspectors, flight attendants, pharmacy technicians, salespersons (retail), and tellers.
SVP Range	(4.0 to < 6.0)
Education	These occupations usually require a high school diploma and may require some vocational training or job-related course work. In some cases, an associate's or bachelor's degree could be needed.

Work_Styles	Work_Styles Definitions
Dependability	Job requires being reliable, responsible, and dependable, and fulfilling obligations.
Attention to Detail	Job requires being careful about detail and thorough in completing work tasks.
Independence	Job requires developing one's own ways of doing things, guiding oneself with little or no supervision, and depending on oneself to get things done.
Cooperation	Job requires being pleasant with others on the job and displaying a good-natured, cooperative attitude.
Integrity	Job requires being honest and ethical.
Adaptability/Flexibility	Job requires being open to change (positive or negative) and to considerable variety in the workplace.
Leadership	Job requires a willingness to lead, take charge, and offer opinions and direction.
Self Control	Job requires maintaining composure, keeping emotions in check, controlling anger, and avoiding aggressive behavior, even in very difficult situations.
Initiative	Job requires a willingness to take on responsibilities and challenges.
Persistence	Job requires persistence in the face of obstacles.
Analytical Thinking	Job requires analyzing information and using logic to address work-related issues and problems.
Innovation	Job requires creativity and alternative thinking to develop new ideas for and answers to work-related problems.
Achievement/Effort	Job requires establishing and maintaining personally challenging achievement goals and exerting effort toward mastering tasks.
Concern for Others	Job requires being sensitive to others' needs and feelings and being understanding and helpful on the job.
Social Orientation	Job requires preferring to work with others rather than alone, and being personally connected with others on the job.
Stress Tolerance	Job requires accepting criticism and dealing calmly and effectively with high stress situations.

51-9082.00 - Medical Appliance Technicians

Construct, fit, maintain, or repair medical supportive devices, such as braces, artificial limbs, joints, arch supports, and other surgical and medical appliances.

Tasks

1) Lay out and mark dimensions of parts, using templates and precision measuring instruments.

2) Bend, form, and shape fabric or material so that it conforms to prescribed contours needed to fabricate structural components.

3) Fit appliances onto patients, and make any necessary adjustments.

4) Read prescriptions or specifications in order to determine the type of product or device to be fabricated, and the materials and tools that will be required.

5) Cover or pad metal or plastic structures and devices, using coverings such as rubber, leather, felt, plastic, or fiberglass.

6) Construct or receive casts or impressions of patients' torsos or limbs for use as cutting and fabrication patterns.

7) Instruct patients in use of prosthetic or orthotic devices.

8) Test medical supportive devices for proper alignment, movement, and biomechanical stability, using meters and alignment fixtures.

9) Polish artificial limbs, braces, and supports, using grinding and buffing wheels.

10) Mix pigments to match patients' skin coloring, according to formulas, and apply mixtures to orthotic or prosthetic devices.

11) Service and repair machinery used in the fabrication of appliances.

12) Make orthotic/prosthetic devices using materials such as thermoplastic and thermosetting materials, metal alloys and leather, and hand and power tools.

13) Take patients' body or limb measurements for use in device construction.

14) Repair, modify, and maintain medical supportive devices, such as artificial limbs, braces, and surgical supports, according to specifications.

51-9083.01 - Precision Lens Grinders and Polishers

Set up and operate variety of machines and equipment to grind and polish lens and other optical elements.

Tasks

1) Adjust lenses and frames in order to correct alignment.

2) Clean finished lenses and eyeglasses, using cloths and solvents.

3) Position and adjust cutting tools to specified curvature, dimensions, and depth of cut.

4) Examine prescriptions, work orders, or broken or used eyeglasses in order to determine specifications for lenses, contact lenses, and other optical elements.

5) Inspect lens blanks in order to detect flaws, verify smoothness of surface, and ensure thickness of coating on lenses.

6) Inspect, weigh, and measure mounted or unmounted lenses after completion in order to verify alignment and conformance to specifications, using precision instruments.

7) Mount and secure lens blanks or optical lenses in holding tools or chucks of cutting, polishing, grinding, or coating machines.

8) Mount, secure, and align finished lenses in frames or optical assemblies, using precision hand tools.

9) Control equipment that coats lenses to alter their reflective qualities.

10) Repair broken parts, using precision hand tools and soldering irons.

11) Lay out lenses and trace lens outlines on glass, using templates.

12) Remove lenses from molds, and separate lenses in containers for further processing or storage.

13) Select lens blanks, molds, tools, and polishing or grinding wheels, according to production specifications.

14) Set dials and start machines to polish lenses, or hold lenses against rotating wheels in order to polish them manually.

15) Set up machines to polish, bevel, edge, and grind lenses, flats, blanks, and other precision optical elements.

16) Shape lenses appropriately so that they can be inserted into frames.

17) Assemble eyeglass frames and attach shields, nose pads, and temple pieces, using pliers, screwdrivers, and drills.

18) Assemble molds used to cast contact lenses.

51-9083.02 - Optical Instrument Assemblers

Assemble optical instruments, such as telescopes, level-transits, and gunsights.

Tasks

1) Insert and screw locking rings into housings in order to hold elements in place; apply cement to locking rings in order to prevent loosening.

2) Record production, inspection, and test data in logs.

3) Paint parts, using brushes and spray guns.

4) Compute sighting instrument distances, using trigonometric formulas.

5) Study work orders, blueprints, and sketches in order to formulate plans and sequences for fabricating optical elements, instruments, and systems.

6) Sight instruments on targets, and read dials in order to determine optical centers of instrument lenses and to verify compliance to focusing power specifications.

7) Position targets in darkroom tunnels, and connect optical instruments to test devices, such as oscilloscopes and collimators.

8) Clean elements and parts, using tissue, cleaning solutions, and air compressors.

9) Fill instrument housings with nitrogen gas in order to minimize corrosive effects on internal optical surfaces, using vacuum pumps.

10) Cement multiple lens assemblies together.

11) Pick up elements, using vacuum-holding devices, and position elements in mounting seats of instrument housings.

12) Mix holding compounds, and mount workpieces or optical elements on holding fixtures.

13) Measure elements and instrument parts in order to verify dimensional specifications, using precision measuring instruments.

14) Measure and mark dimensions and reference points, and lay out stock for machining.

15) Grind and polish optics, using hand tools and polishing cloths.

16) Set up and operate machines in order to assemble structural, mechanical, and optical parts of instruments.

51-9111.00 - Packaging and Filling Machine Operators and Tenders

Operate or tend machines to prepare industrial or consumer products for storage or shipment. Includes cannery workers who pack food products.

Tasks

1) Start machine by engaging controls.

2) Regulate machine flow, speed, or temperature.

3) Stop or reset machines when malfunctions occur, clear machine jams, and report malfunctions to a supervisor.

4) Stock and sort product for packaging or filling machine operation, and replenish packaging supplies, such as wrapping paper, plastic sheet, boxes, cartons, glue, ink, or labels.

5) Supply materials to spindles, conveyors, hoppers, or other feeding devices and unload packaged product.

6) Package the product in the form in which it will be sent out, for example, filling bags with flour from a chute or spout.

7) Count and record finished and rejected packaged items.

8) Monitor the production line, watching for problems such as pile-ups, jams, or glue that isn't sticking properly.

9) Adjust machine components and machine tension and pressure according to size or processing angle of product.

10) Stack finished packaged items, or wrap protective material around each item and pack the items in cartons or containers.

11) Remove finished packaged items from machine and separate rejected items.

12) Sort, grade, weigh, and inspect products, verifying and adjusting product weight or measurement to meet specifications.

13) Clean, oil, and make minor adjustments or repairs to machinery and equipment, such as

opening valves or setting guides.

14) Tend or operate machine that packages product.

15) Secure finished packaged items by hand tying, sewing, gluing, stapling, or attaching fastener.

16) Attach identification labels to finished packaged items, or cut stencils and stencil information on containers, such as lot numbers or shipping destinations.

17) Clean and remove damaged or otherwise inferior materials to prepare raw products for processing.

18) Clean packaging containers, line and pad crates, and/or assemble cartons to prepare for product packing.

19) Inspect and remove defective products and packaging material.

Knowledge	Knowledge Definitions
Production and Processing	Knowledge of raw materials, production processes, quality control, costs, and other techniques for maximizing the effective manufacture and distribution of goods.
Customer and Personal Service	Knowledge of principles and processes for providing customer and personal services. This includes customer needs assessment, meeting quality standards for services, and evaluation of customer satisfaction.
Mechanical	Knowledge of machines and tools, including their designs, uses, repair, and maintenance.
Computers and Electronics	Knowledge of circuit boards, processors, chips, electronic equipment, and computer hardware and software, including applications and programming.
Communications and Media	Knowledge of media production, communication, and dissemination techniques and methods. This includes alternative ways to inform and entertain via written, oral, and visual media.
Education and Training	Knowledge of principles and methods for curriculum and training design, teaching and instruction for individuals and groups, and the measurement of training effects.
English Language	Knowledge of the structure and content of the English language including the meaning and spelling of words, rules of composition, and grammar.
Public Safety and Security	Knowledge of relevant equipment, policies, procedures, and strategies to promote effective local, state, or national security operations for the protection of people, data, property, and institutions.
Psychology	Knowledge of human behavior and performance; individual differences in ability, personality, and interests; learning and motivation; psychological research methods; and the assessment and treatment of behavioral and affective disorders.
Sociology and Anthropology	Knowledge of group behavior and dynamics, societal trends and influences, human migrations, ethnicity, cultures and their history and origins.
Engineering and Technology	Knowledge of the practical application of engineering science and technology. This includes applying principles, techniques, procedures, and equipment to the design and production of various goods and services.
Administration and Management	Knowledge of business and management principles involved in strategic planning, resource allocation, human resources modeling, leadership technique, production methods, and coordination of people and resources.
Personnel and Human Resources	Knowledge of principles and procedures for personnel recruitment, selection, training, compensation and benefits, labor relations and negotiation, and personnel information systems.
Physics	Knowledge and prediction of physical principles, laws, their interrelationships, and applications to understanding fluid, material, and atmospheric dynamics, and mechanical, electrical, atomic and sub-atomic structures and processes.
Mathematics	Knowledge of arithmetic, algebra, geometry, calculus, statistics, and their applications.
Clerical	Knowledge of administrative and clerical procedures and systems such as word processing, managing files and records, stenography and transcription, designing forms, and other office procedures and terminology.
Chemistry	Knowledge of the chemical composition, structure, and properties of substances and of the chemical processes and transformations that they undergo. This includes uses of chemicals and their interactions, danger signs, production techniques, and disposal methods.

Law and Government	Knowledge of laws, legal codes, court procedures, precedents, government regulations, executive orders, agency rules, and the democratic political process.
Transportation	Knowledge of principles and methods for moving people or goods by air, rail, sea, or road, including the relative costs and benefits.
Sales and Marketing	Knowledge of principles and methods for showing, promoting, and selling products or services. This includes marketing strategy and tactics, product demonstration, sales techniques, and sales control systems.
Food Production	Knowledge of techniques and equipment for planting, growing, and harvesting food products (both plant and animal) for consumption, including storage/handling techniques.
Design	Knowledge of design techniques, tools, and principles involved in production of precision technical plans, blueprints, drawings, and models.
Telecommunications	Knowledge of transmission, broadcasting, switching, control, and operation of telecommunications systems.
Medicine and Dentistry	Knowledge of the information and techniques needed to diagnose and treat human injuries, diseases, and deformities. This includes symptoms, treatment alternatives, drug properties and interactions, and preventive health-care measures.
Philosophy and Theology	Knowledge of different philosophical systems and religions. This includes their basic principles, values, ethics, ways of thinking, customs, practices, and their impact on human culture.
Building and Construction	Knowledge of materials, methods, and the tools involved in the construction or repair of houses, buildings, or other structures such as highways and roads.
Economics and Accounting	Knowledge of economic and accounting principles and practices, the financial markets, banking and the analysis and reporting of financial data.
Geography	Knowledge of principles and methods for describing the features of land, sea, and air masses, including their physical characteristics, locations, interrelationships, and distribution of plant, animal, and human life.
Therapy and Counseling	Knowledge of principles, methods, and procedures for diagnosis, treatment, and rehabilitation of physical and mental dysfunctions, and for career counseling and guidance.
Foreign Language	Knowledge of the structure and content of a foreign (non-English) language including the meaning and spelling of words, rules of composition and grammar, and pronunciation.
Biology	Knowledge of plant and animal organisms, their tissues, cells, functions, interdependencies, and interactions with each other and the environment.
Fine Arts	Knowledge of the theory and techniques required to compose, produce, and perform works of music, dance, visual arts, drama, and sculpture.
History and Archeology	Knowledge of historical events and their causes, indicators, and effects on civilizations and cultures.

Skills	**Skills Definitions**
Reading Comprehension	Understanding written sentences and paragraphs in work related documents.
Quality Control Analysis	Conducting tests and inspections of products, services, or processes to evaluate quality or performance.
Operation and Control	Controlling operations of equipment or systems.
Active Listening	Giving full attention to what other people are saying, taking time to understand the points being made, asking questions as appropriate, and not interrupting at inappropriate times.
Instructing	Teaching others how to do something.
Equipment Maintenance	Performing routine maintenance on equipment and determining when and what kind of maintenance is needed.
Coordination	Adjusting actions in relation to others' actions.
Troubleshooting	Determining causes of operating errors and deciding what to do about it.
Time Management	Managing one's own time and the time of others.
Judgment and Decision Making	Considering the relative costs and benefits of potential actions to choose the most appropriate one.
Operation Monitoring	Watching gauges, dials, or other indicators to make sure a machine is working properly.
Learning Strategies	Selecting and using training/instructional methods and procedures appropriate for the situation when learning or teaching new things.
Equipment Selection	Determining the kind of tools and equipment needed to do a job.

Monitoring	Monitoring/Assessing performance of yourself, other individuals, or organizations to make improvements or take corrective action.
Critical Thinking	Using logic and reasoning to identify the strengths and weaknesses of alternative solutions, conclusions or approaches to problems.
Active Learning	Understanding the implications of new information for both current and future problem-solving and decision-making.
Repairing	Repairing machines or systems using the needed tools.
Writing	Communicating effectively in writing as appropriate for the needs of the audience.
Service Orientation	Actively looking for ways to help people.
Management of Personnel Resources	Motivating, developing, and directing people as they work, identifying the best people for the job.
Installation	Installing equipment, machines, wiring, or programs to meet specifications.
Complex Problem Solving	Identifying complex problems and reviewing related information to develop and evaluate options and implement solutions.
Speaking	Talking to others to convey information effectively.
Negotiation	Bringing others together and trying to reconcile differences.
Persuasion	Persuading others to change their minds or behavior.
Mathematics	Using mathematics to solve problems.
Social Perceptiveness	Being aware of others' reactions and understanding why they react as they do.
Management of Material Resources	Obtaining and seeing to the appropriate use of equipment, facilities, and materials needed to do certain work.
Technology Design	Generating or adapting equipment and technology to serve user needs.
Systems Evaluation	Identifying measures or indicators of system performance and the actions needed to improve or correct performance, relative to the goals of the system.
Operations Analysis	Analyzing needs and product requirements to create a design.
Science	Using scientific rules and methods to solve problems.
Systems Analysis	Determining how a system should work and how changes in conditions, operations, and the environment will affect outcomes.
Management of Financial Resources	Determining how money will be spent to get the work done, and accounting for these expenditures.
Programming	Writing computer programs for various purposes.

Ability	**Ability Definitions**
Manual Dexterity	The ability to quickly move your hand, your hand together with your arm, or your two hands to grasp, manipulate, or assemble objects.
Control Precision	The ability to quickly and repeatedly adjust the controls of a machine or a vehicle to exact positions.
Perceptual Speed	The ability to quickly and accurately compare similarities and differences among sets of letters, numbers, objects, pictures, or patterns. The things to be compared may be presented at the same time or one after the other. This ability also includes comparing a presented object with a remembered object.
Near Vision	The ability to see details at close range (within a few feet of the observer).
Problem Sensitivity	The ability to tell when something is wrong or is likely to go wrong. It does not involve solving the problem, only recognizing there is a problem.
Selective Attention	The ability to concentrate on a task over a period of time without being distracted.
Information Ordering	The ability to arrange things or actions in a certain order or pattern according to a specific rule or set of rules (e.g., patterns of numbers, letters, words, pictures, mathematical operations).
Reaction Time	The ability to quickly respond (with the hand, finger, or foot) to a signal (sound, light, picture) when it appears.
Static Strength	The ability to exert maximum muscle force to lift, push, pull, or carry objects.
Arm-Hand Steadiness	The ability to keep your hand and arm steady while moving your arm or while holding your arm and hand in one position.
Inductive Reasoning	The ability to combine pieces of information to form general rules or conclusions (includes finding a relationship among seemingly unrelated events).
Response Orientation	The ability to choose quickly between two or more movements in response to two or more different signals (lights, sounds, pictures). It includes the speed with which the correct response is started with the hand, foot, or other body part.

Ability	Definition
Flexibility of Closure	The ability to identify or detect a known pattern (a figure, object, word, or sound) that is hidden in other distracting material.
Extent Flexibility	The ability to bend, stretch, twist, or reach with your body, arms, and/or legs.
Deductive Reasoning	The ability to apply general rules to specific problems to produce answers that make sense.
Finger Dexterity	The ability to make precisely coordinated movements of the fingers of one or both hands to grasp, manipulate, or assemble very small objects.
Trunk Strength	The ability to use your abdominal and lower back muscles to support part of the body repeatedly or continuously over time without 'giving out' or fatiguing.
Multilimb Coordination	The ability to coordinate two or more limbs (for example, two arms, two legs, or one leg and one arm) while sitting, standing, or lying down. It does not involve performing the activities while the whole body is in motion.
Written Comprehension	The ability to read and understand information and ideas presented in writing.
Oral Comprehension	The ability to listen to and understand information and ideas presented through spoken words and sentences.
Category Flexibility	The ability to generate or use different sets of rules for combining or grouping things in different ways.
Far Vision	The ability to see details at a distance.
Depth Perception	The ability to judge which of several objects is closer or farther away from you, or to judge the distance between you and an object.
Visual Color Discrimination	The ability to match or detect differences between colors, including shades of color and brightness.
Number Facility	The ability to add, subtract, multiply, or divide quickly and correctly.
Hearing Sensitivity	The ability to detect or tell the differences between sounds that vary in pitch and loudness.
Visualization	The ability to imagine how something will look after it is moved around or when its parts are moved or rearranged.
Oral Expression	The ability to communicate information and ideas in speaking so others will understand.
Speed of Closure	The ability to quickly make sense of, combine, and organize information into meaningful patterns.
Rate Control	The ability to time your movements or the movement of a piece of equipment in anticipation of changes in the speed and/or direction of a moving object or scene.
Speech Recognition	The ability to identify and understand the speech of another person.
Stamina	The ability to exert yourself physically over long periods of time without getting winded or out of breath.
Wrist-Finger Speed	The ability to make fast, simple, repeated movements of the fingers, hands, and wrists.
Auditory Attention	The ability to focus on a single source of sound in the presence of other distracting sounds.
Speed of Limb Movement	The ability to quickly move the arms and legs.
Dynamic Strength	The ability to exert muscle force repeatedly or continuously over time. This involves muscular endurance and resistance to muscle fatigue.
Speech Clarity	The ability to speak clearly so others can understand you.
Memorization	The ability to remember information such as words, numbers, pictures, and procedures.
Time Sharing	The ability to shift back and forth between two or more activities or sources of information (such as speech, sounds, touch, or other sources).
Written Expression	The ability to communicate information and ideas in writing so others will understand.
Peripheral Vision	The ability to see objects or movement of objects to one's side when the eyes are looking ahead.
Originality	The ability to come up with unusual or clever ideas about a given topic or situation, or to develop creative ways to solve a problem.
Spatial Orientation	The ability to know your location in relation to the environment or to know where other objects are in relation to you.
Fluency of Ideas	The ability to come up with a number of ideas about a topic (the number of ideas is important, not their quality, correctness, or creativity).
Gross Body Coordination	The ability to coordinate the movement of your arms, legs, and torso together when the whole body is in motion.
Gross Body Equilibrium	The ability to keep or regain your body balance or stay upright when in an unstable position.
Mathematical Reasoning	The ability to choose the right mathematical methods or formulas to solve a problem.

Ability	Definition
Sound Localization	The ability to tell the direction from which a sound originated.
Dynamic Flexibility	The ability to quickly and repeatedly bend, stretch, twist, or reach out with your body, arms, and/or legs.
Night Vision	The ability to see under low light conditions.
Glare Sensitivity	The ability to see objects in the presence of glare or bright lighting.
Explosive Strength	The ability to use short bursts of muscle force to propel oneself (as in jumping or sprinting), or to throw an object.

Work_Activity	Work_Activity Definitions
Communicating with Supervisors, Peers, or Subordin	Providing information to supervisors, co-workers, and subordinates by telephone, in written form, e-mail, or in person.
Controlling Machines and Processes	Using either control mechanisms or direct physical activity to operate machines or processes (not including computers or vehicles).
Inspecting Equipment, Structures, or Material	Inspecting equipment, structures, or materials to identify the cause of errors or other problems or defects.
Making Decisions and Solving Problems	Analyzing information and evaluating results to choose the best solution and solve problems.
Evaluating Information to Determine Compliance wit	Using relevant information and individual judgment to determine whether events or processes comply with laws, regulations, or standards.
Scheduling Work and Activities	Scheduling events, programs, and activities, as well as the work of others.
Handling and Moving Objects	Using hands and arms in handling, installing, positioning, and moving materials, and manipulating things.
Repairing and Maintaining Mechanical Equipment	Servicing, repairing, adjusting, and testing machines, devices, moving parts, and equipment that operate primarily on the basis of mechanical (not electronic) principles.
Performing General Physical Activities	Performing physical activities that require considerable use of your arms and legs and moving your whole body, such as climbing, lifting, balancing, walking, stooping, and handling of materials.
Operating Vehicles, Mechanized Devices, or Equipme	Running, maneuvering, navigating, or driving vehicles or mechanized equipment, such as forklifts, passenger vehicles, aircraft, or water craft.
Thinking Creatively	Developing, designing, or creating new applications, ideas, relationships, systems, or products, including artistic contributions.
Updating and Using Relevant Knowledge	Keeping up-to-date technically and applying new knowledge to your job.
Getting Information	Observing, receiving, and otherwise obtaining information from all relevant sources.
Identifying Objects, Actions, and Events	Identifying information by categorizing, estimating, recognizing differences or similarities, and detecting changes in circumstances or events.
Processing Information	Compiling, coding, categorizing, calculating, tabulating, auditing, or verifying information or data.
Organizing, Planning, and Prioritizing Work	Developing specific goals and plans to prioritize, organize, and accomplish your work.
Repairing and Maintaining Electronic Equipment	Servicing, repairing, calibrating, regulating, fine-tuning, or testing machines, devices, and equipment that operate primarily on the basis of electrical or electronic (not mechanical) principles.
Analyzing Data or Information	Identifying the underlying principles, reasons, or facts of information by breaking down information or data into separate parts.
Estimating the Quantifiable Characteristics of Pro	Estimating sizes, distances, and quantities; or determining time, costs, resources, or materials needed to perform a work activity.
Developing Objectives and Strategies	Establishing long-range objectives and specifying the strategies and actions to achieve them.
Documenting/Recording Information	Entering, transcribing, recording, storing, or maintaining information in written or electronic/magnetic form.
Coordinating the Work and Activities of Others	Getting members of a group to work together to accomplish tasks.
Monitor Processes, Materials, or Surroundings	Monitoring and reviewing information from materials, events, or the environment, to detect or assess problems.
Judging the Qualities of Things, Services, or Peop	Assessing the value, importance, or quality of things or people.
Training and Teaching Others	Identifying the educational needs of others, developing formal educational or training programs or classes, and teaching or instructing others.

Establishing and Maintaining Interpersonal Relatio	Developing constructive and cooperative working relationships with others, and maintaining them over time.
Monitoring and Controlling Resources	Monitoring and controlling resources and overseeing the spending of money.
Interpreting the Meaning of Information for Others	Translating or explaining what information means and how it can be used.
Developing and Building Teams	Encouraging and building mutual trust, respect, and cooperation among team members.
Interacting With Computers	Using computers and computer systems (including hardware and software) to program, write software, set up functions, enter data, or process information.
Provide Consultation and Advice to Others	Providing guidance and expert advice to management or other groups on technical, systems-, or process-related topics.
Resolving Conflicts and Negotiating with Others	Handling complaints, settling disputes, and resolving grievances and conflicts, or otherwise negotiating with others.
Assisting and Caring for Others	Providing personal assistance, medical attention, emotional support, or other personal care to others such as coworkers, customers, or patients.
Communicating with Persons Outside Organization	Communicating with people outside the organization, representing the organization to customers, the public, government, and other external sources. This information can be exchanged in person, in writing, or by telephone or e-mail.
Coaching and Developing Others	Identifying the developmental needs of others and coaching, mentoring, or otherwise helping others to improve their knowledge or skills.
Guiding, Directing, and Motivating Subordinates	Providing guidance and direction to subordinates, including setting performance standards and monitoring performance.
Drafting, Laying Out, and Specifying Technical Dev	Providing documentation, detailed instructions, drawings, or specifications to tell others about how devices, parts, equipment, or structures are to be fabricated, constructed, assembled, modified, maintained, or used.
Performing Administrative Activities	Performing day-to-day administrative tasks such as maintaining information files and processing paperwork.
Performing for or Working Directly with the Public	Performing for people or dealing directly with the public. This includes serving customers in restaurants and stores, and receiving clients or guests.
Staffing Organizational Units	Recruiting, interviewing, selecting, hiring, and promoting employees in an organization.
Selling or Influencing Others	Convincing others to buy merchandise/goods or to otherwise change their minds or actions.

Work_Context	Work_Context Definitions
Face-to-Face Discussions	How often do you have to have face-to-face discussions with individuals or teams in this job?
Spend Time Using Your Hands to Handle, Control, or	How much does this job require using your hands to handle, control, or feel objects, tools or controls?
Exposed to Hazardous Equipment	How often does this job require exposure to hazardous equipment?
Spend Time Standing	How much does this job require standing?
Exposed to Contaminants	How often does this job require working exposed to contaminants (such as pollutants, gases, dust or odors)?
Sounds, Noise Levels Are Distracting or Uncomforta	How often does this job require working exposed to sounds and noise levels that are distracting or uncomfortable?
Wear Common Protective or Safety Equipment such as	How much does this job require wearing common protective or safety equipment such as safety shoes, glasses, gloves, hard hats or live jackets?
Spend Time Making Repetitive Motions	How much does this job require making repetitive motions?
Exposed to Hazardous Conditions	How often does this job require exposure to hazardous conditions?
Freedom to Make Decisions	How much decision making freedom, without supervision, does the job offer?
Importance of Being Exact or Accurate	How important is being very exact or highly accurate in performing this job?
Frequency of Decision Making	How frequently is the worker required to make decisions that affect other people, the financial resources, and/or the image and reputation of the organization?
Time Pressure	How often does this job require the worker to meet strict deadlines?
Contact With Others	How much does this job require the worker to be in contact with others (face-to-face, by telephone, or otherwise) in order to perform it?
Spend Time Bending or Twisting the Body	How much does this job require bending or twisting your body?

Indoors, Not Environmentally Controlled	How often does this job require working indoors in non-controlled environmental conditions (e.g., warehouse without heat)?
Impact of Decisions on Co-workers or Company Resul	How do the decisions an employee makes impact the results of co-workers, clients or the company?
Structured versus Unstructured Work	To what extent is this job structured for the worker, rather than allowing the worker to determine tasks, priorities, and goals?
Importance of Repeating Same Tasks	How important is repeating the same physical activities (e.g., key entry) or mental activities (e.g., checking entries in a ledger) over and over, without stopping, to performing this job?
Physical Proximity	To what extent does this job require the worker to perform job tasks in close physical proximity to other people?
Pace Determined by Speed of Equipment	How important is it to this job that the pace is determined by the speed of equipment or machinery? (This does not refer to keeping busy at all times on this job.)
Work With Work Group or Team	How important is it to work with others in a group or team in this job?
Responsible for Others' Health and Safety	How much responsibility is there for the health and safety of others in this job?
Exposed to Minor Burns, Cuts, Bites, or Stings	How often does this job require exposure to minor burns, cuts, bites, or stings?
Degree of Automation	How automated is the job?
Responsibility for Outcomes and Results	How responsible is the worker for work outcomes and results of other workers?
Exposed to High Places	How often does this job require exposure to high places?
Spend Time Walking and Running	How much does this job require walking and running?
Indoors, Environmentally Controlled	How often does this job require working indoors in environmentally controlled conditions?
Telephone	How often do you have telephone conversations in this job?
Coordinate or Lead Others	How important is it to coordinate or lead others in accomplishing work activities in this job?
Consequence of Error	How serious would the result usually be if the worker made a mistake that was not readily correctable?
Very Hot or Cold Temperatures	How often does this job require working in very hot (above 90 F degrees) or very cold (below 32 F degrees) temperatures?
In an Enclosed Vehicle or Equipment	How often does this job require working in a closed vehicle or equipment (e.g., car)?
In an Open Vehicle or Equipment	How often does this job require working in an open vehicle or equipment (e.g., tractor)?
Deal With External Customers	How important is it to work with external customers or the public in this job?
Deal With Unpleasant or Angry People	How frequently does the worker have to deal with unpleasant, angry, or discourteous individuals as part of the job requirements?
Level of Competition	To what extent does this job require the worker to compete or to be aware of competitive pressures?
Spend Time Sitting	How much does this job require sitting?
Letters and Memos	How often does the job require written letters and memos?
Frequency of Conflict Situations	How often are there conflict situations the employee has to face in this job?
Spend Time Climbing Ladders, Scaffolds, or Poles	How much does this job require climbing ladders, scaffolds, or poles?
Wear Specialized Protective or Safety Equipment su	How much does this job require wearing specialized protective or safety equipment such as breathing apparatus, safety harness, full protection suits, or radiation protection?
Outdoors, Under Cover	How often does this job require working outdoors, under cover (e.g., structure with roof but no walls)?
Spend Time Kneeling, Crouching, Stooping, or Crawl	How much does this job require kneeling, crouching, stooping, or crawling?
Exposed to Whole Body Vibration	How often does this job require exposure to whole body vibration (e.g., operate a jackhammer)?
Extremely Bright or Inadequate Lighting	How often does this job require working in extremely bright or inadequate lighting conditions?
Deal With Physically Aggressive People	How frequently does this job require the worker to deal with physical aggression of violent individuals?
Spend Time Keeping or Regaining Balance	How much does this job require keeping or regaining your balance?
Cramped Work Space, Awkward Positions	How often does this job require working in cramped work spaces that requires getting into awkward positions?
Outdoors, Exposed to Weather	How often does this job require working outdoors, exposed to all weather conditions?
Public Speaking	How often do you have to perform public speaking in this job?
Electronic Mail	How often do you use electronic mail in this job?
Exposed to Radiation	How often does this job require exposure to radiation?

Exposed to Disease or Infections	How often does this job require exposure to disease/infections?

Job Zone Component	Job Zone Component Definitions
Title	Job Zone Two: Some Preparation Needed
Overall Experience	Some previous work-related skill, knowledge, or experience may be helpful in these occupations, but usually is not needed. For example, a drywall installer might benefit from experience installing drywall, but an inexperienced person could still learn to be an installer with little difficulty.
Job Training	Employees in these occupations need anywhere from a few months to one year of working with experienced employees.
Job Zone Examples	These occupations often involve using your knowledge and skills to help others. Examples include drywall installers, fire inspectors, flight attendants, pharmacy technicians, salespersons (retail), and tellers.
SVP Range	(4.0 to < 6.0)
Education	These occupations usually require a high school diploma and may require some vocational training or job-related course work. In some cases, an associate's or bachelor's degree could be needed.

Work_Styles	Work_Styles Definitions
Attention to Detail	Job requires being careful about detail and thorough in completing work tasks.
Integrity	Job requires being honest and ethical.
Dependability	Job requires being reliable, responsible, and dependable, and fulfilling obligations.
Cooperation	Job requires being pleasant with others on the job and displaying a good-natured, cooperative attitude.
Innovation	Job requires creativity and alternative thinking to develop new ideas for and answers to work-related problems.
Self Control	Job requires maintaining composure, keeping emotions in check, controlling anger, and avoiding aggressive behavior, even in very difficult situations.
Adaptability/Flexibility	Job requires being open to change (positive or negative) and to considerable variety in the workplace.
Concern for Others	Job requires being sensitive to others' needs and feelings and being understanding and helpful on the job.
Initiative	Job requires a willingness to take on responsibilities and challenges.
Independence	Job requires developing one's own ways of doing things, guiding oneself with little or no supervision, and depending on oneself to get things done.
Persistence	Job requires persistence in the face of obstacles.
Stress Tolerance	Job requires accepting criticism and dealing calmly and effectively with high stress situations.
Analytical Thinking	Job requires analyzing information and using logic to address work-related issues and problems.
Achievement/Effort	Job requires establishing and maintaining personally challenging achievement goals and exerting effort toward mastering tasks.
Leadership	Job requires a willingness to lead, take charge, and offer opinions and direction.
Social Orientation	Job requires preferring to work with others rather than alone, and being personally connected with others on the job.

51-9122.00 - Painters, Transportation Equipment

Operate or tend painting machines to paint surfaces of transportation equipment, such as automobiles, buses, trucks, trains, boats, and airplanes.

Tasks

1) Set up portable equipment such as ventilators, exhaust units, ladders, and scaffolding.

2) Lay out logos, symbols, or designs on painted surfaces, according to blueprint specifications, using measuring instruments, stencils, and patterns.

3) Apply designs, lettering, or other identifying or decorative items to finished products, using paint brushes or paint sprayers.

4) Allow the sprayed product to dry, and then touch up any spots that may have been missed.

5) Adjust controls on infrared ovens, heat lamps, portable ventilators, and exhaust units in order to speed the drying of vehicles between coats.

6) Spray prepared surfaces with specified amounts of primers and decorative or finish coatings.

7) Apply rust-resistant undercoats, and caulk and seal seams.

8) Fill small dents and scratches with body fillers, and smooth surfaces in order to prepare vehicles for painting.

9) Select paint according to company requirements, and match colors of paint following specified color charts.

10) Buff and wax the finished paintwork.

11) Disassemble, clean, and reassemble sprayers and power equipment, using solvents, wire brushes, and cloths for cleaning duties.

12) Apply primer over any repairs made to vehicle surfaces.

13) Sand vehicle surfaces between coats of paint and/or primer in order to remove flaws and enhance adhesion for subsequent coats.

14) Mix paints to match color specifications or vehicles' original colors, then stir and thin the paints, using spatulas or power mixing equipment.

15) Paint by hand areas that cannot be reached with a spray gun, or those that need retouching, using brushes.

16) Remove grease, dirt, paint, and rust from vehicle surfaces in preparation for paint application, using abrasives, solvents, brushes, blowtorches, washing tanks, or sandblasters.

17) Remove accessories from vehicles, such as chrome or mirrors, and mask other surfaces with tape or paper in order to protect them from paint.

18) Pour paint into spray guns, and adjust nozzles and paint mixes in order to get the proper paint flow and coating thickness.

19) Sand the final finish, and apply sealer once a vehicle has dried properly.

20) Operate lifting and moving devices in order to move equipment or materials so that areas to be painted are accessible.

21) Monitor painting operations in order to identify flaws such as blisters and streaks so that their causes can be corrected.

22) Verify paint consistency, using a viscosity meter.

23) Dispose of hazardous waste in an appropriate manner.

51-9131.00 - Photographic Process Workers

Perform precision work involved in photographic processing, such as editing photographic negatives and prints, using photo-mechanical, chemical, or computerized methods.

Tasks

1) Mount cameras on tripods or stands, and load prescribed types and sizes of film in cameras.

2) Produce color or black-and-white photographs, negatives, and slides, applying standard photographic reproduction techniques and procedures.

3) Cut negatives and put them in order.

4) Reprint originals to enlarge them, or in sections to be pieced together.

5) Apply paint to retouch or enhance negatives or photographs, using airbrushes, pens, artists' brushes, cotton swabs, or gloved fingers.

6) Ink borders or lettering on illustrations, using pens, brushes, or drafting instruments.

7) Color photographs to produce natural, lifelike appearances, using oil colors.

8) Paint negatives with retouching mediums to ensure that retouching pencils will mark surfaces of negatives.

9) Read work orders to determine required processes, techniques, materials, and equipment.

10) Rub erasers or cloths over photographs to reduce gloss, remove debris, or prepare specified areas of illustrations for highlighting.

11) Thread film strips through densitometers, and expose film to light to determine density of film and necessary color corrections.

12) Produce timed prints with separate densities and color settings for each scene of a production.

13) Thread film strips through sensitometers, expose film to light, and read gauges to assess

light sensitivity.

14) Select lens assemblies according to sizes and types of negatives or photographs to be printed.

15) Trim edges of prints to enhance appearance, using scissors or paper cutters.

16) Create work prints according to customer specifications and lab protocols.

17) Examine quality of film fades and dissolves, and evaluate potential color corrections, using color analyzers.

18) Examine developed prints for defects such as broken lines, spots, and blurs.

19) Set automatic timers, lens openings, and printer carriages to specified focus and exposure times, and start exposure in order to duplicate originals, photographs, or negatives.

20) Clean and organize darkrooms, and maintain darkroom equipment.

21) Expose film strips to progressively timed lights to compare effects of various exposure times.

22) Immerse film, negatives, paper, or prints in developing solutions, fixing solutions, and water in order to complete photographic development processes.

23) Evaluate film and negatives to determine characteristics such as sensitivity to light, density, and exposure time required for printing.

24) Examine drawings, negatives, or photographic prints to determine coloring, shading, accenting, and other changes required for retouching or restoration.

25) Cut out masking templates, using shears, and position templates on pictures to mask selected areas.

26) Measure material to be copied, and compute percentages of enlargement or reproduction necessary, using rules, charts, or percentage scales.

27) Place sensitized paper in frames of projection printers, photostats, or other reproduction machines.

28) Correct color work prints to adjust for outdoor filming.

29) Shade negatives or photographs with pencils to smooth facial contours, soften highlights, and conceal blemishes, stray hairs, or wrinkles.

30) Mix developing and fixing solutions according to established formulas.

31) Place identification on film as necessary.

32) Record test data from film that has been examined, and route film to film developers and film printers for further processing.

33) Mount original photographs, negatives, or other printed material in holders or vacuum frames beneath lights.

34) Dry prints or negatives, using sponges and/or squeegees, mechanical air dryers, or drying cabinets.

35) Mix ink or paint solutions, according to color specifications, color charts, and desired consistencies.

51-9132.00 - Photographic Processing Machine Operators

Operate photographic processing machines, such as photographic printing machines, film developing machines, and mounting presses.

Tasks

1) Maintain records such as quantities and types of processing completed, rate of materials usage, and customer charges.

2) Insert processed negatives and prints into envelopes so that they can be returned to customers.

3) Inspect film or circuit patterns on photographic plates to locate any defects; discard defective products or repair them, using cleaning solutions and hand tools.

4) Load circuit boards, racks or rolls of film, negatives, and/or printing paper into processing or printing machines.

5) Measure and mix chemicals to prepare solutions for processing, according to formulas.

6) Place film in labeled containers, or number film for identification, by hand or by using numbering machines.

7) Fill tanks of processing machines with solutions such as developer, dyes, stop-baths, fixers, bleaches, and washes.

8) Set and adjust machine controls, according to specifications, type of operation, and material requirements.

9) Read work orders and examine negatives and film in order to determine machine settings and processing requirements.

10) Sort film to be developed according to criteria such as film type or completion date.

11) Clean and maintain photoprocessing equipment, using cleaning and rinsing solutions and ultrasonic equipment.

12) Operate special equipment to perform tasks such as transferring film to videotape or producing photographic enlargements.

13) Retouch photographic negatives or original prints to correct defects.

14) Splice broken or separated film, and mount film on reels.

15) Monitor equipment operation to detect malfunctions.

16) Start and operate machines to prepare circuit boards and to expose, develop, etch, fix, wash, dry, and print film or plates.

51-9141.00 - Semiconductor Processors

Perform any or all of the following functions in the manufacture of electronic semiconductors: load semiconductor material into furnace; saw formed ingots into segments; load individual segment into crystal growing chamber and monitor controls; locate crystal axis in ingot using x-ray equipment and saw ingots into wafers; clean, polish, and load wafers into series of special purpose furnaces, chemical baths, and equipment used to form circuitry and change conductive properties.

Tasks

1) Measure and weigh amounts of crystal growing materials, mix and grind materials, load materials into container, and monitor processing procedures to help identify crystal growing problems.

2) Manipulate valves, switches, and buttons, or key commands into control panels to start semiconductor processing cycles.

3) Locate crystal axis of ingot, and draw orientation lines on ingot, using x-ray equipment, drill, and sanding machine.

4) Load semiconductor material into furnace.

5) Etch, lap, polish, or grind wafers or ingots to form circuitry and change conductive properties, using etching, lapping, polishing, or grinding equipment.

6) Load and unload equipment chambers and transport finished product to storage or to area for further processing.

7) Connect reactor to computer, using hand tools and power tools.

8) Maintain processing, production, and inspection information and reports.

9) Operate saw to cut remelt into sections of specified size or to cut ingots into wafers.

10) Clean semiconductor wafers using cleaning equipment, such as chemical baths, automatic wafer cleaners, or blow-off wands.

11) Calculate etching time based on thickness of material to be removed from wafers or crystals.

12) Mount crystal ingots or wafers on blocks or plastic laminate, using special mounting devices, to facilitate their positioning in the holding fixtures of sawing, drilling, grinding or sanding equipment.

13) Scribe or separate wafers into dice.

14) Inspect materials, components, or products for surface defects and measure circuitry, using electronic test equipment, precision measuring instruments, microscope, and standard procedures.

15) Inspect equipment for leaks, diagnose malfunctions, and request repairs.

16) Place semiconductor wafers in processing containers or equipment holders, using vacuum wand or tweezers.

17) Set, adjust, and readjust computerized or mechanical equipment controls to regulate power level, temperature, vacuum, and rotation speed of furnace, according to crystal growing specifications.

18) Stamp, etch, or scribe identifying information on finished component according to specifications.

19) Study work orders, instructions, formulas, and processing charts to determine specifications and sequence of operations.

20) Clean and maintain equipment, including replacing etching and rinsing solutions and cleaning bath containers and work area.

1179

21) Align photo mask pattern on photoresist layer, expose pattern to ultraviolet light, and develop pattern, using specialized equipment.

22) Count, sort, and weigh processed items.

23) Attach ampoule to diffusion pump to remove air from ampoule, and seal ampoule, using blowtorch.

51-9191.00 - Cementing and Gluing Machine Operators and Tenders

Operate or tend cementing and gluing machines to join items for further processing or to form a completed product. Processes include joining veneer sheets into plywood; gluing paper; joining rubber and rubberized fabric parts, plastic, simulated leather, or other materials.

Tasks

1) Fill machines with glue, cement, or adhesives.

2) Remove and stack completed materials or products, and restock materials to be joined.

3) Read work orders and communicate with coworkers in order to determine machine and equipment settings and adjustments, and supply and product specifications.

4) Perform test production runs and make adjustments as necessary to ensure that completed products meet standards and specifications.

5) Observe gauges, meters, and control panels to obtain information about equipment temperatures and pressures, or the speed of feeders or conveyors.

6) Mount or load material such as paper, plastic, wood, or rubber in feeding mechanisms of cementing or gluing machines.

7) Monitor machine operations to detect malfunctions; report or resolve problems.

8) Adjust machine components according to specifications such as widths, lengths, and thickness of materials and amounts of glue, cement, or adhesive required.

9) Depress pedals to lower electrodes that heat and seal edges of material.

10) Remove jammed materials from machines and readjust components as necessary to resume normal operations.

11) Align and position materials being joined in order to ensure accurate application of adhesive or heat sealing.

12) Clean and maintain gluing and cementing machines, using solutions, lubricants, brushes, and scrapers.

13) Start machines, and turn valves or move controls to feed, admit, apply, or transfer materials and adhesives, and to adjust temperature, pressure, and time settings.

14) Measure and mix ingredients to prepare glue.

15) Transport materials, supplies, and finished products between storage and work areas, using forklifts.

16) Examine and measure completed materials or products to verify conformance to specifications, using measuring devices such as tape measures, gauges, or calipers.

51-9192.00 - Cleaning, Washing, and Metal Pickling Equipment Operators and Tenders

Operate or tend machines to wash or clean products, such as barrels or kegs, glass items, tin plate, food, pulp, coal, plastic, or rubber, to remove impurities.

Tasks

1) Operate or tend machines to wash and remove impurities from items such as barrels or kegs, glass products, tin plate surfaces, dried fruit, pulp, animal stock, coal, manufactured articles, plastic, or rubber.

2) Draw samples for laboratory analysis, or test solutions for conformance to specifications, such as acidity or specific gravity.

3) Set controls to regulate temperature and length of cycles, and start conveyors, pumps, agitators, and machines.

4) Measure, weigh, or mix cleaning solutions, using measuring tanks, calibrated rods or suction tubes.

5) Add specified amounts of chemicals to equipment at required times to maintain solution levels and concentrations.

6) Drain, clean, and refill machines or tanks at designated intervals, using cleaning solutions or water.

7) Load machines with objects to be processed, then unload objects after cleaning and place them on conveyors or racks.

8) Examine and inspect machines to detect malfunctions.

9) Observe machine operations, gauges, or thermometers, and adjust controls to maintain specified conditions.

10) Record gauge readings, materials used, processing times, and/or test results in production logs.

51-9193.00 - Cooling and Freezing Equipment Operators and Tenders

Operate or tend equipment, such as cooling and freezing units, refrigerators, batch freezers, and freezing tunnels, to cool or freeze products, food, blood plasma, and chemicals.

Tasks

1) Start machinery such as pumps, feeders, or conveyors, and turn valves in order to heat, admit, or transfer products, refrigerants, or mixes.

2) Correct machinery malfunctions by performing actions such as removing jams, and inform supervisors of malfunctions as necessary.

3) Insert forming fixtures, and start machines that cut frozen products into measured portions or specified shapes.

4) Measure or weigh specified amounts of ingredients or materials, and load them into tanks, vats, hoppers, or other equipment.

5) Place or position containers into equipment, and remove containers after completion of cooling or freezing processes.

6) Start agitators to blend contents, or start beater, scraper, and expeller blades to mix contents with air and prevent sticking.

7) Monitor pressure gauges, ammeters, flowmeters, thermometers, or products, and adjust controls to maintain specified conditions, such as feed rate, product consistency, temperature, air pressure, and machine speed.

8) Stir material with spoons or paddles in order to mix ingredients or allow even cooling and prevent coagulation.

9) Weigh packages and adjust freezer air valves or switches on filler heads in order to obtain specified amounts of product in each container.

10) Activate mechanical rakes in order to regulate flow of ice from storage bins to vats.

11) Assemble equipment, and attach pipes, fittings, or valves, using hand tools.

12) Inspect and flush lines with solutions or steam, and spray equipment with sterilizing solutions.

13) Record temperatures, amounts of materials processed, and/or test results on report forms.

14) Sample and test product characteristics such as specific gravity, acidity, and sugar content, using hydrometers, pH meters, or refractometers.

15) Scrape, dislodge, or break excess frost, ice, or frozen product from equipment in order to prevent accumulation, using hands and hand tools.

16) Position molds on conveyors, and measure and adjust level of fill, using depth gauges.

17) Load and position wrapping paper, sticks, bags, or cartons into dispensing machines.

18) Adjust machine or freezer speed and air intake in order to obtain desired consistency and amount of product.

51-9196.00 - Paper Goods Machine Setters, Operators, and Tenders

Set up, operate, or tend paper goods machines that perform a variety of functions, such as converting, sawing, corrugating, banding, wrapping, boxing, stitching, forming, or sealing paper or paperboard sheets into products.

Tasks

1) Monitor finished cartons as they drop from forming machines into rotating hoppers and then into gravity feed chutes, in order to prevent jamming.

2) Disassemble machines to maintain, repair, or replace broken or worn parts, using hand or power tools.

3) Stamp products with information such as dates, using hand stamps or automatic stamping devices.

4) Lift tote boxes of finished cartons, and dump cartons into feed hoppers.

5) Start machines and move controls to regulate tension on pressure rolls, to synchronize speed of machine components, and to adjust temperatures of glue or paraffin.

6) Remove finished cores, and stack or place them on conveyors for transfer to other work areas.

7) Observe operation of various machines to detect and correct machine malfunctions such as improper forming, glue flow, or pasteboard tension.

8) Measure, space, and set saw blades, cutters, and perforators, according to product specifications.

9) Load automatic stapling mechanisms.

10) Install attachments to machines for gluing, folding, printing, or cutting.

11) Fill glue and paraffin reservoirs, and position rollers to dispense glue onto paperboard.

12) Examine completed work to detect defects and verify conformance to work orders, and adjust machinery as necessary to correct production problems.

13) Adjust guide assemblies, forming bars, and folding mechanisms according to specifications, using hand tools.

14) Cut products to specified dimensions, using hand or power cutters.

51-9197.00 - Tire Builders

Operate machines to build tires from rubber components.

Tasks

1) Roll hand rollers over rebuilt casings, exerting pressure to ensure adhesion between camelbacks and casings.

2) Measure tires to determine mold size requirements.

3) Place tires into molds for new tread.

4) Inspect worn tires for faults, cracks, cuts and nail holes, and to determine if tires are suitable for retreading.

5) Clean and paint completed tires.

6) Build semi-raw rubber treads onto buffed tire casings in order to prepare tires for vulcanization in recapping or retreading processes.

7) Wind chafers and breakers onto plies.

8) Depress pedals to collapse drums after processing is complete.

9) Cut plies at splice points, and press ends together to form continuous bands.

10) Brush or spray solvents onto plies to ensure adhesion, and repeat process as specified, alternating direction of each ply to strengthen tires.

11) Align treads with guides, start drums to wind treads onto plies, and slice ends.

12) Start rollers that bond tread and plies as drums revolve.

13) Activate bead setters that press prefabricated beads onto plies.

14) Select camelbacks according to specified tire widths and tread thicknesses, and whether tires are to be retreaded or recapped.

15) Spray tires with vulcanizing cement.

16) Trim excess rubber and imperfections during retreading processes.

17) Depress pedals to rotate drums, and wind specified numbers of plies around drums to form tire bodies.

18) Place rebuilt casings in molds for vulcanization processes.

19) Position ply stitcher rollers and drums according to width of stock, using hand tools and gauges.

20) Position rollers that turn ply edges under and over beads, or use steel rods to turn ply edges.

21) Pull plies from supply racks, and align plies with edges of drums.

22) Fit inner tubes and final layers of rubber onto tires.

23) Roll camelbacks onto casings by hand, and cut camelbacks, using knives.

24) Rub cement sticks on drum edges to provide adhesive surfaces for plies.

53-1011.00 - Aircraft Cargo Handling Supervisors

Direct ground crew in the loading, unloading, securing, and staging of aircraft cargo or baggage. Determine the quantity and orientation of cargo and compute aircraft center of gravity. May accompany aircraft as member of flight crew and monitor and handle cargo in flight, and assist and brief passengers on safety and emergency procedures.

Tasks

1) Brief aircraft passengers on safety and emergency procedures.

2) Determine the quantity and orientation of cargo, and compute an aircraft's center of gravity.

3) Distribute cargo in such a manner that space use is maximized.

4) Calculate load weights for different aircraft compartments, using charts and computers.

5) Accompany aircraft as a member of the flight crew in order to monitor and handle cargo in flight.

53-1021.00 - First-Line Supervisors/Managers of Helpers, Laborers, and Material Movers, Hand

Supervise and coordinate the activities of helpers, laborers, or material movers.

Tasks

1) Resolve personnel problems, complaints, and formal grievances when possible, or refer them to higher-level supervisors for resolution.

2) Quote prices to customers.

3) Collaborate with workers and managers to solve work-related problems.

4) Assess training needs of staff; then arrange for or provide appropriate instruction.

5) Evaluate employee performance, and prepare performance appraisals.

6) Plan work schedules and assign duties to maintain adequate staffing levels, to ensure that activities are performed effectively, and to respond to fluctuating workloads.

7) Conduct staff meetings to relay general information or to address specific topics such as safety.

8) Provide assistance in balancing books, tracking, monitoring, and projecting a unit's budget needs, and in developing unit policies and procedures.

9) Perform the same work duties as those whom they supervise, and/or perform more difficult or skilled tasks or assist in their performance.

10) Review work throughout the work process and at completion, in order to ensure that it has been performed properly.

11) Recommend or initiate personnel actions such as promotions, transfers, and disciplinary measures.

12) Estimate material, time, and staffing requirements for a given project, based on work orders, job specifications, and experience.

13) Inventory supplies, and requisition or purchase additional items as necessary.

14) Transmit and explain work orders to laborers.

15) Inspect equipment for wear and for conformance to specifications.

16) Inform designated employees or departments of items loaded, and problems encountered.

17) Counsel employees in work-related activities, personal growth, and career development.

18) Check specifications of materials loaded or unloaded against information contained in work orders.

19) Participate in the hiring process by reviewing credentials, conducting interviews, and/or making hiring decisions or recommendations.

20) Inspect job sites to determine the extent of maintenance or repairs needed.

21) Examine freight to determine loading sequences.

22) Prepare and maintain work records and reports that include information such as employee time and wages, daily receipts, and inspection results.

53-1031.00 - First-Line Supervisors/Managers of Transportation and Material-Moving Machine and Vehicle Operators

Directly supervise and coordinate activities of transportation and material-moving machine and vehicle operators and helpers.

Tasks

1) Direct workers in transportation or related services, such as pumping, moving, storing, and loading/unloading of materials or people.

2) Requisition needed personnel, supplies, equipment, parts, or repair services.

3) Recommend or implement personnel actions such as employee selection, evaluation, and rewards or disciplinary actions.

4) Prepare, compile, and submit reports on work activities, operations, production, and work-related accidents.

5) Plan work assignments and equipment allocations in order to meet transportation, operations, or production goals.

6) Monitor field work to ensure that it is being performed properly and that materials are being used as they should be.

7) Maintain or verify records of time, materials, expenditures, and crew activities.

8) Interpret transportation and tariff regulations, shipping orders, safety regulations, and company policies and procedures for workers.

9) Compute and estimate cash, payroll, transportation, personnel, and storage requirements.

10) Enforce safety rules and regulations.

11) Plan and establish transportation routes.

12) Review orders, production schedules, blueprints, and shipping/receiving notices to determine work sequences and material shipping dates, types, volumes, and destinations.

13) Provide workers with assistance in performing tasks such as coupling railroad cars or loading vehicles.

14) Perform or schedule repairs and preventive maintenance of vehicles and other equipment.

15) Inspect or test materials, stock, vehicles, equipment, and facilities to ensure that they are safe, free of defects, and meet specifications.

16) Examine, measure, and weigh cargo or materials to determine specific handling requirements.

17) Drive vehicles or operate machines or equipment to complete work assignments or to assist workers.

18) Dispatch personnel and vehicles in respond to telephone or radio reports of emergencies.

19) Recommend and implement measures to improve worker motivation, equipment performance, work methods, and customer services.

20) Confer with customers, supervisors, contractors, and other personnel to exchange information and to resolve problems.

21) Explain and demonstrate work tasks to new workers, or assign workers to more experienced workers for further training.

53-2011.00 - Airline Pilots, Copilots, and Flight Engineers

Pilot and navigate the flight of multi-engine aircraft in regularly scheduled service for the transport of passengers and cargo. Requires Federal Air Transport rating and certification in specific aircraft type used.

Tasks

1) Monitor engine operation, fuel consumption, and functioning of aircraft systems during flights.

2) Contact control towers for takeoff clearances, arrival instructions, and other information, using radio equipment.

3) Direct activities of aircraft crews during flights.

4) File instrument flight plans with air traffic control to ensure that flights are coordinated with other air traffic.

5) Inspect aircraft for defects and malfunctions, according to pre-flight checklists.

6) Make announcements regarding flights, using public address systems.

7) Test and evaluate the performance of new aircraft.

8) Coordinate flight activities with ground crews and air-traffic control, and inform crew members of flight and test procedures.

9) Record in log books information such as flight times, distances flown, and fuel consumption.

10) Load smaller aircraft, handling passenger luggage and supervising refueling.

11) Start engines, operate controls, and pilot airplanes to transport passengers, mail, or freight, while adhering to flight plans, regulations, and procedures.

12) Evaluate other pilots or pilot-license applicants for proficiency.

13) Order changes in fuel supplies, loads, routes, or schedules to ensure safety of flights.

14) Check passenger and cargo distributions and fuel amounts, to ensure that weight and balance specifications are met.

15) Work as part of a flight team with other crew members, especially during takeoffs and landings.

16) Confer with flight dispatchers and weather forecasters to keep abreast of flight conditions.

17) Choose routes, altitudes, and speeds that will provide the fastest, safest, and smoothest flights.

18) Brief crews about flight details such as destinations, duties, and responsibilities.

19) Perform minor maintenance work, or arrange for major maintenance.

20) Monitor gauges, warning devices, and control panels to verify aircraft performance and to regulate engine speed.

21) Conduct in-flight tests and evaluations at specified altitudes and in all types of weather, in order to determine the receptivity and other characteristics of equipment and systems.

22) Plan and formulate flight activities and test schedules, and prepare flight evaluation reports.

23) Respond to and report in-flight emergencies and malfunctions.

24) Use instrumentation to guide flights when visibility is poor.

25) Steer aircraft along planned routes with the assistance of autopilot and flight management computers.

53-2012.00 - Commercial Pilots

Pilot and navigate the flight of small fixed or rotary winged aircraft, primarily for the transport of cargo and passengers. Requires Commercial Rating.

Tasks

1) Conduct in-flight tests and evaluations at specified altitudes and in all types of weather, in order to determine the receptivity and other characteristics of equipment and systems.

2) Plan and formulate flight activities and test schedules, and prepare flight evaluation reports.

3) Write specified information in flight records, such as flight times, altitudes flown, and fuel consumption.

4) Teach company regulations and procedures to other pilots.

5) Obtain and review data such as load weights, fuel supplies, weather conditions, and flight schedules in order to determine flight plans, and to see if changes might be necessary.

6) Supervise other crew members.

7) Perform minor aircraft maintenance and repair work, or arrange for major maintenance.

8) Fly with other pilots or pilot-license applicants to evaluate their proficiency.

9) Order changes in fuel supplies, loads, routes, or schedules to ensure safety of flights.

10) Consider airport altitudes, outside temperatures, plane weights, and wind speeds and directions in order to calculate the speed needed to become airborne.

11) Check the flight performance of new and experimental planes.

12) Instruct other pilots and student pilots in aircraft operations.

13) Plan flights, following government and company regulations, using aeronautical charts and navigation instruments.

14) Coordinate flight activities with ground crews and air-traffic control, and inform crew members of flight and test procedures.

15) Check baggage or cargo to ensure that it has been loaded correctly.

16) Co-pilot aircraft, or perform captain's duties if required.

17) Check aircraft prior to flights to ensure that the engines, controls, instruments, and other systems are functioning properly.

18) Choose routes, altitudes, and speeds that will provide the fastest, safest, and smoothest flights.

19) Contact control towers for takeoff clearances, arrival instructions, and other information, using radio equipment.

20) Monitor engine operation, fuel consumption, and functioning of aircraft systems during flights.

21) Use instrumentation to pilot aircraft when visibility is poor.

22) Request changes in altitudes or routes as circumstances dictate.

23) Rescue and evacuate injured persons.

24) Start engines, operate controls, and pilot airplanes to transport passengers, mail, or freight, while adhering to flight plans, regulations, and procedures.

25) File instrument flight plans with air traffic control so that flights can be coordinated with other air traffic.

53-2021.00 - Air Traffic Controllers

Control air traffic on and within vicinity of airport and movement of air traffic between altitude sectors and control centers according to established procedures and policies. Authorize, regulate, and control commercial airline flights according to government or company regulations to expedite and ensure flight safety.

Tasks

1) Conduct pre-flight briefings on weather conditions, suggested routes, altitudes, indications of turbulence, and other flight safety information.

2) Analyze factors such as weather reports, fuel requirements, and maps in order to determine air routes.

3) Determine the timing and procedures for flight vector changes.

4) Direct ground traffic, including taxiing aircraft, maintenance and baggage vehicles, and airport workers.

5) Direct pilots to runways when space is available, or direct them to maintain a traffic pattern until there is space for them to land.

6) Alert airport emergency services in cases of emergency and when aircraft are experiencing difficulties.

7) Inspect, adjust, and control radio equipment and airport lights.

8) Initiate and coordinate searches for missing aircraft.

9) Inform pilots about nearby planes as well as potentially hazardous conditions such as weather, speed and direction of wind, and visibility problems.

10) Monitor aircraft within a specific airspace, using radar, computer equipment, and visual references.

11) Monitor and direct the movement of aircraft within an assigned air space and on the ground at airports to minimize delays and maximize safety.

12) Review records and reports for clarity and completeness, and maintain records and reports as required under federal law.

13) Maintain radio and telephone contact with adjacent control towers, terminal control units, and other area control centers in order to coordinate aircraft movement.

14) Issue landing and take-off authorizations and instructions.

15) Complete daily activity reports and keep records of messages from aircraft.

16) Provide flight path changes or directions to emergency landing fields for pilots traveling in bad weather or in emergency situations.

17) Organize flight plans and traffic management plans to prepare for planes about to enter assigned airspace.

18) Transfer control of departing flights to traffic control centers and accept control of arriving flights.

19) Contact pilots by radio to provide meteorological, navigational, and other information.

20) Compile information about flights from flight plans, pilot reports, radar, and observations.

21) Relay to control centers such air traffic information as courses, altitudes, and expected arrival times.

53-2022.00 - Airfield Operations Specialists

Ensure the safe takeoff and landing of commercial and military aircraft. Duties include coordination between air-traffic control and maintenance personnel; dispatching; using airfield landing and navigational aids; implementing airfield safety procedures; monitoring and maintaining flight records; and applying knowledge of weather information.

Tasks

1) Provide aircrews with information and services needed for airfield management and flight planning.

2) Use airfield landing and navigational aids and digital data terminal communications equipment to perform duties.

3) Receive and post weather information and flight plan data such as air routes and arrival and departure times.

4) Check military flight plans with civilian agencies.

5) Procure, produce, and provide information on the safe operation of aircraft, such as flight planning publications, operations publications, charts and maps, and weather information.

6) Coordinate communications between air-traffic control and maintenance personnel.

7) Relay departure, arrival, delay, aircraft and airfield status, and other pertinent information to upline controlling agencies.

8) Post visual display boards and status boards.

9) Coordinate changes to flight itineraries with appropriate Air Traffic Control (ATC) agencies.

10) Plan and coordinate airfield construction.

11) Anticipate aircraft equipment needs for air evacuation and cargo flights.

12) Perform and supervise airfield management activities, which may include mobile airfield management functions.

13) Train operations staff.

14) Implement airfield safety procedures to ensure a safe operating environment for personnel and aircraft operation.

15) Store and provide receipts for aircrew weapons and classified materials.

16) Monitor the arrival, parking, refueling, loading, and departure of all aircraft.

17) Coordinate with agencies such as air traffic control, civil engineers, and command posts to ensure support of airfield management activities.

18) Conduct departure and arrival briefings.

19) Collaborate with others to plan flight schedules and air crew assignments.

20) Coordinate with agencies to meet aircrew requirements for billeting, messing, refueling, ground transportation, and transient aircraft maintenance.

21) Maintain air-to-ground and point-to-point radio contact with aircraft commanders.

22) Maintain flight and events logs, air crew flying records, and flight operations records of incoming and outgoing flights.

53-3011.00 - Ambulance Drivers and Attendants, Except Emergency Medical Technicians

Drive ambulance or assist ambulance driver in transporting sick, injured, or convalescent persons. Assist in lifting patients.

Tasks

1) Report facts concerning accidents or emergencies to hospital personnel or law enforcement

officials.

2) Accompany and assist emergency medical technicians on calls.

3) Restrain or shackle violent patients.

4) Drive ambulances or assist ambulance drivers in transporting sick, injured, or convalescent persons.

5) Place patients on stretchers, and load stretchers into ambulances, usually with assistance from other attendants.

6) Administer first aid such as bandaging, splinting, and administering oxygen.

7) Replace supplies and disposable items on ambulances.

8) Remove and replace soiled linens and equipment in order to maintain sanitary conditions.

53-3021.00 - Bus Drivers, Transit and Intercity

Drive bus or motor coach, including regular route operations, charters, and private carriage. May assist passengers with baggage. May collect fares or tickets.

Tasks

1) Park vehicles at loading areas so that passengers can board.

2) Drive vehicles over specified routes or to specified destinations according to time schedules in order to transport passengers, complying with traffic regulations.

3) Inspect vehicles, and check gas, oil, and water levels prior to departure.

4) Advise passengers to be seated and orderly while on vehicles.

5) Report delays or accidents.

6) Assist passengers with baggage and collect tickets or cash fares.

7) Load and unload baggage in baggage compartments.

8) Record cash receipts and ticket fares.

9) Make minor repairs to vehicle and change tires.

Knowledge	Knowledge Definitions
Transportation	Knowledge of principles and methods for moving people or goods by air, rail, sea, or road, including the relative costs and benefits.
Customer and Personal Service	Knowledge of principles and processes for providing customer and personal services. This includes customer needs assessment, meeting quality standards for services, and evaluation of customer satisfaction.
Public Safety and Security	Knowledge of relevant equipment, policies, procedures, and strategies to promote effective local, state, or national security operations for the protection of people, data, property, and institutions.
Geography	Knowledge of principles and methods for describing the features of land, sea, and air masses, including their physical characteristics, locations, interrelationships, and distribution of plant, animal, and human life.
Law and Government	Knowledge of laws, legal codes, court procedures, precedents, government regulations, executive orders, agency rules, and the democratic political process.
Psychology	Knowledge of human behavior and performance; individual differences in ability, personality, and interests; learning and motivation; psychological research methods; and the assessment and treatment of behavioral and affective disorders.
English Language	Knowledge of the structure and content of the English language including the meaning and spelling of words, rules of composition, and grammar.
Mechanical	Knowledge of machines and tools, including their designs, uses, repair, and maintenance.
Mathematics	Knowledge of arithmetic, algebra, geometry, calculus, statistics, and their applications.
Telecommunications	Knowledge of transmission, broadcasting, switching, control, and operation of telecommunications systems.
Administration and Management	Knowledge of business and management principles involved in strategic planning, resource allocation, human resources modeling, leadership technique, production methods, and coordination of people and resources.

Communications and Media	Knowledge of media production, communication, and dissemination techniques and methods. This includes alternative ways to inform and entertain via written, oral, and visual media.
Sociology and Anthropology	Knowledge of group behavior and dynamics, societal trends and influences, human migrations, ethnicity, cultures and their history and origins.
History and Archeology	Knowledge of historical events and their causes, indicators, and effects on civilizations and cultures.
Clerical	Knowledge of administrative and clerical procedures and systems such as word processing, managing files and records, stenography and transcription, designing forms, and other office procedures and terminology.
Sales and Marketing	Knowledge of principles and methods for showing, promoting, and selling products or services. This includes marketing strategy and tactics, product demonstration, sales techniques, and sales control systems.
Philosophy and Theology	Knowledge of different philosophical systems and religions. This includes their basic principles, values, ethics, ways of thinking, customs, practices, and their impact on human culture.
Computers and Electronics	Knowledge of circuit boards, processors, chips, electronic equipment, and computer hardware and software, including applications and programming.
Education and Training	Knowledge of principles and methods for curriculum and training design, teaching and instruction for individuals and groups, and the measurement of training effects.
Medicine and Dentistry	Knowledge of the information and techniques needed to diagnose and treat human injuries, diseases, and deformities. This includes symptoms, treatment alternatives, drug properties and interactions, and preventive health-care measures.
Therapy and Counseling	Knowledge of principles, methods, and procedures for diagnosis, treatment, and rehabilitation of physical and mental dysfunctions, and for career counseling and guidance.
Engineering and Technology	Knowledge of the practical application of engineering science and technology. This includes applying principles, techniques, procedures, and equipment to the design and production of various goods and services.
Foreign Language	Knowledge of the structure and content of a foreign (non-English) language including the meaning and spelling of words, rules of composition and grammar, and pronunciation.
Chemistry	Knowledge of the chemical composition, structure, and properties of substances and of the chemical processes and transformations that they undergo. This includes uses of chemicals and their interactions, danger signs, production techniques, and disposal methods.
Economics and Accounting	Knowledge of economic and accounting principles and practices, the financial markets, banking and the analysis and reporting of financial data.
Physics	Knowledge and prediction of physical principles, laws, their interrelationships, and applications to understanding fluid, material, and atmospheric dynamics, and mechanical, electrical, atomic and sub-atomic structures and processes.
Personnel and Human Resources	Knowledge of principles and procedures for personnel recruitment, selection, training, compensation and benefits, labor relations and negotiation, and personnel information systems.
Fine Arts	Knowledge of the theory and techniques required to compose, produce, and perform works of music, dance, visual arts, drama, and sculpture.
Building and Construction	Knowledge of materials, methods, and the tools involved in the construction or repair of houses, buildings, or other structures such as highways and roads.
Biology	Knowledge of plant and animal organisms, their tissues, cells, functions, interdependencies, and interactions with each other and the environment.
Food Production	Knowledge of techniques and equipment for planting, growing, and harvesting food products (both plant and animal) for consumption, including storage/handling techniques.
Design	Knowledge of design techniques, tools, and principles involved in production of precision technical plans, blueprints, drawings, and models.
Production and Processing	Knowledge of raw materials, production processes, quality control, costs, and other techniques for maximizing the effective manufacture and distribution of goods.

Skills	Skills Definitions
Active Listening	Giving full attention to what other people are saying, taking time to understand the points being made, asking questions as appropriate, and not interrupting at inappropriate times.
Operation Monitoring	Watching gauges, dials, or other indicators to make sure a machine is working properly.
Social Perceptiveness	Being aware of others' reactions and understanding why they react as they do.
Equipment Maintenance	Performing routine maintenance on equipment and determining when and what kind of maintenance is needed.
Operation and Control	Controlling operations of equipment or systems.
Reading Comprehension	Understanding written sentences and paragraphs in work related documents.
Coordination	Adjusting actions in relation to others' actions.
Time Management	Managing one's own time and the time of others.
Speaking	Talking to others to convey information effectively.
Service Orientation	Actively looking for ways to help people.
Critical Thinking	Using logic and reasoning to identify the strengths and weaknesses of alternative solutions, conclusions or approaches to problems.
Negotiation	Bringing others together and trying to reconcile differences.
Troubleshooting	Determining causes of operating errors and deciding what to do about it.
Writing	Communicating effectively in writing as appropriate for the needs of the audience.
Judgment and Decision Making	Considering the relative costs and benefits of potential actions to choose the most appropriate one.
Mathematics	Using mathematics to solve problems.
Learning Strategies	Selecting and using training/instructional methods and procedures appropriate for the situation when learning or teaching new things.
Instructing	Teaching others how to do something.
Equipment Selection	Determining the kind of tools and equipment needed to do a job.
Monitoring	Monitoring/Assessing performance of yourself, other individuals, or organizations to make improvements or take corrective action.
Systems Evaluation	Identifying measures or indicators of system performance and the actions needed to improve or correct performance, relative to the goals of the system.
Active Learning	Understanding the implications of new information for both current and future problem-solving and decision-making.
Repairing	Repairing machines or systems using the needed tools.
Persuasion	Persuading others to change their minds or behavior.
Systems Analysis	Determining how a system should work and how changes in conditions, operations, and the environment will affect outcomes.
Complex Problem Solving	Identifying complex problems and reviewing related information to develop and evaluate options and implement solutions.
Management of Personnel Resources	Motivating, developing, and directing people as they work, identifying the best people for the job.
Quality Control Analysis	Conducting tests and inspections of products, services, or processes to evaluate quality or performance.
Installation	Installing equipment, machines, wiring, or programs to meet specifications.
Management of Financial Resources	Determining how money will be spent to get the work done, and accounting for these expenditures.
Management of Material Resources	Obtaining and seeing to the appropriate use of equipment, facilities, and materials needed to do certain work.
Operations Analysis	Analyzing needs and product requirements to create a design.
Technology Design	Generating or adapting equipment and technology to serve user needs.
Programming	Writing computer programs for various purposes.
Science	Using scientific rules and methods to solve problems.

Ability	Ability Definitions
Near Vision	The ability to see details at close range (within a few feet of the observer).
Far Vision	The ability to see details at a distance.
Depth Perception	The ability to judge which of several objects is closer or farther away from you, or to judge the distance between you and an object.
Reaction Time	The ability to quickly respond (with the hand, finger, or foot) to a signal (sound, light, picture) when it appears.

Problem Sensitivity	The ability to tell when something is wrong or is likely to go wrong. It does not involve solving the problem, only recognizing there is a problem.
Control Precision	The ability to quickly and repeatedly adjust the controls of a machine or a vehicle to exact positions.
Selective Attention	The ability to concentrate on a task over a period of time without being distracted.
Response Orientation	The ability to choose quickly between two or more movements in response to two or more different signals (lights, sounds, pictures). It includes the speed with which the correct response is started with the hand, foot, or other body part.
Spatial Orientation	The ability to know your location in relation to the environment or to know where other objects are in relation to you.
Night Vision	The ability to see under low light conditions.
Oral Comprehension	The ability to listen to and understand information and ideas presented through spoken words and sentences.
Time Sharing	The ability to shift back and forth between two or more activities or sources of information (such as speech, sounds, touch, or other sources).
Multilimb Coordination	The ability to coordinate two or more limbs (for example, two arms, two legs, or one leg and one arm) while sitting, standing, or lying down. It does not involve performing the activities while the whole body is in motion.
Oral Expression	The ability to communicate information and ideas in speaking so others will understand.
Peripheral Vision	The ability to see objects or movement of objects to one's side when the eyes are looking ahead.
Rate Control	The ability to time your movements or the movement of a piece of equipment in anticipation of changes in the speed and/or direction of a moving object or scene.
Speech Clarity	The ability to speak clearly so others can understand you.
Speech Recognition	The ability to identify and understand the speech of another person.
Glare Sensitivity	The ability to see objects in the presence of glare or bright lighting.
Arm-Hand Steadiness	The ability to keep your hand and arm steady while moving your arm or while holding your arm and hand in one position.
Visual Color Discrimination	The ability to match or detect differences between colors, including shades of color and brightness.
Written Comprehension	The ability to read and understand information and ideas presented in writing.
Deductive Reasoning	The ability to apply general rules to specific problems to produce answers that make sense.
Inductive Reasoning	The ability to combine pieces of information to form general rules or conclusions (includes finding a relationship among seemingly unrelated events).
Hearing Sensitivity	The ability to detect or tell the differences between sounds that vary in pitch and loudness.
Flexibility of Closure	The ability to identify or detect a known pattern (a figure, object, word, or sound) that is hidden in other distracting material.
Perceptual Speed	The ability to quickly and accurately compare similarities and differences among sets of letters, numbers, objects, pictures, or patterns. The things to be compared may be presented at the same time or one after the other. This ability also includes comparing a presented object with a remembered object.
Static Strength	The ability to exert maximum muscle force to lift, push, pull, or carry objects.
Sound Localization	The ability to tell the direction from which a sound originated.
Information Ordering	The ability to arrange things or actions in a certain order or pattern according to a specific rule or set of rules (e.g., patterns of numbers, letters, words, pictures, mathematical operations).
Manual Dexterity	The ability to quickly move your hand, your hand together with your arm, or your two hands to grasp, manipulate, or assemble objects.
Trunk Strength	The ability to use your abdominal and lower back muscles to support part of the body repeatedly or continuously over time without 'giving out' or fatiguing.
Auditory Attention	The ability to focus on a single source of sound in the presence of other distracting sounds.
Written Expression	The ability to communicate information and ideas in writing so others will understand.
Extent Flexibility	The ability to bend, stretch, twist, or reach with your body, arms, and/or legs.
Number Facility	The ability to add, subtract, multiply, or divide quickly and correctly.

Finger Dexterity	The ability to make precisely coordinated movements of the fingers of one or both hands to grasp, manipulate, or assemble very small objects.
Gross Body Coordination	The ability to coordinate the movement of your arms, legs, and torso together when the whole body is in motion.
Speed of Limb Movement	The ability to quickly move the arms and legs.
Category Flexibility	The ability to generate or use different sets of rules for combining or grouping things in different ways.
Originality	The ability to come up with unusual or clever ideas about a given topic or situation, or to develop creative ways to solve a problem.
Speed of Closure	The ability to quickly make sense of, combine, and organize information into meaningful patterns.
Visualization	The ability to imagine how something will look after it is moved around or when its parts are moved or rearranged.
Wrist-Finger Speed	The ability to make fast, simple, repeated movements of the fingers, hands, and wrists.
Fluency of Ideas	The ability to come up with a number of ideas about a topic (the number of ideas is important, not their quality, correctness, or creativity).
Mathematical Reasoning	The ability to choose the right mathematical methods or formulas to solve a problem.
Memorization	The ability to remember information such as words, numbers, pictures, and procedures.
Stamina	The ability to exert yourself physically over long periods of time without getting winded or out of breath.
Dynamic Strength	The ability to exert muscle force repeatedly or continuously over time. This involves muscular endurance and resistance to muscle fatigue.
Gross Body Equilibrium	The ability to keep or regain your body balance or stay upright when in an unstable position.
Explosive Strength	The ability to use short bursts of muscle force to propel oneself (as in jumping or sprinting), or to throw an object.
Dynamic Flexibility	The ability to quickly and repeatedly bend, stretch, twist, or reach out with your body, arms, and/or legs.

Work_Activity	Work_Activity Definitions
Operating Vehicles, Mechanized Devices, or Equipme	Running, maneuvering, navigating, or driving vehicles or mechanized equipment, such as forklifts, passenger vehicles, aircraft, or water craft.
Getting Information	Observing, receiving, and otherwise obtaining information from all relevant sources.
Inspecting Equipment, Structures, or Material	Inspecting equipment, structures, or materials to identify the cause of errors or other problems or defects.
Identifying Objects, Actions, and Events	Identifying information by categorizing, estimating, recognizing differences or similarities, and detecting changes in circumstances or events.
Performing for or Working Directly with the Public	Performing for people or dealing directly with the public. This includes serving customers in restaurants and stores, and receiving clients or guests.
Making Decisions and Solving Problems	Analyzing information and evaluating results to choose the best solution and solve problems.
Communicating with Supervisors, Peers, or Subordin	Providing information to supervisors, co-workers, and subordinates by telephone, in written form, e-mail, or in person.
Communicating with Persons Outside Organization	Communicating with people outside the organization, representing the organization to customers, the public, government, and other external sources. This information can be exchanged in person, in writing, or by telephone or e-mail.
Updating and Using Relevant Knowledge	Keeping up-to-date technically and applying new knowledge to your job.
Assisting and Caring for Others	Providing personal assistance, medical attention, emotional support, or other personal care to others such as coworkers, customers, or patients.
Documenting/Recording Information	Entering, transcribing, recording, storing, or maintaining information in written or electronic/magnetic form.
Establishing and Maintaining Interpersonal Relatio	Developing constructive and cooperative working relationships with others, and maintaining them over time.
Monitor Processes, Materials, or Surroundings	Monitoring and reviewing information from materials, events, or the environment, to detect or assess problems.
Evaluating Information to Determine Compliance wit	Using relevant information and individual judgment to determine whether events or processes comply with laws, regulations, or standards.
Handling and Moving Objects	Using hands and arms in handling, installing, positioning, and moving materials, and manipulating things.

Performing General Physical Activities	Performing physical activities that require considerable use of your arms and legs and moving your whole body, such as climbing, lifting, balancing, walking, stooping, and handling of materials.
Judging the Qualities of Things, Services, or Peop	Assessing the value, importance, or quality of things or people.
Thinking Creatively	Developing, designing, or creating new applications, ideas, relationships, systems, or products, including artistic contributions.
Estimating the Quantifiable Characteristics of Pro	Estimating sizes, distances, and quantities; or determining time, costs, resources, or materials needed to perform a work activity.
Organizing, Planning, and Prioritizing Work	Developing specific goals and plans to prioritize, organize, and accomplish your work.
Interpreting the Meaning of Information for Others	Translating or explaining what information means and how it can be used.
Coordinating the Work and Activities of Others	Getting members of a group to work together to accomplish tasks.
Controlling Machines and Processes	Using either control mechanisms or direct physical activity to operate machines or processes (not including computers or vehicles).
Performing Administrative Activities	Performing day-to-day administrative tasks such as maintaining information files and processing paperwork.
Processing Information	Compiling, coding, categorizing, calculating, tabulating, auditing, or verifying information or data.
Provide Consultation and Advice to Others	Providing guidance and expert advice to management or other groups on technical, systems-, or process-related topics.
Resolving Conflicts and Negotiating with Others	Handling complaints, settling disputes, and resolving grievances and conflicts, or otherwise negotiating with others.
Developing Objectives and Strategies	Establishing long-range objectives and specifying the strategies and actions to achieve them.
Analyzing Data or Information	Identifying the underlying principles, reasons, or facts of information by breaking down information or data into separate parts.
Developing and Building Teams	Encouraging and building mutual trust, respect, and cooperation among team members.
Guiding, Directing, and Motivating Subordinates	Providing guidance and direction to subordinates, including setting performance standards and monitoring performance.
Scheduling Work and Activities	Scheduling events, programs, and activities, as well as the work of others.
Repairing and Maintaining Mechanical Equipment	Servicing, repairing, adjusting, and testing machines, devices, moving parts, and equipment that operate primarily on the basis of mechanical (not electronic) principles.
Coaching and Developing Others	Identifying the developmental needs of others and coaching, mentoring, or otherwise helping others to improve their knowledge or skills.
Training and Teaching Others	Identifying the educational needs of others, developing formal educational or training programs or classes, and teaching or instructing others.
Selling or Influencing Others	Convincing others to buy merchandise/goods or to otherwise change their minds or actions.
Monitoring and Controlling Resources	Monitoring and controlling resources and overseeing the spending of money.
Drafting, Laying Out, and Specifying Technical Dev	Providing documentation, detailed instructions, drawings, or specifications to tell others about how devices, parts, equipment, or structures are to be fabricated, constructed, assembled, modified, maintained, or used.
Repairing and Maintaining Electronic Equipment	Servicing, repairing, calibrating, regulating, fine-tuning, or testing machines, devices, and equipment that operate primarily on the basis of electrical or electronic (not mechanical) principles.
Staffing Organizational Units	Recruiting, interviewing, selecting, hiring, and promoting employees in an organization.
Interacting With Computers	Using computers and computer systems (including hardware and software) to program, write software, set up functions, enter data, or process information.

Work_Context	Work_Context Definitions
In an Enclosed Vehicle or Equipment	How often does this job require working in a closed vehicle or equipment (e.g., car)?
Contact With Others	How much does this job require the worker to be in contact with others (face-to-face, by telephone, or otherwise) in order to perform it?
Frequency of Decision Making	How frequently is the worker required to make decisions that affect other people, the financial resources, and/or the image and reputation of the organization?

Impact of Decisions on Co-workers or Company Resul	How do the decisions an employee makes impact the results of co-workers, clients or the company?
Deal With External Customers	How important is it to work with external customers or the public in this job?
Sounds. Noise Levels Are Distracting or Uncomforta	How often does this job require working exposed to sounds and noise levels that are distracting or uncomfortable?
Freedom to Make Decisions	How much decision making freedom, without supervision, does the job offer?
Spend Time Using Your Hands to Handle. Control, or	How much does this job require using your hands to handle, control, or feel objects, tools or controls?
Time Pressure	How often does this job require the worker to meet strict deadlines?
Physical Proximity	To what extent does this job require the worker to perform job tasks in close physical proximity to other people?
Work With Work Group or Team	How important is it to work with others in a group or team in this job?
Importance of Being Exact or Accurate	How important is being very exact or highly accurate in performing this job?
Spend Time Sitting	How much does this job require sitting?
Face-to-Face Discussions	How often do you have to have face-to-face discussions with individuals or teams in this job?
Importance of Repeating Same Tasks	How important is repeating the same physical activities (e.g., key entry) or mental activities (e.g., checking entries in a ledger) over and over, without stopping, to performing this job?
Spend Time Making Repetitive Motions	How much does this job require making repetitive motions?
Responsible for Others' Health and Safety	How much responsibility is there for the health and safety of others in this job?
Exposed to Contaminants	How often does this job require working exposed to contaminants (such as pollutants, gases, dust or odors)?
Consequence of Error	How serious would the result usually be if the worker made a mistake that was not readily correctable?
Coordinate or Lead Others	How important is it to coordinate or lead others in accomplishing work activities in this job?
Telephone	How often do you have telephone conversations in this job?
Deal With Unpleasant or Angry People	How frequently does the worker have to deal with unpleasant, angry, or discourteous individuals as part of the job requirements?
Outdoors, Exposed to Weather	How often does this job require working outdoors, exposed to all weather conditions?
Frequency of Conflict Situations	How often are there conflict situations the employee has to face in this job?
Structured versus Unstructured Work	To what extent is this job structured for the worker, rather than allowing the worker to determine tasks, priorities, and goals?
Pace Determined by Speed of Equipment	How important is it to this job that the pace is determined by the speed of equipment or machinery? (This does not refer to keeping busy at all times on this job.)
Very Hot or Cold Temperatures	How often does this job require working in very hot (above 90 F degrees) or very cold (below 32 F degrees) temperatures?
Extremely Bright or Inadequate Lighting	How often does this job require working in extremely bright or inadequate lighting conditions?
Level of Competition	To what extent does this job require the worker to compete or to be aware of competitive pressures?
Responsibility for Outcomes and Results	How responsible is the worker for work outcomes and results of other workers?
Exposed to Disease or Infections	How often does this job require exposure to disease/infections?
Spend Time Bending or Twisting the Body	How much does this job require bending or twisting your body?
Indoors, Not Environmentally Controlled	How often does this job require working indoors in non-controlled environmental conditions (e.g., warehouse without heat)?
Public Speaking	How often do you have to perform public speaking in this job?
Letters and Memos	How often does the job require written letters and memos?
Deal With Physically Aggressive People	How frequently does this job require the worker to deal with physical aggression of violent individuals?
Outdoors, Under Cover	How often does this job require working outdoors, under cover (e.g., structure with roof but no walls)?
Cramped Work Space, Awkward Positions	How often does this job require working in cramped work spaces that requires getting into awkward positions?
Spend Time Standing	How much does this job require standing?
Degree of Automation	How automated is the job?
Exposed to Minor Burns, Cuts, Bites, or Stings	How often does this job require exposure to minor burns, cuts, bites, or stings?

Wear Specialized Protective or Safety Equipment su	How much does this job require wearing specialized protective or safety equipment such as breathing apparatus, safety harness, full protection suits, or radiation protection?
Indoors, Environmentally Controlled	How often does this job require working indoors in environmentally controlled conditions?
Exposed to Whole Body Vibration	How often does this job require exposure to whole body vibration (e.g., operate a jackhammer)?
Electronic Mail	How often do you use electronic mail in this job?
Spend Time Kneeling, Crouching, Stooping, or Crawl	How much does this job require kneeling, crouching, stooping, or crawling?
Exposed to Hazardous Conditions	How often does this job require exposure to hazardous conditions?
Spend Time Walking and Running	How much does this job require walking and running?
In an Open Vehicle or Equipment	How often does this job require working in an open vehicle or equipment (e.g., tractor)?
Wear Common Protective or Safety Equipment such as	How much does this job require wearing common protective or safety equipment such as safety shoes, glasses, gloves, hard hats or live jackets?
Spend Time Keeping or Regaining Balance	How much does this job require keeping or regaining your balance?
Exposed to Hazardous Equipment	How often does this job require exposure to hazardous equipment?
Spend Time Climbing Ladders, Scaffolds, or Poles	How much does this job require climbing ladders, scaffolds, or poles?
Exposed to High Places	How often does this job require exposure to high places?
Exposed to Radiation	How often does this job require exposure to radiation?

Job Zone Component	Job Zone Component Definitions
Title	Job Zone Two: Some Preparation Needed
	Some previous work-related skill, knowledge, or experience may be helpful in these occupations, but usually is not needed.
Overall Experience	For example, a drywall installer might benefit from experience installing drywall, but an inexperienced person could still learn to be an installer with little difficulty.
Job Training	Employees in these occupations need anywhere from a few months to one year of working with experienced employees. These occupations often involve using your knowledge and
Job Zone Examples	skills to help others. Examples include drywall installers, fire inspectors, flight attendants, pharmacy technicians, salespersons (retail), and tellers.
SVP Range	(4.0 to < 6.0)
Education	These occupations usually require a high school diploma and may require some vocational training or job-related course work. In some cases, an associate's or bachelor's degree could be needed.

Work_Styles	Work_Styles Definitions
Self Control	Job requires maintaining composure, keeping emotions in check, controlling anger, and avoiding aggressive behavior, even in very difficult situations.
Cooperation	Job requires being pleasant with others on the job and displaying a good-natured, cooperative attitude.
Dependability	Job requires being reliable, responsible, and dependable, and fulfilling obligations.
Concern for Others	Job requires being sensitive to others' needs and feelings and being understanding and helpful on the job.
Integrity	Job requires being honest and ethical.
Attention to Detail	Job requires being careful about detail and thorough in completing work tasks.
Stress Tolerance	Job requires accepting criticism and dealing calmly and effectively with high stress situations.
Initiative	Job requires a willingness to take on responsibilities and challenges.
Independence	Job requires developing one's own ways of doing things, guiding oneself with little or no supervision, and depending on oneself to get things done.
Social Orientation	Job requires preferring to work with others rather than alone, and being personally connected with others on the job.
Leadership	Job requires a willingness to lead, take charge, and offer opinions and direction.
Adaptability/Flexibility	Job requires being open to change (positive or negative) and to considerable variety in the workplace.

Persistence	Job requires persistence in the face of obstacles.
Analytical Thinking	Job requires analyzing information and using logic to address work-related issues and problems.
Innovation	Job requires creativity and alternative thinking to develop new ideas for and answers to work-related problems.
Achievement/Effort	Job requires establishing and maintaining personally challenging achievement goals and exerting effort toward mastering tasks.

53-3022.00 - Bus Drivers, School

Transport students or special clients, such as the elderly or persons with disabilities. Ensure adherence to safety rules. May assist passengers in boarding or exiting.

Tasks

1) Report delays, accidents, or other traffic and transportation situations, using telephones or mobile two-way radios.

2) Report any bus malfunctions or needed repairs.

3) Prepare and submit reports that may include the number of passengers or trips, hours worked, mileage, fuel consumption, and/or fares received.

4) Make minor repairs to vehicles.

5) Read maps, and follow written and verbal geographic directions.

6) Maintain knowledge of first-aid procedures.

7) Regulate heating, lighting, and ventilation systems for passenger comfort.

8) Pick up and drop off students at regularly scheduled neighborhood locations, following strict time schedules.

9) Follow safety rules as students are boarding and exiting buses, and as they cross streets near bus stops.

10) Comply with traffic regulations in order to operate vehicles in a safe and courteous manner.

11) Check the condition of a vehicle's tires, brakes, windshield wipers, lights, oil, fuel, water, and safety equipment to ensure that everything is in working order.

12) Drive gasoline, diesel, or electrically powered multi-passenger vehicles to transport students between neighborhoods, schools, and school activities.

13) Escort small children across roads and highways.

14) Maintain order among pupils during trips, in order to ensure safety.

53-3031.00 - Driver/Sales Workers

Drive truck or other vehicle over established routes or within an established territory and sell goods, such as food products, including restaurant take-out items, or pick up and deliver items, such as laundry. May also take orders and collect payments. Includes newspaper delivery drivers.

Tasks

1) Collect money from customers, make change, and record transactions on customer receipts.

2) Inform regular customers of new products or services and price changes.

3) Record sales or delivery information on daily sales or delivery record.

4) Write customer orders and sales contracts according to company guidelines.

5) Arrange merchandise and sales promotion displays, or issue sales promotion materials to customers.

6) Drive trucks in order to deliver such items as food, medical supplies, or newspapers.

7) Call on prospective customers in order to explain company services and to solicit new business.

8) Review lists of dealers, customers, or station drops and load trucks.

9) Sell food specialties, such as sandwiches and beverages, to office workers and patrons of sports events.

10) Maintain trucks and food-dispensing equipment and clean inside of machines that dispense food or beverages.

11) Collect coins from vending machines, refill machines, and remove aged merchandise.

Knowledge	Knowledge Definitions
English Language	Knowledge of the structure and content of the English language including the meaning and spelling of words, rules of composition, and grammar.
Customer and Personal Service	Knowledge of principles and processes for providing customer and personal services. This includes customer needs assessment, meeting quality standards for services, and evaluation of customer satisfaction.
Mathematics	Knowledge of arithmetic, algebra, geometry, calculus, statistics, and their applications.
Public Safety and Security	Knowledge of relevant equipment, policies, procedures, and strategies to promote effective local, state, or national security operations for the protection of people, data, property, and institutions.
Transportation	Knowledge of principles and methods for moving people or goods by air, rail, sea, or road, including the relative costs and benefits.
Sales and Marketing	Knowledge of principles and methods for showing, promoting, and selling products or services. This includes marketing strategy and tactics, product demonstration, sales techniques, and sales control systems.
Production and Processing	Knowledge of raw materials, production processes, quality control, costs, and other techniques for maximizing the effective manufacture and distribution of goods.
Education and Training	Knowledge of principles and methods for curriculum and training design, teaching and instruction for individuals and groups, and the measurement of training effects.
Administration and Management	Knowledge of business and management principles involved in strategic planning, resource allocation, human resources modeling, leadership technique, production methods, and coordination of people and resources.
Computers and Electronics	Knowledge of circuit boards, processors, chips, electronic equipment, and computer hardware and software, including applications and programming.
Geography	Knowledge of principles and methods for describing the features of land, sea, and air masses, including their physical characteristics, locations, interrelationships, and distribution of plant, animal, and human life.
Food Production	Knowledge of techniques and equipment for planting, growing, and harvesting food products (both plant and animal) for consumption, including storage/handling techniques.
Clerical	Knowledge of administrative and clerical procedures and systems such as word processing, managing files and records, stenography and transcription, designing forms, and other office procedures and terminology.
Telecommunications	Knowledge of transmission, broadcasting, switching, control, and operation of telecommunications systems.
Chemistry	Knowledge of the chemical composition, structure, and properties of substances and of the chemical processes and transformations that they undergo. This includes uses of chemicals and their interactions, danger signs, production techniques, and disposal methods.
Engineering and Technology	Knowledge of the practical application of engineering science and technology. This includes applying principles, techniques, procedures, and equipment to the design and production of various goods and services.
Mechanical	Knowledge of machines and tools, including their designs, uses, repair, and maintenance.
Communications and Media	Knowledge of media production, communication, and dissemination techniques and methods. This includes alternative ways to inform and entertain via written, oral, and visual media.
Law and Government	Knowledge of laws, legal codes, court procedures, precedents, government regulations, executive orders, agency rules, and the democratic political process.
Personnel and Human Resources	Knowledge of principles and procedures for personnel recruitment, selection, training, compensation and benefits, labor relations and negotiation, and personnel information systems.
Design	Knowledge of design techniques, tools, and principles involved in production of precision technical plans, blueprints, drawings, and models.

Economics and Accounting	Knowledge of economic and accounting principles and practices. the financial markets. banking and the analysis and reporting of financial data.
Biology	Knowledge of plant and animal organisms. their tissues, cells. functions, interdependencies. and interactions with each other and the environment.
Psychology	Knowledge of human behavior and performance; individual differences in ability. personality. and interests; learning and motivation; psychological research methods; and the assessment and treatment of behavioral and affective disorders.
Sociology and Anthropology	Knowledge of group behavior and dynamics, societal trends and influences. human migrations. ethnicity. cultures and their history and origins.
Physics	Knowledge and prediction of physical principles, laws, their interrelationships, and applications to understanding fluid, material, and atmospheric dynamics, and mechanical, electrical, atomic and sub- atomic structures and processes.
Medicine and Dentistry	Knowledge of the information and techniques needed to diagnose and treat human injuries, diseases, and deformities. This includes symptoms, treatment alternatives, drug properties and interactions, and preventive health-care measures.
Foreign Language	Knowledge of the structure and content of a foreign (non-English) language including the meaning and spelling of words, rules of composition and grammar, and pronunciation.
Building and Construction	Knowledge of materials, methods, and the tools involved in the construction or repair of houses, buildings, or other structures such as highways and roads.
Philosophy and Theology	Knowledge of different philosophical systems and religions. This includes their basic principles, values, ethics, ways of thinking, customs, practices, and their impact on human culture.
Fine Arts	Knowledge of the theory and techniques required to compose, produce, and perform works of music. dance, visual arts, drama, and sculpture.
History and Archeology	Knowledge of historical events and their causes, indicators, and effects on civilizations and cultures.
Therapy and Counseling	Knowledge of principles, methods, and procedures for diagnosis, treatment, and rehabilitation of physical and mental dysfunctions, and for career counseling and guidance.

Skills	Skills Definitions
Active Listening	Giving full attention to what other people are saying, taking time to understand the points being made, asking questions as appropriate, and not interrupting at inappropriate times.
Speaking	Talking to others to convey information effectively.
Social Perceptiveness	Being aware of others' reactions and understanding why they react as they do.
Critical Thinking	Using logic and reasoning to identify the strengths and weaknesses of alternative solutions, conclusions or approaches to problems.
Coordination	Adjusting actions in relation to others' actions.
Time Management	Managing one's own time and the time of others.
Service Orientation	Actively looking for ways to help people.
Active Learning	Understanding the implications of new information for both current and future problem-solving and decision-making.
Reading Comprehension	Understanding written sentences and paragraphs in work related documents.
Mathematics	Using mathematics to solve problems.
Persuasion	Persuading others to change their minds or behavior.
Negotiation	Bringing others together and trying to reconcile differences.
Learning Strategies	Selecting and using training/instructional methods and procedures appropriate for the situation when learning or teaching new things.
Judgment and Decision Making	Considering the relative costs and benefits of potential actions to choose the most appropriate one.
Monitoring	Monitoring/Assessing performance of yourself, other individuals, or organizations to make improvements or take corrective action.
Writing	Communicating effectively in writing as appropriate for the needs of the audience.
Troubleshooting	Determining causes of operating errors and deciding what to do about it.
Instructing	Teaching others how to do something.
Equipment Selection	Determining the kind of tools and equipment needed to do a job.
Quality Control Analysis	Conducting tests and inspections of products, services, or processes to evaluate quality or performance.

Complex Problem Solving	Identifying complex problems and reviewing related information to develop and evaluate options and implement solutions.
Equipment Maintenance	Performing routine maintenance on equipment and determining when and what kind of maintenance is needed.
Operation Monitoring	Watching gauges, dials, or other indicators to make sure a machine is working properly.
Management of Material Resources	Obtaining and seeing to the appropriate use of equipment. facilities. and materials needed to do certain work.
Management of Personnel Resources	Motivating, developing, and directing people as they work, identifying the best people for the job.
Operations Analysis	Analyzing needs and product requirements to create a design.
Systems Evaluation	Identifying measures or indicators of system performance and the actions needed to improve or correct performance. relative to the goals of the system.
Installation	Installing equipment, machines, wiring, or programs to meet specifications.
Operation and Control	Controlling operations of equipment or systems.
Technology Design	Generating or adapting equipment and technology to serve user needs.
Science	Using scientific rules and methods to solve problems.
Repairing	Repairing machines or systems using the needed tools.
Systems Analysis	Determining how a system should work and how changes in conditions, operations, and the environment will affect outcomes.
Management of Financial Resources	Determining how money will be spent to get the work done. and accounting for these expenditures.
Programming	Writing computer programs for various purposes.

Ability	Ability Definitions
Oral Comprehension	The ability to listen to and understand information and ideas presented through spoken words and sentences.
Near Vision	The ability to see details at close range (within a few feet of the observer).
Oral Expression	The ability to communicate information and ideas in speaking so others will understand.
Speech Clarity	The ability to speak clearly so others can understand you.
Written Expression	The ability to communicate information and ideas in writing so others will understand.
Written Comprehension	The ability to read and understand information and ideas presented in writing.
Number Facility	The ability to add, subtract, multiply, or divide quickly and correctly.
Speech Recognition	The ability to identify and understand the speech of another person.
Inductive Reasoning	The ability to combine pieces of information to form general rules or conclusions (includes finding a relationship among seemingly unrelated events).
Depth Perception	The ability to judge which of several objects is closer or farther away from you, or to judge the distance between you and an object.
Problem Sensitivity	The ability to tell when something is wrong or is likely to go wrong. It does not involve solving the problem, only recognizing there is a problem.
Far Vision	The ability to see details at a distance.
Multilimb Coordination	The ability to coordinate two or more limbs (for example, two arms, two legs, or one leg and one arm) while sitting, standing, or lying down. It does not involve performing the activities while the whole body is in motion.
Control Precision	The ability to quickly and repeatedly adjust the controls of a machine or a vehicle to exact positions.
Spatial Orientation	The ability to know your location in relation to the environment or to know where other objects are in relation to you.
Selective Attention	The ability to concentrate on a task over a period of time without being distracted.
Deductive Reasoning	The ability to apply general rules to specific problems to produce answers that make sense.
Mathematical Reasoning	The ability to choose the right mathematical methods or formulas to solve a problem.
Manual Dexterity	The ability to quickly move your hand, your hand together with your arm, or your two hands to grasp, manipulate, or assemble objects.
Arm-Hand Steadiness	The ability to keep your hand and arm steady while moving your arm or while holding your arm and hand in one position.
Flexibility of Closure	The ability to identify or detect a known pattern (a figure, object, word, or sound) that is hidden in other distracting material.

Information Ordering	The ability to arrange things or actions in a certain order or pattern according to a specific rule or set of rules (e.g., patterns of numbers, letters, words, pictures, mathematical operations).
Reaction Time	The ability to quickly respond (with the hand, finger, or foot) to a signal (sound, light, picture) when it appears.
Time Sharing	The ability to shift back and forth between two or more activities or sources of information (such as speech, sounds, touch, or other sources).
Perceptual Speed	The ability to quickly and accurately compare similarities and differences among sets of letters, numbers, objects, pictures, or patterns. The things to be compared may be presented at the same time or one after the other. This ability also includes comparing a presented object with a remembered object.
Finger Dexterity	The ability to make precisely coordinated movements of the fingers of one or both hands to grasp, manipulate, or assemble very small objects.
Static Strength	The ability to exert maximum muscle force to lift, push, pull, or carry objects.
Originality	The ability to come up with unusual or clever ideas about a given topic or situation, or to develop creative ways to solve a problem.
Category Flexibility	The ability to generate or use different sets of rules for combining or grouping things in different ways.
Visual Color Discrimination	The ability to match or detect differences between colors, including shades of color and brightness.
Trunk Strength	The ability to use your abdominal and lower back muscles to support part of the body repeatedly or continuously over time without 'giving out' or fatiguing.
Response Orientation	The ability to choose quickly between two or more movements in response to two or more different signals (lights, sounds, pictures). It includes the speed with which the correct response is started with the hand, foot, or other body part.
Visualization	The ability to imagine how something will look after it is moved around or when its parts are moved or rearranged.
Fluency of Ideas	The ability to come up with a number of ideas about a topic (the number of ideas is important, not their quality, correctness, or creativity).
Memorization	The ability to remember information such as words, numbers, pictures, and procedures.
Peripheral Vision	The ability to see objects or movement of objects to one's side when the eyes are looking ahead.
Hearing Sensitivity	The ability to detect or tell the differences between sounds that vary in pitch and loudness.
Glare Sensitivity	The ability to see objects in the presence of glare or bright lighting.
Speed of Closure	The ability to quickly make sense of, combine, and organize information into meaningful patterns.
Rate Control	The ability to time your movements or the movement of a piece of equipment in anticipation of changes in the speed and/or direction of a moving object or scene.
Night Vision	The ability to see under low light conditions.
Gross Body Coordination	The ability to coordinate the movement of your arms, legs, and torso together when the whole body is in motion.
Dynamic Strength	The ability to exert muscle force repeatedly or continuously over time. This involves muscular endurance and resistance to muscle fatigue.
Extent Flexibility	The ability to bend, stretch, twist, or reach with your body, arms, and/or legs.
Auditory Attention	The ability to focus on a single source of sound in the presence of other distracting sounds.
Sound Localization	The ability to tell the direction from which a sound originated.
Stamina	The ability to exert yourself physically over long periods of time without getting winded or out of breath.
Speed of Limb Movement	The ability to quickly move the arms and legs.
Wrist-Finger Speed	The ability to make fast, simple, repeated movements of the fingers, hands, and wrists.
Gross Body Equilibrium	The ability to keep or regain your body balance or stay upright when in an unstable position.
Explosive Strength	The ability to use short bursts of muscle force to propel oneself (as in jumping or sprinting), or to throw an object.
Dynamic Flexibility	The ability to quickly and repeatedly bend, stretch, twist, or reach out with your body, arms, and/or legs.

Work_Activity	Work_Activity Definitions
Communicating with Persons Outside Organization	Communicating with people outside the organization, representing the organization to customers, the public, government, and other external sources. This information can be exchanged in person, in writing, or by telephone or e-mail.
Getting Information	Observing, receiving, and otherwise obtaining information from all relevant sources.
Selling or Influencing Others	Convincing others to buy merchandise/goods or to otherwise change their minds or actions.
Identifying Objects, Actions, and Events	Identifying information by categorizing, estimating, recognizing differences or similarities, and detecting changes in circumstances or events.
Monitor Processes, Materials, or Surroundings	Monitoring and reviewing information from materials, events, or the environment, to detect or assess problems.
Communicating with Supervisors, Peers, or Subordin	Providing information to supervisors, co-workers, and subordinates by telephone, in written form, e-mail, or in person.
Operating Vehicles, Mechanized Devices, or Equipme	Running, maneuvering, navigating, or driving vehicles or mechanized equipment, such as forklifts, passenger vehicles, aircraft, or water craft.
Performing for or Working Directly with the Public	Performing for people or dealing directly with the public. This includes serving customers in restaurants and stores, and receiving clients or guests.
Handling and Moving Objects	Using hands and arms in handling, installing, positioning, and moving materials, and manipulating things.
Establishing and Maintaining Interpersonal Relatio	Developing constructive and cooperative working relationships with others, and maintaining them over time.
Organizing, Planning, and Prioritizing Work	Developing specific goals and plans to prioritize, organize, and accomplish your work.
Performing General Physical Activities	Performing physical activities that require considerable use of your arms and legs and moving your whole body, such as climbing, lifting, balancing, walking, stooping, and handling of materials.
Controlling Machines and Processes	Using either control mechanisms or direct physical activity to operate machines or processes (not including computers or vehicles).
Judging the Qualities of Things, Services, or Peop	Assessing the value, importance, or quality of things or people.
Analyzing Data or Information	Identifying the underlying principles, reasons, or facts of information by breaking down information or data into separate parts.
Inspecting Equipment, Structures, or Material	Inspecting equipment, structures, or materials to identify the cause of errors or other problems or defects.
Scheduling Work and Activities	Scheduling events, programs, and activities, as well as the work of others.
Estimating the Quantifiable Characteristics of Pro	Estimating sizes, distances, and quantities; or determining time, costs, resources, or materials needed to perform a work activity.
Interacting With Computers	Using computers and computer systems (including hardware and software) to program, write software, set up functions, enter data, or process information.
Thinking Creatively	Developing, designing, or creating new applications, ideas, relationships, systems, or products, including artistic contributions.
Processing Information	Compiling, coding, categorizing, calculating, tabulating, auditing, or verifying information or data.
Training and Teaching Others	Identifying the educational needs of others, developing formal educational or training programs or classes, and teaching or instructing others.
Documenting/Recording Information	Entering, transcribing, recording, storing, or maintaining information in written or electronic/magnetic form.
Making Decisions and Solving Problems	Analyzing information and evaluating results to choose the best solution and solve problems.
Evaluating Information to Determine Compliance wit	Using relevant information and individual judgment to determine whether events or processes comply with laws, regulations, or standards.
Developing and Building Teams	Encouraging and building mutual trust, respect, and cooperation among team members.
Updating and Using Relevant Knowledge	Keeping up-to-date technically and applying new knowledge to your job.
Assisting and Caring for Others	Providing personal assistance, medical attention, emotional support, or other personal care to others such as coworkers, customers, or patients.
Resolving Conflicts and Negotiating with Others	Handling complaints, settling disputes, and resolving grievances and conflicts, or otherwise negotiating with others.

Coordinating the Work and Activities of Others	Getting members of a group to work together to accomplish tasks.
Developing Objectives and Strategies	Establishing long-range objectives and specifying the strategies and actions to achieve them.
Monitoring and Controlling Resources	Monitoring and controlling resources and overseeing the spending of money.
Coaching and Developing Others	Identifying the developmental needs of others and coaching, mentoring, or otherwise helping others to improve their knowledge or skills.
Interpreting the Meaning of Information for Others	Translating or explaining what information means and how it can be used.
Provide Consultation and Advice to Others	Providing guidance and expert advice to management or other groups on technical, systems-, or process-related topics.
Staffing Organizational Units	Recruiting, interviewing, selecting, hiring, and promoting employees in an organization.
Repairing and Maintaining Electronic Equipment	Servicing, repairing, calibrating, regulating, fine-tuning, or testing machines, devices, and equipment that operate primarily on the basis of electrical or electronic (not mechanical) principles.
Guiding, Directing, and Motivating Subordinates	Providing guidance and direction to subordinates, including setting performance standards and monitoring performance.
Repairing and Maintaining Mechanical Equipment	Servicing, repairing, adjusting, and testing machines, devices, moving parts, and equipment that operate primarily on the basis of mechanical (not electronic) principles.
Drafting, Laying Out, and Specifying Technical Dev	Providing documentation, detailed instructions, drawings, or specifications to tell others about how devices, parts, equipment, or structures are to be fabricated, constructed, assembled, modified, maintained, or used.
Performing Administrative Activities	Performing day-to-day administrative tasks such as maintaining information files and processing paperwork.

Work_Context	**Work_Context Definitions**
In an Enclosed Vehicle or Equipment	How often does this job require working in a closed vehicle or equipment (e.g., car)?
Telephone	How often do you have telephone conversations in this job?
Face-to-Face Discussions	How often do you have to have face-to-face discussions with individuals or teams in this job?
Impact of Decisions on Co-workers or Company Resul	How do the decisions an employee makes impact the results of co-workers, clients or the company?
Deal With External Customers	How important is it to work with external customers or the public in this job?
Contact With Others	How much does this job require the worker to be in contact with others (face-to-face, by telephone, or otherwise) in order to perform it?
Work With Work Group or Team	How important is it to work with others in a group or team in this job?
Frequency of Decision Making	How frequently is the worker required to make decisions that affect other people, the financial resources, and/or the image and reputation of the organization?
Physical Proximity	To what extent does this job require the worker to perform job tasks in close physical proximity to other people?
Outdoors, Exposed to Weather	How often does this job require working outdoors, exposed to all weather conditions?
Freedom to Make Decisions	How much decision making freedom, without supervision, does the job offer?
Structured versus Unstructured Work	To what extent is this job structured for the worker, rather than allowing the worker to determine tasks, priorities, and goals?
Importance of Being Exact or Accurate	How important is being very exact or highly accurate in performing this job?
Spend Time Using Your Hands to Handle, Control, or	How much does this job require using your hands to handle, control, or feel objects, tools or controls?
Time Pressure	How often does this job require the worker to meet strict deadlines?
Very Hot or Cold Temperatures	How often does this job require working in very hot (above 90 F degrees) or very cold (below 32 F degrees) temperatures?
Indoors, Environmentally Controlled	How often does this job require working indoors in environmentally controlled conditions?
Deal With Unpleasant or Angry People	How frequently does the worker have to deal with unpleasant, angry, or discourteous individuals as part of the job requirements?
Spend Time Making Repetitive Motions	How much does this job require making repetitive motions?
Consequence of Error	How serious would the result usually be if the worker made a mistake that was not readily correctable?
Spend Time Sitting	How much does this job require sitting?

Frequency of Conflict Situations	How often are there conflict situations the employee has to face in this job?
Level of Competition	To what extent does this job require the worker to compete or to be aware of competitive pressures?
Spend Time Standing	How much does this job require standing?
Indoors, Not Environmentally Controlled	How often does this job require working indoors in non-controlled environmental conditions (e.g., warehouse without heat)?
Importance of Repeating Same Tasks	How important is repeating the same physical activities (e.g., key entry) or mental activities (e.g., checking entries in a ledger) over and over, without stopping, to performing this job?
Exposed to Minor Burns, Cuts, Bites, or Stings	How often does this job require exposure to minor burns, cuts, bites, or stings?
Spend Time Walking and Running	How much does this job require walking and running?
Coordinate or Lead Others	How important is it to coordinate or lead others in accomplishing work activities in this job?
Outdoors, Under Cover	How often does this job require working outdoors, under cover (e.g., structure with roof but no walls)?
Responsible for Others' Health and Safety	How much responsibility is there for the health and safety of others in this job?
Spend Time Bending or Twisting the Body	How much does this job require bending or twisting your body?
Sounds, Noise Levels Are Distracting or Uncomforta	How often does this job require working exposed to sounds and noise levels that are distracting or uncomfortable?
Letters and Memos	How often does the job require written letters and memos?
Wear Specialized Protective or Safety Equipment su	How much does this job require wearing specialized protective or safety equipment such as breathing apparatus, safety harness, full protection suits, or radiation protection?
Degree of Automation	How automated is the job?
Responsibility for Outcomes and Results	How responsible is the worker for work outcomes and results of other workers?
Cramped Work Space, Awkward Positions	How often does this job require working in cramped work spaces that requires getting into awkward positions?
Electronic Mail	How often do you use electronic mail in this job?
Pace Determined by Speed of Equipment	How important is it to this job that the pace is determined by the speed of equipment or machinery? (This does not refer to keeping busy at all times on this job.)
Extremely Bright or Inadequate Lighting	How often does this job require working in extremely bright or inadequate lighting conditions?
Spend Time Kneeling, Crouching, Stooping, or Crawl	How much does this job require kneeling, crouching, stooping, or crawling?
Exposed to Contaminants	How often does this job require working exposed to contaminants (such as pollutants, gases, dust or odors)?
Spend Time Keeping or Regaining Balance	How much does this job require keeping or regaining your balance?
Wear Common Protective or Safety Equipment such as	How much does this job require wearing common protective or safety equipment such as safety shoes, glasses, gloves, hard hats or life jackets?
Deal With Physically Aggressive People	How frequently does this job require the worker to deal with physical aggression of violent individuals?
Exposed to Hazardous Equipment	How often does this job require exposure to hazardous equipment?
Exposed to Disease or Infections	How often does this job require exposure to disease/infections?
Exposed to High Places	How often does this job require exposure to high places?
Spend Time Climbing Ladders, Scaffolds, or Poles	How much does this job require climbing ladders, scaffolds, or poles?
Exposed to Whole Body Vibration	How often does this job require exposure to whole body vibration (e.g., operate a jackhammer)?
Public Speaking	How often do you have to perform public speaking in this job?
In an Open Vehicle or Equipment	How often does this job require working in an open vehicle or equipment (e.g., tractor)?
Exposed to Radiation	How often does this job require exposure to radiation?
Exposed to Hazardous Conditions	How often does this job require exposure to hazardous conditions?

Job Zone Component	**Job Zone Component Definitions**
Title	Job Zone One: Little or No Preparation Needed
Overall Experience	No previous work-related skill, knowledge, or experience is needed for these occupations. For example, a person can become a general office clerk even if he/she has never worked in an office before.

Job Training	Employees in these occupations need anywhere from a few days to a few months of training. Usually, an experienced worker could show you how to do the job.
Job Zone Examples	These occupations involve following instructions and helping others. Examples include bus drivers, forest and conservation workers, general office clerks, home health aides, and waiters/waitresses.
SVP Range	(Below 4.0)
Education	These occupations may require a high school diploma or GED certificate. Some may require a formal training course to obtain a license.

Work_Styles	Work_Styles Definitions
Dependability	Job requires being reliable, responsible, and dependable, and fulfilling obligations.
Attention to Detail	Job requires being careful about detail and thorough in completing work tasks.
Self Control	Job requires maintaining composure, keeping emotions in check, controlling anger, and avoiding aggressive behavior, even in very difficult situations.
Integrity	Job requires being honest and ethical.
Cooperation	Job requires being pleasant with others on the job and displaying a good-natured, cooperative attitude.
Independence	Job requires developing one's own ways of doing things, guiding oneself with little or no supervision, and depending on oneself to get things done.
Adaptability/Flexibility	Job requires being open to change (positive or negative) and to considerable variety in the workplace.
Stress Tolerance	Job requires accepting criticism and dealing calmly and effectively with high stress situations.
Concern for Others	Job requires being sensitive to others' needs and feelings and being understanding and helpful on the job.
Social Orientation	Job requires preferring to work with others rather than alone, and being personally connected with others on the job.
Initiative	Job requires a willingness to take on responsibilities and challenges.
Achievement/Effort	Job requires establishing and maintaining personally challenging achievement goals and exerting effort toward mastering tasks.
Leadership	Job requires a willingness to lead, take charge, and offer opinions and direction.
Persistence	Job requires persistence in the face of obstacles.
Innovation	Job requires creativity and alternative thinking to develop new ideas for and answers to work-related problems.
Analytical Thinking	Job requires analyzing information and using logic to address work-related issues and problems.

53-3032.00 - Truck Drivers, Heavy and Tractor-Trailer

Drive a tractor-trailer combination or a truck with a capacity of at least 26,000 GVW, to transport and deliver goods, livestock, or materials in liquid, loose, or packaged form. May be required to unload truck. May require use of automated routing equipment. Requires commercial drivers' license.

Tasks

1) Check conditions of trailers after contents have been unloaded to ensure that there has been no damage.

2) Follow appropriate safety procedures when transporting dangerous goods.

3) Climb ladders to inspect loads after loading is complete, in order to ensure that cargo is secure.

4) Collect delivery instructions from appropriate sources, verifying instructions and routes.

5) Couple and uncouple trailers by changing trailer jack positions, connecting or disconnecting air and electrical lines, and manipulating fifth-wheel locks.

6) Obtain receipts or signatures when loads are delivered, and collect payment for services when required.

7) Drive trucks to weigh stations before and after loading and along routes, in order to document weights and to comply with state regulations.

8) Operate equipment such as truck cab computers, CB radios, and telephones to exchange necessary information with bases, supervisors, or other drivers.

9) Give directions to laborers who are packing goods and moving them onto trailers.

10) Secure cargo for transport, using ropes, blocks, chain, binders, and/or covers.

11) Check vehicles before driving them to ensure that mechanical, safety, and emergency equipment is in good working order.

12) Crank trailer landing gear up and down to safely secure vehicles.

13) Check all load-related documentation to ensure that it is complete and accurate.

14) Follow special procedures related to specific cargo, such as checking refrigeration systems when carrying frozen foods, or providing food and water when carrying livestock.

15) Perform emergency roadside repairs such as changing tires and installing light bulbs, tire chains, and spark plugs.

16) Drive trucks with capacities greater than 3 tons, including tractor-trailer combinations, in order to transport and deliver products, livestock, or other materials.

17) Perform basic vehicle maintenance tasks such as adding oil, fuel, and radiator fluid, or performing minor repairs.

18) Install and remove special equipment such as tire chains, grader blades, plow blades, and sanders.

19) Maintain logs of working hours and of vehicle service and repair status, following applicable state and federal regulations.

20) Operate trucks equipped with snowplows and sander attachments to maintain roads in winter weather.

21) Place empty carts and pallets in trailers so they will be available to facilitate placement and movement of goods.

22) Read and interpret maps in order to determine vehicle routes.

23) Remove any debris from trailers after loading is completed.

24) Wrap goods using pads, packing paper, and containers, and secure loads to trailer walls, using straps.

25) Hire other drivers to transport cargo on portions of routes, such as return trips.

26) Report vehicle defects, accidents, traffic violations, or damage to the vehicles.

27) Load and unload trucks, or help others with loading and unloading, operating any special loading-related equipment on vehicles and using other equipment as necessary.

28) Maneuver trucks into loading or unloading positions, following signals from loading crew as needed; check that vehicle position is correct and any special loading equipment is properly positioned.

29) Collaborate with other drivers as part of a driving team on some trips.

30) Inventory and inspect goods to be moved, in order to determine quantities and conditions.

53-3033.00 - Truck Drivers, Light or Delivery Services

Drive a truck or van with a capacity of under 26,000 GVW, primarily to deliver or pick up merchandise or to deliver packages within a specified area. May require use of automatic routing or location software. May load and unload truck.

Tasks

1) Inspect and maintain vehicle supplies and equipment, such as gas, oil, water, tires, lights, and brakes in order to ensure that vehicles are in proper working condition.

2) Turn in receipts and money received from deliveries.

3) Report delays, accidents, or other traffic and transportation situations to bases or other vehicles, using telephones or mobile two-way radios.

4) Report any mechanical problems encountered with vehicles.

5) Present bills and receipts, and collect payments for goods delivered or loaded.

6) Perform emergency repairs such as changing tires or installing light bulbs, fuses, tire chains, and spark plugs.

7) Obey traffic laws, and follow established traffic and transportation procedures.

8) Verify the contents of inventory loads against shipping papers.

9) Drive vehicles with capacities under three tons in order to transport materials to and from specified destinations such as railroad stations, plants, residences and offices, or within industrial yards.

10) Use and maintain the tools and equipment found on commercial vehicles, such as weighing and measuring devices.

11) Sell and keep records of sales for products from truck inventory.

12) Read maps, and follow written and verbal geographic directions.

13) Drive trucks equipped with public address systems through city streets in order to broadcast announcements for advertising or publicity purposes.

14) Maintain records such as vehicle logs, records of cargo, or billing statements in accordance with regulations.

53-3041.00 - Taxi Drivers and Chauffeurs

Drive automobiles, vans, or limousines to transport passengers. May occasionally carry cargo.

Tasks

1) Notify dispatchers or company mechanics of vehicle problems.

2) Communicate with dispatchers by radio, telephone, or computer in order to exchange information and receive requests for passenger service.

3) Provide passengers with assistance entering and exiting vehicles, and help them with any luggage.

4) Perform routine vehicle maintenance, such as regulating tire pressure and adding gasoline, oil, and water.

5) Drive taxicabs, limousines, company cars, or privately owned vehicles in order to transport passengers.

6) Pick up passengers at prearranged locations, at taxi stands, or by cruising streets in high traffic areas.

7) Vacuum and clean interiors, and wash and polish exteriors of automobiles.

8) Complete accident reports when necessary.

9) Follow regulations governing taxi operation and ensure that passengers follow safety regulations.

10) Record name, date, and taxi identification information on trip sheets, along with trip information such as time and place of pickup and drop-off, and total fee.

11) Arrange to pick up particular customers or groups on a regular schedule.

12) Provide passengers with information about the local area and points of interest, and/or give advice on hotels and restaurants.

13) Perform minor vehicle repairs such as cleaning spark plugs, or take vehicles to mechanics for servicing.

14) Pick up or meet employers according to requests, appointments, or schedules.

15) Collect fares or vouchers from passengers); and make change and/or issue receipts, as necessary.

16) Operate vans with special equipment, such as wheelchair lifts to transport people with special needs.

17) Determine fares based on trip distances and times, using taximeters and fee schedules, and announce fares to passengers.

18) Turn the taximeter on when passengers enter the cab, and turn it off when they reach the final destination.

19) Perform errands for customers or employers, such as delivering or picking up mail and packages.

20) Report to taxicab services or garages in order to receive vehicle assignments.

Knowledge	Knowledge Definitions
Customer and Personal Service	Knowledge of principles and processes for providing customer and personal services. This includes customer needs assessment, meeting quality standards for services, and evaluation of customer satisfaction.
Public Safety and Security	Knowledge of relevant equipment, policies, procedures, and strategies to promote effective local, state, or national security operations for the protection of people, data, property, and institutions.
English Language	Knowledge of the structure and content of the English language including the meaning and spelling of words, rules of composition, and grammar.
Transportation	Knowledge of principles and methods for moving people or goods by air, rail, sea, or road, including the relative costs and benefits.
Administration and Management	Knowledge of business and management principles involved in strategic planning, resource allocation, human resources modeling, leadership technique, production methods, and coordination of people and resources.
Economics and Accounting	Knowledge of economic and accounting principles and practices, the financial markets, banking and the analysis and reporting of financial data.
Clerical	Knowledge of administrative and clerical procedures and systems such as word processing, managing files and records, stenography and transcription, designing forms, and other office procedures and terminology.
Sales and Marketing	Knowledge of principles and methods for showing, promoting, and selling products or services. This includes marketing strategy and tactics, product demonstration, sales techniques, and sales control systems.
Personnel and Human Resources	Knowledge of principles and procedures for personnel recruitment, selection, training, compensation and benefits, labor relations and negotiation, and personnel information systems.
Telecommunications	Knowledge of transmission, broadcasting, switching, control, and operation of telecommunications systems.
Mathematics	Knowledge of arithmetic, algebra, geometry, calculus, statistics, and their applications.
Education and Training	Knowledge of principles and methods for curriculum and training design, teaching and instruction for individuals and groups, and the measurement of training effects.
Mechanical	Knowledge of machines and tools, including their designs, uses, repair, and maintenance.
Psychology	Knowledge of human behavior and performance; individual differences in ability, personality, and interests; learning and motivation; psychological research methods; and the assessment and treatment of behavioral and affective disorders.
Law and Government	Knowledge of laws, legal codes, court procedures, precedents, government regulations, executive orders, agency rules, and the democratic political process.
Geography	Knowledge of principles and methods for describing the features of land, sea, and air masses, including their physical characteristics, locations, interrelationships, and distribution of plant, animal, and human life.
Communications and Media	Knowledge of media production, communication, and dissemination techniques and methods. This includes alternative ways to inform and entertain via written, oral, and visual media.
Foreign Language	Knowledge of the structure and content of a foreign (non-English) language including the meaning and spelling of words, rules of composition and grammar, and pronunciation.
Sociology and Anthropology	Knowledge of group behavior and dynamics, societal trends and influences, human migrations, ethnicity, cultures and their history and origins.
Computers and Electronics	Knowledge of circuit boards, processors, chips, electronic equipment, and computer hardware and software, including applications and programming.
Production and Processing	Knowledge of raw materials, production processes, quality control, costs, and other techniques for maximizing the effective manufacture and distribution of goods.
Philosophy and Theology	Knowledge of different philosophical systems and religions. This includes their basic principles, values, ethics, ways of thinking, customs, practices, and their impact on human culture.
Medicine and Dentistry	Knowledge of the information and techniques needed to diagnose and treat human injuries, diseases, and deformities. This includes symptoms, treatment alternatives, drug properties and interactions, and preventive health-care measures.
History and Archeology	Knowledge of historical events and their causes, indicators, and effects on civilizations and cultures.
Therapy and Counseling	Knowledge of principles, methods, and procedures for diagnosis, treatment, and rehabilitation of physical and mental dysfunctions, and for career counseling and guidance.
Food Production	Knowledge of techniques and equipment for planting, growing, and harvesting food products (both plant and animal) for consumption, including storage/handling techniques.
Engineering and Technology	Knowledge of the practical application of engineering science and technology. This includes applying principles, techniques, procedures, and equipment to the design and production of various goods and services.
Biology	Knowledge of plant and animal organisms, their tissues, cells, functions, interdependencies, and interactions with each other and the environment.

Design	Knowledge of design techniques, tools, and principles involved in production of precision technical plans, blueprints, drawings, and models.
Building and Construction	Knowledge of materials, methods, and the tools involved in the construction or repair of houses, buildings, or other structures such as highways and roads.
Fine Arts	Knowledge of the theory and techniques required to compose, produce, and perform works of music, dance, visual arts, drama, and sculpture.
Chemistry	Knowledge of the chemical composition, structure, and properties of substances and of the chemical processes and transformations that they undergo. This includes uses of chemicals and their interactions, danger signs, production techniques, and disposal methods.
Physics	Knowledge and prediction of physical principles, laws, their interrelationships, and applications to understanding fluid, material, and atmospheric dynamics, and mechanical, electrical, atomic and sub- atomic structures and processes.

Skills	Skills Definitions
Time Management	Managing one's own time and the time of others.
Equipment Maintenance	Performing routine maintenance on equipment and determining when and what kind of maintenance is needed.
Social Perceptiveness	Being aware of others' reactions and understanding why they react as they do.
Mathematics	Using mathematics to solve problems.
Active Listening	Giving full attention to what other people are saying, taking time to understand the points being made, asking questions as appropriate, and not interrupting at inappropriate times.
Active Learning	Understanding the implications of new information for both current and future problem-solving and decision-making.
Operation and Control	Controlling operations of equipment or systems.
Critical Thinking	Using logic and reasoning to identify the strengths and weaknesses of alternative solutions, conclusions or approaches to problems.
Service Orientation	Actively looking for ways to help people.
Speaking	Talking to others to convey information effectively.
Reading Comprehension	Understanding written sentences and paragraphs in work related documents.
Instructing	Teaching others how to do something.
Operation Monitoring	Watching gauges, dials, or other indicators to make sure a machine is working properly.
Learning Strategies	Selecting and using training/instructional methods and procedures appropriate for the situation when learning or teaching new things.
Coordination	Adjusting actions in relation to others' actions.
Troubleshooting	Determining causes of operating errors and deciding what to do about it.
Equipment Selection	Determining the kind of tools and equipment needed to do a job.
Installation	Installing equipment, machines, wiring, or programs to meet specifications.
Writing	Communicating effectively in writing as appropriate for the needs of the audience.
Negotiation	Bringing others together and trying to reconcile differences.
Management of Financial Resources	Determining how money will be spent to get the work done, and accounting for these expenditures.
Judgment and Decision Making	Considering the relative costs and benefits of potential actions to choose the most appropriate one.
Monitoring	Monitoring/Assessing performance of yourself, other individuals, or organizations to make improvements or take corrective action.
Repairing	Repairing machines or systems using the needed tools.
Management of Personnel Resources	Motivating, developing, and directing people as they work, identifying the best people for the job.
Complex Problem Solving	Identifying complex problems and reviewing related information to develop and evaluate options and implement solutions.
Quality Control Analysis	Conducting tests and inspections of products, services, or processes to evaluate quality or performance.
Technology Design	Generating or adapting equipment and technology to serve user needs.
Persuasion	Persuading others to change their minds or behavior.
Management of Material Resources	Obtaining and seeing to the appropriate use of equipment, facilities, and materials needed to do certain work.
Operations Analysis	Analyzing needs and product requirements to create a design.

Systems Analysis	Determining how a system should work and how changes in conditions, operations, and the environment will affect outcomes.
Systems Evaluation	Identifying measures or indicators of system performance and the actions needed to improve or correct performance, relative to the goals of the system.
Programming	Writing computer programs for various purposes.
Science	Using scientific rules and methods to solve problems.

Ability	Ability Definitions
Response Orientation	The ability to choose quickly between two or more movements in response to two or more different signals (lights, sounds, pictures). It includes the speed with which the correct response is started with the hand, foot, or other body part.
Reaction Time	The ability to quickly respond (with the hand, finger, or foot) to a signal (sound, light, picture) when it appears.
Far Vision	The ability to see details at a distance.
Oral Comprehension	The ability to listen to and understand information and ideas presented through spoken words and sentences.
Time Sharing	The ability to shift back and forth between two or more activities or sources of information (such as speech, sounds, touch, or other sources).
Problem Sensitivity	The ability to tell when something is wrong or is likely to go wrong. It does not involve solving the problem, only recognizing there is a problem.
Night Vision	The ability to see under low light conditions.
Near Vision	The ability to see details at close range (within a few feet of the observer).
Control Precision	The ability to quickly and repeatedly adjust the controls of a machine or a vehicle to exact positions.
Oral Expression	The ability to communicate information and ideas in speaking so others will understand.
Spatial Orientation	The ability to know your location in relation to the environment or to know where other objects are in relation to you.
Depth Perception	The ability to judge which of several objects is closer or farther away from you, or to judge the distance between you and an object.
Peripheral Vision	The ability to see objects or movement of objects to one's side when the eyes are looking ahead.
Deductive Reasoning	The ability to apply general rules to specific problems to produce answers that make sense.
Speech Recognition	The ability to identify and understand the speech of another person.
Speech Clarity	The ability to speak clearly so others can understand you.
Selective Attention	The ability to concentrate on a task over a period of time without being distracted.
Glare Sensitivity	The ability to see objects in the presence of glare or bright lighting.
Inductive Reasoning	The ability to combine pieces of information to form general rules or conclusions (includes finding a relationship among seemingly unrelated events).
Multilimb Coordination	The ability to coordinate two or more limbs (for example, two arms, two legs, or one leg and one arm) while sitting, standing, or lying down. It does not involve performing the activities while the whole body is in motion.
Rate Control	The ability to time your movements or the movement of a piece of equipment in anticipation of changes in the speed and/or direction of a moving object or scene.
Hearing Sensitivity	The ability to detect or tell the differences between sounds that vary in pitch and loudness.
Flexibility of Closure	The ability to identify or detect a known pattern (a figure, object, word, or sound) that is hidden in other distracting material.
Written Expression	The ability to communicate information and ideas in writing so others will understand.
Arm-Hand Steadiness	The ability to keep your hand and arm steady while moving your arm or while holding your arm and hand in one position.
Visual Color Discrimination	The ability to match or detect differences between colors, including shades of color and brightness.
Auditory Attention	The ability to focus on a single source of sound in the presence of other distracting sounds.
Information Ordering	The ability to arrange things or actions in a certain order or pattern according to a specific rule or set of rules (e.g., patterns of numbers, letters, words, pictures, mathematical operations).
Written Comprehension	The ability to read and understand information and ideas presented in writing.

Manual Dexterity	The ability to quickly move your hand, your hand together with your arm, or your two hands to grasp, manipulate, or assemble objects.
Sound Localization	The ability to tell the direction from which a sound originated.
Static Strength	The ability to exert maximum muscle force to lift, push, pull, or carry objects.
Perceptual Speed	The ability to quickly and accurately compare similarities and differences among sets of letters, numbers, objects, pictures, or patterns. The things to be compared may be presented at the same time or one after the other. This ability also includes comparing a presented object with a remembered object.
Finger Dexterity	The ability to make precisely coordinated movements of the fingers of one or both hands to grasp, manipulate, or assemble very small objects.
Category Flexibility	The ability to generate or use different sets of rules for combining or grouping things in different ways.
Visualization	The ability to imagine how something will look after it is moved around or when its parts are moved or rearranged.
Speed of Closure	The ability to quickly make sense of, combine, and organize information into meaningful patterns.
Trunk Strength	The ability to use your abdominal and lower back muscles to support part of the body repeatedly or continuously over time without 'giving out' or fatiguing.
Number Facility	The ability to add, subtract, multiply, or divide quickly and correctly.
Fluency of Ideas	The ability to come up with a number of ideas about a topic (the number of ideas is important, not their quality, correctness, or creativity).
Speed of Limb Movement	The ability to quickly move the arms and legs.
Gross Body Coordination	The ability to coordinate the movement of your arms, legs, and torso together when the whole body is in motion.
Originality	The ability to come up with unusual or clever ideas about a given topic or situation, or to develop creative ways to solve a problem.
Mathematical Reasoning	The ability to choose the right mathematical methods or formulas to solve a problem.
Extent Flexibility	The ability to bend, stretch, twist, or reach with your body, arms, and/or legs.
Memorization	The ability to remember information such as words, numbers, pictures, and procedures.
Stamina	The ability to exert yourself physically over long periods of time without getting winded or out of breath.
Dynamic Strength	The ability to exert muscle force repeatedly or continuously over time. This involves muscular endurance and resistance to muscle fatigue.
Gross Body Equilibrium	The ability to keep or regain your body balance or stay upright when in an unstable position.
Dynamic Flexibility	The ability to quickly and repeatedly bend, stretch, twist, or reach out with your body, arms, and/or legs.
Wrist-Finger Speed	The ability to make fast, simple, repeated movements of the fingers, hands, and wrists.
Explosive Strength	The ability to use short bursts of muscle force to propel oneself (as in jumping or sprinting), or to throw an object.

Work_Activity	Work_Activity Definitions
Operating Vehicles, Mechanized Devices, or Equipme	Running, maneuvering, navigating, or driving vehicles or mechanized equipment, such as forklifts, passenger vehicles, aircraft, or water craft.
Inspecting Equipment, Structures, or Material	Inspecting equipment, structures, or materials to identify the cause of errors or other problems or defects.
Performing for or Working Directly with the Public	Performing for people or dealing directly with the public. This includes serving customers in restaurants and stores, and receiving clients or guests.
Assisting and Caring for Others	Providing personal assistance, medical attention, emotional support, or other personal care to others such as coworkers, customers, or patients.
Monitor Processes, Materials, or Surroundings	Monitoring and reviewing information from materials, events, or the environment, to detect or assess problems.
Judging the Qualities of Things, Services, or Peop	Assessing the value, importance, or quality of things or people.
Communicating with Supervisors, Peers, or Subordin	Providing information to supervisors, co-workers, and subordinates by telephone, in written form, e-mail, or in person.
Handling and Moving Objects	Using hands and arms in handling, installing, positioning, and moving materials, and manipulating things.

Getting Information	Observing, receiving, and otherwise obtaining information from all relevant sources.
Performing General Physical Activities	Performing physical activities that require considerable use of your arms and legs and moving your whole body, such as climbing, lifting, balancing, walking, stooping, and handling of materials.
Making Decisions and Solving Problems	Analyzing information and evaluating results to choose the best solution and solve problems.
Estimating the Quantifiable Characteristics of Pro	Estimating sizes, distances, and quantities; or determining time, costs, resources, or materials needed to perform a work activity.
Establishing and Maintaining Interpersonal Relatio	Developing constructive and cooperative working relationships with others, and maintaining them over time.
Communicating with Persons Outside Organization	Communicating with people outside the organization, representing the organization to customers, the public, government, and other external sources. This information can be exchanged in person, in writing, or by telephone or e-mail.
Identifying Objects, Actions, and Events	Identifying information by categorizing, estimating, recognizing differences or similarities, and detecting changes in circumstances or events.
Evaluating Information to Determine Compliance wit	Using relevant information and individual judgment to determine whether events or processes comply with laws, regulations, or standards.
Resolving Conflicts and Negotiating with Others	Handling complaints, settling disputes, and resolving grievances and conflicts, or otherwise negotiating with others.
Organizing, Planning, and Prioritizing Work	Developing specific goals and plans to prioritize, organize, and accomplish your work.
Updating and Using Relevant Knowledge	Keeping up-to-date technically and applying new knowledge to your job.
Developing and Building Teams	Encouraging and building mutual trust, respect, and cooperation among team members.
Documenting/Recording Information	Entering, transcribing, recording, storing, or maintaining information in written or electronic/magnetic form.
Interpreting the Meaning of Information for Others	Translating or explaining what information means and how it can be used.
Controlling Machines and Processes	Using either control mechanisms or direct physical activity to operate machines or processes (not including computers or vehicles).
Processing Information	Compiling, coding, categorizing, calculating, tabulating, auditing, or verifying information or data.
Developing Objectives and Strategies	Establishing long-range objectives and specifying the strategies and actions to achieve them.
Coordinating the Work and Activities of Others	Getting members of a group to work together to accomplish tasks.
Coaching and Developing Others	Identifying the developmental needs of others and coaching, mentoring, or otherwise helping others to improve their knowledge or skills.
Analyzing Data or Information	Identifying the underlying principles, reasons, or facts of information by breaking down information or data into separate parts.
Thinking Creatively	Developing, designing, or creating new applications, ideas, relationships, systems, or products, including artistic contributions.
Performing Administrative Activities	Performing day-to-day administrative tasks such as maintaining information files and processing paperwork.
Scheduling Work and Activities	Scheduling events, programs, and activities, as well as the work of others.
Selling or Influencing Others	Convincing others to buy merchandise/goods or to otherwise change their minds or actions.
Training and Teaching Others	Identifying the educational needs of others, developing formal educational or training programs or classes, and teaching or instructing others.
Provide Consultation and Advice to Others	Providing guidance and expert advice to management or other groups on technical, systems-, or process-related topics.
Monitoring and Controlling Resources	Monitoring and controlling resources and overseeing the spending of money.
Guiding, Directing, and Motivating Subordinates	Providing guidance and direction to subordinates, including setting performance standards and monitoring performance.
Repairing and Maintaining Mechanical Equipment	Servicing, repairing, adjusting, and testing machines, devices, moving parts, and equipment that operate primarily on the basis of mechanical (not electronic) principles.
Interacting With Computers	Using computers and computer systems (including hardware and software) to program, write software, set up functions, enter data, or process information.
Staffing Organizational Units	Recruiting, interviewing, selecting, hiring, and promoting employees in an organization.

Repairing and Maintaining Electronic Equipment	Servicing, repairing, calibrating, regulating, fine-tuning, or testing machines, devices, and equipment that operate primarily on the basis of electrical or electronic (not mechanical) principles.	Very Hot or Cold Temperatures	How often does this job require working in very hot (above 90 F degrees) or very cold (below 32 F degrees) temperatures?
Drafting, Laying Out, and Specifying Technical Dev	Providing documentation, detailed instructions, drawings, or specifications to tell others about how devices, parts, equipment, or structures are to be fabricated, constructed, assembled, modified, maintained, or used.	Indoors, Environmentally Controlled	How often does this job require working indoors in environmentally controlled conditions?
		Cramped Work Space, Awkward Positions	How often does this job require working in cramped work spaces that requires getting into awkward positions?
Work_Context	**Work_Context Definitions**	Letters and Memos	How often does the job require written letters and memos?
In an Enclosed Vehicle or Equipment	How often does this job require working in a closed vehicle or equipment (e.g., car)?	Deal With Physically Aggressive People	How frequently does this job require the worker to deal with physical aggression of violent individuals?
Impact of Decisions on Co-workers or Company Resul	How do the decisions an employee makes impact the results of co-workers, clients or the company?	Exposed to Minor Burns, Cuts, Bites, or Stings	How often does this job require exposure to minor burns, cuts, bites, or stings?
Importance of Being Exact or Accurate	How important is being very exact or highly accurate in performing this job?	Exposed to Hazardous Conditions	How often does this job require exposure to hazardous conditions?
Contact With Others	How much does this job require the worker to be in contact with others (face-to-face, by telephone, or otherwise) in order to perform it?	Spend Time Walking and Running	How much does this job require walking and running?
Consequence of Error	How serious would the result usually be if the worker made a mistake that was not readily correctable?	Indoors, Not Environmentally Controlled	How often does this job require working indoors in non-controlled environmental conditions (e.g., warehouse without heat)?
Time Pressure	How often does this job require the worker to meet strict deadlines?	Degree of Automation	How automated is the job?
Structured versus Unstructured Work	To what extent is this job structured for the worker, rather than allowing the worker to determine tasks, priorities, and goals?	Pace Determined by Speed of Equipment	How important is it to this job that the pace is determined by the speed of equipment or machinery? (This does not refer to keeping busy at all times on this job.)
Spend Time Sitting	How much does this job require sitting?	Public Speaking	How often do you have to perform public speaking in this job?
Frequency of Decision Making	How frequently is the worker required to make decisions that affect other people, the financial resources, and/or the image and reputation of the organization?	Electronic Mail	How often do you use electronic mail in this job?
		Spend Time Kneeling, Crouching, Stooping, or Crawl	How much does this job require kneeling, crouching, stooping, or crawling?
Freedom to Make Decisions	How much decision making freedom, without supervision, does the job offer?	Wear Specialized Protective or Safety Equipment su	How much does this job require wearing specialized protective or safety equipment such as breathing apparatus, safety harness, full protection suits, or radiation protection?
Face-to-Face Discussions	How often do you have to have face-to-face discussions with individuals or teams in this job?	Exposed to Whole Body Vibration	How often does this job require exposure to whole body vibration (e.g., operate a jackhammer)?
Spend Time Using Your Hands to Handle, Control, or	How much does this job require using your hands to handle, control, or feel objects, tools or controls?	Spend Time Keeping or Regaining Balance	How much does this job require keeping or regaining your balance?
Deal With External Customers	How important is it to work with external customers or the public in this job?	Exposed to Hazardous Equipment	How often does this job require exposure to hazardous equipment?
Telephone	How often do you have telephone conversations in this job?	In an Open Vehicle or Equipment	How often does this job require working in an open vehicle or equipment (e.g., tractor)?
Exposed to Contaminants	How often does this job require working exposed to contaminants (such as pollutants, gases, dust or odors)?	Wear Common Protective or Safety Equipment such as	How much does this job require wearing common protective or safety equipment such as safety shoes, glasses, gloves, hard hats or life jackets?
Responsible for Others' Health and Safety	How much responsibility is there for the health and safety of others in this job?	Spend Time Climbing Ladders, Scaffolds, or Poles	How much does this job require climbing ladders, scaffolds, or poles?
Physical Proximity	To what extent does this job require the worker to perform job tasks in close physical proximity to other people?	Exposed to High Places	How often does this job require exposure to high places?
Outdoors, Exposed to Weather	How often does this job require working outdoors, exposed to all weather conditions?	Exposed to Radiation	How often does this job require exposure to radiation?
Work With Work Group or Team	How important is it to work with others in a group or team in this job?		
Extremely Bright or Inadequate Lighting	How often does this job require working in extremely bright or inadequate lighting conditions?	**Job Zone Component**	**Job Zone Component Definitions**
Level of Competition	To what extent does this job require the worker to compete or to be aware of competitive pressures?	Title	Job Zone One: Little or No Preparation Needed
Deal With Unpleasant or Angry People	How frequently does the worker have to deal with unpleasant, angry, or discourteous individuals as part of the job requirements?	Overall Experience	No previous work-related skill, knowledge, or experience is needed for these occupations. For example, a person can become a general office clerk even if he/she has never worked in an office before.
Frequency of Conflict Situations	How often are there conflict situations the employee has to face in this job?	Job Training	Employees in these occupations need anywhere from a few days to a few months of training. Usually, an experienced worker could show you how to do the job.
Responsibility for Outcomes and Results	How responsible is the worker for work outcomes and results of other workers?	Job Zone Examples	These occupations involve following instructions and helping others. Examples include bus drivers, forest and conservation workers, general office clerks, home health aides, and waiters/waitresses.
Coordinate or Lead Others	How important is it to coordinate or lead others in accomplishing work activities in this job?	SVP Range	(Below 4.0)
Importance of Repeating Same Tasks	How important is repeating the same physical activities (e.g., key entry) or mental activities (e.g., checking entries in a ledger) over and over, without stopping, to performing this job?	Education	These occupations may require a high school diploma or GED certificate. Some may require a formal training course to obtain a license.
Exposed to Disease or Infections	How often does this job require exposure to disease/infections?		
Sounds, Noise Levels Are Distracting or Uncomforta	How often does this job require working exposed to sounds and noise levels that are distracting or uncomfortable?	**Work_Styles**	**Work_Styles Definitions**
Spend Time Making Repetitive Motions	How much does this job require making repetitive motions?	Dependability	Job requires being reliable, responsible, and dependable, and fulfilling obligations.
Outdoors, Under Cover	How often does this job require working outdoors, under cover (e.g., structure with roof but no walls)?	Adaptability/Flexibility	Job requires being open to change (positive or negative) and to considerable variety in the workplace.
Spend Time Standing	How much does this job require standing?	Self Control	Job requires maintaining composure, keeping emotions in check, controlling anger, and avoiding aggressive behavior, even in very difficult situations.
Spend Time Bending or Twisting the Body	How much does this job require bending or twisting your body?	Attention to Detail	Job requires being careful about detail and thorough in completing work tasks.

Stress Tolerance	Job requires accepting criticism and dealing calmly and effectively with high stress situations.
Integrity	Job requires being honest and ethical.
Independence	Job requires developing one's own ways of doing things, guiding oneself with little or no supervision, and depending on oneself to get things done.
Concern for Others	Job requires being sensitive to others' needs and feelings and being understanding and helpful on the job.
Cooperation	Job requires being pleasant with others on the job and displaying a good-natured, cooperative attitude.
Initiative	Job requires a willingness to take on responsibilities and challenges.
Persistence	Job requires persistence in the face of obstacles.
Achievement/Effort	Job requires establishing and maintaining personally challenging achievement goals and exerting effort toward mastering tasks.
Leadership	Job requires a willingness to lead, take charge, and offer opinions and direction.
Social Orientation	Job requires preferring to work with others rather than alone, and being personally connected with others on the job.
Innovation	Job requires creativity and alternative thinking to develop new ideas for and answers to work-related problems.
Analytical Thinking	Job requires analyzing information and using logic to address work-related issues and problems.

53-4011.00 - Locomotive Engineers

Drive electric, diesel-electric, steam, or gas-turbine-electric locomotives to transport passengers or freight. Interpret train orders, electronic or manual signals, and railroad rules and regulations.

Tasks

1) Interpret train orders, signals, and railroad rules and regulations that govern the operation of locomotives.

2) Prepare reports regarding any problems encountered, such as accidents, signaling problems, unscheduled stops, or delays.

3) Monitor train loading procedures to ensure that freight and rolling stock are loaded or unloaded without damage.

4) Inspect locomotives after runs to detect damaged or defective equipment.

5) Drive diesel-electric rail-detector cars to transport rail-flaw-detecting machines over tracks.

6) Check to ensure that documentation, including procedure manuals and logbooks, is in the driver's cab and available for staff use.

7) Call out train signals to assistants in order to verify meanings.

8) Operate locomotives to transport freight or passengers between stations, and to assemble and disassemble trains within rail yards.

9) Monitor gauges and meters that measure speed, amperage, battery charge, and air pressure in brakelines and in main reservoirs.

10) Respond to emergency conditions or breakdowns, following applicable safety procedures and rules.

11) Confer with conductors or traffic control center personnel via radiophones to issue or receive information concerning stops, delays, or oncoming trains.

12) Inspect locomotives to verify adequate fuel, sand, water, and other supplies before each run, and to check for mechanical problems.

13) Observe tracks to detect obstructions.

14) Check to ensure that brake examination tests are conducted at shunting stations.

53-4012.00 - Locomotive Firers

Monitor locomotive instruments and watch for dragging equipment, obstacles on rights-of-way, and train signals during run. Watch for and relay traffic signals from yard workers to yard engineer in railroad yard.

Tasks

1) Observe train signals along routes and verify their meanings for engineers.

2) Signal other workers to set brakes and to throw track switches when switching cars from trains to way stations.

3) Monitor oil, temperature, and pressure gauges on dashboards to determine if engines are operating safely and efficiently.

4) Receive signals from workers in rear of train and relay that information to engineers.

5) Inspect locomotives to detect damaged or worn parts.

6) Operate locomotives in emergency situations.

7) Observe tracks from left sides of locomotives to detect obstructions on tracks.

8) Check to see that trains are equipped with supplies such as fuel, water, and sand.

9) Start diesel engines to warm engines before runs.

53-4013.00 - Rail Yard Engineers, Dinkey Operators, and Hostlers

Drive switching or other locomotive or dinkey engines within railroad yard, industrial plant, quarry, construction project, or similar location.

Tasks

1) Apply and release hand brakes.

2) Drive engines within railroad yards or other establishments to couple, uncouple, or switch railroad cars.

3) Read switching instructions and daily car schedules to determine work to be performed, or receive orders from yard conductors.

4) Drive locomotives to and from various stations in roundhouses to have locomotives cleaned, serviced, repaired, or supplied.

5) Confer with conductors and other workers via radio-telephones or computers to exchange switching information.

6) Provide assistance in aligning drawbars, using available equipment to lift, pull, or push on the drawbars.

7) Receive, relay, and act upon instructions and inquiries from train operations and customer service center personnel.

8) Observe and respond to wayside and cab signals, including color light signals, position signals, torpedoes, flags, and hot box detectors.

9) Operate track switches, derails, automatic switches, and retarders to change routing of train or cars.

10) Operate and control dinkey engines to transport and shunt cars at industrial or mine sites.

11) Signal crew members for movement of engines or trains, using lanterns, hand signals, radios, or telephones.

12) Inspect engines before and after use to ensure proper operation.

13) Observe water levels and oil, air, and steam pressure gauges in order to ensure proper operation of equipment.

14) Couple and uncouple air hoses and electrical connections between cars.

15) Inspect the condition of stationary trains, rolling stock, and equipment.

16) Inspect track for defects such as broken rails and switch malfunctions.

17) Operate flatcars equipped with derricks or railcars to transport personnel or equipment.

18) Provide assistance in the installation or repair of rails and ties.

19) Record numbers of cars available, numbers of cars sent to repair stations, and types of service needed.

20) Report arrival and departure times, train delays, work order completion, and time on duty.

21) Ride on moving cars by holding onto grab irons and standing on ladder steps.

22) Spot cars for loading and unloading at customer locations.

23) Perform routine repair and maintenance duties.

24) Pull knuckles to open them for coupling.

53-4021.00 - Railroad Brake, Signal, and Switch Operators

Operate railroad track switches. Couple or uncouple rolling stock to make up or break up trains. Signal engineers by hand or flagging. May inspect couplings, air hoses, journal boxes, and hand brakes.

Tasks

1) Signal locomotive engineers to start or stop trains when coupling or uncoupling cars, using hand signals, lanterns, or radio communication.

2) Open and close ventilation doors.

3) Connect air hoses to cars, using wrenches.

4) Make minor repairs to couplings, air hoses, and journal boxes, using hand tools.

5) Observe signals from other crewmembers so that work activities can be coordinated.

6) Pull or push track switches to reroute cars.

7) Raise levers to couple and uncouple cars for makeup and breakup of trains.

8) Ride atop cars that have been shunted, and turn handwheels to control speeds or stop cars at specified positions.

9) Inspect couplings, air hoses, journal boxes, and handbrakes to ensure that they are securely fastened and functioning properly.

10) Collect tickets, fares, and passes from passengers.

11) Receive oral or written instructions from yardmasters or yard conductors indicating track assignments and cars to be switched.

12) Operate and drive locomotives, diesel switch engines, dinkey engines, flatcars, and railcars in train yards and at industrial sites.

13) Answer questions from passengers concerning train rules, stations, and timetable information.

14) Open and close chute gates to load and unload cars.

15) Monitor oil, air, and steam pressure gauges, and make sure water levels are adequate.

16) Record numbers of cars available, numbers of cars sent to repair stations, and types of service needed.

17) Refuel and lubricate engines.

18) Set flares, flags, lanterns, or torpedoes in front and at rear of trains during emergency stops in order to warn oncoming trains.

19) Adjust controls to regulate air-conditioning, heating, and lighting on trains for comfort of passengers.

20) Attach cables to cars being hoisted by cables or chains in mines, quarries, or industrial plants.

21) Watch for and relay traffic signals to start and stop cars during shunting.

22) Provide passengers with assistance entering and exiting trains.

23) Place passengers' baggage in racks above seats on trains.

24) Repair and install rails and ties.

25) Inspect tracks, cars, and engines for defects and to determine service needs, sending engines and cars for repairs as necessary.

53-4031.00 - Railroad Conductors and Yardmasters

Conductors coordinate activities of train crew on passenger or freight train. Coordinate activities of switch-engine crew within yard of railroad, industrial plant, or similar location. Yardmasters coordinate activities of workers engaged in railroad traffic operations, such as the makeup or breakup of trains, yard switching, and review train schedules and switching orders.

Tasks

1) Direct and instruct workers engaged in yard activities, such as switching tracks, coupling and uncoupling cars, and routing inbound and outbound traffic.

2) Record departure and arrival times, messages, tickets and revenue collected, and passenger accommodations and destinations.

3) Instruct workers to regulate air-conditioning, lighting, and heating in passenger cars in order to ensure passengers' comfort.

4) Keep records of the contents and destination of each train car, and make sure that cars are added or removed at proper points on routes.

5) Observe lights on panelboards to monitor and chart locations of trains, and to estimate arrival times.

6) Observe yard traffic to determine tracks available to accommodate inbound and outbound traffic.

7) Confirm routes and destination information for freight cars.

8) Verify accuracy of timekeeping instruments with engineers to ensure trains depart on time.

9) Supervise workers in the inspection and maintenance of mechanical equipment in order to ensure efficient and safe train operation.

10) Receive instructions from dispatchers regarding trains' routes, timetables, and cargoes.

11) Review schedules, switching orders, way bills, and shipping records to obtain cargo loading and unloading information and to plan work.

12) Signal engineers to begin train runs, stop trains, or change speed, using telecommunications equipment or hand signals.

13) Instruct workers to set warning signals in front and at rear of trains during emergency stops.

14) Confer with engineers regarding train routes, timetables, and cargoes, and to discuss alternative routes when there are rail defects or obstructions.

15) Operate controls to activate track switches and traffic signals.

16) Inspect freight cars for compliance with sealing procedures, and record car numbers and seal numbers.

17) Inspect each car periodically during runs.

18) Document and prepare reports of accidents, unscheduled stops, or delays.

19) Arrange for the removal of defective cars from trains at stations or stops.

20) Supervise and coordinate crew activities to transport freight and passengers and to provide boarding, porter, maid, and meal services to passengers.

21) Answer passengers' inquiries and announce information such as approaching train stops.

22) Collect tickets, fares, or passes from passengers.

23) Direct engineers to move cars to fit planned train configurations, combining or separating cars to make up or break up trains.

53-4041.00 - Subway and Streetcar Operators

Operate subway or elevated suburban train with no separate locomotive, or electric-powered streetcar to transport passengers. May handle fares.

Tasks

1) Monitor lights indicating obstructions or other trains ahead and watch for car and truck traffic at crossings to stay alert to potential hazards.

2) Greet passengers, provide information, and answer questions concerning fares, schedules, transfers, and routings.

3) Attend meetings on driver and passenger safety in order to learn ways in which job performance might be affected.

4) Collect fares from passengers, and issue change and transfers.

5) Complete reports, including shift summaries and incident or accident reports.

6) Report delays, mechanical problems, and emergencies to supervisors or dispatchers, using radios.

7) Operate controls to open and close transit vehicle doors.

8) Make announcements to passengers, such as notifications of upcoming stops or schedule delays.

9) Drive and control rail-guided public transportation, such as subways, elevated trains, and electric-powered streetcars, trams, or trolleys, in order to transport passengers.

10) Record transactions and coin receptor readings in order to verify the amount of money collected.

11) Regulate vehicle speed and the time spent at each stop, in order to maintain schedules.

53-5022.00 - Motorboat Operators

Operate small motor-driven boats to carry passengers and freight between ships, or ship to shore. May patrol harbors and beach areas. May assist in navigational activities.

Tasks

1) Maintain desired courses, using compasses or electronic navigational aids.

2) Follow safety procedures in order to ensure the protection of passengers, cargo, and vessels.

3) Arrange repairs, fuel, and supplies for vessels.

4) Clean boats and repair hulls and superstructures, using hand tools, paint, and brushes.

5) Position booms around docked ships.

6) Tow, push, or guide other boats, barges, logs, or rafts.

7) Operate engine throttles and steering mechanisms in order to guide boats on desired courses.

8) Direct safety operations in emergency situations.

9) Perform general labor duties such as repairing booms.

10) Report any observed navigational hazards to authorities.

11) Take depth soundings in turning basins.

12) Oversee operation of vessels used for carrying passengers, motor vehicles, or goods across rivers, harbors, lakes, and coastal waters.

13) Issue directions for loading, unloading, and seating in boats.

14) Secure boats to docks with mooring lines, and cast off lines to enable departure.

15) Organize and direct the activities of crew members.

16) Maintain equipment such as range markers, fire extinguishers, boat fenders, lines, pumps, and fittings.

53-6021.00 - Parking Lot Attendants

Park automobiles or issue tickets for customers in a parking lot or garage. May collect fee.

Tasks

1) Direct motorists to parking areas or parking spaces, using hand signals or flashlights as necessary.

2) Patrol parking areas in order to prevent vehicle damage and vehicle or property thefts.

3) Take numbered tags from customers, locate vehicles, and deliver vehicles, or provide customers with instructions for locating vehicles.

4) Lift, position, and remove barricades in order to open or close parking areas.

5) Greet customers and open their car doors.

6) Issue ticket stubs, or place numbered tags on windshields, and give customers matching tags for locating parked vehicles.

7) Park and retrieve automobiles for customers in parking lots, storage garages, or new car lots.

8) Inspect vehicles in order to detect any damage.

9) Escort customers to their vehicles in order to ensure their safety.

10) Calculate parking charges, and collect fees from customers.

11) Review motorists' identification before allowing them to enter parking facilities.

12) Perform maintenance on cars in storage in order to protect tires, batteries, and exteriors from deterioration.

13) Service vehicles with gas, oil, and water.

Knowledge	Knowledge Definitions
Customer and Personal Service	Knowledge of principles and processes for providing customer and personal services. This includes customer needs assessment, meeting quality standards for services, and evaluation of customer satisfaction.
English Language	Knowledge of the structure and content of the English language including the meaning and spelling of words, rules of composition, and grammar.
Public Safety and Security	Knowledge of relevant equipment, policies, procedures, and strategies to promote effective local, state, or national security operations for the protection of people, data, property, and institutions.
Transportation	Knowledge of principles and methods for moving people or goods by air, rail, sea, or road, including the relative costs and benefits.
Mathematics	Knowledge of arithmetic, algebra, geometry, calculus, statistics, and their applications.
Mechanical	Knowledge of machines and tools, including their designs, uses, repair, and maintenance.
Education and Training	Knowledge of principles and methods for curriculum and training design, teaching and instruction for individuals and groups, and the measurement of training effects.
Psychology	Knowledge of human behavior and performance; individual differences in ability, personality, and interests; learning and motivation; psychological research methods; and the assessment and treatment of behavioral and affective disorders.
Administration and Management	Knowledge of business and management principles involved in strategic planning, resource allocation, human resources modeling, leadership technique, production methods, and coordination of people and resources.
Economics and Accounting	Knowledge of economic and accounting principles and practices, the financial markets, banking and the analysis and reporting of financial data.
Production and Processing	Knowledge of raw materials, production processes, quality control, costs, and other techniques for maximizing the effective manufacture and distribution of goods.
Law and Government	Knowledge of laws, legal codes, court procedures, precedents, government regulations, executive orders, agency rules, and the democratic political process.
Personnel and Human Resources	Knowledge of principles and procedures for personnel recruitment, selection, training, compensation and benefits, labor relations and negotiation, and personnel information systems.
Communications and Media	Knowledge of media production, communication, and dissemination techniques and methods. This includes alternative ways to inform and entertain via written, oral, and visual media.
Clerical	Knowledge of administrative and clerical procedures and systems such as word processing, managing files and records, stenography and transcription, designing forms, and other office procedures and terminology.
Geography	Knowledge of principles and methods for describing the features of land, sea, and air masses, including their physical characteristics, locations, interrelationships, and distribution of plant, animal, and human life.
Foreign Language	Knowledge of the structure and content of a foreign (non-English) language including the meaning and spelling of words, rules of composition and grammar, and pronunciation.
Telecommunications	Knowledge of transmission, broadcasting, switching, control, and operation of telecommunications systems.
Physics	Knowledge and prediction of physical principles, laws, their interrelationships, and applications to understanding fluid, material, and atmospheric dynamics, and mechanical, electrical, atomic and sub-atomic structures and processes.
Sales and Marketing	Knowledge of principles and methods for showing, promoting, and selling products or services. This includes marketing strategy and tactics, product demonstration, sales techniques, and sales control systems.
Therapy and Counseling	Knowledge of principles, methods, and procedures for diagnosis, treatment, and rehabilitation of physical and mental dysfunctions, and for career counseling and guidance.
Design	Knowledge of design techniques, tools, and principles involved in production of precision technical plans, blueprints, drawings, and models.
Engineering and Technology	Knowledge of the practical application of engineering science and technology. This includes applying principles, techniques, procedures, and equipment to the design and production of various goods and services.
Medicine and Dentistry	Knowledge of the information and techniques needed to diagnose and treat human injuries, diseases, and deformities. This includes symptoms, treatment alternatives, drug properties and interactions, and preventive health-care measures.

Sociology and Anthropology	Knowledge of group behavior and dynamics, societal trends and influences, human migrations, ethnicity, cultures and their history and origins.
Biology	Knowledge of plant and animal organisms, their tissues, cells, functions, interdependencies, and interactions with each other and the environment.
Computers and Electronics	Knowledge of circuit boards, processors, chips, electronic equipment, and computer hardware and software, including applications and programming.
Philosophy and Theology	Knowledge of different philosophical systems and religions. This includes their basic principles, values, ethics, ways of thinking, customs, practices, and their impact on human culture.
Chemistry	Knowledge of the chemical composition, structure, and properties of substances and of the chemical processes and transformations that they undergo. This includes uses of chemicals and their interactions, danger signs, production techniques, and disposal methods.
History and Archeology	Knowledge of historical events and their causes, indicators, and effects on civilizations and cultures.
Fine Arts	Knowledge of the theory and techniques required to compose, produce, and perform works of music, dance, visual arts, drama, and sculpture.
Building and Construction	Knowledge of materials, methods, and the tools involved in the construction or repair of houses, buildings, or other structures such as highways and roads.
Food Production	Knowledge of techniques and equipment for planting, growing, and harvesting food products (both plant and animal) for consumption, including storage/handling techniques.

Skills	Skills Definitions
Service Orientation	Actively looking for ways to help people.
Speaking	Talking to others to convey information effectively.
Social Perceptiveness	Being aware of others' reactions and understanding why they react as they do.
Time Management	Managing one's own time and the time of others.
Critical Thinking	Using logic and reasoning to identify the strengths and weaknesses of alternative solutions, conclusions or approaches to problems.
Coordination	Adjusting actions in relation to others' actions.
Instructing	Teaching others how to do something.
Active Listening	Giving full attention to what other people are saying, taking time to understand the points being made, asking questions as appropriate, and not interrupting at inappropriate times.
Judgment and Decision Making	Considering the relative costs and benefits of potential actions to choose the most appropriate one.
Management of Personnel Resources	Motivating, developing, and directing people as they work, identifying the best people for the job.
Learning Strategies	Selecting and using training/instructional methods and procedures appropriate for the situation when learning or teaching new things.
Mathematics	Using mathematics to solve problems.
Reading Comprehension	Understanding written sentences and paragraphs in work related documents.
Monitoring	Monitoring/Assessing performance of yourself, other individuals, or organizations to make improvements or take corrective action.
Negotiation	Bringing others together and trying to reconcile differences.
Systems Evaluation	Identifying measures or indicators of system performance and the actions needed to improve or correct performance, relative to the goals of the system.
Writing	Communicating effectively in writing as appropriate for the needs of the audience.
Active Learning	Understanding the implications of new information for both current and future problem-solving and decision-making.
Complex Problem Solving	Identifying complex problems and reviewing related information to develop and evaluate options and implement solutions.
Equipment Maintenance	Performing routine maintenance on equipment and determining when and what kind of maintenance is needed.
Operations Analysis	Analyzing needs and product requirements to create a design.
Operation and Control	Controlling operations of equipment or systems.
Troubleshooting	Determining causes of operating errors and deciding what to do about it.
Equipment Selection	Determining the kind of tools and equipment needed to do a job.

Systems Analysis	Determining how a system should work and how changes in conditions, operations, and the environment will affect outcomes.
Operation Monitoring	Watching gauges, dials, or other indicators to make sure a machine is working properly.
Management of Material Resources	Obtaining and seeing to the appropriate use of equipment, facilities, and materials needed to do certain work.
Persuasion	Persuading others to change their minds or behavior.
Technology Design	Generating or adapting equipment and technology to serve user needs.
Repairing	Repairing machines or systems using the needed tools.
Management of Financial Resources	Determining how money will be spent to get the work done, and accounting for these expenditures.
Quality Control Analysis	Conducting tests and inspections of products, services, or processes to evaluate quality or performance.
Programming	Writing computer programs for various purposes.
Installation	Installing equipment, machines, wiring, or programs to meet specifications.
Science	Using scientific rules and methods to solve problems.

Ability	Ability Definitions
Problem Sensitivity	The ability to tell when something is wrong or is likely to go wrong. It does not involve solving the problem, only recognizing there is a problem.
Far Vision	The ability to see details at a distance.
Speech Clarity	The ability to speak clearly so others can understand you.
Speech Recognition	The ability to identify and understand the speech of another person.
Oral Expression	The ability to communicate information and ideas in speaking so others will understand.
Near Vision	The ability to see details at close range (within a few feet of the observer).
Oral Comprehension	The ability to listen to and understand information and ideas presented through spoken words and sentences.
Multilimb Coordination	The ability to coordinate two or more limbs (for example, two arms, two legs, or one leg and one arm) while sitting, standing, or lying down. It does not involve performing the activities while the whole body is in motion.
Arm-Hand Steadiness	The ability to keep your hand and arm steady while moving your arm or while holding your arm and hand in one position.
Depth Perception	The ability to judge which of several objects is closer or farther away from you, or to judge the distance between you and an object.
Selective Attention	The ability to concentrate on a task over a period of time without being distracted.
Spatial Orientation	The ability to know your location in relation to the environment or to know where other objects are in relation to you.
Information Ordering	The ability to arrange things or actions in a certain order or pattern according to a specific rule or set of rules (e.g., patterns of numbers, letters, words, pictures, mathematical operations).
Control Precision	The ability to quickly and repeatedly adjust the controls of a machine or a vehicle to exact positions.
Perceptual Speed	The ability to quickly and accurately compare similarities and differences among sets of letters, numbers, objects, pictures, or patterns. The things to be compared may be presented at the same time or one after the other. This ability also includes comparing a presented object with a remembered object.
Deductive Reasoning	The ability to apply general rules to specific problems to produce answers that make sense.
Extent Flexibility	The ability to bend, stretch, twist, or reach with your body, arms, and/or legs.
Stamina	The ability to exert yourself physically over long periods of time without getting winded or out of breath.
Peripheral Vision	The ability to see objects or movement of objects to one's side when the eyes are looking ahead.
Static Strength	The ability to exert maximum muscle force to lift, push, pull, or carry objects.
Gross Body Coordination	The ability to coordinate the movement of your arms, legs, and torso together when the whole body is in motion.
Number Facility	The ability to add, subtract, multiply, or divide quickly and correctly.
Night Vision	The ability to see under low light conditions.
Visualization	The ability to imagine how something will look after it is moved around or when its parts are moved or rearranged.
Trunk Strength	The ability to use your abdominal and lower back muscles to support part of the body repeatedly or continuously over time without 'giving out' or fatiguing.

Manual Dexterity	The ability to quickly move your hand, your hand together with your arm, or your two hands to grasp, manipulate, or assemble objects.
Speed of Limb Movement	The ability to quickly move the arms and legs.
Response Orientation	The ability to choose quickly between two or more movements in response to two or more different signals (lights, sounds, pictures). It includes the speed with which the correct response is started with the hand, foot, or other body part.
Visual Color Discrimination	The ability to match or detect differences between colors, including shades of color and brightness.
Reaction Time	The ability to quickly respond (with the hand, finger, or foot) to a signal (sound, light, picture) when it appears.
Inductive Reasoning	The ability to combine pieces of information to form general rules or conclusions (includes finding a relationship among seemingly unrelated events).
Time Sharing	The ability to shift back and forth between two or more activities or sources of information (such as speech, sounds, touch, or other sources).
Mathematical Reasoning	The ability to choose the right mathematical methods or formulas to solve a problem.
Flexibility of Closure	The ability to identify or detect a known pattern (a figure, object, word, or sound) that is hidden in other distracting material.
Finger Dexterity	The ability to make precisely coordinated movements of the fingers of one or both hands to grasp, manipulate, or assemble very small objects.
Category Flexibility	The ability to generate or use different sets of rules for combining or grouping things in different ways.
Glare Sensitivity	The ability to see objects in the presence of glare or bright lighting.
Speed of Closure	The ability to quickly make sense of, combine, and organize information into meaningful patterns.
Written Expression	The ability to communicate information and ideas in writing so others will understand.
Fluency of Ideas	The ability to come up with a number of ideas about a topic (the number of ideas is important, not their quality, correctness, or creativity).
Written Comprehension	The ability to read and understand information and ideas presented in writing.
Originality	The ability to come up with unusual or clever ideas about a given topic or situation, or to develop creative ways to solve a problem.
Sound Localization	The ability to tell the direction from which a sound originated.
Auditory Attention	The ability to focus on a single source of sound in the presence of other distracting sounds.
Hearing Sensitivity	The ability to detect or tell the differences between sounds that vary in pitch and loudness.
Rate Control	The ability to time your movements or the movement of a piece of equipment in anticipation of changes in the speed and/or direction of a moving object or scene.
Memorization	The ability to remember information such as words, numbers, pictures, and procedures.
Gross Body Equilibrium	The ability to keep or regain your body balance or stay upright when in an unstable position.
Explosive Strength	The ability to use short bursts of muscle force to propel oneself (as in jumping or sprinting), or to throw an object.
Dynamic Strength	The ability to exert muscle force repeatedly or continuously over time. This involves muscular endurance and resistance to muscle fatigue.
Wrist-Finger Speed	The ability to make fast, simple, repeated movements of the fingers, hands, and wrists.
Dynamic Flexibility	The ability to quickly and repeatedly bend, stretch, twist, or reach out with your body, arms, and/or legs.

Work_Activity	Work_Activity Definitions
Performing for or Working Directly with the Public	Performing for people or dealing directly with the public. This includes serving customers in restaurants and stores, and receiving clients or guests.
Handling and Moving Objects	Using hands and arms in handling, installing, positioning, and moving materials, and manipulating things.
Performing General Physical Activities	Performing physical activities that require considerable use of your arms and legs and moving your whole body, such as climbing, lifting, balancing, walking, stooping, and handling of materials.
Operating Vehicles, Mechanized Devices, or Equipme	Running, maneuvering, navigating, or driving vehicles or mechanized equipment, such as forklifts, passenger vehicles, aircraft, or water craft.

Establishing and Maintaining Interpersonal Relatio	Developing constructive and cooperative working relationships with others, and maintaining them over time.
Communicating with Supervisors, Peers, or Subordin	Providing information to supervisors, co-workers, and subordinates by telephone, in written form, e-mail, or in person.
Identifying Objects, Actions, and Events	Identifying information by categorizing, estimating, recognizing differences or similarities, and detecting changes in circumstances or events.
Making Decisions and Solving Problems	Analyzing information and evaluating results to choose the best solution and solve problems.
Communicating with Persons Outside Organization	Communicating with people outside the organization, representing the organization to customers, the public, government, and other external sources. This information can be exchanged in person, in writing, or by telephone or e-mail.
Resolving Conflicts and Negotiating with Others	Handling complaints, settling disputes, and resolving grievances and conflicts, or otherwise negotiating with others.
Coordinating the Work and Activities of Others	Getting members of a group to work together to accomplish tasks.
Developing and Building Teams	Encouraging and building mutual trust, respect, and cooperation among team members.
Monitor Processes, Materials, or Surroundings	Monitoring and reviewing information from materials, events, or the environment, to detect or assess problems.
Estimating the Quantifiable Characteristics of Pro	Estimating sizes, distances, and quantities; or determining time, costs, resources, or materials needed to perform a work activity.
Getting Information	Observing, receiving, and otherwise obtaining information from all relevant sources.
Developing Objectives and Strategies	Establishing long-range objectives and specifying the strategies and actions to achieve them.
Guiding, Directing, and Motivating Subordinates	Providing guidance and direction to subordinates, including setting performance standards and monitoring performance.
Documenting/Recording Information	Entering, transcribing, recording, storing, or maintaining information in written or electronic/magnetic form.
Assisting and Caring for Others	Providing personal assistance, medical attention, emotional support, or other personal care to others such as coworkers, customers, or patients.
Training and Teaching Others	Identifying the educational needs of others, developing formal educational or training programs or classes, and teaching or instructing others.
Processing Information	Compiling, coding, categorizing, calculating, tabulating, auditing, or verifying information or data.
Organizing, Planning, and Prioritizing Work	Developing specific goals and plans to prioritize, organize, and accomplish your work.
Monitoring and Controlling Resources	Monitoring and controlling resources and overseeing the spending of money.
Inspecting Equipment, Structures, or Material	Inspecting equipment, structures, or materials to identify the cause of errors or other problems or defects.
Coaching and Developing Others	Identifying the developmental needs of others and coaching, mentoring, or otherwise helping others to improve their knowledge or skills.
Judging the Qualities of Things, Services, or Peop	Assessing the value, importance, or quality of things or people.
Thinking Creatively	Developing, designing, or creating new applications, ideas, relationships, systems, or products, including artistic contributions.
Selling or Influencing Others	Convincing others to buy merchandise/goods or to otherwise change their minds or actions.
Scheduling Work and Activities	Scheduling events, programs, and activities, as well as the work of others.
Evaluating Information to Determine Compliance wit	Using relevant information and individual judgment to determine whether events or processes comply with laws, regulations, or standards.
Interacting With Computers	Using computers and computer systems (including hardware and software) to program, write software, set up functions, enter data, or process information.
Staffing Organizational Units	Recruiting, interviewing, selecting, hiring, and promoting employees in an organization.
Controlling Machines and Processes	Using either control mechanisms or direct physical activity to operate machines or processes (not including computers or vehicles).
Analyzing Data or Information	Identifying the underlying principles, reasons, or facts of information by breaking down information or data into separate parts.
Interpreting the Meaning of Information for Others	Translating or explaining what information means and how it can be used.

Repairing and Maintaining Electronic Equipment	Servicing, repairing, calibrating, regulating, fine-tuning, or testing machines, devices, and equipment that operate primarily on the basis of electrical or electronic (not mechanical) principles.
Repairing and Maintaining Mechanical Equipment	Servicing, repairing, adjusting, and testing machines, devices, moving parts, and equipment that operate primarily on the basis of mechanical (not electronic) principles.
Updating and Using Relevant Knowledge	Keeping up-to-date technically and applying new knowledge to your job.
Performing Administrative Activities	Performing day-to-day administrative tasks such as maintaining information files and processing paperwork.
Provide Consultation and Advice to Others	Providing guidance and expert advice to management or other groups on technical, systems-, or process-related topics.
Drafting, Laying Out, and Specifying Technical Dev	Providing documentation, detailed instructions, drawings, or specifications to tell others about how devices, parts, equipment, or structures are to be fabricated, constructed, assembled, modified, maintained, or used.

Work_Context — **Work_Context Definitions**

Deal With Unpleasant or Angry People	How frequently does the worker have to deal with unpleasant, angry, or discourteous individuals as part of the job requirements?
Contact With Others	How much does this job require the worker to be in contact with others (face-to-face, by telephone, or otherwise) in order to perform it?
Physical Proximity	To what extent does this job require the worker to perform job tasks in close physical proximity to other people?
Spend Time Making Repetitive Motions	How much does this job require making repetitive motions?
Freedom to Make Decisions	How much decision making freedom, without supervision, does the job offer?
Importance of Being Exact or Accurate	How important is being very exact or highly accurate in performing this job?
Outdoors, Exposed to Weather	How often does this job require working outdoors, exposed to all weather conditions?
Frequency of Decision Making	How frequently is the worker required to make decisions that affect other people, the financial resources, and/or the image and reputation of the organization?
Work With Work Group or Team	How important is it to work with others in a group or team in this job?
Exposed to Contaminants	How often does this job require working exposed to contaminants (such as pollutants, gases, dust or odors)?
Spend Time Walking and Running	How much does this job require walking and running?
Spend Time Standing	How much does this job require standing?
In an Enclosed Vehicle or Equipment	How often does this job require working in a closed vehicle or equipment (e.g., car)?
Deal With External Customers	How important is it to work with external customers or the public in this job?
Very Hot or Cold Temperatures	How often does this job require working in very hot (above 90 F degrees) or very cold (below 32 F degrees) temperatures?
Frequency of Conflict Situations	How often are there conflict situations the employee has to face in this job?
Spend Time Using Your Hands to Handle, Control, or	How much does this job require using your hands to handle, control, or feel objects, tools or controls?
Face-to-Face Discussions	How often do you have to have face-to-face discussions with individuals or teams in this job?
Responsibility for Outcomes and Results	How responsible is the worker for work outcomes and results of other workers?
Spend Time Bending or Twisting the Body	How much does this job require bending or twisting your body?
Impact of Decisions on Co-workers or Company Resul	How do the decisions an employee makes impact the results of co-workers, clients or the company?
Responsible for Others' Health and Safety	How much responsibility is there for the health and safety of others in this job?
Sounds, Noise Levels Are Distracting or Uncomforta	How often does this job require working exposed to sounds and noise levels that are distracting or uncomfortable?
Importance of Repeating Same Tasks	How important is repeating the same physical activities (e.g., key entry) or mental activities (e.g., checking entries in a ledger) over and over, without stopping, to performing this job?
Outdoors, Under Cover	How often does this job require working outdoors, under cover (e.g., structure with roof but no walls)?
Structured versus Unstructured Work	To what extent is this job structured for the worker, rather than allowing the worker to determine tasks, priorities, and goals?

Level of Competition	To what extent does this job require the worker to compete or to be aware of competitive pressures?
Telephone	How often do you have telephone conversations in this job?
Deal With Physically Aggressive People	How frequently does this job require the worker to deal with physical aggression of violent individuals?
Consequence of Error	How serious would the result usually be if the worker made a mistake that was not readily correctable?
Coordinate or Lead Others	How important is it to coordinate or lead others in accomplishing work activities in this job?
Time Pressure	How often does this job require the worker to meet strict deadlines?
Exposed to Hazardous Equipment	How often does this job require exposure to hazardous equipment?
Extremely Bright or Inadequate Lighting	How often does this job require working in extremely bright or inadequate lighting conditions?
Degree of Automation	How automated is the job?
Exposed to Minor Burns, Cuts, Bites, or Stings	How often does this job require exposure to minor burns, cuts, bites, or stings?
Spend Time Sitting	How much does this job require sitting?
Letters and Memos	How often does the job require written letters and memos?
In an Open Vehicle or Equipment	How often does this job require working in an open vehicle or equipment (e.g., tractor)?
Public Speaking	How often do you have to perform public speaking in this job?
Indoors, Not Environmentally Controlled	How often does this job require working indoors in non-controlled environmental conditions (e.g., warehouse without heat)?
Spend Time Keeping or Regaining Balance	How much does this job require keeping or regaining your balance?
Cramped Work Space, Awkward Positions	How often does this job require working in cramped work spaces that requires getting into awkward positions?
Pace Determined by Speed of Equipment	How important is it to this job that the pace is determined by the speed of equipment or machinery? (This does not refer to keeping busy at all times on this job.)
Electronic Mail	How often do you use electronic mail in this job?
Spend Time Kneeling, Crouching, Stooping, or Crawl	How much does this job require kneeling, crouching, stooping, or crawling?
Indoors, Environmentally Controlled	How often does this job require working indoors in environmentally controlled conditions?
Wear Specialized Protective or Safety Equipment su	How much does this job require wearing specialized protective or safety equipment such as breathing apparatus, safety harness, full protection suits, or radiation protection?
Exposed to Disease or Infections	How often does this job require exposure to disease/infections?
Spend Time Climbing Ladders, Scaffolds, or Poles	How much does this job require climbing ladders, scaffolds, or poles?
Exposed to High Places	How often does this job require exposure to high places?
Wear Common Protective or Safety Equipment such as	How much does this job require wearing common protective or safety equipment such as safety shoes, glasses, gloves, hard hats or life jackets?
Exposed to Whole Body Vibration	How often does this job require exposure to whole body vibration (e.g., operate a jackhammer)?
Exposed to Hazardous Conditions	How often does this job require exposure to hazardous conditions?
Exposed to Radiation	How often does this job require exposure to radiation?

Job Zone Component — **Job Zone Component Definitions**

Title	Job Zone One: Little or No Preparation Needed
Overall Experience	No previous work-related skill, knowledge, or experience is needed for these occupations. For example, a person can become a general office clerk even if he/she has never worked in an office before.
Job Training	Employees in these occupations need anywhere from a few days to a few months of training. Usually, an experienced worker could show you how to do the job.
Job Zone Examples	These occupations involve following instructions and helping others. Examples include bus drivers, forest and conservation workers, general office clerks, home health aides, and waiters/waitresses.
SVP Range	(Below 4.0)
Education	These occupations may require a high school diploma or GED certificate. Some may require a formal training course to obtain a license.

Work_Styles	Work_Styles Definitions
Dependability	Job requires being reliable, responsible, and dependable, and fulfilling obligations.
Concern for Others	Job requires being sensitive to others' needs and feelings and being understanding and helpful on the job.
Cooperation	Job requires being pleasant with others on the job and displaying a good-natured, cooperative attitude.
Self Control	Job requires maintaining composure, keeping emotions in check, controlling anger, and avoiding aggressive behavior, even in very difficult situations.
Persistence	Job requires persistence in the face of obstacles.
Integrity	Job requires being honest and ethical.
Attention to Detail	Job requires being careful about detail and thorough in completing work tasks.
Adaptability/Flexibility	Job requires being open to change (positive or negative) and to considerable variety in the workplace.
Initiative	Job requires a willingness to take on responsibilities and challenges.
Leadership	Job requires a willingness to lead, take charge, and offer opinions and direction.
Stress Tolerance	Job requires accepting criticism and dealing calmly and effectively with high stress situations.
Social Orientation	Job requires preferring to work with others rather than alone, and being personally connected with others on the job.
Achievement/Effort	Job requires establishing and maintaining personally challenging achievement goals and exerting effort toward mastering tasks.
Independence	Job requires developing one's own ways of doing things, guiding oneself with little or no supervision, and depending on oneself to get things done.
Analytical Thinking	Job requires analyzing information and using logic to address work-related issues and problems.
Innovation	Job requires creativity and alternative thinking to develop new ideas for and answers to work-related problems.

53-6031.00 - Service Station Attendants

Service automobiles, buses, trucks, boats, and other automotive or marine vehicles with fuel, lubricants, and accessories. Collect payment for services and supplies. May lubricate vehicle, change motor oil, install antifreeze, or replace lights or other accessories, such as windshield wiper blades or fan belts. May repair or replace tires.

Tasks

1) Prepare daily reports of fuel, oil, and accessory sales.

2) Sell prepared food, groceries, and related items.

3) Test and charge batteries.

4) Check air pressure in vehicle tires; and levels of fuel, motor oil, transmission, radiator, battery, and other fluids; and add air, oil, water, or other fluids, as required.

5) Clean parking areas, offices, restrooms, and equipment, and remove trash.

6) Clean windshields, and/or wash and wax vehicles.

7) Collect cash payments from customers and make change, or charge purchases to customers' credit cards and provide customers with receipts.

8) Grease and lubricate vehicles or specified units, such as springs, universal joints, and steering knuckles, using grease guns or spray lubricants.

9) Maintain customer records and follow up periodically with telephone, mail, or personal reminders of service due.

10) Operate car washes.

11) Perform minor repairs such as adjusting brakes, replacing spark plugs, and changing engine oil and filters.

12) Rotate, test, and repair or replace tires.

13) Sell and install accessories, such as batteries, windshield wiper blades, fan belts, bulbs and headlamps.

14) Provide customers with information about local roads and highways.

15) Activate fuel pumps and fill fuel tanks of vehicles with gasoline or diesel fuel to specified levels.

53-6041.00 - Traffic Technicians

Conduct field studies to determine traffic volume, speed, effectiveness of signals, adequacy of lighting, and other factors influencing traffic conditions, under direction of traffic engineer.

Tasks

1) Place and secure automatic counters, using power tools, and retrieve counters after counting periods end.

2) Measure and record the speed of vehicular traffic, using electrical timing devices or radar equipment.

3) Develop plans and long-range strategies for providing adequate parking space.

4) Lay out pavement markings for striping crews.

5) Interview motorists about specific intersections or highways in order to secure information regarding roadway conditions for use in planning.

6) Prepare drawings of proposed signal installations or other control devices, using drafting instruments or computer automated drafting equipment.

7) Compute time settings for traffic signals and speed restrictions, using standard formulas.

8) Operate counters and record data in order to assess the volume, type, and movement of vehicular and pedestrian traffic at specified times.

9) Study factors affecting traffic conditions, such as lighting, and sign and marking visibility, in order to assess their effectiveness.

10) Gather and compile data from hand count sheets, machine count tapes, and radar speed checks, and code data for computer input.

11) Analyze data related to traffic flow, accident rate data, and proposed development in order to determine the most efficient methods to expedite traffic flow.

12) Prepare work orders for repair, maintenance, and changes in traffic systems.

13) Maintain and make minor adjustments and field repairs to equipment used in surveys, including the replacement of parts on traffic data gathering devices.

14) Study traffic delays by noting times of delays, the numbers of vehicles affected, and vehicle speed through the delay area.

15) Plan, design, and improve components of traffic control systems in order to accommodate current and projected traffic, and to increase usability and efficiency.

16) Prepare graphs, charts, diagrams, and other aids in order to illustrate observations and conclusions.

17) Provide technical supervision regarding traffic control devices to other traffic technicians and laborers.

18) Review traffic control/barricade plans in order to issue permits for parades and other special events and for construction work that affects rights-of-way, providing assistance with plan preparation or revision as necessary.

19) Visit development and work sites in order to determine projects' effect on traffic and the adequacy of plans to control traffic and maintain safety, and to suggest traffic control measures.

20) Interact with the public in order to answer traffic-related questions, respond to complaints and requests, or to discuss traffic control ordinances, plans, policies, and procedures.

21) Monitor street and utility projects for compliance to traffic control permit conditions.

22) Establish procedures for street closures and for repair or construction projects.

53-6051.01 - Aviation Inspectors

Inspect aircraft, maintenance procedures, air navigational aids, air traffic controls, and communications equipment to ensure conformance with Federal safety regulations.

Tasks

1) Examine aircraft access plates and doors for security.

2) Investigate air accidents and complaints to determine causes.

3) Observe flight activities of pilots to assess flying skills and to ensure conformance to flight and safety regulations.

4) Analyze training programs and conduct oral and written examinations to ensure the competency of persons operating, installing, and repairing aircraft equipment.

5) Approve or deny issuance of certificates of airworthiness.

6) Conduct flight test programs to test equipment, instruments, and systems under a variety of conditions, using both manual and automatic controls.

7) Issue pilots' licenses to individuals meeting standards.

8) Recommend changes in rules, policies, standards, and regulations, based on knowledge of operating conditions, aircraft improvements, and other factors.

9) Prepare and maintain detailed repair, inspection, investigation, and certification records and reports.

10) Inspect work of aircraft mechanics performing maintenance, modification, or repair and overhaul of aircraft and aircraft mechanical systems, in order to ensure adherence to standards and procedures.

11) Inspect new, repaired, or modified aircraft to identify damage or defects, and to assess airworthiness and conformance to standards, using checklists, hand tools, and test instruments.

12) Recommend replacement, repair, or modification of aircraft equipment.

13) Examine maintenance records and flight logs to determine if service and maintenance checks and overhauls were performed at prescribed intervals.

14) Start aircraft, and observe gauges, meters, and other instruments to detect evidence of malfunctions.

15) Examine landing gear, tires, and exteriors of fuselage, wings, and engines for evidence of damage or corrosion, and to determine whether repairs are needed.

53-7011.00 - Conveyor Operators and Tenders

Control or tend conveyors or conveyor systems that move materials or products to and from stockpiles, processing stations, departments, or vehicles. May control speed and routing of materials or products.

Tasks

1) Measure dimensions of bundles, using rulers, and cut battens to required sizes, using power saws.

2) Distribute materials, supplies, and equipment to work stations, using lifts and trucks.

3) Operate consoles to control automatic palletizing equipment.

4) Record production data such as weights, types, quantities, and storage locations of materials, as well as equipment performance problems and downtime.

5) Repair or replace equipment components or parts such as blades, rolls, and pumps.

6) Stop equipment or machinery and clear jams, using poles, bars, and hand tools, or remove damaged materials from conveyors.

7) Clean, sterilize, and maintain equipment, machinery, and work stations, using hand tools, shovels, brooms, chemicals, hoses, and lubricants.

8) Affix identifying information to materials or products, using hand tools.

9) Thread strapping through strapping tools; then secure battens with strapping to form protective pallets around extrusions.

10) Position deflector bars, gates, chutes, or spouts to divert flow of materials from one conveyor onto another conveyor.

11) Collect samples of materials or products, checking them to ensure conformance to specifications or sending them to laboratories for analysis.

12) Join sections of conveyor frames at temporary working areas, and connect power units.

13) Load, unload, or adjust materials or products on conveyors by hand, by using lifts, hoists, and scoops, or by opening gates, chutes, or hoppers.

14) Manipulate controls, levers, and valves to start pumps, auxiliary equipment, or conveyors, and to adjust equipment positions, speeds, timing, and material flows.

15) Observe packages moving along conveyors in order to identify packages and to detect defective packaging.

16) Press console buttons to deflect packages to predetermined accumulators or reject lines.

17) Read production and delivery schedules, and confer with supervisors, to determine sorting and transfer procedures, arrangement of packages on pallets, and destinations of loaded pallets.

18) Inform supervisors of equipment malfunctions that need to be addressed.

19) Operate elevator systems in conjunction with conveyor systems.

20) Contact workers in work stations or other departments to request movement of materials, products, or machinery, or to notify them of incoming shipments and their estimated delivery times.

21) Weigh or measure materials and products, using scales or other measuring instruments, or read scales on conveyors that continually weigh products, in order to verify specified tonnages and prevent overloads.

22) Observe conveyor operations and monitor lights, dials, and gauges, in order to maintain specified operating levels and to detect equipment malfunctions.

53-7021.00 - Crane and Tower Operators

Operate mechanical boom and cable or tower and cable equipment to lift and move materials, machines, or products in many directions.

Tasks

1) Move levers, depress foot pedals, and turn dials to operate cranes, cherry pickers, electromagnets, or other moving equipment for lifting, moving, and placing loads.

2) Direct helpers engaged in placing blocking and outrigging under cranes.

3) Load and unload bundles from trucks, and move containers to storage bins, using moving equipment.

4) Weigh bundles, using floor scales, and record weights for company records.

5) Clean, lubricate, and maintain mechanisms such as cables, pulleys, and grappling devices, making repairs as necessary.

6) Inspect and adjust crane mechanisms and lifting accessories in order to prevent malfunctions and damage.

7) Direct truck drivers backing vehicles into loading bays, and cover, uncover, and secure loads for delivery.

8) Inspect cables and grappling devices for wear, and install or replace cables as needed.

9) Review daily work and delivery schedules to determine orders, sequences of deliveries, and special loading instructions.

10) Determine load weights and check them against lifting capacities in order to prevent overload.

53-7041.00 - Hoist and Winch Operators

Operate or tend hoists or winches to lift and pull loads using power-operated cable equipment.

Tasks

1) Move levers, pedals, and throttles in order to stop, start, and regulate speeds of hoist or winch drums in response to hand, bell, buzzer, telephone, loud-speaker, or whistle signals, or by observing dial indicators or cable marks.

2) Signal and assist other workers loading or unloading materials.

3) Start engines of hoists or winches and use levers and pedals to wind or unwind cable on drums.

4) Select loads or materials according to weight and size specifications.

5) Move or reposition hoists, winches, loads and materials, manually or using equipment and machines such as trucks, cars, and hand trucks.

6) Attach, fasten, and disconnect cables or lines to loads, materials, and equipment, using hand tools.

7) Operate compressed air, diesel, electric, gasoline, or steam-driven hoists or winches in order to control movement of cableways, cages, derricks, draglines, loaders, railcars, or skips.

8) Repair, maintain, and adjust equipment, using hand tools.

9) Apply hand or foot brakes and move levers to lock hoists or winches.

10) Oil winch drums so that cables will wind smoothly.

11) Tend auxiliary equipment such as jacks, slings, cables, or stop blocks, in order to facilitate moving items or materials for further processing.

12) Climb ladders in order to position and setup vehicle-mounted derricks.

Knowledge	Knowledge Definitions
Mechanical	Knowledge of machines and tools, including their designs, uses, repair, and maintenance.
Customer and Personal Service	Knowledge of principles and processes for providing customer and personal services. This includes customer needs assessment, meeting quality standards for services, and evaluation of customer satisfaction.
English Language	Knowledge of the structure and content of the English language including the meaning and spelling of words, rules of composition, and grammar.
Public Safety and Security	Knowledge of relevant equipment, policies, procedures, and strategies to promote effective local, state, or national security operations for the protection of people, data, property, and institutions.
Transportation	Knowledge of principles and methods for moving people or goods by air, rail, sea, or road, including the relative costs and benefits.
Administration and Management	Knowledge of business and management principles involved in strategic planning, resource allocation, human resources modeling, leadership technique, production methods, and coordination of people and resources.
Engineering and Technology	Knowledge of the practical application of engineering science and technology. This includes applying principles, techniques, procedures, and equipment to the design and production of various goods and services.
Education and Training	Knowledge of principles and methods for curriculum and training design, teaching and instruction for individuals and groups, and the measurement of training effects.
Mathematics	Knowledge of arithmetic, algebra, geometry, calculus, statistics, and their applications.
Production and Processing	Knowledge of raw materials, production processes, quality control, costs, and other techniques for maximizing the effective manufacture and distribution of goods.
Physics	Knowledge and prediction of physical principles, laws, their interrelationships, and applications to understanding fluid, material, and atmospheric dynamics, and mechanical, electrical, atomic and sub-atomic structures and processes.
Design	Knowledge of design techniques, tools, and principles involved in production of precision technical plans, blueprints, drawings, and models.
Building and Construction	Knowledge of materials, methods, and the tools involved in the construction or repair of houses, buildings, or other structures such as highways and roads.
Personnel and Human Resources	Knowledge of principles and procedures for personnel recruitment, selection, training, compensation and benefits, labor relations and negotiation, and personnel information systems.
Computers and Electronics	Knowledge of circuit boards, processors, chips, electronic equipment, and computer hardware and software, including applications and programming.
Telecommunications	Knowledge of transmission, broadcasting, switching, control, and operation of telecommunications systems.
Chemistry	Knowledge of the chemical composition, structure, and properties of substances and of the chemical processes and transformations that they undergo. This includes uses of chemicals and their interactions, danger signs, production techniques, and disposal methods.
Law and Government	Knowledge of laws, legal codes, court procedures, precedents, government regulations, executive orders, agency rules, and the democratic political process.
Medicine and Dentistry	Knowledge of the information and techniques needed to diagnose and treat human injuries, diseases, and deformities. This includes symptoms, treatment alternatives, drug properties and interactions, and preventive health-care measures.
Clerical	Knowledge of administrative and clerical procedures and systems such as word processing, managing files and records, stenography and transcription, designing forms, and other office procedures and terminology.
Sales and Marketing	Knowledge of principles and methods for showing, promoting, and selling products or services. This includes marketing strategy and tactics, product demonstration, sales techniques, and sales control systems.
Therapy and Counseling	Knowledge of principles, methods, and procedures for diagnosis, treatment, and rehabilitation of physical and mental dysfunctions, and for career counseling and guidance.
Communications and Media	Knowledge of media production, communication, and dissemination techniques and methods. This includes alternative ways to inform and entertain via written, oral, and visual media.
Economics and Accounting	Knowledge of economic and accounting principles and practices, the financial markets, banking and the analysis and reporting of financial data.
Psychology	Knowledge of human behavior and performance; individual differences in ability, personality, and interests; learning and motivation; psychological research methods; and the assessment and treatment of behavioral and affective disorders.
Geography	Knowledge of principles and methods for describing the features of land, sea, and air masses, including their physical characteristics, locations, interrelationships, and distribution of plant, animal, and human life.
Sociology and Anthropology	Knowledge of group behavior and dynamics, societal trends and influences, human migrations, ethnicity, cultures and their history and origins.
Biology	Knowledge of plant and animal organisms, their tissues, cells, functions, interdependencies, and interactions with each other and the environment.
Foreign Language	Knowledge of the structure and content of a foreign (non-English) language including the meaning and spelling of words, rules of composition and grammar, and pronunciation.
History and Archeology	Knowledge of historical events and their causes, indicators, and effects on civilizations and cultures.
Food Production	Knowledge of techniques and equipment for planting, growing, and harvesting food products (both plant and animal) for consumption, including storage/handling techniques.
Fine Arts	Knowledge of the theory and techniques required to compose, produce, and perform works of music, dance, visual arts, drama, and sculpture.
Philosophy and Theology	Knowledge of different philosophical systems and religions. This includes their basic principles, values, ethics, ways of thinking, customs, practices, and their impact on human culture.

Skills	Skills Definitions
Operation and Control	Controlling operations of equipment or systems.
Coordination	Adjusting actions in relation to others' actions.
Reading Comprehension	Understanding written sentences and paragraphs in work related documents.
Speaking	Talking to others to convey information effectively.
Judgment and Decision Making	Considering the relative costs and benefits of potential actions to choose the most appropriate one.
Repairing	Repairing machines or systems using the needed tools.
Operation Monitoring	Watching gauges, dials, or other indicators to make sure a machine is working properly.
Critical Thinking	Using logic and reasoning to identify the strengths and weaknesses of alternative solutions, conclusions or approaches to problems.
Equipment Maintenance	Performing routine maintenance on equipment and determining when and what kind of maintenance is needed.
Time Management	Managing one's own time and the time of others.
Troubleshooting	Determining causes of operating errors and deciding what to do about it.
Equipment Selection	Determining the kind of tools and equipment needed to do a job.
Mathematics	Using mathematics to solve problems.
Complex Problem Solving	Identifying complex problems and reviewing related information to develop and evaluate options and implement solutions.
Learning Strategies	Selecting and using training/instructional methods and procedures appropriate for the situation when learning or teaching new things.
Writing	Communicating effectively in writing as appropriate for the needs of the audience.
Active Listening	Giving full attention to what other people are saying, taking time to understand the points being made, asking questions as appropriate, and not interrupting at inappropriate times.
Active Learning	Understanding the implications of new information for both current and future problem-solving and decision-making.
Management of Personnel Resources	Motivating, developing, and directing people as they work, identifying the best people for the job.
Monitoring	Monitoring/Assessing performance of yourself, other individuals, or organizations to make improvements or take corrective action.

Management of Financial Resources	Determining how money will be spent to get the work done, and accounting for these expenditures.
Quality Control Analysis	Conducting tests and inspections of products, services, or processes to evaluate quality or performance.
Social Perceptiveness	Being aware of others' reactions and understanding why they react as they do.
Instructing	Teaching others how to do something.
Technology Design	Generating or adapting equipment and technology to serve user needs.
Science	Using scientific rules and methods to solve problems.
Management of Material Resources	Obtaining and seeing to the appropriate use of equipment, facilities, and materials needed to do certain work.
Systems Evaluation	Identifying measures or indicators of system performance and the actions needed to improve or correct performance, relative to the goals of the system.
Systems Analysis	Determining how a system should work and how changes in conditions, operations, and the environment will affect outcomes.
Installation	Installing equipment, machines, wiring, or programs to meet specifications.
Persuasion	Persuading others to change their minds or behavior.
Negotiation	Bringing others together and trying to reconcile differences.
Service Orientation	Actively looking for ways to help people.
Operations Analysis	Analyzing needs and product requirements to create a design.
Programming	Writing computer programs for various purposes.

Ability	Ability Definitions
Problem Sensitivity	The ability to tell when something is wrong or is likely to go wrong. It does not involve solving the problem, only recognizing there is a problem.
Reaction Time	The ability to quickly respond (with the hand, finger, or foot) to a signal (sound, light, picture) when it appears.
Arm-Hand Steadiness	The ability to keep your hand and arm steady while moving your arm or while holding your arm and hand in one position.
Depth Perception	The ability to judge which of several objects is closer or farther away from you, or to judge the distance between you and an object.
Control Precision	The ability to quickly and repeatedly adjust the controls of a machine or a vehicle to exact positions.
Multilimb Coordination	The ability to coordinate two or more limbs (for example, two arms, two legs, or one leg and one arm) while sitting, standing, or lying down. It does not involve performing the activities while the whole body is in motion.
Near Vision	The ability to see details at close range (within a few feet of the observer).
Oral Comprehension	The ability to listen to and understand information and ideas presented through spoken words and sentences.
Manual Dexterity	The ability to quickly move your hand, your hand together with your arm, or your two hands to grasp, manipulate, or assemble objects.
Oral Expression	The ability to communicate information and ideas in speaking so others will understand.
Speech Recognition	The ability to identify and understand the speech of another person.
Selective Attention	The ability to concentrate on a task over a period of time without being distracted.
Deductive Reasoning	The ability to apply general rules to specific problems to produce answers that make sense.
Far Vision	The ability to see details at a distance.
Rate Control	The ability to time your movements or the movement of a piece of equipment in anticipation of changes in the speed and/or direction of a moving object or scene.
Hearing Sensitivity	The ability to detect or tell the differences between sounds that vary in pitch and loudness.
Speech Clarity	The ability to speak clearly so others can understand you.
Visualization	The ability to imagine how something will look after it is moved around or when its parts are moved or rearranged.
Perceptual Speed	The ability to quickly and accurately compare similarities and differences among sets of letters, numbers, objects, pictures, or patterns. The things to be compared may be presented at the same time or one after the other. This ability also includes comparing a presented object with a remembered object.
Inductive Reasoning	The ability to combine pieces of information to form general rules or conclusions (includes finding a relationship among seemingly unrelated events).

Finger Dexterity	The ability to make precisely coordinated movements of the fingers of one or both hands to grasp, manipulate, or assemble very small objects.
Information Ordering	The ability to arrange things or actions in a certain order or pattern according to a specific rule or set of rules (e.g., patterns of numbers, letters, words, pictures, mathematical operations).
Extent Flexibility	The ability to bend, stretch, twist, or reach with your body, arms, and/or legs.
Gross Body Equilibrium	The ability to keep or regain your body balance or stay upright when in an unstable position.
Category Flexibility	The ability to generate or use different sets of rules for combining or grouping things in different ways.
Response Orientation	The ability to choose quickly between two or more movements in response to two or more different signals (lights, sounds, pictures). It includes the speed with which the correct response is started with the hand, foot, or other body part.
Auditory Attention	The ability to focus on a single source of sound in the presence of other distracting sounds.
Visual Color Discrimination	The ability to match or detect differences between colors, including shades of color and brightness.
Written Comprehension	The ability to read and understand information and ideas presented in writing.
Flexibility of Closure	The ability to identify or detect a known pattern (a figure, object, word, or sound) that is hidden in other distracting material.
Spatial Orientation	The ability to know your location in relation to the environment or to know where other objects are in relation to you.
Sound Localization	The ability to tell the direction from which a sound originated.
Time Sharing	The ability to shift back and forth between two or more activities or sources of information (such as speech, sounds, touch, or other sources).
Speed of Limb Movement	The ability to quickly move the arms and legs.
Fluency of Ideas	The ability to come up with a number of ideas about a topic (the number of ideas is important, not their quality, correctness, or creativity).
Static Strength	The ability to exert maximum muscle force to lift, push, pull, or carry objects.
Trunk Strength	The ability to use your abdominal and lower back muscles to support part of the body repeatedly or continuously over time without 'giving out' or fatiguing.
Speed of Closure	The ability to quickly make sense of, combine, and organize information into meaningful patterns.
Written Expression	The ability to communicate information and ideas in writing so others will understand.
Peripheral Vision	The ability to see objects or movement of objects to one's side when the eyes are looking ahead.
Memorization	The ability to remember information such as words, numbers, pictures, and procedures.
Originality	The ability to come up with unusual or clever ideas about a given topic or situation, or to develop creative ways to solve a problem.
Glare Sensitivity	The ability to see objects in the presence of glare or bright lighting.
Number Facility	The ability to add, subtract, multiply, or divide quickly and correctly.
Wrist-Finger Speed	The ability to make fast, simple, repeated movements of the fingers, hands, and wrists.
Gross Body Coordination	The ability to coordinate the movement of your arms, legs, and torso together when the whole body is in motion.
Stamina	The ability to exert yourself physically over long periods of time without getting winded or out of breath.
Mathematical Reasoning	The ability to choose the right mathematical methods or formulas to solve a problem.
Dynamic Strength	The ability to exert muscle force repeatedly or continuously over time. This involves muscular endurance and resistance to muscle fatigue.
Night Vision	The ability to see under low light conditions.
Dynamic Flexibility	The ability to quickly and repeatedly bend, stretch, twist, or reach out with your body, arms, and/or legs.
Explosive Strength	The ability to use short bursts of muscle force to propel oneself (as in jumping or sprinting), or to throw an object.

Work_Activity	Work_Activity Definitions
Repairing and Maintaining Mechanical Equipment	Servicing, repairing, adjusting, and testing machines, devices, moving parts, and equipment that operate primarily on the basis of mechanical (not electronic) principles.

Handling and Moving Objects	Using hands and arms in handling. installing. positioning, and moving materials. and manipulating things.
Getting Information	Observing. receiving. and otherwise obtaining information from all relevant sources.
Operating Vehicles, Mechanized Devices, or Equipme	Running. maneuvering, navigating, or driving vehicles or mechanized equipment, such as forklifts. passenger vehicles. aircraft, or water craft.
Controlling Machines and Processes	Using either control mechanisms or direct physical activity to operate machines or processes (not including computers or vehicles).
Monitor Processes. Materials. or Surroundings	Monitoring and reviewing information from materials. events, or the environment, to detect or assess problems.
Communicating with Supervisors, Peers. or Subordin	Providing information to supervisors. co-workers. and subordinates by telephone, in written form. e-mail. or in person.
Inspecting Equipment, Structures, or Material	Inspecting equipment, structures, or materials to identify the cause of errors or other problems or defects.
Organizing, Planning, and Prioritizing Work	Developing specific goals and plans to prioritize. organize. and accomplish your work.
Identifying Objects, Actions, and Events	Identifying information by categorizing. estimating. recognizing differences or similarities. and detecting changes in circumstances or events.
Making Decisions and Solving Problems	Analyzing information and evaluating results to choose the best solution and solve problems.
Guiding, Directing, and Motivating Subordinates	Providing guidance and direction to subordinates. including setting performance standards and monitoring performance.
Training and Teaching Others	Identifying the educational needs of others. developing formal educational or training programs or classes. and teaching or instructing others.
Judging the Qualities of Things, Services, or Peop	Assessing the value, importance, or quality of things or people.
Interpreting the Meaning of Information for Others	Translating or explaining what information means and how it can be used.
Processing Information	Compiling. coding, categorizing, calculating. tabulating, auditing, or verifying information or data.
Documenting/Recording Information	Entering, transcribing, recording, storing. or maintaining information in written or electronic/magnetic form.
Developing Objectives and Strategies	Establishing long-range objectives and specifying the strategies and actions to achieve them.
Estimating the Quantifiable Characteristics of Pro	Estimating sizes, distances, and quantities: or determining time, costs, resources, or materials needed to perform a work activity.
Developing and Building Teams	Encouraging and building mutual trust. respect. and cooperation among team members.
Performing General Physical Activities	Performing physical activities that require considerable use of your arms and legs and moving your whole body, such as climbing, lifting, balancing, walking, stooping, and handling of materials.
Updating and Using Relevant Knowledge	Keeping up-to-date technically and applying new knowledge to your job.
Assisting and Caring for Others	Providing personal assistance, medical attention, emotional support, or other personal care to others such as coworkers, customers, or patients.
Monitoring and Controlling Resources	Monitoring and controlling resources and overseeing the spending of money.
Establishing and Maintaining Interpersonal Relatio	Developing constructive and cooperative working relationships with others, and maintaining them over time.
Evaluating Information to Determine Compliance wit	Using relevant information and individual judgment to determine whether events or processes comply with laws, regulations, or standards.
Coaching and Developing Others	Identifying the developmental needs of others and coaching, mentoring, or otherwise helping others to improve their knowledge or skills.
Analyzing Data or Information	Identifying the underlying principles. reasons. or facts of information by breaking down information or data into separate parts.
Coordinating the Work and Activities of Others	Getting members of a group to work together to accomplish tasks.
Repairing and Maintaining Electronic Equipment	Servicing, repairing, calibrating. regulating. fine-tuning. or testing machines, devices, and equipment that operate primarily on the basis of electrical or electronic (not mechanical) principles.
Thinking Creatively	Developing, designing, or creating new applications, ideas, relationships, systems, or products. including artistic contributions.
Drafting, Laying Out, and Specifying Technical Dev	Providing documentation. detailed instructions, drawings, or specifications to tell others about how devices, parts, equipment. or structures are to be fabricated, constructed, assembled, modified. maintained, or used.
Resolving Conflicts and Negotiating with Others	Handling complaints. settling disputes, and resolving grievances and conflicts. or otherwise negotiating with others.
Interacting With Computers	Using computers and computer systems (including hardware and software) to program, write software, set up functions, enter data, or process information.
Scheduling Work and Activities	Scheduling events. programs. and activities, as well as the work of others.
Provide Consultation and Advice to Others	Providing guidance and expert advice to management or other groups on technical. systems , or process-related topics.
Selling or Influencing Others	Convincing others to buy merchandise/goods or to otherwise change their minds or actions.
Performing for or Working Directly with the Public	Performing for people or dealing directly with the public. This includes serving customers in restaurants and stores, and receiving clients or guests.
Communicating with Persons Outside Organization	Communicating with people outside the organization, representing the organization to customers, the public, government, and other external sources. This information can be exchanged in person. in writing, or by telephone or e-mail.
Performing Administrative Activities	Performing day-to-day administrative tasks such as maintaining information files and processing paperwork.
Staffing Organizational Units	Recruiting. interviewing, selecting, hiring, and promoting employees in an organization.

Work_Context	Work_Context Definitions
Wear Common Protective or Safety Equipment such as	How much does this job require wearing common protective or safety equipment such as safety shoes, glasses, gloves, hard hats or live jackets?
Sounds, Noise Levels Are Distracting or Uncomforta	How often does this job require working exposed to sounds and noise levels that are distracting or uncomfortable?
Spend Time Using Your Hands to Handle, Control, or	How much does this job require using your hands to handle, control, or feel objects, tools or controls?
Responsible for Others' Health and Safety	How much responsibility is there for the health and safety of others in this job?
Importance of Being Exact or Accurate	How important is being very exact or highly accurate in performing this job?
Face-to-Face Discussions	How often do you have to have face-to-face discussions with individuals or teams in this job?
Time Pressure	How often does this job require the worker to meet strict deadlines?
Work With Work Group or Team	How important is it to work with others in a group or team in this job?
Freedom to Make Decisions	How much decision making freedom, without supervision, does the job offer?
Exposed to Hazardous Equipment	How often does this job require exposure to hazardous equipment?
Exposed to Contaminants	How often does this job require working exposed to contaminants (such as pollutants, gases, dust or odors)?
Impact of Decisions on Co-workers or Company Resul	How do the decisions an employee makes impact the results of co-workers, clients or the company?
Frequency of Decision Making	How frequently is the worker required to make decisions that affect other people, the financial resources, and/or the image and reputation of the organization?
Exposed to High Places	How often does this job require exposure to high places?
Structured versus Unstructured Work	To what extent is this job structured for the worker, rather than allowing the worker to determine tasks, priorities, and goals?
Spend Time Making Repetitive Motions	How much does this job require making repetitive motions?
Consequence of Error	How serious would the result usually be if the worker made a mistake that was not readily correctable?
Spend Time Bending or Twisting the Body	How much does this job require bending or twisting your body?
Pace Determined by Speed of Equipment	How important is it to this job that the pace is determined by the speed of equipment or machinery? (This does not refer to keeping busy at all times on this job.)
Cramped Work Space, Awkward Positions	How often does this job require working in cramped work spaces that requires getting into awkward positions?
In an Enclosed Vehicle or Equipment	How often does this job require working in a closed vehicle or equipment (e.g., car)?
Exposed to Hazardous Conditions	How often does this job require exposure to hazardous conditions?

1207

Contact With Others	How much does this job require the worker to be in contact with others (face-to-face, by telephone, or otherwise) in order to perform it?
Exposed to Whole Body Vibration	How often does this job require exposure to whole body vibration (e.g., operate a jackhammer)?
Very Hot or Cold Temperatures	How often does this job require working in very hot (above 90 F degrees) or very cold (below 32 F degrees) temperatures?
Indoors, Not Environmentally Controlled	How often does this job require working indoors in non-controlled environmental conditions (e.g., warehouse without heat)?
Spend Time Sitting	How much does this job require sitting?
Importance of Repeating Same Tasks	How important is repeating the same physical activities (e.g., key entry) or mental activities (e.g., checking entries in a ledger) over and over, without stopping, to performing this job?
Deal With Unpleasant or Angry People	How frequently does the worker have to deal with unpleasant, angry, or discourteous individuals as part of the job requirements?
Coordinate or Lead Others	How important is it to coordinate or lead others in accomplishing work activities in this job?
Extremely Bright or Inadequate Lighting	How often does this job require working in extremely bright or inadequate lighting conditions?
Physical Proximity	To what extent does this job require the worker to perform job tasks in close physical proximity to other people?
Frequency of Conflict Situations	How often are there conflict situations the employee has to face in this job?
Spend Time Walking and Running	How much does this job require walking and running?
In an Open Vehicle or Equipment	How often does this job require working in an open vehicle or equipment (e.g., tractor)?
Responsibility for Outcomes and Results	How responsible is the worker for work outcomes and results of other workers?
Spend Time Keeping or Regaining Balance	How much does this job require keeping or regaining your balance?
Outdoors, Exposed to Weather	How often does this job require working outdoors, exposed to all weather conditions?
Level of Competition	To what extent does this job require the worker to compete or to be aware of competitive pressures?
Exposed to Minor Burns, Cuts, Bites, or Stings	How often does this job require exposure to minor burns, cuts, bites, or stings?
Telephone	How often do you have telephone conversations in this job?
Wear Specialized Protective or Safety Equipment su	How much does this job require wearing specialized protective or safety equipment such as breathing apparatus, safety harness, full protection suits, or radiation protection?
Spend Time Standing	How much does this job require standing?
Degree of Automation	How automated is the job?
Deal With External Customers	How important is it to work with external customers or the public in this job?
Outdoors, Under Cover	How often does this job require working outdoors, under cover (e.g., structure with roof but no walls)?
Letters and Memos	How often does the job require written letters and memos?
Spend Time Climbing Ladders, Scaffolds, or Poles	How much does this job require climbing ladders, scaffolds, or poles?
Spend Time Kneeling, Crouching, Stooping, or Crawl	How much does this job require kneeling, crouching, stooping, or crawling?
Deal With Physically Aggressive People	How frequently does this job require the worker to deal with physical aggression of violent individuals?
Public Speaking	How often do you have to perform public speaking in this job?
Indoors, Environmentally Controlled	How often does this job require working indoors in environmentally controlled conditions?
Electronic Mail	How often do you use electronic mail in this job?
Exposed to Radiation	How often does this job require exposure to radiation?
Exposed to Disease or Infections	How often does this job require exposure to disease/infections?

Job Zone Component	Job Zone Component Definitions
Title	Job Zone Two: Some Preparation Needed
Overall Experience	Some previous work-related skill, knowledge, or experience may be helpful in these occupations, but usually is not needed. For example, a drywall installer might benefit from experience installing drywall, but an inexperienced person could still learn to be an installer with little difficulty.
Job Training	Employees in these occupations need anywhere from a few months to one year of working with experienced employees.

Job Zone Examples	These occupations often involve using your knowledge and skills to help others. Examples include drywall installers, fire inspectors, flight attendants, pharmacy technicians, salespersons (retail), and tellers.
SVP Range	(4.0 to < 6.0)
Education	These occupations usually require a high school diploma and may require some vocational training or job-related course work. In some cases, an associate's or bachelor's degree could be needed.

Work_Styles	Work_Styles Definitions
Independence	Job requires developing one's own ways of doing things, guiding oneself with little or no supervision, and depending on oneself to get things done.
Initiative	Job requires a willingness to take on responsibilities and challenges.
Dependability	Job requires being reliable, responsible, and dependable, and fulfilling obligations.
Attention to Detail	Job requires being careful about detail and thorough in completing work tasks.
Cooperation	Job requires being pleasant with others on the job and displaying a good-natured, cooperative attitude.
Persistence	Job requires persistence in the face of obstacles.
Concern for Others	Job requires being sensitive to others' needs and feelings and being understanding and helpful on the job.
Adaptability/Flexibility	Job requires being open to change (positive or negative) and to considerable variety in the workplace.
Stress Tolerance	Job requires accepting criticism and dealing calmly and effectively with high stress situations.
Self Control	Job requires maintaining composure, keeping emotions in check, controlling anger, and avoiding aggressive behavior, even in very difficult situations.
Achievement/Effort	Job requires establishing and maintaining personally challenging achievement goals and exerting effort toward mastering tasks.
Analytical Thinking	Job requires analyzing information and using logic to address work-related issues and problems.
Innovation	Job requires creativity and alternative thinking to develop new ideas for and answers to work-related problems.
Integrity	Job requires being honest and ethical.
Social Orientation	Job requires preferring to work with others rather than alone, and being personally connected with others on the job.
Leadership	Job requires a willingness to lead, take charge, and offer opinions and direction.

53-7051.00 - Industrial Truck and Tractor Operators

Operate industrial trucks or tractors equipped to move materials around a warehouse, storage yard, factory, construction site, or similar location.

Tasks

1) Manually load or unload materials onto or off pallets, skids, platforms, cars, or lifting devices.

2) Position lifting devices under, over, or around loaded pallets, skids, and boxes, and secure material or products for transport to designated areas.

3) Move controls to drive gasoline- or electric-powered trucks, cars, or tractors and transport materials between loading, processing, and storage areas.

4) Perform routine maintenance on vehicles and auxiliary equipment, such as cleaning, lubricating, recharging batteries, fueling, or replacing liquefied-gas tank.

5) Weigh materials or products, and record weight and other production data on tags or labels.

6) Operate or tend automatic stacking, loading, packaging, or cutting machines.

7) Hook tow trucks to trailer hitches and fasten attachments, such as graders, plows, rollers, and winch cables to tractors, using hitchpins.

8) Signal workers to discharge, dump, or level materials.

9) Turn valves and open chutes in order to dump, spray, or release materials from dump cars or storage bins into hoppers.

Knowledge	Knowledge Definitions
Transportation	Knowledge of principles and methods for moving people or goods by air, rail, sea, or road, including the relative costs and benefits.
Mathematics	Knowledge of arithmetic, algebra, geometry, calculus, statistics, and their applications.
English Language	Knowledge of the structure and content of the English language including the meaning and spelling of words, rules of composition, and grammar.
Mechanical	Knowledge of machines and tools, including their designs, uses, repair, and maintenance.
Customer and Personal Service	Knowledge of principles and processes for providing customer and personal services. This includes customer needs assessment, meeting quality standards for services, and evaluation of customer satisfaction.
Administration and Management	Knowledge of business and management principles involved in strategic planning, resource allocation, human resources modeling, leadership technique, production methods, and coordination of people and resources.
Education and Training	Knowledge of principles and methods for curriculum and training design, teaching and instruction for individuals and groups, and the measurement of training effects.
Production and Processing	Knowledge of raw materials, production processes, quality control, costs, and other techniques for maximizing the effective manufacture and distribution of goods.
Public Safety and Security	Knowledge of relevant equipment, policies, procedures, and strategies to promote effective local, state, or national security operations for the protection of people, data, property, and institutions.
Clerical	Knowledge of administrative and clerical procedures and systems such as word processing, managing files and records, stenography and transcription, designing forms, and other office procedures and terminology.
Computers and Electronics	Knowledge of circuit boards, processors, chips, electronic equipment, and computer hardware and software, including applications and programming.
Telecommunications	Knowledge of transmission, broadcasting, switching, control, and operation of telecommunications systems.
Chemistry	Knowledge of the chemical composition, structure, and properties of substances and of the chemical processes and transformations that they undergo. This includes uses of chemicals and their interactions, danger signs, production techniques, and disposal methods.
Economics and Accounting	Knowledge of economic and accounting principles and practices, the financial markets, banking and the analysis and reporting of financial data.
Psychology	Knowledge of human behavior and performance; individual differences in ability, personality, and interests; learning and motivation; psychological research methods; and the assessment and treatment of behavioral and affective disorders.
Geography	Knowledge of principles and methods for describing the features of land, sea, and air masses, including their physical characteristics, locations, interrelationships, and distribution of plant, animal, and human life.
Building and Construction	Knowledge of materials, methods, and the tools involved in the construction or repair of houses, buildings, or other structures such as highways and roads.
Physics	Knowledge and prediction of physical principles, laws, their interrelationships, and applications to understanding fluid, material, and atmospheric dynamics, and mechanical, electrical, atomic and sub-atomic structures and processes.
Law and Government	Knowledge of laws, legal codes, court procedures, precedents, government regulations, executive orders, agency rules, and the democratic political process.
Communications and Media	Knowledge of media production, communication, and dissemination techniques and methods. This includes alternative ways to inform and entertain via written, oral, and visual media.
Foreign Language	Knowledge of the structure and content of a foreign (non-English) language including the meaning and spelling of words, rules of composition and grammar, and pronunciation.
Sales and Marketing	Knowledge of principles and methods for showing, promoting, and selling products or services. This includes marketing strategy and tactics, product demonstration, sales techniques, and sales control systems.
Sociology and Anthropology	Knowledge of group behavior and dynamics, societal trends and influences, human migrations, ethnicity, cultures and their history and origins.
Design	Knowledge of design techniques, tools, and principles involved in production of precision technical plans, blueprints, drawings, and models.
Engineering and Technology	Knowledge of the practical application of engineering science and technology. This includes applying principles, techniques, procedures, and equipment to the design and production of various goods and services.
Personnel and Human Resources	Knowledge of principles and procedures for personnel recruitment, selection, training, compensation and benefits, labor relations and negotiation, and personnel information systems.
Philosophy and Theology	Knowledge of different philosophical systems and religions. This includes their basic principles, values, ethics, ways of thinking, customs, practices, and their impact on human culture.
Therapy and Counseling	Knowledge of principles, methods, and procedures for diagnosis, treatment, and rehabilitation of physical and mental dysfunctions, and for career counseling and guidance.
History and Archeology	Knowledge of historical events and their causes, indicators, and effects on civilizations and cultures.
Food Production	Knowledge of techniques and equipment for planting, growing, and harvesting food products (both plant and animal) for consumption, including storage/handling techniques.
Medicine and Dentistry	Knowledge of the information and techniques needed to diagnose and treat human injuries, diseases, and deformities. This includes symptoms, treatment alternatives, drug properties and interactions, and preventive health-care measures.
Biology	Knowledge of plant and animal organisms, their tissues, cells, functions, interdependencies, and interactions with each other and the environment.
Fine Arts	Knowledge of the theory and techniques required to compose, produce, and perform works of music, dance, visual arts, drama, and sculpture.

Skills	Skills Definitions
Mathematics	Using mathematics to solve problems.
Active Listening	Giving full attention to what other people are saying, taking time to understand the points being made, asking questions as appropriate, and not interrupting at inappropriate times.
Reading Comprehension	Understanding written sentences and paragraphs in work related documents.
Equipment Maintenance	Performing routine maintenance on equipment and determining when and what kind of maintenance is needed.
Operation and Control	Controlling operations of equipment or systems.
Instructing	Teaching others how to do something.
Operation Monitoring	Watching gauges, dials, or other indicators to make sure a machine is working properly.
Critical Thinking	Using logic and reasoning to identify the strengths and weaknesses of alternative solutions, conclusions or approaches to problems.
Time Management	Managing one's own time and the time of others.
Equipment Selection	Determining the kind of tools and equipment needed to do a job.
Coordination	Adjusting actions in relation to others' actions.
Judgment and Decision Making	Considering the relative costs and benefits of potential actions to choose the most appropriate one.
Speaking	Talking to others to convey information effectively.
Active Learning	Understanding the implications of new information for both current and future problem-solving and decision-making.
Social Perceptiveness	Being aware of others' reactions and understanding why they react as they do.
Learning Strategies	Selecting and using training/instructional methods and procedures appropriate for the situation when learning or teaching new things.
Writing	Communicating effectively in writing as appropriate for the needs of the audience.
Quality Control Analysis	Conducting tests and inspections of products, services, or processes to evaluate quality or performance.
Repairing	Repairing machines or systems using the needed tools.
Troubleshooting	Determining causes of operating errors and deciding what to do about it.
Systems Analysis	Determining how a system should work and how changes in conditions, operations, and the environment will affect outcomes.

Monitoring	Monitoring/Assessing performance of yourself, other individuals, or organizations to make improvements or take corrective action.
Service Orientation	Actively looking for ways to help people.
Negotiation	Bringing others together and trying to reconcile differences.
Systems Evaluation	Identifying measures or indicators of system performance and the actions needed to improve or correct performance, relative to the goals of the system.
Complex Problem Solving	Identifying complex problems and reviewing related information to develop and evaluate options and implement solutions.
Technology Design	Generating or adapting equipment and technology to serve user needs.
Management of Personnel Resources	Motivating, developing, and directing people as they work, identifying the best people for the job.
Management of Material Resources	Obtaining and seeing to the appropriate use of equipment, facilities, and materials needed to do certain work.
Persuasion	Persuading others to change their minds or behavior.
Management of Financial Resources	Determining how money will be spent to get the work done, and accounting for these expenditures.
Operations Analysis	Analyzing needs and product requirements to create a design.
Installation	Installing equipment, machines, wiring, or programs to meet specifications.
Science	Using scientific rules and methods to solve problems.
Programming	Writing computer programs for various purposes.

Ability	Ability Definitions
Arm-Hand Steadiness	The ability to keep your hand and arm steady while moving your arm or while holding your arm and hand in one position.
Multilimb Coordination	The ability to coordinate two or more limbs (for example, two arms, two legs, or one leg and one arm) while sitting, standing, or lying down. It does not involve performing the activities while the whole body is in motion.
Depth Perception	The ability to judge which of several objects is closer or farther away from you, or to judge the distance between you and an object.
Static Strength	The ability to exert maximum muscle force to lift, push, pull, or carry objects.
Control Precision	The ability to quickly and repeatedly adjust the controls of a machine or a vehicle to exact positions.
Trunk Strength	The ability to use your abdominal and lower back muscles to support part of the body repeatedly or continuously over time without 'giving out' or fatiguing.
Manual Dexterity	The ability to quickly move your hand, your hand together with your arm, or your two hands to grasp, manipulate, or assemble objects.
Stamina	The ability to exert yourself physically over long periods of time without getting winded or out of breath.
Extent Flexibility	The ability to bend, stretch, twist, or reach with your body, arms, and/or legs.
Far Vision	The ability to see details at a distance.
Dynamic Strength	The ability to exert muscle force repeatedly or continuously over time. This involves muscular endurance and resistance to muscle fatigue.
Oral Comprehension	The ability to listen to and understand information and ideas presented through spoken words and sentences.
Response Orientation	The ability to choose quickly between two or more movements in response to two or more different signals (lights, sounds, pictures). It includes the speed with which the correct response is started with the hand, foot, or other body part.
Rate Control	The ability to time your movements or the movement of a piece of equipment in anticipation of changes in the speed and/or direction of a moving object or scene.
Near Vision	The ability to see details at close range (within a few feet of the observer).
Selective Attention	The ability to concentrate on a task over a period of time without being distracted.
Problem Sensitivity	The ability to tell when something is wrong or is likely to go wrong. It does not involve solving the problem, only recognizing there is a problem.
Finger Dexterity	The ability to make precisely coordinated movements of the fingers of one or both hands to grasp, manipulate, or assemble very small objects.
Spatial Orientation	The ability to know your location in relation to the environment or to know where other objects are in relation to you.
Reaction Time	The ability to quickly respond (with the hand, finger, or foot) to a signal (sound, light, picture) when it appears.

Peripheral Vision	The ability to see objects or movement of objects to one's side when the eyes are looking ahead.
Oral Expression	The ability to communicate information and ideas in speaking so others will understand.
Speech Clarity	The ability to speak clearly so others can understand you.
Deductive Reasoning	The ability to apply general rules to specific problems to produce answers that make sense.
Written Comprehension	The ability to read and understand information and ideas presented in writing.
Flexibility of Closure	The ability to identify or detect a known pattern (a figure, object, word, or sound) that is hidden in other distracting material.
Inductive Reasoning	The ability to combine pieces of information to form general rules or conclusions (includes finding a relationship among seemingly unrelated events).
Speed of Limb Movement	The ability to quickly move the arms and legs.
Gross Body Coordination	The ability to coordinate the movement of your arms, legs, and torso together when the whole body is in motion.
Speech Recognition	The ability to identify and understand the speech of another person.
Time Sharing	The ability to shift back and forth between two or more activities or sources of information (such as speech, sounds, touch, or other sources).
Perceptual Speed	The ability to quickly and accurately compare similarities and differences among sets of letters, numbers, objects, pictures, or patterns. The things to be compared may be presented at the same time or one after the other. This ability also includes comparing a presented object with a remembered object.
Night Vision	The ability to see under low light conditions.
Visualization	The ability to imagine how something will look after it is moved around or when its parts are moved or rearranged.
Information Ordering	The ability to arrange things or actions in a certain order or pattern according to a specific rule or set of rules (e.g., patterns of numbers, letters, words, pictures, mathematical operations).
Category Flexibility	The ability to generate or use different sets of rules for combining or grouping things in different ways.
Visual Color Discrimination	The ability to match or detect differences between colors, including shades of color and brightness.
Gross Body Equilibrium	The ability to keep or regain your body balance or stay upright when in an unstable position.
Hearing Sensitivity	The ability to detect or tell the differences between sounds that vary in pitch and loudness.
Auditory Attention	The ability to focus on a single source of sound in the presence of other distracting sounds.
Glare Sensitivity	The ability to see objects in the presence of glare or bright lighting.
Written Expression	The ability to communicate information and ideas in writing so others will understand.
Sound Localization	The ability to tell the direction from which a sound originated.
Originality	The ability to come up with unusual or clever ideas about a given topic or situation, or to develop creative ways to solve a problem.
Mathematical Reasoning	The ability to choose the right mathematical methods or formulas to solve a problem.
Wrist-Finger Speed	The ability to make fast, simple, repeated movements of the fingers, hands, and wrists.
Speed of Closure	The ability to quickly make sense of, combine, and organize information into meaningful patterns.
Fluency of Ideas	The ability to come up with a number of ideas about a topic (the number of ideas is important, not their quality, correctness, or creativity).
Memorization	The ability to remember information such as words, numbers, pictures, and procedures.
Number Facility	The ability to add, subtract, multiply, or divide quickly and correctly.
Dynamic Flexibility	The ability to quickly and repeatedly bend, stretch, twist, or reach out with your body, arms, and/or legs.
Explosive Strength	The ability to use short bursts of muscle force to propel oneself (as in jumping or sprinting), or to throw an object.

Work_Activity	Work_Activity Definitions
Operating Vehicles, Mechanized Devices, or Equipme	Running, maneuvering, navigating, or driving vehicles or mechanized equipment, such as forklifts, passenger vehicles, aircraft, or water craft.
Handling and Moving Objects	Using hands and arms in handling, installing, positioning, and moving materials, and manipulating things.

Getting Information	Observing, receiving, and otherwise obtaining information from all relevant sources.
Performing General Physical Activities	Performing physical activities that require considerable use of your arms and legs and moving your whole body, such as climbing, lifting, balancing, walking, stooping, and handling of materials.
Identifying Objects, Actions, and Events	Identifying information by categorizing, estimating, recognizing differences or similarities, and detecting changes in circumstances or events.
Controlling Machines and Processes	Using either control mechanisms or direct physical activity to operate machines or processes (not including computers or vehicles).
Inspecting Equipment, Structures, or Material	Inspecting equipment, structures, or materials to identify the cause of errors or other problems or defects.
Establishing and Maintaining Interpersonal Relatio	Developing constructive and cooperative working relationships with others, and maintaining them over time.
Making Decisions and Solving Problems	Analyzing information and evaluating results to choose the best solution and solve problems.
Documenting/Recording Information	Entering, transcribing, recording, storing, or maintaining information in written or electronic/magnetic form.
Communicating with Supervisors, Peers, or Subordin	Providing information to supervisors, co-workers, and subordinates by telephone, in written form, e-mail, or in person.
Interacting With Computers	Using computers and computer systems (including hardware and software) to program, write software, set up functions, enter data, or process information.
Monitor Processes, Materials, or Surroundings	Monitoring and reviewing information from materials, events, or the environment, to detect or assess problems.
Organizing, Planning, and Prioritizing Work	Developing specific goals and plans to prioritize, organize, and accomplish your work.
Judging the Qualities of Things, Services, or Peop	Assessing the value, importance, or quality of things or people.
Training and Teaching Others	Identifying the educational needs of others, developing formal educational or training programs or classes, and teaching or instructing others.
Thinking Creatively	Developing, designing, or creating new applications, ideas, relationships, systems, or products, including artistic contributions.
Evaluating Information to Determine Compliance wit	Using relevant information and individual judgment to determine whether events or processes comply with laws, regulations, or standards.
Updating and Using Relevant Knowledge	Keeping up-to-date technically and applying new knowledge to your job.
Guiding, Directing, and Motivating Subordinates	Providing guidance and direction to subordinates, including setting performance standards and monitoring performance.
Scheduling Work and Activities	Scheduling events, programs, and activities, as well as the work of others.
Estimating the Quantifiable Characteristics of Pro	Estimating sizes, distances, and quantities; or determining time, costs, resources, or materials needed to perform a work activity.
Performing for or Working Directly with the Public	Performing for people or dealing directly with the public. This includes serving customers in restaurants and stores, and receiving clients or guests.
Resolving Conflicts and Negotiating with Others	Handling complaints, settling disputes, and resolving grievances and conflicts, or otherwise negotiating with others.
Processing Information	Compiling, coding, categorizing, calculating, tabulating, auditing, or verifying information or data.
Assisting and Caring for Others	Providing personal assistance, medical attention, emotional support, or other personal care to others such as coworkers, customers, or patients.
Coordinating the Work and Activities of Others	Getting members of a group to work together to accomplish tasks.
Developing and Building Teams	Encouraging and building mutual trust, respect, and cooperation among team members.
Communicating with Persons Outside Organization	Communicating with people outside the organization, representing the organization to customers, the public, government, and other external sources. This information can be exchanged in person, in writing, or by telephone or e-mail.
Coaching and Developing Others	Identifying the developmental needs of others and coaching, mentoring, or otherwise helping others to improve their knowledge or skills.
Interpreting the Meaning of Information for Others	Translating or explaining what information means and how it can be used.
Selling or Influencing Others	Convincing others to buy merchandise/goods or to otherwise change their minds or actions.
Developing Objectives and Strategies	Establishing long-range objectives and specifying the strategies and actions to achieve them.
Performing Administrative Activities	Performing day-to-day administrative tasks such as maintaining information files and processing paperwork.
Monitoring and Controlling Resources	Monitoring and controlling resources and overseeing the spending of money.
Analyzing Data or Information	Identifying the underlying principles, reasons, or facts of information by breaking down information or data into separate parts.
Provide Consultation and Advice to Others	Providing guidance and expert advice to management or other groups on technical, systems-, or process-related topics.
Repairing and Maintaining Electronic Equipment	Servicing, repairing, calibrating, regulating, fine-tuning, or testing machines, devices, and equipment that operate primarily on the basis of electrical or electronic (not mechanical) principles.
Repairing and Maintaining Mechanical Equipment	Servicing, repairing, adjusting, and testing machines, devices, moving parts, and equipment that operate primarily on the basis of mechanical (not electronic) principles.
Staffing Organizational Units	Recruiting, interviewing, selecting, hiring, and promoting employees in an organization.
Drafting, Laying Out, and Specifying Technical Dev	Providing documentation, detailed instructions, drawings, or specifications to tell others about how devices, parts, equipment, or structures are to be fabricated, constructed, assembled, modified, maintained, or used.

Work_Context	Work_Context Definitions
Spend Time Using Your Hands to Handle, Control, or	How much does this job require using your hands to handle, control, or feel objects, tools or controls?
Importance of Being Exact or Accurate	How important is being very exact or highly accurate in performing this job?
Time Pressure	How often does this job require the worker to meet strict deadlines?
Indoors, Not Environmentally Controlled	How often does this job require working indoors in non-controlled environmental conditions (e.g., warehouse without heat)?
Sounds, Noise Levels Are Distracting or Uncomforta	How often does this job require working exposed to sounds and noise levels that are distracting or uncomfortable?
Face-to-Face Discussions	How often do you have to have face-to-face discussions with individuals or teams in this job?
Work With Work Group or Team	How important is it to work with others in a group or team in this job?
Responsible for Others' Health and Safety	How much responsibility is there for the health and safety of others in this job?
Exposed to Contaminants	How often does this job require working exposed to contaminants (such as pollutants, gases, dust or odors)?
Contact With Others	How much does this job require the worker to be in contact with others (face-to-face, by telephone, or otherwise) in order to perform it?
Freedom to Make Decisions	How much decision making freedom, without supervision, does the job offer?
In an Open Vehicle or Equipment	How often does this job require working in an open vehicle or equipment (e.g., tractor)?
Wear Common Protective or Safety Equipment such as	How much does this job require wearing common protective or safety equipment such as safety shoes, glasses, gloves, hard hats or live jackets?
Frequency of Decision Making	How frequently is the worker required to make decisions that affect other people, the financial resources, and/or the image and reputation of the organization?
Structured versus Unstructured Work	To what extent is this job structured for the worker, rather than allowing the worker to determine tasks, priorities, and goals?
Very Hot or Cold Temperatures	How often does this job require working in very hot (above 90 F degrees) or very cold (below 32 F degrees) temperatures?
Spend Time Bending or Twisting the Body	How much does this job require bending or twisting your body?
Spend Time Standing	How much does this job require standing?
Impact of Decisions on Co-workers or Company Resul	How do the decisions an employee makes impact the results of co-workers, clients or the company?
Spend Time Walking and Running	How much does this job require walking and running?
Exposed to Hazardous Equipment	How often does this job require exposure to hazardous equipment?
Extremely Bright or Inadequate Lighting	How often does this job require working in extremely bright or inadequate lighting conditions?
Responsibility for Outcomes and Results	How responsible is the worker for work outcomes and results of other workers?

Spend Time Making Repetitive Motions	How much does this job require making repetitive motions?
Physical Proximity	To what extent does this job require the worker to perform job tasks in close physical proximity to other people?
Indoors, Environmentally Controlled	How often does this job require working indoors in environmentally controlled conditions?
Telephone	How often do you have telephone conversations in this job?
Importance of Repeating Same Tasks	How important is repeating the same physical activities (e.g., key entry) or mental activities (e.g., checking entries in a ledger) over and over, without stopping, to performing this job?
Consequence of Error	How serious would the result usually be if the worker made a mistake that was not readily correctable?
Cramped Work Space, Awkward Positions	How often does this job require working in cramped work spaces that requires getting into awkward positions?
Deal With Unpleasant or Angry People	How frequently does the worker have to deal with unpleasant, angry, or discourteous individuals as part of the job requirements?
Spend Time Sitting	How much does this job require sitting?
Exposed to Minor Burns, Cuts, Bites, or Stings	How often does this job require exposure to minor burns, cuts, bites, or stings?
Coordinate or Lead Others	How important is it to coordinate or lead others in accomplishing work activities in this job?
Exposed to High Places	How often does this job require exposure to high places?
Pace Determined by Speed of Equipment	How important is it to this job that the pace is determined by the speed of equipment or machinery? (This does not refer to keeping busy at all times on this job.)
Outdoors, Exposed to Weather	How often does this job require working outdoors, exposed to all weather conditions?
Exposed to Whole Body Vibration	How often does this job require exposure to whole body vibration (e.g., operate a jackhammer)?
Level of Competition	To what extent does this job require the worker to compete or to be aware of competitive pressures?
Frequency of Conflict Situations	How often are there conflict situations the employee has to face in this job?
Deal With External Customers	How important is it to work with external customers or the public in this job?
Wear Specialized Protective or Safety Equipment su	How much does this job require wearing specialized protective or safety equipment such as breathing apparatus, safety harness, full protection suits, or radiation protection?
Letters and Memos	How often does the job require written letters and memos?
Spend Time Kneeling, Crouching, Stooping, or Crawl	How much does this job require kneeling, crouching, stooping, or crawling?
Degree of Automation	How automated is the job?
Outdoors, Under Cover	How often does this job require working outdoors, under cover (e.g., structure with roof but no walls)?
In an Enclosed Vehicle or Equipment	How often does this job require working in a closed vehicle or equipment (e.g., car)?
Spend Time Climbing Ladders, Scaffolds, or Poles	How much does this job require climbing ladders, scaffolds, or poles?
Public Speaking	How often do you have to perform public speaking in this job?
Deal With Physically Aggressive People	How frequently does this job require the worker to deal with physical aggression of violent individuals?
Exposed to Hazardous Conditions	How often does this job require exposure to hazardous conditions?
Spend Time Keeping or Regaining Balance	How much does this job require keeping or regaining your balance?
Electronic Mail	How often do you use electronic mail in this job?
Exposed to Disease or Infections	How often does this job require exposure to disease/infections?
Exposed to Radiation	How often does this job require exposure to radiation?

Job Zone Component	Job Zone Component Definitions
Title	Job Zone Two: Some Preparation Needed
Overall Experience	Some previous work-related skill, knowledge, or experience may be helpful in these occupations, but usually is not needed. For example, a drywall installer might benefit from experience installing drywall, but an inexperienced person could still learn to be an installer with little difficulty.
Job Training	Employees in these occupations need anywhere from a few months to one year of working with experienced employees.
Job Zone Examples	These occupations often involve using your knowledge and skills to help others. Examples include drywall installers, fire inspectors, flight attendants, pharmacy technicians, salespersons (retail), and tellers.

SVP Range	(4.0 to < 6.0)
Education	These occupations usually require a high school diploma and may require some vocational training or job-related course work. In some cases, an associate's or bachelor's degree could be needed.

Work_Styles	Work_Styles Definitions
Dependability	Job requires being reliable, responsible, and dependable, and fulfilling obligations.
Self Control	Job requires maintaining composure, keeping emotions in check, controlling anger, and avoiding aggressive behavior, even in very difficult situations.
Attention to Detail	Job requires being careful about detail and thorough in completing work tasks.
Cooperation	Job requires being pleasant with others on the job and displaying a good-natured, cooperative attitude.
Independence	Job requires developing one's own ways of doing things, guiding oneself with little or no supervision, and depending on oneself to get things done.
Initiative	Job requires a willingness to take on responsibilities and challenges.
Stress Tolerance	Job requires accepting criticism and dealing calmly and effectively with high stress situations.
Adaptability/Flexibility	Job requires being open to change (positive or negative) and to considerable variety in the workplace.
Integrity	Job requires being honest and ethical.
Persistence	Job requires persistence in the face of obstacles.
Analytical Thinking	Job requires analyzing information and using logic to address work-related issues and problems.
Concern for Others	Job requires being sensitive to others' needs and feelings and being understanding and helpful on the job.
Achievement/Effort	Job requires establishing and maintaining personally challenging achievement goals and exerting effort toward mastering tasks.
Innovation	Job requires creativity and alternative thinking to develop new ideas for and answers to work-related problems.
Leadership	Job requires a willingness to lead, take charge, and offer opinions and direction.
Social Orientation	Job requires preferring to work with others rather than alone, and being personally connected with others on the job.

53-7061.00 - Cleaners of Vehicles and Equipment

Wash or otherwise clean vehicles, machinery, and other equipment. Use such materials as water, cleaning agents, brushes, cloths, and hoses.

Tasks

1) Inspect parts, equipment, and vehicles for cleanliness, damage, and compliance with standards or regulations.

2) Pre-soak or rinse machine parts, equipment, or vehicles by immersing objects in cleaning solutions or water, manually or using hoists.

3) Clean and polish vehicle windows.

4) Scrub, scrape, or spray machine parts, equipment, or vehicles, using scrapers, brushes, clothes, cleaners, disinfectants, insecticides, acid, abrasives, vacuums, and hoses.

5) Press buttons to activate cleaning equipment or machines.

6) Turn valves or handles on equipment in order to regulate pressure and flow of water, air, steam, or abrasives from sprayer nozzles.

7) Rinse objects and place them on drying racks; or use cloth, squeegees, or air compressors to dry surfaces.

8) Mix cleaning solutions, abrasive compositions, and other compounds, according to formulas.

9) Drive vehicles to and from workshops and/or customers' workplaces or homes.

10) Monitor operation of cleaning machines, and stop machines or notify supervisors when malfunctions occur.

11) Lubricate machinery, vehicles, and equipment, and perform minor repairs and adjustments, using hand tools.

12) Maintain inventories of supplies.

13) Turn valves or disconnect hoses in order to eliminate water, cleaning solutions, or vapors from machinery or tanks.

14) Connect hoses and lines to pumps and other equipment.

15) Disassemble and reassemble machines or equipment; or remove and reattach vehicle parts and trim, using hand tools.

16) Apply paints, dyes, polishes, reconditioners, waxes, and masking materials to vehicles in order to preserve, protect, or restore color and condition.

17) Transport materials, equipment, or supplies to and from work areas, using carts or hoists.

18) Clean the plastic work inside cars, using paintbrushes.

19) Collect and test samples of cleaning solutions and vapors.

20) Fit boot spoilers, side skirts, and mud flaps to cars.

Knowledge	Knowledge Definitions
Public Safety and Security	Knowledge of relevant equipment, policies, procedures, and strategies to promote effective local, state, or national security operations for the protection of people, data, property, and institutions.
Customer and Personal Service	Knowledge of principles and processes for providing customer and personal services. This includes customer needs assessment, meeting quality standards for services, and evaluation of customer satisfaction.
Transportation	Knowledge of principles and methods for moving people or goods by air, rail, sea, or road, including the relative costs and benefits.
Mechanical	Knowledge of machines and tools, including their designs, uses, repair, and maintenance.
Administration and Management	Knowledge of business and management principles involved in strategic planning, resource allocation, human resources modeling, leadership technique, production methods, and coordination of people and resources.
English Language	Knowledge of the structure and content of the English language including the meaning and spelling of words, rules of composition, and grammar.
Education and Training	Knowledge of principles and methods for curriculum and training design, teaching and instruction for individuals and groups, and the measurement of training effects.
Mathematics	Knowledge of arithmetic, algebra, geometry, calculus, statistics, and their applications.
Chemistry	Knowledge of the chemical composition, structure, and properties of substances and of the chemical processes and transformations that they undergo. This includes uses of chemicals and their interactions, danger signs, production techniques, and disposal methods.
Production and Processing	Knowledge of raw materials, production processes, quality control, costs, and other techniques for maximizing the effective manufacture and distribution of goods.
Economics and Accounting	Knowledge of economic and accounting principles and practices, the financial markets, banking and the analysis and reporting of financial data.
Psychology	Knowledge of human behavior and performance; individual differences in ability, personality, and interests; learning and motivation; psychological research methods; and the assessment and treatment of behavioral and affective disorders.
Personnel and Human Resources	Knowledge of principles and procedures for personnel recruitment, selection, training, compensation and benefits, labor relations and negotiation, and personnel information systems.
Clerical	Knowledge of administrative and clerical procedures and systems such as word processing, managing files and records, stenography and transcription, designing forms, and other office procedures and terminology.
Building and Construction	Knowledge of materials, methods, and the tools involved in the construction or repair of houses, buildings, or other structures such as highways and roads.
Sales and Marketing	Knowledge of principles and methods for showing, promoting, and selling products or services. This includes marketing strategy and tactics, product demonstration, sales techniques, and sales control systems.
Engineering and Technology	Knowledge of the practical application of engineering science and technology. This includes applying principles, techniques, procedures, and equipment to the design and production of various goods and services.

Law and Government	Knowledge of laws, legal codes, court procedures, precedents, government regulations, executive orders, agency rules, and the democratic political process.
Physics	Knowledge and prediction of physical principles, laws, their interrelationships, and applications to understanding fluid, material, and atmospheric dynamics, and mechanical, electrical, atomic and sub-atomic structures and processes.
Design	Knowledge of design techniques, tools, and principles involved in production of precision technical plans, blueprints, drawings, and models.
Communications and Media	Knowledge of media production, communication, and dissemination techniques and methods. This includes alternative ways to inform and entertain via written, oral, and visual media.
Computers and Electronics	Knowledge of circuit boards, processors, chips, electronic equipment, and computer hardware and software, including applications and programming.
Medicine and Dentistry	Knowledge of the information and techniques needed to diagnose and treat human injuries, diseases, and deformities. This includes symptoms, treatment alternatives, drug properties and interactions, and preventive health-care measures.
Sociology and Anthropology	Knowledge of group behavior and dynamics, societal trends and influences, human migrations, ethnicity, cultures and their history and origins.
Biology	Knowledge of plant and animal organisms, their tissues, cells, functions, interdependencies, and interactions with each other and the environment.
Food Production	Knowledge of techniques and equipment for planting, growing, and harvesting food products (both plant and animal) for consumption, including storage/handling techniques.
Telecommunications	Knowledge of transmission, broadcasting, switching, control, and operation of telecommunications systems.
Geography	Knowledge of principles and methods for describing the features of land, sea, and air masses, including their physical characteristics, locations, interrelationships, and distribution of plant, animal, and human life.
History and Archeology	Knowledge of historical events and their causes, indicators, and effects on civilizations and cultures.
Therapy and Counseling	Knowledge of principles, methods, and procedures for diagnosis, treatment, and rehabilitation of physical and mental dysfunctions, and for career counseling and guidance.
Foreign Language	Knowledge of the structure and content of a foreign (non-English) language including the meaning and spelling of words, rules of composition and grammar, and pronunciation.
Philosophy and Theology	Knowledge of different philosophical systems and religions. This includes their basic principles, values, ethics, ways of thinking, customs, practices, and their impact on human culture.
Fine Arts	Knowledge of the theory and techniques required to compose, produce, and perform works of music, dance, visual arts, drama, and sculpture.

Skills	Skills Definitions
Equipment Maintenance	Performing routine maintenance on equipment and determining when and what kind of maintenance is needed.
Active Listening	Giving full attention to what other people are saying, taking time to understand the points being made, asking questions as appropriate, and not interrupting at inappropriate times.
Time Management	Managing one's own time and the time of others.
Coordination	Adjusting actions in relation to others' actions.
Instructing	Teaching others how to do something.
Quality Control Analysis	Conducting tests and inspections of products, services, or processes to evaluate quality or performance.
Troubleshooting	Determining causes of operating errors and deciding what to do about it.
Equipment Selection	Determining the kind of tools and equipment needed to do a job.
Speaking	Talking to others to convey information effectively.
Social Perceptiveness	Being aware of others' reactions and understanding why they react as they do.
Active Learning	Understanding the implications of new information for both current and future problem-solving and decision-making.
Judgment and Decision Making	Considering the relative costs and benefits of potential actions to choose the most appropriate one.
Monitoring	Monitoring/Assessing performance of yourself, other individuals, or organizations to make improvements or take corrective action.

Critical Thinking	Using logic and reasoning to identify the strengths and weaknesses of alternative solutions, conclusions or approaches to problems.
Repairing	Repairing machines or systems using the needed tools.
Operation and Control	Controlling operations of equipment or systems.
Learning Strategies	Selecting and using training/instructional methods and procedures appropriate for the situation when learning or teaching new things.
Installation	Installing equipment, machines, wiring, or programs to meet specifications.
Management of Material Resources	Obtaining and seeing to the appropriate use of equipment, facilities, and materials needed to do certain work.
Reading Comprehension	Understanding written sentences and paragraphs in work related documents.
Service Orientation	Actively looking for ways to help people.
Operation Monitoring	Watching gauges, dials, or other indicators to make sure a machine is working properly.
Writing	Communicating effectively in writing as appropriate for the needs of the audience.
Complex Problem Solving	Identifying complex problems and reviewing related information to develop and evaluate options and implement solutions.
Management of Personnel Resources	Motivating, developing, and directing people as they work, identifying the best people for the job.
Systems Analysis	Determining how a system should work and how changes in conditions, operations, and the environment will affect outcomes.
Operations Analysis	Analyzing needs and product requirements to create a design.
Negotiation	Bringing others together and trying to reconcile differences.
Technology Design	Generating or adapting equipment and technology to serve user needs.
Management of Financial Resources	Determining how money will be spent to get the work done, and accounting for these expenditures.
Persuasion	Persuading others to change their minds or behavior.
Mathematics	Using mathematics to solve problems.
Systems Evaluation	Identifying measures or indicators of system performance and the actions needed to improve or correct performance, relative to the goals of the system.
Science	Using scientific rules and methods to solve problems.
Programming	Writing computer programs for various purposes.

Ability	Ability Definitions
Near Vision	The ability to see details at close range (within a few feet of the observer).
Multilimb Coordination	The ability to coordinate two or more limbs (for example, two arms, two legs, or one leg and one arm) while sitting, standing, or lying down. It does not involve performing the activities while the whole body is in motion.
Manual Dexterity	The ability to quickly move your hand, your hand together with your arm, or your two hands to grasp, manipulate, or assemble objects.
Control Precision	The ability to quickly and repeatedly adjust the controls of a machine or a vehicle to exact positions.
Information Ordering	The ability to arrange things or actions in a certain order or pattern according to a specific rule or set of rules (e.g., patterns of numbers, letters, words, pictures, mathematical operations).
Trunk Strength	The ability to use your abdominal and lower back muscles to support part of the body repeatedly or continuously over time without 'giving out' or fatiguing.
Problem Sensitivity	The ability to tell when something is wrong or is likely to go wrong. It does not involve solving the problem, only recognizing there is a problem.
Depth Perception	The ability to judge which of several objects is closer or farther away from you, or to judge the distance between you and an object.
Arm-Hand Steadiness	The ability to keep your hand and arm steady while moving your arm or while holding your arm and hand in one position.
Deductive Reasoning	The ability to apply general rules to specific problems to produce answers that make sense.
Extent Flexibility	The ability to bend, stretch, twist, or reach with your body, arms, and/or legs.
Stamina	The ability to exert yourself physically over long periods of time without getting winded or out of breath.
Oral Expression	The ability to communicate information and ideas in speaking so others will understand.
Gross Body Coordination	The ability to coordinate the movement of your arms, legs, and torso together when the whole body is in motion.

Speech Recognition	The ability to identify and understand the speech of another person.
Inductive Reasoning	The ability to combine pieces of information to form general rules or conclusions (includes finding a relationship among seemingly unrelated events).
Speech Clarity	The ability to speak clearly so others can understand you.
Oral Comprehension	The ability to listen to and understand information and ideas presented through spoken words and sentences.
Dynamic Strength	The ability to exert muscle force repeatedly or continuously over time. This involves muscular endurance and resistance to muscle fatigue.
Far Vision	The ability to see details at a distance.
Category Flexibility	The ability to generate or use different sets of rules for combining or grouping things in different ways.
Written Comprehension	The ability to read and understand information and ideas presented in writing.
Finger Dexterity	The ability to make precisely coordinated movements of the fingers of one or both hands to grasp, manipulate, or assemble very small objects.
Visualization	The ability to imagine how something will look after it is moved around or when its parts are moved or rearranged.
Static Strength	The ability to exert maximum muscle force to lift, push, pull, or carry objects.
Selective Attention	The ability to concentrate on a task over a period of time without being distracted.
Rate Control	The ability to time your movements or the movement of a piece of equipment in anticipation of changes in the speed and/or direction of a moving object or scene.
Reaction Time	The ability to quickly respond (with the hand, finger, or foot) to a signal (sound, light, picture) when it appears.
Speed of Limb Movement	The ability to quickly move the arms and legs.
Response Orientation	The ability to choose quickly between two or more movements in response to two or more different signals (lights, sounds, pictures). It includes the speed with which the correct response is started with the hand, foot, or other body part.
Wrist-Finger Speed	The ability to make fast, simple, repeated movements of the fingers, hands, and wrists.
Memorization	The ability to remember information such as words, numbers, pictures, and procedures.
Perceptual Speed	The ability to quickly and accurately compare similarities and differences among sets of letters, numbers, objects, pictures, or patterns. The things to be compared may be presented at the same time or one after the other. This ability also includes comparing a presented object with a remembered object.
Flexibility of Closure	The ability to identify or detect a known pattern (a figure, object, word, or sound) that is hidden in other distracting material.
Fluency of Ideas	The ability to come up with a number of ideas about a topic (the number of ideas is important, not their quality, correctness, or creativity).
Number Facility	The ability to add, subtract, multiply, or divide quickly and correctly.
Spatial Orientation	The ability to know your location in relation to the environment or to know where other objects are in relation to you.
Time Sharing	The ability to shift back and forth between two or more activities or sources of information (such as speech, sounds, touch, or other sources).
Glare Sensitivity	The ability to see objects in the presence of glare or bright lighting.
Auditory Attention	The ability to focus on a single source of sound in the presence of other distracting sounds.
Visual Color Discrimination	The ability to match or detect differences between colors, including shades of color and brightness.
Speed of Closure	The ability to quickly make sense of, combine, and organize information into meaningful patterns.
Peripheral Vision	The ability to see objects or movement of objects to one's side when the eyes are looking ahead.
Gross Body Equilibrium	The ability to keep or regain your body balance or stay upright when in an unstable position.
Originality	The ability to come up with unusual or clever ideas about a given topic or situation, or to develop creative ways to solve a problem.
Written Expression	The ability to communicate information and ideas in writing so others will understand.
Hearing Sensitivity	The ability to detect or tell the differences between sounds that vary in pitch and loudness.
Mathematical Reasoning	The ability to choose the right mathematical methods or formulas to solve a problem.

Sound Localization	The ability to tell the direction from which a sound originated.
Explosive Strength	The ability to use short bursts of muscle force to propel oneself (as in jumping or sprinting), or to throw an object.
Night Vision	The ability to see under low light conditions.
Dynamic Flexibility	The ability to quickly and repeatedly bend, stretch, twist, or reach out with your body, arms, and/or legs.

Work_Activity	Work_Activity Definitions
Operating Vehicles, Mechanized Devices, or Equipme	Running, maneuvering, navigating, or driving vehicles or mechanized equipment, such as forklifts, passenger vehicles, aircraft, or water craft.
Inspecting Equipment, Structures, or Material	Inspecting equipment, structures, or materials to identify the cause of errors or other problems or defects.
Controlling Machines and Processes	Using either control mechanisms or direct physical activity to operate machines or processes (not including computers or vehicles).
Repairing and Maintaining Mechanical Equipment	Servicing, repairing, adjusting, and testing machines, devices, moving parts, and equipment that operate primarily on the basis of mechanical (not electronic) principles.
Handling and Moving Objects	Using hands and arms in handling, installing, positioning, and moving materials, and manipulating things.
Getting Information	Observing, receiving, and otherwise obtaining information from all relevant sources.
Establishing and Maintaining Interpersonal Relatio	Developing constructive and cooperative working relationships with others, and maintaining them over time.
Performing General Physical Activities	Performing physical activities that require considerable use of your arms and legs and moving your whole body, such as climbing, lifting, balancing, walking, stooping, and handling of materials.
Assisting and Caring for Others	Providing personal assistance, medical attention, emotional support, or other personal care to others such as coworkers, customers, or patients.
Communicating with Supervisors, Peers, or Subordin	Providing information to supervisors, co-workers, and subordinates by telephone, in written form, e-mail, or in person.
Identifying Objects, Actions, and Events	Identifying information by categorizing, estimating, recognizing differences or similarities, and detecting changes in circumstances or events.
Making Decisions and Solving Problems	Analyzing information and evaluating results to choose the best solution and solve problems.
Monitor Processes, Materials, or Surroundings	Monitoring and reviewing information from materials, events, or the environment, to detect or assess problems.
Updating and Using Relevant Knowledge	Keeping up-to-date technically and applying new knowledge to your job.
Performing for or Working Directly with the Public	Performing for people or dealing directly with the public. This includes serving customers in restaurants and stores, and receiving clients or guests.
Communicating with Persons Outside Organization	Communicating with people outside the organization, representing the organization to customers, the public, government, and other external sources. This information can be exchanged in person, in writing, or by telephone or e-mail.
Organizing, Planning, and Prioritizing Work	Developing specific goals and plans to prioritize, organize, and accomplish your work.
Developing Objectives and Strategies	Establishing long-range objectives and specifying the strategies and actions to achieve them.
Coordinating the Work and Activities of Others	Getting members of a group to work together to accomplish tasks.
Resolving Conflicts and Negotiating with Others	Handling complaints, settling disputes, and resolving grievances and conflicts, or otherwise negotiating with others.
Estimating the Quantifiable Characteristics of Pro	Estimating sizes, distances, and quantities; or determining time, costs, resources, or materials needed to perform a work activity.
Repairing and Maintaining Electronic Equipment	Servicing, repairing, calibrating, regulating, fine-tuning, or testing machines, devices, and equipment that operate primarily on the basis of electrical or electronic (not mechanical) principles.
Training and Teaching Others	Identifying the educational needs of others, developing formal educational or training programs or classes, and teaching or instructing others.
Thinking Creatively	Developing, designing, or creating new applications, ideas, relationships, systems, or products, including artistic contributions.
Evaluating Information to Determine Compliance wit	Using relevant information and individual judgment to determine whether events or processes comply with laws, regulations, or standards.

Judging the Qualities of Things, Services, or Peop	Assessing the value, importance, or quality of things or people.
Developing and Building Teams	Encouraging and building mutual trust, respect, and cooperation among team members.
Scheduling Work and Activities	Scheduling events, programs, and activities, as well as the work of others.
Selling or Influencing Others	Convincing others to buy merchandise/goods or to otherwise change their minds or actions.
Interpreting the Meaning of Information for Others	Translating or explaining what information means and how it can be used.
Processing Information	Compiling, coding, categorizing, calculating, tabulating, auditing, or verifying information or data.
Monitoring and Controlling Resources	Monitoring and controlling resources and overseeing the spending of money.
Analyzing Data or Information	Identifying the underlying principles, reasons, or facts of information by breaking down information or data into separate parts.
Coaching and Developing Others	Identifying the developmental needs of others and coaching, mentoring, or otherwise helping others to improve their knowledge or skills.
Guiding, Directing, and Motivating Subordinates	Providing guidance and direction to subordinates, including setting performance standards and monitoring performance.
Documenting/Recording Information	Entering, transcribing, recording, storing, or maintaining information in written or electronic/magnetic form.
Provide Consultation and Advice to Others	Providing guidance and expert advice to management or other groups on technical, systems-, or process-related topics.
Interacting With Computers	Using computers and computer systems (including hardware and software) to program, write software, set up functions, enter data, or process information.
Performing Administrative Activities	Performing day-to-day administrative tasks such as maintaining information files and processing paperwork.
Staffing Organizational Units	Recruiting, interviewing, selecting, hiring, and promoting employees in an organization.
Drafting, Laying Out, and Specifying Technical Dev	Providing documentation, detailed instructions, drawings, or specifications to tell others about how devices, parts, equipment, or structures are to be fabricated, constructed, assembled, modified, maintained, or used.

Work_Context	Work_Context Definitions
In an Enclosed Vehicle or Equipment	How often does this job require working in a closed vehicle or equipment (e.g., car)?
Exposed to Contaminants	How often does this job require working exposed to contaminants (such as pollutants, gases, dust or odors)?
Spend Time Standing	How much does this job require standing?
Wear Common Protective or Safety Equipment such as	How much does this job require wearing common protective or safety equipment such as safety shoes, glasses, gloves, hard hats or live jackets?
Sounds, Noise Levels Are Distracting or Uncomforta	How much does this job require working exposed to sounds and noise levels that are distracting or uncomfortable?
Time Pressure	How often does this job require the worker to meet strict deadlines?
Freedom to Make Decisions	How much decision making freedom, without supervision, does the job offer?
Contact With Others	How much does this job require the worker to be in contact with others (face-to-face, by telephone, or otherwise) in order to perform it?
Physical Proximity	To what extent does this job require the worker to perform job tasks in close physical proximity to other people?
Spend Time Walking and Running	How much does this job require walking and running?
Outdoors, Exposed to Weather	How often does this job require working outdoors, exposed to all weather conditions?
Impact of Decisions on Co-workers or Company Resul	How do the decisions an employee makes impact the results of co-workers, clients or the company?
Spend Time Making Repetitive Motions	How much does this job require making repetitive motions?
Spend Time Using Your Hands to Handle, Control, or	How much does this job require using your hands to handle, control, or feel objects, tools or controls?
Responsible for Others' Health and Safety	How much responsibility is there for the health and safety of others in this job?
Spend Time Bending or Twisting the Body	How much does this job require bending or twisting your body?
Structured versus Unstructured Work	To what extent is this job structured for the worker, rather than allowing the worker to determine tasks, priorities, and goals?
Telephone	How often do you have telephone conversations in this job?

Face-to-Face Discussions	How often do you have to have face-to-face discussions with individuals or teams in this job?
Coordinate or Lead Others	How important is it to coordinate or lead others in accomplishing work activities in this job?
Work With Work Group or Team	How important is it to work with others in a group or team in this job?
Exposed to Hazardous Equipment	How often does this job require exposure to hazardous equipment?
Importance of Being Exact or Accurate	How important is being very exact or highly accurate in performing this job?
Responsibility for Outcomes and Results	How responsible is the worker for work outcomes and results of other workers?
Exposed to Hazardous Conditions	How often does this job require exposure to hazardous conditions?
Indoors, Not Environmentally Controlled	How often does this job require working indoors in non-controlled environmental conditions (e.g., warehouse without heat)?
Deal With External Customers	How important is it to work with external customers or the public in this job?
Extremely Bright or Inadequate Lighting	How often does this job require working in extremely bright or inadequate lighting conditions?
Very Hot or Cold Temperatures	How often does this job require working in very hot (above 90 F degrees) or very cold (below 32 F degrees) temperatures?
Frequency of Decision Making	How frequently is the worker required to make decisions that affect other people, the financial resources, and/or the image and reputation of the organization?
Exposed to Minor Burns, Cuts, Bites, or Stings	How often does this job require exposure to minor burns, cuts, bites, or stings?
Indoors, Environmentally Controlled	How often does this job require working indoors in environmentally controlled conditions?
In an Open Vehicle or Equipment	How often does this job require working in an open vehicle or equipment (e.g., tractor)?
Spend Time Kneeling, Crouching, Stooping, or Crawl	How much does this job require kneeling, crouching, stooping or crawling?
Importance of Repeating Same Tasks	How important is repeating the same physical activities (e.g., key entry) or mental activities (e.g., checking entries in a ledger) over and over, without stopping, to performing this job?
Level of Competition	To what extent does this job require the worker to compete or to be aware of competitive pressures?
Cramped Work Space, Awkward Positions	How often does this job require working in cramped work spaces that requires getting into awkward positions?
Consequence of Error	How serious would the result usually be if the worker made a mistake that was not readily correctable?
Deal With Unpleasant or Angry People	How frequently does the worker have to deal with unpleasant, angry, or discourteous individuals as part of the job requirements?
Frequency of Conflict Situations	How often are there conflict situations the employee has to face in this job?
Pace Determined by Speed of Equipment	How important is it to this job that the pace is determined by the speed of equipment or machinery? (This does not refer to keeping busy at all times on this job.)
Spend Time Climbing Ladders, Scaffolds, or Poles	How much does this job require climbing ladders, scaffolds, or poles?
Spend Time Keeping or Regaining Balance	How much does this job require keeping or regaining your balance?
Spend Time Sitting	How much does this job require sitting?
Exposed to High Places	How often does this job require exposure to high places?
Outdoors, Under Cover	How often does this job require working outdoors, under cover (e.g., structure with roof but no walls)?
Letters and Memos	How often does the job require written letters and memos?
Degree of Automation	How automated is the job?
Wear Specialized Protective or Safety Equipment su	How much does this job require wearing specialized protective or safety equipment such as breathing apparatus, safety harness, full protection suits, or radiation protection?
Public Speaking	How often do you have to perform public speaking in this job?
Exposed to Whole Body Vibration	How often does this job require exposure to whole body vibration (e.g., operate a jackhammer)?
Exposed to Disease or Infections	How often does this job require exposure to disease/infections?
Electronic Mail	How often do you use electronic mail in this job?
Deal With Physically Aggressive People	How frequently does this job require the worker to deal with physical aggression of violent individuals?
Exposed to Radiation	How often does this job require exposure to radiation?

Job Zone Component	Job Zone Component Definitions
Title	Job Zone One: Little or No Preparation Needed
Overall Experience	No previous work-related skill, knowledge, or experience is needed for these occupations. For example, a person can become a general office clerk even if he/she has never worked in an office before.
Job Training	Employees in these occupations need anywhere from a few days to a few months of training. Usually, an experienced worker could show you how to do the job.
Job Zone Examples	These occupations involve following instructions and helping others. Examples include bus drivers, forest and conservation workers, general office clerks, home health aides, and waiters/waitresses.
SVP Range	(Below 4.0)
Education	These occupations may require a high school diploma or GED certificate. Some may require a formal training course to obtain a license.

Work_Styles	Work_Styles Definitions
Dependability	Job requires being reliable, responsible, and dependable, and fulfilling obligations.
Attention to Detail	Job requires being careful about detail and thorough in completing work tasks.
Integrity	Job requires being honest and ethical.
Independence	Job requires developing one's own ways of doing things, guiding oneself with little or no supervision, and depending on oneself to get things done.
Initiative	Job requires a willingness to take on responsibilities and challenges.
Cooperation	Job requires being pleasant with others on the job and displaying a good-natured, cooperative attitude.
Self Control	Job requires maintaining composure, keeping emotions in check, controlling anger, and avoiding aggressive behavior, even in very difficult situations.
Adaptability/Flexibility	Job requires being open to change (positive or negative) and to considerable variety in the workplace.
Stress Tolerance	Job requires accepting criticism and dealing calmly and effectively with high stress situations.
Leadership	Job requires a willingness to lead, take charge, and offer opinions and direction.
Concern for Others	Job requires being sensitive to others' needs and feelings and being understanding and helpful on the job.
Achievement/Effort	Job requires establishing and maintaining personally challenging achievement goals and exerting effort toward mastering tasks.
Innovation	Job requires creativity and alternative thinking to develop new ideas for and answers to work-related problems.
Social Orientation	Job requires preferring to work with others rather than alone, and being personally connected with others on the job.
Analytical Thinking	Job requires analyzing information and using logic to address work-related issues and problems.
Persistence	Job requires persistence in the face of obstacles.

53-7062.00 - Laborers and Freight, Stock, and Material Movers, Hand

Manually move freight, stock, or other materials or perform other unskilled general labor. Includes all unskilled manual laborers not elsewhere classified.

Tasks

1) Attach slings, hooks, and other devices to lift cargo and guide loads.

2) Read work orders or receive oral instructions to determine work assignments and material and equipment needs.

3) Lay tracks for camera dollies and cranes, and carry or push around dollies and cranes as instructed.

4) Sew canvas and other materials to make and repair tents, tarps, scrims, and backings, using sewing machines.

5) Build braces and otherwise lash and shore cargo in ships' holds, in order to prevent shifting

during voyages.

6) Adjust or replace equipment parts such as rollers, belts, plugs, and caps, using hand tools.

7) Adjust controls to raise and lower scenery and stage curtains during performances, following cues.

8) Wash out cargo containers and storage areas.

9) Shovel material such as gravel, ice, or spilled concrete into containers or bins, or onto conveyors.

10) Bundle and band material such as fodder and tobacco leaves, using banding machines.

11) Record numbers of units handled and moved, using daily production sheets or work tickets.

12) Move freight, stock, and other materials to and from storage and production areas, loading docks, delivery vehicles, ships, and containers, by hand or using trucks, tractors, and other equipment.

13) Load and unload ship cargo, using winches and other hoisting devices.

14) Connect hoses and operate equipment to move liquid materials into and out of storage tanks on vessels.

15) Carry needed tools and supplies from storage or trucks, and return them after use.

16) Pack containers and re-pack damaged containers.

17) Rig and dismantle props and equipment such as frames, scaffolding, platforms, or backdrops, using hand tools.

18) Guide loads being lifted in order to prevent swinging.

19) Stack cargo in locations such as transit sheds or in holds of ships as directed, using pallets or cargo boards.

20) Assemble product containers and crates, using hand tools and precut lumber.

21) Connect electrical equipment to power sources so that it can be tested before use.

22) Attach identifying tags to containers, or mark them with identifying information.

23) Sort cargo before loading and unloading.

24) Erect tents and canopies to protect crews and equipment from weather.

25) Secure and release mooring lines of ships.

26) Set up the equipment needed to produce special lighting and sound effects during performances.

27) Install protective devices, such as bracing, padding, or strapping, to prevent shifting or damage to items being transported.

28) Check out, rent, or requisition all equipment needed for productions or for set construction.

29) Carry out general yard duties such as performing shunting on railway lines.

30) Direct spouts and position receptacles such as bins, carts, and containers so they can be loaded.

31) Adjust controls to guide, position and move equipment such as cranes, booms, and cameras.

53-7064.00 - Packers and Packagers, Hand

Pack or package by hand a wide variety of products and materials.

Tasks

1) Mark and label containers, container tags, or products, using marking tools.

2) Clean containers, materials, supplies, or work areas, using cleaning solutions and hand tools.

3) Record product, packaging, and order information on specified forms and records.

4) Remove completed or defective products or materials, placing them on moving equipment such as conveyors or in specified areas such as loading docks.

5) Seal containers or materials, using glues, fasteners, nails, and hand tools.

6) Examine and inspect containers, materials, and products in order to ensure that packing specifications are met.

7) Transport packages to customers' vehicles.

8) Load materials and products into package processing equipment.

9) Assemble, line, and pad cartons, crates, and containers, using hand tools.

10) Obtain, move, and sort products, materials, containers, and orders, using hand tools.

11) Place or pour products or materials into containers, using hand tools and equipment, or fill containers from spouts or chutes.

Knowledge	Knowledge Definitions
Production and Processing	Knowledge of raw materials, production processes, quality control, costs, and other techniques for maximizing the effective manufacture and distribution of goods.
Customer and Personal Service	Knowledge of principles and processes for providing customer and personal services. This includes customer needs assessment, meeting quality standards for services, and evaluation of customer satisfaction.
Mathematics	Knowledge of arithmetic, algebra, geometry, calculus, statistics, and their applications.
Education and Training	Knowledge of principles and methods for curriculum and training design, teaching and instruction for individuals and groups, and the measurement of training effects.
English Language	Knowledge of the structure and content of the English language including the meaning and spelling of words, rules of composition, and grammar.
Public Safety and Security	Knowledge of relevant equipment, policies, procedures, and strategies to promote effective local, state, or national security operations for the protection of people, data, property, and institutions.
Administration and Management	Knowledge of business and management principles involved in strategic planning, resource allocation, human resources modeling, leadership technique, production methods, and coordination of people and resources.
Clerical	Knowledge of administrative and clerical procedures and systems such as word processing, managing files and records, stenography and transcription, designing forms, and other office procedures and terminology.
Food Production	Knowledge of techniques and equipment for planting, growing, and harvesting food products (both plant and animal) for consumption, including storage/handling techniques.
Transportation	Knowledge of principles and methods for moving people or goods by air, rail, sea, or road, including the relative costs and benefits.
Mechanical	Knowledge of machines and tools, including their designs, uses, repair, and maintenance.
Design	Knowledge of design techniques, tools, and principles involved in production of precision technical plans, blueprints, drawings, and models.
Sales and Marketing	Knowledge of principles and methods for showing, promoting, and selling products or services. This includes marketing strategy and tactics, product demonstration, sales techniques, and sales control systems.
Communications and Media	Knowledge of media production, communication, and dissemination techniques and methods. This includes alternative ways to inform and entertain via written, oral, and visual media.
Personnel and Human Resources	Knowledge of principles and procedures for personnel recruitment, selection, training, compensation and benefits, labor relations and negotiation, and personnel information systems.
Building and Construction	Knowledge of materials, methods, and the tools involved in the construction or repair of houses, buildings, or other structures such as highways and roads.
Economics and Accounting	Knowledge of economic and accounting principles and practices, the financial markets, banking and the analysis and reporting of financial data.
Law and Government	Knowledge of laws, legal codes, court procedures, precedents, government regulations, executive orders, agency rules, and the democratic political process.
Psychology	Knowledge of human behavior and performance; individual differences in ability, personality, and interests; learning and motivation; psychological research methods; and the assessment and treatment of behavioral and affective disorders.
Engineering and Technology	Knowledge of the practical application of engineering science and technology. This includes applying principles, techniques, procedures, and equipment to the design and production of various goods and services.
Computers and Electronics	Knowledge of circuit boards, processors, chips, electronic equipment, and computer hardware and software, including applications and programming.

Geography	Knowledge of principles and methods for describing the features of land, sea, and air masses, including their physical characteristics, locations, interrelationships, and distribution of plant, animal, and human life.
Physics	Knowledge and prediction of physical principles, laws, their interrelationships, and applications to understanding fluid, material, and atmospheric dynamics, and mechanical, electrical, atomic and sub- atomic structures and processes.
Chemistry	Knowledge of the chemical composition, structure, and properties of substances and of the chemical processes and transformations that they undergo. This includes uses of chemicals and their interactions, danger signs, production techniques, and disposal methods.
Telecommunications	Knowledge of transmission, broadcasting, switching, control, and operation of telecommunications systems.
Sociology and Anthropology	Knowledge of group behavior and dynamics, societal trends and influences, human migrations, ethnicity, cultures and their history and origins.
Foreign Language	Knowledge of the structure and content of a foreign (non-English) language including the meaning and spelling of words, rules of composition and grammar, and pronunciation.
History and Archeology	Knowledge of historical events and their causes, indicators, and effects on civilizations and cultures.
Biology	Knowledge of plant and animal organisms, their tissues, cells, functions, interdependencies, and interactions with each other and the environment.
Philosophy and Theology	Knowledge of different philosophical systems and religions. This includes their basic principles, values, ethics, ways of thinking, customs, practices, and their impact on human culture.
Therapy and Counseling	Knowledge of principles, methods, and procedures for diagnosis, treatment, and rehabilitation of physical and mental dysfunctions, and for career counseling and guidance.
Fine Arts	Knowledge of the theory and techniques required to compose, produce, and perform works of music, dance, visual arts, drama, and sculpture.
Medicine and Dentistry	Knowledge of the information and techniques needed to diagnose and treat human injuries, diseases, and deformities. This includes symptoms, treatment alternatives, drug properties and interactions, and preventive health-care measures.

Skills	**Skills Definitions**
Active Listening	Giving full attention to what other people are saying, taking time to understand the points being made, asking questions as appropriate, and not interrupting at inappropriate times.
Coordination	Adjusting actions in relation to others' actions.
Speaking	Talking to others to convey information effectively.
Learning Strategies	Selecting and using training/instructional methods and procedures appropriate for the situation when learning or teaching new things.
Reading Comprehension	Understanding written sentences and paragraphs in work related documents.
Social Perceptiveness	Being aware of others' reactions and understanding why they react as they do.
Active Learning	Understanding the implications of new information for both current and future problem-solving and decision-making.
Monitoring	Monitoring/Assessing performance of yourself, other individuals, or organizations to make improvements or take corrective action.
Service Orientation	Actively looking for ways to help people.
Time Management	Managing one's own time and the time of others.
Mathematics	Using mathematics to solve problems.
Instructing	Teaching others how to do something.
Quality Control Analysis	Conducting tests and inspections of products, services, or processes to evaluate quality or performance.
Critical Thinking	Using logic and reasoning to identify the strengths and weaknesses of alternative solutions, conclusions or approaches to problems.
Persuasion	Persuading others to change their minds or behavior.
Management of Personnel Resources	Motivating, developing, and directing people as they work, identifying the best people for the job.
Judgment and Decision Making	Considering the relative costs and benefits of potential actions to choose the most appropriate one.
Operation and Control	Controlling operations of equipment or systems.
Negotiation	Bringing others together and trying to reconcile differences.
Equipment Maintenance	Performing routine maintenance on equipment and determining when and what kind of maintenance is needed.

Operation Monitoring	Watching gauges, dials, or other indicators to make sure a machine is working properly.
Troubleshooting	Determining causes of operating errors and deciding what to do about it.
Equipment Selection	Determining the kind of tools and equipment needed to do a job.
Writing	Communicating effectively in writing as appropriate for the needs of the audience.
Complex Problem Solving	Identifying complex problems and reviewing related information to develop and evaluate options and implement solutions.
Repairing	Repairing machines or systems using the needed tools.
Systems Evaluation	Identifying measures or indicators of system performance and the actions needed to improve or correct performance, relative to the goals of the system.
Installation	Installing equipment, machines, wiring, or programs to meet specifications.
Systems Analysis	Determining how a system should work and how changes in conditions, operations, and the environment will affect outcomes.
Management of Material Resources	Obtaining and seeing to the appropriate use of equipment, facilities, and materials needed to do certain work.
Science	Using scientific rules and methods to solve problems.
Technology Design	Generating or adapting equipment and technology to serve user needs.
Operations Analysis	Analyzing needs and product requirements to create a design.
Management of Financial Resources	Determining how money will be spent to get the work done, and accounting for these expenditures.
Programming	Writing computer programs for various purposes.

Ability	**Ability Definitions**
Manual Dexterity	The ability to quickly move your hand, your hand together with your arm, or your two hands to grasp, manipulate, or assemble objects.
Multilimb Coordination	The ability to coordinate two or more limbs (for example, two arms, two legs, or one leg and one arm) while sitting, standing, or lying down. It does not involve performing the activities while the whole body is in motion.
Near Vision	The ability to see details at close range (within a few feet of the observer).
Trunk Strength	The ability to use your abdominal and lower back muscles to support part of the body repeatedly or continuously over time without 'giving out' or fatiguing.
Speech Clarity	The ability to speak clearly so others can understand you.
Oral Expression	The ability to communicate information and ideas in speaking so others will understand.
Oral Comprehension	The ability to listen to and understand information and ideas presented through spoken words and sentences.
Speech Recognition	The ability to identify and understand the speech of another person.
Problem Sensitivity	The ability to tell when something is wrong or is likely to go wrong. It does not involve solving the problem, only recognizing there is a problem.
Information Ordering	The ability to arrange things or actions in a certain order or pattern according to a specific rule or set of rules (e.g., patterns of numbers, letters, words, pictures, mathematical operations).
Arm-Hand Steadiness	The ability to keep your hand and arm steady while moving your arm or while holding your arm and hand in one position.
Static Strength	The ability to exert maximum muscle force to lift, push, pull, or carry objects.
Stamina	The ability to exert yourself physically over long periods of time without getting winded or out of breath.
Written Expression	The ability to communicate information and ideas in writing so others will understand.
Deductive Reasoning	The ability to apply general rules to specific problems to produce answers that make sense.
Selective Attention	The ability to concentrate on a task over a period of time without being distracted.
Extent Flexibility	The ability to bend, stretch, twist, or reach with your body, arms, and/or legs.
Category Flexibility	The ability to generate or use different sets of rules for combining or grouping things in different ways.
Finger Dexterity	The ability to make precisely coordinated movements of the fingers of one or both hands to grasp, manipulate, or assemble very small objects.
Gross Body Coordination	The ability to coordinate the movement of your arms, legs, and torso together when the whole body is in motion.

Inductive Reasoning	The ability to combine pieces of information to form general rules or conclusions (includes finding a relationship among seemingly unrelated events).
Depth Perception	The ability to judge which of several objects is closer or farther away from you, or to judge the distance between you and an object.
Control Precision	The ability to quickly and repeatedly adjust the controls of a machine or a vehicle to exact positions.
Dynamic Strength	The ability to exert muscle force repeatedly or continuously over time. This involves muscular endurance and resistance to muscle fatigue.
Written Comprehension	The ability to read and understand information and ideas presented in writing.
Number Facility	The ability to add, subtract, multiply, or divide quickly and correctly.
Speed of Limb Movement	The ability to quickly move the arms and legs.
Wrist-Finger Speed	The ability to make fast, simple, repeated movements of the fingers, hands, and wrists.
Perceptual Speed	The ability to quickly and accurately compare similarities and differences among sets of letters, numbers, objects, pictures, or patterns. The things to be compared may be presented at the same time or one after the other. This ability also includes comparing a presented object with a remembered object.
Auditory Attention	The ability to focus on a single source of sound in the presence of other distracting sounds.
Rate Control	The ability to time your movements or the movement of a piece of equipment in anticipation of changes in the speed and/or direction of a moving object or scene.
Flexibility of Closure	The ability to identify or detect a known pattern (a figure, object, word, or sound) that is hidden in other distracting material.
Memorization	The ability to remember information such as words, numbers, pictures, and procedures.
Time Sharing	The ability to shift back and forth between two or more activities or sources of information (such as speech, sounds, touch, or other sources).
Far Vision	The ability to see details at a distance.
Speed of Closure	The ability to quickly make sense of, combine, and organize information into meaningful patterns.
Visualization	The ability to imagine how something will look after it is moved around or when its parts are moved or rearranged.
Gross Body Equilibrium	The ability to keep or regain your body balance or stay upright when in an unstable position.
Reaction Time	The ability to quickly respond (with the hand, finger, or foot) to a signal (sound, light, picture) when it appears.
Visual Color Discrimination	The ability to match or detect differences between colors, including shades of color and brightness.
Dynamic Flexibility	The ability to quickly and repeatedly bend, stretch, twist, or reach out with your body, arms, and/or legs.
Fluency of Ideas	The ability to come up with a number of ideas about a topic (the number of ideas is important, not their quality, correctness, or creativity).
Response Orientation	The ability to choose quickly between two or more movements in response to two or more different signals (lights, sounds, pictures). It includes the speed with which the correct response is started with the hand, foot, or other body part.
Spatial Orientation	The ability to know your location in relation to the environment or to know where other objects are in relation to you.
Explosive Strength	The ability to use short bursts of muscle force to propel oneself (as in jumping or sprinting), or to throw an object.
Hearing Sensitivity	The ability to detect or tell the differences between sounds that vary in pitch and loudness.
Mathematical Reasoning	The ability to choose the right mathematical methods or formulas to solve a problem.
Originality	The ability to come up with unusual or clever ideas about a given topic or situation, or to develop creative ways to solve a problem.
Sound Localization	The ability to tell the direction from which a sound originated.
Peripheral Vision	The ability to see objects or movement of objects to one's side when the eyes are looking ahead.
Glare Sensitivity	The ability to see objects in the presence of glare or bright lighting.
Night Vision	The ability to see under low light conditions.

Work_Activity	Work_Activity Definitions
Handling and Moving Objects	Using hands and arms in handling, installing, positioning, and moving materials, and manipulating things.
Performing General Physical Activities	Performing physical activities that require considerable use of your arms and legs and moving your whole body, such as climbing, lifting, balancing, walking, stooping, and handling of materials.
Communicating with Supervisors, Peers, or Subordin	Providing information to supervisors, co-workers, and subordinates by telephone, in written form, e-mail, or in person.
Establishing and Maintaining Interpersonal Relatio	Developing constructive and cooperative working relationships with others, and maintaining them over time.
Identifying Objects, Actions, and Events	Identifying information by categorizing, estimating, recognizing differences or similarities, and detecting changes in circumstances or events.
Getting Information	Observing, receiving, and otherwise obtaining information from all relevant sources.
Judging the Qualities of Things, Services, or Peop	Assessing the value, importance, or quality of things or people.
Assisting and Caring for Others	Providing personal assistance, medical attention, emotional support, or other personal care to others such as coworkers, customers, or patients.
Inspecting Equipment, Structures, or Material	Inspecting equipment, structures, or materials to identify the cause of errors or other problems or defects.
Making Decisions and Solving Problems	Analyzing information and evaluating results to choose the best solution and solve problems.
Organizing, Planning, and Prioritizing Work	Developing specific goals and plans to prioritize, organize, and accomplish your work.
Controlling Machines and Processes	Using either control mechanisms or direct physical activity to operate machines or processes (not including computers or vehicles).
Coaching and Developing Others	Identifying the developmental needs of others and coaching, mentoring, or otherwise helping others to improve their knowledge or skills.
Performing for or Working Directly with the Public	Performing for people or dealing directly with the public. This includes serving customers in restaurants and stores, and receiving clients or guests.
Monitor Processes, Materials, or Surroundings	Monitoring and reviewing information from materials, events, or the environment, to detect or assess problems.
Developing and Building Teams	Encouraging and building mutual trust, respect, and cooperation among team members.
Coordinating the Work and Activities of Others	Getting members of a group to work together to accomplish tasks.
Evaluating Information to Determine Compliance wit	Using relevant information and individual judgment to determine whether events or processes comply with laws, regulations, or standards.
Training and Teaching Others	Identifying the educational needs of others, developing formal educational or training programs or classes, and teaching or instructing others.
Interpreting the Meaning of Information for Others	Translating or explaining what information means and how it can be used.
Performing Administrative Activities	Performing day-to-day administrative tasks such as maintaining information files and processing paperwork.
Documenting/Recording Information	Entering, transcribing, recording, storing, or maintaining information in written or electronic/magnetic form.
Estimating the Quantifiable Characteristics of Pro	Estimating sizes, distances, and quantities; or determining time, costs, resources, or materials needed to perform a work activity.
Resolving Conflicts and Negotiating with Others	Handling complaints, settling disputes, and resolving grievances and conflicts, or otherwise negotiating with others.
Updating and Using Relevant Knowledge	Keeping up-to-date technically and applying new knowledge to your job.
Provide Consultation and Advice to Others	Providing guidance and expert advice to management or other groups on technical, systems-, or process-related topics.
Thinking Creatively	Developing, designing, or creating new applications, ideas, relationships, systems, or products, including artistic contributions.
Processing Information	Compiling, coding, categorizing, calculating, tabulating, auditing, or verifying information or data.
Interacting With Computers	Using computers and computer systems (including hardware and software) to program, write software, set up functions, enter data, or process information.
Analyzing Data or Information	Identifying the underlying principles, reasons, or facts of information by breaking down information or data into separate parts.
Scheduling Work and Activities	Scheduling events, programs, and activities, as well as the work of others.

Communicating with Persons Outside Organization	Communicating with people outside the organization, representing the organization to customers, the public, government, and other external sources. This information can be exchanged in person, in writing, or by telephone or e-mail.
Guiding, Directing, and Motivating Subordinates	Providing guidance and direction to subordinates, including setting performance standards and monitoring performance.
Repairing and Maintaining Mechanical Equipment	Servicing, repairing, adjusting, and testing machines, devices, moving parts, and equipment that operate primarily on the basis of mechanical (not electronic) principles.
Selling or Influencing Others	Convincing others to buy merchandise/goods or to otherwise change their minds or actions.
Monitoring and Controlling Resources	Monitoring and controlling resources and overseeing the spending of money.
Operating Vehicles, Mechanized Devices, or Equipme	Running, maneuvering, navigating, or driving vehicles or mechanized equipment, such as forklifts, passenger vehicles, aircraft, or water craft.
Developing Objectives and Strategies	Establishing long-range objectives and specifying the strategies and actions to achieve them.
Drafting, Laying Out, and Specifying Technical Dev	Providing documentation, detailed instructions, drawings, or specifications to tell others about how devices, parts, equipment, or structures are to be fabricated, constructed, assembled, modified, maintained, or used.
Repairing and Maintaining Electronic Equipment	Servicing, repairing, calibrating, regulating, fine-tuning, or testing machines, devices, and equipment that operate primarily on the basis of electrical or electronic (not mechanical) principles.
Staffing Organizational Units	Recruiting, interviewing, selecting, hiring, and promoting employees in an organization.

Work_Context	Work_Context Definitions
Spend Time Standing	How much does this job require standing?
Spend Time Using Your Hands to Handle, Control, or	How much does this job require using your hands to handle, control, or feel objects, tools or controls?
Indoors, Environmentally Controlled	How often does this job require working indoors in environmentally controlled conditions?
Contact With Others	How much does this job require the worker to be in contact with others (face-to-face, by telephone, or otherwise) in order to perform it?
Face-to-Face Discussions	How often do you have to have face-to-face discussions with individuals or teams in this job?
Spend Time Making Repetitive Motions	How much does this job require making repetitive motions?
Physical Proximity	To what extent does this job require the worker to perform job tasks in close physical proximity to other people?
Work With Work Group or Team	How important is it to work with others in a group or team in this job?
Time Pressure	How often does this job require the worker to meet strict deadlines?
Spend Time Walking and Running	How much does this job require walking and running?
Sounds, Noise Levels Are Distracting or Uncomforta	How often does this job require working exposed to sounds and noise levels that are distracting or uncomfortable?
Deal With External Customers	How important is it to work with external customers or the public in this job?
Coordinate or Lead Others	How important is it to coordinate or lead others in accomplishing work activities in this job?
Importance of Being Exact or Accurate	How important is being very exact or highly accurate in performing this job?
Importance of Repeating Same Tasks	How important is repeating the same physical activities (e.g., key entry) or mental activities (e.g., checking entries in a ledger) over and over, without stopping, to performing this job?
Wear Common Protective or Safety Equipment such as	How much does this job require wearing common protective or safety equipment such as safety shoes, glasses, gloves, hard hats or live jackets?
Structured versus Unstructured Work	To what extent is this job structured for the worker, rather than allowing the worker to determine tasks, priorities, and goals?
Exposed to Contaminants	How often does this job require working exposed to contaminants (such as pollutants, gases, dust or odors)?
Freedom to Make Decisions	How much decision making freedom, without supervision, does the job offer?
Spend Time Bending or Twisting the Body	How much does this job require bending or twisting your body?
Impact of Decisions on Co-workers or Company Resul	How do the decisions an employee makes impact the results of co-workers, clients or the company?

Frequency of Decision Making	How frequently is the worker required to make decisions that affect other people, the financial resources, and/or the image and reputation of the organization?
Indoors, Not Environmentally Controlled	How often does this job require working indoors in non-controlled environmental conditions (e.g., warehouse without heat)?
Very Hot or Cold Temperatures	How often does this job require working in very hot (above 90 F degrees) or very cold (below 32 F degrees) temperatures?
Pace Determined by Speed of Equipment	How important is it to this job that the pace is determined by the speed of equipment or machinery? (This does not refer to keeping busy at all times on this job.)
Exposed to Hazardous Equipment	How often does this job require exposure to hazardous equipment?
Responsible for Others' Health and Safety	How much responsibility is there for the health and safety of others in this job?
Responsibility for Outcomes and Results	How responsible is the worker for work outcomes and results of other workers?
Deal With Unpleasant or Angry People	How frequently does the worker have to deal with unpleasant, angry, or discourteous individuals as part of the job requirements?
Telephone	How often do you have telephone conversations in this job?
Outdoors, Exposed to Weather	How often does this job require working outdoors, exposed to all weather conditions?
Exposed to Hazardous Conditions	How often does this job require exposure to hazardous conditions?
Frequency of Conflict Situations	How often are there conflict situations the employee has to face in this job?
Cramped Work Space, Awkward Positions	How often does this job require working in cramped work spaces that requires getting into awkward positions?
Extremely Bright or Inadequate Lighting	How often does this job require working in extremely bright or inadequate lighting conditions?
Level of Competition	To what extent does this job require the worker to compete or to be aware of competitive pressures?
Exposed to Minor Burns, Cuts, Bites, or Stings	How often does this job require exposure to minor burns, cuts, bites, or stings?
Consequence of Error	How serious would the result usually be if the worker made a mistake that was not readily correctable?
Spend Time Sitting	How much does this job require sitting?
Public Speaking	How often do you have to perform public speaking in this job?
Letters and Memos	How often does the job require written letters and memos?
Exposed to Disease or Infections	How often does this job require exposure to disease/infections?
Spend Time Keeping or Regaining Balance	How much does this job require keeping or regaining your balance?
Degree of Automation	How automated is the job?
Wear Specialized Protective or Safety Equipment su	How much does this job require wearing specialized protective or safety equipment such as breathing apparatus, safety harness, full protection suits, or radiation protection?
Spend Time Kneeling, Crouching, Stooping, or Crawl	How much does this job require kneeling, crouching, stooping, or crawling?
In an Open Vehicle or Equipment	How often does this job require working in an open vehicle or equipment (e.g., tractor)?
Electronic Mail	How often do you use electronic mail in this job?
Outdoors, Under Cover	How often does this job require working outdoors, under cover (e.g., structure with roof but no walls)?
Exposed to High Places	How often does this job require exposure to high places?
Spend Time Climbing Ladders, Scaffolds, or Poles	How much does this job require climbing ladders, scaffolds, or poles?
In an Enclosed Vehicle or Equipment	How often does this job require working in a closed vehicle or equipment (e.g., car)?
Deal With Physically Aggressive People	How frequently does this job require the worker to deal with physical aggression of violent individuals?
Exposed to Whole Body Vibration	How often does this job require exposure to whole body vibration (e.g., operate a jackhammer)?
Exposed to Radiation	How often does this job require exposure to radiation?

Job Zone Component	Job Zone Component Definitions
Title	Job Zone One: Little or No Preparation Needed
Overall Experience	No previous work-related skill, knowledge, or experience is needed for these occupations. For example, a person can become a general office clerk even if he/she has never worked in an office before.

Job Training	Employees in these occupations need anywhere from a few days to a few months of training. Usually, an experienced worker could show you how to do the job.
Job Zone Examples	These occupations involve following instructions and helping others. Examples include bus drivers, forest and conservation workers, general office clerks, home health aides, and waiters/waitresses.
SVP Range	(Below 4.0)
Education	These occupations may require a high school diploma or GED certificate. Some may require a formal training course to obtain a license.

Work_Styles	Work_Styles Definitions
Attention to Detail	Job requires being careful about detail and thorough in completing work tasks.
Dependability	Job requires being reliable, responsible, and dependable, and fulfilling obligations.
Cooperation	Job requires being pleasant with others on the job and displaying a good-natured, cooperative attitude.
Self Control	Job requires maintaining composure, keeping emotions in check, controlling anger, and avoiding aggressive behavior, even in very difficult situations.
Stress Tolerance	Job requires accepting criticism and dealing calmly and effectively with high stress situations.
Concern for Others	Job requires being sensitive to others' needs and feelings and being understanding and helpful on the job.
Integrity	Job requires being honest and ethical.
Independence	Job requires developing one's own ways of doing things, guiding oneself with little or no supervision, and depending on oneself to get things done.
Adaptability/Flexibility	Job requires being open to change (positive or negative) and to considerable variety in the workplace.
Analytical Thinking	Job requires analyzing information and using logic to address work-related issues and problems.
Social Orientation	Job requires preferring to work with others rather than alone, and being personally connected with others on the job.
Initiative	Job requires a willingness to take on responsibilities and challenges.
Innovation	Job requires creativity and alternative thinking to develop new ideas for and answers to work-related problems.
Achievement/Effort	Job requires establishing and maintaining personally challenging achievement goals and exerting effort toward mastering tasks.
Persistence	Job requires persistence in the face of obstacles.
Leadership	Job requires a willingness to lead, take charge, and offer opinions and direction.

53-7071.00 - Gas Compressor and Gas Pumping Station Operators

Operate steam, gas, electric motor, or internal combustion engine driven compressors. Transmit, compress, or recover gases, such as butane, nitrogen, hydrogen, and natural gas.

Tasks

1) Read gas meters, and maintain records of the amounts of gas received and dispensed from holders.

2) Move controls and turn valves to start compressor engines, pumps, and auxiliary equipment.

3) Monitor meters and pressure gauges to determine consumption rate variations, temperatures, and pressures.

4) Maintain each station by performing general housekeeping duties such as painting, washing, and cleaning.

5) Record instrument readings and operational changes in operating logs.

6) Connect pipelines between pumps and containers that are being filled or emptied.

7) Clean, lubricate, and adjust equipment, and replace filters and gaskets, using hand tools.

8) Turn knobs or switches to regulate pressures.

9) Respond to problems by adjusting control room equipment, and/or instructing other personnel to adjust equipment at problem locations or in other control areas.

10) Take samples of gases and conduct chemical tests in order to determine gas quality and sulfur or moisture content, or send samples to laboratories for analysis.

11) Operate power-driven pumps that transfer liquids, semi-liquids, gases, or powdered materials.

12) Adjust valves and equipment to obtain specified performance.

53-7072.00 - Pump Operators, Except Wellhead Pumpers

Tend, control, or operate power-driven, stationary, or portable pumps and manifold systems to transfer gases, oil, other liquids, slurries, or powdered materials to and from various vessels and processes.

Tasks

1) Tend auxiliary equipment such as water treatment and refrigeration units, and heat exchangers.

2) Read operating schedules or instructions or receive verbal orders, in order to determine amounts to be pumped.

3) Record operating data such as products and quantities pumped, stocks used, gauging results, and operating times.

4) Tend vessels that store substances such as gases, liquids, slurries, or powdered materials, checking levels of substances by using calibrated rods or by reading mercury gauges and tank charts.

5) Collect and deliver sample solutions for laboratory analysis.

6) Turn valves and start pumps to start or regulate flows of substances such as gases, liquids, slurries, or powdered materials.

7) Pump two or more materials into one tank to blend mixtures.

8) Plan movement of products through lines to processing, storage, and shipping units, utilizing knowledge of interconnections and capacities of pipelines, valve manifolds, pumps, and tankage.

9) Test materials and solutions, using testing equipment.

10) Connect hoses and pipelines to pumps and vessels prior to material transfer, using hand tools.

11) Monitor gauges and flowmeters and inspect equipment to ensure that tank levels, temperatures, chemical amounts, and pressures are at specified levels, reporting abnormalities as necessary.

12) Add chemicals and solutions to tanks to ensure that specifications are met.

13) Communicate with other workers, using signals, radios, or telephones, to start and stop flows of materials or substances.

53-7073.00 - Wellhead Pumpers

Operate power pumps and auxiliary equipment to produce flow of oil or gas from wells in oil field.

Tasks

1) Monitor control panels during pumping operations in order to ensure that materials are being pumped at the correct pressure, density, rate, and concentration.

2) Perform routine maintenance on vehicles and equipment.

3) Repair gas and oil meters and gauges.

4) Unload and assemble pipes and pumping equipment, using hand tools.

5) Attach pumps and hoses to wellheads.

6) Open valves to return compressed gas to bottoms of specified wells in order to repressurize them and force oil to surface.

7) Supervise oil pumpers and other workers engaged in producing oil from wells.

8) Start compressor engines, and divert oil from storage tanks into compressor units and auxiliary equipment in order to recover natural gas from oil.

9) Prepare trucks and equipment necessary for the type of pumping service required.

10) Drive trucks in order to transport high-pressure pumping equipment, and chemicals, fluids, or gases to be pumped into wells.

11) Mix acids, chemicals, or dry cement as required for a specific job.

12) Control pumping and blending equipment to acidize, cement, or fracture gas or oil wells and permeable rock formations.

Knowledge	Knowledge Definitions
Mechanical	Knowledge of machines and tools, including their designs, uses, repair, and maintenance.
Mathematics	Knowledge of arithmetic, algebra, geometry, calculus, statistics, and their applications.
Production and Processing	Knowledge of raw materials, production processes, quality control, costs, and other techniques for maximizing the effective manufacture and distribution of goods.
Public Safety and Security	Knowledge of relevant equipment, policies, procedures, and strategies to promote effective local, state, or national security operations for the protection of people, data, property, and institutions.
English Language	Knowledge of the structure and content of the English language including the meaning and spelling of words, rules of composition, and grammar.
Administration and Management	Knowledge of business and management principles involved in strategic planning, resource allocation, human resources modeling, leadership technique, production methods, and coordination of people and resources.
Computers and Electronics	Knowledge of circuit boards, processors, chips, electronic equipment, and computer hardware and software, including applications and programming.
Physics	Knowledge and prediction of physical principles, laws, their interrelationships, and applications to understanding fluid, material, and atmospheric dynamics, and mechanical, electrical, atomic and sub- atomic structures and processes.
Engineering and Technology	Knowledge of the practical application of engineering science and technology. This includes applying principles, techniques, procedures, and equipment to the design and production of various goods and services.
Chemistry	Knowledge of the chemical composition, structure, and properties of substances and of the chemical processes and transformations that they undergo. This includes uses of chemicals and their interactions, danger signs, production techniques, and disposal methods.
Design	Knowledge of design techniques, tools, and principles involved in production of precision technical plans, blueprints, drawings, and models.
Customer and Personal Service	Knowledge of principles and processes for providing customer and personal services. This includes customer needs assessment, meeting quality standards for services, and evaluation of customer satisfaction.
Transportation	Knowledge of principles and methods for moving people or goods by air, rail, sea, or road, including the relative costs and benefits.
Education and Training	Knowledge of principles and methods for curriculum and training design, teaching and instruction for individuals and groups, and the measurement of training effects.
Clerical	Knowledge of administrative and clerical procedures and systems such as word processing, managing files and records, stenography and transcription, designing forms, and other office procedures and terminology.
Law and Government	Knowledge of laws, legal codes, court procedures, precedents, government regulations, executive orders, agency rules, and the democratic political process.
Building and Construction	Knowledge of materials, methods, and the tools involved in the construction or repair of houses, buildings, or other structures such as highways and roads.
Telecommunications	Knowledge of transmission, broadcasting, switching, control, and operation of telecommunications systems.
Economics and Accounting	Knowledge of economic and accounting principles and practices, the financial markets, banking and the analysis and reporting of financial data.
Personnel and Human Resources	Knowledge of principles and procedures for personnel recruitment, selection, training, compensation and benefits, labor relations and negotiation, and personnel information systems.
Geography	Knowledge of principles and methods for describing the features of land, sea, and air masses, including their physical characteristics, locations, interrelationships, and distribution of plant, animal, and human life.
Communications and Media	Knowledge of media production, communication, and dissemination techniques and methods. This includes alternative ways to inform and entertain via written, oral, and visual media.
Biology	Knowledge of plant and animal organisms, their tissues, cells, functions, interdependencies, and interactions with each other and the environment.
Psychology	Knowledge of human behavior and performance; individual differences in ability, personality, and interests; learning and motivation; psychological research methods; and the assessment and treatment of behavioral and affective disorders.
Sales and Marketing	Knowledge of principles and methods for showing, promoting, and selling products or services. This includes marketing strategy and tactics, product demonstration, sales techniques, and sales control systems.
Medicine and Dentistry	Knowledge of the information and techniques needed to diagnose and treat human injuries, diseases, and deformities. This includes symptoms, treatment alternatives, drug properties and interactions, and preventive health-care measures.
Sociology and Anthropology	Knowledge of group behavior and dynamics, societal trends and influences, human migrations, ethnicity, cultures and their history and origins.
Therapy and Counseling	Knowledge of principles, methods, and procedures for diagnosis, treatment, and rehabilitation of physical and mental dysfunctions, and for career counseling and guidance.
Philosophy and Theology	Knowledge of different philosophical systems and religions. This includes their basic principles, values, ethics, ways of thinking, customs, practices, and their impact on human culture.
History and Archeology	Knowledge of historical events and their causes, indicators, and effects on civilizations and cultures.
Foreign Language	Knowledge of the structure and content of a foreign (non-English) language including the meaning and spelling of words, rules of composition and grammar, and pronunciation.
Food Production	Knowledge of techniques and equipment for planting, growing, and harvesting food products (both plant and animal) for consumption, including storage/handling techniques.
Fine Arts	Knowledge of the theory and techniques required to compose, produce, and perform works of music, dance, visual arts, drama, and sculpture.

Skills	Skills Definitions
Operation Monitoring	Watching gauges, dials, or other indicators to make sure a machine is working properly.
Equipment Maintenance	Performing routine maintenance on equipment and determining when and what kind of maintenance is needed.
Repairing	Repairing machines or systems using the needed tools.
Operation and Control	Controlling operations of equipment or systems.
Troubleshooting	Determining causes of operating errors and deciding what to do about it.
Equipment Selection	Determining the kind of tools and equipment needed to do a job.
Mathematics	Using mathematics to solve problems.
Active Listening	Giving full attention to what other people are saying, taking time to understand the points being made, asking questions as appropriate, and not interrupting at inappropriate times.
Active Learning	Understanding the implications of new information for both current and future problem-solving and decision-making.
Critical Thinking	Using logic and reasoning to identify the strengths and weaknesses of alternative solutions, conclusions or approaches to problems.
Speaking	Talking to others to convey information effectively.
Installation	Installing equipment, machines, wiring, or programs to meet specifications.
Reading Comprehension	Understanding written sentences and paragraphs in work related documents.
Writing	Communicating effectively in writing as appropriate for the needs of the audience.
Judgment and Decision Making	Considering the relative costs and benefits of potential actions to choose the most appropriate one.
Systems Evaluation	Identifying measures or indicators of system performance and the actions needed to improve or correct performance, relative to the goals of the system.
Systems Analysis	Determining how a system should work and how changes in conditions, operations, and the environment will affect outcomes.

Learning Strategies	Selecting and using training/instructional methods and procedures appropriate for the situation when learning or teaching new things.
Complex Problem Solving	Identifying complex problems and reviewing related information to develop and evaluate options and implement solutions.
Time Management	Managing one's own time and the time of others.
Coordination	Adjusting actions in relation to others' actions.
Monitoring	Monitoring/Assessing performance of yourself, other individuals, or organizations to make improvements or take corrective action.
Instructing	Teaching others how to do something.
Operations Analysis	Analyzing needs and product requirements to create a design.
Quality Control Analysis	Conducting tests and inspections of products, services, or processes to evaluate quality or performance.
Management of Material Resources	Obtaining and seeing to the appropriate use of equipment, facilities, and materials needed to do certain work.
Technology Design	Generating or adapting equipment and technology to serve user needs.
Science	Using scientific rules and methods to solve problems.
Service Orientation	Actively looking for ways to help people.
Social Perceptiveness	Being aware of others' reactions and understanding why they react as they do.
Negotiation	Bringing others together and trying to reconcile differences.
Management of Personnel Resources	Motivating, developing, and directing people as they work, identifying the best people for the job.
Persuasion	Persuading others to change their minds or behavior.
Management of Financial Resources	Determining how money will be spent to get the work done, and accounting for these expenditures.
Programming	Writing computer programs for various purposes.

Ability	Ability Definitions
Problem Sensitivity	The ability to tell when something is wrong or is likely to go wrong. It does not involve solving the problem, only recognizing there is a problem.
Near Vision	The ability to see details at close range (within a few feet of the observer).
Control Precision	The ability to quickly and repeatedly adjust the controls of a machine or a vehicle to exact positions.
Multilimb Coordination	The ability to coordinate two or more limbs (for example, two arms, two legs, or one leg and one arm) while sitting, standing, or lying down. It does not involve performing the activities while the whole body is in motion.
Reaction Time	The ability to quickly respond (with the hand, finger, or foot) to a signal (sound, light, picture) when it appears.
Deductive Reasoning	The ability to apply general rules to specific problems to produce answers that make sense.
Oral Expression	The ability to communicate information and ideas in speaking so others will understand.
Oral Comprehension	The ability to listen to and understand information and ideas presented through spoken words and sentences.
Arm-Hand Steadiness	The ability to keep your hand and arm steady while moving your arm or while holding your arm and hand in one position.
Perceptual Speed	The ability to quickly and accurately compare similarities and differences among sets of letters, numbers, objects, pictures, or patterns. The things to be compared may be presented at the same time or one after the other. This ability also includes comparing a presented object with a remembered object.
Manual Dexterity	The ability to quickly move your hand, your hand together with your arm, or your two hands to grasp, manipulate, or assemble objects.
Speech Recognition	The ability to identify and understand the speech of another person.
Static Strength	The ability to exert maximum muscle force to lift, push, pull, or carry objects.
Information Ordering	The ability to arrange things or actions in a certain order or pattern according to a specific rule or set of rules (e.g., patterns of numbers, letters, words, pictures, mathematical operations).
Speech Clarity	The ability to speak clearly so others can understand you.
Inductive Reasoning	The ability to combine pieces of information to form general rules or conclusions (includes finding a relationship among seemingly unrelated events).
Selective Attention	The ability to concentrate on a task over a period of time without being distracted.
Gross Body Equilibrium	The ability to keep or regain your body balance or stay upright when in an unstable position.

Written Comprehension	The ability to read and understand information and ideas presented in writing.
Written Expression	The ability to communicate information and ideas in writing so others will understand.
Category Flexibility	The ability to generate or use different sets of rules for combining or grouping things in different ways.
Finger Dexterity	The ability to make precisely coordinated movements of the fingers of one or both hands to grasp, manipulate, or assemble very small objects.
Trunk Strength	The ability to use your abdominal and lower back muscles to support part of the body repeatedly or continuously over time without 'giving out' or fatiguing.
Gross Body Coordination	The ability to coordinate the movement of your arms, legs, and torso together when the whole body is in motion.
Extent Flexibility	The ability to bend, stretch, twist, or reach with your body, arms, and/or legs.
Response Orientation	The ability to choose quickly between two or more movements in response to two or more different signals (lights, sounds, pictures). It includes the speed with which the correct response is started with the hand, foot, or other body part.
Auditory Attention	The ability to focus on a single source of sound in the presence of other distracting sounds.
Stamina	The ability to exert yourself physically over long periods of time without getting winded or out of breath.
Dynamic Strength	The ability to exert muscle force repeatedly or continuously over time. This involves muscular endurance and resistance to muscle fatigue.
Visualization	The ability to imagine how something will look after it is moved around or when its parts are moved or rearranged.
Far Vision	The ability to see details at a distance.
Depth Perception	The ability to judge which of several objects is closer or farther away from you, or to judge the distance between you and an object.
Rate Control	The ability to time your movements or the movement of a piece of equipment in anticipation of changes in the speed and/or direction of a moving object or scene.
Hearing Sensitivity	The ability to detect or tell the differences between sounds that vary in pitch and loudness.
Memorization	The ability to remember information such as words, numbers, pictures, and procedures.
Flexibility of Closure	The ability to identify or detect a known pattern (a figure, object, word, or sound) that is hidden in other distracting material.
Time Sharing	The ability to shift back and forth between two or more activities or sources of information (such as speech, sounds, touch, or other sources).
Visual Color Discrimination	The ability to match or detect differences between colors, including shades of color and brightness.
Wrist-Finger Speed	The ability to make fast, simple, repeated movements of the fingers, hands, and wrists.
Originality	The ability to come up with unusual or clever ideas about a given topic or situation, or to develop creative ways to solve a problem.
Glare Sensitivity	The ability to see objects in the presence of glare or bright lighting.
Speed of Limb Movement	The ability to quickly move the arms and legs.
Fluency of Ideas	The ability to come up with a number of ideas about a topic (the number of ideas is important, not their quality, correctness, or creativity).
Peripheral Vision	The ability to see objects or movement of objects to one's side when the eyes are looking ahead.
Number Facility	The ability to add, subtract, multiply, or divide quickly and correctly.
Speed of Closure	The ability to quickly make sense of, combine, and organize information into meaningful patterns.
Spatial Orientation	The ability to know your location in relation to the environment or to know where other objects are in relation to you.
Mathematical Reasoning	The ability to choose the right mathematical methods or formulas to solve a problem.
Night Vision	The ability to see under low light conditions.
Dynamic Flexibility	The ability to quickly and repeatedly bend, stretch, twist, or reach out with your body, arms, and/or legs.
Explosive Strength	The ability to use short bursts of muscle force to propel oneself (as in jumping or sprinting), or to throw an object.
Sound Localization	The ability to tell the direction from which a sound originated.

Work_Activity	Work_Activity Definitions
Operating Vehicles, Mechanized Devices, or Equipme	Running, maneuvering, navigating, or driving vehicles or mechanized equipment, such as forklifts, passenger vehicles, aircraft, or water craft.
Inspecting Equipment, Structures, or Material	Inspecting equipment, structures, or materials to identify the cause of errors or other problems or defects.
Controlling Machines and Processes	Using either control mechanisms or direct physical activity to operate machines or processes (not including computers or vehicles).
Documenting/Recording Information	Entering, transcribing, recording, storing, or maintaining information in written or electronic/magnetic form.
Performing General Physical Activities	Performing physical activities that require considerable use of your arms and legs and moving your whole body, such as climbing, lifting, balancing, walking, stooping, and handling of materials.
Communicating with Supervisors, Peers, or Subordin	Providing information to supervisors, co-workers, and subordinates by telephone, in written form, e-mail, or in person.
Repairing and Maintaining Mechanical Equipment	Servicing, repairing, adjusting, and testing machines, devices, moving parts, and equipment that operate primarily on the basis of mechanical (not electronic) principles.
Monitor Processes, Materials, or Surroundings	Monitoring and reviewing information from materials, events, or the environment, to detect or assess problems.
Identifying Objects, Actions, and Events	Identifying information by categorizing, estimating, recognizing differences or similarities, and detecting changes in circumstances or events.
Handling and Moving Objects	Using hands and arms in handling, installing, positioning, and moving materials, and manipulating things.
Making Decisions and Solving Problems	Analyzing information and evaluating results to choose the best solution and solve problems.
Getting Information	Observing, receiving, and otherwise obtaining information from all relevant sources.
Updating and Using Relevant Knowledge	Keeping up-to-date technically and applying new knowledge to your job.
Evaluating Information to Determine Compliance wit	Using relevant information and individual judgment to determine whether events or processes comply with laws, regulations, or standards.
Organizing, Planning, and Prioritizing Work	Developing specific goals and plans to prioritize, organize, and accomplish your work.
Processing Information	Compiling, coding, categorizing, calculating, tabulating, auditing, or verifying information or data.
Repairing and Maintaining Electronic Equipment	Servicing, repairing, calibrating, regulating, fine-tuning, or testing machines, devices, and equipment that operate primarily on the basis of electrical or electronic (not mechanical) principles.
Establishing and Maintaining Interpersonal Relatio	Developing constructive and cooperative working relationships with others, and maintaining them over time.
Analyzing Data or Information	Identifying the underlying principles, reasons, or facts of information by breaking down information or data into separate parts.
Communicating with Persons Outside Organization	Communicating with people outside the organization, representing the organization to customers, the public, government, and other external sources. This information can be exchanged in person, in writing, or by telephone or e-mail.
Judging the Qualities of Things, Services, or Peop	Assessing the value, importance, or quality of things or people.
Estimating the Quantifiable Characteristics of Pro	Estimating sizes, distances, and quantities; or determining time, costs, resources, or materials needed to perform a work activity.
Scheduling Work and Activities	Scheduling events, programs, and activities, as well as the work of others.
Interpreting the Meaning of Information for Others	Translating or explaining what information means and how it can be used.
Thinking Creatively	Developing, designing, or creating new applications, ideas, relationships, systems, or products, including artistic contributions.
Monitoring and Controlling Resources	Monitoring and controlling resources and overseeing the spending of money.
Assisting and Caring for Others	Providing personal assistance, medical attention, emotional support, or other personal care to others such as coworkers, customers, or patients.
Coordinating the Work and Activities of Others	Getting members of a group to work together to accomplish tasks.
Performing Administrative Activities	Performing day-to-day administrative tasks such as maintaining information files and processing paperwork.

Developing Objectives and Strategies	Establishing long-range objectives and specifying the strategies and actions to achieve them.
Interacting With Computers	Using computers and computer systems (including hardware and software) to program, write software, set up functions, enter data, or process information.
Developing and Building Teams	Encouraging and building mutual trust, respect, and cooperation among team members.
Resolving Conflicts and Negotiating with Others	Handling complaints, settling disputes, and resolving grievances and conflicts, or otherwise negotiating with others.
Guiding, Directing, and Motivating Subordinates	Providing guidance and direction to subordinates, including setting performance standards and monitoring performance.
Coaching and Developing Others	Identifying the developmental needs of others and coaching, mentoring, or otherwise helping others to improve their knowledge or skills.
Training and Teaching Others	Identifying the educational needs of others, developing formal educational or training programs or classes, and teaching or instructing others.
Drafting, Laying Out, and Specifying Technical Dev	Providing documentation, detailed instructions, drawings, or specifications to tell others about how devices, parts, equipment, or structures are to be fabricated, constructed, assembled, modified, maintained, or used.
Provide Consultation and Advice to Others	Providing guidance and expert advice to management or other groups on technical, systems-, or process-related topics.
Performing for or Working Directly with the Public	Performing for people or dealing directly with the public. This includes serving customers in restaurants and stores, and receiving clients or guests.
Selling or Influencing Others	Convincing others to buy merchandise/goods or to otherwise change their minds or actions.
Staffing Organizational Units	Recruiting, interviewing, selecting, hiring, and promoting employees in an organization.

Work_Context	Work_Context Definitions
In an Enclosed Vehicle or Equipment	How often does this job require working in a closed vehicle or equipment (e.g., car)?
Outdoors, Exposed to Weather	How often does this job require working outdoors, exposed to all weather conditions?
Exposed to Contaminants	How often does this job require working exposed to contaminants (such as pollutants, gases, dust or odors)?
Face-to-Face Discussions	How often do you have to have face-to-face discussions with individuals or teams in this job?
Telephone	How often do you have telephone conversations in this job?
Wear Common Protective or Safety Equipment such as	How much does this job require wearing common protective or safety equipment such as safety shoes, glasses, gloves, hard hats or live jackets?
Exposed to Hazardous Equipment	How often does this job require exposure to hazardous equipment?
Frequency of Decision Making	How frequently is the worker required to make decisions that affect other people, the financial resources, and/or the image and reputation of the organization?
Very Hot or Cold Temperatures	How often does this job require working in very hot (above 90 F degrees) or very cold (below 32 F degrees) temperatures?
Exposed to Hazardous Conditions	How often does this job require exposure to hazardous conditions?
Exposed to High Places	How often does this job require exposure to high places?
Impact of Decisions on Co-workers or Company Resul	How do the decisions an employee makes impact the results of co-workers, clients or the company?
Freedom to Make Decisions	How much decision making freedom, without supervision, does the job offer?
Sounds, Noise Levels Are Distracting or Uncomforta	How often does this job require working exposed to sounds and noise levels that are distracting or uncomfortable?
Structured versus Unstructured Work	To what extent is this job structured for the worker, rather than allowing the worker to determine tasks, priorities, and goals?
Consequence of Error	How serious would the result usually be if the worker made a mistake that was not readily correctable?
Contact With Others	How often does this job require the worker to be in contact with others (face-to-face, by telephone, or otherwise) in order to perform it?
Importance of Being Exact or Accurate	How important is being very exact or highly accurate in performing this job?
Time Pressure	How often does this job require the worker to meet strict deadlines?
Spend Time Using Your Hands to Handle, Control, or	How much does this job require using your hands to handle, control, or feel objects, tools or controls?
Spend Time Standing	How much does this job require standing?

Work With Work Group or Team	How important is it to work with others in a group or team in this job?
Indoors, Not Environmentally Controlled	How often does this job require working indoors in non-controlled environmental conditions (e.g., warehouse without heat)?
Responsible for Others' Health and Safety	How much responsibility is there for the health and safety of others in this job?
Exposed to Minor Burns, Cuts, Bites, or Stings	How often does this job require exposure to minor burns, cuts, bites, or stings?
Importance of Repeating Same Tasks	How important is repeating the same physical activities (e.g., key entry) or mental activities (e.g., checking entries in a ledger) over and over, without stopping, to performing this job?
Responsibility for Outcomes and Results	How responsible is the worker for work outcomes and results of other workers?
Letters and Memos	How often does the job require written letters and memos?
Electronic Mail	How often do you use electronic mail in this job?
Pace Determined by Speed of Equipment	How important is it to this job that the pace is determined by the speed of equipment or machinery? (This does not refer to keeping busy at all times on this job.)
Coordinate or Lead Others	How important is it to coordinate or lead others in accomplishing work activities in this job?
Degree of Automation	How automated is the job?
Outdoors, Under Cover	How often does this job require working outdoors, under cover (e.g., structure with roof but no walls)?
Level of Competition	To what extent does this job require the worker to compete or to be aware of competitive pressures?
Cramped Work Space, Awkward Positions	How often does this job require working in cramped work spaces that requires getting into awkward positions?
Deal With External Customers	How important is it to work with external customers or the public in this job?
Spend Time Bending or Twisting the Body	How much does this job require bending or twisting your body?
Spend Time Walking and Running	How much does this job require walking and running?
Spend Time Climbing Ladders, Scaffolds, or Poles	How much does this job require climbing ladders, scaffolds, or poles?
Extremely Bright or Inadequate Lighting	How often does this job require working in extremely bright or inadequate lighting conditions?
Physical Proximity	To what extent does this job require the worker to perform job tasks in close physical proximity to other people?
Spend Time Sitting	How much does this job require sitting?
Deal With Unpleasant or Angry People	How frequently does the worker have to deal with unpleasant, angry, or discourteous individuals as part of the job requirements?
Spend Time Making Repetitive Motions	How much does this job require making repetitive motions?
Frequency of Conflict Situations	How often are there conflict situations the employee has to face in this job?
In an Open Vehicle or Equipment	How often does this job require working in an open vehicle or equipment (e.g., tractor)?
Spend Time Kneeling, Crouching, Stooping, or Crawl	How much does this job require kneeling, crouching, stooping, or crawling?
Public Speaking	How often do you have to perform public speaking in this job?
Spend Time Keeping or Regaining Balance	How much does this job require keeping or regaining your balance?
Exposed to Whole Body Vibration	How often does this job require exposure to whole body vibration (e.g., operate a jackhammer)?
Indoors, Environmentally Controlled	How often does this job require working indoors in environmentally controlled conditions?
Wear Specialized Protective or Safety Equipment su	How much does this job require wearing specialized protective or safety equipment such as breathing apparatus, safety harness, full protection suits, or radiation protection?
Deal With Physically Aggressive People	How frequently does this job require the worker to deal with physical aggression of violent individuals?
Exposed to Radiation	How often does this job require exposure to radiation?
Exposed to Disease or Infections	How often does this job require exposure to disease/infections?

Job Zone Component	Job Zone Component Definitions
Title	Job Zone Two: Some Preparation Needed

Overall Experience	Some previous work-related skill, knowledge, or experience may be helpful in these occupations, but usually is not needed. For example, a drywall installer might benefit from experience installing drywall, but an inexperienced person could still learn to be an installer with little difficulty.
Job Training	Employees in these occupations need anywhere from a few months to one year of working with experienced employees.
Job Zone Examples	These occupations often involve using your knowledge and skills to help others. Examples include drywall installers, fire inspectors, flight attendants, pharmacy technicians, salespersons (retail), and tellers.
SVP Range	(4.0 to < 6.0)
Education	These occupations usually require a high school diploma and may require some vocational training or job-related course work. In some cases, an associate's or bachelor's degree could be needed.

Work_Styles	Work_Styles Definitions
Dependability	Job requires being reliable, responsible, and dependable, and fulfilling obligations.
Independence	Job requires developing one's own ways of doing things, guiding oneself with little or no supervision, and depending on oneself to get things done.
Integrity	Job requires being honest and ethical.
Attention to Detail	Job requires being careful about detail and thorough in completing work tasks.
Adaptability/Flexibility	Job requires being open to change (positive or negative) and to considerable variety in the workplace.
Analytical Thinking	Job requires analyzing information and using logic to address work-related issues and problems.
Cooperation	Job requires being pleasant with others on the job and displaying a good-natured, cooperative attitude.
Concern for Others	Job requires being sensitive to others' needs and feelings and being understanding and helpful on the job.
Self Control	Job requires maintaining composure, keeping emotions in check, controlling anger, and avoiding aggressive behavior, even in very difficult situations.
Initiative	Job requires a willingness to take on responsibilities and challenges.
Persistence	Job requires persistence in the face of obstacles.
Stress Tolerance	Job requires accepting criticism and dealing calmly and effectively with high stress situations.
Achievement/Effort	Job requires establishing and maintaining personally challenging achievement goals and exerting effort toward mastering tasks.
Innovation	Job requires creativity and alternative thinking to develop new ideas for and answers to work-related problems.
Leadership	Job requires a willingness to lead, take charge, and offer opinions and direction.
Social Orientation	Job requires preferring to work with others rather than alone, and being personally connected with others on the job.

53-7111.00 - Shuttle Car Operators

Operate diesel or electric-powered shuttle car in underground mine to transport materials from working face to mine cars or conveyor.

Tasks

1) Control conveyors that run the entire length of shuttle cars in order to distribute loads as loading progresses.

2) Clean, fuel, and service equipment, and repair and replace parts as necessary.

3) Observe hand signals, grade stakes, or other markings when operating machines.

4) Monitor loading processes in order to ensure that materials are loaded according to specifications.

5) Guide and stop cars by switching, applying brakes, or placing scotches (wooden wedges) between wheels and rails.

6) Maintain records of materials moved.

7) Read written instructions or confer with supervisors about schedules and materials to be moved.

8) Direct other workers to move stakes, place blocks, position anchors or cables, or move materials.

9) Move mine cars into position for loading and unloading, using pinchbars inserted under car wheels to position cars under loading spouts.

10) Measure, weigh, or verify levels of rock, gravel, or other excavated material in order to prevent equipment overloads.

11) Push or ride cars down slopes, or hook cars to cables and control cable drum brakes, in order to ease cars down inclines.

12) Open and close bottom doors of cars in order to dump contents.

Knowledge	Knowledge Definitions
Mechanical	Knowledge of machines and tools, including their designs, uses, repair, and maintenance.
Law and Government	Knowledge of laws, legal codes, court procedures, precedents, government regulations, executive orders, agency rules, and the democratic political process.
Transportation	Knowledge of principles and methods for moving people or goods by air, rail, sea, or road, including the relative costs and benefits.
Administration and Management	Knowledge of business and management principles involved in strategic planning, resource allocation, human resources modeling, leadership technique, production methods, and coordination of people and resources.
Education and Training	Knowledge of principles and methods for curriculum and training design, teaching and instruction for individuals and groups, and the measurement of training effects.
Chemistry	Knowledge of the chemical composition, structure, and properties of substances and of the chemical processes and transformations that they undergo. This includes uses of chemicals and their interactions, danger signs, production techniques, and disposal methods.
Psychology	Knowledge of human behavior and performance; individual differences in ability, personality, and interests; learning and motivation; psychological research methods; and the assessment and treatment of behavioral and affective disorders.
English Language	Knowledge of the structure and content of the English language including the meaning and spelling of words, rules of composition, and grammar.
Mathematics	Knowledge of arithmetic, algebra, geometry, calculus, statistics, and their applications.
Public Safety and Security	Knowledge of relevant equipment, policies, procedures, and strategies to promote effective local, state, or national security operations for the protection of people, data, property, and institutions.
Personnel and Human Resources	Knowledge of principles and procedures for personnel recruitment, selection, training, compensation and benefits, labor relations and negotiation, and personnel information systems.
Engineering and Technology	Knowledge of the practical application of engineering science and technology. This includes applying principles, techniques, procedures, and equipment to the design and production of various goods and services.
Production and Processing	Knowledge of raw materials, production processes, quality control, costs, and other techniques for maximizing the effective manufacture and distribution of goods.
Building and Construction	Knowledge of materials, methods, and the tools involved in the construction or repair of houses, buildings, or other structures such as highways and roads.
Design	Knowledge of design techniques, tools, and principles involved in production of precision technical plans, blueprints, drawings, and models.
Customer and Personal Service	Knowledge of principles and processes for providing customer and personal services. This includes customer needs assessment, meeting quality standards for services, and evaluation of customer satisfaction.
Physics	Knowledge and prediction of physical principles, laws, their interrelationships, and applications to understanding fluid, material, and atmospheric dynamics, and mechanical, electrical, atomic and sub- atomic structures and processes.
Communications and Media	Knowledge of media production, communication, and dissemination techniques and methods. This includes alternative ways to inform and entertain via written, oral, and visual media.
Medicine and Dentistry	Knowledge of the information and techniques needed to diagnose and treat human injuries, diseases, and deformities. This includes symptoms, treatment alternatives, drug properties and interactions, and preventive health-care measures.
Geography	Knowledge of principles and methods for describing the features of land, sea, and air masses, including their physical characteristics, locations, interrelationships, and distribution of plant, animal, and human life.
Biology	Knowledge of plant and animal organisms, their tissues, cells, functions, interdependencies, and interactions with each other and the environment.
Therapy and Counseling	Knowledge of principles, methods, and procedures for diagnosis, treatment, and rehabilitation of physical and mental dysfunctions, and for career counseling and guidance.
Telecommunications	Knowledge of transmission, broadcasting, switching, control, and operation of telecommunications systems.
Economics and Accounting	Knowledge of economic and accounting principles and practices, the financial markets, banking and the analysis and reporting of financial data.
Philosophy and Theology	Knowledge of different philosophical systems and religions. This includes their basic principles, values, ethics, ways of thinking, customs, practices, and their impact on human culture.
Clerical	Knowledge of administrative and clerical procedures and systems such as word processing, managing files and records, stenography and transcription, designing forms, and other office procedures and terminology.
Sociology and Anthropology	Knowledge of group behavior and dynamics, societal trends and influences, human migrations, ethnicity, cultures and their history and origins.
Sales and Marketing	Knowledge of principles and methods for showing, promoting, and selling products or services. This includes marketing strategy and tactics, product demonstration, sales techniques, and sales control systems.
Computers and Electronics	Knowledge of circuit boards, processors, chips, electronic equipment, and computer hardware and software, including applications and programming.
History and Archeology	Knowledge of historical events and their causes, indicators, and effects on civilizations and cultures.
Fine Arts	Knowledge of the theory and techniques required to compose, produce, and perform works of music, dance, visual arts, drama, and sculpture.
Foreign Language	Knowledge of the structure and content of a foreign (non-English) language including the meaning and spelling of words, rules of composition and grammar, and pronunciation.
Food Production	Knowledge of techniques and equipment for planting, growing, and harvesting food products (both plant and animal) for consumption, including storage/handling techniques.

Skills	Skills Definitions
Active Listening	Giving full attention to what other people are saying, taking time to understand the points being made, asking questions as appropriate, and not interrupting at inappropriate times.
Equipment Maintenance	Performing routine maintenance on equipment and determining when and what kind of maintenance is needed.
Operation and Control	Controlling operations of equipment or systems.
Coordination	Adjusting actions in relation to others' actions.
Speaking	Talking to others to convey information effectively.
Operation Monitoring	Watching gauges, dials, or other indicators to make sure a machine is working properly.
Learning Strategies	Selecting and using training/instructional methods and procedures appropriate for the situation when learning or teaching new things.
Active Learning	Understanding the implications of new information for both current and future problem-solving and decision-making.
Equipment Selection	Determining the kind of tools and equipment needed to do a job.
Critical Thinking	Using logic and reasoning to identify the strengths and weaknesses of alternative solutions, conclusions or approaches to problems.
Social Perceptiveness	Being aware of others' reactions and understanding why they react as they do.
Instructing	Teaching others how to do something.
Repairing	Repairing machines or systems using the needed tools.
Troubleshooting	Determining causes of operating errors and deciding what to do about it.

Judgment and Decision Making	Considering the relative costs and benefits of potential actions to choose the most appropriate one.
Time Management	Managing one's own time and the time of others.
Monitoring	Monitoring/Assessing performance of yourself, other individuals, or organizations to make improvements or take corrective action.
Installation	Installing equipment, machines, wiring, or programs to meet specifications.
Service Orientation	Actively looking for ways to help people.
Quality Control Analysis	Conducting tests and inspections of products, services, or processes to evaluate quality or performance.
Systems Analysis	Determining how a system should work and how changes in conditions, operations, and the environment will affect outcomes.
Negotiation	Bringing others together and trying to reconcile differences.
Systems Evaluation	Identifying measures or indicators of system performance and the actions needed to improve or correct performance, relative to the goals of the system.
Complex Problem Solving	Identifying complex problems and reviewing related information to develop and evaluate options and implement solutions.
Reading Comprehension	Understanding written sentences and paragraphs in work related documents.
Management of Material Resources	Obtaining and seeing to the appropriate use of equipment, facilities, and materials needed to do certain work.
Technology Design	Generating or adapting equipment and technology to serve user needs.
Persuasion	Persuading others to change their minds or behavior.
Operations Analysis	Analyzing needs and product requirements to create a design.
Science	Using scientific rules and methods to solve problems.
Management of Personnel Resources	Motivating, developing, and directing people as they work, identifying the best people for the job.
Writing	Communicating effectively in writing as appropriate for the needs of the audience.
Management of Financial Resources	Determining how money will be spent to get the work done, and accounting for these expenditures.
Mathematics	Using mathematics to solve problems.
Programming	Writing computer programs for various purposes.

Ability	Ability Definitions
Control Precision	The ability to quickly and repeatedly adjust the controls of a machine or a vehicle to exact positions.
Manual Dexterity	The ability to quickly move your hand, your hand together with your arm, or your two hands to grasp, manipulate, or assemble objects.
Multilimb Coordination	The ability to coordinate two or more limbs (for example, two arms, two legs, or one leg and one arm) while sitting, standing, or lying down. It does not involve performing the activities while the whole body is in motion.
Near Vision	The ability to see details at close range (within a few feet of the observer).
Reaction Time	The ability to quickly respond (with the hand, finger, or foot) to a signal (sound, light, picture) when it appears.
Depth Perception	The ability to judge which of several objects is closer or farther away from you, or to judge the distance between you and an object.
Rate Control	The ability to time your movements or the movement of a piece of equipment in anticipation of changes in the speed and/or direction of a moving object or scene.
Problem Sensitivity	The ability to tell when something is wrong or is likely to go wrong. It does not involve solving the problem, only recognizing there is a problem.
Oral Comprehension	The ability to listen to and understand information and ideas presented through spoken words and sentences.
Oral Expression	The ability to communicate information and ideas in speaking so others will understand.
Far Vision	The ability to see details at a distance.
Arm-Hand Steadiness	The ability to keep your hand and arm steady while moving your arm or while holding your arm and hand in one position.
Response Orientation	The ability to choose quickly between two or more movements in response to two or more different signals (lights, sounds, pictures). It includes the speed with which the correct response is started with the hand, foot, or other body part.
Static Strength	The ability to exert maximum muscle force to lift, push, pull, or carry objects.
Extent Flexibility	The ability to bend, stretch, twist, or reach with your body, arms, and/or legs.

Deductive Reasoning	The ability to apply general rules to specific problems to produce answers that make sense.
Speech Clarity	The ability to speak clearly so others can understand you.
Selective Attention	The ability to concentrate on a task over a period of time without being distracted.
Speech Recognition	The ability to identify and understand the speech of another person.
Spatial Orientation	The ability to know your location in relation to the environment or to know where other objects are in relation to you.
Visualization	The ability to imagine how something will look after it is moved around or when its parts are moved or rearranged.
Time Sharing	The ability to shift back and forth between two or more activities or sources of information (such as speech, sounds, touch, or other sources).
Inductive Reasoning	The ability to combine pieces of information to form general rules or conclusions (includes finding a relationship among seemingly unrelated events).
Information Ordering	The ability to arrange things or actions in a certain order or pattern according to a specific rule or set of rules (e.g., patterns of numbers, letters, words, pictures, mathematical operations).
Written Comprehension	The ability to read and understand information and ideas presented in writing.
Perceptual Speed	The ability to quickly and accurately compare similarities and differences among sets of letters, numbers, objects, pictures, or patterns. The things to be compared may be presented at the same time or one after the other. This ability also includes comparing a presented object with a remembered object.
Gross Body Coordination	The ability to coordinate the movement of your arms, legs, and torso together when the whole body is in motion.
Written Expression	The ability to communicate information and ideas in writing so others will understand.
Finger Dexterity	The ability to make precisely coordinated movements of the fingers of one or both hands to grasp, manipulate, or assemble very small objects.
Trunk Strength	The ability to use your abdominal and lower back muscles to support part of the body repeatedly or continuously over time without 'giving out' or fatiguing.
Auditory Attention	The ability to focus on a single source of sound in the presence of other distracting sounds.
Glare Sensitivity	The ability to see objects in the presence of glare or bright lighting.
Stamina	The ability to exert yourself physically over long periods of time without getting winded or out of breath.
Dynamic Strength	The ability to exert muscle force repeatedly or continuously over time. This involves muscular endurance and resistance to muscle fatigue.
Category Flexibility	The ability to generate or use different sets of rules for combining or grouping things in different ways.
Night Vision	The ability to see under low light conditions.
Hearing Sensitivity	The ability to detect or tell the differences between sounds that vary in pitch and loudness.
Originality	The ability to come up with unusual or clever ideas about a given topic or situation, or to develop creative ways to solve a problem.
Speed of Limb Movement	The ability to quickly move the arms and legs.
Peripheral Vision	The ability to see objects or movement of objects to one's side when the eyes are looking ahead.
Wrist-Finger Speed	The ability to make fast, simple, repeated movements of the fingers, hands, and wrists.
Visual Color Discrimination	The ability to match or detect differences between colors, including shades of color and brightness.
Mathematical Reasoning	The ability to choose the right mathematical methods or formulas to solve a problem.
Fluency of Ideas	The ability to come up with a number of ideas about a topic (the number of ideas is important, not their quality, correctness, or creativity).
Flexibility of Closure	The ability to identify or detect a known pattern (a figure, object, word, or sound) that is hidden in other distracting material.
Gross Body Equilibrium	The ability to keep or regain your body balance or stay upright when in an unstable position.
Memorization	The ability to remember information such as words, numbers, pictures, and procedures.
Number Facility	The ability to add, subtract, multiply, or divide quickly and correctly.
Speed of Closure	The ability to quickly make sense of, combine, and organize information into meaningful patterns.

Explosive Strength	The ability to use short bursts of muscle force to propel oneself (as in jumping or sprinting), or to throw an object.
Dynamic Flexibility	The ability to quickly and repeatedly bend, stretch, twist, or reach out with your body, arms, and/or legs.
Sound Localization	The ability to tell the direction from which a sound originated.

Work_Activity	Work_Activity Definitions
Controlling Machines and Processes	Using either control mechanisms or direct physical activity to operate machines or processes (not including computers or vehicles).
Operating Vehicles, Mechanized Devices, or Equipme	Running, maneuvering, navigating, or driving vehicles or mechanized equipment, such as forklifts, passenger vehicles, aircraft, or water craft.
Inspecting Equipment, Structures, or Material	Inspecting equipment, structures, or materials to identify the cause of errors or other problems or defects.
Monitor Processes, Materials, or Surroundings	Monitoring and reviewing information from materials, events, or the environment, to detect or assess problems.
Evaluating Information to Determine Compliance wit	Using relevant information and individual judgment to determine whether events or processes comply with laws, regulations, or standards.
Communicating with Supervisors, Peers, or Subordin	Providing information to supervisors, co-workers, and subordinates by telephone, in written form, e-mail, or in person.
Identifying Objects, Actions, and Events	Identifying information by categorizing, estimating, recognizing differences or similarities, and detecting changes in circumstances or events.
Handling and Moving Objects	Using hands and arms in handling, installing, positioning, and moving materials, and manipulating things.
Repairing and Maintaining Mechanical Equipment	Servicing, repairing, adjusting, and testing machines, devices, moving parts, and equipment that operate primarily on the basis of mechanical (not electronic) principles.
Performing General Physical Activities	Performing physical activities that require considerable use of your arms and legs and moving your whole body, such as climbing, lifting, balancing, walking, stooping, and handling of materials.
Establishing and Maintaining Interpersonal Relatio	Developing constructive and cooperative working relationships with others, and maintaining them over time.
Making Decisions and Solving Problems	Analyzing information and evaluating results to choose the best solution and solve problems.
Getting Information	Observing, receiving, and otherwise obtaining information from all relevant sources.
Assisting and Caring for Others	Providing personal assistance, medical attention, emotional support, or other personal care to others such as coworkers, customers, or patients.
Developing and Building Teams	Encouraging and building mutual trust, respect, and cooperation among team members.
Interpreting the Meaning of Information for Others	Translating or explaining what information means and how it can be used.
Thinking Creatively	Developing, designing, or creating new applications, ideas, relationships, systems, or products, including artistic contributions.
Training and Teaching Others	Identifying the educational needs of others, developing formal educational or training programs or classes, and teaching or instructing others.
Organizing, Planning, and Prioritizing Work	Developing specific goals and plans to prioritize, organize, and accomplish your work.
Updating and Using Relevant Knowledge	Keeping up-to-date technically and applying new knowledge to your job.
Coordinating the Work and Activities of Others	Getting members of a group to work together to accomplish tasks.
Estimating the Quantifiable Characteristics of Pro	Estimating sizes, distances, and quantities; or determining time, costs, resources, or materials needed to perform a work activity.
Judging the Qualities of Things, Services, or Peop	Assessing the value, importance, or quality of things or people.
Repairing and Maintaining Electronic Equipment	Servicing, repairing, calibrating, regulating, fine-tuning, or testing machines, devices, and equipment that operate primarily on the basis of electrical or electronic (not mechanical) principles.
Developing Objectives and Strategies	Establishing long-range objectives and specifying the strategies and actions to achieve them.
Scheduling Work and Activities	Scheduling events, programs, and activities, as well as the work of others.
Guiding, Directing, and Motivating Subordinates	Providing guidance and direction to subordinates, including setting performance standards and monitoring performance.

Processing Information	Compiling, coding, categorizing, calculating, tabulating, auditing, or verifying information or data.
Coaching and Developing Others	Identifying the developmental needs of others and coaching, mentoring, or otherwise helping others to improve their knowledge or skills.
Analyzing Data or Information	Identifying the underlying principles, reasons, or facts of information by breaking down information or data into separate parts.
Resolving Conflicts and Negotiating with Others	Handling complaints, settling disputes, and resolving grievances and conflicts, or otherwise negotiating with others.
Drafting, Laying Out, and Specifying Technical Dev	Providing documentation, detailed instructions, drawings, or specifications to tell others about how devices, parts, equipment, or structures are to be fabricated, constructed, assembled, modified, maintained, or used.
Provide Consultation and Advice to Others	Providing guidance and expert advice to management or other groups on technical, systems-, or process-related topics.
Communicating with Persons Outside Organization	Communicating with people outside the organization, representing the organization to customers, the public, government, and other external sources. This information can be exchanged in person, in writing, or by telephone or e-mail.
Documenting/Recording Information	Entering, transcribing, recording, storing, or maintaining information in written or electronic/magnetic form.
Monitoring and Controlling Resources	Monitoring and controlling resources and overseeing the spending of money.
Selling or Influencing Others	Convincing others to buy merchandise/goods or to otherwise change their minds or actions.
Performing for or Working Directly with the Public	Performing for people or dealing directly with the public. This includes serving customers in restaurants and stores, and receiving clients or guests.
Staffing Organizational Units	Recruiting, interviewing, selecting, hiring, and promoting employees in an organization.
Performing Administrative Activities	Performing day-to-day administrative tasks such as maintaining information files and processing paperwork.
Interacting With Computers	Using computers and computer systems (including hardware and software) to program, write software, set up functions, enter data, or process information.

Work_Context	Work_Context Definitions
Exposed to Contaminants	How often does this job require working exposed to contaminants (such as pollutants, gases, dust or odors)?
Wear Common Protective or Safety Equipment such as	How much does this job require wearing common protective or safety equipment such as safety shoes, glasses, gloves, hard hats or live jackets?
Sounds, Noise Levels Are Distracting or Uncomforta	How much does this job require working exposed to sounds and noise levels that are distracting or uncomfortable?
Spend Time Using Your Hands to Handle, Control, or	How much does this job require using your hands to handle, control, or feel objects, tools or controls?
Spend Time Making Repetitive Motions	How much does this job require making repetitive motions?
Exposed to Hazardous Equipment	How often does this job require exposure to hazardous equipment?
Cramped Work Space, Awkward Positions	How often does this job require working in cramped work spaces that requires getting into awkward positions?
Spend Time Sitting	How much does this job require sitting?
Face-to-Face Discussions	How often do you have to have face-to-face discussions with individuals or teams in this job?
Exposed to Whole Body Vibration	How often does this job require exposure to whole body vibration (e.g., operate a jackhammer)?
Consequence of Error	How serious would the result usually be if the worker made a mistake that was not readily correctable?
Exposed to Hazardous Conditions	How often does this job require exposure to hazardous conditions?
Work With Work Group or Team	How important is it to work with others in a group or team in this job?
Pace Determined by Speed of Equipment	How important is it to this job that the pace is determined by the speed of equipment or machinery? (This does not refer to keeping busy at all times on this job.)
Responsible for Others' Health and Safety	How much responsibility is there for the health and safety of others in this job?
Frequency of Decision Making	How frequently is the worker required to make decisions that affect other people, the financial resources, and/or the image and reputation of the organization?
In an Open Vehicle or Equipment	How often does this job require working in an open vehicle or equipment (e.g., tractor)?
Extremely Bright or Inadequate Lighting	How often does this job require working in extremely bright or inadequate lighting conditions?

Impact of Decisions on Co-workers or Company Resul	How do the decisions an employee makes impact the results of co-workers, clients or the company?
Contact With Others	How much does this job require the worker to be in contact with others (face-to-face, by telephone, or otherwise) in order to perform it?
Time Pressure	How often does this job require the worker to meet strict deadlines?
Importance of Being Exact or Accurate	How important is being very exact or highly accurate in performing this job?
Freedom to Make Decisions	How much decision making freedom, without supervision, does the job offer?
Coordinate or Lead Others	How important is it to coordinate or lead others in accomplishing work activities in this job?
Deal With Unpleasant or Angry People	How frequently does the worker have to deal with unpleasant, angry, or discourteous individuals as part of the job requirements?
Spend Time Bending or Twisting the Body	How much does this job require bending or twisting your body?
Physical Proximity	To what extent does this job require the worker to perform job tasks in close physical proximity to other people?
Level of Competition	To what extent does this job require the worker to compete or to be aware of competitive pressures?
Exposed to Minor Burns, Cuts, Bites, or Stings	How often does this job require exposure to minor burns, cuts, bites, or stings?
Structured versus Unstructured Work	To what extent is this job structured for the worker, rather than allowing the worker to determine tasks, priorities, and goals?
Responsibility for Outcomes and Results	How responsible is the worker for work outcomes and results of other workers?
Indoors, Not Environmentally Controlled	How often does this job require working indoors in non-controlled environmental conditions (e.g., warehouse without heat)?
Degree of Automation	How automated is the job?
Importance of Repeating Same Tasks	How important is repeating the same physical activities (e.g., key entry) or mental activities (e.g., checking entries in a ledger) over and over, without stopping, to performing this job?
Frequency of Conflict Situations	How often are there conflict situations the employee has to face in this job?
Spend Time Standing	How much does this job require standing?
Spend Time Walking and Running	How much does this job require walking and running?
Wear Specialized Protective or Safety Equipment su	How much does this job require wearing specialized protective or safety equipment such as breathing apparatus, safety harness, full protection suits, or radiation protection?
Spend Time Kneeling, Crouching, Stooping, or Crawl	How much does this job require kneeling, crouching, stooping or crawling?
In an Enclosed Vehicle or Equipment	How often does this job require working in a closed vehicle or equipment (e.g., car)?
Very Hot or Cold Temperatures	How often does this job require working in very hot (above 90 F degrees) or very cold (below 32 F degrees) temperatures?
Telephone	How often do you have telephone conversations in this job?
Spend Time Keeping or Regaining Balance	How much does this job require keeping or regaining your balance?
Exposed to High Places	How often does this job require exposure to high places?
Deal With Physically Aggressive People	How frequently does this job require the worker to deal with physical aggression of violent individuals?
Letters and Memos	How often does the job require written letters and memos?
Public Speaking	How often do you have to perform public speaking in this job?
Exposed to Disease or Infections	How often does this job require exposure to disease/infections?
Indoors, Environmentally Controlled	How often does this job require working indoors in environmentally controlled conditions?
Outdoors, Under Cover	How often does this job require working outdoors, under cover (e.g., structure with roof but no walls)?
Spend Time Climbing Ladders, Scaffolds, or Poles	How much does this job require climbing ladders, scaffolds, or poles?
Outdoors, Exposed to Weather	How often does this job require working outdoors, exposed to all weather conditions?
Deal With External Customers	How important is it to work with external customers or the public in this job?
Exposed to Radiation	How often does this job require exposure to radiation?
Electronic Mail	How often do you use electronic mail in this job?

Job Zone Component	Job Zone Component Definitions
Title	Job Zone Two: Some Preparation Needed
Overall Experience	Some previous work-related skill, knowledge, or experience may be helpful in these occupations, but usually is not needed. For example, a drywall installer might benefit from experience installing drywall, but an inexperienced person could still learn to be an installer with little difficulty.
Job Training	Employees in these occupations need anywhere from a few months to one year of working with experienced employees.
Job Zone Examples	These occupations often involve using your knowledge and skills to help others. Examples include drywall installers, fire inspectors, flight attendants, pharmacy technicians, salespersons (retail), and tellers.
SVP Range	(4.0 to < 6.0)
Education	These occupations usually require a high school diploma and may require some vocational training or job-related course work. In some cases, an associate's or bachelor's degree could be needed.

Work_Styles	Work_Styles Definitions
Dependability	Job requires being reliable, responsible, and dependable, and fulfilling obligations.
Cooperation	Job requires being pleasant with others on the job and displaying a good-natured, cooperative attitude.
Self Control	Job requires maintaining composure, keeping emotions in check, controlling anger, and avoiding aggressive behavior, even in very difficult situations.
Stress Tolerance	Job requires accepting criticism and dealing calmly and effectively with high stress situations.
Concern for Others	Job requires being sensitive to others' needs and feelings and being understanding and helpful on the job.
Persistence	Job requires persistence in the face of obstacles.
Initiative	Job requires a willingness to take on responsibilities and challenges.
Achievement/Effort	Job requires establishing and maintaining personally challenging achievement goals and exerting effort toward mastering tasks.
Independence	Job requires developing one's own ways of doing things, guiding oneself with little or no supervision, and depending on oneself to get things done.
Integrity	Job requires being honest and ethical.
Adaptability/Flexibility	Job requires being open to change (positive or negative) and to considerable variety in the workplace.
Social Orientation	Job requires preferring to work with others rather than alone, and being personally connected with others on the job.
Attention to Detail	Job requires being careful about detail and thorough in completing work tasks.
Innovation	Job requires creativity and alternative thinking to develop new ideas for and answers to work-related problems.
Analytical Thinking	Job requires analyzing information and using logic to address work-related issues and problems.
Leadership	Job requires a willingness to lead, take charge, and offer opinions and direction.

53-7121.00 - Tank Car, Truck, and Ship Loaders

Load and unload chemicals and bulk solids, such as coal, sand, and grain into or from tank cars, trucks, or ships using material moving equipment. May perform a variety of other tasks relating to shipment of products. May gauge or sample shipping tanks and test them for leaks.

Tasks

1) Operate conveyors and equipment to transfer grain or other materials from transportation vehicles.

2) Observe positions of cars passing loading spouts, and swing spouts into the correct positions at the appropriate times.

3) Lower gauge rods into tanks or read meters, in order to verify contents, temperatures, and volumes of liquid loads.

4) Record operating data such as products and quantities pumped, gauge readings, and operating times, manually or using computers.

5) Check conditions and weights of vessels to ensure cleanliness and compliance with loading procedures.

6) Verify tank car, barge, or truck load numbers to ensure car placement accuracy based on written or verbal instructions.

7) Monitor product movement to and from storage tanks, coordinating activities with other workers to ensure constant product flow.

8) Connect ground cables to carry off static electricity when unloading tanker cars.

9) Remove and replace tank car dome caps, or direct other workers in their removal and replacement.

10) Seal outlet valves on tank cars, barges, and trucks.

11) Unload cars containing liquids by connecting hoses to outlet plugs and pumping compressed air into cars to force liquids into storage tanks.

12) Perform general warehouse activities, such as opening containers and crates, filling warehouse orders, assisting in taking inventory, and weighing and checking materials.

13) Operate ship loading and unloading equipment, conveyors, hoists, and other specialized material handling equipment such as railroad tank car unloading equipment.

14) Clean interiors of tank cars or tank trucks, using mechanical spray nozzles.

15) Operate industrial trucks, tractors, loaders and other equipment to transport materials to and from transportation vehicles and loading docks, and to store and retrieve materials in warehouses.

16) Start pumps and adjust valves or cables in order to regulate the flow of products to vessels, utilizing knowledge of loading procedures.

17) Copy and attach load specifications to loaded tanks.

18) Test vessels for leaks, damage, and defects, and repair or replace defective parts as necessary.

Table II

O*NET™—SOC Proposed 8.0 Definitions by Code Number

Caveat: **These Proposed 8.0 Definitions are *not* effective yet and subject to changes and additions, but are presented in advance for informational purposes only.**

11-9012.00 - Farmers and Ranchers

On an ownership or rental basis, operate farms, ranches, greenhouses, nurseries, timber tracts, or other agricultural production establishments which produce crops, horticultural specialties, livestock, poultry, finfish, shellfish, or animal specialties. May plant, cultivate, harvest, perform post-harvest activities, and market crops and livestock; may hire, train, and supervise farm workers or supervise a farm labor contractor; may prepare cost, production, and other records. May maintain and operate machinery and perform physical work.

Tasks

11-9012.00 - Farmers and Ranchers

On an ownership or rental basis, operate farms, ranches, greenhouses, nurseries, timber tracts, or other agricultural production establishments which produce crops, horticultural specialties, livestock, poultry, finfish, shellfish, or animal specialties. May plant, cultivate, harvest, perform post-harvest activities, and market crops and livestock; may hire, train, and supervise farm workers or supervise a farm labor contractor; may prepare cost, production, and other records. May maintain and operate machinery and perform physical work.

Tasks

1) Clean and disinfect buildings and yards, and remove manure.

2) Perform crop production duties such as planning, tilling, planting, fertilizing, cultivating, spraying, and harvesting.

3) Plan crop activities based on factors such as crop maturity and weather conditions.

4) Purchase and store livestock feed.

5) Remove lower quality or older animals from herds and purchase other livestock to replace culled animals.

6) Transport grain to silos for storage, and burn or bale any straw that is left behind.

7) Keep hens in order to produce table eggs for eating or fertile eggs for breeding.

8) Assemble, position, and secure structures such as trellises, beehives, or fences, using hand tools.

9) Clean and sanitize milking equipment, storage tanks, collection cups, and cows' udders, or ensure that procedures are followed to maintain sanitary conditions for handling of milk.

10) Buy or sell futures contracts, or price products in advance of future sales so that risk is limited and/or profit is increased.

11) Grow out-of-season or early crops in greenhouses or cold-frame beds, or bud and graft plant stock.

12) Assist in animal births, and care for newborn livestock.

13) Operate dairy farms that produce bulk milk.

14) Select animals for market, and provide transportation of livestock to market.

15) Maintain pastures or grazing lands to ensure that animals have enough feed, employing pasture-conservation measures such as arranging rotational grazing.

16) Select and purchase supplies and equipment such as seed, fertilizers, and farm machinery.

17) Maintain colonies of bees to produce honey and hive byproducts, pollinate crops, and/or produce queens and bees for sale.

18) Maintain financial, tax, production, and employee records.

19) Maintain facilities such as fencing, water supplies, and outdoor housing and wind shelters.

20) Lubricate, adjust, and make minor repairs to farm equipment, using oilcans, grease guns, and hand tools.

21) Hire, train, and direct workers engaged in planting, cultivating, irrigating, harvesting, and marketing crops, and in raising livestock.

22) Demonstrate and explain farm work techniques and safety regulations to workers.

23) Herd cattle, using horses or all-terrain vehicles.

24) Monitor crops as they grow in order to ensure that they are growing properly and are free from diseases and contaminants.

25) Negotiate and arrange with buyers for the sale, storage, and shipment of crops.

26) Milk cows, using milking machinery.

27) Manage and oversee the day-to-day running of farms raising poultry or pigs for the production of meat and breeding stock.

28) Install and shift irrigation systems to irrigate fields evenly or according to crop need.

29) Harvest crops, and collect specialty products such as royal jelly, wax, pollen, and honey from bee colonies.

30) Evaluate product marketing alternatives, then promote and market farm products, acting as the sales agent for livestock and crops.

31) Determine types and quantities of crops or livestock to be raised, according to factors such as market conditions, federal program availability, and soil conditions.

32) Destroy diseased or superfluous crops.

33) Control the spread of disease and parasites in herds, by using vaccination and medication, and by separating sick animals.

34) Clean, grade, and package crops for marketing.

35) Obtain financing from lenders to purchase machinery, fertilizer, livestock, and feed.

11-9031.00 - Education Administrators, Preschool and Child Care Center/Program

Plan, direct, or coordinate the academic and nonacademic activities of preschool and child care centers or programs.

Tasks

1) Prepare and maintain attendance, activity, planning, accounting, or personnel reports and records for officials and agencies, or direct preparation and maintenance activities.

2) Recruit, hire, train, and evaluate primary and supplemental staff, and recommend personnel actions for programs and services.

3) Plan, direct, and monitor instructional methods and content of educational, vocational, or student activity programs.

4) Monitor students' progress, and provide students and teachers with assistance in resolving any problems.

5) Teach classes or courses, and/or provide direct care to children.

6) Determine the scope of educational program offerings, and prepare drafts of program schedules and descriptions, in order to estimate staffing and facility requirements.

7) Direct and coordinate activities of teachers or administrators at daycare centers, schools, public agencies, and/or institutions.

8) Determine allocations of funds for staff, supplies, materials, and equipment, and authorize purchases.

9) Review and interpret government codes, and develop procedures to meet codes and to ensure facility safety, security, and maintenance.

10) Review and evaluate new and current programs to determine their efficiency, effectiveness, and compliance with state, local, and federal regulations; recommend any necessary modifications.

11) Inform businesses, community groups, and governmental agencies about educational needs, available programs, and program policies.

12) Prepare and submit budget requests or grant proposals to solicit program funding.

13) Collect and analyze survey data, regulatory information, and demographic and employment trends, in order to forecast enrollment patterns and the need for curriculum changes.

14) Organize and direct committees of specialists, volunteers, and staff to provide technical and advisory assistance for programs.

15) Write articles, manuals, and other publications, and assist in the distribution of promotional literature about programs and facilities.

16) Confer with parents and staff to discuss educational activities and policies, and students' behavioral or learning problems.

Knowledge	Knowledge Definitions
Personnel and Human Resources	Knowledge of principles and procedures for personnel recruitment, selection, training, compensation and benefits, labor relations and negotiation, and personnel information systems.
Customer and Personal Service	Knowledge of principles and processes for providing customer and personal services. This includes customer needs assessment, meeting quality standards for services, and evaluation of customer satisfaction.

Administration and Management	Knowledge of business and management principles involved in strategic planning, resource allocation, human resources modeling, leadership technique, production methods, and coordination of people and resources.
Education and Training	Knowledge of principles and methods for curriculum and training design, teaching and instruction for individuals and groups, and the measurement of training effects.
English Language	Knowledge of the structure and content of the English language including the meaning and spelling of words, rules of composition, and grammar.
Clerical	Knowledge of administrative and clerical procedures and systems such as word processing, managing files and records, stenography and transcription, designing forms, and other office procedures and terminology.
Psychology	Knowledge of human behavior and performance; individual differences in ability, personality, and interests; learning and motivation; psychological research methods; and the assessment and treatment of behavioral and affective disorders.
Public Safety and Security	Knowledge of relevant equipment, policies, procedures, and strategies to promote effective local, state, or national security operations for the protection of people, data, property, and institutions.
Economics and Accounting	Knowledge of economic and accounting principles and practices, the financial markets, banking and the analysis and reporting of financial data.
Law and Government	Knowledge of laws, legal codes, court procedures, precedents, government regulations, executive orders, agency rules, and the democratic political process.
Sociology and Anthropology	Knowledge of group behavior and dynamics, societal trends and influences, human migrations, ethnicity, cultures and their history and origins.
Computers and Electronics	Knowledge of circuit boards, processors, chips, electronic equipment, and computer hardware and software, including applications and programming.
Sales and Marketing	Knowledge of principles and methods for showing, promoting, and selling products or services. This includes marketing strategy and tactics, product demonstration, sales techniques, and sales control systems.
Communications and Media	Knowledge of media production, communication, and dissemination techniques and methods. This includes alternative ways to inform and entertain via written, oral, and visual media.
Therapy and Counseling	Knowledge of principles, methods, and procedures for diagnosis, treatment, and rehabilitation of physical and mental dysfunctions, and for career counseling and guidance.
Philosophy and Theology	Knowledge of different philosophical systems and religions. This includes their basic principles, values, ethics, ways of thinking, customs, practices, and their impact on human culture.
Medicine and Dentistry	Knowledge of the information and techniques needed to diagnose and treat human injuries, diseases, and deformities. This includes symptoms, treatment alternatives, drug properties and interactions, and preventive health-care measures.
Mathematics	Knowledge of arithmetic, algebra, geometry, calculus, statistics, and their applications.
Fine Arts	Knowledge of the theory and techniques required to compose, produce, and perform works of music, dance, visual arts, drama, and sculpture.
History and Archeology	Knowledge of historical events and their causes, indicators, and effects on civilizations and cultures.
Production and Processing	Knowledge of raw materials, production processes, quality control, costs, and other techniques for maximizing the effective manufacture and distribution of goods.
Foreign Language	Knowledge of the structure and content of a foreign (non-English) language including the meaning and spelling of words, rules of composition and grammar, and pronunciation.
Transportation	Knowledge of principles and methods for moving people or goods by air, rail, sea, or road, including the relative costs and benefits.
Telecommunications	Knowledge of transmission, broadcasting, switching, control, and operation of telecommunications systems.
Geography	Knowledge of principles and methods for describing the features of land, sea, and air masses, including their physical characteristics, locations, interrelationships, and distribution of plant, animal, and human life.
Mechanical	Knowledge of machines and tools, including their designs, uses, repair, and maintenance.
Chemistry	Knowledge of the chemical composition, structure, and properties of substances and of the chemical processes and transformations that they undergo. This includes uses of chemicals and their interactions, danger signs, production techniques, and disposal methods.
Engineering and Technology	Knowledge of the practical application of engineering science and technology. This includes applying principles, techniques, procedures, and equipment to the design and production of various goods and services.
Building and Construction	Knowledge of materials, methods, and the tools involved in the construction or repair of houses, buildings, or other structures such as highways and roads.
Food Production	Knowledge of techniques and equipment for planting, growing, and harvesting food products (both plant and animal) for consumption, including storage/handling techniques.
Biology	Knowledge of plant and animal organisms, their tissues, cells, functions, interdependencies, and interactions with each other and the environment.
Physics	Knowledge and prediction of physical principles, laws, their interrelationships, and applications to understanding fluid, material, and atmospheric dynamics, and mechanical, electrical, atomic and sub-atomic structures and processes.
Design	Knowledge of design techniques, tools, and principles involved in production of precision technical plans, blueprints, drawings, and models.

Skills	Skills Definitions
Social Perceptiveness	Being aware of others' reactions and understanding why they react as they do.
Active Listening	Giving full attention to what other people are saying, taking time to understand the points being made, asking questions as appropriate, and not interrupting at inappropriate times.
Speaking	Talking to others to convey information effectively.
Time Management	Managing one's own time and the time of others.
Monitoring	Monitoring/Assessing performance of yourself, other individuals, or organizations to make improvements or take corrective action.
Reading Comprehension	Understanding written sentences and paragraphs in work related documents.
Management of Personnel Resources	Motivating, developing, and directing people as they work, identifying the best people for the job.
Judgment and Decision Making	Considering the relative costs and benefits of potential actions to choose the most appropriate one.
Instructing	Teaching others how to do something.
Learning Strategies	Selecting and using training/instructional methods and procedures appropriate for the situation when learning or teaching new things.
Critical Thinking	Using logic and reasoning to identify the strengths and weaknesses of alternative solutions, conclusions or approaches to problems.
Active Learning	Understanding the implications of new information for both current and future problem-solving and decision-making.
Writing	Communicating effectively in writing as appropriate for the needs of the audience.
Service Orientation	Actively looking for ways to help people.
Management of Financial Resources	Determining how money will be spent to get the work done, and accounting for these expenditures.
Coordination	Adjusting actions in relation to others' actions.
Persuasion	Persuading others to change their minds or behavior.
Negotiation	Bringing others together and trying to reconcile differences.
Management of Material Resources	Obtaining and seeing to the appropriate use of equipment, facilities, and materials needed to do certain work.
Complex Problem Solving	Identifying complex problems and reviewing related information to develop and evaluate options and implement solutions.
Mathematics	Using mathematics to solve problems.
Equipment Selection	Determining the kind of tools and equipment needed to do a job.
Troubleshooting	Determining causes of operating errors and deciding what to do about it.
Systems Evaluation	Identifying measures or indicators of system performance and the actions needed to improve or correct performance, relative to the goals of the system.
Operations Analysis	Analyzing needs and product requirements to create a design.
Quality Control Analysis	Conducting tests and inspections of products, services, or processes to evaluate quality or performance.
Equipment Maintenance	Performing routine maintenance on equipment and determining when and what kind of maintenance is needed.

Technology Design	Generating or adapting equipment and technology to serve user needs.
Systems Analysis	Determining how a system should work and how changes in conditions, operations, and the environment will affect outcomes.
Repairing	Repairing machines or systems using the needed tools.
Installation	Installing equipment, machines, wiring, or programs to meet specifications.
Operation and Control	Controlling operations of equipment or systems.
Science	Using scientific rules and methods to solve problems.
Operation Monitoring	Watching gauges, dials, or other indicators to make sure a machine is working properly.
Programming	Writing computer programs for various purposes.

Ability	Ability Definitions
Oral Expression	The ability to communicate information and ideas in speaking so others will understand.
Problem Sensitivity	The ability to tell when something is wrong or is likely to go wrong. It does not involve solving the problem, only recognizing there is a problem.
Oral Comprehension	The ability to listen to and understand information and ideas presented through spoken words and sentences.
Speech Clarity	The ability to speak clearly so others can understand you.
Speech Recognition	The ability to identify and understand the speech of another person.
Inductive Reasoning	The ability to combine pieces of information to form general rules or conclusions (includes finding a relationship among seemingly unrelated events).
Written Comprehension	The ability to read and understand information and ideas presented in writing.
Written Expression	The ability to communicate information and ideas in writing so others will understand.
Originality	The ability to come up with unusual or clever ideas about a given topic or situation, or to develop creative ways to solve a problem.
Deductive Reasoning	The ability to apply general rules to specific problems to produce answers that make sense.
Fluency of Ideas	The ability to come up with a number of ideas about a topic (the number of ideas is important, not their quality, correctness, or creativity).
Near Vision	The ability to see details at close range (within a few feet of the observer).
Information Ordering	The ability to arrange things or actions in a certain order or pattern according to a specific rule or set of rules (e.g., patterns of numbers, letters, words, pictures, mathematical operations).
Selective Attention	The ability to concentrate on a task over a period of time without being distracted.
Category Flexibility	The ability to generate or use different sets of rules for combining or grouping things in different ways.
Far Vision	The ability to see details at a distance.
Speed of Closure	The ability to quickly make sense of, combine, and organize information into meaningful patterns.
Time Sharing	The ability to shift back and forth between two or more activities or sources of information (such as speech, sounds, touch, or other sources).
Flexibility of Closure	The ability to identify or detect a known pattern (a figure, object, word, or sound) that is hidden in other distracting material.
Perceptual Speed	The ability to quickly and accurately compare similarities and differences among sets of letters, numbers, objects, pictures, or patterns. The things to be compared may be presented at the same time or one after the other. This ability also includes comparing a presented object with a remembered object.
Visual Color Discrimination	The ability to match or detect differences between colors, including shades of color and brightness.
Number Facility	The ability to add, subtract, multiply, or divide quickly and correctly.
Memorization	The ability to remember information such as words, numbers, pictures, and procedures.
Finger Dexterity	The ability to make precisely coordinated movements of the fingers of one or both hands to grasp, manipulate, or assemble very small objects.
Visualization	The ability to imagine how something will look after it is moved around or when its parts are moved or rearranged.
Mathematical Reasoning	The ability to choose the right mathematical methods or formulas to solve a problem.
Hearing Sensitivity	The ability to detect or tell the differences between sounds that vary in pitch and loudness.

Auditory Attention	The ability to focus on a single source of sound in the presence of other distracting sounds.
Depth Perception	The ability to judge which of several objects is closer or farther away from you, or to judge the distance between you and an object.
Multilimb Coordination	The ability to coordinate two or more limbs (for example, two arms, two legs, or one leg and one arm) while sitting, standing, or lying down. It does not involve performing the activities while the whole body is in motion.
Static Strength	The ability to exert maximum muscle force to lift, push, pull, or carry objects.
Trunk Strength	The ability to use your abdominal and lower back muscles to support part of the body repeatedly or continuously over time without 'giving out' or fatiguing.
Arm-Hand Steadiness	The ability to keep your hand and arm steady while moving your arm or while holding your arm and hand in one position.
Stamina	The ability to exert yourself physically over long periods of time without getting winded or out of breath.
Manual Dexterity	The ability to quickly move your hand, your hand together with your arm, or your two hands to grasp, manipulate, or assemble objects.
Control Precision	The ability to quickly and repeatedly adjust the controls of a machine or a vehicle to exact positions.
Gross Body Coordination	The ability to coordinate the movement of your arms, legs, and torso together when the whole body is in motion.
Speed of Limb Movement	The ability to quickly move the arms and legs.
Extent Flexibility	The ability to bend, stretch, twist, or reach with your body, arms, and/or legs.
Dynamic Strength	The ability to exert muscle force repeatedly or continuously over time. This involves muscular endurance and resistance to muscle fatigue.
Gross Body Equilibrium	The ability to keep or regain your body balance or stay upright when in an unstable position.
Spatial Orientation	The ability to know your location in relation to the environment or to know where other objects are in relation to you.
Wrist-Finger Speed	The ability to make fast, simple, repeated movements of the fingers, hands, and wrists.
Response Orientation	The ability to choose quickly between two or more movements in response to two or more different signals (lights, sounds, pictures). It includes the speed with which the correct response is started with the hand, foot, or other body part.
Night Vision	The ability to see under low light conditions.
Rate Control	The ability to time your movements or the movement of a piece of equipment in anticipation of changes in the speed and/or direction of a moving object or scene.
Peripheral Vision	The ability to see objects or movement of objects to one's side when the eyes are looking ahead.
Glare Sensitivity	The ability to see objects in the presence of glare or bright lighting.
Dynamic Flexibility	The ability to quickly and repeatedly bend, stretch, twist, or reach out with your body, arms, and/or legs.
Sound Localization	The ability to tell the direction from which a sound originated.
Explosive Strength	The ability to use short bursts of muscle force to propel oneself (as in jumping or sprinting), or to throw an object.
Reaction Time	The ability to quickly respond (with the hand, finger, or foot) to a signal (sound, light, picture) when it appears.

Work_Activity	Work_Activity Definitions
Developing and Building Teams	Encouraging and building mutual trust, respect, and cooperation among team members.
Making Decisions and Solving Problems	Analyzing information and evaluating results to choose the best solution and solve problems.
Communicating with Supervisors, Peers, or Subordin	Providing information to supervisors, co-workers, and subordinates by telephone, in written form, e-mail, or in person.
Coordinating the Work and Activities of Others	Getting members of a group to work together to accomplish tasks.
Performing for or Working Directly with the Public	Performing for people or dealing directly with the public. This includes serving customers in restaurants and stores, and receiving clients or guests.
Performing Administrative Activities	Performing day-to-day administrative tasks such as maintaining information files and processing paperwork.
Getting Information	Observing, receiving, and otherwise obtaining information from all relevant sources.
Resolving Conflicts and Negotiating with Others	Handling complaints, settling disputes, and resolving grievances and conflicts, or otherwise negotiating with others.
Establishing and Maintaining Interpersonal Relatio	Developing constructive and cooperative working relationships with others, and maintaining them over time.

Documenting/Recording Information	Entering, transcribing, recording, storing, or maintaining information in written or electronic/magnetic form.
Judging the Qualities of Things, Services, or Peop	Assessing the value, importance, or quality of things or people.
Monitor Processes, Materials, or Surroundings	Monitoring and reviewing information from materials, events, or the environment, to detect or assess problems.
Evaluating Information to Determine Compliance wit	Using relevant information and individual judgment to determine whether events or processes comply with laws, regulations, or standards.
Communicating with Persons Outside Organization	Communicating with people outside the organization, representing the organization to customers, the public, government, and other external sources. This information can be exchanged in person, in writing, or by telephone or e-mail.
Scheduling Work and Activities	Scheduling events, programs, and activities, as well as the work of others.
Organizing, Planning, and Prioritizing Work	Developing specific goals and plans to prioritize, organize, and accomplish your work.
Guiding, Directing, and Motivating Subordinates	Providing guidance and direction to subordinates, including setting performance standards and monitoring performance.
Thinking Creatively	Developing, designing, or creating new applications, ideas, relationships, systems, or products, including artistic contributions.
Assisting and Caring for Others	Providing personal assistance, medical attention, emotional support, or other personal care to others such as coworkers, customers, or patients.
Staffing Organizational Units	Recruiting, interviewing, selecting, hiring, and promoting employees in an organization.
Developing Objectives and Strategies	Establishing long-range objectives and specifying the strategies and actions to achieve them.
Monitoring and Controlling Resources	Monitoring and controlling resources and overseeing the spending of money.
Coaching and Developing Others	Identifying the developmental needs of others and coaching, mentoring, or otherwise helping others to improve their knowledge or skills.
Identifying Objects, Actions, and Events	Identifying information by categorizing, estimating, recognizing differences or similarities, and detecting changes in circumstances or events.
Training and Teaching Others	Identifying the educational needs of others, developing formal educational or training programs or classes, and teaching or instructing others.
Updating and Using Relevant Knowledge	Keeping up-to-date technically and applying new knowledge to your job.
Processing Information	Compiling, coding, categorizing, calculating, tabulating, auditing, or verifying information or data.
Interpreting the Meaning of Information for Others	Translating or explaining what information means and how it can be used.
Inspecting Equipment, Structures, or Material	Inspecting equipment, structures, or materials to identify the cause of errors or other problems or defects.
Interacting With Computers	Using computers and computer systems (including hardware and software) to program, write software, set up functions, enter data, or process information.
Analyzing Data or Information	Identifying the underlying principles, reasons, or facts of information by breaking down information or data into separate parts.
Provide Consultation and Advice to Others	Providing guidance and expert advice to management or other groups on technical, systems-, or process-related topics.
Performing General Physical Activities	Performing physical activities that require considerable use of your arms and legs and moving your whole body, such as climbing, lifting, balancing, walking, stooping, and handling of materials.
Handling and Moving Objects	Using hands and arms in handling, installing, positioning, and moving materials, and manipulating things.
Selling or Influencing Others	Convincing others to buy merchandise/goods or to otherwise change their minds or actions.
Estimating the Quantifiable Characteristics of Pro	Estimating sizes, distances, and quantities; or determining time, costs, resources, or materials needed to perform a work activity.
Operating Vehicles, Mechanized Devices, or Equipme	Running, maneuvering, navigating, or driving vehicles or mechanized equipment, such as forklifts, passenger vehicles, aircraft, or water craft.
Controlling Machines and Processes	Using either control mechanisms or direct physical activity to operate machines or processes (not including computers or vehicles).
Repairing and Maintaining Electronic Equipment	Servicing, repairing, calibrating, regulating, fine-tuning, or testing machines, devices, and equipment that operate primarily on the basis of electrical or electronic (not mechanical) principles.
Repairing and Maintaining Mechanical Equipment	Servicing, repairing, adjusting, and testing machines, devices, moving parts, and equipment that operate primarily on the basis of mechanical (not electronic) principles.
Drafting, Laying Out, and Specifying Technical Dev	Providing documentation, detailed instructions, drawings, or specifications to tell others about how devices, parts, equipment, or structures are to be fabricated, constructed, assembled, modified, maintained, or used.

Work Context	Work_Context Definitions
Contact With Others	How much does this job require the worker to be in contact with others (face-to-face, by telephone, or otherwise) in order to perform it?
Face-to-Face Discussions	How often do you have to have face-to-face discussions with individuals or teams in this job?
Telephone	How often do you have telephone conversations in this job?
Work With Work Group or Team	How important is it to work with others in a group or team in this job?
Structured versus Unstructured Work	To what extent is this job structured for the worker, rather than allowing the worker to determine tasks, priorities, and goals?
Freedom to Make Decisions	How much decision making freedom, without supervision, does the job offer?
Responsibility for Outcomes and Results	How responsible is the worker for work outcomes and results of other workers?
Deal With External Customers	How important is it to work with external customers or the public in this job?
Responsible for Others' Health and Safety	How much responsibility is there for the health and safety of others in this job?
Letters and Memos	How often does the job require written letters and memos?
Impact of Decisions on Co-workers or Company Resul	How do the decisions an employee makes impact the results of co-workers, clients or the company?
Physical Proximity	To what extent does this job require the worker to perform job tasks in close physical proximity to other people?
Frequency of Decision Making	How frequently is the worker required to make decisions that affect other people, the financial resources, and/or the image and reputation of the organization?
Coordinate or Lead Others	How important is it to coordinate or lead others in accomplishing work activities in this job?
Importance of Being Exact or Accurate	How important is being very exact or highly accurate in performing this job?
Frequency of Conflict Situations	How often are there conflict situations the employee has to face in this job?
Time Pressure	How often does this job require the worker to meet strict deadlines?
Indoors, Environmentally Controlled	How often does this job require working indoors in environmentally controlled conditions?
Electronic Mail	How often do you use electronic mail in this job?
Spend Time Standing	How much does this job require standing?
In an Enclosed Vehicle or Equipment	How often does this job require working in a closed vehicle or equipment (e.g., car)?
Deal With Unpleasant or Angry People	How frequently does the worker have to deal with unpleasant, angry, or discourteous individuals as part of the job requirements?
Spend Time Sitting	How much does this job require sitting?
Consequence of Error	How serious would the result usually be if the worker made a mistake that was not readily correctable?
Sounds, Noise Levels Are Distracting or Uncomforta	How often does this job require working exposed to sounds and noise levels that are distracting or uncomfortable?
Exposed to Disease or Infections	How often does this job require exposure to disease/infections?
Importance of Repeating Same Tasks	How important is repeating the same physical activities (e.g., key entry) or mental activities (e.g., checking entries in a ledger) over and over, without stopping, to performing this job?
Outdoors, Exposed to Weather	How often does this job require working outdoors, exposed to all weather conditions?
Spend Time Walking and Running	How much does this job require walking and running?
Level of Competition	To what extent does this job require the worker to compete or to be aware of competitive pressures?
Public Speaking	How often do you have to perform public speaking in this job?
Spend Time Making Repetitive Motions	How much does this job require making repetitive motions?
Spend Time Kneeling, Crouching, Stooping, or Crawl	How much does this job require kneeling, crouching, stooping or crawling?
Spend Time Bending or Twisting the Body	How much does this job require bending or twisting your body?
Exposed to Contaminants	How often does this job require working exposed to contaminants (such as pollutants, gases, dust or odors)?

Outdoors, Under Cover	How often does this job require working outdoors, under cover (e.g., structure with roof but no walls)?
Exposed to Minor Burns, Cuts, Bites, or Stings	How often does this job require exposure to minor burns, cuts, bites, or stings?
Wear Common Protective or Safety Equipment such as	How much does this job require wearing common protective or safety equipment such as safety shoes, glasses, gloves, hard hats or life jackets?
Spend Time Using Your Hands to Handle, Control, or	How much does this job require using your hands to handle, control, or feel objects, tools or controls?
Very Hot or Cold Temperatures	How often does this job require working in very hot (above 90 F degrees) or very cold (below 32 F degrees) temperatures?
Degree of Automation	How automated is the job?
Deal With Physically Aggressive People	How frequently does this job require the worker to deal with physical aggression of violent individuals?
Spend Time Keeping or Regaining Balance	How much does this job require keeping or regaining your balance?
Extremely Bright or Inadequate Lighting	How often does this job require working in extremely bright or inadequate lighting conditions?
Indoors, Not Environmentally Controlled	How often does this job require working indoors in non-controlled environmental conditions (e.g., warehouse without heat)?
Cramped Work Space, Awkward Positions	How often does this job require working in cramped work spaces that requires getting into awkward positions?
Exposed to Hazardous Conditions	How often does this job require exposure to hazardous conditions?
Wear Specialized Protective or Safety Equipment su	How much does this job require wearing specialized protective or safety equipment such as breathing apparatus, safety harness, full protection suits, or radiation protection?
Exposed to High Places	How often does this job require exposure to high places?
Exposed to Hazardous Equipment	How often does this job require exposure to hazardous equipment?
Pace Determined by Speed of Equipment	How important is it to this job that the pace is determined by the speed of equipment or machinery? (This does not refer to keeping busy at all times on this job.)
In an Open Vehicle or Equipment	How often does this job require working in an open vehicle or equipment (e.g., tractor)?
Exposed to Whole Body Vibration	How often does this job require exposure to whole body vibration (e.g., operate a jackhammer)?
Spend Time Climbing Ladders, Scaffolds, or Poles	How much does this job require climbing ladders, scaffolds, or poles?
Exposed to Radiation	How often does this job require exposure to radiation?

Job Zone Component	Job Zone Component Definitions
Title	Job Zone Four: Considerable Preparation Needed
Overall Experience	A minimum of two to four years of work-related skill, knowledge, or experience is needed for these occupations. For example, an accountant must complete four years of college and work for several years in accounting to be considered qualified.
Job Training	Employees in these occupations usually need several years of work-related experience, on-the-job training, and/or vocational training.
Job Zone Examples	Many of these occupations involve coordinating, supervising, managing, or training others. Examples include accountants, chefs and head cooks, computer programmers, historians, pharmacists, and police detectives.
SVP Range	(7.0 to < 8.0)
Education	Most of these occupations require a four - year bachelor's degree, but some do not.

Work_Styles	Work_Styles Definitions
Dependability	Job requires being reliable, responsible, and dependable, and fulfilling obligations.
Adaptability/Flexibility	Job requires being open to change (positive or negative) and to considerable variety in the workplace.
Leadership	Job requires a willingness to lead, take charge, and offer opinions and direction.
Initiative	Job requires a willingness to take on responsibilities and challenges.
Cooperation	Job requires being pleasant with others on the job and displaying a good-natured, cooperative attitude.
Integrity	Job requires being honest and ethical.

Self Control	Job requires maintaining composure, keeping emotions in check, controlling anger, and avoiding aggressive behavior, even in very difficult situations.
Stress Tolerance	Job requires accepting criticism and dealing calmly and effectively with high stress situations.
Concern for Others	Job requires being sensitive to others' needs and feelings and being understanding and helpful on the job.
Independence	Job requires developing one's own ways of doing things, guiding oneself with little or no supervision, and depending on oneself to get things done.
Social Orientation	Job requires preferring to work with others rather than alone, and being personally connected with others on the job.
Attention to Detail	Job requires being careful about detail and thorough in completing work tasks.
Innovation	Job requires creativity and alternative thinking to develop new ideas for and answers to work-related problems.
Analytical Thinking	Job requires analyzing information and using logic to address work-related issues and problems.
Achievement/Effort	Job requires establishing and maintaining personally challenging achievement goals and exerting effort toward mastering tasks.
Persistence	Job requires persistence in the face of obstacles.

11-9032.00 - Education Administrators, Elementary and Secondary School

Plan, direct, or coordinate the academic, clerical, or auxiliary activities of public or private elementary or secondary level schools.

Tasks

1) Prepare, maintain, or oversee the preparation/maintenance of attendance, activity, planning, or personnel reports and records.

2) Confer with parents and staff to discuss educational activities, policies, and student behavioral or learning problems.

3) Review and approve new programs, or recommend modifications to existing programs, submitting program proposals for school board approval as necessary.

4) Evaluate curricula, teaching methods, and programs to determine their effectiveness, efficiency, and utilization, and to ensure that school activities comply with federal, state, and local regulations.

5) Organize and direct committees of specialists, volunteers, and staff to provide technical and advisory assistance for programs.

6) Direct and coordinate school maintenance services and the use of school facilities.

7) Enforce discipline and attendance rules.

8) Counsel and provide guidance to students regarding personal, academic, vocational, or behavioral issues.

9) Teach classes or courses to students.

10) Observe teaching methods and examine learning materials in order to evaluate and standardize curricula and teaching techniques, and to determine areas where improvement is needed.

11) Recruit, hire, train, and evaluate primary and supplemental staff.

12) Advocate for new schools to be built, or for existing facilities to be repaired or remodeled.

13) Review and interpret government codes, and develop programs to ensure adherence to codes and facility safety, security, and maintenance.

14) Determine allocations of funds for staff, supplies, materials, and equipment, and authorize purchases.

15) Direct and coordinate activities of teachers, administrators, and support staff at schools, public agencies, and institutions.

16) Write articles, manuals, and other publications, and assist in the distribution of promotional literature about facilities and programs.

17) Collaborate with teachers to develop and maintain curriculum standards, develop mission statements, and set performance goals and objectives.

18) Set educational standards and goals, and help establish policies and procedures to carry them out.

19) Plan and develop instructional methods and content for educational, vocational, or student activity programs.

20) Determine the scope of educational program offerings, and prepare drafts of course schedules and descriptions in order to estimate staffing and facility requirements.

21) Establish, coordinate, and oversee particular programs across school districts, such as programs to evaluate student academic achievement.

22) Recommend personnel actions related to programs and services.

23) Collect and analyze survey data, regulatory information, and data on demographic and employment trends to forecast enrollment patterns and curriculum change needs.

24) Develop partnerships with businesses, communities, and other organizations to help meet identified educational needs and to provide school-to-work programs.

Knowledge	Knowledge Definitions
Education and Training	Knowledge of principles and methods for curriculum and training design, teaching and instruction for individuals and groups, and the measurement of training effects.
Administration and Management	Knowledge of business and management principles involved in strategic planning, resource allocation, human resources modeling, leadership technique, production methods, and coordination of people and resources.
English Language	Knowledge of the structure and content of the English language including the meaning and spelling of words, rules of composition, and grammar.
Personnel and Human Resources	Knowledge of principles and procedures for personnel recruitment, selection, training, compensation and benefits, labor relations and negotiation, and personnel information systems.
Customer and Personal Service	Knowledge of principles and processes for providing customer and personal services. This includes customer needs assessment, meeting quality standards for services, and evaluation of customer satisfaction.
Psychology	Knowledge of human behavior and performance; individual differences in ability, personality, and interests; learning and motivation; psychological research methods; and the assessment and treatment of behavioral and affective disorders.
Public Safety and Security	Knowledge of relevant equipment, policies, procedures, and strategies to promote effective local, state, or national security operations for the protection of people, data, property, and institutions.
Law and Government	Knowledge of laws, legal codes, court procedures, precedents, government regulations, executive orders, agency rules, and the democratic political process.
Clerical	Knowledge of administrative and clerical procedures and systems such as word processing, managing files and records, stenography and transcription, designing forms, and other office procedures and terminology.
Therapy and Counseling	Knowledge of principles, methods, and procedures for diagnosis, treatment, and rehabilitation of physical and mental dysfunctions, and for career counseling and guidance.
Mathematics	Knowledge of arithmetic, algebra, geometry, calculus, statistics, and their applications.
Communications and Media	Knowledge of media production, communication, and dissemination techniques and methods. This includes alternative ways to inform and entertain via written, oral, and visual media.
Computers and Electronics	Knowledge of circuit boards, processors, chips, electronic equipment, and computer hardware and software, including applications and programming.
Sociology and Anthropology	Knowledge of group behavior and dynamics, societal trends and influences, human migrations, ethnicity, cultures and their history and origins.
Economics and Accounting	Knowledge of economic and accounting principles and practices, the financial markets, banking and the analysis and reporting of financial data.
Philosophy and Theology	Knowledge of different philosophical systems and religions. This includes their basic principles, values, ethics, ways of thinking, customs, practices, and their impact on human culture.
History and Archeology	Knowledge of historical events and their causes, indicators, and effects on civilizations and cultures.
Telecommunications	Knowledge of transmission, broadcasting, switching, control, and operation of telecommunications systems.
Sales and Marketing	Knowledge of principles and methods for showing, promoting, and selling products or services. This includes marketing strategy and tactics, product demonstration, sales techniques, and sales control systems.
Geography	Knowledge of principles and methods for describing the features of land, sea, and air masses, including their physical characteristics, locations, interrelationships, and distribution of plant, animal, and human life.
Transportation	Knowledge of principles and methods for moving people or goods by air, rail, sea, or road, including the relative costs and benefits.
Fine Arts	Knowledge of the theory and techniques required to compose, produce, and perform works of music, dance, visual arts, drama, and sculpture.
Medicine and Dentistry	Knowledge of the information and techniques needed to diagnose and treat human injuries, diseases, and deformities. This includes symptoms, treatment alternatives, drug properties and interactions, and preventive health-care measures.
Foreign Language	Knowledge of the structure and content of a foreign (non-English) language including the meaning and spelling of words, rules of composition and grammar, and pronunciation.
Production and Processing	Knowledge of raw materials, production processes, quality control, costs, and other techniques for maximizing the effective manufacture and distribution of goods.
Building and Construction	Knowledge of materials, methods, and the tools involved in the construction or repair of houses, buildings, or other structures such as highways and roads.
Chemistry	Knowledge of the chemical composition, structure, and properties of substances and of the chemical processes and transformations that they undergo. This includes uses of chemicals and their interactions, danger signs, production techniques, and disposal methods.
Biology	Knowledge of plant and animal organisms, their tissues, cells, functions, interdependencies, and interactions with each other and the environment.
Design	Knowledge of design techniques, tools, and principles involved in production of precision technical plans, blueprints, drawings, and models.
Mechanical	Knowledge of machines and tools, including their designs, uses, repair, and maintenance.
Engineering and Technology	Knowledge of the practical application of engineering science and technology. This includes applying principles, techniques, procedures, and equipment to the design and production of various goods and services.
Physics	Knowledge and prediction of physical principles, laws, their interrelationships, and applications to understanding fluid, material, and atmospheric dynamics, and mechanical, electrical, atomic and sub-atomic structures and processes.
Food Production	Knowledge of techniques and equipment for planting, growing, and harvesting food products (both plant and animal) for consumption, including storage/handling techniques.

Skills	Skills Definitions
Active Listening	Giving full attention to what other people are saying, taking time to understand the points being made, asking questions as appropriate, and not interrupting at inappropriate times.
Reading Comprehension	Understanding written sentences and paragraphs in work related documents.
Monitoring	Monitoring/Assessing performance of yourself, other individuals, or organizations to make improvements or take corrective action.
Learning Strategies	Selecting and using training/instructional methods and procedures appropriate for the situation when learning or teaching new things.
Management of Personnel Resources	Motivating, developing, and directing people as they work, identifying the best people for the job.
Speaking	Talking to others to convey information effectively.
Critical Thinking	Using logic and reasoning to identify the strengths and weaknesses of alternative solutions, conclusions or approaches to problems.
Time Management	Managing one's own time and the time of others.
Instructing	Teaching others how to do something.
Social Perceptiveness	Being aware of others' reactions and understanding why they react as they do.
Writing	Communicating effectively in writing as appropriate for the needs of the audience.
Coordination	Adjusting actions in relation to others' actions.

Active Learning	Understanding the implications of new information for both current and future problem-solving and decision-making.
Judgment and Decision Making	Considering the relative costs and benefits of potential actions to choose the most appropriate one.
Negotiation	Bringing others together and trying to reconcile differences.
Persuasion	Persuading others to change their minds or behavior.
Complex Problem Solving	Identifying complex problems and reviewing related information to develop and evaluate options and implement solutions.
Service Orientation	Actively looking for ways to help people.
Management of Financial Resources	Determining how money will be spent to get the work done, and accounting for these expenditures.
Systems Evaluation	Identifying measures or indicators of system performance and the actions needed to improve or correct performance, relative to the goals of the system.
Operations Analysis	Analyzing needs and product requirements to create a design.
Management of Material Resources	Obtaining and seeing to the appropriate use of equipment, facilities, and materials needed to do certain work.
Mathematics	Using mathematics to solve problems.
Equipment Selection	Determining the kind of tools and equipment needed to do a job.
Systems Analysis	Determining how a system should work and how changes in conditions, operations, and the environment will affect outcomes.
Quality Control Analysis	Conducting tests and inspections of products, services, or processes to evaluate quality or performance.
Troubleshooting	Determining causes of operating errors and deciding what to do about it.
Technology Design	Generating or adapting equipment and technology to serve user needs.
Science	Using scientific rules and methods to solve problems.
Operation and Control	Controlling operations of equipment or systems.
Operation Monitoring	Watching gauges, dials, or other indicators to make sure a machine is working properly.
Equipment Maintenance	Performing routine maintenance on equipment and determining when and what kind of maintenance is needed.
Installation	Installing equipment, machines, wiring, or programs to meet specifications.
Repairing	Repairing machines or systems using the needed tools.
Programming	Writing computer programs for various purposes.

Ability	**Ability Definitions**
Oral Expression	The ability to communicate information and ideas in speaking so others will understand.
Oral Comprehension	The ability to listen to and understand information and ideas presented through spoken words and sentences.
Written Expression	The ability to communicate information and ideas in writing so others will understand.
Written Comprehension	The ability to read and understand information and ideas presented in writing.
Speech Clarity	The ability to speak clearly so others can understand you.
Problem Sensitivity	The ability to tell when something is wrong or is likely to go wrong. It does not involve solving the problem, only recognizing there is a problem.
Deductive Reasoning	The ability to apply general rules to specific problems to produce answers that make sense.
Near Vision	The ability to see details at close range (within a few feet of the observer).
Speech Recognition	The ability to identify and understand the speech of another person.
Inductive Reasoning	The ability to combine pieces of information to form general rules or conclusions (includes finding a relationship among seemingly unrelated events).
Fluency of Ideas	The ability to come up with a number of ideas about a topic (the number of ideas is important, not their quality, correctness, or creativity).
Originality	The ability to come up with unusual or clever ideas about a given topic or situation, or to develop creative ways to solve a problem.
Information Ordering	The ability to arrange things or actions in a certain order or pattern according to a specific rule or set of rules (e.g., patterns of numbers, letters, words, pictures, mathematical operations).
Category Flexibility	The ability to generate or use different sets of rules for combining or grouping things in different ways.
Selective Attention	The ability to concentrate on a task over a period of time without being distracted.

Mathematical Reasoning	The ability to choose the right mathematical methods or formulas to solve a problem.
Time Sharing	The ability to shift back and forth between two or more activities or sources of information (such as speech, sounds, touch, or other sources).
Memorization	The ability to remember information such as words, numbers, pictures, and procedures.
Flexibility of Closure	The ability to identify or detect a known pattern (a figure, object, word, or sound) that is hidden in other distracting material.
Far Vision	The ability to see details at a distance.
Number Facility	The ability to add, subtract, multiply, or divide quickly and correctly.
Perceptual Speed	The ability to quickly and accurately compare similarities and differences among sets of letters, numbers, objects, pictures, or patterns. The things to be compared may be presented at the same time or one after the other. This ability also includes comparing a presented object with a remembered object.
Auditory Attention	The ability to focus on a single source of sound in the presence of other distracting sounds.
Trunk Strength	The ability to use your abdominal and lower back muscles to support part of the body repeatedly or continuously over time without 'giving out' or fatiguing.
Speed of Closure	The ability to quickly make sense of, combine, and organize information into meaningful patterns.
Stamina	The ability to exert yourself physically over long periods of time without getting winded or out of breath.
Visualization	The ability to imagine how something will look after it is moved around or when its parts are moved or rearranged.
Gross Body Coordination	The ability to coordinate the movement of your arms, legs, and torso together when the whole body is in motion.
Finger Dexterity	The ability to make precisely coordinated movements of the fingers of one or both hands to grasp, manipulate, or assemble very small objects.
Static Strength	The ability to exert maximum muscle force to lift, push, pull, or carry objects.
Response Orientation	The ability to choose quickly between two or more movements in response to two or more different signals (lights, sounds, pictures). It includes the speed with which the correct response is started with the hand, foot, or other body part.
Visual Color Discrimination	The ability to match or detect differences between colors, including shades of color and brightness.
Reaction Time	The ability to quickly respond (with the hand, finger, or foot) to a signal (sound, light, picture) when it appears.
Speed of Limb Movement	The ability to quickly move the arms and legs.
Gross Body Equilibrium	The ability to keep or regain your body balance or stay upright when in an unstable position.
Explosive Strength	The ability to use short bursts of muscle force to propel oneself (as in jumping or sprinting), or to throw an object.
Hearing Sensitivity	The ability to detect or tell the differences between sounds that vary in pitch and loudness.
Depth Perception	The ability to judge which of several objects is closer or farther away from you, or to judge the distance between you and an object.
Rate Control	The ability to time your movements or the movement of a piece of equipment in anticipation of changes in the speed and/or direction of a moving object or scene.
Peripheral Vision	The ability to see objects or movement of objects to one's side when the eyes are looking ahead.
Arm-Hand Steadiness	The ability to keep your hand and arm steady while moving your arm or while holding your arm and hand in one position.
Spatial Orientation	The ability to know your location in relation to the environment or to know where other objects are in relation to you.
Dynamic Flexibility	The ability to quickly and repeatedly bend, stretch, twist, or reach out with your body, arms, and/or legs.
Control Precision	The ability to quickly and repeatedly adjust the controls of a machine or a vehicle to exact positions.
Multilimb Coordination	The ability to coordinate two or more limbs (for example, two arms, two legs, or one leg and one arm) while sitting, standing, or lying down. It does not involve performing the activities while the whole body is in motion.
Dynamic Strength	The ability to exert muscle force repeatedly or continuously over time. This involves muscular endurance and resistance to muscle fatigue.
Extent Flexibility	The ability to bend, stretch, twist, or reach with your body, arms, and/or legs.

Manual Dexterity	The ability to quickly move your hand, your hand together with your arm, or your two hands to grasp, manipulate, or assemble objects.
Glare Sensitivity	The ability to see objects in the presence of glare or bright lighting.
Night Vision	The ability to see under low light conditions.
Wrist-Finger Speed	The ability to make fast, simple, repeated movements of the fingers, hands, and wrists.
Sound Localization	The ability to tell the direction from which a sound originated.

Work_Activity	Work_Activity Definitions
Establishing and Maintaining Interpersonal Relatio	Developing constructive and cooperative working relationships with others, and maintaining them over time.
Making Decisions and Solving Problems	Analyzing information and evaluating results to choose the best solution and solve problems.
Communicating with Supervisors, Peers, or Subordin	Providing information to supervisors, co-workers, and subordinates by telephone, in written form, e-mail, or in person.
Getting Information	Observing, receiving, and otherwise obtaining information from all relevant sources.
Performing Administrative Activities	Performing day-to-day administrative tasks such as maintaining information files and processing paperwork.
Developing and Building Teams	Encouraging and building mutual trust, respect, and cooperation among team members.
Organizing, Planning, and Prioritizing Work	Developing specific goals and plans to prioritize, organize, and accomplish your work.
Resolving Conflicts and Negotiating with Others	Handling complaints, settling disputes, and resolving grievances and conflicts, or otherwise negotiating with others.
Coordinating the Work and Activities of Others	Getting members of a group to work together to accomplish tasks.
Guiding, Directing, and Motivating Subordinates	Providing guidance and direction to subordinates, including setting performance standards and monitoring performance.
Evaluating Information to Determine Compliance wit	Using relevant information and individual judgment to determine whether events or processes comply with laws, regulations, or standards.
Coaching and Developing Others	Identifying the developmental needs of others and coaching, mentoring, or otherwise helping others to improve their knowledge or skills.
Judging the Qualities of Things, Services, or Peop	Assessing the value, importance, or quality of things or people.
Developing Objectives and Strategies	Establishing long-range objectives and specifying the strategies and actions to achieve them.
Training and Teaching Others	Identifying the educational needs of others, developing formal educational or training programs or classes, and teaching or instructing others.
Interacting With Computers	Using computers and computer systems (including hardware and software) to program, write software, set up functions, enter data, or process information.
Communicating with Persons Outside Organization	Communicating with people outside the organization, representing the organization to customers, the public, government, and other external sources. This information can be exchanged in person, in writing, or by telephone or e-mail.
Scheduling Work and Activities	Scheduling events, programs, and activities, as well as the work of others.
Updating and Using Relevant Knowledge	Keeping up-to-date technically and applying new knowledge to your job.
Performing for or Working Directly with the Public	Performing for people or dealing directly with the public. This includes serving customers in restaurants and stores, and receiving clients or guests.
Analyzing Data or Information	Identifying the underlying principles, reasons, or facts of information by breaking down information or data into separate parts.
Processing Information	Compiling, coding, categorizing, calculating, tabulating, auditing, or verifying information or data.
Identifying Objects, Actions, and Events	Identifying information by categorizing, estimating, recognizing differences or similarities, and detecting changes in circumstances or events.
Staffing Organizational Units	Recruiting, interviewing, selecting, hiring, and promoting employees in an organization.
Monitoring and Controlling Resources	Monitoring and controlling resources and overseeing the spending of money.
Thinking Creatively	Developing, designing, or creating new applications, ideas, relationships, systems, or products, including artistic contributions.
Provide Consultation and Advice to Others	Providing guidance and expert advice to management or other groups on technical, systems-, or process-related topics.

Monitor Processes, Materials, or Surroundings	Monitoring and reviewing information from materials, events, or the environment, to detect or assess problems.
Interpreting the Meaning of Information for Others	Translating or explaining what information means and how it can be used.
Documenting/Recording Information	Entering, transcribing, recording, storing, or maintaining information in written or electronic/magnetic form.
Assisting and Caring for Others	Providing personal assistance, medical attention, emotional support, or other personal care to others such as coworkers, customers, or patients.
Estimating the Quantifiable Characteristics of Pro	Estimating sizes, distances, and quantities; or determining time, costs, resources, or materials needed to perform a work activity.
Selling or Influencing Others	Convincing others to buy merchandise/goods or to otherwise change their minds or actions.
Inspecting Equipment, Structures, or Material	Inspecting equipment, structures, or materials to identify the cause of errors or other problems or defects.
Performing General Physical Activities	Performing physical activities that require considerable use of your arms and legs and moving your whole body, such as climbing, lifting, balancing, walking, stooping, and handling of materials.
Handling and Moving Objects	Using hands and arms in handling, installing, positioning, and moving materials, and manipulating things.
Controlling Machines and Processes	Using either control mechanisms or direct physical activity to operate machines or processes (not including computers or vehicles).
Repairing and Maintaining Electronic Equipment	Servicing, repairing, calibrating, regulating, fine-tuning, or testing machines, devices, and equipment that operate primarily on the basis of electrical or electronic (not mechanical) principles.
Repairing and Maintaining Mechanical Equipment	Servicing, repairing, adjusting, and testing machines, devices, moving parts, and equipment that operate primarily on the basis of mechanical (not electronic) principles.
Drafting, Laying Out, and Specifying Technical Dev	Providing documentation, detailed instructions, drawings, or specifications to tell others about how devices, parts, equipment, or structures are to be fabricated, constructed, assembled, modified, maintained, or used.
Operating Vehicles, Mechanized Devices, or Equipme	Running, maneuvering, navigating, or driving vehicles or mechanized equipment, such as forklifts, passenger vehicles, aircraft, or water craft.

Work_Context	Work_Context Definitions
Telephone	How often do you have telephone conversations in this job?
Face-to-Face Discussions	How often do you have to have face-to-face discussions with individuals or teams in this job?
Electronic Mail	How often do you use electronic mail in this job?
Work With Work Group or Team	How important is it to work with others in a group or team in this job?
Contact With Others	How much does this job require the worker to be in contact with others (face-to-face, by telephone, or otherwise) in order to perform it?
Frequency of Decision Making	How frequently is the worker required to make decisions that affect other people, the financial resources, and/or the image and reputation of the organization?
Deal With External Customers	How important is it to work with external customers or the public in this job?
Letters and Memos	How often does the job require written letters and memos?
Structured versus Unstructured Work	To what extent is this job structured for the worker, rather than allowing the worker to determine tasks, priorities, and goals?
Freedom to Make Decisions	How much decision making freedom, without supervision, does the job offer?
Impact of Decisions on Co-workers or Company Resul	How do the decisions an employee makes impact the results of co-workers, clients or the company?
Indoors, Environmentally Controlled	How often does this job require working indoors in environmentally controlled conditions?
Responsibility for Outcomes and Results	How responsible is the worker for work outcomes and results of other workers?
Coordinate or Lead Others	How important is it to coordinate or lead others in accomplishing work activities in this job?
Responsible for Others' Health and Safety	How much responsibility is there for the health and safety of others in this job?
Frequency of Conflict Situations	How often are there conflict situations the employee has to face in this job?
Deal With Unpleasant or Angry People	How frequently does the worker have to deal with unpleasant, angry, or discourteous individuals as part of the job requirements?

Time Pressure	How often does this job require the worker to meet strict deadlines?
Importance of Being Exact or Accurate	How important is being very exact or highly accurate in performing this job?
Public Speaking	How often do you have to perform public speaking in this job?
Level of Competition	To what extent does this job require the worker to compete or to be aware of competitive pressures?
Physical Proximity	To what extent does this job require the worker to perform job tasks in close physical proximity to other people?
Spend Time Standing	How much does this job require standing?
Sounds, Noise Levels Are Distracting or Uncomforta	How often does this job require working exposed to sounds and noise levels that are distracting or uncomfortable?
Spend Time Sitting	How much does this job require sitting?
Consequence of Error	How serious would the result usually be if the worker made a mistake that was not readily correctable?
Spend Time Walking and Running	How much does this job require walking and running?
Deal With Physically Aggressive People	How frequently does this job require the worker to deal with physical aggression of violent individuals?
Importance of Repeating Same Tasks	How important is repeating the same physical activities (e.g., key entry) or mental activities (e.g., checking entries in a ledger) over and over, without stopping, to performing this job?
Outdoors, Exposed to Weather	How often does this job require working outdoors, exposed to all weather conditions?
Exposed to Disease or Infections	How often does this job require exposure to disease/infections?
Indoors, Not Environmentally Controlled	How often does this job require working indoors in non-controlled environmental conditions (e.g., warehouse without heat)?
Degree of Automation	How automated is the job?
Very Hot or Cold Temperatures	How often does this job require working in very hot (above 90 F degrees) or very cold (below 32 F degrees) temperatures?
Exposed to Contaminants	How often does this job require working exposed to contaminants (such as pollutants, gases, dust or odors)?
Spend Time Making Repetitive Motions	How much does this job require making repetitive motions?
In an Enclosed Vehicle or Equipment	How often does this job require working in a closed vehicle or equipment (e.g., car)?
Spend Time Using Your Hands to Handle, Control, or	How much does this job require using your hands to handle, control, or feel objects, tools or controls?
Extremely Bright or Inadequate Lighting	How often does this job require working in extremely bright or inadequate lighting conditions?
Outdoors, Under Cover	How often does this job require working outdoors, under cover (e.g., structure with roof but no walls)?
Exposed to Minor Burns, Cuts, Bites, or Stings	How often does this job require exposure to minor burns, cuts, bites, or stings?
Spend Time Bending or Twisting the Body	How much does this job require bending or twisting your body?
Spend Time Kneeling, Crouching, Stooping, or Crawl	How much does this job require kneeling, crouching, stooping or crawling?
Cramped Work Space, Awkward Positions	How often does this job require working in cramped work spaces that requires getting into awkward positions?
Spend Time Keeping or Regaining Balance	How much does this job require keeping or regaining your balance?
Exposed to Hazardous Equipment	How often does this job require exposure to hazardous equipment?
Wear Common Protective or Safety Equipment such as	How much does this job require wearing common protective or safety equipment such as safety shoes, glasses, gloves, hard hats or life jackets?
Exposed to Hazardous Conditions	How often does this job require exposure to hazardous conditions?
Exposed to High Places	How often does this job require exposure to high places?
Pace Determined by Speed of Equipment	How important is it to this job that the pace is determined by the speed of equipment or machinery? (This does not refer to keeping busy at all times on this job.)
Spend Time Climbing Ladders, Scaffolds, or Poles	How much does this job require climbing ladders, scaffolds, or poles?
In an Open Vehicle or Equipment	How often does this job require working in an open vehicle or equipment (e.g., tractor)?
Exposed to Whole Body Vibration	How often does this job require exposure to whole body vibration (e.g., operate a jackhammer)?
Exposed to Radiation	How often does this job require exposure to radiation?
Wear Specialized Protective or Safety Equipment su	How much does this job require wearing specialized protective or safety equipment such as breathing apparatus, safety harness, full protection suits, or radiation protection?

Job Zone Component	Job Zone Component Definitions
Title	Job Zone Five: Extensive Preparation Needed Extensive skill, knowledge, and experience are needed for these occupations. Many require more than five years of experience.
Overall Experience	For example, surgeons must complete four years of college and an additional five to seven years of specialized medical training to be able to do their job.
Job Training	Employees may need some on-the-job training, but most of these occupations assume that the person will already have the required skills, knowledge, work-related experience, and/or training.
Job Zone Examples	These occupations often involve coordinating, training, supervising, or managing the activities of others to accomplish goals. Very advanced communication and organizational skills are required. Examples include athletic trainers, lawyers, managing editors, physicists, social psychologists, and surgeons.
SVP Range	(8.0 and above)
Education	A bachelor's degree is the minimum formal education required for these occupations. However, many also require graduate school. For example, they may require a master's degree, and some require a Ph.D., M.D., or J.D. (law degree).

Work_Styles	Work_Styles Definitions
Leadership	Job requires a willingness to lead, take charge, and offer opinions and direction.
Dependability	Job requires being reliable, responsible, and dependable, and fulfilling obligations.
Integrity	Job requires being honest and ethical.
Self Control	Job requires maintaining composure, keeping emotions in check, controlling anger, and avoiding aggressive behavior, even in very difficult situations.
Stress Tolerance	Job requires accepting criticism and dealing calmly and effectively with high stress situations.
Cooperation	Job requires being pleasant with others on the job and displaying a good-natured, cooperative attitude.
Initiative	Job requires a willingness to take on responsibilities and challenges.
Attention to Detail	Job requires being careful about detail and thorough in completing work tasks.
Concern for Others	Job requires being sensitive to others' needs and feelings and being understanding and helpful on the job.
Persistence	Job requires persistence in the face of obstacles.
Adaptability/Flexibility	Job requires being open to change (positive or negative) and to considerable variety in the workplace.
Achievement/Effort	Job requires establishing and maintaining personally challenging achievement goals and exerting effort toward mastering tasks.
Social Orientation	Job requires preferring to work with others rather than alone, and being personally connected with others on the job.
Analytical Thinking	Job requires analyzing information and using logic to address work-related issues and problems.
Independence	Job requires developing one's own ways of doing things, guiding oneself with little or no supervision, and depending on oneself to get things done.
Innovation	Job requires creativity and alternative thinking to develop new ideas for and answers to work-related problems.

11-9033.00 - Education Administrators, Postsecondary

Plan, direct, or coordinate research, instructional, student administration and services, and other educational activities at postsecondary institutions, including universities, colleges, and junior and community colleges.

Tasks

1) Represent institutions at community and campus events, in meetings with other institution personnel, and during accreditation processes.

2) Recruit, hire, train, and terminate departmental personnel.

3) Plan, administer, and control budgets, maintain financial records, and produce financial

reports.

4) Establish operational policies and procedures and make any necessary modifications, based on analysis of operations, demographics, and other research information.

5) Provide assistance to faculty and staff in duties such as teaching classes, conducting orientation programs, issuing transcripts, and scheduling events.

6) Confer with other academic staff to explain and formulate admission requirements and course credit policies.

7) Coordinate the production and dissemination of university publications such as course catalogs and class schedules.

8) Review registration statistics, and consult with faculty officials to develop registration policies.

9) Consult with government regulatory and licensing agencies in order to ensure the institution's conformance with applicable standards.

10) Develop curricula, and recommend curricula revisions and additions.

11) Participate in student recruitment, selection, and admission, making admissions recommendations when required to do so.

12) Direct, coordinate, and evaluate the activities of personnel engaged in administering academic institutions, departments, and/or alumni organizations.

13) Direct and participate in institutional fundraising activities, and encourage alumni participation in such activities.

14) Determine course schedules, and coordinate teaching assignments and room assignments in order to ensure optimum use of buildings and equipment.

15) Review student misconduct reports requiring disciplinary action, and counsel students regarding such reports.

16) Appoint individuals to faculty positions, and evaluate their performance.

17) Direct activities of administrative departments such as admissions, registration, and career services.

18) Teach courses within their department.

19) Plan and promote sporting events and social, cultural, and recreational activities.

20) Direct scholarship, fellowship, and loan programs, performing activities such as selecting recipients and distributing aid.

21) Assess and collect tuition and fees.

22) Audit the financial status of student organizations and facility accounts.

23) Negotiate with foundation and industry representatives on issues such as securing loans and determining construction costs and materials.

24) Supervise coaches.

Knowledge	Knowledge Definitions
Administration and Management	Knowledge of business and management principles involved in strategic planning, resource allocation, human resources modeling, leadership technique, production methods, and coordination of people and resources.
English Language	Knowledge of the structure and content of the English language including the meaning and spelling of words, rules of composition, and grammar.
Education and Training	Knowledge of principles and methods for curriculum and training design, teaching and instruction for individuals and groups, and the measurement of training effects.
Customer and Personal Service	Knowledge of principles and processes for providing customer and personal services. This includes customer needs assessment, meeting quality standards for services, and evaluation of customer satisfaction.
Personnel and Human Resources	Knowledge of principles and procedures for personnel recruitment, selection, training, compensation and benefits, labor relations and negotiation, and personnel information systems.
Psychology	Knowledge of human behavior and performance; individual differences in ability, personality, and interests; learning and motivation; psychological research methods; and the assessment and treatment of behavioral and affective disorders.
Computers and Electronics	Knowledge of circuit boards, processors, chips, electronic equipment, and computer hardware and software, including applications and programming.
Sociology and Anthropology	Knowledge of group behavior and dynamics, societal trends and influences, human migrations, ethnicity, cultures and their history and origins.
Clerical	Knowledge of administrative and clerical procedures and systems such as word processing, managing files and records, stenography and transcription, designing forms, and other office procedures and terminology.
Law and Government	Knowledge of laws, legal codes, court procedures, precedents, government regulations, executive orders, agency rules, and the democratic political process.
Communications and Media	Knowledge of media production, communication, and dissemination techniques and methods. This includes alternative ways to inform and entertain via written, oral, and visual media.
Mathematics	Knowledge of arithmetic, algebra, geometry, calculus, statistics, and their applications.
Economics and Accounting	Knowledge of economic and accounting principles and practices, the financial markets, banking and the analysis and reporting of financial data.
Sales and Marketing	Knowledge of principles and methods for showing, promoting, and selling products or services. This includes marketing strategy and tactics, product demonstration, sales techniques, and sales control systems.
Public Safety and Security	Knowledge of relevant equipment, policies, procedures, and strategies to promote effective local, state, or national security operations for the protection of people, data, property, and institutions.
Philosophy and Theology	Knowledge of different philosophical systems and religions. This includes their basic principles, values, ethics, ways of thinking, customs, practices, and their impact on human culture.
Therapy and Counseling	Knowledge of principles, methods, and procedures for diagnosis, treatment, and rehabilitation of physical and mental dysfunctions, and for career counseling and guidance.
History and Archeology	Knowledge of historical events and their causes, indicators, and effects on civilizations and cultures.
Telecommunications	Knowledge of transmission, broadcasting, switching, control, and operation of telecommunications systems.
Geography	Knowledge of principles and methods for describing the features of land, sea, and air masses, including their physical characteristics, locations, interrelationships, and distribution of plant, animal, and human life.
Fine Arts	Knowledge of the theory and techniques required to compose, produce, and perform works of music, dance, visual arts, drama, and sculpture.
Production and Processing	Knowledge of raw materials, production processes, quality control, costs, and other techniques for maximizing the effective manufacture and distribution of goods.
Transportation	Knowledge of principles and methods for moving people or goods by air, rail, sea, or road, including the relative costs and benefits.
Design	Knowledge of design techniques, tools, and principles involved in production of precision technical plans, blueprints, drawings, and models.
Foreign Language	Knowledge of the structure and content of a foreign (non-English) language including the meaning and spelling of words, rules of composition and grammar, and pronunciation.
Building and Construction	Knowledge of materials, methods, and the tools involved in the construction or repair of houses, buildings, or other structures such as highways and roads.
Engineering and Technology	Knowledge of the practical application of engineering science and technology. This includes applying principles, techniques, procedures, and equipment to the design and production of various goods and services.
Mechanical	Knowledge of machines and tools, including their designs, uses, repair, and maintenance.
Medicine and Dentistry	Knowledge of the information and techniques needed to diagnose and treat human injuries, diseases, and deformities. This includes symptoms, treatment alternatives, drug properties and interactions, and preventive health-care measures.
Biology	Knowledge of plant and animal organisms, their tissues, cells, functions, interdependencies, and interactions with each other and the environment.
Chemistry	Knowledge of the chemical composition, structure, and properties of substances and of the chemical processes and transformations that they undergo. This includes uses of chemicals and their interactions, danger signs, production techniques, and disposal methods.

Physics	Knowledge and prediction of physical principles, laws, their interrelationships, and applications to understanding fluid, material, and atmospheric dynamics, and mechanical, electrical, atomic and sub- atomic structures and processes.
Food Production	Knowledge of techniques and equipment for planting, growing, and harvesting food products (both plant and animal) for consumption, including storage/handling techniques.

Skills	Skills Definitions
Active Listening	Giving full attention to what other people are saying, taking time to understand the points being made, asking questions as appropriate, and not interrupting at inappropriate times.
Reading Comprehension	Understanding written sentences and paragraphs in work related documents.
Critical Thinking	Using logic and reasoning to identify the strengths and weaknesses of alternative solutions, conclusions or approaches to problems.
Writing	Communicating effectively in writing as appropriate for the needs of the audience.
Speaking	Talking to others to convey information effectively.
Management of Personnel Resources	Motivating, developing, and directing people as they work, identifying the best people for the job.
Judgment and Decision Making	Considering the relative costs and benefits of potential actions to choose the most appropriate one.
Coordination	Adjusting actions in relation to others' actions.
Time Management	Managing one's own time and the time of others.
Monitoring	Monitoring/Assessing performance of yourself, other individuals, or organizations to make improvements or take corrective action.
Active Learning	Understanding the implications of new information for both current and future problem-solving and decision-making.
Social Perceptiveness	Being aware of others' reactions and understanding why they react as they do.
Service Orientation	Actively looking for ways to help people.
Instructing	Teaching others how to do something.
Complex Problem Solving	Identifying complex problems and reviewing related information to develop and evaluate options and implement solutions.
Learning Strategies	Selecting and using training/instructional methods and procedures appropriate for the situation when learning or teaching new things.
Persuasion	Persuading others to change their minds or behavior.
Management of Financial Resources	Determining how money will be spent to get the work done, and accounting for these expenditures.
Negotiation	Bringing others together and trying to reconcile differences.
Systems Evaluation	Identifying measures or indicators of system performance and the actions needed to improve or correct performance, relative to the goals of the system.
Operations Analysis	Analyzing needs and product requirements to create a design.
Mathematics	Using mathematics to solve problems.
Management of Material Resources	Obtaining and seeing to the appropriate use of equipment, facilities, and materials needed to do certain work.
Systems Analysis	Determining how a system should work and how changes in conditions, operations, and the environment will affect outcomes.
Quality Control Analysis	Conducting tests and inspections of products, services, or processes to evaluate quality or performance.
Equipment Selection	Determining the kind of tools and equipment needed to do a job.
Technology Design	Generating or adapting equipment and technology to serve user needs.
Troubleshooting	Determining causes of operating errors and deciding what to do about it.
Science	Using scientific rules and methods to solve problems.
Operation and Control	Controlling operations of equipment or systems.
Operation Monitoring	Watching gauges, dials, or other indicators to make sure a machine is working properly.
Equipment Maintenance	Performing routine maintenance on equipment and determining when and what kind of maintenance is needed.
Installation	Installing equipment, machines, wiring, or programs to meet specifications.
Programming	Writing computer programs for various purposes.
Repairing	Repairing machines or systems using the needed tools.

Ability	Ability Definitions
Oral Expression	The ability to communicate information and ideas in speaking so others will understand.
Written Comprehension	The ability to read and understand information and ideas presented in writing.
Speech Clarity	The ability to speak clearly so others can understand you.
Problem Sensitivity	The ability to tell when something is wrong or is likely to go wrong. It does not involve solving the problem, only recognizing there is a problem.
Oral Comprehension	The ability to listen to and understand information and ideas presented through spoken words and sentences.
Speech Recognition	The ability to identify and understand the speech of another person.
Deductive Reasoning	The ability to apply general rules to specific problems to produce answers that make sense.
Inductive Reasoning	The ability to combine pieces of information to form general rules or conclusions (includes finding a relationship among seemingly unrelated events).
Written Expression	The ability to communicate information and ideas in writing so others will understand.
Information Ordering	The ability to arrange things or actions in a certain order or pattern according to a specific rule or set of rules (e.g., patterns of numbers, letters, words, pictures, mathematical operations).
Near Vision	The ability to see details at close range (within a few feet of the observer).
Originality	The ability to come up with unusual or clever ideas about a given topic or situation, or to develop creative ways to solve a problem.
Fluency of Ideas	The ability to come up with a number of ideas about a topic (the number of ideas is important, not their quality, correctness, or creativity).
Category Flexibility	The ability to generate or use different sets of rules for combining or grouping things in different ways.
Mathematical Reasoning	The ability to choose the right mathematical methods or formulas to solve a problem.
Number Facility	The ability to add, subtract, multiply, or divide quickly and correctly.
Selective Attention	The ability to concentrate on a task over a period of time without being distracted.
Memorization	The ability to remember information such as words, numbers, pictures, and procedures.
Far Vision	The ability to see details at a distance.
Flexibility of Closure	The ability to identify or detect a known pattern (a figure, object, word, or sound) that is hidden in other distracting material.
Time Sharing	The ability to shift back and forth between two or more activities or sources of information (such as speech, sounds, touch, or other sources).
Visualization	The ability to imagine how something will look after it is moved around or when its parts are moved or rearranged.
Hearing Sensitivity	The ability to detect or tell the differences between sounds that vary in pitch and loudness.
Speed of Closure	The ability to quickly make sense of, combine, and organize information into meaningful patterns.
Perceptual Speed	The ability to quickly and accurately compare similarities and differences among sets of letters, numbers, objects, pictures, or patterns. The things to be compared may be presented at the same time or one after the other. This ability also includes comparing a presented object with a remembered object.
Auditory Attention	The ability to focus on a single source of sound in the presence of other distracting sounds.
Visual Color Discrimination	The ability to match or detect differences between colors, including shades of color and brightness.
Finger Dexterity	The ability to make precisely coordinated movements of the fingers of one or both hands to grasp, manipulate, or assemble very small objects.
Depth Perception	The ability to judge which of several objects is closer or farther away from you, or to judge the distance between you and an object.
Static Strength	The ability to exert maximum muscle force to lift, push, pull, or carry objects.
Trunk Strength	The ability to use your abdominal and lower back muscles to support part of the body repeatedly or continuously over time without 'giving out' or fatiguing.
Explosive Strength	The ability to use short bursts of muscle force to propel oneself (as in jumping or sprinting), or to throw an object.

Reaction Time	The ability to quickly respond (with the hand, finger, or foot) to a signal (sound, light, picture) when it appears.
Gross Body Equilibrium	The ability to keep or regain your body balance or stay upright when in an unstable position.
Gross Body Coordination	The ability to coordinate the movement of your arms, legs, and torso together when the whole body is in motion.
Speed of Limb Movement	The ability to quickly move the arms and legs.
Response Orientation	The ability to choose quickly between two or more movements in response to two or more different signals (lights, sounds, pictures). It includes the speed with which the correct response is started with the hand, foot, or other body part.
Stamina	The ability to exert yourself physically over long periods of time without getting winded or out of breath.
Wrist-Finger Speed	The ability to make fast, simple, repeated movements of the fingers, hands, and wrists.
Dynamic Flexibility	The ability to quickly and repeatedly bend, stretch, twist, or reach out with your body, arms, and/or legs.
Arm-Hand Steadiness	The ability to keep your hand and arm steady while moving your arm or while holding your arm and hand in one position.
Manual Dexterity	The ability to quickly move your hand, your hand together with your arm, or your two hands to grasp, manipulate, or assemble objects.
Control Precision	The ability to quickly and repeatedly adjust the controls of a machine or a vehicle to exact positions.
Rate Control	The ability to time your movements or the movement of a piece of equipment in anticipation of changes in the speed and/or direction of a moving object or scene.
Dynamic Strength	The ability to exert muscle force repeatedly or continuously over time. This involves muscular endurance and resistance to muscle fatigue.
Spatial Orientation	The ability to know your location in relation to the environment or to know where other objects are in relation to you.
Extent Flexibility	The ability to bend, stretch, twist, or reach with your body, arms, and/or legs.
Sound Localization	The ability to tell the direction from which a sound originated.
Night Vision	The ability to see under low light conditions.
Peripheral Vision	The ability to see objects or movement of objects to one's side when the eyes are looking ahead.
Glare Sensitivity	The ability to see objects in the presence of glare or bright lighting.
Multilimb Coordination	The ability to coordinate two or more limbs (for example, two arms, two legs, or one leg and one arm) while sitting, standing, or lying down. It does not involve performing the activities while the whole body is in motion.

Work_Activity	Work_Activity Definitions
Communicating with Supervisors, Peers, or Subordin	Providing information to supervisors, co-workers, and subordinates by telephone, in written form, e-mail, or in person.
Getting Information	Observing, receiving, and otherwise obtaining information from all relevant sources.
Establishing and Maintaining Interpersonal Relatio	Developing constructive and cooperative working relationships with others, and maintaining them over time.
Making Decisions and Solving Problems	Analyzing information and evaluating results to choose the best solution and solve problems.
Organizing, Planning, and Prioritizing Work	Developing specific goals and plans to prioritize, organize, and accomplish your work.
Judging the Qualities of Things, Services, or Peop	Assessing the value, importance, or quality of things or people.
Guiding, Directing, and Motivating Subordinates	Providing guidance and direction to subordinates, including setting performance standards and monitoring performance.
Developing Objectives and Strategies	Establishing long-range objectives and specifying the strategies and actions to achieve them.
Interacting With Computers	Using computers and computer systems (including hardware and software) to program, write software, set up functions, enter data, or process information.
Developing and Building Teams	Encouraging and building mutual trust, respect, and cooperation among team members.
Thinking Creatively	Developing, designing, or creating new applications, ideas, relationships, systems, or products, including artistic contributions.
Updating and Using Relevant Knowledge	Keeping up-to-date technically and applying new knowledge to your job.
Coordinating the Work and Activities of Others	Getting members of a group to work together to accomplish tasks.

Communicating with Persons Outside Organization	Communicating with people outside the organization, representing the organization to customers, the public, government, and other external sources. This information can be exchanged in person, in writing, or by telephone or e-mail.
Resolving Conflicts and Negotiating with Others	Handling complaints, settling disputes, and resolving grievances and conflicts, or otherwise negotiating with others.
Performing Administrative Activities	Performing day-to-day administrative tasks such as maintaining information files and processing paperwork.
Analyzing Data or Information	Identifying the underlying principles, reasons, or facts of information by breaking down information or data into separate parts.
Identifying Objects, Actions, and Events	Identifying information by categorizing, estimating, recognizing differences or similarities, and detecting changes in circumstances or events.
Scheduling Work and Activities	Scheduling events, programs, and activities, as well as the work of others.
Evaluating Information to Determine Compliance wit	Using relevant information and individual judgment to determine whether events or processes comply with laws, regulations, or standards.
Coaching and Developing Others	Identifying the developmental needs of others and coaching, mentoring, or otherwise helping others to improve their knowledge or skills.
Interpreting the Meaning of Information for Others	Translating or explaining what information means and how it can be used.
Monitoring and Controlling Resources	Monitoring and controlling resources and overseeing the spending of money.
Training and Teaching Others	Identifying the educational needs of others, developing formal educational or training programs or classes, and teaching or instructing others.
Processing Information	Compiling, coding, categorizing, calculating, tabulating, auditing, or verifying information or data.
Provide Consultation and Advice to Others	Providing guidance and expert advice to management or other groups on technical, systems-, or process-related topics.
Monitor Processes, Materials, or Surroundings	Monitoring and reviewing information from materials, events, or the environment, to detect or assess problems.
Performing for or Working Directly with the Public	Performing for people or dealing directly with the public. This includes serving customers in restaurants and stores, and receiving clients or guests.
Staffing Organizational Units	Recruiting, interviewing, selecting, hiring, and promoting employees in an organization.
Documenting/Recording Information	Entering, transcribing, recording, storing, or maintaining information in written or electronic/magnetic form.
Selling or Influencing Others	Convincing others to buy merchandise/goods or to otherwise change their minds or actions.
Estimating the Quantifiable Characteristics of Pro	Estimating sizes, distances, and quantities; or determining time, costs, resources, or materials needed to perform a work activity.
Assisting and Caring for Others	Providing personal assistance, medical attention, emotional support, or other personal care to others such as coworkers, customers, or patients.
Inspecting Equipment, Structures, or Material	Inspecting equipment, structures, or materials to identify the cause of errors or other problems or defects.
Performing General Physical Activities	Performing physical activities that require considerable use of your arms and legs and moving your whole body, such as climbing, lifting, balancing, walking, stooping, and handling of materials.
Handling and Moving Objects	Using hands and arms in handling, installing, positioning, and moving materials, and manipulating things.
Controlling Machines and Processes	Using either control mechanisms or direct physical activity to operate machines or processes (not including computers or vehicles).
Operating Vehicles, Mechanized Devices, or Equipme	Running, maneuvering, navigating, or driving vehicles or mechanized equipment, such as forklifts, passenger vehicles, aircraft, or water craft.
Drafting, Laying Out, and Specifying Technical Dev	Providing documentation, detailed instructions, drawings, or specifications to tell others about how devices, parts, equipment, or structures are to be fabricated, constructed, assembled, modified, maintained, or used.
Repairing and Maintaining Electronic Equipment	Servicing, repairing, calibrating, regulating, fine-tuning, or testing machines, devices, and equipment that operate primarily on the basis of electrical or electronic (not mechanical) principles.
Repairing and Maintaining Mechanical Equipment	Servicing, repairing, adjusting, and testing machines, devices, moving parts, and equipment that operate primarily on the basis of mechanical (not electronic) principles.

Work_Context	Work_Context Definitions
Telephone	How often do you have telephone conversations in this job?
Electronic Mail	How often do you use electronic mail in this job?
Face-to-Face Discussions	How often do you have to have face-to-face discussions with individuals or teams in this job?
Structured versus Unstructured Work	To what extent is this job structured for the worker, rather than allowing the worker to determine tasks, priorities, and goals?
Freedom to Make Decisions	How much decision making freedom, without supervision, does the job offer?
Work With Work Group or Team	How important is it to work with others in a group or team in this job?
Contact With Others	How much does this job require the worker to be in contact with others (face-to-face, by telephone, or otherwise) in order to perform it?
Indoors, Environmentally Controlled	How often does this job require working indoors in environmentally controlled conditions?
Letters and Memos	How often does the job require written letters and memos?
Impact of Decisions on Co-workers or Company Resul	How do the decisions an employee makes impact the results of co-workers, clients or the company?
Frequency of Decision Making	How frequently is the worker required to make decisions that affect other people, the financial resources, and/or the image and reputation of the organization?
Coordinate or Lead Others	How important is it to coordinate or lead others in accomplishing work activities in this job?
Responsibility for Outcomes and Results	How responsible is the worker for work outcomes and results of other workers?
Spend Time Sitting	How much does this job require sitting?
Importance of Being Exact or Accurate	How important is being very exact or highly accurate in performing this job?
Deal With External Customers	How important is it to work with external customers or the public in this job?
Time Pressure	How often does this job require the worker to meet strict deadlines?
Frequency of Conflict Situations	How often are there conflict situations the employee has to face in this job?
Public Speaking	How often do you have to perform public speaking in this job?
Level of Competition	To what extent does this job require the worker to compete or to be aware of competitive pressures?
Deal With Unpleasant or Angry People	How frequently does the worker have to deal with unpleasant, angry, or discourteous individuals as part of the job requirements?
Consequence of Error	How serious would the result usually be if the worker made a mistake that was not readily correctable?
Responsible for Others' Health and Safety	How much responsibility is there for the health and safety of others in this job?
Physical Proximity	To what extent does this job require the worker to perform job tasks in close physical proximity to other people?
Importance of Repeating Same Tasks	How important is repeating the same physical activities (e.g., key entry) or mental activities (e.g., checking entries in a ledger) over and over, without stopping, to performing this job?
Sounds, Noise Levels Are Distracting or Uncomforta	How often does this job require working exposed to sounds and noise levels that are distracting or uncomfortable?
Degree of Automation	How automated is the job?
Spend Time Standing	How much does this job require standing?
Spend Time Making Repetitive Motions	How much does this job require making repetitive motions?
In an Enclosed Vehicle or Equipment	How often does this job require working in a closed vehicle or equipment (e.g., car)?
Spend Time Using Your Hands to Handle, Control, or	How much does this job require using your hands to handle, control, or feel objects, tools or controls?
Spend Time Walking and Running	How much does this job require walking and running?
Indoors, Not Environmentally Controlled	How often does this job require working indoors in non-controlled environmental conditions (e.g., warehouse without heat)?
Deal With Physically Aggressive People	How frequently does this job require the worker to deal with physical aggression of violent individuals?
Exposed to Contaminants	How often does this job require working exposed to contaminants (such as pollutants, gases, dust or odors)?
Outdoors, Exposed to Weather	How often does this job require working outdoors, exposed to all weather conditions?
Very Hot or Cold Temperatures	How often does this job require working in very hot (above 90 F degrees) or very cold (below 32 F degrees) temperatures?
Extremely Bright or Inadequate Lighting	How often does this job require working in extremely bright or inadequate lighting conditions?
Exposed to Disease or Infections	How often does this job require exposure to disease/infections?
Spend Time Bending or Twisting the Body	How much does this job require bending or twisting your body?
Outdoors, Under Cover	How often does this job require working outdoors, under cover (e.g., structure with roof but no walls)?
Wear Common Protective or Safety Equipment such as	How much does this job require wearing common protective or safety equipment such as safety shoes, glasses, gloves, hard hats or life jackets?
Exposed to Minor Burns, Cuts, Bites, or Stings	How often does this job require exposure to minor burns, cuts, bites, or stings?
Spend Time Kneeling, Crouching, Stooping, or Crawl	How much does this job require kneeling, crouching, stooping or crawling?
Cramped Work Space, Awkward Positions	How often does this job require working in cramped work spaces that requires getting into awkward positions?
Exposed to Hazardous Equipment	How often does this job require exposure to hazardous equipment?
Exposed to Hazardous Conditions	How often does this job require exposure to hazardous conditions?
Spend Time Keeping or Regaining Balance	How much does this job require keeping or regaining your balance?
Exposed to Radiation	How often does this job require exposure to radiation?
In an Open Vehicle or Equipment	How often does this job require working in an open vehicle or equipment (e.g., tractor)?
Spend Time Climbing Ladders, Scaffolds, or Poles	How much does this job require climbing ladders, scaffolds, or poles?
Exposed to High Places	How often does this job require exposure to high places?
Exposed to Whole Body Vibration	How often does this job require exposure to whole body vibration (e.g., operate a jackhammer)?
Pace Determined by Speed of Equipment	How important is it to this job that the pace is determined by the speed of equipment or machinery? (This does not refer to keeping busy at all times on this job.)
Wear Specialized Protective or Safety Equipment su	How much does this job require wearing specialized protective or safety equipment such as breathing apparatus, safety harness, full protection suits, or radiation protection?

Job Zone Component	Job Zone Component Definitions
Title	Job Zone Five: Extensive Preparation Needed
Overall Experience	Extensive skill, knowledge, and experience are needed for these occupations. Many require more than five years of experience. For example, surgeons must complete four years of college and an additional five to seven years of specialized medical training to be able to do their job.
Job Training	Employees may need some on-the-job training, but most of these occupations assume that the person will already have the required skills, knowledge, work-related experience, and/or training.
Job Zone Examples	These occupations often involve coordinating, training, supervising, or managing the activities of others to accomplish goals. Very advanced communication and organizational skills are required. Examples include athletic trainers, lawyers, managing editors, physicists, social psychologists, and surgeons.
SVP Range	(8.0 and above)
Education	A bachelor's degree is the minimum formal education required for these occupations. However, many also require graduate school. For example, they may require a master's degree, and some require a Ph.D., M.D., or J.D. (law degree).

Work_Styles	Work_Styles Definitions
Integrity	Job requires being honest and ethical.
Dependability	Job requires being reliable, responsible, and dependable, and fulfilling obligations.
Leadership	Job requires a willingness to lead, take charge, and offer opinions and direction.
Cooperation	Job requires being pleasant with others on the job and displaying a good-natured, cooperative attitude.
Initiative	Job requires a willingness to take on responsibilities and challenges.
Self Control	Job requires maintaining composure, keeping emotions in check, controlling anger, and avoiding aggressive behavior, even in very difficult situations.
Persistence	Job requires persistence in the face of obstacles.

Concern for Others	Job requires being sensitive to others' needs and feelings and being understanding and helpful on the job.
Adaptability/Flexibility	Job requires being open to change (positive or negative) and to considerable variety in the workplace.
Attention to Detail	Job requires being careful about detail and thorough in completing work tasks.
Stress Tolerance	Job requires accepting criticism and dealing calmly and effectively with high stress situations.
Analytical Thinking	Job requires analyzing information and using logic to address work-related issues and problems.
Achievement/Effort	Job requires establishing and maintaining personally challenging achievement goals and exerting effort toward mastering tasks.
Independence	Job requires developing one's own ways of doing things, guiding oneself with little or no supervision, and depending on oneself to get things done.
Innovation	Job requires creativity and alternative thinking to develop new ideas for and answers to work-related problems.
Social Orientation	Job requires preferring to work with others rather than alone, and being personally connected with others on the job.

11-9131.00 - Postmasters and Mail Superintendents

Direct and coordinate operational, administrative, management, and supportive services of a U.S. post office; or coordinate activities of workers engaged in postal and related work in assigned post office.

Tasks

1) Resolve customer complaints.

2) Prepare employee work schedules.

3) Prepare and submit detailed and summary reports of post office activities to designated supervisors.

4) Hire and train employees, and evaluate their performance.

5) Negotiate labor disputes.

6) Direct and coordinate operational, management, and supportive services of one or a number of postal facilities.

7) Inform the public of available services, and of postal laws and regulations.

8) Collect rents for post office boxes.

9) Issue and cash money orders.

10) Confer with suppliers to obtain bids for proposed purchases and to requisition supplies; disburse funds according to federal regulations.

11) Select and train postmasters and managers of associate postal units.

Knowledge	Knowledge Definitions
Administration and Management	Knowledge of business and management principles involved in strategic planning, resource allocation, human resources modeling, leadership technique, production methods, and coordination of people and resources.
Customer and Personal Service	Knowledge of principles and processes for providing customer and personal services. This includes customer needs assessment, meeting quality standards for services, and evaluation of customer satisfaction.
English Language	Knowledge of the structure and content of the English language including the meaning and spelling of words, rules of composition, and grammar.
Production and Processing	Knowledge of raw materials, production processes, quality control, costs, and other techniques for maximizing the effective manufacture and distribution of goods.
Public Safety and Security	Knowledge of relevant equipment, policies, procedures, and strategies to promote effective local, state, or national security operations for the protection of people, data, property, and institutions.
Clerical	Knowledge of administrative and clerical procedures and systems such as word processing, managing files and records, stenography and transcription, designing forms, and other office procedures and terminology.

Education and Training	Knowledge of principles and methods for curriculum and training design, teaching and instruction for individuals and groups, and the measurement of training effects.
Personnel and Human Resources	Knowledge of principles and procedures for personnel recruitment, selection, training, compensation and benefits, labor relations and negotiation, and personnel information systems.
Psychology	Knowledge of human behavior and performance; individual differences in ability, personality, and interests; learning and motivation; psychological research methods; and the assessment and treatment of behavioral and affective disorders.
Computers and Electronics	Knowledge of circuit boards, processors, chips, electronic equipment, and computer hardware and software, including applications and programming.
Mathematics	Knowledge of arithmetic, algebra, geometry, calculus, statistics, and their applications.
Economics and Accounting	Knowledge of economic and accounting principles and practices, the financial markets, banking and the analysis and reporting of financial data.
Communications and Media	Knowledge of media production, communication, and dissemination techniques and methods. This includes alternative ways to inform and entertain via written, oral, and visual media.
Transportation	Knowledge of principles and methods for moving people or goods by air, rail, sea, or road, including the relative costs and benefits.
Law and Government	Knowledge of laws, legal codes, court procedures, precedents, government regulations, executive orders, agency rules, and the democratic political process.
Sales and Marketing	Knowledge of principles and methods for showing, promoting, and selling products or services. This includes marketing strategy and tactics, product demonstration, sales techniques, and sales control systems.
Sociology and Anthropology	Knowledge of group behavior and dynamics, societal trends and influences, human migrations, ethnicity, cultures and their history and origins.
Telecommunications	Knowledge of transmission, broadcasting, switching, control, and operation of telecommunications systems.
Therapy and Counseling	Knowledge of principles, methods, and procedures for diagnosis, treatment, and rehabilitation of physical and mental dysfunctions, and for career counseling and guidance.
Geography	Knowledge of principles and methods for describing the features of land, sea, and air masses, including their physical characteristics, locations, interrelationships, and distribution of plant, animal, and human life.
Philosophy and Theology	Knowledge of different philosophical systems and religions. This includes their basic principles, values, ethics, ways of thinking, customs, practices, and their impact on human culture.
Mechanical	Knowledge of machines and tools, including their designs, uses, repair, and maintenance.
Engineering and Technology	Knowledge of the practical application of engineering science and technology. This includes applying principles, techniques, procedures, and equipment to the design and production of various goods and services.
Chemistry	Knowledge of the chemical composition, structure, and properties of substances and of the chemical processes and transformations that they undergo. This includes uses of chemicals and their interactions, danger signs, production techniques, and disposal methods.
History and Archeology	Knowledge of historical events and their causes, indicators, and effects on civilizations and cultures.
Medicine and Dentistry	Knowledge of the information and techniques needed to diagnose and treat human injuries, diseases, and deformities. This includes symptoms, treatment alternatives, drug properties and interactions, and preventive health-care measures.
Design	Knowledge of design techniques, tools, and principles involved in production of precision technical plans, blueprints, drawings, and models.
Biology	Knowledge of plant and animal organisms, their tissues, cells, functions, interdependencies, and interactions with each other and the environment.
Physics	Knowledge and prediction of physical principles, laws, their interrelationships, and applications to understanding fluid, material, and atmospheric dynamics, and mechanical, electrical, atomic and sub- atomic structures and processes.

Foreign Language	Knowledge of the structure and content of a foreign (non-English) language including the meaning and spelling of words, rules of composition and grammar, and pronunciation.
Building and Construction	Knowledge of materials, methods, and the tools involved in the construction or repair of houses, buildings, or other structures such as highways and roads.
Food Production	Knowledge of techniques and equipment for planting, growing, and harvesting food products (both plant and animal) for consumption, including storage/handling techniques.
Fine Arts	Knowledge of the theory and techniques required to compose, produce, and perform works of music, dance, visual arts, drama, and sculpture.

Skills	Skills Definitions
Reading Comprehension	Understanding written sentences and paragraphs in work related documents.
Active Listening	Giving full attention to what other people are saying, taking time to understand the points being made, asking questions as appropriate, and not interrupting at inappropriate times.
Time Management	Managing one's own time and the time of others.
Speaking	Talking to others to convey information effectively.
Monitoring	Monitoring/Assessing performance of yourself, other individuals, or organizations to make improvements or take corrective action.
Coordination	Adjusting actions in relation to others' actions.
Instructing	Teaching others how to do something.
Writing	Communicating effectively in writing as appropriate for the needs of the audience.
Critical Thinking	Using logic and reasoning to identify the strengths and weaknesses of alternative solutions, conclusions or approaches to problems.
Negotiation	Bringing others together and trying to reconcile differences.
Judgment and Decision Making	Considering the relative costs and benefits of potential actions to choose the most appropriate one.
Active Learning	Understanding the implications of new information for both current and future problem-solving and decision-making.
Learning Strategies	Selecting and using training/instructional methods and procedures appropriate for the situation when learning or teaching new things.
Service Orientation	Actively looking for ways to help people.
Management of Personnel Resources	Motivating, developing, and directing people as they work, identifying the best people for the job.
Persuasion	Persuading others to change their minds or behavior.
Social Perceptiveness	Being aware of others' reactions and understanding why they react as they do.
Mathematics	Using mathematics to solve problems.
Complex Problem Solving	Identifying complex problems and reviewing related information to develop and evaluate options and implement solutions.
Management of Financial Resources	Determining how money will be spent to get the work done, and accounting for these expenditures.
Operations Analysis	Analyzing needs and product requirements to create a design
Quality Control Analysis	Conducting tests and inspections of products, services, or processes to evaluate quality or performance.
Management of Material Resources	Obtaining and seeing to the appropriate use of equipment, facilities, and materials needed to do certain work.
Operation Monitoring	Watching gauges, dials, or other indicators to make sure a machine is working properly.
Troubleshooting	Determining causes of operating errors and deciding what to do about it.
Operation and Control	Controlling operations of equipment or systems.
Equipment Selection	Determining the kind of tools and equipment needed to do a job.
Systems Evaluation	Identifying measures or indicators of system performance and the actions needed to improve or correct performance, relative to the goals of the system.
Systems Analysis	Determining how a system should work and how changes in conditions, operations, and the environment will affect outcomes.
Technology Design	Generating or adapting equipment and technology to serve user needs.
Programming	Writing computer programs for various purposes.
Equipment Maintenance	Performing routine maintenance on equipment and determining when and what kind of maintenance is needed.
Installation	Installing equipment, machines, wiring, or programs to meet specifications.
Repairing	Repairing machines or systems using the needed tools.

Science	Using scientific rules and methods to solve problems.

Ability	Ability Definitions
Oral Comprehension	The ability to listen to and understand information and ideas presented through spoken words and sentences.
Problem Sensitivity	The ability to tell when something is wrong or is likely to go wrong. It does not involve solving the problem, only recognizing there is a problem.
Oral Expression	The ability to communicate information and ideas in speaking so others will understand.
Written Comprehension	The ability to read and understand information and ideas presented in writing.
Inductive Reasoning	The ability to combine pieces of information to form general rules or conclusions (includes finding a relationship among seemingly unrelated events).
Information Ordering	The ability to arrange things or actions in a certain order or pattern according to a specific rule or set of rules (e.g., patterns of numbers, letters, words, pictures, mathematical operations).
Deductive Reasoning	The ability to apply general rules to specific problems to produce answers that make sense.
Speech Recognition	The ability to identify and understand the speech of another person.
Speech Clarity	The ability to speak clearly so others can understand you.
Category Flexibility	The ability to generate or use different sets of rules for combining or grouping things in different ways.
Near Vision	The ability to see details at close range (within a few feet of the observer).
Written Expression	The ability to communicate information and ideas in writing so others will understand.
Selective Attention	The ability to concentrate on a task over a period of time without being distracted.
Fluency of Ideas	The ability to come up with a number of ideas about a topic (the number of ideas is important, not their quality, correctness, or creativity).
Originality	The ability to come up with unusual or clever ideas about a given topic or situation, or to develop creative ways to solve a problem.
Perceptual Speed	The ability to quickly and accurately compare similarities and differences among sets of letters, numbers, objects, pictures, or patterns. The things to be compared may be presented at the same time or one after the other. This ability also includes comparing a presented object with a remembered object.
Mathematical Reasoning	The ability to choose the right mathematical methods or formulas to solve a problem.
Finger Dexterity	The ability to make precisely coordinated movements of the fingers of one or both hands to grasp, manipulate, or assemble very small objects.
Number Facility	The ability to add, subtract, multiply, or divide quickly and correctly.
Speed of Closure	The ability to quickly make sense of, combine, and organize information into meaningful patterns.
Time Sharing	The ability to shift back and forth between two or more activities or sources of information (such as speech, sounds, touch, or other sources).
Far Vision	The ability to see details at a distance.
Flexibility of Closure	The ability to identify or detect a known pattern (a figure, object, word, or sound) that is hidden in other distracting material.
Auditory Attention	The ability to focus on a single source of sound in the presence of other distracting sounds.
Memorization	The ability to remember information such as words, numbers, pictures, and procedures.
Hearing Sensitivity	The ability to detect or tell the differences between sounds that vary in pitch and loudness.
Visual Color Discrimination	The ability to match or detect differences between colors, including shades of color and brightness.
Visualization	The ability to imagine how something will look after it is moved around or when its parts are moved or rearranged.
Depth Perception	The ability to judge which of several objects is closer or farther away from you, or to judge the distance between you and an object.
Trunk Strength	The ability to use your abdominal and lower back muscles to support part of the body repeatedly or continuously over time without 'giving out' or fatiguing.
Gross Body Coordination	The ability to coordinate the movement of your arms, legs, and torso together when the whole body is in motion.

Stamina	The ability to exert yourself physically over long periods of time without getting winded or out of breath.
Speed of Limb Movement	The ability to quickly move the arms and legs.
Response Orientation	The ability to choose quickly between two or more movements in response to two or more different signals (lights, sounds, pictures). It includes the speed with which the correct response is started with the hand, foot, or other body part.
Arm-Hand Steadiness	The ability to keep your hand and arm steady while moving your arm or while holding your arm and hand in one position.
Dynamic Strength	The ability to exert muscle force repeatedly or continuously over time. This involves muscular endurance and resistance to muscle fatigue.
Explosive Strength	The ability to use short bursts of muscle force to propel oneself (as in jumping or sprinting), or to throw an object.
Static Strength	The ability to exert maximum muscle force to lift, push, pull, or carry objects.
Wrist-Finger Speed	The ability to make fast, simple, repeated movements of the fingers, hands, and wrists.
Reaction Time	The ability to quickly respond (with the hand, finger, or foot) to a signal (sound, light, picture) when it appears.
Rate Control	The ability to time your movements or the movement of a piece of equipment in anticipation of changes in the speed and/or direction of a moving object or scene.
Dynamic Flexibility	The ability to quickly and repeatedly bend, stretch, twist, or reach out with your body, arms, and/or legs.
Control Precision	The ability to quickly and repeatedly adjust the controls of a machine or a vehicle to exact positions.
Spatial Orientation	The ability to know your location in relation to the environment or to know where other objects are in relation to you.
Multilimb Coordination	The ability to coordinate two or more limbs (for example, two arms, two legs, or one leg and one arm) while sitting, standing, or lying down. It does not involve performing the activities while the whole body is in motion.
Peripheral Vision	The ability to see objects or movement of objects to one's side when the eyes are looking ahead.
Sound Localization	The ability to tell the direction from which a sound originated.
Glare Sensitivity	The ability to see objects in the presence of glare or bright lighting.
Night Vision	The ability to see under low light conditions.
Gross Body Equilibrium	The ability to keep or regain your body balance or stay upright when in an unstable position.
Extent Flexibility	The ability to bend, stretch, twist, or reach with your body, arms, and/or legs.
Manual Dexterity	The ability to quickly move your hand, your hand together with your arm, or your two hands to grasp, manipulate, or assemble objects.

Work_Activity	Work_Activity Definitions
Communicating with Supervisors, Peers, or Subordin	Providing information to supervisors, co-workers, and subordinates by telephone, in written form, e-mail, or in person.
Getting Information	Observing, receiving, and otherwise obtaining information from all relevant sources.
Documenting/Recording Information	Entering, transcribing, recording, storing, or maintaining information in written or electronic/magnetic form.
Making Decisions and Solving Problems	Analyzing information and evaluating results to choose the best solution and solve problems.
Processing Information	Compiling, coding, categorizing, calculating, tabulating, auditing, or verifying information or data.
Interacting With Computers	Using computers and computer systems (including hardware and software) to program, write software, set up functions, enter data, or process information.
Guiding, Directing, and Motivating Subordinates	Providing guidance and direction to subordinates, including setting performance standards and monitoring performance.
Coordinating the Work and Activities of Others	Getting members of a group to work together to accomplish tasks.
Performing Administrative Activities	Performing day-to-day administrative tasks such as maintaining information files and processing paperwork.
Analyzing Data or Information	Identifying the underlying principles, reasons, or facts of information by breaking down information or data into separate parts.
Judging the Qualities of Things, Services, or Peop	Assessing the value, importance, or quality of things or people.
Organizing, Planning, and Prioritizing Work	Developing specific goals and plans to prioritize, organize, and accomplish your work.
Scheduling Work and Activities	Scheduling events, programs, and activities, as well as the work of others.

Interpreting the Meaning of Information for Others	Translating or explaining what information means and how it can be used.
Communicating with Persons Outside Organization	Communicating with people outside the organization, representing the organization to customers, the public, government, and other external sources. This information can be exchanged in person, in writing, or by telephone or e-mail.
Resolving Conflicts and Negotiating with Others	Handling complaints, settling disputes, and resolving grievances and conflicts, or otherwise negotiating with others.
Monitor Processes, Materials, or Surroundings	Monitoring and reviewing information from materials, events, or the environment, to detect or assess problems.
Developing and Building Teams	Encouraging and building mutual trust, respect, and cooperation among team members.
Coaching and Developing Others	Identifying the developmental needs of others and coaching, mentoring, or otherwise helping others to improve their knowledge or skills.
Identifying Objects, Actions, and Events	Identifying information by categorizing, estimating, recognizing differences or similarities, and detecting changes in circumstances or events.
Updating and Using Relevant Knowledge	Keeping up-to-date technically and applying new knowledge to your job.
Evaluating Information to Determine Compliance wit	Using relevant information and individual judgment to determine whether events or processes comply with laws, regulations, or standards.
Training and Teaching Others	Identifying the educational needs of others, developing formal educational or training programs or classes, and teaching or instructing others.
Estimating the Quantifiable Characteristics of Pro	Estimating sizes, distances, and quantities; or determining time, costs, resources, or materials needed to perform a work activity.
Performing for or Working Directly with the Public	Performing for people or dealing directly with the public. This includes serving customers in restaurants and stores, and receiving clients or guests.
Developing Objectives and Strategies	Establishing long-range objectives and specifying the strategies and actions to achieve them.
Monitoring and Controlling Resources	Monitoring and controlling resources and overseeing the spending of money.
Staffing Organizational Units	Recruiting, interviewing, selecting, hiring, and promoting employees in an organization.
Inspecting Equipment, Structures, or Material	Inspecting equipment, structures, or materials to identify the cause of errors or other problems or defects.
Establishing and Maintaining Interpersonal Relatio	Developing constructive and cooperative working relationships with others, and maintaining them over time.
Thinking Creatively	Developing, designing, or creating new applications, ideas, relationships, systems, or products, including artistic contributions.
Assisting and Caring for Others	Providing personal assistance, medical attention, emotional support, or other personal care to others such as coworkers, customers, or patients.
Provide Consultation and Advice to Others	Providing guidance and expert advice to management or other groups on technical, systems-, or process-related topics.
Selling or Influencing Others	Convincing others to buy merchandise/goods or to otherwise change their minds or actions.
Performing General Physical Activities	Performing physical activities that require considerable use of your arms and legs and moving your whole body, such as climbing, lifting, balancing, walking, stooping, and handling of materials.
Controlling Machines and Processes	Using either control mechanisms or direct physical activity to operate machines or processes (not including computers or vehicles).
Operating Vehicles, Mechanized Devices, or Equipme	Running, maneuvering, navigating, or driving vehicles or mechanized equipment, such as forklifts, passenger vehicles, aircraft, or water craft.
Handling and Moving Objects	Using hands and arms in handling, installing, positioning, and moving materials, and manipulating things.
Repairing and Maintaining Electronic Equipment	Servicing, repairing, calibrating, regulating, fine-tuning, or testing machines, devices, and equipment that operate primarily on the basis of electrical or electronic (not mechanical) principles.
Repairing and Maintaining Mechanical Equipment	Servicing, repairing, adjusting, and testing machines, devices, moving parts, and equipment that operate primarily on the basis of mechanical (not electronic) principles.
Drafting, Laying Out, and Specifying Technical Dev	Providing documentation, detailed instructions, drawings, or specifications to tell others about how devices, parts, equipment, or structures are to be fabricated, constructed, assembled, modified, maintained, or used.

Work_Context	Work_Context Definitions
Face-to-Face Discussions	How often do you have to have face-to-face discussions with individuals or teams in this job?
Indoors, Environmentally Controlled	How often does this job require working indoors in environmentally controlled conditions?
Telephone	How often do you have telephone conversations in this job?
Responsible for Others' Health and Safety	How much responsibility is there for the health and safety of others in this job?
Responsibility for Outcomes and Results	How responsible is the worker for work outcomes and results of other workers?
Contact With Others	How much does this job require the worker to be in contact with others (face-to-face, by telephone, or otherwise) in order to perform it?
Electronic Mail	How often do you use electronic mail in this job?
Time Pressure	How often does this job require the worker to meet strict deadlines?
Frequency of Decision Making	How frequently is the worker required to make decisions that affect other people, the financial resources, and/or the image and reputation of the organization?
Work With Work Group or Team	How important is it to work with others in a group or team in this job?
Letters and Memos	How often does the job require written letters and memos?
Freedom to Make Decisions	How much decision making freedom, without supervision, does the job offer?
Coordinate or Lead Others	How important is it to coordinate or lead others in accomplishing work activities in this job?
Deal With External Customers	How important is it to work with external customers or the public in this job?
Public Speaking	How often do you have to perform public speaking in this job?
Impact of Decisions on Co-workers or Company Resul	How do the decisions an employee makes impact the results of co-workers, clients or the company?
Structured versus Unstructured Work	To what extent is this job structured for the worker, rather than allowing the worker to determine tasks, priorities, and goals?
Importance of Being Exact or Accurate	How important is being very exact or highly accurate in performing this job?
Level of Competition	To what extent does this job require the worker to compete or to be aware of competitive pressures?
Deal With Unpleasant or Angry People	How frequently does the worker have to deal with unpleasant, angry, or discourteous individuals as part of the job requirements?
Frequency of Conflict Situations	How often are there conflict situations the employee has to face in this job?
Exposed to Contaminants	How often does this job require working exposed to contaminants (such as pollutants, gases, dust or odors)?
Spend Time Standing	How much does this job require standing?
Importance of Repeating Same Tasks	How important is repeating the same physical activities (e.g., key entry) or mental activities (e.g., checking entries in a ledger) over and over, without stopping, to performing this job?
Physical Proximity	To what extent does this job require the worker to perform job tasks in close physical proximity to other people?
Spend Time Walking and Running	How much does this job require walking and running?
Spend Time Sitting	How much does this job require sitting?
Consequence of Error	How serious would the result usually be if the worker made a mistake that was not readily correctable?
Degree of Automation	How automated is the job?
In an Enclosed Vehicle or Equipment	How often does this job require working in a closed vehicle or equipment (e.g., car)?
Sounds, Noise Levels Are Distracting or Uncomforta	How often does this job require working exposed to sounds and noise levels that are distracting or uncomfortable?
Outdoors, Exposed to Weather	How often does this job require working outdoors, exposed to all weather conditions?
Deal With Physically Aggressive People	How frequently does this job require the worker to deal with physical aggression of violent individuals?
Spend Time Making Repetitive Motions	How much does this job require making repetitive motions?
Pace Determined by Speed of Equipment	How important is it to this job that the pace is determined by the speed of equipment or machinery? (This does not refer to keeping busy at all times on this job.)
Indoors, Not Environmentally Controlled	How often does this job require working indoors in non-controlled environmental conditions (e.g., warehouse without heat)?
Very Hot or Cold Temperatures	How often does this job require working in very hot (above 90 F degrees) or very cold (below 32 F degrees) temperatures?
Spend Time Bending or Twisting the Body	How much does this job require bending or twisting your body?

Exposed to Minor Burns, Cuts, Bites, or Stings	How often does this job require exposure to minor burns, cuts, bites, or stings?
Spend Time Using Your Hands to Handle, Control, or	How much does this job require using your hands to handle, control, or feel objects, tools or controls?
Extremely Bright or Inadequate Lighting	How often does this job require working in extremely bright or inadequate lighting conditions?
Exposed to Hazardous Equipment	How often does this job require exposure to hazardous equipment?
Wear Common Protective or Safety Equipment such as	How much does this job require wearing common protective or safety equipment such as safety shoes, glasses, gloves, hard hats or live jackets?
Outdoors, Under Cover	How often does this job require working outdoors, under cover (e.g., structure with roof but no walls)?
Spend Time Kneeling, Crouching, Stooping, or Crawl	How much does this job require kneeling, crouching, stooping or crawling?
Cramped Work Space, Awkward Positions	How often does this job require working in cramped work spaces that requires getting into awkward positions?
Exposed to High Places	How often does this job require exposure to high places?
Spend Time Keeping or Regaining Balance	How much does this job require keeping or regaining your balance?
Exposed to Hazardous Conditions	How often does this job require exposure to hazardous conditions?
Exposed to Disease or Infections	How often does this job require exposure to disease/infections?
Exposed to Whole Body Vibration	How often does this job require exposure to whole body vibration (e.g., operate a jackhammer)?
In an Open Vehicle or Equipment	How often does this job require working in an open vehicle or equipment (e.g., tractor)?
Spend Time Climbing Ladders, Scaffolds, or Poles	How much does this job require climbing ladders, scaffolds, or poles?
Wear Specialized Protective or Safety Equipment su	How much does this job require wearing specialized protective or safety equipment such as breathing apparatus, safety harness, full protection suits, or radiation protection?
Exposed to Radiation	How often does this job require exposure to radiation?

Job Zone Component	Job Zone Component Definitions
Title	Job Zone Three: Medium Preparation Needed
Overall Experience	Previous work-related skill, knowledge, or experience is required for these occupations. For example, an electrician must have completed three or four years of apprenticeship or several years of vocational training, and often must have passed a licensing exam, in order to perform the job.
Job Training	Employees in these occupations usually need one or two years of training involving both on-the-job experience and informal training with experienced workers.
Job Zone Examples	These occupations usually involve using communication and organizational skills to coordinate, supervise, manage, or train others to accomplish goals. Examples include dental assistants, electricians, fish and game wardens, legal secretaries, personnel recruiters, and recreation workers.
SVP Range	(6.0 to < 7.0)
Education	Most occupations in this zone require training in vocational schools, related on-the-job experience, or an associate's degree. Some may require a bachelor's degree.

Work_Styles	Work_Styles Definitions
Dependability	Job requires being reliable, responsible, and dependable, and fulfilling obligations.
Self Control	Job requires maintaining composure, keeping emotions in check, controlling anger, and avoiding aggressive behavior, even in very difficult situations.
Leadership	Job requires a willingness to lead, take charge, and offer opinions and direction.
Integrity	Job requires being honest and ethical.
Stress Tolerance	Job requires accepting criticism and dealing calmly and effectively with high stress situations.
Cooperation	Job requires being pleasant with others on the job and displaying a good-natured, cooperative attitude.
Adaptability/Flexibility	Job requires being open to change (positive or negative) and to considerable variety in the workplace.
Initiative	Job requires a willingness to take on responsibilities and challenges.

Achievement/Effort	Job requires establishing and maintaining personally challenging achievement goals and exerting effort toward mastering tasks.
Attention to Detail	Job requires being careful about detail and thorough in completing work tasks.
Persistence	Job requires persistence in the face of obstacles.
Concern for Others	Job requires being sensitive to others' needs and feelings and being understanding and helpful on the job.
Independence	Job requires developing one's own ways of doing things, guiding oneself with little or no supervision, and depending on oneself to get things done.
Analytical Thinking	Job requires analyzing information and using logic to address work-related issues and problems.
Social Orientation	Job requires preferring to work with others rather than alone, and being personally connected with others on the job.
Innovation	Job requires creativity and alternative thinking to develop new ideas for and answers to work-related problems.

13-1031.01 - Claims Examiners, Property and Casualty Insurance

Review settled insurance claims to determine that payments and settlements have been made in accordance with company practices and procedures. Report overpayments, underpayments, and other irregularities. Confer with legal counsel on claims requiring litigation.

Tasks

1) Pay and process claims within designated authority level.

2) Contact and/or interview claimants, doctors, medical specialists, or employers to get additional information.

3) Confer with legal counsel on claims requiring litigation.

4) Report overpayments, underpayments, and other irregularities.

5) Examine claims investigated by insurance adjusters, further investigating questionable claims to determine whether to authorize payments.

6) Verify and analyze data used in settling claims to ensure that claims are valid and that settlements are made according to company practices and procedures.

7) Maintain claim files, such as records of settled claims and an inventory of claims requiring detailed analysis.

8) Enter claim payments, reserves and new claims on computer system, inputting concise yet sufficient file documentation.

9) Resolve complex, severe exposure claims, using high service oriented file handling.

10) Adjust reserves and provide reserve recommendations to ensure reserving activities consistent with corporate policies.

11) Present cases and participate in their discussion at claim committee meetings.

12) Communicate with reinsurance brokers to obtain information necessary for processing claims.

13) Conduct detailed bill reviews to implement sound litigation management and expense control.

14) Supervise claims adjusters to ensure that adjusters have followed proper methods.

15) Prepare reports to be submitted to company's data processing department.

Knowledge	Knowledge Definitions
English Language	Knowledge of the structure and content of the English language including the meaning and spelling of words, rules of composition, and grammar.
Customer and Personal Service	Knowledge of principles and processes for providing customer and personal services. This includes customer needs assessment, meeting quality standards for services, and evaluation of customer satisfaction.
Law and Government	Knowledge of laws, legal codes, court procedures, precedents, government regulations, executive orders, agency rules, and the democratic political process.
Clerical	Knowledge of administrative and clerical procedures and systems such as word processing, managing files and records, stenography and transcription, designing forms, and other office procedures and terminology.
Mathematics	Knowledge of arithmetic, algebra, geometry, calculus, statistics, and their applications.
Computers and Electronics	Knowledge of circuit boards, processors, chips, electronic equipment, and computer hardware and software, including applications and programming.
Medicine and Dentistry	Knowledge of the information and techniques needed to diagnose and treat human injuries, diseases, and deformities. This includes symptoms, treatment alternatives, drug properties and interactions, and preventive health-care measures.
Administration and Management	Knowledge of business and management principles involved in strategic planning, resource allocation, human resources modeling, leadership technique, production methods, and coordination of people and resources.
Economics and Accounting	Knowledge of economic and accounting principles and practices, the financial markets, banking and the analysis and reporting of financial data.
Telecommunications	Knowledge of transmission, broadcasting, switching, control, and operation of telecommunications systems.
Education and Training	Knowledge of principles and methods for curriculum and training design, teaching and instruction for individuals and groups, and the measurement of training effects.
Communications and Media	Knowledge of media production, communication, and dissemination techniques and methods. This includes alternative ways to inform and entertain via written, oral, and visual media.
Public Safety and Security	Knowledge of relevant equipment, policies, procedures, and strategies to promote effective local, state, or national security operations for the protection of people, data, property, and institutions.
Psychology	Knowledge of human behavior and performance; individual differences in ability, personality, and interests; learning and motivation; psychological research methods; and the assessment and treatment of behavioral and affective disorders.
Personnel and Human Resources	Knowledge of principles and procedures for personnel recruitment, selection, training, compensation and benefits, labor relations and negotiation, and personnel information systems.
Transportation	Knowledge of principles and methods for moving people or goods by air, rail, sea, or road, including the relative costs and benefits.
Therapy and Counseling	Knowledge of principles, methods, and procedures for diagnosis, treatment, and rehabilitation of physical and mental dysfunctions, and for career counseling and guidance.
Sales and Marketing	Knowledge of principles and methods for showing, promoting, and selling products or services. This includes marketing strategy and tactics, product demonstration, sales techniques, and sales control systems.
Geography	Knowledge of principles and methods for describing the features of land, sea, and air masses, including their physical characteristics, locations, interrelationships, and distribution of plant, animal, and human life.
Production and Processing	Knowledge of raw materials, production processes, quality control, costs, and other techniques for maximizing the effective manufacture and distribution of goods.
Sociology and Anthropology	Knowledge of group behavior and dynamics, societal trends and influences, human migrations, ethnicity, cultures and their history and origins.
Building and Construction	Knowledge of materials, methods, and the tools involved in the construction or repair of houses, buildings, or other structures, such as highways and roads.
Mechanical	Knowledge of machines and tools, including their designs, uses, repair, and maintenance.
History and Archeology	Knowledge of historical events and their causes, indicators, and effects on civilizations and cultures.
Foreign Language	Knowledge of the structure and content of a foreign (non-English) language including the meaning and spelling of words, rules of composition and grammar, and pronunciation.
Biology	Knowledge of plant and animal organisms, their tissues, cells, functions, interdependencies, and interactions with each other and the environment.
Philosophy and Theology	Knowledge of different philosophical systems and religions. This includes their basic principles, values, ethics, ways of thinking, customs, practices, and their impact on human culture.
Physics	Knowledge and prediction of physical principles, laws, their interrelationships, and applications to understanding fluid, material, and atmospheric dynamics, and mechanical, electrical, atomic and sub-atomic structures and processes.

Chemistry	Knowledge of the chemical composition, structure, and properties of substances and of the chemical processes and transformations that they undergo. This includes uses of chemicals and their interactions, danger signs, production techniques, and disposal methods.
Design	Knowledge of design techniques, tools, and principles involved in production of precision technical plans, blueprints, drawings, and models.
Engineering and Technology	Knowledge of the practical application of engineering science and technology. This includes applying principles, techniques, procedures, and equipment to the design and production of various goods and services.
Fine Arts	Knowledge of the theory and techniques required to compose, produce, and perform works of music, dance, visual arts, drama, and sculpture.
Food Production	Knowledge of techniques and equipment for planting, growing, and harvesting food products (both plant and animal) for consumption, including storage/handling techniques.

Skills	Skills Definitions
Reading Comprehension	Understanding written sentences and paragraphs in work related documents.
Judgment and Decision Making	Considering the relative costs and benefits of potential actions to choose the most appropriate one.
Active Listening	Giving full attention to what other people are saying, taking time to understand the points being made, asking questions as appropriate, and not interrupting at inappropriate times.
Writing	Communicating effectively in writing as appropriate for the needs of the audience.
Time Management	Managing one's own time and the time of others.
Critical Thinking	Using logic and reasoning to identify the strengths and weaknesses of alternative solutions, conclusions or approaches to problems.
Speaking	Talking to others to convey information effectively.
Active Learning	Understanding the implications of new information for both current and future problem-solving and decision-making.
Negotiation	Bringing others together and trying to reconcile differences.
Complex Problem Solving	Identifying complex problems and reviewing related information to develop and evaluate options and implement solutions.
Service Orientation	Actively looking for ways to help people.
Monitoring	Monitoring/Assessing performance of yourself, other individuals, or organizations to make improvements or take corrective action.
Instructing	Teaching others how to do something.
Mathematics	Using mathematics to solve problems.
Persuasion	Persuading others to change their minds or behavior.
Learning Strategies	Selecting and using training/instructional methods and procedures appropriate for the situation when learning or teaching new things.
Social Perceptiveness	Being aware of others' reactions and understanding why they react as they do.
Coordination	Adjusting actions in relation to others' actions.
Quality Control Analysis	Conducting tests and inspections of products, services, or processes to evaluate quality or performance.
Management of Personnel Resources	Motivating, developing, and directing people as they work, identifying the best people for the job.
Management of Financial Resources	Determining how money will be spent to get the work done, and accounting for these expenditures.
Systems Evaluation	Identifying measures or indicators of system performance and the actions needed to improve or correct performance, relative to the goals of the system.
Science	Using scientific rules and methods to solve problems.
Management of Material Resources	Obtaining and seeing to the appropriate use of equipment, facilities, and materials needed to do certain work.
Systems Analysis	Determining how a system should work and how changes in conditions, operations, and the environment will affect outcomes.
Operations Analysis	Analyzing needs and product requirements to create a design.
Operation and Control	Controlling operations of equipment or systems.
Technology Design	Generating or adapting equipment and technology to serve user needs.
Troubleshooting	Determining causes of operating errors and deciding what to do about it.
Equipment Selection	Determining the kind of tools and equipment needed to do a job.

Equipment Maintenance	Performing routine maintenance on equipment and determining when and what kind of maintenance is needed.
Repairing	Repairing machines or systems using the needed tools.
Operation Monitoring	Watching gauges, dials, or other indicators to make sure a machine is working properly.
Installation	Installing equipment, machines, wiring, or programs to meet specifications.
Programming	Writing computer programs for various purposes.

Ability	Ability Definitions
Deductive Reasoning	The ability to apply general rules to specific problems to produce answers that make sense.
Oral Expression	The ability to communicate information and ideas in speaking so others will understand.
Oral Comprehension	The ability to listen to and understand information and ideas presented through spoken words and sentences.
Written Comprehension	The ability to read and understand information and ideas presented in writing.
Problem Sensitivity	The ability to tell when something is wrong or is likely to go wrong. It does not involve solving the problem, only recognizing there is a problem.
Inductive Reasoning	The ability to combine pieces of information to form general rules or conclusions (includes finding a relationship among seemingly unrelated events).
Speech Recognition	The ability to identify and understand the speech of another person.
Speech Clarity	The ability to speak clearly so others can understand you.
Information Ordering	The ability to arrange things or actions in a certain order or pattern according to a specific rule or set of rules (e.g., patterns of numbers, letters, words, pictures, mathematical operations).
Written Expression	The ability to communicate information and ideas in writing so others will understand.
Near Vision	The ability to see details at close range (within a few feet of the observer).
Category Flexibility	The ability to generate or use different sets of rules for combining or grouping things in different ways.
Selective Attention	The ability to concentrate on a task over a period of time without being distracted.
Fluency of Ideas	The ability to come up with a number of ideas about a topic (the number of ideas is important, not their quality, correctness, or creativity).
Far Vision	The ability to see details at a distance.
Flexibility of Closure	The ability to identify or detect a known pattern (a figure, object, word, or sound) that is hidden in other distracting material.
Number Facility	The ability to add, subtract, multiply, or divide quickly and correctly.
Perceptual Speed	The ability to quickly and accurately compare similarities and differences among sets of letters, numbers, objects, pictures, or patterns. The things to be compared may be presented at the same time or one after the other. This ability also includes comparing a presented object with a remembered object.
Mathematical Reasoning	The ability to choose the right mathematical methods or formulas to solve a problem.
Speed of Closure	The ability to quickly make sense of, combine, and organize information into meaningful patterns.
Finger Dexterity	The ability to make precisely coordinated movements of the fingers of one or both hands to grasp, manipulate, or assemble very small objects.
Visualization	The ability to imagine how something will look after it is moved around or when its parts are moved or rearranged.
Originality	The ability to come up with unusual or clever ideas about a given topic or situation, or to develop creative ways to solve a problem.
Memorization	The ability to remember information such as words, numbers, pictures, and procedures.
Visual Color Discrimination	The ability to match or detect differences between colors, including shades of color and brightness.
Auditory Attention	The ability to focus on a single source of sound in the presence of other distracting sounds.
Time Sharing	The ability to shift back and forth between two or more activities or sources of information (such as speech, sounds, touch, or other sources).
Hearing Sensitivity	The ability to detect or tell the differences between sounds that vary in pitch and loudness.
Arm-Hand Steadiness	The ability to keep your hand and arm steady while moving your arm or while holding your arm and hand in one position.

Control Precision	The ability to quickly and repeatedly adjust the controls of a machine or a vehicle to exact positions.
Manual Dexterity	The ability to quickly move your hand, your hand together with your arm, or your two hands to grasp, manipulate, or assemble objects.
Depth Perception	The ability to judge which of several objects is closer or farther away from you, or to judge the distance between you and an object.
Wrist-Finger Speed	The ability to make fast, simple, repeated movements of the fingers, hands, and wrists.
Spatial Orientation	The ability to know your location in relation to the environment or to know where other objects are in relation to you.
Rate Control	The ability to time your movements or the movement of a piece of equipment in anticipation of changes in the speed and/or direction of a moving object or scene.
Extent Flexibility	The ability to bend, stretch, twist, or reach with your body, arms, and/or legs.
Stamina	The ability to exert yourself physically over long periods of time without getting winded or out of breath.
Trunk Strength	The ability to use your abdominal and lower back muscles to support part of the body repeatedly or continuously over time without 'giving out' or fatiguing.
Dynamic Strength	The ability to exert muscle force repeatedly or continuously over time. This involves muscular endurance and resistance to muscle fatigue.
Explosive Strength	The ability to use short bursts of muscle force to propel oneself (as in jumping or sprinting), or to throw an object.
Static Strength	The ability to exert maximum muscle force to lift, push, pull, or carry objects.
Reaction Time	The ability to quickly respond (with the hand, finger, or foot) to a signal (sound, light, picture) when it appears.
Dynamic Flexibility	The ability to quickly and repeatedly bend, stretch, twist, or reach out with your body, arms, and/or legs.
Multilimb Coordination	The ability to coordinate two or more limbs (for example, two arms, two legs, or one leg and one arm) while sitting, standing, or lying down. It does not involve performing the activities while the whole body is in motion.
Glare Sensitivity	The ability to see objects in the presence of glare or bright lighting.
Speed of Limb Movement	The ability to quickly move the arms and legs.
Sound Localization	The ability to tell the direction from which a sound originated.
Night Vision	The ability to see under low light conditions.
Peripheral Vision	The ability to see objects or movement of objects to one's side when the eyes are looking ahead.
Gross Body Equilibrium	The ability to keep or regain your body balance or stay upright when in an unstable position.
Gross Body Coordination	The ability to coordinate the movement of your arms, legs, and torso together when the whole body is in motion.
Response Orientation	The ability to choose quickly between two or more movements in response to two or more different signals (lights, sounds, pictures). It includes the speed with which the correct response is started with the hand, foot, or other body part.

Work_Activity	Work_Activity Definitions
Getting Information	Observing, receiving, and otherwise obtaining information from all relevant sources.
Communicating with Persons Outside Organization	Communicating with people outside the organization, representing the organization to customers, the public, government, and other external sources. This information can be exchanged in person, in writing, or by telephone or e-mail.
Interacting With Computers	Using computers and computer systems (including hardware and software) to program, write software, set up functions, enter data, or process information.
Documenting/Recording Information	Entering, transcribing, recording, storing, or maintaining information in written or electronic/magnetic form.
Communicating with Supervisors, Peers, or Subordin	Providing information to supervisors, co-workers, and subordinates by telephone, in written form, e-mail, or in person.
Making Decisions and Solving Problems	Analyzing information and evaluating results to choose the best solution and solve problems.
Establishing and Maintaining Interpersonal Relatio	Developing constructive and cooperative working relationships with others, and maintaining them over time.
Evaluating Information to Determine Compliance wit	Using relevant information and individual judgment to determine whether events or processes comply with laws, regulations, or standards.

Performing Administrative Activities	Performing day-to-day administrative tasks such as maintaining information files and processing paperwork.
Interpreting the Meaning of Information for Others	Translating or explaining what information means and how it can be used.
Processing Information	Compiling, coding, categorizing, calculating, tabulating, auditing, or verifying information or data.
Identifying Objects, Actions, and Events	Identifying information by categorizing, estimating, recognizing differences or similarities, and detecting changes in circumstances or events.
Organizing, Planning, and Prioritizing Work	Developing specific goals and plans to prioritize, organize, and accomplish your work.
Updating and Using Relevant Knowledge	Keeping up-to-date technically and applying new knowledge to your job.
Resolving Conflicts and Negotiating with Others	Handling complaints, settling disputes, and resolving grievances and conflicts, or otherwise negotiating with others.
Analyzing Data or Information	Identifying the underlying principles, reasons, or facts of information by breaking down information or data into separate parts.
Monitor Processes, Materials, or Surroundings	Monitoring and reviewing information from materials, events, or the environment, to detect or assess problems.
Judging the Qualities of Things, Services, or Peop	Assessing the value, importance, or quality of things or people.
Training and Teaching Others	Identifying the educational needs of others, developing formal educational or training programs or classes, and teaching or instructing others.
Provide Consultation and Advice to Others	Providing guidance and expert advice to management or other groups on technical, systems-, or process-related topics.
Developing Objectives and Strategies	Establishing long-range objectives and specifying the strategies and actions to achieve them.
Estimating the Quantifiable Characteristics of Pro	Estimating sizes, distances, and quantities; or determining time, costs, resources, or materials needed to perform a work activity.
Performing for or Working Directly with the Public	Performing for people or dealing directly with the public. This includes serving customers in restaurants and stores, and receiving clients or guests.
Assisting and Caring for Others	Providing personal assistance, medical attention, emotional support, or other personal care to others such as coworkers, customers, or patients.
Coordinating the Work and Activities of Others	Getting members of a group to work together to accomplish tasks.
Coaching and Developing Others	Identifying the developmental needs of others and coaching, mentoring, or otherwise helping others to improve their knowledge or skills.
Inspecting Equipment, Structures, or Material	Inspecting equipment, structures, or materials to identify the cause of errors or other problems or defects.
Guiding, Directing, and Motivating Subordinates	Providing guidance and direction to subordinates, including setting performance standards and monitoring performance.
Developing and Building Teams	Encouraging and building mutual trust, respect, and cooperation among team members.
Selling or Influencing Others	Convincing others to buy merchandise/goods or to otherwise change their minds or actions.
Scheduling Work and Activities	Scheduling events, programs, and activities, as well as the work of others.
Handling and Moving Objects	Using hands and arms in handling, installing, positioning, and moving materials, and manipulating things.
Thinking Creatively	Developing, designing, or creating new applications, ideas, relationships, systems, or products, including artistic contributions.
Monitoring and Controlling Resources	Monitoring and controlling resources and overseeing the spending of money.
Performing General Physical Activities	Performing physical activities that require considerable use of your arms and legs and moving your whole body, such as climbing, lifting, balancing, walking, stooping, and handling of materials.
Controlling Machines and Processes	Using either control mechanisms or direct physical activity to operate machines or processes (not including computers or vehicles).
Staffing Organizational Units	Recruiting, interviewing, selecting, hiring, and promoting employees in an organization.
Operating Vehicles, Mechanized Devices, or Equipme	Running, maneuvering, navigating, or driving vehicles or mechanized equipment, such as forklifts, passenger vehicles, aircraft, or water craft.
Repairing and Maintaining Electronic Equipment	Servicing, repairing, calibrating, regulating, fine-tuning, or testing machines, devices, and equipment that operate primarily on the basis of electrical or electronic (not mechanical) principles.

Drafting, Laying Out, and Specifying Technical Dev	Providing documentation, detailed instructions, drawings, or specifications to tell others about how devices, parts, equipment, or structures are to be fabricated, constructed, assembled, modified, maintained, or used.
Repairing and Maintaining Mechanical Equipment	Servicing, repairing, adjusting, and testing machines, devices, moving parts, and equipment that operate primarily on the basis of mechanical (not electronic) principles.

Work_Context	Work_Context Definitions
Structured versus Unstructured Work	To what extent is this job structured for the worker, rather than allowing the worker to determine tasks, priorities, and goals?
Indoors, Environmentally Controlled	How often does this job require working indoors in environmentally controlled conditions?
Spend Time Sitting	How much does this job require sitting?
Face-to-Face Discussions	How often do you have to have face-to-face discussions with individuals or teams in this job?
Importance of Being Exact or Accurate	How important is being very exact or highly accurate in performing this job?
Contact With Others	How much does this job require the worker to be in contact with others (face-to-face, by telephone, or otherwise) in order to perform it?
Telephone	How often do you have telephone conversations in this job?
Freedom to Make Decisions	How much decision making freedom, without supervision, does the job offer?
Time Pressure	How often does this job require the worker to meet strict deadlines?
Frequency of Decision Making	How frequently is the worker required to make decisions that affect other people, the financial resources, and/or the image and reputation of the organization?
Importance of Repeating Same Tasks	How important is repeating the same physical activities (e.g., key entry) or mental activities (e.g., checking entries in a ledger) over and over, without stopping, to performing this job?
Letters and Memos	How often does the job require written letters and memos?
Impact of Decisions on Co-workers or Company Resul	How do the decisions an employee makes impact the results of co-workers, clients or the company?
Electronic Mail	How often do you use electronic mail in this job?
Deal With External Customers	How important is it to work with external customers or the public in this job?
Work With Work Group or Team	How important is it to work with others in a group or team in this job?
Coordinate or Lead Others	How important is it to coordinate or lead others in accomplishing work activities in this job?
Responsibility for Outcomes and Results	How responsible is the worker for work outcomes and results of other workers?
Level of Competition	To what extent does this job require the worker to compete or to be aware of competitive pressures?
Deal With Unpleasant or Angry People	How frequently does the worker have to deal with unpleasant, angry, or discourteous individuals as part of the job requirements?
Spend Time Using Your Hands to Handle, Control, or	How much does this job require using your hands to handle, control, or feel objects, tools or controls?
Spend Time Making Repetitive Motions	How much does this job require making repetitive motions?
Frequency of Conflict Situations	How often are there conflict situations the employee has to face in this job?
Physical Proximity	To what extent does this job require the worker to perform job tasks in close physical proximity to other people?
Consequence of Error	How serious would the result usually be if the worker made a mistake that was not readily correctable?
Sounds, Noise Levels Are Distracting or Uncomforta	How often does this job require working exposed to sounds and noise levels that are distracting or uncomfortable?
Degree of Automation	How automated is the job?
In an Enclosed Vehicle or Equipment	How often does this job require working in a closed vehicle or equipment (e.g., car)?
Responsible for Others' Health and Safety	How much responsibility is there for the health and safety of others in this job?
Spend Time Standing	How much does this job require standing?
Outdoors, Exposed to Weather	How often does this job require working outdoors, exposed to all weather conditions?
Very Hot or Cold Temperatures	How often does this job require working in very hot (above 90 F degrees) or very cold (below 32 F degrees) temperatures?
Indoors, Not Environmentally Controlled	How often does this job require working indoors in non-controlled environmental conditions (e.g., warehouse without heat)?

Spend Time Walking and Running	How much does this job require walking and running?
Exposed to Contaminants	How often does this job require working exposed to contaminants (such as pollutants, gases, dust or odors)?
Pace Determined by Speed of Equipment	How important is it to this job that the pace is determined by the speed of equipment or machinery? (This does not refer to keeping busy at all times on this job.)
Spend Time Bending or Twisting the Body	How much does this job require bending or twisting your body?
Deal With Physically Aggressive People	How frequently does this job require the worker to deal with physical aggression of violent individuals?
Extremely Bright or Inadequate Lighting	How often does this job require working in extremely bright or inadequate lighting conditions?
Spend Time Keeping or Regaining Balance	How much does this job require keeping or regaining your balance?
Public Speaking	How often do you have to perform public speaking in this job?
Exposed to Radiation	How often does this job require exposure to radiation?
Exposed to High Places	How often does this job require exposure to high places?
Spend Time Kneeling, Crouching, Stooping, or Crawl	How much does this job require kneeling, crouching, stooping or crawling?
Cramped Work Space, Awkward Positions	How often does this job require working in cramped work spaces that requires getting into awkward positions?
Exposed to Minor Burns, Cuts, Bites, or Stings	How often does this job require exposure to minor burns, cuts, bites, or stings?
Spend Time Climbing Ladders, Scaffolds, or Poles	How much does this job require climbing ladders, scaffolds, or poles?
Wear Common Protective or Safety Equipment such as	How much does this job require wearing common protective or safety equipment such as safety shoes, glasses, gloves, hard hats or life jackets?
Outdoors, Under Cover	How often does this job require working outdoors, under cover (e.g., structure with roof but no walls)?
In an Open Vehicle or Equipment	How often does this job require working in an open vehicle or equipment (e.g., tractor)?
Exposed to Hazardous Equipment	How often does this job require exposure to hazardous equipment?
Wear Specialized Protective or Safety Equipment su	How much does this job require wearing specialized protective or safety equipment such as breathing apparatus, safety harness, full protection suits, or radiation protection?
Exposed to Hazardous Conditions	How often does this job require exposure to hazardous conditions?
Exposed to Whole Body Vibration	How often does this job require exposure to whole body vibration (e.g., operate a jackhammer)?
Exposed to Disease or Infections	How often does this job require exposure to disease/infections?

Job Zone Component	Job Zone Component Definitions
Title	Job Zone Three: Medium Preparation Needed
Overall Experience	Previous work-related skill, knowledge, or experience is required for these occupations. For example, an electrician must have completed three or four years of apprenticeship or several years of vocational training, and often must have passed a licensing exam, in order to perform the job.
Job Training	Employees in these occupations usually need one or two years of training involving both on-the-job experience and informal training with experienced workers.
Job Zone Examples	These occupations usually involve using communication and organizational skills to coordinate, supervise, manage, or train others to accomplish goals. Examples include dental assistants, electricians, fish and game wardens, legal secretaries, personnel recruiters, and recreation workers.
SVP Range	(6.0 to < 7.0)
Education	Most occupations in this zone require training in vocational schools, related on-the-job experience, or an associate's degree. Some may require a bachelor's degree.

Work_Styles	Work_Styles Definitions
Dependability	Job requires being reliable, responsible, and dependable, and fulfilling obligations.
Attention to Detail	Job requires being careful about detail and thorough in completing work tasks.
Integrity	Job requires being honest and ethical.
Analytical Thinking	Job requires analyzing information and using logic to address work-related issues and problems.

Adaptability/Flexibility	Job requires being open to change (positive or negative) and to considerable variety in the workplace.
Stress Tolerance	Job requires accepting criticism and dealing calmly and effectively with high stress situations.
Cooperation	Job requires being pleasant with others on the job and displaying a good-natured, cooperative attitude.
Initiative	Job requires a willingness to take on responsibilities and challenges.
Self Control	Job requires maintaining composure, keeping emotions in check, controlling anger, and avoiding aggressive behavior, even in very difficult situations.
Persistence	Job requires persistence in the face of obstacles.
Independence	Job requires developing one's own ways of doing things, guiding oneself with little or no supervision, and depending on oneself to get things done.
Achievement/Effort	Job requires establishing and maintaining personally challenging achievement goals and exerting effort toward mastering tasks.
Concern for Others	Job requires being sensitive to others' needs and feelings and being understanding and helpful on the job.
Leadership	Job requires a willingness to lead, take charge, and offer opinions and direction.
Innovation	Job requires creativity and alternative thinking to develop new ideas for and answers to work-related problems.
Social Orientation	Job requires preferring to work with others rather than alone, and being personally connected with others on the job.

13-1041.01 - Environmental Compliance Inspectors

Inspect and investigate sources of pollution to protect the public and environment and ensure conformance with Federal, State, and local regulations and ordinances.

Tasks

1) Inform health professionals, property owners, and the public about harmful properties and related problems of water pollution and contaminated wastewater.

2) Determine which sites and violation reports to investigate, and coordinate compliance and enforcement activities with other government agencies.

3) Perform laboratory tests on samples collected, such as analyzing the content of contaminated wastewater.

4) Observe and record field conditions, gathering, interpreting, and reporting data such as flow meter readings and chemical levels.

5) Monitor follow-up actions in cases where violations were found, and review compliance monitoring reports.

6) Learn and observe proper safety precautions, rules, regulations, and practices so that unsafe conditions can be recognized and proper safety protocols implemented.

7) Investigate complaints and suspected violations regarding illegal dumping, pollution, pesticides, product quality, or labeling laws.

8) Inspect waste pretreatment, treatment, and disposal facilities and systems for conformance to federal, state, or local regulations.

9) Determine sampling locations and methods, and collect water or wastewater samples for analysis, preserving samples with appropriate containers and preservation methods.

10) Prepare written, oral, tabular, and graphic reports summarizing requirements and regulations, including enforcement and chain of custody documentation.

11) Prepare, organize, and maintain inspection records.

12) Examine permits, licenses, applications, and records to ensure compliance with licensing requirements.

13) Evaluate label information for accuracy and conformance to regulatory requirements.

14) Inform individuals and groups of pollution control regulations and inspection findings, and explain how problems can be corrected.

15) Research and perform calculations related to landscape allowances, discharge volumes, production-based and alternative limits, and wastewater strength classifications, then make recommendations and complete documentation.

16) Interview individuals to determine the nature of suspected violations and to obtain evidence of violations.

17) Maintain and repair materials, worksites, and equipment.

18) Analyze and implement state, federal or local requirements as necessary to maintain approved pretreatment, pollution prevention, and storm water runoff programs.

19) Participate in the development of spill prevention programs and hazardous waste rules and regulations, and recommend corrective actions for hazardous waste problems.

20) Conduct research on hazardous waste management projects in order to determine the magnitude of problems, and treatment or disposal alternatives and costs.

21) Prepare data to calculate sewer service charges and capacity fees.

22) Review and evaluate applications for registration of products containing dangerous materials, or for pollution control discharge permits.

23) Research and keep informed of pertinent information and developments in areas such as EPA laws and regulations.

24) Respond to questions and inquiries, such as those concerning service charges and capacity fees, or refer them to supervisors.

25) Determine the nature of code violations and actions to be taken, and issue written notices of violation; participate in enforcement hearings as necessary.

13-1041.04 - Government Property Inspectors and Investigators

Investigate or inspect government property to ensure compliance with contract agreements and government regulations.

Tasks

1) Testify in court or at administrative proceedings concerning investigation findings.

2) Submit samples of products to government laboratories for testing as required.

3) Coordinate with and assist law enforcement agencies in matters of mutual concern.

4) Recommend legal or administrative action to protect government property.

5) Monitor investigations of suspected offenders to ensure that they are conducted in accordance with constitutional requirements.

6) Locate and interview plaintiffs, witnesses, or representatives of business or government in order to gather facts relevant to inspections or alleged violations.

7) Investigate applications for special licenses or permits, as well as alleged license or permit violations.

8) Collect, identify, evaluate, and preserve case evidence.

9) Inspect government-owned equipment and materials in the possession of private contractors, in order to ensure compliance with contracts and regulations and to prevent misuse.

10) Examine records, reports, and documents in order to establish facts and detect discrepancies.

11) Prepare correspondence, reports of inspections or investigations, and recommendations for action.

13-1041.06 - Coroners

Direct activities such as autopsies, pathological and toxicological analyses, and inquests relating to the investigation of deaths occurring within a legal jurisdiction to determine cause of death or to fix responsibility for accidental, violent, or unexplained deaths.

Tasks

1) Perform medico-legal examinations and autopsies, conducting preliminary examinations of the body in order to identify victims, to locate signs of trauma, and to identify factors that would indicate time of death.

2) Testify at inquests, hearings, and court trials.

3) Arrange for the next of kin to be notified of deaths.

4) Provide information concerning the circumstances of death to relatives of the deceased.

5) Inquire into the cause, manner, and circumstances of human deaths, and establish the identities of deceased persons.

6) Confer with officials of public health and law enforcement agencies in order to coordinate interdepartmental activities.

1254

7) Observe, record, and preserve any objects or personal property related to deaths, including objects such as medication containers and suicide notes.

8) Observe and record the positions and conditions of bodies and of related evidence.

9) Complete death certificates, including the assignment of a cause and manner of death.

10) Interview persons present at death scenes to obtain information useful in determining the manner of death.

11) Direct activities of workers who conduct autopsies, perform pathological and toxicological analyses, and prepare documents for permanent records.

12) Record the disposition of minor children, as well as details of arrangements made for their care.

13) Remove or supervise removal of bodies from death scenes, using the proper equipment and supplies, and arrange for transportation to morgues.

14) Locate and document information regarding the next of kin, including their relationship to the deceased and the status of notification attempts.

15) Coordinate the release of personal effects to authorized persons, and facilitate the disposition of unclaimed corpses and personal effects.

16) Complete reports and forms required to finalize cases.

17) Collect and document any pertinent medical history information.

18) Witness and certify deaths that are the result of a judicial order.

19) Collect wills, burial instructions, and other documentation needed for investigations and for handling of the remains.

13-2081.00 - Tax Examiners, Collectors, and Revenue Agents

Determine tax liability or collect taxes from individuals or business firms according to prescribed laws and regulations.

Tasks

1) Maintain records for each case, including contacts, telephone numbers, and actions taken.

2) Contact taxpayers by mail or telephone in order to address discrepancies and to request supporting documentation.

3) Notify taxpayers of any overpayment or underpayment, and either issue a refund or request further payment.

4) Collect taxes from individuals or businesses according to prescribed laws and regulations.

5) Confer with taxpayers or their representatives in order to discuss the issues, laws, and regulations involved in returns, and to resolve problems with returns.

6) Send notices to taxpayers when accounts are delinquent.

7) Check tax forms in order to verify that names and taxpayer identification numbers are correct, that computations have been performed correctly, and that amounts match those on supporting documentation.

8) Review filed tax returns in order to determine whether claimed tax credits and deductions are allowed by law.

9) Impose payment deadlines on delinquent taxpayers and monitor payments in order to ensure that deadlines are met.

10) Examine and analyze tax assets and liabilities in order to determine resolution of delinquent tax problems.

11) Enter tax return information into computers for processing.

12) Examine accounting systems and records in order to determine whether accounting methods used were appropriate and in compliance with statutory provisions.

13) Conduct independent field audits and investigations of income tax returns in order to verify information and/or to amend tax liabilities.

14) Investigate claims of inability to pay taxes by researching court information for the status of liens, mortgages, or financial statements, or by locating assets through third parties.

15) Determine appropriate methods of debt settlement, such as offers of compromise, wage garnishment, or seizure and sale of property.

16) Prepare briefs, and assist in searching and seizing records in order to prepare charges and documentation for court cases.

17) Review selected tax returns in order to determine the nature and extent of audits to be performed on them.

18) Recommend criminal prosecutions and/or civil penalties.

19) Secure a taxpayer's agreement to discharge a tax assessment, or submit contested determinations to other administrative or judicial conferees for appeals hearings.

20) Process individual and corporate income tax returns, and sales and excise tax returns.

21) Direct service of legal documents, such as subpoenas, warrants, notices of assessment and garnishments.

22) Request that the state or federal revenue service prepare a return on a taxpayer's behalf in cases where taxes have not been filed.

23) Participate in informal appeals hearings on contested cases from other agents.

24) Install systems of recording costs or other financial and budgetary data or provide advice on such systems, based on examination of current financial records.

Knowledge	Knowledge Definitions
Law and Government	Knowledge of laws, legal codes, court procedures, precedents, government regulations, executive orders, agency rules, and the democratic political process.
Customer and Personal Service	Knowledge of principles and processes for providing customer and personal services. This includes customer needs assessment, meeting quality standards for services, and evaluation of customer satisfaction.
English Language	Knowledge of the structure and content of the English language including the meaning and spelling of words, rules of composition, and grammar.
Computers and Electronics	Knowledge of circuit boards, processors, chips, electronic equipment, and computer hardware and software, including applications and programming.
Mathematics	Knowledge of arithmetic, algebra, geometry, calculus, statistics, and their applications.
Clerical	Knowledge of administrative and clerical procedures and systems such as word processing, managing files and records, stenography and transcription, designing forms, and other office procedures and terminology.
Economics and Accounting	Knowledge of economic and accounting principles and practices, the financial markets, banking and the analysis and reporting of financial data.
Education and Training	Knowledge of principles and methods for curriculum and training design, teaching and instruction for individuals and groups, and the measurement of training effects.
Psychology	Knowledge of human behavior and performance; individual differences in ability, personality, and interests; learning and motivation; psychological research methods; and the assessment and treatment of behavioral and affective disorders.
Communications and Media	Knowledge of media production, communication, and dissemination techniques and methods. This includes alternative ways to inform and entertain via written, oral, and visual media.
Production and Processing	Knowledge of raw materials, production processes, quality control, costs, and other techniques for maximizing the effective manufacture and distribution of goods.
Administration and Management	Knowledge of business and management principles involved in strategic planning, resource allocation, human resources modeling, leadership technique, production methods, and coordination of people and resources.
Public Safety and Security	Knowledge of relevant equipment, policies, procedures, and strategies to promote effective local, state, or national security operations for the protection of people, data, property, and institutions.
Telecommunications	Knowledge of transmission, broadcasting, switching, control, and operation of telecommunications systems.
Transportation	Knowledge of principles and methods for moving people or goods by air, rail, sea, or road, including the relative costs and benefits.
Sales and Marketing	Knowledge of principles and methods for showing, promoting, and selling products or services. This includes marketing strategy and tactics, product demonstration, sales techniques, and sales control systems.
Personnel and Human Resources	Knowledge of principles and procedures for personnel recruitment, selection, training, compensation and benefits, labor relations and negotiation, and personnel information systems.
Foreign Language	Knowledge of the structure and content of a foreign (non-English) language including the meaning and spelling of words, rules of composition and grammar, and pronunciation.
Sociology and Anthropology	Knowledge of group behavior and dynamics, societal trends and influences, human migrations, ethnicity, cultures and their history and origins.

Engineering and Technology	Knowledge of the practical application of engineering science and technology. This includes applying principles, techniques, procedures, and equipment to the design and production of various goods and services.
Therapy and Counseling	Knowledge of principles, methods, and procedures for diagnosis, treatment, and rehabilitation of physical and mental dysfunctions, and for career counseling and guidance.
Building and Construction	Knowledge of materials, methods, and the tools involved in the construction or repair of houses, buildings, or other structures such as highways and roads.
Geography	Knowledge of principles and methods for describing the features of land, sea, and air masses, including their physical characteristics, locations, interrelationships, and distribution of plant, animal, and human life.
Design	Knowledge of design techniques, tools, and principles involved in production of precision technical plans, blueprints, drawings, and models.
Mechanical	Knowledge of machines and tools, including their designs, uses, repair, and maintenance.
Philosophy and Theology	Knowledge of different philosophical systems and religions. This includes their basic principles, values, ethics, ways of thinking, customs, practices, and their impact on human culture.
History and Archeology	Knowledge of historical events and their causes, indicators, and effects on civilizations and cultures.
Food Production	Knowledge of techniques and equipment for planting, growing, and harvesting food products (both plant and animal) for consumption, including storage/handling techniques.
Chemistry	Knowledge of the chemical composition, structure, and properties of substances and of the chemical processes and transformations that they undergo. This includes uses of chemicals and their interactions, danger signs, production techniques, and disposal methods.
Physics	Knowledge and prediction of physical principles, laws, their interrelationships, and applications to understanding fluid, material, and atmospheric dynamics, and mechanical, electrical, atomic and sub- atomic structures and processes.
Medicine and Dentistry	Knowledge of the information and techniques needed to diagnose and treat human injuries, diseases, and deformities. This includes symptoms, treatment alternatives, drug properties and interactions, and preventive health-care measures.
Biology	Knowledge of plant and animal organisms, their tissues, cells, functions, interdependencies, and interactions with each other and the environment.
Fine Arts	Knowledge of the theory and techniques required to compose, produce, and perform works of music, dance, visual arts, drama, and sculpture.

Skills	Skills Definitions
Active Listening	Giving full attention to what other people are saying, taking time to understand the points being made, asking questions as appropriate, and not interrupting at inappropriate times.
Mathematics	Using mathematics to solve problems.
Reading Comprehension	Understanding written sentences and paragraphs in work related documents.
Active Learning	Understanding the implications of new information for both current and future problem-solving and decision-making.
Speaking	Talking to others to convey information effectively.
Complex Problem Solving	Identifying complex problems and reviewing related information to develop and evaluate options and implement solutions.
Service Orientation	Actively looking for ways to help people.
Critical Thinking	Using logic and reasoning to identify the strengths and weaknesses of alternative solutions, conclusions or approaches to problems.
Instructing	Teaching others how to do something.
Time Management	Managing one's own time and the time of others.
Learning Strategies	Selecting and using training/instructional methods and procedures appropriate for the situation when learning or teaching new things.
Social Perceptiveness	Being aware of others' reactions and understanding why they react as they do.
Writing	Communicating effectively in writing as appropriate for the needs of the audience.
Judgment and Decision Making	Considering the relative costs and benefits of potential actions to choose the most appropriate one.

Monitoring	Monitoring/Assessing performance of yourself, other individuals, or organizations to make improvements or take corrective action.
Coordination	Adjusting actions in relation to others' actions.
Management of Personnel Resources	Motivating, developing, and directing people as they work, identifying the best people for the job.
Negotiation	Bringing others together and trying to reconcile differences.
Operations Analysis	Analyzing needs and product requirements to create a design.
Persuasion	Persuading others to change their minds or behavior.
Management of Material Resources	Obtaining and seeing to the appropriate use of equipment, facilities, and materials needed to do certain work.
Equipment Selection	Determining the kind of tools and equipment needed to do a job.
Quality Control Analysis	Conducting tests and inspections of products, services, or processes to evaluate quality or performance.
Systems Analysis	Determining how a system should work and how changes in conditions, operations, and the environment will affect outcomes.
Systems Evaluation	Identifying measures or indicators of system performance and the actions needed to improve or correct performance, relative to the goals of the system.
Management of Financial Resources	Determining how money will be spent to get the work done, and accounting for these expenditures.
Troubleshooting	Determining causes of operating errors and deciding what to do about it.
Technology Design	Generating or adapting equipment and technology to serve user needs.
Operation and Control	Controlling operations of equipment or systems.
Installation	Installing equipment, machines, wiring, or programs to meet specifications.
Operation Monitoring	Watching gauges, dials, or other indicators to make sure a machine is working properly.
Equipment Maintenance	Performing routine maintenance on equipment and determining when and what kind of maintenance is needed.
Repairing	Repairing machines or systems using the needed tools.
Science	Using scientific rules and methods to solve problems.
Programming	Writing computer programs for various purposes.

Ability	Ability Definitions
Information Ordering	The ability to arrange things or actions in a certain order or pattern according to a specific rule or set of rules (e.g., patterns of numbers, letters, words, pictures, mathematical operations).
Oral Comprehension	The ability to listen to and understand information and ideas presented through spoken words and sentences.
Deductive Reasoning	The ability to apply general rules to specific problems to produce answers that make sense.
Problem Sensitivity	The ability to tell when something is wrong or is likely to go wrong. It does not involve solving the problem, only recognizing there is a problem.
Written Comprehension	The ability to read and understand information and ideas presented in writing.
Inductive Reasoning	The ability to combine pieces of information to form general rules or conclusions (includes finding a relationship among seemingly unrelated events).
Oral Expression	The ability to communicate information and ideas in speaking so others will understand.
Speech Recognition	The ability to identify and understand the speech of another person.
Near Vision	The ability to see details at close range (within a few feet of the observer).
Speech Clarity	The ability to speak clearly so others can understand you.
Written Expression	The ability to communicate information and ideas in writing so others will understand.
Category Flexibility	The ability to generate or use different sets of rules for combining or grouping things in different ways.
Number Facility	The ability to add, subtract, multiply, or divide quickly and correctly.
Selective Attention	The ability to concentrate on a task over a period of time without being distracted.
Mathematical Reasoning	The ability to choose the right mathematical methods or formulas to solve a problem.
Flexibility of Closure	The ability to identify or detect a known pattern (a figure, object, word, or sound) that is hidden in other distracting material.

Perceptual Speed	The ability to quickly and accurately compare similarities and differences among sets of letters, numbers, objects, pictures, or patterns. The things to be compared may be presented at the same time or one after the other. This ability also includes comparing a presented object with a remembered object.
Originality	The ability to come up with unusual or clever ideas about a given topic or situation, or to develop creative ways to solve a problem.
Finger Dexterity	The ability to make precisely coordinated movements of the fingers of one or both hands to grasp, manipulate, or assemble very small objects.
Speed of Closure	The ability to quickly make sense of, combine, and organize information into meaningful patterns.
Far Vision	The ability to see details at a distance.
Fluency of Ideas	The ability to come up with a number of ideas about a topic (the number of ideas is important, not their quality, correctness, or creativity).
Memorization	The ability to remember information such as words, numbers, pictures, and procedures.
Visualization	The ability to imagine how something will look after it is moved around or when its parts are moved or rearranged.
Time Sharing	The ability to shift back and forth between two or more activities or sources of information (such as speech, sounds, touch, or other sources).
Visual Color Discrimination	The ability to match or detect differences between colors, including shades of color and brightness.
Auditory Attention	The ability to focus on a single source of sound in the presence of other distracting sounds.
Manual Dexterity	The ability to quickly move your hand, your hand together with your arm, or your two hands to grasp, manipulate, or assemble objects.
Hearing Sensitivity	The ability to detect or tell the differences between sounds that vary in pitch and loudness.
Control Precision	The ability to quickly and repeatedly adjust the controls of a machine or a vehicle to exact positions.
Arm-Hand Steadiness	The ability to keep your hand and arm steady while moving your arm or while holding your arm and hand in one position.
Depth Perception	The ability to judge which of several objects is closer or farther away from you, or to judge the distance between you and an object.
Gross Body Coordination	The ability to coordinate the movement of your arms, legs, and torso together when the whole body is in motion.
Wrist-Finger Speed	The ability to make fast, simple, repeated movements of the fingers, hands, and wrists.
Extent Flexibility	The ability to bend, stretch, twist, or reach with your body, arms, and/or legs.
Gross Body Equilibrium	The ability to keep or regain your body balance or stay upright when in an unstable position.
Multilimb Coordination	The ability to coordinate two or more limbs (for example, two arms, two legs, or one leg and one arm) while sitting, standing, or lying down. It does not involve performing the activities while the whole body is in motion.
Response Orientation	The ability to choose quickly between two or more movements in response to two or more different signals (lights, sounds, pictures). It includes the speed with which the correct response is started with the hand, foot, or other body part.
Rate Control	The ability to time your movements or the movement of a piece of equipment in anticipation of changes in the speed and/or direction of a moving object or scene.
Reaction Time	The ability to quickly respond (with the hand, finger, or foot) to a signal (sound, light, picture) when it appears.
Speed of Limb Movement	The ability to quickly move the arms and legs.
Static Strength	The ability to exert maximum muscle force to lift, push, pull, or carry objects.
Explosive Strength	The ability to use short bursts of muscle force to propel oneself (as in jumping or sprinting), or to throw an object.
Dynamic Strength	The ability to exert muscle force repeatedly or continuously over time. This involves muscular endurance and resistance to muscle fatigue.
Stamina	The ability to exert yourself physically over long periods of time without getting winded or out of breath.
Dynamic Flexibility	The ability to quickly and repeatedly bend, stretch, twist, or reach out with your body, arms, and/or legs.
Glare Sensitivity	The ability to see objects in the presence of glare or bright lighting.
Sound Localization	The ability to tell the direction from which a sound originated.
Spatial Orientation	The ability to know your location in relation to the environment or to know where other objects are in relation to you.
Night Vision	The ability to see under low light conditions.
Peripheral Vision	The ability to see objects or movement of objects to one's side when the eyes are looking ahead.
Trunk Strength	The ability to use your abdominal and lower back muscles to support part of the body repeatedly or continuously over time without 'giving out' or fatiguing.

Work_Activity	Work_Activity Definitions
Evaluating Information to Determine Compliance wit	Using relevant information and individual judgment to determine whether events or processes comply with laws, regulations, or standards.
Getting Information	Observing, receiving, and otherwise obtaining information from all relevant sources
Communicating with Persons Outside Organization	Communicating with people outside the organization, representing the organization to customers, the public, government, and other external sources. This information can be exchanged in person, in writing, or by telephone or e-mail.
Communicating with Supervisors, Peers, or Subordin	Providing information to supervisors, co-workers, and subordinates by telephone, in written form, e-mail, or in person.
Updating and Using Relevant Knowledge	Keeping up-to-date technically and applying new knowledge to your job.
Identifying Objects, Actions, and Events	Identifying information by categorizing, estimating, recognizing differences or similarities, and detecting changes in circumstances or events.
Analyzing Data or Information	Identifying the underlying principles, reasons, or facts of information by breaking down information or data into separate parts.
Interacting With Computers	Using computers and computer systems (including hardware and software) to program, write software, set up functions, enter data, or process information.
Organizing, Planning, and Prioritizing Work	Developing specific goals and plans to prioritize, organize, and accomplish your work.
Documenting/Recording Information	Entering, transcribing, recording, storing, or maintaining information in written or electronic/magnetic form.
Performing for or Working Directly with the Public	Performing for people or dealing directly with the public. This includes serving customers in restaurants and stores, and receiving clients or guests.
Processing Information	Compiling, coding, categorizing, calculating, tabulating, auditing, or verifying information or data.
Interpreting the Meaning of Information for Others	Translating or explaining what information means and how it can be used.
Making Decisions and Solving Problems	Analyzing information and evaluating results to choose the best solution and solve problems.
Performing Administrative Activities	Performing day-to-day administrative tasks such as maintaining information files and processing paperwork.
Establishing and Maintaining Interpersonal Relatio	Developing constructive and cooperative working relationships with others, and maintaining them over time.
Training and Teaching Others	Identifying the educational needs of others, developing formal educational or training programs or classes, and teaching or instructing others.
Judging the Qualities of Things, Services, or Peop	Assessing the value, importance, or quality of things or people.
Resolving Conflicts and Negotiating with Others	Handling complaints, settling disputes, and resolving grievances and conflicts, or otherwise negotiating with others.
Developing Objectives and Strategies	Establishing long-range objectives and specifying the strategies and actions to achieve them.
Monitor Processes, Materials, or Surroundings	Monitoring and reviewing information from materials, events, or the environment, to detect or assess problems.
Estimating the Quantifiable Characteristics of Pro	Estimating sizes, distances, and quantities; or determining time, costs, resources, or materials needed to perform a work activity.
Thinking Creatively	Developing, designing, or creating new applications, ideas, relationships, systems, or products, including artistic contributions.
Scheduling Work and Activities	Scheduling events, programs, and activities, as well as the work of others.
Coordinating the Work and Activities of Others	Getting members of a group to work together to accomplish tasks.
Developing and Building Teams	Encouraging and building mutual trust, respect, and cooperation among team members.
Selling or Influencing Others	Convincing others to buy merchandise/goods or to otherwise change their minds or actions.
Provide Consultation and Advice to Others	Providing guidance and expert advice to management or other groups on technical, systems-, or process-related topics.

Assisting and Caring for Others	Providing personal assistance, medical attention, emotional support, or other personal care to others such as coworkers, customers, or patients.
Coaching and Developing Others	Identifying the developmental needs of others and coaching, mentoring, or otherwise helping others to improve their knowledge or skills.
Controlling Machines and Processes	Using either control mechanisms or direct physical activity to operate machines or processes (not including computers or vehicles).
Handling and Moving Objects	Using hands and arms in handling, installing, positioning, and moving materials, and manipulating things.
Staffing Organizational Units	Recruiting, interviewing, selecting, hiring, and promoting employees in an organization.
Operating Vehicles, Mechanized Devices, or Equipme	Running, maneuvering, navigating, or driving vehicles or mechanized equipment, such as forklifts, passenger vehicles, aircraft, or water craft.
Guiding, Directing, and Motivating Subordinates	Providing guidance and direction to subordinates, including setting performance standards and monitoring performance.
Monitoring and Controlling Resources	Monitoring and controlling resources and overseeing the spending of money.
Inspecting Equipment, Structures, or Material	Inspecting equipment, structures, or materials to identify the cause of errors or other problems or defects.
Performing General Physical Activities	Performing physical activities that require considerable use of your arms and legs and moving your whole body, such as climbing, lifting, balancing, walking, stooping, and handling of materials.
Repairing and Maintaining Electronic Equipment	Servicing, repairing, calibrating, regulating, fine-tuning, or testing machines, devices, and equipment that operate primarily on the basis of electrical or electronic (not mechanical) principles.
Repairing and Maintaining Mechanical Equipment	Servicing, repairing, adjusting, and testing machines, devices, moving parts, and equipment that operate primarily on the basis of mechanical (not electronic) principles.
Drafting, Laying Out, and Specifying Technical Dev	Providing documentation, detailed instructions, drawings, or specifications to tell others about how devices, parts, equipment, or structures are to be fabricated, constructed, assembled, modified, maintained, or used.

Work_Context	Work_Context Definitions
Telephone	How often do you have telephone conversations in this job?
Contact With Others	How much does this job require the worker to be in contact with others (face-to-face, by telephone, or otherwise) in order to perform it?
Importance of Being Exact or Accurate	How important is being very exact or highly accurate in performing this job?
Face-to-Face Discussions	How often do you have to have face-to-face discussions with individuals or teams in this job?
Importance of Repeating Same Tasks	How important is repeating the same physical activities (e.g., key entry) or mental activities (e.g., checking entries in a ledger) over and over, without stopping, to performing this job?
Spend Time Sitting	How much does this job require sitting?
Structured versus Unstructured Work	To what extent is this job structured for the worker, rather than allowing the worker to determine tasks, priorities, and goals?
Letters and Memos	How often does the job require written letters and memos?
Frequency of Decision Making	How frequently is the worker required to make decisions that affect other people, the financial resources, and/or the image and reputation of the organization?
Impact of Decisions on Co-workers or Company Resul	How do the decisions an employee makes impact the results of co-workers, clients or the company?
Spend Time Making Repetitive Motions	How much does this job require making repetitive motions?
Deal With External Customers	How important is it to work with external customers or the public in this job?
Electronic Mail	How often do you use electronic mail in this job?
Indoors, Environmentally Controlled	How often does this job require working indoors in environmentally controlled conditions?
Freedom to Make Decisions	How much decision making freedom, without supervision, does the job offer?
Frequency of Conflict Situations	How often are there conflict situations the employee has to face in this job?
Time Pressure	How often does this job require the worker to meet strict deadlines?
Deal With Unpleasant or Angry People	How frequently does the worker have to deal with unpleasant, angry, or discourteous individuals as part of the job requirements?

Work With Work Group or Team	How important is it to work with others in a group or team in this job?
Physical Proximity	To what extent does this job require the worker to perform job tasks in close physical proximity to other people?
Sounds, Noise Levels Are Distracting or Uncomforta	How often does this job require working exposed to sounds and noise levels that are distracting or uncomfortable?
Spend Time Using Your Hands to Handle, Control, or	How much does this job require using your hands to handle, control, or feel objects, tools or controls?
In an Enclosed Vehicle or Equipment	How often does this job require working in a closed vehicle or equipment (e.g., car)?
Degree of Automation	How automated is the job?
Level of Competition	To what extent does this job require the worker to compete or to be aware of competitive pressures?
Consequence of Error	How serious would the result usually be if the worker made a mistake that was not readily correctable?
Exposed to Contaminants	How often does this job require working exposed to contaminants (such as pollutants, gases, dust or odors)?
Coordinate or Lead Others	How important is it to coordinate or lead others in accomplishing work activities in this job?
Responsible for Others' Health and Safety	How much responsibility is there for the health and safety of others in this job?
Responsibility for Outcomes and Results	How responsible is the worker for work outcomes and results of other workers?
Spend Time Standing	How much does this job require standing?
Very Hot or Cold Temperatures	How often does this job require working in very hot (above 90 F degrees) or very cold (below 32 F degrees) temperatures?
Spend Time Walking and Running	How much does this job require walking and running?
Public Speaking	How often do you have to perform public speaking in this job?
Extremely Bright or Inadequate Lighting	How often does this job require working in extremely bright or inadequate lighting conditions?
Deal With Physically Aggressive People	How frequently does this job require the worker to deal with physical aggression of violent individuals?
Cramped Work Space, Awkward Positions	How often does this job require working in cramped work spaces that requires getting into awkward positions?
Pace Determined by Speed of Equipment	How important is it to this job that the pace is determined by the speed of equipment or machinery? (This does not refer to keeping busy at all times on this job.)
Spend Time Bending or Twisting the Body	How much does this job require bending or twisting your body?
Indoors, Not Environmentally Controlled	How often does this job require working indoors in non-controlled environmental conditions (e.g., warehouse without heat)?
Exposed to Disease or Infections	How often does this job require exposure to disease/infections?
Outdoors, Exposed to Weather	How often does this job require working outdoors, exposed to all weather conditions?
Exposed to Minor Burns, Cuts, Bites, or Stings	How often does this job require exposure to minor burns, cuts, bites, or stings?
Spend Time Kneeling, Crouching, Stooping, or Crawl	How much does this job require kneeling, crouching, stooping, or crawling?
Outdoors, Under Cover	How often does this job require working outdoors, under cover (e.g., structure with roof but no walls)?
Exposed to Hazardous Conditions	How often does this job require exposure to hazardous conditions?
Wear Common Protective or Safety Equipment such as	How much does this job require wearing common protective or safety equipment such as safety shoes, glasses, gloves, hard hats or live jackets?
Exposed to Hazardous Equipment	How often does this job require exposure to hazardous equipment?
Exposed to High Places	How often does this job require exposure to high places?
Exposed to Radiation	How often does this job require exposure to radiation?
Exposed to Whole Body Vibration	How often does this job require exposure to whole body vibration (e.g., operate a jackhammer)?
Wear Specialized Protective or Safety Equipment su	How much does this job require wearing specialized protective or safety equipment such as breathing apparatus, safety harness, full protection suits, or radiation protection?
In an Open Vehicle or Equipment	How often does this job require working in an open vehicle or equipment (e.g., tractor)?
Spend Time Climbing Ladders, Scaffolds, or Poles	How much does this job require climbing ladders, scaffolds, or poles?
Spend Time Keeping or Regaining Balance	How much does this job require keeping or regaining your balance?

1258

Job Zone Component	Job Zone Component Definitions
Title	Job Zone Three: Medium Preparation Needed
Overall Experience	Previous work-related skill, knowledge, or experience is required for these occupations. For example, an electrician must have completed three or four years of apprenticeship or several years of vocational training, and often must have passed a licensing exam, in order to perform the job.
Job Training	Employees in these occupations usually need one or two years of training involving both on-the-job experience and informal training with experienced workers.
Job Zone Examples	These occupations usually involve using communication and organizational skills to coordinate, supervise, manage, or train others to accomplish goals. Examples include dental assistants, electricians, fish and game wardens, legal secretaries, personnel recruiters, and recreation workers.
SVP Range	(6.0 to < 7.0)
Education	Most occupations in this zone require training in vocational schools, related on-the-job experience, or an associate's degree. Some may require a bachelor's degree.

Work_Styles	Work_Styles Definitions
Integrity	Job requires being honest and ethical.
Attention to Detail	Job requires being careful about detail and thorough in completing work tasks.
Dependability	Job requires being reliable, responsible, and dependable, and fulfilling obligations.
Self Control	Job requires maintaining composure, keeping emotions in check, controlling anger, and avoiding aggressive behavior, even in very difficult situations.
Adaptability/Flexibility	Job requires being open to change (positive or negative) and to considerable variety in the workplace.
Cooperation	Job requires being pleasant with others on the job and displaying a good-natured, cooperative attitude.
Independence	Job requires developing one's own ways of doing things, guiding oneself with little or no supervision, and depending on oneself to get things done.
Analytical Thinking	Job requires analyzing information and using logic to address work-related issues and problems.
Stress Tolerance	Job requires accepting criticism and dealing calmly and effectively with high stress situations.
Concern for Others	Job requires being sensitive to others' needs and feelings and being understanding and helpful on the job.
Initiative	Job requires a willingness to take on responsibilities and challenges.
Innovation	Job requires creativity and alternative thinking to develop new ideas for and answers to work-related problems.
Achievement/Effort	Job requires establishing and maintaining personally challenging achievement goals and exerting effort toward mastering tasks.
Persistence	Job requires persistence in the face of obstacles.
Social Orientation	Job requires preferring to work with others rather than alone, and being personally connected with others on the job.
Leadership	Job requires a willingness to lead, take charge, and offer opinions and direction.

15-1011.00 - Computer and Information Scientists, Research

Conduct research into fundamental computer and information science as theorists, designers, or inventors. Solve or develop solutions to problems in the field of computer hardware and software.

Tasks

1) Evaluate project plans and proposals to assess feasibility issues.

2) Maintain network hardware and software, direct network security measures, and monitor networks to ensure availability to system users.

3) Participate in multidisciplinary projects in areas such as virtual reality, human-computer interaction, or robotics.

4) Meet with managers, vendors, and others to solicit cooperation and resolve problems.

5) Direct daily operations of departments, coordinating project activities with other departments.

6) Develop performance standards, and evaluate work in light of established standards.

7) Assign or schedule tasks in order to meet work priorities and goals.

8) Consult with users, management, vendors, and technicians to determine computing needs and system requirements.

9) Conduct logical analyses of business, scientific, engineering, and other technical problems, formulating mathematical models of problems for solution by computers.

10) Apply theoretical expertise and innovation to create or apply new technology, such as adapting principles for applying computers to new uses.

11) Analyze problems to develop solutions involving computer hardware and software.

12) Participate in staffing decisions and direct training of subordinates.

13) Approve, prepare, monitor, and adjust operational budgets.

14) Develop and interpret organizational goals, policies, and procedures.

15-1071.01 - Computer Security Specialists

Plan, coordinate, and implement security measures for information systems to regulate access to computer data files and prevent unauthorized modification, destruction, or disclosure of information.

Tasks

1) Confer with users to discuss issues such as computer data access needs, security violations, and programming changes.

2) Document computer security and emergency measures policies, procedures, and tests.

3) Coordinate implementation of computer system plan with establishment personnel and outside vendors.

4) Train users and promote security awareness to ensure system security and to improve server and network efficiency.

5) Monitor current reports of computer viruses to determine when to update virus protection systems.

6) Monitor use of data files and regulate access to safeguard information in computer files.

7) Review violations of computer security procedures and discuss procedures with violators to ensure violations are not repeated.

8) Perform risk assessments and execute tests of data processing system to ensure functioning of data processing activities and security measures.

9) Modify computer security files to incorporate new software, correct errors, or change individual access status.

10) Encrypt data transmissions and erect firewalls to conceal confidential information as it is being transmitted and to keep out tainted digital transfers.

11) Maintain permanent fleet cryptologic and carry-on direct support systems required in special land, sea surface and subsurface operations.

Knowledge	Knowledge Definitions
Computers and Electronics	Knowledge of circuit boards, processors, chips, electronic equipment, and computer hardware and software, including applications and programming.
Customer and Personal Service	Knowledge of principles and processes for providing customer and personal services. This includes customer needs assessment, meeting quality standards for services, and evaluation of customer satisfaction.
Administration and Management	Knowledge of business and management principles involved in strategic planning, resource allocation, human resources modeling, leadership technique, production methods, and coordination of people and resources.
Engineering and Technology	Knowledge of the practical application of engineering science and technology. This includes applying principles, techniques, procedures, and equipment to the design and production of various goods and services.
Telecommunications	Knowledge of transmission, broadcasting, switching, control, and operation of telecommunications systems.
Education and Training	Knowledge of principles and methods for curriculum and training design, teaching and instruction for individuals and groups, and the measurement of training effects.
English Language	Knowledge of the structure and content of the English language including the meaning and spelling of words, rules of composition, and grammar.

Law and Government	Knowledge of laws. legal codes. court procedures. precedents. government regulations. executive orders. agency rules. and the democratic political process.	Medicine and Dentistry	Knowledge of the information and techniques needed to diagnose and treat human injuries. diseases. and deformities. This includes symptoms. treatment alternatives. drug properties and interactions, and preventive health-care measures.
Public Safety and Security	Knowledge of relevant equipment, policies, procedures. and strategies to promote effective local. state. or national security operations for the protection of people. data. property, and institutions.	Biology	Knowledge of plant and animal organisms. their tissues. cells, functions, interdependencies. and interactions with each other and the environment.
Communications and Media	Knowledge of media production. communication. and dissemination techniques and methods. This includes alternative ways to inform and entertain via written, oral. and visual media.	Food Production	Knowledge of techniques and equipment for planting, growing, and harvesting food products (both plant and animal) for consumption, including storage/handling techniques.
Economics and Accounting	Knowledge of economic and accounting principles and practices, the financial markets, banking and the analysis and reporting of financial data.	**Skills**	**Skills Definitions**
Design	Knowledge of design techniques, tools, and principles involved in production of precision technical plans, blueprints, drawings. and models.	Reading Comprehension	Understanding written sentences and paragraphs in work related documents.
Production and Processing	Knowledge of raw materials, production processes, quality control, costs, and other techniques for maximizing the effective manufacture and distribution of goods.	Active Learning	Understanding the implications of new information for both current and future problem-solving and decision-making.
Personnel and Human Resources	Knowledge of principles and procedures for personnel recruitment, selection. training. compensation and benefits. labor relations and negotiation. and personnel information systems.	Systems Evaluation	Identifying measures or indicators of system performance and the actions needed to improve or correct performance, relative to the goals of the system.
Clerical	Knowledge of administrative and clerical procedures and systems such as word processing, managing files and records, stenography and transcription, designing forms, and other office procedures and terminology.	Critical Thinking	Using logic and reasoning to identify the strengths and weaknesses of alternative solutions. conclusions or approaches to problems.
Mathematics	Knowledge of arithmetic, algebra, geometry, calculus, statistics, and their applications.	Active Listening	Giving full attention to what other people are saying, taking time to understand the points being made. asking questions as appropriate, and not interrupting at inappropriate times.
Sales and Marketing	Knowledge of principles and methods for showing, promoting. and selling products or services. This includes marketing strategy and tactics, product demonstration, sales techniques, and sales control systems.	Time Management	Managing one's own time and the time of others.
		Systems Analysis	Determining how a system should work and how changes in conditions, operations, and the environment will affect outcomes.
Therapy and Counseling	Knowledge of principles, methods, and procedures for diagnosis, treatment, and rehabilitation of physical and mental dysfunctions, and for career counseling and guidance.	Troubleshooting	Determining causes of operating errors and deciding what to do about it.
Psychology	Knowledge of human behavior and performance; individual differences in ability, personality, and interests; learning and motivation; psychological research methods; and the assessment and treatment of behavioral and affective disorders.	Judgment and Decision Making	Considering the relative costs and benefits of potential actions to choose the most appropriate one.
		Writing	Communicating effectively in writing as appropriate for the needs of the audience.
Sociology and Anthropology	Knowledge of group behavior and dynamics, societal trends and influences, human migrations, ethnicity, cultures and their history and origins.	Management of Material Resources	Obtaining and seeing to the appropriate use of equipment, facilities, and materials needed to do certain work.
		Operations Analysis	Analyzing needs and product requirements to create a design.
Transportation	Knowledge of principles and methods for moving people or goods by air, rail, sea, or road, including the relative costs and benefits.	Technology Design	Generating or adapting equipment and technology to serve user needs.
Building and Construction	Knowledge of materials, methods, and the tools involved in construction or repair of houses, buildings, or other structures such as highways and roads.	Monitoring	Monitoring/Assessing performance of yourself, other individuals, or organizations to make improvements or take corrective action.
		Speaking	Talking to others to convey information effectively.
Geography	Knowledge of principles and methods for describing the features of land, sea, and air masses, including their physical characteristics, locations, interrelationships, and distribution of plant, animal, and human life.	Instructing	Teaching others how to do something.
		Complex Problem Solving	Identifying complex problems and reviewing related information to develop and evaluate options and implement solutions.
Mechanical	Knowledge of machines and tools, including their designs, uses, repair, and maintenance.	Management of Personnel Resources	Motivating, developing, and directing people as they work, identifying the best people for the job.
History and Archeology	Knowledge of historical events and their causes, indicators, and effects on civilizations and cultures.	Coordination	Adjusting actions in relation to others' actions.
Physics	Knowledge and prediction of physical principles, laws, their interrelationships, and applications to understanding fluid, material, and atmospheric dynamics, and mechanical, electrical, atomic and sub- atomic structures and processes.	Installation	Installing equipment, machines, wiring, or programs to meet specifications.
		Repairing	Repairing machines or systems using the needed tools.
		Management of Financial Resources	Determining how money will be spent to get the work done, and accounting for these expenditures.
Foreign Language	Knowledge of the structure and content of a foreign (non-English) language including the meaning and spelling of words, rules of composition and grammar, and pronunciation.	Equipment Maintenance	Performing routine maintenance on equipment and determining when and what kind of maintenance is needed.
Philosophy and Theology	Knowledge of different philosophical systems and religions. This includes their basic principles, values, ethics, ways of thinking, customs, practices, and their impact on human culture.	Learning Strategies	Selecting and using training/instructional methods and procedures appropriate for the situation when learning or teaching new things.
		Equipment Selection	Determining the kind of tools and equipment needed to do a job.
Fine Arts	Knowledge of the theory and techniques required to compose, produce, and perform works of music, dance, visual arts, drama, and sculpture.	Service Orientation	Actively looking for ways to help people.
		Negotiation	Bringing others together and trying to reconcile differences.
Chemistry	Knowledge of the chemical composition, structure, and properties of substances and of the chemical processes and transformations that they undergo. This includes uses of chemicals and their interactions, danger signs, production techniques, and disposal methods.	Operation Monitoring	Watching gauges, dials, or other indicators to make sure a machine is working properly.
		Operation and Control	Controlling operations of equipment or systems.
		Quality Control Analysis	Conducting tests and inspections of products, services, or processes to evaluate quality or performance.
		Social Perceptiveness	Being aware of others' reactions and understanding why they react as they do.
		Mathematics	Using mathematics to solve problems.
		Programming	Writing computer programs for various purposes.
		Persuasion	Persuading others to change their minds or behavior.
		Science	Using scientific rules and methods to solve problems.

Ability	Ability Definitions
Problem Sensitivity	The ability to tell when something is wrong or is likely to go wrong. It does not involve solving the problem, only recognizing there is a problem.
Inductive Reasoning	The ability to combine pieces of information to form general rules or conclusions (includes finding a relationship among seemingly unrelated events).
Near Vision	The ability to see details at close range (within a few feet of the observer).
Oral Comprehension	The ability to listen to and understand information and ideas presented through spoken words and sentences.
Oral Expression	The ability to communicate information and ideas in speaking so others will understand.
Deductive Reasoning	The ability to apply general rules to specific problems to produce answers that make sense.
Written Comprehension	The ability to read and understand information and ideas presented in writing.
Information Ordering	The ability to arrange things or actions in a certain order or pattern according to a specific rule or set of rules (e.g., patterns of numbers, letters, words, pictures, mathematical operations).
Finger Dexterity	The ability to make precisely coordinated movements of the fingers of one or both hands to grasp, manipulate, or assemble very small objects.
Selective Attention	The ability to concentrate on a task over a period of time without being distracted.
Speech Clarity	The ability to speak clearly so others can understand you.
Category Flexibility	The ability to generate or use different sets of rules for combining or grouping things in different ways.
Written Expression	The ability to communicate information and ideas in writing so others will understand.
Speech Recognition	The ability to identify and understand the speech of another person.
Originality	The ability to come up with unusual or clever ideas about a given topic or situation, or to develop creative ways to solve a problem.
Fluency of Ideas	The ability to come up with a number of ideas about a topic (the number of ideas is important, not their quality, correctness, or creativity).
Visualization	The ability to imagine how something will look after it is moved around or when its parts are moved or rearranged.
Flexibility of Closure	The ability to identify or detect a known pattern (a figure, object, word, or sound) that is hidden in other distracting material.
Perceptual Speed	The ability to quickly and accurately compare similarities and differences among sets of letters, numbers, objects, pictures, or patterns. The things to be compared may be presented at the same time or one after the other. This ability also includes comparing a presented object with a remembered object.
Memorization	The ability to remember information such as words, numbers, pictures, and procedures.
Speed of Closure	The ability to quickly make sense of, combine, and organize information into meaningful patterns.
Far Vision	The ability to see details at a distance.
Control Precision	The ability to quickly and repeatedly adjust the controls of a machine or a vehicle to exact positions.
Mathematical Reasoning	The ability to choose the right mathematical methods or formulas to solve a problem.
Visual Color Discrimination	The ability to match or detect differences between colors, including shades of color and brightness.
Number Facility	The ability to add, subtract, multiply, or divide quickly and correctly.
Arm-Hand Steadiness	The ability to keep your hand and arm steady while moving your arm or while holding your arm and hand in one position.
Manual Dexterity	The ability to quickly move your hand, your hand together with your arm, or your two hands to grasp, manipulate, or assemble objects.
Hearing Sensitivity	The ability to detect or tell the differences between sounds that vary in pitch and loudness.
Time Sharing	The ability to shift back and forth between two or more activities or sources of information (such as speech, sounds, touch, or other sources).
Depth Perception	The ability to judge which of several objects is closer or farther away from you, or to judge the distance between you and an object.
Auditory Attention	The ability to focus on a single source of sound in the presence of other distracting sounds.

Ability	Ability Definitions
Wrist-Finger Speed	The ability to make fast, simple, repeated movements of the fingers, hands, and wrists.
Multilimb Coordination	The ability to coordinate two or more limbs (for example, two arms, two legs, or one leg and one arm) while sitting, standing, or lying down. It does not involve performing the activities while the whole body is in motion.
Rate Control	The ability to time your movements or the movement of a piece of equipment in anticipation of changes in the speed and/or direction of a moving object or scene.
Reaction Time	The ability to quickly respond (with the hand, finger, or foot) to a signal (sound, light, picture) when it appears.
Response Orientation	The ability to choose quickly between two or more movements in response to two or more different signals (lights, sounds, pictures). It includes the speed with which the correct response is started with the hand, foot, or other body part.
Peripheral Vision	The ability to see objects or movement of objects to one's side when the eyes are looking ahead.
Spatial Orientation	The ability to know your location in relation to the environment or to know where other objects are in relation to you.
Extent Flexibility	The ability to bend, stretch, twist, or reach with your body, arms, and/or legs.
Stamina	The ability to exert yourself physically over long periods of time without getting winded or out of breath.
Gross Body Equilibrium	The ability to keep or regain your body balance or stay upright when in an unstable position.
Gross Body Coordination	The ability to coordinate the movement of your arms, legs, and torso together when the whole body is in motion.
Dynamic Strength	The ability to exert muscle force repeatedly or continuously over time. This involves muscular endurance and resistance to muscle fatigue.
Dynamic Flexibility	The ability to quickly and repeatedly bend, stretch, twist, or reach out with your body, arms, and/or legs.
Explosive Strength	The ability to use short bursts of muscle force to propel oneself (as in jumping or sprinting), or to throw an object.
Static Strength	The ability to exert maximum muscle force to lift, push, pull, or carry objects.
Night Vision	The ability to see under low light conditions.
Sound Localization	The ability to tell the direction from which a sound originated.
Glare Sensitivity	The ability to see objects in the presence of glare or bright lighting.
Speed of Limb Movement	The ability to quickly move the arms and legs.
Trunk Strength	The ability to use your abdominal and lower back muscles to support part of the body repeatedly or continuously over time without 'giving out' or fatiguing.

Work_Activity	Work_Activity Definitions
Interacting With Computers	Using computers and computer systems (including hardware and software) to program, write software, set up functions, enter data, or process information.
Updating and Using Relevant Knowledge	Keeping up-to-date technically and applying new knowledge to your job.
Getting Information	Observing, receiving, and otherwise obtaining information from all relevant sources.
Making Decisions and Solving Problems	Analyzing information and evaluating results to choose the best solution and solve problems.
Thinking Creatively	Developing, designing, or creating new applications, ideas, relationships, systems, or products, including artistic contributions.
Communicating with Supervisors, Peers, or Subordin	Providing information to supervisors, co-workers, and subordinates by telephone, in written form, e-mail, or in person.
Processing Information	Compiling, coding, categorizing, calculating, tabulating, auditing, or verifying information or data.
Analyzing Data or Information	Identifying the underlying principles, reasons, or facts of information by breaking down information or data into separate parts.
Organizing, Planning, and Prioritizing Work	Developing specific goals and plans to prioritize, organize, and accomplish your work.
Documenting/Recording Information	Entering, transcribing, recording, storing, or maintaining information in written or electronic/magnetic form.
Evaluating Information to Determine Compliance wit	Using relevant information and individual judgment to determine whether events or processes comply with laws, regulations, or standards.
Identifying Objects, Actions, and Events	Identifying information by categorizing, estimating, recognizing differences or similarities, and detecting changes in circumstances or events.

Developing Objectives and Strategies	Establishing long-range objectives and specifying the strategies and actions to achieve them.
Judging the Qualities of Things, Services, or Peop	Assessing the value, importance, or quality of things or people.
Scheduling Work and Activities	Scheduling events, programs, and activities, as well as the work of others.
Repairing and Maintaining Electronic Equipment	Servicing, repairing, calibrating, regulating, fine-tuning, or testing machines, devices, and equipment that operate primarily on the basis of electrical or electronic (not mechanical) principles.
Establishing and Maintaining Interpersonal Relatio	Developing constructive and cooperative working relationships with others, and maintaining them over time.
Interpreting the Meaning of Information for Others	Translating or explaining what information means and how it can be used.
Communicating with Persons Outside Organization	Communicating with people outside the organization, representing the organization to customers, the public, government, and other external sources. This information can be exchanged in person, in writing, or by telephone or e-mail.
Monitor Processes, Materials, or Surroundings	Monitoring and reviewing information from materials, events, or the environment, to detect or assess problems.
Provide Consultation and Advice to Others	Providing guidance and expert advice to management or other groups on technical, systems-, or process-related topics.
Controlling Machines and Processes	Using either control mechanisms or direct physical activity to operate machines or processes (not including computers or vehicles).
Training and Teaching Others	Identifying the educational needs of others, developing formal educational or training programs or classes, and teaching or instructing others.
Drafting, Laying Out, and Specifying Technical Dev	Providing documentation, detailed instructions, drawings, or specifications to tell others about how devices, parts, equipment, or structures are to be fabricated, constructed, assembled, modified, maintained, or used.
Coordinating the Work and Activities of Others	Getting members of a group to work together to accomplish tasks.
Assisting and Caring for Others	Providing personal assistance, medical attention, emotional support, or other personal care to others such as coworkers, customers, or patients.
Performing Administrative Activities	Performing day-to-day administrative tasks such as maintaining information files and processing paperwork.
Monitoring and Controlling Resources	Monitoring and controlling resources and overseeing the spending of money.
Developing and Building Teams	Encouraging and building mutual trust, respect, and cooperation among team members.
Coaching and Developing Others	Identifying the developmental needs of others and coaching, mentoring, or otherwise helping others to improve their knowledge or skills.
Resolving Conflicts and Negotiating with Others	Handling complaints, settling disputes, and resolving grievances and conflicts, or otherwise negotiating with others.
Repairing and Maintaining Mechanical Equipment	Servicing, repairing, adjusting, and testing machines, devices, moving parts, and equipment that operate primarily on the basis of mechanical (not electronic) principles.
Inspecting Equipment, Structures, or Material	Inspecting equipment, structures, or materials to identify the cause of errors or other problems or defects.
Performing General Physical Activities	Performing physical activities that require considerable use of your arms and legs and moving your whole body, such as climbing, lifting, balancing, walking, stooping, and handling of materials.
Handling and Moving Objects	Using hands and arms in handling, installing, positioning, and moving materials, and manipulating things.
Selling or Influencing Others	Convincing others to buy merchandise/goods or to otherwise change their minds or actions.
Guiding, Directing, and Motivating Subordinates	Providing guidance and direction to subordinates, including setting performance standards and monitoring performance.
Estimating the Quantifiable Characteristics of Pro	Estimating sizes, distances, and quantities; or determining time, costs, resources, or materials needed to perform a work activity.
Operating Vehicles, Mechanized Devices, or Equipme	Running, maneuvering, navigating, or driving vehicles or mechanized equipment, such as forklifts, passenger vehicles, aircraft, or water craft.
Staffing Organizational Units	Recruiting, interviewing, selecting, hiring, and promoting employees in an organization.
Performing for or Working Directly with the Public	Performing for people or dealing directly with the public. This includes serving customers in restaurants and stores, and receiving clients or guests.

Work_Context	Work_Context Definitions
Electronic Mail	How often do you use electronic mail in this job?
Telephone	How often do you have telephone conversations in this job?
Face-to-Face Discussions	How often do you have to have face-to-face discussions with individuals or teams in this job?
Contact With Others	How much does this job require the worker to be in contact with others (face-to-face, by telephone, or otherwise) in order to perform it?
Structured versus Unstructured Work	To what extent is this job structured for the worker, rather than allowing the worker to determine tasks, priorities, and goals?
Spend Time Sitting	How much does this job require sitting?
Indoors, Environmentally Controlled	How often does this job require working indoors in environmentally controlled conditions?
Importance of Being Exact or Accurate	How important is being very exact or highly accurate in performing this job?
Deal With External Customers	How important is it to work with external customers or the public in this job?
Impact of Decisions on Co-workers or Company Resul	How do the decisions an employee makes impact the results of co-workers, clients or the company?
Freedom to Make Decisions	How much decision making freedom, without supervision, does the job offer?
Time Pressure	How often does this job require the worker to meet strict deadlines?
Frequency of Decision Making	How frequently is the worker required to make decisions that affect other people, the financial resources, and/or the image and reputation of the organization?
Work With Work Group or Team	How important is it to work with others in a group or team in this job?
Physical Proximity	To what extent does this job require the worker to perform job tasks in close physical proximity to other people?
Coordinate or Lead Others	How important is it to coordinate or lead others in accomplishing work activities in this job?
Consequence of Error	How serious would the result usually be if the worker made a mistake that was not readily correctable?
In an Enclosed Vehicle or Equipment	How often does this job require working in a closed vehicle or equipment (e.g., car)?
Letters and Memos	How often does the job require written letters and memos?
Deal With Unpleasant or Angry People	How frequently does the worker have to deal with unpleasant, angry, or discourteous individuals as part of the job requirements?
Level of Competition	To what extent does this job require the worker to compete or to be aware of competitive pressures?
Importance of Repeating Same Tasks	How important is repeating the same physical activities (e.g., key entry) or mental activities (e.g., checking entries in a ledger) over and over, without stopping, to performing this job?
Spend Time Using Your Hands to Handle, Control, or	How much does this job require using your hands to handle, control, or feel objects, tools or controls?
Frequency of Conflict Situations	How often are there conflict situations the employee has to face in this job?
Responsibility for Outcomes and Results	How responsible is the worker for work outcomes and results of other workers?
Spend Time Making Repetitive Motions	How much does this job require making repetitive motions?
Degree of Automation	How automated is the job?
Spend Time Standing	How much does this job require standing?
Spend Time Kneeling, Crouching, Stooping, or Crawl	How much does this job require kneeling, crouching, stooping, or crawling?
Cramped Work Space, Awkward Positions	How often does this job require working in cramped work spaces that requires getting into awkward positions?
In an Open Vehicle or Equipment	How often does this job require working in an open vehicle or equipment (e.g., tractor)?
Public Speaking	How often do you have to perform public speaking in this job?
Spend Time Walking and Running	How much does this job require walking and running?
Exposed to Minor Burns, Cuts, Bites, or Stings	How often does this job require exposure to minor burns, cuts, bites, or stings?
Sounds, Noise Levels Are Distracting or Uncomforta	How often does this job require working exposed to sounds and noise levels that are distracting or uncomfortable?
Deal With Physically Aggressive People	How frequently does this job require the worker to deal with physical aggression of violent individuals?
Responsible for Others' Health and Safety	How much responsibility is there for the health and safety of others in this job?
Exposed to Contaminants	How often does this job require working exposed to contaminants (such as pollutants, gases, dust or odors)?

Spend Time Bending or Twisting the Body	How much does this job require bending or twisting your body?
Indoors, Not Environmentally Controlled	How often does this job require working indoors in non-controlled environmental conditions (e.g., warehouse without heat)?
Outdoors, Exposed to Weather	How often does this job require working outdoors, exposed to all weather conditions?
Very Hot or Cold Temperatures	How often does this job require working in very hot (above 90 F degrees) or very cold (below 32 F degrees) temperatures?
Outdoors, Under Cover	How often does this job require working outdoors, under cover (e.g., structure with roof but no walls)?
Extremely Bright or Inadequate Lighting	How often does this job require working in extremely bright or inadequate lighting conditions?
Spend Time Keeping or Regaining Balance	How much does this job require keeping or regaining your balance?
Exposed to Hazardous Conditions	How often does this job require exposure to hazardous conditions?
Spend Time Climbing Ladders, Scaffolds, or Poles	How much does this job require climbing ladders, scaffolds, or poles?
Exposed to High Places	How often does this job require exposure to high places?
Pace Determined by Speed of Equipment	How important is it to this job that the pace is determined by the speed of equipment or machinery? (This does not refer to keeping busy at all times on this job).
Wear Common Protective or Safety Equipment such as	How much does this job require wearing common protective or safety equipment such as safety shoes, glasses, gloves, hard hats or life jackets?
Exposed to Whole Body Vibration	How often does this job require exposure to whole body vibration (e.g., operate a jackhammer)?
Exposed to Radiation	How often does this job require exposure to radiation?
Exposed to Disease or Infections	How often does this job require exposure to disease/infections?
Wear Specialized Protective or Safety Equipment su	How much does this job require wearing specialized protective or safety equipment such as breathing apparatus, safety harness, full protection suits, or radiation protection?
Exposed to Hazardous Equipment	How often does this job require exposure to hazardous equipment?

Job Zone Component	Job Zone Component Definitions
Title	Job Zone Four: Considerable Preparation Needed
Overall Experience	A minimum of two to four years of work-related skill, knowledge, or experience is needed for these occupations. For example, an accountant must complete four years of college and work for several years in accounting to be considered qualified.
Job Training	Employees in these occupations usually need several years of work-related experience, on-the-job training, and/or vocational training.
Job Zone Examples	Many of these occupations involve coordinating, supervising, managing, or training others. Examples include accountants, chefs and head cooks, computer programmers, historians, pharmacists, and police detectives.
SVP Range	(7.0 to < 8.0)
Education	Most of these occupations require a four - year bachelor's degree, but some do not.

Work_Styles	Work_Styles Definitions
Integrity	Job requires being honest and ethical.
Initiative	Job requires a willingness to take on responsibilities and challenges.
Dependability	Job requires being reliable, responsible, and dependable, and fulfilling obligations.
Persistence	Job requires persistence in the face of obstacles.
Stress Tolerance	Job requires accepting criticism and dealing calmly and effectively with high stress situations.
Attention to Detail	Job requires being careful about detail and thorough in completing work tasks.
Self Control	Job requires maintaining composure, keeping emotions in check, controlling anger, and avoiding aggressive behavior, even in very difficult situations.
Achievement/Effort	Job requires establishing and maintaining personally challenging achievement goals and exerting effort toward mastering tasks.
Cooperation	Job requires being pleasant with others on the job and displaying a good-natured, cooperative attitude.

Adaptability/Flexibility	Job requires being open to change (positive or negative) and to considerable variety in the workplace.
Analytical Thinking	Job requires analyzing information and using logic to address work-related issues and problems.
Concern for Others	Job requires being sensitive to others' needs and feelings and being understanding and helpful on the job.
Leadership	Job requires a willingness to lead, take charge, and offer opinions and direction.
Innovation	Job requires creativity and alternative thinking to develop new ideas for and answers to work-related problems.
Independence	Job requires developing one's own ways of doing things, guiding oneself with little or no supervision, and depending on oneself to get things done.
Social Orientation	Job requires preferring to work with others rather than alone, and being personally connected with others on the job.

15-2031.00 - Operations Research Analysts

Formulate and apply mathematical modeling and other optimizing methods using a computer to develop and interpret information that assists management with decision making, policy formulation, or other managerial functions. May develop related software, service, or products. Frequently concentrates on collecting and analyzing data and developing decision support software. May develop and supply optimal time, cost, or logistics networks for program evaluation, review, or implementation.

Tasks

1) Study and analyze information about alternative courses of action in order to determine which plan will offer the best outcomes.

2) Specify manipulative or computational methods to be applied to models.

3) Prepare management reports defining and evaluating problems and recommending solutions.

4) Formulate mathematical or simulation models of problems, relating constants and variables, restrictions, alternatives, conflicting objectives, and their numerical parameters.

5) Collaborate with senior managers and decision-makers to identify and solve a variety of problems, and to clarify management objectives.

6) Design, conduct, and evaluate experimental operational models in cases where models cannot be developed from existing data.

7) Define data requirements; then gather and validate information, applying judgment and statistical tests.

8) Collaborate with others in the organization to ensure successful implementation of chosen problem solutions.

9) Break systems into their component parts, assign numerical values to each component, and examine the mathematical relationships between them.

10) Perform validation and testing of models to ensure adequacy; reformulate models as necessary.

11) Analyze information obtained from management in order to conceptualize and define operational problems.

12) Observe the current system in operation, and gather and analyze information about each of the parts of component problems, using a variety of sources.

13) Develop and apply time and cost networks in order to plan, control, and review large projects.

17-2021.00 - Agricultural Engineers

Apply knowledge of engineering technology and biological science to agricultural problems concerned with power and machinery, electrification, structures, soil and water conservation, and processing of agricultural products.

Tasks

1) Design sensing, measuring, and recording devices, and other instrumentation used to study plant or animal life.

2) Test agricultural machinery and equipment to ensure adequate performance.

3) Design agricultural machinery components and equipment, using computer-aided design

technology.

4) Supervise food processing or manufacturing plant operations.

5) Visit sites to observe environmental problems, to consult with contractors, and/or to monitor construction activities.

6) Design structures for crop storage, animal shelter and loading, and animal and crop processing, and supervise their construction.

7) Design food processing plants and related mechanical systems.

8) Plan and direct construction of rural electric-power distribution systems, and irrigation, drainage, and flood control systems for soil and water conservation.

9) Design and supervise environmental and land reclamation projects in agriculture and related industries.

10) Meet with clients, such as district or regional councils, farmers, and developers, to discuss their needs.

11) Provide advice on water quality and issues related to pollution management, river control, and ground and surface water resources.

12) Conduct educational programs that provide farmers or farm cooperative members with information that can help them improve agricultural productivity.

13) Prepare reports, sketches, working drawings, specifications, proposals, and budgets for proposed sites or systems.

Knowledge	Knowledge Definitions
Engineering and Technology	Knowledge of the practical application of engineering science and technology. This includes applying principles, techniques, procedures, and equipment to the design and production of various goods and services.
Design	Knowledge of design techniques, tools, and principles involved in production of precision technical plans, blueprints, drawings, and models.
Physics	Knowledge and prediction of physical principles, laws, their interrelationships, and applications to understanding fluid, material, and atmospheric dynamics, and mechanical, electrical, atomic and sub-atomic structures and processes.
Mathematics	Knowledge of arithmetic, algebra, geometry, calculus, statistics, and their applications.
Food Production	Knowledge of techniques and equipment for planting, growing, and harvesting food products (both plant and animal) for consumption, including storage/handling techniques.
Mechanical	Knowledge of machines and tools, including their designs, uses, repair, and maintenance.
English Language	Knowledge of the structure and content of the English language including the meaning and spelling of words, rules of composition, and grammar.
Production and Processing	Knowledge of raw materials, production processes, quality control, costs, and other techniques for maximizing the effective manufacture and distribution of goods.
Biology	Knowledge of plant and animal organisms, their tissues, cells, functions, interdependencies, and interactions with each other and the environment.
Computers and Electronics	Knowledge of circuit boards, processors, chips, electronic equipment, and computer hardware and software, including applications and programming.
Building and Construction	Knowledge of materials, methods, and the tools involved in the construction or repair of houses, buildings, or other structures such as highways and roads.
Chemistry	Knowledge of the chemical composition, structure, and properties of substances and of the chemical processes and transformations that they undergo. This includes uses of chemicals and their interactions, danger signs, production techniques, and disposal methods.
Customer and Personal Service	Knowledge of principles and processes for providing customer and personal services. This includes customer needs assessment, meeting quality standards for services, and evaluation of customer satisfaction.
Public Safety and Security	Knowledge of relevant equipment, policies, procedures, and strategies to promote effective local, state, or national security operations for the protection of people, data, property, and institutions.
Administration and Management	Knowledge of business and management principles involved in strategic planning, resource allocation, human resources modeling, leadership technique, production methods, and coordination of people and resources.

Geography	Knowledge of principles and methods for describing the features of land, sea, and air masses, including their physical characteristics, locations, interrelationships, and distribution of plant, animal, and human life.
Law and Government	Knowledge of laws, legal codes, court procedures, precedents, government regulations, executive orders, agency rules, and the democratic political process.
Education and Training	Knowledge of principles and methods for curriculum and training design, teaching and instruction for individuals and groups, and the measurement of training effects.
Economics and Accounting	Knowledge of economic and accounting principles and practices, the financial markets, banking and the analysis and reporting of financial data.
Transportation	Knowledge of principles and methods for moving people or goods by air, rail, sea, or road, including the relative costs and benefits.
Sales and Marketing	Knowledge of principles and methods for showing, promoting, and selling products or services. This includes marketing strategy and tactics, product demonstration, sales techniques, and sales control systems.
Psychology	Knowledge of human behavior and performance; individual differences in ability, personality, and interests; learning and motivation; psychological research methods; and the assessment and treatment of behavioral and affective disorders.
Communications and Media	Knowledge of media production, communication, and dissemination techniques and methods. This includes alternative ways to inform and entertain via written, oral, and visual media.
Telecommunications	Knowledge of transmission, broadcasting, switching, control, and operation of telecommunications systems.
Personnel and Human Resources	Knowledge of principles and procedures for personnel recruitment, selection, training, compensation and benefits, labor relations and negotiation, and personnel information systems.
Clerical	Knowledge of administrative and clerical procedures and systems such as word processing, managing files and records, stenography and transcription, designing forms, and other office procedures and terminology.
Sociology and Anthropology	Knowledge of group behavior and dynamics, societal trends and influences, human migrations, ethnicity, cultures and their history and origins.
Foreign Language	Knowledge of the structure and content of a foreign (non-English) language including the meaning and spelling of words, rules of composition and grammar, and pronunciation.
History and Archeology	Knowledge of historical events and their causes, indicators, and effects on civilizations and cultures.
Philosophy and Theology	Knowledge of different philosophical systems and religions. This includes their basic principles, values, ethics, ways of thinking, customs, practices, and their impact on human culture.
Medicine and Dentistry	Knowledge of the information and techniques needed to diagnose and treat human injuries, diseases, and deformities. This includes symptoms, treatment alternatives, drug properties and interactions, and preventive health-care measures.
Therapy and Counseling	Knowledge of principles, methods, and procedures for diagnosis, treatment, and rehabilitation of physical and mental dysfunctions, and for career counseling and guidance.
Fine Arts	Knowledge of the theory and techniques required to compose, produce, and perform works of music, dance, visual arts, drama, and sculpture.

Skills	Skills Definitions
Mathematics	Using mathematics to solve problems.
Science	Using scientific rules and methods to solve problems.
Reading Comprehension	Understanding written sentences and paragraphs in work related documents.
Technology Design	Generating or adapting equipment and technology to serve user needs.
Critical Thinking	Using logic and reasoning to identify the strengths and weaknesses of alternative solutions, conclusions or approaches to problems.
Writing	Communicating effectively in writing as appropriate for the needs of the audience.
Complex Problem Solving	Identifying complex problems and reviewing related information to develop and evaluate options and implement solutions.

Active Learning	Understanding the implications of new information for both current and future problem-solving and decision-making.	Fluency of Ideas	The ability to come up with a number of ideas about a topic (the number of ideas is important, not their quality, correctness, or creativity).
Equipment Selection	Determining the kind of tools and equipment needed to do a job.	Originality	The ability to come up with unusual or clever ideas about a given topic or situation, or to develop creative ways to solve a problem.
Operations Analysis	Analyzing needs and product requirements to create a design.		
Systems Analysis	Determining how a system should work and how changes in conditions, operations, and the environment will affect outcomes.	Speech Recognition	The ability to identify and understand the speech of another person.
		Near Vision	The ability to see details at close range (within a few feet of the observer).
Active Listening	Giving full attention to what other people are saying, taking time to understand the points being made, asking questions as appropriate, and not interrupting at inappropriate times.	Mathematical Reasoning	The ability to choose the right mathematical methods or formulas to solve a problem.
Time Management	Managing one's own time and the time of others.	Number Facility	The ability to add, subtract, multiply, or divide quickly and correctly.
Judgment and Decision Making	Considering the relative costs and benefits of potential actions to choose the most appropriate one.	Flexibility of Closure	The ability to identify or detect a known pattern (a figure, object, word, or sound) that is hidden in other distracting material.
Speaking	Talking to others to convey information effectively.		
Troubleshooting	Determining causes of operating errors and deciding what to do about it.	Selective Attention	The ability to concentrate on a task over a period of time without being distracted.
Systems Evaluation	Identifying measures or indicators of system performance and the actions needed to improve or correct performance, relative to the goals of the system.	Visualization	The ability to imagine how something will look after it is moved around or when its parts are moved or rearranged.
Coordination	Adjusting actions in relation to others' actions.	Perceptual Speed	The ability to quickly and accurately compare similarities and differences among sets of letters, numbers, objects, pictures, or patterns. The things to be compared may be presented at the same time or one after the other. This ability also includes comparing a presented object with a remembered object.
Quality Control Analysis	Conducting tests and inspections of products, services, or processes to evaluate quality or performance.		
Instructing	Teaching others how to do something.		
Management of Financial Resources	Determining how money will be spent to get the work done, and accounting for these expenditures.		
Management of Material Resources	Obtaining and seeing to the appropriate use of equipment, facilities, and materials needed to do certain work.	Finger Dexterity	The ability to make precisely coordinated movements of the fingers of one or both hands to grasp, manipulate, or assemble very small objects.
Programming	Writing computer programs for various purposes.	Visual Color Discrimination	The ability to match or detect differences between colors, including shades of color and brightness.
Monitoring	Monitoring/Assessing performance of yourself, other individuals, or organizations to make improvements or take corrective action.	Speed of Closure	The ability to quickly make sense of, combine, and organize information into meaningful patterns.
Learning Strategies	Selecting and using training/instructional methods and procedures appropriate for the situation when learning or teaching new things.	Depth Perception	The ability to judge which of several objects is closer or farther away from you, or to judge the distance between you and an object.
Social Perceptiveness	Being aware of others' reactions and understanding why they react as they do.	Hearing Sensitivity	The ability to detect or tell the differences between sounds that vary in pitch and loudness.
Management of Personnel Resources	Motivating, developing, and directing people as they work, identifying the best people for the job.	Auditory Attention	The ability to focus on a single source of sound in the presence of other distracting sounds.
Operation and Control	Controlling operations of equipment or systems.	Memorization	The ability to remember information such as words, numbers, pictures, and procedures.
Persuasion	Persuading others to change their minds or behavior.		
Operation Monitoring	Watching gauges, dials, or other indicators to make sure a machine is working properly.	Time Sharing	The ability to shift back and forth between two or more activities or sources of information (such as speech, sounds, touch, or other sources).
Service Orientation	Actively looking for ways to help people.	Control Precision	The ability to quickly and repeatedly adjust the controls of a machine or a vehicle to exact positions.
Installation	Installing equipment, machines, wiring, or programs to meet specifications.		
Negotiation	Bringing others together and trying to reconcile differences.	Multilimb Coordination	The ability to coordinate two or more limbs (for example, two arms, two legs, or one leg and one arm) while sitting, standing, or lying down. It does not involve performing the activities while the whole body is in motion.
Equipment Maintenance	Performing routine maintenance on equipment and determining when and what kind of maintenance is needed.		
Repairing	Repairing machines or systems using the needed tools.	Arm-Hand Steadiness	The ability to keep your hand and arm steady while moving your arm or while holding your arm and hand in one position.

Ability	Ability Definitions
Deductive Reasoning	The ability to apply general rules to specific problems to produce answers that make sense.
Problem Sensitivity	The ability to tell when something is wrong or is likely to go wrong. It does not involve solving the problem, only recognizing there is a problem.
Inductive Reasoning	The ability to combine pieces of information to form general rules or conclusions (includes finding a relationship among seemingly unrelated events).
Oral Expression	The ability to communicate information and ideas in speaking so others will understand.
Oral Comprehension	The ability to listen to and understand information and ideas presented through spoken words and sentences.
Written Comprehension	The ability to read and understand information and ideas presented in writing.
Information Ordering	The ability to arrange things or actions in a certain order or pattern according to a specific rule or set of rules (e.g., patterns of numbers, letters, words, pictures, mathematical operations).
Far Vision	The ability to see details at a distance.
Category Flexibility	The ability to generate or use different sets of rules for combining or grouping things in different ways.
Speech Clarity	The ability to speak clearly so others can understand you.
Written Expression	The ability to communicate information and ideas in writing so others will understand.

Manual Dexterity	The ability to quickly move your hand, your hand together with your arm, or your two hands to grasp, manipulate, or assemble objects.
Reaction Time	The ability to quickly respond (with the hand, finger, or foot) to a signal (sound, light, picture) when it appears.
Wrist-Finger Speed	The ability to make fast, simple, repeated movements of the fingers, hands, and wrists.
Response Orientation	The ability to choose quickly between two or more movements in response to two or more different signals (lights, sounds, pictures). It includes the speed with which the correct response is started with the hand, foot, or other body part.
Rate Control	The ability to time your movements or the movement of a piece of equipment in anticipation of changes in the speed and/or direction of a moving object or scene.
Sound Localization	The ability to tell the direction from which a sound originated.
Gross Body Coordination	The ability to coordinate the movement of your arms, legs, and torso together when the whole body is in motion.
Spatial Orientation	The ability to know your location in relation to the environment or to know where other objects are in relation to you.
Glare Sensitivity	The ability to see objects in the presence of glare or bright lighting.
Dynamic Strength	The ability to exert muscle force repeatedly or continuously over time. This involves muscular endurance and resistance to muscle fatigue.

Trunk Strength	The ability to use your abdominal and lower back muscles to support part of the body repeatedly or continuously over time without 'giving out' or fatiguing.
Peripheral Vision	The ability to see objects or movement of objects to one's side when the eyes are looking ahead.
Night Vision	The ability to see under low light conditions.
Stamina	The ability to exert yourself physically over long periods of time without getting winded or out of breath.
Extent Flexibility	The ability to bend, stretch, twist, or reach with your body, arms, and/or legs.
Dynamic Flexibility	The ability to quickly and repeatedly bend, stretch, twist, or reach out with your body, arms, and/or legs.
Gross Body Equilibrium	The ability to keep or regain your body balance or stay upright when in an unstable position.
Explosive Strength	The ability to use short bursts of muscle force to propel oneself (as in jumping or sprinting), or to throw an object.
Speed of Limb Movement	The ability to quickly move the arms and legs.
Static Strength	The ability to exert maximum muscle force to lift, push, pull, or carry objects.

Work_Activity	Work_Activity Definitions
Interacting With Computers	Using computers and computer systems (including hardware and software) to program, write software, set up functions, enter data, or process information.
Making Decisions and Solving Problems	Analyzing information and evaluating results to choose the best solution and solve problems.
Updating and Using Relevant Knowledge	Keeping up-to-date technically and applying new knowledge to your job.
Thinking Creatively	Developing, designing, or creating new applications, ideas, relationships, systems, or products, including artistic contributions.
Analyzing Data or Information	Identifying the underlying principles, reasons, or facts of information by breaking down information or data into separate parts.
Getting Information	Observing, receiving, and otherwise obtaining information from all relevant sources.
Communicating with Supervisors, Peers, or Subordin	Providing information to supervisors, co-workers, and subordinates by telephone, in written form, e-mail, or in person.
Processing Information	Compiling, coding, categorizing, calculating, tabulating, auditing, or verifying information or data.
Drafting, Laying Out, and Specifying Technical Dev	Providing documentation, detailed instructions, drawings, or specifications to tell others about how devices, parts, equipment, or structures are to be fabricated, constructed, assembled, modified, maintained, or used.
Provide Consultation and Advice to Others	Providing guidance and expert advice to management or other groups on technical, systems-, or process-related topics.
Interpreting the Meaning of Information for Others	Translating or explaining what information means and how it can be used.
Monitor Processes, Materials, or Surroundings	Monitoring and reviewing information from materials, events, or the environment, to detect or assess problems.
Organizing, Planning, and Prioritizing Work	Developing specific goals and plans to prioritize, organize, and accomplish your work.
Evaluating Information to Determine Compliance wit	Using relevant information and individual judgment to determine whether events or processes comply with laws, regulations, or standards.
Identifying Objects, Actions, and Events	Identifying information by categorizing, estimating, recognizing differences or similarities, and detecting changes in circumstances or events.
Inspecting Equipment, Structures, or Material	Inspecting equipment, structures, or materials to identify the cause of errors or other problems or defects.
Communicating with Persons Outside Organization	Communicating with people outside the organization, representing the organization to customers, the public, government, and other external sources. This information can be exchanged in person, in writing, or by telephone or e-mail.
Estimating the Quantifiable Characteristics of Pro	Estimating sizes, distances, and quantities; or determining time, costs, resources, or materials needed to perform a work activity.
Establishing and Maintaining Interpersonal Relatio	Developing constructive and cooperative working relationships with others, and maintaining them over time.
Scheduling Work and Activities	Scheduling events, programs, and activities, as well as the work of others.
Coordinating the Work and Activities of Others	Getting members of a group to work together to accomplish tasks.

Developing and Building Teams	Encouraging and building mutual trust, respect, and cooperation among team members.
Monitoring and Controlling Resources	Monitoring and controlling resources and overseeing the spending of money.
Training and Teaching Others	Identifying the educational needs of others, developing formal educational or training programs or classes, and teaching or instructing others.
Documenting/Recording Information	Entering, transcribing, recording, storing, or maintaining information in written or electronic/magnetic form.
Developing Objectives and Strategies	Establishing long-range objectives and specifying the strategies and actions to achieve them.
Judging the Qualities of Things, Services, or Peop	Assessing the value, importance, or quality of things or people.
Guiding, Directing, and Motivating Subordinates	Providing guidance and direction to subordinates, including setting performance standards and monitoring performance.
Coaching and Developing Others	Identifying the developmental needs of others and coaching, mentoring, or otherwise helping others to improve their knowledge or skills.
Resolving Conflicts and Negotiating with Others	Handling complaints, settling disputes, and resolving grievances and conflicts, or otherwise negotiating with others.
Performing for or Working Directly with the Public	Performing for people or dealing directly with the public. This includes serving customers in restaurants and stores, and receiving clients or guests.
Selling or Influencing Others	Convincing others to buy merchandise/goods or to otherwise change their minds or actions.
Staffing Organizational Units	Recruiting, interviewing, selecting, hiring, and promoting employees in an organization.
Repairing and Maintaining Electronic Equipment	Servicing, repairing, calibrating, regulating, fine-tuning, or testing machines, devices, and equipment that operate primarily on the basis of electrical or electronic (not mechanical) principles.
Controlling Machines and Processes	Using either control mechanisms or direct physical activity to operate machines or processes (not including computers or vehicles).
Performing Administrative Activities	Performing day-to-day administrative tasks such as maintaining information files and processing paperwork.
Operating Vehicles, Mechanized Devices, or Equipme	Running, maneuvering, navigating, or driving vehicles or mechanized equipment, such as forklifts, passenger vehicles, aircraft, or water craft.
Repairing and Maintaining Mechanical Equipment	Servicing, repairing, adjusting, and testing machines, devices, moving parts, and equipment that operate primarily on the basis of mechanical (not electronic) principles.
Handling and Moving Objects	Using hands and arms in handling, installing, positioning, and moving materials, and manipulating things.
Performing General Physical Activities	Performing physical activities that require considerable use of your arms and legs and moving your whole body, such as climbing, lifting, balancing, walking, stooping, and handling of materials.
Assisting and Caring for Others	Providing personal assistance, medical attention, emotional support, or other personal care to others such as coworkers, customers, or patients.

Work_Context	Work_Context Definitions
Electronic Mail	How often do you use electronic mail in this job?
Telephone	How often do you have telephone conversations in this job?
Face-to-Face Discussions	How often do you have to have face-to-face discussions with individuals or teams in this job?
Freedom to Make Decisions	How much decision making freedom, without supervision, does the job offer?
Indoors, Environmentally Controlled	How often does this job require working indoors in environmentally controlled conditions?
Structured versus Unstructured Work	To what extent is this job structured for the worker, rather than allowing the worker to determine tasks, priorities, and goals?
Importance of Being Exact or Accurate	How important is being very exact or highly accurate in performing this job?
Work With Work Group or Team	How important is it to work with others in a group or team in this job?
Impact of Decisions on Co-workers or Company Resul	How do the decisions an employee makes impact the results of co-workers, clients or the company?
Contact With Others	How much does this job require the worker to be in contact with others (face-to-face, by telephone, or otherwise) in order to perform it?
Letters and Memos	How often does the job require written letters and memos?
Frequency of Decision Making	How frequently is the worker required to make decisions that affect other people, the financial resources, and/or the image and reputation of the organization?

Time Pressure	How often does this job require the worker to meet strict deadlines?
Spend Time Sitting	How much does this job require sitting?
Coordinate or Lead Others	How important is it to coordinate or lead others in accomplishing work activities in this job?
In an Enclosed Vehicle or Equipment	How often does this job require working in a closed vehicle or equipment (e.g., car)?
Deal With External Customers	How important is it to work with external customers or the public in this job?
Indoors, Not Environmentally Controlled	How often does this job require working indoors in non-controlled environmental conditions (e.g., warehouse without heat)?
Responsible for Others' Health and Safety	How much responsibility is there for the health and safety of others in this job?
Responsibility for Outcomes and Results	How responsible is the worker for work outcomes and results of other workers?
Consequence of Error	How serious would the result usually be if the worker made a mistake that was not readily correctable?
Level of Competition	To what extent does this job require the worker to compete or to be aware of competitive pressures?
Outdoors, Exposed to Weather	How often does this job require working outdoors, exposed to all weather conditions?
Wear Common Protective or Safety Equipment such as	How much does this job require wearing common protective or safety equipment such as safety shoes, glasses, gloves, hard hats or live jackets?
Outdoors, Under Cover	How often does this job require working outdoors, under cover (e.g., structure with roof but no walls)?
Sounds, Noise Levels Are Distracting or Uncomforta	How often does this job require working exposed to sounds and noise levels that are distracting or uncomfortable?
Public Speaking	How often do you have to perform public speaking in this job?
Physical Proximity	To what extent does this job require the worker to perform job tasks in close physical proximity to other people?
In an Open Vehicle or Equipment	How often does this job require working in an open vehicle or equipment (e.g., tractor)?
Importance of Repeating Same Tasks	How important is repeating the same physical activities (e.g., key entry) or mental activities (e.g., checking entries in a ledger) over and over, without stopping, to performing this job?
Exposed to Hazardous Equipment	How often does this job require exposure to hazardous equipment?
Frequency of Conflict Situations	How often are there conflict situations the employee has to face in this job?
Degree of Automation	How automated is the job?
Exposed to Contaminants	How often does this job require working exposed to contaminants (such as pollutants, gases, dust or odors)?
Deal With Unpleasant or Angry People	How frequently does the worker have to deal with unpleasant, angry, or discourteous individuals as part of the job requirements?
Very Hot or Cold Temperatures	How often does this job require working in very hot (above 90 F degrees) or very cold (below 32 F degrees) temperatures?
Extremely Bright or Inadequate Lighting	How often does this job require working in extremely bright or inadequate lighting conditions?
Spend Time Using Your Hands to Handle, Control, or	How much does this job require using your hands to handle, control, or feel objects, tools or controls?
Exposed to High Places	How often does this job require exposure to high places?
Exposed to Minor Burns, Cuts, Bites, or Stings	How often does this job require exposure to minor burns, cuts, bites, or stings?
Cramped Work Space, Awkward Positions	How often does this job require working in cramped work spaces that requires getting into awkward positions?
Spend Time Standing	How much does this job require standing?
Exposed to Hazardous Conditions	How often does this job require exposure to hazardous conditions?
Spend Time Walking and Running	How much does this job require walking and running?
Spend Time Making Repetitive Motions	How much does this job require making repetitive motions?
Spend Time Bending or Twisting the Body	How much does this job require bending or twisting your body?
Spend Time Kneeling, Crouching, Stooping, or Crawl	How much does this job require kneeling, crouching, stooping or crawling?
Exposed to Whole Body Vibration	How often does this job require exposure to whole body vibration (e.g., operate a jackhammer)?
Exposed to Disease or Infections	How often does this job require exposure to disease/infections?
Pace Determined by Speed of Equipment	How important is it to this job that the pace is determined by the speed of equipment or machinery? (This does not refer to keeping busy at all times on this job.)

Wear Specialized Protective or Safety Equipment su	How much does this job require wearing specialized protective or safety equipment such as breathing apparatus, safety harness, full protection suits, or radiation protection?
Spend Time Climbing Ladders, Scaffolds, or Poles	How much does this job require climbing ladders, scaffolds, or poles?
Spend Time Keeping or Regaining Balance	How much does this job require keeping or regaining your balance?
Deal With Physically Aggressive People	How frequently does this job require the worker to deal with physical aggression of violent individuals?
Exposed to Radiation	How often does this job require exposure to radiation?

Job Zone Component	Job Zone Component Definitions
Title	Job Zone Four: Considerable Preparation Needed
Overall Experience	A minimum of two to four years of work-related skill, knowledge, or experience is needed for these occupations. For example, an accountant must complete four years of college and work for several years in accounting to be considered qualified.
Job Training	Employees in these occupations usually need several years of work-related experience, on-the-job training, and/or vocational training.
Job Zone Examples	Many of these occupations involve coordinating, supervising, managing, or training others. Examples include accountants, chefs and head cooks, computer programmers, historians, pharmacists, and police detectives.
SVP Range	(7.0 to < 8.0)
Education	Most of these occupations require a four - year bachelor's degree, but some do not.

Work_Styles	Work_Styles Definitions
Integrity	Job requires being honest and ethical.
Attention to Detail	Job requires being careful about detail and thorough in completing work tasks.
Analytical Thinking	Job requires analyzing information and using logic to address work-related issues and problems.
Dependability	Job requires being reliable, responsible, and dependable, and fulfilling obligations.
Initiative	Job requires a willingness to take on responsibilities and challenges.
Innovation	Job requires creativity and alternative thinking to develop new ideas for and answers to work-related problems.
Adaptability/Flexibility	Job requires being open to change (positive or negative) and to considerable variety in the workplace.
Independence	Job requires developing one's own ways of doing things, guiding oneself with little or no supervision, and depending on oneself to get things done.
Cooperation	Job requires being pleasant with others on the job and displaying a good-natured, cooperative attitude.
Leadership	Job requires a willingness to lead, take charge, and offer opinions and direction.
Persistence	Job requires persistence in the face of obstacles.
Achievement/Effort	Job requires establishing and maintaining personally challenging achievement goals and exerting effort toward mastering tasks.
Self Control	Job requires maintaining composure, keeping emotions in check, controlling anger, and avoiding aggressive behavior, even in very difficult situations.
Stress Tolerance	Job requires accepting criticism and dealing calmly and effectively with high stress situations.
Concern for Others	Job requires being sensitive to others' needs and feelings and being understanding and helpful on the job.
Social Orientation	Job requires preferring to work with others rather than alone, and being personally connected with others on the job.

17-2072.00 - Electronics Engineers, Except Computer

Research, design, develop, and test electronic components and systems for commercial, industrial, military, or scientific use utilizing knowledge of electronic theory and materials properties. Design electronic circuits and components for use in fields such as telecommunications, aerospace guidance and propulsion control, acoustics, or instruments and controls.

Tasks

1) Evaluate operational systems, prototypes and proposals and recommend repair or design modifications based on factors such as environment, service, cost, and system capabilities.

2) Direct and coordinate activities concerned with manufacture, construction, installation, maintenance, operation, and modification of electronic equipment, products, and systems.

3) Develop and perform operational, maintenance, and testing procedures for electronic products, components, equipment, and systems.

4) Provide technical support and instruction to staff and customers regarding equipment standards, and help solve specific, difficult in-service engineering problems.

5) Determine material and equipment needs and order supplies.

6) Operate computer-assisted engineering and design software and equipment to perform engineering tasks.

7) Inspect electronic equipment, instruments, products, and systems to ensure conformance to specifications, safety standards, and applicable codes and regulations.

8) Prepare engineering sketches and specifications for construction, relocation, and installation of equipment, facilities, products, and systems.

9) Design electronic components and software, products and systems for commercial, industrial, medical, military, and scientific applications.

10) Review and evaluate work of others, inside and outside the organization, to ensure effectiveness, technical adequacy and compatibility in the resolution of complex engineering problems.

11) Analyze system requirements, capacity, cost, and customer needs to determine feasibility of project and develop system plan.

12) Plan and develop applications and modifications for electronic properties used in components, products, and systems, to improve technical performance.

13) Plan and implement research, methodology, and procedures to apply principles of electronic theory to engineering projects.

14) Prepare documentation containing information such as confidential descriptions and specifications of proprietary hardware and software, product development and introduction schedules, product costs, and information about product performance weaknesses.

15) Prepare, review, and maintain maintenance schedules, design documentation and operational reports and charts.

16) Represent employer at conferences, meetings, boards, panels, committees, and working groups to present, explain, and defend findings and recommendations, negotiate compromises and agreements and exchange information.

17) Prepare necessary criteria, procedures, reports, and plans for successful conduct of the program/project with consideration given to site preparation, facility validation, installation, quality assurance and testing.

18) Review or prepare budget and cost estimates for equipment, construction, and installation projects, and control expenditures.

Knowledge

Knowledge	Knowledge Definitions
Engineering and Technology	Knowledge of the practical application of engineering science and technology. This includes applying principles, techniques, procedures, and equipment to the design and production of various goods and services.
Computers and Electronics	Knowledge of circuit boards, processors, chips, electronic equipment, and computer hardware and software, including applications and programming.
Design	Knowledge of design techniques, tools, and principles involved in production of precision technical plans, blueprints, drawings, and models.
Mathematics	Knowledge of arithmetic, algebra, geometry, calculus, statistics, and their applications.
Physics	Knowledge and prediction of physical principles, laws, their interrelationships, and applications to understanding fluid, material, and atmospheric dynamics, and mechanical, electrical, atomic and sub- atomic structures and processes.
Production and Processing	Knowledge of raw materials, production processes, quality control, costs, and other techniques for maximizing the effective manufacture and distribution of goods.
English Language	Knowledge of the structure and content of the English language including the meaning and spelling of words, rules of composition, and grammar.
Customer and Personal Service	Knowledge of principles and processes for providing customer and personal services. This includes customer needs assessment, meeting quality standards for services, and evaluation of customer satisfaction.
Mechanical	Knowledge of machines and tools, including their designs, uses, repair, and maintenance.
Communications and Media	Knowledge of media production, communication, and dissemination techniques and methods. This includes alternative ways to inform and entertain via written, oral, and visual media.
Education and Training	Knowledge of principles and methods for curriculum and training design, teaching and instruction for individuals and groups, and the measurement of training effects.
Telecommunications	Knowledge of transmission, broadcasting, switching, control, and operation of telecommunications systems.
Administration and Management	Knowledge of business and management principles involved in strategic planning, resource allocation, human resources modeling, leadership technique, production methods, and coordination of people and resources.
Clerical	Knowledge of administrative and clerical procedures and systems such as word processing, managing files and records, stenography and transcription, designing forms, and other office procedures and terminology.
Public Safety and Security	Knowledge of relevant equipment, policies, procedures, and strategies to promote effective local, state, or national security operations for the protection of people, data, property, and institutions.
Chemistry	Knowledge of the chemical composition, structure, and properties of substances and of the chemical processes and transformations that they undergo. This includes uses of chemicals and their interactions, danger signs, production techniques, and disposal methods.
Sales and Marketing	Knowledge of principles and methods for showing, promoting, and selling products or services. This includes marketing strategy and tactics, product demonstration, sales techniques, and sales control systems.
Transportation	Knowledge of principles and methods for moving people or goods by air, rail, sea, or road, including the relative costs and benefits.
Building and Construction	Knowledge of materials, methods, and the tools involved in the construction or repair of houses, buildings, or other structures such as highways and roads.
Law and Government	Knowledge of laws, legal codes, court procedures, precedents, government regulations, executive orders, agency rules, and the democratic political process.
Economics and Accounting	Knowledge of economic and accounting principles and practices, the financial markets, banking and the analysis and reporting of financial data.
Psychology	Knowledge of human behavior and performance; individual differences in ability, personality, and interests; learning and motivation; psychological research methods; and the assessment and treatment of behavioral and affective disorders.
Personnel and Human Resources	Knowledge of principles and procedures for personnel recruitment, selection, training, compensation and benefits, labor relations and negotiation, and personnel information systems.
Foreign Language	Knowledge of the structure and content of a foreign (non-English) language including the meaning and spelling of words, rules of composition and grammar, and pronunciation.
Geography	Knowledge of principles and methods for describing the features of land, sea, and air masses, including their physical characteristics, locations, interrelationships, and distribution of plant, animal, and human life.
Therapy and Counseling	Knowledge of principles, methods, and procedures for diagnosis, treatment, and rehabilitation of physical and mental dysfunctions, and for career counseling and guidance.
Sociology and Anthropology	Knowledge of group behavior and dynamics, societal trends and influences, human migrations, ethnicity, cultures and their history and origins.
Biology	Knowledge of plant and animal organisms, their tissues, cells, functions, interdependencies, and interactions with each other and the environment.
Medicine and Dentistry	Knowledge of the information and techniques needed to diagnose and treat human injuries, diseases, and deformities. This includes symptoms, treatment alternatives, drug properties and interactions, and preventive health-care measures.
Philosophy and Theology	Knowledge of different philosophical systems and religions. This includes their basic principles, values, ethics, ways of thinking, customs, practices, and their impact on human culture.
History and Archeology	Knowledge of historical events and their causes, indicators, and effects on civilizations and cultures.

Food Production	Knowledge of techniques and equipment for planting, growing, and harvesting food products (both plant and animal) for consumption, including storage/handling techniques.
Fine Arts	Knowledge of the theory and techniques required to compose, produce, and perform works of music, dance, visual arts, drama, and sculpture.

Skills	Skills Definitions
Reading Comprehension	Understanding written sentences and paragraphs in work related documents.
Complex Problem Solving	Identifying complex problems and reviewing related information to develop and evaluate options and implement solutions.
Troubleshooting	Determining causes of operating errors and deciding what to do about it.
Equipment Selection	Determining the kind of tools and equipment needed to do a job.
Critical Thinking	Using logic and reasoning to identify the strengths and weaknesses of alternative solutions, conclusions or approaches to problems.
Active Learning	Understanding the implications of new information for both current and future problem-solving and decision-making.
Mathematics	Using mathematics to solve problems.
Coordination	Adjusting actions in relation to others' actions.
Active Listening	Giving full attention to what other people are saying, taking time to understand the points being made, asking questions as appropriate, and not interrupting at inappropriate times.
Judgment and Decision Making	Considering the relative costs and benefits of potential actions to choose the most appropriate one.
Writing	Communicating effectively in writing as appropriate for the needs of the audience.
Science	Using scientific rules and methods to solve problems.
Operations Analysis	Analyzing needs and product requirements to create a design.
Technology Design	Generating or adapting equipment and technology to serve user needs.
Speaking	Talking to others to convey information effectively.
Installation	Installing equipment, machines, wiring, or programs to meet specifications.
Instructing	Teaching others how to do something.
Systems Analysis	Determining how a system should work and how changes in conditions, operations, and the environment will affect outcomes.
Time Management	Managing one's own time and the time of others.
Monitoring	Monitoring/Assessing performance of yourself, other individuals, or organizations to make improvements or take corrective action.
Persuasion	Persuading others to change their minds or behavior.
Management of Personnel Resources	Motivating, developing, and directing people as they work, identifying the best people for the job.
Systems Evaluation	Identifying measures or indicators of system performance and the actions needed to improve or correct performance, relative to the goals of the system.
Learning Strategies	Selecting and using training/instructional methods and procedures appropriate for the situation when learning or teaching new things.
Negotiation	Bringing others together and trying to reconcile differences.
Operation Monitoring	Watching gauges, dials, or other indicators to make sure a machine is working properly.
Equipment Maintenance	Performing routine maintenance on equipment and determining when and what kind of maintenance is needed.
Repairing	Repairing machines or systems using the needed tools.
Social Perceptiveness	Being aware of others' reactions and understanding why they react as they do.
Operation and Control	Controlling operations of equipment or systems.
Quality Control Analysis	Conducting tests and inspections of products, services, or processes to evaluate quality or performance.
Management of Financial Resources	Determining how money will be spent to get the work done, and accounting for these expenditures.
Programming	Writing computer programs for various purposes.
Service Orientation	Actively looking for ways to help people.
Management of Material Resources	Obtaining and seeing to the appropriate use of equipment, facilities, and materials needed to do certain work.

Ability	Ability Definitions
Problem Sensitivity	The ability to tell when something is wrong or is likely to go wrong. It does not involve solving the problem, only recognizing there is a problem.
Deductive Reasoning	The ability to apply general rules to specific problems to produce answers that make sense.
Inductive Reasoning	The ability to combine pieces of information to form general rules or conclusions (includes finding a relationship among seemingly unrelated events).
Oral Expression	The ability to communicate information and ideas in speaking so others will understand.
Oral Comprehension	The ability to listen to and understand information and ideas presented through spoken words and sentences.
Written Comprehension	The ability to read and understand information and ideas presented in writing.
Speech Clarity	The ability to speak clearly so others can understand you.
Information Ordering	The ability to arrange things or actions in a certain order or pattern according to a specific rule or set of rules (e.g., patterns of numbers, letters, words, pictures, mathematical operations).
Speech Recognition	The ability to identify and understand the speech of another person.
Visualization	The ability to imagine how something will look after it is moved around or when its parts are moved or rearranged.
Selective Attention	The ability to concentrate on a task over a period of time without being distracted.
Perceptual Speed	The ability to quickly and accurately compare similarities and differences among sets of letters, numbers, objects, pictures, or patterns. The things to be compared may be presented at the same time or one after the other. This ability also includes comparing a presented object with a remembered object.
Visual Color Discrimination	The ability to match or detect differences between colors, including shades of color and brightness.
Category Flexibility	The ability to generate or use different sets of rules for combining or grouping things in different ways.
Finger Dexterity	The ability to make precisely coordinated movements of the fingers of one or both hands to grasp, manipulate, or assemble very small objects.
Flexibility of Closure	The ability to identify or detect a known pattern (a figure, object, word, or sound) that is hidden in other distracting material.
Near Vision	The ability to see details at close range (within a few feet of the observer).
Mathematical Reasoning	The ability to choose the right mathematical methods or formulas to solve a problem.
Memorization	The ability to remember information such as words, numbers, pictures, and procedures.
Written Expression	The ability to communicate information and ideas in writing so others will understand.
Originality	The ability to come up with unusual or clever ideas about a given topic or situation, or to develop creative ways to solve a problem.
Far Vision	The ability to see details at a distance.
Fluency of Ideas	The ability to come up with a number of ideas about a topic (the number of ideas is important, not their quality, correctness, or creativity).
Arm-Hand Steadiness	The ability to keep your hand and arm steady while moving your arm or while holding your arm and hand in one position.
Number Facility	The ability to add, subtract, multiply, or divide quickly and correctly.
Manual Dexterity	The ability to quickly move your hand, your hand together with your arm, or your two hands to grasp, manipulate, or assemble objects.
Depth Perception	The ability to judge which of several objects is closer or farther away from you, or to judge the distance between you and an object.
Hearing Sensitivity	The ability to detect or tell the differences between sounds that vary in pitch and loudness.
Auditory Attention	The ability to focus on a single source of sound in the presence of other distracting sounds.
Speed of Closure	The ability to quickly make sense of, combine, and organize information into meaningful patterns.
Time Sharing	The ability to shift back and forth between two or more activities or sources of information (such as speech, sounds, touch, or other sources).
Control Precision	The ability to quickly and repeatedly adjust the controls of a machine or a vehicle to exact positions.

Reaction Time	The ability to quickly respond (with the hand, finger, or foot) to a signal (sound, light, picture) when it appears.
Response Orientation	The ability to choose quickly between two or more movements in response to two or more different signals (lights, sounds, pictures). It includes the speed with which the correct response is started with the hand, foot, or other body part.
Wrist-Finger Speed	The ability to make fast, simple, repeated movements of the fingers, hands, and wrists.
Multilimb Coordination	The ability to coordinate two or more limbs (for example, two arms, two legs, or one leg and one arm) while sitting, standing, or lying down. It does not involve performing the activities while the whole body is in motion.
Rate Control	The ability to time your movements or the movement of a piece of equipment in anticipation of changes in the speed and/or direction of a moving object or scene.
Spatial Orientation	The ability to know your location in relation to the environment or to know where other objects are in relation to you.
Gross Body Equilibrium	The ability to keep or regain your body balance or stay upright when in an unstable position.
Speed of Limb Movement	The ability to quickly move the arms and legs.
Peripheral Vision	The ability to see objects or movement of objects to one's side when the eyes are looking ahead.
Static Strength	The ability to exert maximum muscle force to lift, push, pull, or carry objects.
Explosive Strength	The ability to use short bursts of muscle force to propel oneself (as in jumping or sprinting), or to throw an object.
Dynamic Strength	The ability to exert muscle force repeatedly or continuously over time. This involves muscular endurance and resistance to muscle fatigue.
Trunk Strength	The ability to use your abdominal and lower back muscles to support part of the body repeatedly or continuously over time without 'giving out' or fatiguing.
Gross Body Coordination	The ability to coordinate the movement of your arms, legs, and torso together when the whole body is in motion.
Night Vision	The ability to see under low light conditions.
Glare Sensitivity	The ability to see objects in the presence of glare or bright lighting.
Stamina	The ability to exert yourself physically over long periods of time without getting winded or out of breath.
Sound Localization	The ability to tell the direction from which a sound originated.
Dynamic Flexibility	The ability to quickly and repeatedly bend, stretch, twist, or reach out with your body, arms, and/or legs.
Extent Flexibility	The ability to bend, stretch, twist, or reach with your body, arms, and/or legs.

Work_Activity	Work_Activity Definitions
Interacting With Computers	Using computers and computer systems (including hardware and software) to program, write software, set up functions, enter data, or process information.
Getting Information	Observing, receiving, and otherwise obtaining information from all relevant sources.
Identifying Objects, Actions, and Events	Identifying information by categorizing, estimating, recognizing differences or similarities, and detecting changes in circumstances or events.
Repairing and Maintaining Electronic Equipment	Servicing, repairing, calibrating, regulating, fine-tuning, or testing machines, devices, and equipment that operate primarily on the basis of electrical or electronic (not mechanical) principles.
Inspecting Equipment, Structures, or Material	Inspecting equipment, structures, or materials to identify the cause of errors or other problems or defects.
Documenting/Recording Information	Entering, transcribing, recording, storing, or maintaining information in written or electronic/magnetic form.
Updating and Using Relevant Knowledge	Keeping up-to-date technically and applying new knowledge to your job.
Making Decisions and Solving Problems	Analyzing information and evaluating results to choose the best solution and solve problems.
Analyzing Data or Information	Identifying the underlying principles, reasons, or facts of information by breaking down information or data into separate parts.
Estimating the Quantifiable Characteristics of Pro	Estimating sizes, distances, and quantities; or determining time, costs, resources, or materials needed to perform a work activity.
Evaluating Information to Determine Compliance wit	Using relevant information and individual judgment to determine whether events or processes comply with laws, regulations, or standards.

Communicating with Supervisors, Peers, or Subordin	Providing information to supervisors, co-workers, and subordinates by telephone, in written form, e-mail, or in person.
Thinking Creatively	Developing, designing, or creating new applications, ideas, relationships, systems, or products, including artistic contributions.
Monitor Processes, Materials, or Surroundings	Monitoring and reviewing information from materials, events, or the environment, to detect or assess problems.
Controlling Machines and Processes	Using either control mechanisms or direct physical activity to operate machines or processes (not including computers or vehicles).
Processing Information	Compiling, coding, categorizing, calculating, tabulating, auditing, or verifying information or data.
Drafting, Laying Out, and Specifying Technical Dev	Providing documentation, detailed instructions, drawings, or specifications to tell others about how devices, parts, equipment, or structures are to be fabricated, constructed, assembled, modified, maintained, or used.
Organizing, Planning, and Prioritizing Work	Developing specific goals and plans to prioritize, organize, and accomplish your work.
Provide Consultation and Advice to Others	Providing guidance and expert advice to management or other groups on technical, systems-, or process-related topics.
Judging the Qualities of Things, Services, or Peop	Assessing the value, importance, or quality of things or people.
Scheduling Work and Activities	Scheduling events, programs, and activities, as well as the work of others.
Developing and Building Teams	Encouraging and building mutual trust, respect, and cooperation among team members.
Establishing and Maintaining Interpersonal Relatio	Developing constructive and cooperative working relationships with others, and maintaining them over time.
Communicating with Persons Outside Organization	Communicating with people outside the organization, representing the organization to customers, the public, government, and other external sources. This information can be exchanged in person, in writing, or by telephone or e-mail.
Coaching and Developing Others	Identifying the developmental needs of others and coaching, mentoring, or otherwise helping others to improve their knowledge or skills.
Training and Teaching Others	Identifying the educational needs of others, developing formal educational or training programs or classes, and teaching or instructing others.
Monitoring and Controlling Resources	Monitoring and controlling resources and overseeing the spending of money.
Developing Objectives and Strategies	Establishing long-range objectives and specifying the strategies and actions to achieve them.
Operating Vehicles, Mechanized Devices, or Equipme	Running, maneuvering, navigating, or driving vehicles or mechanized equipment, such as forklifts, passenger vehicles, aircraft, or water craft.
Interpreting the Meaning of Information for Others	Translating or explaining what information means and how it can be used.
Coordinating the Work and Activities of Others	Getting members of a group to work together to accomplish tasks.
Handling and Moving Objects	Using hands and arms in handling, installing, positioning, and moving materials, and manipulating things.
Performing Administrative Activities	Performing day-to-day administrative tasks such as maintaining information files and processing paperwork.
Repairing and Maintaining Mechanical Equipment	Servicing, repairing, adjusting, and testing machines, devices, moving parts, and equipment that operate primarily on the basis of mechanical (not electronic) principles.
Resolving Conflicts and Negotiating with Others	Handling complaints, settling disputes, and resolving grievances and conflicts, or otherwise negotiating with others.
Assisting and Caring for Others	Providing personal assistance, medical attention, emotional support, or other personal care to others such as coworkers, customers, or patients.
Guiding, Directing, and Motivating Subordinates	Providing guidance and direction to subordinates, including setting performance standards and monitoring performance.
Selling or Influencing Others	Convincing others to buy merchandise/goods or to otherwise change their minds or actions.
Performing General Physical Activities	Performing physical activities that require considerable use of your arms and legs and moving your whole body, such as climbing, lifting, balancing, walking, stooping, and handling of materials.
Staffing Organizational Units	Recruiting, interviewing, selecting, hiring, and promoting employees in an organization.
Performing for or Working Directly with the Public	Performing for people or dealing directly with the public. This includes serving customers in restaurants and stores, and receiving clients or guests.

Work_Context	Work_Context Definitions
Electronic Mail	How often do you use electronic mail in this job?
Face-to-Face Discussions	How often do you have to have face-to-face discussions with individuals or teams in this job?
Indoors, Environmentally Controlled	How often does this job require working indoors in environmentally controlled conditions?
Telephone	How often do you have telephone conversations in this job?
Structured versus Unstructured Work	To what extent is this job structured for the worker, rather than allowing the worker to determine tasks, priorities, and goals?
Freedom to Make Decisions	How much decision making freedom, without supervision, does the job offer?
Spend Time Sitting	How much does this job require sitting?
Work With Work Group or Team	How important is it to work with others in a group or team in this job?
Importance of Being Exact or Accurate	How important is being very exact or highly accurate in performing this job?
Contact With Others	How much does this job require the worker to be in contact with others (face-to-face, by telephone, or otherwise) in order to perform it?
Coordinate or Lead Others	How important is it to coordinate or lead others in accomplishing work activities in this job?
Time Pressure	How often does this job require the worker to meet strict deadlines?
Responsibility for Outcomes and Results	How responsible is the worker for work outcomes and results of other workers?
Impact of Decisions on Co-workers or Company Resul	How do the decisions an employee makes impact the results of co-workers, clients or the company?
Letters and Memos	How often does the job require written letters and memos?
Frequency of Decision Making	How frequently is the worker required to make decisions that affect other people, the financial resources, and/or the image and reputation of the organization?
Sounds, Noise Levels Are Distracting or Uncomforta	How often does this job require working exposed to sounds and noise levels that are distracting or uncomfortable?
Level of Competition	To what extent does this job require the worker to compete or to be aware of competitive pressures?
Consequence of Error	How serious would the result usually be if the worker made a mistake that was not readily correctable?
Wear Common Protective or Safety Equipment such as	How much does this job require wearing common protective or safety equipment such as safety shoes, glasses, gloves, hard hats or live jackets?
Responsible for Others' Health and Safety	How much responsibility is there for the health and safety of others in this job?
Frequency of Conflict Situations	How often are there conflict situations the employee has to face in this job?
Importance of Repeating Same Tasks	How important is repeating the same physical activities (e.g., key entry) or mental activities (e.g., checking entries in a ledger) over and over, without stopping, to performing this job?
Deal With External Customers	How important is it to work with external customers or the public in this job?
Deal With Unpleasant or Angry People	How frequently does the worker have to deal with unpleasant, angry, or discourteous individuals as part of the job requirements?
Physical Proximity	To what extent does this job require the worker to perform job tasks in close physical proximity to other people?
Indoors, Not Environmentally Controlled	How often does this job require working indoors in non-controlled environmental conditions (e.g., warehouse without heat)?
Exposed to Contaminants	How often does this job require working exposed to contaminants (such as pollutants, gases, dust or odors)?
Public Speaking	How often do you have to perform public speaking in this job?
Spend Time Walking and Running	How much does this job require walking and running?
Spend Time Standing	How much does this job require standing?
Exposed to Hazardous Conditions	How often does this job require exposure to hazardous conditions?
Very Hot or Cold Temperatures	How often does this job require working in very hot (above 90 F degrees) or very cold (below 32 F degrees) temperatures?
Spend Time Using Your Hands to Handle, Control, or	How much does this job require using your hands to handle, control, or feel objects, tools or controls?
Pace Determined by Speed of Equipment	How important is it to this job that the pace is determined by the speed of equipment or machinery? (This does not refer to keeping busy at all times on this job.)
Extremely Bright or Inadequate Lighting	How often does this job require working in extremely bright or inadequate lighting conditions?
In an Enclosed Vehicle or Equipment	How often does this job require working in a closed vehicle or equipment (e.g., car)?
Spend Time Making Repetitive Motions	How much does this job require making repetitive motions?
Cramped Work Space, Awkward Positions	How often does this job require working in cramped work spaces that requires getting into awkward positions?
Exposed to Radiation	How often does this job require exposure to radiation?
Outdoors, Under Cover	How often does this job require working outdoors, under cover (e.g., structure with roof but no walls)?
Degree of Automation	How automated is the job?
Outdoors, Exposed to Weather	How often does this job require working outdoors, exposed to all weather conditions?
Spend Time Kneeling, Crouching, Stooping, or Crawl	How much does this job require kneeling, crouching, stooping or crawling?
Spend Time Bending or Twisting the Body	How much does this job require bending or twisting your body?
Exposed to Minor Burns, Cuts, Bites, or Stings	How often does this job require exposure to minor burns, cuts, bites, or stings?
Exposed to Hazardous Equipment	How often does this job require exposure to hazardous equipment?
Spend Time Keeping or Regaining Balance	How much does this job require keeping or regaining your balance?
Exposed to High Places	How often does this job require exposure to high places?
Wear Specialized Protective or Safety Equipment su	How much does this job require wearing specialized protective or safety equipment such as breathing apparatus, safety harness, full protection suits, or radiation protection?
Exposed to Disease or Infections	How often does this job require exposure to disease/infections?
In an Open Vehicle or Equipment	How often does this job require working in an open vehicle or equipment (e.g., tractor)?
Deal With Physically Aggressive People	How frequently does this job require the worker to deal with physical aggression of violent individuals?
Exposed to Whole Body Vibration	How often does this job require exposure to whole body vibration (e.g., operate a jackhammer)?
Spend Time Climbing Ladders, Scaffolds, or Poles	How much does this job require climbing ladders, scaffolds, or poles?

Job Zone Component	Job Zone Component Definitions
Title	Job Zone Four: Considerable Preparation Needed
Overall Experience	A minimum of two to four years of work-related skill, knowledge, or experience is needed for these occupations. For example, an accountant must complete four years of college and work for several years in accounting to be considered qualified.
Job Training	Employees in these occupations usually need several years of work-related experience, on-the-job training, and/or vocational training.
Job Zone Examples	Many of these occupations involve coordinating, supervising, managing, or training others. Examples include accountants, chefs and head cooks, computer programmers, historians, pharmacists, and police detectives.
SVP Range	(7.0 to < 8.0)
Education	Most of these occupations require a four - year bachelor's degree, but some do not.

Work_Styles	Work_Styles Definitions
Attention to Detail	Job requires being careful about detail and thorough in completing work tasks.
Dependability	Job requires being reliable, responsible, and dependable, and fulfilling obligations.
Integrity	Job requires being honest and ethical.
Initiative	Job requires a willingness to take on responsibilities and challenges.
Analytical Thinking	Job requires analyzing information and using logic to address work-related issues and problems.
Innovation	Job requires creativity and alternative thinking to develop new ideas for and answers to work-related problems.
Stress Tolerance	Job requires accepting criticism and dealing calmly and effectively with high stress situations.
Independence	Job requires developing one's own ways of doing things, guiding oneself with little or no supervision, and depending on oneself to get things done.

Cooperation	Job requires being pleasant with others on the job and displaying a good-natured, cooperative attitude.
Persistence	Job requires persistence in the face of obstacles.
Achievement/Effort	Job requires establishing and maintaining personally challenging achievement goals and exerting effort toward mastering tasks.
Adaptability/Flexibility	Job requires being open to change (positive or negative) and to considerable variety in the workplace.
Self Control	Job requires maintaining composure, keeping emotions in check, controlling anger, and avoiding aggressive behavior, even in very difficult situations.
Leadership	Job requires a willingness to lead, take charge, and offer opinions and direction.
Concern for Others	Job requires being sensitive to others' needs and feelings and being understanding and helpful on the job.
Social Orientation	Job requires preferring to work with others rather than alone, and being personally connected with others on the job.

17-2111.01 - Industrial Safety and Health Engineers

Plan, implement, and coordinate safety programs, requiring application of engineering principles and technology, to prevent or correct unsafe environmental working conditions.

Tasks

1) Maintain liaisons with outside organizations, such as fire departments, mutual aid societies, and rescue teams, so that emergency responses can be facilitated.

2) Provide technical advice and guidance to organizations on how to handle health-related problems and make needed changes.

3) Evaluate adequacy of actions taken to correct health inspection violations.

4) Install safety devices on machinery, or direct device installation.

5) Write and revise safety regulations and codes.

6) Plan and conduct industrial hygiene research.

7) Check floors of plants to ensure that they are strong enough to support heavy machinery.

8) Design and build safety equipment.

9) Recommend process and product safety features that will reduce employees' exposure to chemical, physical, and biological work hazards.

10) Interview employers and employees to obtain information about work environments and workplace incidents.

11) Review employee safety programs to determine their adequacy.

12) Review plans and specifications for construction of new machinery or equipment in order to determine if all safety requirements have been met.

13) Compile, analyze, and interpret statistical data related to occupational illnesses and accidents.

14) Conduct or coordinate worker training in areas such as safety laws and regulations, hazardous condition monitoring, and use of safety equipment.

15) Inspect facilities, machinery, and safety equipment in order to identify and correct potential hazards, and to ensure safety regulation compliance.

16) Maintain and apply knowledge of current policies, regulations, and industrial processes.

17) Report or review findings from accident investigations, facilities inspections, or environmental testing.

18) Investigate industrial accidents, injuries, or occupational diseases to determine causes and preventive measures.

19) Conduct or direct testing of air quality, noise, temperature, and/or radiation levels to verify compliance with health and safety regulations.

20) Interpret safety regulations for others interested in industrial safety, such as safety engineers, labor representatives, and safety inspectors.

Knowledge / Knowledge Definitions

Public Safety and Security	Knowledge of relevant equipment, policies, procedures, and strategies to promote effective local, state, or national security operations for the protection of people, data, property, and institutions.
Education and Training	Knowledge of principles and methods for curriculum and training design, teaching and instruction for individuals and groups, and the measurement of training effects.
Administration and Management	Knowledge of business and management principles involved in strategic planning, resource allocation, human resources modeling, leadership technique, production methods, and coordination of people and resources.
Law and Government	Knowledge of laws, legal codes, court procedures, precedents, government regulations, executive orders, agency rules, and the democratic political process.
English Language	Knowledge of the structure and content of the English language including the meaning and spelling of words, rules of composition, and grammar.
Psychology	Knowledge of human behavior and performance; individual differences in ability, personality, and interests; learning and motivation; psychological research methods; and the assessment and treatment of behavioral and affective disorders.
Engineering and Technology	Knowledge of the practical application of engineering science and technology. This includes applying principles, techniques, procedures, and equipment to the design and production of various goods and services.
Mathematics	Knowledge of arithmetic, algebra, geometry, calculus, statistics, and their applications.
Chemistry	Knowledge of the chemical composition, structure, and properties of substances and of the chemical processes and transformations that they undergo. This includes uses of chemicals and their interactions, danger signs, production techniques, and disposal methods.
Customer and Personal Service	Knowledge of principles and processes for providing customer and personal services. This includes customer needs assessment, meeting quality standards for services, and evaluation of customer satisfaction.
Physics	Knowledge and prediction of physical principles, laws, their interrelationships, and applications to understanding fluid, material, and atmospheric dynamics, and mechanical, electrical, atomic and sub-atomic structures and processes.
Personnel and Human Resources	Knowledge of principles and procedures for personnel recruitment, selection, training, compensation and benefits, labor relations and negotiation, and personnel information systems.
Production and Processing	Knowledge of raw materials, production processes, quality control, costs, and other techniques for maximizing the effective manufacture and distribution of goods.
Biology	Knowledge of plant and animal organisms, their tissues, cells, functions, interdependencies, and interactions with each other and the environment.
Mechanical	Knowledge of machines and tools, including their designs, uses, repair, and maintenance.
Building and Construction	Knowledge of materials, methods, and the tools involved in the construction or repair of houses, buildings, or other structures such as highways and roads.
Communications and Media	Knowledge of media production, communication, and dissemination techniques and methods. This includes alternative ways to inform and entertain via written, oral, and visual media.
Design	Knowledge of design techniques, tools, and principles involved in production of precision technical plans, blueprints, drawings, and models.
Computers and Electronics	Knowledge of circuit boards, processors, chips, electronic equipment, and computer hardware and software, including applications and programming.
Economics and Accounting	Knowledge of economic and accounting principles and practices, the financial markets, banking and the analysis and reporting of financial data.
Clerical	Knowledge of administrative and clerical procedures and systems such as word processing, managing files and records, stenography and transcription, designing forms, and other office procedures and terminology.
Sociology and Anthropology	Knowledge of group behavior and dynamics, societal trends and influences, human migrations, ethnicity, cultures and their history and origins.
Sales and Marketing	Knowledge of principles and methods for showing, promoting, and selling products or services. This includes marketing strategy and tactics, product demonstration, sales techniques, and sales control systems.
Transportation	Knowledge of principles and methods for moving people or goods by air, rail, sea, or road, including the relative costs and benefits.

Medicine and Dentistry	Knowledge of the information and techniques needed to diagnose and treat human injuries, diseases, and deformities. This includes symptoms, treatment alternatives, drug properties and interactions, and preventive health-care measures.
Therapy and Counseling	Knowledge of principles, methods, and procedures for diagnosis, treatment, and rehabilitation of physical and mental dysfunctions, and for career counseling and guidance.
Foreign Language	Knowledge of the structure and content of a foreign (non-English) language including the meaning and spelling of words, rules of composition and grammar, and pronunciation.
Philosophy and Theology	Knowledge of different philosophical systems and religions. This includes their basic principles, values, ethics, ways of thinking, customs, practices, and their impact on human culture.
Geography	Knowledge of principles and methods for describing the features of land, sea, and air masses, including their physical characteristics, locations, interrelationships, and distribution of plant, animal, and human life.
Telecommunications	Knowledge of transmission, broadcasting, switching, control, and operation of telecommunications systems.
Food Production	Knowledge of techniques and equipment for planting, growing, and harvesting food products (both plant and animal) for consumption, including storage/handling techniques.
History and Archeology	Knowledge of historical events and their causes, indicators, and effects on civilizations and cultures.
Fine Arts	Knowledge of the theory and techniques required to compose, produce, and perform works of music, dance, visual arts, drama, and sculpture.

Skills	Skills Definitions
Speaking	Talking to others to convey information effectively.
Reading Comprehension	Understanding written sentences and paragraphs in work related documents.
Writing	Communicating effectively in writing as appropriate for the needs of the audience.
Active Listening	Giving full attention to what other people are saying, taking time to understand the points being made, asking questions as appropriate, and not interrupting at inappropriate times.
Persuasion	Persuading others to change their minds or behavior.
Critical Thinking	Using logic and reasoning to identify the strengths and weaknesses of alternative solutions, conclusions or approaches to problems.
Time Management	Managing one's own time and the time of others.
Active Learning	Understanding the implications of new information for both current and future problem-solving and decision-making.
Instructing	Teaching others how to do something.
Negotiation	Bringing others together and trying to reconcile differences.
Monitoring	Monitoring/Assessing performance of yourself, other individuals, or organizations to make improvements or take corrective action.
Judgment and Decision Making	Considering the relative costs and benefits of potential actions to choose the most appropriate one.
Complex Problem Solving	Identifying complex problems and reviewing related information to develop and evaluate options and implement solutions.
Coordination	Adjusting actions in relation to others' actions.
Learning Strategies	Selecting and using training/instructional methods and procedures appropriate for the situation when learning or teaching new things.
Service Orientation	Actively looking for ways to help people.
Social Perceptiveness	Being aware of others' reactions and understanding why they react as they do.
Science	Using scientific rules and methods to solve problems.
Systems Analysis	Determining how a system should work and how changes in conditions, operations, and the environment will affect outcomes.
Equipment Selection	Determining the kind of tools and equipment needed to do a job.
Mathematics	Using mathematics to solve problems.
Management of Personnel Resources	Motivating, developing, and directing people as they work, identifying the best people for the job.
Management of Financial Resources	Determining how money will be spent to get the work done, and accounting for these expenditures.
Systems Evaluation	Identifying measures or indicators of system performance and the actions needed to improve or correct performance, relative to the goals of the system.
Operations Analysis	Analyzing needs and product requirements to create a design.

Troubleshooting	Determining causes of operating errors and deciding what to do about it.
Management of Material Resources	Obtaining and seeing to the appropriate use of equipment, facilities, and materials needed to do certain work.
Technology Design	Generating or adapting equipment and technology to serve user needs.
Quality Control Analysis	Conducting tests and inspections of products, services, or processes to evaluate quality or performance.
Operation Monitoring	Watching gauges, dials, or other indicators to make sure a machine is working properly.
Operation and Control	Controlling operations of equipment or systems.
Installation	Installing equipment, machines, wiring, or programs to meet specifications.
Equipment Maintenance	Performing routine maintenance on equipment and determining when and what kind of maintenance is needed.
Programming	Writing computer programs for various purposes.
Repairing	Repairing machines or systems using the needed tools.

Ability	Ability Definitions
Oral Expression	The ability to communicate information and ideas in speaking so others will understand.
Written Expression	The ability to communicate information and ideas in writing so others will understand.
Problem Sensitivity	The ability to tell when something is wrong or is likely to go wrong. It does not involve solving the problem, only recognizing there is a problem.
Oral Comprehension	The ability to listen to and understand information and ideas presented through spoken words and sentences.
Speech Clarity	The ability to speak clearly so others can understand you.
Inductive Reasoning	The ability to combine pieces of information to form general rules or conclusions (includes finding a relationship among seemingly unrelated events).
Deductive Reasoning	The ability to apply general rules to specific problems to produce answers that make sense.
Originality	The ability to come up with unusual or clever ideas about a given topic or situation, or to develop creative ways to solve a problem.
Speech Recognition	The ability to identify and understand the speech of another person.
Written Comprehension	The ability to read and understand information and ideas presented in writing.
Near Vision	The ability to see details at close range (within a few feet of the observer).
Fluency of Ideas	The ability to come up with a number of ideas about a topic (the number of ideas is important, not their quality, correctness, or creativity).
Information Ordering	The ability to arrange things or actions in a certain order or pattern according to a specific rule or set of rules (e.g., patterns of numbers, letters, words, pictures, mathematical operations).
Category Flexibility	The ability to generate or use different sets of rules for combining or grouping things in different ways.
Selective Attention	The ability to concentrate on a task over a period of time without being distracted.
Far Vision	The ability to see details at a distance.
Flexibility of Closure	The ability to identify or detect a known pattern (a figure, object, word, or sound) that is hidden in other distracting material.
Mathematical Reasoning	The ability to choose the right mathematical methods or formulas to solve a problem.
Hearing Sensitivity	The ability to detect or tell the differences between sounds that vary in pitch and loudness.
Number Facility	The ability to add, subtract, multiply, or divide quickly and correctly.
Perceptual Speed	The ability to quickly and accurately compare similarities and differences among sets of letters, numbers, objects, pictures, or patterns. The things to be compared may be presented at the same time or one after the other. This ability also includes comparing a presented object with a remembered object.
Auditory Attention	The ability to focus on a single source of sound in the presence of other distracting sounds.
Speed of Closure	The ability to quickly make sense of, combine, and organize information into meaningful patterns.
Visualization	The ability to imagine how something will look after it is moved around or when its parts are moved or rearranged.
Depth Perception	The ability to judge which of several objects is closer or farther away from you, or to judge the distance between you and an object.

Visual Color Discrimination	The ability to match or detect differences between colors, including shades of color and brightness.
Memorization	The ability to remember information such as words, numbers, pictures, and procedures.
Time Sharing	The ability to shift back and forth between two or more activities or sources of information (such as speech, sounds, touch, or other sources).
Finger Dexterity	The ability to make precisely coordinated movements of the fingers of one or both hands to grasp, manipulate, or assemble very small objects.
Control Precision	The ability to quickly and repeatedly adjust the controls of a machine or a vehicle to exact positions.
Multilimb Coordination	The ability to coordinate two or more limbs (for example, two arms, two legs, or one leg and one arm) while sitting, standing, or lying down. It does not involve performing the activities while the whole body is in motion.
Trunk Strength	The ability to use your abdominal and lower back muscles to support part of the body repeatedly or continuously over time without 'giving out' or fatiguing.
Reaction Time	The ability to quickly respond (with the hand, finger, or foot) to a signal (sound, light, picture) when it appears.
Gross Body Equilibrium	The ability to keep or regain your body balance or stay upright when in an unstable position.
Gross Body Coordination	The ability to coordinate the movement of your arms, legs, and torso together when the whole body is in motion.
Wrist-Finger Speed	The ability to make fast, simple, repeated movements of the fingers, hands, and wrists.
Stamina	The ability to exert yourself physically over long periods of time without getting winded or out of breath.
Dynamic Strength	The ability to exert muscle force repeatedly or continuously over time. This involves muscular endurance and resistance to muscle fatigue.
Static Strength	The ability to exert maximum muscle force to lift, push, pull, or carry objects.
Spatial Orientation	The ability to know your location in relation to the environment or to know where other objects are in relation to you.
Manual Dexterity	The ability to quickly move your hand, your hand together with your arm, or your two hands to grasp, manipulate, or assemble objects.
Glare Sensitivity	The ability to see objects in the presence of glare or bright lighting.
Response Orientation	The ability to choose quickly between two or more movements in response to two or more different signals (lights, sounds, pictures). It includes the speed with which the correct response is started with the hand, foot, or other body part.
Dynamic Flexibility	The ability to quickly and repeatedly bend, stretch, twist, or reach out with your body, arms, and/or legs.
Explosive Strength	The ability to use short bursts of muscle force to propel oneself (as in jumping or sprinting), or to throw an object.
Speed of Limb Movement	The ability to quickly move the arms and legs.
Arm-Hand Steadiness	The ability to keep your hand and arm steady while moving your arm or while holding your arm and hand in one position.
Night Vision	The ability to see under low light conditions.
Peripheral Vision	The ability to see objects or movement of objects to one's side when the eyes are looking ahead.
Sound Localization	The ability to tell the direction from which a sound originated.
Extent Flexibility	The ability to bend, stretch, twist, or reach with your body, arms, and/or legs.
Rate Control	The ability to time your movements or the movement of a piece of equipment in anticipation of changes in the speed and/or direction of a moving object or scene.

Work_Activity	**Work_Activity Definitions**
Communicating with Supervisors, Peers, or Subordin	Providing information to supervisors, co-workers, and subordinates by telephone, in written form, e-mail, or in person.
Establishing and Maintaining Interpersonal Relatio	Developing constructive and cooperative working relationships with others, and maintaining them over time.
Making Decisions and Solving Problems	Analyzing information and evaluating results to choose the best solution and solve problems.
Updating and Using Relevant Knowledge	Keeping up-to-date technically and applying new knowledge to your job.
Evaluating Information to Determine Compliance wit	Using relevant information and individual judgment to determine whether events or processes comply with laws, regulations, or standards.

Getting Information	Observing, receiving, and otherwise obtaining information from all relevant sources.
Provide Consultation and Advice to Others	Providing guidance and expert advice to management or other groups on technical, systems-, or process-related topics.
Training and Teaching Others	Identifying the educational needs of others, developing formal educational or training programs or classes, and teaching or instructing others.
Developing and Building Teams	Encouraging and building mutual trust, respect, and cooperation among team members.
Interacting With Computers	Using computers and computer systems (including hardware and software) to program, write software, set up functions, enter data, or process information.
Analyzing Data or Information	Identifying the underlying principles, reasons, or facts of information by breaking down information or data into separate parts.
Interpreting the Meaning of Information for Others	Translating or explaining what information means and how it can be used.
Organizing, Planning, and Prioritizing Work	Developing specific goals and plans to prioritize, organize, and accomplish your work.
Monitor Processes, Materials, or Surroundings	Monitoring and reviewing information from materials, events, or the environment, to detect or assess problems.
Communicating with Persons Outside Organization	Communicating with people outside the organization, representing the organization to customers, the public, government, and other external sources. This information can be exchanged in person, in writing, or by telephone or e-mail.
Identifying Objects, Actions, and Events	Identifying information by categorizing, estimating, recognizing differences or similarities, and detecting changes in circumstances or events.
Inspecting Equipment, Structures, or Material	Inspecting equipment, structures, or materials to identify the cause of errors or other problems or defects.
Developing Objectives and Strategies	Establishing long-range objectives and specifying the strategies and actions to achieve them.
Resolving Conflicts and Negotiating with Others	Handling complaints, settling disputes, and resolving grievances and conflicts, or otherwise negotiating with others.
Coordinating the Work and Activities of Others	Getting members of a group to work together to accomplish tasks.
Coaching and Developing Others	Identifying the developmental needs of others and coaching, mentoring, or otherwise helping others to improve their knowledge or skills.
Processing Information	Compiling, coding, categorizing, calculating, tabulating, auditing, or verifying information or data.
Guiding, Directing, and Motivating Subordinates	Providing guidance and direction to subordinates, including setting performance standards and monitoring performance.
Selling or Influencing Others	Convincing others to buy merchandise/goods or to otherwise change their minds or actions.
Thinking Creatively	Developing, designing, or creating new applications, ideas, relationships, systems, or products, including artistic contributions.
Documenting/Recording Information	Entering, transcribing, recording, storing, or maintaining information in written or electronic/magnetic form.
Monitoring and Controlling Resources	Monitoring and controlling resources and overseeing the spending of money.
Judging the Qualities of Things, Services, or Peop	Assessing the value, importance, or quality of things or people.
Estimating the Quantifiable Characteristics of Pro	Estimating sizes, distances, and quantities; or determining time, costs, resources, or materials needed to perform a work activity.
Scheduling Work and Activities	Scheduling events, programs, and activities, as well as the work of others.
Performing Administrative Activities	Performing day-to-day administrative tasks such as maintaining information files and processing paperwork.
Staffing Organizational Units	Recruiting, interviewing, selecting, hiring, and promoting employees in an organization.
Assisting and Caring for Others	Providing personal assistance, medical attention, emotional support, or other personal care to others such as coworkers, customers, or patients.
Drafting, Laying Out, and Specifying Technical Dev	Providing documentation, detailed instructions, drawings, or specifications to tell others about how devices, parts, equipment, or structures are to be fabricated, constructed, assembled, modified, maintained, or used.
Performing for or Working Directly with the Public	Performing for people or dealing directly with the public. This includes serving customers in restaurants and stores, and receiving clients or guests.
Performing General Physical Activities	Performing physical activities that require considerable use of your arms and legs and moving your whole body, such as climbing, lifting, balancing, walking, stooping, and handling of materials.

Operating Vehicles, Mechanized Devices, or Equipme	Running, maneuvering, navigating, or driving vehicles or mechanized equipment, such as forklifts, passenger vehicles, aircraft, or water craft.
Controlling Machines and Processes	Using either control mechanisms or direct physical activity to operate machines or processes (not including computers or vehicles).
Repairing and Maintaining Electronic Equipment	Servicing, repairing, calibrating, regulating, fine-tuning, or testing machines, devices, and equipment that operate primarily on the basis of electrical or electronic (not mechanical) principles.
Handling and Moving Objects	Using hands and arms in handling, installing, positioning, and moving materials, and manipulating things.
Repairing and Maintaining Mechanical Equipment	Servicing, repairing, adjusting, and testing machines, devices, moving parts, and equipment that operate primarily on the basis of mechanical (not electronic) principles.

Work_Context	Work_Context Definitions
Electronic Mail	How often do you use electronic mail in this job?
Telephone	How often do you have telephone conversations in this job?
Face-to-Face Discussions	How often do you have to have face-to-face discussions with individuals or teams in this job?
Contact With Others	How much does this job require the worker to be in contact with others (face-to-face, by telephone, or otherwise) in order to perform it?
Work With Work Group or Team	How important is it to work with others in a group or team in this job?
Structured versus Unstructured Work	To what extent is this job structured for the worker, rather than allowing the worker to determine tasks, priorities, and goals?
Freedom to Make Decisions	How much decision making freedom, without supervision, does the job offer?
Wear Common Protective or Safety Equipment such as	How much does this job require wearing common protective or safety equipment such as safety shoes, glasses, gloves, hard hats or live jackets?
Impact of Decisions on Co-workers or Company Resul	How do the decisions an employee makes impact the results of co-workers, clients or the company?
Letters and Memos	How often does the job require written letters and memos?
Frequency of Decision Making	How frequently is the worker required to make decisions that affect other people, the financial resources, and/or the image and reputation of the organization?
Coordinate or Lead Others	How important is it to coordinate or lead others in accomplishing work activities in this job?
Responsible for Others' Health and Safety	How much responsibility is there for the health and safety of others in this job?
Indoors, Environmentally Controlled	How often does this job require working indoors in environmentally controlled conditions?
Importance of Being Exact or Accurate	How important is being very exact or highly accurate in performing this job?
In an Enclosed Vehicle or Equipment	How often does this job require working in a closed vehicle or equipment (e.g., car)?
Time Pressure	How often does this job require the worker to meet strict deadlines?
Outdoors, Exposed to Weather	How often does this job require working outdoors, exposed to all weather conditions?
Indoors, Not Environmentally Controlled	How often does this job require working indoors in non-controlled environmental conditions (e.g., warehouse without heat)?
Consequence of Error	How serious would the result usually be if the worker made a mistake that was not readily correctable?
Frequency of Conflict Situations	How often are there conflict situations the employee has to face in this job?
Spend Time Sitting	How much does this job require sitting?
Sounds, Noise Levels Are Distracting or Uncomforta	How often does this job require working exposed to sounds and noise levels that are distracting or uncomfortable?
Public Speaking	How often do you have to perform public speaking in this job?
Deal With External Customers	How important is it to work with external customers or the public in this job?
Level of Competition	To what extent does this job require the worker to compete or to be aware of competitive pressures?
Deal With Unpleasant or Angry People	How frequently does the worker have to deal with unpleasant, angry, or discourteous individuals as part of the job requirements?
Physical Proximity	To what extent does this job require the worker to perform job tasks in close physical proximity to other people?
Responsibility for Outcomes and Results	How responsible is the worker for work outcomes and results of other workers?

Exposed to Contaminants	How often does this job require working exposed to contaminants (such as pollutants, gases, dust or odors)?
Very Hot or Cold Temperatures	How often does this job require working in very hot (above 90 F degrees) or very cold (below 32 F degrees) temperatures?
Outdoors, Under Cover	How often does this job require working outdoors, under cover (e.g., structure with roof but no walls)?
Spend Time Standing	How much does this job require standing?
Importance of Repeating Same Tasks	How important is repeating the same physical activities (e.g., key entry) or mental activities (e.g., checking entries in a ledger) over and over, without stopping, to performing this job?
Exposed to Hazardous Equipment	How often does this job require exposure to hazardous equipment?
Exposed to High Places	How often does this job require exposure to high places?
Exposed to Hazardous Conditions	How often does this job require exposure to hazardous conditions?
Wear Specialized Protective or Safety Equipment su	How much does this job require wearing specialized protective or safety equipment such as breathing apparatus, safety harness, full protection suits, or radiation protection?
Extremely Bright or Inadequate Lighting	How often does this job require working in extremely bright or inadequate lighting conditions?
Degree of Automation	How automated is the job?
Cramped Work Space, Awkward Positions	How often does this job require working in cramped work spaces that requires getting into awkward positions?
Spend Time Walking and Running	How much does this job require walking and running?
Spend Time Using Your Hands to Handle, Control, or	How much does this job require using your hands to handle, control, or feel objects, tools or controls?
Spend Time Climbing Ladders, Scaffolds, or Poles	How much does this job require climbing ladders, scaffolds, or poles?
Spend Time Making Repetitive Motions	How much does this job require making repetitive motions?
Exposed to Minor Burns, Cuts, Bites, or Stings	How often does this job require exposure to minor burns, cuts, bites, or stings?
Deal With Physically Aggressive People	How frequently does this job require the worker to deal with physical aggression of violent individuals?
Spend Time Kneeling, Crouching, Stooping, or Crawl	How much does this job require kneeling, crouching, stooping or crawling?
Exposed to Disease or Infections	How often does this job require exposure to disease/infections?
Spend Time Bending or Twisting the Body	How much does this job require bending or twisting your body?
Spend Time Keeping or Regaining Balance	How much does this job require keeping or regaining your balance?
Exposed to Radiation	How often does this job require exposure to radiation?
Pace Determined by Speed of Equipment	How important is it to this job that the pace is determined by the speed of equipment or machinery? (This does not refer to keeping busy at all times on this job.)
In an Open Vehicle or Equipment	How often does this job require working in an open vehicle or equipment (e.g., tractor)?
Exposed to Whole Body Vibration	How often does this job require exposure to whole body vibration (e.g., operate a jackhammer)?

Job Zone Component	Job Zone Component Definitions
Title	Job Zone Four: Considerable Preparation Needed
Overall Experience	A minimum of two to four years of work-related skill, knowledge, or experience is needed for these occupations. For example, an accountant must complete four years of college and work for several years in accounting to be considered qualified.
Job Training	Employees in these occupations usually need several years of work-related experience, on-the-job training, and/or vocational training.
Job Zone Examples	Many of these occupations involve coordinating, supervising, managing, or training others. Examples include accountants, chefs and head cooks, computer programmers, historians, pharmacists, and police detectives.
SVP Range	(7.0 to < 8.0)
Education	Most of these occupations require a four - year bachelor's degree, but some do not.

Work_Styles	Work_Styles Definitions
Integrity	Job requires being honest and ethical.
Dependability	Job requires being reliable, responsible, and dependable, and fulfilling obligations.
Cooperation	Job requires being pleasant with others on the job and displaying a good-natured, cooperative attitude.
Initiative	Job requires a willingness to take on responsibilities and challenges.
Persistence	Job requires persistence in the face of obstacles.
Self Control	Job requires maintaining composure, keeping emotions in check, controlling anger, and avoiding aggressive behavior, even in very difficult situations.
Attention to Detail	Job requires being careful about detail and thorough in completing work tasks.
Leadership	Job requires a willingness to lead, take charge, and offer opinions and direction.
Concern for Others	Job requires being sensitive to others' needs and feelings and being understanding and helpful on the job.
Adaptability/Flexibility	Job requires being open to change (positive or negative) and to considerable variety in the workplace.
Analytical Thinking	Job requires analyzing information and using logic to address work-related issues and problems.
Stress Tolerance	Job requires accepting criticism and dealing calmly and effectively with high stress situations.
Social Orientation	Job requires preferring to work with others rather than alone, and being personally connected with others on the job.
Achievement/Effort	Job requires establishing and maintaining personally challenging achievement goals and exerting effort toward mastering tasks.
Independence	Job requires developing one's own ways of doing things, guiding oneself with little or no supervision, and depending on oneself to get things done.
Innovation	Job requires creativity and alternative thinking to develop new ideas for and answers to work-related problems.

17-2111.02 - Fire-Prevention and Protection Engineers

Research causes of fires, determine fire protection methods, and design or recommend materials or equipment such as structural components or fire-detection equipment to assist organizations in safeguarding life and property against fire, explosion, and related hazards.

Tasks

1) Study the relationships between ignition sources and materials to determine how fires start.

2) Inspect buildings or building designs to determine fire protection system requirements and potential problems in areas such as water supplies, exit locations, and construction materials.

3) Develop plans for the prevention of destruction by fire, wind, and water.

4) Prepare and write reports detailing specific fire prevention and protection issues such as work performed and proposed review schedules.

5) Evaluate fire department performance and the laws and regulations affecting fire prevention or fire safety.

6) Develop training materials, and conduct training sessions on fire protection.

7) Determine causes of fires, and ways in which they could have been prevented.

8) Design fire detection equipment, alarm systems, and fire extinguishing devices and systems.

9) Consult with authorities to discuss safety regulations and to recommend changes as necessary.

10) Conduct research on fire retardants and the fire safety of materials and devices.

11) Advise architects, builders, and other construction personnel on fire prevention equipment and techniques, and on fire code and standard interpretation and compliance.

12) Direct the purchase, modification, installation, maintenance, and operation of fire protection systems.

17-2111.03 - Product Safety Engineers

Develop and conduct tests to evaluate product safety levels and recommend measures to

reduce or eliminate hazards.

Tasks

1) Investigate causes of accidents, injuries, or illnesses related to product usage in order to develop solutions to minimize or prevent recurrence.

2) Evaluate potential health hazards or damage that could occur from product misuse.

3) Conduct research to evaluate safety levels for products.

4) Participate in preparation of product usage and precautionary label instructions.

5) Recommend procedures for detection, prevention, and elimination of physical, chemical, or other product hazards.

17-2161.00 - Nuclear Engineers

Conduct research on nuclear engineering problems or apply principles and theory of nuclear science to problems concerned with release, control, and utilization of nuclear energy and nuclear waste disposal.

Tasks

1) Monitor nuclear facility operations in order to identify any design, construction, or operation practices that violate safety regulations and laws or that could jeopardize the safety of operations.

2) Examine accidents in order to obtain data that can be used to design preventive measures.

3) Write operational instructions to be used in nuclear plant operation and nuclear fuel and waste handling and disposal.

4) Synthesize analyses of test results, and use the results to prepare technical reports of findings and recommendations.

5) Analyze available data and consult with other scientists in order to determine parameters of experimentation and suitability of analytical models.

6) Prepare construction project proposals that include cost estimates, and discuss proposals with interested parties such as vendors, contractors, and nuclear facility review boards.

7) Recommend preventive measures to be taken in the handling of nuclear technology, based on data obtained from operations monitoring or from evaluation of test results.

8) Initiate corrective actions and/or order plant shutdowns in emergency situations.

9) Direct operating and maintenance activities of operational nuclear power plants in order to ensure efficiency and conformity to safety standards.

10) Design and develop nuclear equipment such as reactor cores, radiation shielding, and associated instrumentation and control mechanisms.

11) Design and oversee construction and operation of nuclear reactors and power plants and nuclear fuels reprocessing and reclamation systems.

12) Conduct tests of nuclear fuel behavior and cycles and performance of nuclear machinery and equipment, in order to optimize performance of existing plants.

13) Perform experiments that will provide information about acceptable methods of nuclear material usage, nuclear fuel reclamation, and waste disposal.

14) Design and direct nuclear research projects in order to discover facts, to test or modify theoretical models, or to develop new theoretical models or new uses for current models.

Knowledge	Knowledge Definitions
Engineering and Technology	Knowledge of the practical application of engineering science and technology. This includes applying principles, techniques, procedures, and equipment to the design and production of various goods and services.
Mathematics	Knowledge of arithmetic, algebra, geometry, calculus, statistics, and their applications.
English Language	Knowledge of the structure and content of the English language including the meaning and spelling of words, rules of composition, and grammar.
Mechanical	Knowledge of machines and tools, including their designs, uses, repair, and maintenance.
Physics	Knowledge and prediction of physical principles, laws, their interrelationships, and applications to understanding fluid, material, and atmospheric dynamics, and mechanical, electrical, atomic and sub-atomic structures and processes.

Public Safety and Security	Knowledge of relevant equipment, policies, procedures, and strategies to promote effective local, state, or national security operations for the protection of people, data, property, and institutions.
Design	Knowledge of design techniques, tools, and principles involved in production of precision technical plans, blueprints, drawings, and models.
Computers and Electronics	Knowledge of circuit boards, processors, chips, electronic equipment, and computer hardware and software, including applications and programming.
Law and Government	Knowledge of laws, legal codes, court procedures, precedents, government regulations, executive orders, agency rules, and the democratic political process.
Chemistry	Knowledge of the chemical composition, structure, and properties of substances and of the chemical processes and transformations that they undergo. This includes uses of chemicals and their interactions, danger signs, production techniques, and disposal methods.
Administration and Management	Knowledge of business and management principles involved in strategic planning, resource allocation, human resources modeling, leadership technique, production methods, and coordination of people and resources.
Education and Training	Knowledge of principles and methods for curriculum and training design, teaching and instruction for individuals and groups, and the measurement of training effects.
Telecommunications	Knowledge of transmission, broadcasting, switching, control, and operation of telecommunications systems.
Building and Construction	Knowledge of materials, methods, and the tools involved in the construction or repair of houses, buildings, or other structures such as highways and roads.
Customer and Personal Service	Knowledge of principles and processes for providing customer and personal services. This includes customer needs assessment, meeting quality standards for services, and evaluation of customer satisfaction.
Production and Processing	Knowledge of raw materials, production processes, quality control, costs, and other techniques for maximizing the effective manufacture and distribution of goods.
Clerical	Knowledge of administrative and clerical procedures and systems such as word processing, managing files and records, stenography and transcription, designing forms, and other office procedures and terminology.
Communications and Media	Knowledge of media production, communication, and dissemination techniques and methods. This includes alternative ways to inform and entertain via written, oral, and visual media.
Psychology	Knowledge of human behavior and performance; individual differences in ability, personality, and interests; learning and motivation; psychological research methods; and the assessment and treatment of behavioral and affective disorders.
Economics and Accounting	Knowledge of economic and accounting principles and practices, the financial markets, banking and the analysis and reporting of financial data.
Transportation	Knowledge of principles and methods for moving people or goods by air, rail, sea, or road, including the relative costs and benefits.
Personnel and Human Resources	Knowledge of principles and procedures for personnel recruitment, selection, training, compensation and benefits, labor relations and negotiation, and personnel information systems.
Sales and Marketing	Knowledge of principles and methods for showing, promoting, and selling products or services. This includes marketing strategy and tactics, product demonstration, sales techniques, and sales control systems.
Sociology and Anthropology	Knowledge of group behavior and dynamics, societal trends and influences, human migrations, ethnicity, cultures and their history and origins.
Biology	Knowledge of plant and animal organisms, their tissues, cells, functions, interdependencies, and interactions with each other and the environment.
Medicine and Dentistry	Knowledge of the information and techniques needed to diagnose and treat human injuries, diseases, and deformities. This includes symptoms, treatment alternatives, drug properties and interactions, and preventive health-care measures.
Geography	Knowledge of principles and methods for describing the features of land, sea, and air masses, including their physical characteristics, locations, interrelationships, and distribution of plant, animal, and human life.

History and Archeology	Knowledge of historical events and their causes, indicators, and effects on civilizations and cultures.
Philosophy and Theology	Knowledge of different philosophical systems and religions. This includes their basic principles, values, ethics, ways of thinking, customs, practices, and their impact on human culture.
Therapy and Counseling	Knowledge of principles, methods, and procedures for diagnosis, treatment, and rehabilitation of physical and mental dysfunctions, and for career counseling and guidance.
Foreign Language	Knowledge of the structure and content of a foreign (non-English) language including the meaning and spelling of words, rules of composition and grammar, and pronunciation.
Fine Arts	Knowledge of the theory and techniques required to compose, produce, and perform works of music, dance, visual arts, drama, and sculpture.
Food Production	Knowledge of techniques and equipment for planting, growing, and harvesting food products (both plant and animal) for consumption, including storage/handling techniques.

Skills

Skills Definitions

Active Listening	Giving full attention to what other people are saying, taking time to understand the points being made, asking questions as appropriate, and not interrupting at inappropriate times.
Critical Thinking	Using logic and reasoning to identify the strengths and weaknesses of alternative solutions, conclusions or approaches to problems.
Quality Control Analysis	Conducting tests and inspections of products, services, or processes to evaluate quality or performance.
Operation Monitoring	Watching gauges, dials, or other indicators to make sure a machine is working properly.
Judgment and Decision Making	Considering the relative costs and benefits of potential actions to choose the most appropriate one.
Time Management	Managing one's own time and the time of others.
Troubleshooting	Determining causes of operating errors and deciding what to do about it.
Learning Strategies	Selecting and using training/instructional methods and procedures appropriate for the situation when learning or teaching new things.
Coordination	Adjusting actions in relation to others' actions.
Reading Comprehension	Understanding written sentences and paragraphs in work related documents.
Social Perceptiveness	Being aware of others' reactions and understanding why they react as they do.
Writing	Communicating effectively in writing as appropriate for the needs of the audience.
Instructing	Teaching others how to do something.
Persuasion	Persuading others to change their minds or behavior.
Management of Personnel Resources	Motivating, developing, and directing people as they work, identifying the best people for the job.
Mathematics	Using mathematics to solve problems.
Complex Problem Solving	Identifying complex problems and reviewing related information to develop and evaluate options and implement solutions.
Management of Material Resources	Obtaining and seeing to the appropriate use of equipment, facilities, and materials needed to do certain work.
Science	Using scientific rules and methods to solve problems.
Systems Analysis	Determining how a system should work and how changes in conditions, operations, and the environment will affect outcomes.
Operations Analysis	Analyzing needs and product requirements to create a design.
Active Learning	Understanding the implications of new information for both current and future problem-solving and decision-making.
Systems Evaluation	Identifying measures or indicators of system performance and the actions needed to improve or correct performance, relative to the goals of the system.
Speaking	Talking to others to convey information effectively.
Equipment Maintenance	Performing routine maintenance on equipment and determining when and what kind of maintenance is needed.
Technology Design	Generating or adapting equipment and technology to serve user needs.
Operation and Control	Controlling operations of equipment or systems.
Equipment Selection	Determining the kind of tools and equipment needed to do a job.
Monitoring	Monitoring/Assessing performance of yourself, other individuals, or organizations to make improvements or take corrective action.
Negotiation	Bringing others together and trying to reconcile differences.

Installation	Installing equipment, machines, wiring, or programs to meet specifications.
Service Orientation	Actively looking for ways to help people.
Management of Financial Resources	Determining how money will be spent to get the work done, and accounting for these expenditures.
Repairing	Repairing machines or systems using the needed tools.
Programming	Writing computer programs for various purposes.

Ability	Ability Definitions
Problem Sensitivity	The ability to tell when something is wrong or is likely to go wrong. It does not involve solving the problem, only recognizing there is a problem.
Written Comprehension	The ability to read and understand information and ideas presented in writing.
Oral Comprehension	The ability to listen to and understand information and ideas presented through spoken words and sentences.
Deductive Reasoning	The ability to apply general rules to specific problems to produce answers that make sense.
Speech Clarity	The ability to speak clearly so others can understand you.
Oral Expression	The ability to communicate information and ideas in speaking so others will understand.
Inductive Reasoning	The ability to combine pieces of information to form general rules or conclusions (includes finding a relationship among seemingly unrelated events).
Speech Recognition	The ability to identify and understand the speech of another person.
Information Ordering	The ability to arrange things or actions in a certain order or pattern according to a specific rule or set of rules (e.g., patterns of numbers, letters, words, pictures, mathematical operations).
Written Expression	The ability to communicate information and ideas in writing so others will understand.
Selective Attention	The ability to concentrate on a task over a period of time without being distracted.
Flexibility of Closure	The ability to identify or detect a known pattern (a figure, object, word, or sound) that is hidden in other distracting material.
Near Vision	The ability to see details at close range (within a few feet of the observer).
Mathematical Reasoning	The ability to choose the right mathematical methods or formulas to solve a problem.
Perceptual Speed	The ability to quickly and accurately compare similarities and differences among sets of letters, numbers, objects, pictures, or patterns. The things to be compared may be presented at the same time or one after the other. This ability also includes comparing a presented object with a remembered object.
Category Flexibility	The ability to generate or use different sets of rules for combining or grouping things in different ways.
Number Facility	The ability to add, subtract, multiply, or divide quickly and correctly.
Far Vision	The ability to see details at a distance.
Originality	The ability to come up with unusual or clever ideas about a given topic or situation, or to develop creative ways to solve a problem.
Fluency of Ideas	The ability to come up with a number of ideas about a topic (the number of ideas is important, not their quality, correctness, or creativity).
Visualization	The ability to imagine how something will look after it is moved around or when its parts are moved or rearranged.
Finger Dexterity	The ability to make precisely coordinated movements of the fingers of one or both hands to grasp, manipulate, or assemble very small objects.
Time Sharing	The ability to shift back and forth between two or more activities or sources of information (such as speech, sounds, touch, or other sources).
Speed of Closure	The ability to quickly make sense of, combine, and organize information into meaningful patterns.
Hearing Sensitivity	The ability to detect or tell the differences between sounds that vary in pitch and loudness.
Visual Color Discrimination	The ability to match or detect differences between colors, including shades of color and brightness.
Memorization	The ability to remember information such as words, numbers, pictures, and procedures.
Auditory Attention	The ability to focus on a single source of sound in the presence of other distracting sounds.
Depth Perception	The ability to judge which of several objects is closer or farther away from you, or to judge the distance between you and an object.

Control Precision	The ability to quickly and repeatedly adjust the controls of a machine or a vehicle to exact positions.
Multilimb Coordination	The ability to coordinate two or more limbs (for example, two arms, two legs, or one leg and one arm) while sitting, standing, or lying down. It does not involve performing the activities while the whole body is in motion.
Reaction Time	The ability to quickly respond (with the hand, finger, or foot) to a signal (sound, light, picture) when it appears.
Manual Dexterity	The ability to quickly move your hand, your hand together with your arm, or your two hands to grasp, manipulate, or assemble objects.
Response Orientation	The ability to choose quickly between two or more movements in response to two or more different signals (lights, sounds, pictures). It includes the speed with which the correct response is started with the hand, foot, or other body part.
Sound Localization	The ability to tell the direction from which a sound originated.
Wrist-Finger Speed	The ability to make fast, simple, repeated movements of the fingers, hands, and wrists.
Gross Body Coordination	The ability to coordinate the movement of your arms, legs, and torso together when the whole body is in motion.
Spatial Orientation	The ability to know your location in relation to the environment or to know where other objects are in relation to you.
Extent Flexibility	The ability to bend, stretch, twist, or reach with your body, arms, and/or legs.
Dynamic Flexibility	The ability to quickly and repeatedly bend, stretch, twist, or reach out with your body, arms, and/or legs.
Trunk Strength	The ability to use your abdominal and lower back muscles to support part of the body repeatedly or continuously over time without 'giving out' or fatiguing.
Static Strength	The ability to exert maximum muscle force to lift, push, pull, or carry objects.
Night Vision	The ability to see under low light conditions.
Speed of Limb Movement	The ability to quickly move the arms and legs.
Peripheral Vision	The ability to see objects or movement of objects to one's side when the eyes are looking ahead.
Arm-Hand Steadiness	The ability to keep your hand and arm steady while moving your arm or while holding your arm and hand in one position.
Gross Body Equilibrium	The ability to keep or regain your body balance or stay upright when in an unstable position.
Explosive Strength	The ability to use short bursts of muscle force to propel oneself (as in jumping or sprinting), or to throw an object.
Stamina	The ability to exert yourself physically over long periods of time without getting winded or out of breath.
Rate Control	The ability to time your movements or the movement of a piece of equipment in anticipation of changes in the speed and/or direction of a moving object or scene.
Dynamic Strength	The ability to exert muscle force repeatedly or continuously over time. This involves muscular endurance and resistance to muscle fatigue.
Glare Sensitivity	The ability to see objects in the presence of glare or bright lighting.

Work_Activity	Work_Activity Definitions
Interacting With Computers	Using computers and computer systems (including hardware and software) to program, write software, set up functions, enter data, or process information.
Getting Information	Observing, receiving, and otherwise obtaining information from all relevant sources.
Documenting/Recording Information	Entering, transcribing, recording, storing, or maintaining information in written or electronic/magnetic form.
Evaluating Information to Determine Compliance wit	Using relevant information and individual judgment to determine whether events or processes comply with laws, regulations, or standards.
Communicating with Supervisors, Peers, or Subordin	Providing information to supervisors, co-workers, and subordinates by telephone, in written form, e-mail, or in person.
Analyzing Data or Information	Identifying the underlying principles, reasons, or facts of information by breaking down information or data into separate parts.
Updating and Using Relevant Knowledge	Keeping up-to-date technically and applying new knowledge to your job.
Identifying Objects, Actions, and Events	Identifying information by categorizing, estimating, recognizing differences or similarities, and detecting changes in circumstances or events.
Making Decisions and Solving Problems	Analyzing information and evaluating results to choose the best solution and solve problems.

Processing Information	Compiling, coding, categorizing, calculating, tabulating, auditing, or verifying information or data.
Monitor Processes, Materials, or Surroundings	Monitoring and reviewing information from materials, events, or the environment, to detect or assess problems.
Organizing, Planning, and Prioritizing Work	Developing specific goals and plans to prioritize, organize, and accomplish your work.
Establishing and Maintaining Interpersonal Relatio	Developing constructive and cooperative working relationships with others, and maintaining them over time.
Interpreting the Meaning of Information for Others	Translating or explaining what information means and how it can be used.
Communicating with Persons Outside Organization	Communicating with people outside the organization, representing the organization to customers, the public, government, and other external sources. This information can be exchanged in person, in writing, or by telephone or e-mail.
Provide Consultation and Advice to Others	Providing guidance and expert advice to management or other groups on technical, systems-, or process-related topics.
Scheduling Work and Activities	Scheduling events, programs, and activities, as well as the work of others.
Estimating the Quantifiable Characteristics of Pro	Estimating sizes, distances, and quantities; or determining time, costs, resources, or materials needed to perform a work activity.
Developing and Building Teams	Encouraging and building mutual trust, respect, and cooperation among team members.
Coordinating the Work and Activities of Others	Getting members of a group to work together to accomplish tasks.
Inspecting Equipment, Structures, or Material	Inspecting equipment, structures, or materials to identify the cause of errors or other problems or defects.
Training and Teaching Others	Identifying the educational needs of others, developing formal educational or training programs or classes, and teaching or instructing others.
Judging the Qualities of Things, Services, or Peop	Assessing the value, importance, or quality of things or people.
Coaching and Developing Others	Identifying the developmental needs of others and coaching, mentoring, or otherwise helping others to improve their knowledge or skills.
Resolving Conflicts and Negotiating with Others	Handling complaints, settling disputes, and resolving grievances and conflicts, or otherwise negotiating with others.
Drafting, Laying Out, and Specifying Technical Dev	Providing documentation, detailed instructions, drawings, or specifications to tell others about how devices, parts, equipment, or structures are to be fabricated, constructed, assembled, modified, maintained, or used.
Thinking Creatively	Developing, designing, or creating new applications, ideas, relationships, systems, or products, including artistic contributions.
Developing Objectives and Strategies	Establishing long-range objectives and specifying the strategies and actions to achieve them.
Performing Administrative Activities	Performing day-to-day administrative tasks such as maintaining information files and processing paperwork.
Monitoring and Controlling Resources	Monitoring and controlling resources and overseeing the spending of money.
Guiding, Directing, and Motivating Subordinates	Providing guidance and direction to subordinates, including setting performance standards and monitoring performance.
Performing for or Working Directly with the Public	Performing for people or dealing directly with the public. This includes serving customers in restaurants and stores, and receiving clients or guests.
Selling or Influencing Others	Convincing others to buy merchandise/goods or to otherwise change their minds or actions.
Assisting and Caring for Others	Providing personal assistance, medical attention, emotional support, or other personal care to others such as coworkers, customers, or patients.
Controlling Machines and Processes	Using either control mechanisms or direct physical activity to operate machines or processes (not including computers or vehicles).
Staffing Organizational Units	Recruiting, interviewing, selecting, hiring, and promoting employees in an organization.
Performing General Physical Activities	Performing physical activities that require considerable use of your arms and legs and moving your whole body, such as climbing, lifting, balancing, walking, stooping, and handling of materials.
Repairing and Maintaining Electronic Equipment	Servicing, repairing, calibrating, regulating, fine-tuning, or testing machines, devices, and equipment that operate primarily on the basis of electrical or electronic (not mechanical) principles.
Handling and Moving Objects	Using hands and arms in handling, installing, positioning, and moving materials, and manipulating things.
Repairing and Maintaining Mechanical Equipment	Servicing, repairing, adjusting, and testing machines, devices, moving parts, and equipment that operate primarily on the basis of mechanical (not electronic) principles.
Operating Vehicles, Mechanized Devices, or Equipme	Running, maneuvering, navigating, or driving vehicles or mechanized equipment, such as forklifts, passenger vehicles, aircraft, or water craft.

Work_Context	Work_Context Definitions
Electronic Mail	How often do you use electronic mail in this job?
Indoors, Environmentally Controlled	How often does this job require working indoors in environmentally controlled conditions?
Telephone	How often do you have telephone conversations in this job?
Face-to-Face Discussions	How often do you have to have face-to-face discussions with individuals or teams in this job?
Importance of Being Exact or Accurate	How important is being very exact or highly accurate in performing this job?
Work With Work Group or Team	How important is it to work with others in a group or team in this job?
Structured versus Unstructured Work	To what extent is this job structured for the worker, rather than allowing the worker to determine tasks, priorities, and goals?
Contact With Others	How much does this job require the worker to be in contact with others (face-to-face, by telephone, or otherwise) in order to perform it?
Freedom to Make Decisions	How much decision making freedom, without supervision, does the job offer?
Spend Time Sitting	How much does this job require sitting?
Letters and Memos	How often does the job require written letters and memos?
Impact of Decisions on Co-workers or Company Resul	How do the decisions an employee makes impact the results of co-workers, clients or the company?
Time Pressure	How often does this job require the worker to meet strict deadlines?
Coordinate or Lead Others	How important is it to coordinate or lead others in accomplishing work activities in this job?
Sounds, Noise Levels Are Distracting or Uncomforta	How often does this job require working exposed to sounds and noise levels that are distracting or uncomfortable?
Consequence of Error	How serious would the result usually be if the worker made a mistake that was not readily correctable?
Importance of Repeating Same Tasks	How important is repeating the same physical activities (e.g., key entry) or mental activities (e.g., checking entries in a ledger) over and over, without stopping, to performing this job?
Responsibility for Outcomes and Results	How responsible is the worker for work outcomes and results of other workers?
Frequency of Decision Making	How frequently is the worker required to make decisions that affect other people, the financial resources, and/or the image and reputation of the organization?
Frequency of Conflict Situations	How often are there conflict situations the employee has to face in this job?
Wear Common Protective or Safety Equipment such as	How much does this job require wearing common protective or safety equipment such as safety shoes, glasses, gloves, hard hats or live jackets?
Public Speaking	How often do you have to perform public speaking in this job?
Exposed to Radiation	How often does this job require exposure to radiation?
Physical Proximity	To what extent does this job require the worker to perform job tasks in close physical proximity to other people?
Deal With External Customers	How important is it to work with external customers or the public in this job?
Responsible for Others' Health and Safety	How much responsibility is there for the health and safety of others in this job?
Wear Specialized Protective or Safety Equipment su	How much does this job require wearing specialized protective or safety equipment such as breathing apparatus, safety harness, full protection suits, or radiation protection?
Indoors, Not Environmentally Controlled	How often does this job require working indoors in non-controlled environmental conditions (e.g., warehouse without heat)?
In an Enclosed Vehicle or Equipment	How often does this job require working in a closed vehicle or equipment (e.g., car)?
Very Hot or Cold Temperatures	How often does this job require working in very hot (above 90 F degrees) or very cold (below 32 F degrees) temperatures?
Extremely Bright or Inadequate Lighting	How often does this job require working in extremely bright or inadequate lighting conditions?
Level of Competition	To what extent does this job require the worker to compete or to be aware of competitive pressures?
Spend Time Making Repetitive Motions	How much does this job require making repetitive motions?
Exposed to Contaminants	How often does this job require working exposed to contaminants (such as pollutants, gases, dust or odors)?

Deal With Unpleasant or Angry People	How frequently does the worker have to deal with unpleasant, angry, or discourteous individuals as part of the job requirements?
Spend Time Standing	How much does this job require standing?
Spend Time Walking and Running	How much does this job require walking and running?
Exposed to Hazardous Conditions	How often does this job require exposure to hazardous conditions?
Degree of Automation	How automated is the job?
Cramped Work Space, Awkward Positions	How often does this job require working in cramped work spaces that requires getting into awkward positions?
Spend Time Using Your Hands to Handle, Control, or	How much does this job require using your hands to handle, control, or feel objects, tools or controls?
Outdoors, Exposed to Weather	How often does this job require working outdoors, exposed to all weather conditions?
Outdoors, Under Cover	How often does this job require working outdoors, under cover (e.g., structure with roof but no walls)?
Exposed to High Places	How often does this job require exposure to high places?
Spend Time Climbing Ladders, Scaffolds, or Poles	How much does this job require climbing ladders, scaffolds, or poles?
Spend Time Bending or Twisting the Body	How much does this job require bending or twisting your body?
Exposed to Hazardous Equipment	How often does this job require exposure to hazardous equipment?
Spend Time Kneeling, Crouching, Stooping, or Crawl	How much does this job require kneeling, crouching, stooping, or crawling?
Spend Time Keeping or Regaining Balance	How much does this job require keeping or regaining your balance?
Pace Determined by Speed of Equipment	How important is it to this job that the pace is determined by the speed of equipment or machinery? (This does not refer to keeping busy at all times on this job.)
Exposed to Minor Burns, Cuts, Bites, or Stings	How often does this job require exposure to minor burns, cuts, bites, or stings?
Exposed to Whole Body Vibration	How often does this job require exposure to whole body vibration (e.g., operate a jackhammer)?
Deal With Physically Aggressive People	How frequently does this job require the worker to deal with physical aggression of violent individuals?
Exposed to Disease or Infections	How often does this job require exposure to disease/infections?
In an Open Vehicle or Equipment	How often does this job require working in an open vehicle or equipment (e.g., tractor)?

Job Zone Component	Job Zone Component Definitions
Title	Job Zone Four: Considerable Preparation Needed
Overall Experience	A minimum of two to four years of work-related skill, knowledge, or experience is needed for these occupations. For example, an accountant must complete four years of college and work for several years in accounting to be considered qualified.
Job Training	Employees in these occupations usually need several years of work-related experience, on-the-job training, and/or vocational training.
Job Zone Examples	Many of these occupations involve coordinating, supervising, managing, or training others. Examples include accountants, chefs and head cooks, computer programmers, historians, pharmacists, and police detectives.
SVP Range	(7.0 to < 8.0)
Education	Most of these occupations require a four - year bachelor's degree, but some do not.

Work_Styles	Work_Styles Definitions
Attention to Detail	Job requires being careful about detail and thorough in completing work tasks.
Integrity	Job requires being honest and ethical.
Analytical Thinking	Job requires analyzing information and using logic to address work-related issues and problems.
Stress Tolerance	Job requires accepting criticism and dealing calmly and effectively with high stress situations.
Adaptability/Flexibility	Job requires being open to change (positive or negative) and to considerable variety in the workplace.
Dependability	Job requires being reliable, responsible, and dependable, and fulfilling obligations.

Initiative	Job requires a willingness to take on responsibilities and challenges.
Persistence	Job requires persistence in the face of obstacles.
Self Control	Job requires maintaining composure, keeping emotions in check, controlling anger, and avoiding aggressive behavior, even in very difficult situations.
Cooperation	Job requires being pleasant with others on the job and displaying a good-natured, cooperative attitude.
Independence	Job requires developing one's own ways of doing things, guiding oneself with little or no supervision, and depending on oneself to get things done.
Achievement/Effort	Job requires establishing and maintaining personally challenging achievement goals and exerting effort toward mastering tasks.
Innovation	Job requires creativity and alternative thinking to develop new ideas for and answers to work-related problems.
Leadership	Job requires a willingness to lead, take charge, and offer opinions and direction.
Concern for Others	Job requires being sensitive to others' needs and feelings and being understanding and helpful on the job.
Social Orientation	Job requires preferring to work with others rather than alone, and being personally connected with others on the job.

17-3024.00 - Electro-Mechanical Technicians

Operate, test, and maintain unmanned, automated, servo-mechanical, or electromechanical equipment. May operate unmanned submarines, aircraft, or other equipment at worksites, such as oil rigs, deep ocean exploration, or hazardous waste removal. May assist engineers in testing and designing robotics equipment.

Tasks

1) Verify dimensions and clearances of parts to ensure conformance to specifications, using precision measuring instruments.

2) Develop, test, and program new robots.

3) Repair, rework, and calibrate hydraulic and pneumatic assemblies and systems to meet operational specifications and tolerances.

4) Install electrical and electronic parts and hardware in housings or assemblies, using soldering equipment and hand tools.

5) Align, fit, and assemble component parts, using hand tools, power tools, fixtures, templates, and microscopes.

6) Read blueprints, schematics, diagrams, and technical orders to determine methods and sequences of assembly.

7) Test performance of electromechanical assemblies, using test instruments such as oscilloscopes, electronic voltmeters, and bridges.

8) Analyze and record test results, and prepare written testing documentation.

9) Train others to install, use, and maintain robots.

10) Operate metalworking machines to fabricate housings, jigs, fittings, and fixtures.

17-3031.01 - Surveying Technicians

Adjust and operate surveying instruments, such as the theodolite and electronic distance-measuring equipment, and compile notes, make sketches and enter data into computers.

Tasks

1) Adjust and operate surveying instruments such as prisms, theodolites, and electronic distance-measuring equipment.

2) Set out and recover stakes, marks, and other monumentation.

3) Place and hold measuring tapes when electronic distance-measuring equipment is not used.

4) Perform manual labor, such as cutting brush for lines, carrying stakes, rebar, and other heavy items, and stacking rods.

5) Conduct surveys to ascertain the locations of natural features and human-made structures on the Earth's surface, underground, and underwater, using electronic distance-measuring

equipment and other surveying instruments.

6) Perform calculations to determine earth curvature corrections, atmospheric impacts on measurements, traverse closures and adjustments, azimuths, level runs, and placement of markers.

7) Lay out grids, and determine horizontal and vertical controls.

8) Record survey measurements and descriptive data, using notes, drawings, sketches, and inked tracings.

9) Compile information necessary to stake projects for construction, using engineering plans.

10) Collect information needed to carry out new surveys, using source maps, previous survey data, photographs, computer records, and other relevant information.

11) Position and hold the vertical rods, or targets, that theodolite operators use for sighting in order to measure angles, distances, and elevations.

12) Prepare topographic and contour maps of land surveyed, including site features and other relevant information such as charts, drawings, and survey notes.

13) Compare survey computations with applicable standards in order to determine adequacy of data.

14) Run rods for benches and cross-section elevations.

15) Provide assistance in the development of methods and procedures for conducting field surveys.

16) Maintain equipment and vehicles used by surveying crews.

17) Direct and supervise work of subordinate members of surveying parties.

18) Operate and manage land-information computer systems, performing tasks such as storing data, making inquiries, and producing plots and reports.

Knowledge	Knowledge Definitions
Mathematics	Knowledge of arithmetic, algebra, geometry, calculus, statistics, and their applications.
Engineering and Technology	Knowledge of the practical application of engineering science and technology. This includes applying principles, techniques, procedures, and equipment to the design and production of various goods and services.
Design	Knowledge of design techniques, tools, and principles involved in production of precision technical plans, blueprints, drawings, and models.
Building and Construction	Knowledge of materials, methods, and the tools involved in the construction or repair of houses, buildings, or other structures such as highways and roads.
Computers and Electronics	Knowledge of circuit boards, processors, chips, electronic equipment, and computer hardware and software, including applications and programming.
Geography	Knowledge of principles and methods for describing the features of land, sea, and air masses, including their physical characteristics, locations, interrelationships, and distribution of plant, animal, and human life.
English Language	Knowledge of the structure and content of the English language including the meaning and spelling of words, rules of composition, and grammar.
Law and Government	Knowledge of laws, legal codes, court procedures, precedents, government regulations, executive orders, agency rules, and the democratic political process.
Public Safety and Security	Knowledge of relevant equipment, policies, procedures, and strategies to promote effective local, state, or national security operations for the protection of people, data, property, and institutions.
Education and Training	Knowledge of principles and methods for curriculum and training design, teaching and instruction for individuals and groups, and the measurement of training effects.
Mechanical	Knowledge of machines and tools, including their designs, uses, repair, and maintenance.
Customer and Personal Service	Knowledge of principles and processes for providing customer and personal services. This includes customer needs assessment, meeting quality standards for services, and evaluation of customer satisfaction.
Physics	Knowledge and prediction of physical principles, laws, their interrelationships, and applications to understanding fluid, material, and atmospheric dynamics, and mechanical, electrical, atomic and sub-atomic structures and processes.
Communications and Media	Knowledge of media production, communication, and dissemination techniques and methods. This includes alternative ways to inform and entertain via written, oral, and visual media.
Transportation	Knowledge of principles and methods for moving people or goods by air, rail, sea, or road, including the relative costs and benefits.
Administration and Management	Knowledge of business and management principles involved in strategic planning, resource allocation, human resources modeling, leadership technique, production methods, and coordination of people and resources.
Clerical	Knowledge of administrative and clerical procedures and systems such as word processing, managing files and records, stenography and transcription, designing forms, and other office procedures and terminology.
Telecommunications	Knowledge of transmission, broadcasting, switching, control, and operation of telecommunications systems.
Production and Processing	Knowledge of raw materials, production processes, quality control, costs, and other techniques for maximizing the effective manufacture and distribution of goods.
Therapy and Counseling	Knowledge of principles, methods, and procedures for diagnosis, treatment, and rehabilitation of physical and mental dysfunctions, and for career counseling and guidance.
Personnel and Human Resources	Knowledge of principles and procedures for personnel recruitment, selection, training, compensation and benefits, labor relations and negotiation, and personnel information systems.
Biology	Knowledge of plant and animal organisms, their tissues, cells, functions, interdependencies, and interactions with each other and the environment.
Chemistry	Knowledge of the chemical composition, structure, and properties of substances and of the chemical processes and transformations that they undergo. This includes uses of chemicals and their interactions, danger signs, production techniques, and disposal methods.
Economics and Accounting	Knowledge of economic and accounting principles and practices, the financial markets, banking and the analysis and reporting of financial data.
Foreign Language	Knowledge of the structure and content of a foreign (non-English) language including the meaning and spelling of words, rules of composition and grammar, and pronunciation.
History and Archeology	Knowledge of historical events and their causes, indicators, and effects on civilizations and cultures.
Psychology	Knowledge of human behavior and performance; individual differences in ability, personality, and interests; learning and motivation; psychological research methods; and the assessment and treatment of behavioral and affective disorders.
Sales and Marketing	Knowledge of principles and methods for showing, promoting, and selling products or services. This includes marketing strategy and tactics, product demonstration, sales techniques, and sales control systems.
Philosophy and Theology	Knowledge of different philosophical systems and religions. This includes their basic principles, values, ethics, ways of thinking, customs, practices, and their impact on human culture.
Sociology and Anthropology	Knowledge of group behavior and dynamics, societal trends and influences, human migrations, ethnicity, cultures and their history and origins.
Medicine and Dentistry	Knowledge of the information and techniques needed to diagnose and treat human injuries, diseases, and deformities. This includes symptoms, treatment alternatives, drug properties and interactions, and preventive health-care measures.
Fine Arts	Knowledge of the theory and techniques required to compose, produce, and perform works of music, dance, visual arts, drama, and sculpture.
Food Production	Knowledge of techniques and equipment for planting, growing, and harvesting food products (both plant and animal) for consumption, including storage/handling techniques.

Skills	Skills Definitions
Mathematics	Using mathematics to solve problems.
Active Listening	Giving full attention to what other people are saying, taking time to understand the points being made, asking questions as appropriate, and not interrupting at inappropriate times.
Reading Comprehension	Understanding written sentences and paragraphs in work related documents.
Active Learning	Understanding the implications of new information for both current and future problem-solving and decision-making.
Time Management	Managing one's own time and the time of others.

Critical Thinking	Using logic and reasoning to identify the strengths and weaknesses of alternative solutions, conclusions or approaches to problems.
Coordination	Adjusting actions in relation to others' actions.
Speaking	Talking to others to convey information effectively.
Instructing	Teaching others how to do something.
Equipment Selection	Determining the kind of tools and equipment needed to do a job.
Learning Strategies	Selecting and using training/instructional methods and procedures appropriate for the situation when learning or teaching new things.
Judgment and Decision Making	Considering the relative costs and benefits of potential actions to choose the most appropriate one.
Complex Problem Solving	Identifying complex problems and reviewing related information to develop and evaluate options and implement solutions.
Troubleshooting	Determining causes of operating errors and deciding what to do about it.
Writing	Communicating effectively in writing as appropriate for the needs of the audience.
Quality Control Analysis	Conducting tests and inspections of products, services, or processes to evaluate quality or performance.
Equipment Maintenance	Performing routine maintenance on equipment and determining when and what kind of maintenance is needed.
Social Perceptiveness	Being aware of others' reactions and understanding why they react as they do.
Service Orientation	Actively looking for ways to help people.
Monitoring	Monitoring/Assessing performance of yourself, other individuals, or organizations to make improvements or take corrective action.
Management of Personnel Resources	Motivating, developing, and directing people as they work, identifying the best people for the job.
Science	Using scientific rules and methods to solve problems.
Technology Design	Generating or adapting equipment and technology to serve user needs.
Negotiation	Bringing others together and trying to reconcile differences.
Operation and Control	Controlling operations of equipment or systems.
Persuasion	Persuading others to change their minds or behavior.
Operations Analysis	Analyzing needs and product requirements to create a design.
Management of Material Resources	Obtaining and seeing to the appropriate use of equipment, facilities, and materials needed to do certain work.
Systems Evaluation	Identifying measures or indicators of system performance and the actions needed to improve or correct performance, relative to the goals of the system.
Management of Financial Resources	Determining how money will be spent to get the work done, and accounting for these expenditures.
Systems Analysis	Determining how a system should work and how changes in conditions, operations, and the environment will affect outcomes.
Repairing	Repairing machines or systems using the needed tools.
Operation Monitoring	Watching gauges, dials, or other indicators to make sure a machine is working properly.
Installation	Installing equipment, machines, wiring, or programs to meet specifications.
Programming	Writing computer programs for various purposes.

Ability	Ability Definitions
Problem Sensitivity	The ability to tell when something is wrong or is likely to go wrong. It does not involve solving the problem, only recognizing there is a problem.
Near Vision	The ability to see details at close range (within a few feet of the observer).
Speech Recognition	The ability to identify and understand the speech of another person.
Oral Comprehension	The ability to listen to and understand information and ideas presented through spoken words and sentences.
Far Vision	The ability to see details at a distance.
Speech Clarity	The ability to speak clearly so others can understand you.
Oral Expression	The ability to communicate information and ideas in speaking so others will understand.
Information Ordering	The ability to arrange things or actions in a certain order or pattern according to a specific rule or set of rules (e.g., patterns of numbers, letters, words, pictures, mathematical operations).
Written Comprehension	The ability to read and understand information and ideas presented in writing.
Arm-Hand Steadiness	The ability to keep your hand and arm steady while moving your arm or while holding your arm and hand in one position.

Depth Perception	The ability to judge which of several objects is closer or farther away from you, or to judge the distance between you and an object.
Inductive Reasoning	The ability to combine pieces of information to form general rules or conclusions (includes finding a relationship among seemingly unrelated events).
Deductive Reasoning	The ability to apply general rules to specific problems to produce answers that make sense.
Category Flexibility	The ability to generate or use different sets of rules for combining or grouping things in different ways.
Selective Attention	The ability to concentrate on a task over a period of time without being distracted.
Written Expression	The ability to communicate information and ideas in writing so others will understand.
Perceptual Speed	The ability to quickly and accurately compare similarities and differences among sets of letters, numbers, objects, pictures, or patterns. The things to be compared may be presented at the same time or one after the other. This ability also includes comparing a presented object with a remembered object.
Multilimb Coordination	The ability to coordinate two or more limbs (for example, two arms, two legs, or one leg and one arm) while sitting, standing, or lying down. It does not involve performing the activities while the whole body is in motion.
Control Precision	The ability to quickly and repeatedly adjust the controls of a machine or a vehicle to exact positions.
Manual Dexterity	The ability to quickly move your hand, your hand together with your arm, or your two hands to grasp, manipulate, or assemble objects.
Mathematical Reasoning	The ability to choose the right mathematical methods or formulas to solve a problem.
Number Facility	The ability to add, subtract, multiply, or divide quickly and correctly.
Finger Dexterity	The ability to make precisely coordinated movements of the fingers of one or both hands to grasp, manipulate, or assemble very small objects.
Flexibility of Closure	The ability to identify or detect a known pattern (a figure, object, word, or sound) that is hidden in other distracting material.
Visualization	The ability to imagine how something will look after it is moved around or when its parts are moved or rearranged.
Visual Color Discrimination	The ability to match or detect differences between colors, including shades of color and brightness.
Trunk Strength	The ability to use your abdominal and lower back muscles to support part of the body repeatedly or continuously over time without 'giving out' or fatiguing.
Fluency of Ideas	The ability to come up with a number of ideas about a topic (the number of ideas is important, not their quality, correctness, or creativity).
Spatial Orientation	The ability to know your location in relation to the environment or to know where other objects are in relation to you.
Static Strength	The ability to exert maximum muscle force to lift, push, pull, or carry objects.
Originality	The ability to come up with unusual or clever ideas about a given topic or situation, or to develop creative ways to solve a problem.
Extent Flexibility	The ability to bend, stretch, twist, or reach with your body, arms, and/or legs.
Hearing Sensitivity	The ability to detect or tell the differences between sounds that vary in pitch and loudness.
Auditory Attention	The ability to focus on a single source of sound in the presence of other distracting sounds.
Speed of Closure	The ability to quickly make sense of, combine, and organize information into meaningful patterns.
Dynamic Strength	The ability to exert muscle force repeatedly or continuously over time. This involves muscular endurance and resistance to muscle fatigue.
Memorization	The ability to remember information such as words, numbers, pictures, and procedures.
Time Sharing	The ability to shift back and forth between two or more activities or sources of information (such as speech, sounds, touch, or other sources).
Glare Sensitivity	The ability to see objects in the presence of glare or bright lighting.
Gross Body Coordination	The ability to coordinate the movement of your arms, legs, and torso together when the whole body is in motion.
Reaction Time	The ability to quickly respond (with the hand, finger, or foot) to a signal (sound, light, picture) when it appears.

Response Orientation	The ability to choose quickly between two or more movements in response to two or more different signals (lights, sounds, pictures). It includes the speed with which the correct response is started with the hand, foot, or other body part.
Stamina	The ability to exert yourself physically over long periods of time without getting winded or out of breath.
Gross Body Equilibrium	The ability to keep or regain your body balance or stay upright when in an unstable position.
Speed of Limb Movement	The ability to quickly move the arms and legs.
Wrist-Finger Speed	The ability to make fast, simple, repeated movements of the fingers, hands, and wrists.
Sound Localization	The ability to tell the direction from which a sound originated.
Rate Control	The ability to time your movements or the movement of a piece of equipment in anticipation of changes in the speed and/or direction of a moving object or scene.
Peripheral Vision	The ability to see objects or movement of objects to one's side when the eyes are looking ahead.
Night Vision	The ability to see under low light conditions.
Explosive Strength	The ability to use short bursts of muscle force to propel oneself (as in jumping or sprinting), or to throw an object.
Dynamic Flexibility	The ability to quickly and repeatedly bend, stretch, twist, or reach out with your body, arms, and/or legs.

Work_Activity	Work_Activity Definitions
Getting Information	Observing, receiving, and otherwise obtaining information from all relevant sources.
Performing General Physical Activities	Performing physical activities that require considerable use of your arms and legs and moving your whole body, such as climbing, lifting, balancing, walking, stooping, and handling of materials.
Identifying Objects, Actions, and Events	Identifying information by categorizing, estimating, recognizing differences or similarities, and detecting changes in circumstances or events.
Making Decisions and Solving Problems	Analyzing information and evaluating results to choose the best solution and solve problems.
Documenting/Recording Information	Entering, transcribing, recording, storing, or maintaining information in written or electronic/magnetic form.
Communicating with Supervisors, Peers, or Subordin	Providing information to supervisors, co-workers, and subordinates by telephone, in written form, e-mail, or in person.
Handling and Moving Objects	Using hands and arms in handling, installing, positioning, and moving materials, and manipulating things.
Updating and Using Relevant Knowledge	Keeping up-to-date technically and applying new knowledge to your job.
Processing Information	Compiling, coding, categorizing, calculating, tabulating, auditing, or verifying information or data.
Establishing and Maintaining Interpersonal Relatio	Developing constructive and cooperative working relationships with others, and maintaining them over time.
Analyzing Data or Information	Identifying the underlying principles, reasons, or facts of information by breaking down information or data into separate parts.
Controlling Machines and Processes	Using either control mechanisms or direct physical activity to operate machines or processes (not including computers or vehicles).
Operating Vehicles, Mechanized Devices, or Equipme	Running, maneuvering, navigating, or driving vehicles or mechanized equipment, such as forklifts, passenger vehicles, aircraft, or water craft.
Interacting With Computers	Using computers and computer systems (including hardware and software) to program, write software, set up functions, enter data, or process information.
Evaluating Information to Determine Compliance wit	Using relevant information and individual judgment to determine whether events or processes comply with laws, regulations, or standards.
Interpreting the Meaning of Information for Others	Translating or explaining what information means and how it can be used.
Thinking Creatively	Developing, designing, or creating new applications, ideas, relationships, systems, or products, including artistic contributions.
Estimating the Quantifiable Characteristics of Pro	Estimating sizes, distances, and quantities; or determining time, costs, resources, or materials needed to perform a work activity.
Drafting, Laying Out, and Specifying Technical Dev	Providing documentation, detailed instructions, drawings, or specifications to tell others about how devices, parts, equipment, or structures are to be fabricated, constructed, assembled, modified, maintained, or used.

Communicating with Persons Outside Organization	Communicating with people outside the organization, representing the organization to customers, the public, government, and other external sources. This information can be exchanged in person, in writing, or by telephone or e-mail.
Training and Teaching Others	Identifying the educational needs of others, developing formal educational or training programs or classes, and teaching or instructing others.
Coordinating the Work and Activities of Others	Getting members of a group to work together to accomplish tasks.
Organizing, Planning, and Prioritizing Work	Developing specific goals and plans to prioritize, organize, and accomplish your work.
Resolving Conflicts and Negotiating with Others	Handling complaints, settling disputes, and resolving grievances and conflicts, or otherwise negotiating with others.
Monitor Processes, Materials, or Surroundings	Monitoring and reviewing information from materials, events, or the environment, to detect or assess problems.
Guiding, Directing, and Motivating Subordinates	Providing guidance and direction to subordinates, including setting performance standards and monitoring performance.
Scheduling Work and Activities	Scheduling events, programs, and activities, as well as the work of others.
Inspecting Equipment, Structures, or Material	Inspecting equipment, structures, or materials to identify the cause of errors or other problems or defects.
Coaching and Developing Others	Identifying the developmental needs of others and coaching, mentoring, or otherwise helping others to improve their knowledge or skills.
Judging the Qualities of Things, Services, or Peop	Assessing the value, importance, or quality of things or people.
Performing Administrative Activities	Performing day-to-day administrative tasks such as maintaining information files and processing paperwork.
Developing Objectives and Strategies	Establishing long-range objectives and specifying the strategies and actions to achieve them.
Performing for or Working Directly with the Public	Performing for people or dealing directly with the public. This includes serving customers in restaurants and stores, and receiving clients or guests.
Developing and Building Teams	Encouraging and building mutual trust, respect, and cooperation among team members.
Repairing and Maintaining Electronic Equipment	Servicing, repairing, calibrating, regulating, fine-tuning, or testing machines, devices, and equipment that operate primarily on the basis of electrical or electronic (not mechanical) principles.
Assisting and Caring for Others	Providing personal assistance, medical attention, emotional support, or other personal care to others such as coworkers, customers, or patients.
Provide Consultation and Advice to Others	Providing guidance and expert advice to management or other groups on technical, systems-, or process-related topics.
Monitoring and Controlling Resources	Monitoring and controlling resources and overseeing the spending of money.
Repairing and Maintaining Mechanical Equipment	Servicing, repairing, adjusting, and testing machines, devices, moving parts, and equipment that operate primarily on the basis of mechanical (not electronic) principles.
Staffing Organizational Units	Recruiting, interviewing, selecting, hiring, and promoting employees in an organization.
Selling or Influencing Others	Convincing others to buy merchandise/goods or to otherwise change their minds or actions.

Work_Context	Work_Context Definitions
Face-to-Face Discussions	How often do you have to have face-to-face discussions with individuals or teams in this job?
Spend Time Using Your Hands to Handle, Control, or	How much does this job require using your hands to handle, control, or feel objects, tools or controls?
Outdoors, Exposed to Weather	How often does this job require working outdoors, exposed to all weather conditions?
In an Enclosed Vehicle or Equipment	How often does this job require working in a closed vehicle or equipment (e.g., car)?
Importance of Being Exact or Accurate	How important is being very exact or highly accurate in performing this job?
Work With Work Group or Team	How important is it to work with others in a group or team in this job?
Freedom to Make Decisions	How much decision making freedom, without supervision, does the job offer?
Contact With Others	How much does this job require the worker to be in contact with others (face-to-face, by telephone, or otherwise) in order to perform it?
Importance of Repeating Same Tasks	How important is repeating the same physical activities (e.g., key entry) or mental activities (e.g., checking entries in a ledger) over and over, without stopping, to performing this job?

1283

Exposed to Hazardous Equipment	How often does this job require exposure to hazardous equipment?
Coordinate or Lead Others	How important is it to coordinate or lead others in accomplishing work activities in this job?
Telephone	How often do you have telephone conversations in this job?
Very Hot or Cold Temperatures	How often does this job require working in very hot (above 90 F degrees) or very cold (below 32 F degrees) temperatures?
Extremely Bright or Inadequate Lighting	How often does this job require working in extremely bright or inadequate lighting conditions?
Responsibility for Outcomes and Results	How responsible is the worker for work outcomes and results of other workers?
Exposed to Minor Burns, Cuts, Bites, or Stings	How often does this job require exposure to minor burns, cuts, bites, or stings?
Frequency of Decision Making	How frequently is the worker required to make decisions that affect other people, the financial resources, and/or the image and reputation of the organization?
Time Pressure	How often does this job require the worker to meet strict deadlines?
Electronic Mail	How often do you use electronic mail in this job?
Deal With External Customers	How important is it to work with external customers or the public in this job?
Structured versus Unstructured Work	To what extent is this job structured for the worker, rather than allowing the worker to determine tasks, priorities, and goals?
Spend Time Making Repetitive Motions	How much does this job require making repetitive motions?
Wear Common Protective or Safety Equipment such as	How much does this job require wearing common protective or safety equipment such as safety shoes, glasses, gloves, hard hats or live jackets?
Sounds, Noise Levels Are Distracting or Uncomforta	How often does this job require working exposed to sounds and noise levels that are distracting or uncomfortable?
Exposed to Contaminants	How often does this job require working exposed to contaminants (such as pollutants, gases, dust or odors)?
Spend Time Standing	How much does this job require standing?
Impact of Decisions on Co-workers or Company Resul	How do the decisions an employee makes impact the results of co-workers, clients or the company?
Spend Time Bending or Twisting the Body	How much does this job require bending or twisting your body?
Spend Time Walking and Running	How much does this job require walking and running?
Consequence of Error	How serious would the result usually be if the worker made a mistake that was not readily correctable?
Physical Proximity	To what extent does this job require the worker to perform job tasks in close physical proximity to other people?
Letters and Memos	How often does the job require written letters and memos?
Responsible for Others' Health and Safety	How much responsibility is there for the health and safety of others in this job?
Degree of Automation	How automated is the job?
Deal With Unpleasant or Angry People	How frequently does the worker have to deal with unpleasant, angry, or discourteous individuals as part of the job requirements?
Frequency of Conflict Situations	How often are there conflict situations the employee has to face in this job?
Spend Time Sitting	How much does this job require sitting?
Indoors, Environmentally Controlled	How often does this job require working indoors in environmentally controlled conditions?
Exposed to Hazardous Conditions	How often does this job require exposure to hazardous conditions?
Cramped Work Space, Awkward Positions	How often does this job require working in cramped work spaces that requires getting into awkward positions?
Level of Competition	To what extent does this job require the worker to compete or to be aware of competitive pressures?
Indoors, Not Environmentally Controlled	How often does this job require working indoors in non-controlled environmental conditions (e.g., warehouse without heat)?
Spend Time Kneeling, Crouching, Stooping, or Crawl	How much does this job require kneeling, crouching, stooping or crawling?
Spend Time Keeping or Regaining Balance	How much does this job require keeping or regaining your balance?
Pace Determined by Speed of Equipment	How important is it to this job that the pace is determined by the speed of equipment or machinery? (This does not refer to keeping busy at all times on this job.)
Exposed to High Places	How often does this job require exposure to high places?
In an Open Vehicle or Equipment	How often does this job require working in an open vehicle or equipment (e.g., tractor)?
Exposed to Whole Body Vibration	How often does this job require exposure to whole body vibration (e.g., operate a jackhammer)?

Exposed to Radiation	How often does this job require exposure to radiation?
Exposed to Disease or Infections	How often does this job require exposure to disease/infections?
Deal With Physically Aggressive People	How frequently does this job require the worker to deal with physical aggression of violent individuals?
Outdoors, Under Cover	How often does this job require working outdoors, under cover (e.g., structure with roof but no walls)?
Public Speaking	How often do you have to perform public speaking in this job?
Wear Specialized Protective or Safety Equipment su	How much does this job require wearing specialized protective or safety equipment such as breathing apparatus, safety harness, full protection suits, or radiation protection?
Spend Time Climbing Ladders, Scaffolds, or Poles	How much does this job require climbing ladders, scaffolds, or poles?

Job Zone Component	Job Zone Component Definitions
Title	Job Zone Three: Medium Preparation Needed
Overall Experience	Previous work-related skill, knowledge, or experience is required for these occupations. For example, an electrician must have completed three or four years of apprenticeship or several years of vocational training, and often must have passed a licensing exam, in order to perform the job.
Job Training	Employees in these occupations usually need one or two years of training involving both on-the-job experience and informal training with experienced workers.
Job Zone Examples	These occupations usually involve using communication and organizational skills to coordinate, supervise, manage, or train others to accomplish goals. Examples include dental assistants, electricians, fish and game wardens, legal secretaries, personnel recruiters, and recreation workers.
SVP Range	(6.0 to < 7.0)
Education	Most occupations in this zone require training in vocational schools, related on-the-job experience, or an associate's degree. Some may require a bachelor's degree.

Work_Styles	Work_Styles Definitions
Attention to Detail	Job requires being careful about detail and thorough in completing work tasks.
Dependability	Job requires being reliable, responsible, and dependable, and fulfilling obligations.
Analytical Thinking	Job requires analyzing information and using logic to address work-related issues and problems.
Self Control	Job requires maintaining composure, keeping emotions in check, controlling anger, and avoiding aggressive behavior, even in very difficult situations.
Stress Tolerance	Job requires accepting criticism and dealing calmly and effectively with high stress situations.
Cooperation	Job requires being pleasant with others on the job and displaying a good-natured, cooperative attitude.
Integrity	Job requires being honest and ethical.
Independence	Job requires developing one's own ways of doing things, guiding oneself with little or no supervision, and depending on oneself to get things done.
Leadership	Job requires a willingness to lead, take charge, and offer opinions and direction.
Persistence	Job requires persistence in the face of obstacles.
Adaptability/Flexibility	Job requires being open to change (positive or negative) and to considerable variety in the workplace.
Concern for Others	Job requires being sensitive to others' needs and feelings and being understanding and helpful on the job.
Social Orientation	Job requires preferring to work with others rather than alone, and being personally connected with others on the job.
Initiative	Job requires a willingness to take on responsibilities and challenges.
Innovation	Job requires creativity and alternative thinking to develop new ideas for and answers to work-related problems.
Achievement/Effort	Job requires establishing and maintaining personally challenging achievement goals and exerting effort toward mastering tasks.

19-1011.00 - Animal Scientists

Conduct research in the genetics, nutrition, reproduction, growth, and development of domestic farm animals.

Tasks

1) Study effects of management practices, processing methods, feed, and/or environmental conditions on quality and quantity of animal products, such as eggs and milk.

2) Develop improved practices in feeding, housing, sanitation, and/or parasite and disease control of animals.

3) Determine genetic composition of animal populations and heritability of traits, utilizing principles of genetics.

4) Crossbreed animals with existing strains or cross strains to obtain new combinations of desirable characteristics.

5) Research and control animal selection and breeding practices to increase production efficiency and improve animal quality.

6) Conduct research concerning animal nutrition, breeding, and/or management to improve products or processes.

7) Advise producers about improved products and techniques that could enhance their animal production efforts.

Knowledge	Knowledge Definitions
Biology	Knowledge of plant and animal organisms, their tissues, cells, functions, interdependencies, and interactions with each other and the environment.
Food Production	Knowledge of techniques and equipment for planting, growing, and harvesting food products (both plant and animal) for consumption, including storage/handling techniques.
Chemistry	Knowledge of the chemical composition, structure, and properties of substances and of the chemical processes and transformations that they undergo. This includes uses of chemicals and their interactions, danger signs, production techniques, and disposal methods.
Mathematics	Knowledge of arithmetic, algebra, geometry, calculus, statistics, and their applications.
English Language	Knowledge of the structure and content of the English language including the meaning and spelling of words, rules of composition, and grammar.
Education and Training	Knowledge of principles and methods for curriculum and training design, teaching and instruction for individuals and groups, and the measurement of training effects.
Production and Processing	Knowledge of raw materials, production processes, quality control, costs, and other techniques for maximizing the effective manufacture and distribution of goods.
Computers and Electronics	Knowledge of circuit boards, processors, chips, electronic equipment, and computer hardware and software, including applications and programming.
Communications and Media	Knowledge of media production, communication, and dissemination techniques and methods. This includes alternative ways to inform and entertain via written, oral, and visual media.
Administration and Management	Knowledge of business and management principles involved in strategic planning, resource allocation, human resources modeling, leadership technique, production methods, and coordination of people and resources.
Clerical	Knowledge of administrative and clerical procedures and systems such as word processing, managing files and records, stenography and transcription, designing forms, and other office procedures and terminology.
Law and Government	Knowledge of laws, legal codes, court procedures, precedents, government regulations, executive orders, agency rules, and the democratic political process.
Public Safety and Security	Knowledge of relevant equipment, policies, procedures, and strategies to promote effective local, state, or national security operations for the protection of people, data, property, and institutions.
Customer and Personal Service	Knowledge of principles and processes for providing customer and personal services. This includes customer needs assessment, meeting quality standards for services, and evaluation of customer satisfaction.
Physics	Knowledge and prediction of physical principles, laws, their interrelationships, and applications to understanding fluid, material, and atmospheric dynamics, and mechanical, electrical, atomic and sub-atomic structures and processes.
Engineering and Technology	Knowledge of the practical application of engineering science and technology. This includes applying principles, techniques, procedures, and equipment to the design and production of various goods and services.
Economics and Accounting	Knowledge of economic and accounting principles and practices, the financial markets, banking and the analysis and reporting of financial data.
Personnel and Human Resources	Knowledge of principles and procedures for personnel recruitment, selection, training, compensation and benefits, labor relations and negotiation, and personnel information systems.
Mechanical	Knowledge of machines and tools, including their designs, uses, repair, and maintenance.
Psychology	Knowledge of human behavior and performance; individual differences in ability, personality, and interests; learning and motivation; psychological research methods; and the assessment and treatment of behavioral and affective disorders.
Geography	Knowledge of principles and methods for describing the features of land, sea, and air masses, including their physical characteristics, locations, interrelationships, and distribution of plant, animal, and human life.
Sales and Marketing	Knowledge of principles and methods for showing, promoting, and selling products or services. This includes marketing strategy and tactics, product demonstration, sales techniques, and sales control systems.
Medicine and Dentistry	Knowledge of the information and techniques needed to diagnose and treat human injuries, diseases, and deformities. This includes symptoms, treatment alternatives, drug properties and interactions, and preventive health-care measures.
Transportation	Knowledge of principles and methods for moving people or goods by air, rail, sea, or road, including the relative costs and benefits.
Sociology and Anthropology	Knowledge of group behavior and dynamics, societal trends and influences, human migrations, ethnicity, cultures and their history and origins.
Telecommunications	Knowledge of transmission, broadcasting, switching, control, and operation of telecommunications systems.
Foreign Language	Knowledge of the structure and content of a foreign (non-English) language including the meaning and spelling of words, rules of composition and grammar, and pronunciation.
Building and Construction	Knowledge of materials, methods, and the tools involved in the construction or repair of houses, buildings, or other structures such as highways and roads.
Design	Knowledge of design techniques, tools, and principles involved in production of precision technical plans, blueprints, drawings, and models.
Philosophy and Theology	Knowledge of different philosophical systems and religions. This includes their basic principles, values, ethics, ways of thinking, customs, practices, and their impact on human culture.
History and Archeology	Knowledge of historical events and their causes, indicators, and effects on civilizations and cultures.
Therapy and Counseling	Knowledge of principles, methods, and procedures for diagnosis, treatment, and rehabilitation of physical and mental dysfunctions, and for career counseling and guidance.
Fine Arts	Knowledge of the theory and techniques required to compose, produce, and perform works of music, dance, visual arts, drama, and sculpture.

Skills	Skills Definitions
Science	Using scientific rules and methods to solve problems.
Reading Comprehension	Understanding written sentences and paragraphs in work related documents.
Critical Thinking	Using logic and reasoning to identify the strengths and weaknesses of alternative solutions, conclusions or approaches to problems.
Writing	Communicating effectively in writing as appropriate for the needs of the audience.
Active Learning	Understanding the implications of new information for both current and future problem-solving and decision-making.
Complex Problem Solving	Identifying complex problems and reviewing related information to develop and evaluate options and implement solutions.

Active Listening	Giving full attention to what other people are saying, taking time to understand the points being made, asking questions as appropriate, and not interrupting at inappropriate times.
Speaking	Talking to others to convey information effectively.
Time Management	Managing one's own time and the time of others.
Mathematics	Using mathematics to solve problems.
Instructing	Teaching others how to do something.
Judgment and Decision Making	Considering the relative costs and benefits of potential actions to choose the most appropriate one.
Learning Strategies	Selecting and using training/instructional methods and procedures appropriate for the situation when learning or teaching new things.
Monitoring	Monitoring/Assessing performance of yourself, other individuals, or organizations to make improvements or take corrective action.
Service Orientation	Actively looking for ways to help people.
Persuasion	Persuading others to change their minds or behavior.
Troubleshooting	Determining causes of operating errors and deciding what to do about it.
Coordination	Adjusting actions in relation to others' actions.
Management of Financial Resources	Determining how money will be spent to get the work done, and accounting for these expenditures.
Systems Analysis	Determining how a system should work and how changes in conditions, operations, and the environment will affect outcomes.
Management of Personnel Resources	Motivating, developing, and directing people as they work, identifying the best people for the job.
Management of Material Resources	Obtaining and seeing to the appropriate use of equipment, facilities, and materials needed to do certain work.
Operations Analysis	Analyzing needs and product requirements to create a design.
Equipment Selection	Determining the kind of tools and equipment needed to do a job.
Social Perceptiveness	Being aware of others' reactions and understanding why they react as they do.
Systems Evaluation	Identifying measures or indicators of system performance and the actions needed to improve or correct performance, relative to the goals of the system.
Technology Design	Generating or adapting equipment and technology to serve user needs.
Quality Control Analysis	Conducting tests and inspections of products, services, or processes to evaluate quality or performance.
Negotiation	Bringing others together and trying to reconcile differences.
Operation and Control	Controlling operations of equipment or systems.
Equipment Maintenance	Performing routine maintenance on equipment and determining when and what kind of maintenance is needed.
Programming	Writing computer programs for various purposes.
Operation Monitoring	Watching gauges, dials, or other indicators to make sure a machine is working properly.
Installation	Installing equipment, machines, wiring, or programs to meet specifications.
Repairing	Repairing machines or systems using the needed tools.

Ability	Ability Definitions
Written Comprehension	The ability to read and understand information and ideas presented in writing.
Inductive Reasoning	The ability to combine pieces of information to form general rules or conclusions (includes finding a relationship among seemingly unrelated events).
Oral Comprehension	The ability to listen to and understand information and ideas presented through spoken words and sentences.
Deductive Reasoning	The ability to apply general rules to specific problems to produce answers that make sense.
Oral Expression	The ability to communicate information and ideas in speaking so others will understand.
Written Expression	The ability to communicate information and ideas in writing so others will understand.
Problem Sensitivity	The ability to tell when something is wrong or is likely to go wrong. It does not involve solving the problem, only recognizing there is a problem.
Near Vision	The ability to see details at close range (within a few feet of the observer).
Fluency of Ideas	The ability to come up with a number of ideas about a topic (the number of ideas is important, not their quality, correctness, or creativity).
Originality	The ability to come up with unusual or clever ideas about a given topic or situation, or to develop creative ways to solve a problem.

Speech Recognition	The ability to identify and understand the speech of another person.
Category Flexibility	The ability to generate or use different sets of rules for combining or grouping things in different ways.
Speech Clarity	The ability to speak clearly so others can understand you.
Information Ordering	The ability to arrange things or actions in a certain order or pattern according to a specific rule or set of rules (e.g., patterns of numbers, letters, words, pictures, mathematical operations).
Flexibility of Closure	The ability to identify or detect a known pattern (a figure, object, word, or sound) that is hidden in other distracting material.
Mathematical Reasoning	The ability to choose the right mathematical methods or formulas to solve a problem.
Selective Attention	The ability to concentrate on a task over a period of time without being distracted.
Perceptual Speed	The ability to quickly and accurately compare similarities and differences among sets of letters, numbers, objects, pictures, or patterns. The things to be compared may be presented at the same time or one after the other. This ability also includes comparing a presented object with a remembered object.
Time Sharing	The ability to shift back and forth between two or more activities or sources of information (such as speech, sounds, touch, or other sources).
Number Facility	The ability to add, subtract, multiply, or divide quickly and correctly.
Memorization	The ability to remember information such as words, numbers, pictures, and procedures.
Visualization	The ability to imagine how something will look after it is moved around or when its parts are moved or rearranged.
Speed of Closure	The ability to quickly make sense of, combine, and organize information into meaningful patterns.
Far Vision	The ability to see details at a distance.
Control Precision	The ability to quickly and repeatedly adjust the controls of a machine or a vehicle to exact positions.
Visual Color Discrimination	The ability to match or detect differences between colors, including shades of color and brightness.
Auditory Attention	The ability to focus on a single source of sound in the presence of other distracting sounds.
Depth Perception	The ability to judge which of several objects is closer or farther away from you, or to judge the distance between you and an object.
Hearing Sensitivity	The ability to detect or tell the differences between sounds that vary in pitch and loudness.
Multilimb Coordination	The ability to coordinate two or more limbs (for example, two arms, two legs, or one leg and one arm) while sitting, standing, or lying down. It does not involve performing the activities while the whole body is in motion.
Finger Dexterity	The ability to make precisely coordinated movements of the fingers of one or both hands to grasp, manipulate, or assemble very small objects.
Trunk Strength	The ability to use your abdominal and lower back muscles to support part of the body repeatedly or continuously over time without 'giving out' or fatiguing.
Reaction Time	The ability to quickly respond (with the hand, finger, or foot) to a signal (sound, light, picture) when it appears.
Dynamic Flexibility	The ability to quickly and repeatedly bend, stretch, twist, or reach out with your body, arms, and/or legs.
Extent Flexibility	The ability to bend, stretch, twist, or reach with your body, arms, and/or legs.
Stamina	The ability to exert yourself physically over long periods of time without getting winded or out of breath.
Rate Control	The ability to time your movements or the movement of a piece of equipment in anticipation of changes in the speed and/or direction of a moving object or scene.
Dynamic Strength	The ability to exert muscle force repeatedly or continuously over time. This involves muscular endurance and resistance to muscle fatigue.
Explosive Strength	The ability to use short bursts of muscle force to propel oneself (as in jumping or sprinting), or to throw an object.
Static Strength	The ability to exert maximum muscle force to lift, push, pull, or carry objects.
Speed of Limb Movement	The ability to quickly move the arms and legs.
Gross Body Coordination	The ability to coordinate the movement of your arms, legs, and torso together when the whole body is in motion.
Response Orientation	The ability to choose quickly between two or more movements in response to two or more different signals (lights, sounds, pictures). It includes the speed with which the correct response is started with the hand, foot, or other body part.

Arm-Hand Steadiness	The ability to keep your hand and arm steady while moving your arm or while holding your arm and hand in one position.
Wrist-Finger Speed	The ability to make fast, simple, repeated movements of the fingers, hands, and wrists.
Glare Sensitivity	The ability to see objects in the presence of glare or bright lighting.
Sound Localization	The ability to tell the direction from which a sound originated.
Peripheral Vision	The ability to see objects or movement of objects to one's side when the eyes are looking ahead.
Gross Body Equilibrium	The ability to keep or regain your body balance or stay upright when in an unstable position.
Spatial Orientation	The ability to know your location in relation to the environment or to know where other objects are in relation to you.
Night Vision	The ability to see under low light conditions.
Manual Dexterity	The ability to quickly move your hand, your hand together with your arm, or your two hands to grasp, manipulate, or assemble objects.

Work_Activity	Work_Activity Definitions
Analyzing Data or Information	Identifying the underlying principles, reasons, or facts of information by breaking down information or data into separate parts.
Getting Information	Observing, receiving, and otherwise obtaining information from all relevant sources.
Updating and Using Relevant Knowledge	Keeping up-to-date technically and applying new knowledge to your job.
Making Decisions and Solving Problems	Analyzing information and evaluating results to choose the best solution and solve problems.
Processing Information	Compiling, coding, categorizing, calculating, tabulating, auditing, or verifying information or data.
Interpreting the Meaning of Information for Others	Translating or explaining what information means and how it can be used.
Communicating with Supervisors, Peers, or Subordin	Providing information to supervisors, co-workers, and subordinates by telephone, in written form, e-mail, or in person.
Interacting With Computers	Using computers and computer systems (including hardware and software) to program, write software, set up functions, enter data, or process information.
Communicating with Persons Outside Organization	Communicating with people outside the organization, representing the organization to customers, the public, government, and other external sources. This information can be exchanged in person, in writing, or by telephone or e-mail.
Thinking Creatively	Developing, designing, or creating new applications, ideas, relationships, systems, or products, including artistic contributions.
Identifying Objects, Actions, and Events	Identifying information by categorizing, estimating, recognizing differences or similarities, and detecting changes in circumstances or events.
Training and Teaching Others	Identifying the educational needs of others, developing formal educational or training programs or classes, and teaching or instructing others.
Documenting/Recording Information	Entering, transcribing, recording, storing, or maintaining information in written or electronic/magnetic form.
Developing Objectives and Strategies	Establishing long-range objectives and specifying the strategies and actions to achieve them.
Organizing, Planning, and Prioritizing Work	Developing specific goals and plans to prioritize, organize, and accomplish your work.
Provide Consultation and Advice to Others	Providing guidance and expert advice to management or other groups on technical, systems-, or process-related topics.
Estimating the Quantifiable Characteristics of Pro	Estimating sizes, distances, and quantities; or determining time, costs, resources, or materials needed to perform a work activity.
Monitor Processes, Materials, or Surroundings	Monitoring and reviewing information from materials, events, or the environment, to detect or assess problems.
Establishing and Maintaining Interpersonal Relatio	Developing constructive and cooperative working relationships with others, and maintaining them over time.
Evaluating Information to Determine Compliance wit	Using relevant information and individual judgment to determine whether events or processes comply with laws, regulations, or standards.
Scheduling Work and Activities	Scheduling events, programs, and activities, as well as the work of others.
Coordinating the Work and Activities of Others	Getting members of a group to work together to accomplish tasks.
Monitoring and Controlling Resources	Monitoring and controlling resources and overseeing the spending of money.

Developing and Building Teams	Encouraging and building mutual trust, respect, and cooperation among team members.
Performing for or Working Directly with the Public	Performing for people or dealing directly with the public. This includes serving customers in restaurants and stores, and receiving clients or guests.
Guiding, Directing, and Motivating Subordinates	Providing guidance and direction to subordinates, including setting performance standards and monitoring performance.
Judging the Qualities of Things, Services, or Peop	Assessing the value, importance, or quality of things or people.
Coaching and Developing Others	Identifying the developmental needs of others and coaching, mentoring, or otherwise helping others to improve their knowledge or skills.
Inspecting Equipment, Structures, or Material	Inspecting equipment, structures, or materials to identify the cause of errors or other problems or defects.
Performing Administrative Activities	Performing day-to-day administrative tasks such as maintaining information files and processing paperwork.
Selling or Influencing Others	Convincing others to buy merchandise/goods or to otherwise change their minds or actions.
Staffing Organizational Units	Recruiting, interviewing, selecting, hiring, and promoting employees in an organization.
Resolving Conflicts and Negotiating with Others	Handling complaints, settling disputes, and resolving grievances and conflicts, or otherwise negotiating with others.
Operating Vehicles, Mechanized Devices, or Equipme	Running, maneuvering, navigating, or driving vehicles or mechanized equipment, such as forklifts, passenger vehicles, aircraft, or water craft.
Performing General Physical Activities	Performing physical activities that require considerable use of your arms and legs and moving your whole body, such as climbing, lifting, balancing, walking, stooping, and handling of materials.
Controlling Machines and Processes	Using either control mechanisms or direct physical activity to operate machines or processes (not including computers or vehicles).
Assisting and Caring for Others	Providing personal assistance, medical attention, emotional support, or other personal care to others such as coworkers, customers, or patients.
Handling and Moving Objects	Using hands and arms in handling, installing, positioning, and moving materials, and manipulating things.
Repairing and Maintaining Electronic Equipment	Servicing, repairing, calibrating, regulating, fine-tuning, or testing machines, devices, and equipment that operate primarily on the basis of electrical or electronic (not mechanical) principles.
Drafting, Laying Out, and Specifying Technical Dev	Providing documentation, detailed instructions, drawings, or specifications to tell others about how devices, parts, equipment, or structures are to be fabricated, constructed, assembled, modified, maintained, or used.
Repairing and Maintaining Mechanical Equipment	Servicing, repairing, adjusting, and testing machines, devices, moving parts, and equipment that operate primarily on the basis of mechanical (not electronic) principles.

Work_Context	Work_Context Definitions
Telephone	How often do you have telephone conversations in this job?
Electronic Mail	How often do you use electronic mail in this job?
Freedom to Make Decisions	How much decision making freedom, without supervision, does the job offer?
Structured versus Unstructured Work	To what extent is this job structured for the worker, rather than allowing the worker to determine tasks, priorities, and goals?
Face-to-Face Discussions	How often do you have to have face-to-face discussions with individuals or teams in this job?
Importance of Being Exact or Accurate	How important is being very exact or highly accurate in performing this job?
Letters and Memos	How often does the job require written letters and memos?
Contact With Others	How much does this job require the worker to be in contact with others (face-to-face, by telephone, or otherwise) in order to perform it?
Indoors, Environmentally Controlled	How often does this job require working indoors in environmentally controlled conditions?
Work With Work Group or Team	How important is it to work with others in a group or team in this job?
Impact of Decisions on Co-workers or Company Resul	How do the decisions an employee makes impact the results of co-workers, clients or the company?
Deal With External Customers	How important is it to work with external customers or the public in this job?
In an Enclosed Vehicle or Equipment	How often does this job require working in a closed vehicle or equipment (e.g., car)?
Level of Competition	To what extent does this job require the worker to compete or to be aware of competitive pressures?

Frequency of Decision Making	How frequently is the worker required to make decisions that affect other people, the financial resources, and/or the image and reputation of the organization?
Spend Time Sitting	How much does this job require sitting?
Indoors, Not Environmentally Controlled	How often does this job require working indoors in non-controlled environmental conditions (e.g., warehouse without heat)?
Outdoors, Exposed to Weather	How often does this job require working outdoors, exposed to all weather conditions?
Public Speaking	How often do you have to perform public speaking in this job?
Responsibility for Outcomes and Results	How responsible is the worker for work outcomes and results of other workers?
Coordinate or Lead Others	How important is it to coordinate or lead others in accomplishing work activities in this job?
Time Pressure	How often does this job require the worker to meet strict deadlines?
Outdoors, Under Cover	How often does this job require working outdoors, under cover (e.g., structure with roof but no walls)?
Responsible for Others' Health and Safety	How much responsibility is there for the health and safety of others in this job?
Exposed to Contaminants	How often does this job require working exposed to contaminants (such as pollutants, gases, dust or odors)?
Wear Common Protective or Safety Equipment such as	How much does this job require wearing common protective or safety equipment such as safety shoes, glasses, gloves, hard hats or life jackets?
Consequence of Error	How serious would the result usually be if the worker made a mistake that was not readily correctable?
Degree of Automation	How automated is the job?
Physical Proximity	To what extent does this job require the worker to perform job tasks in close physical proximity to other people?
Very Hot or Cold Temperatures	How often does this job require working in very hot (above 90 F degrees) or very cold (below 32 F degrees) temperatures?
Importance of Repeating Same Tasks	How important is repeating the same physical activities (e.g., key entry) or mental activities (e.g., checking entries in a ledger) over and over, without stopping, to performing this job?
Frequency of Conflict Situations	How often are there conflict situations the employee has to face in this job?
Sounds, Noise Levels Are Distracting or Uncomforta	How often does this job require working exposed to sounds and noise levels that are distracting or uncomfortable?
Spend Time Standing	How much does this job require standing?
Spend Time Using Your Hands to Handle, Control, or	How much does this job require using your hands to handle, control, or feel objects, tools or controls?
In an Open Vehicle or Equipment	How often does this job require working in an open vehicle or equipment (e.g., tractor)?
Exposed to Hazardous Equipment	How often does this job require exposure to hazardous equipment?
Deal With Unpleasant or Angry People	How frequently does the worker have to deal with unpleasant, angry, or discourteous individuals as part of the job requirements?
Exposed to Hazardous Conditions	How often does this job require exposure to hazardous conditions?
Spend Time Walking and Running	How much does this job require walking and running?
Exposed to Minor Burns, Cuts, Bites, or Stings	How often does this job require exposure to minor burns, cuts, bites, or stings?
Extremely Bright or Inadequate Lighting	How often does this job require working in extremely bright or inadequate lighting conditions?
Exposed to Disease or Infections	How often does this job require exposure to disease/infections?
Spend Time Making Repetitive Motions	How much does this job require making repetitive motions?
Cramped Work Space, Awkward Positions	How often does this job require working in cramped work spaces that requires getting into awkward positions?
Wear Specialized Protective or Safety Equipment su	How much does this job require wearing specialized protective or safety equipment such as breathing apparatus, safety harness, full protection suits, or radiation protection?
Spend Time Bending or Twisting the Body	How much does this job require bending or twisting your body?
Exposed to High Places	How often does this job require exposure to high places?
Pace Determined by Speed of Equipment	How important is it to this job that the pace is determined by the speed of equipment or machinery? (This does not refer to keeping busy at all times on this job.)
Exposed to Radiation	How often does this job require exposure to radiation?
Spend Time Kneeling, Crouching, Stooping, or Crawl	How much does this job require kneeling, crouching, stooping, or crawling?
Spend Time Keeping or Regaining Balance	How much does this job require keeping or regaining your balance?
Spend Time Climbing Ladders, Scaffolds, or Poles	How much does this job require climbing ladders, scaffolds, or poles?
Deal With Physically Aggressive People	How frequently does this job require the worker to deal with physical aggression of violent individuals?
Exposed to Whole Body Vibration	How often does this job require exposure to whole body vibration (e.g., operate a jackhammer)?

Job Zone Component	Job Zone Component Definitions
Title	Job Zone Five: Extensive Preparation Needed
Overall Experience	Extensive skill, knowledge, and experience are needed for these occupations. Many require more than five years of experience. For example, surgeons must complete four years of college and an additional five to seven years of specialized medical training to be able to do their job.
Job Training	Employees may need some on-the-job training, but most of these occupations assume that the person will already have the required skills, knowledge, work-related experience, and/or training.
Job Zone Examples	These occupations often involve coordinating, training, supervising, or managing the activities of others to accomplish goals. Very advanced communication and organizational skills are required. Examples include athletic trainers, lawyers, managing editors, phyicists, social psychologists, and surgeons.
SVP Range	(8.0 and above)
Education	A bachelor's degree is the minimum formal education required for these occupations. However, many also require graduate school. For example, they may require a master's degree, and some require a Ph.D., M.D., or J.D. (law degree).

Work_Styles	Work_Styles Definitions
Integrity	Job requires being honest and ethical.
Analytical Thinking	Job requires analyzing information and using logic to address work-related issues and problems.
Initiative	Job requires a willingness to take on responsibilities and challenges.
Attention to Detail	Job requires being careful about detail and thorough in completing work tasks.
Dependability	Job requires being reliable, responsible, and dependable, and fulfilling obligations.
Innovation	Job requires creativity and alternative thinking to develop new ideas for and answers to work-related problems.
Independence	Job requires developing one's own ways of doing things, guiding oneself with little or no supervision, and depending on oneself to get things done.
Achievement/Effort	Job requires establishing and maintaining personally challenging achievement goals and exerting effort toward mastering tasks.
Persistence	Job requires persistence in the face of obstacles.
Adaptability/Flexibility	Job requires being open to change (positive or negative) and to considerable variety in the workplace.
Cooperation	Job requires being pleasant with others on the job and displaying a good-natured, cooperative attitude.
Stress Tolerance	Job requires accepting criticism and dealing calmly and effectively with high stress situations.
Self Control	Job requires maintaining composure, keeping emotions in check, controlling anger, and avoiding aggressive behavior, even in very difficult situations.
Leadership	Job requires a willingness to lead, take charge, and offer opinions and direction.
Concern for Others	Job requires being sensitive to others' needs and feelings and being understanding and helpful on the job.
Social Orientation	Job requires preferring to work with others rather than alone, and being personally connected with others on the job.

19-1041.00 - Epidemiologists

Investigate and describe the determinants and distribution of disease, disability, and other health outcomes and develop the means for prevention and control.

Tasks

1) Plan and direct studies to investigate human or animal disease, preventive methods, and treatments for disease.

2) Provide expertise in the design, management and evaluation of study protocols and health status questionnaires, sample selection and analysis.

3) Investigate diseases or parasites to determine cause and risk factors, progress, life cycle, or mode of transmission.

4) Plan, administer and evaluate health safety standards and programs to improve public health, conferring with health department, industry personnel, physicians and others.

5) Consult with and advise physicians, educators, researchers, government health officials and others regarding medical applications of sciences, such as physics, biology, and chemistry.

6) Supervise professional, technical and clerical personnel.

7) Conduct research to develop methodologies, instrumentation and procedures for medical application, analyzing data and presenting findings.

8) Identify and analyze public health issues related to foodborne parasitic diseases and their impact on public policies or scientific studies or surveys.

9) Teach principles of medicine and medical and laboratory procedures to physicians, residents, students, and technicians.

10) Prepare and analyze samples to study effects of drugs, gases, pesticides, or microorganisms on cell structure and tissue.

11) Standardize drug dosages, methods of immunization, and procedures for manufacture of drugs and medicinal compounds.

Knowledge	Knowledge Definitions
English Language	Knowledge of the structure and content of the English language including the meaning and spelling of words, rules of composition, and grammar.
Mathematics	Knowledge of arithmetic, algebra, geometry, calculus, statistics, and their applications.
Biology	Knowledge of plant and animal organisms, their tissues, cells, functions, interdependencies, and interactions with each other and the environment.
Medicine and Dentistry	Knowledge of the information and techniques needed to diagnose and treat human injuries, diseases, and deformities. This includes symptoms, treatment alternatives, drug properties and interactions, and preventive health-care measures.
Computers and Electronics	Knowledge of circuit boards, processors, chips, electronic equipment, and computer hardware and software, including applications and programming.
Education and Training	Knowledge of principles and methods for curriculum and training design, teaching and instruction for individuals and groups, and the measurement of training effects.
Sociology and Anthropology	Knowledge of group behavior and dynamics, societal trends and influences, human migrations, ethnicity, cultures and their history and origins.
Customer and Personal Service	Knowledge of principles and processes for providing customer and personal services. This includes customer needs assessment, meeting quality standards for services, and evaluation of customer satisfaction.
Administration and Management	Knowledge of business and management principles involved in strategic planning, resource allocation, human resources modeling, leadership technique, production methods, and coordination of people and resources.
Psychology	Knowledge of human behavior and performance; individual differences in ability, personality, and interests; learning and motivation; psychological research methods; and the assessment and treatment of behavioral and affective disorders.
Clerical	Knowledge of administrative and clerical procedures and systems such as word processing, managing files and records, stenography and transcription, designing forms, and other office procedures and terminology.
Law and Government	Knowledge of laws, legal codes, court procedures, precedents, government regulations, executive orders, agency rules, and the democratic political process.
Public Safety and Security	Knowledge of relevant equipment, policies, procedures, and strategies to promote effective local, state, or national security operations for the protection of people, data, property, and institutions.
Communications and Media	Knowledge of media production, communication, and dissemination techniques and methods. This includes alternative ways to inform and entertain via written, oral, and visual media.
Telecommunications	Knowledge of transmission, broadcasting, switching, control, and operation of telecommunications systems.
Therapy and Counseling	Knowledge of principles, methods, and procedures for diagnosis, treatment, and rehabilitation of physical and mental dysfunctions, and for career counseling and guidance.
Chemistry	Knowledge of the chemical composition, structure, and properties of substances and of the chemical processes and transformations that they undergo. This includes uses of chemicals and their interactions, danger signs, production techniques, and disposal methods.
Geography	Knowledge of principles and methods for describing the features of land, sea, and air masses, including their physical characteristics, locations, interrelationships, and distribution of plant, animal, and human life.
Personnel and Human Resources	Knowledge of principles and procedures for personnel recruitment, selection, training, compensation and benefits, labor relations and negotiation, and personnel information systems.
Philosophy and Theology	Knowledge of different philosophical systems and religions. This includes their basic principles, values, ethics, ways of thinking, customs, practices, and their impact on human culture.
Sales and Marketing	Knowledge of principles and methods for showing, promoting, and selling products or services. This includes marketing strategy and tactics, product demonstration, sales techniques, and sales control systems.
Food Production	Knowledge of techniques and equipment for planting, growing, and harvesting food products (both plant and animal) for consumption, including storage/handling techniques.
Transportation	Knowledge of principles and methods for moving people or goods by air, rail, sea, or road, including the relative costs and benefits.
History and Archeology	Knowledge of historical events and their causes, indicators, and effects on civilizations and cultures.
Design	Knowledge of design techniques, tools, and principles involved in production of precision technical plans, blueprints, drawings, and models.
Foreign Language	Knowledge of the structure and content of a foreign (non-English) language including the meaning and spelling of words, rules of composition and grammar, and pronunciation.
Economics and Accounting	Knowledge of economic and accounting principles and practices, the financial markets, banking and the analysis and reporting of financial data.
Engineering and Technology	Knowledge of the practical application of engineering science and technology. This includes applying principles, techniques, procedures, and equipment to the design and production of various goods and services.
Production and Processing	Knowledge of raw materials, production processes, quality control, costs, and other techniques for maximizing the effective manufacture and distribution of goods.
Physics	Knowledge and prediction of physical principles, laws, their interrelationships, and applications to understanding fluid, material, and atmospheric dynamics, and mechanical, electrical, atomic and sub-atomic structures and processes.
Mechanical	Knowledge of machines and tools, including their designs, uses, repair, and maintenance.
Fine Arts	Knowledge of the theory and techniques required to compose, produce, and perform works of music, dance, visual arts, drama, and sculpture.
Building and Construction	Knowledge of materials, methods, and the tools involved in the construction or repair of houses, buildings, or other structures such as highways and roads.

Skills	Skills Definitions
Reading Comprehension	Understanding written sentences and paragraphs in work related documents.
Writing	Communicating effectively in writing as appropriate for the needs of the audience.
Science	Using scientific rules and methods to solve problems.
Active Listening	Giving full attention to what other people are saying, taking time to understand the points being made, asking questions as appropriate, and not interrupting at inappropriate times.

Critical Thinking	Using logic and reasoning to identify the strengths and weaknesses of alternative solutions, conclusions or approaches to problems.
Active Learning	Understanding the implications of new information for both current and future problem-solving and decision-making.
Speaking	Talking to others to convey information effectively.
Time Management	Managing one's own time and the time of others.
Complex Problem Solving	Identifying complex problems and reviewing related information to develop and evaluate options and implement solutions.
Mathematics	Using mathematics to solve problems.
Monitoring	Monitoring/Assessing performance of yourself, other individuals, or organizations to make improvements or take corrective action.
Coordination	Adjusting actions in relation to others' actions.
Learning Strategies	Selecting and using training/instructional methods and procedures appropriate for the situation when learning or teaching new things.
Judgment and Decision Making	Considering the relative costs and benefits of potential actions to choose the most appropriate one.
Social Perceptiveness	Being aware of others' reactions and understanding why they react as they do.
Persuasion	Persuading others to change their minds or behavior.
Instructing	Teaching others how to do something.
Service Orientation	Actively looking for ways to help people.
Quality Control Analysis	Conducting tests and inspections of products, services, or processes to evaluate quality or performance.
Operations Analysis	Analyzing needs and product requirements to create a design.
Negotiation	Bringing others together and trying to reconcile differences.
Troubleshooting	Determining causes of operating errors and deciding what to do about it.
Equipment Selection	Determining the kind of tools and equipment needed to do a job.
Programming	Writing computer programs for various purposes.
Systems Evaluation	Identifying measures or indicators of system performance and the actions needed to improve or correct performance, relative to the goals of the system.
Management of Personnel Resources	Motivating, developing, and directing people as they work, identifying the best people for the job.
Management of Financial Resources	Determining how money will be spent to get the work done, and accounting for these expenditures.
Systems Analysis	Determining how a system should work and how changes in conditions, operations, and the environment will affect outcomes.
Management of Material Resources	Obtaining and seeing to the appropriate use of equipment, facilities, and materials needed to do certain work.
Technology Design	Generating or adapting equipment and technology to serve user needs.
Operation and Control	Controlling operations of equipment or systems.
Operation Monitoring	Watching gauges, dials, or other indicators to make sure a machine is working properly.
Repairing	Repairing machines or systems using the needed tools.
Installation	Installing equipment, machines, wiring, or programs to meet specifications.
Equipment Maintenance	Performing routine maintenance on equipment and determining when and what kind of maintenance is needed.

Ability — Ability Definitions

Inductive Reasoning	The ability to combine pieces of information to form general rules or conclusions (includes finding a relationship among seemingly unrelated events).
Oral Comprehension	The ability to listen to and understand information and ideas presented through spoken words and sentences.
Oral Expression	The ability to communicate information and ideas in speaking so others will understand.
Problem Sensitivity	The ability to tell when something is wrong or is likely to go wrong. It does not involve solving the problem, only recognizing there is a problem.
Deductive Reasoning	The ability to apply general rules to specific problems to produce answers that make sense.
Written Comprehension	The ability to read and understand information and ideas presented in writing.
Written Expression	The ability to communicate information and ideas in writing so others will understand.
Speech Clarity	The ability to speak clearly so others can understand you.
Near Vision	The ability to see details at close range (within a few feet of the observer).

Information Ordering	The ability to arrange things or actions in a certain order or pattern according to a specific rule or set of rules (e.g., patterns of numbers, letters, words, pictures, mathematical operations).
Speech Recognition	The ability to identify and understand the speech of another person.
Category Flexibility	The ability to generate or use different sets of rules for combining or grouping things in different ways.
Mathematical Reasoning	The ability to choose the right mathematical methods or formulas to solve a problem.
Fluency of Ideas	The ability to come up with a number of ideas about a topic (the number of ideas is important, not their quality, correctness, or creativity).
Flexibility of Closure	The ability to identify or detect a known pattern (a figure, object, word, or sound) that is hidden in other distracting material.
Originality	The ability to come up with unusual or clever ideas about a given topic or situation, or to develop creative ways to solve a problem.
Selective Attention	The ability to concentrate on a task over a period of time without being distracted.
Speed of Closure	The ability to quickly make sense of, combine, and organize information into meaningful patterns.
Perceptual Speed	The ability to quickly and accurately compare similarities and differences among sets of letters, numbers, objects, pictures, or patterns. The things to be compared may be presented at the same time or one after the other. This ability also includes comparing a presented object with a remembered object.
Number Facility	The ability to add, subtract, multiply, or divide quickly and correctly.
Far Vision	The ability to see details at a distance.
Memorization	The ability to remember information such as words, numbers, pictures, and procedures.
Auditory Attention	The ability to focus on a single source of sound in the presence of other distracting sounds.
Time Sharing	The ability to shift back and forth between two or more activities or sources of information (such as speech, sounds, touch, or other sources).
Finger Dexterity	The ability to make precisely coordinated movements of the fingers of one or both hands to grasp, manipulate, or assemble very small objects.
Visualization	The ability to imagine how something will look after it is moved around or when its parts are moved or rearranged.
Visual Color Discrimination	The ability to match or detect differences between colors, including shades of color and brightness.
Depth Perception	The ability to judge which of several objects is closer or farther away from you, or to judge the distance between you and an object.
Hearing Sensitivity	The ability to detect or tell the differences between sounds that vary in pitch and loudness.
Trunk Strength	The ability to use your abdominal and lower back muscles to support part of the body repeatedly or continuously over time without 'giving out' or fatiguing.
Arm-Hand Steadiness	The ability to keep your hand and arm steady while moving your arm or while holding your arm and hand in one position.
Manual Dexterity	The ability to quickly move your hand, your hand together with your arm, or your two hands to grasp, manipulate, or assemble objects.
Dynamic Flexibility	The ability to quickly and repeatedly bend, stretch, twist, or reach out with your body, arms, and/or legs.
Peripheral Vision	The ability to see objects or movement of objects to one's side when the eyes are looking ahead.
Glare Sensitivity	The ability to see objects in the presence of glare or bright lighting.
Sound Localization	The ability to tell the direction from which a sound originated.
Gross Body Coordination	The ability to coordinate the movement of your arms, legs, and torso together when the whole body is in motion.
Spatial Orientation	The ability to know your location in relation to the environment or to know where other objects are in relation to you.
Control Precision	The ability to quickly and repeatedly adjust the controls of a machine or a vehicle to exact positions.
Response Orientation	The ability to choose quickly between two or more movements in response to two or more different signals (lights, sounds, pictures). It includes the speed with which the correct response is started with the hand, foot, or other body part.
Rate Control	The ability to time your movements or the movement of a piece of equipment in anticipation of changes in the speed and/or direction of a moving object or scene.

Reaction Time	The ability to quickly respond (with the hand, finger, or foot) to a signal (sound, light, picture) when it appears.
Wrist-Finger Speed	The ability to make fast, simple, repeated movements of the fingers, hands, and wrists.
Static Strength	The ability to exert maximum muscle force to lift, push, pull, or carry objects.
Explosive Strength	The ability to use short bursts of muscle force to propel oneself (as in jumping or sprinting), or to throw an object.
Dynamic Strength	The ability to exert muscle force repeatedly or continuously over time. This involves muscular endurance and resistance to muscle fatigue.
Extent Flexibility	The ability to bend, stretch, twist, or reach with your body, arms, and/or legs.
Stamina	The ability to exert yourself physically over long periods of time without getting winded or out of breath.
Speed of Limb Movement	The ability to quickly move the arms and legs.
Multilimb Coordination	The ability to coordinate two or more limbs (for example, two arms, two legs, or one leg and one arm) while sitting, standing, or lying down. It does not involve performing the activities while the whole body is in motion.
Gross Body Equilibrium	The ability to keep or regain your body balance or stay upright when in an unstable position.
Night Vision	The ability to see under low light conditions.

Work_Activity	Work_Activity Definitions
Getting Information	Observing, receiving, and otherwise obtaining information from all relevant sources.
Updating and Using Relevant Knowledge	Keeping up-to-date technically and applying new knowledge to your job.
Communicating with Supervisors, Peers, or Subordin	Providing information to supervisors, co-workers, and subordinates by telephone, in written form, e-mail, or in person.
Analyzing Data or Information	Identifying the underlying principles, reasons, or facts of information by breaking down information or data into separate parts.
Interacting With Computers	Using computers and computer systems (including hardware and software) to program, write software, set up functions, enter data, or process information.
Processing Information	Compiling, coding, categorizing, calculating, tabulating, auditing, or verifying information or data.
Evaluating Information to Determine Compliance wit	Using relevant information and individual judgment to determine whether events or processes comply with laws, regulations, or standards.
Documenting/Recording Information	Entering, transcribing, recording, storing, or maintaining information in written or electronic/magnetic form.
Organizing, Planning, and Prioritizing Work	Developing specific goals and plans to prioritize, organize, and accomplish your work.
Identifying Objects, Actions, and Events	Identifying information by categorizing, estimating, recognizing differences or similarities, and detecting changes in circumstances or events.
Establishing and Maintaining Interpersonal Relatio	Developing constructive and cooperative working relationships with others, and maintaining them over time.
Interpreting the Meaning of Information for Others	Translating or explaining what information means and how it can be used.
Communicating with Persons Outside Organization	Communicating with people outside the organization, representing the organization to customers, the public, government, and other external sources. This information can be exchanged in person, in writing, or by telephone or e-mail.
Making Decisions and Solving Problems	Analyzing information and evaluating results to choose the best solution and solve problems.
Monitor Processes, Materials, or Surroundings	Monitoring and reviewing information from materials, events, or the environment, to detect or assess problems.
Provide Consultation and Advice to Others	Providing guidance and expert advice to management or other groups on technical, systems-, or process-related topics.
Training and Teaching Others	Identifying the educational needs of others, developing formal educational or training programs or classes, and teaching or instructing others.
Thinking Creatively	Developing, designing, or creating new applications, ideas, relationships, systems, or products, including artistic contributions.
Estimating the Quantifiable Characteristics of Pro	Estimating sizes, distances, and quantities; or determining time, costs, resources, or materials needed to perform a work activity.
Developing Objectives and Strategies	Establishing long-range objectives and specifying the strategies and actions to achieve them.

Scheduling Work and Activities	Scheduling events, programs, and activities, as well as the work of others.
Judging the Qualities of Things, Services, or Peop	Assessing the value, importance, or quality of things or people.
Developing and Building Teams	Encouraging and building mutual trust, respect, and cooperation among team members.
Coordinating the Work and Activities of Others	Getting members of a group to work together to accomplish tasks.
Performing Administrative Activities	Performing day-to-day administrative tasks such as maintaining information files and processing paperwork.
Performing for or Working Directly with the Public	Performing for people or dealing directly with the public. This includes serving customers in restaurants and stores, and receiving clients or guests.
Assisting and Caring for Others	Providing personal assistance, medical attention, emotional support, or other personal care to others such as coworkers, customers, or patients.
Coaching and Developing Others	Identifying the developmental needs of others and coaching, mentoring, or otherwise helping others to improve their knowledge or skills.
Resolving Conflicts and Negotiating with Others	Handling complaints, settling disputes, and resolving grievances and conflicts, or otherwise negotiating with others.
Selling or Influencing Others	Convincing others to buy merchandise/goods or to otherwise change their minds or actions.
Inspecting Equipment, Structures, or Material	Inspecting equipment, structures, or materials to identify the cause of errors or other problems or defects.
Guiding, Directing, and Motivating Subordinates	Providing guidance and direction to subordinates, including setting performance standards and monitoring performance.
Monitoring and Controlling Resources	Monitoring and controlling resources and overseeing the spending of money.
Performing General Physical Activities	Performing physical activities that require considerable use of your arms and legs and moving your whole body, such as climbing, lifting, balancing, walking, stooping, and handling of materials.
Handling and Moving Objects	Using hands and arms in handling, installing, positioning, and moving materials, and manipulating things.
Controlling Machines and Processes	Using either control mechanisms or direct physical activity to operate machines or processes (not including computers or vehicles).
Operating Vehicles, Mechanized Devices, or Equipme	Running, maneuvering, navigating, or driving vehicles or mechanized equipment, such as forklifts, passenger vehicles, aircraft, or water craft.
Staffing Organizational Units	Recruiting, interviewing, selecting, hiring, and promoting employees in an organization.
Repairing and Maintaining Electronic Equipment	Servicing, repairing, calibrating, regulating, fine-tuning, or testing machines, devices, and equipment that operate primarily on the basis of electrical or electronic (not mechanical) principles.
Repairing and Maintaining Mechanical Equipment	Servicing, repairing, adjusting, and testing machines, devices, moving parts, and equipment that operate primarily on the basis of mechanical (not electronic) principles.
Drafting, Laying Out, and Specifying Technical Dev	Providing documentation, detailed instructions, drawings, or specifications to tell others about how devices, parts, equipment, or structures are to be fabricated, constructed, assembled, modified, maintained, or used.

Work_Context	Work_Context Definitions
Electronic Mail	How often do you use electronic mail in this job?
Telephone	How often do you have telephone conversations in this job?
Face-to-Face Discussions	How often do you have to have face-to-face discussions with individuals or teams in this job?
Indoors, Environmentally Controlled	How often does this job require working indoors in environmentally controlled conditions?
Work With Work Group or Team	How important is it to work with others in a group or team in this job?
Structured versus Unstructured Work	To what extent is this job structured for the worker, rather than allowing the worker to determine tasks, priorities, and goals?
Spend Time Sitting	How much does this job require sitting?
Freedom to Make Decisions	How much decision making freedom, without supervision, does the job offer?
Importance of Being Exact or Accurate	How important is being very exact or highly accurate in performing this job?
Contact With Others	How much does this job require the worker to be in contact with others (face-to-face, by telephone, or otherwise) in order to perform it?
Letters and Memos	How often does the job require written letters and memos?

Impact of Decisions on Co-workers or Company Resul	How do the decisions an employee makes impact the results of co-workers, clients or the company?
Coordinate or Lead Others	How important is it to coordinate or lead others in accomplishing work activities in this job?
Responsibility for Outcomes and Results	How responsible is the worker for work outcomes and results of other workers?
Importance of Repeating Same Tasks	How important is repeating the same physical activities (e.g., key entry) or mental activities (e.g., checking entries in a ledger) over and over, without stopping, to performing this job?
Frequency of Decision Making	How frequently is the worker required to make decisions that affect other people, the financial resources, and/or the image and reputation of the organization?
Sounds, Noise Levels Are Distracting or Uncomforta	How often does this job require working exposed to sounds and noise levels that are distracting or uncomfortable?
Deal With External Customers	How important is it to work with external customers or the public in this job?
Time Pressure	How often does this job require the worker to meet strict deadlines?
Spend Time Making Repetitive Motions	How much does this job require making repetitive motions?
Responsible for Others' Health and Safety	How much responsibility is there for the health and safety of others in this job?
Degree of Automation	How automated is the job?
Level of Competition	To what extent does this job require the worker to compete or to be aware of competitive pressures?
Physical Proximity	To what extent does this job require the worker to perform job tasks in close physical proximity to other people?
Consequence of Error	How serious would the result usually be if the worker made a mistake that was not readily correctable?
Frequency of Conflict Situations	How often are there conflict situations the employee has to face in this job?
Public Speaking	How often do you have to perform public speaking in this job?
Deal With Unpleasant or Angry People	How frequently does the worker have to deal with unpleasant, angry, or discourteous individuals as part of the job requirements?
Exposed to Contaminants	How often does this job require working exposed to contaminants (such as pollutants, gases, dust or odors)?
Spend Time Using Your Hands to Handle, Control, or	How much does this job require using your hands to handle, control, or feel objects, tools or controls?
Spend Time Standing	How much does this job require standing?
In an Enclosed Vehicle or Equipment	How often does this job require working in a closed vehicle or equipment (e.g., car)?
Spend Time Walking and Running	How much does this job require walking and running?
Exposed to Disease or Infections	How often does this job require exposure to disease/infections?
Outdoors, Exposed to Weather	How often does this job require working outdoors, exposed to all weather conditions?
Extremely Bright or Inadequate Lighting	How often does this job require working in extremely bright or inadequate lighting conditions?
Very Hot or Cold Temperatures	How often does this job require working in very hot (above 90 F degrees) or very cold (below 32 F degrees) temperatures?
Spend Time Keeping or Regaining Balance	How much does this job require keeping or regaining your balance?
Wear Specialized Protective or Safety Equipment su	How much does this job require wearing specialized protective or safety equipment such as breathing apparatus, safety harness, full protection suits, or radiation protection?
Wear Common Protective or Safety Equipment such as	How much does this job require wearing common protective or safety equipment such as safety shoes, glasses, gloves, hard hats or live jackets?
Deal With Physically Aggressive People	How frequently does this job require the worker to deal with physical aggression of violent individuals?
Outdoors, Under Cover	How often does this job require working outdoors, under cover (e.g., structure with roof but no walls)?
Spend Time Bending or Twisting the Body	How much does this job require bending or twisting your body?
Indoors, Not Environmentally Controlled	How often does this job require working indoors in non-controlled environmental conditions (e.g., warehouse without heat)?
Pace Determined by Speed of Equipment	How important is it to this job that the pace is determined by the speed of equipment or machinery? (This does not refer to keeping busy at all times on this job.)
Exposed to Minor Burns, Cuts, Bites, or Stings	How often does this job require exposure to minor burns, cuts, bites, or stings?
Cramped Work Space, Awkward Positions	How often does this job require working in cramped work spaces that requires getting into awkward positions?

Exposed to Radiation	How often does this job require exposure to radiation?
Spend Time Kneeling, Crouching, Stooping, or Crawl	How much does this job require kneeling, crouching, stooping or crawling?
Exposed to Hazardous Conditions	How often does this job require exposure to hazardous conditions?
Exposed to High Places	How often does this job require exposure to high places?
In an Open Vehicle or Equipment	How often does this job require working in an open vehicle or equipment (e.g., tractor)?
Spend Time Climbing Ladders, Scaffolds, or Poles	How much does this job require climbing ladders, scaffolds, or poles?
Exposed to Hazardous Equipment	How often does this job require exposure to hazardous equipment?
Exposed to Whole Body Vibration	How often does this job require exposure to whole body vibration (e.g., operate a jackhammer)?

Job Zone Component	Job Zone Component Definitions
Title	Job Zone Five: Extensive Preparation Needed
Overall Experience	Extensive skill, knowledge, and experience are needed for these occupations. Many require more than five years of experience. For example, surgeons must complete four years of college and an additional five to seven years of specialized medical training to be able to do their job.
Job Training	Employees may need some on-the-job training, but most of these occupations assume that the person will already have the required skills, knowledge, work-related experience, and/or training.
Job Zone Examples	These occupations often involve coordinating, training, supervising, or managing the activities of others to accomplish goals. Very advanced communication and organizational skills are required. Examples include athletic trainers, lawyers, managing editors, phyicists, social psychologists, and surgeons.
SVP Range	(8.0 and above)
Education	A bachelor's degree is the minimum formal education required for these occupations. However, many also require graduate school. For example, they may require a master's degree, and some require a Ph.D., M.D., or J.D. (law degree).

Work_Styles	Work_Styles Definitions
Analytical Thinking	Job requires analyzing information and using logic to address work-related issues and problems.
Attention to Detail	Job requires being careful about detail and thorough in completing work tasks.
Integrity	Job requires being honest and ethical.
Cooperation	Job requires being pleasant with others on the job and displaying a good-natured, cooperative attitude.
Dependability	Job requires being reliable, responsible, and dependable, and fulfilling obligations.
Initiative	Job requires a willingness to take on responsibilities and challenges.
Achievement/Effort	Job requires establishing and maintaining personally challenging achievement goals and exerting effort toward mastering tasks.
Independence	Job requires developing one's own ways of doing things, guiding oneself with little or no supervision, and depending on oneself to get things done.
Stress Tolerance	Job requires accepting criticism and dealing calmly and effectively with high stress situations.
Persistence	Job requires persistence in the face of obstacles.
Adaptability/Flexibility	Job requires being open to change (positive or negative) and to considerable variety in the workplace.
Self Control	Job requires maintaining composure, keeping emotions in check, controlling anger, and avoiding aggressive behavior, even in very difficult situations.
Leadership	Job requires a willingness to lead, take charge, and offer opinions and direction.
Concern for Others	Job requires being sensitive to others' needs and feelings and being understanding and helpful on the job.
Innovation	Job requires creativity and alternative thinking to develop new ideas for and answers to work-related problems.
Social Orientation	Job requires preferring to work with others rather than alone, and being personally connected with others on the job.

19-2011.00 - Astronomers

Observe, research, and interpret celestial and astronomical phenomena to increase basic knowledge and apply such information to practical problems.

Tasks

1) Study celestial phenomena, using a variety of ground-based and space-borne telescopes and scientific instruments.

2) Teach astronomy or astrophysics.

3) Direct the operations of a planetarium.

4) Develop instrumentation and software for astronomical observation and analysis.

5) Develop and modify astronomy-related programs for public presentation.

6) Present research findings at scientific conferences, and in papers written for scientific journals.

7) Develop theories based on personal observations, or on observations and theories of other astronomers.

8) Collaborate with other astronomers to carry out research projects.

9) Calculate orbits, and determine sizes, shapes, brightness, and motions of different celestial bodies.

10) Analyze research data to determine its significance, using computers.

11) Measure radio, infrared, gamma, and x-ray emissions from extraterrestrial sources.

19-2043.00 - Hydrologists

Research the distribution, circulation, and physical properties of underground and surface waters; study the form and intensity of precipitation, its rate of infiltration into the soil, movement through the earth, and its return to the ocean and atmosphere.

Tasks

1) Evaluate research data in terms of its impact on issues such as soil and water conservation, flood control planning, and water supply forecasting.

2) Coordinate and supervise the work of professional and technical staff, including research assistants, technologists, and technicians.

3) Review applications for site plans and permits, and recommend approval, denial, modification, or further investigative action.

4) Monitor the work of well contractors, exploratory borers, and engineers, in order to enforce rules regarding their activities.

5) Administer programs designed to ensure the proper sealing of abandoned wells.

6) Prepare hydrogeologic evaluations of known or suspected hazardous waste sites and land treatment and feedlot facilities.

7) Investigate complaints or conflicts related to the alteration of public waters, gathering information, recommending alternatives, informing participants of progress, and preparing draft orders.

8) Install, maintain, and calibrate instruments such as those that monitor water levels, rainfall, and sediments.

9) Investigate properties, origins, and activities of glaciers, ice, snow, and permafrost.

10) Compile and evaluate hydrologic information in order to prepare navigational charts and maps, and to predict atmospheric conditions.

11) Develop or modify methods of conducting hydrologic studies.

12) Evaluate data and provide recommendations regarding the feasibility of municipal projects such as hydroelectric power plants, irrigation systems, flood warning systems and waste treatment facilities.

13) Design and conduct scientific hydrogeological investigations to ensure that accurate and appropriate information is available for use in water resource management decisions.

14) Draft final reports describing research results, including illustrations, appendices, maps, and other attachments.

15) Measure and graph phenomena such as lake levels, stream flows, and changes in water volumes.

16) Study and analyze the physical aspects of the Earth in terms of the hydrological components, including atmosphere, hydrosphere, and interior structure.

17) Study and document quantities, distribution, disposition, and development of underground and surface waters.

18) Study public water supply issues, including flood and drought risks, water quality, wastewater, and impacts on wetland habitats.

19) Answer questions and provide technical assistance and information to contractors and/or the public regarding issues such as well drilling, code requirements, hydrology, and geology.

20) Collect and analyze water samples as part of field investigations and/or to validate data from automatic monitors.

21) Apply research findings to help minimize the environmental impacts of pollution, water-borne diseases, erosion, and sedimentation.

22) Design civil works associated with hydrographic activities, and supervise their construction, installation, and maintenance.

23) Conduct research and communicate information to promote the conservation and preservation of water resources.

19-3021.00 - Market Research Analysts

Research market conditions in local, regional, or national areas to determine potential sales of a product or service. May gather information on competitors, prices, sales, and methods of marketing and distribution. May use survey results to create a marketing campaign based on regional preferences and buying habits.

Tasks

1) Prepare reports of findings, illustrating data graphically and translating complex findings into written text.

2) Measure the effectiveness of marketing, advertising, and communications programs and strategies.

3) Gather data on competitors and analyze their prices, sales, and method of marketing and distribution.

4) Forecast and track marketing and sales trends, analyzing collected data.

5) Monitor industry statistics and follow trends in trade literature.

6) Attend staff conferences to provide management with information and proposals concerning the promotion, distribution, design, and pricing of company products or services.

7) Devise and evaluate methods and procedures for collecting data (such as surveys, opinion polls, or questionnaires), or arrange to obtain existing data.

8) Conduct research on consumer opinions and marketing strategies, collaborating with marketing professionals, statisticians, pollsters, and other professionals.

9) Develop and implement procedures for identifying advertising needs.

10) Measure and assess customer and employee satisfaction.

11) Seek and provide information to help companies determine their position in the marketplace.

12) Direct trained survey interviewers.

Knowledge	Knowledge Definitions
Customer and Personal Service	Knowledge of principles and processes for providing customer and personal services. This includes customer needs assessment, meeting quality standards for services, and evaluation of customer satisfaction.
Sales and Marketing	Knowledge of principles and methods for showing, promoting, and selling products or services. This includes marketing strategy and tactics, product demonstration, sales techniques, and sales control systems.
English Language	Knowledge of the structure and content of the English language including the meaning and spelling of words, rules of composition, and grammar.
Administration and Management	Knowledge of business and management principles involved in strategic planning, resource allocation, human resources modeling, leadership technique, production methods, and coordination of people and resources.
Communications and Media	Knowledge of media production, communication, and dissemination techniques and methods. This includes alternative ways to inform and entertain via written, oral, and visual media.

Mathematics	Knowledge of arithmetic, algebra, geometry, calculus, statistics, and their applications.
Computers and Electronics	Knowledge of circuit boards, processors, chips, electronic equipment, and computer hardware and software, including applications and programming.
Economics and Accounting	Knowledge of economic and accounting principles and practices, the financial markets, banking and the analysis and reporting of financial data.
Education and Training	Knowledge of principles and methods for curriculum and training design, teaching and instruction for individuals and groups, and the measurement of training effects.
Clerical	Knowledge of administrative and clerical procedures and systems such as word processing, managing files and records, stenography and transcription, designing forms, and other office procedures and terminology.
Personnel and Human Resources	Knowledge of principles and procedures for personnel recruitment, selection, training, compensation and benefits, labor relations and negotiation, and personnel information systems.
Telecommunications	Knowledge of transmission, broadcasting, switching, control, and operation of telecommunications systems.
Psychology	Knowledge of human behavior and performance; individual differences in ability, personality, and interests; learning and motivation; psychological research methods; and the assessment and treatment of behavioral and affective disorders.
Sociology and Anthropology	Knowledge of group behavior and dynamics, societal trends and influences, human migrations, ethnicity, cultures and their history and origins.
Engineering and Technology	Knowledge of the practical application of engineering science and technology. This includes applying principles, techniques, procedures, and equipment to the design and production of various goods and services.
Law and Government	Knowledge of laws, legal codes, court procedures, precedents, government regulations, executive orders, agency rules, and the democratic political process.
Foreign Language	Knowledge of the structure and content of a foreign (non-English) language including the meaning and spelling of words, rules of composition and grammar, and pronunciation.
Production and Processing	Knowledge of raw materials, production processes, quality control, costs, and other techniques for maximizing the effective manufacture and distribution of goods.
Design	Knowledge of design techniques, tools, and principles involved in production of precision technical plans, blueprints, drawings, and models.
Public Safety and Security	Knowledge of relevant equipment, policies, procedures, and strategies to promote effective local, state, or national security operations for the protection of people, data, property, and institutions.
Geography	Knowledge of principles and methods for describing the features of land, sea, and air masses, including their physical characteristics, locations, interrelationships, and distribution of plant, animal, and human life.
Mechanical	Knowledge of machines and tools, including their designs, uses, repair, and maintenance.
History and Archeology	Knowledge of historical events and their causes, indicators, and effects on civilizations and cultures.
Philosophy and Theology	Knowledge of different philosophical systems and religions. This includes their basic principles, values, ethics, ways of thinking, customs, practices, and their impact on human culture.
Transportation	Knowledge of principles and methods for moving people or goods by air, rail, sea, or road, including the relative costs and benefits.
Fine Arts	Knowledge of the theory and techniques required to compose, produce, and perform works of music, dance, visual arts, drama, and sculpture.
Therapy and Counseling	Knowledge of principles, methods, and procedures for diagnosis, treatment, and rehabilitation of physical and mental dysfunctions, and for career counseling and guidance.
Medicine and Dentistry	Knowledge of the information and techniques needed to diagnose and treat human injuries, diseases, and deformities. This includes symptoms, treatment alternatives, drug properties and interactions, and preventive health-care measures.
Physics	Knowledge and prediction of physical principles, laws, their interrelationships, and applications to understanding fluid, material, and atmospheric dynamics, and mechanical, electrical, atomic and sub- atomic structures and processes.

Chemistry	Knowledge of the chemical composition, structure, and properties of substances and of the chemical processes and transformations that they undergo. This includes uses of chemicals and their interactions, danger signs, production techniques, and disposal methods.
Food Production	Knowledge of techniques and equipment for planting, growing, and harvesting food products (both plant and animal) for consumption, including storage/handling techniques.
Biology	Knowledge of plant and animal organisms, their tissues, cells, functions, interdependencies, and interactions with each other and the environment.
Building and Construction	Knowledge of materials, methods, and the tools involved in the construction or repair of houses, buildings, or other structures such as highways and roads.

Skills	Skills Definitions
Reading Comprehension	Understanding written sentences and paragraphs in work related documents.
Time Management	Managing one's own time and the time of others.
Writing	Communicating effectively in writing as appropriate for the needs of the audience.
Active Listening	Giving full attention to what other people are saying, taking time to understand the points being made, asking questions as appropriate, and not interrupting at inappropriate times.
Coordination	Adjusting actions in relation to others' actions.
Active Learning	Understanding the implications of new information for both current and future problem-solving and decision-making.
Critical Thinking	Using logic and reasoning to identify the strengths and weaknesses of alternative solutions, conclusions or approaches to problems.
Speaking	Talking to others to convey information effectively.
Judgment and Decision Making	Considering the relative costs and benefits of potential actions to choose the most appropriate one.
Negotiation	Bringing others together and trying to reconcile differences.
Social Perceptiveness	Being aware of others' reactions and understanding why they react as they do.
Persuasion	Persuading others to change their minds or behavior.
Complex Problem Solving	Identifying complex problems and reviewing related information to develop and evaluate options and implement solutions.
Learning Strategies	Selecting and using training/instructional methods and procedures appropriate for the situation when learning or teaching new things.
Monitoring	Monitoring/Assessing performance of yourself, other individuals, or organizations to make improvements or take corrective action.
Service Orientation	Actively looking for ways to help people.
Equipment Selection	Determining the kind of tools and equipment needed to do a job.
Instructing	Teaching others how to do something.
Management of Financial Resources	Determining how money will be spent to get the work done, and accounting for these expenditures.
Mathematics	Using mathematics to solve problems.
Quality Control Analysis	Conducting tests and inspections of products, services, or processes to evaluate quality or performance.
Management of Personnel Resources	Motivating, developing, and directing people as they work, identifying the best people for the job.
Operations Analysis	Analyzing needs and product requirements to create a design.
Technology Design	Generating or adapting equipment and technology to serve user needs.
Systems Evaluation	Identifying measures or indicators of system performance and the actions needed to improve or correct performance, relative to the goals of the system.
Science	Using scientific rules and methods to solve problems.
Management of Material Resources	Obtaining and seeing to the appropriate use of equipment, facilities, and materials needed to do certain work.
Troubleshooting	Determining causes of operating errors and deciding what to do about it.
Systems Analysis	Determining how a system should work and how changes in conditions, operations, and the environment will affect outcomes.
Operation and Control	Controlling operations of equipment or systems.
Operation Monitoring	Watching gauges, dials, or other indicators to make sure a machine is working properly.
Programming	Writing computer programs for various purposes.
Installation	Installing equipment, machines, wiring, or programs to meet specifications.

| Equipment Maintenance | Performing routine maintenance on equipment and determining when and what kind of maintenance is needed. |
| Repairing | Repairing machines or systems using the needed tools. |

Ability	**Ability Definitions**
Written Comprehension	The ability to read and understand information and ideas presented in writing.
Written Expression	The ability to communicate information and ideas in writing so others will understand.
Oral Comprehension	The ability to listen to and understand information and ideas presented through spoken words and sentences.
Inductive Reasoning	The ability to combine pieces of information to form general rules or conclusions (includes finding a relationship among seemingly unrelated events).
Oral Expression	The ability to communicate information and ideas in speaking so others will understand.
Deductive Reasoning	The ability to apply general rules to specific problems to produce answers that make sense.
Speech Clarity	The ability to speak clearly so others can understand you.
Near Vision	The ability to see details at close range (within a few feet of the observer).
Problem Sensitivity	The ability to tell when something is wrong or is likely to go wrong. It does not involve solving the problem, only recognizing there is a problem.
Information Ordering	The ability to arrange things or actions in a certain order or pattern according to a specific rule or set of rules (e.g., patterns of numbers, letters, words, pictures, mathematical operations).
Speech Recognition	The ability to identify and understand the speech of another person.
Mathematical Reasoning	The ability to choose the right mathematical methods or formulas to solve a problem.
Category Flexibility	The ability to generate or use different sets of rules for combining or grouping things in different ways.
Originality	The ability to come up with unusual or clever ideas about a given topic or situation, or to develop creative ways to solve a problem.
Selective Attention	The ability to concentrate on a task over a period of time without being distracted.
Fluency of Ideas	The ability to come up with a number of ideas about a topic (the number of ideas is important, not their quality, correctness, or creativity).
Flexibility of Closure	The ability to identify or detect a known pattern (a figure, object, word, or sound) that is hidden in other distracting material.
Speed of Closure	The ability to quickly make sense of, combine, and organize information into meaningful patterns.
Number Facility	The ability to add, subtract, multiply, or divide quickly and correctly.
Trunk Strength	The ability to use your abdominal and lower back muscles to support part of the body repeatedly or continuously over time without 'giving out' or fatiguing.
Perceptual Speed	The ability to quickly and accurately compare similarities and differences among sets of letters, numbers, objects, pictures, or patterns. The things to be compared may be presented at the same time or one after the other. This ability also includes comparing a presented object with a remembered object.
Visualization	The ability to imagine how something will look after it is moved around or when its parts are moved or rearranged.
Memorization	The ability to remember information such as words, numbers, pictures, and procedures.
Far Vision	The ability to see details at a distance.
Finger Dexterity	The ability to make precisely coordinated movements of the fingers of one or both hands to grasp, manipulate, or assemble very small objects.
Time Sharing	The ability to shift back and forth between two or more activities or sources of information (such as speech, sounds, touch, or other sources).
Auditory Attention	The ability to focus on a single source of sound in the presence of other distracting sounds.
Visual Color Discrimination	The ability to match or detect differences between colors, including shades of color and brightness.
Depth Perception	The ability to judge which of several objects is closer or farther away from you, or to judge the distance between you and an object.
Hearing Sensitivity	The ability to detect or tell the differences between sounds that vary in pitch and loudness.

Arm-Hand Steadiness	The ability to keep your hand and arm steady while moving your arm or while holding your arm and hand in one position.
Spatial Orientation	The ability to know your location in relation to the environment or to know where other objects are in relation to you.
Manual Dexterity	The ability to quickly move your hand, your hand together with your arm, or your two hands to grasp, manipulate, or assemble objects.
Gross Body Coordination	The ability to coordinate the movement of your arms, legs, and torso together when the whole body is in motion.
Gross Body Equilibrium	The ability to keep or regain your body balance or stay upright when in an unstable position.
Stamina	The ability to exert yourself physically over long periods of time without getting winded or out of breath.
Night Vision	The ability to see under low light conditions.
Peripheral Vision	The ability to see objects or movement of objects to one's side when the eyes are looking ahead.
Sound Localization	The ability to tell the direction from which a sound originated.
Extent Flexibility	The ability to bend, stretch, twist, or reach with your body, arms, and/or legs.
Control Precision	The ability to quickly and repeatedly adjust the controls of a machine or a vehicle to exact positions.
Glare Sensitivity	The ability to see objects in the presence of glare or bright lighting.
Response Orientation	The ability to choose quickly between two or more movements in response to two or more different signals (lights, sounds, pictures). It includes the speed with which the correct response is started with the hand, foot, or other body part.
Dynamic Flexibility	The ability to quickly and repeatedly bend, stretch, twist, or reach out with your body, arms, and/or legs.
Reaction Time	The ability to quickly respond (with the hand, finger, or foot) to a signal (sound, light, picture) when it appears.
Multilimb Coordination	The ability to coordinate two or more limbs (for example, two arms, two legs, or one leg and one arm) while sitting, standing, or lying down. It does not involve performing the activities while the whole body is in motion.
Wrist-Finger Speed	The ability to make fast, simple, repeated movements of the fingers, hands, and wrists.
Speed of Limb Movement	The ability to quickly move the arms and legs.
Static Strength	The ability to exert maximum muscle force to lift, push, pull, or carry objects.
Explosive Strength	The ability to use short bursts of muscle force to propel oneself (as in jumping or sprinting), or to throw an object.
Dynamic Strength	The ability to exert muscle force repeatedly or continuously over time. This involves muscular endurance and resistance to muscle fatigue.
Rate Control	The ability to time your movements or the movement of a piece of equipment in anticipation of changes in the speed and/or direction of a moving object or scene.

Work_Activity	**Work_Activity Definitions**
Interacting With Computers	Using computers and computer systems (including hardware and software) to program, write software, set up functions, enter data, or process information.
Communicating with Supervisors, Peers, or Subordin	Providing information to supervisors, co-workers, and subordinates by telephone, in written form, e-mail, or in person.
Documenting/Recording Information	Entering, transcribing, recording, storing, or maintaining information in written or electronic/magnetic form.
Updating and Using Relevant Knowledge	Keeping up-to-date technically and applying new knowledge to your job.
Establishing and Maintaining Interpersonal Relatio	Developing constructive and cooperative working relationships with others, and maintaining them over time.
Getting Information	Observing, receiving, and otherwise obtaining information from all relevant sources.
Processing Information	Compiling, coding, categorizing, calculating, tabulating, auditing, or verifying information or data.
Communicating with Persons Outside Organization	Communicating with people outside the organization, representing the organization to customers, the public, government, and other external sources. This information can be exchanged in person, in writing, or by telephone or e-mail.
Making Decisions and Solving Problems	Analyzing information and evaluating results to choose the best solution and solve problems.
Developing Objectives and Strategies	Establishing long-range objectives and specifying the strategies and actions to achieve them.

Analyzing Data or Information	Identifying the underlying principles, reasons, or facts of information by breaking down information or data into separate parts.	Repairing and Maintaining Mechanical Equipment	Servicing, repairing, adjusting, and testing machines, devices, moving parts, and equipment that operate primarily on the basis of mechanical (not electronic) principles.
Interpreting the Meaning of Information for Others	Translating or explaining what information means and how it can be used.	**Work_Context**	**Work_Context Definitions**
Identifying Objects, Actions, and Events	Identifying information by categorizing, estimating, recognizing differences or similarities, and detecting changes in circumstances or events.	Telephone	How often do you have telephone conversations in this job?
Estimating the Quantifiable Characteristics of Pro	Estimating sizes, distances, and quantities; or determining time, costs, resources, or materials needed to perform a work activity.	Electronic Mail	How often do you use electronic mail in this job?
		Structured versus Unstructured Work	To what extent is this job structured for the worker, rather than allowing the worker to determine tasks, priorities, and goals?
Organizing, Planning, and Prioritizing Work	Developing specific goals and plans to prioritize, organize, and accomplish your work.	Importance of Being Exact or Accurate	How important is being very exact or highly accurate in performing this job?
Selling or Influencing Others	Convincing others to buy merchandise/goods or to otherwise change their minds or actions.	Indoors, Environmentally Controlled	How often does this job require working indoors in environmentally controlled conditions?
Judging the Qualities of Things, Services, or Peop	Assessing the value, importance, or quality of things or people.	Spend Time Sitting	How much does this job require sitting?
		Freedom to Make Decisions	How much decision making freedom, without supervision, does the job offer?
Thinking Creatively	Developing, designing, or creating new applications, ideas, relationships, systems, or products, including artistic contributions.	Work With Work Group or Team	How important is it to work with others in a group or team in this job?
Resolving Conflicts and Negotiating with Others	Handling complaints, settling disputes, and resolving grievances and conflicts, or otherwise negotiating with others.	Face-to-Face Discussions	How often do you have to have face-to-face discussions with individuals or teams in this job?
Coordinating the Work and Activities of Others	Getting members of a group to work together to accomplish tasks.	Contact With Others	How much does this job require the worker to be in contact with others (face-to-face, by telephone, or otherwise) in order to perform it?
Performing Administrative Activities	Performing day-to-day administrative tasks such as maintaining information files and processing paperwork.	Time Pressure	How often does this job require the worker to meet strict deadlines?
Provide Consultation and Advice to Others	Providing guidance and expert advice to management or other groups on technical, systems-, or process-related topics.	Letters and Memos	How often does the job require written letters and memos?
Scheduling Work and Activities	Scheduling events, programs, and activities, as well as the work of others.	Responsibility for Outcomes and Results	How responsible is the worker for work outcomes and results of other workers?
Monitor Processes, Materials, or Surroundings	Monitoring and reviewing information from materials, events, or the environment, to detect or assess problems.	Deal With External Customers	How important is it to work with external customers or the public in this job?
Monitoring and Controlling Resources	Monitoring and controlling resources and overseeing the spending of money.	Importance of Repeating Same Tasks	How important is repeating the same physical activities (e.g., key entry) or mental activities (e.g., checking entries in a ledger) over and over, without stopping, to performing this job?
Developing and Building Teams	Encouraging and building mutual trust, respect, and cooperation among team members.	Level of Competition	To what extent does this job require the worker to compete or to be aware of competitive pressures?
Guiding, Directing, and Motivating Subordinates	Providing guidance and direction to subordinates, including setting performance standards and monitoring performance.	Impact of Decisions on Co-workers or Company Resul	How do the decisions an employee makes impact the results of co-workers, clients or the company?
Evaluating Information to Determine Compliance wit	Using relevant information and individual judgment to determine whether events or processes comply with laws, regulations, or standards.	Sounds, Noise Levels Are Distracting or Uncomforta	How often does this job require working exposed to sounds and noise levels that are distracting or uncomfortable?
Coaching and Developing Others	Identifying the developmental needs of others and coaching, mentoring, or otherwise helping others to improve their knowledge or skills.	Frequency of Conflict Situations	How often are there conflict situations the employee has to face in this job?
Training and Teaching Others	Identifying the educational needs of others, developing formal educational or training programs or classes, and teaching or instructing others.	Frequency of Decision Making	How frequently is the worker required to make decisions that affect other people, the financial resources, and/or the image and reputation of the organization?
Assisting and Caring for Others	Providing personal assistance, medical attention, emotional support, or other personal care to others such as coworkers, customers, or patients.	Degree of Automation	How automated is the job?
		Responsible for Others' Health and Safety	How much responsibility is there for the health and safety of others in this job?
Inspecting Equipment, Structures, or Material	Inspecting equipment, structures, or materials to identify the cause of errors or other problems or defects.	Coordinate or Lead Others	How important is it to coordinate or lead others in accomplishing work activities in this job?
Performing for or Working Directly with the Public	Performing for people or dealing directly with the public. This includes serving customers in restaurants and stores, and receiving clients or guests.	Physical Proximity	To what extent does this job require the worker to perform job tasks in close physical proximity to other people?
Staffing Organizational Units	Recruiting, interviewing, selecting, hiring, and promoting employees in an organization.	Deal With Unpleasant or Angry People	How frequently does the worker have to deal with unpleasant, angry, or discourteous individuals as part of the job requirements?
Controlling Machines and Processes	Using either control mechanisms or direct physical activity to operate machines or processes (not including computers or vehicles).	Spend Time Standing	How much does this job require standing?
		Public Speaking	How often do you have to perform public speaking in this job?
Drafting, Laying Out, and Specifying Technical Dev	Providing documentation, detailed instructions, drawings, or specifications to tell others about how devices, parts, equipment, or structures are to be fabricated, constructed, assembled, modified, maintained, or used.	Spend Time Making Repetitive Motions	How much does this job require making repetitive motions?
		Consequence of Error	How serious would the result usually be if the worker made a mistake that was not readily correctable?
Handling and Moving Objects	Using hands and arms in handling, installing, positioning, and moving materials, and manipulating things.	Spend Time Using Your Hands to Handle, Control, or	How much does this job require using your hands to handle, control, or feel objects, tools or controls?
Performing General Physical Activities	Performing physical activities that require considerable use of your arms and legs and moving your whole body, such as climbing, lifting, balancing, walking, stooping, and handling of materials.	Outdoors, Exposed to Weather	How often does this job require working outdoors, exposed to all weather conditions?
		Spend Time Walking and Running	How much does this job require walking and running?
Operating Vehicles, Mechanized Devices, or Equipme	Running, maneuvering, navigating, or driving vehicles or mechanized equipment, such as forklifts, passenger vehicles, aircraft, or water craft.	In an Enclosed Vehicle or Equipment	How often does this job require working in a closed vehicle or equipment (e.g., car)?
		Deal With Physically Aggressive People	How frequently does this job require the worker to deal with physical aggression of violent individuals?
Repairing and Maintaining Electronic Equipment	Servicing, repairing, calibrating, regulating, fine-tuning, or testing machines, devices, and equipment that operate primarily on the basis of electrical or electronic (not mechanical) principles.	Indoors, Not Environmentally Controlled	How often does this job require working indoors in non-controlled environmental conditions (e.g., warehouse without heat)?
		Outdoors, Under Cover	How often does this job require working outdoors, under cover (e.g., structure with roof but no walls)?

Very Hot or Cold Temperatures	How often does this job require working in very hot (above 90 F degrees) or very cold (below 32 F degrees) temperatures?
Spend Time Bending or Twisting the Body	How much does this job require bending or twisting your body?
Cramped Work Space, Awkward Positions	How often does this job require working in cramped work spaces that requires getting into awkward positions?
Pace Determined by Speed of Equipment	How important is it to this job that the pace is determined by the speed of equipment or machinery? (This does not refer to keeping busy at all times on this job.)
Extremely Bright or Inadequate Lighting	How often does this job require working in extremely bright or inadequate lighting conditions?
Wear Common Protective or Safety Equipment such as	How much does this job require wearing common protective or safety equipment such as safety shoes, glasses, gloves, hard hats or live jackets?
Spend Time Kneeling, Crouching, Stooping, or Crawl	How much does this job require kneeling, crouching, stooping or crawling?
Exposed to Contaminants	How often does this job require working exposed to contaminants (such as pollutants, gases, dust or odors)?
Exposed to Hazardous Equipment	How often does this job require exposure to hazardous equipment?
Exposed to Hazardous Conditions	How often does this job require exposure to hazardous conditions?
Exposed to Minor Burns, Cuts, Bites, or Stings	How often does this job require exposure to minor burns, cuts, bites, or stings?
Spend Time Climbing Ladders, Scaffolds, or Poles	How much does this job require climbing ladders, scaffolds, or poles?
Wear Specialized Protective or Safety Equipment su	How much does this job require wearing specialized protective or safety equipment such as breathing apparatus, safety harness, full protection suits, or radiation protection?
Exposed to High Places	How often does this job require exposure to high places?
Exposed to Radiation	How often does this job require exposure to radiation?
Spend Time Keeping or Regaining Balance	How much does this job require keeping or regaining your balance?
Exposed to Whole Body Vibration	How often does this job require exposure to whole body vibration (e.g., operate a jackhammer)?
In an Open Vehicle or Equipment	How often does this job require working in an open vehicle or equipment (e.g., tractor)?
Exposed to Disease or Infections	How often does this job require exposure to disease/infections?

Job Zone Component	Job Zone Component Definitions
Title	Job Zone Four: Considerable Preparation Needed
Overall Experience	A minimum of two to four years of work-related skill, knowledge, or experience is needed for these occupations. For example, an accountant must complete four years of college and work for several years in accounting to be considered qualified.
Job Training	Employees in these occupations usually need several years of work-related experience, on-the-job training, and/or vocational training.
Job Zone Examples	Many of these occupations involve coordinating, supervising, managing, or training others. Examples include accountants, chefs and head cooks, computer programmers, historians, pharmacists, and police detectives.
SVP Range	(7.0 to < 8.0)
Education	Most of these occupations require a four - year bachelor's degree, but some do not.

Work_Styles	Work_Styles Definitions
Initiative	Job requires a willingness to take on responsibilities and challenges.
Achievement/Effort	Job requires establishing and maintaining personally challenging achievement goals and exerting effort toward mastering tasks.
Integrity	Job requires being honest and ethical.
Persistence	Job requires persistence in the face of obstacles.
Attention to Detail	Job requires being careful about detail and thorough in completing work tasks.
Innovation	Job requires creativity and alternative thinking to develop new ideas for and answers to work-related problems.
Dependability	Job requires being reliable, responsible, and dependable, and fulfilling obligations.

Leadership	Job requires a willingness to lead, take charge, and offer opinions and direction.
Stress Tolerance	Job requires accepting criticism and dealing calmly and effectively with high stress situations.
Adaptability/Flexibility	Job requires being open to change (positive or negative) and to considerable variety in the workplace.
Analytical Thinking	Job requires analyzing information and using logic to address work-related issues and problems.
Self Control	Job requires maintaining composure, keeping emotions in check, controlling anger, and avoiding aggressive behavior, even in very difficult situations.
Cooperation	Job requires being pleasant with others on the job and displaying a good-natured, cooperative attitude.
Independence	Job requires developing one's own ways of doing things, guiding oneself with little or no supervision, and depending on oneself to get things done.
Social Orientation	Job requires preferring to work with others rather than alone, and being personally connected with others on the job.
Concern for Others	Job requires being sensitive to others' needs and feelings and being understanding and helpful on the job.

19-3031.01 - Educational Psychologists

Investigate processes of learning and teaching and develop psychological principles and techniques applicable to educational problems.

Tasks

1) Assess an individual child's needs, limitations, and potential, using observation, review of school records, and consultation with parents and school personnel.

2) Compile and interpret students' test results, along with information from teachers and parents, in order to diagnose conditions, and to help assess eligibility for special services.

3) Promote an understanding of child development and its relationship to learning and behavior.

4) Refer students and their families to appropriate community agencies for medical, vocational, or social services.

5) Attend workshops, seminars, and/or professional meetings in order to remain informed of new developments in school psychology.

6) Select, administer, and score psychological tests.

7) Develop individualized educational plans in collaboration with teachers and other staff members.

8) Collaborate with other educational professionals to develop teaching strategies and school programs.

9) Report any pertinent information to the proper authorities in cases of child endangerment, neglect, or abuse.

10) Serve as a resource to help families and schools deal with crises, such as separation and loss.

11) Provide educational programs on topics such as classroom management, teaching strategies, or parenting skills.

12) Maintain student records, including special education reports, confidential records, records of services provided, and behavioral data.

13) Counsel children and families to help solve conflicts and problems in learning and adjustment.

14) Collect and analyze data to evaluate the effectiveness of academic programs and other services, such as behavioral management systems.

15) Initiate and direct efforts to foster tolerance, understanding, and appreciation of diversity in school communities.

16) Design classes and programs to meet the needs of special students.

17) Conduct research to generate new knowledge that can be used to address learning and behavior issues.

Knowledge	Knowledge Definitions
Psychology	Knowledge of human behavior and performance; individual differences in ability, personality, and interests; learning and motivation; psychological research methods; and the assessment and treatment of behavioral and affective disorders.

Therapy and Counseling	Knowledge of principles, methods, and procedures for diagnosis, treatment, and rehabilitation of physical and mental dysfunctions, and for career counseling and guidance.
Education and Training	Knowledge of principles and methods for curriculum and training design, teaching and instruction for individuals and groups, and the measurement of training effects.
English Language	Knowledge of the structure and content of the English language including the meaning and spelling of words, rules of composition, and grammar.
Customer and Personal Service	Knowledge of principles and processes for providing customer and personal services. This includes customer needs assessment, meeting quality standards for services, and evaluation of customer satisfaction.
Sociology and Anthropology	Knowledge of group behavior and dynamics, societal trends and influences, human migrations, ethnicity, cultures and their history and origins.
Mathematics	Knowledge of arithmetic, algebra, geometry, calculus, statistics, and their applications.
Clerical	Knowledge of administrative and clerical procedures and systems such as word processing, managing files and records, stenography and transcription, designing forms, and other office procedures and terminology.
Law and Government	Knowledge of laws, legal codes, court procedures, precedents, government regulations, executive orders, agency rules, and the democratic political process.
Computers and Electronics	Knowledge of circuit boards, processors, chips, electronic equipment, and computer hardware and software, including applications and programming.
Philosophy and Theology	Knowledge of different philosophical systems and religions. This includes their basic principles, values, ethics, ways of thinking, customs, practices, and their impact on human culture.
Administration and Management	Knowledge of business and management principles involved in strategic planning, resource allocation, human resources modeling, leadership technique, production methods, and coordination of people and resources.
Medicine and Dentistry	Knowledge of the information and techniques needed to diagnose and treat human injuries, diseases, and deformities. This includes symptoms, treatment alternatives, drug properties and interactions, and preventive health-care measures.
Public Safety and Security	Knowledge of relevant equipment, policies, procedures, and strategies to promote effective local, state, or national security operations for the protection of people, data, property, and institutions.
Communications and Media	Knowledge of media production, communication, and dissemination techniques and methods. This includes alternative ways to inform and entertain via written, oral, and visual media.
Biology	Knowledge of plant and animal organisms, their tissues, cells, functions, interdependencies, and interactions with each other and the environment.
Foreign Language	Knowledge of the structure and content of a foreign (non-English) language including the meaning and spelling of words, rules of composition and grammar, and pronunciation.
Personnel and Human Resources	Knowledge of principles and procedures for personnel recruitment, selection, training, compensation and benefits, labor relations and negotiation, and personnel information systems.
History and Archeology	Knowledge of historical events and their causes, indicators, and effects on civilizations and cultures.
Transportation	Knowledge of principles and methods for moving people or goods by air, rail, sea, or road, including the relative costs and benefits.
Geography	Knowledge of principles and methods for describing the features of land, sea, and air masses, including their physical characteristics, locations, interrelationships, and distribution of plant, animal, and human life.
Telecommunications	Knowledge of transmission, broadcasting, switching, control, and operation of telecommunications systems.
Fine Arts	Knowledge of the theory and techniques required to compose, produce, and perform works of music, dance, visual arts, drama, and sculpture.
Production and Processing	Knowledge of raw materials, production processes, quality control, costs, and other techniques for maximizing the effective manufacture and distribution of goods.
Sales and Marketing	Knowledge of principles and methods for showing, promoting, and selling products or services. This includes marketing strategy and tactics, product demonstration, sales techniques, and sales control systems.
Chemistry	Knowledge of the chemical composition, structure, and properties of substances and of the chemical processes and transformations that they undergo. This includes uses of chemicals and their interactions, danger signs, production techniques, and disposal methods.
Engineering and Technology	Knowledge of the practical application of engineering science and technology. This includes applying principles, techniques, procedures, and equipment to the design and production of various goods and services.
Design	Knowledge of design techniques, tools, and principles involved in production of precision technical plans, blueprints, drawings, and models.
Economics and Accounting	Knowledge of economic and accounting principles and practices, the financial markets, banking and the analysis and reporting of financial data.
Mechanical	Knowledge of machines and tools, including their designs, uses, repair, and maintenance.
Building and Construction	Knowledge of materials, methods, and the tools involved in the construction or repair of houses, buildings, or other structures such as highways and roads.
Physics	Knowledge and prediction of physical principles, laws, their interrelationships, and applications to understanding fluid, material, and atmospheric dynamics, and mechanical, electrical, atomic and sub- atomic structures and processes.
Food Production	Knowledge of techniques and equipment for planting, growing, and harvesting food products (both plant and animal) for consumption, including storage/handling techniques.

Skills	Skills Definitions
Active Listening	Giving full attention to what other people are saying, taking time to understand the points being made, asking questions as appropriate, and not interrupting at inappropriate times.
Reading Comprehension	Understanding written sentences and paragraphs in work related documents.
Writing	Communicating effectively in writing as appropriate for the needs of the audience.
Social Perceptiveness	Being aware of others' reactions and understanding why they react as they do.
Learning Strategies	Selecting and using training/instructional methods and procedures appropriate for the situation when learning or teaching new things.
Speaking	Talking to others to convey information effectively.
Time Management	Managing one's own time and the time of others.
Critical Thinking	Using logic and reasoning to identify the strengths and weaknesses of alternative solutions, conclusions or approaches to problems.
Active Learning	Understanding the implications of new information for both current and future problem-solving and decision-making.
Negotiation	Bringing others together and trying to reconcile differences.
Coordination	Adjusting actions in relation to others' actions.
Complex Problem Solving	Identifying complex problems and reviewing related information to develop and evaluate options and implement solutions.
Judgment and Decision Making	Considering the relative costs and benefits of potential actions to choose the most appropriate one.
Service Orientation	Actively looking for ways to help people.
Monitoring	Monitoring/Assessing performance of yourself, other individuals, or organizations to make improvements or take corrective action.
Persuasion	Persuading others to change their minds or behavior.
Instructing	Teaching others how to do something.
Equipment Selection	Determining the kind of tools and equipment needed to do a job.
Mathematics	Using mathematics to solve problems.
Science	Using scientific rules and methods to solve problems.
Management of Personnel Resources	Motivating, developing, and directing people as they work, identifying the best people for the job.
Systems Evaluation	Identifying measures or indicators of system performance and the actions needed to improve or correct performance, relative to the goals of the system.
Systems Analysis	Determining how a system should work and how changes in conditions, operations, and the environment will affect outcomes.

Quality Control Analysis	Conducting tests and inspections of products, services, or processes to evaluate quality or performance.
Technology Design	Generating or adapting equipment and technology to serve user needs.
Operations Analysis	Analyzing needs and product requirements to create a design.
Troubleshooting	Determining causes of operating errors and deciding what to do about it.
Management of Material Resources	Obtaining and seeing to the appropriate use of equipment, facilities, and materials needed to do certain work.
Management of Financial Resources	Determining how money will be spent to get the work done, and accounting for these expenditures.
Repairing	Repairing machines or systems using the needed tools.
Installation	Installing equipment, machines, wiring, or programs to meet specifications.
Operation and Control	Controlling operations of equipment or systems.
Equipment Maintenance	Performing routine maintenance on equipment and determining when and what kind of maintenance is needed.
Operation Monitoring	Watching gauges, dials, or other indicators to make sure a machine is working properly.
Programming	Writing computer programs for various purposes.

Ability	**Ability Definitions**
Oral Expression	The ability to communicate information and ideas in speaking so others will understand.
Oral Comprehension	The ability to listen to and understand information and ideas presented through spoken words and sentences.
Written Comprehension	The ability to read and understand information and ideas presented in writing.
Problem Sensitivity	The ability to tell when something is wrong or is likely to go wrong. It does not involve solving the problem, only recognizing there is a problem.
Speech Clarity	The ability to speak clearly so others can understand you.
Inductive Reasoning	The ability to combine pieces of information to form general rules or conclusions (includes finding a relationship among seemingly unrelated events).
Speech Recognition	The ability to identify and understand the speech of another person.
Written Expression	The ability to communicate information and ideas in writing so others will understand.
Deductive Reasoning	The ability to apply general rules to specific problems to produce answers that make sense.
Near Vision	The ability to see details at close range (within a few feet of the observer).
Information Ordering	The ability to arrange things or actions in a certain order or pattern according to a specific rule or set of rules (e.g., patterns of numbers, letters, words, pictures, mathematical operations).
Originality	The ability to come up with unusual or clever ideas about a given topic or situation, or to develop creative ways to solve a problem.
Category Flexibility	The ability to generate or use different sets of rules for combining or grouping things in different ways.
Fluency of Ideas	The ability to come up with a number of ideas about a topic (the number of ideas is important, not their quality, correctness, or creativity).
Selective Attention	The ability to concentrate on a task over a period of time without being distracted.
Mathematical Reasoning	The ability to choose the right mathematical methods or formulas to solve a problem.
Flexibility of Closure	The ability to identify or detect a known pattern (a figure, object, word, or sound) that is hidden in other distracting material.
Speed of Closure	The ability to quickly make sense of, combine, and organize information into meaningful patterns.
Time Sharing	The ability to shift back and forth between two or more activities or sources of information (such as speech, sounds, touch, or other sources).
Number Facility	The ability to add, subtract, multiply, or divide quickly and correctly.
Memorization	The ability to remember information such as words, numbers, pictures, and procedures.
Perceptual Speed	The ability to quickly and accurately compare similarities and differences among sets of letters, numbers, objects, pictures, or patterns. The things to be compared may be presented at the same time or one after the other. This ability also includes comparing a presented object with a remembered object.
Auditory Attention	The ability to focus on a single source of sound in the presence of other distracting sounds.

Far Vision	The ability to see details at a distance.
Finger Dexterity	The ability to make precisely coordinated movements of the fingers of one or both hands to grasp, manipulate, or assemble very small objects.
Visual Color Discrimination	The ability to match or detect differences between colors, including shades of color and brightness.
Visualization	The ability to imagine how something will look after it is moved around or when its parts are moved or rearranged.
Hearing Sensitivity	The ability to detect or tell the differences between sounds that vary in pitch and loudness.
Depth Perception	The ability to judge which of several objects is closer or farther away from you, or to judge the distance between you and an object.
Trunk Strength	The ability to use your abdominal and lower back muscles to support part of the body repeatedly or continuously over time without 'giving out' or fatiguing.
Manual Dexterity	The ability to quickly move your hand, your hand together with your arm, or your two hands to grasp, manipulate, or assemble objects.
Glare Sensitivity	The ability to see objects in the presence of glare or bright lighting.
Peripheral Vision	The ability to see objects or movement of objects to one's side when the eyes are looking ahead.
Night Vision	The ability to see under low light conditions.
Stamina	The ability to exert yourself physically over long periods of time without getting winded or out of breath.
Control Precision	The ability to quickly and repeatedly adjust the controls of a machine or a vehicle to exact positions.
Extent Flexibility	The ability to bend, stretch, twist, or reach with your body, arms, and/or legs.
Arm-Hand Steadiness	The ability to keep your hand and arm steady while moving your arm or while holding your arm and hand in one position.
Sound Localization	The ability to tell the direction from which a sound originated.
Reaction Time	The ability to quickly respond (with the hand, finger, or foot) to a signal (sound, light, picture) when it appears.
Gross Body Equilibrium	The ability to keep or regain your body balance or stay upright when in an unstable position.
Dynamic Flexibility	The ability to quickly and repeatedly bend, stretch, twist, or reach out with your body, arms, and/or legs.
Response Orientation	The ability to choose quickly between two or more movements in response to two or more different signals (lights, sounds, pictures). It includes the speed with which the correct response is started with the hand, foot, or other body part.
Wrist-Finger Speed	The ability to make fast, simple, repeated movements of the fingers, hands, and wrists.
Speed of Limb Movement	The ability to quickly move the arms and legs.
Static Strength	The ability to exert maximum muscle force to lift, push, pull, or carry objects.
Explosive Strength	The ability to use short bursts of muscle force to propel oneself (as in jumping or sprinting), or to throw an object.
Dynamic Strength	The ability to exert muscle force repeatedly or continuously over time. This involves muscular endurance and resistance to muscle fatigue.
Spatial Orientation	The ability to know your location in relation to the environment or to know where other objects are in relation to you.
Rate Control	The ability to time your movements or the movement of a piece of equipment in anticipation of changes in the speed and/or direction of a moving object or scene.
Multilimb Coordination	The ability to coordinate two or more limbs (for example, two arms, two legs, or one leg and one arm) while sitting, standing, or lying down. It does not involve performing the activities while the whole body is in motion.
Gross Body Coordination	The ability to coordinate the movement of your arms, legs, and torso together when the whole body is in motion.

Work_Activity	**Work_Activity Definitions**
Getting Information	Observing, receiving, and otherwise obtaining information from all relevant sources.
Interpreting the Meaning of Information for Others	Translating or explaining what information means and how it can be used.
Making Decisions and Solving Problems	Analyzing information and evaluating results to choose the best solution and solve problems.
Establishing and Maintaining Interpersonal Relatio	Developing constructive and cooperative working relationships with others, and maintaining them over time.

Evaluating Information to Determine Compliance wit	Using relevant information and individual judgment to determine whether events or processes comply with laws, regulations, or standards.
Analyzing Data or Information	Identifying the underlying principles, reasons, or facts of information by breaking down information or data into separate parts.
Communicating with Supervisors, Peers, or Subordin	Providing information to supervisors, co-workers, and subordinates by telephone, in written form, e-mail, or in person.
Updating and Using Relevant Knowledge	Keeping up-to-date technically and applying new knowledge to your job.
Processing Information	Compiling, coding, categorizing, calculating, tabulating, auditing, or verifying information or data.
Identifying Objects, Actions, and Events	Identifying information by categorizing, estimating, recognizing differences or similarities, and detecting changes in circumstances or events.
Assisting and Caring for Others	Providing personal assistance, medical attention, emotional support, or other personal care to others such as coworkers, customers, or patients.
Organizing, Planning, and Prioritizing Work	Developing specific goals and plans to prioritize, organize, and accomplish your work.
Documenting/Recording Information	Entering, transcribing, recording, storing, or maintaining information in written or electronic/magnetic form.
Communicating with Persons Outside Organization	Communicating with people outside the organization, representing the organization to customers, the public, government, and other external sources. This information can be exchanged in person, in writing, or by telephone or e-mail.
Performing for or Working Directly with the Public	Performing for people or dealing directly with the public. This includes serving customers in restaurants and stores, and receiving clients or guests.
Provide Consultation and Advice to Others	Providing guidance and expert advice to management or other groups on technical, systems-, or process-related topics.
Monitor Processes, Materials, or Surroundings	Monitoring and reviewing information from materials, events, or the environment, to detect or assess problems.
Resolving Conflicts and Negotiating with Others	Handling complaints, settling disputes, and resolving grievances and conflicts, or otherwise negotiating with others.
Interacting With Computers	Using computers and computer systems (including hardware and software) to program, write software, set up functions, enter data, or process information.
Developing and Building Teams	Encouraging and building mutual trust, respect, and cooperation among team members.
Judging the Qualities of Things, Services, or Peop	Assessing the value, importance, or quality of things or people.
Developing Objectives and Strategies	Establishing long-range objectives and specifying the strategies and actions to achieve them.
Training and Teaching Others	Identifying the educational needs of others, developing formal educational or training programs or classes, and teaching or instructing others.
Coordinating the Work and Activities of Others	Getting members of a group to work together to accomplish tasks.
Scheduling Work and Activities	Scheduling events, programs, and activities, as well as the work of others.
Thinking Creatively	Developing, designing, or creating new applications, ideas, relationships, systems, or products, including artistic contributions.
Performing Administrative Activities	Performing day-to-day administrative tasks such as maintaining information files and processing paperwork.
Coaching and Developing Others	Identifying the developmental needs of others and coaching, mentoring, or otherwise helping others to improve their knowledge or skills.
Selling or Influencing Others	Convincing others to buy merchandise/goods or to otherwise change their minds or actions.
Estimating the Quantifiable Characteristics of Pro	Estimating sizes, distances, and quantities; or determining time, costs, resources, or materials needed to perform a work activity.
Guiding, Directing, and Motivating Subordinates	Providing guidance and direction to subordinates, including setting performance standards and monitoring performance.
Handling and Moving Objects	Using hands and arms in handling, installing, positioning, and moving materials, and manipulating things.
Performing General Physical Activities	Performing physical activities that require considerable use of your arms and legs and moving your whole body, such as climbing, lifting, balancing, walking, stooping, and handling of materials.
Inspecting Equipment, Structures, or Material	Inspecting equipment, structures, or materials to identify the cause of errors or other problems or defects.
Monitoring and Controlling Resources	Monitoring and controlling resources and overseeing the spending of money.

Operating Vehicles, Mechanized Devices, or Equipme	Running, maneuvering, navigating, or driving vehicles or mechanized equipment, such as forklifts, passenger vehicles, aircraft, or water craft.
Drafting, Laying Out, and Specifying Technical Dev	Providing documentation, detailed instructions, drawings, or specifications to tell others about how devices, parts, equipment, or structures are to be fabricated, constructed, assembled, modified, maintained, or used.
Controlling Machines and Processes	Using either control mechanisms or direct physical activity to operate machines or processes (not including computers or vehicles).
Staffing Organizational Units	Recruiting, interviewing, selecting, hiring, and promoting employees in an organization.
Repairing and Maintaining Electronic Equipment	Servicing, repairing, calibrating, regulating, fine-tuning, or testing machines, devices, and equipment that operate primarily on the basis of electrical or electronic (not mechanical) principles.
Repairing and Maintaining Mechanical Equipment	Servicing, repairing, adjusting, and testing machines, devices, moving parts, and equipment that operate primarily on the basis of mechanical (not electronic) principles.

Work_Context	Work_Context Definitions
Face-to-Face Discussions	How often do you have to have face-to-face discussions with individuals or teams in this job?
Work With Work Group or Team	How important is it to work with others in a group or team in this job?
Contact With Others	How much does this job require the worker to be in contact with others (face-to-face, by telephone, or otherwise) in order to perform it?
Telephone	How often do you have telephone conversations in this job?
Structured versus Unstructured Work	To what extent is this job structured for the worker, rather than allowing the worker to determine tasks, priorities, and goals?
Freedom to Make Decisions	How much decision making freedom, without supervision, does the job offer?
Electronic Mail	How often do you use electronic mail in this job?
Indoors, Environmentally Controlled	How often does this job require working indoors in environmentally controlled conditions?
Spend Time Sitting	How much does this job require sitting?
Letters and Memos	How often does the job require written letters and memos?
Importance of Being Exact or Accurate	How important is being very exact or highly accurate in performing this job?
Time Pressure	How often does this job require the worker to meet strict deadlines?
Impact of Decisions on Co-workers or Company Resul	How do the decisions an employee makes impact the results of co-workers, clients or the company?
Frequency of Decision Making	How frequently is the worker required to make decisions that affect other people, the financial resources, and/or the image and reputation of the organization?
Coordinate or Lead Others	How important is it to coordinate or lead others in accomplishing work activities in this job?
Deal With External Customers	How important is it to work with external customers or the public in this job?
Frequency of Conflict Situations	How often are there conflict situations the employee has to face in this job?
Physical Proximity	To what extent does this job require the worker to perform job tasks in close physical proximity to other people?
Importance of Repeating Same Tasks	How important is repeating the same physical activities (e.g., key entry) or mental activities (e.g., checking entries in a ledger) over and over, without stopping, to performing this job?
Deal With Unpleasant or Angry People	How frequently does the worker have to deal with unpleasant, angry, or discourteous individuals as part of the job requirements?
Consequence of Error	How serious would the result usually be if the worker made a mistake that was not readily correctable?
Exposed to Disease or Infections	How often does this job require exposure to disease/infections?
Sounds, Noise Levels Are Distracting or Uncomforta	How often does this job require working exposed to sounds and noise levels that are distracting or uncomfortable?
Public Speaking	How often do you have to perform public speaking in this job?
Spend Time Making Repetitive Motions	How much does this job require making repetitive motions?
Responsibility for Outcomes and Results	How responsible is the worker for work outcomes and results of other workers?
Deal With Physically Aggressive People	How frequently does this job require the worker to deal with physical aggression of violent individuals?

Spend Time Using Your Hands to Handle, Control, or	How much does this job require using your hands to handle, control, or feel objects, tools or controls?
Level of Competition	To what extent does this job require the worker to compete or to be aware of competitive pressures?
Indoors, Not Environmentally Controlled	How often does this job require working indoors in non-controlled environmental conditions (e.g., warehouse without heat)?
Responsible for Others' Health and Safety	How much responsibility is there for the health and safety of others in this job?
Spend Time Walking and Running	How much does this job require walking and running?
Spend Time Standing	How much does this job require standing?
In an Enclosed Vehicle or Equipment	How often does this job require working in a closed vehicle or equipment (e.g., car)?
Exposed to Contaminants	How often does this job require working exposed to contaminants (such as pollutants, gases, dust or odors)?
Degree of Automation	How automated is the job?
Exposed to Minor Burns, Cuts, Bites, or Stings	How often does this job require exposure to minor burns, cuts, bites, or stings?
Spend Time Bending or Twisting the Body	How much does this job require bending or twisting your body?
Very Hot or Cold Temperatures	How often does this job require working in very hot (above 90 F degrees) or very cold (below 32 F degrees) temperatures?
Extremely Bright or Inadequate Lighting	How often does this job require working in extremely bright or inadequate lighting conditions?
Cramped Work Space, Awkward Positions	How often does this job require working in cramped work spaces that requires getting into awkward positions?
Spend Time Kneeling, Crouching, Stooping, or Crawl	How much does this job require kneeling, crouching, stooping or crawling?
Spend Time Keeping or Regaining Balance	How much does this job require keeping or regaining your balance?
Outdoors, Exposed to Weather	How often does this job require working outdoors, exposed to all weather conditions?
Outdoors, Under Cover	How often does this job require working outdoors, under cover (e.g., structure with roof but no walls)?
Exposed to Hazardous Equipment	How often does this job require exposure to hazardous equipment?
Exposed to Radiation	How often does this job require exposure to radiation?
Spend Time Climbing Ladders, Scaffolds, or Poles	How much does this job require climbing ladders, scaffolds, or poles?
Exposed to Hazardous Conditions	How often does this job require exposure to hazardous conditions?
Wear Common Protective or Safety Equipment such as	How much does this job require wearing common protective or safety equipment such as safety shoes, glasses, gloves, hard hats or live jackets?
Exposed to High Places	How often does this job require exposure to high places?
Wear Specialized Protective or Safety Equipment su	How much does this job require wearing specialized protective or safety equipment such as breathing apparatus, safety harness, full protection suits, or radiation protection?
In an Open Vehicle or Equipment	How often does this job require working in an open vehicle or equipment (e.g., tractor)?
Pace Determined by Speed of Equipment	How important is it to this job that the pace is determined by the speed of equipment or machinery? (This does not refer to keeping busy at all times on this job.)
Exposed to Whole Body Vibration	How often does this job require exposure to whole body vibration (e.g., operate a jackhammer)?

Job Zone Component	Job Zone Component Definitions
Title	Job Zone Five: Extensive Preparation Needed
Overall Experience	Extensive skill, knowledge, and experience are needed for these occupations. Many require more than five years of experience. For example, surgeons must complete four years of college and an additional five to seven years of specialized medical training to be able to do their job.
Job Training	Employees may need some on-the-job training, but most of these occupations assume that the person will already have the required skills, knowledge, work-related experience, and/or training.
Job Zone Examples	These occupations often involve coordinating, training, supervising, or managing the activities of others to accomplish goals. Very advanced communication and organizational skills are required. Examples include athletic trainers, lawyers, managing editors, physicists, social psychologists, and surgeons.

SVP Range	(8.0 and above)
Education	A bachelor's degree is the minimum formal education required for these occupations. However, many also require graduate school. For example, they may require a master's degree, and some require a Ph.D., M.D., or J.D. (law degree).

Work_Styles	Work_Styles Definitions
Cooperation	Job requires being pleasant with others on the job and displaying a good-natured, cooperative attitude.
Concern for Others	Job requires being sensitive to others' needs and feelings and being understanding and helpful on the job.
Integrity	Job requires being honest and ethical.
Dependability	Job requires being reliable, responsible, and dependable, and fulfilling obligations.
Self Control	Job requires maintaining composure, keeping emotions in check, controlling anger, and avoiding aggressive behavior, even in very difficult situations.
Analytical Thinking	Job requires analyzing information and using logic to address work-related issues and problems.
Social Orientation	Job requires preferring to work with others rather than alone, and being personally connected with others on the job.
Independence	Job requires developing one's own ways of doing things, guiding oneself with little or no supervision, and depending on oneself to get things done.
Attention to Detail	Job requires being careful about detail and thorough in completing work tasks.
Stress Tolerance	Job requires accepting criticism and dealing calmly and effectively with high stress situations.
Adaptability/Flexibility	Job requires being open to change (positive or negative) and to considerable variety in the workplace.
Persistence	Job requires persistence in the face of obstacles.
Initiative	Job requires a willingness to take on responsibilities and challenges.
Leadership	Job requires a willingness to lead, take charge, and offer opinions and direction.
Achievement/Effort	Job requires establishing and maintaining personally challenging achievement goals and exerting effort toward mastering tasks.
Innovation	Job requires creativity and alternative thinking to develop new ideas for and answers to work-related problems.

19-3041.00 - Sociologists

Study human society and social behavior by examining the groups and social institutions that people form, as well as various social, religious, political, and business organizations. May study the behavior and interaction of groups, trace their origin and growth, and analyze the influence of group activities on individual members.

Tasks

1) Develop problem intervention procedures, utilizing techniques such as interviews, consultations, role playing, and participant observation of group interactions.

2) Observe group interactions and role affiliations to collect data, identify problems, evaluate progress, and determine the need for additional change.

3) Teach sociology.

4) Collaborate with research workers in other disciplines.

5) Analyze and interpret data in order to increase the understanding of human social behavior.

6) Plan and conduct research to develop and test theories about societal issues such as crime, group relations, poverty, and aging.

7) Collect data about the attitudes, values, and behaviors of people in groups, using observation, interviews, and review of documents.

8) Direct work of statistical clerks, statisticians, and others who compile and evaluate research data.

9) Consult with and advise individuals such as administrators, social workers, and legislators regarding social issues and policies, as well as the implications of research findings.

10) Develop, implement, and evaluate methods of data collection, such as questionnaires or interviews.

11) Prepare publications and reports containing research findings.

Knowledge	Knowledge Definitions
Sociology and Anthropology	Knowledge of group behavior and dynamics, societal trends and influences, human migrations, ethnicity, cultures and their history and origins.
English Language	Knowledge of the structure and content of the English language including the meaning and spelling of words, rules of composition, and grammar.
Mathematics	Knowledge of arithmetic, algebra, geometry, calculus, statistics, and their applications.
Psychology	Knowledge of human behavior and performance; individual differences in ability, personality, and interests; learning and motivation; psychological research methods; and the assessment and treatment of behavioral and affective disorders.
Education and Training	Knowledge of principles and methods for curriculum and training design, teaching and instruction for individuals and groups, and the measurement of training effects.
Computers and Electronics	Knowledge of circuit boards, processors, chips, electronic equipment, and computer hardware and software, including applications and programming.
Law and Government	Knowledge of laws, legal codes, court procedures, precedents, government regulations, executive orders, agency rules, and the democratic political process.
Philosophy and Theology	Knowledge of different philosophical systems and religions. This includes their basic principles, values, ethics, ways of thinking, customs, practices, and their impact on human culture.
Communications and Media	Knowledge of media production, communication, and dissemination techniques and methods. This includes alternative ways to inform and entertain via written, oral, and visual media.
Administration and Management	Knowledge of business and management principles involved in strategic planning, resource allocation, human resources modeling, leadership technique, production methods, and coordination of people and resources.
History and Archeology	Knowledge of historical events and their causes, indicators, and effects on civilizations and cultures.
Geography	Knowledge of principles and methods for describing the features of land, sea, and air masses, including their physical characteristics, locations, interrelationships, and distribution of plant, animal, and human life.
Clerical	Knowledge of administrative and clerical procedures and systems such as word processing, managing files and records, stenography and transcription, designing forms, and other office procedures and terminology.
Customer and Personal Service	Knowledge of principles and processes for providing customer and personal services. This includes customer needs assessment, meeting quality standards for services, and evaluation of customer satisfaction.
Personnel and Human Resources	Knowledge of principles and procedures for personnel recruitment, selection, training, compensation and benefits, labor relations and negotiation, and personnel information systems.
Economics and Accounting	Knowledge of economic and accounting principles and practices, the financial markets, banking and the analysis and reporting of financial data.
Foreign Language	Knowledge of the structure and content of a foreign (non-English) language including the meaning and spelling of words, rules of composition and grammar, and pronunciation.
Sales and Marketing	Knowledge of principles and methods for showing, promoting, and selling products or services. This includes marketing strategy and tactics, product demonstration, sales techniques, and sales control systems.
Therapy and Counseling	Knowledge of principles, methods, and procedures for diagnosis, treatment, and rehabilitation of physical and mental dysfunctions, and for career counseling and guidance.
Biology	Knowledge of plant and animal organisms, their tissues, cells, functions, interdependencies, and interactions with each other and the environment.
Public Safety and Security	Knowledge of relevant equipment, policies, procedures, and strategies to promote effective local, state, or national security operations for the protection of people, data, property, and institutions.
Medicine and Dentistry	Knowledge of the information and techniques needed to diagnose and treat human injuries, diseases, and deformities. This includes symptoms, treatment alternatives, drug properties and interactions, and preventive health-care measures.
Telecommunications	Knowledge of transmission, broadcasting, switching, control, and operation of telecommunications systems.
Fine Arts	Knowledge of the theory and techniques required to compose, produce, and perform works of music, dance, visual arts, drama, and sculpture.
Production and Processing	Knowledge of raw materials, production processes, quality control, costs, and other techniques for maximizing the effective manufacture and distribution of goods.
Transportation	Knowledge of principles and methods for moving people or goods by air, rail, sea, or road, including the relative costs and benefits.
Engineering and Technology	Knowledge of the practical application of engineering science and technology. This includes applying principles, techniques, procedures, and equipment to the design and production of various goods and services.
Design	Knowledge of design techniques, tools, and principles involved in production of precision technical plans, blueprints, drawings, and models.
Physics	Knowledge and prediction of physical principles, laws, their interrelationships, and applications to understanding fluid, material, and atmospheric dynamics, and mechanical, electrical, atomic and sub-atomic structures and processes.
Chemistry	Knowledge of the chemical composition, structure, and properties of substances and of the chemical processes and transformations that they undergo. This includes uses of chemicals and their interactions, danger signs, production techniques, and disposal methods.
Building and Construction	Knowledge of materials, methods, and the tools involved in the construction or repair of houses, buildings, or other structures such as highways and roads.
Food Production	Knowledge of techniques and equipment for planting, growing, and harvesting food products (both plant and animal) for consumption, including storage/handling techniques.
Mechanical	Knowledge of machines and tools, including their designs, uses, repair, and maintenance.

Skills	Skills Definitions
Writing	Communicating effectively in writing as appropriate for the needs of the audience.
Reading Comprehension	Understanding written sentences and paragraphs in work related documents.
Critical Thinking	Using logic and reasoning to identify the strengths and weaknesses of alternative solutions, conclusions or approaches to problems.
Active Learning	Understanding the implications of new information for both current and future problem-solving and decision-making.
Complex Problem Solving	Identifying complex problems and reviewing related information to develop and evaluate options and implement solutions.
Science	Using scientific rules and methods to solve problems.
Time Management	Managing one's own time and the time of others.
Active Listening	Giving full attention to what other people are saying, taking time to understand the points being made, asking questions as appropriate, and not interrupting at inappropriate times.
Speaking	Talking to others to convey information effectively.
Instructing	Teaching others how to do something.
Learning Strategies	Selecting and using training/instructional methods and procedures appropriate for the situation when learning or teaching new things.
Social Perceptiveness	Being aware of others' reactions and understanding why they react as they do.
Judgment and Decision Making	Considering the relative costs and benefits of potential actions to choose the most appropriate one.
Mathematics	Using mathematics to solve problems.
Monitoring	Monitoring/Assessing performance of yourself, other individuals, or organizations to make improvements or take corrective action.
Coordination	Adjusting actions in relation to others' actions.
Management of Financial Resources	Determining how money will be spent to get the work done, and accounting for these expenditures.
Systems Evaluation	Identifying measures or indicators of system performance and the actions needed to improve or correct performance, relative to the goals of the system.
Persuasion	Persuading others to change their minds or behavior.
Management of Personnel Resources	Motivating, developing, and directing people as they work, identifying the best people for the job.

Systems Analysis	Determining how a system should work and how changes in conditions, operations, and the environment will affect outcomes.
Service Orientation	Actively looking for ways to help people.
Negotiation	Bringing others together and trying to reconcile differences.
Programming	Writing computer programs for various purposes.
Quality Control Analysis	Conducting tests and inspections of products, services, or processes to evaluate quality or performance.
Operations Analysis	Analyzing needs and product requirements to create a design.
Management of Material Resources	Obtaining and seeing to the appropriate use of equipment, facilities, and materials needed to do certain work.
Equipment Selection	Determining the kind of tools and equipment needed to do a job.
Troubleshooting	Determining causes of operating errors and deciding what to do about it.
Technology Design	Generating or adapting equipment and technology to serve user needs.
Operation Monitoring	Watching gauges, dials, or other indicators to make sure a machine is working properly.
Operation and Control	Controlling operations of equipment or systems.
Repairing	Repairing machines or systems using the needed tools.
Equipment Maintenance	Performing routine maintenance on equipment and determining when and what kind of maintenance is needed.
Installation	Installing equipment, machines, wiring, or programs to meet specifications.

Ability	Ability Definitions
Written Comprehension	The ability to read and understand information and ideas presented in writing.
Oral Expression	The ability to communicate information and ideas in speaking so others will understand.
Written Expression	The ability to communicate information and ideas in writing so others will understand.
Oral Comprehension	The ability to listen to and understand information and ideas presented through spoken words and sentences.
Speech Clarity	The ability to speak clearly so others can understand you.
Inductive Reasoning	The ability to combine pieces of information to form general rules or conclusions (includes finding a relationship among seemingly unrelated events).
Deductive Reasoning	The ability to apply general rules to specific problems to produce answers that make sense.
Speech Recognition	The ability to identify and understand the speech of another person.
Near Vision	The ability to see details at close range (within a few feet of the observer).
Problem Sensitivity	The ability to tell when something is wrong or is likely to go wrong. It does not involve solving the problem, only recognizing there is a problem.
Originality	The ability to come up with unusual or clever ideas about a given topic or situation, or to develop creative ways to solve a problem.
Information Ordering	The ability to arrange things or actions in a certain order or pattern according to a specific rule or set of rules (e.g., patterns of numbers, letters, words, pictures, mathematical operations).
Mathematical Reasoning	The ability to choose the right mathematical methods or formulas to solve a problem.
Fluency of Ideas	The ability to come up with a number of ideas about a topic (the number of ideas is important, not their quality, correctness, or creativity).
Category Flexibility	The ability to generate or use different sets of rules for combining or grouping things in different ways.
Selective Attention	The ability to concentrate on a task over a period of time without being distracted.
Flexibility of Closure	The ability to identify or detect a known pattern (a figure, object, word, or sound) that is hidden in other distracting material.
Memorization	The ability to remember information such as words, numbers, pictures, and procedures.
Number Facility	The ability to add, subtract, multiply, or divide quickly and correctly.
Time Sharing	The ability to shift back and forth between two or more activities or sources of information (such as speech, sounds, touch, or other sources).
Far Vision	The ability to see details at a distance.
Speed of Closure	The ability to quickly make sense of, combine, and organize information into meaningful patterns.

Visualization	The ability to imagine how something will look after it is moved around or when its parts are moved or rearranged.
Perceptual Speed	The ability to quickly and accurately compare similarities and differences among sets of letters, numbers, objects, pictures, or patterns. The things to be compared may be presented at the same time or one after the other. This ability also includes comparing a presented object with a remembered object.
Auditory Attention	The ability to focus on a single source of sound in the presence of other distracting sounds.
Finger Dexterity	The ability to make precisely coordinated movements of the fingers of one or both hands to grasp, manipulate, or assemble very small objects.
Visual Color Discrimination	The ability to match or detect differences between colors, including shades of color and brightness.
Hearing Sensitivity	The ability to detect or tell the differences between sounds that vary in pitch and loudness.
Depth Perception	The ability to judge which of several objects is closer or farther away from you, or to judge the distance between you and an object.
Trunk Strength	The ability to use your abdominal and lower back muscles to support part of the body repeatedly or continuously over time without 'giving out' or fatiguing.
Gross Body Equilibrium	The ability to keep or regain your body balance or stay upright when in an unstable position.
Explosive Strength	The ability to use short bursts of muscle force to propel oneself (as in jumping or sprinting), or to throw an object.
Static Strength	The ability to exert maximum muscle force to lift, push, pull, or carry objects.
Dynamic Strength	The ability to exert muscle force repeatedly or continuously over time. This involves muscular endurance and resistance to muscle fatigue.
Arm-Hand Steadiness	The ability to keep your hand and arm steady while moving your arm or while holding your arm and hand in one position.
Spatial Orientation	The ability to know your location in relation to the environment or to know where other objects are in relation to you.
Stamina	The ability to exert yourself physically over long periods of time without getting winded or out of breath.
Reaction Time	The ability to quickly respond (with the hand, finger, or foot) to a signal (sound, light, picture) when it appears.
Response Orientation	The ability to choose quickly between two or more movements in response to two or more different signals (lights, sounds, pictures). It includes the speed with which the correct response is started with the hand, foot, or other body part.
Wrist-Finger Speed	The ability to make fast, simple, repeated movements of the fingers, hands, and wrists.
Gross Body Coordination	The ability to coordinate the movement of your arms, legs, and torso together when the whole body is in motion.
Multilimb Coordination	The ability to coordinate two or more limbs (for example, two arms, two legs, or one leg and one arm) while sitting, standing, or lying down. It does not involve performing the activities while the whole body is in motion.
Rate Control	The ability to time your movements or the movement of a piece of equipment in anticipation of changes in the speed and/or direction of a moving object or scene.
Extent Flexibility	The ability to bend, stretch, twist, or reach with your body, arms, and/or legs.
Sound Localization	The ability to tell the direction from which a sound originated.
Manual Dexterity	The ability to quickly move your hand, your hand together with your arm, or your two hands to grasp, manipulate, or assemble objects.
Night Vision	The ability to see under low light conditions.
Control Precision	The ability to quickly and repeatedly adjust the controls of a machine or a vehicle to exact positions.
Peripheral Vision	The ability to see objects or movement of objects to one's side when the eyes are looking ahead.
Glare Sensitivity	The ability to see objects in the presence of glare or bright lighting.
Dynamic Flexibility	The ability to quickly and repeatedly bend, stretch, twist, or reach out with your body, arms, and/or legs.
Speed of Limb Movement	The ability to quickly move the arms and legs.

Work_Activity	Work_Activity Definitions
Getting Information	Observing, receiving, and otherwise obtaining information from all relevant sources.
Analyzing Data or Information	Identifying the underlying principles, reasons, or facts of information by breaking down information or data into separate parts.

Processing Information	Compiling, coding, categorizing, calculating, tabulating, auditing, or verifying information or data.	Handling and Moving Objects	Using hands and arms in handling, installing, positioning, and moving materials, and manipulating things.
Identifying Objects, Actions, and Events	Identifying information by categorizing, estimating, recognizing differences or similarities, and detecting changes in circumstances or events.	Repairing and Maintaining Electronic Equipment	Servicing, repairing, calibrating, regulating, fine-tuning, or testing machines, devices, and equipment that operate primarily on the basis of electrical or electronic (not mechanical) principles.
Thinking Creatively	Developing, designing, or creating new applications, ideas, relationships, systems, or products, including artistic contributions.	Controlling Machines and Processes	Using either control mechanisms or direct physical activity to operate machines or processes (not including computers or vehicles).
Interacting With Computers	Using computers and computer systems (including hardware and software) to program, write software, set up functions, enter data, or process information.	Performing General Physical Activities	Performing physical activities that require considerable use of your arms and legs and moving your whole body, such as climbing, lifting, balancing, walking, stooping, and handling of materials.
Interpreting the Meaning of Information for Others	Translating or explaining what information means and how it can be used.	Operating Vehicles, Mechanized Devices, or Equipme	Running, maneuvering, navigating, or driving vehicles or mechanized equipment, such as forklifts, passenger vehicles, aircraft, or water craft.
Training and Teaching Others	Identifying the educational needs of others, developing formal educational or training programs or classes, and teaching or instructing others.	Drafting, Laying Out, and Specifying Technical Dev	Providing documentation, detailed instructions, drawings, or specifications to tell others about how devices, parts, equipment, or structures are to be fabricated, constructed, assembled, modified, maintained, or used.
Updating and Using Relevant Knowledge	Keeping up-to-date technically and applying new knowledge to your job.	Repairing and Maintaining Mechanical Equipment	Servicing, repairing, adjusting, and testing machines, devices, moving parts, and equipment that operate primarily on the basis of mechanical (not electronic) principles.
Making Decisions and Solving Problems	Analyzing information and evaluating results to choose the best solution and solve problems.		
Communicating with Supervisors, Peers, or Subordin	Providing information to supervisors, co-workers, and subordinates by telephone, in written form, e-mail, or in person.		
		Work_Context	**Work_Context Definitions**
Communicating with Persons Outside Organization	Communicating with people outside the organization, representing the organization to customers, the public, government, and other external sources. This information can be exchanged in person, in writing, or by telephone or e-mail.	Electronic Mail	How often do you use electronic mail in this job?
		Freedom to Make Decisions	How much decision making freedom, without supervision, does the job offer?
Organizing, Planning, and Prioritizing Work	Developing specific goals and plans to prioritize, organize, and accomplish your work.	Face-to-Face Discussions	How often do you have to have face-to-face discussions with individuals or teams in this job?
Estimating the Quantifiable Characteristics of Pro	Estimating sizes, distances, and quantities; or determining time, costs, resources, or materials needed to perform a work activity.	Structured versus Unstructured Work	To what extent is this job structured for the worker, rather than allowing the worker to determine tasks, priorities, and goals?
Developing Objectives and Strategies	Establishing long-range objectives and specifying the strategies and actions to achieve them.	Indoors, Environmentally Controlled	How often does this job require working indoors in environmentally controlled conditions?
Establishing and Maintaining Interpersonal Relatio	Developing constructive and cooperative working relationships with others, and maintaining them over time.	Telephone	How often do you have telephone conversations in this job?
		Spend Time Sitting	How much does this job require sitting?
Coaching and Developing Others	Identifying the developmental needs of others and coaching, mentoring, or otherwise helping others to improve their knowledge or skills.	Work With Work Group or Team	How important is it to work with others in a group or team in this job?
Provide Consultation and Advice to Others	Providing guidance and expert advice to management or other groups on technical, systems-, or process-related topics.	Contact With Others	How much does this job require the worker to be in contact with others (face-to-face, by telephone, or otherwise) in order to perform it?
Documenting/Recording Information	Entering, transcribing, recording, storing, or maintaining information in written or electronic/magnetic form.	Importance of Being Exact or Accurate	How important is being very exact or highly accurate in performing this job?
Coordinating the Work and Activities of Others	Getting members of a group to work together to accomplish tasks.	Level of Competition	To what extent does this job require the worker to compete or to be aware of competitive pressures?
Judging the Qualities of Things, Services, or Peop	Assessing the value, importance, or quality of things or people.	Letters and Memos	How often does the job require written letters and memos?
Scheduling Work and Activities	Scheduling events, programs, and activities, as well as the work of others.	Public Speaking	How often do you have to perform public speaking in this job?
		Coordinate or Lead Others	How important is it to coordinate or lead others in accomplishing work activities in this job?
Guiding, Directing, and Motivating Subordinates	Providing guidance and direction to subordinates, including setting performance standards and monitoring performance.	Responsibility for Outcomes and Results	How responsible is the worker for work outcomes and results of other workers?
Developing and Building Teams	Encouraging and building mutual trust, respect, and cooperation among team members.	Time Pressure	How often does this job require the worker to meet strict deadlines?
Monitor Processes, Materials, or Surroundings	Monitoring and reviewing information from materials, events, or the environment, to detect or assess problems.	Impact of Decisions on Co-workers or Company Resul	How do the decisions an employee makes impact the results of co-workers, clients or the company?
Monitoring and Controlling Resources	Monitoring and controlling resources and overseeing the spending of money.	Deal With External Customers	How important is it to work with external customers or the public in this job?
Performing Administrative Activities	Performing day-to-day administrative tasks such as maintaining information files and processing paperwork.	Frequency of Decision Making	How frequently is the worker required to make decisions that affect other people, the financial resources, and/or the image and reputation of the organization?
Performing for or Working Directly with the Public	Performing for people or dealing directly with the public. This includes serving customers in restaurants and stores, and receiving clients or guests.	Importance of Repeating Same Tasks	How important is repeating the same physical activities (e.g., key entry) or mental activities (e.g., checking entries in a ledger) over and over, without stopping, to performing this job?
Evaluating Information to Determine Compliance wit	Using relevant information and individual judgment to determine whether events or processes comply with laws, regulations, or standards.	Spend Time Making Repetitive Motions	How much does this job require making repetitive motions?
Selling or Influencing Others	Convincing others to buy merchandise/goods or to otherwise change their minds or actions.	Frequency of Conflict Situations	How often are there conflict situations the employee has to face in this job?
Staffing Organizational Units	Recruiting, interviewing, selecting, hiring, and promoting employees in an organization.	Consequence of Error	How serious would the result usually be if the worker made a mistake that was not readily correctable?
Resolving Conflicts and Negotiating with Others	Handling complaints, settling disputes, and resolving grievances and conflicts, or otherwise negotiating with others.	Physical Proximity	To what extent does this job require the worker to perform job tasks in close physical proximity to other people?
Assisting and Caring for Others	Providing personal assistance, medical attention, emotional support, or other personal care to others such as coworkers, customers, or patients.	Deal With Unpleasant or Angry People	How frequently does the worker have to deal with unpleasant, angry, or discourteous individuals as part of the job requirements?
Inspecting Equipment, Structures, Material	Inspecting equipment, structures, or materials to identify the cause of errors or other problems or defects.	Spend Time Standing	How much does this job require standing?

Spend Time Using Your Hands to Handle, Control, or	How much does this job require using your hands to handle, control, or feel objects, tools or controls?
Responsible for Others' Health and Safety	How much responsibility is there for the health and safety of others in this job?
Sounds, Noise Levels Are Distracting or Uncomforta	How often does this job require working exposed to sounds and noise levels that are distracting or uncomfortable?
Degree of Automation	How automated is the job?
In an Enclosed Vehicle or Equipment	How often does this job require working in a closed vehicle or equipment (e.g., car)?
Spend Time Walking and Running	How much does this job require walking and running?
Indoors, Not Environmentally Controlled	How often does this job require working indoors in non-controlled environmental conditions (e.g., warehouse without heat)?
Exposed to Disease or Infections	How often does this job require exposure to disease/infections?
Deal With Physically Aggressive People	How frequently does this job require the worker to deal with physical aggression of violent individuals?
Outdoors, Exposed to Weather	How often does this job require working outdoors, exposed to all weather conditions?
Outdoors, Under Cover	How often does this job require working outdoors, under cover (e.g., structure with roof but no walls)?
Very Hot or Cold Temperatures	How often does this job require working in very hot (above 90 F degrees) or very cold (below 32 F degrees) temperatures?
Extremely Bright or Inadequate Lighting	How often does this job require working in extremely bright or inadequate lighting conditions?
Cramped Work Space, Awkward Positions	How often does this job require working in cramped work spaces that requires getting into awkward positions?
Spend Time Bending or Twisting the Body	How much does this job require bending or twisting your body?
Exposed to Contaminants	How often does this job require working exposed to contaminants (such as pollutants, gases, dust or odors)?
Spend Time Kneeling, Crouching, Stooping, or Crawl	How much does this job require kneeling, crouching, stooping or crawling?
Pace Determined by Speed of Equipment	How important is it to this job that the pace is determined by the speed of equipment or machinery? (This does not refer to keeping busy at all times on this job.)
Spend Time Climbing Ladders, Scaffolds, or Poles	How much does this job require climbing ladders, scaffolds, or poles?
In an Open Vehicle or Equipment	How often does this job require working in an open vehicle or equipment (e.g., tractor)?
Exposed to Radiation	How often does this job require exposure to radiation?
Exposed to Minor Burns, Cuts, Bites, or Stings	How often does this job require exposure to minor burns, cuts, bites, or stings?
Exposed to Hazardous Conditions	How often does this job require exposure to hazardous conditions?
Wear Specialized Protective or Safety Equipment su	How much does this job require wearing specialized protective or safety equipment such as breathing apparatus, safety harness, full protection suits, or radiation protection?
Spend Time Keeping or Regaining Balance	How much does this job require keeping or regaining your balance?
Exposed to Hazardous Equipment	How often does this job require exposure to hazardous equipment?
Exposed to Whole Body Vibration	How often does this job require exposure to whole body vibration (e.g., operate a jackhammer)?
Wear Common Protective or Safety Equipment such as	How much does this job require wearing common protective or safety equipment such as safety shoes, glasses, gloves, hard hats or live jackets?
Exposed to High Places	How often does this job require exposure to high places?

Job Zone Component	Job Zone Component Definitions
Title	Job Zone Five: Extensive Preparation Needed
Overall Experience	Extensive skill, knowledge, and experience are needed for these occupations. Many require more than five years of experience. For example, surgeons must complete four years of college and an additional five to seven years of specialized medical training to be able to do their job.
Job Training	Employees may need some on-the-job training, but most of these occupations assume that the person will already have the required skills, knowledge, work-related experience, and/or training.

Job Zone Examples	These occupations often involve coordinating, training, supervising, or managing the activities of others to accomplish goals. Very advanced communication and organizational skills are required. Examples include athletic trainers, lawyers, managing editors, physicists, social psychologists, and surgeons.
SVP Range	(8.0 and above)
Education	A bachelor's degree is the minimum formal education required for these occupations. However, many also require graduate school. For example, they may require a master's degree, and some require a Ph.D., M.D., or J.D. (law degree).

Work_Styles	Work_Styles Definitions
Analytical Thinking	Job requires analyzing information and using logic to address work-related issues and problems.
Achievement/Effort	Job requires establishing and maintaining personally challenging achievement goals and exerting effort toward mastering tasks.
Independence	Job requires developing one's own ways of doing things, guiding oneself with little or no supervision, and depending on oneself to get things done.
Initiative	Job requires a willingness to take on responsibilities and challenges.
Persistence	Job requires persistence in the face of obstacles.
Integrity	Job requires being honest and ethical.
Innovation	Job requires creativity and alternative thinking to develop new ideas for and answers to work-related problems.
Dependability	Job requires being reliable, responsible, and dependable, and fulfilling obligations.
Attention to Detail	Job requires being careful about detail and thorough in completing work tasks.
Adaptability/Flexibility	Job requires being open to change (positive or negative) and to considerable variety in the workplace.
Stress Tolerance	Job requires accepting criticism and dealing calmly and effectively with high stress situations.
Leadership	Job requires a willingness to lead, take charge, and offer opinions and direction.
Cooperation	Job requires being pleasant with others on the job and displaying a good-natured, cooperative attitude.
Self Control	Job requires maintaining composure, keeping emotions in check, controlling anger, and avoiding aggressive behavior, even in very difficult situations.
Social Orientation	Job requires preferring to work with others rather than alone, and being personally connected with others on the job.
Concern for Others	Job requires being sensitive to others' needs and feelings and being understanding and helpful on the job.

19-3091.01 - Anthropologists

Research or study the origins and physical, social, and cultural development and behavior of humans and the cultures and organizations they have created.

Tasks

1) Identify key individual cultural collaborators, using reputational and positional selection techniques.

2) Formulate general rules that describe and predict the development and behavior of cultures and social institutions.

3) Construct and test data collection methods.

4) Train others in the application of ethnographic research methods to solve problems in organizational effectiveness, communications, technology development, policy-making, and program planning.

5) Develop intervention procedures, utilizing techniques such as individual and focus group interviews, consultations, and participant observation of social interaction.

6) Apply traditional ecological knowledge and assessments of culturally distinctive land and resource management institutions to assist in the resolution of conflicts over habitat protection and resource enhancement.

7) Build and use text-based database management systems to support the analysis of detailed first-hand observational records, or field notes.

8) Create data records for use in describing and analyzing social patterns and processes, using photography, videography, and audio recordings.

9) Collaborate with economic development planners to decide on the implementation of proposed development policies, plans, and programs based on culturally institutionalized barriers and facilitating circumstances.

10) Identify culturally-specific beliefs and practices affecting health status and access to services for distinct populations and communities, in collaboration with medical and public health officials.

11) Conduct participatory action research in communities and organizations to assess how work is done, and to design work systems, technologies, and environments.

12) Enhance the cultural sensitivity of elementary and secondary curricula and classroom interactions in collaboration with educators and teachers.

13) Build geographic information systems (GIS) to record, analyze, and cartographically represent the distribution of languages, cultural and natural resources, land use, and settlement patterns of specific populations.

14) Observe the production, distribution, and consumption of food to identify and mitigate threats to food security.

15) Analyze and characterize user experiences and institutional settings to assist consumer product developers, technology developers, and software engineers with the design of innovative products and services.

16) Organize public exhibits and displays to promote public awareness of diverse and distinctive cultural traditions.

17) Gather and analyze artifacts and skeletal remains in order to increase knowledge of ancient cultures.

18) Examine museum collections of hominid fossils to classify anatomical and physiological variations, and to determine how they fit into evolutionary theory.

19) Participate in forensic activities such as tooth and bone structure identification, in conjunction with police departments and pathologists.

20) Observe and measure bodily variations and physical attributes of different human groups.

21) Advise government agencies, private organizations, and communities regarding proposed programs, plans, and policies and their potential impacts on cultural institutions, organizations, and communities.

22) Write about and present research findings for a variety of specialized and general audiences.

23) Plan and direct research to characterize and compare the economic, demographic, health care, social, political, linguistic, and religious institutions of distinct cultural groups, communities, and organizations.

24) Study archival collections of primary historical sources to help explain the origins and development of cultural patterns.

25) Explain the origins and physical, social, or cultural development of humans, including physical attributes, cultural traditions, beliefs, languages, resource management practices, and settlement patterns.

26) Collect information and make judgments through observation, interviews, and the review of documents.

Knowledge	Knowledge Definitions
Sociology and Anthropology	Knowledge of group behavior and dynamics, societal trends and influences, human migrations, ethnicity, cultures and their history and origins.
English Language	Knowledge of the structure and content of the English language including the meaning and spelling of words, rules of composition, and grammar.
History and Archeology	Knowledge of historical events and their causes, indicators, and effects on civilizations and cultures.
Education and Training	Knowledge of principles and methods for curriculum and training design, teaching and instruction for individuals and groups, and the measurement of training effects.
Foreign Language	Knowledge of the structure and content of a foreign (non-English) language including the meaning and spelling of words, rules of composition and grammar, and pronunciation.
Psychology	Knowledge of human behavior and performance; individual differences in ability, personality, and interests; learning and motivation; psychological research methods; and the assessment and treatment of behavioral and affective disorders.
Philosophy and Theology	Knowledge of different philosophical systems and religions. This includes their basic principles, values, ethics, ways of thinking, customs, practices, and their impact on human culture.

Geography	Knowledge of principles and methods for describing the features of land, sea, and air masses, including their physical characteristics, locations, interrelationships, and distribution of plant, animal, and human life.
Communications and Media	Knowledge of media production, communication, and dissemination techniques and methods. This includes alternative ways to inform and entertain via written, oral, and visual media.
Mathematics	Knowledge of arithmetic, algebra, geometry, calculus, statistics, and their applications.
Law and Government	Knowledge of laws, legal codes, court procedures, precedents, government regulations, executive orders, agency rules, and the democratic political process.
Clerical	Knowledge of administrative and clerical procedures and systems such as word processing, managing files and records, stenography and transcription, designing forms, and other office procedures and terminology.
Administration and Management	Knowledge of business and management principles involved in strategic planning, resource allocation, human resources modeling, leadership technique, production methods, and coordination of people and resources.
Customer and Personal Service	Knowledge of principles and processes for providing customer and personal services. This includes customer needs assessment, meeting quality standards for services, and evaluation of customer satisfaction.
Biology	Knowledge of plant and animal organisms, their tissues, cells, functions, interdependencies, and interactions with each other and the environment.
Computers and Electronics	Knowledge of circuit boards, processors, chips, electronic equipment, and computer hardware and software, including applications and programming.
Personnel and Human Resources	Knowledge of principles and procedures for personnel recruitment, selection, training, compensation and benefits, labor relations and negotiation, and personnel information systems.
Medicine and Dentistry	Knowledge of the information and techniques needed to diagnose and treat human injuries, diseases, and deformities. This includes symptoms, treatment alternatives, drug properties and interactions, and preventive health-care measures.
Economics and Accounting	Knowledge of economic and accounting principles and practices, the financial markets, banking and the analysis and reporting of financial data.
Fine Arts	Knowledge of the theory and techniques required to compose, produce, and perform works of music, dance, visual arts, drama, and sculpture.
Public Safety and Security	Knowledge of relevant equipment, policies, procedures, and strategies to promote effective local, state, or national security operations for the protection of people, data, property, and institutions.
Therapy and Counseling	Knowledge of principles, methods, and procedures for diagnosis, treatment, and rehabilitation of physical and mental dysfunctions, and for career counseling and guidance.
Sales and Marketing	Knowledge of principles and methods for showing, promoting, and selling products or services. This includes marketing strategy and tactics, product demonstration, sales techniques, and sales control systems.
Production and Processing	Knowledge of raw materials, production processes, quality control, costs, and other techniques for maximizing the effective manufacture and distribution of goods.
Telecommunications	Knowledge of transmission, broadcasting, switching, control, and operation of telecommunications systems.
Transportation	Knowledge of principles and methods for moving people or goods by air, rail, sea, or road, including the relative costs and benefits.
Food Production	Knowledge of techniques and equipment for planting, growing, and harvesting food products (both plant and animal) for consumption, including storage/handling techniques.
Chemistry	Knowledge of the chemical composition, structure, and properties of substances and of the chemical processes and transformations that they undergo. This includes uses of chemicals and their interactions, danger signs, production techniques, and disposal methods.
Design	Knowledge of design techniques, tools, and principles involved in production of precision technical plans, blueprints, drawings, and models.

Engineering and Technology	Knowledge of the practical application of engineering science and technology. This includes applying principles, techniques, procedures, and equipment to the design and production of various goods and services.
Building and Construction	Knowledge of materials, methods, and the tools involved in the construction or repair of houses, buildings, or other structures such as highways and roads.
Mechanical	Knowledge of machines and tools, including their designs, uses, repair, and maintenance.
Physics	Knowledge and prediction of physical principles, laws, their interrelationships, and applications to understanding fluid, material, and atmospheric dynamics, and mechanical, electrical, atomic and sub-atomic structures and processes.

Skills	Skills Definitions
Reading Comprehension	Understanding written sentences and paragraphs in work related documents.
Writing	Communicating effectively in writing as appropriate for the needs of the audience.
Critical Thinking	Using logic and reasoning to identify the strengths and weaknesses of alternative solutions, conclusions or approaches to problems.
Active Listening	Giving full attention to what other people are saying, taking time to understand the points being made, asking questions as appropriate, and not interrupting at inappropriate times.
Social Perceptiveness	Being aware of others' reactions and understanding why they react as they do.
Speaking	Talking to others to convey information effectively.
Complex Problem Solving	Identifying complex problems and reviewing related information to develop and evaluate options and implement solutions.
Active Learning	Understanding the implications of new information for both current and future problem-solving and decision-making.
Science	Using scientific rules and methods to solve problems.
Learning Strategies	Selecting and using training/instructional methods and procedures appropriate for the situation when learning or teaching new things.
Judgment and Decision Making	Considering the relative costs and benefits of potential actions to choose the most appropriate one.
Instructing	Teaching others how to do something.
Time Management	Managing one's own time and the time of others.
Monitoring	Monitoring/Assessing performance of yourself, other individuals, or organizations to make improvements or take corrective action.
Coordination	Adjusting actions in relation to others' actions.
Negotiation	Bringing others together and trying to reconcile differences.
Systems Analysis	Determining how a system should work and how changes in conditions, operations, and the environment will affect outcomes.
Systems Evaluation	Identifying measures or indicators of system performance and the actions needed to improve or correct performance, relative to the goals of the system.
Persuasion	Persuading others to change their minds or behavior.
Service Orientation	Actively looking for ways to help people.
Mathematics	Using mathematics to solve problems.
Management of Financial Resources	Determining how money will be spent to get the work done, and accounting for these expenditures.
Management of Personnel Resources	Motivating, developing, and directing people as they work, identifying the best people for the job.
Operations Analysis	Analyzing needs and product requirements to create a design.
Management of Material Resources	Obtaining and seeing to the appropriate use of equipment, facilities, and materials needed to do certain work.
Equipment Selection	Determining the kind of tools and equipment needed to do a job.
Quality Control Analysis	Conducting tests and inspections of products, services, or processes to evaluate quality or performance.
Troubleshooting	Determining causes of operating errors and deciding what to do about it.
Programming	Writing computer programs for various purposes.
Technology Design	Generating or adapting equipment and technology to serve user needs.
Operation and Control	Controlling operations of equipment or systems.
Installation	Installing equipment, machines, wiring, or programs to meet specifications.
Equipment Maintenance	Performing routine maintenance on equipment and determining when and what kind of maintenance is needed.
Repairing	Repairing machines or systems using the needed tools.

Operation Monitoring	Watching gauges, dials, or other indicators to make sure a machine is working properly.

Ability	Ability Definitions
Inductive Reasoning	The ability to combine pieces of information to form general rules or conclusions (includes finding a relationship among seemingly unrelated events).
Written Comprehension	The ability to read and understand information and ideas presented in writing.
Oral Expression	The ability to communicate information and ideas in speaking so others will understand.
Oral Comprehension	The ability to listen to and understand information and ideas presented through spoken words and sentences.
Written Expression	The ability to communicate information and ideas in writing so others will understand.
Deductive Reasoning	The ability to apply general rules to specific problems to produce answers that make sense.
Problem Sensitivity	The ability to tell when something is wrong or is likely to go wrong. It does not involve solving the problem, only recognizing there is a problem.
Speech Clarity	The ability to speak clearly so others can understand you.
Near Vision	The ability to see details at close range (within a few feet of the observer).
Speech Recognition	The ability to identify and understand the speech of another person.
Information Ordering	The ability to arrange things or actions in a certain order or pattern according to a specific rule or set of rules (e.g., patterns of numbers, letters, words, pictures, mathematical operations).
Category Flexibility	The ability to generate or use different sets of rules for combining or grouping things in different ways.
Originality	The ability to come up with unusual or clever ideas about a given topic or situation, or to develop creative ways to solve a problem.
Fluency of Ideas	The ability to come up with a number of ideas about a topic (the number of ideas is important, not their quality, correctness, or creativity).
Selective Attention	The ability to concentrate on a task over a period of time without being distracted.
Flexibility of Closure	The ability to identify or detect a known pattern (a figure, object, word, or sound) that is hidden in other distracting material.
Far Vision	The ability to see details at a distance.
Memorization	The ability to remember information such as words, numbers, pictures, and procedures.
Speed of Closure	The ability to quickly make sense of, combine, and organize information into meaningful patterns.
Mathematical Reasoning	The ability to choose the right mathematical methods or formulas to solve a problem.
Time Sharing	The ability to shift back and forth between two or more activities or sources of information (such as speech, sounds, touch, or other sources).
Visualization	The ability to imagine how something will look after it is moved around or when its parts are moved or rearranged.
Perceptual Speed	The ability to quickly and accurately compare similarities and differences among sets of letters, numbers, objects, pictures, or patterns. The things to be compared may be presented at the same time or one after the other. This ability also includes comparing a presented object with a remembered object.
Number Facility	The ability to add, subtract, multiply, or divide quickly and correctly.
Visual Color Discrimination	The ability to match or detect differences between colors, including shades of color and brightness.
Depth Perception	The ability to judge which of several objects is closer or farther away from you, or to judge the distance between you and an object.
Finger Dexterity	The ability to make precisely coordinated movements of the fingers of one or both hands to grasp, manipulate, or assemble very small objects.
Auditory Attention	The ability to focus on a single source of sound in the presence of other distracting sounds.
Multilimb Coordination	The ability to coordinate two or more limbs (for example, two arms, two legs, or one leg and one arm) while sitting, standing, or lying down. It does not involve performing the activities while the whole body is in motion.
Control Precision	The ability to quickly and repeatedly adjust the controls of a machine or a vehicle to exact positions.

Hearing Sensitivity	The ability to detect or tell the differences between sounds that vary in pitch and loudness.
Trunk Strength	The ability to use your abdominal and lower back muscles to support part of the body repeatedly or continuously over time without 'giving out' or fatiguing.
Gross Body Coordination	The ability to coordinate the movement of your arms, legs, and torso together when the whole body is in motion.
Spatial Orientation	The ability to know your location in relation to the environment or to know where other objects are in relation to you.
Extent Flexibility	The ability to bend, stretch, twist, or reach with your body, arms, and/or legs.
Arm-Hand Steadiness	The ability to keep your hand and arm steady while moving your arm or while holding your arm and hand in one position.
Sound Localization	The ability to tell the direction from which a sound originated.
Peripheral Vision	The ability to see objects or movement of objects to one's side when the eyes are looking ahead.
Night Vision	The ability to see under low light conditions.
Rate Control	The ability to time your movements or the movement of a piece of equipment in anticipation of changes in the speed and/or direction of a moving object or scene.
Manual Dexterity	The ability to quickly move your hand, your hand together with your arm, or your two hands to grasp, manipulate, or assemble objects.
Dynamic Flexibility	The ability to quickly and repeatedly bend, stretch, twist, or reach out with your body, arms, and/or legs.
Stamina	The ability to exert yourself physically over long periods of time without getting winded or out of breath.
Dynamic Strength	The ability to exert muscle force repeatedly or continuously over time. This involves muscular endurance and resistance to muscle fatigue.
Explosive Strength	The ability to use short bursts of muscle force to propel oneself (as in jumping or sprinting), or to throw an object.
Static Strength	The ability to exert maximum muscle force to lift, push, pull, or carry objects.
Speed of Limb Movement	The ability to quickly move the arms and legs.
Wrist-Finger Speed	The ability to make fast, simple, repeated movements of the fingers, hands, and wrists.
Glare Sensitivity	The ability to see objects in the presence of glare or bright lighting.
Reaction Time	The ability to quickly respond (with the hand, finger, or foot) to a signal (sound, light, picture) when it appears.
Gross Body Equilibrium	The ability to keep or regain your body balance or stay upright when in an unstable position.
Response Orientation	The ability to choose quickly between two or more movements in response to two or more different signals (lights, sounds, pictures). It includes the speed with which the correct response is started with the hand, foot, or other body part.

Work_Activity	Work_Activity Definitions
Getting Information	Observing, receiving, and otherwise obtaining information from all relevant sources.
Interpreting the Meaning of Information for Others	Translating or explaining what information means and how it can be used.
Thinking Creatively	Developing, designing, or creating new applications, ideas, relationships, systems, or products, including artistic contributions.
Identifying Objects, Actions, and Events	Identifying information by categorizing, estimating, recognizing differences or similarities, and detecting changes in circumstances or events.
Processing Information	Compiling, coding, categorizing, calculating, tabulating, auditing, or verifying information or data.
Documenting/Recording Information	Entering, transcribing, recording, storing, or maintaining information in written or electronic/magnetic form.
Analyzing Data or Information	Identifying the underlying principles, reasons, or facts of information by breaking down information or data into separate parts.
Organizing, Planning, and Prioritizing Work	Developing specific goals and plans to prioritize, organize, and accomplish your work.
Updating and Using Relevant Knowledge	Keeping up-to-date technically and applying new knowledge to your job.
Establishing and Maintaining Interpersonal Relatio	Developing constructive and cooperative working relationships with others, and maintaining them over time.
Interacting With Computers	Using computers and computer systems (including hardware and software) to program, write software, set up functions, enter data, or process information.

Making Decisions and Solving Problems	Analyzing information and evaluating results to choose the best solution and solve problems.
Communicating with Persons Outside Organization	Communicating with people outside the organization, representing the organization to customers, the public, government, and other external sources. This information can be exchanged in person, in writing, or by telephone or e-mail.
Communicating with Supervisors, Peers, or Subordin	Providing information to supervisors, co-workers, and subordinates by telephone, in written form, e-mail, or in person.
Training and Teaching Others	Identifying the educational needs of others, developing formal educational or training programs or classes, and teaching or instructing others.
Judging the Qualities of Things, Services, or Peop	Assessing the value, importance, or quality of things or people.
Developing Objectives and Strategies	Establishing long-range objectives and specifying the strategies and actions to achieve them.
Provide Consultation and Advice to Others	Providing guidance and expert advice to management or other groups on technical, systems-, or process-related topics.
Scheduling Work and Activities	Scheduling events, programs, and activities, as well as the work of others.
Coaching and Developing Others	Identifying the developmental needs of others and coaching, mentoring, or otherwise helping others to improve their knowledge or skills.
Monitor Processes, Materials, or Surroundings	Monitoring and reviewing information from materials, events, or the environment, to detect or assess problems.
Performing Administrative Activities	Performing day-to-day administrative tasks such as maintaining information files and processing paperwork.
Resolving Conflicts and Negotiating with Others	Handling complaints, settling disputes, and resolving grievances and conflicts, or otherwise negotiating with others.
Coordinating the Work and Activities of Others	Getting members of a group to work together to accomplish tasks.
Guiding, Directing, and Motivating Subordinates	Providing guidance and direction to subordinates, including setting performance standards and monitoring performance.
Developing and Building Teams	Encouraging and building mutual trust, respect, and cooperation among team members.
Monitoring and Controlling Resources	Monitoring and controlling resources and overseeing the spending of money.
Estimating the Quantifiable Characteristics of Pro	Estimating sizes, distances, and quantities; or determining time, costs, resources, or materials needed to perform a work activity.
Evaluating Information to Determine Compliance wit	Using relevant information and individual judgment to determine whether events or processes comply with laws, regulations, or standards.
Performing for or Working Directly with the Public	Performing for people or dealing directly with the public. This includes serving customers in restaurants and stores, and receiving clients or guests.
Assisting and Caring for Others	Providing personal assistance, medical attention, emotional support, or other personal care to others such as coworkers, customers, or patients.
Selling or Influencing Others	Convincing others to buy merchandise/goods or to otherwise change their minds or actions.
Staffing Organizational Units	Recruiting, interviewing, selecting, hiring, and promoting employees in an organization.
Inspecting Equipment, Structures, or Material	Inspecting equipment, structures, or materials to identify the cause of errors or other problems or defects.
Performing General Physical Activities	Performing physical activities that require considerable use of your arms and legs and moving your whole body, such as climbing, lifting, balancing, walking, stooping, and handling of materials.
Handling and Moving Objects	Using hands and arms in handling, installing, positioning, and moving materials, and manipulating things.
Operating Vehicles, Mechanized Devices, or Equipme	Running, maneuvering, navigating, or driving vehicles or mechanized equipment, such as forklifts, passenger vehicles, aircraft, or water craft.
Controlling Machines and Processes	Using either control mechanisms or direct physical activity to operate machines or processes (not including computers or vehicles).
Drafting, Laying Out, and Specifying Technical Dev	Providing documentation, detailed instructions, drawings, or specifications to tell others about how devices, parts, equipment, or structures are to be fabricated, constructed, assembled, modified, maintained, or used.
Repairing and Maintaining Electronic Equipment	Servicing, repairing, calibrating, regulating, fine-tuning, or testing machines, devices, and equipment that operate primarily on the basis of electrical or electronic (not mechanical) principles.

Repairing and Maintaining Mechanical Equipment	Servicing, repairing, adjusting, and testing machines, devices, moving parts, and equipment that operate primarily on the basis of mechanical (not electronic) principles.

Work_Context	Work_Context Definitions
Electronic Mail	How often do you use electronic mail in this job?
Freedom to Make Decisions	How much decision making freedom, without supervision, does the job offer?
Telephone	How often do you have telephone conversations in this job?
Face-to-Face Discussions	How often do you have to have face-to-face discussions with individuals or teams in this job?
Structured versus Unstructured Work	To what extent is this job structured for the worker, rather than allowing the worker to determine tasks, priorities, and goals?
Indoors, Environmentally Controlled	How often does this job require working indoors in environmentally controlled conditions?
Importance of Being Exact or Accurate	How important is being very exact or highly accurate in performing this job?
Contact With Others	How much does this job require the worker to be in contact with others (face-to-face, by telephone, or otherwise) in order to perform it?
Spend Time Sitting	How much does this job require sitting?
Letters and Memos	How often does the job require written letters and memos?
Frequency of Decision Making	How frequently is the worker required to make decisions that affect other people, the financial resources, and/or the image and reputation of the organization?
Public Speaking	How often do you have to perform public speaking in this job?
Work With Work Group or Team	How important is it to work with others in a group or team in this job?
Level of Competition	To what extent does this job require the worker to compete or to be aware of competitive pressures?
Time Pressure	How often does this job require the worker to meet strict deadlines?
Impact of Decisions on Co-workers or Company Resul	How do the decisions an employee makes impact the results of co-workers, clients or the company?
Coordinate or Lead Others	How important is it to coordinate or lead others in accomplishing work activities in this job?
Responsibility for Outcomes and Results	How responsible is the worker for work outcomes and results of other workers?
Indoors, Not Environmentally Controlled	How often does this job require working indoors in non-controlled environmental conditions (e.g., warehouse without heat)?
Deal With External Customers	How important is it to work with external customers or the public in this job?
Frequency of Conflict Situations	How often are there conflict situations the employee has to face in this job?
Spend Time Making Repetitive Motions	How much does this job require making repetitive motions?
Outdoors, Exposed to Weather	How often does this job require working outdoors, exposed to all weather conditions?
Physical Proximity	To what extent does this job require the worker to perform job tasks in close physical proximity to other people?
Deal With Unpleasant or Angry People	How frequently does the worker have to deal with unpleasant, angry, or discourteous individuals as part of the job requirements?
Consequence of Error	How serious would the result usually be if the worker made a mistake that was not readily correctable?
In an Enclosed Vehicle or Equipment	How often does this job require working in a closed vehicle or equipment (e.g., car)?
Importance of Repeating Same Tasks	How important is repeating the same physical activities (e.g., key entry) or mental activities (e.g., checking entries in a ledger) over and over, without stopping, to performing this job?
Responsible for Others' Health and Safety	How much responsibility is there for the health and safety of others in this job?
Sounds, Noise Levels Are Distracting or Uncomforta	How often does this job require working exposed to sounds and noise levels that are distracting or uncomfortable?
Outdoors, Under Cover	How often does this job require working outdoors, under cover (e.g., structure with roof but no walls)?
Spend Time Using Your Hands to Handle, Control, or	How much does this job require using your hands to handle, control, or feel objects, tools or controls?
Very Hot or Cold Temperatures	How often does this job require working in very hot (above 90 F degrees) or very cold (below 32 F degrees) temperatures?
Spend Time Standing	How much does this job require standing?
Exposed to Contaminants	How often does this job require working exposed to contaminants (such as pollutants, gases, dust or odors)?

Extremely Bright or Inadequate Lighting	How often does this job require working in extremely bright or inadequate lighting conditions?
Exposed to Disease or Infections	How often does this job require exposure to disease/infections?
Exposed to Minor Burns, Cuts, Bites, or Stings	How often does this job require exposure to minor burns, cuts, bites, or stings?
Spend Time Walking and Running	How much does this job require walking and running?
Cramped Work Space, Awkward Positions	How often does this job require working in cramped work spaces that requires getting into awkward positions?
Degree of Automation	How automated is the job?
Deal With Physically Aggressive People	How frequently does this job require the worker to deal with physical aggression of violent individuals?
In an Open Vehicle or Equipment	How often does this job require working in an open vehicle or equipment (e.g., tractor)?
Spend Time Kneeling, Crouching, Stooping, or Crawl	How much does this job require kneeling, crouching, stooping or crawling?
Spend Time Bending or Twisting the Body	How much does this job require bending or twisting your body?
Wear Common Protective or Safety Equipment such as	How much does this job require wearing common protective or safety equipment such as safety shoes, glasses, gloves, hard hats or live jackets?
Exposed to Hazardous Equipment	How often does this job require exposure to hazardous equipment?
Exposed to High Places	How often does this job require exposure to high places?
Spend Time Keeping or Regaining Balance	How much does this job require keeping or regaining your balance?
Exposed to Hazardous Conditions	How often does this job require exposure to hazardous conditions?
Wear Specialized Protective or Safety Equipment su	How much does this job require wearing specialized protective or safety equipment such as breathing apparatus, safety harness, full protection suits, or radiation protection?
Exposed to Radiation	How often does this job require exposure to radiation?
Exposed to Whole Body Vibration	How often does this job require exposure to whole body vibration (e.g., operate a jackhammer)?
Spend Time Climbing Ladders, Scaffolds, or Poles	How much does this job require climbing ladders, scaffolds, or poles?
Pace Determined by Speed of Equipment	How important is it to this job that the pace is determined by the speed of equipment or machinery? (This does not refer to keeping busy at all times on this job.)

Job Zone Component	Job Zone Component Definitions
Title	Job Zone Five: Extensive Preparation Needed
Overall Experience	Extensive skill, knowledge, and experience are needed for these occupations. Many require more than five years of experience. For example, surgeons must complete four years of college and an additional five to seven years of specialized medical training to be able to do their job.
Job Training	Employees may need some on-the-job training, but most of these occupations assume that the person will already have the required skills, knowledge, work-related experience, and/or training.
Job Zone Examples	These occupations often involve coordinating, training, supervising, or managing the activities of others to accomplish goals. Very advanced communication and organizational skills are required. Examples include athletic trainers, lawyers, managing editors, physicists, social psychologists, and surgeons.
SVP Range	(8.0 and above)
Education	A bachelor's degree is the minimum formal education required for these occupations. However, many also require graduate school. For example, they may require a master's degree, and some require a Ph.D., M.D., or J.D. (law degree).

Work_Styles	Work_Styles Definitions
Analytical Thinking	Job requires analyzing information and using logic to address work-related issues and problems.
Independence	Job requires developing one's own ways of doing things, guiding oneself with little or no supervision, and depending on oneself to get things done.
Integrity	Job requires being honest and ethical.
Initiative	Job requires a willingness to take on responsibilities and challenges.

Adaptability/Flexibility	Job requires being open to change (positive or negative) and to considerable variety in the workplace.
Dependability	Job requires being reliable, responsible, and dependable, and fulfilling obligations.
Persistence	Job requires persistence in the face of obstacles.
Achievement/Effort	Job requires establishing and maintaining personally challenging achievement goals and exerting effort toward mastering tasks.
Innovation	Job requires creativity and alternative thinking to develop new ideas for and answers to work-related problems.
Self Control	Job requires maintaining composure, keeping emotions in check, controlling anger, and avoiding aggressive behavior, even in very difficult situations.
Attention to Detail	Job requires being careful about detail and thorough in completing work tasks.
Social Orientation	Job requires preferring to work with others rather than alone, and being personally connected with others on the job.
Concern for Others	Job requires being sensitive to others' needs and feelings and being understanding and helpful on the job.
Cooperation	Job requires being pleasant with others on the job and displaying a good-natured, cooperative attitude.
Stress Tolerance	Job requires accepting criticism and dealing calmly and effectively with high stress situations.
Leadership	Job requires a willingness to lead, take charge, and offer opinions and direction.

19-3092.00 - Geographers

Study nature and use of areas of earth's surface, relating and interpreting interactions of physical and cultural phenomena. Conduct research on physical aspects of a region, including land forms, climates, soils, plants and animals, and conduct research on the spatial implications of human activities within a given area, including social characteristics, economic activities, and political organization, as well as researching interdependence between regions at scales ranging from local to global.

Tasks

1) Provide geographical information systems support to the private and public sectors.

2) Study the economic, political, and cultural characteristics of a specific region's population.

3) Develop, operate, and maintain geographical information (GIS) computer systems, including hardware, software, plotters, digitizers, printers, and video cameras.

4) Locate and obtain existing geographic information databases.

5) Analyze geographic distributions of physical and cultural phenomena on local, regional, continental, and/or global scales.

6) Gather and compile geographic data from sources including censuses, field observations, satellite imagery, aerial photographs, and existing maps.

7) Provide consulting services in fields including resource development and management, business location and market area analysis, environmental hazards, regional cultural history, and urban social planning.

8) Collect data on physical characteristics of specified areas, such as geological formations, climates, and vegetation, using surveying or meteorological equipment.

9) Create and modify maps, graphs, and/or diagrams, using geographical information software and related equipment, and principles of cartography such as coordinate systems, longitude, latitude, elevation, topography, and map scales.

10) Write and present reports of research findings.

11) Conduct fieldwork at outdoor sites.

Knowledge	Knowledge Definitions
Geography	Knowledge of principles and methods for describing the features of land, sea, and air masses, including their physical characteristics, locations, interrelationships, and distribution of plant, animal, and human life.
English Language	Knowledge of the structure and content of the English language including the meaning and spelling of words, rules of composition, and grammar.
Sociology and Anthropology	Knowledge of group behavior and dynamics, societal trends and influences, human migrations, ethnicity, cultures and their history and origins.
Education and Training	Knowledge of principles and methods for curriculum and training design, teaching and instruction for individuals and groups, and the measurement of training effects.
Mathematics	Knowledge of arithmetic, algebra, geometry, calculus, statistics, and their applications.
Computers and Electronics	Knowledge of circuit boards, processors, chips, electronic equipment, and computer hardware and software, including applications and programming.
History and Archeology	Knowledge of historical events and their causes, indicators, and effects on civilizations and cultures.
Communications and Media	Knowledge of media production, communication, and dissemination techniques and methods. This includes alternative ways to inform and entertain via written, oral, and visual media.
Biology	Knowledge of plant and animal organisms, their tissues, cells, functions, interdependencies, and interactions with each other and the environment.
Transportation	Knowledge of principles and methods for moving people or goods by air, rail, sea, or road, including the relative costs and benefits.
Administration and Management	Knowledge of business and management principles involved in strategic planning, resource allocation, human resources modeling, leadership technique, production methods, and coordination of people and resources.
Foreign Language	Knowledge of the structure and content of a foreign (non-English) language including the meaning and spelling of words, rules of composition and grammar, and pronunciation.
Physics	Knowledge and prediction of physical principles, laws, their interrelationships, and applications to understanding fluid, material, and atmospheric dynamics, and mechanical, electrical, atomic and sub- atomic structures and processes.
Clerical	Knowledge of administrative and clerical procedures and systems such as word processing, managing files and records, stenography and transcription, designing forms, and other office procedures and terminology.
Law and Government	Knowledge of laws, legal codes, court procedures, precedents, government regulations, executive orders, agency rules, and the democratic political process.
Design	Knowledge of design techniques, tools, and principles involved in production of precision technical plans, blueprints, drawings, and models.
Philosophy and Theology	Knowledge of different philosophical systems and religions. This includes their basic principles, values, ethics, ways of thinking, customs, practices, and their impact on human culture.
Engineering and Technology	Knowledge of the practical application of engineering science and technology. This includes applying principles, techniques, procedures, and equipment to the design and production of various goods and services.
Psychology	Knowledge of human behavior and performance; individual differences in ability, personality, and interests; learning and motivation; psychological research methods; and the assessment and treatment of behavioral and affective disorders.
Customer and Personal Service	Knowledge of principles and processes for providing customer and personal services. This includes customer needs assessment, meeting quality standards for services, and evaluation of customer satisfaction.
Telecommunications	Knowledge of transmission, broadcasting, switching, control, and operation of telecommunications systems.
Chemistry	Knowledge of the chemical composition, structure, and properties of substances and of the chemical processes and transformations that they undergo. This includes uses of chemicals and their interactions, danger signs, production techniques, and disposal methods.
Public Safety and Security	Knowledge of relevant equipment, policies, procedures, and strategies to promote effective local, state, or national security operations for the protection of people, data, property, and institutions.
Personnel and Human Resources	Knowledge of principles and procedures for personnel recruitment, selection, training, compensation and benefits, labor relations and negotiation, and personnel information systems.
Economics and Accounting	Knowledge of economic and accounting principles and practices, the financial markets, banking and the analysis and reporting of financial data.

Sales and Marketing	Knowledge of principles and methods for showing, promoting, and selling products or services. This includes marketing strategy and tactics, product demonstration, sales techniques, and sales control systems.
Medicine and Dentistry	Knowledge of the information and techniques needed to diagnose and treat human injuries, diseases, and deformities. This includes symptoms, treatment alternatives, drug properties and interactions, and preventive health-care measures.
Production and Processing	Knowledge of raw materials, production processes, quality control, costs, and other techniques for maximizing the effective manufacture and distribution of goods.
Mechanical	Knowledge of machines and tools, including their designs, uses, repair, and maintenance.
Food Production	Knowledge of techniques and equipment for planting, growing, and harvesting food products (both plant and animal) for consumption, including storage/handling techniques.
Building and Construction	Knowledge of materials, methods, and the tools involved in the construction or repair of houses, buildings, or other structures such as highways and roads.
Fine Arts	Knowledge of the theory and techniques required to compose, produce, and perform works of music, dance, visual arts, drama, and sculpture.
Therapy and Counseling	Knowledge of principles, methods, and procedures for diagnosis, treatment, and rehabilitation of physical and mental dysfunctions, and for career counseling and guidance.

Skills	**Skills Definitions**
Critical Thinking	Using logic and reasoning to identify the strengths and weaknesses of alternative solutions, conclusions or approaches to problems.
Reading Comprehension	Understanding written sentences and paragraphs in work related documents.
Writing	Communicating effectively in writing as appropriate for the needs of the audience.
Active Learning	Understanding the implications of new information for both current and future problem-solving and decision-making.
Complex Problem Solving	Identifying complex problems and reviewing related information to develop and evaluate options and implement solutions.
Speaking	Talking to others to convey information effectively.
Science	Using scientific rules and methods to solve problems.
Time Management	Managing one's own time and the time of others.
Active Listening	Giving full attention to what other people are saying, taking time to understand the points being made, asking questions as appropriate, and not interrupting at inappropriate times.
Instructing	Teaching others how to do something.
Learning Strategies	Selecting and using training/instructional methods and procedures appropriate for the situation when learning or teaching new things.
Mathematics	Using mathematics to solve problems.
Social Perceptiveness	Being aware of others' reactions and understanding why they react as they do.
Coordination	Adjusting actions in relation to others' actions.
Judgment and Decision Making	Considering the relative costs and benefits of potential actions to choose the most appropriate one.
Monitoring	Monitoring/Assessing performance of yourself, other individuals, or organizations to make improvements or take corrective action.
Equipment Selection	Determining the kind of tools and equipment needed to do a job.
Persuasion	Persuading others to change their minds or behavior.
Management of Financial Resources	Determining how money will be spent to get the work done, and accounting for these expenditures.
Programming	Writing computer programs for various purposes.
Systems Analysis	Determining how a system should work and how changes in conditions, operations, and the environment will affect outcomes.
Management of Personnel Resources	Motivating, developing, and directing people as they work, identifying the best people for the job.
Service Orientation	Actively looking for ways to help people.
Operations Analysis	Analyzing needs and product requirements to create a design.
Negotiation	Bringing others together and trying to reconcile differences.
Technology Design	Generating or adapting equipment and technology to serve user needs.
Management of Material Resources	Obtaining and seeing to the appropriate use of equipment, facilities, and materials needed to do certain work.

Systems Evaluation	Identifying measures or indicators of system performance and the actions needed to improve or correct performance, relative to the goals of the system.
Quality Control Analysis	Conducting tests and inspections of products, services, or processes to evaluate quality or performance.
Troubleshooting	Determining causes of operating errors and deciding what to do about it.
Installation	Installing equipment, machines, wiring, or programs to meet specifications.
Operation and Control	Controlling operations of equipment or systems.
Operation Monitoring	Watching gauges, dials, or other indicators to make sure a machine is working properly.
Equipment Maintenance	Performing routine maintenance on equipment and determining when and what kind of maintenance is needed.
Repairing	Repairing machines or systems using the needed tools.

Ability	**Ability Definitions**
Oral Expression	The ability to communicate information and ideas in speaking so others will understand.
Written Comprehension	The ability to read and understand information and ideas presented in writing.
Written Expression	The ability to communicate information and ideas in writing so others will understand.
Near Vision	The ability to see details at close range (within a few feet of the observer).
Oral Comprehension	The ability to listen to and understand information and ideas presented through spoken words and sentences.
Speech Clarity	The ability to speak clearly so others can understand you.
Inductive Reasoning	The ability to combine pieces of information to form general rules or conclusions (includes finding a relationship among seemingly unrelated events).
Deductive Reasoning	The ability to apply general rules to specific problems to produce answers that make sense.
Problem Sensitivity	The ability to tell when something is wrong or is likely to go wrong. It does not involve solving the problem, only recognizing there is a problem.
Information Ordering	The ability to arrange things or actions in a certain order or pattern according to a specific rule or set of rules (e.g., patterns of numbers, letters, words, pictures, mathematical operations).
Speech Recognition	The ability to identify and understand the speech of another person.
Far Vision	The ability to see details at a distance.
Selective Attention	The ability to concentrate on a task over a period of time without being distracted.
Originality	The ability to come up with unusual or clever ideas about a given topic or situation, or to develop creative ways to solve a problem.
Fluency of Ideas	The ability to come up with a number of ideas about a topic (the number of ideas is important, not their quality, correctness, or creativity).
Visualization	The ability to imagine how something will look after it is moved around or when its parts are moved or rearranged.
Category Flexibility	The ability to generate or use different sets of rules for combining or grouping things in different ways.
Flexibility of Closure	The ability to identify or detect a known pattern (a figure, object, word, or sound) that is hidden in other distracting material.
Mathematical Reasoning	The ability to choose the right mathematical methods or formulas to solve a problem.
Time Sharing	The ability to shift back and forth between two or more activities or sources of information (such as speech, sounds, touch, or other sources).
Number Facility	The ability to add, subtract, multiply, or divide quickly and correctly.
Speed of Closure	The ability to quickly make sense of, combine, and organize information into meaningful patterns.
Memorization	The ability to remember information such as words, numbers, pictures, and procedures.
Perceptual Speed	The ability to quickly and accurately compare similarities and differences among sets of letters, numbers, objects, pictures, or patterns. The things to be compared may be presented at the same time or one after the other. This ability also includes comparing a presented object with a remembered object.
Visual Color Discrimination	The ability to match or detect differences between colors, including shades of color and brightness.

Depth Perception	The ability to judge which of several objects is closer or farther away from you, or to judge the distance between you and an object.
Finger Dexterity	The ability to make precisely coordinated movements of the fingers of one or both hands to grasp, manipulate, or assemble very small objects.
Spatial Orientation	The ability to know your location in relation to the environment or to know where other objects are in relation to you.
Auditory Attention	The ability to focus on a single source of sound in the presence of other distracting sounds.
Hearing Sensitivity	The ability to detect or tell the differences between sounds that vary in pitch and loudness.
Control Precision	The ability to quickly and repeatedly adjust the controls of a machine or a vehicle to exact positions.
Manual Dexterity	The ability to quickly move your hand, your hand together with your arm, or your two hands to grasp, manipulate, or assemble objects.
Trunk Strength	The ability to use your abdominal and lower back muscles to support part of the body repeatedly or continuously over time without 'giving out' or fatiguing.
Multilimb Coordination	The ability to coordinate two or more limbs (for example, two arms, two legs, or one leg and one arm) while sitting, standing, or lying down. It does not involve performing the activities while the whole body is in motion.
Arm-Hand Steadiness	The ability to keep your hand and arm steady while moving your arm or while holding your arm and hand in one position.
Wrist-Finger Speed	The ability to make fast, simple, repeated movements of the fingers, hands, and wrists.
Glare Sensitivity	The ability to see objects in the presence of glare or bright lighting.
Peripheral Vision	The ability to see objects or movement of objects to one's side when the eyes are looking ahead.
Night Vision	The ability to see under low light conditions.
Gross Body Coordination	The ability to coordinate the movement of your arms, legs, and torso together when the whole body is in motion.
Dynamic Flexibility	The ability to quickly and repeatedly bend, stretch, twist, or reach out with your body, arms, and/or legs.
Extent Flexibility	The ability to bend, stretch, twist, or reach with your body, arms, and/or legs.
Stamina	The ability to exert yourself physically over long periods of time without getting winded or out of breath.
Dynamic Strength	The ability to exert muscle force repeatedly or continuously over time. This involves muscular endurance and resistance to muscle fatigue.
Explosive Strength	The ability to use short bursts of muscle force to propel oneself (as in jumping or sprinting), or to throw an object.
Sound Localization	The ability to tell the direction from which a sound originated.
Speed of Limb Movement	The ability to quickly move the arms and legs.
Rate Control	The ability to time your movements or the movement of a piece of equipment in anticipation of changes in the speed and/or direction of a moving object or scene.
Static Strength	The ability to exert maximum muscle force to lift, push, pull, or carry objects.
Response Orientation	The ability to choose quickly between two or more movements in response to two or more different signals (lights, sounds, pictures). It includes the speed with which the correct response is started with the hand, foot, or other body part.
Gross Body Equilibrium	The ability to keep or regain your body balance or stay upright when in an unstable position.
Reaction Time	The ability to quickly respond (with the hand, finger, or foot) to a signal (sound, light, picture) when it appears.

Work_Activity	Work_Activity Definitions
Analyzing Data or Information	Identifying the underlying principles, reasons, or facts of information by breaking down information or data into separate parts.
Getting Information	Observing, receiving, and otherwise obtaining information from all relevant sources.
Interacting With Computers	Using computers and computer systems (including hardware and software) to program, write software, set up functions, enter data, or process information.
Updating and Using Relevant Knowledge	Keeping up-to-date technically and applying new knowledge to your job.
Processing Information	Compiling, coding, categorizing, calculating, tabulating, auditing, or verifying information or data.

Training and Teaching Others	Identifying the educational needs of others, developing formal educational or training programs or classes, and teaching or instructing others.
Interpreting the Meaning of Information for Others	Translating or explaining what information means and how it can be used.
Communicating with Supervisors, Peers, or Subordin	Providing information to supervisors, co-workers, and subordinates by telephone, in written form, e-mail, or in person.
Thinking Creatively	Developing, designing, or creating new applications, ideas, relationships, systems, or products, including artistic contributions.
Making Decisions and Solving Problems	Analyzing information and evaluating results to choose the best solution and solve problems.
Communicating with Persons Outside Organization	Communicating with people outside the organization, representing the organization to customers, the public, government, and other external sources. This information can be exchanged in person, in writing, or by telephone or e-mail.
Identifying Objects, Actions, and Events	Identifying information by categorizing, estimating, recognizing differences or similarities, and detecting changes in circumstances or events.
Organizing, Planning, and Prioritizing Work	Developing specific goals and plans to prioritize, organize, and accomplish your work.
Estimating the Quantifiable Characteristics of Pro	Estimating sizes, distances, and quantities; or determining time, costs, resources, or materials needed to perform a work activity.
Documenting/Recording Information	Entering, transcribing, recording, storing, or maintaining information in written or electronic/magnetic form.
Establishing and Maintaining Interpersonal Relatio	Developing constructive and cooperative working relationships with others, and maintaining them over time.
Monitor Processes, Materials, or Surroundings	Monitoring and reviewing information from materials, events, or the environment, to detect or assess problems.
Judging the Qualities of Things, Services, or Peop	Assessing the value, importance, or quality of things or people.
Provide Consultation and Advice to Others	Providing guidance and expert advice to management or other groups on technical, systems-, or process-related topics.
Developing Objectives and Strategies	Establishing long-range objectives and specifying the strategies and actions to achieve them.
Coordinating the Work and Activities of Others	Getting members of a group to work together to accomplish tasks.
Scheduling Work and Activities	Scheduling events, programs, and activities, as well as the work of others.
Coaching and Developing Others	Identifying the developmental needs of others and coaching, mentoring, or otherwise helping others to improve their knowledge or skills.
Guiding, Directing, and Motivating Subordinates	Providing guidance and direction to subordinates, including setting performance standards and monitoring performance.
Evaluating Information to Determine Compliance wit	Using relevant information and individual judgment to determine whether events or processes comply with laws, regulations, or standards.
Monitoring and Controlling Resources	Monitoring and controlling resources and overseeing the spending of money.
Developing and Building Teams	Encouraging and building mutual trust, respect, and cooperation among team members.
Performing Administrative Activities	Performing day-to-day administrative tasks such as maintaining information files and processing paperwork.
Performing for or Working Directly with the Public	Performing for people or dealing directly with the public. This includes serving customers in restaurants and stores, and receiving clients or guests.
Resolving Conflicts and Negotiating with Others	Handling complaints, settling disputes, and resolving grievances and conflicts, or otherwise negotiating with others.
Staffing Organizational Units	Recruiting, interviewing, selecting, hiring, and promoting employees in an organization.
Selling or Influencing Others	Convincing others to buy merchandise/goods or to otherwise change their minds or actions.
Performing General Physical Activities	Performing physical activities that require considerable use of your arms and legs and moving your whole body, such as climbing, lifting, balancing, walking, stooping, and handling of materials.
Handling and Moving Objects	Using hands and arms in handling, installing, positioning, and moving materials, and manipulating things.
Inspecting Equipment, Structures, or Material	Inspecting equipment, structures, or materials to identify the cause of errors or other problems or defects.
Drafting, Laying Out, and Specifying Technical Dev	Providing documentation, detailed instructions, drawings, or specifications to tell others about how devices, parts, equipment, or structures are to be fabricated, constructed, assembled, modified, maintained, or used.

Operating Vehicles, Mechanized Devices, or Equipme	Running, maneuvering, navigating, or driving vehicles or mechanized equipment, such as forklifts, passenger vehicles, aircraft, or water craft.
Assisting and Caring for Others	Providing personal assistance, medical attention, emotional support, or other personal care to others such as coworkers, customers, or patients.
Repairing and Maintaining Electronic Equipment	Servicing, repairing, calibrating, regulating, fine-tuning, or testing machines, devices, and equipment that operate primarily on the basis of electrical or electronic (not mechanical) principles.
Controlling Machines and Processes	Using either control mechanisms or direct physical activity to operate machines or processes (not including computers or vehicles).
Repairing and Maintaining Mechanical Equipment	Servicing, repairing, adjusting, and testing machines, devices, moving parts, and equipment that operate primarily on the basis of mechanical (not electronic) principles.

Work_Context	Work_Context Definitions
Electronic Mail	How often do you use electronic mail in this job?
Face-to-Face Discussions	How often do you have to have face-to-face discussions with individuals or teams in this job?
Indoors, Environmentally Controlled	How often does this job require working indoors in environmentally controlled conditions?
Telephone	How often do you have telephone conversations in this job?
Freedom to Make Decisions	How much decision making freedom, without supervision, does the job offer?
Structured versus Unstructured Work	To what extent is this job structured for the worker, rather than allowing the worker to determine tasks, priorities, and goals?
Importance of Being Exact or Accurate	How important is being very exact or highly accurate in performing this job?
Letters and Memos	How often does the job require written letters and memos?
Spend Time Sitting	How much does this job require sitting?
Contact With Others	How much does this job require the worker to be in contact with others (face-to-face, by telephone, or otherwise) in order to perform it?
Work With Work Group or Team	How important is it to work with others in a group or team in this job?
Public Speaking	How often do you have to perform public speaking in this job?
Time Pressure	How often does this job require the worker to meet strict deadlines?
Level of Competition	To what extent does this job require the worker to compete or to be aware of competitive pressures?
Impact of Decisions on Co-workers or Company Resul	How do the decisions an employee makes impact the results of co-workers, clients or the company?
Coordinate or Lead Others	How important is it to coordinate or lead others in accomplishing work activities in this job?
Frequency of Decision Making	How frequently is the worker required to make decisions that affect other people, the financial resources, and/or the image and reputation of the organization?
Deal With External Customers	How important is it to work with external customers or the public in this job?
Responsibility for Outcomes and Results	How responsible is the worker for work outcomes and results of other workers?
Importance of Repeating Same Tasks	How important is repeating the same physical activities (e.g., key entry) or mental activities (e.g., checking entries in a ledger) over and over, without stopping, to performing this job?
Consequence of Error	How serious would the result usually be if the worker made a mistake that was not readily correctable?
Physical Proximity	To what extent does this job require the worker to perform job tasks in close physical proximity to other people?
Spend Time Making Repetitive Motions	How much does this job require making repetitive motions?
Frequency of Conflict Situations	How often are there conflict situations the employee has to face in this job?
Outdoors, Exposed to Weather	How often does this job require working outdoors, exposed to all weather conditions?
Degree of Automation	How automated is the job?
Deal With Unpleasant or Angry People	How frequently does the worker have to deal with unpleasant, angry, or discourteous individuals as part of the job requirements?
In an Enclosed Vehicle or Equipment	How often does this job require working in a closed vehicle or equipment (e.g., car)?
Spend Time Standing	How much does this job require standing?
Spend Time Using Your Hands to Handle, Control, or	How much does this job require using your hands to handle, control, or feel objects, tools or controls?

Indoors, Not Environmentally Controlled	How often does this job require working indoors in non-controlled environmental conditions (e.g., warehouse without heat)?
Responsible for Others' Health and Safety	How much responsibility is there for the health and safety of others in this job?
Sounds, Noise Levels Are Distracting or Uncomforta	How often does this job require working exposed to sounds and noise levels that are distracting or uncomfortable?
Outdoors, Under Cover	How often does this job require working outdoors, under cover (e.g., structure with roof but no walls)?
Very Hot or Cold Temperatures	How often does this job require working in very hot (above 90 F degrees) or very cold (below 32 F degrees) temperatures?
Spend Time Walking and Running	How much does this job require walking and running?
Exposed to Contaminants	How often does this job require working exposed to contaminants (such as pollutants, gases, dust or odors)?
Exposed to Minor Burns, Cuts, Bites, or Stings	How often does this job require exposure to minor burns, cuts, bites, or stings?
Wear Common Protective or Safety Equipment such as	How much does this job require wearing common protective or safety equipment such as safety shoes, glasses, gloves, hard hats or live jackets?
Extremely Bright or Inadequate Lighting	How often does this job require working in extremely bright or inadequate lighting conditions?
In an Open Vehicle or Equipment	How often does this job require working in an open vehicle or equipment (e.g., tractor)?
Cramped Work Space, Awkward Positions	How often does this job require working in cramped work spaces that requires getting into awkward positions?
Exposed to High Places	How often does this job require exposure to high places?
Pace Determined by Speed of Equipment	How important is it to this job that the pace is determined by the speed of equipment or machinery? (This does not refer to keeping busy at all times on this job.)
Wear Specialized Protective or Safety Equipment su	How much does this job require wearing specialized protective or safety equipment such as breathing apparatus, safety harness, full protection suits, or radiation protection?
Spend Time Bending or Twisting the Body	How much does this job require bending or twisting your body?
Deal With Physically Aggressive People	How frequently does this job require the worker to deal with physical aggression of violent individuals?
Spend Time Kneeling, Crouching, Stooping, or Crawl	How much does this job require kneeling, crouching, stooping or crawling?
Exposed to Hazardous Equipment	How often does this job require exposure to hazardous equipment?
Spend Time Keeping or Regaining Balance	How much does this job require keeping or regaining your balance?
Spend Time Climbing Ladders, Scaffolds, or Poles	How much does this job require climbing ladders, scaffolds, or poles?
Exposed to Disease or Infections	How often does this job require exposure to disease/infections?
Exposed to Hazardous Conditions	How often does this job require exposure to hazardous conditions?
Exposed to Whole Body Vibration	How often does this job require exposure to whole body vibration (e.g., operate a jackhammer)?
Exposed to Radiation	How often does this job require exposure to radiation?

Job Zone Component	Job Zone Component Definitions
Title	Job Zone Five: Extensive Preparation Needed
Overall Experience	Extensive skill, knowledge, and experience are needed for these occupations. Many require more than five years of experience. For example, surgeons must complete four years of college and an additional five to seven years of specialized medical training to be able to do their job.
Job Training	Employees may need some on-the-job training, but most of these occupations assume that the person will already have the required skills, knowledge, work-related experience, and/or training.
Job Zone Examples	These occupations often involve coordinating, training, supervising, or managing the activities of others to accomplish goals. Very advanced communication and organizational skills are required. Examples include athletic trainers, lawyers, managing editors, phyicists, social psychologists, and surgeons.
SVP Range	(8.0 and above)
Education	A bachelor's degree is the minimum formal education required for these occupations. However, many also require graduate school. For example, they may require a master's degree, and some require a Ph.D., M.D., or J.D. (law degree).

Work_Styles	Work_Styles Definitions
Analytical Thinking	Job requires analyzing information and using logic to address work-related issues and problems.
Integrity	Job requires being honest and ethical.
Attention to Detail	Job requires being careful about detail and thorough in completing work tasks.
Dependability	Job requires being reliable, responsible, and dependable, and fulfilling obligations.
Independence	Job requires developing one's own ways of doing things, guiding oneself with little or no supervision, and depending on oneself to get things done.
Initiative	Job requires a willingness to take on responsibilities and challenges.
Achievement/Effort	Job requires establishing and maintaining personally challenging achievement goals and exerting effort toward mastering tasks.
Persistence	Job requires persistence in the face of obstacles.
Innovation	Job requires creativity and alternative thinking to develop new ideas for and answers to work-related problems.
Adaptability/Flexibility	Job requires being open to change (positive or negative) and to considerable variety in the workplace.
Cooperation	Job requires being pleasant with others on the job and displaying a good-natured, cooperative attitude.
Stress Tolerance	Job requires accepting criticism and dealing calmly and effectively with high stress situations.
Leadership	Job requires a willingness to lead, take charge, and offer opinions and direction.
Self Control	Job requires maintaining composure, keeping emotions in check, controlling anger, and avoiding aggressive behavior, even in very difficult situations.
Concern for Others	Job requires being sensitive to others' needs and feelings and being understanding and helpful on the job.
Social Orientation	Job requires preferring to work with others rather than alone, and being personally connected with others on the job.

19-3094.00 - Political Scientists

Study the origin, development, and operation of political systems. Research a wide range of subjects, such as relations between the United States and foreign countries, the beliefs and institutions of foreign nations, or the politics of small towns or a major metropolis. May study topics, such as public opinion, political decision making, and ideology. May analyze the structure and operation of governments, as well as various political entities. May conduct public opinion surveys, analyze election results, or analyze public documents.

Tasks

1) Forecast political, economic, and social trends.

2) Disseminate research results through academic publications, written reports, or public presentations.

3) Collect, analyze, and interpret data such as election results and public opinion surveys; report on findings, recommendations, and conclusions.

4) Develop and test theories, using information from interviews, newspapers, periodicals, case law, historical papers, polls, and/or statistical sources.

5) Write drafts of legislative proposals, and prepare speeches, correspondence, and policy papers for governmental use.

6) Interpret and analyze policies, public issues, legislation, and/or the operations of governments, businesses, and organizations.

7) Identify issues for research and analysis.

8) Provide media commentary and/or criticism related to public policy and political issues and events.

9) Maintain current knowledge of government policy decisions.

10) Consult with and advise government officials, civic bodies, research agencies, the media, political parties, and others concerned with political issues.

11) Evaluate programs and policies, and make related recommendations to institutions and organizations.

Knowledge	Knowledge Definitions
Law and Government	Knowledge of laws, legal codes, court procedures, precedents, government regulations, executive orders, agency rules, and the democratic political process.
English Language	Knowledge of the structure and content of the English language including the meaning and spelling of words, rules of composition, and grammar.
Education and Training	Knowledge of principles and methods for curriculum and training design, teaching and instruction for individuals and groups, and the measurement of training effects.
History and Archeology	Knowledge of historical events and their causes, indicators, and effects on civilizations and cultures.
Sociology and Anthropology	Knowledge of group behavior and dynamics, societal trends and influences, human migrations, ethnicity, cultures and their history and origins.
Philosophy and Theology	Knowledge of different philosophical systems and religions. This includes their basic principles, values, ethics, ways of thinking, customs, practices, and their impact on human culture.
Geography	Knowledge of principles and methods for describing the features of land, sea, and air masses, including their physical characteristics, locations, interrelationships, and distribution of plant, animal, and human life.
Customer and Personal Service	Knowledge of principles and processes for providing customer and personal services. This includes customer needs assessment, meeting quality standards for services, and evaluation of customer satisfaction.
Communications and Media	Knowledge of media production, communication, and dissemination techniques and methods. This includes alternative ways to inform and entertain via written, oral, and visual media.
Mathematics	Knowledge of arithmetic, algebra, geometry, calculus, statistics, and their applications.
Administration and Management	Knowledge of business and management principles involved in strategic planning, resource allocation, human resources modeling, leadership technique, production methods, and coordination of people and resources.
Computers and Electronics	Knowledge of circuit boards, processors, chips, electronic equipment, and computer hardware and software, including applications and programming.
Foreign Language	Knowledge of the structure and content of a foreign (non-English) language including the meaning and spelling of words, rules of composition and grammar, and pronunciation.
Psychology	Knowledge of human behavior and performance; individual differences in ability, personality, and interests; learning and motivation; psychological research methods; and the assessment and treatment of behavioral and affective disorders.
Clerical	Knowledge of administrative and clerical procedures and systems such as word processing, managing files and records, stenography and transcription, designing forms, and other office procedures and terminology.
Personnel and Human Resources	Knowledge of principles and procedures for personnel recruitment, selection, training, compensation and benefits, labor relations and negotiation, and personnel information systems.
Economics and Accounting	Knowledge of economic and accounting principles and practices, the financial markets, banking and the analysis and reporting of financial data.
Public Safety and Security	Knowledge of relevant equipment, policies, procedures, and strategies to promote effective local, state, or national security operations for the protection of people, data, property, and institutions.
Sales and Marketing	Knowledge of principles and methods for showing, promoting, and selling products or services. This includes marketing strategy and tactics, product demonstration, sales techniques, and sales control systems.
Telecommunications	Knowledge of transmission, broadcasting, switching, control, and operation of telecommunications systems.
Transportation	Knowledge of principles and methods for moving people or goods by air, rail, sea, or road, including the relative costs and benefits.
Production and Processing	Knowledge of raw materials, production processes, quality control, costs, and other techniques for maximizing the effective manufacture and distribution of goods.
Therapy and Counseling	Knowledge of principles, methods, and procedures for diagnosis, treatment, and rehabilitation of physical and mental dysfunctions, and for career counseling and guidance.

Engineering and Technology	Knowledge of the practical application of engineering science and technology. This includes applying principles, techniques, procedures, and equipment to the design and production of various goods and services.
Design	Knowledge of design techniques, tools, and principles involved in production of precision technical plans, blueprints, drawings, and models.
Biology	Knowledge of plant and animal organisms, their tissues, cells, functions, interdependencies, and interactions with each other and the environment.
Fine Arts	Knowledge of the theory and techniques required to compose, produce, and perform works of music, dance, visual arts, drama, and sculpture.
Physics	Knowledge and prediction of physical principles, laws, their interrelationships, and applications to understanding fluid, material, and atmospheric dynamics, and mechanical, electrical, atomic and sub-atomic structures and processes.
Chemistry	Knowledge of the chemical composition, structure, and properties of substances and of the chemical processes and transformations that they undergo. This includes uses of chemicals and their interactions, danger signs, production techniques, and disposal methods.
Mechanical	Knowledge of machines and tools, including their designs, uses, repair, and maintenance.
Medicine and Dentistry	Knowledge of the information and techniques needed to diagnose and treat human injuries, diseases, and deformities. This includes symptoms, treatment alternatives, drug properties and interactions, and preventive health-care measures.
Food Production	Knowledge of techniques and equipment for planting, growing, and harvesting food products (both plant and animal) for consumption, including storage/handling techniques.
Building and Construction	Knowledge of materials, methods, and the tools involved in the construction or repair of houses, buildings, or other structures such as highways and roads.

Skills	Skills Definitions
Reading Comprehension	Understanding written sentences and paragraphs in work related documents.
Writing	Communicating effectively in writing as appropriate for the needs of the audience.
Critical Thinking	Using logic and reasoning to identify the strengths and weaknesses of alternative solutions, conclusions or approaches to problems.
Speaking	Talking to others to convey information effectively.
Instructing	Teaching others how to do something.
Active Learning	Understanding the implications of new information for both current and future problem-solving and decision-making.
Time Management	Managing one's own time and the time of others.
Active Listening	Giving full attention to what other people are saying, taking time to understand the points being made, asking questions as appropriate, and not interrupting at inappropriate times.
Complex Problem Solving	Identifying complex problems and reviewing related information to develop and evaluate options and implement solutions.
Social Perceptiveness	Being aware of others' reactions and understanding why they react as they do.
Learning Strategies	Selecting and using training/instructional methods and procedures appropriate for the situation when learning or teaching new things.
Judgment and Decision Making	Considering the relative costs and benefits of potential actions to choose the most appropriate one.
Monitoring	Monitoring/Assessing performance of yourself, other individuals, or organizations to make improvements or take corrective action.
Persuasion	Persuading others to change their minds or behavior.
Science	Using scientific rules and methods to solve problems.
Coordination	Adjusting actions in relation to others' actions.
Mathematics	Using mathematics to solve problems.
Negotiation	Bringing others together and trying to reconcile differences.
Service Orientation	Actively looking for ways to help people.
Management of Personnel Resources	Motivating, developing, and directing people as they work, identifying the best people for the job.
Systems Evaluation	Identifying measures or indicators of system performance and the actions needed to improve or correct performance, relative to the goals of the system.

Systems Analysis	Determining how a system should work and how changes in conditions, operations, and the environment will affect outcomes.
Management of Financial Resources	Determining how money will be spent to get the work done, and accounting for these expenditures.
Quality Control Analysis	Conducting tests and inspections of products, services, or processes to evaluate quality or performance.
Programming	Writing computer programs for various purposes.
Operations Analysis	Analyzing needs and product requirements to create a design.
Management of Material Resources	Obtaining and seeing to the appropriate use of equipment, facilities, and materials needed to do certain work.
Equipment Selection	Determining the kind of tools and equipment needed to do a job.
Operation and Control	Controlling operations of equipment or systems.
Troubleshooting	Determining causes of operating errors and deciding what to do about it.
Technology Design	Generating or adapting equipment and technology to serve user needs.
Installation	Installing equipment, machines, wiring, or programs to meet specifications.
Equipment Maintenance	Performing routine maintenance on equipment and determining when and what kind of maintenance is needed.
Operation Monitoring	Watching gauges, dials, or other indicators to make sure a machine is working properly.
Repairing	Repairing machines or systems using the needed tools.

Ability	Ability Definitions
Written Comprehension	The ability to read and understand information and ideas presented in writing.
Oral Expression	The ability to communicate information and ideas in speaking so others will understand.
Written Expression	The ability to communicate information and ideas in writing so others will understand.
Inductive Reasoning	The ability to combine pieces of information to form general rules or conclusions (includes finding a relationship among seemingly unrelated events).
Speech Clarity	The ability to speak clearly so others can understand you.
Deductive Reasoning	The ability to apply general rules to specific problems to produce answers that make sense.
Oral Comprehension	The ability to listen to and understand information and ideas presented through spoken words and sentences.
Near Vision	The ability to see details at close range (within a few feet of the observer).
Speech Recognition	The ability to identify and understand the speech of another person.
Problem Sensitivity	The ability to tell when something is wrong or is likely to go wrong. It does not involve solving the problem, only recognizing there is a problem.
Originality	The ability to come up with unusual or clever ideas about a given topic or situation, or to develop creative ways to solve a problem.
Category Flexibility	The ability to generate or use different sets of rules for combining or grouping things in different ways.
Selective Attention	The ability to concentrate on a task over a period of time without being distracted.
Information Ordering	The ability to arrange things or actions in a certain order or pattern according to a specific rule or set of rules (e.g., patterns of numbers, letters, words, pictures, mathematical operations).
Fluency of Ideas	The ability to come up with a number of ideas about a topic (the number of ideas is important, not their quality, correctness, or creativity).
Flexibility of Closure	The ability to identify or detect a known pattern (a figure, object, word, or sound) that is hidden in other distracting material.
Mathematical Reasoning	The ability to choose the right mathematical methods or formulas to solve a problem.
Memorization	The ability to remember information such as words, numbers, pictures, and procedures.
Speed of Closure	The ability to quickly make sense of, combine, and organize information into meaningful patterns.
Time Sharing	The ability to shift back and forth between two or more activities or sources of information (such as speech, sounds, touch, or other sources).
Far Vision	The ability to see details at a distance.
Number Facility	The ability to add, subtract, multiply, or divide quickly and correctly.

Perceptual Speed	The ability to quickly and accurately compare similarities and differences among sets of letters, numbers, objects, pictures, or patterns. The things to be compared may be presented at the same time or one after the other. This ability also includes comparing a presented object with a remembered object.
Visualization	The ability to imagine how something will look after it is moved around or when its parts are moved or rearranged.
Visual Color Discrimination	The ability to match or detect differences between colors, including shades of color and brightness.
Auditory Attention	The ability to focus on a single source of sound in the presence of other distracting sounds.
Finger Dexterity	The ability to make precisely coordinated movements of the fingers of one or both hands to grasp, manipulate, or assemble very small objects.
Hearing Sensitivity	The ability to detect or tell the differences between sounds that vary in pitch and loudness.
Depth Perception	The ability to judge which of several objects is closer or farther away from you, or to judge the distance between you and an object.
Trunk Strength	The ability to use your abdominal and lower back muscles to support part of the body repeatedly or continuously over time without 'giving out' or fatiguing.
Rate Control	The ability to time your movements or the movement of a piece of equipment in anticipation of changes in the speed and/or direction of a moving object or scene.
Peripheral Vision	The ability to see objects or movement of objects to one's side when the eyes are looking ahead.
Response Orientation	The ability to choose quickly between two or more movements in response to two or more different signals (lights, sounds, pictures). It includes the speed with which the correct response is started with the hand, foot, or other body part.
Control Precision	The ability to quickly and repeatedly adjust the controls of a machine or a vehicle to exact positions.
Spatial Orientation	The ability to know your location in relation to the environment or to know where other objects are in relation to you.
Reaction Time	The ability to quickly respond (with the hand, finger, or foot) to a signal (sound, light, picture) when it appears.
Dynamic Strength	The ability to exert muscle force repeatedly or continuously over time. This involves muscular endurance and resistance to muscle fatigue.
Stamina	The ability to exert yourself physically over long periods of time without getting winded or out of breath.
Explosive Strength	The ability to use short bursts of muscle force to propel oneself (as in jumping or sprinting), or to throw an object.
Static Strength	The ability to exert maximum muscle force to lift, push, pull, or carry objects.
Speed of Limb Movement	The ability to quickly move the arms and legs.
Wrist-Finger Speed	The ability to make fast, simple, repeated movements of the fingers, hands, and wrists.
Multilimb Coordination	The ability to coordinate two or more limbs (for example, two arms, two legs, or one leg and one arm) while sitting, standing, or lying down. It does not involve performing the activities while the whole body is in motion.
Extent Flexibility	The ability to bend, stretch, twist, or reach with your body, arms, and/or legs.
Manual Dexterity	The ability to quickly move your hand, your hand together with your arm, or your two hands to grasp, manipulate, or assemble objects.
Arm-Hand Steadiness	The ability to keep your hand and arm steady while moving your arm or while holding your arm and hand in one position.
Glare Sensitivity	The ability to see objects in the presence of glare or bright lighting.
Gross Body Coordination	The ability to coordinate the movement of your arms, legs, and torso together when the whole body is in motion.
Gross Body Equilibrium	The ability to keep or regain your body balance or stay upright when in an unstable position.
Sound Localization	The ability to tell the direction from which a sound originated.
Dynamic Flexibility	The ability to quickly and repeatedly bend, stretch, twist, or reach out with your body, arms, and/or legs.
Night Vision	The ability to see under low light conditions.

Work_Activity	Work_Activity Definitions
Getting Information	Observing, receiving, and otherwise obtaining information from all relevant sources.
Thinking Creatively	Developing, designing, or creating new applications, ideas, relationships, systems, or products, including artistic contributions.
Training and Teaching Others	Identifying the educational needs of others, developing formal educational or training programs or classes, and teaching or instructing others.
Analyzing Data or Information	Identifying the underlying principles, reasons, or facts of information by breaking down information or data into separate parts.
Identifying Objects, Actions, and Events	Identifying information by categorizing, estimating, recognizing differences or similarities, and detecting changes in circumstances or events.
Processing Information	Compiling, coding, categorizing, calculating, tabulating, auditing, or verifying information or data.
Interacting With Computers	Using computers and computer systems (including hardware and software) to program, write software, set up functions, enter data, or process information.
Interpreting the Meaning of Information for Others	Translating or explaining what information means and how it can be used.
Updating and Using Relevant Knowledge	Keeping up-to-date technically and applying new knowledge to your job.
Communicating with Supervisors, Peers, or Subordin	Providing information to supervisors, co-workers, and subordinates by telephone, in written form, e-mail, or in person.
Organizing, Planning, and Prioritizing Work	Developing specific goals and plans to prioritize, organize, and accomplish your work.
Judging the Qualities of Things, Services, or Peop	Assessing the value, importance, or quality of things or people.
Communicating with Persons Outside Organization	Communicating with people outside the organization, representing the organization to customers, the public, government, and other external sources. This information can be exchanged in person, in writing, or by telephone or e-mail.
Making Decisions and Solving Problems	Analyzing information and evaluating results to choose the best solution and solve problems.
Documenting/Recording Information	Entering, transcribing, recording, storing, or maintaining information in written or electronic/magnetic form.
Establishing and Maintaining Interpersonal Relatio	Developing constructive and cooperative working relationships with others, and maintaining them over time.
Evaluating Information to Determine Compliance wit	Using relevant information and individual judgment to determine whether events or processes comply with laws, regulations, or standards.
Estimating the Quantifiable Characteristics of Pro	Estimating sizes, distances, and quantities; or determining time, costs, resources, or materials needed to perform a work activity.
Coaching and Developing Others	Identifying the developmental needs of others and coaching, mentoring, or otherwise helping others to improve their knowledge or skills.
Monitor Processes, Materials, or Surroundings	Monitoring and reviewing information from materials, events, or the environment, to detect or assess problems.
Provide Consultation and Advice to Others	Providing guidance and expert advice to management or other groups on technical, systems-, or process-related topics.
Developing Objectives and Strategies	Establishing long-range objectives and specifying the strategies and actions to achieve them.
Guiding, Directing, and Motivating Subordinates	Providing guidance and direction to subordinates, including setting performance standards and monitoring performance.
Scheduling Work and Activities	Scheduling events, programs, and activities, as well as the work of others.
Staffing Organizational Units	Recruiting, interviewing, selecting, hiring, and promoting employees in an organization.
Performing Administrative Activities	Performing day-to-day administrative tasks such as maintaining information files and processing paperwork.
Resolving Conflicts and Negotiating with Others	Handling complaints, settling disputes, and resolving grievances and conflicts, or otherwise negotiating with others.
Performing for or Working Directly with the Public	Performing for people or dealing directly with the public. This includes serving customers in restaurants and stores, and receiving clients or guests.
Coordinating the Work and Activities of Others	Getting members of a group to work together to accomplish tasks.
Developing and Building Teams	Encouraging and building mutual trust, respect, and cooperation among team members.
Selling or Influencing Others	Convincing others to buy merchandise/goods or to otherwise change their minds or actions.
Monitoring and Controlling Resources	Monitoring and controlling resources and overseeing the spending of money.
Assisting and Caring for Others	Providing personal assistance, medical attention, emotional support, or other personal care to others such as coworkers, customers, or patients.
Inspecting Equipment, Structures, or Material	Inspecting equipment, structures, or materials to identify the cause of errors or other problems or defects.

Handling and Moving Objects	Using hands and arms in handling. installing. positioning. and moving materials. and manipulating things.
Controlling Machines and Processes	Using either control mechanisms or direct physical activity to operate machines or processes (not including computers or vehicles).
Drafting, Laying Out, and Specifying Technical Dev	Providing documentation. detailed instructions. drawings. or specifications to tell others about how devices. parts. equipment, or structures are to be fabricated, constructed, assembled, modified, maintained. or used.
Repairing and Maintaining Electronic Equipment	Servicing, repairing, calibrating. regulating. fine-tuning. or testing machines, devices. and equipment that operate primarily on the basis of electrical or electronic (not mechanical) principles.
Repairing and Maintaining Mechanical Equipment	Servicing, repairing, adjusting, and testing machines. devices. moving parts. and equipment that operate primarily on the basis of mechanical (not electronic) principles.
Performing General Physical Activities	Performing physical activities that require considerable use of your arms and legs and moving your whole body, such as climbing, lifting, balancing, walking, stooping, and handling of materials.
Operating Vehicles, Mechanized Devices, or Equipme	Running, maneuvering, navigating, or driving vehicles or mechanized equipment, such as forklifts. passenger vehicles. aircraft, or water craft.

Work_Context	Work_Context Definitions
Electronic Mail	How often do you use electronic mail in this job?
Freedom to Make Decisions	How much decision making freedom. without supervision, does the job offer?
Structured versus Unstructured Work	To what extent is this job structured for the worker, rather than allowing the worker to determine tasks. priorities. and goals?
Telephone	How often do you have telephone conversations in this job?
Face-to-Face Discussions	How often do you have to have face-to-face discussions with individuals or teams in this job?
Indoors, Environmentally Controlled	How often does this job require working indoors in environmentally controlled conditions?
Spend Time Sitting	How much does this job require sitting?
Letters and Memos	How often does the job require written letters and memos?
Contact With Others	How much does this job require the worker to be in contact with others (face-to-face, by telephone. or otherwise) in order to perform it?
Importance of Being Exact or Accurate	How important is being very exact or highly accurate in performing this job?
Public Speaking	How often do you have to perform public speaking in this job?
Level of Competition	To what extent does this job require the worker to compete or to be aware of competitive pressures?
Time Pressure	How often does this job require the worker to meet strict deadlines?
Impact of Decisions on Co-workers or Company Resul	How do the decisions an employee makes impact the results of co-workers, clients or the company?
Deal With External Customers	How important is it to work with external customers or the public in this job?
Work With Work Group or Team	How important is it to work with others in a group or team in this job?
Coordinate or Lead Others	How important is it to coordinate or lead others in accomplishing work activities in this job?
Frequency of Decision Making	How frequently is the worker required to make decisions that affect other people, the financial resources, and/or the image and reputation of the organization?
Frequency of Conflict Situations	How often are there conflict situations the employee has to face in this job?
Responsibility for Outcomes and Results	How responsible is the worker for work outcomes and results of other workers?
Deal With Unpleasant or Angry People	How frequently does the worker have to deal with unpleasant, angry, or discourteous individuals as part of the job requirements?
Spend Time Making Repetitive Motions	How much does this job require making repetitive motions?
Importance of Repeating Same Tasks	How important is repeating the same physical activities (e.g., key entry) or mental activities (e.g., checking entries in a ledger) over and over, without stopping, to performing this job?
Physical Proximity	To what extent does this job require the worker to perform job tasks in close physical proximity to other people?
Consequence of Error	How serious would the result usually be if the worker made a mistake that was not readily correctable?
Spend Time Standing	How much does this job require standing?

Spend Time Using Your Hands to Handle, Control. or	How much does this job require using your hands to handle. control. or feel objects. tools or controls?
Sounds, Noise Levels Are Distracting or Uncomforta	How often does this job require working exposed to sounds and noise levels that are distracting or uncomfortable?
Degree of Automation	How automated is the job?
Responsible for Others' Health and Safety	How much responsibility is there for the health and safety of others in this job?
Indoors, Not Environmentally Controlled	How often does this job require working indoors in non-controlled environmental conditions (e.g., warehouse without heat)?
Extremely Bright or Inadequate Lighting	How often does this job require working in extremely bright or inadequate lighting conditions?
Exposed to Disease or Infections	How often does this job require exposure to disease/infections?
Deal With Physically Aggressive People	How frequently does this job require the worker to deal with physical aggression of violent individuals?
Spend Time Walking and Running	How much does this job require walking and running?
Very Hot or Cold Temperatures	How often does this job require working in very hot (above 90 F degrees) or very cold (below 32 F degrees) temperatures?
Exposed to Contaminants	How often does this job require working exposed to contaminants (such as pollutants, gases, dust or odors)?
In an Enclosed Vehicle or Equipment	How often does this job require working in a closed vehicle or equipment (e.g., car)?
Cramped Work Space, Awkward Positions	How often does this job require working in cramped work spaces that requires getting into awkward positions?
Outdoors, Under Cover	How often does this job require working outdoors, under cover (e.g., structure with roof but no walls)?
Outdoors, Exposed to Weather	How often does this job require working outdoors, exposed to all weather conditions?
In an Open Vehicle or Equipment	How often does this job require working in an open vehicle or equipment (e.g., tractor)?
Spend Time Keeping or Regaining Balance	How much does this job require keeping or regaining your balance?
Exposed to Hazardous Conditions	How often does this job require exposure to hazardous conditions?
Wear Common Protective or Safety Equipment such as	How much does this job require wearing common protective or safety equipment such as safety shoes, glasses, gloves, hard hats or live jackets?
Spend Time Bending or Twisting the Body	How much does this job require bending or twisting your body?
Wear Specialized Protective or Safety Equipment su	How much does this job require wearing specialized protective or safety equipment such as breathing apparatus, safety harness, full protection suits, or radiation protection?
Exposed to Radiation	How often does this job require exposure to radiation?
Exposed to Hazardous Equipment	How often does this job require exposure to hazardous equipment?
Exposed to Whole Body Vibration	How often does this job require exposure to whole body vibration (e.g., operate a jackhammer)?
Exposed to Minor Burns, Cuts, Bites, or Stings	How often does this job require exposure to minor burns, cuts, bites, or stings?
Pace Determined by Speed of Equipment	How important is it to this job that the pace is determined by the speed of equipment or machinery? (This does not refer to keeping busy at all times on this job.)
Exposed to High Places	How often does this job require exposure to high places?
Spend Time Kneeling, Crouching, Stooping, or Crawl	How much does this job require kneeling, crouching, stooping or crawling?
Spend Time Climbing Ladders, Scaffolds, or Poles	How much does this job require climbing ladders, scaffolds, or poles?

Job Zone Component	Job Zone Component Definitions
Title	Job Zone Five: Extensive Preparation Needed Extensive skill, knowledge, and experience are needed for these occupations. Many require more than five years of experience.
Overall Experience	For example, surgeons must complete four years of college and an additional five to seven years of specialized medical training to be able to do their job.
Job Training	Employees may need some on-the-job training, but most of these occupations assume that the person will already have the required skills, knowledge, work-related experience, and/or training.

Job Zone Examples	These occupations often involve coordinating, training, supervising, or managing the activities of others to accomplish goals. Very advanced communication and organizational skills are required. Examples include athletic trainers, lawyers, managing editors, physicists, social psychologists, and surgeons.
SVP Range	(8.0 and above)
Education	A bachelor's degree is the minimum formal education required for these occupations. However, many also require graduate school. For example, they may require a master's degree, and some require a Ph.D., M.D., or J.D. (law degree).

Work_Styles	Work_Styles Definitions
Analytical Thinking	Job requires analyzing information and using logic to address work-related issues and problems.
Integrity	Job requires being honest and ethical.
Independence	Job requires developing one's own ways of doing things, guiding oneself with little or no supervision, and depending on oneself to get things done.
Achievement/Effort	Job requires establishing and maintaining personally challenging achievement goals and exerting effort toward mastering tasks.
Initiative	Job requires a willingness to take on responsibilities and challenges.
Persistence	Job requires persistence in the face of obstacles.
Dependability	Job requires being reliable, responsible, and dependable, and fulfilling obligations.
Innovation	Job requires creativity and alternative thinking to develop new ideas for and answers to work-related problems.
Attention to Detail	Job requires being careful about detail and thorough in completing work tasks.
Adaptability/Flexibility	Job requires being open to change (positive or negative) and to considerable variety in the workplace.
Stress Tolerance	Job requires accepting criticism and dealing calmly and effectively with high stress situations.
Self Control	Job requires maintaining composure, keeping emotions in check, controlling anger, and avoiding aggressive behavior, even in very difficult situations.
Leadership	Job requires a willingness to lead, take charge, and offer opinions and direction.
Concern for Others	Job requires being sensitive to others' needs and feelings and being understanding and helpful on the job.
Cooperation	Job requires being pleasant with others on the job and displaying a good-natured, cooperative attitude.
Social Orientation	Job requires preferring to work with others rather than alone, and being personally connected with others on the job.

19-4011.01 - Agricultural Technicians

Set up and maintain laboratory and collect and record data to assist scientist in biology or related agricultural science experiments.

Tasks

1) Prepare data summaries, reports, and analyses that include results, charts, and graphs in order to document research findings and results.

2) Collect samples from crops or animals so testing can be performed.

3) Adjust testing equipment, and prepare culture media, following standard procedures.

4) Operate laboratory equipment such as spectrometers, nitrogen determination apparatus, air samplers, centrifuges, and PH meters in order to perform tests.

5) Receive and prepare laboratory samples for analysis, following proper protocols in order to ensure that they will be stored, prepared, and disposed of efficiently and effectively.

6) Measure or weigh ingredients used in testing or for purposes such as animal feed.

7) Operate farm machinery including tractors, plows, mowers, combines, balers, sprayers, earthmoving equipment, and trucks.

8) Maintain and repair agricultural facilities, equipment, and tools in order to ensure operational readiness, safety, and cleanliness.

9) Perform crop production duties such as tilling, hoeing, pruning, weeding, and harvesting crops.

10) Respond to inquiries and requests from the public that do not require specialized scientific knowledge or expertise.

11) Set up laboratory or field equipment, and prepare sites for testing.

12) Transplant trees, vegetables, and/or horticultural plants.

13) Supervise and train agricultural technicians and farm laborers.

14) Prepare and present agricultural demonstrations.

15) Measure and mark plot areas; and plow, disc, level, and otherwise prepare land for cultivated crops, orchards and vineyards.

16) Conduct insect and plant disease surveys.

17) Examine animals and specimens in order to determine the presence of diseases or other problems.

18) Plant seeds in specified areas, and count the resulting plants in order to determine the percentage of seeds that germinated.

19) Supervise pest or weed control operations including locating and identifying pests or weeds, selecting chemicals and application methods, scheduling application, and training operators.

20) Perform general nursery duties such as propagating standard varieties of plant materials, collecting and germinating seeds, maintaining cuttings of plants, and controlling environmental conditions.

21) Devise cultural methods and environmental controls for plants for which guidelines are sketchy or nonexistent.

22) Provide food and water to livestock and laboratory animals, and record details of their food consumption.

23) Provide routine animal care such as taking and recording body measurements, applying identification, and assisting in the birthing process.

Knowledge	Knowledge Definitions
Chemistry	Knowledge of the chemical composition, structure, and properties of substances and of the chemical processes and transformations that they undergo. This includes uses of chemicals and their interactions, danger signs, production techniques, and disposal methods.
Biology	Knowledge of plant and animal organisms, their tissues, cells, functions, interdependencies, and interactions with each other and the environment.
Customer and Personal Service	Knowledge of principles and processes for providing customer and personal services. This includes customer needs assessment, meeting quality standards for services, and evaluation of customer satisfaction.
English Language	Knowledge of the structure and content of the English language including the meaning and spelling of words, rules of composition, and grammar.
Food Production	Knowledge of techniques and equipment for planting, growing, and harvesting food products (both plant and animal) for consumption, including storage/handling techniques.
Education and Training	Knowledge of principles and methods for curriculum and training design, teaching and instruction for individuals and groups, and the measurement of training effects.
Mathematics	Knowledge of arithmetic, algebra, geometry, calculus, statistics, and their applications.
Production and Processing	Knowledge of raw materials, production processes, quality control, costs, and other techniques for maximizing the effective manufacture and distribution of goods.
Clerical	Knowledge of administrative and clerical procedures and systems such as word processing, managing files and records, stenography and transcription, designing forms, and other office procedures and terminology.
Public Safety and Security	Knowledge of relevant equipment, policies, procedures, and strategies to promote effective local, state, or national security operations for the protection of people, data, property, and institutions.
Mechanical	Knowledge of machines and tools, including their designs, uses, repair, and maintenance.
Computers and Electronics	Knowledge of circuit boards, processors, chips, electronic equipment, and computer hardware and software, including applications and programming.
Administration and Management	Knowledge of business and management principles involved in strategic planning, resource allocation, human resources modeling, leadership technique, production methods, and coordination of people and resources.

Engineering and Technology	Knowledge of the practical application of engineering science and technology. This includes applying principles, techniques, procedures, and equipment to the design and production of various goods and services.
Law and Government	Knowledge of laws, legal codes, court procedures, precedents, government regulations, executive orders, agency rules, and the democratic political process.
Personnel and Human Resources	Knowledge of principles and procedures for personnel recruitment, selection, training, compensation and benefits, labor relations and negotiation, and personnel information systems.
Communications and Media	Knowledge of media production, communication, and dissemination techniques and methods. This includes alternative ways to inform and entertain via written, oral, and visual media.
Economics and Accounting	Knowledge of economic and accounting principles and practices, the financial markets, banking and the analysis and reporting of financial data.
Geography	Knowledge of principles and methods for describing the features of land, sea, and air masses, including their physical characteristics, locations, interrelationships, and distribution of plant, animal, and human life.
Design	Knowledge of design techniques, tools, and principles involved in production of precision technical plans, blueprints, drawings, and models.
Transportation	Knowledge of principles and methods for moving people or goods by air, rail, sea, or road, including the relative costs and benefits.
Physics	Knowledge and prediction of physical principles, laws, their interrelationships, and applications to understanding fluid, material, and atmospheric dynamics, and mechanical, electrical, atomic and sub- atomic structures and processes.
Building and Construction	Knowledge of materials, methods, and the tools involved in the construction or repair of houses, buildings, or other structures such as highways and roads.
Psychology	Knowledge of human behavior and performance; individual differences in ability, personality, and interests; learning and motivation; psychological research methods; and the assessment and treatment of behavioral and affective disorders.
Sales and Marketing	Knowledge of principles and methods for showing, promoting, and selling products or services. This includes marketing strategy and tactics, product demonstration, sales techniques, and sales control systems.
Telecommunications	Knowledge of transmission, broadcasting, switching, control, and operation of telecommunications systems.
Sociology and Anthropology	Knowledge of group behavior and dynamics, societal trends and influences, human migrations, ethnicity, cultures and their history and origins.
Therapy and Counseling	Knowledge of principles, methods, and procedures for diagnosis, treatment, and rehabilitation of physical and mental dysfunctions, and for career counseling and guidance.
Fine Arts	Knowledge of the theory and techniques required to compose, produce, and perform works of music, dance, visual arts, drama, and sculpture.
History and Archeology	Knowledge of historical events and their causes, indicators, and effects on civilizations and cultures.
Medicine and Dentistry	Knowledge of the information and techniques needed to diagnose and treat human injuries, diseases, and deformities. This includes symptoms, treatment alternatives, drug properties and interactions, and preventive health-care measures.
Philosophy and Theology	Knowledge of different philosophical systems and religions. This includes their basic principles, values, ethics, ways of thinking, customs, practices, and their impact on human culture.
Foreign Language	Knowledge of the structure and content of a foreign (non-English) language including the meaning and spelling of words, rules of composition and grammar, and pronunciation.

Skills   Skills Definitions

Time Management	Managing one's own time and the time of others.
Reading Comprehension	Understanding written sentences and paragraphs in work related documents.
Science	Using scientific rules and methods to solve problems.
Active Listening	Giving full attention to what other people are saying, taking time to understand the points being made, asking questions as appropriate, and not interrupting at inappropriate times.

Equipment Maintenance	Performing routine maintenance on equipment and determining when and what kind of maintenance is needed.
Active Learning	Understanding the implications of new information for both current and future problem-solving and decision-making.
Monitoring	Monitoring/Assessing performance of yourself, other individuals, or organizations to make improvements or take corrective action.
Critical Thinking	Using logic and reasoning to identify the strengths and weaknesses of alternative solutions, conclusions or approaches to problems.
Troubleshooting	Determining causes of operating errors and deciding what to do about it.
Speaking	Talking to others to convey information effectively.
Instructing	Teaching others how to do something.
Judgment and Decision Making	Considering the relative costs and benefits of potential actions to choose the most appropriate one.
Writing	Communicating effectively in writing as appropriate for the needs of the audience.
Quality Control Analysis	Conducting tests and inspections of products, services, or processes to evaluate quality or performance.
Mathematics	Using mathematics to solve problems.
Coordination	Adjusting actions in relation to others' actions.
Equipment Selection	Determining the kind of tools and equipment needed to do a job.
Operation and Control	Controlling operations of equipment or systems.
Learning Strategies	Selecting and using training/instructional methods and procedures appropriate for the situation when learning or teaching new things.
Complex Problem Solving	Identifying complex problems and reviewing related information to develop and evaluate options and implement solutions.
Operation Monitoring	Watching gauges, dials, or other indicators to make sure a machine is working properly.
Repairing	Repairing machines or systems using the needed tools.
Service Orientation	Actively looking for ways to help people.
Operations Analysis	Analyzing needs and product requirements to create a design.
Social Perceptiveness	Being aware of others' reactions and understanding why they react as they do.
Technology Design	Generating or adapting equipment and technology to serve user needs.
Persuasion	Persuading others to change their minds or behavior.
Installation	Installing equipment, machines, wiring, or programs to meet specifications.
Management of Personnel Resources	Motivating, developing, and directing people as they work, identifying the best people for the job.
Systems Analysis	Determining how a system should work and how changes in conditions, operations, and the environment will affect outcomes.
Management of Material Resources	Obtaining and seeing to the appropriate use of equipment, facilities, and materials needed to do certain work.
Systems Evaluation	Identifying measures or indicators of system performance and the actions needed to improve or correct performance, relative to the goals of the system.
Negotiation	Bringing others together and trying to reconcile differences.
Management of Financial Resources	Determining how money will be spent to get the work done, and accounting for these expenditures.
Programming	Writing computer programs for various purposes.

Ability   Ability Definitions

Problem Sensitivity	The ability to tell when something is wrong or is likely to go wrong. It does not involve solving the problem, only recognizing there is a problem.
Oral Comprehension	The ability to listen to and understand information and ideas presented through spoken words and sentences.
Oral Expression	The ability to communicate information and ideas in speaking so others will understand.
Near Vision	The ability to see details at close range (within a few feet of the observer).
Deductive Reasoning	The ability to apply general rules to specific problems to produce answers that make sense.
Written Expression	The ability to communicate information and ideas in writing so others will understand.
Category Flexibility	The ability to generate or use different sets of rules for combining or grouping things in different ways.
Inductive Reasoning	The ability to combine pieces of information to form general rules or conclusions (includes finding a relationship among seemingly unrelated events).

Written Comprehension	The ability to read and understand information and ideas presented in writing.
Information Ordering	The ability to arrange things or actions in a certain order or pattern according to a specific rule or set of rules (e.g., patterns of numbers, letters, words, pictures, mathematical operations).
Flexibility of Closure	The ability to identify or detect a known pattern (a figure, object, word, or sound) that is hidden in other distracting material.
Speech Clarity	The ability to speak clearly so others can understand you.
Selective Attention	The ability to concentrate on a task over a period of time without being distracted.
Far Vision	The ability to see details at a distance.
Speech Recognition	The ability to identify and understand the speech of another person.
Visualization	The ability to imagine how something will look after it is moved around or when its parts are moved or rearranged.
Manual Dexterity	The ability to quickly move your hand, your hand together with your arm, or your two hands to grasp, manipulate, or assemble objects.
Perceptual Speed	The ability to quickly and accurately compare similarities and differences among sets of letters, numbers, objects, pictures, or patterns. The things to be compared may be presented at the same time or one after the other. This ability also includes comparing a presented object with a remembered object.
Originality	The ability to come up with unusual or clever ideas about a given topic or situation, or to develop creative ways to solve a problem.
Time Sharing	The ability to shift back and forth between two or more activities or sources of information (such as speech, sounds, touch, or other sources).
Arm-Hand Steadiness	The ability to keep your hand and arm steady while moving your arm or while holding your arm and hand in one position.
Mathematical Reasoning	The ability to choose the right mathematical methods or formulas to solve a problem.
Finger Dexterity	The ability to make precisely coordinated movements of the fingers of one or both hands to grasp, manipulate, or assemble very small objects.
Number Facility	The ability to add, subtract, multiply, or divide quickly and correctly.
Fluency of Ideas	The ability to come up with a number of ideas about a topic (the number of ideas is important, not their quality, correctness, or creativity).
Control Precision	The ability to quickly and repeatedly adjust the controls of a machine or a vehicle to exact positions.
Auditory Attention	The ability to focus on a single source of sound in the presence of other distracting sounds.
Depth Perception	The ability to judge which of several objects is closer or farther away from you, or to judge the distance between you and an object.
Trunk Strength	The ability to use your abdominal and lower back muscles to support part of the body repeatedly or continuously over time without 'giving out' or fatiguing.
Static Strength	The ability to exert maximum muscle force to lift, push, pull, or carry objects.
Multilimb Coordination	The ability to coordinate two or more limbs (for example, two arms, two legs, or one leg and one arm) while sitting, standing, or lying down. It does not involve performing the activities while the whole body is in motion.
Speed of Closure	The ability to quickly make sense of, combine, and organize information into meaningful patterns.
Memorization	The ability to remember information such as words, numbers, pictures, and procedures.
Visual Color Discrimination	The ability to match or detect differences between colors, including shades of color and brightness.
Reaction Time	The ability to quickly respond (with the hand, finger, or foot) to a signal (sound, light, picture) when it appears.
Dynamic Strength	The ability to exert muscle force repeatedly or continuously over time. This involves muscular endurance and resistance to muscle fatigue.
Stamina	The ability to exert yourself physically over long periods of time without getting winded or out of breath.
Extent Flexibility	The ability to bend, stretch, twist, or reach with your body, arms, and/or legs.
Rate Control	The ability to time your movements or the movement of a piece of equipment in anticipation of changes in the speed and/or direction of a moving object or scene.
Gross Body Coordination	The ability to coordinate the movement of your arms, legs, and torso together when the whole body is in motion.

Spatial Orientation	The ability to know your location in relation to the environment or to know where other objects are in relation to you.
Speed of Limb Movement	The ability to quickly move the arms and legs.
Hearing Sensitivity	The ability to detect or tell the differences between sounds that vary in pitch and loudness.
Gross Body Equilibrium	The ability to keep or regain your body balance or stay upright when in an unstable position.
Response Orientation	The ability to choose quickly between two or more movements in response to two or more different signals (lights, sounds, pictures). It includes the speed with which the correct response is started with the hand, foot, or other body part.
Wrist-Finger Speed	The ability to make fast, simple, repeated movements of the fingers, hands, and wrists.
Peripheral Vision	The ability to see objects or movement of objects to one's side when the eyes are looking ahead.
Glare Sensitivity	The ability to see objects in the presence of glare or bright lighting.
Night Vision	The ability to see under low light conditions.
Sound Localization	The ability to tell the direction from which a sound originated.
Explosive Strength	The ability to use short bursts of muscle force to propel oneself (as in jumping or sprinting), or to throw an object.
Dynamic Flexibility	The ability to quickly and repeatedly bend, stretch, twist, or reach out with your body, arms, and/or legs.

Work_Activity	Work_Activity Definitions
Communicating with Supervisors, Peers, or Subordin	Providing information to supervisors, co-workers, and subordinates by telephone, in written form, e-mail, or in person.
Documenting/Recording Information	Entering, transcribing, recording, storing, or maintaining information in written or electronic/magnetic form.
Getting Information	Observing, receiving, and otherwise obtaining information from all relevant sources.
Identifying Objects, Actions, and Events	Identifying information by categorizing, estimating, recognizing differences or similarities, and detecting changes in circumstances or events.
Monitor Processes, Materials, or Surroundings	Monitoring and reviewing information from materials, events, or the environment, to detect or assess problems.
Establishing and Maintaining Interpersonal Relatio	Developing constructive and cooperative working relationships with others, and maintaining them over time.
Organizing, Planning, and Prioritizing Work	Developing specific goals and plans to prioritize, organize, and accomplish your work.
Updating and Using Relevant Knowledge	Keeping up-to-date technically and applying new knowledge to your job.
Making Decisions and Solving Problems	Analyzing information and evaluating results to choose the best solution and solve problems.
Processing Information	Compiling, coding, categorizing, calculating, tabulating, auditing, or verifying information or data.
Inspecting Equipment, Structures, or Material	Inspecting equipment, structures, or materials to identify the cause of errors or other problems or defects.
Operating Vehicles, Mechanized Devices, or Equipme	Running, maneuvering, navigating, or driving vehicles or mechanized equipment, such as forklifts, passenger vehicles, aircraft, or water craft.
Performing General Physical Activities	Performing physical activities that require considerable use of your arms and legs and moving your whole body, such as climbing, lifting, balancing, walking, stooping, and handling of materials.
Evaluating Information to Determine Compliance wit	Using relevant information and individual judgment to determine whether events or processes comply with laws, regulations, or standards.
Coordinating the Work and Activities of Others	Getting members of a group to work together to accomplish tasks.
Controlling Machines and Processes	Using either control mechanisms or direct physical activity to operate machines or processes (not including computers or vehicles).
Handling and Moving Objects	Using hands and arms in handling, installing, positioning, and moving materials, and manipulating things.
Interacting With Computers	Using computers and computer systems (including hardware and software) to program, write software, set up functions, enter data, or process information.
Scheduling Work and Activities	Scheduling events, programs, and activities, as well as the work of others.
Training and Teaching Others	Identifying the educational needs of others, developing formal educational or training programs or classes, and teaching or instructing others.

Estimating the Quantifiable Characteristics of Pro	Estimating sizes, distances, and quantities; or determining time, costs, resources, or materials needed to perform a work activity.
Judging the Qualities of Things, Services, or Peop	Assessing the value, importance, or quality of things or people.
Analyzing Data or Information	Identifying the underlying principles, reasons, or facts of information by breaking down information or data into separate parts.
Thinking Creatively	Developing, designing, or creating new applications, ideas, relationships, systems, or products, including artistic contributions.
Interpreting the Meaning of Information for Others	Translating or explaining what information means and how it can be used.
Developing and Building Teams	Encouraging and building mutual trust, respect, and cooperation among team members.
Developing Objectives and Strategies	Establishing long-range objectives and specifying the strategies and actions to achieve them.
Performing Administrative Activities	Performing day-to-day administrative tasks such as maintaining information files and processing paperwork.
Communicating with Persons Outside Organization	Communicating with people outside the organization, representing the organization to customers, the public, government, and other external sources. This information can be exchanged in person, in writing, or by telephone or e-mail.
Repairing and Maintaining Mechanical Equipment	Servicing, repairing, adjusting, and testing machines, devices, moving parts, and equipment that operate primarily on the basis of mechanical (not electronic) principles.
Coaching and Developing Others	Identifying the developmental needs of others and coaching, mentoring, or otherwise helping others to improve their knowledge or skills.
Assisting and Caring for Others	Providing personal assistance, medical attention, emotional support, or other personal care to others such as coworkers, customers, or patients.
Monitoring and Controlling Resources	Monitoring and controlling resources and overseeing the spending of money.
Guiding, Directing, and Motivating Subordinates	Providing guidance and direction to subordinates, including setting performance standards and monitoring performance.
Repairing and Maintaining Electronic Equipment	Servicing, repairing, calibrating, regulating, fine-tuning, or testing machines, devices, and equipment that operate primarily on the basis of electrical or electronic (not mechanical) principles.
Selling or Influencing Others	Convincing others to buy merchandise/goods or to otherwise change their minds or actions.
Provide Consultation and Advice to Others	Providing guidance and expert advice to management or other groups on technical, systems-, or process-related topics.
Performing for or Working Directly with the Public	Performing for people or dealing directly with the public. This includes serving customers in restaurants and stores, and receiving clients or guests.
Drafting, Laying Out, and Specifying Technical Dev	Providing documentation, detailed instructions, drawings, or specifications to tell others about how devices, parts, equipment, or structures are to be fabricated, constructed, assembled, modified, maintained, or used.
Resolving Conflicts and Negotiating with Others	Handling complaints, settling disputes, and resolving grievances and conflicts, or otherwise negotiating with others.
Staffing Organizational Units	Recruiting, interviewing, selecting, hiring, and promoting employees in an organization.

Work_Context	Work_Context Definitions
Importance of Being Exact or Accurate	How important is being very exact or highly accurate in performing this job?
Contact With Others	How much does this job require the worker to be in contact with others (face-to-face, by telephone, or otherwise) in order to perform it?
Work With Work Group or Team	How important is it to work with others in a group or team in this job?
Freedom to Make Decisions	How much decision making freedom, without supervision, does the job offer?
Face-to-Face Discussions	How often do you have to have face-to-face discussions with individuals or teams in this job?
Telephone	How often do you have telephone conversations in this job?
Indoors, Environmentally Controlled	How often does this job require working indoors in environmentally controlled conditions?
Spend Time Using Your Hands to Handle, Control, or	How much does this job require using your hands to handle, control, or feel objects, tools or controls?
Coordinate or Lead Others	How important is it to coordinate or lead others in accomplishing work activities in this job?

Importance of Repeating Same Tasks	How important is repeating the same physical activities (e.g., key entry) or mental activities (e.g., checking entries in a ledger) over and over, without stopping, to performing this job?
Time Pressure	How often does this job require the worker to meet strict deadlines?
Structured versus Unstructured Work	To what extent is this job structured for the worker, rather than allowing the worker to determine tasks, priorities, and goals?
Impact of Decisions on Co-workers or Company Resul	How do the decisions an employee makes impact the results of co-workers, clients or the company?
Frequency of Decision Making	How frequently is the worker required to make decisions that affect other people, the financial resources, and/or the image and reputation of the organization?
Spend Time Standing	How much does this job require standing?
Exposed to Contaminants	How often does this job require working exposed to contaminants (such as pollutants, gases, dust or odors)?
Electronic Mail	How often do you use electronic mail in this job?
Wear Common Protective or Safety Equipment such as	How much does this job require wearing common protective or safety equipment such as safety shoes, glasses, gloves, hard hats or life jackets?
Physical Proximity	To what extent does this job require the worker to perform job tasks in close physical proximity to other people?
Responsible for Others' Health and Safety	How much responsibility is there for the health and safety of others in this job?
Deal With External Customers	How important is it to work with external customers or the public in this job?
Consequence of Error	How serious would the result usually be if the worker made a mistake that was not readily correctable?
Indoors, Not Environmentally Controlled	How often does this job require working indoors in non-controlled environmental conditions (e.g., warehouse without heat)?
Pace Determined by Speed of Equipment	How important is it to this job that the pace is determined by the speed of equipment or machinery? (This does not refer to keeping busy at all times on this job.)
Exposed to Hazardous Conditions	How often does this job require exposure to hazardous conditions?
Letters and Memos	How often does the job require written letters and memos?
Responsibility for Outcomes and Results	How responsible is the worker for work outcomes and results of other workers?
Outdoors, Exposed to Weather	How often does this job require working outdoors, exposed to all weather conditions?
Spend Time Making Repetitive Motions	How much does this job require making repetitive motions?
Frequency of Conflict Situations	How often are there conflict situations the employee has to face in this job?
Spend Time Walking and Running	How much does this job require walking and running?
Very Hot or Cold Temperatures	How often does this job require working in very hot (above 90 F degrees) or very cold (below 32 F degrees) temperatures?
In an Enclosed Vehicle or Equipment	How often does this job require working in a closed vehicle or equipment (e.g., car)?
Sounds, Noise Levels Are Distracting or Uncomforta	How often does this job require working exposed to sounds and noise levels that are distracting or uncomfortable?
Spend Time Sitting	How much does this job require sitting?
Exposed to Hazardous Equipment	How often does this job require exposure to hazardous equipment?
Deal With Unpleasant or Angry People	How frequently does the worker have to deal with unpleasant, angry, or discourteous individuals as part of the job requirements?
Degree of Automation	How automated is the job?
Outdoors, Under Cover	How often does this job require working outdoors, under cover (e.g., structure with roof but no walls)?
In an Open Vehicle or Equipment	How often does this job require working in an open vehicle or equipment (e.g., tractor)?
Exposed to Minor Burns, Cuts, Bites, or Stings	How often does this job require exposure to minor burns, cuts, bites, or stings?
Spend Time Bending or Twisting the Body	How much does this job require bending or twisting your body?
Extremely Bright or Inadequate Lighting	How often does this job require working in extremely bright or inadequate lighting conditions?
Level of Competition	To what extent does this job require the worker to compete or to be aware of competitive pressures?
Cramped Work Space, Awkward Positions	How often does this job require working in cramped work spaces that requires getting into awkward positions?
Exposed to Disease or Infections	How often does this job require exposure to disease/infections?
Exposed to Whole Body Vibration	How often does this job require exposure to whole body vibration (e.g., operate a jackhammer)?

Wear Specialized Protective or Safety Equipment su	How much does this job require wearing specialized protective or safety equipment such as breathing apparatus. safety harness. full protection suits, or radiation protection?
Exposed to High Places	How often does this job require exposure to high places?
Spend Time Kneeling. Crouching. Stooping. or Crawl	How much does this job require kneeling. crouching. stooping. or crawling?
Exposed to Radiation	How often does this job require exposure to radiation?
Public Speaking	How often do you have to perform public speaking in this job?
Spend Time Keeping or Regaining Balance	How much does this job require keeping or regaining your balance?
Spend Time Climbing Ladders. Scaffolds. or Poles	How much does this job require climbing ladders. scaffolds. or poles?
Deal With Physically Aggressive People	How frequently does this job require the worker to deal with physical aggression of violent individuals?

Job Zone Component	Job Zone Component Definitions
Title	Job Zone Three: Medium Preparation Needed
Overall Experience	Previous work-related skill, knowledge. or experience is required for these occupations. For example. an electrician must have completed three or four years of apprenticeship or several years of vocational training, and often must have passed a licensing exam, in order to perform the job.
Job Training	Employees in these occupations usually need one or two years of training involving both on-the-job experience and informal training with experienced workers.
Job Zone Examples	These occupations usually involve using communication and organizational skills to coordinate. supervise. manage. or train others to accomplish goals. Examples include dental assistants. electricians, fish and game wardens, legal secretaries. personnel recruiters, and recreation workers.
SVP Range	(6.0 to < 7.0)
Education	Most occupations in this zone require training in vocational schools, related on-the-job experience, or an associate's degree. Some may require a bachelor's degree.

Work_Styles	Work_Styles Definitions
Attention to Detail	Job requires being careful about detail and thorough in completing work tasks.
Dependability	Job requires being reliable, responsible, and dependable, and fulfilling obligations.
Integrity	Job requires being honest and ethical.
Cooperation	Job requires being pleasant with others on the job and displaying a good-natured, cooperative attitude.
Adaptability/Flexibility	Job requires being open to change (positive or negative) and to considerable variety in the workplace.
Concern for Others	Job requires being sensitive to others' needs and feelings and being understanding and helpful on the job.
Self Control	Job requires maintaining composure, keeping emotions in check, controlling anger, and avoiding aggressive behavior, even in very difficult situations.
Initiative	Job requires a willingness to take on responsibilities and challenges.
Persistence	Job requires persistence in the face of obstacles.
Analytical Thinking	Job requires analyzing information and using logic to address work-related issues and problems.
Stress Tolerance	Job requires accepting criticism and dealing calmly and effectively with high stress situations.
Leadership	Job requires a willingness to lead, take charge, and offer opinions and direction.
Achievement/Effort	Job requires establishing and maintaining personally challenging achievement goals and exerting effort toward mastering tasks.
Social Orientation	Job requires preferring to work with others rather than alone, and being personally connected with others on the job.
Independence	Job requires developing one's own ways of doing things, guiding oneself with little or no supervision, and depending on oneself to get things done.
Innovation	Job requires creativity and alternative thinking to develop new ideas for and answers to work-related problems.

19-4061.01 - City Planning Aides

Compile data from various sources. such as maps. reports. and field and file investigations. for use by city planner in making planning studies.

Tasks

1) Prepare, maintain and update files and records. including land use data and statistics.

2) Participate in and support team planning efforts.

3) Research, compile, analyze and organize information from maps. reports. investigations. and books for use in reports and special projects.

4) Perform clerical duties such as composing, typing and proofreading documents, scheduling appointments and meetings, handling mail and posting public notices.

5) Prepare, develop and maintain maps and databases.

6) Serve as a liaison between planning department and other departments and agencies.

7) Conduct interviews, surveys and site inspections concerning factors that affect land usage, such as zoning, traffic flow and housing.

8) Provide and process zoning and project permits and applications.

9) Prepare reports, using statistics, charts, and graphs, to illustrate planning studies in areas such as population, land use, or zoning.

10) Inspect sites and review plans for minor development permit applications.

11) Perform code enforcement tasks.

Knowledge	Knowledge Definitions
English Language	Knowledge of the structure and content of the English language including the meaning and spelling of words, rules of composition, and grammar.
Geography	Knowledge of principles and methods for describing the features of land, sea, and air masses, including their physical characteristics, locations, interrelationships, and distribution of plant, animal, and human life.
Law and Government	Knowledge of laws, legal codes, court procedures, precedents, government regulations, executive orders, agency rules, and the democratic political process.
Clerical	Knowledge of administrative and clerical procedures and systems such as word processing, managing files and records, stenography and transcription, designing forms, and other office procedures and terminology.
Mathematics	Knowledge of arithmetic, algebra, geometry, calculus, statistics, and their applications.
Customer and Personal Service	Knowledge of principles and processes for providing customer and personal services. This includes customer needs assessment, meeting quality standards for services, and evaluation of customer satisfaction.
Administration and Management	Knowledge of business and management principles involved in strategic planning, resource allocation, human resources modeling, leadership technique, production methods, and coordination of people and resources.
Design	Knowledge of design techniques, tools, and principles involved in production of precision technical plans, blueprints, drawings, and models.
Computers and Electronics	Knowledge of circuit boards, processors, chips, electronic equipment, and computer hardware and software, including applications and programming.
Transportation	Knowledge of principles and methods for moving people or goods by air, rail, sea, or road, including the relative costs and benefits.
Education and Training	Knowledge of principles and methods for curriculum and training design, teaching and instruction for individuals and groups, and the measurement of training effects.
Building and Construction	Knowledge of materials, methods, and the tools involved in the construction or repair of houses, buildings, or other structures such as highways and roads.
Sales and Marketing	Knowledge of principles and methods for showing, promoting, and selling products or services. This includes marketing strategy and tactics, product demonstration, sales techniques, and sales control systems.
Public Safety and Security	Knowledge of relevant equipment, policies, procedures, and strategies to promote effective local, state, or national security operations for the protection of people, data, property, and institutions.

Communications and Media	Knowledge of media production, communication, and dissemination techniques and methods. This includes alternative ways to inform and entertain via written, oral, and visual media.	Speaking	Talking to others to convey information effectively.
		Time Management	Managing one's own time and the time of others.
Economics and Accounting	Knowledge of economic and accounting principles and practices, the financial markets, banking and the analysis and reporting of financial data.	Judgment and Decision Making	Considering the relative costs and benefits of potential actions to choose the most appropriate one.
Sociology and Anthropology	Knowledge of group behavior and dynamics, societal trends and influences, human migrations, ethnicity, cultures and their history and origins.	Critical Thinking	Using logic and reasoning to identify the strengths and weaknesses of alternative solutions, conclusions or approaches to problems.
		Service Orientation	Actively looking for ways to help people.
Psychology	Knowledge of human behavior and performance; individual differences in ability, personality, and interests; learning and motivation; psychological research methods; and the assessment and treatment of behavioral and affective disorders.	Complex Problem Solving	Identifying complex problems and reviewing related information to develop and evaluate options and implement solutions.
		Learning Strategies	Selecting and using training/instructional methods and procedures appropriate for the situation when learning or teaching new things.
Personnel and Human Resources	Knowledge of principles and procedures for personnel recruitment, selection, training, compensation and benefits, labor relations and negotiation, and personnel information systems.	Persuasion	Persuading others to change their minds or behavior.
		Monitoring	Monitoring/Assessing performance of yourself, other individuals, or organizations to make improvements or take corrective action.
Engineering and Technology	Knowledge of the practical application of engineering science and technology. This includes applying principles, techniques, procedures, and equipment to the design and production of various goods and services.	Negotiation	Bringing others together and trying to reconcile differences.
		Instructing	Teaching others how to do something.
		Mathematics	Using mathematics to solve problems.
History and Archeology	Knowledge of historical events and their causes, indicators, and effects on civilizations and cultures.	Equipment Selection	Determining the kind of tools and equipment needed to do a job.
Mechanical	Knowledge of machines and tools, including their designs, uses, repair, and maintenance.	Operations Analysis	Analyzing needs and product requirements to create a design.
		Operation and Control	Controlling operations of equipment or systems.
Foreign Language	Knowledge of the structure and content of a foreign (non-English) language including the meaning and spelling of words, rules of composition and grammar, and pronunciation.	Quality Control Analysis	Conducting tests and inspections of products, services, or processes to evaluate quality or performance.
		Management of Financial Resources	Determining how money will be spent to get the work done, and accounting for these expenditures.
Production and Processing	Knowledge of raw materials, production processes, quality control, costs, and other techniques for maximizing the effective manufacture and distribution of goods.	Systems Analysis	Determining how a system should work and how changes in conditions, operations, and the environment will affect outcomes.
Telecommunications	Knowledge of transmission, broadcasting, switching, control, and operation of telecommunications systems.	Equipment Maintenance	Performing routine maintenance on equipment and determining when and what kind of maintenance is needed.
Physics	Knowledge and prediction of physical principles, laws, their interrelationships, and applications to understanding fluid, material, and atmospheric dynamics, and mechanical, electrical, atomic and sub-atomic structures and processes.	Systems Evaluation	Identifying measures or indicators of system performance and the actions needed to improve or correct performance, relative to the goals of the system.
		Management of Personnel Resources	Motivating, developing, and directing people as they work, identifying the best people for the job.
Biology	Knowledge of plant and animal organisms, their tissues, cells, functions, interdependencies, and interactions with each other and the environment.	Science	Using scientific rules and methods to solve problems.
		Technology Design	Generating or adapting equipment and technology to serve user needs.
Chemistry	Knowledge of the chemical composition, structure, and properties of substances and of the chemical processes and transformations that they undergo. This includes uses of chemicals and their interactions, danger signs, production techniques, and disposal methods.	Management of Material Resources	Obtaining and seeing to the appropriate use of equipment, facilities, and materials needed to do certain work.
		Troubleshooting	Determining causes of operating errors and deciding what to do about it.
		Operation Monitoring	Watching gauges, dials, or other indicators to make sure a machine is working properly.
Philosophy and Theology	Knowledge of different philosophical systems and religions. This includes their basic principles, values, ethics, ways of thinking, customs, practices, and their impact on human culture.	Programming	Writing computer programs for various purposes.
		Installation	Installing equipment, machines, wiring, or programs to meet specifications.
Fine Arts	Knowledge of the theory and techniques required to compose, produce, and perform works of music, dance, visual arts, drama, and sculpture.	Repairing	Repairing machines or systems using the needed tools.

Ability	**Ability Definitions**
Therapy and Counseling	Knowledge of principles, methods, and procedures for diagnosis, treatment, and rehabilitation of physical and mental dysfunctions, and for career counseling and guidance.
Oral Expression	The ability to communicate information and ideas in speaking so others will understand.
Food Production	Knowledge of techniques and equipment for planting, growing, and harvesting food products (both plant and animal) for consumption, including storage/handling techniques.
Information Ordering	The ability to arrange things or actions in a certain order or pattern according to a specific rule or set of rules (e.g., patterns of numbers, letters, words, pictures, mathematical operations).
Medicine and Dentistry	Knowledge of the information and techniques needed to diagnose and treat human injuries, diseases, and deformities. This includes symptoms, treatment alternatives, drug properties and interactions, and preventive health-care measures.
Oral Comprehension	The ability to listen to and understand information and ideas presented through spoken words and sentences.
Written Expression	The ability to communicate information and ideas in writing so others will understand.

Skills	**Skills Definitions**
Problem Sensitivity	The ability to tell when something is wrong or is likely to go wrong. It does not involve solving the problem, only recognizing there is a problem.
Reading Comprehension	Understanding written sentences and paragraphs in work related documents.
Written Comprehension	The ability to read and understand information and ideas presented in writing.
Active Listening	Giving full attention to what other people are saying, taking time to understand the points being made, asking questions as appropriate, and not interrupting at inappropriate times.
Speech Recognition	The ability to identify and understand the speech of another person.
Speech Clarity	The ability to speak clearly so others can understand you.
Writing	Communicating effectively in writing as appropriate for the needs of the audience.
Deductive Reasoning	The ability to apply general rules to specific problems to produce answers that make sense.
Active Learning	Understanding the implications of new information for both current and future problem-solving and decision-making.
Inductive Reasoning	The ability to combine pieces of information to form general rules or conclusions (includes finding a relationship among seemingly unrelated events).
Coordination	Adjusting actions in relation to others' actions.
Social Perceptiveness	Being aware of others' reactions and understanding why they react as they do.

Category Flexibility	The ability to generate or use different sets of rules for combining or grouping things in different ways.
Near Vision	The ability to see details at close range (within a few feet of the observer).
Selective Attention	The ability to concentrate on a task over a period of time without being distracted.
Fluency of Ideas	The ability to come up with a number of ideas about a topic (the number of ideas is important, not their quality, correctness, or creativity).
Far Vision	The ability to see details at a distance.
Originality	The ability to come up with unusual or clever ideas about a given topic or situation, or to develop creative ways to solve a problem.
Finger Dexterity	The ability to make precisely coordinated movements of the fingers of one or both hands to grasp, manipulate, or assemble very small objects.
Flexibility of Closure	The ability to identify or detect a known pattern (a figure, object, word, or sound) that is hidden in other distracting material.
Mathematical Reasoning	The ability to choose the right mathematical methods or formulas to solve a problem.
Visual Color Discrimination	The ability to match or detect differences between colors, including shades of color and brightness.
Number Facility	The ability to add, subtract, multiply, or divide quickly and correctly.
Memorization	The ability to remember information such as words, numbers, pictures, and procedures.
Speed of Closure	The ability to quickly make sense of, combine, and organize information into meaningful patterns.
Time Sharing	The ability to shift back and forth between two or more activities or sources of information (such as speech, sounds, touch, or other sources).
Perceptual Speed	The ability to quickly and accurately compare similarities and differences among sets of letters, numbers, objects, pictures, or patterns. The things to be compared may be presented at the same time or one after the other. This ability also includes comparing a presented object with a remembered object.
Visualization	The ability to imagine how something will look after it is moved around or when its parts are moved or rearranged.
Auditory Attention	The ability to focus on a single source of sound in the presence of other distracting sounds.
Hearing Sensitivity	The ability to detect or tell the differences between sounds that vary in pitch and loudness.
Depth Perception	The ability to judge which of several objects is closer or farther away from you, or to judge the distance between you and an object.
Control Precision	The ability to quickly and repeatedly adjust the controls of a machine or a vehicle to exact positions.
Multilimb Coordination	The ability to coordinate two or more limbs (for example, two arms, two legs, or one leg and one arm) while sitting, standing, or lying down. It does not involve performing the activities while the whole body is in motion.
Trunk Strength	The ability to use your abdominal and lower back muscles to support part of the body repeatedly or continuously over time without 'giving out' or fatiguing.
Response Orientation	The ability to choose quickly between two or more movements in response to two or more different signals (lights, sounds, pictures). It includes the speed with which the correct response is started with the hand, foot, or other body part.
Reaction Time	The ability to quickly respond (with the hand, finger, or foot) to a signal (sound, light, picture) when it appears.
Manual Dexterity	The ability to quickly move your hand, your hand together with your arm, or your two hands to grasp, manipulate, or assemble objects.
Wrist-Finger Speed	The ability to make fast, simple, repeated movements of the fingers, hands, and wrists.
Gross Body Coordination	The ability to coordinate the movement of your arms, legs, and torso together when the whole body is in motion.
Spatial Orientation	The ability to know your location in relation to the environment or to know where other objects are in relation to you.
Gross Body Equilibrium	The ability to keep or regain your body balance or stay upright when in an unstable position.
Dynamic Strength	The ability to exert muscle force repeatedly or continuously over time. This involves muscular endurance and resistance to muscle fatigue.
Static Strength	The ability to exert maximum muscle force to lift, push, pull, or carry objects.
Sound Localization	The ability to tell the direction from which a sound originated.

Speed of Limb Movement	The ability to quickly move the arms and legs.
Night Vision	The ability to see under low light conditions.
Peripheral Vision	The ability to see objects or movement of objects to one's side when the eyes are looking ahead.
Explosive Strength	The ability to use short bursts of muscle force to propel oneself (as in jumping or sprinting), or to throw an object.
Rate Control	The ability to time your movements or the movement of a piece of equipment in anticipation of changes in the speed and/or direction of a moving object or scene.
Glare Sensitivity	The ability to see objects in the presence of glare or bright lighting.
Extent Flexibility	The ability to bend, stretch, twist, or reach with your body, arms, and/or legs.
Arm-Hand Steadiness	The ability to keep your hand and arm steady while moving your arm or while holding your arm and hand in one position.
Stamina	The ability to exert yourself physically over long periods of time without getting winded or out of breath.
Dynamic Flexibility	The ability to quickly and repeatedly bend, stretch, twist, or reach out with your body, arms, and/or legs.

Work_Activity	Work_Activity Definitions
Interacting With Computers	Using computers and computer systems (including hardware and software) to program, write software, set up functions, enter data, or process information.
Organizing, Planning, and Prioritizing Work	Developing specific goals and plans to prioritize, organize, and accomplish your work.
Getting Information	Observing, receiving, and otherwise obtaining information from all relevant sources.
Communicating with Persons Outside Organization	Communicating with people outside the organization, representing the organization to customers, the public, government, and other external sources. This information can be exchanged in person, in writing, or by telephone or e-mail.
Performing for or Working Directly with the Public	Performing for people or dealing directly with the public. This includes serving customers in restaurants and stores, and receiving clients or guests.
Analyzing Data or Information	Identifying the underlying principles, reasons, or facts of information by breaking down information or data into separate parts.
Communicating with Supervisors, Peers, or Subordin	Providing information to supervisors, co-workers, and subordinates by telephone, in written form, e-mail, or in person.
Making Decisions and Solving Problems	Analyzing information and evaluating results to choose the best solution and solve problems.
Identifying Objects, Actions, and Events	Identifying information by categorizing, estimating, recognizing differences or similarities, and detecting changes in circumstances or events.
Updating and Using Relevant Knowledge	Keeping up-to-date technically and applying new knowledge to your job.
Processing Information	Compiling, coding, categorizing, calculating, tabulating, auditing, or verifying information or data.
Establishing and Maintaining Interpersonal Relatio	Developing constructive and cooperative working relationships with others, and maintaining them over time.
Evaluating Information to Determine Compliance wit	Using relevant information and individual judgment to determine whether events or processes comply with laws, regulations, or standards.
Scheduling Work and Activities	Scheduling events, programs, and activities, as well as the work of others.
Monitor Processes, Materials, or Surroundings	Monitoring and reviewing information from materials, events, or the environment, to detect or assess problems.
Documenting/Recording Information	Entering, transcribing, recording, storing, or maintaining information in written or electronic/magnetic form.
Thinking Creatively	Developing, designing, or creating new applications, ideas, relationships, systems, or products, including artistic contributions.
Interpreting the Meaning of Information for Others	Translating or explaining what information means and how it can be used.
Estimating the Quantifiable Characteristics of Pro	Estimating sizes, distances, and quantities; or determining time, costs, resources, or materials needed to perform a work activity.
Resolving Conflicts and Negotiating with Others	Handling complaints, settling disputes, and resolving grievances and conflicts, or otherwise negotiating with others.
Performing Administrative Activities	Performing day-to-day administrative tasks such as maintaining information files and processing paperwork.
Developing Objectives and Strategies	Establishing long-range objectives and specifying the strategies and actions to achieve them.

Judging the Qualities of Things, Services, or Peop	Assessing the value, importance, or quality of things or people.
Coordinating the Work and Activities of Others	Getting members of a group to work together to accomplish tasks.
Coaching and Developing Others	Identifying the developmental needs of others and coaching, mentoring, or otherwise helping others to improve their knowledge or skills.
Inspecting Equipment, Structures, or Material	Inspecting equipment, structures, or materials to identify the cause of errors or other problems or defects.
Training and Teaching Others	Identifying the educational needs of others, developing formal educational or training programs or classes, and teaching or instructing others.
Provide Consultation and Advice to Others	Providing guidance and expert advice to management or other groups on technical, systems-, or process-related topics.
Developing and Building Teams	Encouraging and building mutual trust, respect, and cooperation among team members.
Drafting, Laying Out, and Specifying Technical Dev	Providing documentation, detailed instructions, drawings, or specifications to tell others about how devices, parts, equipment, or structures are to be fabricated, constructed, assembled, modified, maintained, or used.
Assisting and Caring for Others	Providing personal assistance, medical attention, emotional support, or other personal care to others such as coworkers, customers, or patients.
Handling and Moving Objects	Using hands and arms in handling, installing, positioning, and moving materials, and manipulating things.
Controlling Machines and Processes	Using either control mechanisms or direct physical activity to operate machines or processes (not including computers or vehicles).
Repairing and Maintaining Electronic Equipment	Servicing, repairing, calibrating, regulating, fine-tuning, or testing machines, devices, and equipment that operate primarily on the basis of electrical or electronic (not mechanical) principles.
Performing General Physical Activities	Performing physical activities that require considerable use of your arms and legs and moving your whole body, such as climbing, lifting, balancing, walking, stooping, and handling of materials.
Guiding, Directing, and Motivating Subordinates	Providing guidance and direction to subordinates, including setting performance standards and monitoring performance.
Repairing and Maintaining Mechanical Equipment	Servicing, repairing, adjusting, and testing machines, devices, moving parts, and equipment that operate primarily on the basis of mechanical (not electronic) principles.
Monitoring and Controlling Resources	Monitoring and controlling resources and overseeing the spending of money.
Staffing Organizational Units	Recruiting, interviewing, selecting, hiring, and promoting employees in an organization.
Selling or Influencing Others	Convincing others to buy merchandise/goods or to otherwise change their minds or actions.
Operating Vehicles, Mechanized Devices, or Equipme	Running, maneuvering, navigating, or driving vehicles or mechanized equipment, such as forklifts, passenger vehicles, aircraft, or water craft.

Work_Context	Work_Context Definitions
Face-to-Face Discussions	How often do you have to have face-to-face discussions with individuals or teams in this job?
Telephone	How often do you have telephone conversations in this job?
Indoors, Environmentally Controlled	How often does this job require working indoors in environmentally controlled conditions?
Electronic Mail	How often do you use electronic mail in this job?
Structured versus Unstructured Work	To what extent is this job structured for the worker, rather than allowing the worker to determine tasks, priorities, and goals?
Spend Time Sitting	How much does this job require sitting?
Work With Work Group or Team	How important is it to work with others in a group or team in this job?
Contact With Others	How much does this job require the worker to be in contact with others (face-to-face, by telephone, or otherwise) in order to perform it?
Letters and Memos	How often does the job require written letters and memos?
Freedom to Make Decisions	How much decision making freedom, without supervision, does the job offer?
Deal With External Customers	How important is it to work with external customers or the public in this job?
Importance of Being Exact or Accurate	How important is being very exact or highly accurate in performing this job?
Impact of Decisions on Co-workers or Company Resul	How do the decisions an employee makes impact the results of co-workers, clients or the company?

Frequency of Decision Making	How frequently is the worker required to make decisions that affect other people, the financial resources, and/or the image and reputation of the organization?
Time Pressure	How often does this job require the worker to meet strict deadlines?
Coordinate or Lead Others	How important is it to coordinate or lead others in accomplishing work activities in this job?
Level of Competition	To what extent does this job require the worker to compete or to be aware of competitive pressures?
Sounds, Noise Levels Are Distracting or Uncomforta	How often does this job require working exposed to sounds and noise levels that are distracting or uncomfortable?
Deal With Unpleasant or Angry People	How frequently does the worker have to deal with unpleasant, angry, or discourteous individuals as part of the job requirements?
Physical Proximity	To what extent does this job require the worker to perform job tasks in close physical proximity to other people?
Consequence of Error	How serious would the result usually be if the worker made a mistake that was not readily correctable?
Frequency of Conflict Situations	How often are there conflict situations the employee has to face in this job?
Responsibility for Outcomes and Results	How responsible is the worker for work outcomes and results of other workers?
Spend Time Making Repetitive Motions	How much does this job require making repetitive motions?
In an Enclosed Vehicle or Equipment	How often does this job require working in a closed vehicle or equipment (e.g., car)?
Public Speaking	How often do you have to perform public speaking in this job?
Importance of Repeating Same Tasks	How important is repeating the same physical activities (e.g., key entry) or mental activities (e.g., checking entries in a ledger) over and over, without stopping, to performing this job?
Spend Time Using Your Hands to Handle, Control, or	How much does this job require using your hands to handle, control, or feel objects, tools or controls?
Exposed to Contaminants	How often does this job require working exposed to contaminants (such as pollutants, gases, dust or odors)?
Spend Time Standing	How much does this job require standing?
Spend Time Walking and Running	How much does this job require walking and running?
Degree of Automation	How automated is the job?
Responsible for Others' Health and Safety	How much responsibility is there for the health and safety of others in this job?
Extremely Bright or Inadequate Lighting	How often does this job require working in extremely bright or inadequate lighting conditions?
Indoors, Not Environmentally Controlled	How often does this job require working indoors in non-controlled environmental conditions (e.g., warehouse without heat)?
Deal With Physically Aggressive People	How frequently does this job require the worker to deal with physical aggression of violent individuals?
Outdoors, Exposed to Weather	How often does this job require working outdoors, exposed to all weather conditions?
Cramped Work Space, Awkward Positions	How often does this job require working in cramped work spaces that requires getting into awkward positions?
Outdoors, Under Cover	How often does this job require working outdoors, under cover (e.g., structure with roof but no walls)?
Spend Time Bending or Twisting the Body	How much does this job require bending or twisting your body?
Exposed to Minor Burns, Cuts, Bites, or Stings	How often does this job require exposure to minor burns, cuts, bites, or stings?
Very Hot or Cold Temperatures	How often does this job require working in very hot (above 90 F degrees) or very cold (below 32 F degrees) temperatures?
Spend Time Kneeling, Crouching, Stooping, or Crawl	How much does this job require kneeling, crouching, stooping or crawling?
Wear Common Protective or Safety Equipment such as	How much does this job require wearing common protective or safety equipment such as safety shoes, glasses, gloves, hard hats or live jackets?
Pace Determined by Speed of Equipment	How important is it to this job that the pace is determined by the speed of equipment or machinery? (This does not refer to keeping busy at all times on this job.)
Spend Time Keeping or Regaining Balance	How much does this job require keeping or regaining your balance?
Exposed to Disease or Infections	How often does this job require exposure to disease/infections?
Exposed to Radiation	How often does this job require exposure to radiation?
Wear Specialized Protective or Safety Equipment su	How much does this job require wearing specialized protective or safety equipment such as breathing apparatus, safety harness, full protection suits, or radiation protection?

Exposed to Whole Body Vibration	How often does this job require exposure to whole body vibration (e.g., operate a jackhammer)?
Exposed to Hazardous Equipment	How often does this job require exposure to hazardous equipment?
Exposed to Hazardous Conditions	How often does this job require exposure to hazardous conditions?
In an Open Vehicle or Equipment	How often does this job require working in an open vehicle or equipment (e.g., tractor)?
Spend Time Climbing Ladders, Scaffolds, or Poles	How much does this job require climbing ladders, scaffolds, or poles?
Exposed to High Places	How often does this job require exposure to high places?

Job Zone Component	Job Zone Component Definitions
Title	Job Zone Three: Medium Preparation Needed
Overall Experience	Previous work-related skill, knowledge, or experience is required for these occupations. For example, an electrician must have completed three or four years of apprenticeship or several years of vocational training, and often must have passed a licensing exam, in order to perform the job.
Job Training	Employees in these occupations usually need one or two years of training involving both on-the-job experience and informal training with experienced workers.
Job Zone Examples	These occupations usually involve using communication and organizational skills to coordinate, supervise, manage, or train others to accomplish goals. Examples include dental assistants, electricians, fish and game wardens, legal secretaries, personnel recruiters, and recreation workers.
SVP Range	(6.0 to < 7.0)
Education	Most occupations in this zone require training in vocational schools, related on-the-job experience, or an associate's degree. Some may require a bachelor's degree.

Work_Styles	Work_Styles Definitions
Cooperation	Job requires being pleasant with others on the job and displaying a good-natured, cooperative attitude.
Integrity	Job requires being honest and ethical.
Attention to Detail	Job requires being careful about detail and thorough in completing work tasks.
Dependability	Job requires being reliable, responsible, and dependable, and fulfilling obligations.
Concern for Others	Job requires being sensitive to others' needs and feelings and being understanding and helpful on the job.
Self Control	Job requires maintaining composure, keeping emotions in check, controlling anger, and avoiding aggressive behavior, even in very difficult situations.
Initiative	Job requires a willingness to take on responsibilities and challenges.
Persistence	Job requires persistence in the face of obstacles.
Stress Tolerance	Job requires accepting criticism and dealing calmly and effectively with high stress situations.
Analytical Thinking	Job requires analyzing information and using logic to address work-related issues and problems.
Social Orientation	Job requires preferring to work with others rather than alone, and being personally connected with others on the job.
Independence	Job requires developing one's own ways of doing things, guiding oneself with little or no supervision, and depending on oneself to get things done.
Leadership	Job requires a willingness to lead, take charge, and offer opinions and direction.
Adaptability/Flexibility	Job requires being open to change (positive or negative) and to considerable variety in the workplace.
Achievement/Effort	Job requires establishing and maintaining personally challenging achievement goals and exerting effort toward mastering tasks.
Innovation	Job requires creativity and alternative thinking to develop new ideas for and answers to work-related problems.

19-4093.00 - Forest and Conservation Technicians

Compile data pertaining to size, content, condition, and other characteristics of forest tracts, under direction of foresters; train and lead forest workers in forest propagation, fire prevention and suppression. May assist conservation scientists in managing, improving, and protecting rangelands and wildlife habitats, and help provide technical assistance regarding the conservation of soil, water, and related natural resources.

Tasks

1) Manage forest protection activities, including fire control, fire crew training, and coordination of fire detection and public education programs.

2) Patrol park or forest areas to protect resources and prevent damage.

3) Train and lead forest and conservation workers in seasonal activities, such as planting tree seedlings, putting out forest fires and maintaining recreational facilities.

4) Select and mark trees for thinning or logging, drawing detailed plans that include access roads.

5) Survey, measure, and map access roads and forest areas such as burns, cut-over areas, experimental plots, and timber sales sections.

6) Provide forestry education and general information, advice, and recommendations to woodlot owners, community organizations, and the general public.

7) Monitor activities of logging companies and contractors.

8) Thin and space trees and control weeds and undergrowth, using manual tools and chemicals, or supervise workers performing these tasks.

9) Perform reforestation (forest renewal), including nursery and silviculture operations, site preparation, seeding and tree planting programs, cone collection, and tree improvement.

10) Inspect trees and collect samples of plants, seeds, foliage, bark and roots to locate insect and disease damage.

11) Issue fire permits, timber permits and other forest use licenses.

12) Develop and maintain computer databases.

13) Supervise forest nursery operations, timber harvesting, land use activities such as livestock grazing, and disease or insect control programs.

14) Provide technical support to forestry research programs in areas such as tree improvement, seed orchard operations, insect and disease surveys, or experimental forestry and forest engineering research.

15) Plan and supervise construction of access routes and forest roads.

16) Measure distances, clean site-lines, and record data to help survey crews.

17) Keep records of the amount and condition of logs taken to mills.

18) Conduct laboratory or field experiments with plants, animals, insects, diseases and soils.

19) Install gauges, stream flow recorders, and soil moisture measuring instruments, and collect and record data from them to assist with watershed analysis.

Knowledge	Knowledge Definitions
English Language	Knowledge of the structure and content of the English language including the meaning and spelling of words, rules of composition, and grammar.
Geography	Knowledge of principles and methods for describing the features of land, sea, and air masses, including their physical characteristics, locations, interrelationships, and distribution of plant, animal, and human life.
Biology	Knowledge of plant and animal organisms, their tissues, cells, functions, interdependencies, and interactions with each other and the environment.
Law and Government	Knowledge of laws, legal codes, court procedures, precedents, government regulations, executive orders, agency rules, and the democratic political process.
Mathematics	Knowledge of arithmetic, algebra, geometry, calculus, statistics, and their applications.
Administration and Management	Knowledge of business and management principles involved in strategic planning, resource allocation, human resources modeling, leadership technique, production methods, and coordination of people and resources.
Transportation	Knowledge of principles and methods for moving people or goods by air, rail, sea, or road, including the relative costs and benefits.
Mechanical	Knowledge of machines and tools, including their designs, uses, repair, and maintenance.
Public Safety and Security	Knowledge of relevant equipment, policies, procedures, and strategies to promote effective local, state, or national security operations for the protection of people, data, property, and institutions.

1326

Production and Processing	Knowledge of raw materials, production processes, quality control, costs, and other techniques for maximizing the effective manufacture and distribution of goods.
Clerical	Knowledge of administrative and clerical procedures and systems such as word processing, managing files and records, stenography and transcription, designing forms, and other office procedures and terminology.
Education and Training	Knowledge of principles and methods for curriculum and training design, teaching and instruction for individuals and groups, and the measurement of training effects.
Customer and Personal Service	Knowledge of principles and processes for providing customer and personal services. This includes customer needs assessment, meeting quality standards for services, and evaluation of customer satisfaction.
Computers and Electronics	Knowledge of circuit boards, processors, chips, electronic equipment, and computer hardware and software, including applications and programming.
Personnel and Human Resources	Knowledge of principles and procedures for personnel recruitment, selection, training, compensation and benefits, labor relations and negotiation, and personnel information systems.
Building and Construction	Knowledge of materials, methods, and the tools involved in the construction or repair of houses, buildings, or other structures such as highways and roads.
Engineering and Technology	Knowledge of the practical application of engineering science and technology. This includes applying principles, techniques, procedures, and equipment to the design and production of various goods and services.
Economics and Accounting	Knowledge of economic and accounting principles and practices, the financial markets, banking and the analysis and reporting of financial data.
Psychology	Knowledge of human behavior and performance; individual differences in ability, personality, and interests; learning and motivation; psychological research methods; and the assessment and treatment of behavioral and affective disorders.
Physics	Knowledge and prediction of physical principles, laws, their interrelationships, and applications to understanding fluid, material, and atmospheric dynamics, and mechanical, electrical, atomic and sub-atomic structures and processes.
History and Archeology	Knowledge of historical events and their causes, indicators, and effects on civilizations and cultures.
Telecommunications	Knowledge of transmission, broadcasting, switching, control, and operation of telecommunications systems.
Design	Knowledge of design techniques, tools, and principles involved in production of precision technical plans, blueprints, drawings, and models.
Communications and Media	Knowledge of media production, communication, and dissemination techniques and methods. This includes alternative ways to inform and entertain via written, oral, and visual media.
Chemistry	Knowledge of the chemical composition, structure, and properties of substances and of the chemical processes and transformations that they undergo. This includes uses of chemicals and their interactions, danger signs, production techniques, and disposal methods.
Sociology and Anthropology	Knowledge of group behavior and dynamics, societal trends and influences, human migrations, ethnicity, cultures and their history and origins.
Food Production	Knowledge of techniques and equipment for planting, growing, and harvesting food products (both plant and animal) for consumption, including storage/handling techniques.
Medicine and Dentistry	Knowledge of the information and techniques needed to diagnose and treat human injuries, diseases, and deformities. This includes symptoms, treatment alternatives, drug properties and interactions, and preventive health-care measures.
Sales and Marketing	Knowledge of principles and methods for showing, promoting, and selling products or services. This includes marketing strategy and tactics, product demonstration, sales techniques, and sales control systems.
Foreign Language	Knowledge of the structure and content of a foreign (non-English) language including the meaning and spelling of words, rules of composition and grammar, and pronunciation.
Therapy and Counseling	Knowledge of principles, methods, and procedures for diagnosis, treatment, and rehabilitation of physical and mental dysfunctions, and for career counseling and guidance.
Philosophy and Theology	Knowledge of different philosophical systems and religions. This includes their basic principles, values, ethics, ways of thinking, customs, practices, and their impact on human culture.
Fine Arts	Knowledge of the theory and techniques required to compose, produce, and perform works of music, dance, visual arts, drama, and sculpture.

Skills	Skills Definitions
Critical Thinking	Using logic and reasoning to identify the strengths and weaknesses of alternative solutions, conclusions or approaches to problems.
Active Listening	Giving full attention to what other people are saying, taking time to understand the points being made, asking questions as appropriate, and not interrupting at inappropriate times.
Active Learning	Understanding the implications of new information for both current and future problem-solving and decision-making.
Reading Comprehension	Understanding written sentences and paragraphs in work related documents.
Speaking	Talking to others to convey information effectively.
Science	Using scientific rules and methods to solve problems.
Judgment and Decision Making	Considering the relative costs and benefits of potential actions to choose the most appropriate one.
Mathematics	Using mathematics to solve problems.
Time Management	Managing one's own time and the time of others.
Equipment Selection	Determining the kind of tools and equipment needed to do a job.
Writing	Communicating effectively in writing as appropriate for the needs of the audience.
Coordination	Adjusting actions in relation to others' actions.
Instructing	Teaching others how to do something.
Equipment Maintenance	Performing routine maintenance on equipment and determining when and what kind of maintenance is needed.
Learning Strategies	Selecting and using training/instructional methods and procedures appropriate for the situation when learning or teaching new things.
Service Orientation	Actively looking for ways to help people.
Monitoring	Monitoring/Assessing performance of yourself, other individuals, or organizations to make improvements or take corrective action.
Management of Personnel Resources	Motivating, developing, and directing people as they work, identifying the best people for the job.
Complex Problem Solving	Identifying complex problems and reviewing related information to develop and evaluate options and implement solutions.
Operations Analysis	Analyzing needs and product requirements to create a design.
Management of Financial Resources	Determining how money will be spent to get the work done, and accounting for these expenditures.
Social Perceptiveness	Being aware of others' reactions and understanding why they react as they do.
Management of Material Resources	Obtaining and seeing to the appropriate use of equipment, facilities, and materials needed to do certain work.
Operation and Control	Controlling operations of equipment or systems.
Operation Monitoring	Watching gauges, dials, or other indicators to make sure a machine is working properly.
Troubleshooting	Determining causes of operating errors and deciding what to do about it.
Negotiation	Bringing others together and trying to reconcile differences.
Systems Evaluation	Identifying measures or indicators of system performance and the actions needed to improve or correct performance, relative to the goals of the system.
Persuasion	Persuading others to change their minds or behavior.
Repairing	Repairing machines or systems using the needed tools.
Installation	Installing equipment, machines, wiring, or programs to meet specifications.
Systems Analysis	Determining how a system should work and how changes in conditions, operations, and the environment will affect outcomes.
Quality Control Analysis	Conducting tests and inspections of products, services, or processes to evaluate quality or performance.
Technology Design	Generating or adapting equipment and technology to serve user needs.
Programming	Writing computer programs for various purposes.

Ability	Ability Definitions
Oral Comprehension	The ability to listen to and understand information and ideas presented through spoken words and sentences.
Problem Sensitivity	The ability to tell when something is wrong or is likely to go wrong. It does not involve solving the problem, only recognizing there is a problem.
Near Vision	The ability to see details at close range (within a few feet of the observer).
Oral Expression	The ability to communicate information and ideas in speaking so others will understand.
Deductive Reasoning	The ability to apply general rules to specific problems to produce answers that make sense.
Speech Clarity	The ability to speak clearly so others can understand you.
Inductive Reasoning	The ability to combine pieces of information to form general rules or conclusions (includes finding a relationship among seemingly unrelated events).
Speech Recognition	The ability to identify and understand the speech of another person.
Written Comprehension	The ability to read and understand information and ideas presented in writing.
Written Expression	The ability to communicate information and ideas in writing so others will understand.
Category Flexibility	The ability to generate or use different sets of rules for combining or grouping things in different ways.
Selective Attention	The ability to concentrate on a task over a period of time without being distracted.
Information Ordering	The ability to arrange things or actions in a certain order or pattern according to a specific rule or set of rules (e.g., patterns of numbers, letters, words, pictures, mathematical operations).
Far Vision	The ability to see details at a distance.
Manual Dexterity	The ability to quickly move your hand, your hand together with your arm, or your two hands to grasp, manipulate, or assemble objects.
Multilimb Coordination	The ability to coordinate two or more limbs (for example, two arms, two legs, or one leg and one arm) while sitting, standing, or lying down. It does not involve performing the activities while the whole body is in motion.
Arm-Hand Steadiness	The ability to keep your hand and arm steady while moving your arm or while holding your arm and hand in one position.
Visualization	The ability to imagine how something will look after it is moved around or when its parts are moved or rearranged.
Dynamic Strength	The ability to exert muscle force repeatedly or continuously over time. This involves muscular endurance and resistance to muscle fatigue.
Flexibility of Closure	The ability to identify or detect a known pattern (a figure, object, word, or sound) that is hidden in other distracting material.
Spatial Orientation	The ability to know your location in relation to the environment or to know where other objects are in relation to you.
Depth Perception	The ability to judge which of several objects is closer or farther away from you, or to judge the distance between you and an object.
Control Precision	The ability to quickly and repeatedly adjust the controls of a machine or a vehicle to exact positions.
Static Strength	The ability to exert maximum muscle force to lift, push, pull, or carry objects.
Time Sharing	The ability to shift back and forth between two or more activities or sources of information (such as speech, sounds, touch, or other sources).
Fluency of Ideas	The ability to come up with a number of ideas about a topic (the number of ideas is important, not their quality, correctness, or creativity).
Extent Flexibility	The ability to bend, stretch, twist, or reach with your body, arms, and/or legs.
Stamina	The ability to exert yourself physically over long periods of time without getting winded or out of breath.
Originality	The ability to come up with unusual or clever ideas about a given topic or situation, or to develop creative ways to solve a problem.
Speed of Closure	The ability to quickly make sense of, combine, and organize information into meaningful patterns.
Trunk Strength	The ability to use your abdominal and lower back muscles to support part of the body repeatedly or continuously over time without 'giving out' or fatiguing.
Gross Body Coordination	The ability to coordinate the movement of your arms, legs, and torso together when the whole body is in motion.

Finger Dexterity	The ability to make precisely coordinated movements of the fingers of one or both hands to grasp, manipulate, or assemble very small objects.
Mathematical Reasoning	The ability to choose the right mathematical methods or formulas to solve a problem.
Memorization	The ability to remember information such as words, numbers, pictures, and procedures.
Speed of Limb Movement	The ability to quickly move the arms and legs.
Perceptual Speed	The ability to quickly and accurately compare similarities and differences among sets of letters, numbers, objects, pictures, or patterns. The things to be compared may be presented at the same time or one after the other. This ability also includes comparing a presented object with a remembered object.
Visual Color Discrimination	The ability to match or detect differences between colors, including shades of color and brightness.
Response Orientation	The ability to choose quickly between two or more movements in response to two or more different signals (lights, sounds, pictures). It includes the speed with which the correct response is started with the hand, foot, or other body part.
Reaction Time	The ability to quickly respond (with the hand, finger, or foot) to a signal (sound, light, picture) when it appears.
Number Facility	The ability to add, subtract, multiply, or divide quickly and correctly.
Auditory Attention	The ability to focus on a single source of sound in the presence of other distracting sounds.
Gross Body Equilibrium	The ability to keep or regain your body balance or stay upright when in an unstable position.
Peripheral Vision	The ability to see objects or movement of objects to one's side when the eyes are looking ahead.
Wrist-Finger Speed	The ability to make fast, simple, repeated movements of the fingers, hands, and wrists.
Rate Control	The ability to time your movements or the movement of a piece of equipment in anticipation of changes in the speed and/or direction of a moving object or scene.
Hearing Sensitivity	The ability to detect or tell the differences between sounds that vary in pitch and loudness.
Night Vision	The ability to see under low light conditions.
Glare Sensitivity	The ability to see objects in the presence of glare or bright lighting.
Dynamic Flexibility	The ability to quickly and repeatedly bend, stretch, twist, or reach out with your body, arms, and/or legs.
Sound Localization	The ability to tell the direction from which a sound originated.
Explosive Strength	The ability to use short bursts of muscle force to propel oneself (as in jumping or sprinting), or to throw an object.

Work_Activity	Work_Activity Definitions
Performing General Physical Activities	Performing physical activities that require considerable use of your arms and legs and moving your whole body, such as climbing, lifting, balancing, walking, stooping, and handling of materials.
Getting Information	Observing, receiving, and otherwise obtaining information from all relevant sources.
Operating Vehicles, Mechanized Devices, or Equipme	Running, maneuvering, navigating, or driving vehicles or mechanized equipment, such as forklifts, passenger vehicles, aircraft, or water craft.
Communicating with Supervisors, Peers, or Subordin	Providing information to supervisors, co-workers, and subordinates by telephone, in written form, e-mail, or in person.
Making Decisions and Solving Problems	Analyzing information and evaluating results to choose the best solution and solve problems.
Identifying Objects, Actions, and Events	Identifying information by categorizing, estimating, recognizing differences or similarities, and detecting changes in circumstances or events.
Monitor Processes, Materials, or Surroundings	Monitoring and reviewing information from materials, events, or the environment, to detect or assess problems.
Evaluating Information to Determine Compliance wit	Using relevant information and individual judgment to determine whether events or processes comply with laws, regulations, or standards.
Judging the Qualities of Things, Services, or Peop	Assessing the value, importance, or quality of things or people.
Estimating the Quantifiable Characteristics of Pro	Estimating sizes, distances, and quantities; or determining time, costs, resources, or materials needed to perform a work activity.
Handling and Moving Objects	Using hands and arms in handling, installing, positioning, and moving materials, and manipulating things.

		Work_Context	Work_Context Definitions
Inspecting Equipment. Structures, or Material	Inspecting equipment, structures, or materials to identify the cause of errors or other problems or defects.	Telephone	How often do you have telephone conversations in this job?
Organizing, Planning, and Prioritizing Work	Developing specific goals and plans to prioritize, organize, and accomplish your work.	Outdoors, Exposed to Weather	How often does this job require working outdoors, exposed to all weather conditions?
Analyzing Data or Information	Identifying the underlying principles, reasons, or facts of information by breaking down information or data into separate parts.	Face-to-Face Discussions	How often do you have to have face-to-face discussions with individuals or teams in this job?
Updating and Using Relevant Knowledge	Keeping up-to-date technically and applying new knowledge to your job.	In an Enclosed Vehicle or Equipment	How often does this job require working in a closed vehicle or equipment (e.g., car)?
Performing for or Working Directly with the Public	Performing for people or dealing directly with the public. This includes serving customers in restaurants and stores, and receiving clients or guests.	Deal With External Customers	How important is it to work with external customers or the public in this job?
Communicating with Persons Outside Organization	Communicating with people outside the organization, representing the organization to customers, the public, government, and other external sources. This information can be exchanged in person, in writing, or by telephone or e-mail.	Electronic Mail	How often do you use electronic mail in this job?
		Wear Common Protective or Safety Equipment such as	How much does this job require wearing common protective or safety equipment such as safety shoes, glasses, gloves, hard hats or life jackets?
Establishing and Maintaining Interpersonal Relatio	Developing constructive and cooperative working relationships with others, and maintaining them over time.	Work With Work Group or Team	How important is it to work with others in a group or team in this job?
Processing Information	Compiling, coding, categorizing, calculating, tabulating, auditing, or verifying information or data.	Contact With Others	How much does this job require the worker to be in contact with others (face-to-face, by telephone, or otherwise) in order to perform it?
Training and Teaching Others	Identifying the educational needs of others, developing formal educational or training programs or classes, and teaching or instructing others.	Freedom to Make Decisions	How much decision making freedom, without supervision, does the job offer?
Interacting With Computers	Using computers and computer systems (including hardware and software) to program, write software, set up functions, enter data, or process information.	Structured versus Unstructured Work	To what extent is this job structured for the worker, rather than allowing the worker to determine tasks, priorities, and goals?
Interpreting the Meaning of Information for Others	Translating or explaining what information means and how it can be used.	Importance of Being Exact or Accurate	How important is being very exact or highly accurate in performing this job?
Coordinating the Work and Activities of Others	Getting members of a group to work together to accomplish tasks.	Impact of Decisions on Co-workers or Company Resul	How do the decisions an employee makes impact the results of co-workers, clients or the company?
Documenting/Recording Information	Entering, transcribing, recording, storing, or maintaining information in written or electronic/magnetic form.	Exposed to Minor Burns, Cuts, Bites, or Stings	How often does this job require exposure to minor burns, cuts, bites, or stings?
Resolving Conflicts and Negotiating with Others	Handling complaints, settling disputes, and resolving grievances and conflicts, or otherwise negotiating with others.	Letters and Memos	How often does the job require written letters and memos?
Scheduling Work and Activities	Scheduling events, programs, and activities, as well as the work of others.	Responsible for Others' Health and Safety	How much responsibility is there for the health and safety of others in this job?
Guiding, Directing, and Motivating Subordinates	Providing guidance and direction to subordinates, including setting performance standards and monitoring performance.	Frequency of Decision Making	How frequently is the worker required to make decisions that affect other people, the financial resources, and/or the image and reputation of the organization?
Controlling Machines and Processes	Using either control mechanisms or direct physical activity to operate machines or processes (not including computers or vehicles).	Very Hot or Cold Temperatures	How often does this job require working in very hot (above 90 F degrees) or very cold (below 32 F degrees) temperatures?
Thinking Creatively	Developing, designing, or creating new applications, ideas, relationships, systems, or products, including artistic contributions.	Consequence of Error	How serious would the result usually be if the worker made a mistake that was not readily correctable?
		Spend Time Walking and Running	How much does this job require walking and running?
Developing Objectives and Strategies	Establishing long-range objectives and specifying the strategies and actions to achieve them.	Time Pressure	How often does this job require the worker to meet strict deadlines?
Developing and Building Teams	Encouraging and building mutual trust, respect, and cooperation among team members.	Exposed to Hazardous Equipment	How often does this job require exposure to hazardous equipment?
Repairing and Maintaining Mechanical Equipment	Servicing, repairing, adjusting, and testing machines, devices, moving parts, and equipment that operate primarily on the basis of mechanical (not electronic) principles.	Coordinate or Lead Others	How important is it to coordinate or lead others in accomplishing work activities in this job?
Coaching and Developing Others	Identifying the developmental needs of others and coaching, mentoring, or otherwise helping others to improve their knowledge or skills.	Frequency of Conflict Situations	How often are there conflict situations the employee has to face in this job?
Provide Consultation and Advice to Others	Providing guidance and expert advice to management or other groups on technical, systems-, or process-related topics.	Exposed to Contaminants	How often does this job require working exposed to contaminants (such as pollutants, gases, dust or odors)?
Performing Administrative Activities	Performing day-to-day administrative tasks such as maintaining information files and processing paperwork.	Spend Time Standing	How much does this job require standing?
		Sounds, Noise Levels Are Distracting or Uncomforta	How often does this job require working exposed to sounds and noise levels that are distracting or uncomfortable?
Assisting and Caring for Others	Providing personal assistance, medical attention, emotional support, or other personal care to others such as coworkers, customers, or patients.	Responsibility for Outcomes and Results	How responsible is the worker for work outcomes and results of other workers?
Monitoring and Controlling Resources	Monitoring and controlling resources and overseeing the spending of money.	Exposed to Hazardous Conditions	How often does this job require exposure to hazardous conditions?
Selling or Influencing Others	Convincing others to buy merchandise/goods or to otherwise change their minds or actions.	Physical Proximity	To what extent does this job require the worker to perform job tasks in close physical proximity to other people?
Drafting, Laying Out, and Specifying Technical Dev	Providing documentation, detailed instructions, drawings, or specifications to tell others about how devices, parts, equipment, or structures are to be fabricated, constructed, assembled, modified, maintained, or used.	Deal With Unpleasant or Angry People	How frequently does the worker have to deal with unpleasant, angry, or discourteous individuals as part of the job requirements?
Staffing Organizational Units	Recruiting, interviewing, selecting, hiring, and promoting employees in an organization.	Level of Competition	To what extent does this job require the worker to compete or to be aware of competitive pressures?
Repairing and Maintaining Electronic Equipment	Servicing, repairing, calibrating, regulating, fine-tuning, or testing machines, devices, and equipment that operate primarily on the basis of electrical or electronic (not mechanical) principles.	Importance of Repeating Same Tasks	How important is repeating the same physical activities (e.g., key entry) or mental activities (e.g., checking entries in a ledger) over and over, without stopping, to performing this job?
		In an Open Vehicle or Equipment	How often does this job require working in an open vehicle or equipment (e.g., tractor)?
		Indoors, Not Environmentally Controlled	How often does this job require working indoors in non-controlled environmental conditions (e.g., warehouse without heat)?
		Spend Time Bending or Twisting the Body	How much does this job require bending or twisting your body?

Exposed to Whole Body Vibration	How often does this job require exposure to whole body vibration (e.g., operate a jackhammer)?
Indoors, Environmentally Controlled	How often does this job require working indoors in environmentally controlled conditions?
Spend Time Sitting	How much does this job require sitting?
Extremely Bright or Inadequate Lighting	How often does this job require working in extremely bright or inadequate lighting conditions?
Spend Time Using Your Hands to Handle, Control, or	How much does this job require using your hands to handle, control, or feel objects, tools or controls?
Outdoors, Under Cover	How often does this job require working outdoors, under cover (e.g., structure with roof but no walls)?
Cramped Work Space, Awkward Positions	How often does this job require working in cramped work spaces that requires getting into awkward positions?
Spend Time Making Repetitive Motions	How much does this job require making repetitive motions?
Public Speaking	How often do you have to perform public speaking in this job?
Exposed to High Places	How often does this job require exposure to high places?
Wear Specialized Protective or Safety Equipment su	How much does this job require wearing specialized protective or safety equipment such as breathing apparatus, safety harness, full protection suits, or radiation protection?
Spend Time Keeping or Regaining Balance	How much does this job require keeping or regaining your balance?
Spend Time Kneeling, Crouching, Stooping, or Crawl	How much does this job require kneeling, crouching, stooping, or crawling?
Degree of Automation	How automated is the job?
Exposed to Disease or Infections	How often does this job require exposure to disease/infections?
Deal With Physically Aggressive People	How frequently does this job require the worker to deal with physical aggression of violent individuals?
Spend Time Climbing Ladders, Scaffolds, or Poles	How much does this job require climbing ladders, scaffolds, or poles?
Pace Determined by Speed of Equipment	How important is it to this job that the pace is determined by the speed of equipment or machinery? (This does not refer to keeping busy at all times on this job.)
Exposed to Radiation	How often does this job require exposure to radiation?

Job Zone Component	Job Zone Component Definitions
Title	Job Zone Three: Medium Preparation Needed
Overall Experience	Previous work-related skill, knowledge, or experience is required for these occupations. For example, an electrician must have completed three or four years of apprenticeship or several years of vocational training, and often must have passed a licensing exam, in order to perform the job.
Job Training	Employees in these occupations usually need one or two years of training involving both on-the-job experience and informal training with experienced workers.
Job Zone Examples	These occupations usually involve using communication and organizational skills to coordinate, supervise, manage, or train others to accomplish goals. Examples include dental assistants, electricians, fish and game wardens, legal secretaries, personnel recruiters, and recreation workers.
SVP Range	(6.0 to < 7.0)
Education	Most occupations in this zone require training in vocational schools, related on-the-job experience, or an associate's degree. Some may require a bachelor's degree.

Work_Styles	Work_Styles Definitions
Cooperation	Job requires being pleasant with others on the job and displaying a good-natured, cooperative attitude.
Adaptability/Flexibility	Job requires being open to change (positive or negative) and to considerable variety in the workplace.
Attention to Detail	Job requires being careful about detail and thorough in completing work tasks.
Integrity	Job requires being honest and ethical.
Dependability	Job requires being reliable, responsible, and dependable, and fulfilling obligations.
Initiative	Job requires a willingness to take on responsibilities and challenges.
Independence	Job requires developing one's own ways of doing things, guiding oneself with little or no supervision, and depending on oneself to get things done.

Achievement/Effort	Job requires establishing and maintaining personally challenging achievement goals and exerting effort toward mastering tasks.
Leadership	Job requires a willingness to lead, take charge, and offer opinions and direction.
Persistence	Job requires persistence in the face of obstacles.
Analytical Thinking	Job requires analyzing information and using logic to address work-related issues and problems.
Stress Tolerance	Job requires accepting criticism and dealing calmly and effectively with high stress situations.
Self Control	Job requires maintaining composure, keeping emotions in check, controlling anger, and avoiding aggressive behavior, even in very difficult situations.
Concern for Others	Job requires being sensitive to others' needs and feelings and being understanding and helpful on the job.
Innovation	Job requires creativity and alternative thinking to develop new ideas for and answers to work-related problems.
Social Orientation	Job requires preferring to work with others rather than alone, and being personally connected with others on the job.

21-1011.00 - Substance Abuse and Behavioral Disorder Counselors

Counsel and advise individuals with alcohol, tobacco, drug, or other problems, such as gambling and eating disorders. May counsel individuals, families, or groups or engage in prevention programs.

Tasks

1) Provide clients or family members with information about addiction issues and about available services and programs, making appropriate referrals when necessary.

2) Counsel clients and patients, individually and in group sessions, to assist in overcoming dependencies, adjusting to life, and making changes.

3) Intervene as advocate for clients or patients in order to resolve emergency problems in crisis situations.

4) Interview clients, review records, and confer with other professionals in order to evaluate individuals' mental and physical condition, and to determine their suitability for participation in a specific program.

5) Complete and maintain accurate records and reports regarding the patients' histories and progress, services provided, and other required information.

6) Coordinate counseling efforts with mental health professionals and other health professionals such as doctors, nurses, and social workers.

7) Review and evaluate clients' progress in relation to measurable goals described in treatment and care plans.

8) Modify treatment plans to comply with changes in client status.

9) Confer with family members or others close to clients in order to keep them informed of treatment planning and progress.

10) Develop client treatment plans based on research, clinical experience, and client histories.

11) Counsel family members to assist them in understanding, dealing with, and supporting clients or patients.

12) Coordinate activities with courts, probation officers, community services and other post-treatment agencies.

13) Act as liaisons between clients and medical staff.

14) Conduct chemical dependency program orientation sessions.

15) Plan and implement follow-up and aftercare programs for clients to be discharged from treatment programs.

16) Instruct others in program methods, procedures, and functions.

17) Follow progress of discharged patients in order to determine effectiveness of treatments.

18) Develop, implement, and evaluate public education, prevention, and health promotion programs, working in collaboration with organizations, institutions and communities.

19) Supervise and direct other workers providing services to clients or patients.

20) Attend training sessions in order to increase knowledge and skills.

Knowledge	Knowledge Definitions
Therapy and Counseling	Knowledge of principles, methods, and procedures for diagnosis, treatment, and rehabilitation of physical and mental dysfunctions, and for career counseling and guidance.
Psychology	Knowledge of human behavior and performance; individual differences in ability, personality, and interests; learning and motivation; psychological research methods; and the assessment and treatment of behavioral and affective disorders.
Sociology and Anthropology	Knowledge of group behavior and dynamics, societal trends and influences, human migrations, ethnicity, cultures and their history and origins.
Customer and Personal Service	Knowledge of principles and processes for providing customer and personal services. This includes customer needs assessment, meeting quality standards for services, and evaluation of customer satisfaction.
Education and Training	Knowledge of principles and methods for curriculum and training design, teaching and instruction for individuals and groups, and the measurement of training effects.
English Language	Knowledge of the structure and content of the English language including the meaning and spelling of words, rules of composition, and grammar.
Philosophy and Theology	Knowledge of different philosophical systems and religions. This includes their basic principles, values, ethics, ways of thinking, customs, practices, and their impact on human culture.
Administration and Management	Knowledge of business and management principles involved in strategic planning, resource allocation, human resources modeling, leadership technique, production methods, and coordination of people and resources.
Law and Government	Knowledge of laws, legal codes, court procedures, precedents, government regulations, executive orders, agency rules, and the democratic political process.
Clerical	Knowledge of administrative and clerical procedures and systems such as word processing, managing files and records, stenography and transcription, designing forms, and other office procedures and terminology.
Public Safety and Security	Knowledge of relevant equipment, policies, procedures, and strategies to promote effective local, state, or national security operations for the protection of people, data, property, and institutions.
Computers and Electronics	Knowledge of circuit boards, processors, chips, electronic equipment, and computer hardware and software, including applications and programming.
Medicine and Dentistry	Knowledge of the information and techniques needed to diagnose and treat human injuries, diseases, and deformities. This includes symptoms, treatment alternatives, drug properties and interactions, and preventive health-care measures.
Communications and Media	Knowledge of media production, communication, and dissemination techniques and methods. This includes alternative ways to inform and entertain via written, oral, and visual media.
Personnel and Human Resources	Knowledge of principles and procedures for personnel recruitment, selection, training, compensation and benefits, labor relations and negotiation, and personnel information systems.
Sales and Marketing	Knowledge of principles and methods for showing, promoting, and selling products or services. This includes marketing strategy and tactics, product demonstration, sales techniques, and sales control systems.
Mathematics	Knowledge of arithmetic, algebra, geometry, calculus, statistics, and their applications.
Biology	Knowledge of plant and animal organisms, their tissues, cells, functions, interdependencies, and interactions with each other and the environment.
Foreign Language	Knowledge of the structure and content of a foreign (non-English) language including the meaning and spelling of words, rules of composition and grammar, and pronunciation.
History and Archeology	Knowledge of historical events and their causes, indicators, and effects on civilizations and cultures.
Economics and Accounting	Knowledge of economic and accounting principles and practices, the financial markets, banking and the analysis and reporting of financial data.
Transportation	Knowledge of principles and methods for moving people or goods by air, rail, sea, or road, including the relative costs and benefits.
Telecommunications	Knowledge of transmission, broadcasting, switching, control, and operation of telecommunications systems.
Chemistry	Knowledge of the chemical composition, structure, and properties of substances and of the chemical processes and transformations that they undergo. This includes uses of chemicals and their interactions, danger signs, production techniques, and disposal methods.
Production and Processing	Knowledge of raw materials, production processes, quality control, costs, and other techniques for maximizing the effective manufacture and distribution of goods.
Fine Arts	Knowledge of the theory and techniques required to compose, produce, and perform works of music, dance, visual arts, drama, and sculpture.
Geography	Knowledge of principles and methods for describing the features of land, sea, and air masses, including their physical characteristics, locations, interrelationships, and distribution of plant, animal, and human life.
Design	Knowledge of design techniques, tools, and principles involved in production of precision technical plans, blueprints, drawings, and models.
Food Production	Knowledge of techniques and equipment for planting, growing, and harvesting food products (both plant and animal) for consumption, including storage/handling techniques.
Mechanical	Knowledge of machines and tools, including their designs, uses, repair, and maintenance.
Building and Construction	Knowledge of materials, methods, and the tools involved in the construction or repair of houses, buildings, or other structures such as highways and roads.
Engineering and Technology	Knowledge of the practical application of engineering science and technology. This includes applying principles, techniques, procedures, and equipment to the design and production of various goods and services.
Physics	Knowledge and prediction of physical principles, laws, their interrelationships, and applications to understanding fluid, material, and atmospheric dynamics, and mechanical, electrical, atomic and sub-atomic structures and processes.

Skills	Skills Definitions
Active Listening	Giving full attention to what other people are saying, taking time to understand the points being made, asking questions as appropriate, and not interrupting at inappropriate times.
Social Perceptiveness	Being aware of others' reactions and understanding why they react as they do.
Service Orientation	Actively looking for ways to help people.
Time Management	Managing one's own time and the time of others.
Speaking	Talking to others to convey information effectively.
Critical Thinking	Using logic and reasoning to identify the strengths and weaknesses of alternative solutions, conclusions or approaches to problems.
Persuasion	Persuading others to change their minds or behavior.
Reading Comprehension	Understanding written sentences and paragraphs in work related documents.
Instructing	Teaching others how to do something.
Writing	Communicating effectively in writing as appropriate for the needs of the audience.
Coordination	Adjusting actions in relation to others' actions.
Learning Strategies	Selecting and using training/instructional methods and procedures appropriate for the situation when learning or teaching new things.
Active Learning	Understanding the implications of new information for both current and future problem-solving and decision-making.
Monitoring	Monitoring/Assessing performance of yourself, other individuals, or organizations to make improvements or take corrective action.
Complex Problem Solving	Identifying complex problems and reviewing related information to develop and evaluate options and implement solutions.
Negotiation	Bringing others together and trying to reconcile differences.
Judgment and Decision Making	Considering the relative costs and benefits of potential actions to choose the most appropriate one.
Management of Personnel Resources	Motivating, developing, and directing people as they work, identifying the best people for the job.
Quality Control Analysis	Conducting tests and inspections of products, services, or processes to evaluate quality or performance.
Operations Analysis	Analyzing needs and product requirements to create a design.
Systems Evaluation	Identifying measures or indicators of system performance and the actions needed to improve or correct performance, relative to the goals of the system.
Science	Using scientific rules and methods to solve problems.

Management of Financial Resources	Determining how money will be spent to get the work done, and accounting for these expenditures.
Management of Material Resources	Obtaining and seeing to the appropriate use of equipment, facilities, and materials needed to do certain work.
Mathematics	Using mathematics to solve problems.
Equipment Selection	Determining the kind of tools and equipment needed to do a job.
Systems Analysis	Determining how a system should work and how changes in conditions, operations, and the environment will affect outcomes.
Technology Design	Generating or adapting equipment and technology to serve user needs.
Troubleshooting	Determining causes of operating errors and deciding what to do about it.
Operation and Control	Controlling operations of equipment or systems.
Operation Monitoring	Watching gauges, dials, or other indicators to make sure a machine is working properly.
Installation	Installing equipment, machines, wiring, or programs to meet specifications.
Equipment Maintenance	Performing routine maintenance on equipment and determining when and what kind of maintenance is needed.
Repairing	Repairing machines or systems using the needed tools.
Programming	Writing computer programs for various purposes.

Ability	Ability Definitions
Oral Comprehension	The ability to listen to and understand information and ideas presented through spoken words and sentences.
Oral Expression	The ability to communicate information and ideas in speaking so others will understand.
Speech Clarity	The ability to speak clearly so others can understand you.
Problem Sensitivity	The ability to tell when something is wrong or is likely to go wrong. It does not involve solving the problem, only recognizing there is a problem.
Inductive Reasoning	The ability to combine pieces of information to form general rules or conclusions (includes finding a relationship among seemingly unrelated events).
Speech Recognition	The ability to identify and understand the speech of another person.
Deductive Reasoning	The ability to apply general rules to specific problems to produce answers that make sense.
Written Comprehension	The ability to read and understand information and ideas presented in writing.
Written Expression	The ability to communicate information and ideas in writing so others will understand.
Near Vision	The ability to see details at close range (within a few feet of the observer).
Information Ordering	The ability to arrange things or actions in a certain order or pattern according to a specific rule or set of rules (e.g., patterns of numbers, letters, words, pictures, mathematical operations).
Originality	The ability to come up with unusual or clever ideas about a given topic or situation, or to develop creative ways to solve a problem.
Category Flexibility	The ability to generate or use different sets of rules for combining or grouping things in different ways.
Fluency of Ideas	The ability to come up with a number of ideas about a topic (the number of ideas is important, not their quality, correctness, or creativity).
Selective Attention	The ability to concentrate on a task over a period of time without being distracted.
Time Sharing	The ability to shift back and forth between two or more activities or sources of information (such as speech, sounds, touch, or other sources).
Flexibility of Closure	The ability to identify or detect a known pattern (a figure, object, word, or sound) that is hidden in other distracting material.
Memorization	The ability to remember information such as words, numbers, pictures, and procedures.
Speed of Closure	The ability to quickly make sense of, combine, and organize information into meaningful patterns.
Perceptual Speed	The ability to quickly and accurately compare similarities and differences among sets of letters, numbers, objects, pictures, or patterns. The things to be compared may be presented at the same time or one after the other. This ability also includes comparing a presented object with a remembered object.
Far Vision	The ability to see details at a distance.
Mathematical Reasoning	The ability to choose the right mathematical methods or formulas to solve a problem.

Static Strength	The ability to exert maximum muscle force to lift, push, pull, or carry objects.
Reaction Time	The ability to quickly respond (with the hand, finger, or foot) to a signal (sound, light, picture) when it appears.
Number Facility	The ability to add, subtract, multiply, or divide quickly and correctly.
Gross Body Coordination	The ability to coordinate the movement of your arms, legs, and torso together when the whole body is in motion.
Response Orientation	The ability to choose quickly between two or more movements in response to two or more different signals (lights, sounds, pictures). It includes the speed with which the correct response is started with the hand, foot, or other body part.
Visualization	The ability to imagine how something will look after it is moved around or when its parts are moved or rearranged.
Gross Body Equilibrium	The ability to keep or regain your body balance or stay upright when in an unstable position.
Explosive Strength	The ability to use short bursts of muscle force to propel oneself (as in jumping or sprinting), or to throw an object.
Visual Color Discrimination	The ability to match or detect differences between colors, including shades of color and brightness.
Finger Dexterity	The ability to make precisely coordinated movements of the fingers of one or both hands to grasp, manipulate, or assemble very small objects.
Hearing Sensitivity	The ability to detect or tell the differences between sounds that vary in pitch and loudness.
Stamina	The ability to exert yourself physically over long periods of time without getting winded or out of breath.
Auditory Attention	The ability to focus on a single source of sound in the presence of other distracting sounds.
Trunk Strength	The ability to use your abdominal and lower back muscles to support part of the body repeatedly or continuously over time without 'giving out' or fatiguing.
Spatial Orientation	The ability to know your location in relation to the environment or to know where other objects are in relation to you.
Night Vision	The ability to see under low light conditions.
Extent Flexibility	The ability to bend, stretch, twist, or reach with your body, arms, and/or legs.
Dynamic Strength	The ability to exert muscle force repeatedly or continuously over time. This involves muscular endurance and resistance to muscle fatigue.
Speed of Limb Movement	The ability to quickly move the arms and legs.
Wrist-Finger Speed	The ability to make fast, simple, repeated movements of the fingers, hands, and wrists.
Rate Control	The ability to time your movements or the movement of a piece of equipment in anticipation of changes in the speed and/or direction of a moving object or scene.
Multilimb Coordination	The ability to coordinate two or more limbs (for example, two arms, two legs, or one leg and one arm) while sitting, standing, or lying down. It does not involve performing the activities while the whole body is in motion.
Dynamic Flexibility	The ability to quickly and repeatedly bend, stretch, twist, or reach out with your body, arms, and/or legs.
Depth Perception	The ability to judge which of several objects is closer or farther away from you, or to judge the distance between you and an object.
Control Precision	The ability to quickly and repeatedly adjust the controls of a machine or a vehicle to exact positions.
Sound Localization	The ability to tell the direction from which a sound originated.
Arm-Hand Steadiness	The ability to keep your hand and arm steady while moving your arm or while holding your arm and hand in one position.
Glare Sensitivity	The ability to see objects in the presence of glare or bright lighting.
Manual Dexterity	The ability to quickly move your hand, your hand together with your arm, or your two hands to grasp, manipulate, or assemble objects.
Peripheral Vision	The ability to see objects or movement of objects to one's side when the eyes are looking ahead.

Work_Activity	Work_Activity Definitions
Getting Information	Observing, receiving, and otherwise obtaining information from all relevant sources.
Assisting and Caring for Others	Providing personal assistance, medical attention, emotional support, or other personal care to others such as coworkers, customers, or patients.
Establishing and Maintaining Interpersonal Relatio	Developing constructive and cooperative working relationships with others, and maintaining them over time.

Communicating with Supervisors, Peers, or Subordin	Providing information to supervisors, co-workers, and subordinates by telephone, in written form, e-mail, or in person.
Documenting/Recording Information	Entering, transcribing, recording, storing, or maintaining information in written or electronic/magnetic form.
Making Decisions and Solving Problems	Analyzing information and evaluating results to choose the best solution and solve problems.
Organizing, Planning, and Prioritizing Work	Developing specific goals and plans to prioritize, organize, and accomplish your work.
Resolving Conflicts and Negotiating with Others	Handling complaints, settling disputes, and resolving grievances and conflicts, or otherwise negotiating with others.
Evaluating Information to Determine Compliance wit	Using relevant information and individual judgment to determine whether events or processes comply with laws, regulations, or standards.
Communicating with Persons Outside Organization	Communicating with people outside the organization, representing the organization to customers, the public, government, and other external sources. This information can be exchanged in person, in writing, or by telephone or e-mail.
Performing for or Working Directly with the Public	Performing for people or dealing directly with the public. This includes serving customers in restaurants and stores, and receiving clients or guests.
Developing Objectives and Strategies	Establishing long-range objectives and specifying the strategies and actions to achieve them.
Updating and Using Relevant Knowledge	Keeping up-to-date technically and applying new knowledge to your job.
Interpreting the Meaning of Information for Others	Translating or explaining what information means and how it can be used.
Thinking Creatively	Developing, designing, or creating new applications, ideas, relationships, systems, or products, including artistic contributions.
Identifying Objects, Actions, and Events	Identifying information by categorizing, estimating, recognizing differences or similarities, and detecting changes in circumstances or events.
Training and Teaching Others	Identifying the educational needs of others, developing formal educational or training programs or classes, and teaching or instructing others.
Judging the Qualities of Things, Services, or Peop	Assessing the value, importance, or quality of things or people.
Processing Information	Compiling, coding, categorizing, calculating, tabulating, auditing, or verifying information or data.
Scheduling Work and Activities	Scheduling events, programs, and activities, as well as the work of others.
Monitor Processes, Materials, or Surroundings	Monitoring and reviewing information from materials, events, or the environment, to detect or assess problems.
Coaching and Developing Others	Identifying the developmental needs of others and coaching, mentoring, or otherwise helping others to improve their knowledge or skills.
Developing and Building Teams	Encouraging and building mutual trust, respect, and cooperation among team members.
Provide Consultation and Advice to Others	Providing guidance and expert advice to management or other groups on technical, systems-, or process-related topics.
Interacting With Computers	Using computers and computer systems (including hardware and software) to program, write software, set up functions, enter data, or process information.
Selling or Influencing Others	Convincing others to buy merchandise/goods or to otherwise change their minds or actions.
Performing Administrative Activities	Performing day-to-day administrative tasks such as maintaining information files and processing paperwork.
Analyzing Data or Information	Identifying the underlying principles, reasons, or facts of information by breaking down information or data into separate parts.
Coordinating the Work and Activities of Others	Getting members of a group to work together to accomplish tasks.
Guiding, Directing, and Motivating Subordinates	Providing guidance and direction to subordinates, including setting performance standards and monitoring performance.
Estimating the Quantifiable Characteristics of Pro	Estimating sizes, distances, and quantities; or determining time, costs, resources, or materials needed to perform a work activity.
Monitoring and Controlling Resources	Monitoring and controlling resources and overseeing the spending of money.
Staffing Organizational Units	Recruiting, interviewing, selecting, hiring, and promoting employees in an organization.
Performing General Physical Activities	Performing physical activities that require considerable use of your arms and legs and moving your whole body, such as climbing, lifting, balancing, walking, stooping, and handling of materials.
Inspecting Equipment, Structures, or Material	Inspecting equipment, structures, or materials to identify the cause of errors or other problems or defects.
Operating Vehicles, Mechanized Devices, or Equipme	Running, maneuvering, navigating, or driving vehicles or mechanized equipment, such as forklifts, passenger vehicles, aircraft, or water craft.
Handling and Moving Objects	Using hands and arms in handling, installing, positioning, and moving materials, and manipulating things.
Controlling Machines and Processes	Using either control mechanisms or direct physical activity to operate machines or processes (not including computers or vehicles).
Repairing and Maintaining Electronic Equipment	Servicing, repairing, calibrating, regulating, fine-tuning, or testing machines, devices, and equipment that operate primarily on the basis of electrical or electronic (not mechanical) principles.
Drafting, Laying Out, and Specifying Technical Dev	Providing documentation, detailed instructions, drawings, or specifications to tell others about how devices, parts, equipment, or structures are to be fabricated, constructed, assembled, modified, maintained, or used.
Repairing and Maintaining Mechanical Equipment	Servicing, repairing, adjusting, and testing machines, devices, moving parts, and equipment that operate primarily on the basis of mechanical (not electronic) principles.

Work_Context	Work_Context Definitions
Contact With Others	How much does this job require the worker to be in contact with others (face-to-face, by telephone, or otherwise) in order to perform it?
Face-to-Face Discussions	How often do you have to have face-to-face discussions with individuals or teams in this job?
Telephone	How often do you have telephone conversations in this job?
Indoors, Environmentally Controlled	How often does this job require working indoors in environmentally controlled conditions?
Work With Work Group or Team	How important is it to work with others in a group or team in this job?
Freedom to Make Decisions	How much decision making freedom, without supervision, does the job offer?
Structured versus Unstructured Work	To what extent is this job structured for the worker, rather than allowing the worker to determine tasks, priorities, and goals?
Deal With External Customers	How important is it to work with external customers or the public in this job?
Spend Time Sitting	How much does this job require sitting?
Letters and Memos	How often does the job require written letters and memos?
Frequency of Decision Making	How frequently is the worker required to make decisions that affect other people, the financial resources, and/or the image and reputation of the organization?
Impact of Decisions on Co-workers or Company Resul	How do the decisions an employee makes impact the results of co-workers, clients or the company?
Importance of Being Exact or Accurate	How important is being very exact or highly accurate in performing this job?
Coordinate or Lead Others	How important is it to coordinate or lead others in accomplishing work activities in this job?
Time Pressure	How often does this job require the worker to meet strict deadlines?
Electronic Mail	How often do you use electronic mail in this job?
Deal With Unpleasant or Angry People	How frequently does the worker have to deal with unpleasant, angry, or discourteous individuals as part of the job requirements?
Physical Proximity	To what extent does this job require the worker to perform job tasks in close physical proximity to other people?
Exposed to Disease or Infections	How often does this job require exposure to disease/infections?
Frequency of Conflict Situations	How often are there conflict situations the employee has to face in this job?
Importance of Repeating Same Tasks	How important is repeating the same physical activities (e.g., key entry) or mental activities (e.g., checking entries in a ledger) over and over, without stopping, to performing this job?
Responsible for Others' Health and Safety	How much responsibility is there for the health and safety of others in this job?
Public Speaking	How often do you have to perform public speaking in this job?
Deal With Physically Aggressive People	How frequently does this job require the worker to deal with physical aggression of violent individuals?
Responsibility for Outcomes and Results	How responsible is the worker for work outcomes and results of other workers?
Level of Competition	To what extent does this job require the worker to compete or to be aware of competitive pressures?
Consequence of Error	How serious would the result usually be if the worker made a mistake that was not readily correctable?

Sounds, Noise Levels Are Distracting or Uncomforta | How often does this job require working exposed to sounds and noise levels that are distracting or uncomfortable?

Spend Time Using Your Hands to Handle, Control, or | How much does this job require using your hands to handle, control, or feel objects, tools or controls?

Spend Time Making Repetitive Motions | How much does this job require making repetitive motions?

In an Enclosed Vehicle or Equipment | How often does this job require working in a closed vehicle or equipment (e.g., car)?

Spend Time Standing | How much does this job require standing?

Spend Time Walking and Running | How much does this job require walking and running?

Degree of Automation | How automated is the job?

Exposed to Contaminants | How often does this job require working exposed to contaminants (such as pollutants, gases, dust or odors)?

Wear Common Protective or Safety Equipment such as | How often does this job require wearing common protective or safety equipment such as safety shoes, glasses, gloves, hard hats or life jackets?

Extremely Bright or Inadequate Lighting | How often does this job require working in extremely bright or inadequate lighting conditions?

Spend Time Bending or Twisting the Body | How much does this job require bending or twisting your body?

Outdoors, Exposed to Weather | How often does this job require working outdoors, exposed to all weather conditions?

Exposed to Minor Burns, Cuts, Bites, or Stings | How often does this job require exposure to minor burns, cuts, bites, or stings?

Indoors, Not Environmentally Controlled | How often does this job require working indoors in non-controlled environmental conditions (e.g., warehouse without heat)?

Cramped Work Space, Awkward Positions | How often does this job require working in cramped work spaces that requires getting into awkward positions?

Spend Time Kneeling, Crouching, Stooping, or Crawl | How much does this job require kneeling, crouching, stooping, or crawling?

Very Hot or Cold Temperatures | How often does this job require working in very hot (above 90 F degrees) or very cold (below 32 F degrees) temperatures?

Outdoors, Under Cover | How often does this job require working outdoors, under cover (e.g., structure with roof but no walls)?

Pace Determined by Speed of Equipment | How important is it to this job that the pace is determined by the speed of equipment or machinery? (This does not refer to keeping busy at all times on this job.)

Spend Time Keeping or Regaining Balance | How much does this job require keeping or regaining your balance?

Wear Specialized Protective or Safety Equipment su | How much does this job require wearing specialized protective or safety equipment such as breathing apparatus, safety harness, full protection suits, or radiation protection?

Exposed to Whole Body Vibration | How often does this job require exposure to whole body vibration (e.g., operate a jackhammer)?

Exposed to Hazardous Equipment | How often does this job require exposure to hazardous equipment?

Exposed to Hazardous Conditions | How often does this job require exposure to hazardous conditions?

Exposed to Radiation | How often does this job require exposure to radiation?

In an Open Vehicle or Equipment | How often does this job require working in an open vehicle or equipment (e.g., tractor)?

Spend Time Climbing Ladders, Scaffolds, or Poles | How much does this job require climbing ladders, scaffolds, or poles?

Exposed to High Places | How often does this job require exposure to high places?

21-1011.00

Job Zone Component	Job Zone Component Definitions
Title	Job Zone Five: Extensive Preparation Needed
	Extensive skill, knowledge, and experience are needed for these occupations. Many require more than five years of experience.
Overall Experience	For example, surgeons must complete four years of college and an additional five to seven years of specialized medical training to be able to do their job.
Job Training	Employees may need some on-the-job training, but most of these occupations assume that the person will already have the required skills, knowledge, work-related experience, and/or training.
Job Zone Examples	These occupations often involve coordinating, training, supervising, or managing the activities of others to accomplish goals. Very advanced communication and organizational skills are required. Examples include athletic trainers, lawyers, managing editors, physicists, social psychologists, and surgeons.

SVP Range	(8.0 and above)
Education	A bachelor's degree is the minimum formal education required for these occupations. However, many also require graduate school. For example, they may require a master's degree, and some require a Ph.D., M.D., or J.D. (law degree).

Work_Styles	Work_Styles Definitions
Integrity	Job requires being honest and ethical.
Concern for Others	Job requires being sensitive to others' needs and feelings and being understanding and helpful on the job.
Dependability	Job requires being reliable, responsible, and dependable, and fulfilling obligations.
Stress Tolerance	Job requires accepting criticism and dealing calmly and effectively with high stress situations.
Self Control	Job requires maintaining composure, keeping emotions in check, controlling anger, and avoiding aggressive behavior, even in very difficult situations.
Cooperation	Job requires being pleasant with others on the job and displaying a good-natured, cooperative attitude.
Adaptability/Flexibility	Job requires being open to change (positive or negative) and to considerable variety in the workplace.
Initiative	Job requires a willingness to take on responsibilities and challenges.
Persistence	Job requires persistence in the face of obstacles.
Social Orientation	Job requires preferring to work with others rather than alone, and being personally connected with others on the job.
Attention to Detail	Job requires being careful about detail and thorough in completing work tasks.
Leadership	Job requires a willingness to lead, take charge, and offer opinions and direction.
Achievement/Effort	Job requires establishing and maintaining personally challenging achievement goals and exerting effort toward mastering tasks.
Independence	Job requires developing one's own ways of doing things, guiding oneself with little or no supervision, and depending on oneself to get things done.
Analytical Thinking	Job requires analyzing information and using logic to address work-related issues and problems.
Innovation	Job requires creativity and alternative thinking to develop new ideas for and answers to work-related problems.

21-1012.00 - Educational, Vocational, and School Counselors

Counsel individuals and provide group educational and vocational guidance services.

Tasks

1) Attend professional meetings, educational conferences, and teacher training workshops, in order to maintain and improve professional competence.

2) Prepare students for later educational experiences by encouraging them to explore learning opportunities and to persevere with challenging tasks.

3) Meet with other professionals to discuss individual students' needs and progress.

4) Counsel students regarding educational issues such as course and program selection, class scheduling, school adjustment, truancy, study habits, and career planning.

5) Maintain accurate and complete student records as required by laws, district policies, and administrative regulations.

6) Prepare reports on students and activities as required by administration.

7) Counsel individuals to help them understand and overcome personal, social, or behavioral problems affecting their educational or vocational situations.

8) Confer with parents or guardians, teachers, other counselors, and administrators to resolve students' behavioral, academic, and other problems.

9) Collaborate with teachers and administrators in the development, evaluation, and revision of school programs.

10) Address community groups, faculty, and staff members to explain available counseling services.

11) Provide students with information on such topics as college degree programs and admission requirements, financial aid opportunities, trade and technical schools, and apprenticeship programs.

12) Evaluate individuals' abilities, interests, and personality characteristics using tests, records, interviews, and professional sources.

13) Enforce all administration policies and rules governing students.

14) Observe and evaluate students' performance, behavior, social development, and physical health.

15) Encourage students and/or parents to seek additional assistance from mental health professionals when necessary.

16) Teach classes and present self-help or information sessions on subjects related to education and career planning.

17) Provide crisis intervention to students when difficult situations occur at schools.

18) Identify cases involving domestic abuse or other family problems affecting students' development.

19) Conduct follow-up interviews with counselees to determine if their needs have been met.

20) Compile and study occupational, educational, and economic information to assist counselees in determining and carrying out vocational and educational objectives.

21) Meet with parents and guardians to discuss their children's progress, and to determine their priorities for their children and their resource needs.

22) Provide information for teachers and staff members involved in helping students or graduates identify and pursue employment opportunities.

23) Plan and conduct orientation programs and group conferences to promote the adjustment of individuals to new life experiences such as starting college.

24) Instruct individuals in career development techniques such as job search and application strategies, resume writing, and interview skills.

25) Establish and enforce behavioral rules and procedures to maintain order among students.

26) Assess needs for assistance such as rehabilitation, financial aid, or additional vocational training, and refer clients to the appropriate services.

27) Provide special services such as alcohol and drug prevention programs, and classes that teach students to handle conflicts without resorting to violence.

28) Review transcripts to ensure that students meet graduation or college entrance requirements, and write letters of recommendation.

29) Refer students to degree programs based on interests, aptitudes, or educational assessments.

30) Observe children during classroom and play activities to gain additional information about them.

31) Plan and promote career and employment-related programs such as work-experience programs.

32) Establish and supervise peer counseling and peer tutoring programs.

33) Perform administrative duties such as hall and cafeteria monitoring, and bus loading and unloading.

34) Sponsor extracurricular activities such as clubs, student organizations, and academic contests.

35) Refer qualified counselees to employers or employment services for job placement.

36) Provide disabled students with assistive devices, supportive technology, and assistance accessing facilities such as restrooms.

37) Interview clients to obtain information about employment history, educational background, and career goals, and to identify barriers to employment.

38) Provide information to businesses regarding human resource and employment issues.

Knowledge	Knowledge Definitions
Education and Training	Knowledge of principles and methods for curriculum and training design, teaching and instruction for individuals and groups, and the measurement of training effects.
Therapy and Counseling	Knowledge of principles, methods, and procedures for diagnosis, treatment, and rehabilitation of physical and mental dysfunctions, and for career counseling and guidance.
English Language	Knowledge of the structure and content of the English language including the meaning and spelling of words, rules of composition, and grammar.
Psychology	Knowledge of human behavior and performance; individual differences in ability, personality, and interests; learning and motivation; psychological research methods; and the assessment and treatment of behavioral and affective disorders.
Customer and Personal Service	Knowledge of principles and processes for providing customer and personal services. This includes customer needs assessment, meeting quality standards for services, and evaluation of customer satisfaction.
Sociology and Anthropology	Knowledge of group behavior and dynamics, societal trends and influences, human migrations, ethnicity, cultures and their history and origins.
Clerical	Knowledge of administrative and clerical procedures and systems such as word processing, managing files and records, stenography and transcription, designing forms, and other office procedures and terminology.
Computers and Electronics	Knowledge of circuit boards, processors, chips, electronic equipment, and computer hardware and software, including applications and programming.
Administration and Management	Knowledge of business and management principles involved in strategic planning, resource allocation, human resources modeling, leadership technique, production methods, and coordination of people and resources.
Personnel and Human Resources	Knowledge of principles and procedures for personnel recruitment, selection, training, compensation and benefits, labor relations and negotiation, and personnel information systems.
Law and Government	Knowledge of laws, legal codes, court procedures, precedents, government regulations, executive orders, agency rules, and the democratic political process.
Communications and Media	Knowledge of media production, communication, and dissemination techniques and methods. This includes alternative ways to inform and entertain via written, oral, and visual media.
Mathematics	Knowledge of arithmetic, algebra, geometry, calculus, statistics, and their applications.
Public Safety and Security	Knowledge of relevant equipment, policies, procedures, and strategies to promote effective local, state, or national security operations for the protection of people, data, property, and institutions.
Philosophy and Theology	Knowledge of different philosophical systems and religions. This includes their basic principles, values, ethics, ways of thinking, customs, practices, and their impact on human culture.
Sales and Marketing	Knowledge of principles and methods for showing, promoting, and selling products or services. This includes marketing strategy and tactics, product demonstration, sales techniques, and sales control systems.
Foreign Language	Knowledge of the structure and content of a foreign (non-English) language including the meaning and spelling of words, rules of composition and grammar, and pronunciation.
Telecommunications	Knowledge of transmission, broadcasting, switching, control, and operation of telecommunications systems.
History and Archeology	Knowledge of historical events and their causes, indicators, and effects on civilizations and cultures.
Medicine and Dentistry	Knowledge of the information and techniques needed to diagnose and treat human injuries, diseases, and deformities. This includes symptoms, treatment alternatives, drug properties and interactions, and preventive health-care measures.
Fine Arts	Knowledge of the theory and techniques required to compose, produce, and perform works of music, dance, visual arts, drama, and sculpture.
Economics and Accounting	Knowledge of economic and accounting principles and practices, the financial markets, banking and the analysis and reporting of financial data.
Transportation	Knowledge of principles and methods for moving people or goods by air, rail, sea, or road, including the relative costs and benefits.
Geography	Knowledge of principles and methods for describing the features of land, sea, and air masses, including their physical characteristics, locations, interrelationships, and distribution of plant, animal, and human life.
Production and Processing	Knowledge of raw materials, production processes, quality control, costs, and other techniques for maximizing the effective manufacture and distribution of goods.
Engineering and Technology	Knowledge of the practical application of engineering science and technology. This includes applying principles, techniques, procedures, and equipment to the design and production of various goods and services.
Biology	Knowledge of plant and animal organisms, their tissues, cells, functions, interdependencies, and interactions with each other and the environment.

Chemistry	Knowledge of the chemical composition, structure, and properties of substances and of the chemical processes and transformations that they undergo. This includes uses of chemicals and their interactions, danger signs, production techniques, and disposal methods.
Design	Knowledge of design techniques, tools, and principles involved in production of precision technical plans, blueprints, drawings, and models.
Physics	Knowledge and prediction of physical principles, laws, their interrelationships, and applications to understanding fluid, material, and atmospheric dynamics, and mechanical, electrical, atomic and sub- atomic structures and processes.
Mechanical	Knowledge of machines and tools, including their designs, uses, repair, and maintenance.
Food Production	Knowledge of techniques and equipment for planting, growing, and harvesting food products (both plant and animal) for consumption, including storage/handling techniques.
Building and Construction	Knowledge of materials, methods, and the tools involved in the construction or repair of houses, buildings, or other structures such as highways and roads.

Skills	Skills Definitions
Active Listening	Giving full attention to what other people are saying, taking time to understand the points being made, asking questions as appropriate, and not interrupting at inappropriate times.
Social Perceptiveness	Being aware of others' reactions and understanding why they react as they do.
Reading Comprehension	Understanding written sentences and paragraphs in work related documents.
Speaking	Talking to others to convey information effectively.
Service Orientation	Actively looking for ways to help people.
Critical Thinking	Using logic and reasoning to identify the strengths and weaknesses of alternative solutions, conclusions or approaches to problems.
Time Management	Managing one's own time and the time of others.
Writing	Communicating effectively in writing as appropriate for the needs of the audience.
Active Learning	Understanding the implications of new information for both current and future problem-solving and decision-making.
Coordination	Adjusting actions in relation to others' actions.
Instructing	Teaching others how to do something.
Monitoring	Monitoring/Assessing performance of yourself, other individuals, or organizations to make improvements or take corrective action.
Learning Strategies	Selecting and using training/instructional methods and procedures appropriate for the situation when learning or teaching new things.
Negotiation	Bringing others together and trying to reconcile differences.
Persuasion	Persuading others to change their minds or behavior.
Judgment and Decision Making	Considering the relative costs and benefits of potential actions to choose the most appropriate one.
Complex Problem Solving	Identifying complex problems and reviewing related information to develop and evaluate options and implement solutions.
Management of Personnel Resources	Motivating, developing, and directing people as they work, identifying the best people for the job.
Mathematics	Using mathematics to solve problems.
Operations Analysis	Analyzing needs and product requirements to create a design.
Systems Evaluation	Identifying measures or indicators of system performance and the actions needed to improve or correct performance, relative to the goals of the system.
Management of Material Resources	Obtaining and seeing to the appropriate use of equipment, facilities, and materials needed to do certain work.
Management of Financial Resources	Determining how money will be spent to get the work done, and accounting for these expenditures.
Quality Control Analysis	Conducting tests and inspections of products, services, or processes to evaluate quality or performance.
Equipment Selection	Determining the kind of tools and equipment needed to do a job.
Systems Analysis	Determining how a system should work and how changes in conditions, operations, and the environment will affect outcomes
Science	Using scientific rules and methods to solve problems.
Troubleshooting	Determining causes of operating errors and deciding what to do about it.
Technology Design	Generating or adapting equipment and technology to serve user needs.

Operation and Control	Controlling operations of equipment or systems.
Equipment Maintenance	Performing routine maintenance on equipment and determining when and what kind of maintenance is needed.
Installation	Installing equipment, machines, wiring, or programs to meet specifications.
Operation Monitoring	Watching gauges, dials, or other indicators to make sure a machine is working properly.
Repairing	Repairing machines or systems using the needed tools.
Programming	Writing computer programs for various purposes.

Ability	Ability Definitions
Oral Expression	The ability to communicate information and ideas in speaking so others will understand.
Oral Comprehension	The ability to listen to and understand information and ideas presented through spoken words and sentences.
Problem Sensitivity	The ability to tell when something is wrong or is likely to go wrong. It does not involve solving the problem, only recognizing there is a problem.
Speech Clarity	The ability to speak clearly so others can understand you.
Written Expression	The ability to communicate information and ideas in writing so others will understand.
Inductive Reasoning	The ability to combine pieces of information to form general rules or conclusions (includes finding a relationship among seemingly unrelated events).
Deductive Reasoning	The ability to apply general rules to specific problems to produce answers that make sense.
Speech Recognition	The ability to identify and understand the speech of another person.
Written Comprehension	The ability to read and understand information and ideas presented in writing.
Near Vision	The ability to see details at close range (within a few feet of the observer).
Information Ordering	The ability to arrange things or actions in a certain order or pattern according to a specific rule or set of rules (e.g., patterns of numbers, letters, words, pictures, mathematical operations).
Category Flexibility	The ability to generate or use different sets of rules for combining or grouping things in different ways.
Fluency of Ideas	The ability to come up with a number of ideas about a topic (the number of ideas is important, not their quality, correctness, or creativity).
Originality	The ability to come up with unusual or clever ideas about a given topic or situation, or to develop creative ways to solve a problem.
Selective Attention	The ability to concentrate on a task over a period of time without being distracted.
Time Sharing	The ability to shift back and forth between two or more activities or sources of information (such as speech, sounds, touch, or other sources).
Memorization	The ability to remember information such as words, numbers, pictures, and procedures.
Auditory Attention	The ability to focus on a single source of sound in the presence of other distracting sounds.
Flexibility of Closure	The ability to identify or detect a known pattern (a figure, object, word, or sound) that is hidden in other distracting material.
Trunk Strength	The ability to use your abdominal and lower back muscles to support part of the body repeatedly or continuously over time without 'giving out' or fatiguing.
Perceptual Speed	The ability to quickly and accurately compare similarities and differences among sets of letters, numbers, objects, pictures, or patterns. The things to be compared may be presented at the same time or one after the other. This ability also includes comparing a presented object with a remembered object.
Mathematical Reasoning	The ability to choose the right mathematical methods or formulas to solve a problem.
Speed of Closure	The ability to quickly make sense of, combine, and organize information into meaningful patterns.
Number Facility	The ability to add, subtract, multiply, or divide quickly and correctly.
Far Vision	The ability to see details at a distance.
Finger Dexterity	The ability to make precisely coordinated movements of the fingers of one or both hands to grasp, manipulate, or assemble very small objects.
Visualization	The ability to imagine how something will look after it is moved around or when its parts are moved or rearranged.
Hearing Sensitivity	The ability to detect or tell the differences between sounds that vary in pitch and loudness.

Visual Color Discrimination	The ability to match or detect differences between colors, including shades of color and brightness.
Wrist-Finger Speed	The ability to make fast, simple, repeated movements of the fingers, hands, and wrists.
Explosive Strength	The ability to use short bursts of muscle force to propel oneself (as in jumping or sprinting), or to throw an object.
Control Precision	The ability to quickly and repeatedly adjust the controls of a machine or a vehicle to exact positions.
Extent Flexibility	The ability to bend, stretch, twist, or reach with your body, arms, and/or legs.
Response Orientation	The ability to choose quickly between two or more movements in response to two or more different signals (lights, sounds, pictures). It includes the speed with which the correct response is started with the hand, foot, or other body part.
Rate Control	The ability to time your movements or the movement of a piece of equipment in anticipation of changes in the speed and/or direction of a moving object or scene.
Reaction Time	The ability to quickly respond (with the hand, finger, or foot) to a signal (sound, light, picture) when it appears.
Speed of Limb Movement	The ability to quickly move the arms and legs.
Manual Dexterity	The ability to quickly move your hand, your hand together with your arm, or your two hands to grasp, manipulate, or assemble objects.
Gross Body Equilibrium	The ability to keep or regain your body balance or stay upright when in an unstable position.
Dynamic Strength	The ability to exert muscle force repeatedly or continuously over time. This involves muscular endurance and resistance to muscle fatigue.
Dynamic Flexibility	The ability to quickly and repeatedly bend, stretch, twist, or reach out with your body, arms, and/or legs.
Static Strength	The ability to exert maximum muscle force to lift, push, pull, or carry objects.
Spatial Orientation	The ability to know your location in relation to the environment or to know where other objects are in relation to you.
Multilimb Coordination	The ability to coordinate two or more limbs (for example, two arms, two legs, or one leg and one arm) while sitting, standing, or lying down. It does not involve performing the activities while the whole body is in motion.
Night Vision	The ability to see under low light conditions.
Sound Localization	The ability to tell the direction from which a sound originated.
Glare Sensitivity	The ability to see objects in the presence of glare or bright lighting.
Stamina	The ability to exert yourself physically over long periods of time without getting winded or out of breath.
Peripheral Vision	The ability to see objects or movement of objects to one's side when the eyes are looking ahead.
Depth Perception	The ability to judge which of several objects is closer or farther away from you, or to judge the distance between you and an object.
Arm-Hand Steadiness	The ability to keep your hand and arm steady while moving your arm or while holding your arm and hand in one position.
Gross Body Coordination	The ability to coordinate the movement of your arms, legs, and torso together when the whole body is in motion.

Work_Activity	Work_Activity Definitions
Communicating with Supervisors, Peers, or Subordin	Providing information to supervisors, co-workers, and subordinates by telephone, in written form, e-mail, or in person.
Establishing and Maintaining Interpersonal Relatio	Developing constructive and cooperative working relationships with others, and maintaining them over time.
Getting Information	Observing, receiving, and otherwise obtaining information from all relevant sources.
Making Decisions and Solving Problems	Analyzing information and evaluating results to choose the best solution and solve problems.
Assisting and Caring for Others	Providing personal assistance, medical attention, emotional support, or other personal care to others such as coworkers, customers, or patients.
Organizing, Planning, and Prioritizing Work	Developing specific goals and plans to prioritize, organize, and accomplish your work.
Resolving Conflicts and Negotiating with Others	Handling complaints, settling disputes, and resolving grievances and conflicts, or otherwise negotiating with others.
Communicating with Persons Outside Organization	Communicating with people outside the organization, representing the organization to customers, the public, government, and other external sources. This information can be exchanged in person, in writing, or by telephone or e-mail.

Updating and Using Relevant Knowledge	Keeping up-to-date technically and applying new knowledge to your job.
Performing for or Working Directly with the Public	Performing for people or dealing directly with the public. This includes serving customers in restaurants and stores, and receiving clients or guests.
Interacting With Computers	Using computers and computer systems (including hardware and software) to program, write software, set up functions, enter data, or process information.
Training and Teaching Others	Identifying the educational needs of others, developing formal educational or training programs or classes, and teaching or instructing others.
Documenting/Recording Information	Entering, transcribing, recording, storing, or maintaining information in written or electronic/magnetic form.
Interpreting the Meaning of Information for Others	Translating or explaining what information means and how it can be used.
Developing and Building Teams	Encouraging and building mutual trust, respect, and cooperation among team members.
Coaching and Developing Others	Identifying the developmental needs of others and coaching, mentoring, or otherwise helping others to improve their knowledge or skills.
Scheduling Work and Activities	Scheduling events, programs, and activities, as well as the work of others.
Performing Administrative Activities	Performing day-to-day administrative tasks such as maintaining information files and processing paperwork.
Judging the Qualities of Things, Services, or Peop	Assessing the value, importance, or quality of things or people.
Identifying Objects, Actions, and Events	Identifying information by categorizing, estimating, recognizing differences or similarities, and detecting changes in circumstances or events.
Processing Information	Compiling, coding, categorizing, calculating, tabulating, auditing, or verifying information or data.
Analyzing Data or Information	Identifying the underlying principles, reasons, or facts of information by breaking down information or data into separate parts.
Developing Objectives and Strategies	Establishing long-range objectives and specifying the strategies and actions to achieve them.
Thinking Creatively	Developing, designing, or creating new applications, ideas, relationships, systems, or products, including artistic contributions.
Provide Consultation and Advice to Others	Providing guidance and expert advice to management or other groups on technical, systems-, or process-related topics.
Coordinating the Work and Activities of Others	Getting members of a group to work together to accomplish tasks.
Evaluating Information to Determine Compliance wit	Using relevant information and individual judgment to determine whether events or processes comply with laws, regulations, or standards.
Monitor Processes, Materials, or Surroundings	Monitoring and reviewing information from materials, events, or the environment, to detect or assess problems.
Guiding, Directing, and Motivating Subordinates	Providing guidance and direction to subordinates, including setting performance standards and monitoring performance.
Selling or Influencing Others	Convincing others to buy merchandise/goods or to otherwise change their minds or actions.
Estimating the Quantifiable Characteristics of Pro	Estimating sizes, distances, and quantities; or determining time, costs, resources, or materials needed to perform a work activity.
Monitoring and Controlling Resources	Monitoring and controlling resources and overseeing the spending of money.
Staffing Organizational Units	Recruiting, interviewing, selecting, hiring, and promoting employees in an organization.
Inspecting Equipment, Structures, or Material	Inspecting equipment, structures, or materials to identify the cause of errors or other problems or defects.
Performing General Physical Activities	Performing physical activities that require considerable use of your arms and legs and moving your whole body, such as climbing, lifting, balancing, walking, stooping, and handling of materials.
Handling and Moving Objects	Using hands and arms in handling, installing, positioning, and moving materials, and manipulating things.
Controlling Machines and Processes	Using either control mechanisms or direct physical activity to operate machines or processes (not including computers or vehicles).
Operating Vehicles, Mechanized Devices, or Equipme	Running, maneuvering, navigating, or driving vehicles or mechanized equipment, such as forklifts, passenger vehicles, aircraft, or water craft.
Repairing and Maintaining Electronic Equipment	Servicing, repairing, calibrating, regulating, fine-tuning, or testing machines, devices, and equipment that operate primarily on the basis of electrical or electronic (not mechanical) principles.

Drafting, Laying Out, and Specifying Technical Dev	Providing documentation, detailed instructions, drawings, or specifications to tell others about how devices, parts, equipment, or structures are to be fabricated, constructed, assembled, modified, maintained, or used.
Repairing and Maintaining Mechanical Equipment	Servicing, repairing, adjusting, and testing machines, devices, moving parts, and equipment that operate primarily on the basis of mechanical (not electronic) principles.

Work_Context	Work_Context Definitions
Contact With Others	How much does this job require the worker to be in contact with others (face-to-face, by telephone, or otherwise) in order to perform it?
Face-to-Face Discussions	How often do you have to have face-to-face discussions with individuals or teams in this job?
Telephone	How often do you have telephone conversations in this job?
Work With Work Group or Team	How important is it to work with others in a group or team in this job?
Electronic Mail	How often do you use electronic mail in this job?
Indoors, Environmentally Controlled	How often does this job require working indoors in environmentally controlled conditions?
Letters and Memos	How often does the job require written letters and memos?
Structured versus Unstructured Work	To what extent is this job structured for the worker, rather than allowing the worker to determine tasks, priorities, and goals?
Freedom to Make Decisions	How much decision making freedom, without supervision, does the job offer?
Deal With External Customers	How important is it to work with external customers or the public in this job?
Coordinate or Lead Others	How important is it to coordinate or lead others in accomplishing work activities in this job?
Frequency of Conflict Situations	How often are there conflict situations the employee has to face in this job?
Frequency of Decision Making	How frequently is the worker required to make decisions that affect other people, the financial resources, and/or the image and reputation of the organization?
Impact of Decisions on Co-workers or Company Resul	How do the decisions an employee makes impact the results of co-workers, clients or the company?
Importance of Being Exact or Accurate	How important is being very exact or highly accurate in performing this job?
Deal With Unpleasant or Angry People	How frequently does the worker have to deal with unpleasant, angry, or discourteous individuals as part of the job requirements?
Time Pressure	How often does this job require the worker to meet strict deadlines?
Spend Time Sitting	How much does this job require sitting?
Physical Proximity	To what extent does this job require the worker to perform job tasks in close physical proximity to other people?
Public Speaking	How often do you have to perform public speaking in this job?
Importance of Repeating Same Tasks	How important is repeating the same physical activities (e.g., key entry) or mental activities (e.g., checking entries in a ledger) over and over, without stopping, to performing this job?
Responsibility for Outcomes and Results	How responsible is the worker for work outcomes and results of other workers?
Spend Time Standing	How much does this job require standing?
Sounds, Noise Levels Are Distracting or Uncomforta	How often does this job require working exposed to sounds and noise levels that are distracting or uncomfortable?
Consequence of Error	How serious would the result usually be if the worker made a mistake that was not readily correctable?
Level of Competition	To what extent does this job require the worker to compete or to be aware of competitive pressures?
Responsible for Others' Health and Safety	How much responsibility is there for the health and safety of others in this job?
Spend Time Walking and Running	How much does this job require walking and running?
Exposed to Disease or Infections	How often does this job require exposure to disease/infections?
Deal With Physically Aggressive People	How frequently does this job require the worker to deal with physical aggression of violent individuals?
Spend Time Using Your Hands to Handle, Control, or	How much does this job require using your hands to handle, control, or feel objects, tools or controls?
Degree of Automation	How automated is the job?
Spend Time Making Repetitive Motions	How much does this job require making repetitive motions?
Exposed to Contaminants	How often does this job require working exposed to contaminants (such as pollutants, gases, dust or odors)?

Indoors, Not Environmentally Controlled	How often does this job require working indoors in non-controlled environmental conditions (e.g., warehouse without heat)?
Outdoors, Exposed to Weather	How often does this job require working outdoors, exposed to all weather conditions?
Spend Time Bending or Twisting the Body	How much does this job require bending or twisting your body?
Cramped Work Space, Awkward Positions	How often does this job require working in cramped work spaces that requires getting into awkward positions?
Exposed to Minor Burns, Cuts, Bites, or Stings	How often does this job require exposure to minor burns, cuts, bites, or stings?
In an Enclosed Vehicle or Equipment	How often does this job require working in a closed vehicle or equipment (e.g., car)?
Extremely Bright or Inadequate Lighting	How often does this job require working in extremely bright or inadequate lighting conditions?
Very Hot or Cold Temperatures	How often does this job require working in very hot (above 90 F degrees) or very cold (below 32 F degrees) temperatures?
Spend Time Kneeling, Crouching, Stooping, or Crawl	How much does this job require kneeling, crouching, stooping or crawling?
Pace Determined by Speed of Equipment	How important is it to this job that the pace is determined by the speed of equipment or machinery? (This does not refer to keeping busy at all times on this job.)
Outdoors, Under Cover	How often does this job require working outdoors, under cover (e.g., structure with roof but no walls)?
Spend Time Keeping or Regaining Balance	How much does this job require keeping or regaining your balance?
Exposed to Hazardous Equipment	How often does this job require exposure to hazardous equipment?
Wear Common Protective or Safety Equipment such as	How much does this job require wearing common protective or safety equipment such as safety shoes, glasses, gloves, hard hats or live jackets?
Exposed to Hazardous Conditions	How often does this job require exposure to hazardous conditions?
Exposed to Radiation	How often does this job require exposure to radiation?
In an Open Vehicle or Equipment	How often does this job require working in an open vehicle or equipment (e.g., tractor)?
Exposed to Whole Body Vibration	How often does this job require exposure to whole body vibration (e.g., operate a jackhammer)?
Spend Time Climbing Ladders, Scaffolds, or Poles	How much does this job require climbing ladders, scaffolds, or poles?
Wear Specialized Protective or Safety Equipment su	How much does this job require wearing specialized protective or safety equipment such as breathing apparatus, safety harness, full protection suits, or radiation protection?
Exposed to High Places	How often does this job require exposure to high places?

Job Zone Component	Job Zone Component Definitions
Title	Job Zone Five: Extensive Preparation Needed
Overall Experience	Extensive skill, knowledge, and experience are needed for these occupations. Many require more than five years of experience. For example, surgeons must complete four years of college and an additional five to seven years of specialized medical training to be able to do their job.
Job Training	Employees may need some on-the-job training, but most of these occupations assume that the person will already have the required skills, knowledge, work-related experience, and/or training.
Job Zone Examples	These occupations often involve coordinating, training, supervising, or managing the activities of others to accomplish goals. Very advanced communication and organizational skills are required. Examples include athletic trainers, lawyers, managing editors, physicists, social psychologists, and surgeons.
SVP Range	(8.0 and above)
Education	A bachelor's degree is the minimum formal education required for these occupations. However, many also require graduate school. For example, they may require a master's degree, and some require a Ph.D., M.D., or J.D. (law degree).

Work_Styles	Work_Styles Definitions
Integrity	Job requires being honest and ethical.
Concern for Others	Job requires being sensitive to others' needs and feelings and being understanding and helpful on the job.
Cooperation	Job requires being pleasant with others on the job and displaying a good-natured, cooperative attitude.

Self Control	Job requires maintaining composure, keeping emotions in check, controlling anger, and avoiding aggressive behavior, even in very difficult situations.
Dependability	Job requires being reliable, responsible, and dependable, and fulfilling obligations.
Stress Tolerance	Job requires accepting criticism and dealing calmly and effectively with high stress situations.
Attention to Detail	Job requires being careful about detail and thorough in completing work tasks.
Adaptability/Flexibility	Job requires being open to change (positive or negative) and to considerable variety in the workplace.
Initiative	Job requires a willingness to take on responsibilities and challenges.
Social Orientation	Job requires preferring to work with others rather than alone, and being personally connected with others on the job.
Independence	Job requires developing one's own ways of doing things, guiding oneself with little or no supervision, and depending on oneself to get things done.
Persistence	Job requires persistence in the face of obstacles.
Achievement/Effort	Job requires establishing and maintaining personally challenging achievement goals and exerting effort toward mastering tasks.
Leadership	Job requires a willingness to lead, take charge, and offer opinions and direction.
Analytical Thinking	Job requires analyzing information and using logic to address work-related issues and problems.
Innovation	Job requires creativity and alternative thinking to develop new ideas for and answers to work-related problems.

23-1023.00 - Judges, Magistrate Judges, and Magistrates

Arbitrate, advise, adjudicate, or administer justice in a court of law. May sentence defendant in criminal cases according to government statutes. May determine liability of defendant in civil cases. May issue marriage licenses and perform wedding ceremonies.

Tasks

1) Research legal issues and write opinions on the issues.

2) Read documents on pleadings and motions to ascertain facts and issues.

3) Rule on admissibility of evidence and methods of conducting testimony.

4) Preside over hearings and listen to allegations made by plaintiffs to determine whether the evidence supports the charges.

5) Monitor proceedings to ensure that all applicable rules and procedures are followed.

6) Write decisions on cases.

7) Interpret and enforce rules of procedure or establish new rules in situations where there are no procedures already established by law.

8) Settle disputes between opposing attorneys.

9) Award compensation for damages to litigants in civil cases in relation to findings by juries or by the court.

10) Perform wedding ceremonies.

11) Sentence defendants in criminal cases, on conviction by jury, according to applicable government statutes.

12) Conduct preliminary hearings to decide issues such as whether there is reasonable and probable cause to hold defendants in felony cases.

13) Supervise other judges, court officers, and the court's administrative staff.

14) Impose restrictions upon parties in civil cases until trials can be held.

15) Instruct juries on applicable laws, direct juries to deduce the facts from the evidence presented, and hear their verdicts.

16) Rule on custody and access disputes, and enforce court orders regarding custody and support of children.

17) Grant divorces and divide assets between spouses.

18) Participate in judicial tribunals to help resolve disputes.

Knowledge	Knowledge Definitions
Law and Government	Knowledge of laws, legal codes, court procedures, precedents, government regulations, executive orders, agency rules, and the democratic political process.
English Language	Knowledge of the structure and content of the English language including the meaning and spelling of words, rules of composition, and grammar.
Public Safety and Security	Knowledge of relevant equipment, policies, procedures, and strategies to promote effective local, state, or national security operations for the protection of people, data, property, and institutions.
Psychology	Knowledge of human behavior and performance; individual differences in ability, personality, and interests; learning and motivation; psychological research methods; and the assessment and treatment of behavioral and affective disorders.
Customer and Personal Service	Knowledge of principles and processes for providing customer and personal services. This includes customer needs assessment, meeting quality standards for services, and evaluation of customer satisfaction.
Education and Training	Knowledge of principles and methods for curriculum and training design, teaching and instruction for individuals and groups, and the measurement of training effects.
Administration and Management	Knowledge of business and management principles involved in strategic planning, resource allocation, human resources modeling, leadership technique, production methods, and coordination of people and resources.
Therapy and Counseling	Knowledge of principles, methods, and procedures for diagnosis, treatment, and rehabilitation of physical and mental dysfunctions, and for career counseling and guidance.
Personnel and Human Resources	Knowledge of principles and procedures for personnel recruitment, selection, training, compensation and benefits, labor relations and negotiation, and personnel information systems.
Computers and Electronics	Knowledge of circuit boards, processors, chips, electronic equipment, and computer hardware and software, including applications and programming.
Sociology and Anthropology	Knowledge of group behavior and dynamics, societal trends and influences, human migrations, ethnicity, cultures and their history and origins.
Communications and Media	Knowledge of media production, communication, and dissemination techniques and methods. This includes alternative ways to inform and entertain via written, oral, and visual media.
Philosophy and Theology	Knowledge of different philosophical systems and religions. This includes their basic principles, values, ethics, ways of thinking, customs, practices, and their impact on human culture.
Economics and Accounting	Knowledge of economic and accounting principles and practices, the financial markets, banking and the analysis and reporting of financial data.
Clerical	Knowledge of administrative and clerical procedures and systems such as word processing, managing files and records, stenography and transcription, designing forms, and other office procedures and terminology.
Mathematics	Knowledge of arithmetic, algebra, geometry, calculus, statistics, and their applications.
History and Archeology	Knowledge of historical events and their causes, indicators, and effects on civilizations and cultures.
Medicine and Dentistry	Knowledge of the information and techniques needed to diagnose and treat human injuries, diseases, and deformities. This includes symptoms, treatment alternatives, drug properties and interactions, and preventive health-care measures.
Telecommunications	Knowledge of transmission, broadcasting, switching, control, and operation of telecommunications systems.
Transportation	Knowledge of principles and methods for moving people or goods by air, rail, sea, or road, including the relative costs and benefits.
Foreign Language	Knowledge of the structure and content of a foreign (non-English) language including the meaning and spelling of words, rules of composition and grammar, and pronunciation.
Geography	Knowledge of principles and methods for describing the features of land, sea, and air masses, including their physical characteristics, locations, interrelationships, and distribution of plant, animal, and human life.
Biology	Knowledge of plant and animal organisms, their tissues, cells, functions, interdependencies, and interactions with each other and the environment.

Sales and Marketing	Knowledge of principles and methods for showing, promoting, and selling products or services. This includes marketing strategy and tactics, product demonstration, sales techniques, and sales control systems.
Physics	Knowledge and prediction of physical principles, laws, their interrelationships, and applications to understanding fluid, material, and atmospheric dynamics, and mechanical, electrical, atomic and sub- atomic structures and processes.
Chemistry	Knowledge of the chemical composition, structure, and properties of substances and of the chemical processes and transformations that they undergo. This includes uses of chemicals and their interactions, danger signs, production techniques, and disposal methods.
Production and Processing	Knowledge of raw materials, production processes, quality control, costs, and other techniques for maximizing the effective manufacture and distribution of goods.
Building and Construction	Knowledge of materials, methods, and the tools involved in the construction or repair of houses, buildings, or other structures such as highways and roads.
Mechanical	Knowledge of machines and tools, including their designs, uses, repair, and maintenance.
Engineering and Technology	Knowledge of the practical application of engineering science and technology. This includes applying principles, techniques, procedures, and equipment to the design and production of various goods and services.
Fine Arts	Knowledge of the theory and techniques required to compose, produce, and perform works of music, dance, visual arts, drama, and sculpture.
Design	Knowledge of design techniques, tools, and principles involved in production of precision technical plans, blueprints, drawings, and models.
Food Production	Knowledge of techniques and equipment for planting, growing, and harvesting food products (both plant and animal) for consumption, including storage/handling techniques.

Skills	Skills Definitions
Active Listening	Giving full attention to what other people are saying, taking time to understand the points being made, asking questions as appropriate, and not interrupting at inappropriate times.
Reading Comprehension	Understanding written sentences and paragraphs in work related documents.
Judgment and Decision Making	Considering the relative costs and benefits of potential actions to choose the most appropriate one.
Critical Thinking	Using logic and reasoning to identify the strengths and weaknesses of alternative solutions, conclusions or approaches to problems.
Speaking	Talking to others to convey information effectively.
Writing	Communicating effectively in writing as appropriate for the needs of the audience.
Social Perceptiveness	Being aware of others' reactions and understanding why they react as they do.
Active Learning	Understanding the implications of new information for both current and future problem-solving and decision-making.
Time Management	Managing one's own time and the time of others.
Complex Problem Solving	Identifying complex problems and reviewing related information to develop and evaluate options and implement solutions.
Negotiation	Bringing others together and trying to reconcile differences.
Service Orientation	Actively looking for ways to help people.
Persuasion	Persuading others to change their minds or behavior.
Coordination	Adjusting actions in relation to others' actions.
Learning Strategies	Selecting and using training/instructional methods and procedures appropriate for the situation when learning or teaching new things.
Management of Personnel Resources	Motivating, developing, and directing people as they work, identifying the best people for the job.
Instructing	Teaching others how to do something.
Monitoring	Monitoring/Assessing performance of yourself, other individuals, or organizations to make improvements or take corrective action.
Mathematics	Using mathematics to solve problems.
Management of Financial Resources	Determining how money will be spent to get the work done, and accounting for these expenditures.
Operations Analysis	Analyzing needs and product requirements to create a design.
Management of Material Resources	Obtaining and seeing to the appropriate use of equipment, facilities, and materials needed to do certain work.
Science	Using scientific rules and methods to solve problems.

Quality Control Analysis	Conducting tests and inspections of products, services, or processes to evaluate quality or performance.
Systems Evaluation	Identifying measures or indicators of system performance and the actions needed to improve or correct performance, relative to the goals of the system.
Equipment Selection	Determining the kind of tools and equipment needed to do a job.
Troubleshooting	Determining causes of operating errors and deciding what to do about it.
Technology Design	Generating or adapting equipment and technology to serve user needs.
Systems Analysis	Determining how a system should work and how changes in conditions, operations, and the environment will affect outcomes.
Operation and Control	Controlling operations of equipment or systems.
Programming	Writing computer programs for various purposes.
Equipment Maintenance	Performing routine maintenance on equipment and determining when and what kind of maintenance is needed.
Installation	Installing equipment, machines, wiring, or programs to meet specifications.
Operation Monitoring	Watching gauges, dials, or other indicators to make sure a machine is working properly.
Repairing	Repairing machines or systems using the needed tools.

Ability	Ability Definitions
Oral Comprehension	The ability to listen to and understand information and ideas presented through spoken words and sentences.
Deductive Reasoning	The ability to apply general rules to specific problems to produce answers that make sense.
Oral Expression	The ability to communicate information and ideas in speaking so others will understand.
Inductive Reasoning	The ability to combine pieces of information to form general rules or conclusions (includes finding a relationship among seemingly unrelated events).
Written Comprehension	The ability to read and understand information and ideas presented in writing.
Problem Sensitivity	The ability to tell when something is wrong or is likely to go wrong. It does not involve solving the problem, only recognizing there is a problem.
Written Expression	The ability to communicate information and ideas in writing so others will understand.
Speech Recognition	The ability to identify and understand the speech of another person.
Speech Clarity	The ability to speak clearly so others can understand you.
Near Vision	The ability to see details at close range (within a few feet of the observer).
Information Ordering	The ability to arrange things or actions in a certain order or pattern according to a specific rule or set of rules (e.g., patterns of numbers, letters, words, pictures, mathematical operations).
Category Flexibility	The ability to generate or use different sets of rules for combining or grouping things in different ways.
Selective Attention	The ability to concentrate on a task over a period of time without being distracted.
Memorization	The ability to remember information such as words, numbers, pictures, and procedures.
Fluency of Ideas	The ability to come up with a number of ideas about a topic (the number of ideas is important, not their quality, correctness, or creativity).
Flexibility of Closure	The ability to identify or detect a known pattern (a figure, object, word, or sound) that is hidden in other distracting material.
Originality	The ability to come up with unusual or clever ideas about a given topic or situation, or to develop creative ways to solve a problem.
Time Sharing	The ability to shift back and forth between two or more activities or sources of information (such as speech, sounds, touch, or other sources).
Speed of Closure	The ability to quickly make sense of, combine, and organize information into meaningful patterns.
Perceptual Speed	The ability to quickly and accurately compare similarities and differences among sets of letters, numbers, objects, pictures, or patterns. The things to be compared may be presented at the same time or one after the other. This ability also includes comparing a presented object with a remembered object.
Mathematical Reasoning	The ability to choose the right mathematical methods or formulas to solve a problem.
Far Vision	The ability to see details at a distance.

Auditory Attention	The ability to focus on a single source of sound in the presence of other distracting sounds.
Number Facility	The ability to add, subtract, multiply, or divide quickly and correctly.
Visual Color Discrimination	The ability to match or detect differences between colors, including shades of color and brightness.
Visualization	The ability to imagine how something will look after it is moved around or when its parts are moved or rearranged.
Hearing Sensitivity	The ability to detect or tell the differences between sounds that vary in pitch and loudness.
Finger Dexterity	The ability to make precisely coordinated movements of the fingers of one or both hands to grasp, manipulate, or assemble very small objects.
Reaction Time	The ability to quickly respond (with the hand, finger, or foot) to a signal (sound, light, picture) when it appears.
Response Orientation	The ability to choose quickly between two or more movements in response to two or more different signals (lights, sounds, pictures). It includes the speed with which the correct response is started with the hand, foot, or other body part.
Explosive Strength	The ability to use short bursts of muscle force to propel oneself (as in jumping or sprinting), or to throw an object.
Static Strength	The ability to exert maximum muscle force to lift, push, pull, or carry objects.
Gross Body Coordination	The ability to coordinate the movement of your arms, legs, and torso together when the whole body is in motion.
Stamina	The ability to exert yourself physically over long periods of time without getting winded or out of breath.
Gross Body Equilibrium	The ability to keep or regain your body balance or stay upright when in an unstable position.
Trunk Strength	The ability to use your abdominal and lower back muscles to support part of the body repeatedly or continuously over time without 'giving out' or fatiguing.
Night Vision	The ability to see under low light conditions.
Depth Perception	The ability to judge which of several objects is closer or farther away from you, or to judge the distance between you and an object.
Extent Flexibility	The ability to bend, stretch, twist, or reach with your body, arms, and/or legs.
Speed of Limb Movement	The ability to quickly move the arms and legs.
Wrist-Finger Speed	The ability to make fast, simple, repeated movements of the fingers, hands, and wrists.
Dynamic Strength	The ability to exert muscle force repeatedly or continuously over time. This involves muscular endurance and resistance to muscle fatigue.
Multilimb Coordination	The ability to coordinate two or more limbs (for example, two arms, two legs, or one leg and one arm) while sitting, standing, or lying down. It does not involve performing the activities while the whole body is in motion.
Peripheral Vision	The ability to see objects or movement of objects to one's side when the eyes are looking ahead.
Manual Dexterity	The ability to quickly move your hand, your hand together with your arm, or your two hands to grasp, manipulate, or assemble objects.
Arm-Hand Steadiness	The ability to keep your hand and arm steady while moving your arm or while holding your arm and hand in one position.
Sound Localization	The ability to tell the direction from which a sound originated.
Spatial Orientation	The ability to know your location in relation to the environment or to know where other objects are in relation to you.
Dynamic Flexibility	The ability to quickly and repeatedly bend, stretch, twist, or reach out with your body, arms, and/or legs.
Control Precision	The ability to quickly and repeatedly adjust the controls of a machine or a vehicle to exact positions.
Rate Control	The ability to time your movements or the movement of a piece of equipment in anticipation of changes in the speed and/or direction of a moving object or scene.
Glare Sensitivity	The ability to see objects in the presence of glare or bright lighting.

Work_Activity	Work_Activity Definitions
Getting Information	Observing, receiving, and otherwise obtaining information from all relevant sources.
Making Decisions and Solving Problems	Analyzing information and evaluating results to choose the best solution and solve problems.
Performing for or Working Directly with the Public	Performing for people or dealing directly with the public. This includes serving customers in restaurants and stores, and receiving clients or guests.

Judging the Qualities of Things, Services, or Peop	Assessing the value, importance, or quality of things or people.
Identifying Objects, Actions, and Events	Identifying information by categorizing, estimating, recognizing differences or similarities, and detecting changes in circumstances or events.
Resolving Conflicts and Negotiating with Others	Handling complaints, settling disputes, and resolving grievances and conflicts, or otherwise negotiating with others.
Updating and Using Relevant Knowledge	Keeping up-to-date technically and applying new knowledge to your job.
Analyzing Data or Information	Identifying the underlying principles, reasons, or facts of information by breaking down information or data into separate parts.
Interpreting the Meaning of Information for Others	Translating or explaining what information means and how it can be used.
Evaluating Information to Determine Compliance wit	Using relevant information and individual judgment to determine whether events or processes comply with laws, regulations, or standards.
Monitor Processes, Materials, or Surroundings	Monitoring and reviewing information from materials, events, or the environment, to detect or assess problems.
Establishing and Maintaining Interpersonal Relatio	Developing constructive and cooperative working relationships with others, and maintaining them over time.
Communicating with Supervisors, Peers, or Subordin	Providing information to supervisors, co-workers, and subordinates by telephone, in written form, e-mail, or in person.
Documenting/Recording Information	Entering, transcribing, recording, storing, or maintaining information in written or electronic/magnetic form.
Processing Information	Compiling, coding, categorizing, calculating, tabulating, auditing, or verifying information or data.
Communicating with Persons Outside Organization	Communicating with people outside the organization, representing the organization to customers, the public, government, and other external sources. This information can be exchanged in person, in writing, or by telephone or e-mail.
Organizing, Planning, and Prioritizing Work	Developing specific goals and plans to prioritize, organize, and accomplish your work.
Scheduling Work and Activities	Scheduling events, programs, and activities, as well as the work of others.
Coordinating the Work and Activities of Others	Getting members of a group to work together to accomplish tasks.
Thinking Creatively	Developing, designing, or creating new applications, ideas, relationships, systems, or products, including artistic contributions.
Interacting With Computers	Using computers and computer systems (including hardware and software) to program, write software, set up functions, enter data, or process information.
Guiding, Directing, and Motivating Subordinates	Providing guidance and direction to subordinates, including setting performance standards and monitoring performance.
Developing and Building Teams	Encouraging and building mutual trust, respect, and cooperation among team members.
Training and Teaching Others	Identifying the educational needs of others, developing formal educational or training programs or classes, and teaching or instructing others.
Coaching and Developing Others	Identifying the developmental needs of others and coaching, mentoring, or otherwise helping others to improve their knowledge or skills.
Performing Administrative Activities	Performing day-to-day administrative tasks such as maintaining information files and processing paperwork.
Provide Consultation and Advice to Others	Providing guidance and expert advice to management or other groups on technical, systems-, or process-related topics.
Developing Objectives and Strategies	Establishing long-range objectives and specifying the strategies and actions to achieve them.
Estimating the Quantifiable Characteristics of Pro	Estimating sizes, distances, and quantities; or determining time, costs, resources, or materials needed to perform a work activity.
Staffing Organizational Units	Recruiting, interviewing, selecting, hiring, and promoting employees in an organization.
Monitoring and Controlling Resources	Monitoring and controlling resources and overseeing the spending of money.
Assisting and Caring for Others	Providing personal assistance, medical attention, emotional support, or other personal care to others such as coworkers, customers, or patients.
Selling or Influencing Others	Convincing others to buy merchandise/goods or to otherwise change their minds or actions.
Handling and Moving Objects	Using hands and arms in handling, installing, positioning, and moving materials, and manipulating things.
Inspecting Equipment, Structures, or Material	Inspecting equipment, structures, or materials to identify the cause of errors or other problems or defects.

Performing General Physical Activities	Performing physical activities that require considerable use of your arms and legs and moving your whole body, such as climbing, lifting, balancing, walking, stooping, and handling of materials.
Controlling Machines and Processes	Using either control mechanisms or direct physical activity to operate machines or processes (not including computers or vehicles).
Repairing and Maintaining Electronic Equipment	Servicing, repairing, calibrating, regulating, fine-tuning, or testing machines, devices, and equipment that operate primarily on the basis of electrical or electronic (not mechanical) principles.
Drafting, Laying Out, and Specifying Technical Dev	Providing documentation, detailed instructions, drawings, or specifications to tell others about how devices, parts, equipment, or structures are to be fabricated, constructed, assembled, modified, maintained, or used.
Operating Vehicles, Mechanized Devices, or Equipme	Running, maneuvering, navigating, or driving vehicles or mechanized equipment, such as forklifts, passenger vehicles, aircraft, or water craft.
Repairing and Maintaining Mechanical Equipment	Servicing, repairing, adjusting, and testing machines, devices, moving parts, and equipment that operate primarily on the basis of mechanical (not electronic) principles.

Work_Context	Work_Context Definitions
Impact of Decisions on Co-workers or Company Resul	How do the decisions an employee makes impact the results of co-workers, clients or the company?
Spend Time Sitting	How much does this job require sitting?
Face-to-Face Discussions	How often do you have to have face-to-face discussions with individuals or teams in this job?
Telephone	How often do you have telephone conversations in this job?
Importance of Being Exact or Accurate	How important is being very exact or highly accurate in performing this job?
Frequency of Decision Making	How frequently is the worker required to make decisions that affect other people, the financial resources, and/or the image and reputation of the organization?
Indoors, Environmentally Controlled	How often does this job require working indoors in environmentally controlled conditions?
Freedom to Make Decisions	How much decision making freedom, without supervision, does the job offer?
Contact With Others	How much does this job require the worker to be in contact with others (face-to-face, by telephone, or otherwise) in order to perform it?
Structured versus Unstructured Work	To what extent is this job structured for the worker, rather than allowing the worker to determine tasks, priorities, and goals?
Electronic Mail	How often do you use electronic mail in this job?
Letters and Memos	How often does the job require written letters and memos?
Frequency of Conflict Situations	How often are there conflict situations the employee has to face in this job?
Deal With External Customers	How important is it to work with external customers or the public in this job?
Deal With Unpleasant or Angry People	How frequently does the worker have to deal with unpleasant, angry, or discourteous individuals as part of the job requirements?
Responsibility for Outcomes and Results	How responsible is the worker for work outcomes and results of other workers?
Public Speaking	How often do you have to perform public speaking in this job?
Time Pressure	How often does this job require the worker to meet strict deadlines?
Consequence of Error	How serious would the result usually be if the worker made a mistake that was not readily correctable?
Physical Proximity	To what extent does this job require the worker to perform job tasks in close physical proximity to other people?
Work With Work Group or Team	How important is it to work with others in a group or team in this job?
Coordinate or Lead Others	How important is it to coordinate or lead others in accomplishing work activities in this job?
Deal With Physically Aggressive People	How frequently does this job require the worker to deal with physical aggression of violent individuals?
Level of Competition	To what extent does this job require the worker to compete or to be aware of competitive pressures?
Responsible for Others' Health and Safety	How much responsibility is there for the health and safety of others in this job?
Sounds, Noise Levels Are Distracting or Uncomforta	How often does this job require working exposed to sounds and noise levels that are distracting or uncomfortable?
Importance of Repeating Same Tasks	How important is repeating the same physical activities (e.g., key entry) or mental activities (e.g., checking entries in a ledger) over and over, without stopping, to performing this job?

Exposed to Disease or Infections	How often does this job require exposure to disease/infections?
Degree of Automation	How automated is the job?
Exposed to Contaminants	How often does this job require working exposed to contaminants (such as pollutants, gases, dust or odors)?
Spend Time Standing	How much does this job require standing?
Spend Time Making Repetitive Motions	How much does this job require making repetitive motions?
In an Enclosed Vehicle or Equipment	How often does this job require working in a closed vehicle or equipment (e.g., car)?
Spend Time Using Your Hands to Handle, Control, or	How much does this job require using your hands to handle, control, or feel objects, tools or controls?
Spend Time Walking and Running	How much does this job require walking and running?
Spend Time Bending or Twisting the Body	How much does this job require bending or twisting your body?
Extremely Bright or Inadequate Lighting	How often does this job require working in extremely bright or inadequate lighting conditions?
Very Hot or Cold Temperatures	How often does this job require working in very hot (above 90 F degrees) or very cold (below 32 F degrees) temperatures?
Indoors, Not Environmentally Controlled	How often does this job require working indoors in non-controlled environmental conditions (e.g., warehouse without heat)?
Outdoors, Exposed to Weather	How often does this job require working outdoors, exposed to all weather conditions?
Cramped Work Space, Awkward Positions	How often does this job require working in cramped work spaces that requires getting into awkward positions?
Exposed to Minor Burns, Cuts, Bites, or Stings	How often does this job require exposure to minor burns, cuts, bites, or stings?
Spend Time Kneeling, Crouching, Stooping, or Crawl	How much does this job require kneeling, crouching, stooping, or crawling?
Spend Time Keeping or Regaining Balance	How much does this job require keeping or regaining your balance?
Outdoors, Under Cover	How often does this job require working outdoors, under cover (e.g., structure with roof but no walls)?
Exposed to Whole Body Vibration	How often does this job require exposure to whole body vibration (e.g., operate a jackhammer)?
Spend Time Climbing Ladders, Scaffolds, or Poles	How much does this job require climbing ladders, scaffolds, or poles?
Exposed to Hazardous Equipment	How often does this job require exposure to hazardous equipment?
Exposed to Hazardous Conditions	How often does this job require exposure to hazardous conditions?
Wear Common Protective or Safety Equipment such as	How much does this job require wearing common protective or safety equipment such as safety shoes, glasses, gloves, hard hats or live jackets?
Pace Determined by Speed of Equipment	How important is it to this job that the pace is determined by the speed of equipment or machinery? (This does not refer to keeping busy at all times on this job.)
Wear Specialized Protective or Safety Equipment su	How much does this job require wearing specialized protective or safety equipment such as breathing apparatus, safety harness, full protection suits, or radiation protection?
In an Open Vehicle or Equipment	How often does this job require working in an open vehicle or equipment (e.g., tractor)?
Exposed to High Places	How often does this job require exposure to high places?
Exposed to Radiation	How often does this job require exposure to radiation?

Job Zone Component	Job Zone Component Definitions
Title	Job Zone Five: Extensive Preparation Needed
Overall Experience	Extensive skill, knowledge, and experience are needed for these occupations. Many require more than five years of experience. For example, surgeons must complete four years of college and an additional five to seven years of specialized medical training to be able to do their job.
Job Training	Employees may need some on-the-job training, but most of these occupations assume that the person will already have the required skills, knowledge, work-related experience, and/or training.
Job Zone Examples	These occupations often involve coordinating, training, supervising, or managing the activities of others to accomplish goals. Very advanced communication and organizational skills are required. Examples include athletic trainers, lawyers, managing editors, physicists, social psychologists, and surgeons.

Work_Styles	Work_Styles Definitions

SVP Range (8.0 and above)

Education A bachelor's degree is the minimum formal education required for these occupations. However, many also require graduate school. For example, they may require a master's degree, and some require a Ph.D., M.D., or J.D. (law degree).

Work_Styles	Work_Styles Definitions
Integrity	Job requires being honest and ethical.
Dependability	Job requires being reliable, responsible, and dependable, and fulfilling obligations.
Self Control	Job requires maintaining composure, keeping emotions in check, controlling anger, and avoiding aggressive behavior, even in very difficult situations.
Attention to Detail	Job requires being careful about detail and thorough in completing work tasks.
Stress Tolerance	Job requires accepting criticism and dealing calmly and effectively with high stress situations.
Analytical Thinking	Job requires analyzing information and using logic to address work-related issues and problems.
Concern for Others	Job requires being sensitive to others' needs and feelings and being understanding and helpful on the job.
Independence	Job requires developing one's own ways of doing things, guiding oneself with little or no supervision, and depending on oneself to get things done.
Achievement/Effort	Job requires establishing and maintaining personally challenging achievement goals and exerting effort toward mastering tasks.
Leadership	Job requires a willingness to lead, take charge, and offer opinions and direction.
Persistence	Job requires persistence in the face of obstacles.
Cooperation	Job requires being pleasant with others on the job and displaying a good-natured, cooperative attitude.
Initiative	Job requires a willingness to take on responsibilities and challenges.
Adaptability/Flexibility	Job requires being open to change (positive or negative) and to considerable variety in the workplace.
Social Orientation	Job requires preferring to work with others rather than alone, and being personally connected with others on the job.
Innovation	Job requires creativity and alternative thinking to develop new ideas for and answers to work-related problems.

25-1011.00 - Business Teachers, Postsecondary

Teach courses in business administration and management, such as accounting, finance, human resources, labor relations, marketing, and operations research.

Tasks

1) Initiate, facilitate, and moderate classroom discussions.

2) Evaluate and grade students' class work, assignments, and papers.

3) Keep abreast of developments in their field by reading current literature, talking with colleagues, and participating in professional organizations and conferences.

4) Plan, evaluate, and revise curricula, course content, and course materials and methods of instruction.

5) Compile, administer, and grade examinations, or assign this work to others.

6) Advise students on academic and vocational curricula, and on career issues.

7) Collaborate with colleagues to address teaching and research issues.

8) Select and obtain materials and supplies such as textbooks.

9) Maintain regularly scheduled office hours in order to advise and assist students.

10) Participate in campus and community events.

11) Serve on academic or administrative committees that deal with institutional policies, departmental matters, and academic issues.

12) Prepare and deliver lectures to undergraduate and/or graduate students on topics such as financial accounting, principles of marketing, and operations management.

13) Participate in student recruitment, registration, and placement activities.

14) Compile bibliographies of specialized materials for outside reading assignments.

15) Collaborate with members of the business community to improve programs, to develop new programs, and to provide student access to learning opportunities such as internships.

16) Conduct research in a particular field of knowledge, and publish findings in professional journals, books, and/or electronic media.

17) Act as advisers to student organizations.

18) Provide professional consulting services to government and/or industry.

19) Supervise undergraduate and/or graduate teaching, internship, and research work.

20) Perform administrative duties such as serving as department head.

21) Write grant proposals to procure external research funding.

22) Maintain student attendance records, grades, and other required records.

Knowledge	Knowledge Definitions
Education and Training	Knowledge of principles and methods for curriculum and training design, teaching and instruction for individuals and groups, and the measurement of training effects.
English Language	Knowledge of the structure and content of the English language including the meaning and spelling of words, rules of composition, and grammar.
Computers and Electronics	Knowledge of circuit boards, processors, chips, electronic equipment, and computer hardware and software, including applications and programming.
Economics and Accounting	Knowledge of economic and accounting principles and practices, the financial markets, banking and the analysis and reporting of financial data.
Customer and Personal Service	Knowledge of principles and processes for providing customer and personal services. This includes customer needs assessment, meeting quality standards for services, and evaluation of customer satisfaction.
Administration and Management	Knowledge of business and management principles involved in strategic planning, resource allocation, human resources modeling, leadership technique, production methods, and coordination of people and resources.
Mathematics	Knowledge of arithmetic, algebra, geometry, calculus, statistics, and their applications.
Psychology	Knowledge of human behavior and performance; individual differences in ability, personality, and interests; learning and motivation; psychological research methods; and the assessment and treatment of behavioral and affective disorders.
Clerical	Knowledge of administrative and clerical procedures and systems such as word processing, managing files and records, stenography and transcription, designing forms, and other office procedures and terminology.
Communications and Media	Knowledge of media production, communication, and dissemination techniques and methods. This includes alternative ways to inform and entertain via written, oral, and visual media.
Sales and Marketing	Knowledge of principles and methods for showing, promoting, and selling products or services. This includes marketing strategy and tactics, product demonstration, sales techniques, and sales control systems.
Personnel and Human Resources	Knowledge of principles and procedures for personnel recruitment, selection, training, compensation and benefits, labor relations and negotiation, and personnel information systems.
Law and Government	Knowledge of laws, legal codes, court procedures, precedents, government regulations, executive orders, agency rules, and the democratic political process.
Sociology and Anthropology	Knowledge of group behavior and dynamics, societal trends and influences, human migrations, ethnicity, cultures and their history and origins.
Philosophy and Theology	Knowledge of different philosophical systems and religions. This includes their basic principles, values, ethics, ways of thinking, customs, practices, and their impact on human culture.
Production and Processing	Knowledge of raw materials, production processes, quality control, costs, and other techniques for maximizing the effective manufacture and distribution of goods.
Telecommunications	Knowledge of transmission, broadcasting, switching, control, and operation of telecommunications systems.
Therapy and Counseling	Knowledge of principles, methods, and procedures for diagnosis, treatment, and rehabilitation of physical and mental dysfunctions, and for career counseling and guidance.

Public Safety and Security	Knowledge of relevant equipment, policies, procedures, and strategies to promote effective local, state, or national security operations for the protection of people, data, property, and institutions.
History and Archeology	Knowledge of historical events and their causes, indicators, and effects on civilizations and cultures.
Geography	Knowledge of principles and methods for describing the features of land, sea, and air masses, including their physical characteristics, locations, interrelationships, and distribution of plant, animal, and human life.
Engineering and Technology	Knowledge of the practical application of engineering science and technology. This includes applying principles, techniques, procedures, and equipment to the design and production of various goods and services.
Design	Knowledge of design techniques, tools, and principles involved in production of precision technical plans, blueprints, drawings, and models.
Transportation	Knowledge of principles and methods for moving people or goods by air, rail, sea, or road, including the relative costs and benefits.
Fine Arts	Knowledge of the theory and techniques required to compose, produce, and perform works of music, dance, visual arts, drama, and sculpture.
Foreign Language	Knowledge of the structure and content of a foreign (non-English) language including the meaning and spelling of words, rules of composition and grammar, and pronunciation.
Mechanical	Knowledge of machines and tools, including their designs, uses, repair, and maintenance.
Medicine and Dentistry	Knowledge of the information and techniques needed to diagnose and treat human injuries, diseases, and deformities. This includes symptoms, treatment alternatives, drug properties and interactions, and preventive health-care measures.
Food Production	Knowledge of techniques and equipment for planting, growing, and harvesting food products (both plant and animal) for consumption, including storage/handling techniques.
Physics	Knowledge and prediction of physical principles, laws, their interrelationships, and applications to understanding fluid, material, and atmospheric dynamics, and mechanical, electrical, atomic and sub-atomic structures and processes.
Chemistry	Knowledge of the chemical composition, structure, and properties of substances and of the chemical processes and transformations that they undergo. This includes uses of chemicals and their interactions, danger signs, production techniques, and disposal methods.
Biology	Knowledge of plant and animal organisms, their tissues, cells, functions, interdependencies, and interactions with each other and the environment.
Building and Construction	Knowledge of materials, methods, and the tools involved in the construction or repair of houses, buildings, or other structures such as highways and roads.

Skills	Skills Definitions
Instructing	Teaching others how to do something.
Reading Comprehension	Understanding written sentences and paragraphs in work related documents.
Speaking	Talking to others to convey information effectively.
Critical Thinking	Using logic and reasoning to identify the strengths and weaknesses of alternative solutions, conclusions or approaches to problems.
Learning Strategies	Selecting and using training/instructional methods and procedures appropriate for the situation when learning or teaching new things.
Active Listening	Giving full attention to what other people are saying, taking time to understand the points being made, asking questions as appropriate, and not interrupting at inappropriate times.
Active Learning	Understanding the implications of new information for both current and future problem-solving and decision-making.
Writing	Communicating effectively in writing as appropriate for the needs of the audience.
Time Management	Managing one's own time and the time of others.
Monitoring	Monitoring/Assessing performance of yourself, other individuals, or organizations to make improvements or take corrective action.
Social Perceptiveness	Being aware of others' reactions and understanding why they react as they do.
Judgment and Decision Making	Considering the relative costs and benefits of potential actions to choose the most appropriate one.

Complex Problem Solving	Identifying complex problems and reviewing related information to develop and evaluate options and implement solutions.
Mathematics	Using mathematics to solve problems.
Persuasion	Persuading others to change their minds or behavior.
Coordination	Adjusting actions in relation to others' actions.
Service Orientation	Actively looking for ways to help people.
Negotiation	Bringing others together and trying to reconcile differences.
Operations Analysis	Analyzing needs and product requirements to create a design.
Management of Personnel Resources	Motivating, developing, and directing people as they work, identifying the best people for the job.
Systems Evaluation	Identifying measures or indicators of system performance and the actions needed to improve or correct performance, relative to the goals of the system.
Science	Using scientific rules and methods to solve problems.
Quality Control Analysis	Conducting tests and inspections of products, services, or processes to evaluate quality or performance.
Management of Financial Resources	Determining how money will be spent to get the work done, and accounting for these expenditures.
Equipment Selection	Determining the kind of tools and equipment needed to do a job.
Technology Design	Generating or adapting equipment and technology to serve user needs.
Systems Analysis	Determining how a system should work and how changes in conditions, operations, and the environment will affect outcomes.
Troubleshooting	Determining causes of operating errors and deciding what to do about it.
Management of Material Resources	Obtaining and seeing to the appropriate use of equipment, facilities, and materials needed to do certain work.
Programming	Writing computer programs for various purposes.
Operation and Control	Controlling operations of equipment or systems.
Operation Monitoring	Watching gauges, dials, or other indicators to make sure a machine is working properly.
Installation	Installing equipment, machines, wiring, or programs to meet specifications.
Equipment Maintenance	Performing routine maintenance on equipment and determining when and what kind of maintenance is needed.
Repairing	Repairing machines or systems using the needed tools.

Ability	Ability Definitions
Oral Expression	The ability to communicate information and ideas in speaking so others will understand.
Written Comprehension	The ability to read and understand information and ideas presented in writing.
Written Expression	The ability to communicate information and ideas in writing so others will understand.
Oral Comprehension	The ability to listen to and understand information and ideas presented through spoken words and sentences.
Speech Clarity	The ability to speak clearly so others can understand you.
Deductive Reasoning	The ability to apply general rules to specific problems to produce answers that make sense.
Inductive Reasoning	The ability to combine pieces of information to form general rules or conclusions (includes finding a relationship among seemingly unrelated events).
Near Vision	The ability to see details at close range (within a few feet of the observer).
Problem Sensitivity	The ability to tell when something is wrong or is likely to go wrong. It does not involve solving the problem, only recognizing there is a problem.
Selective Attention	The ability to concentrate on a task over a period of time without being distracted.
Information Ordering	The ability to arrange things or actions in a certain order or pattern according to a specific rule or set of rules (e.g., patterns of numbers, letters, words, pictures, mathematical operations).
Speech Recognition	The ability to identify and understand the speech of another person.
Mathematical Reasoning	The ability to choose the right mathematical methods or formulas to solve a problem.
Category Flexibility	The ability to generate or use different sets of rules for combining or grouping things in different ways.
Originality	The ability to come up with unusual or clever ideas about a given topic or situation, or to develop creative ways to solve a problem.
Memorization	The ability to remember information such as words, numbers, pictures, and procedures.

Fluency of Ideas	The ability to come up with a number of ideas about a topic (the number of ideas is important, not their quality, correctness, or creativity).
Time Sharing	The ability to shift back and forth between two or more activities or sources of information (such as speech, sounds, touch, or other sources).
Number Facility	The ability to add, subtract, multiply, or divide quickly and correctly.
Flexibility of Closure	The ability to identify or detect a known pattern (a figure, object, word, or sound) that is hidden in other distracting material.
Far Vision	The ability to see details at a distance.
Speed of Closure	The ability to quickly make sense of, combine, and organize information into meaningful patterns.
Perceptual Speed	The ability to quickly and accurately compare similarities and differences among sets of letters, numbers, objects, pictures, or patterns. The things to be compared may be presented at the same time or one after the other. This ability also includes comparing a presented object with a remembered object.
Visualization	The ability to imagine how something will look after it is moved around or when its parts are moved or rearranged.
Trunk Strength	The ability to use your abdominal and lower back muscles to support part of the body repeatedly or continuously over time without 'giving out' or fatiguing.
Auditory Attention	The ability to focus on a single source of sound in the presence of other distracting sounds.
Visual Color Discrimination	The ability to match or detect differences between colors, including shades of color and brightness.
Finger Dexterity	The ability to make precisely coordinated movements of the fingers of one or both hands to grasp, manipulate, or assemble very small objects.
Hearing Sensitivity	The ability to detect or tell the differences between sounds that vary in pitch and loudness.
Sound Localization	The ability to tell the direction from which a sound originated.
Depth Perception	The ability to judge which of several objects is closer or farther away from you, or to judge the distance between you and an object.
Glare Sensitivity	The ability to see objects in the presence of glare or bright lighting.
Response Orientation	The ability to choose quickly between two or more movements in response to two or more different signals (lights, sounds, pictures). It includes the speed with which the correct response is started with the hand, foot, or other body part.
Explosive Strength	The ability to use short bursts of muscle force to propel oneself (as in jumping or sprinting), or to throw an object.
Static Strength	The ability to exert maximum muscle force to lift, push, pull, or carry objects.
Speed of Limb Movement	The ability to quickly move the arms and legs.
Dynamic Flexibility	The ability to quickly and repeatedly bend, stretch, twist, or reach out with your body, arms, and/or legs.
Stamina	The ability to exert yourself physically over long periods of time without getting winded or out of breath.
Reaction Time	The ability to quickly respond (with the hand, finger, or foot) to a signal (sound, light, picture) when it appears.
Gross Body Coordination	The ability to coordinate the movement of your arms, legs, and torso together when the whole body is in motion.
Dynamic Strength	The ability to exert muscle force repeatedly or continuously over time. This involves muscular endurance and resistance to muscle fatigue.
Multilimb Coordination	The ability to coordinate two or more limbs (for example, two arms, two legs, or one leg and one arm) while sitting, standing, or lying down. It does not involve performing the activities while the whole body is in motion.
Control Precision	The ability to quickly and repeatedly adjust the controls of a machine or a vehicle to exact positions.
Manual Dexterity	The ability to quickly move your hand, your hand together with your arm, or your two hands to grasp, manipulate, or assemble objects.
Spatial Orientation	The ability to know your location in relation to the environment or to know where other objects are in relation to you.
Peripheral Vision	The ability to see objects or movement of objects to one's side when the eyes are looking ahead.
Arm-Hand Steadiness	The ability to keep your hand and arm steady while moving your arm or while holding your arm and hand in one position.
Night Vision	The ability to see under low light conditions.
Gross Body Equilibrium	The ability to keep or regain your body balance or stay upright when in an unstable position.

Rate Control	The ability to time your movements or the movement of a piece of equipment in anticipation of changes in the speed and/or direction of a moving object or scene.
Wrist-Finger Speed	The ability to make fast, simple, repeated movements of the fingers, hands, and wrists.
Extent Flexibility	The ability to bend, stretch, twist, or reach with your body, arms, and/or legs.

Work_Activity	Work_Activity Definitions
Training and Teaching Others	Identifying the educational needs of others, developing formal educational or training programs or classes, and teaching or instructing others.
Updating and Using Relevant Knowledge	Keeping up-to-date technically and applying new knowledge to your job.
Interpreting the Meaning of Information for Others	Translating or explaining what information means and how it can be used.
Interacting With Computers	Using computers and computer systems (including hardware and software) to program, write software, set up functions, enter data, or process information.
Getting Information	Observing, receiving, and otherwise obtaining information from all relevant sources.
Thinking Creatively	Developing, designing, or creating new applications, ideas, relationships, systems, or products, including artistic contributions.
Coaching and Developing Others	Identifying the developmental needs of others and coaching, mentoring, or otherwise helping others to improve their knowledge or skills.
Analyzing Data or Information	Identifying the underlying principles, reasons, or facts of information by breaking down information or data into separate parts.
Establishing and Maintaining Interpersonal Relatio	Developing constructive and cooperative working relationships with others, and maintaining them over time.
Communicating with Supervisors, Peers, or Subordin	Providing information to supervisors, co-workers, and subordinates by telephone, in written form, e-mail, or in person.
Processing Information	Compiling, coding, categorizing, calculating, tabulating, auditing, or verifying information or data.
Judging the Qualities of Things, Services, or Peop	Assessing the value, importance, or quality of things or people.
Organizing, Planning, and Prioritizing Work	Developing specific goals and plans to prioritize, organize, and accomplish your work.
Documenting/Recording Information	Entering, transcribing, recording, storing, or maintaining information in written or electronic/magnetic form.
Identifying Objects, Actions, and Events	Identifying information by categorizing, estimating, recognizing differences or similarities, and detecting changes in circumstances or events.
Making Decisions and Solving Problems	Analyzing information and evaluating results to choose the best solution and solve problems.
Scheduling Work and Activities	Scheduling events, programs, and activities, as well as the work of others.
Developing Objectives and Strategies	Establishing long-range objectives and specifying the strategies and actions to achieve them.
Communicating with Persons Outside Organization	Communicating with people outside the organization, representing the organization to customers, the public, government, and other external sources. This information can be exchanged in person, in writing, or by telephone or e-mail.
Provide Consultation and Advice to Others	Providing guidance and expert advice to management or other groups on technical, systems-, or process-related topics.
Evaluating Information to Determine Compliance wit	Using relevant information and individual judgment to determine whether events or processes comply with laws, regulations, or standards.
Monitor Processes, Materials, or Surroundings	Monitoring and reviewing information from materials, events, or the environment, to detect or assess problems.
Estimating the Quantifiable Characteristics of Pro	Estimating sizes, distances, and quantities; or determining time, costs, resources, or materials needed to perform a work activity.
Performing for or Working Directly with the Public	Performing for people or dealing directly with the public. This includes serving customers in restaurants and stores, and receiving clients or guests.
Performing Administrative Activities	Performing day-to-day administrative tasks such as maintaining information files and processing paperwork.
Developing and Building Teams	Encouraging and building mutual trust, respect, and cooperation among team members.
Coordinating the Work and Activities of Others	Getting members of a group to work together to accomplish tasks.

Selling or Influencing Others	Convincing others to buy merchandise/goods or to otherwise change their minds or actions.
Resolving Conflicts and Negotiating with Others	Handling complaints, settling disputes, and resolving grievances and conflicts, or otherwise negotiating with others.
Guiding, Directing, and Motivating Subordinates	Providing guidance and direction to subordinates, including setting performance standards and monitoring performance.
Assisting and Caring for Others	Providing personal assistance, medical attention, emotional support, or other personal care to others such as coworkers, customers, or patients.
Monitoring and Controlling Resources	Monitoring and controlling resources and overseeing the spending of money.
Staffing Organizational Units	Recruiting, interviewing, selecting, hiring, and promoting employees in an organization.
Performing General Physical Activities	Performing physical activities that require considerable use of your arms and legs and moving your whole body, such as climbing, lifting, balancing, walking, stooping, and handling of materials.
Inspecting Equipment, Structures, or Material	Inspecting equipment, structures, or materials to identify the cause of errors or other problems or defects.
Controlling Machines and Processes	Using either control mechanisms or direct physical activity to operate machines or processes (not including computers or vehicles).
Handling and Moving Objects	Using hands and arms in handling, installing, positioning, and moving materials, and manipulating things.
Repairing and Maintaining Electronic Equipment	Servicing, repairing, calibrating, regulating, fine-tuning, or testing machines, devices, and equipment that operate primarily on the basis of electrical or electronic (not mechanical) principles.
Operating Vehicles, Mechanized Devices, or Equipme	Running, maneuvering, navigating, or driving vehicles or mechanized equipment, such as forklifts, passenger vehicles, aircraft, or water craft.
Drafting, Laying Out, and Specifying Technical Dev	Providing documentation, detailed instructions, drawings, or specifications to tell others about how devices, parts, equipment, or structures are to be fabricated, constructed, assembled, modified, maintained, or used.
Repairing and Maintaining Mechanical Equipment	Servicing, repairing, adjusting, and testing machines, devices, moving parts, and equipment that operate primarily on the basis of mechanical (not electronic) principles.

Work_Context	Work_Context Definitions
Electronic Mail	How often do you use electronic mail in this job?
Freedom to Make Decisions	How much decision making freedom, without supervision, does the job offer?
Indoors, Environmentally Controlled	How often does this job require working indoors in environmentally controlled conditions?
Structured versus Unstructured Work	To what extent is this job structured for the worker, rather than allowing the worker to determine tasks, priorities, and goals?
Face-to-Face Discussions	How often do you have to have face-to-face discussions with individuals or teams in this job?
Public Speaking	How often do you have to perform public speaking in this job?
Telephone	How often do you have telephone conversations in this job?
Contact With Others	How much does this job require the worker to be in contact with others (face-to-face, by telephone, or otherwise) in order to perform it?
Frequency of Decision Making	How frequently is the worker required to make decisions that affect other people, the financial resources, and/or the image and reputation of the organization?
Letters and Memos	How often does the job require written letters and memos?
Deal With External Customers	How important is it to work with external customers or the public in this job?
Time Pressure	How often does this job require the worker to meet strict deadlines?
Importance of Being Exact or Accurate	How important is being very exact or highly accurate in performing this job?
Coordinate or Lead Others	How important is it to coordinate or lead others in accomplishing work activities in this job?
Impact of Decisions on Co-workers or Company Resul	How do the decisions an employee makes impact the results of co-workers, clients or the company?
Work With Work Group or Team	How important is it to work with others in a group or team in this job?
Spend Time Sitting	How much does this job require sitting?
Physical Proximity	To what extent does this job require the worker to perform job tasks in close physical proximity to other people?
Frequency of Conflict Situations	How often are there conflict situations the employee has to face in this job?

Level of Competition	To what extent does this job require the worker to compete or to be aware of competitive pressures?
Responsibility for Outcomes and Results	How responsible is the worker for work outcomes and results of other workers?
Deal With Unpleasant or Angry People	How frequently does the worker have to deal with unpleasant, angry, or discourteous individuals as part of the job requirements?
Spend Time Standing	How much does this job require standing?
Importance of Repeating Same Tasks	How important is repeating the same physical activities (e.g., key entry) or mental activities (e.g., checking entries in a ledger) over and over, without stopping, to performing this job?
Sounds, Noise Levels Are Distracting or Uncomforta	How often does this job require working exposed to sounds and noise levels that are distracting or uncomfortable?
Spend Time Using Your Hands to Handle, Control, or	How much does this job require using your hands to handle, control, or feel objects, tools or controls?
Consequence of Error	How serious would the result usually be if the worker made a mistake that was not readily correctable?
Spend Time Making Repetitive Motions	How much does this job require making repetitive motions?
Responsible for Others' Health and Safety	How much responsibility is there for the health and safety of others in this job?
Degree of Automation	How automated is the job?
Spend Time Walking and Running	How much does this job require walking and running?
Exposed to Disease or Infections	How often does this job require exposure to disease/infections?
Exposed to Contaminants	How often does this job require working exposed to contaminants (such as pollutants, gases, dust or odors)?
In an Enclosed Vehicle or Equipment	How often does this job require working in a closed vehicle or equipment (e.g., car)?
Extremely Bright or Inadequate Lighting	How often does this job require working in extremely bright or inadequate lighting conditions?
Spend Time Bending or Twisting the Body	How much does this job require bending or twisting your body?
Indoors, Not Environmentally Controlled	How often does this job require working indoors in non-controlled environmental conditions (e.g., warehouse without heat)?
Deal With Physically Aggressive People	How frequently does this job require the worker to deal with physical aggression of violent individuals?
Cramped Work Space, Awkward Positions	How often does this job require working in cramped work spaces that requires getting into awkward positions?
Very Hot or Cold Temperatures	How often does this job require working in very hot (above 90 F degrees) or very cold (below 32 F degrees) temperatures?
Outdoors, Exposed to Weather	How often does this job require working outdoors, exposed to all weather conditions?
Outdoors, Under Cover	How often does this job require working outdoors, under cover (e.g., structure with roof but no walls)?
Exposed to Hazardous Equipment	How often does this job require exposure to hazardous equipment?
Spend Time Kneeling, Crouching, Stooping, or Crawl	How much does this job require kneeling, crouching, stooping or crawling?
Exposed to Minor Burns, Cuts, Bites, or Stings	How often does this job require exposure to minor burns, cuts, bites, or stings?
Spend Time Keeping or Regaining Balance	How much does this job require keeping or regaining your balance?
Wear Common Protective or Safety Equipment such as	How much does this job require wearing common protective or safety equipment such as safety shoes, glasses, gloves, hard hats or live jackets?
Pace Determined by Speed of Equipment	How important is it to this job that the pace is determined by the speed of equipment or machinery? (This does not refer to keeping busy at all times on this job.)
Exposed to Radiation	How often does this job require exposure to radiation?
Exposed to Hazardous Conditions	How often does this job require exposure to hazardous conditions?
Exposed to High Places	How often does this job require exposure to high places?
Spend Time Climbing Ladders, Scaffolds, or Poles	How much does this job require climbing ladders, scaffolds, or poles?
Wear Specialized Protective or Safety Equipment su	How much does this job require wearing specialized protective or safety equipment such as breathing apparatus, safety harness, full protection suits, or radiation protection?
In an Open Vehicle or Equipment	How often does this job require working in an open vehicle or equipment (e.g., tractor)?
Exposed to Whole Body Vibration	How often does this job require exposure to whole body vibration (e.g., operate a jackhammer)?

Job Zone Component	Job Zone Component Definitions
Title	Job Zone Five: Extensive Preparation Needed
Overall Experience	Extensive skill, knowledge, and experience are needed for these occupations. Many require more than five years of experience. For example, surgeons must complete four years of college and an additional five to seven years of specialized medical training to be able to do their job.
Job Training	Employees may need some on-the-job training, but most of these occupations assume that the person will already have the required skills, knowledge, work-related experience, and/or training.
Job Zone Examples	These occupations often involve coordinating, training, supervising, or managing the activities of others to accomplish goals. Very advanced communication and organizational skills are required. Examples include athletic trainers, lawyers, managing editors, physicists, social psychologists, and surgeons.
SVP Range	(8.0 and above)
Education	A bachelor's degree is the minimum formal education required for these occupations. However, many also require graduate school. For example, they may require a master's degree, and some require a Ph.D., M.D., or J.D. (law degree).

Work_Styles	Work_Styles Definitions
Integrity	Job requires being honest and ethical.
Dependability	Job requires being reliable, responsible, and dependable, and fulfilling obligations.
Independence	Job requires developing one's own ways of doing things, guiding oneself with little or no supervision, and depending on oneself to get things done.
Self Control	Job requires maintaining composure, keeping emotions in check, controlling anger, and avoiding aggressive behavior, even in very difficult situations.
Attention to Detail	Job requires being careful about detail and thorough in completing work tasks.
Achievement/Effort	Job requires establishing and maintaining personally challenging achievement goals and exerting effort toward mastering tasks.
Analytical Thinking	Job requires analyzing information and using logic to address work-related issues and problems.
Initiative	Job requires a willingness to take on responsibilities and challenges.
Persistence	Job requires persistence in the face of obstacles.
Concern for Others	Job requires being sensitive to others' needs and feelings and being understanding and helpful on the job.
Cooperation	Job requires being pleasant with others on the job and displaying a good-natured, cooperative attitude.
Stress Tolerance	Job requires accepting criticism and dealing calmly and effectively with high stress situations.
Adaptability/Flexibility	Job requires being open to change (positive or negative) and to considerable variety in the workplace.
Leadership	Job requires a willingness to lead, take charge, and offer opinions and direction.
Social Orientation	Job requires preferring to work with others rather than alone, and being personally connected with others on the job.
Innovation	Job requires creativity and alternative thinking to develop new ideas for and answers to work-related problems.

25-1021.00 - Computer Science Teachers, Postsecondary

Teach courses in computer science. May specialize in a field of computer science, such as the design and function of computers or operations and research analysis.

Tasks

1) Keep abreast of developments in their field by reading current literature, talking with colleagues, and participating in professional conferences.

2) Maintain student attendance records, grades, and other required records.

3) Compile, administer, and grade examinations, or assign this work to others.

4) Initiate, facilitate, and moderate classroom discussions.

5) Maintain regularly scheduled office hours in order to advise and assist students.

6) Select and obtain materials and supplies such as textbooks and laboratory equipment.

7) Plan, evaluate, and revise curricula, course content, and course materials and methods of instruction.

8) Advise students on academic and vocational curricula, and on career issues.

9) Collaborate with colleagues to address teaching and research issues.

10) Participate in campus and community events.

11) Serve on academic or administrative committees that deal with institutional policies, departmental matters, and academic issues.

12) Prepare and deliver lectures to undergraduate and/or graduate students on topics such as programming, data structures, and software design.

13) Supervise students' laboratory work.

14) Participate in student recruitment, registration, and placement activities.

15) Act as advisers to student organizations.

16) Compile bibliographies of specialized materials for outside reading assignments.

17) Perform administrative duties such as serving as department head.

18) Write grant proposals to procure external research funding.

19) Supervise undergraduate and/or graduate teaching, internship, and research work.

20) Conduct research in a particular field of knowledge, and publish findings in professional journals, books, and/or electronic media.

21) Provide professional consulting services to government and/or industry.

22) Direct research of other teachers or of graduate students working for advanced academic degrees.

23) Evaluate and grade students' class work, laboratory work, assignments, and papers.

Knowledge	Knowledge Definitions
Computers and Electronics	Knowledge of circuit boards, processors, chips, electronic equipment, and computer hardware and software, including applications and programming.
Education and Training	Knowledge of principles and methods for curriculum and training design, teaching and instruction for individuals and groups, and the measurement of training effects.
English Language	Knowledge of the structure and content of the English language including the meaning and spelling of words, rules of composition, and grammar.
Mathematics	Knowledge of arithmetic, algebra, geometry, calculus, statistics, and their applications.
Telecommunications	Knowledge of transmission, broadcasting, switching, control, and operation of telecommunications systems.
Engineering and Technology	Knowledge of the practical application of engineering science and technology. This includes applying principles, techniques, procedures, and equipment to the design and production of various goods and services.
Customer and Personal Service	Knowledge of principles and processes for providing customer and personal services. This includes customer needs assessment, meeting quality standards for services, and evaluation of customer satisfaction.
Communications and Media	Knowledge of media production, communication, and dissemination techniques and methods. This includes alternative ways to inform and entertain via written, oral, and visual media.
Clerical	Knowledge of administrative and clerical procedures and systems such as word processing, managing files and records, stenography and transcription, designing forms, and other office procedures and terminology.
Administration and Management	Knowledge of business and management principles involved in strategic planning, resource allocation, human resources modeling, leadership technique, production methods, and coordination of people and resources.
Design	Knowledge of design techniques, tools, and principles involved in production of precision technical plans, blueprints, drawings, and models.
Psychology	Knowledge of human behavior and performance; individual differences in ability, personality, and interests; learning and motivation; psychological research methods; and the assessment and treatment of behavioral and affective disorders.
Personnel and Human Resources	Knowledge of principles and procedures for personnel recruitment, selection, training, compensation and benefits, labor relations and negotiation, and personnel information systems.

Sociology and Anthropology	Knowledge of group behavior and dynamics, societal trends and influences, human migrations, ethnicity, cultures and their history and origins.
Public Safety and Security	Knowledge of relevant equipment, policies, procedures, and strategies to promote effective local, state, or national security operations for the protection of people, data, property, and institutions.
Sales and Marketing	Knowledge of principles and methods for showing, promoting, and selling products or services. This includes marketing strategy and tactics, product demonstration, sales techniques, and sales control systems.
Physics	Knowledge and prediction of physical principles, laws, their interrelationships, and applications to understanding fluid, material, and atmospheric dynamics, and mechanical, electrical, atomic and sub- atomic structures and processes.
Law and Government	Knowledge of laws, legal codes, court procedures, precedents, government regulations, executive orders, agency rules, and the democratic political process.
Therapy and Counseling	Knowledge of principles, methods, and procedures for diagnosis, treatment, and rehabilitation of physical and mental dysfunctions, and for career counseling and guidance.
Economics and Accounting	Knowledge of economic and accounting principles and practices, the financial markets, banking and the analysis and reporting of financial data.
Philosophy and Theology	Knowledge of different philosophical systems and religions. This includes their basic principles, values, ethics, ways of thinking, customs, practices, and their impact on human culture.
Production and Processing	Knowledge of raw materials, production processes, quality control, costs, and other techniques for maximizing the effective manufacture and distribution of goods.
Mechanical	Knowledge of machines and tools, including their designs, uses, repair, and maintenance.
Transportation	Knowledge of principles and methods for moving people or goods by air, rail, sea, or road, including the relative costs and benefits.
History and Archeology	Knowledge of historical events and their causes, indicators, and effects on civilizations and cultures.
Geography	Knowledge of principles and methods for describing the features of land, sea, and air masses, including their physical characteristics, locations, interrelationships, and distribution of plant, animal, and human life.
Fine Arts	Knowledge of the theory and techniques required to compose, produce, and perform works of music, dance, visual arts, drama, and sculpture.
Foreign Language	Knowledge of the structure and content of a foreign (non-English) language including the meaning and spelling of words, rules of composition and grammar, and pronunciation.
Chemistry	Knowledge of the chemical composition, structure, and properties of substances and of the chemical processes and transformations that they undergo. This includes uses of chemicals and their interactions, danger signs, production techniques, and disposal methods.
Biology	Knowledge of plant and animal organisms, their tissues, cells, functions, interdependencies, and interactions with each other and the environment.
Building and Construction	Knowledge of materials, methods, and the tools involved in the construction or repair of houses, buildings, or other structures such as highways and roads.
Medicine and Dentistry	Knowledge of the information and techniques needed to diagnose and treat human injuries, diseases, and deformities. This includes symptoms, treatment alternatives, drug properties and interactions, and preventive health-care measures.
Food Production	Knowledge of techniques and equipment for planting, growing, and harvesting food products (both plant and animal) for consumption, including storage/handling techniques.

Skills	**Skills Definitions**
Instructing	Teaching others how to do something.
Critical Thinking	Using logic and reasoning to identify the strengths and weaknesses of alternative solutions, conclusions or approaches to problems.
Speaking	Talking to others to convey information effectively.
Reading Comprehension	Understanding written sentences and paragraphs in work related documents.

Learning Strategies	Selecting and using training/instructional methods and procedures appropriate for the situation when learning or teaching new things.
Active Learning	Understanding the implications of new information for both current and future problem-solving and decision-making.
Active Listening	Giving full attention to what other people are saying, taking time to understand the points being made, asking questions as appropriate, and not interrupting at inappropriate times.
Complex Problem Solving	Identifying complex problems and reviewing related information to develop and evaluate options and implement solutions.
Writing	Communicating effectively in writing as appropriate for the needs of the audience.
Time Management	Managing one's own time and the time of others.
Mathematics	Using mathematics to solve problems.
Programming	Writing computer programs for various purposes.
Monitoring	Monitoring/Assessing performance of yourself, other individuals, or organizations to make improvements or take corrective action.
Technology Design	Generating or adapting equipment and technology to serve user needs.
Social Perceptiveness	Being aware of others' reactions and understanding why they react as they do.
Operations Analysis	Analyzing needs and product requirements to create a design.
Coordination	Adjusting actions in relation to others' actions.
Troubleshooting	Determining causes of operating errors and deciding what to do about it.
Equipment Selection	Determining the kind of tools and equipment needed to do a job.
Service Orientation	Actively looking for ways to help people.
Judgment and Decision Making	Considering the relative costs and benefits of potential actions to choose the most appropriate one.
Science	Using scientific rules and methods to solve problems.
Systems Analysis	Determining how a system should work and how changes in conditions, operations, and the environment will affect outcomes.
Persuasion	Persuading others to change their minds or behavior.
Systems Evaluation	Identifying measures or indicators of system performance and the actions needed to improve or correct performance, relative to the goals of the system.
Installation	Installing equipment, machines, wiring, or programs to meet specifications.
Quality Control Analysis	Conducting tests and inspections of products, services, or processes to evaluate quality or performance.
Management of Personnel Resources	Motivating, developing, and directing people as they work, identifying the best people for the job.
Negotiation	Bringing others together and trying to reconcile differences.
Management of Material Resources	Obtaining and seeing to the appropriate use of equipment, facilities, and materials needed to do certain work.
Management of Financial Resources	Determining how money will be spent to get the work done, and accounting for these expenditures.
Operation and Control	Controlling operations of equipment or systems.
Equipment Maintenance	Performing routine maintenance on equipment and determining when and what kind of maintenance is needed.
Repairing	Repairing machines or systems using the needed tools.
Operation Monitoring	Watching gauges, dials, or other indicators to make sure a machine is working properly.

Ability	**Ability Definitions**
Oral Expression	The ability to communicate information and ideas in speaking so others will understand.
Speech Clarity	The ability to speak clearly so others can understand you.
Written Comprehension	The ability to read and understand information and ideas presented in writing.
Oral Comprehension	The ability to listen to and understand information and ideas presented through spoken words and sentences.
Deductive Reasoning	The ability to apply general rules to specific problems to produce answers that make sense.
Written Expression	The ability to communicate information and ideas in writing so others will understand.
Inductive Reasoning	The ability to combine pieces of information to form general rules or conclusions (includes finding a relationship among seemingly unrelated events).
Information Ordering	The ability to arrange things or actions in a certain order or pattern according to a specific rule or set of rules (e.g., patterns of numbers, letters, words, pictures, mathematical operations).

Problem Sensitivity	The ability to tell when something is wrong or is likely to go wrong. It does not involve solving the problem, only recognizing there is a problem.
Near Vision	The ability to see details at close range (within a few feet of the observer).
Speech Recognition	The ability to identify and understand the speech of another person.
Category Flexibility	The ability to generate or use different sets of rules for combining or grouping things in different ways.
Mathematical Reasoning	The ability to choose the right mathematical methods or formulas to solve a problem.
Originality	The ability to come up with unusual or clever ideas about a given topic or situation, or to develop creative ways to solve a problem.
Selective Attention	The ability to concentrate on a task over a period of time without being distracted.
Fluency of Ideas	The ability to come up with a number of ideas about a topic (the number of ideas is important, not their quality, correctness, or creativity).
Flexibility of Closure	The ability to identify or detect a known pattern (a figure, object, word, or sound) that is hidden in other distracting material.
Memorization	The ability to remember information such as words, numbers, pictures, and procedures.
Speed of Closure	The ability to quickly make sense of, combine, and organize information into meaningful patterns.
Number Facility	The ability to add, subtract, multiply, or divide quickly and correctly.
Finger Dexterity	The ability to make precisely coordinated movements of the fingers of one or both hands to grasp, manipulate, or assemble very small objects.
Far Vision	The ability to see details at a distance.
Time Sharing	The ability to shift back and forth between two or more activities or sources of information (such as speech, sounds, touch, or other sources).
Manual Dexterity	The ability to quickly move your hand, your hand together with your arm, or your two hands to grasp, manipulate, or assemble objects.
Arm-Hand Steadiness	The ability to keep your hand and arm steady while moving your arm or while holding your arm and hand in one position.
Perceptual Speed	The ability to quickly and accurately compare similarities and differences among sets of letters, numbers, objects, pictures, or patterns. The things to be compared may be presented at the same time or one after the other. This ability also includes comparing a presented object with a remembered object.
Trunk Strength	The ability to use your abdominal and lower back muscles to support part of the body repeatedly or continuously over time without 'giving out' or fatiguing.
Visualization	The ability to imagine how something will look after it is moved around or when its parts are moved or rearranged.
Auditory Attention	The ability to focus on a single source of sound in the presence of other distracting sounds.
Control Precision	The ability to quickly and repeatedly adjust the controls of a machine or a vehicle to exact positions.
Visual Color Discrimination	The ability to match or detect differences between colors, including shades of color and brightness.
Depth Perception	The ability to judge which of several objects is closer or farther away from you, or to judge the distance between you and an object.
Hearing Sensitivity	The ability to detect or tell the differences between sounds that vary in pitch and loudness.
Wrist-Finger Speed	The ability to make fast, simple, repeated movements of the fingers, hands, and wrists.
Speed of Limb Movement	The ability to quickly move the arms and legs.
Night Vision	The ability to see under low light conditions.
Stamina	The ability to exert yourself physically over long periods of time without getting winded or out of breath.
Extent Flexibility	The ability to bend, stretch, twist, or reach with your body, arms, and/or legs.
Explosive Strength	The ability to use short bursts of muscle force to propel oneself (as in jumping or sprinting), or to throw an object.
Dynamic Flexibility	The ability to quickly and repeatedly bend, stretch, twist, or reach out with your body, arms, and/or legs.
Gross Body Coordination	The ability to coordinate the movement of your arms, legs, and torso together when the whole body is in motion.
Static Strength	The ability to exert maximum muscle force to lift, push, pull, or carry objects.

Peripheral Vision	The ability to see objects or movement of objects to one's side when the eyes are looking ahead.
Dynamic Strength	The ability to exert muscle force repeatedly or continuously over time. This involves muscular endurance and resistance to muscle fatigue.
Gross Body Equilibrium	The ability to keep or regain your body balance or stay upright when in an unstable position.
Sound Localization	The ability to tell the direction from which a sound originated.
Reaction Time	The ability to quickly respond (with the hand, finger, or foot) to a signal (sound, light, picture) when it appears.
Glare Sensitivity	The ability to see objects in the presence of glare or bright lighting.
Multilimb Coordination	The ability to coordinate two or more limbs (for example, two arms, two legs, or one leg and one arm) while sitting, standing, or lying down. It does not involve performing the activities while the whole body is in motion.
Response Orientation	The ability to choose quickly between two or more movements in response to two or more different signals (lights, sounds, pictures). It includes the speed with which the correct response is started with the hand, foot, or other body part.
Rate Control	The ability to time your movements or the movement of a piece of equipment in anticipation of changes in the speed and/or direction of a moving object or scene.
Spatial Orientation	The ability to know your location in relation to the environment or to know where other objects are in relation to you.

Work_Activity	Work_Activity Definitions
Interacting With Computers	Using computers and computer systems (including hardware and software) to program, write software, set up functions, enter data, or process information.
Training and Teaching Others	Identifying the educational needs of others, developing formal educational or training programs or classes, and teaching or instructing others.
Updating and Using Relevant Knowledge	Keeping up-to-date technically and applying new knowledge to your job.
Getting Information	Observing, receiving, and otherwise obtaining information from all relevant sources.
Thinking Creatively	Developing, designing, or creating new applications, ideas, relationships, systems, or products, including artistic contributions.
Making Decisions and Solving Problems	Analyzing information and evaluating results to choose the best solution and solve problems.
Communicating with Supervisors, Peers, or Subordin	Providing information to supervisors, co-workers, and subordinates by telephone, in written form, e-mail, or in person.
Processing Information	Compiling, coding, categorizing, calculating, tabulating, auditing, or verifying information or data.
Interpreting the Meaning of Information for Others	Translating or explaining what information means and how it can be used.
Coaching and Developing Others	Identifying the developmental needs of others and coaching, mentoring, or otherwise helping others to improve their knowledge or skills.
Organizing, Planning, and Prioritizing Work	Developing specific goals and plans to prioritize, organize, and accomplish your work.
Analyzing Data or Information	Identifying the underlying principles, reasons, or facts of information by breaking down information or data into separate parts.
Establishing and Maintaining Interpersonal Relatio	Developing constructive and cooperative working relationships with others, and maintaining them over time.
Judging the Qualities of Things, Services, or Peop	Assessing the value, importance, or quality of things or people.
Documenting/Recording Information	Entering, transcribing, recording, storing, or maintaining information in written or electronic/magnetic form.
Scheduling Work and Activities	Scheduling events, programs, and activities, as well as the work of others.
Developing Objectives and Strategies	Establishing long-range objectives and specifying the strategies and actions to achieve them.
Provide Consultation and Advice to Others	Providing guidance and expert advice to management or other groups on technical, systems-, or process-related topics.
Identifying Objects, Actions, and Events	Identifying information by categorizing, estimating, recognizing differences or similarities, and detecting changes in circumstances or events.
Performing Administrative Activities	Performing day-to-day administrative tasks such as maintaining information files and processing paperwork.

Performing for or Working Directly with the Public	Performing for people or dealing directly with the public. This includes serving customers in restaurants and stores, and receiving clients or guests.
Monitor Processes, Materials, or Surroundings	Monitoring and reviewing information from materials, events, or the environment, to detect or assess problems.
Evaluating Information to Determine Compliance wit	Using relevant information and individual judgment to determine whether events or processes comply with laws, regulations, or standards.
Communicating with Persons Outside Organization	Communicating with people outside the organization, representing the organization to customers, the public, government, and other external sources. This information can be exchanged in person, in writing, or by telephone or e-mail.
Coordinating the Work and Activities of Others	Getting members of a group to work together to accomplish tasks.
Guiding, Directing, and Motivating Subordinates	Providing guidance and direction to subordinates, including setting performance standards and monitoring performance.
Assisting and Caring for Others	Providing personal assistance, medical attention, emotional support, or other personal care to others such as coworkers, customers, or patients.
Resolving Conflicts and Negotiating with Others	Handling complaints, settling disputes, and resolving grievances and conflicts, or otherwise negotiating with others.
Developing and Building Teams	Encouraging and building mutual trust, respect, and cooperation among team members.
Estimating the Quantifiable Characteristics of Pro	Estimating sizes, distances, and quantities; or determining time, costs, resources, or materials needed to perform a work activity.
Inspecting Equipment, Structures, or Material	Inspecting equipment, structures, or materials to identify the cause of errors or other problems or defects.
Repairing and Maintaining Electronic Equipment	Servicing, repairing, calibrating, regulating, fine-tuning, or testing machines, devices, and equipment that operate primarily on the basis of electrical or electronic (not mechanical) principles.
Selling or Influencing Others	Convincing others to buy merchandise/goods or to otherwise change their minds or actions.
Monitoring and Controlling Resources	Monitoring and controlling resources and overseeing the spending of money.
Drafting, Laying Out, and Specifying Technical Dev	Providing documentation, detailed instructions, drawings, or specifications to tell others about how devices, parts, equipment, or structures are to be fabricated, constructed, assembled, modified, maintained, or used.
Controlling Machines and Processes	Using either control mechanisms or direct physical activity to operate machines or processes (not including computers or vehicles).
Staffing Organizational Units	Recruiting, interviewing, selecting, hiring, and promoting employees in an organization.
Handling and Moving Objects	Using hands and arms in handling, installing, positioning, and moving materials, and manipulating things.
Performing General Physical Activities	Performing physical activities that require considerable use of your arms and legs and moving your whole body, such as climbing, lifting, balancing, walking, stooping, and handling of materials.
Repairing and Maintaining Mechanical Equipment	Servicing, repairing, adjusting, and testing machines, devices, moving parts, and equipment that operate primarily on the basis of mechanical (not electronic) principles.
Operating Vehicles, Mechanized Devices, or Equipme	Running, maneuvering, navigating, or driving vehicles or mechanized equipment, such as forklifts, passenger vehicles, aircraft, or water craft.

Work_Context	**Work_Context Definitions**
Electronic Mail	How often do you use electronic mail in this job?
Indoors, Environmentally Controlled	How often does this job require working indoors in environmentally controlled conditions?
Freedom to Make Decisions	How much decision making freedom, without supervision, does the job offer?
Face-to-Face Discussions	How often do you have to have face-to-face discussions with individuals or teams in this job?
Structured versus Unstructured Work	To what extent is this job structured for the worker, rather than allowing the worker to determine tasks, priorities, and goals?
Public Speaking	How often do you have to perform public speaking in this job?
Contact With Others	How much does this job require the worker to be in contact with others (face-to-face, by telephone, or otherwise) in order to perform it?
Telephone	How often do you have telephone conversations in this job?
Coordinate or Lead Others	How important is it to coordinate or lead others in accomplishing work activities in this job?

Work With Work Group or Team	How important is it to work with others in a group or team in this job?
Importance of Being Exact or Accurate	How important is being very exact or highly accurate in performing this job?
Frequency of Decision Making	How frequently is the worker required to make decisions that affect other people, the financial resources, and/or the image and reputation of the organization?
Time Pressure	How often does this job require the worker to meet strict deadlines?
Letters and Memos	How often does the job require written letters and memos?
Impact of Decisions on Co-workers or Company Resul	How do the decisions an employee makes impact the results of co-workers, clients or the company?
Spend Time Sitting	How much does this job require sitting?
Deal With External Customers	How important is it to work with external customers or the public in this job?
Physical Proximity	To what extent does this job require the worker to perform job tasks in close physical proximity to other people?
Level of Competition	To what extent does this job require the worker to compete or to be aware of competitive pressures?
Importance of Repeating Same Tasks	How important is repeating the same physical activities (e.g., key entry) or mental activities (e.g., checking entries in a ledger) over and over, without stopping, to performing this job?
Spend Time Using Your Hands to Handle, Control, or	How much does this job require using your hands to handle, control, or feel objects, tools or controls?
Frequency of Conflict Situations	How often are there conflict situations the employee has to face in this job?
Deal With Unpleasant or Angry People	How frequently does the worker have to deal with unpleasant, angry, or discourteous individuals as part of the job requirements?
Spend Time Standing	How much does this job require standing?
Responsibility for Outcomes and Results	How responsible is the worker for work outcomes and results of other workers?
Spend Time Making Repetitive Motions	How much does this job require making repetitive motions?
Sounds, Noise Levels Are Distracting or Uncomforta	How often does this job require working exposed to sounds and noise levels that are distracting or uncomfortable?
Consequence of Error	How serious would the result usually be if the worker made a mistake that was not readily correctable?
Responsible for Others' Health and Safety	How much responsibility is there for the health and safety of others in this job?
Degree of Automation	How automated is the job?
Spend Time Walking and Running	How much does this job require walking and running?
Exposed to Contaminants	How often does this job require working exposed to contaminants (such as pollutants, gases, dust or odors)?
Cramped Work Space, Awkward Positions	How often does this job require working in cramped work spaces that requires getting into awkward positions?
Exposed to Disease or Infections	How often does this job require exposure to disease/infections?
Extremely Bright or Inadequate Lighting	How often does this job require working in extremely bright or inadequate lighting conditions?
In an Enclosed Vehicle or Equipment	How often does this job require working in a closed vehicle or equipment (e.g., car)?
Spend Time Bending or Twisting the Body	How much does this job require bending or twisting your body?
Deal With Physically Aggressive People	How frequently does this job require the worker to deal with physical aggression of violent individuals?
Very Hot or Cold Temperatures	How often does this job require working in very hot (above 90 F degrees) or very cold (below 32 F degrees) temperatures?
Indoors, Not Environmentally Controlled	How often does this job require working indoors in non-controlled environmental conditions (e.g., warehouse without heat)?
Pace Determined by Speed of Equipment	How important is it to this job that the pace is determined by the speed of equipment or machinery? (This does not refer to keeping busy at all times on this job.)
Spend Time Kneeling, Crouching, Stooping, or Crawl	How much does this job require kneeling, crouching, stooping or crawling?
Exposed to Minor Burns, Cuts, Bites, or Stings	How often does this job require exposure to minor burns, cuts, bites, or stings?
Exposed to Radiation	How often does this job require exposure to radiation?
Exposed to Hazardous Equipment	How often does this job require exposure to hazardous equipment?
Exposed to Hazardous Conditions	How often does this job require exposure to hazardous conditions?

Outdoors, Exposed to Weather	How often does this job require working outdoors, exposed to all weather conditions?
Outdoors, Under Cover	How often does this job require working outdoors, under cover (e.g., structure with roof but no walls)?
Spend Time Keeping or Regaining Balance	How much does this job require keeping or regaining your balance?
Exposed to High Places	How often does this job require exposure to high places?
Wear Common Protective or Safety Equipment such as	How much does this job require wearing common protective or safety equipment such as safety shoes, glasses, gloves, hard hats or life jackets?
Spend Time Climbing Ladders, Scaffolds, or Poles	How much does this job require climbing ladders, scaffolds, or poles?
In an Open Vehicle or Equipment	How often does this job require working in an open vehicle or equipment (e.g., tractor)?
Exposed to Whole Body Vibration	How often does this job require exposure to whole body vibration (e.g., operate a jackhammer)?
Wear Specialized Protective or Safety Equipment su	How much does this job require wearing specialized protective or safety equipment such as breathing apparatus, safety harness, full protection suits, or radiation protection?

Job Zone Component	Job Zone Component Definitions
Title	Job Zone Five: Extensive Preparation Needed
Overall Experience	Extensive skill, knowledge, and experience are needed for these occupations. Many require more than five years of experience. For example, surgeons must complete four years of college and an additional five to seven years of specialized medical training to be able to do their job.
Job Training	Employees may need some on-the-job training, but most of these occupations assume that the person will already have the required skills, knowledge, work-related experience, and/or training.
Job Zone Examples	These occupations often involve coordinating, training, supervising, or managing the activities of others to accomplish goals. Very advanced communication and organizational skills are required. Examples include athletic trainers, lawyers, managing editors, physicists, social psychologists, and surgeons.
SVP Range	(8.0 and above)
Education	A bachelor's degree is the minimum formal education required for these occupations. However, many also require graduate school. For example, they may require a master's degree, and some require a Ph.D., M.D., or J.D. (law degree).

Work_Styles	Work_Styles Definitions
Dependability	Job requires being reliable, responsible, and dependable, and fulfilling obligations.
Integrity	Job requires being honest and ethical.
Analytical Thinking	Job requires analyzing information and using logic to address work-related issues and problems.
Self Control	Job requires maintaining composure, keeping emotions in check, controlling anger, and avoiding aggressive behavior, even in very difficult situations.
Initiative	Job requires a willingness to take on responsibilities and challenges.
Attention to Detail	Job requires being careful about detail and thorough in completing work tasks.
Independence	Job requires developing one's own ways of doing things, guiding oneself with little or no supervision, and depending on oneself to get things done.
Persistence	Job requires persistence in the face of obstacles.
Concern for Others	Job requires being sensitive to others' needs and feelings and being understanding and helpful on the job.
Adaptability/Flexibility	Job requires being open to change (positive or negative) and to considerable variety in the workplace.
Achievement/Effort	Job requires establishing and maintaining personally challenging achievement goals and exerting effort toward mastering tasks.
Cooperation	Job requires being pleasant with others on the job and displaying a good-natured, cooperative attitude.
Stress Tolerance	Job requires accepting criticism and dealing calmly and effectively with high stress situations.
Leadership	Job requires a willingness to lead, take charge, and offer opinions and direction.
Innovation	Job requires creativity and alternative thinking to develop new ideas for and answers to work-related problems.

Social Orientation	Job requires preferring to work with others rather than alone, and being personally connected with others on the job.

25-1022.00 - Mathematical Science Teachers, Postsecondary

Teach courses pertaining to mathematical concepts, statistics, and actuarial science and to the application of original and standardized mathematical techniques in solving specific problems and situations.

Tasks

1) Maintain student attendance records, grades, and other required records.

2) Compile, administer, and grade examinations, or assign this work to others.

3) Evaluate and grade students' class work, assignments, and papers.

4) Plan, evaluate, and revise curricula, course content, and course materials and methods of instruction.

5) Maintain regularly scheduled office hours in order to advise and assist students.

6) Keep abreast of developments in their field by reading current literature, talking with colleagues, and participating in professional conferences.

7) Select and obtain materials and supplies such as textbooks.

8) Collaborate with colleagues to address teaching and research issues.

9) Initiate, facilitate, and moderate classroom discussions.

10) Advise students on academic and vocational curricula, and on career issues.

11) Participate in campus and community events.

12) Serve on academic or administrative committees that deal with institutional policies, departmental matters, and academic issues.

13) Participate in student recruitment, registration, and placement activities.

14) Prepare and deliver lectures to undergraduate and/or graduate students on topics such as linear algebra, differential equations, and discrete mathematics.

15) Act as advisers to student organizations.

16) Conduct research in a particular field of knowledge, and publish findings in books, professional journals, and/or electronic media.

17) Write grant proposals to procure external research funding.

18) Compile bibliographies of specialized materials for outside reading assignments.

19) Supervise undergraduate and/or graduate teaching, internship, and research work.

20) Perform administrative duties such as serving as department head.

21) Provide professional consulting services to government and/or industry.

Knowledge	Knowledge Definitions
Mathematics	Knowledge of arithmetic, algebra, geometry, calculus, statistics, and their applications.
Education and Training	Knowledge of principles and methods for curriculum and training design, teaching and instruction for individuals and groups, and the measurement of training effects.
English Language	Knowledge of the structure and content of the English language including the meaning and spelling of words, rules of composition, and grammar.
Computers and Electronics	Knowledge of circuit boards, processors, chips, electronic equipment, and computer hardware and software, including applications and programming.
Customer and Personal Service	Knowledge of principles and processes for providing customer and personal services. This includes customer needs assessment, meeting quality standards for services, and evaluation of customer satisfaction.
Physics	Knowledge and prediction of physical principles, laws, their interrelationships, and applications to understanding fluid, material, and atmospheric dynamics, and mechanical, electrical, atomic and sub-atomic structures and processes.
Psychology	Knowledge of human behavior and performance; individual differences in ability, personality, and interests; learning and motivation; psychological research methods; and the assessment and treatment of behavioral and affective disorders.

Clerical	Knowledge of administrative and clerical procedures and systems such as word processing, managing files and records, stenography and transcription, designing forms, and other office procedures and terminology.
Communications and Media	Knowledge of media production, communication, and dissemination techniques and methods. This includes alternative ways to inform and entertain via written, oral, and visual media.
Administration and Management	Knowledge of business and management principles involved in strategic planning, resource allocation, human resources modeling, leadership technique, production methods, and coordination of people and resources.
Engineering and Technology	Knowledge of the practical application of engineering science and technology. This includes applying principles, techniques, procedures, and equipment to the design and production of various goods and services.
Personnel and Human Resources	Knowledge of principles and procedures for personnel recruitment, selection, training, compensation and benefits, labor relations and negotiation, and personnel information systems.
Sociology and Anthropology	Knowledge of group behavior and dynamics, societal trends and influences, human migrations, ethnicity, cultures and their history and origins.
Public Safety and Security	Knowledge of relevant equipment, policies, procedures, and strategies to promote effective local, state, or national security operations for the protection of people, data, property, and institutions.
Chemistry	Knowledge of the chemical composition, structure, and properties of substances and of the chemical processes and transformations that they undergo. This includes uses of chemicals and their interactions, danger signs, production techniques, and disposal methods.
Design	Knowledge of design techniques, tools, and principles involved in production of precision technical plans, blueprints, drawings, and models.
Therapy and Counseling	Knowledge of principles, methods, and procedures for diagnosis, treatment, and rehabilitation of physical and mental dysfunctions, and for career counseling and guidance.
Telecommunications	Knowledge of transmission, broadcasting, switching, control, and operation of telecommunications systems.
Law and Government	Knowledge of laws, legal codes, court procedures, precedents, government regulations, executive orders, agency rules, and the democratic political process.
Biology	Knowledge of plant and animal organisms, their tissues, cells, functions, interdependencies, and interactions with each other and the environment.
Philosophy and Theology	Knowledge of different philosophical systems and religions. This includes their basic principles, values, ethics, ways of thinking, customs, practices, and their impact on human culture.
History and Archeology	Knowledge of historical events and their causes, indicators, and effects on civilizations and cultures.
Sales and Marketing	Knowledge of principles and methods for showing, promoting, and selling products or services. This includes marketing strategy and tactics, product demonstration, sales techniques, and sales control systems.
Production and Processing	Knowledge of raw materials, production processes, quality control, costs, and other techniques for maximizing the effective manufacture and distribution of goods.
Economics and Accounting	Knowledge of economic and accounting principles and practices, the financial markets, banking and the analysis and reporting of financial data.
Geography	Knowledge of principles and methods for describing the features of land, sea, and air masses, including their physical characteristics, locations, interrelationships, and distribution of plant, animal, and human life.
Mechanical	Knowledge of machines and tools, including their designs, uses, repair, and maintenance.
Transportation	Knowledge of principles and methods for moving people or goods by air, rail, sea, or road, including the relative costs and benefits.
Medicine and Dentistry	Knowledge of the information and techniques needed to diagnose and treat human injuries, diseases, and deformities. This includes symptoms, treatment alternatives, drug properties and interactions, and preventive health-care measures.
Foreign Language	Knowledge of the structure and content of a foreign (non-English) language including the meaning and spelling of words, rules of composition and grammar, and pronunciation.

Fine Arts	Knowledge of the theory and techniques required to compose, produce, and perform works of music, dance, visual arts, drama, and sculpture.
Building and Construction	Knowledge of materials, methods, and the tools involved in the construction or repair of houses, buildings, or other structures such as highways and roads.
Food Production	Knowledge of techniques and equipment for planting, growing, and harvesting food products (both plant and animal) for consumption, including storage/handling techniques.

Skills	Skills Definitions
Mathematics	Using mathematics to solve problems.
Instructing	Teaching others how to do something.
Speaking	Talking to others to convey information effectively.
Critical Thinking	Using logic and reasoning to identify the strengths and weaknesses of alternative solutions, conclusions or approaches to problems.
Reading Comprehension	Understanding written sentences and paragraphs in work related documents.
Active Listening	Giving full attention to what other people are saying, taking time to understand the points being made, asking questions as appropriate, and not interrupting at inappropriate times.
Learning Strategies	Selecting and using training/instructional methods and procedures appropriate for the situation when learning or teaching new things.
Active Learning	Understanding the implications of new information for both current and future problem-solving and decision-making.
Monitoring	Monitoring/Assessing performance of yourself, other individuals, or organizations to make improvements or take corrective action.
Time Management	Managing one's own time and the time of others.
Complex Problem Solving	Identifying complex problems and reviewing related information to develop and evaluate options and implement solutions.
Writing	Communicating effectively in writing as appropriate for the needs of the audience.
Social Perceptiveness	Being aware of others' reactions and understanding why they react as they do.
Coordination	Adjusting actions in relation to others' actions.
Service Orientation	Actively looking for ways to help people.
Science	Using scientific rules and methods to solve problems.
Persuasion	Persuading others to change their minds or behavior.
Judgment and Decision Making	Considering the relative costs and benefits of potential actions to choose the most appropriate one.
Equipment Selection	Determining the kind of tools and equipment needed to do a job.
Technology Design	Generating or adapting equipment and technology to serve user needs.
Negotiation	Bringing others together and trying to reconcile differences.
Management of Personnel Resources	Motivating, developing, and directing people as they work, identifying the best people for the job.
Operations Analysis	Analyzing needs and product requirements to create a design.
Quality Control Analysis	Conducting tests and inspections of products, services, or processes to evaluate quality or performance.
Systems Evaluation	Identifying measures or indicators of system performance and the actions needed to improve or correct performance, relative to the goals of the system.
Programming	Writing computer programs for various purposes.
Troubleshooting	Determining causes of operating errors and deciding what to do about it.
Systems Analysis	Determining how a system should work and how changes in conditions, operations, and the environment will affect outcomes.
Management of Financial Resources	Determining how money will be spent to get the work done, and accounting for these expenditures.
Management of Material Resources	Obtaining and seeing to the appropriate use of equipment, facilities, and materials needed to do certain work.
Operation and Control	Controlling operations of equipment or systems.
Installation	Installing equipment, machines, wiring, or programs to meet specifications.
Equipment Maintenance	Performing routine maintenance on equipment and determining when and what kind of maintenance is needed.
Operation Monitoring	Watching gauges, dials, or other indicators to make sure a machine is working properly.
Repairing	Repairing machines or systems using the needed tools.

Ability	Ability Definitions
Oral Expression	The ability to communicate information and ideas in speaking so others will understand.
Mathematical Reasoning	The ability to choose the right mathematical methods or formulas to solve a problem.
Speech Clarity	The ability to speak clearly so others can understand you.
Written Comprehension	The ability to read and understand information and ideas presented in writing.
Inductive Reasoning	The ability to combine pieces of information to form general rules or conclusions (includes finding a relationship among seemingly unrelated events).
Oral Comprehension	The ability to listen to and understand information and ideas presented through spoken words and sentences.
Deductive Reasoning	The ability to apply general rules to specific problems to produce answers that make sense.
Written Expression	The ability to communicate information and ideas in writing so others will understand.
Near Vision	The ability to see details at close range (within a few feet of the observer).
Number Facility	The ability to add, subtract, multiply, or divide quickly and correctly.
Problem Sensitivity	The ability to tell when something is wrong or is likely to go wrong. It does not involve solving the problem, only recognizing there is a problem.
Information Ordering	The ability to arrange things or actions in a certain order or pattern according to a specific rule or set of rules (e.g., patterns of numbers, letters, words, pictures, mathematical operations).
Category Flexibility	The ability to generate or use different sets of rules for combining or grouping things in different ways.
Speech Recognition	The ability to identify and understand the speech of another person.
Selective Attention	The ability to concentrate on a task over a period of time without being distracted.
Originality	The ability to come up with unusual or clever ideas about a given topic or situation, or to develop creative ways to solve a problem.
Fluency of Ideas	The ability to come up with a number of ideas about a topic (the number of ideas is important, not their quality, correctness, or creativity).
Time Sharing	The ability to shift back and forth between two or more activities or sources of information (such as speech, sounds, touch, or other sources).
Memorization	The ability to remember information such as words, numbers, pictures, and procedures.
Flexibility of Closure	The ability to identify or detect a known pattern (a figure, object, word, or sound) that is hidden in other distracting material.
Speed of Closure	The ability to quickly make sense of, combine, and organize information into meaningful patterns.
Far Vision	The ability to see details at a distance.
Perceptual Speed	The ability to quickly and accurately compare similarities and differences among sets of letters, numbers, objects, pictures, or patterns. The things to be compared may be presented at the same time or one after the other. This ability also includes comparing a presented object with a remembered object.
Visualization	The ability to imagine how something will look after it is moved around or when its parts are moved or rearranged.
Trunk Strength	The ability to use your abdominal and lower back muscles to support part of the body repeatedly or continuously over time without 'giving out' or fatiguing.
Auditory Attention	The ability to focus on a single source of sound in the presence of other distracting sounds.
Visual Color Discrimination	The ability to match or detect differences between colors, including shades of color and brightness.
Finger Dexterity	The ability to make precisely coordinated movements of the fingers of one or both hands to grasp, manipulate, or assemble very small objects.
Hearing Sensitivity	The ability to detect or tell the differences between sounds that vary in pitch and loudness.
Depth Perception	The ability to judge which of several objects is closer or farther away from you, or to judge the distance between you and an object.
Sound Localization	The ability to tell the direction from which a sound originated.
Extent Flexibility	The ability to bend, stretch, twist, or reach with your body, arms, and/or legs.

Multilimb Coordination	The ability to coordinate two or more limbs (for example, two arms, two legs, or one leg and one arm) while sitting, standing, or lying down. It does not involve performing the activities while the whole body is in motion.
Wrist-Finger Speed	The ability to make fast, simple, repeated movements of the fingers, hands, and wrists.
Speed of Limb Movement	The ability to quickly move the arms and legs.
Static Strength	The ability to exert maximum muscle force to lift, push, pull, or carry objects.
Control Precision	The ability to quickly and repeatedly adjust the controls of a machine or a vehicle to exact positions.
Explosive Strength	The ability to use short bursts of muscle force to propel oneself (as in jumping or sprinting), or to throw an object.
Stamina	The ability to exert yourself physically over long periods of time without getting winded or out of breath.
Peripheral Vision	The ability to see objects or movement of objects to one's side when the eyes are looking ahead.
Reaction Time	The ability to quickly respond (with the hand, finger, or foot) to a signal (sound, light, picture) when it appears.
Dynamic Strength	The ability to exert muscle force repeatedly or continuously over time. This involves muscular endurance and resistance to muscle fatigue.
Gross Body Equilibrium	The ability to keep or regain your body balance or stay upright when in an unstable position.
Arm-Hand Steadiness	The ability to keep your hand and arm steady while moving your arm or while holding your arm and hand in one position.
Spatial Orientation	The ability to know your location in relation to the environment or to know where other objects are in relation to you.
Dynamic Flexibility	The ability to quickly and repeatedly bend, stretch, twist, or reach out with your body, arms, and/or legs.
Rate Control	The ability to time your movements or the movement of a piece of equipment in anticipation of changes in the speed and/or direction of a moving object or scene.
Response Orientation	The ability to choose quickly between two or more movements in response to two or more different signals (lights, sounds, pictures). It includes the speed with which the correct response is started with the hand, foot, or other body part.
Glare Sensitivity	The ability to see objects in the presence of glare or bright lighting.
Gross Body Coordination	The ability to coordinate the movement of your arms, legs, and torso together when the whole body is in motion.
Night Vision	The ability to see under low light conditions.
Manual Dexterity	The ability to quickly move your hand, your hand together with your arm, or your two hands to grasp, manipulate, or assemble objects.

Work_Activity	Work_Activity Definitions
Training and Teaching Others	Identifying the educational needs of others, developing formal educational or training programs or classes, and teaching or instructing others.
Interpreting the Meaning of Information for Others	Translating or explaining what information means and how it can be used.
Thinking Creatively	Developing, designing, or creating new applications, ideas, relationships, systems, or products, including artistic contributions.
Making Decisions and Solving Problems	Analyzing information and evaluating results to choose the best solution and solve problems.
Interacting With Computers	Using computers and computer systems (including hardware and software) to program, write software, set up functions, enter data, or process information.
Updating and Using Relevant Knowledge	Keeping up-to-date technically and applying new knowledge to your job.
Establishing and Maintaining Interpersonal Relatio	Developing constructive and cooperative working relationships with others, and maintaining them over time.
Coaching and Developing Others	Identifying the developmental needs of others and coaching, mentoring, or otherwise helping others to improve their knowledge or skills.
Getting Information	Observing, receiving, and otherwise obtaining information from all relevant sources.
Organizing, Planning, and Prioritizing Work	Developing specific goals and plans to prioritize, organize, and accomplish your work.
Communicating with Supervisors, Peers, or Subordin	Providing information to supervisors, co-workers, and subordinates by telephone, in written form, e-mail, or in person.
Documenting/Recording Information	Entering, transcribing, recording, storing, or maintaining information in written or electronic/magnetic form.

		Work_Context	Work_Context Definitions

Analyzing Data or Information	Identifying the underlying principles, reasons, or facts of information by breaking down information or data into separate parts.
Processing Information	Compiling, coding, categorizing, calculating, tabulating, auditing, or verifying information or data.
Judging the Qualities of Things, Services, or Peop	Assessing the value, importance, or quality of things or people.
Identifying Objects, Actions, and Events	Identifying information by categorizing, estimating, recognizing differences or similarities, and detecting changes in circumstances or events.
Developing Objectives and Strategies	Establishing long-range objectives and specifying the strategies and actions to achieve them.
Scheduling Work and Activities	Scheduling events, programs, and activities, as well as the work of others.
Performing for or Working Directly with the Public	Performing for people or dealing directly with the public. This includes serving customers in restaurants and stores, and receiving clients or guests.
Monitor Processes, Materials, or Surroundings	Monitoring and reviewing information from materials, events, or the environment, to detect or assess problems.
Evaluating Information to Determine Compliance wit	Using relevant information and individual judgment to determine whether events or processes comply with laws, regulations, or standards.
Provide Consultation and Advice to Others	Providing guidance and expert advice to management or other groups on technical, systems-, or process-related topics.
Coordinating the Work and Activities of Others	Getting members of a group to work together to accomplish tasks.
Communicating with Persons Outside Organization	Communicating with people outside the organization, representing the organization to customers, the public, government, and other external sources. This information can be exchanged in person, in writing, or by telephone or e-mail.
Performing Administrative Activities	Performing day-to-day administrative tasks such as maintaining information files and processing paperwork.
Assisting and Caring for Others	Providing personal assistance, medical attention, emotional support, or other personal care to others such as coworkers, customers, or patients.
Guiding, Directing, and Motivating Subordinates	Providing guidance and direction to subordinates, including setting performance standards and monitoring performance.
Resolving Conflicts and Negotiating with Others	Handling complaints, settling disputes, and resolving grievances and conflicts, or otherwise negotiating with others.
Estimating the Quantifiable Characteristics of Pro	Estimating sizes, distances, and quantities; or determining time, costs, resources, or materials needed to perform a work activity.
Developing and Building Teams	Encouraging and building mutual trust, respect, and cooperation among team members.
Selling or Influencing Others	Convincing others to buy merchandise/goods or to otherwise change their minds or actions.
Inspecting Equipment, Structures, or Material	Inspecting equipment, structures, or materials to identify the cause of errors or other problems or defects.
Performing General Physical Activities	Performing physical activities that require considerable use of your arms and legs and moving your whole body, such as climbing, lifting, balancing, walking, stooping, and handling of materials.
Staffing Organizational Units	Recruiting, interviewing, selecting, hiring, and promoting employees in an organization.
Handling and Moving Objects	Using hands and arms in handling, installing, positioning, and moving materials, and manipulating things.
Monitoring and Controlling Resources	Monitoring and controlling resources and overseeing the spending of money.
Controlling Machines and Processes	Using either control mechanisms or direct physical activity to operate machines or processes (not including computers or vehicles).
Repairing and Maintaining Electronic Equipment	Servicing, repairing, calibrating, regulating, fine-tuning, or testing machines, devices, and equipment that operate primarily on the basis of electrical or electronic (not mechanical) principles.
Drafting, Laying Out, and Specifying Technical Dev	Providing documentation, detailed instructions, drawings, or specifications to tell others about how devices, parts, equipment, or structures are to be fabricated, constructed, assembled, modified, maintained, or used.
Operating Vehicles, Mechanized Devices, or Equipme	Running, maneuvering, navigating, or driving vehicles or mechanized equipment, such as forklifts, passenger vehicles, aircraft, or water craft.
Repairing and Maintaining Mechanical Equipment	Servicing, repairing, adjusting, and testing machines, devices, moving parts, and equipment that operate primarily on the basis of mechanical (not electronic) principles.

Work_Context	Work_Context Definitions
Electronic Mail	How often do you use electronic mail in this job?
Face-to-Face Discussions	How often do you have to have face-to-face discussions with individuals or teams in this job?
Freedom to Make Decisions	How much decision making freedom, without supervision, does the job offer?
Indoors, Environmentally Controlled	How often does this job require working indoors in environmentally controlled conditions?
Structured versus Unstructured Work	To what extent is this job structured for the worker, rather than allowing the worker to determine tasks, priorities, and goals?
Public Speaking	How often do you have to perform public speaking in this job?
Contact With Others	How much does this job require the worker to be in contact with others (face-to-face, by telephone, or otherwise) in order to perform it?
Importance of Being Exact or Accurate	How important is being very exact or highly accurate in performing this job?
Telephone	How often do you have telephone conversations in this job?
Work With Work Group or Team	How important is it to work with others in a group or team in this job?
Frequency of Decision Making	How frequently is the worker required to make decisions that affect other people, the financial resources, and/or the image and reputation of the organization?
Coordinate or Lead Others	How important is it to coordinate or lead others in accomplishing work activities in this job?
Letters and Memos	How often does the job require written letters and memos?
Time Pressure	How often does this job require the worker to meet strict deadlines?
Physical Proximity	To what extent does this job require the worker to perform job tasks in close physical proximity to other people?
Impact of Decisions on Co-workers or Company Resul	How do the decisions an employee makes impact the results of co-workers, clients or the company?
Deal With External Customers	How important is it to work with external customers or the public in this job?
Importance of Repeating Same Tasks	How important is repeating the same physical activities (e.g., key entry) or mental activities (e.g., checking entries in a ledger) over and over, without stopping, to performing this job?
Spend Time Standing	How much does this job require standing?
Spend Time Sitting	How much does this job require sitting?
Level of Competition	To what extent does this job require the worker to compete or to be aware of competitive pressures?
Deal With Unpleasant or Angry People	How frequently does the worker have to deal with unpleasant, angry, or discourteous individuals as part of the job requirements?
Frequency of Conflict Situations	How often are there conflict situations the employee has to face in this job?
Spend Time Using Your Hands to Handle, Control, or	How much does this job require using your hands to handle, control, or feel objects, tools or controls?
Responsibility for Outcomes and Results	How responsible is the worker for work outcomes and results of other workers?
Spend Time Making Repetitive Motions	How much does this job require making repetitive motions?
Sounds, Noise Levels Are Distracting or Uncomforta	How often does this job require working exposed to sounds and noise levels that are distracting or uncomfortable?
Responsible for Others' Health and Safety	How much responsibility is there for the health and safety of others in this job?
Spend Time Walking and Running	How much does this job require walking and running?
Consequence of Error	How serious would the result usually be if the worker made a mistake that was not readily correctable?
Exposed to Contaminants	How often does this job require working exposed to contaminants (such as pollutants, gases, dust or odors)?
Degree of Automation	How automated is the job?
Exposed to Disease or Infections	How often does this job require exposure to disease/infections?
Indoors, Not Environmentally Controlled	How often does this job require working indoors in non-controlled environmental conditions (e.g., warehouse without heat)?
Cramped Work Space, Awkward Positions	How often does this job require working in cramped work spaces that requires getting into awkward positions?
Deal With Physically Aggressive People	How frequently does this job require the worker to deal with physical aggression of violent individuals?
Spend Time Bending or Twisting the Body	How much does this job require bending or twisting your body?
Very Hot or Cold Temperatures	How often does this job require working in very hot (above 90 F degrees) or very cold (below 32 F degrees) temperatures?

Extremely Bright or Inadequate Lighting	How often does this job require working in extremely bright or inadequate lighting conditions?
Spend Time Keeping or Regaining Balance	How much does this job require keeping or regaining your balance?
In an Enclosed Vehicle or Equipment	How often does this job require working in a closed vehicle or equipment (e.g., car)?
Spend Time Climbing Ladders, Scaffolds, or Poles	How much does this job require climbing ladders, scaffolds, or poles?
Outdoors, Exposed to Weather	How often does this job require working outdoors, exposed to all weather conditions?
Outdoors, Under Cover	How often does this job require working outdoors, under cover (e.g., structure with roof but no walls)?
Wear Common Protective or Safety Equipment such as	How much does this job require wearing common protective or safety equipment such as safety shoes, glasses, gloves, hard hats or live jackets?
Pace Determined by Speed of Equipment	How important is it to this job that the pace is determined by the speed of equipment or machinery? (This does not refer to keeping busy at all times on this job.)
Exposed to Minor Burns, Cuts, Bites, or Stings	How often does this job require exposure to minor burns, cuts, bites, or stings?
Exposed to Whole Body Vibration	How often does this job require exposure to whole body vibration (e.g., operate a jackhammer)?
Spend Time Kneeling, Crouching, Stooping, or Crawl	How much does this job require kneeling, crouching, stooping or crawling?
Exposed to High Places	How often does this job require exposure to high places?
Exposed to Radiation	How often does this job require exposure to radiation?
Exposed to Hazardous Conditions	How often does this job require exposure to hazardous conditions?
Exposed to Hazardous Equipment	How often does this job require exposure to hazardous equipment?
Wear Specialized Protective or Safety Equipment su	How much does this job require wearing specialized protective or safety equipment such as breathing apparatus, safety harness, full protection suits, or radiation protection?
In an Open Vehicle or Equipment	How often does this job require working in an open vehicle or equipment (e.g., tractor)?

Job Zone Component	Job Zone Component Definitions
Title	Job Zone Five: Extensive Preparation Needed
	Extensive skill, knowledge, and experience are needed for these occupations. Many require more than five years of experience.
Overall Experience	For example, surgeons must complete four years of college and an additional five to seven years of specialized medical training to be able to do their job.
Job Training	Employees may need some on-the-job training, but most of these occupations assume that the person will already have the required skills, knowledge, work-related experience, and/or training.
Job Zone Examples	These occupations often involve coordinating, training, supervising, or managing the activities of others to accomplish goals. Very advanced communication and organizational skills are required. Examples include athletic trainers, lawyers, managing editors, physicists, social psychologists, and surgeons.
SVP Range	(8.0 and above)
Education	A bachelor's degree is the minimum formal education required for these occupations. However, many also require graduate school. For example, they may require a master's degree, and some require a Ph.D., M.D., or J.D. (law degree).

Work_Styles	Work_Styles Definitions
Dependability	Job requires being reliable, responsible, and dependable, and fulfilling obligations.
Integrity	Job requires being honest and ethical.
Self Control	Job requires maintaining composure, keeping emotions in check, controlling anger, and avoiding aggressive behavior, even in very difficult situations.
Attention to Detail	Job requires being careful about detail and thorough in completing work tasks.
Analytical Thinking	Job requires analyzing information and using logic to address work-related issues and problems.
Independence	Job requires developing one's own ways of doing things, guiding oneself with little or no supervision, and depending on oneself to get things done.

Concern for Others	Job requires being sensitive to others' needs and feelings and being understanding and helpful on the job.
Cooperation	Job requires being pleasant with others on the job and displaying a good-natured, cooperative attitude.
Initiative	Job requires a willingness to take on responsibilities and challenges.
Achievement/Effort	Job requires establishing and maintaining personally challenging achievement goals and exerting effort toward mastering tasks.
Persistence	Job requires persistence in the face of obstacles.
Leadership	Job requires a willingness to lead, take charge, and offer opinions and direction.
Innovation	Job requires creativity and alternative thinking to develop new ideas for and answers to work-related problems.
Stress Tolerance	Job requires accepting criticism and dealing calmly and effectively with high stress situations.
Adaptability/Flexibility	Job requires being open to change (positive or negative) and to considerable variety in the workplace.
Social Orientation	Job requires preferring to work with others rather than alone, and being personally connected with others on the job.

25-1031.00 - Architecture Teachers, Postsecondary

Teach courses in architecture and architectural design, such as architectural environmental design, interior architecture/design, and landscape architecture.

Tasks

1) Prepare course materials such as syllabi, homework assignments, and handouts.

2) Initiate, facilitate, and moderate classroom discussions.

3) Prepare and deliver lectures to undergraduate and/or graduate students on topics such as architectural design methods, aesthetics and design, and structures and materials.

4) Collaborate with colleagues to address teaching and research issues.

5) Maintain regularly scheduled office hours in order to advise and assist students.

6) Participate in campus and community events.

7) Maintain student attendance records, grades, and other required records.

8) Advise students on academic and vocational curricula, and on career issues.

9) Serve on academic or administrative committees that deal with institutional policies, departmental matters, and academic issues.

10) Compile bibliographies of specialized materials for outside reading assignments.

11) Compile, administer, and grade examinations, or assign this work to others.

12) Select and obtain materials and supplies such as textbooks and laboratory equipment.

13) Conduct research in a particular field of knowledge, and publish findings in professional journals, books, and/or electronic media.

14) Participate in student recruitment, registration, and placement activities.

15) Supervise undergraduate and/or graduate teaching, internship, and research work.

16) Write grant proposals to procure external research funding.

17) Act as advisers to student organizations.

18) Provide professional consulting services to government and/or industry.

19) Perform administrative duties such as serving as department head.

20) Plan, evaluate, and revise curricula, course content, and course materials and methods of instruction.

21) Keep abreast of developments in their field by reading current literature, talking with colleagues, and participating in professional conferences.

Knowledge	Knowledge Definitions
Design	Knowledge of design techniques, tools, and principles involved in production of precision technical plans, blueprints, drawings, and models.
Education and Training	Knowledge of principles and methods for curriculum and training design, teaching and instruction for individuals and groups, and the measurement of training effects.

English Language	Knowledge of the structure and content of the English language including the meaning and spelling of words, rules of composition, and grammar.
Building and Construction	Knowledge of materials, methods, and the tools involved in the construction or repair of houses, buildings, or other structures such as highways and roads.
Fine Arts	Knowledge of the theory and techniques required to compose, produce, and perform works of music, dance, visual arts, drama, and sculpture.
History and Archeology	Knowledge of historical events and their causes, indicators, and effects on civilizations and cultures.
Engineering and Technology	Knowledge of the practical application of engineering science and technology. This includes applying principles, techniques, procedures, and equipment to the design and production of various goods and services.
Computers and Electronics	Knowledge of circuit boards, processors, chips, electronic equipment, and computer hardware and software, including applications and programming.
Philosophy and Theology	Knowledge of different philosophical systems and religions. This includes their basic principles, values, ethics, ways of thinking, customs, practices, and their impact on human culture.
Geography	Knowledge of principles and methods for describing the features of land, sea, and air masses, including their physical characteristics, locations, interrelationships, and distribution of plant, animal, and human life.
Communications and Media	Knowledge of media production, communication, and dissemination techniques and methods. This includes alternative ways to inform and entertain via written, oral, and visual media.
Mathematics	Knowledge of arithmetic, algebra, geometry, calculus, statistics, and their applications.
Customer and Personal Service	Knowledge of principles and processes for providing customer and personal services. This includes customer needs assessment, meeting quality standards for services, and evaluation of customer satisfaction.
Public Safety and Security	Knowledge of relevant equipment, policies, procedures, and strategies to promote effective local, state, or national security operations for the protection of people, data, property, and institutions.
Mechanical	Knowledge of machines and tools, including their designs, uses, repair, and maintenance.
Administration and Management	Knowledge of business and management principles involved in strategic planning, resource allocation, human resources modeling, leadership technique, production methods, and coordination of people and resources.
Physics	Knowledge and prediction of physical principles, laws, their interrelationships, and applications to understanding fluid, material, and atmospheric dynamics, and mechanical, electrical, atomic and sub- atomic structures and processes.
Sociology and Anthropology	Knowledge of group behavior and dynamics, societal trends and influences, human migrations, ethnicity, cultures and their history and origins.
Psychology	Knowledge of human behavior and performance; individual differences in ability, personality, and interests; learning and motivation; psychological research methods; and the assessment and treatment of behavioral and affective disorders.
Law and Government	Knowledge of laws, legal codes, court procedures, precedents, government regulations, executive orders, agency rules, and the democratic political process.
Personnel and Human Resources	Knowledge of principles and procedures for personnel recruitment, selection, training, compensation and benefits, labor relations and negotiation, and personnel information systems.
Clerical	Knowledge of administrative and clerical procedures and systems such as word processing, managing files and records, stenography and transcription, designing forms, and other office procedures and terminology.
Transportation	Knowledge of principles and methods for moving people or goods by air, rail, sea, or road, including the relative costs and benefits.
Production and Processing	Knowledge of raw materials, production processes, quality control, costs, and other techniques for maximizing the effective manufacture and distribution of goods.
Sales and Marketing	Knowledge of principles and methods for showing, promoting, and selling products or services. This includes marketing strategy and tactics, product demonstration, sales techniques, and sales control systems.

Economics and Accounting	Knowledge of economic and accounting principles and practices, the financial markets, banking and the analysis and reporting of financial data.
Foreign Language	Knowledge of the structure and content of a foreign (non-English) language including the meaning and spelling of words, rules of composition and grammar, and pronunciation.
Therapy and Counseling	Knowledge of principles, methods, and procedures for diagnosis, treatment, and rehabilitation of physical and mental dysfunctions, and for career counseling and guidance.
Telecommunications	Knowledge of transmission, broadcasting, switching, control, and operation of telecommunications systems.
Chemistry	Knowledge of the chemical composition, structure, and properties of substances and of the chemical processes and transformations that they undergo. This includes uses of chemicals and their interactions, danger signs, production techniques, and disposal methods.
Biology	Knowledge of plant and animal organisms, their tissues, cells, functions, interdependencies, and interactions with each other and the environment.
Medicine and Dentistry	Knowledge of the information and techniques needed to diagnose and treat human injuries, diseases, and deformities. This includes symptoms, treatment alternatives, drug properties and interactions, and preventive health-care measures.
Food Production	Knowledge of techniques and equipment for planting, growing, and harvesting food products (both plant and animal) for consumption, including storage/handling techniques.

Skills	Skills Definitions
Instructing	Teaching others how to do something.
Speaking	Talking to others to convey information effectively.
Critical Thinking	Using logic and reasoning to identify the strengths and weaknesses of alternative solutions, conclusions or approaches to problems.
Active Listening	Giving full attention to what other people are saying, taking time to understand the points being made, asking questions as appropriate, and not interrupting at inappropriate times.
Reading Comprehension	Understanding written sentences and paragraphs in work related documents.
Learning Strategies	Selecting and using training/instructional methods and procedures appropriate for the situation when learning or teaching new things.
Active Learning	Understanding the implications of new information for both current and future problem-solving and decision-making.
Writing	Communicating effectively in writing as appropriate for the needs of the audience.
Time Management	Managing one's own time and the time of others.
Complex Problem Solving	Identifying complex problems and reviewing related information to develop and evaluate options and implement solutions.
Coordination	Adjusting actions in relation to others' actions.
Social Perceptiveness	Being aware of others' reactions and understanding why they react as they do.
Monitoring	Monitoring/Assessing performance of yourself, other individuals, or organizations to make improvements or take corrective action.
Judgment and Decision Making	Considering the relative costs and benefits of potential actions to choose the most appropriate one.
Operations Analysis	Analyzing needs and product requirements to create a design.
Technology Design	Generating or adapting equipment and technology to serve user needs.
Persuasion	Persuading others to change their minds or behavior.
Service Orientation	Actively looking for ways to help people.
Mathematics	Using mathematics to solve problems.
Equipment Selection	Determining the kind of tools and equipment needed to do a job.
Management of Personnel Resources	Motivating, developing, and directing people as they work, identifying the best people for the job.
Science	Using scientific rules and methods to solve problems.
Negotiation	Bringing others together and trying to reconcile differences.
Systems Analysis	Determining how a system should work and how changes in conditions, operations, and the environment will affect outcomes.
Systems Evaluation	Identifying measures or indicators of system performance and the actions needed to improve or correct performance, relative to the goals of the system.
Management of Financial Resources	Determining how money will be spent to get the work done, and accounting for these expenditures.

Quality Control Analysis	Conducting tests and inspections of products, services, or processes to evaluate quality or performance.
Management of Material Resources	Obtaining and seeing to the appropriate use of equipment, facilities, and materials needed to do certain work.
Troubleshooting	Determining causes of operating errors and deciding what to do about it.
Installation	Installing equipment, machines, wiring, or programs to meet specifications.
Programming	Writing computer programs for various purposes.
Equipment Maintenance	Performing routine maintenance on equipment and determining when and what kind of maintenance is needed.
Operation Monitoring	Watching gauges, dials, or other indicators to make sure a machine is working properly.
Operation and Control	Controlling operations of equipment or systems.
Repairing	Repairing machines or systems using the needed tools.

Ability	Ability Definitions
Oral Expression	The ability to communicate information and ideas in speaking so others will understand.
Written Comprehension	The ability to read and understand information and ideas presented in writing.
Speech Clarity	The ability to speak clearly so others can understand you.
Oral Comprehension	The ability to listen to and understand information and ideas presented through spoken words and sentences.
Written Expression	The ability to communicate information and ideas in writing so others will understand.
Inductive Reasoning	The ability to combine pieces of information to form general rules or conclusions (includes finding a relationship among seemingly unrelated events).
Deductive Reasoning	The ability to apply general rules to specific problems to produce answers that make sense.
Near Vision	The ability to see details at close range (within a few feet of the observer).
Problem Sensitivity	The ability to tell when something is wrong or is likely to go wrong. It does not involve solving the problem, only recognizing there is a problem.
Originality	The ability to come up with unusual or clever ideas about a given topic or situation, or to develop creative ways to solve a problem.
Speech Recognition	The ability to identify and understand the speech of another person.
Visualization	The ability to imagine how something will look after it is moved around or when its parts are moved or rearranged.
Fluency of Ideas	The ability to come up with a number of ideas about a topic (the number of ideas is important, not their quality, correctness, or creativity).
Category Flexibility	The ability to generate or use different sets of rules for combining or grouping things in different ways.
Information Ordering	The ability to arrange things or actions in a certain order or pattern according to a specific rule or set of rules (e.g., patterns of numbers, letters, words, pictures, mathematical operations).
Selective Attention	The ability to concentrate on a task over a period of time without being distracted.
Time Sharing	The ability to shift back and forth between two or more activities or sources of information (such as speech, sounds, touch, or other sources).
Mathematical Reasoning	The ability to choose the right mathematical methods or formulas to solve a problem.
Memorization	The ability to remember information such as words, numbers, pictures, and procedures.
Far Vision	The ability to see details at a distance.
Number Facility	The ability to add, subtract, multiply, or divide quickly and correctly.
Flexibility of Closure	The ability to identify or detect a known pattern (a figure, object, word, or sound) that is hidden in other distracting material.
Speed of Closure	The ability to quickly make sense of, combine, and organize information into meaningful patterns.
Visual Color Discrimination	The ability to match or detect differences between colors, including shades of color and brightness.
Trunk Strength	The ability to use your abdominal and lower back muscles to support part of the body repeatedly or continuously over time without 'giving out' or fatiguing.
Auditory Attention	The ability to focus on a single source of sound in the presence of other distracting sounds.

Perceptual Speed	The ability to quickly and accurately compare similarities and differences among sets of letters, numbers, objects, pictures, or patterns. The things to be compared may be presented at the same time or one after the other. This ability also includes comparing a presented object with a remembered object.
Finger Dexterity	The ability to make precisely coordinated movements of the fingers of one or both hands to grasp, manipulate, or assemble very small objects.
Hearing Sensitivity	The ability to detect or tell the differences between sounds that vary in pitch and loudness.
Depth Perception	The ability to judge which of several objects is closer or farther away from you, or to judge the distance between you and an object.
Spatial Orientation	The ability to know your location in relation to the environment or to know where other objects are in relation to you.
Sound Localization	The ability to tell the direction from which a sound originated.
Arm-Hand Steadiness	The ability to keep your hand and arm steady while moving your arm or while holding your arm and hand in one position.
Reaction Time	The ability to quickly respond (with the hand, finger, or foot) to a signal (sound, light, picture) when it appears.
Gross Body Coordination	The ability to coordinate the movement of your arms, legs, and torso together when the whole body is in motion.
Dynamic Flexibility	The ability to quickly and repeatedly bend, stretch, twist, or reach out with your body, arms, and/or legs.
Extent Flexibility	The ability to bend, stretch, twist, or reach with your body, arms, and/or legs.
Stamina	The ability to exert yourself physically over long periods of time without getting winded or out of breath.
Dynamic Strength	The ability to exert muscle force repeatedly or continuously over time. This involves muscular endurance and resistance to muscle fatigue.
Speed of Limb Movement	The ability to quickly move the arms and legs.
Wrist-Finger Speed	The ability to make fast, simple, repeated movements of the fingers, hands, and wrists.
Static Strength	The ability to exert maximum muscle force to lift, push, pull, or carry objects.
Explosive Strength	The ability to use short bursts of muscle force to propel oneself (as in jumping or sprinting), or to throw an object.
Gross Body Equilibrium	The ability to keep or regain your body balance or stay upright when in an unstable position.
Peripheral Vision	The ability to see objects or movement of objects to one's side when the eyes are looking ahead.
Night Vision	The ability to see under low light conditions.
Control Precision	The ability to quickly and repeatedly adjust the controls of a machine or a vehicle to exact positions.
Multilimb Coordination	The ability to coordinate two or more limbs (for example, two arms, two legs, or one leg and one arm) while sitting, standing, or lying down. It does not involve performing the activities while the whole body is in motion.
Manual Dexterity	The ability to quickly move your hand, your hand together with your arm, or your two hands to grasp, manipulate, or assemble objects.
Response Orientation	The ability to choose quickly between two or more movements in response to two or more different signals (lights, sounds, pictures). It includes the speed with which the correct response is started with the hand, foot, or other body part.
Rate Control	The ability to time your movements or the movement of a piece of equipment in anticipation of changes in the speed and/or direction of a moving object or scene.
Glare Sensitivity	The ability to see objects in the presence of glare or bright lighting.

Work_Activity	Work_Activity Definitions
Thinking Creatively	Developing, designing, or creating new applications, ideas, relationships, systems, or products, including artistic contributions.
Training and Teaching Others	Identifying the educational needs of others, developing formal educational or training programs or classes, and teaching or instructing others.
Making Decisions and Solving Problems	Analyzing information and evaluating results to choose the best solution and solve problems.
Getting Information	Observing, receiving, and otherwise obtaining information from all relevant sources.
Updating and Using Relevant Knowledge	Keeping up-to-date technically and applying new knowledge to your job.
Interpreting the Meaning of Information for Others	Translating or explaining what information means and how it can be used.

Coaching and Developing Others	Identifying the developmental needs of others and coaching, mentoring, or otherwise helping others to improve their knowledge or skills.
Organizing, Planning, and Prioritizing Work	Developing specific goals and plans to prioritize, organize, and accomplish your work.
Developing Objectives and Strategies	Establishing long-range objectives and specifying the strategies and actions to achieve them.
Interacting With Computers	Using computers and computer systems (including hardware and software) to program, write software, set up functions, enter data, or process information.
Establishing and Maintaining Interpersonal Relatio	Developing constructive and cooperative working relationships with others, and maintaining them over time.
Identifying Objects, Actions, and Events	Identifying information by categorizing, estimating, recognizing differences or similarities, and detecting changes in circumstances or events.
Judging the Qualities of Things, Services, or Peop	Assessing the value, importance, or quality of things or people.
Communicating with Supervisors, Peers, or Subordin	Providing information to supervisors, co-workers, and subordinates by telephone, in written form, e-mail, or in person.
Scheduling Work and Activities	Scheduling events, programs, and activities, as well as the work of others.
Analyzing Data or Information	Identifying the underlying principles, reasons, or facts of information by breaking down information or data into separate parts.
Coordinating the Work and Activities of Others	Getting members of a group to work together to accomplish tasks.
Documenting/Recording Information	Entering, transcribing, recording, storing, or maintaining information in written or electronic/magnetic form.
Processing Information	Compiling, coding, categorizing, calculating, tabulating, auditing, or verifying information or data.
Developing and Building Teams	Encouraging and building mutual trust, respect, and cooperation among team members.
Provide Consultation and Advice to Others	Providing guidance and expert advice to management or other groups on technical, systems-, or process-related topics.
Communicating with Persons Outside Organization	Communicating with people outside the organization, representing the organization to customers, the public, government, and other external sources. This information can be exchanged in person, in writing, or by telephone or e-mail.
Performing Administrative Activities	Performing day-to-day administrative tasks such as maintaining information files and processing paperwork.
Monitor Processes, Materials, or Surroundings	Monitoring and reviewing information from materials, events, or the environment, to detect or assess problems.
Estimating the Quantifiable Characteristics of Pro	Estimating sizes, distances, and quantities; or determining time, costs, resources, or materials needed to perform a work activity.
Evaluating Information to Determine Compliance wit	Using relevant information and individual judgment to determine whether events or processes comply with laws, regulations, or standards.
Guiding, Directing, and Motivating Subordinates	Providing guidance and direction to subordinates, including setting performance standards and monitoring performance.
Resolving Conflicts and Negotiating with Others	Handling complaints, settling disputes, and resolving grievances and conflicts, or otherwise negotiating with others.
Assisting and Caring for Others	Providing personal assistance, medical attention, emotional support, or other personal care to others such as coworkers, customers, or patients.
Selling or Influencing Others	Convincing others to buy merchandise/goods or to otherwise change their minds or actions.
Drafting, Laying Out, and Specifying Technical Dev	Providing documentation, detailed instructions, drawings, or specifications to tell others about how devices, parts, equipment, or structures are to be fabricated, constructed, assembled, modified, maintained, or used.
Performing for or Working Directly with the Public	Performing for people or dealing directly with the public. This includes serving customers in restaurants and stores, and receiving clients or guests.
Monitoring and Controlling Resources	Monitoring and controlling resources and overseeing the spending of money.
Performing General Physical Activities	Performing physical activities that require considerable use of your arms and legs and moving your whole body, such as climbing, lifting, balancing, walking, stooping, and handling of materials.
Handling and Moving Objects	Using hands and arms in handling, installing, positioning, and moving materials, and manipulating things.
Inspecting Equipment, Structures, or Material	Inspecting equipment, structures, or materials to identify the cause of errors or other problems or defects.

Staffing Organizational Units	Recruiting, interviewing, selecting, hiring, and promoting employees in an organization.
Controlling Machines and Processes	Using either control mechanisms or direct physical activity to operate machines or processes (not including computers or vehicles).
Repairing and Maintaining Electronic Equipment	Servicing, repairing, calibrating, regulating, fine-tuning, or testing machines, devices, and equipment that operate primarily on the basis of electrical or electronic (not mechanical) principles.
Operating Vehicles, Mechanized Devices, or Equipme	Running, maneuvering, navigating, or driving vehicles or mechanized equipment, such as forklifts, passenger vehicles, aircraft, or water craft.
Repairing and Maintaining Mechanical Equipment	Servicing, repairing, adjusting, and testing machines, devices, moving parts, and equipment that operate primarily on the basis of mechanical (not electronic) principles.

Work_Context	Work_Context Definitions
Face-to-Face Discussions	How often do you have to have face-to-face discussions with individuals or teams in this job?
Electronic Mail	How often do you use electronic mail in this job?
Freedom to Make Decisions	How much decision making freedom, without supervision, does the job offer?
Telephone	How often do you have telephone conversations in this job?
Indoors, Environmentally Controlled	How often does this job require working indoors in environmentally controlled conditions?
Structured versus Unstructured Work	To what extent is this job structured for the worker, rather than allowing the worker to determine tasks, priorities, and goals?
Contact With Others	How much does this job require the worker to be in contact with others (face-to-face, by telephone, or otherwise) in order to perform it?
Public Speaking	How often do you have to perform public speaking in this job?
Coordinate or Lead Others	How important is it to coordinate or lead others in accomplishing work activities in this job?
Work With Work Group or Team	How important is it to work with others in a group or team in this job?
Frequency of Decision Making	How frequently is the worker required to make decisions that affect other people, the financial resources, and/or the image and reputation of the organization?
Impact of Decisions on Co-workers or Company Resul	How do the decisions an employee makes impact the results of co-workers, clients or the company?
Letters and Memos	How often does the job require written letters and memos?
Time Pressure	How often does this job require the worker to meet strict deadlines?
Physical Proximity	To what extent does this job require the worker to perform job tasks in close physical proximity to other people?
Deal With External Customers	How important is it to work with external customers or the public in this job?
Importance of Being Exact or Accurate	How important is being very exact or highly accurate in performing this job?
Level of Competition	To what extent does this job require the worker to compete or to be aware of competitive pressures?
Spend Time Sitting	How much does this job require sitting?
Responsibility for Outcomes and Results	How responsible is the worker for work outcomes and results of other workers?
Frequency of Conflict Situations	How often are there conflict situations the employee has to face in this job?
Spend Time Standing	How much does this job require standing?
Deal With Unpleasant or Angry People	How frequently does the worker have to deal with unpleasant, angry, or discourteous individuals as part of the job requirements?
Responsible for Others' Health and Safety	How much responsibility is there for the health and safety of others in this job?
Importance of Repeating Same Tasks	How important is repeating the same physical activities (e.g., key entry) or mental activities (e.g., checking entries in a ledger) over and over, without stopping, to performing this job?
Sounds, Noise Levels Are Distracting or Uncomforta	How often does this job require working exposed to sounds and noise levels that are distracting or uncomfortable?
Extremely Bright or Inadequate Lighting	How often does this job require working in extremely bright or inadequate lighting conditions?
Spend Time Using Your Hands to Handle, Control, or	How much does this job require using your hands to handle, control, or feel objects, tools or controls?
Consequence of Error	How serious would the result usually be if the worker made a mistake that was not readily correctable?
Spend Time Making Repetitive Motions	How much does this job require making repetitive motions?

Exposed to Contaminants	How often does this job require working exposed to contaminants (such as pollutants, gases, dust or odors)?
Spend Time Walking and Running	How much does this job require walking and running?
Outdoors, Exposed to Weather	How often does this job require working outdoors, exposed to all weather conditions?
In an Enclosed Vehicle or Equipment	How often does this job require working in a closed vehicle or equipment (e.g., car)?
Exposed to Disease or Infections	How often does this job require exposure to disease/infections?
Degree of Automation	How automated is the job?
Cramped Work Space, Awkward Positions	How often does this job require working in cramped work spaces that requires getting into awkward positions?
Outdoors, Under Cover	How often does this job require working outdoors, under cover (e.g., structure with roof but no walls)?
Very Hot or Cold Temperatures	How often does this job require working in very hot (above 90 F degrees) or very cold (below 32 F degrees) temperatures?
Indoors, Not Environmentally Controlled	How often does this job require working indoors in non-controlled environmental conditions (e.g., warehouse without heat)?
Spend Time Bending or Twisting the Body	How much does this job require bending or twisting your body?
Exposed to Hazardous Equipment	How often does this job require exposure to hazardous equipment?
Wear Common Protective or Safety Equipment such as	How much does this job require wearing common protective or safety equipment such as safety shoes, glasses, gloves, hard hats or life jackets?
Deal With Physically Aggressive People	How frequently does this job require the worker to deal with physical aggression of violent individuals?
Spend Time Keeping or Regaining Balance	How much does this job require keeping or regaining your balance?
Exposed to Minor Burns, Cuts, Bites, or Stings	How often does this job require exposure to minor burns, cuts, bites, or stings?
Spend Time Kneeling, Crouching, Stooping, or Crawl	How much does this job require kneeling, crouching, stooping or crawling?
Exposed to Radiation	How often does this job require exposure to radiation?
Exposed to High Places	How often does this job require exposure to high places?
Exposed to Hazardous Conditions	How often does this job require exposure to hazardous conditions?
Pace Determined by Speed of Equipment	How important is it to this job that the pace is determined by the speed of equipment or machinery? (This does not refer to keeping busy at all times on this job.)
Spend Time Climbing Ladders, Scaffolds, or Poles	How much does this job require climbing ladders, scaffolds, or poles?
In an Open Vehicle or Equipment	How often does this job require working in an open vehicle or equipment (e.g., tractor)?
Wear Specialized Protective or Safety Equipment su	How much does this job require wearing specialized protective or safety equipment such as breathing apparatus, safety harness, full protection suits, or radiation protection?
Exposed to Whole Body Vibration	How often does this job require exposure to whole body vibration (e.g., operate a jackhammer)?

Job Zone Component	Job Zone Component Definitions
Title	Job Zone Five: Extensive Preparation Needed
Overall Experience	Extensive skill, knowledge, and experience are needed for these occupations. Many require more than five years of experience. For example, surgeons must complete four years of college and an additional five to seven years of specialized medical training to be able to do their job.
Job Training	Employees may need some on-the-job training, but most of these occupations assume that the person will already have the required skills, knowledge, work-related experience, and/or training.
Job Zone Examples	These occupations often involve coordinating, training, supervising, or managing the activities of others to accomplish goals. Very advanced communication and organizational skills are required. Examples include athletic trainers, lawyers, managing editors, phyicists, social psychologists, and surgeons.
SVP Range	(8.0 and above)
Education	A bachelor's degree is the minimum formal education required for these occupations. However, many also require graduate school. For example, they may require a master's degree, and some require a Ph.D., M.D., or J.D. (law degree).

Work_Styles	Work_Styles Definitions
Integrity	Job requires being honest and ethical.
Analytical Thinking	Job requires analyzing information and using logic to address work-related issues and problems.
Dependability	Job requires being reliable, responsible, and dependable, and fulfilling obligations.
Initiative	Job requires a willingness to take on responsibilities and challenges.
Innovation	Job requires creativity and alternative thinking to develop new ideas for and answers to work-related problems.
Leadership	Job requires a willingness to lead, take charge, and offer opinions and direction.
Achievement/Effort	Job requires establishing and maintaining personally challenging achievement goals and exerting effort toward mastering tasks.
Self Control	Job requires maintaining composure, keeping emotions in check, controlling anger, and avoiding aggressive behavior, even in very difficult situations.
Cooperation	Job requires being pleasant with others on the job and displaying a good-natured, cooperative attitude.
Independence	Job requires developing one's own ways of doing things, guiding oneself with little or no supervision, and depending on oneself to get things done.
Persistence	Job requires persistence in the face of obstacles.
Concern for Others	Job requires being sensitive to others' needs and feelings and being understanding and helpful on the job.
Adaptability/Flexibility	Job requires being open to change (positive or negative) and to considerable variety in the workplace.
Stress Tolerance	Job requires accepting criticism and dealing calmly and effectively with high stress situations.
Attention to Detail	Job requires being careful about detail and thorough in completing work tasks.
Social Orientation	Job requires preferring to work with others rather than alone, and being personally connected with others on the job.

25-1032.00 - Engineering Teachers, Postsecondary

Teach courses pertaining to the application of physical laws and principles of engineering for the development of machines, materials, instruments, processes, and services. Includes teachers of subjects, such as chemical, civil, electrical, industrial, mechanical, mineral, and petroleum engineering. Includes both teachers primarily engaged in teaching and those who do a combination of both teaching and research.

Tasks

1) Select and obtain materials and supplies such as textbooks and laboratory equipment.

2) Maintain regularly scheduled office hours in order to advise and assist students.

3) Prepare course materials such as syllabi, homework assignments, and handouts.

4) Evaluate and grade students' class work, laboratory work, assignments, and papers.

5) Compile, administer, and grade examinations, or assign this work to others.

6) Advise students on academic and vocational curricula, and on career issues.

7) Maintain student attendance records, grades, and other required records.

8) Initiate, facilitate, and moderate class discussions.

9) Prepare and deliver lectures to undergraduate and/or graduate students on topics such as mechanics, hydraulics, and robotics.

10) Serve on academic or administrative committees that deal with institutional policies, departmental matters, and academic issues.

11) Conduct research in a particular field of knowledge, and publish findings in professional journals, books, and/or electronic media.

12) Participate in student recruitment, registration, and placement activities.

13) Participate in campus and community events.

14) Write grant proposals to procure external research funding.

15) Supervise undergraduate and/or graduate teaching, internship, and research work.

16) Provide professional consulting services to government and/or industry.

17) Supervise students' laboratory work.

18) Compile bibliographies of specialized materials for outside reading assignments.

19) Act as advisers to student organizations.

20) Perform administrative duties such as serving as department head.

21) Plan, evaluate, and revise curricula, course content, and course materials and methods of instruction.

22) Keep abreast of developments in their field by reading current literature, talking with colleagues, and participating in professional conferences.

Knowledge	Knowledge Definitions
Mathematics	Knowledge of arithmetic, algebra, geometry, calculus, statistics, and their applications.
Engineering and Technology	Knowledge of the practical application of engineering science and technology. This includes applying principles, techniques, procedures, and equipment to the design and production of various goods and services.
English Language	Knowledge of the structure and content of the English language including the meaning and spelling of words, rules of composition, and grammar.
Education and Training	Knowledge of principles and methods for curriculum and training design, teaching and instruction for individuals and groups, and the measurement of training effects.
Physics	Knowledge and prediction of physical principles, laws, their interrelationships, and applications to understanding fluid, material, and atmospheric dynamics, and mechanical, electrical, atomic and sub-atomic structures and processes.
Design	Knowledge of design techniques, tools, and principles involved in production of precision technical plans, blueprints, drawings, and models.
Computers and Electronics	Knowledge of circuit boards, processors, chips, electronic equipment, and computer hardware and software, including applications and programming.
Mechanical	Knowledge of machines and tools, including their designs, uses, repair, and maintenance.
Telecommunications	Knowledge of transmission, broadcasting, switching, control, and operation of telecommunications systems.
Communications and Media	Knowledge of media production, communication, and dissemination techniques and methods. This includes alternative ways to inform and entertain via written, oral, and visual media.
Chemistry	Knowledge of the chemical composition, structure, and properties of substances and of the chemical processes and transformations that they undergo. This includes uses of chemicals and their interactions, danger signs, production techniques, and disposal methods.
Administration and Management	Knowledge of business and management principles involved in strategic planning, resource allocation, human resources modeling, leadership technique, production methods, and coordination of people and resources.
Personnel and Human Resources	Knowledge of principles and procedures for personnel recruitment, selection, training, compensation and benefits, labor relations and negotiation, and personnel information systems.
Clerical	Knowledge of administrative and clerical procedures and systems such as word processing, managing files and records, stenography and transcription, designing forms, and other office procedures and terminology.
Customer and Personal Service	Knowledge of principles and processes for providing customer and personal services. This includes customer needs assessment, meeting quality standards for services, and evaluation of customer satisfaction.
Public Safety and Security	Knowledge of relevant equipment, policies, procedures, and strategies to promote effective local, state, or national security operations for the protection of people, data, property, and institutions.
Biology	Knowledge of plant and animal organisms, their tissues, cells, functions, interdependencies, and interactions with each other and the environment.
Building and Construction	Knowledge of materials, methods, and the tools involved in the construction or repair of houses, buildings, or other structures such as highways and roads.
Economics and Accounting	Knowledge of economic and accounting principles and practices, the financial markets, banking and the analysis and reporting of financial data.
Production and Processing	Knowledge of raw materials, production processes, quality control, costs, and other techniques for maximizing the effective manufacture and distribution of goods.
Psychology	Knowledge of human behavior and performance; individual differences in ability, personality, and interests; learning and motivation; psychological research methods; and the assessment and treatment of behavioral and affective disorders.
Law and Government	Knowledge of laws, legal codes, court procedures, precedents, government regulations, executive orders, agency rules, and the democratic political process.
Sales and Marketing	Knowledge of principles and methods for showing, promoting, and selling products or services. This includes marketing strategy and tactics, product demonstration, sales techniques, and sales control systems.
Geography	Knowledge of principles and methods for describing the features of land, sea, and air masses, including their physical characteristics, locations, interrelationships, and distribution of plant, animal, and human life.
Sociology and Anthropology	Knowledge of group behavior and dynamics, societal trends and influences, human migrations, ethnicity, cultures and their history and origins.
Therapy and Counseling	Knowledge of principles, methods, and procedures for diagnosis, treatment, and rehabilitation of physical and mental dysfunctions, and for career counseling and guidance.
Transportation	Knowledge of principles and methods for moving people or goods by air, rail, sea, or road, including the relative costs and benefits.
History and Archeology	Knowledge of historical events and their causes, indicators, and effects on civilizations and cultures.
Philosophy and Theology	Knowledge of different philosophical systems and religions. This includes their basic principles, values, ethics, ways of thinking, customs, practices, and their impact on human culture.
Medicine and Dentistry	Knowledge of the information and techniques needed to diagnose and treat human injuries, diseases, and deformities. This includes symptoms, treatment alternatives, drug properties and interactions, and preventive health-care measures.
Foreign Language	Knowledge of the structure and content of a foreign (non-English) language including the meaning and spelling of words, rules of composition and grammar, and pronunciation.
Fine Arts	Knowledge of the theory and techniques required to compose, produce, and perform works of music, dance, visual arts, drama, and sculpture.
Food Production	Knowledge of techniques and equipment for planting, growing, and harvesting food products (both plant and animal) for consumption, including storage/handling techniques.

Skills	Skills Definitions
Critical Thinking	Using logic and reasoning to identify the strengths and weaknesses of alternative solutions, conclusions or approaches to problems.
Active Learning	Understanding the implications of new information for both current and future problem-solving and decision-making.
Mathematics	Using mathematics to solve problems.
Speaking	Talking to others to convey information effectively.
Science	Using scientific rules and methods to solve problems.
Complex Problem Solving	Identifying complex problems and reviewing related information to develop and evaluate options and implement solutions.
Writing	Communicating effectively in writing as appropriate for the needs of the audience.
Reading Comprehension	Understanding written sentences and paragraphs in work related documents.
Instructing	Teaching others how to do something.
Active Listening	Giving full attention to what other people are saying, taking time to understand the points being made, asking questions as appropriate, and not interrupting at inappropriate times.
Learning Strategies	Selecting and using training/instructional methods and procedures appropriate for the situation when learning or teaching new things.
Time Management	Managing one's own time and the time of others.
Monitoring	Monitoring/Assessing performance of yourself, other individuals, or organizations to make improvements or take corrective action.
Technology Design	Generating or adapting equipment and technology to serve user needs.
Judgment and Decision Making	Considering the relative costs and benefits of potential actions to choose the most appropriate one.
Social Perceptiveness	Being aware of others' reactions and understanding why they react as they do.

Coordination	Adjusting actions in relation to others' actions.
Persuasion	Persuading others to change their minds or behavior.
Programming	Writing computer programs for various purposes.
Operations Analysis	Analyzing needs and product requirements to create a design.
Equipment Selection	Determining the kind of tools and equipment needed to do a job.
Service Orientation	Actively looking for ways to help people.
Management of Financial Resources	Determining how money will be spent to get the work done, and accounting for these expenditures.
Management of Personnel Resources	Motivating, developing, and directing people as they work, identifying the best people for the job.
Systems Evaluation	Identifying measures or indicators of system performance and the actions needed to improve or correct performance, relative to the goals of the system.
Negotiation	Bringing others together and trying to reconcile differences.
Systems Analysis	Determining how a system should work and how changes in conditions, operations, and the environment will affect outcomes.
Management of Material Resources	Obtaining and seeing to the appropriate use of equipment, facilities, and materials needed to do certain work.
Quality Control Analysis	Conducting tests and inspections of products, services, or processes to evaluate quality or performance.
Troubleshooting	Determining causes of operating errors and deciding what to do about it.
Installation	Installing equipment, machines, wiring, or programs to meet specifications.
Operation Monitoring	Watching gauges, dials, or other indicators to make sure a machine is working properly.
Operation and Control	Controlling operations of equipment or systems.
Equipment Maintenance	Performing routine maintenance on equipment and determining when and what kind of maintenance is needed.
Repairing	Repairing machines or systems using the needed tools.

Ability	Ability Definitions
Oral Expression	The ability to communicate information and ideas in speaking so others will understand.
Oral Comprehension	The ability to listen to and understand information and ideas presented through spoken words and sentences.
Written Comprehension	The ability to read and understand information and ideas presented in writing.
Speech Clarity	The ability to speak clearly so others can understand you.
Written Expression	The ability to communicate information and ideas in writing so others will understand.
Originality	The ability to come up with unusual or clever ideas about a given topic or situation, or to develop creative ways to solve a problem.
Mathematical Reasoning	The ability to choose the right mathematical methods or formulas to solve a problem.
Inductive Reasoning	The ability to combine pieces of information to form general rules or conclusions (includes finding a relationship among seemingly unrelated events).
Speech Recognition	The ability to identify and understand the speech of another person.
Deductive Reasoning	The ability to apply general rules to specific problems to produce answers that make sense.
Problem Sensitivity	The ability to tell when something is wrong or is likely to go wrong. It does not involve solving the problem, only recognizing there is a problem.
Information Ordering	The ability to arrange things or actions in a certain order or pattern according to a specific rule or set of rules (e.g., patterns of numbers, letters, words, pictures, mathematical operations).
Category Flexibility	The ability to generate or use different sets of rules for combining or grouping things in different ways.
Number Facility	The ability to add, subtract, multiply, or divide quickly and correctly.
Near Vision	The ability to see details at close range (within a few feet of the observer).
Fluency of Ideas	The ability to come up with a number of ideas about a topic (the number of ideas is important, not their quality, correctness, or creativity).
Selective Attention	The ability to concentrate on a task over a period of time without being distracted.
Memorization	The ability to remember information such as words, numbers, pictures, and procedures.
Flexibility of Closure	The ability to identify or detect a known pattern (a figure, object, word, or sound) that is hidden in other distracting material.

Time Sharing	The ability to shift back and forth between two or more activities or sources of information (such as speech, sounds, touch, or other sources).
Far Vision	The ability to see details at a distance.
Visualization	The ability to imagine how something will look after it is moved around or when its parts are moved or rearranged.
Finger Dexterity	The ability to make precisely coordinated movements of the fingers of one or both hands to grasp, manipulate, or assemble very small objects.
Speed of Closure	The ability to quickly make sense of, combine, and organize information into meaningful patterns.
Auditory Attention	The ability to focus on a single source of sound in the presence of other distracting sounds.
Perceptual Speed	The ability to quickly and accurately compare similarities and differences among sets of letters, numbers, objects, pictures, or patterns. The things to be compared may be presented at the same time or one after the other. This ability also includes comparing a presented object with a remembered object.
Visual Color Discrimination	The ability to match or detect differences between colors, including shades of color and brightness.
Hearing Sensitivity	The ability to detect or tell the differences between sounds that vary in pitch and loudness.
Depth Perception	The ability to judge which of several objects is closer or farther away from you, or to judge the distance between you and an object.
Trunk Strength	The ability to use your abdominal and lower back muscles to support part of the body repeatedly or continuously over time without 'giving out' or fatiguing.
Gross Body Coordination	The ability to coordinate the movement of your arms, legs, and torso together when the whole body is in motion.
Control Precision	The ability to quickly and repeatedly adjust the controls of a machine or a vehicle to exact positions.
Reaction Time	The ability to quickly respond (with the hand, finger, or foot) to a signal (sound, light, picture) when it appears.
Wrist-Finger Speed	The ability to make fast, simple, repeated movements of the fingers, hands, and wrists.
Speed of Limb Movement	The ability to quickly move the arms and legs.
Static Strength	The ability to exert maximum muscle force to lift, push, pull, or carry objects.
Explosive Strength	The ability to use short bursts of muscle force to propel oneself (as in jumping or sprinting), or to throw an object.
Dynamic Strength	The ability to exert muscle force repeatedly or continuously over time. This involves muscular endurance and resistance to muscle fatigue.
Stamina	The ability to exert yourself physically over long periods of time without getting winded or out of breath.
Dynamic Flexibility	The ability to quickly and repeatedly bend, stretch, twist, or reach out with your body, arms, and/or legs.
Gross Body Equilibrium	The ability to keep or regain your body balance or stay upright when in an unstable position.
Night Vision	The ability to see under low light conditions.
Extent Flexibility	The ability to bend, stretch, twist, or reach with your body, arms, and/or legs.
Rate Control	The ability to time your movements or the movement of a piece of equipment in anticipation of changes in the speed and/or direction of a moving object or scene.
Multilimb Coordination	The ability to coordinate two or more limbs (for example, two arms, two legs, or one leg and one arm) while sitting, standing, or lying down. It does not involve performing the activities while the whole body is in motion.
Sound Localization	The ability to tell the direction from which a sound originated.
Spatial Orientation	The ability to know your location in relation to the environment or to know where other objects are in relation to you.
Arm-Hand Steadiness	The ability to keep your hand and arm steady while moving your arm or while holding your arm and hand in one position.
Glare Sensitivity	The ability to see objects in the presence of glare or bright lighting.
Peripheral Vision	The ability to see objects or movement of objects to one's side when the eyes are looking ahead.
Manual Dexterity	The ability to quickly move your hand, your hand together with your arm, or your two hands to grasp, manipulate, or assemble objects.
Response Orientation	The ability to choose quickly between two or more movements in response to two or more different signals (lights, sounds, pictures). It includes the speed with which the correct response is started with the hand, foot, or other body part.

Work_Activity	Work_Activity Definitions
Training and Teaching Others	Identifying the educational needs of others, developing formal educational or training programs or classes, and teaching or instructing others.
Interacting With Computers	Using computers and computer systems (including hardware and software) to program, write software, set up functions, enter data, or process information.
Thinking Creatively	Developing, designing, or creating new applications, ideas, relationships, systems, or products, including artistic contributions.
Getting Information	Observing, receiving, and otherwise obtaining information from all relevant sources.
Interpreting the Meaning of Information for Others	Translating or explaining what information means and how it can be used.
Updating and Using Relevant Knowledge	Keeping up-to-date technically and applying new knowledge to your job.
Analyzing Data or Information	Identifying the underlying principles, reasons, or facts of information by breaking down information or data into separate parts.
Making Decisions and Solving Problems	Analyzing information and evaluating results to choose the best solution and solve problems.
Coaching and Developing Others	Identifying the developmental needs of others and coaching, mentoring, or otherwise helping others to improve their knowledge or skills.
Identifying Objects, Actions, and Events	Identifying information by categorizing, estimating, recognizing differences or similarities, and detecting changes in circumstances or events.
Organizing, Planning, and Prioritizing Work	Developing specific goals and plans to prioritize, organize, and accomplish your work.
Processing Information	Compiling, coding, categorizing, calculating, tabulating, auditing, or verifying information or data.
Provide Consultation and Advice to Others	Providing guidance and expert advice to management or other groups on technical, systems-, or process-related topics.
Estimating the Quantifiable Characteristics of Pro	Estimating sizes, distances, and quantities; or determining time, costs, resources, or materials needed to perform a work activity.
Communicating with Supervisors, Peers, or Subordin	Providing information to supervisors, co-workers, and subordinates by telephone, in written form, e-mail, or in person.
Monitor Processes, Materials, or Surroundings	Monitoring and reviewing information from materials, events, or the environment, to detect or assess problems.
Judging the Qualities of Things, Services, or Peop	Assessing the value, importance, or quality of things or people.
Documenting/Recording Information	Entering, transcribing, recording, storing, or maintaining information in written or electronic/magnetic form.
Guiding, Directing, and Motivating Subordinates	Providing guidance and direction to subordinates, including setting performance standards and monitoring performance.
Establishing and Maintaining Interpersonal Relatio	Developing constructive and cooperative working relationships with others, and maintaining them over time.
Communicating with Persons Outside Organization	Communicating with people outside the organization, representing the organization to customers, the public, government, and other external sources. This information can be exchanged in person, in writing, or by telephone or e-mail.
Developing Objectives and Strategies	Establishing long-range objectives and specifying the strategies and actions to achieve them.
Scheduling Work and Activities	Scheduling events, programs, and activities, as well as the work of others.
Developing and Building Teams	Encouraging and building mutual trust, respect, and cooperation among team members.
Coordinating the Work and Activities of Others	Getting members of a group to work together to accomplish tasks.
Evaluating Information to Determine Compliance wit	Using relevant information and individual judgment to determine whether events or processes comply with laws, regulations, or standards.
Performing Administrative Activities	Performing day-to-day administrative tasks such as maintaining information files and processing paperwork.
Inspecting Equipment, Structures, or Material	Inspecting equipment, structures, or materials to identify the cause of errors or other problems or defects.
Resolving Conflicts and Negotiating with Others	Handling complaints, settling disputes, and resolving grievances and conflicts, or otherwise negotiating with others.
Assisting and Caring for Others	Providing personal assistance, medical attention, emotional support, or other personal care to others such as coworkers, customers, or patients.
Selling or Influencing Others	Convincing others to buy merchandise/goods or to otherwise change their minds or actions.
Performing for or Working Directly with the Public	Performing for people or dealing directly with the public. This includes serving customers in restaurants and stores, and receiving clients or guests.
Monitoring and Controlling Resources	Monitoring and controlling resources and overseeing the spending of money.
Drafting, Laying Out, and Specifying Technical Dev	Providing documentation, detailed instructions, drawings, or specifications to tell others about how devices, parts, equipment, or structures are to be fabricated, constructed, assembled, modified, maintained, or used.
Controlling Machines and Processes	Using either control mechanisms or direct physical activity to operate machines or processes (not including computers or vehicles).
Performing General Physical Activities	Performing physical activities that require considerable use of your arms and legs and moving your whole body, such as climbing, lifting, balancing, walking, stooping, and handling of materials.
Staffing Organizational Units	Recruiting, interviewing, selecting, hiring, and promoting employees in an organization.
Repairing and Maintaining Electronic Equipment	Servicing, repairing, calibrating, regulating, fine-tuning, or testing machines, devices, and equipment that operate primarily on the basis of electrical or electronic (not mechanical) principles.
Repairing and Maintaining Mechanical Equipment	Servicing, repairing, adjusting, and testing machines, devices, moving parts, and equipment that operate primarily on the basis of mechanical (not electronic) principles.
Handling and Moving Objects	Using hands and arms in handling, installing, positioning, and moving materials, and manipulating things.
Operating Vehicles, Mechanized Devices, or Equipme	Running, maneuvering, navigating, or driving vehicles or mechanized equipment, such as forklifts, passenger vehicles, aircraft, or water craft.

Work_Context	Work_Context Definitions
Electronic Mail	How often do you use electronic mail in this job?
Face-to-Face Discussions	How often do you have to have face-to-face discussions with individuals or teams in this job?
Freedom to Make Decisions	How much decision making freedom, without supervision, does the job offer?
Telephone	How often do you have telephone conversations in this job?
Structured versus Unstructured Work	To what extent is this job structured for the worker, rather than allowing the worker to determine tasks, priorities, and goals?
Indoors, Environmentally Controlled	How often does this job require working indoors in environmentally controlled conditions?
Public Speaking	How often do you have to perform public speaking in this job?
Contact With Others	How much does this job require the worker to be in contact with others (face-to-face, by telephone, or otherwise) in order to perform it?
Work With Work Group or Team	How important is it to work with others in a group or team in this job?
Importance of Being Exact or Accurate	How important is being very exact or highly accurate in performing this job?
Responsibility for Outcomes and Results	How responsible is the worker for work outcomes and results of other workers?
Spend Time Sitting	How much does this job require sitting?
Letters and Memos	How often does the job require written letters and memos?
Impact of Decisions on Co-workers or Company Resul	How do the decisions an employee makes impact the results of co-workers, clients or the company?
Level of Competition	To what extent does this job require the worker to compete or to be aware of competitive pressures?
Coordinate or Lead Others	How important is it to coordinate or lead others in accomplishing work activities in this job?
Time Pressure	How often does this job require the worker to meet strict deadlines?
Frequency of Decision Making	How frequently is the worker required to make decisions that affect other people, the financial resources, and/or the image and reputation of the organization?
Deal With External Customers	How important is it to work with external customers or the public in this job?
Frequency of Conflict Situations	How often are there conflict situations the employee has to face in this job?
Physical Proximity	To what extent does this job require the worker to perform job tasks in close physical proximity to other people?
Responsible for Others' Health and Safety	How much responsibility is there for the health and safety of others in this job?
Consequence of Error	How serious would the result usually be if the worker made a mistake that was not readily correctable?

Importance of Repeating Same Tasks	How important is repeating the same physical activities (e.g., key entry) or mental activities (e.g., checking entries in a ledger) over and over, without stopping, to performing this job?
Deal With Unpleasant or Angry People	How frequently does the worker have to deal with unpleasant, angry, or discourteous individuals as part of the job requirements?
Spend Time Standing	How much does this job require standing?
Spend Time Making Repetitive Motions	How much does this job require making repetitive motions?
Spend Time Using Your Hands to Handle, Control, or	How much does this job require using your hands to handle, control, or feel objects, tools or controls?
Sounds, Noise Levels Are Distracting or Uncomforta	How often does this job require working exposed to sounds and noise levels that are distracting or uncomfortable?
Exposed to Hazardous Conditions	How often does this job require exposure to hazardous conditions?
Wear Common Protective or Safety Equipment such as	How much does this job require wearing common protective or safety equipment such as safety shoes, glasses, gloves, hard hats or live jackets?
Spend Time Walking and Running	How much does this job require walking and running?
Exposed to Contaminants	How often does this job require working exposed to contaminants (such as pollutants, gases, dust or odors)?
Degree of Automation	How automated is the job?
Exposed to Hazardous Equipment	How often does this job require exposure to hazardous equipment?
In an Enclosed Vehicle or Equipment	How often does this job require working in a closed vehicle or equipment (e.g., car)?
Indoors, Not Environmentally Controlled	How often does this job require working indoors in non-controlled environmental conditions (e.g., warehouse without heat)?
Exposed to Minor Burns, Cuts, Bites, or Stings	How often does this job require exposure to minor burns, cuts, bites, or stings?
Outdoors, Exposed to Weather	How often does this job require working outdoors, exposed to all weather conditions?
Very Hot or Cold Temperatures	How often does this job require working in very hot (above 90 F degrees) or very cold (below 32 F degrees) temperatures?
Extremely Bright or Inadequate Lighting	How often does this job require working in extremely bright or inadequate lighting conditions?
Exposed to Disease or Infections	How often does this job require exposure to disease/infections?
Cramped Work Space, Awkward Positions	How often does this job require working in cramped work spaces that requires getting into awkward positions?
Spend Time Bending or Twisting the Body	How much does this job require bending or twisting your body?
Exposed to Radiation	How often does this job require exposure to radiation?
Spend Time Kneeling, Crouching, Stooping, or Crawl	How much does this job require kneeling, crouching, stooping or crawling?
Outdoors, Under Cover	How often does this job require working outdoors, under cover (e.g., structure with roof but no walls)?
Deal With Physically Aggressive People	How frequently does this job require the worker to deal with physical aggression of violent individuals?
Wear Specialized Protective or Safety Equipment su	How much does this job require wearing specialized protective or safety equipment such as breathing apparatus, safety harness, full protection suits, or radiation protection?
Spend Time Keeping or Regaining Balance	How much does this job require keeping or regaining your balance?
Pace Determined by Speed of Equipment	How important is it to this job that the pace is determined by the speed of equipment or machinery? (This does not refer to keeping busy at all times on this job.)
Spend Time Climbing Ladders, Scaffolds, or Poles	How much does this job require climbing ladders, scaffolds, or poles?
Exposed to Whole Body Vibration	How often does this job require exposure to whole body vibration (e.g., operate a jackhammer)?
Exposed to High Places	How often does this job require exposure to high places?
In an Open Vehicle or Equipment	How often does this job require working in an open vehicle or equipment (e.g., tractor)?

Job Zone Component	Job Zone Component Definitions
Title	Job Zone Five: Extensive Preparation Needed

Overall Experience	Extensive skill, knowledge, and experience are needed for these occupations. Many require more than five years of experience. For example, surgeons must complete four years of college and an additional five to seven years of specialized medical training to be able to do their job.
Job Training	Employees may need some on-the-job training, but most of these occupations assume that the person will already have the required skills, knowledge, work-related experience, and/or training.
Job Zone Examples	These occupations often involve coordinating, training, supervising, or managing the activities of others to accomplish goals. Very advanced communication and organizational skills are required. Examples include athletic trainers, lawyers, managing editors, phyicists, social psychologists, and surgeons.
SVP Range	(8.0 and above)
Education	A bachelor's degree is the minimum formal education required for these occupations. However, many also require graduate school. For example, they may require a master's degree, and some require a Ph.D., M.D., or J.D. (law degree).

Work_Styles	Work_Styles Definitions
Analytical Thinking	Job requires analyzing information and using logic to address work-related issues and problems.
Achievement/Effort	Job requires establishing and maintaining personally challenging achievement goals and exerting effort toward mastering tasks.
Initiative	Job requires a willingness to take on responsibilities and challenges.
Integrity	Job requires being honest and ethical.
Independence	Job requires developing one's own ways of doing things, guiding oneself with little or no supervision, and depending on oneself to get things done.
Persistence	Job requires persistence in the face of obstacles.
Leadership	Job requires a willingness to lead, take charge, and offer opinions and direction.
Innovation	Job requires creativity and alternative thinking to develop new ideas for and answers to work-related problems.
Dependability	Job requires being reliable, responsible, and dependable, and fulfilling obligations.
Attention to Detail	Job requires being careful about detail and thorough in completing work tasks.
Self Control	Job requires maintaining composure, keeping emotions in check, controlling anger, and avoiding aggressive behavior, even in very difficult situations.
Stress Tolerance	Job requires accepting criticism and dealing calmly and effectively with high stress situations.
Cooperation	Job requires being pleasant with others on the job and displaying a good-natured, cooperative attitude.
Adaptability/Flexibility	Job requires being open to change (positive or negative) and to considerable variety in the workplace.
Concern for Others	Job requires being sensitive to others' needs and feelings and being understanding and helpful on the job.
Social Orientation	Job requires preferring to work with others rather than alone, and being personally connected with others on the job.

25-1041.00 - Agricultural Sciences Teachers, Postsecondary

Teach courses in the agricultural sciences. Includes teachers of agronomy, dairy sciences, fisheries management, horticultural sciences, poultry sciences, range management, and agricultural soil conservation.

Tasks

1) Collaborate with colleagues to address teaching and research issues.

2) Plan, evaluate, and revise curricula, course content, and course materials and methods of instruction.

3) Participate in campus and community events.

4) Initiate, facilitate, and moderate classroom discussions.

5) Advise students on academic and vocational curricula, and on career issues.

6) Evaluate and grade students' class work, laboratory work, assignments, and papers.

7) Serve on academic or administrative committees that deal with institutional policies, departmental matters, and academic issues.

8) Select and obtain materials and supplies such as textbooks and laboratory equipment.

9) Maintain student attendance records, grades, and other required records.

10) Compile, administer, and grade examinations, or assign this work to others.

11) Supervise laboratory sessions and field work, and coordinate laboratory operations.

12) Participate in student recruitment, registration, and placement activities.

13) Maintain regularly scheduled office hours in order to advise and assist students.

14) Supervise undergraduate and/or graduate teaching, internship, and research work.

15) Write grant proposals to procure external research funding.

16) Conduct research in a particular field of knowledge, and publish findings in professional journals, books, and/or electronic media.

17) Prepare and deliver lectures to undergraduate and/or graduate students on topics such as crop production, plant genetics, and soil chemistry.

18) Act as advisers to student organizations.

19) Compile bibliographies of specialized materials for outside reading assignments.

20) Provide professional consulting services to government and/or industry.

21) Perform administrative duties such as serving as department head.

22) Keep abreast of developments in their field by reading current literature, talking with colleagues, and participating in professional conferences.

Knowledge	Knowledge Definitions
Education and Training	Knowledge of principles and methods for curriculum and training design, teaching and instruction for individuals and groups, and the measurement of training effects.
English Language	Knowledge of the structure and content of the English language including the meaning and spelling of words, rules of composition, and grammar.
Biology	Knowledge of plant and animal organisms, their tissues, cells, functions, interdependencies, and interactions with each other and the environment.
Mathematics	Knowledge of arithmetic, algebra, geometry, calculus, statistics, and their applications.
Computers and Electronics	Knowledge of circuit boards, processors, chips, electronic equipment, and computer hardware and software, including applications and programming.
Communications and Media	Knowledge of media production, communication, and dissemination techniques and methods. This includes alternative ways to inform and entertain via written, oral, and visual media.
Administration and Management	Knowledge of business and management principles involved in strategic planning, resource allocation, human resources modeling, leadership technique, production methods, and coordination of people and resources.
Chemistry	Knowledge of the chemical composition, structure, and properties of substances and of the chemical processes and transformations that they undergo. This includes uses of chemicals and their interactions, danger signs, production techniques, and disposal methods.
Food Production	Knowledge of techniques and equipment for planting, growing, and harvesting food products (both plant and animal) for consumption, including storage/handling techniques.
Personnel and Human Resources	Knowledge of principles and procedures for personnel recruitment, selection, training, compensation and benefits, labor relations and negotiation, and personnel information systems.
Customer and Personal Service	Knowledge of principles and processes for providing customer and personal services. This includes customer needs assessment, meeting quality standards for services, and evaluation of customer satisfaction.
Geography	Knowledge of principles and methods for describing the features of land, sea, and air masses, including their physical characteristics, locations, interrelationships, and distribution of plant, animal, and human life.
Clerical	Knowledge of administrative and clerical procedures and systems such as word processing, managing files and records, stenography and transcription, designing forms, and other office procedures and terminology.

Psychology	Knowledge of human behavior and performance; individual differences in ability, personality, and interests; learning and motivation; psychological research methods; and the assessment and treatment of behavioral and affective disorders.
Public Safety and Security	Knowledge of relevant equipment, policies, procedures, and strategies to promote effective local, state, or national security operations for the protection of people, data, property, and institutions.
Engineering and Technology	Knowledge of the practical application of engineering science and technology. This includes applying principles, techniques, procedures, and equipment to the design and production of various goods and services.
Law and Government	Knowledge of laws, legal codes, court procedures, precedents, government regulations, executive orders, agency rules, and the democratic political process.
Mechanical	Knowledge of machines and tools, including their designs, uses, repair, and maintenance.
Physics	Knowledge and prediction of physical principles, laws, their interrelationships, and applications to understanding fluid, material, and atmospheric dynamics, and mechanical, electrical, atomic and sub-atomic structures and processes.
Sales and Marketing	Knowledge of principles and methods for showing, promoting, and selling products or services. This includes marketing strategy and tactics, product demonstration, sales techniques, and sales control systems.
Economics and Accounting	Knowledge of economic and accounting principles and practices, the financial markets, banking and the analysis and reporting of financial data.
Production and Processing	Knowledge of raw materials, production processes, quality control, costs, and other techniques for maximizing the effective manufacture and distribution of goods.
Sociology and Anthropology	Knowledge of group behavior and dynamics, societal trends and influences, human migrations, ethnicity, cultures and their history and origins.
Telecommunications	Knowledge of transmission, broadcasting, switching, control, and operation of telecommunications systems.
Design	Knowledge of design techniques, tools, and principles involved in production of precision technical plans, blueprints, drawings, and models.
Transportation	Knowledge of principles and methods for moving people or goods by air, rail, sea, or road, including the relative costs and benefits.
Therapy and Counseling	Knowledge of principles, methods, and procedures for diagnosis, treatment, and rehabilitation of physical and mental dysfunctions, and for career counseling and guidance.
History and Archeology	Knowledge of historical events and their causes, indicators, and effects on civilizations and cultures.
Building and Construction	Knowledge of materials, methods, and the tools involved in the construction or repair of houses, buildings, or other structures such as highways and roads.
Philosophy and Theology	Knowledge of different philosophical systems and religions. This includes their basic principles, values, ethics, ways of thinking, customs, practices, and their impact on human culture.
Foreign Language	Knowledge of the structure and content of a foreign (non-English) language including the meaning and spelling of words, rules of composition and grammar, and pronunciation.
Medicine and Dentistry	Knowledge of the information and techniques needed to diagnose and treat human injuries, diseases, and deformities. This includes symptoms, treatment alternatives, drug properties and interactions, and preventive health-care measures.
Fine Arts	Knowledge of the theory and techniques required to compose, produce, and perform works of music, dance, visual arts, drama, and sculpture.

Skills	Skills Definitions
Instructing	Teaching others how to do something.
Reading Comprehension	Understanding written sentences and paragraphs in work related documents.
Writing	Communicating effectively in writing as appropriate for the needs of the audience.
Science	Using scientific rules and methods to solve problems.
Critical Thinking	Using logic and reasoning to identify the strengths and weaknesses of alternative solutions, conclusions or approaches to problems.
Speaking	Talking to others to convey information effectively.

Active Listening	Giving full attention to what other people are saying, taking time to understand the points being made, asking questions as appropriate, and not interrupting at inappropriate times.
Active Learning	Understanding the implications of new information for both current and future problem-solving and decision-making.
Learning Strategies	Selecting and using training/instructional methods and procedures appropriate for the situation when learning or teaching new things.
Time Management	Managing one's own time and the time of others.
Complex Problem Solving	Identifying complex problems and reviewing related information to develop and evaluate options and implement solutions.
Coordination	Adjusting actions in relation to others' actions.
Judgment and Decision Making	Considering the relative costs and benefits of potential actions to choose the most appropriate one.
Monitoring	Monitoring/Assessing performance of yourself, other individuals, or organizations to make improvements or take corrective action.
Mathematics	Using mathematics to solve problems.
Social Perceptiveness	Being aware of others' reactions and understanding why they react as they do.
Equipment Selection	Determining the kind of tools and equipment needed to do a job.
Service Orientation	Actively looking for ways to help people.
Management of Financial Resources	Determining how money will be spent to get the work done, and accounting for these expenditures.
Management of Personnel Resources	Motivating, developing, and directing people as they work, identifying the best people for the job.
Persuasion	Persuading others to change their minds or behavior.
Negotiation	Bringing others together and trying to reconcile differences.
Troubleshooting	Determining causes of operating errors and deciding what to do about it.
Management of Material Resources	Obtaining and seeing to the appropriate use of equipment, facilities, and materials needed to do certain work.
Operations Analysis	Analyzing needs and product requirements to create a design.
Quality Control Analysis	Conducting tests and inspections of products, services, or processes to evaluate quality or performance.
Systems Evaluation	Identifying measures or indicators of system performance and the actions needed to improve or correct performance, relative to the goals of the system.
Systems Analysis	Determining how a system should work and how changes in conditions, operations, and the environment will affect outcomes.
Technology Design	Generating or adapting equipment and technology to serve user needs.
Equipment Maintenance	Performing routine maintenance on equipment and determining when and what kind of maintenance is needed.
Operation and Control	Controlling operations of equipment or systems.
Installation	Installing equipment, machines, wiring, or programs to meet specifications.
Operation Monitoring	Watching gauges, dials, or other indicators to make sure a machine is working properly.
Repairing	Repairing machines or systems using the needed tools.
Programming	Writing computer programs for various purposes.

Ability	Ability Definitions
Oral Expression	The ability to communicate information and ideas in speaking so others will understand.
Speech Clarity	The ability to speak clearly so others can understand you.
Written Expression	The ability to communicate information and ideas in writing so others will understand.
Written Comprehension	The ability to read and understand information and ideas presented in writing.
Oral Comprehension	The ability to listen to and understand information and ideas presented through spoken words and sentences.
Inductive Reasoning	The ability to combine pieces of information to form general rules or conclusions (includes finding a relationship among seemingly unrelated events).
Deductive Reasoning	The ability to apply general rules to specific problems to produce answers that make sense.
Speech Recognition	The ability to identify and understand the speech of another person.
Near Vision	The ability to see details at close range (within a few feet of the observer).
Problem Sensitivity	The ability to tell when something is wrong or is likely to go wrong. It does not involve solving the problem, only recognizing there is a problem.

Originality	The ability to come up with unusual or clever ideas about a given topic or situation, or to develop creative ways to solve a problem.
Fluency of Ideas	The ability to come up with a number of ideas about a topic (the number of ideas is important, not their quality, correctness, or creativity).
Information Ordering	The ability to arrange things or actions in a certain order or pattern according to a specific rule or set of rules (e.g., patterns of numbers, letters, words, pictures, mathematical operations).
Category Flexibility	The ability to generate or use different sets of rules for combining or grouping things in different ways.
Selective Attention	The ability to concentrate on a task over a period of time without being distracted.
Memorization	The ability to remember information such as words, numbers, pictures, and procedures.
Mathematical Reasoning	The ability to choose the right mathematical methods or formulas to solve a problem.
Far Vision	The ability to see details at a distance.
Flexibility of Closure	The ability to identify or detect a known pattern (a figure, object, word, or sound) that is hidden in other distracting material.
Number Facility	The ability to add, subtract, multiply, or divide quickly and correctly.
Time Sharing	The ability to shift back and forth between two or more activities or sources of information (such as speech, sounds, touch, or other sources).
Speed of Closure	The ability to quickly make sense of, combine, and organize information into meaningful patterns.
Trunk Strength	The ability to use your abdominal and lower back muscles to support part of the body repeatedly or continuously over time without 'giving out' or fatiguing.
Control Precision	The ability to quickly and repeatedly adjust the controls of a machine or a vehicle to exact positions.
Perceptual Speed	The ability to quickly and accurately compare similarities and differences among sets of letters, numbers, objects, pictures, or patterns. The things to be compared may be presented at the same time or one after the other. This ability also includes comparing a presented object with a remembered object.
Visualization	The ability to imagine how something will look after it is moved around or when its parts are moved or rearranged.
Auditory Attention	The ability to focus on a single source of sound in the presence of other distracting sounds.
Multilimb Coordination	The ability to coordinate two or more limbs (for example, two arms, two legs, or one leg and one arm) while sitting, standing, or lying down. It does not involve performing the activities while the whole body is in motion.
Depth Perception	The ability to judge which of several objects is closer or farther away from you, or to judge the distance between you and an object.
Finger Dexterity	The ability to make precisely coordinated movements of the fingers of one or both hands to grasp, manipulate, or assemble very small objects.
Hearing Sensitivity	The ability to detect or tell the differences between sounds that vary in pitch and loudness.
Visual Color Discrimination	The ability to match or detect differences between colors, including shades of color and brightness.
Wrist-Finger Speed	The ability to make fast, simple, repeated movements of the fingers, hands, and wrists.
Dynamic Strength	The ability to exert muscle force repeatedly or continuously over time. This involves muscular endurance and resistance to muscle fatigue.
Explosive Strength	The ability to use short bursts of muscle force to propel oneself (as in jumping or sprinting), or to throw an object.
Static Strength	The ability to exert maximum muscle force to lift, push, pull, or carry objects.
Speed of Limb Movement	The ability to quickly move the arms and legs.
Sound Localization	The ability to tell the direction from which a sound originated.
Gross Body Equilibrium	The ability to keep or regain your body balance or stay upright when in an unstable position.
Peripheral Vision	The ability to see objects or movement of objects to one's side when the eyes are looking ahead.
Stamina	The ability to exert yourself physically over long periods of time without getting winded or out of breath.
Reaction Time	The ability to quickly respond (with the hand, finger, or foot) to a signal (sound, light, picture) when it appears.
Dynamic Flexibility	The ability to quickly and repeatedly bend, stretch, twist, or reach out with your body, arms, and/or legs.

Gross Body Coordination	The ability to coordinate the movement of your arms, legs, and torso together when the whole body is in motion.
Rate Control	The ability to time your movements or the movement of a piece of equipment in anticipation of changes in the speed and/or direction of a moving object or scene.
Manual Dexterity	The ability to quickly move your hand, your hand together with your arm, or your two hands to grasp, manipulate, or assemble objects.
Response Orientation	The ability to choose quickly between two or more movements in response to two or more different signals (lights, sounds, pictures). It includes the speed with which the correct response is started with the hand, foot, or other body part.
Night Vision	The ability to see under low light conditions.
Spatial Orientation	The ability to know your location in relation to the environment or to know where other objects are in relation to you.
Glare Sensitivity	The ability to see objects in the presence of glare or bright lighting.
Arm-Hand Steadiness	The ability to keep your hand and arm steady while moving your arm or while holding your arm and hand in one position.
Extent Flexibility	The ability to bend, stretch, twist, or reach with your body, arms, and/or legs.

Work_Activity	Work_Activity Definitions
Updating and Using Relevant Knowledge	Keeping up-to-date technically and applying new knowledge to your job.
Analyzing Data or Information	Identifying the underlying principles, reasons, or facts of information by breaking down information or data into separate parts.
Making Decisions and Solving Problems	Analyzing information and evaluating results to choose the best solution and solve problems.
Interacting With Computers	Using computers and computer systems (including hardware and software) to program, write software, set up functions, enter data, or process information.
Thinking Creatively	Developing, designing, or creating new applications, ideas, relationships, systems, or products, including artistic contributions.
Getting Information	Observing, receiving, and otherwise obtaining information from all relevant sources.
Interpreting the Meaning of Information for Others	Translating or explaining what information means and how it can be used.
Communicating with Supervisors, Peers, or Subordin	Providing information to supervisors, co-workers, and subordinates by telephone, in written form, e-mail, or in person.
Training and Teaching Others	Identifying the educational needs of others, developing formal educational or training programs or classes, and teaching or instructing others.
Organizing, Planning, and Prioritizing Work	Developing specific goals and plans to prioritize, organize, and accomplish your work.
Processing Information	Compiling, coding, categorizing, calculating, tabulating, auditing, or verifying information or data.
Judging the Qualities of Things, Services, or Peop	Assessing the value, importance, or quality of things or people.
Communicating with Persons Outside Organization	Communicating with people outside the organization, representing the organization to customers, the public, government, and other external sources. This information can be exchanged in person, in writing, or by telephone or e-mail.
Establishing and Maintaining Interpersonal Relatio	Developing constructive and cooperative working relationships with others, and maintaining them over time.
Coaching and Developing Others	Identifying the developmental needs of others and coaching, mentoring, or otherwise helping others to improve their knowledge or skills.
Developing Objectives and Strategies	Establishing long-range objectives and specifying the strategies and actions to achieve them.
Documenting/Recording Information	Entering, transcribing, recording, storing, or maintaining information in written or electronic/magnetic form.
Identifying Objects, Actions, and Events	Identifying information by categorizing, estimating, recognizing differences or similarities, and detecting changes in circumstances or events.
Scheduling Work and Activities	Scheduling events, programs, and activities, as well as the work of others.
Monitor Processes, Materials, or Surroundings	Monitoring and reviewing information from materials, events, or the environment, to detect or assess problems.
Guiding, Directing, and Motivating Subordinates	Providing guidance and direction to subordinates, including setting performance standards and monitoring performance.

Estimating the Quantifiable Characteristics of Pro	Estimating sizes, distances, and quantities; or determining time, costs, resources, or materials needed to perform a work activity.
Provide Consultation and Advice to Others	Providing guidance and expert advice to management or other groups on technical, systems-, or process-related topics.
Monitoring and Controlling Resources	Monitoring and controlling resources and overseeing the spending of money.
Coordinating the Work and Activities of Others	Getting members of a group to work together to accomplish tasks.
Developing and Building Teams	Encouraging and building mutual trust, respect, and cooperation among team members.
Performing for or Working Directly with the Public	Performing for people or dealing directly with the public. This includes serving customers in restaurants and stores, and receiving clients or guests.
Selling or Influencing Others	Convincing others to buy merchandise/goods or to otherwise change their minds or actions.
Evaluating Information to Determine Compliance wit	Using relevant information and individual judgment to determine whether events or processes comply with laws, regulations, or standards.
Performing Administrative Activities	Performing day-to-day administrative tasks such as maintaining information files and processing paperwork.
Inspecting Equipment, Structures, or Material	Inspecting equipment, structures, or materials to identify the cause of errors or other problems or defects.
Assisting and Caring for Others	Providing personal assistance, medical attention, emotional support, or other personal care to others such as coworkers, customers, or patients.
Staffing Organizational Units	Recruiting, interviewing, selecting, hiring, and promoting employees in an organization.
Resolving Conflicts and Negotiating with Others	Handling complaints, settling disputes, and resolving grievances and conflicts, or otherwise negotiating with others.
Controlling Machines and Processes	Using either control mechanisms or direct physical activity to operate machines or processes (not including computers or vehicles).
Performing General Physical Activities	Performing physical activities that require considerable use of your arms and legs and moving your whole body, such as climbing, lifting, balancing, walking, stooping, and handling of materials.
Operating Vehicles, Mechanized Devices, or Equipme	Running, maneuvering, navigating, or driving vehicles or mechanized equipment, such as forklifts, passenger vehicles, aircraft, or water craft.
Handling and Moving Objects	Using hands and arms in handling, installing, positioning, and moving materials, and manipulating things.
Repairing and Maintaining Electronic Equipment	Servicing, repairing, calibrating, regulating, fine-tuning, or testing machines, devices, and equipment that operate primarily on the basis of electrical or electronic (not mechanical) principles.
Drafting, Laying Out, and Specifying Technical Dev	Providing documentation, detailed instructions, drawings, or specifications to tell others about how devices, parts, equipment, or structures are to be fabricated, constructed, assembled, modified, maintained, or used.
Repairing and Maintaining Mechanical Equipment	Servicing, repairing, adjusting, and testing machines, devices, moving parts, and equipment that operate primarily on the basis of mechanical (not electronic) principles.

Work_Context	Work_Context Definitions
Face-to-Face Discussions	How often do you have to have face-to-face discussions with individuals or teams in this job?
Freedom to Make Decisions	How much decision making freedom, without supervision, does the job offer?
Telephone	How often do you have telephone conversations in this job?
Electronic Mail	How often do you use electronic mail in this job?
Structured versus Unstructured Work	To what extent is this job structured for the worker, rather than allowing the worker to determine tasks, priorities, and goals?
Contact With Others	How much does this job require the worker to be in contact with others (face-to-face, by telephone, or otherwise) in order to perform it?
Public Speaking	How often do you have to perform public speaking in this job?
Letters and Memos	How often does the job require written letters and memos?
Indoors, Environmentally Controlled	How often does this job require working indoors in environmentally controlled conditions?
Work With Work Group or Team	How important is it to work with others in a group or team in this job?
Importance of Being Exact or Accurate	How important is being very exact or highly accurate in performing this job?
Coordinate or Lead Others	How important is it to coordinate or lead others in accomplishing work activities in this job?

Time Pressure	How often does this job require the worker to meet strict deadlines?
Deal With External Customers	How important is it to work with external customers or the public in this job?
Spend Time Sitting	How much does this job require sitting?
Impact of Decisions on Co-workers or Company Resul	How do the decisions an employee makes impact the results of co-workers, clients or the company?
Responsibility for Outcomes and Results	How responsible is the worker for work outcomes and results of other workers?
Frequency of Decision Making	How frequently is the worker required to make decisions that affect other people, the financial resources, and/or the image and reputation of the organization?
Responsible for Others' Health and Safety	How much responsibility is there for the health and safety of others in this job?
Level of Competition	To what extent does this job require the worker to compete or to be aware of competitive pressures?
In an Enclosed Vehicle or Equipment	How often does this job require working in a closed vehicle or equipment (e.g., car)?
Physical Proximity	To what extent does this job require the worker to perform job tasks in close physical proximity to other people?
Outdoors, Exposed to Weather	How often does this job require working outdoors, exposed to all weather conditions?
Spend Time Standing	How much does this job require standing?
Frequency of Conflict Situations	How often are there conflict situations the employee has to face in this job?
Indoors, Not Environmentally Controlled	How often does this job require working indoors in non-controlled environmental conditions (e.g., warehouse without heat)?
Importance of Repeating Same Tasks	How important is repeating the same physical activities (e.g., key entry) or mental activities (e.g., checking entries in a ledger) over and over, without stopping, to performing this job?
Deal With Unpleasant or Angry People	How frequently does the worker have to deal with unpleasant, angry, or discourteous individuals as part of the job requirements?
Outdoors, Under Cover	How often does this job require working outdoors, under cover (e.g., structure with roof but no walls)?
Spend Time Making Repetitive Motions	How much does this job require making repetitive motions?
Sounds, Noise Levels Are Distracting or Uncomforta	How often does this job require working exposed to sounds and noise levels that are distracting or uncomfortable?
Spend Time Using Your Hands to Handle, Control, or	How much does this job require using your hands to handle, control, or feel objects, tools or controls?
Exposed to Contaminants	How often does this job require working exposed to contaminants (such as pollutants, gases, dust or odors)?
Consequence of Error	How serious would the result usually be if the worker made a mistake that was not readily correctable?
Very Hot or Cold Temperatures	How often does this job require working in very hot (above 90 F degrees) or very cold (below 32 F degrees) temperatures?
Wear Common Protective or Safety Equipment such as	How much does this job require wearing common protective or safety equipment such as safety shoes, glasses, gloves, hard hats or live jackets?
Spend Time Walking and Running	How much does this job require walking and running?
Exposed to Minor Burns, Cuts, Bites, or Stings	How often does this job require exposure to minor burns, cuts, bites, or stings?
Degree of Automation	How automated is the job?
Exposed to Hazardous Equipment	How often does this job require exposure to hazardous equipment?
In an Open Vehicle or Equipment	How often does this job require working in an open vehicle or equipment (e.g., tractor)?
Exposed to Hazardous Conditions	How often does this job require exposure to hazardous conditions?
Extremely Bright or Inadequate Lighting	How often does this job require working in extremely bright or inadequate lighting conditions?
Spend Time Bending or Twisting the Body	How much does this job require bending or twisting your body?
Exposed to Disease or Infections	How often does this job require exposure to disease/infections?
Cramped Work Space, Awkward Positions	How often does this job require working in cramped work spaces that requires getting into awkward positions?
Wear Specialized Protective or Safety Equipment su	How much does this job require wearing specialized protective or safety equipment such as breathing apparatus, safety harness, full protection suits, or radiation protection?
Spend Time Kneeling, Crouching, Stooping, or Crawl	How much does this job require kneeling, crouching, stooping or crawling?

Pace Determined by Speed of Equipment	How important is it to this job that the pace is determined by the speed of equipment or machinery? (This does not refer to keeping busy at all times on this job.)
Exposed to High Places	How often does this job require exposure to high places?
Deal With Physically Aggressive People	How frequently does this job require the worker to deal with physical aggression of violent individuals?
Spend Time Climbing Ladders, Scaffolds, or Poles	How much does this job require climbing ladders, scaffolds, or poles?
Exposed to Whole Body Vibration	How often does this job require exposure to whole body vibration (e.g., operate a jackhammer)?
Spend Time Keeping or Regaining Balance	How much does this job require keeping or regaining your balance?
Exposed to Radiation	How often does this job require exposure to radiation?

Job Zone Component	Job Zone Component Definitions
Title	Job Zone Five: Extensive Preparation Needed
Overall Experience	Extensive skill, knowledge, and experience are needed for these occupations. Many require more than five years of experience. For example, surgeons must complete four years of college and an additional five to seven years of specialized medical training to be able to do their job.
Job Training	Employees may need some on-the-job training, but most of these occupations assume that the person will already have the required skills, knowledge, work-related experience, and/or training.
Job Zone Examples	These occupations often involve coordinating, training, supervising, or managing the activities of others to accomplish goals. Very advanced communication and organizational skills are required. Examples include athletic trainers, lawyers, managing editors, phyicists, social psychologists, and surgeons.
SVP Range	(8.0 and above)
Education	A bachelor's degree is the minimum formal education required for these occupations. However, many also require graduate school. For example, they may require a master's degree, and some require a Ph.D., M.D., or J.D. (law degree).

Work_Styles	Work_Styles Definitions
Integrity	Job requires being honest and ethical.
Dependability	Job requires being reliable, responsible, and dependable, and fulfilling obligations.
Initiative	Job requires a willingness to take on responsibilities and challenges.
Achievement/Effort	Job requires establishing and maintaining personally challenging achievement goals and exerting effort toward mastering tasks.
Analytical Thinking	Job requires analyzing information and using logic to address work-related issues and problems.
Independence	Job requires developing one's own ways of doing things, guiding oneself with little or no supervision, and depending on oneself to get things done.
Attention to Detail	Job requires being careful about detail and thorough in completing work tasks.
Leadership	Job requires a willingness to lead, take charge, and offer opinions and direction.
Cooperation	Job requires being pleasant with others on the job and displaying a good-natured, cooperative attitude.
Persistence	Job requires persistence in the face of obstacles.
Stress Tolerance	Job requires accepting criticism and dealing calmly and effectively with high stress situations.
Self Control	Job requires maintaining composure, keeping emotions in check, controlling anger, and avoiding aggressive behavior, even in very difficult situations.
Innovation	Job requires creativity and alternative thinking to develop new ideas for and answers to work-related problems.
Adaptability/Flexibility	Job requires being open to change (positive or negative) and to considerable variety in the workplace.
Concern for Others	Job requires being sensitive to others' needs and feelings and being understanding and helpful on the job.
Social Orientation	Job requires preferring to work with others rather than alone, and being personally connected with others on the job.

25-1042.00 - Biological Science Teachers, Postsecondary

Teach courses in biological sciences.

Tasks

1) Evaluate and grade students' class work, laboratory work, assignments, and papers.

2) Maintain regularly scheduled office hours in order to advise and assist students.

3) Keep abreast of developments in their field by reading current literature, talking with colleagues, and participating in professional conferences.

4) Compile, administer, and grade examinations, or assign this work to others.

5) Collaborate with colleagues to address teaching and research issues.

6) Prepare and deliver lectures to undergraduate and/or graduate students on topics such as molecular biology, marine biology, and botany.

7) Maintain student attendance records, grades, and other required records.

8) Initiate, facilitate, and moderate classroom discussions.

9) Plan, evaluate, and revise curricula, course content, and course materials and methods of instruction.

10) Select and obtain materials and supplies such as textbooks and laboratory equipment.

11) Advise students on academic and vocational curricula, and on career issues.

12) Participate in campus and community events.

13) Supervise students' laboratory work.

14) Serve on academic or administrative committees that deal with institutional policies, departmental matters, and academic issues.

15) Compile bibliographies of specialized materials for outside reading assignments.

16) Conduct research in a particular field of knowledge, and publish findings in professional journals, books, and/or electronic media.

17) Participate in student recruitment, registration, and placement activities.

18) Supervise undergraduate and/or graduate teaching, internship, and research work.

19) Act as advisers to student organizations.

20) Write grant proposals to procure external research funding.

21) Perform administrative duties such as serving as department head.

22) Provide professional consulting services to government and/or industry.

Knowledge	Knowledge Definitions
Biology	Knowledge of plant and animal organisms, their tissues, cells, functions, interdependencies, and interactions with each other and the environment.
Education and Training	Knowledge of principles and methods for curriculum and training design, teaching and instruction for individuals and groups, and the measurement of training effects.
English Language	Knowledge of the structure and content of the English language including the meaning and spelling of words, rules of composition, and grammar.
Chemistry	Knowledge of the chemical composition, structure, and properties of substances and of the chemical processes and transformations that they undergo. This includes uses of chemicals and their interactions, danger signs, production techniques, and disposal methods.
Mathematics	Knowledge of arithmetic, algebra, geometry, calculus, statistics, and their applications.
Computers and Electronics	Knowledge of circuit boards, processors, chips, electronic equipment, and computer hardware and software, including applications and programming.
Medicine and Dentistry	Knowledge of the information and techniques needed to diagnose and treat human injuries, diseases, and deformities. This includes symptoms, treatment alternatives, drug properties and interactions, and preventive health-care measures.
Clerical	Knowledge of administrative and clerical procedures and systems such as word processing, managing files and records, stenography and transcription, designing forms, and other office procedures and terminology.
Psychology	Knowledge of human behavior and performance; individual differences in ability, personality, and interests; learning and motivation; psychological research methods; and the assessment and treatment of behavioral and affective disorders.
Administration and Management	Knowledge of business and management principles involved in strategic planning, resource allocation, human resources modeling, leadership technique, production methods, and coordination of people and resources.
Communications and Media	Knowledge of media production, communication, and dissemination techniques and methods. This includes alternative ways to inform and entertain via written, oral, and visual media.
Physics	Knowledge and prediction of physical principles, laws, their interrelationships, and applications to understanding fluid, material, and atmospheric dynamics, and mechanical, electrical, atomic and sub-atomic structures and processes.
Customer and Personal Service	Knowledge of principles and processes for providing customer and personal services. This includes customer needs assessment, meeting quality standards for services, and evaluation of customer satisfaction.
Personnel and Human Resources	Knowledge of principles and procedures for personnel recruitment, selection, training, compensation and benefits, labor relations and negotiation, and personnel information systems.
Engineering and Technology	Knowledge of the practical application of engineering science and technology. This includes applying principles, techniques, procedures, and equipment to the design and production of various goods and services.
Geography	Knowledge of principles and methods for describing the features of land, sea, and air masses, including their physical characteristics, locations, interrelationships, and distribution of plant, animal, and human life.
Public Safety and Security	Knowledge of relevant equipment, policies, procedures, and strategies to promote effective local, state, or national security operations for the protection of people, data, property, and institutions.
Sociology and Anthropology	Knowledge of group behavior and dynamics, societal trends and influences, human migrations, ethnicity, cultures and their history and origins.
Therapy and Counseling	Knowledge of principles, methods, and procedures for diagnosis, treatment, and rehabilitation of physical and mental dysfunctions, and for career counseling and guidance.
Philosophy and Theology	Knowledge of different philosophical systems and religions. This includes their basic principles, values, ethics, ways of thinking, customs, practices, and their impact on human culture.
History and Archeology	Knowledge of historical events and their causes, indicators, and effects on civilizations and cultures.
Law and Government	Knowledge of laws, legal codes, court procedures, precedents, government regulations, executive orders, agency rules, and the democratic political process.
Mechanical	Knowledge of machines and tools, including their designs, uses, repair, and maintenance.
Telecommunications	Knowledge of transmission, broadcasting, switching, control, and operation of telecommunications systems.
Design	Knowledge of design techniques, tools, and principles involved in production of precision technical plans, blueprints, drawings, and models.
Foreign Language	Knowledge of the structure and content of a foreign (non-English) language including the meaning and spelling of words, rules of composition and grammar, and pronunciation.
Economics and Accounting	Knowledge of economic and accounting principles and practices, the financial markets, banking and the analysis and reporting of financial data.
Sales and Marketing	Knowledge of principles and methods for showing, promoting, and selling products or services. This includes marketing strategy and tactics, product demonstration, sales techniques, and sales control systems.
Production and Processing	Knowledge of raw materials, production processes, quality control, costs, and other techniques for maximizing the effective manufacture and distribution of goods.
Transportation	Knowledge of principles and methods for moving people or goods by air, rail, sea, or road, including the relative costs and benefits.
Food Production	Knowledge of techniques and equipment for planting, growing, and harvesting food products (both plant and animal) for consumption, including storage/handling techniques.

Fine Arts	Knowledge of the theory and techniques required to compose, produce, and perform works of music, dance, visual arts, drama, and sculpture.
Building and Construction	Knowledge of materials, methods, and the tools involved in the construction or repair of houses, buildings, or other structures such as highways and roads.

Skills	Skills Definitions
Science	Using scientific rules and methods to solve problems.
Instructing	Teaching others how to do something.
Reading Comprehension	Understanding written sentences and paragraphs in work related documents.
Speaking	Talking to others to convey information effectively.
Critical Thinking	Using logic and reasoning to identify the strengths and weaknesses of alternative solutions, conclusions or approaches to problems.
Active Learning	Understanding the implications of new information for both current and future problem-solving and decision-making.
Writing	Communicating effectively in writing as appropriate for the needs of the audience.
Learning Strategies	Selecting and using training/instructional methods and procedures appropriate for the situation when learning or teaching new things.
Active Listening	Giving full attention to what other people are saying, taking time to understand the points being made, asking questions as appropriate, and not interrupting at inappropriate times.
Time Management	Managing one's own time and the time of others.
Monitoring	Monitoring/Assessing performance of yourself, other individuals, or organizations to make improvements or take corrective action.
Complex Problem Solving	Identifying complex problems and reviewing related information to develop and evaluate options and implement solutions.
Judgment and Decision Making	Considering the relative costs and benefits of potential actions to choose the most appropriate one.
Social Perceptiveness	Being aware of others' reactions and understanding why they react as they do.
Coordination	Adjusting actions in relation to others' actions.
Mathematics	Using mathematics to solve problems.
Equipment Selection	Determining the kind of tools and equipment needed to do a job.
Persuasion	Persuading others to change their minds or behavior.
Service Orientation	Actively looking for ways to help people.
Management of Personnel Resources	Motivating, developing, and directing people as they work, identifying the best people for the job.
Negotiation	Bringing others together and trying to reconcile differences.
Quality Control Analysis	Conducting tests and inspections of products, services, or processes to evaluate quality or performance.
Management of Financial Resources	Determining how money will be spent to get the work done, and accounting for these expenditures.
Operations Analysis	Analyzing needs and product requirements to create a design.
Technology Design	Generating or adapting equipment and technology to serve user needs.
Management of Material Resources	Obtaining and seeing to the appropriate use of equipment, facilities, and materials needed to do certain work.
Troubleshooting	Determining causes of operating errors and deciding what to do about it.
Systems Evaluation	Identifying measures or indicators of system performance and the actions needed to improve or correct performance, relative to the goals of the system.
Installation	Installing equipment, machines, wiring, or programs to meet specifications.
Equipment Maintenance	Performing routine maintenance on equipment and determining when and what kind of maintenance is needed.
Operation and Control	Controlling operations of equipment or systems.
Systems Analysis	Determining how a system should work and how changes in conditions, operations, and the environment will affect outcomes.
Operation Monitoring	Watching gauges, dials, or other indicators to make sure a machine is working properly.
Repairing	Repairing machines or systems using the needed tools.
Programming	Writing computer programs for various purposes.

Ability	Ability Definitions
Oral Expression	The ability to communicate information and ideas in speaking so others will understand.
Written Expression	The ability to communicate information and ideas in writing so others will understand.
Oral Comprehension	The ability to listen to and understand information and ideas presented through spoken words and sentences.
Speech Clarity	The ability to speak clearly so others can understand you.
Written Comprehension	The ability to read and understand information and ideas presented in writing.
Inductive Reasoning	The ability to combine pieces of information to form general rules or conclusions (includes finding a relationship among seemingly unrelated events).
Deductive Reasoning	The ability to apply general rules to specific problems to produce answers that make sense.
Speech Recognition	The ability to identify and understand the speech of another person.
Near Vision	The ability to see details at close range (within a few feet of the observer).
Problem Sensitivity	The ability to tell when something is wrong or is likely to go wrong. It does not involve solving the problem, only recognizing there is a problem.
Information Ordering	The ability to arrange things or actions in a certain order or pattern according to a specific rule or set of rules (e.g., patterns of numbers, letters, words, pictures, mathematical operations).
Originality	The ability to come up with unusual or clever ideas about a given topic or situation, or to develop creative ways to solve a problem.
Category Flexibility	The ability to generate or use different sets of rules for combining or grouping things in different ways.
Fluency of Ideas	The ability to come up with a number of ideas about a topic (the number of ideas is important, not their quality, correctness, or creativity).
Selective Attention	The ability to concentrate on a task over a period of time without being distracted.
Mathematical Reasoning	The ability to choose the right mathematical methods or formulas to solve a problem.
Memorization	The ability to remember information such as words, numbers, pictures, and procedures.
Flexibility of Closure	The ability to identify or detect a known pattern (a figure, object, word, or sound) that is hidden in other distracting material.
Time Sharing	The ability to shift back and forth between two or more activities or sources of information (such as speech, sounds, touch, or other sources).
Far Vision	The ability to see details at a distance.
Finger Dexterity	The ability to make precisely coordinated movements of the fingers of one or both hands to grasp, manipulate, or assemble very small objects.
Number Facility	The ability to add, subtract, multiply, or divide quickly and correctly.
Manual Dexterity	The ability to quickly move your hand, your hand together with your arm, or your two hands to grasp, manipulate, or assemble objects.
Visual Color Discrimination	The ability to match or detect differences between colors, including shades of color and brightness.
Visualization	The ability to imagine how something will look after it is moved around or when its parts are moved or rearranged.
Perceptual Speed	The ability to quickly and accurately compare similarities and differences among sets of letters, numbers, objects, pictures, or patterns. The things to be compared may be presented at the same time or one after the other. This ability also includes comparing a presented object with a remembered object.
Speed of Closure	The ability to quickly make sense of, combine, and organize information into meaningful patterns.
Auditory Attention	The ability to focus on a single source of sound in the presence of other distracting sounds.
Control Precision	The ability to quickly and repeatedly adjust the controls of a machine or a vehicle to exact positions.
Trunk Strength	The ability to use your abdominal and lower back muscles to support part of the body repeatedly or continuously over time without 'giving out' or fatiguing.
Arm-Hand Steadiness	The ability to keep your hand and arm steady while moving your arm or while holding your arm and hand in one position.
Depth Perception	The ability to judge which of several objects is closer or farther away from you, or to judge the distance between you and an object.
Hearing Sensitivity	The ability to detect or tell the differences between sounds that vary in pitch and loudness.
Dynamic Flexibility	The ability to quickly and repeatedly bend, stretch, twist, or reach out with your body, arms, and/or legs.

Reaction Time	The ability to quickly respond (with the hand, finger, or foot) to a signal (sound, light, picture) when it appears.
Static Strength	The ability to exert maximum muscle force to lift, push, pull, or carry objects.
Multilimb Coordination	The ability to coordinate two or more limbs (for example, two arms, two legs, or one leg and one arm) while sitting, standing, or lying down. It does not involve performing the activities while the whole body is in motion.
Dynamic Strength	The ability to exert muscle force repeatedly or continuously over time. This involves muscular endurance and resistance to muscle fatigue.
Stamina	The ability to exert yourself physically over long periods of time without getting winded or out of breath.
Explosive Strength	The ability to use short bursts of muscle force to propel oneself (as in jumping or sprinting), or to throw an object.
Extent Flexibility	The ability to bend, stretch, twist, or reach with your body, arms, and/or legs.
Speed of Limb Movement	The ability to quickly move the arms and legs.
Wrist-Finger Speed	The ability to make fast, simple, repeated movements of the fingers, hands, and wrists.
Spatial Orientation	The ability to know your location in relation to the environment or to know where other objects are in relation to you.
Response Orientation	The ability to choose quickly between two or more movements in response to two or more different signals (lights, sounds, pictures). It includes the speed with which the correct response is started with the hand, foot, or other body part.
Peripheral Vision	The ability to see objects or movement of objects to one's side when the eyes are looking ahead.
Rate Control	The ability to time your movements or the movement of a piece of equipment in anticipation of changes in the speed and/or direction of a moving object or scene.
Glare Sensitivity	The ability to see objects in the presence of glare or bright lighting.
Gross Body Equilibrium	The ability to keep or regain your body balance or stay upright when in an unstable position.
Gross Body Coordination	The ability to coordinate the movement of your arms, legs, and torso together when the whole body is in motion.
Sound Localization	The ability to tell the direction from which a sound originated.
Night Vision	The ability to see under low light conditions.

Work_Activity	Work_Activity Definitions
Training and Teaching Others	Identifying the educational needs of others, developing formal educational or training programs or classes, and teaching or instructing others.
Getting Information	Observing, receiving, and otherwise obtaining information from all relevant sources.
Updating and Using Relevant Knowledge	Keeping up-to-date technically and applying new knowledge to your job.
Interpreting the Meaning of Information for Others	Translating or explaining what information means and how it can be used.
Thinking Creatively	Developing, designing, or creating new applications, ideas, relationships, systems, or products, including artistic contributions.
Processing Information	Compiling, coding, categorizing, calculating, tabulating, auditing, or verifying information or data.
Analyzing Data or Information	Identifying the underlying principles, reasons, or facts of information by breaking down information or data into separate parts.
Making Decisions and Solving Problems	Analyzing information and evaluating results to choose the best solution and solve problems.
Interacting With Computers	Using computers and computer systems (including hardware and software) to program, write software, set up functions, enter data, or process information.
Communicating with Supervisors, Peers, or Subordin	Providing information to supervisors, co-workers, and subordinates by telephone, in written form, e-mail, or in person.
Organizing, Planning, and Prioritizing Work	Developing specific goals and plans to prioritize, organize, and accomplish your work.
Identifying Objects, Actions, and Events	Identifying information by categorizing, estimating, recognizing differences or similarities, and detecting changes in circumstances or events.
Documenting/Recording Information	Entering, transcribing, recording, storing, or maintaining information in written or electronic/magnetic form.
Establishing and Maintaining Interpersonal Relatio	Developing constructive and cooperative working relationships with others, and maintaining them over time.

Judging the Qualities of Things. Services. or Peop	Assessing the value, importance, or quality of things or people.
Coaching and Developing Others	Identifying the developmental needs of others and coaching, mentoring, or otherwise helping others to improve their knowledge or skills.
Developing Objectives and Strategies	Establishing long-range objectives and specifying the strategies and actions to achieve them.
Monitor Processes, Materials, or Surroundings	Monitoring and reviewing information from materials, events, or the environment, to detect or assess problems.
Scheduling Work and Activities	Scheduling events, programs, and activities, as well as the work of others.
Estimating the Quantifiable Characteristics of Pro	Estimating sizes, distances, and quantities; or determining time, costs, resources, or materials needed to perform a work activity.
Communicating with Persons Outside Organization	Communicating with people outside the organization, representing the organization to customers, the public, government, and other external sources. This information can be exchanged in person, in writing, or by telephone or e-mail.
Coordinating the Work and Activities of Others	Getting members of a group to work together to accomplish tasks.
Guiding, Directing, and Motivating Subordinates	Providing guidance and direction to subordinates, including setting performance standards and monitoring performance.
Provide Consultation and Advice to Others	Providing guidance and expert advice to management or other groups on technical, systems-, or process-related topics.
Evaluating Information to Determine Compliance wit	Using relevant information and individual judgment to determine whether events or processes comply with laws, regulations, or standards.
Performing for or Working Directly with the Public	Performing for people or dealing directly with the public. This includes serving customers in restaurants and stores, and receiving clients or guests.
Performing Administrative Activities	Performing day-to-day administrative tasks such as maintaining information files and processing paperwork.
Inspecting Equipment, Structures, or Material	Inspecting equipment, structures, or materials to identify the cause of errors or other problems or defects.
Resolving Conflicts and Negotiating with Others	Handling complaints, settling disputes, and resolving grievances and conflicts, or otherwise negotiating with others.
Developing and Building Teams	Encouraging and building mutual trust, respect, and cooperation among team members.
Assisting and Caring for Others	Providing personal assistance, medical attention, emotional support, or other personal care to others such as coworkers, customers, or patients.
Monitoring and Controlling Resources	Monitoring and controlling resources and overseeing the spending of money.
Handling and Moving Objects	Using hands and arms in handling, installing, positioning, and moving materials, and manipulating things.
Selling or Influencing Others	Convincing others to buy merchandise/goods or to otherwise change their minds or actions.
Staffing Organizational Units	Recruiting, interviewing, selecting, hiring, and promoting employees in an organization.
Controlling Machines and Processes	Using either control mechanisms or direct physical activity to operate machines or processes (not including computers or vehicles).
Performing General Physical Activities	Performing physical activities that require considerable use of your arms and legs and moving your whole body, such as climbing, lifting, balancing, walking, stooping, and handling of materials.
Repairing and Maintaining Electronic Equipment	Servicing, repairing, calibrating, regulating, fine-tuning, or testing machines, devices, and equipment that operate primarily on the basis of electrical or electronic (not mechanical) principles.
Repairing and Maintaining Mechanical Equipment	Servicing, repairing, adjusting, and testing machines, devices, moving parts, and equipment that operate primarily on the basis of mechanical (not electronic) principles.
Operating Vehicles, Mechanized Devices, or Equipme	Running, maneuvering, navigating, or driving vehicles or mechanized equipment, such as forklifts, passenger vehicles, aircraft, or water craft.
Drafting, Laying Out, and Specifying Technical Dev	Providing documentation, detailed instructions, drawings, or specifications to tell others about how devices, parts, equipment, or structures are to be fabricated, constructed, assembled, modified, maintained, or used.

Work_Context	Work_Context Definitions
Electronic Mail	How often do you use electronic mail in this job?
Structured versus Unstructured Work	To what extent is this job structured for the worker, rather than allowing the worker to determine tasks, priorities, and goals?

Freedom to Make Decisions	How much decision making freedom, without supervision, does the job offer?
Contact With Others	How much does this job require the worker to be in contact with others (face-to-face, by telephone, or otherwise) in order to perform it?
Face-to-Face Discussions	How often do you have to have face-to-face discussions with individuals or teams in this job?
Indoors, Environmentally Controlled	How often does this job require working indoors in environmentally controlled conditions?
Telephone	How often do you have telephone conversations in this job?
Public Speaking	How often do you have to perform public speaking in this job?
Importance of Being Exact or Accurate	How important is being very exact or highly accurate in performing this job?
Work With Work Group or Team	How important is it to work with others in a group or team in this job?
Time Pressure	How often does this job require the worker to meet strict deadlines?
Impact of Decisions on Co-workers or Company Resul	How do the decisions an employee makes impact the results of co-workers, clients or the company?
Letters and Memos	How often does the job require written letters and memos?
Frequency of Decision Making	How frequently is the worker required to make decisions that affect other people, the financial resources, and/or the image and reputation of the organization?
Coordinate or Lead Others	How important is it to coordinate or lead others in accomplishing work activities in this job?
Level of Competition	To what extent does this job require the worker to compete or to be aware of competitive pressures?
Physical Proximity	To what extent does this job require the worker to perform job tasks in close physical proximity to other people?
Deal With External Customers	How important is it to work with external customers or the public in this job?
Responsible for Others' Health and Safety	How much responsibility is there for the health and safety of others in this job?
Responsibility for Outcomes and Results	How responsible is the worker for work outcomes and results of other workers?
Spend Time Sitting	How much does this job require sitting?
Spend Time Standing	How much does this job require standing?
Exposed to Contaminants	How often does this job require working exposed to contaminants (such as pollutants, gases, dust or odors)?
Frequency of Conflict Situations	How often are there conflict situations the employee has to face in this job?
Deal With Unpleasant or Angry People	How frequently does the worker have to deal with unpleasant, angry, or discourteous individuals as part of the job requirements?
Importance of Repeating Same Tasks	How important is repeating the same physical activities (e.g., key entry) or mental activities (e.g., checking entries in a ledger) over and over, without stopping, to performing this job?
Spend Time Using Your Hands to Handle, Control, or	How much does this job require using your hands to handle, control, or feel objects, tools or controls?
Exposed to Hazardous Conditions	How often does this job require exposure to hazardous conditions?
Wear Common Protective or Safety Equipment such as	How much does this job require wearing common protective or safety equipment such as safety shoes, glasses, gloves, hard hats or live jackets?
Spend Time Making Repetitive Motions	How much does this job require making repetitive motions?
Sounds, Noise Levels Are Distracting or Uncomfort	How often does this job require working exposed to sounds and noise levels that are distracting or uncomfortable?
Consequence of Error	How serious would the result usually be if the worker made a mistake that was not readily correctable?
Exposed to Disease or Infections	How often does this job require exposure to disease/infections?
Spend Time Walking and Running	How much does this job require walking and running?
Indoors, Not Environmentally Controlled	How often does this job require working indoors in non-controlled environmental conditions (e.g., warehouse without heat)?
Exposed to Minor Burns, Cuts, Bites, or Stings	How often does this job require exposure to minor burns, cuts, bites, or stings?
Degree of Automation	How automated is the job?
In an Enclosed Vehicle or Equipment	How often does this job require working in a closed vehicle or equipment (e.g., car)?
Outdoors, Exposed to Weather	How often does this job require working outdoors, exposed to all weather conditions?
Very Hot or Cold Temperatures	How often does this job require working in very hot (above 90 F degrees) or very cold (below 32 F degrees) temperatures?

Extremely Bright or Inadequate Lighting	How often does this job require working in extremely bright or inadequate lighting conditions?
Cramped Work Space, Awkward Positions	How often does this job require working in cramped work spaces that requires getting into awkward positions?
Wear Specialized Protective or Safety Equipment su	How much does this job require wearing specialized protective or safety equipment such as breathing apparatus, safety harness, full protection suits, or radiation protection?
Spend Time Bending or Twisting the Body	How much does this job require bending or twisting your body?
Deal With Physically Aggressive People	How frequently does this job require the worker to deal with physical aggression of violent individuals?
Exposed to Hazardous Equipment	How often does this job require exposure to hazardous equipment?
Outdoors, Under Cover	How often does this job require working outdoors, under cover (e.g., structure with roof but no walls)?
Spend Time Keeping or Regaining Balance	How much does this job require keeping or regaining your balance?
Pace Determined by Speed of Equipment	How important is it to this job that the pace is determined by the speed of equipment or machinery? (This does not refer to keeping busy at all times on this job.)
Spend Time Kneeling, Crouching, Stooping, or Crawl	How much does this job require kneeling, crouching, stooping, or crawling?
Exposed to Radiation	How often does this job require exposure to radiation?
In an Open Vehicle or Equipment	How often does this job require working in an open vehicle or equipment (e.g., tractor)?
Exposed to High Places	How often does this job require exposure to high places?
Exposed to Whole Body Vibration	How often does this job require exposure to whole body vibration (e.g., operate a jackhammer)?
Spend Time Climbing Ladders, Scaffolds, or Poles	How much does this job require climbing ladders, scaffolds, or poles?

Job Zone Component	Job Zone Component Definitions
Title	Job Zone Five: Extensive Preparation Needed
	Extensive skill, knowledge, and experience are needed for these occupations. Many require more than five years of experience.
Overall Experience	For example, surgeons must complete four years of college and an additional five to seven years of specialized medical training to be able to do their job.
Job Training	Employees may need some on-the-job training, but most of these occupations assume that the person will already have the required skills, knowledge, work-related experience, and/or training.
Job Zone Examples	These occupations often involve coordinating, training, supervising, or managing the activities of others to accomplish goals. Very advanced communication and organizational skills are required. Examples include athletic trainers, lawyers, managing editors, phyicists, social psychologists, and surgeons.
SVP Range	(8.0 and above)
Education	A bachelor's degree is the minimum formal education required for these occupations. However, many also require graduate school. For example, they may require a master's degree, and some require a Ph.D., M.D., or J.D. (law degree).

Work_Styles	Work_Styles Definitions
Integrity	Job requires being honest and ethical.
Dependability	Job requires being reliable, responsible, and dependable, and fulfilling obligations.
Analytical Thinking	Job requires analyzing information and using logic to address work-related issues and problems.
Attention to Detail	Job requires being careful about detail and thorough in completing work tasks.
Independence	Job requires developing one's own ways of doing things, guiding oneself with little or no supervision, and depending on oneself to get things done.
Initiative	Job requires a willingness to take on responsibilities and challenges.
Leadership	Job requires a willingness to lead, take charge, and offer opinions and direction.
Self Control	Job requires maintaining composure, keeping emotions in check, controlling anger, and avoiding aggressive behavior, even in very difficult situations.

Achievement/Effort	Job requires establishing and maintaining personally challenging achievement goals and exerting effort toward mastering tasks.
Concern for Others	Job requires being sensitive to others' needs and feelings and being understanding and helpful on the job.
Innovation	Job requires creativity and alternative thinking to develop new ideas for and answers to work-related problems.
Cooperation	Job requires being pleasant with others on the job and displaying a good-natured, cooperative attitude.
Adaptability/Flexibility	Job requires being open to change (positive or negative) and to considerable variety in the workplace.
Persistence	Job requires persistence in the face of obstacles.
Stress Tolerance	Job requires accepting criticism and dealing calmly and effectively with high stress situations.
Social Orientation	Job requires preferring to work with others rather than alone, and being personally connected with others on the job.

25-1043.00 - Forestry and Conservation Science Teachers, Postsecondary

Teach courses in environmental and conservation science.

Tasks

1) Evaluate and grade students' class work, assignments, and papers.

2) Select and obtain materials and supplies such as textbooks and laboratory equipment.

3) Plan, evaluate, and revise curricula, course content, and course materials and methods of instruction.

4) Initiate, facilitate, and moderate classroom discussions.

5) Conduct research in a particular field of knowledge, and publish findings in books, professional journals, and/or electronic media.

6) Prepare course materials such as syllabi, homework assignments, and handouts.

7) Advise students on academic and vocational curricula, and on career issues.

8) Serve on academic or administrative committees that deal with institutional policies, departmental matters, and academic issues.

9) Compile, administer, and grade examinations, or assign this work to others.

10) Maintain student attendance records, grades, and other required records.

11) Write grant proposals to procure external research funding.

12) Prepare and deliver lectures to undergraduate and/or graduate students on topics such as forest resource policy, forest pathology, and mapping.

13) Compile bibliographies of specialized materials for outside reading assignments.

14) Supervise undergraduate and/or graduate teaching, internship, and research work.

15) Supervise students' laboratory and/or field work.

16) Maintain regularly scheduled office hours in order to advise and assist students.

17) Provide professional consulting services to government and/or industry.

18) Participate in student recruitment, registration, and placement activities.

19) Act as advisers to student organizations.

20) Perform administrative duties such as serving as department head.

21) Keep abreast of developments in their field by reading current literature, talking with colleagues, and participating in professional conferences.

22) Collaborate with colleagues to address teaching and research issues.

Knowledge	Knowledge Definitions
English Language	Knowledge of the structure and content of the English language including the meaning and spelling of words, rules of composition, and grammar.
Biology	Knowledge of plant and animal organisms, their tissues, cells, functions, interdependencies, and interactions with each other and the environment.
Mathematics	Knowledge of arithmetic, algebra, geometry, calculus, statistics, and their applications.
Education and Training	Knowledge of principles and methods for curriculum and training design, teaching and instruction for individuals and groups, and the measurement of training effects.
Computers and Electronics	Knowledge of circuit boards, processors, chips, electronic equipment, and computer hardware and software, including applications and programming.
Geography	Knowledge of principles and methods for describing the features of land, sea, and air masses, including their physical characteristics, locations, interrelationships, and distribution of plant, animal, and human life.
Administration and Management	Knowledge of business and management principles involved in strategic planning, resource allocation, human resources modeling, leadership technique, production methods, and coordination of people and resources.
Communications and Media	Knowledge of media production, communication, and dissemination techniques and methods. This includes alternative ways to inform and entertain via written, oral, and visual media.
Physics	Knowledge and prediction of physical principles, laws, their interrelationships, and applications to understanding fluid, material, and atmospheric dynamics, and mechanical, electrical, atomic and sub-atomic structures and processes.
Chemistry	Knowledge of the chemical composition, structure, and properties of substances and of the chemical processes and transformations that they undergo. This includes uses of chemicals and their interactions, danger signs, production techniques, and disposal methods.
Clerical	Knowledge of administrative and clerical procedures and systems such as word processing, managing files and records, stenography and transcription, designing forms, and other office procedures and terminology.
Personnel and Human Resources	Knowledge of principles and procedures for personnel recruitment, selection, training, compensation and benefits, labor relations and negotiation, and personnel information systems.
Customer and Personal Service	Knowledge of principles and processes for providing customer and personal services. This includes customer needs assessment, meeting quality standards for services, and evaluation of customer satisfaction.
Economics and Accounting	Knowledge of economic and accounting principles and practices, the financial markets, banking and the analysis and reporting of financial data.
Law and Government	Knowledge of laws, legal codes, court procedures, precedents, government regulations, executive orders, agency rules, and the democratic political process.
Engineering and Technology	Knowledge of the practical application of engineering science and technology. This includes applying principles, techniques, procedures, and equipment to the design and production of various goods and services.
Sociology and Anthropology	Knowledge of group behavior and dynamics, societal trends and influences, human migrations, ethnicity, cultures and their history and origins.
Psychology	Knowledge of human behavior and performance; individual differences in ability, personality, and interests; learning and motivation; psychological research methods; and the assessment and treatment of behavioral and affective disorders.
History and Archeology	Knowledge of historical events and their causes, indicators, and effects on civilizations and cultures.
Design	Knowledge of design techniques, tools, and principles involved in production of precision technical plans, blueprints, drawings, and models.
Telecommunications	Knowledge of transmission, broadcasting, switching, control, and operation of telecommunications systems.
Mechanical	Knowledge of machines and tools, including their designs, uses, repair, and maintenance.
Sales and Marketing	Knowledge of principles and methods for showing, promoting, and selling products or services. This includes marketing strategy and tactics, product demonstration, sales techniques, and sales control systems.
Public Safety and Security	Knowledge of relevant equipment, policies, procedures, and strategies to promote effective local, state, or national security operations for the protection of people, data, property, and institutions.
Production and Processing	Knowledge of raw materials, production processes, quality control, costs, and other techniques for maximizing the effective manufacture and distribution of goods.
Building and Construction	Knowledge of materials, methods, and the tools involved in the construction or repair of houses, buildings, or other structures such as highways and roads.

Transportation	Knowledge of principles and methods for moving people or goods by air, rail, sea, or road, including the relative costs and benefits.	Troubleshooting	Determining causes of operating errors and deciding what to do about it.
Philosophy and Theology	Knowledge of different philosophical systems and religions. This includes their basic principles, values, ethics, ways of thinking, customs, practices, and their impact on human culture.	Technology Design	Generating or adapting equipment and technology to serve user needs.
		Installation	Installing equipment, machines, wiring, or programs to meet specifications.
Food Production	Knowledge of techniques and equipment for planting, growing, and harvesting food products (both plant and animal) for consumption, including storage/handling techniques.	Programming	Writing computer programs for various purposes.
		Equipment Maintenance	Performing routine maintenance on equipment and determining when and what kind of maintenance is needed.
Foreign Language	Knowledge of the structure and content of a foreign (non-English) language including the meaning and spelling of words, rules of composition and grammar, and pronunciation.	Operation and Control	Controlling operations of equipment or systems.
		Operation Monitoring	Watching gauges, dials, or other indicators to make sure a machine is working properly.
Therapy and Counseling	Knowledge of principles, methods, and procedures for diagnosis, treatment, and rehabilitation of physical and mental dysfunctions, and for career counseling and guidance.	Repairing	Repairing machines or systems using the needed tools.
Medicine and Dentistry	Knowledge of the information and techniques needed to diagnose and treat human injuries, diseases, and deformities. This includes symptoms, treatment alternatives, drug properties and interactions, and preventive health-care measures.	**Ability**	**Ability Definitions**
		Oral Expression	The ability to communicate information and ideas in speaking so others will understand.
Fine Arts	Knowledge of the theory and techniques required to compose, produce, and perform works of music, dance, visual arts, drama, and sculpture.	Speech Clarity	The ability to speak clearly so others can understand you.
		Written Expression	The ability to communicate information and ideas in writing so others will understand.
Skills	**Skills Definitions**	Oral Comprehension	The ability to listen to and understand information and ideas presented through spoken words and sentences.
Instructing	Teaching others how to do something.	Written Comprehension	The ability to read and understand information and ideas presented in writing.
Reading Comprehension	Understanding written sentences and paragraphs in work related documents.	Deductive Reasoning	The ability to apply general rules to specific problems to produce answers that make sense.
Writing	Communicating effectively in writing as appropriate for the needs of the audience.	Inductive Reasoning	The ability to combine pieces of information to form general rules or conclusions (includes finding a relationship among seemingly unrelated events).
Speaking	Talking to others to convey information effectively.	Speech Recognition	The ability to identify and understand the speech of another person.
Critical Thinking	Using logic and reasoning to identify the strengths and weaknesses of alternative solutions, conclusions or approaches to problems.	Problem Sensitivity	The ability to tell when something is wrong or is likely to go wrong. It does not involve solving the problem, only recognizing there is a problem.
Science	Using scientific rules and methods to solve problems.	Near Vision	The ability to see details at close range (within a few feet of the observer).
Active Learning	Understanding the implications of new information for both current and future problem-solving and decision-making.	Originality	The ability to come up with unusual or clever ideas about a given topic or situation, or to develop creative ways to solve a problem.
Learning Strategies	Selecting and using training/instructional methods and procedures appropriate for the situation when learning or teaching new things.	Information Ordering	The ability to arrange things or actions in a certain order or pattern according to a specific rule or set of rules (e.g., patterns of numbers, letters, words, pictures, mathematical operations).
Active Listening	Giving full attention to what other people are saying, taking time to understand the points being made, asking questions as appropriate, and not interrupting at inappropriate times.	Fluency of Ideas	The ability to come up with a number of ideas about a topic (the number of ideas is important, not their quality, correctness, or creativity).
Time Management	Managing one's own time and the time of others.	Selective Attention	The ability to concentrate on a task over a period of time without being distracted.
Complex Problem Solving	Identifying complex problems and reviewing related information to develop and evaluate options and implement solutions.	Category Flexibility	The ability to generate or use different sets of rules for combining or grouping things in different ways.
Mathematics	Using mathematics to solve problems.	Mathematical Reasoning	The ability to choose the right mathematical methods or formulas to solve a problem.
Monitoring	Monitoring/Assessing performance of yourself, other individuals, or organizations to make improvements or take corrective action.	Far Vision	The ability to see details at a distance.
Judgment and Decision Making	Considering the relative costs and benefits of potential actions to choose the most appropriate one.	Memorization	The ability to remember information such as words, numbers, pictures, and procedures.
Coordination	Adjusting actions in relation to others' actions.	Flexibility of Closure	The ability to identify or detect a known pattern (a figure, object, word, or sound) that is hidden in other distracting material.
Management of Financial Resources	Determining how money will be spent to get the work done, and accounting for these expenditures.	Time Sharing	The ability to shift back and forth between two or more activities or sources of information (such as speech, sounds, touch, or other sources).
Social Perceptiveness	Being aware of others' reactions and understanding why they react as they do.	Number Facility	The ability to add, subtract, multiply, or divide quickly and correctly.
Management of Personnel Resources	Motivating, developing, and directing people as they work, identifying the best people for the job.	Speed of Closure	The ability to quickly make sense of, combine, and organize information into meaningful patterns.
Equipment Selection	Determining the kind of tools and equipment needed to do a job.	Perceptual Speed	The ability to quickly and accurately compare similarities and differences among sets of letters, numbers, objects, pictures, or patterns. The things to be compared may be presented at the same time or one after the other. This ability also includes comparing a presented object with a remembered object.
Persuasion	Persuading others to change their minds or behavior.		
Management of Material Resources	Obtaining and seeing to the appropriate use of equipment, facilities, and materials needed to do certain work.	Auditory Attention	The ability to focus on a single source of sound in the presence of other distracting sounds.
Service Orientation	Actively looking for ways to help people.	Visual Color Discrimination	The ability to match or detect differences between colors, including shades of color and brightness.
Systems Analysis	Determining how a system should work and how changes in conditions, operations, and the environment will affect outcomes.	Visualization	The ability to imagine how something will look after it is moved around or when its parts are moved or rearranged.
Negotiation	Bringing others together and trying to reconcile differences.		
Quality Control Analysis	Conducting tests and inspections of products, services, or processes to evaluate quality or performance.		
Systems Evaluation	Identifying measures or indicators of system performance and the actions needed to improve or correct performance, relative to the goals of the system.		
Operations Analysis	Analyzing needs and product requirements to create a design.		

1373

Depth Perception	The ability to judge which of several objects is closer or farther away from you, or to judge the distance between you and an object.
Finger Dexterity	The ability to make precisely coordinated movements of the fingers of one or both hands to grasp, manipulate, or assemble very small objects.
Control Precision	The ability to quickly and repeatedly adjust the controls of a machine or a vehicle to exact positions.
Multilimb Coordination	The ability to coordinate two or more limbs (for example, two arms, two legs, or one leg and one arm) while sitting, standing, or lying down. It does not involve performing the activities while the whole body is in motion.
Hearing Sensitivity	The ability to detect or tell the differences between sounds that vary in pitch and loudness.
Trunk Strength	The ability to use your abdominal and lower back muscles to support part of the body repeatedly or continuously over time without 'giving out' or fatiguing.
Static Strength	The ability to exert maximum muscle force to lift, push, pull, or carry objects.
Explosive Strength	The ability to use short bursts of muscle force to propel oneself (as in jumping or sprinting), or to throw an object.
Peripheral Vision	The ability to see objects or movement of objects to one's side when the eyes are looking ahead.
Dynamic Strength	The ability to exert muscle force repeatedly or continuously over time. This involves muscular endurance and resistance to muscle fatigue.
Stamina	The ability to exert yourself physically over long periods of time without getting winded or out of breath.
Extent Flexibility	The ability to bend, stretch, twist, or reach with your body, arms, and/or legs.
Dynamic Flexibility	The ability to quickly and repeatedly bend, stretch, twist, or reach out with your body, arms, and/or legs.
Gross Body Coordination	The ability to coordinate the movement of your arms, legs, and torso together when the whole body is in motion.
Speed of Limb Movement	The ability to quickly move the arms and legs.
Wrist-Finger Speed	The ability to make fast, simple, repeated movements of the fingers, hands, and wrists.
Night Vision	The ability to see under low light conditions.
Gross Body Equilibrium	The ability to keep or regain your body balance or stay upright when in an unstable position.
Reaction Time	The ability to quickly respond (with the hand, finger, or foot) to a signal (sound, light, picture) when it appears.
Glare Sensitivity	The ability to see objects in the presence of glare or bright lighting.
Rate Control	The ability to time your movements or the movement of a piece of equipment in anticipation of changes in the speed and/or direction of a moving object or scene.
Arm-Hand Steadiness	The ability to keep your hand and arm steady while moving your arm or while holding your arm and hand in one position.
Sound Localization	The ability to tell the direction from which a sound originated.
Response Orientation	The ability to choose quickly between two or more movements in response to two or more different signals (lights, sounds, pictures). It includes the speed with which the correct response is started with the hand, foot, or other body part.
Spatial Orientation	The ability to know your location in relation to the environment or to know where other objects are in relation to you.
Manual Dexterity	The ability to quickly move your hand, your hand together with your arm, or your two hands to grasp, manipulate, or assemble objects.

Work_Activity	Work_Activity Definitions
Thinking Creatively	Developing, designing, or creating new applications, ideas, relationships, systems, or products, including artistic contributions.
Updating and Using Relevant Knowledge	Keeping up-to-date technically and applying new knowledge to your job.
Analyzing Data or Information	Identifying the underlying principles, reasons, or facts of information by breaking down information or data into separate parts.
Getting Information	Observing, receiving, and otherwise obtaining information from all relevant sources.
Interacting With Computers	Using computers and computer systems (including hardware and software) to program, write software, set up functions, enter data, or process information.
Interpreting the Meaning of Information for Others	Translating or explaining what information means and how it can be used.

Identifying Objects, Actions, and Events	Identifying information by categorizing, estimating, recognizing differences or similarities, and detecting changes in circumstances or events.
Training and Teaching Others	Identifying the educational needs of others, developing formal educational or training programs or classes, and teaching or instructing others.
Processing Information	Compiling, coding, categorizing, calculating, tabulating, auditing, or verifying information or data.
Organizing, Planning, and Prioritizing Work	Developing specific goals and plans to prioritize, organize, and accomplish your work.
Making Decisions and Solving Problems	Analyzing information and evaluating results to choose the best solution and solve problems.
Communicating with Persons Outside Organization	Communicating with people outside the organization, representing the organization to customers, the public, government, and other external sources. This information can be exchanged in person, in writing, or by telephone or e-mail.
Monitor Processes, Materials, or Surroundings	Monitoring and reviewing information from materials, events, or the environment, to detect or assess problems.
Estimating the Quantifiable Characteristics of Pro	Estimating sizes, distances, and quantities; or determining time, costs, resources, or materials needed to perform a work activity.
Communicating with Supervisors, Peers, or Subordin	Providing information to supervisors, co-workers, and subordinates by telephone, in written form, e-mail, or in person.
Establishing and Maintaining Interpersonal Relatio	Developing constructive and cooperative working relationships with others, and maintaining them over time.
Provide Consultation and Advice to Others	Providing guidance and expert advice to management or other groups on technical, systems-, or process-related topics.
Developing Objectives and Strategies	Establishing long-range objectives and specifying the strategies and actions to achieve them.
Coaching and Developing Others	Identifying the developmental needs of others and coaching, mentoring, or otherwise helping others to improve their knowledge or skills.
Documenting/Recording Information	Entering, transcribing, recording, storing, or maintaining information in written or electronic/magnetic form.
Scheduling Work and Activities	Scheduling events, programs, and activities, as well as the work of others.
Judging the Qualities of Things, Services, or Peop	Assessing the value, importance, or quality of things or people.
Guiding, Directing, and Motivating Subordinates	Providing guidance and direction to subordinates, including setting performance standards and monitoring performance.
Monitoring and Controlling Resources	Monitoring and controlling resources and overseeing the spending of money.
Coordinating the Work and Activities of Others	Getting members of a group to work together to accomplish tasks.
Developing and Building Teams	Encouraging and building mutual trust, respect, and cooperation among team members.
Performing for or Working Directly with the Public	Performing for people or dealing directly with the public. This includes serving customers in restaurants and stores, and receiving clients or guests.
Evaluating Information to Determine Compliance wit	Using relevant information and individual judgment to determine whether events or processes comply with laws, regulations, or standards.
Performing Administrative Activities	Performing day-to-day administrative tasks such as maintaining information files and processing paperwork.
Resolving Conflicts and Negotiating with Others	Handling complaints, settling disputes, and resolving grievances and conflicts, or otherwise negotiating with others.
Inspecting Equipment, Structures, or Material	Inspecting equipment, structures, or materials to identify the cause of errors or other problems or defects.
Staffing Organizational Units	Recruiting, interviewing, selecting, hiring, and promoting employees in an organization.
Selling or Influencing Others	Convincing others to buy merchandise/goods or to otherwise change their minds or actions.
Performing General Physical Activities	Performing physical activities that require considerable use of your arms and legs and moving your whole body, such as climbing, lifting, balancing, walking, stooping, and handling of materials.
Assisting and Caring for Others	Providing personal assistance, medical attention, emotional support, or other personal care to others such as coworkers, customers, or patients.
Controlling Machines and Processes	Using either control mechanisms or direct physical activity to operate machines or processes (not including computers or vehicles).
Operating Vehicles, Mechanized Devices, or Equipme	Running, maneuvering, navigating, or driving vehicles or mechanized equipment, such as forklifts, passenger vehicles, aircraft, or water craft.

Handling and Moving Objects	Using hands and arms in handling, installing, positioning, and moving materials, and manipulating things.
Drafting, Laying Out, and Specifying Technical Dev	Providing documentation, detailed instructions, drawings, or specifications to tell others about how devices, parts, equipment, or structures are to be fabricated, constructed, assembled, modified, maintained, or used.
Repairing and Maintaining Electronic Equipment	Servicing, repairing, calibrating, regulating, fine-tuning, or testing machines, devices, and equipment that operate primarily on the basis of electrical or electronic (not mechanical) principles.
Repairing and Maintaining Mechanical Equipment	Servicing, repairing, adjusting, and testing machines, devices, moving parts, and equipment that operate primarily on the basis of mechanical (not electronic) principles.

Work_Context	Work_Context Definitions
Electronic Mail	How often do you use electronic mail in this job?
Freedom to Make Decisions	How much decision making freedom, without supervision, does the job offer?
Structured versus Unstructured Work	To what extent is this job structured for the worker, rather than allowing the worker to determine tasks, priorities, and goals?
Telephone	How often do you have telephone conversations in this job?
Face-to-Face Discussions	How often do you have to have face-to-face discussions with individuals or teams in this job?
Work With Work Group or Team	How important is it to work with others in a group or team in this job?
Letters and Memos	How often does the job require written letters and memos?
Public Speaking	How often do you have to perform public speaking in this job?
Contact With Others	How much does this job require the worker to be in contact with others (face-to-face, by telephone, or otherwise) in order to perform it?
Importance of Being Exact or Accurate	How important is being very exact or highly accurate in performing this job?
Spend Time Sitting	How much does this job require sitting?
Indoors, Environmentally Controlled	How often does this job require working indoors in environmentally controlled conditions?
Coordinate or Lead Others	How important is it to coordinate or lead others in accomplishing work activities in this job?
Level of Competition	To what extent does this job require the worker to compete or to be aware of competitive pressures?
Responsibility for Outcomes and Results	How responsible is the worker for work outcomes and results of other workers?
Impact of Decisions on Co-workers or Company Resul	How do the decisions an employee makes impact the results of co-workers, clients or the company?
Time Pressure	How often does this job require the worker to meet strict deadlines?
Frequency of Decision Making	How frequently is the worker required to make decisions that affect other people, the financial resources, and/or the image and reputation of the organization?
Deal With External Customers	How important is it to work with external customers or the public in this job?
Responsible for Others' Health and Safety	How much responsibility is there for the health and safety of others in this job?
Importance of Repeating Same Tasks	How important is repeating the same physical activities (e.g., key entry) or mental activities (e.g., checking entries in a ledger) over and over, without stopping, to performing this job?
Indoors, Not Environmentally Controlled	How often does this job require working indoors in non-controlled environmental conditions (e.g., warehouse without heat)?
In an Enclosed Vehicle or Equipment	How often does this job require working in a closed vehicle or equipment (e.g., car)?
Frequency of Conflict Situations	How often are there conflict situations the employee has to face in this job?
Outdoors, Exposed to Weather	How often does this job require working outdoors, exposed to all weather conditions?
Physical Proximity	To what extent does this job require the worker to perform job tasks in close physical proximity to other people?
Consequence of Error	How serious would the result usually be if the worker made a mistake that was not readily correctable?
Deal With Unpleasant or Angry People	How frequently does the worker have to deal with unpleasant, angry, or discourteous individuals as part of the job requirements?
Spend Time Making Repetitive Motions	How much does this job require making repetitive motions?
Spend Time Standing	How much does this job require standing?
Exposed to Minor Burns, Cuts, Bites, or Stings	How often does this job require exposure to minor burns, cuts, bites, or stings?
Sounds, Noise Levels Are Distracting or Uncomforta	How often does this job require working exposed to sounds and noise levels that are distracting or uncomfortable?
Spend Time Using Your Hands to Handle, Control, or	How much does this job require using your hands to handle, control, or feel objects, tools or controls?
Exposed to Contaminants	How often does this job require working exposed to contaminants (such as pollutants, gases, dust or odors)?
Very Hot or Cold Temperatures	How often does this job require working in very hot (above 90 F degrees) or very cold (below 32 F degrees) temperatures?
Wear Common Protective or Safety Equipment such as	How much does this job require wearing common protective or safety equipment such as safety shoes, glasses, gloves, hard hats or life jackets?
Spend Time Walking and Running	How much does this job require walking and running?
Outdoors, Under Cover	How often does this job require working outdoors, under cover (e.g., structure with roof but no walls)?
Extremely Bright or Inadequate Lighting	How often does this job require working in extremely bright or inadequate lighting conditions?
Degree of Automation	How automated is the job?
Exposed to Hazardous Equipment	How often does this job require exposure to hazardous equipment?
Cramped Work Space, Awkward Positions	How often does this job require working in cramped work spaces that requires getting into awkward positions?
Exposed to Hazardous Conditions	How often does this job require exposure to hazardous conditions?
Spend Time Bending or Twisting the Body	How much does this job require bending or twisting your body?
Deal With Physically Aggressive People	How frequently does this job require the worker to deal with physical aggression of violent individuals?
Exposed to Disease or Infections	How often does this job require exposure to disease/infections?
Spend Time Kneeling, Crouching, Stooping, or Crawl	How much does this job require kneeling, crouching, stooping or crawling?
Wear Specialized Protective or Safety Equipment su	How much does this job require wearing specialized protective or safety equipment such as breathing apparatus, safety harness, full protection suits, or radiation protection?
Exposed to High Places	How often does this job require exposure to high places?
Spend Time Keeping or Regaining Balance	How much does this job require keeping or regaining your balance?
Exposed to Whole Body Vibration	How often does this job require exposure to whole body vibration (e.g., operate a jackhammer)?
Spend Time Climbing Ladders, Scaffolds, or Poles	How much does this job require climbing ladders, scaffolds, or poles?
In an Open Vehicle or Equipment	How often does this job require working in an open vehicle or equipment (e.g., tractor)?
Pace Determined by Speed of Equipment	How important is it to this job that the pace is determined by the speed of equipment or machinery? (This does not refer to keeping busy at all times on this job.)
Exposed to Radiation	How often does this job require exposure to radiation?

Job Zone Component	Job Zone Component Definitions
Title	Job Zone Five: Extensive Preparation Needed
Overall Experience	Extensive skill, knowledge, and experience are needed for these occupations. Many require more than five years of experience. For example, surgeons must complete four years of college and an additional five to seven years of specialized medical training to be able to do their job.
Job Training	Employees may need some on-the-job training, but most of these occupations assume that the person will already have the required skills, knowledge, work-related experience, and/or training.
Job Zone Examples	These occupations often involve coordinating, training, supervising, or managing the activities of others to accomplish goals. Very advanced communication and organizational skills are required. Examples include athletic trainers, lawyers, managing editors, physicists, social psychologists, and surgeons.
SVP Range	(8.0 and above)
Education	A bachelor's degree is the minimum formal education required for these occupations. However, many also require graduate school. For example, they may require a master's degree, and some require a Ph.D., M.D., or J.D. (law degree).

Work_Styles	Work_Styles Definitions
Analytical Thinking	Job requires analyzing information and using logic to address work-related issues and problems.
Integrity	Job requires being honest and ethical.
Achievement/Effort	Job requires establishing and maintaining personally challenging achievement goals and exerting effort toward mastering tasks.
Initiative	Job requires a willingness to take on responsibilities and challenges.
Independence	Job requires developing one's own ways of doing things, guiding oneself with little or no supervision, and depending on oneself to get things done.
Persistence	Job requires persistence in the face of obstacles.
Dependability	Job requires being reliable, responsible, and dependable, and fulfilling obligations.
Attention to Detail	Job requires being careful about detail and thorough in completing work tasks.
Innovation	Job requires creativity and alternative thinking to develop new ideas for and answers to work-related problems.
Leadership	Job requires a willingness to lead, take charge, and offer opinions and direction.
Cooperation	Job requires being pleasant with others on the job and displaying a good-natured, cooperative attitude.
Stress Tolerance	Job requires accepting criticism and dealing calmly and effectively with high stress situations.
Adaptability/Flexibility	Job requires being open to change (positive or negative) and to considerable variety in the workplace.
Self Control	Job requires maintaining composure, keeping emotions in check, controlling anger, and avoiding aggressive behavior, even in very difficult situations.
Concern for Others	Job requires being sensitive to others' needs and feelings and being understanding and helpful on the job.
Social Orientation	Job requires preferring to work with others rather than alone, and being personally connected with others on the job.

25-1051.00 - Atmospheric, Earth, Marine, and Space Sciences Teachers, Postsecondary

Teach courses in the physical sciences, except chemistry and physics.

Tasks

1) Supervise undergraduate and/or graduate teaching, internship, and research work.

2) Select and obtain materials and supplies such as textbooks and laboratory equipment.

3) Conduct research in a particular field of knowledge, and publish findings in professional journals, books, and/or electronic media.

4) Serve on academic or administrative committees that deal with institutional policies, departmental matters, and academic issues.

5) Maintain regularly scheduled office hours in order to advise and assist students.

6) Write grant proposals to procure external research funding.

7) Advise students on academic and vocational curricula, and on career issues.

8) Compile, administer, and grade examinations, or assign this work to others.

9) Prepare course materials such as syllabi, homework assignments, and handouts.

10) Plan, evaluate, and revise curricula, course content, and course materials and methods of instruction.

11) Evaluate and grade students' class work, assignments, and papers.

12) Participate in student recruitment, registration, and placement activities.

13) Maintain student attendance records, grades, and other required records.

14) Participate in campus and community events.

15) Initiate, facilitate, and moderate classroom discussions.

16) Supervise laboratory work and field work.

17) Prepare and deliver lectures to undergraduate and/or graduate students on topics such as structural geology, micrometeorology, and atmospheric thermodynamics.

18) Compile bibliographies of specialized materials for outside reading assignments.

19) Provide professional consulting services to government and/or industry.

20) Perform administrative duties such as serving as department head.

21) Act as advisers to student organizations.

22) Keep abreast of developments in their field by reading current literature, talking with colleagues, and participating in professional conferences.

Knowledge	Knowledge Definitions
Physics	Knowledge and prediction of physical principles, laws, their interrelationships, and applications to understanding fluid, material, and atmospheric dynamics, and mechanical, electrical, atomic and sub- atomic structures and processes.
Mathematics	Knowledge of arithmetic, algebra, geometry, calculus, statistics, and their applications.
Education and Training	Knowledge of principles and methods for curriculum and training design, teaching and instruction for individuals and groups, and the measurement of training effects.
English Language	Knowledge of the structure and content of the English language including the meaning and spelling of words, rules of composition, and grammar.
Computers and Electronics	Knowledge of circuit boards, processors, chips, electronic equipment, and computer hardware and software, including applications and programming.
Geography	Knowledge of principles and methods for describing the features of land, sea, and air masses, including their physical characteristics, locations, interrelationships, and distribution of plant, animal, and human life.
Chemistry	Knowledge of the chemical composition, structure, and properties of substances and of the chemical processes and transformations that they undergo. This includes uses of chemicals and their interactions, danger signs, production techniques, and disposal methods.
Engineering and Technology	Knowledge of the practical application of engineering science and technology. This includes applying principles, techniques, procedures, and equipment to the design and production of various goods and services.
Biology	Knowledge of plant and animal organisms, their tissues, cells, functions, interdependencies, and interactions with each other and the environment.
Communications and Media	Knowledge of media production, communication, and dissemination techniques and methods. This includes alternative ways to inform and entertain via written, oral, and visual media.
Design	Knowledge of design techniques, tools, and principles involved in production of precision technical plans, blueprints, drawings, and models.
Administration and Management	Knowledge of business and management principles involved in strategic planning, resource allocation, human resources modeling, leadership technique, production methods, and coordination of people and resources.
Personnel and Human Resources	Knowledge of principles and procedures for personnel recruitment, selection, training, compensation and benefits, labor relations and negotiation, and personnel information systems.
Customer and Personal Service	Knowledge of principles and processes for providing customer and personal services. This includes customer needs assessment, meeting quality standards for services, and evaluation of customer satisfaction.
Clerical	Knowledge of administrative and clerical procedures and systems such as word processing, managing files and records, stenography and transcription, designing forms, and other office procedures and terminology.
Telecommunications	Knowledge of transmission, broadcasting, switching, control, and operation of telecommunications systems.
Psychology	Knowledge of human behavior and performance; individual differences in ability, personality, and interests; learning and motivation; psychological research methods; and the assessment and treatment of behavioral and affective disorders.
Mechanical	Knowledge of machines and tools, including their designs, uses, repair, and maintenance.
History and Archeology	Knowledge of historical events and their causes, indicators, and effects on civilizations and cultures.
Economics and Accounting	Knowledge of economic and accounting principles and practices, the financial markets, banking and the analysis and reporting of financial data.
Law and Government	Knowledge of laws, legal codes, court procedures, precedents, government regulations, executive orders, agency rules, and the democratic political process.

Sales and Marketing	Knowledge of principles and methods for showing, promoting, and selling products or services. This includes marketing strategy and tactics, product demonstration, sales techniques, and sales control systems.
Foreign Language	Knowledge of the structure and content of a foreign (non-English) language including the meaning and spelling of words, rules of composition and grammar, and pronunciation.
Sociology and Anthropology	Knowledge of group behavior and dynamics, societal trends and influences, human migrations, ethnicity, cultures and their history and origins.
Production and Processing	Knowledge of raw materials, production processes, quality control, costs, and other techniques for maximizing the effective manufacture and distribution of goods.
Public Safety and Security	Knowledge of relevant equipment, policies, procedures, and strategies to promote effective local, state, or national security operations for the protection of people, data, property, and institutions.
Transportation	Knowledge of principles and methods for moving people or goods by air, rail, sea, or road, including the relative costs and benefits.
Therapy and Counseling	Knowledge of principles, methods, and procedures for diagnosis, treatment, and rehabilitation of physical and mental dysfunctions, and for career counseling and guidance.
Philosophy and Theology	Knowledge of different philosophical systems and religions. This includes their basic principles, values, ethics, ways of thinking, customs, practices, and their impact on human culture.
Building and Construction	Knowledge of materials, methods, and the tools involved in the construction or repair of houses, buildings, or other structures such as highways and roads.
Fine Arts	Knowledge of the theory and techniques required to compose, produce, and perform works of music, dance, visual arts, drama, and sculpture.
Medicine and Dentistry	Knowledge of the information and techniques needed to diagnose and treat human injuries, diseases, and deformities. This includes symptoms, treatment alternatives, drug properties and interactions, and preventive health-care measures.
Food Production	Knowledge of techniques and equipment for planting, growing, and harvesting food products (both plant and animal) for consumption, including storage/handling techniques.

Skills	Skills Definitions
Science	Using scientific rules and methods to solve problems.
Reading Comprehension	Understanding written sentences and paragraphs in work related documents.
Instructing	Teaching others how to do something.
Critical Thinking	Using logic and reasoning to identify the strengths and weaknesses of alternative solutions, conclusions or approaches to problems.
Writing	Communicating effectively in writing as appropriate for the needs of the audience.
Complex Problem Solving	Identifying complex problems and reviewing related information to develop and evaluate options and implement solutions.
Active Learning	Understanding the implications of new information for both current and future problem-solving and decision-making.
Speaking	Talking to others to convey information effectively.
Mathematics	Using mathematics to solve problems.
Active Listening	Giving full attention to what other people are saying, taking time to understand the points being made, asking questions as appropriate, and not interrupting at inappropriate times.
Time Management	Managing one's own time and the time of others.
Learning Strategies	Selecting and using training/instructional methods and procedures appropriate for the situation when learning or teaching new things.
Judgment and Decision Making	Considering the relative costs and benefits of potential actions to choose the most appropriate one.
Monitoring	Monitoring/Assessing performance of yourself, other individuals, or organizations to make improvements or take corrective action.
Programming	Writing computer programs for various purposes.
Coordination	Adjusting actions in relation to others' actions.
Management of Financial Resources	Determining how money will be spent to get the work done, and accounting for these expenditures.
Equipment Selection	Determining the kind of tools and equipment needed to do a job.
Management of Personnel Resources	Motivating, developing, and directing people as they work, identifying the best people for the job.
Persuasion	Persuading others to change their minds or behavior.

Social Perceptiveness	Being aware of others' reactions and understanding why they react as they do.
Troubleshooting	Determining causes of operating errors and deciding what to do about it.
Quality Control Analysis	Conducting tests and inspections of products, services, or processes to evaluate quality or performance.
Technology Design	Generating or adapting equipment and technology to serve user needs.
Systems Analysis	Determining how a system should work and how changes in conditions, operations, and the environment will affect outcomes.
Negotiation	Bringing others together and trying to reconcile differences.
Operations Analysis	Analyzing needs and product requirements to create a design.
Service Orientation	Actively looking for ways to help people.
Management of Material Resources	Obtaining and seeing to the appropriate use of equipment, facilities, and materials needed to do certain work.
Systems Evaluation	Identifying measures or indicators of system performance and the actions needed to improve or correct performance, relative to the goals of the system.
Operation Monitoring	Watching gauges, dials, or other indicators to make sure a machine is working properly.
Equipment Maintenance	Performing routine maintenance on equipment and determining when and what kind of maintenance is needed.
Installation	Installing equipment, machines, wiring, or programs to meet specifications.
Operation and Control	Controlling operations of equipment or systems.
Repairing	Repairing machines or systems using the needed tools.

Ability	Ability Definitions
Oral Expression	The ability to communicate information and ideas in speaking so others will understand.
Written Expression	The ability to communicate information and ideas in writing so others will understand.
Written Comprehension	The ability to read and understand information and ideas presented in writing.
Speech Clarity	The ability to speak clearly so others can understand you.
Oral Comprehension	The ability to listen to and understand information and ideas presented through spoken words and sentences.
Deductive Reasoning	The ability to apply general rules to specific problems to produce answers that make sense.
Inductive Reasoning	The ability to combine pieces of information to form general rules or conclusions (includes finding a relationship among seemingly unrelated events).
Speech Recognition	The ability to identify and understand the speech of another person.
Near Vision	The ability to see details at close range (within a few feet of the observer).
Problem Sensitivity	The ability to tell when something is wrong or is likely to go wrong. It does not involve solving the problem, only recognizing there is a problem.
Information Ordering	The ability to arrange things or actions in a certain order or pattern according to a specific rule or set of rules (e.g., patterns of numbers, letters, words, pictures, mathematical operations).
Category Flexibility	The ability to generate or use different sets of rules for combining or grouping things in different ways.
Mathematical Reasoning	The ability to choose the right mathematical methods or formulas to solve a problem.
Originality	The ability to come up with unusual or clever ideas about a given topic or situation, or to develop creative ways to solve a problem.
Selective Attention	The ability to concentrate on a task over a period of time without being distracted.
Fluency of Ideas	The ability to come up with a number of ideas about a topic (the number of ideas is important, not their quality, correctness, or creativity).
Number Facility	The ability to add, subtract, multiply, or divide quickly and correctly.
Flexibility of Closure	The ability to identify or detect a known pattern (a figure, object, word, or sound) that is hidden in other distracting material.
Time Sharing	The ability to shift back and forth between two or more activities or sources of information (such as speech, sounds, touch, or other sources).
Far Vision	The ability to see details at a distance.
Memorization	The ability to remember information such as words, numbers, pictures, and procedures.
Speed of Closure	The ability to quickly make sense of, combine, and organize information into meaningful patterns.

Perceptual Speed	The ability to quickly and accurately compare similarities and differences among sets of letters, numbers, objects, pictures, or patterns. The things to be compared may be presented at the same time or one after the other. This ability also includes comparing a presented object with a remembered object.
Visualization	The ability to imagine how something will look after it is moved around or when its parts are moved or rearranged.
Auditory Attention	The ability to focus on a single source of sound in the presence of other distracting sounds.
Visual Color Discrimination	The ability to match or detect differences between colors, including shades of color and brightness.
Hearing Sensitivity	The ability to detect or tell the differences between sounds that vary in pitch and loudness.
Depth Perception	The ability to judge which of several objects is closer or farther away from you, or to judge the distance between you and an object.
Finger Dexterity	The ability to make precisely coordinated movements of the fingers of one or both hands to grasp, manipulate, or assemble very small objects.
Trunk Strength	The ability to use your abdominal and lower back muscles to support part of the body repeatedly or continuously over time without 'giving out' or fatiguing.
Extent Flexibility	The ability to bend, stretch, twist, or reach with your body, arms, and/or legs.
Gross Body Equilibrium	The ability to keep or regain your body balance or stay upright when in an unstable position.
Explosive Strength	The ability to use short bursts of muscle force to propel oneself (as in jumping or sprinting), or to throw an object.
Stamina	The ability to exert yourself physically over long periods of time without getting winded or out of breath.
Gross Body Coordination	The ability to coordinate the movement of your arms, legs, and torso together when the whole body is in motion.
Dynamic Strength	The ability to exert muscle force repeatedly or continuously over time. This involves muscular endurance and resistance to muscle fatigue.
Dynamic Flexibility	The ability to quickly and repeatedly bend, stretch, twist, or reach out with your body, arms, and/or legs.
Static Strength	The ability to exert maximum muscle force to lift, push, pull, or carry objects.
Speed of Limb Movement	The ability to quickly move the arms and legs.
Reaction Time	The ability to quickly respond (with the hand, finger, or foot) to a signal (sound, light, picture) when it appears.
Rate Control	The ability to time your movements or the movement of a piece of equipment in anticipation of changes in the speed and/or direction of a moving object or scene.
Arm-Hand Steadiness	The ability to keep your hand and arm steady while moving your arm or while holding your arm and hand in one position.
Sound Localization	The ability to tell the direction from which a sound originated.
Response Orientation	The ability to choose quickly between two or more movements in response to two or more different signals (lights, sounds, pictures). It includes the speed with which the correct response is started with the hand, foot, or other body part.
Manual Dexterity	The ability to quickly move your hand, your hand together with your arm, or your two hands to grasp, manipulate, or assemble objects.
Glare Sensitivity	The ability to see objects in the presence of glare or bright lighting.
Peripheral Vision	The ability to see objects or movement of objects to one's side when the eyes are looking ahead.
Night Vision	The ability to see under low light conditions.
Control Precision	The ability to quickly and repeatedly adjust the controls of a machine or a vehicle to exact positions.
Multilimb Coordination	The ability to coordinate two or more limbs (for example, two arms, two legs, or one leg and one arm) while sitting, standing, or lying down. It does not involve performing the activities while the whole body is in motion.
Wrist-Finger Speed	The ability to make fast, simple, repeated movements of the fingers, hands, and wrists.
Spatial Orientation	The ability to know your location in relation to the environment or to know where other objects are in relation to you.

Work_Activity	**Work_Activity Definitions**
Analyzing Data or Information	Identifying the underlying principles, reasons, or facts of information by breaking down information or data into separate parts.
Getting Information	Observing, receiving, and otherwise obtaining information from all relevant sources.

Thinking Creatively	Developing, designing, or creating new applications, ideas, relationships, systems, or products, including artistic contributions.
Interacting With Computers	Using computers and computer systems (including hardware and software) to program, write software, set up functions, enter data, or process information.
Processing Information	Compiling, coding, categorizing, calculating, tabulating, auditing, or verifying information or data.
Training and Teaching Others	Identifying the educational needs of others, developing formal educational or training programs or classes, and teaching or instructing others.
Updating and Using Relevant Knowledge	Keeping up-to-date technically and applying new knowledge to your job.
Making Decisions and Solving Problems	Analyzing information and evaluating results to choose the best solution and solve problems.
Interpreting the Meaning of Information for Others	Translating or explaining what information means and how it can be used.
Identifying Objects, Actions, and Events	Identifying information by categorizing, estimating, recognizing differences or similarities, and detecting changes in circumstances or events.
Estimating the Quantifiable Characteristics of Pro	Estimating sizes, distances, and quantities; or determining time, costs, resources, or materials needed to perform a work activity.
Communicating with Supervisors, Peers, or Subordin	Providing information to supervisors, co-workers, and subordinates by telephone, in written form, e-mail, or in person.
Communicating with Persons Outside Organization	Communicating with people outside the organization, representing the organization to customers, the public, government, and other external sources. This information can be exchanged in person, in writing, or by telephone or e-mail.
Developing Objectives and Strategies	Establishing long-range objectives and specifying the strategies and actions to achieve them.
Judging the Qualities of Things, Services, or Peop	Assessing the value, importance, or quality of things or people.
Documenting/Recording Information	Entering, transcribing, recording, storing, or maintaining information in written or electronic/magnetic form.
Organizing, Planning, and Prioritizing Work	Developing specific goals and plans to prioritize, organize, and accomplish your work.
Guiding, Directing, and Motivating Subordinates	Providing guidance and direction to subordinates, including setting performance standards and monitoring performance.
Monitor Processes, Materials, or Surroundings	Monitoring and reviewing information from materials, events, or the environment, to detect or assess problems.
Establishing and Maintaining Interpersonal Relatio	Developing constructive and cooperative working relationships with others, and maintaining them over time.
Coaching and Developing Others	Identifying the developmental needs of others and coaching, mentoring, or otherwise helping others to improve their knowledge or skills.
Provide Consultation and Advice to Others	Providing guidance and expert advice to management or other groups on technical, systems-, or process-related topics.
Monitoring and Controlling Resources	Monitoring and controlling resources and overseeing the spending of money.
Coordinating the Work and Activities of Others	Getting members of a group to work together to accomplish tasks.
Scheduling Work and Activities	Scheduling events, programs, and activities, as well as the work of others.
Developing and Building Teams	Encouraging and building mutual trust, respect, and cooperation among team members.
Performing Administrative Activities	Performing day-to-day administrative tasks such as maintaining information files and processing paperwork.
Selling or Influencing Others	Convincing others to buy merchandise/goods or to otherwise change their minds or actions.
Resolving Conflicts and Negotiating with Others	Handling complaints, settling disputes, and resolving grievances and conflicts, or otherwise negotiating with others.
Evaluating Information to Determine Compliance wit	Using relevant information and individual judgment to determine whether events or processes comply with laws, regulations, or standards.
Staffing Organizational Units	Recruiting, interviewing, selecting, hiring, and promoting employees in an organization.
Performing for or Working Directly with the Public	Performing for people or dealing directly with the public. This includes serving customers in restaurants and stores, and receiving clients or guests.
Inspecting Equipment, Structures, or Material	Inspecting equipment, structures, or materials to identify the cause of errors or other problems or defects.
Assisting and Caring for Others	Providing personal assistance, medical attention, emotional support, or other personal care to others such as coworkers, customers, or patients.

Controlling Machines and Processes	Using either control mechanisms or direct physical activity to operate machines or processes (not including computers or vehicles).
Performing General Physical Activities	Performing physical activities that require considerable use of your arms and legs and moving your whole body, such as climbing, lifting, balancing, walking, stooping, and handling of materials.
Drafting, Laying Out, and Specifying Technical Dev	Providing documentation, detailed instructions, drawings, or specifications to tell others about how devices, parts, equipment, or structures are to be fabricated, constructed, assembled, modified, maintained, or used.
Repairing and Maintaining Electronic Equipment	Servicing, repairing, calibrating, regulating, fine-tuning, or testing machines, devices, and equipment that operate primarily on the basis of electrical or electronic (not mechanical) principles.
Handling and Moving Objects	Using hands and arms in handling, installing, positioning, and moving materials, and manipulating things.
Repairing and Maintaining Mechanical Equipment	Servicing, repairing, adjusting, and testing machines, devices, moving parts, and equipment that operate primarily on the basis of mechanical (not electronic) principles.
Operating Vehicles, Mechanized Devices, or Equipme	Running, maneuvering, navigating, or driving vehicles or mechanized equipment, such as forklifts, passenger vehicles, aircraft, or water craft.

Work_Context	Work_Context Definitions
Electronic Mail	How often do you use electronic mail in this job?
Face-to-Face Discussions	How often do you have to have face-to-face discussions with individuals or teams in this job?
Structured versus Unstructured Work	To what extent is this job structured for the worker, rather than allowing the worker to determine tasks, priorities, and goals?
Indoors, Environmentally Controlled	How often does this job require working indoors in environmentally controlled conditions?
Freedom to Make Decisions	How much decision making freedom, without supervision, does the job offer?
Telephone	How often do you have telephone conversations in this job?
Importance of Being Exact or Accurate	How important is being very exact or highly accurate in performing this job?
Level of Competition	To what extent does this job require the worker to compete or to be aware of competitive pressures?
Letters and Memos	How often does the job require written letters and memos?
Contact With Others	How often does this job require the worker to be in contact with others (face-to-face, by telephone, or otherwise) in order to perform it?
Spend Time Sitting	How much does this job require sitting?
Public Speaking	How often do you have to perform public speaking in this job?
Work With Work Group or Team	How important is it to work with others in a group or team in this job?
Impact of Decisions on Co-workers or Company Resul	How do the decisions an employee makes impact the results of co-workers, clients or the company?
Coordinate or Lead Others	How important is it to coordinate or lead others in accomplishing work activities in this job?
Time Pressure	How often does this job require the worker to meet strict deadlines?
Frequency of Decision Making	How frequently is the worker required to make decisions that affect other people, the financial resources, and/or the image and reputation of the organization?
Responsibility for Outcomes and Results	How responsible is the worker for work outcomes and results of other workers?
Importance of Repeating Same Tasks	How important is repeating the same physical activities (e.g., key entry) or mental activities (e.g., checking entries in a ledger) over and over, without stopping, to performing this job?
Deal With External Customers	How important is it to work with external customers or the public in this job?
Responsible for Others' Health and Safety	How much responsibility is there for the health and safety of others in this job?
Spend Time Making Repetitive Motions	How much does this job require making repetitive motions?
Consequence of Error	How serious would the result usually be if the worker made a mistake that was not readily correctable?
Spend Time Using Your Hands to Handle, Control, or	How much does this job require using your hands to handle, control, or feel objects, tools or controls?
Sounds, Noise Levels Are Distracting or Uncomforta	How often does this job require working exposed to sounds and noise levels that are distracting or uncomfortable?
Frequency of Conflict Situations	How often are there conflict situations the employee has to face in this job?
Physical Proximity	To what extent does this job require the worker to perform job tasks in close physical proximity to other people?

Spend Time Standing	How much does this job require standing?
Deal With Unpleasant or Angry People	How frequently does the worker have to deal with unpleasant, angry, or discourteous individuals as part of the job requirements?
In an Enclosed Vehicle or Equipment	How often does this job require working in a closed vehicle or equipment (e.g., car)?
Outdoors, Exposed to Weather	How often does this job require working outdoors, exposed to all weather conditions?
Spend Time Walking and Running	How much does this job require walking and running?
Indoors, Not Environmentally Controlled	How often does this job require working indoors in non-controlled environmental conditions (e.g., warehouse without heat)?
Extremely Bright or Inadequate Lighting	How often does this job require working in extremely bright or inadequate lighting conditions?
Exposed to Contaminants	How often does this job require working exposed to contaminants (such as pollutants, gases, dust or odors)?
Very Hot or Cold Temperatures	How often does this job require working in very hot (above 90 F degrees) or very cold (below 32 F degrees) temperatures?
Exposed to Hazardous Equipment	How often does this job require exposure to hazardous equipment?
Exposed to Hazardous Conditions	How often does this job require exposure to hazardous conditions?
Wear Common Protective or Safety Equipment such as	How much does this job require wearing common protective or safety equipment such as safety shoes, glasses, gloves, hard hats or life jackets?
Cramped Work Space, Awkward Positions	How often does this job require working in cramped work spaces that requires getting into awkward positions?
Outdoors, Under Cover	How often does this job require working outdoors, under cover (e.g., structure with roof but no walls)?
Exposed to Minor Burns, Cuts, Bites, or Stings	How often does this job require exposure to minor burns, cuts, bites, or stings?
Degree of Automation	How automated is the job?
Spend Time Bending or Twisting the Body	How much does this job require bending or twisting your body?
Spend Time Kneeling, Crouching, Stooping, or Crawl	How much does this job require kneeling, crouching, stooping or crawling?
Wear Specialized Protective or Safety Equipment su	How much does this job require wearing specialized protective or safety equipment such as breathing apparatus, safety harness, full protection suits, or radiation protection?
Pace Determined by Speed of Equipment	How important is it to this job that the pace is determined by the speed of equipment or machinery? (This does not refer to keeping busy at all times on this job.)
Deal With Physically Aggressive People	How frequently does this job require the worker to deal with physical aggression of violent individuals?
In an Open Vehicle or Equipment	How often does this job require working in an open vehicle or equipment (e.g., tractor)?
Exposed to Radiation	How often does this job require exposure to radiation?
Spend Time Keeping or Regaining Balance	How much does this job require keeping or regaining your balance?
Exposed to High Places	How often does this job require exposure to high places?
Spend Time Climbing Ladders, Scaffolds, or Poles	How much does this job require climbing ladders, scaffolds, or poles?
Exposed to Whole Body Vibration	How often does this job require exposure to whole body vibration (e.g., operate a jackhammer)?
Exposed to Disease or Infections	How often does this job require exposure to disease/infections?

Job Zone Component	Job Zone Component Definitions
Title	Job Zone Five: Extensive Preparation Needed
Overall Experience	Extensive skill, knowledge, and experience are needed for these occupations. Many require more than five years of experience. For example, surgeons must complete four years of college and an additional five to seven years of specialized medical training to be able to do their job.
Job Training	Employees may need some on-the-job training, but most of these occupations assume that the person will already have the required skills, knowledge, work-related experience, and/or training.
Job Zone Examples	These occupations often involve coordinating, training, supervising, or managing the activities of others to accomplish goals. Very advanced communication and organizational skills are required. Examples include athletic trainers, lawyers, managing editors, physicists, social psychologists, and surgeons.
SVP Range	(8.0 and above)

Education	A bachelor's degree is the minimum formal education required for these occupations. However, many also require graduate school. For example, they may require a master's degree, and some require a Ph.D., M.D., or J.D. (law degree).

Work_Styles	Work_Styles Definitions
Analytical Thinking	Job requires analyzing information and using logic to address work-related issues and problems.
Independence	Job requires developing one's own ways of doing things, guiding oneself with little or no supervision, and depending on oneself to get things done.
Achievement/Effort	Job requires establishing and maintaining personally challenging achievement goals and exerting effort toward mastering tasks.
Initiative	Job requires a willingness to take on responsibilities and challenges.
Persistence	Job requires persistence in the face of obstacles.
Innovation	Job requires creativity and alternative thinking to develop new ideas for and answers to work-related problems.
Integrity	Job requires being honest and ethical.
Dependability	Job requires being reliable, responsible, and dependable, and fulfilling obligations.
Leadership	Job requires a willingness to lead, take charge, and offer opinions and direction.
Stress Tolerance	Job requires accepting criticism and dealing calmly and effectively with high stress situations.
Attention to Detail	Job requires being careful about detail and thorough in completing work tasks.
Self Control	Job requires maintaining composure, keeping emotions in check, controlling anger, and avoiding aggressive behavior, even in very difficult situations.
Cooperation	Job requires being pleasant with others on the job and displaying a good-natured, cooperative attitude.
Adaptability/Flexibility	Job requires being open to change (positive or negative) and to considerable variety in the workplace.
Concern for Others	Job requires being sensitive to others' needs and feelings and being understanding and helpful on the job.
Social Orientation	Job requires preferring to work with others rather than alone, and being personally connected with others on the job.

25-1052.00 - Chemistry Teachers, Postsecondary

Teach courses pertaining to the chemical and physical properties and compositional changes of substances. Work may include instruction in the methods of qualitative and quantitative chemical analysis. Includes both teachers primarily engaged in teaching, and those who do a combination of both teaching and research.

Tasks

1) Maintain regularly scheduled office hours in order to advise and assist students.

2) Compile, administer, and grade examinations, or assign this work to others.

3) Select and obtain materials and supplies such as textbooks and laboratory equipment.

4) Plan, evaluate, and revise curricula, course content, and course materials and methods of instruction.

5) Supervise students' laboratory work.

6) Advise students on academic and vocational curricula, and on career issues.

7) Prepare and deliver lectures to undergraduate and/or graduate students on topics such as organic chemistry, analytical chemistry, and chemical separation.

8) Collaborate with colleagues to address teaching and research issues.

9) Initiate, facilitate, and moderate classroom discussions.

10) Participate in campus and community events.

11) Serve on academic or administrative committees that deal with institutional policies, departmental matters, and academic issues.

12) Participate in student recruitment, registration, and placement activities.

13) Prepare and submit required reports related to instruction.

14) Write grant proposals to procure external research funding.

15) Conduct research in a particular field of knowledge, and publish findings in professional journals, books and/or electronic media.

16) Supervise undergraduate and/or graduate teaching, internship, and research work.

17) Compile bibliographies of specialized materials for outside reading assignments.

18) Act as advisers to student organizations.

19) Perform administrative duties such as serving as a department head.

20) Provide professional consulting services to government and/or industry.

21) Prepare course materials such as syllabi, homework assignments, and handouts.

22) Evaluate and grade students' class work, laboratory performance, assignments, and papers.

23) Maintain student attendance records, grades, and other required records.

Knowledge	Knowledge Definitions
Chemistry	Knowledge of the chemical composition, structure, and properties of substances and of the chemical processes and transformations that they undergo. This includes uses of chemicals and their interactions, danger signs, production techniques, and disposal methods.
Education and Training	Knowledge of principles and methods for curriculum and training design, teaching and instruction for individuals and groups, and the measurement of training effects.
English Language	Knowledge of the structure and content of the English language including the meaning and spelling of words, rules of composition, and grammar.
Mathematics	Knowledge of arithmetic, algebra, geometry, calculus, statistics, and their applications.
Physics	Knowledge and prediction of physical principles, laws, their interrelationships, and applications to understanding fluid, material, and atmospheric dynamics, and mechanical, electrical, atomic and sub-atomic structures and processes.
Biology	Knowledge of plant and animal organisms, their tissues, cells, functions, interdependencies, and interactions with each other and the environment.
Computers and Electronics	Knowledge of circuit boards, processors, chips, electronic equipment, and computer hardware and software, including applications and programming.
Engineering and Technology	Knowledge of the practical application of engineering science and technology. This includes applying principles, techniques, procedures, and equipment to the design and production of various goods and services.
Communications and Media	Knowledge of media production, communication, and dissemination techniques and methods. This includes alternative ways to inform and entertain via written, oral, and visual media.
Clerical	Knowledge of administrative and clerical procedures and systems such as word processing, managing files and records, stenography and transcription, designing forms, and other office procedures and terminology.
Psychology	Knowledge of human behavior and performance; individual differences in ability, personality, and interests; learning and motivation; psychological research methods; and the assessment and treatment of behavioral and affective disorders.
Administration and Management	Knowledge of business and management principles involved in strategic planning, resource allocation, human resources modeling, leadership technique, production methods, and coordination of people and resources.
Public Safety and Security	Knowledge of relevant equipment, policies, procedures, and strategies to promote effective local, state, or national security operations for the protection of people, data, property, and institutions.
Mechanical	Knowledge of machines and tools, including their designs, uses, repair, and maintenance.
Customer and Personal Service	Knowledge of principles and processes for providing customer and personal services. This includes customer needs assessment, meeting quality standards for services, and evaluation of customer satisfaction.
Medicine and Dentistry	Knowledge of the information and techniques needed to diagnose and treat human injuries, diseases, and deformities. This includes symptoms, treatment alternatives, drug properties and interactions, and preventive health-care measures.
Personnel and Human Resources	Knowledge of principles and procedures for personnel recruitment, selection, training, compensation and benefits, labor relations and negotiation, and personnel information systems.

Design	Knowledge of design techniques, tools, and principles involved in production of precision technical plans, blueprints, drawings, and models.
Law and Government	Knowledge of laws, legal codes, court procedures, precedents, government regulations, executive orders, agency rules, and the democratic political process.
Sociology and Anthropology	Knowledge of group behavior and dynamics, societal trends and influences, human migrations, ethnicity, cultures and their history and origins.
Geography	Knowledge of principles and methods for describing the features of land, sea, and air masses, including their physical characteristics, locations, interrelationships, and distribution of plant, animal, and human life.
Therapy and Counseling	Knowledge of principles, methods, and procedures for diagnosis, treatment, and rehabilitation of physical and mental dysfunctions, and for career counseling and guidance.
History and Archeology	Knowledge of historical events and their causes, indicators, and effects on civilizations and cultures.
Philosophy and Theology	Knowledge of different philosophical systems and religions. This includes their basic principles, values, ethics, ways of thinking, customs, practices, and their impact on human culture.
Foreign Language	Knowledge of the structure and content of a foreign (non-English) language including the meaning and spelling of words, rules of composition and grammar, and pronunciation.
Sales and Marketing	Knowledge of principles and methods for showing, promoting, and selling products or services. This includes marketing strategy and tactics, product demonstration, sales techniques, and sales control systems.
Telecommunications	Knowledge of transmission, broadcasting, switching, control, and operation of telecommunications systems.
Economics and Accounting	Knowledge of economic and accounting principles and practices, the financial markets, banking and the analysis and reporting of financial data.
Production and Processing	Knowledge of raw materials, production processes, quality control, costs, and other techniques for maximizing the effective manufacture and distribution of goods.
Building and Construction	Knowledge of materials, methods, and the tools involved in the construction or repair of houses, buildings, or other structures such as highways and roads.
Fine Arts	Knowledge of the theory and techniques required to compose, produce, and perform works of music, dance, visual arts, drama, and sculpture.
Transportation	Knowledge of principles and methods for moving people or goods by air, rail, sea, or road, including the relative costs and benefits.
Food Production	Knowledge of techniques and equipment for planting, growing, and harvesting food products (both plant and animal) for consumption, including storage/handling techniques.

Skills | Skills Definitions

Science	Using scientific rules and methods to solve problems.
Instructing	Teaching others how to do something.
Reading Comprehension	Understanding written sentences and paragraphs in work related documents.
Speaking	Talking to others to convey information effectively.
Critical Thinking	Using logic and reasoning to identify the strengths and weaknesses of alternative solutions, conclusions or approaches to problems.
Mathematics	Using mathematics to solve problems.
Active Learning	Understanding the implications of new information for both current and future problem-solving and decision-making.
Writing	Communicating effectively in writing as appropriate for the needs of the audience.
Learning Strategies	Selecting and using training/instructional methods and procedures appropriate for the situation when learning or teaching new things.
Time Management	Managing one's own time and the time of others.
Complex Problem Solving	Identifying complex problems and reviewing related information to develop and evaluate options and implement solutions.
Active Listening	Giving full attention to what other people are saying, taking time to understand the points being made, asking questions as appropriate, and not interrupting at inappropriate times.
Monitoring	Monitoring/Assessing performance of yourself, other individuals, or organizations to make improvements or take corrective action.

Equipment Selection	Determining the kind of tools and equipment needed to do a job.
Social Perceptiveness	Being aware of others' reactions and understanding why they react as they do.
Judgment and Decision Making	Considering the relative costs and benefits of potential actions to choose the most appropriate one.
Coordination	Adjusting actions in relation to others' actions.
Troubleshooting	Determining causes of operating errors and deciding what to do about it.
Persuasion	Persuading others to change their minds or behavior.
Technology Design	Generating or adapting equipment and technology to serve user needs.
Service Orientation	Actively looking for ways to help people.
Management of Material Resources	Obtaining and seeing to the appropriate use of equipment, facilities, and materials needed to do certain work.
Operations Analysis	Analyzing needs and product requirements to create a design.
Equipment Maintenance	Performing routine maintenance on equipment and determining when and what kind of maintenance is needed.
Management of Personnel Resources	Motivating, developing, and directing people as they work, identifying the best people for the job.
Management of Financial Resources	Determining how money will be spent to get the work done, and accounting for these expenditures.
Negotiation	Bringing others together and trying to reconcile differences.
Quality Control Analysis	Conducting tests and inspections of products, services, or processes to evaluate quality or performance.
Systems Evaluation	Identifying measures or indicators of system performance and the actions needed to improve or correct performance, relative to the goals of the system.
Repairing	Repairing machines or systems using the needed tools.
Operation and Control	Controlling operations of equipment or systems.
Installation	Installing equipment, machines, wiring, or programs to meet specifications.
Systems Analysis	Determining how a system should work and how changes in conditions, operations, and the environment will affect outcomes.
Operation Monitoring	Watching gauges, dials, or other indicators to make sure a machine is working properly.
Programming	Writing computer programs for various purposes.

Ability | Ability Definitions

Oral Expression	The ability to communicate information and ideas in speaking so others will understand.
Oral Comprehension	The ability to listen to and understand information and ideas presented through spoken words and sentences.
Written Comprehension	The ability to read and understand information and ideas presented in writing.
Speech Clarity	The ability to speak clearly so others can understand you.
Written Expression	The ability to communicate information and ideas in writing so others will understand.
Deductive Reasoning	The ability to apply general rules to specific problems to produce answers that make sense.
Inductive Reasoning	The ability to combine pieces of information to form general rules or conclusions (includes finding a relationship among seemingly unrelated events).
Near Vision	The ability to see details at close range (within a few feet of the observer).
Problem Sensitivity	The ability to tell when something is wrong or is likely to go wrong. It does not involve solving the problem, only recognizing there is a problem.
Speech Recognition	The ability to identify and understand the speech of another person.
Originality	The ability to come up with unusual or clever ideas about a given topic or situation, or to develop creative ways to solve a problem.
Mathematical Reasoning	The ability to choose the right mathematical methods or formulas to solve a problem.
Information Ordering	The ability to arrange things or actions in a certain order or pattern according to a specific rule or set of rules (e.g., patterns of numbers, letters, words, pictures, mathematical operations).
Selective Attention	The ability to concentrate on a task over a period of time without being distracted.
Category Flexibility	The ability to generate or use different sets of rules for combining or grouping things in different ways.
Memorization	The ability to remember information such as words, numbers, pictures, and procedures.

Fluency of Ideas	The ability to come up with a number of ideas about a topic (the number of ideas is important, not their quality, correctness, or creativity).
Flexibility of Closure	The ability to identify or detect a known pattern (a figure, object, word, or sound) that is hidden in other distracting material.
Number Facility	The ability to add, subtract, multiply, or divide quickly and correctly.
Time Sharing	The ability to shift back and forth between two or more activities or sources of information (such as speech, sounds, touch, or other sources).
Finger Dexterity	The ability to make precisely coordinated movements of the fingers of one or both hands to grasp, manipulate, or assemble very small objects.
Speed of Closure	The ability to quickly make sense of, combine, and organize information into meaningful patterns.
Visualization	The ability to imagine how something will look after it is moved around or when its parts are moved or rearranged.
Far Vision	The ability to see details at a distance.
Perceptual Speed	The ability to quickly and accurately compare similarities and differences among sets of letters, numbers, objects, pictures, or patterns. The things to be compared may be presented at the same time or one after the other. This ability also includes comparing a presented object with a remembered object.
Auditory Attention	The ability to focus on a single source of sound in the presence of other distracting sounds.
Visual Color Discrimination	The ability to match or detect differences between colors, including shades of color and brightness.
Arm-Hand Steadiness	The ability to keep your hand and arm steady while moving your arm or while holding your arm and hand in one position.
Trunk Strength	The ability to use your abdominal and lower back muscles to support part of the body repeatedly or continuously over time without 'giving out' or fatiguing.
Manual Dexterity	The ability to quickly move your hand, your hand together with your arm, or your two hands to grasp, manipulate, or assemble objects.
Depth Perception	The ability to judge which of several objects is closer or farther away from you, or to judge the distance between you and an object.
Hearing Sensitivity	The ability to detect or tell the differences between sounds that vary in pitch and loudness.
Gross Body Coordination	The ability to coordinate the movement of your arms, legs, and torso together when the whole body is in motion.
Dynamic Flexibility	The ability to quickly and repeatedly bend, stretch, twist, or reach out with your body, arms, and/or legs.
Extent Flexibility	The ability to bend, stretch, twist, or reach with your body, arms, and/or legs.
Stamina	The ability to exert yourself physically over long periods of time without getting winded or out of breath.
Reaction Time	The ability to quickly respond (with the hand, finger, or foot) to a signal (sound, light, picture) when it appears.
Rate Control	The ability to time your movements or the movement of a piece of equipment in anticipation of changes in the speed and/or direction of a moving object or scene.
Dynamic Strength	The ability to exert muscle force repeatedly or continuously over time. This involves muscular endurance and resistance to muscle fatigue.
Multilimb Coordination	The ability to coordinate two or more limbs (for example, two arms, two legs, or one leg and one arm) while sitting, standing, or lying down. It does not involve performing the activities while the whole body is in motion.
Control Precision	The ability to quickly and repeatedly adjust the controls of a machine or a vehicle to exact positions.
Response Orientation	The ability to choose quickly between two or more movements in response to two or different signals (lights, sounds, pictures). It includes the speed with which the correct response is started with the hand, foot, or other body part.
Static Strength	The ability to exert maximum muscle force to lift, push, pull, or carry objects.
Spatial Orientation	The ability to know your location in relation to the environment or to know where other objects are in relation to you.
Peripheral Vision	The ability to see objects or movement of objects to one's side when the eyes are looking ahead.
Wrist-Finger Speed	The ability to make fast, simple, repeated movements of the fingers, hands, and wrists.
Explosive Strength	The ability to use short bursts of muscle force to propel oneself (as in jumping or sprinting), or to throw an object.
Night Vision	The ability to see under low light conditions.

Glare Sensitivity	The ability to see objects in the presence of glare or bright lighting.
Sound Localization	The ability to tell the direction from which a sound originated.
Speed of Limb Movement	The ability to quickly move the arms and legs.
Gross Body Equilibrium	The ability to keep or regain your body balance or stay upright when in an unstable position.

Work_Activity	Work_Activity Definitions
Training and Teaching Others	Identifying the educational needs of others, developing formal educational or training programs or classes, and teaching or instructing others.
Interpreting the Meaning of Information for Others	Translating or explaining what information means and how it can be used.
Making Decisions and Solving Problems	Analyzing information and evaluating results to choose the best solution and solve problems.
Getting Information	Observing, receiving, and otherwise obtaining information from all relevant sources.
Interacting With Computers	Using computers and computer systems (including hardware and software) to program, write software, set up functions, enter data, or process information.
Updating and Using Relevant Knowledge	Keeping up-to-date technically and applying new knowledge to your job.
Thinking Creatively	Developing, designing, or creating new applications, ideas, relationships, systems, or products, including artistic contributions.
Analyzing Data or Information	Identifying the underlying principles, reasons, or facts of information by breaking down information or data into separate parts.
Processing Information	Compiling, coding, categorizing, calculating, tabulating, auditing, or verifying information or data.
Identifying Objects, Actions, and Events	Identifying information by categorizing, estimating, recognizing differences or similarities, and detecting changes in circumstances or events.
Documenting/Recording Information	Entering, transcribing, recording, storing, or maintaining information in written or electronic/magnetic form.
Communicating with Supervisors, Peers, or Subordin	Providing information to supervisors, co-workers, and subordinates by telephone, in written form, e-mail, or in person.
Coaching and Developing Others	Identifying the developmental needs of others and coaching, mentoring, or otherwise helping others to improve their knowledge or skills.
Organizing, Planning, and Prioritizing Work	Developing specific goals and plans to prioritize, organize, and accomplish your work.
Judging the Qualities of Things, Services, or Peop	Assessing the value, importance, or quality of things or people.
Establishing and Maintaining Interpersonal Relatio	Developing constructive and cooperative working relationships with others, and maintaining them over time.
Monitor Processes, Materials, or Surroundings	Monitoring and reviewing information from materials, events, or the environment, to detect or assess problems.
Estimating the Quantifiable Characteristics of Pro	Estimating sizes, distances, and quantities; or determining time, costs, resources, or materials needed to perform a work activity.
Scheduling Work and Activities	Scheduling events, programs, and activities, as well as the work of others.
Developing Objectives and Strategies	Establishing long-range objectives and specifying the strategies and actions to achieve them.
Guiding, Directing, and Motivating Subordinates	Providing guidance and direction to subordinates, including setting performance standards and monitoring performance.
Performing for or Working Directly with the Public	Performing for people or dealing directly with the public. This includes serving customers in restaurants and stores, and receiving clients or guests.
Inspecting Equipment, Structures, or Material	Inspecting equipment, structures, or materials to identify the cause of errors or other problems or defects.
Performing Administrative Activities	Performing day-to-day administrative tasks such as maintaining information files and processing paperwork.
Communicating with Persons Outside Organization	Communicating with people outside the organization, representing the organization to customers, the public, government, and other external sources. This information can be exchanged in person, in writing, or by telephone or e-mail.
Coordinating the Work and Activities of Others	Getting members of a group to work together to accomplish tasks.
Evaluating Information to Determine Compliance wit	Using relevant information and individual judgment to determine whether events or processes comply with laws, regulations, or standards.

Provide Consultation and Advice to Others	Providing guidance and expert advice to management or other groups on technical, systems-, or process-related topics.
Monitoring and Controlling Resources	Monitoring and controlling resources and overseeing the spending of money.
Assisting and Caring for Others	Providing personal assistance, medical attention, emotional support, or other personal care to others such as coworkers, customers, or patients.
Developing and Building Teams	Encouraging and building mutual trust, respect, and cooperation among team members.
Resolving Conflicts and Negotiating with Others	Handling complaints, settling disputes, and resolving grievances and conflicts, or otherwise negotiating with others.
Repairing and Maintaining Electronic Equipment	Servicing, repairing, calibrating, regulating, fine-tuning, or testing machines, devices, and equipment that operate primarily on the basis of electrical or electronic (not mechanical) principles.
Controlling Machines and Processes	Using either control mechanisms or direct physical activity to operate machines or processes (not including computers or vehicles).
Staffing Organizational Units	Recruiting, interviewing, selecting, hiring, and promoting employees in an organization.
Handling and Moving Objects	Using hands and arms in handling, installing, positioning, and moving materials, and manipulating things.
Selling or Influencing Others	Convincing others to buy merchandise/goods or to otherwise change their minds or actions.
Performing General Physical Activities	Performing physical activities that require considerable use of your arms and legs and moving your whole body, such as climbing, lifting, balancing, walking, stooping, and handling of materials.
Repairing and Maintaining Mechanical Equipment	Servicing, repairing, adjusting, and testing machines, devices, moving parts, and equipment that operate primarily on the basis of mechanical (not electronic) principles.
Drafting, Laying Out, and Specifying Technical Dev	Providing documentation, detailed instructions, drawings, or specifications to tell others about how devices, parts, equipment, or structures are to be fabricated, constructed, assembled, modified, maintained, or used.
Operating Vehicles, Mechanized Devices, or Equipme	Running, maneuvering, navigating, or driving vehicles or mechanized equipment, such as forklifts, passenger vehicles, aircraft, or water craft.

Work_Context	**Work_Context Definitions**
Electronic Mail	How often do you use electronic mail in this job?
Face-to-Face Discussions	How often do you have to have face-to-face discussions with individuals or teams in this job?
Indoors, Environmentally Controlled	How often does this job require working indoors in environmentally controlled conditions?
Public Speaking	How often do you have to perform public speaking in this job?
Structured versus Unstructured Work	To what extent is this job structured for the worker, rather than allowing the worker to determine tasks, priorities, and goals?
Freedom to Make Decisions	How much decision making freedom, without supervision, does the job offer?
Telephone	How often do you have telephone conversations in this job?
Contact With Others	How much does this job require the worker to be in contact with others (face-to-face, by telephone, or otherwise) in order to perform it?
Responsible for Others' Health and Safety	How much responsibility is there for the health and safety of others in this job?
Exposed to Hazardous Conditions	How often does this job require exposure to hazardous conditions?
Wear Common Protective or Safety Equipment such as	How much does this job require wearing common protective or safety equipment such as safety shoes, glasses, gloves, hard hats or live jackets?
Work With Work Group or Team	How important is it to work with others in a group or team in this job?
Importance of Being Exact or Accurate	How important is being very exact or highly accurate in performing this job?
Time Pressure	How often does this job require the worker to meet strict deadlines?
Exposed to Contaminants	How often does this job require working exposed to contaminants (such as pollutants, gases, dust or odors)?
Letters and Memos	How often does the job require written letters and memos?
Impact of Decisions on Co-workers or Company Resul	How do the decisions an employee makes impact the results of co-workers, clients or the company?
Coordinate or Lead Others	How important is it to coordinate or lead others in accomplishing work activities in this job?

Frequency of Decision Making	How frequently is the worker required to make decisions that affect other people, the financial resources, and/or the image and reputation of the organization?
Deal With External Customers	How important is it to work with external customers or the public in this job?
Spend Time Sitting	How much does this job require sitting?
Consequence of Error	How serious would the result usually be if the worker made a mistake that was not readily correctable?
Responsibility for Outcomes and Results	How responsible is the worker for work outcomes and results of other workers?
Physical Proximity	To what extent does this job require the worker to perform job tasks in close physical proximity to other people?
Level of Competition	To what extent does this job require the worker to compete or to be aware of competitive pressures?
Spend Time Standing	How much does this job require standing?
Deal With Unpleasant or Angry People	How frequently does the worker have to deal with unpleasant, angry, or discourteous individuals as part of the job requirements?
Frequency of Conflict Situations	How often are there conflict situations the employee has to face in this job?
Importance of Repeating Same Tasks	How important is repeating the same physical activities (e.g., key entry) or mental activities (e.g., checking entries in a ledger) over and over, without stopping, to performing this job?
Spend Time Using Your Hands to Handle, Control, or	How much does this job require using your hands to handle, control, or feel objects, tools or controls?
Sounds, Noise Levels Are Distracting or Uncomforta	How often does this job require working exposed to sounds and noise levels that are distracting or uncomfortable?
Exposed to Minor Burns, Cuts, Bites, or Stings	How often does this job require exposure to minor burns, cuts, bites, or stings?
Spend Time Walking and Running	How much does this job require walking and running?
Spend Time Making Repetitive Motions	How much does this job require making repetitive motions?
Degree of Automation	How automated is the job?
Cramped Work Space, Awkward Positions	How often does this job require working in cramped work spaces that requires getting into awkward positions?
Exposed to Hazardous Equipment	How often does this job require exposure to hazardous equipment?
Extremely Bright or Inadequate Lighting	How often does this job require working in extremely bright or inadequate lighting conditions?
Spend Time Bending or Twisting the Body	How much does this job require bending or twisting your body?
Very Hot or Cold Temperatures	How often does this job require working in very hot (above 90 F degrees) or very cold (below 32 F degrees) temperatures?
Exposed to Disease or Infections	How often does this job require exposure to disease/infections?
Indoors, Not Environmentally Controlled	How often does this job require working indoors in non-controlled environmental conditions (e.g., warehouse without heat)?
Exposed to Radiation	How often does this job require exposure to radiation?
Wear Specialized Protective or Safety Equipment su	How much does this job require wearing specialized protective or safety equipment such as breathing apparatus, safety harness, full protection suits, or radiation protection?
In an Enclosed Vehicle or Equipment	How often does this job require working in a closed vehicle or equipment (e.g., car)?
Deal With Physically Aggressive People	How frequently does this job require the worker to deal with physical aggression of violent individuals?
Spend Time Kneeling, Crouching, Stooping, or Crawl	How much does this job require kneeling, crouching, stooping or crawling?
Pace Determined by Speed of Equipment	How important is it to this job that the pace is determined by the speed of equipment or machinery? (This does not refer to keeping busy at all times on this job.)
Spend Time Keeping or Regaining Balance	How much does this job require keeping or regaining your balance?
Outdoors, Exposed to Weather	How often does this job require working outdoors, exposed to all weather conditions?
Spend Time Climbing Ladders, Scaffolds, or Poles	How much does this job require climbing ladders, scaffolds, or poles?
Outdoors, Under Cover	How often does this job require working outdoors, under cover (e.g., structure with roof but no walls)?
In an Open Vehicle or Equipment	How often does this job require working in an open vehicle or equipment (e.g., tractor)?
Exposed to High Places	How often does this job require exposure to high places?
Exposed to Whole Body Vibration	How often does this job require exposure to whole body vibration (e.g., operate a jackhammer)?

5) Evaluate and grade students' class work, laboratory work, assignments, and papers.

6) Conduct research in a particular field of knowledge, and publish findings in professional journals, books, and/or electronic media.

7) Advise students on academic and vocational curricula, and on career issues.

8) Serve on academic or administrative committees that deal with institutional policies, departmental matters, and academic issues.

9) Compile, administer, and grade examinations, or assign this work to others.

10) Write grant proposals to procure external research funding.

11) Select and obtain materials and supplies such as textbooks and laboratory equipment.

12) Maintain student attendance records, grades, and other required records.

13) Maintain regularly scheduled office hours in order to advise and assist students.

14) Participate in campus and community events.

15) Supervise students' laboratory and field work.

16) Compile bibliographies of specialized materials for outside reading assignments.

17) Prepare and deliver lectures to undergraduate and/or graduate students on topics such as hazardous waste management, industrial safety, and environmental toxicology.

18) Participate in student recruitment, registration, and placement activities.

19) Provide professional consulting services to government and/or industry.

20) Perform administrative duties such as serving as department head.

21) Act as advisers to student organizations.

22) Collaborate with colleagues to address teaching and research issues.

Knowledge	Knowledge Definitions
English Language	Knowledge of the structure and content of the English language including the meaning and spelling of words, rules of composition, and grammar.
Education and Training	Knowledge of principles and methods for curriculum and training design, teaching and instruction for individuals and groups, and the measurement of training effects.
Biology	Knowledge of plant and animal organisms, their tissues, cells, functions, interdependencies, and interactions with each other and the environment.
Chemistry	Knowledge of the chemical composition, structure, and properties of substances and of the chemical processes and transformations that they undergo. This includes uses of chemicals and their interactions, danger signs, production techniques, and disposal methods.
Mathematics	Knowledge of arithmetic, algebra, geometry, calculus, statistics, and their applications.
Geography	Knowledge of principles and methods for describing the features of land, sea, and air masses, including their physical characteristics, locations, interrelationships, and distribution of plant, animal, and human life.
Computers and Electronics	Knowledge of circuit boards, processors, chips, electronic equipment, and computer hardware and software, including applications and programming.
Physics	Knowledge and prediction of physical principles, laws, their interrelationships, and applications to understanding fluid, material, and atmospheric dynamics, and mechanical, electrical, atomic and sub-atomic structures and processes.
Administration and Management	Knowledge of business and management principles involved in strategic planning, resource allocation, human resources modeling, leadership technique, production methods, and coordination of people and resources.
Engineering and Technology	Knowledge of the practical application of engineering science and technology. This includes applying principles, techniques, procedures, and equipment to the design and production of various goods and services.
Communications and Media	Knowledge of media production, communication, and dissemination techniques and methods. This includes alternative ways to inform and entertain via written, oral, and visual media.
Psychology	Knowledge of human behavior and performance; individual differences in ability, personality, and interests; learning and motivation; psychological research methods; and the assessment and treatment of behavioral and affective disorders.
Sociology and Anthropology	Knowledge of group behavior and dynamics, societal trends and influences, human migrations, ethnicity, cultures and their history and origins.

Job Zone Component	Job Zone Component Definitions
Title	Job Zone Five: Extensive Preparation Needed
Overall Experience	Extensive skill, knowledge, and experience are needed for these occupations. Many require more than five years of experience. For example, surgeons must complete four years of college and an additional five to seven years of specialized medical training to be able to do their job.
Job Training	Employees may need some on-the-job training, but most of these occupations assume that the person will already have the required skills, knowledge, work-related experience, and/or training.
Job Zone Examples	These occupations often involve coordinating, training, supervising, or managing the activities of others to accomplish goals. Very advanced communication and organizational skills are required. Examples include athletic trainers, lawyers, managing editors, physicists, social psychologists, and surgeons.
SVP Range	(8.0 and above)
Education	A bachelor's degree is the minimum formal education required for these occupations. However, many also require graduate school. For example, they may require a master's degree, and some require a Ph.D., M.D., or J.D. (law degree).

Work_Styles	Work_Styles Definitions
Integrity	Job requires being honest and ethical.
Analytical Thinking	Job requires analyzing information and using logic to address work-related issues and problems.
Dependability	Job requires being reliable, responsible, and dependable, and fulfilling obligations.
Initiative	Job requires a willingness to take on responsibilities and challenges.
Attention to Detail	Job requires being careful about detail and thorough in completing work tasks.
Independence	Job requires developing one's own ways of doing things, guiding oneself with little or no supervision, and depending on oneself to get things done.
Persistence	Job requires persistence in the face of obstacles.
Achievement/Effort	Job requires establishing and maintaining personally challenging achievement goals and exerting effort toward mastering tasks.
Leadership	Job requires a willingness to lead, take charge, and offer opinions and direction.
Cooperation	Job requires being pleasant with others on the job and displaying a good-natured, cooperative attitude.
Innovation	Job requires creativity and alternative thinking to develop new ideas for and answers to work-related problems.
Concern for Others	Job requires being sensitive to others' needs and feelings and being understanding and helpful on the job.
Stress Tolerance	Job requires accepting criticism and dealing calmly and effectively with high stress situations.
Self Control	Job requires maintaining composure, keeping emotions in check, controlling anger, and avoiding aggressive behavior, even in very difficult situations.
Adaptability/Flexibility	Job requires being open to change (positive or negative) and to considerable variety in the workplace.
Social Orientation	Job requires preferring to work with others rather than alone, and being personally connected with others on the job.

25-1053.00 - Environmental Science Teachers, Postsecondary

Teach courses in environmental science.

Tasks

1) Initiate, facilitate, and moderate classroom discussions.

2) Plan, evaluate, and revise curricula, course content, and course materials and methods of instruction.

3) Keep abreast of developments in their field by reading current literature, talking with colleagues, and participating in professional conferences.

4) Supervise undergraduate and/or graduate teaching, internship, and research work.

Personnel and Human Resources	Knowledge of principles and procedures for personnel recruitment, selection, training, compensation and benefits, labor relations and negotiation, and personnel information systems.
Clerical	Knowledge of administrative and clerical procedures and systems such as word processing, managing files and records, stenography and transcription, designing forms, and other office procedures and terminology.
Law and Government	Knowledge of laws, legal codes, court procedures, precedents, government regulations, executive orders, agency rules, and the democratic political process.
History and Archeology	Knowledge of historical events and their causes, indicators, and effects on civilizations and cultures.
Customer and Personal Service	Knowledge of principles and processes for providing customer and personal services. This includes customer needs assessment, meeting quality standards for services, and evaluation of customer satisfaction.
Philosophy and Theology	Knowledge of different philosophical systems and religions. This includes their basic principles, values, ethics, ways of thinking, customs, practices, and their impact on human culture.
Design	Knowledge of design techniques, tools, and principles involved in production of precision technical plans, blueprints, drawings, and models.
Economics and Accounting	Knowledge of economic and accounting principles and practices, the financial markets, banking and the analysis and reporting of financial data.
Medicine and Dentistry	Knowledge of the information and techniques needed to diagnose and treat human injuries, diseases, and deformities. This includes symptoms, treatment alternatives, drug properties and interactions, and preventive health-care measures.
Foreign Language	Knowledge of the structure and content of a foreign (non-English) language including the meaning and spelling of words, rules of composition and grammar, and pronunciation.
Public Safety and Security	Knowledge of relevant equipment, policies, procedures, and strategies to promote effective local, state, or national security operations for the protection of people, data, property, and institutions.
Mechanical	Knowledge of machines and tools, including their designs, uses, repair, and maintenance.
Transportation	Knowledge of principles and methods for moving people or goods by air, rail, sea, or road, including the relative costs and benefits.
Telecommunications	Knowledge of transmission, broadcasting, switching, control, and operation of telecommunications systems.
Sales and Marketing	Knowledge of principles and methods for showing, promoting, and selling products or services. This includes marketing strategy and tactics, product demonstration, sales techniques, and sales control systems.
Therapy and Counseling	Knowledge of principles, methods, and procedures for diagnosis, treatment, and rehabilitation of physical and mental dysfunctions, and for career counseling and guidance.
Production and Processing	Knowledge of raw materials, production processes, quality control, costs, and other techniques for maximizing the effective manufacture and distribution of goods.
Building and Construction	Knowledge of materials, methods, and the tools involved in the construction or repair of houses, buildings, or other structures such as highways and roads.
Fine Arts	Knowledge of the theory and techniques required to compose, produce, and perform works of music, dance, visual arts, drama, and sculpture.
Food Production	Knowledge of techniques and equipment for planting, growing, and harvesting food products (both plant and animal) for consumption, including storage/handling techniques.

Skills	Skills Definitions
Reading Comprehension	Understanding written sentences and paragraphs in work related documents.
Critical Thinking	Using logic and reasoning to identify the strengths and weaknesses of alternative solutions, conclusions or approaches to problems.
Instructing	Teaching others how to do something.
Writing	Communicating effectively in writing as appropriate for the needs of the audience.
Speaking	Talking to others to convey information effectively.
Active Learning	Understanding the implications of new information for both current and future problem-solving and decision-making.

Science	Using scientific rules and methods to solve problems.
Learning Strategies	Selecting and using training/instructional methods and procedures appropriate for the situation when learning or teaching new things.
Active Listening	Giving full attention to what other people are saying, taking time to understand the points being made, asking questions as appropriate, and not interrupting at inappropriate times.
Complex Problem Solving	Identifying complex problems and reviewing related information to develop and evaluate options and implement solutions.
Time Management	Managing one's own time and the time of others.
Mathematics	Using mathematics to solve problems.
Monitoring	Monitoring/Assessing performance of yourself, other individuals, or organizations to make improvements or take corrective action.
Judgment and Decision Making	Considering the relative costs and benefits of potential actions to choose the most appropriate one.
Social Perceptiveness	Being aware of others' reactions and understanding why they react as they do.
Coordination	Adjusting actions in relation to others' actions.
Management of Personnel Resources	Motivating, developing, and directing people as they work, identifying the best people for the job.
Equipment Selection	Determining the kind of tools and equipment needed to do a job.
Persuasion	Persuading others to change their minds or behavior.
Management of Financial Resources	Determining how money will be spent to get the work done, and accounting for these expenditures.
Operations Analysis	Analyzing needs and product requirements to create a design.
Negotiation	Bringing others together and trying to reconcile differences.
Service Orientation	Actively looking for ways to help people.
Systems Analysis	Determining how a system should work and how changes in conditions, operations, and the environment will affect outcomes.
Management of Material Resources	Obtaining and seeing to the appropriate use of equipment, facilities, and materials needed to do certain work.
Troubleshooting	Determining causes of operating errors and deciding what to do about it.
Technology Design	Generating or adapting equipment and technology to serve user needs.
Quality Control Analysis	Conducting tests and inspections of products, services, or processes to evaluate quality or performance.
Systems Evaluation	Identifying measures or indicators of system performance and the actions needed to improve or correct performance, relative to the goals of the system.
Programming	Writing computer programs for various purposes.
Operation and Control	Controlling operations of equipment or systems.
Equipment Maintenance	Performing routine maintenance on equipment and determining when and what kind of maintenance is needed.
Installation	Installing equipment, machines, wiring, or programs to meet specifications.
Operation Monitoring	Watching gauges, dials, or other indicators to make sure a machine is working properly.
Repairing	Repairing machines or systems using the needed tools.

Ability	Ability Definitions
Written Comprehension	The ability to read and understand information and ideas presented in writing.
Oral Expression	The ability to communicate information and ideas in speaking so others will understand.
Written Expression	The ability to communicate information and ideas in writing so others will understand.
Speech Clarity	The ability to speak clearly so others can understand you.
Oral Comprehension	The ability to listen to and understand information and ideas presented through spoken words and sentences.
Deductive Reasoning	The ability to apply general rules to specific problems to produce answers that make sense.
Inductive Reasoning	The ability to combine pieces of information to form general rules or conclusions (includes finding a relationship among seemingly unrelated events).
Near Vision	The ability to see details at close range (within a few feet of the observer).
Speech Recognition	The ability to identify and understand the speech of another person.
Problem Sensitivity	The ability to tell when something is wrong or is likely to go wrong. It does not involve solving the problem, only recognizing there is a problem.

Selective Attention	The ability to concentrate on a task over a period of time without being distracted.
Category Flexibility	The ability to generate or use different sets of rules for combining or grouping things in different ways.
Information Ordering	The ability to arrange things or actions in a certain order or pattern according to a specific rule or set of rules (e.g., patterns of numbers, letters, words, pictures, mathematical operations).
Originality	The ability to come up with unusual or clever ideas about a given topic or situation, or to develop creative ways to solve a problem.
Fluency of Ideas	The ability to come up with a number of ideas about a topic (the number of ideas is important, not their quality, correctness, or creativity).
Mathematical Reasoning	The ability to choose the right mathematical methods or formulas to solve a problem.
Memorization	The ability to remember information such as words, numbers, pictures, and procedures.
Flexibility of Closure	The ability to identify or detect a known pattern (a figure, object, word, or sound) that is hidden in other distracting material.
Speed of Closure	The ability to quickly make sense of, combine, and organize information into meaningful patterns.
Time Sharing	The ability to shift back and forth between two or more activities or sources of information (such as speech, sounds, touch, or other sources).
Number Facility	The ability to add, subtract, multiply, or divide quickly and correctly.
Far Vision	The ability to see details at a distance.
Perceptual Speed	The ability to quickly and accurately compare similarities and differences among sets of letters, numbers, objects, pictures, or patterns. The things to be compared may be presented at the same time or one after the other. This ability also includes comparing a presented object with a remembered object.
Visualization	The ability to imagine how something will look after it is moved around or when its parts are moved or rearranged.
Auditory Attention	The ability to focus on a single source of sound in the presence of other distracting sounds.
Visual Color Discrimination	The ability to match or detect differences between colors, including shades of color and brightness.
Finger Dexterity	The ability to make precisely coordinated movements of the fingers of one or both hands to grasp, manipulate, or assemble very small objects.
Depth Perception	The ability to judge which of several objects is closer or farther away from you, or to judge the distance between you and an object.
Hearing Sensitivity	The ability to detect or tell the differences between sounds that vary in pitch and loudness.
Trunk Strength	The ability to use your abdominal and lower back muscles to support part of the body repeatedly or continuously over time without 'giving out' or fatiguing.
Dynamic Strength	The ability to exert muscle force repeatedly or continuously over time. This involves muscular endurance and resistance to muscle fatigue.
Multilimb Coordination	The ability to coordinate two or more limbs (for example, two arms, two legs, or one leg and one arm) while sitting, standing, or lying down. It does not involve performing the activities while the whole body is in motion.
Response Orientation	The ability to choose quickly between two or more movements in response to two or more different signals (lights, sounds, pictures). It includes the speed with which the correct response is started with the hand, foot, or other body part.
Rate Control	The ability to time your movements or the movement of a piece of equipment in anticipation of changes in the speed and/or direction of a moving object or scene.
Wrist-Finger Speed	The ability to make fast, simple, repeated movements of the fingers, hands, and wrists.
Speed of Limb Movement	The ability to quickly move the arms and legs.
Explosive Strength	The ability to use short bursts of muscle force to propel oneself (as in jumping or sprinting), or to throw an object.
Arm-Hand Steadiness	The ability to keep your hand and arm steady while moving your arm or while holding your arm and hand in one position.
Stamina	The ability to exert yourself physically over long periods of time without getting winded or out of breath.
Reaction Time	The ability to quickly respond (with the hand, finger, or foot) to a signal (sound, light, picture) when it appears.
Control Precision	The ability to quickly and repeatedly adjust the controls of a machine or a vehicle to exact positions.

Static Strength	The ability to exert maximum muscle force to lift, push, pull, or carry objects.
Spatial Orientation	The ability to know your location in relation to the environment or to know where other objects are in relation to you.
Extent Flexibility	The ability to bend, stretch, twist, or reach with your body, arms, and/or legs.
Gross Body Coordination	The ability to coordinate the movement of your arms, legs, and torso together when the whole body is in motion.
Gross Body Equilibrium	The ability to keep or regain your body balance or stay upright when in an unstable position.
Sound Localization	The ability to tell the direction from which a sound originated.
Dynamic Flexibility	The ability to quickly and repeatedly bend, stretch, twist, or reach out with your body, arms, and/or legs.
Night Vision	The ability to see under low light conditions.
Peripheral Vision	The ability to see objects or movement of objects to one's side when the eyes are looking ahead.
Glare Sensitivity	The ability to see objects in the presence of glare or bright lighting.
Manual Dexterity	The ability to quickly move your hand, your hand together with your arm, or your two hands to grasp, manipulate, or assemble objects.

Work_Activity	Work_Activity Definitions
Training and Teaching Others	Identifying the educational needs of others, developing formal educational or training programs or classes, and teaching or instructing others.
Analyzing Data or Information	Identifying the underlying principles, reasons, or facts of information by breaking down information or data into separate parts.
Thinking Creatively	Developing, designing, or creating new applications, ideas, relationships, systems, or products, including artistic contributions.
Getting Information	Observing, receiving, and otherwise obtaining information from all relevant sources.
Updating and Using Relevant Knowledge	Keeping up-to-date technically and applying new knowledge to your job.
Processing Information	Compiling, coding, categorizing, calculating, tabulating, auditing, or verifying information or data.
Making Decisions and Solving Problems	Analyzing information and evaluating results to choose the best solution and solve problems.
Interacting With Computers	Using computers and computer systems (including hardware and software) to program, write software, set up functions, enter data, or process information.
Interpreting the Meaning of Information for Others	Translating or explaining what information means and how it can be used.
Identifying Objects, Actions, and Events	Identifying information by categorizing, estimating, recognizing differences or similarities, and detecting changes in circumstances or events.
Communicating with Persons Outside Organization	Communicating with people outside the organization, representing the organization to customers, the public, government, and other external sources. This information can be exchanged in person, in writing, or by telephone or e-mail.
Organizing, Planning, and Prioritizing Work	Developing specific goals and plans to prioritize, organize, and accomplish your work.
Communicating with Supervisors, Peers, or Subordin	Providing information to supervisors, co-workers, and subordinates by telephone, in written form, e-mail, or in person.
Judging the Qualities of Things, Services, or Peop	Assessing the value, importance, or quality of things or people.
Establishing and Maintaining Interpersonal Relatio	Developing constructive and cooperative working relationships with others, and maintaining them over time.
Developing Objectives and Strategies	Establishing long-range objectives and specifying the strategies and actions to achieve them.
Coaching and Developing Others	Identifying the developmental needs of others and coaching, mentoring, or otherwise helping others to improve their knowledge or skills.
Monitor Processes, Materials, or Surroundings	Monitoring and reviewing information from materials, events, or the environment, to detect or assess problems.
Documenting/Recording Information	Entering, transcribing, recording, storing, or maintaining information in written or electronic/magnetic form.
Estimating the Quantifiable Characteristics of Pro	Estimating sizes, distances, and quantities; or determining time, costs, resources, or materials needed to perform a work activity.
Provide Consultation and Advice to Others	Providing guidance and expert advice to management or other groups on technical, systems-, or process-related topics.

Scheduling Work and Activities	Scheduling events, programs, and activities, as well as the work of others.
Guiding, Directing, and Motivating Subordinates	Providing guidance and direction to subordinates, including setting performance standards and monitoring performance.
Coordinating the Work and Activities of Others	Getting members of a group to work together to accomplish tasks.
Evaluating Information to Determine Compliance wit	Using relevant information and individual judgment to determine whether events or processes comply with laws, regulations, or standards.
Developing and Building Teams	Encouraging and building mutual trust, respect, and cooperation among team members.
Performing Administrative Activities	Performing day-to-day administrative tasks such as maintaining information files and processing paperwork.
Monitoring and Controlling Resources	Monitoring and controlling resources and overseeing the spending of money.
Inspecting Equipment, Structures, or Material	Inspecting equipment, structures, or materials to identify the cause of errors or other problems or defects.
Performing for or Working Directly with the Public	Performing for people or dealing directly with the public. This includes serving customers in restaurants and stores, and receiving clients or guests.
Assisting and Caring for Others	Providing personal assistance, medical attention, emotional support, or other personal care to others such as coworkers, customers, or patients.
Resolving Conflicts and Negotiating with Others	Handling complaints, settling disputes, and resolving grievances and conflicts, or otherwise negotiating with others.
Selling or Influencing Others	Convincing others to buy merchandise/goods or to otherwise change their minds or actions.
Controlling Machines and Processes	Using either control mechanisms or direct physical activity to operate machines or processes (not including computers or vehicles).
Staffing Organizational Units	Recruiting, interviewing, selecting, hiring, and promoting employees in an organization.
Repairing and Maintaining Electronic Equipment	Servicing, repairing, calibrating, regulating, fine-tuning, or testing machines, devices, and equipment that operate primarily on the basis of electrical or electronic (not mechanical) principles.
Performing General Physical Activities	Performing physical activities that require considerable use of your arms and legs and moving your whole body, such as climbing, lifting, balancing, walking, stooping, and handling of materials.
Handling and Moving Objects	Using hands and arms in handling, installing, positioning, and moving materials, and manipulating things.
Drafting, Laying Out, and Specifying Technical Dev	Providing documentation, detailed instructions, drawings, or specifications to tell others about how devices, parts, equipment, or structures are to be fabricated, constructed, assembled, modified, maintained, or used.
Repairing and Maintaining Mechanical Equipment	Servicing, repairing, adjusting, and testing machines, devices, moving parts, and equipment that operate primarily on the basis of mechanical (not electronic) principles.
Operating Vehicles, Mechanized Devices, or Equipme	Running, maneuvering, navigating, or driving vehicles or mechanized equipment, such as forklifts, passenger vehicles, aircraft, or water craft.

Work_Context	Work_Context Definitions
Electronic Mail	How often do you use electronic mail in this job?
Face-to-Face Discussions	How often do you have to have face-to-face discussions with individuals or teams in this job?
Structured versus Unstructured Work	To what extent is this job structured for the worker, rather than allowing the worker to determine tasks, priorities, and goals?
Telephone	How often do you have telephone conversations in this job?
Freedom to Make Decisions	How much decision making freedom, without supervision, does the job offer?
Letters and Memos	How often does the job require written letters and memos?
Contact With Others	How much does this job require the worker to be in contact with others (face-to-face, by telephone, or otherwise) in order to perform it?
Importance of Being Exact or Accurate	How important is being very exact or highly accurate in performing this job?
Work With Work Group or Team	How important is it to work with others in a group or team in this job?
Indoors, Environmentally Controlled	How often does this job require working indoors in environmentally controlled conditions?
Public Speaking	How often do you have to perform public speaking in this job?
Coordinate or Lead Others	How important is it to coordinate or lead others in accomplishing work activities in this job?
Spend Time Sitting	How much does this job require sitting?

Level of Competition	To what extent does this job require the worker to compete or to be aware of competitive pressures?
Impact of Decisions on Co-workers or Company Resul	How do the decisions an employee makes impact the results of co-workers, clients or the company?
Frequency of Decision Making	How frequently is the worker required to make decisions that affect other people, the financial resources, and/or the image and reputation of the organization?
Time Pressure	How often does this job require the worker to meet strict deadlines?
Responsibility for Outcomes and Results	How responsible is the worker for work outcomes and results of other workers?
Deal With External Customers	How important is it to work with external customers or the public in this job?
Frequency of Conflict Situations	How often are there conflict situations the employee has to face in this job?
Responsible for Others' Health and Safety	How much responsibility is there for the health and safety of others in this job?
Physical Proximity	To what extent does this job require the worker to perform job tasks in close physical proximity to other people?
Importance of Repeating Same Tasks	How important is repeating the same physical activities (e.g., key entry) or mental activities (e.g., checking entries in a ledger) over and over, without stopping, to performing this job?
Outdoors, Exposed to Weather	How often does this job require working outdoors, exposed to all weather conditions?
Deal With Unpleasant or Angry People	How frequently does the worker have to deal with unpleasant, angry, or discourteous individuals as part of the job requirements?
Sounds, Noise Levels Are Distracting or Uncomforta	How often does this job require working exposed to sounds and noise levels that are distracting or uncomfortable?
Spend Time Using Your Hands to Handle, Control, or	How much does this job require using your hands to handle, control, or feel objects, tools or controls?
In an Enclosed Vehicle or Equipment	How often does this job require working in a closed vehicle or equipment (e.g., car)?
Consequence of Error	How serious would the result usually be if the worker made a mistake that was not readily correctable?
Spend Time Making Repetitive Motions	How much does this job require making repetitive motions?
Exposed to Contaminants	How often does this job require working exposed to contaminants (such as pollutants, gases, dust or odors)?
Spend Time Standing	How much does this job require standing?
Indoors, Not Environmentally Controlled	How often does this job require working indoors in non-controlled environmental conditions (e.g., warehouse without heat)?
Very Hot or Cold Temperatures	How often does this job require working in very hot (above 90 F degrees) or very cold (below 32 F degrees) temperatures?
Spend Time Walking and Running	How much does this job require walking and running?
Exposed to Minor Burns, Cuts, Bites, or Stings	How often does this job require exposure to minor burns, cuts, bites, or stings?
Degree of Automation	How automated is the job?
Wear Common Protective or Safety Equipment such as	How much does this job require wearing common protective or safety equipment such as safety shoes, glasses, gloves, hard hats or live jackets?
Outdoors, Under Cover	How often does this job require working outdoors, under cover (e.g., structure with roof but no walls)?
Exposed to Hazardous Conditions	How often does this job require exposure to hazardous conditions?
Extremely Bright or Inadequate Lighting	How often does this job require working in extremely bright or inadequate lighting conditions?
Cramped Work Space, Awkward Positions	How often does this job require working in cramped work spaces that requires getting into awkward positions?
Exposed to Hazardous Equipment	How often does this job require exposure to hazardous equipment?
Spend Time Bending or Twisting the Body	How much does this job require bending or twisting your body?
In an Open Vehicle or Equipment	How often does this job require working in an open vehicle or equipment (e.g., tractor)?
Spend Time Kneeling, Crouching, Stooping, or Crawl	How much does this job require kneeling, crouching, stooping or crawling?
Exposed to Disease or Infections	How often does this job require exposure to disease/infections?
Spend Time Climbing Ladders, Scaffolds, or Poles	How much does this job require climbing ladders, scaffolds, or poles?
Exposed to High Places	How often does this job require exposure to high places?

Pace Determined by Speed of Equipment	How important is it to this job that the pace is determined by the speed of equipment or machinery? (This does not refer to keeping busy at all times on this job.)
Spend Time Keeping or Regaining Balance	How much does this job require keeping or regaining your balance?
Exposed to Radiation	How often does this job require exposure to radiation?
Wear Specialized Protective or Safety Equipment su	How much does this job require wearing specialized protective or safety equipment such as breathing apparatus, safety harness, full protection suits, or radiation protection?
Exposed to Whole Body Vibration	How often does this job require exposure to whole body vibration (e.g., operate a jackhammer)?
Deal With Physically Aggressive People	How frequently does this job require the worker to deal with physical aggression of violent individuals?

Job Zone Component	Job Zone Component Definitions
Title	Job Zone Five: Extensive Preparation Needed Extensive skill, knowledge, and experience are needed for these occupations. Many require more than five years of experience.
Overall Experience	For example, surgeons must complete four years of college and an additional five to seven years of specialized medical training to be able to do their job.
Job Training	Employees may need some on-the-job training, but most of these occupations assume that the person will already have the required skills, knowledge, work-related experience, and/or training.
Job Zone Examples	These occupations often involve coordinating, training, supervising, or managing the activities of others to accomplish goals. Very advanced communication and organizational skills are required. Examples include athletic trainers, lawyers, managing editors, physicists, social psychologists, and surgeons.
SVP Range	(8.0 and above)
Education	A bachelor's degree is the minimum formal education required for these occupations. However, many also require graduate school. For example, they may require a master's degree, and some require a Ph.D., M.D., or J.D. (law degree).

Work_Styles	Work_Styles Definitions
Achievement/Effort	Job requires establishing and maintaining personally challenging achievement goals and exerting effort toward mastering tasks.
Analytical Thinking	Job requires analyzing information and using logic to address work-related issues and problems.
Initiative	Job requires a willingness to take on responsibilities and challenges.
Integrity	Job requires being honest and ethical.
Innovation	Job requires creativity and alternative thinking to develop new ideas for and answers to work-related problems.
Independence	Job requires developing one's own ways of doing things, guiding oneself with little or no supervision, and depending on oneself to get things done.
Persistence	Job requires persistence in the face of obstacles.
Dependability	Job requires being reliable, responsible, and dependable, and fulfilling obligations.
Attention to Detail	Job requires being careful about detail and thorough in completing work tasks.
Stress Tolerance	Job requires accepting criticism and dealing calmly and effectively with high stress situations.
Leadership	Job requires a willingness to lead, take charge, and offer opinions and direction.
Adaptability/Flexibility	Job requires being open to change (positive or negative) and to considerable variety in the workplace.
Cooperation	Job requires being pleasant with others on the job and displaying a good-natured, cooperative attitude.
Self Control	Job requires maintaining composure, keeping emotions in check, controlling anger, and avoiding aggressive behavior, even in very difficult situations.
Concern for Others	Job requires being sensitive to others' needs and feelings and being understanding and helpful on the job.
Social Orientation	Job requires preferring to work with others rather than alone, and being personally connected with others on the job.

25-1054.00 - Physics Teachers, Postsecondary

Teach courses pertaining to the laws of matter and energy. Includes both teachers primarily engaged in teaching and those who do a combination of both teaching and research.

Tasks

1) Maintain regularly scheduled office hours in order to advise and assist students.

2) Collaborate with colleagues to address teaching and research issues.

3) Select and obtain materials and supplies such as textbooks and laboratory equipment.

4) Compile, administer, and grade examinations, or assign this work to others.

5) Plan, evaluate, and revise curricula, course content, and course materials and methods of instruction.

6) Keep abreast of developments in their field by reading current literature, talking with colleagues, and participating in professional conferences.

7) Participate in campus and community events.

8) Initiate, facilitate, and moderate classroom discussions.

9) Advise students on academic and vocational curricula, and on career issues.

10) Serve on academic or administrative committees that deal with institutional policies, departmental matters, and academic issues.

11) Supervise students' laboratory work.

12) Prepare and deliver lectures to undergraduate and/or graduate students on topics such as quantum mechanics, particle physics, and optics.

13) Participate in student recruitment, registration, and placement activities.

14) Conduct research in a particular field of knowledge, and publish findings in professional journals, books, and/or electronic media.

15) Supervise undergraduate and/or graduate teaching, internship, and research work.

16) Compile bibliographies of specialized materials for outside reading assignments.

17) Write grant proposals to procure external research funding.

18) Act as advisers to student organizations.

19) Perform administrative duties such as serving as department head.

20) Provide professional consulting services to government and/or industry.

21) Evaluate and grade students' class work, laboratory work, assignments, and papers.

22) Prepare course materials such as syllabi, homework assignments, and handouts.

Knowledge	Knowledge Definitions
Physics	Knowledge and prediction of physical principles, laws, their interrelationships, and applications to understanding fluid, material, and atmospheric dynamics, and mechanical, electrical, atomic and sub-atomic structures and processes.
Mathematics	Knowledge of arithmetic, algebra, geometry, calculus, statistics, and their applications.
Education and Training	Knowledge of principles and methods for curriculum and training design, teaching and instruction for individuals and groups, and the measurement of training effects.
English Language	Knowledge of the structure and content of the English language including the meaning and spelling of words, rules of composition, and grammar.
Computers and Electronics	Knowledge of circuit boards, processors, chips, electronic equipment, and computer hardware and software, including applications and programming.
Engineering and Technology	Knowledge of the practical application of engineering science and technology. This includes applying principles, techniques, procedures, and equipment to the design and production of various goods and services.
Chemistry	Knowledge of the chemical composition, structure, and properties of substances and of the chemical processes and transformations that they undergo. This includes uses of chemicals and their interactions, danger signs, production techniques, and disposal methods.
Design	Knowledge of design techniques, tools, and principles involved in production of precision technical plans, blueprints, drawings, and models.
Mechanical	Knowledge of machines and tools, including their designs, uses, repair, and maintenance.

Communications and Media	Knowledge of media production, communication, and dissemination techniques and methods. This includes alternative ways to inform and entertain via written, oral, and visual media.
Telecommunications	Knowledge of transmission, broadcasting, switching, control, and operation of telecommunications systems.
Clerical	Knowledge of administrative and clerical procedures and systems such as word processing, managing files and records, stenography and transcription, designing forms, and other office procedures and terminology.
Customer and Personal Service	Knowledge of principles and processes for providing customer and personal services. This includes customer needs assessment, meeting quality standards for services, and evaluation of customer satisfaction.
Personnel and Human Resources	Knowledge of principles and procedures for personnel recruitment, selection, training, compensation and benefits, labor relations and negotiation, and personnel information systems.
Psychology	Knowledge of human behavior and performance; individual differences in ability, personality, and interests; learning and motivation; psychological research methods; and the assessment and treatment of behavioral and affective disorders.
Administration and Management	Knowledge of business and management principles involved in strategic planning, resource allocation, human resources modeling, leadership technique, production methods, and coordination of people and resources.
Public Safety and Security	Knowledge of relevant equipment, policies, procedures, and strategies to promote effective local, state, or national security operations for the protection of people, data, property, and institutions.
Biology	Knowledge of plant and animal organisms, their tissues, cells, functions, interdependencies, and interactions with each other and the environment.
Building and Construction	Knowledge of materials, methods, and the tools involved in the construction or repair of houses, buildings, or other structures such as highways and roads.
Philosophy and Theology	Knowledge of different philosophical systems and religions. This includes their basic principles, values, ethics, ways of thinking, customs, practices, and their impact on human culture.
Geography	Knowledge of principles and methods for describing the features of land, sea, and air masses, including their physical characteristics, locations, interrelationships, and distribution of plant, animal, and human life.
Law and Government	Knowledge of laws, legal codes, court procedures, precedents, government regulations, executive orders, agency rules, and the democratic political process.
Therapy and Counseling	Knowledge of principles, methods, and procedures for diagnosis, treatment, and rehabilitation of physical and mental dysfunctions, and for career counseling and guidance.
Production and Processing	Knowledge of raw materials, production processes, quality control, costs, and other techniques for maximizing the effective manufacture and distribution of goods.
Sales and Marketing	Knowledge of principles and methods for showing, promoting, and selling products or services. This includes marketing strategy and tactics, product demonstration, sales techniques, and sales control systems.
Sociology and Anthropology	Knowledge of group behavior and dynamics, societal trends and influences, human migrations, ethnicity, cultures and their history and origins.
Medicine and Dentistry	Knowledge of the information and techniques needed to diagnose and treat human injuries, diseases, and deformities. This includes symptoms, treatment alternatives, drug properties and interactions, and preventive health-care measures.
Transportation	Knowledge of principles and methods for moving people or goods by air, rail, sea, or road, including the relative costs and benefits.
Foreign Language	Knowledge of the structure and content of a foreign (non-English) language including the meaning and spelling of words, rules of composition and grammar, and pronunciation.
Economics and Accounting	Knowledge of economic and accounting principles and practices, the financial markets, banking and the analysis and reporting of financial data.
History and Archeology	Knowledge of historical events and their causes, indicators, and effects on civilizations and cultures.
Fine Arts	Knowledge of the theory and techniques required to compose, produce, and perform works of music, dance, visual arts, drama, and sculpture.

Food Production	Knowledge of techniques and equipment for planting, growing, and harvesting food products (both plant and animal) for consumption, including storage/handling techniques.

Skills	Skills Definitions
Instructing	Teaching others how to do something.
Science	Using scientific rules and methods to solve problems.
Speaking	Talking to others to convey information effectively.
Critical Thinking	Using logic and reasoning to identify the strengths and weaknesses of alternative solutions, conclusions or approaches to problems.
Reading Comprehension	Understanding written sentences and paragraphs in work related documents.
Mathematics	Using mathematics to solve problems.
Active Learning	Understanding the implications of new information for both current and future problem-solving and decision-making.
Writing	Communicating effectively in writing as appropriate for the needs of the audience.
Learning Strategies	Selecting and using training/instructional methods and procedures appropriate for the situation when learning or teaching new things.
Active Listening	Giving full attention to what other people are saying, taking time to understand the points being made, asking questions as appropriate, and not interrupting at inappropriate times.
Complex Problem Solving	Identifying complex problems and reviewing related information to develop and evaluate options and implement solutions.
Monitoring	Monitoring/Assessing performance of yourself, other individuals, or organizations to make improvements or take corrective action.
Time Management	Managing one's own time and the time of others.
Coordination	Adjusting actions in relation to others' actions.
Equipment Selection	Determining the kind of tools and equipment needed to do a job.
Social Perceptiveness	Being aware of others' reactions and understanding why they react as they do.
Judgment and Decision Making	Considering the relative costs and benefits of potential actions to choose the most appropriate one.
Troubleshooting	Determining causes of operating errors and deciding what to do about it.
Persuasion	Persuading others to change their minds or behavior.
Service Orientation	Actively looking for ways to help people.
Technology Design	Generating or adapting equipment and technology to serve user needs.
Operations Analysis	Analyzing needs and product requirements to create a design.
Programming	Writing computer programs for various purposes.
Equipment Maintenance	Performing routine maintenance on equipment and determining when and what kind of maintenance is needed.
Installation	Installing equipment, machines, wiring, or programs to meet specifications.
Management of Financial Resources	Determining how money will be spent to get the work done, and accounting for these expenditures.
Operation and Control	Controlling operations of equipment or systems.
Management of Personnel Resources	Motivating, developing, and directing people as they work, identifying the best people for the job.
Management of Material Resources	Obtaining and seeing to the appropriate use of equipment, facilities, and materials needed to do certain work.
Negotiation	Bringing others together and trying to reconcile differences.
Repairing	Repairing machines or systems using the needed tools.
Quality Control Analysis	Conducting tests and inspections of products, services, or processes to evaluate quality or performance.
Systems Evaluation	Identifying measures or indicators of system performance and the actions needed to improve or correct performance, relative to the goals of the system.
Systems Analysis	Determining how a system should work and how changes in conditions, operations, and the environment will affect outcomes.
Operation Monitoring	Watching gauges, dials, or other indicators to make sure a machine is working properly.

Ability	Ability Definitions
Oral Expression	The ability to communicate information and ideas in speaking so others will understand.
Written Comprehension	The ability to read and understand information and ideas presented in writing.
Speech Clarity	The ability to speak clearly so others can understand you.

Oral Comprehension	The ability to listen to and understand information and ideas presented through spoken words and sentences.
Written Expression	The ability to communicate information and ideas in writing so others will understand.
Deductive Reasoning	The ability to apply general rules to specific problems to produce answers that make sense.
Inductive Reasoning	The ability to combine pieces of information to form general rules or conclusions (includes finding a relationship among seemingly unrelated events).
Near Vision	The ability to see details at close range (within a few feet of the observer).
Problem Sensitivity	The ability to tell when something is wrong or is likely to go wrong. It does not involve solving the problem, only recognizing there is a problem.
Speech Recognition	The ability to identify and understand the speech of another person.
Information Ordering	The ability to arrange things or actions in a certain order or pattern according to a specific rule or set of rules (e.g., patterns of numbers, letters, words, pictures, mathematical operations).
Originality	The ability to come up with unusual or clever ideas about a given topic or situation, or to develop creative ways to solve a problem.
Category Flexibility	The ability to generate or use different sets of rules for combining or grouping things in different ways.
Selective Attention	The ability to concentrate on a task over a period of time without being distracted.
Mathematical Reasoning	The ability to choose the right mathematical methods or formulas to solve a problem.
Fluency of Ideas	The ability to come up with a number of ideas about a topic (the number of ideas is important, not their quality, correctness, or creativity).
Memorization	The ability to remember information such as words, numbers, pictures, and procedures.
Number Facility	The ability to add, subtract, multiply, or divide quickly and correctly.
Flexibility of Closure	The ability to identify or detect a known pattern (a figure, object, word, or sound) that is hidden in other distracting material.
Time Sharing	The ability to shift back and forth between two or more activities or sources of information (such as speech, sounds, touch, or other sources).
Far Vision	The ability to see details at a distance.
Trunk Strength	The ability to use your abdominal and lower back muscles to support part of the body repeatedly or continuously over time without 'giving out' or fatiguing.
Perceptual Speed	The ability to quickly and accurately compare similarities and differences among sets of letters, numbers, objects, pictures, or patterns. The things to be compared may be presented at the same time or one after the other. This ability also includes comparing a presented object with a remembered object.
Visualization	The ability to imagine how something will look after it is moved around or when its parts are moved or rearranged.
Speed of Closure	The ability to quickly make sense of, combine, and organize information into meaningful patterns.
Auditory Attention	The ability to focus on a single source of sound in the presence of other distracting sounds.
Visual Color Discrimination	The ability to match or detect differences between colors, including shades of color and brightness.
Finger Dexterity	The ability to make precisely coordinated movements of the fingers of one or both hands to grasp, manipulate, or assemble very small objects.
Depth Perception	The ability to judge which of several objects is closer or farther away from you, or to judge the distance between you and an object.
Hearing Sensitivity	The ability to detect or tell the differences between sounds that vary in pitch and loudness.
Speed of Limb Movement	The ability to quickly move the arms and legs.
Arm-Hand Steadiness	The ability to keep your hand and arm steady while moving your arm or while holding your arm and hand in one position.
Extent Flexibility	The ability to bend, stretch, twist, or reach with your body, arms, and/or legs.
Stamina	The ability to exert yourself physically over long periods of time without getting winded or out of breath.
Dynamic Strength	The ability to exert muscle force repeatedly or continuously over time. This involves muscular endurance and resistance to muscle fatigue.

Rate Control	The ability to time your movements or the movement of a piece of equipment in anticipation of changes in the speed and/or direction of a moving object or scene.
Static Strength	The ability to exert maximum muscle force to lift, push, pull, or carry objects.
Reaction Time	The ability to quickly respond (with the hand, finger, or foot) to a signal (sound, light, picture) when it appears.
Dynamic Flexibility	The ability to quickly and repeatedly bend, stretch, twist, or reach out with your body, arms, and/or legs.
Multilimb Coordination	The ability to coordinate two or more limbs (for example, two arms, two legs, or one leg and one arm) while sitting, standing, or lying down. It does not involve performing the activities while the whole body is in motion.
Manual Dexterity	The ability to quickly move your hand, your hand together with your arm, or your two hands to grasp, manipulate, or assemble objects.
Glare Sensitivity	The ability to see objects in the presence of glare or bright lighting.
Spatial Orientation	The ability to know your location in relation to the environment or to know where other objects are in relation to you.
Night Vision	The ability to see under low light conditions.
Sound Localization	The ability to tell the direction from which a sound originated.
Gross Body Coordination	The ability to coordinate the movement of your arms, legs, and torso together when the whole body is in motion.
Explosive Strength	The ability to use short bursts of muscle force to propel oneself (as in jumping or sprinting), or to throw an object.
Gross Body Equilibrium	The ability to keep or regain your body balance or stay upright when in an unstable position.
Control Precision	The ability to quickly and repeatedly adjust the controls of a machine or a vehicle to exact positions.
Wrist-Finger Speed	The ability to make fast, simple, repeated movements of the fingers, hands, and wrists.
Response Orientation	The ability to choose quickly between two or more movements in response to two or more different signals (lights, sounds, pictures). It includes the speed with which the correct response is started with the hand, foot, or other body part.
Peripheral Vision	The ability to see objects or movement of objects to one's side when the eyes are looking ahead.

Work_Activity	Work_Activity Definitions
Training and Teaching Others	Identifying the educational needs of others, developing formal educational or training programs or classes, and teaching or instructing others.
Interacting With Computers	Using computers and computer systems (including hardware and software) to program, write software, set up functions, enter data, or process information.
Interpreting the Meaning of Information for Others	Translating or explaining what information means and how it can be used.
Getting Information	Observing, receiving, and otherwise obtaining information from all relevant sources.
Updating and Using Relevant Knowledge	Keeping up-to-date technically and applying new knowledge to your job.
Analyzing Data or Information	Identifying the underlying principles, reasons, or facts of information by breaking down information or data into separate parts.
Organizing, Planning, and Prioritizing Work	Developing specific goals and plans to prioritize, organize, and accomplish your work.
Processing Information	Compiling, coding, categorizing, calculating, tabulating, auditing, or verifying information or data.
Coaching and Developing Others	Identifying the developmental needs of others and coaching, mentoring, or otherwise helping others to improve their knowledge or skills.
Making Decisions and Solving Problems	Analyzing information and evaluating results to choose the best solution and solve problems.
Thinking Creatively	Developing, designing, or creating new applications, ideas, relationships, systems, or products, including artistic contributions.
Communicating with Supervisors, Peers, or Subordin	Providing information to supervisors, co-workers, and subordinates by telephone, in written form, e-mail, or in person.
Documenting/Recording Information	Entering, transcribing, recording, storing, or maintaining information in written or electronic/magnetic form.
Identifying Objects, Actions, and Events	Identifying information by categorizing, estimating, recognizing differences or similarities, and detecting changes in circumstances or events.
Developing Objectives and Strategies	Establishing long-range objectives and specifying the strategies and actions to achieve them.

Establishing and Maintaining Interpersonal Relatio	Developing constructive and cooperative working relationships with others, and maintaining them over time.
Guiding, Directing, and Motivating Subordinates	Providing guidance and direction to subordinates, including setting performance standards and monitoring performance.
Scheduling Work and Activities	Scheduling events, programs, and activities, as well as the work of others.
Judging the Qualities of Things, Services, or Peop	Assessing the value, importance, or quality of things or people.
Coordinating the Work and Activities of Others	Getting members of a group to work together to accomplish tasks.
Monitor Processes, Materials, or Surroundings	Monitoring and reviewing information from materials, events, or the environment, to detect or assess problems.
Communicating with Persons Outside Organization	Communicating with people outside the organization, representing the organization to customers, the public, government, and other external sources. This information can be exchanged in person, in writing, or by telephone or e-mail.
Performing Administrative Activities	Performing day-to-day administrative tasks such as maintaining information files and processing paperwork.
Provide Consultation and Advice to Others	Providing guidance and expert advice to management or other groups on technical, systems-, or process-related topics.
Estimating the Quantifiable Characteristics of Pro	Estimating sizes, distances, and quantities; or determining time, costs, resources, or materials needed to perform a work activity.
Developing and Building Teams	Encouraging and building mutual trust, respect, and cooperation among team members.
Performing for or Working Directly with the Public	Performing for people or dealing directly with the public. This includes serving customers in restaurants and stores, and receiving clients or guests.
Evaluating Information to Determine Compliance wit	Using relevant information and individual judgment to determine whether events or processes comply with laws, regulations, or standards.
Assisting and Caring for Others	Providing personal assistance, medical attention, emotional support, or other personal care to others such as coworkers, customers, or patients.
Monitoring and Controlling Resources	Monitoring and controlling resources and overseeing the spending of money.
Resolving Conflicts and Negotiating with Others	Handling complaints, settling disputes, and resolving grievances and conflicts, or otherwise negotiating with others.
Repairing and Maintaining Electronic Equipment	Servicing, repairing, calibrating, regulating, fine-tuning, or testing machines, devices, and equipment that operate primarily on the basis of electrical or electronic (not mechanical) principles.
Inspecting Equipment, Structures, or Material	Inspecting equipment, structures, or materials to identify the cause of errors or other problems or defects.
Controlling Machines and Processes	Using either control mechanisms or direct physical activity to operate machines or processes (not including computers or vehicles).
Selling or Influencing Others	Convincing others to buy merchandise/goods or to otherwise change their minds or actions.
Drafting, Laying Out, and Specifying Technical Dev	Providing documentation, detailed instructions, drawings, or specifications to tell others about how devices, parts, equipment, or structures are to be fabricated, constructed, assembled, modified, maintained, or used.
Handling and Moving Objects	Using hands and arms in handling, installing, positioning, and moving materials, and manipulating things.
Repairing and Maintaining Mechanical Equipment	Servicing, repairing, adjusting, and testing machines, devices, moving parts, and equipment that operate primarily on the basis of mechanical (not electronic) principles.
Performing General Physical Activities	Performing physical activities that require considerable use of your arms and legs and moving your whole body, such as climbing, lifting, balancing, walking, stooping, and handling of materials.
Staffing Organizational Units	Recruiting, interviewing, selecting, hiring, and promoting employees in an organization.
Operating Vehicles, Mechanized Devices, or Equipme	Running, maneuvering, navigating, or driving vehicles or mechanized equipment, such as forklifts, passenger vehicles, aircraft, or water craft.

Work_Context	Work_Context Definitions
Electronic Mail	How often do you use electronic mail in this job?
Indoors, Environmentally Controlled	How often does this job require working indoors in environmentally controlled conditions?
Freedom to Make Decisions	How much decision making freedom, without supervision, does the job offer?

Face-to-Face Discussions	How often do you have to have face-to-face discussions with individuals or teams in this job?
Public Speaking	How often do you have to perform public speaking in this job?
Contact With Others	How much does this job require the worker to be in contact with others (face-to-face, by telephone, or otherwise) in order to perform it?
Telephone	How often do you have telephone conversations in this job?
Structured versus Unstructured Work	To what extent is this job structured for the worker, rather than allowing the worker to determine tasks, priorities, and goals?
Importance of Being Exact or Accurate	How important is being very exact or highly accurate in performing this job?
Time Pressure	How often does this job require the worker to meet strict deadlines?
Coordinate or Lead Others	How important is it to coordinate or lead others in accomplishing work activities in this job?
Letters and Memos	How often does the job require written letters and memos?
Impact of Decisions on Co-workers or Company Resul	How do the decisions an employee makes impact the results of co-workers, clients or the company?
Work With Work Group or Team	How important is it to work with others in a group or team in this job?
Frequency of Decision Making	How frequently is the worker required to make decisions that affect other people, the financial resources, and/or the image and reputation of the organization?
Spend Time Sitting	How much does this job require sitting?
Level of Competition	To what extent does this job require the worker to compete or to be aware of competitive pressures?
Responsibility for Outcomes and Results	How responsible is the worker for work outcomes and results of other workers?
Deal With External Customers	How important is it to work with external customers or the public in this job?
Physical Proximity	To what extent does this job require the worker to perform job tasks in close physical proximity to other people?
Frequency of Conflict Situations	How often are there conflict situations the employee has to face in this job?
Deal With Unpleasant or Angry People	How frequently does the worker have to deal with unpleasant, angry, or discourteous individuals as part of the job requirements?
Spend Time Standing	How much does this job require standing?
Importance of Repeating Same Tasks	How important is repeating the same physical activities (e.g., key entry) or mental activities (e.g., checking entries in a ledger) over and over, without stopping, to performing this job?
Responsible for Others' Health and Safety	How much responsibility is there for the health and safety of others in this job?
Sounds, Noise Levels Are Distracting or Uncomforta	How often does this job require working exposed to sounds and noise levels that are distracting or uncomfortable?
Consequence of Error	How serious would the result usually be if the worker made a mistake that was not readily correctable?
Spend Time Making Repetitive Motions	How much does this job require making repetitive motions?
Exposed to Contaminants	How often does this job require working exposed to contaminants (such as pollutants, gases, dust or odors)?
Spend Time Using Your Hands to Handle, Control, or	How much does this job require using your hands to handle, control, or feel objects, tools or controls?
Indoors, Not Environmentally Controlled	How often does this job require working indoors in non-controlled environmental conditions (e.g., warehouse without heat)?
Exposed to Hazardous Conditions	How often does this job require exposure to hazardous conditions?
Wear Common Protective or Safety Equipment such as	How much does this job require wearing common protective or safety equipment such as safety shoes, glasses, gloves, hard hats or life jackets?
Exposed to Disease or Infections	How often does this job require exposure to disease/infections?
Exposed to Minor Burns, Cuts, Bites, or Stings	How often does this job require exposure to minor burns, cuts, bites, or stings?
In an Enclosed Vehicle or Equipment	How often does this job require working in a closed vehicle or equipment (e.g., car)?
Spend Time Walking and Running	How much does this job require walking and running?
Extremely Bright or Inadequate Lighting	How often does this job require working in extremely bright or inadequate lighting conditions?
Exposed to Hazardous Equipment	How often does this job require exposure to hazardous equipment?
Degree of Automation	How automated is the job?
Cramped Work Space, Awkward Positions	How often does this job require working in cramped work spaces that requires getting into awkward positions?

Outdoors, Exposed to Weather	How often does this job require working outdoors, exposed to all weather conditions?
Exposed to Radiation	How often does this job require exposure to radiation?
Very Hot or Cold Temperatures	How often does this job require working in very hot (above 90 F degrees) or very cold (below 32 F degrees) temperatures?
Outdoors, Under Cover	How often does this job require working outdoors, under cover (e.g., structure with roof but no walls)?
Spend Time Bending or Twisting the Body	How much does this job require bending or twisting your body?
Wear Specialized Protective or Safety Equipment su	How much does this job require wearing specialized protective or safety equipment such as breathing apparatus, safety harness, full protection suits, or radiation protection?
Spend Time Kneeling, Crouching, Stooping, or Crawl	How much does this job require kneeling, crouching, stooping or crawling?
Pace Determined by Speed of Equipment	How important is it to this job that the pace is determined by the speed of equipment or machinery? (This does not refer to keeping busy at all times on this job.)
Exposed to High Places	How often does this job require exposure to high places?
Spend Time Climbing Ladders, Scaffolds, or Poles	How much does this job require climbing ladders, scaffolds, or poles?
Spend Time Keeping or Regaining Balance	How much does this job require keeping or regaining your balance?
Deal With Physically Aggressive People	How frequently does this job require the worker to deal with physical aggression of violent individuals?
In an Open Vehicle or Equipment	How often does this job require working in an open vehicle or equipment (e.g., tractor)?
Exposed to Whole Body Vibration	How often does this job require exposure to whole body vibration (e.g., operate a jackhammer)?

Job Zone Component	Job Zone Component Definitions
Title	Job Zone Five: Extensive Preparation Needed
Overall Experience	Extensive skill, knowledge, and experience are needed for these occupations. Many require more than five years of experience. For example, surgeons must complete four years of college and an additional five to seven years of specialized medical training to be able to do their job.
Job Training	Employees may need some on-the-job training, but most of these occupations assume that the person will already have the required skills, knowledge, work-related experience, and/or training.
Job Zone Examples	These occupations often involve coordinating, training, supervising, or managing the activities of others to accomplish goals. Very advanced communication and organizational skills are required. Examples include athletic trainers, lawyers, managing editors, phyicists, social psychologists, and surgeons.
SVP Range	(8.0 and above)
Education	A bachelor's degree is the minimum formal education required for these occupations. However, many also require graduate school. For example, they may require a master's degree, and some require a Ph.D., M.D., or J.D. (law degree).

Work_Styles	Work_Styles Definitions
Integrity	Job requires being honest and ethical.
Analytical Thinking	Job requires analyzing information and using logic to address work-related issues and problems.
Independence	Job requires developing one's own ways of doing things, guiding oneself with little or no supervision, and depending on oneself to get things done.
Dependability	Job requires being reliable, responsible, and dependable, and fulfilling obligations.
Attention to Detail	Job requires being careful about detail and thorough in completing work tasks.
Achievement/Effort	Job requires establishing and maintaining personally challenging achievement goals and exerting effort toward mastering tasks.
Innovation	Job requires creativity and alternative thinking to develop new ideas for and answers to work-related problems.
Initiative	Job requires a willingness to take on responsibilities and challenges.
Persistence	Job requires persistence in the face of obstacles.
Self Control	Job requires maintaining composure, keeping emotions in check, controlling anger, and avoiding aggressive behavior, even in very difficult situations.

Concern for Others	Job requires being sensitive to others' needs and feelings and being understanding and helpful on the job.
Cooperation	Job requires being pleasant with others on the job and displaying a good-natured, cooperative attitude.
Leadership	Job requires a willingness to lead, take charge, and offer opinions and direction.
Stress Tolerance	Job requires accepting criticism and dealing calmly and effectively with high stress situations.
Adaptability/Flexibility	Job requires being open to change (positive or negative) and to considerable variety in the workplace.
Social Orientation	Job requires preferring to work with others rather than alone, and being personally connected with others on the job.

25-1061.00 - Anthropology and Archeology Teachers, Postsecondary

Teach courses in anthropology or archeology.

Tasks

1) **Prepare course materials** such as syllabi, homework assignments, and handouts.

2) **Advise students** on academic and vocational curricula, career issues, and laboratory and field research.

3) **Compile bibliographies** of specialized materials for outside reading assignments.

4) **Initiate, facilitate, and moderate** classroom discussions.

5) **Participate** in campus and community events.

6) **Supervise** undergraduate and/or graduate teaching, internship, and research work.

7) **Participate** in student recruitment, registration, and placement activities.

8) **Compile, administer, and grade** examinations, or assign this work to others.

9) **Serve** on academic or administrative committees that deal with institutional policies, departmental matters, and academic issues.

10) **Maintain** student attendance records, grades, and other required records.

11) **Select and obtain** materials and supplies such as textbooks and laboratory equipment.

12) **Write grant proposals** to procure external research funding.

13) **Supervise** students' laboratory or field work.

14) **Prepare and deliver lectures** to undergraduate and/or graduate students on topics such as research methods, urban anthropology, and language and culture.

15) **Act as advisers** to student organizations.

16) **Provide professional consulting services** to government and/or industry.

17) **Perform administrative duties** such as serving as department head.

18) **Conduct research** in a particular field of knowledge, and publish findings in professional journals, books, and/or electronic media.

19) **Plan, evaluate, and revise** curricula, course content, and course materials and methods of instruction.

20) **Maintain** regularly scheduled office hours in order to advise and assist students.

21) **Keep abreast** of developments in their field by reading current literature, talking with colleagues, and participating in professional conferences.

22) **Evaluate and grade** students' class work, assignments, and papers.

Knowledge	Knowledge Definitions
Sociology and Anthropology	Knowledge of group behavior and dynamics, societal trends and influences, human migrations, ethnicity, cultures and their history and origins.
English Language	Knowledge of the structure and content of the English language including the meaning and spelling of words, rules of composition, and grammar.
History and Archeology	Knowledge of historical events and their causes, indicators, and effects on civilizations and cultures.
Education and Training	Knowledge of principles and methods for curriculum and training design, teaching and instruction for individuals and groups, and the measurement of training effects.

Geography	Knowledge of principles and methods for describing the features of land, sea, and air masses, including their physical characteristics, locations, interrelationships, and distribution of plant, animal, and human life.
Foreign Language	Knowledge of the structure and content of a foreign (non-English) language including the meaning and spelling of words, rules of composition and grammar, and pronunciation.
Computers and Electronics	Knowledge of circuit boards, processors, chips, electronic equipment, and computer hardware and software, including applications and programming.
Philosophy and Theology	Knowledge of different philosophical systems and religions. This includes their basic principles, values, ethics, ways of thinking, customs, practices, and their impact on human culture.
Psychology	Knowledge of human behavior and performance; individual differences in ability, personality, and interests; learning and motivation; psychological research methods; and the assessment and treatment of behavioral and affective disorders.
Communications and Media	Knowledge of media production, communication, and dissemination techniques and methods. This includes alternative ways to inform and entertain via written, oral, and visual media.
Mathematics	Knowledge of arithmetic, algebra, geometry, calculus, statistics, and their applications.
Personnel and Human Resources	Knowledge of principles and procedures for personnel recruitment, selection, training, compensation and benefits, labor relations and negotiation, and personnel information systems.
Biology	Knowledge of plant and animal organisms, their tissues, cells, functions, interdependencies, and interactions with each other and the environment.
Clerical	Knowledge of administrative and clerical procedures and systems such as word processing, managing files and records, stenography and transcription, designing forms, and other office procedures and terminology.
Law and Government	Knowledge of laws, legal codes, court procedures, precedents, government regulations, executive orders, agency rules, and the democratic political process.
Administration and Management	Knowledge of business and management principles involved in strategic planning, resource allocation, human resources modeling, leadership technique, production methods, and coordination of people and resources.
Customer and Personal Service	Knowledge of principles and processes for providing customer and personal services. This includes customer needs assessment, meeting quality standards for services, and evaluation of customer satisfaction.
Economics and Accounting	Knowledge of economic and accounting principles and practices, the financial markets, banking and the analysis and reporting of financial data.
Public Safety and Security	Knowledge of relevant equipment, policies, procedures, and strategies to promote effective local, state, or national security operations for the protection of people, data, property, and institutions.
Medicine and Dentistry	Knowledge of the information and techniques needed to diagnose and treat human injuries, diseases, and deformities. This includes symptoms, treatment alternatives, drug properties and interactions, and preventive health-care measures.
Therapy and Counseling	Knowledge of principles, methods, and procedures for diagnosis, treatment, and rehabilitation of physical and mental dysfunctions, and for career counseling and guidance.
Physics	Knowledge and prediction of physical principles, laws, their interrelationships, and applications to understanding fluid, material, and atmospheric dynamics, and mechanical, electrical, atomic and sub- atomic structures and processes.
Chemistry	Knowledge of the chemical composition, structure, and properties of substances and of the chemical processes and transformations that they undergo. This includes uses of chemicals and their interactions, danger signs, production techniques, and disposal methods.
Transportation	Knowledge of principles and methods for moving people or goods by air, rail, sea, or road, including the relative costs and benefits.
Telecommunications	Knowledge of transmission, broadcasting, switching, control, and operation of telecommunications systems.
Mechanical	Knowledge of machines and tools, including their designs, uses, repair, and maintenance.

Fine Arts	Knowledge of the theory and techniques required to compose, produce, and perform works of music, dance, visual arts, drama, and sculpture.
Design	Knowledge of design techniques, tools, and principles involved in production of precision technical plans, blueprints, drawings, and models.
Sales and Marketing	Knowledge of principles and methods for showing, promoting, and selling products or services. This includes marketing strategy and tactics, product demonstration, sales techniques, and sales control systems.
Food Production	Knowledge of techniques and equipment for planting, growing, and harvesting food products (both plant and animal) for consumption, including storage/handling techniques.
Engineering and Technology	Knowledge of the practical application of engineering science and technology. This includes applying principles, techniques, procedures, and equipment to the design and production of various goods and services.
Production and Processing	Knowledge of raw materials, production processes, quality control, costs, and other techniques for maximizing the effective manufacture and distribution of goods.
Building and Construction	Knowledge of materials, methods, and the tools involved in the construction or repair of houses, buildings, or other structures such as highways and roads.

Skills	Skills Definitions
Reading Comprehension	Understanding written sentences and paragraphs in work related documents.
Writing	Communicating effectively in writing as appropriate for the needs of the audience.
Instructing	Teaching others how to do something.
Critical Thinking	Using logic and reasoning to identify the strengths and weaknesses of alternative solutions, conclusions or approaches to problems.
Active Learning	Understanding the implications of new information for both current and future problem-solving and decision-making.
Speaking	Talking to others to convey information effectively.
Active Listening	Giving full attention to what other people are saying, taking time to understand the points being made, asking questions as appropriate, and not interrupting at inappropriate times.
Learning Strategies	Selecting and using training/instructional methods and procedures appropriate for the situation when learning or teaching new things.
Social Perceptiveness	Being aware of others' reactions and understanding why they react as they do.
Complex Problem Solving	Identifying complex problems and reviewing related information to develop and evaluate options and implement solutions.
Science	Using scientific rules and methods to solve problems.
Time Management	Managing one's own time and the time of others.
Monitoring	Monitoring/Assessing performance of yourself, other individuals, or organizations to make improvements or take corrective action.
Persuasion	Persuading others to change their minds or behavior.
Coordination	Adjusting actions in relation to others' actions.
Judgment and Decision Making	Considering the relative costs and benefits of potential actions to choose the most appropriate one.
Negotiation	Bringing others together and trying to reconcile differences.
Service Orientation	Actively looking for ways to help people.
Mathematics	Using mathematics to solve problems.
Management of Financial Resources	Determining how money will be spent to get the work done, and accounting for these expenditures.
Equipment Selection	Determining the kind of tools and equipment needed to do a job.
Management of Personnel Resources	Motivating, developing, and directing people as they work, identifying the best people for the job.
Management of Material Resources	Obtaining and seeing to the appropriate use of equipment, facilities, and materials needed to do certain work.
Operations Analysis	Analyzing needs and product requirements to create a design.
Quality Control Analysis	Conducting tests and inspections of products, services, or processes to evaluate quality or performance.
Technology Design	Generating or adapting equipment and technology to serve user needs.
Systems Analysis	Determining how a system should work and how changes in conditions, operations, and the environment will affect outcomes.

Systems Evaluation	Identifying measures or indicators of system performance and the actions needed to improve or correct performance, relative to the goals of the system.
Operation and Control	Controlling operations of equipment or systems.
Troubleshooting	Determining causes of operating errors and deciding what to do about it.
Installation	Installing equipment, machines, wiring, or programs to meet specifications.
Programming	Writing computer programs for various purposes.
Equipment Maintenance	Performing routine maintenance on equipment and determining when and what kind of maintenance is needed.
Repairing	Repairing machines or systems using the needed tools.
Operation Monitoring	Watching gauges, dials, or other indicators to make sure a machine is working properly.

Ability	Ability Definitions
Oral Expression	The ability to communicate information and ideas in speaking so others will understand.
Written Comprehension	The ability to read and understand information and ideas presented in writing.
Speech Clarity	The ability to speak clearly so others can understand you.
Oral Comprehension	The ability to listen to and understand information and ideas presented through spoken words and sentences.
Inductive Reasoning	The ability to combine pieces of information to form general rules or conclusions (includes finding a relationship among seemingly unrelated events).
Written Expression	The ability to communicate information and ideas in writing so others will understand.
Deductive Reasoning	The ability to apply general rules to specific problems to produce answers that make sense.
Near Vision	The ability to see details at close range (within a few feet of the observer).
Category Flexibility	The ability to generate or use different sets of rules for combining or grouping things in different ways.
Problem Sensitivity	The ability to tell when something is wrong or is likely to go wrong. It does not involve solving the problem, only recognizing there is a problem.
Originality	The ability to come up with unusual or clever ideas about a given topic or situation, or to develop creative ways to solve a problem.
Fluency of Ideas	The ability to come up with a number of ideas about a topic (the number of ideas is important, not their quality, correctness, or creativity).
Speech Recognition	The ability to identify and understand the speech of another person.
Information Ordering	The ability to arrange things or actions in a certain order or pattern according to a specific rule or set of rules (e.g., patterns of numbers, letters, words, pictures, mathematical operations).
Selective Attention	The ability to concentrate on a task over a period of time without being distracted.
Memorization	The ability to remember information such as words, numbers, pictures, and procedures.
Flexibility of Closure	The ability to identify or detect a known pattern (a figure, object, word, or sound) that is hidden in other distracting material.
Time Sharing	The ability to shift back and forth between two or more activities or sources of information (such as speech, sounds, touch, or other sources).
Mathematical Reasoning	The ability to choose the right mathematical methods or formulas to solve a problem.
Far Vision	The ability to see details at a distance.
Visualization	The ability to imagine how something will look after it is moved around or when its parts are moved or rearranged.
Speed of Closure	The ability to quickly make sense of, combine, and organize information into meaningful patterns.
Perceptual Speed	The ability to quickly and accurately compare similarities and differences among sets of letters, numbers, objects, pictures, or patterns. The things to be compared may be presented at the same time or one after the other. This ability also includes comparing a presented object with a remembered object.
Number Facility	The ability to add, subtract, multiply, or divide quickly and correctly.
Auditory Attention	The ability to focus on a single source of sound in the presence of other distracting sounds.
Visual Color Discrimination	The ability to match or detect differences between colors, including shades of color and brightness.

Finger Dexterity	The ability to make precisely coordinated movements of the fingers of one or both hands to grasp, manipulate, or assemble very small objects.
Hearing Sensitivity	The ability to detect or tell the differences between sounds that vary in pitch and loudness.
Depth Perception	The ability to judge which of several objects is closer or farther away from you, or to judge the distance between you and an object.
Trunk Strength	The ability to use your abdominal and lower back muscles to support part of the body repeatedly or continuously over time without 'giving out' or fatiguing.
Dynamic Strength	The ability to exert muscle force repeatedly or continuously over time. This involves muscular endurance and resistance to muscle fatigue.
Dynamic Flexibility	The ability to quickly and repeatedly bend, stretch, twist, or reach out with your body, arms, and/or legs.
Rate Control	The ability to time your movements or the movement of a piece of equipment in anticipation of changes in the speed and/or direction of a moving object or scene.
Extent Flexibility	The ability to bend, stretch, twist, or reach with your body, arms, and/or legs.
Wrist-Finger Speed	The ability to make fast, simple, repeated movements of the fingers, hands, and wrists.
Speed of Limb Movement	The ability to quickly move the arms and legs.
Control Precision	The ability to quickly and repeatedly adjust the controls of a machine or a vehicle to exact positions.
Explosive Strength	The ability to use short bursts of muscle force to propel oneself (as in jumping or sprinting), or to throw an object.
Manual Dexterity	The ability to quickly move your hand, your hand together with your arm, or your two hands to grasp, manipulate, or assemble objects.
Response Orientation	The ability to choose quickly between two or more movements in response to two or more different signals (lights, sounds, pictures). It includes the speed with which the correct response is started with the hand, foot, or other body part.
Static Strength	The ability to exert maximum muscle force to lift, push, pull, or carry objects.
Glare Sensitivity	The ability to see objects in the presence of glare or bright lighting.
Gross Body Coordination	The ability to coordinate the movement of your arms, legs, and torso together when the whole body is in motion.
Multilimb Coordination	The ability to coordinate two or more limbs (for example, two arms, two legs, or one leg and one arm) while sitting, standing, or lying down. It does not involve performing the activities while the whole body is in motion.
Night Vision	The ability to see under low light conditions.
Stamina	The ability to exert yourself physically over long periods of time without getting winded or out of breath.
Sound Localization	The ability to tell the direction from which a sound originated.
Peripheral Vision	The ability to see objects or movement of objects to one's side when the eyes are looking ahead.
Reaction Time	The ability to quickly respond (with the hand, finger, or foot) to a signal (sound, light, picture) when it appears.
Spatial Orientation	The ability to know your location in relation to the environment or to know where other objects are in relation to you.
Arm-Hand Steadiness	The ability to keep your hand and arm steady while moving your arm or while holding your arm and hand in one position.
Gross Body Equilibrium	The ability to keep or regain your body balance or stay upright when in an unstable position.

Work_Activity	Work_Activity Definitions
Training and Teaching Others	Identifying the educational needs of others, developing formal educational or training programs or classes, and teaching or instructing others.
Thinking Creatively	Developing, designing, or creating new applications, ideas, relationships, systems, or products, including artistic contributions.
Getting Information	Observing, receiving, and otherwise obtaining information from all relevant sources.
Updating and Using Relevant Knowledge	Keeping up-to-date technically and applying new knowledge to your job.
Analyzing Data or Information	Identifying the underlying principles, reasons, or facts of information by breaking down information or data into separate parts.
Interacting With Computers	Using computers and computer systems (including hardware and software) to program, write software, set up functions, enter data, or process information.

Processing Information	Compiling, coding, categorizing, calculating, tabulating, auditing, or verifying information or data.
Interpreting the Meaning of Information for Others	Translating or explaining what information means and how it can be used.
Documenting/Recording Information	Entering, transcribing, recording, storing, or maintaining information in written or electronic/magnetic form.
Identifying Objects, Actions, and Events	Identifying information by categorizing, estimating, recognizing differences or similarities, and detecting changes in circumstances or events.
Judging the Qualities of Things, Services, or Peop	Assessing the value, importance, or quality of things or people.
Organizing, Planning, and Prioritizing Work	Developing specific goals and plans to prioritize, organize, and accomplish your work.
Making Decisions and Solving Problems	Analyzing information and evaluating results to choose the best solution and solve problems.
Communicating with Persons Outside Organization	Communicating with people outside the organization, representing the organization to customers, the public, government, and other external sources. This information can be exchanged in person, in writing, or by telephone or e-mail.
Establishing and Maintaining Interpersonal Relatio	Developing constructive and cooperative working relationships with others, and maintaining them over time.
Coaching and Developing Others	Identifying the developmental needs of others and coaching, mentoring, or otherwise helping others to improve their knowledge or skills.
Communicating with Supervisors, Peers, or Subordin	Providing information to supervisors, co-workers, and subordinates by telephone, in written form, e-mail, or in person.
Scheduling Work and Activities	Scheduling events, programs, and activities, as well as the work of others.
Developing Objectives and Strategies	Establishing long-range objectives and specifying the strategies and actions to achieve them.
Provide Consultation and Advice to Others	Providing guidance and expert advice to management or other groups on technical, systems-, or process-related topics.
Evaluating Information to Determine Compliance wit	Using relevant information and individual judgment to determine whether events or processes comply with laws, regulations, or standards.
Performing Administrative Activities	Performing day-to-day administrative tasks such as maintaining information files and processing paperwork.
Monitor Processes, Materials, or Surroundings	Monitoring and reviewing information from materials, events, or the environment, to detect or assess problems.
Guiding, Directing, and Motivating Subordinates	Providing guidance and direction to subordinates, including setting performance standards and monitoring performance.
Coordinating the Work and Activities of Others	Getting members of a group to work together to accomplish tasks.
Developing and Building Teams	Encouraging and building mutual trust, respect, and cooperation among team members.
Assisting and Caring for Others	Providing personal assistance, medical attention, emotional support, or other personal care to others such as coworkers, customers, or patients.
Performing for or Working Directly with the Public	Performing for people or dealing directly with the public. This includes serving customers in restaurants and stores, and receiving clients or guests.
Estimating the Quantifiable Characteristics of Pro	Estimating sizes, distances, and quantities; or determining time, costs, resources, or materials needed to perform a work activity.
Monitoring and Controlling Resources	Monitoring and controlling resources and overseeing the spending of money.
Resolving Conflicts and Negotiating with Others	Handling complaints, settling disputes, and resolving grievances and conflicts, or otherwise negotiating with others.
Staffing Organizational Units	Recruiting, interviewing, selecting, hiring, and promoting employees in an organization.
Selling or Influencing Others	Convincing others to buy merchandise/goods or to otherwise change their minds or actions.
Inspecting Equipment, Structures, or Material	Inspecting equipment, structures, or materials to identify the cause of errors or other problems or defects.
Performing General Physical Activities	Performing physical activities that require considerable use of your arms and legs and moving your whole body, such as climbing, lifting, balancing, walking, stooping, and handling of materials.
Controlling Machines and Processes	Using either control mechanisms or direct physical activity to operate machines or processes (not including computers or vehicles).
Handling and Moving Objects	Using hands and arms in handling, installing, positioning, and moving materials, and manipulating things.
Repairing and Maintaining Electronic Equipment	Servicing, repairing, calibrating, regulating, fine-tuning, or testing machines, devices, and equipment that operate primarily on the basis of electrical or electronic (not mechanical) principles.
Operating Vehicles, Mechanized Devices, or Equipme	Running, maneuvering, navigating, or driving vehicles or mechanized equipment, such as forklifts, passenger vehicles, aircraft, or water craft.
Drafting, Laying Out, and Specifying Technical Dev	Providing documentation, detailed instructions, drawings, or specifications to tell others about how devices, parts, equipment, or structures are to be fabricated, constructed, assembled, modified, maintained, or used.
Repairing and Maintaining Mechanical Equipment	Servicing, repairing, adjusting, and testing machines, devices, moving parts, and equipment that operate primarily on the basis of mechanical (not electronic) principles.

Work_Context	Work_Context Definitions
Electronic Mail	How often do you use electronic mail in this job?
Face-to-Face Discussions	How often do you have to have face-to-face discussions with individuals or teams in this job?
Freedom to Make Decisions	How much decision making freedom, without supervision, does the job offer?
Structured versus Unstructured Work	To what extent is this job structured for the worker, rather than allowing the worker to determine tasks, priorities, and goals?
Contact With Others	How much does this job require the worker to be in contact with others (face-to-face, by telephone, or otherwise) in order to perform it?
Indoors, Environmentally Controlled	How often does this job require working indoors in environmentally controlled conditions?
Telephone	How often do you have telephone conversations in this job?
Public Speaking	How often do you have to perform public speaking in this job?
Letters and Memos	How often does the job require written letters and memos?
Spend Time Sitting	How much does this job require sitting?
Level of Competition	To what extent does this job require the worker to compete or to be aware of competitive pressures?
Time Pressure	How often does this job require the worker to meet strict deadlines?
Impact of Decisions on Co-workers or Company Resul	How do the decisions an employee makes impact the results of co-workers, clients or the company?
Frequency of Decision Making	How frequently is the worker required to make decisions that affect other people, the financial resources, and/or the image and reputation of the organization?
Work With Work Group or Team	How important is it to work with others in a group or team in this job?
Importance of Being Exact or Accurate	How important is being very exact or highly accurate in performing this job?
Coordinate or Lead Others	How important is it to coordinate or lead others in accomplishing work activities in this job?
Physical Proximity	To what extent does this job require the worker to perform job tasks in close physical proximity to other people?
Deal With External Customers	How important is it to work with external customers or the public in this job?
Frequency of Conflict Situations	How often are there conflict situations the employee has to face in this job?
Responsibility for Outcomes and Results	How responsible is the worker for work outcomes and results of other workers?
Spend Time Making Repetitive Motions	How much does this job require making repetitive motions?
Deal With Unpleasant or Angry People	How frequently does the worker have to deal with unpleasant, angry, or discourteous individuals as part of the job requirements?
Sounds, Noise Levels Are Distracting or Uncomforta	How often does this job require working exposed to sounds and noise levels that are distracting or uncomfortable?
Exposed to Contaminants	How often does this job require working exposed to contaminants (such as pollutants, gases, dust or odors)?
Consequence of Error	How serious would the result usually be if the worker made a mistake that was not readily correctable?
Spend Time Standing	How much does this job require standing?
Importance of Repeating Same Tasks	How important is repeating the same physical activities (e.g., key entry) or mental activities (e.g., checking entries in a ledger) over and over, without stopping, to performing this job?
Indoors, Not Environmentally Controlled	How often does this job require working indoors in non-controlled environmental conditions (e.g., warehouse without heat)?
Spend Time Using Your Hands to Handle, Control, or	How much does this job require using your hands to handle, control, or feel objects, tools or controls?

		Work_Styles	Work_Styles Definitions
Responsible for Others' Health and Safety	How much responsibility is there for the health and safety of others in this job?	Analytical Thinking	Job requires analyzing information and using logic to address work-related issues and problems.
Spend Time Walking and Running	How much does this job require walking and running?		
Outdoors, Exposed to Weather	How often does this job require working outdoors, exposed to all weather conditions?	Achievement/Effort	Job requires establishing and maintaining personally challenging achievement goals and exerting effort toward mastering tasks.
In an Enclosed Vehicle or Equipment	How often does this job require working in a closed vehicle or equipment (e.g., car)?	Dependability	Job requires being reliable, responsible, and dependable, and fulfilling obligations.
Outdoors, Under Cover	How often does this job require working outdoors, under cover (e.g., structure with roof but no walls)?	Independence	Job requires developing one's own ways of doing things, guiding oneself with little or no supervision, and depending on oneself to get things done.
Exposed to Disease or Infections	How often does this job require exposure to disease/infections?	Initiative	Job requires a willingness to take on responsibilities and challenges.
Very Hot or Cold Temperatures	How often does this job require working in very hot (above 90 F degrees) or very cold (below 32 F degrees) temperatures?	Persistence	Job requires persistence in the face of obstacles.
Degree of Automation	How automated is the job?	Integrity	Job requires being honest and ethical.
Spend Time Bending or Twisting the Body	How much does this job require bending or twisting your body?	Innovation	Job requires creativity and alternative thinking to develop new ideas for and answers to work-related problems.
Extremely Bright or Inadequate Lighting	How often does this job require working in extremely bright or inadequate lighting conditions?	Stress Tolerance	Job requires accepting criticism and dealing calmly and effectively with high stress situations.
Exposed to Minor Burns, Cuts, Bites, or Stings	How often does this job require exposure to minor burns, cuts, bites, or stings?	Attention to Detail	Job requires being careful about detail and thorough in completing work tasks.
Cramped Work Space, Awkward Positions	How often does this job require working in cramped work spaces that requires getting into awkward positions?	Adaptability/Flexibility	Job requires being open to change (positive or negative) and to considerable variety in the workplace.
Spend Time Kneeling, Crouching, Stooping, or Crawl	How much does this job require kneeling, crouching, stooping, or crawling?	Leadership	Job requires a willingness to lead, take charge, and offer opinions and direction.
Wear Common Protective or Safety Equipment such as	How much does this job require wearing common protective or safety equipment such as safety shoes, glasses, gloves, hard hats or life jackets?	Cooperation	Job requires being pleasant with others on the job and displaying a good-natured, cooperative attitude.
Spend Time Climbing Ladders, Scaffolds, or Poles	How much does this job require climbing ladders, scaffolds, or poles?	Self Control	Job requires maintaining composure, keeping emotions in check, controlling anger, and avoiding aggressive behavior, even in very difficult situations.
In an Open Vehicle or Equipment	How often does this job require working in an open vehicle or equipment (e.g., tractor)?	Concern for Others	Job requires being sensitive to others' needs and feelings and being understanding and helpful on the job.
Exposed to Hazardous Conditions	How often does this job require exposure to hazardous conditions?	Social Orientation	Job requires preferring to work with others rather than alone, and being personally connected with others on the job.
Exposed to Hazardous Equipment	How often does this job require exposure to hazardous equipment?		
Exposed to High Places	How often does this job require exposure to high places?		
Deal With Physically Aggressive People	How frequently does this job require the worker to deal with physical aggression of violent individuals?		
Pace Determined by Speed of Equipment	How important is it to this job that the pace is determined by the speed of equipment or machinery? (This does not refer to keeping busy at all times on this job.)		
Exposed to Radiation	How often does this job require exposure to radiation?		
Exposed to Whole Body Vibration	How often does this job require exposure to whole body vibration (e.g., operate a jackhammer)?		
Spend Time Keeping or Regaining Balance	How much does this job require keeping or regaining your balance?		
Wear Specialized Protective or Safety Equipment su	How much does this job require wearing specialized protective or safety equipment such as breathing apparatus, safety harness, full protection suits, or radiation protection?		

Job Zone Component	Job Zone Component Definitions
Title	Job Zone Five: Extensive Preparation Needed
Overall Experience	Extensive skill, knowledge, and experience are needed for these occupations. Many require more than five years of experience. For example, surgeons must complete four years of college and an additional five to seven years of specialized medical training to be able to do their job.
Job Training	Employees may need some on-the-job training, but most of these occupations assume that the person will already have the required skills, knowledge, work-related experience, and/or training.
Job Zone Examples	These occupations often involve coordinating, training, supervising, or managing the activities of others to accomplish goals. Very advanced communication and organizational skills are required. Examples include athletic trainers, lawyers, managing editors, phyicists, social psychologists, and surgeons.
SVP Range	(8.0 and above)
Education	A bachelor's degree is the minimum formal education required for these occupations. However, many also require graduate school. For example, they may require a master's degree, and some require a Ph.D., M.D., or J.D. (law degree).

25-1062.00 - Area, Ethnic, and Cultural Studies Teachers, Postsecondary

Teach courses pertaining to the culture and development of an area (e.g., Latin America), an ethnic group, or any other group (e.g., women's studies, urban affairs).

Tasks

1) Compile bibliographies of specialized materials for outside reading assignments.

2) Plan, evaluate, and revise curricula, course content, and course materials and methods of instruction.

3) Prepare and deliver lectures to undergraduate and/or graduate students on topics such as race and ethnic relations, gender studies, and cross-cultural perspectives.

4) Maintain student attendance records, grades, and other required records.

5) Serve on academic or administrative committees that deal with institutional policies, departmental matters, and academic issues.

6) Write grant proposals to procure external research funding.

7) Supervise undergraduate and/or graduate teaching, internship, and research work.

8) Participate in student recruitment, registration, and placement activities.

9) Incorporate experiential/site visit components into courses.

10) Act as advisers to student organizations.

11) Perform administrative duties such as serving as department head.

12) Provide professional consulting services to government and/or industry.

13) Prepare course materials such as syllabi, homework assignments, and handouts.

14) Advise students on academic and vocational curricula, and on career issues.

15) Evaluate and grade students' class work, assignments, and papers.

16) Keep abreast of developments in their field by reading current literature, talking with colleagues, and participating in professional conferences.

17) Initiate, facilitate, and moderate classroom discussions.

18) Conduct research in a particular field of knowledge, and publish findings in professional

journals, books, and/or electronic media.

19) Compile, administer, and grade examinations. or assign this work to others.

20) Participate in campus and community events.

21) Maintain regularly scheduled office hours in order to advise and assist students.

22) Collaborate with colleagues to address teaching and research issues.

Knowledge	Knowledge Definitions
English Language	Knowledge of the structure and content of the English language including the meaning and spelling of words, rules of composition, and grammar.
Education and Training	Knowledge of principles and methods for curriculum and training design, teaching and instruction for individuals and groups, and the measurement of training effects.
History and Archeology	Knowledge of historical events and their causes, indicators, and effects on civilizations and cultures.
Foreign Language	Knowledge of the structure and content of a foreign (non-English) language including the meaning and spelling of words, rules of composition and grammar, and pronunciation.
Sociology and Anthropology	Knowledge of group behavior and dynamics, societal trends and influences, human migrations, ethnicity, cultures and their history and origins.
Philosophy and Theology	Knowledge of different philosophical systems and religions. This includes their basic principles, values, ethics, ways of thinking, customs, practices, and their impact on human culture.
Geography	Knowledge of principles and methods for describing the features of land, sea, and air masses, including their physical characteristics, locations, interrelationships, and distribution of plant, animal, and human life.
Communications and Media	Knowledge of media production, communication, and dissemination techniques and methods. This includes alternative ways to inform and entertain via written, oral, and visual media.
Administration and Management	Knowledge of business and management principles involved in strategic planning, resource allocation, human resources modeling, leadership technique, production methods, and coordination of people and resources.
Customer and Personal Service	Knowledge of principles and processes for providing customer and personal services. This includes customer needs assessment, meeting quality standards for services, and evaluation of customer satisfaction.
Clerical	Knowledge of administrative and clerical procedures and systems such as word processing, managing files and records, stenography and transcription, designing forms, and other office procedures and terminology.
Psychology	Knowledge of human behavior and performance; individual differences in ability, personality, and interests; learning and motivation; psychological research methods; and the assessment and treatment of behavioral and affective disorders.
Personnel and Human Resources	Knowledge of principles and procedures for personnel recruitment, selection, training, compensation and benefits, labor relations and negotiation, and personnel information systems.
Fine Arts	Knowledge of the theory and techniques required to compose, produce, and perform works of music, dance, visual arts, drama, and sculpture.
Computers and Electronics	Knowledge of circuit boards, processors, chips, electronic equipment, and computer hardware and software, including applications and programming.
Law and Government	Knowledge of laws, legal codes, court procedures, precedents, government regulations, executive orders, agency rules, and the democratic political process.
Therapy and Counseling	Knowledge of principles, methods, and procedures for diagnosis, treatment, and rehabilitation of physical and mental dysfunctions, and for career counseling and guidance.
Mathematics	Knowledge of arithmetic, algebra, geometry, calculus, statistics, and their applications.
Public Safety and Security	Knowledge of relevant equipment, policies, procedures, and strategies to promote effective local, state, or national security operations for the protection of people, data, property, and institutions.
Sales and Marketing	Knowledge of principles and methods for showing, promoting, and selling products or services. This includes marketing strategy and tactics, product demonstration, sales techniques, and sales control systems.

Economics and Accounting	Knowledge of economic and accounting principles and practices, the financial markets, banking and the analysis and reporting of financial data.
Telecommunications	Knowledge of transmission, broadcasting, switching, control, and operation of telecommunications systems.
Transportation	Knowledge of principles and methods for moving people or goods by air, rail, sea, or road, including the relative costs and benefits.
Medicine and Dentistry	Knowledge of the information and techniques needed to diagnose and treat human injuries, diseases, and deformities. This includes symptoms, treatment alternatives, drug properties and interactions, and preventive health-care measures.
Biology	Knowledge of plant and animal organisms, their tissues, cells, functions, interdependencies, and interactions with each other and the environment.
Chemistry	Knowledge of the chemical composition, structure, and properties of substances and of the chemical processes and transformations that they undergo. This includes uses of chemicals and their interactions, danger signs, production techniques, and disposal methods.
Design	Knowledge of design techniques, tools, and principles involved in production of precision technical plans, blueprints, drawings, and models.
Production and Processing	Knowledge of raw materials, production processes, quality control, costs, and other techniques for maximizing the effective manufacture and distribution of goods.
Mechanical	Knowledge of machines and tools, including their designs, uses, repair, and maintenance.
Physics	Knowledge and prediction of physical principles, laws, their interrelationships, and applications to understanding fluid, material, and atmospheric dynamics, and mechanical, electrical, atomic and sub-atomic structures and processes.
Engineering and Technology	Knowledge of the practical application of engineering science and technology. This includes applying principles, techniques, procedures, and equipment to the design and production of various goods and services.
Building and Construction	Knowledge of materials, methods, and the tools involved in the construction or repair of houses, buildings, or other structures such as highways and roads.
Food Production	Knowledge of techniques and equipment for planting, growing, and harvesting food products (both plant and animal) for consumption, including storage/handling techniques.

Skills	Skills Definitions
Instructing	Teaching others how to do something.
Reading Comprehension	Understanding written sentences and paragraphs in work related documents.
Writing	Communicating effectively in writing as appropriate for the needs of the audience.
Critical Thinking	Using logic and reasoning to identify the strengths and weaknesses of alternative solutions, conclusions or approaches to problems.
Speaking	Talking to others to convey information effectively.
Active Listening	Giving full attention to what other people are saying, taking time to understand the points being made, asking questions as appropriate, and not interrupting at inappropriate times.
Social Perceptiveness	Being aware of others' reactions and understanding why they react as they do.
Active Learning	Understanding the implications of new information for both current and future problem-solving and decision-making.
Learning Strategies	Selecting and using training/instructional methods and procedures appropriate for the situation when learning or teaching new things.
Time Management	Managing one's own time and the time of others.
Persuasion	Persuading others to change their minds or behavior.
Monitoring	Monitoring/Assessing performance of yourself, other individuals, or organizations to make improvements or take corrective action.
Judgment and Decision Making	Considering the relative costs and benefits of potential actions to choose the most appropriate one.
Service Orientation	Actively looking for ways to help people.
Coordination	Adjusting actions in relation to others' actions.
Complex Problem Solving	Identifying complex problems and reviewing related information to develop and evaluate options and implement solutions.
Management of Personnel Resources	Motivating, developing, and directing people as they work, identifying the best people for the job.

Negotiation	Bringing others together and trying to reconcile differences.
Technology Design	Generating or adapting equipment and technology to serve user needs.
Management of Financial Resources	Determining how money will be spent to get the work done, and accounting for these expenditures.
Equipment Selection	Determining the kind of tools and equipment needed to do a job.
Mathematics	Using mathematics to solve problems.
Operations Analysis	Analyzing needs and product requirements to create a design.
Science	Using scientific rules and methods to solve problems.
Quality Control Analysis	Conducting tests and inspections of products, services, or processes to evaluate quality or performance.
Management of Material Resources	Obtaining and seeing to the appropriate use of equipment, facilities, and materials needed to do certain work.
Systems Analysis	Determining how a system should work and how changes in conditions, operations, and the environment will affect outcomes.
Systems Evaluation	Identifying measures or indicators of system performance and the actions needed to improve or correct performance, relative to the goals of the system.
Troubleshooting	Determining causes of operating errors and deciding what to do about it.
Operation and Control	Controlling operations of equipment or systems.
Installation	Installing equipment, machines, wiring, or programs to meet specifications.
Equipment Maintenance	Performing routine maintenance on equipment and determining when and what kind of maintenance is needed.
Programming	Writing computer programs for various purposes.
Operation Monitoring	Watching gauges, dials, or other indicators to make sure a machine is working properly.
Repairing	Repairing machines or systems using the needed tools.

Ability	Ability Definitions
Oral Expression	The ability to communicate information and ideas in speaking so others will understand.
Written Comprehension	The ability to read and understand information and ideas presented in writing.
Oral Comprehension	The ability to listen to and understand information and ideas presented through spoken words and sentences.
Inductive Reasoning	The ability to combine pieces of information to form general rules or conclusions (includes finding a relationship among seemingly unrelated events).
Speech Clarity	The ability to speak clearly so others can understand you.
Written Expression	The ability to communicate information and ideas in writing so others will understand.
Deductive Reasoning	The ability to apply general rules to specific problems to produce answers that make sense.
Near Vision	The ability to see details at close range (within a few feet of the observer).
Originality	The ability to come up with unusual or clever ideas about a given topic or situation, or to develop creative ways to solve a problem.
Problem Sensitivity	The ability to tell when something is wrong or is likely to go wrong. It does not involve solving the problem, only recognizing there is a problem.
Speech Recognition	The ability to identify and understand the speech of another person.
Fluency of Ideas	The ability to come up with a number of ideas about a topic (the number of ideas is important, not their quality, correctness, or creativity).
Category Flexibility	The ability to generate or use different sets of rules for combining or grouping things in different ways.
Information Ordering	The ability to arrange things or actions in a certain order or pattern according to a specific rule or set of rules (e.g., patterns of numbers, letters, words, pictures, mathematical operations).
Selective Attention	The ability to concentrate on a task over a period of time without being distracted.
Memorization	The ability to remember information such as words, numbers, pictures, and procedures.
Time Sharing	The ability to shift back and forth between two or more activities or sources of information (such as speech, sounds, touch, or other sources).
Flexibility of Closure	The ability to identify or detect a known pattern (a figure, object, word, or sound) that is hidden in other distracting material.
Far Vision	The ability to see details at a distance.

Mathematical Reasoning	The ability to choose the right mathematical methods or formulas to solve a problem.
Speed of Closure	The ability to quickly make sense of, combine, and organize information into meaningful patterns.
Perceptual Speed	The ability to quickly and accurately compare similarities and differences among sets of letters, numbers, objects, pictures, or patterns. The things to be compared may be presented at the same time or one after the other. This ability also includes comparing a presented object with a remembered object.
Number Facility	The ability to add, subtract, multiply, or divide quickly and correctly.
Auditory Attention	The ability to focus on a single source of sound in the presence of other distracting sounds.
Visualization	The ability to imagine how something will look after it is moved around or when its parts are moved or rearranged.
Finger Dexterity	The ability to make precisely coordinated movements of the fingers of one or both hands to grasp, manipulate, or assemble very small objects.
Visual Color Discrimination	The ability to match or detect differences between colors, including shades of color and brightness.
Hearing Sensitivity	The ability to detect or tell the differences between sounds that vary in pitch and loudness.
Trunk Strength	The ability to use your abdominal and lower back muscles to support part of the body repeatedly or continuously over time without 'giving out' or fatiguing.
Depth Perception	The ability to judge which of several objects is closer or farther away from you, or to judge the distance between you and an object.
Sound Localization	The ability to tell the direction from which a sound originated.
Stamina	The ability to exert yourself physically over long periods of time without getting winded or out of breath.
Gross Body Coordination	The ability to coordinate the movement of your arms, legs, and torso together when the whole body is in motion.
Rate Control	The ability to time your movements or the movement of a piece of equipment in anticipation of changes in the speed and/or direction of a moving object or scene.
Wrist-Finger Speed	The ability to make fast, simple, repeated movements of the fingers, hands, and wrists.
Speed of Limb Movement	The ability to quickly move the arms and legs.
Static Strength	The ability to exert maximum muscle force to lift, push, pull, or carry objects.
Explosive Strength	The ability to use short bursts of muscle force to propel oneself (as in jumping or sprinting), or to throw an object.
Dynamic Strength	The ability to exert muscle force repeatedly or continuously over time. This involves muscular endurance and resistance to muscle fatigue.
Night Vision	The ability to see under low light conditions.
Multilimb Coordination	The ability to coordinate two or more limbs (for example, two arms, two legs, or one leg and one arm) while sitting, standing, or lying down. It does not involve performing the activities while the whole body is in motion.
Response Orientation	The ability to choose quickly between two or more movements in response to two or more different signals (lights, sounds, pictures). It includes the speed with which the correct response is started with the hand, foot, or other body part.
Manual Dexterity	The ability to quickly move your hand, your hand together with your arm, or your two hands to grasp, manipulate, or assemble objects.
Arm-Hand Steadiness	The ability to keep your hand and arm steady while moving your arm or while holding your arm and hand in one position.
Spatial Orientation	The ability to know your location in relation to the environment or to know where other objects are in relation to you.
Reaction Time	The ability to quickly respond (with the hand, finger, or foot) to a signal (sound, light, picture) when it appears.
Glare Sensitivity	The ability to see objects in the presence of glare or bright lighting.
Extent Flexibility	The ability to bend, stretch, twist, or reach with your body, arms, and/or legs.
Dynamic Flexibility	The ability to quickly and repeatedly bend, stretch, twist, or reach out with your body, arms, and/or legs.
Peripheral Vision	The ability to see objects or movement of objects to one's side when the eyes are looking ahead.
Gross Body Equilibrium	The ability to keep or regain your body balance or stay upright when in an unstable position.
Control Precision	The ability to quickly and repeatedly adjust the controls of a machine or a vehicle to exact positions.

1398

Work_Activity	Work_Activity Definitions
Training and Teaching Others	Identifying the educational needs of others, developing formal educational or training programs or classes, and teaching or instructing others.
Interpreting the Meaning of Information for Others	Translating or explaining what information means and how it can be used.
Getting Information	Observing, receiving, and otherwise obtaining information from all relevant sources.
Updating and Using Relevant Knowledge	Keeping up-to-date technically and applying new knowledge to your job.
Thinking Creatively	Developing, designing, or creating new applications, ideas, relationships, systems, or products, including artistic contributions.
Organizing, Planning, and Prioritizing Work	Developing specific goals and plans to prioritize, organize, and accomplish your work.
Interacting With Computers	Using computers and computer systems (including hardware and software) to program, write software, set up functions, enter data, or process information.
Analyzing Data or Information	Identifying the underlying principles, reasons, or facts of information by breaking down information or data into separate parts.
Processing Information	Compiling, coding, categorizing, calculating, tabulating, auditing, or verifying information or data.
Identifying Objects, Actions, and Events	Identifying information by categorizing, estimating, recognizing differences or similarities, and detecting changes in circumstances or events.
Documenting/Recording Information	Entering, transcribing, recording, storing, or maintaining information in written or electronic/magnetic form.
Making Decisions and Solving Problems	Analyzing information and evaluating results to choose the best solution and solve problems.
Establishing and Maintaining Interpersonal Relatio	Developing constructive and cooperative working relationships with others, and maintaining them over time.
Judging the Qualities of Things, Services, or Peop	Assessing the value, importance, or quality of things or people.
Communicating with Supervisors, Peers, or Subordin	Providing information to supervisors, co-workers, and subordinates by telephone, in written form, e-mail, or in person.
Developing Objectives and Strategies	Establishing long-range objectives and specifying the strategies and actions to achieve them.
Provide Consultation and Advice to Others	Providing guidance and expert advice to management or other groups on technical, systems-, or process-related topics.
Scheduling Work and Activities	Scheduling events, programs, and activities, as well as the work of others.
Coaching and Developing Others	Identifying the developmental needs of others and coaching, mentoring, or otherwise helping others to improve their knowledge or skills.
Communicating with Persons Outside Organization	Communicating with people outside the organization, representing the organization to customers, the public, government, and other external sources. This information can be exchanged in person, in writing, or by telephone or e-mail.
Monitor Processes, Materials, or Surroundings	Monitoring and reviewing information from materials, events, or the environment, to detect or assess problems.
Performing Administrative Activities	Performing day-to-day administrative tasks such as maintaining information files and processing paperwork.
Coordinating the Work and Activities of Others	Getting members of a group to work together to accomplish tasks.
Guiding, Directing, and Motivating Subordinates	Providing guidance and direction to subordinates, including setting performance standards and monitoring performance.
Performing for or Working Directly with the Public	Performing for people or dealing directly with the public. This includes serving customers in restaurants and stores, and receiving clients or guests.
Evaluating Information to Determine Compliance wit	Using relevant information and individual judgment to determine whether events or processes comply with laws, regulations, or standards.
Estimating the Quantifiable Characteristics of Pro	Estimating sizes, distances, and quantities; or determining time, costs, resources, or materials needed to perform a work activity.
Developing and Building Teams	Encouraging and building mutual trust, respect, and cooperation among team members.
Assisting and Caring for Others	Providing personal assistance, medical attention, emotional support, or other personal care to others such as coworkers, customers, or patients.
Resolving Conflicts and Negotiating with Others	Handling complaints, settling disputes, and resolving grievances and conflicts, or otherwise negotiating with others.

Staffing Organizational Units	Recruiting, interviewing, selecting, hiring, and promoting employees in an organization.
Selling or Influencing Others	Convincing others to buy merchandise/goods or to otherwise change their minds or actions.
Monitoring and Controlling Resources	Monitoring and controlling resources and overseeing the spending of money.
Inspecting Equipment, Structures, or Material	Inspecting equipment, structures, or materials to identify the cause of errors or other problems or defects.
Performing General Physical Activities	Performing physical activities that require considerable use of your arms and legs and moving your whole body, such as climbing, lifting, balancing, walking, stooping, and handling of materials.
Controlling Machines and Processes	Using either control mechanisms or direct physical activity to operate machines or processes (not including computers or vehicles).
Handling and Moving Objects	Using hands and arms in handling, installing, positioning, and moving materials, and manipulating things.
Drafting, Laying Out, and Specifying Technical Dev	Providing documentation, detailed instructions, drawings, or specifications to tell others about how devices, parts, equipment, or structures are to be fabricated, constructed, assembled, modified, maintained, or used.
Operating Vehicles, Mechanized Devices, or Equipme	Running, maneuvering, navigating, or driving vehicles or mechanized equipment, such as forklifts, passenger vehicles, aircraft, or water craft.
Repairing and Maintaining Electronic Equipment	Servicing, repairing, calibrating, regulating, fine-tuning, or testing machines, devices, and equipment that operate primarily on the basis of electrical or electronic (not mechanical) principles.
Repairing and Maintaining Mechanical Equipment	Servicing, repairing, adjusting, and testing machines, devices, moving parts, and equipment that operate primarily on the basis of mechanical (not electronic) principles.

Work_Context	Work_Context Definitions
Electronic Mail	How often do you use electronic mail in this job?
Face-to-Face Discussions	How often do you have to have face-to-face discussions with individuals or teams in this job?
Indoors, Environmentally Controlled	How often does this job require working indoors in environmentally controlled conditions?
Freedom to Make Decisions	How much decision making freedom, without supervision, does the job offer?
Telephone	How often do you have telephone conversations in this job?
Contact With Others	How much does this job require the worker to be in contact with others (face-to-face, by telephone, or otherwise) in order to perform it?
Structured versus Unstructured Work	To what extent is this job structured for the worker, rather than allowing the worker to determine tasks, priorities, and goals?
Work With Work Group or Team	How important is it to work with others in a group or team in this job?
Letters and Memos	How often does the job require written letters and memos?
Public Speaking	How often do you have to perform public speaking in this job?
Spend Time Sitting	How much does this job require sitting?
Time Pressure	How often does this job require the worker to meet strict deadlines?
Coordinate or Lead Others	How important is it to coordinate or lead others in accomplishing work activities in this job?
Importance of Being Exact or Accurate	How important is being very exact or highly accurate in performing this job?
Frequency of Decision Making	How frequently is the worker required to make decisions that affect other people, the financial resources, and/or the image and reputation of the organization?
Impact of Decisions on Co-workers or Company Resul	How do the decisions an employee makes impact the results of co-workers, clients or the company?
Level of Competition	To what extent does this job require the worker to compete or to be aware of competitive pressures?
Deal With External Customers	How important is it to work with external customers or the public in this job?
Frequency of Conflict Situations	How often are there conflict situations the employee has to face in this job?
Sounds, Noise Levels Are Distracting or Uncomforta	How often does this job require working exposed to sounds and noise levels that are distracting or uncomfortable?
Responsibility for Outcomes and Results	How responsible is the worker for work outcomes and results of other workers?
Physical Proximity	To what extent does this job require the worker to perform job tasks in close physical proximity to other people?

Deal With Unpleasant or Angry People	How frequently does the worker have to deal with unpleasant, angry, or discourteous individuals as part of the job requirements?
Spend Time Making Repetitive Motions	How much does this job require making repetitive motions?
Importance of Repeating Same Tasks	How important is repeating the same physical activities (e.g., key entry) or mental activities (e.g., checking entries in a ledger) over and over, without stopping, to performing this job?
Spend Time Standing	How much does this job require standing?
Exposed to Contaminants	How often does this job require working exposed to contaminants (such as pollutants, gases, dust or odors)?
Consequence of Error	How serious would the result usually be if the worker made a mistake that was not readily correctable?
Spend Time Using Your Hands to Handle, Control, or	How much does this job require using your hands to handle, control, or feel objects, tools or controls?
Exposed to Disease or Infections	How often does this job require exposure to disease/infections?
Extremely Bright or Inadequate Lighting	How often does this job require working in extremely bright or inadequate lighting conditions?
Spend Time Walking and Running	How much does this job require walking and running?
Degree of Automation	How automated is the job?
Responsible for Others' Health and Safety	How much responsibility is there for the health and safety of others in this job?
Very Hot or Cold Temperatures	How often does this job require working in very hot (above 90 F degrees) or very cold (below 32 F degrees) temperatures?
Indoors, Not Environmentally Controlled	How often does this job require working indoors in non-controlled environmental conditions (e.g., warehouse without heat)?
Deal With Physically Aggressive People	How frequently does this job require the worker to deal with physical aggression of violent individuals?
In an Enclosed Vehicle or Equipment	How often does this job require working in a closed vehicle or equipment (e.g., car)?
Spend Time Bending or Twisting the Body	How much does this job require bending or twisting your body?
Outdoors, Exposed to Weather	How often does this job require working outdoors, exposed to all weather conditions?
Outdoors, Under Cover	How often does this job require working outdoors, under cover (e.g., structure with roof but no walls)?
Cramped Work Space, Awkward Positions	How often does this job require working in cramped work spaces that requires getting into awkward positions?
Wear Common Protective or Safety Equipment such as	How much does this job require wearing common protective or safety equipment such as safety shoes, glasses, gloves, hard hats or live jackets?
Spend Time Kneeling, Crouching, Stooping, or Crawl	How much does this job require kneeling, crouching, stooping or crawling?
Exposed to Minor Burns, Cuts, Bites, or Stings	How often does this job require exposure to minor burns, cuts, bites, or stings?
Spend Time Climbing Ladders, Scaffolds, or Poles	How much does this job require climbing ladders, scaffolds, or poles?
Pace Determined by Speed of Equipment	How important is it to this job that the pace is determined by the speed of equipment or machinery? (This does not refer to keeping busy at all times on this job.)
Exposed to Whole Body Vibration	How often does this job require exposure to whole body vibration (e.g., operate a jackhammer)?
Exposed to Hazardous Conditions	How often does this job require exposure to hazardous conditions?
Exposed to Radiation	How often does this job require exposure to radiation?
Exposed to High Places	How often does this job require exposure to high places?
Exposed to Hazardous Equipment	How often does this job require exposure to hazardous equipment?
In an Open Vehicle or Equipment	How often does this job require working in an open vehicle or equipment (e.g., tractor)?
Spend Time Keeping or Regaining Balance	How much does this job require keeping or regaining your balance?
Wear Specialized Protective or Safety Equipment su	How much does this job require wearing specialized protective or safety equipment such as breathing apparatus, safety harness, full protection suits, or radiation protection?

Job Zone Component	Job Zone Component Definitions
Title	Job Zone Five: Extensive Preparation Needed

Overall Experience	Extensive skill, knowledge, and experience are needed for these occupations. Many require more than five years of experience. For example, surgeons must complete four years of college and an additional five to seven years of specialized medical training to be able to do their job.
Job Training	Employees may need some on-the-job training, but most of these occupations assume that the person will already have the required skills, knowledge, work-related experience, and/or training.
Job Zone Examples	These occupations often involve coordinating, training, supervising, or managing the activities of others to accomplish goals. Very advanced communication and organizational skills are required. Examples include athletic trainers, lawyers, managing editors, phyicists, social psychologists, and surgeons.
SVP Range	(8.0 and above)
Education	A bachelor's degree is the minimum formal education required for these occupations. However, many also require graduate school. For example, they may require a master's degree, and some require a Ph.D., M.D., or J.D. (law degree).

Work_Styles	Work_Styles Definitions
Integrity	Job requires being honest and ethical.
Persistence	Job requires persistence in the face of obstacles.
Leadership	Job requires a willingness to lead, take charge, and offer opinions and direction.
Analytical Thinking	Job requires analyzing information and using logic to address work-related issues and problems.
Initiative	Job requires a willingness to take on responsibilities and challenges.
Achievement/Effort	Job requires establishing and maintaining personally challenging achievement goals and exerting effort toward mastering tasks.
Self Control	Job requires maintaining composure, keeping emotions in check, controlling anger, and avoiding aggressive behavior, even in very difficult situations.
Dependability	Job requires being reliable, responsible, and dependable, and fulfilling obligations.
Independence	Job requires developing one's own ways of doing things, guiding oneself with little or no supervision, and depending on oneself to get things done.
Attention to Detail	Job requires being careful about detail and thorough in completing work tasks.
Cooperation	Job requires being pleasant with others on the job and displaying a good-natured, cooperative attitude.
Social Orientation	Job requires preferring to work with others rather than alone, and being personally connected with others on the job.
Innovation	Job requires creativity and alternative thinking to develop new ideas for and answers to work-related problems.
Concern for Others	Job requires being sensitive to others' needs and feelings and being understanding and helpful on the job.
Stress Tolerance	Job requires accepting criticism and dealing calmly and effectively with high stress situations.
Adaptability/Flexibility	Job requires being open to change (positive or negative) and to considerable variety in the workplace.

25-1063.00 - Economics Teachers, Postsecondary

Teach courses in economics.

Tasks

1) Maintain regularly scheduled office hours in order to advise and assist students.

2) Prepare course materials such as syllabi, homework assignments, and handouts.

3) Evaluate and grade students' class work, assignments, and papers.

4) Compile, administer, and grade examinations, or assign this work to others.

5) Maintain student attendance records, grades, and other required records.

6) Initiate, facilitate, and moderate classroom discussions.

7) Plan, evaluate, and revise curricula, course content, and course materials and methods of instruction.

8) Select and obtain materials and supplies such as textbooks.

9) Collaborate with colleagues to address teaching and research issues.

10) Participate in campus and community events.

11) Serve on academic or administrative committees that deal with institutional policies, departmental matters, and academic issues.

12) Advise students on academic and vocational curricula, and on career issues.

13) Compile bibliographies of specialized materials for outside reading assignments.

14) Participate in student recruitment, registration, and placement activities.

15) Conduct research in a particular field of knowledge, and publish findings in professional journals, books, and/or electronic media.

16) Supervise undergraduate and/or graduate teaching, internship, and research work.

17) Provide professional consulting services to government and/or industry.

18) Act as advisers to student organizations.

19) Write grant proposals to procure external research funding.

20) Perform administrative duties such as serving as department head.

21) Keep abreast of developments in their field by reading current literature, talking with colleagues, and participating in professional conferences.

Knowledge	Knowledge Definitions
Economics and Accounting	Knowledge of economic and accounting principles and practices, the financial markets, banking and the analysis and reporting of financial data.
English Language	Knowledge of the structure and content of the English language including the meaning and spelling of words, rules of composition, and grammar.
Mathematics	Knowledge of arithmetic, algebra, geometry, calculus, statistics, and their applications.
Education and Training	Knowledge of principles and methods for curriculum and training design, teaching and instruction for individuals and groups, and the measurement of training effects.
Computers and Electronics	Knowledge of circuit boards, processors, chips, electronic equipment, and computer hardware and software, including applications and programming.
Law and Government	Knowledge of laws, legal codes, court procedures, precedents, government regulations, executive orders, agency rules, and the democratic political process.
Administration and Management	Knowledge of business and management principles involved in strategic planning, resource allocation, human resources modeling, leadership technique, production methods, and coordination of people and resources.
History and Archeology	Knowledge of historical events and their causes, indicators, and effects on civilizations and cultures.
Psychology	Knowledge of human behavior and performance; individual differences in ability, personality, and interests; learning and motivation; psychological research methods; and the assessment and treatment of behavioral and affective disorders.
Customer and Personal Service	Knowledge of principles and processes for providing customer and personal services. This includes customer needs assessment, meeting quality standards for services, and evaluation of customer satisfaction.
Philosophy and Theology	Knowledge of different philosophical systems and religions. This includes their basic principles, values, ethics, ways of thinking, customs, practices, and their impact on human culture.
Personnel and Human Resources	Knowledge of principles and procedures for personnel recruitment, selection, training, compensation and benefits, labor relations and negotiation, and personnel information systems.
Sociology and Anthropology	Knowledge of group behavior and dynamics, societal trends and influences, human migrations, ethnicity, cultures and their history and origins.
Communications and Media	Knowledge of media production, communication, and dissemination techniques and methods. This includes alternative ways to inform and entertain via written, oral, and visual media.
Geography	Knowledge of principles and methods for describing the features of land, sea, and air masses, including their physical characteristics, locations, interrelationships, and distribution of plant, animal, and human life.
Clerical	Knowledge of administrative and clerical procedures and systems such as word processing, managing files and records, stenography and transcription, designing forms, and other office procedures and terminology.
Sales and Marketing	Knowledge of principles and methods for showing, promoting, and selling products or services. This includes marketing strategy and tactics, product demonstration, sales techniques, and sales control systems.
Production and Processing	Knowledge of raw materials, production processes, quality control, costs, and other techniques for maximizing the effective manufacture and distribution of goods.
Telecommunications	Knowledge of transmission, broadcasting, switching, control, and operation of telecommunications systems.
Transportation	Knowledge of principles and methods for moving people or goods by air, rail, sea, or road, including the relative costs and benefits.
Public Safety and Security	Knowledge of relevant equipment, policies, procedures, and strategies to promote effective local, state, or national security operations for the protection of people, data, property, and institutions.
Foreign Language	Knowledge of the structure and content of a foreign (non-English) language including the meaning and spelling of words, rules of composition and grammar, and pronunciation.
Therapy and Counseling	Knowledge of principles, methods, and procedures for diagnosis, treatment, and rehabilitation of physical and mental dysfunctions, and for career counseling and guidance.
Engineering and Technology	Knowledge of the practical application of engineering science and technology. This includes applying principles, techniques, procedures, and equipment to the design and production of various goods and services.
Design	Knowledge of design techniques, tools, and principles involved in production of precision technical plans, blueprints, drawings, and models.
Physics	Knowledge and prediction of physical principles, laws, their interrelationships, and applications to understanding fluid, material, and atmospheric dynamics, and mechanical, electrical, atomic and sub- atomic structures and processes.
Medicine and Dentistry	Knowledge of the information and techniques needed to diagnose and treat human injuries, diseases, and deformities. This includes symptoms, treatment alternatives, drug properties and interactions, and preventive health-care measures.
Food Production	Knowledge of techniques and equipment for planting, growing, and harvesting food products (both plant and animal) for consumption, including storage/handling techniques.
Biology	Knowledge of plant and animal organisms, their tissues, cells, functions, interdependencies, and interactions with each other and the environment.
Mechanical	Knowledge of machines and tools, including their designs, uses, repair, and maintenance.
Fine Arts	Knowledge of the theory and techniques required to compose, produce, and perform works of music, dance, visual arts, drama, and sculpture.
Building and Construction	Knowledge of materials, methods, and the tools involved in the construction or repair of houses, buildings, or other structures such as highways and roads.
Chemistry	Knowledge of the chemical composition, structure, and properties of substances and of the chemical processes and transformations that they undergo. This includes uses of chemicals and their interactions, danger signs, production techniques, and disposal methods.

Skills	Skills Definitions
Instructing	Teaching others how to do something.
Speaking	Talking to others to convey information effectively.
Reading Comprehension	Understanding written sentences and paragraphs in work related documents.
Critical Thinking	Using logic and reasoning to identify the strengths and weaknesses of alternative solutions, conclusions or approaches to problems.
Writing	Communicating effectively in writing as appropriate for the needs of the audience.
Active Listening	Giving full attention to what other people are saying, taking time to understand the points being made, asking questions as appropriate, and not interrupting at inappropriate times.
Learning Strategies	Selecting and using training/instructional methods and procedures appropriate for the situation when learning or teaching new things.
Time Management	Managing one's own time and the time of others.
Mathematics	Using mathematics to solve problems.
Social Perceptiveness	Being aware of others' reactions and understanding why they react as they do.

Active Learning	Understanding the implications of new information for both current and future problem-solving and decision-making.
Complex Problem Solving	Identifying complex problems and reviewing related information to develop and evaluate options and implement solutions.
Judgment and Decision Making	Considering the relative costs and benefits of potential actions to choose the most appropriate one.
Monitoring	Monitoring/Assessing performance of yourself, other individuals, or organizations to make improvements or take corrective action.
Persuasion	Persuading others to change their minds or behavior.
Coordination	Adjusting actions in relation to others' actions.
Service Orientation	Actively looking for ways to help people.
Science	Using scientific rules and methods to solve problems.
Management of Personnel Resources	Motivating, developing, and directing people as they work, identifying the best people for the job.
Negotiation	Bringing others together and trying to reconcile differences.
Management of Financial Resources	Determining how money will be spent to get the work done, and accounting for these expenditures.
Quality Control Analysis	Conducting tests and inspections of products, services, or processes to evaluate quality or performance.
Equipment Selection	Determining the kind of tools and equipment needed to do a job.
Operations Analysis	Analyzing needs and product requirements to create a design.
Programming	Writing computer programs for various purposes.
Systems Evaluation	Identifying measures or indicators of system performance and the actions needed to improve or correct performance, relative to the goals of the system.
Technology Design	Generating or adapting equipment and technology to serve user needs.
Management of Material Resources	Obtaining and seeing to the appropriate use of equipment, facilities, and materials needed to do certain work.
Systems Analysis	Determining how a system should work and how changes in conditions, operations, and the environment will affect outcomes.
Troubleshooting	Determining causes of operating errors and deciding what to do about it.
Operation and Control	Controlling operations of equipment or systems.
Installation	Installing equipment, machines, wiring, or programs to meet specifications.
Operation Monitoring	Watching gauges, dials, or other indicators to make sure a machine is working properly.
Equipment Maintenance	Performing routine maintenance on equipment and determining when and what kind of maintenance is needed.
Repairing	Repairing machines or systems using the needed tools.

Ability	Ability Definitions
Oral Expression	The ability to communicate information and ideas in speaking so others will understand.
Written Expression	The ability to communicate information and ideas in writing so others will understand.
Oral Comprehension	The ability to listen to and understand information and ideas presented through spoken words and sentences.
Speech Clarity	The ability to speak clearly so others can understand you.
Written Comprehension	The ability to read and understand information and ideas presented in writing.
Deductive Reasoning	The ability to apply general rules to specific problems to produce answers that make sense.
Problem Sensitivity	The ability to tell when something is wrong or is likely to go wrong. It does not involve solving the problem, only recognizing there is a problem.
Number Facility	The ability to add, subtract, multiply, or divide quickly and correctly.
Near Vision	The ability to see details at close range (within a few feet of the observer).
Inductive Reasoning	The ability to combine pieces of information to form general rules or conclusions (includes finding a relationship among seemingly unrelated events).
Speech Recognition	The ability to identify and understand the speech of another person.
Mathematical Reasoning	The ability to choose the right mathematical methods or formulas to solve a problem.
Information Ordering	The ability to arrange things or actions in a certain order or pattern according to a specific rule or set of rules (e.g., patterns of numbers, letters, words, pictures, mathematical operations).

Originality	The ability to come up with unusual or clever ideas about a given topic or situation, or to develop creative ways to solve a problem.
Category Flexibility	The ability to generate or use different sets of rules for combining or grouping things in different ways.
Fluency of Ideas	The ability to come up with a number of ideas about a topic (the number of ideas is important, not their quality, correctness, or creativity).
Flexibility of Closure	The ability to identify or detect a known pattern (a figure, object, word, or sound) that is hidden in other distracting material.
Selective Attention	The ability to concentrate on a task over a period of time without being distracted.
Far Vision	The ability to see details at a distance.
Time Sharing	The ability to shift back and forth between two or more activities or sources of information (such as speech, sounds, touch, or other sources).
Memorization	The ability to remember information such as words, numbers, pictures, and procedures.
Speed of Closure	The ability to quickly make sense of, combine, and organize information into meaningful patterns.
Perceptual Speed	The ability to quickly and accurately compare similarities and differences among sets of letters, numbers, objects, pictures, or patterns. The things to be compared may be presented at the same time or one after the other. This ability also includes comparing a presented object with a remembered object.
Visualization	The ability to imagine how something will look after it is moved around or when its parts are moved or rearranged.
Hearing Sensitivity	The ability to detect or tell the differences between sounds that vary in pitch and loudness.
Finger Dexterity	The ability to make precisely coordinated movements of the fingers of one or both hands to grasp, manipulate, or assemble very small objects.
Auditory Attention	The ability to focus on a single source of sound in the presence of other distracting sounds.
Visual Color Discrimination	The ability to match or detect differences between colors, including shades of color and brightness.
Trunk Strength	The ability to use your abdominal and lower back muscles to support part of the body repeatedly or continuously over time without 'giving out' or fatiguing.
Depth Perception	The ability to judge which of several objects is closer or farther away from you, or to judge the distance between you and an object.
Multilimb Coordination	The ability to coordinate two or more limbs (for example, two arms, two legs, or one leg and one arm) while sitting, standing, or lying down. It does not involve performing the activities while the whole body is in motion.
Control Precision	The ability to quickly and repeatedly adjust the controls of a machine or a vehicle to exact positions.
Extent Flexibility	The ability to bend, stretch, twist, or reach with your body, arms, and/or legs.
Stamina	The ability to exert yourself physically over long periods of time without getting winded or out of breath.
Dynamic Strength	The ability to exert muscle force repeatedly or continuously over time. This involves muscular endurance and resistance to muscle fatigue.
Explosive Strength	The ability to use short bursts of muscle force to propel oneself (as in jumping or sprinting), or to throw an object.
Static Strength	The ability to exert maximum muscle force to lift, push, pull, or carry objects.
Speed of Limb Movement	The ability to quickly move the arms and legs.
Wrist-Finger Speed	The ability to make fast, simple, repeated movements of the fingers, hands, and wrists.
Rate Control	The ability to time your movements or the movement of a piece of equipment in anticipation of changes in the speed and/or direction of a moving object or scene.
Response Orientation	The ability to choose quickly between two or more movements in response to two or more different signals (lights, sounds, pictures). It includes the speed with which the correct response is started with the hand, foot, or other body part.
Manual Dexterity	The ability to quickly move your hand, your hand together with your arm, or your two hands to grasp, manipulate, or assemble objects.
Arm-Hand Steadiness	The ability to keep your hand and arm steady while moving your arm or while holding your arm and hand in one position.
Reaction Time	The ability to quickly respond (with the hand, finger, or foot) to a signal (sound, light, picture) when it appears.

Peripheral Vision	The ability to see objects or movement of objects to one's side when the eyes are looking ahead.
Sound Localization	The ability to tell the direction from which a sound originated.
Dynamic Flexibility	The ability to quickly and repeatedly bend, stretch, twist, or reach out with your body, arms, and/or legs.
Glare Sensitivity	The ability to see objects in the presence of glare or bright lighting.
Gross Body Coordination	The ability to coordinate the movement of your arms, legs, and torso together when the whole body is in motion.
Night Vision	The ability to see under low light conditions.
Spatial Orientation	The ability to know your location in relation to the environment or to know where other objects are in relation to you.
Gross Body Equilibrium	The ability to keep or regain your body balance or stay upright when in an unstable position.

Work_Activity	Work_Activity Definitions
Training and Teaching Others	Identifying the educational needs of others, developing formal educational or training programs or classes, and teaching or instructing others.
Getting Information	Observing, receiving, and otherwise obtaining information from all relevant sources.
Updating and Using Relevant Knowledge	Keeping up-to-date technically and applying new knowledge to your job.
Thinking Creatively	Developing, designing, or creating new applications, ideas, relationships, systems, or products, including artistic contributions.
Analyzing Data or Information	Identifying the underlying principles, reasons, or facts of information by breaking down information or data into separate parts.
Interpreting the Meaning of Information for Others	Translating or explaining what information means and how it can be used.
Interacting With Computers	Using computers and computer systems (including hardware and software) to program, write software, set up functions, enter data, or process information.
Processing Information	Compiling, coding, categorizing, calculating, tabulating, auditing, or verifying information or data.
Making Decisions and Solving Problems	Analyzing information and evaluating results to choose the best solution and solve problems.
Organizing, Planning, and Prioritizing Work	Developing specific goals and plans to prioritize, organize, and accomplish your work.
Communicating with Supervisors, Peers, or Subordin	Providing information to supervisors, co-workers, and subordinates by telephone, in written form, e-mail, or in person.
Establishing and Maintaining Interpersonal Relatio	Developing constructive and cooperative working relationships with others, and maintaining them over time.
Identifying Objects, Actions, and Events	Identifying information by categorizing, estimating, recognizing differences or similarities, and detecting changes in circumstances or events.
Judging the Qualities of Things, Services, or Peop	Assessing the value, importance, or quality of things or people.
Coaching and Developing Others	Identifying the developmental needs of others and coaching, mentoring, or otherwise helping others to improve their knowledge or skills.
Documenting/Recording Information	Entering, transcribing, recording, storing, or maintaining information in written or electronic/magnetic form.
Provide Consultation and Advice to Others	Providing guidance and expert advice to management or other groups on technical, systems-, or process-related topics.
Developing Objectives and Strategies	Establishing long-range objectives and specifying the strategies and actions to achieve them.
Estimating the Quantifiable Characteristics of Pro	Estimating sizes, distances, and quantities; or determining time, costs, resources, or materials needed to perform a work activity.
Communicating with Persons Outside Organization	Communicating with people outside the organization, representing the organization to customers, the public, government, and other external sources. This information can be exchanged in person, in writing, or by telephone or e-mail.
Scheduling Work and Activities	Scheduling events, programs, and activities, as well as the work of others.
Evaluating Information to Determine Compliance wit	Using relevant information and individual judgment to determine whether events or processes comply with laws, regulations, or standards.
Monitor Processes, Materials, or Surroundings	Monitoring and reviewing information from materials, events, or the environment, to detect or assess problems.

Performing for or Working Directly with the Public	Performing for people or dealing directly with the public. This includes serving customers in restaurants and stores, and receiving clients or guests.
Guiding, Directing, and Motivating Subordinates	Providing guidance and direction to subordinates, including setting performance standards and monitoring performance.
Assisting and Caring for Others	Providing personal assistance, medical attention, emotional support, or other personal care to others such as coworkers, customers, or patients.
Performing Administrative Activities	Performing day-to-day administrative tasks such as maintaining information files and processing paperwork.
Resolving Conflicts and Negotiating with Others	Handling complaints, settling disputes, and resolving grievances and conflicts, or otherwise negotiating with others.
Selling or Influencing Others	Convincing others to buy merchandise/goods or to otherwise change their minds or actions.
Coordinating the Work and Activities of Others	Getting members of a group to work together to accomplish tasks.
Developing and Building Teams	Encouraging and building mutual trust, respect, and cooperation among team members.
Monitoring and Controlling Resources	Monitoring and controlling resources and overseeing the spending of money.
Staffing Organizational Units	Recruiting, interviewing, selecting, hiring, and promoting employees in an organization.
Handling and Moving Objects	Using hands and arms in handling, installing, positioning, and moving materials, and manipulating things.
Inspecting Equipment, Structures, or Material	Inspecting equipment, structures, or materials to identify the cause of errors or other problems or defects.
Controlling Machines and Processes	Using either control mechanisms or direct physical activity to operate machines or processes (not including computers or vehicles).
Performing General Physical Activities	Performing physical activities that require considerable use of your arms and legs and moving your whole body, such as climbing, lifting, balancing, walking, stooping, and handling of materials.
Repairing and Maintaining Electronic Equipment	Servicing, repairing, calibrating, regulating, fine-tuning, or testing machines, devices, and equipment that operate primarily on the basis of electrical or electronic (not mechanical) principles.
Operating Vehicles, Mechanized Devices, or Equipme	Running, maneuvering, navigating, or driving vehicles or mechanized equipment, such as forklifts, passenger vehicles, aircraft, or water craft.
Drafting, Laying Out, and Specifying Technical Dev	Providing documentation, detailed instructions, drawings, or specifications to tell others about how devices, parts, equipment, or structures are to be fabricated, constructed, assembled, modified, maintained, or used.
Repairing and Maintaining Mechanical Equipment	Servicing, repairing, adjusting, and testing machines, devices, moving parts, and equipment that operate primarily on the basis of mechanical (not electronic) principles.

Work_Context	Work_Context Definitions
Electronic Mail	How often do you use electronic mail in this job?
Freedom to Make Decisions	How much decision making freedom, without supervision, does the job offer?
Structured versus Unstructured Work	To what extent is this job structured for the worker, rather than allowing the worker to determine tasks, priorities, and goals?
Face-to-Face Discussions	How often do you have to have face-to-face discussions with individuals or teams in this job?
Public Speaking	How often do you have to perform public speaking in this job?
Telephone	How often do you have telephone conversations in this job?
Indoors, Environmentally Controlled	How often does this job require working indoors in environmentally controlled conditions?
Time Pressure	How often does this job require the worker to meet strict deadlines?
Contact With Others	How much does this job require the worker to be in contact with others (face-to-face, by telephone, or otherwise) in order to perform it?
Importance of Being Exact or Accurate	How important is being very exact or highly accurate in performing this job?
Letters and Memos	How often does the job require written letters and memos?
Coordinate or Lead Others	How important is it to coordinate or lead others in accomplishing work activities in this job?
Spend Time Sitting	How much does this job require sitting?
Frequency of Decision Making	How frequently is the worker required to make decisions that affect other people, the financial resources, and/or the image and reputation of the organization?
Impact of Decisions on Co-workers or Company Resul	How do the decisions an employee makes impact the results of co-workers, clients or the company?

Level of Competition	To what extent does this job require the worker to compete or to be aware of competitive pressures?
Deal With External Customers	How important is it to work with external customers or the public in this job?
Work With Work Group or Team	How important is it to work with others in a group or team in this job?
Physical Proximity	To what extent does this job require the worker to perform job tasks in close physical proximity to other people?
Frequency of Conflict Situations	How often are there conflict situations the employee has to face in this job?
Deal With Unpleasant or Angry People	How frequently does the worker have to deal with unpleasant, angry, or discourteous individuals as part of the job requirements?
Spend Time Standing	How much does this job require standing?
Importance of Repeating Same Tasks	How important is repeating the same physical activities (e.g., key entry) or mental activities (e.g., checking entries in a ledger) over and over, without stopping, to performing this job?
Sounds, Noise Levels Are Distracting or Uncomforta	How often does this job require working exposed to sounds and noise levels that are distracting or uncomfortable?
Spend Time Using Your Hands to Handle, Control, or	How much does this job require using your hands to handle, control, or feel objects, tools or controls?
Consequence of Error	How serious would the result usually be if the worker made a mistake that was not readily correctable?
Spend Time Making Repetitive Motions	How much does this job require making repetitive motions?
Responsibility for Outcomes and Results	How responsible is the worker for work outcomes and results of other workers?
Degree of Automation	How automated is the job?
Indoors, Not Environmentally Controlled	How often does this job require working indoors in non-controlled environmental conditions (e.g., warehouse without heat)?
Spend Time Walking and Running	How much does this job require walking and running?
Responsible for Others' Health and Safety	How much responsibility is there for the health and safety of others in this job?
Deal With Physically Aggressive People	How often does this job require the worker to deal with physical aggression of violent individuals?
Exposed to Contaminants	How often does this job require working exposed to contaminants (such as pollutants, gases, dust or odors)?
Very Hot or Cold Temperatures	How often does this job require working in very hot (above 90 F degrees) or very cold (below 32 F degrees) temperatures?
In an Enclosed Vehicle or Equipment	How often does this job require working in a closed vehicle or equipment (e.g., car)?
Exposed to Disease or Infections	How often does this job require exposure to disease/infections?
Outdoors, Exposed to Weather	How often does this job require working outdoors, exposed to all weather conditions?
Extremely Bright or Inadequate Lighting	How often does this job require working in extremely bright or inadequate lighting conditions?
Spend Time Bending or Twisting the Body	How much does this job require bending or twisting your body?
Pace Determined by Speed of Equipment	How important is it to this job that the pace is determined by the speed of equipment or machinery? (This does not refer to keeping busy at all times on this job.)
Cramped Work Space, Awkward Positions	How often does this job require working in cramped work spaces that requires getting into awkward positions?
Outdoors, Under Cover	How often does this job require working outdoors, under cover (e.g., structure with roof but no walls)?
Exposed to Hazardous Equipment	How often does this job require exposure to hazardous equipment?
Exposed to Minor Burns, Cuts, Bites, or Stings	How often does this job require exposure to minor burns, cuts, bites, or stings?
In an Open Vehicle or Equipment	How often does this job require working in an open vehicle or equipment (e.g., tractor)?
Exposed to Radiation	How often does this job require exposure to radiation?
Exposed to Hazardous Conditions	How often does this job require exposure to hazardous conditions?
Exposed to Whole Body Vibration	How often does this job require exposure to whole body vibration (e.g., operate a jackhammer)?
Wear Specialized Protective or Safety Equipment su	How much does this job require wearing specialized protective or safety equipment such as breathing apparatus, safety harness, full protection suits, or radiation protection?
Wear Common Protective or Safety Equipment such as	How much does this job require wearing common protective or safety equipment such as safety shoes, glasses, gloves, hard hats or live jackets?

Spend Time Climbing Ladders. Scaffolds, or Poles	How much does this job require climbing ladders. scaffolds. or poles?
Spend Time Keeping or Regaining Balance	How much does this job require keeping or regaining your balance?
Spend Time Kneeling. Crouching. Stooping, or Crawl	How much does this job require kneeling. crouching. stooping or crawling?
Exposed to High Places	How often does this job require exposure to high places?

Job Zone Component	Job Zone Component Definitions
Title	Job Zone Five: Extensive Preparation Needed
	Extensive skill, knowledge, and experience are needed for these occupations. Many require more than five years of experience.
Overall Experience	For example, surgeons must complete four years of college and an additional five to seven years of specialized medical training to be able to do their job.
	Employees may need some on-the-job training, but most of these occupations assume that the person will already have the required skills, knowledge, work-related experience, and/or training.
Job Training	
	These occupations often involve coordinating, training, supervising, or managing the activities of others to accomplish goals. Very advanced communication and organizational skills are required. Examples include athletic trainers, lawyers, managing editors, phyicists, social psychologists, and surgeons.
Job Zone Examples	
SVP Range	(8.0 and above)
	A bachelor's degree is the minimum formal education required for these occupations. However, many also require graduate school. For example, they may require a master's degree, and some require a Ph.D., M.D., or J.D. (law degree).
Education	

Work_Styles	Work_Styles Definitions
Independence	Job requires developing one's own ways of doing things, guiding oneself with little or no supervision, and depending on oneself to get things done.
Analytical Thinking	Job requires analyzing information and using logic to address work-related issues and problems.
Dependability	Job requires being reliable, responsible, and dependable, and fulfilling obligations.
Integrity	Job requires being honest and ethical.
Achievement/Effort	Job requires establishing and maintaining personally challenging achievement goals and exerting effort toward mastering tasks.
Initiative	Job requires a willingness to take on responsibilities and challenges.
Attention to Detail	Job requires being careful about detail and thorough in completing work tasks.
Persistence	Job requires persistence in the face of obstacles.
Self Control	Job requires maintaining composure, keeping emotions in check, controlling anger, and avoiding aggressive behavior, even in very difficult situations.
Adaptability/Flexibility	Job requires being open to change (positive or negative) and to considerable variety in the workplace.
Leadership	Job requires a willingness to lead, take charge, and offer opinions and direction.
Cooperation	Job requires being pleasant with others on the job and displaying a good-natured, cooperative attitude.
Innovation	Job requires creativity and alternative thinking to develop new ideas for and answers to work-related problems.
Stress Tolerance	Job requires accepting criticism and dealing calmly and effectively with high stress situations.
Concern for Others	Job requires being sensitive to others' needs and feelings and being understanding and helpful on the job.
Social Orientation	Job requires preferring to work with others rather than alone, and being personally connected with others on the job.

25-1064.00 - Geography Teachers, Postsecondary

Teach courses in geography.

Tasks

1) Plan, evaluate, and revise curricula, course content, and course materials and methods of instruction.

2) Prepare and deliver lectures to undergraduate and/or graduate students on topics such as urbanization, environmental systems, and cultural geography.

3) Maintain regularly scheduled office hours in order to advise and assist students.

4) Advise students on academic and vocational curricula, and on career issues.

5) Collaborate with colleagues to address teaching and research issues.

6) Participate in campus and community events.

7) Serve on academic or administrative committees that deal with institutional policies, departmental matters, and academic issues.

8) Compile bibliographies of specialized materials for outside reading assignments.

9) Conduct research in a particular field of knowledge, and publish findings in professional journals, books, and/or electronic media.

10) Supervise students' laboratory and field work.

11) Participate in student recruitment, registration, and placement activities.

12) Supervise undergraduate and/or graduate teaching, internship, and research work.

13) Write grant proposals to procure external research funding.

14) Act as advisers to student organizations.

15) Perform spatial analysis and modeling, using geographic information system techniques.

16) Provide professional consulting services to government and/or industry.

17) Perform administrative duties such as serving as department head.

18) Maintain geographic information systems laboratories, performing duties such as updating software.

19) Select and obtain materials and supplies such as textbooks.

20) Initiate, facilitate, and moderate classroom discussions.

21) Evaluate and grade students' class work, assignments, and papers.

22) Prepare course materials such as syllabi, homework assignments, and handouts.

23) Maintain student attendance records, grades, and other required records.

24) Compile, administer, and grade examinations, or assign this work to others.

Knowledge	Knowledge Definitions
Geography	Knowledge of principles and methods for describing the features of land, sea, and air masses, including their physical characteristics, locations, interrelationships, and distribution of plant, animal, and human life.
English Language	Knowledge of the structure and content of the English language including the meaning and spelling of words, rules of composition, and grammar.
Education and Training	Knowledge of principles and methods for curriculum and training design, teaching and instruction for individuals and groups, and the measurement of training effects.
Sociology and Anthropology	Knowledge of group behavior and dynamics, societal trends and influences, human migrations, ethnicity, cultures and their history and origins.
Computers and Electronics	Knowledge of circuit boards, processors, chips, electronic equipment, and computer hardware and software, including applications and programming.
Mathematics	Knowledge of arithmetic, algebra, geometry, calculus, statistics, and their applications.
History and Archeology	Knowledge of historical events and their causes, indicators, and effects on civilizations and cultures.
Communications and Media	Knowledge of media production, communication, and dissemination techniques and methods. This includes alternative ways to inform and entertain via written, oral, and visual media.
Administration and Management	Knowledge of business and management principles involved in strategic planning, resource allocation, human resources modeling, leadership technique, production methods, and coordination of people and resources.
Customer and Personal Service	Knowledge of principles and processes for providing customer and personal services. This includes customer needs assessment, meeting quality standards for services, and evaluation of customer satisfaction.
Philosophy and Theology	Knowledge of different philosophical systems and religions. This includes their basic principles, values, ethics, ways of thinking, customs, practices, and their impact on human culture.
Clerical	Knowledge of administrative and clerical procedures and systems such as word processing, managing files and records, stenography and transcription, designing forms, and other office procedures and terminology.
Personnel and Human Resources	Knowledge of principles and procedures for personnel recruitment, selection, training, compensation and benefits, labor relations and negotiation, and personnel information systems.
Biology	Knowledge of plant and animal organisms, their tissues, cells, functions, interdependencies, and interactions with each other and the environment.
Design	Knowledge of design techniques, tools, and principles involved in production of precision technical plans, blueprints, drawings, and models.
Psychology	Knowledge of human behavior and performance; individual differences in ability, personality, and interests; learning and motivation; psychological research methods; and the assessment and treatment of behavioral and affective disorders.
Law and Government	Knowledge of laws, legal codes, court procedures, precedents, government regulations, executive orders, agency rules, and the democratic political process.
Physics	Knowledge and prediction of physical principles, laws, their interrelationships, and applications to understanding fluid, material, and atmospheric dynamics, and mechanical, electrical, atomic and sub-atomic structures and processes.
Transportation	Knowledge of principles and methods for moving people or goods by air, rail, sea, or road, including the relative costs and benefits.
Chemistry	Knowledge of the chemical composition, structure, and properties of substances and of the chemical processes and transformations that they undergo. This includes uses of chemicals and their interactions, danger signs, production techniques, and disposal methods.
Foreign Language	Knowledge of the structure and content of a foreign (non-English) language including the meaning and spelling of words, rules of composition and grammar, and pronunciation.
Telecommunications	Knowledge of transmission, broadcasting, switching, control, and operation of telecommunications systems.
Public Safety and Security	Knowledge of relevant equipment, policies, procedures, and strategies to promote effective local, state, or national security operations for the protection of people, data, property, and institutions.
Therapy and Counseling	Knowledge of principles, methods, and procedures for diagnosis, treatment, and rehabilitation of physical and mental dysfunctions, and for career counseling and guidance.
Engineering and Technology	Knowledge of the practical application of engineering science and technology. This includes applying principles, techniques, procedures, and equipment to the design and production of various goods and services.
Fine Arts	Knowledge of the theory and techniques required to compose, produce, and perform works of music, dance, visual arts, drama, and sculpture.
Economics and Accounting	Knowledge of economic and accounting principles and practices, the financial markets, banking and the analysis and reporting of financial data.
Mechanical	Knowledge of machines and tools, including their designs, uses, repair, and maintenance.
Production and Processing	Knowledge of raw materials, production processes, quality control, costs, and other techniques for maximizing the effective manufacture and distribution of goods.
Sales and Marketing	Knowledge of principles and methods for showing, promoting, and selling products or services. This includes marketing strategy and tactics, product demonstration, sales techniques, and sales control systems.
Building and Construction	Knowledge of materials, methods, and the tools involved in the construction or repair of houses, buildings, or other structures such as highways and roads.
Food Production	Knowledge of techniques and equipment for planting, growing, and harvesting food products (both plant and animal) for consumption, including storage/handling techniques.
Medicine and Dentistry	Knowledge of the information and techniques needed to diagnose and treat human injuries, diseases, and deformities. This includes symptoms, treatment alternatives, drug properties and interactions, and preventive health-care measures.

Skills	Skills Definitions
Instructing	Teaching others how to do something.
Speaking	Talking to others to convey information effectively.
Reading Comprehension	Understanding written sentences and paragraphs in work related documents.
Critical Thinking	Using logic and reasoning to identify the strengths and weaknesses of alternative solutions, conclusions or approaches to problems.
Writing	Communicating effectively in writing as appropriate for the needs of the audience.
Active Listening	Giving full attention to what other people are saying, taking time to understand the points being made, asking questions as appropriate, and not interrupting at inappropriate times.
Learning Strategies	Selecting and using training/instructional methods and procedures appropriate for the situation when learning or teaching new things.
Active Learning	Understanding the implications of new information for both current and future problem-solving and decision-making.
Time Management	Managing one's own time and the time of others.
Science	Using scientific rules and methods to solve problems.
Monitoring	Monitoring/Assessing performance of yourself, other individuals, or organizations to make improvements or take corrective action.
Social Perceptiveness	Being aware of others' reactions and understanding why they react as they do.
Complex Problem Solving	Identifying complex problems and reviewing related information to develop and evaluate options and implement solutions.
Judgment and Decision Making	Considering the relative costs and benefits of potential actions to choose the most appropriate one.
Coordination	Adjusting actions in relation to others' actions.
Persuasion	Persuading others to change their minds or behavior.
Service Orientation	Actively looking for ways to help people.
Mathematics	Using mathematics to solve problems.
Equipment Selection	Determining the kind of tools and equipment needed to do a job.
Negotiation	Bringing others together and trying to reconcile differences.
Operations Analysis	Analyzing needs and product requirements to create a design.
Management of Financial Resources	Determining how money will be spent to get the work done, and accounting for these expenditures.
Technology Design	Generating or adapting equipment and technology to serve user needs.
Management of Personnel Resources	Motivating, developing, and directing people as they work, identifying the best people for the job.
Quality Control Analysis	Conducting tests and inspections of products, services, or processes to evaluate quality or performance.
Management of Material Resources	Obtaining and seeing to the appropriate use of equipment, facilities, and materials needed to do certain work.
Systems Analysis	Determining how a system should work and how changes in conditions, operations, and the environment will affect outcomes.
Systems Evaluation	Identifying measures or indicators of system performance and the actions needed to improve or correct performance, relative to the goals of the system.
Troubleshooting	Determining causes of operating errors and deciding what to do about it.
Programming	Writing computer programs for various purposes.
Equipment Maintenance	Performing routine maintenance on equipment and determining when and what kind of maintenance is needed.
Operation and Control	Controlling operations of equipment or systems.
Operation Monitoring	Watching gauges, dials, or other indicators to make sure a machine is working properly.
Repairing	Repairing machines or systems using the needed tools.
Installation	Installing equipment, machines, wiring, or programs to meet specifications.

Ability	Ability Definitions
Oral Expression	The ability to communicate information and ideas in speaking so others will understand.
Speech Clarity	The ability to speak clearly so others can understand you.
Written Comprehension	The ability to read and understand information and ideas presented in writing.
Oral Comprehension	The ability to listen to and understand information and ideas presented through spoken words and sentences.

Written Expression	The ability to communicate information and ideas in writing so others will understand.
Deductive Reasoning	The ability to apply general rules to specific problems to produce answers that make sense.
Inductive Reasoning	The ability to combine pieces of information to form general rules or conclusions (includes finding a relationship among seemingly unrelated events).
Speech Recognition	The ability to identify and understand the speech of another person.
Problem Sensitivity	The ability to tell when something is wrong or is likely to go wrong. It does not involve solving the problem, only recognizing there is a problem.
Near Vision	The ability to see details at close range (within a few feet of the observer).
Fluency of Ideas	The ability to come up with a number of ideas about a topic (the number of ideas is important, not their quality, correctness, or creativity).
Originality	The ability to come up with unusual or clever ideas about a given topic or situation, or to develop creative ways to solve a problem.
Selective Attention	The ability to concentrate on a task over a period of time without being distracted.
Category Flexibility	The ability to generate or use different sets of rules for combining or grouping things in different ways.
Information Ordering	The ability to arrange things or actions in a certain order or pattern according to a specific rule or set of rules (e.g., patterns of numbers, letters, words, pictures, mathematical operations).
Mathematical Reasoning	The ability to choose the right mathematical methods or formulas to solve a problem.
Memorization	The ability to remember information such as words, numbers, pictures, and procedures.
Time Sharing	The ability to shift back and forth between two or more activities or sources of information (such as speech, sounds, touch, or other sources).
Number Facility	The ability to add, subtract, multiply, or divide quickly and correctly.
Flexibility of Closure	The ability to identify or detect a known pattern (a figure, object, word, or sound) that is hidden in other distracting material.
Speed of Closure	The ability to quickly make sense of, combine, and organize information into meaningful patterns.
Far Vision	The ability to see details at a distance.
Visualization	The ability to imagine how something will look after it is moved around or when its parts are moved or rearranged.
Perceptual Speed	The ability to quickly and accurately compare similarities and differences among sets of letters, numbers, objects, pictures, or patterns. The things to be compared may be presented at the same time or one after the other. This ability also includes comparing a presented object with a remembered object.
Trunk Strength	The ability to use your abdominal and lower back muscles to support part of the body repeatedly or continuously over time without 'giving out' or fatiguing.
Hearing Sensitivity	The ability to detect or tell the differences between sounds that vary in pitch and loudness.
Visual Color Discrimination	The ability to match or detect differences between colors, including shades of color and brightness.
Auditory Attention	The ability to focus on a single source of sound in the presence of other distracting sounds.
Finger Dexterity	The ability to make precisely coordinated movements of the fingers of one or both hands to grasp, manipulate, or assemble very small objects.
Spatial Orientation	The ability to know your location in relation to the environment or to know where other objects are in relation to you.
Depth Perception	The ability to judge which of several objects is closer or farther away from you, or to judge the distance between you and an object.
Explosive Strength	The ability to use short bursts of muscle force to propel oneself (as in jumping or sprinting), or to throw an object.
Arm-Hand Steadiness	The ability to keep your hand and arm steady while moving your arm or while holding your arm and hand in one position.
Multilimb Coordination	The ability to coordinate two or more limbs (for example, two arms, two legs, or one leg and one arm) while sitting, standing, or lying down. It does not involve performing the activities while the whole body is in motion.
Extent Flexibility	The ability to bend, stretch, twist, or reach with your body, arms, and/or legs.

Dynamic Strength	The ability to exert muscle force repeatedly or continuously over time. This involves muscular endurance and resistance to muscle fatigue.
Speed of Limb Movement	The ability to quickly move the arms and legs.
Reaction Time	The ability to quickly respond (with the hand, finger, or foot) to a signal (sound, light, picture) when it appears.
Response Orientation	The ability to choose quickly between two or more movements in response to two or more different signals (lights, sounds, pictures). It includes the speed with which the correct response is started with the hand, foot, or other body part.
Control Precision	The ability to quickly and repeatedly adjust the controls of a machine or a vehicle to exact positions.
Manual Dexterity	The ability to quickly move your hand, your hand together with your arm, or your two hands to grasp, manipulate, or assemble objects.
Stamina	The ability to exert yourself physically over long periods of time without getting winded or out of breath.
Night Vision	The ability to see under low light conditions.
Wrist-Finger Speed	The ability to make fast, simple, repeated movements of the fingers, hands, and wrists.
Sound Localization	The ability to tell the direction from which a sound originated.
Glare Sensitivity	The ability to see objects in the presence of glare or bright lighting.
Gross Body Coordination	The ability to coordinate the movement of your arms, legs, and torso together when the whole body is in motion.
Gross Body Equilibrium	The ability to keep or regain your body balance or stay upright when in an unstable position.
Peripheral Vision	The ability to see objects or movement of objects to one's side when the eyes are looking ahead.
Rate Control	The ability to time your movements or the movement of a piece of equipment in anticipation of changes in the speed and/or direction of a moving object or scene.
Dynamic Flexibility	The ability to quickly and repeatedly bend, stretch, twist, or reach out with your body, arms, and/or legs.
Static Strength	The ability to exert maximum muscle force to lift, push, pull, or carry objects.

Work_Activity	Work_Activity Definitions
Training and Teaching Others	Identifying the educational needs of others, developing formal educational or training programs or classes, and teaching or instructing others.
Getting Information	Observing, receiving, and otherwise obtaining information from all relevant sources.
Updating and Using Relevant Knowledge	Keeping up-to-date technically and applying new knowledge to your job.
Thinking Creatively	Developing, designing, or creating new applications, ideas, relationships, systems, or products, including artistic contributions.
Analyzing Data or Information	Identifying the underlying principles, reasons, or facts of information by breaking down information or data into separate parts.
Organizing, Planning, and Prioritizing Work	Developing specific goals and plans to prioritize, organize, and accomplish your work.
Interacting With Computers	Using computers and computer systems (including hardware and software) to program, write software, set up functions, enter data, or process information.
Communicating with Supervisors, Peers, or Subordin	Providing information to supervisors, co-workers, and subordinates by telephone, in written form, e-mail, or in person.
Processing Information	Compiling, coding, categorizing, calculating, tabulating, auditing, or verifying information or data.
Interpreting the Meaning of Information for Others	Translating or explaining what information means and how it can be used.
Establishing and Maintaining Interpersonal Relatio	Developing constructive and cooperative working relationships with others, and maintaining them over time.
Identifying Objects, Actions, and Events	Identifying information by categorizing, estimating, recognizing differences or similarities, and detecting changes in circumstances or events.
Making Decisions and Solving Problems	Analyzing information and evaluating results to choose the best solution and solve problems.
Judging the Qualities of Things, Services, or Peop	Assessing the value, importance, or quality of things or people.
Communicating with Persons Outside Organization	Communicating with people outside the organization, representing the organization to customers, the public, government, and other external sources. This information can be exchanged in person, in writing, or by telephone or e-mail.

Developing Objectives and Strategies	Establishing long-range objectives and specifying the strategies and actions to achieve them.
Documenting/Recording Information	Entering, transcribing, recording, storing, or maintaining information in written or electronic/magnetic form.
Coaching and Developing Others	Identifying the developmental needs of others and coaching, mentoring, or otherwise helping others to improve their knowledge or skills.
Scheduling Work and Activities	Scheduling events, programs, and activities, as well as the work of others.
Performing for or Working Directly with the Public	Performing for people or dealing directly with the public. This includes serving customers in restaurants and stores, and receiving clients or guests.
Estimating the Quantifiable Characteristics of Pro	Estimating sizes, distances, and quantities; or determining time, costs, resources, or materials needed to perform a work activity.
Provide Consultation and Advice to Others	Providing guidance and expert advice to management or other groups on technical, systems-, or process-related topics.
Monitor Processes, Materials, or Surroundings	Monitoring and reviewing information from materials, events, or the environment, to detect or assess problems.
Performing Administrative Activities	Performing day-to-day administrative tasks such as maintaining information files and processing paperwork.
Coordinating the Work and Activities of Others	Getting members of a group to work together to accomplish tasks.
Evaluating Information to Determine Compliance wit	Using relevant information and individual judgment to determine whether events or processes comply with laws, regulations, or standards.
Developing and Building Teams	Encouraging and building mutual trust, respect, and cooperation among team members.
Guiding, Directing, and Motivating Subordinates	Providing guidance and direction to subordinates, including setting performance standards and monitoring performance.
Assisting and Caring for Others	Providing personal assistance, medical attention, emotional support, or other personal care to others such as coworkers, customers, or patients.
Resolving Conflicts and Negotiating with Others	Handling complaints, settling disputes, and resolving grievances and conflicts, or otherwise negotiating with others.
Selling or Influencing Others	Convincing others to buy merchandise/goods or to otherwise change their minds or actions.
Monitoring and Controlling Resources	Monitoring and controlling resources and overseeing the spending of money.
Staffing Organizational Units	Recruiting, interviewing, selecting, hiring, and promoting employees in an organization.
Handling and Moving Objects	Using hands and arms in handling, installing, positioning, and moving materials, and manipulating things.
Inspecting Equipment, Structures, or Material	Inspecting equipment, structures, or materials to identify the cause of errors or other problems or defects.
Controlling Machines and Processes	Using either control mechanisms or direct physical activity to operate machines or processes (not including computers or vehicles).
Performing General Physical Activities	Performing physical activities that require considerable use of your arms and legs and moving your whole body, such as climbing, lifting, balancing, walking, stooping, and handling of materials.
Operating Vehicles, Mechanized Devices, or Equipme	Running, maneuvering, navigating, or driving vehicles or mechanized equipment, such as forklifts, passenger vehicles, aircraft, or water craft.
Drafting, Laying Out, and Specifying Technical Dev	Providing documentation, detailed instructions, drawings, or specifications to tell others about how devices, parts, equipment, or structures are to be fabricated, constructed, assembled, modified, maintained, or used.
Repairing and Maintaining Mechanical Equipment	Servicing, repairing, adjusting, and testing machines, devices, moving parts, and equipment that operate primarily on the basis of mechanical (not electronic) principles.
Repairing and Maintaining Electronic Equipment	Servicing, repairing, calibrating, regulating, fine-tuning, or testing machines, devices, and equipment that operate primarily on the basis of electrical or electronic (not mechanical) principles.

Work_Context	Work_Context Definitions
Electronic Mail	How often do you use electronic mail in this job?
Indoors, Environmentally Controlled	How often does this job require working indoors in environmentally controlled conditions?
Face-to-Face Discussions	How often do you have to have face-to-face discussions with individuals or teams in this job?
Freedom to Make Decisions	How much decision making freedom, without supervision, does the job offer?

1407

Structured versus Unstructured Work	To what extent is this job structured for the worker, rather than allowing the worker to determine tasks, priorities, and goals?
Contact With Others	How much does this job require the worker to be in contact with others (face-to-face, by telephone, or otherwise) in order to perform it?
Telephone	How often do you have telephone conversations in this job?
Public Speaking	How often do you have to perform public speaking in this job?
Coordinate or Lead Others	How important is it to coordinate or lead others in accomplishing work activities in this job?
Importance of Being Exact or Accurate	How important is being very exact or highly accurate in performing this job?
Frequency of Decision Making	How frequently is the worker required to make decisions that affect other people, the financial resources, and/or the image and reputation of the organization?
Impact of Decisions on Co-workers or Company Resul	How do the decisions an employee makes impact the results of co-workers, clients or the company?
Letters and Memos	How often does the job require written letters and memos?
Time Pressure	How often does this job require the worker to meet strict deadlines?
Work With Work Group or Team	How important is it to work with others in a group or team in this job?
Spend Time Sitting	How much does this job require sitting?
Deal With External Customers	How important is it to work with external customers or the public in this job?
Level of Competition	To what extent does this job require the worker to compete or to be aware of competitive pressures?
Physical Proximity	To what extent does this job require the worker to perform job tasks in close physical proximity to other people?
Spend Time Standing	How much does this job require standing?
Responsibility for Outcomes and Results	How responsible is the worker for work outcomes and results of other workers?
Spend Time Making Repetitive Motions	How much does this job require making repetitive motions?
Deal With Unpleasant or Angry People	How frequently does the worker have to deal with unpleasant, angry, or discourteous individuals as part of the job requirements?
Frequency of Conflict Situations	How often are there conflict situations the employee has to face in this job?
Importance of Repeating Same Tasks	How important is repeating the same physical activities (e.g., key entry) or mental activities (e.g., checking entries in a ledger) over and over, without stopping, to performing this job?
Spend Time Using Your Hands to Handle, Control, or	How much does this job require using your hands to handle, control, or feel objects, tools or controls?
Responsible for Others' Health and Safety	How much responsibility is there for the health and safety of others in this job?
Consequence of Error	How serious would the result usually be if the worker made a mistake that was not readily correctable?
Spend Time Walking and Running	How much does this job require walking and running?
Outdoors, Exposed to Weather	How often does this job require working outdoors, exposed to all weather conditions?
Exposed to Contaminants	How often does this job require working exposed to contaminants (such as pollutants, gases, dust or odors)?
Degree of Automation	How automated is the job?
Sounds, Noise Levels Are Distracting or Uncomforta	How often does this job require working exposed to sounds and noise levels that are distracting or uncomfortable?
Indoors, Not Environmentally Controlled	How often does this job require working indoors in non-controlled environmental conditions (e.g., warehouse without heat)?
In an Enclosed Vehicle or Equipment	How often does this job require working in a closed vehicle or equipment (e.g., car)?
Exposed to Disease or Infections	How often does this job require exposure to disease/infections?
Spend Time Bending or Twisting the Body	How much does this job require bending or twisting your body?
Very Hot or Cold Temperatures	How often does this job require working in very hot (above 90 F degrees) or very cold (below 32 F degrees) temperatures?
Wear Common Protective or Safety Equipment such as	How much does this job require wearing common protective or safety equipment such as safety shoes, glasses, gloves, hard hats or live jackets?
Outdoors, Under Cover	How often does this job require working outdoors, under cover (e.g., structure with roof but no walls)?
Exposed to Hazardous Equipment	How often does this job require exposure to hazardous equipment?
Exposed to Minor Burns, Cuts, Bites, or Stings	How often does this job require exposure to minor burns, cuts, bites, or stings?

Cramped Work Space, Awkward Positions	How often does this job require working in cramped work spaces that requires getting into awkward positions?
Exposed to Hazardous Conditions	How often does this job require exposure to hazardous conditions?
Spend Time Kneeling, Crouching, Stooping, or Crawl	How much does this job require kneeling, crouching, stooping or crawling?
Extremely Bright or Inadequate Lighting	How often does this job require working in extremely bright or inadequate lighting conditions?
Exposed to Radiation	How often does this job require exposure to radiation?
Spend Time Keeping or Regaining Balance	How much does this job require keeping or regaining your balance?
Pace Determined by Speed of Equipment	How important is it to this job that the pace is determined by the speed of equipment or machinery? (This does not refer to keeping busy at all times on this job.)
Exposed to High Places	How often does this job require exposure to high places?
Deal With Physically Aggressive People	How frequently does this job require the worker to deal with physical aggression of violent individuals?
Spend Time Climbing Ladders, Scaffolds, or Poles	How much does this job require climbing ladders, scaffolds, or poles?
In an Open Vehicle or Equipment	How often does this job require working in an open vehicle or equipment (e.g., tractor)?
Wear Specialized Protective or Safety Equipment su	How much does this job require wearing specialized protective or safety equipment such as breathing apparatus, safety harness, full protection suits, or radiation protection?
Exposed to Whole Body Vibration	How often does this job require exposure to whole body vibration (e.g., operate a jackhammer)?

Job Zone Component	Job Zone Component Definitions
Title	Job Zone Five: Extensive Preparation Needed
Overall Experience	Extensive skill, knowledge, and experience are needed for these occupations. Many require more than five years of experience. For example, surgeons must complete four years of college and an additional five to seven years of specialized medical training to be able to do their job.
Job Training	Employees may need some on-the-job training, but most of these occupations assume that the person will already have the required skills, knowledge, work-related experience, and/or training.
Job Zone Examples	These occupations often involve coordinating, training, supervising, or managing the activities of others to accomplish goals. Very advanced communication and organizational skills are required. Examples include athletic trainers, lawyers, managing editors, phyicists, social psychologists, and surgeons.
SVP Range	(8.0 and above)
Education	A bachelor's degree is the minimum formal education required for these occupations. However, many also require graduate school. For example, they may require a master's degree, and some require a Ph.D., M.D., or J.D. (law degree).

Work_Styles	Work_Styles Definitions
Integrity	Job requires being honest and ethical.
Independence	Job requires developing one's own ways of doing things, guiding oneself with little or no supervision, and depending on oneself to get things done.
Dependability	Job requires being reliable, responsible, and dependable, and fulfilling obligations.
Analytical Thinking	Job requires analyzing information and using logic to address work-related issues and problems.
Initiative	Job requires a willingness to take on responsibilities and challenges.
Attention to Detail	Job requires being careful about detail and thorough in completing work tasks.
Achievement/Effort	Job requires establishing and maintaining personally challenging achievement goals and exerting effort toward mastering tasks.
Innovation	Job requires creativity and alternative thinking to develop new ideas for and answers to work-related problems.
Leadership	Job requires a willingness to lead, take charge, and offer opinions and direction.
Persistence	Job requires persistence in the face of obstacles.
Concern for Others	Job requires being sensitive to others' needs and feelings and being understanding and helpful on the job.

1408

Adaptability/Flexibility	Job requires being open to change (positive or negative) and to considerable variety in the workplace.
Stress Tolerance	Job requires accepting criticism and dealing calmly and effectively with high stress situations.
Self Control	Job requires maintaining composure, keeping emotions in check, controlling anger, and avoiding aggressive behavior, even in very difficult situations.
Cooperation	Job requires being pleasant with others on the job and displaying a good-natured, cooperative attitude.
Social Orientation	Job requires preferring to work with others rather than alone, and being personally connected with others on the job.

25-1065.00 - Political Science Teachers, Postsecondary

Teach courses in political science, international affairs, and international relations.

Tasks

1) Maintain student attendance records, grades, and other required records.

2) Compile, administer, and grade examinations, or assign this work to others.

3) Select and obtain materials and supplies such as textbooks.

4) Maintain regularly scheduled office hours in order to advise and assist students.

5) Participate in campus and community events.

6) Advise students on academic and vocational curricula, and on career issues.

7) Prepare and deliver lectures to undergraduate and/or graduate students on topics such as classical political thought, international relations, and democracy and citizenship.

8) Serve on academic or administrative committees that deal with institutional policies, departmental matters, and academic issues.

9) Collaborate with colleagues to address teaching and research issues.

10) Compile bibliographies of specialized materials for outside reading assignments.

11) Participate in student recruitment, registration, and placement activities.

12) Conduct research in a particular field of knowledge, and publish findings in professional journals, books, and/or electronic media.

13) Write grant proposals to procure external research funding.

14) Supervise undergraduate and/or graduate teaching, internship, and research work.

15) Act as advisers to student organizations.

16) Perform administrative duties such as serving as department head.

17) Provide professional consulting services to government and/or industry.

18) Prepare course materials such as syllabi, homework assignments, and handouts.

19) Initiate, facilitate, and moderate classroom discussions.

20) Evaluate and grade students' class work, assignments, and papers.

21) Plan, evaluate, and revise curricula, course content, and course materials and methods of instruction.

Knowledge	Knowledge Definitions
Law and Government	Knowledge of laws, legal codes, court procedures, precedents, government regulations, executive orders, agency rules, and the democratic political process.
English Language	Knowledge of the structure and content of the English language including the meaning and spelling of words, rules of composition, and grammar.
Education and Training	Knowledge of principles and methods for curriculum and training design, teaching and instruction for individuals and groups, and the measurement of training effects.
History and Archeology	Knowledge of historical events and their causes, indicators, and effects on civilizations and cultures.
Philosophy and Theology	Knowledge of different philosophical systems and religions. This includes their basic principles, values, ethics, ways of thinking, customs, practices, and their impact on human culture.
Sociology and Anthropology	Knowledge of group behavior and dynamics, societal trends and influences, human migrations, ethnicity, cultures and their history and origins.
Geography	Knowledge of principles and methods for describing the features of land, sea, and air masses, including their physical characteristics, locations, interrelationships, and distribution of plant, animal, and human life.
Communications and Media	Knowledge of media production, communication, and dissemination techniques and methods. This includes alternative ways to inform and entertain via written, oral, and visual media.
Computers and Electronics	Knowledge of circuit boards, processors, chips, electronic equipment, and computer hardware and software, including applications and programming.
Psychology	Knowledge of human behavior and performance; individual differences in ability, personality, and interests; learning and motivation; psychological research methods; and the assessment and treatment of behavioral and affective disorders.
Mathematics	Knowledge of arithmetic, algebra, geometry, calculus, statistics, and their applications.
Clerical	Knowledge of administrative and clerical procedures and systems such as word processing, managing files and records, stenography and transcription, designing forms, and other office procedures and terminology.
Customer and Personal Service	Knowledge of principles and processes for providing customer and personal services. This includes customer needs assessment, meeting quality standards for services, and evaluation of customer satisfaction.
Foreign Language	Knowledge of the structure and content of a foreign (non-English) language including the meaning and spelling of words, rules of composition and grammar, and pronunciation.
Administration and Management	Knowledge of business and management principles involved in strategic planning, resource allocation, human resources modeling, leadership technique, production methods, and coordination of people and resources.
Personnel and Human Resources	Knowledge of principles and procedures for personnel recruitment, selection, training, compensation and benefits, labor relations and negotiation, and personnel information systems.
Therapy and Counseling	Knowledge of principles, methods, and procedures for diagnosis, treatment, and rehabilitation of physical and mental dysfunctions, and for career counseling and guidance.
Economics and Accounting	Knowledge of economic and accounting principles and practices, the financial markets, banking and the analysis and reporting of financial data.
Public Safety and Security	Knowledge of relevant equipment, policies, procedures, and strategies to promote effective local, state, or national security operations for the protection of people, data, property, and institutions.
Telecommunications	Knowledge of transmission, broadcasting, switching, control, and operation of telecommunications systems.
Fine Arts	Knowledge of the theory and techniques required to compose, produce, and perform works of music, dance, visual arts, drama, and sculpture.
Sales and Marketing	Knowledge of principles and methods for showing, promoting, and selling products or services. This includes marketing strategy and tactics, product demonstration, sales techniques, and sales control systems.
Biology	Knowledge of plant and animal organisms, their tissues, cells, functions, interdependencies, and interactions with each other and the environment.
Transportation	Knowledge of principles and methods for moving people or goods by air, rail, sea, or road, including the relative costs and benefits.
Design	Knowledge of design techniques, tools, and principles involved in production of precision technical plans, blueprints, drawings, and models.
Engineering and Technology	Knowledge of the practical application of engineering science and technology. This includes applying principles, techniques, procedures, and equipment to the design and production of various goods and services.
Production and Processing	Knowledge of raw materials, production processes, quality control, costs, and other techniques for maximizing the effective manufacture and distribution of goods.
Medicine and Dentistry	Knowledge of the information and techniques needed to diagnose and treat human injuries, diseases, and deformities. This includes symptoms, treatment alternatives, drug properties and interactions, and preventive health-care measures.

Physics	Knowledge and prediction of physical principles, laws, their interrelationships, and applications to understanding fluid, material, and atmospheric dynamics, and mechanical, electrical, atomic and sub- atomic structures and processes.
Mechanical	Knowledge of machines and tools, including their designs, uses, repair, and maintenance.
Chemistry	Knowledge of the chemical composition, structure, and properties of substances and of the chemical processes and transformations that they undergo. This includes uses of chemicals and their interactions, danger signs, production techniques, and disposal methods.
Building and Construction	Knowledge of materials, methods, and the tools involved in the construction or repair of houses, buildings, or other structures such as highways and roads.
Food Production	Knowledge of techniques and equipment for planting, growing, and harvesting food products (both plant and animal) for consumption, including storage/handling techniques.

Skills	Skills Definitions
Instructing	Teaching others how to do something.
Reading Comprehension	Understanding written sentences and paragraphs in work related documents.
Speaking	Talking to others to convey information effectively.
Critical Thinking	Using logic and reasoning to identify the strengths and weaknesses of alternative solutions, conclusions or approaches to problems.
Writing	Communicating effectively in writing as appropriate for the needs of the audience.
Active Listening	Giving full attention to what other people are saying, taking time to understand the points being made, asking questions as appropriate, and not interrupting at inappropriate times.
Learning Strategies	Selecting and using training/instructional methods and procedures appropriate for the situation when learning or teaching new things.
Active Learning	Understanding the implications of new information for both current and future problem-solving and decision-making.
Time Management	Managing one's own time and the time of others.
Monitoring	Monitoring/Assessing performance of yourself, other individuals, or organizations to make improvements or take corrective action.
Social Perceptiveness	Being aware of others' reactions and understanding why they react as they do.
Complex Problem Solving	Identifying complex problems and reviewing related information to develop and evaluate options and implement solutions.
Persuasion	Persuading others to change their minds or behavior.
Judgment and Decision Making	Considering the relative costs and benefits of potential actions to choose the most appropriate one.
Coordination	Adjusting actions in relation to others' actions.
Service Orientation	Actively looking for ways to help people.
Negotiation	Bringing others together and trying to reconcile differences.
Management of Personnel Resources	Motivating, developing, and directing people as they work, identifying the best people for the job.
Mathematics	Using mathematics to solve problems.
Science	Using scientific rules and methods to solve problems.
Quality Control Analysis	Conducting tests and inspections of products, services, or processes to evaluate quality or performance.
Management of Financial Resources	Determining how money will be spent to get the work done, and accounting for these expenditures.
Operations Analysis	Analyzing needs and product requirements to create a design.
Equipment Selection	Determining the kind of tools and equipment needed to do a job.
Management of Material Resources	Obtaining and seeing to the appropriate use of equipment, facilities, and materials needed to do certain work.
Systems Evaluation	Identifying measures or indicators of system performance and the actions needed to improve or correct performance, relative to the goals of the system.
Technology Design	Generating or adapting equipment and technology to serve user needs.
Systems Analysis	Determining how a system should work and how changes in conditions, operations, and the environment will affect outcomes.
Troubleshooting	Determining causes of operating errors and deciding what to do about it.
Operation and Control	Controlling operations of equipment or systems.
Programming	Writing computer programs for various purposes.

Operation Monitoring	Watching gauges, dials, or other indicators to make sure a machine is working properly.
Equipment Maintenance	Performing routine maintenance on equipment and determining when and what kind of maintenance is needed.
Installation	Installing equipment, machines, wiring, or programs to meet specifications.
Repairing	Repairing machines or systems using the needed tools.

Ability	Ability Definitions
Oral Expression	The ability to communicate information and ideas in speaking so others will understand.
Speech Clarity	The ability to speak clearly so others can understand you.
Oral Comprehension	The ability to listen to and understand information and ideas presented through spoken words and sentences.
Written Expression	The ability to communicate information and ideas in writing so others will understand.
Written Comprehension	The ability to read and understand information and ideas presented in writing.
Inductive Reasoning	The ability to combine pieces of information to form general rules or conclusions (includes finding a relationship among seemingly unrelated events).
Near Vision	The ability to see details at close range (within a few feet of the observer).
Deductive Reasoning	The ability to apply general rules to specific problems to produce answers that make sense.
Speech Recognition	The ability to identify and understand the speech of another person.
Problem Sensitivity	The ability to tell when something is wrong or is likely to go wrong. It does not involve solving the problem, only recognizing there is a problem.
Fluency of Ideas	The ability to come up with a number of ideas about a topic (the number of ideas is important, not their quality, correctness, or creativity).
Information Ordering	The ability to arrange things or actions in a certain order or pattern according to a specific rule or set of rules (e.g., patterns of numbers, letters, words, pictures, mathematical operations).
Originality	The ability to come up with unusual or clever ideas about a given topic or situation, or to develop creative ways to solve a problem.
Category Flexibility	The ability to generate or use different sets of rules for combining or grouping things in different ways.
Selective Attention	The ability to concentrate on a task over a period of time without being distracted.
Memorization	The ability to remember information such as words, numbers, pictures, and procedures.
Time Sharing	The ability to shift back and forth between two or more activities or sources of information (such as speech, sounds, touch, or other sources).
Mathematical Reasoning	The ability to choose the right mathematical methods or formulas to solve a problem.
Far Vision	The ability to see details at a distance.
Flexibility of Closure	The ability to identify or detect a known pattern (a figure, object, word, or sound) that is hidden in other distracting material.
Number Facility	The ability to add, subtract, multiply, or divide quickly and correctly.
Trunk Strength	The ability to use your abdominal and lower back muscles to support part of the body repeatedly or continuously over time without 'giving out' or fatiguing.
Perceptual Speed	The ability to quickly and accurately compare similarities and differences among sets of letters, numbers, objects, pictures, or patterns. The things to be compared may be presented at the same time or one after the other. This ability also includes comparing a presented object with a remembered object.
Speed of Closure	The ability to quickly make sense of, combine, and organize information into meaningful patterns.
Visual Color Discrimination	The ability to match or detect differences between colors, including shades of color and brightness.
Visualization	The ability to imagine how something will look after it is moved around or when its parts are moved or rearranged.
Finger Dexterity	The ability to make precisely coordinated movements of the fingers of one or both hands to grasp, manipulate, or assemble very small objects.
Auditory Attention	The ability to focus on a single source of sound in the presence of other distracting sounds.
Hearing Sensitivity	The ability to detect or tell the differences between sounds that vary in pitch and loudness.

Depth Perception	The ability to judge which of several objects is closer or farther away from you, or to judge the distance between you and an object.
Dynamic Strength	The ability to exert muscle force repeatedly or continuously over time. This involves muscular endurance and resistance to muscle fatigue.
Glare Sensitivity	The ability to see objects in the presence of glare or bright lighting.
Stamina	The ability to exert yourself physically over long periods of time without getting winded or out of breath.
Sound Localization	The ability to tell the direction from which a sound originated.
Peripheral Vision	The ability to see objects or movement of objects to one's side when the eyes are looking ahead.
Night Vision	The ability to see under low light conditions.
Gross Body Equilibrium	The ability to keep or regain your body balance or stay upright when in an unstable position.
Gross Body Coordination	The ability to coordinate the movement of your arms, legs, and torso together when the whole body is in motion.
Extent Flexibility	The ability to bend, stretch, twist, or reach with your body, arms, and/or legs.
Spatial Orientation	The ability to know your location in relation to the environment or to know where other objects are in relation to you.
Explosive Strength	The ability to use short bursts of muscle force to propel oneself (as in jumping or sprinting), or to throw an object.
Static Strength	The ability to exert maximum muscle force to lift, push, pull, or carry objects.
Wrist-Finger Speed	The ability to make fast, simple, repeated movements of the fingers, hands, and wrists.
Dynamic Flexibility	The ability to quickly and repeatedly bend, stretch, twist, or reach out with your body, arms, and/or legs.
Reaction Time	The ability to quickly respond (with the hand, finger, or foot) to a signal (sound, light, picture) when it appears.
Rate Control	The ability to time your movements or the movement of a piece of equipment in anticipation of changes in the speed and/or direction of a moving object or scene.
Response Orientation	The ability to choose quickly between two or more movements in response to two or more different signals (lights, sounds, pictures). It includes the speed with which the correct response is started with the hand, foot, or other body part.
Multilimb Coordination	The ability to coordinate two or more limbs (for example, two arms, two legs, or one leg and one arm) while sitting, standing, or lying down. It does not involve performing the activities while the whole body is in motion.
Speed of Limb Movement	The ability to quickly move the arms and legs.
Arm-Hand Steadiness	The ability to keep your hand and arm steady while moving your arm or while holding your arm and hand in one position.
Manual Dexterity	The ability to quickly move your hand, your hand together with your arm, or your two hands to grasp, manipulate, or assemble objects.
Control Precision	The ability to quickly and repeatedly adjust the controls of a machine or a vehicle to exact positions.

Work_Activity	**Work_Activity Definitions**
Updating and Using Relevant Knowledge	Keeping up-to-date technically and applying new knowledge to your job.
Getting Information	Observing, receiving, and otherwise obtaining information from all relevant sources.
Training and Teaching Others	Identifying the educational needs of others, developing formal educational or training programs or classes, and teaching or instructing others.
Thinking Creatively	Developing, designing, or creating new applications, ideas, relationships, systems, or products, including artistic contributions.
Interpreting the Meaning of Information for Others	Translating or explaining what information means and how it can be used.
Identifying Objects, Actions, and Events	Identifying information by categorizing, estimating, recognizing differences or similarities, and detecting changes in circumstances or events.
Analyzing Data or Information	Identifying the underlying principles, reasons, or facts of information by breaking down information or data into separate parts.
Processing Information	Compiling, coding, categorizing, calculating, tabulating, auditing, or verifying information or data.
Coaching and Developing Others	Identifying the developmental needs of others and coaching, mentoring, or otherwise helping others to improve their knowledge or skills.

Communicating with Supervisors, Peers, or Subordin	Providing information to supervisors, co-workers, and subordinates by telephone, in written form, e-mail, or in person.
Organizing, Planning, and Prioritizing Work	Developing specific goals and plans to prioritize, organize, and accomplish your work.
Judging the Qualities of Things, Services, or Peop	Assessing the value, importance, or quality of things or people.
Interacting With Computers	Using computers and computer systems (including hardware and software) to program, write software, set up functions, enter data, or process information.
Establishing and Maintaining Interpersonal Relatio	Developing constructive and cooperative working relationships with others, and maintaining them over time.
Documenting/Recording Information	Entering, transcribing, recording, storing, or maintaining information in written or electronic/magnetic form.
Making Decisions and Solving Problems	Analyzing information and evaluating results to choose the best solution and solve problems.
Monitor Processes, Materials, or Surroundings	Monitoring and reviewing information from materials, events, or the environment, to detect or assess problems.
Developing Objectives and Strategies	Establishing long-range objectives and specifying the strategies and actions to achieve them.
Performing for or Working Directly with the Public	Performing for people or dealing directly with the public. This includes serving customers in restaurants and stores, and receiving clients or guests.
Scheduling Work and Activities	Scheduling events, programs, and activities, as well as the work of others.
Coordinating the Work and Activities of Others	Getting members of a group to work together to accomplish tasks.
Communicating with Persons Outside Organization	Communicating with people outside the organization, representing the organization to customers, the public, government, and other external sources. This information can be exchanged in person, in writing, or by telephone or e-mail.
Guiding, Directing, and Motivating Subordinates	Providing guidance and direction to subordinates, including setting performance standards and monitoring performance.
Performing Administrative Activities	Performing day-to-day administrative tasks such as maintaining information files and processing paperwork.
Evaluating Information to Determine Compliance wit	Using relevant information and individual judgment to determine whether events or processes comply with laws, regulations, or standards.
Provide Consultation and Advice to Others	Providing guidance and expert advice to management or other groups on technical, systems-, or process-related topics.
Estimating the Quantifiable Characteristics of Pro	Estimating sizes, distances, and quantities; or determining time, costs, resources, or materials needed to perform a work activity.
Assisting and Caring for Others	Providing personal assistance, medical attention, emotional support, or other personal care to others such as coworkers, customers, or patients.
Resolving Conflicts and Negotiating with Others	Handling complaints, settling disputes, and resolving grievances and conflicts, or otherwise negotiating with others.
Developing and Building Teams	Encouraging and building mutual trust, respect, and cooperation among team members.
Monitoring and Controlling Resources	Monitoring and controlling resources and overseeing the spending of money.
Selling or Influencing Others	Convincing others to buy merchandise/goods or to otherwise change their minds or actions.
Staffing Organizational Units	Recruiting, interviewing, selecting, hiring, and promoting employees in an organization.
Inspecting Equipment, Structures, or Material	Inspecting equipment, structures, or materials to identify the cause of errors or other problems or defects.
Controlling Machines and Processes	Using either control mechanisms or direct physical activity to operate machines or processes (not including computers or vehicles).
Performing General Physical Activities	Performing physical activities that require considerable use of your arms and legs and moving your whole body, such as climbing, lifting, balancing, walking, stooping, and handling of materials.
Handling and Moving Objects	Using hands and arms in handling, installing, positioning, and moving materials, and manipulating things.
Drafting, Laying Out, and Specifying Technical Dev	Providing documentation, detailed instructions, drawings, or specifications to tell others about how devices, parts, equipment, or structures are to be fabricated, constructed, assembled, modified, maintained, or used.
Repairing and Maintaining Electronic Equipment	Servicing, repairing, calibrating, regulating, fine-tuning, or testing machines, devices, and equipment that operate primarily on the basis of electrical or electronic (not mechanical) principles.

Operating Vehicles, Mechanized Devices, or Equipme	Running, maneuvering, navigating, or driving vehicles or mechanized equipment, such as forklifts, passenger vehicles, aircraft, or water craft.
Repairing and Maintaining Mechanical Equipment	Servicing, repairing, adjusting, and testing machines, devices, moving parts, and equipment that operate primarily on the basis of mechanical (not electronic) principles.

Work_Context	**Work_Context Definitions**
Electronic Mail	How often do you use electronic mail in this job?
Freedom to Make Decisions	How much decision making freedom, without supervision, does the job offer?
Telephone	How often do you have telephone conversations in this job?
Structured versus Unstructured Work	To what extent is this job structured for the worker, rather than allowing the worker to determine tasks, priorities, and goals?
Face-to-Face Discussions	How often do you have to have face-to-face discussions with individuals or teams in this job?
Contact With Others	How much does this job require the worker to be in contact with others (face-to-face, by telephone, or otherwise) in order to perform it?
Indoors, Environmentally Controlled	How often does this job require working indoors in environmentally controlled conditions?
Public Speaking	How often do you have to perform public speaking in this job?
Coordinate or Lead Others	How important is it to coordinate or lead others in accomplishing work activities in this job?
Letters and Memos	How often does the job require written letters and memos?
Time Pressure	How often does this job require the worker to meet strict deadlines?
Frequency of Decision Making	How frequently is the worker required to make decisions that affect other people, the financial resources, and/or the image and reputation of the organization?
Spend Time Sitting	How much does this job require sitting?
Importance of Being Exact or Accurate	How important is being very exact or highly accurate in performing this job?
Impact of Decisions on Co-workers or Company Resul	How do the decisions an employee makes impact the results of co-workers, clients or the company?
Deal With External Customers	How important is it to work with external customers or the public in this job?
Work With Work Group or Team	How important is it to work with others in a group or team in this job?
Level of Competition	To what extent does this job require the worker to compete or to be aware of competitive pressures?
Physical Proximity	To what extent does this job require the worker to perform job tasks in close physical proximity to other people?
Responsibility for Outcomes and Results	How responsible is the worker for work outcomes and results of other workers?
Frequency of Conflict Situations	How often are there conflict situations the employee has to face in this job?
Deal With Unpleasant or Angry People	How frequently does the worker have to deal with unpleasant, angry, or discourteous individuals as part of the job requirements?
Spend Time Standing	How much does this job require standing?
Importance of Repeating Same Tasks	How important is repeating the same physical activities (e.g., key entry) or mental activities (e.g., checking entries in a ledger) over and over, without stopping, to performing this job?
Sounds, Noise Levels Are Distracting or Uncomforta	How often does this job require working exposed to sounds and noise levels that are distracting or uncomfortable?
Consequence of Error	How serious would the result usually be if the worker made a mistake that was not readily correctable?
Spend Time Making Repetitive Motions	How much does this job require making repetitive motions?
Degree of Automation	How automated is the job?
Responsible for Others' Health and Safety	How much responsibility is there for the health and safety of others in this job?
Exposed to Disease or Infections	How often does this job require exposure to disease/infections?
Spend Time Using Your Hands to Handle, Control, or	How much does this job require using your hands to handle, control, or feel objects, tools or controls?
Spend Time Walking and Running	How much does this job require walking and running?
Indoors, Not Environmentally Controlled	How often does this job require working indoors in non-controlled environmental conditions (e.g., warehouse without heat)?
In an Enclosed Vehicle or Equipment	How often does this job require working in a closed vehicle or equipment (e.g., car)?

Extremely Bright or Inadequate Lighting	How often does this job require working in extremely bright or inadequate lighting conditions?
Very Hot or Cold Temperatures	How often does this job require working in very hot (above 90 F degrees) or very cold (below 32 F degrees) temperatures?
Exposed to Contaminants	How often does this job require working exposed to contaminants (such as pollutants, gases, dust or odors)?
Deal With Physically Aggressive People	How frequently does this job require the worker to deal with physical aggression of violent individuals?
Cramped Work Space, Awkward Positions	How often does this job require working in cramped work spaces that requires getting into awkward positions?
Spend Time Bending or Twisting the Body	How much does this job require bending or twisting your body?
Outdoors, Exposed to Weather	How often does this job require working outdoors, exposed to all weather conditions?
Outdoors, Under Cover	How often does this job require working outdoors, under cover (e.g., structure with roof but no walls)?
Exposed to Whole Body Vibration	How often does this job require exposure to whole body vibration (e.g., operate a jackhammer)?
Pace Determined by Speed of Equipment	How important is it to this job that the pace is determined by the speed of equipment or machinery? (This does not refer to keeping busy at all times on this job.)
Exposed to Minor Burns, Cuts, Bites, or Stings	How often does this job require exposure to minor burns, cuts, bites, or stings?
Exposed to Hazardous Conditions	How often does this job require exposure to hazardous conditions?
Spend Time Keeping or Regaining Balance	How much does this job require keeping or regaining your balance?
Spend Time Kneeling, Crouching, Stooping, or Crawl	How much does this job require kneeling, crouching, stooping, or crawling?
Wear Common Protective or Safety Equipment such as	How much does this job require wearing common protective or safety equipment such as safety shoes, glasses, gloves, hard hats or live jackets?
Exposed to Hazardous Equipment	How often does this job require exposure to hazardous equipment?
In an Open Vehicle or Equipment	How often does this job require working in an open vehicle or equipment (e.g., tractor)?
Exposed to High Places	How often does this job require exposure to high places?
Exposed to Radiation	How often does this job require exposure to radiation?
Spend Time Climbing Ladders, Scaffolds, or Poles	How much does this job require climbing ladders, scaffolds, or poles?
Wear Specialized Protective or Safety Equipment su	How much does this job require wearing specialized protective or safety equipment such as breathing apparatus, safety harness, full protection suits, or radiation protection?

Job Zone Component	**Job Zone Component Definitions**
Title	Job Zone Five: Extensive Preparation Needed
Overall Experience	Extensive skill, knowledge, and experience are needed for these occupations. Many require more than five years of experience. For example, surgeons must complete four years of college and an additional five to seven years of specialized medical training to be able to do their job.
Job Training	Employees may need some on-the-job training, but most of these occupations assume that the person will already have the required skills, knowledge, work-related experience, and/or training.
Job Zone Examples	These occupations often involve coordinating, training, supervising, or managing the activities of others to accomplish goals. Very advanced communication and organizational skills are required. Examples include athletic trainers, lawyers, managing editors, phyicists, social psychologists, and surgeons.
SVP Range	(8.0 and above)
Education	A bachelor's degree is the minimum formal education required for these occupations. However, many also require graduate school. For example, they may require a master's degree, and some require a Ph.D., M.D., or J.D. (law degree).

Work_Styles	**Work_Styles Definitions**
Analytical Thinking	Job requires analyzing information and using logic to address work-related issues and problems.
Integrity	Job requires being honest and ethical.
Independence	Job requires developing one's own ways of doing things, guiding oneself with little or no supervision, and depending on oneself to get things done.

			Knowledge	Knowledge Definitions
Achievement/Effort	Job requires establishing and maintaining personally challenging achievement goals and exerting effort toward mastering tasks.		Psychology	Knowledge of human behavior and performance: individual differences in ability, personality, and interests; learning and motivation; psychological research methods; and the assessment and treatment of behavioral and affective disorders.
Initiative	Job requires a willingness to take on responsibilities and challenges.		English Language	Knowledge of the structure and content of the English language including the meaning and spelling of words, rules of composition, and grammar.
Persistence	Job requires persistence in the face of obstacles.		Education and Training	Knowledge of principles and methods for curriculum and training design, teaching and instruction for individuals and groups, and the measurement of training effects.
Dependability	Job requires being reliable, responsible, and dependable, and fulfilling obligations.			
Innovation	Job requires creativity and alternative thinking to develop new ideas for and answers to work-related problems.		Therapy and Counseling	Knowledge of principles, methods, and procedures for diagnosis, treatment, and rehabilitation of physical and mental dysfunctions, and for career counseling and guidance.
Attention to Detail	Job requires being careful about detail and thorough in completing work tasks.		Sociology and Anthropology	Knowledge of group behavior and dynamics, societal trends and influences, human migrations, ethnicity, cultures and their history and origins.
Self Control	Job requires maintaining composure, keeping emotions in check, controlling anger, and avoiding aggressive behavior, even in very difficult situations.		Mathematics	Knowledge of arithmetic, algebra, geometry, calculus, statistics, and their applications.
Stress Tolerance	Job requires accepting criticism and dealing calmly and effectively with high stress situations.		Computers and Electronics	Knowledge of circuit boards, processors, chips, electronic equipment, and computer hardware and software, including applications and programming.
Concern for Others	Job requires being sensitive to others' needs and feelings and being understanding and helpful on the job.			
Adaptability/Flexibility	Job requires being open to change (positive or negative) and to considerable variety in the workplace.		Philosophy and Theology	Knowledge of different philosophical systems and religions. This includes their basic principles, values, ethics, ways of thinking, customs, practices, and their impact on human culture.
Cooperation	Job requires being pleasant with others on the job and displaying a good-natured, cooperative attitude.			
Leadership	Job requires a willingness to lead, take charge, and offer opinions and direction.		Communications and Media	Knowledge of media production, communication, and dissemination techniques and methods. This includes alternative ways to inform and entertain via written, oral, and visual media.
Social Orientation	Job requires preferring to work with others rather than alone, and being personally connected with others on the job.			
			Customer and Personal Service	Knowledge of principles and processes for providing customer and personal services. This includes customer needs assessment, meeting quality standards for services, and evaluation of customer satisfaction.

25-1066.00 - Psychology Teachers, Postsecondary

Teach courses in psychology, such as child, clinical, and developmental psychology, and psychological counseling.

Tasks

1) Compile, administer, and grade examinations, or assign this work to others.

2) Plan, evaluate, and revise curricula, course content, and course materials and methods of instruction.

3) Initiate, facilitate, and moderate classroom discussions.

4) Maintain student attendance records, grades, and other required records.

5) Select and obtain materials and supplies such as textbooks.

6) Collaborate with colleagues to address teaching and research issues.

7) Advise students on academic and vocational curricula, and on career issues.

0) Maintain regularly scheduled office hours in order to advise and assist students.

9) Prepare and deliver lectures to undergraduate and/or graduate students on topics such as abnormal psychology, cognitive processes, and work motivation.

10) Serve on academic or administrative committees that deal with institutional policies, departmental matters, and academic issues.

11) Compile bibliographies of specialized materials for outside reading assignments.

12) Participate in campus and community events.

13) Conduct research in a particular field of knowledge, and publish findings in professional journals, books, and/or electronic media.

14) Participate in student recruitment, registration, and placement activities.

15) Supervise undergraduate and/or graduate teaching, internship, and research work.

16) Act as advisers to student organizations.

17) Perform administrative duties such as serving as department head.

18) Write grant proposals to procure external research funding.

19) Supervise students' laboratory work.

20) Provide professional consulting services to government and/or industry.

21) Keep abreast of developments in their field by reading current literature, talking with colleagues, and participating in professional conferences.

22) Evaluate and grade students' class work, laboratory work, assignments, and papers.

Knowledge	Knowledge Definitions
Clerical	Knowledge of administrative and clerical procedures and systems such as word processing, managing files and records, stenography and transcription, designing forms, and other office procedures and terminology.
Administration and Management	Knowledge of business and management principles involved in strategic planning, resource allocation, human resources modeling, leadership technique, production methods, and coordination of people and resources.
Biology	Knowledge of plant and animal organisms, their tissues, cells, functions, interdependencies, and interactions with each other and the environment.
Personnel and Human Resources	Knowledge of principles and procedures for personnel recruitment, selection, training, compensation and benefits, labor relations and negotiation, and personnel information systems.
Medicine and Dentistry	Knowledge of the information and techniques needed to diagnose and treat human injuries, diseases, and deformities. This includes symptoms, treatment alternatives, drug properties and interactions, and preventive health-care measures.
Law and Government	Knowledge of laws, legal codes, court procedures, precedents, government regulations, executive orders, agency rules, and the democratic political process.
History and Archeology	Knowledge of historical events and their causes, indicators, and effects on civilizations and cultures.
Public Safety and Security	Knowledge of relevant equipment, policies, procedures, and strategies to promote effective local, state, or national security operations for the protection of people, data, property, and institutions.
Geography	Knowledge of principles and methods for describing the features of land, sea, and air masses, including their physical characteristics, locations, interrelationships, and distribution of plant, animal, and human life.
Sales and Marketing	Knowledge of principles and methods for showing, promoting, and selling products or services. This includes marketing strategy and tactics, product demonstration, sales techniques, and sales control systems.
Economics and Accounting	Knowledge of economic and accounting principles and practices, the financial markets, banking and the analysis and reporting of financial data.
Telecommunications	Knowledge of transmission, broadcasting, switching, control, and operation of telecommunications systems.

1413

Foreign Language	Knowledge of the structure and content of a foreign (non-English) language including the meaning and spelling of words, rules of composition and grammar, and pronunciation.
Design	Knowledge of design techniques, tools, and principles involved in production of precision technical plans, blueprints, drawings, and models.
Fine Arts	Knowledge of the theory and techniques required to compose, produce, and perform works of music, dance, visual arts, drama, and sculpture.
Engineering and Technology	Knowledge of the practical application of engineering science and technology. This includes applying principles, techniques, procedures, and equipment to the design and production of various goods and services.
Chemistry	Knowledge of the chemical composition, structure, and properties of substances and of the chemical processes and transformations that they undergo. This includes uses of chemicals and their interactions, danger signs, production techniques, and disposal methods.
Production and Processing	Knowledge of raw materials, production processes, quality control, costs, and other techniques for maximizing the effective manufacture and distribution of goods.
Physics	Knowledge and prediction of physical principles, laws, their interrelationships, and applications to understanding fluid, material, and atmospheric dynamics, and mechanical, electrical, atomic and sub-atomic structures and processes.
Mechanical	Knowledge of machines and tools, including their designs, uses, repair, and maintenance.
Transportation	Knowledge of principles and methods for moving people or goods by air, rail, sea, or road, including the relative costs and benefits.
Building and Construction	Knowledge of materials, methods, and the tools involved in the construction or repair of houses, buildings, or other structures such as highways and roads.
Food Production	Knowledge of techniques and equipment for planting, growing, and harvesting food products (both plant and animal) for consumption, including storage/handling techniques.

Skills	Skills Definitions
Reading Comprehension	Understanding written sentences and paragraphs in work related documents.
Instructing	Teaching others how to do something.
Speaking	Talking to others to convey information effectively.
Critical Thinking	Using logic and reasoning to identify the strengths and weaknesses of alternative solutions, conclusions or approaches to problems.
Active Listening	Giving full attention to what other people are saying, taking time to understand the points being made, asking questions as appropriate, and not interrupting at inappropriate times.
Active Learning	Understanding the implications of new information for both current and future problem-solving and decision-making.
Learning Strategies	Selecting and using training/instructional methods and procedures appropriate for the situation when learning or teaching new things.
Writing	Communicating effectively in writing as appropriate for the needs of the audience.
Social Perceptiveness	Being aware of others' reactions and understanding why they react as they do.
Time Management	Managing one's own time and the time of others.
Monitoring	Monitoring/Assessing performance of yourself, other individuals, or organizations to make improvements or take corrective action.
Science	Using scientific rules and methods to solve problems.
Judgment and Decision Making	Considering the relative costs and benefits of potential actions to choose the most appropriate one.
Coordination	Adjusting actions in relation to others' actions.
Complex Problem Solving	Identifying complex problems and reviewing related information to develop and evaluate options and implement solutions.
Persuasion	Persuading others to change their minds or behavior.
Service Orientation	Actively looking for ways to help people.
Mathematics	Using mathematics to solve problems.
Negotiation	Bringing others together and trying to reconcile differences.
Systems Evaluation	Identifying measures or indicators of system performance and the actions needed to improve or correct performance, relative to the goals of the system.
Quality Control Analysis	Conducting tests and inspections of products, services, or processes to evaluate quality or performance.

Management of Personnel Resources	Motivating, developing, and directing people as they work, identifying the best people for the job.
Equipment Selection	Determining the kind of tools and equipment needed to do a job.
Operations Analysis	Analyzing needs and product requirements to create a design.
Systems Analysis	Determining how a system should work and how changes in conditions, operations, and the environment will affect outcomes.
Technology Design	Generating or adapting equipment and technology to serve user needs.
Management of Financial Resources	Determining how money will be spent to get the work done, and accounting for these expenditures.
Management of Material Resources	Obtaining and seeing to the appropriate use of equipment, facilities, and materials needed to do certain work.
Troubleshooting	Determining causes of operating errors and deciding what to do about it.
Programming	Writing computer programs for various purposes.
Operation and Control	Controlling operations of equipment or systems.
Installation	Installing equipment, machines, wiring, or programs to meet specifications.
Equipment Maintenance	Performing routine maintenance on equipment and determining when and what kind of maintenance is needed.
Operation Monitoring	Watching gauges, dials, or other indicators to make sure a machine is working properly.
Repairing	Repairing machines or systems using the needed tools.

Ability	Ability Definitions
Oral Expression	The ability to communicate information and ideas in speaking so others will understand.
Oral Comprehension	The ability to listen to and understand information and ideas presented through spoken words and sentences.
Written Expression	The ability to communicate information and ideas in writing so others will understand.
Written Comprehension	The ability to read and understand information and ideas presented in writing.
Speech Clarity	The ability to speak clearly so others can understand you.
Deductive Reasoning	The ability to apply general rules to specific problems to produce answers that make sense.
Inductive Reasoning	The ability to combine pieces of information to form general rules or conclusions (includes finding a relationship among seemingly unrelated events).
Near Vision	The ability to see details at close range (within a few feet of the observer).
Speech Recognition	The ability to identify and understand the speech of another person.
Problem Sensitivity	The ability to tell when something is wrong or is likely to go wrong. It does not involve solving the problem, only recognizing there is a problem.
Originality	The ability to come up with unusual or clever ideas about a given topic or situation, or to develop creative ways to solve a problem.
Category Flexibility	The ability to generate or use different sets of rules for combining or grouping things in different ways.
Fluency of Ideas	The ability to come up with a number of ideas about a topic (the number of ideas is important, not their quality, correctness, or creativity).
Selective Attention	The ability to concentrate on a task over a period of time without being distracted.
Information Ordering	The ability to arrange things or actions in a certain order or pattern according to a specific rule or set of rules (e.g., patterns of numbers, letters, words, pictures, mathematical operations).
Memorization	The ability to remember information such as words, numbers, pictures, and procedures.
Mathematical Reasoning	The ability to choose the right mathematical methods or formulas to solve a problem.
Flexibility of Closure	The ability to identify or detect a known pattern (a figure, object, word, or sound) that is hidden in other distracting material.
Time Sharing	The ability to shift back and forth between two or more activities or sources of information (such as speech, sounds, touch, or other sources).
Speed of Closure	The ability to quickly make sense of, combine, and organize information into meaningful patterns.
Far Vision	The ability to see details at a distance.
Number Facility	The ability to add, subtract, multiply, or divide quickly and correctly.

Trunk Strength	The ability to use your abdominal and lower back muscles to support part of the body repeatedly or continuously over time without 'giving out' or fatiguing.
Perceptual Speed	The ability to quickly and accurately compare similarities and differences among sets of letters, numbers, objects, pictures, or patterns. The things to be compared may be presented at the same time or one after the other. This ability also includes comparing a presented object with a remembered object.
Visualization	The ability to imagine how something will look after it is moved around or when its parts are moved or rearranged.
Finger Dexterity	The ability to make precisely coordinated movements of the fingers of one or both hands to grasp, manipulate, or assemble very small objects.
Auditory Attention	The ability to focus on a single source of sound in the presence of other distracting sounds.
Visual Color Discrimination	The ability to match or detect differences between colors, including shades of color and brightness.
Depth Perception	The ability to judge which of several objects is closer or farther away from you, or to judge the distance between you and an object.
Hearing Sensitivity	The ability to detect or tell the differences between sounds that vary in pitch and loudness.
Response Orientation	The ability to choose quickly between two or more movements in response to two or more different signals (lights, sounds, pictures). It includes the speed with which the correct response is started with the hand, foot, or other body part.
Multilimb Coordination	The ability to coordinate two or more limbs (for example, two arms, two legs, or one leg and one arm) while sitting, standing, or lying down. It does not involve performing the activities while the whole body is in motion.
Speed of Limb Movement	The ability to quickly move the arms and legs.
Rate Control	The ability to time your movements or the movement of a piece of equipment in anticipation of changes in the speed and/or direction of a moving object or scene.
Wrist-Finger Speed	The ability to make fast, simple, repeated movements of the fingers, hands, and wrists.
Static Strength	The ability to exert maximum muscle force to lift, push, pull, or carry objects.
Explosive Strength	The ability to use short bursts of muscle force to propel oneself (as in jumping or sprinting), or to throw an object.
Dynamic Strength	The ability to exert muscle force repeatedly or continuously over time. This involves muscular endurance and resistance to muscle fatigue.
Extent Flexibility	The ability to bend, stretch, twist, or reach with your body, arms, and/or legs.
Glare Sensitivity	The ability to see objects in the presence of glare or bright lighting.
Control Precision	The ability to quickly and repeatedly adjust the controls of a machine or a vehicle to exact positions.
Stamina	The ability to exert yourself physically over long periods of time without getting winded or out of breath.
Gross Body Equilibrium	The ability to keep or regain your body balance or stay upright when in an unstable position.
Arm-Hand Steadiness	The ability to keep your hand and arm steady while moving your arm or while holding your arm and hand in one position.
Dynamic Flexibility	The ability to quickly and repeatedly bend, stretch, twist, or reach out with your body, arms, and/or legs.
Spatial Orientation	The ability to know your location in relation to the environment or to know where other objects are in relation to you.
Peripheral Vision	The ability to see objects or movement of objects to one's side when the eyes are looking ahead.
Gross Body Coordination	The ability to coordinate the movement of your arms, legs, and torso together when the whole body is in motion.
Sound Localization	The ability to tell the direction from which a sound originated.
Night Vision	The ability to see under low light conditions.
Reaction Time	The ability to quickly respond (with the hand, finger, or foot) to a signal (sound, light, picture) when it appears.
Manual Dexterity	The ability to quickly move your hand, your hand together with your arm, or your two hands to grasp, manipulate, or assemble objects.

Work_Activity	Work_Activity Definitions
Training and Teaching Others	Identifying the educational needs of others, developing formal educational or training programs or classes, and teaching or instructing others.
Getting Information	Observing, receiving, and otherwise obtaining information from all relevant sources.

Updating and Using Relevant Knowledge	Keeping up-to-date technically and applying new knowledge to your job.
Interpreting the Meaning of Information for Others	Translating or explaining what information means and how it can be used.
Thinking Creatively	Developing, designing, or creating new applications, ideas, relationships, systems, or products, including artistic contributions.
Making Decisions and Solving Problems	Analyzing information and evaluating results to choose the best solution and solve problems.
Analyzing Data or Information	Identifying the underlying principles, reasons, or facts of information by breaking down information or data into separate parts.
Organizing, Planning, and Prioritizing Work	Developing specific goals and plans to prioritize, organize, and accomplish your work.
Processing Information	Compiling, coding, categorizing, calculating, tabulating, auditing, or verifying information or data.
Interacting With Computers	Using computers and computer systems (including hardware and software) to program, write software, set up functions, enter data, or process information.
Establishing and Maintaining Interpersonal Relatio	Developing constructive and cooperative working relationships with others, and maintaining them over time.
Coaching and Developing Others	Identifying the developmental needs of others and coaching, mentoring, or otherwise helping others to improve their knowledge or skills.
Identifying Objects, Actions, and Events	Identifying information by categorizing, estimating, recognizing differences or similarities, and detecting changes in circumstances or events.
Documenting/Recording Information	Entering, transcribing, recording, storing, or maintaining information in written or electronic/magnetic form.
Communicating with Supervisors, Peers, or Subordin	Providing information to supervisors, co-workers, and subordinates by telephone, in written form, e-mail, or in person.
Judging the Qualities of Things, Services, or Peop	Assessing the value, importance, or quality of things or people.
Developing Objectives and Strategies	Establishing long-range objectives and specifying the strategies and actions to achieve them.
Performing for or Working Directly with the Public	Performing for people or dealing directly with the public. This includes serving customers in restaurants and stores, and receiving clients or guests.
Scheduling Work and Activities	Scheduling events, programs, and activities, as well as the work of others.
Monitor Processes, Materials, or Surroundings	Monitoring and reviewing information from materials, events, or the environment, to detect or assess problems.
Communicating with Persons Outside Organization	Communicating with people outside the organization, representing the organization to customers, the public, government, and other external sources. This information can be exchanged in person, in writing, or by telephone or e-mail.
Evaluating Information to Determine Compliance wit	Using relevant information and individual judgment to determine whether events or processes comply with laws, regulations, or standards.
Assisting and Caring for Others	Providing personal assistance, medical attention, emotional support, or other personal care to others such as coworkers, customers, or patients.
Provide Consultation and Advice to Others	Providing guidance and expert advice to management or other groups on technical, systems-, or process-related topics.
Coordinating the Work and Activities of Others	Getting members of a group to work together to accomplish tasks.
Resolving Conflicts and Negotiating with Others	Handling complaints, settling disputes, and resolving grievances and conflicts, or otherwise negotiating with others.
Guiding, Directing, and Motivating Subordinates	Providing guidance and direction to subordinates, including setting performance standards and monitoring performance.
Performing Administrative Activities	Performing day-to-day administrative tasks such as maintaining information files and processing paperwork.
Estimating the Quantifiable Characteristics of Pro	Estimating sizes, distances, and quantities; or determining time, costs, resources, or materials needed to perform a work activity.
Developing and Building Teams	Encouraging and building mutual trust, respect, and cooperation among team members.
Selling or Influencing Others	Convincing others to buy merchandise/goods or to otherwise change their minds or actions.
Staffing Organizational Units	Recruiting, interviewing, selecting, hiring, and promoting employees in an organization.
Monitoring and Controlling Resources	Monitoring and controlling resources and overseeing the spending of money.
Inspecting Equipment, Structures, or Material	Inspecting equipment, structures, or materials to identify the cause of errors or other problems or defects.

Controlling Machines and Processes	Using either control mechanisms or direct physical activity to operate machines or processes (not including computers or vehicles).
Handling and Moving Objects	Using hands and arms in handling, installing, positioning, and moving materials, and manipulating things.
Performing General Physical Activities	Performing physical activities that require considerable use of your arms and legs and moving your whole body, such as climbing, lifting, balancing, walking, stooping, and handling of materials.
Repairing and Maintaining Electronic Equipment	Servicing, repairing, calibrating, regulating, fine-tuning, or testing machines, devices, and equipment that operate primarily on the basis of electrical or electronic (not mechanical) principles.
Operating Vehicles, Mechanized Devices, or Equipme	Running, maneuvering, navigating, or driving vehicles or mechanized equipment, such as forklifts, passenger vehicles, aircraft, or water craft.
Drafting, Laying Out, and Specifying Technical Dev	Providing documentation, detailed instructions, drawings, or specifications to tell others about how devices, parts, equipment, or structures are to be fabricated, constructed, assembled, modified, maintained, or used.
Repairing and Maintaining Mechanical Equipment	Servicing, repairing, adjusting, and testing machines, devices, moving parts, and equipment that operate primarily on the basis of mechanical (not electronic) principles.

Work_Context	Work_Context Definitions
Freedom to Make Decisions	How much decision making freedom, without supervision, does the job offer?
Face-to-Face Discussions	How often do you have to have face-to-face discussions with individuals or teams in this job?
Electronic Mail	How often do you use electronic mail in this job?
Structured versus Unstructured Work	To what extent is this job structured for the worker, rather than allowing the worker to determine tasks, priorities, and goals?
Indoors, Environmentally Controlled	How often does this job require working indoors in environmentally controlled conditions?
Telephone	How often do you have telephone conversations in this job?
Public Speaking	How often do you have to perform public speaking in this job?
Contact With Others	How much does this job require the worker to be in contact with others (face-to-face, by telephone, or otherwise) in order to perform it?
Time Pressure	How often does this job require the worker to meet strict deadlines?
Coordinate or Lead Others	How important is it to coordinate or lead others in accomplishing work activities in this job?
Importance of Being Exact or Accurate	How important is being very exact or highly accurate in performing this job?
Impact of Decisions on Co-workers or Company Resul	How do the decisions an employee makes impact the results of co-workers, clients or the company?
Frequency of Decision Making	How frequently is the worker required to make decisions that affect other people, the financial resources, and/or the image and reputation of the organization?
Letters and Memos	How often does the job require written letters and memos?
Work With Work Group or Team	How important is it to work with others in a group or team in this job?
Spend Time Sitting	How much does this job require sitting?
Deal With External Customers	How important is it to work with external customers or the public in this job?
Level of Competition	To what extent does this job require the worker to compete or to be aware of competitive pressures?
Physical Proximity	To what extent does this job require the worker to perform job tasks in close physical proximity to other people?
Frequency of Conflict Situations	How often are there conflict situations the employee has to face in this job?
Spend Time Standing	How much does this job require standing?
Deal With Unpleasant or Angry People	How frequently does the worker have to deal with unpleasant, angry, or discourteous individuals as part of the job requirements?
Responsibility for Outcomes and Results	How responsible is the worker for work outcomes and results of other workers?
Importance of Repeating Same Tasks	How important is repeating the same physical activities (e.g., key entry) or mental activities (e.g., checking entries in a ledger) over and over, without stopping, to performing this job?
Sounds, Noise Levels Are Distracting or Uncomforta	How often does this job require working exposed to sounds and noise levels that are distracting or uncomfortable?
Responsible for Others' Health and Safety	How much responsibility is there for the health and safety of others in this job?

Spend Time Making Repetitive Motions	How much does this job require making repetitive motions?
Spend Time Using Your Hands to Handle, Control, or	How much does this job require using your hands to handle, control, or feel objects, tools or controls?
Consequence of Error	How serious would the result usually be if the worker made a mistake that was not readily correctable?
Exposed to Disease or Infections	How often does this job require exposure to disease/infections?
Spend Time Walking and Running	How much does this job require walking and running?
Exposed to Contaminants	How often does this job require working exposed to contaminants (such as pollutants, gases, dust or odors)?
Degree of Automation	How automated is the job?
Indoors, Not Environmentally Controlled	How often does this job require working indoors in non-controlled environmental conditions (e.g., warehouse without heat)?
Extremely Bright or Inadequate Lighting	How often does this job require working in extremely bright or inadequate lighting conditions?
Cramped Work Space, Awkward Positions	How often does this job require working in cramped work spaces that requires getting into awkward positions?
In an Enclosed Vehicle or Equipment	How often does this job require working in a closed vehicle or equipment (e.g., car)?
Very Hot or Cold Temperatures	How often does this job require working in very hot (above 90 F degrees) or very cold (below 32 F degrees) temperatures?
Deal With Physically Aggressive People	How frequently does this job require the worker to deal with physical aggression of violent individuals?
Outdoors, Exposed to Weather	How often does this job require working outdoors, exposed to all weather conditions?
Spend Time Bending or Twisting the Body	How much does this job require bending or twisting your body?
Pace Determined by Speed of Equipment	How important is it to this job that the pace is determined by the speed of equipment or machinery? (This does not refer to keeping busy at all times on this job.)
Exposed to Minor Burns, Cuts, Bites, or Stings	How often does this job require exposure to minor burns, cuts, bites, or stings?
Spend Time Kneeling, Crouching, Stooping, or Crawl	How much does this job require kneeling, crouching, stooping or crawling?
Exposed to Radiation	How often does this job require exposure to radiation?
Exposed to Hazardous Conditions	How often does this job require exposure to hazardous conditions?
Spend Time Keeping or Regaining Balance	How much does this job require keeping or regaining your balance?
Outdoors, Under Cover	How often does this job require working outdoors, under cover (e.g., structure with roof but no walls)?
Wear Common Protective or Safety Equipment such as	How much does this job require wearing common protective or safety equipment such as safety shoes, glasses, gloves, hard hats or live jackets?
Wear Specialized Protective or Safety Equipment su	How much does this job require wearing specialized protective or safety equipment such as breathing apparatus, safety harness, full protection suits, or radiation protection?
Exposed to Whole Body Vibration	How often does this job require exposure to whole body vibration (e.g., operate a jackhammer)?
In an Open Vehicle or Equipment	How often does this job require working in an open vehicle or equipment (e.g., tractor)?
Spend Time Climbing Ladders, Scaffolds, or Poles	How much does this job require climbing ladders, scaffolds, or poles?
Exposed to Hazardous Equipment	How often does this job require exposure to hazardous equipment?
Exposed to High Places	How often does this job require exposure to high places?

Job Zone Component	Job Zone Component Definitions
Title	Job Zone Five: Extensive Preparation Needed
Overall Experience	Extensive skill, knowledge, and experience are needed for these occupations. Many require more than five years of experience. For example, surgeons must complete four years of college and an additional five to seven years of specialized medical training to be able to do their job.
Job Training	Employees may need some on-the-job training, but most of these occupations assume that the person will already have the required skills, knowledge, work-related experience, and/or training.

Job Zone Examples	These occupations often involve coordinating, training, supervising, or managing the activities of others to accomplish goals. Very advanced communication and organizational skills are required. Examples include athletic trainers, lawyers, managing editors, physicists, social psychologists, and surgeons. (8.0 and above)
SVP Range	
Education	A bachelor's degree is the minimum formal education required for these occupations. However, many also require graduate school. For example, they may require a master's degree, and some require a Ph.D., M.D., or J.D. (law degree).

Work_Styles	Work_Styles Definitions
Integrity	Job requires being honest and ethical.
Dependability	Job requires being reliable, responsible, and dependable, and fulfilling obligations.
Initiative	Job requires a willingness to take on responsibilities and challenges.
Independence	Job requires developing one's own ways of doing things, guiding oneself with little or no supervision, and depending on oneself to get things done.
Achievement/Effort	Job requires establishing and maintaining personally challenging achievement goals and exerting effort toward mastering tasks.
Analytical Thinking	Job requires analyzing information and using logic to address work-related issues and problems.
Persistence	Job requires persistence in the face of obstacles.
Self Control	Job requires maintaining composure, keeping emotions in check, controlling anger, and avoiding aggressive behavior, even in very difficult situations.
Concern for Others	Job requires being sensitive to others' needs and feelings and being understanding and helpful on the job.
Attention to Detail	Job requires being careful about detail and thorough in completing work tasks.
Adaptability/Flexibility	Job requires being open to change (positive or negative) and to considerable variety in the workplace.
Innovation	Job requires creativity and alternative thinking to develop new ideas for and answers to work-related problems.
Cooperation	Job requires being pleasant with others on the job and displaying a good-natured, cooperative attitude.
Leadership	Job requires a willingness to lead, take charge, and offer opinions and direction.
Social Orientation	Job requires preferring to work with others rather than alone, and being personally connected with others on the job.
Stress Tolerance	Job requires accepting criticism and dealing calmly and effectively with high stress situations.

25-1067.00 - Sociology Teachers, Postsecondary

Teach courses in sociology.

Tasks

1) Keep abreast of developments in their field by reading current literature, talking with colleagues, and participating in professional conferences.

2) Compile, administer, and grade examinations, or assign this work to others.

3) Maintain regularly scheduled office hours in order to advise and assist students.

4) Plan, evaluate, and revise curricula, course content, and course materials and methods of instruction.

5) Prepare and deliver lectures to undergraduate and/or graduate students on topics such as race and ethnic relations, measurement and data collection, and workplace social relations.

6) Select and obtain materials and supplies such as textbooks and laboratory equipment.

7) Collaborate with colleagues to address teaching and research issues.

8) Participate in campus and community events.

9) Advise students on academic and vocational curricula, and on career issues.

10) Serve on academic or administrative committees that deal with institutional policies, departmental matters, and academic issues.

11) Compile bibliographies of specialized materials for outside reading assignments.

12) Participate in student recruitment, registration, and placement activities.

13) Conduct research in a particular field of knowledge, and publish findings in professional journals, books, and/or electronic media.

14) Supervise undergraduate and/or graduate teaching, internship, and research work.

15) Act as advisers to student organizations.

16) Perform administrative duties such as serving as department head.

17) Supervise students' laboratory and field work.

18) Write grant proposals to procure external research funding.

19) Provide professional consulting services to government and/or industry.

20) Prepare course materials such as syllabi, homework assignments, and handouts.

21) Maintain student attendance records, grades, and other required records.

22) Initiate, facilitate, and moderate classroom discussions.

Knowledge	Knowledge Definitions
Sociology and Anthropology	Knowledge of group behavior and dynamics, societal trends and influences, human migrations, ethnicity, cultures and their history and origins.
English Language	Knowledge of the structure and content of the English language including the meaning and spelling of words, rules of composition, and grammar.
Education and Training	Knowledge of principles and methods for curriculum and training design, teaching and instruction for individuals and groups, and the measurement of training effects.
Psychology	Knowledge of human behavior and performance; individual differences in ability, personality, and interests; learning and motivation; psychological research methods; and the assessment and treatment of behavioral and affective disorders.
History and Archeology	Knowledge of historical events and their causes, indicators, and effects on civilizations and cultures.
Computers and Electronics	Knowledge of circuit boards, processors, chips, electronic equipment, and computer hardware and software, including applications and programming.
Philosophy and Theology	Knowledge of different philosophical systems and religions. This includes their basic principles, values, ethics, ways of thinking, customs, practices, and their impact on human culture.
Mathematics	Knowledge of arithmetic, algebra, geometry, calculus, statistics, and their applications.
Communications and Media	Knowledge of media production, communication, and dissemination techniques and methods. This includes alternative ways to inform and entertain via written, oral, and visual media.
Geography	Knowledge of principles and methods for describing the features of land, sea, and air masses, including their physical characteristics, locations, interrelationships, and distribution of plant, animal, and human life.
Law and Government	Knowledge of laws, legal codes, court procedures, precedents, government regulations, executive orders, agency rules, and the democratic political process.
Clerical	Knowledge of administrative and clerical procedures and systems such as word processing, managing files and records, stenography and transcription, designing forms, and other office procedures and terminology.
Customer and Personal Service	Knowledge of principles and processes for providing customer and personal services. This includes customer needs assessment, meeting quality standards for services, and evaluation of customer satisfaction.
Therapy and Counseling	Knowledge of principles, methods, and procedures for diagnosis, treatment, and rehabilitation of physical and mental dysfunctions, and for career counseling and guidance.
Administration and Management	Knowledge of business and management principles involved in strategic planning, resource allocation, human resources modeling, leadership technique, production methods, and coordination of people and resources.
Personnel and Human Resources	Knowledge of principles and procedures for personnel recruitment, selection, training, compensation and benefits, labor relations and negotiation, and personnel information systems.
Biology	Knowledge of plant and animal organisms, their tissues, cells, functions, interdependencies, and interactions with each other and the environment.
Telecommunications	Knowledge of transmission, broadcasting, switching, control, and operation of telecommunications systems.

Foreign Language	Knowledge of the structure and content of a foreign (non-English) language including the meaning and spelling of words, rules of composition and grammar, and pronunciation.
Public Safety and Security	Knowledge of relevant equipment, policies, procedures, and strategies to promote effective local, state, or national security operations for the protection of people, data, property, and institutions.
Fine Arts	Knowledge of the theory and techniques required to compose, produce, and perform works of music, dance, visual arts, drama, and sculpture.
Sales and Marketing	Knowledge of principles and methods for showing, promoting, and selling products or services. This includes marketing strategy and tactics, product demonstration, sales techniques, and sales control systems.
Economics and Accounting	Knowledge of economic and accounting principles and practices, the financial markets, banking and the analysis and reporting of financial data.
Transportation	Knowledge of principles and methods for moving people or goods by air, rail, sea, or road, including the relative costs and benefits.
Medicine and Dentistry	Knowledge of the information and techniques needed to diagnose and treat human injuries, diseases, and deformities. This includes symptoms, treatment alternatives, drug properties and interactions, and preventive health-care measures.
Chemistry	Knowledge of the chemical composition, structure, and properties of substances and of the chemical processes and transformations that they undergo. This includes uses of chemicals and their interactions, danger signs, production techniques, and disposal methods.
Engineering and Technology	Knowledge of the practical application of engineering science and technology. This includes applying principles, techniques, procedures, and equipment to the design and production of various goods and services.
Production and Processing	Knowledge of raw materials, production processes, quality control, costs, and other techniques for maximizing the effective manufacture and distribution of goods.
Physics	Knowledge and prediction of physical principles, laws, their interrelationships, and applications to understanding fluid, material, and atmospheric dynamics, and mechanical, electrical, atomic and sub- atomic structures and processes.
Food Production	Knowledge of techniques and equipment for planting, growing, and harvesting food products (both plant and animal) for consumption, including storage/handling techniques.
Mechanical	Knowledge of machines and tools, including their designs, uses, repair, and maintenance.
Design	Knowledge of design techniques, tools, and principles involved in production of precision technical plans, blueprints, drawings, and models.
Building and Construction	Knowledge of materials, methods, and the tools involved in the construction or repair of houses, buildings, or other structures such as highways and roads.

Skills	Skills Definitions
Instructing	Teaching others how to do something.
Reading Comprehension	Understanding written sentences and paragraphs in work related documents.
Speaking	Talking to others to convey information effectively.
Writing	Communicating effectively in writing as appropriate for the needs of the audience.
Critical Thinking	Using logic and reasoning to identify the strengths and weaknesses of alternative solutions, conclusions or approaches to problems.
Active Learning	Understanding the implications of new information for both current and future problem-solving and decision-making.
Learning Strategies	Selecting and using training/instructional methods and procedures appropriate for the situation when learning or teaching new things.
Social Perceptiveness	Being aware of others' reactions and understanding why they react as they do.
Active Listening	Giving full attention to what other people are saying, taking time to understand the points being made, asking questions as appropriate, and not interrupting at inappropriate times.
Time Management	Managing one's own time and the time of others.
Monitoring	Monitoring/Assessing performance of yourself, other individuals, or organizations to make improvements or take corrective action.

Complex Problem Solving	Identifying complex problems and reviewing related information to develop and evaluate options and implement solutions.
Persuasion	Persuading others to change their minds or behavior.
Judgment and Decision Making	Considering the relative costs and benefits of potential actions to choose the most appropriate one.
Science	Using scientific rules and methods to solve problems.
Service Orientation	Actively looking for ways to help people.
Coordination	Adjusting actions in relation to others' actions.
Negotiation	Bringing others together and trying to reconcile differences.
Mathematics	Using mathematics to solve problems.
Management of Personnel Resources	Motivating, developing, and directing people as they work, identifying the best people for the job.
Quality Control Analysis	Conducting tests and inspections of products, services, or processes to evaluate quality or performance.
Operations Analysis	Analyzing needs and product requirements to create a design.
Equipment Selection	Determining the kind of tools and equipment needed to do a job.
Systems Evaluation	Identifying measures or indicators of system performance and the actions needed to improve or correct performance, relative to the goals of the system.
Systems Analysis	Determining how a system should work and how changes in conditions, operations, and the environment will affect outcomes.
Management of Financial Resources	Determining how money will be spent to get the work done, and accounting for these expenditures.
Troubleshooting	Determining causes of operating errors and deciding what to do about it.
Management of Material Resources	Obtaining and seeing to the appropriate use of equipment, facilities, and materials needed to do certain work.
Technology Design	Generating or adapting equipment and technology to serve user needs.
Programming	Writing computer programs for various purposes.
Operation and Control	Controlling operations of equipment or systems.
Equipment Maintenance	Performing routine maintenance on equipment and determining when and what kind of maintenance is needed.
Operation Monitoring	Watching gauges, dials, or other indicators to make sure a machine is working properly.
Installation	Installing equipment, machines, wiring, or programs to meet specifications.
Repairing	Repairing machines or systems using the needed tools.

Ability	Ability Definitions
Oral Expression	The ability to communicate information and ideas in speaking so others will understand.
Written Expression	The ability to communicate information and ideas in writing so others will understand.
Written Comprehension	The ability to read and understand information and ideas presented in writing.
Speech Clarity	The ability to speak clearly so others can understand you.
Oral Comprehension	The ability to listen to and understand information and ideas presented through spoken words and sentences.
Deductive Reasoning	The ability to apply general rules to specific problems to produce answers that make sense.
Inductive Reasoning	The ability to combine pieces of information to form general rules or conclusions (includes finding a relationship among seemingly unrelated events).
Near Vision	The ability to see details at close range (within a few feet of the observer).
Speech Recognition	The ability to identify and understand the speech of another person.
Problem Sensitivity	The ability to tell when something is wrong or is likely to go wrong. It does not involve solving the problem, only recognizing there is a problem.
Originality	The ability to come up with unusual or clever ideas about a given topic or situation, or to develop creative ways to solve a problem.
Category Flexibility	The ability to generate or use different sets of rules for combining or grouping things in different ways.
Information Ordering	The ability to arrange things or actions in a certain order or pattern according to a specific rule or set of rules (e.g., patterns of numbers, letters, words, pictures, mathematical operations).
Selective Attention	The ability to concentrate on a task over a period of time without being distracted.
Fluency of Ideas	The ability to come up with a number of ideas about a topic (the number of ideas is important, not their quality, correctness, or creativity).

Memorization	The ability to remember information such as words, numbers, pictures, and procedures.
Time Sharing	The ability to shift back and forth between two or more activities or sources of information (such as speech, sounds, touch, or other sources).
Far Vision	The ability to see details at a distance.
Speed of Closure	The ability to quickly make sense of, combine, and organize information into meaningful patterns.
Mathematical Reasoning	The ability to choose the right mathematical methods or formulas to solve a problem.
Flexibility of Closure	The ability to identify or detect a known pattern (a figure, object, word, or sound) that is hidden in other distracting material.
Number Facility	The ability to add, subtract, multiply, or divide quickly and correctly.
Perceptual Speed	The ability to quickly and accurately compare similarities and differences among sets of letters, numbers, objects, pictures, or patterns. The things to be compared may be presented at the same time or one after the other. This ability also includes comparing a presented object with a remembered object.
Trunk Strength	The ability to use your abdominal and lower back muscles to support part of the body repeatedly or continuously over time without 'giving out' or fatiguing.
Auditory Attention	The ability to focus on a single source of sound in the presence of other distracting sounds.
Visualization	The ability to imagine how something will look after it is moved around or when its parts are moved or rearranged.
Finger Dexterity	The ability to make precisely coordinated movements of the fingers of one or both hands to grasp, manipulate, or assemble very small objects.
Visual Color Discrimination	The ability to match or detect differences between colors, including shades of color and brightness.
Hearing Sensitivity	The ability to detect or tell the differences between sounds that vary in pitch and loudness.
Depth Perception	The ability to judge which of several objects is closer or farther away from you, or to judge the distance between you and an object.
Sound Localization	The ability to tell the direction from which a sound originated.
Control Precision	The ability to quickly and repeatedly adjust the controls of a machine or a vehicle to exact positions.
Multilimb Coordination	The ability to coordinate two or more limbs (for example, two arms, two legs, or one leg and one arm) while sitting, standing, or lying down. It does not involve performing the activities while the whole body is in motion.
Dynamic Strength	The ability to exert muscle force repeatedly or continuously over time. This involves muscular endurance and resistance to muscle fatigue.
Explosive Strength	The ability to use short bursts of muscle force to propel oneself (as in jumping or sprinting), or to throw an object.
Static Strength	The ability to exert maximum muscle force to lift, push, pull, or carry objects.
Speed of Limb Movement	The ability to quickly move the arms and legs.
Wrist-Finger Speed	The ability to make fast, simple, repeated movements of the fingers, hands, and wrists.
Stamina	The ability to exert yourself physically over long periods of time without getting winded or out of breath.
Rate Control	The ability to time your movements or the movement of a piece of equipment in anticipation of changes in the speed and/or direction of a moving object or scene.
Response Orientation	The ability to choose quickly between two or more movements in response to two or more different signals (lights, sounds, pictures). It includes the speed with which the correct response is started with the hand, foot, or other body part.
Night Vision	The ability to see under low light conditions.
Dynamic Flexibility	The ability to quickly and repeatedly bend, stretch, twist, or reach out with your body, arms, and/or legs.
Manual Dexterity	The ability to quickly move your hand, your hand together with your arm, or your two hands to grasp, manipulate, or assemble objects.
Gross Body Equilibrium	The ability to keep or regain your body balance or stay upright when in an unstable position.
Glare Sensitivity	The ability to see objects in the presence of glare or bright lighting.
Peripheral Vision	The ability to see objects or movement of objects to one's side when the eyes are looking ahead.
Reaction Time	The ability to quickly respond (with the hand, finger, or foot) to a signal (sound, light, picture) when it appears.

Spatial Orientation	The ability to know your location in relation to the environment or to know where other objects are in relation to you.
Arm-Hand Steadiness	The ability to keep your hand and arm steady while moving your arm or while holding your arm and hand in one position.
Extent Flexibility	The ability to bend, stretch, twist, or reach with your body, arms, and/or legs.
Gross Body Coordination	The ability to coordinate the movement of your arms, legs, and torso together when the whole body is in motion.

Work_Activity	Work_Activity Definitions
Training and Teaching Others	Identifying the educational needs of others, developing formal educational or training programs or classes, and teaching or instructing others.
Updating and Using Relevant Knowledge	Keeping up-to-date technically and applying new knowledge to your job.
Interpreting the Meaning of Information for Others	Translating or explaining what information means and how it can be used.
Thinking Creatively	Developing, designing, or creating new applications, ideas, relationships, systems, or products, including artistic contributions.
Getting Information	Observing, receiving, and otherwise obtaining information from all relevant sources.
Interacting With Computers	Using computers and computer systems (including hardware and software) to program, write software, set up functions, enter data, or process information.
Analyzing Data or Information	Identifying the underlying principles, reasons, or facts of information by breaking down information or data into separate parts.
Organizing, Planning, and Prioritizing Work	Developing specific goals and plans to prioritize, organize, and accomplish your work.
Communicating with Supervisors, Peers, or Subordin	Providing information to supervisors, co-workers, and subordinates by telephone, in written form, e-mail, or in person.
Identifying Objects, Actions, and Events	Identifying information by categorizing, estimating, recognizing differences or similarities, and detecting changes in circumstances or events.
Processing Information	Compiling, coding, categorizing, calculating, tabulating, auditing, or verifying information or data.
Establishing and Maintaining Interpersonal Relatio	Developing constructive and cooperative working relationships with others, and maintaining them over time.
Coaching and Developing Others	Identifying the developmental needs of others and coaching, mentoring, or otherwise helping others to improve their knowledge or skills.
Judging the Qualities of Things, Services, or Peop	Assessing the value, importance, or quality of things or people.
Making Decisions and Solving Problems	Analyzing information and evaluating results to choose the best solution and solve problems.
Developing Objectives and Strategies	Establishing long-range objectives and specifying the strategies and actions to achieve them.
Documenting/Recording Information	Entering, transcribing, recording, storing, or maintaining information in written or electronic/magnetic form.
Provide Consultation and Advice to Others	Providing guidance and expert advice to management or other groups on technical, systems-, or process-related topics.
Guiding, Directing, and Motivating Subordinates	Providing guidance and direction to subordinates, including setting performance standards and monitoring performance.
Evaluating Information to Determine Compliance wit	Using relevant information and individual judgment to determine whether events or processes comply with laws, regulations, or standards.
Scheduling Work and Activities	Scheduling events, programs, and activities, as well as the work of others.
Performing for or Working Directly with the Public	Performing for people or dealing directly with the public. This includes serving customers in restaurants and stores, and receiving clients or guests.
Monitor Processes, Materials, or Surroundings	Monitoring and reviewing information from materials, events, or the environment, to detect or assess problems.
Communicating with Persons Outside Organization	Communicating with people outside the organization, representing the organization to customers, the public, government, and other external sources. This information can be exchanged in person, in writing, or by telephone or e-mail.
Estimating the Quantifiable Characteristics of Pro	Estimating sizes, distances, and quantities; or determining time, costs, resources, or materials needed to perform a work activity.
Resolving Conflicts and Negotiating with Others	Handling complaints, settling disputes, and resolving grievances and conflicts, or otherwise negotiating with others.

1419

Performing Administrative Activities	Performing day-to-day administrative tasks such as maintaining information files and processing paperwork.
Assisting and Caring for Others	Providing personal assistance, medical attention, emotional support, or other personal care to others such as coworkers, customers, or patients.
Coordinating the Work and Activities of Others	Getting members of a group to work together to accomplish tasks.
Developing and Building Teams	Encouraging and building mutual trust, respect, and cooperation among team members.
Staffing Organizational Units	Recruiting, interviewing, selecting, hiring, and promoting employees in an organization.
Selling or Influencing Others	Convincing others to buy merchandise/goods or to otherwise change their minds or actions.
Monitoring and Controlling Resources	Monitoring and controlling resources and overseeing the spending of money.
Inspecting Equipment, Structures, or Material	Inspecting equipment, structures, or materials to identify the cause of errors or other problems or defects.
Controlling Machines and Processes	Using either control mechanisms or direct physical activity to operate machines or processes (not including computers or vehicles).
Performing General Physical Activities	Performing physical activities that require considerable use of your arms and legs and moving your whole body, such as climbing, lifting, balancing, walking, stooping, and handling of materials.
Handling and Moving Objects	Using hands and arms in handling, installing, positioning, and moving materials, and manipulating things.
Repairing and Maintaining Electronic Equipment	Servicing, repairing, calibrating, regulating, fine-tuning, or testing machines, devices, and equipment that operate primarily on the basis of electrical or electronic (not mechanical) principles.
Operating Vehicles, Mechanized Devices, or Equipme	Running, maneuvering, navigating, or driving vehicles or mechanized equipment, such as forklifts, passenger vehicles, aircraft, or water craft.
Repairing and Maintaining Mechanical Equipment	Servicing, repairing, adjusting, and testing machines, devices, moving parts, and equipment that operate primarily on the basis of mechanical (not electronic) principles.
Drafting, Laying Out, and Specifying Technical Dev	Providing documentation, detailed instructions, drawings, or specifications to tell others about how devices, parts, equipment, or structures are to be fabricated, constructed, assembled, modified, maintained, or used.

Work_Context · Work_Context Definitions

Face-to-Face Discussions	How often do you have to have face-to-face discussions with individuals or teams in this job?
Electronic Mail	How often do you use electronic mail in this job?
Freedom to Make Decisions	How much decision making freedom, without supervision, does the job offer?
Telephone	How often do you have telephone conversations in this job?
Indoors, Environmentally Controlled	How often does this job require working indoors in environmentally controlled conditions?
Contact With Others	How much does this job require the worker to be in contact with others (face-to-face, by telephone, or otherwise) in order to perform it?
Structured versus Unstructured Work	To what extent is this job structured for the worker, rather than allowing the worker to determine tasks, priorities, and goals?
Public Speaking	How often do you have to perform public speaking in this job?
Coordinate or Lead Others	How important is it to coordinate or lead others in accomplishing work activities in this job?
Letters and Memos	How often does the job require written letters and memos?
Work With Work Group or Team	How important is it to work with others in a group or team in this job?
Importance of Being Exact or Accurate	How important is being very exact or highly accurate in performing this job?
Time Pressure	How often does this job require the worker to meet strict deadlines?
Frequency of Decision Making	How frequently is the worker required to make decisions that affect other people, the financial resources, and/or the image and reputation of the organization?
Deal With External Customers	How important is it to work with external customers or the public in this job?
Impact of Decisions on Co-workers or Company Resul	How do the decisions an employee makes impact the results of co-workers, clients or the company?
Spend Time Sitting	How much does this job require sitting?
Physical Proximity	To what extent does this job require the worker to perform job tasks in close physical proximity to other people?

Level of Competition	To what extent does this job require the worker to compete or to be aware of competitive pressures?
Frequency of Conflict Situations	How often are there conflict situations the employee has to face in this job?
Responsibility for Outcomes and Results	How responsible is the worker for work outcomes and results of other workers?
Spend Time Standing	How much does this job require standing?
Deal With Unpleasant or Angry People	How frequently does the worker have to deal with unpleasant, angry, or discourteous individuals as part of the job requirements?
Sounds, Noise Levels Are Distracting or Uncomforta	How often does this job require working exposed to sounds and noise levels that are distracting or uncomfortable?
Importance of Repeating Same Tasks	How important is repeating the same physical activities (e.g., key entry) or mental activities (e.g., checking entries in a ledger) over and over, without stopping, to performing this job?
Responsible for Others' Health and Safety	How much responsibility is there for the health and safety of others in this job?
Consequence of Error	How serious would the result usually be if the worker made a mistake that was not readily correctable?
Spend Time Using Your Hands to Handle, Control, or	How much does this job require using your hands to handle, control, or feel objects, tools or controls?
Spend Time Making Repetitive Motions	How much does this job require making repetitive motions?
Degree of Automation	How automated is the job?
Exposed to Contaminants	How often does this job require working exposed to contaminants (such as pollutants, gases, dust or odors)?
Exposed to Disease or Infections	How often does this job require exposure to disease/infections?
Spend Time Walking and Running	How much does this job require walking and running?
In an Enclosed Vehicle or Equipment	How often does this job require working in a closed vehicle or equipment (e.g., car)?
Deal With Physically Aggressive People	How frequently does this job require the worker to deal with physical aggression of violent individuals?
Indoors, Not Environmentally Controlled	How often does this job require working indoors in non-controlled environmental conditions (e.g., warehouse without heat)?
Very Hot or Cold Temperatures	How often does this job require working in very hot (above 90 F degrees) or very cold (below 32 F degrees) temperatures?
Extremely Bright or Inadequate Lighting	How often does this job require working in extremely bright or inadequate lighting conditions?
Spend Time Bending or Twisting the Body	How much does this job require bending or twisting your body?
Cramped Work Space, Awkward Positions	How often does this job require working in cramped work spaces that requires getting into awkward positions?
Spend Time Keeping or Regaining Balance	How much does this job require keeping or regaining your balance?
Exposed to Minor Burns, Cuts, Bites, or Stings	How often does this job require exposure to minor burns, cuts, bites, or stings?
Spend Time Kneeling, Crouching, Stooping, or Crawl	How much does this job require kneeling, crouching, stooping or crawling?
Pace Determined by Speed of Equipment	How important is it to this job that the pace is determined by the speed of equipment or machinery? (This does not refer to keeping busy at all times on this job.)
Exposed to Radiation	How often does this job require exposure to radiation?
Outdoors, Under Cover	How often does this job require working outdoors, under cover (e.g., structure with roof but no walls)?
Spend Time Climbing Ladders, Scaffolds, or Poles	How much does this job require climbing ladders, scaffolds, or poles?
Outdoors, Exposed to Weather	How often does this job require working outdoors, exposed to all weather conditions?
In an Open Vehicle or Equipment	How often does this job require working in an open vehicle or equipment (e.g., tractor)?
Exposed to High Places	How often does this job require exposure to high places?
Wear Common Protective or Safety Equipment such as	How much does this job require wearing common protective or safety equipment such as safety shoes, glasses, gloves, hard hats or life jackets?
Wear Specialized Protective or Safety Equipment su	How much does this job require wearing specialized protective or safety equipment such as breathing apparatus, safety harness, full protection suits, or radiation protection?
Exposed to Hazardous Equipment	How often does this job require exposure to hazardous equipment?
Exposed to Whole Body Vibration	How often does this job require exposure to whole body vibration (e.g., operate a jackhammer)?

Exposed to Hazardous Conditions	How often does this job require exposure to hazardous conditions?

Job Zone Component	Job Zone Component Definitions
Title	Job Zone Five: Extensive Preparation Needed
Overall Experience	Extensive skill, knowledge, and experience are needed for these occupations. Many require more than five years of experience. For example, surgeons must complete four years of college and an additional five to seven years of specialized medical training to be able to do their job.
Job Training	Employees may need some on-the-job training, but most of these occupations assume that the person will already have the required skills, knowledge, work-related experience, and/or training.
Job Zone Examples	These occupations often involve coordinating, training, supervising, or managing the activities of others to accomplish goals. Very advanced communication and organizational skills are required. Examples include athletic trainers, lawyers, managing editors, phyicists, social psychologists, and surgeons.
SVP Range	(8.0 and above)
Education	A bachelor's degree is the minimum formal education required for these occupations. However, many also require graduate school. For example, they may require a master's degree, and some require a Ph.D., M.D., or J.D. (law degree).

Work_Styles	Work_Styles Definitions
Dependability	Job requires being reliable, responsible, and dependable, and fulfilling obligations.
Analytical Thinking	Job requires analyzing information and using logic to address work-related issues and problems.
Independence	Job requires developing one's own ways of doing things, guiding oneself with little or no supervision, and depending on oneself to get things done.
Integrity	Job requires being honest and ethical.
Initiative	Job requires a willingness to take on responsibilities and challenges.
Achievement/Effort	Job requires establishing and maintaining personally challenging achievement goals and exerting effort toward mastering tasks.
Self Control	Job requires maintaining composure, keeping emotions in check, controlling anger, and avoiding aggressive behavior, even in very difficult situations.
Cooperation	Job requires being pleasant with others on the job and displaying a good-natured, cooperative attitude.
Attention to Detail	Job requires being careful about detail and thorough in completing work tasks.
Persistence	Job requires persistence in the face of obstacles.
Leadership	Job requires a willingness to lead, take charge, and offer opinions and direction.
Stress Tolerance	Job requires accepting criticism and dealing calmly and effectively with high stress situations.
Adaptability/Flexibility	Job requires being open to change (positive or negative) and to considerable variety in the workplace.
Concern for Others	Job requires being sensitive to others' needs and feelings and being understanding and helpful on the job.
Innovation	Job requires creativity and alternative thinking to develop new ideas for and answers to work-related problems.
Social Orientation	Job requires preferring to work with others rather than alone, and being personally connected with others on the job.

25-1071.00 - Health Specialties Teachers, Postsecondary

Teach courses in health specialties, such as veterinary medicine, dentistry, pharmacy, therapy, laboratory technology, and public health.

Tasks

1) Initiate, facilitate, and moderate classroom discussions.

2) Plan, evaluate, and revise curricula, course content, and course materials and methods of instruction.

3) Prepare course materials such as syllabi, homework assignments, and handouts.

4) Participate in campus and community events.

5) Evaluate and grade students' class work, assignments, and papers.

6) Compile, administer, and grade examinations, or assign this work to others.

7) Serve on academic or administrative committees that deal with institutional policies, departmental matters, and academic issues.

8) Conduct research in a particular field of knowledge, and publish findings in professional journals, books, and/or electronic media.

9) Prepare and deliver lectures to undergraduate and/or graduate students on topics such as public health, stress management, and worksite health promotion.

10) Maintain student attendance records, grades, and other required records.

11) Participate in student recruitment, registration, and placement activities.

12) Select and obtain materials and supplies such as textbooks and laboratory equipment.

13) Maintain regularly scheduled office hours in order to advise and assist students.

14) Supervise undergraduate and/or graduate teaching, internship, and research work.

15) Compile bibliographies of specialized materials for outside reading assignments.

16) Write grant proposals to procure external research funding.

17) Act as advisers to student organizations.

18) Provide professional consulting services to government and/or industry.

19) Supervise laboratory sessions.

20) Perform administrative duties such as serving as department head.

21) Keep abreast of developments in their field by reading current literature, talking with colleagues, and participating in professional conferences.

22) Collaborate with colleagues to address teaching and research issues.

Knowledge	Knowledge Definitions
Education and Training	Knowledge of principles and methods for curriculum and training design, teaching and instruction for individuals and groups, and the measurement of training effects.
Medicine and Dentistry	Knowledge of the information and techniques needed to diagnose and treat human injuries, diseases, and deformities. This includes symptoms, treatment alternatives, drug properties and interactions, and preventive health-care measures.
English Language	Knowledge of the structure and content of the English language including the meaning and spelling of words, rules of composition, and grammar.
Biology	Knowledge of plant and animal organisms, their tissues, cells, functions, interdependencies, and interactions with each other and the environment.
Psychology	Knowledge of human behavior and performance; individual differences in ability, personality, and interests; learning and motivation; psychological research methods; and the assessment and treatment of behavioral and affective disorders.
Mathematics	Knowledge of arithmetic, algebra, geometry, calculus, statistics, and their applications.
Customer and Personal Service	Knowledge of principles and processes for providing customer and personal services. This includes customer needs assessment, meeting quality standards for services, and evaluation of customer satisfaction.
Therapy and Counseling	Knowledge of principles, methods, and procedures for diagnosis, treatment, and rehabilitation of physical and mental dysfunctions, and for career counseling and guidance.
Computers and Electronics	Knowledge of circuit boards, processors, chips, electronic equipment, and computer hardware and software, including applications and programming.
Administration and Management	Knowledge of business and management principles involved in strategic planning, resource allocation, human resources modeling, leadership technique, production methods, and coordination of people and resources.
Sociology and Anthropology	Knowledge of group behavior and dynamics, societal trends and influences, human migrations, ethnicity, cultures and their history and origins.
Clerical	Knowledge of administrative and clerical procedures and systems such as word processing, managing files and records, stenography and transcription, designing forms, and other office procedures and terminology.

Chemistry	Knowledge of the chemical composition, structure, and properties of substances and of the chemical processes and transformations that they undergo. This includes uses of chemicals and their interactions, danger signs, production techniques, and disposal methods.
Communications and Media	Knowledge of media production, communication, and dissemination techniques and methods. This includes alternative ways to inform and entertain via written, oral, and visual media.
Public Safety and Security	Knowledge of relevant equipment, policies, procedures, and strategies to promote effective local, state, or national security operations for the protection of people, data, property, and institutions.
Law and Government	Knowledge of laws, legal codes, court procedures, precedents, government regulations, executive orders, agency rules, and the democratic political process.
Personnel and Human Resources	Knowledge of principles and procedures for personnel recruitment, selection, training, compensation and benefits, labor relations and negotiation, and personnel information systems.
Physics	Knowledge and prediction of physical principles, laws, their interrelationships, and applications to understanding fluid, material, and atmospheric dynamics, and mechanical, electrical, atomic and sub-atomic structures and processes.
Philosophy and Theology	Knowledge of different philosophical systems and religions. This includes their basic principles, values, ethics, ways of thinking, customs, practices, and their impact on human culture.
Sales and Marketing	Knowledge of principles and methods for showing, promoting, and selling products or services. This includes marketing strategy and tactics, product demonstration, sales techniques, and sales control systems.
Economics and Accounting	Knowledge of economic and accounting principles and practices, the financial markets, banking and the analysis and reporting of financial data.
Geography	Knowledge of principles and methods for describing the features of land, sea, and air masses, including their physical characteristics, locations, interrelationships, and distribution of plant, animal, and human life.
Engineering and Technology	Knowledge of the practical application of engineering science and technology. This includes applying principles, techniques, procedures, and equipment to the design and production of various goods and services.
History and Archeology	Knowledge of historical events and their causes, indicators, and effects on civilizations and cultures.
Mechanical	Knowledge of machines and tools, including their designs, uses, repair, and maintenance.
Telecommunications	Knowledge of transmission, broadcasting, switching, control, and operation of telecommunications systems.
Design	Knowledge of design techniques, tools, and principles involved in production of precision technical plans, blueprints, drawings, and models.
Transportation	Knowledge of principles and methods for moving people or goods by air, rail, sea, or road, including the relative costs and benefits.
Foreign Language	Knowledge of the structure and content of a foreign (non-English) language including the meaning and spelling of words, rules of composition and grammar, and pronunciation.
Production and Processing	Knowledge of raw materials, production processes, quality control, costs, and other techniques for maximizing the effective manufacture and distribution of goods.
Food Production	Knowledge of techniques and equipment for planting, growing, and harvesting food products (both plant and animal) for consumption, including storage/handling techniques.
Building and Construction	Knowledge of materials, methods, and the tools involved in the construction or repair of houses, buildings, or other structures such as highways and roads.
Fine Arts	Knowledge of the theory and techniques required to compose, produce, and perform works of music, dance, visual arts, drama, and sculpture.

Skills	Skills Definitions
Reading Comprehension	Understanding written sentences and paragraphs in work related documents.
Science	Using scientific rules and methods to solve problems.
Writing	Communicating effectively in writing as appropriate for the needs of the audience.

Instructing	Teaching others how to do something.
Critical Thinking	Using logic and reasoning to identify the strengths and weaknesses of alternative solutions, conclusions or approaches to problems.
Speaking	Talking to others to convey information effectively.
Active Learning	Understanding the implications of new information for both current and future problem-solving and decision-making.
Learning Strategies	Selecting and using training/instructional methods and procedures appropriate for the situation when learning or teaching new things.
Time Management	Managing one's own time and the time of others.
Complex Problem Solving	Identifying complex problems and reviewing related information to develop and evaluate options and implement solutions.
Active Listening	Giving full attention to what other people are saying, taking time to understand the points being made, asking questions as appropriate, and not interrupting at inappropriate times.
Monitoring	Monitoring/Assessing performance of yourself, other individuals, or organizations to make improvements or take corrective action.
Judgment and Decision Making	Considering the relative costs and benefits of potential actions to choose the most appropriate one.
Coordination	Adjusting actions in relation to others' actions.
Social Perceptiveness	Being aware of others' reactions and understanding why they react as they do.
Persuasion	Persuading others to change their minds or behavior.
Mathematics	Using mathematics to solve problems.
Equipment Selection	Determining the kind of tools and equipment needed to do a job.
Service Orientation	Actively looking for ways to help people.
Management of Personnel Resources	Motivating, developing, and directing people as they work, identifying the best people for the job.
Negotiation	Bringing others together and trying to reconcile differences.
Quality Control Analysis	Conducting tests and inspections of products, services, or processes to evaluate quality or performance.
Operations Analysis	Analyzing needs and product requirements to create a design.
Management of Material Resources	Obtaining and seeing to the appropriate use of equipment, facilities, and materials needed to do certain work.
Management of Financial Resources	Determining how money will be spent to get the work done, and accounting for these expenditures.
Systems Evaluation	Identifying measures or indicators of system performance and the actions needed to improve or correct performance, relative to the goals of the system.
Technology Design	Generating or adapting equipment and technology to serve user needs.
Troubleshooting	Determining causes of operating errors and deciding what to do about it.
Operation Monitoring	Watching gauges, dials, or other indicators to make sure a machine is working properly.
Systems Analysis	Determining how a system should work and how changes in conditions, operations, and the environment will affect outcomes.
Operation and Control	Controlling operations of equipment or systems.
Programming	Writing computer programs for various purposes.
Equipment Maintenance	Performing routine maintenance on equipment and determining when and what kind of maintenance is needed.
Installation	Installing equipment, machines, wiring, or programs to meet specifications.
Repairing	Repairing machines or systems using the needed tools.

Ability	Ability Definitions
Oral Expression	The ability to communicate information and ideas in speaking so others will understand.
Written Comprehension	The ability to read and understand information and ideas presented in writing.
Oral Comprehension	The ability to listen to and understand information and ideas presented through spoken words and sentences.
Written Expression	The ability to communicate information and ideas in writing so others will understand.
Speech Clarity	The ability to speak clearly so others can understand you.
Deductive Reasoning	The ability to apply general rules to specific problems to produce answers that make sense.
Inductive Reasoning	The ability to combine pieces of information to form general rules or conclusions (includes finding a relationship among seemingly unrelated events).
Near Vision	The ability to see details at close range (within a few feet of the observer).

Problem Sensitivity	The ability to tell when something is wrong or is likely to go wrong. It does not involve solving the problem, only recognizing there is a problem.
Information Ordering	The ability to arrange things or actions in a certain order or pattern according to a specific rule or set of rules (e.g., patterns of numbers, letters, words, pictures, mathematical operations).
Speech Recognition	The ability to identify and understand the speech of another person.
Selective Attention	The ability to concentrate on a task over a period of time without being distracted.
Originality	The ability to come up with unusual or clever ideas about a given topic or situation, or to develop creative ways to solve a problem.
Category Flexibility	The ability to generate or use different sets of rules for combining or grouping things in different ways.
Fluency of Ideas	The ability to come up with a number of ideas about a topic (the number of ideas is important, not their quality, correctness, or creativity).
Time Sharing	The ability to shift back and forth between two or more activities or sources of information (such as speech, sounds, touch, or other sources).
Flexibility of Closure	The ability to identify or detect a known pattern (a figure, object, word, or sound) that is hidden in other distracting material.
Speed of Closure	The ability to quickly make sense of, combine, and organize information into meaningful patterns.
Mathematical Reasoning	The ability to choose the right mathematical methods or formulas to solve a problem.
Memorization	The ability to remember information such as words, numbers, pictures, and procedures.
Far Vision	The ability to see details at a distance.
Number Facility	The ability to add, subtract, multiply, or divide quickly and correctly.
Visualization	The ability to imagine how something will look after it is moved around or when its parts are moved or rearranged.
Perceptual Speed	The ability to quickly and accurately compare similarities and differences among sets of letters, numbers, objects, pictures, or patterns. The things to be compared may be presented at the same time or one after the other. This ability also includes comparing a presented object with a remembered object.
Auditory Attention	The ability to focus on a single source of sound in the presence of other distracting sounds.
Visual Color Discrimination	The ability to match or detect differences between colors, including shades of color and brightness.
Hearing Sensitivity	The ability to detect or tell the differences between sounds that vary in pitch and loudness.
Finger Dexterity	The ability to make precisely coordinated movements of the fingers of one or both hands to grasp, manipulate, or assemble very small objects.
Trunk Strength	The ability to use your abdominal and lower back muscles to support part of the body repeatedly or continuously over time without 'giving out' or fatiguing.
Depth Perception	The ability to judge which of several objects is closer or farther away from you, or to judge the distance between you and an object.
Response Orientation	The ability to choose quickly between two or more movements in response to two or more different signals (lights, sounds, pictures). It includes the speed with which the correct response is started with the hand, foot, or other body part.
Dynamic Flexibility	The ability to quickly and repeatedly bend, stretch, twist, or reach out with your body, arms, and/or legs.
Arm-Hand Steadiness	The ability to keep your hand and arm steady while moving your arm or while holding your arm and hand in one position.
Spatial Orientation	The ability to know your location in relation to the environment or to know where other objects are in relation to you.
Static Strength	The ability to exert maximum muscle force to lift, push, pull, or carry objects.
Explosive Strength	The ability to use short bursts of muscle force to propel oneself (as in jumping or sprinting), or to throw an object.
Dynamic Strength	The ability to exert muscle force repeatedly or continuously over time. This involves muscular endurance and resistance to muscle fatigue.
Multilimb Coordination	The ability to coordinate two or more limbs (for example, two arms, two legs, or one leg and one arm) while sitting, standing, or lying down. It does not involve performing the activities while the whole body is in motion.
Extent Flexibility	The ability to bend, stretch, twist, or reach with your body, arms, and/or legs.

Gross Body Equilibrium	The ability to keep or regain your body balance or stay upright when in an unstable position.
Stamina	The ability to exert yourself physically over long periods of time without getting winded or out of breath.
Control Precision	The ability to quickly and repeatedly adjust the controls of a machine or a vehicle to exact positions.
Manual Dexterity	The ability to quickly move your hand, your hand together with your arm, or your two hands to grasp, manipulate, or assemble objects.
Speed of Limb Movement	The ability to quickly move the arms and legs.
Glare Sensitivity	The ability to see objects in the presence of glare or bright lighting.
Rate Control	The ability to time your movements or the movement of a piece of equipment in anticipation of changes in the speed and/or direction of a moving object or scene.
Reaction Time	The ability to quickly respond (with the hand, finger, or foot) to a signal (sound, light, picture) when it appears.
Gross Body Coordination	The ability to coordinate the movement of your arms, legs, and torso together when the whole body is in motion.
Night Vision	The ability to see under low light conditions.
Peripheral Vision	The ability to see objects or movement of objects to one's side when the eyes are looking ahead.
Sound Localization	The ability to tell the direction from which a sound originated.
Wrist-Finger Speed	The ability to make fast, simple, repeated movements of the fingers, hands, and wrists.

Work_Activity	Work_Activity Definitions
Training and Teaching Others	Identifying the educational needs of others, developing formal educational or training programs or classes, and teaching or instructing others.
Updating and Using Relevant Knowledge	Keeping up-to-date technically and applying new knowledge to your job.
Getting Information	Observing, receiving, and otherwise obtaining information from all relevant sources.
Making Decisions and Solving Problems	Analyzing information and evaluating results to choose the best solution and solve problems.
Communicating with Supervisors, Peers, or Subordin	Providing information to supervisors, co-workers, and subordinates by telephone, in written form, e-mail, or in person.
Identifying Objects, Actions, and Events	Identifying information by categorizing, estimating, recognizing differences or similarities, and detecting changes in circumstances or events.
Interpreting the Meaning of Information for Others	Translating or explaining what information means and how it can be used.
Establishing and Maintaining Interpersonal Relatio	Developing constructive and cooperative working relationships with others, and maintaining them over time.
Processing Information	Compiling, coding, categorizing, calculating, tabulating, auditing, or verifying information or data.
Analyzing Data or Information	Identifying the underlying principles, reasons, or facts of information by breaking down information or data into separate parts.
Interacting With Computers	Using computers and computer systems (including hardware and software) to program, write software, set up functions, enter data, or process information.
Coaching and Developing Others	Identifying the developmental needs of others and coaching, mentoring, or otherwise helping others to improve their knowledge or skills.
Assisting and Caring for Others	Providing personal assistance, medical attention, emotional support, or other personal care to others such as coworkers, customers, or patients.
Organizing, Planning, and Prioritizing Work	Developing specific goals and plans to prioritize, organize, and accomplish your work.
Judging the Qualities of Things, Services, or Peop	Assessing the value, importance, or quality of things or people.
Thinking Creatively	Developing, designing, or creating new applications, ideas, relationships, systems, or products, including artistic contributions.
Communicating with Persons Outside Organization	Communicating with people outside the organization, representing the organization to customers, the public, government, and other external sources. This information can be exchanged in person, in writing, or by telephone or e-mail.
Documenting/Recording Information	Entering, transcribing, recording, storing, or maintaining information in written or electronic/magnetic form.
Evaluating Information to Determine Compliance wit	Using relevant information and individual judgment to determine whether events or processes comply with laws, regulations, or standards.

Monitor Processes, Materials, or Surroundings	Monitoring and reviewing information from materials, events, or the environment, to detect or assess problems.
Developing Objectives and Strategies	Establishing long-range objectives and specifying the strategies and actions to achieve them.
Provide Consultation and Advice to Others	Providing guidance and expert advice to management or other groups on technical, systems-, or process-related topics.
Coordinating the Work and Activities of Others	Getting members of a group to work together to accomplish tasks.
Scheduling Work and Activities	Scheduling events, programs, and activities, as well as the work of others.
Guiding, Directing, and Motivating Subordinates	Providing guidance and direction to subordinates, including setting performance standards and monitoring performance.
Estimating the Quantifiable Characteristics of Pro	Estimating sizes, distances, and quantities; or determining time, costs, resources, or materials needed to perform a work activity.
Developing and Building Teams	Encouraging and building mutual trust, respect, and cooperation among team members.
Performing for or Working Directly with the Public	Performing for people or dealing directly with the public. This includes serving customers in restaurants and stores, and receiving clients or guests.
Resolving Conflicts and Negotiating with Others	Handling complaints, settling disputes, and resolving grievances and conflicts, or otherwise negotiating with others.
Inspecting Equipment, Structures, or Material	Inspecting equipment, structures, or materials to identify the cause of errors or other problems or defects.
Performing Administrative Activities	Performing day-to-day administrative tasks such as maintaining information files and processing paperwork.
Handling and Moving Objects	Using hands and arms in handling, installing, positioning, and moving materials, and manipulating things.
Monitoring and Controlling Resources	Monitoring and controlling resources and overseeing the spending of money.
Performing General Physical Activities	Performing physical activities that require considerable use of your arms and legs and moving your whole body, such as climbing, lifting, balancing, walking, stooping, and handling of materials.
Selling or Influencing Others	Convincing others to buy merchandise/goods or to otherwise change their minds or actions.
Controlling Machines and Processes	Using either control mechanisms or direct physical activity to operate machines or processes (not including computers or vehicles).
Staffing Organizational Units	Recruiting, interviewing, selecting, hiring, and promoting employees in an organization.
Operating Vehicles, Mechanized Devices, or Equipme	Running, maneuvering, navigating, or driving vehicles or mechanized equipment, such as forklifts, passenger vehicles, aircraft, or water craft.
Repairing and Maintaining Electronic Equipment	Servicing, repairing, calibrating, regulating, fine-tuning, or testing machines, devices, and equipment that operate primarily on the basis of electrical or electronic (not mechanical) principles.
Drafting, Laying Out, and Specifying Technical Dev	Providing documentation, detailed instructions, drawings, or specifications to tell others about how devices, parts, equipment, or structures are to be fabricated, constructed, assembled, modified, maintained, or used.
Repairing and Maintaining Mechanical Equipment	Servicing, repairing, adjusting, and testing machines, devices, moving parts, and equipment that operate primarily on the basis of mechanical (not electronic) principles.

Work_Context	Work_Context Definitions
Electronic Mail	How often do you use electronic mail in this job?
Structured versus Unstructured Work	To what extent is this job structured for the worker, rather than allowing the worker to determine tasks, priorities, and goals?
Indoors, Environmentally Controlled	How often does this job require working indoors in environmentally controlled conditions?
Telephone	How often do you have telephone conversations in this job?
Face-to-Face Discussions	How often do you have to have face-to-face discussions with individuals or teams in this job?
Freedom to Make Decisions	How much decision making freedom, without supervision, does the job offer?
Contact With Others	How often does this job require the worker to be in contact with others (face-to-face, by telephone, or otherwise) in order to perform it?
Work With Work Group or Team	How important is it to work with others in a group or team in this job?
Impact of Decisions on Co-workers or Company Resul	How do the decisions an employee makes impact the results of co-workers, clients or the company?

Importance of Being Exact or Accurate	How important is being very exact or highly accurate in performing this job?
Frequency of Decision Making	How frequently is the worker required to make decisions that affect other people, the financial resources, and/or the image and reputation of the organization?
Letters and Memos	How often does the job require written letters and memos?
Public Speaking	How often do you have to perform public speaking in this job?
Deal With External Customers	How important is it to work with external customers or the public in this job?
Spend Time Sitting	How much does this job require sitting?
Coordinate or Lead Others	How important is it to coordinate or lead others in accomplishing work activities in this job?
Time Pressure	How often does this job require the worker to meet strict deadlines?
Responsibility for Outcomes and Results	How responsible is the worker for work outcomes and results of other workers?
Frequency of Conflict Situations	How often are there conflict situations the employee has to face in this job?
Responsible for Others' Health and Safety	How much responsibility is there for the health and safety of others in this job?
Level of Competition	To what extent does this job require the worker to compete or to be aware of competitive pressures?
Physical Proximity	To what extent does this job require the worker to perform job tasks in close physical proximity to other people?
Deal With Unpleasant or Angry People	How frequently does the worker have to deal with unpleasant, angry, or discourteous individuals as part of the job requirements?
Spend Time Standing	How much does this job require standing?
Exposed to Disease or Infections	How often does this job require exposure to disease/infections?
Spend Time Making Repetitive Motions	How much does this job require making repetitive motions?
Importance of Repeating Same Tasks	How important is repeating the same physical activities (e.g., key entry) or mental activities (e.g., checking entries in a ledger) over and over, without stopping, to performing this job?
Spend Time Using Your Hands to Handle, Control, or	How much does this job require using your hands to handle, control, or feel objects, tools or controls?
Sounds, Noise Levels Are Distracting or Uncomforta	How often does this job require working exposed to sounds and noise levels that are distracting or uncomfortable?
Exposed to Contaminants	How often does this job require working exposed to contaminants (such as pollutants, gases, dust or odors)?
Consequence of Error	How serious would the result usually be if the worker made a mistake that was not readily correctable?
Spend Time Walking and Running	How much does this job require walking and running?
Exposed to Hazardous Conditions	How often does this job require exposure to hazardous conditions?
In an Enclosed Vehicle or Equipment	How often does this job require working in a closed vehicle or equipment (e.g., car)?
Wear Common Protective or Safety Equipment such as	How much does this job require wearing common protective or safety equipment such as safety shoes, glasses, gloves, hard hats or live jackets?
Degree of Automation	How automated is the job?
Cramped Work Space, Awkward Positions	How often does this job require working in cramped work spaces that requires getting into awkward positions?
Indoors, Not Environmentally Controlled	How often does this job require working indoors in non-controlled environmental conditions (e.g., warehouse without heat)?
Exposed to Minor Burns, Cuts, Bites, or Stings	How often does this job require exposure to minor burns, cuts, bites, or stings?
Spend Time Bending or Twisting the Body	How much does this job require bending or twisting your body?
Very Hot or Cold Temperatures	How often does this job require working in very hot (above 90 F degrees) or very cold (below 32 F degrees) temperatures?
Deal With Physically Aggressive People	How frequently does this job require the worker to deal with physical aggression of violent individuals?
Wear Specialized Protective or Safety Equipment su	How much does this job require wearing specialized protective or safety equipment such as breathing apparatus, safety harness, full protection suits, or radiation protection?
Exposed to Radiation	How often does this job require exposure to radiation?
Extremely Bright or Inadequate Lighting	How often does this job require working in extremely bright or inadequate lighting conditions?
Outdoors, Exposed to Weather	How often does this job require working outdoors, exposed to all weather conditions?
Spend Time Kneeling, Crouching, Stooping, or Crawl	How much does this job require kneeling, crouching, stooping or crawling?

Exposed to Hazardous Equipment	How often does this job require exposure to hazardous equipment?
Spend Time Keeping or Regaining Balance	How much does this job require keeping or regaining your balance?
In an Open Vehicle or Equipment	How often does this job require working in an open vehicle or equipment (e.g., tractor)?
Spend Time Climbing Ladders, Scaffolds, or Poles	How much does this job require climbing ladders, scaffolds, or poles?
Outdoors, Under Cover	How often does this job require working outdoors, under cover (e.g., structure with roof but no walls)?
Exposed to High Places	How often does this job require exposure to high places?
Exposed to Whole Body Vibration	How often does this job require exposure to whole body vibration (e.g., operate a jackhammer)?
Pace Determined by Speed of Equipment	How important is it to this job that the pace is determined by the speed of equipment or machinery? (This does not refer to keeping busy at all times on this job.)

Job Zone Component	Job Zone Component Definitions
Title	Job Zone Five: Extensive Preparation Needed
Overall Experience	Extensive skill, knowledge, and experience are needed for these occupations. Many require more than five years of experience. For example, surgeons must complete four years of college and an additional five to seven years of specialized medical training to be able to do their job.
Job Training	Employees may need some on-the-job training, but most of these occupations assume that the person will already have the required skills, knowledge, work-related experience, and/or training.
Job Zone Examples	These occupations often involve coordinating, training, supervising, or managing the activities of others to accomplish goals. Very advanced communication and organizational skills are required. Examples include athletic trainers, lawyers, managing editors, physicists, social psychologists, and surgeons.
SVP Range	(8.0 and above)
Education	A bachelor's degree is the minimum formal education required for these occupations. However, many also require graduate school. For example, they may require a master's degree, and some require a Ph.D., M.D., or J.D. (law degree).

Work_Styles	Work_Styles Definitions
Dependability	Job requires being reliable, responsible, and dependable, and fulfilling obligations.
Initiative	Job requires a willingness to take on responsibilities and challenges.
Integrity	Job requires being honest and ethical.
Analytical Thinking	Job requires analyzing information and using logic to address work-related issues and problems.
Independence	Job requires developing one's own ways of doing things, guiding oneself with little or no supervision, and depending on oneself to get things done.
Stress Tolerance	Job requires accepting criticism and dealing calmly and effectively with high stress situations.
Achievement/Effort	Job requires establishing and maintaining personally challenging achievement goals and exerting effort toward mastering tasks.
Self Control	Job requires maintaining composure, keeping emotions in check, controlling anger, and avoiding aggressive behavior, even in very difficult situations.
Persistence	Job requires persistence in the face of obstacles.
Attention to Detail	Job requires being careful about detail and thorough in completing work tasks.
Concern for Others	Job requires being sensitive to others' needs and feelings and being understanding and helpful on the job.
Adaptability/Flexibility	Job requires being open to change (positive or negative) and to considerable variety in the workplace.
Cooperation	Job requires being pleasant with others on the job and displaying a good-natured, cooperative attitude.
Leadership	Job requires a willingness to lead, take charge, and offer opinions and direction.
Innovation	Job requires creativity and alternative thinking to develop new ideas for and answers to work-related problems.
Social Orientation	Job requires preferring to work with others rather than alone, and being personally connected with others on the job.

25-1072.00 - Nursing Instructors and Teachers, Postsecondary

Demonstrate and teach patient care in classroom and clinical units to nursing students. Includes both teachers primarily engaged in teaching and those who do a combination of both teaching and research.

Tasks

1) Advise students on academic and vocational curricula, and on career issues.

2) Maintain student attendance records, grades, and other required records.

3) Prepare course materials such as syllabi, homework assignments, and handouts.

4) Participate in campus and community events.

5) Assess clinical education needs, and patient and client teaching needs, utilizing a variety of methods.

6) Compile, administer, and grade examinations, or assign this work to others.

7) Compile bibliographies of specialized materials for outside reading assignments.

8) Select and obtain materials and supplies such as textbooks and laboratory equipment.

9) Maintain regularly scheduled office hours in order to advise and assist students.

10) Serve on academic or administrative committees that deal with institutional policies, departmental matters, and academic issues.

11) Prepare and deliver lectures to undergraduate and/or graduate students on topics such as pharmacology, mental health nursing, and community health care practices.

12) Participate in student recruitment, registration, and placement activities.

13) Supervise students' laboratory and clinical work.

14) Supervise undergraduate and/or graduate teaching, internship, and research work.

15) Conduct research in a particular field of knowledge, and publish findings in professional journals, books, and/or electronic media.

16) Write grant proposals to procure external research funding.

17) Act as advisers to student organizations.

18) Coordinate training programs with area universities, clinics, hospitals, health agencies, and/or vocational schools.

19) Demonstrate patient care in clinical units of hospitals.

20) Provide professional consulting services to government and/or industry.

21) Perform administrative duties such as serving as department head.

22) Evaluate and grade students' class work, laboratory and clinic work, assignments, and papers.

23) Keep abreast of developments in their field by reading current literature, talking with colleagues, and participating in professional conferences.

24) Plan, evaluate, and revise curricula, course content, and course materials and methods of instruction.

25) Collaborate with colleagues to address teaching and research issues.

Knowledge	Knowledge Definitions
Education and Training	Knowledge of principles and methods for curriculum and training design, teaching and instruction for individuals and groups, and the measurement of training effects.
English Language	Knowledge of the structure and content of the English language including the meaning and spelling of words, rules of composition, and grammar.
Medicine and Dentistry	Knowledge of the information and techniques needed to diagnose and treat human injuries, diseases, and deformities. This includes symptoms, treatment alternatives, drug properties and interactions, and preventive health-care measures.
Psychology	Knowledge of human behavior and performance; individual differences in ability, personality, and interests; learning and motivation; psychological research methods; and the assessment and treatment of behavioral and affective disorders.
Biology	Knowledge of plant and animal organisms, their tissues, cells, functions, interdependencies, and interactions with each other and the environment.
Sociology and Anthropology	Knowledge of group behavior and dynamics, societal trends and influences, human migrations, ethnicity, cultures and their history and origins.

Therapy and Counseling	Knowledge of principles, methods, and procedures for diagnosis, treatment, and rehabilitation of physical and mental dysfunctions, and for career counseling and guidance.
Customer and Personal Service	Knowledge of principles and processes for providing customer and personal services. This includes customer needs assessment, meeting quality standards for services, and evaluation of customer satisfaction.
Mathematics	Knowledge of arithmetic, algebra, geometry, calculus, statistics, and their applications.
Public Safety and Security	Knowledge of relevant equipment, policies, procedures, and strategies to promote effective local, state, or national security operations for the protection of people, data, property, and institutions.
Administration and Management	Knowledge of business and management principles involved in strategic planning, resource allocation, human resources modeling, leadership technique, production methods, and coordination of people and resources.
Computers and Electronics	Knowledge of circuit boards, processors, chips, electronic equipment, and computer hardware and software, including applications and programming.
Law and Government	Knowledge of laws, legal codes, court procedures, precedents, government regulations, executive orders, agency rules, and the democratic political process.
Philosophy and Theology	Knowledge of different philosophical systems and religions. This includes their basic principles, values, ethics, ways of thinking, customs, practices, and their impact on human culture.
Personnel and Human Resources	Knowledge of principles and procedures for personnel recruitment, selection, training, compensation and benefits, labor relations and negotiation, and personnel information systems.
Clerical	Knowledge of administrative and clerical procedures and systems such as word processing, managing files and records, stenography and transcription, designing forms, and other office procedures and terminology.
Communications and Media	Knowledge of media production, communication, and dissemination techniques and methods. This includes alternative ways to inform and entertain via written, oral, and visual media.
Chemistry	Knowledge of the chemical composition, structure, and properties of substances and of the chemical processes and transformations that they undergo. This includes uses of chemicals and their interactions, danger signs, production techniques, and disposal methods.
Sales and Marketing	Knowledge of principles and methods for showing, promoting, and selling products or services. This includes marketing strategy and tactics, product demonstration, sales techniques, and sales control systems.
History and Archeology	Knowledge of historical events and their causes, indicators, and effects on civilizations and cultures.
Telecommunications	Knowledge of transmission, broadcasting, switching, control, and operation of telecommunications systems.
Physics	Knowledge and prediction of physical principles, laws, their interrelationships, and applications to understanding fluid, material, and atmospheric dynamics, and mechanical, electrical, atomic and sub-atomic structures and processes.
Economics and Accounting	Knowledge of economic and accounting principles and practices, the financial markets, banking and the analysis and reporting of financial data.
Geography	Knowledge of principles and methods for describing the features of land, sea, and air masses, including their physical characteristics, locations, interrelationships, and distribution of plant, animal, and human life.
Engineering and Technology	Knowledge of the practical application of engineering science and technology. This includes applying principles, techniques, procedures, and equipment to the design and production of various goods and services.
Foreign Language	Knowledge of the structure and content of a foreign (non-English) language including the meaning and spelling of words, rules of composition and grammar, and pronunciation.
Mechanical	Knowledge of machines and tools, including their designs, uses, repair, and maintenance.
Production and Processing	Knowledge of raw materials, production processes, quality control, costs, and other techniques for maximizing the effective manufacture and distribution of goods.
Transportation	Knowledge of principles and methods for moving people or goods by air, rail, sea, or road, including the relative costs and benefits.

Fine Arts	Knowledge of the theory and techniques required to compose, produce, and perform works of music, dance, visual arts, drama, and sculpture.
Design	Knowledge of design techniques, tools, and principles involved in production of precision technical plans, blueprints, drawings, and models.
Food Production	Knowledge of techniques and equipment for planting, growing, and harvesting food products (both plant and animal) for consumption, including storage/handling techniques.
Building and Construction	Knowledge of materials, methods, and the tools involved in the construction or repair of houses, buildings, or other structures such as highways and roads.

Skills	Skills Definitions
Reading Comprehension	Understanding written sentences and paragraphs in work related documents.
Instructing	Teaching others how to do something.
Speaking	Talking to others to convey information effectively.
Active Listening	Giving full attention to what other people are saying, taking time to understand the points being made, asking questions as appropriate, and not interrupting at inappropriate times.
Writing	Communicating effectively in writing as appropriate for the needs of the audience.
Critical Thinking	Using logic and reasoning to identify the strengths and weaknesses of alternative solutions, conclusions or approaches to problems.
Science	Using scientific rules and methods to solve problems.
Active Learning	Understanding the implications of new information for both current and future problem-solving and decision-making.
Learning Strategies	Selecting and using training/instructional methods and procedures appropriate for the situation when learning or teaching new things.
Time Management	Managing one's own time and the time of others.
Monitoring	Monitoring/Assessing performance of yourself, other individuals, or organizations to make improvements or take corrective action.
Complex Problem Solving	Identifying complex problems and reviewing related information to develop and evaluate options and implement solutions.
Social Perceptiveness	Being aware of others' reactions and understanding why they react as they do.
Service Orientation	Actively looking for ways to help people.
Judgment and Decision Making	Considering the relative costs and benefits of potential actions to choose the most appropriate one.
Coordination	Adjusting actions in relation to others' actions.
Persuasion	Persuading others to change their minds or behavior.
Negotiation	Bringing others together and trying to reconcile differences.
Mathematics	Using mathematics to solve problems.
Management of Personnel Resources	Motivating, developing, and directing people as they work, identifying the best people for the job.
Management of Financial Resources	Determining how money will be spent to get the work done, and accounting for these expenditures.
Systems Analysis	Determining how a system should work and how changes in conditions, operations, and the environment will affect outcomes.
Quality Control Analysis	Conducting tests and inspections of products, services, or processes to evaluate quality or performance.
Management of Material Resources	Obtaining and seeing to the appropriate use of equipment, facilities, and materials needed to do certain work.
Systems Evaluation	Identifying measures or indicators of system performance and the actions needed to improve or correct performance, relative to the goals of the system.
Operations Analysis	Analyzing needs and product requirements to create a design.
Equipment Selection	Determining the kind of tools and equipment needed to do a job.
Troubleshooting	Determining causes of operating errors and deciding what to do about it.
Technology Design	Generating or adapting equipment and technology to serve user needs.
Operation Monitoring	Watching gauges, dials, or other indicators to make sure a machine is working properly.
Operation and Control	Controlling operations of equipment or systems.
Equipment Maintenance	Performing routine maintenance on equipment and determining when and what kind of maintenance is needed.
Programming	Writing computer programs for various purposes.
Installation	Installing equipment, machines, wiring, or programs to meet specifications.

Repairing	Repairing machines or systems using the needed tools.

Ability	Ability Definitions
Oral Expression	The ability to communicate information and ideas in speaking so others will understand.
Speech Clarity	The ability to speak clearly so others can understand you.
Oral Comprehension	The ability to listen to and understand information and ideas presented through spoken words and sentences.
Written Comprehension	The ability to read and understand information and ideas presented in writing.
Written Expression	The ability to communicate information and ideas in writing so others will understand.
Inductive Reasoning	The ability to combine pieces of information to form general rules or conclusions (includes finding a relationship among seemingly unrelated events).
Deductive Reasoning	The ability to apply general rules to specific problems to produce answers that make sense.
Problem Sensitivity	The ability to tell when something is wrong or is likely to go wrong. It does not involve solving the problem, only recognizing there is a problem.
Near Vision	The ability to see details at close range (within a few feet of the observer).
Information Ordering	The ability to arrange things or actions in a certain order or pattern according to a specific rule or set of rules (e.g., patterns of numbers, letters, words, pictures, mathematical operations).
Speech Recognition	The ability to identify and understand the speech of another person.
Selective Attention	The ability to concentrate on a task over a period of time without being distracted.
Originality	The ability to come up with unusual or clever ideas about a given topic or situation, or to develop creative ways to solve a problem.
Category Flexibility	The ability to generate or use different sets of rules for combining or grouping things in different ways.
Fluency of Ideas	The ability to come up with a number of ideas about a topic (the number of ideas is important, not their quality, correctness, or creativity).
Time Sharing	The ability to shift back and forth between two or more activities or sources of information (such as speech, sounds, touch, or other sources).
Far Vision	The ability to see details at a distance.
Flexibility of Closure	The ability to identify or detect a known pattern (a figure, object, word, or sound) that is hidden in other distracting material.
Mathematical Reasoning	The ability to choose the right mathematical methods or formulas to solve a problem.
Memorization	The ability to remember information such as words, numbers, pictures, and procedures.
Speed of Closure	The ability to quickly make sense of, combine, and organize information into meaningful patterns
Perceptual Speed	The ability to quickly and accurately compare similarities and differences among sets of letters, numbers, objects, pictures, or patterns. The things to be compared may be presented at the same time or one after the other. This ability also includes comparing a presented object with a remembered object.
Number Facility	The ability to add, subtract, multiply, or divide quickly and correctly.
Visual Color Discrimination	The ability to match or detect differences between colors, including shades of color and brightness.
Visualization	The ability to imagine how something will look after it is moved around or when its parts are moved or rearranged.
Trunk Strength	The ability to use your abdominal and lower back muscles to support part of the body repeatedly or continuously over time without 'giving out' or fatiguing.
Arm-Hand Steadiness	The ability to keep your hand and arm steady while moving your arm or while holding your arm and hand in one position.
Finger Dexterity	The ability to make precisely coordinated movements of the fingers of one or both hands to grasp, manipulate, or assemble very small objects.
Control Precision	The ability to quickly and repeatedly adjust the controls of a machine or a vehicle to exact positions.
Auditory Attention	The ability to focus on a single source of sound in the presence of other distracting sounds.
Manual Dexterity	The ability to quickly move your hand, your hand together with your arm, or your two hands to grasp, manipulate, or assemble objects.

Hearing Sensitivity	The ability to detect or tell the differences between sounds that vary in pitch and loudness.
Static Strength	The ability to exert maximum muscle force to lift, push, pull, or carry objects.
Multilimb Coordination	The ability to coordinate two or more limbs (for example, two arms, two legs, or one leg and one arm) while sitting, standing, or lying down. It does not involve performing the activities while the whole body is in motion.
Depth Perception	The ability to judge which of several objects is closer or farther away from you, or to judge the distance between you and an object.
Gross Body Coordination	The ability to coordinate the movement of your arms, legs, and torso together when the whole body is in motion.
Stamina	The ability to exert yourself physically over long periods of time without getting winded or out of breath.
Dynamic Strength	The ability to exert muscle force repeatedly or continuously over time. This involves muscular endurance and resistance to muscle fatigue.
Extent Flexibility	The ability to bend, stretch, twist, or reach with your body, arms, and/or legs.
Gross Body Equilibrium	The ability to keep or regain your body balance or stay upright when in an unstable position.
Wrist-Finger Speed	The ability to make fast, simple, repeated movements of the fingers, hands, and wrists.
Rate Control	The ability to time your movements or the movement of a piece of equipment in anticipation of changes in the speed and/or direction of a moving object or scene.
Glare Sensitivity	The ability to see objects in the presence of glare or bright lighting.
Dynamic Flexibility	The ability to quickly and repeatedly bend, stretch, twist, or reach out with your body, arms, and/or legs.
Explosive Strength	The ability to use short bursts of muscle force to propel oneself (as in jumping or sprinting), or to throw an object.
Speed of Limb Movement	The ability to quickly move the arms and legs.
Reaction Time	The ability to quickly respond (with the hand, finger, or foot) to a signal (sound, light, picture) when it appears.
Night Vision	The ability to see under low light conditions.
Response Orientation	The ability to choose quickly between two or more movements in response to two or more different signals (lights, sounds, pictures). It includes the speed with which the correct response is started with the hand, foot, or other body part.
Sound Localization	The ability to tell the direction from which a sound originated.
Spatial Orientation	The ability to know your location in relation to the environment or to know where other objects are in relation to you.
Peripheral Vision	The ability to see objects or movement of objects to one's side when the eyes are looking ahead.

Work_Activity	Work_Activity Definitions
Updating and Using Relevant Knowledge	Keeping up-to-date technically and applying new knowledge to your job.
Getting Information	Observing, receiving, and otherwise obtaining information from all relevant sources.
Assisting and Caring for Others	Providing personal assistance, medical attention, emotional support, or other personal care to others such as coworkers, customers, or patients.
Training and Teaching Others	Identifying the educational needs of others, developing formal educational or training programs or classes, and teaching or instructing others.
Communicating with Supervisors, Peers, or Subordin	Providing information to supervisors, co-workers, and subordinates by telephone, in written form, e-mail, or in person.
Establishing and Maintaining Interpersonal Relatio	Developing constructive and cooperative working relationships with others, and maintaining them over time.
Interacting With Computers	Using computers and computer systems (including hardware and software) to program, write software, set up functions, enter data, or process information.
Coaching and Developing Others	Identifying the developmental needs of others and coaching, mentoring, or otherwise helping others to improve their knowledge or skills.
Identifying Objects, Actions, and Events	Identifying information by categorizing, estimating, recognizing differences or similarities, and detecting changes in circumstances or events.
Organizing, Planning, and Prioritizing Work	Developing specific goals and plans to prioritize, organize, and accomplish your work.

Evaluating Information to Determine Compliance wit	Using relevant information and individual judgment to determine whether events or processes comply with laws, regulations, or standards.
Judging the Qualities of Things, Services, or Peop	Assessing the value, importance, or quality of things or people.
Making Decisions and Solving Problems	Analyzing information and evaluating results to choose the best solution and solve problems.
Interpreting the Meaning of Information for Others	Translating or explaining what information means and how it can be used.
Thinking Creatively	Developing, designing, or creating new applications, ideas, relationships, systems, or products, including artistic contributions.
Analyzing Data or Information	Identifying the underlying principles, reasons, or facts of information by breaking down information or data into separate parts.
Developing Objectives and Strategies	Establishing long-range objectives and specifying the strategies and actions to achieve them.
Documenting/Recording Information	Entering, transcribing, recording, storing, or maintaining information in written or electronic/magnetic form.
Monitor Processes, Materials, or Surroundings	Monitoring and reviewing information from materials, events, or the environment, to detect or assess problems.
Communicating with Persons Outside Organization	Communicating with people outside the organization, representing the organization to customers, the public, government, and other external sources. This information can be exchanged in person, in writing, or by telephone or e-mail.
Processing Information	Compiling, coding, categorizing, calculating, tabulating, auditing, or verifying information or data.
Coordinating the Work and Activities of Others	Getting members of a group to work together to accomplish tasks.
Scheduling Work and Activities	Scheduling events, programs, and activities, as well as the work of others.
Performing for or Working Directly with the Public	Performing for people or dealing directly with the public. This includes serving customers in restaurants and stores, and receiving clients or guests.
Developing and Building Teams	Encouraging and building mutual trust, respect, and cooperation among team members.
Provide Consultation and Advice to Others	Providing guidance and expert advice to management or other groups on technical, systems-, or process-related topics.
Resolving Conflicts and Negotiating with Others	Handling complaints, settling disputes, and resolving grievances and conflicts, or otherwise negotiating with others.
Guiding, Directing, and Motivating Subordinates	Providing guidance and direction to subordinates, including setting performance standards and monitoring performance.
Estimating the Quantifiable Characteristics of Pro	Estimating sizes, distances, and quantities; or determining time, costs, resources, or materials needed to perform a work activity.
Performing Administrative Activities	Performing day-to-day administrative tasks such as maintaining information files and processing paperwork.
Inspecting Equipment, Structures, or Material	Inspecting equipment, structures, or materials to identify the cause of errors or other problems or defects.
Selling or Influencing Others	Convincing others to buy merchandise/goods or to otherwise change their minds or actions.
Performing General Physical Activities	Performing physical activities that require considerable use of your arms and legs and moving your whole body, such as climbing, lifting, balancing, walking, stooping, and handling of materials.
Monitoring and Controlling Resources	Monitoring and controlling resources and overseeing the spending of money.
Handling and Moving Objects	Using hands and arms in handling, installing, positioning, and moving materials, and manipulating things.
Staffing Organizational Units	Recruiting, interviewing, selecting, hiring, and promoting employees in an organization.
Controlling Machines and Processes	Using either control mechanisms or direct physical activity to operate machines or processes (not including computers or vehicles).
Operating Vehicles, Mechanized Devices, or Equipme	Running, maneuvering, navigating, or driving vehicles or mechanized equipment, such as forklifts, passenger vehicles, aircraft, or water craft.
Drafting, Laying Out, and Specifying Technical Dev	Providing documentation, detailed instructions, drawings, or specifications to tell others about how devices, parts, equipment, or structures are to be fabricated, constructed, assembled, modified, maintained, or used.
Repairing and Maintaining Electronic Equipment	Servicing, repairing, calibrating, regulating, fine-tuning, or testing machines, devices, and equipment that operate primarily on the basis of electrical or electronic (not mechanical) principles.
Repairing and Maintaining Mechanical Equipment	Servicing, repairing, adjusting, and testing machines, devices, moving parts, and equipment that operate primarily on the basis of mechanical (not electronic) principles.

Work_Context	Work_Context Definitions
Electronic Mail	How often do you use electronic mail in this job?
Face-to-Face Discussions	How often do you have to have face-to-face discussions with individuals or teams in this job?
Telephone	How often do you have telephone conversations in this job?
Freedom to Make Decisions	How much decision making freedom, without supervision, does the job offer?
Structured versus Unstructured Work	To what extent is this job structured for the worker, rather than allowing the worker to determine tasks, priorities, and goals?
Indoors, Environmentally Controlled	How often does this job require working indoors in environmentally controlled conditions?
Work With Work Group or Team	How important is it to work with others in a group or team in this job?
Deal With External Customers	How important is it to work with external customers or the public in this job?
Contact With Others	How much does this job require the worker to be in contact with others (face-to-face, by telephone, or otherwise) in order to perform it?
Importance of Being Exact or Accurate	How important is being very exact or highly accurate in performing this job?
Coordinate or Lead Others	How important is it to coordinate or lead others in accomplishing work activities in this job?
Frequency of Decision Making	How frequently is the worker required to make decisions that affect other people, the financial resources, and/or the image and reputation of the organization?
Impact of Decisions on Co-workers or Company Resul	How do the decisions an employee makes impact the results of co-workers, clients or the company?
Letters and Memos	How often does the job require written letters and memos?
Time Pressure	How often does this job require the worker to meet strict deadlines?
Responsibility for Outcomes and Results	How responsible is the worker for work outcomes and results of other workers?
Public Speaking	How often do you have to perform public speaking in this job?
Physical Proximity	To what extent does this job require the worker to perform job tasks in close physical proximity to other people?
Responsible for Others' Health and Safety	How much responsibility is there for the health and safety of others in this job?
Exposed to Disease or Infections	How often does this job require exposure to disease/infections?
Consequence of Error	How serious would the result usually be if the worker made a mistake that was not readily correctable?
Frequency of Conflict Situations	How often are there conflict situations the employee has to face in this job?
Level of Competition	To what extent does this job require the worker to compete or to be aware of competitive pressures?
Spend Time Sitting	How much does this job require sitting?
Deal With Unpleasant or Angry People	How frequently does the worker have to deal with unpleasant, angry, or discourteous individuals as part of the job requirements?
Spend Time Standing	How much does this job require standing?
Importance of Repeating Same Tasks	How important is repeating the same physical activities (e.g., key entry) or mental activities (e.g., checking entries in a ledger) over and over, without stopping, to performing this job?
Wear Common Protective or Safety Equipment such as	How much does this job require wearing common protective or safety equipment such as safety shoes, glasses, gloves, hard hats or live jackets?
Spend Time Using Your Hands to Handle, Control, or	How much does this job require using your hands to handle, control, or feel objects, tools or controls?
Exposed to Contaminants	How often does this job require working exposed to contaminants (such as pollutants, gases, dust or odors)?
Degree of Automation	How automated is the job?
Spend Time Walking and Running	How much does this job require walking and running?
Spend Time Making Repetitive Motions	How much does this job require making repetitive motions?
Sounds, Noise Levels Are Distracting or Uncomforta	How often does this job require working exposed to sounds and noise levels that are distracting or uncomfortable?
Spend Time Bending or Twisting the Body	How much does this job require bending or twisting your body?
In an Enclosed Vehicle or Equipment	How often does this job require working in a closed vehicle or equipment (e.g., car)?

Deal With Physically Aggressive People	How frequently does this job require the worker to deal with physical aggression of violent individuals?
Cramped Work Space, Awkward Positions	How often does this job require working in cramped work spaces that requires getting into awkward positions?
Exposed to Radiation	How often does this job require exposure to radiation?
Extremely Bright or Inadequate Lighting	How often does this job require working in extremely bright or inadequate lighting conditions?
Exposed to Hazardous Conditions	How often does this job require exposure to hazardous conditions?
Pace Determined by Speed of Equipment	How important is it to this job that the pace is determined by the speed of equipment or machinery? (This does not refer to keeping busy at all times on this job.)
Wear Specialized Protective or Safety Equipment su	How much does this job require wearing specialized protective or safety equipment such as breathing apparatus, safety harness, full protection suits, or radiation protection?
Indoors, Not Environmentally Controlled	How often does this job require working indoors in non-controlled environmental conditions (e.g., warehouse without heat)?
Exposed to Minor Burns, Cuts, Bites, or Stings	How often does this job require exposure to minor burns, cuts, bites, or stings?
Spend Time Kneeling, Crouching, Stooping, or Crawl	How much does this job require kneeling, crouching, stooping, or crawling?
Very Hot or Cold Temperatures	How often does this job require working in very hot (above 90 F degrees) or very cold (below 32 F degrees) temperatures?
Outdoors, Exposed to Weather	How often does this job require working outdoors, exposed to all weather conditions?
Exposed to Hazardous Equipment	How often does this job require exposure to hazardous equipment?
Spend Time Keeping or Regaining Balance	How much does this job require keeping or regaining your balance?
Outdoors, Under Cover	How often does this job require working outdoors, under cover (e.g., structure with roof but no walls)?
In an Open Vehicle or Equipment	How often does this job require working in an open vehicle or equipment (e.g., tractor)?
Exposed to High Places	How often does this job require exposure to high places?
Exposed to Whole Body Vibration	How often does this job require exposure to whole body vibration (e.g., operate a jackhammer)?
Spend Time Climbing Ladders, Scaffolds, or Poles	How much does this job require climbing ladders, scaffolds, or poles?

Job Zone Component	Job Zone Component Definitions
Title	Job Zone Five: Extensive Preparation Needed
Overall Experience	Extensive skill, knowledge, and experience are needed for these occupations. Many require more than five years of experience. For example, surgeons must complete four years of college and an additional five to seven years of specialized medical training to be able to do their job.
Job Training	Employees may need some on-the-job training, but most of these occupations assume that the person will already have the required skills, knowledge, work-related experience, and/or training.
Job Zone Examples	These occupations often involve coordinating, training, supervising, or managing the activities of others to accomplish goals. Very advanced communication and organizational skills are required. Examples include athletic trainers, lawyers, managing editors, phyicists, social psychologists, and surgeons. (8.0 and above)
SVP Range	
Education	A bachelor's degree is the minimum formal education required for these occupations. However, many also require graduate school. For example, they may require a master's degree, and some require a Ph.D., M.D., or J.D. (law degree).

Work_Styles	Work_Styles Definitions
Integrity	Job requires being honest and ethical.
Dependability	Job requires being reliable, responsible, and dependable, and fulfilling obligations.
Concern for Others	Job requires being sensitive to others' needs and feelings and being understanding and helpful on the job.
Achievement/Effort	Job requires establishing and maintaining personally challenging achievement goals and exerting effort toward mastering tasks.
Analytical Thinking	Job requires analyzing information and using logic to address work-related issues and problems.

Self Control	Job requires maintaining composure, keeping emotions in check, controlling anger, and avoiding aggressive behavior, even in very difficult situations.
Leadership	Job requires a willingness to lead, take charge, and offer opinions and direction.
Independence	Job requires developing one's own ways of doing things, guiding oneself with little or no supervision, and depending on oneself to get things done.
Cooperation	Job requires being pleasant with others on the job and displaying a good-natured, cooperative attitude.
Stress Tolerance	Job requires accepting criticism and dealing calmly and effectively with high stress situations.
Adaptability/Flexibility	Job requires being open to change (positive or negative) and to considerable variety in the workplace.
Attention to Detail	Job requires being careful about detail and thorough in completing work tasks.
Initiative	Job requires a willingness to take on responsibilities and challenges.
Social Orientation	Job requires preferring to work with others rather than alone, and being personally connected with others on the job.
Innovation	Job requires creativity and alternative thinking to develop new ideas for and answers to work-related problems.
Persistence	Job requires persistence in the face of obstacles.

25-1081.00 - Education Teachers, Postsecondary

Teach courses pertaining to education, such as counseling, curriculum, guidance, instruction, teacher education, and teaching English as a second language.

Tasks

1) Maintain student attendance records, grades, and other required records.

2) Maintain regularly scheduled office hours in order to advise and assist students.

3) Advise students on academic and vocational curricula, and on career issues.

4) Plan, evaluate, and revise curricula, course content, and course materials and methods of instruction.

5) Participate in campus and community events.

6) Collaborate with colleagues to address teaching and research issues.

7) Select and obtain materials and supplies such as textbooks.

8) Compile, administer, and grade examinations, or assign this work to others.

9) Compile bibliographies of specialized materials for outside reading assignments.

10) Prepare and deliver lectures to undergraduate and/or graduate students on topics such as children's literature, learning and development, and reading instruction.

11) Serve on academic or administrative committees that deal with institutional policies, departmental matters, and academic issues.

12) Supervise students' fieldwork, internship, and research work.

13) Conduct research in a particular field of knowledge, and publish findings in professional journals, books, and/or electronic media.

14) Participate in student recruitment, registration, and placement activities.

15) Write grant proposals to procure external research funding.

16) Advise and instruct teachers employed in school systems, by providing activities such as in-service seminars.

17) Act as advisers to student organizations.

18) Perform administrative duties such as serving as department head.

19) Provide professional consulting services to government and/or industry.

20) Prepare course materials such as syllabi, homework assignments, and handouts.

21) Initiate, facilitate, and moderate classroom discussions.

22) Keep abreast of developments in their field by reading current literature, talking with colleagues, and participating in professional conferences.

Knowledge	Knowledge Definitions
Education and Training	Knowledge of principles and methods for curriculum and training design, teaching and instruction for individuals and groups, and the measurement of training effects.

English Language	Knowledge of the structure and content of the English language including the meaning and spelling of words, rules of composition, and grammar.
Psychology	Knowledge of human behavior and performance; individual differences in ability, personality, and interests; learning and motivation; psychological research methods; and the assessment and treatment of behavioral and affective disorders.
Sociology and Anthropology	Knowledge of group behavior and dynamics, societal trends and influences, human migrations, ethnicity, cultures and their history and origins.
Customer and Personal Service	Knowledge of principles and processes for providing customer and personal services. This includes customer needs assessment, meeting quality standards for services, and evaluation of customer satisfaction.
Therapy and Counseling	Knowledge of principles, methods, and procedures for diagnosis, treatment, and rehabilitation of physical and mental dysfunctions, and for career counseling and guidance.
Administration and Management	Knowledge of business and management principles involved in strategic planning, resource allocation, human resources modeling, leadership technique, production methods, and coordination of people and resources.
Law and Government	Knowledge of laws, legal codes, court procedures, precedents, government regulations, executive orders, agency rules, and the democratic political process.
Philosophy and Theology	Knowledge of different philosophical systems and religions. This includes their basic principles, values, ethics, ways of thinking, customs, practices, and their impact on human culture.
Computers and Electronics	Knowledge of circuit boards, processors, chips, electronic equipment, and computer hardware and software, including applications and programming.
Personnel and Human Resources	Knowledge of principles and procedures for personnel recruitment, selection, training, compensation and benefits, labor relations and negotiation, and personnel information systems.
Clerical	Knowledge of administrative and clerical procedures and systems such as word processing, managing files and records, stenography and transcription, designing forms, and other office procedures and terminology.
Communications and Media	Knowledge of media production, communication, and dissemination techniques and methods. This includes alternative ways to inform and entertain via written, oral, and visual media.
Mathematics	Knowledge of arithmetic, algebra, geometry, calculus, statistics, and their applications.
Public Safety and Security	Knowledge of relevant equipment, policies, procedures, and strategies to promote effective local, state, or national security operations for the protection of people, data, property, and institutions.
History and Archeology	Knowledge of historical events and their causes, indicators, and effects on civilizations and cultures.
Sales and Marketing	Knowledge of principles and methods for showing, promoting, and selling products or services. This includes marketing strategy and tactics, product demonstration, sales techniques, and sales control systems.
Foreign Language	Knowledge of the structure and content of a foreign (non-English) language including the meaning and spelling of words, rules of composition and grammar, and pronunciation.
Medicine and Dentistry	Knowledge of the information and techniques needed to diagnose and treat human injuries, diseases, and deformities. This includes symptoms, treatment alternatives, drug properties and interactions, and preventive health-care measures.
Geography	Knowledge of principles and methods for describing the features of land, sea, and air masses, including their physical characteristics, locations, interrelationships, and distribution of plant, animal, and human life.
Transportation	Knowledge of principles and methods for moving people or goods by air, rail, sea, or road, including the relative costs and benefits.
Economics and Accounting	Knowledge of economic and accounting principles and practices, the financial markets, banking and the analysis and reporting of financial data.
Biology	Knowledge of plant and animal organisms, their tissues, cells, functions, interdependencies, and interactions with each other and the environment.
Fine Arts	Knowledge of the theory and techniques required to compose, produce, and perform works of music, dance, visual arts, drama, and sculpture.

Telecommunications	Knowledge of transmission, broadcasting, switching, control, and operation of telecommunications systems.
Production and Processing	Knowledge of raw materials, production processes, quality control, costs, and other techniques for maximizing the effective manufacture and distribution of goods.
Design	Knowledge of design techniques, tools, and principles involved in production of precision technical plans, blueprints, drawings, and models.
Engineering and Technology	Knowledge of the practical application of engineering science and technology. This includes applying principles, techniques, procedures, and equipment to the design and production of various goods and services.
Chemistry	Knowledge of the chemical composition, structure, and properties of substances and of the chemical processes and transformations that they undergo. This includes uses of chemicals and their interactions, danger signs, production techniques, and disposal methods.
Physics	Knowledge and prediction of physical principles, laws, their interrelationships, and applications to understanding fluid, material, and atmospheric dynamics, and mechanical, electrical, atomic and sub-atomic structures and processes.
Food Production	Knowledge of techniques and equipment for planting, growing, and harvesting food products (both plant and animal) for consumption, including storage/handling techniques.
Mechanical	Knowledge of machines and tools, including their designs, uses, repair, and maintenance.
Building and Construction	Knowledge of materials, methods, and the tools involved in the construction or repair of houses, buildings, or other structures such as highways and roads.

Skills	Skills Definitions
Instructing	Teaching others how to do something.
Reading Comprehension	Understanding written sentences and paragraphs in work related documents.
Learning Strategies	Selecting and using training/instructional methods and procedures appropriate for the situation when learning or teaching new things.
Critical Thinking	Using logic and reasoning to identify the strengths and weaknesses of alternative solutions, conclusions or approaches to problems.
Active Listening	Giving full attention to what other people are saying, taking time to understand the points being made, asking questions as appropriate, and not interrupting at inappropriate times.
Writing	Communicating effectively in writing as appropriate for the needs of the audience.
Speaking	Talking to others to convey information effectively.
Active Learning	Understanding the implications of new information for both current and future problem-solving and decision-making.
Time Management	Managing one's own time and the time of others.
Social Perceptiveness	Being aware of others' reactions and understanding why they react as they do.
Monitoring	Monitoring/Assessing performance of yourself, other individuals, or organizations to make improvements or take corrective action.
Complex Problem Solving	Identifying complex problems and reviewing related information to develop and evaluate options and implement solutions.
Coordination	Adjusting actions in relation to others' actions.
Persuasion	Persuading others to change their minds or behavior.
Service Orientation	Actively looking for ways to help people.
Judgment and Decision Making	Considering the relative costs and benefits of potential actions to choose the most appropriate one.
Negotiation	Bringing others together and trying to reconcile differences.
Science	Using scientific rules and methods to solve problems.
Mathematics	Using mathematics to solve problems.
Equipment Selection	Determining the kind of tools and equipment needed to do a job.
Operations Analysis	Analyzing needs and product requirements to create a design.
Systems Evaluation	Identifying measures or indicators of system performance and the actions needed to improve or correct performance, relative to the goals of the system.
Technology Design	Generating or adapting equipment and technology to serve user needs.
Management of Personnel Resources	Motivating, developing, and directing people as they work, identifying the best people for the job.
Quality Control Analysis	Conducting tests and inspections of products, services, or processes to evaluate quality or performance.

Systems Analysis	Determining how a system should work and how changes in conditions, operations, and the environment will affect outcomes.
Management of Material Resources	Obtaining and seeing to the appropriate use of equipment, facilities, and materials needed to do certain work.
Management of Financial Resources	Determining how money will be spent to get the work done, and accounting for these expenditures.
Troubleshooting	Determining causes of operating errors and deciding what to do about it.
Installation	Installing equipment, machines, wiring, or programs to meet specifications.
Operation and Control	Controlling operations of equipment or systems.
Programming	Writing computer programs for various purposes.
Equipment Maintenance	Performing routine maintenance on equipment and determining when and what kind of maintenance is needed.
Repairing	Repairing machines or systems using the needed tools.
Operation Monitoring	Watching gauges, dials, or other indicators to make sure a machine is working properly.

Ability	Ability Definitions
Oral Expression	The ability to communicate information and ideas in speaking so others will understand.
Speech Clarity	The ability to speak clearly so others can understand you.
Written Comprehension	The ability to read and understand information and ideas presented in writing.
Oral Comprehension	The ability to listen to and understand information and ideas presented through spoken words and sentences.
Written Expression	The ability to communicate information and ideas in writing so others will understand.
Deductive Reasoning	The ability to apply general rules to specific problems to produce answers that make sense.
Speech Recognition	The ability to identify and understand the speech of another person.
Near Vision	The ability to see details at close range (within a few feet of the observer).
Problem Sensitivity	The ability to tell when something is wrong or is likely to go wrong. It does not involve solving the problem, only recognizing there is a problem.
Inductive Reasoning	The ability to combine pieces of information to form general rules or conclusions (includes finding a relationship among seemingly unrelated events).
Originality	The ability to come up with unusual or clever ideas about a given topic or situation, or to develop creative ways to solve a problem.
Category Flexibility	The ability to generate or use different sets of rules for combining or grouping things in different ways.
Fluency of Ideas	The ability to come up with a number of ideas about a topic (the number of ideas is important, not their quality, correctness, or creativity).
Information Ordering	The ability to arrange things or actions in a certain order or pattern according to a specific rule or set of rules (e.g., patterns of numbers, letters, words, pictures, mathematical operations).
Selective Attention	The ability to concentrate on a task over a period of time without being distracted.
Time Sharing	The ability to shift back and forth between two or more activities or sources of information (such as speech, sounds, touch, or other sources).
Memorization	The ability to remember information such as words, numbers, pictures, and procedures.
Flexibility of Closure	The ability to identify or detect a known pattern (a figure, object, word, or sound) that is hidden in other distracting material.
Far Vision	The ability to see details at a distance.
Mathematical Reasoning	The ability to choose the right mathematical methods or formulas to solve a problem.
Speed of Closure	The ability to quickly make sense of, combine, and organize information into meaningful patterns.
Number Facility	The ability to add, subtract, multiply, or divide quickly and correctly.
Perceptual Speed	The ability to quickly and accurately compare similarities and differences among sets of letters, numbers, objects, pictures, or patterns. The things to be compared may be presented at the same time or one after the other. This ability also includes comparing a presented object with a remembered object.
Trunk Strength	The ability to use your abdominal and lower back muscles to support part of the body repeatedly or continuously over time without 'giving out' or fatiguing.

Auditory Attention	The ability to focus on a single source of sound in the presence of other distracting sounds.
Finger Dexterity	The ability to make precisely coordinated movements of the fingers of one or both hands to grasp, manipulate, or assemble very small objects.
Visualization	The ability to imagine how something will look after it is moved around or when its parts are moved or rearranged.
Visual Color Discrimination	The ability to match or detect differences between colors, including shades of color and brightness.
Manual Dexterity	The ability to quickly move your hand, your hand together with your arm, or your two hands to grasp, manipulate, or assemble objects.
Control Precision	The ability to quickly and repeatedly adjust the controls of a machine or a vehicle to exact positions.
Arm-Hand Steadiness	The ability to keep your hand and arm steady while moving your arm or while holding your arm and hand in one position.
Depth Perception	The ability to judge which of several objects is closer or farther away from you, or to judge the distance between you and an object.
Hearing Sensitivity	The ability to detect or tell the differences between sounds that vary in pitch and loudness.
Gross Body Coordination	The ability to coordinate the movement of your arms, legs, and torso together when the whole body is in motion.
Wrist-Finger Speed	The ability to make fast, simple, repeated movements of the fingers, hands, and wrists.
Reaction Time	The ability to quickly respond (with the hand, finger, or foot) to a signal (sound, light, picture) when it appears.
Rate Control	The ability to time your movements or the movement of a piece of equipment in anticipation of changes in the speed and/or direction of a moving object or scene.
Response Orientation	The ability to choose quickly between two or more movements in response to two or more different signals (lights, sounds, pictures). It includes the speed with which the correct response is started with the hand, foot, or other body part.
Multilimb Coordination	The ability to coordinate two or more limbs (for example, two arms, two legs, or one leg and one arm) while sitting, standing, or lying down. It does not involve performing the activities while the whole body is in motion.
Dynamic Flexibility	The ability to quickly and repeatedly bend, stretch, twist, or reach out with your body, arms, and/or legs.
Stamina	The ability to exert yourself physically over long periods of time without getting winded or out of breath.
Speed of Limb Movement	The ability to quickly move the arms and legs.
Spatial Orientation	The ability to know your location in relation to the environment or to know where other objects are in relation to you.
Explosive Strength	The ability to use short bursts of muscle force to propel oneself (as in jumping or sprinting), or to throw an object.
Dynamic Strength	The ability to exert muscle force repeatedly or continuously over time. This involves muscular endurance and resistance to muscle fatigue.
Static Strength	The ability to exert maximum muscle force to lift, push, pull, or carry objects.
Glare Sensitivity	The ability to see objects in the presence of glare or bright lighting.
Extent Flexibility	The ability to bend, stretch, twist, or reach with your body, arms, and/or legs.
Gross Body Equilibrium	The ability to keep or regain your body balance or stay upright when in an unstable position.
Sound Localization	The ability to tell the direction from which a sound originated.
Peripheral Vision	The ability to see objects or movement of objects to one's side when the eyes are looking ahead.
Night Vision	The ability to see under low light conditions.

Work_Activity	Work_Activity Definitions
Establishing and Maintaining Interpersonal Relatio	Developing constructive and cooperative working relationships with others, and maintaining them over time.
Getting Information	Observing, receiving, and otherwise obtaining information from all relevant sources.
Training and Teaching Others	Identifying the educational needs of others, developing formal educational or training programs or classes, and teaching or instructing others.
Organizing, Planning, and Prioritizing Work	Developing specific goals and plans to prioritize, organize, and accomplish your work.
Updating and Using Relevant Knowledge	Keeping up-to-date technically and applying new knowledge to your job.

Thinking Creatively	Developing, designing, or creating new applications, ideas, relationships, systems, or products, including artistic contributions.
Interacting With Computers	Using computers and computer systems (including hardware and software) to program, write software, set up functions, enter data, or process information.
Coaching and Developing Others	Identifying the developmental needs of others and coaching, mentoring, or otherwise helping others to improve their knowledge or skills.
Communicating with Supervisors, Peers, or Subordin	Providing information to supervisors, co-workers, and subordinates by telephone, in written form, e-mail, or in person.
Interpreting the Meaning of Information for Others	Translating or explaining what information means and how it can be used.
Analyzing Data or Information	Identifying the underlying principles, reasons, or facts of information by breaking down information or data into separate parts.
Identifying Objects, Actions, and Events	Identifying information by categorizing, estimating, recognizing differences or similarities, and detecting changes in circumstances or events.
Making Decisions and Solving Problems	Analyzing information and evaluating results to choose the best solution and solve problems.
Communicating with Persons Outside Organization	Communicating with people outside the organization, representing the organization to customers, the public, government, and other external sources. This information can be exchanged in person, in writing, or by telephone or e-mail.
Evaluating Information to Determine Compliance wit	Using relevant information and individual judgment to determine whether events or processes comply with laws, regulations, or standards.
Developing Objectives and Strategies	Establishing long-range objectives and specifying the strategies and actions to achieve them.
Provide Consultation and Advice to Others	Providing guidance and expert advice to management or other groups on technical, systems-, or process-related topics.
Documenting/Recording Information	Entering, transcribing, recording, storing, or maintaining information in written or electronic/magnetic form.
Judging the Qualities of Things, Services, or Peop	Assessing the value, importance, or quality of things or people.
Processing Information	Compiling, coding, categorizing, calculating, tabulating, auditing, or verifying information or data.
Developing and Building Teams	Encouraging and building mutual trust, respect, and cooperation among team members.
Scheduling Work and Activities	Scheduling events, programs, and activities, as well as the work of others.
Monitor Processes, Materials, or Surroundings	Monitoring and reviewing information from materials, events, or the environment, to detect or assess problems.
Resolving Conflicts and Negotiating with Others	Handling complaints, settling disputes, and resolving grievances and conflicts, or otherwise negotiating with others.
Coordinating the Work and Activities of Others	Getting members of a group to work together to accomplish tasks.
Guiding, Directing, and Motivating Subordinates	Providing guidance and direction to subordinates, including setting performance standards and monitoring performance.
Assisting and Caring for Others	Providing personal assistance, medical attention, emotional support, or other personal care to others such as coworkers, customers, or patients.
Performing for or Working Directly with the Public	Performing for people or dealing directly with the public. This includes serving customers in restaurants and stores, and receiving clients or guests.
Estimating the Quantifiable Characteristics of Pro	Estimating sizes, distances, and quantities; or determining time, costs, resources, or materials needed to perform a work activity.
Performing Administrative Activities	Performing day-to-day administrative tasks such as maintaining information files and processing paperwork.
Selling or Influencing Others	Convincing others to buy merchandise/goods or to otherwise change their minds or actions.
Monitoring and Controlling Resources	Monitoring and controlling resources and overseeing the spending of money.
Staffing Organizational Units	Recruiting, interviewing, selecting, hiring, and promoting employees in an organization.
Performing General Physical Activities	Performing physical activities that require considerable use of your arms and legs and moving your whole body, such as climbing, lifting, balancing, walking, stooping, and handling of materials.
Inspecting Equipment, Structures, or Material	Inspecting equipment, structures, or materials to identify the cause of errors or other problems or defects.
Handling and Moving Objects	Using hands and arms in handling, installing, positioning, and moving materials, and manipulating things.

Controlling Machines and Processes	Using either control mechanisms or direct physical activity to operate machines or processes (not including computers or vehicles).
Operating Vehicles, Mechanized Devices, or Equipme	Running, maneuvering, navigating, or driving vehicles or mechanized equipment, such as forklifts, passenger vehicles, aircraft, or water craft.
Drafting, Laying Out, and Specifying Technical Dev	Providing documentation, detailed instructions, drawings, or specifications to tell others about how devices, parts, equipment, or structures are to be fabricated, constructed, assembled, modified, maintained, or used.
Repairing and Maintaining Electronic Equipment	Servicing, repairing, calibrating, regulating, fine-tuning, or testing machines, devices, and equipment that operate primarily on the basis of electrical or electronic (not mechanical) principles.
Repairing and Maintaining Mechanical Equipment	Servicing, repairing, adjusting, and testing machines, devices, moving parts, and equipment that operate primarily on the basis of mechanical (not electronic) principles.

Work_Context	Work_Context Definitions
Face-to-Face Discussions	How often do you have to have face-to-face discussions with individuals or teams in this job?
Electronic Mail	How often do you use electronic mail in this job?
Contact With Others	How much does this job require the worker to be in contact with others (face-to-face, by telephone, or otherwise) in order to perform it?
Freedom to Make Decisions	How much decision making freedom, without supervision, does the job offer?
Structured versus Unstructured Work	To what extent is this job structured for the worker, rather than allowing the worker to determine tasks, priorities, and goals?
Telephone	How often do you have telephone conversations in this job?
Public Speaking	How often do you have to perform public speaking in this job?
Work With Work Group or Team	How important is it to work with others in a group or team in this job?
Letters and Memos	How often does the job require written letters and memos?
Indoors, Environmentally Controlled	How often does this job require working indoors in environmentally controlled conditions?
Coordinate or Lead Others	How important is it to coordinate or lead others in accomplishing work activities in this job?
Frequency of Decision Making	How frequently is the worker required to make decisions that affect other people, the financial resources, and/or the image and reputation of the organization?
Impact of Decisions on Co-workers or Company Resul	How do the decisions an employee makes impact the results of co-workers, clients or the company?
Deal With External Customers	How important is it to work with external customers or the public in this job?
Spend Time Sitting	How much does this job require sitting?
Importance of Being Exact or Accurate	How important is being very exact or highly accurate in performing this job?
Time Pressure	How often does this job require the worker to meet strict deadlines?
Physical Proximity	To what extent does this job require the worker to perform job tasks in close physical proximity to other people?
Level of Competition	To what extent does this job require the worker to compete or to be aware of competitive pressures?
Frequency of Conflict Situations	How often are there conflict situations the employee has to face in this job?
Responsibility for Outcomes and Results	How responsible is the worker for work outcomes and results of other workers?
Spend Time Using Your Hands to Handle, Control, or	How much does this job require using your hands to handle, control, or feel objects, tools or controls?
Spend Time Standing	How much does this job require standing?
Deal With Unpleasant or Angry People	How frequently does the worker have to deal with unpleasant, angry, or discourteous individuals as part of the job requirements?
Spend Time Making Repetitive Motions	How much does this job require making repetitive motions?
Importance of Repeating Same Tasks	How important is repeating the same physical activities (e.g., key entry) or mental activities (e.g., checking entries in a ledger) over and over, without stopping, to performing this job?
Sounds, Noise Levels Are Distracting or Uncomforta	How often does this job require working exposed to sounds and noise levels that are distracting or uncomfortable?
Responsible for Others' Health and Safety	How much responsibility is there for the health and safety of others in this job?
In an Enclosed Vehicle or Equipment	How often does this job require working in a closed vehicle or equipment (e.g., car)?

1432

Consequence of Error	How serious would the result usually be if the worker made a mistake that was not readily correctable?
Extremely Bright or Inadequate Lighting	How often does this job require working in extremely bright or inadequate lighting conditions?
Degree of Automation	How automated is the job?
Exposed to Contaminants	How often does this job require working exposed to contaminants (such as pollutants, gases, dust or odors)?
Spend Time Walking and Running	How much does this job require walking and running?
Exposed to Disease or Infections	How often does this job require exposure to disease/infections?
Indoors, Not Environmentally Controlled	How often does this job require working indoors in non-controlled environmental conditions (e.g., warehouse without heat)?
Very Hot or Cold Temperatures	How often does this job require working in very hot (above 90 F degrees) or very cold (below 32 F degrees) temperatures?
Cramped Work Space, Awkward Positions	How often does this job require working in cramped work spaces that requires getting into awkward positions?
Outdoors, Exposed to Weather	How often does this job require working outdoors, exposed to all weather conditions?
Deal With Physically Aggressive People	How frequently does this job require the worker to deal with physical aggression of violent individuals?
Spend Time Bending or Twisting the Body	How much does this job require bending or twisting your body?
Spend Time Kneeling, Crouching, Stooping, or Crawl	How much does this job require kneeling, crouching, stooping or crawling?
Exposed to Minor Burns, Cuts, Bites, or Stings	How often does this job require exposure to minor burns, cuts, bites, or stings?
Outdoors, Under Cover	How often does this job require working outdoors, under cover (e.g., structure with roof but no walls)?
Spend Time Keeping or Regaining Balance	How much does this job require keeping or regaining your balance?
Spend Time Climbing Ladders, Scaffolds, or Poles	How much does this job require climbing ladders, scaffolds, or poles?
Exposed to High Places	How often does this job require exposure to high places?
Wear Common Protective or Safety Equipment such as	How much does this job require wearing common protective or safety equipment such as safety shoes, glasses, gloves, hard hats or life jackets?
Exposed to Hazardous Equipment	How often does this job require exposure to hazardous equipment?
In an Open Vehicle or Equipment	How often does this job require working in an open vehicle or equipment (e.g., tractor)?
Pace Determined by Speed of Equipment	How important is it to this job that the pace is determined by the speed of equipment or machinery? (This does not refer to keeping busy at all times on this job.)
Exposed to Radiation	How often does this job require exposure to radiation?
Exposed to Whole Body Vibration	How often does this job require exposure to whole body vibration (e.g., operate a jackhammer)?
Exposed to Hazardous Conditions	How often does this job require exposure to hazardous conditions?
Wear Specialized Protective or Safety Equipment su	How much does this job require wearing specialized protective or safety equipment such as breathing apparatus, safety harness, full protection suits, or radiation protection?

Job Zone Component	Job Zone Component Definitions
Title	Job Zone Five: Extensive Preparation Needed Extensive skill, knowledge, and experience are needed for these occupations. Many require more than five years of experience.
Overall Experience	For example, surgeons must complete four years of college and an additional five to seven years of specialized medical training to be able to do their job.
Job Training	Employees may need some on-the-job training, but most of these occupations assume that the person will already have the required skills, knowledge, work-related experience, and/or training.
Job Zone Examples	These occupations often involve coordinating, training, supervising, or managing the activities of others to accomplish goals. Very advanced communication and organizational skills are required. Examples include athletic trainers, lawyers, managing editors, physicists, social psychologists, and surgeons.
SVP Range	(8.0 and above)

Education	A bachelor's degree is the minimum formal education required for these occupations. However, many also require graduate school. For example, they may require a master's degree, and some require a Ph.D., M.D., or J.D. (law degree).

Work_Styles	Work_Styles Definitions
Initiative	Job requires a willingness to take on responsibilities and challenges.
Achievement/Effort	Job requires establishing and maintaining personally challenging achievement goals and exerting effort toward mastering tasks.
Analytical Thinking	Job requires analyzing information and using logic to address work-related issues and problems.
Concern for Others	Job requires being sensitive to others' needs and feelings and being understanding and helpful on the job.
Independence	Job requires developing one's own ways of doing things, guiding oneself with little or no supervision, and depending on oneself to get things done.
Dependability	Job requires being reliable, responsible, and dependable, and fulfilling obligations.
Leadership	Job requires a willingness to lead, take charge, and offer opinions and direction.
Integrity	Job requires being honest and ethical.
Adaptability/Flexibility	Job requires being open to change (positive or negative) and to considerable variety in the workplace.
Persistence	Job requires persistence in the face of obstacles.
Cooperation	Job requires being pleasant with others on the job and displaying a good-natured, cooperative attitude.
Self Control	Job requires maintaining composure, keeping emotions in check, controlling anger, and avoiding aggressive behavior, even in very difficult situations.
Stress Tolerance	Job requires accepting criticism and dealing calmly and effectively with high stress situations.
Social Orientation	Job requires preferring to work with others rather than alone, and being personally connected with others on the job.
Innovation	Job requires creativity and alternative thinking to develop new ideas for and answers to work-related problems.
Attention to Detail	Job requires being careful about detail and thorough in completing work tasks.

25-1082.00 - Library Science Teachers, Postsecondary

Teach courses in library science.

Tasks

1) Keep abreast of developments in their field by reading current literature, talking with colleagues, and participating in professional conferences.

2) Initiate, facilitate, and moderate classroom discussions.

3) Select and obtain materials and supplies such as textbooks.

4) Maintain student attendance records, grades, and other required records.

5) Maintain regularly scheduled office hours in order to advise and assist students.

6) Advise students on academic and vocational curricula, and on career issues.

7) Compile, administer, and grade examinations, or assign this work to others.

8) Participate in campus and community events.

9) Compile bibliographies of specialized materials for outside reading assignments.

10) Prepare and deliver lectures to undergraduate and/or graduate students on topics such as collection development, archival methods, and indexing and abstracting.

11) Conduct research in a particular field of knowledge, and publish findings in professional journals, books, and/or electronic media.

12) Serve on academic or administrative committees that deal with institutional policies, departmental matters, and academic issues.

13) Supervise undergraduate and/or graduate teaching, internship, and research work.

14) Write grant proposals to procure external research funding.

15) Participate in student recruitment, registration, and placement activities.

16) Act as advisers to student organizations.

17) Provide professional consulting services to government and/or industry.

18) Perform administrative duties such as serving as department head.

19) Collaborate with colleagues to address teaching and research issues.

20) Prepare course materials such as syllabi, homework assignments, and handouts.

21) Evaluate and grade students' class work, assignments, and papers.

Knowledge	Knowledge Definitions
English Language	Knowledge of the structure and content of the English language including the meaning and spelling of words, rules of composition, and grammar.
Education and Training	Knowledge of principles and methods for curriculum and training design, teaching and instruction for individuals and groups, and the measurement of training effects.
Computers and Electronics	Knowledge of circuit boards, processors, chips, electronic equipment, and computer hardware and software, including applications and programming.
Communications and Media	Knowledge of media production, communication, and dissemination techniques and methods. This includes alternative ways to inform and entertain via written, oral, and visual media.
Customer and Personal Service	Knowledge of principles and processes for providing customer and personal services. This includes customer needs assessment, meeting quality standards for services, and evaluation of customer satisfaction.
Psychology	Knowledge of human behavior and performance; individual differences in ability, personality, and interests; learning and motivation; psychological research methods; and the assessment and treatment of behavioral and affective disorders.
Sociology and Anthropology	Knowledge of group behavior and dynamics, societal trends and influences, human migrations, ethnicity, cultures and their history and origins.
Telecommunications	Knowledge of transmission, broadcasting, switching, control, and operation of telecommunications systems.
Administration and Management	Knowledge of business and management principles involved in strategic planning, resource allocation, human resources modeling, leadership technique, production methods, and coordination of people and resources.
Personnel and Human Resources	Knowledge of principles and procedures for personnel recruitment, selection, training, compensation and benefits, labor relations and negotiation, and personnel information systems.
Mathematics	Knowledge of arithmetic, algebra, geometry, calculus, statistics, and their applications.
Clerical	Knowledge of administrative and clerical procedures and systems such as word processing, managing files and records, stenography and transcription, designing forms, and other office procedures and terminology.
Law and Government	Knowledge of laws, legal codes, court procedures, precedents, government regulations, executive orders, agency rules, and the democratic political process.
Philosophy and Theology	Knowledge of different philosophical systems and religions. This includes their basic principles, values, ethics, ways of thinking, customs, practices, and their impact on human culture.
History and Archeology	Knowledge of historical events and their causes, indicators, and effects on civilizations and cultures.
Sales and Marketing	Knowledge of principles and methods for showing, promoting, and selling products or services. This includes marketing strategy and tactics, product demonstration, sales techniques, and sales control systems.
Design	Knowledge of design techniques, tools, and principles involved in production of precision technical plans, blueprints, drawings, and models.
Therapy and Counseling	Knowledge of principles, methods, and procedures for diagnosis, treatment, and rehabilitation of physical and mental dysfunctions, and for career counseling and guidance.
Geography	Knowledge of principles and methods for describing the features of land, sea, and air masses, including their physical characteristics, locations, interrelationships, and distribution of plant, animal, and human life.
Public Safety and Security	Knowledge of relevant equipment, policies, procedures, and strategies to promote effective local, state, or national security operations for the protection of people, data, property, and institutions.

Foreign Language	Knowledge of the structure and content of a foreign (non-English) language including the meaning and spelling of words, rules of composition and grammar, and pronunciation.
Engineering and Technology	Knowledge of the practical application of engineering science and technology. This includes applying principles, techniques, procedures, and equipment to the design and production of various goods and services.
Fine Arts	Knowledge of the theory and techniques required to compose, produce, and perform works of music, dance, visual arts, drama, and sculpture.
Economics and Accounting	Knowledge of economic and accounting principles and practices, the financial markets, banking and the analysis and reporting of financial data.
Transportation	Knowledge of principles and methods for moving people or goods by air, rail, sea, or road, including the relative costs and benefits.
Production and Processing	Knowledge of raw materials, production processes, quality control, costs, and other techniques for maximizing the effective manufacture and distribution of goods.
Biology	Knowledge of plant and animal organisms, their tissues, cells, functions, interdependencies, and interactions with each other and the environment.
Building and Construction	Knowledge of materials, methods, and the tools involved in the construction or repair of houses, buildings, or other structures such as highways and roads.
Medicine and Dentistry	Knowledge of the information and techniques needed to diagnose and treat human injuries, diseases, and deformities. This includes symptoms, treatment alternatives, drug properties and interactions, and preventive health-care measures.
Mechanical	Knowledge of machines and tools, including their designs, uses, repair, and maintenance.
Physics	Knowledge and prediction of physical principles, laws, their interrelationships, and applications to understanding fluid, material, and atmospheric dynamics, and mechanical, electrical, atomic and sub- atomic structures and processes.
Chemistry	Knowledge of the chemical composition, structure, and properties of substances and of the chemical processes and transformations that they undergo. This includes uses of chemicals and their interactions, danger signs, production techniques, and disposal methods.
Food Production	Knowledge of techniques and equipment for planting, growing, and harvesting food products (both plant and animal) for consumption, including storage/handling techniques.

Skills	Skills Definitions
Instructing	Teaching others how to do something.
Reading Comprehension	Understanding written sentences and paragraphs in work related documents.
Critical Thinking	Using logic and reasoning to identify the strengths and weaknesses of alternative solutions, conclusions or approaches to problems.
Writing	Communicating effectively in writing as appropriate for the needs of the audience.
Speaking	Talking to others to convey information effectively.
Learning Strategies	Selecting and using training/instructional methods and procedures appropriate for the situation when learning or teaching new things.
Active Learning	Understanding the implications of new information for both current and future problem-solving and decision-making.
Active Listening	Giving full attention to what other people are saying, taking time to understand the points being made, asking questions as appropriate, and not interrupting at inappropriate times.
Monitoring	Monitoring/Assessing performance of yourself, other individuals, or organizations to make improvements or take corrective action.
Time Management	Managing one's own time and the time of others.
Social Perceptiveness	Being aware of others' reactions and understanding why they react as they do.
Complex Problem Solving	Identifying complex problems and reviewing related information to develop and evaluate options and implement solutions.
Service Orientation	Actively looking for ways to help people.
Coordination	Adjusting actions in relation to others' actions.
Judgment and Decision Making	Considering the relative costs and benefits of potential actions to choose the most appropriate one.
Persuasion	Persuading others to change their minds or behavior.
Operations Analysis	Analyzing needs and product requirements to create a design.

Technology Design	Generating or adapting equipment and technology to serve user needs.
Negotiation	Bringing others together and trying to reconcile differences.
Equipment Selection	Determining the kind of tools and equipment needed to do a job.
Systems Evaluation	Identifying measures or indicators of system performance and the actions needed to improve or correct performance, relative to the goals of the system.
Mathematics	Using mathematics to solve problems.
Science	Using scientific rules and methods to solve problems.
Systems Analysis	Determining how a system should work and how changes in conditions, operations, and the environment will affect outcomes.
Quality Control Analysis	Conducting tests and inspections of products, services, or processes to evaluate quality or performance.
Management of Personnel Resources	Motivating, developing, and directing people as they work, identifying the best people for the job.
Management of Material Resources	Obtaining and seeing to the appropriate use of equipment, facilities, and materials needed to do certain work.
Management of Financial Resources	Determining how money will be spent to get the work done, and accounting for these expenditures.
Troubleshooting	Determining causes of operating errors and deciding what to do about it.
Programming	Writing computer programs for various purposes.
Operation and Control	Controlling operations of equipment or systems.
Installation	Installing equipment, machines, wiring, or programs to meet specifications.
Operation Monitoring	Watching gauges, dials, or other indicators to make sure a machine is working properly.
Equipment Maintenance	Performing routine maintenance on equipment and determining when and what kind of maintenance is needed.
Repairing	Repairing machines or systems using the needed tools.

Ability	Ability Definitions
Oral Expression	The ability to communicate information and ideas in speaking so others will understand.
Written Comprehension	The ability to read and understand information and ideas presented in writing.
Written Expression	The ability to communicate information and ideas in writing so others will understand.
Oral Comprehension	The ability to listen to and understand information and ideas presented through spoken words and sentences.
Speech Clarity	The ability to speak clearly so others can understand you.
Inductive Reasoning	The ability to combine pieces of information to form general rules or conclusions (includes finding a relationship among seemingly unrelated events).
Deductive Reasoning	The ability to apply general rules to specific problems to produce answers that make sense.
Near Vision	The ability to see details at close range (within a few feet of the observer)
Information Ordering	The ability to arrange things or actions in a certain order or pattern according to a specific rule or set of rules (e.g., patterns of numbers, letters, words, pictures, mathematical operations).
Problem Sensitivity	The ability to tell when something is wrong or is likely to go wrong. It does not involve solving the problem, only recognizing there is a problem.
Speech Recognition	The ability to identify and understand the speech of another person.
Category Flexibility	The ability to generate or use different sets of rules for combining or grouping things in different ways.
Selective Attention	The ability to concentrate on a task over a period of time without being distracted.
Originality	The ability to come up with unusual or clever ideas about a given topic or situation, or to develop creative ways to solve a problem.
Fluency of Ideas	The ability to come up with a number of ideas about a topic (the number of ideas is important, not their quality, correctness, or creativity).
Memorization	The ability to remember information such as words, numbers, pictures, and procedures.
Time Sharing	The ability to shift back and forth between two or more activities or sources of information (such as speech, sounds, touch, or other sources).
Far Vision	The ability to see details at a distance.
Speed of Closure	The ability to quickly make sense of, combine, and organize information into meaningful patterns.

Mathematical Reasoning	The ability to choose the right mathematical methods or formulas to solve a problem.
Flexibility of Closure	The ability to identify or detect a known pattern (a figure, object, word, or sound) that is hidden in other distracting material.
Visualization	The ability to imagine how something will look after it is moved around or when its parts are moved or rearranged.
Perceptual Speed	The ability to quickly and accurately compare similarities and differences among sets of letters, numbers, objects, pictures, or patterns. The things to be compared may be presented at the same time or one after the other. This ability also includes comparing a presented object with a remembered object.
Number Facility	The ability to add, subtract, multiply, or divide quickly and correctly.
Auditory Attention	The ability to focus on a single source of sound in the presence of other distracting sounds.
Visual Color Discrimination	The ability to match or detect differences between colors, including shades of color and brightness.
Finger Dexterity	The ability to make precisely coordinated movements of the fingers of one or both hands to grasp, manipulate, or assemble very small objects.
Hearing Sensitivity	The ability to detect or tell the differences between sounds that vary in pitch and loudness.
Depth Perception	The ability to judge which of several objects is closer or farther away from you, or to judge the distance between you and an object.
Trunk Strength	The ability to use your abdominal and lower back muscles to support part of the body repeatedly or continuously over time without 'giving out' or fatiguing.
Static Strength	The ability to exert maximum muscle force to lift, push, pull, or carry objects.
Manual Dexterity	The ability to quickly move your hand, your hand together with your arm, or your two hands to grasp, manipulate, or assemble objects.
Explosive Strength	The ability to use short bursts of muscle force to propel oneself (as in jumping or sprinting), or to throw an object.
Response Orientation	The ability to choose quickly between two or more movements in response to two or more different signals (lights, sounds, pictures). It includes the speed with which the correct response is started with the hand, foot, or other body part.
Speed of Limb Movement	The ability to quickly move the arms and legs.
Wrist-Finger Speed	The ability to make fast, simple, repeated movements of the fingers, hands, and wrists.
Stamina	The ability to exert yourself physically over long periods of time without getting winded or out of breath.
Rate Control	The ability to time your movements or the movement of a piece of equipment in anticipation of changes in the speed and/or direction of a moving object or scene.
Extent Flexibility	The ability to bend, stretch, twist, or reach with your body, arms, or legs.
Multilimb Coordination	The ability to coordinate two or more limbs (for example, two arms, two legs, or one leg and one arm) while sitting, standing, or lying down. It does not involve performing the activities while the whole body is in motion.
Control Precision	The ability to quickly and repeatedly adjust the controls of a machine or a vehicle to exact positions.
Gross Body Equilibrium	The ability to keep or regain your body balance or stay upright when in an unstable position.
Arm-Hand Steadiness	The ability to keep your hand and arm steady while moving your arm or while holding your arm and hand in one position.
Dynamic Strength	The ability to exert muscle force repeatedly or continuously over time. This involves muscular endurance and resistance to muscle fatigue.
Gross Body Coordination	The ability to coordinate the movement of your arms, legs, and torso together when the whole body is in motion.
Night Vision	The ability to see under low light conditions.
Glare Sensitivity	The ability to see objects in the presence of glare or bright lighting.
Sound Localization	The ability to tell the direction from which a sound originated.
Peripheral Vision	The ability to see objects or movement of objects to one's side when the eyes are looking ahead.
Reaction Time	The ability to quickly respond (with the hand, finger, or foot) to a signal (sound, light, picture) when it appears.
Spatial Orientation	The ability to know your location in relation to the environment or to know where other objects are in relation to you.
Dynamic Flexibility	The ability to quickly and repeatedly bend, stretch, twist, or reach out with your body, arms, and/or legs.

Work_Activity	Work_Activity Definitions
Interacting With Computers	Using computers and computer systems (including hardware and software) to program, write software, set up functions, enter data, or process information.
Training and Teaching Others	Identifying the educational needs of others, developing formal educational or training programs or classes, and teaching or instructing others.
Updating and Using Relevant Knowledge	Keeping up-to-date technically and applying new knowledge to your job.
Getting Information	Observing, receiving, and otherwise obtaining information from all relevant sources.
Interpreting the Meaning of Information for Others	Translating or explaining what information means and how it can be used.
Thinking Creatively	Developing, designing, or creating new applications, ideas, relationships, systems, or products, including artistic contributions.
Analyzing Data or Information	Identifying the underlying principles, reasons, or facts of information by breaking down information or data into separate parts.
Organizing, Planning, and Prioritizing Work	Developing specific goals and plans to prioritize, organize, and accomplish your work.
Processing Information	Compiling, coding, categorizing, calculating, tabulating, auditing, or verifying information or data.
Coaching and Developing Others	Identifying the developmental needs of others and coaching, mentoring, or otherwise helping others to improve their knowledge or skills.
Judging the Qualities of Things, Services, or Peop	Assessing the value, importance, or quality of things or people.
Identifying Objects, Actions, and Events	Identifying information by categorizing, estimating, recognizing differences or similarities, and detecting changes in circumstances or events.
Establishing and Maintaining Interpersonal Relatio	Developing constructive and cooperative working relationships with others, and maintaining them over time.
Making Decisions and Solving Problems	Analyzing information and evaluating results to choose the best solution and solve problems.
Communicating with Supervisors, Peers, or Subordin	Providing information to supervisors, co-workers, and subordinates by telephone, in written form, e-mail, or in person.
Documenting/Recording Information	Entering, transcribing, recording, storing, or maintaining information in written or electronic/magnetic form.
Communicating with Persons Outside Organization	Communicating with people outside the organization, representing the organization to customers, the public, government, and other external sources. This information can be exchanged in person, in writing, or by telephone or e-mail.
Developing Objectives and Strategies	Establishing long-range objectives and specifying the strategies and actions to achieve them.
Provide Consultation and Advice to Others	Providing guidance and expert advice to management or other groups on technical, systems-, or process-related topics.
Scheduling Work and Activities	Scheduling events, programs, and activities, as well as the work of others.
Evaluating Information to Determine Compliance wit	Using relevant information and individual judgment to determine whether events or processes comply with laws, regulations, or standards.
Developing and Building Teams	Encouraging and building mutual trust, respect, and cooperation among team members.
Coordinating the Work and Activities of Others	Getting members of a group to work together to accomplish tasks.
Monitor Processes, Materials, or Surroundings	Monitoring and reviewing information from materials, events, or the environment, to detect or assess problems.
Estimating the Quantifiable Characteristics of Pro	Estimating sizes, distances, and quantities; or determining time, costs, resources, or materials needed to perform a work activity.
Assisting and Caring for Others	Providing personal assistance, medical attention, emotional support, or other personal care to others such as coworkers, customers, or patients.
Performing for or Working Directly with the Public	Performing for people or dealing directly with the public. This includes serving customers in restaurants and stores, and receiving clients or guests.
Performing Administrative Activities	Performing day-to-day administrative tasks such as maintaining information files and processing paperwork.
Resolving Conflicts and Negotiating with Others	Handling complaints, settling disputes, and resolving grievances and conflicts, or otherwise negotiating with others.
Guiding, Directing, and Motivating Subordinates	Providing guidance and direction to subordinates, including setting performance standards and monitoring performance.

Selling or Influencing Others	Convincing others to buy merchandise/goods or to otherwise change their minds or actions.
Inspecting Equipment, Structures, or Material	Inspecting equipment, structures, or materials to identify the cause of errors or other problems or defects.
Monitoring and Controlling Resources	Monitoring and controlling resources and overseeing the spending of money.
Staffing Organizational Units	Recruiting, interviewing, selecting, hiring, and promoting employees in an organization.
Controlling Machines and Processes	Using either control mechanisms or direct physical activity to operate machines or processes (not including computers or vehicles).
Handling and Moving Objects	Using hands and arms in handling, installing, positioning, and moving materials, and manipulating things.
Performing General Physical Activities	Performing physical activities that require considerable use of your arms and legs and moving your whole body, such as climbing, lifting, balancing, walking, stooping, and handling of materials.
Repairing and Maintaining Electronic Equipment	Servicing, repairing, calibrating, regulating, fine-tuning, or testing machines, devices, and equipment that operate primarily on the basis of electrical or electronic (not mechanical) principles.
Drafting, Laying Out, and Specifying Technical Dev	Providing documentation, detailed instructions, drawings, or specifications to tell others about how devices, parts, equipment, or structures are to be fabricated, constructed, assembled, modified, maintained, or used.
Operating Vehicles, Mechanized Devices, or Equipme	Running, maneuvering, navigating, or driving vehicles or mechanized equipment, such as forklifts, passenger vehicles, aircraft, or water craft.
Repairing and Maintaining Mechanical Equipment	Servicing, repairing, adjusting, and testing machines, devices, moving parts, and equipment that operate primarily on the basis of mechanical (not electronic) principles.

Work_Context	Work_Context Definitions
Electronic Mail	How often do you use electronic mail in this job?
Freedom to Make Decisions	How much decision making freedom, without supervision, does the job offer?
Structured versus Unstructured Work	To what extent is this job structured for the worker, rather than allowing the worker to determine tasks, priorities, and goals?
Indoors, Environmentally Controlled	How often does this job require working indoors in environmentally controlled conditions?
Face-to-Face Discussions	How often do you have to have face-to-face discussions with individuals or teams in this job?
Telephone	How often do you have telephone conversations in this job?
Contact With Others	How often does this job require the worker to be in contact with others (face-to-face, by telephone, or otherwise) in order to perform it?
Work With Work Group or Team	How important is it to work with others in a group or team in this job?
Coordinate or Lead Others	How important is it to coordinate or lead others in accomplishing work activities in this job?
Spend Time Sitting	How much does this job require sitting?
Importance of Being Exact or Accurate	How important is being very exact or highly accurate in performing this job?
Letters and Memos	How often does the job require written letters and memos?
Public Speaking	How often do you have to perform public speaking in this job?
Impact of Decisions on Co-workers or Company Resul	How do the decisions an employee makes impact the results of co-workers, clients or the company?
Time Pressure	How often does this job require the worker to meet strict deadlines?
Frequency of Decision Making	How frequently is the worker required to make decisions that affect other people, the financial resources, and/or the image and reputation of the organization?
Deal With External Customers	How important is it to work with external customers or the public in this job?
Level of Competition	To what extent does this job require the worker to compete or to be aware of competitive pressures?
Responsibility for Outcomes and Results	How responsible is the worker for work outcomes and results of other workers?
Frequency of Conflict Situations	How often are there conflict situations the employee has to face in this job?
Spend Time Making Repetitive Motions	How much does this job require making repetitive motions?
Degree of Automation	How automated is the job?
Importance of Repeating Same Tasks	How important is repeating the same physical activities (e.g., key entry) or mental activities (e.g., checking entries in a ledger) over and over, without stopping, to performing this job?

Physical Proximity	To what extent does this job require the worker to perform job tasks in close physical proximity to other people?
Spend Time Using Your Hands to Handle, Control, or	How much does this job require using your hands to handle, control, or feel objects, tools or controls?
Deal With Unpleasant or Angry People	How frequently does the worker have to deal with unpleasant, angry, or discourteous individuals as part of the job requirements?
Spend Time Standing	How much does this job require standing?
Consequence of Error	How serious would the result usually be if the worker made a mistake that was not readily correctable?
Sounds, Noise Levels Are Distracting or Uncomforta	How often does this job require working exposed to sounds and noise levels that are distracting or uncomfortable?
Responsible for Others' Health and Safety	How much responsibility is there for the health and safety of others in this job?
Spend Time Walking and Running	How much does this job require walking and running?
In an Enclosed Vehicle or Equipment	How often does this job require working in a closed vehicle or equipment (e.g., car)?
Indoors, Not Environmentally Controlled	How often does this job require working indoors in non-controlled environmental conditions (e.g., warehouse without heat)?
Extremely Bright or Inadequate Lighting	How often does this job require working in extremely bright or inadequate lighting conditions?
Exposed to Disease or Infections	How often does this job require exposure to disease/infections?
Exposed to Contaminants	How often does this job require working exposed to contaminants (such as pollutants, gases, dust or odors)?
Cramped Work Space, Awkward Positions	How often does this job require working in cramped work spaces that requires getting into awkward positions?
Very Hot or Cold Temperatures	How often does this job require working in very hot (above 90 F degrees) or very cold (below 32 F degrees) temperatures?
Spend Time Bending or Twisting the Body	How much does this job require bending or twisting your body?
Pace Determined by Speed of Equipment	How important is it to this job that the pace is determined by the speed of equipment or machinery? (This does not refer to keeping busy at all times on this job.)
Deal With Physically Aggressive People	How frequently does this job require the worker to deal with physical aggression of violent individuals?
Spend Time Kneeling, Crouching, Stooping, or Crawl	How much does this job require kneeling, crouching, stooping or crawling?
Outdoors, Under Cover	How often does this job require working outdoors, under cover (e.g., structure with roof but no walls)?
Spend Time Keeping or Regaining Balance	How often does this job require keeping or regaining your balance?
Outdoors, Exposed to Weather	How often does this job require working outdoors, exposed to all weather conditions?
Exposed to High Places	How often does this job require exposure to high places?
Exposed to Minor Burns, Cuts, Bites, or Stings	How often does this job require exposure to minor burns, cuts, bites, or stings?
Exposed to Hazardous Conditions	How often does this job require exposure to hazardous conditions?
Exposed to Hazardous Equipment	How often does this job require exposure to hazardous equipment?
Wear Common Protective or Safety Equipment such as	How much does this job require wearing common protective or safety equipment such as safety shoes, glasses, gloves, hard hats or live jackets?
Spend Time Climbing Ladders, Scaffolds, or Poles	How much does this job require climbing ladders, scaffolds, or poles?
In an Open Vehicle or Equipment	How often does this job require working in an open vehicle or equipment (e.g., tractor)?
Exposed to Whole Body Vibration	How often does this job require exposure to whole body vibration (e.g., operate a jackhammer)?
Exposed to Radiation	How often does this job require exposure to radiation?
Wear Specialized Protective or Safety Equipment su	How much does this job require wearing specialized protective or safety equipment such as breathing apparatus, safety harness, full protection suits, or radiation protection?

Job Zone Component Title	Job Zone Component Definitions
Title	Job Zone Five: Extensive Preparation Needed

Overall Experience	Extensive skill, knowledge, and experience are needed for these occupations. Many require more than five years of experience. For example, surgeons must complete four years of college and an additional five to seven years of specialized medical training to be able to do their job.
Job Training	Employees may need some on-the-job training, but most of these occupations assume that the person will already have the required skills, knowledge, work-related experience, and/or training.
Job Zone Examples	These occupations often involve coordinating, training, supervising, or managing the activities of others to accomplish goals. Very advanced communication and organizational skills are required. Examples include athletic trainers, lawyers, managing editors, phyicists, social psychologists, and surgeons.
SVP Range	(8.0 and above)
Education	A bachelor's degree is the minimum formal education required for these occupations. However, many also require graduate school. For example, they may require a master's degree, and some require a Ph.D., M.D., or J.D. (law degree).

Work_Styles	Work_Styles Definitions
Independence	Job requires developing one's own ways of doing things, guiding oneself with little or no supervision, and depending on oneself to get things done.
Integrity	Job requires being honest and ethical.
Initiative	Job requires a willingness to take on responsibilities and challenges.
Achievement/Effort	Job requires establishing and maintaining personally challenging achievement goals and exerting effort toward mastering tasks.
Dependability	Job requires being reliable, responsible, and dependable, and fulfilling obligations.
Analytical Thinking	Job requires analyzing information and using logic to address work-related issues and problems.
Innovation	Job requires creativity and alternative thinking to develop new ideas for and answers to work-related problems.
Persistence	Job requires persistence in the face of obstacles.
Adaptability/Flexibility	Job requires being open to change (positive or negative) and to considerable variety in the workplace.
Attention to Detail	Job requires being careful about detail and thorough in completing work tasks.
Self Control	Job requires maintaining composure, keeping emotions in check, controlling anger, and avoiding aggressive behavior, even in very difficult situations.
Stress Tolerance	Job requires accepting criticism and dealing calmly and effectively with high stress situations.
Leadership	Job requires a willingness to lead, take charge, and offer opinions and direction.
Cooperation	Job requires being pleasant with others on the job and displaying a good-natured, cooperative attitude.
Concern for Others	Job requires being sensitive to others' needs and feelings and being understanding and helpful on the job.
Social Orientation	Job requires preferring to work with others rather than alone, and being personally connected with others on the job.

25-1111.00 - Criminal Justice and Law Enforcement Teachers, Postsecondary

Teach courses in criminal justice, corrections, and law enforcement administration.

Tasks

1) Advise students on academic and vocational curricula, and on career issues.

2) Maintain regularly scheduled office hours in order to advise and assist students.

3) Plan, evaluate, and revise curricula, course content, and course materials and methods of instruction.

4) Collaborate with colleagues to address teaching and research issues.

5) Maintain student attendance records, grades, and other required records.

6) Select and obtain materials and supplies such as textbooks.

7) Compile bibliographies of specialized materials for outside reading assignments.

1437

8) Serve on academic or administrative committees that deal with institutional policies, departmental matters, and academic issues.

9) Prepare and deliver lectures to undergraduate and/or graduate students on topics such as criminal law, defensive policing, and investigation techniques.

10) Conduct research in a particular field of knowledge, and publish findings in professional journals, books, and/or electronic media.

11) Participate in student recruitment, registration, and placement activities.

12) Supervise undergraduate and/or graduate teaching, internship, and research work.

13) Write grant proposals to procure external research funding.

14) Act as advisers to student organizations.

15) Provide professional consulting services to government and/or industry.

16) Perform administrative duties such as serving as department head.

17) Keep abreast of developments in their field by reading current literature, talking with colleagues, and participating in professional conferences.

18) Prepare course materials such as syllabi, homework assignments, and handouts.

19) Compile, administer, and grade examinations, or assign this work to others.

20) Evaluate and grade students' class work, assignments, and papers.

21) Initiate, facilitate, and moderate classroom discussions.

Knowledge	Knowledge Definitions
English Language	Knowledge of the structure and content of the English language including the meaning and spelling of words, rules of composition, and grammar.
Law and Government	Knowledge of laws, legal codes, court procedures, precedents, government regulations, executive orders, agency rules, and the democratic political process.
Education and Training	Knowledge of principles and methods for curriculum and training design, teaching and instruction for individuals and groups, and the measurement of training effects.
Sociology and Anthropology	Knowledge of group behavior and dynamics, societal trends and influences, human migrations, ethnicity, cultures and their history and origins.
Mathematics	Knowledge of arithmetic, algebra, geometry, calculus, statistics, and their applications.
Psychology	Knowledge of human behavior and performance; individual differences in ability, personality, and interests; learning and motivation; psychological research methods; and the assessment and treatment of behavioral and affective disorders.
Computers and Electronics	Knowledge of circuit boards, processors, chips, electronic equipment, and computer hardware and software, including applications and programming.
Philosophy and Theology	Knowledge of different philosophical systems and religions. This includes their basic principles, values, ethics, ways of thinking, customs, practices, and their impact on human culture.
Public Safety and Security	Knowledge of relevant equipment, policies, procedures, and strategies to promote effective local, state, or national security operations for the protection of people, data, property, and institutions.
History and Archeology	Knowledge of historical events and their causes, indicators, and effects on civilizations and cultures.
Administration and Management	Knowledge of business and management principles involved in strategic planning, resource allocation, human resources modeling, leadership technique, production methods, and coordination of people and resources.
Geography	Knowledge of principles and methods for describing the features of land, sea, and air masses, including their physical characteristics, locations, interrelationships, and distribution of plant, animal, and human life.
Therapy and Counseling	Knowledge of principles, methods, and procedures for diagnosis, treatment, and rehabilitation of physical and mental dysfunctions, and for career counseling and guidance.
Communications and Media	Knowledge of media production, communication, and dissemination techniques and methods. This includes alternative ways to inform and entertain via written, oral, and visual media.
Customer and Personal Service	Knowledge of principles and processes for providing customer and personal services. This includes customer needs assessment, meeting quality standards for services, and evaluation of customer satisfaction.
Personnel and Human Resources	Knowledge of principles and procedures for personnel recruitment, selection, training, compensation and benefits, labor relations and negotiation, and personnel information systems.
Clerical	Knowledge of administrative and clerical procedures and systems such as word processing, managing files and records, stenography and transcription, designing forms, and other office procedures and terminology.
Telecommunications	Knowledge of transmission, broadcasting, switching, control, and operation of telecommunications systems.
Economics and Accounting	Knowledge of economic and accounting principles and practices, the financial markets, banking and the analysis and reporting of financial data.
Transportation	Knowledge of principles and methods for moving people or goods by air, rail, sea, or road, including the relative costs and benefits.
Sales and Marketing	Knowledge of principles and methods for showing, promoting, and selling products or services. This includes marketing strategy and tactics, product demonstration, sales techniques, and sales control systems.
Biology	Knowledge of plant and animal organisms, their tissues, cells, functions, interdependencies, and interactions with each other and the environment.
Medicine and Dentistry	Knowledge of the information and techniques needed to diagnose and treat human injuries, diseases, and deformities. This includes symptoms, treatment alternatives, drug properties and interactions, and preventive health-care measures.
Foreign Language	Knowledge of the structure and content of a foreign (non-English) language including the meaning and spelling of words, rules of composition and grammar, and pronunciation.
Engineering and Technology	Knowledge of the practical application of engineering science and technology. This includes applying principles, techniques, procedures, and equipment to the design and production of various goods and services.
Chemistry	Knowledge of the chemical composition, structure, and properties of substances and of the chemical processes and transformations that they undergo. This includes uses of chemicals and their interactions, danger signs, production techniques, and disposal methods.
Fine Arts	Knowledge of the theory and techniques required to compose, produce, and perform works of music, dance, visual arts, drama, and sculpture.
Building and Construction	Knowledge of materials, methods, and the tools involved in the construction or repair of houses, buildings, or other structures such as highways and roads.
Design	Knowledge of design techniques, tools, and principles involved in production of precision technical plans, blueprints, drawings, and models.
Physics	Knowledge and prediction of physical principles, laws, their interrelationships, and applications to understanding fluid, material, and atmospheric dynamics, and mechanical, electrical, atomic and sub-atomic structures and processes.
Production and Processing	Knowledge of raw materials, production processes, quality control, costs, and other techniques for maximizing the effective manufacture and distribution of goods.
Mechanical	Knowledge of machines and tools, including their designs, uses, repair, and maintenance.
Food Production	Knowledge of techniques and equipment for planting, growing, and harvesting food products (both plant and animal) for consumption, including storage/handling techniques.

Skills	Skills Definitions
Reading Comprehension	Understanding written sentences and paragraphs in work related documents.
Writing	Communicating effectively in writing as appropriate for the needs of the audience.
Critical Thinking	Using logic and reasoning to identify the strengths and weaknesses of alternative solutions, conclusions or approaches to problems.
Speaking	Talking to others to convey information effectively.
Instructing	Teaching others how to do something.
Active Learning	Understanding the implications of new information for both current and future problem-solving and decision-making.
Active Listening	Giving full attention to what other people are saying, taking time to understand the points being made, asking questions as appropriate, and not interrupting at inappropriate times.

Learning Strategies	Selecting and using training/instructional methods and procedures appropriate for the situation when learning or teaching new things.
Time Management	Managing one's own time and the time of others.
Complex Problem Solving	Identifying complex problems and reviewing related information to develop and evaluate options and implement solutions.
Judgment and Decision Making	Considering the relative costs and benefits of potential actions to choose the most appropriate one.
Social Perceptiveness	Being aware of others' reactions and understanding why they react as they do.
Monitoring	Monitoring/Assessing performance of yourself, other individuals, or organizations to make improvements or take corrective action.
Coordination	Adjusting actions in relation to others' actions.
Persuasion	Persuading others to change their minds or behavior.
Service Orientation	Actively looking for ways to help people.
Negotiation	Bringing others together and trying to reconcile differences.
Mathematics	Using mathematics to solve problems.
Science	Using scientific rules and methods to solve problems.
Management of Personnel Resources	Motivating, developing, and directing people as they work, identifying the best people for the job.
Management of Financial Resources	Determining how money will be spent to get the work done, and accounting for these expenditures.
Technology Design	Generating or adapting equipment and technology to serve user needs.
Operations Analysis	Analyzing needs and product requirements to create a design.
Equipment Selection	Determining the kind of tools and equipment needed to do a job.
Management of Material Resources	Obtaining and seeing to the appropriate use of equipment, facilities, and materials needed to do certain work.
Systems Evaluation	Identifying measures or indicators of system performance and the actions needed to improve or correct performance, relative to the goals of the system.
Quality Control Analysis	Conducting tests and inspections of products, services, or processes to evaluate quality or performance.
Programming	Writing computer programs for various purposes.
Systems Analysis	Determining how a system should work and how changes in conditions, operations, and the environment will affect outcomes.
Troubleshooting	Determining causes of operating errors and deciding what to do about it.
Operation and Control	Controlling operations of equipment or systems.
Equipment Maintenance	Performing routine maintenance on equipment and determining when and what kind of maintenance is needed.
Installation	Installing equipment, machines, wiring, or programs to meet specifications.
Repairing	Repairing machines or systems using the needed tools.
Operation Monitoring	Watching gauges, dials, or other indicators to make sure a machine is working properly.

Ability	Ability Definitions
Written Comprehension	The ability to read and understand information and ideas presented in writing.
Oral Expression	The ability to communicate information and ideas in speaking so others will understand.
Oral Comprehension	The ability to listen to and understand information and ideas presented through spoken words and sentences.
Inductive Reasoning	The ability to combine pieces of information to form general rules or conclusions (includes finding a relationship among seemingly unrelated events).
Written Expression	The ability to communicate information and ideas in writing so others will understand.
Speech Clarity	The ability to speak clearly so others can understand you.
Deductive Reasoning	The ability to apply general rules to specific problems to produce answers that make sense.
Near Vision	The ability to see details at close range (within a few feet of the observer).
Problem Sensitivity	The ability to tell when something is wrong or is likely to go wrong. It does not involve solving the problem, only recognizing there is a problem.
Speech Recognition	The ability to identify and understand the speech of another person.
Information Ordering	The ability to arrange things or actions in a certain order or pattern according to a specific rule or set of rules (e.g., patterns of numbers, letters, words, pictures, mathematical operations).

Originality	The ability to come up with unusual or clever ideas about a given topic or situation, or to develop creative ways to solve a problem.
Category Flexibility	The ability to generate or use different sets of rules for combining or grouping things in different ways.
Fluency of Ideas	The ability to come up with a number of ideas about a topic (the number of ideas is important, not their quality, correctness, or creativity).
Selective Attention	The ability to concentrate on a task over a period of time without being distracted.
Time Sharing	The ability to shift back and forth between two or more activities or sources of information (such as speech, sounds, touch, or other sources).
Memorization	The ability to remember information such as words, numbers, pictures, and procedures.
Flexibility of Closure	The ability to identify or detect a known pattern (a figure, object, word, or sound) that is hidden in other distracting material.
Speed of Closure	The ability to quickly make sense of, combine, and organize information into meaningful patterns.
Mathematical Reasoning	The ability to choose the right mathematical methods or formulas to solve a problem.
Far Vision	The ability to see details at a distance.
Number Facility	The ability to add, subtract, multiply, or divide quickly and correctly.
Perceptual Speed	The ability to quickly and accurately compare similarities and differences among sets of letters, numbers, objects, pictures, or patterns. The things to be compared may be presented at the same time or one after the other. This ability also includes comparing a presented object with a remembered object.
Visualization	The ability to imagine how something will look after it is moved around or when its parts are moved or rearranged.
Trunk Strength	The ability to use your abdominal and lower back muscles to support part of the body repeatedly or continuously over time without 'giving out' or fatiguing.
Auditory Attention	The ability to focus on a single source of sound in the presence of other distracting sounds.
Finger Dexterity	The ability to make precisely coordinated movements of the fingers of one or both hands to grasp, manipulate, or assemble very small objects.
Visual Color Discrimination	The ability to match or detect differences between colors, including shades of color and brightness.
Hearing Sensitivity	The ability to detect or tell the differences between sounds that vary in pitch and loudness.
Depth Perception	The ability to judge which of several objects is closer or farther away from you, or to judge the distance between you and an object.
Sound Localization	The ability to tell the direction from which a sound originated.
Extent Flexibility	The ability to bend, stretch, twist, or reach with your body, arms, and/or legs.
Rate Control	The ability to time your movements or the movement of a piece of equipment in anticipation of changes in the speed and/or direction of a moving object or scene.
Spatial Orientation	The ability to know your location in relation to the environment or to know where other objects are in relation to you.
Wrist-Finger Speed	The ability to make fast, simple, repeated movements of the fingers, hands, and wrists.
Speed of Limb Movement	The ability to quickly move the arms and legs.
Static Strength	The ability to exert maximum muscle force to lift, push, pull, or carry objects.
Explosive Strength	The ability to use short bursts of muscle force to propel oneself (as in jumping or sprinting), or to throw an object.
Dynamic Flexibility	The ability to quickly and repeatedly bend, stretch, twist, or reach out with your body, arms, and/or legs.
Arm-Hand Steadiness	The ability to keep your hand and arm steady while moving your arm or while holding your arm and hand in one position.
Response Orientation	The ability to choose quickly between two or more movements in response to two or more different signals (lights, sounds, pictures). It includes the speed with which the correct response is started with the hand, foot, or other body part.
Dynamic Strength	The ability to exert muscle force repeatedly or continuously over time. This involves muscular endurance and resistance to muscle fatigue.
Multilimb Coordination	The ability to coordinate two or more limbs (for example, two arms, two legs, or one leg and one arm) while sitting, standing, or lying down. It does not involve performing the activities while the whole body is in motion.

Manual Dexterity	The ability to quickly move your hand, your hand together with your arm, or your two hands to grasp, manipulate, or assemble objects.
Reaction Time	The ability to quickly respond (with the hand, finger, or foot) to a signal (sound, light, picture) when it appears.
Glare Sensitivity	The ability to see objects in the presence of glare or bright lighting.
Gross Body Coordination	The ability to coordinate the movement of your arms, legs, and torso together when the whole body is in motion.
Gross Body Equilibrium	The ability to keep or regain your body balance or stay upright when in an unstable position.
Stamina	The ability to exert yourself physically over long periods of time without getting winded or out of breath.
Peripheral Vision	The ability to see objects or movement of objects to one's side when the eyes are looking ahead.
Night Vision	The ability to see under low light conditions.
Control Precision	The ability to quickly and repeatedly adjust the controls of a machine or a vehicle to exact positions.

Work_Activity	**Work_Activity Definitions**
Training and Teaching Others	Identifying the educational needs of others, developing formal educational or training programs or classes, and teaching or instructing others.
Getting Information	Observing, receiving, and otherwise obtaining information from all relevant sources.
Interpreting the Meaning of Information for Others	Translating or explaining what information means and how it can be used.
Thinking Creatively	Developing, designing, or creating new applications, ideas, relationships, systems, or products, including artistic contributions.
Analyzing Data or Information	Identifying the underlying principles, reasons, or facts of information by breaking down information or data into separate parts.
Updating and Using Relevant Knowledge	Keeping up-to-date technically and applying new knowledge to your job.
Judging the Qualities of Things, Services, or Peop	Assessing the value, importance, or quality of things or people.
Processing Information	Compiling, coding, categorizing, calculating, tabulating, auditing, or verifying information or data.
Organizing, Planning, and Prioritizing Work	Developing specific goals and plans to prioritize, organize, and accomplish your work.
Making Decisions and Solving Problems	Analyzing information and evaluating results to choose the best solution and solve problems.
Establishing and Maintaining Interpersonal Relatio	Developing constructive and cooperative working relationships with others, and maintaining them over time.
Interacting With Computers	Using computers and computer systems (including hardware and software) to program, write software, set up functions, enter data, or process information.
Coaching and Developing Others	Identifying the developmental needs of others and coaching, mentoring, or otherwise helping others to improve their knowledge or skills.
Identifying Objects, Actions, and Events	Identifying information by categorizing, estimating, recognizing differences or similarities, and detecting changes in circumstances or events.
Communicating with Supervisors, Peers, or Subordin	Providing information to supervisors, co-workers, and subordinates by telephone, in written form, e-mail, or in person.
Documenting/Recording Information	Entering, transcribing, recording, storing, or maintaining information in written or electronic/magnetic form.
Developing Objectives and Strategies	Establishing long-range objectives and specifying the strategies and actions to achieve them.
Performing for or Working Directly with the Public	Performing for people or dealing directly with the public. This includes serving customers in restaurants and stores, and receiving clients or guests.
Monitor Processes, Materials, or Surroundings	Monitoring and reviewing information from materials, events, or the environment, to detect or assess problems.
Communicating with Persons Outside Organization	Communicating with people outside the organization, representing the organization to customers, the public, government, and other external sources. This information can be exchanged in person, in writing, or by telephone or e-mail.
Scheduling Work and Activities	Scheduling events, programs, and activities, as well as the work of others.
Provide Consultation and Advice to Others	Providing guidance and expert advice to management or other groups on technical, systems-, or process-related topics.

Evaluating Information to Determine Compliance wit	Using relevant information and individual judgment to determine whether events or processes comply with laws, regulations, or standards.
Coordinating the Work and Activities of Others	Getting members of a group to work together to accomplish tasks.
Performing Administrative Activities	Performing day-to-day administrative tasks such as maintaining information files and processing paperwork.
Estimating the Quantifiable Characteristics of Pro	Estimating sizes, distances, and quantities; or determining time, costs, resources, or materials needed to perform a work activity.
Assisting and Caring for Others	Providing personal assistance, medical attention, emotional support, or other personal care to others such as coworkers, customers, or patients.
Resolving Conflicts and Negotiating with Others	Handling complaints, settling disputes, and resolving grievances and conflicts, or otherwise negotiating with others.
Developing and Building Teams	Encouraging and building mutual trust, respect, and cooperation among team members.
Guiding, Directing, and Motivating Subordinates	Providing guidance and direction to subordinates, including setting performance standards and monitoring performance.
Selling or Influencing Others	Convincing others to buy merchandise/goods or to otherwise change their minds or actions.
Staffing Organizational Units	Recruiting, interviewing, selecting, hiring, and promoting employees in an organization.
Monitoring and Controlling Resources	Monitoring and controlling resources and overseeing the spending of money.
Inspecting Equipment, Structures, or Material	Inspecting equipment, structures, or materials to identify the cause of errors or other problems or defects.
Handling and Moving Objects	Using hands and arms in handling, installing, positioning, and moving materials, and manipulating things.
Controlling Machines and Processes	Using either control mechanisms or direct physical activity to operate machines or processes (not including computers or vehicles).
Performing General Physical Activities	Performing physical activities that require considerable use of your arms and legs and moving your whole body, such as climbing, lifting, balancing, walking, stooping, and handling of materials.
Drafting, Laying Out, and Specifying Technical Dev	Providing documentation, detailed instructions, drawings, or specifications to tell others about how devices, parts, equipment, or structures are to be fabricated, constructed, assembled, modified, maintained, or used.
Operating Vehicles, Mechanized Devices, or Equipme	Running, maneuvering, navigating, or driving vehicles or mechanized equipment, such as forklifts, passenger vehicles, aircraft, or water craft.
Repairing and Maintaining Electronic Equipment	Servicing, repairing, calibrating, regulating, fine-tuning, or testing machines, devices, and equipment that operate primarily on the basis of electrical or electronic (not mechanical) principles.
Repairing and Maintaining Mechanical Equipment	Servicing, repairing, adjusting, and testing machines, devices, moving parts, and equipment that operate primarily on the basis of mechanical (not electronic) principles.

Work_Context	**Work_Context Definitions**
Structured versus Unstructured Work	To what extent is this job structured for the worker, rather than allowing the worker to determine tasks, priorities, and goals?
Freedom to Make Decisions	How much decision making freedom, without supervision, does the job offer?
Electronic Mail	How often do you use electronic mail in this job?
Telephone	How often do you have telephone conversations in this job?
Face-to-Face Discussions	How often do you have to have face-to-face discussions with individuals or teams in this job?
Public Speaking	How often do you have to perform public speaking in this job?
Contact With Others	How much does this job require the worker to be in contact with others (face-to-face, by telephone, or otherwise) in order to perform it?
Indoors, Environmentally Controlled	How often does this job require working indoors in environmentally controlled conditions?
Importance of Being Exact or Accurate	How important is being very exact or highly accurate in performing this job?
Coordinate or Lead Others	How important is it to coordinate or lead others in accomplishing work activities in this job?
Time Pressure	How often does this job require the worker to meet strict deadlines?
Letters and Memos	How often does the job require written letters and memos?
Work With Work Group or Team	How important is it to work with others in a group or team in this job?
Level of Competition	To what extent does this job require the worker to compete or to be aware of competitive pressures?

Frequency of Decision Making	How frequently is the worker required to make decisions that affect other people, the financial resources, and/or the image and reputation of the organization?
Spend Time Sitting	How much does this job require sitting?
Impact of Decisions on Co-workers or Company Resul	How do the decisions an employee makes impact the results of co-workers, clients or the company?
Physical Proximity	To what extent does this job require the worker to perform job tasks in close physical proximity to other people?
Deal With External Customers	How important is it to work with external customers or the public in this job?
Deal With Unpleasant or Angry People	How frequently does the worker have to deal with unpleasant, angry, or discourteous individuals as part of the job requirements?
Spend Time Standing	How much does this job require standing?
Frequency of Conflict Situations	How often are there conflict situations the employee has to face in this job?
Sounds, Noise Levels Are Distracting or Uncomforta	How often does this job require working exposed to sounds and noise levels that are distracting or uncomfortable?
Responsibility for Outcomes and Results	How responsible is the worker for work outcomes and results of other workers?
Importance of Repeating Same Tasks	How important is repeating the same physical activities (e.g., key entry) or mental activities (e.g., checking entries in a ledger) over and over, without stopping, to performing this job?
Responsible for Others' Health and Safety	How much responsibility is there for the health and safety of others in this job?
Degree of Automation	How automated is the job?
Consequence of Error	How serious would the result usually be if the worker made a mistake that was not readily correctable?
Spend Time Making Repetitive Motions	How much does this job require making repetitive motions?
Spend Time Walking and Running	How much does this job require walking and running?
Spend Time Using Your Hands to Handle, Control, or	How much does this job require using your hands to handle, control, or feel objects, tools or controls?
Extremely Bright or Inadequate Lighting	How often does this job require working in extremely bright or inadequate lighting conditions?
In an Enclosed Vehicle or Equipment	How often does this job require working in a closed vehicle or equipment (e.g., car)?
Very Hot or Cold Temperatures	How often does this job require working in very hot (above 90 F degrees) or very cold (below 32 F degrees) temperatures?
Indoors, Not Environmentally Controlled	How often does this job require working indoors in non-controlled environmental conditions (e.g., warehouse without heat)?
Cramped Work Space, Awkward Positions	How often does this job require working in cramped work spaces that requires getting into awkward positions?
Exposed to Disease or Infections	How often does this job require exposure to disease/infections?
Outdoors, Exposed to Weather	How often does this job require working outdoors, exposed to all weather conditions?
Deal With Physically Aggressive People	How frequently does this job require the worker to deal with physical aggression of violent individuals?
Outdoors, Under Cover	How often does this job require working outdoors, under cover (e.g., structure with roof but no walls)?
Spend Time Bending or Twisting the Body	How much does this job require bending or twisting your body?
Exposed to Contaminants	How often does this job require working exposed to contaminants (such as pollutants, gases, dust or odors)?
Spend Time Kneeling, Crouching, Stooping, or Crawl	How much does this job require kneeling, crouching, stooping or crawling?
Exposed to Minor Burns, Cuts, Bites, or Stings	How often does this job require exposure to minor burns, cuts, bites, or stings?
Pace Determined by Speed of Equipment	How important is it to this job that the pace is determined by the speed of equipment or machinery? (This does not refer to keeping busy at all times on this job.)
Spend Time Keeping or Regaining Balance	How much does this job require keeping or regaining your balance?
In an Open Vehicle or Equipment	How often does this job require working in an open vehicle or equipment (e.g., tractor)?
Wear Specialized Protective or Safety Equipment su	How much does this job require wearing specialized protective or safety equipment such as breathing apparatus, safety harness, full protection suits, or radiation protection?
Exposed to Hazardous Conditions	How often does this job require exposure to hazardous conditions?
Exposed to Hazardous Equipment	How often does this job require exposure to hazardous equipment?

Exposed to High Places	How often does this job require exposure to high places?
Exposed to Radiation	How often does this job require exposure to radiation?
Exposed to Whole Body Vibration	How often does this job require exposure to whole body vibration (e.g., operate a jackhammer)?
Spend Time Climbing Ladders, Scaffolds, or Poles	How much does this job require climbing ladders, scaffolds, or poles?
Wear Common Protective or Safety Equipment such as	How much does this job require wearing common protective or safety equipment such as safety shoes, glasses, gloves, hard hats or live jackets?

Job Zone Component	Job Zone Component Definitions
Title	Job Zone Five: Extensive Preparation Needed
Overall Experience	Extensive skill, knowledge, and experience are needed for these occupations. Many require more than five years of experience. For example, surgeons must complete four years of college and an additional five to seven years of specialized medical training to be able to do their job.
Job Training	Employees may need some on-the-job training, but most of these occupations assume that the person will already have the required skills, knowledge, work-related experience, and/or training.
Job Zone Examples	These occupations often involve coordinating, training, supervising, or managing the activities of others to accomplish goals. Very advanced communication and organizational skills are required. Examples include athletic trainers, lawyers, managing editors, phyicists, social psychologists, and surgeons.
SVP Range	(8.0 and above)
Education	A bachelor's degree is the minimum formal education required for these occupations. However, many also require graduate school. For example, they may require a master's degree, and some require a Ph.D., M.D., or J.D. (law degree).

Work_Styles	Work_Styles Definitions
Integrity	Job requires being honest and ethical.
Independence	Job requires developing one's own ways of doing things, guiding oneself with little or no supervision, and depending on oneself to get things done.
Analytical Thinking	Job requires analyzing information and using logic to address work-related issues and problems.
Initiative	Job requires a willingness to take on responsibilities and challenges.
Dependability	Job requires being reliable, responsible, and dependable, and fulfilling obligations.
Attention to Detail	Job requires being careful about detail and thorough in completing work tasks.
Achievement/Effort	Job requires establishing and maintaining personally challenging achievement goals and exerting effort toward mastering tasks.
Innovation	Job requires creativity and alternative thinking to develop new ideas for and answers to work-related problems.
Persistence	Job requires persistence in the face of obstacles.
Leadership	Job requires a willingness to lead, take charge, and offer opinions and direction.
Cooperation	Job requires being pleasant with others on the job and displaying a good-natured, cooperative attitude.
Concern for Others	Job requires being sensitive to others' needs and feelings and being understanding and helpful on the job.
Self Control	Job requires maintaining composure, keeping emotions in check, controlling anger, and avoiding aggressive behavior, even in very difficult situations.
Adaptability/Flexibility	Job requires being open to change (positive or negative) and to considerable variety in the workplace.
Stress Tolerance	Job requires accepting criticism and dealing calmly and effectively with high stress situations.
Social Orientation	Job requires preferring to work with others rather than alone, and being personally connected with others on the job.

25-1112.00 - Law Teachers, Postsecondary

Teach courses in law.

Tasks

1) Compile, administer, and grade examinations, or assign this work to others.

2) Maintain student attendance records, grades, and other required records.

3) Advise students on academic and vocational curricula, and on career issues.

4) Participate in campus and community events.

5) Serve on academic or administrative committees that deal with institutional policies, departmental matters, and academic issues.

6) Maintain regularly scheduled office hours in order to advise and assist students.

7) Prepare and deliver lectures to undergraduate and/or graduate students on topics such as civil procedure, contracts, and torts.

8) Conduct research in a particular field of knowledge, and publish findings in professional journals, books, and/or electronic media.

9) Compile bibliographies of specialized materials for outside reading assignments.

10) Participate in student recruitment, registration, and placement activities.

11) Act as advisers to student organizations.

12) Supervise undergraduate and/or graduate teaching, internship, and research work.

13) Perform administrative duties such as serving as department head.

14) Assign cases for students to hear and try.

15) Provide professional consulting services to government and/or industry.

16) Write grant proposals to procure external research funding.

17) Keep abreast of developments in their field by reading current literature, talking with colleagues, and participating in professional conferences.

18) Evaluate and grade students' class work, assignments, papers, and oral presentations.

19) Prepare course materials such as syllabi, homework assignments, and handouts.

20) Plan, evaluate, and revise curricula, course content, and course materials and methods of instruction.

21) Collaborate with colleagues to address teaching and research issues.

22) Initiate, facilitate, and moderate classroom discussions.

Knowledge	Knowledge Definitions
Law and Government	Knowledge of laws, legal codes, court procedures, precedents, government regulations, executive orders, agency rules, and the democratic political process.
English Language	Knowledge of the structure and content of the English language including the meaning and spelling of words, rules of composition, and grammar.
Education and Training	Knowledge of principles and methods for curriculum and training design, teaching and instruction for individuals and groups, and the measurement of training effects.
Computers and Electronics	Knowledge of circuit boards, processors, chips, electronic equipment, and computer hardware and software, including applications and programming.
Philosophy and Theology	Knowledge of different philosophical systems and religions. This includes their basic principles, values, ethics, ways of thinking, customs, practices, and their impact on human culture.
History and Archeology	Knowledge of historical events and their causes, indicators, and effects on civilizations and cultures.
Communications and Media	Knowledge of media production, communication, and dissemination techniques and methods. This includes alternative ways to inform and entertain via written, oral, and visual media.
Administration and Management	Knowledge of business and management principles involved in strategic planning, resource allocation, human resources modeling, leadership technique, production methods, and coordination of people and resources.
Sociology and Anthropology	Knowledge of group behavior and dynamics, societal trends and influences, human migrations, ethnicity, cultures and their history and origins.
Clerical	Knowledge of administrative and clerical procedures and systems such as word processing, managing files and records, stenography and transcription, designing forms, and other office procedures and terminology.
Psychology	Knowledge of human behavior and performance; individual differences in ability, personality, and interests; learning and motivation; psychological research methods; and the assessment and treatment of behavioral and affective disorders.
Customer and Personal Service	Knowledge of principles and processes for providing customer and personal services. This includes customer needs assessment, meeting quality standards for services, and evaluation of customer satisfaction.
Public Safety and Security	Knowledge of relevant equipment, policies, procedures, and strategies to promote effective local, state, or national security operations for the protection of people, data, property, and institutions.
Personnel and Human Resources	Knowledge of principles and procedures for personnel recruitment, selection, training, compensation and benefits, labor relations and negotiation, and personnel information systems.
Therapy and Counseling	Knowledge of principles, methods, and procedures for diagnosis, treatment, and rehabilitation of physical and mental dysfunctions, and for career counseling and guidance.
Mathematics	Knowledge of arithmetic, algebra, geometry, calculus, statistics, and their applications.
Geography	Knowledge of principles and methods for describing the features of land, sea, and air masses, including their physical characteristics, locations, interrelationships, and distribution of plant, animal, and human life.
Economics and Accounting	Knowledge of economic and accounting principles and practices, the financial markets, banking and the analysis and reporting of financial data.
Fine Arts	Knowledge of the theory and techniques required to compose, produce, and perform works of music, dance, visual arts, drama, and sculpture.
Foreign Language	Knowledge of the structure and content of a foreign (non-English) language including the meaning and spelling of words, rules of composition and grammar, and pronunciation.
Sales and Marketing	Knowledge of principles and methods for showing, promoting, and selling products or services. This includes marketing strategy and tactics, product demonstration, sales techniques, and sales control systems.
Medicine and Dentistry	Knowledge of the information and techniques needed to diagnose and treat human injuries, diseases, and deformities. This includes symptoms, treatment alternatives, drug properties and interactions, and preventive health-care measures.
Telecommunications	Knowledge of transmission, broadcasting, switching, control, and operation of telecommunications systems.
Transportation	Knowledge of principles and methods for moving people or goods by air, rail, sea, or road, including the relative costs and benefits.
Biology	Knowledge of plant and animal organisms, their tissues, cells, functions, interdependencies, and interactions with each other and the environment.
Chemistry	Knowledge of the chemical composition, structure, and properties of substances and of the chemical processes and transformations that they undergo. This includes uses of chemicals and their interactions, danger signs, production techniques, and disposal methods.
Design	Knowledge of design techniques, tools, and principles involved in production of precision technical plans, blueprints, drawings, and models.
Physics	Knowledge and prediction of physical principles, laws, their interrelationships, and applications to understanding fluid, material, and atmospheric dynamics, and mechanical, electrical, atomic and sub-atomic structures and processes.
Production and Processing	Knowledge of raw materials, production processes, quality control, costs, and other techniques for maximizing the effective manufacture and distribution of goods.
Building and Construction	Knowledge of materials, methods, and the tools involved in the construction or repair of houses, buildings, or other structures such as highways and roads.
Engineering and Technology	Knowledge of the practical application of engineering science and technology. This includes applying principles, techniques, procedures, and equipment to the design and production of various goods and services.
Mechanical	Knowledge of machines and tools, including their designs, uses, repair, and maintenance.
Food Production	Knowledge of techniques and equipment for planting, growing, and harvesting food products (both plant and animal) for consumption, including storage/handling techniques.

Skills	Skills Definitions
Instructing	Teaching others how to do something.

Reading Comprehension	Understanding written sentences and paragraphs in work related documents.
Speaking	Talking to others to convey information effectively.
Critical Thinking	Using logic and reasoning to identify the strengths and weaknesses of alternative solutions, conclusions or approaches to problems.
Active Listening	Giving full attention to what other people are saying, taking time to understand the points being made, asking questions as appropriate, and not interrupting at inappropriate times.
Writing	Communicating effectively in writing as appropriate for the needs of the audience.
Time Management	Managing one's own time and the time of others.
Active Learning	Understanding the implications of new information for both current and future problem-solving and decision-making.
Learning Strategies	Selecting and using training/instructional methods and procedures appropriate for the situation when learning or teaching new things.
Monitoring	Monitoring/Assessing performance of yourself, other individuals, or organizations to make improvements or take corrective action.
Persuasion	Persuading others to change their minds or behavior.
Social Perceptiveness	Being aware of others' reactions and understanding why they react as they do.
Complex Problem Solving	Identifying complex problems and reviewing related information to develop and evaluate options and implement solutions.
Judgment and Decision Making	Considering the relative costs and benefits of potential actions to choose the most appropriate one.
Service Orientation	Actively looking for ways to help people.
Coordination	Adjusting actions in relation to others' actions.
Negotiation	Bringing others together and trying to reconcile differences.
Quality Control Analysis	Conducting tests and inspections of products, services, or processes to evaluate quality or performance.
Management of Personnel Resources	Motivating, developing, and directing people as they work, identifying the best people for the job.
Systems Evaluation	Identifying measures or indicators of system performance and the actions needed to improve or correct performance, relative to the goals of the system.
Systems Analysis	Determining how a system should work and how changes in conditions, operations, and the environment will affect outcomes.
Mathematics	Using mathematics to solve problems.
Equipment Selection	Determining the kind of tools and equipment needed to do a job.
Management of Financial Resources	Determining how money will be spent to get the work done, and accounting for these expenditures.
Operations Analysis	Analyzing needs and product requirements to create a design.
Management of Material Resources	Obtaining and seeing to the appropriate use of equipment, facilities, and materials needed to do certain work.
Troubleshooting	Determining causes of operating errors and deciding what to do about it.
Science	Using scientific rules and methods to solve problems.
Technology Design	Generating or adapting equipment and technology to serve user needs.
Operation and Control	Controlling operations of equipment or systems.
Operation Monitoring	Watching gauges, dials, or other indicators to make sure a machine is working properly.
Installation	Installing equipment, machines, wiring, or programs to meet specifications.
Programming	Writing computer programs for various purposes.
Equipment Maintenance	Performing routine maintenance on equipment and determining when and what kind of maintenance is needed.
Repairing	Repairing machines or systems using the needed tools.

Ability	Ability Definitions
Oral Expression	The ability to communicate information and ideas in speaking so others will understand.
Written Comprehension	The ability to read and understand information and ideas presented in writing.
Speech Clarity	The ability to speak clearly so others can understand you.
Oral Comprehension	The ability to listen to and understand information and ideas presented through spoken words and sentences.
Written Expression	The ability to communicate information and ideas in writing so others will understand.
Deductive Reasoning	The ability to apply general rules to specific problems to produce answers that make sense.

Inductive Reasoning	The ability to combine pieces of information to form general rules or conclusions (includes finding a relationship among seemingly unrelated events).
Speech Recognition	The ability to identify and understand the speech of another person.
Near Vision	The ability to see details at close range (within a few feet of the observer).
Problem Sensitivity	The ability to tell when something is wrong or is likely to go wrong. It does not involve solving the problem, only recognizing there is a problem.
Information Ordering	The ability to arrange things or actions in a certain order or pattern according to a specific rule or set of rules (e.g., patterns of numbers, letters, words, pictures, mathematical operations).
Category Flexibility	The ability to generate or use different sets of rules for combining or grouping things in different ways.
Originality	The ability to come up with unusual or clever ideas about a given topic or situation, or to develop creative ways to solve a problem.
Fluency of Ideas	The ability to come up with a number of ideas about a topic (the number of ideas is important, not their quality, correctness, or creativity).
Time Sharing	The ability to shift back and forth between two or more activities or sources of information (such as speech, sounds, touch, or other sources).
Selective Attention	The ability to concentrate on a task over a period of time without being distracted.
Memorization	The ability to remember information such as words, numbers, pictures, and procedures.
Flexibility of Closure	The ability to identify or detect a known pattern (a figure, object, word, or sound) that is hidden in other distracting material.
Mathematical Reasoning	The ability to choose the right mathematical methods or formulas to solve a problem.
Speed of Closure	The ability to quickly make sense of, combine, and organize information into meaningful patterns.
Number Facility	The ability to add, subtract, multiply, or divide quickly and correctly.
Auditory Attention	The ability to focus on a single source of sound in the presence of other distracting sounds.
Perceptual Speed	The ability to quickly and accurately compare similarities and differences among sets of letters, numbers, objects, pictures, or patterns. The things to be compared may be presented at the same time or one after the other. This ability also includes comparing a presented object with a remembered object.
Visualization	The ability to imagine how something will look after it is moved around or when its parts are moved or rearranged.
Far Vision	The ability to see details at a distance.
Finger Dexterity	The ability to make precisely coordinated movements of the fingers of one or both hands to grasp, manipulate, or assemble very small objects.
Visual Color Discrimination	The ability to match or detect differences between colors, including shades of color and brightness.
Hearing Sensitivity	The ability to detect or tell the differences between sounds that vary in pitch and loudness.
Trunk Strength	The ability to use your abdominal and lower back muscles to support part of the body repeatedly or continuously over time without 'giving out' or fatiguing.
Dynamic Strength	The ability to exert muscle force repeatedly or continuously over time. This involves muscular endurance and resistance to muscle fatigue.
Extent Flexibility	The ability to bend, stretch, twist, or reach with your body, arms, and/or legs.
Response Orientation	The ability to choose quickly between two or more movements in response to two or more different signals (lights, sounds, pictures). It includes the speed with which the correct response is started with the hand, foot, or other body part.
Stamina	The ability to exert yourself physically over long periods of time without getting winded or out of breath.
Reaction Time	The ability to quickly respond (with the hand, finger, or foot) to a signal (sound, light, picture) when it appears.
Wrist-Finger Speed	The ability to make fast, simple, repeated movements of the fingers, hands, and wrists.
Speed of Limb Movement	The ability to quickly move the arms and legs.
Explosive Strength	The ability to use short bursts of muscle force to propel oneself (as in jumping or sprinting), or to throw an object.
Night Vision	The ability to see under low light conditions.

Multilimb Coordination	The ability to coordinate two or more limbs (for example, two arms, two legs, or one leg and one arm) while sitting, standing, or lying down. It does not involve performing the activities while the whole body is in motion.
Control Precision	The ability to quickly and repeatedly adjust the controls of a machine or a vehicle to exact positions.
Static Strength	The ability to exert maximum muscle force to lift, push, pull, or carry objects.
Gross Body Coordination	The ability to coordinate the movement of your arms, legs, and torso together when the whole body is in motion.
Arm-Hand Steadiness	The ability to keep your hand and arm steady while moving your arm or while holding your arm and hand in one position.
Spatial Orientation	The ability to know your location in relation to the environment or to know where other objects are in relation to you.
Rate Control	The ability to time your movements or the movement of a piece of equipment in anticipation of changes in the speed and/or direction of a moving object or scene.
Peripheral Vision	The ability to see objects or movement of objects to one's side when the eyes are looking ahead.
Sound Localization	The ability to tell the direction from which a sound originated.
Depth Perception	The ability to judge which of several objects is closer or farther away from you, or to judge the distance between you and an object.
Gross Body Equilibrium	The ability to keep or regain your body balance or stay upright when in an unstable position.
Dynamic Flexibility	The ability to quickly and repeatedly bend, stretch, twist, or reach out with your body, arms, and/or legs.
Glare Sensitivity	The ability to see objects in the presence of glare or bright lighting.
Manual Dexterity	The ability to quickly move your hand, your hand together with your arm, or your two hands to grasp, manipulate, or assemble objects.

Work_Activity	Work_Activity Definitions
Training and Teaching Others	Identifying the educational needs of others, developing formal educational or training programs or classes, and teaching or instructing others.
Getting Information	Observing, receiving, and otherwise obtaining information from all relevant sources.
Interpreting the Meaning of Information for Others	Translating or explaining what information means and how it can be used.
Thinking Creatively	Developing, designing, or creating new applications, ideas, relationships, systems, or products, including artistic contributions.
Establishing and Maintaining Interpersonal Relatio	Developing constructive and cooperative working relationships with others, and maintaining them over time.
Analyzing Data or Information	Identifying the underlying principles, reasons, or facts of information by breaking down information or data into separate parts.
Making Decisions and Solving Problems	Analyzing information and evaluating results to choose the best solution and solve problems.
Communicating with Supervisors, Peers, or Subordin	Providing information to supervisors, co-workers, and subordinates by telephone, in written form, e-mail, or in person.
Updating and Using Relevant Knowledge	Keeping up-to-date technically and applying new knowledge to your job.
Organizing, Planning, and Prioritizing Work	Developing specific goals and plans to prioritize, organize, and accomplish your work.
Judging the Qualities of Things, Services, or Peop	Assessing the value, importance, or quality of things or people.
Identifying Objects, Actions, and Events	Identifying information by categorizing, estimating, recognizing differences or similarities, and detecting changes in circumstances or events.
Coaching and Developing Others	Identifying the developmental needs of others and coaching, mentoring, or otherwise helping others to improve their knowledge or skills.
Evaluating Information to Determine Compliance wit	Using relevant information and individual judgment to determine whether events or processes comply with laws, regulations, or standards.
Interacting With Computers	Using computers and computer systems (including hardware and software) to program, write software, set up functions, enter data, or process information.
Developing Objectives and Strategies	Establishing long-range objectives and specifying the strategies and actions to achieve them.
Processing Information	Compiling, coding, categorizing, calculating, tabulating, auditing, or verifying information or data.

Documenting/Recording Information	Entering, transcribing, recording, storing, or maintaining information in written or electronic/magnetic form.
Monitor Processes, Materials, or Surroundings	Monitoring and reviewing information from materials, events, or the environment, to detect or assess problems.
Communicating with Persons Outside Organization	Communicating with people outside the organization, representing the organization to customers, the public, government, and other external sources. This information can be exchanged in person, in writing, or by telephone or e-mail.
Provide Consultation and Advice to Others	Providing guidance and expert advice to management or other groups on technical, systems-, or process-related topics.
Scheduling Work and Activities	Scheduling events, programs, and activities, as well as the work of others.
Performing Administrative Activities	Performing day-to-day administrative tasks such as maintaining information files and processing paperwork.
Guiding, Directing, and Motivating Subordinates	Providing guidance and direction to subordinates, including setting performance standards and monitoring performance.
Resolving Conflicts and Negotiating with Others	Handling complaints, settling disputes, and resolving grievances and conflicts, or otherwise negotiating with others.
Coordinating the Work and Activities of Others	Getting members of a group to work together to accomplish tasks.
Developing and Building Teams	Encouraging and building mutual trust, respect, and cooperation among team members.
Performing for or Working Directly with the Public	Performing for people or dealing directly with the public. This includes serving customers in restaurants and stores, and receiving clients or guests.
Selling or Influencing Others	Convincing others to buy merchandise/goods or to otherwise change their minds or actions.
Assisting and Caring for Others	Providing personal assistance, medical attention, emotional support, or other personal care to others such as coworkers, customers, or patients.
Estimating the Quantifiable Characteristics of Pro	Estimating sizes, distances, and quantities; or determining time, costs, resources, or materials needed to perform a work activity.
Staffing Organizational Units	Recruiting, interviewing, selecting, hiring, and promoting employees in an organization.
Monitoring and Controlling Resources	Monitoring and controlling resources and overseeing the spending of money.
Inspecting Equipment, Structures, or Material	Inspecting equipment, structures, or materials to identify the cause of errors or other problems or defects.
Controlling Machines and Processes	Using either control mechanisms or direct physical activity to operate machines or processes (not including computers or vehicles).
Handling and Moving Objects	Using hands and arms in handling, installing, positioning, and moving materials, and manipulating things.
Performing General Physical Activities	Performing physical activities that require considerable use of your arms and legs and moving your whole body, such as climbing, lifting, balancing, walking, stooping, and handling of materials.
Drafting, Laying Out, and Specifying Technical Dev	Providing documentation, detailed instructions, drawings, or specifications to tell others about how devices, parts, equipment, or structures are to be fabricated, constructed, assembled, modified, maintained, or used.
Repairing and Maintaining Electronic Equipment	Servicing, repairing, calibrating, regulating, fine-tuning, or testing machines, devices, and equipment that operate primarily on the basis of electrical or electronic (not mechanical) principles.
Repairing and Maintaining Mechanical Equipment	Servicing, repairing, adjusting, and testing machines, devices, moving parts, and equipment that operate primarily on the basis of mechanical (not electronic) principles.
Operating Vehicles, Mechanized Devices, or Equipme	Running, maneuvering, navigating, or driving vehicles or mechanized equipment, such as forklifts, passenger vehicles, aircraft, or water craft.

Work_Context	Work_Context Definitions
Electronic Mail	How often do you use electronic mail in this job?
Face-to-Face Discussions	How often do you have to have face-to-face discussions with individuals or teams in this job?
Structured versus Unstructured Work	To what extent is this job structured for the worker, rather than allowing the worker to determine tasks, priorities, and goals?
Indoors, Environmentally Controlled	How often does this job require working indoors in environmentally controlled conditions?
Freedom to Make Decisions	How much decision making freedom, without supervision, does the job offer?
Telephone	How often do you have telephone conversations in this job?

Contact With Others	How much does this job require the worker to be in contact with others (face-to-face, by telephone, or otherwise) in order to perform it?
Public Speaking	How often do you have to perform public speaking in this job?
Time Pressure	How often does this job require the worker to meet strict deadlines?
Spend Time Sitting	How much does this job require sitting?
Letters and Memos	How often does the job require written letters and memos?
Work With Work Group or Team	How important is it to work with others in a group or team in this job?
Impact of Decisions on Co-workers or Company Resul	How do the decisions an employee makes impact the results of co-workers, clients or the company?
Coordinate or Lead Others	How important is it to coordinate or lead others in accomplishing work activities in this job?
Importance of Being Exact or Accurate	How important is being very exact or highly accurate in performing this job?
Frequency of Decision Making	How frequently is the worker required to make decisions that affect other people, the financial resources, and/or the image and reputation of the organization?
Level of Competition	To what extent does this job require the worker to compete or to be aware of competitive pressures?
Frequency of Conflict Situations	How often are there conflict situations the employee has to face in this job?
Deal With External Customers	How important is it to work with external customers or the public in this job?
Deal With Unpleasant or Angry People	How frequently does the worker have to deal with unpleasant, angry, or discourteous individuals as part of the job requirements?
Physical Proximity	To what extent does this job require the worker to perform job tasks in close physical proximity to other people?
Responsibility for Outcomes and Results	How responsible is the worker for work outcomes and results of other workers?
Importance of Repeating Same Tasks	How important is repeating the same physical activities (e.g., key entry) or mental activities (e.g., checking entries in a ledger) over and over, without stopping, to performing this job?
Spend Time Making Repetitive Motions	How much does this job require making repetitive motions?
Consequence of Error	How serious would the result usually be if the worker made a mistake that was not readily correctable?
Spend Time Standing	How much does this job require standing?
Sounds, Noise Levels Are Distracting or Uncomforta	How often does this job require working exposed to sounds and noise levels that are distracting or uncomfortable?
Spend Time Using Your Hands to Handle, Control, or	How much does this job require using your hands to handle, control, or feel objects, tools or controls?
Degree of Automation	How automated is the job?
Exposed to Disease or Infections	How often does this job require exposure to disease/infections?
Exposed to Contaminants	How often does this job require working exposed to contaminants (such as pollutants, gases, dust or odors)?
Responsible for Others' Health and Safety	How much responsibility is there for the health and safety of others in this job?
Spend Time Walking and Running	How much does this job require walking and running?
Extremely Bright or Inadequate Lighting	How often does this job require working in extremely bright or inadequate lighting conditions?
Deal With Physically Aggressive People	How frequently does this job require the worker to deal with physical aggression of violent individuals?
Outdoors, Exposed to Weather	How often does this job require working outdoors, exposed to all weather conditions?
Very Hot or Cold Temperatures	How often does this job require working in very hot (above 90 F degrees) or very cold (below 32 F degrees) temperatures?
Indoors, Not Environmentally Controlled	How often does this job require working indoors in non-controlled environmental conditions (e.g., warehouse without heat)?
Cramped Work Space, Awkward Positions	How often does this job require working in cramped work spaces that requires getting into awkward positions?
In an Enclosed Vehicle or Equipment	How often does this job require working in a closed vehicle or equipment (e.g., car)?
Spend Time Bending or Twisting the Body	How much does this job require bending or twisting your body?
Outdoors, Under Cover	How often does this job require working outdoors, under cover (e.g., structure with roof but no walls)?
Spend Time Kneeling, Crouching, Stooping, or Crawl	How much does this job require kneeling, crouching, stooping or crawling?

Exposed to Hazardous Conditions	How often does this job require exposure to hazardous conditions?
Exposed to Minor Burns, Cuts, Bites, or Stings	How often does this job require exposure to minor burns, cuts, bites, or stings?
Exposed to Whole Body Vibration	How often does this job require exposure to whole body vibration (e.g., operate a jackhammer)?
Wear Common Protective or Safety Equipment such as	How much does this job require wearing common protective or safety equipment such as safety shoes, glasses, gloves, hard hats or life jackets?
Exposed to Hazardous Equipment	How often does this job require exposure to hazardous equipment?
Spend Time Climbing Ladders, Scaffolds, or Poles	How much does this job require climbing ladders, scaffolds, or poles?
Spend Time Keeping or Regaining Balance	How much does this job require keeping or regaining your balance?
In an Open Vehicle or Equipment	How often does this job require working in an open vehicle or equipment (e.g., tractor)?
Exposed to High Places	How often does this job require exposure to high places?
Pace Determined by Speed of Equipment	How important is it to this job that the pace is determined by the speed of equipment or machinery? (This does not refer to keeping busy at all times on this job.)
Exposed to Radiation	How often does this job require exposure to radiation?
Wear Specialized Protective or Safety Equipment su	How much does this job require wearing specialized protective or safety equipment such as breathing apparatus, safety harness, full protection suits, or radiation protection?

Job Zone Component	Job Zone Component Definitions
Title	Job Zone Five: Extensive Preparation Needed
Overall Experience	Extensive skill, knowledge, and experience are needed for these occupations. Many require more than five years of experience. For example, surgeons must complete four years of college and an additional five to seven years of specialized medical training to be able to do their job.
Job Training	Employees may need some on-the-job training, but most of these occupations assume that the person will already have the required skills, knowledge, work-related experience, and/or training.
Job Zone Examples	These occupations often involve coordinating, training, supervising, or managing the activities of others to accomplish goals. Very advanced communication and organizational skills are required. Examples include athletic trainers, lawyers, managing editors, phyicists, social psychologists, and surgeons.
SVP Range	(8.0 and above)
Education	A bachelor's degree is the minimum formal education required for these occupations. However, many also require graduate school. For example, they may require a master's degree, and some require a Ph.D., M.D., or J.D. (law degree).

Work_Styles	Work_Styles Definitions
Analytical Thinking	Job requires analyzing information and using logic to address work-related issues and problems.
Dependability	Job requires being reliable, responsible, and dependable, and fulfilling obligations.
Independence	Job requires developing one's own ways of doing things, guiding oneself with little or no supervision, and depending on oneself to get things done.
Integrity	Job requires being honest and ethical.
Achievement/Effort	Job requires establishing and maintaining personally challenging achievement goals and exerting effort toward mastering tasks.
Attention to Detail	Job requires being careful about detail and thorough in completing work tasks.
Initiative	Job requires a willingness to take on responsibilities and challenges.
Persistence	Job requires persistence in the face of obstacles.
Self Control	Job requires maintaining composure, keeping emotions in check, controlling anger, and avoiding aggressive behavior, even in very difficult situations.
Innovation	Job requires creativity and alternative thinking to develop new ideas for and answers to work-related problems.
Concern for Others	Job requires being sensitive to others' needs and feelings and being understanding and helpful on the job.
Stress Tolerance	Job requires accepting criticism and dealing calmly and effectively with high stress situations.

Adaptability/Flexibility	Job requires being open to change (positive or negative) and to considerable variety in the workplace.
Leadership	Job requires a willingness to lead, take charge, and offer opinions and direction.
Cooperation	Job requires being pleasant with others on the job and displaying a good-natured, cooperative attitude.
Social Orientation	Job requires preferring to work with others rather than alone, and being personally connected with others on the job.

25-1113.00 - Social Work Teachers, Postsecondary

Teach courses in social work.

Tasks

1) Initiate, facilitate, and moderate classroom discussions.

2) Prepare and deliver lectures to undergraduate and/or graduate students on topics such as family behavior, child and adolescent mental health, and social intervention evaluation.

3) Compile bibliographies of specialized materials for outside reading assignments.

4) Participate in campus and community events.

5) Maintain regularly scheduled office hours in order to advise and assist students.

6) Prepare course materials such as syllabi, homework assignments, and handouts.

7) Maintain student attendance records, grades, and other required records.

8) Serve on academic or administrative committees that deal with institutional policies, departmental matters, and academic issues.

9) Compile, administer, and grade examinations, or assign this work to others.

10) Select and obtain materials and supplies such as textbooks and laboratory equipment.

11) Participate in student recruitment, registration, and placement activities.

12) Supervise undergraduate and/or graduate teaching, internship, and research work.

13) Conduct research in a particular field of knowledge, and publish findings in professional journals, books, and/or electronic media.

14) Supervise students' laboratory and field work.

15) Provide professional consulting services to government and/or industry.

16) Write grant proposals to procure external research funding.

17) Perform administrative duties such as serving as department head.

18) Act as advisers to student organizations.

19) Collaborate with colleagues, and with community agencies, in order to address teaching and research issues.

20) Plan, evaluate, and revise curricula, course content, and course materials and methods of instruction.

21) Keep abreast of developments in their field by reading current literature, talking with colleagues, and participating in professional conferences.

22) Evaluate and grade students' class work, assignments, and papers.

Knowledge	Knowledge Definitions
Education and Training	Knowledge of principles and methods for curriculum and training design, teaching and instruction for individuals and groups, and the measurement of training effects.
English Language	Knowledge of the structure and content of the English language including the meaning and spelling of words, rules of composition, and grammar.
Sociology and Anthropology	Knowledge of group behavior and dynamics, societal trends and influences, human migrations, ethnicity, cultures and their history and origins.
Psychology	Knowledge of human behavior and performance; individual differences in ability, personality, and interests; learning and motivation; psychological research methods; and the assessment and treatment of behavioral and affective disorders.
Therapy and Counseling	Knowledge of principles, methods, and procedures for diagnosis, treatment, and rehabilitation of physical and mental dysfunctions, and for career counseling and guidance.
Philosophy and Theology	Knowledge of different philosophical systems and religions. This includes their basic principles, values, ethics, ways of thinking, customs, practices, and their impact on human culture.
Computers and Electronics	Knowledge of circuit boards, processors, chips, electronic equipment, and computer hardware and software, including applications and programming.
Law and Government	Knowledge of laws, legal codes, court procedures, precedents, government regulations, executive orders, agency rules, and the democratic political process.
Administration and Management	Knowledge of business and management principles involved in strategic planning, resource allocation, human resources modeling, leadership technique, production methods, and coordination of people and resources.
Customer and Personal Service	Knowledge of principles and processes for providing customer and personal services. This includes customer needs assessment, meeting quality standards for services, and evaluation of customer satisfaction.
Mathematics	Knowledge of arithmetic, algebra, geometry, calculus, statistics, and their applications.
Communications and Media	Knowledge of media production, communication, and dissemination techniques and methods. This includes alternative ways to inform and entertain via written, oral, and visual media.
Personnel and Human Resources	Knowledge of principles and procedures for personnel recruitment, selection, training, compensation and benefits, labor relations and negotiation, and personnel information systems.
History and Archeology	Knowledge of historical events and their causes, indicators, and effects on civilizations and cultures.
Clerical	Knowledge of administrative and clerical procedures and systems such as word processing, managing files and records, stenography and transcription, designing forms, and other office procedures and terminology.
Geography	Knowledge of principles and methods for describing the features of land, sea, and air masses, including their physical characteristics, locations, interrelationships, and distribution of plant, animal, and human life.
Sales and Marketing	Knowledge of principles and methods for showing, promoting, and selling products or services. This includes marketing strategy and tactics, product demonstration, sales techniques, and sales control systems.
Foreign Language	Knowledge of the structure and content of a foreign (non-English) language including the meaning and spelling of words, rules of composition and grammar, and pronunciation.
Medicine and Dentistry	Knowledge of the information and techniques needed to diagnose and treat human injuries, diseases, and deformities. This includes symptoms, treatment alternatives, drug properties and interactions, and preventive health-care measures.
Biology	Knowledge of plant and animal organisms, their tissues, cells, functions, interdependencies, and interactions with each other and the environment.
Economics and Accounting	Knowledge of economic and accounting principles and practices, the financial markets, banking and the analysis and reporting of financial data.
Public Safety and Security	Knowledge of relevant equipment, policies, procedures, and strategies to promote effective local, state, or national security operations for the protection of people, data, property, and institutions.
Telecommunications	Knowledge of transmission, broadcasting, switching, control, and operation of telecommunications systems.
Transportation	Knowledge of principles and methods for moving people or goods by air, rail, sea, or road, including the relative costs and benefits.
Fine Arts	Knowledge of the theory and techniques required to compose, produce, and perform works of music, dance, visual arts, drama, and sculpture.
Design	Knowledge of design techniques, tools, and principles involved in production of precision technical plans, blueprints, drawings, and models.
Production and Processing	Knowledge of raw materials, production processes, quality control, costs, and other techniques for maximizing the effective manufacture and distribution of goods.
Engineering and Technology	Knowledge of the practical application of engineering science and technology. This includes applying principles, techniques, procedures, and equipment to the design and production of various goods and services.

Chemistry	Knowledge of the chemical composition, structure, and properties of substances and of the chemical processes and transformations that they undergo. This includes uses of chemicals and their interactions, danger signs, production techniques, and disposal methods.
Mechanical	Knowledge of machines and tools, including their designs, uses, repair, and maintenance.
Food Production	Knowledge of techniques and equipment for planting, growing, and harvesting food products (both plant and animal) for consumption, including storage/handling techniques.
Physics	Knowledge and prediction of physical principles, laws, their interrelationships, and applications to understanding fluid, material, and atmospheric dynamics, and mechanical, electrical, atomic and sub- atomic structures and processes.
Building and Construction	Knowledge of materials, methods, and the tools involved in the construction or repair of houses, buildings, or other structures such as highways and roads.

Skills	Skills Definitions
Reading Comprehension	Understanding written sentences and paragraphs in work related documents.
Instructing	Teaching others how to do something.
Social Perceptiveness	Being aware of others' reactions and understanding why they react as they do.
Active Listening	Giving full attention to what other people are saying, taking time to understand the points being made, asking questions as appropriate, and not interrupting at inappropriate times.
Writing	Communicating effectively in writing as appropriate for the needs of the audience.
Critical Thinking	Using logic and reasoning to identify the strengths and weaknesses of alternative solutions, conclusions or approaches to problems.
Active Learning	Understanding the implications of new information for both current and future problem-solving and decision-making.
Speaking	Talking to others to convey information effectively.
Learning Strategies	Selecting and using training/instructional methods and procedures appropriate for the situation when learning or teaching new things.
Service Orientation	Actively looking for ways to help people.
Complex Problem Solving	Identifying complex problems and reviewing related information to develop and evaluate options and implement solutions.
Coordination	Adjusting actions in relation to others' actions.
Monitoring	Monitoring/Assessing performance of yourself, other individuals, or organizations to make improvements or take corrective action.
Time Management	Managing one's own time and the time of others.
Judgment and Decision Making	Considering the relative costs and benefits of potential actions to choose the most appropriate one.
Negotiation	Bringing others together and trying to reconcile differences.
Persuasion	Persuading others to change their minds or behavior.
Management of Personnel Resources	Motivating, developing, and directing people as they work, identifying the best people for the job.
Operations Analysis	Analyzing needs and product requirements to create a design.
Systems Evaluation	Identifying measures or indicators of system performance and the actions needed to improve or correct performance, relative to the goals of the system.
Science	Using scientific rules and methods to solve problems.
Quality Control Analysis	Conducting tests and inspections of products, services, or processes to evaluate quality or performance.
Management of Financial Resources	Determining how money will be spent to get the work done, and accounting for these expenditures.
Systems Analysis	Determining how a system should work and how changes in conditions, operations, and the environment will affect outcomes.
Mathematics	Using mathematics to solve problems.
Technology Design	Generating or adapting equipment and technology to serve user needs.
Equipment Selection	Determining the kind of tools and equipment needed to do a job.
Management of Material Resources	Obtaining and seeing to the appropriate use of equipment, facilities, and materials needed to do certain work.
Troubleshooting	Determining causes of operating errors and deciding what to do about it.
Programming	Writing computer programs for various purposes.
Operation Monitoring	Watching gauges, dials, or other indicators to make sure a machine is working properly.

Operation and Control	Controlling operations of equipment or systems.
Equipment Maintenance	Performing routine maintenance on equipment and determining when and what kind of maintenance is needed.
Installation	Installing equipment, machines, wiring, or programs to meet specifications.
Repairing	Repairing machines or systems using the needed tools.

Ability	Ability Definitions
Oral Expression	The ability to communicate information and ideas in speaking so others will understand.
Written Comprehension	The ability to read and understand information and ideas presented in writing.
Speech Clarity	The ability to speak clearly so others can understand you.
Written Expression	The ability to communicate information and ideas in writing so others will understand.
Oral Comprehension	The ability to listen to and understand information and ideas presented through spoken words and sentences.
Deductive Reasoning	The ability to apply general rules to specific problems to produce answers that make sense.
Inductive Reasoning	The ability to combine pieces of information to form general rules or conclusions (includes finding a relationship among seemingly unrelated events).
Speech Recognition	The ability to identify and understand the speech of another person.
Near Vision	The ability to see details at close range (within a few feet of the observer).
Originality	The ability to come up with unusual or clever ideas about a given topic or situation, or to develop creative ways to solve a problem.
Problem Sensitivity	The ability to tell when something is wrong or is likely to go wrong. It does not involve solving the problem, only recognizing there is a problem.
Fluency of Ideas	The ability to come up with a number of ideas about a topic (the number of ideas is important, not their quality, correctness, or creativity).
Information Ordering	The ability to arrange things or actions in a certain order or pattern according to a specific rule or set of rules (e.g., patterns of numbers, letters, words, pictures, mathematical operations).
Category Flexibility	The ability to generate or use different sets of rules for combining or grouping things in different ways.
Selective Attention	The ability to concentrate on a task over a period of time without being distracted.
Memorization	The ability to remember information such as words, numbers, pictures, and procedures.
Mathematical Reasoning	The ability to choose the right mathematical methods or formulas to solve a problem.
Far Vision	The ability to see details at a distance.
Time Sharing	The ability to shift back and forth between two or more activities or sources of information (such as speech, sounds, touch, or other sources).
Flexibility of Closure	The ability to identify or detect a known pattern (a figure, object, word, or sound) that is hidden in other distracting material.
Speed of Closure	The ability to quickly make sense of, combine, and organize information into meaningful patterns.
Number Facility	The ability to add, subtract, multiply, or divide quickly and correctly.
Perceptual Speed	The ability to quickly and accurately compare similarities and differences among sets of letters, numbers, objects, pictures, or patterns. The things to be compared may be presented at the same time or one after the other. This ability also includes comparing a presented object with a remembered object.
Visualization	The ability to imagine how something will look after it is moved around or when its parts are moved or rearranged.
Finger Dexterity	The ability to make precisely coordinated movements of the fingers of one or both hands to grasp, manipulate, or assemble very small objects.
Auditory Attention	The ability to focus on a single source of sound in the presence of other distracting sounds.
Visual Color Discrimination	The ability to match or detect differences between colors, including shades of color and brightness.
Hearing Sensitivity	The ability to detect or tell the differences between sounds that vary in pitch and loudness.
Trunk Strength	The ability to use your abdominal and lower back muscles to support part of the body repeatedly or continuously over time without 'giving out' or fatiguing.

Depth Perception	The ability to judge which of several objects is closer or farther away from you, or to judge the distance between you and an object.
Arm-Hand Steadiness	The ability to keep your hand and arm steady while moving your arm or while holding your arm and hand in one position.
Manual Dexterity	The ability to quickly move your hand, your hand together with your arm, or your two hands to grasp, manipulate, or assemble objects.
Spatial Orientation	The ability to know your location in relation to the environment or to know where other objects are in relation to you.
Dynamic Strength	The ability to exert muscle force repeatedly or continuously over time. This involves muscular endurance and resistance to muscle fatigue.
Explosive Strength	The ability to use short bursts of muscle force to propel oneself (as in jumping or sprinting), or to throw an object.
Static Strength	The ability to exert maximum muscle force to lift, push, pull, or carry objects.
Speed of Limb Movement	The ability to quickly move the arms and legs.
Wrist-Finger Speed	The ability to make fast, simple, repeated movements of the fingers, hands, and wrists.
Reaction Time	The ability to quickly respond (with the hand, finger, or foot) to a signal (sound, light, picture) when it appears.
Multilimb Coordination	The ability to coordinate two or more limbs (for example, two arms, two legs, or one leg and one arm) while sitting, standing, or lying down. It does not involve performing the activities while the whole body is in motion.
Control Precision	The ability to quickly and repeatedly adjust the controls of a machine or a vehicle to exact positions.
Peripheral Vision	The ability to see objects or movement of objects to one's side when the eyes are looking ahead.
Dynamic Flexibility	The ability to quickly and repeatedly bend, stretch, twist, or reach out with your body, arms, and/or legs.
Stamina	The ability to exert yourself physically over long periods of time without getting winded or out of breath.
Gross Body Equilibrium	The ability to keep or regain your body balance or stay upright when in an unstable position.
Glare Sensitivity	The ability to see objects in the presence of glare or bright lighting.
Sound Localization	The ability to tell the direction from which a sound originated.
Night Vision	The ability to see under low light conditions.
Rate Control	The ability to time your movements or the movement of a piece of equipment in anticipation of changes in the speed and/or direction of a moving object or scene.
Extent Flexibility	The ability to bend, stretch, twist, or reach with your body, arms, and/or legs.
Response Orientation	The ability to choose quickly between two or more movements in response to two or more different signals (lights, sounds, pictures). It includes the speed with which the correct response is started with the hand, foot, or other body part.
Gross Body Coordination	The ability to coordinate the movement of your arms, legs, and torso together when the whole body is in motion.

Work_Activity	Work_Activity Definitions
Updating and Using Relevant Knowledge	Keeping up-to-date technically and applying new knowledge to your job.
Training and Teaching Others	Identifying the educational needs of others, developing formal educational or training programs or classes, and teaching or instructing others.
Establishing and Maintaining Interpersonal Relatio	Developing constructive and cooperative working relationships with others, and maintaining them over time.
Judging the Qualities of Things, Services, or Peop	Assessing the value, importance, or quality of things or people.
Interpreting the Meaning of Information for Others	Translating or explaining what information means and how it can be used.
Making Decisions and Solving Problems	Analyzing information and evaluating results to choose the best solution and solve problems.
Getting Information	Observing, receiving, and otherwise obtaining information from all relevant sources.
Thinking Creatively	Developing, designing, or creating new applications, ideas, relationships, systems, or products, including artistic contributions.
Organizing, Planning, and Prioritizing Work	Developing specific goals and plans to prioritize, organize, and accomplish your work.
Communicating with Supervisors, Peers, or Subordin	Providing information to supervisors, co-workers, and subordinates by telephone, in written form, e-mail, or in person.

Analyzing Data or Information	Identifying the underlying principles, reasons, or facts of information by breaking down information or data into separate parts.
Interacting With Computers	Using computers and computer systems (including hardware and software) to program, write software, set up functions, enter data, or process information.
Communicating with Persons Outside Organization	Communicating with people outside the organization, representing the organization to customers, the public, government, and other external sources. This information can be exchanged in person, in writing, or by telephone or e-mail.
Coaching and Developing Others	Identifying the developmental needs of others and coaching, mentoring, or otherwise helping others to improve their knowledge or skills.
Documenting/Recording Information	Entering, transcribing, recording, storing, or maintaining information in written or electronic/magnetic form.
Identifying Objects, Actions, and Events	Identifying information by categorizing, estimating, recognizing differences or similarities, and detecting changes in circumstances or events.
Scheduling Work and Activities	Scheduling events, programs, and activities, as well as the work of others.
Developing Objectives and Strategies	Establishing long-range objectives and specifying the strategies and actions to achieve them.
Provide Consultation and Advice to Others	Providing guidance and expert advice to management or other groups on technical, systems-, or process-related topics.
Processing Information	Compiling, coding, categorizing, calculating, tabulating, auditing, or verifying information or data.
Resolving Conflicts and Negotiating with Others	Handling complaints, settling disputes, and resolving grievances and conflicts, or otherwise negotiating with others.
Developing and Building Teams	Encouraging and building mutual trust, respect, and cooperation among team members.
Coordinating the Work and Activities of Others	Getting members of a group to work together to accomplish tasks.
Evaluating Information to Determine Compliance wit	Using relevant information and individual judgment to determine whether events or processes comply with laws, regulations, or standards.
Monitor Processes, Materials, or Surroundings	Monitoring and reviewing information from materials, events, or the environment, to detect or assess problems.
Assisting and Caring for Others	Providing personal assistance, medical attention, emotional support, or other personal care to others such as coworkers, customers, or patients.
Performing Administrative Activities	Performing day-to-day administrative tasks such as maintaining information files and processing paperwork.
Guiding, Directing, and Motivating Subordinates	Providing guidance and direction to subordinates, including setting performance standards and monitoring performance.
Performing for or Working Directly with the Public	Performing for people or dealing directly with the public. This includes serving customers in restaurants and stores, and receiving clients or guests.
Selling or Influencing Others	Convincing others to buy merchandise/goods or to otherwise change their minds or actions.
Estimating the Quantifiable Characteristics of Pro	Estimating sizes, distances, and quantities; or determining time, costs, resources, or materials needed to perform a work activity.
Monitoring and Controlling Resources	Monitoring and controlling resources and overseeing the spending of money.
Staffing Organizational Units	Recruiting, interviewing, selecting, hiring, and promoting employees in an organization.
Inspecting Equipment, Structures, or Material	Inspecting equipment, structures, or materials to identify the cause of errors or other problems or defects.
Operating Vehicles, Mechanized Devices, or Equipme	Running, maneuvering, navigating, or driving vehicles or mechanized equipment, such as forklifts, passenger vehicles, aircraft, or water craft.
Performing General Physical Activities	Performing physical activities that require considerable use of your arms and legs and moving your whole body, such as climbing, lifting, balancing, walking, stooping, and handling of materials.
Controlling Machines and Processes	Using either control mechanisms or direct physical activity to operate machines or processes (not including computers or vehicles).
Handling and Moving Objects	Using hands and arms in handling, installing, positioning, and moving materials, and manipulating things.
Repairing and Maintaining Electronic Equipment	Servicing, repairing, calibrating, regulating, fine-tuning, or testing machines, devices, and equipment that operate primarily on the basis of electrical or electronic (not mechanical) principles.
Repairing and Maintaining Mechanical Equipment	Servicing, repairing, adjusting, and testing machines, devices, moving parts, and equipment that operate primarily on the basis of mechanical (not electronic) principles.

Drafting, Laying Out, and Specifying Technical Dev	Providing documentation, detailed instructions, drawings, or specifications to tell others about how devices, parts, equipment, or structures are to be fabricated, constructed, assembled, modified, maintained, or used.

Work_Context	Work_Context Definitions
Electronic Mail	How often do you use electronic mail in this job?
Freedom to Make Decisions	How much decision making freedom, without supervision, does the job offer?
Telephone	How often do you have telephone conversations in this job?
Structured versus Unstructured Work	To what extent is this job structured for the worker, rather than allowing the worker to determine tasks, priorities, and goals?
Indoors, Environmentally Controlled	How often does this job require working indoors in environmentally controlled conditions?
Face-to-Face Discussions	How often do you have to have face-to-face discussions with individuals or teams in this job?
Contact With Others	How much does this job require the worker to be in contact with others (face-to-face, by telephone, or otherwise) in order to perform it?
Spend Time Sitting	How much does this job require sitting?
Coordinate or Lead Others	How important is it to coordinate or lead others in accomplishing work activities in this job?
Work With Work Group or Team	How important is it to work with others in a group or team in this job?
Letters and Memos	How often does the job require written letters and memos?
Public Speaking	How often do you have to perform public speaking in this job?
Time Pressure	How often does this job require the worker to meet strict deadlines?
Deal With External Customers	How important is it to work with external customers or the public in this job?
Frequency of Decision Making	How frequently is the worker required to make decisions that affect other people, the financial resources, and/or the image and reputation of the organization?
Impact of Decisions on Co-workers or Company Resul	How do the decisions an employee makes impact the results of co-workers, clients or the company?
Importance of Being Exact or Accurate	How important is being very exact or highly accurate in performing this job?
Level of Competition	To what extent does this job require the worker to compete or to be aware of competitive pressures?
Frequency of Conflict Situations	How often are there conflict situations the employee has to face in this job?
Deal With Unpleasant or Angry People	How frequently does the worker have to deal with unpleasant, angry, or discourteous individuals as part of the job requirements?
Responsibility for Outcomes and Results	How responsible is the worker for work outcomes and results of other workers?
Consequence of Error	How serious would the result usually be if the worker made a mistake that was not readily correctable?
Sounds, Noise Levels Are Distracting or Uncomforta	How often does this job require working exposed to sounds and noise levels that are distracting or uncomfortable?
Physical Proximity	To what extent does this job require the worker to perform job tasks in close physical proximity to other people?
Spend Time Standing	How much does this job require standing?
In an Enclosed Vehicle or Equipment	How often does this job require working in a closed vehicle or equipment (e.g., car)?
Responsible for Others' Health and Safety	How much responsibility is there for the health and safety of others in this job?
Spend Time Making Repetitive Motions	How much does this job require making repetitive motions?
Importance of Repeating Same Tasks	How important is repeating the same physical activities (e.g., key entry) or mental activities (e.g., checking entries in a ledger) over and over, without stopping, to performing this job?
Degree of Automation	How automated is the job?
Spend Time Using Your Hands to Handle, Control, or	How much does this job require using your hands to handle, control, or feel objects, tools or controls?
Exposed to Contaminants	How often does this job require working exposed to contaminants (such as pollutants, gases, dust or odors)?
Spend Time Walking and Running	How much does this job require walking and running?
Extremely Bright or Inadequate Lighting	How often does this job require working in extremely bright or inadequate lighting conditions?
Exposed to Disease or Infections	How often does this job require exposure to disease/infections?
Very Hot or Cold Temperatures	How often does this job require working in very hot (above 90 F degrees) or very cold (below 32 F degrees) temperatures?

Deal With Physically Aggressive People	How frequently does this job require the worker to deal with physical aggression of violent individuals?
Indoors, Not Environmentally Controlled	How often does this job require working indoors in non-controlled environmental conditions (e.g., warehouse without heat)?
Outdoors, Exposed to Weather	How often does this job require working outdoors, exposed to all weather conditions?
Cramped Work Space, Awkward Positions	How often does this job require working in cramped work spaces that requires getting into awkward positions?
Outdoors, Under Cover	How often does this job require working outdoors, under cover (e.g., structure with roof but no walls)?
Spend Time Bending or Twisting the Body	How much does this job require bending or twisting your body?
In an Open Vehicle or Equipment	How often does this job require working in an open vehicle or equipment (e.g., tractor)?
Exposed to Minor Burns, Cuts, Bites, or Stings	How often does this job require exposure to minor burns, cuts, bites, or stings?
Pace Determined by Speed of Equipment	How important is it to this job that the pace is determined by the speed of equipment or machinery? (This does not refer to keeping busy at all times on this job.)
Exposed to Hazardous Equipment	How often does this job require exposure to hazardous equipment?
Exposed to Hazardous Conditions	How often does this job require exposure to hazardous conditions?
Wear Common Protective or Safety Equipment such as	How much does this job require wearing common protective or safety equipment such as safety shoes, glasses, gloves, hard hats or life jackets?
Spend Time Kneeling, Crouching, Stooping, or Crawl	How much does this job require kneeling, crouching, stooping or crawling?
Exposed to Whole Body Vibration	How often does this job require exposure to whole body vibration (e.g., operate a jackhammer)?
Exposed to Radiation	How often does this job require exposure to radiation?
Exposed to High Places	How often does this job require exposure to high places?
Spend Time Climbing Ladders, Scaffolds, or Poles	How much does this job require climbing ladders, scaffolds, or poles?
Wear Specialized Protective or Safety Equipment su	How much does this job require wearing specialized protective or safety equipment such as breathing apparatus, safety harness, full protection suits, or radiation protection?
Spend Time Keeping or Regaining Balance	How much does this job require keeping or regaining your balance?

Job Zone Component	Job Zone Component Definitions
Title	Job Zone Five: Extensive Preparation Needed
Overall Experience	Extensive skill, knowledge, and experience are needed for these occupations. Many require more than five years of experience. For example, surgeons must complete four years of college and an additional five to seven years of specialized medical training to be able to do their job.
Job Training	Employees may need some on-the-job training, but most of these occupations assume that the person will already have the required skills, knowledge, work-related experience, and/or training.
Job Zone Examples	These occupations often involve coordinating, training, supervising, or managing the activities of others to accomplish goals. Very advanced communication and organizational skills are required. Examples include athletic trainers, lawyers, managing editors, physicists, social psychologists, and surgeons.
SVP Range	(8.0 and above)
Education	A bachelor's degree is the minimum formal education required for these occupations. However, many also require graduate school. For example, they may require a master's degree, and some require a Ph.D., M.D., or J.D. (law degree).

Work_Styles	Work_Styles Definitions
Integrity	Job requires being honest and ethical.
Dependability	Job requires being reliable, responsible, and dependable, and fulfilling obligations.
Achievement/Effort	Job requires establishing and maintaining personally challenging achievement goals and exerting effort toward mastering tasks.
Initiative	Job requires a willingness to take on responsibilities and challenges.

Analytical Thinking	Job requires analyzing information and using logic to address work-related issues and problems.
Independence	Job requires developing one's own ways of doing things, guiding oneself with little or no supervision, and depending on oneself to get things done.
Self Control	Job requires maintaining composure, keeping emotions in check, controlling anger, and avoiding aggressive behavior, even in very difficult situations.
Persistence	Job requires persistence in the face of obstacles.
Attention to Detail	Job requires being careful about detail and thorough in completing work tasks.
Concern for Others	Job requires being sensitive to others' needs and feelings and being understanding and helpful on the job.
Leadership	Job requires a willingness to lead, take charge, and offer opinions and direction.
Stress Tolerance	Job requires accepting criticism and dealing calmly and effectively with high stress situations.
Innovation	Job requires creativity and alternative thinking to develop new ideas for and answers to work-related problems.
Cooperation	Job requires being pleasant with others on the job and displaying a good-natured, cooperative attitude.
Adaptability/Flexibility	Job requires being open to change (positive or negative) and to considerable variety in the workplace.
Social Orientation	Job requires preferring to work with others rather than alone, and being personally connected with others on the job.

25-1121.00 - Art, Drama, and Music Teachers, Postsecondary

Teach courses in drama, music, and the arts including fine and applied art, such as painting and sculpture, or design and crafts.

Tasks

1) Advise students on academic and vocational curricula, and on career issues.

2) Maintain student attendance records, grades, and other required records.

3) Prepare course materials such as syllabi, homework assignments, and handouts.

4) Prepare students for performances, exams, or assessments.

5) Maintain regularly scheduled office hours in order to advise and assist students.

6) Keep students informed of community events such as plays and concerts.

7) Select and obtain materials and supplies such as textbooks and performance pieces.

8) Initiate, facilitate, and moderate classroom discussions.

9) Participate in campus and community events.

10) Explain and demonstrate artistic techniques.

11) Collaborate with colleagues to address teaching and research issues

12) Participate in student recruitment, registration, and placement activities.

13) Prepare and deliver lectures to undergraduate and/or graduate students on topics such as acting techniques, fundamentals of music, and art history.

14) Compile, administer, and grade examinations, or assign this work to others.

15) Serve on academic or administrative committees that deal with institutional policies, departmental matters, and academic issues.

16) Supervise undergraduate and/or graduate teaching, internship, and research work.

17) Compile bibliographies of specialized materials for outside reading assignments.

18) Conduct research in a particular field of knowledge, and publish findings in professional journals, books, and/or electronic media.

19) Organize performance groups, and direct their rehearsals.

20) Write grant proposals to procure external research funding.

21) Display students' work in schools, galleries, and exhibitions.

22) Act as advisers to student organizations.

23) Perform administrative duties such as serving as department head.

24) Provide professional consulting services to government and/or industry.

25) Plan, evaluate, and revise curricula, course content, and course materials and methods of instruction.

26) Evaluate and grade students' class work, performances, projects, assignments, and papers.

Knowledge	Knowledge Definitions
Fine Arts	Knowledge of the theory and techniques required to compose, produce, and perform works of music, dance, visual arts, drama, and sculpture.
Education and Training	Knowledge of principles and methods for curriculum and training design, teaching and instruction for individuals and groups, and the measurement of training effects.
English Language	Knowledge of the structure and content of the English language including the meaning and spelling of words, rules of composition, and grammar.
Psychology	Knowledge of human behavior and performance; individual differences in ability, personality, and interests; learning and motivation; psychological research methods; and the assessment and treatment of behavioral and affective disorders.
Communications and Media	Knowledge of media production, communication, and dissemination techniques and methods. This includes alternative ways to inform and entertain via written, oral, and visual media.
Philosophy and Theology	Knowledge of different philosophical systems and religions. This includes their basic principles, values, ethics, ways of thinking, customs, practices, and their impact on human culture.
History and Archeology	Knowledge of historical events and their causes, indicators, and effects on civilizations and cultures.
Administration and Management	Knowledge of business and management principles involved in strategic planning, resource allocation, human resources modeling, leadership technique, production methods, and coordination of people and resources.
Customer and Personal Service	Knowledge of principles and processes for providing customer and personal services. This includes customer needs assessment, meeting quality standards for services, and evaluation of customer satisfaction.
Computers and Electronics	Knowledge of circuit boards, processors, chips, electronic equipment, and computer hardware and software, including applications and programming.
Clerical	Knowledge of administrative and clerical procedures and systems such as word processing, managing files and records, stenography and transcription, designing forms, and other office procedures and terminology.
Sociology and Anthropology	Knowledge of group behavior and dynamics, societal trends and influences, human migrations, ethnicity, cultures and their history and origins.
Therapy and Counseling	Knowledge of principles, methods, and procedures for diagnosis, treatment, and rehabilitation of physical and mental dysfunctions, and for career counseling and guidance.
Personnel and Human Resources	Knowledge of principles and procedures for personnel recruitment, selection, training, compensation and benefits, labor relations and negotiation, and personnel information systems.
Foreign Language	Knowledge of the structure and content of a foreign (non-English) language including the meaning and spelling of words, rules of composition and grammar, and pronunciation.
Sales and Marketing	Knowledge of principles and methods for showing, promoting, and selling products or services. This includes marketing strategy and tactics, product demonstration, sales techniques, and sales control systems.
Mathematics	Knowledge of arithmetic, algebra, geometry, calculus, statistics, and their applications.
Design	Knowledge of design techniques, tools, and principles involved in production of precision technical plans, blueprints, drawings, and models.
Law and Government	Knowledge of laws, legal codes, court procedures, precedents, government regulations, executive orders, agency rules, and the democratic political process.
Public Safety and Security	Knowledge of relevant equipment, policies, procedures, and strategies to promote effective local, state, or national security operations for the protection of people, data, property, and institutions.
Production and Processing	Knowledge of raw materials, production processes, quality control, costs, and other techniques for maximizing the effective manufacture and distribution of goods.
Geography	Knowledge of principles and methods for describing the features of land, sea, and air masses, including their physical characteristics, locations, interrelationships, and distribution of plant, animal, and human life.

Telecommunications	Knowledge of transmission, broadcasting, switching, control, and operation of telecommunications systems.
Economics and Accounting	Knowledge of economic and accounting principles and practices, the financial markets, banking and the analysis and reporting of financial data.
Physics	Knowledge and prediction of physical principles, laws, their interrelationships, and applications to understanding fluid, material, and atmospheric dynamics, and mechanical, electrical, atomic and sub-atomic structures and processes.
Engineering and Technology	Knowledge of the practical application of engineering science and technology. This includes applying principles, techniques, procedures, and equipment to the design and production of various goods and services.
Biology	Knowledge of plant and animal organisms, their tissues, cells, functions, interdependencies, and interactions with each other and the environment.
Transportation	Knowledge of principles and methods for moving people or goods by air, rail, sea, or road, including the relative costs and benefits.
Medicine and Dentistry	Knowledge of the information and techniques needed to diagnose and treat human injuries, diseases, and deformities. This includes symptoms, treatment alternatives, drug properties and interactions, and preventive health-care measures.
Mechanical	Knowledge of machines and tools, including their designs, uses, repair, and maintenance.
Building and Construction	Knowledge of materials, methods, and the tools involved in the construction or repair of houses, buildings, or other structures such as highways and roads.
Chemistry	Knowledge of the chemical composition, structure, and properties of substances and of the chemical processes and transformations that they undergo. This includes uses of chemicals and their interactions, danger signs, production techniques, and disposal methods.
Food Production	Knowledge of techniques and equipment for planting, growing, and harvesting food products (both plant and animal) for consumption, including storage/handling techniques.

Skills	**Skills Definitions**
Instructing	Teaching others how to do something.
Speaking	Talking to others to convey information effectively.
Active Listening	Giving full attention to what other people are saying, taking time to understand the points being made, asking questions as appropriate, and not interrupting at inappropriate times.
Reading Comprehension	Understanding written sentences and paragraphs in work related documents.
Critical Thinking	Using logic and reasoning to identify the strengths and weaknesses of alternative solutions, conclusions or approaches to problems.
Learning Strategies	Selecting and using training/instructional methods and procedures appropriate for the situation when learning or teaching new things.
Active Learning	Understanding the implications of new information for both current and future problem-solving and decision-making.
Time Management	Managing one's own time and the time of others.
Social Perceptiveness	Being aware of others' reactions and understanding why they react as they do.
Monitoring	Monitoring/Assessing performance of yourself, other individuals, or organizations to make improvements or take corrective action.
Coordination	Adjusting actions in relation to others' actions.
Persuasion	Persuading others to change their minds or behavior.
Writing	Communicating effectively in writing as appropriate for the needs of the audience.
Complex Problem Solving	Identifying complex problems and reviewing related information to develop and evaluate options and implement solutions.
Service Orientation	Actively looking for ways to help people.
Judgment and Decision Making	Considering the relative costs and benefits of potential actions to choose the most appropriate one.
Negotiation	Bringing others together and trying to reconcile differences.
Management of Personnel Resources	Motivating, developing, and directing people as they work, identifying the best people for the job.
Equipment Selection	Determining the kind of tools and equipment needed to do a job.
Operations Analysis	Analyzing needs and product requirements to create a design.
Quality Control Analysis	Conducting tests and inspections of products, services, or processes to evaluate quality or performance.

Technology Design	Generating or adapting equipment and technology to serve user needs.
Troubleshooting	Determining causes of operating errors and deciding what to do about it.
Management of Material Resources	Obtaining and seeing to the appropriate use of equipment, facilities, and materials needed to do certain work.
Science	Using scientific rules and methods to solve problems.
Management of Financial Resources	Determining how money will be spent to get the work done, and accounting for these expenditures.
Systems Analysis	Determining how a system should work and how changes in conditions, operations, and the environment will affect outcomes.
Systems Evaluation	Identifying measures or indicators of system performance and the actions needed to improve or correct performance, relative to the goals of the system.
Mathematics	Using mathematics to solve problems.
Equipment Maintenance	Performing routine maintenance on equipment and determining when and what kind of maintenance is needed.
Repairing	Repairing machines or systems using the needed tools.
Operation and Control	Controlling operations of equipment or systems.
Installation	Installing equipment, machines, wiring, or programs to meet specifications.
Operation Monitoring	Watching gauges, dials, or other indicators to make sure a machine is working properly.
Programming	Writing computer programs for various purposes.

Ability	**Ability Definitions**
Oral Expression	The ability to communicate information and ideas in speaking so others will understand.
Speech Clarity	The ability to speak clearly so others can understand you.
Written Comprehension	The ability to read and understand information and ideas presented in writing.
Written Expression	The ability to communicate information and ideas in writing so others will understand.
Oral Comprehension	The ability to listen to and understand information and ideas presented through spoken words and sentences.
Originality	The ability to come up with unusual or clever ideas about a given topic or situation, or to develop creative ways to solve a problem.
Problem Sensitivity	The ability to tell when something is wrong or is likely to go wrong. It does not involve solving the problem, only recognizing there is a problem.
Deductive Reasoning	The ability to apply general rules to specific problems to produce answers that make sense.
Inductive Reasoning	The ability to combine pieces of information to form general rules or conclusions (includes finding a relationship among seemingly unrelated events).
Speech Recognition	The ability to identify and understand the speech of another person.
Near Vision	The ability to see details at close range (within a few feet of the observer).
Fluency of Ideas	The ability to come up with a number of ideas about a topic (the number of ideas is important, not their quality, correctness, or creativity).
Information Ordering	The ability to arrange things or actions in a certain order or pattern according to a specific rule or set of rules (e.g., patterns of numbers, letters, words, pictures, mathematical operations).
Selective Attention	The ability to concentrate on a task over a period of time without being distracted.
Category Flexibility	The ability to generate or use different sets of rules for combining or grouping things in different ways.
Visualization	The ability to imagine how something will look after it is moved around or when its parts are moved or rearranged.
Time Sharing	The ability to shift back and forth between two or more activities or sources of information (such as speech, sounds, touch, or other sources).
Flexibility of Closure	The ability to identify or detect a known pattern (a figure, object, word, or sound) that is hidden in other distracting material.
Memorization	The ability to remember information such as words, numbers, pictures, and procedures.
Far Vision	The ability to see details at a distance.
Visual Color Discrimination	The ability to match or detect differences between colors, including shades of color and brightness.
Mathematical Reasoning	The ability to choose the right mathematical methods or formulas to solve a problem.

Speed of Closure	The ability to quickly make sense of, combine, and organize information into meaningful patterns.
Arm-Hand Steadiness	The ability to keep your hand and arm steady while moving your arm or while holding your arm and hand in one position.
Manual Dexterity	The ability to quickly move your hand, your hand together with your arm, or your two hands to grasp, manipulate, or assemble objects.
Trunk Strength	The ability to use your abdominal and lower back muscles to support part of the body repeatedly or continuously over time without 'giving out' or fatiguing.
Number Facility	The ability to add, subtract, multiply, or divide quickly and correctly.
Auditory Attention	The ability to focus on a single source of sound in the presence of other distracting sounds.
Finger Dexterity	The ability to make precisely coordinated movements of the fingers of one or both hands to grasp, manipulate, or assemble very small objects.
Perceptual Speed	The ability to quickly and accurately compare similarities and differences among sets of letters, numbers, objects, pictures, or patterns. The things to be compared may be presented at the same time or one after the other. This ability also includes comparing a presented object with a remembered object.
Multilimb Coordination	The ability to coordinate two or more limbs (for example, two arms, two legs, or one leg and one arm) while sitting, standing, or lying down. It does not involve performing the activities while the whole body is in motion.
Control Precision	The ability to quickly and repeatedly adjust the controls of a machine or a vehicle to exact positions.
Hearing Sensitivity	The ability to detect or tell the differences between sounds that vary in pitch and loudness.
Depth Perception	The ability to judge which of several objects is closer or farther away from you, or to judge the distance between you and an object.
Extent Flexibility	The ability to bend, stretch, twist, or reach with your body, arms, and/or legs.
Static Strength	The ability to exert maximum muscle force to lift, push, pull, or carry objects.
Stamina	The ability to exert yourself physically over long periods of time without getting winded or out of breath.
Gross Body Coordination	The ability to coordinate the movement of your arms, legs, and torso together when the whole body is in motion.
Gross Body Equilibrium	The ability to keep or regain your body balance or stay upright when in an unstable position.
Dynamic Strength	The ability to exert muscle force repeatedly or continuously over time. This involves muscular endurance and resistance to muscle fatigue.
Speed of Limb Movement	The ability to quickly move the arms and legs.
Spatial Orientation	The ability to know your location in relation to the environment or to know where other objects are in relation to you.
Glare Sensitivity	The ability to see objects in the presence of glare or bright lighting.
Night Vision	The ability to see under low light conditions.
Wrist-Finger Speed	The ability to make fast, simple, repeated movements of the fingers, hands, and wrists.
Peripheral Vision	The ability to see objects or movement of objects to one's side when the eyes are looking ahead.
Response Orientation	The ability to choose quickly between two or more movements in response to two or more different signals (lights, sounds, pictures). It includes the speed with which the correct response is started with the hand, foot, or other body part.
Rate Control	The ability to time your movements or the movement of a piece of equipment in anticipation of changes in the speed and/or direction of a moving object or scene.
Reaction Time	The ability to quickly respond (with the hand, finger, or foot) to a signal (sound, light, picture) when it appears.
Dynamic Flexibility	The ability to quickly and repeatedly bend, stretch, twist, or reach out with your body, arms, and/or legs.
Explosive Strength	The ability to use short bursts of muscle force to propel oneself (as in jumping or sprinting), or to throw an object.
Sound Localization	The ability to tell the direction from which a sound originated.

Work_Activity	Work_Activity Definitions
Thinking Creatively	Developing, designing, or creating new applications, ideas, relationships, systems, or products, including artistic contributions.
Training and Teaching Others	Identifying the educational needs of others, developing formal educational or training programs or classes, and teaching or instructing others.
Organizing, Planning, and Prioritizing Work	Developing specific goals and plans to prioritize, organize, and accomplish your work.
Coaching and Developing Others	Identifying the developmental needs of others and coaching, mentoring, or otherwise helping others to improve their knowledge or skills.
Getting Information	Observing, receiving, and otherwise obtaining information from all relevant sources.
Establishing and Maintaining Interpersonal Relatio	Developing constructive and cooperative working relationships with others, and maintaining them over time.
Judging the Qualities of Things, Services, or Peop	Assessing the value, importance, or quality of things or people.
Updating and Using Relevant Knowledge	Keeping up-to-date technically and applying new knowledge to your job.
Making Decisions and Solving Problems	Analyzing information and evaluating results to choose the best solution and solve problems.
Communicating with Supervisors, Peers, or Subordin	Providing information to supervisors, co-workers, and subordinates by telephone, in written form, e-mail, or in person.
Scheduling Work and Activities	Scheduling events, programs, and activities, as well as the work of others.
Developing Objectives and Strategies	Establishing long-range objectives and specifying the strategies and actions to achieve them.
Interpreting the Meaning of Information for Others	Translating or explaining what information means and how it can be used.
Identifying Objects, Actions, and Events	Identifying information by categorizing, estimating, recognizing differences or similarities, and detecting changes in circumstances or events.
Coordinating the Work and Activities of Others	Getting members of a group to work together to accomplish tasks.
Guiding, Directing, and Motivating Subordinates	Providing guidance and direction to subordinates, including setting performance standards and monitoring performance.
Provide Consultation and Advice to Others	Providing guidance and expert advice to management or other groups on technical, systems-, or process-related topics.
Interacting With Computers	Using computers and computer systems (including hardware and software) to program, write software, set up functions, enter data, or process information.
Performing Administrative Activities	Performing day-to-day administrative tasks such as maintaining information files and processing paperwork.
Monitor Processes, Materials, or Surroundings	Monitoring and reviewing information from materials, events, or the environment, to detect or assess problems.
Resolving Conflicts and Negotiating with Others	Handling complaints, settling disputes, and resolving grievances and conflicts, or otherwise negotiating with others.
Documenting/Recording Information	Entering, transcribing, recording, storing, or maintaining information in written or electronic/magnetic form.
Developing and Building Teams	Encouraging and building mutual trust, respect, and cooperation among team members.
Performing for or Working Directly with the Public	Performing for people or dealing directly with the public. This includes serving customers in restaurants and stores, and receiving clients or guests.
Communicating with Persons Outside Organization	Communicating with people outside the organization, representing the organization to customers, the public, government, and other external sources. This information can be exchanged in person, in writing, or by telephone or e-mail.
Evaluating Information to Determine Compliance wit	Using relevant information and individual judgment to determine whether events or processes comply with laws, regulations, or standards.
Assisting and Caring for Others	Providing personal assistance, medical attention, emotional support, or other personal care to others such as coworkers, customers, or patients.
Analyzing Data or Information	Identifying the underlying principles, reasons, or facts of information by breaking down information or data into separate parts.
Processing Information	Compiling, coding, categorizing, calculating, tabulating, auditing, or verifying information or data.
Monitoring and Controlling Resources	Monitoring and controlling resources and overseeing the spending of money.
Performing General Physical Activities	Performing physical activities that require considerable use of your arms and legs and moving your whole body, such as climbing, lifting, balancing, walking, stooping, and handling of materials.
Estimating the Quantifiable Characteristics of Pro	Estimating sizes, distances, and quantities; or determining time, costs, resources, or materials needed to perform a work activity.

Staffing Organizational Units	Recruiting, interviewing, selecting, hiring, and promoting employees in an organization.
Inspecting Equipment, Structures, or Material	Inspecting equipment, structures, or materials to identify the cause of errors or other problems or defects.
Handling and Moving Objects	Using hands and arms in handling, installing, positioning, and moving materials, and manipulating things.
Selling or Influencing Others	Convincing others to buy merchandise/goods or to otherwise change their minds or actions.
Controlling Machines and Processes	Using either control mechanisms or direct physical activity to operate machines or processes (not including computers or vehicles).
Repairing and Maintaining Mechanical Equipment	Servicing, repairing, adjusting, and testing machines, devices, moving parts, and equipment that operate primarily on the basis of mechanical (not electronic) principles.
Repairing and Maintaining Electronic Equipment	Servicing, repairing, calibrating, regulating, fine-tuning, or testing machines, devices, and equipment that operate primarily on the basis of electrical or electronic (not mechanical) principles.
Drafting, Laying Out, and Specifying Technical Dev	Providing documentation, detailed instructions, drawings, or specifications to tell others about how devices, parts, equipment, or structures are to be fabricated, constructed, assembled, modified, maintained, or used.
Operating Vehicles, Mechanized Devices, or Equipme	Running, maneuvering, navigating, or driving vehicles or mechanized equipment, such as forklifts, passenger vehicles, aircraft, or water craft.

Work_Context	Work_Context Definitions
Contact With Others	How much does this job require the worker to be in contact with others (face-to-face, by telephone, or otherwise) in order to perform it?
Indoors, Environmentally Controlled	How often does this job require working indoors in environmentally controlled conditions?
Structured versus Unstructured Work	To what extent is this job structured for the worker, rather than allowing the worker to determine tasks, priorities, and goals?
Electronic Mail	How often do you use electronic mail in this job?
Freedom to Make Decisions	How much decision making freedom, without supervision, does the job offer?
Face-to-Face Discussions	How often do you have to have face-to-face discussions with individuals or teams in this job?
Telephone	How often do you have telephone conversations in this job?
Public Speaking	How often do you have to perform public speaking in this job?
Work With Work Group or Team	How important is it to work with others in a group or team in this job?
Coordinate or Lead Others	How important is it to coordinate or lead others in accomplishing work activities in this job?
Importance of Being Exact or Accurate	How important is being very exact or highly accurate in performing this job?
Letters and Memos	How often does the job require written letters and memos?
Physical Proximity	To what extent does this job require the worker to perform job tasks in close physical proximity to other people?
Spend Time Sitting	How much does this job require sitting?
Time Pressure	How often does this job require the worker to meet strict deadlines?
Level of Competition	To what extent does this job require the worker to compete or to be aware of competitive pressures?
Frequency of Decision Making	How frequently is the worker required to make decisions that affect other people, the financial resources, and/or the image and reputation of the organization?
Impact of Decisions on Co-workers or Company Resul	How do the decisions an employee makes impact the results of co-workers, clients or the company?
Sounds, Noise Levels Are Distracting or Uncomforta	How often does this job require working exposed to sounds and noise levels that are distracting or uncomfortable?
Deal With External Customers	How important is it to work with external customers or the public in this job?
Importance of Repeating Same Tasks	How important is repeating the same physical activities (e.g., key entry) or mental activities (e.g., checking entries in a ledger) over and over, without stopping, to performing this job?
Frequency of Conflict Situations	How often are there conflict situations the employee has to face in this job?
Spend Time Making Repetitive Motions	How much does this job require making repetitive motions?
Responsibility for Outcomes and Results	How responsible is the worker for work outcomes and results of other workers?
Spend Time Using Your Hands to Handle, Control, or	How much does this job require using your hands to handle, control, or feel objects, tools or controls?

Spend Time Standing	How much does this job require standing?
Deal With Unpleasant or Angry People	How frequently does the worker have to deal with unpleasant, angry, or discourteous individuals as part of the job requirements?
Responsible for Others' Health and Safety	How much responsibility is there for the health and safety of others in this job?
Extremely Bright or Inadequate Lighting	How often does this job require working in extremely bright or inadequate lighting conditions?
Exposed to Contaminants	How often does this job require working exposed to contaminants (such as pollutants, gases, dust or odors)?
Consequence of Error	How serious would the result usually be if the worker made a mistake that was not readily correctable?
Indoors, Not Environmentally Controlled	How often does this job require working indoors in non-controlled environmental conditions (e.g., warehouse without heat)?
Spend Time Walking and Running	How much does this job require walking and running?
Spend Time Bending or Twisting the Body	How much does this job require bending or twisting your body?
Exposed to Disease or Infections	How often does this job require exposure to disease/infections?
Exposed to Hazardous Equipment	How often does this job require exposure to hazardous equipment?
Exposed to Minor Burns, Cuts, Bites, or Stings	How often does this job require exposure to minor burns, cuts, bites, or stings?
Wear Common Protective or Safety Equipment such as	How much does this job require wearing common protective or safety equipment such as safety shoes, glasses, gloves, hard hats or life jackets?
Exposed to Hazardous Conditions	How often does this job require exposure to hazardous conditions?
Cramped Work Space, Awkward Positions	How often does this job require working in cramped work spaces that requires getting into awkward positions?
Wear Specialized Protective or Safety Equipment su	How much does this job require wearing specialized protective or safety equipment such as breathing apparatus, safety harness, full protection suits, or radiation protection?
Very Hot or Cold Temperatures	How often does this job require working in very hot (above 90 F degrees) or very cold (below 32 F degrees) temperatures?
Outdoors, Under Cover	How often does this job require working outdoors, under cover (e.g., structure with roof but no walls)?
In an Enclosed Vehicle or Equipment	How often does this job require working in a closed vehicle or equipment (e.g., car)?
Degree of Automation	How automated is the job?
Spend Time Kneeling, Crouching, Stooping, or Crawl	How much does this job require kneeling, crouching, stooping, or crawling?
Outdoors, Exposed to Weather	How often does this job require working outdoors, exposed to all weather conditions?
Spend Time Keeping or Regaining Balance	How much does this job require keeping or regaining your balance?
Deal With Physically Aggressive People	How frequently does this job require the worker to deal with physical aggression of violent individuals?
Exposed to High Places	How often does this job require exposure to high places?
Spend Time Climbing Ladders, Scaffolds, or Poles	How much does this job require climbing ladders, scaffolds, or poles?
Exposed to Radiation	How often does this job require exposure to radiation?
Pace Determined by Speed of Equipment	How important is it to this job that the pace is determined by the speed of equipment or machinery? (This does not refer to keeping busy at all times on this job.)
In an Open Vehicle or Equipment	How often does this job require working in an open vehicle or equipment (e.g., tractor)?
Exposed to Whole Body Vibration	How often does this job require exposure to whole body vibration (e.g., operate a jackhammer)?

Job Zone Component	Job Zone Component Definitions
Title	Job Zone Five: Extensive Preparation Needed
	Extensive skill, knowledge, and experience are needed for these occupations. Many require more than five years of experience.
Overall Experience	For example, surgeons must complete four years of college and an additional five to seven years of specialized medical training to be able to do their job.
Job Training	Employees may need some on-the-job training, but most of these occupations assume that the person will already have the required skills, knowledge, work-related experience, and/or training.

1453

13) Conduct research in a particular field of knowledge, and publish findings in professional journals, books, and/or electronic media.

14) Act as advisers to student organizations.

15) Supervise undergraduate and/or graduate teaching, internship, and research work.

16) Provide professional consulting services to government and/or industry.

17) Write grant proposals to procure external research funding.

18) Perform administrative duties such as serving as department head.

19) Prepare course materials such as syllabi, homework assignments, and handouts.

20) Evaluate and grade students' class work, assignments, and papers.

21) Keep abreast of developments in their field by reading current literature, talking with colleagues, and participating in professional conferences.

Knowledge	Knowledge Definitions
Education and Training	Knowledge of principles and methods for curriculum and training design, teaching and instruction for individuals and groups, and the measurement of training effects.
English Language	Knowledge of the structure and content of the English language including the meaning and spelling of words, rules of composition, and grammar.
Communications and Media	Knowledge of media production, communication, and dissemination techniques and methods. This includes alternative ways to inform and entertain via written, oral, and visual media.
Computers and Electronics	Knowledge of circuit boards, processors, chips, electronic equipment, and computer hardware and software, including applications and programming.
Customer and Personal Service	Knowledge of principles and processes for providing customer and personal services. This includes customer needs assessment, meeting quality standards for services, and evaluation of customer satisfaction.
Psychology	Knowledge of human behavior and performance; individual differences in ability, personality, and interests; learning and motivation; psychological research methods; and the assessment and treatment of behavioral and affective disorders.
Sociology and Anthropology	Knowledge of group behavior and dynamics, societal trends and influences, human migrations, ethnicity, cultures and their history and origins.
Philosophy and Theology	Knowledge of different philosophical systems and religions. This includes their basic principles, values, ethics, ways of thinking, customs, practices, and their impact on human culture.
Clerical	Knowledge of administrative and clerical procedures and systems such as word processing, managing files and records, stenography and transcription, designing forms, and other office procedures and terminology.
Law and Government	Knowledge of laws, legal codes, court procedures, precedents, government regulations, executive orders, agency rules, and the democratic political process.
Fine Arts	Knowledge of the theory and techniques required to compose, produce, and perform works of music, dance, visual arts, drama, and sculpture.
History and Archeology	Knowledge of historical events and their causes, indicators, and effects on civilizations and cultures.
Administration and Management	Knowledge of business and management principles involved in strategic planning, resource allocation, human resources modeling, leadership technique, production methods, and coordination of people and resources.
Telecommunications	Knowledge of transmission, broadcasting, switching, control, and operation of telecommunications systems.
Personnel and Human Resources	Knowledge of principles and procedures for personnel recruitment, selection, training, compensation and benefits, labor relations and negotiation, and personnel information systems.
Mathematics	Knowledge of arithmetic, algebra, geometry, calculus, statistics, and their applications.
Therapy and Counseling	Knowledge of principles, methods, and procedures for diagnosis, treatment, and rehabilitation of physical and mental dysfunctions, and for career counseling and guidance.
Geography	Knowledge of principles and methods for describing the features of land, sea, and air masses, including their physical characteristics, locations, interrelationships, and distribution of plant, animal, and human life.

These occupations often involve coordinating, training, supervising, or managing the activities of others to accomplish goals. Very advanced communication and organizational skills are required. Examples include athletic trainers, lawyers, managing editors, physicists, social psychologists, and surgeons.

Job Zone Examples

SVP Range (8.0 and above)

Education A bachelor's degree is the minimum formal education required for these occupations. However, many also require graduate school. For example, they may require a master's degree, and some require a Ph.D., M.D., or J.D. (law degree).

Work_Styles	Work_Styles Definitions
Integrity	Job requires being honest and ethical.
Dependability	Job requires being reliable, responsible, and dependable, and fulfilling obligations.
Independence	Job requires developing one's own ways of doing things, guiding oneself with little or no supervision, and depending on oneself to get things done.
Self Control	Job requires maintaining composure, keeping emotions in check, controlling anger, and avoiding aggressive behavior, even in very difficult situations.
Concern for Others	Job requires being sensitive to others' needs and feelings and being understanding and helpful on the job.
Attention to Detail	Job requires being careful about detail and thorough in completing work tasks.
Achievement/Effort	Job requires establishing and maintaining personally challenging achievement goals and exerting effort toward mastering tasks.
Initiative	Job requires a willingness to take on responsibilities and challenges.
Cooperation	Job requires being pleasant with others on the job and displaying a good-natured, cooperative attitude.
Innovation	Job requires creativity and alternative thinking to develop new ideas for and answers to work-related problems.
Leadership	Job requires a willingness to lead, take charge, and offer opinions and direction.
Social Orientation	Job requires preferring to work with others rather than alone, and being personally connected with others on the job.
Adaptability/Flexibility	Job requires being open to change (positive or negative) and to considerable variety in the workplace.
Persistence	Job requires persistence in the face of obstacles.
Analytical Thinking	Job requires analyzing information and using logic to address work-related issues and problems.
Stress Tolerance	Job requires accepting criticism and dealing calmly and effectively with high stress situations.

25-1122.00 - Communications Teachers, Postsecondary

Teach courses in communications, such as organizational communications, public relations, radio/television broadcasting, and journalism.

Tasks

1) Compile, administer, and grade examinations, or assign this work to others.

2) Plan, evaluate, and revise curricula, course content, and course materials and methods of instruction.

3) Initiate, facilitate, and moderate classroom discussions.

4) Select and obtain materials and supplies such as textbooks.

5) Maintain regularly scheduled office hours in order to advise and assist students.

6) Advise students on academic and vocational curricula, and on career issues.

7) Participate in campus and community events.

8) Collaborate with colleagues to address teaching and research issues.

9) Prepare and deliver lectures to undergraduate and/or graduate students on topics such as public speaking, media criticism, and oral traditions.

10) Serve on academic or administrative committees that deal with institutional policies, departmental matters, and academic issues.

11) Compile bibliographies of specialized materials for outside reading assignments.

12) Participate in student recruitment, registration, and placement activities.

Sales and Marketing	Knowledge of principles and methods for showing, promoting, and selling products or services. This includes marketing strategy and tactics, product demonstration, sales techniques, and sales control systems.
Public Safety and Security	Knowledge of relevant equipment, policies, procedures, and strategies to promote effective local, state, or national security operations for the protection of people, data, property, and institutions.
Foreign Language	Knowledge of the structure and content of a foreign (non-English) language including the meaning and spelling of words, rules of composition and grammar, and pronunciation.
Economics and Accounting	Knowledge of economic and accounting principles and practices, the financial markets, banking and the analysis and reporting of financial data.
Design	Knowledge of design techniques, tools, and principles involved in production of precision technical plans, blueprints, drawings, and models.
Production and Processing	Knowledge of raw materials, production processes, quality control, costs, and other techniques for maximizing the effective manufacture and distribution of goods.
Engineering and Technology	Knowledge of the practical application of engineering science and technology. This includes applying principles, techniques, procedures, and equipment to the design and production of various goods and services.
Transportation	Knowledge of principles and methods for moving people or goods by air, rail, sea, or road, including the relative costs and benefits.
Medicine and Dentistry	Knowledge of the information and techniques needed to diagnose and treat human injuries, diseases, and deformities. This includes symptoms, treatment alternatives, drug properties and interactions, and preventive health-care measures.
Mechanical	Knowledge of machines and tools, including their designs, uses, repair, and maintenance.
Biology	Knowledge of plant and animal organisms, their tissues, cells, functions, interdependencies, and interactions with each other and the environment.
Physics	Knowledge and prediction of physical principles, laws, their interrelationships, and applications to understanding fluid, material, and atmospheric dynamics, and mechanical, electrical, atomic and sub- atomic structures and processes.
Building and Construction	Knowledge of materials, methods, and the tools involved in the construction or repair of houses, buildings, or other structures such as highways and roads.
Chemistry	Knowledge of the chemical composition, structure, and properties of substances and of the chemical processes and transformations that they undergo. This includes uses of chemicals and their interactions, danger signs, production techniques, and disposal methods.
Food Production	Knowledge of techniques and equipment for planting, growing, and harvesting food products (both plant and animal) for consumption, including storage/handling techniques.

Skills	Skills Definitions
Instructing	Teaching others how to do something.
Active Listening	Giving full attention to what other people are saying, taking time to understand the points being made, asking questions as appropriate, and not interrupting at inappropriate times.
Reading Comprehension	Understanding written sentences and paragraphs in work related documents.
Speaking	Talking to others to convey information effectively.
Writing	Communicating effectively in writing as appropriate for the needs of the audience.
Critical Thinking	Using logic and reasoning to identify the strengths and weaknesses of alternative solutions, conclusions or approaches to problems.
Learning Strategies	Selecting and using training/instructional methods and procedures appropriate for the situation when learning or teaching new things.
Time Management	Managing one's own time and the time of others.
Active Learning	Understanding the implications of new information for both current and future problem-solving and decision-making.
Monitoring	Monitoring/Assessing performance of yourself, other individuals, or organizations to make improvements or take corrective action.
Social Perceptiveness	Being aware of others' reactions and understanding why they react as they do.
Persuasion	Persuading others to change their minds or behavior.

Coordination	Adjusting actions in relation to others' actions.
Judgment and Decision Making	Considering the relative costs and benefits of potential actions to choose the most appropriate one.
Complex Problem Solving	Identifying complex problems and reviewing related information to develop and evaluate options and implement solutions.
Negotiation	Bringing others together and trying to reconcile differences.
Service Orientation	Actively looking for ways to help people.
Management of Personnel Resources	Motivating, developing, and directing people as they work, identifying the best people for the job.
Equipment Selection	Determining the kind of tools and equipment needed to do a job.
Quality Control Analysis	Conducting tests and inspections of products, services, or processes to evaluate quality or performance.
Operations Analysis	Analyzing needs and product requirements to create a design.
Systems Evaluation	Identifying measures or indicators of system performance and the actions needed to improve or correct performance, relative to the goals of the system.
Mathematics	Using mathematics to solve problems.
Troubleshooting	Determining causes of operating errors and deciding what to do about it.
Management of Financial Resources	Determining how money will be spent to get the work done, and accounting for these expenditures.
Management of Material Resources	Obtaining and seeing to the appropriate use of equipment, facilities, and materials needed to do certain work.
Science	Using scientific rules and methods to solve problems.
Technology Design	Generating or adapting equipment and technology to serve user needs.
Systems Analysis	Determining how a system should work and how changes in conditions, operations, and the environment will affect outcomes.
Operation and Control	Controlling operations of equipment or systems.
Equipment Maintenance	Performing routine maintenance on equipment and determining when and what kind of maintenance is needed.
Installation	Installing equipment, machines, wiring, or programs to meet specifications.
Programming	Writing computer programs for various purposes.
Operation Monitoring	Watching gauges, dials, or other indicators to make sure a machine is working properly.
Repairing	Repairing machines or systems using the needed tools.

Ability	Ability Definitions
Oral Expression	The ability to communicate information and ideas in speaking so others will understand.
Speech Clarity	The ability to speak clearly so others can understand you.
Oral Comprehension	The ability to listen to and understand information and ideas presented through spoken words and sentences.
Written Expression	The ability to communicate information and ideas in writing so others will understand.
Written Comprehension	The ability to read and understand information and ideas presented in writing.
Deductive Reasoning	The ability to apply general rules to specific problems to produce answers that make sense.
Inductive Reasoning	The ability to combine pieces of information to form general rules or conclusions (includes finding a relationship among seemingly unrelated events).
Speech Recognition	The ability to identify and understand the speech of another person.
Problem Sensitivity	The ability to tell when something is wrong or is likely to go wrong. It does not involve solving the problem, only recognizing there is a problem.
Near Vision	The ability to see details at close range (within a few feet of the observer).
Fluency of Ideas	The ability to come up with a number of ideas about a topic (the number of ideas is important, not their quality, correctness, or creativity).
Originality	The ability to come up with unusual or clever ideas about a given topic or situation, or to develop creative ways to solve a problem.
Information Ordering	The ability to arrange things or actions in a certain order or pattern according to a specific rule or set of rules (e.g., patterns of numbers, letters, words, pictures, mathematical operations).
Selective Attention	The ability to concentrate on a task over a period of time without being distracted.
Category Flexibility	The ability to generate or use different sets of rules for combining or grouping things in different ways.

Flexibility of Closure	The ability to identify or detect a known pattern (a figure, object, word, or sound) that is hidden in other distracting material.
Memorization	The ability to remember information such as words, numbers, pictures, and procedures.
Time Sharing	The ability to shift back and forth between two or more activities or sources of information (such as speech, sounds, touch, or other sources).
Far Vision	The ability to see details at a distance.
Speed of Closure	The ability to quickly make sense of, combine, and organize information into meaningful patterns.
Mathematical Reasoning	The ability to choose the right mathematical methods or formulas to solve a problem.
Number Facility	The ability to add, subtract, multiply, or divide quickly and correctly.
Perceptual Speed	The ability to quickly and accurately compare similarities and differences among sets of letters, numbers, objects, pictures, or patterns. The things to be compared may be presented at the same time or one after the other. This ability also includes comparing a presented object with a remembered object.
Trunk Strength	The ability to use your abdominal and lower back muscles to support part of the body repeatedly or continuously over time without 'giving out' or fatiguing.
Auditory Attention	The ability to focus on a single source of sound in the presence of other distracting sounds.
Finger Dexterity	The ability to make precisely coordinated movements of the fingers of one or both hands to grasp, manipulate, or assemble very small objects.
Visualization	The ability to imagine how something will look after it is moved around or when its parts are moved or rearranged.
Visual Color Discrimination	The ability to match or detect differences between colors, including shades of color and brightness.
Hearing Sensitivity	The ability to detect or tell the differences between sounds that vary in pitch and loudness.
Depth Perception	The ability to judge which of several objects is closer or farther away from you, or to judge the distance between you and an object.
Dynamic Strength	The ability to exert muscle force repeatedly or continuously over time. This involves muscular endurance and resistance to muscle fatigue.
Response Orientation	The ability to choose quickly between two or more movements in response to two or more different signals (lights, sounds, pictures). It includes the speed with which the correct response is started with the hand, foot, or other body part.
Rate Control	The ability to time your movements or the movement of a piece of equipment in anticipation of changes in the speed and/or direction of a moving object or scene.
Reaction Time	The ability to quickly respond (with the hand, finger, or foot) to a signal (sound, light, picture) when it appears.
Wrist-Finger Speed	The ability to make fast, simple, repeated movements of the fingers, hands, and wrists.
Speed of Limb Movement	The ability to quickly move the arms and legs.
Static Strength	The ability to exert maximum muscle force to lift, push, pull, or carry objects.
Extent Flexibility	The ability to bend, stretch, twist, or reach with your body, arms, and/or legs.
Stamina	The ability to exert yourself physically over long periods of time without getting winded or out of breath.
Manual Dexterity	The ability to quickly move your hand, your hand together with your arm, or your two hands to grasp, manipulate, or assemble objects.
Explosive Strength	The ability to use short bursts of muscle force to propel oneself (as in jumping or sprinting), or to throw an object.
Spatial Orientation	The ability to know your location in relation to the environment or to know where other objects are in relation to you.
Control Precision	The ability to quickly and repeatedly adjust the controls of a machine or a vehicle to exact positions.
Multilimb Coordination	The ability to coordinate two or more limbs (for example, two arms, two legs, or one leg and one arm) while sitting, standing, or lying down. It does not involve performing the activities while the whole body is in motion.
Dynamic Flexibility	The ability to quickly and repeatedly bend, stretch, twist, or reach out with your body, arms, and/or legs.
Gross Body Coordination	The ability to coordinate the movement of your arms, legs, and torso together when the whole body is in motion.
Sound Localization	The ability to tell the direction from which a sound originated.
Gross Body Equilibrium	The ability to keep or regain your body balance or stay upright when in an unstable position.

Glare Sensitivity	The ability to see objects in the presence of glare or bright lighting.
Peripheral Vision	The ability to see objects or movement of objects to one's side when the eyes are looking ahead.
Night Vision	The ability to see under low light conditions.
Arm-Hand Steadiness	The ability to keep your hand and arm steady while moving your arm or while holding your arm and hand in one position.

Work_Activity	Work_Activity Definitions
Training and Teaching Others	Identifying the educational needs of others, developing formal educational or training programs or classes, and teaching or instructing others.
Establishing and Maintaining Interpersonal Relatio	Developing constructive and cooperative working relationships with others, and maintaining them over time.
Organizing, Planning, and Prioritizing Work	Developing specific goals and plans to prioritize, organize, and accomplish your work.
Communicating with Supervisors, Peers, or Subordin	Providing information to supervisors, co-workers, and subordinates by telephone, in written form, e-mail, or in person.
Interpreting the Meaning of Information for Others	Translating or explaining what information means and how it can be used.
Getting Information	Observing, receiving, and otherwise obtaining information from all relevant sources.
Thinking Creatively	Developing, designing, or creating new applications, ideas, relationships, systems, or products, including artistic contributions.
Updating and Using Relevant Knowledge	Keeping up-to-date technically and applying new knowledge to your job.
Interacting With Computers	Using computers and computer systems (including hardware and software) to program, write software, set up functions, enter data, or process information.
Coaching and Developing Others	Identifying the developmental needs of others and coaching, mentoring, or otherwise helping others to improve their knowledge or skills.
Judging the Qualities of Things, Services, or Peop	Assessing the value, importance, or quality of things or people.
Identifying Objects, Actions, and Events	Identifying information by categorizing, estimating, recognizing differences or similarities, and detecting changes in circumstances or events.
Documenting/Recording Information	Entering, transcribing, recording, storing, or maintaining information in written or electronic/magnetic form.
Developing Objectives and Strategies	Establishing long-range objectives and specifying the strategies and actions to achieve them.
Making Decisions and Solving Problems	Analyzing information and evaluating results to choose the best solution and solve problems.
Analyzing Data or Information	Identifying the underlying principles, reasons, or facts of information by breaking down information or data into separate parts.
Scheduling Work and Activities	Scheduling events, programs, and activities, as well as the work of others.
Processing Information	Compiling, coding, categorizing, calculating, tabulating, auditing, or verifying information or data.
Coordinating the Work and Activities of Others	Getting members of a group to work together to accomplish tasks.
Provide Consultation and Advice to Others	Providing guidance and expert advice to management or other groups on technical, systems-, or process-related topics.
Performing for or Working Directly with the Public	Performing for people or dealing directly with the public. This includes serving customers in restaurants and stores, and receiving clients or guests.
Guiding, Directing, and Motivating Subordinates	Providing guidance and direction to subordinates, including setting performance standards and monitoring performance.
Assisting and Caring for Others	Providing personal assistance, medical attention, emotional support, or other personal care to others such as coworkers, customers, or patients.
Evaluating Information to Determine Compliance wit	Using relevant information and individual judgment to determine whether events or processes comply with laws, regulations, or standards.
Resolving Conflicts and Negotiating with Others	Handling complaints, settling disputes, and resolving grievances and conflicts, or otherwise negotiating with others.
Communicating with Persons Outside Organization	Communicating with people outside the organization, representing the organization to customers, the public, government, and other external sources. This information can be exchanged in person, in writing, or by telephone or e-mail.
Performing Administrative Activities	Performing day-to-day administrative tasks such as maintaining information files and processing paperwork.

Developing and Building Teams	Encouraging and building mutual trust, respect, and cooperation among team members.
Monitor Processes, Materials, or Surroundings	Monitoring and reviewing information from materials, events, or the environment, to detect or assess problems.
Estimating the Quantifiable Characteristics of Pro	Estimating sizes, distances, and quantities; or determining time, costs, resources, or materials needed to perform a work activity.
Selling or Influencing Others	Convincing others to buy merchandise/goods or to otherwise change their minds or actions.
Monitoring and Controlling Resources	Monitoring and controlling resources and overseeing the spending of money.
Staffing Organizational Units	Recruiting, interviewing, selecting, hiring, and promoting employees in an organization.
Controlling Machines and Processes	Using either control mechanisms or direct physical activity to operate machines or processes (not including computers or vehicles).
Inspecting Equipment, Structures, or Material	Inspecting equipment, structures, or materials to identify the cause of errors or other problems or defects.
Handling and Moving Objects	Using hands and arms in handling, installing, positioning, and moving materials, and manipulating things.
Performing General Physical Activities	Performing physical activities that require considerable use of your arms and legs and moving your whole body, such as climbing, lifting, balancing, walking, stooping, and handling of materials.
Repairing and Maintaining Electronic Equipment	Servicing, repairing, calibrating, regulating, fine-tuning, or testing machines, devices, and equipment that operate primarily on the basis of electrical or electronic (not mechanical) principles.
Drafting, Laying Out, and Specifying Technical Dev	Providing documentation, detailed instructions, drawings, or specifications to tell others about how devices, parts, equipment, or structures are to be fabricated, constructed, assembled, modified, maintained, or used.
Operating Vehicles, Mechanized Devices, or Equipme	Running, maneuvering, navigating, or driving vehicles or mechanized equipment, such as forklifts, passenger vehicles, aircraft, or water craft.
Repairing and Maintaining Mechanical Equipment	Servicing, repairing, adjusting, and testing machines, devices, moving parts, and equipment that operate primarily on the basis of mechanical (not electronic) principles.

Work_Context	Work_Context Definitions
Electronic Mail	How often do you use electronic mail in this job?
Face-to-Face Discussions	How often do you have to have face-to-face discussions with individuals or teams in this job?
Public Speaking	How often do you have to perform public speaking in this job?
Telephone	How often do you have telephone conversations in this job?
Structured versus Unstructured Work	To what extent is this job structured for the worker, rather than allowing the worker to determine tasks, priorities, and goals?
Contact With Others	How much does this job require the worker to be in contact with others (face-to-face, by telephone, or otherwise) in order to perform it?
Freedom to Make Decisions	How much decision making freedom, without supervision, does the job offer?
Indoors, Environmentally Controlled	How often does this job require working indoors in environmentally controlled conditions?
Work With Work Group or Team	How important is it to work with others in a group or team in this job?
Coordinate or Lead Others	How important is it to coordinate or lead others in accomplishing work activities in this job?
Letters and Memos	How often does the job require written letters and memos?
Time Pressure	How often does this job require the worker to meet strict deadlines?
Frequency of Decision Making	How frequently is the worker required to make decisions that affect other people, the financial resources, and/or the image and reputation of the organization?
Impact of Decisions on Co-workers or Company Resul	How do the decisions an employee makes impact the results of co-workers, clients or the company?
Importance of Being Exact or Accurate	How important is being very exact or highly accurate in performing this job?
Deal With External Customers	How important is it to work with external customers or the public in this job?
Physical Proximity	To what extent does this job require the worker to perform job tasks in close physical proximity to other people?
Frequency of Conflict Situations	How often are there conflict situations the employee has to face in this job?
Spend Time Sitting	How much does this job require sitting?

Deal With Unpleasant or Angry People	How frequently does the worker have to deal with unpleasant, angry, or discourteous individuals as part of the job requirements?
Level of Competition	To what extent does this job require the worker to compete or to be aware of competitive pressures?
Responsibility for Outcomes and Results	How responsible is the worker for work outcomes and results of other workers?
Spend Time Standing	How much does this job require standing?
Sounds, Noise Levels Are Distracting or Uncomforta	How often does this job require working exposed to sounds and noise levels that are distracting or uncomfortable?
Responsible for Others' Health and Safety	How much responsibility is there for the health and safety of others in this job?
Importance of Repeating Same Tasks	How important is repeating the same physical activities (e.g., key entry) or mental activities (e.g., checking entries in a ledger) over and over, without stopping, to performing this job?
Spend Time Using Your Hands to Handle, Control, or	How much does this job require using your hands to handle, control, or feel objects, tools or controls?
Consequence of Error	How serious would the result usually be if the worker made a mistake that was not readily correctable?
Spend Time Making Repetitive Motions	How much does this job require making repetitive motions?
Spend Time Walking and Running	How much does this job require walking and running?
Exposed to Contaminants	How often does this job require working exposed to contaminants (such as pollutants, gases, dust or odors)?
Extremely Bright or Inadequate Lighting	How often does this job require working in extremely bright or inadequate lighting conditions?
Degree of Automation	How automated is the job?
Exposed to Disease or Infections	How often does this job require exposure to disease/infections?
Cramped Work Space, Awkward Positions	How often does this job require working in cramped work spaces that requires getting into awkward positions?
In an Enclosed Vehicle or Equipment	How often does this job require working in a closed vehicle or equipment (e.g., car)?
Indoors, Not Environmentally Controlled	How often does this job require working indoors in non-controlled environmental conditions (e.g., warehouse without heat)?
Deal With Physically Aggressive People	How frequently does this job require the worker to deal with physical aggression of violent individuals?
Very Hot or Cold Temperatures	How often does this job require working in very hot (above 90 F degrees) or very cold (below 32 F degrees) temperatures?
Spend Time Bending or Twisting the Body	How much does this job require bending or twisting your body?
Exposed to Hazardous Conditions	How often does this job require exposure to hazardous conditions?
Outdoors, Exposed to Weather	How often does this job require working outdoors, exposed to all weather conditions?
Exposed to Minor Burns, Cuts, Bites, or Stings	How often does this job require exposure to minor burns, cuts, bites, or stings?
Exposed to Hazardous Equipment	How often does this job require exposure to hazardous equipment?
Spend Time Kneeling, Crouching, Stooping, or Crawl	How much does this job require kneeling, crouching, stooping or crawling?
Pace Determined by Speed of Equipment	How important is it to this job that the pace is determined by the speed of equipment or machinery? (This does not refer to keeping busy at all times on this job.)
Exposed to High Places	How often does this job require exposure to high places?
Outdoors, Under Cover	How often does this job require working outdoors, under cover (e.g., structure with roof but no walls)?
Spend Time Climbing Ladders, Scaffolds, or Poles	How much does this job require climbing ladders, scaffolds, or poles?
Exposed to Radiation	How often does this job require exposure to radiation?
Spend Time Keeping or Regaining Balance	How much does this job require keeping or regaining your balance?
Wear Common Protective or Safety Equipment such as	How much does this job require wearing common protective or safety equipment such as safety shoes, glasses, gloves, hard hats or life jackets?
Exposed to Whole Body Vibration	How often does this job require exposure to whole body vibration (e.g., operate a jackhammer)?
Wear Specialized Protective or Safety Equipment su	How much does this job require wearing specialized protective or safety equipment such as breathing apparatus, safety harness, full protection suits, or radiation protection?
In an Open Vehicle or Equipment	How often does this job require working in an open vehicle or equipment (e.g., tractor)?

Job Zone Component	Job Zone Component Definitions
Title	Job Zone Five: Extensive Preparation Needed
	Extensive skill, knowledge, and experience are needed for these occupations. Many require more than five years of experience.
Overall Experience	For example, surgeons must complete four years of college and an additional five to seven years of specialized medical training to be able to do their job.
Job Training	Employees may need some on-the-job training, but most of these occupations assume that the person will already have the required skills, knowledge, work-related experience, and/or training.
Job Zone Examples	These occupations often involve coordinating, training, supervising, or managing the activities of others to accomplish goals. Very advanced communication and organizational skills are required. Examples include athletic trainers, lawyers, managing editors, physicists, social psychologists, and surgeons.
SVP Range	(8.0 and above)
Education	A bachelor's degree is the minimum formal education required for these occupations. However, many also require graduate school. For example, they may require a master's degree, and some require a Ph.D., M.D., or J.D. (law degree).

Work_Styles	Work_Styles Definitions
Dependability	Job requires being reliable, responsible, and dependable, and fulfilling obligations.
Integrity	Job requires being honest and ethical.
Attention to Detail	Job requires being careful about detail and thorough in completing work tasks.
Independence	Job requires developing one's own ways of doing things, guiding oneself with little or no supervision, and depending on oneself to get things done.
Self Control	Job requires maintaining composure, keeping emotions in check, controlling anger, and avoiding aggressive behavior, even in very difficult situations.
Adaptability/Flexibility	Job requires being open to change (positive or negative) and to considerable variety in the workplace.
Analytical Thinking	Job requires analyzing information and using logic to address work-related issues and problems.
Concern for Others	Job requires being sensitive to others' needs and feelings and being understanding and helpful on the job.
Cooperation	Job requires being pleasant with others on the job and displaying a good-natured, cooperative attitude.
Initiative	Job requires a willingness to take on responsibilities and challenges.
Stress Tolerance	Job requires accepting criticism and dealing calmly and effectively with high stress situations.
Leadership	Job requires a willingness to lead, take charge, and offer opinions and direction.
Persistence	Job requires persistence in the face of obstacles.
Achievement/Effort	Job requires establishing and maintaining personally challenging achievement goals and exerting effort toward mastering tasks.
Innovation	Job requires creativity and alternative thinking to develop new ideas for and answers to work-related problems.
Social Orientation	Job requires preferring to work with others rather than alone, and being personally connected with others on the job.

25-1123.00 - English Language and Literature Teachers, Postsecondary

Teach courses in English language and literature, including linguistics and comparative literature.

Tasks

1) Maintain student attendance records, grades, and other required records.

2) Maintain regularly scheduled office hours in order to advise and assist students.

3) Keep abreast of developments in their field by reading current literature, talking with colleagues, and participating in professional conferences.

4) Participate in campus and community events.

5) Select and obtain materials and supplies such as textbooks.

6) Collaborate with colleagues to address teaching and research issues.

7) Compile, administer, and grade examinations, or assign this work to others.

8) Advise students on academic and vocational curricula, and on career issues.

9) Serve on academic or administrative committees that deal with institutional policies, departmental matters, and academic issues.

10) Prepare and deliver lectures to undergraduate and/or graduate students on topics such as poetry, novel structure, and translation and adaptation.

11) Compile bibliographies of specialized materials for outside reading assignments.

12) Participate in student recruitment, registration, and placement activities.

13) Conduct research in a particular field of knowledge, and publish findings in professional journals, books, and/or electronic media.

14) Act as advisers to student organizations.

15) Supervise undergraduate and/or graduate teaching, internship, and research work.

16) Perform administrative duties such as serving as department head.

17) Provide assistance to students in college writing centers.

18) Write grant proposals to procure external research funding.

19) Provide professional consulting services to government and/or industry.

20) Recruit, train, and supervise student writing instructors.

21) Evaluate and grade students' class work, assignments, and papers.

22) Prepare course materials such as syllabi, homework assignments, and handouts.

23) Initiate, facilitate, and moderate classroom discussions.

Knowledge	Knowledge Definitions
English Language	Knowledge of the structure and content of the English language including the meaning and spelling of words, rules of composition, and grammar.
Education and Training	Knowledge of principles and methods for curriculum and training design, teaching and instruction for individuals and groups, and the measurement of training effects.
Communications and Media	Knowledge of media production, communication, and dissemination techniques and methods. This includes alternative ways to inform and entertain via written, oral, and visual media.
Philosophy and Theology	Knowledge of different philosophical systems and religions. This includes their basic principles, values, ethics, ways of thinking, customs, practices, and their impact on human culture.
Psychology	Knowledge of human behavior and performance; individual differences in ability, personality, and interests; learning and motivation; psychological research methods; and the assessment and treatment of behavioral and affective disorders.
History and Archeology	Knowledge of historical events and their causes, indicators, and effects on civilizations and cultures.
Customer and Personal Service	Knowledge of principles and processes for providing customer and personal services. This includes customer needs assessment, meeting quality standards for services, and evaluation of customer satisfaction.
Fine Arts	Knowledge of the theory and techniques required to compose, produce, and perform works of music, dance, visual arts, drama, and sculpture.
Computers and Electronics	Knowledge of circuit boards, processors, chips, electronic equipment, and computer hardware and software, including applications and programming.
Sociology and Anthropology	Knowledge of group behavior and dynamics, societal trends and influences, human migrations, ethnicity, cultures and their history and origins.
Clerical	Knowledge of administrative and clerical procedures and systems such as word processing, managing files and records, stenography and transcription, designing forms, and other office procedures and terminology.
Administration and Management	Knowledge of business and management principles involved in strategic planning, resource allocation, human resources modeling, leadership technique, production methods, and coordination of people and resources.
Law and Government	Knowledge of laws, legal codes, court procedures, precedents, government regulations, executive orders, agency rules, and the democratic political process.

Therapy and Counseling	Knowledge of principles, methods, and procedures for diagnosis, treatment, and rehabilitation of physical and mental dysfunctions, and for career counseling and guidance.
Geography	Knowledge of principles and methods for describing the features of land, sea, and air masses, including their physical characteristics, locations, interrelationships, and distribution of plant, animal, and human life.
Personnel and Human Resources	Knowledge of principles and procedures for personnel recruitment, selection, training, compensation and benefits, labor relations and negotiation, and personnel information systems.
Foreign Language	Knowledge of the structure and content of a foreign (non-English) language including the meaning and spelling of words, rules of composition and grammar, and pronunciation.
Mathematics	Knowledge of arithmetic, algebra, geometry, calculus, statistics, and their applications.
Telecommunications	Knowledge of transmission, broadcasting, switching, control, and operation of telecommunications systems.
Public Safety and Security	Knowledge of relevant equipment, policies, procedures, and strategies to promote effective local, state, or national security operations for the protection of people, data, property, and institutions.
Sales and Marketing	Knowledge of principles and methods for showing, promoting, and selling products or services. This includes marketing strategy and tactics, product demonstration, sales techniques, and sales control systems.
Economics and Accounting	Knowledge of economic and accounting principles and practices, the financial markets, banking and the analysis and reporting of financial data.
Design	Knowledge of design techniques, tools, and principles involved in production of precision technical plans, blueprints, drawings, and models.
Production and Processing	Knowledge of raw materials, production processes, quality control, costs, and other techniques for maximizing the effective manufacture and distribution of goods.
Transportation	Knowledge of principles and methods for moving people or goods by air, rail, sea, or road, including the relative costs and benefits.
Medicine and Dentistry	Knowledge of the information and techniques needed to diagnose and treat human injuries, diseases, and deformities. This includes symptoms, treatment alternatives, drug properties and interactions, and preventive health-care measures.
Engineering and Technology	Knowledge of the practical application of engineering science and technology. This includes applying principles, techniques, procedures, and equipment to the design and production of various goods and services.
Biology	Knowledge of plant and animal organisms, their tissues, cells, functions, interdependencies, and interactions with each other and the environment.
Mechanical	Knowledge of machines and tools, including their designs, uses, repair, and maintenance.
Physics	Knowledge and prediction of physical principles, laws, their interrelationships, and applications to understanding fluid, material, and atmospheric dynamics, and mechanical, electrical, atomic and sub-atomic structures and processes.
Chemistry	Knowledge of the chemical composition, structure, and properties of substances and of the chemical processes and transformations that they undergo. This includes uses of chemicals and their interactions, danger signs, production techniques, and disposal methods.
Building and Construction	Knowledge of materials, methods, and the tools involved in the construction or repair of houses, buildings, or other structures such as highways and roads.
Food Production	Knowledge of techniques and equipment for planting, growing, and harvesting food products (both plant and animal) for consumption, including storage/handling techniques.

Skills	**Skills Definitions**
Instructing	Teaching others how to do something.
Reading Comprehension	Understanding written sentences and paragraphs in work related documents.
Writing	Communicating effectively in writing as appropriate for the needs of the audience.
Critical Thinking	Using logic and reasoning to identify the strengths and weaknesses of alternative solutions, conclusions or approaches to problems.

Active Listening	Giving full attention to what other people are saying, taking time to understand the points being made, asking questions as appropriate, and not interrupting at inappropriate times.
Speaking	Talking to others to convey information effectively.
Learning Strategies	Selecting and using training/instructional methods and procedures appropriate for the situation when learning or teaching new things.
Active Learning	Understanding the implications of new information for both current and future problem-solving and decision-making.
Social Perceptiveness	Being aware of others' reactions and understanding why they react as they do.
Time Management	Managing one's own time and the time of others.
Monitoring	Monitoring/Assessing performance of yourself, other individuals, or organizations to make improvements or take corrective action.
Persuasion	Persuading others to change their minds or behavior.
Complex Problem Solving	Identifying complex problems and reviewing related information to develop and evaluate options and implement solutions.
Judgment and Decision Making	Considering the relative costs and benefits of potential actions to choose the most appropriate one.
Coordination	Adjusting actions in relation to others' actions.
Service Orientation	Actively looking for ways to help people.
Negotiation	Bringing others together and trying to reconcile differences.
Management of Personnel Resources	Motivating, developing, and directing people as they work, identifying the best people for the job.
Quality Control Analysis	Conducting tests and inspections of products, services, or processes to evaluate quality or performance.
Operations Analysis	Analyzing needs and product requirements to create a design.
Equipment Selection	Determining the kind of tools and equipment needed to do a job.
Technology Design	Generating or adapting equipment and technology to serve user needs.
Systems Evaluation	Identifying measures or indicators of system performance and the actions needed to improve or correct performance, relative to the goals of the system.
Mathematics	Using mathematics to solve problems.
Systems Analysis	Determining how a system should work and how changes in conditions, operations, and the environment will affect outcomes.
Management of Material Resources	Obtaining and seeing to the appropriate use of equipment, facilities, and materials needed to do certain work.
Science	Using scientific rules and methods to solve problems.
Troubleshooting	Determining causes of operating errors and deciding what to do about it.
Management of Financial Resources	Determining how money will be spent to get the work done, and accounting for these expenditures.
Operation and Control	Controlling operations of equipment or systems.
Installation	Installing equipment, machines, wiring, or programs to meet specifications.
Equipment Maintenance	Performing routine maintenance on equipment and determining when and what kind of maintenance is needed.
Operation Monitoring	Watching gauges, dials, or other indicators to make sure a machine is working properly.
Repairing	Repairing machines or systems using the needed tools.
Programming	Writing computer programs for various purposes.

Ability	**Ability Definitions**
Written Comprehension	The ability to read and understand information and ideas presented in writing.
Oral Expression	The ability to communicate information and ideas in speaking so others will understand.
Written Expression	The ability to communicate information and ideas in writing so others will understand.
Oral Comprehension	The ability to listen to and understand information and ideas presented through spoken words and sentences.
Speech Clarity	The ability to speak clearly so others can understand you.
Inductive Reasoning	The ability to combine pieces of information to form general rules or conclusions (includes finding a relationship among seemingly unrelated events).
Deductive Reasoning	The ability to apply general rules to specific problems to produce answers that make sense.
Near Vision	The ability to see details at close range (within a few feet of the observer).
Speech Recognition	The ability to identify and understand the speech of another person.

Problem Sensitivity	The ability to tell when something is wrong or is likely to go wrong. It does not involve solving the problem, only recognizing there is a problem.
Originality	The ability to come up with unusual or clever ideas about a given topic or situation, or to develop creative ways to solve a problem.
Category Flexibility	The ability to generate or use different sets of rules for combining or grouping things in different ways.
Information Ordering	The ability to arrange things or actions in a certain order or pattern according to a specific rule or set of rules (e.g., patterns of numbers, letters, words, pictures, mathematical operations).
Fluency of Ideas	The ability to come up with a number of ideas about a topic (the number of ideas is important, not their quality, correctness, or creativity).
Selective Attention	The ability to concentrate on a task over a period of time without being distracted.
Flexibility of Closure	The ability to identify or detect a known pattern (a figure, object, word, or sound) that is hidden in other distracting material.
Memorization	The ability to remember information such as words, numbers, pictures, and procedures.
Time Sharing	The ability to shift back and forth between two or more activities or sources of information (such as speech, sounds, touch, or other sources).
Far Vision	The ability to see details at a distance.
Speed of Closure	The ability to quickly make sense of, combine, and organize information into meaningful patterns.
Perceptual Speed	The ability to quickly and accurately compare similarities and differences among sets of letters, numbers, objects, pictures, or patterns. The things to be compared may be presented at the same time or one after the other. This ability also includes comparing a presented object with a remembered object.
Visualization	The ability to imagine how something will look after it is moved around or when its parts are moved or rearranged.
Mathematical Reasoning	The ability to choose the right mathematical methods or formulas to solve a problem.
Number Facility	The ability to add, subtract, multiply, or divide quickly and correctly.
Trunk Strength	The ability to use your abdominal and lower back muscles to support part of the body repeatedly or continuously over time without 'giving out' or fatiguing.
Finger Dexterity	The ability to make precisely coordinated movements of the fingers of one or both hands to grasp, manipulate, or assemble very small objects.
Auditory Attention	The ability to focus on a single source of sound in the presence of other distracting sounds.
Hearing Sensitivity	The ability to detect or tell the differences between sounds that vary in pitch and loudness.
Visual Color Discrimination	The ability to match or detect differences between colors, including shades of color and brightness.
Speed of Limb Movement	The ability to quickly move the arms and legs.
Wrist-Finger Speed	The ability to make fast, simple, repeated movements of the fingers, hands, and wrists.
Gross Body Coordination	The ability to coordinate the movement of your arms, legs, and torso together when the whole body is in motion.
Dynamic Flexibility	The ability to quickly and repeatedly bend, stretch, twist, or reach out with your body, arms, and/or legs.
Extent Flexibility	The ability to bend, stretch, twist, or reach with your body, arms, and/or legs.
Stamina	The ability to exert yourself physically over long periods of time without getting winded or out of breath.
Gross Body Equilibrium	The ability to keep or regain your body balance or stay upright when in an unstable position.
Reaction Time	The ability to quickly respond (with the hand, finger, or foot) to a signal (sound, light, picture) when it appears.
Dynamic Strength	The ability to exert muscle force repeatedly or continuously over time. This involves muscular endurance and resistance to muscle fatigue.
Explosive Strength	The ability to use short bursts of muscle force to propel oneself (as in jumping or sprinting), or to throw an object.
Rate Control	The ability to time your movements or the movement of a piece of equipment in anticipation of changes in the speed and/or direction of a moving object or scene.
Static Strength	The ability to exert maximum muscle force to lift, push, pull, or carry objects.

Multilimb Coordination	The ability to coordinate two or more limbs (for example, two arms, two legs, or one leg and one arm) while sitting, standing, or lying down. It does not involve performing the activities while the whole body is in motion.
Night Vision	The ability to see under low light conditions.
Peripheral Vision	The ability to see objects or movement of objects to one's side when the eyes are looking ahead.
Depth Perception	The ability to judge which of several objects is closer or farther away from you, or to judge the distance between you and an object.
Glare Sensitivity	The ability to see objects in the presence of glare or bright lighting.
Spatial Orientation	The ability to know your location in relation to the environment or to know where other objects are in relation to you.
Arm-Hand Steadiness	The ability to keep your hand and arm steady while moving your arm or while holding your arm and hand in one position.
Control Precision	The ability to quickly and repeatedly adjust the controls of a machine or a vehicle to exact positions.
Sound Localization	The ability to tell the direction from which a sound originated.
Manual Dexterity	The ability to quickly move your hand, your hand together with your arm, or your two hands to grasp, manipulate, or assemble objects.
Response Orientation	The ability to choose quickly between two or more movements in response to two or more different signals (lights, sounds, pictures). It includes the speed with which the correct response is started with the hand, foot, or other body part.

Work_Activity	Work_Activity Definitions
Training and Teaching Others	Identifying the educational needs of others, developing formal educational or training programs or classes, and teaching or instructing others.
Thinking Creatively	Developing, designing, or creating new applications, ideas, relationships, systems, or products, including artistic contributions.
Interpreting the Meaning of Information for Others	Translating or explaining what information means and how it can be used.
Communicating with Supervisors, Peers, or Subordin	Providing information to supervisors, co-workers, and subordinates by telephone, in written form, e-mail, or in person.
Getting Information	Observing, receiving, and otherwise obtaining information from all relevant sources.
Organizing, Planning, and Prioritizing Work	Developing specific goals and plans to prioritize, organize, and accomplish your work.
Establishing and Maintaining Interpersonal Relatio	Developing constructive and cooperative working relationships with others, and maintaining them over time.
Making Decisions and Solving Problems	Analyzing information and evaluating results to choose the best solution and solve problems.
Coaching and Developing Others	Identifying the developmental needs of others and coaching, mentoring, or otherwise helping others to improve their knowledge or skills.
Scheduling Work and Activities	Scheduling events, programs, and activities, as well as the work of others.
Interacting With Computers	Using computers and computer systems (including hardware and software) to program, write software, set up functions, enter data, or process information.
Updating and Using Relevant Knowledge	Keeping up-to-date technically and applying new knowledge to your job.
Developing Objectives and Strategies	Establishing long-range objectives and specifying the strategies and actions to achieve them.
Judging the Qualities of Things, Services, or Peop	Assessing the value, importance, or quality of things or people.
Documenting/Recording Information	Entering, transcribing, recording, storing, or maintaining information in written or electronic/magnetic form.
Analyzing Data or Information	Identifying the underlying principles, reasons, or facts of information by breaking down information or data into separate parts.
Identifying Objects, Actions, and Events	Identifying information by categorizing, estimating, recognizing differences or similarities, and detecting changes in circumstances or events.
Performing for or Working Directly with the Public	Performing for people or dealing directly with the public. This includes serving customers in restaurants and stores, and receiving clients or guests.
Coordinating the Work and Activities of Others	Getting members of a group to work together to accomplish tasks.
Processing Information	Compiling, coding, categorizing, calculating, tabulating, auditing, or verifying information or data.

Evaluating Information to Determine Compliance wit	Using relevant information and individual judgment to determine whether events or processes comply with laws, regulations, or standards.
Provide Consultation and Advice to Others	Providing guidance and expert advice to management or other groups on technical, systems-, or process-related topics.
Performing Administrative Activities	Performing day-to-day administrative tasks such as maintaining information files and processing paperwork.
Resolving Conflicts and Negotiating with Others	Handling complaints, settling disputes, and resolving grievances and conflicts, or otherwise negotiating with others.
Communicating with Persons Outside Organization	Communicating with people outside the organization, representing the organization to customers, the public, government, and other external sources. This information can be exchanged in person, in writing, or by telephone or e-mail.
Developing and Building Teams	Encouraging and building mutual trust, respect, and cooperation among team members.
Monitor Processes, Materials, or Surroundings	Monitoring and reviewing information from materials, events, or the environment, to detect or assess problems.
Assisting and Caring for Others	Providing personal assistance, medical attention, emotional support, or other personal care to others such as coworkers, customers, or patients.
Guiding, Directing, and Motivating Subordinates	Providing guidance and direction to subordinates, including setting performance standards and monitoring performance.
Selling or Influencing Others	Convincing others to buy merchandise/goods or to otherwise change their minds or actions.
Estimating the Quantifiable Characteristics of Pro	Estimating sizes, distances, and quantities; or determining time, costs, resources, or materials needed to perform a work activity.
Staffing Organizational Units	Recruiting, interviewing, selecting, hiring, and promoting employees in an organization.
Monitoring and Controlling Resources	Monitoring and controlling resources and overseeing the spending of money.
Inspecting Equipment, Structures, or Material	Inspecting equipment, structures, or materials to identify the cause of errors or other problems or defects.
Controlling Machines and Processes	Using either control mechanisms or direct physical activity to operate machines or processes (not including computers or vehicles).
Handling and Moving Objects	Using hands and arms in handling, installing, positioning, and moving materials, and manipulating things.
Performing General Physical Activities	Performing physical activities that require considerable use of your arms and legs and moving your whole body, such as climbing, lifting, balancing, walking, stooping, and handling of materials.
Drafting, Laying Out, and Specifying Technical Dev	Providing documentation, detailed instructions, drawings, or specifications to tell others about how devices, parts, equipment, or structures are to be fabricated, constructed, assembled, modified, maintained, or used.
Repairing and Maintaining Electronic Equipment	Servicing, repairing, calibrating, regulating, fine-tuning, or testing machines, devices, and equipment that operate primarily on the basis of electrical or electronic (not mechanical) principles.
Operating Vehicles, Mechanized Devices, or Equipme	Running, maneuvering, navigating, or driving vehicles or mechanized equipment, such as forklifts, passenger vehicles, aircraft, or water craft.
Repairing and Maintaining Mechanical Equipment	Servicing, repairing, adjusting, and testing machines, devices, moving parts, and equipment that operate primarily on the basis of mechanical (not electronic) principles.

Work_Context	Work_Context Definitions
Electronic Mail	How often do you use electronic mail in this job?
Face-to-Face Discussions	How often do you have to have face-to-face discussions with individuals or teams in this job?
Freedom to Make Decisions	How much decision making freedom, without supervision, does the job offer?
Structured versus Unstructured Work	To what extent is this job structured for the worker, rather than allowing the worker to determine tasks, priorities, and goals?
Contact With Others	How much does this job require the worker to be in contact with others (face-to-face, by telephone, or otherwise) in order to perform it?
Public Speaking	How often do you have to perform public speaking in this job?
Indoors, Environmentally Controlled	How often does this job require working indoors in environmentally controlled conditions?
Telephone	How often do you have telephone conversations in this job?
Frequency of Decision Making	How frequently is the worker required to make decisions that affect other people, the financial resources, and/or the image and reputation of the organization?

Coordinate or Lead Others	How important is it to coordinate or lead others in accomplishing work activities in this job?
Work With Work Group or Team	How important is it to work with others in a group or team in this job?
Letters and Memos	How often does the job require written letters and memos?
Impact of Decisions on Co-workers or Company Resul	How do the decisions an employee makes impact the results of co-workers, clients or the company?
Physical Proximity	To what extent does this job require the worker to perform job tasks in close physical proximity to other people?
Importance of Being Exact or Accurate	How important is being very exact or highly accurate in performing this job?
Time Pressure	How often does this job require the worker to meet strict deadlines?
Spend Time Sitting	How much does this job require sitting?
Level of Competition	To what extent does this job require the worker to compete or to be aware of competitive pressures?
Deal With External Customers	How important is it to work with external customers or the public in this job?
Frequency of Conflict Situations	How often are there conflict situations the employee has to face in this job?
Deal With Unpleasant or Angry People	How frequently does the worker have to deal with unpleasant, angry, or discourteous individuals as part of the job requirements?
Importance of Repeating Same Tasks	How important is repeating the same physical activities (e.g., key entry) or mental activities (e.g., checking entries in a ledger) over and over, without stopping, to performing this job?
Spend Time Standing	How much does this job require standing?
Responsibility for Outcomes and Results	How responsible is the worker for work outcomes and results of other workers?
Sounds, Noise Levels Are Distracting or Uncomforta	How often does this job require working exposed to sounds and noise levels that are distracting or uncomfortable?
Spend Time Making Repetitive Motions	How much does this job require making repetitive motions?
Spend Time Using Your Hands to Handle, Control, or	How much does this job require using your hands to handle, control, or feel objects, tools or controls?
Exposed to Disease or Infections	How often does this job require exposure to disease/infections?
Consequence of Error	How serious would the result usually be if the worker made a mistake that was not readily correctable?
Degree of Automation	How automated is the job?
Spend Time Walking and Running	How much does this job require walking and running?
Responsible for Others' Health and Safety	How much responsibility is there for the health and safety of others in this job?
Exposed to Contaminants	How often does this job require working exposed to contaminants (such as pollutants, gases, dust or odors)?
Extremely Bright or Inadequate Lighting	How often does this job require working in extremely bright or inadequate lighting conditions?
Indoors, Not Environmentally Controlled	How often does this job require working indoors in non-controlled environmental conditions (e.g., warehouse without heat)?
Spend Time Bending or Twisting the Body	How much does this job require bending or twisting your body?
In an Enclosed Vehicle or Equipment	How often does this job require working in a closed vehicle or equipment (e.g., car)?
Cramped Work Space, Awkward Positions	How often does this job require working in cramped work spaces that requires getting into awkward positions?
Very Hot or Cold Temperatures	How often does this job require working in very hot (above 90 F degrees) or very cold (below 32 F degrees) temperatures?
Deal With Physically Aggressive People	How frequently does this job require the worker to deal with physical aggression of violent individuals?
Exposed to Minor Burns, Cuts, Bites, or Stings	How often does this job require exposure to minor burns, cuts, bites, or stings?
Pace Determined by Speed of Equipment	How important is it to this job that the pace is determined by the speed of equipment or machinery? (This does not refer to keeping busy at all times on this job.)
Spend Time Kneeling, Crouching, Stooping, or Crawl	How much does this job require kneeling, crouching, stooping or crawling?
Spend Time Keeping or Regaining Balance	How much does this job require keeping or regaining your balance?
Outdoors, Exposed to Weather	How often does this job require working outdoors, exposed to all weather conditions?
Outdoors, Under Cover	How often does this job require working outdoors, under cover (e.g., structure with roof but no walls)?
Exposed to Radiation	How often does this job require exposure to radiation?

Exposed to Hazardous Conditions	How often does this job require exposure to hazardous conditions?
Exposed to High Places	How often does this job require exposure to high places?
Exposed to Whole Body Vibration	How often does this job require exposure to whole body vibration (e.g., operate a jackhammer)?
Spend Time Climbing Ladders, Scaffolds, or Poles	How much does this job require climbing ladders, scaffolds, or poles?
Exposed to Hazardous Equipment	How often does this job require exposure to hazardous equipment?
Wear Specialized Protective or Safety Equipment su	How much does this job require wearing specialized protective or safety equipment such as breathing apparatus, safety harness, full protection suits, or radiation protection?
Wear Common Protective or Safety Equipment such as	How much does this job require wearing common protective or safety equipment such as safety shoes, glasses, gloves, hard hats or live jackets?
In an Open Vehicle or Equipment	How often does this job require working in an open vehicle or equipment (e.g., tractor)?

Job Zone Component	Job Zone Component Definitions
Title	Job Zone Five: Extensive Preparation Needed
Overall Experience	Extensive skill, knowledge, and experience are needed for these occupations. Many require more than five years of experience. For example, surgeons must complete four years of college and an additional five to seven years of specialized medical training to be able to do their job.
Job Training	Employees may need some on-the-job training, but most of these occupations assume that the person will already have the required skills, knowledge, work-related experience, and/or training.
Job Zone Examples	These occupations often involve coordinating, training, supervising, or managing the activities of others to accomplish goals. Very advanced communication and organizational skills are required. Examples include athletic trainers, lawyers, managing editors, phyicists, social psychologists, and surgeons.
SVP Range	(8.0 and above)
Education	A bachelor's degree is the minimum formal education required for these occupations. However, many also require graduate school. For example, they may require a master's degree, and some require a Ph.D., M.D., or J.D. (law degree).

Work_Styles	Work_Styles Definitions
Integrity	Job requires being honest and ethical.
Dependability	Job requires being reliable, responsible, and dependable, and fulfilling obligations.
Independence	Job requires developing one's own ways of doing things, guiding oneself with little or no supervision, and depending on oneself to get things done.
Initiative	Job requires a willingness to take on responsibilities and challenges.
Analytical Thinking	Job requires analyzing information and using logic to address work-related issues and problems.
Concern for Others	Job requires being sensitive to others' needs and feelings and being understanding and helpful on the job.
Persistence	Job requires persistence in the face of obstacles.
Achievement/Effort	Job requires establishing and maintaining personally challenging achievement goals and exerting effort toward mastering tasks.
Innovation	Job requires creativity and alternative thinking to develop new ideas for and answers to work-related problems.
Leadership	Job requires a willingness to lead, take charge, and offer opinions and direction.
Attention to Detail	Job requires being careful about detail and thorough in completing work tasks.
Cooperation	Job requires being pleasant with others on the job and displaying a good-natured, cooperative attitude.
Adaptability/Flexibility	Job requires being open to change (positive or negative) and to considerable variety in the workplace.
Self Control	Job requires maintaining composure, keeping emotions in check, controlling anger, and avoiding aggressive behavior, even in very difficult situations.
Social Orientation	Job requires preferring to work with others rather than alone, and being personally connected with others on the job.
Stress Tolerance	Job requires accepting criticism and dealing calmly and effectively with high stress situations.

25-1124.00 - Foreign Language and Literature Teachers, Postsecondary

Teach courses in foreign (i.e., other than English) languages and literature.

Tasks

1) Maintain student attendance records, grades, and other required records.

2) Maintain regularly scheduled office hours in order to advise and assist students.

3) Plan, evaluate, and revise curricula, course content, and course materials and methods of instruction.

4) Initiate, facilitate, and moderate classroom discussions.

5) Keep abreast of developments in their field by reading current literature, talking with colleagues, and participating in professional organizations and activities.

6) Collaborate with colleagues to address teaching and research issues.

7) Select and obtain materials and supplies such as textbooks.

8) Compile, administer, and grade examinations, or assign this work to others.

9) Participate in campus and community events.

10) Advise students on academic and vocational curricula, and on career issues.

11) Serve on academic or administrative committees that deal with institutional policies, departmental matters, and academic issues.

12) Prepare and deliver lectures to undergraduate and/or graduate students on topics such as how to speak and write a foreign language, and the cultural aspects of areas where a particular language is used.

13) Participate in student recruitment, registration, and placement activities.

14) Act as advisers to student organizations.

15) Compile bibliographies of specialized materials for outside reading assignments.

16) Conduct research in a particular field of knowledge, and publish findings in scholarly journals, books, and/or electronic media.

17) Write grant proposals to procure external research funding.

18) Perform administrative duties such as serving as department head.

19) Supervise undergraduate and/or graduate teaching, internship, and research work.

20) Provide professional consulting services to government and/or industry.

21) Prepare course materials such as syllabi, homework assignments, and handouts.

Knowledge	Knowledge Definitions
English Language	Knowledge of the structure and content of the English language including the meaning and spelling of words, rules of composition, and grammar.
Foreign Language	Knowledge of the structure and content of a foreign (non-English) language including the meaning and spelling of words, rules of composition and grammar, and pronunciation.
Education and Training	Knowledge of principles and methods for curriculum and training design, teaching and instruction for individuals and groups, and the measurement of training effects.
History and Archeology	Knowledge of historical events and their causes, indicators, and effects on civilizations and cultures.
Sociology and Anthropology	Knowledge of group behavior and dynamics, societal trends and influences, human migrations, ethnicity, cultures and their history and origins.
Philosophy and Theology	Knowledge of different philosophical systems and religions. This includes their basic principles, values, ethics, ways of thinking, customs, practices, and their impact on human culture.
Psychology	Knowledge of human behavior and performance; individual differences in ability, personality, and interests; learning and motivation; psychological research methods; and the assessment and treatment of behavioral and affective disorders.
Communications and Media	Knowledge of media production, communication, and dissemination techniques and methods. This includes alternative ways to inform and entertain via written, oral, and visual media.

Geography	Knowledge of principles and methods for describing the features of land, sea, and air masses, including their physical characteristics, locations, interrelationships, and distribution of plant, animal, and human life.
Computers and Electronics	Knowledge of circuit boards, processors, chips, electronic equipment, and computer hardware and software, including applications and programming.
Fine Arts	Knowledge of the theory and techniques required to compose, produce, and perform works of music, dance, visual arts, drama, and sculpture.
Clerical	Knowledge of administrative and clerical procedures and systems such as word processing, managing files and records, stenography and transcription, designing forms, and other office procedures and terminology.
Customer and Personal Service	Knowledge of principles and processes for providing customer and personal services. This includes customer needs assessment, meeting quality standards for services, and evaluation of customer satisfaction.
Administration and Management	Knowledge of business and management principles involved in strategic planning, resource allocation, human resources modeling, leadership technique, production methods, and coordination of people and resources.
Law and Government	Knowledge of laws, legal codes, court procedures, precedents, government regulations, executive orders, agency rules, and the democratic political process.
Personnel and Human Resources	Knowledge of principles and procedures for personnel recruitment, selection, training, compensation and benefits, labor relations and negotiation, and personnel information systems.
Therapy and Counseling	Knowledge of principles, methods, and procedures for diagnosis, treatment, and rehabilitation of physical and mental dysfunctions, and for career counseling and guidance.
Mathematics	Knowledge of arithmetic, algebra, geometry, calculus, statistics, and their applications.
Telecommunications	Knowledge of transmission, broadcasting, switching, control, and operation of telecommunications systems.
Public Safety and Security	Knowledge of relevant equipment, policies, procedures, and strategies to promote effective local, state, or national security operations for the protection of people, data, property, and institutions.
Sales and Marketing	Knowledge of principles and methods for showing, promoting, and selling products or services. This includes marketing strategy and tactics, product demonstration, sales techniques, and sales control systems.
Transportation	Knowledge of principles and methods for moving people or goods by air, rail, sea, or road, including the relative costs and benefits.
Economics and Accounting	Knowledge of economic and accounting principles and practices, the financial markets, banking and the analysis and reporting of financial data.
Medicine and Dentistry	Knowledge of the information and techniques needed to diagnose and treat human injuries, diseases, and deformities. This includes symptoms, treatment alternatives, drug properties and interactions, and preventive health-care measures.
Biology	Knowledge of plant and animal organisms, their tissues, cells, functions, interdependencies, and interactions with each other and the environment.
Engineering and Technology	Knowledge of the practical application of engineering science and technology. This includes applying principles, techniques, procedures, and equipment to the design and production of various goods and services.
Design	Knowledge of design techniques, tools, and principles involved in production of precision technical plans, blueprints, drawings, and models.
Mechanical	Knowledge of machines and tools, including their designs, uses, repair, and maintenance.
Production and Processing	Knowledge of raw materials, production processes, quality control, costs, and other techniques for maximizing the effective manufacture and distribution of goods.
Chemistry	Knowledge of the chemical composition, structure, and properties of substances and of the chemical processes and transformations that they undergo. This includes uses of chemicals and their interactions, danger signs, production techniques, and disposal methods.
Building and Construction	Knowledge of materials, methods, and the tools involved in the construction or repair of houses, buildings, or other structures such as highways and roads.
Food Production	Knowledge of techniques and equipment for planting, growing, and harvesting food products (both plant and animal) for consumption, including storage/handling techniques.
Physics	Knowledge and prediction of physical principles, laws, their interrelationships, and applications to understanding fluid, material, and atmospheric dynamics, and mechanical, electrical, atomic and sub-atomic structures and processes.

Skills	Skills Definitions
Instructing	Teaching others how to do something.
Speaking	Talking to others to convey information effectively.
Reading Comprehension	Understanding written sentences and paragraphs in work related documents.
Active Listening	Giving full attention to what other people are saying, taking time to understand the points being made, asking questions as appropriate, and not interrupting at inappropriate times.
Critical Thinking	Using logic and reasoning to identify the strengths and weaknesses of alternative solutions, conclusions or approaches to problems.
Learning Strategies	Selecting and using training/instructional methods and procedures appropriate for the situation when learning or teaching new things.
Writing	Communicating effectively in writing as appropriate for the needs of the audience.
Active Learning	Understanding the implications of new information for both current and future problem-solving and decision-making.
Social Perceptiveness	Being aware of others' reactions and understanding why they react as they do.
Monitoring	Monitoring/Assessing performance of yourself, other individuals, or organizations to make improvements or take corrective action.
Time Management	Managing one's own time and the time of others.
Coordination	Adjusting actions in relation to others' actions.
Judgment and Decision Making	Considering the relative costs and benefits of potential actions to choose the most appropriate one.
Persuasion	Persuading others to change their minds or behavior.
Complex Problem Solving	Identifying complex problems and reviewing related information to develop and evaluate options and implement solutions.
Service Orientation	Actively looking for ways to help people.
Negotiation	Bringing others together and trying to reconcile differences.
Quality Control Analysis	Conducting tests and inspections of products, services, or processes to evaluate quality or performance.
Management of Personnel Resources	Motivating, developing, and directing people as they work, identifying the best people for the job.
Equipment Selection	Determining the kind of tools and equipment needed to do a job.
Mathematics	Using mathematics to solve problems.
Management of Material Resources	Obtaining and seeing to the appropriate use of equipment, facilities, and materials needed to do certain work.
Systems Evaluation	Identifying measures or indicators of system performance and the actions needed to improve or correct performance, relative to the goals of the system.
Management of Financial Resources	Determining how money will be spent to get the work done, and accounting for these expenditures.
Operations Analysis	Analyzing needs and product requirements to create a design.
Troubleshooting	Determining causes of operating errors and deciding what to do about it.
Technology Design	Generating or adapting equipment and technology to serve user needs.
Systems Analysis	Determining how a system should work and how changes in conditions, operations, and the environment will affect outcomes.
Science	Using scientific rules and methods to solve problems.
Operation and Control	Controlling operations of equipment or systems.
Programming	Writing computer programs for various purposes.
Installation	Installing equipment, machines, wiring, or programs to meet specifications.
Operation Monitoring	Watching gauges, dials, or other indicators to make sure a machine is working properly.
Repairing	Repairing machines or systems using the needed tools.
Equipment Maintenance	Performing routine maintenance on equipment and determining when and what kind of maintenance is needed.

Ability	Ability Definitions
Oral Expression	The ability to communicate information and ideas in speaking so others will understand.
Speech Clarity	The ability to speak clearly so others can understand you.
Written Comprehension	The ability to read and understand information and ideas presented in writing.
Oral Comprehension	The ability to listen to and understand information and ideas presented through spoken words and sentences.
Written Expression	The ability to communicate information and ideas in writing so others will understand.
Speech Recognition	The ability to identify and understand the speech of another person.
Inductive Reasoning	The ability to combine pieces of information to form general rules or conclusions (includes finding a relationship among seemingly unrelated events).
Deductive Reasoning	The ability to apply general rules to specific problems to produce answers that make sense.
Near Vision	The ability to see details at close range (within a few feet of the observer).
Problem Sensitivity	The ability to tell when something is wrong or is likely to go wrong. It does not involve solving the problem, only recognizing there is a problem.
Information Ordering	The ability to arrange things or actions in a certain order or pattern according to a specific rule or set of rules (e.g., patterns of numbers, letters, words, pictures, mathematical operations).
Originality	The ability to come up with unusual or clever ideas about a given topic or situation, or to develop creative ways to solve a problem.
Memorization	The ability to remember information such as words, numbers, pictures, and procedures.
Category Flexibility	The ability to generate or use different sets of rules for combining or grouping things in different ways.
Fluency of Ideas	The ability to come up with a number of ideas about a topic (the number of ideas is important, not their quality, correctness, or creativity).
Selective Attention	The ability to concentrate on a task over a period of time without being distracted.
Flexibility of Closure	The ability to identify or detect a known pattern (a figure, object, word, or sound) that is hidden in other distracting material.
Time Sharing	The ability to shift back and forth between two or more activities or sources of information (such as speech, sounds, touch, or other sources).
Speed of Closure	The ability to quickly make sense of, combine, and organize information into meaningful patterns.
Far Vision	The ability to see details at a distance.
Mathematical Reasoning	The ability to choose the right mathematical methods or formulas to solve a problem.
Auditory Attention	The ability to focus on a single source of sound in the presence of other distracting sounds.
Number Facility	The ability to add, subtract, multiply, or divide quickly and correctly.
Perceptual Speed	The ability to quickly and accurately compare similarities and differences among sets of letters, numbers, objects, pictures, or patterns. The things to be compared may be presented at the same time or one after the other. This ability also includes comparing a presented object with a remembered object.
Visualization	The ability to imagine how something will look after it is moved around or when its parts are moved or rearranged.
Trunk Strength	The ability to use your abdominal and lower back muscles to support part of the body repeatedly or continuously over time without 'giving out' or fatiguing.
Hearing Sensitivity	The ability to detect or tell the differences between sounds that vary in pitch and loudness.
Finger Dexterity	The ability to make precisely coordinated movements of the fingers of one or both hands to grasp, manipulate, or assemble very small objects.
Visual Color Discrimination	The ability to match or detect differences between colors, including shades of color and brightness.
Rate Control	The ability to time your movements or the movement of a piece of equipment in anticipation of changes in the speed and/or direction of a moving object or scene.
Response Orientation	The ability to choose quickly between two or more movements in response to two or more different signals (lights, sounds, pictures). It includes the speed with which the correct response is started with the hand, foot, or other body part.

Multilimb Coordination	The ability to coordinate two or more limbs (for example. two arms, two legs, or one leg and one arm) while sitting, standing, or lying down. It does not involve performing the activities while the whole body is in motion.
Extent Flexibility	The ability to bend, stretch, twist, or reach with your body, arms, and/or legs.
Stamina	The ability to exert yourself physically over long periods of time without getting winded or out of breath.
Dynamic Strength	The ability to exert muscle force repeatedly or continuously over time. This involves muscular endurance and resistance to muscle fatigue.
Explosive Strength	The ability to use short bursts of muscle force to propel oneself (as in jumping or sprinting), or to throw an object.
Static Strength	The ability to exert maximum muscle force to lift, push, pull, or carry objects.
Speed of Limb Movement	The ability to quickly move the arms and legs.
Wrist-Finger Speed	The ability to make fast, simple, repeated movements of the fingers, hands, and wrists.
Reaction Time	The ability to quickly respond (with the hand, finger, or foot) to a signal (sound, light, picture) when it appears.
Dynamic Flexibility	The ability to quickly and repeatedly bend, stretch, twist, or reach out with your body, arms, and/or legs.
Depth Perception	The ability to judge which of several objects is closer or farther away from you, or to judge the distance between you and an object.
Control Precision	The ability to quickly and repeatedly adjust the controls of a machine or a vehicle to exact positions.
Arm-Hand Steadiness	The ability to keep your hand and arm steady while moving your arm or while holding your arm and hand in one position.
Night Vision	The ability to see under low light conditions.
Sound Localization	The ability to tell the direction from which a sound originated.
Glare Sensitivity	The ability to see objects in the presence of glare or bright lighting.
Peripheral Vision	The ability to see objects or movement of objects to one's side when the eyes are looking ahead.
Gross Body Coordination	The ability to coordinate the movement of your arms, legs, and torso together when the whole body is in motion.
Spatial Orientation	The ability to know your location in relation to the environment or to know where other objects are in relation to you.
Gross Body Equilibrium	The ability to keep or regain your body balance or stay upright when in an unstable position.
Manual Dexterity	The ability to quickly move your hand, your hand together with your arm, or your two hands to grasp, manipulate, or assemble objects.

Work_Activity	Work_Activity Definitions
Training and Teaching Others	Identifying the educational needs of others, developing formal educational or training programs or classes, and teaching or instructing others.
Thinking Creatively	Developing, designing, or creating new applications, ideas, relationships, systems, or products, including artistic contributions.
Getting Information	Observing, receiving, and otherwise obtaining information from all relevant sources.
Organizing, Planning, and Prioritizing Work	Developing specific goals and plans to prioritize, organize, and accomplish your work.
Coaching and Developing Others	Identifying the developmental needs of others and coaching, mentoring, or otherwise helping others to improve their knowledge or skills.
Interpreting the Meaning of Information for Others	Translating or explaining what information means and how it can be used.
Establishing and Maintaining Interpersonal Relatio	Developing constructive and cooperative working relationships with others, and maintaining them over time.
Judging the Qualities of Things, Services, or Peop	Assessing the value, importance, or quality of things or people.
Communicating with Supervisors, Peers, or Subordin	Providing information to supervisors, co-workers, and subordinates by telephone, in written form, e-mail, or in person.
Updating and Using Relevant Knowledge	Keeping up-to-date technically and applying new knowledge to your job.
Documenting/Recording Information	Entering, transcribing, recording, storing, or maintaining information in written or electronic/magnetic form.
Developing Objectives and Strategies	Establishing long-range objectives and specifying the strategies and actions to achieve them.
Making Decisions and Solving Problems	Analyzing information and evaluating results to choose the best solution and solve problems.

Analyzing Data or Information	Identifying the underlying principles, reasons, or facts of information by breaking down information or data into separate parts.	

Work_Context	**Work_Context Definitions**
Electronic Mail	How often do you use electronic mail in this job?

Analyzing Data or Information	Identifying the underlying principles, reasons, or facts of information by breaking down information or data into separate parts.
Performing for or Working Directly with the Public	Performing for people or dealing directly with the public. This includes serving customers in restaurants and stores, and receiving clients or guests.
Processing Information	Compiling, coding, categorizing, calculating, tabulating, auditing, or verifying information or data.
Interacting With Computers	Using computers and computer systems (including hardware and software) to program, write software, set up functions, enter data, or process information.
Identifying Objects, Actions, and Events	Identifying information by categorizing, estimating, recognizing differences or similarities, and detecting changes in circumstances or events.
Evaluating Information to Determine Compliance wit	Using relevant information and individual judgment to determine whether events or processes comply with laws, regulations, or standards.
Coordinating the Work and Activities of Others	Getting members of a group to work together to accomplish tasks.
Assisting and Caring for Others	Providing personal assistance, medical attention, emotional support, or other personal care to others such as coworkers, customers, or patients.
Scheduling Work and Activities	Scheduling events, programs, and activities, as well as the work of others.
Guiding, Directing, and Motivating Subordinates	Providing guidance and direction to subordinates, including setting performance standards and monitoring performance.
Developing and Building Teams	Encouraging and building mutual trust, respect, and cooperation among team members.
Provide Consultation and Advice to Others	Providing guidance and expert advice to management or other groups on technical, systems-, or process-related topics.
Communicating with Persons Outside Organization	Communicating with people outside the organization, representing the organization to customers, the public, government, and other external sources. This information can be exchanged in person, in writing, or by telephone or e-mail.
Monitor Processes, Materials, or Surroundings	Monitoring and reviewing information from materials, events, or the environment, to detect or assess problems.
Performing Administrative Activities	Performing day-to-day administrative tasks such as maintaining information files and processing paperwork.
Resolving Conflicts and Negotiating with Others	Handling complaints, settling disputes, and resolving grievances and conflicts, or otherwise negotiating with others.
Selling or Influencing Others	Convincing others to buy merchandise/goods or to otherwise change their minds or actions.
Estimating the Quantifiable Characteristics of Pro	Estimating sizes, distances, and quantities; or determining time, costs, resources, or materials needed to perform a work activity.
Staffing Organizational Units	Recruiting, interviewing, selecting, hiring, and promoting employees in an organization.
Inspecting Equipment, Structures, or Material	Inspecting equipment, structures, or materials to identify the cause of errors or other problems or defects.
Monitoring and Controlling Resources	Monitoring and controlling resources and overseeing the spending of money.
Performing General Physical Activities	Performing physical activities that require considerable use of your arms and legs and moving your whole body, such as climbing, lifting, balancing, walking, stooping, and handling of materials.
Handling and Moving Objects	Using hands and arms in handling, installing, positioning, and moving materials, and manipulating things.
Controlling Machines and Processes	Using either control mechanisms or direct physical activity to operate machines or processes (not including computers or vehicles).
Operating Vehicles, Mechanized Devices, or Equipme	Running, maneuvering, navigating, or driving vehicles or mechanized equipment, such as forklifts, passenger vehicles, aircraft, or water craft.
Repairing and Maintaining Electronic Equipment	Servicing, repairing, calibrating, regulating, fine-tuning, or testing machines, devices, and equipment that operate primarily on the basis of electrical or electronic (not mechanical) principles.
Drafting, Laying Out, and Specifying Technical Dev	Providing documentation, detailed instructions, drawings, or specifications to tell others about how devices, parts, equipment, or structures are to be fabricated, constructed, assembled, modified, maintained, or used.
Repairing and Maintaining Mechanical Equipment	Servicing, repairing, adjusting, and testing machines, devices, moving parts, and equipment that operate primarily on the basis of mechanical (not electronic) principles.

Work_Context	**Work_Context Definitions**
Electronic Mail	How often do you use electronic mail in this job?
Face-to-Face Discussions	How often do you have to have face-to-face discussions with individuals or teams in this job?
Freedom to Make Decisions	How much decision making freedom, without supervision, does the job offer?
Indoors, Environmentally Controlled	How often does this job require working indoors in environmentally controlled conditions?
Contact With Others	How much does this job require the worker to be in contact with others (face-to-face, by telephone, or otherwise) in order to perform it?
Structured versus Unstructured Work	To what extent is this job structured for the worker, rather than allowing the worker to determine tasks, priorities, and goals?
Telephone	How often do you have telephone conversations in this job?
Public Speaking	How often do you have to perform public speaking in this job?
Coordinate or Lead Others	How important is it to coordinate or lead others in accomplishing work activities in this job?
Work With Work Group or Team	How important is it to work with others in a group or team in this job?
Letters and Memos	How often does the job require written letters and memos?
Time Pressure	How often does this job require the worker to meet strict deadlines?
Impact of Decisions on Co-workers or Company Resul	How do the decisions an employee makes impact the results of co-workers, clients or the company?
Importance of Being Exact or Accurate	How important is being very exact or highly accurate in performing this job?
Frequency of Decision Making	How frequently is the worker required to make decisions that affect other people, the financial resources, and/or the image and reputation of the organization?
Physical Proximity	To what extent does this job require the worker to perform job tasks in close physical proximity to other people?
Level of Competition	To what extent does this job require the worker to compete or to be aware of competitive pressures?
Spend Time Sitting	How much does this job require sitting?
Deal With External Customers	How important is it to work with external customers or the public in this job?
Frequency of Conflict Situations	How often are there conflict situations the employee has to face in this job?
Spend Time Standing	How much does this job require standing?
Responsibility for Outcomes and Results	How responsible is the worker for work outcomes and results of other workers?
Deal With Unpleasant or Angry People	How frequently does the worker have to deal with unpleasant, angry, or discourteous individuals as part of the job requirements?
Sounds, Noise Levels Are Distracting or Uncomforta	How often does this job require working exposed to sounds and noise levels that are distracting or uncomfortable?
Importance of Repeating Same Tasks	How important is repeating the same physical activities (e.g., key entry) or mental activities (e.g., checking entries in a ledger) over and over, without stopping, to performing this job?
Spend Time Making Repetitive Motions	How much does this job require making repetitive motions?
Spend Time Using Your Hands to Handle, Control, or	How much does this job require using your hands to handle, control, or feel objects, tools or controls?
Consequence of Error	How serious would the result usually be if the worker made a mistake that was not readily correctable?
Exposed to Disease or Infections	How often does this job require exposure to disease/infections?
Spend Time Walking and Running	How much does this job require walking and running?
Indoors, Not Environmentally Controlled	How often does this job require working indoors in non-controlled environmental conditions (e.g., warehouse without heat)?
Responsible for Others' Health and Safety	How much responsibility is there for the health and safety of others in this job?
Degree of Automation	How automated is the job?
Very Hot or Cold Temperatures	How often does this job require working in very hot (above 90 F degrees) or very cold (below 32 F degrees) temperatures?
Deal With Physically Aggressive People	How frequently does this job require the worker to deal with physical aggression of violent individuals?
Extremely Bright or Inadequate Lighting	How often does this job require working in extremely bright or inadequate lighting conditions?
Exposed to Contaminants	How often does this job require working exposed to contaminants (such as pollutants, gases, dust or odors)?
In an Enclosed Vehicle or Equipment	How often does this job require working in a closed vehicle or equipment (e.g., car)?

Spend Time Bending or Twisting the Body	How much does this job require bending or twisting your body?
Cramped Work Space, Awkward Positions	How often does this job require working in cramped work spaces that requires getting into awkward positions?
Spend Time Keeping or Regaining Balance	How much does this job require keeping or regaining your balance?
Pace Determined by Speed of Equipment	How important is it to this job that the pace is determined by the speed of equipment or machinery? (This does not refer to keeping busy at all times on this job.)
Outdoors, Exposed to Weather	How often does this job require working outdoors, exposed to all weather conditions?
Spend Time Kneeling, Crouching, Stooping, or Crawl	How much does this job require kneeling, crouching, stooping, or crawling?
Exposed to Minor Burns, Cuts, Bites, or Stings	How often does this job require exposure to minor burns, cuts, bites, or stings?
Outdoors, Under Cover	How often does this job require working outdoors, under cover (e.g., structure with roof but no walls)?
Spend Time Climbing Ladders, Scaffolds, or Poles	How much does this job require climbing ladders, scaffolds, or poles?
Exposed to Hazardous Conditions	How often does this job require exposure to hazardous conditions?
Exposed to Hazardous Equipment	How often does this job require exposure to hazardous equipment?
Exposed to Whole Body Vibration	How often does this job require exposure to whole body vibration (e.g., operate a jackhammer)?
Wear Specialized Protective or Safety Equipment su	How much does this job require wearing specialized protective or safety equipment such as breathing apparatus, safety harness, full protection suits, or radiation protection?
Exposed to High Places	How often does this job require exposure to high places?
In an Open Vehicle or Equipment	How often does this job require working in an open vehicle or equipment (e.g., tractor)?
Wear Common Protective or Safety Equipment such as	How much does this job require wearing common protective or safety equipment such as safety shoes, glasses, gloves, hard hats or live jackets?
Exposed to Radiation	How often does this job require exposure to radiation?

Job Zone Component	Job Zone Component Definitions
Title	Job Zone Five: Extensive Preparation Needed
	Extensive skill, knowledge, and experience are needed for these occupations. Many require more than five years of experience.
Overall Experience	For example, surgeons must complete four years of college and an additional five to seven years of specialized medical training to be able to do their job.
Job Training	Employees may need some on-the-job training, but most of these occupations assume that the person will already have the required skills, knowledge, work-related experience, and/or training.
Job Zone Examples	These occupations often involve coordinating, training, supervising, or managing the activities of others to accomplish goals. Very advanced communication and organizational skills are required. Examples include athletic trainers, lawyers, managing editors, physicists, social psychologists, and surgeons.
SVP Range	(8.0 and above)
Education	A bachelor's degree is the minimum formal education required for these occupations. However, many also require graduate school. For example, they may require a master's degree, and some require a Ph.D., M.D., or J.D. (law degree).

Work_Styles	Work_Styles Definitions
Dependability	Job requires being reliable, responsible, and dependable, and fulfilling obligations.
Integrity	Job requires being honest and ethical.
Independence	Job requires developing one's own ways of doing things, guiding oneself with little or no supervision, and depending on oneself to get things done.
Self Control	Job requires maintaining composure, keeping emotions in check, controlling anger, and avoiding aggressive behavior, even in very difficult situations.
Attention to Detail	Job requires being careful about detail and thorough in completing work tasks.
Initiative	Job requires a willingness to take on responsibilities and challenges.
Persistence	Job requires persistence in the face of obstacles.

Analytical Thinking	Job requires analyzing information and using logic to address work-related issues and problems.
Concern for Others	Job requires being sensitive to others' needs and feelings and being understanding and helpful on the job.
Cooperation	Job requires being pleasant with others on the job and displaying a good-natured, cooperative attitude.
Achievement/Effort	Job requires establishing and maintaining personally challenging achievement goals and exerting effort toward mastering tasks.
Stress Tolerance	Job requires accepting criticism and dealing calmly and effectively with high stress situations.
Social Orientation	Job requires preferring to work with others rather than alone, and being personally connected with others on the job.
Adaptability/Flexibility	Job requires being open to change (positive or negative) and to considerable variety in the workplace.
Leadership	Job requires a willingness to lead, take charge, and offer opinions and direction.
Innovation	Job requires creativity and alternative thinking to develop new ideas for and answers to work-related problems.

25-1125.00 - History Teachers, Postsecondary

Teach courses in human history and historiography.

Tasks

1) Maintain student attendance records, grades, and other required records.

2) Plan, evaluate, and revise curricula, course content, and course materials and methods of instruction.

3) Prepare and deliver lectures to undergraduate and/or graduate students on topics such as ancient history, postwar civilizations, and the history of third-world countries.

4) Compile, administer, and grade examinations, or assign this work to others.

5) Participate in campus and community events.

6) Select and obtain materials and supplies such as textbooks.

7) Maintain regularly scheduled office hours in order to advise and assist students.

8) Collaborate with colleagues to address teaching and research issues.

9) Advise students on academic and vocational curricula, and on career issues.

10) Serve on academic or administrative committees that deal with institutional policies, departmental matters, and academic issues.

11) Conduct research in a particular field of knowledge, and publish findings in professional journals, books, and/or electronic media.

12) Compile bibliographies of specialized materials for outside reading assignments.

13) Participate in student recruitment, registration, and placement activities.

14) Write grant proposals to procure external research funding.

15) Act as advisers to student organizations.

16) Supervise undergraduate and/or graduate teaching, internship, and research work.

17) Provide professional consulting services to government, educational institutions, and/or industry.

18) Perform administrative duties such as serving as department head.

19) Initiate, facilitate, and moderate classroom discussions.

20) Evaluate and grade students' class work, assignments, and papers.

21) Prepare course materials such as syllabi, homework assignments, and handouts.

Knowledge	Knowledge Definitions
History and Archeology	Knowledge of historical events and their causes, indicators, and effects on civilizations and cultures.
English Language	Knowledge of the structure and content of the English language including the meaning and spelling of words, rules of composition, and grammar.
Education and Training	Knowledge of principles and methods for curriculum and training design, teaching and instruction for individuals and groups, and the measurement of training effects.

Geography	Knowledge of principles and methods for describing the features of land, sea, and air masses, including their physical characteristics, locations, interrelationships, and distribution of plant, animal, and human life.	Physics	Knowledge and prediction of physical principles, laws, their interrelationships, and applications to understanding fluid, material, and atmospheric dynamics, and mechanical, electrical, atomic and sub- atomic structures and processes.
Philosophy and Theology	Knowledge of different philosophical systems and religions. This includes their basic principles, values, ethics, ways of thinking, customs, practices, and their impact on human culture.	Production and Processing	Knowledge of raw materials, production processes, quality control, costs, and other techniques for maximizing the effective manufacture and distribution of goods.
Sociology and Anthropology	Knowledge of group behavior and dynamics, societal trends and influences, human migrations, ethnicity, cultures and their history and origins.	Engineering and Technology	Knowledge of the practical application of engineering science and technology. This includes applying principles, techniques, procedures, and equipment to the design and production of various goods and services.
Law and Government	Knowledge of laws, legal codes, court procedures, precedents, government regulations, executive orders, agency rules, and the democratic political process.	Chemistry	Knowledge of the chemical composition, structure, and properties of substances and of the chemical processes and transformations that they undergo. This includes uses of chemicals and their interactions, danger signs, production techniques, and disposal methods.
Computers and Electronics	Knowledge of circuit boards, processors, chips, electronic equipment, and computer hardware and software, including applications and programming.	Mechanical	Knowledge of machines and tools, including their designs, uses, repair, and maintenance.
Communications and Media	Knowledge of media production, communication, and dissemination techniques and methods. This includes alternative ways to inform and entertain via written, oral, and visual media.	Building and Construction	Knowledge of materials, methods, and the tools involved in the construction or repair of houses, buildings, or other structures such as highways and roads.
Foreign Language	Knowledge of the structure and content of a foreign (non-English) language including the meaning and spelling of words, rules of composition and grammar, and pronunciation.	Food Production	Knowledge of techniques and equipment for planting, growing, and harvesting food products (both plant and animal) for consumption, including storage/handling techniques.
Psychology	Knowledge of human behavior and performance; individual differences in ability, personality, and interests; learning and motivation; psychological research methods; and the assessment and treatment of behavioral and affective disorders.	**Skills**	**Skills Definitions**
Clerical	Knowledge of administrative and clerical procedures and systems such as word processing, managing files and records, stenography and transcription, designing forms, and other office procedures and terminology.	Reading Comprehension	Understanding written sentences and paragraphs in work related documents.
		Instructing	Teaching others how to do something.
		Speaking	Talking to others to convey information effectively.
Fine Arts	Knowledge of the theory and techniques required to compose, produce, and perform works of music, dance, visual arts, drama, and sculpture.	Writing	Communicating effectively in writing as appropriate for the needs of the audience.
Customer and Personal Service	Knowledge of principles and processes for providing customer and personal services. This includes customer needs assessment, meeting quality standards for services, and evaluation of customer satisfaction.	Critical Thinking	Using logic and reasoning to identify the strengths and weaknesses of alternative solutions, conclusions or approaches to problems.
Administration and Management	Knowledge of business and management principles involved in strategic planning, resource allocation, human resources modeling, leadership technique, production methods, and coordination of people and resources.	Active Listening	Giving full attention to what other people are saying, taking time to understand the points being made, asking questions as appropriate, and not interrupting at inappropriate times.
Personnel and Human Resources	Knowledge of principles and procedures for personnel recruitment, selection, training, compensation and benefits, labor relations and negotiation, and personnel information systems.	Learning Strategies	Selecting and using training/instructional methods and procedures appropriate for the situation when learning or teaching new things.
Mathematics	Knowledge of arithmetic, algebra, geometry, calculus, statistics, and their applications.	Active Learning	Understanding the implications of new information for both current and future problem-solving and decision-making.
Telecommunications	Knowledge of transmission, broadcasting, switching, control, and operation of telecommunications systems.	Social Perceptiveness	Being aware of others' reactions and understanding why they react as they do.
Therapy and Counseling	Knowledge of principles, methods, and procedures for diagnosis, treatment, and rehabilitation of physical and mental dysfunctions, and for career counseling and guidance.	Time Management	Managing one's own time and the time of others.
		Monitoring	Monitoring/Assessing performance of yourself, other individuals, or organizations to make improvements or take corrective action.
Transportation	Knowledge of principles and methods for moving people or goods by air, rail, sea, or road, including the relative costs and benefits.	Persuasion	Persuading others to change their minds or behavior.
		Coordination	Adjusting actions in relation to others' actions.
Economics and Accounting	Knowledge of economic and accounting principles and practices, the financial markets, banking and the analysis and reporting of financial data.	Judgment and Decision Making	Considering the relative costs and benefits of potential actions to choose the most appropriate one.
		Service Orientation	Actively looking for ways to help people.
Public Safety and Security	Knowledge of relevant equipment, policies, procedures, and strategies to promote effective local, state, or national security operations for the protection of people, data, property, and institutions.	Complex Problem Solving	Identifying complex problems and reviewing related information to develop and evaluate options and implement solutions.
		Negotiation	Bringing others together and trying to reconcile differences.
Sales and Marketing	Knowledge of principles and methods for showing, promoting, and selling products or services. This includes marketing strategy and tactics, product demonstration, sales techniques, and sales control systems.	Management of Personnel Resources	Motivating, developing, and directing people as they work, identifying the best people for the job.
		Quality Control Analysis	Conducting tests and inspections of products, services, or processes to evaluate quality or performance.
Biology	Knowledge of plant and animal organisms, their tissues, cells, functions, interdependencies, and interactions with each other and the environment.	Operations Analysis	Analyzing needs and product requirements to create a design.
		Equipment Selection	Determining the kind of tools and equipment needed to do a job.
Medicine and Dentistry	Knowledge of the information and techniques needed to diagnose and treat human injuries, diseases, and deformities. This includes symptoms, treatment alternatives, drug properties and interactions, and preventive health-care measures.	Management of Material Resources	Obtaining and seeing to the appropriate use of equipment, facilities, and materials needed to do certain work.
		Mathematics	Using mathematics to solve problems.
		Management of Financial Resources	Determining how money will be spent to get the work done, and accounting for these expenditures.
Design	Knowledge of design techniques, tools, and principles involved in production of precision technical plans, blueprints, drawings, and models.	Systems Evaluation	Identifying measures or indicators of system performance and the actions needed to improve or correct performance, relative to the goals of the system.
		Science	Using scientific rules and methods to solve problems.
		Systems Analysis	Determining how a system should work and how changes in conditions, operations, and the environment will affect outcomes.

1467

Troubleshooting	Determining causes of operating errors and deciding what to do about it.	
Technology Design	Generating or adapting equipment and technology to serve user needs.	
Operation and Control	Controlling operations of equipment or systems.	
Installation	Installing equipment, machines, wiring, or programs to meet specifications.	
Operation Monitoring	Watching gauges, dials, or other indicators to make sure a machine is working properly.	
Programming	Writing computer programs for various purposes.	
Repairing	Repairing machines or systems using the needed tools.	
Equipment Maintenance	Performing routine maintenance on equipment and determining when and what kind of maintenance is needed.	

Ability	Ability Definitions
Oral Expression	The ability to communicate information and ideas in speaking so others will understand.
Written Comprehension	The ability to read and understand information and ideas presented in writing.
Oral Comprehension	The ability to listen to and understand information and ideas presented through spoken words and sentences.
Written Expression	The ability to communicate information and ideas in writing so others will understand.
Speech Clarity	The ability to speak clearly so others can understand you.
Inductive Reasoning	The ability to combine pieces of information to form general rules or conclusions (includes finding a relationship among seemingly unrelated events).
Deductive Reasoning	The ability to apply general rules to specific problems to produce answers that make sense.
Near Vision	The ability to see details at close range (within a few feet of the observer).
Problem Sensitivity	The ability to tell when something is wrong or is likely to go wrong. It does not involve solving the problem, only recognizing there is a problem.
Speech Recognition	The ability to identify and understand the speech of another person.
Information Ordering	The ability to arrange things or actions in a certain order or pattern according to a specific rule or set of rules (e.g., patterns of numbers, letters, words, pictures, mathematical operations).
Category Flexibility	The ability to generate or use different sets of rules for combining or grouping things in different ways.
Originality	The ability to come up with unusual or clever ideas about a given topic or situation, or to develop creative ways to solve a problem.
Selective Attention	The ability to concentrate on a task over a period of time without being distracted.
Memorization	The ability to remember information such as words, numbers, pictures, and procedures.
Fluency of Ideas	The ability to come up with a number of ideas about a topic (the number of ideas is important, not their quality, correctness, or creativity).
Far Vision	The ability to see details at a distance.
Time Sharing	The ability to shift back and forth between two or more activities or sources of information (such as speech, sounds, touch, or other sources).
Mathematical Reasoning	The ability to choose the right mathematical methods or formulas to solve a problem.
Speed of Closure	The ability to quickly make sense of, combine, and organize information into meaningful patterns.
Flexibility of Closure	The ability to identify or detect a known pattern (a figure, object, word, or sound) that is hidden in other distracting material.
Number Facility	The ability to add, subtract, multiply, or divide quickly and correctly.
Trunk Strength	The ability to use your abdominal and lower back muscles to support part of the body repeatedly or continuously over time without 'giving out' or fatiguing.
Auditory Attention	The ability to focus on a single source of sound in the presence of other distracting sounds.
Perceptual Speed	The ability to quickly and accurately compare similarities and differences among sets of letters, numbers, objects, pictures, or patterns. The things to be compared may be presented at the same time or one after the other. This ability also includes comparing a presented object with a remembered object.
Visualization	The ability to imagine how something will look after it is moved around or when its parts are moved or rearranged.

Finger Dexterity	The ability to make precisely coordinated movements of the fingers of one or both hands to grasp, manipulate, or assemble very small objects.
Visual Color Discrimination	The ability to match or detect differences between colors, including shades of color and brightness.
Hearing Sensitivity	The ability to detect or tell the differences between sounds that vary in pitch and loudness.
Manual Dexterity	The ability to quickly move your hand, your hand together with your arm, or your two hands to grasp, manipulate, or assemble objects.
Wrist-Finger Speed	The ability to make fast, simple, repeated movements of the fingers, hands, and wrists.
Control Precision	The ability to quickly and repeatedly adjust the controls of a machine or a vehicle to exact positions.
Dynamic Strength	The ability to exert muscle force repeatedly or continuously over time. This involves muscular endurance and resistance to muscle fatigue.
Explosive Strength	The ability to use short bursts of muscle force to propel oneself (as in jumping or sprinting), or to throw an object.
Stamina	The ability to exert yourself physically over long periods of time without getting winded or out of breath.
Speed of Limb Movement	The ability to quickly move the arms and legs.
Static Strength	The ability to exert maximum muscle force to lift, push, pull, or carry objects.
Reaction Time	The ability to quickly respond (with the hand, finger, or foot) to a signal (sound, light, picture) when it appears.
Rate Control	The ability to time your movements or the movement of a piece of equipment in anticipation of changes in the speed and/or direction of a moving object or scene.
Multilimb Coordination	The ability to coordinate two or more limbs (for example, two arms, two legs, or one leg and one arm) while sitting, standing, or lying down. It does not involve performing the activities while the whole body is in motion.
Arm-Hand Steadiness	The ability to keep your hand and arm steady while moving your arm or while holding your arm and hand in one position.
Glare Sensitivity	The ability to see objects in the presence of glare or bright lighting.
Response Orientation	The ability to choose quickly between two or more movements in response to two or more different signals (lights, sounds, pictures). It includes the speed with which the correct response is started with the hand, foot, or other body part.
Depth Perception	The ability to judge which of several objects is closer or farther away from you, or to judge the distance between you and an object.
Gross Body Coordination	The ability to coordinate the movement of your arms, legs, and torso together when the whole body is in motion.
Extent Flexibility	The ability to bend, stretch, twist, or reach with your body, arms, and/or legs.
Sound Localization	The ability to tell the direction from which a sound originated.
Gross Body Equilibrium	The ability to keep or regain your body balance or stay upright when in an unstable position.
Night Vision	The ability to see under low light conditions.
Peripheral Vision	The ability to see objects or movement of objects to one's side when the eyes are looking ahead.
Spatial Orientation	The ability to know your location in relation to the environment or to know where other objects are in relation to you.
Dynamic Flexibility	The ability to quickly and repeatedly bend, stretch, twist, or reach out with your body, arms, and/or legs.

Work_Activity	Work_Activity Definitions
Interpreting the Meaning of Information for Others	Translating or explaining what information means and how it can be used.
Training and Teaching Others	Identifying the educational needs of others, developing formal educational or training programs or classes, and teaching or instructing others.
Getting Information	Observing, receiving, and otherwise obtaining information from all relevant sources.
Updating and Using Relevant Knowledge	Keeping up-to-date technically and applying new knowledge to your job.
Identifying Objects, Actions, and Events	Identifying information by categorizing, estimating, recognizing differences or similarities, and detecting changes in circumstances or events.
Thinking Creatively	Developing, designing, or creating new applications, ideas, relationships, systems, or products, including artistic contributions.

Analyzing Data or Information	Identifying the underlying principles, reasons, or facts of information by breaking down information or data into separate parts.
Communicating with Supervisors, Peers, or Subordin	Providing information to supervisors, co-workers, and subordinates by telephone, in written form, e-mail, or in person.
Organizing, Planning, and Prioritizing Work	Developing specific goals and plans to prioritize, organize, and accomplish your work.
Establishing and Maintaining Interpersonal Relatio	Developing constructive and cooperative working relationships with others, and maintaining them over time.
Interacting With Computers	Using computers and computer systems (including hardware and software) to program, write software, set up functions, enter data, or process information.
Judging the Qualities of Things, Services, or Peop	Assessing the value, importance, or quality of things or people.
Making Decisions and Solving Problems	Analyzing information and evaluating results to choose the best solution and solve problems.
Developing Objectives and Strategies	Establishing long-range objectives and specifying the strategies and actions to achieve them.
Processing Information	Compiling, coding, categorizing, calculating, tabulating, auditing, or verifying information or data.
Documenting/Recording Information	Entering, transcribing, recording, storing, or maintaining information in written or electronic/magnetic form.
Coaching and Developing Others	Identifying the developmental needs of others and coaching, mentoring, or otherwise helping others to improve their knowledge or skills.
Scheduling Work and Activities	Scheduling events, programs, and activities, as well as the work of others.
Communicating with Persons Outside Organization	Communicating with people outside the organization, representing the organization to customers, the public, government, and other external sources. This information can be exchanged in person, in writing, or by telephone or e-mail.
Provide Consultation and Advice to Others	Providing guidance and expert advice to management or other groups on technical, systems-, or process-related topics.
Monitor Processes, Materials, or Surroundings	Monitoring and reviewing information from materials, events, or the environment, to detect or assess problems.
Performing for or Working Directly with the Public	Performing for people or dealing directly with the public. This includes serving customers in restaurants and stores, and receiving clients or guests.
Assisting and Caring for Others	Providing personal assistance, medical attention, emotional support, or other personal care to others such as coworkers, customers, or patients.
Performing Administrative Activities	Performing day-to-day administrative tasks such as maintaining information files and processing paperwork.
Evaluating Information to Determine Compliance wit	Using relevant information and individual judgment to determine whether events or processes comply with laws, regulations, or standards.
Coordinating the Work and Activities of Others	Getting members of a group to work together to accomplish tasks.
Resolving Conflicts and Negotiating with Others	Handling complaints, settling disputes, and resolving grievances and conflicts, or otherwise negotiating with others.
Guiding, Directing, and Motivating Subordinates	Providing guidance and direction to subordinates, including setting performance standards and monitoring performance.
Developing and Building Teams	Encouraging and building mutual trust, respect, and cooperation among team members.
Selling or Influencing Others	Convincing others to buy merchandise/goods or to otherwise change their minds or actions.
Estimating the Quantifiable Characteristics of Pro	Estimating sizes, distances, and quantities; or determining time, costs, resources, or materials needed to perform a work activity.
Monitoring and Controlling Resources	Monitoring and controlling resources and overseeing the spending of money.
Staffing Organizational Units	Recruiting, interviewing, selecting, hiring, and promoting employees in an organization.
Performing General Physical Activities	Performing physical activities that require considerable use of your arms and legs and moving your whole body, such as climbing, lifting, balancing, walking, stooping, and handling of materials.
Inspecting Equipment, Structures, or Material	Inspecting equipment, structures, or materials to identify the cause of errors or other problems or defects.
Controlling Machines and Processes	Using either control mechanisms or direct physical activity to operate machines or processes (not including computers or vehicles).
Handling and Moving Objects	Using hands and arms in handling, installing, positioning, and moving materials, and manipulating things.
Repairing and Maintaining Electronic Equipment	Servicing, repairing, calibrating, regulating, fine-tuning, or testing machines, devices, and equipment that operate primarily on the basis of electrical or electronic (not mechanical) principles.
Drafting, Laying Out, and Specifying Technical Dev	Providing documentation, detailed instructions, drawings, or specifications to tell others about how devices, parts, equipment, or structures are to be fabricated, constructed, assembled, modified, maintained, or used.
Operating Vehicles, Mechanized Devices, or Equipme	Running, maneuvering, navigating, or driving vehicles or mechanized equipment, such as forklifts, passenger vehicles, aircraft, or water craft.
Repairing and Maintaining Mechanical Equipment	Servicing, repairing, adjusting, and testing machines, devices, moving parts, and equipment that operate primarily on the basis of mechanical (not electronic) principles.

Work_Context	Work_Context Definitions
Freedom to Make Decisions	How much decision making freedom, without supervision, does the job offer?
Structured versus Unstructured Work	To what extent is this job structured for the worker, rather than allowing the worker to determine tasks, priorities, and goals?
Electronic Mail	How often do you use electronic mail in this job?
Face-to-Face Discussions	How often do you have to have face-to-face discussions with individuals or teams in this job?
Public Speaking	How often do you have to perform public speaking in this job?
Contact With Others	How much does this job require the worker to be in contact with others (face-to-face, by telephone, or otherwise) in order to perform it?
Telephone	How often do you have telephone conversations in this job?
Indoors, Environmentally Controlled	How often does this job require working indoors in environmentally controlled conditions?
Letters and Memos	How often does the job require written letters and memos?
Frequency of Decision Making	How frequently is the worker required to make decisions that affect other people, the financial resources, and/or the image and reputation of the organization?
Impact of Decisions on Co-workers or Company Resul	How do the decisions an employee makes impact the results of co-workers, clients or the company?
Importance of Being Exact or Accurate	How important is being very exact or highly accurate in performing this job?
Time Pressure	How often does this job require the worker to meet strict deadlines?
Coordinate or Lead Others	How important is it to coordinate or lead others in accomplishing work activities in this job?
Work With Work Group or Team	How important is it to work with others in a group or team in this job?
Deal With External Customers	How important is it to work with external customers or the public in this job?
Spend Time Sitting	How much does this job require sitting?
Level of Competition	To what extent does this job require the worker to compete or to be aware of competitive pressures?
Physical Proximity	To what extent does this job require the worker to perform job tasks in close physical proximity to other people?
Frequency of Conflict Situations	How often are there conflict situations the employee has to face in this job?
Spend Time Standing	How much does this job require standing?
Deal With Unpleasant or Angry People	How frequently does the worker have to deal with unpleasant, angry, or discourteous individuals as part of the job requirements?
Importance of Repeating Same Tasks	How important is repeating the same physical activities (e.g., key entry) or mental activities (e.g., checking entries in a ledger) over and over, without stopping, to performing this job?
Sounds, Noise Levels Are Distracting or Uncomforta	How often does this job require working exposed to sounds and noise levels that are distracting or uncomfortable?
Responsibility for Outcomes and Results	How responsible is the worker for work outcomes and results of other workers?
Consequence of Error	How serious would the result usually be if the worker made a mistake that was not readily correctable?
Spend Time Making Repetitive Motions	How much does this job require making repetitive motions?
Spend Time Using Your Hands to Handle, Control, or	How much does this job require using your hands to handle, control, or feel objects, tools or controls?
Exposed to Disease or Infections	How often does this job require exposure to disease/infections?
Indoors, Not Environmentally Controlled	How often does this job require working indoors in non-controlled environmental conditions (e.g., warehouse without heat)?

Degree of Automation	How automated is the job?
Responsible for Others' Health and Safety	How much responsibility is there for the health and safety of others in this job?
Spend Time Walking and Running	How much does this job require walking and running?
Exposed to Contaminants	How often does this job require working exposed to contaminants (such as pollutants, gases, dust or odors)?
Extremely Bright or Inadequate Lighting	How often does this job require working in extremely bright or inadequate lighting conditions?
In an Enclosed Vehicle or Equipment	How often does this job require working in a closed vehicle or equipment (e.g., car)?
Deal With Physically Aggressive People	How frequently does this job require the worker to deal with physical aggression of violent individuals?
Very Hot or Cold Temperatures	How often does this job require working in very hot (above 90 F degrees) or very cold (below 32 F degrees) temperatures?
Cramped Work Space, Awkward Positions	How often does this job require working in cramped work spaces that requires getting into awkward positions?
Spend Time Bending or Twisting the Body	How much does this job require bending or twisting your body?
Outdoors, Exposed to Weather	How much does this job require working outdoors, exposed to all weather conditions?
Spend Time Kneeling, Crouching, Stooping, or Crawl	How much does this job require kneeling, crouching, stooping, or crawling?
Exposed to Radiation	How often does this job require exposure to radiation?
Exposed to Whole Body Vibration	How often does this job require exposure to whole body vibration (e.g., operate a jackhammer)?
Outdoors, Under Cover	How often does this job require working outdoors, under cover (e.g., structure with roof but no walls)?
Pace Determined by Speed of Equipment	How important is it to this job that the pace is determined by the speed of equipment or machinery? (This does not refer to keeping busy at all times on this job.)
Exposed to Minor Burns, Cuts, Bites, or Stings	How often does this job require exposure to minor burns, cuts, bites, or stings?
In an Open Vehicle or Equipment	How often does this job require working in an open vehicle or equipment (e.g., tractor)?
Wear Common Protective or Safety Equipment such as	How much does this job require wearing common protective or safety equipment such as safety shoes, glasses, gloves, hard hats or life jackets?
Spend Time Keeping or Regaining Balance	How much does this job require keeping or regaining your balance?
Exposed to Hazardous Equipment	How often does this job require exposure to hazardous equipment?
Exposed to Hazardous Conditions	How often does this job require exposure to hazardous conditions?
Exposed to High Places	How often does this job require exposure to high places?
Spend Time Climbing Ladders, Scaffolds, or Poles	How much does this job require climbing ladders, scaffolds, or poles?
Wear Specialized Protective or Safety Equipment su	How much does this job require wearing specialized protective or safety equipment such as breathing apparatus, safety harness, full protection suits, or radiation protection?

Job Zone Component	Job Zone Component Definitions
Title	Job Zone Five: Extensive Preparation Needed
	Extensive skill, knowledge, and experience are needed for these occupations. Many require more than five years of experience.
Overall Experience	For example, surgeons must complete four years of college and an additional five to seven years of specialized medical training to be able to do their job.
Job Training	Employees may need some on-the-job training, but most of these occupations assume that the person will already have the required skills, knowledge, work-related experience, and/or training.
Job Zone Examples	These occupations often involve coordinating, training, supervising, or managing the activities of others to accomplish goals. Very advanced communication and organizational skills are required. Examples include athletic trainers, lawyers, managing editors, physicists, social psychologists, and surgeons.
SVP Range	(8.0 and above)
Education	A bachelor's degree is the minimum formal education required for these occupations. However, many also require graduate school. For example, they may require a master's degree, and some require a Ph.D., M.D., or J.D. (law degree).

Work_Styles	Work_Styles Definitions
Integrity	Job requires being honest and ethical.
Independence	Job requires developing one's own ways of doing things, guiding oneself with little or no supervision, and depending on oneself to get things done.
Analytical Thinking	Job requires analyzing information and using logic to address work-related issues and problems.
Dependability	Job requires being reliable, responsible, and dependable, and fulfilling obligations.
Achievement/Effort	Job requires establishing and maintaining personally challenging achievement goals and exerting effort toward mastering tasks.
Initiative	Job requires a willingness to take on responsibilities and challenges.
Persistence	Job requires persistence in the face of obstacles.
Self Control	Job requires maintaining composure, keeping emotions in check, controlling anger, and avoiding aggressive behavior, even in very difficult situations.
Concern for Others	Job requires being sensitive to others' needs and feelings and being understanding and helpful on the job.
Attention to Detail	Job requires being careful about detail and thorough in completing work tasks.
Innovation	Job requires creativity and alternative thinking to develop new ideas for and answers to work-related problems.
Cooperation	Job requires being pleasant with others on the job and displaying a good-natured, cooperative attitude.
Leadership	Job requires a willingness to lead, take charge, and offer opinions and direction.
Stress Tolerance	Job requires accepting criticism and dealing calmly and effectively with high stress situations.
Adaptability/Flexibility	Job requires being open to change (positive or negative) and to considerable variety in the workplace.
Social Orientation	Job requires preferring to work with others rather than alone, and being personally connected with others on the job.

25-1126.00 - Philosophy and Religion Teachers, Postsecondary

Teach courses in philosophy, religion, and theology.

Tasks

1) Plan, evaluate, and revise curricula, course content, and course materials and methods of instruction.

2) Maintain student attendance records, grades, and other required records.

3) Prepare and deliver lectures to undergraduate and/or graduate students on topics such as ethics, logic, and contemporary religious thought.

4) Compile, administer, and grade examinations, or assign this work to others.

5) Select and obtain materials and supplies such as textbooks.

6) Collaborate with colleagues to address teaching and research issues.

7) Participate in campus and community events.

8) Advise students on academic and vocational curricula, and on career issues.

9) Maintain regularly scheduled office hours in order to advise and assist students.

10) Serve on academic or administrative committees that deal with institutional policies, departmental matters, and academic issues.

11) Compile bibliographies of specialized materials for outside reading assignments.

12) Conduct research in a particular field of knowledge, and publish findings in professional journals, books, and/or electronic media.

13) Participate in student recruitment, registration, and placement activities.

14) Act as advisers to student organizations.

15) Perform administrative duties such as serving as department head.

16) Supervise undergraduate and/or graduate teaching, internship, and research work.

17) Write grant proposals to procure external research funding.

18) Provide professional consulting services to government and/or industry.

19) Keep abreast of developments in their field by reading current literature, talking with colleagues, and participating in professional conferences.

20) Prepare course materials such as syllabi, homework assignments, and handouts.

21) Initiate, facilitate, and moderate classroom discussions.

Knowledge	Knowledge Definitions
Philosophy and Theology	Knowledge of different philosophical systems and religions. This includes their basic principles, values, ethics, ways of thinking, customs, practices, and their impact on human culture.
English Language	Knowledge of the structure and content of the English language including the meaning and spelling of words, rules of composition, and grammar.
Education and Training	Knowledge of principles and methods for curriculum and training design, teaching and instruction for individuals and groups, and the measurement of training effects.
History and Archeology	Knowledge of historical events and their causes, indicators, and effects on civilizations and cultures.
Computers and Electronics	Knowledge of circuit boards, processors, chips, electronic equipment, and computer hardware and software, including applications and programming.
Sociology and Anthropology	Knowledge of group behavior and dynamics, societal trends and influences, human migrations, ethnicity, cultures and their history and origins.
Psychology	Knowledge of human behavior and performance; individual differences in ability, personality, and interests; learning and motivation; psychological research methods; and the assessment and treatment of behavioral and affective disorders.
Foreign Language	Knowledge of the structure and content of a foreign (non-English) language including the meaning and spelling of words, rules of composition and grammar, and pronunciation.
Customer and Personal Service	Knowledge of principles and processes for providing customer and personal services. This includes customer needs assessment, meeting quality standards for services, and evaluation of customer satisfaction.
Communications and Media	Knowledge of media production, communication, and dissemination techniques and methods. This includes alternative ways to inform and entertain via written, oral, and visual media.
Clerical	Knowledge of administrative and clerical procedures and systems such as word processing, managing files and records, stenography and transcription, designing forms, and other office procedures and terminology.
Administration and Management	Knowledge of business and management principles involved in strategic planning, resource allocation, human resources modeling, leadership technique, production methods, and coordination of people and resources.
Therapy and Counseling	Knowledge of principles, methods, and procedures for diagnosis, treatment, and rehabilitation of physical and mental dysfunctions, and for career counseling and guidance.
Geography	Knowledge of principles and methods for describing the features of land, sea, and air masses, including their physical characteristics, locations, interrelationships, and distribution of plant, animal, and human life.
Personnel and Human Resources	Knowledge of principles and procedures for personnel recruitment, selection, training, compensation and benefits, labor relations and negotiation, and personnel information systems.
Law and Government	Knowledge of laws, legal codes, court procedures, precedents, government regulations, executive orders, agency rules, and the democratic political process.
Mathematics	Knowledge of arithmetic, algebra, geometry, calculus, statistics, and their applications.
Fine Arts	Knowledge of the theory and techniques required to compose, produce, and perform works of music, dance, visual arts, drama, and sculpture.
Telecommunications	Knowledge of transmission, broadcasting, switching, control, and operation of telecommunications systems.
Sales and Marketing	Knowledge of principles and methods for showing, promoting, and selling products or services. This includes marketing strategy and tactics, product demonstration, sales techniques, and sales control systems.
Biology	Knowledge of plant and animal organisms, their tissues, cells, functions, interdependencies, and interactions with each other and the environment.
Transportation	Knowledge of principles and methods for moving people or goods by air, rail, sea, or road, including the relative costs and benefits.

Public Safety and Security	Knowledge of relevant equipment, policies, procedures, and strategies to promote effective local, state, or national security operations for the protection of people, data, property, and institutions.
Economics and Accounting	Knowledge of economic and accounting principles and practices, the financial markets, banking and the analysis and reporting of financial data.
Production and Processing	Knowledge of raw materials, production processes, quality control, costs, and other techniques for maximizing the effective manufacture and distribution of goods.
Physics	Knowledge and prediction of physical principles, laws, their interrelationships, and applications to understanding fluid, material, and atmospheric dynamics, and mechanical, electrical, atomic and sub-atomic structures and processes.
Engineering and Technology	Knowledge of the practical application of engineering science and technology. This includes applying principles, techniques, procedures, and equipment to the design and production of various goods and services.
Design	Knowledge of design techniques, tools, and principles involved in production of precision technical plans, blueprints, drawings, and models.
Medicine and Dentistry	Knowledge of the information and techniques needed to diagnose and treat human injuries, diseases, and deformities. This includes symptoms, treatment alternatives, drug properties and interactions, and preventive health-care measures.
Chemistry	Knowledge of the chemical composition, structure, and properties of substances and of the chemical processes and transformations that they undergo. This includes uses of chemicals and their interactions, danger signs, production techniques, and disposal methods.
Building and Construction	Knowledge of materials, methods, and the tools involved in the construction or repair of houses, buildings, or other structures such as highways and roads.
Mechanical	Knowledge of machines and tools, including their designs, uses, repair, and maintenance.
Food Production	Knowledge of techniques and equipment for planting, growing, and harvesting food products (both plant and animal) for consumption, including storage/handling techniques.

Skills	Skills Definitions
Reading Comprehension	Understanding written sentences and paragraphs in work related documents.
Instructing	Teaching others how to do something.
Speaking	Talking to others to convey information effectively.
Critical Thinking	Using logic and reasoning to identify the strengths and weaknesses of alternative solutions, conclusions or approaches to problems.
Writing	Communicating effectively in writing as appropriate for the needs of the audience.
Active Listening	Giving full attention to what other people are saying, taking time to understand the points being made, asking questions as appropriate, and not interrupting at inappropriate times.
Learning Strategies	Selecting and using training/instructional methods and procedures appropriate for the situation when learning or teaching new things.
Active Learning	Understanding the implications of new information for both current and future problem-solving and decision-making.
Social Perceptiveness	Being aware of others' reactions and understanding why they react as they do.
Time Management	Managing one's own time and the time of others.
Monitoring	Monitoring/Assessing performance of yourself, other individuals, or organizations to make improvements or take corrective action.
Persuasion	Persuading others to change their minds or behavior.
Complex Problem Solving	Identifying complex problems and reviewing related information to develop and evaluate options and implement solutions.
Judgment and Decision Making	Considering the relative costs and benefits of potential actions to choose the most appropriate one.
Service Orientation	Actively looking for ways to help people.
Coordination	Adjusting actions in relation to others' actions.
Negotiation	Bringing others together and trying to reconcile differences.
Management of Personnel Resources	Motivating, developing, and directing people as they work, identifying the best people for the job.
Science	Using scientific rules and methods to solve problems.
Mathematics	Using mathematics to solve problems.

Management of Financial Resources	Determining how money will be spent to get the work done, and accounting for these expenditures.
Quality Control Analysis	Conducting tests and inspections of products, services, or processes to evaluate quality or performance.
Systems Evaluation	Identifying measures or indicators of system performance and the actions needed to improve or correct performance, relative to the goals of the system.
Operations Analysis	Analyzing needs and product requirements to create a design.
Management of Material Resources	Obtaining and seeing to the appropriate use of equipment, facilities, and materials needed to do certain work.
Systems Analysis	Determining how a system should work and how changes in conditions, operations, and the environment will affect outcomes.
Equipment Selection	Determining the kind of tools and equipment needed to do a job.
Technology Design	Generating or adapting equipment and technology to serve user needs.
Operation and Control	Controlling operations of equipment or systems.
Troubleshooting	Determining causes of operating errors and deciding what to do about it.
Programming	Writing computer programs for various purposes.
Equipment Maintenance	Performing routine maintenance on equipment and determining when and what kind of maintenance is needed.
Repairing	Repairing machines or systems using the needed tools.
Operation Monitoring	Watching gauges, dials, or other indicators to make sure a machine is working properly.
Installation	Installing equipment, machines, wiring, or programs to meet specifications.

Ability	Ability Definitions
Oral Expression	The ability to communicate information and ideas in speaking so others will understand.
Written Comprehension	The ability to read and understand information and ideas presented in writing.
Speech Clarity	The ability to speak clearly so others can understand you.
Written Expression	The ability to communicate information and ideas in writing so others will understand.
Oral Comprehension	The ability to listen to and understand information and ideas presented through spoken words and sentences.
Inductive Reasoning	The ability to combine pieces of information to form general rules or conclusions (includes finding a relationship among seemingly unrelated events).
Deductive Reasoning	The ability to apply general rules to specific problems to produce answers that make sense.
Near Vision	The ability to see details at close range (within a few feet of the observer).
Problem Sensitivity	The ability to tell when something is wrong or is likely to go wrong. It does not involve solving the problem, only recognizing there is a problem.
Speech Recognition	The ability to identify and understand the speech of another person.
Originality	The ability to come up with unusual or clever ideas about a given topic or situation, or to develop creative ways to solve a problem.
Selective Attention	The ability to concentrate on a task over a period of time without being distracted.
Information Ordering	The ability to arrange things or actions in a certain order or pattern according to a specific rule or set of rules (e.g., patterns of numbers, letters, words, pictures, mathematical operations).
Fluency of Ideas	The ability to come up with a number of ideas about a topic (the number of ideas is important, not their quality, correctness, or creativity).
Category Flexibility	The ability to generate or use different sets of rules for combining or grouping things in different ways.
Memorization	The ability to remember information such as words, numbers, pictures, and procedures.
Time Sharing	The ability to shift back and forth between two or more activities or sources of information (such as speech, sounds, touch, or other sources).
Mathematical Reasoning	The ability to choose the right mathematical methods or formulas to solve a problem.
Speed of Closure	The ability to quickly make sense of, combine, and organize information into meaningful patterns.
Far Vision	The ability to see details at a distance.
Flexibility of Closure	The ability to identify or detect a known pattern (a figure, object, word, or sound) that is hidden in other distracting material.

Trunk Strength	The ability to use your abdominal and lower back muscles to support part of the body repeatedly or continuously over time without 'giving out' or fatiguing.
Number Facility	The ability to add, subtract, multiply, or divide quickly and correctly.
Perceptual Speed	The ability to quickly and accurately compare similarities and differences among sets of letters, numbers, objects, pictures, or patterns. The things to be compared may be presented at the same time or one after the other. This ability also includes comparing a presented object with a remembered object.
Visualization	The ability to imagine how something will look after it is moved around or when its parts are moved or rearranged.
Auditory Attention	The ability to focus on a single source of sound in the presence of other distracting sounds.
Finger Dexterity	The ability to make precisely coordinated movements of the fingers of one or both hands to grasp, manipulate, or assemble very small objects.
Visual Color Discrimination	The ability to match or detect differences between colors, including shades of color and brightness.
Control Precision	The ability to quickly and repeatedly adjust the controls of a machine or a vehicle to exact positions.
Hearing Sensitivity	The ability to detect or tell the differences between sounds that vary in pitch and loudness.
Arm-Hand Steadiness	The ability to keep your hand and arm steady while moving your arm or while holding your arm and hand in one position.
Manual Dexterity	The ability to quickly move your hand, your hand together with your arm, or your two hands to grasp, manipulate, or assemble objects.
Explosive Strength	The ability to use short bursts of muscle force to propel oneself (as in jumping or sprinting), or to throw an object.
Stamina	The ability to exert yourself physically over long periods of time without getting winded or out of breath.
Response Orientation	The ability to choose quickly between two or more movements in response to two or more different signals (lights, sounds, pictures). It includes the speed with which the correct response is started with the hand, foot, or other body part.
Rate Control	The ability to time your movements or the movement of a piece of equipment in anticipation of changes in the speed and/or direction of a moving object or scene.
Reaction Time	The ability to quickly respond (with the hand, finger, or foot) to a signal (sound, light, picture) when it appears.
Wrist-Finger Speed	The ability to make fast, simple, repeated movements of the fingers, hands, and wrists.
Multilimb Coordination	The ability to coordinate two or more limbs (for example, two arms, two legs, or one leg and one arm) while sitting, standing, or lying down. It does not involve performing the activities while the whole body is in motion.
Static Strength	The ability to exert maximum muscle force to lift, push, pull, or carry objects.
Gross Body Equilibrium	The ability to keep or regain your body balance or stay upright when in an unstable position.
Dynamic Strength	The ability to exert muscle force repeatedly or continuously over time. This involves muscular endurance and resistance to muscle fatigue.
Dynamic Flexibility	The ability to quickly and repeatedly bend, stretch, twist, or reach out with your body, arms, and/or legs.
Gross Body Coordination	The ability to coordinate the movement of your arms, legs, and torso together when the whole body is in motion.
Spatial Orientation	The ability to know your location in relation to the environment or to know where other objects are in relation to you.
Night Vision	The ability to see under low light conditions.
Peripheral Vision	The ability to see objects or movement of objects to one's side when the eyes are looking ahead.
Depth Perception	The ability to judge which of several objects is closer or farther away from you, or to judge the distance between you and an object.
Glare Sensitivity	The ability to see objects in the presence of glare or bright lighting.
Sound Localization	The ability to tell the direction from which a sound originated.
Speed of Limb Movement	The ability to quickly move the arms and legs.
Extent Flexibility	The ability to bend, stretch, twist, or reach with your body, arms, and/or legs.

Work_Activity	Work_Activity Definitions
Training and Teaching Others	Identifying the educational needs of others, developing formal educational or training programs or classes, and teaching or instructing others.

Thinking Creatively	Developing, designing, or creating new applications, ideas, relationships, systems, or products, including artistic contributions.
Interpreting the Meaning of Information for Others	Translating or explaining what information means and how it can be used.
Getting Information	Observing, receiving, and otherwise obtaining information from all relevant sources.
Establishing and Maintaining Interpersonal Relatio	Developing constructive and cooperative working relationships with others, and maintaining them over time.
Updating and Using Relevant Knowledge	Keeping up-to-date technically and applying new knowledge to your job.
Organizing, Planning, and Prioritizing Work	Developing specific goals and plans to prioritize, organize, and accomplish your work.
Judging the Qualities of Things, Services, or Peop	Assessing the value, importance, or quality of things or people.
Communicating with Supervisors, Peers, or Subordin	Providing information to supervisors, co-workers, and subordinates by telephone, in written form, e-mail, or in person.
Coaching and Developing Others	Identifying the developmental needs of others and coaching, mentoring, or otherwise helping others to improve their knowledge or skills.
Analyzing Data or Information	Identifying the underlying principles, reasons, or facts of information by breaking down information or data into separate parts.
Interacting With Computers	Using computers and computer systems (including hardware and software) to program, write software, set up functions, enter data, or process information.
Developing Objectives and Strategies	Establishing long-range objectives and specifying the strategies and actions to achieve them.
Making Decisions and Solving Problems	Analyzing information and evaluating results to choose the best solution and solve problems.
Identifying Objects, Actions, and Events	Identifying information by categorizing, estimating, recognizing differences or similarities, and detecting changes in circumstances or events.
Communicating with Persons Outside Organization	Communicating with people outside the organization, representing the organization to customers, the public, government, and other external sources. This information can be exchanged in person, in writing, or by telephone or e-mail.
Documenting/Recording Information	Entering, transcribing, recording, storing, or maintaining information in written or electronic/magnetic form.
Performing for or Working Directly with the Public	Performing for people or dealing directly with the public. This includes serving customers in restaurants and stores, and receiving clients or guests.
Guiding, Directing, and Motivating Subordinates	Providing guidance and direction to subordinates, including setting performance standards and monitoring performance.
Processing Information	Compiling, coding, categorizing, calculating, tabulating, auditing, or verifying information or data.
Provide Consultation and Advice to Others	Providing guidance and expert advice to management or other groups on technical, systems-, or process-related topics.
Resolving Conflicts and Negotiating with Others	Handling complaints, settling disputes, and resolving grievances and conflicts, or otherwise negotiating with others.
Scheduling Work and Activities	Scheduling events, programs, and activities, as well as the work of others.
Assisting and Caring for Others	Providing personal assistance, medical attention, emotional support, or other personal care to others such as coworkers, customers, or patients.
Monitor Processes, Materials, or Surroundings	Monitoring and reviewing information from materials, events, or the environment, to detect or assess problems.
Coordinating the Work and Activities of Others	Getting members of a group to work together to accomplish tasks.
Developing and Building Teams	Encouraging and building mutual trust, respect, and cooperation among team members.
Performing Administrative Activities	Performing day-to-day administrative tasks such as maintaining information files and processing paperwork.
Evaluating Information to Determine Compliance wit	Using relevant information and individual judgment to determine whether events or processes comply with laws, regulations, or standards.
Selling or Influencing Others	Convincing others to buy merchandise/goods or to otherwise change their minds or actions.
Estimating the Quantifiable Characteristics of Pro	Estimating sizes, distances, and quantities; or determining time, costs, resources, or materials needed to perform a work activity.
Monitoring and Controlling Resources	Monitoring and controlling resources and overseeing the spending of money.
Staffing Organizational Units	Recruiting, interviewing, selecting, hiring, and promoting employees in an organization.

Controlling Machines and Processes	Using either control mechanisms or direct physical activity to operate machines or processes (not including computers or vehicles).
Inspecting Equipment, Structures, or Material	Inspecting equipment, structures, or materials to identify the cause of errors or other problems or defects.
Performing General Physical Activities	Performing physical activities that require considerable use of your arms and legs and moving your whole body, such as climbing, lifting, balancing, walking, stooping, and handling of materials.
Handling and Moving Objects	Using hands and arms in handling, installing, positioning, and moving materials, and manipulating things.
Operating Vehicles, Mechanized Devices, or Equipme	Running, maneuvering, navigating, or driving vehicles or mechanized equipment, such as forklifts, passenger vehicles, aircraft, or water craft.
Repairing and Maintaining Electronic Equipment	Servicing, repairing, calibrating, regulating, fine-tuning, or testing machines, devices, and equipment that operate primarily on the basis of electrical or electronic (not mechanical) principles.
Drafting, Laying Out, and Specifying Technical Dev	Providing documentation, detailed instructions, drawings, or specifications to tell others about how devices, parts, equipment, or structures are to be fabricated, constructed, assembled, modified, maintained, or used.
Repairing and Maintaining Mechanical Equipment	Servicing, repairing, adjusting, and testing machines, devices, moving parts, and equipment that operate primarily on the basis of mechanical (not electronic) principles.

Work_Context	Work_Context Definitions
Electronic Mail	How often do you use electronic mail in this job?
Structured versus Unstructured Work	To what extent is this job structured for the worker, rather than allowing the worker to determine tasks, priorities, and goals?
Freedom to Make Decisions	How much decision making freedom, without supervision, does the job offer?
Face-to-Face Discussions	How often do you have to have face-to-face discussions with individuals or teams in this job?
Contact With Others	How much does this job require the worker to be in contact with others (face-to-face, by telephone, or otherwise) in order to perform it?
Public Speaking	How often do you have to perform public speaking in this job?
Indoors, Environmentally Controlled	How often does this job require working indoors in environmentally controlled conditions?
Telephone	How often do you have telephone conversations in this job?
Impact of Decisions on Co-workers or Company Resul	How do the decisions an employee makes impact the results of co-workers, clients or the company?
Importance of Being Exact or Accurate	How important is being very exact or highly accurate in performing this job?
Time Pressure	How often does this job require the worker to meet strict deadlines?
Frequency of Decision Making	How frequently is the worker required to make decisions that affect other people, the financial resources, and/or the image and reputation of the organization?
Work With Work Group or Team	How important is it to work with others in a group or team in this job?
Letters and Memos	How often does the job require written letters and memos?
Coordinate or Lead Others	How important is it to coordinate or lead others in accomplishing work activities in this job?
Spend Time Sitting	How much does this job require sitting?
Level of Competition	To what extent does this job require the worker to compete or to be aware of competitive pressures?
Deal With External Customers	How important is it to work with external customers or the public in this job?
Physical Proximity	To what extent does this job require the worker to perform job tasks in close physical proximity to other people?
Responsibility for Outcomes and Results	How responsible is the worker for work outcomes and results of other workers?
Frequency of Conflict Situations	How often are there conflict situations the employee has to face in this job?
Spend Time Standing	How much does this job require standing?
Deal With Unpleasant or Angry People	How frequently does the worker have to deal with unpleasant, angry, or discourteous individuals as part of the job requirements?
Consequence of Error	How serious would the result usually be if the worker made a mistake that was not readily correctable?
Sounds, Noise Levels Are Distracting or Uncomforta	How often does this job require working exposed to sounds and noise levels that are distracting or uncomfortable?

Spend Time Using Your Hands to Handle, Control, or	How much does this job require using your hands to handle, control, or feel objects, tools or controls?
Importance of Repeating Same Tasks	How important is repeating the same physical activities (e.g., key entry) or mental activities (e.g., checking entries in a ledger) over and over, without stopping, to performing this job?
Spend Time Making Repetitive Motions	How much does this job require making repetitive motions?
Responsible for Others' Health and Safety	How much responsibility is there for the health and safety of others in this job?
Spend Time Walking and Running	How much does this job require walking and running?
Exposed to Disease or Infections	How often does this job require exposure to disease/infections?
Indoors, Not Environmentally Controlled	How often does this job require working indoors in non-controlled environmental conditions (e.g., warehouse without heat)?
Extremely Bright or Inadequate Lighting	How often does this job require working in extremely bright or inadequate lighting conditions?
Degree of Automation	How automated is the job?
In an Enclosed Vehicle or Equipment	How often does this job require working in a closed vehicle or equipment (e.g., car)?
Exposed to Contaminants	How often does this job require working exposed to contaminants (such as pollutants, gases, dust or odors)?
Deal With Physically Aggressive People	How frequently does this job require the worker to deal with physical aggression of violent individuals?
Very Hot or Cold Temperatures	How often does this job require working in very hot (above 90 F degrees) or very cold (below 32 F degrees) temperatures?
Outdoors, Exposed to Weather	How often does this job require working outdoors, exposed to all weather conditions?
Spend Time Bending or Twisting the Body	How much does this job require bending or twisting your body?
Exposed to Minor Burns, Cuts, Bites, or Stings	How often does this job require exposure to minor burns, cuts, bites, or stings?
Pace Determined by Speed of Equipment	How important is it to this job that the pace is determined by the speed of equipment or machinery? (This does not refer to keeping busy at all times on this job.)
Cramped Work Space, Awkward Positions	How often does this job require working in cramped work spaces that requires getting into awkward positions?
Spend Time Kneeling, Crouching, Stooping, or Crawl	How much does this job require kneeling, crouching, stooping, or crawling?
Outdoors, Under Cover	How often does this job require working outdoors, under cover (e.g., structure with roof but no walls)?
Spend Time Keeping or Regaining Balance	How much does this job require keeping or regaining your balance?
Exposed to Hazardous Conditions	How often does this job require exposure to hazardous conditions?
Exposed to Whole Body Vibration	How often does this job require exposure to whole body vibration (e.g., operate a jackhammer)?
Spend Time Climbing Ladders, Scaffolds, or Poles	How much does this job require climbing ladders, scaffolds, or poles?
Exposed to Hazardous Equipment	How often does this job require exposure to hazardous equipment?
In an Open Vehicle or Equipment	How often does this job require working in an open vehicle or equipment (e.g., tractor)?
Exposed to High Places	How often does this job require exposure to high places?
Wear Common Protective or Safety Equipment such as	How much does this job require wearing common protective or safety equipment such as safety shoes, glasses, gloves, hard hats or live jackets?
Wear Specialized Protective or Safety Equipment su	How much does this job require wearing specialized protective or safety equipment such as breathing apparatus, safety harness, full protection suits, or radiation protection?
Exposed to Radiation	How often does this job require exposure to radiation?

Job Zone Component	Job Zone Component Definitions
Title	Job Zone Five: Extensive Preparation Needed
Overall Experience	Extensive skill, knowledge, and experience are needed for these occupations. Many require more than five years of experience. For example, surgeons must complete four years of college and an additional five to seven years of specialized medical training to be able to do their job.

Job Training	Employees may need some on-the-job training, but most of these occupations assume that the person will already have the required skills, knowledge, work-related experience, and/or training.
Job Zone Examples	These occupations often involve coordinating, training, supervising, or managing the activities of others to accomplish goals. Very advanced communication and organizational skills are required. Examples include athletic trainers, lawyers, managing editors, phyicists, social psychologists, and surgeons.
SVP Range	(8.0 and above)
Education	A bachelor's degree is the minimum formal education required for these occupations. However, many also require graduate school. For example, they may require a master's degree, and some require a Ph.D., M.D., or J.D. (law degree).

Work_Styles	Work_Styles Definitions
Integrity	Job requires being honest and ethical.
Dependability	Job requires being reliable, responsible, and dependable, and fulfilling obligations.
Independence	Job requires developing one's own ways of doing things, guiding oneself with little or no supervision, and depending on oneself to get things done.
Analytical Thinking	Job requires analyzing information and using logic to address work-related issues and problems.
Attention to Detail	Job requires being careful about detail and thorough in completing work tasks.
Achievement/Effort	Job requires establishing and maintaining personally challenging achievement goals and exerting effort toward mastering tasks.
Cooperation	Job requires being pleasant with others on the job and displaying a good-natured, cooperative attitude.
Concern for Others	Job requires being sensitive to others' needs and feelings and being understanding and helpful on the job.
Initiative	Job requires a willingness to take on responsibilities and challenges.
Self Control	Job requires maintaining composure, keeping emotions in check, controlling anger, and avoiding aggressive behavior, even in very difficult situations.
Persistence	Job requires persistence in the face of obstacles.
Leadership	Job requires a willingness to lead, take charge, and offer opinions and direction.
Innovation	Job requires creativity and alternative thinking to develop new ideas for and answers to work-related problems.
Stress Tolerance	Job requires accepting criticism and dealing calmly and effectively with high stress situations.
Adaptability/Flexibility	Job requires being open to change (positive or negative) and to considerable variety in the workplace.
Social Orientation	Job requires preferring to work with others rather than alone, and being personally connected with others on the job.

25-1192.00 - Home Economics Teachers, Postsecondary

Teach courses in child care, family relations, finance, nutrition, and related subjects as pertaining to home management.

Tasks

1) Plan, evaluate, and revise curricula, course content, and course materials and methods of instruction.

2) Maintain student attendance records, grades, and other required records.

3) Keep abreast of developments in their field by reading current literature, talking with colleagues, and participating in professional conferences.

4) Select and obtain materials and supplies such as textbooks.

5) Maintain regularly scheduled office hours in order to advise and assist students.

6) Collaborate with colleagues to address teaching and research issues.

7) Participate in campus and community events.

8) Serve on academic or administrative committees that deal with institutional policies, departmental matters, and academic issues.

9) Prepare and deliver lectures to undergraduate and/or graduate students on topics such as

food science, nutrition, and child care.

10) Compile bibliographies of specialized materials for outside reading assignments.

11) Participate in student recruitment, registration, and placement activities.

12) Conduct research in a particular field of knowledge, and publish findings in professional journals, books, and/or electronic media.

13) Act as advisers to student organizations.

14) Supervise undergraduate and/or graduate teaching, internship, and research work.

15) Write grant proposals to procure external research funding.

16) Provide professional consulting services to government and/or industry.

17) Perform administrative duties such as serving as department head.

18) Advise students on academic and vocational curricula, and on career issues.

19) Initiate, facilitate, and moderate classroom discussions.

20) Compile, administer, and grade examinations, or assign this work to others.

21) Prepare course materials such as syllabi, homework assignments, and handouts.

Knowledge	Knowledge Definitions
Education and Training	Knowledge of principles and methods for curriculum and training design, teaching and instruction for individuals and groups, and the measurement of training effects.
English Language	Knowledge of the structure and content of the English language including the meaning and spelling of words, rules of composition, and grammar.
Psychology	Knowledge of human behavior and performance; individual differences in ability, personality, and interests; learning and motivation; psychological research methods; and the assessment and treatment of behavioral and affective disorders.
Customer and Personal Service	Knowledge of principles and processes for providing customer and personal services. This includes customer needs assessment, meeting quality standards for services, and evaluation of customer satisfaction.
Sociology and Anthropology	Knowledge of group behavior and dynamics, societal trends and influences, human migrations, ethnicity, cultures and their history and origins.
Administration and Management	Knowledge of business and management principles involved in strategic planning, resource allocation, human resources modeling, leadership technique, production methods, and coordination of people and resources.
Computers and Electronics	Knowledge of circuit boards, processors, chips, electronic equipment, and computer hardware and software, including applications and programming.
Communications and Media	Knowledge of media production, communication, and dissemination techniques and methods. This includes alternative ways to inform and entertain via written, oral, and visual media.
Therapy and Counseling	Knowledge of principles, methods, and procedures for diagnosis, treatment, and rehabilitation of physical and mental dysfunctions, and for career counseling and guidance.
Philosophy and Theology	Knowledge of different philosophical systems and religions. This includes their basic principles, values, ethics, ways of thinking, customs, practices, and their impact on human culture.
Clerical	Knowledge of administrative and clerical procedures and systems such as word processing, managing files and records, stenography and transcription, designing forms, and other office procedures and terminology.
Mathematics	Knowledge of arithmetic, algebra, geometry, calculus, statistics, and their applications.
Law and Government	Knowledge of laws, legal codes, court procedures, precedents, government regulations, executive orders, agency rules, and the democratic political process.
Sales and Marketing	Knowledge of principles and methods for showing, promoting, and selling products or services. This includes marketing strategy and tactics, product demonstration, sales techniques, and sales control systems.
Personnel and Human Resources	Knowledge of principles and procedures for personnel recruitment, selection, training, compensation and benefits, labor relations and negotiation, and personnel information systems.
Public Safety and Security	Knowledge of relevant equipment, policies, procedures, and strategies to promote effective local, state, or national security operations for the protection of people, data, property, and institutions.

History and Archeology	Knowledge of historical events and their causes, indicators, and effects on civilizations and cultures.
Design	Knowledge of design techniques, tools, and principles involved in production of precision technical plans, blueprints, drawings, and models.
Biology	Knowledge of plant and animal organisms, their tissues, cells, functions, interdependencies, and interactions with each other and the environment.
Geography	Knowledge of principles and methods for describing the features of land, sea, and air masses, including their physical characteristics, locations, interrelationships, and distribution of plant, animal, and human life.
Chemistry	Knowledge of the chemical composition, structure, and properties of substances and of the chemical processes and transformations that they undergo. This includes uses of chemicals and their interactions, danger signs, production techniques, and disposal methods.
Economics and Accounting	Knowledge of economic and accounting principles and practices, the financial markets, banking and the analysis and reporting of financial data.
Production and Processing	Knowledge of raw materials, production processes, quality control, costs, and other techniques for maximizing the effective manufacture and distribution of goods.
Food Production	Knowledge of techniques and equipment for planting, growing, and harvesting food products (both plant and animal) for consumption, including storage/handling techniques.
Medicine and Dentistry	Knowledge of the information and techniques needed to diagnose and treat human injuries, diseases, and deformities. This includes symptoms, treatment alternatives, drug properties and interactions, and preventive health-care measures.
Telecommunications	Knowledge of transmission, broadcasting, switching, control, and operation of telecommunications systems.
Building and Construction	Knowledge of materials, methods, and the tools involved in the construction or repair of houses, buildings, or other structures such as highways and roads.
Engineering and Technology	Knowledge of the practical application of engineering science and technology. This includes applying principles, techniques, procedures, and equipment to the design and production of various goods and services.
Fine Arts	Knowledge of the theory and techniques required to compose, produce, and perform works of music, dance, visual arts, drama, and sculpture.
Foreign Language	Knowledge of the structure and content of a foreign (non-English) language including the meaning and spelling of words, rules of composition and grammar, and pronunciation.
Transportation	Knowledge of principles and methods for moving people or goods by air, rail, sea, or road, including the relative costs and benefits.
Mechanical	Knowledge of machines and tools, including their designs, uses, repair, and maintenance.
Physics	Knowledge and prediction of physical principles, laws, their interrelationships, and applications to understanding fluid, material, and atmospheric dynamics, and mechanical, electrical, atomic and sub-atomic structures and processes.

Skills	Skills Definitions
Instructing	Teaching others how to do something.
Speaking	Talking to others to convey information effectively.
Reading Comprehension	Understanding written sentences and paragraphs in work related documents.
Critical Thinking	Using logic and reasoning to identify the strengths and weaknesses of alternative solutions, conclusions or approaches to problems.
Writing	Communicating effectively in writing as appropriate for the needs of the audience.
Active Learning	Understanding the implications of new information for both current and future problem-solving and decision-making.
Active Listening	Giving full attention to what other people are saying, taking time to understand the points being made, asking questions as appropriate, and not interrupting at inappropriate times.
Learning Strategies	Selecting and using training/instructional methods and procedures appropriate for the situation when learning or teaching new things.
Time Management	Managing one's own time and the time of others.
Monitoring	Monitoring/Assessing performance of yourself, other individuals, or organizations to make improvements or take corrective action.

Social Perceptiveness	Being aware of others' reactions and understanding why they react as they do.
Service Orientation	Actively looking for ways to help people.
Coordination	Adjusting actions in relation to others' actions.
Judgment and Decision Making	Considering the relative costs and benefits of potential actions to choose the most appropriate one.
Persuasion	Persuading others to change their minds or behavior.
Complex Problem Solving	Identifying complex problems and reviewing related information to develop and evaluate options and implement solutions.
Negotiation	Bringing others together and trying to reconcile differences.
Science	Using scientific rules and methods to solve problems.
Operations Analysis	Analyzing needs and product requirements to create a design.
Equipment Selection	Determining the kind of tools and equipment needed to do a job.
Mathematics	Using mathematics to solve problems.
Management of Financial Resources	Determining how money will be spent to get the work done, and accounting for these expenditures.
Management of Personnel Resources	Motivating, developing, and directing people as they work, identifying the best people for the job.
Management of Material Resources	Obtaining and seeing to the appropriate use of equipment, facilities, and materials needed to do certain work.
Quality Control Analysis	Conducting tests and inspections of products, services, or processes to evaluate quality or performance.
Systems Evaluation	Identifying measures or indicators of system performance and the actions needed to improve or correct performance, relative to the goals of the system.
Technology Design	Generating or adapting equipment and technology to serve user needs.
Systems Analysis	Determining how a system should work and how changes in conditions, operations, and the environment will affect outcomes.
Operation and Control	Controlling operations of equipment or systems.
Troubleshooting	Determining causes of operating errors and deciding what to do about it.
Equipment Maintenance	Performing routine maintenance on equipment and determining when and what kind of maintenance is needed.
Repairing	Repairing machines or systems using the needed tools.
Installation	Installing equipment, machines, wiring, or programs to meet specifications.
Operation Monitoring	Watching gauges, dials, or other indicators to make sure a machine is working properly.
Programming	Writing computer programs for various purposes.

Ability	Ability Definitions
Oral Expression	The ability to communicate information and ideas in speaking so others will understand.
Oral Comprehension	The ability to listen to and understand information and ideas presented through spoken words and sentences.
Written Comprehension	The ability to read and understand information and ideas presented in writing.
Speech Clarity	The ability to speak clearly so others can understand you.
Inductive Reasoning	The ability to combine pieces of information to form general rules or conclusions (includes finding a relationship among seemingly unrelated events).
Written Expression	The ability to communicate information and ideas in writing so others will understand.
Near Vision	The ability to see details at close range (within a few feet of the observer).
Problem Sensitivity	The ability to tell when something is wrong or is likely to go wrong. It does not involve solving the problem, only recognizing there is a problem.
Deductive Reasoning	The ability to apply general rules to specific problems to produce answers that make sense.
Speech Recognition	The ability to identify and understand the speech of another person.
Category Flexibility	The ability to generate or use different sets of rules for combining or grouping things in different ways.
Information Ordering	The ability to arrange things or actions in a certain order or pattern according to a specific rule or set of rules (e.g., patterns of numbers, letters, words, pictures, mathematical operations).
Originality	The ability to come up with unusual or clever ideas about a given topic or situation, or to develop creative ways to solve a problem.
Fluency of Ideas	The ability to come up with a number of ideas about a topic (the number of ideas is important, not their quality, correctness, or creativity).

Selective Attention	The ability to concentrate on a task over a period of time without being distracted.
Time Sharing	The ability to shift back and forth between two or more activities or sources of information (such as speech, sounds, touch, or other sources).
Mathematical Reasoning	The ability to choose the right mathematical methods or formulas to solve a problem.
Memorization	The ability to remember information such as words, numbers, pictures, and procedures.
Far Vision	The ability to see details at a distance.
Speed of Closure	The ability to quickly make sense of, combine, and organize information into meaningful patterns.
Flexibility of Closure	The ability to identify or detect a known pattern (a figure, object, word, or sound) that is hidden in other distracting material.
Visualization	The ability to imagine how something will look after it is moved around or when its parts are moved or rearranged.
Number Facility	The ability to add, subtract, multiply, or divide quickly and correctly.
Perceptual Speed	The ability to quickly and accurately compare similarities and differences among sets of letters, numbers, objects, pictures, or patterns. The things to be compared may be presented at the same time or one after the other. This ability also includes comparing a presented object with a remembered object.
Trunk Strength	The ability to use your abdominal and lower back muscles to support part of the body repeatedly or continuously over time without 'giving out' or fatiguing.
Auditory Attention	The ability to focus on a single source of sound in the presence of other distracting sounds.
Finger Dexterity	The ability to make precisely coordinated movements of the fingers of one or both hands to grasp, manipulate, or assemble very small objects.
Visual Color Discrimination	The ability to match or detect differences between colors, including shades of color and brightness.
Hearing Sensitivity	The ability to detect or tell the differences between sounds that vary in pitch and loudness.
Depth Perception	The ability to judge which of several objects is closer or farther away from you, or to judge the distance between you and an object.
Spatial Orientation	The ability to know your location in relation to the environment or to know where other objects are in relation to you.
Wrist-Finger Speed	The ability to make fast, simple, repeated movements of the fingers, hands, and wrists.
Glare Sensitivity	The ability to see objects in the presence of glare or bright lighting.
Gross Body Equilibrium	The ability to keep or regain your body balance or stay upright when in an unstable position.
Night Vision	The ability to see under low light conditions.
Peripheral Vision	The ability to see objects or movement of objects to one's side when the eyes are looking ahead.
Manual Dexterity	The ability to quickly move your hand, your hand together with your arm, or your two hands to grasp, manipulate, or assemble objects.
Arm-Hand Steadiness	The ability to keep your hand and arm steady while moving your arm or while holding your arm and hand in one position.
Sound Localization	The ability to tell the direction from which a sound originated.
Speed of Limb Movement	The ability to quickly move the arms and legs.
Multilimb Coordination	The ability to coordinate two or more limbs (for example, two arms, two legs, or one leg and one arm) while sitting, standing, or lying down. It does not involve performing the activities while the whole body is in motion.
Explosive Strength	The ability to use short bursts of muscle force to propel oneself (as in jumping or sprinting), or to throw an object.
Control Precision	The ability to quickly and repeatedly adjust the controls of a machine or a vehicle to exact positions.
Response Orientation	The ability to choose quickly between two or more movements in response to two or more different signals (lights, sounds, pictures). It includes the speed with which the correct response is started with the hand, foot, or other body part.
Gross Body Coordination	The ability to coordinate the movement of your arms, legs, and torso together when the whole body is in motion.
Dynamic Flexibility	The ability to quickly and repeatedly bend, stretch, twist, or reach out with your body, arms, and/or legs.
Extent Flexibility	The ability to bend, stretch, twist, or reach with your body, arms, and/or legs.
Stamina	The ability to exert yourself physically over long periods of time without getting winded or out of breath.

Reaction Time	The ability to quickly respond (with the hand, finger, or foot) to a signal (sound, light, picture) when it appears.
Static Strength	The ability to exert maximum muscle force to lift, push, pull, or carry objects.
Dynamic Strength	The ability to exert muscle force repeatedly or continuously over time. This involves muscular endurance and resistance to muscle fatigue.
Rate Control	The ability to time your movements or the movement of a piece of equipment in anticipation of changes in the speed and/or direction of a moving object or scene.

Work_Activity	**Work_Activity Definitions**
Training and Teaching Others	Identifying the educational needs of others, developing formal educational or training programs or classes, and teaching or instructing others.
Updating and Using Relevant Knowledge	Keeping up-to-date technically and applying new knowledge to your job.
Communicating with Supervisors, Peers, or Subordin	Providing information to supervisors, co-workers, and subordinates by telephone, in written form, e-mail, or in person.
Interpreting the Meaning of Information for Others	Translating or explaining what information means and how it can be used.
Coaching and Developing Others	Identifying the developmental needs of others and coaching, mentoring, or otherwise helping others to improve their knowledge or skills.
Interacting With Computers	Using computers and computer systems (including hardware and software) to program, write software, set up functions, enter data, or process information.
Judging the Qualities of Things, Services, or Peop	Assessing the value, importance, or quality of things or people.
Organizing, Planning, and Prioritizing Work	Developing specific goals and plans to prioritize, organize, and accomplish your work.
Making Decisions and Solving Problems	Analyzing information and evaluating results to choose the best solution and solve problems.
Establishing and Maintaining Interpersonal Relatio	Developing constructive and cooperative working relationships with others, and maintaining them over time.
Processing Information	Compiling, coding, categorizing, calculating, tabulating, auditing, or verifying information or data.
Documenting/Recording Information	Entering, transcribing, recording, storing, or maintaining information in written or electronic/magnetic form.
Provide Consultation and Advice to Others	Providing guidance and expert advice to management or other groups on technical, systems-, or process-related topics.
Getting Information	Observing, receiving, and otherwise obtaining information from all relevant sources.
Thinking Creatively	Developing, designing, or creating new applications, ideas, relationships, systems, or products, including artistic contributions.
Analyzing Data or Information	Identifying the underlying principles, reasons, or facts of information by breaking down information or data into separate parts.
Performing for or Working Directly with the Public	Performing for people or dealing directly with the public. This includes serving customers in restaurants and stores, and receiving clients or guests.
Developing Objectives and Strategies	Establishing long-range objectives and specifying the strategies and actions to achieve them.
Scheduling Work and Activities	Scheduling events, programs, and activities, as well as the work of others.
Identifying Objects, Actions, and Events	Identifying information by categorizing, estimating, recognizing differences or similarities, and detecting changes in circumstances or events.
Developing and Building Teams	Encouraging and building mutual trust, respect, and cooperation among team members.
Communicating with Persons Outside Organization	Communicating with people outside the organization, representing the organization to customers, the public, government, and other external sources. This information can be exchanged in person, in writing, or by telephone or e-mail.
Evaluating Information to Determine Compliance wit	Using relevant information and individual judgment to determine whether events or processes comply with laws, regulations, or standards.
Assisting and Caring for Others	Providing personal assistance, medical attention, emotional support, or other personal care to others such as coworkers, customers, or patients.
Resolving Conflicts and Negotiating with Others	Handling complaints, settling disputes, and resolving grievances and conflicts, or otherwise negotiating with others.
Coordinating the Work and Activities of Others	Getting members of a group to work together to accomplish tasks.

Monitor Processes, Materials, or Surroundings	Monitoring and reviewing information from materials, events, or the environment, to detect or assess problems.
Performing Administrative Activities	Performing day-to-day administrative tasks such as maintaining information files and processing paperwork.
Guiding, Directing, and Motivating Subordinates	Providing guidance and direction to subordinates, including setting performance standards and monitoring performance.
Estimating the Quantifiable Characteristics of Pro	Estimating sizes, distances, and quantities; or determining time, costs, resources, or materials needed to perform a work activity.
Monitoring and Controlling Resources	Monitoring and controlling resources and overseeing the spending of money.
Selling or Influencing Others	Convincing others to buy merchandise/goods or to otherwise change their minds or actions.
Staffing Organizational Units	Recruiting, interviewing, selecting, hiring, and promoting employees in an organization.
Inspecting Equipment, Structures, or Material	Inspecting equipment, structures, or materials to identify the cause of errors or other problems or defects.
Performing General Physical Activities	Performing physical activities that require considerable use of your arms and legs and moving your whole body, such as climbing, lifting, balancing, walking, stooping, and handling of materials.
Controlling Machines and Processes	Using either control mechanisms or direct physical activity to operate machines or processes (not including computers or vehicles).
Handling and Moving Objects	Using hands and arms in handling, installing, positioning, and moving materials, and manipulating things.
Drafting, Laying Out, and Specifying Technical Dev	Providing documentation, detailed instructions, drawings, or specifications to tell others about how devices, parts, equipment, or structures are to be fabricated, constructed, assembled, modified, maintained, or used.
Repairing and Maintaining Electronic Equipment	Servicing, repairing, calibrating, regulating, fine-tuning, or testing machines, devices, and equipment that operate primarily on the basis of electrical or electronic (not mechanical) principles.
Repairing and Maintaining Mechanical Equipment	Servicing, repairing, adjusting, and testing machines, devices, moving parts, and equipment that operate primarily on the basis of mechanical (not electronic) principles.
Operating Vehicles, Mechanized Devices, or Equipme	Running, maneuvering, navigating, or driving vehicles or mechanized equipment, such as forklifts, passenger vehicles, aircraft, or water craft.

Work_Context	**Work_Context Definitions**
Structured versus Unstructured Work	To what extent is this job structured for the worker, rather than allowing the worker to determine tasks, priorities, and goals?
Electronic Mail	How often do you use electronic mail in this job?
Face-to-Face Discussions	How often do you have to have face-to-face discussions with individuals or teams in this job?
Contact With Others	How much does this job require the worker to be in contact with others (face-to-face, by telephone, or otherwise) in order to perform it?
Indoors, Environmentally Controlled	How often does this job require working indoors in environmentally controlled conditions?
Freedom to Make Decisions	How much decision making freedom, without supervision, does the job offer?
Telephone	How often do you have telephone conversations in this job?
Public Speaking	How often do you have to perform public speaking in this job?
Work With Work Group or Team	How important is it to work with others in a group or team in this job?
Frequency of Decision Making	How frequently is the worker required to make decisions that affect other people, the financial resources, and/or the image and reputation of the organization?
Letters and Memos	How often does the job require written letters and memos?
Impact of Decisions on Co-workers or Company Resul	How do the decisions an employee makes impact the results of co-workers, clients or the company?
Coordinate or Lead Others	How important is it to coordinate or lead others in accomplishing work activities in this job?
Time Pressure	How often does this job require the worker to meet strict deadlines?
Deal With External Customers	How important is it to work with external customers or the public in this job?
Importance of Being Exact or Accurate	How important is being very exact or highly accurate in performing this job?
Physical Proximity	To what extent does this job require the worker to perform job tasks in close physical proximity to other people?
Spend Time Sitting	How much does this job require sitting?

Level of Competition	To what extent does this job require the worker to compete or to be aware of competitive pressures?
Frequency of Conflict Situations	How often are there conflict situations the employee has to face in this job?
Deal With Unpleasant or Angry People	How frequently does the worker have to deal with unpleasant, angry, or discourteous individuals as part of the job requirements?
Spend Time Standing	How much does this job require standing?
Responsibility for Outcomes and Results	How responsible is the worker for work outcomes and results of other workers?
Responsible for Others' Health and Safety	How much responsibility is there for the health and safety of others in this job?
Spend Time Making Repetitive Motions	How much does this job require making repetitive motions?
Importance of Repeating Same Tasks	How important is repeating the same physical activities (e.g., key entry) or mental activities (e.g., checking entries in a ledger) over and over, without stopping, to performing this job?
Sounds, Noise Levels Are Distracting or Uncomforta	How often does this job require working exposed to sounds and noise levels that are distracting or uncomfortable?
Spend Time Using Your Hands to Handle, Control, or	How much does this job require using your hands to handle, control, or feel objects, tools or controls?
Consequence of Error	How serious would the result usually be if the worker made a mistake that was not readily correctable?
Spend Time Walking and Running	How much does this job require walking and running?
In an Enclosed Vehicle or Equipment	How often does this job require working in a closed vehicle or equipment (e.g., car)?
Degree of Automation	How automated is the job?
Cramped Work Space, Awkward Positions	How often does this job require working in cramped work spaces that requires getting into awkward positions?
Exposed to Contaminants	How often does this job require working exposed to contaminants (such as pollutants, gases, dust or odors)?
Exposed to Disease or Infections	How often does this job require exposure to disease/infections?
Deal With Physically Aggressive People	How frequently does this job require the worker to deal with physical aggression of violent individuals?
Spend Time Keeping or Regaining Balance	How much does this job require keeping or regaining your balance?
Extremely Bright or Inadequate Lighting	How often does this job require working in extremely bright or inadequate lighting conditions?
Indoors, Not Environmentally Controlled	How often does this job require working indoors in non-controlled environmental conditions (e.g., warehouse without heat)?
Spend Time Bending or Twisting the Body	How much does this job require bending or twisting your body?
Outdoors, Under Cover	How often does this job require working outdoors, under cover (e.g., structure with roof but no walls)?
Outdoors, Exposed to Weather	How often does this job require working outdoors, exposed to all weather conditions?
Exposed to Minor Burns, Cuts, Bites, or Stings	How often does this job require exposure to minor burns, cuts, bites, or stings?
Very Hot or Cold Temperatures	How often does this job require working in very hot (above 90 F degrees) or very cold (below 32 F degrees) temperatures?
Spend Time Kneeling, Crouching, Stooping, or Crawl	How much does this job require kneeling, crouching, stooping or crawling?
Exposed to Hazardous Conditions	How often does this job require exposure to hazardous conditions?
In an Open Vehicle or Equipment	How often does this job require working in an open vehicle or equipment (e.g., tractor)?
Exposed to High Places	How often does this job require exposure to high places?
Exposed to Radiation	How often does this job require exposure to radiation?
Wear Common Protective or Safety Equipment such as	How much does this job require wearing common protective or safety equipment such as safety shoes, glasses, gloves, hard hats or life jackets?
Exposed to Hazardous Equipment	How often does this job require exposure to hazardous equipment?
Spend Time Climbing Ladders, Scaffolds, or Poles	How much does this job require climbing ladders, scaffolds, or poles?
Pace Determined by Speed of Equipment	How important is it to this job that the pace is determined by the speed of equipment or machinery? (This does not refer to keeping busy at all times on this job.)
Exposed to Whole Body Vibration	How often does this job require exposure to whole body vibration (e.g., operate a jackhammer)?

Wear Specialized Protective or Safety Equipment su	How much does this job require wearing specialized protective or safety equipment such as breathing apparatus, safety harness, full protection suits, or radiation protection?

Job Zone Component	Job Zone Component Definitions
Title	Job Zone Five: Extensive Preparation Needed
	Extensive skill, knowledge, and experience are needed for these occupations. Many require more than five years of experience.
Overall Experience	For example, surgeons must complete four years of college and an additional five to seven years of specialized medical training to be able to do their job.
Job Training	Employees may need some on-the-job training, but most of these occupations assume that the person will already have the required skills, knowledge, work-related experience, and/or training.
Job Zone Examples	These occupations often involve coordinating, training, supervising, or managing the activities of others to accomplish goals. Very advanced communication and organizational skills are required. Examples include athletic trainers, lawyers, managing editors, phyicists, social psychologists, and surgeons.
SVP Range	(8.0 and above)
Education	A bachelor's degree is the minimum formal education required for these occupations. However, many also require graduate school. For example, they may require a master's degree, and some require a Ph.D., M.D., or J.D. (law degree).

Work_Styles	Work_Styles Definitions
Integrity	Job requires being honest and ethical.
Dependability	Job requires being reliable, responsible, and dependable, and fulfilling obligations.
Cooperation	Job requires being pleasant with others on the job and displaying a good-natured, cooperative attitude.
Concern for Others	Job requires being sensitive to others' needs and feelings and being understanding and helpful on the job.
Initiative	Job requires a willingness to take on responsibilities and challenges.
Attention to Detail	Job requires being careful about detail and thorough in completing work tasks.
Independence	Job requires developing one's own ways of doing things, guiding oneself with little or no supervision, and depending on oneself to get things done.
Self Control	Job requires maintaining composure, keeping emotions in check, controlling anger, and avoiding aggressive behavior, even in very difficult situations.
Achievement/Effort	Job requires establishing and maintaining personally challenging achievement goals and exerting effort toward mastering tasks.
Persistence	Job requires persistence in the face of obstacles.
Innovation	Job requires creativity and alternative thinking to develop new ideas for and answers to work-related problems.
Analytical Thinking	Job requires analyzing information and using logic to address work-related issues and problems.
Social Orientation	Job requires preferring to work with others rather than alone, and being personally connected with others on the job.
Adaptability/Flexibility	Job requires being open to change (positive or negative) and to considerable variety in the workplace.
Leadership	Job requires a willingness to lead, take charge, and offer opinions and direction.
Stress Tolerance	Job requires accepting criticism and dealing calmly and effectively with high stress situations.

25-1193.00 - Recreation and Fitness Studies Teachers, Postsecondary

Teach courses pertaining to recreation, leisure, and fitness studies, including exercise physiology and facilities management.

Tasks

1) Maintain regularly scheduled office hours in order to advise and assist students.

2) Keep abreast of developments in their field by reading current literature, talking with

colleagues, and participating in professional conferences.

3) Compile, administer, and grade examinations, or assign this work to others.

4) Prepare course materials such as syllabi, homework assignments, and handouts.

5) Plan, evaluate, and revise curricula, course content, and course materials and methods of instruction.

6) Select and obtain materials and supplies such as textbooks.

7) Initiate, facilitate, and moderate classroom discussions.

8) Advise students on academic and vocational curricula, and on career issues.

9) Serve on academic or administrative committees that deal with institutional policies, departmental matters, and academic issues.

10) Collaborate with colleagues to address teaching and research issues.

11) Participate in student recruitment, registration, and placement activities.

12) Compile bibliographies of specialized materials for outside reading assignments.

13) Prepare and deliver lectures to undergraduate and/or graduate students on topics such as anatomy, therapeutic recreation, and conditioning theory.

14) Supervise undergraduate and/or graduate teaching, internship, and research work.

15) Conduct research in a particular field of knowledge, and publish findings in professional journals, books, and/or electronic media.

16) Prepare students to act as sports coaches.

17) Act as advisers to student organizations.

18) Perform administrative duties such as serving as department heads.

19) Write grant proposals to procure external research funding.

20) Provide professional consulting services to government and/or industry.

21) Participate in campus and community events.

22) Maintain student attendance records, grades, and other required records.

Knowledge	Knowledge Definitions
Education and Training	Knowledge of principles and methods for curriculum and training design, teaching and instruction for individuals and groups, and the measurement of training effects.
English Language	Knowledge of the structure and content of the English language including the meaning and spelling of words, rules of composition, and grammar.
Psychology	Knowledge of human behavior and performance; individual differences in ability, personality, and interests; learning and motivation; psychological research methods; and the assessment and treatment of behavioral and affective disorders.
Customer and Personal Service	Knowledge of principles and processes for providing customer and personal services. This includes customer needs assessment, meeting quality standards for services, and evaluation of customer satisfaction.
Administration and Management	Knowledge of business and management principles involved in strategic planning, resource allocation, human resources modeling, leadership technique, production methods, and coordination of people and resources.
Computers and Electronics	Knowledge of circuit boards, processors, chips, electronic equipment, and computer hardware and software, including applications and programming.
Personnel and Human Resources	Knowledge of principles and procedures for personnel recruitment, selection, training, compensation and benefits, labor relations and negotiation, and personnel information systems.
Clerical	Knowledge of administrative and clerical procedures and systems such as word processing, managing files and records, stenography and transcription, designing forms, and other office procedures and terminology.
Mathematics	Knowledge of arithmetic, algebra, geometry, calculus, statistics, and their applications.
Medicine and Dentistry	Knowledge of the information and techniques needed to diagnose and treat human injuries, diseases, and deformities. This includes symptoms, treatment alternatives, drug properties and interactions, and preventive health-care measures.
Communications and Media	Knowledge of media production, communication, and dissemination techniques and methods. This includes alternative ways to inform and entertain via written, oral, and visual media.
Public Safety and Security	Knowledge of relevant equipment, policies, procedures, and strategies to promote effective local, state, or national security operations for the protection of people, data, property, and institutions.
Sociology and Anthropology	Knowledge of group behavior and dynamics, societal trends and influences, human migrations, ethnicity, cultures and their history and origins.
Therapy and Counseling	Knowledge of principles, methods, and procedures for diagnosis, treatment, and rehabilitation of physical and mental dysfunctions, and for career counseling and guidance.
Sales and Marketing	Knowledge of principles and methods for showing, promoting, and selling products or services. This includes marketing strategy and tactics, product demonstration, sales techniques, and sales control systems.
Biology	Knowledge of plant and animal organisms, their tissues, cells, functions, interdependencies, and interactions with each other and the environment.
Philosophy and Theology	Knowledge of different philosophical systems and religions. This includes their basic principles, values, ethics, ways of thinking, customs, practices, and their impact on human culture.
Law and Government	Knowledge of laws, legal codes, court procedures, precedents, government regulations, executive orders, agency rules, and the democratic political process.
History and Archeology	Knowledge of historical events and their causes, indicators, and effects on civilizations and cultures.
Economics and Accounting	Knowledge of economic and accounting principles and practices, the financial markets, banking and the analysis and reporting of financial data.
Physics	Knowledge and prediction of physical principles, laws, their interrelationships, and applications to understanding fluid, material, and atmospheric dynamics, and mechanical, electrical, atomic and sub-atomic structures and processes.
Telecommunications	Knowledge of transmission, broadcasting, switching, control, and operation of telecommunications systems.
Chemistry	Knowledge of the chemical composition, structure, and properties of substances and of the chemical processes and transformations that they undergo. This includes uses of chemicals and their interactions, danger signs, production techniques, and disposal methods.
Geography	Knowledge of principles and methods for describing the features of land, sea, and air masses, including their physical characteristics, locations, interrelationships, and distribution of plant, animal, and human life.
Transportation	Knowledge of principles and methods for moving people or goods by air, rail, sea, or road, including the relative costs and benefits.
Engineering and Technology	Knowledge of the practical application of engineering science and technology. This includes applying principles, techniques, procedures, and equipment to the design and production of various goods and services.
Design	Knowledge of design techniques, tools, and principles involved in production of precision technical plans, blueprints, drawings, and models.
Production and Processing	Knowledge of raw materials, production processes, quality control, costs, and other techniques for maximizing the effective manufacture and distribution of goods.
Mechanical	Knowledge of machines and tools, including their designs, uses, repair, and maintenance.
Foreign Language	Knowledge of the structure and content of a foreign (non-English) language including the meaning and spelling of words, rules of composition and grammar, and pronunciation.
Fine Arts	Knowledge of the theory and techniques required to compose, produce, and perform works of music, dance, visual arts, drama, and sculpture.
Building and Construction	Knowledge of materials, methods, and the tools involved in the construction or repair of houses, buildings, or other structures such as highways and roads.
Food Production	Knowledge of techniques and equipment for planting, growing, and harvesting food products (both plant and animal) for consumption, including storage/handling techniques.

Skills	Skills Definitions
Instructing	Teaching others how to do something.
Speaking	Talking to others to convey information effectively.

Active Listening	Giving full attention to what other people are saying, taking time to understand the points being made, asking questions as appropriate, and not interrupting at inappropriate times.
Learning Strategies	Selecting and using training/instructional methods and procedures appropriate for the situation when learning or teaching new things.
Reading Comprehension	Understanding written sentences and paragraphs in work related documents.
Time Management	Managing one's own time and the time of others.
Active Learning	Understanding the implications of new information for both current and future problem-solving and decision-making.
Writing	Communicating effectively in writing as appropriate for the needs of the audience.
Monitoring	Monitoring/Assessing performance of yourself, other individuals, or organizations to make improvements or take corrective action.
Critical Thinking	Using logic and reasoning to identify the strengths and weaknesses of alternative solutions, conclusions or approaches to problems.
Social Perceptiveness	Being aware of others' reactions and understanding why they react as they do.
Coordination	Adjusting actions in relation to others' actions.
Judgment and Decision Making	Considering the relative costs and benefits of potential actions to choose the most appropriate one.
Service Orientation	Actively looking for ways to help people.
Persuasion	Persuading others to change their minds or behavior.
Science	Using scientific rules and methods to solve problems.
Complex Problem Solving	Identifying complex problems and reviewing related information to develop and evaluate options and implement solutions.
Equipment Selection	Determining the kind of tools and equipment needed to do a job.
Management of Personnel Resources	Motivating, developing, and directing people as they work, identifying the best people for the job.
Negotiation	Bringing others together and trying to reconcile differences.
Mathematics	Using mathematics to solve problems.
Management of Financial Resources	Determining how money will be spent to get the work done, and accounting for these expenditures.
Management of Material Resources	Obtaining and seeing to the appropriate use of equipment, facilities, and materials needed to do certain work.
Technology Design	Generating or adapting equipment and technology to serve user needs.
Operations Analysis	Analyzing needs and product requirements to create a design.
Quality Control Analysis	Conducting tests and inspections of products, services, or processes to evaluate quality or performance.
Troubleshooting	Determining causes of operating errors and deciding what to do about it.
Systems Evaluation	Identifying measures or indicators of system performance and the actions needed to improve or correct performance, relative to the goals of the system.
Equipment Maintenance	Performing routine maintenance on equipment and determining when and what kind of maintenance is needed.
Operation and Control	Controlling operations of equipment or systems.
Systems Analysis	Determining how a system should work and how changes in conditions, operations, and the environment will affect outcomes.
Installation	Installing equipment, machines, wiring, or programs to meet specifications.
Repairing	Repairing machines or systems using the needed tools.
Operation Monitoring	Watching gauges, dials, or other indicators to make sure a machine is working properly.
Programming	Writing computer programs for various purposes.

Ability	Ability Definitions
Oral Expression	The ability to communicate information and ideas in speaking so others will understand.
Speech Clarity	The ability to speak clearly so others can understand you.
Written Comprehension	The ability to read and understand information and ideas presented in writing.
Oral Comprehension	The ability to listen to and understand information and ideas presented through spoken words and sentences.
Written Expression	The ability to communicate information and ideas in writing so others will understand.
Inductive Reasoning	The ability to combine pieces of information to form general rules or conclusions (includes finding a relationship among seemingly unrelated events).

Near Vision	The ability to see details at close range (within a few feet of the observer).
Deductive Reasoning	The ability to apply general rules to specific problems to produce answers that make sense.
Problem Sensitivity	The ability to tell when something is wrong or is likely to go wrong. It does not involve solving the problem, only recognizing there is a problem.
Speech Recognition	The ability to identify and understand the speech of another person.
Originality	The ability to come up with unusual or clever ideas about a given topic or situation, or to develop creative ways to solve a problem.
Fluency of Ideas	The ability to come up with a number of ideas about a topic (the number of ideas is important, not their quality, correctness, or creativity).
Information Ordering	The ability to arrange things or actions in a certain order or pattern according to a specific rule or set of rules (e.g., patterns of numbers, letters, words, pictures, mathematical operations).
Category Flexibility	The ability to generate or use different sets of rules for combining or grouping things in different ways.
Selective Attention	The ability to concentrate on a task over a period of time without being distracted.
Time Sharing	The ability to shift back and forth between two or more activities or sources of information (such as speech, sounds, touch, or other sources).
Memorization	The ability to remember information such as words, numbers, pictures, and procedures.
Speed of Closure	The ability to quickly make sense of, combine, and organize information into meaningful patterns.
Far Vision	The ability to see details at a distance.
Flexibility of Closure	The ability to identify or detect a known pattern (a figure, object, word, or sound) that is hidden in other distracting material.
Mathematical Reasoning	The ability to choose the right mathematical methods or formulas to solve a problem.
Trunk Strength	The ability to use your abdominal and lower back muscles to support part of the body repeatedly or continuously over time without 'giving out' or fatiguing.
Number Facility	The ability to add, subtract, multiply, or divide quickly and correctly.
Perceptual Speed	The ability to quickly and accurately compare similarities and differences among sets of letters, numbers, objects, pictures, or patterns. The things to be compared may be presented at the same time or one after the other. This ability also includes comparing a presented object with a remembered object.
Visualization	The ability to imagine how something will look after it is moved around or when its parts are moved or rearranged.
Auditory Attention	The ability to focus on a single source of sound in the presence of other distracting sounds.
Depth Perception	The ability to judge which of several objects is closer or farther away from you, or to judge the distance between you and an object.
Multilimb Coordination	The ability to coordinate two or more limbs (for example, two arms, two legs, or one leg and one arm) while sitting, standing, or lying down. It does not involve performing the activities while the whole body is in motion.
Stamina	The ability to exert yourself physically over long periods of time without getting winded or out of breath.
Control Precision	The ability to quickly and repeatedly adjust the controls of a machine or a vehicle to exact positions.
Extent Flexibility	The ability to bend, stretch, twist, or reach with your body, arms, and/or legs.
Dynamic Strength	The ability to exert muscle force repeatedly or continuously over time. This involves muscular endurance and resistance to muscle fatigue.
Gross Body Equilibrium	The ability to keep or regain your body balance or stay upright when in an unstable position.
Static Strength	The ability to exert maximum muscle force to lift, push, pull, or carry objects.
Visual Color Discrimination	The ability to match or detect differences between colors, including shades of color and brightness.
Gross Body Coordination	The ability to coordinate the movement of your arms, legs, and torso together when the whole body is in motion.
Finger Dexterity	The ability to make precisely coordinated movements of the fingers of one or both hands to grasp, manipulate, or assemble very small objects.
Arm-Hand Steadiness	The ability to keep your hand and arm steady while moving your arm or while holding your arm and hand in one position.

Hearing Sensitivity	The ability to detect or tell the differences between sounds that vary in pitch and loudness.
Sound Localization	The ability to tell the direction from which a sound originated.
Night Vision	The ability to see under low light conditions.
Rate Control	The ability to time your movements or the movement of a piece of equipment in anticipation of changes in the speed and/or direction of a moving object or scene.
Wrist-Finger Speed	The ability to make fast, simple, repeated movements of the fingers, hands, and wrists.
Speed of Limb Movement	The ability to quickly move the arms and legs.
Explosive Strength	The ability to use short bursts of muscle force to propel oneself (as in jumping or sprinting), or to throw an object.
Peripheral Vision	The ability to see objects or movement of objects to one's side when the eyes are looking ahead.
Glare Sensitivity	The ability to see objects in the presence of glare or bright lighting.
Response Orientation	The ability to choose quickly between two or more movements in response to two or more different signals (lights, sounds, pictures). It includes the speed with which the correct response is started with the hand, foot, or other body part.
Manual Dexterity	The ability to quickly move your hand, your hand together with your arm, or your two hands to grasp, manipulate, or assemble objects.
Spatial Orientation	The ability to know your location in relation to the environment or to know where other objects are in relation to you.
Dynamic Flexibility	The ability to quickly and repeatedly bend, stretch, twist, or reach out with your body, arms, and/or legs.
Reaction Time	The ability to quickly respond (with the hand, finger, or foot) to a signal (sound, light, picture) when it appears.

Work_Activity	Work_Activity Definitions
Training and Teaching Others	Identifying the educational needs of others, developing formal educational or training programs or classes, and teaching or instructing others.
Coaching and Developing Others	Identifying the developmental needs of others and coaching, mentoring, or otherwise helping others to improve their knowledge or skills.
Updating and Using Relevant Knowledge	Keeping up-to-date technically and applying new knowledge to your job.
Getting Information	Observing, receiving, and otherwise obtaining information from all relevant sources.
Organizing, Planning, and Prioritizing Work	Developing specific goals and plans to prioritize, organize, and accomplish your work.
Establishing and Maintaining Interpersonal Relatio	Developing constructive and cooperative working relationships with others, and maintaining them over time.
Communicating with Supervisors, Peers, or Subordin	Providing information to supervisors, co-workers, and subordinates by telephone, in written form, e-mail, or in person.
Thinking Creatively	Developing, designing, or creating new applications, ideas, relationships, systems, or products, including artistic contributions.
Interacting With Computers	Using computers and computer systems (including hardware and software) to program, write software, set up functions, enter data, or process information.
Making Decisions and Solving Problems	Analyzing information and evaluating results to choose the best solution and solve problems.
Developing Objectives and Strategies	Establishing long-range objectives and specifying the strategies and actions to achieve them.
Documenting/Recording Information	Entering, transcribing, recording, storing, or maintaining information in written or electronic/magnetic form.
Identifying Objects, Actions, and Events	Identifying information by categorizing, estimating, recognizing differences or similarities, and detecting changes in circumstances or events.
Interpreting the Meaning of Information for Others	Translating or explaining what information means and how it can be used.
Judging the Qualities of Things, Services, or Peop	Assessing the value, importance, or quality of things or people.
Communicating with Persons Outside Organization	Communicating with people outside the organization, representing the organization to customers, the public, government, and other external sources. This information can be exchanged in person, in writing, or by telephone or e-mail.
Scheduling Work and Activities	Scheduling events, programs, and activities, as well as the work of others.

Performing General Physical Activities	Performing physical activities that require considerable use of your arms and legs and moving your whole body, such as climbing, lifting, balancing, walking, stooping, and handling of materials.
Guiding, Directing, and Motivating Subordinates	Providing guidance and direction to subordinates, including setting performance standards and monitoring performance.
Analyzing Data or Information	Identifying the underlying principles, reasons, or facts of information by breaking down information or data into separate parts.
Processing Information	Compiling, coding, categorizing, calculating, tabulating, auditing, or verifying information or data.
Provide Consultation and Advice to Others	Providing guidance and expert advice to management or other groups on technical, systems-, or process-related topics.
Performing for or Working Directly with the Public	Performing for people or dealing directly with the public. This includes serving customers in restaurants and stores, and receiving clients or guests.
Developing and Building Teams	Encouraging and building mutual trust, respect, and cooperation among team members.
Coordinating the Work and Activities of Others	Getting members of a group to work together to accomplish tasks.
Performing Administrative Activities	Performing day-to-day administrative tasks such as maintaining information files and processing paperwork.
Assisting and Caring for Others	Providing personal assistance, medical attention, emotional support, or other personal care to others such as coworkers, customers, or patients.
Evaluating Information to Determine Compliance wit	Using relevant information and individual judgment to determine whether events or processes comply with laws, regulations, or standards.
Monitor Processes, Materials, or Surroundings	Monitoring and reviewing information from materials, events, or the environment, to detect or assess problems.
Resolving Conflicts and Negotiating with Others	Handling complaints, settling disputes, and resolving grievances and conflicts, or otherwise negotiating with others.
Monitoring and Controlling Resources	Monitoring and controlling resources and overseeing the spending of money.
Selling or Influencing Others	Convincing others to buy merchandise/goods or to otherwise change their minds or actions.
Inspecting Equipment, Structures, or Material	Inspecting equipment, structures, or materials to identify the cause of errors or other problems or defects.
Estimating the Quantifiable Characteristics of Pro	Estimating sizes, distances, and quantities; or determining time, costs, resources, or materials needed to perform a work activity.
Staffing Organizational Units	Recruiting, interviewing, selecting, hiring, and promoting employees in an organization.
Handling and Moving Objects	Using hands and arms in handling, installing, positioning, and moving materials, and manipulating things.
Controlling Machines and Processes	Using either control mechanisms or direct physical activity to operate machines or processes (not including computers or vehicles).
Operating Vehicles, Mechanized Devices, or Equipm	Running, maneuvering, navigating, or driving vehicles or mechanized equipment, such as forklifts, passenger vehicles, aircraft, or water craft.
Repairing and Maintaining Mechanical Equipment	Servicing, repairing, adjusting, and testing machines, devices, moving parts, and equipment that operate primarily on the basis of mechanical (not electronic) principles.
Drafting, Laying Out, and Specifying Technical Dev	Providing documentation, detailed instructions, drawings, or specifications to tell others about how devices, parts, equipment, or structures are to be fabricated, constructed, assembled, modified, maintained, or used.
Repairing and Maintaining Electronic Equipment	Servicing, repairing, calibrating, regulating, fine-tuning, or testing machines, devices, and equipment that operate primarily on the basis of electrical or electronic (not mechanical) principles.

Work_Context	Work_Context Definitions
Electronic Mail	How often do you use electronic mail in this job?
Telephone	How often do you have telephone conversations in this job?
Face-to-Face Discussions	How often do you have to have face-to-face discussions with individuals or teams in this job?
Freedom to Make Decisions	How much decision making freedom, without supervision, does the job offer?
Structured versus Unstructured Work	To what extent is this job structured for the worker, rather than allowing the worker to determine tasks, priorities, and goals?
Contact With Others	How much does this job require the worker to be in contact with others (face-to-face, by telephone, or otherwise) in order to perform it?
Public Speaking	How often do you have to perform public speaking in this job?

Indoors, Environmentally Controlled	How often does this job require working indoors in environmentally controlled conditions?	Spend Time Kneeling, Crouching, Stooping, or Crawl	How much does this job require kneeling, crouching, stooping, or crawling?
Work With Work Group or Team	How important is it to work with others in a group or team in this job?	Exposed to Hazardous Equipment	How often does this job require exposure to hazardous equipment?
Coordinate or Lead Others	How important is it to coordinate or lead others in accomplishing work activities in this job?	Exposed to Hazardous Conditions	How often does this job require exposure to hazardous conditions?
Letters and Memos	How often does the job require written letters and memos?	Cramped Work Space, Awkward Positions	How often does this job require working in cramped work spaces that requires getting into awkward positions?
Impact of Decisions on Co-workers or Company Resul	How do the decisions an employee makes impact the results of co-workers, clients or the company?	Wear Specialized Protective or Safety Equipment su	How much does this job require wearing specialized protective or safety equipment such as breathing apparatus, safety harness, full protection suits, or radiation protection?
Time Pressure	How often does this job require the worker to meet strict deadlines?	In an Open Vehicle or Equipment	How often does this job require working in an open vehicle or equipment (e.g., tractor)?
Frequency of Decision Making	How frequently is the worker required to make decisions that affect other people, the financial resources, and/or the image and reputation of the organization?	Exposed to High Places	How often does this job require exposure to high places?
Importance of Being Exact or Accurate	How important is being very exact or highly accurate in performing this job?	Spend Time Climbing Ladders, Scaffolds, or Poles	How much does this job require climbing ladders, scaffolds, or poles?
Deal With External Customers	How important is it to work with external customers or the public in this job?	Exposed to Radiation	How often does this job require exposure to radiation?
Responsible for Others' Health and Safety	How much responsibility is there for the health and safety of others in this job?	Pace Determined by Speed of Equipment	How important is it to this job that the pace is determined by the speed of equipment or machinery? (This does not refer to keeping busy at all times on this job.)
Physical Proximity	To what extent does this job require the worker to perform job tasks in close physical proximity to other people?	Exposed to Whole Body Vibration	How often does this job require exposure to whole body vibration (e.g., operate a jackhammer)?
Frequency of Conflict Situations	How often are there conflict situations the employee has to face in this job?		
Level of Competition	To what extent does this job require the worker to compete or to be aware of competitive pressures?		

Responsibility for Outcomes and Results	How responsible is the worker for work outcomes and results of other workers?	Title	Job Zone Five: Extensive Preparation Needed
Outdoors, Exposed to Weather	How often does this job require working outdoors, exposed to all weather conditions?	Overall Experience	Extensive skill, knowledge, and experience are needed for these occupations. Many require more than five years of experience. For example, surgeons must complete four years of college and an additional five to seven years of specialized medical training to be able to do their job.
Deal With Unpleasant or Angry People	How frequently does the worker have to deal with unpleasant, angry, or discourteous individuals as part of the job requirements?	Job Training	Employees may need some on-the-job training, but most of these occupations assume that the person will already have the required skills, knowledge, work-related experience, and/or training.
Spend Time Standing	How much does this job require standing?		
Spend Time Sitting	How much does this job require sitting?		
Sounds, Noise Levels Are Distracting or Uncomforta	How often does this job require working exposed to sounds and noise levels that are distracting or uncomfortable?	Job Zone Examples	These occupations often involve coordinating, training, supervising, or managing the activities of others to accomplish goals. Very advanced communication and organizational skills are required. Examples include athletic trainers, lawyers, managing editors, physicists, social psychologists, and surgeons.
Indoors, Not Environmentally Controlled	How often does this job require working indoors in non-controlled environmental conditions (e.g., warehouse without heat)?	SVP Range	(8.0 and above)
Importance of Repeating Same Tasks	How important is repeating the same physical activities (e.g., key entry) or mental activities (e.g., checking entries in a ledger) over and over, without stopping, to performing this job?	Education	A bachelor's degree is the minimum formal education required for these occupations. However, many also require graduate school. For example, they may require a master's degree, and some require a Ph.D., M.D., or J.D. (law degree).
Consequence of Error	How serious would the result usually be if the worker made a mistake that was not readily correctable?		
In an Enclosed Vehicle or Equipment	How often does this job require working in a closed vehicle or equipment (e.g., car)?		

Spend Time Walking and Running	How much does this job require walking and running?	Dependability	Job requires being reliable, responsible, and dependable, and fulfilling obligations.
Spend Time Using Your Hands to Handle, Control, or	How much does this job require using your hands to handle, control, or feel objects, tools or controls?	Integrity	Job requires being honest and ethical.
Exposed to Disease or Infections	How often does this job require exposure to disease/infections?	Cooperation	Job requires being pleasant with others on the job and displaying a good-natured, cooperative attitude.
Spend Time Making Repetitive Motions	How much does this job require making repetitive motions?	Leadership	Job requires a willingness to lead, take charge, and offer opinions and direction.
Exposed to Contaminants	How often does this job require working exposed to contaminants (such as pollutants, gases, dust or odors)?	Self Control	Job requires maintaining composure, keeping emotions in check, controlling anger, and avoiding aggressive behavior, even in very difficult situations.
Very Hot or Cold Temperatures	How often does this job require working in very hot (above 90 F degrees) or very cold (below 32 F degrees) temperatures?	Initiative	Job requires a willingness to take on responsibilities and challenges.
Extremely Bright or Inadequate Lighting	How often does this job require working in extremely bright or inadequate lighting conditions?	Independence	Job requires developing one's own ways of doing things, guiding oneself with little or no supervision, and depending on oneself to get things done.
Degree of Automation	How automated is the job?		
Spend Time Bending or Twisting the Body	How much does this job require bending or twisting your body?	Concern for Others	Job requires being sensitive to others' needs and feelings and being understanding and helpful on the job.
Exposed to Minor Burns, Cuts, Bites, or Stings	How often does this job require exposure to minor burns, cuts, bites, or stings?	Stress Tolerance	Job requires accepting criticism and dealing calmly and effectively with high stress situations.
Outdoors, Under Cover	How often does this job require working outdoors, under cover (e.g., structure with roof but no walls)?	Achievement/Effort	Job requires establishing and maintaining personally challenging achievement goals and exerting effort toward mastering tasks.
Spend Time Keeping or Regaining Balance	How much does this job require keeping or regaining your balance?	Social Orientation	Job requires preferring to work with others rather than alone, and being personally connected with others on the job.
Wear Common Protective or Safety Equipment such as	How much does this job require wearing common protective or safety equipment such as safety shoes, glasses, gloves, hard hats or live jackets?	Persistence	Job requires persistence in the face of obstacles.
Deal With Physically Aggressive People	How frequently does this job require the worker to deal with physical aggression of violent individuals?	Adaptability/Flexibility	Job requires being open to change (positive or negative) and to considerable variety in the workplace.

Attention to Detail	Job requires being careful about detail and thorough in completing work tasks.
Analytical Thinking	Job requires analyzing information and using logic to address work-related issues and problems.
Innovation	Job requires creativity and alternative thinking to develop new ideas for and answers to work-related problems.

25-1194.00 - Vocational Education Teachers Postsecondary

Teach or instruct vocational or occupational subjects at the postsecondary level (but at less than the baccalaureate) to students who have graduated or left high school. Includes correspondence school instructors; industrial, commercial and government training instructors; and adult education teachers and instructors who prepare persons to operate industrial machinery and equipment and transportation and communications equipment. Teaching may take place in public or private schools whose primary business is education or in a school associated with an organization whose primary business is other than education.

Tasks

1) Observe and evaluate students' work to determine progress, provide feedback, and make suggestions for improvement.

2) Determine training needs of students or workers.

3) Provide individualized instruction and tutorial and/or remedial instruction.

4) Present lectures and conduct discussions to increase students' knowledge and competence, using visual aids such as graphs, charts, videotapes, and slides.

5) Administer oral, written, or performance tests in order to measure progress, and to evaluate training effectiveness.

6) Participate in conferences, seminars, and training sessions to keep abreast of developments in the field; and integrate relevant information into training programs.

7) Prepare outlines of instructional programs and training schedules, and establish course goals.

8) Select and assemble books, materials, supplies, and equipment for training, courses, or projects.

9) Supervise and monitor students' use of tools and equipment.

10) Develop curricula, and plan course content and methods of instruction.

11) Develop teaching aids such as instructional software, multimedia visual aids, or study materials.

12) Supervise independent or group projects, field placements, laboratory work, or other training.

13) Conduct on-the-job training, classes, or training sessions to teach and demonstrate principles, techniques, procedures, and/or methods of designated subjects.

14) Advise students on course selection, career decisions, and other academic and vocational concerns.

15) Integrate academic and vocational curricula so that students can obtain a variety of skills.

16) Serve on faculty and school committees concerned with budgeting, curriculum revision, and course and diploma requirements.

17) Arrange for lectures by experts in designated fields.

18) Review enrollment applications, and correspond with applicants to obtain additional information.

Knowledge	Knowledge Definitions
Education and Training	Knowledge of principles and methods for curriculum and training design, teaching and instruction for individuals and groups, and the measurement of training effects.
Customer and Personal Service	Knowledge of principles and processes for providing customer and personal services. This includes customer needs assessment, meeting quality standards for services, and evaluation of customer satisfaction.
English Language	Knowledge of the structure and content of the English language including the meaning and spelling of words, rules of composition, and grammar.
Mathematics	Knowledge of arithmetic, algebra, geometry, calculus, statistics, and their applications.
Computers and Electronics	Knowledge of circuit boards, processors, chips, electronic equipment, and computer hardware and software, including applications and programming.
Psychology	Knowledge of human behavior and performance; individual differences in ability, personality, and interests; learning and motivation; psychological research methods; and the assessment and treatment of behavioral and affective disorders.
Mechanical	Knowledge of machines and tools, including their designs, uses, repair, and maintenance.
Administration and Management	Knowledge of business and management principles involved in strategic planning, resource allocation, human resources modeling, leadership technique, production methods, and coordination of people and resources.
Public Safety and Security	Knowledge of relevant equipment, policies, procedures, and strategies to promote effective local, state, or national security operations for the protection of people, data, property, and institutions.
Personnel and Human Resources	Knowledge of principles and procedures for personnel recruitment, selection, training, compensation and benefits, labor relations and negotiation, and personnel information systems.
Design	Knowledge of design techniques, tools, and principles involved in production of precision technical plans, blueprints, drawings, and models.
Clerical	Knowledge of administrative and clerical procedures and systems such as word processing, managing files and records, stenography and transcription, designing forms, and other office procedures and terminology.
Engineering and Technology	Knowledge of the practical application of engineering science and technology. This includes applying principles, techniques, procedures, and equipment to the design and production of various goods and services.
Communications and Media	Knowledge of media production, communication, and dissemination techniques and methods. This includes alternative ways to inform and entertain via written, oral, and visual media.
Sales and Marketing	Knowledge of principles and methods for showing, promoting, and selling products or services. This includes marketing strategy and tactics, product demonstration, sales techniques, and sales control systems.
Therapy and Counseling	Knowledge of principles, methods, and procedures for diagnosis, treatment, and rehabilitation of physical and mental dysfunctions, and for career counseling and guidance.
Law and Government	Knowledge of laws, legal codes, court procedures, precedents, government regulations, executive orders, agency rules, and the democratic political process.
Production and Processing	Knowledge of raw materials, production processes, quality control, costs, and other techniques for maximizing the effective manufacture and distribution of goods.
Physics	Knowledge and prediction of physical principles, laws, their interrelationships, and applications to understanding fluid, material, and atmospheric dynamics, and mechanical, electrical, atomic and sub-atomic structures and processes.
Chemistry	Knowledge of the chemical composition, structure, and properties of substances and of the chemical processes and transformations that they undergo. This includes uses of chemicals and their interactions, danger signs, production techniques, and disposal methods.
Sociology and Anthropology	Knowledge of group behavior and dynamics, societal trends and influences, human migrations, ethnicity, cultures and their history and origins.
Telecommunications	Knowledge of transmission, broadcasting, switching, control, and operation of telecommunications systems.
Building and Construction	Knowledge of materials, methods, and the tools involved in the construction or repair of houses, buildings, or other structures such as highways and roads.
Economics and Accounting	Knowledge of economic and accounting principles and practices, the financial markets, banking and the analysis and reporting of financial data.
Medicine and Dentistry	Knowledge of the information and techniques needed to diagnose and treat human injuries, diseases, and deformities. This includes symptoms, treatment alternatives, drug properties and interactions, and preventive health-care measures.
Biology	Knowledge of plant and animal organisms, their tissues, cells, functions, interdependencies, and interactions with each other and the environment.
Transportation	Knowledge of principles and methods for moving people or goods by air, rail, sea, or road, including the relative costs and benefits.

Philosophy and Theology	Knowledge of different philosophical systems and religions. This includes their basic principles, values, ethics, ways of thinking, customs, practices, and their impact on human culture.
History and Archeology	Knowledge of historical events and their causes, indicators, and effects on civilizations and cultures.
Geography	Knowledge of principles and methods for describing the features of land, sea, and air masses, including their physical characteristics, locations, interrelationships, and distribution of plant, animal, and human life.
Fine Arts	Knowledge of the theory and techniques required to compose, produce, and perform works of music, dance, visual arts, drama, and sculpture.
Foreign Language	Knowledge of the structure and content of a foreign (non-English) language including the meaning and spelling of words, rules of composition and grammar, and pronunciation.
Food Production	Knowledge of techniques and equipment for planting, growing, and harvesting food products (both plant and animal) for consumption, including storage/handling techniques.

Skills	Skills Definitions
Instructing	Teaching others how to do something.
Speaking	Talking to others to convey information effectively.
Reading Comprehension	Understanding written sentences and paragraphs in work related documents.
Active Listening	Giving full attention to what other people are saying, taking time to understand the points being made, asking questions as appropriate, and not interrupting at inappropriate times.
Active Learning	Understanding the implications of new information for both current and future problem-solving and decision-making.
Learning Strategies	Selecting and using training/instructional methods and procedures appropriate for the situation when learning or teaching new things.
Time Management	Managing one's own time and the time of others.
Critical Thinking	Using logic and reasoning to identify the strengths and weaknesses of alternative solutions, conclusions or approaches to problems.
Service Orientation	Actively looking for ways to help people.
Social Perceptiveness	Being aware of others' reactions and understanding why they react as they do.
Writing	Communicating effectively in writing as appropriate for the needs of the audience.
Judgment and Decision Making	Considering the relative costs and benefits of potential actions to choose the most appropriate one.
Monitoring	Monitoring/Assessing performance of yourself, other individuals, or organizations to make improvements or take corrective action.
Complex Problem Solving	Identifying complex problems and reviewing related information to develop and evaluate options and implement solutions.
Coordination	Adjusting actions in relation to others' actions.
Mathematics	Using mathematics to solve problems.
Persuasion	Persuading others to change their minds or behavior.
Equipment Selection	Determining the kind of tools and equipment needed to do a job.
Negotiation	Bringing others together and trying to reconcile differences.
Troubleshooting	Determining causes of operating errors and deciding what to do about it.
Science	Using scientific rules and methods to solve problems.
Management of Personnel Resources	Motivating, developing, and directing people as they work, identifying the best people for the job.
Operations Analysis	Analyzing needs and product requirements to create a design.
Equipment Maintenance	Performing routine maintenance on equipment and determining when and what kind of maintenance is needed.
Management of Material Resources	Obtaining and seeing to the appropriate use of equipment, facilities, and materials needed to do certain work.
Technology Design	Generating or adapting equipment and technology to serve user needs.
Quality Control Analysis	Conducting tests and inspections of products, services, or processes to evaluate quality or performance.
Operation and Control	Controlling operations of equipment or systems.
Management of Financial Resources	Determining how money will be spent to get the work done, and accounting for these expenditures.
Installation	Installing equipment, machines, wiring, or programs to meet specifications.
Repairing	Repairing machines or systems using the needed tools.

Operation Monitoring	Watching gauges, dials, or other indicators to make sure a machine is working properly.
Systems Evaluation	Identifying measures or indicators of system performance and the actions needed to improve or correct performance, relative to the goals of the system.
Systems Analysis	Determining how a system should work and how changes in conditions, operations, and the environment will affect outcomes.
Programming	Writing computer programs for various purposes.

Ability	Ability Definitions
Oral Expression	The ability to communicate information and ideas in speaking so others will understand.
Speech Clarity	The ability to speak clearly so others can understand you.
Oral Comprehension	The ability to listen to and understand information and ideas presented through spoken words and sentences.
Written Comprehension	The ability to read and understand information and ideas presented in writing.
Problem Sensitivity	The ability to tell when something is wrong or is likely to go wrong. It does not involve solving the problem, only recognizing there is a problem.
Speech Recognition	The ability to identify and understand the speech of another person.
Written Expression	The ability to communicate information and ideas in writing so others will understand.
Near Vision	The ability to see details at close range (within a few feet of the observer).
Deductive Reasoning	The ability to apply general rules to specific problems to produce answers that make sense.
Information Ordering	The ability to arrange things or actions in a certain order or pattern according to a specific rule or set of rules (e.g., patterns of numbers, letters, words, pictures, mathematical operations).
Inductive Reasoning	The ability to combine pieces of information to form general rules or conclusions (includes finding a relationship among seemingly unrelated events).
Originality	The ability to come up with unusual or clever ideas about a given topic or situation, or to develop creative ways to solve a problem.
Selective Attention	The ability to concentrate on a task over a period of time without being distracted.
Category Flexibility	The ability to generate or use different sets of rules for combining or grouping things in different ways.
Fluency of Ideas	The ability to come up with a number of ideas about a topic (the number of ideas is important, not their quality, correctness, or creativity).
Arm-Hand Steadiness	The ability to keep your hand and arm steady while moving your arm or while holding your arm and hand in one position.
Manual Dexterity	The ability to quickly move your hand, your hand together with your arm, or your two hands to grasp, manipulate, or assemble objects.
Far Vision	The ability to see details at a distance.
Finger Dexterity	The ability to make precisely coordinated movements of the fingers of one or both hands to grasp, manipulate, or assemble very small objects.
Flexibility of Closure	The ability to identify or detect a known pattern (a figure, object, word, or sound) that is hidden in other distracting material.
Memorization	The ability to remember information such as words, numbers, pictures, and procedures.
Trunk Strength	The ability to use your abdominal and lower back muscles to support part of the body repeatedly or continuously over time without 'giving out' or fatiguing.
Time Sharing	The ability to shift back and forth between two or more activities or sources of information (such as speech, sounds, touch, or other sources).
Mathematical Reasoning	The ability to choose the right mathematical methods or formulas to solve a problem.
Multilimb Coordination	The ability to coordinate two or more limbs (for example, two arms, two legs, or one leg and one arm) while sitting, standing, or lying down. It does not involve performing the activities while the whole body is in motion.
Auditory Attention	The ability to focus on a single source of sound in the presence of other distracting sounds.
Visualization	The ability to imagine how something will look after it is moved around or when its parts are moved or rearranged.
Number Facility	The ability to add, subtract, multiply, or divide quickly and correctly.

Gross Body Coordination	The ability to coordinate the movement of your arms, legs, and torso together when the whole body is in motion.
Static Strength	The ability to exert maximum muscle force to lift, push, pull, or carry objects.
Speed of Closure	The ability to quickly make sense of, combine, and organize information into meaningful patterns.
Control Precision	The ability to quickly and repeatedly adjust the controls of a machine or a vehicle to exact positions.
Stamina	The ability to exert yourself physically over long periods of time without getting winded or out of breath.
Perceptual Speed	The ability to quickly and accurately compare similarities and differences among sets of letters, numbers, objects, pictures, or patterns. The things to be compared may be presented at the same time or one after the other. This ability also includes comparing a presented object with a remembered object.
Visual Color Discrimination	The ability to match or detect differences between colors, including shades of color and brightness.
Speed of Limb Movement	The ability to quickly move the arms and legs.
Depth Perception	The ability to judge which of several objects is closer or farther away from you, or to judge the distance between you and an object.
Dynamic Strength	The ability to exert muscle force repeatedly or continuously over time. This involves muscular endurance and resistance to muscle fatigue.
Hearing Sensitivity	The ability to detect or tell the differences between sounds that vary in pitch and loudness.
Extent Flexibility	The ability to bend, stretch, twist, or reach with your body, arms, and/or legs.
Response Orientation	The ability to choose quickly between two or more movements in response to two or more different signals (lights, sounds, pictures). It includes the speed with which the correct response is started with the hand, foot, or other body part.
Sound Localization	The ability to tell the direction from which a sound originated.
Reaction Time	The ability to quickly respond (with the hand, finger, or foot) to a signal (sound, light, picture) when it appears.
Rate Control	The ability to time your movements or the movement of a piece of equipment in anticipation of changes in the speed and/or direction of a moving object or scene.
Gross Body Equilibrium	The ability to keep or regain your body balance or stay upright when in an unstable position.
Spatial Orientation	The ability to know your location in relation to the environment or to know where other objects are in relation to you.
Wrist-Finger Speed	The ability to make fast, simple, repeated movements of the fingers, hands, and wrists.
Glare Sensitivity	The ability to see objects in the presence of glare or bright lighting.
Peripheral Vision	The ability to see objects or movement of objects to one's side when the eyes are looking ahead.
Dynamic Flexibility	The ability to quickly and repeatedly bend, stretch, twist, or reach out with your body, arms, and/or legs.
Night Vision	The ability to see under low light conditions.
Explosive Strength	The ability to use short bursts of muscle force to propel oneself (as in jumping or sprinting), or to throw an object.

Work_Activity	Work_Activity Definitions
Training and Teaching Others	Identifying the educational needs of others, developing formal educational or training programs or classes, and teaching or instructing others.
Updating and Using Relevant Knowledge	Keeping up-to-date technically and applying new knowledge to your job.
Making Decisions and Solving Problems	Analyzing information and evaluating results to choose the best solution and solve problems.
Coaching and Developing Others	Identifying the developmental needs of others and coaching, mentoring, or otherwise helping others to improve their knowledge or skills.
Interpreting the Meaning of Information for Others	Translating or explaining what information means and how it can be used.
Getting Information	Observing, receiving, and otherwise obtaining information from all relevant sources.
Communicating with Supervisors, Peers, or Subordin	Providing information to supervisors, co-workers, and subordinates by telephone, in written form, e-mail, or in person.
Organizing, Planning, and Prioritizing Work	Developing specific goals and plans to prioritize, organize, and accomplish your work.
Establishing and Maintaining Interpersonal Relatio	Developing constructive and cooperative working relationships with others, and maintaining them over time.

Evaluating Information to Determine Compliance wit	Using relevant information and individual judgment to determine whether events or processes comply with laws, regulations, or standards.
Thinking Creatively	Developing, designing, or creating new applications, ideas, relationships, systems, or products, including artistic contributions.
Documenting/Recording Information	Entering, transcribing, recording, storing, or maintaining information in written or electronic/magnetic form.
Judging the Qualities of Things, Services, or Peop	Assessing the value, importance, or quality of things or people.
Inspecting Equipment, Structures, or Material	Inspecting equipment, structures, or materials to identify the cause of errors or other problems or defects.
Performing for or Working Directly with the Public	Performing for people or dealing directly with the public. This includes serving customers in restaurants and stores, and receiving clients or guests.
Performing Administrative Activities	Performing day-to-day administrative tasks such as maintaining information files and processing paperwork.
Interacting With Computers	Using computers and computer systems (including hardware and software) to program, write software, set up functions, enter data, or process information.
Guiding, Directing, and Motivating Subordinates	Providing guidance and direction to subordinates, including setting performance standards and monitoring performance.
Communicating with Persons Outside Organization	Communicating with people outside the organization, representing the organization to customers, the public, government, and other external sources. This information can be exchanged in person, in writing, or by telephone or e-mail.
Coordinating the Work and Activities of Others	Getting members of a group to work together to accomplish tasks.
Identifying Objects, Actions, and Events	Identifying information by categorizing, estimating, recognizing differences or similarities, and detecting changes in circumstances or events.
Resolving Conflicts and Negotiating with Others	Handling complaints, settling disputes, and resolving grievances and conflicts, or otherwise negotiating with others.
Monitor Processes, Materials, or Surroundings	Monitoring and reviewing information from materials, events, or the environment, to detect or assess problems.
Assisting and Caring for Others	Providing personal assistance, medical attention, emotional support, or other personal care to others such as coworkers, customers, or patients.
Developing Objectives and Strategies	Establishing long-range objectives and specifying the strategies and actions to achieve them.
Processing Information	Compiling, coding, categorizing, calculating, tabulating, auditing, or verifying information or data.
Scheduling Work and Activities	Scheduling events, programs, and activities, as well as the work of others.
Provide Consultation and Advice to Others	Providing guidance and expert advice to management or other groups on technical, systems-, or process-related topics.
Developing and Building Teams	Encouraging and building mutual trust, respect, and cooperation among team members.
Selling or Influencing Others	Convincing others to buy merchandise/goods or to otherwise change their minds or actions.
Analyzing Data or Information	Identifying the underlying principles, reasons, or facts of information by breaking down information or data into separate parts.
Performing General Physical Activities	Performing physical activities that require considerable use of your arms and legs and moving your whole body, such as climbing, lifting, balancing, walking, stooping, and handling of materials.
Handling and Moving Objects	Using hands and arms in handling, installing, positioning, and moving materials, and manipulating things.
Monitoring and Controlling Resources	Monitoring and controlling resources and overseeing the spending of money.
Repairing and Maintaining Electronic Equipment	Servicing, repairing, calibrating, regulating, fine-tuning, or testing machines, devices, and equipment that operate primarily on the basis of electrical or electronic (not mechanical) principles.
Estimating the Quantifiable Characteristics of Pro	Estimating sizes, distances, and quantities; or determining time, costs, resources, or materials needed to perform a work activity.
Controlling Machines and Processes	Using either control mechanisms or direct physical activity to operate machines or processes (not including computers or vehicles).
Repairing and Maintaining Mechanical Equipment	Servicing, repairing, adjusting, and testing machines, devices, moving parts, and equipment that operate primarily on the basis of mechanical (not electronic) principles.
Operating Vehicles, Mechanized Devices, or Equipme	Running, maneuvering, navigating, or driving vehicles or mechanized equipment, such as forklifts, passenger vehicles, aircraft, or water craft.

Drafting, Laying Out, and Specifying Technical Dev	Providing documentation, detailed instructions, drawings, or specifications to tell others about how devices, parts, equipment, or structures are to be fabricated, constructed, assembled, modified, maintained, or used.
Staffing Organizational Units	Recruiting, interviewing, selecting, hiring, and promoting employees in an organization.

Work_Context	**Work_Context Definitions**
Face-to-Face Discussions	How often do you have to have face-to-face discussions with individuals or teams in this job?
Contact With Others	How much does this job require the worker to be in contact with others (face-to-face, by telephone, or otherwise) in order to perform it?
Freedom to Make Decisions	How much decision making freedom, without supervision, does the job offer?
Structured versus Unstructured Work	To what extent is this job structured for the worker, rather than allowing the worker to determine tasks, priorities, and goals?
Telephone	How often do you have telephone conversations in this job?
Impact of Decisions on Co-workers or Company Resul	How do the decisions an employee makes impact the results of co-workers, clients or the company?
Public Speaking	How often do you have to perform public speaking in this job?
Work With Work Group or Team	How important is it to work with others in a group or team in this job?
Importance of Being Exact or Accurate	How important is being very exact or highly accurate in performing this job?
Frequency of Decision Making	How frequently is the worker required to make decisions that affect other people, the financial resources, and/or the image and reputation of the organization?
Physical Proximity	To what extent does this job require the worker to perform job tasks in close physical proximity to other people?
Coordinate or Lead Others	How important is it to coordinate or lead others in accomplishing work activities in this job?
Indoors, Environmentally Controlled	How often does this job require working indoors in environmentally controlled conditions?
Electronic Mail	How often do you use electronic mail in this job?
Letters and Memos	How often does the job require written letters and memos?
Time Pressure	How often does this job require the worker to meet strict deadlines?
Responsible for Others' Health and Safety	How much responsibility is there for the health and safety of others in this job?
Responsibility for Outcomes and Results	How responsible is the worker for work outcomes and results of other workers?
Spend Time Standing	How much does this job require standing?
Deal With External Customers	How important is it to work with external customers or the public in this job?
Importance of Repeating Same Tasks	How important is repeating the same physical activities (e.g., key entry) or mental activities (e.g., checking entries in a ledger) over and over, without stopping, to performing this job?
Deal With Unpleasant or Angry People	How frequently does the worker have to deal with unpleasant, angry, or discourteous individuals as part of the job requirements?
Spend Time Using Your Hands to Handle, Control, or	How much does this job require using your hands to handle, control, or feel objects, tools or controls?
Frequency of Conflict Situations	How often are there conflict situations the employee has to face in this job?
Level of Competition	To what extent does this job require the worker to compete or to be aware of competitive pressures?
Exposed to Contaminants	How often does this job require working exposed to contaminants (such as pollutants, gases, dust or odors)?
Sounds, Noise Levels Are Distracting or Uncomforta	How often does this job require working exposed to sounds and noise levels that are distracting or uncomfortable?
Spend Time Making Repetitive Motions	How much does this job require making repetitive motions?
Wear Common Protective or Safety Equipment such as	How much does this job require wearing common protective or safety equipment such as safety shoes, glasses, gloves, hard hats or life jackets?
Spend Time Sitting	How much does this job require sitting?
Spend Time Walking and Running	How much does this job require walking and running?
Consequence of Error	How serious would the result usually be if the worker made a mistake that was not readily correctable?
Degree of Automation	How automated is the job?
Spend Time Bending or Twisting the Body	How much does this job require bending or twisting your body?

Exposed to Disease or Infections	How often does this job require exposure to disease/infections?
Exposed to Minor Burns, Cuts, Bites, or Stings	How often does this job require exposure to minor burns, cuts, bites, or stings?
Cramped Work Space, Awkward Positions	How often does this job require working in cramped work spaces that requires getting into awkward positions?
Deal With Physically Aggressive People	How frequently does this job require the worker to deal with physical aggression of violent individuals?
Exposed to Hazardous Conditions	How often does this job require exposure to hazardous conditions?
Indoors, Not Environmentally Controlled	How often does this job require working indoors in non-controlled environmental conditions (e.g., warehouse without heat)?
In an Enclosed Vehicle or Equipment	How often does this job require working in a closed vehicle or equipment (e.g., car)?
Exposed to Hazardous Equipment	How often does this job require exposure to hazardous equipment?
Extremely Bright or Inadequate Lighting	How often does this job require working in extremely bright or inadequate lighting conditions?
Very Hot or Cold Temperatures	How often does this job require working in very hot (above 90 F degrees) or very cold (below 32 F degrees) temperatures?
Spend Time Kneeling, Crouching, Stooping, or Crawl	How much does this job require kneeling, crouching, stooping, or crawling?
Spend Time Keeping or Regaining Balance	How much does this job require keeping or regaining your balance?
Outdoors, Exposed to Weather	How often does this job require working outdoors, exposed to all weather conditions?
Pace Determined by Speed of Equipment	How important is it to this job that the pace is determined by the speed of equipment or machinery? (This does not refer to keeping busy at all times on this job.)
Exposed to Radiation	How often does this job require exposure to radiation?
Outdoors, Under Cover	How often does this job require working outdoors, under cover (e.g., structure with roof but no walls)?
Wear Specialized Protective or Safety Equipment su	How much does this job require wearing specialized protective or safety equipment such as breathing apparatus, safety harness, full protection suits, or radiation protection?
Spend Time Climbing Ladders, Scaffolds, or Poles	How much does this job require climbing ladders, scaffolds, or poles?
In an Open Vehicle or Equipment	How often does this job require working in an open vehicle or equipment (e.g., tractor)?
Exposed to High Places	How often does this job require exposure to high places?
Exposed to Whole Body Vibration	How often does this job require exposure to whole body vibration (e.g., operate a jackhammer)?

Job Zone Component	**Job Zone Component Definitions**
Title	Job Zone Four: Considerable Preparation Needed
Overall Experience	A minimum of two to four years of work-related skill, knowledge, or experience is needed for these occupations. For example, an accountant must complete four years of college and work for several years in accounting to be considered qualified.
Job Training	Employees in these occupations usually need several years of work-related experience, on-the-job training, and/or vocational training.
Job Zone Examples	Many of these occupations involve coordinating, supervising, managing, or training others. Examples include accountants, chefs and head cooks, computer programmers, historians, pharmacists, and police detectives.
SVP Range	(7.0 to < 8.0)
Education	Most of these occupations require a four - year bachelor's degree, but some do not.

Work_Styles	**Work_Styles Definitions**
Dependability	Job requires being reliable, responsible, and dependable, and fulfilling obligations.
Integrity	Job requires being honest and ethical.
Leadership	Job requires a willingness to lead, take charge, and offer opinions and direction.
Attention to Detail	Job requires being careful about detail and thorough in completing work tasks.
Cooperation	Job requires being pleasant with others on the job and displaying a good-natured, cooperative attitude.

Independence	Job requires developing one's own ways of doing things, guiding oneself with little or no supervision, and depending on oneself to get things done.
Self Control	Job requires maintaining composure, keeping emotions in check, controlling anger, and avoiding aggressive behavior, even in very difficult situations.
Adaptability/Flexibility	Job requires being open to change (positive or negative) and to considerable variety in the workplace.
Concern for Others	Job requires being sensitive to others' needs and feelings and being understanding and helpful on the job.
Initiative	Job requires a willingness to take on responsibilities and challenges.
Stress Tolerance	Job requires accepting criticism and dealing calmly and effectively with high stress situations.
Innovation	Job requires creativity and alternative thinking to develop new ideas for and answers to work-related problems.
Achievement/Effort	Job requires establishing and maintaining personally challenging achievement goals and exerting effort toward mastering tasks.
Persistence	Job requires persistence in the face of obstacles.
Analytical Thinking	Job requires analyzing information and using logic to address work-related issues and problems.
Social Orientation	Job requires preferring to work with others rather than alone, and being personally connected with others on the job.

25-2011.00 - Preschool Teachers, Except Special Education

Instruct children (normally up to 5 years of age) in activities designed to promote social, physical, and intellectual growth needed for primary school in preschool, day care center, or other child development facility. May be required to hold State certification.

Tasks

1) Provide a variety of materials and resources for children to explore, manipulate and use, both in learning activities and in imaginative play.

2) Organize and label materials, and display students' work in a manner appropriate for their ages and perceptual skills.

3) Demonstrate activities to children.

4) Attend professional meetings, educational conferences, and teacher training workshops in order to maintain and improve professional competence.

5) Prepare materials and classrooms for class activities.

6) Observe and evaluate children's performance, behavior, social development, and physical health.

7) Teach basic skills such as color, shape, number and letter recognition, personal hygiene, and social skills.

8) Read books to entire classes or to small groups.

9) Organize and lead activities designed to promote physical, mental and social development, such as games, arts and crafts, music, storytelling, and field trips.

10) Assimilate arriving children to the school environment by greeting them, helping them remove outerwear, and selecting activities of interest to them.

11) Establish clear objectives for all lessons, units, and projects, and communicate those objectives to children.

12) Teach proper eating habits and personal hygiene.

13) Attend staff meetings, and serve on committees as required.

14) Arrange indoor and outdoor space to facilitate creative play, motor-skill activities, and safety.

15) Adapt teaching methods and instructional materials to meet students' varying needs and interests.

16) Serve meals and snacks in accordance with nutritional guidelines.

17) Identify children showing signs of emotional, developmental, or health-related problems, and discuss them with supervisors, parents or guardians, and child development specialists.

18) Enforce all administration policies and rules governing students.

19) Meet with parents and guardians to discuss their children's progress and needs, determine their priorities for their children, and suggest ways that they can promote learning and development.

20) Plan and conduct activities for a balanced program of instruction, demonstration, and work time that provides students with opportunities to observe, question, and investigate.

21) Plan and supervise class projects, field trips, visits by guests, or other experiential activities, and guide students in learning from those activities.

22) Prepare reports on students and activities as required by administration.

23) Confer with other staff members to plan and schedule lessons promoting learning, following approved curricula.

24) Collaborate with other teachers and administrators in the development, evaluation, and revision of preschool programs.

25) Maintain accurate and complete student records as required by laws, district policies, and administrative regulations.

26) Meet with other professionals to discuss individual students' needs and progress.

27) Select, store, order, issue, and inventory classroom equipment, materials, and supplies.

28) Attend to children's basic needs by feeding them, dressing them, and changing their diapers.

29) Supervise, evaluate, and plan assignments for teacher assistants and volunteers.

30) Administer tests to help determine children's developmental levels, needs, and potential.

31) Prepare and implement remedial programs for students requiring extra help.

32) Perform administrative duties such as hall and cafeteria monitoring, and bus loading and unloading.

33) Provide disabled students with assistive devices, supportive technology, and assistance accessing facilities such as restrooms.

Knowledge	Knowledge Definitions
Customer and Personal Service	Knowledge of principles and processes for providing customer and personal services. This includes customer needs assessment, meeting quality standards for services, and evaluation of customer satisfaction.
Psychology	Knowledge of human behavior and performance; individual differences in ability, personality, and interests; learning and motivation; psychological research methods; and the assessment and treatment of behavioral and affective disorders.
Education and Training	Knowledge of principles and methods for curriculum and training design, teaching and instruction for individuals and groups, and the measurement of training effects.
English Language	Knowledge of the structure and content of the English language including the meaning and spelling of words, rules of composition, and grammar.
Public Safety and Security	Knowledge of relevant equipment, policies, procedures, and strategies to promote effective local, state, or national security operations for the protection of people, data, property, and institutions.
Administration and Management	Knowledge of business and management principles involved in strategic planning, resource allocation, human resources modeling, leadership technique, production methods, and coordination of people and resources.
Sociology and Anthropology	Knowledge of group behavior and dynamics, societal trends and influences, human migrations, ethnicity, cultures and their history and origins.
Clerical	Knowledge of administrative and clerical procedures and systems such as word processing, managing files and records, stenography and transcription, designing forms, and other office procedures and terminology.
Philosophy and Theology	Knowledge of different philosophical systems and religions. This includes their basic principles, values, ethics, ways of thinking, customs, practices, and their impact on human culture.
Medicine and Dentistry	Knowledge of the information and techniques needed to diagnose and treat human injuries, diseases, and deformities. This includes symptoms, treatment alternatives, drug properties and interactions, and preventive health-care measures.
Computers and Electronics	Knowledge of circuit boards, processors, chips, electronic equipment, and computer hardware and software, including applications and programming.
Communications and Media	Knowledge of media production, communication, and dissemination techniques and methods. This includes alternative ways to inform and entertain via written, oral, and visual media.

Personnel and Human Resources	Knowledge of principles and procedures for personnel recruitment, selection, training, compensation and benefits, labor relations and negotiation, and personnel information systems.
Law and Government	Knowledge of laws, legal codes, court procedures, precedents, government regulations, executive orders, agency rules, and the democratic political process.
Therapy and Counseling	Knowledge of principles, methods, and procedures for diagnosis, treatment, and rehabilitation of physical and mental dysfunctions, and for career counseling and guidance.
Mathematics	Knowledge of arithmetic, algebra, geometry, calculus, statistics, and their applications.
Fine Arts	Knowledge of the theory and techniques required to compose, produce, and perform works of music, dance, visual arts, drama, and sculpture.
Foreign Language	Knowledge of the structure and content of a foreign (non-English) language including the meaning and spelling of words, rules of composition and grammar, and pronunciation.
Geography	Knowledge of principles and methods for describing the features of land, sea, and air masses, including their physical characteristics, locations, interrelationships, and distribution of plant, animal, and human life.
History and Archeology	Knowledge of historical events and their causes, indicators, and effects on civilizations and cultures.
Telecommunications	Knowledge of transmission, broadcasting, switching, control, and operation of telecommunications systems.
Transportation	Knowledge of principles and methods for moving people or goods by air, rail, sea, or road, including the relative costs and benefits.
Biology	Knowledge of plant and animal organisms, their tissues, cells, functions, interdependencies, and interactions with each other and the environment.
Design	Knowledge of design techniques, tools, and principles involved in production of precision technical plans, blueprints, drawings, and models.
Economics and Accounting	Knowledge of economic and accounting principles and practices, the financial markets, banking and the analysis and reporting of financial data.
Sales and Marketing	Knowledge of principles and methods for showing, promoting, and selling products or services. This includes marketing strategy and tactics, product demonstration, sales techniques, and sales control systems.
Food Production	Knowledge of techniques and equipment for planting, growing, and harvesting food products (both plant and animal) for consumption, including storage/handling techniques.
Chemistry	Knowledge of the chemical composition, structure, and properties of substances and of the chemical processes and transformations that they undergo. This includes uses of chemicals and their interactions, danger signs, production techniques, and disposal methods.
Engineering and Technology	Knowledge of the practical application of engineering science and technology. This includes applying principles, techniques, procedures, and equipment to the design and production of various goods and services.
Production and Processing	Knowledge of raw materials, production processes, quality control, costs, and other techniques for maximizing the effective manufacture and distribution of goods.
Mechanical	Knowledge of machines and tools, including their designs, uses, repair, and maintenance.
Physics	Knowledge and prediction of physical principles, laws, their interrelationships, and applications to understanding fluid, material, and atmospheric dynamics, and mechanical, electrical, atomic and sub-atomic structures and processes.
Building and Construction	Knowledge of materials, methods, and the tools involved in the construction or repair of houses, buildings, or other structures such as highways and roads.

Skills	Skills Definitions
Active Listening	Giving full attention to what other people are saying, taking time to understand the points being made, asking questions as appropriate, and not interrupting at inappropriate times.
Instructing	Teaching others how to do something.
Speaking	Talking to others to convey information effectively.
Reading Comprehension	Understanding written sentences and paragraphs in work related documents.

Learning Strategies	Selecting and using training/instructional methods and procedures appropriate for the situation when learning or teaching new things.
Writing	Communicating effectively in writing as appropriate for the needs of the audience.
Social Perceptiveness	Being aware of others' reactions and understanding why they react as they do.
Time Management	Managing one's own time and the time of others.
Critical Thinking	Using logic and reasoning to identify the strengths and weaknesses of alternative solutions, conclusions or approaches to problems.
Monitoring	Monitoring/Assessing performance of yourself, other individuals, or organizations to make improvements or take corrective action.
Service Orientation	Actively looking for ways to help people.
Active Learning	Understanding the implications of new information for both current and future problem-solving and decision-making.
Negotiation	Bringing others together and trying to reconcile differences.
Coordination	Adjusting actions in relation to others' actions.
Judgment and Decision Making	Considering the relative costs and benefits of potential actions to choose the most appropriate one.
Persuasion	Persuading others to change their minds or behavior.
Management of Personnel Resources	Motivating, developing, and directing people as they work, identifying the best people for the job.
Complex Problem Solving	Identifying complex problems and reviewing related information to develop and evaluate options and implement solutions.
Management of Material Resources	Obtaining and seeing to the appropriate use of equipment, facilities, and materials needed to do certain work.
Mathematics	Using mathematics to solve problems.
Equipment Selection	Determining the kind of tools and equipment needed to do a job.
Science	Using scientific rules and methods to solve problems.
Operations Analysis	Analyzing needs and product requirements to create a design.
Operation and Control	Controlling operations of equipment or systems.
Management of Financial Resources	Determining how money will be spent to get the work done, and accounting for these expenditures.
Systems Evaluation	Identifying measures or indicators of system performance and the actions needed to improve or correct performance, relative to the goals of the system.
Troubleshooting	Determining causes of operating errors and deciding what to do about it.
Technology Design	Generating or adapting equipment and technology to serve user needs.
Systems Analysis	Determining how a system should work and how changes in conditions, operations, and the environment will affect outcomes.
Equipment Maintenance	Performing routine maintenance on equipment and determining when and what kind of maintenance is needed.
Installation	Installing equipment, machines, wiring, or programs to meet specifications.
Programming	Writing computer programs for various purposes.
Quality Control Analysis	Conducting tests and inspections of products, services, or processes to evaluate quality or performance.
Repairing	Repairing machines or systems using the needed tools.
Operation Monitoring	Watching gauges, dials, or other indicators to make sure a machine is working properly.

Ability	Ability Definitions
Oral Expression	The ability to communicate information and ideas in speaking so others will understand.
Speech Clarity	The ability to speak clearly so others can understand you.
Speech Recognition	The ability to identify and understand the speech of another person.
Problem Sensitivity	The ability to tell when something is wrong or is likely to go wrong. It does not involve solving the problem, only recognizing there is a problem.
Originality	The ability to come up with unusual or clever ideas about a given topic or situation, or to develop creative ways to solve a problem.
Oral Comprehension	The ability to listen to and understand information and ideas presented through spoken words and sentences.
Fluency of Ideas	The ability to come up with a number of ideas about a topic (the number of ideas is important, not their quality, correctness, or creativity).
Deductive Reasoning	The ability to apply general rules to specific problems to produce answers that make sense.

1488

Written Comprehension	The ability to read and understand information and ideas presented in writing.
Written Expression	The ability to communicate information and ideas in writing so others will understand.
Category Flexibility	The ability to generate or use different sets of rules for combining or grouping things in different ways.
Near Vision	The ability to see details at close range (within a few feet of the observer).
Information Ordering	The ability to arrange things or actions in a certain order or pattern according to a specific rule or set of rules (e.g., patterns of numbers, letters, words, pictures, mathematical operations).
Inductive Reasoning	The ability to combine pieces of information to form general rules or conclusions (includes finding a relationship among seemingly unrelated events).
Selective Attention	The ability to concentrate on a task over a period of time without being distracted.
Auditory Attention	The ability to focus on a single source of sound in the presence of other distracting sounds.
Memorization	The ability to remember information such as words, numbers, pictures, and procedures.
Speed of Closure	The ability to quickly make sense of, combine, and organize information into meaningful patterns.
Flexibility of Closure	The ability to identify or detect a known pattern (a figure, object, word, or sound) that is hidden in other distracting material.
Hearing Sensitivity	The ability to detect or tell the differences between sounds that vary in pitch and loudness.
Far Vision	The ability to see details at a distance.
Perceptual Speed	The ability to quickly and accurately compare similarities and differences among sets of letters, numbers, objects, pictures, or patterns. The things to be compared may be presented at the same time or one after the other. This ability also includes comparing a presented object with a remembered object.
Time Sharing	The ability to shift back and forth between two or more activities or sources of information (such as speech, sounds, touch, or other sources).
Visualization	The ability to imagine how something will look after it is moved around or when its parts are moved or rearranged.
Number Facility	The ability to add, subtract, multiply, or divide quickly and correctly.
Visual Color Discrimination	The ability to match or detect differences between colors, including shades of color and brightness.
Trunk Strength	The ability to use your abdominal and lower back muscles to support part of the body repeatedly or continuously over time without 'giving out' or fatiguing.
Extent Flexibility	The ability to bend, stretch, twist, or reach with your body, arms, and/or legs.
Finger Dexterity	The ability to make precisely coordinated movements of the fingers of one or both hands to grasp, manipulate, or assemble very small objects.
Arm-Hand Steadiness	The ability to keep your hand and arm steady while moving your arm or while holding your arm and hand in one position.
Gross Body Coordination	The ability to coordinate the movement of your arms, legs, and torso together when the whole body is in motion.
Static Strength	The ability to exert maximum muscle force to lift, push, pull, or carry objects.
Multilimb Coordination	The ability to coordinate two or more limbs (for example, two arms, two legs, or one leg and one arm) while sitting, standing, or lying down. It does not involve performing the activities while the whole body is in motion.
Dynamic Strength	The ability to exert muscle force repeatedly or continuously over time. This involves muscular endurance and resistance to muscle fatigue.
Stamina	The ability to exert yourself physically over long periods of time without getting winded or out of breath.
Manual Dexterity	The ability to quickly move your hand, your hand together with your arm, or your two hands to grasp, manipulate, or assemble objects.
Depth Perception	The ability to judge which of several objects is closer or farther away from you, or to judge the distance between you and an object.
Mathematical Reasoning	The ability to choose the right mathematical methods or formulas to solve a problem.
Speed of Limb Movement	The ability to quickly move the arms and legs.
Gross Body Equilibrium	The ability to keep or regain your body balance or stay upright when in an unstable position.
Control Precision	The ability to quickly and repeatedly adjust the controls of a machine or a vehicle to exact positions.

Response Orientation	The ability to choose quickly between two or more movements in response to two or more different signals (lights, sounds, pictures). It includes the speed with which the correct response is started with the hand, foot, or other body part.
Sound Localization	The ability to tell the direction from which a sound originated.
Peripheral Vision	The ability to see objects or movement of objects to one's side when the eyes are looking ahead.
Wrist-Finger Speed	The ability to make fast, simple, repeated movements of the fingers, hands, and wrists.
Reaction Time	The ability to quickly respond (with the hand, finger, or foot) to a signal (sound, light, picture) when it appears.
Night Vision	The ability to see under low light conditions.
Explosive Strength	The ability to use short bursts of muscle force to propel oneself (as in jumping or sprinting), or to throw an object.
Glare Sensitivity	The ability to see objects in the presence of glare or bright lighting.
Spatial Orientation	The ability to know your location in relation to the environment or to know where other objects are in relation to you.
Dynamic Flexibility	The ability to quickly and repeatedly bend, stretch, twist, or reach out with your body, arms, and/or legs.
Rate Control	The ability to time your movements or the movement of a piece of equipment in anticipation of changes in the speed and/or direction of a moving object or scene.

Work_Activity	Work_Activity Definitions
Assisting and Caring for Others	Providing personal assistance, medical attention, emotional support, or other personal care to others such as coworkers, customers, or patients.
Thinking Creatively	Developing, designing, or creating new applications, ideas, relationships, systems, or products, including artistic contributions.
Establishing and Maintaining Interpersonal Relatio	Developing constructive and cooperative working relationships with others, and maintaining them over time.
Communicating with Supervisors, Peers, or Subordin	Providing information to supervisors, co-workers, and subordinates by telephone, in written form, e-mail, or in person.
Getting Information	Observing, receiving, and otherwise obtaining information from all relevant sources.
Organizing, Planning, and Prioritizing Work	Developing specific goals and plans to prioritize, organize, and accomplish your work.
Resolving Conflicts and Negotiating with Others	Handling complaints, settling disputes, and resolving grievances and conflicts, or otherwise negotiating with others.
Training and Teaching Others	Identifying the educational needs of others, developing formal educational or training programs or classes, and teaching or instructing others.
Making Decisions and Solving Problems	Analyzing information and evaluating results to choose the best solution and solve problems.
Evaluating Information to Determine Compliance wit	Using relevant information and individual judgment to determine whether events or processes comply with laws, regulations, or standards.
Coordinating the Work and Activities of Others	Getting members of a group to work together to accomplish tasks.
Scheduling Work and Activities	Scheduling events, programs, and activities, as well as the work of others.
Performing General Physical Activities	Performing physical activities that require considerable use of your arms and legs and moving your whole body, such as climbing, lifting, balancing, walking, stooping, and handling of materials.
Inspecting Equipment, Structures, or Material	Inspecting equipment, structures, or materials to identify the cause of errors or other problems or defects.
Communicating with Persons Outside Organization	Communicating with people outside the organization, representing the organization to customers, the public, government, and other external sources. This information can be exchanged in person, in writing, or by telephone or e-mail.
Performing for or Working Directly with the Public	Performing for people or dealing directly with the public. This includes serving customers in restaurants and stores, and receiving clients or guests.
Coaching and Developing Others	Identifying the developmental needs of others and coaching, mentoring, or otherwise helping others to improve their knowledge or skills.
Developing and Building Teams	Encouraging and building mutual trust, respect, and cooperation among team members.
Monitor Processes, Materials, or Surroundings	Monitoring and reviewing information from materials, events, or the environment, to detect or assess problems.

Judging the Qualities of Things, Services, or Peop	Assessing the value, importance, or quality of things or people.
Identifying Objects, Actions, and Events	Identifying information by categorizing, estimating, recognizing differences or similarities, and detecting changes in circumstances or events.
Documenting/Recording Information	Entering, transcribing, recording, storing, or maintaining information in written or electronic/magnetic form.
Updating and Using Relevant Knowledge	Keeping up-to-date technically and applying new knowledge to your job.
Developing Objectives and Strategies	Establishing long-range objectives and specifying the strategies and actions to achieve them.
Guiding, Directing, and Motivating Subordinates	Providing guidance and direction to subordinates, including setting performance standards and monitoring performance.
Handling and Moving Objects	Using hands and arms in handling, installing, positioning, and moving materials, and manipulating things.
Processing Information	Compiling, coding, categorizing, calculating, tabulating, auditing, or verifying information or data.
Interpreting the Meaning of Information for Others	Translating or explaining what information means and how it can be used.
Provide Consultation and Advice to Others	Providing guidance and expert advice to management or other groups on technical, systems-, or process-related topics.
Estimating the Quantifiable Characteristics of Pro	Estimating sizes, distances, and quantities; or determining time, costs, resources, or materials needed to perform a work activity.
Analyzing Data or Information	Identifying the underlying principles, reasons, or facts of information by breaking down information or data into separate parts.
Performing Administrative Activities	Performing day-to-day administrative tasks such as maintaining information files and processing paperwork.
Interacting With Computers	Using computers and computer systems (including hardware and software) to program, write software, set up functions, enter data, or process information.
Selling or Influencing Others	Convincing others to buy merchandise/goods or to otherwise change their minds or actions.
Staffing Organizational Units	Recruiting, interviewing, selecting, hiring, and promoting employees in an organization.
Controlling Machines and Processes	Using either control mechanisms or direct physical activity to operate machines or processes (not including computers or vehicles).
Monitoring and Controlling Resources	Monitoring and controlling resources and overseeing the spending of money.
Operating Vehicles, Mechanized Devices, or Equipme	Running, maneuvering, navigating, or driving vehicles or mechanized equipment, such as forklifts, passenger vehicles, aircraft, or water craft.
Repairing and Maintaining Electronic Equipment	Servicing, repairing, calibrating, regulating, fine-tuning, or testing machines, devices, and equipment that operate primarily on the basis of electrical or electronic (not mechanical) principles.
Repairing and Maintaining Mechanical Equipment	Servicing, repairing, adjusting, and testing machines, devices, moving parts, and equipment that operate primarily on the basis of mechanical (not electronic) principles.
Drafting, Laying Out, and Specifying Technical Dev	Providing documentation, detailed instructions, drawings, or specifications to tell others about how devices, parts, equipment, or structures are to be fabricated, constructed, assembled, modified, maintained, or used.

Work_Context	Work_Context Definitions
Contact With Others	How much does this job require the worker to be in contact with others (face-to-face, by telephone, or otherwise) in order to perform it?
Work With Work Group or Team	How important is it to work with others in a group or team in this job?
Physical Proximity	To what extent does this job require the worker to perform job tasks in close physical proximity to other people?
Face-to-Face Discussions	How often do you have to have face-to-face discussions with individuals or teams in this job?
Freedom to Make Decisions	How much decision making freedom, without supervision, does the job offer?
Structured versus Unstructured Work	To what extent is this job structured for the worker, rather than allowing the worker to determine tasks, priorities, and goals?
Telephone	How often do you have telephone conversations in this job?
Spend Time Standing	How much does this job require standing?
Coordinate or Lead Others	How important is it to coordinate or lead others in accomplishing work activities in this job?
Impact of Decisions on Co-workers or Company Resul	How do the decisions an employee makes impact the results of co-workers, clients or the company?

Letters and Memos	How often does the job require written letters and memos?
Indoors, Environmentally Controlled	How often does this job require working indoors in environmentally controlled conditions?
Frequency of Decision Making	How frequently is the worker required to make decisions that affect other people, the financial resources, and/or the image and reputation of the organization?
Deal With External Customers	How important is it to work with external customers or the public in this job?
Spend Time Bending or Twisting the Body	How much does this job require bending or twisting your body?
Spend Time Walking and Running	How much does this job require walking and running?
Importance of Being Exact or Accurate	How important is being very exact or highly accurate in performing this job?
Outdoors, Exposed to Weather	How often does this job require working outdoors, exposed to all weather conditions?
Spend Time Kneeling, Crouching, Stooping, or Crawl	How much does this job require kneeling, crouching, stooping, or crawling?
Spend Time Making Repetitive Motions	How much does this job require making repetitive motions?
Exposed to Disease or Infections	How often does this job require exposure to disease/infections?
Deal With Unpleasant or Angry People	How frequently does the worker have to deal with unpleasant, angry, or discourteous individuals as part of the job requirements?
Responsible for Others' Health and Safety	How much responsibility is there for the health and safety of others in this job?
Frequency of Conflict Situations	How often are there conflict situations the employee has to face in this job?
Consequence of Error	How serious would the result usually be if the worker made a mistake that was not readily correctable?
Time Pressure	How often does this job require the worker to meet strict deadlines?
Spend Time Using Your Hands to Handle, Control, or	How much does this job require using your hands to handle, control, or feel objects, tools or controls?
Sounds, Noise Levels Are Distracting or Uncomforta	How often does this job require working exposed to sounds and noise levels that are distracting or uncomfortable?
Responsibility for Outcomes and Results	How responsible is the worker for work outcomes and results of other workers?
Spend Time Sitting	How much does this job require sitting?
Exposed to Minor Burns, Cuts, Bites, or Stings	How often does this job require exposure to minor burns, cuts, bites, or stings?
Importance of Repeating Same Tasks	How important is repeating the same physical activities (e.g., key entry) or mental activities (e.g., checking entries in a ledger) over and over, without stopping, to performing this job?
Exposed to Contaminants	How often does this job require working exposed to contaminants (such as pollutants, gases, dust or odors)?
Public Speaking	How often do you have to perform public speaking in this job?
Level of Competition	To what extent does this job require the worker to compete or to be aware of competitive pressures?
Wear Common Protective or Safety Equipment such as	How much does this job require wearing common protective or safety equipment such as safety shoes, glasses, gloves, hard hats or live jackets?
Spend Time Keeping or Regaining Balance	How much does this job require keeping or regaining your balance?
Deal With Physically Aggressive People	How frequently does this job require the worker to deal with physical aggression of violent individuals?
Degree of Automation	How automated is the job?
Electronic Mail	How often do you use electronic mail in this job?
Very Hot or Cold Temperatures	How often does this job require working in very hot (above 90 F degrees) or very cold (below 32 F degrees) temperatures?
In an Enclosed Vehicle or Equipment	How often does this job require working in a closed vehicle or equipment (e.g., car)?
Outdoors, Under Cover	How often does this job require working outdoors, under cover (e.g., structure with roof but no walls)?
Indoors, Not Environmentally Controlled	How often does this job require working indoors in non-controlled environmental conditions (e.g., warehouse without heat)?
Cramped Work Space, Awkward Positions	How often does this job require working in cramped work spaces that requires getting into awkward positions?
Extremely Bright or Inadequate Lighting	How often does this job require working in extremely bright or inadequate lighting conditions?
Pace Determined by Speed of Equipment	How important is it to this job that the pace is determined by the speed of equipment or machinery? (This does not refer to keeping busy at all times on this job.)

Spend Time Climbing Ladders, Scaffolds, or Poles	How much does this job require climbing ladders, scaffolds, or poles?
Exposed to Radiation	How often does this job require exposure to radiation?
Exposed to High Places	How often does this job require exposure to high places?
Wear Specialized Protective or Safety Equipment su	How much does this job require wearing specialized protective or safety equipment such as breathing apparatus, safety harness, full protection suits, or radiation protection?
Exposed to Hazardous Conditions	How often does this job require exposure to hazardous conditions?
Exposed to Whole Body Vibration	How often does this job require exposure to whole body vibration (e.g., operate a jackhammer)?
Exposed to Hazardous Equipment	How often does this job require exposure to hazardous equipment?
In an Open Vehicle or Equipment	How often does this job require working in an open vehicle or equipment (e.g., tractor)?

Job Zone Component	Job Zone Component Definitions
Title	Job Zone Three: Medium Preparation Needed
Overall Experience	Previous work-related skill, knowledge, or experience is required for these occupations. For example, an electrician must have completed three or four years of apprenticeship or several years of vocational training, and often must have passed a licensing exam, in order to perform the job.
Job Training	Employees in these occupations usually need one or two years of training involving both on-the-job experience and informal training with experienced workers.
Job Zone Examples	These occupations usually involve using communication and organizational skills to coordinate, supervise, manage, or train others to accomplish goals. Examples include dental assistants, electricians, fish and game wardens, legal secretaries, personnel recruiters, and recreation workers.
SVP Range	(6.0 to < 7.0)
Education	Most occupations in this zone require training in vocational schools, related on-the-job experience, or an associate's degree. Some may require a bachelor's degree.

Work_Styles	Work_Styles Definitions
Self Control	Job requires maintaining composure, keeping emotions in check, controlling anger, and avoiding aggressive behavior, even in very difficult situations.
Dependability	Job requires being reliable, responsible, and dependable, and fulfilling obligations.
Concern for Others	Job requires being sensitive to others' needs and feelings and being understanding and helpful on the job.
Integrity	Job requires being honest and ethical.
Cooperation	Job requires being pleasant with others on the job and displaying a good-natured, cooperative attitude.
Social Orientation	Job requires preferring to work with others rather than alone, and being personally connected with others on the job.
Adaptability/Flexibility	Job requires being open to change (positive or negative) and to considerable variety in the workplace.
Stress Tolerance	Job requires accepting criticism and dealing calmly and effectively with high stress situations.
Leadership	Job requires a willingness to lead, take charge, and offer opinions and direction.
Initiative	Job requires a willingness to take on responsibilities and challenges.
Innovation	Job requires creativity and alternative thinking to develop new ideas for and answers to work-related problems.
Independence	Job requires developing one's own ways of doing things, guiding oneself with little or no supervision, and depending on oneself to get things done.
Attention to Detail	Job requires being careful about detail and thorough in completing work tasks.
Persistence	Job requires persistence in the face of obstacles.
Achievement/Effort	Job requires establishing and maintaining personally challenging achievement goals and exerting effort toward mastering tasks.
Analytical Thinking	Job requires analyzing information and using logic to address work-related issues and problems.

25-2012.00 - Kindergarten Teachers, Except Special Education

Teach elemental natural and social science, personal hygiene, music, art, and literature to children from 4 to 6 years old. Promote physical, mental, and social development. May be required to hold State certification.

Tasks

1) Prepare children for later grades by encouraging them to explore learning opportunities and to persevere with challenging tasks.

2) Confer with other staff members to plan and schedule lessons promoting learning, following approved curricula.

3) Prepare objectives and outlines for courses of study, following curriculum guidelines or requirements of states and schools.

4) Organize and label materials and display children's work in a manner appropriate for their sizes and perceptual skills.

5) Establish and enforce rules for behavior, and policies and procedures to maintain order among students.

6) Identify children showing signs of emotional, developmental, or health-related problems, and discuss them with supervisors, parents or guardians, and child development specialists.

7) Instruct and monitor students in the use and care of equipment and materials, in order to prevent injuries and damage.

8) Select, store, order, issue, and inventory classroom equipment, materials, and supplies.

9) Collaborate with other teachers and administrators in the development, evaluation, and revision of kindergarten programs.

10) Prepare materials, classrooms, and other indoor and outdoor spaces to facilitate creative play, learning and motor-skill activities, and safety.

11) Use computers, audiovisual aids, and other equipment and materials to supplement presentations.

12) Involve parent volunteers and older students in children's activities, in order to facilitate involvement in focused, complex play.

13) Assimilate arriving children to the school environment by greeting them, helping them remove outerwear, and selecting activities of interest to them.

14) Prepare and implement remedial programs for students requiring extra help.

15) Prepare, administer, and grade tests and assignments to evaluate children's progress.

16) Prepare for assigned classes, and show written evidence of preparation upon request of immediate supervisors.

17) Guide and counsel students with adjustment and/or academic problems, or special academic interests.

18) Supervise, evaluate, and plan assignments for teacher assistants and volunteers.

19) Perform administrative duties such as assisting in school libraries, hall and cafeteria monitoring, and bus loading and unloading.

20) Administer standardized ability and achievement tests, and interpret results to determine children's developmental levels and needs.

21) Provide disabled students with assistive devices, supportive technology, and assistance accessing facilities such as restrooms.

22) Plan and supervise class projects, field trips, visits by guests, or other experiential activities, and guide students in learning from those activities.

23) Meet with parents and guardians to discuss their children's progress, and to determine their priorities for their children and their resource needs.

24) Maintain accurate and complete student records, and prepare reports on children and activities, as required by laws, district policies, and administrative regulations.

25) Teach basic skills such as color, shape, number and letter recognition, personal hygiene, and social skills.

26) Attend professional meetings, educational conferences, and teacher training workshops in order to maintain and improve professional competence.

27) Provide a variety of materials and resources for children to explore, manipulate, and use, both in learning activities and in imaginative play.

28) Observe and evaluate children's performance, behavior, social development, and physical health.

29) Instruct students individually and in groups, adapting teaching methods to meet students' varying needs and interests.

30) Demonstrate activities to children.

31) Attend staff meetings, and serve on committees as required.

32) Organize and lead activities designed to promote physical, mental, and social development such as games, arts and crafts, music, and storytelling.

33) Confer with parents or guardians, other teachers, counselors, and administrators to resolve students' behavioral and academic problems.

34) Plan and conduct activities for a balanced program of instruction, demonstration, and work time that provides students with opportunities to observe, question, and investigate.

35) Establish clear objectives for all lessons, units, and projects, and communicate those objectives to children.

36) Read books to entire classes or to small groups.

Knowledge	Knowledge Definitions
English Language	Knowledge of the structure and content of the English language including the meaning and spelling of words, rules of composition, and grammar.
Education and Training	Knowledge of principles and methods for curriculum and training design, teaching and instruction for individuals and groups, and the measurement of training effects.
Psychology	Knowledge of human behavior and performance; individual differences in ability, personality, and interests; learning and motivation; psychological research methods; and the assessment and treatment of behavioral and affective disorders.
Mathematics	Knowledge of arithmetic, algebra, geometry, calculus, statistics, and their applications.
Sociology and Anthropology	Knowledge of group behavior and dynamics, societal trends and influences, human migrations, ethnicity, cultures and their history and origins.
Geography	Knowledge of principles and methods for describing the features of land, sea, and air masses, including their physical characteristics, locations, interrelationships, and distribution of plant, animal, and human life.
History and Archeology	Knowledge of historical events and their causes, indicators, and effects on civilizations and cultures.
Public Safety and Security	Knowledge of relevant equipment, policies, procedures, and strategies to promote effective local, state, or national security operations for the protection of people, data, property, and institutions.
Customer and Personal Service	Knowledge of principles and processes for providing customer and personal services. This includes customer needs assessment, meeting quality standards for services, and evaluation of customer satisfaction.
Computers and Electronics	Knowledge of circuit boards, processors, chips, electronic equipment, and computer hardware and software, including applications and programming.
Communications and Media	Knowledge of media production, communication, and dissemination techniques and methods. This includes alternative ways to inform and entertain via written, oral, and visual media.
Administration and Management	Knowledge of business and management principles involved in strategic planning, resource allocation, human resources modeling, leadership technique, production methods, and coordination of people and resources.
Therapy and Counseling	Knowledge of principles, methods, and procedures for diagnosis, treatment, and rehabilitation of physical and mental dysfunctions, and for career counseling and guidance.
Philosophy and Theology	Knowledge of different philosophical systems and religions. This includes their basic principles, values, ethics, ways of thinking, customs, practices, and their impact on human culture.
Clerical	Knowledge of administrative and clerical procedures and systems such as word processing, managing files and records, stenography and transcription, designing forms, and other office procedures and terminology.
Fine Arts	Knowledge of the theory and techniques required to compose, produce, and perform works of music, dance, visual arts, drama, and sculpture.
Biology	Knowledge of plant and animal organisms, their tissues, cells, functions, interdependencies, and interactions with each other and the environment.
Medicine and Dentistry	Knowledge of the information and techniques needed to diagnose and treat human injuries, diseases, and deformities. This includes symptoms, treatment alternatives, drug properties and interactions, and preventive health-care measures.
Law and Government	Knowledge of laws, legal codes, court procedures, precedents, government regulations, executive orders, agency rules, and the democratic political process.
Foreign Language	Knowledge of the structure and content of a foreign (non-English) language including the meaning and spelling of words, rules of composition and grammar, and pronunciation.
Personnel and Human Resources	Knowledge of principles and procedures for personnel recruitment, selection, training, compensation and benefits, labor relations and negotiation, and personnel information systems.
Transportation	Knowledge of principles and methods for moving people or goods by air, rail, sea, or road, including the relative costs and benefits.
Telecommunications	Knowledge of transmission, broadcasting, switching, control, and operation of telecommunications systems.
Design	Knowledge of design techniques, tools, and principles involved in production of precision technical plans, blueprints, drawings, and models.
Chemistry	Knowledge of the chemical composition, structure, and properties of substances and of the chemical processes and transformations that they undergo. This includes uses of chemicals and their interactions, danger signs, production techniques, and disposal methods.
Physics	Knowledge and prediction of physical principles, laws, their interrelationships, and applications to understanding fluid, material, and atmospheric dynamics, and mechanical, electrical, atomic and sub-atomic structures and processes.
Sales and Marketing	Knowledge of principles and methods for showing, promoting, and selling products or services. This includes marketing strategy and tactics, product demonstration, sales techniques, and sales control systems.
Food Production	Knowledge of techniques and equipment for planting, growing, and harvesting food products (both plant and animal) for consumption, including storage/handling techniques.
Production and Processing	Knowledge of raw materials, production processes, quality control, costs, and other techniques for maximizing the effective manufacture and distribution of goods.
Engineering and Technology	Knowledge of the practical application of engineering science and technology. This includes applying principles, techniques, procedures, and equipment to the design and production of various goods and services.
Economics and Accounting	Knowledge of economic and accounting principles and practices, the financial markets, banking and the analysis and reporting of financial data.
Mechanical	Knowledge of machines and tools, including their designs, uses, repair, and maintenance.
Building and Construction	Knowledge of materials, methods, and the tools involved in the construction or repair of houses, buildings, or other structures such as highways and roads.

Skills	Skills Definitions
Instructing	Teaching others how to do something.
Reading Comprehension	Understanding written sentences and paragraphs in work related documents.
Speaking	Talking to others to convey information effectively.
Monitoring	Monitoring/Assessing performance of yourself, other individuals, or organizations to make improvements or take corrective action.
Learning Strategies	Selecting and using training/instructional methods and procedures appropriate for the situation when learning or teaching new things.
Active Listening	Giving full attention to what other people are saying, taking time to understand the points being made, asking questions as appropriate, and not interrupting at inappropriate times.
Time Management	Managing one's own time and the time of others.
Writing	Communicating effectively in writing as appropriate for the needs of the audience.
Active Learning	Understanding the implications of new information for both current and future problem-solving and decision-making.
Social Perceptiveness	Being aware of others' reactions and understanding why they react as they do.
Critical Thinking	Using logic and reasoning to identify the strengths and weaknesses of alternative solutions, conclusions or approaches to problems.
Coordination	Adjusting actions in relation to others' actions.
Mathematics	Using mathematics to solve problems.
Service Orientation	Actively looking for ways to help people.

Complex Problem Solving	Identifying complex problems and reviewing related information to develop and evaluate options and implement solutions.
Persuasion	Persuading others to change their minds or behavior.
Negotiation	Bringing others together and trying to reconcile differences.
Science	Using scientific rules and methods to solve problems.
Judgment and Decision Making	Considering the relative costs and benefits of potential actions to choose the most appropriate one.
Equipment Selection	Determining the kind of tools and equipment needed to do a job.
Management of Material Resources	Obtaining and seeing to the appropriate use of equipment, facilities, and materials needed to do certain work.
Management of Personnel Resources	Motivating, developing, and directing people as they work, identifying the best people for the job.
Technology Design	Generating or adapting equipment and technology to serve user needs.
Operations Analysis	Analyzing needs and product requirements to create a design.
Systems Evaluation	Identifying measures or indicators of system performance and the actions needed to improve or correct performance, relative to the goals of the system.
Management of Financial Resources	Determining how money will be spent to get the work done, and accounting for these expenditures.
Quality Control Analysis	Conducting tests and inspections of products, services, or processes to evaluate quality or performance.
Troubleshooting	Determining causes of operating errors and deciding what to do about it.
Systems Analysis	Determining how a system should work and how changes in conditions, operations, and the environment will affect outcomes.
Operation and Control	Controlling operations of equipment or systems.
Equipment Maintenance	Performing routine maintenance on equipment and determining when and what kind of maintenance is needed.
Repairing	Repairing machines or systems using the needed tools.
Installation	Installing equipment, machines, wiring, or programs to meet specifications.
Programming	Writing computer programs for various purposes.
Operation Monitoring	Watching gauges, dials, or other indicators to make sure a machine is working properly.

Ability	**Ability Definitions**
Speech Recognition	The ability to identify and understand the speech of another person.
Oral Expression	The ability to communicate information and ideas in speaking so others will understand.
Speech Clarity	The ability to speak clearly so others can understand you.
Oral Comprehension	The ability to listen to and understand information and ideas presented through spoken words and sentences.
Deductive Reasoning	The ability to apply general rules to specific problems to produce answers that make sense.
Written Expression	The ability to communicate information and ideas in writing so others will understand.
Problem Sensitivity	The ability to tell when something is wrong or is likely to go wrong. It does not involve solving the problem, only recognizing there is a problem.
Information Ordering	The ability to arrange things or actions in a certain order or pattern according to a specific rule or set of rules (e.g., patterns of numbers, letters, words, pictures, mathematical operations).
Near Vision	The ability to see details at close range (within a few feet of the observer).
Inductive Reasoning	The ability to combine pieces of information to form general rules or conclusions (includes finding a relationship among seemingly unrelated events).
Fluency of Ideas	The ability to come up with a number of ideas about a topic (the number of ideas is important, not their quality, correctness, or creativity).
Written Comprehension	The ability to read and understand information and ideas presented in writing.
Originality	The ability to come up with unusual or clever ideas about a given topic or situation, or to develop creative ways to solve a problem.
Category Flexibility	The ability to generate or use different sets of rules for combining or grouping things in different ways.
Selective Attention	The ability to concentrate on a task over a period of time without being distracted.
Far Vision	The ability to see details at a distance.

Flexibility of Closure	The ability to identify or detect a known pattern (a figure, object, word, or sound) that is hidden in other distracting material.
Time Sharing	The ability to shift back and forth between two or more activities or sources of information (such as speech, sounds, touch, or other sources).
Perceptual Speed	The ability to quickly and accurately compare similarities and differences among sets of letters, numbers, objects, pictures, or patterns. The things to be compared may be presented at the same time or one after the other. This ability also includes comparing a presented object with a remembered object.
Auditory Attention	The ability to focus on a single source of sound in the presence of other distracting sounds.
Speed of Closure	The ability to quickly make sense of, combine, and organize information into meaningful patterns.
Memorization	The ability to remember information such as words, numbers, pictures, and procedures.
Hearing Sensitivity	The ability to detect or tell the differences between sounds that vary in pitch and loudness.
Visual Color Discrimination	The ability to match or detect differences between colors, including shades of color and brightness.
Visualization	The ability to imagine how something will look after it is moved around or when its parts are moved or rearranged.
Mathematical Reasoning	The ability to choose the right mathematical methods or formulas to solve a problem.
Number Facility	The ability to add, subtract, multiply, or divide quickly and correctly.
Finger Dexterity	The ability to make precisely coordinated movements of the fingers of one or both hands to grasp, manipulate, or assemble very small objects.
Arm-Hand Steadiness	The ability to keep your hand and arm steady while moving your arm or while holding your arm and hand in one position.
Multilimb Coordination	The ability to coordinate two or more limbs (for example, two arms, two legs, or one leg and one arm) while sitting, standing, or lying down. It does not involve performing the activities while the whole body is in motion.
Trunk Strength	The ability to use your abdominal and lower back muscles to support part of the body repeatedly or continuously over time without 'giving out' or fatiguing.
Depth Perception	The ability to judge which of several objects is closer or farther away from you, or to judge the distance between you and an object.
Stamina	The ability to exert yourself physically over long periods of time without getting winded or out of breath.
Extent Flexibility	The ability to bend, stretch, twist, or reach with your body, arms, and/or legs.
Gross Body Coordination	The ability to coordinate the movement of your arms, legs, and torso together when the whole body is in motion.
Dynamic Strength	The ability to exert muscle force repeatedly or continuously over time. This involves muscular endurance and resistance to muscle fatigue.
Static Strength	The ability to exert maximum muscle force to lift, push, pull, or carry objects.
Speed of Limb Movement	The ability to quickly move the arms and legs.
Gross Body Equilibrium	The ability to keep or regain your body balance or stay upright when in an unstable position.
Response Orientation	The ability to choose quickly between two or more movements in response to two or more different signals (lights, sounds, pictures). It includes the speed with which the correct response is started with the hand, foot, or other body part.
Control Precision	The ability to quickly and repeatedly adjust the controls of a machine or a vehicle to exact positions.
Sound Localization	The ability to tell the direction from which a sound originated.
Wrist-Finger Speed	The ability to make fast, simple, repeated movements of the fingers, hands, and wrists.
Reaction Time	The ability to quickly respond (with the hand, finger, or foot) to a signal (sound, light, picture) when it appears.
Manual Dexterity	The ability to quickly move your hand, your hand together with your arm, or your two hands to grasp, manipulate, or assemble objects.
Peripheral Vision	The ability to see objects or movement of objects to one's side when the eyes are looking ahead.
Dynamic Flexibility	The ability to quickly and repeatedly bend, stretch, twist, or reach out with your body, arms, and/or legs.
Spatial Orientation	The ability to know your location in relation to the environment or to know where other objects are in relation to you.
Explosive Strength	The ability to use short bursts of muscle force to propel oneself (as in jumping or sprinting), or to throw an object.

Glare Sensitivity	The ability to see objects in the presence of glare or bright lighting.
Rate Control	The ability to time your movements or the movement of a piece of equipment in anticipation of changes in the speed and/or direction of a moving object or scene.
Night Vision	The ability to see under low light conditions.

Work_Activity	Work_Activity Definitions
Training and Teaching Others	Identifying the educational needs of others, developing formal educational or training programs or classes, and teaching or instructing others.
Developing Objectives and Strategies	Establishing long-range objectives and specifying the strategies and actions to achieve them.
Organizing, Planning, and Prioritizing Work	Developing specific goals and plans to prioritize, organize, and accomplish your work.
Making Decisions and Solving Problems	Analyzing information and evaluating results to choose the best solution and solve problems.
Evaluating Information to Determine Compliance wit	Using relevant information and individual judgment to determine whether events or processes comply with laws, regulations, or standards.
Updating and Using Relevant Knowledge	Keeping up-to-date technically and applying new knowledge to your job.
Coaching and Developing Others	Identifying the developmental needs of others and coaching, mentoring, or otherwise helping others to improve their knowledge or skills.
Thinking Creatively	Developing, designing, or creating new applications, ideas, relationships, systems, or products, including artistic contributions.
Getting Information	Observing, receiving, and otherwise obtaining information from all relevant sources.
Establishing and Maintaining Interpersonal Relatio	Developing constructive and cooperative working relationships with others, and maintaining them over time.
Monitor Processes, Materials, or Surroundings	Monitoring and reviewing information from materials, events, or the environment, to detect or assess problems.
Communicating with Supervisors, Peers, or Subordin	Providing information to supervisors, co-workers, and subordinates by telephone, in written form, e-mail, or in person.
Identifying Objects, Actions, and Events	Identifying information by categorizing, estimating, recognizing differences or similarities, and detecting changes in circumstances or events.
Scheduling Work and Activities	Scheduling events, programs, and activities, as well as the work of others.
Assisting and Caring for Others	Providing personal assistance, medical attention, emotional support, or other personal care to others such as coworkers, customers, or patients.
Documenting/Recording Information	Entering, transcribing, recording, storing, or maintaining information in written or electronic/magnetic form.
Communicating with Persons Outside Organization	Communicating with people outside the organization, representing the organization to customers, the public, government, and other external sources. This information can be exchanged in person, in writing, or by telephone or e-mail.
Interpreting the Meaning of Information for Others	Translating or explaining what information means and how it can be used.
Resolving Conflicts and Negotiating with Others	Handling complaints, settling disputes, and resolving grievances and conflicts, or otherwise negotiating with others.
Developing and Building Teams	Encouraging and building mutual trust, respect, and cooperation among team members.
Processing Information	Compiling, coding, categorizing, calculating, tabulating, auditing, or verifying information or data.
Coordinating the Work and Activities of Others	Getting members of a group to work together to accomplish tasks.
Judging the Qualities of Things, Services, or Peop	Assessing the value, importance, or quality of things or people.
Interacting With Computers	Using computers and computer systems (including hardware and software) to program, write software, set up functions, enter data, or process information.
Performing for or Working Directly with the Public	Performing for people or dealing directly with the public. This includes serving customers in restaurants and stores, and receiving clients or guests.
Analyzing Data or Information	Identifying the underlying principles, reasons, or facts of information by breaking down information or data into separate parts.
Guiding, Directing, and Motivating Subordinates	Providing guidance and direction to subordinates, including setting performance standards and monitoring performance.

Performing Administrative Activities	Performing day-to-day administrative tasks such as maintaining information files and processing paperwork.
Performing General Physical Activities	Performing physical activities that require considerable use of your arms and legs and moving your whole body, such as climbing, lifting, balancing, walking, stooping, and handling of materials.
Provide Consultation and Advice to Others	Providing guidance and expert advice to management or other groups on technical, systems-, or process-related topics.
Inspecting Equipment, Structures, or Material	Inspecting equipment, structures, or materials to identify the cause of errors or other problems or defects.
Estimating the Quantifiable Characteristics of Pro	Estimating sizes, distances, and quantities; or determining time, costs, resources, or materials needed to perform a work activity.
Handling and Moving Objects	Using hands and arms in handling, installing, positioning, and moving materials, and manipulating things.
Monitoring and Controlling Resources	Monitoring and controlling resources and overseeing the spending of money.
Selling or Influencing Others	Convincing others to buy merchandise/goods or to otherwise change their minds or actions.
Controlling Machines and Processes	Using either control mechanisms or direct physical activity to operate machines or processes (not including computers or vehicles).
Staffing Organizational Units	Recruiting, interviewing, selecting, hiring, and promoting employees in an organization.
Drafting, Laying Out, and Specifying Technical Dev	Providing documentation, detailed instructions, drawings, or specifications to tell others about how devices, parts, equipment, or structures are to be fabricated, constructed, assembled, modified, maintained, or used.
Operating Vehicles, Mechanized Devices, or Equipme	Running, maneuvering, navigating, or driving vehicles or mechanized equipment, such as forklifts, passenger vehicles, aircraft, or water craft.
Repairing and Maintaining Electronic Equipment	Servicing, repairing, calibrating, regulating, fine-tuning, or testing machines, devices, and equipment that operate primarily on the basis of electrical or electronic (not mechanical) principles.
Repairing and Maintaining Mechanical Equipment	Servicing, repairing, adjusting, and testing machines, devices, moving parts, and equipment that operate primarily on the basis of mechanical (not electronic) principles.

Work_Context	Work_Context Definitions
Contact With Others	How much does this job require the worker to be in contact with others (face-to-face, by telephone, or otherwise) in order to perform it?
Face-to-Face Discussions	How often do you have to have face-to-face discussions with individuals or teams in this job?
Work With Work Group or Team	How important is it to work with others in a group or team in this job?
Indoors, Environmentally Controlled	How often does this job require working indoors in environmentally controlled conditions?
Physical Proximity	To what extent does this job require the worker to perform job tasks in close physical proximity to other people?
Freedom to Make Decisions	How much decision making freedom, without supervision, does the job offer?
Coordinate or Lead Others	How important is it to coordinate or lead others in accomplishing work activities in this job?
Letters and Memos	How often does the job require written letters and memos?
Impact of Decisions on Co-workers or Company Resul	How do the decisions an employee makes impact the results of co-workers, clients or the company?
Frequency of Decision Making	How frequently is the worker required to make decisions that affect other people, the financial resources, and/or the image and reputation of the organization?
Structured versus Unstructured Work	To what extent is this job structured for the worker, rather than allowing the worker to determine tasks, priorities, and goals?
Electronic Mail	How often do you use electronic mail in this job?
Deal With External Customers	How important is it to work with external customers or the public in this job?
Telephone	How often do you have telephone conversations in this job?
Spend Time Standing	How much does this job require standing?
Importance of Being Exact or Accurate	How important is being very exact or highly accurate in performing this job?
Public Speaking	How often do you have to perform public speaking in this job?
Time Pressure	How often does this job require the worker to meet strict deadlines?
Frequency of Conflict Situations	How often are there conflict situations the employee has to face in this job?

Responsible for Others' Health and Safety	How much responsibility is there for the health and safety of others in this job?
Exposed to Disease or Infections	How often does this job require exposure to disease/infections?
Deal With Unpleasant or Angry People	How frequently does the worker have to deal with unpleasant, angry, or discourteous individuals as part of the job requirements?
Responsibility for Outcomes and Results	How responsible is the worker for work outcomes and results of other workers?
Sounds, Noise Levels Are Distracting or Uncomforta	How often does this job require working exposed to sounds and noise levels that are distracting or uncomfortable?
Spend Time Walking and Running	How much does this job require walking and running?
Level of Competition	To what extent does this job require the worker to compete or to be aware of competitive pressures?
Spend Time Sitting	How much does this job require sitting?
Importance of Repeating Same Tasks	How important is repeating the same physical activities (e.g., key entry) or mental activities (e.g., checking entries in a ledger) over and over, without stopping, to performing this job?
Spend Time Using Your Hands to Handle, Control, or	How much does this job require using your hands to handle, control, or feel objects, tools or controls?
Consequence of Error	How serious would the result usually be if the worker made a mistake that was not readily correctable?
Spend Time Bending or Twisting the Body	How much does this job require bending or twisting your body?
Exposed to Contaminants	How often does this job require working exposed to contaminants (such as pollutants, gases, dust or odors)?
Spend Time Kneeling, Crouching, Stooping, or Crawl	How much does this job require kneeling, crouching, stooping or crawling?
Outdoors, Exposed to Weather	How often does this job require working outdoors, exposed to all weather conditions?
Spend Time Making Repetitive Motions	How much does this job require making repetitive motions?
Indoors, Not Environmentally Controlled	How often does this job require working indoors in non-controlled environmental conditions (e.g., warehouse without heat)?
Deal With Physically Aggressive People	How frequently does this job require the worker to deal with physical aggression of violent individuals?
Exposed to Minor Burns, Cuts, Bites, or Stings	How often does this job require exposure to minor burns, cuts, bites, or stings?
Very Hot or Cold Temperatures	How often does this job require working in very hot (above 90 F degrees) or very cold (below 32 F degrees) temperatures?
Degree of Automation	How automated is the job?
Cramped Work Space, Awkward Positions	How often does this job require working in cramped work spaces that requires getting into awkward positions?
Extremely Bright or Inadequate Lighting	How often does this job require working in extremely bright or inadequate lighting conditions?
Spend Time Keeping or Regaining Balance	How much does this job require keeping or regaining your balance?
Outdoors, Under Cover	How often does this job require working outdoors, under cover (e.g., structure with roof but no walls)?
In an Enclosed Vehicle or Equipment	How often does this job require working in a closed vehicle or equipment (e.g., car)?
Wear Common Protective or Safety Equipment such as	How often does this job require wearing common protective or safety equipment such as safety shoes, glasses, gloves, hard hats or live jackets?
Pace Determined by Speed of Equipment	How important is it to this job that the pace is determined by the speed of equipment or machinery? (This does not refer to keeping busy at all times on this job.)
Exposed to Hazardous Equipment	How often does this job require exposure to hazardous equipment?
Wear Specialized Protective or Safety Equipment su	How much does this job require wearing specialized protective or safety equipment such as breathing apparatus, safety harness, full protection suits, or radiation protection?
Exposed to Radiation	How often does this job require exposure to radiation?
Spend Time Climbing Ladders, Scaffolds, or Poles	How much does this job require climbing ladders, scaffolds, or poles?
In an Open Vehicle or Equipment	How often does this job require working in an open vehicle or equipment (e.g., tractor)?
Exposed to Whole Body Vibration	How often does this job require exposure to whole body vibration (e.g., operate a jackhammer)?
Exposed to Hazardous Conditions	How often does this job require exposure to hazardous conditions?
Exposed to High Places	How often does this job require exposure to high places?

Job Zone Component	Job Zone Component Definitions
Title	Job Zone Four: Considerable Preparation Needed
Overall Experience	A minimum of two to four years of work-related skill, knowledge, or experience is needed for these occupations. For example, an accountant must complete four years of college and work for several years in accounting to be considered qualified.
Job Training	Employees in these occupations usually need several years of work-related experience, on-the-job training, and/or vocational training.
Job Zone Examples	Many of these occupations involve coordinating, supervising, managing, or training others. Examples include accountants, chefs and head cooks, computer programmers, historians, pharmacists, and police detectives.
SVP Range	(7.0 to < 8.0)
Education	Most of these occupations require a four - year bachelor's degree, but some do not.

Work_Styles	Work_Styles Definitions
Dependability	Job requires being reliable, responsible, and dependable, and fulfilling obligations.
Self Control	Job requires maintaining composure, keeping emotions in check, controlling anger, and avoiding aggressive behavior, even in very difficult situations.
Cooperation	Job requires being pleasant with others on the job and displaying a good-natured, cooperative attitude.
Concern for Others	Job requires being sensitive to others' needs and feelings and being understanding and helpful on the job.
Integrity	Job requires being honest and ethical.
Social Orientation	Job requires preferring to work with others rather than alone, and being personally connected with others on the job.
Initiative	Job requires a willingness to take on responsibilities and challenges.
Stress Tolerance	Job requires accepting criticism and dealing calmly and effectively with high stress situations.
Adaptability/Flexibility	Job requires being open to change (positive or negative) and to considerable variety in the workplace.
Persistence	Job requires persistence in the face of obstacles.
Achievement/Effort	Job requires establishing and maintaining personally challenging achievement goals and exerting effort toward mastering tasks.
Attention to Detail	Job requires being careful about detail and thorough in completing work tasks.
Leadership	Job requires a willingness to lead, take charge, and offer opinions and direction.
Innovation	Job requires creativity and alternative thinking to develop new ideas for and answers to work-related problems.
Independence	Job requires developing one's own ways of doing things, guiding oneself with little or no supervision, and depending on oneself to get things done.
Analytical Thinking	Job requires analyzing information and using logic to address work-related issues and problems.

25-2021.00 - Elementary School Teachers, Except Special Education

Teach pupils in public or private schools at the elementary level basic academic, social, and other formative skills.

Tasks

1) Adapt teaching methods and instructional materials to meet students' varying needs and interests.

2) Attend professional meetings, educational conferences, and teacher training workshops in order to maintain and improve professional competence.

3) Organize and label materials, and display students' work.

4) Plan and supervise class projects, field trips, visits by guest speakers or other experiential activities, and guide students in learning from those activities.

5) Collaborate with other teachers and administrators in the development, evaluation, and revision of elementary school programs.

6) Prepare materials and classrooms for class activities.

7) Read books to entire classes or small groups.

8) Instruct students individually and in groups, using various teaching methods such as lectures, discussions, and demonstrations.

9) Enforce administration policies and rules governing students.

10) Establish clear objectives for all lessons, units, and projects, and communicate those objectives to students.

11) Confer with other staff members to plan and schedule lessons promoting learning, following approved curricula.

12) Meet with parents and guardians to discuss their children's progress, and to determine their priorities for their children and their resource needs.

13) Plan and conduct activities for a balanced program of instruction, demonstration, and work time that provides students with opportunities to observe, question, and investigate.

14) Prepare students for later grades by encouraging them to explore learning opportunities and to persevere with challenging tasks.

15) Prepare, administer, and grade tests and assignments in order to evaluate students' progress.

16) Assign and grade class work and homework.

17) Provide a variety of materials and resources for children to explore, manipulate and use, both in learning activities and in imaginative play.

18) Prepare reports on students and activities as required by administration.

19) Maintain accurate and complete student records as required by laws, district policies, and administrative regulations.

20) Use computers, audiovisual aids, and other equipment and materials to supplement presentations.

21) Organize and lead activities designed to promote physical, mental and social development, such as games, arts and crafts, music, and storytelling.

22) Guide and counsel students with adjustment and/or academic problems, or special academic interests.

23) Select, store, order, issue, and inventory classroom equipment, materials, and supplies.

24) Prepare objectives and outlines for courses of study, following curriculum guidelines or requirements of states and schools.

25) Prepare for assigned classes, and show written evidence of preparation upon request of immediate supervisors.

26) Instruct and monitor students in the use and care of equipment and materials, in order to prevent injuries and damage.

27) Prepare and implement remedial programs for students requiring extra help.

28) Administer standardized ability and achievement tests, and interpret results to determine student strengths and areas of need.

29) Involve parent volunteers and older students in children's activities, in order to facilitate involvement in focused, complex play.

30) Perform administrative duties such as assisting in school libraries, hall and cafeteria monitoring, and bus loading and unloading.

31) Supervise, evaluate, and plan assignments for teacher assistants and volunteers.

32) Sponsor extracurricular activities such as clubs, student organizations, and academic contests.

33) Provide disabled students with assistive devices, supportive technology, and assistance accessing facilities such as restrooms.

34) Establish and enforce rules for behavior and procedures for maintaining order among the students for whom they are responsible.

35) Attend staff meetings, and serve on committees as required.

36) Meet with other professionals to discuss individual students' needs and progress.

37) Observe and evaluate students' performance, behavior, social development, and physical health.

Knowledge	Knowledge Definitions
English Language	Knowledge of the structure and content of the English language including the meaning and spelling of words, rules of composition, and grammar.
Education and Training	Knowledge of principles and methods for curriculum and training design, teaching and instruction for individuals and groups, and the measurement of training effects.
Mathematics	Knowledge of arithmetic, algebra, geometry, calculus, statistics, and their applications.
Psychology	Knowledge of human behavior and performance; individual differences in ability, personality, and interests; learning and motivation; psychological research methods; and the assessment and treatment of behavioral and affective disorders.
Geography	Knowledge of principles and methods for describing the features of land, sea, and air masses, including their physical characteristics, locations, interrelationships, and distribution of plant, animal, and human life.
History and Archeology	Knowledge of historical events and their causes, indicators, and effects on civilizations and cultures.
Public Safety and Security	Knowledge of relevant equipment, policies, procedures, and strategies to promote effective local, state, or national security operations for the protection of people, data, property, and institutions.
Computers and Electronics	Knowledge of circuit boards, processors, chips, electronic equipment, and computer hardware and software, including applications and programming.
Customer and Personal Service	Knowledge of principles and processes for providing customer and personal services. This includes customer needs assessment, meeting quality standards for services, and evaluation of customer satisfaction.
Clerical	Knowledge of administrative and clerical procedures and systems such as word processing, managing files and records, stenography and transcription, designing forms, and other office procedures and terminology.
Sociology and Anthropology	Knowledge of group behavior and dynamics, societal trends and influences, human migrations, ethnicity, cultures and their history and origins.
Administration and Management	Knowledge of business and management principles involved in strategic planning, resource allocation, human resources modeling, leadership technique, production methods, and coordination of people and resources.
Communications and Media	Knowledge of media production, communication, and dissemination techniques and methods. This includes alternative ways to inform and entertain via written, oral, and visual media.
Therapy and Counseling	Knowledge of principles, methods, and procedures for diagnosis, treatment, and rehabilitation of physical and mental dysfunctions, and for career counseling and guidance.
Law and Government	Knowledge of laws, legal codes, court procedures, precedents, government regulations, executive orders, agency rules, and the democratic political process.
Biology	Knowledge of plant and animal organisms, their tissues, cells, functions, interdependencies, and interactions with each other and the environment.
Philosophy and Theology	Knowledge of different philosophical systems and religions. This includes their basic principles, values, ethics, ways of thinking, customs, practices, and their impact on human culture.
Personnel and Human Resources	Knowledge of principles and procedures for personnel recruitment, selection, training, compensation and benefits, labor relations and negotiation, and personnel information systems.
Fine Arts	Knowledge of the theory and techniques required to compose, produce, and perform works of music, dance, visual arts, drama, and sculpture.
Medicine and Dentistry	Knowledge of the information and techniques needed to diagnose and treat human injuries, diseases, and deformities. This includes symptoms, treatment alternatives, drug properties and interactions, and preventive health-care measures.
Foreign Language	Knowledge of the structure and content of a foreign (non-English) language including the meaning and spelling of words, rules of composition and grammar, and pronunciation.
Transportation	Knowledge of principles and methods for moving people or goods by air, rail, sea, or road, including the relative costs and benefits.
Telecommunications	Knowledge of transmission, broadcasting, switching, control, and operation of telecommunications systems.
Chemistry	Knowledge of the chemical composition, structure, and properties of substances and of the chemical processes and transformations that they undergo. This includes uses of chemicals and their interactions, danger signs, production techniques, and disposal methods.

Physics	Knowledge and prediction of physical principles, laws, their interrelationships, and applications to understanding fluid, material, and atmospheric dynamics, and mechanical, electrical, atomic and sub- atomic structures and processes.	Systems Evaluation	Identifying measures or indicators of system performance and the actions needed to improve or correct performance, relative to the goals of the system.
Production and Processing	Knowledge of raw materials, production processes, quality control, costs, and other techniques for maximizing the effective manufacture and distribution of goods.	Systems Analysis	Determining how a system should work and how changes in conditions, operations, and the environment will affect outcomes.
Design	Knowledge of design techniques, tools, and principles involved in production of precision technical plans, blueprints, drawings, and models.	Management of Financial Resources	Determining how money will be spent to get the work done, and accounting for these expenditures.
Engineering and Technology	Knowledge of the practical application of engineering science and technology. This includes applying principles, techniques, procedures, and equipment to the design and production of various goods and services.	Troubleshooting	Determining causes of operating errors and deciding what to do about it.
		Operation and Control	Controlling operations of equipment or systems.
		Installation	Installing equipment, machines, wiring, or programs to meet specifications.
Food Production	Knowledge of techniques and equipment for planting, growing, and harvesting food products (both plant and animal) for consumption, including storage/handling techniques.	Equipment Maintenance	Performing routine maintenance on equipment and determining when and what kind of maintenance is needed.
Mechanical	Knowledge of machines and tools, including their designs, uses, repair, and maintenance.	Operation Monitoring	Watching gauges, dials, or other indicators to make sure a machine is working properly.
Sales and Marketing	Knowledge of principles and methods for showing, promoting, and selling products or services. This includes marketing strategy and tactics, product demonstration, sales techniques, and sales control systems.	Programming	Writing computer programs for various purposes.
		Repairing	Repairing machines or systems using the needed tools.
Economics and Accounting	Knowledge of economic and accounting principles and practices, the financial markets, banking and the analysis and reporting of financial data.	**Ability**	**Ability Definitions**
		Problem Sensitivity	The ability to tell when something is wrong or is likely to go wrong. It does not involve solving the problem, only recognizing there is a problem.
Building and Construction	Knowledge of materials, methods, and the tools involved in the construction or repair of houses, buildings, or other structures such as highways and roads.	Oral Comprehension	The ability to listen to and understand information and ideas presented through spoken words and sentences.
Skills	**Skills Definitions**	Oral Expression	The ability to communicate information and ideas in speaking so others will understand.
Instructing	Teaching others how to do something.	Speech Clarity	The ability to speak clearly so others can understand you.
Speaking	Talking to others to convey information effectively.	Written Comprehension	The ability to read and understand information and ideas presented in writing.
Reading Comprehension	Understanding written sentences and paragraphs in work related documents.	Speech Recognition	The ability to identify and understand the speech of another person.
Learning Strategies	Selecting and using training/instructional methods and procedures appropriate for the situation when learning or teaching new things.	Written Expression	The ability to communicate information and ideas in writing so others will understand.
Active Listening	Giving full attention to what other people are saying, taking time to understand the points being made, asking questions as appropriate, and not interrupting at inappropriate times.	Inductive Reasoning	The ability to combine pieces of information to form general rules or conclusions (includes finding a relationship among seemingly unrelated events).
Monitoring	Monitoring/Assessing performance of yourself, other individuals, or organizations to make improvements or take corrective action.	Deductive Reasoning	The ability to apply general rules to specific problems to produce answers that make sense.
Time Management	Managing one's own time and the time of others.	Fluency of Ideas	The ability to come up with a number of ideas about a topic (the number of ideas is important, not their quality, correctness, or creativity).
Active Learning	Understanding the implications of new information for both current and future problem-solving and decision-making.	Information Ordering	The ability to arrange things or actions in a certain order or pattern according to a specific rule or set of rules (e.g., patterns of numbers, letters, words, pictures, mathematical operations).
Writing	Communicating effectively in writing as appropriate for the needs of the audience.	Originality	The ability to come up with unusual or clever ideas about a given topic or situation, or to develop creative ways to solve a problem.
Critical Thinking	Using logic and reasoning to identify the strengths and weaknesses of alternative solutions, conclusions or approaches to problems.	Near Vision	The ability to see details at close range (within a few feet of the observer).
Social Perceptiveness	Being aware of others' reactions and understanding why they react as they do.	Category Flexibility	The ability to generate or use different sets of rules for combining or grouping things in different ways.
Service Orientation	Actively looking for ways to help people.	Selective Attention	The ability to concentrate on a task over a period of time without being distracted.
Mathematics	Using mathematics to solve problems.	Flexibility of Closure	The ability to identify or detect a known pattern (a figure, object, word, or sound) that is hidden in other distracting material.
Coordination	Adjusting actions in relation to others' actions.	Far Vision	The ability to see details at a distance.
Persuasion	Persuading others to change their minds or behavior.	Time Sharing	The ability to shift back and forth between two or more activities or sources of information (such as speech, sounds, touch, or other sources).
Negotiation	Bringing others together and trying to reconcile differences.		
Judgment and Decision Making	Considering the relative costs and benefits of potential actions to choose the most appropriate one.	Mathematical Reasoning	The ability to choose the right mathematical methods or formulas to solve a problem.
Complex Problem Solving	Identifying complex problems and reviewing related information to develop and evaluate options and implement solutions.	Visualization	The ability to imagine how something will look after it is moved around or when its parts are moved or rearranged.
Science	Using scientific rules and methods to solve problems.	Auditory Attention	The ability to focus on a single source of sound in the presence of other distracting sounds.
Equipment Selection	Determining the kind of tools and equipment needed to do a job.	Memorization	The ability to remember information such as words, numbers, pictures, and procedures.
Management of Personnel Resources	Motivating, developing, and directing people as they work, identifying the best people for the job.	Hearing Sensitivity	The ability to detect or tell the differences between sounds that vary in pitch and loudness.
Operations Analysis	Analyzing needs and product requirements to create a design.	Number Facility	The ability to add, subtract, multiply, or divide quickly and correctly.
Quality Control Analysis	Conducting tests and inspections of products, services, or processes to evaluate quality or performance.	Visual Color Discrimination	The ability to match or detect differences between colors, including shades of color and brightness.
Technology Design	Generating or adapting equipment and technology to serve user needs.		
Management of Material Resources	Obtaining and seeing to the appropriate use of equipment, facilities, and materials needed to do certain work.		

Finger Dexterity	The ability to make precisely coordinated movements of the fingers of one or both hands to grasp, manipulate, or assemble very small objects.
Perceptual Speed	The ability to quickly and accurately compare similarities and differences among sets of letters, numbers, objects, pictures, or patterns. The things to be compared may be presented at the same time or one after the other. This ability also includes comparing a presented object with a remembered object.
Speed of Closure	The ability to quickly make sense of, combine, and organize information into meaningful patterns.
Trunk Strength	The ability to use your abdominal and lower back muscles to support part of the body repeatedly or continuously over time without 'giving out' or fatiguing.
Stamina	The ability to exert yourself physically over long periods of time without getting winded or out of breath.
Extent Flexibility	The ability to bend, stretch, twist, or reach with your body, arms, and/or legs.
Static Strength	The ability to exert maximum muscle force to lift, push, pull, or carry objects.
Multilimb Coordination	The ability to coordinate two or more limbs (for example, two arms, two legs, or one leg and one arm) while sitting, standing, or lying down. It does not involve performing the activities while the whole body is in motion.
Gross Body Coordination	The ability to coordinate the movement of your arms, legs, and torso together when the whole body is in motion.
Arm-Hand Steadiness	The ability to keep your hand and arm steady while moving your arm or while holding your arm and hand in one position.
Gross Body Equilibrium	The ability to keep or regain your body balance or stay upright when in an unstable position.
Speed of Limb Movement	The ability to quickly move the arms and legs.
Dynamic Strength	The ability to exert muscle force repeatedly or continuously over time. This involves muscular endurance and resistance to muscle fatigue.
Sound Localization	The ability to tell the direction from which a sound originated.
Response Orientation	The ability to choose quickly between two or more movements in response to two or more different signals (lights, sounds, pictures). It includes the speed with which the correct response is started with the hand, foot, or other body part.
Manual Dexterity	The ability to quickly move your hand, your hand together with your arm, or your two hands to grasp, manipulate, or assemble objects.
Wrist-Finger Speed	The ability to make fast, simple, repeated movements of the fingers, hands, and wrists.
Spatial Orientation	The ability to know your location in relation to the environment or to know where other objects are in relation to you.
Control Precision	The ability to quickly and repeatedly adjust the controls of a machine or a vehicle to exact positions.
Explosive Strength	The ability to use short bursts of muscle force to propel oneself (as in jumping or sprinting), or to throw an object.
Reaction Time	The ability to quickly respond (with the hand, finger, or foot) to a signal (sound, light, picture) when it appears.
Rate Control	The ability to time your movements or the movement of a piece of equipment in anticipation of changes in the speed and/or direction of a moving object or scene.
Night Vision	The ability to see under low light conditions.
Peripheral Vision	The ability to see objects or movement of objects to one's side when the eyes are looking ahead.
Depth Perception	The ability to judge which of several objects is closer or farther away from you, or to judge the distance between you and an object.
Dynamic Flexibility	The ability to quickly and repeatedly bend, stretch, twist, or reach out with your body, arms, and/or legs.
Glare Sensitivity	The ability to see objects in the presence of glare or bright lighting.

Work_Activity	**Work_Activity Definitions**
Training and Teaching Others	Identifying the educational needs of others, developing formal educational or training programs or classes, and teaching or instructing others.
Organizing, Planning, and Prioritizing Work	Developing specific goals and plans to prioritize, organize, and accomplish your work.
Establishing and Maintaining Interpersonal Relatio	Developing constructive and cooperative working relationships with others, and maintaining them over time.
Getting Information	Observing, receiving, and otherwise obtaining information from all relevant sources.

Communicating with Supervisors, Peers, or Subordin	Providing information to supervisors, co-workers, and subordinates by telephone, in written form, e-mail, or in person.
Thinking Creatively	Developing, designing, or creating new applications, ideas, relationships, systems, or products, including artistic contributions.
Coaching and Developing Others	Identifying the developmental needs of others and coaching, mentoring, or otherwise helping others to improve their knowledge or skills.
Making Decisions and Solving Problems	Analyzing information and evaluating results to choose the best solution and solve problems.
Developing Objectives and Strategies	Establishing long-range objectives and specifying the strategies and actions to achieve them.
Updating and Using Relevant Knowledge	Keeping up-to-date technically and applying new knowledge to your job.
Documenting/Recording Information	Entering, transcribing, recording, storing, or maintaining information in written or electronic/magnetic form.
Evaluating Information to Determine Compliance wit	Using relevant information and individual judgment to determine whether events or processes comply with laws, regulations, or standards.
Assisting and Caring for Others	Providing personal assistance, medical attention, emotional support, or other personal care to others such as coworkers, customers, or patients.
Resolving Conflicts and Negotiating with Others	Handling complaints, settling disputes, and resolving grievances and conflicts, or otherwise negotiating with others.
Identifying Objects, Actions, and Events	Identifying information by categorizing, estimating, recognizing differences or similarities, and detecting changes in circumstances or events.
Developing and Building Teams	Encouraging and building mutual trust, respect, and cooperation among team members.
Processing Information	Compiling, coding, categorizing, calculating, tabulating, auditing, or verifying information or data.
Monitor Processes, Materials, or Surroundings	Monitoring and reviewing information from materials, events, or the environment, to detect or assess problems.
Coordinating the Work and Activities of Others	Getting members of a group to work together to accomplish tasks.
Scheduling Work and Activities	Scheduling events, programs, and activities, as well as the work of others.
Interpreting the Meaning of Information for Others	Translating or explaining what information means and how it can be used.
Judging the Qualities of Things, Services, or Peop	Assessing the value, importance, or quality of things or people.
Performing for or Working Directly with the Public	Performing for people or dealing directly with the public. This includes serving customers in restaurants and stores, and receiving clients or guests.
Interacting With Computers	Using computers and computer systems (including hardware and software) to program, write software, set up functions, enter data, or process information.
Analyzing Data or Information	Identifying the underlying principles, reasons, or facts of information by breaking down information or data into separate parts.
Communicating with Persons Outside Organization	Communicating with people outside the organization, representing the organization to customers, the public, government, and other external sources. This information can be exchanged in person, in writing, or by telephone or e-mail.
Performing Administrative Activities	Performing day-to-day administrative tasks such as maintaining information files and processing paperwork.
Guiding, Directing, and Motivating Subordinates	Providing guidance and direction to subordinates, including setting performance standards and monitoring performance.
Provide Consultation and Advice to Others	Providing guidance and expert advice to management or other groups on technical, systems-, or process-related topics.
Performing General Physical Activities	Performing physical activities that require considerable use of your arms and legs and moving your whole body, such as climbing, lifting, balancing, walking, stooping, and handling of materials.
Handling and Moving Objects	Using hands and arms in handling, installing, positioning, and moving materials, and manipulating things.
Estimating the Quantifiable Characteristics of Pro	Estimating sizes, distances, and quantities; or determining time, costs, resources, or materials needed to perform a work activity.
Monitoring and Controlling Resources	Monitoring and controlling resources and overseeing the spending of money.
Inspecting Equipment, Structures, or Material	Inspecting equipment, structures, or materials to identify the cause of errors or other problems or defects.
Selling or Influencing Others	Convincing others to buy merchandise/goods or to otherwise change their minds or actions.

Controlling Machines and Processes	Using either control mechanisms or direct physical activity to operate machines or processes (not including computers or vehicles).
Staffing Organizational Units	Recruiting, interviewing, selecting, hiring, and promoting employees in an organization.
Repairing and Maintaining Electronic Equipment	Servicing, repairing, calibrating, regulating, fine-tuning, or testing machines, devices, and equipment that operate primarily on the basis of electrical or electronic (not mechanical) principles.
Operating Vehicles, Mechanized Devices, or Equipme	Running, maneuvering, navigating, or driving vehicles or mechanized equipment, such as forklifts, passenger vehicles, aircraft, or water craft.
Drafting, Laying Out, and Specifying Technical Dev	Providing documentation, detailed instructions, drawings, or specifications to tell others about how devices, parts, equipment, or structures are to be fabricated, constructed, assembled, modified, maintained, or used.
Repairing and Maintaining Mechanical Equipment	Servicing, repairing, adjusting, and testing machines, devices, moving parts, and equipment that operate primarily on the basis of mechanical (not electronic) principles.

Work_Context	Work_Context Definitions
Face-to-Face Discussions	How often do you have to have face-to-face discussions with individuals or teams in this job?
Contact With Others	How much does this job require the worker to be in contact with others (face-to-face, by telephone, or otherwise) in order to perform it?
Physical Proximity	To what extent does this job require the worker to perform job tasks in close physical proximity to other people?
Work With Work Group or Team	How important is it to work with others in a group or team in this job?
Freedom to Make Decisions	How much decision making freedom, without supervision, does the job offer?
Spend Time Standing	How much does this job require standing?
Indoors, Environmentally Controlled	How often does this job require working indoors in environmentally controlled conditions?
Electronic Mail	How often do you use electronic mail in this job?
Letters and Memos	How often does the job require written letters and memos?
Frequency of Decision Making	How frequently is the worker required to make decisions that affect other people, the financial resources, and/or the image and reputation of the organization?
Importance of Being Exact or Accurate	How important is being very exact or highly accurate in performing this job?
Telephone	How often do you have telephone conversations in this job?
Impact of Decisions on Co-workers or Company Resul	How do the decisions an employee makes impact the results of co-workers, clients or the company?
Structured versus Unstructured Work	To what extent is this job structured for the worker, rather than allowing the worker to determine tasks, priorities, and goals?
Deal With External Customers	How important is it to work with external customers or the public in this job?
Coordinate or Lead Others	How important is it to coordinate or lead others in accomplishing work activities in this job?
Time Pressure	How often does this job require the worker to meet strict deadlines?
Public Speaking	How often do you have to perform public speaking in this job?
Frequency of Conflict Situations	How often are there conflict situations the employee has to face in this job?
Exposed to Disease or Infections	How often does this job require exposure to disease/infections?
Sounds, Noise Levels Are Distracting or Uncomforta	How often does this job require working exposed to sounds and noise levels that are distracting or uncomfortable?
Deal With Unpleasant or Angry People	How frequently does the worker have to deal with unpleasant, angry, or discourteous individuals as part of the job requirements?
Spend Time Walking and Running	How much does this job require walking and running?
Importance of Repeating Same Tasks	How important is repeating the same physical activities (e.g., key entry) or mental activities (e.g., checking entries in a ledger) over and over, without stopping, to performing this job?
Level of Competition	To what extent does this job require the worker to compete or to be aware of competitive pressures?
Responsible for Others' Health and Safety	How much responsibility is there for the health and safety of others in this job?
Responsibility for Outcomes and Results	How responsible is the worker for work outcomes and results of other workers?
Outdoors, Exposed to Weather	How often does this job require working outdoors, exposed to all weather conditions?

Indoors, Not Environmentally Controlled	How often does this job require working indoors in non-controlled environmental conditions (e.g., warehouse without heat)?
Spend Time Kneeling, Crouching, Stooping, or Crawl	How much does this job require kneeling, crouching, stooping or crawling?
Spend Time Making Repetitive Motions	How much does this job require making repetitive motions?
Consequence of Error	How serious would the result usually be if the worker made a mistake that was not readily correctable?
Spend Time Sitting	How much does this job require sitting?
Exposed to Contaminants	How often does this job require working exposed to contaminants (such as pollutants, gases, dust or odors)?
Spend Time Bending or Twisting the Body	How much does this job require bending or twisting your body?
Very Hot or Cold Temperatures	How often does this job require working in very hot (above 90 F degrees) or very cold (below 32 F degrees) temperatures?
Extremely Bright or Inadequate Lighting	How often does this job require working in extremely bright or inadequate lighting conditions?
Deal With Physically Aggressive People	How frequently does this job require the worker to deal with physical aggression of violent individuals?
Exposed to Minor Burns, Cuts, Bites, or Stings	How often does this job require exposure to minor burns, cuts, bites, or stings?
Spend Time Using Your Hands to Handle, Control, or	How much does this job require using your hands to handle, control, or feel objects, tools or controls?
Cramped Work Space, Awkward Positions	How often does this job require working in cramped work spaces that requires getting into awkward positions?
Degree of Automation	How automated is the job?
Wear Common Protective or Safety Equipment such as	How much does this job require wearing common protective or safety equipment such as safety shoes, glasses, gloves, hard hats or live jackets?
Spend Time Keeping or Regaining Balance	How much does this job require keeping or regaining your balance?
Outdoors, Under Cover	How often does this job require working outdoors, under cover (e.g., structure with roof but no walls)?
In an Enclosed Vehicle or Equipment	How often does this job require working in a closed vehicle or equipment (e.g., car)?
Exposed to Hazardous Equipment	How often does this job require exposure to hazardous equipment?
Exposed to High Places	How often does this job require exposure to high places?
Spend Time Climbing Ladders, Scaffolds, or Poles	How much does this job require climbing ladders, scaffolds, or poles?
Exposed to Whole Body Vibration	How often does this job require exposure to whole body vibration (e.g., operate a jackhammer)?
Exposed to Hazardous Conditions	How often does this job require exposure to hazardous conditions?
Pace Determined by Speed of Equipment	How important is it to this job that the pace is determined by the speed of equipment or machinery? (This does not refer to keeping busy at all times on this job.)
In an Open Vehicle or Equipment	How often does this job require working in an open vehicle or equipment (e.g., tractor)?
Wear Specialized Protective or Safety Equipment su	How much does this job require wearing specialized protective or safety equipment such as breathing apparatus, safety harness, full protection suits, or radiation protection?
Exposed to Radiation	How often does this job require exposure to radiation?

Job Zone Component	Job Zone Component Definitions
Title	Job Zone Four: Considerable Preparation Needed
Overall Experience	A minimum of two to four years of work-related skill, knowledge, or experience is needed for these occupations. For example, an accountant must complete four years of college and work for several years in accounting to be considered qualified.
Job Training	Employees in these occupations usually need several years of work-related experience, on-the-job training, and/or vocational training.
Job Zone Examples	Many of these occupations involve coordinating, supervising, managing, or training others. Examples include accountants, chefs and head cooks, computer programmers, historians, pharmacists, and police detectives.
SVP Range	(7.0 to < 8.0)
Education	Most of these occupations require a four - year bachelor's degree, but some do not.

Work_Styles	Work_Styles Definitions
Self Control	Job requires maintaining composure, keeping emotions in check, controlling anger, and avoiding aggressive behavior, even in very difficult situations.
Concern for Others	Job requires being sensitive to others' needs and feelings and being understanding and helpful on the job.
Dependability	Job requires being reliable, responsible, and dependable, and fulfilling obligations.
Integrity	Job requires being honest and ethical.
Cooperation	Job requires being pleasant with others on the job and displaying a good-natured, cooperative attitude.
Persistence	Job requires persistence in the face of obstacles.
Initiative	Job requires a willingness to take on responsibilities and challenges.
Adaptability/Flexibility	Job requires being open to change (positive or negative) and to considerable variety in the workplace.
Stress Tolerance	Job requires accepting criticism and dealing calmly and effectively with high stress situations.
Achievement/Effort	Job requires establishing and maintaining personally challenging achievement goals and exerting effort toward mastering tasks.
Attention to Detail	Job requires being careful about detail and thorough in completing work tasks.
Social Orientation	Job requires preferring to work with others rather than alone, and being personally connected with others on the job.
Leadership	Job requires a willingness to lead, take charge, and offer opinions and direction.
Independence	Job requires developing one's own ways of doing things, guiding oneself with little or no supervision, and depending on oneself to get things done.
Innovation	Job requires creativity and alternative thinking to develop new ideas for and answers to work-related problems.
Analytical Thinking	Job requires analyzing information and using logic to address work-related issues and problems.

25-2022.00 - Middle School Teachers, Except Special and Vocational Education

Teach students in public or private schools in one or more subjects at the middle, intermediate, or junior high level, which falls between elementary and senior high school as defined by applicable State laws and regulations.

Tasks

1) Adapt teaching methods and instructional materials to meet students' varying needs and interests.

2) Attend professional meetings, educational conferences, and teacher training workshops in order to maintain and improve professional competence.

3) Prepare students for later grades by encouraging them to explore learning opportunities and to persevere with challenging tasks.

4) Prepare materials and classrooms for class activities.

5) Plan and conduct activities for a balanced program of instruction, demonstration, and work time that provides students with opportunities to observe, question, and investigate.

6) Establish clear objectives for all lessons, units, and projects, and communicate these objectives to students.

7) Confer with parents or guardians, other teachers, counselors, and administrators in order to resolve students' behavioral and academic problems.

8) Prepare, administer, and grade tests and assignments in order to evaluate students' progress.

9) Meet with parents and guardians to discuss their children's progress, and to determine their priorities for their children and their resource needs.

10) Use computers, audiovisual aids, and other equipment and materials to supplement presentations.

11) Prepare objectives and outlines for courses of study, following curriculum guidelines or requirements of states and schools.

12) Prepare for assigned classes, and show written evidence of preparation upon request of immediate supervisors.

13) Observe and evaluate students' performance, behavior, social development, and physical health.

14) Maintain accurate, complete, and correct student records as required by laws, district policies, and administrative regulations.

15) Confer with other staff members to plan and schedule lessons promoting learning, following approved curricula.

16) Enforce all administration policies and rules governing students.

17) Prepare reports on students and activities as required by administration.

18) Collaborate with other teachers and administrators in the development, evaluation, and revision of middle school programs.

19) Guide and counsel students with adjustment and/or academic problems, or special academic interests.

20) Assign lessons and correct homework.

21) Select, store, order, issue, and inventory classroom equipment, materials, and supplies.

22) Organize and label materials, and display students' work.

23) Instruct through lectures, discussions, and demonstrations in one or more subjects such as English, mathematics, or social studies.

24) Plan and supervise class projects, field trips, visits by guest speakers or other experiential activities, and guide students in learning from such activities.

25) Perform administrative duties such as assisting in school libraries, hall and cafeteria monitoring, and bus loading and unloading.

26) Administer standardized ability and achievement tests, and interpret results to determine student strengths and areas of need.

27) Prepare and implement remedial programs for students requiring extra help.

28) Instruct and monitor students in the use and care of equipment and materials, in order to prevent injury and damage.

29) Sponsor extracurricular activities such as clubs, student organizations, and academic contests.

30) Organize and supervise games and other recreational activities to promote physical, mental, and social development.

31) Provide disabled students with assistive devices, supportive technology, and assistance accessing facilities such as restrooms.

32) Supervise, evaluate, and plan assignments for teacher assistants and volunteers.

33) Meet with other professionals to discuss individual students' needs and progress.

34) Attend staff meetings, and serve on staff committees as required.

Knowledge	Knowledge Definitions
Education and Training	Knowledge of principles and methods for curriculum and training design, teaching and instruction for individuals and groups, and the measurement of training effects.
English Language	Knowledge of the structure and content of the English language including the meaning and spelling of words, rules of composition, and grammar.
Psychology	Knowledge of human behavior and performance; individual differences in ability, personality, and interests; learning and motivation; psychological research methods; and the assessment and treatment of behavioral and affective disorders.
Computers and Electronics	Knowledge of circuit boards, processors, chips, electronic equipment, and computer hardware and software, including applications and programming.
Sociology and Anthropology	Knowledge of group behavior and dynamics, societal trends and influences, human migrations, ethnicity, cultures and their history and origins.
Mathematics	Knowledge of arithmetic, algebra, geometry, calculus, statistics, and their applications.
Customer and Personal Service	Knowledge of principles and processes for providing customer and personal services. This includes customer needs assessment, meeting quality standards for services, and evaluation of customer satisfaction.
Clerical	Knowledge of administrative and clerical procedures and systems such as word processing, managing files and records, stenography and transcription, designing forms, and other office procedures and terminology.
Administration and Management	Knowledge of business and management principles involved in strategic planning, resource allocation, human resources modeling, leadership technique, production methods, and coordination of people and resources.

Communications and Media	Knowledge of media production, communication, and dissemination techniques and methods. This includes alternative ways to inform and entertain via written, oral, and visual media.
Public Safety and Security	Knowledge of relevant equipment, policies, procedures, and strategies to promote effective local, state, or national security operations for the protection of people, data, property, and institutions.
Geography	Knowledge of principles and methods for describing the features of land, sea, and air masses, including their physical characteristics, locations, interrelationships, and distribution of plant, animal, and human life.
Therapy and Counseling	Knowledge of principles, methods, and procedures for diagnosis, treatment, and rehabilitation of physical and mental dysfunctions, and for career counseling and guidance.
History and Archeology	Knowledge of historical events and their causes, indicators, and effects on civilizations and cultures.
Law and Government	Knowledge of laws, legal codes, court procedures, precedents, government regulations, executive orders, agency rules, and the democratic political process.
Philosophy and Theology	Knowledge of different philosophical systems and religions. This includes their basic principles, values, ethics, ways of thinking, customs, practices, and their impact on human culture.
Personnel and Human Resources	Knowledge of principles and procedures for personnel recruitment, selection, training, compensation and benefits, labor relations and negotiation, and personnel information systems.
Fine Arts	Knowledge of the theory and techniques required to compose, produce, and perform works of music, dance, visual arts, drama, and sculpture.
Biology	Knowledge of plant and animal organisms, their tissues, cells, functions, interdependencies, and interactions with each other and the environment.
Foreign Language	Knowledge of the structure and content of a foreign (non-English) language including the meaning and spelling of words, rules of composition and grammar, and pronunciation.
Medicine and Dentistry	Knowledge of the information and techniques needed to diagnose and treat human injuries, diseases, and deformities. This includes symptoms, treatment alternatives, drug properties and interactions, and preventive health-care measures.
Telecommunications	Knowledge of transmission, broadcasting, switching, control, and operation of telecommunications systems.
Chemistry	Knowledge of the chemical composition, structure, and properties of substances and of the chemical processes and transformations that they undergo. This includes uses of chemicals and their interactions, danger signs, production techniques, and disposal methods.
Physics	Knowledge and prediction of physical principles, laws, their interrelationships, and applications to understanding fluid, material, and atmospheric dynamics, and mechanical, electrical, atomic and sub- atomic structures and processes.
Transportation	Knowledge of principles and methods for moving people or goods by air, rail, sea, or road, including the relative costs and benefits.
Sales and Marketing	Knowledge of principles and methods for showing, promoting, and selling products or services. This includes marketing strategy and tactics, product demonstration, sales techniques, and sales control systems.
Engineering and Technology	Knowledge of the practical application of engineering science and technology. This includes applying principles, techniques, procedures, and equipment to the design and production of various goods and services.
Economics and Accounting	Knowledge of economic and accounting principles and practices, the financial markets, banking and the analysis and reporting of financial data.
Design	Knowledge of design techniques, tools, and principles involved in production of precision technical plans, blueprints, drawings, and models.
Production and Processing	Knowledge of raw materials, production processes, quality control, costs, and other techniques for maximizing the effective manufacture and distribution of goods.
Mechanical	Knowledge of machines and tools, including their designs, uses, repair, and maintenance.
Building and Construction	Knowledge of materials, methods, and the tools involved in the construction or repair of houses, buildings, or other structures such as highways and roads.

Food Production	Knowledge of techniques and equipment for planting, growing, and harvesting food products (both plant and animal) for consumption, including storage/handling techniques.

Skills	Skills Definitions
Instructing	Teaching others how to do something.
Speaking	Talking to others to convey information effectively.
Learning Strategies	Selecting and using training/instructional methods and procedures appropriate for the situation when learning or teaching new things.
Active Listening	Giving full attention to what other people are saying, taking time to understand the points being made, asking questions as appropriate, and not interrupting at inappropriate times.
Reading Comprehension	Understanding written sentences and paragraphs in work related documents.
Time Management	Managing one's own time and the time of others.
Monitoring	Monitoring/Assessing performance of yourself, other individuals, or organizations to make improvements or take corrective action.
Social Perceptiveness	Being aware of others' reactions and understanding why they react as they do.
Critical Thinking	Using logic and reasoning to identify the strengths and weaknesses of alternative solutions, conclusions or approaches to problems.
Active Learning	Understanding the implications of new information for both current and future problem-solving and decision-making.
Writing	Communicating effectively in writing as appropriate for the needs of the audience.
Coordination	Adjusting actions in relation to others' actions.
Service Orientation	Actively looking for ways to help people.
Persuasion	Persuading others to change their minds or behavior.
Complex Problem Solving	Identifying complex problems and reviewing related information to develop and evaluate options and implement solutions.
Negotiation	Bringing others together and trying to reconcile differences.
Judgment and Decision Making	Considering the relative costs and benefits of potential actions to choose the most appropriate one.
Mathematics	Using mathematics to solve problems.
Science	Using scientific rules and methods to solve problems.
Equipment Selection	Determining the kind of tools and equipment needed to do a job.
Management of Personnel Resources	Motivating, developing, and directing people as they work, identifying the best people for the job.
Management of Material Resources	Obtaining and seeing to the appropriate use of equipment, facilities, and materials needed to do certain work.
Operations Analysis	Analyzing needs and product requirements to create a design.
Quality Control Analysis	Conducting tests and inspections of products, services, or processes to evaluate quality or performance.
Technology Design	Generating or adapting equipment and technology to serve user needs.
Troubleshooting	Determining causes of operating errors and deciding what to do about it.
Management of Financial Resources	Determining how money will be spent to get the work done, and accounting for these expenditures.
Systems Evaluation	Identifying measures or indicators of system performance and the actions needed to improve or correct performance, relative to the goals of the system.
Systems Analysis	Determining how a system should work and how changes in conditions, operations, and the environment will affect outcomes.
Operation and Control	Controlling operations of equipment or systems.
Equipment Maintenance	Performing routine maintenance on equipment and determining when and what kind of maintenance is needed.
Installation	Installing equipment, machines, wiring, or programs to meet specifications.
Repairing	Repairing machines or systems using the needed tools.
Operation Monitoring	Watching gauges, dials, or other indicators to make sure a machine is working properly.
Programming	Writing computer programs for various purposes.

Ability	Ability Definitions
Oral Expression	The ability to communicate information and ideas in speaking so others will understand.
Oral Comprehension	The ability to listen to and understand information and ideas presented through spoken words and sentences.
Speech Clarity	The ability to speak clearly so others can understand you.
Speech Recognition	The ability to identify and understand the speech of another person.

Problem Sensitivity	The ability to tell when something is wrong or is likely to go wrong. It does not involve solving the problem, only recognizing there is a problem.
Written Comprehension	The ability to read and understand information and ideas presented in writing.
Written Expression	The ability to communicate information and ideas in writing so others will understand.
Originality	The ability to come up with unusual or clever ideas about a given topic or situation, or to develop creative ways to solve a problem.
Deductive Reasoning	The ability to apply general rules to specific problems to produce answers that make sense.
Inductive Reasoning	The ability to combine pieces of information to form general rules or conclusions (includes finding a relationship among seemingly unrelated events).
Information Ordering	The ability to arrange things or actions in a certain order or pattern according to a specific rule or set of rules (e.g., patterns of numbers, letters, words, pictures, mathematical operations).
Near Vision	The ability to see details at close range (within a few feet of the observer).
Category Flexibility	The ability to generate or use different sets of rules for combining or grouping things in different ways.
Selective Attention	The ability to concentrate on a task over a period of time without being distracted.
Fluency of Ideas	The ability to come up with a number of ideas about a topic (the number of ideas is important, not their quality, correctness, or creativity).
Far Vision	The ability to see details at a distance.
Mathematical Reasoning	The ability to choose the right mathematical methods or formulas to solve a problem.
Time Sharing	The ability to shift back and forth between two or more activities or sources of information (such as speech, sounds, touch, or other sources).
Perceptual Speed	The ability to quickly and accurately compare similarities and differences among sets of letters, numbers, objects, pictures, or patterns. The things to be compared may be presented at the same time or one after the other. This ability also includes comparing a presented object with a remembered object.
Speed of Closure	The ability to quickly make sense of, combine, and organize information into meaningful patterns.
Flexibility of Closure	The ability to identify or detect a known pattern (a figure, object, word, or sound) that is hidden in other distracting material.
Memorization	The ability to remember information such as words, numbers, pictures, and procedures.
Auditory Attention	The ability to focus on a single source of sound in the presence of other distracting sounds.
Visual Color Discrimination	The ability to match or detect differences between colors, including shades of color and brightness.
Number Facility	The ability to add, subtract, multiply, or divide quickly and correctly.
Visualization	The ability to imagine how something will look after it is moved around or when its parts are moved or rearranged.
Hearing Sensitivity	The ability to detect or tell the differences between sounds that vary in pitch and loudness.
Trunk Strength	The ability to use your abdominal and lower back muscles to support part of the body repeatedly or continuously over time without 'giving out' or fatiguing.
Stamina	The ability to exert yourself physically over long periods of time without getting winded or out of breath.
Depth Perception	The ability to judge which of several objects is closer or farther away from you, or to judge the distance between you and an object.
Finger Dexterity	The ability to make precisely coordinated movements of the fingers of one or both hands to grasp, manipulate, or assemble very small objects.
Gross Body Coordination	The ability to coordinate the movement of your arms, legs, and torso together when the whole body is in motion.
Arm-Hand Steadiness	The ability to keep your hand and arm steady while moving your arm or while holding your arm and hand in one position.
Dynamic Strength	The ability to exert muscle force repeatedly or continuously over time. This involves muscular endurance and resistance to muscle fatigue.
Extent Flexibility	The ability to bend, stretch, twist, or reach with your body, arms, and/or legs.
Static Strength	The ability to exert maximum muscle force to lift, push, pull, or carry objects.
Multilimb Coordination	The ability to coordinate two or more limbs (for example, two arms, two legs, or one leg and one arm) while sitting, standing, or lying down. It does not involve performing the activities while the whole body is in motion.
Gross Body Equilibrium	The ability to keep or regain your body balance or stay upright when in an unstable position.
Speed of Limb Movement	The ability to quickly move the arms and legs.
Wrist-Finger Speed	The ability to make fast, simple, repeated movements of the fingers, hands, and wrists.
Sound Localization	The ability to tell the direction from which a sound originated.
Control Precision	The ability to quickly and repeatedly adjust the controls of a machine or a vehicle to exact positions.
Reaction Time	The ability to quickly respond (with the hand, finger, or foot) to a signal (sound, light, picture) when it appears.
Peripheral Vision	The ability to see objects or movement of objects to one's side when the eyes are looking ahead.
Explosive Strength	The ability to use short bursts of muscle force to propel oneself (as in jumping or sprinting), or to throw an object.
Dynamic Flexibility	The ability to quickly and repeatedly bend, stretch, twist, or reach out with your body, arms, and/or legs.
Response Orientation	The ability to choose quickly between two or more movements in response to two or more different signals (lights, sounds, pictures). It includes the speed with which the correct response is started with the hand, foot, or other body part.
Night Vision	The ability to see under low light conditions.
Spatial Orientation	The ability to know your location in relation to the environment or to know where other objects are in relation to you.
Glare Sensitivity	The ability to see objects in the presence of glare or bright lighting.
Manual Dexterity	The ability to quickly move your hand, your hand together with your arm, or your two hands to grasp, manipulate, or assemble objects.
Rate Control	The ability to time your movements or the movement of a piece of equipment in anticipation of changes in the speed and/or direction of a moving object or scene.

Work_Activity	Work_Activity Definitions
Training and Teaching Others	Identifying the educational needs of others, developing formal educational or training programs or classes, and teaching or instructing others.
Organizing, Planning, and Prioritizing Work	Developing specific goals and plans to prioritize, organize, and accomplish your work.
Coaching and Developing Others	Identifying the developmental needs of others and coaching, mentoring, or otherwise helping others to improve their knowledge or skills.
Establishing and Maintaining Interpersonal Relatio	Developing constructive and cooperative working relationships with others, and maintaining them over time.
Making Decisions and Solving Problems	Analyzing information and evaluating results to choose the best solution and solve problems.
Thinking Creatively	Developing, designing, or creating new applications, ideas, relationships, systems, or products, including artistic contributions.
Developing Objectives and Strategies	Establishing long-range objectives and specifying the strategies and actions to achieve them.
Getting Information	Observing, receiving, and otherwise obtaining information from all relevant sources.
Updating and Using Relevant Knowledge	Keeping up-to-date technically and applying new knowledge to your job.
Communicating with Supervisors, Peers, or Subordin	Providing information to supervisors, co-workers, and subordinates by telephone, in written form, e-mail, or in person.
Documenting/Recording Information	Entering, transcribing, recording, storing, or maintaining information in written or electronic/magnetic form.
Monitor Processes, Materials, or Surroundings	Monitoring and reviewing information from materials, events, or the environment, to detect or assess problems.
Assisting and Caring for Others	Providing personal assistance, medical attention, emotional support, or other personal care to others such as coworkers, customers, or patients.
Evaluating Information to Determine Compliance wit	Using relevant information and individual judgment to determine whether events or processes comply with laws, regulations, or standards.
Processing Information	Compiling, coding, categorizing, calculating, tabulating, auditing, or verifying information or data.
Interpreting the Meaning of Information for Others	Translating or explaining what information means and how it can be used.

Interacting With Computers	Using computers and computer systems (including hardware and software) to program, write software, set up functions, enter data, or process information.
Coordinating the Work and Activities of Others	Getting members of a group to work together to accomplish tasks.
Identifying Objects, Actions, and Events	Identifying information by categorizing, estimating, recognizing differences or similarities, and detecting changes in circumstances or events.
Developing and Building Teams	Encouraging and building mutual trust, respect, and cooperation among team members.
Resolving Conflicts and Negotiating with Others	Handling complaints, settling disputes, and resolving grievances and conflicts, or otherwise negotiating with others.
Communicating with Persons Outside Organization	Communicating with people outside the organization, representing the organization to customers, the public, government, and other external sources. This information can be exchanged in person, in writing, or by telephone or e-mail.
Scheduling Work and Activities	Scheduling events, programs, and activities, as well as the work of others.
Judging the Qualities of Things, Services, or Peop	Assessing the value, importance, or quality of things or people.
Performing for or Working Directly with the Public	Performing for people or dealing directly with the public. This includes serving customers in restaurants and stores, and receiving clients or guests.
Analyzing Data or Information	Identifying the underlying principles, reasons, or facts of information by breaking down information or data into separate parts.
Guiding, Directing, and Motivating Subordinates	Providing guidance and direction to subordinates, including setting performance standards and monitoring performance.
Performing Administrative Activities	Performing day-to-day administrative tasks such as maintaining information files and processing paperwork.
Provide Consultation and Advice to Others	Providing guidance and expert advice to management or other groups on technical, systems-, or process-related topics.
Estimating the Quantifiable Characteristics of Pro	Estimating sizes, distances, and quantities; or determining time, costs, resources, or materials needed to perform a work activity.
Selling or Influencing Others	Convincing others to buy merchandise/goods or to otherwise change their minds or actions.
Performing General Physical Activities	Performing physical activities that require considerable use of your arms and legs and moving your whole body, such as climbing, lifting, balancing, walking, stooping, and handling of materials.
Inspecting Equipment, Structures, or Material	Inspecting equipment, structures, or materials to identify the cause of errors or other problems or defects.
Handling and Moving Objects	Using hands and arms in handling, installing, positioning, and moving materials, and manipulating things.
Monitoring and Controlling Resources	Monitoring and controlling resources and overseeing the spending of money.
Controlling Machines and Processes	Using either control mechanisms or direct physical activity to operate machines or processes (not including computers or vehicles).
Repairing and Maintaining Electronic Equipment	Servicing, repairing, calibrating, regulating, fine-tuning, or testing machines, devices, and equipment that operate primarily on the basis of electrical or electronic (not mechanical) principles.
Staffing Organizational Units	Recruiting, interviewing, selecting, hiring, and promoting employees in an organization.
Drafting, Laying Out, and Specifying Technical Dev	Providing documentation, detailed instructions, drawings, or specifications to tell others about how devices, parts, equipment, or structures are to be fabricated, constructed, assembled, modified, maintained, or used.
Repairing and Maintaining Mechanical Equipment	Servicing, repairing, adjusting, and testing machines, devices, moving parts, and equipment that operate primarily on the basis of mechanical (not electronic) principles.
Operating Vehicles, Mechanized Devices, or Equipme	Running, maneuvering, navigating, or driving vehicles or mechanized equipment, such as forklifts, passenger vehicles, aircraft, or water craft.

Work_Context	Work_Context Definitions
Face-to-Face Discussions	How often do you have to have face-to-face discussions with individuals or teams in this job?
Contact With Others	How much does this job require the worker to be in contact with others (face-to-face, by telephone, or otherwise) in order to perform it?
Work With Work Group or Team	How important is it to work with others in a group or team in this job?
Physical Proximity	To what extent does this job require the worker to perform job tasks in close physical proximity to other people?

Frequency of Decision Making	How frequently is the worker required to make decisions that affect other people, the financial resources, and/or the image and reputation of the organization?
Freedom to Make Decisions	How much decision making freedom, without supervision, does the job offer?
Public Speaking	How often do you have to perform public speaking in this job?
Electronic Mail	How often do you use electronic mail in this job?
Indoors, Environmentally Controlled	How often does this job require working indoors in environmentally controlled conditions?
Coordinate or Lead Others	How important is it to coordinate or lead others in accomplishing work activities in this job?
Structured versus Unstructured Work	To what extent is this job structured for the worker, rather than allowing the worker to determine tasks, priorities, and goals?
Impact of Decisions on Co-workers or Company Resul	How do the decisions an employee makes impact the results of co-workers, clients or the company?
Spend Time Standing	How much does this job require standing?
Frequency of Conflict Situations	How often are there conflict situations the employee has to face in this job?
Telephone	How often do you have telephone conversations in this job?
Deal With External Customers	How important is it to work with external customers or the public in this job?
Time Pressure	How often does this job require the worker to meet strict deadlines?
Importance of Being Exact or Accurate	How important is being very exact or highly accurate in performing this job?
Letters and Memos	How often does the job require written letters and memos?
Deal With Unpleasant or Angry People	How frequently does the worker have to deal with unpleasant, angry, or discourteous individuals as part of the job requirements?
Responsible for Others' Health and Safety	How much responsibility is there for the health and safety of others in this job?
Sounds, Noise Levels Are Distracting or Uncomforta	How often does this job require working exposed to sounds and noise levels that are distracting or uncomfortable?
Responsibility for Outcomes and Results	How responsible is the worker for work outcomes and results of other workers?
Importance of Repeating Same Tasks	How important is repeating the same physical activities (e.g., key entry) or mental activities (e.g., checking entries in a ledger) over and over, without stopping, to performing this job?
Spend Time Walking and Running	How much does this job require walking and running?
Exposed to Disease or Infections	How often does this job require exposure to disease/infections?
Spend Time Using Your Hands to Handle, Control, or	How much does this job require using your hands to handle, control, or feel objects, tools or controls?
Exposed to Contaminants	How often does this job require working exposed to contaminants (such as pollutants, gases, dust or odors)?
Level of Competition	To what extent does this job require the worker to compete or to be aware of competitive pressures?
Consequence of Error	How serious would the result usually be if the worker made a mistake that was not readily correctable?
Spend Time Making Repetitive Motions	How much does this job require making repetitive motions?
Indoors, Not Environmentally Controlled	How often does this job require working indoors in non-controlled environmental conditions (e.g., warehouse without heat)?
Deal With Physically Aggressive People	How frequently does this job require the worker to deal with physical aggression of violent individuals?
Spend Time Sitting	How much does this job require sitting?
Spend Time Bending or Twisting the Body	How much does this job require bending or twisting your body?
Exposed to Minor Burns, Cuts, Bites, or Stings	How often does this job require exposure to minor burns, cuts, bites, or stings?
Outdoors, Exposed to Weather	How often does this job require working outdoors, exposed to all weather conditions?
Very Hot or Cold Temperatures	How often does this job require working in very hot (above 90 F degrees) or very cold (below 32 F degrees) temperatures?
Degree of Automation	How automated is the job?
Spend Time Kneeling, Crouching, Stooping, or Crawl	How much does this job require kneeling, crouching, stooping, or crawling?
Extremely Bright or Inadequate Lighting	How often does this job require working in extremely bright or inadequate lighting conditions?
Wear Common Protective or Safety Equipment such as	How much does this job require wearing common protective or safety equipment such as safety shoes, glasses, gloves, hard hats or live jackets?
Cramped Work Space, Awkward Positions	How often does this job require working in cramped work spaces that requires getting into awkward positions?

Spend Time Keeping or Regaining Balance	How much does this job require keeping or regaining your balance?
Outdoors, Under Cover	How often does this job require working outdoors, under cover (e.g., structure with roof but no walls)?
Exposed to Hazardous Equipment	How often does this job require exposure to hazardous equipment?
In an Enclosed Vehicle or Equipment	How often does this job require working in a closed vehicle or equipment (e.g., car)?
Exposed to Hazardous Conditions	How often does this job require exposure to hazardous conditions?
Pace Determined by Speed of Equipment	How important is it to this job that the pace is determined by the speed of equipment or machinery? (This does not refer to keeping busy at all times on this job.)
Exposed to Whole Body Vibration	How often does this job require exposure to whole body vibration (e.g., operate a jackhammer)?
Wear Specialized Protective or Safety Equipment su	How much does this job require wearing specialized protective or safety equipment such as breathing apparatus, safety harness, full protection suits, or radiation protection?
Exposed to High Places	How often does this job require exposure to high places?
In an Open Vehicle or Equipment	How often does this job require working in an open vehicle or equipment (e.g., tractor)?
Spend Time Climbing Ladders, Scaffolds, or Poles	How much does this job require climbing ladders, scaffolds, or poles?
Exposed to Radiation	How often does this job require exposure to radiation?

| Innovation | Job requires creativity and alternative thinking to develop new ideas for and answers to work-related problems. |
| Analytical Thinking | Job requires analyzing information and using logic to address work-related issues and problems. |

25-2023.00 - Vocational Education Teachers, Middle School

Teach or instruct vocational or occupational subjects at the middle school level.

Tasks

1) Attend staff meetings, and serve on committees as required.

2) Instruct and monitor students in the use and care of equipment and materials, in order to prevent injuries and damage.

3) Enforce all administration policies and rules governing students.

4) Prepare objectives and outlines for courses of study, following curriculum guidelines or requirements of states and schools.

5) Plan and conduct activities for a balanced program of instruction, demonstration, and work time that provides students with opportunities to observe, question, and investigate.

6) Use computers, audiovisual aids, and other equipment and materials to supplement presentations.

7) Assign and grade class work and homework.

8) Maintain accurate and complete student records as required by laws, district policies, and administrative regulations.

9) Prepare reports on students and activities as required by administration.

10) Observe and evaluate students' performance, behavior, social development, and physical health.

11) Perform administrative duties such as assisting in school libraries, hall and cafeteria monitoring, and bus loading and unloading.

12) Collaborate with other teachers and administrators in the development, evaluation, and revision of middle school programs.

13) Confer with other staff members to plan and schedule lessons promoting learning, following approved curricula.

14) Guide and counsel students with adjustment and/or academic problems, or special academic interests.

15) Plan and supervise class projects, field trips, visits by guest speakers or other experiential activities, and guide students in learning from those activities.

16) Prepare and implement remedial programs for students requiring extra help.

17) Sponsor extracurricular activities such as clubs, student organizations, and academic contests.

18) Provide disabled students with assistive devices, supportive technology, and assistance accessing facilities such as restrooms.

19) Prepare, administer, and grade tests and assignments to evaluate students' progress.

20) Establish and enforce rules for behavior and procedures for maintaining order among the students for whom they are responsible.

21) Establish clear objectives for all lessons, units, and projects, and communicate those objectives to students.

22) Instruct students individually and in groups, using various teaching methods such as lectures, discussions, and demonstrations.

23) Prepare students for later educational experiences by encouraging them to explore learning opportunities and to persevere with challenging tasks.

24) Confer with parents or guardians, other teachers, counselors, and administrators in order to resolve students' behavioral and academic problems.

25) Meet with parents and guardians to discuss their children's progress, and to determine their priorities for their children and their resource needs.

26) Prepare for assigned classes, and show written evidence of preparation upon request of immediate supervisors.

27) Meet with other professionals to discuss individual students' needs and progress.

28) Adapt teaching methods and instructional materials to meet students' varying needs and interests.

29) Attend professional meetings, educational conferences, and teacher training workshops in

Job Zone Component	Job Zone Component Definitions
Title	Job Zone Four: Considerable Preparation Needed
Overall Experience	A minimum of two to four years of work-related skill, knowledge, or experience is needed for these occupations. For example, an accountant must complete four years of college and work for several years in accounting to be considered qualified.
Job Training	Employees in these occupations usually need several years of work-related experience, on-the-job training, and/or vocational training.
Job Zone Examples	Many of these occupations involve coordinating, supervising, managing, or training others. Examples include accountants, chefs and head cooks, computer programmers, historians, pharmacists, and police detectives.
SVP Range	(7.0 to < 8.0)
Education	Most of these occupations require a four - year bachelor's degree, but some do not.

Work_Styles	Work_Styles Definitions
Dependability	Job requires being reliable, responsible, and dependable, and fulfilling obligations.
Integrity	Job requires being honest and ethical.
Self Control	Job requires maintaining composure, keeping emotions in check, controlling anger, and avoiding aggressive behavior, even in very difficult situations.
Stress Tolerance	Job requires accepting criticism and dealing calmly and effectively with high stress situations.
Concern for Others	Job requires being sensitive to others' needs and feelings and being understanding and helpful on the job.
Adaptability/Flexibility	Job requires being open to change (positive or negative) and to considerable variety in the workplace.
Cooperation	Job requires being pleasant with others on the job and displaying a good-natured, cooperative attitude.
Persistence	Job requires persistence in the face of obstacles.
Initiative	Job requires a willingness to take on responsibilities and challenges.
Leadership	Job requires a willingness to lead, take charge, and offer opinions and direction.
Attention to Detail	Job requires being careful about detail and thorough in completing work tasks.
Social Orientation	Job requires preferring to work with others rather than alone, and being personally connected with others on the job.
Achievement/Effort	Job requires establishing and maintaining personally challenging achievement goals and exerting effort toward mastering tasks.
Independence	Job requires developing one's own ways of doing things, guiding oneself with little or no supervision, and depending on oneself to get things done.

order to maintain and improve professional competence.

30) Prepare materials and classrooms for class activities.

Knowledge	Knowledge Definitions
Education and Training	Knowledge of principles and methods for curriculum and training design, teaching and instruction for individuals and groups, and the measurement of training effects.
English Language	Knowledge of the structure and content of the English language including the meaning and spelling of words, rules of composition, and grammar.
Psychology	Knowledge of human behavior and performance; individual differences in ability, personality, and interests; learning and motivation; psychological research methods; and the assessment and treatment of behavioral and affective disorders.
Computers and Electronics	Knowledge of circuit boards, processors, chips, electronic equipment, and computer hardware and software, including applications and programming.
Customer and Personal Service	Knowledge of principles and processes for providing customer and personal services. This includes customer needs assessment, meeting quality standards for services, and evaluation of customer satisfaction.
Clerical	Knowledge of administrative and clerical procedures and systems such as word processing, managing files and records, stenography and transcription, designing forms, and other office procedures and terminology.
Administration and Management	Knowledge of business and management principles involved in strategic planning, resource allocation, human resources modeling, leadership technique, production methods, and coordination of people and resources.
Mathematics	Knowledge of arithmetic, algebra, geometry, calculus, statistics, and their applications.
Communications and Media	Knowledge of media production, communication, and dissemination techniques and methods. This includes alternative ways to inform and entertain via written, oral, and visual media.
Sociology and Anthropology	Knowledge of group behavior and dynamics, societal trends and influences, human migrations, ethnicity, cultures and their history and origins.
Public Safety and Security	Knowledge of relevant equipment, policies, procedures, and strategies to promote effective local, state, or national security operations for the protection of people, data, property, and institutions.
Mechanical	Knowledge of machines and tools, including their designs, uses, repair, and maintenance.
Law and Government	Knowledge of laws, legal codes, court procedures, precedents, government regulations, executive orders, agency rules, and the democratic political process.
Design	Knowledge of design techniques, tools, and principles involved in production of precision technical plans, blueprints, drawings, and models.
Engineering and Technology	Knowledge of the practical application of engineering science and technology. This includes applying principles, techniques, procedures, and equipment to the design and production of various goods and services.
Therapy and Counseling	Knowledge of principles, methods, and procedures for diagnosis, treatment, and rehabilitation of physical and mental dysfunctions, and for career counseling and guidance.
Telecommunications	Knowledge of transmission, broadcasting, switching, control, and operation of telecommunications systems.
History and Archeology	Knowledge of historical events and their causes, indicators, and effects on civilizations and cultures.
Production and Processing	Knowledge of raw materials, production processes, quality control, costs, and other techniques for maximizing the effective manufacture and distribution of goods.
Geography	Knowledge of principles and methods for describing the features of land, sea, and air masses, including their physical characteristics, locations, interrelationships, and distribution of plant, animal, and human life.
Personnel and Human Resources	Knowledge of principles and procedures for personnel recruitment, selection, training, compensation and benefits, labor relations and negotiation, and personnel information systems.
Building and Construction	Knowledge of materials, methods, and the tools involved in the construction or repair of houses, buildings, or other structures such as highways and roads.
Biology	Knowledge of plant and animal organisms, their tissues, cells, functions, interdependencies, and interactions with each other and the environment.
Transportation	Knowledge of principles and methods for moving people or goods by air, rail, sea, or road, including the relative costs and benefits.
Philosophy and Theology	Knowledge of different philosophical systems and religions. This includes their basic principles, values, ethics, ways of thinking, customs, practices, and their impact on human culture.
Medicine and Dentistry	Knowledge of the information and techniques needed to diagnose and treat human injuries, diseases, and deformities. This includes symptoms, treatment alternatives, drug properties and interactions, and preventive health-care measures.
Sales and Marketing	Knowledge of principles and methods for showing, promoting, and selling products or services. This includes marketing strategy and tactics, product demonstration, sales techniques, and sales control systems.
Chemistry	Knowledge of the chemical composition, structure, and properties of substances and of the chemical processes and transformations that they undergo. This includes uses of chemicals and their interactions, danger signs, production techniques, and disposal methods.
Food Production	Knowledge of techniques and equipment for planting, growing, and harvesting food products (both plant and animal) for consumption, including storage/handling techniques.
Physics	Knowledge and prediction of physical principles, laws, their interrelationships, and applications to understanding fluid, material, and atmospheric dynamics, and mechanical, electrical, atomic and sub-atomic structures and processes.
Economics and Accounting	Knowledge of economic and accounting principles and practices, the financial markets, banking and the analysis and reporting of financial data.
Fine Arts	Knowledge of the theory and techniques required to compose, produce, and perform works of music, dance, visual arts, drama, and sculpture.
Foreign Language	Knowledge of the structure and content of a foreign (non-English) language including the meaning and spelling of words, rules of composition and grammar, and pronunciation.

Skills	Skills Definitions
Instructing	Teaching others how to do something.
Speaking	Talking to others to convey information effectively.
Learning Strategies	Selecting and using training/instructional methods and procedures appropriate for the situation when learning or teaching new things.
Reading Comprehension	Understanding written sentences and paragraphs in work related documents.
Active Listening	Giving full attention to what other people are saying, taking time to understand the points being made, asking questions as appropriate, and not interrupting at inappropriate times.
Time Management	Managing one's own time and the time of others.
Monitoring	Monitoring/Assessing performance of yourself, other individuals, or organizations to make improvements or take corrective action.
Social Perceptiveness	Being aware of others' reactions and understanding why they react as they do.
Active Learning	Understanding the implications of new information for both current and future problem-solving and decision-making.
Coordination	Adjusting actions in relation to others' actions.
Writing	Communicating effectively in writing as appropriate for the needs of the audience.
Critical Thinking	Using logic and reasoning to identify the strengths and weaknesses of alternative solutions, conclusions or approaches to problems.
Persuasion	Persuading others to change their minds or behavior.
Service Orientation	Actively looking for ways to help people.
Equipment Selection	Determining the kind of tools and equipment needed to do a job.
Judgment and Decision Making	Considering the relative costs and benefits of potential actions to choose the most appropriate one.
Mathematics	Using mathematics to solve problems.
Complex Problem Solving	Identifying complex problems and reviewing related information to develop and evaluate options and implement solutions.
Troubleshooting	Determining causes of operating errors and deciding what to do about it.
Technology Design	Generating or adapting equipment and technology to serve user needs.
Negotiation	Bringing others together and trying to reconcile differences.
Management of Material Resources	Obtaining and seeing to the appropriate use of equipment, facilities, and materials needed to do certain work.

Management of Personnel Resources	Motivating, developing, and directing people as they work, identifying the best people for the job.
Equipment Maintenance	Performing routine maintenance on equipment and determining when and what kind of maintenance is needed.
Management of Financial Resources	Determining how money will be spent to get the work done, and accounting for these expenditures.
Science	Using scientific rules and methods to solve problems.
Repairing	Repairing machines or systems using the needed tools.
Operation and Control	Controlling operations of equipment or systems.
Installation	Installing equipment, machines, wiring, or programs to meet specifications.
Quality Control Analysis	Conducting tests and inspections of products, services, or processes to evaluate quality or performance.
Operations Analysis	Analyzing needs and product requirements to create a design.
Operation Monitoring	Watching gauges, dials, or other indicators to make sure a machine is working properly.
Systems Evaluation	Identifying measures or indicators of system performance and the actions needed to improve or correct performance, relative to the goals of the system.
Systems Analysis	Determining how a system should work and how changes in conditions, operations, and the environment will affect outcomes.
Programming	Writing computer programs for various purposes.

Ability	Ability Definitions
Oral Expression	The ability to communicate information and ideas in speaking so others will understand.
Oral Comprehension	The ability to listen to and understand information and ideas presented through spoken words and sentences.
Problem Sensitivity	The ability to tell when something is wrong or is likely to go wrong. It does not involve solving the problem, only recognizing there is a problem.
Speech Clarity	The ability to speak clearly so others can understand you.
Speech Recognition	The ability to identify and understand the speech of another person.
Written Expression	The ability to communicate information and ideas in writing so others will understand.
Deductive Reasoning	The ability to apply general rules to specific problems to produce answers that make sense.
Inductive Reasoning	The ability to combine pieces of information to form general rules or conclusions (includes finding a relationship among seemingly unrelated events).
Written Comprehension	The ability to read and understand information and ideas presented in writing.
Fluency of Ideas	The ability to come up with a number of ideas about a topic (the number of ideas is important, not their quality, correctness, or creativity).
Category Flexibility	The ability to generate or use different sets of rules for combining or grouping things in different ways.
Near Vision	The ability to see details at close range (within a few feet of the observer).
Originality	The ability to come up with unusual or clever ideas about a given topic or situation, or to develop creative ways to solve a problem.
Information Ordering	The ability to arrange things or actions in a certain order or pattern according to a specific rule or set of rules (e.g., patterns of numbers, letters, words, pictures, mathematical operations).
Selective Attention	The ability to concentrate on a task over a period of time without being distracted.
Far Vision	The ability to see details at a distance.
Flexibility of Closure	The ability to identify or detect a known pattern (a figure, object, word, or sound) that is hidden in other distracting material.
Time Sharing	The ability to shift back and forth between two or more activities or sources of information (such as speech, sounds, touch, or other sources).
Visualization	The ability to imagine how something will look after it is moved around or when its parts are moved or rearranged.
Perceptual Speed	The ability to quickly and accurately compare similarities and differences among sets of letters, numbers, objects, pictures, or patterns. The things to be compared may be presented at the same time or one after the other. This ability also includes comparing a presented object with a remembered object.
Hearing Sensitivity	The ability to detect or tell the differences between sounds that vary in pitch and loudness.
Memorization	The ability to remember information such as words, numbers, pictures, and procedures.

Speed of Closure	The ability to quickly make sense of, combine, and organize information into meaningful patterns.
Auditory Attention	The ability to focus on a single source of sound in the presence of other distracting sounds.
Finger Dexterity	The ability to make precisely coordinated movements of the fingers of one or both hands to grasp, manipulate, or assemble very small objects.
Mathematical Reasoning	The ability to choose the right mathematical methods or formulas to solve a problem.
Trunk Strength	The ability to use your abdominal and lower back muscles to support part of the body repeatedly or continuously over time without 'giving out' or fatiguing.
Visual Color Discrimination	The ability to match or detect differences between colors, including shades of color and brightness.
Number Facility	The ability to add, subtract, multiply, or divide quickly and correctly.
Gross Body Coordination	The ability to coordinate the movement of your arms, legs, and torso together when the whole body is in motion.
Extent Flexibility	The ability to bend, stretch, twist, or reach with your body, arms, and/or legs.
Static Strength	The ability to exert maximum muscle force to lift, push, pull, or carry objects.
Depth Perception	The ability to judge which of several objects is closer or farther away from you, or to judge the distance between you and an object.
Multilimb Coordination	The ability to coordinate two or more limbs (for example, two arms, two legs, or one leg and one arm) while sitting, standing, or lying down. It does not involve performing the activities while the whole body is in motion.
Arm-Hand Steadiness	The ability to keep your hand and arm steady while moving your arm or while holding your arm and hand in one position.
Response Orientation	The ability to choose quickly between two or more movements in response to two or more different signals (lights, sounds, pictures). It includes the speed with which the correct response is started with the hand, foot, or other body part.
Dynamic Strength	The ability to exert muscle force repeatedly or continuously over time. This involves muscular endurance and resistance to muscle fatigue.
Speed of Limb Movement	The ability to quickly move the arms and legs.
Stamina	The ability to exert yourself physically over long periods of time without getting winded or out of breath.
Manual Dexterity	The ability to quickly move your hand, your hand together with your arm, or your two hands to grasp, manipulate, or assemble objects.
Gross Body Equilibrium	The ability to keep or regain your body balance or stay upright when in an unstable position.
Control Precision	The ability to quickly and repeatedly adjust the controls of a machine or a vehicle to exact positions.
Wrist-Finger Speed	The ability to make fast, simple, repeated movements of the fingers, hands, and wrists.
Reaction Time	The ability to quickly respond (with the hand, finger, or foot) to a signal (sound, light, picture) when it appears.
Rate Control	The ability to time your movements or the movement of a piece of equipment in anticipation of changes in the speed and/or direction of a moving object or scene.
Dynamic Flexibility	The ability to quickly and repeatedly bend, stretch, twist, or reach out with your body, arms, and/or legs.
Glare Sensitivity	The ability to see objects in the presence of glare or bright lighting.
Night Vision	The ability to see under low light conditions.
Peripheral Vision	The ability to see objects or movement of objects to one's side when the eyes are looking ahead.
Explosive Strength	The ability to use short bursts of muscle force to propel oneself (as in jumping or sprinting), or to throw an object.
Sound Localization	The ability to tell the direction from which a sound originated.
Spatial Orientation	The ability to know your location in relation to the environment or to know where other objects are in relation to you.

Work_Activity	Work_Activity Definitions
Training and Teaching Others	Identifying the educational needs of others, developing formal educational or training programs or classes, and teaching or instructing others.
Organizing, Planning, and Prioritizing Work	Developing specific goals and plans to prioritize, organize, and accomplish your work.
Getting Information	Observing, receiving, and otherwise obtaining information from all relevant sources.

Coaching and Developing Others	Identifying the developmental needs of others and coaching, mentoring, or otherwise helping others to improve their knowledge or skills.
Thinking Creatively	Developing, designing, or creating new applications, ideas, relationships, systems, or products, including artistic contributions.
Developing Objectives and Strategies	Establishing long-range objectives and specifying the strategies and actions to achieve them.
Identifying Objects, Actions, and Events	Identifying information by categorizing, estimating, recognizing differences or similarities, and detecting changes in circumstances or events.
Updating and Using Relevant Knowledge	Keeping up-to-date technically and applying new knowledge to your job.
Making Decisions and Solving Problems	Analyzing information and evaluating results to choose the best solution and solve problems.
Establishing and Maintaining Interpersonal Relatio	Developing constructive and cooperative working relationships with others, and maintaining them over time.
Communicating with Supervisors, Peers, or Subordin	Providing information to supervisors, co-workers, and subordinates by telephone, in written form, e-mail, or in person.
Judging the Qualities of Things, Services, or Peop	Assessing the value, importance, or quality of things or people.
Interacting With Computers	Using computers and computer systems (including hardware and software) to program, write software, set up functions, enter data, or process information.
Coordinating the Work and Activities of Others	Getting members of a group to work together to accomplish tasks.
Monitor Processes, Materials, or Surroundings	Monitoring and reviewing information from materials, events, or the environment, to detect or assess problems.
Scheduling Work and Activities	Scheduling events, programs, and activities, as well as the work of others.
Interpreting the Meaning of Information for Others	Translating or explaining what information means and how it can be used.
Evaluating Information to Determine Compliance wit	Using relevant information and individual judgment to determine whether events or processes comply with laws, regulations, or standards.
Guiding, Directing, and Motivating Subordinates	Providing guidance and direction to subordinates, including setting performance standards and monitoring performance.
Resolving Conflicts and Negotiating with Others	Handling complaints, settling disputes, and resolving grievances and conflicts, or otherwise negotiating with others.
Developing and Building Teams	Encouraging and building mutual trust, respect, and cooperation among team members.
Communicating with Persons Outside Organization	Communicating with people outside the organization, representing the organization to customers, the public, government, and other external sources. This information can be exchanged in person, in writing, or by telephone or e-mail.
Processing Information	Compiling, coding, categorizing, calculating, tabulating, auditing, or verifying information or data.
Assisting and Caring for Others	Providing personal assistance, medical attention, emotional support, or other personal care to others such as coworkers, customers, or patients.
Documenting/Recording Information	Entering, transcribing, recording, storing, or maintaining information in written or electronic/magnetic form.
Inspecting Equipment, Structures, or Material	Inspecting equipment, structures, or materials to identify the cause of errors or other problems or defects.
Performing for or Working Directly with the Public	Performing for people or dealing directly with the public. This includes serving customers in restaurants and stores, and receiving clients or guests.
Controlling Machines and Processes	Using either control mechanisms or direct physical activity to operate machines or processes (not including computers or vehicles).
Analyzing Data or Information	Identifying the underlying principles, reasons, or facts of information by breaking down information or data into separate parts.
Performing General Physical Activities	Performing physical activities that require considerable use of your arms and legs and moving your whole body, such as climbing, lifting, balancing, walking, stooping, and handling of materials.
Handling and Moving Objects	Using hands and arms in handling, installing, positioning, and moving materials, and manipulating things.
Performing Administrative Activities	Performing day-to-day administrative tasks such as maintaining information files and processing paperwork.
Monitoring and Controlling Resources	Monitoring and controlling resources and overseeing the spending of money.
Provide Consultation and Advice to Others	Providing guidance and expert advice to management or other groups on technical, systems-, or process-related topics.

Estimating the Quantifiable Characteristics of Pro	Estimating sizes, distances, and quantities; or determining time, costs, resources, or materials needed to perform a work activity.
Repairing and Maintaining Mechanical Equipment	Servicing, repairing, adjusting, and testing machines, devices, moving parts, and equipment that operate primarily on the basis of mechanical (not electronic) principles.
Selling or Influencing Others	Convincing others to buy merchandise/goods or to otherwise change their minds or actions.
Drafting, Laying Out, and Specifying Technical Dev	Providing documentation, detailed instructions, drawings, or specifications to tell others about how devices, parts, equipment, or structures are to be fabricated, constructed, assembled, modified, maintained, or used.
Repairing and Maintaining Electronic Equipment	Servicing, repairing, calibrating, regulating, fine-tuning, or testing machines, devices, and equipment that operate primarily on the basis of electrical or electronic (not mechanical) principles.
Staffing Organizational Units	Recruiting, interviewing, selecting, hiring, and promoting employees in an organization.
Operating Vehicles, Mechanized Devices, or Equipme	Running, maneuvering, navigating, or driving vehicles or mechanized equipment, such as forklifts, passenger vehicles, aircraft, or water craft.

Work_Context	Work_Context Definitions
Face-to-Face Discussions	How often do you have to have face-to-face discussions with individuals or teams in this job?
Contact With Others	How much does this job require the worker to be in contact with others (face-to-face, by telephone, or otherwise) in order to perform it?
Indoors, Environmentally Controlled	How often does this job require working indoors in environmentally controlled conditions?
Freedom to Make Decisions	How much decision making freedom, without supervision, does the job offer?
Physical Proximity	To what extent does this job require the worker to perform job tasks in close physical proximity to other people?
Electronic Mail	How often do you use electronic mail in this job?
Frequency of Decision Making	How frequently is the worker required to make decisions that affect other people, the financial resources, and/or the image and reputation of the organization?
Structured versus Unstructured Work	To what extent is this job structured for the worker, rather than allowing the worker to determine tasks, priorities, and goals?
Coordinate or Lead Others	How important is it to coordinate or lead others in accomplishing work activities in this job?
Spend Time Standing	How much does this job require standing?
Work With Work Group or Team	How important is it to work with others in a group or team in this job?
Public Speaking	How often do you have to perform public speaking in this job?
Impact of Decisions on Co-workers or Company Resul	How do the decisions an employee makes impact the results of co-workers, clients or the company?
Deal With External Customers	How important is it to work with external customers or the public in this job?
Frequency of Conflict Situations	How often are there conflict situations the employee has to face in this job?
Telephone	How often do you have telephone conversations in this job?
Deal With Unpleasant or Angry People	How frequently does the worker have to deal with unpleasant, angry, or discourteous individuals as part of the job requirements?
Responsible for Others' Health and Safety	How much responsibility is there for the health and safety of others in this job?
Letters and Memos	How often does the job require written letters and memos?
Importance of Being Exact or Accurate	How important is being very exact or highly accurate in performing this job?
Time Pressure	How often does this job require the worker to meet strict deadlines?
Sounds, Noise Levels Are Distracting or Uncomforta	How often does this job require working exposed to sounds and noise levels that are distracting or uncomfortable?
Spend Time Using Your Hands to Handle, Control, or	How much does this job require using your hands to handle, control, or feel objects, tools or controls?
Importance of Repeating Same Tasks	How important is repeating the same physical activities (e.g., key entry) or mental activities (e.g., checking entries in a ledger) over and over, without stopping, to performing this job?
Responsibility for Outcomes and Results	How responsible is the worker for work outcomes and results of other workers?
Spend Time Walking and Running	How much does this job require walking and running?
Exposed to Contaminants	How often does this job require working exposed to contaminants (such as pollutants, gases, dust or odors)?

		Work_Styles	Work_Styles Definitions
Exposed to Disease or Infections	How often does this job require exposure to disease/infections?	Self Control	Job requires maintaining composure, keeping emotions in check, controlling anger, and avoiding aggressive behavior, even in very difficult situations.
Consequence of Error	How serious would the result usually be if the worker made a mistake that was not readily correctable?	Integrity	Job requires being honest and ethical.
Level of Competition	To what extent does this job require the worker to compete or to be aware of competitive pressures?	Dependability	Job requires being reliable, responsible, and dependable, and fulfilling obligations.
Spend Time Making Repetitive Motions	How much does this job require making repetitive motions?	Stress Tolerance	Job requires accepting criticism and dealing calmly and effectively with high stress situations.
Deal With Physically Aggressive People	How frequently does this job require the worker to deal with physical aggression of violent individuals?	Cooperation	Job requires being pleasant with others on the job and displaying a good-natured, cooperative attitude.
Wear Common Protective or Safety Equipment such as	How much does this job require wearing common protective or safety equipment such as safety shoes, glasses, gloves, hard hats or live jackets?	Concern for Others	Job requires being sensitive to others' needs and feelings and being understanding and helpful on the job.
Exposed to Hazardous Equipment	How often does this job require exposure to hazardous equipment?	Attention to Detail	Job requires being careful about detail and thorough in completing work tasks.
Exposed to Minor Burns, Cuts, Bites, or Stings	How often does this job require exposure to minor burns, cuts, bites, or stings?	Innovation	Job requires creativity and alternative thinking to develop new ideas for and answers to work-related problems.
Indoors, Not Environmentally Controlled	How often does this job require working indoors in non-controlled environmental conditions (e.g., warehouse without heat)?	Persistence	Job requires persistence in the face of obstacles.
Spend Time Sitting	How much does this job require sitting?	Initiative	Job requires a willingness to take on responsibilities and challenges.
Degree of Automation	How automated is the job?	Leadership	Job requires a willingness to lead, take charge, and offer opinions and direction.
Spend Time Bending or Twisting the Body	How much does this job require bending or twisting your body?	Adaptability/Flexibility	Job requires being open to change (positive or negative) and to considerable variety in the workplace.
Very Hot or Cold Temperatures	How often does this job require working in very hot (above 90 F degrees) or very cold (below 32 F degrees) temperatures?	Independence	Job requires developing one's own ways of doing things, guiding oneself with little or no supervision, and depending on oneself to get things done.
Pace Determined by Speed of Equipment	How important is it to this job that the pace is determined by the speed of equipment or machinery? (This does not refer to keeping busy at all times on this job.)	Achievement/Effort	Job requires establishing and maintaining personally challenging achievement goals and exerting effort toward mastering tasks.
Outdoors, Exposed to Weather	How often does this job require working outdoors, exposed to all weather conditions?	Social Orientation	Job requires preferring to work with others rather than alone, and being personally connected with others on the job.
Spend Time Kneeling, Crouching, Stooping, or Crawl	How much does this job require kneeling, crouching, stooping or crawling?	Analytical Thinking	Job requires analyzing information and using logic to address work-related issues and problems.
Cramped Work Space, Awkward Positions	How often does this job require working in cramped work spaces that requires getting into awkward positions?		
In an Enclosed Vehicle or Equipment	How often does this job require working in a closed vehicle or equipment (e.g., car)?		
Outdoors, Under Cover	How often does this job require working outdoors, under cover (e.g., structure with roof but no walls)?		
Exposed to Hazardous Conditions	How often does this job require exposure to hazardous conditions?		
Spend Time Keeping or Regaining Balance	How much does this job require keeping or regaining your balance?		
Extremely Bright or Inadequate Lighting	How often does this job require working in extremely bright or inadequate lighting conditions?		
Spend Time Climbing Ladders, Scaffolds, or Poles	How much does this job require climbing ladders, scaffolds, or poles?		
Exposed to High Places	How often does this job require exposure to high places?		
In an Open Vehicle or Equipment	How often does this job require working in an open vehicle or equipment (e.g., tractor)?		
Exposed to Radiation	How often does this job require exposure to radiation?		
Exposed to Whole Body Vibration	How often does this job require exposure to whole body vibration (e.g., operate a jackhammer)?		
Wear Specialized Protective or Safety Equipment su	How much does this job require wearing specialized protective or safety equipment such as breathing apparatus, safety harness, full protection suits, or radiation protection?		

25-2031.00 - Secondary School Teachers, Except Special and Vocational Education

Instruct students in secondary public or private schools in one or more subjects at the secondary level, such as English, mathematics, or social studies. May be designated according to subject matter specialty, such as typing instructors, commercial teachers, or English teachers.

Tasks

1) Adapt teaching methods and instructional materials to meet students' varying needs and interests.

2) Prepare, administer, and grade tests and assignments to evaluate students' progress.

3) Attend professional meetings, educational conferences, and teacher training workshops in order to maintain and improve professional competence.

4) Establish clear objectives for all lessons, units, and projects, and communicate those objectives to students.

5) Confer with parents or guardians, other teachers, counselors, and administrators in order to resolve students' behavioral and academic problems.

6) Prepare materials and classrooms for class activities.

7) Meet with other professionals to discuss individual students' needs and progress.

8) Plan and conduct activities for a balanced program of instruction, demonstration, and work time that provides students with opportunities to observe, question, and investigate.

9) Select, store, order, issue, and inventory classroom equipment, materials, and supplies.

10) Meet with parents and guardians to discuss their children's progress, and to determine their priorities for their children and their resource needs.

11) Enforce all administration policies and rules governing students.

12) Maintain accurate and complete student records as required by laws, district policies, and administrative regulations.

13) Confer with other staff members to plan and schedule lessons promoting learning, following approved curricula.

14) Guide and counsel students with adjustment and/or academic problems, or special academic interests.

Job Zone Component	Job Zone Component Definitions
Title	Job Zone Four: Considerable Preparation Needed
Overall Experience	A minimum of two to four years of work-related skill, knowledge, or experience is needed for these occupations. For example, an accountant must complete four years of college and work for several years in accounting to be considered qualified.
Job Training	Employees in these occupations usually need several years of work-related experience, on-the-job training, and/or vocational training.
Job Zone Examples	Many of these occupations involve coordinating, supervising, managing, or training others. Examples include accountants, chefs and head cooks, computer programmers, historians, pharmacists, and police detectives.
SVP Range	(7.0 to < 8.0)
Education	Most of these occupations require a four - year bachelor's degree, but some do not.

15) Assign and grade class work and homework.

16) Prepare for assigned classes, and show written evidence of preparation upon request of immediate supervisors.

17) Prepare reports on students and activities as required by administration.

18) Prepare objectives and outlines for courses of study, following curriculum guidelines or requirements of states and schools.

19) Instruct through lectures, discussions, and demonstrations in one or more subjects such as English, mathematics, or social studies.

20) Plan and supervise class projects, field trips, visits by guest speakers, or other experiential activities, and guide students in learning from those activities.

21) Observe and evaluate students' performance, behavior, social development, and physical health.

22) Collaborate with other teachers and administrators in the development, evaluation, and revision of secondary school programs.

23) Perform administrative duties such as assisting in school libraries, hall and cafeteria monitoring, and bus loading and unloading.

24) Sponsor extracurricular activities such as clubs, student organizations, and academic contests.

25) Administer standardized ability and achievement tests, and interpret results to determine students' strengths and areas of need.

26) Prepare and implement remedial programs for students requiring extra help.

27) Instruct and monitor students in the use and care of equipment and materials, in order to prevent injuries and damage.

28) Provide disabled students with assistive devices, supportive technology, and assistance accessing facilities such as restrooms.

29) Attend staff meetings, and serve on committees as required.

30) Use computers, audiovisual aids, and other equipment and materials to supplement presentations.

31) Establish and enforce rules for behavior and procedures for maintaining order among the students for whom they are responsible.

Knowledge	Knowledge Definitions
Education and Training	Knowledge of principles and methods for curriculum and training design, teaching and instruction for individuals and groups, and the measurement of training effects.
English Language	Knowledge of the structure and content of the English language including the meaning and spelling of words, rules of composition, and grammar.
Psychology	Knowledge of human behavior and performance; individual differences in ability, personality, and interests; learning and motivation; psychological research methods; and the assessment and treatment of behavioral and affective disorders.
Sociology and Anthropology	Knowledge of group behavior and dynamics, societal trends and influences, human migrations, ethnicity, cultures and their history and origins.
Clerical	Knowledge of administrative and clerical procedures and systems such as word processing, managing files and records, stenography and transcription, designing forms, and other office procedures and terminology
Customer and Personal Service	Knowledge of principles and processes for providing customer and personal services. This includes customer needs assessment, meeting quality standards for services, and evaluation of customer satisfaction.
Mathematics	Knowledge of arithmetic, algebra, geometry, calculus, statistics, and their applications.
Computers and Electronics	Knowledge of circuit boards, processors, chips, electronic equipment, and computer hardware and software, including applications and programming.
History and Archeology	Knowledge of historical events and their causes, indicators, and effects on civilizations and cultures.
Law and Government	Knowledge of laws, legal codes, court procedures, precedents, government regulations, executive orders, agency rules, and the democratic political process.
Public Safety and Security	Knowledge of relevant equipment, policies, procedures, and strategies to promote effective local, state, or national security operations for the protection of people, data, property, and institutions.
Philosophy and Theology	Knowledge of different philosophical systems and religions. This includes their basic principles, values, ethics, ways of thinking, customs, practices, and their impact on human culture.

Administration and Management	Knowledge of business and management principles involved in strategic planning, resource allocation, human resources modeling, leadership technique, production methods, and coordination of people and resources.
Communications and Media	Knowledge of media production, communication, and dissemination techniques and methods. This includes alternative ways to inform and entertain via written, oral, and visual media.
Geography	Knowledge of principles and methods for describing the features of land, sea, and air masses, including their physical characteristics, locations, interrelationships, and distribution of plant, animal, and human life.
Therapy and Counseling	Knowledge of principles, methods, and procedures for diagnosis, treatment, and rehabilitation of physical and mental dysfunctions, and for career counseling and guidance.
Fine Arts	Knowledge of the theory and techniques required to compose, produce, and perform works of music, dance, visual arts, drama, and sculpture.
Foreign Language	Knowledge of the structure and content of a foreign (non-English) language including the meaning and spelling of words, rules of composition and grammar, and pronunciation.
Personnel and Human Resources	Knowledge of principles and procedures for personnel recruitment, selection, training, compensation and benefits, labor relations and negotiation, and personnel information systems.
Telecommunications	Knowledge of transmission, broadcasting, switching, control, and operation of telecommunications systems.
Physics	Knowledge and prediction of physical principles, laws, their interrelationships, and applications to understanding fluid, material, and atmospheric dynamics, and mechanical, electrical, atomic and sub-atomic structures and processes.
Transportation	Knowledge of principles and methods for moving people or goods by air, rail, sea, or road, including the relative costs and benefits.
Chemistry	Knowledge of the chemical composition, structure, and properties of substances and of the chemical processes and transformations that they undergo. This includes uses of chemicals and their interactions, danger signs, production techniques, and disposal methods.
Sales and Marketing	Knowledge of principles and methods for showing, promoting, and selling products or services. This includes marketing strategy and tactics, product demonstration, sales techniques, and sales control systems.
Economics and Accounting	Knowledge of economic and accounting principles and practices, the financial markets, banking and the analysis and reporting of financial data.
Medicine and Dentistry	Knowledge of the information and techniques needed to diagnose and treat human injuries, diseases, and deformities. This includes symptoms, treatment alternatives, drug properties and interactions, and preventive health-care measures.
Biology	Knowledge of plant and animal organisms, their tissues, cells, functions, interdependencies, and interactions with each other and the environment.
Engineering and Technology	Knowledge of the practical application of engineering science and technology. This includes applying principles, techniques, procedures, and equipment to the design and production of various goods and services.
Production and Processing	Knowledge of raw materials, production processes, quality control, costs, and other techniques for maximizing the effective manufacture and distribution of goods.
Design	Knowledge of design techniques, tools, and principles involved in production of precision technical plans, blueprints, drawings, and models.
Mechanical	Knowledge of machines and tools, including their designs, uses, repair, and maintenance.
Building and Construction	Knowledge of materials, methods, and the tools involved in the construction or repair of houses, buildings, or other structures such as highways and roads.
Food Production	Knowledge of techniques and equipment for planting, growing, and harvesting food products (both plant and animal) for consumption, including storage/handling techniques.

Skills	Skills Definitions
Instructing	Teaching others how to do something.
Learning Strategies	Selecting and using training/instructional methods and procedures appropriate for the situation when learning or teaching new things.

Monitoring	Monitoring/Assessing performance of yourself, other individuals, or organizations to make improvements or take corrective action.
Speaking	Talking to others to convey information effectively.
Time Management	Managing one's own time and the time of others.
Active Listening	Giving full attention to what other people are saying, taking time to understand the points being made, asking questions as appropriate, and not interrupting at inappropriate times.
Active Learning	Understanding the implications of new information for both current and future problem-solving and decision-making.
Social Perceptiveness	Being aware of others' reactions and understanding why they react as they do.
Critical Thinking	Using logic and reasoning to identify the strengths and weaknesses of alternative solutions, conclusions or approaches to problems.
Reading Comprehension	Understanding written sentences and paragraphs in work related documents.
Writing	Communicating effectively in writing as appropriate for the needs of the audience.
Persuasion	Persuading others to change their minds or behavior.
Judgment and Decision Making	Considering the relative costs and benefits of potential actions to choose the most appropriate one.
Coordination	Adjusting actions in relation to others' actions.
Complex Problem Solving	Identifying complex problems and reviewing related information to develop and evaluate options and implement solutions.
Service Orientation	Actively looking for ways to help people.
Negotiation	Bringing others together and trying to reconcile differences.
Mathematics	Using mathematics to solve problems.
Management of Personnel Resources	Motivating, developing, and directing people as they work, identifying the best people for the job.
Equipment Selection	Determining the kind of tools and equipment needed to do a job.
Management of Material Resources	Obtaining and seeing to the appropriate use of equipment, facilities, and materials needed to do certain work.
Operations Analysis	Analyzing needs and product requirements to create a design.
Technology Design	Generating or adapting equipment and technology to serve user needs.
Science	Using scientific rules and methods to solve problems.
Quality Control Analysis	Conducting tests and inspections of products, services, or processes to evaluate quality or performance.
Troubleshooting	Determining causes of operating errors and deciding what to do about it.
Management of Financial Resources	Determining how money will be spent to get the work done, and accounting for these expenditures.
Systems Evaluation	Identifying measures or indicators of system performance and the actions needed to improve or correct performance, relative to the goals of the system.
Systems Analysis	Determining how a system should work and how changes in conditions, operations, and the environment will affect outcomes.
Equipment Maintenance	Performing routine maintenance on equipment and determining when and what kind of maintenance is needed.
Operation and Control	Controlling operations of equipment or systems.
Installation	Installing equipment, machines, wiring, or programs to meet specifications.
Repairing	Repairing machines or systems using the needed tools.
Programming	Writing computer programs for various purposes.
Operation Monitoring	Watching gauges, dials, or other indicators to make sure a machine is working properly.

Ability	Ability Definitions
Oral Expression	The ability to communicate information and ideas in speaking so others will understand.
Speech Clarity	The ability to speak clearly so others can understand you.
Speech Recognition	The ability to identify and understand the speech of another person.
Oral Comprehension	The ability to listen to and understand information and ideas presented through spoken words and sentences.
Problem Sensitivity	The ability to tell when something is wrong or is likely to go wrong. It does not involve solving the problem, only recognizing there is a problem.
Written Expression	The ability to communicate information and ideas in writing so others will understand.
Inductive Reasoning	The ability to combine pieces of information to form general rules or conclusions (includes finding a relationship among seemingly unrelated events).
Written Comprehension	The ability to read and understand information and ideas presented in writing.

Deductive Reasoning	The ability to apply general rules to specific problems to produce answers that make sense.
Originality	The ability to come up with unusual or clever ideas about a given topic or situation, or to develop creative ways to solve a problem.
Information Ordering	The ability to arrange things or actions in a certain order or pattern according to a specific rule or set of rules (e.g., patterns of numbers, letters, words, pictures, mathematical operations).
Fluency of Ideas	The ability to come up with a number of ideas about a topic (the number of ideas is important, not their quality, correctness, or creativity).
Category Flexibility	The ability to generate or use different sets of rules for combining or grouping things in different ways.
Near Vision	The ability to see details at close range (within a few feet of the observer).
Selective Attention	The ability to concentrate on a task over a period of time without being distracted.
Far Vision	The ability to see details at a distance.
Flexibility of Closure	The ability to identify or detect a known pattern (a figure, object, word, or sound) that is hidden in other distracting material.
Auditory Attention	The ability to focus on a single source of sound in the presence of other distracting sounds.
Perceptual Speed	The ability to quickly and accurately compare similarities and differences among sets of letters, numbers, objects, pictures, or patterns. The things to be compared may be presented at the same time or one after the other. This ability also includes comparing a presented object with a remembered object.
Speed of Closure	The ability to quickly make sense of, combine, and organize information into meaningful patterns.
Finger Dexterity	The ability to make precisely coordinated movements of the fingers of one or both hands to grasp, manipulate, or assemble very small objects.
Time Sharing	The ability to shift back and forth between two or more activities or sources of information (such as speech, sounds, touch, or other sources).
Hearing Sensitivity	The ability to detect or tell the differences between sounds that vary in pitch and loudness.
Memorization	The ability to remember information such as words, numbers, pictures, and procedures.
Visualization	The ability to imagine how something will look after it is moved around or when its parts are moved or rearranged.
Visual Color Discrimination	The ability to match or detect differences between colors, including shades of color and brightness.
Number Facility	The ability to add, subtract, multiply, or divide quickly and correctly.
Mathematical Reasoning	The ability to choose the right mathematical methods or formulas to solve a problem.
Trunk Strength	The ability to use your abdominal and lower back muscles to support part of the body repeatedly or continuously over time without 'giving out' or fatiguing.
Gross Body Coordination	The ability to coordinate the movement of your arms, legs, and torso together when the whole body is in motion.
Arm-Hand Steadiness	The ability to keep your hand and arm steady while moving your arm or while holding your arm and hand in one position.
Multilimb Coordination	The ability to coordinate two or more limbs (for example, two arms, two legs, or one leg and one arm) while sitting, standing, or lying down. It does not involve performing the activities while the whole body is in motion.
Stamina	The ability to exert yourself physically over long periods of time without getting winded or out of breath.
Static Strength	The ability to exert maximum muscle force to lift, push, pull, or carry objects.
Dynamic Strength	The ability to exert muscle force repeatedly or continuously over time. This involves muscular endurance and resistance to muscle fatigue.
Depth Perception	The ability to judge which of several objects is closer or farther away from you, or to judge the distance between you and an object.
Speed of Limb Movement	The ability to quickly move the arms and legs.
Gross Body Equilibrium	The ability to keep or regain your body balance or stay upright when in an unstable position.
Manual Dexterity	The ability to quickly move your hand, your hand together with your arm, or your two hands to grasp, manipulate, or assemble objects.
Extent Flexibility	The ability to bend, stretch, twist, or reach with your body, arms, and/or legs.
Dynamic Flexibility	The ability to quickly and repeatedly bend, stretch, twist, or reach out with your body, arms, and/or legs.

Response Orientation	The ability to choose quickly between two or more movements in response to two or more different signals (lights, sounds, pictures). It includes the speed with which the correct response is started with the hand, foot, or other body part.
Wrist-Finger Speed	The ability to make fast, simple, repeated movements of the fingers, hands, and wrists.
Reaction Time	The ability to quickly respond (with the hand, finger, or foot) to a signal (sound, light, picture) when it appears.
Peripheral Vision	The ability to see objects or movement of objects to one's side when the eyes are looking ahead.
Glare Sensitivity	The ability to see objects in the presence of glare or bright lighting.
Sound Localization	The ability to tell the direction from which a sound originated.
Spatial Orientation	The ability to know your location in relation to the environment or to know where other objects are in relation to you.
Rate Control	The ability to time your movements or the movement of a piece of equipment in anticipation of changes in the speed and/or direction of a moving object or scene.
Night Vision	The ability to see under low light conditions.
Control Precision	The ability to quickly and repeatedly adjust the controls of a machine or a vehicle to exact positions.
Explosive Strength	The ability to use short bursts of muscle force to propel oneself (as in jumping or sprinting), or to throw an object.

Work_Activity	Work_Activity Definitions
Establishing and Maintaining Interpersonal Relatio	Developing constructive and cooperative working relationships with others, and maintaining them over time.
Communicating with Supervisors, Peers, or Subordin	Providing information to supervisors, co-workers, and subordinates by telephone, in written form, e-mail, or in person.
Organizing, Planning, and Prioritizing Work	Developing specific goals and plans to prioritize, organize, and accomplish your work.
Getting Information	Observing, receiving, and otherwise obtaining information from all relevant sources.
Identifying Objects, Actions, and Events	Identifying information by categorizing, estimating, recognizing differences or similarities, and detecting changes in circumstances or events.
Making Decisions and Solving Problems	Analyzing information and evaluating results to choose the best solution and solve problems.
Coaching and Developing Others	Identifying the developmental needs of others and coaching, mentoring, or otherwise helping others to improve their knowledge or skills.
Training and Teaching Others	Identifying the educational needs of others, developing formal educational or training programs or classes, and teaching or instructing others.
Thinking Creatively	Developing, designing, or creating new applications, ideas, relationships, systems, or products, including artistic contributions.
Updating and Using Relevant Knowledge	Keeping up-to-date technically and applying new knowledge to your job.
Evaluating Information to Determine Compliance wit	Using relevant information and individual judgment to determine whether events or processes comply with laws, regulations, or standards.
Coordinating the Work and Activities of Others	Getting members of a group to work together to accomplish tasks.
Performing Administrative Activities	Performing day-to-day administrative tasks such as maintaining information files and processing paperwork.
Interacting With Computers	Using computers and computer systems (including hardware and software) to program, write software, set up functions, enter data, or process information.
Performing for or Working Directly with the Public	Performing for people or dealing directly with the public. This includes serving customers in restaurants and stores, and receiving clients or guests.
Interpreting the Meaning of Information for Others	Translating or explaining what information means and how it can be used.
Monitor Processes, Materials, or Surroundings	Monitoring and reviewing information from materials, events, or the environment, to detect or assess problems.
Documenting/Recording Information	Entering, transcribing, recording, storing, or maintaining information in written or electronic/magnetic form.
Resolving Conflicts and Negotiating with Others	Handling complaints, settling disputes, and resolving grievances and conflicts, or otherwise negotiating with others.
Analyzing Data or Information	Identifying the underlying principles, reasons, or facts of information by breaking down information or data into separate parts.
Scheduling Work and Activities	Scheduling events, programs, and activities, as well as the work of others.

Developing and Building Teams	Encouraging and building mutual trust, respect, and cooperation among team members.
Developing Objectives and Strategies	Establishing long-range objectives and specifying the strategies and actions to achieve them.
Judging the Qualities of Things, Services, or Peop	Assessing the value, importance, or quality of things or people.
Assisting and Caring for Others	Providing personal assistance, medical attention, emotional support, or other personal care to others such as coworkers, customers, or patients.
Communicating with Persons Outside Organization	Communicating with people outside the organization, representing the organization to customers, the public, government, and other external sources. This information can be exchanged in person, in writing, or by telephone or e-mail.
Processing Information	Compiling, coding, categorizing, calculating, tabulating, auditing, or verifying information or data.
Guiding, Directing, and Motivating Subordinates	Providing guidance and direction to subordinates, including setting performance standards and monitoring performance.
Performing General Physical Activities	Performing physical activities that require considerable use of your arms and legs and moving your whole body, such as climbing, lifting, balancing, walking, stooping, and handling of materials.
Provide Consultation and Advice to Others	Providing guidance and expert advice to management or other groups on technical, systems-, or process-related topics.
Monitoring and Controlling Resources	Monitoring and controlling resources and overseeing the spending of money.
Inspecting Equipment, Structures, or Material	Inspecting equipment, structures, or materials to identify the cause of errors or other problems or defects.
Handling and Moving Objects	Using hands and arms in handling, installing, positioning, and moving materials, and manipulating things.
Estimating the Quantifiable Characteristics of Pro	Estimating sizes, distances, and quantities; or determining time, costs, resources, or materials needed to perform a work activity.
Selling or Influencing Others	Convincing others to buy merchandise/goods or to otherwise change their minds or actions.
Controlling Machines and Processes	Using either control mechanisms or direct physical activity to operate machines or processes (not including computers or vehicles).
Staffing Organizational Units	Recruiting, interviewing, selecting, hiring, and promoting employees in an organization.
Repairing and Maintaining Electronic Equipment	Servicing, repairing, calibrating, regulating, fine-tuning, or testing machines, devices, and equipment that operate primarily on the basis of electrical or electronic (not mechanical) principles.
Repairing and Maintaining Mechanical Equipment	Servicing, repairing, adjusting, and testing machines, devices, moving parts, and equipment that operate primarily on the basis of mechanical (not electronic) principles.
Drafting, Laying Out, and Specifying Technical Dev	Providing documentation, detailed instructions, drawings, or specifications to tell others about how devices, parts, equipment, or structures are to be fabricated, constructed, assembled, modified, maintained, or used.
Operating Vehicles, Mechanized Devices, or Equipme	Running, maneuvering, navigating, or driving vehicles or mechanized equipment, such as forklifts, passenger vehicles, aircraft, or water craft.

Work_Context	Work_Context Definitions
Face-to-Face Discussions	How often do you have to have face-to-face discussions with individuals or teams in this job?
Public Speaking	How often do you have to perform public speaking in this job?
Contact With Others	How much does this job require the worker to be in contact with others (face-to-face, by telephone, or otherwise) in order to perform it?
Indoors, Environmentally Controlled	How often does this job require working indoors in environmentally controlled conditions?
Electronic Mail	How often do you use electronic mail in this job?
Freedom to Make Decisions	How much decision making freedom, without supervision, does the job offer?
Structured versus Unstructured Work	To what extent is this job structured for the worker, rather than allowing the worker to determine tasks, priorities, and goals?
Work With Work Group or Team	How important is it to work with others in a group or team in this job?
Spend Time Standing	How much does this job require standing?
Importance of Being Exact or Accurate	How important is being very exact or highly accurate in performing this job?
Coordinate or Lead Others	How important is it to coordinate or lead others in accomplishing work activities in this job?
Physical Proximity	To what extent does this job require the worker to perform job tasks in close physical proximity to other people?
Time Pressure	How often does this job require the worker to meet strict deadlines?

Telephone	How often do you have telephone conversations in this job?
Frequency of Conflict Situations	How often are there conflict situations the employee has to face in this job?
Letters and Memos	How often does the job require written letters and memos?
Frequency of Decision Making	How frequently is the worker required to make decisions that affect other people, the financial resources, and/or the image and reputation of the organization?
Deal With Unpleasant or Angry People	How frequently does the worker have to deal with unpleasant, angry, or discourteous individuals as part of the job requirements?
Impact of Decisions on Co-workers or Company Resul	How do the decisions an employee makes impact the results of co-workers, clients or the company?
Deal With External Customers	How important is it to work with external customers or the public in this job?
Sounds, Noise Levels Are Distracting or Uncomforta	How often does this job require working exposed to sounds and noise levels that are distracting or uncomfortable?
Importance of Repeating Same Tasks	How important is repeating the same physical activities (e.g., key entry) or mental activities (e.g., checking entries in a ledger) over and over, without stopping, to performing this job?
Responsibility for Outcomes and Results	How responsible is the worker for work outcomes and results of other workers?
Responsible for Others' Health and Safety	How much responsibility is there for the health and safety of others in this job?
Exposed to Disease or Infections	How often does this job require exposure to disease/infections?
Exposed to Contaminants	How often does this job require working exposed to contaminants (such as pollutants, gases, dust or odors)?
Spend Time Walking and Running	How much does this job require walking and running?
Spend Time Sitting	How much does this job require sitting?
Level of Competition	To what extent does this job require the worker to compete or to be aware of competitive pressures?
Spend Time Using Your Hands to Handle, Control, or	How much does this job require using your hands to handle, control, or feel objects, tools or controls?
Indoors, Not Environmentally Controlled	How often does this job require working indoors in non-controlled environmental conditions (e.g., warehouse without heat)?
Spend Time Making Repetitive Motions	How much does this job require making repetitive motions?
Consequence of Error	How serious would the result usually be if the worker made a mistake that was not readily correctable?
Deal With Physically Aggressive People	How frequently does this job require the worker to deal with physical aggression of violent individuals?
Degree of Automation	How automated is the job?
Very Hot or Cold Temperatures	How often does this job require working in very hot (above 90 F degrees) or very cold (below 32 F degrees) temperatures?
Outdoors, Exposed to Weather	How often does this job require working outdoors, exposed to all weather conditions?
Spend Time Bending or Twisting the Body	How much does this job require bending or twisting your body?
Exposed to Minor Burns, Cuts, Bites, or Stings	How often does this job require exposure to minor burns, cuts, bites, or stings?
Cramped Work Space, Awkward Positions	How often does this job require working in cramped work spaces that requires getting into awkward positions?
In an Enclosed Vehicle or Equipment	How often does this job require working in a closed vehicle or equipment (e.g., car)?
Wear Common Protective or Safety Equipment such as	How much does this job require wearing common protective or safety equipment such as safety shoes, glasses, gloves, hard hats or life jackets?
Exposed to Hazardous Equipment	How often does this job require exposure to hazardous equipment?
Pace Determined by Speed of Equipment	How important is it to this job that the pace is determined by the speed of equipment or machinery? (This does not refer to keeping busy at all times on this job.)
Exposed to Hazardous Conditions	How often does this job require exposure to hazardous conditions?
Spend Time Kneeling, Crouching, Stooping, or Crawl	How much does this job require kneeling, crouching, stooping, or crawling?
Spend Time Keeping or Regaining Balance	How much does this job require keeping or regaining your balance?
Extremely Bright or Inadequate Lighting	How often does this job require working in extremely bright or inadequate lighting conditions?
Outdoors, Under Cover	How often does this job require working outdoors, under cover (e.g., structure with roof but no walls)?

In an Open Vehicle or Equipment	How often does this job require working in an open vehicle or equipment (e.g., tractor)?
Exposed to High Places	How often does this job require exposure to high places?
Wear Specialized Protective or Safety Equipment su	How much does this job require wearing specialized protective or safety equipment such as breathing apparatus, safety harness, full protection suits, or radiation protection?
Spend Time Climbing Ladders, Scaffolds, or Poles	How much does this job require climbing ladders, scaffolds, or poles?
Exposed to Radiation	How often does this job require exposure to radiation?
Exposed to Whole Body Vibration	How often does this job require exposure to whole body vibration (e.g., operate a jackhammer)?

Job Zone Component	Job Zone Component Definitions
Title	Job Zone Four: Considerable Preparation Needed
Overall Experience	A minimum of two to four years of work-related skill, knowledge, or experience is needed for these occupations. For example, an accountant must complete four years of college and work for several years in accounting to be considered qualified.
Job Training	Employees in these occupations usually need several years of work-related experience, on-the-job training, and/or vocational training.
Job Zone Examples	Many of these occupations involve coordinating, supervising, managing, or training others. Examples include accountants, chefs and head cooks, computer programmers, historians, pharmacists, and police detectives.
SVP Range	(7.0 to < 8.0)
Education	Most of these occupations require a four-year bachelor's degree, but some do not.

Work_Styles	Work_Styles Definitions
Integrity	Job requires being honest and ethical.
Dependability	Job requires being reliable, responsible, and dependable, and fulfilling obligations.
Self Control	Job requires maintaining composure, keeping emotions in check, controlling anger, and avoiding aggressive behavior, even in very difficult situations.
Concern for Others	Job requires being sensitive to others' needs and feelings and being understanding and helpful on the job.
Stress Tolerance	Job requires accepting criticism and dealing calmly and effectively with high stress situations.
Social Orientation	Job requires preferring to work with others rather than alone, and being personally connected with others on the job.
Persistence	Job requires persistence in the face of obstacles.
Leadership	Job requires a willingness to lead, take charge, and offer opinions and direction.
Initiative	Job requires a willingness to take on responsibilities and challenges.
Cooperation	Job requires being pleasant with others on the job and displaying a good-natured, cooperative attitude.
Adaptability/Flexibility	Job requires being open to change (positive or negative) and to considerable variety in the workplace.
Attention to Detail	Job requires being careful about detail and thorough in completing work tasks.
Achievement/Effort	Job requires establishing and maintaining personally challenging achievement goals and exerting effort toward mastering tasks.
Analytical Thinking	Job requires analyzing information and using logic to address work-related issues and problems.
Innovation	Job requires creativity and alternative thinking to develop new ideas for and answers to work-related problems.
Independence	Job requires developing one's own ways of doing things, guiding oneself with little or no supervision, and depending on oneself to get things done.

25-2032.00 - Vocational Education Teachers, Secondary School

Teach or instruct vocational or occupational subjects at the secondary school level.

Tasks

1) Prepare reports on students and activities as required by administration.

2) Keep informed about trends in education and subject matter specialties.

3) Meet with other professionals to discuss individual students' needs and progress.

4) Maintain accurate and complete student records as required by law, district policy, and administrative regulations.

5) Instruct students individually and in groups, using various teaching methods such as lectures, discussions, and demonstrations.

6) Plan and conduct activities for a balanced program of instruction, demonstration, and work time that provides students with opportunities to observe, question, and investigate.

7) Prepare materials and classroom for class activities.

8) Enforce all administration policies and rules governing students.

9) Use computers, audiovisual aids, and other equipment and materials to supplement presentations.

10) Observe and evaluate students' performance, behavior, social development, and physical health.

11) Confer with parents or guardians, other teachers, counselors, and administrators in order to resolve students' behavioral and academic problems.

12) Establish and enforce rules for behavior and procedures for maintaining order among the students for whom they are responsible.

13) Select, order, store, issue, and inventory classroom equipment, materials, and supplies.

14) Attend staff meetings, and serve on committees as required.

15) Assign and grade class work and homework.

16) Prepare objectives and outlines for courses of study, following curriculum guidelines or requirements of states and schools.

17) Prepare students for later grades by encouraging them to explore learning opportunities and to persevere with challenging tasks.

18) Plan and supervise class projects, field trips, visits by guest speakers or other experiential activities, and guide students in learning from those activities.

19) Instruct and monitor students the in use and care of equipment and materials, in order to prevent injury and damage.

20) Confer with other staff members to plan and schedule lessons promoting learning, following approved curricula.

21) Instruct students in the knowledge and skills required in a specific occupation or occupational field, using a systematic plan of lectures, discussions, audiovisual presentations, and laboratory, shop and field studies.

22) Collaborate with other teachers and administrators in the development, evaluation, and revision of secondary school programs.

23) Guide and counsel students with adjustment and/or academic problems, or special academic interests.

24) Sponsor extracurricular activities such as clubs, student organizations, and academic contests.

25) Perform administrative duties such as assisting in school libraries, hall and cafeteria monitoring, and bus loading and unloading.

26) Plan and supervise work-experience programs in businesses, industrial shops, and school laboratories.

27) Prepare and implement remedial programs for students requiring extra help.

28) Place students in jobs or make referrals to job placement services.

29) Provide disabled students with assistive devices, supportive technology, and assistance accessing facilities such as restrooms.

30) Establish clear objectives for all lessons, units, and projects, and communicate those objectives to students.

31) Attend professional meetings, educational conferences, and teacher training workshops in order to maintain and improve professional competence.

32) Meet with parents and guardians to discuss their children's progress, and to determine their priorities for their children and their resource needs.

Knowledge / Knowledge Definitions

Knowledge	Knowledge Definitions
Education and Training	Knowledge of principles and methods for curriculum and training design, teaching and instruction for individuals and groups, and the measurement of training effects.
English Language	Knowledge of the structure and content of the English language including the meaning and spelling of words, rules of composition, and grammar.
Mathematics	Knowledge of arithmetic, algebra, geometry, calculus, statistics, and their applications.
Computers and Electronics	Knowledge of circuit boards, processors, chips, electronic equipment, and computer hardware and software, including applications and programming.
Clerical	Knowledge of administrative and clerical procedures and systems such as word processing, managing files and records, stenography and transcription, designing forms, and other office procedures and terminology.
Customer and Personal Service	Knowledge of principles and processes for providing customer and personal services. This includes customer needs assessment, meeting quality standards for services, and evaluation of customer satisfaction.
Psychology	Knowledge of human behavior and performance; individual differences in ability, personality, and interests; learning and motivation; psychological research methods; and the assessment and treatment of behavioral and affective disorders.
Public Safety and Security	Knowledge of relevant equipment, policies, procedures, and strategies to promote effective local, state, or national security operations for the protection of people, data, property, and institutions.
Administration and Management	Knowledge of business and management principles involved in strategic planning, resource allocation, human resources modeling, leadership technique, production methods, and coordination of people and resources.
Mechanical	Knowledge of machines and tools, including their designs, uses, repair, and maintenance.
Design	Knowledge of design techniques, tools, and principles involved in production of precision technical plans, blueprints, drawings, and models.
Engineering and Technology	Knowledge of the practical application of engineering science and technology. This includes applying principles, techniques, procedures, and equipment to the design and production of various goods and services.
Communications and Media	Knowledge of media production, communication, and dissemination techniques and methods. This includes alternative ways to inform and entertain via written, oral, and visual media.
Production and Processing	Knowledge of raw materials, production processes, quality control, costs, and other techniques for maximizing the effective manufacture and distribution of goods.
Therapy and Counseling	Knowledge of principles, methods, and procedures for diagnosis, treatment, and rehabilitation of physical and mental dysfunctions, and for career counseling and guidance.
Personnel and Human Resources	Knowledge of principles and procedures for personnel recruitment, selection, training, compensation and benefits, labor relations and negotiation, and personnel information systems.
Building and Construction	Knowledge of materials, methods, and the tools involved in the construction or repair of houses, buildings, or other structures such as highways and roads.
Sociology and Anthropology	Knowledge of group behavior and dynamics, societal trends and influences, human migrations, ethnicity, cultures and their history and origins.
Economics and Accounting	Knowledge of economic and accounting principles and practices, the financial markets, banking and the analysis and reporting of financial data.
Telecommunications	Knowledge of transmission, broadcasting, switching, control, and operation of telecommunications systems.
Law and Government	Knowledge of laws, legal codes, court procedures, precedents, government regulations, executive orders, agency rules, and the democratic political process.
Sales and Marketing	Knowledge of principles and methods for showing, promoting, and selling products or services. This includes marketing strategy and tactics, product demonstration, sales techniques, and sales control systems.
Physics	Knowledge and prediction of physical principles, laws, their interrelationships, and applications to understanding fluid, material, and atmospheric dynamics, and mechanical, electrical, atomic and sub-atomic structures and processes.
Chemistry	Knowledge of the chemical composition, structure, and properties of substances and of the chemical processes and transformations that they undergo. This includes uses of chemicals and their interactions, danger signs, production techniques, and disposal methods.

Transportation	Knowledge of principles and methods for moving people or goods by air, rail, sea, or road, including the relative costs and benefits.
Philosophy and Theology	Knowledge of different philosophical systems and religions. This includes their basic principles, values, ethics, ways of thinking, customs, practices, and their impact on human culture.
Geography	Knowledge of principles and methods for describing the features of land, sea, and air masses, including their physical characteristics, locations, interrelationships, and distribution of plant, animal, and human life.
Biology	Knowledge of plant and animal organisms, their tissues, cells, functions, interdependencies, and interactions with each other and the environment.
Fine Arts	Knowledge of the theory and techniques required to compose, produce, and perform works of music, dance, visual arts, drama, and sculpture.
History and Archeology	Knowledge of historical events and their causes, indicators, and effects on civilizations and cultures.
Food Production	Knowledge of techniques and equipment for planting, growing, and harvesting food products (both plant and animal) for consumption, including storage/handling techniques.
Medicine and Dentistry	Knowledge of the information and techniques needed to diagnose and treat human injuries, diseases, and deformities. This includes symptoms, treatment alternatives, drug properties and interactions, and preventive health-care measures.
Foreign Language	Knowledge of the structure and content of a foreign (non-English) language including the meaning and spelling of words, rules of composition and grammar, and pronunciation.

Skills	**Skills Definitions**
Instructing	Teaching others how to do something.
Speaking	Talking to others to convey information effectively.
Reading Comprehension	Understanding written sentences and paragraphs in work related documents.
Active Listening	Giving full attention to what other people are saying, taking time to understand the points being made, asking questions as appropriate, and not interrupting at inappropriate times.
Time Management	Managing one's own time and the time of others.
Learning Strategies	Selecting and using training/instructional methods and procedures appropriate for the situation when learning or teaching new things.
Monitoring	Monitoring/Assessing performance of yourself, other individuals, or organizations to make improvements or take corrective action.
Social Perceptiveness	Being aware of others' reactions and understanding why they react as they do.
Active Learning	Understanding the implications of new information for both current and future problem-solving and decision-making.
Critical Thinking	Using logic and reasoning to identify the strengths and weaknesses of alternative solutions, conclusions or approaches to problems.
Writing	Communicating effectively in writing as appropriate for the needs of the audience.
Judgment and Decision Making	Considering the relative costs and benefits of potential actions to choose the most appropriate one.
Service Orientation	Actively looking for ways to help people.
Coordination	Adjusting actions in relation to others' actions.
Persuasion	Persuading others to change their minds or behavior.
Equipment Selection	Determining the kind of tools and equipment needed to do a job.
Complex Problem Solving	Identifying complex problems and reviewing related information to develop and evaluate options and implement solutions.
Mathematics	Using mathematics to solve problems.
Management of Personnel Resources	Motivating, developing, and directing people as they work, identifying the best people for the job.
Negotiation	Bringing others together and trying to reconcile differences.
Management of Material Resources	Obtaining and seeing to the appropriate use of equipment, facilities, and materials needed to do certain work.
Technology Design	Generating or adapting equipment and technology to serve user needs.
Management of Financial Resources	Determining how money will be spent to get the work done, and accounting for these expenditures.
Troubleshooting	Determining causes of operating errors and deciding what to do about it.

Equipment Maintenance	Performing routine maintenance on equipment and determining when and what kind of maintenance is needed.
Science	Using scientific rules and methods to solve problems.
Operations Analysis	Analyzing needs and product requirements to create a design.
Installation	Installing equipment, machines, wiring, or programs to meet specifications.
Repairing	Repairing machines or systems using the needed tools.
Operation and Control	Controlling operations of equipment or systems.
Quality Control Analysis	Conducting tests and inspections of products, services, or processes to evaluate quality or performance.
Systems Evaluation	Identifying measures or indicators of system performance and the actions needed to improve or correct performance, relative to the goals of the system.
Operation Monitoring	Watching gauges, dials, or other indicators to make sure a machine is working properly.
Systems Analysis	Determining how a system should work and how changes in conditions, operations, and the environment will affect outcomes.
Programming	Writing computer programs for various purposes.

Ability	**Ability Definitions**
Oral Expression	The ability to communicate information and ideas in speaking so others will understand.
Oral Comprehension	The ability to listen to and understand information and ideas presented through spoken words and sentences.
Speech Recognition	The ability to identify and understand the speech of another person.
Speech Clarity	The ability to speak clearly so others can understand you.
Problem Sensitivity	The ability to tell when something is wrong or is likely to go wrong. It does not involve solving the problem, only recognizing there is a problem.
Written Comprehension	The ability to read and understand information and ideas presented in writing.
Written Expression	The ability to communicate information and ideas in writing so others will understand.
Deductive Reasoning	The ability to apply general rules to specific problems to produce answers that make sense.
Near Vision	The ability to see details at close range (within a few feet of the observer).
Inductive Reasoning	The ability to combine pieces of information to form general rules or conclusions (includes finding a relationship among seemingly unrelated events).
Category Flexibility	The ability to generate or use different sets of rules for combining or grouping things in different ways.
Information Ordering	The ability to arrange things or actions in a certain order or pattern according to a specific rule or set of rules (e.g., patterns of numbers, letters, words, pictures, mathematical operations).
Fluency of Ideas	The ability to come up with a number of ideas about a topic (the number of ideas is important, not their quality, correctness, or creativity).
Originality	The ability to come up with unusual or clever ideas about a given topic or situation, or to develop creative ways to solve a problem.
Selective Attention	The ability to concentrate on a task over a period of time without being distracted.
Flexibility of Closure	The ability to identify or detect a known pattern (a figure, object, word, or sound) that is hidden in other distracting material.
Far Vision	The ability to see details at a distance.
Perceptual Speed	The ability to quickly and accurately compare similarities and differences among sets of letters, numbers, objects, pictures, or patterns. The things to be compared may be presented at the same time or one after the other. This ability also includes comparing a presented object with a remembered object.
Visualization	The ability to imagine how something will look after it is moved around or when its parts are moved or rearranged.
Time Sharing	The ability to shift back and forth between two or more activities or sources of information (such as speech, sounds, touch, or other sources).
Arm-Hand Steadiness	The ability to keep your hand and arm steady while moving your arm or while holding your arm and hand in one position.
Memorization	The ability to remember information such as words, numbers, pictures, and procedures.
Speed of Closure	The ability to quickly make sense of, combine, and organize information into meaningful patterns.
Hearing Sensitivity	The ability to detect or tell the differences between sounds that vary in pitch and loudness.

Visual Color Discrimination	The ability to match or detect differences between colors, including shades of color and brightness.
Mathematical Reasoning	The ability to choose the right mathematical methods or formulas to solve a problem.
Number Facility	The ability to add, subtract, multiply, or divide quickly and correctly.
Stamina	The ability to exert yourself physically over long periods of time without getting winded or out of breath.
Auditory Attention	The ability to focus on a single source of sound in the presence of other distracting sounds.
Finger Dexterity	The ability to make precisely coordinated movements of the fingers of one or both hands to grasp, manipulate, or assemble very small objects.
Manual Dexterity	The ability to quickly move your hand, your hand together with your arm, or your two hands to grasp, manipulate, or assemble objects.
Multilimb Coordination	The ability to coordinate two or more limbs (for example, two arms, two legs, or one leg and one arm) while sitting, standing, or lying down. It does not involve performing the activities while the whole body is in motion.
Trunk Strength	The ability to use your abdominal and lower back muscles to support part of the body repeatedly or continuously over time without 'giving out' or fatiguing.
Response Orientation	The ability to choose quickly between two or more movements in response to two or more different signals (lights, sounds, pictures). It includes the speed with which the correct response is started with the hand, foot, or other body part.
Extent Flexibility	The ability to bend, stretch, twist, or reach with your body, arms, and/or legs.
Depth Perception	The ability to judge which of several objects is closer or farther away from you, or to judge the distance between you and an object.
Gross Body Coordination	The ability to coordinate the movement of your arms, legs, and torso together when the whole body is in motion.
Static Strength	The ability to exert maximum muscle force to lift, push, pull, or carry objects.
Gross Body Equilibrium	The ability to keep or regain your body balance or stay upright when in an unstable position.
Control Precision	The ability to quickly and repeatedly adjust the controls of a machine or a vehicle to exact positions.
Speed of Limb Movement	The ability to quickly move the arms and legs.
Wrist-Finger Speed	The ability to make fast, simple, repeated movements of the fingers, hands, and wrists.
Dynamic Strength	The ability to exert muscle force repeatedly or continuously over time. This involves muscular endurance and resistance to muscle fatigue.
Rate Control	The ability to time your movements or the movement of a piece of equipment in anticipation of changes in the speed and/or direction of a moving object or scene.
Reaction Time	The ability to quickly respond (with the hand, finger, or foot) to a signal (sound, light, picture) when it appears.
Explosive Strength	The ability to use short bursts of muscle force to propel oneself (as in jumping or sprinting), or to throw an object.
Sound Localization	The ability to tell the direction from which a sound originated.
Spatial Orientation	The ability to know your location in relation to the environment or to know where other objects are in relation to you.
Glare Sensitivity	The ability to see objects in the presence of glare or bright lighting.
Night Vision	The ability to see under low light conditions.
Dynamic Flexibility	The ability to quickly and repeatedly bend, stretch, twist, or reach out with your body, arms, and/or legs.
Peripheral Vision	The ability to see objects or movement of objects to one's side when the eyes are looking ahead.

Work_Activity	Work_Activity Definitions
Training and Teaching Others	Identifying the educational needs of others, developing formal educational or training programs or classes, and teaching or instructing others.
Coaching and Developing Others	Identifying the developmental needs of others and coaching, mentoring, or otherwise helping others to improve their knowledge or skills.
Organizing, Planning, and Prioritizing Work	Developing specific goals and plans to prioritize, organize, and accomplish your work.
Getting Information	Observing, receiving, and otherwise obtaining information from all relevant sources.
Updating and Using Relevant Knowledge	Keeping up-to-date technically and applying new knowledge to your job.

Documenting/Recording Information	Entering, transcribing, recording, storing, or maintaining information in written or electronic/magnetic form.
Guiding, Directing, and Motivating Subordinates	Providing guidance and direction to subordinates, including setting performance standards and monitoring performance.
Interacting With Computers	Using computers and computer systems (including hardware and software) to program, write software, set up functions, enter data, or process information.
Communicating with Supervisors, Peers, or Subordin	Providing information to supervisors, co-workers, and subordinates by telephone, in written form, e-mail, or in person.
Establishing and Maintaining Interpersonal Relatio	Developing constructive and cooperative working relationships with others, and maintaining them over time.
Making Decisions and Solving Problems	Analyzing information and evaluating results to choose the best solution and solve problems.
Scheduling Work and Activities	Scheduling events, programs, and activities, as well as the work of others.
Resolving Conflicts and Negotiating with Others	Handling complaints, settling disputes, and resolving grievances and conflicts, or otherwise negotiating with others.
Identifying Objects, Actions, and Events	Identifying information by categorizing, estimating, recognizing differences or similarities, and detecting changes in circumstances or events.
Thinking Creatively	Developing, designing, or creating new applications, ideas, relationships, systems, or products, including artistic contributions.
Developing Objectives and Strategies	Establishing long-range objectives and specifying the strategies and actions to achieve them.
Communicating with Persons Outside Organization	Communicating with people outside the organization, representing the organization to customers, the public, government, and other external sources. This information can be exchanged in person, in writing, or by telephone or e-mail.
Evaluating Information to Determine Compliance wit	Using relevant information and individual judgment to determine whether events or processes comply with laws, regulations, or standards.
Coordinating the Work and Activities of Others	Getting members of a group to work together to accomplish tasks.
Judging the Qualities of Things, Services, or Peop	Assessing the value, importance, or quality of things or people.
Processing Information	Compiling, coding, categorizing, calculating, tabulating, auditing, or verifying information or data.
Performing for or Working Directly with the Public	Performing for people or dealing directly with the public. This includes serving customers in restaurants and stores, and receiving clients or guests.
Developing and Building Teams	Encouraging and building mutual trust, respect, and cooperation among team members.
Assisting and Caring for Others	Providing personal assistance, medical attention, emotional support, or other personal care to others such as coworkers, customers, or patients.
Monitor Processes, Materials, or Surroundings	Monitoring and reviewing information from materials, events, or the environment, to detect or assess problems.
Interpreting the Meaning of Information for Others	Translating or explaining what information means and how it can be used.
Inspecting Equipment, Structures, or Material	Inspecting equipment, structures, or materials to identify the cause of errors or other problems or defects.
Provide Consultation and Advice to Others	Providing guidance and expert advice to management or other groups on technical, systems-, or process-related topics.
Analyzing Data or Information	Identifying the underlying principles, reasons, or facts of information by breaking down information or data into separate parts.
Performing Administrative Activities	Performing day-to-day administrative tasks such as maintaining information files and processing paperwork.
Monitoring and Controlling Resources	Monitoring and controlling resources and overseeing the spending of money.
Controlling Machines and Processes	Using either control mechanisms or direct physical activity to operate machines or processes (not including computers or vehicles).
Estimating the Quantifiable Characteristics of Pro	Estimating sizes, distances, and quantities; or determining time, costs, resources, or materials needed to perform a work activity.
Handling and Moving Objects	Using hands and arms in handling, installing, positioning, and moving materials, and manipulating things.
Repairing and Maintaining Mechanical Equipment	Servicing, repairing, adjusting, and testing machines, devices, moving parts, and equipment that operate primarily on the basis of mechanical (not electronic) principles.

Performing General Physical Activities	Performing physical activities that require considerable use of your arms and legs and moving your whole body, such as climbing, lifting, balancing, walking, stooping, and handling of materials.
Selling or Influencing Others	Convincing others to buy merchandise/goods or to otherwise change their minds or actions.
Repairing and Maintaining Electronic Equipment	Servicing, repairing, calibrating, regulating, fine-tuning, or testing machines, devices, and equipment that operate primarily on the basis of electrical or electronic (not mechanical) principles.
Drafting, Laying Out, and Specifying Technical Dev	Providing documentation, detailed instructions, drawings, or specifications to tell others about how devices, parts, equipment, or structures are to be fabricated, constructed, assembled, modified, maintained, or used.
Operating Vehicles, Mechanized Devices, or Equipme	Running, maneuvering, navigating, or driving vehicles or mechanized equipment, such as forklifts, passenger vehicles, aircraft, or water craft.
Staffing Organizational Units	Recruiting, interviewing, selecting, hiring, and promoting employees in an organization.

Work_Context	Work_Context Definitions
Contact With Others	How much does this job require the worker to be in contact with others (face-to-face, by telephone, or otherwise) in order to perform it?
Face-to-Face Discussions	How often do you have to have face-to-face discussions with individuals or teams in this job?
Freedom to Make Decisions	How much decision making freedom, without supervision, does the job offer?
Physical Proximity	To what extent does this job require the worker to perform job tasks in close physical proximity to other people?
Structured versus Unstructured Work	To what extent is this job structured for the worker, rather than allowing the worker to determine tasks, priorities, and goals?
Frequency of Decision Making	How frequently is the worker required to make decisions that affect other people, the financial resources, and/or the image and reputation of the organization?
Electronic Mail	How often do you use electronic mail in this job?
Indoors, Environmentally Controlled	How often does this job require working indoors in environmentally controlled conditions?
Telephone	How often do you have telephone conversations in this job?
Work With Work Group or Team	How important is it to work with others in a group or team in this job?
Spend Time Standing	How much does this job require standing?
Public Speaking	How often do you have to perform public speaking in this job?
Coordinate or Lead Others	How important is it to coordinate or lead others in accomplishing work activities in this job?
Responsible for Others' Health and Safety	How much responsibility is there for the health and safety of others in this job?
Importance of Being Exact or Accurate	How important is being very exact or highly accurate in performing this job?
Impact of Decisions on Co-workers or Company Resul	How do the decisions an employee makes impact the results of co-workers, clients or the company?
Frequency of Conflict Situations	How often are there conflict situations the employee has to face in this job?
Deal With Unpleasant or Angry People	How frequently does the worker have to deal with unpleasant, angry, or discourteous individuals as part of the job requirements?
Deal With External Customers	How important is it to work with external customers or the public in this job?
Letters and Memos	How often does the job require written letters and memos?
Time Pressure	How often does this job require the worker to meet strict deadlines?
Sounds, Noise Levels Are Distracting or Uncomforta	How often does this job require working exposed to sounds and noise levels that are distracting or uncomfortable?
Responsibility for Outcomes and Results	How responsible is the worker for work outcomes and results of other workers?
Spend Time Using Your Hands to Handle, Control, or	How much does this job require using your hands to handle, control, or feel objects, tools or controls?
Importance of Repeating Same Tasks	How important is repeating the same physical activities (e.g., key entry) or mental activities (e.g., checking entries in a ledger) over and over, without stopping, to performing this job?
Exposed to Contaminants	How often does this job require working exposed to contaminants (such as pollutants, gases, dust or odors)?
Exposed to Disease or Infections	How often does this job require exposure to disease/infections?

Consequence of Error	How serious would the result usually be if the worker made a mistake that was not readily correctable?
Spend Time Walking and Running	How much does this job require walking and running?
Deal With Physically Aggressive People	How frequently does this job require the worker to deal with physical aggression of violent individuals?
Spend Time Making Repetitive Motions	How much does this job require making repetitive motions?
Level of Competition	To what extent does this job require the worker to compete or to be aware of competitive pressures?
Wear Common Protective or Safety Equipment such as	How much does this job require wearing common protective or safety equipment such as safety shoes, glasses, gloves, hard hats or live jackets?
Spend Time Sitting	How much does this job require sitting?
Exposed to Minor Burns, Cuts, Bites, or Stings	How often does this job require exposure to minor burns, cuts, bites, or stings?
Degree of Automation	How automated is the job?
Spend Time Bending or Twisting the Body	How much does this job require bending or twisting your body?
Indoors, Not Environmentally Controlled	How often does this job require working indoors in non-controlled environmental conditions (e.g., warehouse without heat)?
Extremely Bright or Inadequate Lighting	How often does this job require working in extremely bright or inadequate lighting conditions?
Exposed to Hazardous Equipment	How often does this job require exposure to hazardous equipment?
Outdoors, Exposed to Weather	How often does this job require working outdoors, exposed to all weather conditions?
Very Hot or Cold Temperatures	How often does this job require working in very hot (above 90 F degrees) or very cold (below 32 F degrees) temperatures?
Cramped Work Space, Awkward Positions	How often does this job require working in cramped work spaces that requires getting into awkward positions?
Spend Time Kneeling, Crouching, Stooping, or Crawl	How much does this job require kneeling, crouching, stooping or crawling?
In an Enclosed Vehicle or Equipment	How often does this job require working in a closed vehicle or equipment (e.g., car)?
Exposed to Hazardous Conditions	How often does this job require exposure to hazardous conditions?
Spend Time Keeping or Regaining Balance	How much does this job require keeping or regaining your balance?
Pace Determined by Speed of Equipment	How important is it to this job that the pace is determined by the speed of equipment or machinery? (This does not refer to keeping busy at all times on this job.)
Outdoors, Under Cover	How often does this job require working outdoors, under cover (e.g., structure with roof but no walls)?
Wear Specialized Protective or Safety Equipment su	How much does this job require wearing specialized protective or safety equipment such as breathing apparatus, safety harness, full protection suits, or radiation protection?
Exposed to High Places	How often does this job require exposure to high places?
Spend Time Climbing Ladders, Scaffolds, or Poles	How much does this job require climbing ladders, scaffolds, or poles?
Exposed to Radiation	How often does this job require exposure to radiation?
In an Open Vehicle or Equipment	How often does this job require working in an open vehicle or equipment (e.g., tractor)?
Exposed to Whole Body Vibration	How often does this job require exposure to whole body vibration (e.g., operate a jackhammer)?

Job Zone Component	Job Zone Component Definitions
Title	Job Zone Four: Considerable Preparation Needed
Overall Experience	A minimum of two to four years of work-related skill, knowledge, or experience is needed for these occupations. For example, an accountant must complete four years of college and work for several years in accounting to be considered qualified.
Job Training	Employees in these occupations usually need several years of work-related experience, on-the-job training, and/or vocational training.
Job Zone Examples	Many of these occupations involve coordinating, supervising, managing, or training others. Examples include accountants, chefs and head cooks, computer programmers, historians, pharmacists, and police detectives.
SVP Range	(7.0 to < 8.0)
Education	Most of these occupations require a four - year bachelor's degree, but some do not.

Work_Styles	Work_Styles Definitions
Integrity	Job requires being honest and ethical.
Dependability	Job requires being reliable, responsible, and dependable, and fulfilling obligations.
Self Control	Job requires maintaining composure, keeping emotions in check, controlling anger, and avoiding aggressive behavior, even in very difficult situations.
Stress Tolerance	Job requires accepting criticism and dealing calmly and effectively with high stress situations.
Concern for Others	Job requires being sensitive to others' needs and feelings and being understanding and helpful on the job.
Leadership	Job requires a willingness to lead, take charge, and offer opinions and direction.
Cooperation	Job requires being pleasant with others on the job and displaying a good-natured, cooperative attitude.
Initiative	Job requires a willingness to take on responsibilities and challenges.
Persistence	Job requires persistence in the face of obstacles.
Adaptability/Flexibility	Job requires being open to change (positive or negative) and to considerable variety in the workplace.
Attention to Detail	Job requires being careful about detail and thorough in completing work tasks.
Innovation	Job requires creativity and alternative thinking to develop new ideas for and answers to work-related problems.
Independence	Job requires developing one's own ways of doing things, guiding oneself with little or no supervision, and depending on oneself to get things done.
Achievement/Effort	Job requires establishing and maintaining personally challenging achievement goals and exerting effort toward mastering tasks.
Analytical Thinking	Job requires analyzing information and using logic to address work-related issues and problems.
Social Orientation	Job requires preferring to work with others rather than alone, and being personally connected with others on the job.

25-2041.00 - Special Education Teachers, Preschool, Kindergarten, and Elementary School

Teach elementary and preschool school subjects to educationally and physically handicapped students. Includes teachers who specialize and work with audibly and visually handicapped students and those who teach basic academic and life processes skills to the mentally impaired.

Tasks

1) Attend staff meetings, and serve on committees as required.

2) Attend professional meetings, educational conferences, and teacher training workshops in order to maintain and improve professional competence.

3) Teach socially acceptable behavior, employing techniques such as behavior modification and positive reinforcement.

4) Confer with other staff members to plan and schedule lessons promoting learning, following approved curricula.

5) Establish and enforce rules for behavior and policies and procedures to maintain order among the students for whom they are responsible.

6) Meet with parents and guardians to discuss their children's progress, and to determine their priorities for their children and their resource needs.

7) Confer with parents, administrators, testing specialists, social workers, and professionals to develop individual educational plans designed to promote students' educational, physical, and social development.

8) Confer with parents or guardians, teachers, counselors, and administrators in order to resolve students' behavioral and academic problems.

9) Plan and conduct activities for a balanced program of instruction, demonstration, and work time that provides students with opportunities to observe, question, and investigate.

10) Observe and evaluate students' performance, behavior, social development, and physical health.

11) Establish clear objectives for all lessons, units, and projects, and communicate those objectives to students.

12) Instruct students in academic subjects, using a variety of techniques such as phonetics, multisensory learning, and repetition, in order to reinforce learning and to meet students'

varying needs and interests.

13) Organize and label materials, and display students' work in a manner appropriate for their eye levels and perceptual skills.

14) Prepare classrooms for class activities and provide a variety of materials and resources for children to explore, manipulate, and use, both in learning activities and imaginative play.

15) Employ special educational strategies and techniques during instruction to improve the development of sensory- and perceptual-motor skills, language, cognition, and memory.

16) Prepare for assigned classes, and show written evidence of preparation upon request of immediate supervisors.

17) Select, store, order, issue, and inventory classroom equipment, materials, and supplies.

18) Administer standardized ability and achievement tests, and interpret results to determine students' strengths and areas of need.

19) Prepare students for later grades by encouraging them to explore learning opportunities and to persevere with challenging tasks.

20) Prepare, administer, and grade tests and assignments to evaluate students' progress.

21) Prepare objectives and outlines for courses of study, following curriculum guidelines or requirements of states and schools.

22) Supervise, evaluate, and plan assignments for teacher assistants and volunteers.

23) Use computers, audiovisual aids, and other equipment and materials to supplement presentations.

24) Develop and implement strategies to meet the needs of students with a variety of handicapping conditions.

25) Organize and supervise games and other recreational activities to promote physical, mental, and social development.

26) Modify the general education curriculum for special-needs students based upon a variety of instructional techniques and technologies.

27) Teach students personal development skills such as goal setting, independence, and self-advocacy.

28) Perform administrative duties such as assisting in school libraries, hall and cafeteria monitoring, and bus loading and unloading.

29) Guide and counsel students with adjustment and/or academic problems, or special academic interests.

30) Collaborate with other teachers and administrators in the development, evaluation, and revision of preschool, kindergarten, or elementary school programs.

31) Instruct students in daily living skills required for independent maintenance and self-sufficiency, such as hygiene, safety, and food preparation.

32) Coordinate placement of students with special needs into mainstream classes.

33) Meet with parents to provide guidance in using community resources, and to teach skills for dealing with students' impairments.

34) Monitor teachers and teacher assistants to ensure that they adhere to inclusive special education program requirements.

35) Instruct and monitor students in the use and care of equipment and materials, in order to prevent injuries and damage.

36) Plan and supervise class projects, field trips, visits by guest speakers, or other experiential activities, and guide students in learning from those activities.

37) Provide assistive devices, supportive technology, and assistance accessing facilities such as restrooms.

38) Visit schools to tutor students with sensory impairments, and to consult with teachers regarding students' special needs.

39) Provide interpretation and transcription of regular classroom materials through Braille and sign language.

Knowledge	Knowledge Definitions
English Language	Knowledge of the structure and content of the English language including the meaning and spelling of words, rules of composition, and grammar.
Education and Training	Knowledge of principles and methods for curriculum and training design, teaching and instruction for individuals and groups, and the measurement of training effects.
Psychology	Knowledge of human behavior and performance; individual differences in ability, personality, and interests; learning and motivation; psychological research methods; and the assessment and treatment of behavioral and affective disorders.
Mathematics	Knowledge of arithmetic, algebra, geometry, calculus, statistics, and their applications.

Customer and Personal Service	Knowledge of principles and processes for providing customer and personal services. This includes customer needs assessment, meeting quality standards for services, and evaluation of customer satisfaction.
Computers and Electronics	Knowledge of circuit boards, processors, chips, electronic equipment, and computer hardware and software, including applications and programming.
Therapy and Counseling	Knowledge of principles, methods, and procedures for diagnosis, treatment, and rehabilitation of physical and mental dysfunctions, and for career counseling and guidance.
Clerical	Knowledge of administrative and clerical procedures and systems such as word processing, managing files and records, stenography and transcription, designing forms, and other office procedures and terminology.
Sociology and Anthropology	Knowledge of group behavior and dynamics, societal trends and influences, human migrations, ethnicity, cultures and their history and origins.
Public Safety and Security	Knowledge of relevant equipment, policies, procedures, and strategies to promote effective local, state, or national security operations for the protection of people, data, property, and institutions.
Administration and Management	Knowledge of business and management principles involved in strategic planning, resource allocation, human resources modeling, leadership technique, production methods, and coordination of people and resources.
Law and Government	Knowledge of laws, legal codes, court procedures, precedents, government regulations, executive orders, agency rules, and the democratic political process.
Geography	Knowledge of principles and methods for describing the features of land, sea, and air masses, including their physical characteristics, locations, interrelationships, and distribution of plant, animal, and human life.
Philosophy and Theology	Knowledge of different philosophical systems and religions. This includes their basic principles, values, ethics, ways of thinking, customs, practices, and their impact on human culture.
Communications and Media	Knowledge of media production, communication, and dissemination techniques and methods. This includes alternative ways to inform and entertain via written, oral, and visual media.
History and Archeology	Knowledge of historical events and their causes, indicators, and effects on civilizations and cultures.
Medicine and Dentistry	Knowledge of the information and techniques needed to diagnose and treat human injuries, diseases, and deformities. This includes symptoms, treatment alternatives, drug properties and interactions, and preventive health-care measures.
Fine Arts	Knowledge of the theory and techniques required to compose, produce, and perform works of music, dance, visual arts, drama, and sculpture.
Biology	Knowledge of plant and animal organisms, their tissues, cells, functions, interdependencies, and interactions with each other and the environment.
Personnel and Human Resources	Knowledge of principles and procedures for personnel recruitment, selection, training, compensation and benefits, labor relations and negotiation, and personnel information systems.
Telecommunications	Knowledge of transmission, broadcasting, switching, control, and operation of telecommunications systems.
Design	Knowledge of design techniques, tools, and principles involved in production of precision technical plans, blueprints, drawings, and models.
Transportation	Knowledge of principles and methods for moving people or goods by air, rail, sea, or road, including the relative costs and benefits.
Foreign Language	Knowledge of the structure and content of a foreign (non-English) language including the meaning and spelling of words, rules of composition and grammar, and pronunciation.
Chemistry	Knowledge of the chemical composition, structure, and properties of substances and of the chemical processes and transformations that they undergo. This includes uses of chemicals and their interactions, danger signs, production techniques, and disposal methods.
Engineering and Technology	Knowledge of the practical application of engineering science and technology. This includes applying principles, techniques, procedures, and equipment to the design and production of various goods and services.
Economics and Accounting	Knowledge of economic and accounting principles and practices, the financial markets, banking and the analysis and reporting of financial data.

Production and Processing	Knowledge of raw materials, production processes, quality control, costs, and other techniques for maximizing the effective manufacture and distribution of goods.
Food Production	Knowledge of techniques and equipment for planting, growing, and harvesting food products (both plant and animal) for consumption, including storage/handling techniques.
Sales and Marketing	Knowledge of principles and methods for showing, promoting, and selling products or services. This includes marketing strategy and tactics, product demonstration, sales techniques, and sales control systems.
Mechanical	Knowledge of machines and tools, including their designs, uses, repair, and maintenance.
Physics	Knowledge and prediction of physical principles, laws, their interrelationships, and applications to understanding fluid, material, and atmospheric dynamics, and mechanical, electrical, atomic and sub-atomic structures and processes.
Building and Construction	Knowledge of materials, methods, and the tools involved in the construction or repair of houses, buildings, or other structures such as highways and roads.

Skills	Skills Definitions
Instructing	Teaching others how to do something.
Active Listening	Giving full attention to what other people are saying, taking time to understand the points being made, asking questions as appropriate, and not interrupting at inappropriate times.
Learning Strategies	Selecting and using training/instructional methods and procedures appropriate for the situation when learning or teaching new things.
Reading Comprehension	Understanding written sentences and paragraphs in work related documents.
Time Management	Managing one's own time and the time of others.
Monitoring	Monitoring/Assessing performance of yourself, other individuals, or organizations to make improvements or take corrective action.
Speaking	Talking to others to convey information effectively.
Social Perceptiveness	Being aware of others' reactions and understanding why they react as they do.
Writing	Communicating effectively in writing as appropriate for the needs of the audience.
Coordination	Adjusting actions in relation to others' actions.
Active Learning	Understanding the implications of new information for both current and future problem-solving and decision-making.
Critical Thinking	Using logic and reasoning to identify the strengths and weaknesses of alternative solutions, conclusions or approaches to problems.
Service Orientation	Actively looking for ways to help people.
Negotiation	Bringing others together and trying to reconcile differences.
Complex Problem Solving	Identifying complex problems and reviewing related information to develop and evaluate options and implement solutions.
Mathematics	Using mathematics to solve problems.
Judgment and Decision Making	Considering the relative costs and benefits of potential actions to choose the most appropriate one.
Persuasion	Persuading others to change their minds or behavior.
Equipment Selection	Determining the kind of tools and equipment needed to do a job.
Management of Personnel Resources	Motivating, developing, and directing people as they work, identifying the best people for the job.
Management of Material Resources	Obtaining and seeing to the appropriate use of equipment, facilities, and materials needed to do certain work.
Quality Control Analysis	Conducting tests and inspections of products, services, or processes to evaluate quality or performance.
Technology Design	Generating or adapting equipment and technology to serve user needs.
Science	Using scientific rules and methods to solve problems.
Operations Analysis	Analyzing needs and product requirements to create a design.
Systems Evaluation	Identifying measures or indicators of system performance and the actions needed to improve or correct performance, relative to the goals of the system.
Management of Financial Resources	Determining how money will be spent to get the work done, and accounting for these expenditures.
Systems Analysis	Determining how a system should work and how changes in conditions, operations, and the environment will affect outcomes.
Troubleshooting	Determining causes of operating errors and deciding what to do about it.
Operation and Control	Controlling operations of equipment or systems.
Installation	Installing equipment, machines, wiring, or programs to meet specifications.

Equipment Maintenance	Performing routine maintenance on equipment and determining when and what kind of maintenance is needed.
Repairing	Repairing machines or systems using the needed tools.
Programming	Writing computer programs for various purposes.
Operation Monitoring	Watching gauges, dials, or other indicators to make sure a machine is working properly.

Ability	Ability Definitions
Oral Expression	The ability to communicate information and ideas in speaking so others will understand.
Speech Clarity	The ability to speak clearly so others can understand you.
Speech Recognition	The ability to identify and understand the speech of another person.
Problem Sensitivity	The ability to tell when something is wrong or is likely to go wrong. It does not involve solving the problem, only recognizing there is a problem.
Oral Comprehension	The ability to listen to and understand information and ideas presented through spoken words and sentences.
Inductive Reasoning	The ability to combine pieces of information to form general rules or conclusions (includes finding a relationship among seemingly unrelated events).
Deductive Reasoning	The ability to apply general rules to specific problems to produce answers that make sense.
Written Comprehension	The ability to read and understand information and ideas presented in writing.
Information Ordering	The ability to arrange things or actions in a certain order or pattern according to a specific rule or set of rules (e.g., patterns of numbers, letters, words, pictures, mathematical operations).
Near Vision	The ability to see details at close range (within a few feet of the observer).
Written Expression	The ability to communicate information and ideas in writing so others will understand.
Fluency of Ideas	The ability to come up with a number of ideas about a topic (the number of ideas is important, not their quality, correctness, or creativity).
Category Flexibility	The ability to generate or use different sets of rules for combining or grouping things in different ways.
Originality	The ability to come up with unusual or clever ideas about a given topic or situation, or to develop creative ways to solve a problem.
Selective Attention	The ability to concentrate on a task over a period of time without being distracted.
Far Vision	The ability to see details at a distance.
Flexibility of Closure	The ability to identify or detect a known pattern (a figure, object, word, or sound) that is hidden in other distracting material.
Speed of Closure	The ability to quickly make sense of, combine, and organize information into meaningful patterns.
Memorization	The ability to remember information such as words, numbers, pictures, and procedures.
Time Sharing	The ability to shift back and forth between two or more activities or sources of information (such as speech, sounds, touch, or other sources).
Auditory Attention	The ability to focus on a single source of sound in the presence of other distracting sounds.
Perceptual Speed	The ability to quickly and accurately compare similarities and differences among sets of letters, numbers, objects, pictures, or patterns. The things to be compared may be presented at the same time or one after the other. This ability also includes comparing a presented object with a remembered object.
Number Facility	The ability to add, subtract, multiply, or divide quickly and correctly.
Visualization	The ability to imagine how something will look after it is moved around or when its parts are moved or rearranged.
Finger Dexterity	The ability to make precisely coordinated movements of the fingers of one or both hands to grasp, manipulate, or assemble very small objects.
Hearing Sensitivity	The ability to detect or tell the differences between sounds that vary in pitch and loudness.
Visual Color Discrimination	The ability to match or detect differences between colors, including shades of color and brightness.
Mathematical Reasoning	The ability to choose the right mathematical methods or formulas to solve a problem.
Trunk Strength	The ability to use your abdominal and lower back muscles to support part of the body repeatedly or continuously over time without 'giving out' or fatiguing.
Static Strength	The ability to exert maximum muscle force to lift, push, pull, or carry objects.

Arm-Hand Steadiness	The ability to keep your hand and arm steady while moving your arm or while holding your arm and hand in one position.
Stamina	The ability to exert yourself physically over long periods of time without getting winded or out of breath.
Gross Body Coordination	The ability to coordinate the movement of your arms, legs, and torso together when the whole body is in motion.
Multilimb Coordination	The ability to coordinate two or more limbs (for example, two arms, two legs, or one leg and one arm) while sitting, standing, or lying down. It does not involve performing the activities while the whole body is in motion.
Gross Body Equilibrium	The ability to keep or regain your body balance or stay upright when in an unstable position.
Extent Flexibility	The ability to bend, stretch, twist, or reach with your body, arms, and/or legs.
Dynamic Strength	The ability to exert muscle force repeatedly or continuously over time. This involves muscular endurance and resistance to muscle fatigue.
Response Orientation	The ability to choose quickly between two or more movements in response to two or more different signals (lights, sounds, pictures). It includes the speed with which the correct response is started with the hand, foot, or other body part.
Speed of Limb Movement	The ability to quickly move the arms and legs.
Depth Perception	The ability to judge which of several objects is closer or farther away from you, or to judge the distance between you and an object.
Manual Dexterity	The ability to quickly move your hand, your hand together with your arm, or your two hands to grasp, manipulate, or assemble objects.
Explosive Strength	The ability to use short bursts of muscle force to propel oneself (as in jumping or sprinting), or to throw an object.
Reaction Time	The ability to quickly respond (with the hand, finger, or foot) to a signal (sound, light, picture) when it appears.
Rate Control	The ability to time your movements or the movement of a piece of equipment in anticipation of changes in the speed and/or direction of a moving object or scene.
Wrist-Finger Speed	The ability to make fast, simple, repeated movements of the fingers, hands, and wrists.
Control Precision	The ability to quickly and repeatedly adjust the controls of a machine or a vehicle to exact positions.
Night Vision	The ability to see under low light conditions.
Sound Localization	The ability to tell the direction from which a sound originated.
Spatial Orientation	The ability to know your location in relation to the environment or to know where other objects are in relation to you.
Dynamic Flexibility	The ability to quickly and repeatedly bend, stretch, twist, or reach out with your body, arms, and/or legs.
Glare Sensitivity	The ability to see objects in the presence of glare or bright lighting.
Peripheral Vision	The ability to see objects or movement of objects to one's side when the eyes are looking ahead.

Work_Activity	Work_Activity Definitions
Developing Objectives and Strategies	Establishing long-range objectives and specifying the strategies and actions to achieve them.
Organizing, Planning, and Prioritizing Work	Developing specific goals and plans to prioritize, organize, and accomplish your work.
Establishing and Maintaining Interpersonal Relatio	Developing constructive and cooperative working relationships with others, and maintaining them over time.
Training and Teaching Others	Identifying the educational needs of others, developing formal educational or training programs or classes, and teaching or instructing others.
Making Decisions and Solving Problems	Analyzing information and evaluating results to choose the best solution and solve problems.
Getting Information	Observing, receiving, and otherwise obtaining information from all relevant sources.
Documenting/Recording Information	Entering, transcribing, recording, storing, or maintaining information in written or electronic/magnetic form.
Thinking Creatively	Developing, designing, or creating new applications, ideas, relationships, systems, or products, including artistic contributions.
Communicating with Supervisors, Peers, or Subordin	Providing information to supervisors, co-workers, and subordinates by telephone, in written form, e-mail, or in person.
Assisting and Caring for Others	Providing personal assistance, medical attention, emotional support, or other personal care to others such as coworkers, customers, or patients.
Updating and Using Relevant Knowledge	Keeping up-to-date technically and applying new knowledge to your job.

Identifying Objects, Actions, and Events	Identifying information by categorizing, estimating, recognizing differences or similarities, and detecting changes in circumstances or events.
Evaluating Information to Determine Compliance wit	Using relevant information and individual judgment to determine whether events or processes comply with laws, regulations, or standards.
Monitor Processes, Materials, or Surroundings	Monitoring and reviewing information from materials, events, or the environment, to detect or assess problems.
Coaching and Developing Others	Identifying the developmental needs of others and coaching, mentoring, or otherwise helping others to improve their knowledge or skills.
Scheduling Work and Activities	Scheduling events, programs, and activities, as well as the work of others.
Analyzing Data or Information	Identifying the underlying principles, reasons, or facts of information by breaking down information or data into separate parts.
Resolving Conflicts and Negotiating with Others	Handling complaints, settling disputes, and resolving grievances and conflicts, or otherwise negotiating with others.
Developing and Building Teams	Encouraging and building mutual trust, respect, and cooperation among team members.
Processing Information	Compiling, coding, categorizing, calculating, tabulating, auditing, or verifying information or data.
Judging the Qualities of Things, Services, or Peop	Assessing the value, importance, or quality of things or people.
Coordinating the Work and Activities of Others	Getting members of a group to work together to accomplish tasks.
Interpreting the Meaning of Information for Others	Translating or explaining what information means and how it can be used.
Interacting With Computers	Using computers and computer systems (including hardware and software) to program, write software, set up functions, enter data, or process information.
Communicating with Persons Outside Organization	Communicating with people outside the organization, representing the organization to customers, the public, government, and other external sources. This information can be exchanged in person, in writing, or by telephone or e-mail.
Guiding, Directing, and Motivating Subordinates	Providing guidance and direction to subordinates, including setting performance standards and monitoring performance.
Performing Administrative Activities	Performing day-to-day administrative tasks such as maintaining information files and processing paperwork.
Performing for or Working Directly with the Public	Performing for people or dealing directly with the public. This includes serving customers in restaurants and stores, and receiving clients or guests.
Provide Consultation and Advice to Others	Providing guidance and expert advice to management or other groups on technical, systems-, or process-related topics.
Performing General Physical Activities	Performing physical activities that require considerable use of your arms and legs and moving your whole body, such as climbing, lifting, balancing, walking, stooping, and handling of materials.
Estimating the Quantifiable Characteristics of Pro	Estimating sizes, distances, and quantities; or determining time, costs, resources, or materials needed to perform a work activity.
Inspecting Equipment, Structures, or Material	Inspecting equipment, structures, or materials to identify the cause of errors or other problems or defects.
Monitoring and Controlling Resources	Monitoring and controlling resources and overseeing the spending of money.
Handling and Moving Objects	Using hands and arms in handling, installing, positioning, and moving materials, and manipulating things.
Selling or Influencing Others	Convincing others to buy merchandise/goods or to otherwise change their minds or actions.
Controlling Machines and Processes	Using either control mechanisms or direct physical activity to operate machines or processes (not including computers or vehicles).
Staffing Organizational Units	Recruiting, interviewing, selecting, hiring, and promoting employees in an organization.
Repairing and Maintaining Electronic Equipment	Servicing, repairing, calibrating, regulating, fine-tuning, or testing machines, devices, and equipment that operate primarily on the basis of electrical or electronic (not mechanical) principles.
Operating Vehicles, Mechanized Devices, or Equipme	Running, maneuvering, navigating, or driving vehicles or mechanized equipment, such as forklifts, passenger vehicles, aircraft, or water craft.
Drafting, Laying Out, and Specifying Technical Dev	Providing documentation, detailed instructions, drawings, or specifications to tell others about how devices, parts, equipment, or structures are to be fabricated, constructed, assembled, modified, maintained, or used.
Repairing and Maintaining Mechanical Equipment	Servicing, repairing, adjusting, and testing machines, devices, moving parts, and equipment that operate primarily on the basis of mechanical (not electronic) principles.

Work_Context	Work_Context Definitions
Contact With Others	How much does this job require the worker to be in contact with others (face-to-face, by telephone, or otherwise) in order to perform it?
Face-to-Face Discussions	How often do you have to have face-to-face discussions with individuals or teams in this job?
Work With Work Group or Team	How important is it to work with others in a group or team in this job?
Freedom to Make Decisions	How much decision making freedom, without supervision, does the job offer?
Structured versus Unstructured Work	To what extent is this job structured for the worker, rather than allowing the worker to determine tasks, priorities, and goals?
Physical Proximity	To what extent does this job require the worker to perform job tasks in close physical proximity to other people?
Telephone	How often do you have telephone conversations in this job?
Indoors, Environmentally Controlled	How often does this job require working indoors in environmentally controlled conditions?
Electronic Mail	How often do you use electronic mail in this job?
Letters and Memos	How often does the job require written letters and memos?
Impact of Decisions on Co-workers or Company Resul	How do the decisions an employee makes impact the results of co-workers, clients or the company?
Spend Time Standing	How much does this job require standing?
Frequency of Decision Making	How frequently is the worker required to make decisions that affect other people, the financial resources, and/or the image and reputation of the organization?
Coordinate or Lead Others	How important is it to coordinate or lead others in accomplishing work activities in this job?
Time Pressure	How often does this job require the worker to meet strict deadlines?
Deal With External Customers	How important is it to work with external customers or the public in this job?
Importance of Being Exact or Accurate	How important is being very exact or highly accurate in performing this job?
Frequency of Conflict Situations	How often are there conflict situations the employee has to face in this job?
Public Speaking	How often do you have to perform public speaking in this job?
Sounds, Noise Levels Are Distracting or Uncomforta	How often does this job require working exposed to sounds and noise levels that are distracting or uncomfortable?
Deal With Unpleasant or Angry People	How frequently does the worker have to deal with unpleasant, angry, or discourteous individuals as part of the job requirements?
Responsible for Others' Health and Safety	How much responsibility is there for the health and safety of others in this job?
Responsibility for Outcomes and Results	How responsible is the worker for work outcomes and results of other workers?
Spend Time Using Your Hands to Handle, Control, or	How much does this job require using your hands to handle, control, or feel objects, tools or controls?
Spend Time Sitting	How much does this job require sitting?
Spend Time Walking and Running	How much does this job require walking and running?
Consequence of Error	How serious would the result usually be if the worker made a mistake that was not readily correctable?
Exposed to Disease or Infections	How often does this job require exposure to disease/infections?
Importance of Repeating Same Tasks	How important is repeating the same physical activities (e.g., key entry) or mental activities (e.g., checking entries in a ledger) over and over, without stopping, to performing this job?
Spend Time Making Repetitive Motions	How much does this job require making repetitive motions?
Spend Time Kneeling, Crouching, Stooping, or Crawl	How much does this job require kneeling, crouching, stooping, or crawling?
Spend Time Bending or Twisting the Body	How much does this job require bending or twisting your body?
Exposed to Contaminants	How often does this job require working exposed to contaminants (such as pollutants, gases, dust or odors)?
Level of Competition	To what extent does this job require the worker to compete or to be aware of competitive pressures?
Deal With Physically Aggressive People	How frequently does this job require the worker to deal with physical aggression of violent individuals?
Indoors, Not Environmentally Controlled	How often does this job require working indoors in non-controlled environmental conditions (e.g., warehouse without heat)?
Very Hot or Cold Temperatures	How often does this job require working in very hot (above 90 F degrees) or very cold (below 32 F degrees) temperatures?

Outdoors, Exposed to Weather	How often does this job require working outdoors, exposed to all weather conditions?
Exposed to Minor Burns, Cuts, Bites, or Stings	How often does this job require exposure to minor burns, cuts, bites, or stings?
Cramped Work Space, Awkward Positions	How often does this job require working in cramped work spaces that requires getting into awkward positions?
Degree of Automation	How automated is the job?
Spend Time Keeping or Regaining Balance	How much does this job require keeping or regaining your balance?
Extremely Bright or Inadequate Lighting	How often does this job require working in extremely bright or inadequate lighting conditions?
Wear Common Protective or Safety Equipment such as	How much does this job require wearing common protective or safety equipment such as safety shoes, glasses, gloves, hard hats or life jackets?
In an Enclosed Vehicle or Equipment	How often does this job require working in a closed vehicle or equipment (e.g., car)?
Exposed to Hazardous Equipment	How often does this job require exposure to hazardous equipment?
Outdoors, Under Cover	How often does this job require working outdoors, under cover (e.g., structure with roof but no walls)?
Pace Determined by Speed of Equipment	How important is it to this job that the pace is determined by the speed of equipment or machinery? (This does not refer to keeping busy at all times on this job.)
Wear Specialized Protective or Safety Equipment su	How much does this job require wearing specialized protective or safety equipment such as breathing apparatus, safety harness, full protection suits, or radiation protection?
Exposed to Hazardous Conditions	How often does this job require exposure to hazardous conditions?
Spend Time Climbing Ladders, Scaffolds, or Poles	How much does this job require climbing ladders, scaffolds, or poles?
Exposed to Whole Body Vibration	How often does this job require exposure to whole body vibration (e.g., operate a jackhammer)?
Exposed to High Places	How often does this job require exposure to high places?
Exposed to Radiation	How often does this job require exposure to radiation?
In an Open Vehicle or Equipment	How often does this job require working in an open vehicle or equipment (e.g., tractor)?

Job Zone Component	Job Zone Component Definitions
Title	Job Zone Four: Considerable Preparation Needed
Overall Experience	A minimum of two to four years of work-related skill, knowledge, or experience is needed for these occupations. For example, an accountant must complete four years of college and work for several years in accounting to be considered qualified.
Job Training	Employees in these occupations usually need several years of work-related experience, on-the-job training, and/or vocational training.
Job Zone Examples	Many of these occupations involve coordinating, supervising, managing, or training others. Examples include accountants, chefs and head cooks, computer programmers, historians, pharmacists, and police detectives.
SVP Range	(7.0 to < 8.0)
Education	Most of these occupations require a four - year bachelor's degree, but some do not.

Work_Styles	Work_Styles Definitions
Integrity	Job requires being honest and ethical.
Dependability	Job requires being reliable, responsible, and dependable, and fulfilling obligations.
Cooperation	Job requires being pleasant with others on the job and displaying a good-natured, cooperative attitude.
Self Control	Job requires maintaining composure, keeping emotions in check, controlling anger, and avoiding aggressive behavior, even in very difficult situations.
Concern for Others	Job requires being sensitive to others' needs and feelings and being understanding and helpful on the job.
Adaptability/Flexibility	Job requires being open to change (positive or negative) and to considerable variety in the workplace.
Initiative	Job requires a willingness to take on responsibilities and challenges.
Persistence	Job requires persistence in the face of obstacles.
Social Orientation	Job requires preferring to work with others rather than alone, and being personally connected with others on the job.

Stress Tolerance	Job requires accepting criticism and dealing calmly and effectively with high stress situations.
Attention to Detail	Job requires being careful about detail and thorough in completing work tasks.
Leadership	Job requires a willingness to lead, take charge, and offer opinions and direction.
Innovation	Job requires creativity and alternative thinking to develop new ideas for and answers to work-related problems.
Independence	Job requires developing one's own ways of doing things, guiding oneself with little or no supervision, and depending on oneself to get things done.
Achievement/Effort	Job requires establishing and maintaining personally challenging achievement goals and exerting effort toward mastering tasks.
Analytical Thinking	Job requires analyzing information and using logic to address work-related issues and problems.

25-2042.00 - Special Education Teachers, Middle School

Teach middle school subjects to educationally and physically handicapped students. Includes teachers who specialize and work with audibly and visually handicapped students and those who teach basic academic and life processes skills to the mentally impaired.

Tasks

1) Meet with parents and guardians to discuss their children's progress, and to determine their priorities for their children and their resource needs.

2) Confer with parents, administrators, testing specialists, social workers, and professionals to develop individual educational plans designed to promote students' educational, physical, and social development.

3) Prepare materials and classrooms for class activities.

4) Maintain accurate and complete student records, and prepare reports on children and activities, as required by laws, district policies, and administrative regulations.

5) Employ special educational strategies and techniques during instruction to improve the development of sensory- and perceptual-motor skills, language, cognition, and memory.

6) Attend staff meetings, and serve on committees as required.

7) Observe and evaluate students' performance, behavior, social development, and physical health.

8) Modify the general education curriculum for special-needs students based upon a variety of instructional techniques and instructional technology.

9) Teach socially acceptable behavior, employing techniques such as behavior modification and positive reinforcement.

10) Develop and implement strategies to meet the needs of students with a variety of handicapping conditions.

11) Establish clear objectives for all lessons, units, and projects, and communicate those objectives to students.

12) Prepare, administer, and grade tests and assignments to evaluate students' progress.

13) Use computers, audiovisual aids, and other equipment and materials to supplement presentations.

14) Prepare for assigned classes, and show written evidence of preparation upon request of immediate supervisors.

15) Plan and conduct activities for a balanced program of instruction, demonstration, and work time that provides students with opportunities to observe, question, and investigate.

16) Organize and label materials, and display students' work.

17) Meet with parents and guardians to provide guidance in using community resources, and to teach skills for dealing with students' impairments.

18) Confer with other staff members to plan and schedule lessons promoting learning, following approved curricula.

19) Administer standardized ability and achievement tests, and interpret results to determine students' strengths and areas of need.

20) Coordinate placement of students with special needs into mainstream classes.

21) Select, store, order, issue, and inventory classroom equipment, materials, and supplies.

22) Instruct through lectures, discussions, and demonstrations in one or more subjects such as English, mathematics, or social studies.

23) Teach students personal development skills such as goal setting, independence, and self-advocacy.

24) Guide and counsel students with adjustment and/or academic problems, or special academic interests.

25) Plan and supervise class projects, field trips, visits by guest speakers, or other experiential activities, and guide students in learning from those activities.

26) Prepare objectives and outlines for courses of study, following curriculum guidelines or requirements of states and schools.

27) Instruct and monitor students in the use and care of equipment and materials, in order to prevent injuries and damage.

28) Perform administrative duties such as assisting in school libraries, hall and cafeteria monitoring, and bus loading and unloading.

29) Monitor teachers and teacher assistants to ensure that they adhere to inclusive special education program requirements.

30) Organize and supervise games and other recreational activities to promote physical, mental, and social development.

31) Supervise, evaluate, and plan assignments for teacher assistants and volunteers.

32) Instruct students in daily living skills required for independent maintenance and self-sufficiency, such as hygiene, safety, and food preparation.

33) Sponsor extracurricular activities such as clubs, student organizations, and academic contests.

34) Provide assistive devices, supportive technology, and assistance accessing facilities such as restrooms.

35) Provide additional instruction in vocational areas.

36) Visit schools to tutor students with sensory impairments, and to consult with teachers regarding students' special needs.

37) Provide interpretation and transcription of regular classroom materials through Braille and sign language.

38) Confer with parents or guardians, other teachers, counselors, and administrators in order to resolve students' behavioral and academic problems.

39) Attend professional meetings, educational conferences, and teacher training workshops in order to maintain and improve professional competence.

Knowledge	Knowledge Definitions
English Language	Knowledge of the structure and content of the English language including the meaning and spelling of words, rules of composition, and grammar.
Education and Training	Knowledge of principles and methods for curriculum and training design, teaching and instruction for individuals and groups, and the measurement of training effects.
Psychology	Knowledge of human behavior and performance; individual differences in ability, personality, and interests; learning and motivation; psychological research methods; and the assessment and treatment of behavioral and affective disorders.
Mathematics	Knowledge of arithmetic, algebra, geometry, calculus, statistics, and their applications.
Customer and Personal Service	Knowledge of principles and processes for providing customer and personal services. This includes customer needs assessment, meeting quality standards for services, and evaluation of customer satisfaction.
Computers and Electronics	Knowledge of circuit boards, processors, chips, electronic equipment, and computer hardware and software, including applications and programming.
Clerical	Knowledge of administrative and clerical procedures and systems such as word processing, managing files and records, stenography and transcription, designing forms, and other office procedures and terminology.
Geography	Knowledge of principles and methods for describing the features of land, sea, and air masses, including their physical characteristics, locations, interrelationships, and distribution of plant, animal, and human life.
History and Archeology	Knowledge of historical events and their causes, indicators, and effects on civilizations and cultures.
Therapy and Counseling	Knowledge of principles, methods, and procedures for diagnosis, treatment, and rehabilitation of physical and mental dysfunctions, and for career counseling and guidance.
Sociology and Anthropology	Knowledge of group behavior and dynamics, societal trends and influences, human migrations, ethnicity, cultures and their history and origins.
Administration and Management	Knowledge of business and management principles involved in strategic planning, resource allocation, human resources modeling, leadership technique, production methods, and coordination of people and resources.
Public Safety and Security	Knowledge of relevant equipment, policies, procedures, and strategies to promote effective local, state, or national security operations for the protection of people, data, property, and institutions.
Law and Government	Knowledge of laws, legal codes, court procedures, precedents, government regulations, executive orders, agency rules, and the democratic political process.
Communications and Media	Knowledge of media production, communication, and dissemination techniques and methods. This includes alternative ways to inform and entertain via written, oral, and visual media.
Philosophy and Theology	Knowledge of different philosophical systems and religions. This includes their basic principles, values, ethics, ways of thinking, customs, practices, and their impact on human culture.
Biology	Knowledge of plant and animal organisms, their tissues, cells, functions, interdependencies, and interactions with each other and the environment.
Personnel and Human Resources	Knowledge of principles and procedures for personnel recruitment, selection, training, compensation and benefits, labor relations and negotiation, and personnel information systems.
Medicine and Dentistry	Knowledge of the information and techniques needed to diagnose and treat human injuries, diseases, and deformities. This includes symptoms, treatment alternatives, drug properties and interactions, and preventive health-care measures.
Transportation	Knowledge of principles and methods for moving people or goods by air, rail, sea, or road, including the relative costs and benefits.
Chemistry	Knowledge of the chemical composition, structure, and properties of substances and of the chemical processes and transformations that they undergo. This includes uses of chemicals and their interactions, danger signs, production techniques, and disposal methods.
Telecommunications	Knowledge of transmission, broadcasting, switching, control, and operation of telecommunications systems.
Physics	Knowledge and prediction of physical principles, laws, their interrelationships, and applications to understanding fluid, material, and atmospheric dynamics, and mechanical, electrical, atomic and sub-atomic structures and processes.
Fine Arts	Knowledge of the theory and techniques required to compose, produce, and perform works of music, dance, visual arts, drama, and sculpture.
Foreign Language	Knowledge of the structure and content of a foreign (non-English) language including the meaning and spelling of words, rules of composition and grammar, and pronunciation.
Economics and Accounting	Knowledge of economic and accounting principles and practices, the financial markets, banking and the analysis and reporting of financial data.
Design	Knowledge of design techniques, tools, and principles involved in production of precision technical plans, blueprints, drawings, and models.
Sales and Marketing	Knowledge of principles and methods for showing, promoting, and selling products or services. This includes marketing strategy and tactics, product demonstration, sales techniques, and sales control systems.
Production and Processing	Knowledge of raw materials, production processes, quality control, costs, and other techniques for maximizing the effective manufacture and distribution of goods.
Mechanical	Knowledge of machines and tools, including their designs, uses, repair, and maintenance.
Engineering and Technology	Knowledge of the practical application of engineering science and technology. This includes applying principles, techniques, procedures, and equipment to the design and production of various goods and services.
Food Production	Knowledge of techniques and equipment for planting, growing, and harvesting food products (both plant and animal) for consumption, including storage/handling techniques.
Building and Construction	Knowledge of materials, methods, and the tools involved in the construction or repair of houses, buildings, or other structures such as highways and roads.

Skills	Skills Definitions
Instructing	Teaching others how to do something.
Learning Strategies	Selecting and using training/instructional methods and procedures appropriate for the situation when learning or teaching new things.
Reading Comprehension	Understanding written sentences and paragraphs in work related documents.
Active Listening	Giving full attention to what other people are saying, taking time to understand the points being made, asking questions as appropriate, and not interrupting at inappropriate times.
Speaking	Talking to others to convey information effectively.
Monitoring	Monitoring/Assessing performance of yourself, other individuals, or organizations to make improvements or take corrective action.
Time Management	Managing one's own time and the time of others.
Social Perceptiveness	Being aware of others' reactions and understanding why they react as they do.
Active Learning	Understanding the implications of new information for both current and future problem-solving and decision-making.
Writing	Communicating effectively in writing as appropriate for the needs of the audience.
Critical Thinking	Using logic and reasoning to identify the strengths and weaknesses of alternative solutions, conclusions or approaches to problems.
Coordination	Adjusting actions in relation to others' actions.
Service Orientation	Actively looking for ways to help people.
Mathematics	Using mathematics to solve problems.
Negotiation	Bringing others together and trying to reconcile differences.
Persuasion	Persuading others to change their minds or behavior.
Judgment and Decision Making	Considering the relative costs and benefits of potential actions to choose the most appropriate one.
Complex Problem Solving	Identifying complex problems and reviewing related information to develop and evaluate options and implement solutions.
Management of Personnel Resources	Motivating, developing, and directing people as they work, identifying the best people for the job.
Science	Using scientific rules and methods to solve problems.
Equipment Selection	Determining the kind of tools and equipment needed to do a job.
Management of Material Resources	Obtaining and seeing to the appropriate use of equipment, facilities, and materials needed to do certain work.
Operations Analysis	Analyzing needs and product requirements to create a design.
Technology Design	Generating or adapting equipment and technology to serve user needs.
Quality Control Analysis	Conducting tests and inspections of products, services, or processes to evaluate quality or performance.
Troubleshooting	Determining causes of operating errors and deciding what to do about it.
Systems Evaluation	Identifying measures or indicators of system performance and the actions needed to improve or correct performance, relative to the goals of the system.
Management of Financial Resources	Determining how money will be spent to get the work done, and accounting for these expenditures.
Operation and Control	Controlling operations of equipment or systems.
Systems Analysis	Determining how a system should work and how changes in conditions, operations, and the environment will affect outcomes.
Equipment Maintenance	Performing routine maintenance on equipment and determining when and what kind of maintenance is needed.
Installation	Installing equipment, machines, wiring, or programs to meet specifications.
Programming	Writing computer programs for various purposes.
Operation Monitoring	Watching gauges, dials, or other indicators to make sure a machine is working properly.
Repairing	Repairing machines or systems using the needed tools.

Ability	Ability Definitions
Oral Expression	The ability to communicate information and ideas in speaking so others will understand.
Speech Clarity	The ability to speak clearly so others can understand you.
Oral Comprehension	The ability to listen to and understand information and ideas presented through spoken words and sentences.
Speech Recognition	The ability to identify and understand the speech of another person.
Problem Sensitivity	The ability to tell when something is wrong or is likely to go wrong. It does not involve solving the problem, only recognizing there is a problem.
Inductive Reasoning	The ability to combine pieces of information to form general rules or conclusions (includes finding a relationship among seemingly unrelated events).
Deductive Reasoning	The ability to apply general rules to specific problems to produce answers that make sense.
Written Comprehension	The ability to read and understand information and ideas presented in writing.
Written Expression	The ability to communicate information and ideas in writing so others will understand.
Information Ordering	The ability to arrange things or actions in a certain order or pattern according to a specific rule or set of rules (e.g., patterns of numbers, letters, words, pictures, mathematical operations).
Near Vision	The ability to see details at close range (within a few feet of the observer).
Originality	The ability to come up with unusual or clever ideas about a given topic or situation, or to develop creative ways to solve a problem.
Category Flexibility	The ability to generate or use different sets of rules for combining or grouping things in different ways.
Fluency of Ideas	The ability to come up with a number of ideas about a topic (the number of ideas is important, not their quality, correctness, or creativity).
Selective Attention	The ability to concentrate on a task over a period of time without being distracted.
Flexibility of Closure	The ability to identify or detect a known pattern (a figure, object, word, or sound) that is hidden in other distracting material.
Speed of Closure	The ability to quickly make sense of, combine, and organize information into meaningful patterns.
Perceptual Speed	The ability to quickly and accurately compare similarities and differences among sets of letters, numbers, objects, pictures, or patterns. The things to be compared may be presented at the same time or one after the other. This ability also includes comparing a presented object with a remembered object.
Far Vision	The ability to see details at a distance.
Visualization	The ability to imagine how something will look after it is moved around or when its parts are moved or rearranged.
Time Sharing	The ability to shift back and forth between two or more activities or sources of information (such as speech, sounds, touch, or other sources).
Finger Dexterity	The ability to make precisely coordinated movements of the fingers of one or both hands to grasp, manipulate, or assemble very small objects.
Number Facility	The ability to add, subtract, multiply, or divide quickly and correctly.
Mathematical Reasoning	The ability to choose the right mathematical methods or formulas to solve a problem.
Visual Color Discrimination	The ability to match or detect differences between colors, including shades of color and brightness.
Auditory Attention	The ability to focus on a single source of sound in the presence of other distracting sounds.
Memorization	The ability to remember information such as words, numbers, pictures, and procedures.
Depth Perception	The ability to judge which of several objects is closer or farther away from you, or to judge the distance between you and an object.
Hearing Sensitivity	The ability to detect or tell the differences between sounds that vary in pitch and loudness.
Trunk Strength	The ability to use your abdominal and lower back muscles to support part of the body repeatedly or continuously over time without 'giving out' or fatiguing.
Stamina	The ability to exert yourself physically over long periods of time without getting winded or out of breath.
Static Strength	The ability to exert maximum muscle force to lift, push, pull, or carry objects.
Gross Body Equilibrium	The ability to keep or regain your body balance or stay upright when in an unstable position.
Gross Body Coordination	The ability to coordinate the movement of your arms, legs, and torso together when the whole body is in motion.
Reaction Time	The ability to quickly respond (with the hand, finger, or foot) to a signal (sound, light, picture) when it appears.
Explosive Strength	The ability to use short bursts of muscle force to propel oneself (as in jumping or sprinting), or to throw an object.

Response Orientation	The ability to choose quickly between two or more movements in response to two or more different signals (lights, sounds, pictures). It includes the speed with which the correct response is started with the hand, foot, or other body part.
Speed of Limb Movement	The ability to quickly move the arms and legs.
Arm-Hand Steadiness	The ability to keep your hand and arm steady while moving your arm or while holding your arm and hand in one position.
Extent Flexibility	The ability to bend, stretch, twist, or reach with your body, arms, and/or legs.
Peripheral Vision	The ability to see objects or movement of objects to one's side when the eyes are looking ahead.
Night Vision	The ability to see under low light conditions.
Glare Sensitivity	The ability to see objects in the presence of glare or bright lighting.
Sound Localization	The ability to tell the direction from which a sound originated.
Control Precision	The ability to quickly and repeatedly adjust the controls of a machine or a vehicle to exact positions.
Dynamic Flexibility	The ability to quickly and repeatedly bend, stretch, twist, or reach out with your body, arms, and/or legs.
Spatial Orientation	The ability to know your location in relation to the environment or to know where other objects are in relation to you.
Manual Dexterity	The ability to quickly move your hand, your hand together with your arm, or your two hands to grasp, manipulate, or assemble objects.
Multilimb Coordination	The ability to coordinate two or more limbs (for example, two arms, two legs, or one leg and one arm) while sitting, standing, or lying down. It does not involve performing the activities while the whole body is in motion.
Rate Control	The ability to time your movements or the movement of a piece of equipment in anticipation of changes in the speed and/or direction of a moving object or scene.
Dynamic Strength	The ability to exert muscle force repeatedly or continuously over time. This involves muscular endurance and resistance to muscle fatigue.
Wrist-Finger Speed	The ability to make fast, simple, repeated movements of the fingers, hands, and wrists.

Work_Activity	Work_Activity Definitions
Training and Teaching Others	Identifying the educational needs of others, developing formal educational or training programs or classes, and teaching or instructing others.
Getting Information	Observing, receiving, and otherwise obtaining information from all relevant sources.
Developing Objectives and Strategies	Establishing long-range objectives and specifying the strategies and actions to achieve them.
Communicating with Supervisors, Peers, or Subordin	Providing information to supervisors, co-workers, and subordinates by telephone, in written form, e-mail, or in person.
Establishing and Maintaining Interpersonal Relatio	Developing constructive and cooperative working relationships with others, and maintaining them over time.
Evaluating Information to Determine Compliance wit	Using relevant information and individual judgment to determine whether events or processes comply with laws, regulations, or standards.
Organizing, Planning, and Prioritizing Work	Developing specific goals and plans to prioritize, organize, and accomplish your work.
Making Decisions and Solving Problems	Analyzing information and evaluating results to choose the best solution and solve problems.
Coaching and Developing Others	Identifying the developmental needs of others and coaching, mentoring, or otherwise helping others to improve their knowledge or skills.
Documenting/Recording Information	Entering, transcribing, recording, storing, or maintaining information in written or electronic/magnetic form.
Assisting and Caring for Others	Providing personal assistance, medical attention, emotional support, or other personal care to others such as coworkers, customers, or patients.
Thinking Creatively	Developing, designing, or creating new applications, ideas, relationships, systems, or products, including artistic contributions.
Interpreting the Meaning of Information for Others	Translating or explaining what information means and how it can be used.
Coordinating the Work and Activities of Others	Getting members of a group to work together to accomplish tasks.
Updating and Using Relevant Knowledge	Keeping up-to-date technically and applying new knowledge to your job.
Developing and Building Teams	Encouraging and building mutual trust, respect, and cooperation among team members.

Resolving Conflicts and Negotiating with Others	Handling complaints, settling disputes, and resolving grievances and conflicts, or otherwise negotiating with others.
Identifying Objects, Actions, and Events	Identifying information by categorizing, estimating, recognizing differences or similarities, and detecting changes in circumstances or events.
Interacting With Computers	Using computers and computer systems (including hardware and software) to program, write software, set up functions, enter data, or process information.
Analyzing Data or Information	Identifying the underlying principles, reasons, or facts of information by breaking down information or data into separate parts.
Monitor Processes, Materials, or Surroundings	Monitoring and reviewing information from materials, events, or the environment, to detect or assess problems.
Processing Information	Compiling, coding, categorizing, calculating, tabulating, auditing, or verifying information or data.
Communicating with Persons Outside Organization	Communicating with people outside the organization, representing the organization to customers, the public, government, and other external sources. This information can be exchanged in person, in writing, or by telephone or e-mail.
Performing Administrative Activities	Performing day-to-day administrative tasks such as maintaining information files and processing paperwork.
Scheduling Work and Activities	Scheduling events, programs, and activities, as well as the work of others.
Judging the Qualities of Things, Services, or Peop	Assessing the value, importance, or quality of things or people.
Performing for or Working Directly with the Public	Performing for people or dealing directly with the public. This includes serving customers in restaurants and stores, and receiving clients or guests.
Guiding, Directing, and Motivating Subordinates	Providing guidance and direction to subordinates, including setting performance standards and monitoring performance.
Provide Consultation and Advice to Others	Providing guidance and expert advice to management or other groups on technical, systems-, or process-related topics.
Estimating the Quantifiable Characteristics of Pro	Estimating sizes, distances, and quantities; or determining time, costs, resources, or materials needed to perform a work activity.
Inspecting Equipment, Structures, or Material	Inspecting equipment, structures, or materials to identify the cause of errors or other problems or defects.
Selling or Influencing Others	Convincing others to buy merchandise/goods or to otherwise change their minds or actions.
Performing General Physical Activities	Performing physical activities that require considerable use of your arms and legs and moving your whole body, such as climbing, lifting, balancing, walking, stooping, and handling of materials.
Handling and Moving Objects	Using hands and arms in handling, installing, positioning, and moving materials, and manipulating things.
Monitoring and Controlling Resources	Monitoring and controlling resources and overseeing the spending of money.
Controlling Machines and Processes	Using either control mechanisms or direct physical activity to operate machines or processes (not including computers or vehicles).
Staffing Organizational Units	Recruiting, interviewing, selecting, hiring, and promoting employees in an organization.
Operating Vehicles, Mechanized Devices, or Equipme	Running, maneuvering, navigating, or driving vehicles or mechanized equipment, such as forklifts, passenger vehicles, aircraft, or water craft.
Repairing and Maintaining Electronic Equipment	Servicing, repairing, calibrating, regulating, fine-tuning, or testing machines, devices, and equipment that operate primarily on the basis of electrical or electronic (not mechanical) principles.
Drafting, Laying Out, and Specifying Technical Dev	Providing documentation, detailed instructions, drawings, or specifications to tell others about how devices, parts, equipment, or structures are to be fabricated, constructed, assembled, modified, maintained, or used.
Repairing and Maintaining Mechanical Equipment	Servicing, repairing, adjusting, and testing machines, devices, moving parts, and equipment that operate primarily on the basis of mechanical (not electronic) principles.

Work_Context	Work_Context Definitions
Face-to-Face Discussions	How often do you have to have face-to-face discussions with individuals or teams in this job?
Contact With Others	How much does this job require the worker to be in contact with others (face-to-face, by telephone, or otherwise) in order to perform it?
Work With Work Group or Team	How important is it to work with others in a group or team in this job?
Electronic Mail	How often do you use electronic mail in this job?

Structured versus Unstructured Work	To what extent is this job structured for the worker, rather than allowing the worker to determine tasks, priorities, and goals?
Coordinate or Lead Others	How important is it to coordinate or lead others in accomplishing work activities in this job?
Telephone	How often do you have telephone conversations in this job?
Physical Proximity	To what extent does this job require the worker to perform job tasks in close physical proximity to other people?
Freedom to Make Decisions	How much decision making freedom, without supervision, does the job offer?
Letters and Memos	How often does the job require written letters and memos?
Frequency of Decision Making	How frequently is the worker required to make decisions that affect other people, the financial resources, and/or the image and reputation of the organization?
Indoors, Environmentally Controlled	How often does this job require working indoors in environmentally controlled conditions?
Frequency of Conflict Situations	How often are there conflict situations the employee has to face in this job?
Time Pressure	How often does this job require the worker to meet strict deadlines?
Deal With External Customers	How important is it to work with external customers or the public in this job?
Impact of Decisions on Co-workers or Company Resul	How do the decisions an employee makes impact the results of co-workers, clients or the company?
Deal With Unpleasant or Angry People	How frequently does the worker have to deal with unpleasant, angry, or discourteous individuals as part of the job requirements?
Importance of Being Exact or Accurate	How important is being very exact or highly accurate in performing this job?
Spend Time Standing	How much does this job require standing?
Public Speaking	How often do you have to perform public speaking in this job?
Sounds, Noise Levels Are Distracting or Uncomforta	How often does this job require working exposed to sounds and noise levels that are distracting or uncomfortable?
Responsible for Others' Health and Safety	How much responsibility is there for the health and safety of others in this job?
Responsibility for Outcomes and Results	How responsible is the worker for work outcomes and results of other workers?
Exposed to Disease or Infections	How often does this job require exposure to disease/infections?
Importance of Repeating Same Tasks	How important is repeating the same physical activities (e.g., key entry) or mental activities (e.g., checking entries in a ledger) over and over, without stopping, to performing this job?
Deal With Physically Aggressive People	How frequently does this job require the worker to deal with physical aggression of violent individuals?
Spend Time Walking and Running	How much does this job require walking and running?
Consequence of Error	How serious would the result usually be if the worker made a mistake that was not readily correctable?
Spend Time Sitting	How much does this job require sitting?
Level of Competition	To what extent does this job require the worker to compete or to be aware of competitive pressures?
Spend Time Using Your Hands to Handle, Control, or	How much does this job require using your hands to handle, control, or feel objects, tools or controls?
Exposed to Contaminants	How often does this job require working exposed to contaminants (such as pollutants, gases, dust or odors)?
Spend Time Making Repetitive Motions	How much does this job require making repetitive motions?
Indoors, Not Environmentally Controlled	How often does this job require working indoors in non-controlled environmental conditions (e.g., warehouse without heat)?
Spend Time Bending or Twisting the Body	How much does this job require bending or twisting your body?
Exposed to Minor Burns, Cuts, Bites, or Stings	How often does this job require exposure to minor burns, cuts, bites, or stings?
Outdoors, Exposed to Weather	How often does this job require working outdoors, exposed to all weather conditions?
Extremely Bright or Inadequate Lighting	How often does this job require working in extremely bright or inadequate lighting conditions?
Very Hot or Cold Temperatures	How often does this job require working in very hot (above 90 F degrees) or very cold (below 32 F degrees) temperatures?
Degree of Automation	How automated is the job?
Spend Time Kneeling, Crouching, Stooping, or Crawl	How much does this job require kneeling, crouching, stooping or crawling?
In an Enclosed Vehicle or Equipment	How often does this job require working in a closed vehicle or equipment (e.g., car)?

Outdoors, Under Cover	How often does this job require working outdoors, under cover (e.g., structure with roof but no walls)?
Cramped Work Space, Awkward Positions	How often does this job require working in cramped work spaces that requires getting into awkward positions?
Spend Time Keeping or Regaining Balance	How much does this job require keeping or regaining your balance?
Wear Common Protective or Safety Equipment such as	How much does this job require wearing common protective or safety equipment such as safety shoes, glasses, gloves, hard hats or life jackets?
Exposed to Hazardous Conditions	How often does this job require exposure to hazardous conditions?
Exposed to Hazardous Equipment	How often does this job require exposure to hazardous equipment?
Pace Determined by Speed of Equipment	How important is it to this job that the pace is determined by the speed of equipment or machinery? (This does not refer to keeping busy at all times on this job.)
Spend Time Climbing Ladders, Scaffolds, or Poles	How much does this job require climbing ladders, scaffolds, or poles?
Exposed to Radiation	How often does this job require exposure to radiation?
Exposed to High Places	How often does this job require exposure to high places?
In an Open Vehicle or Equipment	How often does this job require working in an open vehicle or equipment (e.g., tractor)?
Wear Specialized Protective or Safety Equipment su	How much does this job require wearing specialized protective or safety equipment such as breathing apparatus, safety harness, full protection suits, or radiation protection?
Exposed to Whole Body Vibration	How often does this job require exposure to whole body vibration (e.g., operate a jackhammer)?

Job Zone Component	Job Zone Component Definitions
Title	Job Zone Four: Considerable Preparation Needed
Overall Experience	A minimum of two to four years of work-related skill, knowledge, or experience is needed for these occupations. For example, an accountant must complete four years of college and work for several years in accounting to be considered qualified.
Job Training	Employees in these occupations usually need several years of work-related experience, on-the-job training, and/or vocational training.
Job Zone Examples	Many of these occupations involve coordinating, supervising, managing, or training others. Examples include accountants, chefs and head cooks, computer programmers, historians, pharmacists, and police detectives.
SVP Range	(7.0 to < 8.0)
Education	Most of these occupations require a four - year bachelor's degree, but some do not.

Work_Styles	Work_Styles Definitions
Integrity	Job requires being honest and ethical.
Dependability	Job requires being reliable, responsible, and dependable and fulfilling obligations.
Self Control	Job requires maintaining composure, keeping emotions in check, controlling anger, and avoiding aggressive behavior, even in very difficult situations.
Concern for Others	Job requires being sensitive to others' needs and feelings and being understanding and helpful on the job.
Cooperation	Job requires being pleasant with others on the job and displaying a good-natured, cooperative attitude.
Stress Tolerance	Job requires accepting criticism and dealing calmly and effectively with high stress situations.
Adaptability/Flexibility	Job requires being open to change (positive or negative) and to considerable variety in the workplace.
Social Orientation	Job requires preferring to work with others rather than alone, and being personally connected with others on the job.
Persistence	Job requires persistence in the face of obstacles.
Attention to Detail	Job requires being careful about detail and thorough in completing work tasks.
Initiative	Job requires a willingness to take on responsibilities and challenges.
Achievement/Effort	Job requires establishing and maintaining personally challenging achievement goals and exerting effort toward mastering tasks.
Innovation	Job requires creativity and alternative thinking to develop new ideas for and answers to work-related problems.

Leadership	Job requires a willingness to lead, take charge, and offer opinions and direction.
Independence	Job requires developing one's own ways of doing things, guiding oneself with little or no supervision, and depending on oneself to get things done.
Analytical Thinking	Job requires analyzing information and using logic to address work-related issues and problems.

25-2043.00 - Special Education Teachers, Secondary School

Teach secondary school subjects to educationally and physically handicapped students. Includes teachers who specialize and work with audibly and visually handicapped students and those who teach basic academic and life processes skills to the mentally impaired.

Tasks

1) Confer with parents or guardians, other teachers, counselors, and administrators in order to resolve students' behavioral and academic problems.

2) Teach personal development skills such as goal setting, independence, and self-advocacy.

3) Establish and enforce rules for behavior and policies and procedures to maintain order among students.

4) Establish clear objectives for all lessons, units, and projects, and communicate those objectives to students.

5) Prepare students for later grades by encouraging them to explore learning opportunities and to persevere with challenging tasks.

6) Plan and conduct activities for a balanced program of instruction, demonstration, and work time that provides students with opportunities to observe, question, and investigate.

7) Observe and evaluate students' performance, behavior, social development, and physical health.

8) Guide and counsel students with adjustment and/or academic problems, or special academic interests.

9) Prepare materials and classrooms for class activities.

10) Teach socially acceptable behavior, employing techniques such as behavior modification and positive reinforcement.

11) Use computers, audiovisual aids, and other equipment and materials to supplement presentations.

12) Meet with parents and guardians to provide guidance in using community resources, and to teach skills for dealing with students' impairments.

13) Prepare, administer, and grade tests and assignments to evaluate students' progress.

14) Modify the general education curriculum for special-needs students, based upon a variety of instructional techniques and technologies.

15) Employ special educational strategies and techniques during instruction to improve the development of sensory- and perceptual-motor skills, language, cognition, and memory.

16) Confer with other staff members to plan and schedule lessons promoting learning, following approved curricula.

17) Coordinate placement of students with special needs into mainstream classes.

18) Develop and implement strategies to meet the needs of students with a variety of handicapping conditions.

19) Instruct through lectures, discussions, and demonstrations in one or more subjects such as English, mathematics, or social studies.

20) Select, store, order, issue, and inventory classroom equipment, materials, and supplies.

21) Prepare objectives and outlines for courses of study, following curriculum guidelines or requirements of states and schools.

22) Prepare for assigned classes, and show written evidence of preparation upon request of immediate supervisors.

23) Administer standardized ability and achievement tests, and interpret results to determine students' strengths and areas of need.

24) Collaborate with other teachers and administrators in the development, evaluation, and revision of secondary school programs.

25) Plan and supervise class projects, field trips, visits by guest speakers, or other experiential activities, and guide students in learning from those activities.

26) Provide additional instruction in vocational areas.

27) Monitor teachers and teacher assistants to ensure that they adhere to inclusive special education program requirements.

28) Perform administrative duties such as assisting in school libraries, hall and cafeteria monitoring, and bus loading and unloading.

29) Instruct students in daily living skills required for independent maintenance and self-sufficiency, such as hygiene, safety, and food preparation.

30) Instruct and monitor students in the use and care of equipment and materials, in order to prevent injuries and damage.

31) Sponsor extracurricular activities such as clubs, student organizations, and academic contests.

32) Provide assistive devices, supportive technology, and assistance accessing facilities such as restrooms.

33) Visit schools to tutor students with sensory impairments, and to consult with teachers regarding students' special needs.

34) Provide interpretation and transcription of regular classroom materials through Braille and sign language.

35) Confer with parents, administrators, testing specialists, social workers, and professionals to develop individual educational plans designed to promote students' educational, physical, and social development.

36) Attend professional meetings, educational conferences, and teacher training workshops to maintain and improve professional competence.

37) Meet with parents and guardians to discuss their children's progress, and to determine their priorities for their children and their resource needs.

38) Meet with other professionals to discuss individual students' needs and progress.

39) Maintain accurate and complete student records, and prepare reports on children and activities, as required by laws, district policies, and administrative regulations.

Knowledge	Knowledge Definitions
English Language	Knowledge of the structure and content of the English language including the meaning and spelling of words, rules of composition, and grammar.
Education and Training	Knowledge of principles and methods for curriculum and training design, teaching and instruction for individuals and groups, and the measurement of training effects.
Psychology	Knowledge of human behavior and performance; individual differences in ability, personality, and interests; learning and motivation; psychological research methods; and the assessment and treatment of behavioral and affective disorders.
Mathematics	Knowledge of arithmetic, algebra, geometry, calculus, statistics, and their applications.
Therapy and Counseling	Knowledge of principles, methods, and procedures for diagnosis, treatment, and rehabilitation of physical and mental dysfunctions, and for career counseling and guidance.
Customer and Personal Service	Knowledge of principles and processes for providing customer and personal services. This includes customer needs assessment, meeting quality standards for services, and evaluation of customer satisfaction.
History and Archeology	Knowledge of historical events and their causes, indicators, and effects on civilizations and cultures.
Clerical	Knowledge of administrative and clerical procedures and systems such as word processing, managing files and records, stenography and transcription, designing forms, and other office procedures and terminology.
Sociology and Anthropology	Knowledge of group behavior and dynamics, societal trends and influences, human migrations, ethnicity, cultures and their history and origins.
Computers and Electronics	Knowledge of circuit boards, processors, chips, electronic equipment, and computer hardware and software, including applications and programming.
Geography	Knowledge of principles and methods for describing the features of land, sea, and air masses, including their physical characteristics, locations, interrelationships, and distribution of plant, animal, and human life.
Administration and Management	Knowledge of business and management principles involved in strategic planning, resource allocation, human resources modeling, leadership technique, production methods, and coordination of people and resources.
Law and Government	Knowledge of laws, legal codes, court procedures, precedents, government regulations, executive orders, agency rules, and the democratic political process.

Public Safety and Security	Knowledge of relevant equipment, policies, procedures, and strategies to promote effective local, state, or national security operations for the protection of people, data, property, and institutions.
Philosophy and Theology	Knowledge of different philosophical systems and religions. This includes their basic principles, values, ethics, ways of thinking, customs, practices, and their impact on human culture.
Personnel and Human Resources	Knowledge of principles and procedures for personnel recruitment, selection, training, compensation and benefits, labor relations and negotiation, and personnel information systems.
Biology	Knowledge of plant and animal organisms, their tissues, cells, functions, interdependencies, and interactions with each other and the environment.
Communications and Media	Knowledge of media production, communication, and dissemination techniques and methods. This includes alternative ways to inform and entertain via written, oral, and visual media.
Medicine and Dentistry	Knowledge of the information and techniques needed to diagnose and treat human injuries, diseases, and deformities. This includes symptoms, treatment alternatives, drug properties and interactions, and preventive health-care measures.
Fine Arts	Knowledge of the theory and techniques required to compose, produce, and perform works of music, dance, visual arts, drama, and sculpture.
Foreign Language	Knowledge of the structure and content of a foreign (non-English) language including the meaning and spelling of words, rules of composition and grammar, and pronunciation.
Chemistry	Knowledge of the chemical composition, structure, and properties of substances and of the chemical processes and transformations that they undergo. This includes uses of chemicals and their interactions, danger signs, production techniques, and disposal methods.
Telecommunications	Knowledge of transmission, broadcasting, switching, control, and operation of telecommunications systems.
Physics	Knowledge and prediction of physical principles, laws, their interrelationships, and applications to understanding fluid, material, and atmospheric dynamics, and mechanical, electrical, atomic and sub- atomic structures and processes.
Transportation	Knowledge of principles and methods for moving people or goods by air, rail, sea, or road, including the relative costs and benefits.
Economics and Accounting	Knowledge of economic and accounting principles and practices, the financial markets, banking and the analysis and reporting of financial data.
Food Production	Knowledge of techniques and equipment for planting, growing, and harvesting food products (both plant and animal) for consumption, including storage/handling techniques.
Sales and Marketing	Knowledge of principles and methods for showing, promoting, and selling products or services. This includes marketing strategy and tactics, product demonstration, sales techniques, and sales control systems.
Production and Processing	Knowledge of raw materials, production processes, quality control, costs, and other techniques for maximizing the effective manufacture and distribution of goods.
Mechanical	Knowledge of machines and tools, including their designs, uses, repair, and maintenance.
Design	Knowledge of design techniques, tools, and principles involved in production of precision technical plans, blueprints, drawings, and models.
Engineering and Technology	Knowledge of the practical application of engineering science and technology. This includes applying principles, techniques, procedures, and equipment to the design and production of various goods and services.
Building and Construction	Knowledge of materials, methods, and the tools involved in the construction or repair of houses, buildings, or other structures such as highways and roads.

Skills	Skills Definitions
Instructing	Teaching others how to do something.
Learning Strategies	Selecting and using training/instructional methods and procedures appropriate for the situation when learning or teaching new things.
Reading Comprehension	Understanding written sentences and paragraphs in work related documents.
Speaking	Talking to others to convey information effectively.

Time Management	Managing one's own time and the time of others.
Active Listening	Giving full attention to what other people are saying, taking time to understand the points being made, asking questions as appropriate, and not interrupting at inappropriate times.
Social Perceptiveness	Being aware of others' reactions and understanding why they react as they do.
Writing	Communicating effectively in writing as appropriate for the needs of the audience.
Monitoring	Monitoring/Assessing performance of yourself, other individuals, or organizations to make improvements or take corrective action.
Critical Thinking	Using logic and reasoning to identify the strengths and weaknesses of alternative solutions, conclusions or approaches to problems.
Coordination	Adjusting actions in relation to others' actions.
Active Learning	Understanding the implications of new information for both current and future problem-solving and decision-making.
Service Orientation	Actively looking for ways to help people.
Persuasion	Persuading others to change their minds or behavior.
Negotiation	Bringing others together and trying to reconcile differences.
Judgment and Decision Making	Considering the relative costs and benefits of potential actions to choose the most appropriate one.
Complex Problem Solving	Identifying complex problems and reviewing related information to develop and evaluate options and implement solutions.
Mathematics	Using mathematics to solve problems.
Management of Personnel Resources	Motivating, developing, and directing people as they work, identifying the best people for the job.
Equipment Selection	Determining the kind of tools and equipment needed to do a job.
Science	Using scientific rules and methods to solve problems.
Operations Analysis	Analyzing needs and product requirements to create a design.
Technology Design	Generating or adapting equipment and technology to serve user needs.
Management of Material Resources	Obtaining and seeing to the appropriate use of equipment, facilities, and materials needed to do certain work.
Troubleshooting	Determining causes of operating errors and deciding what to do about it.
Systems Evaluation	Identifying measures or indicators of system performance and the actions needed to improve or correct performance, relative to the goals of the system.
Quality Control Analysis	Conducting tests and inspections of products, services, or processes to evaluate quality or performance.
Management of Financial Resources	Determining how money will be spent to get the work done, and accounting for these expenditures.
Operation and Control	Controlling operations of equipment or systems.
Systems Analysis	Determining how a system should work and how changes in conditions, operations, and the environment will affect outcomes.
Equipment Maintenance	Performing routine maintenance on equipment and determining when and what kind of maintenance is needed.
Installation	Installing equipment, machines, wiring, or programs to meet specifications.
Repairing	Repairing machines or systems using the needed tools.
Programming	Writing computer programs for various purposes.
Operation Monitoring	Watching gauges, dials, or other indicators to make sure a machine is working properly.

Ability	Ability Definitions
Oral Expression	The ability to communicate information and ideas in speaking so others will understand.
Oral Comprehension	The ability to listen to and understand information and ideas presented through spoken words and sentences.
Speech Clarity	The ability to speak clearly so others can understand you.
Problem Sensitivity	The ability to tell when something is wrong or is likely to go wrong. It does not involve solving the problem, only recognizing there is a problem.
Written Comprehension	The ability to read and understand information and ideas presented in writing.
Written Expression	The ability to communicate information and ideas in writing so others will understand.
Deductive Reasoning	The ability to apply general rules to specific problems to produce answers that make sense.
Originality	The ability to come up with unusual or clever ideas about a given topic or situation, or to develop creative ways to solve a problem.

Near Vision	The ability to see details at close range (within a few feet of the observer).
Speech Recognition	The ability to identify and understand the speech of another person.
Inductive Reasoning	The ability to combine pieces of information to form general rules or conclusions (includes finding a relationship among seemingly unrelated events).
Information Ordering	The ability to arrange things or actions in a certain order or pattern according to a specific rule or set of rules (e.g., patterns of numbers, letters, words, pictures, mathematical operations).
Fluency of Ideas	The ability to come up with a number of ideas about a topic (the number of ideas is important, not their quality, correctness, or creativity).
Selective Attention	The ability to concentrate on a task over a period of time without being distracted.
Time Sharing	The ability to shift back and forth between two or more activities or sources of information (such as speech, sounds, touch, or other sources).
Category Flexibility	The ability to generate or use different sets of rules for combining or grouping things in different ways.
Far Vision	The ability to see details at a distance.
Memorization	The ability to remember information such as words, numbers, pictures, and procedures.
Number Facility	The ability to add, subtract, multiply, or divide quickly and correctly.
Mathematical Reasoning	The ability to choose the right mathematical methods or formulas to solve a problem.
Flexibility of Closure	The ability to identify or detect a known pattern (a figure, object, word, or sound) that is hidden in other distracting material.
Speed of Closure	The ability to quickly make sense of, combine, and organize information into meaningful patterns.
Auditory Attention	The ability to focus on a single source of sound in the presence of other distracting sounds.
Visualization	The ability to imagine how something will look after it is moved around or when its parts are moved or rearranged.
Visual Color Discrimination	The ability to match or detect differences between colors, including shades of color and brightness.
Trunk Strength	The ability to use your abdominal and lower back muscles to support part of the body repeatedly or continuously over time without 'giving out' or fatiguing.
Hearing Sensitivity	The ability to detect or tell the differences between sounds that vary in pitch and loudness.
Perceptual Speed	The ability to quickly and accurately compare similarities and differences among sets of letters, numbers, objects, pictures, or patterns. The things to be compared may be presented at the same time or one after the other. This ability also includes comparing a presented object with a remembered object.
Finger Dexterity	The ability to make precisely coordinated movements of the fingers of one or both hands to grasp, manipulate, or assemble very small objects.
Static Strength	The ability to exert maximum muscle force to lift, push, pull, or carry objects.
Explosive Strength	The ability to use short bursts of muscle force to propel oneself (as in jumping or sprinting), or to throw an object.
Stamina	The ability to exert yourself physically over long periods of time without getting winded or out of breath.
Gross Body Coordination	The ability to coordinate the movement of your arms, legs, and torso together when the whole body is in motion.
Reaction Time	The ability to quickly respond (with the hand, finger, or foot) to a signal (sound, light, picture) when it appears.
Gross Body Equilibrium	The ability to keep or regain your body balance or stay upright when in an unstable position.
Depth Perception	The ability to judge which of several objects is closer or farther away from you, or to judge the distance between you and an object.
Response Orientation	The ability to choose quickly between two or more movements in response to two or more different signals (lights, sounds, pictures). It includes the speed with which the correct response is started with the hand, foot, or other body part.
Wrist-Finger Speed	The ability to make fast, simple, repeated movements of the fingers, hands, and wrists.
Multilimb Coordination	The ability to coordinate two or more limbs (for example, two arms, two legs, or one leg and one arm) while sitting, standing, or lying down. It does not involve performing the activities while the whole body is in motion.

Rate Control	The ability to time your movements or the movement of a piece of equipment in anticipation of changes in the speed and/or direction of a moving object or scene.
Manual Dexterity	The ability to quickly move your hand, your hand together with your arm, or your two hands to grasp, manipulate, or assemble objects.
Arm-Hand Steadiness	The ability to keep your hand and arm steady while moving your arm or while holding your arm and hand in one position.
Speed of Limb Movement	The ability to quickly move the arms and legs.
Dynamic Strength	The ability to exert muscle force repeatedly or continuously over time. This involves muscular endurance and resistance to muscle fatigue.
Sound Localization	The ability to tell the direction from which a sound originated.
Glare Sensitivity	The ability to see objects in the presence of glare or bright lighting.
Spatial Orientation	The ability to know your location in relation to the environment or to know where other objects are in relation to you.
Control Precision	The ability to quickly and repeatedly adjust the controls of a machine or a vehicle to exact positions.
Dynamic Flexibility	The ability to quickly and repeatedly bend, stretch, twist, or reach out with your body, arms, and/or legs.
Peripheral Vision	The ability to see objects or movement of objects to one's side when the eyes are looking ahead.
Night Vision	The ability to see under low light conditions.
Extent Flexibility	The ability to bend, stretch, twist, or reach with your body, arms, and/or legs.

Work_Activity	Work_Activity Definitions
Establishing and Maintaining Interpersonal Relatio	Developing constructive and cooperative working relationships with others, and maintaining them over time.
Communicating with Supervisors, Peers, or Subordin	Providing information to supervisors, co-workers, and subordinates by telephone, in written form, e-mail, or in person.
Training and Teaching Others	Identifying the educational needs of others, developing formal educational or training programs or classes, and teaching or instructing others.
Organizing, Planning, and Prioritizing Work	Developing specific goals and plans to prioritize, organize, and accomplish your work.
Documenting/Recording Information	Entering, transcribing, recording, storing, or maintaining information in written or electronic/magnetic form.
Getting Information	Observing, receiving, and otherwise obtaining information from all relevant sources.
Making Decisions and Solving Problems	Analyzing information and evaluating results to choose the best solution and solve problems.
Resolving Conflicts and Negotiating with Others	Handling complaints, settling disputes, and resolving grievances and conflicts, or otherwise negotiating with others.
Thinking Creatively	Developing, designing, or creating new applications, ideas, relationships, systems, or products, including artistic contributions.
Updating and Using Relevant Knowledge	Keeping up-to-date technically and applying new knowledge to your job.
Developing Objectives and Strategies	Establishing long-range objectives and specifying the strategies and actions to achieve them.
Monitor Processes, Materials, or Surroundings	Monitoring and reviewing information from materials, events, or the environment, to detect or assess problems.
Interpreting the Meaning of Information for Others	Translating or explaining what information means and how it can be used.
Evaluating Information to Determine Compliance wit	Using relevant information and individual judgment to determine whether events or processes comply with laws, regulations, or standards.
Coaching and Developing Others	Identifying the developmental needs of others and coaching, mentoring, or otherwise helping others to improve their knowledge or skills.
Assisting and Caring for Others	Providing personal assistance, medical attention, emotional support, or other personal care to others such as coworkers, customers, or patients.
Judging the Qualities of Things, Services, or Peop	Assessing the value, importance, or quality of things or people.
Communicating with Persons Outside Organization	Communicating with people outside the organization, representing the organization to customers, the public, government, and other external sources. This information can be exchanged in person, in writing, or by telephone or e-mail.
Identifying Objects, Actions, and Events	Identifying information by categorizing, estimating, recognizing differences or similarities, and detecting changes in circumstances or events.

Scheduling Work and Activities	Scheduling events, programs, and activities, as well as the work of others.
Interacting With Computers	Using computers and computer systems (including hardware and software) to program, write software, set up functions, enter data, or process information.
Processing Information	Compiling, coding, categorizing, calculating, tabulating, auditing, or verifying information or data.
Developing and Building Teams	Encouraging and building mutual trust, respect, and cooperation among team members.
Analyzing Data or Information	Identifying the underlying principles, reasons, or facts of information by breaking down information or data into separate parts.
Guiding, Directing, and Motivating Subordinates	Providing guidance and direction to subordinates, including setting performance standards and monitoring performance.
Performing for or Working Directly with the Public	Performing for people or dealing directly with the public. This includes serving customers in restaurants and stores, and receiving clients or guests.
Coordinating the Work and Activities of Others	Getting members of a group to work together to accomplish tasks.
Provide Consultation and Advice to Others	Providing guidance and expert advice to management or other groups on technical, systems-, or process-related topics.
Performing Administrative Activities	Performing day-to-day administrative tasks such as maintaining information files and processing paperwork.
Selling or Influencing Others	Convincing others to buy merchandise/goods or to otherwise change their minds or actions.
Estimating the Quantifiable Characteristics of Pro	Estimating sizes, distances, and quantities; or determining time, costs, resources, or materials needed to perform a work activity.
Inspecting Equipment, Structures, or Material	Inspecting equipment, structures, or materials to identify the cause of errors or other problems or defects.
Monitoring and Controlling Resources	Monitoring and controlling resources and overseeing the spending of money.
Performing General Physical Activities	Performing physical activities that require considerable use of your arms and legs and moving your whole body, such as climbing, lifting, balancing, walking, stooping, and handling of materials.
Handling and Moving Objects	Using hands and arms in handling, installing, positioning, and moving materials, and manipulating things.
Controlling Machines and Processes	Using either control mechanisms or direct physical activity to operate machines or processes (not including computers or vehicles).
Staffing Organizational Units	Recruiting, interviewing, selecting, hiring, and promoting employees in an organization.
Drafting, Laying Out, and Specifying Technical Dev	Providing documentation, detailed instructions, drawings, or specifications to tell others about how devices, parts, equipment, or structures are to be fabricated, constructed, assembled, modified, maintained, or used.
Operating Vehicles, Mechanized Devices, or Equipme	Running, maneuvering, navigating, or driving vehicles or mechanized equipment, such as forklifts, passenger vehicles, aircraft, or water craft.
Repairing and Maintaining Electronic Equipment	Servicing, repairing, calibrating, regulating, fine-tuning, or testing machines, devices, and equipment that operate primarily on the basis of electrical or electronic (not mechanical) principles.
Repairing and Maintaining Mechanical Equipment	Servicing, repairing, adjusting, and testing machines, devices, moving parts, and equipment that operate primarily on the basis of mechanical (not electronic) principles.

Work_Context　　　　　Work_Context Definitions

Face-to-Face Discussions	How often do you have to have face-to-face discussions with individuals or teams in this job?
Contact With Others	How much does this job require the worker to be in contact with others (face-to-face, by telephone, or otherwise) in order to perform it?
Telephone	How often do you have telephone conversations in this job?
Physical Proximity	To what extent does this job require the worker to perform job tasks in close physical proximity to other people?
Work With Work Group or Team	How important is it to work with others in a group or team in this job?
Coordinate or Lead Others	How important is it to coordinate or lead others in accomplishing work activities in this job?
Electronic Mail	How often do you use electronic mail in this job?
Frequency of Decision Making	How frequently is the worker required to make decisions that affect other people, the financial resources, and/or the image and reputation of the organization?
Freedom to Make Decisions	How much decision making freedom, without supervision, does the job offer?

Frequency of Conflict Situations	How often are there conflict situations the employee has to face in this job?
Structured versus Unstructured Work	To what extent is this job structured for the worker, rather than allowing the worker to determine tasks, priorities, and goals?
Indoors, Environmentally Controlled	How often does this job require working indoors in environmentally controlled conditions?
Deal With Unpleasant or Angry People	How frequently does the worker have to deal with unpleasant, angry, or discourteous individuals as part of the job requirements?
Letters and Memos	How often does the job require written letters and memos?
Public Speaking	How often do you have to perform public speaking in this job?
Time Pressure	How often does this job require the worker to meet strict deadlines?
Impact of Decisions on Co-workers or Company Resul	How do the decisions an employee makes impact the results of co-workers, clients or the company?
Deal With External Customers	How important is it to work with external customers or the public in this job?
Importance of Being Exact or Accurate	How important is being very exact or highly accurate in performing this job?
Spend Time Standing	How much does this job require standing?
Sounds, Noise Levels Are Distracting or Uncomforta	How often does this job require working exposed to sounds and noise levels that are distracting or uncomfortable?
Responsibility for Outcomes and Results	How responsible is the worker for work outcomes and results of other workers?
Responsible for Others' Health and Safety	How much responsibility is there for the health and safety of others in this job?
Deal With Physically Aggressive People	How frequently does this job require the worker to deal with physical aggression of violent individuals?
Importance of Repeating Same Tasks	How important is repeating the same physical activities (e.g., key entry) or mental activities (e.g., checking entries in a ledger) over and over, without stopping, to performing this job?
Spend Time Sitting	How much does this job require sitting?
Level of Competition	To what extent does this job require the worker to compete or to be aware of competitive pressures?
Exposed to Disease or Infections	How often does this job require exposure to disease/infections?
Consequence of Error	How serious would the result usually be if the worker made a mistake that was not readily correctable?
Spend Time Using Your Hands to Handle, Control, or	How much does this job require using your hands to handle, control, or feel objects, tools or controls?
Exposed to Contaminants	How often does this job require working exposed to contaminants (such as pollutants, gases, dust or odors)?
Spend Time Making Repetitive Motions	How much does this job require making repetitive motions?
Spend Time Walking and Running	How much does this job require walking and running?
Indoors, Not Environmentally Controlled	How often does this job require working indoors in non-controlled environmental conditions (e.g., warehouse without heat)?
Extremely Bright or Inadequate Lighting	How often does this job require working in extremely bright or inadequate lighting conditions?
Very Hot or Cold Temperatures	How often does this job require working in very hot (above 90 F degrees) or very cold (below 32 F degrees) temperatures?
Outdoors, Exposed to Weather	How often does this job require working outdoors, exposed to all weather conditions?
Degree of Automation	How automated is the job?
Spend Time Bending or Twisting the Body	How much does this job require bending or twisting your body?
In an Enclosed Vehicle or Equipment	How often does this job require working in a closed vehicle or equipment (e.g., car)?
Exposed to Minor Burns, Cuts, Bites, or Stings	How often does this job require exposure to minor burns, cuts, bites, or stings?
Spend Time Kneeling, Crouching, Stooping, or Crawl	How much does this job require kneeling, crouching, stooping or crawling?
Spend Time Keeping or Regaining Balance	How much does this job require keeping or regaining your balance?
Wear Common Protective or Safety Equipment such as	How much does this job require wearing common protective or safety equipment such as safety shoes, glasses, gloves, hard hats or live jackets?
Outdoors, Under Cover	How often does this job require working outdoors, under cover (e.g., structure with roof but no walls)?
Cramped Work Space, Awkward Positions	How often does this job require working in cramped work spaces that requires getting into awkward positions?

1529

Pace Determined by Speed of Equipment	How important is it to this job that the pace is determined by the speed of equipment or machinery? (This does not refer to keeping busy at all times on this job.)
In an Open Vehicle or Equipment	How often does this job require working in an open vehicle or equipment (e.g., tractor)?
Exposed to High Places	How often does this job require exposure to high places?
Spend Time Climbing Ladders, Scaffolds, or Poles	How much does this job require climbing ladders, scaffolds, or poles?
Exposed to Hazardous Equipment	How often does this job require exposure to hazardous equipment?
Exposed to Hazardous Conditions	How often does this job require exposure to hazardous conditions?
Exposed to Whole Body Vibration	How often does this job require exposure to whole body vibration (e.g., operate a jackhammer)?
Wear Specialized Protective or Safety Equipment su	How much does this job require wearing specialized protective or safety equipment such as breathing apparatus, safety harness, full protection suits, or radiation protection?
Exposed to Radiation	How often does this job require exposure to radiation?

Job Zone Component	Job Zone Component Definitions
Title	Job Zone Four: Considerable Preparation Needed
Overall Experience	A minimum of two to four years of work-related skill, knowledge, or experience is needed for these occupations. For example, an accountant must complete four years of college and work for several years in accounting to be considered qualified.
Job Training	Employees in these occupations usually need several years of work-related experience, on-the-job training, and/or vocational training.
Job Zone Examples	Many of these occupations involve coordinating, supervising, managing, or training others. Examples include accountants, chefs and head cooks, computer programmers, historians, pharmacists, and police detectives.
SVP Range	(7.0 to < 8.0)
Education	Most of these occupations require a four - year bachelor's degree, but some do not.

Work_Styles	Work_Styles Definitions
Self Control	Job requires maintaining composure, keeping emotions in check, controlling anger, and avoiding aggressive behavior, even in very difficult situations.
Adaptability/Flexibility	Job requires being open to change (positive or negative) and to considerable variety in the workplace.
Stress Tolerance	Job requires accepting criticism and dealing calmly and effectively with high stress situations.
Integrity	Job requires being honest and ethical.
Cooperation	Job requires being pleasant with others on the job and displaying a good-natured, cooperative attitude.
Concern for Others	Job requires being sensitive to others' needs and feelings and being understanding and helpful on the job.
Dependability	Job requires being reliable, responsible, and dependable, and fulfilling obligations.
Social Orientation	Job requires preferring to work with others rather than alone, and being personally connected with others on the job.
Persistence	Job requires persistence in the face of obstacles.
Attention to Detail	Job requires being careful about detail and thorough in completing work tasks.
Initiative	Job requires a willingness to take on responsibilities and challenges.
Leadership	Job requires a willingness to lead, take charge, and offer opinions and direction.
Independence	Job requires developing one's own ways of doing things, guiding oneself with little or no supervision, and depending on oneself to get things done.
Achievement/Effort	Job requires establishing and maintaining personally challenging achievement goals and exerting effort toward mastering tasks.
Innovation	Job requires creativity and alternative thinking to develop new ideas for and answers to work-related problems.
Analytical Thinking	Job requires analyzing information and using logic to address work-related issues and problems.

25-3011.00 - Adult Literacy, Remedial Education, and GED

Teachers and Instructors

Teach or instruct out-of-school youths and adults in remedial education classes, preparatory classes for the General Educational Development test, literacy, or English as a Second Language. Teaching may or may not take place in a traditional educational institution.

Tasks

1) Adapt teaching methods and instructional materials to meet students' varying needs, abilities, and interests.

2) Prepare students for further education by encouraging them to explore learning opportunities and to persevere with challenging tasks.

3) Attend professional meetings, conferences, and workshops in order to maintain and improve professional competence.

4) Instruct students individually and in groups, using various teaching methods such as lectures, discussions, and demonstrations.

5) Prepare materials and classrooms for class activities.

6) Establish clear objectives for all lessons, units, and projects, and communicate those objectives to students.

7) Observe students to determine qualifications, limitations, abilities, interests, and other individual characteristics.

8) Plan and conduct activities for a balanced program of instruction, demonstration, and work time that provides students with opportunities to observe, question, and investigate.

9) Conduct classes, workshops, and demonstrations to teach principles, techniques, or methods in subjects such as basic English language skills, life skills, and workforce entry skills.

10) Establish and enforce rules for behavior and procedures for maintaining order among the students for whom they are responsible.

11) Attend staff meetings, and serve on committees as required.

12) Enforce administration policies and rules governing students.

13) Prepare objectives and outlines for courses of study, following curriculum guidelines or requirements of states and schools.

14) Collaborate with other teachers and professionals in the development of instructional programs.

15) Meet with other professionals to discuss individual students' needs and progress.

16) Guide and counsel students with adjustment and/or academic problems, or special academic interests.

17) Use computers, audiovisual aids, and other equipment and materials to supplement presentations.

18) Review instructional content, methods, and student evaluations to assess strengths and weaknesses, and to develop recommendations for course revision, development, or elimination.

19) Confer with other staff members to plan and schedule lessons that promote learning, following approved curricula.

20) Select, order, and issue books, materials, and supplies for courses or projects.

21) Prepare and administer written, oral, and performance tests, and issue grades in accordance with performance.

22) Assign and grade class work and homework.

23) Prepare reports on students and activities as required by administration.

24) Prepare and implement remedial programs for students requiring extra help.

25) Register, orient, and assess new students according to standards and procedures.

26) Prepare for assigned classes, and show written evidence of preparation upon request of immediate supervisors.

27) Provide information, guidance, and preparation for the General Equivalency Diploma (GED) examination.

28) Advise students on internships, prospective employers, and job placement services.

29) Participate in publicity planning, community awareness efforts, and student recruitment.

30) Plan and supervise class projects, field trips, visits by guest speakers, contests, or other experiential activities, and guide students in learning from those activities.

31) Provide disabled students with assistive devices, supportive technology, and assistance accessing facilities such as restrooms.

32) Select and schedule class times to ensure maximum attendance.

33) Confer with leaders of government and community groups to coordinate student training or to find opportunities for students to fulfill curriculum requirements.

34) Write instructional articles on designated subjects.

35) Observe and evaluate the performance of other instructors.

36) Train and assist tutors and community literacy volunteers.

37) Write grants to obtain program funding.

38) Observe and evaluate students' work to determine progress and make suggestions for improvement.

Knowledge	Knowledge Definitions
English Language	Knowledge of the structure and content of the English language including the meaning and spelling of words, rules of composition, and grammar.
Education and Training	Knowledge of principles and methods for curriculum and training design, teaching and instruction for individuals and groups, and the measurement of training effects.
Psychology	Knowledge of human behavior and performance; individual differences in ability, personality, and interests; learning and motivation; psychological research methods; and the assessment and treatment of behavioral and affective disorders.
Mathematics	Knowledge of arithmetic, algebra, geometry, calculus, statistics, and their applications.
Customer and Personal Service	Knowledge of principles and processes for providing customer and personal services. This includes customer needs assessment, meeting quality standards for services, and evaluation of customer satisfaction.
Clerical	Knowledge of administrative and clerical procedures and systems such as word processing, managing files and records, stenography and transcription, designing forms, and other office procedures and terminology.
Sociology and Anthropology	Knowledge of group behavior and dynamics, societal trends and influences, human migrations, ethnicity, cultures and their history and origins.
Computers and Electronics	Knowledge of circuit boards, processors, chips, electronic equipment, and computer hardware and software, including applications and programming.
Administration and Management	Knowledge of business and management principles involved in strategic planning, resource allocation, human resources modeling, leadership technique, production methods, and coordination of people and resources.
Geography	Knowledge of principles and methods for describing the features of land, sea, and air masses, including their physical characteristics, locations, interrelationships, and distribution of plant, animal, and human life.
Therapy and Counseling	Knowledge of principles, methods, and procedures for diagnosis, treatment, and rehabilitation of physical and mental dysfunctions, and for career counseling and guidance.
History and Archeology	Knowledge of historical events and their causes, indicators, and effects on civilizations and cultures.
Communications and Media	Knowledge of media production, communication, and dissemination techniques and methods. This includes alternative ways to inform and entertain via written, oral, and visual media.
Public Safety and Security	Knowledge of relevant equipment, policies, procedures, and strategies to promote effective local, state, or national security operations for the protection of people, data, property, and institutions.
Law and Government	Knowledge of laws, legal codes, court procedures, precedents, government regulations, executive orders, agency rules, and the democratic political process.
Personnel and Human Resources	Knowledge of principles and procedures for personnel recruitment, selection, training, compensation and benefits, labor relations and negotiation, and personnel information systems.
Foreign Language	Knowledge of the structure and content of a foreign (non-English) language including the meaning and spelling of words, rules of composition and grammar, and pronunciation.
Philosophy and Theology	Knowledge of different philosophical systems and religions. This includes their basic principles, values, ethics, ways of thinking, customs, practices, and their impact on human culture.
Biology	Knowledge of plant and animal organisms, their tissues, cells, functions, interdependencies, and interactions with each other and the environment.
Transportation	Knowledge of principles and methods for moving people or goods by air, rail, sea, or road, including the relative costs and benefits.
Fine Arts	Knowledge of the theory and techniques required to compose, produce, and perform works of music, dance, visual arts, drama, and sculpture.
Chemistry	Knowledge of the chemical composition, structure, and properties of substances and of the chemical processes and transformations that they undergo. This includes uses of chemicals and their interactions, danger signs, production techniques, and disposal methods.
Telecommunications	Knowledge of transmission, broadcasting, switching, control, and operation of telecommunications systems.
Sales and Marketing	Knowledge of principles and methods for showing, promoting, and selling products or services. This includes marketing strategy and tactics, product demonstration, sales techniques, and sales control systems.
Physics	Knowledge and prediction of physical principles, laws, their interrelationships, and applications to understanding fluid, material, and atmospheric dynamics, and mechanical, electrical, atomic and sub- atomic structures and processes.
Economics and Accounting	Knowledge of economic and accounting principles and practices, the financial markets, banking and the analysis and reporting of financial data.
Medicine and Dentistry	Knowledge of the information and techniques needed to diagnose and treat human injuries, diseases, and deformities. This includes symptoms, treatment alternatives, drug properties and interactions, and preventive health-care measures.
Engineering and Technology	Knowledge of the practical application of engineering science and technology. This includes applying principles, techniques, procedures, and equipment to the design and production of various goods and services.
Mechanical	Knowledge of machines and tools, including their designs, uses, repair, and maintenance.
Production and Processing	Knowledge of raw materials, production processes, quality control, costs, and other techniques for maximizing the effective manufacture and distribution of goods.
Design	Knowledge of design techniques, tools, and principles involved in production of precision technical plans, blueprints, drawings, and models.
Food Production	Knowledge of techniques and equipment for planting, growing, and harvesting food products (both plant and animal) for consumption, including storage/handling techniques.
Building and Construction	Knowledge of materials, methods, and the tools involved in the construction or repair of houses, buildings, or other structures such as highways and roads.

Skills	Skills Definitions
Instructing	Teaching others how to do something.
Reading Comprehension	Understanding written sentences and paragraphs in work related documents.
Speaking	Talking to others to convey information effectively.
Active Listening	Giving full attention to what other people are saying, taking time to understand the points being made, asking questions as appropriate, and not interrupting at inappropriate times.
Learning Strategies	Selecting and using training/instructional methods and procedures appropriate for the situation when learning or teaching new things.
Monitoring	Monitoring/Assessing performance of yourself, other individuals, or organizations to make improvements or take corrective action.
Social Perceptiveness	Being aware of others' reactions and understanding why they react as they do.
Active Learning	Understanding the implications of new information for both current and future problem-solving and decision-making.
Writing	Communicating effectively in writing as appropriate for the needs of the audience.
Coordination	Adjusting actions in relation to others' actions.
Service Orientation	Actively looking for ways to help people.
Critical Thinking	Using logic and reasoning to identify the strengths and weaknesses of alternative solutions, conclusions or approaches to problems.
Time Management	Managing one's own time and the time of others.
Persuasion	Persuading others to change their minds or behavior.
Mathematics	Using mathematics to solve problems.
Negotiation	Bringing others together and trying to reconcile differences.
Complex Problem Solving	Identifying complex problems and reviewing related information to develop and evaluate options and implement solutions.
Judgment and Decision Making	Considering the relative costs and benefits of potential actions to choose the most appropriate one.

Equipment Selection	Determining the kind of tools and equipment needed to do a job.
Science	Using scientific rules and methods to solve problems.
Operations Analysis	Analyzing needs and product requirements to create a design.
Management of Personnel Resources	Motivating, developing, and directing people as they work, identifying the best people for the job.
Technology Design	Generating or adapting equipment and technology to serve user needs.
Quality Control Analysis	Conducting tests and inspections of products, services, or processes to evaluate quality or performance.
Management of Material Resources	Obtaining and seeing to the appropriate use of equipment, facilities, and materials needed to do certain work.
Systems Evaluation	Identifying measures or indicators of system performance and the actions needed to improve or correct performance, relative to the goals of the system.
Troubleshooting	Determining causes of operating errors and deciding what to do about it.
Systems Analysis	Determining how a system should work and how changes in conditions, operations, and the environment will affect outcomes.
Operation and Control	Controlling operations of equipment or systems.
Management of Financial Resources	Determining how money will be spent to get the work done, and accounting for these expenditures.
Installation	Installing equipment, machines, wiring, or programs to meet specifications.
Equipment Maintenance	Performing routine maintenance on equipment and determining when and what kind of maintenance is needed.
Programming	Writing computer programs for various purposes.
Operation Monitoring	Watching gauges, dials, or other indicators to make sure a machine is working properly.
Repairing	Repairing machines or systems using the needed tools.

Ability	Ability Definitions
Speech Clarity	The ability to speak clearly so others can understand you.
Oral Expression	The ability to communicate information and ideas in speaking so others will understand.
Oral Comprehension	The ability to listen to and understand information and ideas presented through spoken words and sentences.
Problem Sensitivity	The ability to tell when something is wrong or is likely to go wrong. It does not involve solving the problem, only recognizing there is a problem.
Written Comprehension	The ability to read and understand information and ideas presented in writing.
Speech Recognition	The ability to identify and understand the speech of another person.
Deductive Reasoning	The ability to apply general rules to specific problems to produce answers that make sense.
Near Vision	The ability to see details at close range (within a few feet of the observer).
Information Ordering	The ability to arrange things or actions in a certain order or pattern according to a specific rule or set of rules (e.g., patterns of numbers, letters, words, pictures, mathematical operations).
Fluency of Ideas	The ability to come up with a number of ideas about a topic (the number of ideas is important, not their quality, correctness, or creativity).
Originality	The ability to come up with unusual or clever ideas about a given topic or situation, or to develop creative ways to solve a problem.
Written Expression	The ability to communicate information and ideas in writing so others will understand.
Inductive Reasoning	The ability to combine pieces of information to form general rules or conclusions (includes finding a relationship among seemingly unrelated events).
Category Flexibility	The ability to generate or use different sets of rules for combining or grouping things in different ways.
Selective Attention	The ability to concentrate on a task over a period of time without being distracted.
Perceptual Speed	The ability to quickly and accurately compare similarities and differences among sets of letters, numbers, objects, pictures, or patterns. The things to be compared may be presented at the same time or one after the other. This ability also includes comparing a presented object with a remembered object.
Far Vision	The ability to see details at a distance.
Flexibility of Closure	The ability to identify or detect a known pattern (a figure, object, word, or sound) that is hidden in other distracting material.
Time Sharing	The ability to shift back and forth between two or more activities or sources of information (such as speech, sounds, touch, or other sources).

Visualization	The ability to imagine how something will look after it is moved around or when its parts are moved or rearranged.
Auditory Attention	The ability to focus on a single source of sound in the presence of other distracting sounds.
Memorization	The ability to remember information such as words, numbers, pictures, and procedures.
Number Facility	The ability to add, subtract, multiply, or divide quickly and correctly.
Mathematical Reasoning	The ability to choose the right mathematical methods or formulas to solve a problem.
Visual Color Discrimination	The ability to match or detect differences between colors, including shades of color and brightness.
Hearing Sensitivity	The ability to detect or tell the differences between sounds that vary in pitch and loudness.
Speed of Closure	The ability to quickly make sense of, combine, and organize information into meaningful patterns.
Finger Dexterity	The ability to make precisely coordinated movements of the fingers of one or both hands to grasp, manipulate, or assemble very small objects.
Trunk Strength	The ability to use your abdominal and lower back muscles to support part of the body repeatedly or continuously over time without 'giving out' or fatiguing.
Sound Localization	The ability to tell the direction from which a sound originated.
Gross Body Coordination	The ability to coordinate the movement of your arms, legs, and torso together when the whole body is in motion.
Extent Flexibility	The ability to bend, stretch, twist, or reach with your body, arms, and/or legs.
Wrist-Finger Speed	The ability to make fast, simple, repeated movements of the fingers, hands, and wrists.
Rate Control	The ability to time your movements or the movement of a piece of equipment in anticipation of changes in the speed and/or direction of a moving object or scene.
Control Precision	The ability to quickly and repeatedly adjust the controls of a machine or a vehicle to exact positions.
Speed of Limb Movement	The ability to quickly move the arms and legs.
Arm-Hand Steadiness	The ability to keep your hand and arm steady while moving your arm or while holding your arm and hand in one position.
Spatial Orientation	The ability to know your location in relation to the environment or to know where other objects are in relation to you.
Gross Body Equilibrium	The ability to keep or regain your body balance or stay upright when in an unstable position.
Multilimb Coordination	The ability to coordinate two or more limbs (for example, two arms, two legs, or one leg and one arm) while sitting, standing, or lying down. It does not involve performing the activities while the whole body is in motion.
Night Vision	The ability to see under low light conditions.
Dynamic Flexibility	The ability to quickly and repeatedly bend, stretch, twist, or reach out with your body, arms, and/or legs.
Peripheral Vision	The ability to see objects or movement of objects to one's side when the eyes are looking ahead.
Reaction Time	The ability to quickly respond (with the hand, finger, or foot) to a signal (sound, light, picture) when it appears.
Depth Perception	The ability to judge which of several objects is closer or farther away from you, or to judge the distance between you and an object.
Static Strength	The ability to exert maximum muscle force to lift, push, pull, or carry objects.
Glare Sensitivity	The ability to see objects in the presence of glare or bright lighting.
Dynamic Strength	The ability to exert muscle force repeatedly or continuously over time. This involves muscular endurance and resistance to muscle fatigue.
Stamina	The ability to exert yourself physically over long periods of time without getting winded or out of breath.
Response Orientation	The ability to choose quickly between two or more movements in response to two or more different signals (lights, sounds, pictures). It includes the speed with which the correct response is started with the hand, foot, or other body part.
Manual Dexterity	The ability to quickly move your hand, your hand together with your arm, or your two hands to grasp, manipulate, or assemble objects.
Explosive Strength	The ability to use short bursts of muscle force to propel oneself (as in jumping or sprinting), or to throw an object.

Work_Activity	Work_Activity Definitions
Training and Teaching Others	Identifying the educational needs of others, developing formal educational or training programs or classes, and teaching or instructing others.

Establishing and Maintaining Interpersonal Relatio	Developing constructive and cooperative working relationships with others, and maintaining them over time.
Coaching and Developing Others	Identifying the developmental needs of others and coaching, mentoring, or otherwise helping others to improve their knowledge or skills.
Getting Information	Observing, receiving, and otherwise obtaining information from all relevant sources.
Communicating with Supervisors, Peers, or Subordin	Providing information to supervisors, co-workers, and subordinates by telephone, in written form, e-mail, or in person.
Interpreting the Meaning of Information for Others	Translating or explaining what information means and how it can be used.
Making Decisions and Solving Problems	Analyzing information and evaluating results to choose the best solution and solve problems.
Organizing, Planning, and Prioritizing Work	Developing specific goals and plans to prioritize, organize, and accomplish your work.
Assisting and Caring for Others	Providing personal assistance, medical attention, emotional support, or other personal care to others such as coworkers, customers, or patients.
Thinking Creatively	Developing, designing, or creating new applications, ideas, relationships, systems, or products, including artistic contributions.
Identifying Objects, Actions, and Events	Identifying information by categorizing, estimating, recognizing differences or similarities, and detecting changes in circumstances or events.
Developing Objectives and Strategies	Establishing long-range objectives and specifying the strategies and actions to achieve them.
Documenting/Recording Information	Entering, transcribing, recording, storing, or maintaining information in written or electronic/magnetic form.
Monitor Processes, Materials, or Surroundings	Monitoring and reviewing information from materials, events, or the environment, to detect or assess problems.
Evaluating Information to Determine Compliance wit	Using relevant information and individual judgment to determine whether events or processes comply with laws, regulations, or standards.
Judging the Qualities of Things, Services, or Peop	Assessing the value, importance, or quality of things or people.
Updating and Using Relevant Knowledge	Keeping up-to-date technically and applying new knowledge to your job.
Performing for or Working Directly with the Public	Performing for people or dealing directly with the public. This includes serving customers in restaurants and stores, and receiving clients or guests.
Scheduling Work and Activities	Scheduling events, programs, and activities, as well as the work of others.
Coordinating the Work and Activities of Others	Getting members of a group to work together to accomplish tasks.
Developing and Building Teams	Encouraging and building mutual trust, respect, and cooperation among team members.
Communicating with Persons Outside Organization	Communicating with people outside the organization, representing the organization to customers, the public, government, and other external sources. This information can be exchanged in person, in writing, or by telephone or e-mail.
Interacting With Computers	Using computers and computer systems (including hardware and software) to program, write software, set up functions, enter data, or process information.
Processing Information	Compiling, coding, categorizing, calculating, tabulating, auditing, or verifying information or data.
Performing Administrative Activities	Performing day-to-day administrative tasks such as maintaining information files and processing paperwork.
Provide Consultation and Advice to Others	Providing guidance and expert advice to management or other groups on technical, systems-, or process-related topics.
Analyzing Data or Information	Identifying the underlying principles, reasons, or facts of information by breaking down information or data into separate parts.
Resolving Conflicts and Negotiating with Others	Handling complaints, settling disputes, and resolving grievances and conflicts, or otherwise negotiating with others.
Guiding, Directing, and Motivating Subordinates	Providing guidance and direction to subordinates, including setting performance standards and monitoring performance.
Selling or Influencing Others	Convincing others to buy merchandise/goods or to otherwise change their minds or actions.
Estimating the Quantifiable Characteristics of Pro	Estimating sizes, distances, and quantities; or determining time, costs, resources, or materials needed to perform a work activity.
Inspecting Equipment, Structures, or Material	Inspecting equipment, structures, or materials to identify the cause of errors or other problems or defects.

Performing General Physical Activities	Performing physical activities that require considerable use of your arms and legs and moving your whole body, such as climbing, lifting, balancing, walking, stooping, and handling of materials.
Monitoring and Controlling Resources	Monitoring and controlling resources and overseeing the spending of money.
Handling and Moving Objects	Using hands and arms in handling, installing, positioning, and moving materials, and manipulating things.
Controlling Machines and Processes	Using either control mechanisms or direct physical activity to operate machines or processes (not including computers or vehicles).
Repairing and Maintaining Electronic Equipment	Servicing, repairing, calibrating, regulating, fine-tuning, or testing machines, devices, and equipment that operate primarily on the basis of electrical or electronic (not mechanical) principles.
Repairing and Maintaining Mechanical Equipment	Servicing, repairing, adjusting, and testing machines, devices, moving parts, and equipment that operate primarily on the basis of mechanical (not electronic) principles.
Drafting, Laying Out, and Specifying Technical Dev	Providing documentation, detailed instructions, drawings, or specifications to tell others about how devices, parts, equipment, or structures are to be fabricated, constructed, assembled, modified, maintained, or used.
Operating Vehicles, Mechanized Devices, or Equipme	Running, maneuvering, navigating, or driving vehicles or mechanized equipment, such as forklifts, passenger vehicles, aircraft, or water craft.
Staffing Organizational Units	Recruiting, interviewing, selecting, hiring, and promoting employees in an organization.

Work_Context	Work_Context Definitions
Contact With Others	How much does this job require the worker to be in contact with others (face-to-face, by telephone, or otherwise) in order to perform it?
Face-to-Face Discussions	How often do you have to have face-to-face discussions with individuals or teams in this job?
Freedom to Make Decisions	How much decision making freedom, without supervision, does the job offer?
Structured versus Unstructured Work	To what extent is this job structured for the worker, rather than allowing the worker to determine tasks, priorities, and goals?
Physical Proximity	To what extent does this job require the worker to perform job tasks in close physical proximity to other people?
Indoors, Environmentally Controlled	How often does this job require working indoors in environmentally controlled conditions?
Work With Work Group or Team	How important is it to work with others in a group or team in this job?
Deal With External Customers	How important is it to work with external customers or the public in this job?
Coordinate or Lead Others	How important is it to coordinate or lead others in accomplishing work activities in this job?
Public Speaking	How often do you have to perform public speaking in this job?
Frequency of Decision Making	How frequently is the worker required to make decisions that affect other people, the financial resources, and/or the image and reputation of the organization?
Impact of Decisions on Co-workers or Company Resul	How do the decisions an employee makes impact the results of co-workers, clients or the company?
Telephone	How often do you have telephone conversations in this job?
Importance of Being Exact or Accurate	How important is being very exact or highly accurate in performing this job?
Spend Time Standing	How much does this job require standing?
Time Pressure	How often does this job require the worker to meet strict deadlines?
Letters and Memos	How often does the job require written letters and memos?
Spend Time Sitting	How much does this job require sitting?
Electronic Mail	How often do you use electronic mail in this job?
Sounds, Noise Levels Are Distracting or Uncomforta	How often does this job require working exposed to sounds and noise levels that are distracting or uncomfortable?
Deal With Unpleasant or Angry People	How frequently does the worker have to deal with unpleasant, angry, or discourteous individuals as part of the job requirements?
Frequency of Conflict Situations	How often are there conflict situations the employee has to face in this job?
Importance of Repeating Same Tasks	How important is repeating the same physical activities (e.g., key entry) or mental activities (e.g., checking entries in a ledger) over and over, without stopping, to performing this job?
Responsibility for Outcomes and Results	How responsible is the worker for work outcomes and results of other workers?
Responsible for Others' Health and Safety	How much responsibility is there for the health and safety of others in this job?

Spend Time Using Your Hands to Handle, Control, or	How much does this job require using your hands to handle, control, or feel objects, tools or controls?
Level of Competition	To what extent does this job require the worker to compete or to be aware of competitive pressures?
Exposed to Contaminants	How often does this job require working exposed to contaminants (such as pollutants, gases, dust or odors)?
Spend Time Making Repetitive Motions	How much does this job require making repetitive motions?
Indoors, Not Environmentally Controlled	How often does this job require working indoors in non-controlled environmental conditions (e.g., warehouse without heat)?
Degree of Automation	How automated is the job?
Exposed to Disease or Infections	How often does this job require exposure to disease/infections?
Spend Time Walking and Running	How much does this job require walking and running?
Consequence of Error	How serious would the result usually be if the worker made a mistake that was not readily correctable?
Spend Time Bending or Twisting the Body	How much does this job require bending or twisting your body?
Deal With Physically Aggressive People	How frequently does this job require the worker to deal with physical aggression of violent individuals?
Extremely Bright or Inadequate Lighting	How often does this job require working in extremely bright or inadequate lighting conditions?
Very Hot or Cold Temperatures	How often does this job require working in very hot (above 90 F degrees) or very cold (below 32 F degrees) temperatures?
Cramped Work Space, Awkward Positions	How often does this job require working in cramped work spaces that requires getting into awkward positions?
In an Enclosed Vehicle or Equipment	How often does this job require working in a closed vehicle or equipment (e.g., car)?
Spend Time Kneeling, Crouching, Stooping, or Crawl	How much does this job require kneeling, crouching, stooping or crawling?
Pace Determined by Speed of Equipment	How important is it to this job that the pace is determined by the speed of equipment or machinery? (This does not refer to keeping busy at all times on this job.)
Exposed to Minor Burns, Cuts, Bites, or Stings	How often does this job require exposure to minor burns, cuts, bites, or stings?
Wear Common Protective or Safety Equipment such as	How much does this job require wearing common protective or safety equipment such as safety shoes, glasses, gloves, hard hats or live jackets?
Outdoors, Exposed to Weather	How often does this job require working outdoors, exposed to all weather conditions?
Spend Time Keeping or Regaining Balance	How much does this job require keeping or regaining your balance?
Outdoors, Under Cover	How often does this job require working outdoors, under cover (e.g., structure with roof but no walls)?
Exposed to Hazardous Equipment	How often does this job require exposure to hazardous equipment?
In an Open Vehicle or Equipment	How often does this job require working in an open vehicle or equipment (e.g., tractor)?
Spend Time Climbing Ladders, Scaffolds, or Poles	How much does this job require climbing ladders, scaffolds, or poles?
Exposed to Hazardous Conditions	How often does this job require exposure to hazardous conditions?
Exposed to Radiation	How often does this job require exposure to radiation?
Exposed to High Places	How often does this job require exposure to high places?
Exposed to Whole Body Vibration	How often does this job require exposure to whole body vibration (e.g., operate a jackhammer)?
Wear Specialized Protective or Safety Equipment su	How much does this job require wearing specialized protective or safety equipment such as breathing apparatus, safety harness, full protection suits, or radiation protection?

Job Zone Component	Job Zone Component Definitions
Title	Job Zone Four: Considerable Preparation Needed
Overall Experience	A minimum of two to four years of work-related skill, knowledge, or experience is needed for these occupations. For example, an accountant must complete four years of college and work for several years in accounting to be considered qualified.
Job Training	Employees in these occupations usually need several years of work-related experience, on-the-job training, and/or vocational training.

Job Zone Examples	Many of these occupations involve coordinating, supervising, managing, or training others. Examples include accountants, chefs and head cooks, computer programmers, historians, pharmacists, and police detectives.
SVP Range	(7.0 to < 8.0)
Education	Most of these occupations require a four - year bachelor's degree, but some do not.

Work_Styles	Work_Styles Definitions
Integrity	Job requires being honest and ethical.
Concern for Others	Job requires being sensitive to others' needs and feelings and being understanding and helpful on the job.
Dependability	Job requires being reliable, responsible, and dependable, and fulfilling obligations.
Self Control	Job requires maintaining composure, keeping emotions in check, controlling anger, and avoiding aggressive behavior, even in very difficult situations.
Cooperation	Job requires being pleasant with others on the job and displaying a good-natured, cooperative attitude.
Social Orientation	Job requires preferring to work with others rather than alone, and being personally connected with others on the job.
Initiative	Job requires a willingness to take on responsibilities and challenges.
Adaptability/Flexibility	Job requires being open to change (positive or negative) and to considerable variety in the workplace.
Attention to Detail	Job requires being careful about detail and thorough in completing work tasks.
Stress Tolerance	Job requires accepting criticism and dealing calmly and effectively with high stress situations.
Independence	Job requires developing one's own ways of doing things, guiding oneself with little or no supervision, and depending on oneself to get things done.
Achievement/Effort	Job requires establishing and maintaining personally challenging achievement goals and exerting effort toward mastering tasks.
Persistence	Job requires persistence in the face of obstacles.
Leadership	Job requires a willingness to lead, take charge, and offer opinions and direction.
Innovation	Job requires creativity and alternative thinking to develop new ideas for and answers to work-related problems.
Analytical Thinking	Job requires analyzing information and using logic to address work-related issues and problems.

25-9021.00 - Farm and Home Management Advisors

Advise, instruct, and assist individuals and families engaged in agriculture, agricultural-related processes, or home economics activities. Demonstrate procedures and apply research findings to solve problems; instruct and train in product development, sales, and the utilization of machinery and equipment to promote general welfare. Includes county agricultural agents, feed and farm management advisers, home economists, and extension service advisors.

Tasks

1) Act as an advocate for farmers or farmers' groups.

2) Set and monitor production targets.

3) Provide direct assistance to farmers by performing activities such as purchasing or selling products and supplies, supervising properties, and collecting soil and herbage samples for testing.

4) Organize, advise, and participate in community activities and organizations such as county and state fair events and 4-H Clubs.

5) Collaborate with social service and health care professionals in order to advise individuals and families on home management practices such as budget planning, meal preparation, and time management.

6) Conduct classes or deliver lectures on subjects such as nutrition, home management, and farming techniques.

7) Advise farmers and demonstrate techniques in areas such as feeding and health maintenance of livestock, growing and harvesting practices, and financial planning.

8) Maintain records of services provided and the effects of advice given.

9) Research information requested by farmers.

10) Collect and evaluate data in order to determine community program needs.

11) Collaborate with producers in order to diagnose and prevent management and production problems.

12) Conduct agricultural research, analyze data, and prepare research reports.

13) Prepare and distribute leaflets, pamphlets, and visual aids for educational and informational purposes.

14) Schedule and make regular visits to farmers.

25-9031.00 - Instructional Coordinators

Develop instructional material, coordinate educational content, and incorporate current technology in specialized fields that provide guidelines to educators and instructors for developing curricula and conducting courses.

Tasks

1) Conduct or participate in workshops, committees, and conferences designed to promote the intellectual, social, and physical welfare of students.

2) Recommend, order, or authorize purchase of instructional materials, supplies, equipment, and visual aids designed to meet student educational needs and district standards.

3) Research, evaluate, and prepare recommendations on curricula, instructional methods, and materials for school systems.

4) Observe work of teaching staff in order to evaluate performance, and to recommend changes that could strengthen teaching skills.

5) Advise teaching and administrative staff in curriculum development, use of materials and equipment, and implementation of state and federal programs and procedures.

6) Confer with members of educational committees and advisory groups to obtain knowledge of subject areas, and to relate curriculum materials to specific subjects, individual student needs, and occupational areas.

7) Prepare grant proposals, budgets, and program policies and goals, or assist in their preparation.

8) Organize production and design of curriculum materials.

9) Address public audiences to explain program objectives and to elicit support.

10) Update the content of educational programs to ensure that students are being trained with equipment and processes that are technologically current.

11) Develop instructional materials to be used by educators and instructors.

12) Interpret and enforce provisions of state education codes, and rules and regulations of state education boards.

13) Develop tests, questionnaires, and procedures that measure the effectiveness of curricula, and use these tools to determine whether program objectives are being met.

14) Prepare or approve manuals, guidelines, and reports on state educational policies and practices for distribution to school districts.

15) Advise and teach students.

16) Develop classroom-based and distance learning training courses, using needs assessments and skill level analyses.

17) Coordinate activities of workers engaged in cataloging, distributing, and maintaining educational materials and equipment in curriculum libraries and laboratories.

18) Inspect instructional equipment to determine if repairs are needed; authorize necessary repairs.

Knowledge	Knowledge Definitions
Education and Training	Knowledge of principles and methods for curriculum and training design, teaching and instruction for individuals and groups, and the measurement of training effects.
English Language	Knowledge of the structure and content of the English language including the meaning and spelling of words, rules of composition, and grammar.
Administration and Management	Knowledge of business and management principles involved in strategic planning, resource allocation, human resources modeling, leadership technique, production methods, and coordination of people and resources.
Customer and Personal Service	Knowledge of principles and processes for providing customer and personal services. This includes customer needs assessment, meeting quality standards for services, and evaluation of customer satisfaction.
Psychology	Knowledge of human behavior and performance; individual differences in ability, personality, and interests; learning and motivation; psychological research methods; and the assessment and treatment of behavioral and affective disorders.
Computers and Electronics	Knowledge of circuit boards, processors, chips, electronic equipment, and computer hardware and software, including applications and programming.
Mathematics	Knowledge of arithmetic, algebra, geometry, calculus, statistics, and their applications.
Personnel and Human Resources	Knowledge of principles and procedures for personnel recruitment, selection, training, compensation and benefits, labor relations and negotiation, and personnel information systems.
Communications and Media	Knowledge of media production, communication, and dissemination techniques and methods. This includes alternative ways to inform and entertain via written, oral, and visual media.
Clerical	Knowledge of administrative and clerical procedures and systems such as word processing, managing files and records, stenography and transcription, designing forms, and other office procedures and terminology.
Sociology and Anthropology	Knowledge of group behavior and dynamics, societal trends and influences, human migrations, ethnicity, cultures and their history and origins.
Law and Government	Knowledge of laws, legal codes, court procedures, precedents, government regulations, executive orders, agency rules, and the democratic political process.
Public Safety and Security	Knowledge of relevant equipment, policies, procedures, and strategies to promote effective local, state, or national security operations for the protection of people, data, property, and institutions.
Therapy and Counseling	Knowledge of principles, methods, and procedures for diagnosis, treatment, and rehabilitation of physical and mental dysfunctions, and for career counseling and guidance.
Telecommunications	Knowledge of transmission, broadcasting, switching, control, and operation of telecommunications systems.
Economics and Accounting	Knowledge of economic and accounting principles and practices, the financial markets, banking and the analysis and reporting of financial data.
Sales and Marketing	Knowledge of principles and methods for showing, promoting, and selling products or services. This includes marketing strategy and tactics, product demonstration, sales techniques, and sales control systems.
Philosophy and Theology	Knowledge of different philosophical systems and religions. This includes their basic principles, values, ethics, ways of thinking, customs, practices, and their impact on human culture.
Geography	Knowledge of principles and methods for describing the features of land, sea, and air masses, including their physical characteristics, locations, interrelationships, and distribution of plant, animal, and human life.
History and Archeology	Knowledge of historical events and their causes, indicators, and effects on civilizations and cultures.
Fine Arts	Knowledge of the theory and techniques required to compose, produce, and perform works of music, dance, visual arts, drama, and sculpture.
Foreign Language	Knowledge of the structure and content of a foreign (non-English) language including the meaning and spelling of words, rules of composition and grammar, and pronunciation.
Engineering and Technology	Knowledge of the practical application of engineering science and technology. This includes applying principles, techniques, procedures, and equipment to the design and production of various goods and services.
Production and Processing	Knowledge of raw materials, production processes, quality control, costs, and other techniques for maximizing the effective manufacture and distribution of goods.
Medicine and Dentistry	Knowledge of the information and techniques needed to diagnose and treat human injuries, diseases, and deformities. This includes symptoms, treatment alternatives, drug properties and interactions, and preventive health-care measures.
Transportation	Knowledge of principles and methods for moving people or goods by air, rail, sea, or road, including the relative costs and benefits.

Design	Knowledge of design techniques, tools, and principles involved in production of precision technical plans, blueprints, drawings, and models.
Mechanical	Knowledge of machines and tools, including their designs, uses, repair, and maintenance.
Physics	Knowledge and prediction of physical principles, laws, their interrelationships, and applications to understanding fluid, material, and atmospheric dynamics, and mechanical, electrical, atomic and sub- atomic structures and processes.
Chemistry	Knowledge of the chemical composition, structure, and properties of substances and of the chemical processes and transformations that they undergo. This includes uses of chemicals and their interactions, danger signs, production techniques, and disposal methods.
Biology	Knowledge of plant and animal organisms, their tissues, cells, functions, interdependencies, and interactions with each other and the environment.
Building and Construction	Knowledge of materials, methods, and the tools involved in the construction or repair of houses, buildings, or other structures such as highways and roads.
Food Production	Knowledge of techniques and equipment for planting, growing, and harvesting food products (both plant and animal) for consumption, including storage/handling techniques.

Skills	Skills Definitions
Reading Comprehension	Understanding written sentences and paragraphs in work related documents.
Active Listening	Giving full attention to what other people are saying, taking time to understand the points being made, asking questions as appropriate, and not interrupting at inappropriate times.
Critical Thinking	Using logic and reasoning to identify the strengths and weaknesses of alternative solutions, conclusions or approaches to problems.
Learning Strategies	Selecting and using training/instructional methods and procedures appropriate for the situation when learning or teaching new things.
Instructing	Teaching others how to do something.
Active Learning	Understanding the implications of new information for both current and future problem-solving and decision-making.
Writing	Communicating effectively in writing as appropriate for the needs of the audience.
Time Management	Managing one's own time and the time of others.
Speaking	Talking to others to convey information effectively.
Monitoring	Monitoring/Assessing performance of yourself, other individuals, or organizations to make improvements or take corrective action.
Coordination	Adjusting actions in relation to others' actions.
Social Perceptiveness	Being aware of others' reactions and understanding why they react as they do.
Complex Problem Solving	Identifying complex problems and reviewing related information to develop and evaluate options and implement solutions.
Service Orientation	Actively looking for ways to help people.
Persuasion	Persuading others to change their minds or behavior.
Judgment and Decision Making	Considering the relative costs and benefits of potential actions to choose the most appropriate one.
Management of Financial Resources	Determining how money will be spent to get the work done, and accounting for these expenditures.
Management of Personnel Resources	Motivating, developing, and directing people as they work, identifying the best people for the job.
Negotiation	Bringing others together and trying to reconcile differences.
Mathematics	Using mathematics to solve problems.
Equipment Selection	Determining the kind of tools and equipment needed to do a job.
Management of Material Resources	Obtaining and seeing to the appropriate use of equipment, facilities, and materials needed to do certain work.
Operations Analysis	Analyzing needs and product requirements to create a design.
Systems Evaluation	Identifying measures or indicators of system performance and the actions needed to improve or correct performance, relative to the goals of the system.
Systems Analysis	Determining how a system should work and how changes in conditions, operations, and the environment will affect outcomes.
Quality Control Analysis	Conducting tests and inspections of products, services, or processes to evaluate quality or performance.
Science	Using scientific rules and methods to solve problems.

Troubleshooting	Determining causes of operating errors and deciding what to do about it.
Technology Design	Generating or adapting equipment and technology to serve user needs.
Operation and Control	Controlling operations of equipment or systems.
Operation Monitoring	Watching gauges, dials, or other indicators to make sure a machine is working properly.
Repairing	Repairing machines or systems using the needed tools.
Installation	Installing equipment, machines, wiring, or programs to meet specifications.
Equipment Maintenance	Performing routine maintenance on equipment and determining when and what kind of maintenance is needed.
Programming	Writing computer programs for various purposes.

Ability	Ability Definitions
Oral Comprehension	The ability to listen to and understand information and ideas presented through spoken words and sentences.
Inductive Reasoning	The ability to combine pieces of information to form general rules or conclusions (includes finding a relationship among seemingly unrelated events).
Oral Expression	The ability to communicate information and ideas in speaking so others will understand.
Problem Sensitivity	The ability to tell when something is wrong or is likely to go wrong. It does not involve solving the problem, only recognizing there is a problem.
Speech Clarity	The ability to speak clearly so others can understand you.
Speech Recognition	The ability to identify and understand the speech of another person.
Deductive Reasoning	The ability to apply general rules to specific problems to produce answers that make sense.
Written Comprehension	The ability to read and understand information and ideas presented in writing.
Information Ordering	The ability to arrange things or actions in a certain order or pattern according to a specific rule or set of rules (e.g., patterns of numbers, letters, words, pictures, mathematical operations).
Written Expression	The ability to communicate information and ideas in writing so others will understand.
Near Vision	The ability to see details at close range (within a few feet of the observer).
Originality	The ability to come up with unusual or clever ideas about a given topic or situation, or to develop creative ways to solve a problem.
Fluency of Ideas	The ability to come up with a number of ideas about a topic (the number of ideas is important, not their quality, correctness, or creativity).
Category Flexibility	The ability to generate or use different sets of rules for combining or grouping things in different ways.
Selective Attention	The ability to concentrate on a task over a period of time without being distracted.
Far Vision	The ability to see details at a distance.
Number Facility	The ability to add, subtract, multiply, or divide quickly and correctly.
Time Sharing	The ability to shift back and forth between two or more activities or sources of information (such as speech, sounds, touch, or other sources).
Flexibility of Closure	The ability to identify or detect a known pattern (a figure, object, word, or sound) that is hidden in other distracting material.
Finger Dexterity	The ability to make precisely coordinated movements of the fingers of one or both hands to grasp, manipulate, or assemble very small objects.
Speed of Closure	The ability to quickly make sense of, combine, and organize information into meaningful patterns.
Mathematical Reasoning	The ability to choose the right mathematical methods or formulas to solve a problem.
Visualization	The ability to imagine how something will look after it is moved around or when its parts are moved or rearranged.
Perceptual Speed	The ability to quickly and accurately compare similarities and differences among sets of letters, numbers, objects, pictures, or patterns. The things to be compared may be presented at the same time or one after the other. This ability also includes comparing a presented object with a remembered object.
Hearing Sensitivity	The ability to detect or tell the differences between sounds that vary in pitch and loudness.
Memorization	The ability to remember information such as words, numbers, pictures, and procedures.

Visual Color Discrimination	The ability to match or detect differences between colors, including shades of color and brightness.
Auditory Attention	The ability to focus on a single source of sound in the presence of other distracting sounds.
Depth Perception	The ability to judge which of several objects is closer or farther away from you, or to judge the distance between you and an object.
Control Precision	The ability to quickly and repeatedly adjust the controls of a machine or a vehicle to exact positions.
Manual Dexterity	The ability to quickly move your hand, your hand together with your arm, or your two hands to grasp, manipulate, or assemble objects.
Multilimb Coordination	The ability to coordinate two or more limbs (for example, two arms, two legs, or one leg and one arm) while sitting, standing, or lying down. It does not involve performing the activities while the whole body is in motion.
Arm-Hand Steadiness	The ability to keep your hand and arm steady while moving your arm or while holding your arm and hand in one position.
Gross Body Coordination	The ability to coordinate the movement of your arms, legs, and torso together when the whole body is in motion.
Sound Localization	The ability to tell the direction from which a sound originated.
Response Orientation	The ability to choose quickly between two or more movements in response to two or more different signals (lights, sounds, pictures). It includes the speed with which the correct response is started with the hand, foot, or other body part.
Reaction Time	The ability to quickly respond (with the hand, finger, or foot) to a signal (sound, light, picture) when it appears.
Wrist-Finger Speed	The ability to make fast, simple, repeated movements of the fingers, hands, and wrists.
Dynamic Strength	The ability to exert muscle force repeatedly or continuously over time. This involves muscular endurance and resistance to muscle fatigue.
Glare Sensitivity	The ability to see objects in the presence of glare or bright lighting.
Dynamic Flexibility	The ability to quickly and repeatedly bend, stretch, twist, or reach out with your body, arms, and/or legs.
Extent Flexibility	The ability to bend, stretch, twist, or reach with your body, arms, and/or legs.
Speed of Limb Movement	The ability to quickly move the arms and legs.
Stamina	The ability to exert yourself physically over long periods of time without getting winded or out of breath.
Trunk Strength	The ability to use your abdominal and lower back muscles to support part of the body repeatedly or continuously over time without 'giving out' or fatiguing.
Static Strength	The ability to exert maximum muscle force to lift, push, pull, or carry objects.
Spatial Orientation	The ability to know your location in relation to the environment or to know where other objects are in relation to you.
Rate Control	The ability to time your movements or the movement of a piece of equipment in anticipation of changes in the speed and/or direction of a moving object or scene.
Explosive Strength	The ability to use short bursts of muscle force to propel oneself (as in jumping or sprinting), or to throw an object.
Peripheral Vision	The ability to see objects or movement of objects to one's side when the eyes are looking ahead.
Gross Body Equilibrium	The ability to keep or regain your body balance or stay upright when in an unstable position.
Night Vision	The ability to see under low light conditions.

Work_Activity	Work_Activity Definitions
Communicating with Supervisors, Peers, or Subordin	Providing information to supervisors, co-workers, and subordinates by telephone, in written form, e-mail, or in person.
Organizing, Planning, and Prioritizing Work	Developing specific goals and plans to prioritize, organize, and accomplish your work.
Establishing and Maintaining Interpersonal Relatio	Developing constructive and cooperative working relationships with others, and maintaining them over time.
Getting Information	Observing, receiving, and otherwise obtaining information from all relevant sources.
Updating and Using Relevant Knowledge	Keeping up-to-date technically and applying new knowledge to your job.
Making Decisions and Solving Problems	Analyzing information and evaluating results to choose the best solution and solve problems.
Training and Teaching Others	Identifying the educational needs of others, developing formal educational or training programs or classes, and teaching or instructing others.

Interacting With Computers	Using computers and computer systems (including hardware and software) to program, write software, set up functions, enter data, or process information.
Coaching and Developing Others	Identifying the developmental needs of others and coaching, mentoring, or otherwise helping others to improve their knowledge or skills.
Analyzing Data or Information	Identifying the underlying principles, reasons, or facts of information by breaking down information or data into separate parts.
Provide Consultation and Advice to Others	Providing guidance and expert advice to management or other groups on technical, systems-, or process-related topics.
Processing Information	Compiling, coding, categorizing, calculating, tabulating, auditing, or verifying information or data.
Scheduling Work and Activities	Scheduling events, programs, and activities, as well as the work of others.
Thinking Creatively	Developing, designing, or creating new applications, ideas, relationships, systems, or products, including artistic contributions.
Evaluating Information to Determine Compliance wit	Using relevant information and individual judgment to determine whether events or processes comply with laws, regulations, or standards.
Developing Objectives and Strategies	Establishing long-range objectives and specifying the strategies and actions to achieve them.
Interpreting the Meaning of Information for Others	Translating or explaining what information means and how it can be used.
Identifying Objects, Actions, and Events	Identifying information by categorizing, estimating, recognizing differences or similarities, and detecting changes in circumstances or events.
Monitor Processes, Materials, or Surroundings	Monitoring and reviewing information from materials, events, or the environment, to detect or assess problems.
Documenting/Recording Information	Entering, transcribing, recording, storing, or maintaining information in written or electronic/magnetic form.
Developing and Building Teams	Encouraging and building mutual trust, respect, and cooperation among team members.
Judging the Qualities of Things, Services, or Peop	Assessing the value, importance, or quality of things or people.
Performing Administrative Activities	Performing day-to-day administrative tasks such as maintaining information files and processing paperwork.
Communicating with Persons Outside Organization	Communicating with people outside the organization, representing the organization to customers, the public, government, and other external sources. This information can be exchanged in person, in writing, or by telephone or e-mail.
Guiding, Directing, and Motivating Subordinates	Providing guidance and direction to subordinates, including setting performance standards and monitoring performance.
Resolving Conflicts and Negotiating with Others	Handling complaints, settling disputes, and resolving grievances and conflicts, or otherwise negotiating with others.
Monitoring and Controlling Resources	Monitoring and controlling resources and overseeing the spending of money.
Performing for or Working Directly with the Public	Performing for people or dealing directly with the public. This includes serving customers in restaurants and stores, and receiving clients or guests.
Estimating the Quantifiable Characteristics of Pro	Estimating sizes, distances, and quantities; or determining time, costs, resources, or materials needed to perform a work activity.
Coordinating the Work and Activities of Others	Getting members of a group to work together to accomplish tasks.
Assisting and Caring for Others	Providing personal assistance, medical attention, emotional support, or other personal care to others such as coworkers, customers, or patients.
Staffing Organizational Units	Recruiting, interviewing, selecting, hiring, and promoting employees in an organization.
Inspecting Equipment, Structures, or Material	Inspecting equipment, structures, or materials to identify the cause of errors or other problems or defects.
Selling or Influencing Others	Convincing others to buy merchandise/goods or to otherwise change their minds or actions.
Handling and Moving Objects	Using hands and arms in handling, installing, positioning, and moving materials, and manipulating things.
Repairing and Maintaining Electronic Equipment	Servicing, repairing, calibrating, regulating, fine-tuning, or testing machines, devices, and equipment that operate primarily on the basis of electrical or electronic (not mechanical) principles.
Operating Vehicles, Mechanized Devices, or Equipme	Running, maneuvering, navigating, or driving vehicles or mechanized equipment, such as forklifts, passenger vehicles, aircraft, or water craft.

Drafting, Laying Out, and Specifying Technical Dev	Providing documentation, detailed instructions, drawings, or specifications to tell others about how devices, parts, equipment, or structures are to be fabricated, constructed, assembled, modified, maintained, or used.
Controlling Machines and Processes	Using either control mechanisms or direct physical activity to operate machines or processes (not including computers or vehicles).
Performing General Physical Activities	Performing physical activities that require considerable use of your arms and legs and moving your whole body, such as climbing, lifting, balancing, walking, stooping, and handling of materials.
Repairing and Maintaining Mechanical Equipment	Servicing, repairing, adjusting, and testing machines, devices, moving parts, and equipment that operate primarily on the basis of mechanical (not electronic) principles.

Work_Context	Work_Context Definitions
Face-to-Face Discussions	How often do you have to have face-to-face discussions with individuals or teams in this job?
Work With Work Group or Team	How important is it to work with others in a group or team in this job?
Electronic Mail	How often do you use electronic mail in this job?
Telephone	How often do you have telephone conversations in this job?
Contact With Others	How much does this job require the worker to be in contact with others (face-to-face, by telephone, or otherwise) in order to perform it?
Freedom to Make Decisions	How much decision making freedom, without supervision, does the job offer?
Structured versus Unstructured Work	To what extent is this job structured for the worker, rather than allowing the worker to determine tasks, priorities, and goals?
Letters and Memos	How often does the job require written letters and memos?
Frequency of Decision Making	How frequently is the worker required to make decisions that affect other people, the financial resources, and/or the image and reputation of the organization?
Impact of Decisions on Co-workers or Company Resul	How do the decisions an employee makes impact the results of co-workers, clients or the company?
Coordinate or Lead Others	How important is it to coordinate or lead others in accomplishing work activities in this job?
Indoors, Environmentally Controlled	How often does this job require working indoors in environmentally controlled conditions?
Responsibility for Outcomes and Results	How responsible is the worker for work outcomes and results of other workers?
Importance of Being Exact or Accurate	How important is being very exact or highly accurate in performing this job?
Time Pressure	How often does this job require the worker to meet strict deadlines?
Deal With External Customers	How important is it to work with external customers or the public in this job?
Spend Time Sitting	How much does this job require sitting?
Public Speaking	How often do you have to perform public speaking in this job?
Frequency of Conflict Situations	How often are there conflict situations the employee has to face in this job?
Physical Proximity	To what extent does this job require the worker to perform job tasks in close physical proximity to other people?
Deal With Unpleasant or Angry People	How frequently does the worker have to deal with unpleasant, angry, or discourteous individuals as part of the job requirements?
Level of Competition	To what extent does this job require the worker to compete or to be aware of competitive pressures?
Responsible for Others' Health and Safety	How much responsibility is there for the health and safety of others in this job?
In an Enclosed Vehicle or Equipment	How often does this job require working in a closed vehicle or equipment (e.g., car)?
Consequence of Error	How serious would the result usually be if the worker made a mistake that was not readily correctable?
Spend Time Using Your Hands to Handle, Control, or	How much does this job require using your hands to handle, control, or feel objects, tools or controls?
Spend Time Standing	How much does this job require standing?
Importance of Repeating Same Tasks	How important is repeating the same physical activities (e.g., key entry) or mental activities (e.g., checking entries in a ledger) over and over, without stopping, to performing this job?
Degree of Automation	How automated is the job?
Spend Time Walking and Running	How much does this job require walking and running?
Exposed to Contaminants	How often does this job require working exposed to contaminants (such as pollutants, gases, dust or odors)?

Sounds, Noise Levels Are Distracting or Uncomforta	How often does this job require working exposed to sounds and noise levels that are distracting or uncomfortable?
Spend Time Making Repetitive Motions	How much does this job require making repetitive motions?
Indoors, Not Environmentally Controlled	How often does this job require working indoors in non-controlled environmental conditions (e.g., warehouse without heat)?
Deal With Physically Aggressive People	How frequently does this job require the worker to deal with physical aggression of violent individuals?
Exposed to Disease or Infections	How often does this job require exposure to disease/infections?
Outdoors, Exposed to Weather	How often does this job require working outdoors, exposed to all weather conditions?
Outdoors, Under Cover	How often does this job require working outdoors, under cover (e.g., structure with roof but no walls)?
Very Hot or Cold Temperatures	How often does this job require working in very hot (above 90 F degrees) or very cold (below 32 F degrees) temperatures?
Spend Time Bending or Twisting the Body	How much does this job require bending or twisting your body?
Spend Time Kneeling, Crouching, Stooping, or Crawl	How much does this job require kneeling, crouching, stooping, or crawling?
Wear Common Protective or Safety Equipment such as	How much does this job require wearing common protective or safety equipment such as safety shoes, glasses, gloves, hard hats or live jackets?
Exposed to Hazardous Equipment	How often does this job require exposure to hazardous equipment?
Cramped Work Space, Awkward Positions	How often does this job require working in cramped work spaces that requires getting into awkward positions?
Extremely Bright or Inadequate Lighting	How often does this job require working in extremely bright or inadequate lighting conditions?
Exposed to Minor Burns, Cuts, Bites, or Stings	How often does this job require exposure to minor burns, cuts, bites, or stings?
Pace Determined by Speed of Equipment	How important is it to this job that the pace is determined by the speed of equipment or machinery? (This does not refer to keeping busy at all times on this job.)
Exposed to Hazardous Conditions	How often does this job require exposure to hazardous conditions?
Spend Time Keeping or Regaining Balance	How much does this job require keeping or regaining your balance?
Exposed to Radiation	How often does this job require exposure to radiation?
Wear Specialized Protective or Safety Equipment su	How much does this job require wearing specialized protective or safety equipment such as breathing apparatus, safety harness, full protection suits, or radiation protection?
In an Open Vehicle or Equipment	How often does this job require working in an open vehicle or equipment (e.g., tractor)?
Exposed to Whole Body Vibration	How often does this job require exposure to whole body vibration (e.g., operate a jackhammer)?
Exposed to High Places	How often does this job require exposure to high places?
Spend Time Climbing Ladders, Scaffolds, or Poles	How much does this job require climbing ladders, scaffolds, or poles?

Job Zone Component	Job Zone Component Definitions
Title	Job Zone Five: Extensive Preparation Needed
Overall Experience	Extensive skill, knowledge, and experience are needed for these occupations. Many require more than five years of experience. For example, surgeons must complete four years of college and an additional five to seven years of specialized medical training to be able to do their job.
Job Training	Employees may need some on-the-job training, but most of these occupations assume that the person will already have the required skills, knowledge, work-related experience, and/or training.
Job Zone Examples	These occupations often involve coordinating, training, supervising, or managing the activities of others to accomplish goals. Very advanced communication and organizational skills are required. Examples include athletic trainers, lawyers, managing editors, phyicists, social psychologists, and surgeons.
SVP Range	(8.0 and above)
Education	A bachelor's degree is the minimum formal education required for these occupations. However, many also require graduate school. For example, they may require a master's degree, and some require a Ph.D., M.D., or J.D. (law degree).

Work_Styles	Work_Styles Definitions

Leadership	Job requires a willingness to lead, take charge, and offer opinions and direction.
Cooperation	Job requires being pleasant with others on the job and displaying a good-natured, cooperative attitude.
Initiative	Job requires a willingness to take on responsibilities and challenges.
Dependability	Job requires being reliable, responsible, and dependable, and fulfilling obligations.
Self Control	Job requires maintaining composure, keeping emotions in check, controlling anger, and avoiding aggressive behavior, even in very difficult situations.
Concern for Others	Job requires being sensitive to others' needs and feelings and being understanding and helpful on the job.
Adaptability/Flexibility	Job requires being open to change (positive or negative) and to considerable variety in the workplace.
Achievement/Effort	Job requires establishing and maintaining personally challenging achievement goals and exerting effort toward mastering tasks.
Integrity	Job requires being honest and ethical.
Persistence	Job requires persistence in the face of obstacles.
Independence	Job requires developing one's own ways of doing things, guiding oneself with little or no supervision, and depending on oneself to get things done.
Attention to Detail	Job requires being careful about detail and thorough in completing work tasks.
Analytical Thinking	Job requires analyzing information and using logic to address work-related issues and problems.
Stress Tolerance	Job requires accepting criticism and dealing calmly and effectively with high stress situations.
Innovation	Job requires creativity and alternative thinking to develop new ideas for and answers to work-related problems.
Social Orientation	Job requires preferring to work with others rather than alone, and being personally connected with others on the job.

27-1012.00 - Craft Artists

Create or reproduce hand-made objects for sale and exhibition using a variety of techniques, such as welding, weaving, pottery, and needlecraft.

Tasks

1) Develop concepts or creative ideas for craft objects.

2) Apply finishes to objects being crafted.

3) Cut, shape, fit, join, mold, or otherwise process materials, using hand tools, power tools, and/or machinery.

4) Fabricate patterns or templates to guide craft production.

5) Create prototypes or models of objects to be crafted.

6) Develop designs using specialized computer software.

7) Select materials for use based on strength, color, texture, balance, weight, size, malleability and other characteristics.

8) Set specifications for materials, dimensions, and finishes.

9) Sketch or draw objects to be crafted.

10) Develop product packaging, display and pricing strategies.

11) Advertise products and work, using media such as internet advertising and brochures.

12) Attend craft shows to market products.

13) Confer with customers to assess customer needs or obtain feedback.

14) Research craft trends, venues, and customer buying patterns in order to inspire designs and marketing strategies.

27-1014.00 - Multi-Media Artists and Animators

Create special effects, animation, or other visual images using film, video, computers, or other electronic tools and media for use in products or creations, such as computer games, movies, music videos, and commercials.

Tasks

1) Design complex graphics and animation, using independent judgment, creativity, and computer equipment.

2) Make objects or characters appear lifelike by manipulating light, color, texture, shadow, and transparency, and/or manipulating static images to give the illusion of motion.

3) Create pen-and-paper images to be scanned, edited, colored, textured or animated by computer.

4) Create basic designs, drawings, and illustrations for product labels, cartons, direct mail, or television.

5) Create two-dimensional and three-dimensional images depicting objects in motion or illustrating a process, using computer animation or modeling programs.

6) Assemble, typeset, scan and produce digital camera-ready art or film negatives and printer's proofs.

7) Script, plan, and create animated narrative sequences under tight deadlines, using computer software and hand drawing techniques.

8) Apply story development, directing, cinematography, and editing to animation to create storyboards that show the flow of the animation and map out key scenes and characters.

9) Participate in design and production of multimedia campaigns, handling budgeting and scheduling, and assisting with such responsibilities as production coordination, background design and progress tracking.

10) Convert real objects to animated objects through modeling, using techniques such as optical scanning.

11) Use models to simulate the behavior of animated objects in the finished sequence.

12) Implement and maintain configuration control systems.

13) Create and install special effects as required by the script, mixing chemicals and fabricating needed parts from wood, metal, plaster, and clay.

Knowledge	Knowledge Definitions
Fine Arts	Knowledge of the theory and techniques required to compose, produce, and perform works of music, dance, visual arts, drama, and sculpture.
Design	Knowledge of design techniques, tools, and principles involved in production of precision technical plans, blueprints, drawings, and models.
Computers and Electronics	Knowledge of circuit boards, processors, chips, electronic equipment, and computer hardware and software, including applications and programming.
Communications and Media	Knowledge of media production, communication, and dissemination techniques and methods. This includes alternative ways to inform and entertain via written, oral, and visual media.
English Language	Knowledge of the structure and content of the English language including the meaning and spelling of words, rules of composition, and grammar.
Mathematics	Knowledge of arithmetic, algebra, geometry, calculus, statistics, and their applications.
Customer and Personal Service	Knowledge of principles and processes for providing customer and personal services. This includes customer needs assessment, meeting quality standards for services, and evaluation of customer satisfaction.
Administration and Management	Knowledge of business and management principles involved in strategic planning, resource allocation, human resources modeling, leadership technique, production methods, and coordination of people and resources.
Education and Training	Knowledge of principles and methods for curriculum and training design, teaching and instruction for individuals and groups, and the measurement of training effects.
Sales and Marketing	Knowledge of principles and methods for showing, promoting, and selling products or services. This includes marketing strategy and tactics, product demonstration, sales techniques, and sales control systems.
Clerical	Knowledge of administrative and clerical procedures and systems such as word processing, managing files and records, stenography and transcription, designing forms, and other office procedures and terminology.
Engineering and Technology	Knowledge of the practical application of engineering science and technology. This includes applying principles, techniques, procedures, and equipment to the design and production of various goods and services.

Physics	Knowledge and prediction of physical principles, laws, their interrelationships, and applications to understanding fluid, material, and atmospheric dynamics, and mechanical, electrical, atomic and sub- atomic structures and processes.
Psychology	Knowledge of human behavior and performance; individual differences in ability, personality, and interests; learning and motivation; psychological research methods; and the assessment and treatment of behavioral and affective disorders.
Production and Processing	Knowledge of raw materials, production processes, quality control, costs, and other techniques for maximizing the effective manufacture and distribution of goods.
Economics and Accounting	Knowledge of economic and accounting principles and practices, the financial markets, banking and the analysis and reporting of financial data.
Sociology and Anthropology	Knowledge of group behavior and dynamics, societal trends and influences, human migrations, ethnicity, cultures and their history and origins.
Mechanical	Knowledge of machines and tools, including their designs, uses, repair, and maintenance.
Philosophy and Theology	Knowledge of different philosophical systems and religions. This includes their basic principles, values, ethics, ways of thinking, customs, practices, and their impact on human culture.
Telecommunications	Knowledge of transmission, broadcasting, switching, control, and operation of telecommunications systems.
Public Safety and Security	Knowledge of relevant equipment, policies, procedures, and strategies to promote effective local, state, or national security operations for the protection of people, data, property, and institutions.
Transportation	Knowledge of principles and methods for moving people or goods by air, rail, sea, or road, including the relative costs and benefits.
History and Archeology	Knowledge of historical events and their causes, indicators, and effects on civilizations and cultures.
Personnel and Human Resources	Knowledge of principles and procedures for personnel recruitment, selection, training, compensation and benefits, labor relations and negotiation, and personnel information systems.
Geography	Knowledge of principles and methods for describing the features of land, sea, and air masses, including their physical characteristics, locations, interrelationships, and distribution of plant, animal, and human life.
Building and Construction	Knowledge of materials, methods, and the tools involved in the construction or repair of houses, buildings, or other structures such as highways and roads.
Law and Government	Knowledge of laws, legal codes, court procedures, precedents, government regulations, executive orders, agency rules, and the democratic political process.
Biology	Knowledge of plant and animal organisms, their tissues, cells, functions, interdependencies, and interactions with each other and the environment.
Medicine and Dentistry	Knowledge of the information and techniques needed to diagnose and treat human injuries, diseases, and deformities. This includes symptoms, treatment alternatives, drug properties and interactions, and preventive health-care measures.
Therapy and Counseling	Knowledge of principles, methods, and procedures for diagnosis, treatment, and rehabilitation of physical and mental dysfunctions, and for career counseling and guidance.
Foreign Language	Knowledge of the structure and content of a foreign (non-English) language including the meaning and spelling of words, rules of composition and grammar, and pronunciation.
Chemistry	Knowledge of the chemical composition, structure, and properties of substances and of the chemical processes and transformations that they undergo. This includes uses of chemicals and their interactions, danger signs, production techniques, and disposal methods.
Food Production	Knowledge of techniques and equipment for planting, growing, and harvesting food products (both plant and animal) for consumption, including storage/handling techniques.

Skills	Skills Definitions
Active Listening	Giving full attention to what other people are saying, taking time to understand the points being made, asking questions as appropriate, and not interrupting at inappropriate times.
Time Management	Managing one's own time and the time of others.
Reading Comprehension	Understanding written sentences and paragraphs in work related documents.

Active Learning	Understanding the implications of new information for both current and future problem-solving and decision-making.
Operations Analysis	Analyzing needs and product requirements to create a design.
Judgment and Decision Making	Considering the relative costs and benefits of potential actions to choose the most appropriate one.
Speaking	Talking to others to convey information effectively.
Writing	Communicating effectively in writing as appropriate for the needs of the audience.
Critical Thinking	Using logic and reasoning to identify the strengths and weaknesses of alternative solutions, conclusions or approaches to problems.
Learning Strategies	Selecting and using training/instructional methods and procedures appropriate for the situation when learning or teaching new things.
Technology Design	Generating or adapting equipment and technology to serve user needs.
Complex Problem Solving	Identifying complex problems and reviewing related information to develop and evaluate options and implement solutions.
Coordination	Adjusting actions in relation to others' actions.
Mathematics	Using mathematics to solve problems.
Equipment Selection	Determining the kind of tools and equipment needed to do a job.
Science	Using scientific rules and methods to solve problems.
Monitoring	Monitoring/Assessing performance of yourself, other individuals, or organizations to make improvements or take corrective action.
Persuasion	Persuading others to change their minds or behavior.
Quality Control Analysis	Conducting tests and inspections of products, services, or processes to evaluate quality or performance.
Troubleshooting	Determining causes of operating errors and deciding what to do about it.
Service Orientation	Actively looking for ways to help people.
Social Perceptiveness	Being aware of others' reactions and understanding why they react as they do.
Systems Evaluation	Identifying measures or indicators of system performance and the actions needed to improve or correct performance, relative to the goals of the system.
Instructing	Teaching others how to do something.
Programming	Writing computer programs for various purposes.
Negotiation	Bringing others together and trying to reconcile differences.
Systems Analysis	Determining how a system should work and how changes in conditions, operations, and the environment will affect outcomes.
Operation and Control	Controlling operations of equipment or systems.
Management of Personnel Resources	Motivating, developing, and directing people as they work, identifying the best people for the job.
Installation	Installing equipment, machines, wiring, or programs to meet specifications.
Management of Material Resources	Obtaining and seeing to the appropriate use of equipment, facilities, and materials needed to do certain work.
Equipment Maintenance	Performing routine maintenance on equipment and determining when and what kind of maintenance is needed.
Management of Financial Resources	Determining how money will be spent to get the work done, and accounting for these expenditures.
Operation Monitoring	Watching gauges, dials, or other indicators to make sure a machine is working properly.
Repairing	Repairing machines or systems using the needed tools.

Ability	Ability Definitions
Inductive Reasoning	The ability to combine pieces of information to form general rules or conclusions (includes finding a relationship among seemingly unrelated events).
Near Vision	The ability to see details at close range (within a few feet of the observer).
Visualization	The ability to imagine how something will look after it is moved around or when its parts are moved or rearranged.
Fluency of Ideas	The ability to come up with a number of ideas about a topic (the number of ideas is important, not their quality, correctness, or creativity).
Problem Sensitivity	The ability to tell when something is wrong or is likely to go wrong. It does not involve solving the problem, only recognizing there is a problem.
Written Comprehension	The ability to read and understand information and ideas presented in writing.
Speech Clarity	The ability to speak clearly so others can understand you.

Information Ordering	The ability to arrange things or actions in a certain order or pattern according to a specific rule or set of rules (e.g., patterns of numbers, letters, words, pictures, mathematical operations).
Originality	The ability to come up with unusual or clever ideas about a given topic or situation, or to develop creative ways to solve a problem.
Oral Comprehension	The ability to listen to and understand information and ideas presented through spoken words and sentences.
Oral Expression	The ability to communicate information and ideas in speaking so others will understand.
Deductive Reasoning	The ability to apply general rules to specific problems to produce answers that make sense.
Category Flexibility	The ability to generate or use different sets of rules for combining or grouping things in different ways.
Selective Attention	The ability to concentrate on a task over a period of time without being distracted.
Speech Recognition	The ability to identify and understand the speech of another person.
Written Expression	The ability to communicate information and ideas in writing so others will understand.
Visual Color Discrimination	The ability to match or detect differences between colors, including shades of color and brightness.
Arm-Hand Steadiness	The ability to keep your hand and arm steady while moving your arm or while holding your arm and hand in one position.
Finger Dexterity	The ability to make precisely coordinated movements of the fingers of one or both hands to grasp, manipulate, or assemble very small objects.
Manual Dexterity	The ability to quickly move your hand, your hand together with your arm, or your two hands to grasp, manipulate, or assemble objects.
Perceptual Speed	The ability to quickly and accurately compare similarities and differences among sets of letters, numbers, objects, pictures, or patterns. The things to be compared may be presented at the same time or one after the other. This ability also includes comparing a presented object with a remembered object.
Flexibility of Closure	The ability to identify or detect a known pattern (a figure, object, word, or sound) that is hidden in other distracting material.
Number Facility	The ability to add, subtract, multiply, or divide quickly and correctly.
Memorization	The ability to remember information such as words, numbers, pictures, and procedures.
Mathematical Reasoning	The ability to choose the right mathematical methods or formulas to solve a problem.
Control Precision	The ability to quickly and repeatedly adjust the controls of a machine or a vehicle to exact positions.
Far Vision	The ability to see details at a distance.
Depth Perception	The ability to judge which of several objects is closer or farther away from you, or to judge the distance between you and an object.
Speed of Closure	The ability to quickly make sense of, combine, and organize information into meaningful patterns.
Auditory Attention	The ability to focus on a single source of sound in the presence of other distracting sounds.
Time Sharing	The ability to shift back and forth between two or more activities or sources of information (such as speech, sounds, touch, or other sources).
Hearing Sensitivity	The ability to detect or tell the differences between sounds that vary in pitch and loudness.
Trunk Strength	The ability to use your abdominal and lower back muscles to support part of the body repeatedly or continuously over time without 'giving out' or fatiguing.
Extent Flexibility	The ability to bend, stretch, twist, or reach with your body, arms, and/or legs.
Response Orientation	The ability to choose quickly between two or more movements in response to two or more different signals (lights, sounds, pictures). It includes the speed with which the correct response is started with the hand, foot, or other body part.
Wrist-Finger Speed	The ability to make fast, simple, repeated movements of the fingers, hands, and wrists.
Rate Control	The ability to time your movements or the movement of a piece of equipment in anticipation of changes in the speed and/or direction of a moving object or scene.
Spatial Orientation	The ability to know your location in relation to the environment or to know where other objects are in relation to you.
Stamina	The ability to exert yourself physically over long periods of time without getting winded or out of breath.
Speed of Limb Movement	The ability to quickly move the arms and legs.

Explosive Strength	The ability to use short bursts of muscle force to propel oneself (as in jumping or sprinting), or to throw an object.
Dynamic Strength	The ability to exert muscle force repeatedly or continuously over time. This involves muscular endurance and resistance to muscle fatigue.
Gross Body Equilibrium	The ability to keep or regain your body balance or stay upright when in an unstable position.
Dynamic Flexibility	The ability to quickly and repeatedly bend, stretch, twist, or reach out with your body, arms, and/or legs.
Gross Body Coordination	The ability to coordinate the movement of your arms, legs, and torso together when the whole body is in motion.
Multilimb Coordination	The ability to coordinate two or more limbs (for example, two arms, two legs, or one leg and one arm) while sitting, standing, or lying down. It does not involve performing the activities while the whole body is in motion.
Static Strength	The ability to exert maximum muscle force to lift, push, pull, or carry objects.
Reaction Time	The ability to quickly respond (with the hand, finger, or foot) to a signal (sound, light, picture) when it appears.
Night Vision	The ability to see under low light conditions.
Glare Sensitivity	The ability to see objects in the presence of glare or bright lighting.
Sound Localization	The ability to tell the direction from which a sound originated.
Peripheral Vision	The ability to see objects or movement of objects to one's side when the eyes are looking ahead.

Work_Activity	Work_Activity Definitions
Thinking Creatively	Developing, designing, or creating new applications, ideas, relationships, systems, or products, including artistic contributions.
Getting Information	Observing, receiving, and otherwise obtaining information from all relevant sources.
Interacting With Computers	Using computers and computer systems (including hardware and software) to program, write software, set up functions, enter data, or process information.
Updating and Using Relevant Knowledge	Keeping up-to-date technically and applying new knowledge to your job.
Making Decisions and Solving Problems	Analyzing information and evaluating results to choose the best solution and solve problems.
Organizing, Planning, and Prioritizing Work	Developing specific goals and plans to prioritize, organize, and accomplish your work.
Establishing and Maintaining Interpersonal Relatio	Developing constructive and cooperative working relationships with others, and maintaining them over time.
Communicating with Supervisors, Peers, or Subordin	Providing information to supervisors, co-workers, and subordinates by telephone, in written form, e-mail, or in person.
Judging the Qualities of Things, Services, or Peop	Assessing the value, importance, or quality of things or people.
Communicating with Persons Outside Organization	Communicating with people outside the organization, representing the organization to customers, the public, government, and other external sources. This information can be exchanged in person, in writing, or by telephone or e-mail.
Interpreting the Meaning of Information for Others	Translating or explaining what information means and how it can be used.
Estimating the Quantifiable Characteristics of Pro	Estimating sizes, distances, and quantities; or determining time, costs, resources, or materials needed to perform a work activity.
Identifying Objects, Actions, and Events	Identifying information by categorizing, estimating, recognizing differences or similarities, and detecting changes in circumstances or events.
Processing Information	Compiling, coding, categorizing, calculating, tabulating, auditing, or verifying information or data.
Developing and Building Teams	Encouraging and building mutual trust, respect, and cooperation among team members.
Scheduling Work and Activities	Scheduling events, programs, and activities, as well as the work of others.
Coordinating the Work and Activities of Others	Getting members of a group to work together to accomplish tasks.
Analyzing Data or Information	Identifying the underlying principles, reasons, or facts of information by breaking down information or data into separate parts.
Monitor Processes, Materials, or Surroundings	Monitoring and reviewing information from materials, events, or the environment, to detect or assess problems.

Training and Teaching Others	Identifying the educational needs of others, developing formal educational or training programs or classes, and teaching or instructing others.
Coaching and Developing Others	Identifying the developmental needs of others and coaching, mentoring, or otherwise helping others to improve their knowledge or skills.
Provide Consultation and Advice to Others	Providing guidance and expert advice to management or other groups on technical, systems-, or process-related topics.
Developing Objectives and Strategies	Establishing long-range objectives and specifying the strategies and actions to achieve them.
Documenting/Recording Information	Entering, transcribing, recording, storing, or maintaining information in written or electronic/magnetic form.
Resolving Conflicts and Negotiating with Others	Handling complaints, settling disputes, and resolving grievances and conflicts, or otherwise negotiating with others.
Performing Administrative Activities	Performing day-to-day administrative tasks such as maintaining information files and processing paperwork.
Guiding, Directing, and Motivating Subordinates	Providing guidance and direction to subordinates, including setting performance standards and monitoring performance.
Evaluating Information to Determine Compliance wit	Using relevant information and individual judgment to determine whether events or processes comply with laws, regulations, or standards.
Monitoring and Controlling Resources	Monitoring and controlling resources and overseeing the spending of money.
Selling or Influencing Others	Convincing others to buy merchandise/goods or to otherwise change their minds or actions.
Drafting, Laying Out, and Specifying Technical Dev	Providing documentation, detailed instructions, drawings, or specifications to tell others about how devices, parts, equipment, or structures are to be fabricated, constructed, assembled, modified, maintained, or used.
Repairing and Maintaining Electronic Equipment	Servicing, repairing, calibrating, regulating, fine-tuning, or testing machines, devices, and equipment that operate primarily on the basis of electrical or electronic (not mechanical) principles.
Inspecting Equipment, Structures, or Material	Inspecting equipment, structures, or materials to identify the cause of errors or other problems or defects.
Handling and Moving Objects	Using hands and arms in handling, installing, positioning, and moving materials, and manipulating things.
Assisting and Caring for Others	Providing personal assistance, medical attention, emotional support, or other personal care to others such as coworkers, customers, or patients.
Controlling Machines and Processes	Using either control mechanisms or direct physical activity to operate machines or processes (not including computers or vehicles).
Performing for or Working Directly with the Public	Performing for people or dealing directly with the public. This includes serving customers in restaurants and stores, and receiving clients or guests.
Staffing Organizational Units	Recruiting, interviewing, selecting, hiring, and promoting employees in an organization.
Repairing and Maintaining Mechanical Equipment	Servicing, repairing, adjusting, and testing machines, devices, moving parts, and equipment that operate primarily on the basis of mechanical (not electronic) principles.
Performing General Physical Activities	Performing physical activities that require considerable use of your arms and legs and moving your whole body, such as climbing, lifting, balancing, walking, stooping, and handling of materials.
Operating Vehicles, Mechanized Devices, or Equipme	Running, maneuvering, navigating, or driving vehicles or mechanized equipment, such as forklifts, passenger vehicles, aircraft, or water craft.

Work_Context	Work_Context Definitions
Indoors, Environmentally Controlled	How often does this job require working indoors in environmentally controlled conditions?
Electronic Mail	How often do you use electronic mail in this job?
Spend Time Using Your Hands to Handle, Control, or	How much does this job require using your hands to handle, control, or feel objects, tools or controls?
Spend Time Sitting	How much does this job require sitting?
Time Pressure	How often does this job require the worker to meet strict deadlines?
Spend Time Making Repetitive Motions	How much does this job require making repetitive motions?
Telephone	How often do you have telephone conversations in this job?
Face-to-Face Discussions	How often do you have to have face-to-face discussions with individuals or teams in this job?
Work With Work Group or Team	How important is it to work with others in a group or team in this job?

Contact With Others	How much does this job require the worker to be in contact with others (face-to-face, by telephone, or otherwise) in order to perform it?
Importance of Repeating Same Tasks	How important is repeating the same physical activities (e.g., key entry) or mental activities (e.g., checking entries in a ledger) over and over, without stopping, to performing this job?
Importance of Being Exact or Accurate	How important is being very exact or highly accurate in performing this job?
Freedom to Make Decisions	How much decision making freedom, without supervision, does the job offer?
Structured versus Unstructured Work	To what extent is this job structured for the worker, rather than allowing the worker to determine tasks, priorities, and goals?
Letters and Memos	How often does the job require written letters and memos?
Frequency of Decision Making	How frequently is the worker required to make decisions that affect other people, the financial resources, and/or the image and reputation of the organization?
Physical Proximity	To what extent does this job require the worker to perform job tasks in close physical proximity to other people?
Coordinate or Lead Others	How important is it to coordinate or lead others in accomplishing work activities in this job?
Impact of Decisions on Co-workers or Company Resul	How do the decisions an employee makes impact the results of co-workers, clients or the company?
Sounds, Noise Levels Are Distracting or Uncomforta	How often does this job require working exposed to sounds and noise levels that are distracting or uncomfortable?
Responsibility for Outcomes and Results	How responsible is the worker for work outcomes and results of other workers?
Frequency of Conflict Situations	How often are there conflict situations the employee has to face in this job?
Deal With External Customers	How important is it to work with external customers or the public in this job?
Level of Competition	To what extent does this job require the worker to compete or to be aware of competitive pressures?
Degree of Automation	How automated is the job?
Consequence of Error	How serious would the result usually be if the worker made a mistake that was not readily correctable?
Deal With Unpleasant or Angry People	How frequently does the worker have to deal with unpleasant, angry, or discourteous individuals as part of the job requirements?
Pace Determined by Speed of Equipment	How important is it to this job that the pace is determined by the speed of equipment or machinery? (This does not refer to keeping busy at all times on this job.)
Public Speaking	How often do you have to perform public speaking in this job?
Spend Time Standing	How much does this job require standing?
Responsible for Others' Health and Safety	How much responsibility is there for the health and safety of others in this job?
Spend Time Walking and Running	How much does this job require walking and running?
Exposed to Contaminants	How often does this job require working exposed to contaminants (such as pollutants, gases, dust or odors)?
Exposed to Radiation	How often does this job require exposure to radiation?
Cramped Work Space, Awkward Positions	How often does this job require working in cramped work spaces that requires getting into awkward positions?
Spend Time Kneeling, Crouching, Stooping, or Crawl	How much does this job require kneeling, crouching, stooping or crawling?
Outdoors, Under Cover	How often does this job require working outdoors, under cover (e.g., structure with roof but no walls)?
Outdoors, Exposed to Weather	How often does this job require working outdoors, exposed to all weather conditions?
In an Enclosed Vehicle or Equipment	How often does this job require working in a closed vehicle or equipment (e.g., car)?
Deal With Physically Aggressive People	How frequently does this job require the worker to deal with physical aggression of violent individuals?
Exposed to Minor Burns, Cuts, Bites, or Stings	How often does this job require exposure to minor burns, cuts, bites, or stings?
Spend Time Bending or Twisting the Body	How much does this job require bending or twisting your body?
Exposed to High Places	How often does this job require exposure to high places?
Exposed to Hazardous Equipment	How often does this job require exposure to hazardous equipment?
Extremely Bright or Inadequate Lighting	How often does this job require working in extremely bright or inadequate lighting conditions?
In an Open Vehicle or Equipment	How often does this job require working in an open vehicle or equipment (e.g., tractor)?
Spend Time Keeping or Regaining Balance	How much does this job require keeping or regaining your balance?

27-1021.00 - Commercial and Industrial Designers

Develop and design manufactured products, such as cars, home appliances, and children's toys. Combine artistic talent with research on product use, marketing, and materials to create the most functional and appealing product design.

Tasks

1) Confer with engineering, marketing, production, and/or sales departments, or with customers, to establish and evaluate design concepts for manufactured products.

2) Modify and refine designs, using working models, to conform with customer specifications, production limitations, or changes in design trends.

3) Present designs and reports to customers or design committees for approval, and discuss need for modification.

4) Direct and coordinate the fabrication of models or samples and the drafting of working drawings and specification sheets from sketches.

5) Evaluate feasibility of design ideas, based on factors such as appearance, safety, function, serviceability, budget, production costs/methods, and market characteristics.

6) Read publications, attend showings, and study competing products and design styles and motifs to obtain perspective and generate design concepts.

7) Coordinate the look and function of product lines.

8) Participate in new product planning or market research, including studying the potential need for new products.

9) Investigate product characteristics such as the product's safety and handling qualities, its market appeal, how efficiently it can be produced, and ways of distributing, using and maintaining it.

10) Supervise assistants' work throughout the design process.

11) Research production specifications, costs, production materials and manufacturing methods, and provide cost estimates and itemized production requirements.

12) Design graphic material for use as ornamentation, illustration, or advertising on manufactured materials and packaging or containers.

13) Fabricate models or samples in paper, wood, glass, fabric, plastic, metal, or other materials, using hand and/or power tools.

14) Develop manufacturing procedures and monitor the manufacture of their designs in a factory to improve operations and product quality.

15) Advise corporations on issues involving corporate image projects or problems.

16) Develop industrial standards and regulatory guidelines.

Indoors, Not Environmentally Controlled	How often does this job require working indoors in non-controlled environmental conditions (e.g., warehouse without heat)?
Very Hot or Cold Temperatures	How often does this job require working in very hot (above 90 F degrees) or very cold (below 32 F degrees) temperatures?
Wear Common Protective or Safety Equipment such as	How much does this job require wearing common protective or safety equipment such as safety shoes, glasses, gloves, hard hats or life jackets?
Exposed to Disease or Infections	How often does this job require exposure to disease/infections?
Wear Specialized Protective or Safety Equipment su	How much does this job require wearing specialized protective or safety equipment such as breathing apparatus, safety harness, full protection suits, or radiation protection?
Exposed to Hazardous Conditions	How often does this job require exposure to hazardous conditions?
Exposed to Whole Body Vibration	How often does this job require exposure to whole body vibration (e.g., operate a jackhammer)?
Spend Time Climbing Ladders, Scaffolds, or Poles	How much does this job require climbing ladders, scaffolds, or poles?

Job Zone Component	Job Zone Component Definitions
Title	Job Zone Four: Considerable Preparation Needed
Overall Experience	A minimum of two to four years of work-related skill, knowledge, or experience is needed for these occupations. For example, an accountant must complete four years of college and work for several years in accounting to be considered qualified.
Job Training	Employees in these occupations usually need several years of work-related experience, on-the-job training, and/or vocational training.
Job Zone Examples	Many of these occupations involve coordinating, supervising, managing, or training others. Examples include accountants, chefs and head cooks, computer programmers, historians, pharmacists, and police detectives.
SVP Range	(7.0 to < 8.0)
Education	Most of these occupations require a four - year bachelor's degree, but some do not.

Work_Styles	Work_Styles Definitions
Attention to Detail	Job requires being careful about detail and thorough in completing work tasks.
Dependability	Job requires being reliable, responsible, and dependable, and fulfilling obligations.
Adaptability/Flexibility	Job requires being open to change (positive or negative) and to considerable variety in the workplace.
Stress Tolerance	Job requires accepting criticism and dealing calmly and effectively with high stress situations.
Cooperation	Job requires being pleasant with others on the job and displaying a good-natured, cooperative attitude.
Achievement/Effort	Job requires establishing and maintaining personally challenging achievement goals and exerting effort toward mastering tasks.
Initiative	Job requires a willingness to take on responsibilities and challenges.
Independence	Job requires developing one's own ways of doing things, guiding oneself with little or no supervision, and depending on oneself to get things done.
Innovation	Job requires creativity and alternative thinking to develop new ideas for and answers to work-related problems.
Persistence	Job requires persistence in the face of obstacles.
Self Control	Job requires maintaining composure, keeping emotions in check, controlling anger, and avoiding aggressive behavior, even in very difficult situations.
Analytical Thinking	Job requires analyzing information and using logic to address work-related issues and problems.
Concern for Others	Job requires being sensitive to others' needs and feelings and being understanding and helpful on the job.
Leadership	Job requires a willingness to lead, take charge, and offer opinions and direction.
Integrity	Job requires being honest and ethical.
Social Orientation	Job requires preferring to work with others rather than alone, and being personally connected with others on the job.

Knowledge	Knowledge Definitions
Design	Knowledge of design techniques, tools, and principles involved in production of precision technical plans, blueprints, drawings, and models.
Engineering and Technology	Knowledge of the practical application of engineering science and technology. This includes applying principles, techniques, procedures, and equipment to the design and production of various goods and services.
Mathematics	Knowledge of arithmetic, algebra, geometry, calculus, statistics, and their applications.
English Language	Knowledge of the structure and content of the English language including the meaning and spelling of words, rules of composition, and grammar.
Production and Processing	Knowledge of raw materials, production processes, quality control, costs, and other techniques for maximizing the effective manufacture and distribution of goods.
Administration and Management	Knowledge of business and management principles involved in strategic planning, resource allocation, human resources modeling, leadership technique, production methods, and coordination of people and resources.
Computers and Electronics	Knowledge of circuit boards, processors, chips, electronic equipment, and computer hardware and software, including applications and programming.
Clerical	Knowledge of administrative and clerical procedures and systems such as word processing, managing files and records, stenography and transcription, designing forms, and other office procedures and terminology.

Customer and Personal Service	Knowledge of principles and processes for providing customer and personal services. This includes customer needs assessment, meeting quality standards for services, and evaluation of customer satisfaction.
Mechanical	Knowledge of machines and tools, including their designs, uses, repair, and maintenance.
Physics	Knowledge and prediction of physical principles, laws, their interrelationships, and applications to understanding fluid, material, and atmospheric dynamics, and mechanical, electrical, atomic and sub- atomic structures and processes.
Sales and Marketing	Knowledge of principles and methods for showing, promoting, and selling products or services. This includes marketing strategy and tactics, product demonstration, sales techniques, and sales control systems.
Education and Training	Knowledge of principles and methods for curriculum and training design, teaching and instruction for individuals and groups, and the measurement of training effects.
Law and Government	Knowledge of laws, legal codes, court procedures, precedents, government regulations, executive orders, agency rules, and the democratic political process.
Public Safety and Security	Knowledge of relevant equipment, policies, procedures, and strategies to promote effective local, state, or national security operations for the protection of people, data, property, and institutions.
Economics and Accounting	Knowledge of economic and accounting principles and practices, the financial markets, banking and the analysis and reporting of financial data.
Chemistry	Knowledge of the chemical composition, structure, and properties of substances and of the chemical processes and transformations that they undergo. This includes uses of chemicals and their interactions, danger signs, production techniques, and disposal methods.
Personnel and Human Resources	Knowledge of principles and procedures for personnel recruitment, selection, training, compensation and benefits, labor relations and negotiation, and personnel information systems.
Communications and Media	Knowledge of media production, communication, and dissemination techniques and methods. This includes alternative ways to inform and entertain via written, oral, and visual media.
Psychology	Knowledge of human behavior and performance; individual differences in ability, personality, and interests; learning and motivation; psychological research methods; and the assessment and treatment of behavioral and affective disorders.
Building and Construction	Knowledge of materials, methods, and the tools involved in the construction or repair of houses, buildings, or other structures such as highways and roads.
Fine Arts	Knowledge of the theory and techniques required to compose, produce, and perform works of music, dance, visual arts, drama, and sculpture.
Sociology and Anthropology	Knowledge of group behavior and dynamics, societal trends and influences, human migrations, ethnicity, cultures and their history and origins.
Transportation	Knowledge of principles and methods for moving people or goods by air, rail, sea, or road, including the relative costs and benefits.
Telecommunications	Knowledge of transmission, broadcasting, switching, control, and operation of telecommunications systems.
Foreign Language	Knowledge of the structure and content of a foreign (non-English) language including the meaning and spelling of words, rules of composition and grammar, and pronunciation.
Biology	Knowledge of plant and animal organisms, their tissues, cells, functions, interdependencies, and interactions with each other and the environment.
Geography	Knowledge of principles and methods for describing the features of land, sea, and air masses, including their physical characteristics, locations, interrelationships, and distribution of plant, animal, and human life.
Philosophy and Theology	Knowledge of different philosophical systems and religions. This includes their basic principles, values, ethics, ways of thinking, customs, practices, and their impact on human culture.
Therapy and Counseling	Knowledge of principles, methods, and procedures for diagnosis, treatment, and rehabilitation of physical and mental dysfunctions, and for career counseling and guidance.

Medicine and Dentistry	Knowledge of the information and techniques needed to diagnose and treat human injuries, diseases, and deformities. This includes symptoms, treatment alternatives, drug properties and interactions, and preventive health-care measures.
History and Archeology	Knowledge of historical events and their causes, indicators, and effects on civilizations and cultures.
Food Production	Knowledge of techniques and equipment for planting, growing, and harvesting food products (both plant and animal) for consumption, including storage/handling techniques.

Skills	Skills Definitions
Time Management	Managing one's own time and the time of others.
Active Listening	Giving full attention to what other people are saying, taking time to understand the points being made, asking questions as appropriate, and not interrupting at inappropriate times.
Reading Comprehension	Understanding written sentences and paragraphs in work related documents.
Mathematics	Using mathematics to solve problems.
Judgment and Decision Making	Considering the relative costs and benefits of potential actions to choose the most appropriate one.
Operations Analysis	Analyzing needs and product requirements to create a design.
Troubleshooting	Determining causes of operating errors and deciding what to do about it.
Writing	Communicating effectively in writing as appropriate for the needs of the audience.
Critical Thinking	Using logic and reasoning to identify the strengths and weaknesses of alternative solutions, conclusions or approaches to problems.
Active Learning	Understanding the implications of new information for both current and future problem-solving and decision-making.
Equipment Selection	Determining the kind of tools and equipment needed to do a job.
Speaking	Talking to others to convey information effectively.
Instructing	Teaching others how to do something.
Technology Design	Generating or adapting equipment and technology to serve user needs.
Complex Problem Solving	Identifying complex problems and reviewing related information to develop and evaluate options and implement solutions.
Coordination	Adjusting actions in relation to others' actions.
Quality Control Analysis	Conducting tests and inspections of products, services, or processes to evaluate quality or performance.
Monitoring	Monitoring/Assessing performance of yourself, other individuals, or organizations to make improvements or take corrective action.
Learning Strategies	Selecting and using training/instructional methods and procedures appropriate for the situation when learning or teaching new things.
Installation	Installing equipment, machines, wiring, or programs to meet specifications.
Negotiation	Bringing others together and trying to reconcile differences.
Systems Evaluation	Identifying measures or indicators of system performance and the actions needed to improve or correct performance, relative to the goals of the system.
Service Orientation	Actively looking for ways to help people.
Persuasion	Persuading others to change their minds or behavior.
Social Perceptiveness	Being aware of others' reactions and understanding why they react as they do.
Management of Personnel Resources	Motivating, developing, and directing people as they work, identifying the best people for the job.
Science	Using scientific rules and methods to solve problems.
Systems Analysis	Determining how a system should work and how changes in conditions, operations, and the environment will affect outcomes.
Management of Material Resources	Obtaining and seeing to the appropriate use of equipment, facilities, and materials needed to do certain work.
Operation Monitoring	Watching gauges, dials, or other indicators to make sure a machine is working properly.
Operation and Control	Controlling operations of equipment or systems.
Programming	Writing computer programs for various purposes.
Equipment Maintenance	Performing routine maintenance on equipment and determining when and what kind of maintenance is needed.
Repairing	Repairing machines or systems using the needed tools.
Management of Financial Resources	Determining how money will be spent to get the work done, and accounting for these expenditures.

Ability	Ability Definitions
Oral Comprehension	The ability to listen to and understand information and ideas presented through spoken words and sentences.
Oral Expression	The ability to communicate information and ideas in speaking so others will understand.
Fluency of Ideas	The ability to come up with a number of ideas about a topic (the number of ideas is important, not their quality, correctness, or creativity).
Originality	The ability to come up with unusual or clever ideas about a given topic or situation, or to develop creative ways to solve a problem.
Deductive Reasoning	The ability to apply general rules to specific problems to produce answers that make sense.
Written Comprehension	The ability to read and understand information and ideas presented in writing.
Near Vision	The ability to see details at close range (within a few feet of the observer).
Problem Sensitivity	The ability to tell when something is wrong or is likely to go wrong. It does not involve solving the problem, only recognizing there is a problem.
Information Ordering	The ability to arrange things or actions in a certain order or pattern according to a specific rule or set of rules (e.g., patterns of numbers, letters, words, pictures, mathematical operations).
Inductive Reasoning	The ability to combine pieces of information to form general rules or conclusions (includes finding a relationship among seemingly unrelated events).
Speech Recognition	The ability to identify and understand the speech of another person.
Visualization	The ability to imagine how something will look after it is moved around or when its parts are moved or rearranged.
Speech Clarity	The ability to speak clearly so others can understand you.
Category Flexibility	The ability to generate or use different sets of rules for combining or grouping things in different ways.
Finger Dexterity	The ability to make precisely coordinated movements of the fingers of one or both hands to grasp, manipulate, or assemble very small objects.
Selective Attention	The ability to concentrate on a task over a period of time without being distracted.
Written Expression	The ability to communicate information and ideas in writing so others will understand.
Far Vision	The ability to see details at a distance.
Perceptual Speed	The ability to quickly and accurately compare similarities and differences among sets of letters, numbers, objects, pictures, or patterns. The things to be compared may be presented at the same time or one after the other. This ability also includes comparing a presented object with a remembered object.
Visual Color Discrimination	The ability to match or detect differences between colors, including shades of color and brightness.
Flexibility of Closure	The ability to identify or detect a known pattern (a figure, object, word, or sound) that is hidden in other distracting material.
Number Facility	The ability to add, subtract, multiply, or divide quickly and correctly.
Mathematical Reasoning	The ability to choose the right mathematical methods or formulas to solve a problem.
Time Sharing	The ability to shift back and forth between two or more activities or sources of information (such as speech, sounds, touch, or other sources).
Speed of Closure	The ability to quickly make sense of, combine, and organize information into meaningful patterns.
Memorization	The ability to remember information such as words, numbers, pictures, and procedures.
Depth Perception	The ability to judge which of several objects is closer or farther away from you, or to judge the distance between you and an object.
Auditory Attention	The ability to focus on a single source of sound in the presence of other distracting sounds.
Arm-Hand Steadiness	The ability to keep your hand and arm steady while moving your arm or while holding your arm and hand in one position.
Manual Dexterity	The ability to quickly move your hand, your hand together with your arm, or your two hands to grasp, manipulate, or assemble objects.
Control Precision	The ability to quickly and repeatedly adjust the controls of a machine or a vehicle to exact positions.
Hearing Sensitivity	The ability to detect or tell the differences between sounds that vary in pitch and loudness.

Response Orientation	The ability to choose quickly between two or more movements in response to two or more different signals (lights, sounds, pictures). It includes the speed with which the correct response is started with the hand, foot, or other body part.
Reaction Time	The ability to quickly respond (with the hand, finger, or foot) to a signal (sound, light, picture) when it appears.
Explosive Strength	The ability to use short bursts of muscle force to propel oneself (as in jumping or sprinting), or to throw an object.
Wrist-Finger Speed	The ability to make fast, simple, repeated movements of the fingers, hands, and wrists.
Extent Flexibility	The ability to bend, stretch, twist, or reach with your body, arms, and/or legs.
Gross Body Coordination	The ability to coordinate the movement of your arms, legs, and torso together when the whole body is in motion.
Spatial Orientation	The ability to know your location in relation to the environment or to know where other objects are in relation to you.
Glare Sensitivity	The ability to see objects in the presence of glare or bright lighting.
Sound Localization	The ability to tell the direction from which a sound originated.
Night Vision	The ability to see under low light conditions.
Dynamic Flexibility	The ability to quickly and repeatedly bend, stretch, twist, or reach out with your body, arms, and/or legs.
Speed of Limb Movement	The ability to quickly move the arms and legs.
Stamina	The ability to exert yourself physically over long periods of time without getting winded or out of breath.
Trunk Strength	The ability to use your abdominal and lower back muscles to support part of the body repeatedly or continuously over time without 'giving out' or fatiguing.
Multilimb Coordination	The ability to coordinate two or more limbs (for example, two arms, two legs, or one leg and one arm) while sitting, standing, or lying down. It does not involve performing the activities while the whole body is in motion.
Dynamic Strength	The ability to exert muscle force repeatedly or continuously over time. This involves muscular endurance and resistance to muscle fatigue.
Static Strength	The ability to exert maximum muscle force to lift, push, pull, or carry objects.
Rate Control	The ability to time your movements or the movement of a piece of equipment in anticipation of changes in the speed and/or direction of a moving object or scene.
Gross Body Equilibrium	The ability to keep or regain your body balance or stay upright when in an unstable position.
Peripheral Vision	The ability to see objects or movement of objects to one's side when the eyes are looking ahead.

Work Activity	Work_Activity Definitions
Getting Information	Observing, receiving, and otherwise obtaining information from all relevant sources.
Interacting With Computers	Using computers and computer systems (including hardware and software) to program, write software, set up functions, enter data, or process information.
Thinking Creatively	Developing, designing, or creating new applications, ideas, relationships, systems, or products, including artistic contributions.
Updating and Using Relevant Knowledge	Keeping up-to-date technically and applying new knowledge to your job.
Communicating with Supervisors, Peers, or Subordin	Providing information to supervisors, co-workers, and subordinates by telephone, in written form, e-mail, or in person.
Identifying Objects, Actions, and Events	Identifying information by categorizing, estimating, recognizing differences or similarities, and detecting changes in circumstances or events.
Making Decisions and Solving Problems	Analyzing information and evaluating results to choose the best solution and solve problems.
Establishing and Maintaining Interpersonal Relatio	Developing constructive and cooperative working relationships with others, and maintaining them over time.
Documenting/Recording Information	Entering, transcribing, recording, storing, or maintaining information in written or electronic/magnetic form.
Organizing, Planning, and Prioritizing Work	Developing specific goals and plans to prioritize, organize, and accomplish your work.
Monitor Processes, Materials, or Surroundings	Monitoring and reviewing information from materials, events, or the environment, to detect or assess problems.

Drafting, Laying Out, and Specifying Technical Dev	Providing documentation, detailed instructions, drawings, or specifications to tell others about how devices, parts, equipment, or structures are to be fabricated, constructed, assembled, modified, maintained, or used.
Interpreting the Meaning of Information for Others	Translating or explaining what information means and how it can be used.
Processing Information	Compiling, coding, categorizing, calculating, tabulating, auditing, or verifying information or data.
Evaluating Information to Determine Compliance wit	Using relevant information and individual judgment to determine whether events or processes comply with laws, regulations, or standards.
Judging the Qualities of Things, Services, or Peop	Assessing the value, importance, or quality of things or people.
Communicating with Persons Outside Organization	Communicating with people outside the organization, representing the organization to customers, the public, government, and other external sources. This information can be exchanged in person, in writing, or by telephone or e-mail.
Analyzing Data or Information	Identifying the underlying principles, reasons, or facts of information by breaking down information or data into separate parts.
Estimating the Quantifiable Characteristics of Pro	Estimating sizes, distances, and quantities; or determining time, costs, resources, or materials needed to perform a work activity.
Performing Administrative Activities	Performing day-to-day administrative tasks such as maintaining information files and processing paperwork.
Inspecting Equipment, Structures, or Material	Inspecting equipment, structures, or materials to identify the cause of errors or other problems or defects.
Provide Consultation and Advice to Others	Providing guidance and expert advice to management or other groups on technical, systems-, or process-related topics.
Developing and Building Teams	Encouraging and building mutual trust, respect, and cooperation among team members.
Training and Teaching Others	Identifying the educational needs of others, developing formal educational or training programs or classes, and teaching or instructing others.
Scheduling Work and Activities	Scheduling events, programs, and activities, as well as the work of others.
Coordinating the Work and Activities of Others	Getting members of a group to work together to accomplish tasks.
Developing Objectives and Strategies	Establishing long-range objectives and specifying the strategies and actions to achieve them.
Selling or Influencing Others	Convincing others to buy merchandise/goods or to otherwise change their minds or actions.
Coaching and Developing Others	Identifying the developmental needs of others and coaching, mentoring, or otherwise helping others to improve their knowledge or skills.
Resolving Conflicts and Negotiating with Others	Handling complaints, settling disputes, and resolving grievances and conflicts, or otherwise negotiating with others.
Monitoring and Controlling Resources	Monitoring and controlling resources and overseeing the spending of money.
Guiding, Directing, and Motivating Subordinates	Providing guidance and direction to subordinates, including setting performance standards and monitoring performance.
Assisting and Caring for Others	Providing personal assistance, medical attention, emotional support, or other personal care to others such as coworkers, customers, or patients.
Controlling Machines and Processes	Using either control mechanisms or direct physical activity to operate machines or processes (not including computers or vehicles).
Performing General Physical Activities	Performing physical activities that require considerable use of your arms and legs and moving your whole body, such as climbing, lifting, balancing, walking, stooping, and handling of materials.
Repairing and Maintaining Electronic Equipment	Servicing, repairing, calibrating, regulating, fine-tuning, or testing machines, devices, and equipment that operate primarily on the basis of electrical or electronic (not mechanical) principles.
Handling and Moving Objects	Using hands and arms in handling, installing, positioning, and moving materials, and manipulating things.
Repairing and Maintaining Mechanical Equipment	Servicing, repairing, adjusting, and testing machines, devices, moving parts, and equipment that operate primarily on the basis of mechanical (not electronic) principles.
Operating Vehicles, Mechanized Devices, or Equipme	Running, maneuvering, navigating, or driving vehicles or mechanized equipment, such as forklifts, passenger vehicles, aircraft, or water craft.
Performing for or Working Directly with the Public	Performing for people or dealing directly with the public. This includes serving customers in restaurants and stores, and receiving clients or guests.
Staffing Organizational Units	Recruiting, interviewing, selecting, hiring, and promoting employees in an organization.

Work_Context	Work_Context Definitions
Indoors, Environmentally Controlled	How often does this job require working indoors in environmentally controlled conditions?
Face-to-Face Discussions	How often do you have to have face-to-face discussions with individuals or teams in this job?
Electronic Mail	How often do you use electronic mail in this job?
Spend Time Sitting	How much does this job require sitting?
Importance of Being Exact or Accurate	How important is being very exact or highly accurate in performing this job?
Time Pressure	How often does this job require the worker to meet strict deadlines?
Work With Work Group or Team	How important is it to work with others in a group or team in this job?
Freedom to Make Decisions	How much decision making freedom, without supervision, does the job offer?
Contact With Others	How much does this job require the worker to be in contact with others (face-to-face, by telephone, or otherwise) in order to perform it?
Telephone	How often do you have telephone conversations in this job?
Structured versus Unstructured Work	To what extent is this job structured for the worker, rather than allowing the worker to determine tasks, priorities, and goals?
Importance of Repeating Same Tasks	How important is repeating the same physical activities (e.g., key entry) or mental activities (e.g., checking entries in a ledger) over and over, without stopping, to performing this job?
Impact of Decisions on Co-workers or Company Resul	How do the decisions an employee makes impact the results of co-workers, clients or the company?
Spend Time Making Repetitive Motions	How much does this job require making repetitive motions?
Frequency of Decision Making	How frequently is the worker required to make decisions that affect other people, the financial resources, and/or the image and reputation of the organization?
Level of Competition	To what extent does this job require the worker to compete or to be aware of competitive pressures?
Coordinate or Lead Others	How important is it to coordinate or lead others in accomplishing work activities in this job?
Spend Time Using Your Hands to Handle, Control, or	How much does this job require using your hands to handle, control, or feel objects, tools or controls?
Letters and Memos	How often does the job require written letters and memos?
Responsibility for Outcomes and Results	How responsible is the worker for work outcomes and results of other workers?
Wear Common Protective or Safety Equipment such as	How much does this job require wearing common protective or safety equipment such as safety shoes, glasses, gloves, hard hats or live jackets?
Sounds, Noise Levels Are Distracting or Uncomforta	How often does this job require working exposed to sounds and noise levels that are distracting or uncomfortable?
Deal With External Customers	How important is it to work with external customers or the public in this job?
Frequency of Conflict Situations	How often are there conflict situations the employee has to face in this job?
Indoors, Not Environmentally Controlled	How often does this job require working indoors in non-controlled environmental conditions (e.g., warehouse without heat)?
Deal With Unpleasant or Angry People	How frequently does the worker have to deal with unpleasant, angry, or discourteous individuals as part of the job requirements?
Physical Proximity	To what extent does this job require the worker to perform job tasks in close physical proximity to other people?
Spend Time Standing	How much does this job require standing?
Spend Time Walking and Running	How much does this job require walking and running?
Degree of Automation	How automated is the job?
Exposed to Contaminants	How often does this job require working exposed to contaminants (such as pollutants, gases, dust or odors)?
In an Enclosed Vehicle or Equipment	How often does this job require working in a closed vehicle or equipment (e.g., car)?
Consequence of Error	How serious would the result usually be if the worker made a mistake that was not readily correctable?
Exposed to Hazardous Equipment	How often does this job require exposure to hazardous equipment?
Responsible for Others' Health and Safety	How much responsibility is there for the health and safety of others in this job?
Public Speaking	How often do you have to perform public speaking in this job?

Pace Determined by Speed of Equipment	How important is it to this job that the pace is determined by the speed of equipment or machinery? (This does not refer to keeping busy at all times on this job.)
Exposed to Hazardous Conditions	How often does this job require exposure to hazardous conditions?
Spend Time Bending or Twisting the Body	How much does this job require bending or twisting your body?
Outdoors. Exposed to Weather	How often does this job require working outdoors, exposed to all weather conditions?
Cramped Work Space, Awkward Positions	How often does this job require working in cramped work spaces that requires getting into awkward positions?
Spend Time Kneeling. Crouching. Stooping, or Crawl	How much does this job require kneeling, crouching, stooping or crawling?
Extremely Bright or Inadequate Lighting	How often does this job require working in extremely bright or inadequate lighting conditions?
Exposed to Minor Burns, Cuts, Bites, or Stings	How often does this job require exposure to minor burns, cuts, bites, or stings?
Very Hot or Cold Temperatures	How often does this job require working in very hot (above 90 F degrees) or very cold (below 32 F degrees) temperatures?
Deal With Physically Aggressive People	How frequently does this job require the worker to deal with physical aggression of violent individuals?
Spend Time Climbing Ladders, Scaffolds, or Poles	How much does this job require climbing ladders, scaffolds, or poles?
Exposed to High Places	How often does this job require exposure to high places?
Exposed to Radiation	How often does this job require exposure to radiation?
Outdoors. Under Cover	How often does this job require working outdoors, under cover (e.g., structure with roof but no walls)?
Spend Time Keeping or Regaining Balance	How much does this job require keeping or regaining your balance?
In an Open Vehicle or Equipment	How often does this job require working in an open vehicle or equipment (e.g., tractor)?
Wear Specialized Protective or Safety Equipment su	How much does this job require wearing specialized protective or safety equipment such as breathing apparatus, safety harness, full protection suits, or radiation protection?
Exposed to Disease or Infections	How often does this job require exposure to disease/infections?
Exposed to Whole Body Vibration	How often does this job require exposure to whole body vibration (e.g., operate a jackhammer)?

Job Zone Component	Job Zone Component Definitions
Title	Job Zone Four: Considerable Preparation Needed
Overall Experience	A minimum of two to four years of work-related skill, knowledge, or experience is needed for these occupations. For example, an accountant must complete four years of college and work for several years in accounting to be considered qualified.
Job Training	Employees in these occupations usually need several years of work-related experience, on-the-job training, and/or vocational training.
Job Zone Examples	Many of these occupations involve coordinating, supervising, managing, or training others. Examples include accountants, chefs and head cooks, computer programmers, historians, pharmacists, and police detectives.
SVP Range	(7.0 to < 8.0)
Education	Most of these occupations require a four - year bachelor's degree, but some do not.

Work_Styles	Work_Styles Definitions
Attention to Detail	Job requires being careful about detail and thorough in completing work tasks.
Dependability	Job requires being reliable, responsible, and dependable, and fulfilling obligations.
Analytical Thinking	Job requires analyzing information and using logic to address work-related issues and problems.
Integrity	Job requires being honest and ethical.
Initiative	Job requires a willingness to take on responsibilities and challenges.
Cooperation	Job requires being pleasant with others on the job and displaying a good-natured, cooperative attitude.
Independence	Job requires developing one's own ways of doing things, guiding oneself with little or no supervision, and depending on oneself to get things done.
Persistence	Job requires persistence in the face of obstacles.

Innovation	Job requires creativity and alternative thinking to develop new ideas for and answers to work-related problems.
Adaptability/Flexibility	Job requires being open to change (positive or negative) and to considerable variety in the workplace.
Achievement/Effort	Job requires establishing and maintaining personally challenging achievement goals and exerting effort toward mastering tasks.
Stress Tolerance	Job requires accepting criticism and dealing calmly and effectively with high stress situations.
Self Control	Job requires maintaining composure, keeping emotions in check, controlling anger, and avoiding aggressive behavior, even in very difficult situations.
Leadership	Job requires a willingness to lead, take charge, and offer opinions and direction.
Concern for Others	Job requires being sensitive to others' needs and feelings and being understanding and helpful on the job.
Social Orientation	Job requires preferring to work with others rather than alone, and being personally connected with others on the job.

27-2032.00 - Choreographers

Create and teach dance. May direct and stage presentations.

Tasks

1) Read and study story lines and musical scores to determine how to translate ideas and moods into dance movements.

2) Teach students, dancers, and other performers about rhythm and interpretive movement.

3) Design dances for individual dancers, dance companies, musical theatre, opera, fashion shows, film, television productions and special events, and for dancers ranging from beginners to professionals.

4) Coordinate production music with music directors.

5) Seek influences from other art forms such as theatre, the visual arts, and architecture.

6) Design sets, lighting, costumes, and other artistic elements of productions, in collaboration with cast members.

7) Experiment with different types of dancers, steps, dances, and placements, testing ideas informally to get feedback from dancers.

8) Direct rehearsals to instruct dancers in how to use dance steps, and in techniques to achieve desired effects.

9) Record dance movements and their technical aspects, using a technical understanding of the patterns and formations of choreography.

10) Re-stage traditional dances and works in dance companies' repertoires, developing new interpretations.

11) Advise dancers on how to stand and move properly, teaching correct dance techniques to help prevent injuries.

12) Assess students' dancing abilities to determine where improvement or change is needed.

13) Audition performers for one or more dance parts.

14) Choose the music, sound effects, or spoken narrative to accompany a dance.

15) Direct and stage dance presentations for various forms of entertainment.

16) Develop ideas for creating dances, keeping notes and sketches to record influences.

17) Manage dance schools, or assist in their management.

29-1011.00 - Chiropractors

Adjust spinal column and other articulations of the body to correct abnormalities of the human body believed to be caused by interference with the nervous system. Examine patient to determine nature and extent of disorder. Manipulate spine or other involved area. May utilize supplementary measures, such as exercise, rest, water, light, heat, and nutritional therapy.

Tasks

1) Obtain and record patients' medical histories.

2) Counsel patients about nutrition, exercise, sleeping habits, stress management, and other matters.

3) Maintain accurate case histories of patients.

4) Arrange for diagnostic x-rays to be taken.

5) Advise patients about recommended courses of treatment.

6) Analyze x-rays in order to locate the sources of patients' difficulties and to rule out fractures or diseases as sources of problems.

7) Evaluate the functioning of the neuromuscularskeletal system and the spine using systems of chiropractic diagnosis.

8) Diagnose health problems by reviewing patients' health and medical histories; questioning, observing and examining patients; and interpreting x-rays.

9) Perform a series of manual adjustments to the spine, or other articulations of the body, in order to correct the musculoskeletal system.

10) Suggest and apply the use of supports such as straps, tapes, bandages, and braces if necessary.

Knowledge	Knowledge Definitions
Medicine and Dentistry	Knowledge of the information and techniques needed to diagnose and treat human injuries, diseases, and deformities. This includes symptoms, treatment alternatives, drug properties and interactions, and preventive health-care measures.
Customer and Personal Service	Knowledge of principles and processes for providing customer and personal services. This includes customer needs assessment, meeting quality standards for services, and evaluation of customer satisfaction.
English Language	Knowledge of the structure and content of the English language including the meaning and spelling of words, rules of composition, and grammar.
Therapy and Counseling	Knowledge of principles, methods, and procedures for diagnosis, treatment, and rehabilitation of physical and mental dysfunctions, and for career counseling and guidance.
Biology	Knowledge of plant and animal organisms, their tissues, cells, functions, interdependencies, and interactions with each other and the environment.
Psychology	Knowledge of human behavior and performance; individual differences in ability, personality, and interests; learning and motivation; psychological research methods; and the assessment and treatment of behavioral and affective disorders.
Administration and Management	Knowledge of business and management principles involved in strategic planning, resource allocation, human resources modeling, leadership technique, production methods, and coordination of people and resources.
Education and Training	Knowledge of principles and methods for curriculum and training design, teaching and instruction for individuals and groups, and the measurement of training effects.
Clerical	Knowledge of administrative and clerical procedures and systems such as word processing, managing files and records, stenography and transcription, designing forms, and other office procedures and terminology.
Sales and Marketing	Knowledge of principles and methods for showing, promoting, and selling products or services. This includes marketing strategy and tactics, product demonstration, sales techniques, and sales control systems.
Economics and Accounting	Knowledge of economic and accounting principles and practices, the financial markets, banking and the analysis and reporting of financial data.
Personnel and Human Resources	Knowledge of principles and procedures for personnel recruitment, selection, training, compensation and benefits, labor relations and negotiation, and personnel information systems.
Law and Government	Knowledge of laws, legal codes, court procedures, precedents, government regulations, executive orders, agency rules, and the democratic political process.
Sociology and Anthropology	Knowledge of group behavior and dynamics, societal trends and influences, human migrations, ethnicity, cultures and their history and origins.
Computers and Electronics	Knowledge of circuit boards, processors, chips, electronic equipment, and computer hardware and software, including applications and programming.
Public Safety and Security	Knowledge of relevant equipment, policies, procedures, and strategies to promote effective local, state, or national security operations for the protection of people, data, property, and institutions.

Communications and Media	Knowledge of media production, communication, and dissemination techniques and methods. This includes alternative ways to inform and entertain via written, oral, and visual media.
Chemistry	Knowledge of the chemical composition, structure, and properties of substances and of the chemical processes and transformations that they undergo. This includes uses of chemicals and their interactions, danger signs, production techniques, and disposal methods.
Mathematics	Knowledge of arithmetic, algebra, geometry, calculus, statistics, and their applications.
Physics	Knowledge and prediction of physical principles, laws, their interrelationships, and applications to understanding fluid, material, and atmospheric dynamics, and mechanical, electrical, atomic and sub- atomic structures and processes.
Philosophy and Theology	Knowledge of different philosophical systems and religions. This includes their basic principles, values, ethics, ways of thinking, customs, practices, and their impact on human culture.
Foreign Language	Knowledge of the structure and content of a foreign (non-English) language including the meaning and spelling of words, rules of composition and grammar, and pronunciation.
Production and Processing	Knowledge of raw materials, production processes, quality control, costs, and other techniques for maximizing the effective manufacture and distribution of goods.
Telecommunications	Knowledge of transmission, broadcasting, switching, control, and operation of telecommunications systems.
Engineering and Technology	Knowledge of the practical application of engineering science and technology. This includes applying principles, techniques, procedures, and equipment to the design and production of various goods and services.
Mechanical	Knowledge of machines and tools, including their designs, uses, repair, and maintenance.
History and Archeology	Knowledge of historical events and their causes, indicators, and effects on civilizations and cultures.
Transportation	Knowledge of principles and methods for moving people or goods by air, rail, sea, or road, including the relative costs and benefits.
Design	Knowledge of design techniques, tools, and principles involved in production of precision technical plans, blueprints, drawings, and models.
Fine Arts	Knowledge of the theory and techniques required to compose, produce, and perform works of music, dance, visual arts, drama, and sculpture.
Geography	Knowledge of principles and methods for describing the features of land, sea, and air masses, including their physical characteristics, locations, interrelationships, and distribution of plant, animal, and human life.
Food Production	Knowledge of techniques and equipment for planting, growing, and harvesting food products (both plant and animal) for consumption, including storage/handling techniques.
Building and Construction	Knowledge of materials, methods, and the tools involved in the construction or repair of houses, buildings, or other structures such as highways and roads.

Skills	Skills Definitions
Active Listening	Giving full attention to what other people are saying, taking time to understand the points being made, asking questions as appropriate, and not interrupting at inappropriate times.
Reading Comprehension	Understanding written sentences and paragraphs in work related documents.
Speaking	Talking to others to convey information effectively.
Critical Thinking	Using logic and reasoning to identify the strengths and weaknesses of alternative solutions, conclusions or approaches to problems.
Service Orientation	Actively looking for ways to help people.
Active Learning	Understanding the implications of new information for both current and future problem-solving and decision-making.
Social Perceptiveness	Being aware of others' reactions and understanding why they react as they do.
Instructing	Teaching others how to do something.
Time Management	Managing one's own time and the time of others.
Science	Using scientific rules and methods to solve problems.
Persuasion	Persuading others to change their minds or behavior.
Writing	Communicating effectively in writing as appropriate for the needs of the audience.

Monitoring	Monitoring/Assessing performance of yourself, other individuals, or organizations to make improvements or take corrective action.
Judgment and Decision Making	Considering the relative costs and benefits of potential actions to choose the most appropriate one.
Coordination	Adjusting actions in relation to others' actions.
Learning Strategies	Selecting and using training/instructional methods and procedures appropriate for the situation when learning or teaching new things.
Complex Problem Solving	Identifying complex problems and reviewing related information to develop and evaluate options and implement solutions.
Management of Financial Resources	Determining how money will be spent to get the work done, and accounting for these expenditures.
Management of Personnel Resources	Motivating, developing, and directing people as they work, identifying the best people for the job.
Equipment Selection	Determining the kind of tools and equipment needed to do a job.
Negotiation	Bringing others together and trying to reconcile differences.
Quality Control Analysis	Conducting tests and inspections of products, services, or processes to evaluate quality or performance.
Mathematics	Using mathematics to solve problems.
Management of Material Resources	Obtaining and seeing to the appropriate use of equipment, facilities, and materials needed to do certain work.
Operations Analysis	Analyzing needs and product requirements to create a design.
Troubleshooting	Determining causes of operating errors and deciding what to do about it.
Systems Evaluation	Identifying measures or indicators of system performance and the actions needed to improve or correct performance, relative to the goals of the system.
Equipment Maintenance	Performing routine maintenance on equipment and determining when and what kind of maintenance is needed.
Operation and Control	Controlling operations of equipment or systems.
Technology Design	Generating or adapting equipment and technology to serve user needs.
Operation Monitoring	Watching gauges, dials, or other indicators to make sure a machine is working properly.
Systems Analysis	Determining how a system should work and how changes in conditions, operations, and the environment will affect outcomes.
Repairing	Repairing machines or systems using the needed tools.
Installation	Installing equipment, machines, wiring, or programs to meet specifications.
Programming	Writing computer programs for various purposes.

Ability	Ability Definitions
Problem Sensitivity	The ability to tell when something is wrong or is likely to go wrong. It does not involve solving the problem, only recognizing there is a problem.
Oral Expression	The ability to communicate information and ideas in speaking so others will understand.
Oral Comprehension	The ability to listen to and understand information and ideas presented through spoken words and sentences.
Speech Clarity	The ability to speak clearly so others can understand you.
Inductive Reasoning	The ability to combine pieces of information to form general rules or conclusions (includes finding a relationship among seemingly unrelated events).
Speech Recognition	The ability to identify and understand the speech of another person.
Deductive Reasoning	The ability to apply general rules to specific problems to produce answers that make sense.
Near Vision	The ability to see details at close range (within a few feet of the observer).
Arm-Hand Steadiness	The ability to keep your hand and arm steady while moving your arm or while holding your arm and hand in one position.
Written Comprehension	The ability to read and understand information and ideas presented in writing.
Manual Dexterity	The ability to quickly move your hand, your hand together with your arm, or your two hands to grasp, manipulate, or assemble objects.
Selective Attention	The ability to concentrate on a task over a period of time without being distracted.
Written Expression	The ability to communicate information and ideas in writing so others will understand.
Finger Dexterity	The ability to make precisely coordinated movements of the fingers of one or both hands to grasp, manipulate, or assemble very small objects.

Information Ordering	The ability to arrange things or actions in a certain order or pattern according to a specific rule or set of rules (e.g., patterns of numbers, letters, words, pictures, mathematical operations).
Category Flexibility	The ability to generate or use different sets of rules for combining or grouping things in different ways.
Flexibility of Closure	The ability to identify or detect a known pattern (a figure, object, word, or sound) that is hidden in other distracting material.
Multilimb Coordination	The ability to coordinate two or more limbs (for example, two arms, two legs, or one leg and one arm) while sitting, standing, or lying down. It does not involve performing the activities while the whole body is in motion.
Static Strength	The ability to exert maximum muscle force to lift, push, pull, or carry objects.
Far Vision	The ability to see details at a distance.
Originality	The ability to come up with unusual or clever ideas about a given topic or situation, or to develop creative ways to solve a problem.
Extent Flexibility	The ability to bend, stretch, twist, or reach with your body, arms, and/or legs.
Dynamic Strength	The ability to exert muscle force repeatedly or continuously over time. This involves muscular endurance and resistance to muscle fatigue.
Visualization	The ability to imagine how something will look after it is moved around or when its parts are moved or rearranged.
Speed of Closure	The ability to quickly make sense of, combine, and organize information into meaningful patterns.
Time Sharing	The ability to shift back and forth between two or more activities or sources of information (such as speech, sounds, touch, or other sources).
Trunk Strength	The ability to use your abdominal and lower back muscles to support part of the body repeatedly or continuously over time without 'giving out' or fatiguing.
Fluency of Ideas	The ability to come up with a number of ideas about a topic (the number of ideas is important, not their quality, correctness, or creativity).
Perceptual Speed	The ability to quickly and accurately compare similarities and differences among sets of letters, numbers, objects, pictures, or patterns. The things to be compared may be presented at the same time or one after the other. This ability also includes comparing a presented object with a remembered object.
Gross Body Coordination	The ability to coordinate the movement of your arms, legs, and torso together when the whole body is in motion.
Control Precision	The ability to quickly and repeatedly adjust the controls of a machine or a vehicle to exact positions.
Stamina	The ability to exert yourself physically over long periods of time without getting winded or out of breath.
Visual Color Discrimination	The ability to match or detect differences between colors, including shades of color and brightness.
Memorization	The ability to remember information such as words, numbers, pictures, and procedures.
Mathematical Reasoning	The ability to choose the right mathematical methods or formulas to solve a problem.
Number Facility	The ability to add, subtract, multiply, or divide quickly and correctly.
Gross Body Equilibrium	The ability to keep or regain your body balance or stay upright when in an unstable position.
Hearing Sensitivity	The ability to detect or tell the differences between sounds that vary in pitch and loudness.
Auditory Attention	The ability to focus on a single source of sound in the presence of other distracting sounds.
Depth Perception	The ability to judge which of several objects is closer or farther away from you, or to judge the distance between you and an object.
Wrist-Finger Speed	The ability to make fast, simple, repeated movements of the fingers, hands, and wrists.
Response Orientation	The ability to choose quickly between two or more movements in response to two or more different signals (lights, sounds, pictures). It includes the speed with which the correct response is started with the hand, foot, or other body part.
Dynamic Flexibility	The ability to quickly and repeatedly bend, stretch, twist, or reach out with your body, arms, and/or legs.
Spatial Orientation	The ability to know your location in relation to the environment or to know where other objects are in relation to you.
Peripheral Vision	The ability to see objects or movement of objects to one's side when the eyes are looking ahead.
Sound Localization	The ability to tell the direction from which a sound originated.
Night Vision	The ability to see under low light conditions.

Explosive Strength	The ability to use short bursts of muscle force to propel oneself (as in jumping or sprinting), or to throw an object.
Rate Control	The ability to time your movements or the movement of a piece of equipment in anticipation of changes in the speed and/or direction of a moving object or scene.
Reaction Time	The ability to quickly respond (with the hand, finger, or foot) to a signal (sound, light, picture) when it appears.
Speed of Limb Movement	The ability to quickly move the arms and legs.
Glare Sensitivity	The ability to see objects in the presence of glare or bright lighting.

Work_Activity	Work_Activity Definitions
Assisting and Caring for Others	Providing personal assistance, medical attention, emotional support, or other personal care to others such as coworkers, customers, or patients.
Performing for or Working Directly with the Public	Performing for people or dealing directly with the public. This includes serving customers in restaurants and stores, and receiving clients or guests.
Getting Information	Observing, receiving, and otherwise obtaining information from all relevant sources.
Making Decisions and Solving Problems	Analyzing information and evaluating results to choose the best solution and solve problems.
Documenting/Recording Information	Entering, transcribing, recording, storing, or maintaining information in written or electronic/magnetic form.
Establishing and Maintaining Interpersonal Relatio	Developing constructive and cooperative working relationships with others, and maintaining them over time.
Updating and Using Relevant Knowledge	Keeping up-to-date technically and applying new knowledge to your job.
Identifying Objects, Actions, and Events	Identifying information by categorizing, estimating, recognizing differences or similarities, and detecting changes in circumstances or events.
Processing Information	Compiling, coding, categorizing, calculating, tabulating, auditing, or verifying information or data.
Performing General Physical Activities	Performing physical activities that require considerable use of your arms and legs and moving your whole body, such as climbing, lifting, balancing, walking, stooping, and handling of materials.
Evaluating Information to Determine Compliance wit	Using relevant information and individual judgment to determine whether events or processes comply with laws, regulations, or standards.
Interpreting the Meaning of Information for Others	Translating or explaining what information means and how it can be used.
Communicating with Persons Outside Organization	Communicating with people outside the organization, representing the organization to customers, the public, government, and other external sources. This information can be exchanged in person, in writing, or by telephone or e-mail.
Performing Administrative Activities	Performing day-to-day administrative tasks such as maintaining information files and processing paperwork.
Handling and Moving Objects	Using hands and arms in handling, installing, positioning, and moving materials, and manipulating things.
Selling or Influencing Others	Convincing others to buy merchandise/goods or to otherwise change their minds or actions.
Organizing, Planning, and Prioritizing Work	Developing specific goals and plans to prioritize, organize, and accomplish your work.
Analyzing Data or Information	Identifying the underlying principles, reasons, or facts of information by breaking down information or data into separate parts.
Monitoring and Controlling Resources	Monitoring and controlling resources and overseeing the spending of money.
Developing Objectives and Strategies	Establishing long-range objectives and specifying the strategies and actions to achieve them.
Judging the Qualities of Things, Services, or Peop	Assessing the value, importance, or quality of things or people.
Provide Consultation and Advice to Others	Providing guidance and expert advice to management or other groups on technical, systems-, or process-related topics.
Interacting With Computers	Using computers and computer systems (including hardware and software) to program, write software, set up functions, enter data, or process information.
Monitor Processes, Materials, or Surroundings	Monitoring and reviewing information from materials, events, or the environment, to detect or assess problems.
Communicating with Supervisors, Peers, or Subordin	Providing information to supervisors, co-workers, and subordinates by telephone, in written form, e-mail, or in person.

Training and Teaching Others	Identifying the educational needs of others, developing formal educational or training programs or classes, and teaching or instructing others.
Scheduling Work and Activities	Scheduling events, programs, and activities, as well as the work of others.
Coaching and Developing Others	Identifying the developmental needs of others and coaching, mentoring, or otherwise helping others to improve their knowledge or skills.
Resolving Conflicts and Negotiating with Others	Handling complaints, settling disputes, and resolving grievances and conflicts, or otherwise negotiating with others.
Thinking Creatively	Developing, designing, or creating new applications, ideas, relationships, systems, or products, including artistic contributions.
Coordinating the Work and Activities of Others	Getting members of a group to work together to accomplish tasks.
Inspecting Equipment, Structures, or Material	Inspecting equipment, structures, or materials to identify the cause of errors or other problems or defects.
Guiding, Directing, and Motivating Subordinates	Providing guidance and direction to subordinates, including setting performance standards and monitoring performance.
Developing and Building Teams	Encouraging and building mutual trust, respect, and cooperation among team members.
Estimating the Quantifiable Characteristics of Pro	Estimating sizes, distances, and quantities; or determining time, costs, resources, or materials needed to perform a work activity.
Staffing Organizational Units	Recruiting, interviewing, selecting, hiring, and promoting employees in an organization.
Controlling Machines and Processes	Using either control mechanisms or direct physical activity to operate machines or processes (not including computers or vehicles).
Repairing and Maintaining Electronic Equipment	Servicing, repairing, calibrating, regulating, fine-tuning, or testing machines, devices, and equipment that operate primarily on the basis of electrical or electronic (not mechanical) principles.
Repairing and Maintaining Mechanical Equipment	Servicing, repairing, adjusting, and testing machines, devices, moving parts, and equipment that operate primarily on the basis of mechanical (not electronic) principles.
Operating Vehicles, Mechanized Devices, or Equipme	Running, maneuvering, navigating, or driving vehicles or mechanized equipment, such as forklifts, passenger vehicles, aircraft, or water craft.
Drafting, Laying Out, and Specifying Technical Dev	Providing documentation, detailed instructions, drawings, or specifications to tell others about how devices, parts, equipment, or structures are to be fabricated, constructed, assembled, modified, maintained, or used.

Work_Context	Work_Context Definitions
Physical Proximity	To what extent does this job require the worker to perform job tasks in close physical proximity to other people?
Indoors, Environmentally Controlled	How often does this job require working indoors in environmentally controlled conditions?
Structured versus Unstructured Work	To what extent is this job structured for the worker, rather than allowing the worker to determine tasks, priorities, and goals?
Freedom to Make Decisions	How much decision making freedom, without supervision, does the job offer?
Face-to-Face Discussions	How often do you have to have face-to-face discussions with individuals or teams in this job?
Telephone	How often do you have telephone conversations in this job?
Contact With Others	How much does this job require the worker to be in contact with others (face-to-face, by telephone, or otherwise) in order to perform it?
Importance of Being Exact or Accurate	How important is being very exact or highly accurate in performing this job?
Impact of Decisions on Co-workers or Company Resul	How do the decisions an employee makes impact the results of co-workers, clients or the company?
Frequency of Decision Making	How frequently is the worker required to make decisions that affect other people, the financial resources, and/or the image and reputation of the organization?
Deal With External Customers	How important is it to work with external customers or the public in this job?
Letters and Memos	How often does the job require written letters and memos?
Responsibility for Outcomes and Results	How responsible is the worker for work outcomes and results of other workers?
Spend Time Standing	How much does this job require standing?
Importance of Repeating Same Tasks	How important is repeating the same physical activities (e.g., key entry) or mental activities (e.g., checking entries in a ledger) over and over, without stopping, to performing this job?

Spend Time Using Your Hands to Handle, Control, or	How much does this job require using your hands to handle, control, or feel objects, tools or controls?
Exposed to Disease or Infections	How often does this job require exposure to disease/infections?
Work With Work Group or Team	How important is it to work with others in a group or team in this job?
Spend Time Making Repetitive Motions	How much does this job require making repetitive motions?
Responsible for Others' Health and Safety	How much responsibility is there for the health and safety of others in this job?
Spend Time Bending or Twisting the Body	How much does this job require bending or twisting your body?
Electronic Mail	How often do you use electronic mail in this job?
Coordinate or Lead Others	How important is it to coordinate or lead others in accomplishing work activities in this job?
Level of Competition	To what extent does this job require the worker to compete or to be aware of competitive pressures?
Time Pressure	How often does this job require the worker to meet strict deadlines?
Consequence of Error	How serious would the result usually be if the worker made a mistake that was not readily correctable?
Frequency of Conflict Situations	How often are there conflict situations the employee has to face in this job?
Deal With Unpleasant or Angry People	How frequently does the worker have to deal with unpleasant, angry, or discourteous individuals as part of the job requirements?
Exposed to Radiation	How often does this job require exposure to radiation?
Public Speaking	How often do you have to perform public speaking in this job?
Spend Time Walking and Running	How much does this job require walking and running?
Spend Time Sitting	How much does this job require sitting?
Spend Time Kneeling, Crouching, Stooping, or Crawl	How much does this job require kneeling, crouching, stooping or crawling?
Degree of Automation	How automated is the job?
Spend Time Keeping or Regaining Balance	How much does this job require keeping or regaining your balance?
Exposed to Contaminants	How often does this job require working exposed to contaminants (such as pollutants, gases, dust or odors)?
Wear Common Protective or Safety Equipment such as	How much does this job require wearing common protective or safety equipment such as safety shoes, glasses, gloves, hard hats or live jackets?
Exposed to Minor Burns, Cuts, Bites, or Stings	How often does this job require exposure to minor burns, cuts, bites, or stings?
Pace Determined by Speed of Equipment	How important is it to this job that the pace is determined by the speed of equipment or machinery? (This does not refer to keeping busy at all times on this job.)
Wear Specialized Protective or Safety Equipment su	How much does this job require wearing specialized protective or safety equipment such as breathing apparatus, safety harness, full protection suits, or radiation protection?
Exposed to Hazardous Conditions	How often does this job require exposure to hazardous conditions?
Deal With Physically Aggressive People	How frequently does this job require the worker to deal with physical aggression of violent individuals?
Sounds, Noise Levels Are Distracting or Uncomforta	How often does this job require working exposed to sounds and noise levels that are distracting or uncomfortable?
Cramped Work Space, Awkward Positions	How often does this job require working in cramped work spaces that requires getting into awkward positions?
In an Enclosed Vehicle or Equipment	How often does this job require working in a closed vehicle or equipment (e.g., car)?
Outdoors, Under Cover	How often does this job require working outdoors, under cover (e.g., structure with roof but no walls)?
Exposed to Hazardous Equipment	How often does this job require exposure to hazardous equipment?
Outdoors, Exposed to Weather	How often does this job require working outdoors, exposed to all weather conditions?
Exposed to Whole Body Vibration	How often does this job require exposure to whole body vibration (e.g., operate a jackhammer)?
Indoors, Not Environmentally Controlled	How often does this job require working indoors in non-controlled environmental conditions (e.g., warehouse without heat)?
Very Hot or Cold Temperatures	How often does this job require working in very hot (above 90 F degrees) or very cold (below 32 F degrees) temperatures?
Exposed to High Places	How often does this job require exposure to high places?
Extremely Bright or Inadequate Lighting	How often does this job require working in extremely bright or inadequate lighting conditions?

Spend Time Climbing Ladders, Scaffolds, or Poles	How much does this job require climbing ladders, scaffolds, or poles?
In an Open Vehicle or Equipment	How often does this job require working in an open vehicle or equipment (e.g., tractor)?

Job Zone Component	Job Zone Component Definitions
Title	Job Zone Five: Extensive Preparation Needed
Overall Experience	Extensive skill, knowledge, and experience are needed for these occupations. Many require more than five years of experience. For example, surgeons must complete four years of college and an additional five to seven years of specialized medical training to be able to do their job.
Job Training	Employees may need some on-the-job training, but most of these occupations assume that the person will already have the required skills, knowledge, work-related experience, and/or training.
Job Zone Examples	These occupations often involve coordinating, training, supervising, or managing the activities of others to accomplish goals. Very advanced communication and organizational skills are required. Examples include athletic trainers, lawyers, managing editors, physicists, social psychologists, and surgeons.
SVP Range	(8.0 and above)
Education	A bachelor's degree is the minimum formal education required for these occupations. However, many also require graduate school. For example, they may require a master's degree, and some require a Ph.D., M.D., or J.D. (law degree).

Work_Styles	Work_Styles Definitions
Concern for Others	Job requires being sensitive to others' needs and feelings and being understanding and helpful on the job.
Integrity	Job requires being honest and ethical.
Dependability	Job requires being reliable, responsible, and dependable, and fulfilling obligations.
Attention to Detail	Job requires being careful about detail and thorough in completing work tasks.
Independence	Job requires developing one's own ways of doing things, guiding oneself with little or no supervision, and depending on oneself to get things done.
Cooperation	Job requires being pleasant with others on the job and displaying a good-natured, cooperative attitude.
Self Control	Job requires maintaining composure, keeping emotions in check, controlling anger, and avoiding aggressive behavior, even in very difficult situations.
Initiative	Job requires a willingness to take on responsibilities and challenges.
Stress Tolerance	Job requires accepting criticism and dealing calmly and effectively with high stress situations.
Leadership	Job requires a willingness to lead, take charge, and offer opinions and direction.
Analytical Thinking	Job requires analyzing information and using logic to address work-related issues and problems.
Achievement/Effort	Job requires establishing and maintaining personally challenging achievement goals and exerting effort toward mastering tasks.
Persistence	Job requires persistence in the face of obstacles.
Social Orientation	Job requires preferring to work with others rather than alone, and being personally connected with others on the job.
Adaptability/Flexibility	Job requires being open to change (positive or negative) and to considerable variety in the workplace.
Innovation	Job requires creativity and alternative thinking to develop new ideas for and answers to work-related problems.

29-1021.00 - Dentists, General

Diagnose and treat diseases, injuries, and malformations of teeth and gums and related oral structures. May treat diseases of nerve, pulp, and other dental tissues affecting vitality of teeth.

Tasks

1) Design, make, and fit prosthodontic appliances such as space maintainers, bridges, and dentures, or write fabrication instructions or prescriptions for denturists and dental technicians.

2) Eliminate irritating margins of fillings and correct occlusions, using dental instruments.

3) Treat exposure of pulp by pulp capping, removal of pulp from pulp chamber, or root canal, using dental instruments.

4) Analyze and evaluate dental needs to determine changes and trends in patterns of dental disease.

5) Apply fluoride and sealants to teeth.

6) Bleach, clean or polish teeth to restore natural color.

7) Manage business, employing and supervising staff and handling paperwork and insurance claims.

8) Fill pulp chamber and canal with endodontic materials.

9) Perform oral and periodontal surgery on the jaw or mouth.

10) Produce and evaluate dental health educational materials.

11) Plan, organize, and maintain dental health programs.

12) Remove diseased tissue using surgical instruments.

13) Formulate plan of treatment for patient's teeth and mouth tissue.

14) Use masks, gloves and safety glasses to protect themselves and their patients from infectious diseases.

15) Diagnose and treat diseases, injuries, and malformations of teeth, gums and related oral structures, and provide preventive and corrective services.

16) Write prescriptions for antibiotics and other medications.

17) Examine teeth, gums, and related tissues, using dental instruments, x-rays, and other diagnostic equipment, to evaluate dental health, diagnose diseases or abnormalities, and plan appropriate treatments.

18) Advise and instruct patients regarding preventive dental care, the causes and treatment of dental problems, and oral health care services.

19) Use air turbine and hand instruments, dental appliances and surgical implements.

Knowledge	Knowledge Definitions
Medicine and Dentistry	Knowledge of the information and techniques needed to diagnose and treat human injuries, diseases, and deformities. This includes symptoms, treatment alternatives, drug properties and interactions, and preventive health-care measures.
Biology	Knowledge of plant and animal organisms, their tissues, cells, functions, interdependencies, and interactions with each other and the environment.
English Language	Knowledge of the structure and content of the English language including the meaning and spelling of words, rules of composition, and grammar.
Customer and Personal Service	Knowledge of principles and processes for providing customer and personal services. This includes customer needs assessment, meeting quality standards for services, and evaluation of customer satisfaction.
Psychology	Knowledge of human behavior and performance; individual differences in ability, personality, and interests; learning and motivation; psychological research methods; and the assessment and treatment of behavioral and affective disorders.
Administration and Management	Knowledge of business and management principles involved in strategic planning, resource allocation, human resources modeling, leadership technique, production methods, and coordination of people and resources.
Education and Training	Knowledge of principles and methods for curriculum and training design, teaching and instruction for individuals and groups, and the measurement of training effects.
Sales and Marketing	Knowledge of principles and methods for showing, promoting, and selling products or services. This includes marketing strategy and tactics, product demonstration, sales techniques, and sales control systems.
Chemistry	Knowledge of the chemical composition, structure, and properties of substances and of the chemical processes and transformations that they undergo. This includes uses of chemicals and their interactions, danger signs, production techniques, and disposal methods.
Economics and Accounting	Knowledge of economic and accounting principles and practices, the financial markets, banking and the analysis and reporting of financial data.
Engineering and Technology	Knowledge of the practical application of engineering science and technology. This includes applying principles, techniques, procedures, and equipment to the design and production of various goods and services.
Law and Government	Knowledge of laws, legal codes, court procedures, precedents, government regulations, executive orders, agency rules, and the democratic political process.
Mechanical	Knowledge of machines and tools, including their designs, uses, repair, and maintenance.
Clerical	Knowledge of administrative and clerical procedures and systems such as word processing, managing files and records, stenography and transcription, designing forms, and other office procedures and terminology.
Mathematics	Knowledge of arithmetic, algebra, geometry, calculus, statistics, and their applications.
Personnel and Human Resources	Knowledge of principles and procedures for personnel recruitment, selection, training, compensation and benefits, labor relations and negotiation, and personnel information systems.
Design	Knowledge of design techniques, tools, and principles involved in production of precision technical plans, blueprints, drawings, and models.
Sociology and Anthropology	Knowledge of group behavior and dynamics, societal trends and influences, human migrations, ethnicity, cultures and their history and origins.
Production and Processing	Knowledge of raw materials, production processes, quality control, costs, and other techniques for maximizing the effective manufacture and distribution of goods.
Therapy and Counseling	Knowledge of principles, methods, and procedures for diagnosis, treatment, and rehabilitation of physical and mental dysfunctions, and for career counseling and guidance.
Physics	Knowledge and prediction of physical principles, laws, their interrelationships, and applications to understanding fluid, material, and atmospheric dynamics, and mechanical, electrical, atomic and sub-atomic structures and processes.
Computers and Electronics	Knowledge of circuit boards, processors, chips, electronic equipment, and computer hardware and software, including applications and programming.
Telecommunications	Knowledge of transmission, broadcasting, switching, control, and operation of telecommunications systems.
Public Safety and Security	Knowledge of relevant equipment, policies, procedures, and strategies to promote effective local, state, or national security operations for the protection of people, data, property, and institutions.
Communications and Media	Knowledge of media production, communication, and dissemination techniques and methods. This includes alternative ways to inform and entertain via written, oral, and visual media.
Building and Construction	Knowledge of materials, methods, and the tools involved in the construction or repair of houses, buildings, or other structures such as highways and roads.
Philosophy and Theology	Knowledge of different philosophical systems and religions. This includes their basic principles, values, ethics, ways of thinking, customs, practices, and their impact on human culture.
Food Production	Knowledge of techniques and equipment for planting, growing, and harvesting food products (both plant and animal) for consumption, including storage/handling techniques.
Transportation	Knowledge of principles and methods for moving people or goods by air, rail, sea, or road, including the relative costs and benefits.
Foreign Language	Knowledge of the structure and content of a foreign (non-English) language including the meaning and spelling of words, rules of composition and grammar, and pronunciation.
Fine Arts	Knowledge of the theory and techniques required to compose, produce, and perform works of music, dance, visual arts, drama, and sculpture.
History and Archeology	Knowledge of historical events and their causes, indicators, and effects on civilizations and cultures.
Geography	Knowledge of principles and methods for describing the features of land, sea, and air masses, including their physical characteristics, locations, interrelationships, and distribution of plant, animal, and human life.

Skills	Skills Definitions
Science	Using scientific rules and methods to solve problems.
Active Listening	Giving full attention to what other people are saying, taking time to understand the points being made, asking questions as appropriate, and not interrupting at inappropriate times.
Critical Thinking	Using logic and reasoning to identify the strengths and weaknesses of alternative solutions, conclusions or approaches to problems.
Complex Problem Solving	Identifying complex problems and reviewing related information to develop and evaluate options and implement solutions.
Reading Comprehension	Understanding written sentences and paragraphs in work related documents.
Judgment and Decision Making	Considering the relative costs and benefits of potential actions to choose the most appropriate one.
Equipment Selection	Determining the kind of tools and equipment needed to do a job.
Time Management	Managing one's own time and the time of others.
Instructing	Teaching others how to do something.
Active Learning	Understanding the implications of new information for both current and future problem-solving and decision-making.
Service Orientation	Actively looking for ways to help people.
Coordination	Adjusting actions in relation to others' actions.
Management of Financial Resources	Determining how money will be spent to get the work done, and accounting for these expenditures.
Speaking	Talking to others to convey information effectively.
Persuasion	Persuading others to change their minds or behavior.
Troubleshooting	Determining causes of operating errors and deciding what to do about it.
Monitoring	Monitoring/Assessing performance of yourself, other individuals, or organizations to make improvements or take corrective action.
Social Perceptiveness	Being aware of others' reactions and understanding why they react as they do.
Learning Strategies	Selecting and using training/instructional methods and procedures appropriate for the situation when learning or teaching new things.
Management of Material Resources	Obtaining and seeing to the appropriate use of equipment, facilities, and materials needed to do certain work.
Management of Personnel Resources	Motivating, developing, and directing people as they work, identifying the best people for the job.
Writing	Communicating effectively in writing as appropriate for the needs of the audience.
Operations Analysis	Analyzing needs and product requirements to create a design.
Quality Control Analysis	Conducting tests and inspections of products, services, or processes to evaluate quality or performance.
Equipment Maintenance	Performing routine maintenance on equipment and determining when and what kind of maintenance is needed.
Negotiation	Bringing others together and trying to reconcile differences.
Technology Design	Generating or adapting equipment and technology to serve user needs.
Mathematics	Using mathematics to solve problems.
Systems Evaluation	Identifying measures or indicators of system performance and the actions needed to improve or correct performance, relative to the goals of the system
Operation and Control	Controlling operations of equipment or systems.
Installation	Installing equipment, machines, wiring, or programs to meet specifications.
Operation Monitoring	Watching gauges, dials, or other indicators to make sure a machine is working properly.
Repairing	Repairing machines or systems using the needed tools.
Systems Analysis	Determining how a system should work and how changes in conditions, operations, and the environment will affect outcomes.
Programming	Writing computer programs for various purposes.

Ability	Ability Definitions
Problem Sensitivity	The ability to tell when something is wrong or is likely to go wrong. It does not involve solving the problem, only recognizing there is a problem.
Inductive Reasoning	The ability to combine pieces of information to form general rules or conclusions (includes finding a relationship among seemingly unrelated events).
Oral Comprehension	The ability to listen to and understand information and ideas presented through spoken words and sentences.
Oral Expression	The ability to communicate information and ideas in speaking so others will understand.
Speech Clarity	The ability to speak clearly so others can understand you.
Speech Recognition	The ability to identify and understand the speech of another person.
Deductive Reasoning	The ability to apply general rules to specific problems to produce answers that make sense.
Near Vision	The ability to see details at close range (within a few feet of the observer).
Written Comprehension	The ability to read and understand information and ideas presented in writing.
Control Precision	The ability to quickly and repeatedly adjust the controls of a machine or a vehicle to exact positions.
Information Ordering	The ability to arrange things or actions in a certain order or pattern according to a specific rule or set of rules (e.g., patterns of numbers, letters, words, pictures, mathematical operations).
Written Expression	The ability to communicate information and ideas in writing so others will understand.
Finger Dexterity	The ability to make precisely coordinated movements of the fingers of one or both hands to grasp, manipulate, or assemble very small objects.
Category Flexibility	The ability to generate or use different sets of rules for combining or grouping things in different ways.
Arm-Hand Steadiness	The ability to keep your hand and arm steady while moving your arm or while holding your arm and hand in one position.
Perceptual Speed	The ability to quickly and accurately compare similarities and differences among sets of letters, numbers, objects, pictures, or patterns. The things to be compared may be presented at the same time or one after the other. This ability also includes comparing a presented object with a remembered object.
Visualization	The ability to imagine how something will look after it is moved around or when its parts are moved or rearranged.
Flexibility of Closure	The ability to identify or detect a known pattern (a figure, object, word, or sound) that is hidden in other distracting material.
Fluency of Ideas	The ability to come up with a number of ideas about a topic (the number of ideas is important, not their quality, correctness, or creativity).
Selective Attention	The ability to concentrate on a task over a period of time without being distracted.
Originality	The ability to come up with unusual or clever ideas about a given topic or situation, or to develop creative ways to solve a problem.
Far Vision	The ability to see details at a distance.
Manual Dexterity	The ability to quickly move your hand, your hand together with your arm, or your two hands to grasp, manipulate, or assemble objects.
Visual Color Discrimination	The ability to match or detect differences between colors, including shades of color and brightness.
Depth Perception	The ability to judge which of several objects is closer or farther away from you, or to judge the distance between you and an object.
Number Facility	The ability to add, subtract, multiply, or divide quickly and correctly.
Time Sharing	The ability to shift back and forth between two or more activities or sources of information (such as speech, sounds, touch, or other sources).
Multilimb Coordination	The ability to coordinate two or more limbs (for example, two arms, two legs, or one leg and one arm) while sitting, standing, or lying down. It does not involve performing the activities while the whole body is in motion.
Auditory Attention	The ability to focus on a single source of sound in the presence of other distracting sounds.
Mathematical Reasoning	The ability to choose the right mathematical methods or formulas to solve a problem.
Speed of Closure	The ability to quickly make sense of, combine, and organize information into meaningful patterns.
Hearing Sensitivity	The ability to detect or tell the differences between sounds that vary in pitch and loudness.
Extent Flexibility	The ability to bend, stretch, twist, or reach with your body, arms, and/or legs.
Memorization	The ability to remember information such as words, numbers, pictures, and procedures.
Wrist-Finger Speed	The ability to make fast, simple, repeated movements of the fingers, hands, and wrists.
Reaction Time	The ability to quickly respond (with the hand, finger, or foot) to a signal (sound, light, picture) when it appears.

Response Orientation	The ability to choose quickly between two or more movements in response to two or more different signals (lights, sounds, pictures). It includes the speed with which the correct response is started with the hand, foot, or other body part.
Rate Control	The ability to time your movements or the movement of a piece of equipment in anticipation of changes in the speed and/or direction of a moving object or scene.
Static Strength	The ability to exert maximum muscle force to lift, push, pull, or carry objects.
Glare Sensitivity	The ability to see objects in the presence of glare or bright lighting.
Speed of Limb Movement	The ability to quickly move the arms and legs.
Trunk Strength	The ability to use your abdominal and lower back muscles to support part of the body repeatedly or continuously over time without 'giving out' or fatiguing.
Sound Localization	The ability to tell the direction from which a sound originated.
Gross Body Equilibrium	The ability to keep or regain your body balance or stay upright when in an unstable position.
Stamina	The ability to exert yourself physically over long periods of time without getting winded or out of breath.
Dynamic Strength	The ability to exert muscle force repeatedly or continuously over time. This involves muscular endurance and resistance to muscle fatigue.
Peripheral Vision	The ability to see objects or movement of objects to one's side when the eyes are looking ahead.
Gross Body Coordination	The ability to coordinate the movement of your arms, legs, and torso together when the whole body is in motion.
Night Vision	The ability to see under low light conditions.
Spatial Orientation	The ability to know your location in relation to the environment or to know where other objects are in relation to you.
Dynamic Flexibility	The ability to quickly and repeatedly bend, stretch, twist, or reach out with your body, arms, and/or legs.
Explosive Strength	The ability to use short bursts of muscle force to propel oneself (as in jumping or sprinting), or to throw an object.

Work_Activity	Work_Activity Definitions
Making Decisions and Solving Problems	Analyzing information and evaluating results to choose the best solution and solve problems.
Updating and Using Relevant Knowledge	Keeping up-to-date technically and applying new knowledge to your job.
Assisting and Caring for Others	Providing personal assistance, medical attention, emotional support, or other personal care to others such as coworkers, customers, or patients.
Getting Information	Observing, receiving, and otherwise obtaining information from all relevant sources.
Documenting/Recording Information	Entering, transcribing, recording, storing, or maintaining information in written or electronic/magnetic form.
Performing for or Working Directly with the Public	Performing for people or dealing directly with the public. This includes serving customers in restaurants and stores, and receiving clients or guests.
Thinking Creatively	Developing, designing, or creating new applications, ideas, relationships, systems, or products, including artistic contributions.
Guiding, Directing, and Motivating Subordinates	Providing guidance and direction to subordinates, including setting performance standards and monitoring performance.
Organizing, Planning, and Prioritizing Work	Developing specific goals and plans to prioritize, organize, and accomplish your work.
Processing Information	Compiling, coding, categorizing, calculating, tabulating, auditing, or verifying information or data.
Training and Teaching Others	Identifying the educational needs of others, developing formal educational or training programs or classes, and teaching or instructing others.
Communicating with Supervisors, Peers, or Subordin	Providing information to supervisors, co-workers, or subordinates by telephone, in written form, e-mail, or in person.
Monitor Processes, Materials, or Surroundings	Monitoring and reviewing information from materials, events, or the environment, to detect or assess problems.
Establishing and Maintaining Interpersonal Relatio	Developing constructive and cooperative working relationships with others, and maintaining them over time.
Identifying Objects, Actions, and Events	Identifying information by categorizing, estimating, recognizing differences or similarities, and detecting changes in circumstances or events.
Controlling Machines and Processes	Using either control mechanisms or direct physical activity to operate machines or processes (not including computers or vehicles).

Coaching and Developing Others	Identifying the developmental needs of others and coaching, mentoring, or otherwise helping others to improve their knowledge or skills.
Judging the Qualities of Things, Services, or Peop	Assessing the value, importance, or quality of things or people.
Evaluating Information to Determine Compliance wit	Using relevant information and individual judgment to determine whether events or processes comply with laws, regulations, or standards.
Interpreting the Meaning of Information for Others	Translating or explaining what information means and how it can be used.
Coordinating the Work and Activities of Others	Getting members of a group to work together to accomplish tasks.
Developing and Building Teams	Encouraging and building mutual trust, respect, and cooperation among team members.
Monitoring and Controlling Resources	Monitoring and controlling resources and overseeing the spending of money.
Developing Objectives and Strategies	Establishing long-range objectives and specifying the strategies and actions to achieve them.
Estimating the Quantifiable Characteristics of Pro	Estimating sizes, distances, and quantities; or determining time, costs, resources, or materials needed to perform a work activity.
Scheduling Work and Activities	Scheduling events, programs, and activities, as well as the work of others.
Inspecting Equipment, Structures, or Material	Inspecting equipment, structures, or materials to identify the cause of errors or other problems or defects.
Provide Consultation and Advice to Others	Providing guidance and expert advice to management or other groups on technical, systems-, or process-related topics.
Resolving Conflicts and Negotiating with Others	Handling complaints, settling disputes, and resolving grievances and conflicts, or otherwise negotiating with others.
Performing Administrative Activities	Performing day-to-day administrative tasks such as maintaining information files and processing paperwork.
Selling or Influencing Others	Convincing others to buy merchandise/goods or to otherwise change their minds or actions.
Analyzing Data or Information	Identifying the underlying principles, reasons, or facts of information by breaking down information or data into separate parts.
Handling and Moving Objects	Using hands and arms in handling, installing, positioning, and moving materials, and manipulating things.
Staffing Organizational Units	Recruiting, interviewing, selecting, hiring, and promoting employees in an organization.
Communicating with Persons Outside Organization	Communicating with people outside the organization, representing the organization to customers, the public, government, and other external sources. This information can be exchanged in person, in writing, or by telephone or e-mail.
Performing General Physical Activities	Performing physical activities that require considerable use of your arms and legs and moving your whole body, such as climbing, lifting, balancing, walking, stooping, and handling of materials.
Interacting With Computers	Using computers and computer systems (including hardware and software) to program, write software, set up functions, enter data, or process information.
Operating Vehicles, Mechanized Devices, or Equipme	Running, maneuvering, navigating, or driving vehicles or mechanized equipment, such as forklifts, passenger vehicles, aircraft, or water craft.
Repairing and Maintaining Mechanical Equipment	Servicing, repairing, adjusting, and testing machines, devices, moving parts, and equipment that operate primarily on the basis of mechanical (not electronic) principles.
Repairing and Maintaining Electronic Equipment	Servicing, repairing, calibrating, regulating, fine-tuning, or testing machines, devices, and equipment that operate primarily on the basis of electrical or electronic (not mechanical) principles.
Drafting, Laying Out, and Specifying Technical Dev	Providing documentation, detailed instructions, drawings, or specifications to tell others about how devices, parts, equipment, or structures are to be fabricated, constructed, assembled, modified, maintained, or used.

Work_Context	Work_Context Definitions
Spend Time Using Your Hands to Handle, Control, or	How much does this job require using your hands to handle, control, or feel objects, tools or controls?
Wear Common Protective or Safety Equipment such as	How much does this job require wearing common protective or safety equipment such as safety shoes, glasses, gloves, hard hats or life jackets?
Importance of Being Exact or Accurate	How important is being very exact or highly accurate in performing this job?
Physical Proximity	To what extent does this job require the worker to perform job tasks in close physical proximity to other people?

Freedom to Make Decisions	How much decision making freedom, without supervision, does the job offer?
Exposed to Disease or Infections	How often does this job require exposure to disease/infections?
Structured versus Unstructured Work	To what extent is this job structured for the worker, rather than allowing the worker to determine tasks, priorities, and goals?
Face-to-Face Discussions	How often do you have to have face-to-face discussions with individuals or teams in this job?
Frequency of Decision Making	How frequently is the worker required to make decisions that affect other people, the financial resources, and/or the image and reputation of the organization?
Responsible for Others' Health and Safety	How much responsibility is there for the health and safety of others in this job?
Work With Work Group or Team	How important is it to work with others in a group or team in this job?
Indoors, Environmentally Controlled	How often does this job require working indoors in environmentally controlled conditions?
Impact of Decisions on Co-workers or Company Resul	How do the decisions an employee makes impact the results of co-workers, clients or the company?
Exposed to Radiation	How often does this job require exposure to radiation?
Responsibility for Outcomes and Results	How responsible is the worker for work outcomes and results of other workers?
Deal With External Customers	How important is it to work with external customers or the public in this job?
Contact With Others	How much does this job require the worker to be in contact with others (face-to-face, by telephone, or otherwise) in order to perform it?
Spend Time Sitting	How much does this job require sitting?
Telephone	How often do you have telephone conversations in this job?
Exposed to Contaminants	How often does this job require working exposed to contaminants (such as pollutants, gases, dust or odors)?
Spend Time Making Repetitive Motions	How much does this job require making repetitive motions?
Consequence of Error	How serious would the result usually be if the worker made a mistake that was not readily correctable?
Letters and Memos	How often does the job require written letters and memos?
Importance of Repeating Same Tasks	How important is repeating the same physical activities (e.g., key entry) or mental activities (e.g., checking entries in a ledger) over and over, without stopping, to performing this job?
Spend Time Bending or Twisting the Body	How much does this job require bending or twisting your body?
Exposed to Hazardous Conditions	How often does this job require exposure to hazardous conditions?
Coordinate or Lead Others	How important is it to coordinate or lead others in accomplishing work activities in this job?
Time Pressure	How often does this job require the worker to meet strict deadlines?
Level of Competition	To what extent does this job require the worker to compete or to be aware of competitive pressures?
Frequency of Conflict Situations	How often are there conflict situations the employee has to face in this job?
Deal With Unpleasant or Angry People	How frequently does the worker have to deal with unpleasant, angry, or discourteous individuals as part of the job requirements?
Sounds, Noise Levels Are Distracting or Uncomforta	How often does this job require working exposed to sounds and noise levels that are distracting or uncomfortable?
Cramped Work Space, Awkward Positions	How often does this job require working in cramped work spaces that requires getting into awkward positions?
Extremely Bright or Inadequate Lighting	How often does this job require working in extremely bright or inadequate lighting conditions?
Wear Specialized Protective or Safety Equipment su	How much does this job require wearing specialized protective or safety equipment such as breathing apparatus, safety harness, full protection suits, or radiation protection?
Exposed to Hazardous Equipment	How often does this job require exposure to hazardous equipment?
Exposed to Minor Burns, Cuts, Bites, or Stings	How often does this job require exposure to minor burns, cuts, bites, or stings?
Electronic Mail	How often do you use electronic mail in this job?
Public Speaking	How often do you have to perform public speaking in this job?
Spend Time Standing	How much does this job require standing?
Pace Determined by Speed of Equipment	How important is it to this job that the pace is determined by the speed of equipment or machinery? (This does not refer to keeping busy at all times on this job.)
Deal With Physically Aggressive People	How frequently does this job require the worker to deal with physical aggression of violent individuals?
Degree of Automation	How automated is the job?

Spend Time Walking and Running	How much does this job require walking and running?
Exposed to Whole Body Vibration	How often does this job require exposure to whole body vibration (e.g., operate a jackhammer)?
Indoors, Not Environmentally Controlled	How often does this job require working indoors in non-controlled environmental conditions (e.g., warehouse without heat)?
Spend Time Kneeling, Crouching, Stooping, or Crawl	How much does this job require kneeling, crouching, stooping or crawling?
Very Hot or Cold Temperatures	How often does this job require working in very hot (above 90 F degrees) or very cold (below 32 F degrees) temperatures?
Outdoors, Exposed to Weather	How often does this job require working outdoors, exposed to all weather conditions?
Spend Time Climbing Ladders, Scaffolds, or Poles	How much does this job require climbing ladders, scaffolds, or poles?
Spend Time Keeping or Regaining Balance	How much does this job require keeping or regaining your balance?
Exposed to High Places	How often does this job require exposure to high places?
Outdoors, Under Cover	How often does this job require working outdoors, under cover (e.g., structure with roof but no walls)?
In an Open Vehicle or Equipment	How often does this job require working in an open vehicle or equipment (e.g., tractor)?
In an Enclosed Vehicle or Equipment	How often does this job require working in a closed vehicle or equipment (e.g., car)?

Job Zone Component	Job Zone Component Definitions
Title	Job Zone Five: Extensive Preparation Needed
Overall Experience	Extensive skill, knowledge, and experience are needed for these occupations. Many require more than five years of experience. For example, surgeons must complete four years of college and an additional five to seven years of specialized medical training to be able to do their job.
Job Training	Employees may need some on-the-job training, but most of these occupations assume that the person will already have the required skills, knowledge, work-related experience, and/or training.
Job Zone Examples	These occupations often involve coordinating, training, supervising, or managing the activities of others to accomplish goals. Very advanced communication and organizational skills are required. Examples include athletic trainers, lawyers, managing editors, phyicists, social psychologists, and surgeons.
SVP Range	(8.0 and above)
Education	A bachelor's degree is the minimum formal education required for these occupations. However, many also require graduate school. For example, they may require a master's degree, and some require a Ph.D., M.D., or J.D. (law degree).

Work_Styles	Work_Styles Definitions
Integrity	Job requires being honest and ethical.
Attention to Detail	Job requires being careful about detail and thorough in completing work tasks.
Dependability	Job requires being reliable, responsible, and dependable, and fulfilling obligations.
Cooperation	Job requires being pleasant with others on the job and displaying a good-natured, cooperative attitude.
Self Control	Job requires maintaining composure, keeping emotions in check, controlling anger, and avoiding aggressive behavior, even in very difficult situations.
Concern for Others	Job requires being sensitive to others' needs and feelings and being understanding and helpful on the job.
Independence	Job requires developing one's own ways of doing things, guiding oneself with little or no supervision, and depending on oneself to get things done.
Stress Tolerance	Job requires accepting criticism and dealing calmly and effectively with high stress situations.
Initiative	Job requires a willingness to take on responsibilities and challenges.
Leadership	Job requires a willingness to lead, take charge, and offer opinions and direction.
Innovation	Job requires creativity and alternative thinking to develop new ideas for and answers to work-related problems.
Adaptability/Flexibility	Job requires being open to change (positive or negative) and to considerable variety in the workplace.

Analytical Thinking	Job requires analyzing information and using logic to address work-related issues and problems.
Social Orientation	Job requires preferring to work with others rather than alone, and being personally connected with others on the job.
Persistence	Job requires persistence in the face of obstacles.
Achievement/Effort	Job requires establishing and maintaining personally challenging achievement goals and exerting effort toward mastering tasks.

29-2053.00 - Psychiatric Technicians

Care for mentally impaired or emotionally disturbed individuals, following physician instructions and hospital procedures. Monitor patients' physical and emotional well-being and report to medical staff. May participate in rehabilitation and treatment programs, help with personal hygiene, and administer oral medications and hypodermic injections.

Tasks

1) Encourage patients to develop work skills and to participate in social, recreational, and other therapeutic activities that enhance interpersonal skills and develop social relationships.

2) Restrain violent, potentially violent, or suicidal patients by verbal or physical means as required.

3) Develop and teach strategies to promote client wellness and independence.

4) Collaborate with and assist doctors, psychologists, and rehabilitation therapists working with mentally disturbed, or developmentally disabled patients in order to treat, rehabilitate, and return patients to the community.

5) Aid patients in performing tasks such as bathing and keeping beds, clothing and living areas clean.

6) Provide nursing, psychiatric and personal care to mentally ill, emotionally disturbed or mentally retarded patients.

7) Take and record measures of patients' physical condition, using devices such as thermometers and blood pressure gauges.

8) Lead prescribed individual or group therapy sessions as part of specific therapeutic procedures.

9) Interview new patients to complete admission forms, to assess their mental health status and to obtain their mental health and treatment history.

10) Administer oral medications and hypodermic injections, following physician's prescriptions and hospital procedures.

11) Issue medications from dispensary and maintain records in accordance with specified procedures.

12) Contact patients' relatives to arrange family conferences.

13) Monitor patients' physical and emotional well-being and report unusual behavior or physical ailments to medical staff.

Knowledge	Knowledge Definitions
Psychology	Knowledge of human behavior and performance; individual differences in ability, personality, and interests; learning and motivation; psychological research methods; and the assessment and treatment of behavioral and affective disorders.
English Language	Knowledge of the structure and content of the English language including the meaning and spelling of words, rules of composition, and grammar.
Therapy and Counseling	Knowledge of principles, methods, and procedures for diagnosis, treatment, and rehabilitation of physical and mental dysfunctions, and for career counseling and guidance.
Public Safety and Security	Knowledge of relevant equipment, policies, procedures, and strategies to promote effective local, state, or national security operations for the protection of people, data, property, and institutions.
Customer and Personal Service	Knowledge of principles and processes for providing customer and personal services. This includes customer needs assessment, meeting quality standards for services, and evaluation of customer satisfaction.
Education and Training	Knowledge of principles and methods for curriculum and training design, teaching and instruction for individuals and groups, and the measurement of training effects.

Medicine and Dentistry	Knowledge of the information and techniques needed to diagnose and treat human injuries, diseases, and deformities. This includes symptoms, treatment alternatives, drug properties and interactions, and preventive health-care measures.
Sociology and Anthropology	Knowledge of group behavior and dynamics, societal trends and influences, human migrations, ethnicity, cultures and their history and origins.
Mathematics	Knowledge of arithmetic, algebra, geometry, calculus, statistics, and their applications.
Transportation	Knowledge of principles and methods for moving people or goods by air, rail, sea, or road, including the relative costs and benefits.
Computers and Electronics	Knowledge of circuit boards, processors, chips, electronic equipment, and computer hardware and software, including applications and programming.
Philosophy and Theology	Knowledge of different philosophical systems and religions. This includes their basic principles, values, ethics, ways of thinking, customs, practices, and their impact on human culture.
Clerical	Knowledge of administrative and clerical procedures and systems such as word processing, managing files and records, stenography and transcription, designing forms, and other office procedures and terminology.
Telecommunications	Knowledge of transmission, broadcasting, switching, control, and operation of telecommunications systems.
Law and Government	Knowledge of laws, legal codes, court procedures, precedents, government regulations, executive orders, agency rules, and the democratic political process.
Foreign Language	Knowledge of the structure and content of a foreign (non-English) language including the meaning and spelling of words, rules of composition and grammar, and pronunciation.
Administration and Management	Knowledge of business and management principles involved in strategic planning, resource allocation, human resources modeling, leadership technique, production methods, and coordination of people and resources.
Chemistry	Knowledge of the chemical composition, structure, and properties of substances and of the chemical processes and transformations that they undergo. This includes uses of chemicals and their interactions, danger signs, production techniques, and disposal methods.
Communications and Media	Knowledge of media production, communication, and dissemination techniques and methods. This includes alternative ways to inform and entertain via written, oral, and visual media.
Personnel and Human Resources	Knowledge of principles and procedures for personnel recruitment, selection, training, compensation and benefits, labor relations and negotiation, and personnel information systems.
Biology	Knowledge of plant and animal organisms, their tissues, cells, functions, interdependencies, and interactions with each other and the environment.
Geography	Knowledge of principles and methods for describing the features of land, sea, and air masses, including their physical characteristics, locations, interrelationships, and distribution of plant, animal, and human life.
Fine Arts	Knowledge of the theory and techniques required to compose, produce, and perform works of music, dance, visual arts, drama, and sculpture.
History and Archeology	Knowledge of historical events and their causes, indicators, and effects on civilizations and cultures.
Economics and Accounting	Knowledge of economic and accounting principles and practices, the financial markets, banking and the analysis and reporting of financial data.
Food Production	Knowledge of techniques and equipment for planting, growing, and harvesting food products (both plant and animal) for consumption, including storage/handling techniques.
Production and Processing	Knowledge of raw materials, production processes, quality control, costs, and other techniques for maximizing the effective manufacture and distribution of goods.
Engineering and Technology	Knowledge of the practical application of engineering science and technology. This includes applying principles, techniques, procedures, and equipment to the design and production of various goods and services.
Mechanical	Knowledge of machines and tools, including their designs, uses, repair, and maintenance.

Physics	Knowledge and prediction of physical principles, laws, their interrelationships, and applications to understanding fluid, material, and atmospheric dynamics, and mechanical, electrical, atomic and sub- atomic structures and processes.
Design	Knowledge of design techniques, tools, and principles involved in production of precision technical plans, blueprints, drawings, and models.
Building and Construction	Knowledge of materials, methods, and the tools involved in the construction or repair of houses, buildings, or other structures such as highways and roads.
Sales and Marketing	Knowledge of principles and methods for showing, promoting, and selling products or services. This includes marketing strategy and tactics, product demonstration, sales techniques, and sales control systems.

Skills   Skills Definitions

Active Listening	Giving full attention to what other people are saying, taking time to understand the points being made, asking questions as appropriate, and not interrupting at inappropriate times.
Writing	Communicating effectively in writing as appropriate for the needs of the audience.
Reading Comprehension	Understanding written sentences and paragraphs in work related documents.
Social Perceptiveness	Being aware of others' reactions and understanding why they react as they do.
Speaking	Talking to others to convey information effectively.
Instructing	Teaching others how to do something.
Critical Thinking	Using logic and reasoning to identify the strengths and weaknesses of alternative solutions, conclusions or approaches to problems.
Service Orientation	Actively looking for ways to help people.
Monitoring	Monitoring/Assessing performance of yourself, other individuals, or organizations to make improvements or take corrective action.
Learning Strategies	Selecting and using training/instructional methods and procedures appropriate for the situation when learning or teaching new things.
Active Learning	Understanding the implications of new information for both current and future problem-solving and decision-making.
Negotiation	Bringing others together and trying to reconcile differences.
Coordination	Adjusting actions in relation to others' actions.
Persuasion	Persuading others to change their minds or behavior.
Judgment and Decision Making	Considering the relative costs and benefits of potential actions to choose the most appropriate one.
Time Management	Managing one's own time and the time of others.
Complex Problem Solving	Identifying complex problems and reviewing related information to develop and evaluate options and implement solutions.
Equipment Selection	Determining the kind of tools and equipment needed to do a job.
Science	Using scientific rules and methods to solve problems.
Mathematics	Using mathematics to solve problems.
Management of Personnel Resources	Motivating, developing, and directing people as they work, identifying the best people for the job.
Systems Evaluation	Identifying measures or indicators of system performance and the actions needed to improve or correct performance, relative to the goals of the system.
Troubleshooting	Determining causes of operating errors and deciding what to do about it.
Management of Material Resources	Obtaining and seeing to the appropriate use of equipment, facilities, and materials needed to do certain work.
Operation and Control	Controlling operations of equipment or systems.
Systems Analysis	Determining how a system should work and how changes in conditions, operations, and the environment will affect outcomes.
Quality Control Analysis	Conducting tests and inspections of products, services, or processes to evaluate quality or performance.
Technology Design	Generating or adapting equipment and technology to serve user needs.
Operation Monitoring	Watching gauges, dials, or other indicators to make sure a machine is working properly.
Management of Financial Resources	Determining how money will be spent to get the work done, and accounting for these expenditures.
Installation	Installing equipment, machines, wiring, or programs to meet specifications.
Operations Analysis	Analyzing needs and product requirements to create a design.
Programming	Writing computer programs for various purposes.

Repairing	Repairing machines or systems using the needed tools.
Equipment Maintenance	Performing routine maintenance on equipment and determining when and what kind of maintenance is needed.

Ability   Ability Definitions

Problem Sensitivity	The ability to tell when something is wrong or is likely to go wrong. It does not involve solving the problem, only recognizing there is a problem.
Oral Comprehension	The ability to listen to and understand information and ideas presented through spoken words and sentences.
Speech Recognition	The ability to identify and understand the speech of another person.
Oral Expression	The ability to communicate information and ideas in speaking so others will understand.
Speech Clarity	The ability to speak clearly so others can understand you.
Deductive Reasoning	The ability to apply general rules to specific problems to produce answers that make sense.
Information Ordering	The ability to arrange things or actions in a certain order or pattern according to a specific rule or set of rules (e.g., patterns of numbers, letters, words, pictures, mathematical operations).
Inductive Reasoning	The ability to combine pieces of information to form general rules or conclusions (includes finding a relationship among seemingly unrelated events).
Near Vision	The ability to see details at close range (within a few feet of the observer).
Written Expression	The ability to communicate information and ideas in writing so others will understand.
Written Comprehension	The ability to read and understand information and ideas presented in writing.
Category Flexibility	The ability to generate or use different sets of rules for combining or grouping things in different ways.
Selective Attention	The ability to concentrate on a task over a period of time without being distracted.
Originality	The ability to come up with unusual or clever ideas about a given topic or situation, or to develop creative ways to solve a problem.
Fluency of Ideas	The ability to come up with a number of ideas about a topic (the number of ideas is important, not their quality, correctness, or creativity).
Far Vision	The ability to see details at a distance.
Perceptual Speed	The ability to quickly and accurately compare similarities and differences among sets of letters, numbers, objects, pictures, or patterns. The things to be compared may be presented at the same time or one after the other. This ability also includes comparing a presented object with a remembered object.
Flexibility of Closure	The ability to identify or detect a known pattern (a figure, object, word, or sound) that is hidden in other distracting material.
Time Sharing	The ability to shift back and forth between two or more activities or sources of information (such as speech, sounds, touch, or other sources).
Visual Color Discrimination	The ability to match or detect differences between colors, including shades of color and brightness.
Hearing Sensitivity	The ability to detect or tell the differences between sounds that vary in pitch and loudness.
Stamina	The ability to exert yourself physically over long periods of time without getting winded or out of breath.
Speed of Closure	The ability to quickly make sense of, combine, and organize information into meaningful patterns.
Static Strength	The ability to exert maximum muscle force to lift, push, pull, or carry objects.
Finger Dexterity	The ability to make precisely coordinated movements of the fingers of one or both hands to grasp, manipulate, or assemble very small objects.
Gross Body Coordination	The ability to coordinate the movement of your arms, legs, and torso together when the whole body is in motion.
Trunk Strength	The ability to use your abdominal and lower back muscles to support part of the body repeatedly or continuously over time without 'giving out' or fatiguing.
Auditory Attention	The ability to focus on a single source of sound in the presence of other distracting sounds.
Arm-Hand Steadiness	The ability to keep your hand and arm steady while moving your arm or while holding your arm and hand in one position.
Response Orientation	The ability to choose quickly between two or more movements in response to two or more different signals (lights, sounds, pictures). It includes the speed with which the correct response is started with the hand, foot, or other body part.

Multilimb Coordination	The ability to coordinate two or more limbs (for example, two arms, two legs, or one leg and one arm) while sitting, standing, or lying down. It does not involve performing the activities while the whole body is in motion.	Monitor Processes, Materials, or Surroundings	Monitoring and reviewing information from materials, events, or the environment, to detect or assess problems.
Reaction Time	The ability to quickly respond (with the hand, finger, or foot) to a signal (sound, light, picture) when it appears.	Evaluating Information to Determine Compliance wit	Using relevant information and individual judgment to determine whether events or processes comply with laws, regulations, or standards.
Manual Dexterity	The ability to quickly move your hand, your hand together with your arm, or your two hands to grasp, manipulate, or assemble objects.	Organizing, Planning, and Prioritizing Work	Developing specific goals and plans to prioritize, organize, and accomplish your work.
Visualization	The ability to imagine how something will look after it is moved around or when its parts are moved or rearranged.	Developing Objectives and Strategies	Establishing long-range objectives and specifying the strategies and actions to achieve them.
Gross Body Equilibrium	The ability to keep or regain your body balance or stay upright when in an unstable position.	Coordinating the Work and Activities of Others	Getting members of a group to work together to accomplish tasks.
Extent Flexibility	The ability to bend, stretch, twist, or reach with your body, arms, and/or legs.	Guiding, Directing, and Motivating Subordinates	Providing guidance and direction to subordinates, including setting performance standards and monitoring performance.
Memorization	The ability to remember information such as words, numbers, pictures, and procedures.	Processing Information	Compiling, coding, categorizing, calculating, tabulating, auditing, or verifying information or data.
Dynamic Strength	The ability to exert muscle force repeatedly or continuously over time. This involves muscular endurance and resistance to muscle fatigue.	Scheduling Work and Activities	Scheduling events, programs, and activities, as well as the work of others.
Explosive Strength	The ability to use short bursts of muscle force to propel oneself (as in jumping or sprinting), or to throw an object.	Developing and Building Teams	Encouraging and building mutual trust, respect, and cooperation among team members.
Speed of Limb Movement	The ability to quickly move the arms and legs.	Training and Teaching Others	Identifying the educational needs of others, developing formal educational or training programs or classes, and teaching or instructing others.
Depth Perception	The ability to judge which of several objects is closer or farther away from you, or to judge the distance between you and an object.	Performing Administrative Activities	Performing day-to-day administrative tasks such as maintaining information files and processing paperwork.
Control Precision	The ability to quickly and repeatedly adjust the controls of a machine or a vehicle to exact positions.	Updating and Using Relevant Knowledge	Keeping up-to-date technically and applying new knowledge to your job.
Spatial Orientation	The ability to know your location in relation to the environment or to know where other objects are in relation to you.	Analyzing Data or Information	Identifying the underlying principles, reasons, or facts of information by breaking down information or data into separate parts.
Peripheral Vision	The ability to see objects or movement of objects to one's side when the eyes are looking ahead.	Judging the Qualities of Things, Services, or Peop	Assessing the value, importance, or quality of things or people.
Number Facility	The ability to add, subtract, multiply, or divide quickly and correctly.	Interpreting the Meaning of Information for Others	Translating or explaining what information means and how it can be used.
Glare Sensitivity	The ability to see objects in the presence of glare or bright lighting.	Thinking Creatively	Developing, designing, or creating new applications, ideas, relationships, systems, or products, including artistic contributions.
Night Vision	The ability to see under low light conditions.		
Rate Control	The ability to time your movements or the movement of a piece of equipment in anticipation of changes in the speed and/or direction of a moving object or scene.	Communicating with Persons Outside Organization	Communicating with people outside the organization, representing the organization to customers, the public, government, and other external sources. This information can be exchanged in person, in writing, or by telephone or e-mail.
Sound Localization	The ability to tell the direction from which a sound originated.		
Mathematical Reasoning	The ability to choose the right mathematical methods or formulas to solve a problem.	Operating Vehicles, Mechanized Devices, or Equipme	Running, maneuvering, navigating, or driving vehicles or mechanized equipment, such as forklifts, passenger vehicles, aircraft, or water craft.
Dynamic Flexibility	The ability to quickly and repeatedly bend, stretch, twist, or reach out with your body, arms, and/or legs.	Handling and Moving Objects	Using hands and arms in handling, installing, positioning, and moving materials, and manipulating things.
Wrist-Finger Speed	The ability to make fast, simple, repeated movements of the fingers, hands, and wrists.	Inspecting Equipment, Structures, or Material	Inspecting equipment, structures, or materials to identify the cause of errors or other problems or defects.

Work_Activity	**Work_Activity Definitions**	Provide Consultation and Advice to Others	Providing guidance and expert advice to management or other groups on technical, systems-, or process-related topics.
Documenting/Recording Information	Entering, transcribing, recording, storing, or maintaining information in written or electronic/magnetic form.	Interacting With Computers	Using computers and computer systems (including hardware and software) to program, write software, set up functions, enter data, or process information.
Communicating with Supervisors, Peers, or Subordin	Providing information to supervisors, co-workers, and subordinates by telephone, in written form, e-mail, or in person.	Performing for or Working Directly with the Public	Performing for people or dealing directly with the public. This includes serving customers in restaurants and stores, and receiving clients or guests.
Resolving Conflicts and Negotiating with Others	Handling complaints, settling disputes, and resolving grievances and conflicts, or otherwise negotiating with others.	Monitoring and Controlling Resources	Monitoring and controlling resources and overseeing the spending of money.
Assisting and Caring for Others	Providing personal assistance, medical attention, emotional support, or other personal care to others such as coworkers, customers, or patients.	Estimating the Quantifiable Characteristics of Pro	Estimating sizes, distances, and quantities; or determining time, costs, resources, or materials needed to perform a work activity.
Getting Information	Observing, receiving, and otherwise obtaining information from all relevant sources.	Selling or Influencing Others	Convincing others to buy merchandise/goods or to otherwise change their minds or actions.
Making Decisions and Solving Problems	Analyzing information and evaluating results to choose the best solution and solve problems.	Repairing and Maintaining Electronic Equipment	Servicing, repairing, calibrating, regulating, fine-tuning, or testing machines, devices, and equipment that operate primarily on the basis of electrical or electronic (not mechanical) principles.
Identifying Objects, Actions, and Events	Identifying information by categorizing, estimating, recognizing differences or similarities, and detecting changes in circumstances or events.		
Establishing and Maintaining Interpersonal Relatio	Developing constructive and cooperative working relationships with others, and maintaining them over time.	Drafting, Laying Out, and Specifying Technical Dev	Providing documentation, detailed instructions, drawings, or specifications to tell others about how devices, parts, equipment, or structures are to be fabricated, constructed, assembled, modified, or used.
Coaching and Developing Others	Identifying the developmental needs of others and coaching, mentoring, or otherwise helping them to improve their knowledge or skills.	Staffing Organizational Units	Recruiting, interviewing, selecting, hiring, and promoting employees in an organization.
Performing General Physical Activities	Performing physical activities that require considerable use of your arms and legs and moving your whole body, such as climbing, lifting, balancing, walking, stooping, and handling of materials.	Controlling Machines and Processes	Using either control mechanisms or direct physical activity to operate machines or processes (not including computers or vehicles).

Repairing and Maintaining Mechanical Equipment	Servicing, repairing, adjusting, and testing machines, devices, moving parts, and equipment that operate primarily on the basis of mechanical (not electronic) principles.

Work_Context	**Work_Context Definitions**
Contact With Others	How much does this job require the worker to be in contact with others (face-to-face, by telephone, or otherwise) in order to perform it?
Exposed to Disease or Infections	How often does this job require exposure to disease/infections?
Face-to-Face Discussions	How often do you have to have face-to-face discussions with individuals or teams in this job?
Deal With Unpleasant or Angry People	How frequently does the worker have to deal with unpleasant, angry, or discourteous individuals as part of the job requirements?
Work With Work Group or Team	How important is it to work with others in a group or team in this job?
Physical Proximity	To what extent does this job require the worker to perform job tasks in close physical proximity to other people?
Deal With Physically Aggressive People	How frequently does this job require the worker to deal with physical aggression of violent individuals?
Indoors, Environmentally Controlled	How often does this job require working indoors in environmentally controlled conditions?
Telephone	How often do you have telephone conversations in this job?
Time Pressure	How often does this job require the worker to meet strict deadlines?
Importance of Being Exact or Accurate	How important is being very exact or highly accurate in performing this job?
Responsible for Others' Health and Safety	How much responsibility is there for the health and safety of others in this job?
Wear Common Protective or Safety Equipment such as	How much does this job require wearing common protective or safety equipment such as safety shoes, glasses, gloves, hard hats or live jackets?
Freedom to Make Decisions	How much decision making freedom, without supervision, does the job offer?
Structured versus Unstructured Work	To what extent is this job structured for the worker, rather than allowing the worker to determine tasks, priorities, and goals?
Letters and Memos	How often does the job require written letters and memos?
Deal With External Customers	How important is it to work with external customers or the public in this job?
Frequency of Decision Making	How frequently is the worker required to make decisions that affect other people, the financial resources, and/or the image and reputation of the organization?
Spend Time Standing	How much does this job require standing?
Importance of Repeating Same Tasks	How important is repeating the same physical activities (e.g., key entry) or mental activities (e.g., checking entries in a ledger) over and over, without stopping, to performing this job?
Frequency of Conflict Situations	How often are there conflict situations the employee has to face in this job?
Exposed to Contaminants	How often does this job require working exposed to contaminants (such as pollutants, gases, dust or odors)?
Coordinate or Lead Others	How important is it to coordinate or lead others in accomplishing work activities in this job?
Spend Time Bending or Twisting the Body	How much does this job require bending or twisting your body?
Sounds, Noise Levels Are Distracting or Uncomforta	How often does this job require working exposed to sounds and noise levels that are distracting or uncomfortable?
Consequence of Error	How serious would the result usually be if the worker made a mistake that was not readily correctable?
Impact of Decisions on Co-workers or Company Resul	How do the decisions an employee makes impact the results of co-workers, clients or the company?
Spend Time Walking and Running	How much does this job require walking and running?
Responsibility for Outcomes and Results	How responsible is the worker for work outcomes and results of other workers?
Level of Competition	To what extent does this job require the worker to compete or to be aware of competitive pressures?
Spend Time Making Repetitive Motions	How much does this job require making repetitive motions?
Public Speaking	How often do you have to perform public speaking in this job?
Spend Time Sitting	How much does this job require sitting?
Spend Time Using Your Hands to Handle, Control, or	How much does this job require using your hands to handle, control, or feel objects, tools or controls?
Electronic Mail	How often do you use electronic mail in this job?
Degree of Automation	How automated is the job?

Spend Time Kneeling, Crouching, Stooping, or Crawl	How much does this job require kneeling, crouching, stooping or crawling?
In an Enclosed Vehicle or Equipment	How often does this job require working in a closed vehicle or equipment (e.g., car)?
Cramped Work Space, Awkward Positions	How often does this job require working in cramped work spaces that requires getting into awkward positions?
Very Hot or Cold Temperatures	How often does this job require working in very hot (above 90 F degrees) or very cold (below 32 F degrees) temperatures?
Spend Time Keeping or Regaining Balance	How much does this job require keeping or regaining your balance?
Extremely Bright or Inadequate Lighting	How often does this job require working in extremely bright or inadequate lighting conditions?
Exposed to Minor Burns, Cuts, Bites, or Stings	How often does this job require exposure to minor burns, cuts, bites, or stings?
Wear Specialized Protective or Safety Equipment su	How much does this job require wearing specialized protective or safety equipment such as breathing apparatus, safety harness, full protection suits, or radiation protection?
Indoors, Not Environmentally Controlled	How often does this job require working indoors in non-controlled environmental conditions (e.g., warehouse without heat)?
Outdoors, Exposed to Weather	How often does this job require working outdoors, exposed to all weather conditions?
Outdoors, Under Cover	How often does this job require working outdoors, under cover (e.g., structure with roof but no walls)?
Exposed to Hazardous Conditions	How often does this job require exposure to hazardous conditions?
Exposed to Radiation	How often does this job require exposure to radiation?
In an Open Vehicle or Equipment	How often does this job require working in an open vehicle or equipment (e.g., tractor)?
Exposed to Hazardous Equipment	How often does this job require exposure to hazardous equipment?
Exposed to High Places	How often does this job require exposure to high places?
Exposed to Whole Body Vibration	How often does this job require exposure to whole body vibration (e.g., operate a jackhammer)?
Spend Time Climbing Ladders, Scaffolds, or Poles	How much does this job require climbing ladders, scaffolds, or poles?
Pace Determined by Speed of Equipment	How important is it to this job that the pace is determined by the speed of equipment or machinery? (This does not refer to keeping busy at all times on this job.)

Job Zone Component	**Job Zone Component Definitions**
Title	Job Zone Three: Medium Preparation Needed
Overall Experience	Previous work-related skill, knowledge, or experience is required for these occupations. For example, an electrician must have completed three or four years of apprenticeship or several years of vocational training, and often must have passed a licensing exam, in order to perform the job.
Job Training	Employees in these occupations usually need one or two years of training involving both on-the-job experience and informal training with experienced workers.
Job Zone Examples	These occupations usually involve using communication and organizational skills to coordinate, supervise, manage, or train others to accomplish goals. Examples include dental assistants, electricians, fish and game wardens, legal secretaries, personnel recruiters, and recreation workers.
SVP Range	(6.0 to < 7.0)
Education	Most occupations in this zone require training in vocational schools, related on-the-job experience, or an associate's degree. Some may require a bachelor's degree.

Work_Styles	**Work_Styles Definitions**
Dependability	Job requires being reliable, responsible, and dependable, and fulfilling obligations.
Cooperation	Job requires being pleasant with others on the job and displaying a good-natured, cooperative attitude.
Concern for Others	Job requires being sensitive to others' needs and feelings and being understanding and helpful on the job.
Initiative	Job requires a willingness to take on responsibilities and challenges.
Self Control	Job requires maintaining composure, keeping emotions in check, controlling anger, and avoiding aggressive behavior, even in very difficult situations.

Leadership	Job requires a willingness to lead, take charge, and offer opinions and direction.
Adaptability/Flexibility	Job requires being open to change (positive or negative) and to considerable variety in the workplace.
Stress Tolerance	Job requires accepting criticism and dealing calmly and effectively with high stress situations.
Integrity	Job requires being honest and ethical.
Social Orientation	Job requires preferring to work with others rather than alone, and being personally connected with others on the job.
Attention to Detail	Job requires being careful about detail and thorough in completing work tasks.
Persistence	Job requires persistence in the face of obstacles.
Independence	Job requires developing one's own ways of doing things, guiding oneself with little or no supervision, and depending on oneself to get things done.
Analytical Thinking	Job requires analyzing information and using logic to address work-related issues and problems.
Achievement/Effort	Job requires establishing and maintaining personally challenging achievement goals and exerting effort toward mastering tasks.
Innovation	Job requires creativity and alternative thinking to develop new ideas for and answers to work-related problems.

29-9011.00 - Occupational Health and Safety Specialists

Review, evaluate, and analyze work environments and design programs and procedures to control, eliminate, and prevent disease or injury caused by chemical, physical, and biological agents or ergonomic factors. May conduct inspections and enforce adherence to laws and regulations governing the health and safety of individuals. May be employed in the public or private sector.

Tasks

1) Develop and maintain hygiene programs such as noise surveys, continuous atmosphere monitoring, ventilation surveys, and asbestos management plans.

2) Coordinate right-to-know programs regarding hazardous chemicals and other substances.

3) Prepare hazardous, radioactive, and mixed waste samples for transportation and storage by treating, compacting, packaging, and labeling them.

4) Conduct safety training and education programs, and demonstrate the use of safety equipment.

5) Conduct audits at hazardous waste sites or industrial sites, and participate in hazardous waste site investigations.

6) Collect samples of hazardous materials, or arrange for sample collection.

7) Order suspension of activities that pose threats to workers' health and safety.

8) Inspect and evaluate workplace environments, equipment, and practices, in order to ensure compliance with safety standards and government regulations.

9) Collect samples of dust, gases, vapors, and other potentially toxic materials for analysis.

10) Maintain and update emergency response plans and procedures.

11) Investigate accidents to identify causes and to determine how such accidents might be prevented in the future.

12) Investigate health-related complaints, and inspect facilities to ensure that they comply with public health legislation and regulations.

13) Investigate the adequacy of ventilation, exhaust equipment, lighting, and other conditions that could affect employee health, comfort, or performance.

14) Collaborate with engineers and physicians to institute control and remedial measures for hazardous and potentially hazardous conditions or equipment.

15) Perform laboratory analyses and physical inspections of samples in order to detect disease or to assess purity or cleanliness.

16) Maintain inventories of hazardous materials and hazardous wastes, using waste tracking systems to ensure that materials are handled properly.

17) Provide new-employee health and safety orientations, and develop materials for these presentations.

18) Recommend measures to help protect workers from potentially hazardous work methods, processes, or materials.

19) Inspect specified areas to ensure the presence of fire prevention equipment, safety equipment, and first-aid supplies.

29-9012.00 - Occupational Health and Safety Technicians

Collect data on work environments for analysis by occupational health and safety specialists. Implement and conduct evaluation of programs designed to limit chemical, physical, biological, and ergonomic risks to workers.

Tasks

1) Prepare and calibrate equipment used to collect and analyze samples.

2) Plan emergency response drills.

3) Maintain logbooks of daily activities, including areas visited and activities performed.

4) Maintain all required records and documentation.

5) Help direct rescue and firefighting operations in the event of a fire or an explosion.

6) Evaluate situations where a worker has refused to work on the grounds that danger or potential harm exists, and determine how such situations should be handled.

7) Educate the public about health issues, and enforce health legislation in order to prevent disease, to promote health, and to help people understand health protection procedures and regulations.

8) Supply, operate, and maintain personal protective equipment.

9) Prepare and review specifications and orders for the purchase of safety equipment, ensuring that proper features are present and that items conform to health and safety standards.

10) Confer with school and state authorities and community groups to develop health standards and programs.

11) Verify that safety equipment such as hearing protection and respirators is available to employees, and monitor their use of such equipment to ensure proper fit and use.

12) Test workplaces for environmental hazards such as exposure to radiation, chemical and biological hazards, and excessive noise.

13) Report the results of environmental contaminant analyses, and recommend corrective measures to be applied.

14) Review physicians' reports, and conduct worker studies in order to determine whether specific instances of disease or illness are job-related.

15) Provide consultation to organizations or agencies on the application of safety principles, practices, and techniques in the workplace.

16) Prepare documents to be used in legal proceedings, testifying in such proceedings when necessary.

17) Conduct fire drills, and inspect fire suppression systems and portable fire systems to ensure that they are in working order.

18) Conduct interviews to obtain information and evidence regarding communicable diseases or violations of health and sanitation regulations.

19) Review records and reports concerning laboratory results, staffing, floor plans, fire inspections, and sanitation in order to gather information for the development and enforcement of safety activities.

33-2021.02 - Fire Investigators

Conduct investigations to determine causes of fires and explosions.

Tasks

1) Analyze evidence and other information to determine probable cause of fire or explosion.

2) Examine fire sites and collect evidence such as glass, metal fragments, charred wood, and accelerant residue for use in determining the cause of a fire.

3) Package collected pieces of evidence in securely closed containers such as bags, crates, or boxes, in order to protect them.

4) Prepare and maintain reports of investigation results, and records of convicted arsonists and arson suspects.

5) Instruct children about the dangers of fire.

6) Testify in court cases involving fires, suspected arson, and false alarms.

7) Subpoena and interview witnesses, property owners, and building occupants to obtain information and sworn testimony.

8) Swear out warrants, and arrest and process suspected arsonists.

9) Test sites and materials to establish facts, such as burn patterns and flash points of materials, using test equipment.

10) Conduct internal investigation to determine negligence and violation of laws and regulations by fire department employees.

11) Dust evidence or portions of fire scenes for latent fingerprints.

Knowledge	Knowledge Definitions
Public Safety and Security	Knowledge of relevant equipment, policies, procedures, and strategies to promote effective local, state, or national security operations for the protection of people, data, property, and institutions.
Law and Government	Knowledge of laws, legal codes, court procedures, precedents, government regulations, executive orders, agency rules, and the democratic political process.
Building and Construction	Knowledge of materials, methods, and the tools involved in the construction or repair of houses, buildings, or other structures such as highways and roads.
English Language	Knowledge of the structure and content of the English language including the meaning and spelling of words, rules of composition, and grammar.
Mechanical	Knowledge of machines and tools, including their designs, uses, repair, and maintenance.
Psychology	Knowledge of human behavior and performance; individual differences in ability, personality, and interests; learning and motivation; psychological research methods; and the assessment and treatment of behavioral and affective disorders.
Clerical	Knowledge of administrative and clerical procedures and systems such as word processing, managing files and records, stenography and transcription, designing forms, and other office procedures and terminology.
Administration and Management	Knowledge of business and management principles involved in strategic planning, resource allocation, human resources modeling, leadership technique, production methods, and coordination of people and resources.
Customer and Personal Service	Knowledge of principles and processes for providing customer and personal services. This includes customer needs assessment, meeting quality standards for services, and evaluation of customer satisfaction.
Chemistry	Knowledge of the chemical composition, structure, and properties of substances and of the chemical processes and transformations that they undergo. This includes uses of chemicals and their interactions, danger signs, production techniques, and disposal methods.
Education and Training	Knowledge of principles and methods for curriculum and training design, teaching and instruction for individuals and groups, and the measurement of training effects.
Physics	Knowledge and prediction of physical principles, laws, their interrelationships, and applications to understanding fluid, material, and atmospheric dynamics, and mechanical, electrical, atomic and sub- atomic structures and processes.
Personnel and Human Resources	Knowledge of principles and procedures for personnel recruitment, selection, training, compensation and benefits, labor relations and negotiation, and personnel information systems.
Mathematics	Knowledge of arithmetic, algebra, geometry, calculus, statistics, and their applications.
Engineering and Technology	Knowledge of the practical application of engineering science and technology. This includes applying principles, techniques, procedures, and equipment to the design and production of various goods and services.
Sociology and Anthropology	Knowledge of group behavior and dynamics, societal trends and influences, human migrations, ethnicity, cultures and their history and origins.
Communications and Media	Knowledge of media production, communication, and dissemination techniques and methods. This includes alternative ways to inform and entertain via written, oral, and visual media.
Computers and Electronics	Knowledge of circuit boards, processors, chips, electronic equipment, and computer hardware and software, including applications and programming.
Design	Knowledge of design techniques, tools, and principles involved in production of precision technical plans, blueprints, drawings, and models.
Economics and Accounting	Knowledge of economic and accounting principles and practices, the financial markets, banking and the analysis and reporting of financial data.
Transportation	Knowledge of principles and methods for moving people or goods by air, rail, sea, or road, including the relative costs and benefits.
Philosophy and Theology	Knowledge of different philosophical systems and religions. This includes their basic principles, values, ethics, ways of thinking, customs, practices, and their impact on human culture.
Therapy and Counseling	Knowledge of principles, methods, and procedures for diagnosis, treatment, and rehabilitation of physical and mental dysfunctions, and for career counseling and guidance.
Telecommunications	Knowledge of transmission, broadcasting, switching, control, and operation of telecommunications systems.
Sales and Marketing	Knowledge of principles and methods for showing, promoting, and selling products or services. This includes marketing strategy and tactics, product demonstration, sales techniques, and sales control systems.
Geography	Knowledge of principles and methods for describing the features of land, sea, and air masses, including their physical characteristics, locations, interrelationships, and distribution of plant, animal, and human life.
Production and Processing	Knowledge of raw materials, production processes, quality control, costs, and other techniques for maximizing the effective manufacture and distribution of goods.
Medicine and Dentistry	Knowledge of the information and techniques needed to diagnose and treat human injuries, diseases, and deformities. This includes symptoms, treatment alternatives, drug properties and interactions, and preventive health-care measures.
Foreign Language	Knowledge of the structure and content of a foreign (non-English) language including the meaning and spelling of words, rules of composition and grammar, and pronunciation.
Biology	Knowledge of plant and animal organisms, their tissues, cells, functions, interdependencies, and interactions with each other and the environment.
History and Archeology	Knowledge of historical events and their causes, indicators, and effects on civilizations and cultures.
Food Production	Knowledge of techniques and equipment for planting, growing, and harvesting food products (both plant and animal) for consumption, including storage/handling techniques.
Fine Arts	Knowledge of the theory and techniques required to compose, produce, and perform works of music, dance, visual arts, drama, and sculpture.

Skills	Skills Definitions
Active Listening	Giving full attention to what other people are saying, taking time to understand the points being made, asking questions as appropriate, and not interrupting at inappropriate times.
Judgment and Decision Making	Considering the relative costs and benefits of potential actions to choose the most appropriate one.
Critical Thinking	Using logic and reasoning to identify the strengths and weaknesses of alternative solutions, conclusions or approaches to problems.
Writing	Communicating effectively in writing as appropriate for the needs of the audience.
Instructing	Teaching others how to do something.
Equipment Selection	Determining the kind of tools and equipment needed to do a job.
Complex Problem Solving	Identifying complex problems and reviewing related information to develop and evaluate options and implement solutions.
Speaking	Talking to others to convey information effectively.
Active Learning	Understanding the implications of new information for both current and future problem-solving and decision-making.
Reading Comprehension	Understanding written sentences and paragraphs in work related documents.
Coordination	Adjusting actions in relation to others' actions.
Social Perceptiveness	Being aware of others' reactions and understanding why they react as they do.
Monitoring	Monitoring/Assessing performance of yourself, other individuals, or organizations to make improvements or take corrective action.
Equipment Maintenance	Performing routine maintenance on equipment and determining when and what kind of maintenance is needed.
Management of Personnel Resources	Motivating, developing, and directing people as they work, identifying the best people for the job.

Time Management	Managing one's own time and the time of others.
Science	Using scientific rules and methods to solve problems.
Service Orientation	Actively looking for ways to help people.
Negotiation	Bringing others together and trying to reconcile differences.
Learning Strategies	Selecting and using training/instructional methods and procedures appropriate for the situation when learning or teaching new things.
Operation and Control	Controlling operations of equipment or systems.
Persuasion	Persuading others to change their minds or behavior.
Troubleshooting	Determining causes of operating errors and deciding what to do about it.
Operations Analysis	Analyzing needs and product requirements to create a design.
Systems Analysis	Determining how a system should work and how changes in conditions, operations, and the environment will affect outcomes.
Systems Evaluation	Identifying measures or indicators of system performance and the actions needed to improve or correct performance, relative to the goals of the system.
Operation Monitoring	Watching gauges, dials, or other indicators to make sure a machine is working properly.
Technology Design	Generating or adapting equipment and technology to serve user needs.
Mathematics	Using mathematics to solve problems.
Management of Material Resources	Obtaining and seeing to the appropriate use of equipment, facilities, and materials needed to do certain work.
Repairing	Repairing machines or systems using the needed tools.
Management of Financial Resources	Determining how money will be spent to get the work done, and accounting for these expenditures.
Installation	Installing equipment, machines, wiring, or programs to meet specifications.
Quality Control Analysis	Conducting tests and inspections of products, services, or processes to evaluate quality or performance.
Programming	Writing computer programs for various purposes.

Ability	Ability Definitions
Inductive Reasoning	The ability to combine pieces of information to form general rules or conclusions (includes finding a relationship among seemingly unrelated events).
Deductive Reasoning	The ability to apply general rules to specific problems to produce answers that make sense.
Problem Sensitivity	The ability to tell when something is wrong or is likely to go wrong. It does not involve solving the problem, only recognizing there is a problem.
Flexibility of Closure	The ability to identify or detect a known pattern (a figure, object, word, or sound) that is hidden in other distracting material.
Near Vision	The ability to see details at close range (within a few feet of the observer).
Information Ordering	The ability to arrange things or actions in a certain order or pattern according to a specific rule or set of rules (e.g., patterns of numbers, letters, words, pictures, mathematical operations).
Oral Comprehension	The ability to listen to and understand information and ideas presented through spoken words and sentences.
Written Comprehension	The ability to read and understand information and ideas presented in writing.
Oral Expression	The ability to communicate information and ideas in speaking so others will understand.
Speech Clarity	The ability to speak clearly so others can understand you.
Written Expression	The ability to communicate information and ideas in writing so others will understand.
Speech Recognition	The ability to identify and understand the speech of another person.
Category Flexibility	The ability to generate or use different sets of rules for combining or grouping things in different ways.
Fluency of Ideas	The ability to come up with a number of ideas about a topic (the number of ideas is important, not their quality, correctness, or creativity).
Visualization	The ability to imagine how something will look after it is moved around or when its parts are moved or rearranged.
Far Vision	The ability to see details at a distance.
Originality	The ability to come up with unusual or clever ideas about a given topic or situation, or to develop creative ways to solve a problem.
Selective Attention	The ability to concentrate on a task over a period of time without being distracted.
Control Precision	The ability to quickly and repeatedly adjust the controls of a machine or a vehicle to exact positions.

Finger Dexterity	The ability to make precisely coordinated movements of the fingers of one or both hands to grasp, manipulate, or assemble very small objects.
Manual Dexterity	The ability to quickly move your hand, your hand together with your arm, or your two hands to grasp, manipulate, or assemble objects.
Arm-Hand Steadiness	The ability to keep your hand and arm steady while moving your arm or while holding your arm and hand in one position.
Multilimb Coordination	The ability to coordinate two or more limbs (for example, two arms, two legs, or one leg and one arm) while sitting, standing, or lying down. It does not involve performing the activities while the whole body is in motion.
Time Sharing	The ability to shift back and forth between two or more activities or sources of information (such as speech, sounds, touch, or other sources).
Static Strength	The ability to exert maximum muscle force to lift, push, pull, or carry objects.
Speed of Closure	The ability to quickly make sense of, combine, and organize information into meaningful patterns.
Perceptual Speed	The ability to quickly and accurately compare similarities and differences among sets of letters, numbers, objects, pictures, or patterns. The things to be compared may be presented at the same time or one after the other. This ability also includes comparing a presented object with a remembered object.
Depth Perception	The ability to judge which of several objects is closer or farther away from you, or to judge the distance between you and an object.
Reaction Time	The ability to quickly respond (with the hand, finger, or foot) to a signal (sound, light, picture) when it appears.
Auditory Attention	The ability to focus on a single source of sound in the presence of other distracting sounds.
Visual Color Discrimination	The ability to match or detect differences between colors, including shades of color and brightness.
Trunk Strength	The ability to use your abdominal and lower back muscles to support part of the body repeatedly or continuously over time without 'giving out' or fatiguing.
Extent Flexibility	The ability to bend, stretch, twist, or reach with your body, arms, and/or legs.
Hearing Sensitivity	The ability to detect or tell the differences between sounds that vary in pitch and loudness.
Rate Control	The ability to time your movements or the movement of a piece of equipment in anticipation of changes in the speed and/or direction of a moving object or scene.
Mathematical Reasoning	The ability to choose the right mathematical methods or formulas to solve a problem.
Dynamic Strength	The ability to exert muscle force repeatedly or continuously over time. This involves muscular endurance and resistance to muscle fatigue.
Number Facility	The ability to add, subtract, multiply, or divide quickly and correctly.
Spatial Orientation	The ability to know your location in relation to the environment or to know where other objects are in relation to you.
Glare Sensitivity	The ability to see objects in the presence of glare or bright lighting.
Stamina	The ability to exert yourself physically over long periods of time without getting winded or out of breath.
Memorization	The ability to remember information such as words, numbers, pictures, and procedures.
Response Orientation	The ability to choose quickly between two or more movements in response to two or more different signals (lights, sounds, pictures). It includes the speed with which the correct response is started with the hand, foot, or other body part.
Night Vision	The ability to see under low light conditions.
Gross Body Coordination	The ability to coordinate the movement of your arms, legs, and torso together when the whole body is in motion.
Peripheral Vision	The ability to see objects or movement of objects to one's side when the eyes are looking ahead.
Gross Body Equilibrium	The ability to keep or regain your body balance or stay upright when in an unstable position.
Speed of Limb Movement	The ability to quickly move the arms and legs.
Sound Localization	The ability to tell the direction from which a sound originated.
Wrist-Finger Speed	The ability to make fast, simple, repeated movements of the fingers, hands, and wrists.
Dynamic Flexibility	The ability to quickly and repeatedly bend, stretch, twist, or reach out with your body, arms, and/or legs.
Explosive Strength	The ability to use short bursts of muscle force to propel oneself (as in jumping or sprinting), or to throw an object.

Work_Activity	Work_Activity Definitions
Identifying Objects, Actions, and Events	Identifying information by categorizing, estimating, recognizing differences or similarities, and detecting changes in circumstances or events.
Getting Information	Observing, receiving, and otherwise obtaining information from all relevant sources.
Inspecting Equipment, Structures, or Material	Inspecting equipment, structures, or materials to identify the cause of errors or other problems or defects.
Documenting/Recording Information	Entering, transcribing, recording, storing, or maintaining information in written or electronic/magnetic form.
Performing for or Working Directly with the Public	Performing for people or dealing directly with the public. This includes serving customers in restaurants and stores, and receiving clients or guests.
Updating and Using Relevant Knowledge	Keeping up to date technically and applying new knowledge to your job.
Making Decisions and Solving Problems	Analyzing information and evaluating results to choose the best solution and solve problems.
Communicating with Persons Outside Organization	Communicating with people outside the organization, representing the organization to customers, the public, government, and other external sources. This information can be exchanged in person, in writing, or by telephone or e-mail.
Monitor Processes, Materials, or Surroundings	Monitoring and reviewing information from materials, events, or the environment, to detect or assess problems.
Processing Information	Compiling, coding, categorizing, calculating, tabulating, auditing, or verifying information or data.
Evaluating Information to Determine Compliance wit	Using relevant information and individual judgment to determine whether events or processes comply with laws, regulations, or standards.
Interpreting the Meaning of Information for Others	Translating or explaining what information means and how it can be used.
Communicating with Supervisors, Peers, or Subordin	Providing information to supervisors, co-workers, and subordinates by telephone, in written form, e-mail, or in person.
Analyzing Data or Information	Identifying the underlying principles, reasons, or facts of information by breaking down information or data into separate parts.
Establishing and Maintaining Interpersonal Relatio	Developing constructive and cooperative working relationships with others, and maintaining them over time.
Operating Vehicles, Mechanized Devices, or Equipme	Running, maneuvering, navigating, or driving vehicles or mechanized equipment, such as forklifts, passenger vehicles, aircraft, or water craft.
Performing General Physical Activities	Performing physical activities that require considerable use of your arms and legs and moving your whole body, such as climbing, lifting, balancing, walking, stooping, and handling of materials.
Handling and Moving Objects	Using hands and arms in handling, installing, positioning, and moving materials, and manipulating things.
Estimating the Quantifiable Characteristics of Pro	Estimating sizes, distances, and quantities; or determining time, costs, resources, or materials needed to perform a work activity.
Judging the Qualities of Things, Services, or Peop	Assessing the value, importance, or quality of things or people.
Performing Administrative Activities	Performing day-to-day administrative tasks such as maintaining information files and processing paperwork.
Thinking Creatively	Developing, designing, or creating new applications, ideas, relationships, systems, or products, including artistic contributions.
Training and Teaching Others	Identifying the educational needs of others, developing formal educational or training programs or classes, and teaching or instructing others.
Provide Consultation and Advice to Others	Providing guidance and expert advice to management or other groups on technical, systems-, or process-related topics.
Organizing, Planning, and Prioritizing Work	Developing specific goals and plans to prioritize, organize, and accomplish your work.
Interacting With Computers	Using computers and computer systems (including hardware and software) to program, write software, set up functions, enter data, or process information.
Developing Objectives and Strategies	Establishing long-range objectives and specifying the strategies and actions to achieve them.
Scheduling Work and Activities	Scheduling events, programs, and activities, as well as the work of others.
Coordinating the Work and Activities of Others	Getting members of a group to work together to accomplish tasks.
Assisting and Caring for Others	Providing personal assistance, medical attention, emotional support, or other personal care to others such as coworkers, customers, or patients.
Guiding, Directing, and Motivating Subordinates	Providing guidance and direction to subordinates, including setting performance standards and monitoring performance.
Developing and Building Teams	Encouraging and building mutual trust, respect, and cooperation among team members.
Resolving Conflicts and Negotiating with Others	Handling complaints, settling disputes, and resolving grievances and conflicts, or otherwise negotiating with others.
Controlling Machines and Processes	Using either control mechanisms or direct physical activity to operate machines or processes (not including computers or vehicles).
Monitoring and Controlling Resources	Monitoring and controlling resources and overseeing the spending of money.
Coaching and Developing Others	Identifying the developmental needs of others and coaching, mentoring, or otherwise helping others to improve their knowledge or skills.
Drafting, Laying Out, and Specifying Technical Dev	Providing documentation, detailed instructions, drawings, or specifications to tell others about how devices, parts, equipment, or structures are to be fabricated, constructed, assembled, modified, maintained, or used.
Selling or Influencing Others	Convincing others to buy merchandise/goods or to otherwise change their minds or actions.
Repairing and Maintaining Mechanical Equipment	Servicing, repairing, adjusting, and testing machines, devices, moving parts, and equipment that operate primarily on the basis of mechanical (not electronic) principles.
Staffing Organizational Units	Recruiting, interviewing, selecting, hiring, and promoting employees in an organization.
Repairing and Maintaining Electronic Equipment	Servicing, repairing, calibrating, regulating, fine-tuning, or testing machines, devices, and equipment that operate primarily on the basis of electrical or electronic (not mechanical) principles.

Work_Context	Work_Context Definitions
Freedom to Make Decisions	How much decision making freedom, without supervision, does the job offer?
Structured versus Unstructured Work	To what extent is this job structured for the worker, rather than allowing the worker to determine tasks, priorities, and goals?
Telephone	How often do you have telephone conversations in this job?
Face-to-Face Discussions	How often do you have to have face-to-face discussions with individuals or teams in this job?
Contact With Others	How much does this job require the worker to be in contact with others (face-to-face, by telephone, or otherwise) in order to perform it?
Electronic Mail	How often do you use electronic mail in this job?
Work With Work Group or Team	How important is it to work with others in a group or team in this job?
Importance of Being Exact or Accurate	How important is being very exact or highly accurate in performing this job?
Time Pressure	How often does this job require the worker to meet strict deadlines?
Letters and Memos	How often does the job require written letters and memos?
Responsible for Others' Health and Safety	How much responsibility is there for the health and safety of others in this job?
Coordinate or Lead Others	How important is it to coordinate or lead others in accomplishing work activities in this job?
Exposed to Hazardous Equipment	How often does this job require exposure to hazardous equipment?
Exposed to Contaminants	How often does this job require working exposed to contaminants (such as pollutants, gases, dust or odors)?
Sounds, Noise Levels Are Distracting or Uncomforta	How often does this job require working exposed to sounds and noise levels that are distracting or uncomfortable?
Indoors, Environmentally Controlled	How often does this job require working indoors in environmentally controlled conditions?
Responsibility for Outcomes and Results	How responsible is the worker for work outcomes and results of other workers?
Impact of Decisions on Co-workers or Company Resul	How do the decisions an employee makes impact the results of co-workers, clients or the company?
Deal With External Customers	How important is it to work with external customers or the public in this job?
Exposed to Hazardous Conditions	How often does this job require exposure to hazardous conditions?
Frequency of Decision Making	How frequently is the worker required to make decisions that affect other people, the financial resources, and/or the image and reputation of the organization?

In an Enclosed Vehicle or Equipment	How often does this job require working in a closed vehicle or equipment (e.g., car)?
Physical Proximity	To what extent does this job require the worker to perform job tasks in close physical proximity to other people?
Spend Time Using Your Hands to Handle, Control, or	How much does this job require using your hands to handle, control, or feel objects, tools or controls?
Wear Common Protective or Safety Equipment such as	How much does this job require wearing common protective or safety equipment such as safety shoes, glasses, gloves, hard hats or live jackets?
Importance of Repeating Same Tasks	How important is repeating the same physical activities (e.g., key entry) or mental activities (e.g., checking entries in a ledger) over and over, without stopping, to performing this job?
Frequency of Conflict Situations	How often are there conflict situations the employee has to face in this job?
Outdoors, Exposed to Weather	How often does this job require working outdoors, exposed to all weather conditions?
Consequence of Error	How serious would the result usually be if the worker made a mistake that was not readily correctable?
Spend Time Standing	How much does this job require standing?
Level of Competition	To what extent does this job require the worker to compete or to be aware of competitive pressures?
Exposed to Minor Burns, Cuts, Bites, or Stings	How often does this job require exposure to minor burns, cuts, bites, or stings?
Indoors, Not Environmentally Controlled	How often does this job require working indoors in non-controlled environmental conditions (e.g., warehouse without heat)?
Deal With Unpleasant or Angry People	How frequently does the worker have to deal with unpleasant, angry, or discourteous individuals as part of the job requirements?
Extremely Bright or Inadequate Lighting	How often does this job require working in extremely bright or inadequate lighting conditions?
Very Hot or Cold Temperatures	How often does this job require working in very hot (above 90 F degrees) or very cold (below 32 F degrees) temperatures?
Spend Time Sitting	How much does this job require sitting?
Spend Time Making Repetitive Motions	How much does this job require making repetitive motions?
Cramped Work Space, Awkward Positions	How often does this job require working in cramped work spaces that requires getting into awkward positions?
Pace Determined by Speed of Equipment	How important is it to this job that the pace is determined by the speed of equipment or machinery? (This does not refer to keeping busy at all times on this job.)
Spend Time Walking and Running	How much does this job require walking and running?
Exposed to Disease or Infections	How often does this job require exposure to disease/infections?
Degree of Automation	How automated is the job?
Exposed to High Places	How often does this job require exposure to high places?
Spend Time Bending or Twisting the Body	How much does this job require bending or twisting your body?
Outdoors, Under Cover	How often does this job require working outdoors, under cover (e.g., structure with roof but no walls)?
Wear Specialized Protective or Safety Equipment su	How much does this job require wearing specialized protective or safety equipment such as breathing apparatus, safety harness, full protection suits, or radiation protection?
Deal With Physically Aggressive People	How frequently does this job require the worker to deal with physical aggression of violent individuals?
Public Speaking	How often do you have to perform public speaking in this job?
Spend Time Kneeling, Crouching, Stooping, or Crawl	How much does this job require kneeling, crouching, stooping or crawling?
Spend Time Climbing Ladders, Scaffolds, or Poles	How much does this job require climbing ladders, scaffolds, or poles?
Spend Time Keeping or Regaining Balance	How much does this job require keeping or regaining your balance?
In an Open Vehicle or Equipment	How often does this job require working in an open vehicle or equipment (e.g., tractor)?
Exposed to Radiation	How often does this job require exposure to radiation?
Exposed to Whole Body Vibration	How often does this job require exposure to whole body vibration (e.g., operate a jackhammer)?

Job Zone Component	Job Zone Component Definitions
Title	Job Zone Three: Medium Preparation Needed

Overall Experience	Previous work-related skill, knowledge, or experience is required for these occupations. For example, an electrician must have completed three or four years of apprenticeship or several years of vocational training, and often must have passed a licensing exam, in order to perform the job.
Job Training	Employees in these occupations usually need one or two years of training involving both on-the-job experience and informal training with experienced workers.
Job Zone Examples	These occupations usually involve using communication and organizational skills to coordinate, supervise, manage, or train others to accomplish goals. Examples include dental assistants, electricians, fish and game wardens, legal secretaries, personnel recruiters, and recreation workers.
SVP Range	(6.0 to < 7.0)
Education	Most occupations in this zone require training in vocational schools, related on-the-job experience, or an associate's degree. Some may require a bachelor's degree.

Work_Styles	Work_Styles Definitions
Integrity	Job requires being honest and ethical.
Dependability	Job requires being reliable, responsible, and dependable, and fulfilling obligations.
Attention to Detail	Job requires being careful about detail and thorough in completing work tasks.
Analytical Thinking	Job requires analyzing information and using logic to address work-related issues and problems.
Initiative	Job requires a willingness to take on responsibilities and challenges.
Self Control	Job requires maintaining composure, keeping emotions in check, controlling anger, and avoiding aggressive behavior, even in very difficult situations.
Stress Tolerance	Job requires accepting criticism and dealing calmly and effectively with high stress situations.
Persistence	Job requires persistence in the face of obstacles.
Leadership	Job requires a willingness to lead, take charge, and offer opinions and direction.
Concern for Others	Job requires being sensitive to others' needs and feelings and being understanding and helpful on the job.
Independence	Job requires developing one's own ways of doing things, guiding oneself with little or no supervision, and depending on oneself to get things done.
Adaptability/Flexibility	Job requires being open to change (positive or negative) and to considerable variety in the workplace.
Cooperation	Job requires being pleasant with others on the job and displaying a good-natured, cooperative attitude.
Social Orientation	Job requires preferring to work with others rather than alone, and being personally connected with others on the job.
Achievement/Effort	Job requires establishing and maintaining personally challenging achievement goals and exerting effort toward mastering tasks.
Innovation	Job requires creativity and alternative thinking to develop new ideas for and answers to work-related problems.

33-3031.00 - Fish and Game Wardens

Patrol assigned area to prevent fish and game law violations. Investigate reports of damage to crops or property by wildlife. Compile biological data.

Tasks

1) Provide advice and information to park and reserve visitors.

2) Promote and provide hunter and trapper safety training.

3) Address schools, civic groups, sporting clubs, and the media to disseminate information concerning wildlife conservation and regulations.

4) Survey areas and compile figures of bag counts of hunters in order to determine the effectiveness of control measures.

5) Supervise the activities of seasonal workers.

6) Patrol assigned areas by car, boat, airplane, horse, or on foot, to enforce game, fish, or boating laws and to manage wildlife programs, lakes, or land.

7) Provide assistance to other local law enforcement agencies as required.

8) Serve warrants, make arrests, and compile and present evidence for court actions.

9) Protect and preserve native wildlife, plants, and ecosystems.

10) Recommend revisions or changes in hunting and trapping regulations or seasons and in animal management programs so that wildlife balances and habitats can be maintained.

11) Issue licenses, permits, and other documentation.

12) Perform facilities maintenance work such as constructing or repairing structures, and controlling weeds and pests.

13) Participate in search-and-rescue operations and in firefighting efforts.

14) Document and detail the extent of crop, property, or habitat damage, and make financial loss estimates and compensation recommendations.

15) Seize equipment used in fish and game law violations, and arrange for disposition of fish or game illegally taken or possessed.

16) Investigate hunting accidents and reports of fish and game law violations, and issue warnings or citations and file reports as necessary.

17) Investigate crop, property, or habitat damage or destruction, or instances of water pollution, in order to determine causes and to advise property owners of preventive measures.

18) Design and implement control measures to prevent or counteract damage caused by wildlife or people.

19) Collect royalties assessed on fish, wildlife and timber resources.

20) Inspect commercial operations relating to fish and wildlife, recreation, and protected areas.

33-9092.00 - Lifeguards, Ski Patrol, and Other Recreational Protective Service Workers

Monitor recreational areas, such as pools, beaches, or ski slopes to provide assistance and protection to participants.

Tasks

1) Rescue distressed persons, using rescue techniques and equipment.

2) Examine injured persons, and administer first aid or cardiopulmonary resuscitation if necessary, utilizing training and medical supplies and equipment.

3) Instruct participants in skiing, swimming, or other recreational activities, and provide safety precaution information.

4) Inspect recreational facilities for cleanliness.

5) Warn recreational participants of inclement weather, unsafe areas, or illegal conduct.

6) Complete and maintain records of weather and beach conditions, emergency medical treatments performed, and other relevant incident information.

7) Inspect recreational equipment, such as rope tows, T-bars, J-bars, and chair lifts, for safety hazards and damage or wear.

8) Provide assistance with staff selection, training, and supervision.

9) Provide assistance in the safe use of equipment such as ski lifts.

10) Participate in recreational demonstrations to entertain resort guests.

11) Observe activities in assigned areas, using binoculars in order to detect hazards, disturbances, or safety infractions.

12) Operate underwater recovery units.

13) Patrol or monitor recreational areas such as trails, slopes, and swimming areas, on foot, in vehicles, or from towers.

Knowledge	Knowledge Definitions
Public Safety and Security	Knowledge of relevant equipment, policies, procedures, and strategies to promote effective local, state, or national security operations for the protection of people, data, property, and institutions.
Customer and Personal Service	Knowledge of principles and processes for providing customer and personal services. This includes customer needs assessment, meeting quality standards for services, and evaluation of customer satisfaction.
Medicine and Dentistry	Knowledge of the information and techniques needed to diagnose and treat human injuries, diseases, and deformities. This includes symptoms, treatment alternatives, drug properties and interactions, and preventive health-care measures.
Education and Training	Knowledge of principles and methods for curriculum and training design, teaching and instruction for individuals and groups, and the measurement of training effects.
Administration and Management	Knowledge of business and management principles involved in strategic planning, resource allocation, human resources modeling, leadership technique, production methods, and coordination of people and resources.
Psychology	Knowledge of human behavior and performance; individual differences in ability, personality, and interests; learning and motivation; psychological research methods; and the assessment and treatment of behavioral and affective disorders.
Chemistry	Knowledge of the chemical composition, structure, and properties of substances and of the chemical processes and transformations that they undergo. This includes uses of chemicals and their interactions, danger signs, production techniques, and disposal methods.
Personnel and Human Resources	Knowledge of principles and procedures for personnel recruitment, selection, training, compensation and benefits, labor relations and negotiation, and personnel information systems.
English Language	Knowledge of the structure and content of the English language including the meaning and spelling of words, rules of composition, and grammar.
Communications and Media	Knowledge of media production, communication, and dissemination techniques and methods. This includes alternative ways to inform and entertain via written, oral, and visual media.
Therapy and Counseling	Knowledge of principles, methods, and procedures for diagnosis, treatment, and rehabilitation of physical and mental dysfunctions, and for career counseling and guidance.
Sales and Marketing	Knowledge of principles and methods for showing, promoting, and selling products or services. This includes marketing strategy and tactics, product demonstration, sales techniques, and sales control systems.
Philosophy and Theology	Knowledge of different philosophical systems and religions. This includes their basic principles, values, ethics, ways of thinking, customs, practices, and their impact on human culture.
Mechanical	Knowledge of machines and tools, including their designs, uses, repair, and maintenance.
Law and Government	Knowledge of laws, legal codes, court procedures, precedents, government regulations, executive orders, agency rules, and the democratic political process.
Clerical	Knowledge of administrative and clerical procedures and systems such as word processing, managing files and records, stenography and transcription, designing forms, and other office procedures and terminology.
Mathematics	Knowledge of arithmetic, algebra, geometry, calculus, statistics, and their applications.
Computers and Electronics	Knowledge of circuit boards, processors, chips, electronic equipment, and computer hardware and software, including applications and programming.
Sociology and Anthropology	Knowledge of group behavior and dynamics, societal trends and influences, human migrations, ethnicity, cultures and their history and origins.
Economics and Accounting	Knowledge of economic and accounting principles and practices, the financial markets, banking and the analysis and reporting of financial data.
Production and Processing	Knowledge of raw materials, production processes, quality control, costs, and other techniques for maximizing the effective manufacture and distribution of goods.
Transportation	Knowledge of principles and methods for moving people or goods by air, rail, sea, or road, including the relative costs and benefits.
Telecommunications	Knowledge of transmission, broadcasting, switching, control, and operation of telecommunications systems.
Engineering and Technology	Knowledge of the practical application of engineering science and technology. This includes applying principles, techniques, procedures, and equipment to the design and production of various goods and services.
Physics	Knowledge and prediction of physical principles, laws, their interrelationships, and applications to understanding fluid, material, and atmospheric dynamics, and mechanical, electrical, atomic and sub-atomic structures and processes.
Biology	Knowledge of plant and animal organisms, their tissues, cells, functions, interdependencies, and interactions with each other and the environment.

Foreign Language	Knowledge of the structure and content of a foreign (non-English) language including the meaning and spelling of words, rules of composition and grammar, and pronunciation.
Design	Knowledge of design techniques, tools, and principles involved in production of precision technical plans, blueprints, drawings, and models.
Geography	Knowledge of principles and methods for describing the features of land, sea, and air masses, including their physical characteristics, locations, interrelationships, and distribution of plant, animal, and human life.
Food Production	Knowledge of techniques and equipment for planting, growing, and harvesting food products (both plant and animal) for consumption, including storage/handling techniques.
History and Archeology	Knowledge of historical events and their causes, indicators, and effects on civilizations and cultures.
Building and Construction	Knowledge of materials, methods, and the tools involved in the construction or repair of houses, buildings, or other structures such as highways and roads.
Fine Arts	Knowledge of the theory and techniques required to compose, produce, and perform works of music, dance, visual arts, drama, and sculpture.

Skills	**Skills Definitions**
Active Listening	Giving full attention to what other people are saying, taking time to understand the points being made, asking questions as appropriate, and not interrupting at inappropriate times.
Monitoring	Monitoring/Assessing performance of yourself, other individuals, or organizations to make improvements or take corrective action.
Instructing	Teaching others how to do something.
Social Perceptiveness	Being aware of others' reactions and understanding why they react as they do.
Speaking	Talking to others to convey information effectively.
Service Orientation	Actively looking for ways to help people.
Critical Thinking	Using logic and reasoning to identify the strengths and weaknesses of alternative solutions, conclusions or approaches to problems.
Judgment and Decision Making	Considering the relative costs and benefits of potential actions to choose the most appropriate one.
Learning Strategies	Selecting and using training/instructional methods and procedures appropriate for the situation when learning or teaching new things.
Time Management	Managing one's own time and the time of others.
Coordination	Adjusting actions in relation to others' actions.
Operation Monitoring	Watching gauges, dials, or other indicators to make sure a machine is working properly.
Reading Comprehension	Understanding written sentences and paragraphs in work related documents.
Science	Using scientific rules and methods to solve problems.
Active Learning	Understanding the implications of new information for both current and future problem-solving and decision-making.
Equipment Maintenance	Performing routine maintenance on equipment and determining when and what kind of maintenance is needed.
Operation and Control	Controlling operations of equipment or systems.
Management of Personnel Resources	Motivating, developing, and directing people as they work, identifying the best people for the job.
Negotiation	Bringing others together and trying to reconcile differences.
Equipment Selection	Determining the kind of tools and equipment needed to do a job.
Management of Material Resources	Obtaining and seeing to the appropriate use of equipment, facilities, and materials needed to do certain work.
Repairing	Repairing machines or systems using the needed tools.
Persuasion	Persuading others to change their minds or behavior.
Complex Problem Solving	Identifying complex problems and reviewing related information to develop and evaluate options and implement solutions.
Quality Control Analysis	Conducting tests and inspections of products, services, or processes to evaluate quality or performance.
Technology Design	Generating or adapting equipment and technology to serve user needs.
Writing	Communicating effectively in writing as appropriate for the needs of the audience.
Troubleshooting	Determining causes of operating errors and deciding what to do about it.
Mathematics	Using mathematics to solve problems.

Systems Evaluation	Identifying measures or indicators of system performance and the actions needed to improve or correct performance, relative to the goals of the system.
Operations Analysis	Analyzing needs and product requirements to create a design.
Systems Analysis	Determining how a system should work and how changes in conditions, operations, and the environment will affect outcomes.
Management of Financial Resources	Determining how money will be spent to get the work done, and accounting for these expenditures.
Installation	Installing equipment, machines, wiring, or programs to meet specifications.
Programming	Writing computer programs for various purposes.

Ability	**Ability Definitions**
Problem Sensitivity	The ability to tell when something is wrong or is likely to go wrong. It does not involve solving the problem, only recognizing there is a problem.
Oral Expression	The ability to communicate information and ideas in speaking so others will understand.
Oral Comprehension	The ability to listen to and understand information and ideas presented through spoken words and sentences.
Far Vision	The ability to see details at a distance.
Deductive Reasoning	The ability to apply general rules to specific problems to produce answers that make sense.
Speech Recognition	The ability to identify and understand the speech of another person.
Speech Clarity	The ability to speak clearly so others can understand you.
Inductive Reasoning	The ability to combine pieces of information to form general rules or conclusions (includes finding a relationship among seemingly unrelated events).
Information Ordering	The ability to arrange things or actions in a certain order or pattern according to a specific rule or set of rules (e.g., patterns of numbers, letters, words, pictures, mathematical operations).
Near Vision	The ability to see details at close range (within a few feet of the observer).
Selective Attention	The ability to concentrate on a task over a period of time without being distracted.
Flexibility of Closure	The ability to identify or detect a known pattern (a figure, object, word, or sound) that is hidden in other distracting material.
Speed of Closure	The ability to quickly make sense of, combine, and organize information into meaningful patterns.
Stamina	The ability to exert yourself physically over long periods of time without getting winded or out of breath.
Written Expression	The ability to communicate information and ideas in writing so others will understand.
Static Strength	The ability to exert maximum muscle force to lift, push, pull, or carry objects.
Time Sharing	The ability to shift back and forth between two or more activities or sources of information (such as speech, sounds, touch, or other sources).
Trunk Strength	The ability to use your abdominal and lower back muscles to support part of the body repeatedly or continuously over time without 'giving out' or fatiguing.
Gross Body Coordination	The ability to coordinate the movement of your arms, legs, and torso together when the whole body is in motion.
Category Flexibility	The ability to generate or use different sets of rules for combining or grouping things in different ways.
Multilimb Coordination	The ability to coordinate two or more limbs (for example, two arms, two legs, or one leg and one arm) while sitting, standing, or lying down. It does not involve performing the activities while the whole body is in motion.
Written Comprehension	The ability to read and understand information and ideas presented in writing.
Auditory Attention	The ability to focus on a single source of sound in the presence of other distracting sounds.
Perceptual Speed	The ability to quickly and accurately compare similarities and differences among sets of letters, numbers, objects, pictures, or patterns. The things to be compared may be presented at the same time or one after the other. This ability also includes comparing a presented object with a remembered object.
Speed of Limb Movement	The ability to quickly move the arms and legs.
Fluency of Ideas	The ability to come up with a number of ideas about a topic (the number of ideas is important, not their quality, correctness, or creativity).
Arm-Hand Steadiness	The ability to keep your hand and arm steady while moving your arm or while holding your arm and hand in one position.
Memorization	The ability to remember information such as words, numbers, pictures, and procedures.

Depth Perception	The ability to judge which of several objects is closer or farther away from you, or to judge the distance between you and an object.
Visual Color Discrimination	The ability to match or detect differences between colors, including shades of color and brightness.
Reaction Time	The ability to quickly respond (with the hand, finger, or foot) to a signal (sound, light, picture) when it appears.
Originality	The ability to come up with unusual or clever ideas about a given topic or situation, or to develop creative ways to solve a problem.
Dynamic Strength	The ability to exert muscle force repeatedly or continuously over time. This involves muscular endurance and resistance to muscle fatigue.
Extent Flexibility	The ability to bend, stretch, twist, or reach with your body, arms, and/or legs.
Hearing Sensitivity	The ability to detect or tell the differences between sounds that vary in pitch and loudness.
Visualization	The ability to imagine how something will look after it is moved around or when its parts are moved or rearranged.
Gross Body Equilibrium	The ability to keep or regain your body balance or stay upright when in an unstable position.
Response Orientation	The ability to choose quickly between two or more movements in response to two or more different signals (lights, sounds, pictures). It includes the speed with which the correct response is started with the hand, foot, or other body part.
Night Vision	The ability to see under low light conditions.
Glare Sensitivity	The ability to see objects in the presence of glare or bright lighting.
Number Facility	The ability to add, subtract, multiply, or divide quickly and correctly.
Manual Dexterity	The ability to quickly move your hand, your hand together with your arm, or your two hands to grasp, manipulate, or assemble objects.
Spatial Orientation	The ability to know your location in relation to the environment or to know where other objects are in relation to you.
Rate Control	The ability to time your movements or the movement of a piece of equipment in anticipation of changes in the speed and/or direction of a moving object or scene.
Explosive Strength	The ability to use short bursts of muscle force to propel oneself (as in jumping or sprinting), or to throw an object.
Finger Dexterity	The ability to make precisely coordinated movements of the fingers of one or both hands to grasp, manipulate, or assemble very small objects.
Sound Localization	The ability to tell the direction from which a sound originated.
Peripheral Vision	The ability to see objects or movement of objects to one's side when the eyes are looking ahead.
Control Precision	The ability to quickly and repeatedly adjust the controls of a machine or a vehicle to exact positions.
Mathematical Reasoning	The ability to choose the right mathematical methods or formulas to solve a problem.
Dynamic Flexibility	The ability to quickly and repeatedly bend, stretch, twist, or reach out with your body, arms, and/or legs.
Wrist-Finger Speed	The ability to make fast, simple, repeated movements of the fingers, hands, and wrists.

Work_Activity	Work_Activity Definitions
Making Decisions and Solving Problems	Analyzing information and evaluating results to choose the best solution and solve problems.
Identifying Objects, Actions, and Events	Identifying information by categorizing, estimating, recognizing differences or similarities, and detecting changes in circumstances or events.
Monitor Processes, Materials, or Surroundings	Monitoring and reviewing information from materials, events, or the environment, to detect or assess problems.
Assisting and Caring for Others	Providing personal assistance, medical attention, emotional support, or other personal care to others such as,coworkers, customers, or patients.
Communicating with Supervisors, Peers, or Subordin	Providing information to supervisors, co-workers, and subordinates by telephone, in written form, e-mail, or in person.
Performing for or Working Directly with the Public	Performing for people or dealing directly with the public. This includes serving customers in restaurants and stores, and receiving clients or guests.
Performing General Physical Activities	Performing physical activities that require considerable use of your arms and legs and moving your whole body, such as climbing, lifting, balancing, walking, stooping, and handling of materials.
Getting Information	Observing, receiving, and otherwise obtaining information from all relevant sources.

Updating and Using Relevant Knowledge	Keeping up-to-date technically and applying new knowledge to your job.
Inspecting Equipment, Structures, or Material	Inspecting equipment, structures, or materials to identify the cause of errors or other problems or defects.
Resolving Conflicts and Negotiating with Others	Handling complaints, settling disputes, and resolving grievances and conflicts, or otherwise negotiating with others.
Scheduling Work and Activities	Scheduling events, programs, and activities, as well as the work of others.
Processing Information	Compiling, coding, categorizing, calculating, tabulating, auditing, or verifying information or data.
Judging the Qualities of Things, Services, or Peop	Assessing the value, importance, or quality of things or people.
Training and Teaching Others	Identifying the educational needs of others, developing formal educational or training programs or classes, and teaching or instructing others.
Establishing and Maintaining Interpersonal Relatio	Developing constructive and cooperative working relationships with others, and maintaining them over time.
Documenting/Recording Information	Entering, transcribing, recording, storing, or maintaining information in written or electronic/magnetic form.
Communicating with Persons Outside Organization	Communicating with people outside the organization, representing the organization to customers, the public, government, and other external sources. This information can be exchanged in person, in writing, or by telephone or e-mail.
Developing Objectives and Strategies	Establishing long-range objectives and specifying the strategies and actions to achieve them.
Coordinating the Work and Activities of Others	Getting members of a group to work together to accomplish tasks.
Coaching and Developing Others	Identifying the developmental needs of others and coaching, mentoring, or otherwise helping others to improve their knowledge or skills.
Interpreting the Meaning of Information for Others	Translating or explaining what information means and how it can be used.
Estimating the Quantifiable Characteristics of Pro	Estimating sizes, distances, and quantities; or determining time, costs, resources, or materials needed to perform a work activity.
Monitoring and Controlling Resources	Monitoring and controlling resources and overseeing the spending of money.
Developing and Building Teams	Encouraging and building mutual trust, respect, and cooperation among team members.
Provide Consultation and Advice to Others	Providing guidance and expert advice to management or other groups on technical, systems-, or process-related topics.
Organizing, Planning, and Prioritizing Work	Developing specific goals and plans to prioritize, organize, and accomplish your work.
Evaluating Information to Determine Compliance wit	Using relevant information and individual judgment to determine whether events or processes comply with laws, regulations, or standards.
Thinking Creatively	Developing, designing, or creating new applications, ideas, relationships, systems, or products, including artistic contributions.
Analyzing Data or Information	Identifying the underlying principles, reasons, or facts of information by breaking down information or data into separate parts.
Guiding, Directing, and Motivating Subordinates	Providing guidance and direction to subordinates, including setting performance standards and monitoring performance.
Handling and Moving Objects	Using hands and arms in handling, installing, positioning, and moving materials, and manipulating things.
Performing Administrative Activities	Performing day-to-day administrative tasks such as maintaining information files and processing paperwork.
Operating Vehicles, Mechanized Devices, or Equipme	Running, maneuvering, navigating, or driving vehicles or mechanized equipment, such as forklifts, passenger vehicles, aircraft, or water craft.
Controlling Machines and Processes	Using either control mechanisms or direct physical activity to operate machines or processes (not including computers or vehicles).
Drafting, Laying Out, and Specifying Technical Dev	Providing documentation, detailed instructions, drawings, or specifications to tell others about how devices, parts, equipment, or structures are to be fabricated, constructed, assembled, modified, maintained, or used.
Repairing and Maintaining Mechanical Equipment	Servicing, repairing, adjusting, and testing machines, devices, moving parts, and equipment that operate primarily on the basis of mechanical (not electronic) principles.
Selling or Influencing Others	Convincing others to buy merchandise/goods or to otherwise change their minds or actions.
Staffing Organizational Units	Recruiting, interviewing, selecting, hiring, and promoting employees in an organization.
Interacting With Computers	Using computers and computer systems (including hardware and software) to program, write software, set up functions, enter data, or process information.

Repairing and Maintaining Electronic Equipment	Servicing, repairing, calibrating, regulating, fine-tuning, or testing machines, devices, and equipment that operate primarily on the basis of electrical or electronic (not mechanical) principles.	Very Hot or Cold Temperatures	How often does this job require working in very hot (above 90 F degrees) or very cold (below 32 F degrees) temperatures?

Work_Context	**Work_Context Definitions**
Contact With Others	How much does this job require the worker to be in contact with others (face-to-face, by telephone, or otherwise) in order to perform it?
Responsible for Others' Health and Safety	How much responsibility is there for the health and safety of others in this job?
Face-to-Face Discussions	How often do you have to have face-to-face discussions with individuals or teams in this job?
Work With Work Group or Team	How important is it to work with others in a group or team in this job?
Coordinate or Lead Others	How important is it to coordinate or lead others in accomplishing work activities in this job?
Deal With External Customers	How important is it to work with external customers or the public in this job?
Freedom to Make Decisions	How much decision making freedom, without supervision, does the job offer?
Physical Proximity	To what extent does this job require the worker to perform job tasks in close physical proximity to other people?
Consequence of Error	How serious would the result usually be if the worker made a mistake that was not readily correctable?
Indoors, Environmentally Controlled	How often does this job require working indoors in environmentally controlled conditions?
Sounds, Noise Levels Are Distracting or Uncomforta	How often does this job require working exposed to sounds and noise levels that are distracting or uncomfortable?
Spend Time Sitting	How much does this job require sitting?
Frequency of Decision Making	How frequently is the worker required to make decisions that affect other people, the financial resources, and/or the image and reputation of the organization?
Importance of Being Exact or Accurate	How important is being very exact or highly accurate in performing this job?
Structured versus Unstructured Work	To what extent is this job structured for the worker, rather than allowing the worker to determine tasks, priorities, and goals?
Wear Common Protective or Safety Equipment such as	How much does this job require wearing common protective or safety equipment such as safety shoes, glasses, gloves, hard hats or live jackets?
Deal With Unpleasant or Angry People	How frequently does the worker have to deal with unpleasant, angry, or discourteous individuals as part of the job requirements?
Public Speaking	How often do you have to perform public speaking in this job?
Telephone	How often do you have telephone conversations in this job?
Exposed to Minor Burns, Cuts, Bites, or Stings	How often does this job require exposure to minor burns, cuts, bites, or stings?
Impact of Decisions on Co-workers or Company Resul	How do the decisions an employee makes impact the results of co-workers, clients or the company?
Spend Time Walking and Running	How much does this job require walking and running?
Spend Time Making Repetitive Motions	How much does this job require making repetitive motions?
Frequency of Conflict Situations	How often are there conflict situations the employee has to face in this job?
Spend Time Standing	How much does this job require standing?
Exposed to Hazardous Conditions	How often does this job require exposure to hazardous conditions?
Exposed to Contaminants	How often does this job require working exposed to contaminants (such as pollutants, gases, dust or odors)?
Responsibility for Outcomes and Results	How responsible is the worker for work outcomes and results of other workers?
Exposed to Disease or Infections	How often does this job require exposure to disease/infections?
Importance of Repeating Same Tasks	How important is repeating the same physical activities (e.g., key entry) or mental activities (e.g., checking entries in a ledger) over and over, without stopping, to performing this job?
Spend Time Bending or Twisting the Body	How much does this job require bending or twisting your body?
Spend Time Keeping or Regaining Balance	How much does this job require keeping or regaining your balance?
Letters and Memos	How often does the job require written letters and memos?
Outdoors, Exposed to Weather	How often does this job require working outdoors, exposed to all weather conditions?
Indoors, Not Environmentally Controlled	How often does this job require working indoors in non-controlled environmental conditions (e.g., warehouse without heat)?

Very Hot or Cold Temperatures	How often does this job require working in very hot (above 90 F degrees) or very cold (below 32 F degrees) temperatures?
Exposed to High Places	How often does this job require exposure to high places?
Wear Specialized Protective or Safety Equipment su	How much does this job require wearing specialized protective or safety equipment such as breathing apparatus, safety harness, full protection suits, or radiation protection?
Extremely Bright or Inadequate Lighting	How often does this job require working in extremely bright or inadequate lighting conditions?
Level of Competition	To what extent does this job require the worker to compete or to be aware of competitive pressures?
Outdoors, Under Cover	How often does this job require working outdoors, under cover (e.g., structure with roof but no walls)?
Spend Time Using Your Hands to Handle, Control, or	How much does this job require using your hands to handle, control, or feel objects, tools or controls?
Cramped Work Space, Awkward Positions	How often does this job require working in cramped work spaces that requires getting into awkward positions?
Exposed to Radiation	How often does this job require exposure to radiation?
Time Pressure	How often does this job require the worker to meet strict deadlines?
Exposed to Hazardous Equipment	How often does this job require exposure to hazardous equipment?
Spend Time Climbing Ladders, Scaffolds, or Poles	How much does this job require climbing ladders, scaffolds, or poles?
Spend Time Kneeling, Crouching, Stooping, or Crawl	How much does this job require kneeling, crouching, stooping, or crawling?
Electronic Mail	How often do you use electronic mail in this job?
Deal With Physically Aggressive People	How frequently does this job require the worker to deal with physical aggression of violent individuals?
In an Open Vehicle or Equipment	How often does this job require working in an open vehicle or equipment (e.g., tractor)?
In an Enclosed Vehicle or Equipment	How often does this job require working in a closed vehicle or equipment (e.g., car)?
Degree of Automation	How automated is the job?
Pace Determined by Speed of Equipment	How important is it to this job that the pace is determined by the speed of equipment or machinery? (This does not refer to keeping busy at all times on this job.)
Exposed to Whole Body Vibration	How often does this job require exposure to whole body vibration (e.g., operate a jackhammer)?

Job Zone Component	**Job Zone Component Definitions**
Title	Job Zone One: Little or No Preparation Needed
Overall Experience	No previous work-related skill, knowledge, or experience is needed for these occupations. For example, a person can become a general office clerk even if he/she has never worked in an office before.
Job Training	Employees in these occupations need anywhere from a few days to a few months of training. Usually, an experienced worker could show you how to do the job.
Job Zone Examples	These occupations involve following instructions and helping others. Examples include bus drivers, forest and conservation workers, general office clerks, home health aides, and waiters/waitresses.
SVP Range	(Below 4.0)
Education	These occupations may require a high school diploma or GED certificate. Some may require a formal training course to obtain a license.

Work_Styles	**Work_Styles Definitions**
Dependability	Job requires being reliable, responsible, and dependable, and fulfilling obligations.
Self Control	Job requires maintaining composure, keeping emotions in check, controlling anger, and avoiding aggressive behavior, even in very difficult situations.
Cooperation	Job requires being pleasant with others on the job and displaying a good-natured, cooperative attitude.
Stress Tolerance	Job requires accepting criticism and dealing calmly and effectively with high stress situations.
Concern for Others	Job requires being sensitive to others' needs and feelings and being understanding and helpful on the job.
Leadership	Job requires a willingness to lead, take charge, and offer opinions and direction.
Social Orientation	Job requires preferring to work with others rather than alone, and being personally connected with others on the job.

Attention to Detail	Job requires being careful about detail and thorough in completing work tasks.
Integrity	Job requires being honest and ethical.
Initiative	Job requires a willingness to take on responsibilities and challenges.
Adaptability/Flexibility	Job requires being open to change (positive or negative) and to considerable variety in the workplace.
Independence	Job requires developing one's own ways of doing things, guiding oneself with little or no supervision, and depending on oneself to get things done.
Achievement/Effort	Job requires establishing and maintaining personally challenging achievement goals and exerting effort toward mastering tasks.
Analytical Thinking	Job requires analyzing information and using logic to address work-related issues and problems.
Persistence	Job requires persistence in the face of obstacles.
Innovation	Job requires creativity and alternative thinking to develop new ideas for and answers to work-related problems.

35-2011.00 - Cooks, Fast Food

Prepare and cook food in a fast food restaurant with a limited menu. Duties of the cooks are limited to preparation of a few basic items and normally involve operating large-volume single-purpose cooking equipment.

Tasks

1) Maintain sanitation, health, and safety standards in work areas.

2) Verify that prepared food meets requirements for quality and quantity.

3) Operate large-volume cooking equipment such as grills, deep-fat fryers, or griddles.

4) Cook the exact number of items ordered by each customer, working on several different orders simultaneously.

5) Measure ingredients required for specific food items being prepared.

6) Read food order slips or receive verbal instructions as to food required by patron, and prepare and cook food according to instructions.

7) Cook and package batches of food, such as hamburgers and fried chicken, which are prepared to order or kept warm until sold.

8) Wash, cut, and prepare foods designated for cooking.

9) Serve orders to customers at windows, counters, or tables.

10) Take food and drink orders and receive payment from customers.

11) Prepare specialty foods such as pizzas, fish and chips, sandwiches, and tacos, following specific methods that usually require short preparation time.

12) Mix ingredients such as pancake or waffle batters.

13) Pre-cook items such as bacon, in order to prepare them for later use.

14) Order and take delivery of supplies.

15) Prepare dough, following recipe.

16) Schedule activities and equipment use with managers, using information about daily menus to help coordinate cooking times.

17) Prepare and serve beverages such as coffee and fountain drinks.

18) Clean food preparation areas, cooking surfaces, and utensils.

Knowledge	Knowledge Definitions
Customer and Personal Service	Knowledge of principles and processes for providing customer and personal services. This includes customer needs assessment, meeting quality standards for services, and evaluation of customer satisfaction.
Food Production	Knowledge of techniques and equipment for planting, growing, and harvesting food products (both plant and animal) for consumption, including storage/handling techniques.
Production and Processing	Knowledge of raw materials, production processes, quality control, costs, and other techniques for maximizing the effective manufacture and distribution of goods.
Personnel and Human Resources	Knowledge of principles and procedures for personnel recruitment, selection, training, compensation and benefits, labor relations and negotiation, and personnel information systems.
Sales and Marketing	Knowledge of principles and methods for showing, promoting, and selling products or services. This includes marketing strategy and tactics, product demonstration, sales techniques, and sales control systems.
English Language	Knowledge of the structure and content of the English language including the meaning and spelling of words, rules of composition, and grammar.
Administration and Management	Knowledge of business and management principles involved in strategic planning, resource allocation, human resources modeling, leadership technique, production methods, and coordination of people and resources.
Education and Training	Knowledge of principles and methods for curriculum and training design, teaching and instruction for individuals and groups, and the measurement of training effects.
Clerical	Knowledge of administrative and clerical procedures and systems such as word processing, managing files and records, stenography and transcription, designing forms, and other office procedures and terminology.
Mathematics	Knowledge of arithmetic, algebra, geometry, calculus, statistics, and their applications.
Mechanical	Knowledge of machines and tools, including their designs, uses, repair, and maintenance.
Public Safety and Security	Knowledge of relevant equipment, policies, procedures, and strategies to promote effective local, state, or national security operations for the protection of people, data, property, and institutions.
Engineering and Technology	Knowledge of the practical application of engineering science and technology. This includes applying principles, techniques, procedures, and equipment to the design and production of various goods and services.
Economics and Accounting	Knowledge of economic and accounting principles and practices, the financial markets, banking and the analysis and reporting of financial data.
Telecommunications	Knowledge of transmission, broadcasting, switching, control, and operation of telecommunications systems.
Transportation	Knowledge of principles and methods for moving people or goods by air, rail, sea, or road, including the relative costs and benefits.
Law and Government	Knowledge of laws, legal codes, court procedures, precedents, government regulations, executive orders, agency rules, and the democratic political process.
Building and Construction	Knowledge of materials, methods, and the tools involved in the construction or repair of houses, buildings, or other structures such as highways and roads.
Foreign Language	Knowledge of the structure and content of a foreign (non-English) language including the meaning and spelling of words, rules of composition and grammar, and pronunciation.
Computers and Electronics	Knowledge of circuit boards, processors, chips, electronic equipment, and computer hardware and software, including applications and programming.
Communications and Media	Knowledge of media production, communication, and dissemination techniques and methods. This includes alternative ways to inform and entertain via written, oral, and visual media.
Chemistry	Knowledge of the chemical composition, structure, and properties of substances and of the chemical processes and transformations that they undergo. This includes uses of chemicals and their interactions, danger signs, production techniques, and disposal methods.
Design	Knowledge of design techniques, tools, and principles involved in production of precision technical plans, blueprints, drawings, and models.
Physics	Knowledge and prediction of physical principles, laws, their interrelationships, and applications to understanding fluid, material, and atmospheric dynamics, and mechanical, electrical, atomic and sub-atomic structures and processes.
Sociology and Anthropology	Knowledge of group behavior and dynamics, societal trends and influences, human migrations, ethnicity, cultures and their history and origins.
Medicine and Dentistry	Knowledge of the information and techniques needed to diagnose and treat human injuries, diseases, and deformities. This includes symptoms, treatment alternatives, drug properties and interactions, and preventive health-care measures.
Geography	Knowledge of principles and methods for describing the features of land, sea, and air masses, including their physical characteristics, locations, interrelationships, and distribution of plant, animal, and human life.

Therapy and Counseling	Knowledge of principles, methods, and procedures for diagnosis, treatment, and rehabilitation of physical and mental dysfunctions, and for career counseling and guidance.
Psychology	Knowledge of human behavior and performance; individual differences in ability, personality, and interests; learning and motivation; psychological research methods; and the assessment and treatment of behavioral and affective disorders.
Biology	Knowledge of plant and animal organisms, their tissues, cells, functions, interdependencies, and interactions with each other and the environment.
History and Archeology	Knowledge of historical events and their causes, indicators, and effects on civilizations and cultures.
Fine Arts	Knowledge of the theory and techniques required to compose, produce, and perform works of music, dance, visual arts, drama, and sculpture.
Philosophy and Theology	Knowledge of different philosophical systems and religions. This includes their basic principles, values, ethics, ways of thinking, customs, practices, and their impact on human culture.

Skills	Skills Definitions
Active Listening	Giving full attention to what other people are saying, taking time to understand the points being made, asking questions as appropriate, and not interrupting at inappropriate times.
Speaking	Talking to others to convey information effectively.
Reading Comprehension	Understanding written sentences and paragraphs in work related documents.
Service Orientation	Actively looking for ways to help people.
Instructing	Teaching others how to do something.
Social Perceptiveness	Being aware of others' reactions and understanding why they react as they do.
Mathematics	Using mathematics to solve problems.
Critical Thinking	Using logic and reasoning to identify the strengths and weaknesses of alternative solutions, conclusions or approaches to problems.
Learning Strategies	Selecting and using training/instructional methods and procedures appropriate for the situation when learning or teaching new things.
Monitoring	Monitoring/Assessing performance of yourself, other individuals, or organizations to make improvements or take corrective action.
Judgment and Decision Making	Considering the relative costs and benefits of potential actions to choose the most appropriate one.
Equipment Selection	Determining the kind of tools and equipment needed to do a job.
Writing	Communicating effectively in writing as appropriate for the needs of the audience.
Time Management	Managing one's own time and the time of others.
Active Learning	Understanding the implications of new information for both current and future problem-solving and decision-making.
Troubleshooting	Determining causes of operating errors and deciding what to do about it.
Operation and Control	Controlling operations of equipment or systems.
Systems Evaluation	Identifying measures or indicators of system performance and the actions needed to improve or correct performance, relative to the goals of the system.
Coordination	Adjusting actions in relation to others' actions.
Complex Problem Solving	Identifying complex problems and reviewing related information to develop and evaluate options and implement solutions.
Systems Analysis	Determining how a system should work and how changes in conditions, operations, and the environment will affect outcomes.
Management of Material Resources	Obtaining and seeing to the appropriate use of equipment, facilities, and materials needed to do certain work.
Quality Control Analysis	Conducting tests and inspections of products, services, or processes to evaluate quality or performance.
Management of Personnel Resources	Motivating, developing, and directing people as they work, identifying the best people for the job.
Equipment Maintenance	Performing routine maintenance on equipment and determining when and what kind of maintenance is needed.
Installation	Installing equipment, machines, wiring, or programs to meet specifications.
Management of Financial Resources	Determining how money will be spent to get the work done, and accounting for these expenditures.
Persuasion	Persuading others to change their minds or behavior.

Operation Monitoring	Watching gauges, dials, or other indicators to make sure a machine is working properly.
Operations Analysis	Analyzing needs and product requirements to create a design.
Negotiation	Bringing others together and trying to reconcile differences.
Technology Design	Generating or adapting equipment and technology to serve user needs.
Repairing	Repairing machines or systems using the needed tools.
Science	Using scientific rules and methods to solve problems.
Programming	Writing computer programs for various purposes.

Ability	Ability Definitions
Oral Comprehension	The ability to listen to and understand information and ideas presented through spoken words and sentences.
Oral Expression	The ability to communicate information and ideas in speaking so others will understand.
Trunk Strength	The ability to use your abdominal and lower back muscles to support part of the body repeatedly or continuously over time without 'giving out' or fatiguing.
Speech Recognition	The ability to identify and understand the speech of another person.
Information Ordering	The ability to arrange things or actions in a certain order or pattern according to a specific rule or set of rules (e.g., patterns of numbers, letters, words, pictures, mathematical operations).
Manual Dexterity	The ability to quickly move your hand, your hand together with your arm, or your two hands to grasp, manipulate, or assemble objects.
Written Comprehension	The ability to read and understand information and ideas presented in writing.
Near Vision	The ability to see details at close range (within a few feet of the observer).
Speech Clarity	The ability to speak clearly so others can understand you.
Problem Sensitivity	The ability to tell when something is wrong or is likely to go wrong. It does not involve solving the problem, only recognizing there is a problem.
Selective Attention	The ability to concentrate on a task over a period of time without being distracted.
Stamina	The ability to exert yourself physically over long periods of time without getting winded or out of breath.
Arm-Hand Steadiness	The ability to keep your hand and arm steady while moving your arm or while holding your arm and hand in one position.
Deductive Reasoning	The ability to apply general rules to specific problems to produce answers that make sense.
Control Precision	The ability to quickly and repeatedly adjust the controls of a machine or a vehicle to exact positions.
Time Sharing	The ability to shift back and forth between two or more activities or sources of information (such as speech, sounds, touch, or other sources).
Static Strength	The ability to exert maximum muscle force to lift, push, pull, or carry objects.
Multilimb Coordination	The ability to coordinate two or more limbs (for example, two arms, two legs, or one leg and one arm) while sitting, standing, or lying down. It does not involve performing the activities while the whole body is in motion.
Inductive Reasoning	The ability to combine pieces of information to form general rules or conclusions (includes finding a relationship among seemingly unrelated events).
Gross Body Coordination	The ability to coordinate the movement of your arms, legs, and torso together when the whole body is in motion.
Written Expression	The ability to communicate information and ideas in writing so others will understand.
Number Facility	The ability to add, subtract, multiply, or divide quickly and correctly.
Category Flexibility	The ability to generate or use different sets of rules for combining or grouping things in different ways.
Auditory Attention	The ability to focus on a single source of sound in the presence of other distracting sounds.
Extent Flexibility	The ability to bend, stretch, twist, or reach with your body, arms, and/or legs.
Reaction Time	The ability to quickly respond (with the hand, finger, or foot) to a signal (sound, light, picture) when it appears.
Memorization	The ability to remember information such as words, numbers, pictures, and procedures.
Mathematical Reasoning	The ability to choose the right mathematical methods or formulas to solve a problem.
Speed of Limb Movement	The ability to quickly move the arms and legs.
Wrist-Finger Speed	The ability to make fast, simple, repeated movements of the fingers, hands, and wrists.

Fluency of Ideas	The ability to come up with a number of ideas about a topic (the number of ideas is important, not their quality, correctness, or creativity).
Finger Dexterity	The ability to make precisely coordinated movements of the fingers of one or both hands to grasp, manipulate, or assemble very small objects.
Rate Control	The ability to time your movements or the movement of a piece of equipment in anticipation of changes in the speed and/or direction of a moving object or scene.
Visualization	The ability to imagine how something will look after it is moved around or when its parts are moved or rearranged.
Far Vision	The ability to see details at a distance.
Response Orientation	The ability to choose quickly between two or more movements in response to two or more different signals (lights, sounds, pictures). It includes the speed with which the correct response is started with the hand, foot, or other body part.
Originality	The ability to come up with unusual or clever ideas about a given topic or situation, or to develop creative ways to solve a problem.
Dynamic Strength	The ability to exert muscle force repeatedly or continuously over time. This involves muscular endurance and resistance to muscle fatigue.
Perceptual Speed	The ability to quickly and accurately compare similarities and differences among sets of letters, numbers, objects, pictures, or patterns. The things to be compared may be presented at the same time or one after the other. This ability also includes comparing a presented object with a remembered object.
Speed of Closure	The ability to quickly make sense of, combine, and organize information into meaningful patterns.
Hearing Sensitivity	The ability to detect or tell the differences between sounds that vary in pitch and loudness.
Visual Color Discrimination	The ability to match or detect differences between colors, including shades of color and brightness.
Flexibility of Closure	The ability to identify or detect a known pattern (a figure, object, word, or sound) that is hidden in other distracting material.
Depth Perception	The ability to judge which of several objects is closer or farther away from you, or to judge the distance between you and an object.
Gross Body Equilibrium	The ability to keep or regain your body balance or stay upright when in an unstable position.
Explosive Strength	The ability to use short bursts of muscle force to propel oneself (as in jumping or sprinting), or to throw an object.
Dynamic Flexibility	The ability to quickly and repeatedly bend, stretch, twist, or reach out with your body, arms, and/or legs.
Sound Localization	The ability to tell the direction from which a sound originated.
Spatial Orientation	The ability to know your location in relation to the environment or to know where other objects are in relation to you.
Peripheral Vision	The ability to see objects or movement of objects to one's side when the eyes are looking ahead.
Glare Sensitivity	The ability to see objects in the presence of glare or bright lighting.
Night Vision	The ability to see under low light conditions.

Work_Activity	Work_Activity Definitions
Getting Information	Observing, receiving, and otherwise obtaining information from all relevant sources.
Judging the Qualities of Things, Services, or Peop	Assessing the value, importance, or quality of things or people.
Performing General Physical Activities	Performing physical activities that require considerable use of your arms and legs and moving your whole body, such as climbing, lifting, balancing, walking, stooping, and handling of materials.
Monitor Processes, Materials, or Surroundings	Monitoring and reviewing information from materials, events, or the environment, to detect or assess problems.
Communicating with Supervisors, Peers, or Subordin	Providing information to supervisors, co-workers, and subordinates by telephone, in written form, e-mail, or in person.
Performing for or Working Directly with the Public	Performing for people or dealing directly with the public. This includes serving customers in restaurants and stores, and receiving clients or guests.
Inspecting Equipment, Structures, or Material	Inspecting equipment, structures, or materials to identify the cause of errors or other problems or defects.
Handling and Moving Objects	Using hands and arms in handling, installing, positioning, and moving materials, and manipulating things.

Organizing, Planning, and Prioritizing Work	Developing specific goals and plans to prioritize, organize, and accomplish your work.
Scheduling Work and Activities	Scheduling events, programs, and activities, as well as the work of others.
Making Decisions and Solving Problems	Analyzing information and evaluating results to choose the best solution and solve problems.
Resolving Conflicts and Negotiating with Others	Handling complaints, settling disputes, and resolving grievances and conflicts, or otherwise negotiating with others.
Training and Teaching Others	Identifying the educational needs of others, developing formal educational or training programs or classes, and teaching or instructing others.
Evaluating Information to Determine Compliance wit	Using relevant information and individual judgment to determine whether events or processes comply with laws, regulations, or standards.
Controlling Machines and Processes	Using either control mechanisms or direct physical activity to operate machines or processes (not including computers or vehicles).
Coaching and Developing Others	Identifying the developmental needs of others and coaching, mentoring, or otherwise helping others to improve their knowledge or skills.
Developing and Building Teams	Encouraging and building mutual trust, respect, and cooperation among team members.
Identifying Objects, Actions, and Events	Identifying information by categorizing, estimating, recognizing differences or similarities, and detecting changes in circumstances or events.
Establishing and Maintaining Interpersonal Relatio	Developing constructive and cooperative working relationships with others, and maintaining them over time.
Estimating the Quantifiable Characteristics of Pro	Estimating sizes, distances, and quantities; or determining time, costs, resources, or materials needed to perform a work activity.
Selling or Influencing Others	Convincing others to buy merchandise/goods or to otherwise change their minds or actions.
Thinking Creatively	Developing, designing, or creating new applications, ideas, relationships, systems, or products, including artistic contributions.
Updating and Using Relevant Knowledge	Keeping up-to-date technically and applying new knowledge to your job.
Coordinating the Work and Activities of Others	Getting members of a group to work together to accomplish tasks.
Interpreting the Meaning of Information for Others	Translating or explaining what information means and how it can be used.
Assisting and Caring for Others	Providing personal assistance, medical attention, emotional support, or other personal care to others such as coworkers, customers, or patients.
Processing Information	Compiling, coding, categorizing, calculating, tabulating, auditing, or verifying information or data.
Guiding, Directing, and Motivating Subordinates	Providing guidance and direction to subordinates, including setting performance standards and monitoring performance.
Staffing Organizational Units	Recruiting, interviewing, selecting, hiring, and promoting employees in an organization.
Monitoring and Controlling Resources	Monitoring and controlling resources and overseeing the spending of money.
Documenting/Recording Information	Entering, transcribing, recording, storing, or maintaining information in written or electronic/magnetic form.
Communicating with Persons Outside Organization	Communicating with people outside the organization, representing the organization to customers, the public, government, and other external sources. This information can be exchanged in person, in writing, or by telephone or e-mail.
Analyzing Data or Information	Identifying the underlying principles, reasons, or facts of information by breaking down information or data into separate parts.
Interacting With Computers	Using computers and computer systems (including hardware and software) to program, write software, set up functions, enter data, or process information.
Drafting, Laying Out, and Specifying Technical Dev	Providing documentation, detailed instructions, drawings, or specifications to tell others about how devices, parts, equipment, or structures are to be fabricated, constructed, assembled, modified, maintained, or used.
Developing Objectives and Strategies	Establishing long-range objectives and specifying the strategies and actions to achieve them.
Performing Administrative Activities	Performing day-to-day administrative tasks such as maintaining information files and processing paperwork.
Provide Consultation and Advice to Others	Providing guidance and expert advice to management or other groups on technical, systems-, or process-related topics.
Repairing and Maintaining Mechanical Equipment	Servicing, repairing, adjusting, and testing machines, devices, moving parts, and equipment that operate primarily on the basis of mechanical (not electronic) principles.

Repairing and Maintaining Electronic Equipment	Servicing, repairing, calibrating, regulating, fine-tuning, or testing machines, devices, and equipment that operate primarily on the basis of electrical or electronic (not mechanical) principles.
Operating Vehicles, Mechanized Devices, or Equipme	Running, maneuvering, navigating, or driving vehicles or mechanized equipment, such as forklifts, passenger vehicles, aircraft, or water craft.

Work_Context	Work_Context Definitions
Spend Time Standing	How much does this job require standing?
Physical Proximity	To what extent does this job require the worker to perform job tasks in close physical proximity to other people?
Indoors, Environmentally Controlled	How often does this job require working indoors in environmentally controlled conditions?
Spend Time Walking and Running	How much does this job require walking and running?
Work With Work Group or Team	How important is it to work with others in a group or team in this job?
Contact With Others	How much does this job require the worker to be in contact with others (face-to-face, by telephone, or otherwise) in order to perform it?
Level of Competition	To what extent does this job require the worker to compete or to be aware of competitive pressures?
Structured versus Unstructured Work	To what extent is this job structured for the worker, rather than allowing the worker to determine tasks, priorities, and goals?
Importance of Being Exact or Accurate	How important is being very exact or highly accurate in performing this job?
Freedom to Make Decisions	How much decision making freedom, without supervision, does the job offer?
Deal With Unpleasant or Angry People	How frequently does the worker have to deal with unpleasant, angry, or discourteous individuals as part of the job requirements?
Face-to-Face Discussions	How often do you have to have face-to-face discussions with individuals or teams in this job?
Exposed to Minor Burns, Cuts, Bites, or Stings	How often does this job require exposure to minor burns, cuts, bites, or stings?
Telephone	How often do you have telephone conversations in this job?
Spend Time Making Repetitive Motions	How much does this job require making repetitive motions?
Spend Time Using Your Hands to Handle, Control, or	How much does this job require using your hands to handle, control, or feel objects, tools or controls?
Coordinate or Lead Others	How important is it to coordinate or lead others in accomplishing work activities in this job?
Spend Time Bending or Twisting the Body	How much does this job require bending or twisting your body?
Frequency of Decision Making	How frequently is the worker required to make decisions that affect other people, the financial resources, and/or the image and reputation of the organization?
Frequency of Conflict Situations	How often are there conflict situations the employee has to face in this job?
Time Pressure	How often does this job require the worker to meet strict deadlines?
Sounds, Noise Levels Are Distracting or Uncomforta	How often does this job require working exposed to sounds and noise levels that are distracting or uncomfortable?
Deal With External Customers	How important is it to work with external customers or the public in this job?
Impact of Decisions on Co-workers or Company Resul	How do the decisions an employee makes impact the results of co-workers, clients or the company?
Pace Determined by Speed of Equipment	How important is it to this job that the pace is determined by the speed of equipment or machinery? (This does not refer to keeping busy at all times on this job.)
Responsible for Others' Health and Safety	How much responsibility is there for the health and safety of others in this job?
Outdoors, Exposed to Weather	How often does this job require working outdoors, exposed to all weather conditions?
Responsibility for Outcomes and Results	How responsible is the worker for work outcomes and results of other workers?
Deal With Physically Aggressive People	How frequently does this job require the worker to deal with physical aggression of violent individuals?
Degree of Automation	How automated is the job?
Importance of Repeating Same Tasks	How important is repeating the same physical activities (e.g., key entry) or mental activities (e.g., checking entries in a ledger) over and over, without stopping, to performing this job?
Letters and Memos	How often does the job require written letters and memos?

Exposed to Contaminants	How often does this job require working exposed to contaminants (such as pollutants, gases, dust or odors)?
Spend Time Kneeling, Crouching, Stooping, or Crawl	How much does this job require kneeling, crouching, stooping or crawling?
Spend Time Sitting	How much does this job require sitting?
Very Hot or Cold Temperatures	How often does this job require working in very hot (above 90 F degrees) or very cold (below 32 F degrees) temperatures?
Spend Time Keeping or Regaining Balance	How much does this job require keeping or regaining your balance?
Consequence of Error	How serious would the result usually be if the worker made a mistake that was not readily correctable?
Cramped Work Space, Awkward Positions	How often does this job require working in cramped work spaces that requires getting into awkward positions?
Wear Common Protective or Safety Equipment such as	How much does this job require wearing common protective or safety equipment such as safety shoes, glasses, gloves, hard hats or live jackets?
In an Open Vehicle or Equipment	How often does this job require working in an open vehicle or equipment (e.g., tractor)?
In an Enclosed Vehicle or Equipment	How often does this job require working in a closed vehicle or equipment (e.g., car)?
Public Speaking	How often do you have to perform public speaking in this job?
Outdoors, Under Cover	How often does this job require working outdoors, under cover (e.g., structure with roof but no walls)?
Exposed to Hazardous Equipment	How often does this job require exposure to hazardous equipment?
Exposed to Whole Body Vibration	How often does this job require exposure to whole body vibration (e.g., operate a jackhammer)?
Exposed to Disease or Infections	How often does this job require exposure to disease/infections?
Exposed to Radiation	How often does this job require exposure to radiation?
Spend Time Climbing Ladders, Scaffolds, or Poles	How much does this job require climbing ladders, scaffolds, or poles?
Wear Specialized Protective or Safety Equipment su	How much does this job require wearing specialized protective or safety equipment such as breathing apparatus, safety harness, full protection suits, or radiation protection?
Exposed to High Places	How often does this job require exposure to high places?
Electronic Mail	How often do you use electronic mail in this job?
Extremely Bright or Inadequate Lighting	How often does this job require working in extremely bright or inadequate lighting conditions?
Indoors, Not Environmentally Controlled	How often does this job require working indoors in non-controlled environmental conditions (e.g., warehouse without heat)?
Exposed to Hazardous Conditions	How often does this job require exposure to hazardous conditions?

Job Zone Component	Job Zone Component Definitions
Title	Job Zone One: Little or No Preparation Needed
Overall Experience	No previous work-related skill, knowledge, or experience is needed for these occupations. For example, a person can become a general office clerk even if he/she has never worked in an office before.
Job Training	Employees in these occupations need anywhere from a few days to a few months of training. Usually, an experienced worker could show you how to do the job.
Job Zone Examples	These occupations involve following instructions and helping others. Examples include bus drivers, forest and conservation workers, general office clerks, home health aides, and waiters/waitresses.
SVP Range	(Below 4.0)
Education	These occupations may require a high school diploma or GED certificate. Some may require a formal training course to obtain a license.

Work_Styles	Work_Styles Definitions
Stress Tolerance	Job requires accepting criticism and dealing calmly and effectively with high stress situations.
Initiative	Job requires a willingness to take on responsibilities and challenges.
Cooperation	Job requires being pleasant with others on the job and displaying a good-natured, cooperative attitude.
Dependability	Job requires being reliable, responsible, and dependable, and fulfilling obligations.

Self Control	Job requires maintaining composure, keeping emotions in check, controlling anger, and avoiding aggressive behavior, even in very difficult situations.
Concern for Others	Job requires being sensitive to others' needs and feelings and being understanding and helpful on the job.
Achievement/Effort	Job requires establishing and maintaining personally challenging achievement goals and exerting effort toward mastering tasks.
Adaptability/Flexibility	Job requires being open to change (positive or negative) and to considerable variety in the workplace.
Social Orientation	Job requires preferring to work with others rather than alone, and being personally connected with others on the job.
Persistence	Job requires persistence in the face of obstacles.
Attention to Detail	Job requires being careful about detail and thorough in completing work tasks.
Integrity	Job requires being honest and ethical.
Independence	Job requires developing one's own ways of doing things, guiding oneself with little or no supervision, and depending on oneself to get things done.
Leadership	Job requires a willingness to lead, take charge, and offer opinions and direction.
Analytical Thinking	Job requires analyzing information and using logic to address work-related issues and problems.
Innovation	Job requires creativity and alternative thinking to develop new ideas for and answers to work-related problems.

35-2013.00 - Cooks, Private Household

Prepare meals in private homes.

Tasks

1) Create and explore new cuisines.

2) Stock, organize, and clean kitchens and cooking utensils.

3) Travel with employers to vacation homes to provide meal preparation at those locations.

4) Direct the operation and organization of kitchens and all food-related activities, including the presentation and serving of food.

5) Plan and prepare food for parties, holiday meals, luncheons, special functions, and other social events.

6) Plan menus according to employers' needs and diet restrictions.

7) Specialize in preparing fancy dishes and/or food for special diets.

8) Serve meals and snacks to employing families and their guests.

9) Shop for or order food and kitchen supplies and equipment.

10) Prepare meals in private homes according to employers' recipes or tastes, handling all meals for the family and possibly for other household staff.

37-3012.00 - Pesticide Handlers, Sprayers, and Applicators, Vegetation

Mix or apply pesticides, herbicides, fungicides, or insecticides through sprays, dusts, vapors, soil incorporation or chemical application on trees, shrubs, lawns, or botanical crops. Usually requires specific training and State or Federal certification.

Tasks

1) Lift, push, and swing nozzles, hoses, and tubes in order to direct spray over designated areas.

2) Clean and service machinery to ensure operating efficiency, using water, gasoline, lubricants, and/or hand tools.

3) Connect hoses and nozzles selected according to terrain, distribution pattern requirements, types of infestations, and velocities.

4) Start motors and engage machinery, such as sprayer agitators and pumps or portable spray equipment.

5) Fill sprayer tanks with water and chemicals, according to formulas.

6) Provide driving instructions to truck drivers to ensure complete coverage of designated

areas, using hand and horn signals.

7) Plant grass with seed spreaders, and operate straw blowers to cover seeded areas with mixtures of asphalt and straw.

8) Cover areas to specified depths with pesticides, applying knowledge of weather conditions, droplet sizes, elevation-to-distance ratios, and obstructions.

37-3013.00 - Tree Trimmers and Pruners

Cut away dead or excess branches from trees or shrubs to maintain right-of-way for roads, sidewalks, or utilities, or to improve appearance, health, and value of tree. Prune or treat trees or shrubs using handsaws, pruning hooks, sheers, and clippers. May use truck-mounted lifts and power pruners. May fill cavities in trees to promote healing and prevent deterioration.

Tasks

1) Climb trees, using climbing hooks and belts, or climb ladders to gain access to work areas.

2) Clear sites, streets, and grounds of woody and herbaceous materials, such as tree stumps and fallen trees and limbs.

3) Clean, sharpen, and lubricate tools and equipment.

4) Cable, brace, tie, bolt, stake, and guy trees and branches to provide support.

5) Hoist tools and equipment to tree trimmers, and lower branches with ropes or block and tackle.

6) Install lightning protection on trees.

7) Split logs or wooden blocks into bolts, pickets, posts, or stakes, using hand tools such as ax wedges, sledgehammers, and mallets.

8) Plan and develop budgets for tree work, and estimate the monetary value of trees.

9) Provide information to the public regarding trees, such as advice on tree care.

10) Scrape decayed matter from cavities in trees and fill holes with cement to promote healing and to prevent further deterioration.

11) Collect debris and refuse from tree trimming and removal operations into piles, using shovels, rakes or other tools.

12) Transplant and remove trees and shrubs, and prepare trees for moving.

13) Load debris and refuse onto trucks and haul it away for disposal.

14) Operate boom trucks, loaders, stump chippers, brush chippers, tractors, power saws, trucks, sprayers, and other equipment and tools.

15) Inspect trees to determine if they have diseases or pest problems.

16) Trim jagged stumps, using saws or pruning shears.

17) Harvest tanbark by cutting rings and slits in bark and stripping bark from trees, using spuds or axes.

18) Operate shredding and chipping equipment, and feed limbs and brush into the machines.

19) Apply tar or other protective substances to cut surfaces to seal surfaces, and to protect them from fungi and insects.

20) Trim, top, and reshape trees to achieve attractive shapes or to remove low-hanging branches.

21) Prune, cut down, fertilize, and spray trees as directed by tree surgeons.

22) Spray trees to treat diseased or unhealthy trees, including mixing chemicals and calibrating spray equipment.

23) Water, root-feed, and fertilize trees.

24) Supervise others engaged in tree trimming work and train lower-level employees.

25) Cut away dead and excess branches from trees, or clear branches around power lines, using climbing equipment or buckets of extended truck booms, and/or chainsaws, hooks, handsaws, shears, and clippers.

39-2021.00 - Nonfarm Animal Caretakers

Feed, water, groom, bathe, exercise, or otherwise care for pets and other nonfarm animals, such as dogs, cats, ornamental fish or birds, zoo animals, and mice. Work in settings such as kennels, animal shelters, zoos, circuses, and aquariums. May keep records of feedings, treatments, and animals received or discharged. May clean, disinfect, and repair cages, pens, or fish tanks.

Tasks

1) Respond to questions from patrons, and provide information about animals, such as behavior, habitat, breeding habits, or facility activities.

2) Examine and observe animals in order to detect signs of illness, disease, or injury.

3) Answer telephones and schedule appointments.

4) Feed and water animals according to schedules and feeding instructions.

5) Perform animal grooming duties such as washing, brushing, clipping, and trimming coats, cutting nails, and cleaning ears.

6) Provide treatment to sick or injured animals, or contact veterinarians in order to secure treatment.

7) Order, unload, and store feed and supplies.

8) Exercise animals in order to maintain their physical and mental health.

9) Collect and record animal information such as weight, size, physical condition, treatments received, medications given, and food intake.

10) Mix food, liquid formulas, medications, or food supplements according to instructions, prescriptions, and knowledge of animal species.

11) Install, maintain, and repair animal care facility equipment such as infrared lights, feeding devices, and cages.

12) Discuss with clients their pets' grooming needs.

13) Find homes for stray or unwanted animals.

14) Transfer animals between enclosures in order to facilitate breeding, birthing, shipping, or rearrangement of exhibits.

15) Observe and caution children petting and feeding animals in designated areas in order to ensure the safety of humans and animals.

16) Adjust controls to regulate specified temperature and humidity of animal quarters, nurseries, or exhibit areas.

17) Train animals to perform certain tasks.

18) Anesthetize and inoculate animals, according to instructions.

19) Sell pet food and supplies.

20) Clean and disinfect surgical equipment.

21) Teach obedience classes.

22) Saddle and shoe animals.

Knowledge	Knowledge Definitions
Customer and Personal Service	Knowledge of principles and processes for providing customer and personal services. This includes customer needs assessment, meeting quality standards for services, and evaluation of customer satisfaction.
English Language	Knowledge of the structure and content of the English language including the meaning and spelling of words, rules of composition, and grammar.
Administration and Management	Knowledge of business and management principles involved in strategic planning, resource allocation, human resources modeling, leadership technique, production methods, and coordination of people and resources.
Public Safety and Security	Knowledge of relevant equipment, policies, procedures, and strategies to promote effective local, state, or national security operations for the protection of people, data, property, and institutions.
Biology	Knowledge of plant and animal organisms, their tissues, cells, functions, interdependencies, and interactions with each other and the environment.
Clerical	Knowledge of administrative and clerical procedures and systems such as word processing, managing files and records, stenography and transcription, designing forms, and other office procedures and terminology.
Education and Training	Knowledge of principles and methods for curriculum and training design, teaching and instruction for individuals and groups, and the measurement of training effects.
Psychology	Knowledge of human behavior and performance; individual differences in ability, personality, and interests; learning and motivation; psychological research methods; and the assessment and treatment of behavioral and affective disorders.
Mechanical	Knowledge of machines and tools, including their designs, uses, repair, and maintenance.
Sales and Marketing	Knowledge of principles and methods for showing, promoting, and selling products or services. This includes marketing strategy and tactics, product demonstration, sales techniques, and sales control systems.
Mathematics	Knowledge of arithmetic, algebra, geometry, calculus, statistics, and their applications.
Law and Government	Knowledge of laws, legal codes, court procedures, precedents, government regulations, executive orders, agency rules, and the democratic political process.
Telecommunications	Knowledge of transmission, broadcasting, switching, control, and operation of telecommunications systems.
Personnel and Human Resources	Knowledge of principles and procedures for personnel recruitment, selection, training, compensation and benefits, labor relations and negotiation, and personnel information systems.
Production and Processing	Knowledge of raw materials, production processes, quality control, costs, and other techniques for maximizing the effective manufacture and distribution of goods.
Medicine and Dentistry	Knowledge of the information and techniques needed to diagnose and treat human injuries, diseases, and deformities. This includes symptoms, treatment alternatives, drug properties and interactions, and preventive health-care measures.
Economics and Accounting	Knowledge of economic and accounting principles and practices, the financial markets, banking and the analysis and reporting of financial data.
Communications and Media	Knowledge of media production, communication, and dissemination techniques and methods. This includes alternative ways to inform and entertain via written, oral, and visual media.
Computers and Electronics	Knowledge of circuit boards, processors, chips, electronic equipment, and computer hardware and software, including applications and programming.
Chemistry	Knowledge of the chemical composition, structure, and properties of substances and of the chemical processes and transformations that they undergo. This includes uses of chemicals and their interactions, danger signs, production techniques, and disposal methods.
Transportation	Knowledge of principles and methods for moving people or goods by air, rail, sea, or road, including the relative costs and benefits.
Geography	Knowledge of principles and methods for describing the features of land, sea, and air masses, including their physical characteristics, locations, interrelationships, and distribution of plant, animal, and human life.
Sociology and Anthropology	Knowledge of group behavior and dynamics, societal trends and influences, human migrations, ethnicity, cultures and their history and origins.
Building and Construction	Knowledge of materials, methods, and the tools involved in the construction or repair of houses, buildings, or other structures such as highways and roads.
Therapy and Counseling	Knowledge of principles, methods, and procedures for diagnosis, treatment, and rehabilitation of physical and mental dysfunctions, and for career counseling and guidance.
Food Production	Knowledge of techniques and equipment for planting, growing, and harvesting food products (both plant and animal) for consumption, including storage/handling techniques.
Foreign Language	Knowledge of the structure and content of a foreign (non-English) language including the meaning and spelling of words, rules of composition and grammar, and pronunciation.
Engineering and Technology	Knowledge of the practical application of engineering science and technology. This includes applying principles, techniques, procedures, and equipment to the design and production of various goods and services.
Philosophy and Theology	Knowledge of different philosophical systems and religions. This includes their basic principles, values, ethics, ways of thinking, customs, practices, and their impact on human culture.
Physics	Knowledge and prediction of physical principles, laws, their interrelationships, and applications to understanding fluid, material, and atmospheric dynamics, and mechanical, electrical, atomic and sub-atomic structures and processes.
Fine Arts	Knowledge of the theory and techniques required to compose, produce, and perform works of music, dance, visual arts, drama, and sculpture.
History and Archeology	Knowledge of historical events and their causes, indicators, and effects on civilizations and cultures.

Design	Knowledge of design techniques, tools, and principles involved in production of precision technical plans, blueprints, drawings, and models.

Skills	Skills Definitions
Active Listening	Giving full attention to what other people are saying, taking time to understand the points being made, asking questions as appropriate, and not interrupting at inappropriate times.
Time Management	Managing one's own time and the time of others.
Speaking	Talking to others to convey information effectively.
Social Perceptiveness	Being aware of others' reactions and understanding why they react as they do.
Coordination	Adjusting actions in relation to others' actions.
Reading Comprehension	Understanding written sentences and paragraphs in work related documents.
Judgment and Decision Making	Considering the relative costs and benefits of potential actions to choose the most appropriate one.
Instructing	Teaching others how to do something.
Equipment Selection	Determining the kind of tools and equipment needed to do a job.
Critical Thinking	Using logic and reasoning to identify the strengths and weaknesses of alternative solutions, conclusions or approaches to problems.
Persuasion	Persuading others to change their minds or behavior.
Active Learning	Understanding the implications of new information for both current and future problem-solving and decision-making.
Equipment Maintenance	Performing routine maintenance on equipment and determining when and what kind of maintenance is needed.
Monitoring	Monitoring/Assessing performance of yourself, other individuals, or organizations to make improvements or take corrective action.
Learning Strategies	Selecting and using training/instructional methods and procedures appropriate for the situation when learning or teaching new things.
Service Orientation	Actively looking for ways to help people.
Management of Material Resources	Obtaining and seeing to the appropriate use of equipment, facilities, and materials needed to do certain work.
Complex Problem Solving	Identifying complex problems and reviewing related information to develop and evaluate options and implement solutions.
Mathematics	Using mathematics to solve problems.
Management of Financial Resources	Determining how money will be spent to get the work done, and accounting for these expenditures.
Writing	Communicating effectively in writing as appropriate for the needs of the audience.
Quality Control Analysis	Conducting tests and inspections of products, services, or processes to evaluate quality or performance.
Negotiation	Bringing others together and trying to reconcile differences.
Management of Personnel Resources	Motivating, developing, and directing people as they work, identifying the best people for the job.
Repairing	Repairing machines or systems using the needed tools.
Troubleshooting	Determining causes of operating errors and deciding what to do about it.
Operations Analysis	Analyzing needs and product requirements to create a design.
Systems Evaluation	Identifying measures or indicators of system performance and the actions needed to improve or correct performance, relative to the goals of the system.
Installation	Installing equipment, machines, wiring, or programs to meet specifications.
Science	Using scientific rules and methods to solve problems.
Operation Monitoring	Watching gauges, dials, or other indicators to make sure a machine is working properly.
Technology Design	Generating or adapting equipment and technology to serve user needs.
Operation and Control	Controlling operations of equipment or systems.
Systems Analysis	Determining how a system should work and how changes in conditions, operations, and the environment will affect outcomes.
Programming	Writing computer programs for various purposes.

Ability	Ability Definitions
Oral Expression	The ability to communicate information and ideas in speaking so others will understand.
Speech Recognition	The ability to identify and understand the speech of another person.
Problem Sensitivity	The ability to tell when something is wrong or is likely to go wrong. It does not involve solving the problem, only recognizing there is a problem.
Oral Comprehension	The ability to listen to and understand information and ideas presented through spoken words and sentences.
Speech Clarity	The ability to speak clearly so others can understand you.
Inductive Reasoning	The ability to combine pieces of information to form general rules or conclusions (includes finding a relationship among seemingly unrelated events).
Deductive Reasoning	The ability to apply general rules to specific problems to produce answers that make sense.
Information Ordering	The ability to arrange things or actions in a certain order or pattern according to a specific rule or set of rules (e.g., patterns of numbers, letters, words, pictures, mathematical operations).
Near Vision	The ability to see details at close range (within a few feet of the observer).
Static Strength	The ability to exert maximum muscle force to lift, push, pull, or carry objects.
Arm-Hand Steadiness	The ability to keep your hand and arm steady while moving your arm or while holding your arm and hand in one position.
Written Comprehension	The ability to read and understand information and ideas presented in writing.
Selective Attention	The ability to concentrate on a task over a period of time without being distracted.
Stamina	The ability to exert yourself physically over long periods of time without getting winded or out of breath.
Trunk Strength	The ability to use your abdominal and lower back muscles to support part of the body repeatedly or continuously over time without 'giving out' or fatiguing.
Category Flexibility	The ability to generate or use different sets of rules for combining or grouping things in different ways.
Multilimb Coordination	The ability to coordinate two or more limbs (for example, two arms, two legs, or one leg and one arm) while sitting, standing, or lying down. It does not involve performing the activities while the whole body is in motion.
Far Vision	The ability to see details at a distance.
Manual Dexterity	The ability to quickly move your hand, your hand together with your arm, or your two hands to grasp, manipulate, or assemble objects.
Written Expression	The ability to communicate information and ideas in writing so others will understand.
Flexibility of Closure	The ability to identify or detect a known pattern (a figure, object, word, or sound) that is hidden in other distracting material.
Auditory Attention	The ability to focus on a single source of sound in the presence of other distracting sounds.
Speed of Closure	The ability to quickly make sense of, combine, and organize information into meaningful patterns.
Originality	The ability to come up with unusual or clever ideas about a given topic or situation, or to develop creative ways to solve a problem.
Perceptual Speed	The ability to quickly and accurately compare similarities and differences among sets of letters, numbers, objects, pictures, or patterns. The things to be compared may be presented at the same time or one after the other. This ability also includes comparing a presented object with a remembered object.
Visual Color Discrimination	The ability to match or detect differences between colors, including shades of color and brightness.
Finger Dexterity	The ability to make precisely coordinated movements of the fingers of one or both hands to grasp, manipulate, or assemble very small objects.
Extent Flexibility	The ability to bend, stretch, twist, or reach with your body, arms, and/or legs.
Depth Perception	The ability to judge which of several objects is closer or farther away from you, or to judge the distance between you and an object.
Visualization	The ability to imagine how something will look after it is moved around or when its parts are moved or rearranged.
Fluency of Ideas	The ability to come up with a number of ideas about a topic (the number of ideas is important, not their quality, correctness, or creativity).
Control Precision	The ability to quickly and repeatedly adjust the controls of a machine or a vehicle to exact positions.
Gross Body Coordination	The ability to coordinate the movement of your arms, legs, and torso together when the whole body is in motion.
Number Facility	The ability to add, subtract, multiply, or divide quickly and correctly.

Time Sharing	The ability to shift back and forth between two or more activities or sources of information (such as speech, sounds, touch, or other sources).
Speed of Limb Movement	The ability to quickly move the arms and legs.
Mathematical Reasoning	The ability to choose the right mathematical methods or formulas to solve a problem.
Hearing Sensitivity	The ability to detect or tell the differences between sounds that vary in pitch and loudness.
Reaction Time	The ability to quickly respond (with the hand, finger, or foot) to a signal (sound, light, picture) when it appears.
Response Orientation	The ability to choose quickly between two or more movements in response to two or more different signals (lights, sounds, pictures). It includes the speed with which the correct response is started with the hand, foot, or other body part.
Memorization	The ability to remember information such as words, numbers, pictures, and procedures.
Dynamic Strength	The ability to exert muscle force repeatedly or continuously over time. This involves muscular endurance and resistance to muscle fatigue.
Sound Localization	The ability to tell the direction from which a sound originated.
Peripheral Vision	The ability to see objects or movement of objects to one's side when the eyes are looking ahead.
Gross Body Equilibrium	The ability to keep or regain your body balance or stay upright when in an unstable position.
Rate Control	The ability to time your movements or the movement of a piece of equipment in anticipation of changes in the speed and/or direction of a moving object or scene.
Spatial Orientation	The ability to know your location in relation to the environment or to know where other objects are in relation to you.
Glare Sensitivity	The ability to see objects in the presence of glare or bright lighting.
Night Vision	The ability to see under low light conditions.
Explosive Strength	The ability to use short bursts of muscle force to propel oneself (as in jumping or sprinting), or to throw an object.
Wrist-Finger Speed	The ability to make fast, simple, repeated movements of the fingers, hands, and wrists.
Dynamic Flexibility	The ability to quickly and repeatedly bend, stretch, twist, or reach out with your body, arms, and/or legs.

Work_Activity	Work_Activity Definitions
Handling and Moving Objects	Using hands and arms in handling, installing, positioning, and moving materials, and manipulating things.
Performing General Physical Activities	Performing physical activities that require considerable use of your arms and legs and moving your whole body, such as climbing, lifting, balancing, walking, stooping, and handling of materials.
Performing for or Working Directly with the Public	Performing for people or dealing directly with the public. This includes serving customers in restaurants and stores, and receiving clients or guests.
Communicating with Supervisors, Peers, or Subordin	Providing information to supervisors, co-workers, and subordinates by telephone, in written form, e-mail, or in person.
Updating and Using Relevant Knowledge	Keeping up-to-date technically and applying new knowledge to your job.
Communicating with Persons Outside Organization	Communicating with people outside the organization, representing the organization to customers, the public, government, and other external sources. This information can be exchanged in person, in writing, or by telephone or e-mail.
Establishing and Maintaining Interpersonal Relatio	Developing constructive and cooperative working relationships with others, and maintaining them over time.
Making Decisions and Solving Problems	Analyzing information and evaluating results to choose the best solution and solve problems.
Getting Information	Observing, receiving, and otherwise obtaining information from all relevant sources.
Resolving Conflicts and Negotiating with Others	Handling complaints, settling disputes, and resolving grievances and conflicts, or otherwise negotiating with others.
Identifying Objects, Actions, and Events	Identifying information by categorizing, estimating, recognizing differences or similarities, and detecting changes in circumstances or events.
Organizing, Planning, and Prioritizing Work	Developing specific goals and plans to prioritize, organize, and accomplish your work.
Monitor Processes, Materials, or Surroundings	Monitoring and reviewing information from materials, events, or the environment, to detect or assess problems.
Documenting/Recording Information	Entering, transcribing, recording, storing, or maintaining information in written or electronic/magnetic form.

Judging the Qualities of Things, Services, or Peop	Assessing the value, importance, or quality of things or people.
Assisting and Caring for Others	Providing personal assistance, medical attention, emotional support, or other personal care to others such as coworkers, customers, or patients.
Evaluating Information to Determine Compliance wit	Using relevant information and individual judgment to determine whether events or processes comply with laws, regulations, or standards.
Coaching and Developing Others	Identifying the developmental needs of others and coaching, mentoring, or otherwise helping others to improve their knowledge or skills.
Thinking Creatively	Developing, designing, or creating new applications, ideas, relationships, systems, or products, including artistic contributions.
Inspecting Equipment, Structures, or Material	Inspecting equipment, structures, or materials to identify the cause of errors or other problems or defects.
Estimating the Quantifiable Characteristics of Pro	Estimating sizes, distances, and quantities; or determining time, costs, resources, or materials needed to perform a work activity.
Processing Information	Compiling, coding, categorizing, calculating, tabulating, auditing, or verifying information or data.
Scheduling Work and Activities	Scheduling events, programs, and activities, as well as the work of others.
Coordinating the Work and Activities of Others	Getting members of a group to work together to accomplish tasks.
Performing Administrative Activities	Performing day-to-day administrative tasks such as maintaining information files and processing paperwork.
Interpreting the Meaning of Information for Others	Translating or explaining what information means and how it can be used.
Operating Vehicles, Mechanized Devices, or Equipme	Running, maneuvering, navigating, or driving vehicles or mechanized equipment, such as forklifts, passenger vehicles, aircraft, or water craft.
Selling or Influencing Others	Convincing others to buy merchandise/goods or to otherwise change their minds or actions.
Guiding, Directing, and Motivating Subordinates	Providing guidance and direction to subordinates, including setting performance standards and monitoring performance.
Analyzing Data or Information	Identifying the underlying principles, reasons, or facts of information by breaking down information or data into separate parts.
Training and Teaching Others	Identifying the educational needs of others, developing formal educational or training programs or classes, and teaching or instructing others.
Monitoring and Controlling Resources	Monitoring and controlling resources and overseeing the spending of money.
Provide Consultation and Advice to Others	Providing guidance and expert advice to management or other groups on technical, systems-, or process-related topics.
Developing Objectives and Strategies	Establishing long-range objectives and specifying the strategies and actions to achieve them.
Developing and Building Teams	Encouraging and building mutual trust, respect, and cooperation among team members.
Repairing and Maintaining Mechanical Equipment	Servicing, repairing, adjusting, and testing machines, devices, moving parts, and equipment that operate primarily on the basis of mechanical (not electronic) principles.
Interacting With Computers	Using computers and computer systems (including hardware and software) to program, write software, set up functions, enter data, or process information.
Controlling Machines and Processes	Using either control mechanisms or direct physical activity to operate machines or processes (not including computers or vehicles).
Staffing Organizational Units	Recruiting, interviewing, selecting, hiring, and promoting employees in an organization.
Repairing and Maintaining Electronic Equipment	Servicing, repairing, calibrating, regulating, fine-tuning, or testing machines, devices, and equipment that operate primarily on the basis of electrical or electronic (not mechanical) principles.
Drafting, Laying Out, and Specifying Technical Dev	Providing documentation, detailed instructions, drawings, or specifications to tell others about how devices, parts, equipment, or structures are to be fabricated, constructed, assembled, modified, maintained, or used.

Work_Context	Work_Context Definitions
Face-to-Face Discussions	How often do you have to have face-to-face discussions with individuals or teams in this job?
Freedom to Make Decisions	How much decision making freedom, without supervision, does the job offer?

Contact With Others	How much does this job require the worker to be in contact with others (face-to-face, by telephone, or otherwise) in order to perform it?
Telephone	How often do you have telephone conversations in this job?
Frequency of Decision Making	How frequently is the worker required to make decisions that affect other people, the financial resources, and/or the image and reputation of the organization?
Structured versus Unstructured Work	To what extent is this job structured for the worker, rather than allowing the worker to determine tasks, priorities, and goals?
Outdoors, Exposed to Weather	How often does this job require working outdoors, exposed to all weather conditions?
Spend Time Standing	How much does this job require standing?
Indoors, Environmentally Controlled	How often does this job require working indoors in environmentally controlled conditions?
Sounds, Noise Levels Are Distracting or Uncomforta	How often does this job require working exposed to sounds and noise levels that are distracting or uncomfortable?
Exposed to Contaminants	How often does this job require working exposed to contaminants (such as pollutants, gases, dust or odors)?
Impact of Decisions on Co-workers or Company Resul	How do the decisions an employee makes impact the results of co-workers, clients or the company?
Exposed to Minor Burns, Cuts, Bites, or Stings	How often does this job require exposure to minor burns, cuts, bites, or stings?
Work With Work Group or Team	How important is it to work with others in a group or team in this job?
Importance of Being Exact or Accurate	How important is being very exact or highly accurate in performing this job?
Physical Proximity	To what extent does this job require the worker to perform job tasks in close physical proximity to other people?
Spend Time Using Your Hands to Handle, Control, or	How much does this job require using your hands to handle, control, or feel objects, tools or controls?
Spend Time Walking and Running	How much does this job require walking and running?
Responsibility for Outcomes and Results	How responsible is the worker for work outcomes and results of other workers?
Deal With External Customers	How important is it to work with external customers or the public in this job?
Responsible for Others' Health and Safety	How much responsibility is there for the health and safety of others in this job?
Consequence of Error	How serious would the result usually be if the worker made a mistake that was not readily correctable?
Letters and Memos	How often does the job require written letters and memos?
Spend Time Making Repetitive Motions	How much does this job require making repetitive motions?
Time Pressure	How often does this job require the worker to meet strict deadlines?
Outdoors, Under Cover	How often does this job require working outdoors, under cover (e.g., structure with roof but no walls)?
Very Hot or Cold Temperatures	How often does this job require working in very hot (above 90 F degrees) or very cold (below 32 F degrees) temperatures?
Spend Time Bending or Twisting the Body	How much does this job require bending or twisting your body?
Coordinate or Lead Others	How important is it to coordinate or lead others in accomplishing work activities in this job?
Importance of Repeating Same Tasks	How important is repeating the same physical activities (e.g., key entry) or mental activities (e.g., checking entries in a ledger) over and over, without stopping, to performing this job?
Deal With Unpleasant or Angry People	How frequently does the worker have to deal with unpleasant, angry, or discourteous individuals as part of the job requirements?
Exposed to Disease or Infections	How often does this job require exposure to disease/infections?
Indoors, Not Environmentally Controlled	How often does this job require working indoors in non-controlled environmental conditions (e.g., warehouse without heat)?
Frequency of Conflict Situations	How often are there conflict situations the employee has to face in this job?
Wear Common Protective or Safety Equipment such as	How much does this job require wearing common protective or safety equipment such as safety shoes, glasses, gloves, hard hats or life jackets?
In an Enclosed Vehicle or Equipment	How often does this job require working in a closed vehicle or equipment (e.g., car)?
Spend Time Kneeling, Crouching, Stooping, or Crawl	How much does this job require kneeling, crouching, stooping or crawling?
Level of Competition	To what extent does this job require the worker to compete or to be aware of competitive pressures?

Cramped Work Space, Awkward Positions	How often does this job require working in cramped work spaces that requires getting into awkward positions?
In an Open Vehicle or Equipment	How often does this job require working in an open vehicle or equipment (e.g., tractor)?
Public Speaking	How often do you have to perform public speaking in this job?
Spend Time Sitting	How much does this job require sitting?
Extremely Bright or Inadequate Lighting	How often does this job require working in extremely bright or inadequate lighting conditions?
Exposed to Hazardous Equipment	How often does this job require exposure to hazardous equipment?
Deal With Physically Aggressive People	How frequently does this job require the worker to deal with physical aggression of violent individuals?
Electronic Mail	How often do you use electronic mail in this job?
Spend Time Keeping or Regaining Balance	How much does this job require keeping or regaining your balance?
Degree of Automation	How automated is the job?
Exposed to Hazardous Conditions	How often does this job require exposure to hazardous conditions?
Exposed to High Places	How often does this job require exposure to high places?
Wear Specialized Protective or Safety Equipment su	How much does this job require wearing specialized protective or safety equipment such as breathing apparatus, safety harness, full protection suits, or radiation protection?
Spend Time Climbing Ladders, Scaffolds, or Poles	How much does this job require climbing ladders, scaffolds, or poles?
Pace Determined by Speed of Equipment	How important is it to this job that the pace is determined by the speed of equipment or machinery? (This does not refer to keeping busy at all times on this job.)
Exposed to Whole Body Vibration	How often does this job require exposure to whole body vibration (e.g., operate a jackhammer)?
Exposed to Radiation	How often does this job require exposure to radiation?

Job Zone Component	Job Zone Component Definitions
Title	Job Zone Two: Some Preparation Needed
Overall Experience	Some previous work-related skill, knowledge, or experience may be helpful in these occupations, but usually is not needed. For example, a drywall installer might benefit from experience installing drywall, but an inexperienced person could still learn to be an installer with little difficulty.
Job Training	Employees in these occupations need anywhere from a few months to one year of working with experienced employees.
Job Zone Examples	These occupations often involve using your knowledge and skills to help others. Examples include drywall installers, fire inspectors, flight attendants, pharmacy technicians, salespersons (retail), and tellers.
SVP Range	(4.0 to < 6.0)
Education	These occupations usually require a high school diploma and may require some vocational training or job-related course work. In some cases, an associate's or bachelor's degree could be needed.

Work_Styles	Work_Styles Definitions
Dependability	Job requires being reliable, responsible, and dependable, and fulfilling obligations.
Cooperation	Job requires being pleasant with others on the job and displaying a good-natured, cooperative attitude.
Attention to Detail	Job requires being careful about detail and thorough in completing work tasks.
Integrity	Job requires being honest and ethical.
Self Control	Job requires maintaining composure, keeping emotions in check, controlling anger, and avoiding aggressive behavior, even in very difficult situations.
Independence	Job requires developing one's own ways of doing things, guiding oneself with little or no supervision, and depending on oneself to get things done.
Stress Tolerance	Job requires accepting criticism and dealing calmly and effectively with high stress situations.
Adaptability/Flexibility	Job requires being open to change (positive or negative) and to considerable variety in the workplace.
Initiative	Job requires a willingness to take on responsibilities and challenges.
Concern for Others	Job requires being sensitive to others' needs and feelings and being understanding and helpful on the job.
Persistence	Job requires persistence in the face of obstacles.

Social Orientation	Job requires preferring to work with others rather than alone, and being personally connected with others on the job.
Achievement/Effort	Job requires establishing and maintaining personally challenging achievement goals and exerting effort toward mastering tasks.
Innovation	Job requires creativity and alternative thinking to develop new ideas for and answers to work-related problems.
Leadership	Job requires a willingness to lead, take charge, and offer opinions and direction.
Analytical Thinking	Job requires analyzing information and using logic to address work-related issues and problems.

39-3031.00 - Ushers, Lobby Attendants, and Ticket Takers

Assist patrons at entertainment events by performing duties, such as collecting admission tickets and passes from patrons, assisting in finding seats, searching for lost articles, and locating such facilities as rest rooms and telephones.

Tasks

1) Greet patrons attending entertainment events.

2) Provide assistance with patrons' special needs, such as helping those with wheelchairs.

3) Search for lost articles or for parents of lost children.

4) Guide patrons to exits or provide other instructions or assistance in case of emergency.

5) Maintain order and ensure adherence to safety rules.

6) Sell and collect admission tickets and passes from patrons at entertainment events.

7) Refuse admittance to undesirable persons or persons without tickets or passes.

8) Examine tickets or passes to verify authenticity, using criteria such as color and date issued.

9) Settle seating disputes and help solve other customer concerns.

10) Assist patrons in finding seats, lighting the way with flashlights if necessary.

11) Distribute programs to patrons.

12) Count and record number of tickets collected.

13) Give door checks to patrons who are temporarily leaving establishments.

14) Operate refreshment stands during intermission or obtain refreshments for press box patrons during performances.

15) Work with others to change advertising displays.

16) Manage informational kiosk and display of event signs and posters.

17) Verify credentials of patrons desiring entrance into press-box and permit only authorized persons to enter.

18) Page individuals wanted at the box office.

19) Manage inventory and sale of artist merchandise.

20) Schedule and manage volunteer usher corps.

Knowledge	Knowledge Definitions
Customer and Personal Service	Knowledge of principles and processes for providing customer and personal services. This includes customer needs assessment, meeting quality standards for services, and evaluation of customer satisfaction.
English Language	Knowledge of the structure and content of the English language including the meaning and spelling of words, rules of composition, and grammar.
Mathematics	Knowledge of arithmetic, algebra, geometry, calculus, statistics, and their applications.
Sales and Marketing	Knowledge of principles and methods for showing, promoting, and selling products or services. This includes marketing strategy and tactics, product demonstration, sales techniques, and sales control systems.
Computers and Electronics	Knowledge of circuit boards, processors, chips, electronic equipment, and computer hardware and software, including applications and programming.
Food Production	Knowledge of techniques and equipment for planting, growing, and harvesting food products (both plant and animal) for consumption, including storage/handling techniques.

Communications and Media	Knowledge of media production, communication, and dissemination techniques and methods. This includes alternative ways to inform and entertain via written, oral, and visual media.
Administration and Management	Knowledge of business and management principles involved in strategic planning, resource allocation, human resources modeling, leadership technique, production methods, and coordination of people and resources.
Clerical	Knowledge of administrative and clerical procedures and systems such as word processing, managing files and records, stenography and transcription, designing forms, and other office procedures and terminology.
Psychology	Knowledge of human behavior and performance; individual differences in ability, personality, and interests; learning and motivation; psychological research methods; and the assessment and treatment of behavioral and affective disorders.
Public Safety and Security	Knowledge of relevant equipment, policies, procedures, and strategies to promote effective local, state, or national security operations for the protection of people, data, property, and institutions.
Economics and Accounting	Knowledge of economic and accounting principles and practices, the financial markets, banking and the analysis and reporting of financial data.
History and Archeology	Knowledge of historical events and their causes, indicators, and effects on civilizations and cultures.
Telecommunications	Knowledge of transmission, broadcasting, switching, control, and operation of telecommunications systems.
Personnel and Human Resources	Knowledge of principles and procedures for personnel recruitment, selection, training, compensation and benefits, labor relations and negotiation, and personnel information systems.
Foreign Language	Knowledge of the structure and content of a foreign (non-English) language including the meaning and spelling of words, rules of composition and grammar, and pronunciation.
Education and Training	Knowledge of principles and methods for curriculum and training design, teaching and instruction for individuals and groups, and the measurement of training effects.
Geography	Knowledge of principles and methods for describing the features of land, sea, and air masses, including their physical characteristics, locations, interrelationships, and distribution of plant, animal, and human life.
Law and Government	Knowledge of laws, legal codes, court procedures, precedents, government regulations, executive orders, agency rules, and the democratic political process.
Mechanical	Knowledge of machines and tools, including their designs, uses, repair, and maintenance.
Fine Arts	Knowledge of the theory and techniques required to compose, produce, and perform works of music, dance, visual arts, drama, and sculpture.
Production and Processing	Knowledge of raw materials, production processes, quality control, costs, and other techniques for maximizing the effective manufacture and distribution of goods.
Transportation	Knowledge of principles and methods for moving people or goods by air, rail, sea, or road, including the relative costs and benefits.
Sociology and Anthropology	Knowledge of group behavior and dynamics, societal trends and influences, human migrations, ethnicity, cultures and their history and origins.
Chemistry	Knowledge of the chemical composition, structure, and properties of substances and of the chemical processes and transformations that they undergo. This includes uses of chemicals and their interactions, danger signs, production techniques, and disposal methods.
Medicine and Dentistry	Knowledge of the information and techniques needed to diagnose and treat human injuries, diseases, and deformities. This includes symptoms, treatment alternatives, drug properties and interactions, and preventive health-care measures.
Philosophy and Theology	Knowledge of different philosophical systems and religions. This includes their basic principles, values, ethics, ways of thinking, customs, practices, and their impact on human culture.
Physics	Knowledge and prediction of physical principles, laws, their interrelationships, and applications to understanding fluid, material, and atmospheric dynamics, and mechanical, electrical, atomic and sub- atomic structures and processes.
Therapy and Counseling	Knowledge of principles, methods, and procedures for diagnosis, treatment, and rehabilitation of physical and mental dysfunctions, and for career counseling and guidance.

Engineering and Technology	Knowledge of the practical application of engineering science and technology. This includes applying principles, techniques, procedures, and equipment to the design and production of various goods and services.
Design	Knowledge of design techniques, tools, and principles involved in production of precision technical plans, blueprints, drawings, and models.
Biology	Knowledge of plant and animal organisms, their tissues, cells, functions, interdependencies, and interactions with each other and the environment.
Building and Construction	Knowledge of materials, methods, and the tools involved in the construction or repair of houses, buildings, or other structures such as highways and roads.

Skills	Skills Definitions
Active Listening	Giving full attention to what other people are saying, taking time to understand the points being made, asking questions as appropriate, and not interrupting at inappropriate times.
Speaking	Talking to others to convey information effectively.
Social Perceptiveness	Being aware of others' reactions and understanding why they react as they do.
Service Orientation	Actively looking for ways to help people.
Coordination	Adjusting actions in relation to others' actions.
Mathematics	Using mathematics to solve problems.
Reading Comprehension	Understanding written sentences and paragraphs in work related documents.
Instructing	Teaching others how to do something.
Learning Strategies	Selecting and using training/instructional methods and procedures appropriate for the situation when learning or teaching new things.
Active Learning	Understanding the implications of new information for both current and future problem-solving and decision-making.
Monitoring	Monitoring/Assessing performance of yourself, other individuals, or organizations to make improvements or take corrective action.
Time Management	Managing one's own time and the time of others.
Persuasion	Persuading others to change their minds or behavior.
Troubleshooting	Determining causes of operating errors and deciding what to do about it.
Operation and Control	Controlling operations of equipment or systems.
Critical Thinking	Using logic and reasoning to identify the strengths and weaknesses of alternative solutions, conclusions or approaches to problems.
Judgment and Decision Making	Considering the relative costs and benefits of potential actions to choose the most appropriate one.
Repairing	Repairing machines or systems using the needed tools.
Writing	Communicating effectively in writing as appropriate for the needs of the audience.
Negotiation	Bringing others together and trying to reconcile differences.
Complex Problem Solving	Identifying complex problems and reviewing related information to develop and evaluate options and implement solutions.
Equipment Selection	Determining the kind of tools and equipment needed to do a job.
Equipment Maintenance	Performing routine maintenance on equipment and determining when and what kind of maintenance is needed.
Management of Material Resources	Obtaining and seeing to the appropriate use of equipment, facilities, and materials needed to do certain work.
Operation Monitoring	Watching gauges, dials, or other indicators to make sure a machine is working properly.
Management of Personnel Resources	Motivating, developing, and directing people as they work, identifying the best people for the job.
Installation	Installing equipment, machines, wiring, or programs to meet specifications.
Quality Control Analysis	Conducting tests and inspections of products, services, or processes to evaluate quality or performance.
Science	Using scientific rules and methods to solve problems.
Operations Analysis	Analyzing needs and product requirements to create a design.
Systems Analysis	Determining how a system should work and how changes in conditions, operations, and the environment will affect outcomes.
Management of Financial Resources	Determining how money will be spent to get the work done, and accounting for these expenditures.
Technology Design	Generating or adapting equipment and technology to serve user needs.

Systems Evaluation	Identifying measures or indicators of system performance and the actions needed to improve or correct performance, relative to the goals of the system.
Programming	Writing computer programs for various purposes.

Ability	Ability Definitions
Speech Clarity	The ability to speak clearly so others can understand you.
Oral Expression	The ability to communicate information and ideas in speaking so others will understand.
Oral Comprehension	The ability to listen to and understand information and ideas presented through spoken words and sentences.
Problem Sensitivity	The ability to tell when something is wrong or is likely to go wrong. It does not involve solving the problem, only recognizing there is a problem.
Speech Recognition	The ability to identify and understand the speech of another person.
Inductive Reasoning	The ability to combine pieces of information to form general rules or conclusions (includes finding a relationship among seemingly unrelated events).
Near Vision	The ability to see details at close range (within a few feet of the observer).
Deductive Reasoning	The ability to apply general rules to specific problems to produce answers that make sense.
Written Comprehension	The ability to read and understand information and ideas presented in writing.
Selective Attention	The ability to concentrate on a task over a period of time without being distracted.
Information Ordering	The ability to arrange things or actions in a certain order or pattern according to a specific rule or set of rules (e.g., patterns of numbers, letters, words, pictures, mathematical operations).
Finger Dexterity	The ability to make precisely coordinated movements of the fingers of one or both hands to grasp, manipulate, or assemble very small objects.
Flexibility of Closure	The ability to identify or detect a known pattern (a figure, object, word, or sound) that is hidden in other distracting material.
Perceptual Speed	The ability to quickly and accurately compare similarities and differences among sets of letters, numbers, objects, pictures, or patterns. The things to be compared may be presented at the same time or one after the other. This ability also includes comparing a presented object with a remembered object.
Trunk Strength	The ability to use your abdominal and lower back muscles to support part of the body repeatedly or continuously over time without 'giving out' or fatiguing.
Category Flexibility	The ability to generate or use different sets of rules for combining or grouping things in different ways.
Far Vision	The ability to see details at a distance.
Visual Color Discrimination	The ability to match or detect differences between colors, including shades of color and brightness.
Manual Dexterity	The ability to quickly move your hand, your hand together with your arm, or your two hands to grasp, manipulate, or assemble objects.
Time Sharing	The ability to shift back and forth between two or more activities or sources of information (such as speech, sounds, touch, or other sources).
Originality	The ability to come up with unusual or clever ideas about a given topic or situation, or to develop creative ways to solve a problem.
Fluency of Ideas	The ability to come up with a number of ideas about a topic (the number of ideas is important, not their quality, correctness, or creativity).
Arm-Hand Steadiness	The ability to keep your hand and arm steady while moving your arm or while holding your arm and hand in one position.
Number Facility	The ability to add, subtract, multiply, or divide quickly and correctly.
Static Strength	The ability to exert maximum muscle force to lift, push, pull, or carry objects.
Written Expression	The ability to communicate information and ideas in writing so others will understand.
Multilimb Coordination	The ability to coordinate two or more limbs (for example, two arms, two legs, or one leg and one arm) while sitting, standing, or lying down. It does not involve performing the activities while the whole body is in motion.
Auditory Attention	The ability to focus on a single source of sound in the presence of other distracting sounds.
Hearing Sensitivity	The ability to detect or tell the differences between sounds that vary in pitch and loudness.

Speed of Closure	The ability to quickly make sense of, combine, and organize information into meaningful patterns.
Visualization	The ability to imagine how something will look after it is moved around or when its parts are moved or rearranged.
Mathematical Reasoning	The ability to choose the right mathematical methods or formulas to solve a problem.
Extent Flexibility	The ability to bend, stretch, twist, or reach with your body, arms, and/or legs.
Memorization	The ability to remember information such as words, numbers, pictures, and procedures.
Depth Perception	The ability to judge which of several objects is closer or farther away from you, or to judge the distance between you and an object.
Gross Body Coordination	The ability to coordinate the movement of your arms, legs, and torso together when the whole body is in motion.
Gross Body Equilibrium	The ability to keep or regain your body balance or stay upright when in an unstable position.
Stamina	The ability to exert yourself physically over long periods of time without getting winded or out of breath.
Control Precision	The ability to quickly and repeatedly adjust the controls of a machine or a vehicle to exact positions.
Dynamic Strength	The ability to exert muscle force repeatedly or continuously over time. This involves muscular endurance and resistance to muscle fatigue.
Spatial Orientation	The ability to know your location in relation to the environment or to know where other objects are in relation to you.
Night Vision	The ability to see under low light conditions.
Wrist-Finger Speed	The ability to make fast, simple, repeated movements of the fingers, hands, and wrists.
Response Orientation	The ability to choose quickly between two or more movements in response to two or more different signals (lights, sounds, pictures). It includes the speed with which the correct response is started with the hand, foot, or other body part.
Reaction Time	The ability to quickly respond (with the hand, finger, or foot) to a signal (sound, light, picture) when it appears.
Peripheral Vision	The ability to see objects or movement of objects to one's side when the eyes are looking ahead.
Speed of Limb Movement	The ability to quickly move the arms and legs.
Glare Sensitivity	The ability to see objects in the presence of glare or bright lighting.
Sound Localization	The ability to tell the direction from which a sound originated.
Dynamic Flexibility	The ability to quickly and repeatedly bend, stretch, twist, or reach out with your body, arms, and/or legs.
Explosive Strength	The ability to use short bursts of muscle force to propel oneself (as in jumping or sprinting), or to throw an object.
Rate Control	The ability to time your movements or the movement of a piece of equipment in anticipation of changes in the speed and/or direction of a moving object or scene.

Work_Activity	**Work_Activity Definitions**
Performing for or Working Directly with the Public	Performing for people or dealing directly with the public. This includes serving customers in restaurants and stores, and receiving clients or guests.
Getting Information	Observing, receiving, and otherwise obtaining information from all relevant sources.
Making Decisions and Solving Problems	Analyzing information and evaluating results to choose the best solution and solve problems.
Assisting and Caring for Others	Providing personal assistance, medical attention, emotional support, or other personal care to others such as coworkers, customers, or patients.
Communicating with Persons Outside Organization	Communicating with people outside the organization, representing the organization to customers, the public, government, and other external sources. This information can be exchanged in person, in writing, or by telephone or e-mail.
Interacting With Computers	Using computers and computer systems (including hardware and software) to program, write software, set up functions, enter data, or process information.
Communicating with Supervisors, Peers, or Subordin	Providing information to supervisors, co-workers, and subordinates by telephone, in written form, e-mail, or in person.
Judging the Qualities of Things, Services, or Peop	Assessing the value, importance, or quality of things or people.
Coordinating the Work and Activities of Others	Getting members of a group to work together to accomplish tasks.
Developing and Building Teams	Encouraging and building mutual trust, respect, and cooperation among team members.

Monitor Processes, Materials, or Surroundings	Monitoring and reviewing information from materials, events, or the environment, to detect or assess problems.
Establishing and Maintaining Interpersonal Relatio	Developing constructive and cooperative working relationships with others, and maintaining them over time.
Identifying Objects, Actions, and Events	Identifying information by categorizing, estimating, recognizing differences or similarities, and detecting changes in circumstances or events.
Evaluating Information to Determine Compliance wit	Using relevant information and individual judgment to determine whether events or processes comply with laws, regulations, or standards.
Resolving Conflicts and Negotiating with Others	Handling complaints, settling disputes, and resolving grievances and conflicts, or otherwise negotiating with others.
Inspecting Equipment, Structures, or Material	Inspecting equipment, structures, or materials to identify the cause of errors or other problems or defects.
Processing Information	Compiling, coding, categorizing, calculating, tabulating, auditing, or verifying information or data.
Handling and Moving Objects	Using hands and arms in handling, installing, positioning, and moving materials, and manipulating things.
Performing General Physical Activities	Performing physical activities that require considerable use of your arms and legs and moving your whole body, such as climbing, lifting, balancing, walking, stooping, and handling of materials.
Scheduling Work and Activities	Scheduling events, programs, and activities, as well as the work of others.
Organizing, Planning, and Prioritizing Work	Developing specific goals and plans to prioritize, organize, and accomplish your work.
Developing Objectives and Strategies	Establishing long-range objectives and specifying the strategies and actions to achieve them.
Selling or Influencing Others	Convincing others to buy merchandise/goods or to otherwise change their minds or actions.
Analyzing Data or Information	Identifying the underlying principles, reasons, or facts of information by breaking down information or data into separate parts.
Updating and Using Relevant Knowledge	Keeping up-to-date technically and applying new knowledge to your job.
Performing Administrative Activities	Performing day-to-day administrative tasks such as maintaining information files and processing paperwork.
Training and Teaching Others	Identifying the educational needs of others, developing formal educational or training programs or classes, and teaching or instructing others.
Coaching and Developing Others	Identifying the developmental needs of others and coaching, mentoring, or otherwise helping others to improve their knowledge or skills.
Thinking Creatively	Developing, designing, or creating new applications, ideas, relationships, systems, or products, including artistic contributions.
Interpreting the Meaning of Information for Others	Translating or explaining what information means and how it can be used.
Estimating the Quantifiable Characteristics of Pro	Estimating sizes, distances, and quantities; or determining time, costs, resources, or materials needed to perform a work activity.
Documenting/Recording Information	Entering, transcribing, recording, storing, or maintaining information in written or electronic/magnetic form.
Guiding, Directing, and Motivating Subordinates	Providing guidance and direction to subordinates, including setting performance standards and monitoring performance.
Monitoring and Controlling Resources	Monitoring and controlling resources and overseeing the spending of money.
Provide Consultation and Advice to Others	Providing guidance and expert advice to management or other groups on technical, systems-, or process-related topics.
Controlling Machines and Processes	Using either control mechanisms or direct physical activity to operate machines or processes (not including computers or vehicles).
Staffing Organizational Units	Recruiting, interviewing, selecting, hiring, and promoting employees in an organization.
Operating Vehicles, Mechanized Devices, or Equipme	Running, maneuvering, navigating, or driving vehicles or mechanized equipment, such as forklifts, passenger vehicles, aircraft, or water craft.
Repairing and Maintaining Electronic Equipment	Servicing, repairing, calibrating, regulating, fine-tuning, or testing machines, devices, and equipment that operate primarily on the basis of electrical or electronic (not mechanical) principles.
Repairing and Maintaining Mechanical Equipment	Servicing, repairing, adjusting, and testing machines, devices, moving parts, and equipment that operate primarily on the basis of mechanical (not electronic) principles.

Drafting, Laying Out, and Specifying Technical Dev	Providing documentation, detailed instructions, drawings, or specifications to tell others about how devices, parts, equipment, or structures are to be fabricated, constructed, assembled, modified, maintained, or used.

Work_Context	Work_Context Definitions
Contact With Others	How much does this job require the worker to be in contact with others (face-to-face, by telephone, or otherwise) in order to perform it?
Face-to-Face Discussions	How often do you have to have face-to-face discussions with individuals or teams in this job?
Indoors, Environmentally Controlled	How often does this job require working indoors in environmentally controlled conditions?
Physical Proximity	To what extent does this job require the worker to perform job tasks in close physical proximity to other people?
Importance of Being Exact or Accurate	How important is being very exact or highly accurate in performing this job?
Spend Time Standing	How much does this job require standing?
Deal With External Customers	How important is it to work with external customers or the public in this job?
Spend Time Using Your Hands to Handle, Control, or	How much does this job require using your hands to handle, control, or feel objects, tools or controls?
Telephone	How often do you have telephone conversations in this job?
Deal With Unpleasant or Angry People	How frequently does the worker have to deal with unpleasant, angry, or discourteous individuals as part of the job requirements?
Work With Work Group or Team	How important is it to work with others in a group or team in this job?
Spend Time Making Repetitive Motions	How much does this job require making repetitive motions?
Frequency of Decision Making	How frequently is the worker required to make decisions that affect other people, the financial resources, and/or the image and reputation of the organization?
Importance of Repeating Same Tasks	How important is repeating the same physical activities (e.g., key entry) or mental activities (e.g., checking entries in a ledger) over and over, without stopping, to performing this job?
Time Pressure	How often does this job require the worker to meet strict deadlines?
Impact of Decisions on Co-workers or Company Resul	How do the decisions an employee makes impact the results of co-workers, clients or the company?
Freedom to Make Decisions	How much decision making freedom, without supervision, does the job offer?
Frequency of Conflict Situations	How often are there conflict situations the employee has to face in this job?
Public Speaking	How often do you have to perform public speaking in this job?
Spend Time Walking and Running	How much does this job require walking and running?
Spend Time Sitting	How much does this job require sitting?
Structured versus Unstructured Work	To what extent is this job structured for the worker, rather than allowing the worker to determine tasks, priorities, and goals?
Sounds, Noise Levels Are Distracting or Uncomforta	How often does this job require working exposed to sounds and noise levels that are distracting or uncomfortable?
Exposed to Minor Burns, Cuts, Bites, or Stings	How often does this job require exposure to minor burns, cuts, bites, or stings?
Coordinate or Lead Others	How important is it to coordinate or lead others in accomplishing work activities in this job?
Outdoors, Exposed to Weather	How often does this job require working outdoors, exposed to all weather conditions?
Level of Competition	To what extent does this job require the worker to compete or to be aware of competitive pressures?
Extremely Bright or Inadequate Lighting	How often does this job require working in extremely bright or inadequate lighting conditions?
Responsible for Others' Health and Safety	How much responsibility is there for the health and safety of others in this job?
Outdoors, Under Cover	How often does this job require working outdoors, under cover (e.g., structure with roof but no walls)?
Consequence of Error	How serious would the result usually be if the worker made a mistake that was not readily correctable?
Degree of Automation	How automated is the job?
Spend Time Bending or Twisting the Body	How much does this job require bending or twisting your body?
Very Hot or Cold Temperatures	How often does this job require working in very hot (above 90 F degrees) or very cold (below 32 F degrees) temperatures?
Responsibility for Outcomes and Results	How responsible is the worker for work outcomes and results of other workers?
Deal With Physically Aggressive People	How frequently does this job require the worker to deal with physical aggression of violent individuals?
Spend Time Kneeling, Crouching, Stooping, or Crawl	How much does this job require kneeling, crouching, stooping or crawling?
Letters and Memos	How often does the job require written letters and memos?
Exposed to Hazardous Equipment	How often does this job require exposure to hazardous equipment?
Exposed to Contaminants	How often does this job require working exposed to contaminants (such as pollutants, gases, dust or odors)?
Electronic Mail	How often do you use electronic mail in this job?
Indoors, Not Environmentally Controlled	How often does this job require working indoors in non-controlled environmental conditions (e.g., warehouse without heat)?
Cramped Work Space, Awkward Positions	How often does this job require working in cramped work spaces that requires getting into awkward positions?
Pace Determined by Speed of Equipment	How important is it to this job that the pace is determined by the speed of equipment or machinery? (This does not refer to keeping busy at all times on this job.)
In an Enclosed Vehicle or Equipment	How often does this job require working in a closed vehicle or equipment (e.g., car)?
Spend Time Keeping or Regaining Balance	How much does this job require keeping or regaining your balance?
Spend Time Climbing Ladders, Scaffolds, or Poles	How much does this job require climbing ladders, scaffolds, or poles?
Exposed to High Places	How often does this job require exposure to high places?
Exposed to Hazardous Conditions	How often does this job require exposure to hazardous conditions?
Exposed to Disease or Infections	How often does this job require exposure to disease/infections?
In an Open Vehicle or Equipment	How often does this job require working in an open vehicle or equipment (e.g., tractor)?
Wear Specialized Protective or Safety Equipment su	How much does this job require wearing specialized protective or safety equipment such as breathing apparatus, safety harness, full protection suits, or radiation protection?
Wear Common Protective or Safety Equipment such as	How much does this job require wearing common protective or safety equipment such as safety shoes, glasses, gloves, hard hats or live jackets?
Exposed to Whole Body Vibration	How often does this job require exposure to whole body vibration (e.g., operate a jackhammer)?
Exposed to Radiation	How often does this job require exposure to radiation?

3

Job Zone Component	Job Zone Component Definitions
Title	Job Zone One: Little or No Preparation Needed
Overall Experience	No previous work-related skill, knowledge, or experience is needed for these occupations. For example, a person can become a general office clerk even if he/she has never worked in an office before.
Job Training	Employees in these occupations need anywhere from a few days to a few months of training. Usually, an experienced worker could show you how to do the job.
Job Zone Examples	These occupations involve following instructions and helping others. Examples include bus drivers, forest and conservation workers, general office clerks, home health aides, and waiters/waitresses.
SVP Range	(Below 4.0)
Education	These occupations may require a high school diploma or GED certificate. Some may require a formal training course to obtain a license.

Work_Styles	Work_Styles Definitions
Integrity	Job requires being honest and ethical.
Dependability	Job requires being reliable, responsible, and dependable, and fulfilling obligations.
Cooperation	Job requires being pleasant with others on the job and displaying a good-natured, cooperative attitude.
Self Control	Job requires maintaining composure, keeping emotions in check, controlling anger, and avoiding aggressive behavior, even in very difficult situations.
Concern for Others	Job requires being sensitive to others' needs and feelings and being understanding and helpful on the job.
Social Orientation	Job requires preferring to work with others rather than alone, and being personally connected with others on the job.

Independence	Job requires developing one's own ways of doing things, guiding oneself with little or no supervision, and depending on oneself to get things done.
Attention to Detail	Job requires being careful about detail and thorough in completing work tasks.
Adaptability/Flexibility	Job requires being open to change (positive or negative) and to considerable variety in the workplace.
Stress Tolerance	Job requires accepting criticism and dealing calmly and effectively with high stress situations.
Initiative	Job requires a willingness to take on responsibilities and challenges.
Persistence	Job requires persistence in the face of obstacles.
Achievement/Effort	Job requires establishing and maintaining personally challenging achievement goals and exerting effort toward mastering tasks.
Leadership	Job requires a willingness to lead, take charge, and offer opinions and direction.
Innovation	Job requires creativity and alternative thinking to develop new ideas for and answers to work-related problems.
Analytical Thinking	Job requires analyzing information and using logic to address work-related issues and problems.

39-3091.00 - Amusement and Recreation Attendants

Perform variety of attending duties at amusement or recreation facility. May schedule use of recreation facilities, maintain and provide equipment to participants of sporting events or recreational pursuits, or operate amusement concessions and rides.

Tasks

1) Monitor activities to ensure adherence to rules and safety procedures, and arrange for the removal of unruly patrons.

2) Record details of attendance, sales, receipts, reservations, and repair activities.

3) Keep informed of shut-down and emergency evacuation procedures.

4) Maintain inventories of equipment, storing and retrieving items and assembling and disassembling equipment as necessary.

5) Sell tickets and collect fees from customers.

6) Clean sporting equipment, vehicles, rides, booths, facilities, and grounds.

7) Inspect equipment to detect wear and damage and perform minor repairs, adjustments and maintenance tasks such as oiling parts.

8) Rent, sell, or issue sporting equipment and supplies such as bowling shoes, golf balls, swimming suits, and beach chairs.

9) Verify, collect, or punch tickets before admitting patrons to venues such as amusement parks and rides.

10) Direct patrons to rides, seats, or attractions.

11) Schedule the use of recreation facilities such as golf courses, tennis courts, bowling alleys, and softball diamonds.

12) Tend amusement booths in parks, carnivals, or stadiums, performing duties such as conducting games, photographing patrons, and awarding prizes.

13) Operate, drive, or explain the use of mechanical riding devices or other automatic equipment in amusement parks, carnivals, or recreation areas.

14) Sell and serve refreshments to customers.

15) Provide assistance to patrons entering or exiting amusement rides, boats, or ski lifts, or mounting or dismounting animals.

16) Announce and describe amusement park attractions to patrons in order to entice customers to games and other entertainment.

17) Fasten safety devices for patrons, or provide them with directions for fastening devices.

18) Operate machines to clean, smooth, and prepare the ice surfaces of rinks for activities such as skating, hockey, and curling.

Knowledge	Knowledge Definitions
Customer and Personal Service	Knowledge of principles and processes for providing customer and personal services. This includes customer needs assessment, meeting quality standards for services, and evaluation of customer satisfaction.
Public Safety and Security	Knowledge of relevant equipment, policies, procedures, and strategies to promote effective local, state, or national security operations for the protection of people, data, property, and institutions.
English Language	Knowledge of the structure and content of the English language including the meaning and spelling of words, rules of composition, and grammar.
Administration and Management	Knowledge of business and management principles involved in strategic planning, resource allocation, human resources modeling, leadership technique, production methods, and coordination of people and resources.
Psychology	Knowledge of human behavior and performance; individual differences in ability, personality, and interests; learning and motivation; psychological research methods; and the assessment and treatment of behavioral and affective disorders.
Clerical	Knowledge of administrative and clerical procedures and systems such as word processing, managing files and records, stenography and transcription, designing forms, and other office procedures and terminology.
Sales and Marketing	Knowledge of principles and methods for showing, promoting, and selling products or services. This includes marketing strategy and tactics, product demonstration, sales techniques, and sales control systems.
Education and Training	Knowledge of principles and methods for curriculum and training design, teaching and instruction for individuals and groups, and the measurement of training effects.
Mathematics	Knowledge of arithmetic, algebra, geometry, calculus, statistics, and their applications.
Economics and Accounting	Knowledge of economic and accounting principles and practices, the financial markets, banking and the analysis and reporting of financial data.
Medicine and Dentistry	Knowledge of the information and techniques needed to diagnose and treat human injuries, diseases, and deformities. This includes symptoms, treatment alternatives, drug properties and interactions, and preventive health-care measures.
Personnel and Human Resources	Knowledge of principles and procedures for personnel recruitment, selection, training, compensation and benefits, labor relations and negotiation, and personnel information systems.
Sociology and Anthropology	Knowledge of group behavior and dynamics, societal trends and influences, human migrations, ethnicity, cultures and their history and origins.
Communications and Media	Knowledge of media production, communication, and dissemination techniques and methods. This includes alternative ways to inform and entertain via written, oral, and visual media.
Therapy and Counseling	Knowledge of principles, methods, and procedures for diagnosis, treatment, and rehabilitation of physical and mental dysfunctions, and for career counseling and guidance.
Fine Arts	Knowledge of the theory and techniques required to compose, produce, and perform works of music, dance, visual arts, drama, and sculpture.
Philosophy and Theology	Knowledge of different philosophical systems and religions. This includes their basic principles, values, ethics, ways of thinking, customs, practices, and their impact on human culture.
Computers and Electronics	Knowledge of circuit boards, processors, chips, electronic equipment, and computer hardware and software, including applications and programming.
Mechanical	Knowledge of machines and tools, including their designs, uses, repair, and maintenance.
History and Archeology	Knowledge of historical events and their causes, indicators, and effects on civilizations and cultures.
Telecommunications	Knowledge of transmission, broadcasting, switching, control, and operation of telecommunications systems.
Chemistry	Knowledge of the chemical composition, structure, and properties of substances and of the chemical processes and transformations that they undergo. This includes uses of chemicals and their interactions, danger signs, production techniques, and disposal methods.
Production and Processing	Knowledge of raw materials, production processes, quality control, costs, and other techniques for maximizing the effective manufacture and distribution of goods.
Law and Government	Knowledge of laws, legal codes, court procedures, precedents, government regulations, executive orders, agency rules, and the democratic political process.

Transportation	Knowledge of principles and methods for moving people or goods by air, rail, sea, or road, including the relative costs and benefits.
Engineering and Technology	Knowledge of the practical application of engineering science and technology. This includes applying principles, techniques, procedures, and equipment to the design and production of various goods and services.
Geography	Knowledge of principles and methods for describing the features of land, sea, and air masses, including their physical characteristics, locations, interrelationships, and distribution of plant, animal, and human life.
Food Production	Knowledge of techniques and equipment for planting, growing, and harvesting food products (both plant and animal) for consumption, including storage/handling techniques.
Design	Knowledge of design techniques, tools, and principles involved in production of precision technical plans, blueprints, drawings, and models.
Foreign Language	Knowledge of the structure and content of a foreign (non-English) language including the meaning and spelling of words, rules of composition and grammar, and pronunciation.
Building and Construction	Knowledge of materials, methods, and the tools involved in the construction or repair of houses, buildings, or other structures such as highways and roads.
Biology	Knowledge of plant and animal organisms, their tissues, cells, functions, interdependencies, and interactions with each other and the environment.
Physics	Knowledge and prediction of physical principles, laws, their interrelationships, and applications to understanding fluid, material, and atmospheric dynamics, and mechanical, electrical, atomic and sub- atomic structures and processes.

Skills	**Skills Definitions**
Active Listening	Giving full attention to what other people are saying, taking time to understand the points being made, asking questions as appropriate, and not interrupting at inappropriate times.
Speaking	Talking to others to convey information effectively.
Coordination	Adjusting actions in relation to others' actions.
Reading Comprehension	Understanding written sentences and paragraphs in work related documents.
Writing	Communicating effectively in writing as appropriate for the needs of the audience.
Social Perceptiveness	Being aware of others' reactions and understanding why they react as they do.
Critical Thinking	Using logic and reasoning to identify the strengths and weaknesses of alternative solutions, conclusions or approaches to problems.
Instructing	Teaching others how to do something.
Learning Strategies	Selecting and using training/instructional methods and procedures appropriate for the situation when learning or teaching new things.
Service Orientation	Actively looking for ways to help people.
Time Management	Managing one's own time and the time of others.
Monitoring	Monitoring/Assessing performance of yourself, other individuals, or organizations to make improvements or take corrective action.
Mathematics	Using mathematics to solve problems.
Active Learning	Understanding the implications of new information for both current and future problem-solving and decision-making.
Persuasion	Persuading others to change their minds or behavior.
Equipment Selection	Determining the kind of tools and equipment needed to do a job.
Negotiation	Bringing others together and trying to reconcile differences.
Operation and Control	Controlling operations of equipment or systems.
Judgment and Decision Making	Considering the relative costs and benefits of potential actions to choose the most appropriate one.
Complex Problem Solving	Identifying complex problems and reviewing related information to develop and evaluate options and implement solutions.
Management of Personnel Resources	Motivating, developing, and directing people as they work, identifying the best people for the job.
Systems Evaluation	Identifying measures or indicators of system performance and the actions needed to improve or correct performance, relative to the goals of the system.
Troubleshooting	Determining causes of operating errors and deciding what to do about it.
Technology Design	Generating or adapting equipment and technology to serve user needs.

Management of Material Resources	Obtaining and seeing to the appropriate use of equipment, facilities, and materials needed to do certain work.
Operations Analysis	Analyzing needs and product requirements to create a design.
Operation Monitoring	Watching gauges, dials, or other indicators to make sure a machine is working properly.
Equipment Maintenance	Performing routine maintenance on equipment and determining when and what kind of maintenance is needed.
Repairing	Repairing machines or systems using the needed tools.
Systems Analysis	Determining how a system should work and how changes in conditions, operations, and the environment will affect outcomes.
Science	Using scientific rules and methods to solve problems.
Management of Financial Resources	Determining how money will be spent to get the work done, and accounting for these expenditures.
Installation	Installing equipment, machines, wiring, or programs to meet specifications.
Quality Control Analysis	Conducting tests and inspections of products, services, or processes to evaluate quality or performance.
Programming	Writing computer programs for various purposes.

Ability	**Ability Definitions**
Oral Expression	The ability to communicate information and ideas in speaking so others will understand.
Speech Clarity	The ability to speak clearly so others can understand you.
Problem Sensitivity	The ability to tell when something is wrong or is likely to go wrong. It does not involve solving the problem, only recognizing there is a problem.
Oral Comprehension	The ability to listen to and understand information and ideas presented through spoken words and sentences.
Speech Recognition	The ability to identify and understand the speech of another person.
Near Vision	The ability to see details at close range (within a few feet of the observer).
Deductive Reasoning	The ability to apply general rules to specific problems to produce answers that make sense.
Inductive Reasoning	The ability to combine pieces of information to form general rules or conclusions (includes finding a relationship among seemingly unrelated events).
Written Expression	The ability to communicate information and ideas in writing so others will understand.
Control Precision	The ability to quickly and repeatedly adjust the controls of a machine or a vehicle to exact positions.
Far Vision	The ability to see details at a distance.
Written Comprehension	The ability to read and understand information and ideas presented in writing.
Manual Dexterity	The ability to quickly move your hand, your hand together with your arm, or your two hands to grasp, manipulate, or assemble objects.
Multilimb Coordination	The ability to coordinate two or more limbs (for example, two arms, two legs, or one leg and one arm) while sitting, standing, or lying down. It does not involve performing the activities while the whole body is in motion.
Selective Attention	The ability to concentrate on a task over a period of time without being distracted.
Information Ordering	The ability to arrange things or actions in a certain order or pattern according to a specific rule or set of rules (e.g., patterns of numbers, letters, words, pictures, mathematical operations).
Response Orientation	The ability to choose quickly between two or more movements in response to two or more different signals (lights, sounds, pictures). It includes the speed with which the correct response is started with the hand, foot, or other body part.
Memorization	The ability to remember information such as words, numbers, pictures, and procedures.
Number Facility	The ability to add, subtract, multiply, or divide quickly and correctly.
Category Flexibility	The ability to generate or use different sets of rules for combining or grouping things in different ways.
Trunk Strength	The ability to use your abdominal and lower back muscles to support part of the body repeatedly or continuously over time without 'giving out' or fatiguing.
Fluency of Ideas	The ability to come up with a number of ideas about a topic (the number of ideas is important, not their quality, correctness, or creativity).

Depth Perception	The ability to judge which of several objects is closer or farther away from you, or to judge the distance between you and an object.
Spatial Orientation	The ability to know your location in relation to the environment or to know where other objects are in relation to you.
Arm-Hand Steadiness	The ability to keep your hand and arm steady while moving your arm or while holding your arm and hand in one position.
Reaction Time	The ability to quickly respond (with the hand, finger, or foot) to a signal (sound, light, picture) when it appears.
Perceptual Speed	The ability to quickly and accurately compare similarities and differences among sets of letters, numbers, objects, pictures, or patterns. The things to be compared may be presented at the same time or one after the other. This ability also includes comparing a presented object with a remembered object.
Originality	The ability to come up with unusual or clever ideas about a given topic or situation, or to develop creative ways to solve a problem.
Static Strength	The ability to exert maximum muscle force to lift, push, pull, or carry objects.
Flexibility of Closure	The ability to identify or detect a known pattern (a figure, object, word, or sound) that is hidden in other distracting material.
Time Sharing	The ability to shift back and forth between two or more activities or sources of information (such as speech, sounds, touch, or other sources).
Visualization	The ability to imagine how something will look after it is moved around or when its parts are moved or rearranged.
Speed of Closure	The ability to quickly make sense of, combine, and organize information into meaningful patterns.
Auditory Attention	The ability to focus on a single source of sound in the presence of other distracting sounds.
Extent Flexibility	The ability to bend, stretch, twist, or reach with your body, arms, and/or legs.
Stamina	The ability to exert yourself physically over long periods of time without getting winded or out of breath.
Rate Control	The ability to time your movements or the movement of a piece of equipment in anticipation of changes in the speed and/or direction of a moving object or scene.
Mathematical Reasoning	The ability to choose the right mathematical methods or formulas to solve a problem.
Gross Body Coordination	The ability to coordinate the movement of your arms, legs, and torso together when the whole body is in motion.
Finger Dexterity	The ability to make precisely coordinated movements of the fingers of one or both hands to grasp, manipulate, or assemble very small objects.
Dynamic Strength	The ability to exert muscle force repeatedly or continuously over time. This involves muscular endurance and resistance to muscle fatigue.
Peripheral Vision	The ability to see objects or movement of objects to one's side when the eyes are looking ahead.
Gross Body Equilibrium	The ability to keep or regain your body balance or stay upright when in an unstable position.
Speed of Limb Movement	The ability to quickly move the arms and legs.
Visual Color Discrimination	The ability to match or detect differences between colors, including shades of color and brightness.
Night Vision	The ability to see under low light conditions.
Explosive Strength	The ability to use short bursts of muscle force to propel oneself (as in jumping or sprinting), or to throw an object.
Hearing Sensitivity	The ability to detect or tell the differences between sounds that vary in pitch and loudness.
Sound Localization	The ability to tell the direction from which a sound originated.
Glare Sensitivity	The ability to see objects in the presence of glare or bright lighting.
Wrist-Finger Speed	The ability to make fast, simple, repeated movements of the fingers, hands, and wrists.
Dynamic Flexibility	The ability to quickly and repeatedly bend, stretch, twist, or reach out with your body, arms, and/or legs.

Work_Activity	Work_Activity Definitions
Establishing and Maintaining Interpersonal Relatio	Developing constructive and cooperative working relationships with others, and maintaining them over time.
Communicating with Supervisors, Peers, or Subordin	Providing information to supervisors, co-workers, and subordinates by telephone, in written form, e-mail, or in person.
Inspecting Equipment, Structures, or Material	Inspecting equipment, structures, or materials to identify the cause of errors or other problems or defects.

Getting Information	Observing, receiving, and otherwise obtaining information from all relevant sources.
Performing for or Working Directly with the Public	Performing for people or dealing directly with the public. This includes serving customers in restaurants and stores, and receiving clients or guests.
Performing General Physical Activities	Performing physical activities that require considerable use of your arms and legs and moving your whole body, such as climbing, lifting, balancing, walking, stooping, and handling of materials.
Assisting and Caring for Others	Providing personal assistance, medical attention, emotional support, or other personal care to others such as coworkers, customers, or patients.
Coordinating the Work and Activities of Others	Getting members of a group to work together to accomplish tasks.
Monitor Processes, Materials, or Surroundings	Monitoring and reviewing information from materials, events, or the environment, to detect or assess problems.
Scheduling Work and Activities	Scheduling events, programs, and activities, as well as the work of others.
Operating Vehicles, Mechanized Devices, or Equipme	Running, maneuvering, navigating, or driving vehicles or mechanized equipment, such as forklifts, passenger vehicles, aircraft, or water craft.
Developing and Building Teams	Encouraging and building mutual trust, respect, and cooperation among team members.
Evaluating Information to Determine Compliance wit	Using relevant information and individual judgment to determine whether events or processes comply with laws, regulations, or standards.
Judging the Qualities of Things, Services, or Peop	Assessing the value, importance, or quality of things or people.
Training and Teaching Others	Identifying the educational needs of others, developing formal educational or training programs or classes, and teaching or instructing others.
Organizing, Planning, and Prioritizing Work	Developing specific goals and plans to prioritize, organize, and accomplish your work.
Handling and Moving Objects	Using hands and arms in handling, installing, positioning, and moving materials, and manipulating things.
Coaching and Developing Others	Identifying the developmental needs of others and coaching, mentoring, or otherwise helping others to improve their knowledge or skills.
Identifying Objects, Actions, and Events	Identifying information by categorizing, estimating, recognizing differences or similarities, and detecting changes in circumstances or events.
Updating and Using Relevant Knowledge	Keeping up-to-date technically and applying new knowledge to your job.
Communicating with Persons Outside Organization	Communicating with people outside the organization, representing the organization to customers, the public, government, and other external sources. This information can be exchanged in person, in writing, or by telephone or e-mail.
Resolving Conflicts and Negotiating with Others	Handling complaints, settling disputes, and resolving grievances and conflicts, or otherwise negotiating with others.
Making Decisions and Solving Problems	Analyzing information and evaluating results to choose the best solution and solve problems.
Developing Objectives and Strategies	Establishing long range objectives and specifying the strategies and actions to achieve them.
Performing Administrative Activities	Performing day-to-day administrative tasks such as maintaining information files and processing paperwork.
Thinking Creatively	Developing, designing, or creating new applications, ideas, relationships, systems, or products, including artistic contributions.
Estimating the Quantifiable Characteristics of Pro	Estimating sizes, distances, and quantities; or determining time, costs, resources, or materials needed to perform a work activity.
Processing Information	Compiling, coding, categorizing, calculating, tabulating, auditing, or verifying information or data.
Guiding, Directing, and Motivating Subordinates	Providing guidance and direction to subordinates, including setting performance standards and monitoring performance.
Staffing Organizational Units	Recruiting, interviewing, selecting, hiring, and promoting employees in an organization.
Documenting/Recording Information	Entering, transcribing, recording, storing, or maintaining information in written or electronic/magnetic form.
Analyzing Data or Information	Identifying the underlying principles, reasons, or facts of information by breaking down information or data into separate parts.
Interpreting the Meaning of Information for Others	Translating or explaining what information means and how it can be used.
Controlling Machines and Processes	Using either control mechanisms or direct physical activity to operate machines or processes (not including computers or vehicles).

Interacting With Computers	Using computers and computer systems (including hardware and software) to program, write software, set up functions, enter data, or process information.
Selling or Influencing Others	Convincing others to buy merchandise/goods or to otherwise change their minds or actions.
Monitoring and Controlling Resources	Monitoring and controlling resources and overseeing the spending of money.
Provide Consultation and Advice to Others	Providing guidance and expert advice to management or other groups on technical, systems-, or process-related topics.
Repairing and Maintaining Mechanical Equipment	Servicing, repairing, adjusting, and testing machines, devices, moving parts, and equipment that operate primarily on the basis of mechanical (not electronic) principles.
Repairing and Maintaining Electronic Equipment	Servicing, repairing, calibrating, regulating, fine-tuning, or testing machines, devices, and equipment that operate primarily on the basis of electrical or electronic (not mechanical) principles.
Drafting, Laying Out, and Specifying Technical Dev	Providing documentation, detailed instructions, drawings, or specifications to tell others about how devices, parts, equipment, or structures are to be fabricated, constructed, assembled, modified, maintained, or used.

Work_Context	Work_Context Definitions
Face-to-Face Discussions	How often do you have to have face-to-face discussions with individuals or teams in this job?
Contact With Others	How much does this job require the worker to be in contact with others (face-to-face, by telephone, or otherwise) in order to perform it?
Physical Proximity	To what extent does this job require the worker to perform job tasks in close physical proximity to other people?
Freedom to Make Decisions	How much decision making freedom, without supervision, does the job offer?
Deal With External Customers	How important is it to work with external customers or the public in this job?
Frequency of Decision Making	How frequently is the worker required to make decisions that affect other people, the financial resources, and/or the image and reputation of the organization?
Telephone	How often do you have telephone conversations in this job?
Structured versus Unstructured Work	To what extent is this job structured for the worker, rather than allowing the worker to determine tasks, priorities, and goals?
Work With Work Group or Team	How important is it to work with others in a group or team in this job?
Indoors, Environmentally Controlled	How often does this job require working indoors in environmentally controlled conditions?
Impact of Decisions on Co-workers or Company Resul	How do the decisions an employee makes impact the results of co-workers, clients or the company?
Frequency of Conflict Situations	How often are there conflict situations the employee has to face in this job?
Deal With Unpleasant or Angry People	How frequently does the worker have to deal with unpleasant, angry, or discourteous individuals as part of the job requirements?
Coordinate or Lead Others	How important is it to coordinate or lead others in accomplishing work activities in this job?
Spend Time Using Your Hands to Handle, Control, or	How much does this job require using your hands to handle, control, or feel objects, tools or controls?
Responsible for Others' Health and Safety	How much responsibility is there for the health and safety of others in this job?
Spend Time Sitting	How much does this job require sitting?
Sounds, Noise Levels Are Distracting or Uncomforta	How often does this job require working exposed to sounds and noise levels that are distracting or uncomfortable?
Outdoors, Exposed to Weather	How often does this job require working outdoors, exposed to all weather conditions?
Importance of Being Exact or Accurate	How important is being very exact or highly accurate in performing this job?
Spend Time Standing	How much does this job require standing?
Letters and Memos	How often does the job require written letters and memos?
Exposed to Contaminants	How often does this job require working exposed to contaminants (such as pollutants, gases, dust or odors)?
Responsibility for Outcomes and Results	How responsible is the worker for work outcomes and results of other workers?
In an Enclosed Vehicle or Equipment	How often does this job require working in a closed vehicle or equipment (e.g., car)?
Deal With Physically Aggressive People	How frequently does this job require the worker to deal with physical aggression of violent individuals?
Exposed to Minor Burns, Cuts, Bites, or Stings	How often does this job require exposure to minor burns, cuts, bites, or stings?

Spend Time Making Repetitive Motions	How much does this job require making repetitive motions?
Electronic Mail	How often do you use electronic mail in this job?
Time Pressure	How often does this job require the worker to meet strict deadlines?
Very Hot or Cold Temperatures	How often does this job require working in very hot (above 90 F degrees) or very cold (below 32 F degrees) temperatures?
Importance of Repeating Same Tasks	How important is repeating the same physical activities (e.g., key entry) or mental activities (e.g., checking entries in a ledger) over and over, without stopping, to performing this job?
Extremely Bright or Inadequate Lighting	How often does this job require working in extremely bright or inadequate lighting conditions?
Spend Time Walking and Running	How much does this job require walking and running?
Public Speaking	How often do you have to perform public speaking in this job?
Spend Time Bending or Twisting the Body	How much does this job require bending or twisting your body?
Consequence of Error	How serious would the result usually be if the worker made a mistake that was not readily correctable?
Level of Competition	To what extent does this job require the worker to compete or to be aware of competitive pressures?
Degree of Automation	How automated is the job?
Indoors, Not Environmentally Controlled	How often does this job require working indoors in non-controlled environmental conditions (e.g., warehouse without heat)?
Spend Time Kneeling, Crouching, Stooping, or Crawl	How much does this job require kneeling, crouching, stooping or crawling?
In an Open Vehicle or Equipment	How often does this job require working in an open vehicle or equipment (e.g., tractor)?
Exposed to Hazardous Equipment	How often does this job require exposure to hazardous equipment?
Wear Common Protective or Safety Equipment such as	How much does this job require wearing common protective or safety equipment such as safety shoes, glasses, gloves, hard hats or life jackets?
Exposed to Hazardous Conditions	How often does this job require exposure to hazardous conditions?
Outdoors, Under Cover	How often does this job require working outdoors, under cover (e.g., structure with roof but no walls)?
Spend Time Climbing Ladders, Scaffolds, or Poles	How much does this job require climbing ladders, scaffolds, or poles?
Exposed to Whole Body Vibration	How often does this job require exposure to whole body vibration (e.g., operate a jackhammer)?
Cramped Work Space, Awkward Positions	How often does this job require working in cramped work spaces that requires getting into awkward positions?
Exposed to Disease or Infections	How often does this job require exposure to disease/infections?
Exposed to High Places	How often does this job require exposure to high places?
Spend Time Keeping or Regaining Balance	How much does this job require keeping or regaining your balance?
Pace Determined by Speed of Equipment	How important is it to this job that the pace is determined by the speed of equipment or machinery? (This does not refer to keeping busy at all times on this job.)
Exposed to Radiation	How often does this job require exposure to radiation?
Wear Specialized Protective or Safety Equipment su	How much does this job require wearing specialized protective or safety equipment such as breathing apparatus, safety harness, full protection suits, or radiation protection?

Job Zone Component	Job Zone Component Definitions
Title	Job Zone One: Little or No Preparation Needed
Overall Experience	No previous work-related skill, knowledge, or experience is needed for these occupations. For example, a person can become a general office clerk even if he/she has never worked in an office before.
Job Training	Employees in these occupations need anywhere from a few days to a few months of training. Usually, an experienced worker could show you how to do the job.
Job Zone Examples	These occupations involve following instructions and helping others. Examples include bus drivers, forest and conservation workers, general office clerks, home health aides, and waiters/waitresses.
SVP Range	(Below 4.0)
Education	These occupations may require a high school diploma or GED certificate. Some may require a formal training course to obtain a license.

Work_Styles	Work_Styles Definitions
Dependability	Job requires being reliable, responsible, and dependable, and fulfilling obligations.
Cooperation	Job requires being pleasant with others on the job and displaying a good-natured, cooperative attitude.
Self Control	Job requires maintaining composure, keeping emotions in check, controlling anger, and avoiding aggressive behavior, even in very difficult situations.
Concern for Others	Job requires being sensitive to others' needs and feelings and being understanding and helpful on the job.
Integrity	Job requires being honest and ethical.
Attention to Detail	Job requires being careful about detail and thorough in completing work tasks.
Independence	Job requires developing one's own ways of doing things, guiding oneself with little or no supervision, and depending on oneself to get things done.
Social Orientation	Job requires preferring to work with others rather than alone, and being personally connected with others on the job.
Adaptability/Flexibility	Job requires being open to change (positive or negative) and to considerable variety in the workplace.
Initiative	Job requires a willingness to take on responsibilities and challenges.
Stress Tolerance	Job requires accepting criticism and dealing calmly and effectively with high stress situations.
Leadership	Job requires a willingness to lead, take charge, and offer opinions and direction.
Persistence	Job requires persistence in the face of obstacles.
Achievement/Effort	Job requires establishing and maintaining personally challenging achievement goals and exerting effort toward mastering tasks.
Innovation	Job requires creativity and alternative thinking to develop new ideas for and answers to work-related problems.
Analytical Thinking	Job requires analyzing information and using logic to address work-related issues and problems.

39-6032.00 - Transportation Attendants, Except Flight Attendants and Baggage Porters

Provide services to ensure the safety and comfort of passengers aboard ships, buses, trains, or within the station or terminal. Perform duties, such as greeting passengers, explaining the use of safety equipment, serving meals or beverages, or answering questions related to travel.

Tasks

1) Perform equipment safety checks prior to departure.

2) Open and close doors for passengers.

3) Transport baggage or coordinate transportation between assigned rooms, terminals, and/or platforms.

4) Inspect kitchens and dining areas to ensure adherence to sanitation requirements.

5) Distribute sports and game equipment, magazines, newspapers, pillows, blankets, and other items to passengers and guests.

6) Adjust window shades and seat cushions at the request of passengers.

7) Clean rooms and bathroom facilities, change linens, and replenish supplies in washrooms.

8) Explain and demonstrate safety procedures and safety equipment use.

9) Signal transportation operators to stop or to proceed.

10) Respond to passengers' questions, requests, or complaints.

11) Provide customers with information on routes, gates, prices, timetables, and/or terminals and concourses.

12) Provide boarding assistance to elderly, sick, or injured people.

13) Issue and collect passenger boarding passes and transfers, tearing or punching tickets as necessary to prevent reuse.

14) Greet passengers boarding transportation equipment, and announce routes and stops.

15) Count and verify tickets and seat reservations, and record numbers of passengers boarding and disembarking.

16) Collect fares from passengers and provide change in return.

17) Determine and/or facilitate seating arrangements.

39-9041.00 - Residential Advisors

Coordinate activities for residents of boarding schools, college fraternities or sororities, college dormitories, or similar establishments. Order supplies and determine need for maintenance, repairs, and furnishings. May maintain household records and assign rooms. May refer residents to counseling resources if needed.

Tasks

1) Communicate with other staff to resolve problems with individual students.

2) Determine the need for facility maintenance and repair, and notify appropriate personnel.

3) Enforce rules and regulations to ensure the smooth and orderly operation of dormitory programs.

4) Make regular rounds to ensure that residents and areas are safe and secure.

5) Observe students in order to detect and report unusual behavior.

6) Administer, coordinate, or recommend disciplinary and corrective actions.

7) Counsel students in the handling of issues such as family, financial, and educational problems.

8) Hold regular meetings with each assigned unit.

9) Direct and participate in on- and off-campus recreational activities for residents of institutions, boarding schools, fraternities or sororities, children's homes, or similar establishments.

10) Provide emergency first aid and summon medical assistance when necessary.

11) Develop program plans for individuals or assist in plan development.

12) Collaborate with counselors to develop counseling programs that address the needs of individual students.

13) Confer with medical personnel to better understand the backgrounds and needs of individual residents.

14) Provide requested information on students' progress and the development of case plans.

15) Chaperone group-sponsored trips and social functions.

16) Compile information such as residents' daily activities and the quantities of supplies used to prepare required reports.

17) Supervise students' housekeeping work to ensure that it is done properly.

18) Assign rooms to students.

19) Inventory, pack, and remove items left behind by former residents.

20) Order supplies for facilities.

21) Process contract cancellations for students who are unable to follow residence hall policies and procedures.

22) Answer telephones, and route calls or deliver messages.

23) Accompany and supervise students during meals.

24) Supervise participants in work-study programs.

25) Supervise the activities of housekeeping personnel.

26) Provide transportation and/or escort for expeditions such as shopping trips or visits to doctors or dentists.

27) Sort and distribute mail.

Knowledge	Knowledge Definitions
Psychology	Knowledge of human behavior and performance; individual differences in ability, personality, and interests; learning and motivation; psychological research methods; and the assessment and treatment of behavioral and affective disorders.
Customer and Personal Service	Knowledge of principles and processes for providing customer and personal services. This includes customer needs assessment, meeting quality standards for services, and evaluation of customer satisfaction.
Public Safety and Security	Knowledge of relevant equipment, policies, procedures, and strategies to promote effective local, state, or national security operations for the protection of people, data, property, and institutions.

Therapy and Counseling	Knowledge of principles, methods, and procedures for diagnosis, treatment, and rehabilitation of physical and mental dysfunctions, and for career counseling and guidance.
Administration and Management	Knowledge of business and management principles involved in strategic planning, resource allocation, human resources modeling, leadership technique, production methods, and coordination of people and resources.
English Language	Knowledge of the structure and content of the English language including the meaning and spelling of words, rules of composition, and grammar.
Sociology and Anthropology	Knowledge of group behavior and dynamics, societal trends and influences, human migrations, ethnicity, cultures and their history and origins.
Personnel and Human Resources	Knowledge of principles and procedures for personnel recruitment, selection, training, compensation and benefits, labor relations and negotiation, and personnel information systems.
Education and Training	Knowledge of principles and methods for curriculum and training design, teaching and instruction for individuals and groups, and the measurement of training effects.
Philosophy and Theology	Knowledge of different philosophical systems and religions. This includes their basic principles, values, ethics, ways of thinking, customs, practices, and their impact on human culture.
Communications and Media	Knowledge of media production, communication, and dissemination techniques and methods. This includes alternative ways to inform and entertain via written, oral, and visual media.
Clerical	Knowledge of administrative and clerical procedures and systems such as word processing, managing files and records, stenography and transcription, designing forms, and other office procedures and terminology.
Computers and Electronics	Knowledge of circuit boards, processors, chips, electronic equipment, and computer hardware and software, including applications and programming.
Law and Government	Knowledge of laws, legal codes, court procedures, precedents, government regulations, executive orders, agency rules, and the democratic political process.
Sales and Marketing	Knowledge of principles and methods for showing, promoting, and selling products or services. This includes marketing strategy and tactics, product demonstration, sales techniques, and sales control systems.
Medicine and Dentistry	Knowledge of the information and techniques needed to diagnose and treat human injuries, diseases, and deformities. This includes symptoms, treatment alternatives, drug properties and interactions, and preventive health-care measures.
Telecommunications	Knowledge of transmission, broadcasting, switching, control, and operation of telecommunications systems.
Mathematics	Knowledge of arithmetic, algebra, geometry, calculus, statistics, and their applications.
Economics and Accounting	Knowledge of economic and accounting principles and practices, the financial markets, banking and the analysis and reporting of financial data.
Fine Arts	Knowledge of the theory and techniques required to compose, produce, and perform works of music, dance, visual arts, drama, and sculpture.
Design	Knowledge of design techniques, tools, and principles involved in production of precision technical plans, blueprints, drawings, and models.
Mechanical	Knowledge of machines and tools, including their designs, uses, repair, and maintenance.
Foreign Language	Knowledge of the structure and content of a foreign (non-English) language including the meaning and spelling of words, rules of composition and grammar, and pronunciation.
Transportation	Knowledge of principles and methods for moving people or goods by air, rail, sea, or road, including the relative costs and benefits.
Chemistry	Knowledge of the chemical composition, structure, and properties of substances and of the chemical processes and transformations that they undergo. This includes uses of chemicals and their interactions, danger signs, production techniques, and disposal methods.
Geography	Knowledge of principles and methods for describing the features of land, sea, and air masses, including their physical characteristics, locations, interrelationships, and distribution of plant, animal, and human life.
History and Archeology	Knowledge of historical events and their causes, indicators, and effects on civilizations and cultures.

Engineering and Technology	Knowledge of the practical application of engineering science and technology. This includes applying principles, techniques, procedures, and equipment to the design and production of various goods and services.
Physics	Knowledge and prediction of physical principles, laws, their interrelationships, and applications to understanding fluid, material, and atmospheric dynamics, and mechanical, electrical, atomic and sub- atomic structures and processes.
Building and Construction	Knowledge of materials, methods, and the tools involved in the construction or repair of houses, buildings, or other structures such as highways and roads.
Biology	Knowledge of plant and animal organisms, their tissues, cells, functions, interdependencies, and interactions with each other and the environment.
Production and Processing	Knowledge of raw materials, production processes, quality control, costs, and other techniques for maximizing the effective manufacture and distribution of goods.
Food Production	Knowledge of techniques and equipment for planting, growing, and harvesting food products (both plant and animal) for consumption, including storage/handling techniques.

Skills	Skills Definitions
Active Listening	Giving full attention to what other people are saying, taking time to understand the points being made, asking questions as appropriate, and not interrupting at inappropriate times.
Social Perceptiveness	Being aware of others' reactions and understanding why they react as they do.
Time Management	Managing one's own time and the time of others.
Monitoring	Monitoring/Assessing performance of yourself, other individuals, or organizations to make improvements or take corrective action.
Speaking	Talking to others to convey information effectively.
Critical Thinking	Using logic and reasoning to identify the strengths and weaknesses of alternative solutions, conclusions or approaches to problems.
Active Learning	Understanding the implications of new information for both current and future problem-solving and decision-making.
Service Orientation	Actively looking for ways to help people.
Coordination	Adjusting actions in relation to others' actions.
Reading Comprehension	Understanding written sentences and paragraphs in work related documents.
Judgment and Decision Making	Considering the relative costs and benefits of potential actions to choose the most appropriate one.
Instructing	Teaching others how to do something.
Writing	Communicating effectively in writing as appropriate for the needs of the audience.
Negotiation	Bringing others together and trying to reconcile differences.
Management of Personnel Resources	Motivating, developing, and directing people as they work, identifying the best people for the job.
Persuasion	Persuading others to change their minds or behavior.
Learning Strategies	Selecting and using training/instructional methods and procedures appropriate for the situation when learning or teaching new things.
Complex Problem Solving	Identifying complex problems and reviewing related information to develop and evaluate options and implement solutions.
Management of Financial Resources	Determining how money will be spent to get the work done, and accounting for these expenditures.
Management of Material Resources	Obtaining and seeing to the appropriate use of equipment, facilities, and materials needed to do certain work.
Systems Evaluation	Identifying measures or indicators of system performance and the actions needed to improve or correct performance, relative to the goals of the system.
Operations Analysis	Analyzing needs and product requirements to create a design.
Quality Control Analysis	Conducting tests and inspections of products, services, or processes to evaluate quality or performance.
Systems Analysis	Determining how a system should work and how changes in conditions, operations, and the environment will affect outcomes.
Mathematics	Using mathematics to solve problems.
Troubleshooting	Determining causes of operating errors and deciding what to do about it.
Equipment Maintenance	Performing routine maintenance on equipment and determining when and what kind of maintenance is needed.
Equipment Selection	Determining the kind of tools and equipment needed to do a job.

Technology Design	Generating or adapting equipment and technology to serve user needs.
Repairing	Repairing machines or systems using the needed tools.
Programming	Writing computer programs for various purposes.
Operation and Control	Controlling operations of equipment or systems.
Installation	Installing equipment, machines, wiring, or programs to meet specifications.
Operation Monitoring	Watching gauges, dials, or other indicators to make sure a machine is working properly.
Science	Using scientific rules and methods to solve problems.

Ability	Ability Definitions
Problem Sensitivity	The ability to tell when something is wrong or is likely to go wrong. It does not involve solving the problem, only recognizing there is a problem.
Oral Expression	The ability to communicate information and ideas in speaking so others will understand.
Speech Clarity	The ability to speak clearly so others can understand you.
Speech Recognition	The ability to identify and understand the speech of another person.
Oral Comprehension	The ability to listen to and understand information and ideas presented through spoken words and sentences.
Written Comprehension	The ability to read and understand information and ideas presented in writing.
Information Ordering	The ability to arrange things or actions in a certain order or pattern according to a specific rule or set of rules (e.g., patterns of numbers, letters, words, pictures, mathematical operations).
Deductive Reasoning	The ability to apply general rules to specific problems to produce answers that make sense.
Inductive Reasoning	The ability to combine pieces of information to form general rules or conclusions (includes finding a relationship among seemingly unrelated events).
Near Vision	The ability to see details at close range (within a few feet of the observer).
Written Expression	The ability to communicate information and ideas in writing so others will understand.
Selective Attention	The ability to concentrate on a task over a period of time without being distracted.
Category Flexibility	The ability to generate or use different sets of rules for combining or grouping things in different ways.
Originality	The ability to come up with unusual or clever ideas about a given topic or situation, or to develop creative ways to solve a problem.
Fluency of Ideas	The ability to come up with a number of ideas about a topic (the number of ideas is important, not their quality, correctness, or creativity).
Flexibility of Closure	The ability to identify or detect a known pattern (a figure, object, word, or sound) that is hidden in other distracting material.
Time Sharing	The ability to shift back and forth between two or more activities or sources of information (such as speech, sounds, touch, or other sources).
Speed of Closure	The ability to quickly make sense of, combine, and organize information into meaningful patterns.
Far Vision	The ability to see details at a distance.
Perceptual Speed	The ability to quickly and accurately compare similarities and differences among sets of letters, numbers, objects, pictures, or patterns. The things to be compared may be presented at the same time or one after the other. This ability also includes comparing a presented object with a remembered object.
Hearing Sensitivity	The ability to detect or tell the differences between sounds that vary in pitch and loudness.
Visualization	The ability to imagine how something will look after it is moved around or when its parts are moved or rearranged.
Finger Dexterity	The ability to make precisely coordinated movements of the fingers of one or both hands to grasp, manipulate, or assemble very small objects.
Auditory Attention	The ability to focus on a single source of sound in the presence of other distracting sounds.
Number Facility	The ability to add, subtract, multiply, or divide quickly and correctly.
Memorization	The ability to remember information such as words, numbers, pictures, and procedures.
Mathematical Reasoning	The ability to choose the right mathematical methods or formulas to solve a problem.
Visual Color Discrimination	The ability to match or detect differences between colors, including shades of color and brightness.

Trunk Strength	The ability to use your abdominal and lower back muscles to support part of the body repeatedly or continuously over time without 'giving out' or fatiguing.
Gross Body Coordination	The ability to coordinate the movement of your arms, legs, and torso together when the whole body is in motion.
Depth Perception	The ability to judge which of several objects is closer or farther away from you, or to judge the distance between you and an object.
Gross Body Equilibrium	The ability to keep or regain your body balance or stay upright when in an unstable position.
Spatial Orientation	The ability to know your location in relation to the environment or to know where other objects are in relation to you.
Response Orientation	The ability to choose quickly between two or more movements in response to two or more different signals (lights, sounds, pictures). It includes the speed with which the correct response is started with the hand, foot, or other body part.
Glare Sensitivity	The ability to see objects in the presence of glare or bright lighting.
Static Strength	The ability to exert maximum muscle force to lift, push, pull, or carry objects.
Night Vision	The ability to see under low light conditions.
Stamina	The ability to exert yourself physically over long periods of time without getting winded or out of breath.
Dynamic Flexibility	The ability to quickly and repeatedly bend, stretch, twist, or reach out with your body, arms, and/or legs.
Reaction Time	The ability to quickly respond (with the hand, finger, or foot) to a signal (sound, light, picture) when it appears.
Extent Flexibility	The ability to bend, stretch, twist, or reach with your body, arms, and/or legs.
Control Precision	The ability to quickly and repeatedly adjust the controls of a machine or a vehicle to exact positions.
Arm-Hand Steadiness	The ability to keep your hand and arm steady while moving your arm or while holding your arm and hand in one position.
Wrist-Finger Speed	The ability to make fast, simple, repeated movements of the fingers, hands, and wrists.
Dynamic Strength	The ability to exert muscle force repeatedly or continuously over time. This involves muscular endurance and resistance to muscle fatigue.
Manual Dexterity	The ability to quickly move your hand, your hand together with your arm, or your two hands to grasp, manipulate, or assemble objects.
Rate Control	The ability to time your movements or the movement of a piece of equipment in anticipation of changes in the speed and/or direction of a moving object or scene.
Explosive Strength	The ability to use short bursts of muscle force to propel oneself (as in jumping or sprinting), or to throw an object.
Sound Localization	The ability to tell the direction from which a sound originated.
Peripheral Vision	The ability to see objects or movement of objects to one's side when the eyes are looking ahead.
Multilimb Coordination	The ability to coordinate two or more limbs (for example, two arms, two legs, or one leg and one arm) while sitting, standing, or lying down. It does not involve performing the activities while the whole body is in motion.
Speed of Limb Movement	The ability to quickly move the arms and legs.

Work_Activity	Work_Activity Definitions
Communicating with Supervisors, Peers, or Subordin	Providing information to supervisors, co-workers, and subordinates by telephone, in written form, e-mail, or in person.
Establishing and Maintaining Interpersonal Relatio	Developing constructive and cooperative working relationships with others, and maintaining them over time.
Getting Information	Observing, receiving, and otherwise obtaining information from all relevant sources.
Developing and Building Teams	Encouraging and building mutual trust, respect, and cooperation among team members.
Making Decisions and Solving Problems	Analyzing information and evaluating results to choose the best solution and solve problems.
Organizing, Planning, and Prioritizing Work	Developing specific goals and plans to prioritize, organize, and accomplish your work.
Resolving Conflicts and Negotiating with Others	Handling complaints, settling disputes, and resolving grievances and conflicts, or otherwise negotiating with others.
Identifying Objects, Actions, and Events	Identifying information by categorizing, estimating, recognizing differences or similarities, and detecting changes in circumstances or events.

Assisting and Caring for Others	Providing personal assistance, medical attention, emotional support, or other personal care to others such as coworkers, customers, or patients.
Thinking Creatively	Developing, designing, or creating new applications, ideas, relationships, systems, or products, including artistic contributions.
Coordinating the Work and Activities of Others	Getting members of a group to work together to accomplish tasks.
Scheduling Work and Activities	Scheduling events, programs, and activities, as well as the work of others.
Coaching and Developing Others	Identifying the developmental needs of others and coaching, mentoring, or otherwise helping others to improve their knowledge or skills.
Guiding, Directing, and Motivating Subordinates	Providing guidance and direction to subordinates, including setting performance standards and monitoring performance.
Judging the Qualities of Things, Services, or Peop	Assessing the value, importance, or quality of things or people.
Documenting/Recording Information	Entering, transcribing, recording, storing, or maintaining information in written or electronic/magnetic form.
Performing Administrative Activities	Performing day-to-day administrative tasks such as maintaining information files and processing paperwork.
Provide Consultation and Advice to Others	Providing guidance and expert advice to management or other groups on technical, systems-, or process-related topics.
Monitor Processes, Materials, or Surroundings	Monitoring and reviewing information from materials, events, or the environment, to detect or assess problems.
Training and Teaching Others	Identifying the educational needs of others, developing formal educational or training programs or classes, and teaching or instructing others.
Evaluating Information to Determine Compliance wit	Using relevant information and individual judgment to determine whether events or processes comply with laws, regulations, or standards.
Updating and Using Relevant Knowledge	Keeping up-to-date technically and applying new knowledge to your job.
Interacting With Computers	Using computers and computer systems (including hardware and software) to program, write software, set up functions, enter data, or process information.
Developing Objectives and Strategies	Establishing long-range objectives and specifying the strategies and actions to achieve them.
Interpreting the Meaning of Information for Others	Translating or explaining what information means and how it can be used.
Processing Information	Compiling, coding, categorizing, calculating, tabulating, auditing, or verifying information or data.
Staffing Organizational Units	Recruiting, interviewing, selecting, hiring, and promoting employees in an organization.
Monitoring and Controlling Resources	Monitoring and controlling resources and overseeing the spending of money.
Communicating with Persons Outside Organization	Communicating with people outside the organization, representing the organization to customers, the public, government, and other external sources. This information can be exchanged in person, in writing, or by telephone or e-mail.
Performing for or Working Directly with the Public	Performing for people or dealing directly with the public. This includes serving customers in restaurants and stores, and receiving clients or guests.
Analyzing Data or Information	Identifying the underlying principles, reasons, or facts of information by breaking down information or data into separate parts.
Estimating the Quantifiable Characteristics of Pro	Estimating sizes, distances, and quantities; or determining time, costs, resources, or materials needed to perform a work activity.
Inspecting Equipment, Structures, or Material	Inspecting equipment, structures, or materials to identify the cause of errors or other problems or defects.
Selling or Influencing Others	Convincing others to buy merchandise/goods or to otherwise change their minds or actions.
Performing General Physical Activities	Performing physical activities that require considerable use of your arms and legs and moving your whole body, such as climbing, lifting, balancing, walking, stooping, and handling of materials.
Handling and Moving Objects	Using hands and arms in handling, installing, positioning, and moving materials, and manipulating things.
Operating Vehicles, Mechanized Devices, or Equipme	Running, maneuvering, navigating, or driving vehicles or mechanized equipment, such as forklifts, passenger vehicles, aircraft, or water craft.
Controlling Machines and Processes	Using either control mechanisms or direct physical activity to operate machines or processes (not including computers or vehicles).
Drafting, Laying Out, and Specifying Technical Dev	Providing documentation, detailed instructions, drawings, or specifications to tell others about how devices, parts, equipment, or structures are to be fabricated, constructed, assembled, modified, maintained, or used.
Repairing and Maintaining Electronic Equipment	Servicing, repairing, calibrating, regulating, fine-tuning, or testing machines, devices, and equipment that operate primarily on the basis of electrical or electronic (not mechanical) principles.
Repairing and Maintaining Mechanical Equipment	Servicing, repairing, adjusting, and testing machines, devices, moving parts, and equipment that operate primarily on the basis of mechanical (not electronic) principles.

Work_Context	Work_Context Definitions
Face-to-Face Discussions	How often do you have to have face-to-face discussions with individuals or teams in this job?
Contact With Others	How much does this job require the worker to be in contact with others (face-to-face, by telephone, or otherwise) in order to perform it?
Work With Work Group or Team	How important is it to work with others in a group or team in this job?
Telephone	How often do you have telephone conversations in this job?
Electronic Mail	How often do you use electronic mail in this job?
Frequency of Conflict Situations	How often are there conflict situations the employee has to face in this job?
Freedom to Make Decisions	How much decision making freedom, without supervision, does the job offer?
Indoors, Environmentally Controlled	How often does this job require working indoors in environmentally controlled conditions?
Structured versus Unstructured Work	To what extent is this job structured for the worker, rather than allowing the worker to determine tasks, priorities, and goals?
Responsible for Others' Health and Safety	How much responsibility is there for the health and safety of others in this job?
Impact of Decisions on Co-workers or Company Resul	How do the decisions an employee makes impact the results of co-workers, clients or the company?
Letters and Memos	How often does the job require written letters and memos?
Responsibility for Outcomes and Results	How responsible is the worker for work outcomes and results of other workers?
Deal With External Customers	How important is it to work with external customers or the public in this job?
Coordinate or Lead Others	How important is it to coordinate or lead others in accomplishing work activities in this job?
Deal With Unpleasant or Angry People	How frequently does the worker have to deal with unpleasant, angry, or discourteous individuals as part of the job requirements?
Frequency of Decision Making	How frequently is the worker required to make decisions that affect other people, the financial resources, and/or the image and reputation of the organization?
Time Pressure	How often does this job require the worker to meet strict deadlines?
Spend Time Sitting	How much does this job require sitting?
Physical Proximity	To what extent does this job require the worker to perform job tasks in close physical proximity to other people?
Public Speaking	How often do you have to perform public speaking in this job?
Sounds, Noise Levels Are Distracting or Uncomforta	How often does this job require working exposed to sounds and noise levels that are distracting or uncomfortable?
Importance of Being Exact or Accurate	How important is being very exact or highly accurate in performing this job?
Spend Time Standing	How much does this job require standing?
Level of Competition	To what extent does this job require the worker to compete or to be aware of competitive pressures?
Deal With Physically Aggressive People	How frequently does this job require the worker to deal with physical aggression of violent individuals?
Consequence of Error	How serious would the result usually be if the worker made a mistake that was not readily correctable?
Importance of Repeating Same Tasks	How important is repeating the same physical activities (e.g., key entry) or mental activities (e.g., checking entries in a ledger) over and over, without stopping, to performing this job?
Spend Time Walking and Running	How much does this job require walking and running?
Degree of Automation	How automated is the job?
Indoors, Not Environmentally Controlled	How often does this job require working indoors in non-controlled environmental conditions (e.g., warehouse without heat)?
Outdoors, Exposed to Weather	How often does this job require working outdoors, exposed to all weather conditions?

In an Enclosed Vehicle or Equipment	How often does this job require working in a closed vehicle or equipment (e.g., car)?
Exposed to Contaminants	How often does this job require working exposed to contaminants (such as pollutants, gases, dust or odors)?
Spend Time Making Repetitive Motions	How much does this job require making repetitive motions?
Spend Time Using Your Hands to Handle, Control, or	How much does this job require using your hands to handle, control, or feel objects, tools or controls?
Exposed to Disease or Infections	How often does this job require exposure to disease/infections?
Extremely Bright or Inadequate Lighting	How often does this job require working in extremely bright or inadequate lighting conditions?
Exposed to Minor Burns, Cuts, Bites, or Stings	How often does this job require exposure to minor burns, cuts, bites, or stings?
Outdoors, Under Cover	How often does this job require working outdoors, under cover (e.g., structure with roof but no walls)?
Very Hot or Cold Temperatures	How often does this job require working in very hot (above 90 F degrees) or very cold (below 32 F degrees) temperatures?
Spend Time Kneeling, Crouching, Stooping, or Crawl	How much does this job require kneeling, crouching, stooping or crawling?
Cramped Work Space, Awkward Positions	How often does this job require working in cramped work spaces that requires getting into awkward positions?
Spend Time Bending or Twisting the Body	How much does this job require bending or twisting your body?
Wear Common Protective or Safety Equipment such as	How much does this job require wearing common protective or safety equipment such as safety shoes, glasses, gloves, hard hats or life jackets?
Spend Time Keeping or Regaining Balance	How much does this job require keeping or regaining your balance?
Exposed to Whole Body Vibration	How often does this job require exposure to whole body vibration (e.g., operate a jackhammer)?
Pace Determined by Speed of Equipment	How important is it to this job that the pace is determined by the speed of equipment or machinery? (This does not refer to keeping busy at all times on this job.)
Spend Time Climbing Ladders, Scaffolds, or Poles	How much does this job require climbing ladders, scaffolds, or poles?
Exposed to Hazardous Conditions	How often does this job require exposure to hazardous conditions?
Exposed to High Places	How often does this job require exposure to high places?
In an Open Vehicle or Equipment	How often does this job require working in an open vehicle or equipment (e.g., tractor)?
Wear Specialized Protective or Safety Equipment su	How much does this job require wearing specialized protective or safety equipment such as breathing apparatus, safety harness, full protection suits, or radiation protection?
Exposed to Hazardous Equipment	How often does this job require exposure to hazardous equipment?
Exposed to Radiation	How often does this job require exposure to radiation?

Job Zone Component	Job Zone Component Definitions
Title	Job Zone Three: Medium Preparation Needed
Overall Experience	Previous work-related skill, knowledge, or experience is required for these occupations. For example, an electrician must have completed three or four years of apprenticeship or several years of vocational training, and often must have passed a licensing exam, in order to perform the job.
Job Training	Employees in these occupations usually need one or two years of training involving both on-the-job experience and informal training with experienced workers.
Job Zone Examples	These occupations usually involve using communication and organizational skills to coordinate, supervise, manage, or train others to accomplish goals. Examples include dental assistants, electricians, fish and game wardens, legal secretaries, personnel recruiters, and recreation workers.
SVP Range	(6.0 to < 7.0)
Education	Most occupations in this zone require training in vocational schools, related on-the-job experience, or an associate's degree. Some may require a bachelor's degree.

Work_Styles	Work_Styles Definitions
Concern for Others	Job requires being sensitive to others' needs and feelings and being understanding and helpful on the job.

Dependability	Job requires being reliable, responsible, and dependable, and fulfilling obligations.
Integrity	Job requires being honest and ethical.
Self Control	Job requires maintaining composure, keeping emotions in check, controlling anger, and avoiding aggressive behavior, even in very difficult situations.
Leadership	Job requires a willingness to lead, take charge, and offer opinions and direction.
Social Orientation	Job requires preferring to work with others rather than alone, and being personally connected with others on the job.
Cooperation	Job requires being pleasant with others on the job and displaying a good-natured, cooperative attitude.
Initiative	Job requires a willingness to take on responsibilities and challenges.
Adaptability/Flexibility	Job requires being open to change (positive or negative) and to considerable variety in the workplace.
Stress Tolerance	Job requires accepting criticism and dealing calmly and effectively with high stress situations.
Persistence	Job requires persistence in the face of obstacles.
Attention to Detail	Job requires being careful about detail and thorough in completing work tasks.
Independence	Job requires developing one's own ways of doing things, guiding oneself with little or no supervision, and depending on oneself to get things done.
Achievement/Effort	Job requires establishing and maintaining personally challenging achievement goals and exerting effort toward mastering tasks.
Analytical Thinking	Job requires analyzing information and using logic to address work-related issues and problems.
Innovation	Job requires creativity and alternative thinking to develop new ideas for and answers to work-related problems.

41-2012.00 - Gaming Change Persons and Booth Cashiers

Exchange coins and tokens for patrons' money. May issue payoffs and obtain customer's signature on receipt when winnings exceed the amount held in the slot machine. May operate a booth in the slot machine area and furnish change persons with money bank at the start of the shift, or count and audit money in drawers.

Tasks

1) Exchange money, credit, and casino chips, and make change for customers.

2) Keep accurate records of monetary exchanges, authorization forms, and transaction reconciliations.

3) Work in and monitor an assigned area on the casino floor where slot machines are located.

4) Listen for jackpot alarm bells and issue payoffs to winners.

5) Maintain cage security according to rules.

6) Obtain customers' signatures on receipts when winnings exceed the amount held in a slot machine.

7) Reconcile daily summaries of transactions to balance books.

8) Sell gambling chips, tokens, or tickets to patrons, or to other workers for resale to patrons.

9) Calculate the value of chips won or lost by players.

10) Furnish change persons with a money bank at the start of each shift.

11) Accept credit applications and verify credit references in order to provide check-cashing authorization or to establish house credit accounts.

Knowledge	Knowledge Definitions
Customer and Personal Service	Knowledge of principles and processes for providing customer and personal services. This includes customer needs assessment, meeting quality standards for services, and evaluation of customer satisfaction.
Mathematics	Knowledge of arithmetic, algebra, geometry, calculus, statistics, and their applications.
English Language	Knowledge of the structure and content of the English language including the meaning and spelling of words, rules of composition, and grammar.

Public Safety and Security	Knowledge of relevant equipment. policies. procedures, and strategies to promote effective local. state. or national security operations for the protection of people. data, property. and institutions.
Computers and Electronics	Knowledge of circuit boards, processors, chips, electronic equipment, and computer hardware and software, including applications and programming.
Administration and Management	Knowledge of business and management principles involved in strategic planning. resource allocation. human resources modeling, leadership technique. production methods, and coordination of people and resources.
Economics and Accounting	Knowledge of economic and accounting principles and practices. the financial markets. banking and the analysis and reporting of financial data.
Sales and Marketing	Knowledge of principles and methods for showing, promoting, and selling products or services. This includes marketing strategy and tactics, product demonstration, sales techniques, and sales control systems.
Engineering and Technology	Knowledge of the practical application of engineering science and technology. This includes applying principles, techniques, procedures, and equipment to the design and production of various goods and services.
Clerical	Knowledge of administrative and clerical procedures and systems such as word processing. managing files and records, stenography and transcription. designing forms, and other office procedures and terminology.
Personnel and Human Resources	Knowledge of principles and procedures for personnel recruitment, selection, training. compensation and benefits, labor relations and negotiation, and personnel information systems.
Psychology	Knowledge of human behavior and performance; individual differences in ability. personality. and interests; learning and motivation; psychological research methods; and the assessment and treatment of behavioral and affective disorders.
Food Production	Knowledge of techniques and equipment for planting, growing, and harvesting food products (both plant and animal) for consumption, including storage/handling techniques.
Law and Government	Knowledge of laws, legal codes, court procedures, precedents, government regulations, executive orders, agency rules, and the democratic political process.
Production and Processing	Knowledge of raw materials, production processes, quality control, costs, and other techniques for maximizing the effective manufacture and distribution of goods.
Education and Training	Knowledge of principles and methods for curriculum and training design, teaching and instruction for individuals and groups, and the measurement of training effects.
Foreign Language	Knowledge of the structure and content of a foreign (non-English) language including the meaning and spelling of words, rules of composition and grammar, and pronunciation.
Sociology and Anthropology	Knowledge of group behavior and dynamics, societal trends and influences, human migrations, ethnicity, cultures and their history and origins.
Mechanical	Knowledge of machines and tools, including their designs, uses, repair, and maintenance.
Design	Knowledge of design techniques, tools, and principles involved in production of precision technical plans, blueprints, drawings, and models.
Communications and Media	Knowledge of media production, communication, and dissemination techniques and methods. This includes alternative ways to inform and entertain via written, oral, and visual media.
Telecommunications	Knowledge of transmission, broadcasting, switching, control, and operation of telecommunications systems.
Geography	Knowledge of principles and methods for describing the features of land, sea, and air masses, including their physical characteristics, locations, interrelationships, and distribution of plant, animal, and human life.
Medicine and Dentistry	Knowledge of the information and techniques needed to diagnose and treat human injuries, diseases, and deformities. This includes symptoms, treatment alternatives, drug properties and interactions, and preventive health-care measures.
Philosophy and Theology	Knowledge of different philosophical systems and religions. This includes their basic principles, values, ethics, ways of thinking, customs, practices, and their impact on human culture.
Transportation	Knowledge of principles and methods for moving people or goods by air, rail, sea, or road, including the relative costs and benefits.

Building and Construction	Knowledge of materials, methods, and the tools involved in the construction or repair of houses, buildings, or other structures such as highways and roads.
Therapy and Counseling	Knowledge of principles, methods, and procedures for diagnosis, treatment, and rehabilitation of physical and mental dysfunctions, and for career counseling and guidance.
Physics	Knowledge and prediction of physical principles, laws, their interrelationships, and applications to understanding fluid, material, and atmospheric dynamics, and mechanical, electrical, atomic and sub- atomic structures and processes.
Chemistry	Knowledge of the chemical composition, structure, and properties of substances and of the chemical processes and transformations that they undergo. This includes uses of chemicals and their interactions, danger signs, production techniques, and disposal methods.
History and Archeology	Knowledge of historical events and their causes, indicators, and effects on civilizations and cultures.
Fine Arts	Knowledge of the theory and techniques required to compose, produce, and perform works of music, dance, visual arts, drama, and sculpture.
Biology	Knowledge of plant and animal organisms, their tissues, cells, functions. interdependencies, and interactions with each other and the environment.

Skills	Skills Definitions
Mathematics	Using mathematics to solve problems.
Active Listening	Giving full attention to what other people are saying, taking time to understand the points being made, asking questions as appropriate, and not interrupting at inappropriate times.
Speaking	Talking to others to convey information effectively.
Social Perceptiveness	Being aware of others' reactions and understanding why they react as they do.
Learning Strategies	Selecting and using training/instructional methods and procedures appropriate for the situation when learning or teaching new things.
Time Management	Managing one's own time and the time of others.
Reading Comprehension	Understanding written sentences and paragraphs in work related documents.
Service Orientation	Actively looking for ways to help people.
Critical Thinking	Using logic and reasoning to identify the strengths and weaknesses of alternative solutions, conclusions or approaches to problems.
Writing	Communicating effectively in writing as appropriate for the needs of the audience.
Active Learning	Understanding the implications of new information for both current and future problem-solving and decision-making.
Judgment and Decision Making	Considering the relative costs and benefits of potential actions to choose the most appropriate one.
Instructing	Teaching others how to do something.
Troubleshooting	Determining causes of operating errors and deciding what to do about it.
Management of Financial Resources	Determining how money will be spent to get the work done, and accounting for these expenditures.
Repairing	Repairing machines or systems using the needed tools.
Coordination	Adjusting actions in relation to others' actions.
Monitoring	Monitoring/Assessing performance of yourself, other individuals, or organizations to make improvements or take corrective action.
Management of Material Resources	Obtaining and seeing to the appropriate use of equipment, facilities, and materials needed to do certain work.
Equipment Maintenance	Performing routine maintenance on equipment and determining when and what kind of maintenance is needed.
Operation Monitoring	Watching gauges, dials, or other indicators to make sure a machine is working properly.
Management of Personnel Resources	Motivating, developing, and directing people as they work, identifying the best people for the job.
Complex Problem Solving	Identifying complex problems and reviewing related information to develop and evaluate options and implement solutions.
Equipment Selection	Determining the kind of tools and equipment needed to do a job.
Systems Analysis	Determining how a system should work and how changes in conditions, operations, and the environment will affect outcomes.
Negotiation	Bringing others together and trying to reconcile differences.
Persuasion	Persuading others to change their minds or behavior.
Operation and Control	Controlling operations of equipment or systems.

Installation	Installing equipment, machines, wiring, or programs to meet specifications.
Quality Control Analysis	Conducting tests and inspections of products, services, or processes to evaluate quality or performance.
Technology Design	Generating or adapting equipment and technology to serve user needs.
Systems Evaluation	Identifying measures or indicators of system performance and the actions needed to improve or correct performance, relative to the goals of the system.
Programming	Writing computer programs for various purposes.
Operations Analysis	Analyzing needs and product requirements to create a design.
Science	Using scientific rules and methods to solve problems.

Ability	Ability Definitions
Oral Comprehension	The ability to listen to and understand information and ideas presented through spoken words and sentences.
Oral Expression	The ability to communicate information and ideas in speaking so others will understand.
Near Vision	The ability to see details at close range (within a few feet of the observer).
Selective Attention	The ability to concentrate on a task over a period of time without being distracted.
Speech Recognition	The ability to identify and understand the speech of another person.
Number Facility	The ability to add, subtract, multiply, or divide quickly and correctly.
Speech Clarity	The ability to speak clearly so others can understand you.
Hearing Sensitivity	The ability to detect or tell the differences between sounds that vary in pitch and loudness.
Information Ordering	The ability to arrange things or actions in a certain order or pattern according to a specific rule or set of rules (e.g., patterns of numbers, letters, words, pictures, mathematical operations).
Problem Sensitivity	The ability to tell when something is wrong or is likely to go wrong. It does not involve solving the problem, only recognizing there is a problem.
Mathematical Reasoning	The ability to choose the right mathematical methods or formulas to solve a problem.
Inductive Reasoning	The ability to combine pieces of information to form general rules or conclusions (includes finding a relationship among seemingly unrelated events).
Deductive Reasoning	The ability to apply general rules to specific problems to produce answers that make sense.
Far Vision	The ability to see details at a distance.
Finger Dexterity	The ability to make precisely coordinated movements of the fingers of one or both hands to grasp, manipulate, or assemble very small objects.
Written Comprehension	The ability to read and understand information and ideas presented in writing.
Arm-Hand Steadiness	The ability to keep your hand and arm steady while moving your arm or while holding your arm and hand in one position.
Category Flexibility	The ability to generate or use different sets of rules for combining or grouping things in different ways.
Auditory Attention	The ability to focus on a single source of sound in the presence of other distracting sounds.
Flexibility of Closure	The ability to identify or detect a known pattern (a figure, object, word, or sound) that is hidden in other distracting material.
Written Expression	The ability to communicate information and ideas in writing so others will understand.
Visual Color Discrimination	The ability to match or detect differences between colors, including shades of color and brightness.
Manual Dexterity	The ability to quickly move your hand, your hand together with your arm, or your two hands to grasp, manipulate, or assemble objects.
Speed of Closure	The ability to quickly make sense of, combine, and organize information into meaningful patterns.
Perceptual Speed	The ability to quickly and accurately compare similarities and differences among sets of letters, numbers, objects, pictures, or patterns. The things to be compared may be presented at the same time or one after the other. This ability also includes comparing a presented object with a remembered object.
Time Sharing	The ability to shift back and forth between two or more activities or sources of information (such as speech, sounds, touch, or other sources).
Trunk Strength	The ability to use your abdominal and lower back muscles to support part of the body repeatedly or continuously over time without 'giving out' or fatiguing.

Control Precision	The ability to quickly and repeatedly adjust the controls of a machine or a vehicle to exact positions.
Extent Flexibility	The ability to bend, stretch, twist, or reach with your body, arms, and/or legs.
Depth Perception	The ability to judge which of several objects is closer or farther away from you, or to judge the distance between you and an object.
Wrist-Finger Speed	The ability to make fast, simple, repeated movements of the fingers, hands, and wrists.
Stamina	The ability to exert yourself physically over long periods of time without getting winded or out of breath.
Response Orientation	The ability to choose quickly between two or more movements in response to two or more different signals (lights, sounds, pictures). It includes the speed with which the correct response is started with the hand, foot, or other body part.
Gross Body Coordination	The ability to coordinate the movement of your arms, legs, and torso together when the whole body is in motion.
Visualization	The ability to imagine how something will look after it is moved around or when its parts are moved or rearranged.
Originality	The ability to come up with unusual or clever ideas about a given topic or situation, or to develop creative ways to solve a problem.
Fluency of Ideas	The ability to come up with a number of ideas about a topic (the number of ideas is important, not their quality, correctness, or creativity).
Memorization	The ability to remember information such as words, numbers, pictures, and procedures.
Static Strength	The ability to exert maximum muscle force to lift, push, pull, or carry objects.
Multilimb Coordination	The ability to coordinate two or more limbs (for example, two arms, two legs, or one leg and one arm) while sitting, standing, or lying down. It does not involve performing the activities while the whole body is in motion.
Gross Body Equilibrium	The ability to keep or regain your body balance or stay upright when in an unstable position.
Speed of Limb Movement	The ability to quickly move the arms and legs.
Reaction Time	The ability to quickly respond (with the hand, finger, or foot) to a signal (sound, light, picture) when it appears.
Rate Control	The ability to time your movements or the movement of a piece of equipment in anticipation of changes in the speed and/or direction of a moving object or scene.
Dynamic Strength	The ability to exert muscle force repeatedly or continuously over time. This involves muscular endurance and resistance to muscle fatigue.
Sound Localization	The ability to tell the direction from which a sound originated.
Spatial Orientation	The ability to know your location in relation to the environment or to know where other objects are in relation to you.
Peripheral Vision	The ability to see objects or movement of objects to one's side when the eyes are looking ahead.
Night Vision	The ability to see under low light conditions.
Dynamic Flexibility	The ability to quickly and repeatedly bend, stretch, twist, or reach out with your body, arms, and/or legs.
Explosive Strength	The ability to use short bursts of muscle force to propel oneself (as in jumping or sprinting), or to throw an object.
Glare Sensitivity	The ability to see objects in the presence of glare or bright lighting.

Work_Activity	Work_Activity Definitions
Performing for or Working Directly with the Public	Performing for people or dealing directly with the public. This includes serving customers in restaurants and stores, and receiving clients or guests.
Communicating with Supervisors, Peers, or Subordin	Providing information to supervisors, co-workers, and subordinates by telephone, in written form, e-mail, or in person.
Establishing and Maintaining Interpersonal Relatio	Developing constructive and cooperative working relationships with others, and maintaining them over time.
Documenting/Recording Information	Entering, transcribing, recording, storing, or maintaining information in written or electronic/magnetic form.
Identifying Objects, Actions, and Events	Identifying information by categorizing, estimating, recognizing differences or similarities, and detecting changes in circumstances or events.
Getting Information	Observing, receiving, and otherwise obtaining information from all relevant sources.
Evaluating Information to Determine Compliance wit	Using relevant information and individual judgment to determine whether events or processes comply with laws, regulations, or standards.

Resolving Conflicts and Negotiating with Others	Handling complaints, settling disputes, and resolving grievances and conflicts, or otherwise negotiating with others.
Assisting and Caring for Others	Providing personal assistance, medical attention, emotional support, or other personal care to others such as coworkers, customers, or patients.
Communicating with Persons Outside Organization	Communicating with people outside the organization, representing the organization to customers, the public, government, and other external sources. This information can be exchanged in person, in writing, or by telephone or e-mail.
Judging the Qualities of Things, Services, or Peop	Assessing the value, importance, or quality of things or people.
Processing Information	Compiling, coding, categorizing, calculating, tabulating, auditing, or verifying information or data.
Making Decisions and Solving Problems	Analyzing information and evaluating results to choose the best solution and solve problems.
Interpreting the Meaning of Information for Others	Translating or explaining what information means and how it can be used.
Inspecting Equipment, Structures, or Material	Inspecting equipment, structures, or materials to identify the cause of errors or other problems or defects.
Monitor Processes, Materials, or Surroundings	Monitoring and reviewing information from materials, events, or the environment, to detect or assess problems.
Performing General Physical Activities	Performing physical activities that require considerable use of your arms and legs and moving your whole body, such as climbing, lifting, balancing, walking, stooping, and handling of materials.
Repairing and Maintaining Mechanical Equipment	Servicing, repairing, adjusting, and testing machines, devices, moving parts, and equipment that operate primarily on the basis of mechanical (not electronic) principles.
Controlling Machines and Processes	Using either control mechanisms or direct physical activity to operate machines or processes (not including computers or vehicles).
Monitoring and Controlling Resources	Monitoring and controlling resources and overseeing the spending of money.
Selling or Influencing Others	Convincing others to buy merchandise/goods or to otherwise change their minds or actions.
Organizing, Planning, and Prioritizing Work	Developing specific goals and plans to prioritize, organize, and accomplish your work.
Updating and Using Relevant Knowledge	Keeping up-to-date technically and applying new knowledge to your job.
Training and Teaching Others	Identifying the educational needs of others, developing formal educational or training programs or classes, and teaching or instructing others.
Handling and Moving Objects	Using hands and arms in handling, installing, positioning, and moving materials, and manipulating things.
Guiding, Directing, and Motivating Subordinates	Providing guidance and direction to subordinates, including setting performance standards and monitoring performance.
Developing and Building Teams	Encouraging and building mutual trust, respect, and cooperation among team members.
Performing Administrative Activities	Performing day-to-day administrative tasks such as maintaining information files and processing paperwork.
Analyzing Data or Information	Identifying the underlying principles, reasons, or facts of information by breaking down information or data into separate parts.
Estimating the Quantifiable Characteristics of Pro	Estimating sizes, distances, and quantities; or determining time, costs, resources, or materials needed to perform a work activity.
Coordinating the Work and Activities of Others	Getting members of a group to work together to accomplish tasks.
Provide Consultation and Advice to Others	Providing guidance and expert advice to management or other groups on technical, systems-, or process-related topics.
Repairing and Maintaining Electronic Equipment	Servicing, repairing, calibrating, regulating, fine-tuning, or testing machines, devices, and equipment that operate primarily on the basis of electrical or electronic (not mechanical) principles.
Interacting With Computers	Using computers and computer systems (including hardware and software) to program, write software, set up functions, enter data, or process information.
Thinking Creatively	Developing, designing, or creating new applications, ideas, relationships, systems, or products, including artistic contributions.
Scheduling Work and Activities	Scheduling events, programs, and activities, as well as the work of others.
Coaching and Developing Others	Identifying the developmental needs of others and coaching, mentoring, or otherwise helping others to improve their knowledge or skills.
Developing Objectives and Strategies	Establishing long-range objectives and specifying the strategies and actions to achieve them.

Staffing Organizational Units	Recruiting, interviewing, selecting, hiring, and promoting employees in an organization.
Operating Vehicles, Mechanized Devices, or Equipme	Running, maneuvering, navigating, or driving vehicles or mechanized equipment, such as forklifts, passenger vehicles, aircraft, or water craft.
Drafting, Laying Out, and Specifying Technical Dev	Providing documentation, detailed instructions, drawings, or specifications to tell others about how devices, parts, equipment, or structures are to be fabricated, constructed, assembled, modified, maintained, or used.

Work_Context	Work_Context Definitions
Indoors, Environmentally Controlled	How often does this job require working indoors in environmentally controlled conditions?
Contact With Others	How much does this job require the worker to be in contact with others (face-to-face, by telephone, or otherwise) in order to perform it?
Importance of Being Exact or Accurate	How important is being very exact or highly accurate in performing this job?
Sounds, Noise Levels Are Distracting or Uncomforta	How often does this job require working exposed to sounds and noise levels that are distracting or uncomfortable?
Deal With External Customers	How important is it to work with external customers or the public in this job?
Spend Time Standing	How much does this job require standing?
Spend Time Walking and Running	How much does this job require walking and running?
Physical Proximity	To what extent does this job require the worker to perform job tasks in close physical proximity to other people?
Deal With Unpleasant or Angry People	How frequently does the worker have to deal with unpleasant, angry, or discourteous individuals as part of the job requirements?
Work With Work Group or Team	How important is it to work with others in a group or team in this job?
Face-to-Face Discussions	How often do you have to have face-to-face discussions with individuals or teams in this job?
Spend Time Using Your Hands to Handle, Control, or	How much does this job require using your hands to handle, control, or feel objects, tools or controls?
Importance of Repeating Same Tasks	How important is repeating the same physical activities (e.g., key entry) or mental activities (e.g., checking entries in a ledger) over and over, without stopping, to performing this job?
Structured versus Unstructured Work	To what extent is this job structured for the worker, rather than allowing the worker to determine tasks, priorities, and goals?
Freedom to Make Decisions	How much decision making freedom, without supervision, does the job offer?
Frequency of Decision Making	How frequently is the worker required to make decisions that affect other people, the financial resources, and/or the image and reputation of the organization?
Letters and Memos	How often does the job require written letters and memos?
Impact of Decisions on Co-workers or Company Resul	How do the decisions an employee makes impact the results of co-workers, clients or the company?
Telephone	How often do you have telephone conversations in this job?
Consequence of Error	How serious would the result usually be if the worker made a mistake that was not readily correctable?
Spend Time Bending or Twisting the Body	How much does this job require bending or twisting your body?
Responsible for Others' Health and Safety	How much responsibility is there for the health and safety of others in this job?
Time Pressure	How often does this job require the worker to meet strict deadlines?
Frequency of Conflict Situations	How often are there conflict situations the employee has to face in this job?
Spend Time Making Repetitive Motions	How much does this job require making repetitive motions?
Responsibility for Outcomes and Results	How responsible is the worker for work outcomes and results of other workers?
Exposed to Contaminants	How often does this job require working exposed to contaminants (such as pollutants, gases, dust or odors)?
Coordinate or Lead Others	How important is it to coordinate or lead others in accomplishing work activities in this job?
Spend Time Keeping or Regaining Balance	How much does this job require keeping or regaining your balance?
Spend Time Kneeling, Crouching, Stooping, or Crawl	How much does this job require kneeling, crouching, stooping or crawling?
Level of Competition	To what extent does this job require the worker to compete or to be aware of competitive pressures?

Exposed to Minor Burns, Cuts, Bites, or Stings	How often does this job require exposure to minor burns, cuts, bites, or stings?
Pace Determined by Speed of Equipment	How important is it to this job that the pace is determined by the speed of equipment or machinery? (This does not refer to keeping busy at all times on this job.)
Wear Common Protective or Safety Equipment such as	How much does this job require wearing common protective or safety equipment such as safety shoes, glasses, gloves, hard hats or life jackets?
Degree of Automation	How automated is the job?
Extremely Bright or Inadequate Lighting	How often does this job require working in extremely bright or inadequate lighting conditions?
Electronic Mail	How often do you use electronic mail in this job?
Cramped Work Space, Awkward Positions	How often does this job require working in cramped work spaces that requires getting into awkward positions?
Deal With Physically Aggressive People	How frequently does this job require the worker to deal with physical aggression of violent individuals?
Public Speaking	How often do you have to perform public speaking in this job?
Spend Time Sitting	How much does this job require sitting?
Exposed to Disease or Infections	How often does this job require exposure to disease/infections?
Exposed to High Places	How often does this job require exposure to high places?
Very Hot or Cold Temperatures	How often does this job require working in very hot (above 90 F degrees) or very cold (below 32 F degrees) temperatures?
Indoors, Not Environmentally Controlled	How often does this job require working indoors in non-controlled environmental conditions (e.g., warehouse without heat)?
Outdoors, Exposed to Weather	How often does this job require working outdoors, exposed to all weather conditions?
Wear Specialized Protective or Safety Equipment su	How much does this job require wearing specialized protective or safety equipment such as breathing apparatus, safety harness, full protection suits, or radiation protection?
Spend Time Climbing Ladders, Scaffolds, or Poles	How much does this job require climbing ladders, scaffolds, or poles?
Exposed to Hazardous Conditions	How often does this job require exposure to hazardous conditions?
Outdoors, Under Cover	How often does this job require working outdoors, under cover (e.g., structure with roof but no walls)?
Exposed to Hazardous Equipment	How often does this job require exposure to hazardous equipment?
In an Enclosed Vehicle or Equipment	How often does this job require working in a closed vehicle or equipment (e.g., car)?
In an Open Vehicle or Equipment	How often does this job require working in an open vehicle or equipment (e.g., tractor)?
Exposed to Whole Body Vibration	How often does this job require exposure to whole body vibration (e.g., operate a jackhammer)?
Exposed to Radiation	How often does this job require exposure to radiation?

Job Zone Component	Job Zone Component Definitions
Title	Job Zone Two: Some Preparation Needed
Overall Experience	Some previous work-related skill, knowledge, or experience may be helpful in these occupations, but usually is not needed. For example, a drywall installer might benefit from experience installing drywall, but an inexperienced person could still learn to be an installer with little difficulty.
Job Training	Employees in these occupations need anywhere from a few months to one year of working with experienced employees.
Job Zone Examples	These occupations often involve using your knowledge and skills to help others. Examples include drywall installers, fire inspectors, flight attendants, pharmacy technicians, salespersons (retail), and tellers.
SVP Range	(4.0 to < 6.0)
Education	These occupations usually require a high school diploma and may require some vocational training or job-related course work. In some cases, an associate's or bachelor's degree could be needed.

Work_Styles	Work_Styles Definitions
Dependability	Job requires being reliable, responsible, and dependable, and fulfilling obligations.
Cooperation	Job requires being pleasant with others on the job and displaying a good-natured, cooperative attitude.
Attention to Detail	Job requires being careful about detail and thorough in completing work tasks.
Integrity	Job requires being honest and ethical.

Self Control	Job requires maintaining composure, keeping emotions in check, controlling anger, and avoiding aggressive behavior, even in very difficult situations.
Stress Tolerance	Job requires accepting criticism and dealing calmly and effectively with high stress situations.
Social Orientation	Job requires preferring to work with others rather than alone, and being personally connected with others on the job.
Concern for Others	Job requires being sensitive to others' needs and feelings and being understanding and helpful on the job.
Independence	Job requires developing one's own ways of doing things, guiding oneself with little or no supervision, and depending on oneself to get things done.
Initiative	Job requires a willingness to take on responsibilities and challenges.
Leadership	Job requires a willingness to lead, take charge, and offer opinions and direction.
Analytical Thinking	Job requires analyzing information and using logic to address work-related issues and problems.
Adaptability/Flexibility	Job requires being open to change (positive or negative) and to considerable variety in the workplace.
Persistence	Job requires persistence in the face of obstacles.
Achievement/Effort	Job requires establishing and maintaining personally challenging achievement goals and exerting effort toward mastering tasks.
Innovation	Job requires creativity and alternative thinking to develop new ideas for and answers to work-related problems.

41-9012.00 - Models

Model garments and other apparel to display clothing before prospective buyers at fashion shows, private showings, retail establishments, or photographer. May pose for photos to be used for advertising purposes. May pose as subject for paintings, sculptures, and other types of artistic expression.

Tasks

1) Record rates of pay and durations of jobs on vouchers.

2) Pose as directed, or strike suitable interpretive poses for promoting and selling merchandise or fashions during appearances, filming, or photo sessions.

3) Gather information from agents concerning the pay, dates, times, provisions, and lengths of jobs.

4) Wear character costumes and impersonate characters portrayed to amuse children and adults.

5) Display clothing and merchandise in commercials, advertisements, and/or fashion shows.

6) Report job completions to agencies and obtain information about future appointments.

7) Pose for artists and photographers.

8) Dress in sample or completed garments, and select accessories.

9) Stand, turn, and walk to demonstrate features of garments for observers at fashion shows, private showings, and retail establishments.

10) Work closely with photographers, fashion coordinators, directors, producers, stylists, make-up artists, other models, and clients to produce the desired looks, and to finish photo shoots on schedule.

11) Hand out samples or gifts, demonstrate products, and converse with children and adults while dressed in costume.

12) Assemble and maintain portfolios, print composite cards, and travel to go-sees to obtain jobs.

13) Make many quick changes backstage during fashion shows and yet maintain poised appearance before audiences.

14) Promote products and services in television commercials, on film, or in videos.

15) Inform prospective purchasers about models, numbers, and prices of garments, the garments' designers, and where garments can be purchased.

16) Follow strict routines of diet, sleep, and exercise to maintain appearance.

43-3021.03 - Billing, Posting, and Calculating Machine Operators

Operate machines that automatically perform mathematical processes, such as addition, subtraction, multiplication, and division, to calculate and record billing, accounting, statistical, and other numerical data. Duties include operating special billing machines to prepare statements, bills, and invoices, and operating bookkeeping machines to copy and post data, make computations, and compile records of transactions.

Tasks

1) Clean machines, and replace ribbons, film, and tape.

2) Operate bookkeeping machines to copy and post data, make computations, and compile records of transactions.

3) Maintain ledgers and registers, posting charges and refunds to individual funds, and computing and verifying balances.

4) Reconcile and post receipts for cash received by various departments.

5) Balance and reconcile batch control totals with source documents or computer listings in order to locate errors, encode correct amounts, or prepare correction records.

6) Prepare transmittal reports for changes to assessment and tax rolls, redemption file changes, and for warrants, deposits, and invoices.

7) Verify and post to ledgers purchase orders, reports of goods received, invoices, paid vouchers, and other information.

8) Verify completeness and accuracy of original documents such as business property statements, tax rolls, invoices, bonds and coupons, and redemption certificates.

9) Encode and add amounts of transaction documents, such as checks or money orders, using encoding machines.

10) Operate special billing machines to prepare statements, bills, and invoices.

11) Sort and list items for proof or collection.

12) Compute payroll and retirement amounts, applying knowledge of payroll deductions, actuarial tables, disability factors, and survivor allowances.

13) Assign purchase order numbers to invoices, requisitions, and formal and informal bids.

14) Compile, code, and verify requisition, production, statistical, mileage, and other reports which require specialized knowledge in selecting the totals used.

15) Bundle sorted documents to prepare those drawn on other banks for collection.

16) Train other calculating machine operators, and review their work.

17) Transcribe data from office records, using specified forms, billing machines, and transcribing machines.

18) Compute monies due on personal and real property, inventories, redemption payments and other amounts, applying specialized knowledge of tax rates, formulas, interest rates, and other relevant information.

19) Transfer data from machines, such as encoding machines, to computers.

20) Send completed bills to billing clerks for information verification.

21) Sort and microfilm transaction documents, such as checks, using sorting machines.

22) Observe operation of sorters to locate documents that machines cannot read, and manually record amounts of these documents.

Knowledge

Knowledge	Knowledge Definitions
Clerical	Knowledge of administrative and clerical procedures and systems such as word processing, managing files and records, stenography and transcription, designing forms, and other office procedures and terminology.
Economics and Accounting	Knowledge of economic and accounting principles and practices, the financial markets, banking and the analysis and reporting of financial data.
English Language	Knowledge of the structure and content of the English language including the meaning and spelling of words, rules of composition, and grammar.
Personnel and Human Resources	Knowledge of principles and procedures for personnel recruitment, selection, training, compensation and benefits, labor relations and negotiation, and personnel information systems.
Computers and Electronics	Knowledge of circuit boards, processors, chips, electronic equipment, and computer hardware and software, including applications and programming.
Telecommunications	Knowledge of transmission, broadcasting, switching, control, and operation of telecommunications systems.
Administration and Management	Knowledge of business and management principles involved in strategic planning, resource allocation, human resources modeling, leadership technique, production methods, and coordination of people and resources.
Mathematics	Knowledge of arithmetic, algebra, geometry, calculus, statistics, and their applications.
Customer and Personal Service	Knowledge of principles and processes for providing customer and personal services. This includes customer needs assessment, meeting quality standards for services, and evaluation of customer satisfaction.
Communications and Media	Knowledge of media production, communication, and dissemination techniques and methods. This includes alternative ways to inform and entertain via written, oral, and visual media.
Production and Processing	Knowledge of raw materials, production processes, quality control, costs, and other techniques for maximizing the effective manufacture and distribution of goods.
Education and Training	Knowledge of principles and methods for curriculum and training design, teaching and instruction for individuals and groups, and the measurement of training effects.
Law and Government	Knowledge of laws, legal codes, court procedures, precedents, government regulations, executive orders, agency rules, and the democratic political process.
Public Safety and Security	Knowledge of relevant equipment, policies, procedures, and strategies to promote effective local, state, or national security operations for the protection of people, data, property, and institutions.
Medicine and Dentistry	Knowledge of the information and techniques needed to diagnose and treat human injuries, diseases, and deformities. This includes symptoms, treatment alternatives, drug properties and interactions, and preventive health-care measures.
Transportation	Knowledge of principles and methods for moving people or goods by air, rail, sea, or road, including the relative costs and benefits.
Sales and Marketing	Knowledge of principles and methods for showing, promoting, and selling products or services. This includes marketing strategy and tactics, product demonstration, sales techniques, and sales control systems.
Chemistry	Knowledge of the chemical composition, structure, and properties of substances and of the chemical processes and transformations that they undergo. This includes uses of chemicals and their interactions, danger signs, production techniques, and disposal methods.
Psychology	Knowledge of human behavior and performance; individual differences in ability, personality, and interests; learning and motivation; psychological research methods; and the assessment and treatment of behavioral and affective disorders.
Engineering and Technology	Knowledge of the practical application of engineering science and technology. This includes applying principles, techniques, procedures, and equipment to the design and production of various goods and services.
Physics	Knowledge and prediction of physical principles, laws, their interrelationships, and applications to understanding fluid, material, and atmospheric dynamics, and mechanical, electrical, atomic and sub-atomic structures and processes.
Therapy and Counseling	Knowledge of principles, methods, and procedures for diagnosis, treatment, and rehabilitation of physical and mental dysfunctions, and for career counseling and guidance.
Food Production	Knowledge of techniques and equipment for planting, growing, and harvesting food products (both plant and animal) for consumption, including storage/handling techniques.
Mechanical	Knowledge of machines and tools, including their designs, uses, repair, and maintenance.
Foreign Language	Knowledge of the structure and content of a foreign (non-English) language including the meaning and spelling of words, rules of composition and grammar, and pronunciation.
Biology	Knowledge of plant and animal organisms, their tissues, cells, functions, interdependencies, and interactions with each other and the environment.
Sociology and Anthropology	Knowledge of group behavior and dynamics, societal trends and influences, human migrations, ethnicity, cultures and their history and origins.
Building and Construction	Knowledge of materials, methods, and the tools involved in the construction or repair of houses, buildings, or other structures such as highways and roads.

Geography	Knowledge of principles and methods for describing the features of land, sea, and air masses. including their physical characteristics, locations, interrelationships, and distribution of plant, animal, and human life.
Philosophy and Theology	Knowledge of different philosophical systems and religions. This includes their basic principles, values, ethics, ways of thinking, customs, practices, and their impact on human culture.
Design	Knowledge of design techniques, tools, and principles involved in production of precision technical plans, blueprints, drawings, and models.
Fine Arts	Knowledge of the theory and techniques required to compose, produce, and perform works of music, dance, visual arts, drama, and sculpture.
History and Archeology	Knowledge of historical events and their causes, indicators, and effects on civilizations and cultures.

Skills	Skills Definitions
Active Listening	Giving full attention to what other people are saying, taking time to understand the points being made, asking questions as appropriate, and not interrupting at inappropriate times.
Reading Comprehension	Understanding written sentences and paragraphs in work related documents.
Writing	Communicating effectively in writing as appropriate for the needs of the audience.
Mathematics	Using mathematics to solve problems.
Speaking	Talking to others to convey information effectively.
Active Learning	Understanding the implications of new information for both current and future problem-solving and decision-making.
Time Management	Managing one's own time and the time of others.
Instructing	Teaching others how to do something.
Critical Thinking	Using logic and reasoning to identify the strengths and weaknesses of alternative solutions, conclusions or approaches to problems.
Learning Strategies	Selecting and using training/instructional methods and procedures appropriate for the situation when learning or teaching new things.
Negotiation	Bringing others together and trying to reconcile differences.
Persuasion	Persuading others to change their minds or behavior.
Monitoring	Monitoring/Assessing performance of yourself, other individuals, or organizations to make improvements or take corrective action.
Coordination	Adjusting actions in relation to others' actions.
Judgment and Decision Making	Considering the relative costs and benefits of potential actions to choose the most appropriate one.
Social Perceptiveness	Being aware of others' reactions and understanding why they react as they do.
Management of Financial Resources	Determining how money will be spent to get the work done, and accounting for these expenditures.
Service Orientation	Actively looking for ways to help people.
Equipment Selection	Determining the kind of tools and equipment needed to do a job.
Management of Personnel Resources	Motivating, developing, and directing people as they work, identifying the best people for the job.
Complex Problem Solving	Identifying complex problems and reviewing related information to develop and evaluate options and implement solutions.
Operation and Control	Controlling operations of equipment or systems.
Operations Analysis	Analyzing needs and product requirements to create a design.
Equipment Maintenance	Performing routine maintenance on equipment and determining when and what kind of maintenance is needed.
Quality Control Analysis	Conducting tests and inspections of products, services, or processes to evaluate quality or performance.
Systems Evaluation	Identifying measures or indicators of system performance and the actions needed to improve or correct performance, relative to the goals of the system.
Technology Design	Generating or adapting equipment and technology to serve user needs.
Installation	Installing equipment, machines, wiring, or programs to meet specifications.
Programming	Writing computer programs for various purposes.
Troubleshooting	Determining causes of operating errors and deciding what to do about it.
Management of Material Resources	Obtaining and seeing to the appropriate use of equipment, facilities, and materials needed to do certain work.
Operation Monitoring	Watching gauges, dials, or other indicators to make sure a machine is working properly.

Repairing	Repairing machines or systems using the needed tools.
Systems Analysis	Determining how a system should work and how changes in conditions, operations, and the environment will affect outcomes.
Science	Using scientific rules and methods to solve problems.

Ability	Ability Definitions
Information Ordering	The ability to arrange things or actions in a certain order or pattern according to a specific rule or set of rules (e.g., patterns of numbers, letters, words, pictures, mathematical operations).
Mathematical Reasoning	The ability to choose the right mathematical methods or formulas to solve a problem.
Near Vision	The ability to see details at close range (within a few feet of the observer).
Oral Expression	The ability to communicate information and ideas in speaking so others will understand.
Oral Comprehension	The ability to listen to and understand information and ideas presented through spoken words and sentences.
Written Comprehension	The ability to read and understand information and ideas presented in writing.
Speech Clarity	The ability to speak clearly so others can understand you.
Speech Recognition	The ability to identify and understand the speech of another person.
Number Facility	The ability to add, subtract, multiply, or divide quickly and correctly.
Deductive Reasoning	The ability to apply general rules to specific problems to produce answers that make sense.
Written Expression	The ability to communicate information and ideas in writing so others will understand.
Inductive Reasoning	The ability to combine pieces of information to form general rules or conclusions (includes finding a relationship among seemingly unrelated events).
Category Flexibility	The ability to generate or use different sets of rules for combining or grouping things in different ways.
Problem Sensitivity	The ability to tell when something is wrong or is likely to go wrong. It does not involve solving the problem, only recognizing there is a problem.
Selective Attention	The ability to concentrate on a task over a period of time without being distracted.
Perceptual Speed	The ability to quickly and accurately compare similarities and differences among sets of letters, numbers, objects, pictures, or patterns. The things to be compared may be presented at the same time or one after the other. This ability also includes comparing a presented object with a remembered object.
Speed of Closure	The ability to quickly make sense of, combine, and organize information into meaningful patterns.
Control Precision	The ability to quickly and repeatedly adjust the controls of a machine or a vehicle to exact positions.
Flexibility of Closure	The ability to identify or detect a known pattern (a figure, object, word, or sound) that is hidden in other distracting material.
Manual Dexterity	The ability to quickly move your hand, your hand together with your arm, or your two hands to grasp, manipulate, or assemble objects.
Memorization	The ability to remember information such as words, numbers, pictures, and procedures.
Fluency of Ideas	The ability to come up with a number of ideas about a topic (the number of ideas is important, not their quality, correctness, or creativity).
Wrist-Finger Speed	The ability to make fast, simple, repeated movements of the fingers, hands, and wrists.
Time Sharing	The ability to shift back and forth between two or more activities or sources of information (such as speech, sounds, touch, or other sources).
Arm-Hand Steadiness	The ability to keep your hand and arm steady while moving your arm or while holding your arm and hand in one position.
Finger Dexterity	The ability to make precisely coordinated movements of the fingers of one or both hands to grasp, manipulate, or assemble very small objects.
Visualization	The ability to imagine how something will look after it is moved around or when its parts are moved or rearranged.
Auditory Attention	The ability to focus on a single source of sound in the presence of other distracting sounds.
Originality	The ability to come up with unusual or clever ideas about a given topic or situation, or to develop creative ways to solve a problem.
Far Vision	The ability to see details at a distance.

Trunk Strength	The ability to use your abdominal and lower back muscles to support part of the body repeatedly or continuously over time without 'giving out' or fatiguing.
Visual Color Discrimination	The ability to match or detect differences between colors, including shades of color and brightness.
Static Strength	The ability to exert maximum muscle force to lift, push, pull, or carry objects.
Depth Perception	The ability to judge which of several objects is closer or farther away from you, or to judge the distance between you and an object.
Hearing Sensitivity	The ability to detect or tell the differences between sounds that vary in pitch and loudness.
Speed of Limb Movement	The ability to quickly move the arms and legs.
Multilimb Coordination	The ability to coordinate two or more limbs (for example, two arms, two legs, or one leg and one arm) while sitting, standing, or lying down. It does not involve performing the activities while the whole body is in motion.
Stamina	The ability to exert yourself physically over long periods of time without getting winded or out of breath.
Night Vision	The ability to see under low light conditions.
Gross Body Equilibrium	The ability to keep or regain your body balance or stay upright when in an unstable position.
Rate Control	The ability to time your movements or the movement of a piece of equipment in anticipation of changes in the speed and/or direction of a moving object or scene.
Reaction Time	The ability to quickly respond (with the hand, finger, or foot) to a signal (sound, light, picture) when it appears.
Explosive Strength	The ability to use short bursts of muscle force to propel oneself (as in jumping or sprinting), or to throw an object.
Dynamic Strength	The ability to exert muscle force repeatedly or continuously over time. This involves muscular endurance and resistance to muscle fatigue.
Dynamic Flexibility	The ability to quickly and repeatedly bend, stretch, twist, or reach out with your body, arms, and/or legs.
Spatial Orientation	The ability to know your location in relation to the environment or to know where other objects are in relation to you.
Response Orientation	The ability to choose quickly between two or more movements in response to two or more different signals (lights, sounds, pictures). It includes the speed with which the correct response is started with the hand, foot, or other body part.
Glare Sensitivity	The ability to see objects in the presence of glare or bright lighting.
Gross Body Coordination	The ability to coordinate the movement of your arms, legs, and torso together when the whole body is in motion.
Peripheral Vision	The ability to see objects or movement of objects to one's side when the eyes are looking ahead.
Extent Flexibility	The ability to bend, stretch, twist, or reach with your body, arms, and/or legs.
Sound Localization	The ability to tell the direction from which a sound originated.

Work_Activity — Work_Activity Definitions

Interacting With Computers	Using computers and computer systems (including hardware and software) to program, write software, set up functions, enter data, or process information.
Processing Information	Compiling, coding, categorizing, calculating, tabulating, auditing, or verifying information or data.
Getting Information	Observing, receiving, and otherwise obtaining information from all relevant sources.
Communicating with Supervisors, Peers, or Subordin	Providing information to supervisors, co-workers, and subordinates by telephone, in written form, e-mail, or in person.
Organizing, Planning, and Prioritizing Work	Developing specific goals and plans to prioritize, organize, and accomplish your work.
Communicating with Persons Outside Organization	Communicating with people outside the organization, representing the organization to customers, the public, government, and other external sources. This information can be exchanged in person, in writing, or by telephone or e-mail.
Updating and Using Relevant Knowledge	Keeping up-to-date technically and applying new knowledge to your job.
Establishing and Maintaining Interpersonal Relatio	Developing constructive and cooperative working relationships with others, and maintaining them over time.
Making Decisions and Solving Problems	Analyzing information and evaluating results to choose the best solution and solve problems.
Documenting/Recording Information	Entering, transcribing, recording, storing, or maintaining information in written or electronic/magnetic form.

Identifying Objects, Actions, and Events	Identifying information by categorizing, estimating, recognizing differences or similarities, and detecting changes in circumstances or events.
Resolving Conflicts and Negotiating with Others	Handling complaints, settling disputes, and resolving grievances and conflicts, or otherwise negotiating with others.
Performing for or Working Directly with the Public	Performing for people or dealing directly with the public. This includes serving customers in restaurants and stores, and receiving clients or guests.
Monitor Processes, Materials, or Surroundings	Monitoring and reviewing information from materials, events, or the environment, to detect or assess problems.
Performing Administrative Activities	Performing day-to-day administrative tasks such as maintaining information files and processing paperwork.
Analyzing Data or Information	Identifying the underlying principles, reasons, or facts of information by breaking down information or data into separate parts.
Coordinating the Work and Activities of Others	Getting members of a group to work together to accomplish tasks.
Scheduling Work and Activities	Scheduling events, programs, and activities, as well as the work of others.
Training and Teaching Others	Identifying the educational needs of others, developing formal educational or training programs or classes, and teaching or instructing others.
Judging the Qualities of Things, Services, or Peop	Assessing the value, importance, or quality of things or people.
Evaluating Information to Determine Compliance wit	Using relevant information and individual judgment to determine whether events or processes comply with laws, regulations, or standards.
Thinking Creatively	Developing, designing, or creating new applications, ideas, relationships, systems, or products, including artistic contributions.
Assisting and Caring for Others	Providing personal assistance, medical attention, emotional support, or other personal care to others such as coworkers, customers, or patients.
Estimating the Quantifiable Characteristics of Pro	Estimating sizes, distances, and quantities; or determining time, costs, resources, or materials needed to perform a work activity.
Interpreting the Meaning of Information for Others	Translating or explaining what information means and how it can be used.
Developing Objectives and Strategies	Establishing long-range objectives and specifying the strategies and actions to achieve them.
Provide Consultation and Advice to Others	Providing guidance and expert advice to management or other groups on technical, systems-, or process-related topics.
Developing and Building Teams	Encouraging and building mutual trust, respect, and cooperation among team members.
Coaching and Developing Others	Identifying the developmental needs of others and coaching, mentoring, or otherwise helping others to improve their knowledge or skills.
Inspecting Equipment, Structures, or Material	Inspecting equipment, structures, or materials to identify the cause of errors or other problems or defects.
Handling and Moving Objects	Using hands and arms in handling, installing, positioning, and moving materials, and manipulating things.
Guiding, Directing, and Motivating Subordinates	Providing guidance and direction to subordinates, including setting performance standards and monitoring performance.
Selling or Influencing Others	Convincing others to buy merchandise/goods or to otherwise change their minds or actions.
Monitoring and Controlling Resources	Monitoring and controlling resources and overseeing the spending of money.
Performing General Physical Activities	Performing physical activities that require considerable use of your arms and legs and moving your whole body, such as climbing, lifting, balancing, walking, stooping, and handling of materials.
Staffing Organizational Units	Recruiting, interviewing, selecting, hiring, and promoting employees in an organization.
Controlling Machines and Processes	Using either control mechanisms or direct physical activity to operate machines or processes (not including computers or vehicles).
Drafting, Laying Out, and Specifying Technical Dev	Providing documentation, detailed instructions, drawings, or specifications to tell others about how devices, parts, equipment, or structures are to be fabricated, constructed, assembled, modified, maintained, or used.
Repairing and Maintaining Electronic Equipment	Servicing, repairing, calibrating, regulating, fine-tuning, or testing machines, devices, and equipment that operate primarily on the basis of electrical or electronic (not mechanical) principles.
Repairing and Maintaining Mechanical Equipment	Servicing, repairing, adjusting, and testing machines, devices, moving parts, and equipment that operate primarily on the basis of mechanical (not electronic) principles.

Operating Vehicles, Mechanized Devices, or Equipme	Running, maneuvering, navigating, or driving vehicles or mechanized equipment, such as forklifts, passenger vehicles, aircraft, or water craft.

Work_Context	**Work_Context Definitions**
Telephone	How often do you have telephone conversations in this job?
Importance of Repeating Same Tasks	How important is repeating the same physical activities (e.g., key entry) or mental activities (e.g., checking entries in a ledger) over and over, without stopping, to performing this job?
Contact With Others	How much does this job require the worker to be in contact with others (face-to-face, by telephone, or otherwise) in order to perform it?
Importance of Being Exact or Accurate	How important is being very exact or highly accurate in performing this job?
Indoors, Environmentally Controlled	How often does this job require working indoors in environmentally controlled conditions?
Face-to-Face Discussions	How often do you have to have face-to-face discussions with individuals or teams in this job?
Letters and Memos	How often does the job require written letters and memos?
Spend Time Sitting	How much does this job require sitting?
Work With Work Group or Team	How important is it to work with others in a group or team in this job?
Frequency of Conflict Situations	How often are there conflict situations the employee has to face in this job?
Deal With Unpleasant or Angry People	How frequently does the worker have to deal with unpleasant, angry, or discourteous individuals as part of the job requirements?
Deal With External Customers	How important is it to work with external customers or the public in this job?
Level of Competition	To what extent does this job require the worker to compete or to be aware of competitive pressures?
Structured versus Unstructured Work	To what extent is this job structured for the worker, rather than allowing the worker to determine tasks, priorities, and goals?
Spend Time Using Your Hands to Handle, Control, or	How much does this job require using your hands to handle, control, or feel objects, tools or controls?
Spend Time Making Repetitive Motions	How much does this job require making repetitive motions?
Frequency of Decision Making	How frequently is the worker required to make decisions that affect other people, the financial resources, and/or the image and reputation of the organization?
Electronic Mail	How often do you use electronic mail in this job?
Impact of Decisions on Co-workers or Company Resul	How do the decisions an employee makes impact the results of co-workers, clients or the company?
Time Pressure	How often does this job require the worker to meet strict deadlines?
Freedom to Make Decisions	How much decision making freedom, without supervision, does the job offer?
Exposed to Contaminants	How often does this job require working exposed to contaminants (such as pollutants, gases, dust or odors)?
Sounds, Noise Levels Are Distracting or Uncomforta	How often does this job require working exposed to sounds and noise levels that are distracting or uncomfortable?
Physical Proximity	To what extent does this job require the worker to perform job tasks in close physical proximity to other people?
Coordinate or Lead Others	How important is it to coordinate or lead others in accomplishing work activities in this job?
Responsibility for Outcomes and Results	How responsible is the worker for work outcomes and results of other workers?
Extremely Bright or Inadequate Lighting	How often does this job require working in extremely bright or inadequate lighting conditions?
Degree of Automation	How automated is the job?
Spend Time Standing	How much does this job require standing?
Consequence of Error	How serious would the result usually be if the worker made a mistake that was not readily correctable?
Responsible for Others' Health and Safety	How much responsibility is there for the health and safety of others in this job?
Very Hot or Cold Temperatures	How often does this job require working in very hot (above 90 F degrees) or very cold (below 32 F degrees) temperatures?
Exposed to Minor Burns, Cuts, Bites, or Stings	How often does this job require exposure to minor burns, cuts, bites, or stings?
Exposed to Disease or Infections	How often does this job require exposure to disease/infections?
Wear Common Protective or Safety Equipment such as	How much does this job require wearing common protective or safety equipment such as safety shoes, glasses, gloves, hard hats or life jackets?

Spend Time Bending or Twisting the Body	How much does this job require bending or twisting your body?
Cramped Work Space, Awkward Positions	How often does this job require working in cramped work spaces that requires getting into awkward positions?
Public Speaking	How often do you have to perform public speaking in this job?
In an Enclosed Vehicle or Equipment	How often does this job require working in a closed vehicle or equipment (e.g., car)?
Pace Determined by Speed of Equipment	How important is it to this job that the pace is determined by the speed of equipment or machinery? (This does not refer to keeping busy at all times on this job.)
Spend Time Walking and Running	How much does this job require walking and running?
Outdoors, Exposed to Weather	How often does this job require working outdoors, exposed to all weather conditions?
Exposed to Radiation	How often does this job require exposure to radiation?
Indoors, Not Environmentally Controlled	How often does this job require working indoors in non-controlled environmental conditions (e.g., warehouse without heat)?
Exposed to Hazardous Equipment	How often does this job require exposure to hazardous equipment?
Spend Time Climbing Ladders, Scaffolds, or Poles	How much does this job require climbing ladders, scaffolds, or poles?
Exposed to High Places	How often does this job require exposure to high places?
Spend Time Kneeling, Crouching, Stooping, or Crawl	How much does this job require kneeling, crouching, stooping or crawling?
Spend Time Keeping or Regaining Balance	How much does this job require keeping or regaining your balance?
Deal With Physically Aggressive People	How frequently does this job require the worker to deal with physical aggression of violent individuals?
Exposed to Hazardous Conditions	How often does this job require exposure to hazardous conditions?
Outdoors, Under Cover	How often does this job require working outdoors, under cover (e.g., structure with roof but no walls)?
In an Open Vehicle or Equipment	How often does this job require working in an open vehicle or equipment (e.g., tractor)?
Exposed to Whole Body Vibration	How often does this job require exposure to whole body vibration (e.g., operate a jackhammer)?
Wear Specialized Protective or Safety Equipment su	How much does this job require wearing specialized protective or safety equipment such as breathing apparatus, safety harness, full protection suits, or radiation protection?

Job Zone Component	**Job Zone Component Definitions**
Title	Job Zone Two: Some Preparation Needed
Overall Experience	Some previous work-related skill, knowledge, or experience may be helpful in these occupations, but usually is not needed. For example, a drywall installer might benefit from experience installing drywall, but an inexperienced person could still learn to be an installer with little difficulty.
Job Training	Employees in these occupations need anywhere from a few months to one year of working with experienced employees. These occupations often involve using your knowledge and skills to help others.
Job Zone Examples	Examples include drywall installers, fire inspectors, flight attendants, pharmacy technicians, salespersons (retail), and tellers.
SVP Range	(4.0 to < 6.0)
Education	These occupations usually require a high school diploma and may require some vocational training or job-related course work. In some cases, an associate's or bachelor's degree could be needed.

Work_Styles	**Work_Styles Definitions**
Dependability	Job requires being reliable, responsible, and dependable, and fulfilling obligations.
Self Control	Job requires maintaining composure, keeping emotions in check, controlling anger, and avoiding aggressive behavior, even in very difficult situations.
Stress Tolerance	Job requires accepting criticism and dealing calmly and effectively with high stress situations.
Attention to Detail	Job requires being careful about detail and thorough in completing work tasks.
Integrity	Job requires being honest and ethical.
Cooperation	Job requires being pleasant with others on the job and displaying a good-natured, cooperative attitude.

Initiative	Job requires a willingness to take on responsibilities and challenges.
Concern for Others	Job requires being sensitive to others' needs and feelings and being understanding and helpful on the job.
Persistence	Job requires persistence in the face of obstacles.
Independence	Job requires developing one's own ways of doing things, guiding oneself with little or no supervision, and depending on oneself to get things done.
Achievement/Effort	Job requires establishing and maintaining personally challenging achievement goals and exerting effort toward mastering tasks.
Adaptability/Flexibility	Job requires being open to change (positive or negative) and to considerable variety in the workplace.
Innovation	Job requires creativity and alternative thinking to develop new ideas for and answers to work-related problems.
Analytical Thinking	Job requires analyzing information and using logic to address work-related issues and problems.
Social Orientation	Job requires preferring to work with others rather than alone, and being personally connected with others on the job.
Leadership	Job requires a willingness to lead, take charge, and offer opinions and direction.

43-5021.00 - Couriers and Messengers

Pick up and carry messages, documents, packages, and other items between offices or departments within an establishment or to other business concerns, traveling by foot, bicycle, motorcycle, automobile, or public conveyance.

Tasks

1) Plan and follow the most efficient routes for delivering goods.

2) Unload and sort items collected along delivery routes.

3) Receive messages or materials to be delivered, and information on recipients, such as names, addresses, telephone numbers, and delivery instructions, communicated via telephone, two-way radio, or in person.

4) Load vehicles with listed goods, ensuring goods are loaded correctly and taking precautions with hazardous goods.

5) Sort items to be delivered according to the delivery route.

6) Deliver messages and items, such as newspapers, documents, and packages, between establishment departments, and to other establishments and private homes.

7) Perform routine maintenance on delivery vehicles, such as monitoring fluid levels and replenishing fuel.

8) Record information, such as items received and delivered and recipients' responses to messages.

9) Obtain signatures and payments, or arrange for recipients to make payments.

10) Call by telephone in order to deliver verbal messages.

11) Check with home offices after completed deliveries, in order to confirm deliveries and collections and to receive instructions for other deliveries.

12) Open, sort, and distribute incoming mail.

13) Perform general office or clerical work such as filing materials, operating duplicating machines, or running errands.

14) Unload goods from large trucks, and load them onto smaller delivery vehicles.

15) Collect, seal, and stamp outgoing mail, using postage meters and envelope sealers.

Knowledge	Knowledge Definitions
Transportation	Knowledge of principles and methods for moving people or goods by air, rail, sea, or road, including the relative costs and benefits.
Customer and Personal Service	Knowledge of principles and processes for providing customer and personal services. This includes customer needs assessment, meeting quality standards for services, and evaluation of customer satisfaction.
English Language	Knowledge of the structure and content of the English language including the meaning and spelling of words, rules of composition, and grammar.
Public Safety and Security	Knowledge of relevant equipment, policies, procedures, and strategies to promote effective local, state, or national security operations for the protection of people, data, property, and institutions.
Geography	Knowledge of principles and methods for describing the features of land, sea, and air masses, including their physical characteristics, locations, interrelationships, and distribution of plant, animal, and human life.
Administration and Management	Knowledge of business and management principles involved in strategic planning, resource allocation, human resources modeling, leadership technique, production methods, and coordination of people and resources.
Mathematics	Knowledge of arithmetic, algebra, geometry, calculus, statistics, and their applications.
Communications and Media	Knowledge of media production, communication, and dissemination techniques and methods. This includes alternative ways to inform and entertain via written, oral, and visual media.
Law and Government	Knowledge of laws, legal codes, court procedures, precedents, government regulations, executive orders, agency rules, and the democratic political process.
Clerical	Knowledge of administrative and clerical procedures and systems such as word processing, managing files and records, stenography and transcription, designing forms, and other office procedures and terminology.
Telecommunications	Knowledge of transmission, broadcasting, switching, control, and operation of telecommunications systems.
Personnel and Human Resources	Knowledge of principles and procedures for personnel recruitment, selection, training, compensation and benefits, labor relations and negotiation, and personnel information systems.
Production and Processing	Knowledge of raw materials, production processes, quality control, costs, and other techniques for maximizing the effective manufacture and distribution of goods.
Mechanical	Knowledge of machines and tools, including their designs, uses, repair, and maintenance.
Psychology	Knowledge of human behavior and performance; individual differences in ability, personality, and interests; learning and motivation; psychological research methods; and the assessment and treatment of behavioral and affective disorders.
Education and Training	Knowledge of principles and methods for curriculum and training design, teaching and instruction for individuals and groups, and the measurement of training effects.
Food Production	Knowledge of techniques and equipment for planting, growing, and harvesting food products (both plant and animal) for consumption, including storage/handling techniques.
Computers and Electronics	Knowledge of circuit boards, processors, chips, electronic equipment, and computer hardware and software, including applications and programming.
Medicine and Dentistry	Knowledge of the information and techniques needed to diagnose and treat human injuries, diseases, and deformities. This includes symptoms, treatment alternatives, drug properties and interactions, and preventive health-care measures.
Physics	Knowledge and prediction of physical principles, laws, their interrelationships, and applications to understanding fluid, material, and atmospheric dynamics, and mechanical, electrical, atomic and sub-atomic structures and processes.
Engineering and Technology	Knowledge of the practical application of engineering science and technology. This includes applying principles, techniques, procedures, and equipment to the design and production of various goods and services.
Sociology and Anthropology	Knowledge of group behavior and dynamics, societal trends and influences, human migrations, ethnicity, cultures and their history and origins.
Economics and Accounting	Knowledge of economic and accounting principles and practices, the financial markets, banking and the analysis and reporting of financial data.
Chemistry	Knowledge of the chemical composition, structure, and properties of substances and of the chemical processes and transformations that they undergo. This includes uses of chemicals and their interactions, danger signs, production techniques, and disposal methods.
Philosophy and Theology	Knowledge of different philosophical systems and religions. This includes their basic principles, values, ethics, ways of thinking, customs, practices, and their impact on human culture.

Biology	Knowledge of plant and animal organisms, their tissues, cells, functions, interdependencies, and interactions with each other and the environment.
Foreign Language	Knowledge of the structure and content of a foreign (non-English) language including the meaning and spelling of words, rules of composition and grammar, and pronunciation.
Sales and Marketing	Knowledge of principles and methods for showing, promoting, and selling products or services. This includes marketing strategy and tactics, product demonstration, sales techniques, and sales control systems.
Therapy and Counseling	Knowledge of principles, methods, and procedures for diagnosis, treatment, and rehabilitation of physical and mental dysfunctions, and for career counseling and guidance.
History and Archeology	Knowledge of historical events and their causes, indicators, and effects on civilizations and cultures.
Building and Construction	Knowledge of materials, methods, and the tools involved in the construction or repair of houses, buildings, or other structures such as highways and roads.
Design	Knowledge of design techniques, tools, and principles involved in production of precision technical plans, blueprints, drawings, and models.
Fine Arts	Knowledge of the theory and techniques required to compose, produce, and perform works of music, dance, visual arts, drama, and sculpture.

Skills	Skills Definitions
Reading Comprehension	Understanding written sentences and paragraphs in work related documents.
Coordination	Adjusting actions in relation to others' actions.
Time Management	Managing one's own time and the time of others.
Active Listening	Giving full attention to what other people are saying, taking time to understand the points being made, asking questions as appropriate, and not interrupting at inappropriate times.
Instructing	Teaching others how to do something.
Speaking	Talking to others to convey information effectively.
Learning Strategies	Selecting and using training/instructional methods and procedures appropriate for the situation when learning or teaching new things.
Service Orientation	Actively looking for ways to help people.
Equipment Maintenance	Performing routine maintenance on equipment and determining when and what kind of maintenance is needed.
Critical Thinking	Using logic and reasoning to identify the strengths and weaknesses of alternative solutions, conclusions or approaches to problems.
Active Learning	Understanding the implications of new information for both current and future problem-solving and decision-making.
Troubleshooting	Determining causes of operating errors and deciding what to do about it.
Social Perceptiveness	Being aware of others' reactions and understanding why they react as they do.
Judgment and Decision Making	Considering the relative costs and benefits of potential actions to choose the most appropriate one.
Persuasion	Persuading others to change their minds or behavior.
Monitoring	Monitoring/Assessing performance of yourself, other individuals, or organizations to make improvements or take corrective action.
Operation and Control	Controlling operations of equipment or systems.
Equipment Selection	Determining the kind of tools and equipment needed to do a job.
Operation Monitoring	Watching gauges, dials, or other indicators to make sure a machine is working properly.
Writing	Communicating effectively in writing as appropriate for the needs of the audience.
Mathematics	Using mathematics to solve problems.
Technology Design	Generating or adapting equipment and technology to serve user needs.
Negotiation	Bringing others together and trying to reconcile differences.
Complex Problem Solving	Identifying complex problems and reviewing related information to develop and evaluate options and implement solutions.
Systems Analysis	Determining how a system should work and how changes in conditions, operations, and the environment will affect outcomes.
Systems Evaluation	Identifying measures or indicators of system performance and the actions needed to improve or correct performance, relative to the goals of the system.
Repairing	Repairing machines or systems using the needed tools.

Quality Control Analysis	Conducting tests and inspections of products, services, or processes to evaluate quality or performance.
Management of Material Resources	Obtaining and seeing to the appropriate use of equipment, facilities, and materials needed to do certain work.
Operations Analysis	Analyzing needs and product requirements to create a design.
Science	Using scientific rules and methods to solve problems.
Management of Personnel Resources	Motivating, developing, and directing people as they work, identifying the best people for the job.
Installation	Installing equipment, machines, wiring, or programs to meet specifications.
Programming	Writing computer programs for various purposes.
Management of Financial Resources	Determining how money will be spent to get the work done, and accounting for these expenditures.

Ability	Ability Definitions
Oral Comprehension	The ability to listen to and understand information and ideas presented through spoken words and sentences.
Multilimb Coordination	The ability to coordinate two or more limbs (for example, two arms, two legs, or one leg and one arm) while sitting, standing, or lying down. It does not involve performing the activities while the whole body is in motion.
Oral Expression	The ability to communicate information and ideas in speaking so others will understand.
Speech Recognition	The ability to identify and understand the speech of another person.
Speech Clarity	The ability to speak clearly so others can understand you.
Near Vision	The ability to see details at close range (within a few feet of the observer).
Problem Sensitivity	The ability to tell when something is wrong or is likely to go wrong. It does not involve solving the problem, only recognizing there is a problem.
Manual Dexterity	The ability to quickly move your hand, your hand together with your arm, or your two hands to grasp, manipulate, or assemble objects.
Written Expression	The ability to communicate information and ideas in writing so others will understand.
Control Precision	The ability to quickly and repeatedly adjust the controls of a machine or a vehicle to exact positions.
Inductive Reasoning	The ability to combine pieces of information to form general rules or conclusions (includes finding a relationship among seemingly unrelated events).
Deductive Reasoning	The ability to apply general rules to specific problems to produce answers that make sense.
Information Ordering	The ability to arrange things or actions in a certain order or pattern according to a specific rule or set of rules (e.g., patterns of numbers, letters, words, pictures, mathematical operations).
Arm-Hand Steadiness	The ability to keep your hand and arm steady while moving your arm or while holding your arm and hand in one position.
Finger Dexterity	The ability to make precisely coordinated movements of the fingers of one or both hands to grasp, manipulate, or assemble very small objects.
Written Comprehension	The ability to read and understand information and ideas presented in writing.
Far Vision	The ability to see details at a distance.
Depth Perception	The ability to judge which of several objects is closer or farther away from you, or to judge the distance between you and an object.
Category Flexibility	The ability to generate or use different sets of rules for combining or grouping things in different ways.
Trunk Strength	The ability to use your abdominal and lower back muscles to support part of the body repeatedly or continuously over time without 'giving out' or fatiguing.
Response Orientation	The ability to choose quickly between two or more movements in response to two or more different signals (lights, sounds, pictures). It includes the speed with which the correct response is started with the hand, foot, or other body part.
Stamina	The ability to exert yourself physically over long periods of time without getting winded or out of breath.
Spatial Orientation	The ability to know your location in relation to the environment or to know where other objects are in relation to you.
Selective Attention	The ability to concentrate on a task over a period of time without being distracted.
Static Strength	The ability to exert maximum muscle force to lift, push, pull, or carry objects.

Perceptual Speed	The ability to quickly and accurately compare similarities and differences among sets of letters, numbers, objects, pictures, or patterns. The things to be compared may be presented at the same time or one after the other. This ability also includes comparing a presented object with a remembered object.	Communicating with Persons Outside Organization	Communicating with people outside the organization, representing the organization to customers, the public, government, and other external sources. This information can be exchanged in person, in writing, or by telephone or e-mail.
Gross Body Coordination	The ability to coordinate the movement of your arms, legs, and torso together when the whole body is in motion.	Communicating with Supervisors, Peers, or Subordin	Providing information to supervisors, co-workers, and subordinates by telephone, in written form, e-mail, or in person.
Time Sharing	The ability to shift back and forth between two or more activities or sources of information (such as speech, sounds, touch, or other sources).	Processing Information	Compiling, coding, categorizing, calculating, tabulating, auditing, or verifying information or data.
Visualization	The ability to imagine how something will look after it is moved around or when its parts are moved or rearranged.	Organizing, Planning, and Prioritizing Work	Developing specific goals and plans to prioritize, organize, and accomplish your work.
Speed of Limb Movement	The ability to quickly move the arms and legs.	Monitor Processes, Materials, or Surroundings	Monitoring and reviewing information from materials, events, or the environment, to detect or assess problems.
Extent Flexibility	The ability to bend, stretch, twist, or reach with your body, arms, and/or legs.		
Reaction Time	The ability to quickly respond (with the hand, finger, or foot) to a signal (sound, light, picture) when it appears.	Identifying Objects, Actions, and Events	Identifying information by categorizing, estimating, recognizing differences or similarities, and detecting changes in circumstances or events.
Flexibility of Closure	The ability to identify or detect a known pattern (a figure, object, word, or sound) that is hidden in other distracting material.	Establishing and Maintaining Interpersonal Relatio	Developing constructive and cooperative working relationships with others, and maintaining them over time.
Glare Sensitivity	The ability to see objects in the presence of glare or bright lighting.	Performing for or Working Directly with the Public	Performing for people or dealing directly with the public. This includes serving customers in restaurants and stores, and receiving clients or guests.
Originality	The ability to come up with unusual or clever ideas about a given topic or situation, or to develop creative ways to solve a problem.	Estimating the Quantifiable Characteristics of Pro	Estimating sizes, distances, and quantities; or determining time, costs, resources, or materials needed to perform a work activity.
Night Vision	The ability to see under low light conditions.	Updating and Using Relevant Knowledge	Keeping up-to-date technically and applying new knowledge to your job.
Rate Control	The ability to time your movements or the movement of a piece of equipment in anticipation of changes in the speed and/or direction of a moving object or scene.	Evaluating Information to Determine Compliance wit	Using relevant information and individual judgment to determine whether events or processes comply with laws, regulations, or standards.
Dynamic Strength	The ability to exert muscle force repeatedly or continuously over time. This involves muscular endurance and resistance to muscle fatigue.	Assisting and Caring for Others	Providing personal assistance, medical attention, emotional support, or other personal care to others such as coworkers, customers, or patients.
Auditory Attention	The ability to focus on a single source of sound in the presence of other distracting sounds.	Making Decisions and Solving Problems	Analyzing information and evaluating results to choose the best solution and solve problems.
Fluency of Ideas	The ability to come up with a number of ideas about a topic (the number of ideas is important, not their quality, correctness, or creativity).	Inspecting Equipment, Structures, or Material	Inspecting equipment, structures, or materials to identify the cause of errors or other problems or defects.
Visual Color Discrimination	The ability to match or detect differences between colors, including shades of color and brightness.	Performing Administrative Activities	Performing day-to-day administrative tasks such as maintaining information files and processing paperwork.
Number Facility	The ability to add, subtract, multiply, or divide quickly and correctly.	Judging the Qualities of Things, Services, or Peop	Assessing the value, importance, or quality of things or people.
Gross Body Equilibrium	The ability to keep or regain your body balance or stay upright when in an unstable position.	Resolving Conflicts and Negotiating with Others	Handling complaints, settling disputes, and resolving grievances and conflicts, or otherwise negotiating with others.
Speed of Closure	The ability to quickly make sense of, combine, and organize information into meaningful patterns.	Developing Objectives and Strategies	Establishing long-range objectives and specifying the strategies and actions to achieve them.
Sound Localization	The ability to tell the direction from which a sound originated.	Analyzing Data or Information	Identifying the underlying principles, reasons, or facts of information by breaking down information or data into separate parts.
Mathematical Reasoning	The ability to choose the right mathematical methods or formulas to solve a problem.		
Peripheral Vision	The ability to see objects or movement of objects to one's side when the eyes are looking ahead.	Scheduling Work and Activities	Scheduling events, programs, and activities, as well as the work of others.
Memorization	The ability to remember information such as words, numbers, pictures, and procedures.	Training and Teaching Others	Identifying the educational needs of others, developing formal educational or training programs or classes, and teaching or instructing others.
Hearing Sensitivity	The ability to detect or tell the differences between sounds that vary in pitch and loudness.	Thinking Creatively	Developing, designing, or creating new applications, ideas, relationships, systems, or products, including artistic contributions.
Dynamic Flexibility	The ability to quickly and repeatedly bend, stretch, twist, or reach out with your body, arms, and/or legs.	Interpreting the Meaning of Information for Others	Translating or explaining what information means and how it can be used.
Wrist-Finger Speed	The ability to make fast, simple, repeated movements of the fingers, hands, and wrists.	Developing and Building Teams	Encouraging and building mutual trust, respect, and cooperation among team members.
Explosive Strength	The ability to use short bursts of muscle force to propel oneself (as in jumping or sprinting), or to throw an object.	Guiding, Directing, and Motivating Subordinates	Providing guidance and direction to subordinates, including setting performance standards and monitoring performance.
Work_Activity	**Work_Activity Definitions**	Coaching and Developing Others	Identifying the developmental needs of others and coaching, mentoring, or otherwise helping others to improve their knowledge or skills.
Operating Vehicles, Mechanized Devices, or Equipme	Running, maneuvering, navigating, or driving vehicles or mechanized equipment, such as forklifts, passenger vehicles, aircraft, or water craft.	Coordinating the Work and Activities of Others	Getting members of a group to work together to accomplish tasks.
Performing General Physical Activities	Performing physical activities that require considerable use of your arms and legs and moving your whole body, such as climbing, lifting, balancing, walking, stooping, and handling of materials.	Provide Consultation and Advice to Others	Providing guidance and expert advice to management or other groups on technical, systems-, or process-related topics.
Handling and Moving Objects	Using hands and arms in handling, installing, positioning, and moving materials, and manipulating things.	Interacting With Computers	Using computers and computer systems (including hardware and software) to program, write software, set up functions, enter data, or process information.
Getting Information	Observing, receiving, and otherwise obtaining information from all relevant sources.	Monitoring and Controlling Resources	Monitoring and controlling resources and overseeing the spending of money.
Documenting/Recording Information	Entering, transcribing, recording, storing, or maintaining information in written or electronic/magnetic form.		

Drafting, Laying Out, and Specifying Technical Dev	Providing documentation, detailed instructions, drawings, or specifications to tell others about how devices, parts, equipment, or structures are to be fabricated, constructed, assembled, modified, maintained, or used.
Controlling Machines and Processes	Using either control mechanisms or direct physical activity to operate machines or processes (not including computers or vehicles).
Repairing and Maintaining Mechanical Equipment	Servicing, repairing, adjusting, and testing machines, devices, moving parts, and equipment that operate primarily on the basis of mechanical (not electronic) principles.
Staffing Organizational Units	Recruiting, interviewing, selecting, hiring, and promoting employees in an organization.
Selling or Influencing Others	Convincing others to buy merchandise/goods or to otherwise change their minds or actions.
Repairing and Maintaining Electronic Equipment	Servicing, repairing, calibrating, regulating, fine-tuning, or testing machines, devices, and equipment that operate primarily on the basis of electrical or electronic (not mechanical) principles.

Work_Context	**Work_Context Definitions**
Contact With Others	How much does this job require the worker to be in contact with others (face-to-face, by telephone, or otherwise) in order to perform it?
Face-to-Face Discussions	How often do you have to have face-to-face discussions with individuals or teams in this job?
Importance of Being Exact or Accurate	How important is being very exact or highly accurate in performing this job?
Outdoors, Exposed to Weather	How often does this job require working outdoors, exposed to all weather conditions?
Time Pressure	How often does this job require the worker to meet strict deadlines?
In an Enclosed Vehicle or Equipment	How often does this job require working in a closed vehicle or equipment (e.g., car)?
Freedom to Make Decisions	How much decision making freedom, without supervision, does the job offer?
Frequency of Decision Making	How frequently is the worker required to make decisions that affect other people, the financial resources, and/or the image and reputation of the organization?
Physical Proximity	To what extent does this job require the worker to perform job tasks in close physical proximity to other people?
Deal With External Customers	How important is it to work with external customers or the public in this job?
Spend Time Walking and Running	How much does this job require walking and running?
Spend Time Using Your Hands to Handle, Control, or	How much does this job require using your hands to handle, control, or feel objects, tools or controls?
Structured versus Unstructured Work	To what extent is this job structured for the worker, rather than allowing the worker to determine tasks, priorities, and goals?
Impact of Decisions on Co-workers or Company Resul	How do the decisions an employee makes impact the results of co-workers, clients or the company?
Telephone	How often do you have telephone conversations in this job?
Deal With Unpleasant or Angry People	How frequently does the worker have to deal with unpleasant, angry, or discourteous individuals as part of the job requirements?
Spend Time Standing	How much does this job require standing?
Very Hot or Cold Temperatures	How often does this job require working in very hot (above 90 F degrees) or very cold (below 32 F degrees) temperatures?
Spend Time Making Repetitive Motions	How much does this job require making repetitive motions?
Coordinate or Lead Others	How important is it to coordinate or lead others in accomplishing work activities in this job?
Exposed to Contaminants	How often does this job require working exposed to contaminants (such as pollutants, gases, dust or odors)?
Sounds, Noise Levels Are Distracting or Uncomforta	How often does this job require working exposed to sounds and noise levels that are distracting or uncomfortable?
Work With Work Group or Team	How important is it to work with others in a group or team in this job?
Spend Time Bending or Twisting the Body	How much does this job require bending or twisting your body?
Indoors, Environmentally Controlled	How often does this job require working indoors in environmentally controlled conditions?
Wear Common Protective or Safety Equipment such as	How much does this job require wearing common protective or safety equipment such as safety shoes, glasses, gloves, hard hats or live jackets?

Consequence of Error	How serious would the result usually be if the worker made a mistake that was not readily correctable?
Frequency of Conflict Situations	How often are there conflict situations the employee has to face in this job?
Exposed to Disease or Infections	How often does this job require exposure to disease/infections?
Letters and Memos	How often does the job require written letters and memos?
Spend Time Sitting	How much does this job require sitting?
Importance of Repeating Same Tasks	How important is repeating the same physical activities (e.g., key entry) or mental activities (e.g., checking entries in a ledger) over and over, without stopping, to performing this job?
Exposed to Minor Burns, Cuts, Bites, or Stings	How often does this job require exposure to minor burns, cuts, bites, or stings?
Level of Competition	To what extent does this job require the worker to compete or to be aware of competitive pressures?
Electronic Mail	How often do you use electronic mail in this job?
Cramped Work Space, Awkward Positions	How often does this job require working in cramped work spaces that requires getting into awkward positions?
Responsibility for Outcomes and Results	How responsible is the worker for work outcomes and results of other workers?
Spend Time Kneeling, Crouching, Stooping, or Crawl	How much does this job require kneeling, crouching, stooping or crawling?
Extremely Bright or Inadequate Lighting	How often does this job require working in extremely bright or inadequate lighting conditions?
Responsible for Others' Health and Safety	How much responsibility is there for the health and safety of others in this job?
Pace Determined by Speed of Equipment	How important is it to this job that the pace is determined by the speed of equipment or machinery? (This does not refer to keeping busy at all times on this job.)
Degree of Automation	How automated is the job?
Spend Time Keeping or Regaining Balance	How much does this job require keeping or regaining your balance?
Exposed to Hazardous Equipment	How often does this job require exposure to hazardous equipment?
Outdoors, Under Cover	How often does this job require working outdoors, under cover (e.g., structure with roof but no walls)?
Deal With Physically Aggressive People	How frequently does this job require the worker to deal with physical aggression of violent individuals?
In an Open Vehicle or Equipment	How often does this job require working in an open vehicle or equipment (e.g., tractor)?
Public Speaking	How often do you have to perform public speaking in this job?
Exposed to Hazardous Conditions	How often does this job require exposure to hazardous conditions?
Indoors, Not Environmentally Controlled	How often does this job require working indoors in non-controlled environmental conditions (e.g., warehouse without heat)?
Exposed to Radiation	How often does this job require exposure to radiation?
Wear Specialized Protective or Safety Equipment su	How much does this job require wearing specialized protective or safety equipment such as breathing apparatus, safety harness, full protection suits, or radiation protection?
Exposed to Whole Body Vibration	How often does this job require exposure to whole body vibration (e.g., operate a jackhammer)?
Exposed to High Places	How often does this job require exposure to high places?
Spend Time Climbing Ladders, Scaffolds, or Poles	How much does this job require climbing ladders, scaffolds, or poles?

Job Zone Component	**Job Zone Component Definitions**
Title	Job Zone Two: Some Preparation Needed
Overall Experience	Some previous work-related skill, knowledge, or experience may be helpful in these occupations, but usually is not needed. For example, a drywall installer might benefit from experience installing drywall, but an inexperienced person could still learn to be an installer with little difficulty.
Job Training	Employees in these occupations need anywhere from a few months to one year of working with experienced employees.
Job Zone Examples	These occupations often involve using your knowledge and skills to help others. Examples include drywall installers, fire inspectors, flight attendants, pharmacy technicians, salespersons (retail), and tellers.
SVP Range	(4.0 to < 6.0)
Education	These occupations usually require a high school diploma and may require some vocational training or job-related course work. In some cases, an associate's or bachelor's degree could be needed.

Work_Styles	Work_Styles Definitions
Dependability	Job requires being reliable, responsible, and dependable, and fulfilling obligations.
Cooperation	Job requires being pleasant with others on the job and displaying a good-natured, cooperative attitude.
Independence	Job requires developing one's own ways of doing things, guiding oneself with little or no supervision, and depending on oneself to get things done.
Concern for Others	Job requires being sensitive to others' needs and feelings and being understanding and helpful on the job.
Integrity	Job requires being honest and ethical.
Self Control	Job requires maintaining composure, keeping emotions in check, controlling anger, and avoiding aggressive behavior, even in very difficult situations.
Attention to Detail	Job requires being careful about detail and thorough in completing work tasks.
Stress Tolerance	Job requires accepting criticism and dealing calmly and effectively with high stress situations.
Adaptability/Flexibility	Job requires being open to change (positive or negative) and to considerable variety in the workplace.
Achievement/Effort	Job requires establishing and maintaining personally challenging achievement goals and exerting effort toward mastering tasks.
Social Orientation	Job requires preferring to work with others rather than alone, and being personally connected with others on the job.
Initiative	Job requires a willingness to take on responsibilities and challenges.
Persistence	Job requires persistence in the face of obstacles.
Innovation	Job requires creativity and alternative thinking to develop new ideas for and answers to work-related problems.
Analytical Thinking	Job requires analyzing information and using logic to address work-related issues and problems.
Leadership	Job requires a willingness to lead, take charge, and offer opinions and direction.

43-5061.00 - Production, Planning, and Expediting Clerks

Coordinate and expedite the flow of work and materials within or between departments of an establishment according to production schedule. Duties include reviewing and distributing production, work, and shipment schedules; conferring with department supervisors to determine progress of work and completion dates; and compiling reports on progress of work, inventory levels, costs, and production problems.

Tasks

1) Establish and prepare product construction directions and locations, and information on required tools, materials, and equipment, numbers of workers needed, and cost projections.

2) Maintain files such as maintenance records, bills of lading, and cost reports.

3) Plan production commitments and timetables for business units, specific programs, and/or jobs, using sales forecasts.

4) Provide documentation and information to account for delays, difficulties, and changes to cost estimates.

5) Review documents such as production schedules, work orders, and staffing tables to determine personnel and materials requirements, and material priorities.

6) Compile and prepare documentation related to production sequences, transportation, personnel schedules, and purchase, maintenance, and repair orders.

7) Arrange for delivery, assembly, and distribution of supplies and parts in order to expedite flow of materials and meet production schedules.

8) Record production data, including volume produced, consumption of raw materials, and quality control measures.

9) Requisition and maintain inventories of materials and supplies necessary to meet production demands.

10) Examine documents, materials, and products, and monitor work processes, in order to assess completeness, accuracy, and conformance to standards and specifications.

11) Confer with establishment personnel, vendors, and customers to coordinate production and shipping activities, and to resolve complaints or eliminate delays.

12) Compile information, such as production rates and progress, materials inventories,

materials used, and customer information, so that status reports can be completed.

13) Confer with department supervisors and other personnel to assess progress and discuss needed changes.

14) Calculate figures such as required amounts of labor and materials, manufacturing costs, and wages, using pricing schedules, adding machines, calculators, or computers.

15) Revise production schedules when required due to design changes, labor or material shortages, backlogs, or other interruptions, collaborating with management, marketing, sales, production, and engineering.

16) Contact suppliers to verify shipment details.

43-5111.00 - Weighers, Measurers, Checkers, and Samplers, Recordkeeping

Weigh, measure, and check materials, supplies, and equipment for the purpose of keeping relevant records. Duties are primarily clerical by nature.

Tasks

1) Transport materials, products, or samples to processing, shipping, or storage areas, manually or using conveyors, pumps, or hand trucks.

2) Inspect products and examination records to determine the number of defects per worker and the reasons for examiners' rejections.

3) Examine products or materials, parts, subassemblies, and packaging for damage, defects, or shortages, using specification sheets, gauges, and standards charts.

4) Document quantity, quality, type, weight, test result data, and value of materials or products, in order to maintain shipping, receiving, and production records and files.

5) Count or estimate quantities of materials, parts, or products received or shipped.

6) Compare product labels, tags, or tickets, shipping manifests, purchase orders, and bills of lading to verify accuracy of shipment contents, quality specifications, and/or weights.

7) Collect product samples and prepare them for laboratory analysis or testing.

8) Fill orders for products and samples, following order tickets, and forward or mail items.

9) Remove from stock products or loads not meeting quality standards, and notify supervisors or appropriate departments of discrepancies or shortages.

10) Collect or prepare measurement, weight, or identification labels; and attach them to products.

11) Compute product totals and charges for shipments.

12) Examine or prepare plans, layouts, or drawings of facilities or finished products to identify storage locations or to verify parts assemblies.

13) Maintain, monitor, and clean work areas, such as recycling collection sites, drop boxes, counters and windows, and areas around scale houses.

14) Prepare measurement tables and conversion charts, using standard formulas.

15) Signal or instruct other workers to weigh, move, or check products.

16) Sort products or materials into predetermined sequences or groupings for display, packing, shipping, or storage.

17) Weigh or measure materials, equipment, or products to maintain relevant records, using volume meters, scales, rules, and/or calipers.

18) Maintain financial records, such as accounts of daily collections and billings, and records of receipts issued.

19) Unload or unpack incoming shipments.

20) Operate scalehouse computers to obtain weight information about incoming shipments such as those from waste haulers.

21) Store samples of finished products in labeled cartons and record their location.

22) Inspect incoming loads of waste to identify contents and to screen for the presence of specific regulated or hazardous wastes.

43-9081.00 - Proofreaders and Copy Markers

Read transcript or proof type setup to detect and mark for correction any grammatical, typographical, or compositional errors.

Tasks

1) Compare information or figures on one record against same data on other records, or with original copy, to detect errors.

2) Read corrected copies or proofs in order to ensure that all corrections have been made.

3) Mark copy to indicate and correct errors in type, arrangement, grammar, punctuation, or spelling, using standard printers' marks.

4) Route proofs with marked corrections to authors, editors, typists, or typesetters for correction and/or reprinting.

5) Read proof sheets aloud, calling out punctuation marks and spelling unusual words and proper names.

6) Measure dimensions, spacing, and positioning of page elements (copy and illustrations) in order to verify conformance to specifications, using printer's ruler.

7) Correct or record omissions, errors, or inconsistencies found.

Knowledge	Knowledge Definitions
English Language	Knowledge of the structure and content of the English language including the meaning and spelling of words, rules of composition, and grammar.
Communications and Media	Knowledge of media production, communication, and dissemination techniques and methods. This includes alternative ways to inform and entertain via written, oral, and visual media.
Philosophy and Theology	Knowledge of different philosophical systems and religions. This includes their basic principles, values, ethics, ways of thinking, customs, practices, and their impact on human culture.
Computers and Electronics	Knowledge of circuit boards, processors, chips, electronic equipment, and computer hardware and software, including applications and programming.
Clerical	Knowledge of administrative and clerical procedures and systems such as word processing, managing files and records, stenography and transcription, designing forms, and other office procedures and terminology.
Geography	Knowledge of principles and methods for describing the features of land, sea, and air masses, including their physical characteristics, locations, interrelationships, and distribution of plant, animal, and human life.
Administration and Management	Knowledge of business and management principles involved in strategic planning, resource allocation, human resources modeling, leadership technique, production methods, and coordination of people and resources.
Education and Training	Knowledge of principles and methods for curriculum and training design, teaching and instruction for individuals and groups, and the measurement of training effects.
Psychology	Knowledge of human behavior and performance; individual differences in ability, personality, and interests; learning and motivation; psychological research methods; and the assessment and treatment of behavioral and affective disorders.
Personnel and Human Resources	Knowledge of principles and procedures for personnel recruitment, selection, training, compensation and benefits, labor relations and negotiation, and personnel information systems.
History and Archeology	Knowledge of historical events and their causes, indicators, and effects on civilizations and cultures.
Law and Government	Knowledge of laws, legal codes, court procedures, precedents, government regulations, executive orders, agency rules, and the democratic political process.
Telecommunications	Knowledge of transmission, broadcasting, switching, control, and operation of telecommunications systems.
Foreign Language	Knowledge of the structure and content of a foreign (non-English) language including the meaning and spelling of words, rules of composition and grammar, and pronunciation.
Mathematics	Knowledge of arithmetic, algebra, geometry, calculus, statistics, and their applications.
Sociology and Anthropology	Knowledge of group behavior and dynamics, societal trends and influences, human migrations, ethnicity, cultures and their history and origins.
Customer and Personal Service	Knowledge of principles and processes for providing customer and personal services. This includes customer needs assessment, meeting quality standards for services, and evaluation of customer satisfaction.
Fine Arts	Knowledge of the theory and techniques required to compose, produce, and perform works of music, dance, visual arts, drama, and sculpture.
Design	Knowledge of design techniques, tools, and principles involved in production of precision technical plans, blueprints, drawings, and models.
Sales and Marketing	Knowledge of principles and methods for showing, promoting, and selling products or services. This includes marketing strategy and tactics, product demonstration, sales techniques, and sales control systems.
Production and Processing	Knowledge of raw materials, production processes, quality control, costs, and other techniques for maximizing the effective manufacture and distribution of goods.
Transportation	Knowledge of principles and methods for moving people or goods by air, rail, sea, or road, including the relative costs and benefits.
Public Safety and Security	Knowledge of relevant equipment, policies, procedures, and strategies to promote effective local, state, or national security operations for the protection of people, data, property, and institutions.
Economics and Accounting	Knowledge of economic and accounting principles and practices, the financial markets, banking and the analysis and reporting of financial data.
Therapy and Counseling	Knowledge of principles, methods, and procedures for diagnosis, treatment, and rehabilitation of physical and mental dysfunctions, and for career counseling and guidance.
Medicine and Dentistry	Knowledge of the information and techniques needed to diagnose and treat human injuries, diseases, and deformities. This includes symptoms, treatment alternatives, drug properties and interactions, and preventive health-care measures.
Biology	Knowledge of plant and animal organisms, their tissues, cells, functions, interdependencies, and interactions with each other and the environment.
Chemistry	Knowledge of the chemical composition, structure, and properties of substances and of the chemical processes and transformations that they undergo. This includes uses of chemicals and their interactions, danger signs, production techniques, and disposal methods.
Engineering and Technology	Knowledge of the practical application of engineering science and technology. This includes applying principles, techniques, procedures, and equipment to the design and production of various goods and services.
Physics	Knowledge and prediction of physical principles, laws, their interrelationships, and applications to understanding fluid, material, and atmospheric dynamics, and mechanical, electrical, atomic and sub-atomic structures and processes.
Mechanical	Knowledge of machines and tools, including their designs, uses, repair, and maintenance.
Building and Construction	Knowledge of materials, methods, and the tools involved in the construction or repair of houses, buildings, or other structures such as highways and roads.
Food Production	Knowledge of techniques and equipment for planting, growing, and harvesting food products (both plant and animal) for consumption, including storage/handling techniques.

Skills	Skills Definitions
Reading Comprehension	Understanding written sentences and paragraphs in work related documents.
Time Management	Managing one's own time and the time of others.
Writing	Communicating effectively in writing as appropriate for the needs of the audience.
Active Listening	Giving full attention to what other people are saying, taking time to understand the points being made, asking questions as appropriate, and not interrupting at inappropriate times.
Monitoring	Monitoring/Assessing performance of yourself, other individuals, or organizations to make improvements or take corrective action.
Social Perceptiveness	Being aware of others' reactions and understanding why they react as they do.
Critical Thinking	Using logic and reasoning to identify the strengths and weaknesses of alternative solutions, conclusions or approaches to problems.
Coordination	Adjusting actions in relation to others' actions.
Judgment and Decision Making	Considering the relative costs and benefits of potential actions to choose the most appropriate one.
Active Learning	Understanding the implications of new information for both current and future problem-solving and decision-making.
Service Orientation	Actively looking for ways to help people.
Speaking	Talking to others to convey information effectively.

Learning Strategies	Selecting and using training/instructional methods and procedures appropriate for the situation when learning or teaching new things.
Persuasion	Persuading others to change their minds or behavior.
Negotiation	Bringing others together and trying to reconcile differences.
Operations Analysis	Analyzing needs and product requirements to create a design.
Instructing	Teaching others how to do something.
Quality Control Analysis	Conducting tests and inspections of products, services, or processes to evaluate quality or performance.
Mathematics	Using mathematics to solve problems.
Troubleshooting	Determining causes of operating errors and deciding what to do about it.
Complex Problem Solving	Identifying complex problems and reviewing related information to develop and evaluate options and implement solutions.
Installation	Installing equipment, machines, wiring, or programs to meet specifications.
Systems Analysis	Determining how a system should work and how changes in conditions, operations, and the environment will affect outcomes.
Systems Evaluation	Identifying measures or indicators of system performance and the actions needed to improve or correct performance, relative to the goals of the system.
Equipment Selection	Determining the kind of tools and equipment needed to do a job.
Management of Personnel Resources	Motivating, developing, and directing people as they work, identifying the best people for the job.
Operation and Control	Controlling operations of equipment or systems.
Operation Monitoring	Watching gauges, dials, or other indicators to make sure a machine is working properly.
Technology Design	Generating or adapting equipment and technology to serve user needs.
Management of Material Resources	Obtaining and seeing to the appropriate use of equipment, facilities, and materials needed to do certain work.
Equipment Maintenance	Performing routine maintenance on equipment and determining when and what kind of maintenance is needed.
Science	Using scientific rules and methods to solve problems.
Management of Financial Resources	Determining how money will be spent to get the work done, and accounting for these expenditures.
Repairing	Repairing machines or systems using the needed tools.
Programming	Writing computer programs for various purposes.

Ability	**Ability Definitions**
Written Comprehension	The ability to read and understand information and ideas presented in writing.
Near Vision	The ability to see details at close range (within a few feet of the observer).
Written Expression	The ability to communicate information and ideas in writing so others will understand.
Oral Expression	The ability to communicate information and ideas in speaking so others will understand.
Oral Comprehension	The ability to listen to and understand information and ideas presented through spoken words and sentences.
Perceptual Speed	The ability to quickly and accurately compare similarities and differences among sets of letters, numbers, objects, pictures, or patterns. The things to be compared may be presented at the same time or one after the other. This ability also includes comparing a presented object with a remembered object.
Problem Sensitivity	The ability to tell when something is wrong or is likely to go wrong. It does not involve solving the problem, only recognizing there is a problem.
Information Ordering	The ability to arrange things or actions in a certain order or pattern according to a specific rule or set of rules (e.g., patterns of numbers, letters, words, pictures, mathematical operations).
Deductive Reasoning	The ability to apply general rules to specific problems to produce answers that make sense.
Speech Recognition	The ability to identify and understand the speech of another person.
Speech Clarity	The ability to speak clearly so others can understand you.
Inductive Reasoning	The ability to combine pieces of information to form general rules or conclusions (includes finding a relationship among seemingly unrelated events).
Selective Attention	The ability to concentrate on a task over a period of time without being distracted.
Category Flexibility	The ability to generate or use different sets of rules for combining or grouping things in different ways.

Flexibility of Closure	The ability to identify or detect a known pattern (a figure, object, word, or sound) that is hidden in other distracting material.
Originality	The ability to come up with unusual or clever ideas about a given topic or situation, or to develop creative ways to solve a problem.
Memorization	The ability to remember information such as words, numbers, pictures, and procedures.
Fluency of Ideas	The ability to come up with a number of ideas about a topic (the number of ideas is important, not their quality, correctness, or creativity).
Visualization	The ability to imagine how something will look after it is moved around or when its parts are moved or rearranged.
Manual Dexterity	The ability to quickly move your hand, your hand together with your arm, or your two hands to grasp, manipulate, or assemble objects.
Finger Dexterity	The ability to make precisely coordinated movements of the fingers of one or both hands to grasp, manipulate, or assemble very small objects.
Mathematical Reasoning	The ability to choose the right mathematical methods or formulas to solve a problem.
Time Sharing	The ability to shift back and forth between two or more activities or sources of information (such as speech, sounds, touch, or other sources).
Speed of Closure	The ability to quickly make sense of, combine, and organize information into meaningful patterns.
Arm-Hand Steadiness	The ability to keep your hand and arm steady while moving your arm or while holding your arm and hand in one position.
Number Facility	The ability to add, subtract, multiply, or divide quickly and correctly.
Control Precision	The ability to quickly and repeatedly adjust the controls of a machine or a vehicle to exact positions.
Visual Color Discrimination	The ability to match or detect differences between colors, including shades of color and brightness.
Auditory Attention	The ability to focus on a single source of sound in the presence of other distracting sounds.
Far Vision	The ability to see details at a distance.
Hearing Sensitivity	The ability to detect or tell the differences between sounds that vary in pitch and loudness.
Trunk Strength	The ability to use your abdominal and lower back muscles to support part of the body repeatedly or continuously over time without 'giving out' or fatiguing.
Explosive Strength	The ability to use short bursts of muscle force to propel oneself (as in jumping or sprinting), or to throw an object.
Peripheral Vision	The ability to see objects or movement of objects to one's side when the eyes are looking ahead.
Dynamic Strength	The ability to exert muscle force repeatedly or continuously over time. This involves muscular endurance and resistance to muscle fatigue.
Wrist-Finger Speed	The ability to make fast, simple, repeated movements of the fingers, hands, and wrists.
Gross Body Equilibrium	The ability to keep or regain your body balance or stay upright when in an unstable position.
Gross Body Coordination	The ability to coordinate the movement of your arms, legs, and torso together when the whole body is in motion.
Dynamic Flexibility	The ability to quickly and repeatedly bend, stretch, twist, or reach out with your body, arms, and/or legs.
Stamina	The ability to exert yourself physically over long periods of time without getting winded or out of breath.
Reaction Time	The ability to quickly respond (with the hand, finger, or foot) to a signal (sound, light, picture) when it appears.
Glare Sensitivity	The ability to see objects in the presence of glare or bright lighting.
Extent Flexibility	The ability to bend, stretch, twist, or reach with your body, arms, and/or legs.
Sound Localization	The ability to tell the direction from which a sound originated.
Night Vision	The ability to see under low light conditions.
Speed of Limb Movement	The ability to quickly move the arms and legs.
Depth Perception	The ability to judge which of several objects is closer or farther away from you, or to judge the distance between you and an object.
Spatial Orientation	The ability to know your location in relation to the environment or to know where other objects are in relation to you.
Response Orientation	The ability to choose quickly between two or more movements in response to two or more different signals (lights, sounds, pictures). It includes the speed with which the correct response is started with the hand, foot, or other body part.

Multilimb Coordination	The ability to coordinate two or more limbs (for example, two arms, two legs, or one leg and one arm) while sitting, standing, or lying down. It does not involve performing the activities while the whole body is in motion.
Static Strength	The ability to exert maximum muscle force to lift, push, pull, or carry objects.
Rate Control	The ability to time your movements or the movement of a piece of equipment in anticipation of changes in the speed and/or direction of a moving object or scene.

Work_Activity	Work_Activity Definitions
Communicating with Supervisors, Peers, or Subordin	Providing information to supervisors, co-workers, and subordinates by telephone, in written form, e-mail, or in person.
Establishing and Maintaining Interpersonal Relatio	Developing constructive and cooperative working relationships with others, and maintaining them over time.
Organizing, Planning, and Prioritizing Work	Developing specific goals and plans to prioritize, organize, and accomplish your work.
Judging the Qualities of Things, Services, or Peop	Assessing the value, importance, or quality of things or people.
Getting Information	Observing, receiving, and otherwise obtaining information from all relevant sources.
Interacting With Computers	Using computers and computer systems (including hardware and software) to program, write software, set up functions, enter data, or process information.
Thinking Creatively	Developing, designing, or creating new applications, ideas, relationships, systems, or products, including artistic contributions.
Interpreting the Meaning of Information for Others	Translating or explaining what information means and how it can be used.
Training and Teaching Others	Identifying the educational needs of others, developing formal educational or training programs or classes, and teaching or instructing others.
Coaching and Developing Others	Identifying the developmental needs of others and coaching, mentoring, or otherwise helping others to improve their knowledge or skills.
Identifying Objects, Actions, and Events	Identifying information by categorizing, estimating, recognizing differences or similarities, and detecting changes in circumstances or events.
Performing Administrative Activities	Performing day-to-day administrative tasks such as maintaining information files and processing paperwork.
Updating and Using Relevant Knowledge	Keeping up-to-date technically and applying new knowledge to your job.
Monitor Processes, Materials, or Surroundings	Monitoring and reviewing information from materials, events, or the environment, to detect or assess problems.
Analyzing Data or Information	Identifying the underlying principles, reasons, or facts of information by breaking down information or data into separate parts.
Selling or Influencing Others	Convincing others to buy merchandise/goods or to otherwise change their minds or actions.
Documenting/Recording Information	Entering, transcribing, recording, storing, or maintaining information in written or electronic/magnetic form.
Developing Objectives and Strategies	Establishing long-range objectives and specifying the strategies and actions to achieve them.
Making Decisions and Solving Problems	Analyzing information and evaluating results to choose the best solution and solve problems.
Scheduling Work and Activities	Scheduling events, programs, and activities, as well as the work of others.
Developing and Building Teams	Encouraging and building mutual trust, respect, and cooperation among team members.
Assisting and Caring for Others	Providing personal assistance, medical attention, emotional support, or other personal care to others such as coworkers, customers, or patients.
Processing Information	Compiling, coding, categorizing, calculating, tabulating, auditing, or verifying information or data.
Coordinating the Work and Activities of Others	Getting members of a group to work together to accomplish tasks.
Evaluating Information to Determine Compliance wit	Using relevant information and individual judgment to determine whether events or processes comply with laws, regulations, or standards.
Guiding, Directing, and Motivating Subordinates	Providing guidance and direction to subordinates, including setting performance standards and monitoring performance.
Estimating the Quantifiable Characteristics of Pro	Estimating sizes, distances, and quantities; or determining time, costs, resources, or materials needed to perform a work activity.

Communicating with Persons Outside Organization	Communicating with people outside the organization, representing the organization to customers, the public, government, and other external sources. This information can be exchanged in person, in writing, or by telephone or e-mail.
Resolving Conflicts and Negotiating with Others	Handling complaints, settling disputes, and resolving grievances and conflicts, or otherwise negotiating with others.
Provide Consultation and Advice to Others	Providing guidance and expert advice to management or other groups on technical, systems-, or process-related topics.
Performing for or Working Directly with the Public	Performing for people or dealing directly with the public. This includes serving customers in restaurants and stores, and receiving clients or guests.
Drafting, Laying Out, and Specifying Technical Dev	Providing documentation, detailed instructions, drawings, or specifications to tell others about how devices, parts, equipment, or structures are to be fabricated, constructed, assembled, modified, maintained, or used.
Handling and Moving Objects	Using hands and arms in handling, installing, positioning, and moving materials, and manipulating things.
Controlling Machines and Processes	Using either control mechanisms or direct physical activity to operate machines or processes (not including computers or vehicles).
Inspecting Equipment, Structures, or Material	Inspecting equipment, structures, or materials to identify the cause of errors or other problems or defects.
Performing General Physical Activities	Performing physical activities that require considerable use of your arms and legs and moving your whole body, such as climbing, lifting, balancing, walking, stooping, and handling of materials.
Monitoring and Controlling Resources	Monitoring and controlling resources and overseeing the spending of money.
Repairing and Maintaining Electronic Equipment	Servicing, repairing, calibrating, regulating, fine-tuning, or testing machines, devices, and equipment that operate primarily on the basis of electrical or electronic (not mechanical) principles.
Operating Vehicles, Mechanized Devices, or Equipme	Running, maneuvering, navigating, or driving vehicles or mechanized equipment, such as forklifts, passenger vehicles, aircraft, or water craft.
Staffing Organizational Units	Recruiting, interviewing, selecting, hiring, and promoting employees in an organization.
Repairing and Maintaining Mechanical Equipment	Servicing, repairing, adjusting, and testing machines, devices, moving parts, and equipment that operate primarily on the basis of mechanical (not electronic) principles.

Work_Context	Work_Context Definitions
Importance of Being Exact or Accurate	How important is being very exact or highly accurate in performing this job?
Spend Time Sitting	How much does this job require sitting?
Indoors, Environmentally Controlled	How often does this job require working indoors in environmentally controlled conditions?
Contact With Others	How much does this job require the worker to be in contact with others (face-to-face, by telephone, or otherwise) in order to perform it?
Telephone	How often do you have telephone conversations in this job?
Electronic Mail	How often do you use electronic mail in this job?
Work With Work Group or Team	How important is it to work with others in a group or team in this job?
Face-to-Face Discussions	How often do you have to have face-to-face discussions with individuals or teams in this job?
Importance of Repeating Same Tasks	How important is repeating the same physical activities (e.g., key entry) or mental activities (e.g., checking entries in a ledger) over and over, without stopping, to performing this job?
Spend Time Making Repetitive Motions	How much does this job require making repetitive motions?
Frequency of Decision Making	How frequently is the worker required to make decisions that affect other people, the financial resources, and/or the image and reputation of the organization?
Impact of Decisions on Co-workers or Company Resul	How do the decisions an employee makes impact the results of co-workers, clients or the company?
Time Pressure	How often does this job require the worker to meet strict deadlines?
Letters and Memos	How often does the job require written letters and memos?
Spend Time Using Your Hands to Handle, Control, or	How much does this job require using your hands to handle, control, or feel objects, tools or controls?
Freedom to Make Decisions	How much decision making freedom, without supervision, does the job offer?
Structured versus Unstructured Work	To what extent is this job structured for the worker, rather than allowing the worker to determine tasks, priorities, and goals?

Coordinate or Lead Others	How important is it to coordinate or lead others in accomplishing work activities in this job?
Consequence of Error	How serious would the result usually be if the worker made a mistake that was not readily correctable?
Physical Proximity	To what extent does this job require the worker to perform job tasks in close physical proximity to other people?
Deal With Unpleasant or Angry People	How frequently does the worker have to deal with unpleasant, angry, or discourteous individuals as part of the job requirements?
Level of Competition	To what extent does this job require the worker to compete or to be aware of competitive pressures?
Responsibility for Outcomes and Results	How responsible is the worker for work outcomes and results of other workers?
Deal With External Customers	How important is it to work with external customers or the public in this job?
Sounds, Noise Levels Are Distracting or Uncomforta	How often does this job require working exposed to sounds and noise levels that are distracting or uncomfortable?
Public Speaking	How often do you have to perform public speaking in this job?
Degree of Automation	How automated is the job?
Frequency of Conflict Situations	How often are there conflict situations the employee has to face in this job?
Spend Time Bending or Twisting the Body	How much does this job require bending or twisting your body?
Exposed to Contaminants	How often does this job require working exposed to contaminants (such as pollutants, gases, dust or odors)?
Spend Time Standing	How much does this job require standing?
Spend Time Walking and Running	How much does this job require walking and running?
Cramped Work Space, Awkward Positions	How often does this job require working in cramped work spaces that requires getting into awkward positions?
Pace Determined by Speed of Equipment	How important is it to this job that the pace is determined by the speed of equipment or machinery? (This does not refer to keeping busy at all times on this job.)
Responsible for Others' Health and Safety	How much responsibility is there for the health and safety of others in this job?
Extremely Bright or Inadequate Lighting	How often does this job require working in extremely bright or inadequate lighting conditions?
Outdoors, Exposed to Weather	How often does this job require working outdoors, exposed to all weather conditions?
In an Enclosed Vehicle or Equipment	How often does this job require working in a closed vehicle or equipment (e.g., car)?
Very Hot or Cold Temperatures	How often does this job require working in very hot (above 90 F degrees) or very cold (below 32 F degrees) temperatures?
Spend Time Kneeling, Crouching, Stooping, or Crawl	How much does this job require kneeling, crouching, stooping or crawling?
Exposed to Minor Burns, Cuts, Bites, or Stings	How often does this job require exposure to minor burns, cuts, bites, or stings?
Spend Time Keeping or Regaining Balance	How much does this job require keeping or regaining your balance?
Indoors, Not Environmentally Controlled	How often does this job require working indoors in non-controlled environmental conditions (e.g., warehouse without heat)?
Deal With Physically Aggressive People	How frequently does this job require the worker to deal with physical aggression of violent individuals?
Exposed to Radiation	How often does this job require exposure to radiation?
Spend Time Climbing Ladders, Scaffolds, or Poles	How much does this job require climbing ladders, scaffolds, or poles?
Exposed to Hazardous Equipment	How often does this job require exposure to hazardous equipment?
Exposed to Disease or Infections	How often does this job require exposure to disease/infections?
Exposed to Whole Body Vibration	How often does this job require exposure to whole body vibration (e.g., operate a jackhammer)?
Outdoors, Under Cover	How often does this job require working outdoors, under cover (e.g., structure with roof but no walls)?
Wear Common Protective or Safety Equipment such as	How often does this job require wearing common protective or safety equipment such as safety shoes, glasses, gloves, hard hats or life jackets?
In an Open Vehicle or Equipment	How often does this job require working in an open vehicle or equipment (e.g., tractor)?
Wear Specialized Protective or Safety Equipment su	How much does this job require wearing specialized protective or safety equipment such as breathing apparatus, safety harness, full protection suits, or radiation protection?
Exposed to Hazardous Conditions	How often does this job require exposure to hazardous conditions?
Exposed to High Places	How often does this job require exposure to high places?

Job Zone Component	Job Zone Component Definitions
Title	Job Zone Four: Considerable Preparation Needed
Overall Experience	A minimum of two to four years of work-related skill, knowledge, or experience is needed for these occupations. For example, an accountant must complete four years of college and work for several years in accounting to be considered qualified.
Job Training	Employees in these occupations usually need several years of work-related experience, on-the-job training, and/or vocational training.
Job Zone Examples	Many of these occupations involve coordinating, supervising, managing, or training others. Examples include accountants, chefs and head cooks, computer programmers, historians, pharmacists, and police detectives.
SVP Range	(7.0 to < 8.0)
Education	Most of these occupations require a four - year bachelor's degree, but some do not.

Work_Styles	Work_Styles Definitions
Attention to Detail	Job requires being careful about detail and thorough in completing work tasks.
Dependability	Job requires being reliable, responsible, and dependable, and fulfilling obligations.
Cooperation	Job requires being pleasant with others on the job and displaying a good-natured, cooperative attitude.
Integrity	Job requires being honest and ethical.
Initiative	Job requires a willingness to take on responsibilities and challenges.
Concern for Others	Job requires being sensitive to others' needs and feelings and being understanding and helpful on the job.
Stress Tolerance	Job requires accepting criticism and dealing calmly and effectively with high stress situations.
Leadership	Job requires a willingness to lead, take charge, and offer opinions and direction.
Independence	Job requires developing one's own ways of doing things, guiding oneself with little or no supervision, and depending on oneself to get things done.
Self Control	Job requires maintaining composure, keeping emotions in check, controlling anger, and avoiding aggressive behavior, even in very difficult situations.
Persistence	Job requires persistence in the face of obstacles.
Achievement/Effort	Job requires establishing and maintaining personally challenging achievement goals and exerting effort toward mastering tasks.
Adaptability/Flexibility	Job requires being open to change (positive or negative) and to considerable variety in the workplace.
Social Orientation	Job requires preferring to work with others rather than alone, and being personally connected with others on the job.
Analytical Thinking	Job requires analyzing information and using logic to address work-related issues and problems.
Innovation	Job requires creativity and alternative thinking to develop new ideas for and answers to work-related problems.

45-1012.00 - Farm Labor Contractors

Recruit, hire, furnish, and supervise seasonal or temporary agricultural laborers for a fee. May transport, house, and provide meals for workers.

Tasks

1) Direct and transport workers to appropriate work sites.

2) Recruit and hire agricultural workers.

3) Supervise the work of contracted employees.

4) Provide food, drinking water, and field sanitation facilities to contracted workers.

5) Pay wages of contracted farm laborers.

6) Employ foremen to deal directly with workers when recruiting, hiring, instructing, assigning tasks, and enforcing work rules.

7) Furnish tools for employee use.

45-2041.00 - Graders and Sorters, Agricultural Products

Grade, sort, or classify unprocessed food and other agricultural products by size, weight, color, or condition.

Tasks

1) Examine product fibers through microscopes to determine maturity and spirality of fibers.

2) Record grade and/or identification numbers on tags or on shipping, receiving, or sales sheets.

3) Place products in containers according to grade and mark grades on containers.

4) Discard inferior or defective products and/or foreign matter, and place acceptable products in containers for further processing.

5) Grade and sort products according to factors such as color, species, length, width, appearance, feel, smell, and quality to ensure correct processing and usage.

6) Weigh products or estimate their weight, visually or by feel.

45-2091.00 - Agricultural Equipment Operators

Drive and control farm equipment to till soil and to plant, cultivate, and harvest crops. May perform tasks, such as crop baling or hay bucking. May operate stationary equipment to perform post-harvest tasks, such as husking, shelling, threshing, and ginning.

Tasks

1) Irrigate soil, using portable pipes or ditch systems, and maintain ditches or pipes and pumps.

2) Observe and listen to machinery operation to detect equipment malfunctions.

3) Mix specified materials or chemicals, and dump solutions, powders, or seeds into planter or sprayer machinery.

4) Position boxes or attach bags at discharge ends of machinery to catch products, removing and closing full containers.

5) Manipulate controls to set, activate, and adjust mechanisms on machinery.

6) Load hoppers, containers, or conveyors to feed machines with products, using forklifts, transfer augers, suction gates, shovels, or pitchforks.

7) Load and unload crops or containers of materials, manually or using conveyors, handtrucks, forklifts, or transfer augers.

8) Guide products on conveyors to regulate flow through machines, and to discard diseased or rotten products.

9) Direct and monitor the activities of work crews engaged in planting, weeding, or harvesting activities.

10) Adjust, repair, and service farm machinery and notify supervisors when machinery malfunctions.

11) Walk beside or ride on planting machines while inserting plants in planter mechanisms at specified intervals.

12) Attach farm implements such as plows, discs, sprayers, or harvesters to tractors, using bolts and hand tools.

13) Operate towed machines such as seed drills or manure spreaders to plant, fertilize, dust, and spray crops.

14) Spray fertilizer or pesticide solutions to control insects, fungus and weed growth, and diseases, using hand sprayers.

15) Drive trucks to haul crops, supplies, tools, or farm workers.

16) Weigh crop-filled containers, and record weights and other identifying information.

45-2092.01 - Nursery Workers

Work in nursery facilities or at customer location planting, cultivating, harvesting, and transplanting trees, shrubs, or plants.

Tasks

1) Maintain inventory, ordering materials as required.

2) Record information about plants and plant growth.

3) Provide information and advice to the public regarding the selection, purchase, and care of products.

4) Sow grass seed, or plant plugs of grass.

5) Maintain and repair irrigation and climate control systems.

6) Clean work areas, and maintain grounds and landscaping.

7) Tie and bunch flowers, plants, shrubs, and trees; wrap their roots; and pack them into boxes to fill orders.

8) Regulate greenhouse conditions, and indoor and outdoor irrigation systems.

9) Move containerized shrubs, plants, and trees, using wheelbarrows or tractors.

10) Haul and spread topsoil, fertilizer, peat moss, and other materials to condition soil, using wheelbarrows or carts and shovels.

11) Operate tractors and other machinery and equipment to fertilize, cultivate, harvest, and spray fields and plants.

12) Dig, cut, and transplant seedlings, cuttings, trees, and shrubs.

13) Trap and destroy pests such as moles, gophers, and mice, using pesticides.

14) Sell and deliver plants and flowers to customers.

15) Cut, roll, and stack sod.

16) Dig, rake, and screen soil; and fill cold frames and hot beds in preparation for planting.

17) Dip cut flowers into disinfectant, count them into bunches, and place them in boxes to prepare them for storage and shipping.

18) Feel plants' leaves and note their coloring to detect the presence of insects or disease.

19) Fill growing tanks with water.

20) Graft plants and trees into different rootstock to reduce disease by inserting and tying buds into incisions in rootstock.

21) Fold and staple corrugated forms to make boxes used for packing horticultural products.

22) Inspect plants and bud ties to assess quality.

23) Plant, spray, weed, fertilize, and water plants, shrubs, and trees, using hand tools and gardening tools.

45-2092.02 - General Farmworkers

Apply pesticides, herbicides, and fertilizer to crops and livestock; plant, maintain, and harvest food crops; and tend livestock and poultry. Repair farm buildings and fences. Duties may include: operating milking machines and other dairy processing equipment; supervising seasonal help; irrigating crops; and hauling livestock products to market.

Tasks

1) Set up and operate irrigation equipment.

2) Clear and maintain irrigation ditches.

3) Repair and maintain farm vehicles, implements, and mechanical equipment.

4) Direct and monitor the work of casual and seasonal help during planting and harvesting.

5) Identify plants, pests, and weeds to determine the selection and application of pesticides and fertilizers.

6) Apply pesticides, herbicides or fertilizers to crops.

7) Participate in the inspection, grading, sorting, storage, and post-harvest treatment of crops.

8) Load agricultural products into trucks, and drive trucks to market or storage facilities.

9) Inform farmers or farm managers of crop progress.

10) Harvest fruits and vegetables by hand.

11) Record information about crops, such as pesticide use, yields, or costs.

12) Repair farm buildings, fences, and other structures.

13) Dig and plant seeds, or transplant seedlings by hand.

45-2093.00 - Farmworkers, Farm and Ranch Animals

Attend to live farm, ranch, or aquacultural animals that may include cattle, sheep, swine, goats, horses and other equines, poultry, finfish, shellfish, and bees. Attend to animals produced for animal products, such as meat, fur, skins, feathers, eggs, milk, and honey. Duties may include feeding, watering, herding, grazing, castrating, branding, de-beaking, weighing, catching, and loading animals. May maintain records on animals; examine animals to detect diseases and injuries; assist in birth deliveries; and administer medications, vaccinations, or insecticides as appropriate. May clean and maintain animal housing areas.

Tasks

1) Groom, clip, trim, and/or castrate animals; dock ears and tails; and/or shear coats to collect hair.

2) Herd livestock to pastures for grazing or to scales, trucks, or other enclosures.

3) Spray livestock with disinfectants and insecticides; or dip or bathe animals.

4) Drive trucks, tractors, and other equipment to distribute feed to animals.

5) Mark livestock to identify ownership and grade, using brands, tags, paint, or tattoos.

6) Mix feed, additives, and medicines in prescribed portions.

7) Examine animals to detect illness, injury, or disease, and to check physical characteristics, such as rate of weight gain.

8) Feed and water livestock; and monitor food and water supplies.

9) Order food for animals, and arrange for its delivery.

10) Milk animals such as cows and goats, by hand or using milking machines.

11) Protect herds from predators, using trained dogs.

12) Maintain growth, feeding, production, and cost records.

13) Clean stalls, pens, and equipment, using disinfectant solutions, brushes, shovels, water hoses, and/or pumps.

14) Provide medical treatment, such as administering medications and vaccinations; or arrange for veterinarians to provide more extensive treatment.

15) Trim and shear poultry beaks, toes, and wings using debeaking machines, heated hand shears, or hot wires.

16) Patrol grazing lands on horseback or using all-terrain vehicles.

17) Move equipment, poultry, or livestock from one location to another, manually or using trucks or carts.

18) Inspect, maintain, and repair equipment, machinery, buildings, pens, yards, and fences.

19) Collect, inspect, and place eggs in incubators; operate machines for egg washing, candling, and grading; and pack eggs in cartons.

20) Shift animals between grazing areas to ensure that they have sufficient access to food.

21) Segregate animals according to weight, age, color, and physical condition.

45-3011.00 - Fishers and Related Fishing Workers

Use nets, fishing rods, traps, or other equipment to catch and gather fish or other aquatic animals from rivers, lakes, or oceans, for human consumption or other uses. May haul game onto ship.

Tasks

1) Estimate costs of operations and plan fishing season budgets accordingly.

2) Maintain engines, fishing gear, and other on-board equipment; and perform minor repairs.

3) Attach nets, slings, hooks, blades, and/or lifting devices to cables, booms, hoists, and/or dredges.

4) Monitor distribution of proceeds from sales of catches to ensure that crew members receive their prearranged portions.

5) Hire qualified crew members, and assign their duties.

6) Interpret weather and vessel conditions to determine appropriate responses.

7) Direct fishing operations, and supervise fishing crew members.

8) Wash decks, conveyors, knives, and other equipment, using brushes, detergents, and water.

9) Steer vessels and operate navigational instruments.

10) Stand lookout for schools of fish, and for steering and engine-room watches.

11) Compute positions and plot courses on charts to navigate vessels, using instruments such as compasses, sextants, and charts.

12) Signal other workers to move, hoist, and position loads.

13) Share fishing expertise through activities such as writing for fishing magazines, hosting television shows, or testing and endorsing fishing equipment.

14) Sort, pack, and store catch in holds with salt and ice.

15) Pull and guide nets, traps, and lines onto vessels, by hand or using hoisting equipment.

16) Locate fish, using fish-finding equipment.

17) Connect accessories such as floats, weights, flags, lights, or markers to nets, lines, or traps.

18) Harvest marine life for human or animal consumption, using diving or dredging equipment, traps, barges, rods, reels, and/or tackle.

19) Club or gaff large fish to enable hauling them into fishing vessel.

20) Load and unload vessel equipment and supplies, by hand or using hoisting equipment.

21) Transport fish to processing plants or to buyers.

22) Plan fishing operations, establishing the fish to be sought, the fishing location, the method of capture, and the duration of the trip.

23) Put fishing equipment into the water and anchor or tow equipment, according to the fishing method used.

24) Remove catches from fishing equipment and measure them to ensure compliance with legal size.

25) Return undesirable or illegal catches to the water.

26) Record in logbooks specifics of fishing activities such as dates, harvest areas, yields, and weather and sea conditions.

27) Operate rowboats, dinghies, and/or skiffs to transport fishers, divers, and/or sponge hookers; or to tow and position fishing equipment.

28) Sell catches by contacting and negotiating with buyers or by sending catches to fish auctions.

29) Participate in wildlife management, disease control, and research activities.

45-4011.00 - Forest and Conservation Workers

Under supervision, perform manual labor necessary to develop, maintain, or protect forest, forested areas, and woodlands through such activities as raising and transporting tree seedlings; combating insects, pests, and diseases harmful to trees; and building erosion and water control structures and leaching of forest soil. Includes forester aides, seedling pullers, and tree planters.

Tasks

1) Check equipment to ensure that it is operating properly.

2) Fight forest fires or perform prescribed burning tasks under the direction of fire suppression officers or forestry technicians.

3) Perform fire protection and suppression duties such as constructing fire breaks and disposing of brush.

4) Identify diseased or undesirable trees, and remove them, using power saws or hand saws.

5) Select and cut trees according to markings or sizes, types, and grades.

6) Thin and space trees, using power thinning saws.

7) Sort and separate tree seedlings, discarding substandard seedlings, according to standard charts and verbal instructions.

8) Maintain tallies of trees examined and counted during tree marking and measuring efforts.

9) Select tree seedlings, prepare the ground, and plant the trees in reforestation areas, using manual planting tools.

10) Operate a skidder, bulldozer or other prime mover to pull a variety of scarification or site preparation equipment over areas to be regenerated.

11) Drag cut trees from cutting areas and load trees onto trucks.

12) Explain and enforce regulations regarding camping, vehicle use, fires, use of building and sanitation.

13) Erect signs and fences, using posthole diggers, shovels, or other hand tools.

14) Spray or inject vegetation with insecticides to kill insects and to protect against disease, and with herbicides to reduce competing vegetation.

15) Provide assistance to forest survey crews by clearing site-lines, holding measuring tools, and setting stakes.

16) Examine and grade trees according to standard charts, and staple color-coded grade tags to limbs.

17) Gather, package, and deliver forest products to buyers.

18) Prune or shear tree tops and limbs in order to control growth, increase density, and improve shape.

19) Maintain campsites and recreational areas, replenishing firewood and other supplies, and cleaning kitchens and restrooms.

20) Sow and harvest cover crops such as alfalfa.

Knowledge	Knowledge Definitions
Mathematics	Knowledge of arithmetic, algebra, geometry, calculus, statistics, and their applications.
Geography	Knowledge of principles and methods for describing the features of land, sea, and air masses, including their physical characteristics, locations, interrelationships, and distribution of plant, animal, and human life.
Biology	Knowledge of plant and animal organisms, their tissues, cells, functions, interdependencies, and interactions with each other and the environment.
Administration and Management	Knowledge of business and management principles involved in strategic planning, resource allocation, human resources modeling, leadership technique, production methods, and coordination of people and resources.
Customer and Personal Service	Knowledge of principles and processes for providing customer and personal services. This includes customer needs assessment, meeting quality standards for services, and evaluation of customer satisfaction.
English Language	Knowledge of the structure and content of the English language including the meaning and spelling of words, rules of composition, and grammar.
Law and Government	Knowledge of laws, legal codes, court procedures, precedents, government regulations, executive orders, agency rules, and the democratic political process.
Personnel and Human Resources	Knowledge of principles and procedures for personnel recruitment, selection, training, compensation and benefits, labor relations and negotiation, and personnel information systems.
Computers and Electronics	Knowledge of circuit boards, processors, chips, electronic equipment, and computer hardware and software, including applications and programming.
Clerical	Knowledge of administrative and clerical procedures and systems such as word processing, managing files and records, stenography and transcription, designing forms, and other office procedures and terminology.
Transportation	Knowledge of principles and methods for moving people or goods by air, rail, sea, or road, including the relative costs and benefits.
Mechanical	Knowledge of machines and tools, including their designs, uses, repair, and maintenance.
Production and Processing	Knowledge of raw materials, production processes, quality control, costs, and other techniques for maximizing the effective manufacture and distribution of goods.
Public Safety and Security	Knowledge of relevant equipment, policies, procedures, and strategies to promote effective local, state, or national security operations for the protection of people, data, property, and institutions.
Economics and Accounting	Knowledge of economic and accounting principles and practices, the financial markets, banking and the analysis and reporting of financial data.
Sales and Marketing	Knowledge of principles and methods for showing, promoting, and selling products or services. This includes marketing strategy and tactics, product demonstration, sales techniques, and sales control systems.
Engineering and Technology	Knowledge of the practical application of engineering science and technology. This includes applying principles, techniques, procedures, and equipment to the design and production of various goods and services.
Education and Training	Knowledge of principles and methods for curriculum and training design, teaching and instruction for individuals and groups, and the measurement of training effects.
Sociology and Anthropology	Knowledge of group behavior and dynamics, societal trends and influences, human migrations, ethnicity, cultures and their history and origins.
Psychology	Knowledge of human behavior and performance; individual differences in ability, personality, and interests; learning and motivation; psychological research methods; and the assessment and treatment of behavioral and affective disorders.
Telecommunications	Knowledge of transmission, broadcasting, switching, control, and operation of telecommunications systems.
Design	Knowledge of design techniques, tools, and principles involved in production of precision technical plans, blueprints, drawings, and models.
Building and Construction	Knowledge of materials, methods, and the tools involved in the construction or repair of houses, buildings, or other structures such as highways and roads.
Chemistry	Knowledge of the chemical composition, structure, and properties of substances and of the chemical processes and transformations that they undergo. This includes uses of chemicals and their interactions, danger signs, production techniques, and disposal methods.
Physics	Knowledge and prediction of physical principles, laws, their interrelationships, and applications to understanding fluid, material, and atmospheric dynamics, and mechanical, electrical, atomic and sub- atomic structures and processes.
History and Archeology	Knowledge of historical events and their causes, indicators, and effects on civilizations and cultures.
Communications and Media	Knowledge of media production, communication, and dissemination techniques and methods. This includes alternative ways to inform and entertain via written, oral, and visual media.
Therapy and Counseling	Knowledge of principles, methods, and procedures for diagnosis, treatment, and rehabilitation of physical and mental dysfunctions, and for career counseling and guidance.
Foreign Language	Knowledge of the structure and content of a foreign (non-English) language including the meaning and spelling of words, rules of composition and grammar, and pronunciation.
Food Production	Knowledge of techniques and equipment for planting, growing, and harvesting food products (both plant and animal) for consumption, including storage/handling techniques.
Medicine and Dentistry	Knowledge of the information and techniques needed to diagnose and treat human injuries, diseases, and deformities. This includes symptoms, treatment alternatives, drug properties and interactions, and preventive health-care measures.
Philosophy and Theology	Knowledge of different philosophical systems and religions. This includes their basic principles, values, ethics, ways of thinking, customs, practices, and their impact on human culture.
Fine Arts	Knowledge of the theory and techniques required to compose, produce, and perform works of music, dance, visual arts, drama, and sculpture.

Skills	Skills Definitions
Equipment Selection	Determining the kind of tools and equipment needed to do a job.
Active Listening	Giving full attention to what other people are saying, taking time to understand the points being made, asking questions as appropriate, and not interrupting at inappropriate times.
Coordination	Adjusting actions in relation to others' actions.
Writing	Communicating effectively in writing as appropriate for the needs of the audience.
Monitoring	Monitoring/Assessing performance of yourself, other individuals, or organizations to make improvements or take corrective action.
Critical Thinking	Using logic and reasoning to identify the strengths and weaknesses of alternative solutions, conclusions or approaches to problems.
Judgment and Decision Making	Considering the relative costs and benefits of potential actions to choose the most appropriate one.
Reading Comprehension	Understanding written sentences and paragraphs in work related documents.
Time Management	Managing one's own time and the time of others.
Troubleshooting	Determining causes of operating errors and deciding what to do about it.
Persuasion	Persuading others to change their minds or behavior.

Mathematics	Using mathematics to solve problems.
Quality Control Analysis	Conducting tests and inspections of products, services, or processes to evaluate quality or performance.
Instructing	Teaching others how to do something.
Complex Problem Solving	Identifying complex problems and reviewing related information to develop and evaluate options and implement solutions.
Active Learning	Understanding the implications of new information for both current and future problem-solving and decision-making.
Management of Personnel Resources	Motivating, developing, and directing people as they work, identifying the best people for the job.
Science	Using scientific rules and methods to solve problems.
Speaking	Talking to others to convey information effectively.
Negotiation	Bringing others together and trying to reconcile differences.
Service Orientation	Actively looking for ways to help people.
Learning Strategies	Selecting and using training/instructional methods and procedures appropriate for the situation when learning or teaching new things.
Management of Material Resources	Obtaining and seeing to the appropriate use of equipment, facilities, and materials needed to do certain work.
Operation and Control	Controlling operations of equipment or systems.
Equipment Maintenance	Performing routine maintenance on equipment and determining when and what kind of maintenance is needed.
Social Perceptiveness	Being aware of others' reactions and understanding why they react as they do.
Management of Financial Resources	Determining how money will be spent to get the work done, and accounting for these expenditures.
Operations Analysis	Analyzing needs and product requirements to create a design.
Systems Evaluation	Identifying measures or indicators of system performance and the actions needed to improve or correct performance, relative to the goals of the system.
Technology Design	Generating or adapting equipment and technology to serve user needs.
Operation Monitoring	Watching gauges, dials, or other indicators to make sure a machine is working properly.
Repairing	Repairing machines or systems using the needed tools.
Systems Analysis	Determining how a system should work and how changes in conditions, operations, and the environment will affect outcomes.
Installation	Installing equipment, machines, wiring, or programs to meet specifications.
Programming	Writing computer programs for various purposes.

Ability	Ability Definitions
Problem Sensitivity	The ability to tell when something is wrong or is likely to go wrong. It does not involve solving the problem, only recognizing there is a problem.
Near Vision	The ability to see details at close range (within a few feet of the observer).
Deductive Reasoning	The ability to apply general rules to specific problems to produce answers that make sense.
Static Strength	The ability to exert maximum muscle force to lift, push, pull, or carry objects.
Arm-Hand Steadiness	The ability to keep your hand and arm steady while moving your arm or while holding your arm and hand in one position.
Information Ordering	The ability to arrange things or actions in a certain order or pattern according to a specific rule or set of rules (e.g., patterns of numbers, letters, words, pictures, mathematical operations).
Manual Dexterity	The ability to quickly move your hand, your hand together with your arm, or your two hands to grasp, manipulate, or assemble objects.
Oral Comprehension	The ability to listen to and understand information and ideas presented through spoken words and sentences.
Oral Expression	The ability to communicate information and ideas in speaking so others will understand.
Multilimb Coordination	The ability to coordinate two or more limbs (for example, two arms, two legs, or one leg and one arm) while sitting, standing, or lying down. It does not involve performing the activities while the whole body is in motion.
Category Flexibility	The ability to generate or use different sets of rules for combining or grouping things in different ways.
Speech Clarity	The ability to speak clearly so others can understand you.
Selective Attention	The ability to concentrate on a task over a period of time without being distracted.
Inductive Reasoning	The ability to combine pieces of information to form general rules or conclusions (includes finding a relationship among seemingly unrelated events).

Speech Recognition	The ability to identify and understand the speech of another person.
Written Comprehension	The ability to read and understand information and ideas presented in writing.
Flexibility of Closure	The ability to identify or detect a known pattern (a figure, object, word, or sound) that is hidden in other distracting material.
Perceptual Speed	The ability to quickly and accurately compare similarities and differences among sets of letters, numbers, objects, pictures, or patterns. The things to be compared may be presented at the same time or one after the other. This ability also includes comparing a presented object with a remembered object.
Depth Perception	The ability to judge which of several objects is closer or farther away from you, or to judge the distance between you and an object.
Control Precision	The ability to quickly and repeatedly adjust the controls of a machine or a vehicle to exact positions.
Trunk Strength	The ability to use your abdominal and lower back muscles to support part of the body repeatedly or continuously over time without 'giving out' or fatiguing.
Far Vision	The ability to see details at a distance.
Visual Color Discrimination	The ability to match or detect differences between colors, including shades of color and brightness.
Dynamic Strength	The ability to exert muscle force repeatedly or continuously over time. This involves muscular endurance and resistance to muscle fatigue.
Spatial Orientation	The ability to know your location in relation to the environment or to know where other objects are in relation to you.
Finger Dexterity	The ability to make precisely coordinated movements of the fingers of one or both hands to grasp, manipulate, or assemble very small objects.
Fluency of Ideas	The ability to come up with a number of ideas about a topic (the number of ideas is important, not their quality, correctness, or creativity).
Reaction Time	The ability to quickly respond (with the hand, finger, or foot) to a signal (sound, light, picture) when it appears.
Extent Flexibility	The ability to bend, stretch, twist, or reach with your body, arms, and/or legs.
Written Expression	The ability to communicate information and ideas in writing so others will understand.
Stamina	The ability to exert yourself physically over long periods of time without getting winded or out of breath.
Hearing Sensitivity	The ability to detect or tell the differences between sounds that vary in pitch and loudness.
Originality	The ability to come up with unusual or clever ideas about a given topic or situation, or to develop creative ways to solve a problem.
Time Sharing	The ability to shift back and forth between two or more activities or sources of information (such as speech, sounds, touch, or other sources).
Visualization	The ability to imagine how something will look after it is moved around or when its parts are moved or rearranged.
Gross Body Coordination	The ability to coordinate the movement of your arms, legs, and torso together when the whole body is in motion.
Number Facility	The ability to add, subtract, multiply, or divide quickly and correctly.
Response Orientation	The ability to choose quickly between two or more movements in response to two or more different signals (lights, sounds, pictures). It includes the speed with which the correct response is started with the hand, foot, or other body part.
Rate Control	The ability to time your movements or the movement of a piece of equipment in anticipation of changes in the speed and/or direction of a moving object or scene.
Speed of Closure	The ability to quickly make sense of, combine, and organize information into meaningful patterns.
Mathematical Reasoning	The ability to choose the right mathematical methods or formulas to solve a problem.
Speed of Limb Movement	The ability to quickly move the arms and legs.
Auditory Attention	The ability to focus on a single source of sound in the presence of other distracting sounds.
Glare Sensitivity	The ability to see objects in the presence of glare or bright lighting.
Peripheral Vision	The ability to see objects or movement of objects to one's side when the eyes are looking ahead.
Memorization	The ability to remember information such as words, numbers, pictures, and procedures.
Sound Localization	The ability to tell the direction from which a sound originated.

Wrist-Finger Speed	The ability to make fast, simple, repeated movements of the fingers, hands, and wrists.
Gross Body Equilibrium	The ability to keep or regain your body balance or stay upright when in an unstable position.
Night Vision	The ability to see under low light conditions.
Explosive Strength	The ability to use short bursts of muscle force to propel oneself (as in jumping or sprinting), or to throw an object.
Dynamic Flexibility	The ability to quickly and repeatedly bend, stretch, twist, or reach out with your body, arms, and/or legs.

Work_Activity	Work_Activity Definitions
Evaluating Information to Determine Compliance wit	Using relevant information and individual judgment to determine whether events or processes comply with laws, regulations, or standards.
Making Decisions and Solving Problems	Analyzing information and evaluating results to choose the best solution and solve problems.
Coordinating the Work and Activities of Others	Getting members of a group to work together to accomplish tasks.
Performing General Physical Activities	Performing physical activities that require considerable use of your arms and legs and moving your whole body, such as climbing, lifting, balancing, walking, stooping, and handling of materials.
Communicating with Supervisors, Peers, or Subordin	Providing information to supervisors, co-workers, and subordinates by telephone, in written form, e-mail, or in person.
Identifying Objects, Actions, and Events	Identifying information by categorizing, estimating, recognizing differences or similarities, and detecting changes in circumstances or events.
Operating Vehicles, Mechanized Devices, or Equipme	Running, maneuvering, navigating, or driving vehicles or mechanized equipment, such as forklifts, passenger vehicles, aircraft, or water craft.
Organizing, Planning, and Prioritizing Work	Developing specific goals and plans to prioritize, organize, and accomplish your work.
Guiding, Directing, and Motivating Subordinates	Providing guidance and direction to subordinates, including setting performance standards and monitoring performance.
Judging the Qualities of Things, Services, or Peop	Assessing the value, importance, or quality of things or people.
Training and Teaching Others	Identifying the educational needs of others, developing formal educational or training programs or classes, and teaching or instructing others.
Handling and Moving Objects	Using hands and arms in handling, installing, positioning, and moving materials, and manipulating things.
Estimating the Quantifiable Characteristics of Pro	Estimating sizes, distances, and quantities; or determining time, costs, resources, or materials needed to perform a work activity.
Monitor Processes, Materials, or Surroundings	Monitoring and reviewing information from materials, events, or the environment, to detect or assess problems.
Establishing and Maintaining Interpersonal Relatio	Developing constructive and cooperative working relationships with others, and maintaining them over time.
Inspecting Equipment, Structures, or Material	Inspecting equipment, structures, or materials to identify the cause of errors or other problems or defects.
Developing Objectives and Strategies	Establishing long-range objectives and specifying the strategies and actions to achieve them.
Thinking Creatively	Developing, designing, or creating new applications, ideas, relationships, systems, or products, including artistic contributions.
Getting Information	Observing, receiving, and otherwise obtaining information from all relevant sources.
Scheduling Work and Activities	Scheduling events, programs, and activities, as well as the work of others.
Processing Information	Compiling, coding, categorizing, calculating, tabulating, auditing, or verifying information or data.
Communicating with Persons Outside Organization	Communicating with people outside the organization, representing the organization to customers, the public, government, and other external sources. This information can be exchanged in person, in writing, or by telephone or e-mail.
Performing for or Working Directly with the Public	Performing for people or dealing directly with the public. This includes serving customers in restaurants and stores, and receiving clients or guests.
Updating and Using Relevant Knowledge	Keeping up-to-date technically and applying new knowledge to your job.
Documenting/Recording Information	Entering, transcribing, recording, storing, or maintaining information in written or electronic/magnetic form.

Coaching and Developing Others	Identifying the developmental needs of others and coaching, mentoring, or otherwise helping others to improve their knowledge or skills.
Analyzing Data or Information	Identifying the underlying principles, reasons, or facts of information by breaking down information or data into separate parts.
Controlling Machines and Processes	Using either control mechanisms or direct physical activity to operate machines or processes (not including computers or vehicles).
Monitoring and Controlling Resources	Monitoring and controlling resources and overseeing the spending of money.
Resolving Conflicts and Negotiating with Others	Handling complaints, settling disputes, and resolving grievances and conflicts, or otherwise negotiating with others.
Developing and Building Teams	Encouraging and building mutual trust, respect, and cooperation among team members.
Provide Consultation and Advice to Others	Providing guidance and expert advice to management or other groups on technical, systems-, or process-related topics.
Performing Administrative Activities	Performing day-to-day administrative tasks such as maintaining information files and processing paperwork.
Staffing Organizational Units	Recruiting, interviewing, selecting, hiring, and promoting employees in an organization.
Interacting With Computers	Using computers and computer systems (including hardware and software) to program, write software, set up functions, enter data, or process information.
Repairing and Maintaining Mechanical Equipment	Servicing, repairing, adjusting, and testing machines, devices, moving parts, and equipment that operate primarily on the basis of mechanical (not electronic) principles.
Interpreting the Meaning of Information for Others	Translating or explaining what information means and how it can be used.
Drafting, Laying Out, and Specifying Technical Dev	Providing documentation, detailed instructions, drawings, or specifications to tell others about how devices, parts, equipment, or structures are to be fabricated, constructed, assembled, modified, maintained, or used.
Assisting and Caring for Others	Providing personal assistance, medical attention, emotional support, or other personal care to others such as coworkers, customers, or patients.
Selling or Influencing Others	Convincing others to buy merchandise/goods or to otherwise change their minds or actions.
Repairing and Maintaining Electronic Equipment	Servicing, repairing, calibrating, regulating, fine-tuning, or testing machines, devices, and equipment that operate primarily on the basis of electrical or electronic (not mechanical) principles.

Work_Context	Work_Context Definitions
Face-to-Face Discussions	How often do you have to have face-to-face discussions with individuals or teams in this job?
Freedom to Make Decisions	How much decision making freedom, without supervision, does the job offer?
Structured versus Unstructured Work	To what extent is this job structured for the worker, rather than allowing the worker to determine tasks, priorities, and goals?
Telephone	How often do you have telephone conversations in this job?
Importance of Being Exact or Accurate	How important is being very exact or highly accurate in performing this job?
Outdoors, Exposed to Weather	How often does this job require working outdoors, exposed to all weather conditions?
Level of Competition	To what extent does this job require the worker to compete or to be aware of competitive pressures?
Responsibility for Outcomes and Results	How responsible is the worker for work outcomes and results of other workers?
Consequence of Error	How serious would the result usually be if the worker made a mistake that was not readily correctable?
Work With Work Group or Team	How important is it to work with others in a group or team in this job?
Wear Common Protective or Safety Equipment such as	How much does this job require wearing common protective or safety equipment such as safety shoes, glasses, gloves, hard hats or live jackets?
Impact of Decisions on Co-workers or Company Resul	How do the decisions an employee makes impact the results of co-workers, clients or the company?
Exposed to Minor Burns, Cuts, Bites, or Stings	How often does this job require exposure to minor burns, cuts, bites, or stings?
Spend Time Making Repetitive Motions	How much does this job require making repetitive motions?
Spend Time Using Your Hands to Handle, Control, or	How much does this job require using your hands to handle, control, or feel objects, tools or controls?

Responsible for Others' Health and Safety	How much responsibility is there for the health and safety of others in this job?
Very Hot or Cold Temperatures	How often does this job require working in very hot (above 90 F degrees) or very cold (below 32 F degrees) temperatures?
Contact With Others	How much does this job require the worker to be in contact with others (face-to-face, by telephone, or otherwise) in order to perform it?
Sounds, Noise Levels Are Distracting or Uncomforta	How often does this job require working exposed to sounds and noise levels that are distracting or uncomfortable?
Exposed to Contaminants	How often does this job require working exposed to contaminants (such as pollutants, gases, dust or odors)?
Exposed to Hazardous Equipment	How often does this job require exposure to hazardous equipment?
Exposed to Hazardous Conditions	How often does this job require exposure to hazardous conditions?
In an Open Vehicle or Equipment	How often does this job require working in an open vehicle or equipment (e.g., tractor)?
Coordinate or Lead Others	How important is it to coordinate or lead others in accomplishing work activities in this job?
Cramped Work Space, Awkward Positions	How often does this job require working in cramped work spaces that requires getting into awkward positions?
Frequency of Decision Making	How frequently is the worker required to make decisions that affect other people, the financial resources, and/or the image and reputation of the organization?
Pace Determined by Speed of Equipment	How important is it to this job that the pace is determined by the speed of equipment or machinery? (This does not refer to keeping busy at all times on this job.)
Exposed to Whole Body Vibration	How often does this job require exposure to whole body vibration (e.g., operate a jackhammer)?
Importance of Repeating Same Tasks	How important is repeating the same physical activities (e.g., key entry) or mental activities (e.g., checking entries in a ledger) over and over, without stopping, to performing this job?
Letters and Memos	How often does the job require written letters and memos?
In an Enclosed Vehicle or Equipment	How often does this job require working in a closed vehicle or equipment (e.g., car)?
Electronic Mail	How often do you use electronic mail in this job?
Spend Time Standing	How much does this job require standing?
Spend Time Walking and Running	How much does this job require walking and running?
Spend Time Sitting	How much does this job require sitting?
Deal With External Customers	How important is it to work with external customers or the public in this job?
Time Pressure	How often does this job require the worker to meet strict deadlines?
Wear Specialized Protective or Safety Equipment su	How much does this job require wearing specialized protective or safety equipment such as breathing apparatus, safety harness, full protection suits, or radiation protection?
Frequency of Conflict Situations	How often are there conflict situations the employee has to face in this job?
Extremely Bright or Inadequate Lighting	How often does this job require working in extremely bright or inadequate lighting conditions?
Indoors, Environmentally Controlled	How often does this job require working indoors in environmentally controlled conditions?
Degree of Automation	How automated is the job?
Indoors, Not Environmentally Controlled	How often does this job require working indoors in non-controlled environmental conditions (e.g., warehouse without heat)?
Physical Proximity	To what extent does this job require the worker to perform job tasks in close physical proximity to other people?
Deal With Unpleasant or Angry People	How frequently does the worker have to deal with unpleasant, angry, or discourteous individuals as part of the job requirements?
Spend Time Bending or Twisting the Body	How much does this job require bending or twisting your body?
Exposed to High Places	How often does this job require exposure to high places?
Outdoors, Under Cover	How often does this job require working outdoors, under cover (e.g., structure with roof but no walls)?
Spend Time Kneeling, Crouching, Stooping, or Crawl	How much does this job require kneeling, crouching, stooping or crawling?
Spend Time Keeping or Regaining Balance	How much does this job require keeping or regaining your balance?
Public Speaking	How often do you have to perform public speaking in this job?
Spend Time Climbing Ladders, Scaffolds, or Poles	How much does this job require climbing ladders, scaffolds, or poles?
Exposed to Radiation	How often does this job require exposure to radiation?

Deal With Physically Aggressive People	How frequently does this job require the worker to deal with physical aggression of violent individuals?
Exposed to Disease or Infections	How often does this job require exposure to disease/infections?

Job Zone Component — Job Zone Component Definitions

Job Zone Component	Job Zone Component Definitions
Title	Job Zone Three: Medium Preparation Needed
Overall Experience	Previous work-related skill, knowledge, or experience is required for these occupations. For example, an electrician must have completed three or four years of apprenticeship or several years of vocational training, and often must have passed a licensing exam, in order to perform the job.
Job Training	Employees in these occupations usually need one or two years of training involving both on-the-job experience and informal training with experienced workers.
Job Zone Examples	These occupations usually involve using communication and organizational skills to coordinate, supervise, manage, or train others to accomplish goals. Examples include dental assistants, electricians, fish and game wardens, legal secretaries, personnel recruiters, and recreation workers.
SVP Range	(6.0 to < 7.0)
Education	Most occupations in this zone require training in vocational schools, related on-the-job experience, or an associate's degree. Some may require a bachelor's degree.

Work_Styles — Work_Styles Definitions

Work_Styles	Work_Styles Definitions
Dependability	Job requires being reliable, responsible, and dependable, and fulfilling obligations.
Integrity	Job requires being honest and ethical.
Cooperation	Job requires being pleasant with others on the job and displaying a good-natured, cooperative attitude.
Adaptability/Flexibility	Job requires being open to change (positive or negative) and to considerable variety in the workplace.
Initiative	Job requires a willingness to take on responsibilities and challenges.
Leadership	Job requires a willingness to lead, take charge, and offer opinions and direction.
Attention to Detail	Job requires being careful about detail and thorough in completing work tasks.
Self Control	Job requires maintaining composure, keeping emotions in check, controlling anger, and avoiding aggressive behavior, even in very difficult situations.
Independence	Job requires developing one's own ways of doing things, guiding oneself with little or no supervision, and depending on oneself to get things done.
Analytical Thinking	Job requires analyzing information and using logic to address work-related issues and problems.
Concern for Others	Job requires being sensitive to others' needs and feelings and being understanding and helpful on the job.
Innovation	Job requires creativity and alternative thinking to develop new ideas for and answers to work-related problems.
Stress Tolerance	Job requires accepting criticism and dealing calmly and effectively with high stress situations.
Achievement/Effort	Job requires establishing and maintaining personally challenging achievement goals and exerting effort toward mastering tasks.
Persistence	Job requires persistence in the face of obstacles.
Social Orientation	Job requires preferring to work with others rather than alone, and being personally connected with others on the job.

47-2043.00 - Floor Sanders and Finishers

Scrape and sand wooden floors to smooth surfaces using floor scraper and floor sanding machine, and apply coats of finish.

Tasks

1) Scrape and sand floor edges and areas inaccessible to floor sanders, using scrapers, disk-type sanders, and sandpaper.

2) Guide sanding machines over surfaces of floors until surfaces are smooth.

3) Attach sandpaper to rollers of sanding machines.

4) Inspect floors for smoothness.

5) Apply filler compound and coats of finish to floors in order to seal wood.

47-2051.00 - Cement Masons and Concrete Finishers

Smooth and finish surfaces of poured concrete, such as floors, walks, sidewalks, roads, or curbs using a variety of hand and power tools. Align forms for sidewalks, curbs, or gutters; patch voids; use saws to cut expansion joints.

Tasks

1) Spread, level, and smooth concrete, using rake, shovel, hand or power trowel, hand or power screed, and float.

2) Signal truck driver to position truck to facilitate pouring concrete, and move chute to direct concrete on forms.

3) Check the forms that hold the concrete to see that they are properly constructed.

4) Produce rough concrete surface, using broom.

5) Wet surface to prepare for bonding, fill holes and cracks with grout or slurry, and smooth, using trowel.

6) Set the forms that hold concrete to the desired pitch and depth, and align them.

7) Cut out damaged areas, drill holes for reinforcing rods, and position reinforcing rods to repair concrete, using power saw and drill.

8) Clean chipped area, using wire brush, and feel and observe surface to determine if it is rough or uneven.

9) Apply hardening and sealing compounds to cure surface of concrete, and waterproof or restore surface.

10) Monitor how the wind, heat, or cold affect the curing of the concrete throughout the entire process.

11) Chip, scrape, and grind high spots, ridges, and rough projections to finish concrete, using pneumatic chisels, power grinders, or hand tools.

12) Direct the casting of the concrete and supervise laborers who use shovels or special tools to spread it.

13) Wet concrete surface, and rub with stone to smooth surface and obtain specified finish.

14) Operate power vibrator to compact concrete.

15) Mix cement, sand, and water to produce concrete, grout, or slurry, using hoe, trowel, tamper, scraper, or concrete-mixing machine.

16) Install anchor bolts, steel plates, door sills and other fixtures in freshly poured concrete and/or pattern or stamp the surface to provide a decorative finish.

17) Build wooden molds, and clamp molds around area to be repaired, using hand tools.

18) Waterproof or restore concrete surfaces, using appropriate compounds.

19) Apply muriatic acid to clean surface, and rinse with water.

20) Polish surface, using polishing or surfacing machine.

21) Fabricate concrete beams, columns, and panels.

22) Sprinkle colored marble or stone chips, powdered steel, or coloring powder over surface to produce prescribed finish.

23) Push roller over surface to embed chips in surface.

24) Cut metal division strips, and press them into terrazzo base so that top edges form desired design or pattern.

25) Spread roofing paper on surface of foundation, and spread concrete onto roofing paper with trowel to form terrazzo base.

Knowledge	Knowledge Definitions
Building and Construction	Knowledge of materials, methods, and the tools involved in the construction or repair of houses, buildings, or other structures such as highways and roads.
Administration and Management	Knowledge of business and management principles involved in strategic planning, resource allocation, human resources modeling, leadership technique, production methods, and coordination of people and resources.
English Language	Knowledge of the structure and content of the English language including the meaning and spelling of words, rules of composition, and grammar.
Public Safety and Security	Knowledge of relevant equipment, policies, procedures, and strategies to promote effective local, state, or national security operations for the protection of people, data, property, and institutions.
Mechanical	Knowledge of machines and tools, including their designs, uses, repair, and maintenance.
Education and Training	Knowledge of principles and methods for curriculum and training design, teaching and instruction for individuals and groups, and the measurement of training effects.
Design	Knowledge of design techniques, tools, and principles involved in production of precision technical plans, blueprints, drawings, and models.
Mathematics	Knowledge of arithmetic, algebra, geometry, calculus, statistics, and their applications.
Medicine and Dentistry	Knowledge of the information and techniques needed to diagnose and treat human injuries, diseases, and deformities. This includes symptoms, treatment alternatives, drug properties and interactions, and preventive health-care measures.
Production and Processing	Knowledge of raw materials, production processes, quality control, costs, and other techniques for maximizing the effective manufacture and distribution of goods.
Customer and Personal Service	Knowledge of principles and processes for providing customer and personal services. This includes customer needs assessment, meeting quality standards for services, and evaluation of customer satisfaction.
Engineering and Technology	Knowledge of the practical application of engineering science and technology. This includes applying principles, techniques, procedures, and equipment to the design and production of various goods and services.
Psychology	Knowledge of human behavior and performance; individual differences in ability, personality, and interests; learning and motivation; psychological research methods; and the assessment and treatment of behavioral and affective disorders.
Personnel and Human Resources	Knowledge of principles and procedures for personnel recruitment, selection, training, compensation and benefits, labor relations and negotiation, and personnel information systems.
Law and Government	Knowledge of laws, legal codes, court procedures, precedents, government regulations, executive orders, agency rules, and the democratic political process.
Transportation	Knowledge of principles and methods for moving people or goods by air, rail, sea, or road, including the relative costs and benefits.
Economics and Accounting	Knowledge of economic and accounting principles and practices, the financial markets, banking and the analysis and reporting of financial data.
Clerical	Knowledge of administrative and clerical procedures and systems such as word processing, managing files and records, stenography and transcription, designing forms, and other office procedures and terminology.
Telecommunications	Knowledge of transmission, broadcasting, switching, control, and operation of telecommunications systems.
Sociology and Anthropology	Knowledge of group behavior and dynamics, societal trends and influences, human migrations, ethnicity, cultures and their history and origins.
Geography	Knowledge of principles and methods for describing the features of land, sea, and air masses, including their physical characteristics, locations, interrelationships, and distribution of plant, animal, and human life.
Communications and Media	Knowledge of media production, communication, and dissemination techniques and methods. This includes alternative ways to inform and entertain via written, oral, and visual media.
Sales and Marketing	Knowledge of principles and methods for showing, promoting, and selling products or services. This includes marketing strategy and tactics, product demonstration, sales techniques, and sales control systems.
Foreign Language	Knowledge of the structure and content of a foreign (non-English) language including the meaning and spelling of words, rules of composition and grammar, and pronunciation.
Therapy and Counseling	Knowledge of principles, methods, and procedures for diagnosis, treatment, and rehabilitation of physical and mental dysfunctions, and for career counseling and guidance.

Fine Arts	Knowledge of the theory and techniques required to compose, produce, and perform works of music, dance, visual arts, drama, and sculpture.
Chemistry	Knowledge of the chemical composition, structure, and properties of substances and of the chemical processes and transformations that they undergo. This includes uses of chemicals and their interactions, danger signs, production techniques, and disposal methods.
Food Production	Knowledge of techniques and equipment for planting, growing, and harvesting food products (both plant and animal) for consumption, including storage/handling techniques.
History and Archeology	Knowledge of historical events and their causes, indicators, and effects on civilizations and cultures.
Biology	Knowledge of plant and animal organisms, their tissues, cells, functions, interdependencies, and interactions with each other and the environment.
Computers and Electronics	Knowledge of circuit boards, processors, chips, electronic equipment, and computer hardware and software, including applications and programming.
Philosophy and Theology	Knowledge of different philosophical systems and religions. This includes their basic principles, values, ethics, ways of thinking, customs, practices, and their impact on human culture.
Physics	Knowledge and prediction of physical principles, laws, their interrelationships, and applications to understanding fluid, material, and atmospheric dynamics, and mechanical, electrical, atomic and sub- atomic structures and processes.

Skills	Skills Definitions
Coordination	Adjusting actions in relation to others' actions.
Mathematics	Using mathematics to solve problems.
Active Listening	Giving full attention to what other people are saying, taking time to understand the points being made, asking questions as appropriate, and not interrupting at inappropriate times.
Critical Thinking	Using logic and reasoning to identify the strengths and weaknesses of alternative solutions, conclusions or approaches to problems.
Active Learning	Understanding the implications of new information for both current and future problem-solving and decision-making.
Complex Problem Solving	Identifying complex problems and reviewing related information to develop and evaluate options and implement solutions.
Equipment Selection	Determining the kind of tools and equipment needed to do a job.
Time Management	Managing one's own time and the time of others.
Equipment Maintenance	Performing routine maintenance on equipment and determining when and what kind of maintenance is needed.
Speaking	Talking to others to convey information effectively.
Learning Strategies	Selecting and using training/instructional methods and procedures appropriate for the situation when learning or teaching new things.
Social Perceptiveness	Being aware of others' reactions and understanding why they react as they do.
Instructing	Teaching others how to do something.
Reading Comprehension	Understanding written sentences and paragraphs in work related documents.
Persuasion	Persuading others to change their minds or behavior.
Repairing	Repairing machines or systems using the needed tools.
Installation	Installing equipment, machines, wiring, or programs to meet specifications.
Judgment and Decision Making	Considering the relative costs and benefits of potential actions to choose the most appropriate one.
Monitoring	Monitoring/Assessing performance of yourself, other individuals, or organizations to make improvements or take corrective action.
Troubleshooting	Determining causes of operating errors and deciding what to do about it.
Operations Analysis	Analyzing needs and product requirements to create a design.
Writing	Communicating effectively in writing as appropriate for the needs of the audience.
Management of Personnel Resources	Motivating, developing, and directing people as they work, identifying the best people for the job.
Service Orientation	Actively looking for ways to help people.
Operation and Control	Controlling operations of equipment or systems.
Negotiation	Bringing others together and trying to reconcile differences.
Technology Design	Generating or adapting equipment and technology to serve user needs.

Management of Material Resources	Obtaining and seeing to the appropriate use of equipment, facilities, and materials needed to do certain work.
Operation Monitoring	Watching gauges, dials, or other indicators to make sure a machine is working properly.
Science	Using scientific rules and methods to solve problems.
Management of Financial Resources	Determining how money will be spent to get the work done, and accounting for these expenditures.
Quality Control Analysis	Conducting tests and inspections of products, services, or processes to evaluate quality or performance.
Systems Analysis	Determining how a system should work and how changes in conditions, operations, and the environment will affect outcomes.
Programming	Writing computer programs for various purposes.
Systems Evaluation	Identifying measures or indicators of system performance and the actions needed to improve or correct performance, relative to the goals of the system.

Ability	Ability Definitions
Control Precision	The ability to quickly and repeatedly adjust the controls of a machine or a vehicle to exact positions.
Problem Sensitivity	The ability to tell when something is wrong or is likely to go wrong. It does not involve solving the problem, only recognizing there is a problem.
Arm-Hand Steadiness	The ability to keep your hand and arm steady while moving your arm or while holding your arm and hand in one position.
Manual Dexterity	The ability to quickly move your hand, your hand together with your arm, or your two hands to grasp, manipulate, or assemble objects.
Extent Flexibility	The ability to bend, stretch, twist, or reach with your body, arms, and/or legs.
Speech Clarity	The ability to speak clearly so others can understand you.
Information Ordering	The ability to arrange things or actions in a certain order or pattern according to a specific rule or set of rules (e.g., patterns of numbers, letters, words, pictures, mathematical operations).
Deductive Reasoning	The ability to apply general rules to specific problems to produce answers that make sense.
Oral Expression	The ability to communicate information and ideas in speaking so others will understand.
Multilimb Coordination	The ability to coordinate two or more limbs (for example, two arms, two legs, or one leg and one arm) while sitting, standing, or lying down. It does not involve performing the activities while the whole body is in motion.
Oral Comprehension	The ability to listen to and understand information and ideas presented through spoken words and sentences.
Inductive Reasoning	The ability to combine pieces of information to form general rules or conclusions (includes finding a relationship among seemingly unrelated events).
Visualization	The ability to imagine how something will look after it is moved around or when its parts are moved or rearranged.
Near Vision	The ability to see details at close range (within a few feet of the observer).
Selective Attention	The ability to concentrate on a task over a period of time without being distracted.
Depth Perception	The ability to judge which of several objects is closer or farther away from you, or to judge the distance between you and an object.
Speech Recognition	The ability to identify and understand the speech of another person.
Far Vision	The ability to see details at a distance.
Trunk Strength	The ability to use your abdominal and lower back muscles to support part of the body repeatedly or continuously over time without 'giving out' or fatiguing.
Static Strength	The ability to exert maximum muscle force to lift, push, pull, or carry objects.
Finger Dexterity	The ability to make precisely coordinated movements of the fingers of one or both hands to grasp, manipulate, or assemble very small objects.
Flexibility of Closure	The ability to identify or detect a known pattern (a figure, object, word, or sound) that is hidden in other distracting material.
Stamina	The ability to exert yourself physically over long periods of time without getting winded or out of breath.
Category Flexibility	The ability to generate or use different sets of rules for combining or grouping things in different ways.
Reaction Time	The ability to quickly respond (with the hand, finger, or foot) to a signal (sound, light, picture) when it appears.

Perceptual Speed	The ability to quickly and accurately compare similarities and differences among sets of letters, numbers, objects, pictures, or patterns. The things to be compared may be presented at the same time or one after the other. This ability also includes comparing a presented object with a remembered object.
Auditory Attention	The ability to focus on a single source of sound in the presence of other distracting sounds.
Dynamic Strength	The ability to exert muscle force repeatedly or continuously over time. This involves muscular endurance and resistance to muscle fatigue.
Visual Color Discrimination	The ability to match or detect differences between colors, including shades of color and brightness.
Gross Body Coordination	The ability to coordinate the movement of your arms, legs, and torso together when the whole body is in motion.
Hearing Sensitivity	The ability to detect or tell the differences between sounds that vary in pitch and loudness.
Gross Body Equilibrium	The ability to keep or regain your body balance or stay upright when in an unstable position.
Speed of Limb Movement	The ability to quickly move the arms and legs.
Rate Control	The ability to time your movements or the movement of a piece of equipment in anticipation of changes in the speed and/or direction of a moving object or scene.
Fluency of Ideas	The ability to come up with a number of ideas about a topic (the number of ideas is important, not their quality, correctness, or creativity).
Time Sharing	The ability to shift back and forth between two or more activities or sources of information (such as speech, sounds, touch, or other sources).
Number Facility	The ability to add, subtract, multiply, or divide quickly and correctly.
Originality	The ability to come up with unusual or clever ideas about a given topic or situation, or to develop creative ways to solve a problem.
Spatial Orientation	The ability to know your location in relation to the environment or to know where other objects are in relation to you.
Written Comprehension	The ability to read and understand information and ideas presented in writing.
Glare Sensitivity	The ability to see objects in the presence of glare or bright lighting.
Response Orientation	The ability to choose quickly between two or more movements in response to two or more different signals (lights, sounds, pictures). It includes the speed with which the correct response is started with the hand, foot, or other body part.
Memorization	The ability to remember information such as words, numbers, pictures, and procedures.
Sound Localization	The ability to tell the direction from which a sound originated.
Written Expression	The ability to communicate information and ideas in writing so others will understand.
Mathematical Reasoning	The ability to choose the right mathematical methods or formulas to solve a problem.
Speed of Closure	The ability to quickly make sense of, combine, and organize information into meaningful patterns.
Peripheral Vision	The ability to see objects or movement of objects to one's side when the eyes are looking ahead.
Night Vision	The ability to see under low light conditions.
Dynamic Flexibility	The ability to quickly and repeatedly bend, stretch, twist, or reach out with your body, arms, and/or legs.
Explosive Strength	The ability to use short bursts of muscle force to propel oneself (as in jumping or sprinting), or to throw an object.
Wrist-Finger Speed	The ability to make fast, simple, repeated movements of the fingers, hands, and wrists.

Work_Activity	Work_Activity Definitions
Inspecting Equipment, Structures, or Material	Inspecting equipment, structures, or materials to identify the cause of errors or other problems or defects.
Getting Information	Observing, receiving, and otherwise obtaining information from all relevant sources.
Monitor Processes, Materials, or Surroundings	Monitoring and reviewing information from materials, events, or the environment, to detect or assess problems.
Performing General Physical Activities	Performing physical activities that require considerable use of your arms and legs and moving your whole body, such as climbing, lifting, balancing, walking, stooping, and handling of materials.
Making Decisions and Solving Problems	Analyzing information and evaluating results to choose the best solution and solve problems.

Evaluating Information to Determine Compliance wit	Using relevant information and individual judgment to determine whether events or processes comply with laws, regulations, or standards.
Handling and Moving Objects	Using hands and arms in handling, installing, positioning, and moving materials, and manipulating things.
Operating Vehicles, Mechanized Devices, or Equipme	Running, maneuvering, navigating, or driving vehicles or mechanized equipment, such as forklifts, passenger vehicles, aircraft, or water craft.
Thinking Creatively	Developing, designing, or creating new applications, ideas, relationships, systems, or products, including artistic contributions.
Estimating the Quantifiable Characteristics of Pro	Estimating sizes, distances, and quantities; or determining time, costs, resources, or materials needed to perform a work activity.
Communicating with Supervisors, Peers, or Subordin	Providing information to supervisors, co-workers, and subordinates by telephone, in written form, e-mail, or in person.
Updating and Using Relevant Knowledge	Keeping up-to-date technically and applying new knowledge to your job.
Identifying Objects, Actions, and Events	Identifying information by categorizing, estimating, recognizing differences or similarities, and detecting changes in circumstances or events.
Processing Information	Compiling, coding, categorizing, calculating, tabulating, auditing, or verifying information or data.
Repairing and Maintaining Mechanical Equipment	Servicing, repairing, adjusting, and testing machines, devices, moving parts, and equipment that operate primarily on the basis of mechanical (not electronic) principles.
Training and Teaching Others	Identifying the educational needs of others, developing formal educational or training programs or classes, and teaching or instructing others.
Controlling Machines and Processes	Using either control mechanisms or direct physical activity to operate machines or processes (not including computers or vehicles).
Scheduling Work and Activities	Scheduling events, programs, and activities, as well as the work of others.
Establishing and Maintaining Interpersonal Relatio	Developing constructive and cooperative working relationships with others, and maintaining them over time.
Organizing, Planning, and Prioritizing Work	Developing specific goals and plans to prioritize, organize, and accomplish your work.
Judging the Qualities of Things, Services, or Peop	Assessing the value, importance, or quality of things or people.
Assisting and Caring for Others	Providing personal assistance, medical attention, emotional support, or other personal care to others such as coworkers, customers, or patients.
Interpreting the Meaning of Information for Others	Translating or explaining what information means and how it can be used.
Coordinating the Work and Activities of Others	Getting members of a group to work together to accomplish tasks.
Communicating with Persons Outside Organization	Communicating with people outside the organization, representing the organization to customers, the public, government, and other external sources. This information can be exchanged in person, in writing, or by telephone or e-mail.
Performing for or Working Directly with the Public	Performing for people or dealing directly with the public. This includes serving customers in restaurants and stores, and receiving clients or guests.
Developing Objectives and Strategies	Establishing long-range objectives and specifying the strategies and actions to achieve them.
Repairing and Maintaining Electronic Equipment	Servicing, repairing, calibrating, regulating, fine-tuning, or testing machines, devices, and equipment that operate primarily on the basis of electrical or electronic (not mechanical) principles.
Developing and Building Teams	Encouraging and building mutual trust, respect, and cooperation among team members.
Resolving Conflicts and Negotiating with Others	Handling complaints, settling disputes, and resolving grievances and conflicts, or otherwise negotiating with others.
Analyzing Data or Information	Identifying the underlying principles, reasons, or facts of information by breaking down information or data into separate parts.
Monitoring and Controlling Resources	Monitoring and controlling resources and overseeing the spending of money.
Guiding, Directing, and Motivating Subordinates	Providing guidance and direction to subordinates, including setting performance standards and monitoring performance.
Coaching and Developing Others	Identifying the developmental needs of others and coaching, mentoring, or otherwise helping others to improve their knowledge or skills.
Performing Administrative Activities	Performing day-to-day administrative tasks such as maintaining information files and processing paperwork.

Selling or Influencing Others	Convincing others to buy merchandise/goods or to otherwise change their minds or actions.
Drafting, Laying Out, and Specifying Technical Dev	Providing documentation, detailed instructions, drawings, or specifications to tell others about how devices, parts, equipment, or structures are to be fabricated, constructed, assembled, modified, maintained, or used.
Interacting With Computers	Using computers and computer systems (including hardware and software) to program, write software, set up functions, enter data, or process information.
Documenting/Recording Information	Entering, transcribing, recording, storing, or maintaining information in written or electronic/magnetic form.
Provide Consultation and Advice to Others	Providing guidance and expert advice to management or other groups on technical, systems-, or process-related topics.
Staffing Organizational Units	Recruiting, interviewing, selecting, hiring, and promoting employees in an organization.

Work_Context	Work_Context Definitions
Outdoors, Exposed to Weather	How often does this job require working outdoors, exposed to all weather conditions?
Face-to-Face Discussions	How often do you have to have face-to-face discussions with individuals or teams in this job?
Wear Common Protective or Safety Equipment such as	How much does this job require wearing common protective or safety equipment such as safety shoes, glasses, gloves, hard hats or live jackets?
Spend Time Using Your Hands to Handle, Control, or	How much does this job require using your hands to handle, control, or feel objects, tools or controls?
Spend Time Standing	How much does this job require standing?
Impact of Decisions on Co-workers or Company Resul	How do the decisions an employee makes impact the results of co-workers, clients or the company?
Exposed to Hazardous Equipment	How often does this job require exposure to hazardous equipment?
Frequency of Decision Making	How frequently is the worker required to make decisions that affect other people, the financial resources, and/or the image and reputation of the organization?
Telephone	How often do you have telephone conversations in this job?
In an Open Vehicle or Equipment	How often does this job require working in an open vehicle or equipment (e.g., tractor)?
Sounds, Noise Levels Are Distracting or Uncomforta	How often does this job require working exposed to sounds and noise levels that are distracting or uncomfortable?
Work With Work Group or Team	How important is it to work with others in a group or team in this job?
Responsible for Others' Health and Safety	How much responsibility is there for the health and safety of others in this job?
Responsibility for Outcomes and Results	How responsible is the worker for work outcomes and results of other workers?
Freedom to Make Decisions	How much decision making freedom, without supervision, does the job offer?
In an Enclosed Vehicle or Equipment	How often does this job require working in a closed vehicle or equipment (e.g., car)?
Physical Proximity	To what extent does this job require the worker to perform job tasks in close physical proximity to other people?
Spend Time Bending or Twisting the Body	How much does this job require bending or twisting your body?
Structured versus Unstructured Work	To what extent is this job structured for the worker, rather than allowing the worker to determine tasks, priorities, and goals?
Exposed to Whole Body Vibration	How often does this job require exposure to whole body vibration (e.g., operate a jackhammer)?
Importance of Being Exact or Accurate	How important is being very exact or highly accurate in performing this job?
Time Pressure	How often does this job require the worker to meet strict deadlines?
Very Hot or Cold Temperatures	How often does this job require working in very hot (above 90 F degrees) or very cold (below 32 F degrees) temperatures?
Exposed to Contaminants	How often does this job require working exposed to contaminants (such as pollutants, gases, dust or odors)?
Contact With Others	How much does this job require the worker to be in contact with others (face-to-face, by telephone, or otherwise) in order to perform it?
Spend Time Making Repetitive Motions	How much does this job require making repetitive motions?
Indoors, Not Environmentally Controlled	How often does this job require working indoors in non-controlled environmental conditions (e.g., warehouse without heat)?
Extremely Bright or Inadequate Lighting	How often does this job require working in extremely bright or inadequate lighting conditions?

Coordinate or Lead Others	How important is it to coordinate or lead others in accomplishing work activities in this job?
Consequence of Error	How serious would the result usually be if the worker made a mistake that was not readily correctable?
Exposed to Minor Burns, Cuts, Bites, or Stings	How often does this job require exposure to minor burns, cuts, bites, or stings?
Pace Determined by Speed of Equipment	How important is it to this job that the pace is determined by the speed of equipment or machinery? (This does not refer to keeping busy at all times on this job.)
Spend Time Walking and Running	How much does this job require walking and running?
Spend Time Kneeling, Crouching, Stooping, or Crawl	How much does this job require kneeling, crouching, stooping or crawling?
Cramped Work Space, Awkward Positions	How often does this job require working in cramped work spaces that requires getting into awkward positions?
Level of Competition	To what extent does this job require the worker to compete or to be aware of competitive pressures?
Deal With External Customers	How important is it to work with external customers or the public in this job?
Importance of Repeating Same Tasks	How important is repeating the same physical activities (e.g., key entry) or mental activities (e.g., checking entries in a ledger) over and over, without stopping, to performing this job?
Exposed to High Places	How often does this job require exposure to high places?
Frequency of Conflict Situations	How often are there conflict situations the employee has to face in this job?
Spend Time Keeping or Regaining Balance	How much does this job require keeping or regaining your balance?
Deal With Unpleasant or Angry People	How frequently does the worker have to deal with unpleasant, angry, or discourteous individuals as part of the job requirements?
Indoors, Environmentally Controlled	How often does this job require working indoors in environmentally controlled conditions?
Outdoors, Under Cover	How often does this job require working outdoors, under cover (e.g., structure with roof but no walls)?
Exposed to Radiation	How often does this job require exposure to radiation?
Letters and Memos	How often does the job require written letters and memos?
Exposed to Hazardous Conditions	How often does this job require exposure to hazardous conditions?
Degree of Automation	How automated is the job?
Spend Time Sitting	How much does this job require sitting?
Wear Specialized Protective or Safety Equipment su	How much does this job require wearing specialized protective or safety equipment such as breathing apparatus, safety harness, full protection suits, or radiation protection?
Exposed to Disease or Infections	How often does this job require exposure to disease/infections?
Spend Time Climbing Ladders, Scaffolds, or Poles	How much does this job require climbing ladders, scaffolds, or poles?
Electronic Mail	How often do you use electronic mail in this job?
Public Speaking	How often do you have to perform public speaking in this job?
Deal With Physically Aggressive People	How frequently does this job require the worker to deal with physical aggression of violent individuals?

Job Zone Component	Job Zone Component Definitions
Title	Job Zone Three: Medium Preparation Needed
Overall Experience	Previous work-related skill, knowledge, or experience is required for these occupations. For example, an electrician must have completed three or four years of apprenticeship or several years of vocational training, and often must have passed a licensing exam, in order to perform the job.
Job Training	Employees in these occupations usually need one or two years of training involving both on-the-job experience and informal training with experienced workers.
Job Zone Examples	These occupations usually involve using communication and organizational skills to coordinate, supervise, manage, or train others to accomplish goals. Examples include dental assistants, electricians, fish and game wardens, legal secretaries, personnel recruiters, and recreation workers.
SVP Range	(6.0 to < 7.0)
Education	Most occupations in this zone require training in vocational schools, related on-the-job experience, or an associate's degree. Some may require a bachelor's degree.

Work_Styles	Work_Styles Definitions

Self Control	Job requires maintaining composure, keeping emotions in check, controlling anger, and avoiding aggressive behavior, even in very difficult situations.
Integrity	Job requires being honest and ethical.
Cooperation	Job requires being pleasant with others on the job and displaying a good-natured, cooperative attitude.
Attention to Detail	Job requires being careful about detail and thorough in completing work tasks.
Dependability	Job requires being reliable, responsible, and dependable, and fulfilling obligations.
Concern for Others	Job requires being sensitive to others' needs and feelings and being understanding and helpful on the job.
Adaptability/Flexibility	Job requires being open to change (positive or negative) and to considerable variety in the workplace.
Innovation	Job requires creativity and alternative thinking to develop new ideas for and answers to work-related problems.
Initiative	Job requires a willingness to take on responsibilities and challenges.
Independence	Job requires developing one's own ways of doing things, guiding oneself with little or no supervision, and depending on oneself to get things done.
Social Orientation	Job requires preferring to work with others rather than alone, and being personally connected with others on the job.
Leadership	Job requires a willingness to lead, take charge, and offer opinions and direction.
Analytical Thinking	Job requires analyzing information and using logic to address work-related issues and problems.
Achievement/Effort	Job requires establishing and maintaining personally challenging achievement goals and exerting effort toward mastering tasks.
Stress Tolerance	Job requires accepting criticism and dealing calmly and effectively with high stress situations.
Persistence	Job requires persistence in the face of obstacles.

47-2061.00 - Construction Laborers

Perform tasks involving physical labor at building, highway, and heavy construction projects, tunnel and shaft excavations, and demolition sites. May operate hand and power tools of all types: air hammers, earth tampers, cement mixers, small mechanical hoists, surveying and measuring equipment, and a variety of other equipment and instruments. May clean and prepare sites, dig trenches, set braces to support the sides of excavations, erect scaffolding, clean up rubble and debris, and remove asbestos, lead, and other hazardous waste materials. May assist other craft workers.

Tasks

1) Measure, mark, and record openings and distances to lay out areas where construction work will be performed.

2) Shovel cement and other materials into portable cement mixers; and mix, pour, and spread concrete.

3) Lubricate, clean, and repair machinery, equipment, and tools.

4) Tend pumps, compressors, and generators to provide power for tools, machinery, and equipment, or to heat and move materials such as asphalt.

5) Tend machines that pump concrete, grout, cement, sand, plaster or stucco through spray-guns for application to ceilings and walls.

6) Identify, pack, and transport hazardous and/or radioactive materials.

7) Dig ditches or trenches, backfill excavations, and compact and level earth to grade specifications, using picks, shovels, pneumatic tampers, and rakes.

8) Use computers and other input devices to control robotic pipe cutters and cleaners.

9) Position, join, align, and seal structural components, such as concrete wall sections and pipes.

10) Place, consolidate, and protect case-in-place concrete or masonry structures.

11) Mop, brush, or spread paints, cleaning solutions, or other compounds over surfaces to clean them or to provide protection.

12) Operate jackhammers and drills to break up concrete or pavement.

13) Spray materials such as water, sand, steam, vinyl, paint, or stucco through hoses to clean, coat, or seal surfaces.

14) Apply caulking compounds by hand or using caulking guns.

15) Build and position forms for pouring concrete, and dismantle forms after use, using saws, hammers, nails, or bolts.

16) Control traffic passing near, in, and around work zones.

17) Erect and disassemble scaffolding, shoring, braces, traffic barricades, ramps, and other temporary structures.

18) Grind, scrape, sand, or polish surfaces such as concrete, marble, terrazzo, or wood flooring, using abrasive tools or machines.

19) Operate, read, and maintain air monitoring and other sampling devices in confined and/or hazardous environments.

20) Load, unload, and identify building materials, machinery, and tools, and distribute them to the appropriate locations, according to project plans and specifications.

21) Smooth and finish freshly poured cement or concrete, using floats, trowels, screeds, or powered cement finishing tools.

22) Mix ingredients to create compounds for covering or cleaning surfaces.

23) Clean and prepare construction sites to eliminate possible hazards.

24) Provide assistance to craft workers, such as carpenters, plasterers, and masons.

25) Raze buildings and salvage useful materials.

26) Read and interpret plans, instructions, and specifications to determine work activities.

27) Transport and set explosives for tunnel, shaft, and road construction.

28) Install sewer, water, and storm drain pipes, using pipe-laying machinery and laser guidance equipment.

47-2072.00 - Pile-Driver Operators

Operate pile drivers mounted on skids, barges, crawler treads, or locomotive cranes to drive pilings for retaining walls, bulkheads, and foundations of structures, such as buildings, bridges, and piers.

Tasks

1) Move hand and foot levers of hoisting equipment to position piling leads, hoist piling into leads, and position hammers over pilings.

2) Clean, lubricate, and refill equipment.

3) Conduct pre-operational checks on equipment to ensure proper functioning.

4) Drive pilings to provide support for buildings or other structures, using heavy equipment with a pile driver head.

47-2082.00 - Tapers

Seal joints between plasterboard or other wallboard to prepare wall surface for painting or papering.

Tasks

1) Mix sealing compounds by hand or with portable electric mixers.

2) Press paper tape over joints to embed tape into sealing compound and to seal joints.

3) Countersink nails or screws below surfaces of walls before applying sealing compounds, using hammers or screwdrivers.

4) Sand or patch nicks or cracks in plasterboard or wallboard.

5) Remove extra compound after surfaces have been covered sufficiently.

6) Spread and smooth cementing material over tape, using trowels or floating machines to blend joints with wall surfaces.

7) Install metal molding at wall corners to secure wallboard.

8) Sand rough spots of dried cement between applications of compounds.

9) Seal joints between plasterboard or other wallboard in order to prepare wall surfaces for painting or papering.

10) Spread sealing compound between boards or panels and over cracks, holes, and nail and screw heads, using trowels, broadknives, or spatulas.

11) Select the correct sealing compound or tape.

12) Use mechanical applicators that spread compounds and embed tape in one operation.

13) Apply additional coats to fill in holes and make surfaces smooth.

14) Check adhesives to ensure that they will work and will remain durable.

47-2121.00 - Glaziers

Install glass in windows, skylights, store fronts, and display cases, or on surfaces, such as building fronts, interior walls, ceilings, and tabletops.

Tasks

1) Fabricate and install metal sashes and moldings for glass installation, using aluminum or steel framing.

2) Grind and polish glass, and smooth edges when necessary.

3) Measure and mark outlines or patterns on glass to indicate cutting lines.

4) Score glass with cutters' wheels, breaking off excess glass by hand or with notched tools.

5) Install pre-assembled metal or wood frameworks for windows or doors to be fitted with glass panels, using hand tools.

6) Determine plumb of walls or ceilings, using plumb-lines and levels.

7) Set glass doors into frames, and bolt metal hinges, handles, locks, and other hardware to attach doors to frames and walls.

8) Cut, fit, install, repair, and replace glass and glass substitutes, such as plastic and aluminum, in building interiors or exteriors and in furniture or other products.

9) Secure mirrors in position, using mastic cement, putty, bolts, or screws.

10) Fasten glass panes into wood sashes or frames with clips, points, or moldings, adding weather seals or putty around pane edges to seal joints.

11) Drive trucks to installation sites, and unload mirrors, glass equipment, and tools.

12) Cut and remove broken glass prior to installing replacement glass.

13) Assemble and cement sections of stained glass together.

14) Cut, assemble, fit, and attach metal-framed glass enclosures for showers, bathtubs, display cases, skylights, solariums, and other structures.

15) Prepare glass for cutting by resting it on rack edges or against cutting tables, and brushing thin layer of oil along cutting lines or dipping cutting tools in oil.

16) Select the type and color of glass or mirror according to specifications.

17) Read and interpret blueprints and specifications to determine size, shape, color, type, and thickness of glass, location of framing, installation procedures, and staging and scaffolding materials required.

18) Assemble, erect, and dismantle scaffolds, rigging, and hoisting equipment.

19) Confer with customers to determine project requirements and to provide cost estimates.

20) Create patterns on glass by etching, sandblasting, or painting designs.

21) Operate cranes or hoists with suction cups to lift large, heavy pieces of glass.

22) Pack spaces between moldings and glass with glazing compounds, and trim excess material with glazing knives.

23) Measure, cut, fit, and press anti-glare adhesive film to glass, or spray glass with tinting solution to prevent light glare.

24) Measure mirrors and dimensions of areas to be covered in order to determine work procedures.

25) Cut and attach mounting strips, metal or wood moldings, rubber gaskets, or metal clips to surfaces in preparation for mirror installation.

26) Move furniture to clear work sites, and cover floors and furnishings with drop cloths.

47-2131.00 - Insulation Workers, Floor, Ceiling, and Wall

Line and cover structures with insulating materials. May work with batt, roll, or blown insulation materials.

Tasks

1) Prepare surfaces for insulation application by brushing or spreading on adhesives, cement, or asphalt, or by attaching metal pins to surfaces.

2) Fit, wrap, staple, or glue insulating materials to structures or surfaces, using hand tools or wires.

3) Measure and cut insulation for covering surfaces, using tape measures, handsaws, power saws, knives, or scissors.

4) Move controls, buttons, or levers to start blowers and regulate flow of materials through nozzles.

5) Remove old insulation such as asbestos, following safety procedures.

6) Cover and line structures with blown or rolled forms of materials to insulate against cold, heat, or moisture, using saws, knives, rasps, trowels, blowers, and other tools and implements.

7) Read blueprints and select appropriate insulation, based on space characteristics and the heat retaining or excluding characteristics of the material.

8) Fill blower hoppers with insulating materials.

9) Cover, seal, or finish insulated surfaces or access holes with plastic covers, canvas ships, sealants, tape, cement or asphalt mastic.

47-2132.00 - Insulation Workers, Mechanical

Apply insulating materials to pipes or ductwork, or other mechanical systems in order to help control and maintain temperature.

Tasks

1) Install sheet metal around insulated pipes with screws in order to protect the insulation from weather conditions or physical damage.

2) Fit insulation around obstructions, and shape insulating materials and protective coverings as required.

3) Determine the amounts and types of insulation needed, and methods of installation, based on factors such as location, surface shape, and equipment use.

4) Cover, seal, and finish insulated surfaces or access holes with plastic covers, canvas ships, sealant, tape, cement, or asphalt mastic.

5) Apply, remove, and repair insulation on industrial equipment, pipes, ductwork, or other mechanical systems such as heat exchangers, tanks, and vessels, to help control noise and maintain temperatures.

6) Distribute insulating materials evenly into small spaces within floors, ceilings, or walls, using blowers and hose attachments or cement mortar.

7) Prepare surfaces for insulation application by brushing or spreading on adhesives, cement, or asphalt, or by attaching metal pins to surfaces.

8) Move controls, buttons, or levers to start blowers, and to regulate flow of materials through nozzles.

9) Remove or seal off old asbestos insulation, following safety procedures.

10) Read blueprints and specifications to determine job requirements.

11) Measure and cut insulation for covering surfaces, using tape measures, handsaws, knives, and scissors.

12) Select appropriate insulation such as fiberglass, Styrofoam, or cork, based on the heat retaining or excluding characteristics of the material.

47-2141.00 - Painters, Construction and Maintenance

Paint walls, equipment, buildings, bridges, and other structural surfaces, using brushes, rollers, and spray guns. May remove old paint to prepare surface prior to painting. May mix colors or oils to obtain desired color or consistency.

Tasks

1) Smooth surfaces, using sandpaper, scrapers, brushes, steel wool, and/or sanding machines.

2) Remove old finishes by stripping, sanding, wire brushing, burning, or using water and/or abrasive blasting.

3) Remove fixtures such as pictures, door knobs, lamps, and electric switch covers prior to painting.

4) Select and purchase tools and finishes for surfaces to be covered, considering durability, ease of handling, methods of application, and customers' wishes.

5) Wash and treat surfaces with oil, turpentine, mildew remover, or other preparations, and sand rough spots to ensure that finishes will adhere properly.

6) Waterproof buildings, using waterproofers and caulking.

7) Use special finishing techniques such as sponging, ragging, layering, or faux finishing.

8) Spray or brush hot plastics or pitch onto surfaces.

9) Cut stencils, and brush and spray lettering and decorations on surfaces.

10) Read work orders or receive instructions from supervisors or homeowners in order to determine work requirements.

11) Erect scaffolding and swing gates, or set up ladders, to work above ground level.

12) Apply paint, stain, varnish, enamel, and other finishes to equipment, buildings, bridges, and/or other structures, using brushes, spray guns, or rollers.

13) Polish final coats to specified finishes.

14) Mix and match colors of paint, stain, or varnish with oil and thinning and drying additives in order to obtain desired colors and consistencies.

15) Fill cracks, holes, and joints with caulk, putty, plaster, or other fillers, using caulking guns or putty knives.

16) Cover surfaces with dropcloths or masking tape and paper to protect surfaces during painting.

17) Calculate amounts of required materials and estimate costs, based on surface measurements and/or work orders.

18) Bake finishes on painted and enameled articles, using baking ovens.

47-2142.00 - Paperhangers

Cover interior walls and ceilings of rooms with decorative wallpaper or fabric, or attach advertising posters on surfaces, such as walls and billboards. Duties include removing old materials from surface to be papered.

Tasks

1) Remove old paper, using water, steam machines, or solvents and scrapers.

2) Measure and cut strips from rolls of wallpaper or fabric, using shears or razors.

3) Cover interior walls and ceilings of rooms with decorative wallpaper or fabric, using hand tools.

4) Check finished wallcoverings for proper alignment, pattern matching, and neatness of seams.

5) Apply thinned glue to waterproof porous surfaces, using brushes, rollers, or pasting machines.

6) Staple or tack advertising posters onto fences, walls, billboards, or poles.

7) Apply sizing to seal surfaces and maximize adhesion of coverings to surfaces.

8) Mark vertical guidelines on walls to align strips, using plumb bobs and chalklines.

9) Place strips or sections of paper on surfaces, aligning section edges and patterns.

10) Measure surfaces and/or review work orders to estimate the quantities of materials needed.

11) Remove paint, varnish, dirt, and grease from surfaces, using paint remover and water soda solutions.

12) Set up equipment such as pasteboards and scaffolds.

13) Smooth strips or sections of paper with brushes or rollers to remove wrinkles and bubbles and to smooth joints.

14) Smooth rough spots on walls and ceilings, using sandpaper.

15) Trim excess material at ceilings or baseboards, using knives.

16) Trim rough edges from strips, using straightedges and trimming knives.

17) Apply acetic acid to damp plaster to prevent lime from bleeding through paper.

18) Mix paste, using paste powder and water, and brush paste onto surfaces.

19) Apply adhesives to the backs of paper strips, using brushes, or dunk strips of prepasted

wallcovering in water; wiping off any excess adhesive.

47-2151.00 - Pipelayers

Lay pipe for storm or sanitation sewers, drains, and water mains. Perform any combination of the following tasks: grade trenches or culverts, position pipe, or seal joints.

Tasks

1) Grade and level trench bases, using tamping machines and hand tools.

2) Train others in pipe-laying, and provide supervision.

3) Check slopes for conformance to requirements, using levels or lasers.

4) Connect pipe pieces and seal joints, using welding equipment, cement, or glue.

5) Cut pipes to required lengths.

6) Install and use instruments such as lasers, grade rods, and transit levels.

7) Lay out pipe routes, following written instructions or blueprints, and coordinating layouts with supervisors.

8) Cover pipes with earth or other materials.

9) Operate mechanized equipment such as pickup trucks, rollers, tandem dump trucks, front-end loaders, and backhoes.

10) Dig trenches to desired or required depths, by hand or using trenching tools.

11) Align and position pipes to prepare them for welding or sealing.

12) Locate existing pipes needing repair or replacement, using magnetic or radio indicators.

13) Install and repair sanitary and stormwater sewer structures and pipe systems.

47-2181.00 - Roofers

Cover roofs of structures with shingles, slate, asphalt, aluminum, wood, and related materials. May spray roofs, sidings, and walls with material to bind, seal, insulate, or soundproof sections of structures.

Tasks

1) Install, repair, or replace single-ply roofing systems, using waterproof sheet materials such as modified plastics, elastomeric, or other asphaltic compositions.

2) Cut roofing paper to size using knives; and nail or staple roofing paper to roofs in overlapping strips to form bases for other materials.

3) Apply gravel or pebbles over top layers of roofs, using rakes or stiff-bristled brooms.

4) Apply plastic coatings and membranes, fiberglass, or felt over sloped roofs before applying shingles.

5) Inspect problem roofs to determine the best procedures for repairing them.

6) Install partially overlapping layers of material over roof insulation surfaces, determining distance of roofing material overlap using chalklines, gauges on shingling hatchets, or lines on shingles.

7) Install vapor barriers and/or layers of insulation on the roof decks of flat roofs, and seal the seams.

8) Cut felt, shingles, and strips of flashing; and fit them into angles formed by walls, vents, and intersecting roof surfaces.

9) Set up scaffolding to provide safe access to roofs.

10) Cover exposed nailheads with roofing cement or caulking to prevent water leakage and rust.

11) Align roofing materials with edges of roofs.

12) Mop or pour hot asphalt or tar onto roof bases.

13) Spray roofs, sidings, and walls with material to bind, seal, insulate, or soundproof sections of structures, using spray guns, air compressors, and heaters.

14) Glaze top layers to make a smooth finish, or embed gravel in the bitumen for rough surfaces.

15) Clean and maintain equipment.

16) Estimate roofing materials and labor required to complete jobs, and provide price quotes.

17) Waterproof and damp-proof walls, floors, roofs, foundations, and basements by painting or spraying surfaces with waterproof coatings, or by attaching waterproofing membranes to surfaces.

18) Remove snow, water, or debris from roofs prior to applying roofing materials.

19) Hammer and chisel away rough spots or remove them with rubbing bricks to prepare surfaces for waterproofing.

20) Cover roofs and exterior walls of structures with slate, asphalt, aluminum, wood, gravel, gypsum, and/or related materials, using brushes, knives, punches, hammers and other tools.

21) Cement or nail flashing-strips of metal or shingle over joints to make them watertight.

22) Apply alternate layers of hot asphalt or tar and roofing paper to roofs, according to specification.

47-2211.00 - Sheet Metal Workers

Fabricate, assemble, install, and repair sheet metal products and equipment, such as ducts, control boxes, drainpipes, and furnace casings. Work may involve any of the following: setting up and operating fabricating machines to cut, bend, and straighten sheet metal; shaping metal over anvils, blocks, or forms using hammer operating soldering and welding equipment to join sheet metal parts inspecting, assembling, and smoothing seams and joints of burred surfaces.

Tasks

1) Lay out, measure, and mark dimensions and reference lines on material, such as roofing panels, according to drawings or templates, using calculators, scribes, dividers, squares, and rulers.

2) Fasten seams and joints together with welds, bolts, cement, rivets, solder, caulks, metal drive clips, and bonds in order to assemble components into products or to repair sheet metal items.

3) Determine project requirements, including scope, assembly sequences, and required methods and materials, according to blueprints, drawings, and written or verbal instructions.

4) Install assemblies, such as flashing, pipes, tubes, heating and air conditioning ducts, furnace casings, rain gutters, and down spouts, in supportive frameworks.

5) Trim, file, grind, deburr, buff, and smooth surfaces, seams, and joints of assembled parts, using hand tools and portable power tools.

6) Maintain equipment, making repairs and modifications when necessary.

7) Fabricate or alter parts at construction sites, using shears, hammers, punches, and drills.

8) Maneuver completed units into position for installation, and anchor the units.

9) Shape metal material over anvils, blocks, or other forms, using hand tools.

10) Finish parts, using hacksaws, and hand, rotary, or squaring shears.

11) Transport prefabricated parts to construction sites for assembly and installation.

12) Select gauges and types of sheet metal or non-metallic material, according to product specifications.

13) Convert blueprints into shop drawings to be followed in the construction and assembly of sheet metal products.

14) Inspect individual parts, assemblies, and installations for conformance to specifications and building codes, using measuring instruments such as calipers, scales, and micrometers.

15) Develop and lay out patterns that use materials most efficiently, using computerized metalworking equipment to experiment with different layouts.

16) Fasten roof panel edges and machine-made molding to structures, nailing or welding pieces into place.

17) Secure metal roof panels in place, then interlock and fasten grooved panel edges.

Knowledge	Knowledge Definitions
Mechanical	Knowledge of machines and tools, including their designs, uses, repair, and maintenance.
Mathematics	Knowledge of arithmetic, algebra, geometry, calculus, statistics, and their applications.
Building and Construction	Knowledge of materials, methods, and the tools involved in the construction or repair of houses, buildings, or other structures such as highways and roads.
Design	Knowledge of design techniques, tools, and principles involved in production of precision technical plans, blueprints, drawings, and models.
Production and Processing	Knowledge of raw materials, production processes, quality control, costs, and other techniques for maximizing the effective manufacture and distribution of goods.
Customer and Personal Service	Knowledge of principles and processes for providing customer and personal services. This includes customer needs assessment, meeting quality standards for services, and evaluation of customer satisfaction.
English Language	Knowledge of the structure and content of the English language including the meaning and spelling of words, rules of composition, and grammar.
Physics	Knowledge and prediction of physical principles, laws, their interrelationships, and applications to understanding fluid, material, and atmospheric dynamics, and mechanical, electrical, atomic and sub-atomic structures and processes.
Administration and Management	Knowledge of business and management principles involved in strategic planning, resource allocation, human resources modeling, leadership technique, production methods, and coordination of people and resources.
Engineering and Technology	Knowledge of the practical application of engineering science and technology. This includes applying principles, techniques, procedures, and equipment to the design and production of various goods and services.
Education and Training	Knowledge of principles and methods for curriculum and training design, teaching and instruction for individuals and groups, and the measurement of training effects.
Public Safety and Security	Knowledge of relevant equipment, policies, procedures, and strategies to promote effective local, state, or national security operations for the protection of people, data, property, and institutions.
Computers and Electronics	Knowledge of circuit boards, processors, chips, electronic equipment, and computer hardware and software, including applications and programming.
Personnel and Human Resources	Knowledge of principles and procedures for personnel recruitment, selection, training, compensation and benefits, labor relations and negotiation, and personnel information systems.
Transportation	Knowledge of principles and methods for moving people or goods by air, rail, sea, or road, including the relative costs and benefits.
Economics and Accounting	Knowledge of economic and accounting principles and practices, the financial markets, banking and the analysis and reporting of financial data.
Telecommunications	Knowledge of transmission, broadcasting, switching, control, and operation of telecommunications systems.
Chemistry	Knowledge of the chemical composition, structure, and properties of substances and of the chemical processes and transformations that they undergo. This includes uses of chemicals and their interactions, danger signs, production techniques, and disposal methods.
Sales and Marketing	Knowledge of principles and methods for showing, promoting, and selling products or services. This includes marketing strategy and tactics, product demonstration, sales techniques, and sales control systems.
Law and Government	Knowledge of laws, legal codes, court procedures, precedents, government regulations, executive orders, agency rules, and the democratic political process.
Geography	Knowledge of principles and methods for describing the features of land, sea, and air masses, including their physical characteristics, locations, interrelationships, and distribution of plant, animal, and human life.
Clerical	Knowledge of administrative and clerical procedures and systems such as word processing, managing files and records, stenography and transcription, designing forms, and other office procedures and terminology.
Psychology	Knowledge of human behavior and performance; individual differences in ability, personality, and interests; learning and motivation; psychological research methods; and the assessment and treatment of behavioral and affective disorders.
Communications and Media	Knowledge of media production, communication, and dissemination techniques and methods. This includes alternative ways to inform and entertain via written, oral, and visual media.
Therapy and Counseling	Knowledge of principles, methods, and procedures for diagnosis, treatment, and rehabilitation of physical and mental dysfunctions, and for career counseling and guidance.

Medicine and Dentistry	Knowledge of the information and techniques needed to diagnose and treat human injuries, diseases, and deformities. This includes symptoms, treatment alternatives, drug properties and interactions, and preventive health-care measures.
Fine Arts	Knowledge of the theory and techniques required to compose, produce, and perform works of music, dance, visual arts, drama, and sculpture.
Biology	Knowledge of plant and animal organisms, their tissues, cells, functions, interdependencies, and interactions with each other and the environment.
History and Archeology	Knowledge of historical events and their causes, indicators, and effects on civilizations and cultures.
Food Production	Knowledge of techniques and equipment for planting, growing, and harvesting food products (both plant and animal) for consumption, including storage/handling techniques.
Foreign Language	Knowledge of the structure and content of a foreign (non-English) language including the meaning and spelling of words, rules of composition and grammar, and pronunciation.
Sociology and Anthropology	Knowledge of group behavior and dynamics, societal trends and influences, human migrations, ethnicity, cultures and their history and origins.
Philosophy and Theology	Knowledge of different philosophical systems and religions. This includes their basic principles, values, ethics, ways of thinking, customs, practices, and their impact on human culture.

Skills	Skills Definitions
Mathematics	Using mathematics to solve problems.
Active Listening	Giving full attention to what other people are saying, taking time to understand the points being made, asking questions as appropriate, and not interrupting at inappropriate times.
Installation	Installing equipment, machines, wiring, or programs to meet specifications.
Equipment Selection	Determining the kind of tools and equipment needed to do a job.
Instructing	Teaching others how to do something.
Coordination	Adjusting actions in relation to others' actions.
Writing	Communicating effectively in writing as appropriate for the needs of the audience.
Critical Thinking	Using logic and reasoning to identify the strengths and weaknesses of alternative solutions, conclusions or approaches to problems.
Reading Comprehension	Understanding written sentences and paragraphs in work related documents.
Speaking	Talking to others to convey information effectively.
Active Learning	Understanding the implications of new information for both current and future problem-solving and decision-making.
Judgment and Decision Making	Considering the relative costs and benefits of potential actions to choose the most appropriate one.
Learning Strategies	Selecting and using training/instructional methods and procedures appropriate for the situation when learning or teaching new things.
Equipment Maintenance	Performing routine maintenance on equipment and determining when and what kind of maintenance is needed.
Time Management	Managing one's own time and the time of others.
Troubleshooting	Determining causes of operating errors and deciding what to do about it.
Monitoring	Monitoring/Assessing performance of yourself, other individuals, or organizations to make improvements or take corrective action.
Management of Material Resources	Obtaining and seeing to the appropriate use of equipment, facilities, and materials needed to do certain work.
Technology Design	Generating or adapting equipment and technology to serve user needs.
Persuasion	Persuading others to change their minds or behavior.
Service Orientation	Actively looking for ways to help people.
Repairing	Repairing machines or systems using the needed tools.
Complex Problem Solving	Identifying complex problems and reviewing related information to develop and evaluate options and implement solutions.
Negotiation	Bringing others together and trying to reconcile differences.
Social Perceptiveness	Being aware of others' reactions and understanding why they react as they do.
Quality Control Analysis	Conducting tests and inspections of products, services, or processes to evaluate quality or performance.

Systems Analysis	Determining how a system should work and how changes in conditions, operations, and the environment will affect outcomes.
Systems Evaluation	Identifying measures or indicators of system performance and the actions needed to improve or correct performance, relative to the goals of the system.
Management of Personnel Resources	Motivating, developing, and directing people as they work, identifying the best people for the job.
Science	Using scientific rules and methods to solve problems.
Operation and Control	Controlling operations of equipment or systems.
Operations Analysis	Analyzing needs and product requirements to create a design.
Operation Monitoring	Watching gauges, dials, or other indicators to make sure a machine is working properly.
Programming	Writing computer programs for various purposes.
Management of Financial Resources	Determining how money will be spent to get the work done, and accounting for these expenditures.

Ability	Ability Definitions
Near Vision	The ability to see details at close range (within a few feet of the observer).
Manual Dexterity	The ability to quickly move your hand, your hand together with your arm, or your two hands to grasp, manipulate, or assemble objects.
Selective Attention	The ability to concentrate on a task over a period of time without being distracted.
Oral Comprehension	The ability to listen to and understand information and ideas presented through spoken words and sentences.
Information Ordering	The ability to arrange things or actions in a certain order or pattern according to a specific rule or set of rules (e.g., patterns of numbers, letters, words, pictures, mathematical operations).
Problem Sensitivity	The ability to tell when something is wrong or is likely to go wrong. It does not involve solving the problem, only recognizing there is a problem.
Static Strength	The ability to exert maximum muscle force to lift, push, pull, or carry objects.
Arm-Hand Steadiness	The ability to keep your hand and arm steady while moving your arm or while holding your arm and hand in one position.
Control Precision	The ability to quickly and repeatedly adjust the controls of a machine or a vehicle to exact positions.
Visualization	The ability to imagine how something will look after it is moved around or when its parts are moved or rearranged.
Deductive Reasoning	The ability to apply general rules to specific problems to produce answers that make sense.
Oral Expression	The ability to communicate information and ideas in speaking so others will understand.
Dynamic Strength	The ability to exert muscle force repeatedly or continuously over time. This involves muscular endurance and resistance to muscle fatigue.
Finger Dexterity	The ability to make precisely coordinated movements of the fingers of one or both hands to grasp, manipulate, or assemble very small objects.
Written Comprehension	The ability to read and understand information and ideas presented in writing.
Trunk Strength	The ability to use your abdominal and lower back muscles to support part of the body repeatedly or continuously over time without 'giving out' or fatiguing.
Speech Recognition	The ability to identify and understand the speech of another person.
Inductive Reasoning	The ability to combine pieces of information to form general rules or conclusions (includes finding a relationship among seemingly unrelated events).
Perceptual Speed	The ability to quickly and accurately compare similarities and differences among sets of letters, numbers, objects, pictures, or patterns. The things to be compared may be presented at the same time or one after the other. This ability also includes comparing a presented object with a remembered object.
Speech Clarity	The ability to speak clearly so others can understand you.
Extent Flexibility	The ability to bend, stretch, twist, or reach with your body, arms, and/or legs.
Category Flexibility	The ability to generate or use different sets of rules for combining or grouping things in different ways.
Multilimb Coordination	The ability to coordinate two or more limbs (for example, two arms, two legs, or one leg and one arm) while sitting, standing, or lying down. It does not involve performing the activities while the whole body is in motion.
Gross Body Equilibrium	The ability to keep or regain your body balance or stay upright when in an unstable position.

Written Expression	The ability to communicate information and ideas in writing so others will understand.
Gross Body Coordination	The ability to coordinate the movement of your arms, legs, and torso together when the whole body is in motion.
Originality	The ability to come up with unusual or clever ideas about a given topic or situation, or to develop creative ways to solve a problem.
Stamina	The ability to exert yourself physically over long periods of time without getting winded or out of breath.
Far Vision	The ability to see details at a distance.
Auditory Attention	The ability to focus on a single source of sound in the presence of other distracting sounds.
Depth Perception	The ability to judge which of several objects is closer or farther away from you, or to judge the distance between you and an object.
Fluency of Ideas	The ability to come up with a number of ideas about a topic (the number of ideas is important, not their quality, correctness, or creativity).
Time Sharing	The ability to shift back and forth between two or more activities or sources of information (such as speech, sounds, touch, or other sources).
Reaction Time	The ability to quickly respond (with the hand, finger, or foot) to a signal (sound, light, picture) when it appears.
Speed of Limb Movement	The ability to quickly move the arms and legs.
Flexibility of Closure	The ability to identify or detect a known pattern (a figure, object, word, or sound) that is hidden in other distracting material.
Explosive Strength	The ability to use short bursts of muscle force to propel oneself (as in jumping or sprinting), or to throw an object.
Response Orientation	The ability to choose quickly between two or more movements in response to two or more different signals (lights, sounds, pictures). It includes the speed with which the correct response is started with the hand, foot, or other body part.
Number Facility	The ability to add, subtract, multiply, or divide quickly and correctly.
Speed of Closure	The ability to quickly make sense of, combine, and organize information into meaningful patterns.
Visual Color Discrimination	The ability to match or detect differences between colors, including shades of color and brightness.
Mathematical Reasoning	The ability to choose the right mathematical methods or formulas to solve a problem.
Memorization	The ability to remember information such as words, numbers, pictures, and procedures.
Glare Sensitivity	The ability to see objects in the presence of glare or bright lighting.
Rate Control	The ability to time your movements or the movement of a piece of equipment in anticipation of changes in the speed and/or direction of a moving object or scene.
Spatial Orientation	The ability to know your location in relation to the environment or to know where other objects are in relation to you.
Wrist-Finger Speed	The ability to make fast, simple, repeated movements of the fingers, hands, and wrists.
Hearing Sensitivity	The ability to detect or tell the differences between sounds that vary in pitch and loudness.
Peripheral Vision	The ability to see objects or movement of objects to one's side when the eyes are looking ahead.
Dynamic Flexibility	The ability to quickly and repeatedly bend, stretch, twist, or reach out with your body, arms, and/or legs.
Night Vision	The ability to see under low light conditions.
Sound Localization	The ability to tell the direction from which a sound originated.

Work_Activity	**Work_Activity Definitions**
Handling and Moving Objects	Using hands and arms in handling, installing, positioning, and moving materials, and manipulating things.
Performing General Physical Activities	Performing physical activities that require considerable use of your arms and legs and moving your whole body, such as climbing, lifting, balancing, walking, stooping, and handling of materials.
Inspecting Equipment, Structures, or Material	Inspecting equipment, structures, or materials to identify the cause of errors or other problems or defects.
Making Decisions and Solving Problems	Analyzing information and evaluating results to choose the best solution and solve problems.
Getting Information	Observing, receiving, and otherwise obtaining information from all relevant sources.
Communicating with Supervisors, Peers, or Subordin	Providing information to supervisors, co-workers, and subordinates by telephone, in written form, e-mail, or in person.

Identifying Objects, Actions, and Events	Identifying information by categorizing, estimating, recognizing differences or similarities, and detecting changes in circumstances or events.
Controlling Machines and Processes	Using either control mechanisms or direct physical activity to operate machines or processes (not including computers or vehicles).
Operating Vehicles, Mechanized Devices, or Equipme	Running, maneuvering, navigating, or driving vehicles or mechanized equipment, such as forklifts, passenger vehicles, aircraft, or water craft.
Thinking Creatively	Developing, designing, or creating new applications, ideas, relationships, systems, or products, including artistic contributions.
Training and Teaching Others	Identifying the educational needs of others, developing formal educational or training programs or classes, and teaching or instructing others.
Organizing, Planning, and Prioritizing Work	Developing specific goals and plans to prioritize, organize, and accomplish your work.
Drafting, Laying Out, and Specifying Technical Dev	Providing documentation, detailed instructions, drawings, or specifications to tell others about how devices, parts, equipment, or structures are to be fabricated, constructed, assembled, modified, maintained, or used.
Monitor Processes, Materials, or Surroundings	Monitoring and reviewing information from materials, events, or the environment, to detect or assess problems.
Updating and Using Relevant Knowledge	Keeping up-to-date technically and applying new knowledge to your job.
Judging the Qualities of Things, Services, or Peop	Assessing the value, importance, or quality of things or people.
Evaluating Information to Determine Compliance wit	Using relevant information and individual judgment to determine whether events or processes comply with laws, regulations, or standards.
Coaching and Developing Others	Identifying the developmental needs of others and coaching, mentoring, or otherwise helping others to improve their knowledge or skills.
Coordinating the Work and Activities of Others	Getting members of a group to work together to accomplish tasks.
Repairing and Maintaining Mechanical Equipment	Servicing, repairing, adjusting, and testing machines, devices, moving parts, and equipment that operate primarily on the basis of mechanical (not electronic) principles.
Guiding, Directing, and Motivating Subordinates	Providing guidance and direction to subordinates, including setting performance standards and monitoring performance.
Establishing and Maintaining Interpersonal Relatio	Developing constructive and cooperative working relationships with others, and maintaining them over time.
Communicating with Persons Outside Organization	Communicating with people outside the organization, representing the organization to customers, the public, government, and other external sources. This information can be exchanged in person, in writing, or by telephone or e-mail.
Estimating the Quantifiable Characteristics of Pro	Estimating sizes, distances, and quantities; or determining time, costs, resources, or materials needed to perform a work activity.
Interpreting the Meaning of Information for Others	Translating or explaining what information means and how it can be used.
Processing Information	Compiling, coding, categorizing, calculating, tabulating, auditing, or verifying information or data.
Developing Objectives and Strategies	Establishing long-range objectives and specifying the strategies and actions to achieve them.
Developing and Building Teams	Encouraging and building mutual trust, respect, and cooperation among team members.
Assisting and Caring for Others	Providing personal assistance, medical attention, emotional support, or other personal care to others such as coworkers, customers, or patients.
Scheduling Work and Activities	Scheduling events, programs, and activities, as well as the work of others.
Performing for or Working Directly with the Public	Performing for people or dealing directly with the public. This includes serving customers in restaurants and stores, and receiving clients or guests.
Resolving Conflicts and Negotiating with Others	Handling complaints, settling disputes, and resolving grievances and conflicts, or otherwise negotiating with others.
Documenting/Recording Information	Entering, transcribing, recording, storing, or maintaining information in written or electronic/magnetic form.
Analyzing Data or Information	Identifying the underlying principles, reasons, or facts of information by breaking down information or data into separate parts.
Provide Consultation and Advice to Others	Providing guidance and expert advice to management or other groups on technical, systems-, or process-related topics.
Monitoring and Controlling Resources	Monitoring and controlling resources and overseeing the spending of money.

Performing Administrative Activities	Performing day-to-day administrative tasks such as maintaining information files and processing paperwork.
Interacting With Computers	Using computers and computer systems (including hardware and software) to program, write software, set up functions, enter data, or process information.
Selling or Influencing Others	Convincing others to buy merchandise/goods or to otherwise change their minds or actions.
Repairing and Maintaining Electronic Equipment	Servicing, repairing, calibrating, regulating, fine-tuning, or testing machines, devices, and equipment that operate primarily on the basis of electrical or electronic (not mechanical) principles.
Staffing Organizational Units	Recruiting, interviewing, selecting, hiring, and promoting employees in an organization.

Work_Context	Work_Context Definitions
Wear Common Protective or Safety Equipment such as	How much does this job require wearing common protective or safety equipment such as safety shoes, glasses, gloves, hard hats or live jackets?
Face-to-Face Discussions	How often do you have to have face-to-face discussions with individuals or teams in this job?
Sounds, Noise Levels Are Distracting or Uncomforta	How often does this job require working exposed to sounds and noise levels that are distracting or uncomfortable?
Contact With Others	How much does this job require the worker to be in contact with others (face-to-face, by telephone, or otherwise) in order to perform it?
Spend Time Standing	How much does this job require standing?
Spend Time Using Your Hands to Handle, Control, or	How much does this job require using your hands to handle, control, or feel objects, tools or controls?
Exposed to Hazardous Equipment	How often does this job require exposure to hazardous equipment?
Importance of Being Exact or Accurate	How important is being very exact or highly accurate in performing this job?
Work With Work Group or Team	How important is it to work with others in a group or team in this job?
Freedom to Make Decisions	How much decision making freedom, without supervision, does the job offer?
Exposed to Minor Burns, Cuts, Bites, or Stings	How often does this job require exposure to minor burns, cuts, bites, or stings?
Time Pressure	How often does this job require the worker to meet strict deadlines?
Telephone	How often do you have telephone conversations in this job?
Frequency of Decision Making	How frequently is the worker required to make decisions that affect other people, the financial resources, and/or the image and reputation of the organization?
Exposed to Contaminants	How often does this job require working exposed to contaminants (such as pollutants, gases, dust or odors)?
Structured versus Unstructured Work	To what extent is this job structured for the worker, rather than allowing the worker to determine tasks, priorities, and goals?
Responsibility for Outcomes and Results	How responsible is the worker for work outcomes and results of other workers?
Outdoors, Exposed to Weather	How often does this job require working outdoors, exposed to all weather conditions?
Indoors, Not Environmentally Controlled	How often does this job require working indoors in non-controlled environmental conditions (e.g., warehouse without heat)?
Responsible for Others' Health and Safety	How much responsibility is there for the health and safety of others in this job?
Very Hot or Cold Temperatures	How often does this job require working in very hot (above 90 F degrees) or very cold (below 32 F degrees) temperatures?
Impact of Decisions on Co-workers or Company Resul	How do the decisions an employee makes impact the results of co-workers, clients or the company?
Physical Proximity	To what extent does this job require the worker to perform job tasks in close physical proximity to other people?
Extremely Bright or Inadequate Lighting	How often does this job require working in extremely bright or inadequate lighting conditions?
Spend Time Walking and Running	How much does this job require walking and running?
Consequence of Error	How serious would the result usually be if the worker made a mistake that was not readily correctable?
Spend Time Bending or Twisting the Body	How much does this job require bending or twisting your body?
Coordinate or Lead Others	How important is it to coordinate or lead others in accomplishing work activities in this job?
Level of Competition	To what extent does this job require the worker to compete or to be aware of competitive pressures?

Exposed to High Places	How often does this job require exposure to high places?
Deal With External Customers	How important is it to work with external customers or the public in this job?
Cramped Work Space, Awkward Positions	How often does this job require working in cramped work spaces that requires getting into awkward positions?
Importance of Repeating Same Tasks	How important is repeating the same physical activities (e.g., key entry) or mental activities (e.g., checking entries in a ledger) over and over, without stopping, to performing this job?
Frequency of Conflict Situations	How often are there conflict situations the employee has to face in this job?
Indoors, Environmentally Controlled	How often does this job require working indoors in environmentally controlled conditions?
Spend Time Making Repetitive Motions	How much does this job require making repetitive motions?
Letters and Memos	How often does the job require written letters and memos?
In an Enclosed Vehicle or Equipment	How often does this job require working in a closed vehicle or equipment (e.g., car)?
Outdoors, Under Cover	How often does this job require working outdoors, under cover (e.g., structure with roof but no walls)?
Deal With Unpleasant or Angry People	How frequently does the worker have to deal with unpleasant, angry, or discourteous individuals as part of the job requirements?
Spend Time Kneeling, Crouching, Stooping, or Crawl	How much does this job require kneeling, crouching, stooping, or crawling?
Spend Time Climbing Ladders, Scaffolds, or Poles	How much does this job require climbing ladders, scaffolds, or poles?
Pace Determined by Speed of Equipment	How important is it to this job that the pace is determined by the speed of equipment or machinery? (This does not refer to keeping busy at all times on this job.)
In an Open Vehicle or Equipment	How often does this job require working in an open vehicle or equipment (e.g., tractor)?
Spend Time Keeping or Regaining Balance	How much does this job require keeping or regaining your balance?
Wear Specialized Protective or Safety Equipment su	How much does this job require wearing specialized protective or safety equipment such as breathing apparatus, safety harness, full protection suits, or radiation protection?
Degree of Automation	How automated is the job?
Exposed to Hazardous Conditions	How often does this job require exposure to hazardous conditions?
Public Speaking	How often do you have to perform public speaking in this job?
Exposed to Whole Body Vibration	How often does this job require exposure to whole body vibration (e.g., operate a jackhammer)?
Electronic Mail	How often do you use electronic mail in this job?
Spend Time Sitting	How much does this job require sitting?
Deal With Physically Aggressive People	How frequently does this job require the worker to deal with physical aggression of violent individuals?
Exposed to Disease or Infections	How often does this job require exposure to disease/infections?
Exposed to Radiation	How often does this job require exposure to radiation?

Job Zone Component	Job Zone Component Definitions
Title	Job Zone Two: Some Preparation Needed
Overall Experience	Some previous work-related skill, knowledge, or experience may be helpful in these occupations, but usually is not needed. For example, a drywall installer might benefit from experience installing drywall, but an inexperienced person could still learn to be an installer with little difficulty.
Job Training	Employees in these occupations need anywhere from a few months to one year of working with experienced employees.
Job Zone Examples	These occupations often involve using your knowledge and skills to help others. Examples include drywall installers, fire inspectors, flight attendants, pharmacy technicians, salespersons (retail), and tellers.
SVP Range	(4.0 to < 6.0)
Education	These occupations usually require a high school diploma and may require some vocational training or job-related course work. In some cases, an associate's or bachelor's degree could be needed.

Work_Styles	Work_Styles Definitions
Dependability	Job requires being reliable, responsible, and dependable, and fulfilling obligations.

Attention to Detail	Job requires being careful about detail and thorough in completing work tasks.
Cooperation	Job requires being pleasant with others on the job and displaying a good-natured, cooperative attitude.
Initiative	Job requires a willingness to take on responsibilities and challenges.
Self Control	Job requires maintaining composure, keeping emotions in check, controlling anger, and avoiding aggressive behavior, even in very difficult situations.
Integrity	Job requires being honest and ethical.
Independence	Job requires developing one's own ways of doing things, guiding oneself with little or no supervision, and depending on oneself to get things done.
Analytical Thinking	Job requires analyzing information and using logic to address work-related issues and problems.
Stress Tolerance	Job requires accepting criticism and dealing calmly and effectively with high stress situations.
Achievement/Effort	Job requires establishing and maintaining personally challenging achievement goals and exerting effort toward mastering tasks.
Persistence	Job requires persistence in the face of obstacles.
Innovation	Job requires creativity and alternative thinking to develop new ideas for and answers to work-related problems.
Leadership	Job requires a willingness to lead, take charge, and offer opinions and direction.
Concern for Others	Job requires being sensitive to others' needs and feelings and being understanding and helpful on the job.
Adaptability/Flexibility	Job requires being open to change (positive or negative) and to considerable variety in the workplace.
Social Orientation	Job requires preferring to work with others rather than alone, and being personally connected with others on the job.

47-3011.00 - Helpers--Brickmasons, Blockmasons, Stonemasons, and Tile and Marble Setters

Help brickmasons, blockmasons, stonemasons, or tile and marble setters by performing duties of lesser skill. Duties include using, supplying or holding materials or tools, and cleaning work area and equipment.

Tasks

1) Apply caulk, sealants, or other agents to installed surfaces.

2) Apply grout between joints of bricks or tiles, using grouting trowels.

3) Erect scaffolding or other installation structures.

4) Provide assistance in the preparation, installation, repair, and/or rebuilding of tile, brick, or stone surfaces.

5) Remove damaged tile, brick, or mortar, and clean and prepare surfaces, using pliers, hammers, chisels, drills, wire brushes, and metal wire anchors.

6) Mix mortar, plaster, and grout, manually or using machines, according to standard formulas.

7) Arrange and store materials, machines, tools, and equipment.

8) Correct surface imperfections or fill chipped, cracked or broken bricks or tiles, using fillers, adhesives, and grouting materials.

9) Transport materials, tools, and machines to installation sites, manually or using conveyance equipment.

10) Select or locate and supply materials to masons for installation, following drawings or numbered sequences.

11) Remove excess grout and residue from tile or brick joints, using sponges or trowels.

12) Move or position materials such as marble slabs, using cranes, hoists, or dollies.

13) Clean installation surfaces, equipment, tools, work sites, and storage areas, using water, chemical solutions, oxygen lances, or polishing machines.

14) Cut materials to specified sizes for installation, using power saws or tile cutters.

47-3014.00 - Helpers--Painters, Paperhangers, Plasterers, and Stucco Masons

Help painters, paperhangers, plasterers, or stucco masons by performing duties of lesser skill. Duties include using, supplying or holding materials or tools, and cleaning work area and equipment.

Tasks

1) Remove articles such as cabinets, metal furniture, and paint containers from stripping tanks after prescribed periods of time.

2) Pour specified amounts of chemical solutions into stripping tanks.

3) Place articles to be stripped into stripping tanks.

4) Supply or hold tools and materials.

5) Smooth surfaces of articles to be painted, using sanding and buffing tools and equipment.

6) Perform support duties to assist painters, paperhangers, plasterers, or masons.

7) Mix plaster, and carry plaster to plasterers.

8) Fill cracks or breaks in surfaces of plaster articles or areas with putty or epoxy compounds.

9) Clean work areas and equipment.

10) Apply protective coverings such as masking tape to articles or areas that could be damaged or stained by work processes.

47-3016.00 - Helpers--Roofers

Help roofers by performing duties of lesser skill. Duties include using, supplying or holding materials or tools, and cleaning work area and equipment.

Tasks

1) Sweep and clean roofs to prepare them for the application of new roofing materials.

2) Unload materials and tools from work trucks, and unroll roofing as directed.

3) Apply shingles, gravel, or asphalt over the top layer of tar to protect the roofing material.

4) Set ladders, scaffolds, and hoists in place for taking supplies to roofs.

5) Attach sheets of metal to roof boards or building frameworks when installing metal roofs.

6) Clear drains and downspouts, and clean gutters.

7) Cover roofs with layers of roofing felt or asphalt strips before installing tile, slate, or composition materials.

8) Locate worn or torn areas in roofs.

9) Remove old roofing materials.

10) Hoist tar and roofing materials to roofs, using ropes and pulleys, or carry materials up ladders.

11) Provide assistance to skilled roofers installing and repairing roofs, flashings, and surfaces.

12) Maintain tools and equipment.

13) Clean work areas and equipment.

14) Chop tar into small pieces, and heat chopped tar in kettles.

15) Check to ensure that completed roofs are watertight.

16) Attach roofing paper and composition shingles, using nails.

17) Place tiles, nail them to roof boards, and cover nailheads with roofing cement.

47-4031.00 - Fence Erectors

Erect and repair metal and wooden fences and fence gates around highways, industrial establishments, residences, or farms, using hand and power tools.

Tasks

1) Set metal or wooden posts in upright positions in postholes.

2) Attach fence rail supports to posts, using hammers and pliers.

3) Attach rails or tension wire along bottoms of posts to form fencing frames.

4) Complete top fence rails of metal fences by connecting tube sections, using metal sleeves.

5) Construct and repair barriers, retaining walls, trellises, and other types of fences, walls, and gates.

6) Dig postholes, using spades, posthole diggers, or power-driven augers.

7) Erect alternate panel, basket weave, and louvered fences.

8) Establish the location for a fence, and gather information needed to ensure that there are no electric cables or water lines in the area.

9) Measure and lay out fence lines and mark posthole positions, following instructions, drawings, or specifications.

10) Make rails for fences, by sawing lumber or by cutting metal tubing to required lengths.

11) Align posts, using lines or by sighting, and verify vertical alignment of posts, using plumb bobs or spirit levels.

12) Blast rock formations and rocky areas with dynamite to facilitate posthole digging.

13) Discuss fencing needs with customers, and estimate and quote prices.

14) Stretch wire, wire mesh, or chain link fencing between posts, and attach fencing to frames.

15) Nail top and bottom rails to fence posts, or insert them in slots on posts.

16) Insert metal tubing through rail supports.

17) Weld metal parts together, using portable gas welding equipment.

18) Assemble gates, and fasten gates into position, using hand tools.

19) Nail pointed slats to rails to construct picket fences.

47-5013.00 - Service Unit Operators, Oil, Gas, and Mining

Operate equipment to increase oil flow from producing wells or to remove stuck pipe, casing, tools, or other obstructions from drilling wells. May also perform similar services in mining exploration operations.

Tasks

1) Confer with other personnel in order to gather information regarding pipe and tool sizes, and borehole conditions in wells.

2) Observe load variations on strain gauges, mud pumps, and motor pressure indicators; and listen to engines, rotary chains, and other equipment in order to detect faulty operations or unusual well conditions.

3) Drive truck-mounted units to well sites.

4) Thread cables through pulleys in derricks and connect hydraulic lines, using hand tools.

5) Close and seal wells no longer in use.

6) Install pressure-control devices onto well heads.

7) Operate controls that raise derricks and level rigs.

8) Quote prices to customers; and prepare reports of services rendered, tools used, and time required so that bills can be produced.

9) Analyze conditions of unserviceable wells in order to determine actions to be taken to improve well conditions.

10) Interpret instrument readings in order to ascertain the depth of obstruction.

11) Plan fishing methods and select tools for removing obstacles, such as liners, broken casing, screens, and drill pipe, from wells.

12) Direct lowering of specialized equipment to point of obstruction, and push switches or pull levers in order to back-off or sever pipes by chemical or explosive action.

13) Assemble and lower detection instruments into wells with obstructions.

14) Perforate well casings or sidewalls of boreholes with explosive charges.

15) Direct drilling crews performing such activities as assembling and connecting pipe, applying weights to drill pipes, and drilling around lodged obstacles.

16) Assemble and operate sound-wave generating and detecting mechanisms in order to determine well fluid levels.

Knowledge

Knowledge	Knowledge Definitions
Mechanical	Knowledge of machines and tools, including their designs, uses, repair, and maintenance.
Customer and Personal Service	Knowledge of principles and processes for providing customer and personal services. This includes customer needs assessment, meeting quality standards for services, and evaluation of customer satisfaction.
English Language	Knowledge of the structure and content of the English language including the meaning and spelling of words, rules of composition, and grammar.
Public Safety and Security	Knowledge of relevant equipment, policies, procedures, and strategies to promote effective local, state, or national security operations for the protection of people, data, property, and institutions.
Transportation	Knowledge of principles and methods for moving people or goods by air, rail, sea, or road, including the relative costs and benefits.
Administration and Management	Knowledge of business and management principles involved in strategic planning, resource allocation, human resources modeling, leadership technique, production methods, and coordination of people and resources.
Mathematics	Knowledge of arithmetic, algebra, geometry, calculus, statistics, and their applications.
Engineering and Technology	Knowledge of the practical application of engineering science and technology. This includes applying principles, techniques, procedures, and equipment to the design and production of various goods and services.
Physics	Knowledge and prediction of physical principles, laws, their interrelationships, and applications to understanding fluid, material, and atmospheric dynamics, and mechanical, electrical, atomic and sub-atomic structures and processes.
Computers and Electronics	Knowledge of circuit boards, processors, chips, electronic equipment, and computer hardware and software, including applications and programming.
Education and Training	Knowledge of principles and methods for curriculum and training design, teaching and instruction for individuals and groups, and the measurement of training effects.
Production and Processing	Knowledge of raw materials, production processes, quality control, costs, and other techniques for maximizing the effective manufacture and distribution of goods.
Law and Government	Knowledge of laws, legal codes, court procedures, precedents, government regulations, executive orders, agency rules, and the democratic political process.
Chemistry	Knowledge of the chemical composition, structure, and properties of substances and of the chemical processes and transformations that they undergo. This includes uses of chemicals and their interactions, danger signs, production techniques, and disposal methods.
Psychology	Knowledge of human behavior and performance; individual differences in ability, personality, and interests; learning and motivation; psychological research methods; and the assessment and treatment of behavioral and affective disorders.
Telecommunications	Knowledge of transmission, broadcasting, switching, control, and operation of telecommunications systems.
Personnel and Human Resources	Knowledge of principles and procedures for personnel recruitment, selection, training, compensation and benefits, labor relations and negotiation, and personnel information systems.
Foreign Language	Knowledge of the structure and content of a foreign (non-English) language including the meaning and spelling of words, rules of composition and grammar, and pronunciation.
Building and Construction	Knowledge of materials, methods, and the tools involved in the construction or repair of houses, buildings, or other structures such as highways and roads.
Sales and Marketing	Knowledge of principles and methods for showing, promoting, and selling products or services. This includes marketing strategy and tactics, product demonstration, sales techniques, and sales control systems.
Clerical	Knowledge of administrative and clerical procedures and systems such as word processing, managing files and records, stenography and transcription, designing forms, and other office procedures and terminology.
Design	Knowledge of design techniques, tools, and principles involved in production of precision technical plans, blueprints, drawings, and models.
Geography	Knowledge of principles and methods for describing the features of land, sea, and air masses, including their physical characteristics, locations, interrelationships, and distribution of plant, animal, and human life.

Economics and Accounting	Knowledge of economic and accounting principles and practices, the financial markets, banking and the analysis and reporting of financial data.
Communications and Media	Knowledge of media production, communication, and dissemination techniques and methods. This includes alternative ways to inform and entertain via written, oral, and visual media.
Sociology and Anthropology	Knowledge of group behavior and dynamics, societal trends and influences, human migrations, ethnicity, cultures and their history and origins.
Medicine and Dentistry	Knowledge of the information and techniques needed to diagnose and treat human injuries, diseases, and deformities. This includes symptoms, treatment alternatives, drug properties and interactions, and preventive health-care measures.
Therapy and Counseling	Knowledge of principles, methods, and procedures for diagnosis, treatment, and rehabilitation of physical and mental dysfunctions, and for career counseling and guidance.
Biology	Knowledge of plant and animal organisms, their tissues, cells, functions, interdependencies, and interactions with each other and the environment.
Philosophy and Theology	Knowledge of different philosophical systems and religions. This includes their basic principles, values, ethics, ways of thinking, customs, practices, and their impact on human culture.
Food Production	Knowledge of techniques and equipment for planting, growing, and harvesting food products (both plant and animal) for consumption, including storage/handling techniques.
History and Archeology	Knowledge of historical events and their causes, indicators, and effects on civilizations and cultures.
Fine Arts	Knowledge of the theory and techniques required to compose, produce, and perform works of music, dance, visual arts, drama, and sculpture.

Skills	Skills Definitions
Equipment Maintenance	Performing routine maintenance on equipment and determining when and what kind of maintenance is needed.
Active Listening	Giving full attention to what other people are saying, taking time to understand the points being made, asking questions as appropriate, and not interrupting at inappropriate times.
Operation Monitoring	Watching gauges, dials, or other indicators to make sure a machine is working properly.
Troubleshooting	Determining causes of operating errors and deciding what to do about it.
Equipment Selection	Determining the kind of tools and equipment needed to do a job.
Repairing	Repairing machines or systems using the needed tools.
Operation and Control	Controlling operations of equipment or systems.
Coordination	Adjusting actions in relation to others' actions.
Instructing	Teaching others how to do something.
Time Management	Managing one's own time and the time of others.
Judgment and Decision Making	Considering the relative costs and benefits of potential actions to choose the most appropriate one.
Active Learning	Understanding the implications of new information for both current and future problem-solving and decision-making.
Mathematics	Using mathematics to solve problems.
Speaking	Talking to others to convey information effectively.
Critical Thinking	Using logic and reasoning to identify the strengths and weaknesses of alternative solutions, conclusions or approaches to problems.
Reading Comprehension	Understanding written sentences and paragraphs in work related documents.
Installation	Installing equipment, machines, wiring, or programs to meet specifications.
Service Orientation	Actively looking for ways to help people.
Monitoring	Monitoring/Assessing performance of yourself, other individuals, or organizations to make improvements or take corrective action.
Complex Problem Solving	Identifying complex problems and reviewing related information to develop and evaluate options and implement solutions.
Writing	Communicating effectively in writing as appropriate for the needs of the audience.
Learning Strategies	Selecting and using training/instructional methods and procedures appropriate for the situation when learning or teaching new things.
Management of Material Resources	Obtaining and seeing to the appropriate use of equipment, facilities, and materials needed to do certain work.

Operations Analysis	Analyzing needs and product requirements to create a design.
Management of Personnel Resources	Motivating, developing, and directing people as they work, identifying the best people for the job.
Quality Control Analysis	Conducting tests and inspections of products, services, or processes to evaluate quality or performance.
Systems Analysis	Determining how a system should work and how changes in conditions, operations, and the environment will affect outcomes.
Persuasion	Persuading others to change their minds or behavior.
Social Perceptiveness	Being aware of others' reactions and understanding why they react as they do.
Negotiation	Bringing others together and trying to reconcile differences.
Systems Evaluation	Identifying measures or indicators of system performance and the actions needed to improve or correct performance, relative to the goals of the system.
Technology Design	Generating or adapting equipment and technology to serve user needs.
Science	Using scientific rules and methods to solve problems.
Management of Financial Resources	Determining how money will be spent to get the work done, and accounting for these expenditures.
Programming	Writing computer programs for various purposes.

Ability	Ability Definitions
Problem Sensitivity	The ability to tell when something is wrong or is likely to go wrong. It does not involve solving the problem, only recognizing there is a problem.
Control Precision	The ability to quickly and repeatedly adjust the controls of a machine or a vehicle to exact positions.
Multilimb Coordination	The ability to coordinate two or more limbs (for example, two arms, two legs, or one leg and one arm) while sitting, standing, or lying down. It does not involve performing the activities while the whole body is in motion.
Arm-Hand Steadiness	The ability to keep your hand and arm steady while moving your arm or while holding your arm and hand in one position.
Near Vision	The ability to see details at close range (within a few feet of the observer).
Hearing Sensitivity	The ability to detect or tell the differences between sounds that vary in pitch and loudness.
Depth Perception	The ability to judge which of several objects is closer or farther away from you, or to judge the distance between you and an object.
Reaction Time	The ability to quickly respond (with the hand, finger, or foot) to a signal (sound, light, picture) when it appears.
Inductive Reasoning	The ability to combine pieces of information to form general rules or conclusions (includes finding a relationship among seemingly unrelated events).
Selective Attention	The ability to concentrate on a task over a period of time without being distracted.
Speech Clarity	The ability to speak clearly so others can understand you.
Oral Expression	The ability to communicate information and ideas in speaking so others will understand.
Perceptual Speed	The ability to quickly and accurately compare similarities and differences among sets of letters, numbers, objects, pictures, or patterns. The things to be compared may be presented at the same time or one after the other. This ability also includes comparing a presented object with a remembered object.
Oral Comprehension	The ability to listen to and understand information and ideas presented through spoken words and sentences.
Speech Recognition	The ability to identify and understand the speech of another person.
Visual Color Discrimination	The ability to match or detect differences between colors, including shades of color and brightness.
Deductive Reasoning	The ability to apply general rules to specific problems to produce answers that make sense.
Far Vision	The ability to see details at a distance.
Manual Dexterity	The ability to quickly move your hand, your hand together with your arm, or your two hands to grasp, manipulate, or assemble objects.
Gross Body Equilibrium	The ability to keep or regain your body balance or stay upright when in an unstable position.
Written Comprehension	The ability to read and understand information and ideas presented in writing.
Auditory Attention	The ability to focus on a single source of sound in the presence of other distracting sounds.
Visualization	The ability to imagine how something will look after it is moved around or when its parts are moved or rearranged.

Information Ordering	The ability to arrange things or actions in a certain order or pattern according to a specific rule or set of rules (e.g., patterns of numbers, letters, words, pictures, mathematical operations).
Category Flexibility	The ability to generate or use different sets of rules for combining or grouping things in different ways.
Flexibility of Closure	The ability to identify or detect a known pattern (a figure, object, word, or sound) that is hidden in other distracting material.
Extent Flexibility	The ability to bend, stretch, twist, or reach with your body, arms, and/or legs.
Static Strength	The ability to exert maximum muscle force to lift, push, pull, or carry objects.
Written Expression	The ability to communicate information and ideas in writing so others will understand.
Trunk Strength	The ability to use your abdominal and lower back muscles to support part of the body repeatedly or continuously over time without 'giving out' or fatiguing.
Gross Body Coordination	The ability to coordinate the movement of your arms, legs, and torso together when the whole body is in motion.
Speed of Closure	The ability to quickly make sense of, combine, and organize information into meaningful patterns.
Response Orientation	The ability to choose quickly between two or more movements in response to two or more different signals (lights, sounds, pictures). It includes the speed with which the correct response is started with the hand, foot, or other body part.
Rate Control	The ability to time your movements or the movement of a piece of equipment in anticipation of changes in the speed and/or direction of a moving object or scene.
Time Sharing	The ability to shift back and forth between two or more activities or sources of information (such as speech, sounds, touch, or other sources).
Wrist-Finger Speed	The ability to make fast, simple, repeated movements of the fingers, hands, and wrists.
Speed of Limb Movement	The ability to quickly move the arms and legs.
Finger Dexterity	The ability to make precisely coordinated movements of the fingers of one or both hands to grasp, manipulate, or assemble very small objects.
Dynamic Strength	The ability to exert muscle force repeatedly or continuously over time. This involves muscular endurance and resistance to muscle fatigue.
Stamina	The ability to exert yourself physically over long periods of time without getting winded or out of breath.
Number Facility	The ability to add, subtract, multiply, or divide quickly and correctly.
Mathematical Reasoning	The ability to choose the right mathematical methods or formulas to solve a problem.
Spatial Orientation	The ability to know your location in relation to the environment or to know where other objects are in relation to you.
Originality	The ability to come up with unusual or clever ideas about a given topic or situation, or to develop creative ways to solve a problem.
Sound Localization	The ability to tell the direction from which a sound originated.
Memorization	The ability to remember information such as words, numbers, pictures, and procedures.
Fluency of Ideas	The ability to come up with a number of ideas about a topic (the number of ideas is important, not their quality, correctness, or creativity).
Glare Sensitivity	The ability to see objects in the presence of glare or bright lighting.
Night Vision	The ability to see under low light conditions.
Peripheral Vision	The ability to see objects or movement of objects to one's side when the eyes are looking ahead.
Explosive Strength	The ability to use short bursts of muscle force to propel oneself (as in jumping or sprinting), or to throw an object.
Dynamic Flexibility	The ability to quickly and repeatedly bend, stretch, twist, or reach out with your body, arms, and/or legs.

Work_Activity	Work_Activity Definitions
Operating Vehicles, Mechanized Devices, or Equipme	Running, maneuvering, navigating, or driving vehicles or mechanized equipment, such as forklifts, passenger vehicles, aircraft, or water craft.
Inspecting Equipment, Structures, or Material	Inspecting equipment, structures, or materials to identify the cause of errors or other problems or defects.
Getting Information	Observing, receiving, and otherwise obtaining information from all relevant sources.

Controlling Machines and Processes	Using either control mechanisms or direct physical activity to operate machines or processes (not including computers or vehicles).
Handling and Moving Objects	Using hands and arms in handling, installing, positioning, and moving materials, and manipulating things.
Communicating with Supervisors, Peers, or Subordin	Providing information to supervisors, co-workers, and subordinates by telephone, in written form, e-mail, or in person.
Repairing and Maintaining Mechanical Equipment	Servicing, repairing, adjusting, and testing machines, devices, moving parts, and equipment that operate primarily on the basis of mechanical (not electronic) principles.
Identifying Objects, Actions, and Events	Identifying information by categorizing, estimating, recognizing differences or similarities, and detecting changes in circumstances or events.
Performing General Physical Activities	Performing physical activities that require considerable use of your arms and legs and moving your whole body, such as climbing, lifting, balancing, walking, stooping, and handling of materials.
Monitor Processes, Materials, or Surroundings	Monitoring and reviewing information from materials, events, or the environment, to detect or assess problems.
Making Decisions and Solving Problems	Analyzing information and evaluating results to choose the best solution and solve problems.
Communicating with Persons Outside Organization	Communicating with people outside the organization, representing the organization to customers, the public, government, and other external sources. This information can be exchanged in person, in writing, or by telephone or e-mail.
Coordinating the Work and Activities of Others	Getting members of a group to work together to accomplish tasks.
Developing and Building Teams	Encouraging and building mutual trust, respect, and cooperation among team members.
Establishing and Maintaining Interpersonal Relatio	Developing constructive and cooperative working relationships with others, and maintaining them over time.
Updating and Using Relevant Knowledge	Keeping up-to-date technically and applying new knowledge to your job.
Training and Teaching Others	Identifying the educational needs of others, developing formal educational or training programs or classes, and teaching or instructing others.
Evaluating Information to Determine Compliance wit	Using relevant information and individual judgment to determine whether events or processes comply with laws, regulations, or standards.
Documenting/Recording Information	Entering, transcribing, recording, storing, or maintaining information in written or electronic/magnetic form.
Guiding, Directing, and Motivating Subordinates	Providing guidance and direction to subordinates, including setting performance standards and monitoring performance.
Judging the Qualities of Things, Services, or Peop	Assessing the value, importance, or quality of things or people.
Estimating the Quantifiable Characteristics of Pro	Estimating sizes, distances, and quantities; or determining time, costs, resources, or materials needed to perform a work activity.
Processing Information	Compiling, coding, categorizing, calculating, tabulating, auditing, or verifying information or data.
Analyzing Data or Information	Identifying the underlying principles, reasons, or facts of information by breaking down information or data into separate parts.
Coaching and Developing Others	Identifying the developmental needs of others and coaching, mentoring, or otherwise helping others to improve their knowledge or skills.
Performing Administrative Activities	Performing day-to-day administrative tasks such as maintaining information files and processing paperwork.
Organizing, Planning, and Prioritizing Work	Developing specific goals and plans to prioritize, organize, and accomplish your work.
Interacting With Computers	Using computers and computer systems (including hardware and software) to program, write software, set up functions, enter data, or process information.
Scheduling Work and Activities	Scheduling events, programs, and activities, as well as the work of others.
Resolving Conflicts and Negotiating with Others	Handling complaints, settling disputes, and resolving grievances and conflicts, or otherwise negotiating with others.
Monitoring and Controlling Resources	Monitoring and controlling resources and overseeing the spending of money.
Thinking Creatively	Developing, designing, or creating new applications, ideas, relationships, systems, or products, including artistic contributions.
Interpreting the Meaning of Information for Others	Translating or explaining what information means and how it can be used.

Provide Consultation and Advice to Others	Providing guidance and expert advice to management or other groups on technical, systems-, or process-related topics.
Developing Objectives and Strategies	Establishing long-range objectives and specifying the strategies and actions to achieve them.
Assisting and Caring for Others	Providing personal assistance, medical attention, emotional support, or other personal care to others such as coworkers, customers, or patients.
Drafting, Laying Out, and Specifying Technical Dev	Providing documentation, detailed instructions, drawings, or specifications to tell others about how devices, parts, equipment, or structures are to be fabricated, constructed, assembled, modified, maintained, or used.
Selling or Influencing Others	Convincing others to buy merchandise/goods or to otherwise change their minds or actions.
Repairing and Maintaining Electronic Equipment	Servicing, repairing, calibrating, regulating, fine-tuning, or testing machines, devices, and equipment that operate primarily on the basis of electrical or electronic (not mechanical) principles.
Staffing Organizational Units	Recruiting, interviewing, selecting, hiring, and promoting employees in an organization.
Performing for or Working Directly with the Public	Performing for people or dealing directly with the public. This includes serving customers in restaurants and stores, and receiving clients or guests.

Work_Context	Work_Context Definitions
Outdoors, Exposed to Weather	How often does this job require working outdoors, exposed to all weather conditions?
Wear Common Protective or Safety Equipment such as	How much does this job require wearing common protective or safety equipment such as safety shoes, glasses, gloves, hard hats or live jackets?
Face-to-Face Discussions	How often do you have to have face-to-face discussions with individuals or teams in this job?
Work With Work Group or Team	How important is it to work with others in a group or team in this job?
Exposed to Contaminants	How often does this job require working exposed to contaminants (such as pollutants, gases, dust or odors)?
Contact With Others	How much does this job require the worker to be in contact with others (face-to-face, by telephone, or otherwise) in order to perform it?
Sounds, Noise Levels Are Distracting or Uncomforta	How often does this job require working exposed to sounds and noise levels that are distracting or uncomfortable?
Responsible for Others' Health and Safety	How much responsibility is there for the health and safety of others in this job?
Telephone	How often do you have telephone conversations in this job?
Very Hot or Cold Temperatures	How often does this job require working in very hot (above 90 F degrees) or very cold (below 32 F degrees) temperatures?
Spend Time Using Your Hands to Handle, Control, or	How much does this job require using your hands to handle, control, or feel objects, tools or controls?
Exposed to Hazardous Conditions	How often does this job require exposure to hazardous conditions?
Frequency of Decision Making	How frequently is the worker required to make decisions that affect other people, the financial resources, and/or the image and reputation of the organization?
Importance of Being Exact or Accurate	How important is being very exact or highly accurate in performing this job?
Consequence of Error	How serious would the result usually be if the worker made a mistake that was not readily correctable?
Responsibility for Outcomes and Results	How responsible is the worker for work outcomes and results of other workers?
Exposed to Hazardous Equipment	How often does this job require exposure to hazardous equipment?
Impact of Decisions on Co-workers or Company Resul	How do the decisions an employee makes impact the results of co-workers, clients or the company?
In an Enclosed Vehicle or Equipment	How often does this job require working in a closed vehicle or equipment (e.g., car)?
Importance of Repeating Same Tasks	How important is repeating the same physical activities (e.g., key entry) or mental activities (e.g., checking entries in a ledger) over and over, without stopping, to performing this job?
Spend Time Making Repetitive Motions	How much does this job require making repetitive motions?
In an Open Vehicle or Equipment	How often does this job require working in an open vehicle or equipment (e.g., tractor)?
Indoors, Not Environmentally Controlled	How often does this job require working indoors in non-controlled environmental conditions (e.g., warehouse without heat)?
Spend Time Standing	How much does this job require standing?

Extremely Bright or Inadequate Lighting	How often does this job require working in extremely bright or inadequate lighting conditions?
Physical Proximity	To what extent does this job require the worker to perform job tasks in close physical proximity to other people?
Spend Time Bending or Twisting the Body	How much does this job require bending or twisting your body?
Freedom to Make Decisions	How much decision making freedom, without supervision, does the job offer?
Time Pressure	How often does this job require the worker to meet strict deadlines?
Structured versus Unstructured Work	To what extent is this job structured for the worker, rather than allowing the worker to determine tasks, priorities, and goals?
Exposed to Minor Burns, Cuts, Bites, or Stings	How often does this job require exposure to minor burns, cuts, bites, or stings?
Exposed to High Places	How often does this job require exposure to high places?
Coordinate or Lead Others	How important is it to coordinate or lead others in accomplishing work activities in this job?
Pace Determined by Speed of Equipment	How important is it to this job that the pace is determined by the speed of equipment or machinery? (This does not refer to keeping busy at all times on this job.)
Level of Competition	To what extent does this job require the worker to compete or to be aware of competitive pressures?
Frequency of Conflict Situations	How often are there conflict situations the employee has to face in this job?
Deal With External Customers	How important is it to work with external customers or the public in this job?
Cramped Work Space, Awkward Positions	How often does this job require working in cramped work spaces that requires getting into awkward positions?
Deal With Unpleasant or Angry People	How frequently does the worker have to deal with unpleasant, angry, or discourteous individuals as part of the job requirements?
Spend Time Walking and Running	How much does this job require walking and running?
Letters and Memos	How often does the job require written letters and memos?
Spend Time Keeping or Regaining Balance	How much does this job require keeping or regaining your balance?
Exposed to Whole Body Vibration	How often does this job require exposure to whole body vibration (e.g., operate a jackhammer)?
Spend Time Climbing Ladders, Scaffolds, or Poles	How much does this job require climbing ladders, scaffolds, or poles?
Wear Specialized Protective or Safety Equipment su	How much does this job require wearing specialized protective or safety equipment such as breathing apparatus, safety harness, full protection suits, or radiation protection?
Spend Time Kneeling, Crouching, Stooping, or Crawl	How much does this job require kneeling, crouching, stooping or crawling?
Degree of Automation	How automated is the job?
Electronic Mail	How often do you use electronic mail in this job?
Spend Time Sitting	How much does this job require sitting?
Outdoors, Under Cover	How often does this job require working outdoors, under cover (e.g., structure with roof but no walls)?
Public Speaking	How often do you have to perform public speaking in this job?
Deal With Physically Aggressive People	How frequently does this job require the worker to deal with physical aggression of violent individuals?
Exposed to Radiation	How often does this job require exposure to radiation?
Indoors, Environmentally Controlled	How often does this job require working indoors in environmentally controlled conditions?
Exposed to Disease or Infections	How often does this job require exposure to disease/infections?

Job Zone Component	Job Zone Component Definitions
Title	Job Zone Two: Some Preparation Needed
Overall Experience	Some previous work-related skill, knowledge, or experience may be helpful in these occupations, but usually is not needed. For example, a drywall installer might benefit from experience installing drywall, but an inexperienced person could still learn to be an installer with little difficulty.
Job Training	Employees in these occupations need anywhere from a few months to one year of working with experienced employees.
Job Zone Examples	These occupations often involve using your knowledge and skills to help others. Examples include drywall installers, fire inspectors, flight attendants, pharmacy technicians, salespersons (retail), and tellers.
SVP Range	(4.0 to < 6.0)

Education	These occupations usually require a high school diploma and may require some vocational training or job-related course work. In some cases, an associate's or bachelor's degree could be needed.

Work_Styles	Work_Styles Definitions
Dependability	Job requires being reliable, responsible, and dependable, and fulfilling obligations.
Attention to Detail	Job requires being careful about detail and thorough in completing work tasks.
Cooperation	Job requires being pleasant with others on the job and displaying a good-natured, cooperative attitude.
Self Control	Job requires maintaining composure, keeping emotions in check, controlling anger, and avoiding aggressive behavior, even in very difficult situations.
Integrity	Job requires being honest and ethical.
Initiative	Job requires a willingness to take on responsibilities and challenges.
Concern for Others	Job requires being sensitive to others' needs and feelings and being understanding and helpful on the job.
Adaptability/Flexibility	Job requires being open to change (positive or negative) and to considerable variety in the workplace.
Leadership	Job requires a willingness to lead, take charge, and offer opinions and direction.
Social Orientation	Job requires preferring to work with others rather than alone, and being personally connected with others on the job.
Stress Tolerance	Job requires accepting criticism and dealing calmly and effectively with high stress situations.
Achievement/Effort	Job requires establishing and maintaining personally challenging achievement goals and exerting effort toward mastering tasks.
Independence	Job requires developing one's own ways of doing things, guiding oneself with little or no supervision, and depending on oneself to get things done.
Persistence	Job requires persistence in the face of obstacles.
Analytical Thinking	Job requires analyzing information and using logic to address work-related issues and problems.
Innovation	Job requires creativity and alternative thinking to develop new ideas for and answers to work-related problems.

47-5031.00 - Explosives Workers, Ordnance Handling Experts, and Blasters

Place and detonate explosives to demolish structures or to loosen, remove, or displace earth, rock, or other materials. May perform specialized handling, storage, and accounting procedures. Includes seismograph shooters.

Tasks

1) Connect electrical wire to primers, and cover charges or fill blast holes with clay, drill chips, sand, or other material.

2) Cut specified lengths of primacord and attach primers to cord ends.

3) Assemble and position equipment, explosives, and blasting caps in holes at specified depths, or load perforating guns or torpedoes with explosives.

4) Compile and keep gun and explosives records in compliance with local and federal laws.

5) Repair and service blasting, shooting, and automotive equipment, and electrical wiring and instruments, using hand tools.

6) Maintain inventory levels, ordering new supplies as necessary.

7) Repair electrical instruments, using electricians' hand tools.

8) Insert, pack, and pour explosives, such as dynamite, ammonium nitrate, black powder, or slurries into blast holes; then shovel drill cuttings, admit water into boreholes, and tamp material to compact charges.

9) Place explosive charges in holes or other spots; then detonate explosives to demolish structures or to loosen, remove, or displace earth, rock, or other materials.

10) Set up and operate equipment such as hoists, jackhammers, or drills, in order to bore charge holes.

11) Signal hoist operators to lower torpedoes or sample-taking guns into wells and to raise equipment for sampling from blast holes after detonation.

12) Tie specified lengths of delaying fuses into patterns in order to time sequences of explosions.

13) Insert waterproof sealers, bullets, and/or powder charges into guns, and screw gun ports back into place.

14) Move and store inventories of explosives, loaded perforating guns, and other materials, according to established safety procedures.

15) Set up and operate short-wave radio or field telephone equipment to transmit and receive blast information.

16) Verify detonation of charges by observing control panels, or by listening for the sounds of blasts.

17) Measure depths of drilled blast holes, using weighted tape measures.

18) Mark patterns, locations, and depths of charge holes for drilling, and issue drilling instructions.

19) Lower perforating guns into wells, using hoists; then use measuring devices and instrument panels to position guns in correct positions for taking samples.

20) Light fuses, drop detonating devices into wells or boreholes, or activate firing devices with plungers, dials, or buttons, in order to set off single or multiple blasts.

21) Lay primacord between rows of charged blast holes, and tie cord into main lines to form blast patterns.

22) Obtain samples of earth from sidewalls of well boreholes, using electrically exploding devices.

23) Place safety cones around blast areas to alert other workers of danger zones, and signal workers as necessary to ensure that they clear blast sites prior to explosions.

24) Clean, gauge, and lubricate gun ports.

25) Connect gun chambers to electric detonating devices, and operate controls at panelboards, in order to detonate charges in guns or to ignite chemical charges.

26) Drive trucks to transport explosives and blasting equipment to blasting sites.

27) Examine blast areas to determine amounts and kinds of explosive charges needed and to ensure that safety laws are observed.

28) Observe odometers, weight indicators, and instrument panels in trucks in order to position guns at predetermined points in wells.

47-5041.00 - Continuous Mining Machine Operators

Operate self-propelled mining machines that rip coal, metal and nonmetal ores, rock, stone, or sand from the face and load it onto conveyors or into shuttle cars in a continuous operation.

Tasks

1) Determine locations, boundaries, and depths of holes or channels to be cut.

2) Move controls to start and regulate movement of conveyors, and to start and position drill cutters or torches.

3) Drive machines into position at working faces.

4) Move levers to raise and lower hydraulic safety bars that support roofs above machines until other workers complete their framing.

5) Observe and listen to equipment operation to detect binding or stoppage of tools and other equipment malfunctions.

6) Reposition machines to make additional holes or cuts.

7) Install casings to prevent cave-ins.

8) Guide and assist crews laying track and resetting supports and blocking.

9) Start machines to gather coal and convey it to floors or shuttle cars.

47-5042.00 - Mine Cutting and Channeling Machine Operators

Operate machinery--such as longwall shears, plows, and cutting machines--to cut or channel along the face or seams of coal mines, stone quarries, or other mining surfaces to facilitate blasting, separating, or removing minerals or materials from mines or from the earth's surface.

Tasks

1) Observe indicator lights and gauges, and listen to machine operation in order to detect binding or stoppage of tools or other equipment problems.

2) Reposition machines and move controls in order to make additional holes or cuts.

3) Position jacks, timbers, or roof supports, and install casings, in order to prevent cave-ins.

4) Cut entries between rooms and haulage-ways.

5) Press buttons to activate conveyor belts, and push or pull chain handles to regulate conveyor movement so that material can be moved or loaded into dinkey cars or dump trucks.

6) Drive mobile, truck-mounted, or track-mounted drilling or cutting machine in mines and quarries or on construction sites.

7) Move planer levers to control and adjust the movement of equipment, the speed, height, and depth of cuts, and to rotate swivel cutting booms.

8) Remove debris such as loose shale from channels and planer travel areas.

9) Determine locations, boundaries, and depths of holes or channels to be cut.

10) Move controls to start and position drill cutters or torches, and to advance tools into mines or quarry faces in order to complete horizontal or vertical cuts.

11) Cut slots along working faces of coal, salt, or other non-metal deposits in order to facilitate blasting, by moving levers to start the machine and to control the vertical reciprocating drills.

12) Advance plow blades through coal strata by remote control, according to electronic or radio signals from the tailer.

13) Signal crewmembers to adjust the speed of equipment to the rate of installation of roof supports, and to adjust the speed of conveyors to the volume of coal.

14) Free jams in planer hoppers, using metal pinch bars.

15) Charge and set off explosives in blasting holes.

16) Guide and assist crews in laying track for machines and resetting planer rails, supports, and blocking, using jacks, shovels, sledges, picks, and pinch bars.

17) Monitor movement of shale along conveyors from hoppers to trucks or railcars.

18) Signal that machine plow blades are properly positioned, using electronic buzzers or two-way radios.

19) Signal truck drivers to position their vehicles for receiving shale from planer hoppers.

20) Cut and move shale from open pits.

Knowledge

Knowledge	Knowledge Definitions
Mechanical	Knowledge of machines and tools, including their designs, uses, repair, and maintenance.
Public Safety and Security	Knowledge of relevant equipment, policies, procedures, and strategies to promote effective local, state, or national security operations for the protection of people, data, property, and institutions.
Law and Government	Knowledge of laws, legal codes, court procedures, precedents, government regulations, executive orders, agency rules, and the democratic political process.
Education and Training	Knowledge of principles and methods for curriculum and training design, teaching and instruction for individuals and groups, and the measurement of training effects.
English Language	Knowledge of the structure and content of the English language including the meaning and spelling of words, rules of composition, and grammar.
Physics	Knowledge and prediction of physical principles, laws, their interrelationships, and applications to understanding fluid, material, and atmospheric dynamics, and mechanical, electrical, atomic and sub-atomic structures and processes.
Administration and Management	Knowledge of business and management principles involved in strategic planning, resource allocation, human resources modeling, leadership technique, production methods, and coordination of people and resources.
Medicine and Dentistry	Knowledge of the information and techniques needed to diagnose and treat human injuries, diseases, and deformities. This includes symptoms, treatment alternatives, drug properties and interactions, and preventive health-care measures.
Transportation	Knowledge of principles and methods for moving people or goods by air, rail, sea, or road, including the relative costs and benefits.
Production and Processing	Knowledge of raw materials, production processes, quality control, costs, and other techniques for maximizing the effective manufacture and distribution of goods.
Engineering and Technology	Knowledge of the practical application of engineering science and technology. This includes applying principles, techniques, procedures, and equipment to the design and production of various goods and services.
Mathematics	Knowledge of arithmetic, algebra, geometry, calculus, statistics, and their applications.
Chemistry	Knowledge of the chemical composition, structure, and properties of substances and of the chemical processes and transformations that they undergo. This includes uses of chemicals and their interactions, danger signs, production techniques, and disposal methods.
Building and Construction	Knowledge of materials, methods, and the tools involved in the construction or repair of houses, buildings, or other structures such as highways and roads.
Psychology	Knowledge of human behavior and performance; individual differences in ability, personality, and interests; learning and motivation; psychological research methods; and the assessment and treatment of behavioral and affective disorders.
Design	Knowledge of design techniques, tools, and principles involved in production of precision technical plans, blueprints, drawings, and models.
Personnel and Human Resources	Knowledge of principles and procedures for personnel recruitment, selection, training, compensation and benefits, labor relations and negotiation, and personnel information systems.
Telecommunications	Knowledge of transmission, broadcasting, switching, control, and operation of telecommunications systems.
Computers and Electronics	Knowledge of circuit boards, processors, chips, electronic equipment, and computer hardware and software, including applications and programming.
Sales and Marketing	Knowledge of principles and methods for showing, promoting, and selling products or services. This includes marketing strategy and tactics, product demonstration, sales techniques, and sales control systems.
Geography	Knowledge of principles and methods for describing the features of land, sea, and air masses, including their physical characteristics, locations, interrelationships, and distribution of plant, animal, and human life.
Communications and Media	Knowledge of media production, communication, and dissemination techniques and methods. This includes alternative ways to inform and entertain via written, oral, and visual media.
Clerical	Knowledge of administrative and clerical procedures and systems such as word processing, managing files and records, stenography and transcription, designing forms, and other office procedures and terminology.
Customer and Personal Service	Knowledge of principles and processes for providing customer and personal services. This includes customer needs assessment, meeting quality standards for services, and evaluation of customer satisfaction.
Biology	Knowledge of plant and animal organisms, their tissues, cells, functions, interdependencies, and interactions with each other and the environment.
Economics and Accounting	Knowledge of economic and accounting principles and practices, the financial markets, banking and the analysis and reporting of financial data.
Therapy and Counseling	Knowledge of principles, methods, and procedures for diagnosis, treatment, and rehabilitation of physical and mental dysfunctions, and for career counseling and guidance.
Philosophy and Theology	Knowledge of different philosophical systems and religions. This includes their basic principles, values, ethics, ways of thinking, customs, practices, and their impact on human culture.
Food Production	Knowledge of techniques and equipment for planting, growing, and harvesting food products (both plant and animal) for consumption, including storage/handling techniques.
Sociology and Anthropology	Knowledge of group behavior and dynamics, societal trends and influences, human migrations, ethnicity, cultures and their history and origins.
History and Archeology	Knowledge of historical events and their causes, indicators, and effects on civilizations and cultures.
Fine Arts	Knowledge of the theory and techniques required to compose, produce, and perform works of music, dance, visual arts, drama, and sculpture.
Foreign Language	Knowledge of the structure and content of a foreign (non-English) language including the meaning and spelling of words, rules of composition and grammar, and pronunciation.

Skills	Skills Definitions
Active Listening	Giving full attention to what other people are saying, taking time to understand the points being made, asking questions as appropriate, and not interrupting at inappropriate times.
Equipment Maintenance	Performing routine maintenance on equipment and determining when and what kind of maintenance is needed.
Operation and Control	Controlling operations of equipment or systems.
Speaking	Talking to others to convey information effectively.
Coordination	Adjusting actions in relation to others' actions.
Critical Thinking	Using logic and reasoning to identify the strengths and weaknesses of alternative solutions, conclusions or approaches to problems.
Judgment and Decision Making	Considering the relative costs and benefits of potential actions to choose the most appropriate one.
Troubleshooting	Determining causes of operating errors and deciding what to do about it.
Repairing	Repairing machines or systems using the needed tools.
Operation Monitoring	Watching gauges, dials, or other indicators to make sure a machine is working properly.
Equipment Selection	Determining the kind of tools and equipment needed to do a job.
Instructing	Teaching others how to do something.
Active Learning	Understanding the implications of new information for both current and future problem-solving and decision-making.
Learning Strategies	Selecting and using training/instructional methods and procedures appropriate for the situation when learning or teaching new things.
Reading Comprehension	Understanding written sentences and paragraphs in work related documents.
Systems Analysis	Determining how a system should work and how changes in conditions, operations, and the environment will affect outcomes.
Social Perceptiveness	Being aware of others' reactions and understanding why they react as they do.
Time Management	Managing one's own time and the time of others.
Service Orientation	Actively looking for ways to help people.
Installation	Installing equipment, machines, wiring, or programs to meet specifications.
Monitoring	Monitoring/Assessing performance of yourself, other individuals, or organizations to make improvements or take corrective action.
Technology Design	Generating or adapting equipment and technology to serve user needs.
Mathematics	Using mathematics to solve problems.
Systems Evaluation	Identifying measures or indicators of system performance and the actions needed to improve or correct performance, relative to the goals of the system.
Management of Material Resources	Obtaining and seeing to the appropriate use of equipment, facilities, and materials needed to do certain work.
Management of Personnel Resources	Motivating, developing, and directing people as they work, identifying the best people for the job.
Complex Problem Solving	Identifying complex problems and reviewing related information to develop and evaluate options and implement solutions.
Quality Control Analysis	Conducting tests and inspections of products, services, or processes to evaluate quality or performance.
Writing	Communicating effectively in writing as appropriate for the needs of the audience.
Negotiation	Bringing others together and trying to reconcile differences.
Persuasion	Persuading others to change their minds or behavior.
Science	Using scientific rules and methods to solve problems.
Operations Analysis	Analyzing needs and product requirements to create a design.
Management of Financial Resources	Determining how money will be spent to get the work done, and accounting for these expenditures.
Programming	Writing computer programs for various purposes.

Ability	Ability Definitions
Control Precision	The ability to quickly and repeatedly adjust the controls of a machine or a vehicle to exact positions.
Multilimb Coordination	The ability to coordinate two or more limbs (for example, two arms, two legs, or one leg and one arm) while sitting, standing, or lying down. It does not involve performing the activities while the whole body is in motion.
Problem Sensitivity	The ability to tell when something is wrong or is likely to go wrong. It does not involve solving the problem, only recognizing there is a problem.
Arm-Hand Steadiness	The ability to keep your hand and arm steady while moving your arm or while holding your arm and hand in one position.
Reaction Time	The ability to quickly respond (with the hand, finger, or foot) to a signal (sound, light, picture) when it appears.
Rate Control	The ability to time your movements or the movement of a piece of equipment in anticipation of changes in the speed and/or direction of a moving object or scene.
Depth Perception	The ability to judge which of several objects is closer or farther away from you, or to judge the distance between you and an object.
Hearing Sensitivity	The ability to detect or tell the differences between sounds that vary in pitch and loudness.
Deductive Reasoning	The ability to apply general rules to specific problems to produce answers that make sense.
Manual Dexterity	The ability to quickly move your hand, your hand together with your arm, or your two hands to grasp, manipulate, or assemble objects.
Oral Comprehension	The ability to listen to and understand information and ideas presented through spoken words and sentences.
Near Vision	The ability to see details at close range (within a few feet of the observer).
Response Orientation	The ability to choose quickly between two or more movements in response to two or more different signals (lights, sounds, pictures). It includes the speed with which the correct response is started with the hand, foot, or other body part.
Static Strength	The ability to exert maximum muscle force to lift, push, pull, or carry objects.
Far Vision	The ability to see details at a distance.
Inductive Reasoning	The ability to combine pieces of information to form general rules or conclusions (includes finding a relationship among seemingly unrelated events).
Speech Recognition	The ability to identify and understand the speech of another person.
Trunk Strength	The ability to use your abdominal and lower back muscles to support part of the body repeatedly or continuously over time without 'giving out' or fatiguing.
Auditory Attention	The ability to focus on a single source of sound in the presence of other distracting sounds.
Category Flexibility	The ability to generate or use different sets of rules for combining or grouping things in different ways.
Extent Flexibility	The ability to bend, stretch, twist, or reach with your body, arms, and/or legs.
Perceptual Speed	The ability to quickly and accurately compare similarities and differences among sets of letters, numbers, objects, pictures, or patterns. The things to be compared may be presented at the same time or one after the other. This ability also includes comparing a presented object with a remembered object.
Information Ordering	The ability to arrange things or actions in a certain order or pattern according to a specific rule or set of rules (e.g., patterns of numbers, letters, words, pictures, mathematical operations).
Finger Dexterity	The ability to make precisely coordinated movements of the fingers of one or both hands to grasp, manipulate, or assemble very small objects.
Speech Clarity	The ability to speak clearly so others can understand you.
Oral Expression	The ability to communicate information and ideas in speaking so others will understand.
Stamina	The ability to exert yourself physically over long periods of time without getting winded or out of breath.
Visual Color Discrimination	The ability to match or detect differences between colors, including shades of color and brightness.
Selective Attention	The ability to concentrate on a task over a period of time without being distracted.
Flexibility of Closure	The ability to identify or detect a known pattern (a figure, object, word, or sound) that is hidden in other distracting material.
Visualization	The ability to imagine how something will look after it is moved around or when its parts are moved or rearranged.
Speed of Limb Movement	The ability to quickly move the arms and legs.
Sound Localization	The ability to tell the direction from which a sound originated.
Speed of Closure	The ability to quickly make sense of, combine, and organize information into meaningful patterns.
Glare Sensitivity	The ability to see objects in the presence of glare or bright lighting.
Time Sharing	The ability to shift back and forth between two or more activities or sources of information (such as speech, sounds, touch, or other sources).
Spatial Orientation	The ability to know your location in relation to the environment or to know where other objects are in relation to you.

Gross Body Coordination	The ability to coordinate the movement of your arms, legs, and torso together when the whole body is in motion.
Fluency of Ideas	The ability to come up with a number of ideas about a topic (the number of ideas is important, not their quality, correctness, or creativity).
Dynamic Strength	The ability to exert muscle force repeatedly or continuously over time. This involves muscular endurance and resistance to muscle fatigue.
Wrist-Finger Speed	The ability to make fast, simple, repeated movements of the fingers, hands, and wrists.
Memorization	The ability to remember information such as words, numbers, pictures, and procedures.
Number Facility	The ability to add, subtract, multiply, or divide quickly and correctly.
Gross Body Equilibrium	The ability to keep or regain your body balance or stay upright when in an unstable position.
Night Vision	The ability to see under low light conditions.
Written Expression	The ability to communicate information and ideas in writing so others will understand.
Originality	The ability to come up with unusual or clever ideas about a given topic or situation, or to develop creative ways to solve a problem.
Peripheral Vision	The ability to see objects or movement of objects to one's side when the eyes are looking ahead.
Written Comprehension	The ability to read and understand information and ideas presented in writing.
Mathematical Reasoning	The ability to choose the right mathematical methods or formulas to solve a problem.
Dynamic Flexibility	The ability to quickly and repeatedly bend, stretch, twist, or reach out with your body, arms, and/or legs.
Explosive Strength	The ability to use short bursts of muscle force to propel oneself (as in jumping or sprinting), or to throw an object.

Work_Activity	Work_Activity Definitions
Controlling Machines and Processes	Using either control mechanisms or direct physical activity to operate machines or processes (not including computers or vehicles).
Identifying Objects, Actions, and Events	Identifying information by categorizing, estimating, recognizing differences or similarities, and detecting changes in circumstances or events.
Inspecting Equipment, Structures, or Material	Inspecting equipment, structures, or materials to identify the cause of errors or other problems or defects.
Operating Vehicles, Mechanized Devices, or Equipme	Running, maneuvering, navigating, or driving vehicles or mechanized equipment, such as forklifts, passenger vehicles, aircraft, or water craft.
Monitor Processes, Materials, or Surroundings	Monitoring and reviewing information from materials, events, or the environment, to detect or assess problems.
Repairing and Maintaining Mechanical Equipment	Servicing, repairing, adjusting, and testing machines, devices, moving parts, and equipment that operate primarily on the basis of mechanical (not electronic) principles.
Handling and Moving Objects	Using hands and arms in handling, installing, positioning, and moving materials, and manipulating things.
Communicating with Supervisors, Peers, or Subordin	Providing information to supervisors, co-workers, and subordinates by telephone, in written form, e-mail, or in person.
Performing General Physical Activities	Performing physical activities that require considerable use of your arms and legs and moving your whole body, such as climbing, lifting, balancing, walking, stooping, and handling of materials.
Evaluating Information to Determine Compliance wit	Using relevant information and individual judgment to determine whether events or processes comply with laws, regulations, or standards.
Getting Information	Observing, receiving, and otherwise obtaining information from all relevant sources.
Updating and Using Relevant Knowledge	Keeping up-to-date technically and applying new knowledge to your job.
Making Decisions and Solving Problems	Analyzing information and evaluating results to choose the best solution and solve problems.
Repairing and Maintaining Electronic Equipment	Servicing, repairing, calibrating, regulating, fine-tuning, or testing machines, devices, and equipment that operate primarily on the basis of electrical or electronic (not mechanical) principles.
Estimating the Quantifiable Characteristics of Pro	Estimating sizes, distances, and quantities; or determining time, costs, resources, or materials needed to perform a work activity.

Assisting and Caring for Others	Providing personal assistance, medical attention, emotional support, or other personal care to others such as coworkers, customers, or patients.
Training and Teaching Others	Identifying the educational needs of others, developing formal educational or training programs or classes, and teaching or instructing others.
Organizing, Planning, and Prioritizing Work	Developing specific goals and plans to prioritize, organize, and accomplish your work.
Judging the Qualities of Things, Services, or Peop	Assessing the value, importance, or quality of things or people.
Establishing and Maintaining Interpersonal Relatio	Developing constructive and cooperative working relationships with others, and maintaining them over time.
Developing Objectives and Strategies	Establishing long-range objectives and specifying the strategies and actions to achieve them.
Coaching and Developing Others	Identifying the developmental needs of others and coaching, mentoring, or otherwise helping others to improve their knowledge or skills.
Coordinating the Work and Activities of Others	Getting members of a group to work together to accomplish tasks.
Developing and Building Teams	Encouraging and building mutual trust, respect, and cooperation among team members.
Interpreting the Meaning of Information for Others	Translating or explaining what information means and how it can be used.
Thinking Creatively	Developing, designing, or creating new applications, ideas, relationships, systems, or products, including artistic contributions.
Processing Information	Compiling, coding, categorizing, calculating, tabulating, auditing, or verifying information or data.
Analyzing Data or Information	Identifying the underlying principles, reasons, or facts of information by breaking down information or data into separate parts.
Provide Consultation and Advice to Others	Providing guidance and expert advice to management or other groups on technical, systems-, or process-related topics.
Resolving Conflicts and Negotiating with Others	Handling complaints, settling disputes, and resolving grievances and conflicts, or otherwise negotiating with others.
Guiding, Directing, and Motivating Subordinates	Providing guidance and direction to subordinates, including setting performance standards and monitoring performance.
Scheduling Work and Activities	Scheduling events, programs, and activities, as well as the work of others.
Monitoring and Controlling Resources	Monitoring and controlling resources and overseeing the spending of money.
Communicating with Persons Outside Organization	Communicating with people outside the organization, representing the organization to customers, the public, government, and other external sources. This information can be exchanged in person, in writing, or by telephone or e-mail.
Documenting/Recording Information	Entering, transcribing, recording, storing, or maintaining information in written or electronic/magnetic form.
Selling or Influencing Others	Convincing others to buy merchandise/goods or to otherwise change their minds or actions.
Drafting, Laying Out, and Specifying Technical Dev	Providing documentation, detailed instructions, drawings, or specifications to tell others about how devices, parts, equipment, or structures are to be fabricated, constructed, assembled, modified, maintained, or used.
Performing Administrative Activities	Performing day-to-day administrative tasks such as maintaining information files and processing paperwork.
Staffing Organizational Units	Recruiting, interviewing, selecting, hiring, and promoting employees in an organization.
Interacting With Computers	Using computers and computer systems (including hardware and software) to program, write software, set up functions, enter data, or process information.
Performing for or Working Directly with the Public	Performing for people or dealing directly with the public. This includes serving customers in restaurants and stores, and receiving clients or guests.

Work_Context	Work_Context Definitions
Wear Common Protective or Safety Equipment such as	How much does this job require wearing common protective or safety equipment such as safety shoes, glasses, gloves, hard hats or live jackets?
Exposed to Contaminants	How often does this job require working exposed to contaminants (such as pollutants, gases, dust or odors)?
Exposed to Hazardous Equipment	How often does this job require exposure to hazardous equipment?
Spend Time Using Your Hands to Handle, Control, or	How much does this job require using your hands to handle, control, or feel objects, tools or controls?

Sounds, Noise Levels Are Distracting or Uncomforta	How often does this job require working exposed to sounds and noise levels that are distracting or uncomfortable?
Contact With Others	How much does this job require the worker to be in contact with others (face-to-face, by telephone, or otherwise) in order to perform it?
Face-to-Face Discussions	How often do you have to have face-to-face discussions with individuals or teams in this job?
Exposed to Hazardous Conditions	How often does this job require exposure to hazardous conditions?
Spend Time Making Repetitive Motions	How much does this job require making repetitive motions?
Pace Determined by Speed of Equipment	How important is it to this job that the pace is determined by the speed of equipment or machinery? (This docs not refer to keeping busy at all times on this job.)
Work With Work Group or Team	How important is it to work with others in a group or team in this job?
Cramped Work Space, Awkward Positions	How often does this job require working in cramped work spaces that requires getting into awkward positions?
Frequency of Decision Making	How frequently is the worker required to make decisions that affect other people, the financial resources, and/or the image and reputation of the organization?
Responsible for Others' Health and Safety	How much responsibility is there for the health and safety of others in this job?
Impact of Decisions on Co-workers or Company Resul	How do the decisions an employee makes impact the results of co-workers, clients or the company?
Extremely Bright or Inadequate Lighting	How often does this job require working in extremely bright or inadequate lighting conditions?
Freedom to Make Decisions	How much decision making freedom, without supervision, does the job offer?
Importance of Being Exact or Accurate	How important is being very exact or highly accurate in performing this job?
Spend Time Standing	How much does this job require standing?
Spend Time Bending or Twisting the Body	How much does this job require bending or twisting your body?
Structured versus Unstructured Work	To what extent is this job structured for the worker, rather than allowing the worker to determine tasks, priorities, and goals?
Consequence of Error	How serious would the result usually be if the worker made a mistake that was not readily correctable?
Wear Specialized Protective or Safety Equipment su	How much does this job require wearing specialized protective or safety equipment such as breathing apparatus, safety harness, full protection suits, or radiation protection?
Exposed to Whole Body Vibration	How often does this job require exposure to whole body vibration (e.g., operate a jackhammer)?
Spend Time Walking and Running	How much does this job require walking and running?
Exposed to Minor Burns, Cuts, Bites, or Stings	How often does this job require exposure to minor burns, cuts, bites, or stings?
Spend Time Kneeling, Crouching, Stooping, or Crawl	How much does this job require kneeling, crouching, stooping or crawling?
In an Open Vehicle or Equipment	How often does this job require working in an open vehicle or equipment (e.g., tractor)?
Deal With Unpleasant or Angry People	How frequently does the worker have to deal with unpleasant, angry, or discourteous individuals as part of the job requirements?
Level of Competition	To what extent does this job require the worker to compete or to be aware of competitive pressures?
Physical Proximity	To what extent does this job require the worker to perform job tasks in close physical proximity to other people?
Coordinate or Lead Others	How important is it to coordinate or lead others in accomplishing work activities in this job?
Time Pressure	How often does this job require the worker to meet strict deadlines?
Degree of Automation	How automated is the job?
Responsibility for Outcomes and Results	How responsible is the worker for work outcomes and results of other workers?
Frequency of Conflict Situations	How often are there conflict situations the employee has to face in this job?
Importance of Repeating Same Tasks	How important is repeating the same physical activities (e.g., key entry) or mental activities (e.g., checking entries in a ledger) over and over, without stopping, to performing this job?
Very Hot or Cold Temperatures	How often does this job require working in very hot (above 90 F degrees) or very cold (below 32 F degrees) temperatures?
Indoors, Not Environmentally Controlled	How often does this job require working indoors in non-controlled environmental conditions (e.g., warehouse without heat)?
Telephone	How often do you have telephone conversations in this job?

Spend Time Sitting	How much does this job require sitting?
In an Enclosed Vehicle or Equipment	How much does this job require working in a closed vehicle or equipment (e.g., car)?
Spend Time Keeping or Regaining Balance	How much does this job require keeping or regaining your balance?
Outdoors, Exposed to Weather	How often does this job require working outdoors, exposed to all weather conditions?
Letters and Memos	How often does the job require written letters and memos?
Exposed to High Places	How often does this job require exposure to high places?
Outdoors, Under Cover	How often does this job require working outdoors, under cover (e.g., structure with roof but no walls)?
Public Speaking	How often do you have to perform public speaking in this job?
Deal With Physically Aggressive People	How frequently does this job require the worker to deal with physical aggression of violent individuals?
Indoors, Environmentally Controlled	How often does this job require working indoors in environmentally controlled conditions?
Deal With External Customers	How important is it to work with external customers or the public in this job?
Spend Time Climbing Ladders, Scaffolds, or Poles	How much does this job require climbing ladders, scaffolds, or poles?
Electronic Mail	How often do you use electronic mail in this job?
Exposed to Radiation	How often does this job require exposure to radiation?
Exposed to Disease or Infections	How often does this job require exposure to disease/infections?

Job Zone Component	Job Zone Component Definitions
Title	Job Zone Two: Some Preparation Needed
Overall Experience	Some previous work-related skill, knowledge, or experience may be helpful in these occupations, but usually is not needed. For example, a drywall installer might benefit from experience installing drywall, but an inexperienced person could still learn to be an installer with little difficulty.
Job Training	Employees in these occupations need anywhere from a few months to one year of working with experienced employees.
Job Zone Examples	These occupations often involve using your knowledge and skills to help others. Examples include drywall installers, fire inspectors, flight attendants, pharmacy technicians, salespersons (retail), and tellers.
SVP Range	(4.0 to < 6.0)
Education	These occupations usually require a high school diploma and may require some vocational training or job-related course work. In some cases, an associate's or bachelor's degree could be needed.

Work_Styles	Work_Styles Definitions
Dependability	Job requires being reliable, responsible, and dependable, and fulfilling obligations.
Initiative	Job requires a willingness to take on responsibilities and challenges.
Self Control	Job requires maintaining composure, keeping emotions in check, controlling anger, and avoiding aggressive behavior, even in very difficult situations.
Cooperation	Job requires being pleasant with others on the job and displaying a good-natured, cooperative attitude.
Attention to Detail	Job requires being careful about detail and thorough in completing work tasks.
Persistence	Job requires persistence in the face of obstacles.
Stress Tolerance	Job requires accepting criticism and dealing calmly and effectively with high stress situations.
Adaptability/Flexibility	Job requires being open to change (positive or negative) and to considerable variety in the workplace.
Analytical Thinking	Job requires analyzing information and using logic to address work-related issues and problems.
Integrity	Job requires being honest and ethical.
Concern for Others	Job requires being sensitive to others' needs and feelings and being understanding and helpful on the job.
Social Orientation	Job requires preferring to work with others rather than alone, and being personally connected with others on the job.
Achievement/Effort	Job requires establishing and maintaining personally challenging achievement goals and exerting effort toward mastering tasks.
Independence	Job requires developing one's own ways of doing things, guiding oneself with little or no supervision, and depending on oneself to get things done.

| Leadership | Job requires a willingness to lead, take charge, and offer opinions and direction. |
| Innovation | Job requires creativity and alternative thinking to develop new ideas for and answers to work-related problems. |

47-5051.00 - Rock Splitters, Quarry

Separate blocks of rough dimension stone from quarry mass using jackhammer and wedges.

Tasks

1) Remove pieces of stone from larger masses, using jackhammers, wedges, and other tools.

2) Set charges of explosives to split rock.

3) Mark dimensions or outlines on stone prior to cutting, using rules and chalklines.

4) Locate grain line patterns to determine how rocks will split when cut.

5) Insert wedges and feathers into holes, and drive wedges with sledgehammers to split stone sections from masses.

6) Drill holes into sides of stones broken from masses, insert dogs or attach slings, and direct removal of stones.

7) Drill holes along outlines, using jackhammers.

8) Cut grooves along outlines, using chisels.

47-5071.00 - Roustabouts, Oil and Gas

Assemble or repair oil field equipment using hand and power tools. Perform other tasks as needed.

Tasks

1) Unscrew or tighten pipes, casing, tubing, and pump rods, using hand and power wrenches and tongs.

2) Dig drainage ditches around wells and storage tanks.

3) Clean up spilled oil by bailing it into barrels.

4) Walk flow lines to locate leaks, using electronic detectors and making visual inspections.

5) Dismantle and repair oil field machinery, boilers, and steam engine parts, using hand tools and power tools.

6) Bolt together pump and engine parts.

7) Keep pipe deck and main deck areas clean and tidy.

8) Supply equipment to rig floors as requested, and provide assistance to roughnecks.

9) Cut down and remove trees and brush to clear drill sites, in order to reduce fire hazards, and to make way for roads to sites.

10) Guide cranes to move loads about decks.

11) Dig holes, set forms, and mix and pour concrete into forms in order to make foundations for wood or steel derricks.

12) Bolt or nail together wood or steel framework in order to erect derricks.

Knowledge	Knowledge Definitions
Mechanical	Knowledge of machines and tools, including their designs, uses, repair, and maintenance.
Public Safety and Security	Knowledge of relevant equipment, policies, procedures, and strategies to promote effective local, state, or national security operations for the protection of people, data, property, and institutions.
Production and Processing	Knowledge of raw materials, production processes, quality control, costs, and other techniques for maximizing the effective manufacture and distribution of goods.
English Language	Knowledge of the structure and content of the English language including the meaning and spelling of words, rules of composition, and grammar.
Transportation	Knowledge of principles and methods for moving people or goods by air, rail, sea, or road, including the relative costs and benefits.
Physics	Knowledge and prediction of physical principles, laws, their interrelationships, and applications to understanding fluid, material, and atmospheric dynamics, and mechanical, electrical, atomic and sub- atomic structures and processes.
Mathematics	Knowledge of arithmetic, algebra, geometry, calculus, statistics, and their applications.
Chemistry	Knowledge of the chemical composition, structure, and properties of substances and of the chemical processes and transformations that they undergo. This includes uses of chemicals and their interactions, danger signs, production techniques, and disposal methods.
Engineering and Technology	Knowledge of the practical application of engineering science and technology. This includes applying principles, techniques, procedures, and equipment to the design and production of various goods and services.
Administration and Management	Knowledge of business and management principles involved in strategic planning, resource allocation, human resources modeling, leadership technique, production methods, and coordination of people and resources.
Education and Training	Knowledge of principles and methods for curriculum and training design, teaching and instruction for individuals and groups, and the measurement of training effects.
Design	Knowledge of design techniques, tools, and principles involved in production of precision technical plans, blueprints, drawings, and models.
Building and Construction	Knowledge of materials, methods, and the tools involved in the construction or repair of houses, buildings, or other structures such as highways and roads.
Law and Government	Knowledge of laws, legal codes, court procedures, precedents, government regulations, executive orders, agency rules, and the democratic political process.
Communications and Media	Knowledge of media production, communication, and dissemination techniques and methods. This includes alternative ways to inform and entertain via written, oral, and visual media.
Personnel and Human Resources	Knowledge of principles and procedures for personnel recruitment, selection, training, compensation and benefits, labor relations and negotiation, and personnel information systems.
Customer and Personal Service	Knowledge of principles and processes for providing customer and personal services. This includes customer needs assessment, meeting quality standards for services, and evaluation of customer satisfaction.
Psychology	Knowledge of human behavior and performance; individual differences in ability, personality, and interests; learning and motivation; psychological research methods; and the assessment and treatment of behavioral and affective disorders.
Clerical	Knowledge of administrative and clerical procedures and systems such as word processing, managing files and records, stenography and transcription, designing forms, and other office procedures and terminology.
Medicine and Dentistry	Knowledge of the information and techniques needed to diagnose and treat human injuries, diseases, and deformities. This includes symptoms, treatment alternatives, drug properties and interactions, and preventive health-care measures.
Economics and Accounting	Knowledge of economic and accounting principles and practices, the financial markets, banking and the analysis and reporting of financial data.
Telecommunications	Knowledge of transmission, broadcasting, switching, control, and operation of telecommunications systems.
Geography	Knowledge of principles and methods for describing the features of land, sea, and air masses, including their physical characteristics, locations, interrelationships, and distribution of plant, animal, and human life.
Sales and Marketing	Knowledge of principles and methods for showing, promoting, and selling products or services. This includes marketing strategy and tactics, product demonstration, sales techniques, and sales control systems.
Biology	Knowledge of plant and animal organisms, their tissues, cells, functions, interdependencies, and interactions with each other and the environment.
Computers and Electronics	Knowledge of circuit boards, processors, chips, electronic equipment, and computer hardware and software, including applications and programming.
Therapy and Counseling	Knowledge of principles, methods, and procedures for diagnosis, treatment, and rehabilitation of physical and mental dysfunctions, and for career counseling and guidance.

Foreign Language	Knowledge of the structure and content of a foreign (non-English) language including the meaning and spelling of words, rules of composition and grammar, and pronunciation.
Food Production	Knowledge of techniques and equipment for planting, growing, and harvesting food products (both plant and animal) for consumption, including storage/handling techniques.
Fine Arts	Knowledge of the theory and techniques required to compose, produce, and perform works of music, dance, visual arts, drama, and sculpture.
Sociology and Anthropology	Knowledge of group behavior and dynamics, societal trends and influences, human migrations, ethnicity, cultures and their history and origins.
History and Archeology	Knowledge of historical events and their causes, indicators, and effects on civilizations and cultures.
Philosophy and Theology	Knowledge of different philosophical systems and religions. This includes their basic principles, values, ethics, ways of thinking, customs, practices, and their impact on human culture.

Skills	Skills Definitions
Active Listening	Giving full attention to what other people are saying, taking time to understand the points being made, asking questions as appropriate, and not interrupting at inappropriate times.
Equipment Maintenance	Performing routine maintenance on equipment and determining when and what kind of maintenance is needed.
Repairing	Repairing machines or systems using the needed tools.
Coordination	Adjusting actions in relation to others' actions.
Operation Monitoring	Watching gauges, dials, or other indicators to make sure a machine is working properly.
Troubleshooting	Determining causes of operating errors and deciding what to do about it.
Active Learning	Understanding the implications of new information for both current and future problem-solving and decision-making.
Equipment Selection	Determining the kind of tools and equipment needed to do a job.
Installation	Installing equipment, machines, wiring, or programs to meet specifications.
Critical Thinking	Using logic and reasoning to identify the strengths and weaknesses of alternative solutions, conclusions or approaches to problems.
Mathematics	Using mathematics to solve problems.
Speaking	Talking to others to convey information effectively.
Operation and Control	Controlling operations of equipment or systems.
Time Management	Managing one's own time and the time of others.
Monitoring	Monitoring/Assessing performance of yourself, other individuals, or organizations to make improvements or take corrective action.
Learning Strategies	Selecting and using training/instructional methods and procedures appropriate for the situation when learning or teaching new things.
Instructing	Teaching others how to do something.
Reading Comprehension	Understanding written sentences and paragraphs in work related documents.
Writing	Communicating effectively in writing as appropriate for the needs of the audience.
Quality Control Analysis	Conducting tests and inspections of products, services, or processes to evaluate quality or performance.
Systems Analysis	Determining how a system should work and how changes in conditions, operations, and the environment will affect outcomes.
Judgment and Decision Making	Considering the relative costs and benefits of potential actions to choose the most appropriate one.
Service Orientation	Actively looking for ways to help people.
Complex Problem Solving	Identifying complex problems and reviewing related information to develop and evaluate options and implement solutions.
Social Perceptiveness	Being aware of others' reactions and understanding why they react as they do.
Science	Using scientific rules and methods to solve problems.
Systems Evaluation	Identifying measures or indicators of system performance and the actions needed to improve or correct performance, relative to the goals of the system.
Technology Design	Generating or adapting equipment and technology to serve user needs.
Operations Analysis	Analyzing needs and product requirements to create a design.
Negotiation	Bringing others together and trying to reconcile differences.
Persuasion	Persuading others to change their minds or behavior.

Management of Material Resources	Obtaining and seeing to the appropriate use of equipment, facilities, and materials needed to do certain work.
Management of Personnel Resources	Motivating, developing, and directing people as they work, identifying the best people for the job.
Management of Financial Resources	Determining how money will be spent to get the work done, and accounting for these expenditures.
Programming	Writing computer programs for various purposes.

Ability	Ability Definitions
Control Precision	The ability to quickly and repeatedly adjust the controls of a machine or a vehicle to exact positions.
Near Vision	The ability to see details at close range (within a few feet of the observer).
Multilimb Coordination	The ability to coordinate two or more limbs (for example, two arms, two legs, or one leg and one arm) while sitting, standing, or lying down. It does not involve performing the activities while the whole body is in motion.
Manual Dexterity	The ability to quickly move your hand, your hand together with your arm, or your two hands to grasp, manipulate, or assemble objects.
Problem Sensitivity	The ability to tell when something is wrong or is likely to go wrong. It does not involve solving the problem, only recognizing there is a problem.
Arm-Hand Steadiness	The ability to keep your hand and arm steady while moving your arm or while holding your arm and hand in one position.
Depth Perception	The ability to judge which of several objects is closer or farther away from you, or to judge the distance between you and an object.
Static Strength	The ability to exert maximum muscle force to lift, push, pull, or carry objects.
Far Vision	The ability to see details at a distance.
Finger Dexterity	The ability to make precisely coordinated movements of the fingers of one or both hands to grasp, manipulate, or assemble very small objects.
Speech Recognition	The ability to identify and understand the speech of another person.
Oral Comprehension	The ability to listen to and understand information and ideas presented through spoken words and sentences.
Oral Expression	The ability to communicate information and ideas in speaking so others will understand.
Deductive Reasoning	The ability to apply general rules to specific problems to produce answers that make sense.
Inductive Reasoning	The ability to combine pieces of information to form general rules or conclusions (includes finding a relationship among seemingly unrelated events).
Extent Flexibility	The ability to bend, stretch, twist, or reach with your body, arms, and/or legs.
Category Flexibility	The ability to generate or use different sets of rules for combining or grouping things in different ways.
Hearing Sensitivity	The ability to detect or tell the differences between sounds that vary in pitch and loudness.
Reaction Time	The ability to quickly respond (with the hand, finger, or foot) to a signal (sound, light, picture) when it appears.
Flexibility of Closure	The ability to identify or detect a known pattern (a figure, object, word, or sound) that is hidden in other distracting material.
Information Ordering	The ability to arrange things or actions in a certain order or pattern according to a specific rule or set of rules (e.g., patterns of numbers, letters, words, pictures, mathematical operations).
Visualization	The ability to imagine how something will look after it is moved around or when its parts are moved or rearranged.
Speech Clarity	The ability to speak clearly so others can understand you.
Written Comprehension	The ability to read and understand information and ideas presented in writing.
Gross Body Equilibrium	The ability to keep or regain your body balance or stay upright when in an unstable position.
Trunk Strength	The ability to use your abdominal and lower back muscles to support part of the body repeatedly or continuously over time without 'giving out' or fatiguing.
Stamina	The ability to exert yourself physically over long periods of time without getting winded or out of breath.
Selective Attention	The ability to concentrate on a task over a period of time without being distracted.
Response Orientation	The ability to choose quickly between two or more movements in response to two or more different signals (lights, sounds, pictures). It includes the speed with which the correct response is started with the hand, foot, or other body part.

Time Sharing	The ability to shift back and forth between two or more activities or sources of information (such as speech, sounds, touch, or other sources).
Visual Color Discrimination	The ability to match or detect differences between colors, including shades of color and brightness.
Perceptual Speed	The ability to quickly and accurately compare similarities and differences among sets of letters, numbers, objects, pictures, or patterns. The things to be compared may be presented at the same time or one after the other. This ability also includes comparing a presented object with a remembered object.
Auditory Attention	The ability to focus on a single source of sound in the presence of other distracting sounds.
Rate Control	The ability to time your movements or the movement of a piece of equipment in anticipation of changes in the speed and/or direction of a moving object or scene.
Gross Body Coordination	The ability to coordinate the movement of your arms, legs, and torso together when the whole body is in motion.
Glare Sensitivity	The ability to see objects in the presence of glare or bright lighting.
Dynamic Strength	The ability to exert muscle force repeatedly or continuously over time. This involves muscular endurance and resistance to muscle fatigue.
Wrist-Finger Speed	The ability to make fast, simple, repeated movements of the fingers, hands, and wrists.
Originality	The ability to come up with unusual or clever ideas about a given topic or situation, or to develop creative ways to solve a problem.
Peripheral Vision	The ability to see objects or movement of objects to one's side when the eyes are looking ahead.
Speed of Closure	The ability to quickly make sense of, combine, and organize information into meaningful patterns.
Speed of Limb Movement	The ability to quickly move the arms and legs.
Memorization	The ability to remember information such as words, numbers, pictures, and procedures.
Written Expression	The ability to communicate information and ideas in writing so others will understand.
Spatial Orientation	The ability to know your location in relation to the environment or to know where other objects are in relation to you.
Fluency of Ideas	The ability to come up with a number of ideas about a topic (the number of ideas is important, not their quality, correctness, or creativity).
Sound Localization	The ability to tell the direction from which a sound originated.
Night Vision	The ability to see under low light conditions.
Number Facility	The ability to add, subtract, multiply, or divide quickly and correctly.
Mathematical Reasoning	The ability to choose the right mathematical methods or formulas to solve a problem.
Dynamic Flexibility	The ability to quickly and repeatedly bend, stretch, twist, or reach out with your body, arms, and/or legs
Explosive Strength	The ability to use short bursts of muscle force to propel oneself (as in jumping or sprinting), or to throw an object.

Work_Activity	Work_Activity Definitions
Handling and Moving Objects	Using hands and arms in handling, installing, positioning, and moving materials, and manipulating things.
Inspecting Equipment, Structures, or Material	Inspecting equipment, structures, or materials to identify the cause of errors or other problems or defects.
Getting Information	Observing, receiving, and otherwise obtaining information from all relevant sources.
Performing General Physical Activities	Performing physical activities that require considerable use of your arms and legs and moving your whole body, such as climbing, lifting, balancing, walking, stooping, and handling of materials.
Identifying Objects, Actions, and Events	Identifying information by categorizing, estimating, recognizing differences or similarities, and detecting changes in circumstances or events.
Operating Vehicles, Mechanized Devices, or Equipme	Running, maneuvering, navigating, or driving vehicles or mechanized equipment, such as forklifts, passenger vehicles, aircraft, or water craft.
Making Decisions and Solving Problems	Analyzing information and evaluating results to choose the best solution and solve problems.
Monitor Processes, Materials, or Surroundings	Monitoring and reviewing information from materials, events, or the environment, to detect or assess problems.
Controlling Machines and Processes	Using either control mechanisms or direct physical activity to operate machines or processes (not including computers or vehicles).

Repairing and Maintaining Mechanical Equipment	Servicing, repairing, adjusting, and testing machines, devices, moving parts, and equipment that operate primarily on the basis of mechanical (not electronic) principles.
Communicating with Supervisors, Peers, or Subordin	Providing information to supervisors, co-workers, and subordinates by telephone, in written form, e-mail, or in person.
Estimating the Quantifiable Characteristics of Pro	Estimating sizes, distances, and quantities; or determining time, costs, resources, or materials needed to perform a work activity.
Analyzing Data or Information	Identifying the underlying principles, reasons, or facts of information by breaking down information or data into separate parts.
Processing Information	Compiling, coding, categorizing, calculating, tabulating, auditing, or verifying information or data.
Training and Teaching Others	Identifying the educational needs of others, developing formal educational or training programs or classes, and teaching or instructing others.
Judging the Qualities of Things, Services, or Peop	Assessing the value, importance, or quality of things or people.
Evaluating Information to Determine Compliance wit	Using relevant information and individual judgment to determine whether events or processes comply with laws, regulations, or standards.
Establishing and Maintaining Interpersonal Relatio	Developing constructive and cooperative working relationships with others, and maintaining them over time.
Scheduling Work and Activities	Scheduling events, programs, and activities, as well as the work of others.
Thinking Creatively	Developing, designing, or creating new applications, ideas, relationships, systems, or products, including artistic contributions.
Coordinating the Work and Activities of Others	Getting members of a group to work together to accomplish tasks.
Developing Objectives and Strategies	Establishing long-range objectives and specifying the strategies and actions to achieve them.
Assisting and Caring for Others	Providing personal assistance, medical attention, emotional support, or other personal care to others such as coworkers, customers, or patients.
Documenting/Recording Information	Entering, transcribing, recording, storing, or maintaining information in written or electronic/magnetic form.
Updating and Using Relevant Knowledge	Keeping up-to-date technically and applying new knowledge to your job.
Guiding, Directing, and Motivating Subordinates	Providing guidance and direction to subordinates, including setting performance standards and monitoring performance.
Interpreting the Meaning of Information for Others	Translating or explaining what information means and how it can be used.
Developing and Building Teams	Encouraging and building mutual trust, respect, and cooperation among team members.
Repairing and Maintaining Electronic Equipment	Servicing, repairing, calibrating, regulating, fine-tuning, or testing machines, devices, and equipment that operate primarily on the basis of electrical or electronic (not mechanical) principles.
Organizing, Planning, and Prioritizing Work	Developing specific goals and plans to prioritize, organize, and accomplish your work.
Coaching and Developing Others	Identifying the developmental needs of others and coaching, mentoring, or otherwise helping others to improve their knowledge or skills.
Drafting, Laying Out, and Specifying Technical Dev	Providing documentation, detailed instructions, drawings, or specifications to tell others about how devices, parts, equipment, or structures are to be fabricated, constructed, assembled, modified, maintained, or used.
Communicating with Persons Outside Organization	Communicating with people outside the organization, representing the organization to customers, the public, government, and other external sources. This information can be exchanged in person, in writing, or by telephone or e-mail.
Monitoring and Controlling Resources	Monitoring and controlling resources and overseeing the spending of money.
Performing for or Working Directly with the Public	Performing for people or dealing directly with the public. This includes serving customers in restaurants and stores, and receiving clients or guests.
Resolving Conflicts and Negotiating with Others	Handling complaints, settling disputes, and resolving grievances and conflicts, or otherwise negotiating with others.
Interacting With Computers	Using computers and computer systems (including hardware and software) to program, write software, set up functions, enter data, or process information.
Provide Consultation and Advice to Others	Providing guidance and expert advice to management or other groups on technical, systems-, or process-related topics.
Selling or Influencing Others	Convincing others to buy merchandise/goods or to otherwise change their minds or actions.

| Staffing Organizational Units | Recruiting, interviewing, selecting, hiring, and promoting employees in an organization. |
| Performing Administrative Activities | Performing day-to-day administrative tasks such as maintaining information files and processing paperwork. |

Work_Context	Work_Context Definitions
Wear Common Protective or Safety Equipment such as	How much does this job require wearing common protective or safety equipment such as safety shoes, glasses, gloves, hard hats or live jackets?
Outdoors, Exposed to Weather	How often does this job require working outdoors, exposed to all weather conditions?
Face-to-Face Discussions	How often do you have to have face-to-face discussions with individuals or teams in this job?
Spend Time Using Your Hands to Handle, Control, or	How much does this job require using your hands to handle, control, or feel objects, tools or controls?
Spend Time Standing	How much does this job require standing?
Very Hot or Cold Temperatures	How often does this job require working in very hot (above 90 F degrees) or very cold (below 32 F degrees) temperatures?
Contact With Others	How much does this job require the worker to be in contact with others (face-to-face, by telephone, or otherwise) in order to perform it?
Exposed to Contaminants	How often does this job require working exposed to contaminants (such as pollutants, gases, dust or odors)?
Physical Proximity	To what extent does this job require the worker to perform job tasks in close physical proximity to other people?
Exposed to Hazardous Conditions	How often does this job require exposure to hazardous conditions?
Exposed to Hazardous Equipment	How often does this job require exposure to hazardous equipment?
Sounds, Noise Levels Are Distracting or Uncomforta	How often does this job require working exposed to sounds and noise levels that are distracting or uncomfortable?
Work With Work Group or Team	How important is it to work with others in a group or team in this job?
Telephone	How often do you have telephone conversations in this job?
Exposed to High Places	How often does this job require exposure to high places?
In an Enclosed Vehicle or Equipment	How often does this job require working in a closed vehicle or equipment (e.g., car)?
In an Open Vehicle or Equipment	How often does this job require working in an open vehicle or equipment (e.g., tractor)?
Importance of Being Exact or Accurate	How important is being very exact or highly accurate in performing this job?
Responsible for Others' Health and Safety	How much responsibility is there for the health and safety of others in this job?
Time Pressure	How often does this job require the worker to meet strict deadlines?
Consequence of Error	How serious would the result usually be if the worker made a mistake that was not readily correctable?
Exposed to Minor Burns, Cuts, Bites, or Stings	How often does this job require exposure to minor burns, cuts, bites, or stings?
Cramped Work Space, Awkward Positions	How often does this job require working in cramped work spaces that requires getting into awkward positions?
Spend Time Making Repetitive Motions	How much does this job require making repetitive motions?
Spend Time Bending or Twisting the Body	How much does this job require bending or twisting your body?
Spend Time Walking and Running	How much does this job require walking and running?
Impact of Decisions on Co-workers or Company Resul	How do the decisions an employee makes impact the results of co-workers, clients or the company?
Responsibility for Outcomes and Results	How responsible is the worker for work outcomes and results of other workers?
Frequency of Decision Making	How frequently is the worker required to make decisions that affect other people, the financial resources, and/or the image and reputation of the organization?
Coordinate or Lead Others	How important is it to coordinate or lead others in accomplishing work activities in this job?
Outdoors, Under Cover	How often does this job require working outdoors, under cover (e.g., structure with roof but no walls)?
Structured versus Unstructured Work	To what extent is this job structured for the worker, rather than allowing the worker to determine tasks, priorities, and goals?
Extremely Bright or Inadequate Lighting	How often does this job require working in extremely bright or inadequate lighting conditions?
Letters and Memos	How often does the job require written letters and memos?

Wear Specialized Protective or Safety Equipment su	How much does this job require wearing specialized protective or safety equipment such as breathing apparatus, safety harness, full protection suits, or radiation protection?
Level of Competition	To what extent does this job require the worker to compete or to be aware of competitive pressures?
Freedom to Make Decisions	How much decision making freedom, without supervision, does the job offer?
Spend Time Climbing Ladders, Scaffolds, or Poles	How much does this job require climbing ladders, scaffolds, or poles?
Indoors, Not Environmentally Controlled	How often does this job require working indoors in non-controlled environmental conditions (e.g., warehouse without heat)?
Spend Time Kneeling, Crouching, Stooping, or Crawl	How much does this job require kneeling, crouching, stooping or crawling?
Spend Time Keeping or Regaining Balance	How much does this job require keeping or regaining your balance?
Importance of Repeating Same Tasks	How important is repeating the same physical activities (e.g., key entry) or mental activities (e.g., checking entries in a ledger) over and over, without stopping, to performing this job?
Pace Determined by Speed of Equipment	How important is it to this job that the pace is determined by the speed of equipment or machinery? (This does not refer to keeping busy at all times on this job.)
Deal With Unpleasant or Angry People	How frequently does the worker have to deal with unpleasant, angry, or discourteous individuals as part of the job requirements?
Deal With External Customers	How important is it to work with external customers or the public in this job?
Frequency of Conflict Situations	How often are there conflict situations the employee has to face in this job?
Exposed to Whole Body Vibration	How often does this job require exposure to whole body vibration (e.g., operate a jackhammer)?
Exposed to Radiation	How often does this job require exposure to radiation?
Spend Time Sitting	How much does this job require sitting?
Degree of Automation	How automated is the job?
Deal With Physically Aggressive People	How frequently does this job require the worker to deal with physical aggression of violent individuals?
Public Speaking	How often do you have to perform public speaking in this job?
Electronic Mail	How often do you use electronic mail in this job?
Indoors, Environmentally Controlled	How often does this job require working indoors in environmentally controlled conditions?
Exposed to Disease or Infections	How often does this job require exposure to disease/infections?

Job Zone Component	Job Zone Component Definitions
Title	Job Zone Two: Some Preparation Needed
Overall Experience	Some previous work-related skill, knowledge, or experience may be helpful in these occupations, but usually is not needed. For example, a drywall installer might benefit from experience installing drywall, but an inexperienced person could still learn to be an installer with little difficulty.
Job Training	Employees in these occupations need anywhere from a few months to one year of working with experienced employees.
Job Zone Examples	These occupations often involve using your knowledge and skills to help others. Examples include drywall installers, fire inspectors, flight attendants, pharmacy technicians, salespersons (retail), and tellers.
SVP Range	(4.0 to < 6.0)
Education	These occupations usually require a high school diploma and may require some vocational training or job-related course work. In some cases, an associate's or bachelor's degree could be needed.

Work_Styles	Work_Styles Definitions
Attention to Detail	Job requires being careful about detail and thorough in completing work tasks.
Concern for Others	Job requires being sensitive to others' needs and feelings and being understanding and helpful on the job.
Dependability	Job requires being reliable, responsible, and dependable, and fulfilling obligations.
Cooperation	Job requires being pleasant with others on the job and displaying a good-natured, cooperative attitude.
Leadership	Job requires a willingness to lead, take charge, and offer opinions and direction.

Self Control	Job requires maintaining composure, keeping emotions in check, controlling anger, and avoiding aggressive behavior, even in very difficult situations.
Independence	Job requires developing one's own ways of doing things, guiding oneself with little or no supervision, and depending on oneself to get things done.
Initiative	Job requires a willingness to take on responsibilities and challenges.
Innovation	Job requires creativity and alternative thinking to develop new ideas for and answers to work-related problems.
Social Orientation	Job requires preferring to work with others rather than alone, and being personally connected with others on the job.
Stress Tolerance	Job requires accepting criticism and dealing calmly and effectively with high stress situations.
Adaptability/Flexibility	Job requires being open to change (positive or negative) and to considerable variety in the workplace.
Persistence	Job requires persistence in the face of obstacles.
Integrity	Job requires being honest and ethical.
Analytical Thinking	Job requires analyzing information and using logic to address work-related issues and problems.
Achievement/Effort	Job requires establishing and maintaining personally challenging achievement goals and exerting effort toward mastering tasks.

49-2021.00 - Radio Mechanics

Test or repair mobile or stationary radio transmitting and receiving equipment and two-way radio communications systems used in ship-to-shore communications and found in service and emergency vehicles.

Tasks

1) Monitor radio range stations to detect transmission flaws and adjust controls to eliminate flaws.

2) Test emergency transmitters to ensure their readiness for immediate use.

3) Calibrate and align components, using scales, gauges, and other measuring instruments.

4) Remove and replace defective components and parts such as conductors, resistors, semiconductors, and integrated circuits, using soldering irons, wire cutters, and hand tools.

5) Test equipment functions such as signal strength and quality, transmission capacity, interference, and signal delay, using equipment such as oscilloscopes, circuit analyzers, frequency meters, and wattmeters.

6) Examine malfunctioning radio equipment to locate defects such as loose connections, broken wires, or burned-out components, using schematic diagrams and test equipment.

7) Clean and lubricate motor generators.

8) Mount equipment on transmission towers and in vehicles such as ships or ambulances.

9) Turn setscrews to adjust receivers for maximum sensitivity and transmitters for maximum output.

10) Install, adjust, and repair stationary and mobile radio transmitting and receiving equipment and two-way radio communication systems.

11) Repair circuits, wiring, and soldering, using soldering irons and hand tools to install parts and adjust connections.

12) Test batteries, using hydrometers and ammeters, and charge batteries as necessary.

49-2096.00 - Electronic Equipment Installers and Repairers, Motor Vehicles

Install, diagnose, or repair communications, sound, security, or navigation equipment in motor vehicles.

Tasks

1) Splice wires with knives or cutting pliers, and solder connections to fixtures and equipment.

2) Record results of diagnostic tests.

3) Remove seats, carpeting, and interiors of doors; add sound-absorbing material in empty spaces; and reinstall interior parts.

4) Cut openings and drill holes for fixtures and equipment, using electric drills and routers.

5) Inspect and test electrical or electronic systems to locate and diagnose malfunctions, using visual inspections and testing instruments such as oscilloscopes and voltmeters.

6) Install equipment and accessories such as stereos, navigation equipment, communication equipment, and security systems.

7) Diagnose or repair problems with electronic equipment, such as sound, navigation, communication, and security equipment, in motor vehicles.

8) Replace and clean electrical or electronic components.

9) Run new speaker and electrical cables.

10) Build fiberglass or wooden enclosures for sound components, and fit them to automobile dimensions.

11) Confer with customers to determine the nature of malfunctions.

49-2097.00 - Electronic Home Entertainment Equipment Installers and Repairers

Repair, adjust, or install audio or television receivers, stereo systems, camcorders, video systems, or other electronic home entertainment equipment.

Tasks

1) Keep records of work orders and test and maintenance reports.

2) Compute cost estimates for labor and materials.

3) Read and interpret electronic circuit diagrams, function block diagrams, specifications, engineering drawings, and service manuals.

4) Install, service, and repair electronic equipment or instruments such as televisions, radios, and videocassette recorders.

5) Disassemble entertainment equipment and repair or replace loose, worn, or defective components and wiring, using hand tools and soldering irons.

6) Confer with customers to determine the nature of problems or to explain repairs.

7) Tune or adjust equipment and instruments to obtain optimum visual or auditory reception, according to specifications, manuals, and drawings.

8) Calibrate and test equipment, and locate circuit and component faults, using hand and power tools and measuring and testing instruments such as resistance meters and oscilloscopes.

9) Instruct customers on the safe and proper use of equipment.

10) Position or mount speakers, and wire speakers to consoles.

49-3041.00 - Farm Equipment Mechanics

Diagnose, adjust, repair, or overhaul farm machinery and vehicles, such as tractors, harvesters, dairy equipment, and irrigation systems.

Tasks

1) Dismantle defective machines for repair, using hand tools.

2) Examine and listen to equipment, read inspection reports, and confer with customers to locate and diagnose malfunctions.

3) Install and repair agricultural irrigation, plumbing, and sprinkler systems.

4) Maintain, repair, and overhaul farm machinery and vehicles, such as tractors, harvesters, and irrigation systems.

5) Reassemble machines and equipment following repair; test operation; and make adjustments as necessary.

6) Repair or replace defective parts, using hand tools, milling and woodworking machines, lathes, welding equipment, grinders, or saws.

7) Test and replace electrical components and wiring, using test meters, soldering equipment, and hand tools.

8) Drive trucks to haul tools and equipment for on-site repair of large machinery.

9) Fabricate new metal parts, using drill presses, engine lathes, and other machine tools.

10) Record details of repairs made and parts used.

11) Calculate bills according to record of repairs made, labor time, and parts used.

12) Clean and lubricate parts.

13) Repair bent or torn sheet metal.

49-3053.00 - Outdoor Power Equipment and Other Small Engine Mechanics

Diagnose, adjust, repair, or overhaul small engines used to power lawn mowers, chain saws, and related equipment.

Tasks

1) Reassemble engines after repair or maintenance work is complete.

2) Obtain problem descriptions from customers, and prepare cost estimates for repairs.

3) Remove engines from equipment, and position and bolt engines to repair stands.

4) Repair and maintain gasoline engines used to power equipment such as portable saws, lawn mowers, generators, and compressors.

5) Repair or replace defective parts such as magnetos, water pumps, gears, pistons, and carburetors, using hand tools.

6) Replace motors.

7) Perform routine maintenance such as cleaning and oiling parts, honing cylinders, and tuning ignition systems.

8) Test and inspect engines to determine malfunctions, to locate missing and broken parts, and to verify repairs, using diagnostic instruments.

9) Grind, ream, rebore, and retap parts to obtain specified clearances, using grinders, lathes, taps, reamers, boring machines, and micrometers.

10) Record repairs made, time spent, and parts used.

11) Adjust points, valves, carburetors, distributors, and spark plug gaps, using feeler gauges.

12) Show customers how to maintain equipment.

13) Dismantle engines, using hand tools, and examine parts for defects.

49-3091.00 - Bicycle Repairers

Repair and service bicycles.

Tasks

1) Assemble new bicycles.

2) Shape replacement parts, using bench grinders.

3) Repair holes in tire tubes, using scrapers and patches.

4) Paint bicycle frames, using spray guns or brushes.

5) Weld broken or cracked frames together, using oxyacetylene torches and welding rods.

6) Align wheels.

7) Install, repair, and replace equipment or accessories, such as handlebars, stands, lights, and seats.

8) Install and adjust speed and gear mechanisms.

Knowledge	Knowledge Definitions
Customer and Personal Service	Knowledge of principles and processes for providing customer and personal services. This includes customer needs assessment, meeting quality standards for services, and evaluation of customer satisfaction.
Mechanical	Knowledge of machines and tools, including their designs, uses, repair, and maintenance.
English Language	Knowledge of the structure and content of the English language including the meaning and spelling of words, rules of composition, and grammar.
Engineering and Technology	Knowledge of the practical application of engineering science and technology. This includes applying principles, techniques, procedures, and equipment to the design and production of various goods and services.
Design	Knowledge of design techniques, tools, and principles involved in production of precision technical plans, blueprints, drawings, and models.
Sales and Marketing	Knowledge of principles and methods for showing, promoting, and selling products or services. This includes marketing strategy and tactics, product demonstration, sales techniques, and sales control systems.
Transportation	Knowledge of principles and methods for moving people or goods by air, rail, sea, or road, including the relative costs and benefits.
Mathematics	Knowledge of arithmetic, algebra, geometry, calculus, statistics, and their applications.
Building and Construction	Knowledge of materials, methods, and the tools involved in the construction or repair of houses, buildings, or other structures such as highways and roads.
Administration and Management	Knowledge of business and management principles involved in strategic planning, resource allocation, human resources modeling, leadership technique, production methods, and coordination of people and resources.
Production and Processing	Knowledge of raw materials, production processes, quality control, costs, and other techniques for maximizing the effective manufacture and distribution of goods.
Economics and Accounting	Knowledge of economic and accounting principles and practices, the financial markets, banking and the analysis and reporting of financial data.
Personnel and Human Resources	Knowledge of principles and procedures for personnel recruitment, selection, training, compensation and benefits, labor relations and negotiation, and personnel information systems.
Physics	Knowledge and prediction of physical principles, laws, their interrelationships, and applications to understanding fluid, material, and atmospheric dynamics, and mechanical, electrical, atomic and sub-atomic structures and processes.
Education and Training	Knowledge of principles and methods for curriculum and training design, teaching and instruction for individuals and groups, and the measurement of training effects.
Public Safety and Security	Knowledge of relevant equipment, policies, procedures, and strategies to promote effective local, state, or national security operations for the protection of people, data, property, and institutions.
Communications and Media	Knowledge of media production, communication, and dissemination techniques and methods. This includes alternative ways to inform and entertain via written, oral, and visual media.
Clerical	Knowledge of administrative and clerical procedures and systems such as word processing, managing files and records, stenography and transcription, designing forms, and other office procedures and terminology.
Computers and Electronics	Knowledge of circuit boards, processors, chips, electronic equipment, and computer hardware and software, including applications and programming.
Chemistry	Knowledge of the chemical composition, structure, and properties of substances and of the chemical processes and transformations that they undergo. This includes uses of chemicals and their interactions, danger signs, production techniques, and disposal methods.
Telecommunications	Knowledge of transmission, broadcasting, switching, control, and operation of telecommunications systems.
Psychology	Knowledge of human behavior and performance; individual differences in ability, personality, and interests; learning and motivation; psychological research methods; and the assessment and treatment of behavioral and affective disorders.
Law and Government	Knowledge of laws, legal codes, court procedures, precedents, government regulations, executive orders, agency rules, and the democratic political process.
Geography	Knowledge of principles and methods for describing the features of land, sea, and air masses, including their physical characteristics, locations, interrelationships, and distribution of plant, animal, and human life.
Biology	Knowledge of plant and animal organisms, their tissues, cells, functions, interdependencies, and interactions with each other and the environment.

Foreign Language	Knowledge of the structure and content of a foreign (non-English) language including the meaning and spelling of words, rules of composition and grammar, and pronunciation.
Food Production	Knowledge of techniques and equipment for planting, growing, and harvesting food products (both plant and animal) for consumption, including storage/handling techniques.
Sociology and Anthropology	Knowledge of group behavior and dynamics, societal trends and influences, human migrations, ethnicity, cultures and their history and origins.
Therapy and Counseling	Knowledge of principles, methods, and procedures for diagnosis, treatment, and rehabilitation of physical and mental dysfunctions, and for career counseling and guidance.
Medicine and Dentistry	Knowledge of the information and techniques needed to diagnose and treat human injuries, diseases, and deformities. This includes symptoms, treatment alternatives, drug properties and interactions, and preventive health-care measures.
Philosophy and Theology	Knowledge of different philosophical systems and religions. This includes their basic principles, values, ethics, ways of thinking, customs, practices, and their impact on human culture.
Fine Arts	Knowledge of the theory and techniques required to compose, produce, and perform works of music, dance, visual arts, drama, and sculpture.
History and Archeology	Knowledge of historical events and their causes, indicators, and effects on civilizations and cultures.

Skills	Skills Definitions
Repairing	Repairing machines or systems using the needed tools.
Troubleshooting	Determining causes of operating errors and deciding what to do about it.
Installation	Installing equipment, machines, wiring, or programs to meet specifications.
Speaking	Talking to others to convey information effectively.
Judgment and Decision Making	Considering the relative costs and benefits of potential actions to choose the most appropriate one.
Active Listening	Giving full attention to what other people are saying, taking time to understand the points being made, asking questions as appropriate, and not interrupting at inappropriate times.
Time Management	Managing one's own time and the time of others.
Service Orientation	Actively looking for ways to help people.
Reading Comprehension	Understanding written sentences and paragraphs in work related documents.
Equipment Maintenance	Performing routine maintenance on equipment and determining when and what kind of maintenance is needed.
Equipment Selection	Determining the kind of tools and equipment needed to do a job.
Quality Control Analysis	Conducting tests and inspections of products, services, or processes to evaluate quality or performance.
Coordination	Adjusting actions in relation to others' actions
Instructing	Teaching others how to do something.
Critical Thinking	Using logic and reasoning to identify the strengths and weaknesses of alternative solutions, conclusions or approaches to problems.
Active Learning	Understanding the implications of new information for both current and future problem-solving and decision-making.
Operations Analysis	Analyzing needs and product requirements to create a design.
Social Perceptiveness	Being aware of others' reactions and understanding why they react as they do.
Persuasion	Persuading others to change their minds or behavior.
Management of Material Resources	Obtaining and seeing to the appropriate use of equipment, facilities, and materials needed to do certain work.
Mathematics	Using mathematics to solve problems.
Complex Problem Solving	Identifying complex problems and reviewing related information to develop and evaluate options and implement solutions.
Learning Strategies	Selecting and using training/instructional methods and procedures appropriate for the situation when learning or teaching new things.
Writing	Communicating effectively in writing as appropriate for the needs of the audience.
Monitoring	Monitoring/Assessing performance of yourself, other individuals, or organizations to make improvements or take corrective action.
Systems Analysis	Determining how a system should work and how changes in conditions, operations, and the environment will affect outcomes.

Systems Evaluation	Identifying measures or indicators of system performance and the actions needed to improve or correct performance, relative to the goals of the system.
Operation and Control	Controlling operations of equipment or systems.
Science	Using scientific rules and methods to solve problems.
Technology Design	Generating or adapting equipment and technology to serve user needs.
Management of Personnel Resources	Motivating, developing, and directing people as they work, identifying the best people for the job.
Negotiation	Bringing others together and trying to reconcile differences.
Operation Monitoring	Watching gauges, dials, or other indicators to make sure a machine is working properly.
Management of Financial Resources	Determining how money will be spent to get the work done, and accounting for these expenditures.
Programming	Writing computer programs for various purposes.

Ability	Ability Definitions
Manual Dexterity	The ability to quickly move your hand, your hand together with your arm, or your two hands to grasp, manipulate, or assemble objects.
Finger Dexterity	The ability to make precisely coordinated movements of the fingers of one or both hands to grasp, manipulate, or assemble very small objects.
Visualization	The ability to imagine how something will look after it is moved around or when its parts are moved or rearranged.
Problem Sensitivity	The ability to tell when something is wrong or is likely to go wrong. It does not involve solving the problem, only recognizing there is a problem.
Near Vision	The ability to see details at close range (within a few feet of the observer).
Information Ordering	The ability to arrange things or actions in a certain order or pattern according to a specific rule or set of rules (e.g., patterns of numbers, letters, words, pictures, mathematical operations).
Arm-Hand Steadiness	The ability to keep your hand and arm steady while moving your arm or while holding your arm and hand in one position.
Speech Clarity	The ability to speak clearly so others can understand you.
Oral Comprehension	The ability to listen to and understand information and ideas presented through spoken words and sentences.
Deductive Reasoning	The ability to apply general rules to specific problems to produce answers that make sense.
Speech Recognition	The ability to identify and understand the speech of another person.
Oral Expression	The ability to communicate information and ideas in speaking so others will understand.
Selective Attention	The ability to concentrate on a task over a period of time without being distracted.
Inductive Reasoning	The ability to combine pieces of information to form general rules or conclusions (includes finding a relationship among seemingly unrelated events).
Trunk Strength	The ability to use your abdominal and lower back muscles to support part of the body repeatedly or continuously over time without 'giving out' or fatiguing.
Category Flexibility	The ability to generate or use different sets of rules for combining or grouping things in different ways.
Depth Perception	The ability to judge which of several objects is closer or farther away from you, or to judge the distance between you and an object.
Control Precision	The ability to quickly and repeatedly adjust the controls of a machine or a vehicle to exact positions.
Written Comprehension	The ability to read and understand information and ideas presented in writing.
Originality	The ability to come up with unusual or clever ideas about a given topic or situation, or to develop creative ways to solve a problem.
Multilimb Coordination	The ability to coordinate two or more limbs (for example, two arms, two legs, or one leg and one arm) while sitting, standing, or lying down. It does not involve performing the activities while the whole body is in motion.
Extent Flexibility	The ability to bend, stretch, twist, or reach with your body, arms, and/or legs.
Visual Color Discrimination	The ability to match or detect differences between colors, including shades of color and brightness.
Perceptual Speed	The ability to quickly and accurately compare similarities and differences among sets of letters, numbers, objects, pictures, or patterns. The things to be compared may be presented at the same time or one after the other. This ability also includes comparing a presented object with a remembered object.

Written Expression	The ability to communicate information and ideas in writing so others will understand.
Far Vision	The ability to see details at a distance.
Static Strength	The ability to exert maximum muscle force to lift, push, pull, or carry objects.
Time Sharing	The ability to shift back and forth between two or more activities or sources of information (such as speech, sounds, touch, or other sources).
Flexibility of Closure	The ability to identify or detect a known pattern (a figure, object, word, or sound) that is hidden in other distracting material.
Speed of Closure	The ability to quickly make sense of, combine, and organize information into meaningful patterns.
Fluency of Ideas	The ability to come up with a number of ideas about a topic (the number of ideas is important, not their quality, correctness, or creativity).
Memorization	The ability to remember information such as words, numbers, pictures, and procedures.
Auditory Attention	The ability to focus on a single source of sound in the presence of other distracting sounds.
Wrist-Finger Speed	The ability to make fast, simple, repeated movements of the fingers, hands, and wrists.
Hearing Sensitivity	The ability to detect or tell the differences between sounds that vary in pitch and loudness.
Number Facility	The ability to add, subtract, multiply, or divide quickly and correctly.
Speed of Limb Movement	The ability to quickly move the arms and legs.
Rate Control	The ability to time your movements or the movement of a piece of equipment in anticipation of changes in the speed and/or direction of a moving object or scene.
Response Orientation	The ability to choose quickly between two or more movements in response to two or more different signals (lights, sounds, pictures). It includes the speed with which the correct response is started with the hand, foot, or other body part.
Gross Body Equilibrium	The ability to keep or regain your body balance or stay upright when in an unstable position.
Reaction Time	The ability to quickly respond (with the hand, finger, or foot) to a signal (sound, light, picture) when it appears.
Dynamic Strength	The ability to exert muscle force repeatedly or continuously over time. This involves muscular endurance and resistance to muscle fatigue.
Peripheral Vision	The ability to see objects or movement of objects to one's side when the eyes are looking ahead.
Night Vision	The ability to see under low light conditions.
Sound Localization	The ability to tell the direction from which a sound originated.
Mathematical Reasoning	The ability to choose the right mathematical methods or formulas to solve a problem.
Stamina	The ability to exert yourself physically over long periods of time without getting winded or out of breath.
Gross Body Coordination	The ability to coordinate the movement of your arms, legs, and torso together when the whole body is in motion.
Glare Sensitivity	The ability to see objects in the presence of glare or bright lighting.
Spatial Orientation	The ability to know your location in relation to the environment or to know where other objects are in relation to you.
Explosive Strength	The ability to use short bursts of muscle force to propel oneself (as in jumping or sprinting), or to throw an object.
Dynamic Flexibility	The ability to quickly and repeatedly bend, stretch, twist, or reach out with your body, arms, and/or legs.

Work_Activity	Work_Activity Definitions
Repairing and Maintaining Mechanical Equipment	Servicing, repairing, adjusting, and testing machines, devices, moving parts, and equipment that operate primarily on the basis of mechanical (not electronic) principles.
Making Decisions and Solving Problems	Analyzing information and evaluating results to choose the best solution and solve problems.
Selling or Influencing Others	Convincing others to buy merchandise/goods or to otherwise change their minds or actions.
Performing for or Working Directly with the Public	Performing for people or dealing directly with the public. This includes serving customers in restaurants and stores, and receiving clients or guests.
Communicating with Persons Outside Organization	Communicating with people outside the organization, representing the organization to customers, the public, government, and other external sources. This information can be exchanged in person, in writing, or by telephone or e-mail.
Documenting/Recording Information	Entering, transcribing, recording, storing, or maintaining information in written or electronic/magnetic form.

Inspecting Equipment, Structures, or Material	Inspecting equipment, structures, or materials to identify the cause of errors or other problems or defects.
Identifying Objects, Actions, and Events	Identifying information by categorizing, estimating, recognizing differences or similarities, and detecting changes in circumstances or events.
Communicating with Supervisors, Peers, or Subordin	Providing information to supervisors, co-workers, and subordinates by telephone, in written form, e-mail, or in person.
Updating and Using Relevant Knowledge	Keeping up-to-date technically and applying new knowledge to your job.
Getting Information	Observing, receiving, and otherwise obtaining information from all relevant sources.
Monitoring and Controlling Resources	Monitoring and controlling resources and overseeing the spending of money.
Monitor Processes, Materials, or Surroundings	Monitoring and reviewing information from materials, events, or the environment, to detect or assess problems.
Handling and Moving Objects	Using hands and arms in handling, installing, positioning, and moving materials, and manipulating things.
Thinking Creatively	Developing, designing, or creating new applications, ideas, relationships, systems, or products, including artistic contributions.
Analyzing Data or Information	Identifying the underlying principles, reasons, or facts of information by breaking down information or data into separate parts.
Organizing, Planning, and Prioritizing Work	Developing specific goals and plans to prioritize, organize, and accomplish your work.
Coaching and Developing Others	Identifying the developmental needs of others and coaching, mentoring, or otherwise helping others to improve their knowledge or skills.
Interpreting the Meaning of Information for Others	Translating or explaining what information means and how it can be used.
Processing Information	Compiling, coding, categorizing, calculating, tabulating, auditing, or verifying information or data.
Operating Vehicles, Mechanized Devices, or Equipme	Running, maneuvering, navigating, or driving vehicles or mechanized equipment, such as forklifts, passenger vehicles, aircraft, or water craft.
Estimating the Quantifiable Characteristics of Pro	Estimating sizes, distances, and quantities; or determining time, costs, resources, or materials needed to perform a work activity.
Controlling Machines and Processes	Using either control mechanisms or direct physical activity to operate machines or processes (not including computers or vehicles).
Judging the Qualities of Things, Services, or Peop	Assessing the value, importance, or quality of things or people.
Scheduling Work and Activities	Scheduling events, programs, and activities, as well as the work of others.
Training and Teaching Others	Identifying the educational needs of others, developing formal educational or training programs or classes, and teaching or instructing others.
Performing General Physical Activities	Performing physical activities that require considerable use of your arms and legs and moving your whole body, such as climbing, lifting, balancing, walking, stooping, and handling of materials.
Provide Consultation and Advice to Others	Providing guidance and expert advice to management or other groups on technical, systems-, or process-related topics.
Establishing and Maintaining Interpersonal Relatio	Developing constructive and cooperative working relationships with others, and maintaining them over time.
Guiding, Directing, and Motivating Subordinates	Providing guidance and direction to subordinates, including setting performance standards and monitoring performance.
Resolving Conflicts and Negotiating with Others	Handling complaints, settling disputes, and resolving grievances and conflicts, or otherwise negotiating with others.
Performing Administrative Activities	Performing day-to-day administrative tasks such as maintaining information files and processing paperwork.
Evaluating Information to Determine Compliance wit	Using relevant information and individual judgment to determine whether events or processes comply with laws, regulations, or standards.
Developing and Building Teams	Encouraging and building mutual trust, respect, and cooperation among team members.
Coordinating the Work and Activities of Others	Getting members of a group to work together to accomplish tasks.
Developing Objectives and Strategies	Establishing long-range objectives and specifying the strategies and actions to achieve them.
Assisting and Caring for Others	Providing personal assistance, medical attention, emotional support, or other personal care to others such as coworkers, customers, or patients.

Interacting With Computers	Using computers and computer systems (including hardware and software) to program, write software, set up functions, enter data, or process information.
Drafting, Laying Out, and Specifying Technical Dev	Providing documentation, detailed instructions, drawings, or specifications to tell others about how devices, parts, equipment, or structures are to be fabricated, constructed, assembled, modified, maintained, or used.
Repairing and Maintaining Electronic Equipment	Servicing, repairing, calibrating, regulating, fine-tuning, or testing machines, devices, and equipment that operate primarily on the basis of electrical or electronic (not mechanical) principles.
Staffing Organizational Units	Recruiting, interviewing, selecting, hiring, and promoting employees in an organization.

Work_Context	Work_Context Definitions
Telephone	How often do you have telephone conversations in this job?
Indoors, Environmentally Controlled	How often does this job require working indoors in environmentally controlled conditions?
Deal With External Customers	How important is it to work with external customers or the public in this job?
Freedom to Make Decisions	How much decision making freedom, without supervision, does the job offer?
Spend Time Standing	How much does this job require standing?
Spend Time Using Your Hands to Handle, Control, or	How much does this job require using your hands to handle, control, or feel objects, tools or controls?
Structured versus Unstructured Work	To what extent is this job structured for the worker, rather than allowing the worker to determine tasks, priorities, and goals?
Face-to-Face Discussions	How often do you have to have face-to-face discussions with individuals or teams in this job?
Impact of Decisions on Co-workers or Company Resul	How do the decisions an employee makes impact the results of co-workers, clients or the company?
Frequency of Decision Making	How frequently is the worker required to make decisions that affect other people, the financial resources, and/or the image and reputation of the organization?
Contact With Others	How much does this job require the worker to be in contact with others (face-to-face, by telephone, or otherwise) in order to perform it?
Time Pressure	How often does this job require the worker to meet strict deadlines?
Exposed to Contaminants	How often does this job require working exposed to contaminants (such as pollutants, gases, dust or odors)?
Importance of Being Exact or Accurate	How important is being very exact or highly accurate in performing this job?
Physical Proximity	To what extent does this job require the worker to perform job tasks in close physical proximity to other people?
Responsibility for Outcomes and Results	How responsible is the worker for work outcomes and results of other workers?
Sounds, Noise Levels Are Distracting or Uncomforta	How often does this job require working exposed to sounds and noise levels that are distracting or uncomfortable?
Work With Work Group or Team	How important is it to work with others in a group or team in this job?
Wear Common Protective or Safety Equipment such as	How much does this job require wearing common protective or safety equipment such as safety shoes, glasses, gloves, hard hats or live jackets?
Exposed to Minor Burns, Cuts, Bites, or Stings	How often does this job require exposure to minor burns, cuts, bites, or stings?
Deal With Unpleasant or Angry People	How frequently does the worker have to deal with unpleasant, angry, or discourteous individuals as part of the job requirements?
Importance of Repeating Same Tasks	How important is repeating the same physical activities (e.g., key entry) or mental activities (e.g., checking entries in a ledger) over and over, without stopping, to performing this job?
Consequence of Error	How serious would the result usually be if the worker made a mistake that was not readily correctable?
Exposed to Hazardous Equipment	How often does this job require exposure to hazardous equipment?
Electronic Mail	How often do you use electronic mail in this job?
Level of Competition	To what extent does this job require the worker to compete or to be aware of competitive pressures?
Frequency of Conflict Situations	How often are there conflict situations the employee has to face in this job?
Cramped Work Space, Awkward Positions	How often does this job require working in cramped work spaces that requires getting into awkward positions?
Coordinate or Lead Others	How important is it to coordinate or lead others in accomplishing work activities in this job?

Responsible for Others' Health and Safety	How much responsibility is there for the health and safety of others in this job?
Exposed to High Places	How often does this job require exposure to high places?
Letters and Memos	How often does the job require written letters and memos?
Spend Time Walking and Running	How much does this job require walking and running?
Spend Time Bending or Twisting the Body	How much does this job require bending or twisting your body?
Very Hot or Cold Temperatures	How often does this job require working in very hot (above 90 F degrees) or very cold (below 32 F degrees) temperatures?
Exposed to Hazardous Conditions	How often does this job require exposure to hazardous conditions?
Spend Time Making Repetitive Motions	How much does this job require making repetitive motions?
Spend Time Keeping or Regaining Balance	How much does this job require keeping or regaining your balance?
Extremely Bright or Inadequate Lighting	How often does this job require working in extremely bright or inadequate lighting conditions?
Spend Time Kneeling, Crouching, Stooping, or Crawl	How much does this job require kneeling, crouching, stooping, or crawling?
Indoors, Not Environmentally Controlled	How often does this job require working indoors in non-controlled environmental conditions (e.g., warehouse without heat)?
Wear Specialized Protective or Safety Equipment su	How much does this job require wearing specialized protective or safety equipment such as breathing apparatus, safety harness, full protection suits, or radiation protection?
In an Enclosed Vehicle or Equipment	How often does this job require working in a closed vehicle or equipment (e.g., car)?
Public Speaking	How often do you have to perform public speaking in this job?
Exposed to Radiation	How often does this job require exposure to radiation?
Outdoors, Exposed to Weather	How often does this job require working outdoors, exposed to all weather conditions?
Spend Time Sitting	How much does this job require sitting?
Spend Time Climbing Ladders, Scaffolds, or Poles	How much does this job require climbing ladders, scaffolds, or poles?
Degree of Automation	How automated is the job?
Exposed to Disease or Infections	How often does this job require exposure to disease/infections?
Outdoors, Under Cover	How often does this job require working outdoors, under cover (e.g., structure with roof but no walls)?
Deal With Physically Aggressive People	How frequently does this job require the worker to deal with physical aggression of violent individuals?
In an Open Vehicle or Equipment	How often does this job require working in an open vehicle or equipment (e.g., tractor)?
Exposed to Whole Body Vibration	How often does this job require exposure to whole body vibration (e.g., operate a jackhammer)?
Pace Determined by Speed of Equipment	How important is it to this job that the pace is determined by the speed of equipment or machinery? (This does not refer to keeping busy at all times on this job.)

Job Zone Component	Job Zone Component Definitions
Title	Job Zone Two: Some Preparation Needed
Overall Experience	Some previous work-related skill, knowledge, or experience may be helpful in these occupations, but usually is not needed. For example, a drywall installer might benefit from experience installing drywall, but an inexperienced person could still learn to be an installer with little difficulty.
Job Training	Employees in these occupations need anywhere from a few months to one year of working with experienced employees.
Job Zone Examples	These occupations often involve using your knowledge and skills to help others. Examples include drywall installers, fire inspectors, flight attendants, pharmacy technicians, salespersons (retail), and tellers.
SVP Range	(4.0 to < 6.0)
Education	These occupations usually require a high school diploma and may require some vocational training or job-related course work. In some cases, an associate's or bachelor's degree could be needed.

Work_Styles	Work_Styles Definitions
Cooperation	Job requires being pleasant with others on the job and displaying a good-natured, cooperative attitude.
Attention to Detail	Job requires being careful about detail and thorough in completing work tasks.

Initiative	Job requires a willingness to take on responsibilities and challenges.
Dependability	Job requires being reliable, responsible, and dependable, and fulfilling obligations.
Achievement/Effort	Job requires establishing and maintaining personally challenging achievement goals and exerting effort toward mastering tasks.
Analytical Thinking	Job requires analyzing information and using logic to address work-related issues and problems.
Self Control	Job requires maintaining composure, keeping emotions in check, controlling anger, and avoiding aggressive behavior, even in very difficult situations.
Persistence	Job requires persistence in the face of obstacles.
Independence	Job requires developing one's own ways of doing things, guiding oneself with little or no supervision, and depending on oneself to get things done.
Adaptability/Flexibility	Job requires being open to change (positive or negative) and to considerable variety in the workplace.
Stress Tolerance	Job requires accepting criticism and dealing calmly and effectively with high stress situations.
Leadership	Job requires a willingness to lead, take charge, and offer opinions and direction.
Integrity	Job requires being honest and ethical.
Concern for Others	Job requires being sensitive to others' needs and feelings and being understanding and helpful on the job.
Innovation	Job requires creativity and alternative thinking to develop new ideas for and answers to work-related problems.
Social Orientation	Job requires preferring to work with others rather than alone, and being personally connected with others on the job.

49-3092.00 - Recreational Vehicle Service Technicians

Diagnose, inspect, adjust, repair, or overhaul recreational vehicles including travel trailers. May specialize in maintaining gas, electrical, hydraulic, plumbing, or chassis/towing systems as well as repairing generators, appliances, and interior components.

Tasks

1) Confer with customers, read work orders, and examine vehicles needing repair in order to determine the nature and extent of damage.

2) Connect electrical systems to outside power sources, and activate switches to test the operation of appliances and light fixtures.

3) Inspect recreational vehicles to diagnose problems, then perform necessary adjustment, repair, or overhaul.

4) Remove damaged exterior panels, and repair and replace structural frame members.

5) Repair leaks with caulking compound, or replace pipes, using pipe wrenches.

6) Repair plumbing and propane gas lines, using caulking compounds and plastic or copper pipe.

7) Open and close doors, windows, and drawers to test their operation, trimming edges to fit as necessary.

8) Refinish wood surfaces on cabinets, doors, moldings, and floors, using power sanders, putty, spray equipment, brushes, paints, or varnishes.

9) Reset hardware, using chisels, mallets, and screwdrivers.

10) Seal open sides of modular units to prepare them for shipment, using polyethylene sheets, nails, and hammers.

11) Connect water hoses to inlet pipes of plumbing systems, and test operation of toilets and sinks.

12) Locate and repair frayed wiring, broken connections, or incorrect wiring, using ohmmeters, soldering irons, tape, and hand tools.

13) List parts needed, estimate costs, and plan work procedures, using parts lists, technical manuals, and diagrams.

49-9041.00 - Industrial Machinery Mechanics

Repair, install, adjust, or maintain industrial production and processing machinery or refinery and pipeline distribution systems.

Tasks

1) Analyze test results, machine error messages, and information obtained from operators in order to diagnose equipment problems.

2) Record parts and materials used, and order or requisition new parts and materials as necessary.

3) Enter codes and instructions to program computer-controlled machinery.

4) Demonstrate equipment functions and features to machine operators.

5) Cut and weld metal to repair broken metal parts, fabricate new parts, and assemble new equipment.

6) Study blueprints and manufacturers' manuals to determine correct installation and operation of machinery.

7) Repair and replace broken or malfunctioning components of machinery and equipment.

8) Repair and maintain the operating condition of industrial production and processing machinery and equipment.

9) Reassemble equipment after completion of inspections, testing, or repairs.

10) Operate newly repaired machinery and equipment to verify the adequacy of repairs.

11) Examine parts for defects such as breakage and excessive wear.

12) Clean, lubricate, and adjust parts, equipment, and machinery.

13) Observe and test the operation of machinery and equipment in order to diagnose malfunctions, using voltmeters and other testing devices.

14) Disassemble machinery and equipment to remove parts and make repairs.

49-9043.00 - Maintenance Workers, Machinery

Lubricate machinery, change parts, or perform other routine machinery maintenance.

Tasks

1) Inventory and requisition machine parts, equipment, and other supplies so that stock can be maintained and replenished.

2) Measure, mix, prepare, and test chemical solutions used to clean or repair machinery and equipment.

3) Install, replace, or change machine parts and attachments, according to production specifications.

4) Dismantle machines and remove parts for repair, using hand tools, chain falls, jacks, cranes, or hoists.

5) Clean machines and machine parts, using cleaning solvents, cloths, air guns, hoses, vacuums, or other equipment.

6) Transport machine parts, tools, equipment, and other material between work areas and storage, using cranes, hoists, or dollies.

7) Inspect or test damaged machine parts, and mark defective areas or advise supervisors of repair needs.

8) Set up and operate machines, and adjust controls to regulate operations.

9) Lubricate or apply adhesives or other materials to machines, machine parts, or other equipment, according to specified procedures.

10) Replace, empty, or replenish machine and equipment containers such as gas tanks or boxes.

11) Collect and discard worn machine parts and other refuse in order to maintain machinery and work areas.

12) Read work orders and specifications to determine machines and equipment requiring repair or maintenance.

13) Collaborate with other workers to repair or move machines, machine parts, or equipment.

14) Start machines and observe mechanical operation to determine efficiency and to detect problems.

15) Replace or repair metal, wood, leather, glass, or other lining in machines, or in equipment compartments or containers.

16) Remove hardened material from machines or machine parts, using abrasives, power and hand tools, jackhammers, sledgehammers, or other equipment.

17) Record production, repair, and machine maintenance information.

49-9093.00 - Fabric Menders, Except Garment

Repair tears, holes, and other defects in fabrics, such as draperies, linens, parachutes, and tents.

Tasks

1) Pull knots to the wrong sides of garments, using hooks.

2) Patch holes, sew tears and ripped seams, or darn defects in items, using needles and thread or sewing machines.

3) Check repaired and repacked survival equipment to ensure that it meets specifications.

4) Stamp grommets into canvas, using mallets and punches or eyelet machines.

5) Spread out articles or materials and examine them for holes, tears, worn areas, and other defects.

6) Sew labels and emblems onto articles for identification.

7) Sew fringe, tassels, and ruffles onto drapes and curtains, and buttons and trimming onto garments.

8) Repair holes by weaving thread over them, using needles.

9) Replace defective shrouds, and splice connections between shrouds and harnesses, using hand tools.

10) Clean stains from fabric or garments, using spray guns and cleaning fluid.

11) Operate sewing machines to restitch defective seams, sew up holes, or replace components of fabric articles.

12) Trim edges of cut or torn fabric, using scissors or knives, and stitch trimmed edges together.

13) Re-knit runs and replace broken threads, using latch needles.

49-9094.00 - Locksmiths and Safe Repairers

Repair and open locks; make keys; change locks and safe combinations; and install and repair safes.

Tasks

1) Cut new or duplicate keys, using keycutting machines.

2) Disassemble mechanical or electrical locking devices, and repair or replace worn tumblers, springs, and other parts, using hand tools.

3) Move picklocks in cylinders in order to open door locks without keys.

4) Keep records of company locks and keys.

5) Repair and adjust safes, vault doors, and vault components, using hand tools, lathes, drill presses, and welding and acetylene cutting apparatus.

6) Open safe locks by drilling.

7) Install safes, vault doors, and deposit boxes according to blueprints, using equipment such as powered drills, taps, dies, truck cranes, and dollies.

8) Remove interior and exterior finishes on safes and vaults, and spray on new finishes.

Knowledge	Knowledge Definitions
Customer and Personal Service	Knowledge of principles and processes for providing customer and personal services. This includes customer needs assessment, meeting quality standards for services, and evaluation of customer satisfaction.
Administration and Management	Knowledge of business and management principles involved in strategic planning, resource allocation, human resources modeling, leadership technique, production methods, and coordination of people and resources.
Clerical	Knowledge of administrative and clerical procedures and systems such as word processing, managing files and records, stenography and transcription, designing forms, and other office procedures and terminology.
Public Safety and Security	Knowledge of relevant equipment, policies, procedures, and strategies to promote effective local, state, or national security operations for the protection of people, data, property, and institutions.
Mechanical	Knowledge of machines and tools, including their designs, uses, repair, and maintenance.
Sales and Marketing	Knowledge of principles and methods for showing, promoting, and selling products or services. This includes marketing strategy and tactics, product demonstration, sales techniques, and sales control systems.
Mathematics	Knowledge of arithmetic, algebra, geometry, calculus, statistics, and their applications.
English Language	Knowledge of the structure and content of the English language including the meaning and spelling of words, rules of composition, and grammar.
Law and Government	Knowledge of laws, legal codes, court procedures, precedents, government regulations, executive orders, agency rules, and the democratic political process.
Engineering and Technology	Knowledge of the practical application of engineering science and technology. This includes applying principles, techniques, procedures, and equipment to the design and production of various goods and services.
Education and Training	Knowledge of principles and methods for curriculum and training design, teaching and instruction for individuals and groups, and the measurement of training effects.
Computers and Electronics	Knowledge of circuit boards, processors, chips, electronic equipment, and computer hardware and software, including applications and programming.
Economics and Accounting	Knowledge of economic and accounting principles and practices, the financial markets, banking and the analysis and reporting of financial data.
Design	Knowledge of design techniques, tools, and principles involved in production of precision technical plans, blueprints, drawings, and models.
Personnel and Human Resources	Knowledge of principles and procedures for personnel recruitment, selection, training, compensation and benefits, labor relations and negotiation, and personnel information systems.
Production and Processing	Knowledge of raw materials, production processes, quality control, costs, and other techniques for maximizing the effective manufacture and distribution of goods.
Telecommunications	Knowledge of transmission, broadcasting, switching, control, and operation of telecommunications systems.
Foreign Language	Knowledge of the structure and content of a foreign (non-English) language including the meaning and spelling of words, rules of composition and grammar, and pronunciation.
Communications and Media	Knowledge of media production, communication, and dissemination techniques and methods. This includes alternative ways to inform and entertain via written, oral, and visual media.
Psychology	Knowledge of human behavior and performance; individual differences in ability, personality, and interests; learning and motivation; psychological research methods; and the assessment and treatment of behavioral and affective disorders.
Building and Construction	Knowledge of materials, methods, and the tools involved in the construction or repair of houses, buildings, or other structures such as highways and roads.
Transportation	Knowledge of principles and methods for moving people or goods by air, rail, sea, or road, including the relative costs and benefits.
Physics	Knowledge and prediction of physical principles, laws, their interrelationships, and applications to understanding fluid, material, and atmospheric dynamics, and mechanical, electrical, atomic and sub-atomic structures and processes.
Philosophy and Theology	Knowledge of different philosophical systems and religions. This includes their basic principles, values, ethics, ways of thinking, customs, practices, and their impact on human culture.
Sociology and Anthropology	Knowledge of group behavior and dynamics, societal trends and influences, human migrations, ethnicity, cultures and their history and origins.
Geography	Knowledge of principles and methods for describing the features of land, sea, and air masses, including their physical characteristics, locations, interrelationships, and distribution of plant, animal, and human life.
Therapy and Counseling	Knowledge of principles, methods, and procedures for diagnosis, treatment, and rehabilitation of physical and mental dysfunctions, and for career counseling and guidance.
History and Archeology	Knowledge of historical events and their causes, indicators, and effects on civilizations and cultures.

Chemistry	Knowledge of the chemical composition, structure, and properties of substances and of the chemical processes and transformations that they undergo. This includes uses of chemicals and their interactions, danger signs, production techniques, and disposal methods.
Medicine and Dentistry	Knowledge of the information and techniques needed to diagnose and treat human injuries, diseases, and deformities. This includes symptoms, treatment alternatives, drug properties and interactions, and preventive health-care measures.
Fine Arts	Knowledge of the theory and techniques required to compose, produce, and perform works of music, dance, visual arts, drama, and sculpture.
Food Production	Knowledge of techniques and equipment for planting, growing, and harvesting food products (both plant and animal) for consumption, including storage/handling techniques.
Biology	Knowledge of plant and animal organisms, their tissues, cells, functions, interdependencies, and interactions with each other and the environment.

Skills	Skills Definitions
Installation	Installing equipment, machines, wiring, or programs to meet specifications.
Repairing	Repairing machines or systems using the needed tools.
Equipment Selection	Determining the kind of tools and equipment needed to do a job.
Troubleshooting	Determining causes of operating errors and deciding what to do about it.
Equipment Maintenance	Performing routine maintenance on equipment and determining when and what kind of maintenance is needed.
Active Listening	Giving full attention to what other people are saying, taking time to understand the points being made, asking questions as appropriate, and not interrupting at inappropriate times.
Reading Comprehension	Understanding written sentences and paragraphs in work related documents.
Service Orientation	Actively looking for ways to help people.
Time Management	Managing one's own time and the time of others.
Active Learning	Understanding the implications of new information for both current and future problem-solving and decision-making.
Speaking	Talking to others to convey information effectively.
Mathematics	Using mathematics to solve problems.
Critical Thinking	Using logic and reasoning to identify the strengths and weaknesses of alternative solutions, conclusions or approaches to problems.
Coordination	Adjusting actions in relation to others' actions.
Complex Problem Solving	Identifying complex problems and reviewing related information to develop and evaluate options and implement solutions.
Learning Strategies	Selecting and using training/instructional methods and procedures appropriate for the situation when learning or teaching new things.
Judgment and Decision Making	Considering the relative costs and benefits of potential actions to choose the most appropriate one.
Management of Material Resources	Obtaining and seeing to the appropriate use of equipment, facilities, and materials needed to do certain work.
Social Perceptiveness	Being aware of others' reactions and understanding why they react as they do.
Management of Financial Resources	Determining how money will be spent to get the work done, and accounting for these expenditures.
Persuasion	Persuading others to change their minds or behavior.
Monitoring	Monitoring/Assessing performance of yourself, other individuals, or organizations to make improvements or take corrective action.
Technology Design	Generating or adapting equipment and technology to serve user needs.
Writing	Communicating effectively in writing as appropriate for the needs of the audience.
Instructing	Teaching others how to do something.
Operations Analysis	Analyzing needs and product requirements to create a design.
Systems Analysis	Determining how a system should work and how changes in conditions, operations, and the environment will affect outcomes.
Operation and Control	Controlling operations of equipment or systems.
Operation Monitoring	Watching gauges, dials, or other indicators to make sure a machine is working properly.
Negotiation	Bringing others together and trying to reconcile differences.
Quality Control Analysis	Conducting tests and inspections of products, services, or processes to evaluate quality or performance.

Management of Personnel Resources	Motivating, developing, and directing people as they work, identifying the best people for the job.
Systems Evaluation	Identifying measures or indicators of system performance and the actions needed to improve or correct performance, relative to the goals of the system.
Programming	Writing computer programs for various purposes.
Science	Using scientific rules and methods to solve problems.

Ability	Ability Definitions
Arm-Hand Steadiness	The ability to keep your hand and arm steady while moving your arm or while holding your arm and hand in one position.
Finger Dexterity	The ability to make precisely coordinated movements of the fingers of one or both hands to grasp, manipulate, or assemble very small objects.
Near Vision	The ability to see details at close range (within a few feet of the observer).
Manual Dexterity	The ability to quickly move your hand, your hand together with your arm, or your two hands to grasp, manipulate, or assemble objects.
Control Precision	The ability to quickly and repeatedly adjust the controls of a machine or a vehicle to exact positions.
Deductive Reasoning	The ability to apply general rules to specific problems to produce answers that make sense.
Multilimb Coordination	The ability to coordinate two or more limbs (for example, two arms, two legs, or one leg and one arm) while sitting, standing, or lying down. It does not involve performing the activities while the whole body is in motion.
Oral Comprehension	The ability to listen to and understand information and ideas presented through spoken words and sentences.
Speech Clarity	The ability to speak clearly so others can understand you.
Problem Sensitivity	The ability to tell when something is wrong or is likely to go wrong. It does not involve solving the problem, only recognizing there is a problem.
Depth Perception	The ability to judge which of several objects is closer or farther away from you, or to judge the distance between you and an object.
Speech Recognition	The ability to identify and understand the speech of another person.
Information Ordering	The ability to arrange things or actions in a certain order or pattern according to a specific rule or set of rules (e.g., patterns of numbers, letters, words, pictures, mathematical operations).
Inductive Reasoning	The ability to combine pieces of information to form general rules or conclusions (includes finding a relationship among seemingly unrelated events).
Hearing Sensitivity	The ability to detect or tell the differences between sounds that vary in pitch and loudness.
Oral Expression	The ability to communicate information and ideas in speaking so others will understand.
Selective Attention	The ability to concentrate on a task over a period of time without being distracted.
Written Expression	The ability to communicate information and ideas in writing so others will understand.
Visualization	The ability to imagine how something will look after it is moved around or when its parts are moved or rearranged.
Written Comprehension	The ability to read and understand information and ideas presented in writing.
Flexibility of Closure	The ability to identify or detect a known pattern (a figure, object, word, or sound) that is hidden in other distracting material.
Speed of Closure	The ability to quickly make sense of, combine, and organize information into meaningful patterns.
Glare Sensitivity	The ability to see objects in the presence of glare or bright lighting.
Fluency of Ideas	The ability to come up with a number of ideas about a topic (the number of ideas is important, not their quality, correctness, or creativity).
Category Flexibility	The ability to generate or use different sets of rules for combining or grouping things in different ways.
Visual Color Discrimination	The ability to match or detect differences between colors, including shades of color and brightness.
Extent Flexibility	The ability to bend, stretch, twist, or reach with your body, arms, and/or legs.
Originality	The ability to come up with unusual or clever ideas about a given topic or situation, or to develop creative ways to solve a problem.
Reaction Time	The ability to quickly respond (with the hand, finger, or foot) to a signal (sound, light, picture) when it appears.

Time Sharing	The ability to shift back and forth between two or more activities or sources of information (such as speech, sounds, touch, or other sources).
Far Vision	The ability to see details at a distance.
Perceptual Speed	The ability to quickly and accurately compare similarities and differences among sets of letters, numbers, objects, pictures, or patterns. The things to be compared may be presented at the same time or one after the other. This ability also includes comparing a presented object with a remembered object.
Rate Control	The ability to time your movements or the movement of a piece of equipment in anticipation of changes in the speed and/or direction of a moving object or scene.
Memorization	The ability to remember information such as words, numbers, pictures, and procedures.
Response Orientation	The ability to choose quickly between two or more movements in response to two or more different signals (lights, sounds, pictures). It includes the speed with which the correct response is started with the hand, foot, or other body part.
Number Facility	The ability to add, subtract, multiply, or divide quickly and correctly.
Speed of Limb Movement	The ability to quickly move the arms and legs.
Auditory Attention	The ability to focus on a single source of sound in the presence of other distracting sounds.
Trunk Strength	The ability to use your abdominal and lower back muscles to support part of the body repeatedly or continuously over time without 'giving out' or fatiguing.
Wrist-Finger Speed	The ability to make fast, simple, repeated movements of the fingers, hands, and wrists.
Mathematical Reasoning	The ability to choose the right mathematical methods or formulas to solve a problem.
Static Strength	The ability to exert maximum muscle force to lift, push, pull, or carry objects.
Gross Body Coordination	The ability to coordinate the movement of your arms, legs, and torso together when the whole body is in motion.
Sound Localization	The ability to tell the direction from which a sound originated.
Peripheral Vision	The ability to see objects or movement of objects to one's side when the eyes are looking ahead.
Night Vision	The ability to see under low light conditions.
Spatial Orientation	The ability to know your location in relation to the environment or to know where other objects are in relation to you.
Stamina	The ability to exert yourself physically over long periods of time without getting winded or out of breath.
Dynamic Strength	The ability to exert muscle force repeatedly or continuously over time. This involves muscular endurance and resistance to muscle fatigue.
Gross Body Equilibrium	The ability to keep or regain your body balance or stay upright when in an unstable position.
Explosive Strength	The ability to use short bursts of muscle force to propel oneself (as in jumping or sprinting), or to throw an object.
Dynamic Flexibility	The ability to quickly and repeatedly bend, stretch, twist, or reach out with your body, arms, and/or legs.

Work_Activity	Work_Activity Definitions
Updating and Using Relevant Knowledge	Keeping up-to-date technically and applying new knowledge to your job.
Performing for or Working Directly with the Public	Performing for people or dealing directly with the public. This includes serving customers in restaurants and stores, and receiving clients or guests.
Getting Information	Observing, receiving, and otherwise obtaining information from all relevant sources.
Controlling Machines and Processes	Using either control mechanisms or direct physical activity to operate machines or processes (not including computers or vehicles).
Operating Vehicles, Mechanized Devices, or Equipme	Running, maneuvering, navigating, or driving vehicles or mechanized equipment, such as forklifts, passenger vehicles, aircraft, or water craft.
Communicating with Persons Outside Organization	Communicating with people outside the organization, representing the organization to customers, the public, government, and other external sources. This information can be exchanged in person, in writing, or by telephone or e-mail.
Selling or Influencing Others	Convincing others to buy merchandise/goods or to otherwise change their minds or actions.
Making Decisions and Solving Problems	Analyzing information and evaluating results to choose the best solution and solve problems.
Establishing and Maintaining Interpersonal Relatio	Developing constructive and cooperative working relationships with others, and maintaining them over time.

Evaluating Information to Determine Compliance wit	Using relevant information and individual judgment to determine whether events or processes comply with laws, regulations, or standards.
Documenting/Recording Information	Entering, transcribing, recording, storing, or maintaining information in written or electronic/magnetic form.
Inspecting Equipment, Structures, or Material	Inspecting equipment, structures, or materials to identify the cause of errors or other problems or defects.
Identifying Objects, Actions, and Events	Identifying information by categorizing, estimating, recognizing differences or similarities, and detecting changes in circumstances or events.
Repairing and Maintaining Mechanical Equipment	Servicing, repairing, adjusting, and testing machines, devices, moving parts, and equipment that operate primarily on the basis of mechanical (not electronic) principles.
Communicating with Supervisors, Peers, or Subordin	Providing information to supervisors, co-workers, and subordinates by telephone, in written form, e-mail, or in person.
Organizing, Planning, and Prioritizing Work	Developing specific goals and plans to prioritize, organize, and accomplish your work.
Performing General Physical Activities	Performing physical activities that require considerable use of your arms and legs and moving your whole body, such as climbing, lifting, balancing, walking, stooping, and handling of materials.
Scheduling Work and Activities	Scheduling events, programs, and activities, as well as the work of others.
Handling and Moving Objects	Using hands and arms in handling, installing, positioning, and moving materials, and manipulating things.
Thinking Creatively	Developing, designing, or creating new applications, ideas, relationships, systems, or products, including artistic contributions.
Resolving Conflicts and Negotiating with Others	Handling complaints, settling disputes, and resolving grievances and conflicts, or otherwise negotiating with others.
Monitoring and Controlling Resources	Monitoring and controlling resources and overseeing the spending of money.
Performing Administrative Activities	Performing day-to-day administrative tasks such as maintaining information files and processing paperwork.
Provide Consultation and Advice to Others	Providing guidance and expert advice to management or other groups on technical, systems-, or process-related topics.
Processing Information	Compiling, coding, categorizing, calculating, tabulating, auditing, or verifying information or data.
Estimating the Quantifiable Characteristics of Pro	Estimating sizes, distances, and quantities; or determining time, costs, resources, or materials needed to perform a work activity.
Assisting and Caring for Others	Providing personal assistance, medical attention, emotional support, or other personal care to others such as coworkers, customers, or patients.
Training and Teaching Others	Identifying the educational needs of others, developing formal educational or training programs or classes, and teaching or instructing others.
Developing Objectives and Strategies	Establishing long-range objectives and specifying the strategies and actions to achieve them.
Coordinating the Work and Activities of Others	Getting members of a group to work together to accomplish tasks.
Monitor Processes, Materials, or Surroundings	Monitoring and reviewing information from materials, events, or the environment, to detect or assess problems.
Interpreting the Meaning of Information for Others	Translating or explaining what information means and how it can be used.
Interacting With Computers	Using computers and computer systems (including hardware and software) to program, write software, set up functions, enter data, or process information.
Analyzing Data or Information	Identifying the underlying principles, reasons, or facts of information by breaking down information or data into separate parts.
Judging the Qualities of Things, Services, or Peop	Assessing the value, importance, or quality of things or people.
Coaching and Developing Others	Identifying the developmental needs of others and coaching, mentoring, or otherwise helping others to improve their knowledge or skills.
Developing and Building Teams	Encouraging and building mutual trust, respect, and cooperation among team members.
Drafting, Laying Out, and Specifying Technical Dev	Providing documentation, detailed instructions, drawings, or specifications to tell others about how devices, parts, equipment, or structures are to be fabricated, constructed, assembled, modified, maintained, or used.
Guiding, Directing, and Motivating Subordinates	Providing guidance and direction to subordinates, including setting performance standards and monitoring performance.

Repairing and Maintaining Electronic Equipment	Servicing, repairing, calibrating, regulating, fine-tuning, or testing machines, devices, and equipment that operate primarily on the basis of electrical or electronic (not mechanical) principles.
Staffing Organizational Units	Recruiting, interviewing, selecting, hiring, and promoting employees in an organization.

Work_Context	**Work_Context Definitions**
Telephone	How often do you have telephone conversations in this job?
Face-to-Face Discussions	How often do you have to have face-to-face discussions with individuals or teams in this job?
Freedom to Make Decisions	How much decision making freedom, without supervision, does the job offer?
Spend Time Using Your Hands to Handle, Control, or	How much does this job require using your hands to handle, control, or feel objects, tools or controls?
Contact With Others	How much does this job require the worker to be in contact with others (face-to-face, by telephone, or otherwise) in order to perform it?
Outdoors, Exposed to Weather	How often does this job require working outdoors, exposed to all weather conditions?
Structured versus Unstructured Work	To what extent is this job structured for the worker, rather than allowing the worker to determine tasks, priorities, and goals?
Frequency of Decision Making	How frequently is the worker required to make decisions that affect other people, the financial resources, and/or the image and reputation of the organization?
Importance of Being Exact or Accurate	How important is being very exact or highly accurate in performing this job?
Impact of Decisions on Co-workers or Company Resul	How do the decisions an employee makes impact the results of co-workers, clients or the company?
In an Enclosed Vehicle or Equipment	How often does this job require working in a closed vehicle or equipment (e.g., car)?
Extremely Bright or Inadequate Lighting	How often does this job require working in extremely bright or inadequate lighting conditions?
Indoors, Environmentally Controlled	How often does this job require working indoors in environmentally controlled conditions?
Time Pressure	How often does this job require the worker to meet strict deadlines?
Deal With External Customers	How important is it to work with external customers or the public in this job?
Letters and Memos	How often does the job require written letters and memos?
Outdoors, Under Cover	How often does this job require working outdoors, under cover (e.g., structure with roof but no walls)?
Sounds, Noise Levels Are Distracting or Uncomforta	How often does this job require working exposed to sounds and noise levels that are distracting or uncomfortable?
Spend Time Standing	How much does this job require standing?
Indoors, Not Environmentally Controlled	How often does this job require working indoors in non-controlled environmental conditions (e.g., warehouse without heat)?
Physical Proximity	To what extent does this job require the worker to perform job tasks in close physical proximity to other people?
Very Hot or Cold Temperatures	How often does this job require working in very hot (above 90 F degrees) or very cold (below 32 F degrees) temperatures?
Deal With Unpleasant or Angry People	How frequently does the worker have to deal with unpleasant, angry, or discourteous individuals as part of the job requirements?
Exposed to Hazardous Equipment	How often does this job require exposure to hazardous equipment?
Importance of Repeating Same Tasks	How important is repeating the same physical activities (e.g., key entry) or mental activities (e.g., checking entries in a ledger) over and over, without stopping, to performing this job?
Cramped Work Space, Awkward Positions	How often does this job require working in cramped work spaces that requires getting into awkward positions?
Spend Time Walking and Running	How much does this job require walking and running?
Wear Common Protective or Safety Equipment such as	How much does this job require wearing common protective or safety equipment such as safety shoes, glasses, gloves, hard hats or live jackets?
Coordinate or Lead Others	How important is it to coordinate or lead others in accomplishing work activities in this job?
Exposed to Minor Burns, Cuts, Bites, or Stings	How often does this job require exposure to minor burns, cuts, bites, or stings?
Responsibility for Outcomes and Results	How responsible is the worker for work outcomes and results of other workers?
Exposed to Contaminants	How often does this job require working exposed to contaminants (such as pollutants, gases, dust or odors)?

Level of Competition	To what extent does this job require the worker to compete or to be aware of competitive pressures?
Work With Work Group or Team	How important is it to work with others in a group or team in this job?
Frequency of Conflict Situations	How often are there conflict situations the employee has to face in this job?
Spend Time Kneeling, Crouching, Stooping, or Crawl	How much does this job require kneeling, crouching, stooping or crawling?
Spend Time Bending or Twisting the Body	How much does this job require bending or twisting your body?
Consequence of Error	How serious would the result usually be if the worker made a mistake that was not readily correctable?
Spend Time Making Repetitive Motions	How much does this job require making repetitive motions?
Responsible for Others' Health and Safety	How much responsibility is there for the health and safety of others in this job?
Spend Time Sitting	How much does this job require sitting?
Electronic Mail	How often do you use electronic mail in this job?
Degree of Automation	How automated is the job?
Spend Time Keeping or Regaining Balance	How much does this job require keeping or regaining your balance?
Deal With Physically Aggressive People	How frequently does this job require the worker to deal with physical aggression of violent individuals?
Exposed to High Places	How often does this job require exposure to high places?
Exposed to Hazardous Conditions	How often does this job require exposure to hazardous conditions?
Exposed to Disease or Infections	How often does this job require exposure to disease/infections?
Spend Time Climbing Ladders, Scaffolds, or Poles	How much does this job require climbing ladders, scaffolds, or poles?
Pace Determined by Speed of Equipment	How important is it to this job that the pace is determined by the speed of equipment or machinery? (This does not refer to keeping busy at all times on this job.)
In an Open Vehicle or Equipment	How often does this job require working in an open vehicle or equipment (e.g., tractor)?
Public Speaking	How often do you have to perform public speaking in this job?
Wear Specialized Protective or Safety Equipment su	How much does this job require wearing specialized protective or safety equipment such as breathing apparatus, safety harness, full protection suits, or radiation protection?
Exposed to Whole Body Vibration	How often does this job require exposure to whole body vibration (e.g., operate a jackhammer)?
Exposed to Radiation	How often does this job require exposure to radiation?

Job Zone Component	**Job Zone Component Definitions**
Title	Job Zone Two: Some Preparation Needed
Overall Experience	Some previous work-related skill, knowledge, or experience may be helpful in these occupations, but usually is not needed. For example, a drywall installer might benefit from experience installing drywall, but an inexperienced person could still learn to be an installer with little difficulty.
Job Training	Employees in these occupations need anywhere from a few months to one year of working with experienced employees.
Job Zone Examples	These occupations often involve using your knowledge and skills to help others. Examples include drywall installers, fire inspectors, flight attendants, pharmacy technicians, salespersons (retail), and tellers.
SVP Range	(4.0 to < 6.0)
Education	These occupations usually require a high school diploma and may require some vocational training or job-related course work. In some cases, an associate's or bachelor's degree could be needed.

Work_Styles	**Work_Styles Definitions**
Integrity	Job requires being honest and ethical.
Dependability	Job requires being reliable, responsible, and dependable, and fulfilling obligations.
Attention to Detail	Job requires being careful about detail and thorough in completing work tasks.
Independence	Job requires developing one's own ways of doing things, guiding oneself with little or no supervision, and depending on oneself to get things done.
Self Control	Job requires maintaining composure, keeping emotions in check, controlling anger, and avoiding aggressive behavior, even in very difficult situations.

Cooperation	Job requires being pleasant with others on the job and displaying a good-natured, cooperative attitude.
Persistence	Job requires persistence in the face of obstacles.
Innovation	Job requires creativity and alternative thinking to develop new ideas for and answers to work-related problems.
Analytical Thinking	Job requires analyzing information and using logic to address work-related issues and problems.
Initiative	Job requires a willingness to take on responsibilities and challenges.
Stress Tolerance	Job requires accepting criticism and dealing calmly and effectively with high stress situations.
Leadership	Job requires a willingness to lead, take charge, and offer opinions and direction.
Concern for Others	Job requires being sensitive to others' needs and feelings and being understanding and helpful on the job.
Achievement/Effort	Job requires establishing and maintaining personally challenging achievement goals and exerting effort toward mastering tasks.
Adaptability/Flexibility	Job requires being open to change (positive or negative) and to considerable variety in the workplace.
Social Orientation	Job requires preferring to work with others rather than alone, and being personally connected with others on the job.

49-9095.00 - Manufactured Building and Mobile Home Installers

Move or install mobile homes or prefabricated buildings.

Tasks

1) Reset hardware, using chisels, mallets, and screwdrivers.

2) Confer with customers or read work orders to determine the nature and extent of damage to units.

3) Inspect, examine, and test the operation of parts or systems to evaluate operating condition and to determine if repairs are needed.

4) Seal open sides of modular units to prepare them for shipment, using polyethylene sheets, nails, and hammers.

5) Locate and repair frayed wiring, broken connections, or incorrect wiring, using ohmmeters, soldering irons, tape, and hand tools.

6) Remove damaged exterior panels, repair and replace structural frame members, and seal leaks, using hand tools.

7) Open and close doors, windows, and drawers to test their operation; and trim edges to fit, using jackplanes or drawknives.

8) Move and set up mobile homes or prefabricated buildings on owners' lots or at mobile home parks.

9) Install, repair, and replace units, fixtures, appliances, and other items and systems in mobile and modular homes, prefabricated buildings, or travel trailers, using hand tools or power tools.

10) Connect water hoses to inlet pipes of plumbing systems, and test operation of plumbing fixtures.

11) Connect electrical systems to outside power sources and activate switches to test the operation of appliances and light fixtures.

12) List parts needed, estimate costs, and plan work procedures, using parts lists, technical manuals, and diagrams.

13) Refinish wood surfaces on cabinets, doors, moldings, and floors, using power sanders, putty, spray equipment, brushes, paints, or varnishes.

51-2021.00 - Coil Winders, Tapers, and Finishers

Wind wire coils used in electrical components, such as resistors and transformers, and in electrical equipment and instruments, such as field cores, bobbins, armature cores, electrical motors, generators, and control equipment.

49-9095.00 - Manufactured Building and Mobile Home Installers

Tasks

1) Stop machines to remove completed components, using hand tools.

2) Operate or tend wire-coiling machines to wind wire coils used in electrical components such as resistors and transformers, and in electrical equipment and instruments such as bobbins and generators.

3) Apply solutions or paints to wired electrical components, using hand tools; and bake components.

4) Select and load materials such as workpieces, objects, and machine parts onto equipment used in coiling processes.

5) Line slots with sheet insulation, and insert coils into slots.

6) Disassemble and assemble motors, and repair and maintain electrical components and machinery parts, using hand tools.

7) Attach, alter, and trim materials such as wire, insulation, and coils, using hand tools.

8) Cut, strip, and bend wire leads at ends of coils, using pliers and wire scrapers.

9) Examine and test wired electrical components such as motors, armatures, and stators, using measuring devices; and record test results.

10) Review work orders and specifications to determine materials needed and types of parts to be processed.

51-2022.00 - Electrical and Electronic Equipment Assemblers

Assemble or modify electrical or electronic equipment, such as computers, test equipment telemetering systems, electric motors, and batteries.

Tasks

1) Measure and adjust voltages to specified values to determine operational accuracy of instruments.

2) Pack finished assemblies for shipment and transport them to storage areas, using hoists or handtrucks.

3) Adjust, repair, or replace electrical or electronic component parts to correct defects and to ensure conformance to specifications.

4) Explain assembly procedures or techniques to other workers.

5) Assemble electrical or electronic systems and support structures; and install components, units, subassemblies, wiring, and assembly casings, using rivets, bolts, soldering and micro-welding equipment.

6) Drill and tap holes in specified equipment locations to mount control units, and to provide openings for elements, wiring, and instruments.

7) Fabricate and form parts, coils, and structures according to specifications, using drills, calipers, cutters, and saws.

8) Paint structures as specified, using paint sprayers.

9) Inspect and test wiring installations, assemblies, and circuits for resistance factors and for operation; and record results.

10) Mark and tag components so that stock inventory can be tracked and identified.

11) Position, align, and adjust workpieces and electrical parts to facilitate wiring and assembly.

12) Confer with supervisors or engineers to plan and review work activities, and to resolve production problems.

13) Distribute materials, supplies, and subassemblies to work areas.

14) Instruct customers in the installation, repair, and maintenance of products.

15) Clean parts, using cleaning solutions, air hoses, and cloths.

16) Complete, review, and maintain production, time, and component waste reports.

51-2023.00 - Electromechanical Equipment Assemblers

Assemble or modify electromechanical equipment or devices, such as servomechanisms, gyros, dynamometers, magnetic drums, tape drives, brakes, control linkage, actuators, and appliances.

Tasks

1) Operate or tend automated assembling equipment, such as robotics and fixed automation equipment.

2) Attach name plates and mark identifying information on parts.

3) Read blueprints and specifications to determine component parts and assembly sequences of electromechanical units.

4) Operate small cranes to transport or position large parts.

5) Disassemble units to replace parts or to crate them for shipping.

6) Measure parts to determine tolerances, using precision measuring instruments such as micrometers, calipers, and verniers.

7) Pack or fold insulation between panels.

8) Position, align, and adjust parts for proper fit and assembly.

9) Inspect, test, and adjust completed units to ensure that units meet specifications, tolerances, and customer order requirements.

10) File, lap, and buff parts to fit, using hand and power tools.

11) Drill, tap, ream, countersink, and spot-face bolt holes in parts, using drill presses and portable power drills.

12) Connect cables, tubes, and wiring, according to specifications.

13) Clean and lubricate parts and subassemblies, using grease paddles or oilcans.

51-2093.00 - Timing Device Assemblers, Adjusters, and Calibrators

Perform precision assembling or adjusting, within narrow tolerances, of timing devices, such as watches, clocks, or chronometers.

Tasks

1) Bend parts, such as hairsprings, pallets, barrel covers, and bridges, to correct deficiencies in truing or endshake, using tweezers.

2) Examine and adjust hairspring assemblies to ensure horizontal and circular alignment of hairsprings, using calipers, loupes, and watchmakers' tools.

3) Clean and lubricate timepiece parts and assemblies, using solvents, buff sticks, and oil.

4) Disassemble timepieces such as watches, clocks, and chronometers so that repairs can be made.

5) Mount hairsprings and balance wheel assemblies between jaws of truing calipers.

6) Bend inner coils of springs away from or toward collets, using tweezers, in order to locate centers of collets in centers of springs, and to correct errors resulting from faulty colleting of coils.

7) Test operation and fit of timepiece parts and subassemblies, using electronic testing equipment, tweezers, watchmakers' tools, and loupes.

8) Review blueprints, sketches, or work orders to gather information about tasks to be completed.

9) Replace specified parts to repair malfunctioning timepieces, using watchmakers' tools, loupes, and holding fixtures.

10) Assemble and install components of timepieces to complete mechanisms, using watchmakers' tools and loupes.

11) Turn wheels of calipers and examine springs, using loupes, to determine if center coils appear as perfect circles.

12) Adjust sizes or positioning of timepiece parts to achieve specified fit or function, using calipers, fixtures, and loupes.

13) Tighten or replace loose jewels, using watchmakers' tools.

14) Estimate spaces between collets and first inner coils in order to determine if spaces are within acceptable limits.

15) Observe operation of timepiece parts and subassemblies to determine accuracy of movement, and to diagnose causes of defects.

16) Examine components of timepieces such as watches, clocks, or chronometers for defects, using loupes or microscopes.

51-4012.00 - Numerical Tool and Process Control

Programmers

Develop programs to control machining or processing of parts by automatic machine tools, equipment, or systems.

Tasks

1) Modify existing programs to enhance efficiency.

2) Enter computer commands to store or retrieve parts patterns, graphic displays, or programs that transfer data to other media.

3) Align and secure pattern film on reference tables of optical programmers, and observe enlarger scope views of printed circuit boards.

4) Write instruction sheets and cutter lists for a machine's controller in order to guide setup and encode numerical control tapes.

5) Revise programs and/or tapes to eliminate errors, and retest programs to check that problems have been solved.

6) Prepare geometric layouts from graphic displays, using computer-assisted drafting software or drafting instruments and graph paper.

7) Compare encoded tapes or computer printouts with original part specifications and blueprints to verify accuracy of instructions.

8) Enter coordinates of hole locations into program memories by depressing pedals or buttons of programmers.

9) Determine the sequence of machine operations, and select the proper cutting tools needed to machine workpieces into the desired shapes.

10) Draw machine tool paths on pattern film, using colored markers and following guidelines for tool speed and efficiency.

11) Sort shop orders into groups to maximize materials utilization and minimize machine setup time.

12) Observe machines on trial runs or conduct computer simulations to ensure that programs and machinery will function properly and produce items that meet specifications.

13) Determine reference points, machine cutting paths, or hole locations, and compute angular and linear dimensions, radii, and curvatures.

14) Analyze job orders, drawings, blueprints, specifications, printed circuit board pattern films, and design data in order to calculate dimensions, tool selection, machine speeds, and feed rates.

51-4032.00 - Drilling and Boring Machine Tool Setters, Operators, and Tenders, Metal and Plastic

Set up, operate, or tend drilling machines to drill, bore, ream, mill, or countersink metal or plastic work pieces.

Tasks

1) Move machine controls to lower tools to workpieces and to engage automatic feeds.

2) Install tools in spindles.

3) Lay out reference lines and machining locations on work, using layout tools, and applying knowledge of shop math and layout techniques.

4) Position and secure workpieces on tables, using bolts, jigs, clamps, shims, or other holding devices.

5) Change worn cutting tools, using wrenches.

6) Operate single- or multiple-spindle drill presses to bore holes so that machining operations can be performed on metal or plastic workpieces.

7) Lift workpieces onto work tables either manually or with hoists, or direct crane operators to lift and position workpieces.

8) Sharpen cutting tools, using bench grinders.

9) Establish zero reference points on workpieces, such as at the intersections of two edges or over hole locations.

10) Verify conformance of machined work to specifications, using measuring instruments such as calipers, micrometers, and fixed and telescoping gauges.

11) Turn valves and direct flow of coolants or cutting oil over cutting areas.

12) Study machining instructions, job orders, and blueprints to determine dimensional and finish specifications, sequences of operations, setups, and tooling requirements.

13) Select and set cutting speeds, feed rates, depths of cuts, and cutting tools according to machining instructions or knowledge of metal properties.

14) Verify that workpiece reference lines are parallel to the axis of table rotation, using dial indicators mounted in spindles.

15) Operate tracing attachments to duplicate contours from templates or models.

16) Observe drilling or boring machine operations to detect any problems.

51-4034.00 - Lathe and Turning Machine Tool Setters, Operators, and Tenders, Metal and Plastic

Set up, operate, or tend lathe and turning machines to turn, bore, thread, form, or face metal or plastic materials, such as wire, rod, or bar stock.

Tasks

1) Turn valve handles to direct the flow of coolant onto work areas or to coat disks with spinning compounds.

2) Select cutting tools and tooling instructions, according to written specifications or knowledge of metal properties and shop mathematics.

3) Mount attachments, such as relieving or tracing attachments, to perform operations such as duplicating contours of templates or trimming workpieces.

4) Compute unspecified dimensions and machine settings, using knowledge of metal properties and shop mathematics.

5) Study blueprints, layouts or charts, and job orders for information on specifications and tooling instructions, and to determine material requirements and operational sequences.

6) Start lath or turning machines and observe operations to ensure that specifications are met.

7) Crank machines through cycles, stopping to adjust tool positions and machine controls to ensure specified timing, clearances, and tolerances.

8) Adjust machine controls and change tool settings in order to keep dimensions within specified tolerances.

9) Move controls to set cutting speeds and depths and feed rates, and to position tools in relation to workpieces.

10) Lift metal stock or workpieces manually or using hoists, and position and secure them in machines, using fasteners and hand tools.

11) Install holding fixtures, cams, gears, and stops to control stock and tool movement, using hand tools, power tools, and measuring instruments.

12) Inspect sample workpieces to verify conformance with specifications, using instruments such as gauges, micrometers, and dial indicators.

13) Position, secure, and align cutting tools in toolholders on machines, using hand tools, and verify their positions with measuring instruments.

14) Replace worn tools, and sharpen dull cutting tools and dies using bench grinders or cutter-grinding machines.

51-4035.00 - Milling and Planing Machine Setters, Operators, and Tenders, Metal and Plastic

Set up, operate, or tend milling or planing machines to mill, plane, shape, groove, or profile metal or plastic work pieces.

Tasks

1) Move controls to set cutting specifications, to position cutting tools and workpieces in relation to each other, and to start machines.

2) Position and secure workpieces on machines, using holding devices, measuring instruments, hand tools, and hoists.

3) Verify alignment of workpieces on machines, using measuring instruments such as rules, gauges, or calipers.

4) Compute dimensions, tolerances, and angles of workpieces or machines, according to specifications and knowledge of metal properties and shop mathematics.

5) Remove workpieces from machines, and check to ensure that they conform to specifications, using measuring instruments such as microscopes, gauges, calipers, and micrometers.

6) Make templates or cutting tools.

7) Mount attachments and tools such as pantographs, engravers, or routers to perform other operations such as drilling or boring.

8) Record production output.

9) Select cutting speeds, feed rates, and depths of cuts, applying knowledge of metal properties and shop mathematics.

10) Select and install cutting tools and other accessories according to specifications, using hand tools or power tools.

11) Move cutters or material manually or by turning handwheels, or engage automatic feeding mechanisms to mill workpieces to specifications.

12) Study blueprints, layouts, sketches, or work orders to assess workpiece specifications and to determine tooling instructions, tools and materials needed, and sequences of operations.

13) Observe milling or planing machine operation and adjust controls to ensure conformance with specified tolerances.

14) Replace worn tools, using hand tools, and sharpen dull tools, using bench grinders.

51-4061.00 - Model Makers, Metal and Plastic

Set up and operate machines, such as lathes, milling and engraving machines, and jig borers to make working models of metal or plastic objects.

Tasks

1) Assemble mechanical, electrical, and electronic components into models or prototypes, using hand tools, power tools, and fabricating machines.

2) Drill, countersink, and ream holes in parts and assemblies for bolts, screws, and other fasteners, using power tools.

3) Grind, file, and sand parts to finished dimensions.

4) Lay out and mark reference points and dimensions on materials, using measuring instruments and drawing or scribing tools.

5) Study blueprints, drawings, and sketches to determine material dimensions, required equipment, and operations sequences.

6) Consult and confer with engineering personnel to discuss developmental problems and to recommend product modifications.

7) Record specifications, production operations, and final dimensions of models for use in establishing operating standards and procedures.

8) Wire and solder electrical and electronic connections and components.

9) Set up and operate machines such as lathes, drill presses, punch presses, or bandsaws to fabricate prototypes or models.

10) Inspect and test products to verify conformance to specifications, using precision measuring instruments or circuit testers.

11) Align, fit, and join parts, using bolts and screws or by welding or gluing.

12) Cut, shape, and form metal parts, using lathes, power saws, snips, power brakes and shears, files, and mallets.

13) Devise and construct tools, dies, molds, jigs, and fixtures, or modify existing tools and equipment.

51-4062.00 - Patternmakers, Metal and Plastic

Lay out, machine, fit, and assemble castings and parts to metal or plastic foundry patterns, core boxes, or match plates.

Tasks

1) Apply plastic-impregnated fabrics or coats of sealing wax or lacquer to patterns that will be used to produce plastic.

2) Paint or lacquer patterns.

3) Mark identification numbers or symbols onto patterns or templates.

1651

4) Construct platforms, fixtures, and jigs for holding and placing patterns.

5) Repair and rework templates and patterns.

6) Verify conformance of patterns or template dimensions to specifications, using measuring instruments such as calipers, scales, and micrometers.

7) Set up and operate machine tools, such as milling machines, lathes, drill presses, and grinders, in order to machine castings or patterns.

8) Select pattern materials such as wood, resin, and fiberglass.

9) Assemble pattern sections, using hand tools, bolts, screws, rivets, glue, and/or welding equipment.

10) Design and create templates, patterns, or coreboxes according to work orders, sample parts, or mockups.

11) Read and interpret blueprints or drawings of parts to be cast or patterns to be made; then compute dimensions and plan operational sequences.

12) Clean and finish patterns or templates, using emery cloths, files, scrapers, and power grinders.

13) Lay out and draw or scribe patterns onto material, using compasses, protractors, rulers, scribes, or other instruments.

51-6041.00 - Shoe and Leather Workers and Repairers

Construct, decorate, or repair leather and leather-like products, such as luggage, shoes, and saddles.

Tasks

1) Estimate the costs of requested products or services such as custom footwear or footwear repair, and receive payment from customers.

2) Attach insoles to shoe lasts, affix shoe uppers, and apply heels and outsoles.

3) Make, modify, and repair orthopedic or therapeutic footwear according to doctors' prescriptions, or modify existing footwear for people with foot problems and special needs.

4) Read prescriptions or specifications, and take measurements to establish the type of product to be made, using calipers, tape measures, or rules.

5) Check the texture, color, and strength of leather to ensure that it is adequate for a particular purpose.

6) Prepare inserts, heel pads, and lifts from casts of customers' feet.

7) Nail heel and toe cleats onto shoes.

8) Repair or replace soles, heels, and other parts of footwear, using sewing, buffing and other shoe repair machines, materials, and equipment.

9) Inspect articles for defects, and remove damaged or worn parts, using hand tools.

10) Select materials and patterns, and trace patterns onto materials to be cut out.

11) Dress and otherwise finish boots or shoes, as by trimming the edges of new soles and heels to the shoe shape.

12) Draw patterns, using measurements, designs, plaster casts, or customer specifications, and position or outline patterns on work pieces.

13) Shape shoe heels with a knife, and sand them on a buffing wheel for smoothness.

14) Cut, insert, position, and secure paddings, cushioning, and/or linings, using stitches or glue.

15) Stretch shoes, first dampening parts; then inserting and twisting parts, using an adjustable stretcher.

16) Clean and polish shoes.

17) Measure customers for fit, and discuss with them the type of footwear to be made, recommending details such as leather quality.

18) Construct, decorate, or repair leather products according to specifications, using sewing machines, needles and thread, leather lacing, glue, clamps, hand tools, and/or rivets.

19) Re-sew seams, and replace handles and linings of suitcases or handbags.

20) Drill or punch holes; then insert or attach metal rings, handles, and fastening hardware such as buckles.

21) Dye, soak, polish, paint, stamp, stitch, stain, buff, or engrave leather or other materials to obtain desired effects, decorations, or shapes.

22) Place shoes on lasts to remove soles and heels, using knives and/or pliers.

23) Repair and recondition leather products such as trunks, luggage, shoes, saddles, belts, purses, and baseball gloves.

24) Cement, nail, or sew soles and heels to shoes.

25) Cut out parts following patterns or outlines, using knives, shears, scissors, or machine presses.

26) Attach accessories or ornamentation to decorate or protect products.

51-6042.00 - Shoe Machine Operators and Tenders

Operate or tend a variety of machines to join, decorate, reinforce, or finish shoes and shoe parts.

Tasks

1) Remove and examine shoes, shoe parts, and designs to verify conformance to specifications such as proper embedding of stitches in channels.

2) Operate or tend machines to join, decorate, reinforce, or finish shoes and shoe parts.

3) Lower levers to open guides for passing wire along and through machine feeders; then raise levers to close guides, and turn knobs to adjust wire tension.

4) Fill shuttle spools with thread from a machine's bobbin-winder by pressing a foot-treadle.

5) Draw thread through machine guide slots, needles, and presser-feet in preparation for stitching, or load rolls of wire through machine axles.

6) Staple sides of shoes, pressing a foot-treadle to position and hold each shoe under the feeder of the machine.

7) Select and insert cassettes into consoles of stitching machines in order to stitch decorative designs onto shoe parts.

8) Hammer loose staples for proper attachment.

9) Cut excess thread or material from shoe parts, using scissors or knives.

10) Turn setscrews on needle bars, and position required numbers of needles in stitching machines.

11) Switch on machines, then lower pressure feet or rollers to secure parts and start machine stitching, using hand, foot, or knee controls.

12) Perform routine equipment maintenance such as cleaning and lubricating machines or replacing broken needles.

13) Turn screws to regulate size of staples.

14) Collect shoe parts from conveyer belts or racks and place them in machinery such as ovens or on molds for dressing, returning them to conveyers or racks to send them to the next work station.

15) Study work orders and/or shoe part tags to obtain information about workloads, specifications, and the types of materials to be used.

16) Select and place spools of thread or pre-wound bobbins into shuttles, or onto spindles or loupers of stitching machines.

17) Position dies on material in a manner that will obtain the maximum number of parts from each portion of material.

18) Align parts to be stitched, following seams, edges, or markings, before positioning them under needles.

19) Load hot-melt plastic rod glue through reactivator axles, using wrenches, then switch on reactivators, setting temperature and timers to heat glue to specifications.

20) Turn knobs to adjust stitch length and thread tension.

51-6061.00 - Textile Bleaching and Dyeing Machine Operators and Tenders

Operate or tend machines to bleach, shrink, wash, dye, or finish textiles or synthetic or glass fibers.

Tasks

1) Inspect machinery to determine necessary adjustments and repairs.

2) Study guides, charts, and specification sheets, and confer with supervisors to determine machine setup requirements.

3) Test solutions used to process textile goods to detect variations from standards.

4) Thread ends of cloth or twine through specified sections of equipment prior to processing.

5) Confer with coworkers to get information about order details, processing plans, or problems that occur.

6) Prepare dyeing machines for production runs, and conduct test runs of machines to ensure their proper operation.

7) Ravel seams that connect cloth ends when processing is completed.

8) Monitor factors such as temperatures and dye flow rates to ensure that they are within specified ranges.

9) Mount rolls of cloth on machines, using hoists, or place textile goods in machines or pieces of equipment.

10) Notify supervisors or mechanics of equipment malfunctions.

11) Perform machine maintenance, such as cleaning and oiling equipment; and repair or replace worn or defective parts.

12) Record production information such as fabric yardage processed, temperature readings, fabric tensions, and machine speeds.

13) Install, level, and align components such as gears, chains, dies, cutters, and needles.

14) Weigh ingredients to be mixed together for use in textile processing.

15) Start and control machines and equipment to wash, bleach, dye, or otherwise process and finish fabric, yarn, thread, and/or other textile goods.

16) Add dyes, water, detergents, or chemicals to tanks to dilute or strengthen solutions, according to established formulas and solution test results.

17) Remove dyed articles from tanks and machines for drying and further processing.

18) Examine and feel products to identify defects and variations from coloring and other processing standards.

19) Soak specified textile products for designated times.

20) Creel machines with bobbins or twine.

21) Key in processing instructions to program electronic equipment.

22) Sew ends of cloth together, by hand or using machines, to form endless lengths of cloth to facilitate processing.

23) Adjust equipment controls to maintain specified heat, tension, and speed.

51-6062.00 - Textile Cutting Machine Setters, Operators, and Tenders

Set up, operate, or tend machines that cut textiles.

Tasks

1) Study guides, samples, charts, and specification sheets; or confer with supervisors or engineering staff to determine setup requirements.

2) Adjust cutting techniques to types of fabrics and styles of garments.

3) Adjust machine controls, such as heating mechanisms, tensions, and/or speeds to produce specified products.

4) Inspect products to ensure that specifications are met and to determine whether machines require adjustment.

5) Install, level, and align components, such as gears, chains, guides, dies, cutters, and/or needles to set up machinery for operation.

6) Operate machines for test runs to verify adjustments and to obtain product samples.

7) Repair or replace worn or defective parts or components, using hand tools.

8) Place patterns on top of layers of fabric and cut fabric following patterns, using electric or manual knives, cutters, or computer numerically controlled cutting devices.

9) Confer with coworkers to obtain information about orders, processes, or problems.

10) Stop machines when specified amounts of product have been produced.

11) Thread yarn, thread, or fabric through guides, needles, and rollers of machines.

12) Clean, oil, and lubricate machines, using air hoses, cleaning solutions, rags, oilcans, and grease guns.

13) Inspect machinery to determine whether repairs are needed.

14) Program electronic equipment.

15) Record information about work completed and machine settings.

16) Start machines, monitor operations, and make adjustments as needed.

17) Operate machines to cut multiple layers of fabric into parts for articles such as canvas goods, house furnishings, garments, hats, or stuffed toys.

51-6063.00 - Textile Knitting and Weaving Machine Setters, Operators, and Tenders

Set up, operate, or tend machines that knit, loop, weave, or draw in textiles.

Tasks

1) Set up, or set up and operate textile machines that perform textile processing and manufacturing operations such as winding, twisting, knitting, weaving, bonding, and/or stretching.

2) Confer with co-workers to obtain information about orders, processes, or problems.

3) Clean, oil, and lubricate machines, using air hoses, cleaning solutions, rags, oil cans, and/or grease guns.

4) Thread yarn, thread, and fabric through guides, needles, and rollers of machines for weaving, knitting, or other processing.

5) Study guides, loom patterns, samples, charts, and/or specification sheets, or confer with supervisors or engineering staff to determine setup requirements.

6) Observe woven cloth to detect weaving defects.

7) Start machines, monitor operations, and make adjustments as needed.

8) Remove defects in cloth by cutting and pulling out filling.

9) Operate machines for test runs to verify adjustments and to obtain product samples.

10) Wash and blend wool, yarn, or cloth.

11) Repair or replace worn or defective needles and other components, using hand tools.

12) Record information about work completed and machine settings.

13) Notify supervisors or repair staff of mechanical malfunctions.

14) Inspect machinery to determine whether repairs are needed.

15) Examine looms to determine causes of loom stoppage, such as warp filling, harness breaks, or mechanical defects.

16) Adjust machine heating mechanisms, tensions, and speeds to produce specified products.

17) Inspect products to ensure that specifications are met and to determine if machines need adjustment.

18) Install, level, and align machine components such as gears, chains, guides, dies, cutters, and/or needles to set up machinery for operation.

19) Stop machines when specified amounts of product have been produced.

51-6064.00 - Textile Winding, Twisting, and Drawing Out Machine Setters, Operators, and Tenders

Set up, operate, or tend machines that wind or twist textiles; or draw out and combine sliver, such as wool, hemp, or synthetic fibers.

Tasks

1) Clean, oil, and lubricate machines, using air hoses, cleaning solutions, rags, oilcans, and grease guns.

2) Stop machines when specified amount of products has been produced.

3) Notify supervisors or mechanics of equipment malfunctions.

4) Tend machines that twist together two or more strands of yarn or insert additional twists into single strands of yarn to increase strength, smoothness, and/or uniformity of yarn.

5) Repair or replace worn or defective parts or components, using hand tools.

6) Tend spinning frames that draw out and twist roving or sliver into yarn.

7) Thread yarn, thread, and/or fabric through guides, needles, and rollers of machines.

8) Unwind lengths of yarn, thread, or twine from spools and wind onto bobbins.

9) Inspect machinery to determine whether repairs are needed.

10) Record production data such as numbers and types of bobbins wound.

11) Tend machines with multiple winding units that wind thread onto shuttle bobbins for use on sewing machines or other kinds of bobbins for sole-stitching, knitting, or weaving machinery.

12) Tend machines that wind wire onto bobbins, preparatory to formation of wire netting used in reinforcing sheet glass.

13) Inspect products to verify that they meet specifications and to determine whether machine adjustment is needed.

14) Start machines, monitor operation, and make adjustments as needed.

15) Replace depleted supply packages with full packages.

16) Remove spindles from machines and bobbins from spindles.

17) Observe operations to detect defects, malfunctions, or supply shortages.

18) Operate machines for test runs to verify adjustments and to obtain product samples.

19) Observe bobbins as they are winding; and cut threads to remove loaded bobbins, using knives.

20) Study guides, samples, charts, and specification sheets, or confer with supervisors or engineering staff to determine setup requirements.

21) Install, level, and align machine components such as gears, chains, guides, dies, cutters, and/or needles to set up machinery for operation.

22) Adjust machine settings such as speed or tension to produce products that meet specifications.

23) Place bobbins on spindles and insert spindles into bobbin-winding machines.

51-6092.00 - Fabric and Apparel Patternmakers

Draw and construct sets of precision master fabric patterns or layouts. May also mark and cut fabrics and apparel.

Tasks

1) Compute dimensions of patterns according to sizes, considering stretching of material.

2) Draw details on outlined parts to indicate where parts are to be joined, as well as the positions of pleats, pockets, buttonholes, and other features, using computers or drafting instruments.

3) Position and cut out master or sample patterns, using scissors and knives, or print out copies of patterns, using computers.

4) Discuss design specifications with designers, and convert their original models of garments into patterns of separate parts that can be laid out on a length of fabric.

5) Trace outlines of paper onto cardboard patterns, and cut patterns into parts to make templates.

6) Mark samples and finished patterns with information such as garment size, section, style, identification, and sewing instructions.

7) Draw outlines of pattern parts by adapting or copying existing patterns, or by drafting new patterns.

8) Test patterns by making and fitting sample garments.

9) Determine the best layout of pattern pieces to minimize waste of material, and mark fabric accordingly.

10) Create a paper pattern from which to mass-produce a design concept.

11) Create a master pattern for each size within a range of garment sizes, using charts, drafting instruments, computers, and/or grading devices.

12) Examine sketches, sample articles, and design specifications to determine quantities, shapes, and sizes of pattern parts, and to determine the amount of material or fabric required to make a product.

51-6093.00 - Upholsterers

Make, repair, or replace upholstery for household furniture or transportation vehicles.

Tasks

1) Stretch webbing and fabric, using webbing stretchers.

2) Attach bindings or apply solutions to edges of cut material to prevent raveling.

3) Adjust or replace webbing, padding, and/or springs, and secure them in place.

4) Fit, install, and secure material on frames, using hand tools, power tools, glue, cement, and/or staples.

5) Make, restore, and/or create custom upholstered furniture, using hand tools and knowledge of fabrics and upholstery methods.

6) Collaborate with interior designers to decorate rooms and coordinate furnishing fabrics.

7) Operate sewing machines or sew upholstery by hand to seam cushions and join various sections of covering material.

8) Discuss upholstery fabrics, colors, and styles with customers, and provide cost estimates.

9) Make, repair, and/or replace automobile upholstery and convertible and vinyl tops, using knowledge of fabric and upholstery methods.

10) Read work orders, and apply knowledge and experience with materials in order to determine types and amounts of materials required to cover workpieces.

11) Measure and cut new covering materials, using patterns and measuring and cutting instruments, following sketches and design specifications.

12) Attach fasteners, grommets, buttons, buckles, ornamental trim, and other accessories to covers or frames, using hand tools.

13) Pick up and deliver furniture.

14) Repair furniture frames and refinish exposed wood.

15) Remove covering, webbing, padding, and/or defective springs from workpieces, using hand tools such as hammers and tack pullers.

16) Design upholstery cover patterns and cutting plans, based on sketches, customer descriptions, or blueprints.

17) Examine furniture frames, upholstery, springs, and webbing to locate defects.

18) Draw cutting lines on material following patterns, templates, sketches, or blueprints, using chalk, pencils, paint, or other methods.

19) Build furniture up with loose fiber stuffing, cotton, felt, and/or foam padding to form smooth rounded surfaces.

20) Sew rips or tears in material, or create tufting, using needles and thread.

21) Interweave and fasten strips of webbing to the backs and undersides of furniture, using small hand tools and fasteners.

51-7011.00 - Cabinetmakers and Bench Carpenters

Cut, shape, and assemble wooden articles or set up and operate a variety of woodworking machines, such as power saws, jointers, and mortisers to surface, cut, or shape lumber or to fabricate parts for wood products.

Tasks

1) Install hardware such as hinges, handles, catches, and drawer pulls, using hand tools.

2) Dip, brush, or spray assembled articles with protective or decorative finishes such as stain, varnish, paint, or lacquer.

3) Bore holes for insertion of screws or dowels, by hand or using boring machines.

4) Perform final touch-ups with sandpaper and steel wool.

5) Match materials for color, grain, and texture, giving attention to knots and other features of the wood.

6) Establish the specifications of articles to be constructed or repaired, and plan the methods and operations for shaping and assembling parts, based on blueprints, drawings, diagrams, or oral or written instructions.

7) Measure and mark dimensions of parts on paper or lumber stock prior to cutting, following blueprints, to ensure a tight fit and quality product.

8) Set up and operate machines, including power saws, jointers, mortisers, tenoners, molders, and shapers, to cut, mold, and shape woodstock and wood substitutes.

9) Estimate the amounts, types, and costs of needed materials.

10) Attach parts and subassemblies together to form completed units, using glue, dowels, nails, screws, and/or clamps.

11) Cut timber to the right size and shape and trim parts of joints to ensure a snug fit, using hand tools such as planes, chisels, or wood files.

12) Apply masonite, formica, and vinyl surfacing materials.

13) Repair or alter wooden furniture, cabinetry, fixtures, paneling, and other pieces.

14) Trim, sand, and scrape surfaces and joints to prepare articles for finishing.

15) Reinforce joints with nails or other fasteners to prepare articles for finishing.

16) Design furniture, using computer-aided drawing programs.

17) Discuss projects with customers, and draw up detailed specifications.

18) Verify dimensions, and check the quality and fit of pieces in order to ensure adherence to specifications.

19) Program computers to operate machinery.

51-7021.00 - Furniture Finishers

Shape, finish, and refinish damaged, worn, or used furniture or new high-grade furniture to specified color or finish.

Tasks

1) Mix finish ingredients to obtain desired colors or shades.

2) Remove old finishes and damaged or deteriorated parts, using hand tools, stripping tools, sandpaper, steel wool, abrasives, solvents, and/or dip baths.

3) Paint metal surfaces electrostatically, or by using a spray gun or other painting equipment.

4) Treat warped or stained surfaces to restore original contours and colors.

5) Fill and smooth cracks or depressions, remove marks and imperfections, and repair broken parts, using plastic or wood putty, glue, nails, and/or screws.

6) Examine furniture to determine the extent of damage or deterioration, and to decide on the best method for repair or restoration.

7) Disassemble items to prepare them for finishing, using hand tools.

8) Brush, spray, or hand-rub finishing ingredients, such as paint, oil, stain, or wax, onto and into wood grain; then apply lacquer or other sealers.

9) Stencil, gild, emboss, mark, or paint designs or borders to reproduce the original appearance of restored pieces, or to decorate new pieces.

10) Follow blueprints to produce specific designs.

11) Brush bleaching agents on wood surfaces to restore natural color.

12) Spread graining ink over metal portions of furniture in order to simulate wood-grain finish.

13) Remove excess solvent, using cloths soaked in paint thinner.

14) Remove accessories prior to finishing, and mask areas that should not be exposed to finishing processes or substances.

15) Select appropriate finishing ingredients such as paint, stain, lacquer, shellac, or varnish, depending on factors such as wood hardness and surface type.

16) Wash surfaces to prepare them for finish application.

17) Confer with customers to determine furniture colors and/or finishes.

18) Design, create, and decorate entire pieces or specific parts of furniture, such as draws for cabinets.

19) Distress surfaces with woodworking tools or abrasives before staining to create an antique appearance, or rub surfaces to bring out highlights and shadings.

20) Recommend woods, colors, finishes, and furniture styles, using knowledge of wood products, fashions, and styles.

21) Replace or refurbish upholstery of items, using tacks, adhesives, softeners, solvents, stains, or polish.

51-7031.00 - Model Makers, Wood

Construct full-size and scale wooden precision models of products. Includes wood jig builders and loft workers.

Tasks

1) Build jigs that can be used as guides for assembling oversized or special types of box shooks.

2) Fit, fasten, and assemble wood parts together to form patterns, models, or sections, using glue, nails, dowels, bolts, screws, and other fasteners.

3) Set up, operate, and adjust a variety of woodworking machines such as bandsaws and planers to cut and shape sections, parts, and patterns, according to specifications.

4) Construct wooden models, patterns, templates, full scale mock-ups, and molds for parts of products and production tools.

5) Issue patterns to designated machine operators.

6) Fabricate work aids such as scrapers or templates.

7) Read blueprints, drawings, or written specifications, and consult with designers to determine sizes and shapes of patterns and required machine setups.

8) Trim, smooth, and shape surfaces, and plane, shave, file, scrape, and sand models to attain specified shapes, using hand tools.

9) Plan, lay out, and draw outlines of units, sectional patterns, or full-scale mock-ups of products.

10) Finish patterns or models with protective or decorative coatings such as shellac, lacquer, or wax.

11) Maintain pattern records for reference.

12) Mark identifying information on patterns, parts, and templates to indicate assembly methods and details.

13) Verify dimensions and contours of models during hand-forming processes, using templates and measuring devices.

51-7032.00 - Patternmakers, Wood

Plan, lay out, and construct wooden unit or sectional patterns used in forming sand molds for castings.

Tasks

1) Lay out patterns on wood stock and draw outlines of units, sectional patterns, or full-scale mock-ups of products, based on blueprint specifications and sketches, and using marking and measuring devices.

2) Fit, fasten, and assemble wood parts together to form patterns, models, or sections, using glue, nails, dowels, bolts, and screws.

3) Divide patterns into sections according to shapes of castings to facilitate removal of patterns from molds.

4) Correct patterns to compensate for defects in castings.

5) Verify dimensions of completed patterns, using templates, straightedges, calipers, and/or protractors.

6) Trim, smooth, and shape surfaces, and plane, shave, file, scrape, and sand models to attain specified shapes, using hand tools.

7) Set up, operate, and adjust a variety of woodworking machines such as bandsaws and lathes to cut and shape sections, parts, and patterns, according to specifications.

8) Collect and store patterns and lumber.

9) Construct wooden models, templates, full scale mock-ups, jigs, and/or molds for shaping parts of products.

10) Maintain pattern records for reference.

11) Select lumber to be used for patterns.

12) Estimate costs for patternmaking jobs.

13) Mark identifying information such as colors or codes on patterns, parts, and templates to indicate assembly methods.

14) Issue patterns to designated machine operators.

15) Inventory equipment and supplies, ordering parts and tools as necessary.

16) Finish completed products or models with shellac, lacquer, wax, or paint.

17) Repair broken or damaged patterns.

18) Compute dimensions, areas, volumes, and weights.

19) Glue fillets along interior angles of patterns.

51-9021.00 - Crushing, Grinding, and Polishing Machine Setters, Operators, and Tenders

Set up, operate, or tend machines to crush, grind, or polish materials, such as coal, glass, grain, stone, food, or rubber.

Tasks

1) Notify supervisors of needed repairs.

2) Test samples of materials or products to ensure compliance with specifications, using test equipment.

3) Observe operation of equipment to ensure continuity of flow, safety, and efficient operation, and to detect malfunctions.

4) Inspect chains, belts, and scrolls for signs of wear.

5) Mark bins as to types of mixtures stored.

6) Add or mix chemicals and ingredients for processing, using hand tools or other devices.

7) Break mixtures to size, using picks.

8) Load materials into machinery and equipment, using hand tools.

9) Dislodge and clear jammed materials or other items from machinery and equipment, using hand tools.

10) Tend accessory equipment such as pumps and conveyors in order to move materials or ingredients through production processes.

11) Transfer materials, supplies, and products between work areas, using moving equipment and hand tools.

12) Turn valves to regulate the moisture contents of materials.

13) Set mill gauges to specified fineness of grind.

14) Reject defective products and readjust equipment to eliminate problems.

15) Weigh or measure materials, ingredients, and/or products at specified intervals to ensure conformance to requirements.

16) Read work orders to determine production specifications and information.

17) Examine materials, ingredients, or products visually or with hands, in order to ensure conformance to established standards.

18) Record data from operations, testing, and production on specified forms.

19) Clean work areas.

20) Clean, adjust and maintain equipment, using hand tools.

21) Collect samples of materials or products for laboratory testing.

51-9022.00 - Grinding and Polishing Workers, Hand

Grind, sand, or polish, using hand tools or hand-held power tools, a variety of metal, wood, stone, clay, plastic, or glass objects.

Tasks

1) Trim, scrape, or deburr objects or parts, using chisels, scrapers, and other hand tools and equipment.

2) Verify quality of finished workpieces by inspecting them, comparing them to templates, measuring their dimensions, or testing them in working machinery.

3) Apply solutions and chemicals to equipment, objects, or parts, using hand tools.

4) Clean brass particles from files by drawing file cards through file grooves.

5) Mark defects such as knotholes, cracks, and splits for repair.

6) Repair and maintain equipment, objects, or parts, using hand tools.

7) Spread emery powder or other polishing compounds on stone, or wet stone surfaces using hoses, then guide buffing wheels over stone to polish surfaces.

8) Wash grit from stone, using hoses.

9) Select files or other abrasives, according to materials, sizes and shapes of workpieces, amount of stock to be removed, finishes specified, and steps in finishing processes.

10) Fill cracks or imperfections in marble with wax that matches the stone color.

11) Load and adjust workpieces onto equipment or work tables, using hand tools.

12) File grooved, contoured, and irregular surfaces of metal objects, such as metalworking dies and machine parts, to conform to templates, other parts, layouts, or blueprint specifications.

13) Remove completed workpieces from equipment or work tables, using hand tools, and place workpieces in containers.

14) Move controls to adjust, start, or stop equipment during grinding and polishing processes.

15) Measure and mark equipment, objects, or parts to ensure grinding and polishing standards are met.

16) Transfer equipment, objects, or parts to specified work areas, using moving devices.

17) Grind, sand, clean, or polish objects or parts to correct defects or to prepare surfaces for further finishing, using hand tools and power tools.

18) Study blueprints or layouts to determine how to lay out workpieces or saw out templates.

19) Sharpen abrasive grinding tools, using machines and hand tools.

51-9031.00 - Cutters and Trimmers, Hand

Use hand tools or hand-held power tools to cut and trim a variety of manufactured items, such as carpet, fabric, stone, glass, or rubber.

Tasks

1) Fold or shape materials before or after cutting them.

2) Position templates or measure materials to locate specified points of cuts or to obtain maximum yields, using rules, scales, or patterns.

3) Transport items to work or storage areas, using carts.

4) Stack cut items and load them on racks or conveyors or onto trucks.

5) Cut, shape, and trim materials, such as textiles, food, glass, stone, and metal, using knives, scissors, and other hand tools, portable power tools, or bench-mounted tools.

6) Mark cutting lines around patterns or templates, or follow layout points, using squares, rules, and straightedges, and chalk, pencils, or scribes.

7) Mark or discard items with defects such as spots, stains, scars, snags, chips, scratches, or unacceptable shapes or finishes.

8) Trim excess material or cut threads off finished products, such as cutting loose ends of plastic off a manufactured toy for a smoother finish.

9) Read work orders to determine dimensions, cutting locations, and quantities to cut.

10) Route items to provide cutouts for parts, using portable routers, grinders, and hand tools.

11) Count or weigh and bundle items.

12) Mark identification numbers, trademarks, grades, marketing data, sizes, or model numbers on products.

13) Replace or sharpen dulled cutting tools such as saws.

14) Unroll, lay out, attach, or mount materials or items on cutting tables or machines.

15) Adjust guides and stops to control depths and widths of cuts.

16) Separate materials or products according to size, weight, type, condition, color, or shade.

17) Clean, treat, buff, or polish finished items, using grinders, brushes, chisels, and cleaning solutions and polishing materials.

51-9081.00 - Dental Laboratory Technicians

Construct and repair full or partial dentures or dental appliances.

Tasks

1) Test appliances for conformance to specifications and accuracy of occlusion, using articulators and micrometers.

2) Fabricate, alter, and repair dental devices such as dentures, crowns, bridges, inlays, and appliances for straightening teeth.

3) Melt metals or mix plaster, porcelain, or acrylic pastes; and pour materials into molds or over frameworks in order to form dental prostheses or apparatus.

4) Remove excess metal or porcelain, and polish surfaces of prostheses or frameworks, using polishing machines.

5) Place tooth models on apparatus that mimics bite and movement of patient's jaw to evaluate functionality of model.

6) Create a model of patient's mouth by pouring plaster into a dental impression and allowing plaster to set.

7) Prepare metal surfaces for bonding with porcelain to create artificial teeth, using small hand tools.

8) Build and shape wax teeth, using small hand instruments and information from observations or dentists' specifications.

9) Apply porcelain paste or wax over prosthesis frameworks or setups, using brushes and spatulas.

10) Train and supervise other dental technicians or dental laboratory bench workers.

11) Load newly constructed teeth into porcelain furnaces in order to bake the porcelain onto the metal framework.

12) Fill chipped or low spots in surfaces of devices, using acrylic resins.

13) Shape and solder wire and metal frames or bands for dental products, using soldering irons and hand tools.

14) Prepare wax bite-blocks and impression trays for use.

15) Rebuild or replace linings, wire sections, and missing teeth in order to repair dentures.

16) Mold wax over denture set-ups in order to form the full contours of artificial gums.

Knowledge	Knowledge Definitions
Medicine and Dentistry	Knowledge of the information and techniques needed to diagnose and treat human injuries, diseases, and deformities. This includes symptoms, treatment alternatives, drug properties and interactions, and preventive health-care measures.
Production and Processing	Knowledge of raw materials, production processes, quality control, costs, and other techniques for maximizing the effective manufacture and distribution of goods.
Customer and Personal Service	Knowledge of principles and processes for providing customer and personal services. This includes customer needs assessment, meeting quality standards for services, and evaluation of customer satisfaction.
Design	Knowledge of design techniques, tools, and principles involved in production of precision technical plans, blueprints, drawings, and models.
Education and Training	Knowledge of principles and methods for curriculum and training design, teaching and instruction for individuals and groups, and the measurement of training effects.
English Language	Knowledge of the structure and content of the English language including the meaning and spelling of words, rules of composition, and grammar.
Administration and Management	Knowledge of business and management principles involved in strategic planning, resource allocation, human resources modeling, leadership technique, production methods, and coordination of people and resources.
Mechanical	Knowledge of machines and tools, including their designs, uses, repair, and maintenance.
Engineering and Technology	Knowledge of the practical application of engineering science and technology. This includes applying principles, techniques, procedures, and equipment to the design and production of various goods and services.
Chemistry	Knowledge of the chemical composition, structure, and properties of substances and of the chemical processes and transformations that they undergo. This includes uses of chemicals and their interactions, danger signs, production techniques, and disposal methods.
Physics	Knowledge and prediction of physical principles, laws, their interrelationships, and applications to understanding fluid, material, and atmospheric dynamics, and mechanical, electrical, atomic and sub- atomic structures and processes.
Sales and Marketing	Knowledge of principles and methods for showing, promoting, and selling products or services. This includes marketing strategy and tactics, product demonstration, sales techniques, and sales control systems.
Fine Arts	Knowledge of the theory and techniques required to compose, produce, and perform works of music, dance, visual arts, drama, and sculpture.
Mathematics	Knowledge of arithmetic, algebra, geometry, calculus, statistics, and their applications.
Public Safety and Security	Knowledge of relevant equipment, policies, procedures, and strategies to promote effective local, state, or national security operations for the protection of people, data, property, and institutions.
Economics and Accounting	Knowledge of economic and accounting principles and practices, the financial markets, banking and the analysis and reporting of financial data.
Personnel and Human Resources	Knowledge of principles and procedures for personnel recruitment, selection, training, compensation and benefits, labor relations and negotiation, and personnel information systems.
Clerical	Knowledge of administrative and clerical procedures and systems such as word processing, managing files and records, stenography and transcription, designing forms, and other office procedures and terminology.
Transportation	Knowledge of principles and methods for moving people or goods by air, rail, sea, or road, including the relative costs and benefits.
Building and Construction	Knowledge of materials, methods, and the tools involved in the construction or repair of houses, buildings, or other structures such as highways and roads.
Communications and Media	Knowledge of media production, communication, and dissemination techniques and methods. This includes alternative ways to inform and entertain via written, oral, and visual media.
Computers and Electronics	Knowledge of circuit boards, processors, chips, electronic equipment, and computer hardware and software, including applications and programming.
Psychology	Knowledge of human behavior and performance; individual differences in ability, personality, and interests; learning and motivation; psychological research methods; and the assessment and treatment of behavioral and affective disorders.
Telecommunications	Knowledge of transmission, broadcasting, switching, control, and operation of telecommunications systems.
Law and Government	Knowledge of laws, legal codes, court procedures, precedents, government regulations, executive orders, agency rules, and the democratic political process.
Sociology and Anthropology	Knowledge of group behavior and dynamics, societal trends and influences, human migrations, ethnicity, cultures and their history and origins.
Therapy and Counseling	Knowledge of principles, methods, and procedures for diagnosis, treatment, and rehabilitation of physical and mental dysfunctions, and for career counseling and guidance.
Biology	Knowledge of plant and animal organisms, their tissues, cells, functions, interdependencies, and interactions with each other and the environment.
Foreign Language	Knowledge of the structure and content of a foreign (non-English) language including the meaning and spelling of words, rules of composition and grammar, and pronunciation.
Philosophy and Theology	Knowledge of different philosophical systems and religions. This includes their basic principles, values, ethics, ways of thinking, customs, practices, and their impact on human culture.
Food Production	Knowledge of techniques and equipment for planting, growing, and harvesting food products (both plant and animal) for consumption, including storage/handling techniques.
Geography	Knowledge of principles and methods for describing the features of land, sea, and air masses, including their physical characteristics, locations, interrelationships, and distribution of plant, animal, and human life.
History and Archeology	Knowledge of historical events and their causes, indicators, and effects on civilizations and cultures.

Skills	Skills Definitions
Reading Comprehension	Understanding written sentences and paragraphs in work related documents.
Time Management	Managing one's own time and the time of others.
Equipment Selection	Determining the kind of tools and equipment needed to do a job.
Active Learning	Understanding the implications of new information for both current and future problem-solving and decision-making.
Speaking	Talking to others to convey information effectively.
Active Listening	Giving full attention to what other people are saying, taking time to understand the points being made, asking questions as appropriate, and not interrupting at inappropriate times.
Coordination	Adjusting actions in relation to others' actions.

Learning Strategies	Selecting and using training/instructional methods and procedures appropriate for the situation when learning or teaching new things.
Critical Thinking	Using logic and reasoning to identify the strengths and weaknesses of alternative solutions, conclusions or approaches to problems.
Quality Control Analysis	Conducting tests and inspections of products, services, or processes to evaluate quality or performance.
Equipment Maintenance	Performing routine maintenance on equipment and determining when and what kind of maintenance is needed.
Troubleshooting	Determining causes of operating errors and deciding what to do about it.
Management of Material Resources	Obtaining and seeing to the appropriate use of equipment, facilities, and materials needed to do certain work.
Monitoring	Monitoring/Assessing performance of yourself, other individuals, or organizations to make improvements or take corrective action.
Operations Analysis	Analyzing needs and product requirements to create a design.
Complex Problem Solving	Identifying complex problems and reviewing related information to develop and evaluate options and implement solutions.
Judgment and Decision Making	Considering the relative costs and benefits of potential actions to choose the most appropriate one.
Instructing	Teaching others how to do something.
Operation Monitoring	Watching gauges, dials, or other indicators to make sure a machine is working properly.
Repairing	Repairing machines or systems using the needed tools.
Operation and Control	Controlling operations of equipment or systems.
Service Orientation	Actively looking for ways to help people.
Social Perceptiveness	Being aware of others' reactions and understanding why they react as they do.
Technology Design	Generating or adapting equipment and technology to serve user needs.
Science	Using scientific rules and methods to solve problems.
Installation	Installing equipment, machines, wiring, or programs to meet specifications.
Writing	Communicating effectively in writing as appropriate for the needs of the audience.
Systems Evaluation	Identifying measures or indicators of system performance and the actions needed to improve or correct performance, relative to the goals of the system.
Systems Analysis	Determining how a system should work and how changes in conditions, operations, and the environment will affect outcomes.
Mathematics	Using mathematics to solve problems.
Management of Personnel Resources	Motivating, developing, and directing people as they work, identifying the best people for the job.
Negotiation	Bringing others together and trying to reconcile differences.
Management of Financial Resources	Determining how money will be spent to get the work done, and accounting for these expenditures.
Persuasion	Persuading others to change their minds or behavior.
Programming	Writing computer programs for various purposes.

Ability	Ability Definitions
Problem Sensitivity	The ability to tell when something is wrong or is likely to go wrong. It does not involve solving the problem, only recognizing there is a problem.
Near Vision	The ability to see details at close range (within a few feet of the observer).
Information Ordering	The ability to arrange things or actions in a certain order or pattern according to a specific rule or set of rules (e.g., patterns of numbers, letters, words, pictures, mathematical operations).
Arm-Hand Steadiness	The ability to keep your hand and arm steady while moving your arm or while holding your arm and hand in one position.
Oral Comprehension	The ability to listen to and understand information and ideas presented through spoken words and sentences.
Selective Attention	The ability to concentrate on a task over a period of time without being distracted.
Speech Recognition	The ability to identify and understand the speech of another person.
Manual Dexterity	The ability to quickly move your hand, your hand together with your arm, or your two hands to grasp, manipulate, or assemble objects.
Inductive Reasoning	The ability to combine pieces of information to form general rules or conclusions (includes finding a relationship among seemingly unrelated events).

Deductive Reasoning	The ability to apply general rules to specific problems to produce answers that make sense.
Written Comprehension	The ability to read and understand information and ideas presented in writing.
Oral Expression	The ability to communicate information and ideas in speaking so others will understand.
Control Precision	The ability to quickly and repeatedly adjust the controls of a machine or a vehicle to exact positions.
Category Flexibility	The ability to generate or use different sets of rules for combining or grouping things in different ways.
Finger Dexterity	The ability to make precisely coordinated movements of the fingers of one or both hands to grasp, manipulate, or assemble very small objects.
Flexibility of Closure	The ability to identify or detect a known pattern (a figure, object, word, or sound) that is hidden in other distracting material.
Perceptual Speed	The ability to quickly and accurately compare similarities and differences among sets of letters, numbers, objects, pictures, or patterns. The things to be compared may be presented at the same time or one after the other. This ability also includes comparing a presented object with a remembered object.
Speech Clarity	The ability to speak clearly so others can understand you.
Visualization	The ability to imagine how something will look after it is moved around or when its parts are moved or rearranged.
Auditory Attention	The ability to focus on a single source of sound in the presence of other distracting sounds.
Hearing Sensitivity	The ability to detect or tell the differences between sounds that vary in pitch and loudness.
Far Vision	The ability to see details at a distance.
Multilimb Coordination	The ability to coordinate two or more limbs (for example, two arms, two legs, or one leg and one arm) while sitting, standing, or lying down. It does not involve performing the activities while the whole body is in motion.
Depth Perception	The ability to judge which of several objects is closer or farther away from you, or to judge the distance between you and an object.
Originality	The ability to come up with unusual or clever ideas about a given topic or situation, or to develop creative ways to solve a problem.
Written Expression	The ability to communicate information and ideas in writing so others will understand.
Time Sharing	The ability to shift back and forth between two or more activities or sources of information (such as speech, sounds, touch, or other sources).
Wrist-Finger Speed	The ability to make fast, simple, repeated movements of the fingers, hands, and wrists.
Visual Color Discrimination	The ability to match or detect differences between colors, including shades of color and brightness.
Response Orientation	The ability to choose quickly between two or more movements in response to two or more different signals (lights, sounds, pictures). It includes the speed with which the correct response is started with the hand, foot, or other body part.
Reaction Time	The ability to quickly respond (with the hand, finger, or foot) to a signal (sound, light, picture) when it appears.
Fluency of Ideas	The ability to come up with a number of ideas about a topic (the number of ideas is important, not their quality, correctness, or creativity).
Number Facility	The ability to add, subtract, multiply, or divide quickly and correctly.
Speed of Closure	The ability to quickly make sense of, combine, and organize information into meaningful patterns.
Mathematical Reasoning	The ability to choose the right mathematical methods or formulas to solve a problem.
Rate Control	The ability to time your movements or the movement of a piece of equipment in anticipation of changes in the speed and/or direction of a moving object or scene.
Memorization	The ability to remember information such as words, numbers, pictures, and procedures.
Static Strength	The ability to exert maximum muscle force to lift, push, pull, or carry objects.
Night Vision	The ability to see under low light conditions.
Spatial Orientation	The ability to know your location in relation to the environment or to know where other objects are in relation to you.
Speed of Limb Movement	The ability to quickly move the arms and legs.
Stamina	The ability to exert yourself physically over long periods of time without getting winded or out of breath.
Extent Flexibility	The ability to bend, stretch, twist, or reach with your body, arms, and/or legs.

Dynamic Flexibility	The ability to quickly and repeatedly bend, stretch, twist, or reach out with your body, arms, and/or legs.
Gross Body Coordination	The ability to coordinate the movement of your arms, legs, and torso together when the whole body is in motion.
Gross Body Equilibrium	The ability to keep or regain your body balance or stay upright when in an unstable position.
Trunk Strength	The ability to use your abdominal and lower back muscles to support part of the body repeatedly or continuously over time without 'giving out' or fatiguing.
Peripheral Vision	The ability to see objects or movement of objects to one's side when the eyes are looking ahead.
Dynamic Strength	The ability to exert muscle force repeatedly or continuously over time. This involves muscular endurance and resistance to muscle fatigue.
Glare Sensitivity	The ability to see objects in the presence of glare or bright lighting.
Sound Localization	The ability to tell the direction from which a sound originated.
Explosive Strength	The ability to use short bursts of muscle force to propel oneself (as in jumping or sprinting), or to throw an object.

Work_Activity	Work_Activity Definitions
Getting Information	Observing, receiving, and otherwise obtaining information from all relevant sources.
Organizing, Planning, and Prioritizing Work	Developing specific goals and plans to prioritize, organize, and accomplish your work.
Communicating with Supervisors, Peers, or Subordin	Providing information to supervisors, co-workers, and subordinates by telephone, in written form, e-mail, or in person.
Monitor Processes, Materials, or Surroundings	Monitoring and reviewing information from materials, events, or the environment, to detect or assess problems.
Controlling Machines and Processes	Using either control mechanisms or direct physical activity to operate machines or processes (not including computers or vehicles).
Making Decisions and Solving Problems	Analyzing information and evaluating results to choose the best solution and solve problems.
Establishing and Maintaining Interpersonal Relatio	Developing constructive and cooperative working relationships with others, and maintaining them over time.
Inspecting Equipment, Structures, or Material	Inspecting equipment, structures, or materials to identify the cause of errors or other problems or defects.
Thinking Creatively	Developing, designing, or creating new applications, ideas, relationships, systems, or products, including artistic contributions.
Identifying Objects, Actions, and Events	Identifying information by categorizing, estimating, recognizing differences or similarities, and detecting changes in circumstances or events.
Judging the Qualities of Things, Services, or Peop	Assessing the value, importance, or quality of things or people.
Processing Information	Compiling, coding, categorizing, calculating, tabulating, auditing, or verifying information or data.
Estimating the Quantifiable Characteristics of Pro	Estimating sizes, distances, and quantities; or determining time, costs, resources, or materials needed to perform a work activity.
Scheduling Work and Activities	Scheduling events, programs, and activities, as well as the work of others.
Updating and Using Relevant Knowledge	Keeping up-to-date technically and applying new knowledge to your job.
Interpreting the Meaning of Information for Others	Translating or explaining what information means and how it can be used.
Handling and Moving Objects	Using hands and arms in handling, installing, positioning, and moving materials, and manipulating things.
Training and Teaching Others	Identifying the educational needs of others, developing formal educational or training programs or classes, and teaching or instructing others.
Coordinating the Work and Activities of Others	Getting members of a group to work together to accomplish tasks.
Analyzing Data or Information	Identifying the underlying principles, reasons, or facts of information by breaking down information or data into separate parts.
Communicating with Persons Outside Organization	Communicating with people outside the organization, representing the organization to customers, the public, government, and other external sources. This information can be exchanged in person, in writing, or by telephone or e-mail.
Evaluating Information to Determine Compliance wit	Using relevant information and individual judgment to determine whether events or processes comply with laws, regulations, or standards.

Coaching and Developing Others	Identifying the developmental needs of others and coaching, mentoring, or otherwise helping others to improve their knowledge or skills.
Guiding, Directing, and Motivating Subordinates	Providing guidance and direction to subordinates, including setting performance standards and monitoring performance.
Documenting/Recording Information	Entering, transcribing, recording, storing, or maintaining information in written or electronic/magnetic form.
Developing Objectives and Strategies	Establishing long-range objectives and specifying the strategies and actions to achieve them.
Provide Consultation and Advice to Others	Providing guidance and expert advice to management or other groups on technical, systems-, or process-related topics.
Developing and Building Teams	Encouraging and building mutual trust, respect, and cooperation among team members.
Assisting and Caring for Others	Providing personal assistance, medical attention, emotional support, or other personal care to others such as coworkers, customers, or patients.
Monitoring and Controlling Resources	Monitoring and controlling resources and overseeing the spending of money.
Repairing and Maintaining Mechanical Equipment	Servicing, repairing, adjusting, and testing machines, devices, moving parts, and equipment that operate primarily on the basis of mechanical (not electronic) principles.
Resolving Conflicts and Negotiating with Others	Handling complaints, settling disputes, and resolving grievances and conflicts, or otherwise negotiating with others.
Performing General Physical Activities	Performing physical activities that require considerable use of your arms and legs and moving your whole body, such as climbing, lifting, balancing, walking, stooping, and handling of materials.
Repairing and Maintaining Electronic Equipment	Servicing, repairing, calibrating, regulating, fine-tuning, or testing machines, devices, and equipment that operate primarily on the basis of electrical or electronic (not mechanical) principles.
Drafting, Laying Out, and Specifying Technical Dev	Providing documentation, detailed instructions, drawings, or specifications to tell others about how devices, parts, equipment, or structures are to be fabricated, constructed, assembled, modified, maintained, or used.
Selling or Influencing Others	Convincing others to buy merchandise/goods or to otherwise change their minds or actions.
Performing Administrative Activities	Performing day-to-day administrative tasks such as maintaining information files and processing paperwork.
Interacting With Computers	Using computers and computer systems (including hardware and software) to program, write software, set up functions, enter data, or process information.
Operating Vehicles, Mechanized Devices, or Equipme	Running, maneuvering, navigating, or driving vehicles or mechanized equipment, such as forklifts, passenger vehicles, aircraft, or water craft.
Staffing Organizational Units	Recruiting, interviewing, selecting, hiring, and promoting employees in an organization.
Performing for or Working Directly with the Public	Performing for people or dealing directly with the public. This includes serving customers in restaurants and stores, and receiving clients or guests.

Work_Context	Work_Context Definitions
Spend Time Using Your Hands to Handle, Control, or	How much does this job require using your hands to handle, control, or feel objects, tools or controls?
Time Pressure	How often does this job require the worker to meet strict deadlines?
Indoors, Environmentally Controlled	How often does this job require working indoors in environmentally controlled conditions?
Importance of Being Exact or Accurate	How important is being very exact or highly accurate in performing this job?
Exposed to Contaminants	How often does this job require working exposed to contaminants (such as pollutants, gases, dust or odors)?
Wear Common Protective or Safety Equipment such as	How much does this job require wearing common protective or safety equipment such as safety shoes, glasses, gloves, hard hats or live jackets?
Face-to-Face Discussions	How often do you have to have face-to-face discussions with individuals or teams in this job?
Structured versus Unstructured Work	To what extent is this job structured for the worker, rather than allowing the worker to determine tasks, priorities, and goals?
Freedom to Make Decisions	How much decision making freedom, without supervision, does the job offer?
Spend Time Sitting	How much does this job require sitting?
Work With Work Group or Team	How important is it to work with others in a group or team in this job?
Spend Time Making Repetitive Motions	How much does this job require making repetitive motions?

Impact of Decisions on Co-workers or Company Resul	How do the decisions an employee makes impact the results of co-workers, clients or the company?
Frequency of Decision Making	How frequently is the worker required to make decisions that affect other people, the financial resources, and/or the image and reputation of the organization?
Contact With Others	How much does this job require the worker to be in contact with others (face-to-face, by telephone, or otherwise) in order to perform it?
Sounds, Noise Levels Are Distracting or Uncomforta	How often does this job require working exposed to sounds and noise levels that are distracting or uncomfortable?
Physical Proximity	To what extent does this job require the worker to perform job tasks in close physical proximity to other people?
Coordinate or Lead Others	How important is it to coordinate or lead others in accomplishing work activities in this job?
Exposed to Minor Burns, Cuts, Bites, or Stings	How often does this job require exposure to minor burns, cuts, bites, or stings?
Responsibility for Outcomes and Results	How responsible is the worker for work outcomes and results of other workers?
Telephone	How often do you have telephone conversations in this job?
Importance of Repeating Same Tasks	How important is repeating the same physical activities (e.g., key entry) or mental activities (e.g., checking entries in a ledger) over and over, without stopping, to performing this job?
Exposed to Hazardous Conditions	How often does this job require exposure to hazardous conditions?
Level of Competition	To what extent does this job require the worker to compete or to be aware of competitive pressures?
Exposed to Disease or Infections	How often does this job require exposure to disease/infections?
Responsible for Others' Health and Safety	How much responsibility is there for the health and safety of others in this job?
Deal With External Customers	How important is it to work with external customers or the public in this job?
Exposed to Hazardous Equipment	How often does this job require exposure to hazardous equipment?
Deal With Unpleasant or Angry People	How frequently does the worker have to deal with unpleasant, angry, or discourteous individuals as part of the job requirements?
Frequency of Conflict Situations	How often are there conflict situations the employee has to face in this job?
Letters and Memos	How often does the job require written letters and memos?
Consequence of Error	How serious would the result usually be if the worker made a mistake that was not readily correctable?
Spend Time Standing	How much does this job require standing?
Spend Time Bending or Twisting the Body	How much does this job require bending or twisting your body?
Pace Determined by Speed of Equipment	How important is it to this job that the pace is determined by the speed of equipment or machinery? (This does not refer to keeping busy at all times on this job.)
Wear Specialized Protective or Safety Equipment su	How much does this job require wearing specialized protective or safety equipment such as breathing apparatus, safety harness, full protection suits, or radiation protection?
Very Hot or Cold Temperatures	How often does this job require working in very hot (above 90 F degrees) or very cold (below 32 F degrees) temperatures?
Spend Time Walking and Running	How much does this job require walking and running?
Electronic Mail	How often do you use electronic mail in this job?
Public Speaking	How often do you have to perform public speaking in this job?
Degree of Automation	How automated is the job?
Spend Time Kneeling, Crouching, Stooping, or Crawl	How much does this job require kneeling, crouching, stooping or crawling?
Extremely Bright or Inadequate Lighting	How often does this job require working in extremely bright or inadequate lighting conditions?
In an Enclosed Vehicle or Equipment	How often does this job require working in a closed vehicle or equipment (e.g., car)?
Deal With Physically Aggressive People	How frequently does this job require the worker to deal with physical aggression of violent individuals?
Cramped Work Space, Awkward Positions	How often does this job require working in cramped work spaces that requires getting into awkward positions?
Exposed to Radiation	How often does this job require exposure to radiation?
Outdoors, Exposed to Weather	How often does this job require working outdoors, exposed to all weather conditions?
Spend Time Keeping or Regaining Balance	How much does this job require keeping or regaining your balance?
Exposed to Whole Body Vibration	How often does this job require exposure to whole body vibration (e.g., operate a jackhammer)?
Exposed to High Places	How often does this job require exposure to high places?

Spend Time Climbing Ladders, Scaffolds, or Poles	How much does this job require climbing ladders, scaffolds, or poles?
Outdoors, Under Cover	How often does this job require working outdoors, under cover (e.g., structure with roof but no walls)?
Indoors, Not Environmentally Controlled	How often does this job require working indoors in non-controlled environmental conditions (e.g., warehouse without heat)?
In an Open Vehicle or Equipment	How often does this job require working in an open vehicle or equipment (e.g., tractor)?

Job Zone Component	Job Zone Component Definitions
Title	Job Zone Two: Some Preparation Needed
Overall Experience	Some previous work-related skill, knowledge, or experience may be helpful in these occupations, but usually is not needed. For example, a drywall installer might benefit from experience installing drywall, but an inexperienced person could still learn to be an installer with little difficulty.
Job Training	Employees in these occupations need anywhere from a few months to one year of working with experienced employees.
Job Zone Examples	These occupations often involve using your knowledge and skills to help others. Examples include drywall installers, fire inspectors, flight attendants, pharmacy technicians, salespersons (retail), and tellers.
SVP Range	(4.0 to < 6.0)
Education	These occupations usually require a high school diploma and may require some vocational training or job-related course work. In some cases, an associate's or bachelor's degree could be needed.

Work_Styles	Work_Styles Definitions
Attention to Detail	Job requires being careful about detail and thorough in completing work tasks.
Dependability	Job requires being reliable, responsible, and dependable, and fulfilling obligations.
Cooperation	Job requires being pleasant with others on the job and displaying a good-natured, cooperative attitude.
Independence	Job requires developing one's own ways of doing things, guiding oneself with little or no supervision, and depending on oneself to get things done.
Achievement/Effort	Job requires establishing and maintaining personally challenging achievement goals and exerting effort toward mastering tasks.
Stress Tolerance	Job requires accepting criticism and dealing calmly and effectively with high stress situations.
Integrity	Job requires being honest and ethical.
Persistence	Job requires persistence in the face of obstacles.
Adaptability/Flexibility	Job requires being open to change (positive or negative) and to considerable variety in the workplace.
Analytical Thinking	Job requires analyzing information and using logic to address work-related issues and problems.
Initiative	Job requires a willingness to take on responsibilities and challenges.
Self Control	Job requires maintaining composure, keeping emotions in check, controlling anger, and avoiding aggressive behavior, even in very difficult situations.
Concern for Others	Job requires being sensitive to others' needs and feelings and being understanding and helpful on the job.
Innovation	Job requires creativity and alternative thinking to develop new ideas for and answers to work-related problems.
Leadership	Job requires a willingness to lead, take charge, and offer opinions and direction.
Social Orientation	Job requires preferring to work with others rather than alone, and being personally connected with others on the job.

51-9123.00 - Painting, Coating, and Decorating Workers

Paint, coat, or decorate articles, such as furniture, glass, plateware, pottery, jewelry, cakes, toys, books, or leather.

Tasks

1) Position and glue decorative pieces in cutout sections of workpieces, following patterns.

2) Place coated workpieces in ovens or dryers for specified times in order to dry or harden finishes.

3) Melt or heat coating materials to specified temperatures.

4) Cut out sections in surfaces of materials to be inlaid with decorative pieces, using patterns and knives or scissors.

5) Conceal blemishes in workpieces, such as nicks and dents, using fillers such as putty.

6) Clean surfaces of workpieces in preparation for coating, using cleaning fluids, solvents, brushes, scrapers, steam, sandpaper, or cloth.

7) Select and mix ingredients to prepare coating substances according to specifications, using paddles or mechanical mixers.

8) Rinse, drain, or wipe coated workpieces to remove excess coating material or to facilitate setting of finish coats on workpieces.

9) Read job orders and inspect workpieces to determine work procedures and materials required.

10) Immerse workpieces into coating materials for specified times.

11) Examine finished surfaces of workpieces to verify conformance to specifications; then retouch any defective areas.

12) Apply coatings, such as paint, ink, or lacquer, to protect or decorate workpiece surfaces, using spray guns, pens, or brushes.

51-9195.04 - Glass Blowers, Molders, Benders, and Finishers

Shape molten glass according to patterns.

Tasks

1) Dip ends of blowpipes into molten glass to collect gobs on pipe heads, or cut gobs from molten glass, using shears.

2) Record manufacturing information such as quantities, sizes, and types of goods produced.

3) Repair broken scrolls by replacing them with new sections of tubing.

4) Place glass into dies or molds of presses, and control presses to form products such as glassware components or optical blanks.

5) Place electrodes in tube ends and heat them with glass burners to fuse them into place.

6) Place rubber hoses on ends of tubing, and charge tubing with gas.

7) Inspect, weigh, and measure products to verify conformance to specifications, using instruments such as micrometers, calipers, magnifiers, and rulers.

8) Set up and adjust machine press stroke lengths and pressures, and regulate oven temperatures according to glass types to be processed.

9) Heat glass to pliable stage, using gas flames or ovens, and rotating glass to heat it uniformly.

10) Superimpose bent tubing on asbestos patterns to ensure accuracy.

11) Develop sketches of glass products into blueprint specifications, applying knowledge of glass technology and glass blowing.

12) Operate and maintain finishing machines to grind, drill, sand, bevel, decorate, wash, and/or polish glass or glass products.

13) Operate electric kilns that heat glass sheets and molds to the shape and curve of metal jigs.

14) Design and create glass objects, using blowpipes and artisans' hand tools and equipment.

15) Shape, bend, or join sections of glass, using paddles, pressing and flattening hand tools, or cork.

16) Cut lengths of tubing to specified sizes, using files or cutting wheels.

17) Determine types and quantities of glass required to fabricate products.

18) Strike necks of finished articles to separate articles from blowpipes.

19) Blow tubing into specified shapes to prevent glass from collapsing, using compressed air or own breath, or blow and rotate gathers in molds or on boards to obtain final shapes.

53-5021.01 - Ship and Boat Captains

Command vessels in oceans, bays, lakes, rivers, and coastal waters.

Tasks

1) Measure depths of water, using depth-measuring equipment.

2) Arrange for ships to be fueled, restocked with supplies, and/or repaired.

3) Assign watches and living quarters to crew members.

4) Signal crew members or deckhands to rig tow lines, open or close gates and ramps, and pull guard chains across entries.

5) Monitor the loading and discharging of cargo or passengers.

6) Maintain records of daily activities, personnel reports, ship positions and movements, ports of call, weather and sea conditions, pollution control efforts, and/or cargo and passenger status.

7) Inspect vessels to ensure efficient and safe operation of vessels and equipment, and conformance to regulations.

8) Compute positions, set courses, and determine speeds, by using charts, area plotting sheets, compasses, sextants, and knowledge of local conditions.

9) Direct and coordinate crew members or workers performing activities such as loading and unloading cargo, steering vessels, operating engines, and operating, maintaining, and repairing ship equipment.

10) Sort logs, form log booms, and salvage lost logs.

11) Maintain boats and equipment on board, such as engines, winches, navigational systems, fire extinguishers, and life preservers.

12) Steer and operate vessels, using radios, depth finders, radars, lights, buoys, and lighthouses.

13) Calculate sightings of land, using electronic sounding devices, and following contour lines on charts.

14) Perform various marine duties such as checking for oil spills or other pollutants around ports and harbors, and patrolling beaches.

15) Contact buyers to sell cargo such as fish.

16) Tow and maneuver barges, or signal tugboats to tow barges to destinations.

17) Signal passing vessels, using whistles, flashing lights, flags, and radios.

18) Resolve questions or problems with customs officials.

19) Read gauges to verify sufficient levels of hydraulic fluid, air pressure, and oxygen.

20) Purchase supplies and equipment.

21) Interview and hire crew members.

53-5021.02 - Mates- Ship, Boat, and Barge

Supervise and coordinate activities of crew aboard ships, boats, barges, or dredges.

Tasks

1) Observe water from ships' mastheads in order to advise on navigational direction.

2) Supervise crew members in the repair or replacement of defective gear and equipment.

3) Stand watches on vessels during specified periods while vessels are under way.

4) Arrange for ships to be stocked, fueled, and repaired.

5) Steer vessels, utilizing navigational devices such as compasses and sextons, and navigational aids such as lighthouses and buoys.

6) Inspect equipment such as cargo-handling gear, lifesaving equipment, visual-signaling equipment, and fishing, towing, or dredging gear, in order to detect problems.

7) Assume command of vessels in the event that ships' masters become incapacitated.

8) Participate in activities related to maintenance of vessel security.

9) Supervise crews in cleaning and maintaining decks, superstructures, and bridges.

10) Observe loading and unloading of cargo and equipment to ensure that handling and storage are performed according to specifications.

53-5021.03 - Pilots, Ship

Command ships to steer them into and out of harbors, estuaries, straits, and sounds, and on rivers, lakes, and bays. Must be licensed by U.S. Coast Guard with limitations indicating class and tonnage of vessels for which license is valid and route and waters that may be piloted.

Tasks

1) Prevent ships under their navigational control from engaging in unsafe operations.

2) Make nautical maps.

3) Give directions to crew members who are steering ships.

4) Direct courses and speeds of ships, based on specialized knowledge of local winds, weather, water depths, tides, currents, and hazards.

5) Consult maps, charts, weather reports, and navigation equipment to determine and direct ship movements.

6) Oversee cargo storage on or below decks.

7) Provide assistance in maritime rescue operations.

8) Report to appropriate authorities any violations of federal or state pilotage laws.

9) Operate amphibious craft during troop landings.

10) Set ships' courses that avoid reefs, outlying shoals, and other hazards, utilizing navigational aids such as lighthouses and buoys.

11) Maintain ship logs.

12) Serve as a vessel's docking master upon arrival at a port and when at a berth.

13) Maintain and repair boats and equipment.

14) Learn to operate new technology systems and procedures, through the use of instruction, simulators, and models.

15) Advise ships' masters on harbor rules and customs procedures.

16) Relieve crew members on tugs and launches.

17) Steer ships into and out of berths, or signal tugboat captains to berth and unberth ships.

18) Operate ship-to-shore radios to exchange information needed for ship operations.

53-5031.00 - Ship Engineers

Supervise and coordinate activities of crew engaged in operating and maintaining engines, boilers, deck machinery, and electrical, sanitary, and refrigeration equipment aboard ship.

Tasks

1) Maintain electrical power, heating, ventilation, refrigeration, water, and sewerage systems.

2) Operate and maintain off-loading liquid pumps and valves.

3) Record orders for changes in ship speed and direction, and note gauge readings and test data, such as revolutions per minute and voltage output, in engineering logs and bellbooks.

4) Fabricate engine replacement parts such as valves, stay rods, and bolts, using metalworking machinery.

5) Order and receive engine room's stores such as oil and spare parts; maintain inventories and record usage of supplies.

6) Maintain and repair engines, electric motors, pumps, winches and other mechanical and electrical equipment, or assist other crew members with maintenance and repair duties.

7) Perform and participate in emergency drills as required.

8) Monitor engine, machinery, and equipment indicators when vessels are underway, and report abnormalities to appropriate shipboard staff.

9) Perform general marine vessel maintenance and repair work such as repairing leaks, finishing interiors, refueling, and maintaining decks.

10) Supervise the activities of marine engine technicians engaged in the maintenance and repair of mechanical and electrical marine vessels, and inspect their work to ensure that it is performed properly.

11) Act as a liaison between a ship's captain and shore personnel to ensure that schedules and budgets are maintained and that the ship is operated safely and efficiently.

12) Clean engine parts, and keep engine rooms clean.

13) Start engines to propel ships, and regulate engines and power transmissions to control speeds of ships, according to directions from captains or bridge computers.

14) Maintain complete records of engineering department activities, including machine operations.

15) Install engine controls, propeller shafts, and propellers.

16) Monitor and test operations of engines and other equipment so that malfunctions and their causes can be identified.

53-6011.00 - Bridge and Lock Tenders

Operate and tend bridges, canal locks, and lighthouses to permit marine passage on inland waterways, near shores, and at danger points in waterway passages. May supervise such operations. Includes drawbridge operators, lock tenders and operators, and slip bridge operators.

Tasks

1) Prepare accident reports.

2) Direct movements of vessels in locks or bridge areas, using signals, telecommunication equipment, or loudspeakers.

3) Control machinery to open and close canal locks and dams, railroad or highway drawbridges, or horizontally or vertically adjustable bridges.

4) Move levers to activate traffic signals, navigation lights, and alarms.

5) Observe approaching vessels to determine size and speed, and listen for whistle signals indicating desire to pass.

6) Inspect canal and bridge equipment, and areas such as roadbeds for damage or defects, reporting problems to supervisors as necessary.

7) Write and submit maintenance work requisitions.

8) Maintain and guard stations in bridges to check waterways for boat traffic.

9) Clean and lubricate equipment, and make minor repairs and adjustments.

10) Log data such as water levels and weather conditions.

11) Check that bridges are clear of vehicles and pedestrians prior to opening.

12) Raise drawbridges and observe passage of water traffic, then lower drawbridges and raise automobile gates.

13) Stop automobile and pedestrian traffic on bridges, and lower automobile gates prior to moving bridges.

14) Attach ropes or cable lines to bits on lock decks or wharfs to secure vessels.

15) Turn valves to increase or decrease water levels in locks.

16) Add and remove balance weights to bridge mechanisms as necessary.

17) Operate lighthouses to assist marine passage near shores and dangerous waters.

18) Perform maintenance duties such as sweeping, painting, and yard work to keep facilities clean and in order.

19) Observe position and progress of vessels to ensure best utilization of lock spaces or bridge opening spaces.

Knowledge	Knowledge Definitions
Public Safety and Security	Knowledge of relevant equipment, policies, procedures, and strategies to promote effective local, state, or national security operations for the protection of people, data, property, and institutions.
English Language	Knowledge of the structure and content of the English language including the meaning and spelling of words, rules of composition, and grammar.
Education and Training	Knowledge of principles and methods for curriculum and training design, teaching and instruction for individuals and groups, and the measurement of training effects.
Telecommunications	Knowledge of transmission, broadcasting, switching, control, and operation of telecommunications systems.
Transportation	Knowledge of principles and methods for moving people or goods by air, rail, sea, or road, including the relative costs and benefits.
Customer and Personal Service	Knowledge of principles and processes for providing customer and personal services. This includes customer needs assessment, meeting quality standards for services, and evaluation of customer satisfaction.

Psychology	Knowledge of human behavior and performance; individual differences in ability, personality, and interests; learning and motivation; psychological research methods; and the assessment and treatment of behavioral and affective disorders.
Mechanical	Knowledge of machines and tools, including their designs, uses, repair, and maintenance.
Law and Government	Knowledge of laws, legal codes, court procedures, precedents, government regulations, executive orders, agency rules, and the democratic political process.
Personnel and Human Resources	Knowledge of principles and procedures for personnel recruitment, selection, training, compensation and benefits, labor relations and negotiation, and personnel information systems.
Clerical	Knowledge of administrative and clerical procedures and systems such as word processing, managing files and records, stenography and transcription, designing forms, and other office procedures and terminology.
Communications and Media	Knowledge of media production, communication, and dissemination techniques and methods. This includes alternative ways to inform and entertain via written, oral, and visual media.
Administration and Management	Knowledge of business and management principles involved in strategic planning, resource allocation, human resources modeling, leadership technique, production methods, and coordination of people and resources.
Mathematics	Knowledge of arithmetic, algebra, geometry, calculus, statistics, and their applications.
Geography	Knowledge of principles and methods for describing the features of land, sea, and air masses, including their physical characteristics, locations, interrelationships, and distribution of plant, animal, and human life.
Computers and Electronics	Knowledge of circuit boards, processors, chips, electronic equipment, and computer hardware and software, including applications and programming.
Engineering and Technology	Knowledge of the practical application of engineering science and technology. This includes applying principles, techniques, procedures, and equipment to the design and production of various goods and services.
Medicine and Dentistry	Knowledge of the information and techniques needed to diagnose and treat human injuries, diseases, and deformities. This includes symptoms, treatment alternatives, drug properties and interactions, and preventive health-care measures.
Chemistry	Knowledge of the chemical composition, structure, and properties of substances and of the chemical processes and transformations that they undergo. This includes uses of chemicals and their interactions, danger signs, production techniques, and disposal methods.
Building and Construction	Knowledge of materials, methods, and the tools involved in the construction or repair of houses, buildings, or other structures such as highways and roads.
Therapy and Counseling	Knowledge of principles, methods, and procedures for diagnosis, treatment, and rehabilitation of physical and mental dysfunctions, and for career counseling and guidance.
Design	Knowledge of design techniques, tools, and principles involved in production of precision technical plans, blueprints, drawings, and models.
Biology	Knowledge of plant and animal organisms, their tissues, cells, functions, interdependencies, and interactions with each other and the environment.
Sociology and Anthropology	Knowledge of group behavior and dynamics, societal trends and influences, human migrations, ethnicity, cultures and their history and origins.
Physics	Knowledge and prediction of physical principles, laws, their interrelationships, and applications to understanding fluid, material, and atmospheric dynamics, and mechanical, electrical, atomic and sub-atomic structures and processes.
Foreign Language	Knowledge of the structure and content of a foreign (non-English) language including the meaning and spelling of words, rules of composition and grammar, and pronunciation.
Economics and Accounting	Knowledge of economic and accounting principles and practices, the financial markets, banking and the analysis and reporting of financial data.
Philosophy and Theology	Knowledge of different philosophical systems and religions. This includes their basic principles, values, ethics, ways of thinking, customs, practices, and their impact on human culture.
History and Archeology	Knowledge of historical events and their causes, indicators, and effects on civilizations and cultures.

Production and Processing	Knowledge of raw materials, production processes, quality control, costs, and other techniques for maximizing the effective manufacture and distribution of goods.
Sales and Marketing	Knowledge of principles and methods for showing, promoting, and selling products or services. This includes marketing strategy and tactics, product demonstration, sales techniques, and sales control systems.
Food Production	Knowledge of techniques and equipment for planting, growing, and harvesting food products (both plant and animal) for consumption, including storage/handling techniques.
Fine Arts	Knowledge of the theory and techniques required to compose, produce, and perform works of music, dance, visual arts, drama, and sculpture.

Skills	Skills Definitions
Operation and Control	Controlling operations of equipment or systems.
Instructing	Teaching others how to do something.
Active Listening	Giving full attention to what other people are saying, taking time to understand the points being made, asking questions as appropriate, and not interrupting at inappropriate times.
Reading Comprehension	Understanding written sentences and paragraphs in work related documents.
Speaking	Talking to others to convey information effectively.
Writing	Communicating effectively in writing as appropriate for the needs of the audience.
Operation Monitoring	Watching gauges, dials, or other indicators to make sure a machine is working properly.
Equipment Maintenance	Performing routine maintenance on equipment and determining when and what kind of maintenance is needed.
Social Perceptiveness	Being aware of others' reactions and understanding why they react as they do.
Troubleshooting	Determining causes of operating errors and deciding what to do about it.
Learning Strategies	Selecting and using training/instructional methods and procedures appropriate for the situation when learning or teaching new things.
Judgment and Decision Making	Considering the relative costs and benefits of potential actions to choose the most appropriate one.
Service Orientation	Actively looking for ways to help people.
Coordination	Adjusting actions in relation to others' actions.
Monitoring	Monitoring/Assessing performance of yourself, other individuals, or organizations to make improvements or take corrective action.
Critical Thinking	Using logic and reasoning to identify the strengths and weaknesses of alternative solutions, conclusions or approaches to problems.
Time Management	Managing one's own time and the time of others.
Active Learning	Understanding the implications of new information for both current and future problem-solving and decision-making.
Persuasion	Persuading others to change their minds or behavior.
Mathematics	Using mathematics to solve problems.
Negotiation	Bringing others together and trying to reconcile differences.
Systems Analysis	Determining how a system should work and how changes in conditions, operations, and the environment will affect outcomes.
Management of Personnel Resources	Motivating, developing, and directing people as they work, identifying the best people for the job.
Technology Design	Generating or adapting equipment and technology to serve user needs.
Repairing	Repairing machines or systems using the needed tools.
Systems Evaluation	Identifying measures or indicators of system performance and the actions needed to improve or correct performance, relative to the goals of the system.
Complex Problem Solving	Identifying complex problems and reviewing related information to develop and evaluate options and implement solutions.
Equipment Selection	Determining the kind of tools and equipment needed to do a job.
Management of Material Resources	Obtaining and seeing to the appropriate use of equipment, facilities, and materials needed to do certain work.
Quality Control Analysis	Conducting tests and inspections of products, services, or processes to evaluate quality or performance.
Installation	Installing equipment, machines, wiring, or programs to meet specifications.
Operations Analysis	Analyzing needs and product requirements to create a design.
Programming	Writing computer programs for various purposes.

Management of Financial Resources	Determining how money will be spent to get the work done, and accounting for these expenditures.
Science	Using scientific rules and methods to solve problems.

Ability	Ability Definitions
Speech Clarity	The ability to speak clearly so others can understand you.
Problem Sensitivity	The ability to tell when something is wrong or is likely to go wrong. It does not involve solving the problem, only recognizing there is a problem.
Control Precision	The ability to quickly and repeatedly adjust the controls of a machine or a vehicle to exact positions.
Speech Recognition	The ability to identify and understand the speech of another person.
Depth Perception	The ability to judge which of several objects is closer or farther away from you, or to judge the distance between you and an object.
Near Vision	The ability to see details at close range (within a few feet of the observer).
Arm-Hand Steadiness	The ability to keep your hand and arm steady while moving your arm or while holding your arm and hand in one position.
Selective Attention	The ability to concentrate on a task over a period of time without being distracted.
Inductive Reasoning	The ability to combine pieces of information to form general rules or conclusions (includes finding a relationship among seemingly unrelated events).
Deductive Reasoning	The ability to apply general rules to specific problems to produce answers that make sense.
Oral Expression	The ability to communicate information and ideas in speaking so others will understand.
Oral Comprehension	The ability to listen to and understand information and ideas presented through spoken words and sentences.
Information Ordering	The ability to arrange things or actions in a certain order or pattern according to a specific rule or set of rules (e.g., patterns of numbers, letters, words, pictures, mathematical operations).
Written Comprehension	The ability to read and understand information and ideas presented in writing.
Written Expression	The ability to communicate information and ideas in writing so others will understand.
Multilimb Coordination	The ability to coordinate two or more limbs (for example, two arms, two legs, or one leg and one arm) while sitting, standing, or lying down. It does not involve performing the activities while the whole body is in motion.
Far Vision	The ability to see details at a distance.
Hearing Sensitivity	The ability to detect or tell the differences between sounds that vary in pitch and loudness.
Category Flexibility	The ability to generate or use different sets of rules for combining or grouping things in different ways.
Auditory Attention	The ability to focus on a single source of sound in the presence of other distracting sounds.
Manual Dexterity	The ability to quickly move your hand, your hand together with your arm, or your two hands to grasp, manipulate, or assemble objects.
Finger Dexterity	The ability to make precisely coordinated movements of the fingers of one or both hands to grasp, manipulate, or assemble very small objects.
Reaction Time	The ability to quickly respond (with the hand, finger, or foot) to a signal (sound, light, picture) when it appears.
Response Orientation	The ability to choose quickly between two or more movements in response to two or more different signals (lights, sounds, pictures). It includes the speed with which the correct response is started with the hand, foot, or other body part.
Perceptual Speed	The ability to quickly and accurately compare similarities and differences among sets of letters, numbers, objects, pictures, or patterns. The things to be compared may be presented at the same time or one after the other. This ability also includes comparing a presented object with a remembered object.
Rate Control	The ability to time your movements or the movement of a piece of equipment in anticipation of changes in the speed and/or direction of a moving object or scene.
Flexibility of Closure	The ability to identify or detect a known pattern (a figure, object, word, or sound) that is hidden in other distracting material.
Time Sharing	The ability to shift back and forth between two or more activities or sources of information (such as speech, sounds, touch, or other sources).
Visual Color Discrimination	The ability to match or detect differences between colors, including shades of color and brightness.

Glare Sensitivity	The ability to see objects in the presence of glare or bright lighting.
Originality	The ability to come up with unusual or clever ideas about a given topic or situation, or to develop creative ways to solve a problem.
Visualization	The ability to imagine how something will look after it is moved around or when its parts are moved or rearranged.
Speed of Closure	The ability to quickly make sense of, combine, and organize information into meaningful patterns.
Sound Localization	The ability to tell the direction from which a sound originated.
Number Facility	The ability to add, subtract, multiply, or divide quickly and correctly.
Memorization	The ability to remember information such as words, numbers, pictures, and procedures.
Gross Body Equilibrium	The ability to keep or regain your body balance or stay upright when in an unstable position.
Trunk Strength	The ability to use your abdominal and lower back muscles to support part of the body repeatedly or continuously over time without 'giving out' or fatiguing.
Fluency of Ideas	The ability to come up with a number of ideas about a topic (the number of ideas is important, not their quality, correctness, or creativity).
Wrist-Finger Speed	The ability to make fast, simple, repeated movements of the fingers, hands, and wrists.
Gross Body Coordination	The ability to coordinate the movement of your arms, legs, and torso together when the whole body is in motion.
Static Strength	The ability to exert maximum muscle force to lift, push, pull, or carry objects.
Speed of Limb Movement	The ability to quickly move the arms and legs.
Dynamic Strength	The ability to exert muscle force repeatedly or continuously over time. This involves muscular endurance and resistance to muscle fatigue.
Spatial Orientation	The ability to know your location in relation to the environment or to know where other objects are in relation to you.
Night Vision	The ability to see under low light conditions.
Extent Flexibility	The ability to bend, stretch, twist, or reach with your body, arms, and/or legs.
Stamina	The ability to exert yourself physically over long periods of time without getting winded or out of breath.
Mathematical Reasoning	The ability to choose the right mathematical methods or formulas to solve a problem.
Peripheral Vision	The ability to see objects or movement of objects to one's side when the eyes are looking ahead.
Explosive Strength	The ability to use short bursts of muscle force to propel oneself (as in jumping or sprinting), or to throw an object.
Dynamic Flexibility	The ability to quickly and repeatedly bend, stretch, twist, or reach out with your body, arms, and/or legs.

Work_Activity	Work_Activity Definitions
Performing for or Working Directly with the Public	Performing for people or dealing directly with the public. This includes serving customers in restaurants and stores, and receiving clients or guests.
Training and Teaching Others	Identifying the educational needs of others, developing formal educational or training programs or classes, and teaching or instructing others.
Documenting/Recording Information	Entering, transcribing, recording, storing, or maintaining information in written or electronic/magnetic form.
Controlling Machines and Processes	Using either control mechanisms or direct physical activity to operate machines or processes (not including computers or vehicles).
Inspecting Equipment, Structures, or Material	Inspecting equipment, structures, or materials to identify the cause of errors or other problems or defects.
Communicating with Supervisors, Peers, or Subordin	Providing information to supervisors, co-workers, and subordinates by telephone, in written form, e-mail, or in person.
Getting Information	Observing, receiving, and otherwise obtaining information from all relevant sources.
Establishing and Maintaining Interpersonal Relatio	Developing constructive and cooperative working relationships with others, and maintaining them over time.
Communicating with Persons Outside Organization	Communicating with people outside the organization, representing the organization to customers, the public, government, and other external sources. This information can be exchanged in person, in writing, or by telephone or e-mail.
Making Decisions and Solving Problems	Analyzing information and evaluating results to choose the best solution and solve problems.

Monitor Processes, Materials, or Surroundings	Monitoring and reviewing information from materials, events, or the environment, to detect or assess problems.
Performing Administrative Activities	Performing day-to-day administrative tasks such as maintaining information files and processing paperwork.
Performing General Physical Activities	Performing physical activities that require considerable use of your arms and legs and moving your whole body, such as climbing, lifting, balancing, walking, stooping, and handling of materials.
Coaching and Developing Others	Identifying the developmental needs of others and coaching, mentoring, or otherwise helping others to improve their knowledge or skills.
Identifying Objects, Actions, and Events	Identifying information by categorizing, estimating, recognizing differences or similarities, and detecting changes in circumstances or events.
Evaluating Information to Determine Compliance wit	Using relevant information and individual judgment to determine whether events or processes comply with laws, regulations, or standards.
Assisting and Caring for Others	Providing personal assistance, medical attention, emotional support, or other personal care to others such as coworkers, customers, or patients.
Coordinating the Work and Activities of Others	Getting members of a group to work together to accomplish tasks.
Handling and Moving Objects	Using hands and arms in handling, installing, positioning, and moving materials, and manipulating things.
Interpreting the Meaning of Information for Others	Translating or explaining what information means and how it can be used.
Resolving Conflicts and Negotiating with Others	Handling complaints, settling disputes, and resolving grievances and conflicts, or otherwise negotiating with others.
Processing Information	Compiling, coding, categorizing, calculating, tabulating, auditing, or verifying information or data.
Developing and Building Teams	Encouraging and building mutual trust, respect, and cooperation among team members.
Repairing and Maintaining Mechanical Equipment	Servicing, repairing, adjusting, and testing machines, devices, moving parts, and equipment that operate primarily on the basis of mechanical (not electronic) principles.
Operating Vehicles, Mechanized Devices, or Equipme	Running, maneuvering, navigating, or driving vehicles or mechanized equipment, such as forklifts, passenger vehicles, aircraft, or water craft.
Judging the Qualities of Things, Services, or Peop	Assessing the value, importance, or quality of things or people.
Estimating the Quantifiable Characteristics of Pro	Estimating sizes, distances, and quantities; or determining time, costs, resources, or materials needed to perform a work activity.
Provide Consultation and Advice to Others	Providing guidance and expert advice to management or other groups on technical, systems-, or process-related topics.
Guiding, Directing, and Motivating Subordinates	Providing guidance and direction to subordinates, including setting performance standards and monitoring performance.
Organizing, Planning, and Prioritizing Work	Developing specific goals and plans to prioritize, organize, and accomplish your work.
Scheduling Work and Activities	Scheduling events, programs, and activities, as well as the work of others.
Updating and Using Relevant Knowledge	Keeping up-to-date technically and applying new knowledge to your job.
Analyzing Data or Information	Identifying the underlying principles, reasons, or facts of information by breaking down information or data into separate parts.
Staffing Organizational Units	Recruiting, interviewing, selecting, hiring, and promoting employees in an organization.
Developing Objectives and Strategies	Establishing long-range objectives and specifying the strategies and actions to achieve them.
Selling or Influencing Others	Convincing others to buy merchandise/goods or to otherwise change their minds or actions.
Thinking Creatively	Developing, designing, or creating new applications, ideas, relationships, systems, or products, including artistic contributions.
Repairing and Maintaining Electronic Equipment	Servicing, repairing, calibrating, regulating, fine-tuning, or testing machines, devices, and equipment that operate primarily on the basis of electrical or electronic (not mechanical) principles.
Monitoring and Controlling Resources	Monitoring and controlling resources and overseeing the spending of money.
Interacting With Computers	Using computers and computer systems (including hardware and software) to program, write software, set up functions, enter data, or process information.
Drafting, Laying Out, and Specifying Technical Dev	Providing documentation, detailed instructions, drawings, or specifications to tell others about how devices, parts, equipment, or structures are to be fabricated, constructed, assembled, modified, maintained, or used.

Work_Context	Work_Context Definitions
Telephone	How often do you have telephone conversations in this job?
Freedom to Make Decisions	How much decision making freedom, without supervision, does the job offer?
Indoors, Environmentally Controlled	How often does this job require working indoors in environmentally controlled conditions?
Face-to-Face Discussions	How often do you have to have face-to-face discussions with individuals or teams in this job?
Spend Time Using Your Hands to Handle, Control, or	How much does this job require using your hands to handle, control, or feel objects, tools or controls?
Sounds, Noise Levels Are Distracting or Uncomforta	How often does this job require working exposed to sounds and noise levels that are distracting or uncomfortable?
Outdoors, Exposed to Weather	How often does this job require working outdoors, exposed to all weather conditions?
Contact With Others	How much does this job require the worker to be in contact with others (face-to-face, by telephone, or otherwise) in order to perform it?
Importance of Being Exact or Accurate	How important is being very exact or highly accurate in performing this job?
Structured versus Unstructured Work	To what extent is this job structured for the worker, rather than allowing the worker to determine tasks, priorities, and goals?
Frequency of Decision Making	How frequently is the worker required to make decisions that affect other people, the financial resources, and/or the image and reputation of the organization?
Consequence of Error	How serious would the result usually be if the worker made a mistake that was not readily correctable?
Wear Common Protective or Safety Equipment such as	How much does this job require wearing common protective or safety equipment such as safety shoes, glasses, gloves, hard hats or live jackets?
Importance of Repeating Same Tasks	How important is repeating the same physical activities (e.g., key entry) or mental activities (e.g., checking entries in a ledger) over and over, without stopping, to performing this job?
Responsible for Others' Health and Safety	How much responsibility is there for the health and safety of others in this job?
Deal With External Customers	How important is it to work with external customers or the public in this job?
Impact of Decisions on Co-workers or Company Resul	How do the decisions an employee makes impact the results of co-workers, clients or the company?
Spend Time Standing	How much does this job require standing?
Deal With Unpleasant or Angry People	How frequently does the worker have to deal with unpleasant, angry, or discourteous individuals as part of the job requirements?
Time Pressure	How often does this job require the worker to meet strict deadlines?
Degree of Automation	How automated is the job?
Letters and Memos	How often does the job require written letters and memos?
Pace Determined by Speed of Equipment	How important is it to this job that the pace is determined by the speed of equipment or machinery? (This does not refer to keeping busy at all times on this job.)
Spend Time Sitting	How much does this job require sitting?
Very Hot or Cold Temperatures	How often does this job require working in very hot (above 90 F degrees) or very cold (below 32 F degrees) temperatures?
Work With Work Group or Team	How important is it to work with others in a group or team in this job?
Spend Time Making Repetitive Motions	How much does this job require making repetitive motions?
Exposed to Minor Burns, Cuts, Bites, or Stings	How often does this job require exposure to minor burns, cuts, bites, or stings?
Exposed to Contaminants	How often does this job require working exposed to contaminants (such as pollutants, gases, dust or odors)?
Coordinate or Lead Others	How important is it to coordinate or lead others in accomplishing work activities in this job?
Spend Time Walking and Running	How much does this job require walking and running?
Exposed to High Places	How often does this job require exposure to high places?
Exposed to Hazardous Equipment	How often does this job require exposure to hazardous equipment?
Responsibility for Outcomes and Results	How responsible is the worker for work outcomes and results of other workers?

Outdoors, Under Cover	How often does this job require working outdoors, under cover (e.g., structure with roof but no walls)?
Indoors, Not Environmentally Controlled	How often does this job require working indoors in non-controlled environmental conditions (e.g., warehouse without heat)?
Frequency of Conflict Situations	How often are there conflict situations the employee has to face in this job?
Extremely Bright or Inadequate Lighting	How often does this job require working in extremely bright or inadequate lighting conditions?
Public Speaking	How often do you have to perform public speaking in this job?
Physical Proximity	To what extent does this job require the worker to perform job tasks in close physical proximity to other people?
Level of Competition	To what extent does this job require the worker to compete or to be aware of competitive pressures?
Spend Time Bending or Twisting the Body	How much does this job require bending or twisting your body?
Exposed to Hazardous Conditions	How often does this job require exposure to hazardous conditions?
Deal With Physically Aggressive People	How frequently does this job require the worker to deal with physical aggression of violent individuals?
Electronic Mail	How often do you use electronic mail in this job?
In an Open Vehicle or Equipment	How often does this job require working in an open vehicle or equipment (e.g., tractor)?
In an Enclosed Vehicle or Equipment	How often does this job require working in a closed vehicle or equipment (e.g., car)?
Spend Time Keeping or Regaining Balance	How much does this job require keeping or regaining your balance?
Spend Time Climbing Ladders, Scaffolds, or Poles	How much does this job require climbing ladders, scaffolds, or poles?
Cramped Work Space, Awkward Positions	How often does this job require working in cramped work spaces that requires getting into awkward positions?
Wear Specialized Protective or Safety Equipment su	How much does this job require wearing specialized protective or safety equipment such as breathing apparatus, safety harness, full protection suits, or radiation protection?
Exposed to Radiation	How often does this job require exposure to radiation?
Exposed to Disease or Infections	How often does this job require exposure to disease/infections?
Exposed to Whole Body Vibration	How often does this job require exposure to whole body vibration (e.g., operate a jackhammer)?
Spend Time Kneeling, Crouching, Stooping, or Crawl	How much does this job require kneeling, crouching, stooping or crawling?

Job Zone Component	Job Zone Component Definitions
Title	Job Zone One: Little or No Preparation Needed
Overall Experience	No previous work-related skill, knowledge, or experience is needed for these occupations. For example, a person can become a general office clerk even if he/she has never worked in an office before.
Job Training	Employees in these occupations need anywhere from a few days to a few months of training. Usually, an experienced worker could show you how to do the job.
Job Zone Examples	These occupations involve following instructions and helping others. Examples include bus drivers, forest and conservation workers, general office clerks, home health aides, and waiters/waitresses.
SVP Range	(Below 4.0)
Education	These occupations may require a high school diploma or GED certificate. Some may require a formal training course to obtain a license.

Work_Styles	Work_Styles Definitions
Dependability	Job requires being reliable, responsible, and dependable, and fulfilling obligations.
Self Control	Job requires maintaining composure, keeping emotions in check, controlling anger, and avoiding aggressive behavior, even in very difficult situations.
Cooperation	Job requires being pleasant with others on the job and displaying a good-natured, cooperative attitude.
Attention to Detail	Job requires being careful about detail and thorough in completing work tasks.
Stress Tolerance	Job requires accepting criticism and dealing calmly and effectively with high stress situations.
Integrity	Job requires being honest and ethical.

Concern for Others	Job requires being sensitive to others' needs and feelings and being understanding and helpful on the job.
Independence	Job requires developing one's own ways of doing things, guiding oneself with little or no supervision, and depending on oneself to get things done.
Adaptability/Flexibility	Job requires being open to change (positive or negative) and to considerable variety in the workplace.
Initiative	Job requires a willingness to take on responsibilities and challenges.
Persistence	Job requires persistence in the face of obstacles.
Achievement/Effort	Job requires establishing and maintaining personally challenging achievement goals and exerting effort toward mastering tasks.
Leadership	Job requires a willingness to lead, take charge, and offer opinions and direction.
Social Orientation	Job requires preferring to work with others rather than alone, and being personally connected with others on the job.
Analytical Thinking	Job requires analyzing information and using logic to address work-related issues and problems.
Innovation	Job requires creativity and alternative thinking to develop new ideas for and answers to work-related problems.

53-7031.00 - Dredge Operators

Operate dredge to remove sand, gravel, or other materials from lakes, rivers, or streams; and to excavate and maintain navigable channels in waterways.

Tasks

1) Start power winches that draw in or let out cables to change positions of dredges, or pull in and let out cables manually.

2) Move levers to position dredges for excavation, to engage hydraulic pumps, to raise and lower suction booms, and to control rotation of cutterheads.

3) Lower anchor poles to verify depths of excavations, using winches, or scan depth gauges to determine depths of excavations.

4) Direct or assist workers placing shore anchors and cables, laying additional pipes from dredges to shore, and pumping water from pontoons.

5) Pump water to clear machinery pipelines.

53-7033.00 - Loading Machine Operators, Underground Mining

Operate underground loading machine to load coal, ore, or rock into shuttle or mine car or onto conveyors. Loading equipment may include power shovels, hoisting engines equipped with cable-drawn scraper or scoop, or machines equipped with gathering arms and conveyor.

Tasks

1) Move trailing electrical cables clear of obstructions, using rubber safety gloves.

2) Drive machines into piles of material blasted from working faces.

3) Operate levers to move conveyor booms or shovels so that mine contents such as coal, rock, and ore can be placed into cars or onto conveyors.

4) Signal workers to move loaded cars.

5) Start conveyor booms and gathering-arm motors, and operate winches to position cars under boom-conveyors for loading.

6) Stop gathering arms when cars are full.

7) Inspect boarding and locking of open-top box cars and wedging of side-drop and hopper cars in order to prevent loss of material in transit.

8) Notify switching departments to deliver specific types of cars.

9) Observe and record car numbers, carriers, customers, tonnages, and grades and conditions of material.

10) Oil, lubricate, and adjust conveyors, crushers, and other equipment, using hand tools and lubricating equipment.

11) Pry off loose material from roofs and move it into the paths of machines, using crowbars.

12) Replace hydraulic hoses, headlight bulbs, and gathering-arm teeth.

13) Estimate and record amounts of material in bins.

14) Clean hoppers, and clean spillage from tracks, walks, driveways, and conveyor decking.

53-7063.00 - Machine Feeders and Offbearers

Feed materials into or remove materials from machines or equipment that is automatic or tended by other workers.

Tasks

1) Weigh or measure materials or products to ensure conformance to specifications.

2) Record production and operational data, such as amount of materials processed.

3) Clean and maintain machinery, equipment, and work areas to ensure proper functioning and safe working conditions.

4) Fasten, package, or stack materials and products, using hand tools and fastening equipment.

5) Identify and mark materials, products, and samples, following instructions.

6) Open and close gates of belt and pneumatic conveyors on machines that are fed directly from preceding machines.

7) Load materials and products into machines and equipment, or onto conveyors, using hand tools and moving devices.

8) Inspect materials and products for defects, and to ensure conformance to specifications.

9) Remove materials and products from machines and equipment, and place them in boxes, trucks or conveyors, using hand tools and moving devices.

10) Transfer materials and products to and from machinery and equipment, using industrial trucks or hand trucks.

11) Add chemicals, solutions, or ingredients to machines or equipment as required by the manufacturing process.

12) Push dual control buttons and move controls in order to start, stop, or adjust machinery and equipment.

53-7081.00 - Refuse and Recyclable Material Collectors

Collect and dump refuse or recyclable materials from containers into truck. May drive truck.

Tasks

1) Communicate with dispatchers concerning delays, unsafe sites, accidents, equipment breakdowns, and other maintenance problems.

2) Drive to disposal sites to empty trucks that have been filled.

3) Drive trucks along established routes through residential streets and alleys, or through business and industrial areas.

4) Fill out any needed reports for defective equipment.

5) Refuel trucks and add other necessary fluids, such as oil.

6) Keep informed of road and weather conditions to determine how routes will be affected.

7) Clean trucks and compactor bodies after routes have been completed.

8) Operate equipment that compresses the collected refuse.

9) Dismount garbage trucks to collect garbage and remount trucks to ride to the next collection point.

10) Operate automated or semi-automated hoisting devices that raise refuse bins and dump contents into openings in truck bodies.

11) Tag garbage or recycling containers to inform customers of problems such as excess garbage or inclusion of items that are not permitted.

12) Organize schedules for refuse collection.

13) Sort items set out for recycling and throw materials into designated truck compartments.

14) Provide quotes for refuse collection contracts.

Knowledge	Knowledge Definitions
Customer and Personal Service	Knowledge of principles and processes for providing customer and personal services. This includes customer needs assessment, meeting quality standards for services, and evaluation of customer satisfaction.
Transportation	Knowledge of principles and methods for moving people or goods by air, rail, sea, or road, including the relative costs and benefits.
Public Safety and Security	Knowledge of relevant equipment, policies, procedures, and strategies to promote effective local, state, or national security operations for the protection of people, data, property, and institutions.
English Language	Knowledge of the structure and content of the English language including the meaning and spelling of words, rules of composition, and grammar.
Mechanical	Knowledge of machines and tools, including their designs, uses, repair, and maintenance.
Education and Training	Knowledge of principles and methods for curriculum and training design, teaching and instruction for individuals and groups, and the measurement of training effects.
Personnel and Human Resources	Knowledge of principles and procedures for personnel recruitment, selection, training, compensation and benefits, labor relations and negotiation, and personnel information systems.
Production and Processing	Knowledge of raw materials, production processes, quality control, costs, and other techniques for maximizing the effective manufacture and distribution of goods.
Administration and Management	Knowledge of business and management principles involved in strategic planning, resource allocation, human resources modeling, leadership technique, production methods, and coordination of people and resources.
Telecommunications	Knowledge of transmission, broadcasting, switching, control, and operation of telecommunications systems.
Law and Government	Knowledge of laws, legal codes, court procedures, precedents, government regulations, executive orders, agency rules, and the democratic political process.
Clerical	Knowledge of administrative and clerical procedures and systems such as word processing, managing files and records, stenography and transcription, designing forms, and other office procedures and terminology.
Sales and Marketing	Knowledge of principles and methods for showing, promoting, and selling products or services. This includes marketing strategy and tactics, product demonstration, sales techniques, and sales control systems.
Communications and Media	Knowledge of media production, communication, and dissemination techniques and methods. This includes alternative ways to inform and entertain via written, oral, and visual media.
Mathematics	Knowledge of arithmetic, algebra, geometry, calculus, statistics, and their applications.
Economics and Accounting	Knowledge of economic and accounting principles and practices, the financial markets, banking and the analysis and reporting of financial data.
Physics	Knowledge and prediction of physical principles, laws, their interrelationships, and applications to understanding fluid, material, and atmospheric dynamics, and mechanical, electrical, atomic and sub-atomic structures and processes.
Foreign Language	Knowledge of the structure and content of a foreign (non-English) language including the meaning and spelling of words, rules of composition and grammar, and pronunciation.
Geography	Knowledge of principles and methods for describing the features of land, sea, and air masses, including their physical characteristics, locations, interrelationships, and distribution of plant, animal, and human life.
Engineering and Technology	Knowledge of the practical application of engineering science and technology. This includes applying principles, techniques, procedures, and equipment to the design and production of various goods and services.
Food Production	Knowledge of techniques and equipment for planting, growing, and harvesting food products (both plant and animal) for consumption, including storage/handling techniques.
Psychology	Knowledge of human behavior and performance; individual differences in ability, personality, and interests; learning and motivation; psychological research methods; and the assessment and treatment of behavioral and affective disorders.

Medicine and Dentistry	Knowledge of the information and techniques needed to diagnose and treat human injuries, diseases, and deformities. This includes symptoms, treatment alternatives, drug properties and interactions. and preventive health-care measures.
Computers and Electronics	Knowledge of circuit boards, processors, chips, electronic equipment, and computer hardware and software, including applications and programming.
Chemistry	Knowledge of the chemical composition, structure, and properties of substances and of the chemical processes and transformations that they undergo. This includes uses of chemicals and their interactions, danger signs, production techniques, and disposal methods.
Design	Knowledge of design techniques, tools, and principles involved in production of precision technical plans, blueprints, drawings, and models.
Building and Construction	Knowledge of materials, methods, and the tools involved in the construction or repair of houses, buildings, or other structures such as highways and roads.
Therapy and Counseling	Knowledge of principles, methods, and procedures for diagnosis, treatment, and rehabilitation of physical and mental dysfunctions, and for career counseling and guidance.
Biology	Knowledge of plant and animal organisms, their tissues, cells, functions, interdependencies, and interactions with each other and the environment.
Sociology and Anthropology	Knowledge of group behavior and dynamics, societal trends and influences, human migrations, ethnicity, cultures and their history and origins.
Philosophy and Theology	Knowledge of different philosophical systems and religions. This includes their basic principles, values, ethics, ways of thinking, customs, practices, and their impact on human culture.
History and Archeology	Knowledge of historical events and their causes, indicators, and effects on civilizations and cultures.
Fine Arts	Knowledge of the theory and techniques required to compose, produce, and perform works of music, dance, visual arts, drama, and sculpture.

Skills	Skills Definitions
Active Listening	Giving full attention to what other people are saying, taking time to understand the points being made, asking questions as appropriate, and not interrupting at inappropriate times.
Coordination	Adjusting actions in relation to others' actions.
Equipment Maintenance	Performing routine maintenance on equipment and determining when and what kind of maintenance is needed.
Critical Thinking	Using logic and reasoning to identify the strengths and weaknesses of alternative solutions, conclusions or approaches to problems.
Reading Comprehension	Understanding written sentences and paragraphs in work related documents.
Social Perceptiveness	Being aware of others' reactions and understanding why they react as they do.
Operation and Control	Controlling operations of equipment or systems.
Learning Strategies	Selecting and using training/instructional methods and procedures appropriate for the situation when learning or teaching new things.
Speaking	Talking to others to convey information effectively.
Monitoring	Monitoring/Assessing performance of yourself, other individuals, or organizations to make improvements or take corrective action.
Operation Monitoring	Watching gauges, dials, or other indicators to make sure a machine is working properly.
Judgment and Decision Making	Considering the relative costs and benefits of potential actions to choose the most appropriate one.
Instructing	Teaching others how to do something.
Time Management	Managing one's own time and the time of others.
Troubleshooting	Determining causes of operating errors and deciding what to do about it.
Active Learning	Understanding the implications of new information for both current and future problem-solving and decision-making.
Equipment Selection	Determining the kind of tools and equipment needed to do a job.
Repairing	Repairing machines or systems using the needed tools.
Writing	Communicating effectively in writing as appropriate for the needs of the audience.
Complex Problem Solving	Identifying complex problems and reviewing related information to develop and evaluate options and implement solutions.

Negotiation	Bringing others together and trying to reconcile differences.
Systems Analysis	Determining how a system should work and how changes in conditions, operations, and the environment will affect outcomes.
Service Orientation	Actively looking for ways to help people.
Management of Material Resources	Obtaining and seeing to the appropriate use of equipment, facilities, and materials needed to do certain work.
Persuasion	Persuading others to change their minds or behavior.
Mathematics	Using mathematics to solve problems.
Management of Personnel Resources	Motivating, developing, and directing people as they work. identifying the best people for the job.
Systems Evaluation	Identifying measures or indicators of system performance and the actions needed to improve or correct performance. relative to the goals of the system.
Management of Financial Resources	Determining how money will be spent to get the work done, and accounting for these expenditures.
Quality Control Analysis	Conducting tests and inspections of products, services, or processes to evaluate quality or performance.
Technology Design	Generating or adapting equipment and technology to serve user needs.
Operations Analysis	Analyzing needs and product requirements to create a design.
Installation	Installing equipment, machines, wiring, or programs to meet specifications.
Science	Using scientific rules and methods to solve problems.
Programming	Writing computer programs for various purposes.

Ability	Ability Definitions
Multilimb Coordination	The ability to coordinate two or more limbs (for example, two arms, two legs, or one leg and one arm) while sitting, standing, or lying down. It does not involve performing the activities while the whole body is in motion.
Control Precision	The ability to quickly and repeatedly adjust the controls of a machine or a vehicle to exact positions.
Near Vision	The ability to see details at close range (within a few feet of the observer).
Oral Expression	The ability to communicate information and ideas in speaking so others will understand.
Depth Perception	The ability to judge which of several objects is closer or farther away from you, or to judge the distance between you and an object.
Oral Comprehension	The ability to listen to and understand information and ideas presented through spoken words and sentences.
Speech Recognition	The ability to identify and understand the speech of another person.
Problem Sensitivity	The ability to tell when something is wrong or is likely to go wrong. It does not involve solving the problem, only recognizing there is a problem.
Static Strength	The ability to exert maximum muscle force to lift, push, pull, or carry objects.
Manual Dexterity	The ability to quickly move your hand, your hand together with your arm, or your two hands to grasp, manipulate, or assemble objects.
Arm-Hand Steadiness	The ability to keep your hand and arm steady while moving your arm or while holding your arm and hand in one position.
Inductive Reasoning	The ability to combine pieces of information to form general rules or conclusions (includes finding a relationship among seemingly unrelated events).
Information Ordering	The ability to arrange things or actions in a certain order or pattern according to a specific rule or set of rules (e.g., patterns of numbers, letters, words, pictures, mathematical operations).
Written Comprehension	The ability to read and understand information and ideas presented in writing.
Speech Clarity	The ability to speak clearly so others can understand you.
Selective Attention	The ability to concentrate on a task over a period of time without being distracted.
Reaction Time	The ability to quickly respond (with the hand, finger, or foot) to a signal (sound, light, picture) when it appears.
Far Vision	The ability to see details at a distance.
Deductive Reasoning	The ability to apply general rules to specific problems to produce answers that make sense.
Flexibility of Closure	The ability to identify or detect a known pattern (a figure, object, word, or sound) that is hidden in other distracting material.
Extent Flexibility	The ability to bend, stretch, twist, or reach with your body, arms, and/or legs.
Stamina	The ability to exert yourself physically over long periods of time without getting winded or out of breath.

Category Flexibility	The ability to generate or use different sets of rules for combining or grouping things in different ways.
Hearing Sensitivity	The ability to detect or tell the differences between sounds that vary in pitch and loudness.
Spatial Orientation	The ability to know your location in relation to the environment or to know where other objects are in relation to you.
Rate Control	The ability to time your movements or the movement of a piece of equipment in anticipation of changes in the speed and/or direction of a moving object or scene.
Perceptual Speed	The ability to quickly and accurately compare similarities and differences among sets of letters, numbers, objects, pictures, or patterns. The things to be compared may be presented at the same time or one after the other. This ability also includes comparing a presented object with a remembered object.
Speed of Limb Movement	The ability to quickly move the arms and legs.
Trunk Strength	The ability to use your abdominal and lower back muscles to support part of the body repeatedly or continuously over time without 'giving out' or fatiguing.
Gross Body Coordination	The ability to coordinate the movement of your arms, legs, and torso together when the whole body is in motion.
Visual Color Discrimination	The ability to match or detect differences between colors, including shades of color and brightness.
Response Orientation	The ability to choose quickly between two or more movements in response to two or more different signals (lights, sounds, pictures). It includes the speed with which the correct response is started with the hand, foot, or other body part.
Finger Dexterity	The ability to make precisely coordinated movements of the fingers of one or both hands to grasp, manipulate, or assemble very small objects.
Glare Sensitivity	The ability to see objects in the presence of glare or bright lighting.
Night Vision	The ability to see under low light conditions.
Dynamic Strength	The ability to exert muscle force repeatedly or continuously over time. This involves muscular endurance and resistance to muscle fatigue.
Peripheral Vision	The ability to see objects or movement of objects to one's side when the eyes are looking ahead.
Visualization	The ability to imagine how something will look after it is moved around or when its parts are moved or rearranged.
Gross Body Equilibrium	The ability to keep or regain your body balance or stay upright when in an unstable position.
Written Expression	The ability to communicate information and ideas in writing so others will understand.
Auditory Attention	The ability to focus on a single source of sound in the presence of other distracting sounds.
Time Sharing	The ability to shift back and forth between two or more activities or sources of information (such as speech, sounds, touch, or other sources).
Wrist-Finger Speed	The ability to make fast, simple, repeated movements of the fingers, hands, and wrists.
Sound Localization	The ability to tell the direction from which a sound originated.
Speed of Closure	The ability to quickly make sense of, combine, and organize information into meaningful patterns.
Memorization	The ability to remember information such as words, numbers, pictures, and procedures.
Fluency of Ideas	The ability to come up with a number of ideas about a topic (the number of ideas is important, not their quality, correctness, or creativity).
Originality	The ability to come up with unusual or clever ideas about a given topic or situation, or to develop creative ways to solve a problem.
Explosive Strength	The ability to use short bursts of muscle force to propel oneself (as in jumping or sprinting), or to throw an object.
Number Facility	The ability to add, subtract, multiply, or divide quickly and correctly.
Dynamic Flexibility	The ability to quickly and repeatedly bend, stretch, twist, or reach out with your body, arms, and/or legs.
Mathematical Reasoning	The ability to choose the right mathematical methods or formulas to solve a problem.

Work_Activity	Work_Activity Definitions
Operating Vehicles, Mechanized Devices, or Equipme	Running, maneuvering, navigating, or driving vehicles or mechanized equipment, such as forklifts, passenger vehicles, aircraft, or water craft.
Inspecting Equipment, Structures, or Material	Inspecting equipment, structures, or materials to identify the cause of errors or other problems or defects.

Performing General Physical Activities	Performing physical activities that require considerable use of your arms and legs and moving your whole body, such as climbing, lifting, balancing, walking, stooping, and handling of materials.
Communicating with Supervisors, Peers, or Subordin	Providing information to supervisors, co-workers, and subordinates by telephone, in written form, e-mail, or in person.
Handling and Moving Objects	Using hands and arms in handling, installing, positioning, and moving materials, and manipulating things.
Controlling Machines and Processes	Using either control mechanisms or direct physical activity to operate machines or processes (not including computers or vehicles).
Identifying Objects, Actions, and Events	Identifying information by categorizing, estimating, recognizing differences or similarities, and detecting changes in circumstances or events.
Getting Information	Observing, receiving, and otherwise obtaining information from all relevant sources.
Performing for or Working Directly with the Public	Performing for people or dealing directly with the public. This includes serving customers in restaurants and stores, and receiving clients or guests.
Making Decisions and Solving Problems	Analyzing information and evaluating results to choose the best solution and solve problems.
Repairing and Maintaining Mechanical Equipment	Servicing, repairing, adjusting, and testing machines, devices, moving parts, and equipment that operate primarily on the basis of mechanical (not electronic) principles.
Evaluating Information to Determine Compliance wit	Using relevant information and individual judgment to determine whether events or processes comply with laws, regulations, or standards.
Monitor Processes, Materials, or Surroundings	Monitoring and reviewing information from materials, events, or the environment, to detect or assess problems.
Organizing, Planning, and Prioritizing Work	Developing specific goals and plans to prioritize, organize, and accomplish your work.
Communicating with Persons Outside Organization	Communicating with people outside the organization, representing the organization to customers, the public, government, and other external sources. This information can be exchanged in person, in writing, or by telephone or e-mail.
Establishing and Maintaining Interpersonal Relatio	Developing constructive and cooperative working relationships with others, and maintaining them over time.
Judging the Qualities of Things, Services, or Peop	Assessing the value, importance, or quality of things or people.
Documenting/Recording Information	Entering, transcribing, recording, storing, or maintaining information in written or electronic/magnetic form.
Processing Information	Compiling, coding, categorizing, calculating, tabulating, auditing, or verifying information or data.
Resolving Conflicts and Negotiating with Others	Handling complaints, settling disputes, and resolving grievances and conflicts, or otherwise negotiating with others.
Scheduling Work and Activities	Scheduling events, programs, and activities, as well as the work of others.
Assisting and Caring for Others	Providing personal assistance, medical attention, emotional support, or other personal care to others such as coworkers, customers, or patients.
Estimating the Quantifiable Characteristics of Pro	Estimating sizes, distances, and quantities; or determining time, costs, resources, or materials needed to perform a work activity.
Developing and Building Teams	Encouraging and building mutual trust, respect, and cooperation among team members.
Interpreting the Meaning of Information for Others	Translating or explaining what information means and how it can be used.
Coordinating the Work and Activities of Others	Getting members of a group to work together to accomplish tasks.
Coaching and Developing Others	Identifying the developmental needs of others and coaching, mentoring, or otherwise helping others to improve their knowledge or skills.
Developing Objectives and Strategies	Establishing long-range objectives and specifying the strategies and actions to achieve them.
Thinking Creatively	Developing, designing, or creating new applications, ideas, relationships, systems, or products, including artistic contributions.
Updating and Using Relevant Knowledge	Keeping up-to-date technically and applying new knowledge to your job.
Guiding, Directing, and Motivating Subordinates	Providing guidance and direction to subordinates, including setting performance standards and monitoring performance.
Training and Teaching Others	Identifying the educational needs of others, developing formal educational or training programs or classes, and teaching or instructing others.

Analyzing Data or Information	Identifying the underlying principles, reasons, or facts of information by breaking down information or data into separate parts.
Repairing and Maintaining Electronic Equipment	Servicing, repairing, calibrating, regulating, fine-tuning, or testing machines, devices, and equipment that operate primarily on the basis of electrical or electronic (not mechanical) principles.
Monitoring and Controlling Resources	Monitoring and controlling resources and overseeing the spending of money.
Provide Consultation and Advice to Others	Providing guidance and expert advice to management or other groups on technical, systems-, or process-related topics.
Selling or Influencing Others	Convincing others to buy merchandise/goods or to otherwise change their minds or actions.
Performing Administrative Activities	Performing day-to-day administrative tasks such as maintaining information files and processing paperwork.
Drafting, Laying Out, and Specifying Technical Dev	Providing documentation, detailed instructions, drawings, or specifications to tell others about how devices, parts, equipment, or structures are to be fabricated, constructed, assembled, modified, maintained, or used.
Interacting With Computers	Using computers and computer systems (including hardware and software) to program, write software, set up functions, enter data, or process information.
Staffing Organizational Units	Recruiting, interviewing, selecting, hiring, and promoting employees in an organization.

Work_Context	**Work_Context Definitions**
Outdoors, Exposed to Weather	How often does this job require working outdoors, exposed to all weather conditions?
Wear Common Protective or Safety Equipment such as	How much does this job require wearing common protective or safety equipment such as safety shoes, glasses, gloves, hard hats or live jackets?
In an Enclosed Vehicle or Equipment	How often does this job require working in a closed vehicle or equipment (e.g., car)?
Exposed to Contaminants	How often does this job require working exposed to contaminants (such as pollutants, gases, dust or odors)?
Spend Time Making Repetitive Motions	How much does this job require making repetitive motions?
Spend Time Using Your Hands to Handle, Control, or	How much does this job require using your hands to handle, control, or feel objects, tools or controls?
Impact of Decisions on Co-workers or Company Resul	How do the decisions an employee makes impact the results of co-workers, clients or the company?
Frequency of Decision Making	How frequently is the worker required to make decisions that affect other people, the financial resources, and/or the image and reputation of the organization?
Freedom to Make Decisions	How much decision making freedom, without supervision, does the job offer?
Sounds, Noise Levels Are Distracting or Uncomforta	How often does this job require working exposed to sounds and noise levels that are distracting or uncomfortable?
Face-to-Face Discussions	How often do you have to have face-to-face discussions with individuals or teams in this job?
Importance of Being Exact or Accurate	How important is being very exact or highly accurate in performing this job?
Consequence of Error	How serious would the result usually be if the worker made a mistake that was not readily correctable?
Spend Time Bending or Twisting the Body	How much does this job require bending or twisting your body?
Very Hot or Cold Temperatures	How often does this job require working in very hot (above 90 F degrees) or very cold (below 32 F degrees) temperatures?
Exposed to Hazardous Equipment	How often does this job require exposure to hazardous equipment?
Time Pressure	How often does this job require the worker to meet strict deadlines?
Deal With External Customers	How important is it to work with external customers or the public in this job?
Work With Work Group or Team	How important is it to work with others in a group or team in this job?
Structured versus Unstructured Work	To what extent is this job structured for the worker, rather than allowing the worker to determine tasks, priorities, and goals?
Exposed to Minor Burns, Cuts, Bites, or Stings	How often does this job require exposure to minor burns, cuts, bites, or stings?
Contact With Others	How much does this job require the worker to be in contact with others (face-to-face, by telephone, or otherwise) in order to perform it?
Exposed to Disease or Infections	How often does this job require exposure to disease/infections?

Responsible for Others' Health and Safety	How much responsibility is there for the health and safety of others in this job?
Spend Time Sitting	How much does this job require sitting?
Importance of Repeating Same Tasks	How important is repeating the same physical activities (e.g., key entry) or mental activities (e.g., checking entries in a ledger) over and over, without stopping, to performing this job?
Spend Time Walking and Running	How much does this job require walking and running?
Spend Time Standing	How much does this job require standing?
Deal With Unpleasant or Angry People	How frequently does the worker have to deal with unpleasant, angry, or discourteous individuals as part of the job requirements?
Pace Determined by Speed of Equipment	How important is it to this job that the pace is determined by the speed of equipment or machinery? (This does not refer to keeping busy at all times on this job.)
Degree of Automation	How automated is the job?
Level of Competition	To what extent does this job require the worker to compete or to be aware of competitive pressures?
Coordinate or Lead Others	How important is it to coordinate or lead others in accomplishing work activities in this job?
Extremely Bright or Inadequate Lighting	How often does this job require working in extremely bright or inadequate lighting conditions?
Frequency of Conflict Situations	How often are there conflict situations the employee has to face in this job?
Exposed to Whole Body Vibration	How often does this job require exposure to whole body vibration (e.g., operate a jackhammer)?
Spend Time Kneeling, Crouching, Stooping, or Crawl	How much does this job require kneeling, crouching, stooping or crawling?
Telephone	How often do you have telephone conversations in this job?
Cramped Work Space, Awkward Positions	How often does this job require working in cramped work spaces that requires getting into awkward positions?
Letters and Memos	How often does the job require written letters and memos?
Responsibility for Outcomes and Results	How responsible is the worker for work outcomes and results of other workers?
Exposed to Hazardous Conditions	How often does this job require exposure to hazardous conditions?
In an Open Vehicle or Equipment	How often does this job require working in an open vehicle or equipment (e.g., tractor)?
Outdoors, Under Cover	How often does this job require working outdoors, under cover (e.g., structure with roof but no walls)?
Indoors, Not Environmentally Controlled	How often does this job require working indoors in non-controlled environmental conditions (e.g., warehouse without heat)?
Exposed to High Places	How often does this job require exposure to high places?
Physical Proximity	To what extent does this job require the worker to perform job tasks in close physical proximity to other people?
Public Speaking	How often do you have to perform public speaking in this job?
Spend Time Keeping or Regaining Balance	How much does this job require keeping or regaining your balance?
Wear Specialized Protective or Safety Equipment su	How much does this job require wearing specialized protective or safety equipment such as breathing apparatus, safety harness, full protection suits, or radiation protection?
Spend Time Climbing Ladders, Scaffolds, or Poles	How much does this job require climbing ladders, scaffolds, or poles?
Indoors, Environmentally Controlled	How often does this job require working indoors in environmentally controlled conditions?
Deal With Physically Aggressive People	How frequently does this job require the worker to deal with physical aggression of violent individuals?
Electronic Mail	How often do you use electronic mail in this job?
Exposed to Radiation	How often does this job require exposure to radiation?

Job Zone Component	**Job Zone Component Definitions**
Title	Job Zone Two: Some Preparation Needed
Overall Experience	Some previous work-related skill, knowledge, or experience may be helpful in these occupations, but usually is not needed. For example, a drywall installer might benefit from experience installing drywall, but an inexperienced person could still learn to be an installer with little difficulty.
Job Training	Employees in these occupations need anywhere from a few months to one year of working with experienced employees.
Job Zone Examples	These occupations often involve using your knowledge and skills to help others. Examples include drywall installers, fire inspectors, flight attendants, pharmacy technicians, salespersons (retail), and tellers.
SVP Range	(4.0 to < 6.0)

Education	These occupations usually require a high school diploma and may require some vocational training or job-related course work. In some cases, an associate's or bachelor's degree could be needed.

Work_Styles	Work_Styles Definitions
Dependability	Job requires being reliable, responsible, and dependable, and fulfilling obligations.
Self Control	Job requires maintaining composure, keeping emotions in check, controlling anger, and avoiding aggressive behavior, even in very difficult situations.
Cooperation	Job requires being pleasant with others on the job and displaying a good-natured, cooperative attitude.
Stress Tolerance	Job requires accepting criticism and dealing calmly and effectively with high stress situations.
Attention to Detail	Job requires being careful about detail and thorough in completing work tasks.
Persistence	Job requires persistence in the face of obstacles.
Achievement/Effort	Job requires establishing and maintaining personally challenging achievement goals and exerting effort toward mastering tasks.
Concern for Others	Job requires being sensitive to others' needs and feelings and being understanding and helpful on the job.
Initiative	Job requires a willingness to take on responsibilities and challenges.
Integrity	Job requires being honest and ethical.
Independence	Job requires developing one's own ways of doing things, guiding oneself with little or no supervision, and depending on oneself to get things done.
Adaptability/Flexibility	Job requires being open to change (positive or negative) and to considerable variety in the workplace.
Leadership	Job requires a willingness to lead, take charge, and offer opinions and direction.
Analytical Thinking	Job requires analyzing information and using logic to address work-related issues and problems.
Innovation	Job requires creativity and alternative thinking to develop new ideas for and answers to work-related problems.
Social Orientation	Job requires preferring to work with others rather than alone, and being personally connected with others on the job.